P9-CDZ-429

THE NIV COMPLETE CONCORDANCE

THE NIV COMPLETE CONCORDANCE

The Complete English Concordance to the New International Version

Edward W. Goodrick &
John R. Kohlenberger III

ZONDERVAN PUBLISHING HOUSE
OF THE ZONDERVAN CORPORATION
GRAND RAPIDS, MICHIGAN 49506

THE NIV COMPLETE CONCORDANCE

Grand Rapids, Michigan

Library of Congress Cataloging in Publication Data

Goodrick, Edward W 1913-

The NIV complete concordance.

1. Bible—Concordances, English—New International.
I. Kohlenberger, John R. II. Title.
BS425.G6 220.5'2 80-28401
ISBN 0-310-43650-8

Printed in the United States of America

PREFACE

The NIV Complete Concordance is the first concordance available for studying the English text of the New International Version Bible. Like other concordances it is one of the most basic tools of Bible study. It is a special index—an alphabetical listing of the words used in the text of the Bible: each word entry is followed by the Scripture references as well as by a brief excerpt from the context in which the word occurs. Thus, a concordance may be used to do word studies, locate and trace biblical themes, and find forgotten references to verses.

In the past, concordances have been produced in different sizes and with different features. Exhaustive concordances list every occurrence of *every* word in the Bible, no matter how minor or insignificant the word. While exhaustive concordances are valuable reference works containing a wealth of information, they are not handy reference tools. Their large size and great bulk make them difficult to carry and awkward to use. At the other extreme are the greatly abridged concordances commonly placed in the back of a Bible. The convenience of having a small concordance bound with a Bible is indisputable, but the relatively small number of entries greatly restricts the usefulness of the abridged concordance.

There is a middle ground between these two extremes occupied by the *NIV Complete Concordance*. This concordance is appropriately spoken of as "complete" because it lists *all* the references for *every* word indexed. In other words, for every entry word every occurrence of that word from Genesis through Revelation is given. In a very few instances this might not appear to be true, though in fact it is. In the English language there are some completely different words with the same spelling. When one of these words was chosen to be indexed and the other, spelled in the same way, was eliminated, it will appear that every occurrence of the word is not given. But in reality, all the references of every indexed word of the same spelling *and meaning* are listed. There are twelve instances of this:

HIGH is indexed only in the sense of "God MOST HIGH" (the name Elyon).
JUST is indexed in "He was a just man," but omitted in "I just remembered."
LEAVES is indexed in "tree leaves," but omitted in "He leaves his coat."
LEFT is indexed in "left, not right," but omitted in "He left town."
MIGHT is indexed in "with all his might," but omitted in "He might go."
MINE is indexed in "the gold mine," but omitted in "The house is mine."
ON is indexed when a proper noun, but omitted in "on the housetop."
OWN is indexed in "I own a house," but omitted in "one's own house."
PUT is indexed when a proper noun, but omitted in "He put it down."
STILL is indexed in "the still small voice," but omitted in "He is still here."
WELL is indexed in "The well was deep," and in "He is well, not sick," but omitted in "well done."
WILL is indexed in "do God's will," but omitted when used as an auxiliary verb.

But this is a complete, not an exhaustive, concordance. While every reference is given for every word indexed, not every NIV word is indexed. Every *key* word in the NIV is indexed, and only those that would have a very limited value in a concordance are omitted. For example, most adverbs and prepositions are not indexed, nor are the definite and indefinite articles *(a, an,* and *the).* All NIV words not indexed in this concordance are listed alphabetically in the appendix (see page 1041).

As in any index, all NIV word entries are listed in alphabetical order; however, the alphabetical order is interrupted by punctuation (in particular, hyphens and apostrophes), keeping together words closest to their root word. For example, note the order in this sequence: BROTHER, BROTHER-IN-LAW, BROTHER'S, BROTHERHOOD, BROTHERLY, BROTHERS. In this same connection, the alphabetized word entries are always single words (or hyphenated word combinations), rather than phrases (such as "power of God," "in power," "my power," which appear in some existing concordances).

Another helpful feature of the *NIV Complete Concordance* is the system of cross-references. Variant spellings due to number, tense, compound forms, etc., of an entry word follow the entry in parentheses. For example, the entry CRUCIFY is followed by (CRUCIFIED CRUCIFYING). Here the cross-references refer the reader to the variant forms found in the NIV of the root word CRUCIFY. The entries CRUCIFIED and CRUCIFYING are both followed by (CRUCIFY), referring back to the root word.

Each variant spelling of a word cross-references back to its root. The entry for the root word also cross-references to all the variant spellings. Word groups closely related to the root are also included in this method of cross-referencing. For example, the entry HEART includes the cross-references HEARTS as well as HARD-HEARTED and WHOLEHEARTEDLY. In this way, one can often do a topical study as well as a word study. Most entries, however, are not cross-referenced to their negative forms (such as those using the prefix "un" or the suffix "less"). Thus, BLAME and BLAMELESS are not cross-referenced to each other, nor are END and ENDLESS.

Two of the names of God have a special feature that should be noted. The Hebrew name *Adonai* is usually translated "Lord" when referring to God. The proper name of God, *Yahweh,* is translated "LORD." The former is printed with a capital followed by lower-case letters (Lord) and the latter with a capital letter followed by small capitals (LORD). In this manner they are distinguished in the printed text of the NIV. However, since all the letters of the entry words in the concordance are capitalized, both entry words *(Lord* and *LORD)* look the same. To eliminate this confusion, "Lord" is marked with an asterisk(*) and "LORD" with a dagger (†). Both entries also include explanatory footnotes.

Another significant feature of the *NIV Complete Concordance* is the one-line context that follows each reference under the indexed entry words. The excerpted context was selected to show how the entry word was used in each occurrence. The italicized first letter of the entry word represents that word to conserve space and allow for a longer context excerpt.

Two words listed in the concordance have all their occurrences listed, but not all their contexts. The word SELAH, a musical or poetic notation, never has a context; thus, only its references are listed. This is also true of the word AMEN, which is most often an isolated statement.

Sometimes an indexed entry word will occur more than once in the quoted context line. To achieve an accurate count of the number of times a word occurs, one should scan the contexts to see how many letters are italicized. For instance, "holy" occurs three times in the famous songs of Isaiah 6:3 and Revelation 4:8, but each occurrence is indicated in one context line as "*H, h, h.*"

Because this concordance is based on the NIV, the excerpted contexts following the references contain all the marks of punctuation included in the NIV text. One unusual symbol is the "half bracket" (⌊ ⌋). These symbols mark the words that are not in the original languages but have been inserted by the translators for clarity. For example, Ecclesiastes

7:28 includes the word ⌊upright⌋ to clarify the meaning. Consequently, the context given for Ecclesiastes 7:28 under UPRIGHT reads, "I found one ⌊*u*⌋ man." This is a good translation in the context, but the half brackets indicate that this word was supplied by the translators rather than by the Hebrew text.

The *NIV Complete Concordance* is a remarkable example of biblical scholars making use of computer technology. What would manually have taken years to produce was accomplished in less than two years. And the accuracy of this computer-produced concordance far exceeds what would have been possible by conventional methods. Through a complex series of programs devised by the biblical scholars and computer analysts, the computer automatically counted the width of each letter so that the contexts would not exceed the line length. By this economy, the concordance indexes many more words per page. Through an ingenious algorithm, constructed by the chief computer analyst, the computer selected the words for each of the 250,000 references. The computer also selected, sorted, arranged, alphabetized, and merged the indexed word entries and 250,000 reference entries and contexts. In the final step, another computer following the instructions of a master tape set over 10,500,000 characters on 257,000 lines on 1,039 three-column pages of concordance in nine and one-half hours!

Edward W. Goodrick and John R. Kohlenberger III were the innovative scholars who dared to think that biblical scholarship and computer science could successfully produce a concordance. Computer services, analysis, programming, and the computer were supplied by the Control Data Corporation of Minneapolis, Minnesota. Without the dedicated services of their Portland, Oregon staff consisting of Bob Lind, Barbara Perz, and especially the chief analyst, Dennis Thomas, the project could not have been completed in so short a time nor with such professional results.

Finally, Bernie Maron, Project Manager of Auto-graphics, Inc. of Monterey Park, California, played a key role. Using the master tape produced by the Portland group, the Auto-graphics team, led by Bernie, performed the phenomenal job of typesetting this work by computer. The members of these smoothly functioning teams are pioneers in a new application of computer science and technology.

In 1737 Alexander Cruden completed his famous concordance of the King James Version Bible. The closing words of his preface to the first edition are just as appropriate for the *NIV Complete Concordance:*

> I conclude this preface with praying that God, who hath graciously enabled me to bring this large work to a conclusion, would render it useful to those who seriously and carefully search the scriptures; and grant that the sacred writings, which are so important and highly worthy of esteem, may meet with all that affection and regard which they deserve. May those who profess to believe the scriptures to be a Revelation from God, apply themselves to the reading and study of them; and may they, by the Holy Spirit of God, who indited [inspired] the scriptures, be made wise to salvation through faith which is in Christ Jesus, Amen.

The Publisher
April 1981

IN MEMORY OF
DR. EDWIN H. PALMER

ACKNOWLEDGEMENTS

Many organizations and people have joined forces to produce this concordance.

We applaud the indispensible skills and pioneering computer work of the Portland, Oregon branch of the Control Data Corporation, specifically analysts Bob Lind, Barbara Perz, and especially their principal analyst, Dennis Thomas. We also thank the staff and management of the Scientific Computer Center at Techtronix, Inc. of Beaverton, Oregon, and of the Milne Computer Center at Oregon State University of Corvallis for their services and cooperation.

We commend the typesetting skills of Auto-graphics, Inc. of Monterey Park, California, especially the cheerful cooperation of Bernie Maron in setting the entire concordance from our computer tapes within the span of a single week. We also gratefully acknowledge the painstaking proofreading of Frederick and Mildred Tripp.

We must express our affection and gratitude to the people of the Zondervan Publishing House for their willingness to support a rather large project with not inconsiderable funds, especially to Executive Vice-President Bob De Vries for his vision and faith in the project and its executors, and to editors Paul Hillman, Stan Gundry, and Doris Rikkers for their invaluable interaction and working-out of details.

Finally, we laud the diligent and sacrificial labors of the translators and editors of the New International Version, who spent more than a decade in producing that magnificent translation for the building-up of the Church and to the glory of God. But especially, the selfless and devoted energies of their Executive Secretary, Dr. Edwin H. Palmer, must be singled out. From the commencement of the activities relating to the NIV in 1968 to his untimely passing on September 16, 1980, Dr. Palmer was the organizing and driving force behind the NIV. It is to his memory that this Concordance, the first of the major study tools based on the NIV, is dedicated.

Edward W. Goodrick
John R. Kohlenberger III

ABBREVIATIONS FOR THE BOOKS OF THE BIBLE

Genesis	Ge
Exodus	Ex
Leviticus	Lev
Numbers	Nu
Deuteronomy	Dt
Joshua	Jos
Judges	Jdg
Ruth	Ru
1 Samuel	1Sa
2 Samuel	2Sa
1 Kings	1Ki
2 Kings	2Ki
1 Chronicles	1Ch
2 Chronicles	2Ch
Ezra	Ezr
Nehemiah	Ne
Esther	Est
Job	Job
Psalms	Ps
Proverbs	Pr
Ecclesiastes	Ecc
Song of Songs	SS
Isaiah	Isa
Jeremiah	Jer
Lamentations	La
Ezekiel	Eze
Daniel	Da
Hosea	Hos
Joel	Joel
Amos	Am
Obadiah	Ob
Jonah	Jnh
Micah	Mic
Nahum	Na
Habbakuk	Hab
Zephaniah	Zep
Haggai	Hag
Zechariah	Zec
Malachi	Mal
Matthew	Mt
Mark	Mk
Luke	Lk
John	Jn
Acts	Ac
Romans	Ro
1 Corinthians	1Co
2 Corinthians	2Co
Galatians	Gal
Ephesians	Eph
Philippians	Php
Colossians	Col
1 Thessalonians	1Th
2 Thessalonians	2Th
1 Timothy	1Ti
2 Timothy	2Ti
Titus	Tit
Philemon	Phm
Hebrews	Heb
James	Jas
1 Peter	1Pe
2 Peter	2Pe
1 John	1Jn
2 John	2Jn
3 John	3Jn
Jude	Jude
Revelation	Rev

AARON (AARON'S AARONIC)

Ex 4: 14 about your brother, *A* the Levite?
4: 27 The LORD said to *A*, "Go
4: 28 Then Moses told *A* everything
4: 29 *A* brought together all the elders
4: 30 *A* told them everything the LORD
5: 1 Afterward Moses and *A* went
5: 4 king of Egypt said, "Moses and *A*,
5: 20 and *A* waiting to meet them,
6: 13 to Moses and *A* about the Israelites
6: 20 who bore him *A* and Moses.
6: 23 *A* married Elisheba, daughter
6: 25 Eleazar son of *A* married one
6: 26 It was this same *A* and Moses
6: 27 It was the same Moses and *A*.
7: 1 and your brother *A* will be your
7: 2 your brother *A* is to tell Pharaoh
7: 6 and *A* did just as the LORD
7: 7 *A* eighty-three when they spoke
7: 8 The LORD said to Moses and *A*,
7: 9 'Perform a miracle,' then say to *A*,
7: 10 Moses and *A* went to Pharaoh
7: 10 *A* threw his staff down in front
7: 19 The LORD said to Moses, "Tell *A*,
7: 20 and *A* did just as the LORD had
7: 22 he would not listen to Moses and *A*
8: 5 the LORD said to Moses, "Tell *A*,
8: 6 So *A* stretched out his hand
8: 8 Pharaoh summoned Moses and *A*
8: 12 After Moses and *A* left Pharaoh,
8: 15 would not listen to Moses and *A*,
8: 16 the LORD said to Moses, "Tell *A*,
8: 17 and when *A* stretched out his hand
8: 25 Pharaoh summoned Moses and *A*
9: 8 the LORD said to Moses and *A*,
9: 12 he would not listen to Moses and *A*
9: 27 Pharaoh summoned Moses and *A*.
10: 3 So Moses and *A* went to Pharaoh
10: 8 *A* were brought back to Pharaoh.
10: 11 and *A* were driven out
10: 16 quickly summoned Moses and *A*
11: 10 and *A* performed all these wonders
12: 1 said to Moses and *A* in Egypt,
12: 28 LORD commanded Moses and *A*.
12: 31 Pharaoh summoned Moses and *A*
12: 43 The LORD said to Moses and *A*,
12: 50 had commanded Moses and *A*.
16: 2 grumbled against Moses and *A*.
16: 6 and *A* said to all the Israelites,
16: 9 Then Moses told *A*, "Say
16: 10 While *A* was speaking
16: 33 So Moses said to *A*, "Take a jar
16: 34 *A* put the manna in front
17: 10 *A* and Hur went to the top
17: 12 *A* and Hur held his hands up—
18: 12 *A* came with all the elders of Israel
19: 24 Go down and bring *A* up with you
24: 1 you and *A*, Nadab and Abihu,
24: 9 Moses and *A*, Nadab and Abihu,
24: 14 *A* and Hur are with you,
27: 21 *A* and his sons are
28: 1 "Have *A* your brother brought
28: 2 garments for your brother *A*,
28: 3 are to make garments for *A*,
28: 4 garments for your brother *A*
28: 12 *A* is to bear the names
28: 29 Whenever *A* enters the Holy Place,
28: 30 Thus *A* will always bear the means
28: 35 *A* must wear it when he ministers.
28: 41 clothes on your brother *A*
28: 43 *A* and his sons must wear them
28: 43 is to be a lasting ordinance for *A*
29: 4 Then bring *A* and his sons
29: 5 and dress *A* with the tunic,
29: 9 In this way you shall ordain *A*
29: 9 Then tie sashes on *A* and his sons.
29: 10 *A* and his sons shall lay their hands
29: 15 *A* and his sons shall lay their hands
29: 19 *A* and his sons shall lay their hands
29: 20 it on the lobes of the right ears of *A*
29: 21 sprinkle it on *A* and his garments
29: 24 Put all these in the hands of *A*
29: 27 the ordination ram that belong to *A*
29: 28 share from the Israelites for *A*
29: 32 *A* and his sons are to eat the meat
29: 35 "Do for *A* and his sons everything I
29: 44 and the altar and will consecrate *A*

Ex 30: 7 "*A* must burn fragrant incense
30: 10 Once a year *A* shall make
30: 19 *A* and his sons are
30: 21 is to be a lasting ordinance for *A*
30: 30 "Anoint *A* and his sons
31: 10 sacred garments for *A* the priest
32: 1 they gathered around *A* and said,
32: 2 *A* answered them, "Take
32: 3 earrings and brought them to *A*.
32: 5 When *A* saw this, he built an altar
32: 21 to *A*, "What did these people do
32: 22 be angry, my lord," *A* answered.
32: 25 and that *A* had let them get out
32: 35 did with the calf *A* had made.
34: 30 When *A* and all the Israelites saw
34: 31 so *A* and all the leaders
35: 19 sacred garments for *A* the priest
38: 21 the direction of Ithamar son of *A*,
39: 1 also made sacred garments for *A*,
39: 27 For *A* and his sons, they made
39: 41 sacred garments for *A* the priest
40: 12 "Bring *A* and his sons
40: 13 dress *A* in the sacred garments,
40: 31 and *A* and his sons used it
Lev 1: 7 The sons of *A* the priest are
2: 3 of the grain offering belongs to *A*
2: 10 of the grain offering belongs to *A*
6: 9 Give *A* and his sons this command:
6: 16 *A* and his sons shall eat the rest of it
6: 18 male descendant of *A* may eat it.
6: 20 "This is the offering *A*
6: 25 said to Moses, "Say to *A*
7: 10 belongs equally to all the sons of *A*.
7: 31 the breast belongs to *A* and his sons
7: 33 The son of *A* who offers the blood
7: 34 and have given them to *A* the priest
7: 35 by fire that were allotted to *A*
8: 2 "Bring *A* and his sons, their
8: 6 Then Moses brought *A*
8: 7 He put the tunic on *A*, tied the sash
8: 14 and *A* and his sons laid their hands
8: 18 and *A* and his sons laid their hands
8: 22 and *A* and his sons laid their hands
8: 27 He put all these in the hands of *A*
8: 30 he consecrated *A* and his garments
8: 30 them on *A* and his garments
8: 31 Moses then said to *A* and his sons,
8: 31 saying, '*A* and his sons are to eat it.'
8: 36 So *A* and his sons did everything
9: 1 the eighth day Moses summoned *A*
9: 2 He said to *A*, "Take a bull calf
9: 7 Moses said to *A*, "Come
9: 8 So *A* came to the altar
9: 15 *A* then brought the offering that
9: 20 then *A* burned the fat on the altar.
9: 21 *A* waved the breasts and the right
9: 22 Then *A* lifted his hands
9: 23 and *A* then went into the Tent
10: 3 *A* remained silent.
10: 3 said to *A*, "This is what the LORD
10: 6 said to *A* and his sons Eleazar
10: 8 Then the LORD said to *A*,
10: 12 said to *A* and his remaining sons,
10: 19 *A* replied to Moses, "Today they
11: 1 The LORD said to Moses and *A*,
13: 1 The LORD said to Moses and *A*,
13: 2 he must be brought to *A* the priest
14: 33 The LORD said to Moses and *A*,
15: 1 The LORD said to Moses and *A*,
16: 1 of the two sons of *A* who died
16: 2 "Tell your brother *A* not
16: 3 "This is how *A* is to enter
16: 6 "*A* is to offer the bull
16: 9 *A* shall bring the goat whose lot
16: 11 "*A* shall bring the bull
16: 17 of Meeting from the time *A* goes
16: 20 "When *A* has finished making
16: 23 *A* is to go into the Tent of Meeting
17: 2 "Speak to *A* and his sons
21: 1 the sons of *A*, and say to them:
21: 17 said to Moses, "Say to *A*:
21: 21 of *A* the priest who has any defect
21: 24 Moses told this to *A* and his sons
22: 2 "Tell *A* and his sons to treat
22: 4 of *A* has an infectious skin disease
22: 18 "Speak to *A* and his sons
24: 3 *A* is to tend the lamps
24: 9 It belongs to *A* and his sons,

Nu 1: 3 *A* are to number by their divisions
1: 17 *A* took these men whose names
1: 44 *A* and the twelve leaders of Israel,
2: 1 The LORD said to Moses and *A*:
3: 1 is the account of the family of *A*
3: 2 sons of *A* were Nadab the firstborn
3: 4 during the lifetime of their father *A*
3: 6 and present them to *A* the priest
3: 9 Give the Levites to *A* and his sons;
3: 10 Appoint *A* and his sons to serve
3: 32 of the Levites was Eleazar son of *A*,
3: 38 and *A* and his sons were to camp
3: 39 and *A* according to their clans,
3: 48 of the additional Israelites to *A*
3: 51 gave the redemption money to *A*
4: 1 The LORD said to Moses and *A*:
4: 5 *A* and his sons are to go in
4: 15 "After *A* and his sons have finished
4: 16 "Eleazar son of *A*, the priest,
4: 17 The LORD said to Moses and *A*,
4: 19 *A* and his sons are to go
4: 27 to be done under the direction of *A*
4: 28 the direction of Ithamar son of *A*,
4: 33 the direction of Ithamar son of *A*,
4: 34 *A* and the leaders
4: 37 and *A* counted them according
4: 41 and *A* counted them according
4: 45 and *A* counted them according
4: 46 *A* and the leaders of Israel counted
6: 23 The LORD said to Moses, "Tell *A*
7: 8 the direction of Ithamar son of *A*,
8: 2 "Speak to *A* and say to him,
8: 3 *A* did so; he set up the lamps
8: 11 *A* is to present the Levites
8: 13 the Levites stand in front of *A*
8: 19 have given the Levites as gifts to *A*
8: 20 *A* and the whole Israelite
8: 21 Then *A* presented them
8: 22 Meeting under the supervision of *A*
9: 6 to Moses and *A* that same day
10: 8 "The sons of *A*, the priests,
12: 1 and *A* began to talk against Moses
12: 4 once the LORD said to Moses, *A*
12: 5 and summoned *A* and Miriam.
12: 10 *A* turned toward her and saw that
13: 26 They came back to Moses and *A*
14: 2 grumbled against Moses and *A*,
14: 5 and *A* fell facedown in front
14: 26 The LORD said to Moses and *A*:
15: 33 and *A* and the whole assembly,
16: 3 as a group to oppose Moses and *A*
16: 11 Who is *A* that you should grumble
16: 16 tomorrow—you and they and *A*.
16: 17 and *A* are to present your censers
16: 18 and *A* at the entrance to the Tent
16: 20 The LORD said to Moses and *A*,
16: 22 But Moses and *A* fell facedown
16: 37 "Tell Eleazar son of *A*, the priest,
16: 40 a descendant of *A* should come
16: 41 grumbled against Moses and *A*.
16: 42 and *A* and turned toward the Tent
16: 43 and *A* went to the front of the Tent
16: 46 Moses said to *A*, "Take your censer
16: 47 So *A* did as Moses said,
16: 47 but *A* offered the incense
16: 50 Then *A* returned to Moses
18: 1 The LORD said to *A*, "You,
18: 8 Then the LORD said to *A*,
18: 20 to *A*, "You will have no inheritance
18: 28 LORD's portion to *A* the priest.
19: 1 The LORD said to Moses and *A*:
20: 2 in opposition to Moses and *A*.
20: 6 and *A* went from the assembly
20: 8 your brother *A* gather the assembly
20: 10 *A* gathered the assembly together
20: 12 the LORD said to Moses and *A*,
20: 23 the LORD said to Moses and *A*,
20: 24 "*A* will be gathered to his people.
20: 25 Get *A* and his son Eleazar
20: 26 for *A* will be gathered to his people;
20: 28 And *A* died there on top
20: 29 learned that *A* had died,
25: 7 the son of *A*, the priest, saw this,
25: 11 son of Eleazar, the son of *A*,
26: 1 said to Moses and Eleazar son of *A*,
26: 9 rebelled against Moses and *A*
26: 59 To Amram she bore *A*, Moses
26: 60 *A* was the father of Nadab

Nu 26: 64 *A* the priest when they counted
27: 13 your people, as your brother *A* was,
33: 1 the leadership of Moses and *A*.
33: 38 the LORD's command *A* the priest
33: 39 *A* was a hundred and twenty-three
Dt 9: 20 but at that time I prayed for *A* too.
9: 20 enough with *A* to destroy him,
10: 6 There *A* died and was buried,
32: 50 your brother *A* died on Mount Hor
Jos 21: 4 of *A* the priest were allotted
21: 10 to the descendants of *A* who were
21: 13 of *A* the priest they gave Hebron
21: 19 the descendants of *A*, were thirteen
24: 5 " 'Then I sent Moses and *A*,
24: 33 And Eleazar son of *A* died
Jdg 20: 28 the son of *A*, ministering before it.)
1Sa 12: 6 who appointed Moses and *A*
12: 8 and the LORD sent Moses and *A*,
1Ch 6: 3 The children of Amram: *A*,
6: 3 The sons of *A*: Nadab, Abihu,
6: 49 But *A* and his descendants were
6: 50 These were the descendants of *A*:
6: 54 to the descendants of *A* who were
6: 57 of *A* were given Hebron (a city
12: 27 of the family of *A*, with 3,700
15: 4 together the descendants of *A*
23: 13 The sons of Amram: *A* and Moses.
23: 13 *A* was set apart, he and his
23: 32 brothers the descendants of *A*,
24: 1 The sons of *A* were Nadab, Abihu,
24: 1 were the divisions of the sons of *A*:
24: 19 for them by their forefather *A*,
24: 31 brothers the descendants of *A* did,
27: 17 over *A*: Zadok; over Judah: Elihu,
2Ch 13: 9 the sons of *A*, and the Levites,
13: 10 who serve the LORD are sons of *A*,
26: 18 of *A*, who have been consecrated
29: 21 the priests, the descendants of *A*,
31: 19 the priests, the descendants of *A*,
35: 14 the priests, the descendants of *A*,
Ezr 7: 5 the son of *A* the chief priest—
Ne 10: 38 A priest descended from *A* is
12: 47 portion for the descendants of *A*.
Ps 77: 20 by the hand of Moses and *A*.
99: 6 and *A* were among his priests,
105: 26 and *A*, whom he had chosen.
106: 16 of *A*, who was consecrated
115: 10 O house of *A*, trust in the LORD—
115: 12 he will bless the house of *A*,
118: 3 Let the house of *A* say:
135: 19 O house of *A*, praise the LORD;
Mic 6: 4 also *A* and Miriam.
Lk 1: 5 was also a descendant of *A*.
Ac 7: 40 They told *A*, 'Make us gods who
Heb 5: 4 called by God, just as *A* was.
7: 11 not in the order of *A*? For

AARON'S (AARON)

Ex 7: 12 *A* staff swallowed up their staffs.
15: 20 Miriam the prophetess, *A* sister,
28: 30 be over *A* heart whenever he enters
28: 38 It will be on *A* forehead continually
28: 38 It will be on *A* forehead,
28: 40 sashes and headbands for *A* sons,
29: 26 breast of the ram for *A* ordination,
29: 29 "*A* sacred garments will belong
Lev 1: 5 then *A* sons the priests shall bring
1: 8 *A* sons the priests shall arrange
1: 11 *A* sons the priests shall sprinkle its
2: 2 and take it to *A* sons the priests.
3: 2 *A* sons the priests shall sprinkle
3: 5 *A* sons are to burn it on the altar
3: 8 Then *A* sons shall sprinkle its blood
3: 13 Then *A* sons shall sprinkle its blood
6: 14 *A* sons are to bring it
8: 9 he placed the turban on *A* head
8: 12 some of the anointing oil on *A* head
8: 13 Then he brought *A* sons forward,
8: 23 and put it on the lobe of *A* right ear,
8: 24 Moses also brought *A* sons forward
10: 1 *A* sons Nadab and Abihu took their
10: 4 sons of *A* uncle Uzziel,
10: 16 *A* remaining sons, and asked,
Nu 3: 3 Those were the names of *A* sons,
17: 3 On the staff of Levi write *A* name,
17: 6 and *A* staff was among them.
17: 8 the Testimony and saw that *A* staff,
17: 10 "Put back *A* staff in front
Nu 20: 26 Remove *A* garments and put them
20: 28 Moses removed *A* garments
1Ch 23: 28 was to help *A* descendants
Ps 133: 2 running down on *A* beard,
Heb 9: 4 of manna, *A* rod that had budded,

AARONIC (AARON)

2Ch 35: 14 for themselves and for the *A* priests

ABADDON

Rev 9: 11 whose name in Hebrew is *A*,

ABAGTHA

Est 1: 10 Biztha, Harbona, Bigtha, *A*,

ABANA

2Ki 5: 12 Are not *A* and Pharpar, the rivers

ABANDON (ABANDONED ABANDONS)

Dt 4: 31 he will not *a* or destroy you
Jos 10: 6 at Gilgal: "Do not *a* your servants.
1Ki 6: 13 and will not *a* my people Israel."
2Ch 12: 5 therefore, I now *a* you to Shishak
Ne 9: 19 compassion you did not *a* them
9: 31 an end to them or *a* them,
Ps 16: 10 you will not *a* me to the grave,
138: 8 do not *a* the works of your hands.
Jer 12: 7 *a* my inheritance;
48: 28 *A* your towns and dwell
Eze 27: 29 will *a* their ships;
Ac 2: 27 you will not *a* me to the grave,
1Ti 4: 1 in later times some will *a* the faith

ABANDONED (ABANDON)

Ge 24: 27 who has not *a* his kindness
Dt 29: 25 because this people *a* the covenant
32: 15 He *a* the God who made him
Jdg 4: 15 and Sisera *a* his chariot
5: 6 in the days of Jael, the roads were *a*
6: 13 But now the LORD has *a* us
1Sa 30: 13 My master *a* me when I became ill
31: 7 they *a* their towns and fled.
2Sa 5: 21 The Philistines *a* their idols there,
1Ki 18: 18 You have *a* the LORD's
2Ki 7: 7 fled in the dusk and *a* their tents
1Ch 10: 7 they *a* their towns and fled.
14: 12 Philistines had *a* their gods there,
2Ch 11: 14 Levites even *a* their pasturelands
12: 1 and all Israel with him *a* the law
12: 5 'You have *a* me; therefore,
16: 5 building Ramah and *a* his work.
24: 18 They *a* the temple of the LORD,
Ne 9: 28 Then you *a* them to the hand
Job 18: 4 is the earth to be *a* for your sake?
Ps 78: 60 He *a* the tabernacle of Shiloh,
Isa 2: 6 You have *a* your people,
10: 14 as men gather *a* eggs,
17: 9 will be like places *a* to thickets
27: 10 an *a* settlement, forsaken like
32: 14 The fortress will be *a*,
54: 7 "For a brief moment I *a* you,
Jer 7: 29 and *a* this generation that is
49: 25 the city of renown not been *a*,
La 2: 7 and *a* his sanctuary.
Mic 5: 3 Therefore Israel will be *a*
Zep 2: 4 Gaza will be *a*
Ac 2: 31 that he was not *a* to the grave,
Ro 1: 27 *a* natural relations with women
2Co 4: 9 persecuted, but not *a*; struck down,
Jude : 6 of authority but *a* their own home

ABANDONS (ABANDON)

Jn 10: 12 he *a* the sheep and runs away.

ABARIM

Nu 27: 12 Go up this mountain in the *A* range
33: 47 and camped in the mountains of *A*,
33: 48 They left the mountains of *A*
Dt 32: 49 "Go up into the *A* Range
Jer 22: 20 cry out from *A*,

ABASHED

Isa 24: 23 moon will be *a*, the sun ashamed;

ABBA

Mk 14: 36 "*A*, Father," he said, "everything is
Ro 8: 15 And by him we cry, "*A*, Father."
Gal 4: 6 the Spirit who calls out, "*A*, Father

ABDA

1Ki 4: 6 Adoniram son of *A*— in charge
Ne 11: 17 among his associates; and *A* son

ABDEEL

Jer 36: 26 and Shelemiah son of *A*

ABDI

1Ch 6: 44 the son of *A*, the son of Malluch,
2Ch 29: 12 Kish son of *A* and Azariah son
Ezr 10: 26 Mattaniah, Zechariah, Jehiel, *A*,

ABDIEL

1Ch 5: 15 Ahi son of *A*, the son of Guni,

ABDOMEN

Nu 5: 21 to waste away and your *a* to swell.
5: 22 body so that your *a* swells
5: 27 her *a* will swell and her thigh waste

ABDON

Jos 19: 28 It went to *A*, Rehob, Hammon
21: 30 Mishal, *A*, Helkath and Rehob,
Jdg 12: 13 After him, *A* son of Hillel,
12: 15 Then *A* son of Hillel died,
1Ch 6: 74 *A*, Hukok and Rehob, together
8: 23 Ishpan, Eber, Eliel, *A*, Zicri, Hanan
8: 30 and his firstborn son was *A*,
9: 36 and his firstborn son was *A*,
2Ch 34: 20 son of Shaphan, *A* son of Micah,

ABEDNEGO

Da 1: 7 Meshach; and to Azariah, *A*.
2: 49 *A* administrators over the province
3: 12 Shadrach, Meshach and *A*—
3: 13 Shadrach, Meshach and *A*.
3: 14 Shadrach, Meshach and *A*,
3: 16 Meshach and *A* replied to the king,
3: 19 and *A*, and his attitude
3: 20 and *A* and throw them
3: 22 and *A*, and these three men,
3: 26 and *A* came out of the fire,
3: 26 "Shadrach, Meshach and *A*,
3: 28 God of Shadrach, Meshach and *A*,
3: 29 Meshach and *A* be cut into pieces
3: 30 and *A* in the province of Babylon.

ABEL

Ge 4: 2 *A* kept flocks, and Cain worked
4: 2 she gave birth to his brother *A*.
4: 4 The LORD looked with favor on *A*
4: 4 *A* brought fat portions from some
4: 8 Cain attacked his brother *A*
4: 8 Now Cain said to his brother *A*,
4: 9 "Where is your brother *A*?"
4: 25 me another child in place of *A*,
2Sa 20: 18 'Get your answer at *A*,'
Mt 23: 35 blood of righteous *A* to the blood
Lk 11: 51 from the blood of *A* to the blood
Heb 11: 4 By faith *A* offered God a better
12: 24 word than the blood of *A*.

ABEL BETH MAACAH (ABEL BETHMAACAH)

2Sa 20: 14 through all the tribes of Israel to *A*
20: 15 came and besieged Sheba in *A*.
2Ki 15: 29 *A*, Janoah, Kedesh and Hazor.

ABEL BETHMAACAH (ABEL BETH MAACAH)

1Ki 15: 20 *A* and all Kinnereth in addition to

ABEL KERAMIM

Jdg 11: 33 the vicinity of Minnith, as far as *A*.

ABEL MAIM

2Ch 16: 4 They conquered Ijon, Dan, *A*

ABEL MEHOLAH

Jdg 7: 22 far as the border of *A* near Tabbath.
1Ki 4: 12 from Beth Shan to *A*
19: 16 Elisha son of Shaphat from *A*

ABEL MIZRAIM

Ge 50: 11 place near the Jordan is called *A*.

ABEL SHITTIM

Nu 33: 49 Jordan from Beth Jeshimoth to *A*.

ABHOR (ABHORRED ABHORRENT ABHORS)
Lev 26: 11 among you, and I will not *a* you.
26: 15 reject my decrees and *a* my laws
26: 30 of your idols, and I will *a* you.
26: 44 I will not reject them or *a* them so
Dt 7: 26 Utterly *a* and detest it,
23: 7 Do not *a* an Edomite,
23: 7 Do not *a* an Egyptian,
Ps 26: 5 I *a* the assembly of evildoers
119:163 I hate and *a* falsehood
139: 21 and *a* those who rise up against you
Am 6: 8 "I *a* the pride of Jacob
Ro 2: 22 You who *a* idols, do you rob

ABHORRED (ABHOR)
Lev 20: 23 they did all these things, I *a* them.
26: 43 rejected my laws and *a* my decrees.
Ps 106: 40 and *a* his inheritance.
Isa 49: 7 to him who was despised and *a*

ABHORRENT (ABHOR)
Jer 15: 4 I will make them *a*
24: 9 I will make them *a* and an offense
29: 18 and will make them *a* to all
34: 17 I will make you *a* to all

ABHORS (ABHOR)
Ps 5: 6 the LORD *a*.
Pr 11: 1 The LORD *a* dishonest scales,

ABI-ALBON
2Sa 23: 31 *A* the Arbathite, Azmaveth

ABIASAPH
Ex 6: 24 Korah were Assir, Elkanah and *A*.

ABIATHAR
1Sa 22: 20 But *A*, a son of Ahimelech son
22: 22 Then David said to *A*: "That day,
23: 6 *A* son of Ahimelech had brought
23: 9 to *A* the priest, "Bring the ephod."
30: 7 Then David said to *A* the priest,
30: 7 *A* brought it to him, and David
2Sa 8: 17 Ahimelech son of *A* were priests;
15: 24 and *A* offered sacrifices
15: 27 Ahimaaz and Jonathan son of *A*.
15: 27 and *A* take your two sons with you.
15: 29 and *A* took the ark of God back
15: 35 the priests Zadok and *A* be there
15: 36 of Zadok and Jonathan son of *A*.
17: 15 Hushai told Zadok and *A*,
19: 11 sent this message to Zadok and *A*,
20: 25 Zadok and *A* were priests;
1Ki 1: 7 of Zeruiah and with *A* the priest,
1: 19 *A* the priest and Joab
1: 25 of the army and *A* the priest.
1: 42 son of *A* the priest arrived.
2: 22 for him and for *A* the priest
2: 26 To *A* the priest the king said,
2: 27 So Solomon removed *A*
2: 35 replaced *A* with Zadok the priest.
4: 4 commander in chief; Zadok and *A*
1Ch 15: 11 Zadok and *A* the priests,
18: 16 Ahimelech son of *A* were priests;
24: 6 Ahimelech son of *A* and the heads
27: 34 son of Benaiah and by *A*.
Mk 2: 26 In the days of *A* the high priest,

ABIB
Ex 13: 4 in the month of *A*, you are leaving.
23: 15 time in the month of *A*,
34: 18 time in the month of *A*,
Dt 16: 1 Observe the month of *A*
16: 1 the month of *A* he brought you out

ABIDA
Ge 25: 4 Epher, Hanoch, *A* and Eldaah.
1Ch 1: 33 Epher, Hanoch, *A* and Eldaah.

ABIDAN
Nu 1: 11 from Benjamin, *A* son of Gideoni;
2: 22 of Benjamin is *A* son of Gideoni.
7: 60 On the ninth day *A* son of Gideoni,
7: 65 the offering of *A* son of Gideoni.
10: 24 and *A* son of Gideoni was

ABIEL
1Sa 9: 1 whose name was Kish son of *A*,
14: 51 Abner's father Ner were sons of *A*.
1Ch 11: 32 *A* the Arbathite, Azmaveth

ABIEZER (ABIEZRITE ABIEZRITES)
Jos 17: 2 the clans of *A*, Helek, Asriel,
Jdg 8: 2 than the full grape harvest of *A*?
2Sa 23: 27 *A* from Anathoth, Mebunnai
1Ch 7: 18 gave birth to Ishhod, *A*
11: 28 *A* from Anathoth, Sibbecai
27: 12 was *A* the Anathothite,

ABIEZRITE (ABIEZER)
Jdg 6: 11 that belonged to Joash the *A*,

ABIEZRITES (ABIEZER)
Jdg 6: 24 stands in Ophrah of the *A*.
6: 34 summoning the *A* to follow him.
8: 32 Joash in Ophrah of the *A*.

ABIGAIL
1Sa 25: 3 and his wife's name was *A*.
25: 14 of the servants told Nabal's wife *A*:
25: 18 *A* lost no time.
25: 23 to him!" When *A* saw David,
25: 32 David said to *A*, "Praise be
25: 36 When *A* went to Nabal, he was
25: 39 Then David sent word to *A*,
25: 40 went to Carmel and said to *A*,
25: 42 *A* quickly got on a donkey and,
27: 3 of Jezreel and *A* of Carmel,
30: 5 Ahinoam of Jezreel and *A*,
2Sa 2: 2 Ahinoam of Jezreel and *A*,
3: 3 Kileab the son of *A* the widow
17: 25 an Israelite who had married *A*,
1Ch 2: 16 Their sisters were Zeruiah and *A*.
2: 17 *A* was the mother of Amasa,
3: 1 Daniel the son of *A* of Carmel;

ABIHAIL
Nu 3: 35 Merarite clans was Zuriel son of *A*;
1Ch 2: 29 Abishur's wife was named *A*,
5: 14 These were the sons of *A* son
2Ch 11: 18 of David's son Jerimoth and of *A*,
Est 2: 15 the daughter of his uncle *A*) to go
9: 29 So Queen Esther, daughter of *A*,

ABIHU
Ex 6: 23 and she bore him Nadab and *A*,
24: 1 you and Aaron, Nadab and *A*,
24: 9 Moses and Aaron, Nadab and *A*,
28: 1 along with his sons Nadab and *A*,
Lev 10: 1 sons Nadab and *A* took their
Nu 3: 2 were Nadab the firstborn and *A*,
3: 4 and *A*, however, fell dead
26: 60 was the father of Nadab and *A*,
26: 61 *A* died when they made an offering
1Ch 6: 3 Nadab, *A*, Eleazar and Ithamar.
24: 1 The sons of Aaron were Nadab, *A*,
24: 2 and *A* died before their father did,

ABIHUD
1Ch 8: 3 Addar, Gera, *A*, Abishua, Naaman,

ABIJAH (ABIJAH'S)
1Sa 8: 2 and the name of his second was *A*,
1Ki 14: 1 At that time *A* son
14: 31 And *A* his son succeeded him
15: 1 *A* became king of Judah,
15: 7 There was war between *A*
15: 8 And *A* rested with his fathers
2Ki 18: 2 His mother's name was *A* daughter
1Ch 2: 24 *A* the wife of Hezron bore him
3: 10 son was Rehoboam, *A* his son,
6: 28 the firstborn and *A* the second son.
7: 8 Elioenai, Omri, Jeremoth, *A*,
24: 10 the eighth to *A*, the ninth to Jeshua
2Ch 11: 20 who bore him *A*, Attai, Ziza
11: 22 Rehoboam appointed *A* son
12: 16 And *A* his son succeeded him
13: 1 reign of Jeroboam, *A* became king
13: 2 There was war between *A*
13: 3 *A* went into battle with a force
13: 4 *A* stood on Mount Zemaraim,
13: 15 and all Israel before *A* and Judah.
13: 17 *A* and his men inflicted heavy
13: 19 *A* pursued Jeroboam and took

2Ch 13: 20 power during the time of *A*.
13: 21 But *A* grew in strength.
14: 1 And *A* rested with his fathers
29: 1 His mother's name was *A* daughter
Ne 10: 7 Baruch, Meshullam, *A*, Mijamin,
12: 4 Iddo, Ginnethon, *A*, Mijamin,
Mt 1: 7 the father of *A*, *A* the father of Asa,
Lk 1: 5 to the priestly division of *A*;

ABIJAH'S (ABIJAH)
1Ki 15: 6 Jeroboam throughout *A* lifetime.
15: 7 As for the other events of *A* reign,
2Ch 13: 22 The other events of *A* reign,
Ne 12: 17 of Ginnethon's, Meshullam; of *A*,

ABILENE
Lk 3: 1 and Lysanias tetrarch of *A*—

ABILITY (ABLE)
Ge 47: 6 of any among them with special *a*,
Ex 31: 3 *a* and knowledge in all kinds
35: 31 *a* and knowledge in all kinds
35: 34 tribe of Dan, the *a* to teach others.
36: 1 and *a* to know how to carry out all
36: 2 to whom the LORD had given *a*
Dt 8: 18 for it is he who gives you the *a*
Ezr 2: 69 According to their *a* they gave
Da 5: 12 and also the *a* to interpret dreams,
Mt 25: 15 one talent, each according to his *a*.
Ac 8: 19 also this *a* so that everyone
11: 29 disciples, each according to his *a*,
1Co 12: 10 to another the *a* to distinguish
12: 10 to another the *a* to speak
2Co 1: 8 far beyond our *a* to endure,
8: 3 were able, and even beyond their *a*.

ABIMAEL
Ge 10: 28 Diklah, Obal, *A*, Sheba, Ophir,
1Ch 1: 22 Diklah, Obal, *A*, Sheba, Ophir,

ABIMELECH (ABIMELECH'S)
Ge 20: 2 *A* king of Gerar sent for Sarah
20: 3 came to *A* in a dream one night
20: 4 Now *A* had not gone near her,
20: 8 the next morning *A* summoned all
20: 9 Then *A* called Abraham in and said
20: 10 *A* asked Abraham, "What was your
20: 14 Then *A* brought sheep and cattle
20: 15 And *A* said, "My land is before you
20: 17 prayed to God, and God healed *A*,
21: 22 At that time *A* and Phicol
21: 25 Abraham complained to *A* about
21: 26 *A* said, "I don't know who has done
21: 27 and cattle and gave them to *A*,
21: 29 the flock, and *A* asked Abraham,
21: 32 *A* and Phicol the commander
26: 1 and Isaac went to *A* king
26: 8 *A* king of the Philistines looked
26: 9 So *A* summoned Isaac and said,
26: 10 *A* said, "What is this you have done
26: 11 So *A* gave orders to all the people:
26: 16 Then *A* said to Isaac, "Move away
26: 26 *A* had come to him from Gerar,
Jdg 8: 31 bore him a son, whom he named *A*.
9: 1 *A* son of Jerub-Baal went
9: 3 they were inclined to follow *A*,
9: 4 and *A* used them to hire reckless
9: 6 in Shechem to crown *A* king.
9: 16 faith when you made *A* king,
9: 18 made *A*, the son of his slave girl,
9: 19 may *A* be your joy, and may you be
9: 20 consume *A*!" Then Jotham fled,
9: 20 let fire come out from *A*
9: 21 he was afraid of his brother *A*.
9: 22 After *A* had governed Israel three
9: 23 God sent an evil spirit between *A*
9: 23 who acted treacherously against *A*.
9: 24 avenged on their brother *A*
9: 25 and this was reported to *A*.
9: 27 and drinking, they cursed *A*.
9: 28 father! Why should we serve *A*?
9: 28 "Who is *A*, and who is Shechem,
9: 29 to *A*, 'Call out your whole army!' "
9: 31 cover he sent messengers to *A*,
9: 34 *A* and all his troops set out by night
9: 35 as *A* and his soldiers came out
9: 38 'Who is *A* that we should be subject
9: 39 citizens of Shechem and fought *A*.

Jdg 9: 40 *A* chased him, and many fell
9: 41 *A* stayed in Arumah, and Zebul
9: 42 and this was reported to *A*.
9: 44 *A* and the companies
9: 45 All that day *A* pressed his attack
9: 47 When *A* heard that they had
9: 49 men cut branches and followed *A*.
9: 50 Next *A* went to Thebez
9: 52 *A* went to the tower and stormed it.
9: 55 the Israelites saw that *A* was dead,
9: 56 the wickedness that *A* had done
10: 1 After the time of *A* a man
2Sa 11: 21 Who killed *A* son of Jerub-Besheth

ABIMELECH'S (ABIMELECH)

Ge 20: 18 up every womb in *A* household
21: 25 of water that *A* servants had seized.

ABINADAB (ABINADAB'S)

1Sa 16: 8 Jesse called *A* and had him pass
17: 13 the second, *A*; and the third,
31: 2 they killed his sons Jonathan, *A*
2Sa 6: 3 Uzzah and Ahio, sons of *A*,
6: 3 and brought it from the house of *A*,
1Ch 2: 13 the second son was *A*, the third
8: 33 Malki-Shua, *A* and Esh-Baal.
9: 39 Malki-Shua, *A* and Esh-Baal.
10: 2 they killed his sons Jonathan, *A*

ABINADAB'S (ABINADAB)

1Sa 7: 1 They took it to *A* house on the hill
1Ch 13: 7 of God from *A* house on a new cart,

ABINOAM

Jdg 4: 6 for Barak son of *A* from Kedesh
4: 12 of *A* had gone up to Mount Tabor,
5: 1 and Barak son of *A* sang this song:
5: 12 captive your captives, O son of *A*.

ABIRAM

Nu 16: 1 Dathan and *A*, sons of Eliab,
16: 12 Moses summoned Dathan and *A*,
16: 24 tents of Korah, Dathan and *A*.' "
16: 25 and went to Dathan and *A*,
16: 27 Dathan and *A* had come out
16: 27 the tents of Korah, Dathan and *A*.
26: 9 Eliab were Nemuel, Dathan and *A*.
26: 9 *A* were the community officials
Dt 11: 6 and what he did to Dathan and *A*,
1Ki 16: 34 at the cost of his firstborn son *A*,
Ps 106: 17 it buried the company of *A*.

ABISHAG

1Ki 1: 3 for a beautiful girl and found *A*,
1: 15 where *A* the Shunammite was
2: 17 to give me *A* the Shunammite
2: 21 "Let *A* the Shunammite be given
2: 22 do you request *A* the Shunammite

ABISHAI

1Sa 26: 6 Ahimelech the Hittite and *A* son
26: 6 to Saul?" "I'll go with you," said *A*.
26: 7 and *A* went to the army by night,
26: 8 *A* said to David, "Today God has
26: 9 said to *A*, "Don't destroy him!
2Sa 2: 18 sons of Zeruiah were there: Joab, *A*
2: 24 But Joab and *A* pursued Abner,
3: 30 and his brother *A* murdered Abner
10: 10 the command of *A* his brother
10: 14 they fled before *A* and went
16: 9 *A* son of Zeruiah said to the king,
16: 11 said to *A* and all his officials,
18: 2 a third under Joab's brother *A* son
18: 5 The king commanded Joab, *A*
18: 12 the king commanded you and *A*
19: 21 Then *A* son of Zeruiah said,
20: 6 David said to *A*, "Now Sheba son
20: 7 out under the command of *A*.
20: 10 his brother *A* pursued Sheba son
21: 17 But *A* son of Zeruiah came
23: 18 *A* the brother of Joab son
1Ch 2: 16 Zeruiah's three sons were *A*,
11: 20 *A* the brother of Joab was chief
18: 12 *A* son of Zeruiah struck
19: 11 the command of *A* his brother,
19: 15 they too fled before his brother *A*

ABISHALOM

1Ki 15: 2 name was Maacah daughter of *A*.
15: 10 name was Maacah daughter of *A*.

ABISHUA

1Ch 6: 5 father of *A*, *A* the father of Bukki,
6: 50 Phinehas his son, *A* his son,
8: 4 Gera, Abihud, *A*, Naaman, Ahoah,
Ezr 7: 5 the son of *A*, the son of Phinehas,

ABISHUR (ABISHUR'S)

1Ch 2: 28 sons of Shammai: Nadab and *A*.

ABISHUR'S (ABISHUR)

1Ch 2: 29 *A* wife was named Abihail,

ABITAL

2Sa 3: 4 Shephatiah the son of *A*;
1Ch 3: 3 Shephatiah the son of *A*;

ABITUB

1Ch 8: 11 By Hushim he had *A* and Elpaal.

ABIUD

Mt 1: 13 father of *A*, *A* the father of Eliakim,

ABLAZE

Dt 5: 23 while the mountain was *a* with fire,
9: 15 mountain while it was *a* with fire.
Job 41: 21 His breath sets coals *a*,
Ps 83: 14 or a flame sets the mountains *a*,
Isa 9: 18 it sets the forest thickets *a*,
30: 33 sets it *a*.
33: 12 cut thornbushes they will be set *a*."
43: 2 the flames will not set you *a*.
50: 11 and of the torches you have set *a*.
64: 2 As when fire sets twigs *a*
Da 7: 9 and its wheels were all *a*.
Rev 8: 8 all *a*, was thrown into the sea.

ABLE (ABILITY ABLE-BODIED ENABLE ENABLED ENABLES ENABLING)

Ge 13: 6 were so great that they were not *a*
14: 23 so that you will never be *a* to say,
45: 3 But his brothers were not *a*
Ex 7: 18 the Egyptians will not be *a*
18: 23 you will be *a* to stand the strain,
Lev 26: 26 ten women will be *a*
26: 37 So you will not be *a* to stand
Nu 1: 3 or more who are *a* to serve
1: 20 or more who were *a* to serve
1: 22 or more who were *a* to serve
1: 24 or more who were *a* to serve
1: 26 or more who were *a* to serve
1: 28 or more who were *a* to serve
1: 30 or more who were *a* to serve
1: 32 or more who were *a* to serve
1: 34 or more who were *a* to serve
1: 36 or more who were *a* to serve
1: 38 or more who were *a* to serve
1: 40 or more who were *a* to serve
1: 42 or more who were *a* to serve
1: 45 or more who were *a* to serve
5: 28 and will be *a* to have children.
14: 16 'The LORD was not *a*
22: 6 Perhaps then I will be *a*
22: 11 Perhaps then I will be *a*
22: 37 Am I really not *a* to reward you?"
26: 2 or more who are *a* to serve
Dt 7: 24 No one will be *a* to stand up
9: 28 'Because the LORD was not *a*
11: 25 No man will be *a* to stand
31: 2 and I am no longer *a* to lead you.
Jos 1: 5 No one will be *a* to stand up
10: 8 of them will be *a* to withstand you
17: 12 Yet the Manassites were not *a*
22: 27 your descendants will not be *a*
23: 9 to this day no one has been *a*
24: 19 "You are not *a* to serve the LORD.
Jdg 2: 14 whom they were no longer *a*
8: 3 What was I *a* to do compared
1Sa 17: 9 If he is *a* to fight and kill me,
17: 33 "You are not *a* to go out
1Ki 3: 9 For who is *a* to govern this great
2Ki 2: 16 "we your servants have fifty *a* men.
9: 37 so that no one will be *a* to say,
18: 35 gods of these countries has been *a*
1Ch 9: 13 They were *a* men, responsible
12: 2 and were *a* to shoot arrows
12: 8 ready for battle and *a*
26: 7 and Semakiah were also *a* men.
26: 9 who were *a* men—18 in all.
26: 30 seventeen hundred *a* men—
26: 32 who were *a* men and heads
29: 14 that we should be *a* to give
2Ch 1: 10 for who is *a* to govern this great
2: 6 who is *a* to build a temple for him,
13: 3 eight hundred thousand *a* troops.
13: 3 hundred thousand *a* fighting men,
13: 17 casualties among Israel's *a* men.
20: 37 and were not *a* to set sail to trade.
25: 5 *a* to handle the spear and shield.
30: 3 They had not been *a* to celebrate it
32: 13 the gods of those nations ever *a*
32: 14 my fathers destroyed has been *a*
32: 15 or kingdom has been *a*
Ne 8: 2 and all who were *a* to understand.
10: 28 daughters who are *a* to understand
Job 41: 10 Who then is *a* to stand against me?
Ps 36: 12 thrown down, not *a* to rise!
Isa 36: 20 gods of these countries has been *a*
Eze 7: 19 and gold will not be *a* to save them
Da 2: 26 "Are you *a* to tell me what I saw
2: 47 for you were *a* to reveal this
3: 15 what god will be *a* to rescue you
3: 17 the God we serve is *a* to save us
4: 37 walk in pride he is *a* to humble.
5: 16 Now I have heard that you are *a*
6: 20 been *a* to rescue you from the lions
11: 16 no one will be *a* to stand
11: 25 but he will not be *a* to stand
Hos 5: 13 But he is not *a* to cure you,
5: 13 not *a* to heal your sores.
Zep 1: 18 will be *a* to save them
Mt 9: 28 "Do you believe that I am *a*
18: 25 Since he was not *a* to pay,
26: 61 'I am *a* to destroy the temple
Mk 3: 20 his disciples were not even *a* to eat.
6: 19 she was not *a* to, because Herod
Lk 1: 20 not *a* to speak until the day this
8: 19 but they were not *a* to get near him
13: 24 will try to enter and will not be *a* to
14: 29 he lays the foundation and is not *a*
14: 30 to build and was not *a* to finish.'
14: 31 he is *a* with ten thousand men
14: 32 If he is not *a*, he will send
21: 15 none of your adversaries will be *a*
21: 36 and pray that you may be *a*
21: 36 and that you may be *a* to stand
Jn 18: 28 they wanted to be *a*
Ac 5: 39 you will not be *a* to stop these men;
15: 10 our fathers have been *a* to bear?
19: 40 In that case we would not be *a*
22: 13 And at that very moment I was *a*
24: 8 him yourself you will be *a*
27: 16 we were hardly *a* to make
Ro 8: 39 will be *a* to separate us
11: 23 for God is *a* to graft them in again.
12: 2 Then you will be *a* to test
14: 4 for the Lord is *a* to make him stand
16: 25 to him who is *a* to establish you
1Co 12: 28 of healing, those *a* to help others,
2Co 8: 3 they gave as much as they were *a*,
9: 8 God is *a* to make all grace abound
Eph 3: 4 you will be *a* to understand my
3: 20 him who is *a* to do immeasurably
6: 13 you may be *a* to stand your ground,
Php 1: 10 so that you may be *a*
1Ti 3: 2 respectable, hospitable, *a* to teach,
2Ti 1: 12 and am convinced that he is *a*
2: 24 kind to everyone, *a* to teach,
3: 7 never *a* to acknowledge the truth.
3: 15 which are *a* to make you wise
Heb 2: 18 he is *a* to help those who are being
3: 19 we see that they were not *a* to enter
5: 2 He is *a* to deal gently
7: 25 he is *a* to save completely
9: 9 sacrifices being offered were not *a*
Jas 3: 2 *a* to keep his whole body in check.
4: 12 the one who is *a* to save
2Pe 1: 15 my departure you will always be *a*
Jude : 24 To him who is *a* to keep you
Rev 5: 5 He is *a* to open the scroll

ABLE-BODIED (ABLE)

Dt 3: 18 all your *a* men, armed for battle,

2Sa 24: 9 hundred thousand *a* men who
1Ch 5: 18 *a* men who could handle shield

ABNER (ABNER'S)

1Sa 14: 50 of Saul's army was *A* son of Ner,
17: 55 commander of the army, "*A*,
17: 55 he said to *A*, commander
17: 55 son is that young man?" *A* replied,
17: 57 *A* took him and brought him
20: 25 and *A* sat next to Saul,
26: 5 He saw where Saul and *A* son
26: 7 *A* and the soldiers were lying
26: 14 going to answer me, *A*?" *A* replied,
26: 14 to the army and to *A* son of Ner,
2Sa 2: 8 Meanwhile, *A* son of Ner,
2: 12 *A* son of Ner, together
2: 14 *A* said to Joab, "Let's have some
2: 17 and *A* and the men of Israel were
2: 19 He chased *A*, turning neither
2: 20 *A* looked behind him and asked,
2: 21 *A* said to him, "Turn aside
2: 22 *A* warned Asahel, "Stop chasing
2: 23 so *A* thrust the butt of his spear
2: 24 But Joab and Abishai pursued *A*,
2: 25 men of Benjamin rallied behind *A*.
2: 26 *A* called out to Joab, "Must
2: 29 All that night *A* and his men
2: 30 Joab returned from pursuing *A*
2: 31 sixty Benjamites who were with *A*.
3: 6 *A* had been strengthening his own
3: 7 And Ish-Bosheth said to *A*,
3: 8 *A* was very angry because of what
3: 9 May God deal with *A*, be it ever
3: 11 dare to say another word to *A*,
3: 12 *A* sent messengers on his behalf
3: 16 *A* said to him, "Go back home!"
3: 17 *A* conferred with the elders
3: 19 *A* also spoke to the Benjamites
3: 20 When *A*, who had twenty men
3: 21 So David sent *A* away,
3: 21 Then *A* said to David, "Let me go
3: 22 But *A* was no longer with David
3: 23 he was told that *A* son
3: 24 have you done? Look, *A* came
3: 25 he is gone! You know *A* son of Ner;
3: 26 and sent messengers after *A*,
3: 27 Now when *A* returned to Hebron,
3: 28 concerning the blood of *A* son
3: 30 his brother Abishai murdered *A*
3: 31 walk in mourning in front of *A*."
3: 32 They buried *A* in Hebron,
3: 33 The king sang this lament for *A*:
3: 33 "Should *A* have died as the lawless
3: 37 part in the murder of *A* son of Ner.
4: 1 son of Saul heard that *A* had died
1Ki 2: 5 *A* son of Ner and Amasa son
2: 32 Both of them—*A* son of Ner,
1Ch 26: 28 *A* son of Ner and Joab son
27: 21 Jaasiel son of *A*; over Dan:

ABNER'S (ABNER)

1Sa 14: 51 *A* father Ner were sons of Abiel.
2Sa 3: 32 and the king wept aloud at *A* tomb.
4: 12 and buried it in *A* tomb at Hebron.

ABOARD (BOARD)

Eze 27: 8 O Tyre, were *a* as your seamen.
Jnh 1: 3 he went *a* and sailed for Tarshish
Jn 21: 11 Simon Peter climbed *a*
Ac 20: 13 where we were going to take Paul *a*
20: 14 we took him *a* and went
21: 6 we went *a* the ship, and they
27: 17 When the men had hoisted it *a*,

ABODE

Job 38: 19 "What is the way to the *a* of light?
Isa 33: 20 a peaceful *a*, a tent that will not be

ABOLISH (ABOLISHED ABOLISHING)

Da 11: 31 and will *a* the daily sacrifice.
Hos 2: 18 I will *a* from the land,
Mt 5: 17 I have not come to *a* them
5: 17 that I have come to *a* the Law

ABOLISHED (ABOLISH)

Da 12: 11 the time that the daily sacrifice is *a*
Gal 5: 11 the offense of the cross has been *a*.

ABOLISHING (ABOLISH)

Eph 2: 15 by *a* in his flesh the law

ABOMINABLE (ABOMINATION)

Isa 66: 17 and rats and other *a* things—
Jer 32: 34 They set up their *a* idols
Rev 17: 4 filled with *a* things and the filth

ABOMINATION (ABOMINABLE ABOMINATIONS)

Da 11: 31 set up the *a* that causes desolation.
12: 11 *a* that causes desolation is set up,
Mt 24: 15 the holy place 'the *a* that causes
Mk 13: 14 you see 'the *a* that causes

ABOMINATIONS (ABOMINATION)

Pr 26: 25 for seven *a* fill his heart.
Isa 66: 3 and their souls delight in their *a*;
Da 9: 27 who causes desolation will place *a*
Rev 17: 5 AND OF THE *A* OF THE EARTH.

ABOUND (ABOUNDING ABOUNDS)

2Ki 9: 22 of your mother Jezebel *a*?"
Ps 4: 7 when their grain and new wine *a*.
72: 7 prosperity will *a* till the moon is no
72: 16 Let grain *a* throughout the land;
2Co 9: 8 able to make all grace *a* to you,
9: 8 you will *a* in every good work.
Php 1: 9 that your love may *a* more

ABOUNDING (ABOUND)

Ex 34: 6 slow to anger, *a* in love
Nu 14: 18 *a* in love and forgiving sin
Dt 33: 23 "Naphtali is *a* with the favor
Ne 9: 17 slow to anger and *a* in love.
Ps 86: 5 *a* in love to all who call to you.
86: 15 slow to anger, *a* in love
103: 8 slow to anger, *a* in love.
Pr 8: 24 when there were no springs *a*
Joel 2: 13 slow to anger and *a* in love,
Jnh 4: 2 slow to anger and *a* in love,

ABOUNDS (ABOUND)

Hab 1: 3 there is strife, and conflict *a*.

ABRAHAM (ABRAHAM'S ABRAM ABRAM'S)

Ge 17: 5 your name will be *A*,
17: 9 Then God said to *A*, "As for you,
17: 15 said to *A*, "As for Sarai your wife,
17: 17 *A* fell facedown; he laughed
17: 18 age of ninety?" And *A* said to God,
17: 22 he had finished speaking with *A*,
17: 23 On that very day *A* took his son
17: 24 *A* was ninety-nine years old
17: 26 *A* and his son Ishmael were both
18: 1 The LORD appeared to *A*
18: 2 *A* looked up and saw three men
18: 6 So *A* hurried into the tent to Sarah.
18: 11 *A* and Sarah were already old
18: 13 Then the LORD said to *A*,
18: 16 and *A* walked along with them
18: 17 Shall I hide from *A* what I am about
18: 18 *A* will surely become a great
18: 19 for *A* what he has promised him."
18: 22 but *A* remained standing
18: 23 Then *A* approached him and said:
18: 27 Then *A* spoke up again:
18: 31 *A* said, "Now that I have been
18: 33 had finished speaking with *A*,
18: 33 he left, and *A* returned home.
19: 27 Early the next morning *A* got up
19: 29 of the plain, he remembered *A*,
20: 1 Now *A* moved on from there
20: 2 and there *A* said of his wife Sarah,
20: 9 Then Abimelech called *A* in
20: 10 Abimelech asked *A*, "What was
20: 11 *A* replied, "I said to myself,
20: 14 female slaves and gave them to *A*,
20: 17 Then *A* prayed to God,
21: 2 and bore a son to *A* in his old age,
21: 3 *A* gave the name Isaac
21: 4 *A* circumcised him, as God
21: 5 *A* was a hundred years old
21: 7 said to *A* that Sarah would nurse
21: 8 Isaac was weaned *A* held a great
21: 9 borne to *A* was mocking,
21: 10 and she said to *A*, "Get rid
Ge 21: 11 The matter distressed *A* greatly
21: 14 the next morning *A* took some food
21: 22 commander of his forces said to *A*,
21: 24 *A* said, "I swear it."
21: 25 *A* complained to Abimelech about
21: 27 So *A* brought sheep and cattle
21: 28 *A* set apart seven ewe lambs
21: 29 the flock, and Abimelech asked *A*,
21: 33 *A* planted a tamarisk tree
21: 34 And *A* stayed in the land
22: 1 He said to him, "*A*!" "Here I am,"
22: 1 Some time later God tested *A*.
22: 3 Early the next morning *A* got up
22: 4 On the third day *A* looked up
22: 6 *A* took the wood for the burnt
22: 7 Father?" "Yes, my son?" *A* replied.
22: 7 spoke up and said to his father *A*,
22: 8 for the burnt offering?" *A* answered
22: 9 *A* built an altar there and arranged
22: 11 "*A*! *A*!" "Here I am," he replied.
22: 13 *A* looked up and there
22: 14 So *A* called that place "The LORD
22: 15 The angel of the LORD called to *A*
22: 19 And *A* stayed in Beersheba.
22: 19 Then *A* returned to his servants,
22: 20 Some time later *A* was told,
23: 2 and *A* went to mourn for Sarah
23: 3 *A* rose from beside his dead wife
23: 5 The Hittites replied to *A*, "Sir,
23: 7 Then *A* rose and bowed
23: 10 and he replied to *A* in the hearing
23: 12 *A* bowed down before the people
23: 14 Ephron answered *A*, "Listen to me,
23: 16 *A* agreed to Ephron's terms
23: 18 was deeded to *A* as his property
23: 19 Afterward *A* buried his wife Sarah
23: 20 deeded to *A* by the Hittites
24: 1 *A* was now old and well advanced
24: 6 take my son back there," *A* said.
24: 9 under the thigh of his master *A*
24: 12 and show kindness to my master *A*.
24: 12 of my master *A*, give me success
24: 27 LORD, the God of my master *A*,
24: 42 God of my master *A*, if you will,
24: 48 LORD, the God of my master *A*,
25: 1 *A* took another wife, whose name
25: 5 *A* left everything he owned to Isaac
25: 7 *A* lived a hundred and seventy-five
25: 8 Then *A* breathed his last
25: 10 There *A* was buried
25: 10 the field *A* had bought
25: 12 Hagar the Egyptian, bore to *A*.
25: 19 *A* became the father of Isaac,
26: 3 the oath I swore to your father *A*.
26: 5 because *A* obeyed me and kept my
26: 15 dug in the time of his father *A*,
26: 18 dug in the time of his father *A*,
26: 18 had stopped up after *A* died,
26: 24 for the sake of my servant *A*."
26: 24 "I am the God of your father *A*.
28: 4 an alien, the land God gave to *A*."
28: 4 your descendants the blessing of *A*,
28: 9 and daughter of Ishmael son of *A*,
28: 13 the God of your father *A*
31: 42 the God of *A* and the Fear of Isaac,
31: 53 May the God of *A* and the God
32: 9 "O God of my father *A*, God
35: 12 The land I gave to *A* and Isaac I
35: 27 where *A* and Isaac had stayed.
48: 15 *A* and Isaac walked,
48: 16 and the names of my fathers *A*
49: 30 which *A* bought as a burial place
49: 31 There *A* and his wife Sarah were
50: 13 which *A* had bought as a burial
50: 24 the land he promised on oath to *A*,
Ex 2: 24 remembered his covenant with *A*,
3: 6 the God of *A*, the God of Isaac
3: 15 of your fathers—the God of *A*,
3: 16 the God of *A*, Isaac and Jacob,
4: 5 of their fathers—the God of *A*,
6: 3 I appeared to *A*, to Isaac
6: 8 with uplifted hand to give to *A*,
32: 13 Remember your servants *A*,
33: 1 to the land I promised on oath to *A*,
Lev 26: 42 with Isaac and my covenant with *A*
Nu 32: 11 the land I promised on oath to *A*,
Dt 1: 8 to *A*, Isaac and Jacob—
6: 10 to *A*, Isaac and Jacob, to give you

Dt 9: 5 swore to your fathers, to *A*,
9: 27 Remember your servants *A*,
29: 13 and as he swore to your fathers, *A*,
30: 20 swore to give to your fathers, *A*,
34: 4 is the land I promised on oath to *A*,
Jos 24: 2 including Terah the father of *A*
24: 3 I took your father *A* from the land
1Ki 18: 36 God of *A*, Isaac and Israel,
2Ki 13: 23 because of his covenant with *A*,
1Ch 1: 27 Terah and Abram (that is, *A*).
1: 28 The sons of *A:* Isaac and Ishmael.
1: 34 *A* was the father of Isaac.
16: 16 the covenant he made with *A*,
29: 18 God of our fathers *A*, Isaac
2Ch 20: 7 to the descendants of *A* your friend
30: 6 the God of *A*, Isaac and Israel,
Ne 9: 7 of the Chaldeans and named him *A*
Ps 47: 9 as the people of the God of *A*,
105: 6 O descendants of *A* his servant,
105: 9 the covenant he made with *A*,
105: 42 given to his servant *A*.
Isa 29: 22 who redeemed *A*, says to the house
41: 8 you descendants of *A* my friend,
51: 2 look to *A*, your father,
63: 16 though *A* does not know us
Jer 33: 26 to rule over the descendants of *A*,
Eze 33: 24 '*A* was only one man, yet he
Mic 7: 20 and show mercy to *A*,
Mt 1: 1 the son of *A: A* was the father
1: 17 generations in all from *A* to David,
3: 9 God can raise up children for *A*.
3: 9 'We have *A* as our father.'
8: 11 places at the feast with *A*,
22: 32 I am the God of *A*, the God of Isaac
Mk 12: 26 I am the God of *A*, the God of Isaac
Lk 1: 55 to *A* and his descendants forever,
1: 73 the oath he swore to our father *A:*
3: 8 God can raise up children for *A*.
3: 8 'We have *A* as our father.'
3: 34 the son of Isaac, the son of *A*,
13: 16 not this woman, a daughter of *A*,
13: 28 gnashing of teeth, when you see *A*,
16: 23 he looked up and saw *A* far away,
16: 24 So he called to him, 'Father *A*,
16: 25 *A* replied, 'Son, remember that
16: 29 "*A* replied, 'They have Moses
16: 30 father *A*,' he said, 'but if someone
19: 9 because this man, too, is a son of *A*.
20: 37 for he calls the Lord 'the God of *A*,
Jn 8: 39 then you would do the things *A* did
8: 39 "*A* is our father," they answered.
8: 40 *A* did not do such things.
8: 52 *A* died and so did the prophets,
8: 53 Are you greater than our father *A?*
8: 56 Your father *A* rejoiced
8: 57 "and you have seen *A!*" "I tell you
8: 58 "before *A* was born,
Ac 3: 13 The God of *A*, Isaac and Jacob,
3: 25 to *A*, 'Through your offspring all
7: 2 to our father *A* while he was still
7: 5 though at that time *A* had no child.
7: 8 And *A* became the father of Isaac
7: 8 Then he gave *A* the covenant
7: 16 in the tomb that *A* had bought
7: 17 for God to fulfill his promise to *A*,
7: 32 the God of *A*, Isaac and Jacob.'
13: 26 of *A*, and you God-fearing Gentiles
Ro 4: 1 What then shall we say that *A*,
4: 2 If, in fact, *A* was justified by works,
4: 3 Scripture say? "*A* believed God,
4: 12 of the faith that our father *A* had
4: 13 It was not through law that *A*
4: 16 to those who are of the faith of *A*.
4: 18 *A* in hope believed
11: 1 a descendant of *A*, from the tribe
Gal 3: 6 Consider *A:* "He believed God,
3: 7 who believe are children of *A*.
3: 8 the gospel in advance to *A:*
3: 9 have faith are blessed along with *A*,
3: 14 to *A* might come to the Gentiles
3: 16 The promises were spoken to *A*
3: 18 it to *A* through a promise.
4: 22 it is written that *A* had two sons,
Heb 6: 13 When God made his promise to *A*,
6: 15 *A* received what was promised.
7: 1 He met *A* returning from the defeat
7: 2 *A* gave him a tenth of everything.
7: 4 Even the patriarch *A* gave him
Heb 7: 5 brothers are descended from *A*.
7: 6 yet he collected a tenth from *A*
7: 9 paid the tenth through *A*,
7: 10 because when Melchizedek met *A*,
11: 8 By faith *A*, when called to go
11: 11 By faith *A*, even though he was past
11: 17 By faith *A*, when God tested him,
11: 19 *A* reasoned that God could raise
Jas 2: 21 our ancestor *A* considered
2: 23 that says, "*A* believed God,
1Pe 3: 6 who obeyed *A* and called him her

ABRAHAM'S (ABRAHAM)

Ge 17: 27 And every male in *A* household,
20: 18 household because of *A* wife Sarah.
22: 23 sons to *A* brother Nahor.
24: 15 the wife of *A* brother Nahor.
24: 34 So he said, "I am *A* servant.
24: 52 When *A* servant heard what they
24: 59 and *A* servant and his men.
25: 11 After *A* death, God blessed his son
25: 12 is the account of *A* son Ishmael,
25: 19 This is the account of *A* son Isaac.
26: 1 besides the earlier famine of *A* time
1Ch 1: 32 *A* concubine: Zimran, Jokshan,
Lk 16: 22 the angels carried him to *A* side.
Jn 8: 33 "We are *A* descendants
8: 37 I know you are *A* descendants.
8: 39 If you were *A* children," said Jesus,
Ro 4: 9 been saying that *A* faith was
4: 16 guaranteed to all *A* offspring—
9: 7 are they all *A* children.
9: 8 who are regarded as *A* offspring.
2Co 11: 22 Are they *A* descendants? So am I.
Gal 3: 29 then you are *A* seed, and heirs
Heb 2: 16 angels he helps, but *A* descendants.

ABRAM (ABRAHAM)

Ge 11: 26 he became the father of *A*,
11: 27 Terah became the father of *A*,
11: 29 *A* and Nahor both married.
11: 31 Sarai, the wife of his son *A*,
11: 31 took his son *A*, his grandson Lot
12: 1 The LORD had said to *A*,
12: 4 *A* left, as the LORD had told him;
12: 4 *A* was seventy-five years old
12: 6 *A* traveled through the land as far
12: 7 the LORD appeared to *A* and said,
12: 9 Then *A* set out and continued
12: 10 *A* went down to Egypt to live there
12: 14 When *A* came to Egypt,
12: 16 He treated *A* well for her sake,
12: 16 and *A* acquired sheep and cattle,
12: 18 So Pharaoh summoned *A*.
12: 20 Then Pharaoh gave orders about *A*
13: 1 So *A* went up from Egypt
13: 2 *A* had become very wealthy
13: 4 There *A* called on the name
13: 5 who was moving about with *A*,
13: 8 *A* said to Lot, "Let's not have any
13: 12 *A* lived in the land of Canaan,
13: 14 The LORD said to *A*
13: 18 *A* moved his tents and went to live
14: 13 *A* was living near the great trees
14: 13 all of whom were allied with *A*.
14: 13 and reported this to *A* the Hebrew.
14: 14 When *A* heard that his relative had
14: 15 During the night *A* divided his men
14: 17 *A* returned from defeating
14: 19 God Most High, and he blessed *A*,
14: 19 "Blessed be *A* by God Most High,
14: 20 *A* gave him a tenth of everything.
14: 21 The king of Sodom said to *A*,
14: 22 But *A* said to the king of Sodom,
14: 23 able to say, 'I made *A* rich.'
15: 1 of the LORD came to *A* in a vision:
15: 1 "Do not be afraid, *A*.
15: 2 But *A* said, "O Sovereign LORD,
15: 3 *A* said, "You have given me no
15: 6 *A* believed the LORD,
15: 8 But *A* said, "O Sovereign LORD,
15: 10 *A* brought all these to him,
15: 11 the carcasses, but *A* drove them
15: 12 As the sun was setting, *A* fell
15: 18 LORD made a covenant with *A*
16: 2 *A* agreed to what Sarai said.
16: 2 said to *A*, "The LORD has kept me
16: 3 So after *A* had been living
Ge 16: 5 said to *A*, "You are responsible
16: 6 is in your hands," *A* said.
16: 15 So Hagar bore *A* a son,
16: 15 and *A* gave the name Ishmael
16: 16 *A* was eighty-six years old
17: 1 When *A* was ninety-nine years old,
17: 3 *A* fell facedown, and God said
17: 5 No longer will you be called *A;*
1Ch 1: 27 Nahor, Terah and *A* (that is,
Ne 9: 7 who chose *A* and brought him out

ABRAM'S (ABRAHAM)

Ge 11: 29 The name of *A* wife was Sarai,
12: 17 household because of *A* wife Sarai.
13: 7 arose between *A* herdsmen
14: 12 They also carried off *A* nephew Lot
16: 1 *A* wife, had borne him no children.

ABROAD

Ps 41: 6 then he goes out and spreads it *a*.
112: 9 He has scattered *a* his gifts
SS 4: 16 that its fragrance may spread *a*.
2Co 9: 9 "He has scattered *a* his gifts

ABRONAH

Nu 33: 34 left Jotbathah and camped at *A*.
33: 35 They left *A* and camped

ABSALOM (ABSALOM'S)

2Sa 3: 3 *A* the son of Maacah daughter
13: 1 sister of *A* son of David.
13: 20 Her brother *A* said to her,
13: 22 *A* never said a word to Amnon,
13: 24 *A* went to the king and said,
13: 25 Although *A* urged him, he still
13: 26 Then *A* said, "If not, please let my
13: 27 go with you?" But *A* urged him,
13: 28 *A* ordered his men, "Listen!
13: 29 did to Amnon what *A* had ordered.
13: 30 "*A* has struck down all the king's
13: 34 Meanwhile, *A* had fled.
13: 37 *A* fled and went to Talmai son
13: 38 After *A* fled and went to Geshur,
13: 39 spirit of the king longed to go to *A*,
14: 1 that the king's heart longed for *A*.
14: 21 Go, bring back the young man *A*."
14: 23 and brought *A* back to Jerusalem.
14: 24 So *A* went to his own house
14: 25 for his handsome appearance as *A*.
14: 27 and a daughter were born to *A*.
14: 28 *A* lived two years in Jerusalem
14: 29 *A* sent for Joab in order to send him
14: 32 field on fire?" *A* said to Joab,
14: 33 And the king kissed *A*.
14: 33 Then the king summoned *A*,
15: 1 *A* provided himself with a chariot
15: 2 *A* would call out to him, "What
15: 3 Then *A* would say to him, "Look,
15: 4 And *A* would add, "If only I were
15: 5 *A* would reach out his hand,
15: 6 *A* behaved in this way
15: 7 *A* said to the king, "Let me go
15: 10 Then *A* sent secret messengers
15: 10 then say, '*A* is king in Hebron.' "
15: 11 Jerusalem had accompanied *A*.
15: 12 While *A* was offering sacrifices,
15: 13 the men of Israel are with *A*."
15: 14 or none of us will escape from *A*.
15: 19 Go back and stay with King *A*.
15: 31 is among the conspirators with *A*."
15: 34 return to the city and say to *A*,
15: 37 as *A* was entering the city.
16: 8 the kingdom over to your son *A*.
16: 15 *A* and all the men of Israel came
16: 16 went to *A* and said to him,
16: 17 live the king!" *A* asked Hushai,
16: 18 said to *A*, "No, the one chosen
16: 20 *A* said to Ahithophel, "Give us
16: 22 So they pitched a tent for *A*
16: 23 and *A* regarded all of Ahithophel's
17: 1 said to *A*, "I would choose twelve
17: 4 This plan seemed good to *A*
17: 5 But *A* said, "Summon
17: 6 When Hushai came to him, *A* said,
17: 7 to *A*, "The advice Ahithophel has
17: 9 among the troops who follow *A*.'
17: 14 *A* and all the men of Israel said,
17: 14 in order to bring disaster on *A*.

2Sa 17:15 "Ahithophel has advised *A*
17:18 a young man saw them and told *A*.
17:24 and *A* crossed the Jordan
17:25 *A* had appointed Amasa
17:26 *A* camped in the land of Gilead.
18: 5 king giving orders concerning *A*
18: 5 with the young man *A* for my sake
18: 9 *A* happened to meet David's men.
18:10 "I just saw *A* hanging in an oak tree
18:12 'Protect the young man *A*
18:14 heart while *A* was still alive
18:15 armor-bearers surrounded *A*,
18:17 They took *A*, threw him
18:18 During his lifetime *A* had taken
18:29 "Is the young man *A* safe?"
18:32 "Is the young man *A* safe?"
18:33 O *A*, my son, my son!" Joab was
18:33 "O my son *A!* My son, my son *A!*
19: 1 is weeping and mourning for *A*."
19: 4 "O my son *A!* O *A*, my son, my son
19: 6 pleased if *A* were alive today
19: 9 has fled the country because of *A*;
19:10 and *A*, whom we anointed to rule
20: 6 will do us more harm than *A* did.
1Ki 1: 6 and was born next after *A*.)
2: 7 when I fled from your brother *A*.
2:28 with Adonijah though not with *A*,
1Ch 3: 2 *A* the son of Maacah daughter
2Ch 11:20 he married Maacah daughter of *A*,
11:21 daughter of *A* more than any

ABSALOM'S (ABSALOM)

2Sa 13: 4 with Tamar, my brother *A* sister."
13:20 Tamar lived in her brother *A* house
13:23 *A* sheepshearers were at Baal
13:29 So *A* men did to Amnon what
13:32 has been *A* expressed intention
14:30 So *A* servants set the field on fire.
14:31 Then Joab did go to *A* house
15:12 and *A* following kept on increasing.
17:20 When *A* men came to the woman
18: 9 *A* head got caught in the tree.
18:14 and plunged them into *A* heart
18:18 it is called *A* Monument to this day

ABSENCE (ABSENT)

Ac 24:17 "After an *a* of several years,
Php 1:27 or only hear about you in my *a*,
2:12 but now much more in my *a*—

ABSENT (ABSENCE)

Pr 10:19 When words are many, sin is not *a*,
2Co 10:11 are in our letters when we are *a*,
13: 2 it while *a*: On my return I will not
13:10 I write these things when I am *a*,
Col 2: 5 though I am *a* from you in body,

ABSOLUTE

1Ti 5: 2 women as sisters, with *a* purity.

ABSTAIN (ABSTAINED ABSTAINS)

Ex 19:15 *A* from sexual relations."
Nu 6: 3 he must *a* from wine and other
Ac 15:20 them to *a* from food polluted
15:29 You are to *a* from food sacrificed
21:25 our decision that they should *a*
1Ti 4: 3 order them to *a* from certain foods,
1Pe 2:11 to *a* from sinful desires,

ABSTAINED (ABSTAIN)

Ex 31:17 on the seventh day he *a* from work

ABSTAINS (ABSTAIN)

Ro 14: 6 thanks to God; and he who *a*,

ABUNDANCE (ABUNDANT)

Ge 27:28 an *a* of grain and new wine.
41:29 Seven years of great *a* are coming
41:30 all the *a* in Egypt will be forgotten,
41:31 The *a* in the land will not be
41:34 Egypt during the seven years of *a*.
41:47 of *a* the land produced plentifully.
41:48 in those seven years of *a* in Egypt
41:53 The seven years of *a* in Egypt came
Dt 33:19 they will feast on the *a* of the seas,
1Ch 29:16 for all this *a* that we have provided
29:21 other sacrifices in *a* for all Israel.
2Ch 29:35 There were burnt offerings in *a*,
Ne 9:25 olive groves and fruit trees in *a*.
Job 36:31 and provides food in *a*.
Ps 36: 8 They feast on the *a* of your house;
65:11 and your carts overflow with *a*.
66:12 but you brought us to a place of *a*.
73:10 and drink up waters in *a*.
Pr 20:15 Gold there is, and rubies in *a*,
Ecc 5:12 but the *a* of a rich man
Isa 7:22 of the *a* of the milk they give,
30:33 with an *a* of fire and wood;
33:23 Then an *a* of spoils will be divided
66:11 and delight in her overflowing *a*."
Jer 2:22 and use an *a* of soap,
31:14 I will satisfy the priests with *a*,
40:12 And they harvested an *a* of wine
Mt 13:12 given more, and he will have an *a*.
25:29 given more, and he will have an *a*.
Lk 12:15 consist in the *a* of his possessions."
1Pe 1: 2 Grace and peace be yours in *a*.
2Pe 1: 2 yours in *a* through the knowledge
Jude : 2 peace and love be yours in *a*.

ABUNDANT (ABUNDANCE)

Nu 24: 7 their seed will have *a* water.
Dt 28:11 will grant you *a* prosperity—
32: 2 like *a* rain on tender plants.
2Ch 11:23 He gave them *a* provisions
Ne 5:18 every ten days an *a* supply of wine
9:37 its *a* harvest goes to the kings you
Est 1: 7 the royal wine was *a*, in keeping
Job 36:28 and *a* showers fall on mankind.
Ps 68: 9 You gave *a* showers, O God;
78:15 gave them water as *a* as the seas;
132:15 I will bless her with *a* provisions;
145: 7 will celebrate your *a* goodness
Pr 12:11 works his land will have *a* food,
13:23 man's field may produce *a* food,
14: 4 of an ox comes an *a* harvest.
28:19 works his land will have *a* food,
Isa 23:18 for *a* food and fine clothes.
Jer 33: 6 and will let them enjoy *a* peace
33: 9 and will tremble at the *a* prosperity
Eze 17: 5 planted it like a willow by *a* water,
17: 8 planted in good soil by *a* water
19:10 because of *a* water.
31: 5 spreading because of *a* waters.
31: 7 down to *a* waters.
31: 9 beautiful with *a* branches,
31:15 and its *a* waters were restrained.
32:13 cattle from beside *a* waters
Da 4:12 Its leaves were beautiful, its fruit *a*,
4:21 with beautiful leaves and *a* fruit,
Joel 2:23 He sends you *a* showers,
Ro 5:17 who receive God's *a* provision

ABUSE (ABUSED ABUSIVE)

1Sa 31: 4 and run me through and *a* me."
1Ch 10: 4 fellows will come and *a* me."
Ps 55:10 malice and *a* are within it.
Pr 9: 7 rebukes a wicked man incurs *a*.
1Pe 4: 4 of dissipation, and they heap *a*

ABUSED (ABUSE)

Jdg 19:25 and *a* her throughout the night,

ABUSIVE (ABUSE)

Ac 18: 6 Jews opposed Paul and became *a*,
2Ti 3: 2 *a*, disobedient to their parents,

ABUTTED

Eze 40:18 It *a* the sides of the gateways

ABYSS

Lk 8:31 not to order them to go into the *A*.
Rev 9: 1 the key to the shaft of the *A*.
9: 2 When he opened the *A*, smoke rose
9: 2 darkened by the smoke from the *A*.
9:11 king over them the angel of the *A*,
11: 7 up from the *A* will attack them,
17: 8 and will come up out of the *A*
20: 1 having the key to the *A*
20: 3 He threw him into the *A*,

ACACIA (ACACIAS)

Ex 25: 5 *a* wood; olive oil for the light;
25:10 Have them make a chest of *a* wood
25:13 Then make poles of *a* wood
25:23 "Make a table of *a* wood—
25:28 Make the poles of *a* wood,
26:15 "Make upright frames of *a* wood
26:26 "Also make crossbars of *a* wood:
26:32 on four posts of *a* wood overlaid
26:37 and five posts of *a* wood overlaid
27: 1 "Build an altar of *a* wood,
27: 6 Make poles of *a* wood for the altar
30: 1 "Make an altar of *a* wood
30: 5 Make the poles of *a* wood
35: 7 *a* wood; olive oil for the light;
35:24 and everyone who had *a* wood
36:20 of *a* wood for the tabernacle.
36:31 also made crossbars of *a* wood:
36:36 They made four posts of *a* wood
37: 1 Bezalel made the ark of *a* wood—
37: 4 Then he made poles of *a* wood
37:10 They made the table of *a* wood—
37:15 the table were made of *a* wood
37:25 the altar of incense out of *a* wood.
37:28 They made the poles of *a* wood
38: 1 altar of burnt offering of *a* wood,
38: 6 They made the poles of *a* wood
Dt 10: 3 So I made the ark out of *a* wood
Isa 41:19 the cedar and the *a*, the myrtle

ACACIAS (ACACIA)

Joel 3:18 and will water the valley of *a*.

ACBOR

Ge 36:38 son of *A* succeeded him
36:39 When Baal-Hanan son of *A* died,
2Ki 22:12 son of Shaphan, *A* son of Micaiah,
22:14 Hilkiah the priest, Ahikam, *A*,
1Ch 1:49 son of *A* succeeded him
Jer 26:22 sent Elnathan son of *A* to Egypt,
36:12 Elnathan son of *A*, Gemariah son

ACCENT

Mt 26:73 for your *a* gives you away."

ACCEPT (ACCEPTABLE ACCEPTANCE ACCEPTED ACCEPTING ACCEPTS)

Ge 14:23 oath that I will *a* nothing belonging
14:24 I will *a* nothing but what my men
21:30 *A* these seven lambs from my hand
23:13 *A* it from me so I can bury my dead
33:10 in your eyes, *a* this gift from me.
33:11 Please *a* the present that was
Ex 22:11 The owner is to *a* this,
23: 8 "Do not *a* a bribe,
Lev 22:25 and you must not *a* such animals
26:23 things you do not *a* my correction
Nu 7: 5 said to Moses, "*A* these from them,
16:15 LORD, "Do not *a* their offering
32:30 they must *a* their possession
35:31 " 'Do not *a* a ransom for the life
35:32 " 'Do not *a* a ransom
Dt 16:19 Do not *a* a bribe, for a bribe blinds
20:11 If they *a* and open their gates,
21: 8 *A* this atonement for your people
1Sa 2:15 he won't *a* boiled meat from you,
10: 4 which you will *a* from them.
26:19 then may he *a* an offering.
2Sa 24:23 May the LORD your God *a* you."
2Ki 5:15 Please *a* now a gift
5:16 whom I serve, I will not *a* a thing."
5:23 He urged Gehazi to *a* them,
5:26 or to *a* clothes, olive groves,
Est 4: 4 but he would not *a* them.
Job 2:10 Shall we *a* good from God,
22:22 *A* instruction from his mouth
42: 8 and I will *a* his prayer and not deal
Ps 15: 5 not *a* a bribe against the innocent.
20: 3 and *a* your burnt offerings.
119:108 *A*, O LORD, the willing praise
Pr 1:25 and would not *a* my rebuke,
1:30 since they would not *a* my advice
2: 1 My son, if you *a* my words
4:10 Listen, my son, *a* what I say,
6:35 He will not *a* any compensation;
10: 8 The wise in heart *a* commands,
19:20 Listen to advice and *a* instruction,
Ecc 5:19 to *a* his lot and be happy
Isa 29:24 who complain will *a* instruction."
Jer 14:10 So the LORD does not *a* them;
14:12 grain offerings, I will not *a* them.
Eze 20:40 serve me, and there I will *a* them.
20:41 I will *a* you as fragrant incense

Eze 22: 12 In you men *a* bribes to shed blood;
43: 27 I will *a* you, declares the Sovereign
Da 4: 27 O king, be pleased to *a* my advice:
Am 5: 22 I will not *a* them.
Zep 3: 7 and *a* correction!'
Mal 1: 8 Would he *a* you?" says the LORD
1: 9 will he *a* you?"—says the LORD
1: 10 I will *a* no offering from your hands
1: 13 should I *a* them from your hands?"
Mt 11: 14 And if you are willing to *a* it,
19: 11 "Not everyone can *a* this teaching,
19: 12 The one who can *a* this should *a* it
Mk 4: 20 *a* it, and produce a crop—
Jn 3: 11 you people do not *a* our testimony.
5: 34 Not that I *a* human testimony;
5: 41 "I do not *a* praise from men,
5: 43 do not *a* me; but if someone else
5: 43 in his own name, you will *a* him.
5: 44 if you *a* praise from one another,
6: 60 Who can *a* it?" Aware that his
12: 48 me and does not *a* my words;
14: 17 The world cannot *a* him,
Ac 16: 21 unlawful for us Romans to *a*
22: 18 they will not *a* your testimony
Ro 14: 1 *A* him whose faith is weak,
15: 7 *A* one another, then, just
1Co 2: 14 the Spirit does not *a* the things that
16: 11 then, should refuse to *a* him.
Jas 1: 21 humbly *a* the word planted in you,
1Jn 5: 9 We *a* man's testimony,

ACCEPTABLE (ACCEPT)

Ex 28: 38 so that they will be *a* to the LORD.
Lev 1: 3 so that it will be *a* to the LORD.
22: 21 without defect or blemish to be *a*.
22: 27 it will be *a* as an offering made
27: 9 he vowed is an animal that is *a*
27: 11 one that is not *a* as an offering
Jdg 14: 3 "Isn't there an *a* woman
Pr 21: 3 is more *a* to the LORD
Isa 58: 5 a day *a* to the LORD?
Jer 6: 20 Your burnt offerings are not *a*;
Mal 1: 14 is the cheat who has an *a* male
3: 4 Jerusalem will be *a* to the LORD,
Ro 15: 16 might become an offering *a*
15: 31 service in Jerusalem may be *a*
2Co 8: 12 the gift is *a* according
Php 4: 18 an *a* sacrifice, pleasing to God.
1Pe 2: 5 offering spiritual sacrifices *a*

ACCEPTANCE (ACCEPT)

Ro 11: 15 what will their *a* be but life
1Ti 1: 15 saying that deserves full *a*:
4: 9 saying that deserves full *a*

ACCEPTED (ACCEPT)

Ge 4: 7 will you not be *a*? But if you do not
33: 11 because Jacob insisted, Esau *a* it.
Lev 1: 4 and it will be *a* on his behalf
7: 18 on the third day, it will not be *a*.
19: 5 it in such a way that it will be *a*
19: 7 it is impure and will not be *a*.
22: 19 or goats in order that it may be *a*
22: 20 it will not be *a* on your behalf.
22: 23 but it will not be *a* in fulfillment
22: 25 They will not be *a* on your behalf,
22: 29 it in such a way that it will be *a*
23: 11 so it will be *a* on your behalf;
Nu 31: 51 and Eleazar the priest *a*
31: 54 and Eleazar the priest *a* the gold
Jdg 13: 23 would not have *a* a burnt offering
1Sa 8: 3 and *a* bribes and perverted justice.
12: 3 From whose hand have I *a* a bribe
25: 35 David *a* from her hand what she
Job 42: 9 and the LORD *a* Job's prayer.
Isa 56: 7 will be *a* on my altar;
60: 7 they will be *a* as offerings
Lk 4: 24 "no prophet is *a* in his home town.
Jn 3: 33 man who has *a* it has certified that
17: 8 you gave me and they *a* them.
Ac 2: 41 Those who *a* his message were
8: 14 heard that Samaria had *a* the word
15: 8 showed that he *a* them
Ro 10: 16 all the Israelites *a* the good news.
14: 3 for God has *a* him.
15: 7 another, then, just as Christ *a* you,
2Co 11: 4 gospel from the one you *a*,
Gal 1: 9 you a gospel other than what you *a*,
1Th 2: 13 you *a* it not as the word of men,
Heb 10: 34 and joyfully *a* the confiscation

ACCEPTING (ACCEPT)

2Ki 5: 20 by not *a* from him what he brought.
Isa 33: 15 and keeps his hand from *a* bribes,

ACCEPTS (ACCEPT)

Dt 10: 17 shows no partiality and *a* no bribes.
27: 25 "Cursed is the man who *a* a bribe
Ps 6: 9 the LORD *a* my prayer.
Pr 17: 23 A wicked man *a* a bribe in secret
Mic 7: 3 the judge *a* bribes,
Zep 3: 2 she *a* no correction.
Mal 2: 13 or *a* them with pleasure
Jn 3: 32 but no one *a* his testimony.
13: 20 whoever *a* anyone I send *a* me;
13: 20 whoever *a* me *a* the one who sent
Ac 10: 35 *a* men from every nation who fear
Heb 12: 6 he punishes everyone he *a* as a son
Jas 1: 27 Religion that God our Father *a*

ACCESS

Est 1: 14 and Media who had special *a*
Ro 5: 2 through whom we have gained *a*
Eph 2: 18 For through him we both have *a*

ACCESSORIES

Ex 25: 39 for the lampstand and all these *a*.
30: 27 and its *a*, the altar of incense,
31: 8 pure gold lampstand and all its *a*,
35: 14 is for light with its *a*,
37: 24 all its *a* from one talent of pure gold
39: 37 with its row of lamps and all its *a*,
Nu 4: 10 and all its *a* in a covering of hides

ACCLAIM (ACCLAMATION)

Ps 89: 15 those who have learned to *a* you,
Isa 24: 14 the west they *a* the LORD's

ACCLAMATION (ACCLAIM)

2Ch 15: 14 an oath to the LORD with loud *a*,

ACCO

Jdg 1: 31 Asher drive out those living in *A*

ACCOMPANIED (ACCOMPANY)

Ge 50: 7 All Pharaoh's officials *a* him—
Ru 1: 22 So Naomi returned from Moab *a*
1Sa 10: 26 *a* by valiant men whose hearts God
2Sa 15: 11 from Jerusalem had *a* Absalom.
15: 18 six hundred Gittites who had *a* him
1Ki 20: 1 *A* by thirty-two kings
1Ch 15: 16 *a* by musical instruments: lyres,
25: 1 *a* by harps, lyres and cymbals.
2Ch 5: 12 They were *a* by 120 priests
5: 13 *A* by trumpets, cymbals
29: 27 *a* by trumpets and the instruments
29: 35 the drink offerings that *a* the burnt
30: 21 *a* by the LORD's instruments
Jer 17: 25 *a* by the men of Judah
22: 4 *a* by their officials and their people.
Mk 6: 1 to his home town, *a* by his disciples
16: 20 word by the signs that *a* it.
Jn 19: 39 He was *a* by Nicodemus, the man
Ac 17: 15 The men who *a* Paul brought him
18: 18 and sailed for Syria, *a* by Priscilla
20: 4 He was *a* by Sopater son of Pyrrhus
20: 38 Then they *a* him to the ship.
21: 5 and children *a* us out of the city,
21: 16 of the disciples from Caesarea *a* us
1Co 10: 4 from the spiritual rock that *a* them,
Jas 2: 17 if it is not *a* by action, is dead.

ACCOMPANIES (ACCOMPANY)

Isa 40: 10 and his recompense *a* him.
62: 11 and his recompense *a* him.' "
2Co 9: 13 obedience that *a* your confession

ACCOMPANY (ACCOMPANIED ACCOMPANIES ACCOMPANYING)

Ge 33: 12 "Let us be on our way; I'll *a* you."
Dt 28: 2 *a* you if you obey the LORD your
1Sa 28: 1 your men will *a* me in the army."
Ne 10: 38 from Aaron is to *a* the Levites
Est 5: 12 to *a* the king to the banquet she
Ecc 8: 15 Then joy will *a* him in his work all
Mk 16: 17 these signs will *a* those who believe
1Co 16: 4 for me to go also, they will *a* me.
2Co 8: 19 chosen by the churches to *a* us
Heb 6: 9 your case—things that *a* salvation.

ACCOMPANYING (ACCOMPANY)

Nu 28: 7 The *a* drink offering is

ACCOMPLICE

Pr 29: 24 The *a* of a thief is his own enemy;

ACCOMPLISH (ACCOMPLISHED ACCOMPLISHES ACCOMPLISHING)

Ge 50: 20 good to *a* what is now being done,
Dt 9: 5 to *a* what he swore to your fathers,
2Ki 8: 13 a mere dog, *a* such a feat?"
19: 31 of the LORD Almighty will *a* this.
Ecc 2: 2 And what does pleasure *a*?"
Isa 9: 7 will *a* this.
37: 32 will *a* this.
44: 28 and will *a* all that I please;
55: 11 but will *a* what I desire
Jer 48: 30 "and her boasts *a* nothing.
Rev 17: 17 it into their hearts to *a* his purpose

ACCOMPLISHED (ACCOMPLISH)

Jdg 8: 2 "What have I *a* compared to you?
Isa 26: 12 all that we have *a* you have done
Mt 5: 18 from the Law until everything is *a*.
Lk 1: 45 the Lord has said to her will be *a*!"
Ro 15: 18 what Christ has *a* through me
Eph 3: 11 to his eternal purpose which he *a*
Rev 10: 7 the mystery of God will be *a*,

ACCOMPLISHES (ACCOMPLISH)

Jer 23: 20 back until he fully *a*
30: 24 back until he fully *a*

ACCOMPLISHING (ACCOMPLISH)

2Ki 10: 30 have done well in *a* what is right
Jn 11: 47 "What are we *a*?" they asked.

ACCORD (ACCORDED)

Nu 24: 13 not do anything of my own *a*,
2Ki 10: 15 "Are you in *a* with me,
Jer 5: 5 But with one *a* they too had broken
Jn 10: 18 but I lay it down of my own *a*.
12: 49 For I did not speak of my own *a*,
Tit 2: 1 is in *a* with sound doctrine.

ACCORDED (ACCORD)

Ge 45: 13 my father about all the honor *a* me

ACCOUNT (ACCOUNTABLE ACCOUNTED ACCOUNTING ACCOUNTS)

Ge 2: 4 This is the *a* of the heavens
5: 1 This is the written *a* of Adam's line
6: 9 This is the *a* of Noah.
10: 1 This is the *a* of Shem, Ham
11: 10 This is the *a* of Shem.
11: 27 This is the *a* of Terah.
25: 12 This is the *a* of Abraham's son
25: 19 This is the *a* of Abraham's son
26: 7 of this place might kill me on *a*
26: 9 I thought I might lose my life on *a*
36: 1 This is the *a* of Esau (that is, Edom
36: 9 This is the *a* of Esau the father
37: 2 This is the *a* of Jacob.
Ex 12: 4 having taken into *a* the number
Nu 3: 1 This is the *a* of the family of Aaron
6: 7 himself ceremonially unclean on *a*
9: 6 unclean on *a* of a dead body.
13: 27 They gave Moses this *a*: "We went
Dt 9: 4 it is on *a* of the wickedness
9: 5 but on *a* of the wickedness
18: 19 I myself will call him to *a*.
Jos 22: 23 may the LORD himself call us to *a*.
1Sa 17: 32 heart on *a* of this Philistine;
20: 16 LORD call David's enemies to *a*."
23: 10 and destroy the town on *a* of me.
2Sa 11: 18 Joab sent David a full *a*
11: 19 have finished giving the king this *a*
13: 2 of illness on *a* of his sister Tamar,
21: 1 on *a* of Saul and his blood-stained
1Ki 9: 15 Here is the *a* of the forced labor
11: 27 Here is the *a* of how he rebelled
2Ki 22: 7 But they need not *a* for the money
1Ch 27: 24 on Israel on *a* of this numbering,
2Ch 24: 22 LORD see this and call you to *a*."

2Ch 24:27 *a* of his sons, the many prophecies
Est 10: 2 with a full *a* of the greatness
Job 31:14 will I answer when called to *a*?
31:37 I would give him an *a*
Ps 10:13 "He won't call me to *a*"?
10:15 call him to *a* for his wickedness
56: 7 On no *a* let them escape;
Ecc 3:15 and God will call the past to *a*.
Isa 2:22 Of what *a* is he?
23:13 this people that is now of no *a*!
Eze 16:14 the nations on *a* of your beauty,
28:17 proud on *a* of your beauty,
Mt 10:18 On my *a* you will be brought
11: 6 man who does not fall away on *a*
12:36 to give *a* on the day of judgment
26:31 night you will all fall away on *a*
26:33 "Even if all fall away on *a* of you,
Mk 12:26 in the *a* of the bush, how God said
13: 9 On *a* of me you will stand
Lk 1: 1 have undertaken to draw up an *a*
1: 3 to me to write an orderly *a* for you,
7:23 man who does not fall away on *a*
16: 2 Give an *a* of your management,
20:37 But in the *a* of the bush,
21:12 governors, and all on *a* of my name
Jn 12:11 for on *a* of him many
Ac 4: 9 called to *a* today for an act
19:40 able to *a* for this commotion,
Ro 5:13 But sin is not taken into *a*
11:28 loved on *a* of the patriarchs,
11:28 they are enemies on your *a*;
14:12 each of us will give an *a* of himself
1Co 6: 4 even men of little *a* in the church!
2Co 7:12 on *a* of the one who did the wrong
Php 1:26 in Christ Jesus will overflow on *a*
4:17 for what may be credited to your *a*.
Heb 4:13 of him to whom we must give *a*.
13:17 as men who must give an *a*.
1Pe 4: 5 But they will have to give *a*
1Jn 2:12 your sins have been forgiven on *a*
Rev 16:21 they cursed God on *a* of the plague

ACCOUNTABLE (ACCOUNT)

Eze 3:18 and I will hold you *a* for his blood.
3:20 and I will hold you *a* for his blood.
33: 6 but I will hold the watchman *a*
33: 8 and I will hold you *a* for his blood.
34:10 and will hold them *a* for my flock.
Da 6: 2 The satraps were made *a* to them
Jnh 1:14 Do not hold us *a* for killing
Ro 3:19 and the whole world held *a* to God.

ACCOUNTED (ACCOUNT)

Ezr 8:34 Everything was *a* for by number

ACCOUNTING (ACCOUNT)

Ge 9: 5 I will demand an *a*
9: 5 I will demand an *a* for the life
9: 5 lifeblood I will surely demand an *a*.
42:22 we must give an *a* for his blood."
2Ki 12:15 They did not require an *a*

ACCOUNTS (ACCOUNT)

Job 21:29 Have you paid no regard to their *a*
Mt 18:23 to settle *a* with his servants.
25:19 servants returned and settled *a*

ACCREDITED (CREDIT)

Ac 2:22 of Nazareth was a man *a* by God

ACCUMULATE (ACCUMULATED)

Dt 17:17 He must not *a* large amounts

ACCUMULATED (ACCUMULATE)

Ge 12: 5 all the possessions they had *a*
31:18 along with all the goods he had *a*
1Ki 10:26 Solomon *a* chariots and horses;
2Ch 1:14 Solomon *a* chariots and horses;

ACCURATE (ACCURATELY)

Dt 25:15 You must have *a* and honest
Pr 11: 1 but *a* weights are his delight.
Eze 45:10 *a* scales, an *a* ephah and an *a* bath.
Ac 23:15 wanting more *a* information about
23:20 wanting more *a* information about

ACCURATELY (ACCURATE)

Ac 18:25 fervor and taught about Jesus *a*,

ACCURSED (CURSE)

Nu 5:27 will become *a* among her people.
2Ki 22:19 that they would become *a*
Isa 65:20 will be considered *a*
Mic 6:10 and the short ephah, which is *a*?
2Pe 2:14 experts in greed—an *a* brood!

ACCUSATION (ACCUSE)

Ezr 4: 6 they lodged an *a* against the people
Mic 6: 2 Hear, O mountains, the LORD's *a*;
Ac 23:29 I found that the *a* had to do
24: 9 in the *a*, asserting that these things
Col 1:22 without blemish and free from *a*—
1Ti 5:19 Do not entertain an *a*
Jude : 9 to bring a slanderous *a* against him,

ACCUSATIONS (ACCUSE)

Ps 35:20 but devise false *a*
Ac 26: 2 against all the *a* of the Jews,
2Pe 2:11 do not bring slanderous *a*

ACCUSE (ACCUSATION ACCUSATIONS ACCUSED ACCUSER ACCUSERS ACCUSES ACCUSING)

Dt 19:16 the stand to *a* a man of a crime,
1Sa 22:15 Let not the king *a* your servant
2Sa 3: 8 Yet now you *a* me
Ps 50:21 and *a* you to your face.
103: 9 He will not always *a*,
109: 4 for my friendship they *a* me,
Pr 3:30 Do not *a* a man for no reason—
Isa 57:16 I will not *a* forever,
Hos 4: 4 let no man *a* another,
Zec 3: 1 standing at his right side to *a* him.
Mt 12:10 Looking for a reason to *a* Jesus,
Mk 3: 2 looking for a reason to *a* Jesus,
Lk 3:14 and don't *a* people falsely—
6: 7 looking for a reason to *a* Jesus,
23: 2 And they began to *a* him, saying,
Jn 5:45 "But do not think I will *a* you
10:36 Why then do you *a* me
1Pe 2:12 though they *a* you of doing wrong,

ACCUSED (ACCUSE)

Nu 35:12 so that a person *a* of murder may
35:25 assembly must protect the one *a*
35:26 if the *a* ever goes outside the limits
35:27 the avenger of blood may kill the *a*
35:28 The *a* must stay in his city of refuge
Dt 19:15 to convict a man *a* of any crime
Jos 20: 5 they must not surrender the one *a*,
21:13 city of refuge for one *a* of murder),
21:21 city of refuge for one *a* of murder)
21:27 city of refuge for one *a* of murder)
21:32 city of refuge for one *a* of murder),
21:38 city of refuge for one *a* of murder),
Ne 5: 7 and then *a* the nobles and officials.
Da 6:24 who had falsely *a* Daniel were
Mt 27:12 When he was *a* by the chief priests
Mk 15: 3 The chief priests *a* him
Lk 16: 1 a rich man whose manager was *a*
Ac 22:30 out exactly why Paul was being *a*

ACCUSER (ACCUSE)

Job 31:35 let my *a* put his indictment
Ps 109: 6 let an *a* stand at his right hand.
Isa 50: 8 Who is my *a*?
Jn 5:45 Your *a* is Moses, on whom your
Rev 12:10 For the *a* of our brothers,

ACCUSERS (ACCUSE)

Ps 71:13 May my *a* perish in shame;
109:20 be the LORD's payment to my *a*,
109:25 I am an object of scorn to my *a*;
109:29 My *a* will be clothed with disgrace
Jer 18:19 hear what my *a* are saying!
Ac 23:30 also ordered his *a* to present
23:35 case when your *a* get here."
24:12 My *a* did not find me arguing
25:16 man before he has faced his *a*
25:18 When his *a* got up to speak,

ACCUSES (ACCUSE)

Job 40: 2 Let him who *a* God answer him!"
Isa 54:17 will refute every tongue that *a* you.
Rev 12:10 who *a* them before our God day

ACCUSING (ACCUSE)

Mt 27:13 how many things they are *a* you
Mk 15: 4 how many things they are *a* you
Lk 23:10 standing there, vehemently *a* him.
Jn 8: 6 in order to have a basis for *a* him.
Ac 23:28 to know why they were *a* him,
26: 7 of this hope that the Jews are *a* me.
Ro 2:15 and their thoughts now *a*,

ACCUSTOMED (CUSTOM)

Jer 2:24 a wild donkey *a* to the desert,
13:23 who are *a* to doing evil.
1Co 8: 7 Some people are still so *a*

ACHAIA

Ac 18:12 While Gallio was proconsul of *A*,
18:27 When Apollos wanted to go to *A*,
19:21 passing through Macedonia and *A*.
Ro 15:26 and *A* were pleased to make
1Co 16:15 were the first converts in *A*,
2Co 1: 1 with all the saints throughout *A*:
9: 2 you in *A* were ready to give;
11:10 regions of *A* will stop this boasting
1Th 1: 7 the believers in Macedonia and *A*.
1: 8 only in Macedonia and *A*—

ACHAICUS

1Co 16:17 Fortunatus and *A* arrived,

ACHAN (ACHAR)

Jos 7: 1 *A* son of Carmi, the son of Zimri,
7:18 *A* son of Carmi, the son of Zimri,
7:19 Then Joshua said to *A*, "My son,
7:20 *A* replied, "It is true! I have sinned
7:24 with all Israel, took *A* son of Zerah,
7:26 Over *A* they heaped up a large pile
22:20 When *A* son of Zerah acted

ACHAR (ACHAN)

1Ch 2: 7 *A*, who brought disaster on Israel

ACHE

Pr 14:13 Even in laughter the heart may *a*,

ACHIEVE (ACHIEVED ACHIEVEMENT ACHIEVEMENTS ACHIEVING)

Job 5:12 so that their hands *a* no success.
Ecc 2:11 and what I had toiled to *a*,
Isa 55:11 *a* the purpose for which I sent it.
Da 11:24 and will *a* what neither his fathers

ACHIEVED (ACHIEVE)

1Ki 9: 1 and had *a* all he had desired to do,
16:27 what he did and the things he *a*,
22:45 the things he *a* and his military

ACHIEVEMENT (ACHIEVE)

Ecc 4: 4 and all *a* spring from man's envy

ACHIEVEMENTS (ACHIEVE)

1Ki 10: 6 in my own country about your *a*
15:23 all his *a*, all he did and the cities he
16: 5 reign, what he did and his *a*,
2Ki 10:34 reign, all he did, and all his *a*,
13: 8 of Jehoahaz, all he did and his *a*,
13:12 and his *a*, including his war
14:15 and his *a*, including his war
14:28 all he did, and his military *a*,
20:20 all his *a* and how he made the pool
2Ch 9: 5 in my own country about your *a*

ACHIEVING (ACHIEVE)

2Co 4:17 and momentary troubles are *a*

ACHISH

1Sa 21:10 and went to *A* king of Gath.
21:11 But the servants of *A* said to him,
21:12 afraid of *A* king of Gath.
21:14 *A* said to his servants, "Look
27: 2 went over to *A* son of Maoch king
27: 3 and his men settled in Gath with *A*.
27: 5 said to *A*, "If I have found favor
27: 6 So on that day *A* gave him Ziklag,
27: 9 Then he returned to *A*.
27:10 When *A* asked, "Where did you go
27:12 *A* trusted David and said to himself
28: 1 *A* said to David, "You must
28: 2 *A* replied, "Very well, I will make

1Sa 29: 2 marching at the rear with *A*.
29: 3 *A* replied, "Is this not
29: 6 So *A* called David and said to him,
29: 9 *A* answered, "I know that
1Ki 2: 39 ran off to *A* son of Maacah,
2: 40 and went to *A* at Gath in search

ACHOR
Jos 7: 24 all that he had, to the Valley of *A*.
7: 26 has been called the Valley of *A* ever
15: 7 up to Debir from the Valley of *A*
Isa 65: 10 and the Valley of *A* a resting place
Hos 2: 15 of *A* a door of hope.

ACKNOWLEDGE (ACKNOWLEDGED ACKNOWLEDGES ACKNOWLEDGMENT)
Dt 4: 39 *A* and take to heart this day that
21: 17 He must *a* the son
33: 9 or *a* his own children,
1Ch 28: 9 my son Solomon, *a* the God
Ps 79: 6 that do not *a* you,
87: 4 Babylon among those who *a* me—
Pr 3: 6 in all your ways *a* him,
Isa 19: 21 in that day they will *a* the LORD.
29: 23 they will *a* the holiness
33: 13 you who are near, *a* my power!
45: 4 though you do not *a* me.
59: 12 and we *a* our iniquities:
61: 9 All who see them will *a*
63: 16 or Israel *a* us;
Jer 3: 13 Only *a* your guilt—
9: 3 they do not *a* me,"
9: 6 in their deceit they refuse to *a* me,"
10: 25 that do not *a* you,
14: 20 O LORD, we *a* our wickedness
Eze 12: 16 go they may *a* all their detestable
Da 4: 25 until you *a* that the Most High is
4: 26 you when you *a* that Heaven rules.
4: 32 until you *a* that the Most High is
11: 39 will greatly honor those who *a* him.
Hos 2: 20 and you will *a* the LORD.
5: 4 they do not *a* the LORD.
6: 3 Let us *a* the LORD;
6: 3 let us press on to *a* him.
8: 2 'O our God, we *a* you!'
13: 4 You shall *a* no God but me,
Mt 10: 32 *a* him before my Father in heaven.
Lk 12: 8 *a* him before the angels of God.
Ac 23: 8 but the Pharisees *a* them all.)
24: 3 we *a* this with profound gratitude.
1Co 14: 37 let him *a* that what I am writing
2Ti 3: 7 but never able to *a* the truth.
1Jn 4: 3 spirit that does not *a* Jesus is not
2Jn : 7 who do not *a* Jesus Christ
Rev 3: 5 will *a* his name before my Father
3: 9 and *a* that I have loved you.

ACKNOWLEDGED (ACKNOWLEDGE)
Lev 22: 32 I must be *a* as holy by the Israelites
1Ch 29: 22 Then they *a* Solomon son of David
Ps 32: 5 Then I *a* my sin to you
Isa 45: 5 though you have not *a* me,
Da 5: 21 until he *a* that the Most High God
Hos 2: 8 She has not *a* that I was the one
Lk 7: 29 *a* that God's way was right,
Jn 9: 22 that anyone who *a* that Jesus was

ACKNOWLEDGES (ACKNOWLEDGE)
Ps 91: 14 for he *a* my name.
Mt 10: 32 "Whoever *a* me before men,
Lk 12: 8 whoever *a* me before men,
1Jn 2: 23 whoever *a* the Son has the Father
4: 2 Every spirit that *a* that Jesus Christ
4: 15 If anyone *a* that Jesus is the Son

ACKNOWLEDGMENT (ACKNOWLEDGE)
Hos 4: 1 no *a* of God in the land.
6: 6 *a* of God rather than burnt

ACQUAINTANCE (ACQUAINTANCES ACQUAINTED)
Php 4: 15 early days of your *a* with the gospel

ACQUAINTANCES (ACQUAINTANCE)
Job 19: 13 my *a* are completely estranged

ACQUAINTED (ACQUAINTANCE)
Ac 24: 22 who was well *a* with the Way,
26: 3 you are well *a* with all the Jewish
Gal 1: 18 up to Jerusalem to get *a* with Peter
Heb 5: 13 is not *a* with the teaching about

ACQUIRE (ACQUIRED ACQUIRES ACQUIRING)
Ge 34: 10 trade in it, and *a* property in it."
Lev 25: 28 But if he does not *a* the means
Dt 17: 16 must not *a* great numbers of horses
Ru 4: 5 you *a* the dead man's widow,
Ne 5: 16 for the work; we did not *a* any land.

ACQUIRED (ACQUIRE)
Ge 12: 5 the people they had *a* in Haran,
12: 16 and Abram *a* sheep and cattle,
36: 6 all the goods he had *a* in Canaan,
46: 6 and the possessions they had *a*
47: 27 They *a* property there
Nu 31: 50 the gold articles each of us *a*—
Jos 22: 9 which they had *a* in accordance
Ru 4: 10 I have also *a* Ruth the Moabitess,
2Ch 32: 29 and *a* great numbers of flocks
Ecc 2: 8 I *a* men and women singers,
Isa 15: 7 the wealth they have *a*
Jer 48: 36 The wealth they *a* is gone.
Rev 3: 17 I have *a* wealth and do not need

ACQUIRES (ACQUIRE)
Lev 25: 26 *a* sufficient means to redeem it,
Pr 18: 15 of the discerning *a* knowledge;

ACQUIRING (ACQUIRE)
Pr 1: 3 for *a* a disciplined and prudent life,

ACQUIT (ACQUITTED ACQUITTING)
Ex 23: 7 to death, for I will not *a* the guilty.
Isa 5: 23 who *a* the guilty for a bribe,
Mic 6: 11 I *a* a man with dishonest scales,

ACQUITTED (ACQUIT)
Mt 12: 37 For by your words you will be *a*,

ACQUITTING (ACQUIT)
Dt 25: 1 *a* the innocent and condemning
Pr 17: 15 *A* the guilty and condemning

ACRE (TEN-ACRE)
1Sa 14: 14 men in an area of about half an *a*.

ACSAH
Jos 15: 16 "I will give my daughter *A*
15: 17 so Caleb gave his daughter *A*
Jdg 1: 12 "I will give my daughter *A*
1: 13 so Caleb gave his daughter *A*
1Ch 2: 49 Caleb's daughter was *A*.

ACSHAPH
Jos 11: 1 to the kings of Shimron and *A*,
12: 20 one the king of *A* one the king
19: 25 Hali, Beten, *A*, Allammelech,

ACT (ACTED ACTING ACTION ACTIONS ACTIVE ACTIVITY ACTS)
Ex 8: 29 does not *a* deceitfully again
Lev 20: 21 it is an *a* of impurity; he has
Nu 5: 13 she has not been caught in the *a*),
23: 19 Does he speak and then not *a*?
Dt 17: 10 You must *a* according
17: 11 *A* according to the law they teach
24: 13 as a righteous *a* in the sight
Jdg 20: 6 and disgraceful *a* in Israel.
1Sa 14: 6 Perhaps the LORD will *a*
2Sa 6: 7 because of his irreverent *a*;
14: 2 *A* like a woman who has spent
1Ki 8: 32 then hear from heaven and *a*.
8: 39 *a*; deal with each man according
21: 7 "Is this how you *a* as king
2Ch 6: 23 then hear from heaven and *a*.
19: 11 *A* with courage, and may
24: 5 But the Levites did not *a* at once.
Ezr 10: 14 Let our officials *a* for the whole
Ne 5: 15 for God I did not *a* like that.
Ps 119: 126 It is time for you to *a*, O LORD;
Pr 3: 27 when it is in your power to *a*.
Isa 43: 13 When I *a*, who can reverse it?"
52: 13 See, my servant will *a* wisely;

Jer 6: 28 they all *a* corruptly.
42: 5 us if we do not *a* in accordance
Eze 24: 14 The time has come for me to *a*.
Da 9: 19 O Lord, hear and *a*! For your sake,
11: 23 with him, he will *a* deceitfully,
Mic 6: 8 To *a* justly and to love mercy
Zep 3: 7 eager to *a* corruptly in all they did.
Jn 8: 4 caught in the *a* of adultery.
Ac 4: 9 today for an *a* of kindness shown
Ro 5: 18 also the result of one *a*
2Co 8: 6 also to completion this *a* of grace
10: 6 to punish every *a* of disobedience,
12: 18 Did we not *a* in the same spirit
Php 2: 13 to *a* according to his good purpose.
Col 4: 5 in the way you *a* toward outsiders;
2Th 1: 11 every *a* prompted by your faith.
Jas 2: 12 and *a* as those who are going

ACTED (ACT)
Dt 32: 5 They have *a* corruptly toward him;
Jos 7: 1 But the Israelites *a* unfaithfully
22: 20 son of Zerah *a* unfaithfully
22: 31 you have not *a* unfaithfully
Jdg 9: 16 "Now if you have *a* honorably
9: 19 if then you have *a* honorably
9: 23 who *a* treacherously
15: 7 to them, "Since you've *a* like this,
1Sa 13: 13 "You *a* foolishly," Samuel said.
21: 13 in their hands he *a* like a madman,
26: 21 Surely I have *a* like a fool
1Ki 8: 47 done wrong, we have *a* wickedly';
20: 25 with them and *a* accordingly.
2Ki 12: 15 they *a* with complete honesty.
22: 13 they have not *a* in accordance
2Ch 6: 37 have done wrong and *a* wickedly';
11: 23 He *a* wisely, dispersing some
25: 4 but *a* in accordance with what is
34: 21 they have not *a* in accordance
Ne 1: 7 We have *a* very wickedly
9: 33 you have *a* faithfully,
Ps 106: 6 have done wrong and *a* wickedly.
Isa 48: 3 then suddenly I *a*, and they came
Jer 38: 9 these men have *a* wickedly
Eze 25: 15 'Because the Philistines *a*
Lk 16: 8 because he had *a* shrewdly.
24: 28 Jesus *a* as if he were going farther.
Ac 3: 17 I know that you *a* in ignorance,
1Ti 1: 13 I *a* in ignorance and unbelief.

ACTING (ACT)
2Sa 12: 21 "Why are you *a* this way?
2Ki 10: 19 Jehu was *a* deceptively in order
22: 7 because they are *a* faithfully."
Eze 16: 30 do all these things, *a* like a brazen
Mal 2: 14 the LORD is *a* as the witness
Ro 14: 15 you are no longer *a* in love.
1Co 3: 3 Are you not *a* like mere men?
7: 36 If anyone thinks he is *a* improperly
Gal 2: 14 When I saw that they were not *a*

ACTION (ACT)
Jer 32: 39 them singleness of heart and *a*,
Da 11: 28 He will take *a* against it
Lk 23: 51 consented to their decision and *a*.
Ac 7: 22 and was powerful in speech and *a*.
2Co 9: 2 has stirred most of them to *a*.
Jas 2: 17 if it is not accompanied by *a*,
1Pe 1: 13 minds for *a*; be self-controlled;

ACTIONS (ACT)
Pr 20: 11 Even a child is known by his *a*,
Isa 66: 18 of their *a* and their imaginations,
Jer 4: 18 "Your own conduct and *a*
7: 3 says: Reform your ways and your *a*
7: 5 your *a* and deal with each other
18: 11 and reform your ways and your *a*.'
26: 13 Now reform your ways and your *a*
35: 15 wicked ways and reform your *a*;
44: 22 no longer endure your wicked *a*
44: 25 by your *a* what you promised
Eze 14: 22 you see their conduct and their *a*,
14: 23 you see their conduct and their *a*,
20: 43 all the *a* by which you have defiled
24: 14 to your conduct and your *a*,
36: 17 it by their conduct and their *a*.
36: 19 to their conduct and their *a*.
Mt 11: 19 wisdom is proved right by her *a*."
2Co 10: 11 be in our *a* when we are present.

2Co 11: 15 end will be what their *a* deserve.
Gal 6: 4 Each one should test his own *a*.
Tit 1: 16 but by their *a* they deny him.
Jas 2: 22 and his *a* were working together,
1Jn 3: 12 Because his own *a* were evil
3: 18 or tongue but with *a* and in truth.

ACTIVE (ACT)

Phm : 6 I pray that you may be *a*
Heb 4: 12 For the word of God is living and *a*

ACTIVITY (ACT)

Ne 11: 23 which regulated their daily *a*.
Ecc 3: 1 a season for every *a* under heaven:
3: 17 for there will be a time for every *a*,
Ac 5: 38 For if their purpose or *a* is
2Co 10: 15 of *a* among you will greatly expand

ACTS (ACT)

Ex 6: 6 and with mighty *a* of judgment.
7: 4 with mighty *a* of judgment I will
Jdg 5: 11 They recite the righteous *a*
5: 11 the righteous *a* of his warriors
1Sa 12: 7 as to all the righteous *a* performed
1Ch 16: 9 tell of all his wonderful *a*.
2Ch 32: 32 and his *a* of devotion are written
35: 26 events of Josiah's reign and his *a*
Est 10: 2 And all his *a* of power and might,
Ps 71: 16 proclaim your mighty *a*,
71: 24 tell of your righteous *a*
105: 2 tell of all his wonderful *a*.
106: 2 Who can proclaim the mighty *a*
145: 4 they will tell of your mighty *a*.
145: 12 all men may know of your mighty *a*
150: 2 Praise him for his *a* of power;
Pr 12: 10 kindest *a* of the wicked are cruel.
13: 16 Every prudent man *a* out
Isa 59: 6 and *a* of violence are in their hands
64: 4 who *a* on behalf of those who wait
64: 6 all our righteous *a* are like filthy
Jer 13: 27 I have seen your detestable *a*
29: 26 any madman who *a* like a prophet
Eze 22: 9 shrines and commit lewd *a*.
Da 9: 16 in keeping with all your righteous *a*
Mic 6: 5 that you may know the righteous *a*
Mt 6: 1 not to do your '*a* of righteousness'
Jn 7: 4 wants to become a public figure *a*
Ro 1: 27 Men committed indecent *a*
Gal 5: 19 *a* of the sinful nature are obvious:
Heb 6: 1 of repentance from *a* that lead
9: 14 our consciences from *a* that lead
10: 17 "Their sins and lawless *a*
Jude : 15 of all the ungodly *a* they have done
Rev 15: 4 for your righteous *a* have been
19: 8 for the righteous *a* of the saints.)

ACZIB

Jos 15: 44 Nezib, Keilah, *A* and Mareshah—
19: 29 out at the sea in the region of *A*,
Jdg 1: 31 or Sidon or Ahlab or *A* or Helbah
Mic 1: 14 The town of *A* will prove deceptive

ADADAH

Jos 15: 22 Kinah, Dimonah, *A*, Kedesh,

ADAH

Ge 4: 19 one named *A* and the other Zillah.
4: 20 *A* gave birth to Jabal; he was
4: 23 "*A* and Zillah, listen to me;
36: 2 *A* daughter of Elon the Hittite,
36: 4 *A* bore Eliphaz to Esau, Basemath
36: 10 the son of Esau's wife *A*, and Reuel
36: 12 were grandsons of Esau's wife *A*.
36: 16 they were grandsons of *A*.

ADAIAH

2Ki 22: 1 name was Jedidah daughter of *A*;
1Ch 6: 41 the son of *A*, the son of Ethan,
8: 21 Zabdi, Elienai, Zillethai, Eliel, *A*,
9: 12 *A* son of Jeroham, the son
2Ch 23: 1 son of *A*, and Elishaphat son
Ezr 10: 29 Meshullam, Malluch, *A*, Jashub,
10: 39 Nathan, *A*, Macnadebai,
Ne 11: 5 the son of *A*, the son of Joiarib,
11: 12 men; *A* son of Jeroham,

ADALIA

Est 9: 8 Aspatha, Poratha, *A*, Aridatha,

ADAM (ADAM'S)

Ge 2: 20 for *A* no suitable helper was found.
3: 17 To *A* he said, "Because you
3: 20 *A* named his wife Eve,
3: 21 God made garments of skin for *A*
4: 1 *A* lay with his wife Eve,
4: 25 *A* lay with his wife again,
5: 3 When *A* had lived 130 years,
5: 4 *A* lived 800 years and had other
5: 5 Altogether, *A* lived 930 years,
Jos 3: 16 at a town called *A* in the vicinity
1Ch 1: 1 *A*, Seth, Enosh, Kenan, Mahalalel,
Hos 6: 7 Like *A*, they have broken
Lk 3: 38 the son of Seth, the son of *A*,
Ro 5: 14 did *A*, who was a pattern of the one
5: 14 from the time of *A* to the time
1Co 15: 22 in *A* all die, so in Christ all will be
15: 45 first man *A* became a living being";
15: 45 the last *A*, a life-giving spirit.
1Ti 2: 13 For *A* was formed first, then Eve.
2: 14 And *A* was not the one deceived;
Jude : 14 Enoch, the seventh from *A*,

ADAM'S (ADAM)

Ge 5: 1 is the written account of *A* line.

ADAMAH

Jos 19: 36 Rakkath, Kinnereth, *A*, Ramah,

ADAMI NEKEB

Jos 19: 33 passing *A* and Jabneel to Lakkum

ADAR

Ezr 6: 15 on the third day of the month *A*,
Est 3: 7 the twelfth month, the month of *A*.
3: 13 of *A*, and to plunder their goods.
8: 12 the twelfth month, the month of *A*.
9: 1 the twelfth month, the month of *A*,
9: 15 day of the month of *A*,
9: 17 day of the month of *A*,
9: 19 the fourteenth of the month of *A*
9: 21 fifteenth days of the month of *A*

ADBEEL

Ge 25: 13 Kedar, *A*, Mibsam, Mishma,
1Ch 1: 29 Kedar, *A*, Mibsam, Mishma,

ADD (ADDED ADDING ADDITION ADDITIONAL ADDS)

Ge 30: 24 "May the LORD *a*
Lev 2: 13 *a* salt to all your offerings.
5: 16 *a* a fifth of the value to that
6: 5 *a* a fifth of the value to it
6: 12 morning the priest is to *a* firewood
22: 14 and *a* a fifth of the value to it.
27: 13 he must *a* a fifth to its value.
27: 15 he must *a* a fifth to its value,
27: 19 he must *a* a fifth to its value,
27: 31 he must *a* a fifth of the value to it.
Nu 5: 7 *a* one fifth to it and give it all
Dt 4: 2 Do not *a* to what I command you
12: 32 do not *a* to it or take away from it.
20: 8 officers shall *a*, "Is any man afraid
2Sa 15: 4 Absalom would *a*, "If only I were
2Ki 20: 6 I will *a* fifteen years to your life.
1Ch 22: 14 And you may *a* to them.
2Ch 28: 13 Do you intend to *a* to our sin
Pr 1: 5 let the wise listen and *a*
9: 9 he will *a* to his learning.
30: 6 Do not *a* to his words,
Isa 5: 8 Woe to you who *a* house to house
29: 1 *A* year to year
38: 5 I will *a* fifteen years to your life.
Jer 7: 21 *a* your burnt offerings
30: 19 I will *a* to their numbers,
Eze 16: 43 Did you not *a* lewdness
Mt 6: 27 by worrying can *a* a single hour
Lk 12: 25 by worrying can *a* a single hour
Gal 3: 15 or *a* to a human covenant that has
2Pe 1: 5 make every effort to *a*
Rev 22: 18 God will *a* to him the plagues

ADDAR

Jos 15: 3 Then it ran past Hezron up to *A*
1Ch 8: 3 *A*, Gera, Abihud, Abishua,

ADDED (ADD)

Ge 16: 10 The angel *a*, "I will
21: 7 And she *a*, "Who would have said
24: 25 she *a*, "We have plenty of straw
30: 28 He *a*, "Name your wages,
38: 25 she *a*, "See if you recognize whose
Ex 12: 34 dough before the yeast was *a*,
Lev 10: 1 put fire in them and *a* incense;
Nu 36: 3 *a* to that of the tribe they marry
36: 4 their inheritance will be *a* to that
Dt 5: 22 darkness; and he *a* nothing more.
Jdg 19: 13 He *a*, "Come, let's try
Ru 2: 20 She *a*, "That man is our close
3: 17 Boaz had done for her and *a*,
1Sa 12: 19 for we have *a* to all our other sins
26: 18 he *a*, "Why is my lord pursuing his
2Sa 19: 35 should your servant be an *a* burden
1Ki 2: 14 he *a*, "I have something to say
22: 28 Then he *a*, "Mark my words,
2Ch 2: 12 Hiram *a*: "Praise be to the LORD,
18: 27 Then he *a*, "Mark my words,
Est 5: 12 "And that's not all," Haman *a*.
Pr 9: 11 and years will be *a* to your life.
Ecc 3: 14 nothing can be *a* to it and nothing
Jer 36: 32 many similar words were *a* to them
40: 5 turned to go, Nebuzaradan *a*,
44: 19 The women *a*, "When we burned
45: 3 The LORD has *a* sorrow
Zec 1: 15 but they *a* to the calamity.'
5: 6 And he *a*, "This is the iniquity
Lk 3: 20 things he had done, Herod *a* this
Jn 1: 51 He then *a*, "I tell you the truth,
Ac 1: 26 so he was *a* to the eleven apostles.
2: 41 and about three thousand were *a*
2: 47 Lord *a* to their number daily those
5: 14 and were *a* to their number.
Ro 5: 20 The law was *a* so that the trespass
Gal 2: 6 those men *a* nothing
3: 19 It was *a* because of transgressions
Rev 19: 9 he *a*, "These are the true words

ADDER (ADDERS)

Job 20: 16 the fangs of an *a* will kill him.
Isa 59: 5 when one is broken, an *a* is hatched

ADDERS (ADDER)

Isa 30: 6 of *a* and darting snakes,

ADDI

Lk 3: 28 the son of *A*, the son of Cosam,

ADDICTED

Tit 2: 3 to be slanderers or *a* to much wine,

ADDING (ADD)

Lev 27: 27 at its set value, *a* a fifth of the value
2Sa 14: 11 of blood from *a* to the destruction,
1Ki 11: 25 *a* to the trouble caused by Hadad.
Ezr 10: 10 have married foreign women, *a*
Ecc 7: 27 "*A* one thing to another

ADDITION (ADD)

Ge 28: 9 in *a* to the wives he already had
Lev 9: 17 in *a* to the morning's burnt offering
23: 38 These offerings are in *a* to those
23: 38 in *a* to your gifts and whatever you
Nu 6: 21 in *a* to whatever else he can afford.
16: 49 in *a* to those who had died
28: 10 in *a* to the regular burnt offering
28: 23 Prepare these in *a*
28: 24 is to be prepared in *a*
28: 31 in *a* to the regular burnt offering
29: 6 These are in *a* to the monthly
29: 11 in *a* to the sin offering
29: 16 in *a* to the regular burnt offering
29: 19 in *a* to the regular burnt offering
29: 22 in *a* to the regular burnt offering
29: 25 in *a* to the regular burnt offering
29: 28 in *a* to the regular burnt offering
29: 31 in *a* to the regular burnt offering
29: 34 in *a* to the regular burnt offering
29: 38 in *a* to the regular burnt offering
29: 39 "'In *a* to what you vow
35: 6 In *a*, give them forty-two other
Dt 29: 1 in *a* to the covenant he had made
Jos 13: 22 In *a* to those slain in battle,
Jdg 20: 15 in *a* to seven hundred chosen men
1Ki 5: 11 in *a* to twenty thousand baths
15: 20 and all Kinnereth in *a* to Naphtali.
2Ch 31: 16 In *a*, they distributed

Ezr 1: 6 in *a* to all the freewill offerings.
Ne 5: 15 of silver from them in *a* to food
Ecc 12: 12 my son, of anything in *a* to them.
Eze 16: 23 In *a* to all your other wickedness,
39: 14 go throughout the land and, in *a*
44: 7 In *a* to all your other detestable
Lk 24: 22 In *a*, some of our women amazed
2Co 7: 13 In *a* to our own encouragement,
8: 22 In *a*, we are sending
Eph 6: 16 In *a* to all this, take up the shield

ADDITIONAL (ADD)

Ge 43: 22 brought *a* silver with us to buy food
Ex 26: 12 As for the *a* length
Nu 3: 48 of the *a* Israelites to Aaron

ADDON

Ezr 2: 59 Kerub, *A* and Immer,
Ne 7: 61 Kerub, *A* and Immer,

ADDRESS (ADDRESSED ADDRESSES)

Dt 20: 2 shall come forward and *a* the army.
Ac 12: 21 delivered a public *a* to the people.
1Co 3: 1 I could not *a* you as spiritual but

ADDRESSED (ADDRESS)

Ac 2: 14 raised his voice and *a* the crowd:
5: 35 Then he *a* them: "Men of Israel,
15: 7 Peter got up and *a* them: "Brothers

ADDRESSES (ADDRESS)

Heb 12: 5 word of encouragement that *a* you

ADDS (ADD)

Job 34: 37 To his sin he *a* rebellion;
Pr 10: 22 and he *a* no trouble to it.
10: 27 of the LORD *a* length to life,
Heb 10: 17 Then he *a*:
Rev 22: 18 If anyone *a* anything to them,

ADHERE

2Ki 17: 34 *a* to the decrees and ordinances,

ADIEL

1Ch 4: 36 Jeshohaiah, Asaiah, *A*, Jesimiel,
9: 12 and Maasai son of *A*, the son
27: 25 Azmaveth son of *A* was in charge

ADIN

Ezr 2: 15 of *A* 454
8: 6 of the descendants of *A*, Ebed son
Ne 7: 20 of *A* 655
10: 16 Adonijah, Bigvai, *A*, Ater,

ADINA

1Ch 11: 42 *A* son of Shiza the Reubenite,

ADITHAIM

Jos 15: 36 *A* and Gederah (or Gederothaim

ADJOURNED

Ac 24: 22 with the Way, *a* the proceedings.

ADLAI

1Ch 27: 29 Shaphat son of *A* was in charge

ADMAH

Ge 10: 19 Gomorrah, *A* and Zeboiim,
14: 2 Shinab king of *A*, Shemeber king
14: 8 king of Gomorrah, the king of *A*,
Dt 29: 23 *A* and Zeboiim, which the LORD
Hos 11: 8 How can I treat you like *A*?

ADMATHA

Est 1: 14 Carshena, Shethar, *A*, Tarshish,

ADMINISTER (ADMINISTERED ADMINISTERING ADMINISTRATION ADMINISTRATOR ADMINISTRATORS)

1Ki 3: 28 wisdom from God to *a* justice.
2Ch 19: 8 of Israelite families to *a* the law
Ezr 7: 25 judges to *a* justice to all the people
Jer 21: 12 " '*A* justice every morning;
Zec 7: 9 Almighty says: '*A* true justice;
2Co 8: 19 which we *a* in order
8: 20 of the way we *a* this liberal gift.

ADMINISTERED (ADMINISTER)

Heb 11: 33 conquered kingdoms, *a* justice,

ADMINISTERING (ADMINISTER)

1Ki 3: 11 but for discernment in *a* justice,
1Pe 4: 10 faithfully *a* God's grace

ADMINISTRATION (ADMINISTER)

1Co 12: 28 with gifts of *a*, and those speaking
Eph 3: 2 Surely you have heard about the *a*
3: 9 to everyone the *a* of this mystery,

ADMINISTRATOR (ADMINISTER)

2Ki 10: 5 So the palace *a*, the city governor,
18: 18 Eliakim son of Hilkiah the palace *a*
18: 37 Eliakim son of Hilkiah the palace *a*
19: 2 He sent Eliakim the palace *a*,
Isa 36: 3 Eliakim son of Hilkiah the palace *a*
36: 22 Eliakim son of Hilkiah the palace *a*
37: 2 He sent Eliakim the palace *a*,

ADMINISTRATORS (ADMINISTER)

2Ch 35: 8 and Jehiel, the *a* of God's temple,
Est 9: 3 and the king's *a* helped the Jews,
Da 2: 49 and Abednego *a* over the province
6: 2 with three *a* over them, one
6: 3 distinguished himself among the *a*
6: 4 the *a* and the satraps tried
6: 6 So the *a* and the satraps went
6: 7 The royal *a*, prefects, satraps,

ADMIRABLE

Php 4: 8 whatever is lovely, whatever is *a*—

ADMIT (ADMITTED)

Jos 20: 4 they are to *a* him into their city
Job 27: 5 I will never *a* you are in the right;
40: 14 Then I myself will *a* to you
Isa 48: 6 Will you not *a* them?
Hos 5: 15 until they *a* their guilt.
Ac 24: 14 I *a* that I worship the God
2Co 11: 21 To my shame I *a* that we were too

ADMITTED (ADMIT)

Ne 13: 1 or Moabite should ever be *a*
Heb 11: 13 And they *a* that they were aliens

ADMONISH (ADMONISHED ADMONISHING ADMONITION)

Col 3: 16 and *a* one another with all wisdom,
1Th 5: 12 you in the Lord and who *a* you.

ADMONISHED (ADMONISH)

Ne 9: 26 who had *a* them in order
9: 30 By your Spirit you *a* them

ADMONISHING (ADMONISH)

Col 1: 28 *a* and teaching everyone

ADMONITION (ADMONISH)

Mal 2: 1 And now this *a* is for you, O priests
2: 4 know that I have sent you this *a*

ADNA

Ezr 10: 30 *A*, Kelal, Benaiah, Maaseiah,
Ne 12: 15 of Harim's, *A*; of Meremoth's,

ADNAH

1Ch 12: 20 *A*, Jozabad, Jediael, Michael,
2Ch 17: 14 *A* the commander, with 300,000

ADONI-BEZEK

Jdg 1: 5 It was there that they found *A*
1: 6 *A* fled, but they chased him
1: 7 Then *A* said, "Seventy kings

ADONI-ZEDEK

Jos 10: 1 *A* king of Jerusalem heard that
10: 3 So *A* king of Jerusalem appealed

ADONIJAH (ADONIJAH'S)

2Sa 3: 4 the fourth, *A* the son of Haggith;
1Ki 1: 5 *A*, whose mother was Haggith,
1: 7 *A* conferred with Joab son
1: 8 special guard did not join *A*.
1: 9 *A* then sacrificed sheep, cattle
1: 11 "Have you not heard that *A*,
1: 13 Why then has *A* become king?'
1: 18 But now *A* has become king,
1: 24 declared that *A* shall be king
1: 25 'Long live King *A*!' But me your
1: 41 *A* and all the guests who were
1: 42 *A* said, "Come in.
1: 50 But *A*, in fear of Solomon,
1: 51 "*A* is afraid of King Solomon
1: 53 And *A* came and bowed
2: 13 Now *A*, the son of Haggith,
2: 19 Solomon to speak to him for *A*,
2: 21 in marriage to your brother *A*."
2: 22 Abishag the Shunammite for *A*?
2: 23 if *A* does not pay with his life
2: 24 *A* shall be put to death today!"
2: 25 and he struck down *A* and he died.
2: 28 who had conspired with *A*
1Ch 3: 2 the fourth, *A* the son of Haggith;
2Ch 17: 8 Shemiramoth, Jehonathan, *A*,
Ne 10: 16 Azgad, Bebai, *A*, Bigvai, Adin,

ADONIJAH'S (ADONIJAH)

1Ki 1: 49 all *A* guests rose in alarm

ADONIKAM

Ezr 2: 13 of *A* 666
8: 13 the descendants of *A*, the last ones,
Ne 7: 18 of *A* 667

ADONIRAM

2Sa 20: 24 *A* was in charge of forced labor;
1Ki 4: 6 of the palace; *A* son of Abda—
5: 14 *A* was in charge of the forced labor.
12: 18 King Rehoboam sent out *A*,
2Ch 10: 18 King Rehoboam sent out *A*,

ADOPT (ADOPTED ADOPTION)

Job 15: 5 you *a* the tongue of the crafty.

ADOPTED (ADOPT)

Est 2: 15 for Esther (the girl Mordecai had *a*
Ps 106: 35 and *a* their customs.
Eph 1: 5 In love he predestined us to be *a*

ADOPTION (ADOPT)

Ro 8: 23 as we wait eagerly for our *a* as sons,
9: 4 Theirs is the *a* as sons; theirs

ADORAIM

2Ch 11: 9 Mareshah, Ziph, *A*, Lachish,

ADORE

SS 1: 4 How right they are to *a* you!

ADORN (ADORNED ADORNMENT ADORNS)

Job 40: 10 Then *a* yourself with glory
Ps 144: 12 carved to *a* a palace.
Pr 1: 9 and a chain to *a* your neck.
Isa 60: 7 and I will *a* my glorious temple.
60: 13 to *a* the place of my sanctuary;
Jer 4: 30 You *a* yourself in vain.
10: 4 They *a* it with silver and gold;

ADORNED (ADORN)

2Sa 1: 24 who *a* your garments
2Ch 3: 6 *a* the temple with precious stones.
Ps 45: 8 from palaces *a* with ivory
Eze 16: 11 I *a* you with jewelry: I put bracelets
16: 13 So you were *a* with gold and silver;
28: 13 every precious stone *a* you:
Hos 10: 1 he *a* his sacred stones.
Am 3: 15 the houses *a* with ivory will be
Lk 21: 5 about how the temple was *a*

ADORNMENT (ADORN)

1Pe 3: 3 should not come from outward *a*,

ADORNS (ADORN)

Ps 93: 5 holiness *a* your house
Isa 61: 10 as a bride *a* herself with her jewels.
61: 10 bridegroom *a* his head like a priest,

ADRAMMELECH

2Ki 17: 31 sacrifices to *A* and Anammelech,
19: 37 his sons *A* and Sharezer cut him
Isa 37: 38 his sons *A* and Sharezer cut him

ADRAMYTTIUM

Ac 27: 2 a ship from *A* about to sail

ADRIATIC
Ac 27: 27 were still being driven across the *A*

ADRIEL
1Sa 18: 19 given in marriage to *A* of Meholah.
2Sa 21: 8 whom she had borne to *A* son

ADULLAM (ADULLAMITE)
Ge 38: 1 stay with a man of *A* named Hirah.
Jos 12: 15 one the king of *A* one the king
15: 35 Enam, Jarmuth, *A*, Socoh, Azekah,
1Sa 22: 1 and escaped to the cave of *A*.
2Sa 23: 13 down to David at the cave of *A*,
1Ch 11: 15 David to the rock at the cave of *A*,
2Ch 11: 7 Beth Zur, Soco, *A*, Gath,
Ne 11: 30 Zanoah, *A* and their villages,
Mic 1: 15 will come to *A*.

ADULLAMITE (ADULLAM)
Ge 38: 12 and his friend Hirah the *A* went
38: 20 goat by his friend the *A* in order

ADULTERER (ADULTERY)
Lev 20: 10 both the *a* and the adulteress must
Job 24: 15 The eye of the *a* watches for dusk;
Heb 13: 4 for God will judge the *a*

ADULTERERS (ADULTERY)
Ps 50: 18 you throw in your lot with *a*.
Isa 57: 3 you offspring of *a* and prostitutes!
Jer 9: 2 for they are all *a*,
23: 10 The land is full of *a*;
Hos 7: 4 They are all *a*,
Mal 3: 5 quick to testify against sorcerers, *a*
Lk 18: 11 *a*—or even like this tax collector.
1Co 6: 9 idolaters nor *a* nor male prostitutes
1Ti 1: 10 for murderers, for *a* and perverts,

ADULTERESS (ADULTERY)
Lev 20: 10 and the *a* must be put to death.
Pr 2: 16 It will save you also from the *a*,
5: 3 For the lips of an *a* drip honey,
5: 20 be captivated, my son, by an *a*?
6: 26 and the *a* preys upon your very life
7: 5 they will keep you from the *a*,
22: 14 The mouth of an *a* is a deep pit;
30: 20 "This is the way of an *a*:
Hos 3: 1 she is loved by another and is an *a*
Ro 7: 3 from that law and is not an *a*,
7: 3 is still alive, she is called an *a*.

ADULTERIES (ADULTERY)
Jer 3: 8 sent her away because of all her *a*.
13: 27 your *a* and lustful neighings,
Rev 14: 8 the maddening wine of her *a*."
17: 2 intoxicated with the wine of her *a*."
17: 4 things and the filth of her *a*.
18: 3 the maddening wine of her *a*.
19: 2 who corrupted the earth by her *a*.

ADULTEROUS (ADULTERY)
Eze 6: 9 have been grieved by their *a* hearts,
16: 32 " 'You *a* wife! You prefer strangers
23: 45 because they are *a* and blood is
Hos 1: 2 take to yourself an *a* wife
2: 2 Let her remove the *a* look
Mt 12: 39 *a* generation asks for a miraculous
16: 4 and *a* generation looks
Mk 8: 38 in this *a* and sinful generation,
Jas 4: 4 You *a* people, don't you know that

ADULTERY (ADULTERER ADULTERERS ADULTERESS ADULTERIES ADULTEROUS)
Ex 20: 14 "You shall not commit *a*.
Lev 20: 10 " 'If a man commits *a*
Dt 5: 18 "You shall not commit *a*.
Pr 6: 32 who commits *a* lacks judgment;
Jer 3: 6 and has committed *a* there.
3: 8 she also went out and committed *a*.
3: 9 committed *a* with stone and wood.
5: 7 yet they committed *a*
7: 9 and murder, commit *a* and perjury,
23: 14 They commit *a* and live a lie.
29: 23 they have committed *a*
Eze 16: 38 of women who commit *a*
23: 37 They committed *a* with their idols;
23: 37 for they have committed *a*
23: 43 I said about the one worn out by *a*,
23: 45 of women who commit *a*
Hos 1: 2 guilty of the vilest *a* in departing
2: 4 because they are the children of *a*.
4: 2 stealing and *a*;
4: 13 and your daughters-in-law to *a*.
4: 14 when they commit *a*,
4: 15 "Though you commit *a*, O Israel,
Mt 5: 27 that it was said, 'Do not commit *a*.'
5: 28 lustfully has already committed *a*
5: 32 a woman so divorced commits *a*.
5: 32 causes her to commit *a*,
15: 19 murder, *a*, sexual immorality, theft
19: 9 marries another woman commits *a*
19: 18 do not commit *a*, do not steal,
Mk 7: 21 theft, murder, *a*, greed, malice,
10: 11 marries another woman commits *a*
10: 12 another man, she commits *a*."
10: 19 do not commit *a*, do not steal,
Lk 16: 18 a divorced woman commits *a*.
16: 18 marries another woman commits *a*
18: 20 'Do not commit *a*, do not murder,
Jn 8: 3 brought in a woman caught in *a*.
8: 4 woman was caught in the act of *a*.
Ro 2: 22 do you commit *a*? You who abhor
2: 22 that people should not commit *a*,
13: 9 "Do not commit *a*," "Do not
Jas 2: 11 If you do not commit *a*
2: 11 "Do not commit *a*," also said,
2Pe 2: 14 full of *a*, they never stop sinning;
Rev 2: 22 I will make those who commit *a*
17: 2 the kings of the earth committed *a*
18: 3 of the earth committed *a* with her,
18: 9 of the earth who committed *a*

ADULTS
1Co 14: 20 but in your thinking be *a*.

ADUMMIM
Jos 15: 7 the Pass of *A* south of the gorge.
18: 17 faces the Pass of *A*, and

ADVANCE (ADVANCED ADVANCES ADVANCING)
Dt 1: 7 and *a* into the hill country
Jos 6: 7 "*A*! March around the city,
8: 5 all those with me will *a* on the city,
Jdg 4: 15 At Barak's *a*, the LORD routed
9: 33 at sunrise, *a* against the city.
2Sa 22: 30 With your help I can *a*
Job 19: 12 His troops *a* in force;
30: 14 They *a* as through a gaping breach;
Ps 18: 29 With your help I can *a*
27: 2 When evil men *a* against me
Pr 30: 27 yet they *a* together in ranks;
Eze 38: 16 You will *a* against my people Israel
Da 11: 13 he will *a* with a huge army fully
Joel 3: 12 let them *a* into the Valley
Hab 1: 9 Their hordes *a* like a desert wind
Ro 9: 23 whom he prepared in *a* for glory—
2Co 9: 5 urge the brothers to visit you in *a*
Gal 3: 8 and announced the gospel in *a*
Eph 2: 10 which God prepared in *a* for us
Php 1: 12 has really served to *a* the gospel.

ADVANCED (ADVANCE)
Ge 18: 11 Sarah were already old and well *a*
24: 1 Abraham was now old and well *a*
Jos 13: 1 When Joshua was old and well *a*
23: 1 by then old and well *a* in years,
23: 2 "I am old and well *a* in years.
Jdg 1: 10 They *a* against the Canaanites
1: 11 From there they *a*
11: 29 there he *a* against the Ammonites.
1Sa 17: 12 in Saul's time he was old and well *a*
2Sa 10: 13 and the troops with him *a*
1Ki 1: 1 King David was old and well *a*
20: 21 king of Israel *a* and overpowered
2Ki 24: 10 king of Babylon *a* on Jerusalem
1Ch 19: 14 and the troops with him *a*
19: 17 he *a* against them and formed his
Job 32: 7 *a* years should teach wisdom.'
Ps 18: 12 of his presence clouds *a*,
48: 4 when they *a* together,

ADVANCES (ADVANCE)
Jer 4: 13 Look! He *a* like the clouds,
46: 22 as the enemy *a* in force;
Na 2: 1 An attacker *a* against you,

ADVANCING (ADVANCE)
1Ki 20: 17 "Men are *a* from Samaria."
Eze 38: 9 *a* like a storm; you will be like
Mt 11: 12 of heaven has been forcefully *a*,
Gal 1: 14 I was *a* in Judaism

ADVANTAGE
Ex 22: 22 "Do not take *a* of a widow
Lev 25: 14 do not take *a* of each other.
25: 17 Do not take *a* of each other,
Dt 24: 14 Do not take *a* of a hired man who is
Ecc 3: 19 man has no *a* over the animal.
6: 8 What *a* has a wise man
7: 12 but the *a* of knowledge is this:
Isa 30: 5 who bring neither help nor *a*,
Ro 3: 1 What *a*, then, is there
2Co 11: 20 or exploits you or takes *a* of you
1Th 4: 6 should wrong his brother or take *a*
Heb 13: 17 for that would be of no *a* to you.
Jude : 16 and flatter others for their own *a*.

ADVENTURERS
Jdg 9: 4 used them to hire reckless *a*,
11: 3 a group of *a* gathered around him

ADVERSARIES (ADVERSARY)
Dt 32: 41 I will take vengeance on my *a*
2Sa 19: 22 This day you have become my *a*!
22: 40 you made my *a* bow at my feet.
Job 27: 7 my *a* like the unjust!
Ps 18: 39 you made my *a* bow at my feet.
44: 7 you put our *a* to shame.
44: 10 and our *a* have plundered us.
74: 23 Do not ignore the clamor of your *a*,
89: 23 and strike down his *a*.
92: 11 eyes have seen the defeat of my *a*;
106: 11 The waters covered their *a*;
139: 20 your *a* misuse your name.
Da 4: 19 and its meaning to your *a*!
Lk 21: 15 none of your *a* will be able

ADVERSARY (ADVERSARIES ADVERSITY)
Dt 32: 27 lest the *a* misunderstand
1Ki 5: 4 and there is no *a* or disaster.
11: 14 up against Solomon an *a*,
11: 23 up against Solomon another *a*,
11: 25 Rezon was Israel's *a* as long
Est 7: 6 *a* and enemy is this vile Haman."
Mt 5: 25 with your *a* who is taking you
Lk 12: 58 with your *a* to the magistrate,
18: 3 'Grant me justice against my *a*.'

ADVERSITY (ADVERSARY)
Pr 17: 17 and a brother is born for *a*.
Isa 30: 20 the Lord gives you the bread of *a*

ADVICE (ADVISE)
Ex 18: 19 and I will give you some *a*,
Nu 31: 16 the ones who followed Balaam's *a*
2Sa 15: 34 me by frustrating Ahithophel's *a*.
16: 20 to Ahithophel, "Give us your *a*.
16: 23 all of Ahithophel's *a*.
16: 23 those days the *a* Ahithophel gave
17: 6 "Ahithophel has given this *a*.
17: 7 *a* Ahithophel has given is not good
17: 14 The *a* of Hushai the Arkite is better
17: 14 determined to frustrate the good *a*
17: 23 saw that his *a* had not been
20: 22 to all the people with her wise *a*,
1Ki 12: 8 rejected the *a* the elders
12: 9 He asked them, "What is your *a*?
12: 13 Rejecting the *a* given him
12: 14 he followed the *a* of the young men
12: 28 After seeking *a*, the king made two
2Ch 10: 8 rejected the *a* the elders
10: 9 He asked them, "What is your *a*?
10: 13 Rejecting the *a* of the elders,
10: 14 he followed the *a* of the young men
Est 1: 21 his nobles were pleased with this *a*,
2: 4 This *a* appealed to the king,
Job 26: 3 What *a* you have offered to one
Pr 1: 25 since you ignored all my *a*
1: 30 since they would not accept my *a*
12: 5 but the *a* of the wicked is deceitful.
12: 15 but a wise man listens to *a*.

Pr 13: 10 in those who take *a*.
19: 20 Listen to *a* and accept instruction,
20: 18 Make plans by seeking *a;*
Isa 19: 11 of Pharaoh give senseless *a*.
Eze 11: 2 and giving wicked *a* in this city.
21: 10 have despised the rod and all *a*.
Da 4: 27 O king, be pleased to accept my *a:*
Ac 27: 11 followed the *a* of the pilot
27: 21 you should have taken my *a* not
2Co 8: 10 And here is my *a* about what is best

ADVISABLE (ADVISE)

1Co 16: 4 If it seems *a* for me to go also,

ADVISE (ADVICE ADVISABLE ADVISED ADVISER ADVISERS)

2Sa 17: 11 I *a* you: Let all Israel, from Dan
1Ki 1: 12 let me *a* you how you can save
12: 6 "How would you *a* me
2Ch 10: 6 "How would you *a* me
Ac 5: 38 in the present case I *a* you:

ADVISED (ADVISE)

2Sa 17: 15 but I have *a* them to do so and so.
17: 15 "Ahithophel has *a* Absalom
17: 21 Ahithophel has *a* such
1Ki 20: 23 officials of the king of Aram *a* him,
Jn 18: 14 the one who had *a* the Jews that it

ADVISER (ADVISE)

Ge 26: 26 with Ahuzzath his personal *a*
1Ki 4: 5 a priest and personal *a* to the king;
2Ch 25: 16 "Have we appointed you an *a*

ADVISERS (ADVISE)

2Sa 8: 18 and David's sons were royal *a*.
2Ki 25: 19 of the fighting men and five royal *a*
2Ch 22: 4 father's death they became his *a*,
25: 17 king of Judah consulted his *a*,
Ezr 7: 14 his seven *a* to inquire about Judah
7: 15 his *a* have freely given to the God
7: 28 his *a* and all the king's powerful
8: 25 his *a*, his officials and all Israel
Est 6: 13 His *a* and his wife Zeresh said
Job 12: 20 He silences the lips of trusted *a*
Pr 11: 14 but many *a* make victory sure.
15: 22 but with many *a* they succeed.
24: 6 and for victory many *a*.
Jer 52: 25 fighting men, and seven royal *a*.
Da 3: 2 prefects, governors, *a*, treasurers,
3: 3 prefects, governors, *a*, treasurers,
3: 24 feet in amazement and asked his *a*,
3: 27 and royal *a* crowded around them.
4: 36 My *a* and nobles sought me out,
6: 7 *a* and governors have all agreed

ADVOCATE (ADVOCATING)

Job 16: 19 my *a* is on high.

ADVOCATING (ADVOCATE)

Ac 16: 21 an uproar by *a* customs unlawful
17: 18 "He seems to be *a* foreign gods."

AENEAS

Ac 9: 33 There he found a man named *A*,
9: 34 Immediately *A* got up.
9: 34 "*A*," Peter said to him, "Jesus

AENON

Jn 3: 23 also was baptizing at *A* near Salim,

AFFECT (AFFECTED AFFECTS)

Job 35: 6 If you sin, how does that *a* him?

AFFECTED (AFFECT)

Lev 13: 50 isolate the *a* article for seven days.
13: 55 After the *a* article has been washed
13: 55 whether the mildew has *a* one side

AFFECTION

Dt 7: 7 The LORD did not set his *a* on you
10: 15 Yet the LORD set his *a*
Eze 24: 21 of your eyes, the object of your *a*.
2Co 6: 12 We are not withholding our *a*
7: 15 And his *a* for you is all the greater
Php 1: 8 all of you with the *a* of Christ Jesus.

AFFECTS (AFFECT)

Job 35: 8 Your wickedness *a* only a man like

AFFIRM (REAFFIRM)

1Ti 1: 7 or what they so confidently *a*.

AFFIXING (FIX)

Ne 9: 38 our priests are *a* their seals to it."

AFFLICT (AFFLICTED AFFLICTING AFFLICTION AFFLICTIONS)

Lev 26: 24 will *a* you for your sins seven times
Dt 28: 27 The LORD will *a* you
28: 28 The LORD will *a* you
28: 35 The LORD will *a* your knees
Ps 55: 19 will hear them and *a* them—*Selah*
Na 1: 12 I will *a* you no more.

AFFLICTED (AFFLICT)

Dt 29: 22 with which the LORD has *a* it.
Jos 24: 5 and I *a* the Egyptians by what I did
Jdg 2: 18 those who oppressed and *a* them.
Ru 1: 21 me Naomi? The LORD has *a* me;
1Sa 5: 6 upon them and *a* them with tumors
5: 9 He *a* the people of the city,
5: 12 Those who did not die were *a*
1Ki 8: 35 their sin because you have *a* them,
2Ki 15: 5 The LORD *a* the king with leprosy
17: 20 he *a* them and gave them
2Ch 6: 26 their sin because you have *a* them,
16: 12 year of his reign Asa was *a*
21: 18 the LORD *a* Jehoram
26: 20 because the LORD had *a* him.
Job 2: 7 and *a* Job with painful sores
30: 11 has unstrung my bow and *a* me,
36: 6 but gives the *a* their rights.
Ps 9: 12 he does not ignore the cry of the *a*.
9: 18 nor the hope of the *a* ever perish.
10: 17 O LORD, the desire of the *a;*
22: 24 the suffering of the *a* one;
25: 16 for I am lonely and *a*.
34: 2 let the *a* hear and rejoice.
72: 2 your *a* ones with justice.
72: 4 He will defend the *a*
72: 12 the *a* who have no one to help.
74: 19 of your *a* people forever.
76: 9 to save all the *a* of the land.
88: 15 From my youth I have been *a*
90: 15 many days as you have *a* us,
116: 10 "I am greatly *a*."
119: 67 Before I was *a* I went astray,
119: 71 It was good for me to be *a*
119: 75 and in faithfulness you have *a* me.
Isa 1: 5 your whole heart *a*.
14: 32 in her his *a* people will find refuge
49: 13 will have compassion on his *a* ones.
51: 21 Therefore hear this, you *a* one,
53: 4 smitten by him, and *a*.
53: 7 He was oppressed and *a*,
54: 11 "O *a* city, lashed by storms
Jer 14: 19 Why have you *a* us
Na 1: 12 Although I have *a* you, ⌞O Judah,⌟
Zec 11: 11 and so the *a* of the flock who were

AFFLICTING (AFFLICT)

2Sa 24: 16 to the angel who was *a* the people,

AFFLICTION (AFFLICT)

Dt 16: 3 bread of *a*, because you left Egypt
Job 10: 15 and drowned in my *a*.
36: 8 held fast by cords of *a*,
36: 15 he speaks to them in their *a*.
36: 21 which you seem to prefer to *a*.
Ps 25: 18 Look upon my *a* and my distress
31: 7 for you saw my *a*
31: 10 my strength fails because of my *a*,
107: 17 *a* because of their iniquities.
107: 41 he lifted the needy out of their *a*
119: 92 I would have perished in my *a*.
Ecc 5: 17 with great frustration, *a* and anger.
Isa 30: 20 of adversity and the water of *a*,
48: 10 in the furnace of *a*.
La 1: 3 After *a* and harsh labor,
1: 7 In the days of her *a* and wandering
1: 9 "Look, O LORD, on my *a*,
3: 1 I am the man who has seen *a*
3: 19 I remember my *a* and my
3: 33 For he does not willingly bring *a*
Ro 12: 12 patient in *a*, faithful in prayer.

AFFLICTIONS (AFFLICT)

Lev 26: 21 I will multiply your *a* seven times
1Ki 8: 38 aware of the *a* of his own heart,
2Ch 6: 29 each one aware of his *a* and pains,
Col 1: 24 lacking in regard to Christ's *a*,
Rev 2: 9 I know your *a* and your poverty—

AFFORD (AFFORDED)

Lev 5: 7 " 'If he cannot *a* a lamb, he is
5: 11 he cannot *a* two doves
12: 8 " 'If she cannot *a* a lamb, she is
14: 21 he is poor and cannot *a* these,
14: 22 two young pigeons, which he can *a*
14: 30 which the person can *a*, one
14: 32 who cannot *a* the regular offerings
27: 8 the man making the vow can *a*.
Nu 6: 21 addition to whatever else he can *a*.

AFFORDED (AFFORD)

Ro 7: 8 seizing the opportunity *a*
7: 11 seizing the opportunity *a*

AFIRE (FIRE)

Dt 32: 22 and set *a* the foundations

AFLAME (FLAME)

Isa 13: 8 their faces *a*.

AFOOT

Ac 14: 5 There was a plot *a*

AFRAID (FEAR)

Ge 3: 10 and I was *a* because I was naked;
15: 1 "Do not be *a*, Abram.
18: 15 Sarah was *a*, so she lied and said,
19: 30 for he was *a* to stay in Zoar.
20: 8 happened, they were very much *a*.
21: 17 is the matter, Hagar? Do not be *a;*
26: 7 he was *a* to say, "She is my wife."
26: 24 Do not be *a*, for I am with you;
28: 17 He was *a* and said, "How awesome
31: 31 Jacob answered Laban, "I was *a*,
32: 11 for I am *a* he will come
35: 17 "Don't be *a*, for you have another
42: 4 he was *a* that harm might come
43: 23 "Don't be *a*.
46: 3 "Do not be *a* to go down to Egypt,
50: 19 Joseph said to them, "Don't be *a*.
50: 21 So then, don't be *a*.
Ex 2: 14 Then Moses was *a* and thought,
3: 6 because he was *a* to look at God.
14: 13 answered the people, "Do not be *a*.
20: 20 said to the people, "Do not be *a*.
34: 30 and they were *a* to come near him.
Lev 26: 6 and no one will make you *a*.
Nu 12: 8 Why then were you not *a*
14: 9 And do not be *a* of the people
14: 9 Do not be *a* of them."
21: 34 said to Moses, "Do not be *a* of him,
Dt 1: 17 Do not be *a* of any man,
1: 21 Do not be *a;* do not be discouraged
1: 29 "Do not be terrified; do not be *a*
2: 4 They will be *a* of you, but be very
3: 2 said to me, "Do not be *a* of him,
3: 22 Do not be *a* of them; the LORD
5: 5 because you were *a* of the fire
7: 18 drive them out?" But do not be *a*
13: 11 Then all Israel will hear and be *a*,
17: 13 All the people will hear and be *a*,
18: 22 Do not be *a* of him.
19: 20 people will hear of this and be *a*,
20: 1 do not be *a* of them,
20: 3 Do not be faint-hearted or *a;*
20: 8 "Is any man *a* or faint-hearted?
21: 21 All Israel will hear of it and be *a*.
31: 6 Do not be *a* or terrified
31: 8 Do not be *a;* do not be discouraged
Jos 8: 1 Do not be *a;* do not be discouraged.
10: 8 to Joshua, "Do not be *a* of them;
10: 25 Do not be *a;* do not be discouraged.
11: 6 to Joshua, "Do not be *a* of them,
Jdg 4: 18 Don't be *a*."
6: 23 said to him, "Peace! Do not be *a*.
6: 27 But because he was *a* of his family
7: 10 If you are *a* to attack, go
8: 20 he was only a boy and was *a*.
9: 21 he was *a* of his brother Abimelech.
Ru 3: 11 And now, my daughter, don't be *a*.

1Sa 3: 15 He was *a* to tell Eli the vision,
4: 7 the camp, the Philistines were *a*.
7: 7 were *a* because of the Philistines.
12: 20 "Do not be *a*," Samuel replied.
15: 24 I was *a* of the people and so I gave
18: 12 Saul was *a* of David,
18: 15 how successful he was, he was *a*
18: 29 Saul became still more *a* of him,
21: 12 was very much *a* of Achish king
22: 23 don't be *a;* the man who is seeking
23: 3 to him, "Here in Judah we are *a*.
23: 17 "Don't be *a*," he said.
28: 5 he was *a;* terror filled his heart.
28: 13 The king said to her, "Don't be *a*.
2Sa 1: 14 "Why were you not *a*
3: 11 to Abner, because he was *a* of him.
6: 9 David was *a* of the LORD that day
9: 7 "Don't be *a*," David said to him,
10: 19 So the Arameans were *a*
12: 18 David's servants were *a*
13: 28 Don't be *a*.
14: 15 the people have made me *a*.
1Ki 1: 51 "Adonijah is *a* of King Solomon
17: 13 Elijah said to her, "Don't be *a*.
19: 3 Elijah was *a* and ran for his life.
2Ki 1: 15 down with him; do not be *a* of him
6: 16 Don't be *a*," the prophet answered.
19: 6 Do not be *a* of what you have
25: 24 "Do not be *a* of the Babylonian
1Ch 13: 12 David was *a* of God that day
21: 30 he was *a* of the sword of the angel
22: 13 Do not be *a* or discouraged.
28: 20 Do not be *a* or discouraged,
2Ch 20: 15 'Do not be *a* or discouraged
20: 17 Do not be *a;* do not be discouraged.
32: 7 Do not be *a* or discouraged
32: 18 and make them *a* in order
Ezr 4: 4 and make them *a* to go on building.
Ne 2: 2 I was very much *a*, but I said
4: 14 of the people, "Don't be *a* of them.
Est 9: 2 of all the other nationalities were *a*
Job 6: 21 see something dreadful and are *a*.
11: 19 with no one to make you *a*,
39: 22 He laughs at fear, *a* of nothing;
Ps 27: 1 of whom shall I be *a?*
56: 3 When I am *a*,
56: 4 in God I trust; I will not be *a*.
56: 11 in God I trust; I will not be *a*
118: 6 is with me; I will not be *a*.
Pr 3: 24 lie down, you will not be *a;*
Ecc 9: 2 with those who are *a* to take them.
12: 5 when men are *a* of heights
Isa 7: 4 careful, keep calm and don't be *a*.
10: 24 do not be *a* of the Assyrians,
12: 2 I will trust and not be *a*.
17: 2 with no one to make them *a*.
20: 5 and boasted in Egypt will be *a*
37: 6 Do not be *a* of what you have
40: 9 lift it up, do not be *a;*
41: 14 Do not be *a*, O worm Jacob,
43: 5 Do not be *a*, for I am with you;
44: 2 Do not be *a*, O Jacob, my servant,
44: 8 Do not tremble, do not be *a*.
54: 4 "Do not be *a;* you will not suffer
Jer 1: 8 Do not be *a* of them, for I am
23: 4 they will no longer be *a* or terrified,
30: 10 and no one will make him *a*.
38: 19 "I am *a* of the Jews who have gone
40: 9 "Do not be *a* to serve
41: 18 They were *a* of them
42: 11 Do not be *a* of him, declares
42: 11 Do not be *a* of the king of Babylon,
46: 27 and no one will make him *a*.
51: 46 Do not lose heart or be *a*
Eze 2: 6 Do not be *a* of what they say
2: 6 Do not be *a*, though briers
2: 6 do not be *a* of them or their words.
3: 9 Do not be *a* of them or terrified
34: 28 and no one will make them *a*.
39: 26 land with no one to make them *a*.
Da 1: 10 "I am *a* of my lord the king,
4: 5 I had a dream that made me *a*.
10: 12 Then he continued, "Do not be *a*,
10: 19 "Do not be *a*, O man highly
Joel 2: 21 Be not *a*, O land;
2: 22 Be not *a*, O wild animals,
Jnh 1: 5 the sailors were *a* and each cried
Mic 4: 4 and no one will make them *a*,
Mic 7: 17 and will be *a* of you.
Zep 3: 13 and no one will make them *a*."
Zec 8: 13 Do not be *a*, but let your hands be
8: 15 Do not be *a*.
Mt 1: 20 do not be *a* to take Mary home
2: 22 place of his father Herod, he was *a*
8: 26 You of little faith, why are you so *a*
10: 26 of his household! "So do not be *a*
10: 28 Do not be *a* of those who kill
10: 28 be *a* of the one who can destroy
10: 31 So don't be *a;* you are worth more
14: 5 but he was *a* of the people,
14: 27 Don't be *a*."
14: 30 he was *a* and, beginning to sink,
17: 7 "Don't be *a*."
21: 26 'From men'—we are *a*
21: 46 but they were *a* of the crowd
25: 25 So I was *a* and went out
28: 4 The guards were so *a*
28: 5 said to the women, "Do not be *a*,
28: 8 from the tomb, *a* yet filled with joy,
28: 10 Jesus said to them, "Do not be *a*.
Mk 4: 40 so *a?* Do you still have no faith?"
5: 15 in his right mind; and they were *a*.
5: 36 "Don't be *a;* just believe."
6: 50 Don't be *a*."
9: 32 and were *a* to ask him about it.
10: 32 while those who followed were *a*.
12: 12 But they were *a* of the crowd;
16: 8 to anyone, because they were *a*.
Lk 1: 13 "Do not be *a*, Zechariah; your
1: 30 "Do not be *a*, Mary, you have
2: 10 said to them, "Do not be *a*.
5: 10 Jesus said to Simon, "Don't be *a;*
8: 35 in his right mind; and they were *a*.
8: 50 Jesus said to Jairus, "Don't be *a;*
9: 34 and they were *a* as they entered
9: 45 and they were *a* to ask him about it.
12: 4 do not be *a* of those who kill
12: 7 Don't be *a;* you are worth more
12: 32 "Do not be *a*, little flock,
19: 21 I was *a* of you, because you are
20: 19 But they were *a* of the people.
22: 2 for they were *a* of the people.
Jn 6: 20 he said to them, "It is I; don't be *a*
9: 22 because they were *a* of the Jews,
12: 15 "Do not be *a*, O Daughter of Zion;
14: 27 hearts be troubled and do not be *a*.
19: 8 even more *a*, and he went back
Ac 9: 26 but they were all *a* of him,
18: 9 "Do not be *a;* keep on speaking,
23: 10 the commander was *a* Paul would
24: 25 Felix was *a* and said, "That's
27: 24 beside me and said, 'Do not be *a*,
Ro 11: 20 Do not be arrogant, but be *a*.
13: 4 be *a*, for he does not bear the sword
2Co 11: 3 But I am *a* that just as Eve was
12: 20 For I am *a* that when I come I may
12: 21 I am *a* that when I come again my
Gal 2: 12 he was *a* of those who belonged
1Th 3: 5 I was *a* that in some way
Heb 11: 23 they were not *a* of the king's edict.
13: 6 Lord is my helper; I will not be *a*.
2Pe 2: 10 these men are not *a*
Rev 1: 17 hand on me and said: "Do not be *a*.
2: 10 Do not be *a* of what you are about

AFTERBIRTH

Dt 28: 57 or daughter the *a* from her womb

AFTERNOON

Jdg 19: 8 Wait till *a!*" So the two
Lk 9: 12 Late in the *a* the Twelve came
Ac 3: 1 time of prayer—at three in the *a*.
10: 3 three in the *a* he had a vision.
10: 30 at this hour, at three in the *a*.

AGABUS

Ac 11: 28 named *A*, stood up
21: 10 a prophet named *A* came

AGAG (AGAGITE)

Nu 24: 7 "Their king will be greater than *A;*
1Sa 15: 8 He took *A* king of the Amalekites
15: 9 But Saul and the army spared *A*
15: 20 and brought back *A* their king.
15: 32 Bring me *A* king of the Amalekites
15: 32 *A* came to him confidently,
1Sa 15: 33 And Samuel put *A* to death

AGAGITE (AGAG)

Est 3: 1 son of Hammedatha, the *A*,
3: 10 the *A*, the enemy of the Jews,
8: 3 to the evil plan of Haman the *A*,
8: 5 the *A*, devised and wrote
9: 24 son of Hammedatha, the *A*,

AGATE

Ex 28: 19 in the third row a jacinth, an *a*
39: 12 in the third row a jacinth, an *a*

AGE (AGE-OLD AGED AGES AGING)

Ge 15: 15 and be buried at a good old *a*.
17: 17 a child at the *a* of ninety?"
18: 11 and Sarah was past the *a*
21: 2 bore a son to Abraham in his old *a*,
21: 7 have borne him a son in his old *a*."
24: 36 has borne him a son in her old *a*,
25: 8 his last and died at a good old *a*,
37: 3 born to him in his old *a;*
44: 20 born to him in his old *a*
48: 10 eyes were failing because of old *a*,
50: 26 Joseph died at the *a* of a hundred
Nu 4: 3 thirty to fifty years of *a* who come
4: 23 thirty to fifty years of *a* who come
4: 30 thirty to fifty years of *a* who come
4: 35 thirty to fifty years of *a* who came
4: 39 thirty to fifty years of *a* who came
4: 43 thirty to fifty years of *a* who came
4: 47 thirty to fifty years of *a* who came
8: 25 at the *a* of fifty, they must retire
Jos 5: 4 all the men of military *a*—
5: 6 of military *a* when they left Egypt
24: 29 died at the *a* of a hundred and ten.
Jdg 2: 8 died at the *a* of a hundred and ten.
8: 32 son of Joash died at a good old *a*
Ru 4: 15 and sustain you in your old *a*.
2Sa 19: 32 a very old man, eighty years of *a*.
1Ki 14: 4 his sight was gone because of his *a*.
15: 23 In his old *a*, however, his feet
1Ch 29: 28 a good old *a*, having enjoyed long
2Ch 24: 15 and he died at the *a* of a hundred
Ezr 3: 8 Levites twenty years of *a*
Job 32: 7 I thought, '*A* should speak;
Ps 92: 14 They will still bear fruit in old *a*,
Isa 46: 4 Even to your old *a* and gray hairs
Da 1: 10 than the other young men your *a?*
5: 31 at the *a* of sixty-two.
Zec 8: 4 and women of ripe old *a* will sit
8: 4 with cane in hand because of his *a*.
Mt 12: 32 either in this *a* or in the *a* to come.
13: 39 The harvest is the end of the *a*,
13: 40 so it will be at the end of the *a*.
13: 49 be at the end of the *a*.
24: 3 and of the end of the *a?*"
28: 20 to the very end of the *a*."
Mk 10: 30 as much in this present *a* (homes,
10: 30 persecutions) and in the *a* to come,
Lk 1: 36 going to have a child in her old *a*,
18: 30 and, in the *a* to come, eternal life."
18: 30 many times as much in this *a*
20: 34 "The people of this *a* marry
20: 35 worthy of taking part in that *a*
Jn 9: 21 He is of *a;* he will speak for himself
9: 23 why his parents said, "He is of *a;*
1Co 1: 20 Where is the philosopher of this *a?*
2: 6 of this *a* or of the rulers of this *a*,
2: 8 of the rulers of this *a* understood it,
3: 18 wise by the standards of this *a*,
2Co 4: 4 god of this *a* has blinded the minds
Gal 1: 4 to rescue us from the present evil *a*,
1: 14 beyond many Jews of my own *a*
Eph 1: 21 not only in the present *a* but
1Ti 6: 19 a firm foundation for the coming *a*,
Tit 2: 12 and godly lives in this present *a*,
Heb 6: 5 and the powers of the coming *a*,
11: 11 even though he was past *a*—

AGE-OLD (AGE)

Ge 49: 26 than the bounty of the *a* hills.
Jdg 5: 21 the *a* river, the river Kishon.
Isa 58: 12 and will raise up the *a* foundations;
Hab 3: 6 and the *a* hills collapsed.

AGED (AGE)

Ge 43: 27 "How is your *a* father you told me

Ge 44: 20 we answered, 'We have an *a* father,
Lev 19: 32 " 'Rise in the presence of the *a*,
1Ki 1: 15 went to see the *a* king in his room,
2Ch 36: 17 nor young woman, old man or *a*.
Job 12: 12 Is not wisdom found among the *a*?
15: 10 The gray-haired and the *a* are
32: 9 not only the *a* who understand
Pr 17: 6 children are a crown to the *a*,
Isa 25: 6 a banquet of *a* wine—
47: 6 Even on the *a*

AGEE

2Sa 23: 11 Shammah son of *A* the Hararite.

AGENT

Ne 11: 24 was the king's *a* in all affairs
Ro 13: 4 an *a* of wrath to bring punishment

AGES (AGE)

Ge 43: 33 before him in the order of their *a*,
Lev 27: 3 of a male between the *a* of twenty
27: 5 a person between the *a* of five
Isa 45: 17 to *a* everlasting.
Joel 2: 2 nor ever will be in *a* to come.
Ac 15: 18 that have been known for *a*.
Ro 16: 25 the mystery hidden for long *a* past,
1Co 10: 11 the fulfillment of the *a* has come.
Eph 2: 7 that in the coming *a* he might show
3: 9 which for *a* past was kept hidden
Col 1: 26 that has been kept hidden for *a*
Heb 9: 26 all at the end of the *a* to do away
Jude : 25 before all *a*, now and forevermore!
Rev 15: 3 King of the *a*.

AGGRESSION (AGGRESSIVE AGGRESSOR)

Isa 14: 6 nations with relentless *a*.

AGGRESSIVE (AGGRESSION)

Isa 18: 2 an *a* nation of strange speech,
18: 7 an *a* nation of strange speech,

AGGRESSOR (AGGRESSION)

Isa 16: 4 the *a* will vanish from the land.

AGHAST

Job 26: 11 *a* at his rebuke.
Isa 13: 8 They will look *a* at each other,

AGING (AGE)

Heb 8: 13 is obsolete and *a* will soon

AGITATING (AGITATORS)

Ac 17: 13 *a* the crowds and stirring them up.

AGITATORS (AGITATING)

Gal 5: 12 for those *a*, I wish they would go

AGONY

Ps 6: 2 heal me, for my bones are in *a*.
42: 10 My bones suffer mortal *a*
Jer 4: 19 Oh, the *a* of my heart!
Eze 30: 16 Pelusium will writhe in *a*.
Mic 4: 10 Writhe in *a*, O Daughter of Zion,
Zec 9: 5 Gaza will writhe in *a*,
Lk 16: 24 because I am in *a* in this fire.'
16: 25 is comforted here and you are in *a*.
Ac 2: 24 freeing him from the *a* of death,
Rev 9: 5 the *a* they suffered was like that
16: 10 Men gnawed their tongues in *a*

AGREE (AGREED AGREEING AGREEMENT AGREEMENTS AGREES)

Ge 34: 17 if you will not *a* to be circumcised,
2Sa 14: 16 Perhaps the king will *a*
1Ki 20: 8 listen to him or *a* to his demands."
22: 13 Let your word *a* with theirs,
2Ch 18: 12 Let your word *a* with theirs,
Mt 18: 19 on earth *a* about anything you ask
20: 13 Didn't you *a* to work for a denarius
Mk 14: 56 but their statements did not *a*.
14: 59 then their testimony did not *a*.
Ac 5: 9 "How could you *a* to test the Spirit
Ro 7: 16 want to do, I *a* that the law is good.
1Co 1: 10 that all of you *a* with one another
Php 4: 2 with Syntyche to *a* with each other
1Ti 6: 3 does not *a* to the sound instruction

AGREED (AGREE)

Ge 16: 2 Abram *a* to what Sarai said.
23: 16 Abraham *a* to Ephron's terms
30: 34 "*A*," said Laban.
34: 24 out of the city gate *a* with Hamor
37: 27 His brothers *a*.
Ex 2: 21 Moses *a* to stay with the man,
Jos 2: 21 "*A*," she replied.
Jdg 15: 13 "*A*," they answered.
17: 11 So the Levite *a* to live with him,
1Ki 15: 20 Ben-Hadad *a* with King Asa
20: 25 He *a* with them and acted
2Ki 12: 8 The priests *a* that they would not
1Ch 13: 4 The whole assembly *a* to do this,
2Ch 16: 4 Ben-Hadad *a* with King Asa
20: 36 He *a* with him to construct a fleet
30: 23 The whole assembly then *a*
Est 9: 23 Jews *a* to continue the celebration
Jer 34: 10 They *a*, and set them free.
34: 10 into this covenant *a* that they
Da 1: 14 So he *a* to this and tested them
6: 7 governors have all *a* that the king
Am 3: 3 unless they have *a* to do so?
Mt 20: 2 He *a* to pay them a denarius
Lk 22: 5 They were delighted and *a*
Ac 15: 25 So we all *a* to choose some men
23: 20 "The Jews have *a* to ask you
Gal 2: 9 They *a* that we should go

AGREEING (AGREE)

Rev 17: 17 to accomplish his purpose by *a*

AGREEMENT (AGREE)

Ge 26: 28 to be a sworn *a* between us'—
2Sa 3: 12 "Whose land is it? Make an *a*
3: 13 "I will make an *a* with you.
Ne 9: 38 we are making a binding *a*,
Job 2: 11 and met together by *a* to go
41: 4 Will he make an *a* with you
Isa 28: 15 with the grave we have made an *a*.
28: 18 your *a* with the grave will not stand
Da 11: 23 After coming to an *a* with him,
Ac 15: 15 of the prophets are in *a* with this,
2Co 6: 16 What *a* is there between the temple
1Jn 5: 8 the blood; and the three are in *a*.

AGREEMENTS (AGREE)

Hos 10: 4 and make *a*;

AGREES (AGREE)

Ac 7: 42 This *a* with what is written
24: 14 I believe everything that *a*
1Co 4: 17 which *a* with what I teach

AGRIPPA

Ac 25: 13 A few days later King *A*
25: 22 *A* said to Festus, "I would like
25: 23 The next day *A* and Bernice came
25: 24 "King *A*, and all who are present
25: 26 and especially before you, King *A*,
26: 1 Then *A* said to Paul, "You have
26: 2 and began his defense: "King *A*,
26: 19 King *A*, I was not disobedient
26: 27 King *A*, do you believe
26: 28 *A* said to Paul, "Do you think that
26: 32 *A* said to Festus, "This man could

AGROUND (GROUND)

Ac 27: 17 Fearing that they would run *a*
27: 26 we must run *a* on some island."
27: 39 to run the ship *a* if they could.
27: 41 the ship struck a sandbar and ran *a*.

AGUR

Pr 30: 1 The sayings of *A* son of Jakeh—

AHAB (AHAB'S)

1Ki 16: 28 And *A* his son succeeded him
16: 29 *A* son of Omri became king
16: 30 *A* son of Omri did more evil
16: 33 *A* also made an Asherah pole
17: 1 said to *A*, "As the LORD,
18: 1 "Go and present yourself to *A*,
18: 2 Elijah went to present himself to *A*.
18: 3 and *A* had summoned Obadiah,
18: 5 *A* had said to Obadiah, "Go
18: 6 *A* going in one direction
18: 9 over to *A* to be put to death?
18: 12 and tell *A* and he doesn't find you,
18: 15 surely present myself to *A* today."
18: 16 So Obadiah went to meet *A*
18: 16 and *A* went to meet Elijah.
18: 20 *A* sent word throughout all Israel
18: 41 And Elijah said to *A*, "Go,
18: 42 So *A* went off to eat and drink,
18: 44 So Elijah said, "Go and tell *A*,
18: 45 came on and *A* rode off to Jezreel.
18: 46 he ran ahead of *A* all the way
19: 1 *A* told Jezebel everything Elijah
20: 2 into the city to *A* king of Israel,
20: 10 sent another message to *A*:
20: 13 a prophet came to *A* king
20: 14 "But who will do this?" asked *A*.
20: 15 So *A* summoned the young officers
20: 33 *A* had him come up into his chariot
20: 34 *A* said, "On the basis
21: 1 to the palace of *A* king of Samaria.
21: 2 *A* said to Naboth, "Let me have
21: 4 So *A* went home, sullen and angry
21: 15 stoned to death, she said to *A*,
21: 16 When *A* heard that Naboth was
21: 18 "Go down to meet *A* king of Israel,
21: 20 yes, yours!' " *A* said to Elijah,
21: 21 and cut off from *A* every last male
21: 24 belonging to *A* who die in the city,
21: 25 (There was never a man like *A*,
21: 27 When *A* heard these words,
21: 29 you noticed how *A* has humbled
22: 20 'Who will lure *A*
22: 40 of Israel? *A* rested with his fathers.
22: 41 year of *A* king of Israel.
22: 49 son of *A* said to Jehoshaphat,
22: 51 Ahaziah son of *A* became king
2Ki 3: 1 Joram son of *A* became king
3: 5 But after *A* died, the king
8: 16 of Joram son of *A* king of Israel,
8: 18 as the house of *A* had done,
8: 18 for he married a daughter of *A*.
8: 25 of Joram son of *A* king of Israel,
8: 27 as the house of *A* had done,
8: 27 in the ways of the house of *A*
8: 28 went with Joram son of *A* to war
8: 29 to Jezreel to see Joram son of *A*,
9: 7 the house of *A* your master,
9: 8 I will cut off from *A* every last male
9: 8 The whole house of *A* will perish.
9: 9 the house of *A* like the house
9: 25 in chariots behind *A* his father
9: 29 year of Joram son of *A*,
10: 1 seventy sons of the house of *A*.
10: 10 against the house of *A* will fail.
10: 11 who remained of the house of *A*,
10: 18 "*A* served Baal a little; Jehu will
10: 30 to the house of *A* all I had in mind
21: 3 as *A* king of Israel had done.
21: 13 used against the house of *A*.
2Ch 18: 1 himself with *A* by marriage.
18: 2 *A* slaughtered many sheep
18: 2 went down to visit *A* in Samaria.
18: 3 *A* king of Israel asked Jehoshaphat
18: 19 'Who will lure *A* king of Israel
21: 6 as the house of *A* had done,
21: 6 for he married a daughter of *A*.
21: 13 just as the house of *A* did.
22: 3 in the ways of the house of *A*,
22: 4 as the house of *A* had done,
22: 5 with Joram son of *A* king of Israel
22: 6 to Jezreel to see Joram son of *A*
22: 7 anointed to destroy the house of *A*.
22: 8 judgment on the house of *A*,
Jer 29: 21 says about *A* son of Kolaiah
29: 22 treat you like Zedekiah and *A*,

AHAB'S (AHAB)

1Ki 16: 34 In *A* time, Hiel of Bethel rebuilt
21: 8 So she wrote letters in *A* name,
22: 39 As for the other events of *A* reign,
2Ki 1: 1 After *A* death, Moab rebelled
8: 27 related by marriage to *A* family.
10: 1 and to the guardians of *A* children.
10: 17 all who were left there of *A* family;
Mic 6: 16 and all the practices of *A* house,

AHARAH

1Ch 8: 1 Ashbel the second son, *A* the third,

AHARHEL

1Ch 4: 8 and of the clans of *A* son of Harum.

AHASBAI

2Sa 23: 34 Eliphelet son of *A* the Maacathite,

AHAVA

Ezr 8: 15 at the canal that flows toward *A*,
8: 21 by the *A* Canal, I proclaimed a fast,
8: 31 out from the *A* Canal to go

AHAZ

2Ki 15: 38 And *A* his son succeeded him
16: 1 *A* son of Jotham king
16: 2 *A* was twenty years old
16: 5 against Jerusalem and besieged *A*,
16: 7 *A* sent messengers to say
16: 8 *A* took the silver and gold found
16: 10 Then King *A* went to Damascus
16: 11 all the plans that King *A* had sent
16: 11 finished it before King *A* returned.
16: 15 King *A* then gave these orders
16: 16 did just as King *A* had ordered.
16: 17 King *A* took away the side panels
16: 19 the other events of the reign of *A*,
16: 20 *A* rested with his fathers
17: 1 year of *A* king of Judah,
18: 1 Hezekiah son of *A* king
20: 11 gone down on the stairway of *A*.
23: 12 the roof near the upper room of *A*,
1Ch 3: 13 Jotham his son, *A* his son,
8: 35 Pithon, Melech, Tarea and *A*.
8: 36 *A* was the father of Jehoaddah,
9: 41 Pithon, Melech, Tahrea and *A*.
9: 42 *A* was the father of Jadah,
2Ch 27: 9 And *A* his son succeeded him
28: 1 *A* was twenty years old
28: 16 At that time King *A* sent
28: 19 because of *A* king of Israel,
28: 21 *A* took some of the things
28: 22 time of trouble King *A* became
28: 24 *A* gathered together
28: 27 *A* rested with his fathers
29: 19 the articles that King *A* removed
Isa 1: 1 *A* and Hezekiah, kings of Judah.
7: 1 When *A* son of Jotham, the son
7: 2 of *A* and his people were shaken,
7: 3 to meet *A* at the end
7: 10 Again the LORD spoke to *A*,
7: 12 But *A* said, ''I will not ask;
14: 28 came in the year King *A* died:
38: 8 gone down on the stairway of *A*.' ''
Hos 1: 1 *A* and Hezekiah, kings of Judah,
Mic 1: 1 *A* and Hezekiah, kings of Judah—
Mt 1: 9 of *A*, *A* the father of Hezekiah,

AHAZIAH (AHAZIAH'S)

1Ki 22: 40 And *A* his son succeeded him
22: 49 At that time *A* son of Ahab said
22: 51 *A* son of Ahab became king
2Ki 1: 2 *A* had fallen through the lattice
1: 17 Because *A* had no son, Joram
8: 24 And *A* his son succeeded him
8: 25 *A* son of Jehoram king
8: 26 *A* was twenty-two years old
8: 28 *A* went with Joram son of Ahab
8: 29 Then *A* son of Jehoram king
9: 16 and *A* king of Judah had gone
9: 21 and *A* king of Judah rode out,
9: 23 calling out to *A*, ''Treachery, *A*!''
9: 27 When *A* king of Judah saw what
9: 29 *A* had become king of Judah.)
10: 13 They said, ''We are relatives of *A*,
10: 13 relatives of *A* king of Judah
11: 1 of *A* saw that her son was dead,
11: 2 of King Jehoram and sister of *A*,
11: 2 son of *A* and stole him away
12: 18 Jehoshaphat, Jehoram and *A*,
13: 1 of Joash son of *A* king of Judah,
14: 13 the son of Joash, the son of *A*,
1Ch 3: 11 Jehoram his son, *A* his son,
2Ch 20: 35 an alliance with *A* king of Israel,
20: 37 you have made an alliance with *A*,
21: 17 Not a son was left to him except *A*,
22: 1 So *A* son of Jehoram king
22: 1 The people of Jerusalem made *A*,
22: 2 *A* was twenty-two years old
22: 6 Then *A* son of Jehoram king
2Ch 22: 7 When *A* arrived, he went out
22: 8 who had been attending *A*,
22: 9 He then went in search of *A*,
22: 9 in the house of *A* powerful enough
22: 10 of *A* saw that her son was dead,
22: 11 son of *A* and stole him away
25: 23 the son of Joash, the son of *A*,

AHAZIAH'S (AHAZIAH)

2Ki 1: 18 for all the other events of *A* reign,
2Ch 22: 7 God brought about *A* downfall.
22: 7 Through *A* visit to Joram,
22: 8 and the sons of *A* relatives,
22: 11 of the priest Jehoiada, was *A* sister,

AHBAN

1Ch 2: 29 who bore him *A* and Molid.

AHER

1Ch 7: 12 the Hushites the descendants of *A*.

AHI

1Ch 5: 15 *A* son of Abdiel, the son of Guni,
7: 34 The sons of Shomer: *A*, Rohgah,

AHIAH

Ne 10: 26 Hashabnah, Maaseiah, *A*, Hanan,

AHIAM

2Sa 23: 33 *A* son of Sharar the Hararite,
1Ch 11: 35 *A* son of Sacar the Hararite,

AHIAN

1Ch 7: 19 *A*, Shechem, Likhi and Aniam.

AHIEZER

Nu 1: 12 from Dan, *A* son of Ammishaddai;
2: 25 of Dan is *A* son of Ammishaddai.
7: 66 On the tenth day *A* son
7: 71 offering of *A* son of Ammishaddai.
10: 25 *A* son of Ammishaddai was
1Ch 12: 3 *A* their chief and Joash the sons

AHIHUD

Nu 34: 27 tribe of Issachar; *A* son of Shelomi,
1Ch 8: 7 who was the father of Uzza and *A*.

AHIJAH (AHIJAH'S)

1Sa 14: 3 among whom was *A*, who was
14: 18 Saul said to *A*, ''Bring the ark
1Ki 4: 3 Elihoreph and *A*, sons of Shisha—
11: 29 *A* the prophet of Shiloh met him
11: 30 *A* took hold of the new cloak he
12: 15 of Nebat through *A* the Shilonite.
14: 2 *A* the prophet is there—the one
14: 4 *A* could not see; his sight was gone
14: 5 But the LORD had told *A*,
14: 6 So when *A* heard the sound
14: 18 through his servant the prophet *A*.
15: 27 Baasha son of *A* of the house
15: 29 through his servant *A* the Shilonite
15: 33 Baasha son of *A* became king
21: 22 and that of Baasha son of *A*,
2Ki 9: 9 like the house of Baasha son of *A*.
1Ch 2: 25 Bunah, Oren, Ozem and *A*.
8: 7 *A*, and Gera, who deported them
11: 36 the Mekerathite, *A* the Pelonite,
2Ch 9: 29 in the prophecy of *A* the Shilonite
10: 15 of Nebat through *A* the Shilonite.

AHIJAH'S (AHIJAH)

1Ki 14: 4 and went to *A* house in Shiloh.

AHIKAM

2Ki 22: 12 *A* son of Shaphan, Acbor son
22: 14 Hilkiah the priest, *A*, Acbor,
25: 22 appointed Gedaliah son of *A*,
2Ch 34: 20 to Hilkiah, *A* son of Shaphan,
Jer 26: 24 *A* son of Shaphan supported
39: 14 him over to Gedaliah son of *A*,
40: 5 ''Go back to Gedaliah son of *A*,
40: 6 to Gedaliah son of *A* at Mizpah
40: 7 had appointed Gedaliah son of *A*
40: 9 Gedaliah son of *A*, the son
40: 11 had appointed Gedaliah son of *A*,
40: 14 son of *A* did not believe them.
40: 16 But Gedaliah son of *A* said
41: 1 to Gedaliah son of *A* at Mizpah.
Jer 41: 2 struck down Gedaliah son of *A*,
41: 6 ''Come to Gedaliah son of *A*.''
41: 10 had appointed Gedaliah son of *A*.
41: 16 assassinated Gedaliah son of *A*:
41: 18 had killed Gedaliah son of *A*,
43: 6 left with Gedaliah son of *A*,

AHILUD

2Sa 8: 16 Jehoshaphat son of *A* was recorder;
20: 24 Jehoshaphat son of *A* was recorder;
1Ki 4: 3 Jehoshaphat son of *A*— recorder;
4: 12 Baana son of *A*— in Taanach
1Ch 18: 15 Jehoshaphat son of *A* was recorder;

AHIMAAZ

1Sa 14: 50 name was Ahinoam daughter of *A*.
2Sa 15: 27 with your son *A* and Jonathan son
15: 36 *A* son of Zadok and Jonathan son
17: 17 Jonathan and *A* were staying
17: 20 ''Where are *A* and Jonathan?''
18: 19 Now *A* son of Zadok said,
18: 22 *A* son of Zadok again said to Joab,
18: 23 Then *A* ran by way of the plain
18: 27 me that the first one runs like *A* son
18: 28 Then *A* called out to the king,
18: 29 *A* answered, ''I saw great confusion
1Ki 4: 15 son of Iddo—in Mahanaim; *A*—
1Ch 6: 9 father of *A*, *A* the father of Azariah,
6: 53 Zadok his son and *A* his son.

AHIMAN

Nu 13: 22 where *A*, Sheshai and Talmai,
Jos 15: 14 *A* and Talmai—descendants
Jdg 1: 10 defeated Sheshai, *A* and Talmai.
1Ch 9: 17 Talmon, *A* and their brothers,

AHIMELECH

1Sa 21: 1 David went to Nob, to *A* the priest.
21: 1 *A* trembled when he met him,
21: 2 David answered *A* the priest,
21: 8 David asked *A*, ''Don't you have
22: 9 of Jesse come to *A* son of Ahitub
22: 10 *A* inquired of the LORD for him;
22: 11 sent for the priest *A* son of Ahitub
22: 14 as he does today?'' *A* answered
22: 16 *A*, you and your father's whole
22: 20 Abiathar, a son of *A* son of Ahitub,
23: 6 son of *A* had brought the ephod
26: 6 David then asked *A* the Hittite
30: 7 the son of *A*, ''Bring me the ephod
2Sa 8: 17 and *A* son of Abiathar were priests;
1Ch 18: 16 and *A* son of Abiathar were priests;
24: 3 and *A* a descendant of Ithamar,
24: 6 *A* son of Abiathar and the heads
24: 31 of King David and of Zadok, *A*,

AHIMOTH

1Ch 6: 25 Amasai, *A*, Elkanah his son,

AHINADAB

1Ki 4: 14 *A* son of Iddo—in Mahanaim;

AHINOAM

1Sa 14: 50 His wife's name was *A* daughter
25: 43 David had also married *A*
27: 3 *A* of Jezreel and Abigail of Carmel,
30: 5 two wives had been captured—*A*
2Sa 2: 2 with his two wives, *A* of Jezreel
3: 2 firstborn was Amnon the son of *A*
1Ch 3: 1 firstborn was Amnon the son of *A*

AHIO

2Sa 6: 3 Uzzah and *A*, sons of Abinadab,
6: 4 and *A* was walking in front of it.
1Ch 8: 14 *A*, Shashak, Jeremoth, Zebadiah,
8: 31 Gedor, *A*, Zeker and Mikloth,
9: 37 Gedor, *A*, Zechariah and Mikloth.
13: 7 with Uzzah and *A* guiding it.

AHIRA

Nu 1: 15 from Naphtali, *A* son of Enan.''
2: 29 of Naphtali is *A* son of Enan.
7: 78 On the twelfth day *A* son of Enan,
7: 83 This was the offering of *A* son
10: 27 and *A* son of Enan was

AHIRAM (AHIRAMITE)

Nu 26: 38 through *A*, the Ahiramite clan;

AHIRAMITE (AHIRAM)

Nu 26: 38 through Ahiram, the *A* clan;

AHISAMACH

Ex 31: 6 I have appointed Oholiab son of *A*,
35: 34 both him and Oholiab son of *A*,
38: 23 with him was Oholiab son of *A*,

AHISHAHAR

1Ch 7: 10 Kenaanah, Zethan, Tarshish and *A*.

AHISHAR

1Ki 4: 6 *A*— in charge of the palace;

AHITHOPHEL (AHITHOPHEL'S)

2Sa 15: 12 he also sent for *A* the Gilonite,
15: 31 "*A* is among the conspirators
16: 15 to Jerusalem, and *A* was with him.
16: 20 said to *A*, "Give us your advice.
16: 21 *A* answered, "Lie with your
16: 23 days the advice *A* gave was like
17: 1 *A* said to Absalom, "I would
17: 6 Absalom said, "*A* has given this
17: 7 advice *A* has given is not good this
17: 14 of *A* in order to bring disaster
17: 14 the Arkite is better than that of *A*."
17: 15 "*A* has advised Absalom
17: 21 *A* has advised such and such
17: 23 When *A* saw that his advice had
23: 34 Eliam son of *A* the Gilonite,
1Ch 27: 33 *A* was the king's counselor.
27: 34 *A* was succeeded by Jehoiada son

AHITHOPHEL'S (AHITHOPHEL)

2Sa 15: 31 turn *A* counsel into foolishness."
15: 34 me by frustrating *A* advice.
16: 23 Absalom regarded all of *A* advice.

AHITUB

1Sa 14: 3 a son of Ichabod's brother *A* son
22: 9 to Ahimelech son of *A* at Nob.
22: 11 for the priest Ahimelech son of *A*
22: 12 Saul said, "Listen now, son of *A*."
22: 20 a son of Ahimelech son of *A*,
2Sa 8: 17 Zadok son of *A* and Ahimelech son
1Ch 6: 8 father of *A*, *A* the father of Zadok,
6: 12 father of *A*, *A* the father of Zadok,
6: 52 Amariah his son, *A* his son,
9: 11 the son of Meraioth, the son of *A*,
18: 16 Zadok son of *A* and Ahimelech son
Ezr 7: 2 the son of *A*, the son of Amariah,
Ne 11: 11 the son of *A*, supervisor

AHLAB

Jdg 1: 31 or Sidon or *A* or Aczib or Helbah

AHLAI

1Ch 2: 31 Sheshan was the father of *A*.
11: 41 Uriah the Hittite, Zabad son of *A*,

AHOAH

1Ch 8: 4 Abishua, Naaman, *A*, Gera,

AHOHITE

2Sa 23: 9 was Eleazar son of Dodai the *A*.
23: 28 Zalmon the *A*, Maharai
1Ch 11: 12 was Eleazar son of Dodai the *A*,
11: 29 Ilai the *A*, Maharai
27: 4 second month was Dodai the *A*;

AHUMAI

1Ch 4: 2 Jahath the father of *A* and Lahad.

AHUZZAM

1Ch 4: 6 Naarah bore him *A*, Hepher,

AHUZZATH

Ge 26: 26 with *A* his personal adviser

AHZAI

Ne 11: 13 the son of *A*, the son

AI

Ge 12: 8 on the west and *A* on the east.
13: 3 *A* where his tent had been earlier
Jos 7: 2 Joshua sent men from Jericho to *A*,
7: 2 the men went up and spied out *A*.
7: 3 have to go up against *A*.
7: 4 they were routed by the men of *A*,
8: 1 into your hands the king of *A*,
8: 1 with you, and go up and attack *A*.
8: 2 You shall do to *A* and its king
8: 3 whole army moved out to attack *A*.
8: 9 lay in wait between Bethel and *A*,
8: 9 of *A*— but Joshua spent that night
8: 10 of Israel marched before them to *A*.
8: 11 They set up camp north of *A*,
8: 12 in ambush between Bethel and *A*,
8: 14 When the king of *A* saw this,
8: 16 All the men of *A* were called
8: 17 Not a man remained in *A*
8: 18 held out his javelin toward *A*.
8: 18 out toward *A* the javelin that is
8: 20 The men of *A* looked back
8: 21 and attacked the men of *A*.
8: 23 But they took the king of *A* alive
8: 24 all the Israelites returned to *A*
8: 24 had finished killing all the men of *A*
8: 25 fell that day—all the people of *A*.
8: 26 had destroyed all who lived in *A*.
8: 28 So Joshua burned *A* and made it
8: 29 He hung the king of *A* on a tree
9: 3 Joshua had done to Jericho and *A*,
10: 1 doing to *A* and its king
10: 1 heard that Joshua had taken *A*
10: 2 than *A*, and all its men were good
12: 9 of *A* (near Bethel) one the king
Ezr 2: 28 of Bethel and *A* 223
Ne 7: 32 of Bethel and *A* 123
Jer 49: 3 O Heshbon, for *A* is destroyed!

AIAH (AIAH'S)

Ge 36: 24 The sons of Zibeon: *A* and Anah.
2Sa 3: 7 named Rizpah daughter of *A*.
21: 10 daughter of *A* took sackcloth
1Ch 1: 40 The sons of Zibeon: *A* and Anah.

AIAH'S (AIAH)

2Sa 21: 8 the two sons of *A* daughter Rizpah,
21: 11 was told what *A* daughter Rizpah,

AIATH

Isa 10: 28 They enter *A*;

AID (AIDE)

Ge 50: 24 But God will surely come to your *a*
50: 25 "God will surely come to your *a*,
Ex 13: 19 "God will surely come to your *a*,
Ru 1: 6 come to the *a* of his people
Ps 35: 2 arise and come to my *a*.
60: 11 Give us *a* against the enemy,
106: 4 come to my *a* when you save them,
108: 12 Give us *a* against the enemy,
Isa 38: 14 troubled; O Lord, come to my *a*!"
Php 4: 16 you sent me *a* again and again

AIDE (AID)

Ex 24: 13 Moses set out with Joshua his *a*,
33: 11 but his young *a* Joshua son
Nu 11: 28 who had been Moses' *a* since youth
Jos 1: 1 Moses' *a*: "Moses my servant is
Ne 6: 5 Sanballat sent his *a* to me

AIJA

Ne 11: 31 *A*, Bethel and its settlements,

AIJALON

Jos 10: 12 O moon, over the Valley of *A*."
19: 42 Shaalabbin, *A*, Ithlah, Elon,
21: 24 *A* and Gath Rimmon, together
Jdg 1: 35 also to hold out in Mount Heres, *A*
12: 12 and was buried in *A* in the land
1Sa 14: 31 the Philistines from Micmash to *A*,
1Ch 6: 69 Beth Horon, *A* and Gath Rimmon,
8: 13 of families of those living in *A*
2Ch 11: 10 Azekah, Zorah, *A* and Hebron.
28: 18 Beth Shemesh, *A* and Gederoth,

AILS

Job 16: 3 What *a* you that you keep

AIM

Ps 21: 12 backs when you *a* at them
64: 3 *a* their words like deadly arrows.
1Co 7: 34 Her *a* is to be devoted to the Lord
2Co 13: 11 *A* for perfection, listen

AIN

Nu 34: 11 to Riblah on the east side of *A*
Jos 15: 32 Lebaoth, Shilhim, *A* and Rimmon
19: 7 *A*, Rimmon, Ether and Ashan—
21: 16 Eshtemoa, Holon, Debir, *A*,
1Ch 4: 32 *A*, Rimmon, Token and Ashan—

AIR (AIRING MIDAIR)

Ge 1: 26 of the sea and the birds of the *a*,
1: 28 birds of the *a* and over every living
1: 30 of the *a* and all the creatures that
2: 19 of the field and all the birds of the *a*
2: 20 the birds of the *a* and all the beasts
6: 7 of the *a*— for I am grieved that I
7: 23 and the birds of the *a* were wiped
9: 2 the earth and all the birds of the *a*,
Ex 9: 8 it into the *a* in the presence
9: 10 Moses tossed it into the *a*,
Dt 4: 17 or any bird that flies in the *a*,
28: 26 food for all the birds of the *a*
1Sa 17: 44 flesh to the birds of the *a*
17: 46 army to the birds of the *a*
2Sa 21: 10 birds of the *a* touch them by day
1Ki 14: 11 and the birds of the *a* will feed
16: 4 and the birds of the *a* will feed
21: 24 and the birds of the *a* will feed
Job 12: 7 of the *a*, and they will tell you;
28: 21 even from the birds of the *a*.
35: 11 wiser than the birds of the *a*?'
41: 16 that no *a* can pass between.
Ps 8: 8 the birds of the *a*,
79: 2 as food to the birds of the *a*,
104: 12 The birds of the *a* nest
Ecc 10: 20 bird of the *a* may carry your words,
Jer 7: 33 food for the birds of the *a*
9: 10 The birds of the *a* have fled
15: 3 the birds of the *a* and the beasts
16: 4 food for the birds of the *a*
19: 7 as food to the birds of the *a*
34: 20 food for the birds of the *a*
Eze 29: 5 of the earth and the birds of the *a*.
31: 6 All the birds of the *a*
31: 13 All the birds of the *a* settled
32: 4 the birds of the *a* settle on you
38: 20 the birds of the *a*, the beasts
Da 2: 38 of the field and the birds of the *a*.
4: 12 and the birds of the *a* lived
4: 21 in its branches for the birds of the *a*
Hos 2: 18 of the field and the birds of the *a*
4: 3 of the field and the birds of the *a*
7: 12 down like birds of the *a*.
Zep 1: 3 I will sweep away the birds of the *a*
Mt 6: 26 Look at the birds of the *a*;
8: 20 and birds of the *a* have nests,
13: 32 so that the birds of the *a* come
Mk 4: 32 of the *a* can perch in its shade."
Lk 8: 5 and the birds of the *a* ate it up.
9: 58 and birds of the *a* have nests,
13: 19 and the birds of the *a* perched
Ac 10: 12 of the earth and birds of the *a*.
11: 6 reptiles, and birds of the *a*.
22: 23 and flinging dust into the *a*,
1Co 9: 26 not fight like a man beating the *a*.
14: 9 You will just be speaking into the *a*
Eph 2: 2 of the ruler of the kingdom of the *a*,
1Th 4: 17 clouds to meet the Lord in the *a*.
Rev 16: 17 poured out his bowl into the *a*,

AIRING (AIR)

Pr 18: 2 but delights in *a* his own opinions.

AKAN

Ge 36: 27 of Ezer: Bilhan, Zaavan and *A*.
1Ch 1: 42 of Ezer: Bilhan, Zaavan and *A*.

AKELDAMA

Ac 1: 19 field in their language *A*,

AKIM

Mt 1: 14 father of *A*, *A* the father of Eliud,

AKKAD

Ge 10: 10 Erech, *A* and Calneh, in Shinar.

AKKUB

1Ch 3: 24 Eliashib, Pelaiah, *A*, Johanan,
9: 17 The gatekeepers: Shallum, *A*,
Ezr 2: 42 of Shallum, Ater, Talmon, *A*,

Ezr 2:45 Lebanah, Hagabah, *A*, Hagab,
Ne 7:45 of Shallum, Ater, Talmon, *A*,
8: 7 Sherebiah, Jamin, *A*, Shabbethai,
11:19 *A*, Talmon and their associates,
12:25 *A* were gatekeepers who guarded

ALABASTER

Mt 26: 7 came to him with an *a* jar
Mk 14: 3 a woman came with an *a* jar
Lk 7:37 she brought an *a* jar of perfume,

ALAMOTH

1Ch 15:20 to play the lyres according to *a*,

ALARM (ALARMED)

1Ki 1:49 all Adonijah's guests rose in *a*
Job 33: 7 No fear of me should *a* you,
Ps 31:22 In my *a* I said,
Da 4:19 the dream or its meaning *a* you."
11:44 the east and the north will *a* him,
Joel 2: 1 sound the *a* on my holy hill.
2Co 7:11 indignation, what *a*, what longing,

ALARMED (ALARM)

Jos 10: 2 his people were very much *a* at this
2Sa 4: 1 courage, and all Israel became *a*.
2Ch 20: 3 *A*, Jehoshaphat resolved to inquire
Job 40:23 When the river rages, he is not *a*;
Da 4:19 for a time, and his thoughts *a* him.
5:10 "Don't be *a*! Don't look so pale!
Mt 24: 6 but see to it that you are not *a*.
Mk 13: 7 and rumors of wars, do not be *a*.
16: 5 on the right side, and they were *a*.
16: 6 "Don't be *a*," he said.
Ac 16:38 were Roman citizens, they were *a*.
20:10 "Don't be *a*," he said.
22:29 The commander himself was *a*
2Th 2: 2 not to become easily unsettled or *a*

ALCOVE (ALCOVES)

Eze 40:12 of each *a* was a wall one cubit high,
40:13 wall of one *a* to the top of

ALCOVES (ALCOVE)

Eze 40: 7 between the *a* were five cubits
40: 7 *a* for the guards were one rod long
40:10 Inside the east gate were three *a*
40:12 and the *a* were six cubits square.
40:16 The *a* and the projecting walls
40:21 Its *a*— three on each side—
40:29 Its *a*, its projecting walls
40:33 Its *a*, its projecting walls
40:36 as did its *a*, its projecting walls

ALEMETH

1Ch 6:60 *A* and Anathoth, together
7: 8 Jeremoth, Abijah, Anathoth and *A*.
8:36 Jehoaddah was the father of *A*,
9:42 Jadah was the father of *A*,

ALERT

Jos 8: 4 All of you be on the *a*.
Ps 17:11 with eyes *a*, to throw me
Isa 21: 7 fully *a*."
21: 7 let him be *a*,
Mk 13:33 Be *a*! You do not know
Eph 6:18 be *a* and always keep on praying
1Th 5: 6 but let us be *a* and self-controlled.
1Pe 5: 8 Be self-controlled and *a*.

ALEXANDER

Mk 15:21 Simon, the father of *A* and Rufus,
Ac 4: 6 *A* and the other men
19:33 The Jews pushed *A* to the front,
1Ti 1:20 them are Hymenaeus and *A*,
2Ti 4:14 *A* the metalworker did me a great

ALEXANDRIA (ALEXANDRIAN)

Ac 6: 9 Jews of Cyrene and *A* as well
18:24 a native of *A*, came to Ephesus.

ALEXANDRIAN (ALEXANDRIA)

Ac 27: 6 centurion found an *A* ship sailing
28:11 was an *A* ship with the figurehead

ALGUM (ALGUMWOOD ALMUGWOOD)

2Ch 2: 8 pine and *a* logs from Lebanon,

ALGUMWOOD (ALGUM)

2Ch 9:10 also brought *a* and precious stones.
9:11 The king used the *a* to make steps

ALIEN (ALIEN'S ALIENATE ALIENATED ALIENS)

Ge 17: 8 of Canaan, where you are now an *a*
19: 9 "This fellow came here as an *a*,
21:23 *a* the same kindness I have shown
23: 4 I am an *a* and a stranger among you
28: 4 land where you now live as an *a*,
Ex 2:22 "I have become an *a*
12:19 whether he is an *a* or native-born.
12:48 "An *a* living among you who wants
12:49 and to the *a* living among you."
18: 3 "I have become an *a*
20:10 nor the *a* within your gates.
22:21 "Do not mistreat an *a*
23: 9 not oppress an *a*; you yourselves
23:12 and the *a* as well, may be refreshed.
Lev 16:29 or an *a* living among you—
17: 8 or any *a* living among them who
17:10 any *a* living among them who eats
17:12 nor may an *a* living among you eat
17:13 any *a* living among you who hunts
17:15 Anyone, whether native-born or *a*,
19:10 Leave them for the poor and the *a*.
19:33 " 'When an *a* lives with you
19:34 *a* living with you must be treated
20: 2 any *a* living in Israel who gives any
22:18 an Israelite or an *a* living in Israel
23:22 Leave them for the poor and the *a*.
24:16 Whether an *a* or native-born,
24:22 are to have the same law for the *a*
25:35 as you would an *a* or a temporary
25:47 himself to the *a* living among you
25:47 " 'If an *a* or a temporary resident
Nu 9:14 An *a* living among you who wants
9:14 have the same regulations for the *a*
15:14 whenever an *a* or anyone else
15:15 and for the *a* living among you;
15:15 and the *a* shall be the same
15:16 and to the *a* living among you.' "
15:29 he is a native-born Israelite or an *a*.
15:30 whether native-born or *a*,
Dt 1:16 or between one of them and an *a*.
5:14 nor the *a* within your gates,
10:18 and loves the *a*, giving him food
14:21 it to an *a* living in any
23: 7 you lived as an *a* in his country.
24:14 or an *a* living in one of your towns.
24:17 not deprive the *a* or the fatherless
24:19 Leave it for the *a*, the fatherless
24:20 Leave what remains for the *a*,
24:21 Leave what remains for the *a*,
26:12 the *a*, the fatherless and the widow,
26:13 the *a*, the fatherless and the widow,
27:19 who withholds justice from the *a*,
28:43 *a* who lives among you will rise
Jos 20: 9 or any *a* living among them who
Jdg 19:12 We won't go into an *a* city,
2Sa 1:13 "I am the son of an *a*, an Amalekite
Job 15:19 when no *a* passed among them):
19:15 they look upon me as an *a*.
Ps 39:12 For I dwell with you as an *a*,
69: 8 an *a* to my own mother's sons;
81: 9 you shall not bow down to an *a* god
94: 6 They slay the widow and the *a*;
105:23 an *a* in the land of Ham.
146: 9 The LORD watches over the *a*
Isa 28:21 and perform his task, his *a* task.
Jer 7: 6 if you do not oppress the *a*,
22: 3 Do no wrong or violence to the *a*,
Eze 14: 7 or any *a* living in Israel separates
22: 7 in you they have oppressed the *a*
22:29 and needy and mistreat the *a*,
47:23 In whatever tribe the *a* settles,
Hos 8:12 they regarded them as something *a*
Zec 7:10 or the fatherless, the *a* or the poor.

ALIEN'S (ALIEN)

Lev 25:47 or to a member of the *a* clan,

ALIENATE (ALIEN)

Gal 4:17 is to *a* you ⌊from us⌋,

ALIENATED (ALIEN)

Job 19:13 "He has *a* my brothers from me;
Gal 5: 4 by law have been *a* from Christ;
Col 1:21 Once you were *a* from God

ALIENS (ALIEN)

Ex 6: 4 of Canaan, where they lived as *a*.
22:21 for you were *a* in Egypt.
23: 9 because you were *a* in Egypt.
23: 9 know how it feels to be *a*,
Lev 18:26 the *a* living among you must not do
19:34 yourself, for you were *a* in Egypt.
25:23 and you are but *a* and my tenants.
Nu 15:26 the *a* living among them will be
19:10 and for the *a* living among them.
35:15 *a* and any other people living
Dt 10:19 for you yourselves were *a* in Egypt.
10:19 you are to love those who are *a*,
14:29 inheritance of their own) and the *a*,
16:11 Levites in your towns, and the *a*,
16:14 and the Levites, the *a*,
26:11 and the *a* among you shall rejoice
29:11 *a* living in your camps who chop
31:12 and the *a* living in your towns—
Jos 8:33 All Israel, *a* and citizens alike,
8:35 and the *a* who lived among them.
2Sa 4: 3 have lived there as *a* to this day.
1Ch 22: 2 to assemble the *a* living in Israel,
29:15 We are *a* and strangers
2Ch 2:17 of all the *a* who were in Israel,
30:25 including the *a* who had come
Isa 14: 1 *A* will join them
61: 5 *A* will shepherd your flocks;
La 5: 2 has been turned over to *a*,
Eze 47:22 and for the *a* who have settled
Mal 3: 5 and deprive *a* of justice,
Eph 2:19 you are no longer foreigners and *a*,
Heb 11:13 they admitted that they were *a*
1Pe 2:11 as *a* and strangers in the world,

ALIVE (LIVE)

Ge 6:19 female, to keep them *a* with you.
6:20 come to you to be kept *a*.
7: 3 to keep their various kinds *a*
11:28 While his father Terah was still *a*,
43:28 "Your servant our father is still *a*
45:26 They told him, "Joseph is still *a*!
45:28 My son Joseph is still *a*.
46:30 seen for myself that you are still *a*."
Ex 4:18 to see if any of them are still *a*."
22: 4 "If the stolen animal is found *a*
Lev 16:10 the scapegoat shall be presented *a*
Nu 16:30 and they go down *a* into the grave,
16:33 They went down *a* into the grave,
Dt 4: 4 LORD your God are still *a* today.
5: 3 with all of us who are *a* here today.
6:24 always prosper and be kept *a*,
20:16 do not leave *a* anything that
31:27 the LORD while I am still *a*
Jos 8:23 But they took the king of Ai *a*
14:10 has kept me *a* for forty-five years
1Sa 2: 6 LORD brings death and makes *a*;
14:36 and let us not leave one of them *a*."
15: 8 king of the Amalekites *a*,
25:22 if by morning I leave *a* one male
25:34 to Nabal would have been left *a*
27: 9 he did not leave a man or woman *a*,
27:11 or woman *a* to be brought to Gath,
2Sa 1: 9 the throes of death, but I'm still *a*."
12:21 While the child was *a*, you fasted
12:22 "While the child was still *a*,
17:12 nor any of his men will be left *a*.
18:14 heart while Absalom was still *a*
19: 6 pleased if Absalom were *a* today
1Ki 3:23 No! Your son is dead and mine is *a*
3:23 'My son is *a* and your son is dead,'
3:26 woman whose son was *a* was filled
17:23 your son is *a*!" Then the woman
18: 5 and mules *a* so we will not have
20:18 out for war, take them *a*."
20:18 take them *a*; if they have come out
20:32 "Is he still *a*? He is my brother."
21:15 He is no longer *a*, but dead."
2Ki 7:12 and then we will take them *a*
10:14 they took them *a* and slaughtered
10:14 "Take them *a*!" he ordered.
2Ch 25:12 also captured ten thousand men *a*,
Ne 5: 2 in order for us to eat and stay *a*,
Job 36: 6 He does not keep the wicked *a*
Ps 22:29 who cannot keep themselves *a*.

Ps 33: 19 and keep them *a* in famine.
55: 15 let them go down *a* to the grave,
124: 3 they would have swallowed us *a;*
Pr 1: 12 let's swallow them *a*, like the grave,
Ecc 4: 2 who are still *a*.
Isa 7: 21 a man will keep *a* a young cow
La 1: 11 food to keep themselves *a*.
1: 19 food to keep themselves *a*.
Mt 27: 63 he was still *a* that deceiver said,
Mk 16: 11 When they heard that Jesus was *a*
Lk 15: 24 of mine was dead and is *a* again;
15: 32 of yours was dead and is *a* again;
20: 38 but of the living, for to him all are *a*
24: 23 vision of angels, who said he was *a*.
Jn 21: 22 him to remain *a* until I return,
21: 23 him to remain *a* until I return,
Ac 1: 3 convincing proofs that he was *a*.
9: 41 and presented her to them *a*.
20: 10 "He's *a!*" Then he went upstairs
20: 12 people took the young man home *a*
25: 19 Jesus who Paul claimed was *a*.
Ro 6: 11 but *a* to God in Christ Jesus.
7: 2 to her husband as long as he is *a*,
7: 3 man while her husband is still *a*,
7: 9 Once I was *a* apart from law;
8: 10 yet your spirit is *a*
1Co 15: 22 so in Christ all will be made *a*.
2Co 4: 11 For we who are *a* are always being
Eph 2: 5 made us *a* with Christ
Col 2: 13 God made you *a* with Christ.
1Th 4: 15 we tell you that we who are still *a*,
4: 17 we who are still *a* and are left will
1Pe 3: 18 death in the body but made *a*
Rev 1: 18 and behold I am *a* for ever and ever
3: 1 you have a reputation of being *a*,
19: 20 The two of them were thrown *a*

ALL-NIGHT (NIGHT)

Jos 10: 9 After an *a* march from Gilgal,

ALL-SURPASSING (SURPASS)

2Co 4: 7 clay to show that this *a* power is

ALLAMMELECH

Jos 19: 26 Acshaph, *A*, Amad and Mishal.

ALLEGIANCE (ALLY)

1Ki 12: 27 they will again give their *a*
Isa 19: 18 swear *a* to the LORD Almighty.
Eze 21: 23 to those who have sworn *a* to him,

ALLEGORY

Eze 17: 2 set forth an *a* and tell the house

ALLEYS

Lk 14: 21 into the streets and *a* of the town

ALLIANCE (ALLY)

1Ki 3: 1 Solomon made an *a*
2Ch 20: 35 king of Judah made an *a*
20: 37 "Because you have made an *a*
Ps 83: 5 they form an *a* against you—
Isa 30: 1 forming an *a*, but not by my Spirit,
Jer 50: 9 an *a* of great nations from the land
Da 11: 6 the king of the North to make an *a*,
11: 17 and will make an *a* with the king

ALLIED (ALLY)

Ge 14: 5 and the kings *a* with him went out
14: 13 all of whom were *a* with Abram.
14: 17 Kedorlaomer and the kings *a*
Jos 13: 21 and Reba—princes *a* with Sihon—
1Ki 20: 16 and the 32 kings *a* with him were
2Ch 18: 1 and he *a* himself with Ahab
Ps 94: 20 Can a corrupt throne be *a* with you
Isa 7: 2 "Aram has *a* itself with Ephraim";

ALLIES (ALLY)

1Ch 5: 20 and all their *a* over to them,
Jer 13: 21 you cultivated as your special *a?*
22: 20 for all your *a* are crushed.
22: 22 and your *a* will go into exile.
30: 14 All your *a* have forgotten you;
La 1: 19 "I called to my *a*
Eze 30: 6 " 'The *a* of Egypt will fall
31: 17 in its shade, its *a* among the nations
32: 21 say of Egypt and her *a*,
Da 11: 6 some years, they will become *a*.

Ob : 7 All your *a* will force you
Na 3: 9 Put and Libya were among her *a*.

ALLOCATE

Jos 13: 6 Be sure to *a* this land to Israel

ALLON

1Ch 4: 37 the son of *A*, the son of Jedaiah,

ALLON BACUTH

Ge 35: 8 So it was named *A*.

ALLOT (ALLOTMENT ALLOTS ALLOTTED ALLOTTING)

Eze 45: 1 " 'When you *a* the land
47: 22 You are to *a* it as an inheritance
48: 29 "This is the land you are to *a*

ALLOTMENT (ALLOT)

Ge 47: 22 because they received a regular *a*
47: 22 from the *a* Pharaoh gave them.
Dt 12: 12 who have no *a* or inheritance
14: 27 for they have no *a* or inheritance
14: 29 so that the Levites (who have no *a*
18: 1 are to have no *a* or inheritance
Jos 15: 1 The *a* for the tribe of Judah,
16: 1 The *a* for Joseph began
17: 1 This was the *a* for the tribe
17: 2 this *a* was for the rest of the people
17: 14 "Why have you given us only one *a*
17: 17 You will have not only one *a*
Eze 48: 13 the Levites will have an *a* 25,000

ALLOTS (ALLOT)

Job 20: 29 Such is the fate God *a* the wicked,
21: 17 the fate God *a* in his anger?
27: 13 "Here is the fate God *a*
Isa 34: 17 He *a* their portions;

ALLOTTED (ALLOT)

Lev 7: 35 LORD by fire that were *a* to Aaron
Nu 26: 53 "The land is to be *a* to them
34: 2 the land that will be *a* to you
36: 3 And so part of the inheritance *a*
Dt 32: 9 Jacob his *a* inheritance.
Jos 14: 1 clans of Israel *a* to them.
18: 11 Their *a* territory lay
19: 49 the land into its *a* portions,
21: 4 the priest were *a* thirteen towns
21: 5 descendants were *a* ten towns
21: 6 of Gershon were *a* thirteen towns
21: 8 the Israelites *a* to the Levites these
21: 9 Simeon they *a* the following towns
21: 20 clans of the Levites were *a* towns
21: 40 All the towns *a* to the Merarite
23: 4 Remember how I have *a*
24: 33 which had been *a* to his son
Jdg 1: 3 up with us into the territory *a* to us,
1Sa 18: 26 So before the *a* time elapsed,
1Ch 6: 54 the locations of their settlements *a*
6: 61 descendants were *a* ten towns
6: 62 were *a* thirteen towns
6: 63 were *a* twelve towns
6: 65 Benjamin they *a* the previously
Ne 5: 14 nor my brothers ate the food *a*
5: 18 I never demanded the food *a*
Job 7: 3 so I have been *a* months of futility,
21: 21 when his *a* months come to an end?
Ps 78: 55 and *a* their lands to them
125: 3 over the land *a* to the righteous,
Eze 47: 22 are to be *a* an inheritance
Da 12: 13 rise to receive your *a* inheritance."

ALLOTTING (ALLOT)

Ne 9: 22 *a* to them even the remotest

ALLOW (ALLOWANCE ALLOWED ALLOWING ALLOWS)

Ex 10: 25 "You must *a* us to have sacrifices
22: 18 "Do not *a* a sorceress to live.
Nu 33: 55 those you *a* to remain will become
35: 32 of refuge and so *a* him to go back
Jdg 6: 39 *A* me one more test with the fleece.
1Sa 16: 22 "*A* David to remain in my service,
24: 7 and did not *a* them to attack Saul.
2Ch 20: 10 territory you would not *a* Israel
Job 11: 14 and *a* no evil to dwell in your tent,
Ps 132: 4 I will *a* no sleep to my eyes,

Pr 6: 4 *A* no sleep to your eyes,
Jer 13: 14 I will *a* no pity or mercy
Eze 45: 8 but will *a* the house of Israel
Mk 5: 12 "Send us among the pigs; *a* us to go
11: 16 and would not *a* anyone
Lk 4: 41 and would not *a* them to speak,
Ac 16: 7 Spirit of Jesus would not *a* them to.
27: 7 When the wind did not *a* us
Ro 14: 16 Do not *a* what you consider good

ALLOWANCE (ALLOW)

2Ki 25: 30 king gave Jehoiachin a regular *a*
Jer 52: 34 gave Jehoiachin a regular *a*
Lk 12: 42 servants to give them their food *a*

ALLOWED (ALLOW)

Ge 3: 22 He must not be *a* to reach out his
31: 7 God has not *a* him to harm me.
46: 34 you will be *a* to settle in the region
48: 11 and now God has *a* me
Lev 11: 39 " 'If an animal that you are *a*
Nu 31: 15 Have you *a* all the women to live?"
Dt 7: 22 You will not be *a* to eliminate them
24: 4 is not *a* to marry her again
Jdg 2: 23 The LORD had *a* those nations
3: 28 they *a* no one to cross over.
2Sa 8: 2 and the third length was *a* to live.
1Ki 1: 48 who has *a* my eyes
1Ch 16: 21 He *a* no man to oppress them;
2Ch 25: 13 and had not *a* to take part
34: 11 of Judah had *a* to fall into ruin.
Est 1: 8 king's command each guest was *a*
4: 2 in sackcloth was *a* to enter it.
Job 31: 30 I have not *a* my mouth to sin
Ps 105: 14 He *a* no one to oppress them;
Eze 33: 12 will not be *a* to live
Da 7: 12 were *a* to live for a period of time.)
Ac 27: 3 *a* him to go to his friends
28: 4 Justice has not *a* him to live."
28: 16 Paul was *a* to live by himself,
1Co 14: 34 They are not *a* to speak,

ALLOWING (ALLOW)

Lev 22: 16 present to the LORD by *a* them
Jdg 1: 34 not *a* them to come

ALLOWS (ALLOW)

Ex 21: 22 husband demands and the court *a*.
Ro 14: 2 One man's faith *a* him

ALLURE (ALLURING)

Hos 2: 14 Therefore I am now going to *a* her;

ALLURING (ALLURE)

Na 3: 4 *a*, the mistress of sorceries,

ALLY (ALLEGIANCE ALLIANCE ALLIED ALLIES)

Jos 23: 12 and *a* yourselves with the survivors
Isa 48: 14 The LORD's chosen *a*

ALMIGHTY (MIGHT)

Ge 17: 1 "I am God *A;* walk before me
28: 3 May God *A* bless you and make
35: 11 "I am God *A;* be fruitful
43: 14 And may God *A* grant you mercy
48: 3 "God *A* appeared to me at Luz
49: 25 because of the *A*, who blesses you
Ex 6: 3 to Isaac and to Jacob as God *A*,
Nu 24: 4 who sees a vision from the *A*,
24: 16 who sees a vision from the *A*,
Ru 1: 20 the *A* has made my life very bitter.
1: 21 the *A* has brought misfortune
1Sa 1: 3 sacrifice to the LORD *A* at Shiloh,
1: 11 made a vow, saying, "O LORD *A*,
4: 4 of the covenant of the LORD *A*,
15: 2 This is what the LORD *A* says:
17: 45 you in the name of the LORD *A*,
2Sa 5: 10 the LORD God *A* was with him.
6: 2 the name of the LORD *A*,
6: 18 in the name of the LORD *A*.
7: 8 'This is what the LORD *A* says:
7: 26 'The LORD *A* is God over Israel!'
7: 27 "O LORD *A*, God of Israel,
1Ki 18: 15 "As the LORD *A* lives, whom I
19: 10 zealous for the LORD God *A*.
19: 14 zealous for the LORD God *A*.
2Ki 3: 14 "As surely as the LORD *A* lives,

2Ki 19:31 of the LORD *A* will accomplish
1Ch 11: 9 because the LORD *A* was with him
17: 7 'This is what the LORD *A* says:
17:24 The LORD *A*, the God over Israel,
Job 5:17 not despise the discipline of the *A*.
6: 4 The arrows of the *A* are in me,
6:14 though he forsakes the fear of the *A*
8: 3 Does the *A* pervert what is right?
8: 5 and plead with the *A*,
11: 7 Can you probe the limits of the *A*?
13: 3 But I desire to speak to the *A*
15:25 and vaunts himself against the *A*,
21:15 Who is the *A*, that we should serve
21:20 let him drink of the wrath of the *A*.
22: 3 What pleasure would it give the *A*
22:17 What can the *A* do to us?'
22:23 to the *A*, you will be restored:
22:25 then the *A* will be your gold,
22:26 then you will find delight in the *A*
23:16 the *A* has terrified me.
24: 1 "Why does the *A* not set times
27: 2 the *A*, who has made me taste
27:10 Will he find delight in the *A*?
27:11 the ways of the *A* I will not conceal.
27:13 a ruthless man receives from the *A*:
29: 5 when the *A* was still with me
31: 2 his heritage from the *A* on high?
31:35 my defense—let the *A* answer me;
32: 8 of the *A*, that gives him
33: 4 the breath of the *A* gives me life.
34:10 from the *A* to do wrong.
34:12 that the *A* would pervert justice.
35:13 the *A* pays no attention to it.
37:23 The *A* is beyond our reach
40: 2 contends with the *A* correct him?
Ps 24:10 The LORD *A*—
46: 7 The LORD *A* is with us;
46:11 The LORD *A* is with us;
48: 8 seen in the city of the LORD *A*,
59: 5 O LORD God *A*, the God of Israel,
68:14 When the *A* scattered the kings
69: 6 O Lord, the LORD *A*;
80: 4 O LORD God *A*,
80: 7 Restore us, O God *A*;
80:14 Return to us, O God *A*!
80:19 Restore us, O LORD God *A*;
84: 1 O LORD *A*!
84: 3 O LORD *A*, my King and my God.
84: 8 Hear my prayer, O LORD God *A*;
84:12 O LORD *A*,
89: 8 O LORD God *A*, who is like you?
91: 1 will rest in the shadow of the *A*.
Isa 1: 9 Unless the LORD *A*
1:24 Therefore the Lord, the LORD *A*,
2:12 The LORD *A* has a day in store
3: 1 the LORD *A*,
3:15 declares the Lord, the LORD *A*.
5: 7 The vineyard of the LORD *A*
5: 9 The LORD *A* has declared
5:16 the LORD *A* will be exalted
5:24 rejected the law of the LORD *A*
6: 3 "Holy, holy, holy is the LORD *A*;
6: 5 have seen the King, the LORD *A*."
8:13 The LORD *A* is the one you are
8:18 in Israel from the LORD *A*,
9: 7 The zeal of the LORD *A*
9:13 nor have they sought the LORD *A*
9:19 By the wrath of the LORD *A*
10:16 Therefore, the Lord, the LORD *A*,
10:23 the LORD *A*, will carry out
10:24 this is what the Lord, the LORD *A*,
10:26 The LORD *A* will lash them
10:33 See, the Lord, the LORD *A*,
13: 4 The LORD *A* is mustering
13: 6 come like destruction from the *A*.
13:13 place at the wrath of the LORD *A*,
14:22 declares the LORD *A*.
14:23 declares the LORD *A*.
14:24 The LORD *A* has sworn,
14:27 For the LORD *A* has purposed,
17: 3 declares the LORD *A*.
18: 7 place of the Name of the LORD *A*.
18: 7 will be brought to the LORD *A*
19: 4 declares the Lord, the LORD *A*.
19:12 what the LORD *A*
19:16 hand that the LORD *A* raises
19:17 of what the LORD *A* is planning
19:18 swear allegiance to the LORD *A*.

Isa 19:20 witness to the LORD *A* in the land
19:25 The LORD *A* will bless them,
21:10 heard from the LORD *A*,
22: 5 The Lord, the LORD *A*, has a day
22:12 The Lord, the LORD *A*,
22:14 The LORD *A* has revealed this
22:14 says the Lord, the LORD *A*.
22:15 This is what the Lord, the LORD *A*
22:25 In that day," declares the LORD *A*
23: 9 The LORD *A* planned it,
24:23 for the LORD *A* will reign
25: 6 the LORD *A* will prepare
28: 5 In that day the LORD *A*
28:22 the LORD *A*, has told me
28:29 comes from the LORD *A*,
29: 6 the LORD *A* will come
31: 4 so the LORD *A* will come down
31: 5 the LORD *A* will shield Jerusalem;
37:16 "O LORD *A*, God of Israel,
37:32 The zeal of the LORD *A*
39: 5 "Hear the word of the LORD *A*:
44: 6 and Redeemer, the LORD *A*:
45:13 says the LORD *A*."
47: 4 the LORD *A* is his name—
48: 2 the LORD *A* is his name:
51:15 the LORD *A* is his name.
54: 5 the LORD *A* is his name—
Jer 2:19 declares the Lord, the LORD *A*.
5:14 this is what the LORD God *A* says:
6: 6 This is what the LORD *A* says:
6: 9 This is what the LORD *A* says:
7: 3 This is what the LORD *A*,
7:21 " 'This is what the LORD *A*,
8: 3 to life, declares the LORD *A*.'
9: 7 this is what the LORD *A* says:
9:15 this is what the LORD *A*, the God
9:17 This is what the LORD *A* says:
10:16 the LORD *A* is his name.
11:17 The LORD *A*, who planted you,
11:20 But, O LORD *A*, you who judge
11:22 this is what the LORD *A* says:
15:16 O LORD God *A*.
16: 9 For this is what the LORD *A*,
19: 3 This is what the LORD *A*,
19:11 'This is what the LORD *A* says:
19:15 "This is what the LORD *A*,
20:12 O LORD *A*, you who examine
23:15 what the LORD *A* says concerning
23:16 This is what the LORD *A* says:
23:36 of the living God, the LORD *A*,
25: 8 Therefore the LORD *A* says this:
25:27 'This is what the LORD *A*,
25:28 'This is what the LORD *A* says:
25:29 on the earth, declares the LORD *A*
25:32 This is what the LORD *A* says:
26:18 'This is what the LORD *A* says:
27: 4 'This is what the LORD *A*,
27:18 plead with the LORD *A* that
27:19 is what the LORD *A* says about
27:21 this is what the LORD *A*, the God
28: 2 "This is what the LORD *A*,
28:14 This is what the LORD *A*,
29: 4 This is what the LORD *A*,
29: 8 this is what the LORD *A*, the God
29:17 yes, this is what the LORD *A* says:
29:21 This is what the LORD *A*,
29:25 "This is what the LORD *A*,
30: 8 In that day,' declares the LORD *A*
31:23 This is what the LORD *A*,
31:35 the LORD *A* is his name:
32:14 'This is what the LORD *A*,
32:15 For this is what the LORD *A*,
32:18 whose name is the LORD *A*,
33:11 "Give thanks to the LORD *A*,
33:12 "This is what the LORD *A* says:
35:13 "This is what the LORD *A*,
35:17 this is what the LORD God *A*,
35:18 "This is what the LORD *A*,
35:19 this is what the LORD *A*, the God
38:17 "This is what the LORD God *A*,
39:16 'This is what the LORD *A*,
42:15 This is what the LORD *A*,
42:18 This is what the LORD *A*,
43:10 'This is what the LORD *A*,
44: 2 "This is what the LORD *A*,
44: 7 Now this is what the LORD God *A*
44:11 this is what the LORD *A*, the God
44:25 This is what the LORD *A*,

Jer 46:10 the LORD *A*, will offer sacrifice
46:10 to the LORD, the LORD *A*—
46:18 whose name is the LORD *A*,
46:25 The LORD *A*, the God of Israel,
48: 1 This is what the LORD *A*,
48:15 whose name is the LORD *A*.
49: 5 declares the Lord, the LORD *A*.
49: 7 This is what the LORD *A* says:
49:26 declares the LORD *A*.
49:35 This is what the LORD *A* says:
50:18 Therefore this is what the LORD *A*
50:25 the Sovereign LORD *A* has work
50:31 declares the Lord, the LORD *A*,
50:33 This is what the LORD *A* says:
50:34 the LORD *A* is his name.
51: 5 by their God, the LORD *A*,
51:14 The LORD *A* has sworn by himself
51:19 The LORD *A* is his name.
51:33 This is what the LORD *A*,
51:57 whose name is the LORD *A*.
51:58 This is what the LORD *A* says:
Eze 1:24 the voice of the *A*, like the tumult
10: 5 voice of God *A* when he speaks.
Hos 12: 5 the LORD God *A*,
Joel 1:15 come like destruction from the *A*.
Am 3:13 the Lord, the LORD God *A*.
4:13 the LORD God *A* is his name.
5:14 the LORD God *A* will be with you,
5:15 the LORD God *A* will have mercy
5:16 what the Lord, the LORD God *A*,
5:27 the LORD, whose name is God *A*.
6: 8 the LORD God *A* declares:
6:14 For the LORD God *A* declares,
9: 5 The Lord, the LORD *A*,
Mic 4: 4 for the LORD *A* has spoken.
Na 2:13 declares the LORD *A*.
3: 5 you," declares the LORD *A*.
Hab 2:13 Has not the LORD *A* determined
Zep 2: 9 declares the LORD *A*, the God
2:10 the people of the LORD *A*.
Hag 1: 2 This is what the LORD *A* says:
1: 5 Now this is what the LORD *A* says
1: 7 This is what the LORD *A* says:
1: 9 Why?" declares the LORD *A*.
1:14 work on the house of the LORD *A*,
2: 4 with you,' declares the LORD *A*.
2: 6 "This is what the LORD *A* says:
2: 7 with glory,' says the LORD *A*.
2: 8 is mine,' declares the LORD *A*.
2: 9 former house,' says the LORD *A*.
2: 9 peace,' declares the LORD *A*."
2:11 "This is what the LORD *A* says:
2:23 declares the LORD *A*, 'I will take
2:23 you,' declares the LORD *A*."
Zec 1: 3 This is what the LORD *A* says:
1: 3 return to you,' says the LORD *A*.
1: 3 to me,' declares the LORD *A*.
1: 4 This is what the LORD *A* says:
1: 6 'The LORD *A* has done
1:12 of the LORD said, "LORD *A*,
1:14 This is what the LORD *A* says:
1:16 Jerusalem,' declares the LORD *A*.
1:17 This is what the LORD *A* says:
2: 8 For this is what the LORD *A* says:
2: 9 that the LORD *A* has sent me.
2:11 that the LORD *A* has sent me
3: 7 "This is what the LORD *A* says:
3: 9 on it,' says the LORD *A*,
3:10 fig tree,' declares the LORD *A*."
4: 6 by my Spirit,' says the LORD *A*.
4: 9 that the LORD *A* has sent me
5: 4 LORD *A* declares, 'I will send it
6:12 him this is what the LORD *A* says:
6:15 that the LORD *A* has sent me
7: 3 priests of the house of the LORD *A*
7: 4 word of the LORD *A* came to me:
7: 9 "This is what the LORD *A* says:
7:12 So the LORD *A* was very angry.
7:12 words that the LORD *A* had sent
7:13 not listen,' says the LORD *A*.
8: 1 word of the LORD *A* came to me.
8: 2 This is what the LORD *A* says:
8: 3 of the LORD *A* will be called
8: 4 This is what the LORD *A* says:
8: 6 This is what the LORD *A* says:
8: 6 to me?" declares the LORD *A*.
8: 7 This is what the LORD *A* says:
8: 9 This is what the LORD *A* says:

Zec 8: 9 laid for the house of the LORD *A*,
8: 11 in the past," declares the LORD *A*.
8: 14 This is what the LORD *A* says:
8: 14 says the LORD *A*,
8: 18 word of the LORD *A* came to me.
8: 19 This is what the LORD *A* says:
8: 20 This is what the LORD *A* says:
8: 21 the LORD and seek the LORD *A*.
8: 22 to Jerusalem to seek the LORD *A*
8: 23 This is what the LORD *A* says:
9: 15 and the LORD *A* will shield them.
10: 3 for the LORD *A* will care
12: 5 because the LORD *A* is their God.'
13: 2 no more," declares the LORD *A*.
13: 7 declares the LORD *A*.
14: 16 the LORD *A*, and to celebrate
14: 17 LORD *A*, they will have no rain.
14: 21 Judah will be holy to the LORD *A*,
14: 21 in the house of the LORD *A*.
Mal 1: 4 But this is what the LORD *A* says:
1: 6 due me?" says the LORD *A*.
1: 8 he accept you?" says the LORD *A*.
1: 9 accept you?"—says the LORD *A*.
1: 10 with you," says the LORD *A*,
1: 11 the nations," says the LORD *A*.
1: 13 says the LORD *A*.
1: 14 a great king," says the LORD *A*,
2: 2 says the LORD *A*, "I will send
2: 4 may continue," says the LORD *A*.
2: 7 he is the messenger of the LORD *A*
2: 8 with Levi," says the LORD *A*.
2: 12 he brings offerings to the LORD *A*.
2: 16 his garment," says the LORD *A*.
3: 1 will come," says the LORD *A*.
3: 5 do not fear me," says the LORD *A*.
3: 7 return to you," says the LORD *A*.
3: 10 Test me in this," says the LORD *A*,
3: 11 cast their fruit," says the LORD *A*.
3: 12 delightful land," says the LORD *A*.
3: 14 mourners before the LORD *A*?
3: 17 will be mine," says the LORD *A*,
4: 1 them on fire," says the LORD *A*.
4: 3 these things," says the LORD *A*.
Ro 9: 29 "Unless the Lord *A*
2Co 6: 18 daughters, says the Lord *A*."
Jas 5: 4 reached the ears of the Lord *A*.
Rev 1: 8 and who is to come, the *A*."
4: 8 holy is the Lord God *A*, who was,
11: 17 thanks to you, Lord God *A*,
15: 3 Lord God *A*.
16: 7 "Yes, Lord God *A*,
16: 14 battle on the great day of God *A*.
19: 6 For our Lord God *A* reigns.
19: 15 of the fury of the wrath of God *A*.
21: 22 because the Lord God *A*

ALMODAD

Ge 10: 26 Joktan was the father of *A*, Sheleph
1Ch 1: 20 Joktan was the father of *A*, Sheleph

ALMON

Jos 21: 18 *A*, together with their pasturelands

ALMON DIBLATHAIM

Nu 33: 46 left Dibon Gad and camped at *A*.
33: 47 They left *A* and camped in

ALMOND (ALMONDS)

Ge 30: 37 *a* and plane trees and made white
Ex 25: 33 Three cups shaped like *a* flowers
25: 34 be four cups shaped like *a* flowers
37: 19 Three cups shaped like *a* flowers
37: 20 four cups shaped like *a* flowers
Ecc 12: 5 when the *a* tree blossoms
Jer 1: 11 "I see the branch of an *a* tree,"

ALMONDS (ALMOND)

Ge 43: 11 some pistachio nuts and *a*.
Nu 17: 8 blossomed and produced *a*.

ALMUGWOOD (ALGUM)

1Ki 10: 11 they brought great cargoes of *a*
10: 12 The king used the *a*
10: 12 much *a* has never been imported

ALOES

Nu 24: 6 like *a* planted by the LORD,
Ps 45: 8 are fragrant with myrrh and *a*
Pr 7: 17 with myrrh, *a* and cinnamon.
SS 4: 14 with myrrh and *a*
Jn 19: 39 brought a mixture of myrrh and *a*,

ALOOF

Job 21: 16 so I stand *a* from the counsel
22: 18 so I stand *a* from the counsel
Ob : 11 On the day you stood *a*

ALOTH

1Ki 4: 16 in *A*; Jehoshaphat son of Paruah—

ALOUD

Ge 27: 38 my father!" Then Esau wept *a*.
29: 11 kissed Rachel and began to weep *a*.
Nu 14: 1 raised their voices and wept *a*.
Jdg 2: 4 people wept *a*, and they called that
Ru 1: 9 and they wept *a* and said to her,
1Sa 11: 4 to the people, they all wept *a*.
24: 16 David my son?" And he wept *a*.
30: 4 his men wept *a* until they had no
2Sa 3: 32 the king wept *a* at Abner's tomb.
13: 19 went away, weeping *a* as she went.
15: 23 The whole countryside wept *a*
19: 4 king covered his face and cried *a*,
Ezr 3: 12 wept *a* when they saw
Ne 8: 3 He read it *a* from daybreak
13: 1 of Moses was read *a* in the hearing
Job 2: 12 him; they began to weep *a*,
Ps 3: 4 To the LORD I cry *a*,
26: 7 proclaiming *a* your praise
81: 1 shout *a* to the God of Jacob!
95: 1 let us shout *a* to the Rock
142: 1 I cry *a* to the LORD;
Pr 1: 20 Wisdom calls *a* in the street,
2: 3 and cry *a* for understanding,
8: 3 at the entrances, she cries *a*:
Isa 12: 6 Shout *a* and sing for joy, people
33: 7 their brave men cry *a* in the streets;
44: 23 shout *a*, O earth beneath.
58: 1 "Shout it *a*, do not hold back.
Jer 4: 5 Cry *a* and say:
51: 61 see that you read all these words *a*.
Mic 4: 9 Why do you now cry *a*—
Zep 3: 14 shout *a*, O Israel!
Gal 4: 27 break forth and cry *a*,

ALPHA

Rev 1: 8 "I am the *A* and the Omega,"
21: 6 I am the *A* and the Omega,
22: 13 I am the *A* and the Omega,

ALPHAEUS

Mt 10: 3 James son of *A*, and Thaddaeus;
Mk 2: 14 he saw Levi son of *A* sitting
3: 18 James son of *A*, Thaddaeus,
Lk 6: 15 Matthew, Thomas, James son of *A*,
Ac 1: 13 son of *A* and Simon the Zealot,

ALTAR (ALTARS)

Ge 8: 20 Then Noah built an *a* to the LORD
12: 7 So he built an *a* there to the LORD
12: 8 There he built an *a* to the LORD
13: 4 and where he had first built an *a*.
13: 18 where he built an *a* to the LORD.
22: 9 Abraham built an *a* there
22: 9 his son Isaac and laid him on the *a*,
26: 25 Isaac built an *a* there and called
33: 20 he set up an *a* and called it El
35: 1 and build an *a* there to God,
35: 3 where I will build an *a* to God,
35: 7 There he built an *a*, and he called
Ex 17: 15 Moses built an *a* and called it
20: 24 " 'Make an *a* of earth for me
20: 25 If you make an *a* of stones for me,
20: 26 And do not go up to my *a* on steps,
21: 14 take him away from my *a*
24: 4 and built an *a* at the foot
24: 6 the other half he sprinkled on the *a*
27: 1 "Build an *a* of acacia wood,
27: 2 and overlay the *a* with bronze.
27: 2 and the *a* are of one piece,
27: 5 the *a* so that it is halfway up the *a*.
27: 6 poles of acacia wood for the *a*
27: 7 sides of the *a* when it is carried.
27: 8 Make the *a* hollow, out of boards.
28: 43 or approach the *a* to minister
29: 12 the horns of the *a* with your finger,
Ex 29: 12 the rest of it at the base of the *a*.
29: 13 them, and burn them on the *a*.
29: 16 sprinkle it against the *a* on all sides.
29: 18 Then burn the entire ram on the *a*.
29: 20 blood against the *a* on all sides.
29: 21 take some of the blood on the *a*
29: 25 and burn them on the *a*
29: 36 Purify the *a* by making atonement
29: 37 Then the *a* will be most holy,
29: 37 days make atonement for the *a*
29: 38 to offer on the *a* regularly each day
29: 44 the *a* and will consecrate Aaron
30: 1 "Make an *a* of acacia wood
30: 4 rings for the *a* below the molding—
30: 6 Put the *a* in front of the curtain that
30: 7 incense on the *a* every morning
30: 9 offer on this *a* any other incense
30: 18 the Tent of Meeting and the *a*,
30: 20 Also, when they approach the *a*
30: 27 its accessories, the *a* of incense,
30: 28 the *a* of burnt offering
31: 8 all its accessories, the *a* of incense,
31: 9 the *a* of burnt offering
32: 5 he built an *a* in front of the calf
35: 15 the *a* of incense with its poles,
35: 16 the *a* of burnt offering
37: 25 They made the *a* of incense out
38: 1 They built the *a* of burnt offering
38: 2 and the *a* were of one piece,
38: 2 they overlaid the *a* with bronze.
38: 4 They made a grating for the *a*,
38: 4 under its ledge, halfway up the *a*.
38: 7 on the sides of the *a* for carrying it.
38: 30 the bronze *a* with its bronze grating
39: 38 the gold *a*, the anointing oil,
39: 39 the bronze *a* with its bronze grating
40: 5 Place the gold *a* of incense in front
40: 6 "Place the *a* of burnt offering
40: 7 and the *a* and put water in it.
40: 10 Then anoint the *a* of burnt offering
40: 10 consecrate the *a*, and it will be
40: 26 Moses placed the gold *a*
40: 29 He set the *a* of burnt offering
40: 30 and the *a* and put water in it
40: 32 of Meeting or approached the *a*,
40: 33 around the tabernacle and *a*
Lev 1: 5 sprinkle it against the *a* on all sides
1: 7 are to put fire on the *a*
1: 8 the burning wood that is on the *a*.
1: 9 the priest is to burn all of it on the *a*
1: 11 blood against the *a* on all sides.
1: 11 side of the *a* before the LORD,
1: 12 the burning wood that is on the *a*.
1: 13 to bring all of it and burn it on the *a*
1: 15 The priest shall bring it to the *a*,
1: 15 off the head and burn it on the *a*;
1: 15 out on the side of the *a*.
1: 16 throw it to the east side of the *a*,
1: 17 is on the fire on the *a*.
2: 2 as a memorial portion on the *a*,
2: 8 the priest, who shall take it to the *a*.
2: 9 burn it on the *a* as an offering made
2: 12 they are not to be offered on the *a*
3: 2 the blood against the *a* on all sides.
3: 5 are to burn it on the *a* on top
3: 8 blood against the *a* on all sides.
3: 11 The priest shall burn them on the *a*
3: 13 blood against the *a* on all sides.
3: 16 The priest shall burn them on the *a*
4: 7 the base of the *a* of burnt offering
4: 7 the blood on the horns of the *a*
4: 10 them on the *a* of burnt offering.
4: 18 blood on the horns of the *a* that is
4: 18 the base of the *a* of burnt offering
4: 19 the fat from it and burn it on the *a*,
4: 25 of the blood at the base of the *a*.
4: 25 the horns of the *a* of burnt offering
4: 26 He shall burn all the fat on the *a*
4: 30 of the blood at the base of the *a*.
4: 30 the horns of the *a* of burnt offering
4: 31 and the priest shall burn it on the *a*
4: 34 of the blood at the base of the *a*.
4: 34 the horns of the *a* of burnt offering
4: 35 it on the *a* on top of the offerings
5: 9 offering against the side of the *a*;
5: 9 out at the base of the *a*.
5: 12 and burn it on the *a* on top
6: 9 fire must be kept burning on the *a*.

Lev 6: 9 is to remain on the *a* hearth
6: 10 and place them beside the *a*.
6: 10 that the fire has consumed on the *a*
6: 12 fire on the *a* must be kept burning;
6: 13 burning on the *a* continuously;
6: 14 before the LORD, in front of the *a*.
6: 15 burn the memorial portion on the *a*
7: 2 sprinkled against the *a* on all sides.
7: 5 The priest shall burn them on the *a*
7: 31 priest shall burn the fat on the *a*,
8: 11 anointing the *a* and all its utensils
8: 11 of the oil on the *a* seven times,
8: 15 of the blood at the base of the *a*.
8: 15 the horns of the *a* to purify the *a*.
8: 16 their fat, and burned it on the *a*.
8: 19 the blood against the *a* on all sides.
8: 21 and burned the whole ram on the *a*
8: 24 blood against the *a* on all sides.
8: 28 and burned them on the *a* on top
8: 30 and some of the blood from the *a*
9: 7 to the *a* and sacrifice your sin
9: 8 to the *a* and slaughtered the calf
9: 9 and put it on the horns of the *a*;
9: 9 out at the base of the *a*.
9: 10 On the *a* he burned the fat,
9: 12 it against the *a* on all sides.
9: 13 and he burned them on the *a*.
9: 14 top of the burnt offering on the *a*.
9: 17 and burned it on the *a* in addition
9: 18 it against the *a* on all sides.
9: 20 then Aaron burned the fat on the *a*.
9: 24 and the fat portions on the *a*.
10: 12 without yeast beside the *a*
14: 20 burnt offering and offer it on the *a*,
16: 12 coals from the *a* before the LORD
16: 18 and put it on all the horns of the *a*.
16: 18 to the *a* that is before the LORD
16: 20 the Tent of Meeting and the *a*,
16: 25 the fat of the sin offering on the *a*.
16: 33 for the Tent of Meeting and the *a*,
17: 6 blood against the *a* of the LORD
17: 11 atonement for yourselves on the *a*;
21: 23 near the curtain or approach the *a*,
22: 22 Do not place any of these on the *a*
Nu 3: 26 surrounding the tabernacle and *a*,
4: 11 "Over the gold *a* they are
4: 13 the ashes from the bronze *a*
4: 14 used for ministering at the *a*,
4: 26 surrounding the tabernacle and *a*,
5: 25 the LORD and bring it to the *a*.
5: 26 offering and burn it on the *a*;
7: 1 anointed and consecrated the *a*
7: 10 When the *a* was anointed,
7: 10 and presented them before the *a*.
7: 11 for the dedication of the *a*."
7: 84 of the *a* when it was anointed:
7: 88 of the *a* after it was anointed.
16: 38 into sheets to overlay the *a*,
16: 39 hammered out to overlay the *a*,
16: 46 along with fire from the *a*,
18: 3 of the sanctuary or the *a*,
18: 5 the care of the sanctuary and the *a*,
18: 7 with everything at the *a*
18: 17 Sprinkle their blood on the *a*
23: 2 offered a bull and a ram on each *a*.
23: 4 and on each *a* I have offered a bull
23: 14 offered a bull and a ram on each *a*.
23: 30 offered a bull and a ram on each *a*.
Dt 12: 27 beside the *a* of the LORD your
12: 27 on the *a* of the LORD your God,
16: 21 pole beside the *a* you build
26: 4 it down in front of the *a*
27: 5 an *a* to the LORD your God, an *a*
27: 6 Build the *a* of the LORD your God
33: 10 whole burnt offerings on your *a*.
Jos 8: 30 on Mount Ebal an *a* to the LORD,
8: 31 an *a* of uncut stones,
9: 27 and for the *a* of the LORD
22: 10 built an imposing *a* there
22: 11 heard that they had built the *a*
22: 16 build yourselves an *a* in rebellion
22: 19 than the *a* of the LORD our God.
22: 19 us by building an *a* for yourselves,
22: 23 If we have built our own *a*
22: 26 'Let us get ready and build an *a*—
22: 28 at the replica of the LORD's *a*,
22: 29 by building an *a* for burnt offerings,
22: 29 than the *a* of the LORD our God

Jos 22: 34 the Gadites gave the *a* this name:
Jdg 6: 24 So Gideon built an *a* to the LORD
6: 25 Tear down your father's *a* to Baal
6: 26 Then build a proper kind of *a*
6: 28 sacrificed on the newly built *a*!
6: 28 there was Baal's *a*, demolished,
6: 30 he has broken down Baal's *a*
6: 31 when someone breaks down his *a*."
6: 32 because he broke down Baal's *a*.
13: 20 up from the *a* toward heaven,
21: 4 the next day the people built an *a*
1Sa 2: 28 to go up to my *a*, to burn incense,
2: 33 off from my *a* will be spared only
7: 17 he built an *a* there to the LORD.
14: 35 Then Saul built an *a* to the LORD;
2Sa 24: 18 and build an *a* to the LORD
24: 21 "so I can build an *a* to the LORD,
24: 25 David built an *a* to the LORD
1Ki 1: 50 and took hold of the horns of the *a*.
1: 51 is clinging to the horns of the *a*.
1: 53 they brought him down from the *a*.
2: 28 and took hold of the horns of the *a*.
2: 29 of the LORD and was beside the *a*.
3: 4 thousand burnt offerings on that *a*.
6: 20 and he also overlaid the *a* of cedar.
6: 22 with gold the *a* that belonged
7: 48 the golden *a*; the golden table
8: 22 stood before the *a* of the LORD
8: 31 oath before your *a* in this temple,
8: 54 from before the *a* of the LORD,
8: 64 bronze *a* before the LORD was too
9: 25 offerings on the *a* he had built
12: 32 and offered sacrifices on the *a*.
12: 33 sacrifices on the *a* he had built
12: 33 went up to the *a* to make offerings.
13: 1 by the *a* to make an offering.
13: 2 out against the *a* by the word
13: 2 "O *a*, *a*! This is what the LORD
13: 3 The *a* will be split apart
13: 4 out against the *a* at Bethel,
13: 4 stretched out his hand from the *a*
13: 5 the *a* was split apart and its ashes
13: 32 the LORD against the *a* in Bethel
16: 32 He set up an *a* for Baal
18: 26 around the *a* they had made.
18: 30 and he repaired the *a* of the LORD
18: 32 With the stones he built an *a*
18: 35 The water ran down around the *a*
2Ki 11: 11 near the *a* and the temple,
12: 9 it beside the *a*, on the right side
16: 10 He saw an *a* in Damascus
16: 10 to Uriah the priest a sketch of the *a*
16: 11 So Uriah the priest built an *a*
16: 12 from Damascus and saw the *a*,
16: 13 of his fellowship offerings on the *a*.
16: 14 The bronze *a* that stood
16: 14 from between the new *a*
16: 14 put it on the north side of the new *a*
16: 15 But I will use the bronze *a*
16: 15 Sprinkle on the *a* all the blood
16: 15 the large new *a*, offer the morning
18: 22 before this *a* in Jerusalem"?
23: 9 at the *a* of the LORD in Jerusalem,
23: 15 Even the *a* at Bethel, the high place
23: 15 even that *a* and high place he
23: 16 and burned on the *a* to defile it,
23: 17 and pronounced against the *a*
1Ch 6: 49 offerings on the *a* of burnt offering
6: 49 on the *a* of incense in connection
16: 40 on the *a* of burnt offering regularly,
21: 18 and build an *a* to the LORD
21: 22 so I can build an *a* to the LORD,
21: 26 David built an *a* to the LORD
21: 26 heaven on the *a* of burnt offering.
21: 29 and the *a* of burnt offering were
22: 1 the *a* of burnt offering for Israel."
28: 18 gold for the *a* of incense.
2Ch 1: 5 the bronze *a* that Bezalel son of Uri
1: 6 to the bronze *a* before the LORD
4: 1 made a bronze *a* twenty cubits
4: 19 the golden *a*; the tables
5: 12 stood on the east side of the *a*,
6: 12 stood before the *a* of the LORD
6: 22 oath before your *a* in this temple,
7: 7 bronze *a* he had made could not
7: 9 dedication of the *a* for seven days
8: 12 On the *a* of the LORD that he had
15: 8 He repaired the *a* of the LORD

2Ch 23: 10 near the *a* and the temple,
26: 16 to burn incense on the *a* of incense.
26: 19 presence before the incense *a*
29: 18 the *a* of burnt offering
29: 19 now in front of the LORD's *a*."
29: 21 these on the *a* of the LORD.
29: 22 and sprinkled their blood on the *a*.
29: 22 and sprinkled their blood on the *a*;
29: 22 the blood and sprinkled it on the *a*;
29: 24 blood on the *a* for a sin offering
29: 27 the burnt offering on the *a*.
32: 12 'You must worship before one *a*
33: 16 he restored the *a* of the LORD
35: 16 offerings on the *a* of the LORD,
Ezr 3: 2 to build the *a* of the God of Israel
3: 3 they built the *a* on its foundation
7: 17 them on the *a* of the temple
Ne 10: 34 on the *a* of the LORD our God,
Ps 26: 6 and go about your *a*, O LORD,
43: 4 Then will I go to the *a* of God,
51: 19 then bulls will be offered on your *a*.
84: 3 a place near your *a*,
118: 27 up to the horns of the *a*.
Isa 6: 6 taken with tongs from the *a*.
19: 19 In that day there will be an *a*
27: 9 When he makes all the *a* stones
29: 2 she will be to me like an *a* hearth.
36: 7 "You must worship before this *a*"?
40: 16 Lebanon is not sufficient for *a* fires,
56: 7 will be accepted on my *a*;
60: 7 be accepted as offerings on my *a*,
La 2: 7 The Lord has rejected his *a*
Eze 8: 5 of the gate of the *a* I saw this idol
8: 16 between the portico and the *a*,
9: 2 and stood beside the bronze *a*.
40: 46 priests who have charge of the *a*.
40: 47 the *a* was in front of the temple.
41: 22 was a wooden *a* three cubits high
43: 13 And this is the height of the *a*:
43: 13 of the *a* in long cubits,
43: 15 The *a* hearth is four cubits high,
43: 16 *a* hearth is square, twelve cubits
43: 17 The steps of the *a* face east."
43: 18 and sprinkling blood upon the *a*
43: 20 and put it on the four horns of the *a*
43: 20 and so purify the *a* and make
43: 22 and the *a* is to be purified
43: 26 are to make atonement for the *a*
43: 27 and fellowship offerings on the *a*.
45: 19 corners of the upper ledge of the *a*
47: 1 side of the temple, south of the *a*.
Joel 1: 13 you who minister before the *a*.
2: 17 the temple porch and the *a*.
Am 2: 8 They lie down beside every *a*
3: 14 the horns of the *a* will be cut off
9: 1 I saw the Lord standing by the *a*,
Zec 9: 15 for sprinkling the corners of the *a*.
14: 20 the sacred bowls in front of the *a*.
Mal 1: 7 "You place defiled food on my *a*.
1: 10 not light useless fires on my *a*!
2: 13 You flood the LORD's *a* with tears
Mt 5: 23 if you are offering your gift at the *a*
5: 24 your gift there in front of the *a*.
23: 18 'If anyone swears by the *a*,
23: 19 or the *a* that makes the gift sacred?
23: 20 he who swears by the *a* swears by it
23: 35 between the temple and the *a*.
Lk 1: 11 at the right side of the *a* of incense.
11: 51 who was killed between the *a*
Ac 17: 23 found an *a* with this inscription:
1Co 9: 13 and those who serve at the *a* share
9: 13 share in what is offered on the *a*?
10: 18 the sacrifices participate in the *a*?
Heb 7: 13 that tribe has ever served at the *a*.
9: 4 which had the golden *a* of incense
13: 10 We have an *a* from which those
Jas 2: 21 he offered his son Isaac on the *a*?
Rev 6: 9 I saw under the *a* the souls
8: 3 censer, came and stood at the *a*.
8: 3 on the golden *a* before the throne.
8: 5 filled it with fire from the *a*,
9: 13 of the golden *a* that is before God.
11: 1 the temple of God and the *a*,
14: 18 came from the *a* and called
16: 7 And I heard the *a* respond:

ALTARS (ALTAR)

Ex 34: 13 down their *a*, smash their sacred

Lev 26: 30 cut down your incense *a*
Nu 3: 31 the table, the lampstand, the *a*,
23: 1 said, "Build me seven *a* here,
23: 4 said, "I have prepared seven *a*,
23: 14 there he built seven *a* and offered
23: 29 said, "Build me seven *a* here,
Dt 7: 5 down their *a*, smash their sacred
12: 3 down their *a*, smash their sacred
Jdg 2: 2 but you shall break down their *a*.'
1Ki 19: 10 covenant, broken down your *a*,
19: 14 covenant, broken down your *a*,
2Ki 11: 18 They smashed the *a* and idols
11: 18 the priest of Baal in front of the *a*.
18: 22 places and *a* Hezekiah removed,
21: 3 he also erected *a* to Baal
21: 4 He built *a* in the temple
21: 5 he built *a* to all the starry hosts.
23: 12 He pulled down the *a* the kings
23: 12 and the *a* Manasseh had built
23: 20 priests of those high places on the *a*
2Ch 14: 3 He removed the foreign *a*
14: 5 incense *a* in every town in Judah,
23: 17 They smashed the *a* and idols
23: 17 the priest of Baal in front of the *a*.
28: 24 and set up *a* at every street corner
30: 14 They removed the *a* in Jerusalem
30: 14 and cleared away the incense *a*
31: 1 and the *a* throughout Judah
32: 12 this god's high places and *a*,
33: 3 he also erected *a* to the Baals
33: 4 He built *a* in the temple
33: 5 he built *a* to all the starry hosts.
33: 15 as all the *a* he had built
34: 4 Under his direction the *a*
34: 4 to pieces the incense *a* that were
34: 5 the bones of the priests on their *a*,
34: 7 and cut to pieces all the incense *a*
34: 7 down the *a* and the Asherah poles
Isa 17: 8 They will not look to the *a*,
17: 8 incense *a* their fingers have made.
27: 9 no Asherah poles or incense *a*
36: 7 places and *a* Hezekiah removed,
65: 3 and burning incense on *a* of brick;
Jer 11: 13 and the *a* you have set up
17: 1 and on the horns of their *a*.
17: 2 their *a* and Asherah poles
Eze 6: 4 Your *a* will be demolished
6: 4 your incense *a* will be smashed;
6: 5 scatter your bones around your *a*.
6: 6 so that your *a* will be laid waste
6: 6 your incense *a* broken down,
6: 13 among their idols around their *a*,
Hos 8: 11 these have become *a* for sinning.
8: 11 "Though Ephraim built many *a*
10: 1 he built more *a*;
10: 2 The LORD will demolish their *a*
10: 8 and cover their *a*.
12: 11 Their *a* will be like piles of stones
Am 3: 14 I will destroy the *a* of Bethel;
Ro 11: 3 prophets and torn down your *a*;

ALTER (ALTERED)

Ps 89: 34 or *a* what my lips have uttered.

ALTERED (ALTER)

Da 6: 8 it in writing so that it cannot be *a*—

ALTERNATE (ALTERNATED)

Ex 28: 34 are to *a* around the hem

ALTERNATED (ALTERNATE)

Ex 39: 26 pomegranates *a* around the hem
Eze 41: 18 Palm trees *a* with cherubim.

ALUSH

Nu 33: 13 left Dophkah and camped at *A*.
33: 14 They left *A* and camped

ALVAH

Ge 36: 40 Timna, *A*, Jetheth, Oholibamah,
1Ch 1: 51 Timna, *A*, Jetheth, Oholibamah,

ALVAN

Ge 36: 23 The sons of Shobal: *A*, Manahath,
1Ch 1: 40 The sons of Shobal: *A*, Manahath,

ALWAYS

Ge 26: 29 molest you but *a* treated you well
Ex 19: 9 and will *a* put their trust in you."
28: 30 Thus Aaron will *a* bear the means
29: 28 This is *a* to be the regular share
Lev 25: 32 " 'The Levites *a* have the right
Nu 22: 30 which you have *a* ridden,
Dt 5: 29 and keep all my commands *a*,
6: 24 so that we might *a* prosper
11: 1 his laws and his commands *a*.
12: 28 so that it may *a* go well with you
14: 23 to revere the LORD your God *a*.
15: 11 There will *a* be poor people
18: 5 minister in the LORD's name *a*.
19: 9 and to walk *a* in his ways—
28: 13 you will *a* be at the top, never
Jos 4: 24 so that you might *a* fear the LORD
1Sa 1: 22 LORD, and he will live there *a*."
2: 35 minister before my anointed one *a*.
7: 17 But he *a* went back to Ramah,
2Sa 9: 7 and you will *a* eat at my table."
9: 10 grandson of your master, will *a* eat
9: 13 because he *a* ate at the king's table,
1Ki 5: 1 he had *a* been on friendly terms
9: 3 and my heart will *a* be there.
11: 36 my servant may *a* have a lamp
12: 7 they will *a* be your servants."
22: 8 anything good about me, but *a* bad.
2Ki 17: 37 You must *a* be careful
1Ch 16: 11 seek his face *a*.
2Ch 7: 16 and my heart will *a* be there.
10: 7 they will *a* be your servants."
18: 7 anything good about me, but *a* bad.
Job 31: 32 for my door was *a* open
Ps 9: 18 the needy will not *a* be forgotten,
10: 5 His ways are *a* prosperous;
10: 6 I'll *a* be happy and never have
16: 8 I have set the LORD *a* before me.
34: 1 his praise will *a* be on my lips.
35: 27 may they *a* say, "The LORD be
37: 26 They are *a* generous and lend
37: 27 then you will *a* live securely.
40: 11 your truth *a* protect me.
40: 16 who love your salvation *a* say,
51: 3 and my sin is *a* before me.
56: 5 they are *a* plotting to harm me.
70: 4 who love your salvation *a* say,
71: 3 to which I can *a* go;
71: 14 But as for me, I will *a* have hope;
73: 12 *a* carefree, they increase in wealth.
73: 23 Yet I am *a* with you;
103: 9 He will not *a* accuse,
105: 4 seek his face *a*.
109: 15 May their sins *a* remain
119: 44 I will *a* obey your law,
119:117 I will *a* have regard
119:132 you *a* do to those who love your
Pr 5: 19 may her breasts satisfy you *a*,
6: 14 he *a* stirs up dissension.
8: 30 rejoicing *a* in his presence,
23: 7 who is *a* thinking about the cost.
23: 17 *a* be zealous for the fear
28: 14 is the man who *a* fears the LORD,
29: 14 his throne will *a* be secure.
Ecc 9: 8 *A* be clothed in white,
9: 8 and *a* anoint your head with oil.
Isa 57: 16 nor will I *a* be angry,
58: 11 The LORD will guide you *a*;
60: 11 Your gates will *a* stand open,
Jer 3: 5 will you *a* be angry?
8: 5 Why does Jerusalem *a* turn away?
12: 1 You are *a* righteous, O LORD,
12: 2 You are *a* on their lips
17: 8 its leaves are *a* green.
32: 39 so that they will *a* fear me
35: 7 any of these things, but must *a* live
La 5: 20 Why do you *a* forget us?
Hos 7: 2 they are *a* before me.
12: 6 and wait for your God *a*.
Mal 1: 4 a people *a* under the wrath
Mt 18: 10 angels in heaven *a* see the face
26: 11 The poor you will *a* have with you,
26: 11 but you will not *a* have me.
28: 20 And surely I will be with you *a*,
Mk 14: 7 But you will not *a* have me.
14: 7 The poor you will *a* have with you,
Lk 15: 31 the father said, 'you are *a* with me,
18: 1 show them that they should *a* pray
21: 36 Be *a* on the watch, and pray that
Jn 5: 17 "My Father is *a* at his work
Jn 8: 29 for I *a* do what pleases him."
11: 42 I knew that you *a* hear me,
12: 8 You will *a* have the poor
12: 8 but you will not *a* have me."
18: 20 "I *a* taught in synagogues
Ac 2: 25 " 'I saw the Lord *a* before me.
7: 51 You *a* resist the Holy Spirit!
9: 36 who was *a* doing good
24: 16 So I strive *a* to keep my conscience
Ro 15: 20 It has *a* been my ambition
1Co 1: 4 I *a* thank God for you
13: 7 *a* protects, *a* trusts, *a* hopes, *a*
15: 58 *A* give yourselves fully to the work
2Co 1: 19 but in him it has *a* been "Yes."
2: 14 *a* leads us in triumphal procession
4: 10 We *a* carry around in our body
4: 11 we who are alive are *a* being given
5: 6 Therefore we are *a* confident
6: 10 sorrowful, yet *a* rejoicing; poor,
Gal 4: 18 to be so *a* and not just when I am
Eph 5: 20 *a* giving thanks to God the Father
6: 18 *a* keep on praying for all the saints.
Php 1: 4 *a* pray with joy because of your
1: 20 *a* Christ will be exalted in my body,
2: 12 friends, as you have *a* obeyed—
4: 4 Rejoice in the Lord *a*.
Col 1: 3 We *a* thank God, the Father
4: 6 Let your conversation be *a* full
4: 12 He is *a* wrestling in prayer for you,
1Th 1: 2 We *a* thank God for all of you,
2: 16 In this way they *a* heap up their
3: 6 us that you *a* have pleasant
5: 15 but *a* try to be kind to each other
5: 16 Be joyful *a*; pray continually;
2Th 1: 3 We ought *a* to thank God for you,
2: 13 we ought *a* to thank God for you,
2Ti 3: 7 *a* learning but never able
Tit 1: 12 "Cretans are *a* liars, evil brutes,
Phm : 4 I *a* thank my God as I remember
Heb 3: 10 'Their hearts are *a* going astray,
7: 25 he *a* lives to intercede for them.
1Pe 3: 15 *A* be prepared to give an answer
2Pe 1: 12 I will *a* remind you of these things,
1: 15 my departure you will *a* be able

AMAD

Jos 19: 26 Allammelech, *A* and Mishal.

AMAL

1Ch 7: 35 Zophah, Imna, Shelesh and *A*.

AMALEK (AMALEKITE AMALEKITES)

Ge 36: 12 named Timna, who bore him *A*.
36: 16 Kenaz, Korah, Gatam and *A*.
Nu 24: 20 Then Balaam saw *A* and uttered his
24: 20 "*A* was first among the nations,
Dt 25: 19 memory of *A* from under heaven.
Jdg 5: 14 Ephraim, whose roots were in *A*;
1Sa 15: 5 Saul went to the city of *A*
2Sa 8: 12 and the Philistines, and *A*.
1Ch 1: 36 Gatam and Kenaz; by Timna: *A*.
18: 11 and the Philistines, and *A*.
Ps 83: 7 Gebal, Ammon and *A*,

AMALEKITE (AMALEK)

Ex 17: 13 So Joshua overcame the *A* army
1Sa 30: 13 I am an Egyptian, the slave of an *A*.
2Sa 1: 8 Who are you?' " 'An *A*,' I answered
1: 13 "I am the son of an alien, an *A*,"

AMALEKITES (AMALEK)

Ge 14: 7 the whole territory of the *A*,
Ex 17: 8 *A* came and attacked the Israelites
17: 9 of our men and go out to fight the *A*
17: 10 So Joshua fought the *A*
17: 11 his hands, the *A* were winning.
17: 14 of the *A* from under heaven."
17: 16 war against the *A* from generation
Nu 13: 29 *A* live in the Negev; the Hittites,
14: 25 Since the *A* and Canaanites are
14: 43 for the *A* and Canaanites will face
14: 45 the *A* and Canaanites who lived
Dt 25: 17 Remember what the *A* did to you
Jdg 3: 13 Getting the Ammonites and *A*
6: 3 *A* and other eastern peoples
6: 33 *A* and other eastern peoples joined
7: 12 *A* and all the other eastern peoples
10: 12 *A* and the Maonites oppressed you

Jdg 12: 15 in the hill country of the *A*.
1Sa 14: 48 valiantly and defeated the *A*,
15: 2 'I will punish the *A*
15: 3 attack the *A* and totally destroy
15: 6 Kenites moved away from the *A*.
15: 6 leave the *A* so that I do not destroy
15: 7 Saul attacked the *A* all the way
15: 8 He took Agag king of the *A* alive,
15: 15 soldiers brought them from the *A*;
15: 18 those wicked people, the *A*;
15: 20 I completely destroyed the *A*
15: 32 "Bring me Agag king of the *A*."
27: 8 Geshurites, the Girzites and the *A*.
28: 18 out his fierce wrath against the *A*,
30: 1 Now the *A* had raided the Negev
30: 18 everything the *A* had taken,
2Sa 1: 1 returned from defeating the *A*
1Ch 4: 43 killed the remaining *A* who had

AMAM

Jos 15: 26 Hazor), *A*, Shema, Moladah,

AMANA

SS 4: 8 Descend from the crest of *A*,

AMARIAH (AMARIAH'S)

1Ch 6: 7 father of *A*, *A* the father of Ahitub,
6: 11 father of *A*, *A* the father of Ahitub,
6: 52 Meraioth his son, *A* his son,
23: 19 Jeriah the first, *A* the second,
24: 23 Jeriah the first, *A* the second,
2Ch 19: 11 "*A* the chief priest will be over you
31: 15 *A* and Shecaniah assisted him
Ezr 7: 3 the son of *A*, the son of Azariah,
10: 42 Shemariah, Shallum, *A* and Joseph.
Ne 10: 3 Jeremiah, Pashhur, *A*, Malkijah,
11: 4 the son of *A*, the son of Shephatiah,
12: 2 Jeremiah, Ezra, *A*, Malluch,
Zep 1: 1 the son of *A*, the son of Hezekiah,

AMARIAH'S (AMARIAH)

Ne 12: 13 Meshullam; of *A*, Jehohanan;

AMASA

2Sa 17: 25 Absalom had appointed *A*
17: 25 *A* was the son of a man named
19: 13 to *A*, 'Are you not my own flesh
20: 4 said to *A*, "Summon the men
20: 5 when *A* went to summon Judah,
20: 8 in Gibeon, *A* came to meet them.
20: 9 Joab said to *A*, "How are you,
20: 9 Then Joab took *A* by the beard
20: 10 *A* was not on his guard
20: 10 being stabbed again, *A* died.
20: 11 One of Joab's men stood beside *A*
20: 12 *A* lay wallowing in his blood
20: 12 who came up to *A* stopped,
20: 13 After *A* had been removed
1Ki 2: 5 son of Ner and *A* son of Jether.
2: 32 of Israel's army, and *A* son
1Ch 2: 17 Abigail was the mother of *A*,
2Ch 28: 12 of Shallum, and *A* son of Hadlai—

AMASAI

1Ch 6: 25 The descendants of Elkanah: *A*,
6: 35 the son of *A*, the son of Elkanah,
12: 18 Then the Spirit came upon *A*,
15: 24 Joshaphat, Nethanel, *A*, Zechariah
2Ch 29: 12 Mahath son of *A* and Joel son

AMASHSAI

Ne 11: 13 242 men; *A* son of Azarel,

AMASIAH

2Ch 17: 16 with 280,000; next, *A* son of Zicri,

AMASSED (AMASSES)

Ecc 2: 8 I *a* silver and gold for myself,
Eze 28: 4 and *a* gold and silver

AMASSES (AMASSED)

Pr 28: 8 *a* it for another, who will be kind

AMAZED (AMAZEMENT)

Isa 29: 9 Be stunned and *a*,
Hab 1: 5 and be utterly *a*.
Mt 7: 28 the crowds were *a* at his teaching,
8: 27 The men were *a* and asked,
9: 33 The crowd was *a* and said,
13: 54 in their synagogue, and they were *a*
15: 31 The people were *a*
21: 20 the disciples saw this, they were *a*.
22: 22 When they heard this, they were *a*.
Mk 1: 22 The people were *a* at his teaching,
1: 27 all so *a* that they asked each other,
2: 12 This *a* everyone and they praised
5: 20 And all the people were *a*.
6: 2 and many who heard him were *a*.
6: 6 And he was *a* at their lack of faith.
6: 51 They were completely *a*,
10: 24 The disciples were *a* at his words.
10: 26 The disciples were even more *a*,
11: 18 because the whole crowd was *a*
12: 17 And they were *a* at him.
15: 5 made no reply, and Pilate was *a*.
Lk 2: 18 and all who heard it were *a*
2: 47 Everyone who heard him was *a*
4: 22 were *a* at the gracious words that
4: 32 They were *a* at his teaching,
4: 36 All the people were *a* and said
5: 26 Everyone was *a* and gave praise
7: 9 When Jesus heard this, he was *a*
9: 43 they were all *a* at the greatness
11: 14 dumb spoke, and the crowd was *a*.
24: 22 some of our women *a* us.
Jn 5: 28 "Do not be *a* at this,
7: 15 The Jews were *a* and asked,
Ac 2: 7 Utterly *a*, they asked: "Are not all
2: 12 *A* and perplexed, they asked one
7: 31 When he saw this, he was *a*
8: 9 and *a* all the people of Samaria.
8: 11 he had *a* them for a long time
13: 12 for he was *a* at the teaching about

AMAZEMENT (AMAZED AMAZING)

Da 3: 24 leaped to his feet in *a*
Mt 27: 14 to the great *a* of the governor.
Mk 7: 37 People were overwhelmed with *a*.
Lk 8: 25 and *a* they asked one another,
24: 41 not believe it because of joy and *a*,
Jn 5: 20 to your *a* he will show him
Ac 3: 10 *a* at what had happened to him.

AMAZIAH (AMAZIAH'S)

2Ki 12: 21 And *A* his son succeeded him
13: 12 war against *A* king of Judah,
14: 1 *A* son of Joash king of Judah began
14: 8 *A* sent messengers to Jehoash son
14: 9 of Israel replied to *A* king of Judah:
14: 11 *A* king of Judah faced each other
14: 11 *A*, however, would not listen,
14: 13 of Israel captured *A* king of Judah,
14: 15 war against *A* king of Judah,
14: 17 *A* son of Joash king of Judah lived
14: 21 king in place of his father *A*.
14: 22 it to Judah after *A* rested
14: 23 year of *A* son of Joash king
15: 1 Azariah son of *A* king
15: 3 just as his father *A* had done.
1Ch 3: 12 *A* his son, Azariah his son,
4: 34 Jamlech, Joshah son of *A*, Joel,
6: 45 the son of *A*, the son of Hilkiah,
2Ch 24: 27 And *A* his son succeeded him
25: 1 *A* was twenty-five years old
25: 5 *A* called the people
25: 9 *A* asked the man of God,
25: 10 So *A* dismissed the troops who had
25: 11 *A* then marshaled his strength
25: 13 the troops that *A* had sent back
25: 14 When *A* returned
25: 15 of the LORD burned against *A*,
25: 17 After *A* king of Judah consulted his
25: 18 of Israel replied to *A* king of Judah:
25: 20 *A*, however, would not listen,
25: 21 *A* king of Judah faced each other
25: 23 of Israel captured *A* king of Judah,
25: 25 *A* son of Joash king of Judah lived
25: 27 From the time that *A* turned away
26: 1 king in place of his father *A*.
26: 2 it to Judah after *A* rested
26: 4 just as his father *A* had done.
Am 7: 10 Then *A* the priest of Bethel sent
7: 12 Then *A* said to Amos, "Get out,
7: 14 Amos answered *A*, "I was neither

AMAZIAH'S (AMAZIAH)

2Ki 14: 18 As for the other events of *A* reign,
2Ch 25: 26 As for the other events of *A* reign,

AMAZING (AMAZEMENT)

Jos 3: 5 the LORD will do *a* things
Jdg 13: 19 And the LORD did an *a* thing
Pr 30: 18 are three things that are too *a*

AMBASSADOR (AMBASSADORS)

Eph 6: 20 for which I am an *a* in chains.

AMBASSADORS (AMBASSADOR)

Isa 57: 9 You sent your *a* far away;
2Co 5: 20 We are therefore Christ's *a*,

AMBITION

Ro 15: 20 It has always been my *a*
Gal 5: 20 fits of rage, selfish *a*, dissensions,
Php 1: 17 preach Christ out of selfish *a*,
2: 3 Do nothing out of selfish *a*
1Th 4: 11 Make it your *a* to lead a quiet life,
Jas 3: 14 and selfish *a* in your hearts,
3: 16 where you have envy and selfish *a*,

AMBUSH (AMBUSHES)

Jos 8: 2 Set an *a* behind the city."
8: 4 You are to set an *a* behind the city.
8: 7 you are to rise up from *a*
8: 9 and they went to the place of *a*
8: 12 and set them in *a* between Bethel
8: 13 of the city and the *a* to the west
8: 14 did not know that an *a* had been set
8: 19 the men in the *a* rose quickly
8: 21 Israel saw that the *a* had taken
8: 22 The men of the *a* also came out
Jdg 9: 25 men on the hilltops to *a*
9: 43 into three companies and set an *a*
20: 29 Then Israel set an *a* around Gibeah
20: 33 and the Israelite *a* charged out
20: 36 they relied on the *a* they had set
20: 37 been in *a* made a sudden dash
20: 38 with the *a* that they should send up
1Sa 15: 5 the city of Amalek and set an *a*
2Ch 13: 13 of Judah the *a* was behind them.
Ps 10: 8 from *a* he murders the innocent,
64: 4 They shoot from *a*
Jer 51: 12 prepare an *a*!
Hos 6: 9 As marauders lie in *a* for a man,
Ac 23: 21 of them are waiting in *a* for him.
25: 3 for they were preparing an *a*

AMBUSHES (AMBUSH)

2Ch 20: 22 the LORD set *a* against the men

AMEN

Dt 27:15-26; 1Ki 1:36; 1Ch 16:36; Ne 5:13; 8:6; Ps 41:13; 72:19; 89:52; 106:48; Jer 11:5; 28:6; Ro 1:25; 9:5; 11:36; 15:33; 16:27; 1Co 14:16; 16:24; 2Co 1:20; Gal 1:5; 6:18; Eph 3:21; Php 4:20,23; 1Ti 1:17; 6:16; 2Ti 4:18; Heb 13:21; 1Pe 4:11; 5:11; 2Pe 3:18; Jude :25; Rev 1:6,7; 3:14; 5:14; 7:12; 19:4; 22:20,21

AMENDS

2Sa 21: 3 How shall I make *a*
Job 20: 10 His children must make *a*
Pr 14: 9 Fools mock at making *a* for sin.

AMETHYST

Ex 28: 19 an *a*; in the fourth row a chrysolite,
39: 12 an *a*; in the fourth row a chrysolite,
Rev 21: 20 eleventh jacinth, and the twelfth *a*.

AMI

Ezr 2: 57 and *A* The temple servants

AMITTAI

2Ki 14: 25 through his servant Jonah son of *A*,
Jnh 1: 1 came to Jonah son of *A*:

AMMAH

2Sa 2: 24 they came to the hill of *A*,

AMMIEL

Nu 13: 12 the tribe of Dan, *A* son of Gemalli;
2Sa 9: 4 at the house of Makir son of *A* in Lo
9: 5 the house of Makir son of *A*.
17: 27 and Makir son of *A* from Lo

1Ch 3: 5 were by Bathsheba daughter of *A*.
26: 5 Nethanel the fifth, *A* the sixth,

AMMIHUD

Nu 1: 10 Elishama son of *A*; from Manasseh,
2: 18 of Ephraim is Elishama son of *A*.
7: 48 the seventh day Elishama son of *A*,
7: 53 the offering of Elishama son of *A*.
10: 22 Elishama son of *A* was in command
34: 20 Shemuel son of *A*, from the tribe
34: 28 Pedahel son of *A*, the leader
2Sa 13: 37 and went to Talmai son of *A*,
1Ch 7: 26 *A* his son, Elishama his son,
9: 4 Uthai son of *A*, the son of Omri,

AMMINADAB

Ex 6: 23 daughter of *A* and sister
Nu 1: 7 Nahshon son of *A*; from Issachar,
2: 3 of Judah is Nahshon son of *A*.
7: 12 son of *A* of the tribe of Judah.
7: 17 the offering of Nahshon son of *A*.
10: 14 Nahshon son of *A* was in command
Ru 4: 19 of *A*, *A* the father of Nahshon,
1Ch 2: 10 Ram was the father of *A*,
2: 10 and *A* the father of Nahshon,
6: 22 descendants of Kohath: *A* his son,
15: 10 *A* the leader and 112 relatives.
15: 11 Shemaiah, Eliel and *A* the Levites.
Mt 1: 4 of *A*, *A* the father of Nahshon,
Lk 3: 33 the son of *A*, the son of Ram,

AMMISHADDAI

Nu 1: 12 Ahiezer son of *A*; from Asher,
2: 25 people of Dan is Ahiezer son of *A*.
7: 66 On the tenth day Ahiezer son of *A*,
7: 71 the offering of Ahiezer son of *A*.
10: 25 Ahiezer son of *A* was in command.

AMMIZABAD

1Ch 27: 6 His son *A* was in charge

AMMON (AMMONITE AMMONITES)

Jdg 11: 28 of *A*, however, paid no attention
11: 33 Thus Israel subdued *A*.
2Ki 23: 13 god of the people of *A*.
2Ch 20: 10 "But now here are men from *A*,
20: 22 ambushes against the men of *A*
20: 23 The men of *A* and Moab rose up
Ne 13: 23 married women from Ashdod, *A*
Ps 83: 7 Gebal, *A* and Amalek,
Jer 9: 26 *A*, Moab and all who live
25: 21 Moab and *A*; all the kings of Tyre
27: 3 to the kings of Edom, Moab, *A*,
40: 11 When all the Jews in Moab, *A*,
Eze 25: 5 *A* into a resting place for sheep.
Da 11: 41 the leaders of *A* will be delivered
Am 1: 13 "For three sins of *A*,

AMMONITE (AMMON)

Dt 23: 3 No *A* or Moabite or any
Jos 13: 25 half the *A* country as far as Aroer,
Jdg 11: 12 to the *A* king with the question:
11: 14 sent back messengers to the *A* king,
1Sa 11: 1 Nahash the *A* went up
11: 2 But Nahash the *A* replied,
2Sa 10: 3 *A* nobles said to Hanun their lord,
12: 31 He did this to all the *A* towns.
23: 37 Zelek the *A*, Naharai
1Ki 14: 21 name was Naamah; she was an *A*.
14: 31 name was Naamah; she was an *A*.
2Ki 24: 2 Moabite and *A* raiders against him.
1Ch 11: 39 Zelek the *A*, Naharai the Berothite,
19: 3 the *A* nobles said to Hanun,
20: 3 David did this to all the *A* towns.
2Ch 12: 13 name was Naamah; she was an *A*.
24: 26 son of Shimeath an *A* woman,
Ne 2: 10 Tobiah the *A* official heard about
2: 19 Tobiah the *A* official and Geshem
4: 3 Tobiah the *A*, who was at his side,
13: 1 there it was found written that no *A*

AMMONITES (AMMON)

Ge 19: 38 he is the father of the *A* of today.
Nu 21: 24 as the *A*, because their border was
Dt 2: 19 come to the *A*, do not harass them
2: 19 of any land belonging to the *A*.
2: 20 the *A* called them Zamzummites.
2: 21 them from before the *A*,
2: 37 on any of the land of the *A*,
3: 11 It is still in Rabbah of the *A*.)
3: 16 River, which is the border of the *A*.
Jos 12: 2 which is the border of the *A*.
13: 10 out to the border of the *A*.
Jdg 3: 13 Getting the *A* and Amalekites
10: 6 the gods of the *A* and the gods
10: 7 hands of the Philistines and the *A*,
10: 9 The *A* also crossed the Jordan
10: 11 the Amorites, the *A*, the Philistines
10: 17 When the *A* were called to arms
10: 18 against the *A* will be the head
11: 4 when the *A* made war on Israel,
11: 6 so we can fight the *A*."
11: 8 come with us to fight the *A*,
11: 9 you take me back to fight the *A*
11: 13 king of the *A* answered Jephthah's
11: 15 land of Moab or the land of the *A*.
11: 27 between the Israelites and the *A*."
11: 29 there he advanced against the *A*.
11: 30 "If you give the *A* into my hands,
11: 31 from the *A* will be the LORD's,
11: 32 Jephthah went over to fight the *A*,
11: 36 you of your enemies, the *A*.
12: 1 go to fight the *A* without calling us
12: 2 in a great struggle with the *A*,
12: 3 and crossed over to fight the *A*,
1Sa 11: 10 said to the *A*, "Tomorrow we will
11: 11 broke into the camp of the *A*
12: 12 of the *A* was moving against you,
14: 47 the *A*, Edom, the kings of Zobah,
2Sa 8: 12 Moab, the *A* and the Philistines,
10: 1 of time, the king of the *A* died,
10: 2 came to the land of the *A*,
10: 6 When the *A* realized that they had
10: 8 The *A* came out and drew up
10: 10 and deployed them against the *A*.
10: 11 but if the *A* are too strong for you,
10: 14 Joab returned from fighting the *A*
10: 14 When the *A* saw that the Arameans
10: 19 afraid to help the *A* anymore.
11: 1 They destroyed the *A* and besieged
12: 9 him with the sword of the *A*.
12: 26 fought against Rabbah of the *A*
17: 27 of Nahash from Rabbah of the *A*,
1Ki 11: 1 *A*, Edomites, Sidonians
11: 5 Molech the detestable god of the *A*
11: 7 the detestable god of the *A*.
11: 33 and Molech the god of the *A*,
1Ch 18: 11 Moab, the *A* and the Philistines,
19: 1 Nahash king of the *A* died,
19: 2 land of the *A* to express sympathy
19: 6 When the *A* realized that they had
19: 6 and the *A* sent a thousand talents
19: 7 while the *A* were mustered
19: 9 The *A* came out and drew up
19: 11 they were deployed against the *A*.
19: 12 but if the *A* are too strong for you,
19: 15 When the *A* saw that the Arameans
19: 19 willing to help the *A* anymore.
20: 1 He laid waste the land of the *A*
2Ch 20: 1 *A* with some of the Meunites came
26: 8 The *A* brought tribute to Uzziah,
27: 5 That year the *A* paid him
27: 5 *A* brought him the same amount
27: 5 war on the king of the *A*
Ezr 9: 1 Perizzites, Jebusites, *A*, Moabites,
Ne 4: 7 the *A* and the men
Isa 11: 14 and the *A* will be subject to them.
Jer 40: 14 king of the *A* has sent Ishmael son
41: 10 and set out to cross over to the *A*.
41: 15 from Johanan and fled to the *A*.
49: 1 Concerning the *A*: This is what
49: 2 cry against Rabbah of the *A*;
49: 6 I will restore the fortunes of the *A*,"
Eze 21: 20 to come against Rabbah of the *A*
21: 28 Sovereign LORD says about the *A*
25: 2 set your face against the *A*
25: 10 along with the *A* to the people
25: 10 so that the *A* will not be
Zep 2: 8 and the taunts of the *A*,
2: 9 the *A* like Gomorrah—

AMNON (AMNON'S)

2Sa 3: 2 His firstborn was *A* the son
13: 1 *A* son of David fell in love
13: 2 *A* became frustrated to the point
13: 3 *A* had a friend named Jonadab son
13: 4 He asked *A*, "Why do you,
13: 4 *A* said to him, "I'm in love
13: 6 *A* lay down and pretended to be ill.
13: 6 came to see him, *A* said to him,
13: 7 "Go to the house of your brother *A*
13: 8 went to the house of her brother *A*,
13: 9 Send everyone out of here," *A* said.
13: 10 *A* said to Tamar, "Bring the food
13: 10 it to her brother *A* in his bedroom.
13: 15 *A* hated her with intense hatred.
13: 15 *A* said to her, "Get up and get out
13: 20 "Has that *A*, your brother,
13: 22 Absalom never said a word to *A*,
13: 22 he hated *A* because he had
13: 26 please let my brother *A* come
13: 27 so he sent with him *A* and the rest
13: 28 When *A* is in high spirits
13: 28 'Strike *A* down,' then kill him.
13: 29 to *A* what Absalom had ordered.
13: 32 all the princes; only *A* is dead.
13: 32 since the day *A* raped his sister
13: 33 Only *A* is dead."
1Ch 3: 1 The firstborn was *A* the son
4: 20 The sons of Shimon: *A*, Rinnah,

AMNON'S (AMNON)

2Sa 13: 39 was consoled concerning *A* death.

AMOK (AMOK'S)

Ne 12: 7 Sallu, *A*, Hilkiah and Jedaiah.

AMOK'S (AMOK)

Ne 12: 20 Kallai; of *A*, Eber; of Hilkiah's,

AMON (AMON'S)

1Ki 22: 26 and send him back to *A* the ruler
2Ki 21: 18 And *A* his son succeeded him
21: 19 *A* was twenty-two years old
21: 24 all who had plotted against King *A*,
1Ch 3: 14 Manasseh his son, *A* his son,
2Ch 18: 25 and send him back to *A* the ruler
33: 20 And *A* his son succeeded him
33: 21 *A* was twenty-two years old
33: 22 *A* worshiped and offered sacrifices
33: 23 before the LORD; *A* increased his
33: 25 all who had plotted against King *A*,
Ne 7: 59 and *A* The temple servants
Jer 1: 2 of Josiah son of *A* king of Judah,
25: 3 of Josiah son of *A* king of Judah
46: 25 punishment on *A* god of Thebes,
Zep 1: 1 of Josiah son of *A* king of Judah:
Mt 1: 10 father of *A*, *A* the father of Josiah,

AMON'S (AMON)

2Ki 21: 23 *A* officials conspired against him
21: 25 As for the other events of *A* reign,
2Ch 33: 24 *A* officials conspired against him

AMORITE (AMORITES)

Ge 14: 13 the great trees of Mamre the *A*,
Nu 21: 13 desert extending into *A* territory.
Dt 2: 24 given into your hand Sihon the *A*,
4: 47 the two *A* kings east of the Jordan.
Jos 5: 1 Now when all the *A* kings west
10: 6 all the *A* kings from the hill country
24: 12 before you—also the two *A* kings.
Eze 16: 3 father was an *A* and your mother
16: 45 was a Hittite and your father an *A*.
Am 2: 9 "I destroyed the *A* before them,

AMORITES (AMORITE)

Ge 10: 16 Jebusites, *A*, Girgashites, Hivites,
14: 7 the *A* who were living in Hazezon
15: 16 of the *A* has not yet reached its full
15: 21 Rephaites, *A*, Canaanites,
48: 22 took from the *A* with my sword
Ex 3: 8 *A*, Perizzites, Hivites and Jebusites
3: 17 *A*, Perizzites, Hivites and Jebusites
13: 5 Hittites, *A*, Hivites and Jebusites—
23: 23 bring you into the land of the *A*,
33: 2 *A*, Hittites, Perizzites, Hivites
34: 11 I will drive out before you the *A*,
Nu 13: 29 and *A* live in the hill country;
21: 13 between Moab and the *A*.
21: 21 to say to Sihon king of the *A*:
21: 25 captured all the cities of the *A*
21: 26 the city of Sihon king of the *A*,
21: 29 as captives to Sihon king of the *A*.

Nu 21:31 So Israel settled in the land of the *A*
21:32 drove out the *A* who were there.
21:34 did to Sihon king of the *A*,
22: 2 all that Israel had done to the *A*.
32:33 the kingdom of Sihon king of the *A*
32:39 drove out the *A* who were there.
Dt 1: 4 had defeated Sihon king of the *A*,
1: 7 into the hill country of the *A*;
1:19 of the *A* through all that vast
1:20 reached the hill country of the *A*,
1:27 the hands of the *A* to destroy us.
1:44 *A* who lived in those hills came out
3: 2 did to Sihon king of the *A*,
3: 8 kings of the *A* the territory east
3: 9 by the Sidonians; the *A* call it Senir
4:46 in the land of Sihon king of the *A*,
7: 1 Girgashites, *A*, Canaanites,
20:17 the Hittites, *A*, Canaanites,
31: 4 kings of the *A*, whom he destroyed
Jos 2:10 kings of the *A* east of the Jordan,
3:10 Girgashites, *A* and Jebusites.
7: 7 the hands of the *A* to destroy us?
9: 1 *A*, Canaanites, Perizzites,
9:10 kings of the *A* east of the Jordan—
10: 5 Then the five kings of the *A*—
10:12 On the day the LORD gave the *A*
11: 3 to the *A*, Hittites, Perizzites
12: 2 Sihon king of the *A*, who reigned
12: 8 *A*, Canaanites, Perizzites,
13: 4 the region of the *A*, the area
13:10 all the towns of Sihon king of the *A*,
13:21 realm of Sihon king of the *A*,
24: 8 to the land of the *A* who lived east
24:11 as did also the *A*, Perizzites,
24:15 of the *A*, in whose land you are
24:18 including the *A*, who lived
Jdg 1:34 The *A* confined the Danites
1:35 And the *A* were determined
1:36 The boundary of the *A* was
3: 5 *A*, Perizzites, Hivites and Jebusites
6:10 do not worship the gods of the *A*,
10: 8 Jordan in Gilead, the land of the *A*.
10:11 "When the Egyptians, the *A*,
11:19 messengers to Sihon king of the *A*,
11:21 of the *A* who lived in that country,
11:23 has driven the *A* out
1Sa 7:14 peace between Israel and the *A*.
2Sa 21: 2 but were survivors of the *A*;
1Ki 4:19 (the country of Sihon king of the *A*
9:20 All the people left from the *A*,
21:26 like the *A* the LORD drove out
2Ki 21:11 evil than the *A* who preceded him
1Ch 1:14 Jebusites, *A*, Girgashites, Hivites,
2Ch 8: 7 left from the Hittites, *A*,
Ezr 9: 1 Moabites, Egyptians and *A*.
Ne 9: 8 *A*, Perizzites, Jebusites
Ps 135:11 Sihon king of the *A*,
136:19 Sihon king of the *A*
Am 2:10 desert to give you the land of the *A*.

AMOS

Am 1: 1 The words of *A*, one
7: 8 do you see, *A*?" "A plumb line,"
7:10 "*A* is raising a conspiracy
7:11 For this is what *A* is saying:
7:12 Then Amaziah said to *A*, "Get out,
7:14 *A* answered Amaziah, "I was
8: 2 "What do you see, *A*?" he asked.
Lk 3:25 the son of Mattathias, the son of *A*,

AMOUNT (AMOUNTED AMOUNTS)

Ge 43:12 Take double the *a* of silver
43:15 men took the gifts and double the *a*
Ex 12: 4 to determine the *a* of lamb needed
38:24 The total *a* of the gold
Lev 25: 8 sabbaths of years *a* to a period
27: 8 poor to pay the specified *a*,
27:16 to the *a* of seed required for it—
1Sa 30:16 of the great *a* of plunder they had
2Ki 12:10 they saw that there was a large *a*
12:11 When the *a* had been determined,
1Ch 22: 3 He provided a large *a* of iron
2Ch 14:13 carried off a large *a* of plunder.
20:25 among them a great *a* of equipment
24:11 and collected a great *a* of money.
24:11 they saw that there was a large *a*
27: 5 brought him the same *a*
31: 5 They brought a great *a*, a tithe
31:10 and this great *a* is left over."
Est 4: 7 including the exact *a*
Isa 41:29 Their deeds *a* to nothing;
Da 1: 5 The king assigned them a daily *a*
Mt 13:33 and mixed into a large *a* of flour
Lk 13:21 and mixed into a large *a* of flour
19: 8 I will pay back four times the *a*."

AMOUNTED (AMOUNT)

Ru 2:17 and it *a* to about an ephah.
2Ch 4:18 these things that Solomon made *a*
29:33 as sacrifices *a* to six hundred bulls

AMOUNTS (AMOUNT)

Ex 30:34 pure frankincense, all in equal *a*,
38:21 These are the *a* of the materials
Dt 17:17 He must not accumulate large *a*
Mk 12:41 Many rich people threw in large *a*.
2Co 10:10 and his speaking *a* to nothing."

AMOZ

2Ki 19: 2 to the prophet Isaiah son of *A*.
19:20 Isaiah son of *A* sent a message
20: 1 The prophet Isaiah son of *A* went
2Ch 26:22 by the prophet Isaiah son of *A*.
32:20 son of *A* cried out in prayer
32:32 of the prophet Isaiah son of *A*
Isa 1: 1 son of *A* saw during the reigns
2: 1 son of *A* saw concerning Judah
13: 1 Babylon that Isaiah son of *A* saw:
20: 2 spoke through Isaiah son of *A*.
37: 2 to the prophet Isaiah son of *A*.
37:21 Isaiah son of *A* sent a message
38: 1 The prophet Isaiah son of *A* went

AMPHIPOLIS

Ac 17: 1 When they had passed through *A*

AMPLIATUS

Ro 16: 8 Greet *A*, whom I love in the Lord.

AMRAM (AMRAM'S AMRAMITES)

Ex 6:18 The sons of Kohath were *A*, Izhar,
6:20 *A* lived 137 years.
6:20 *A* married his father's sister
Nu 3:19 The Kohathite clans: *A*, Izhar,
26:58 (Kohath was the forefather of *A*;
26:59 To *A* she bore Aaron, Moses
1Ch 6: 2 The sons of Kohath: *A*, Izhar,
6: 3 The children of *A*: Aaron,
6:18 The sons of Kohath: *A*, Izhar,
23:12 The sons of Kohath: *A*, Izhar,
23:13 The sons of *A*: Aaron and Moses.
24:20 from the sons of *A*: Shubael;
Ezr 10:34 Maadai, *A* and Uel, Benaiah,

AMRAM'S (AMRAM)

Nu 26:59 the name of *A* wife was Jochebed,

AMRAMITES (AMRAM)

Nu 3:27 belonged the clans of the *A*,
1Ch 26:23 From the *A*, the Izharites,

AMRAPHEL

Ge 14: 1 At this time *A* king of Shinar,
14: 9 *A* king of Shinar and Arioch king

AMZI

1Ch 6:46 the son of *A*, the son of Bani,
Ne 11:12 the son of *A*, the son of Zechariah,

ANAB

Jos 11:21 from Hebron, Debir and *A*,
15:50 *A*, Eshtemoh, Anim, Goshen,

ANAH

Ge 36: 2 and Oholibamah daughter of *A*
36:14 wife Oholibamah daughter of *A*
36:18 wife Oholibamah daughter of *A*.
36:20 Lotan, Shobal, Zibeon, *A*, Dishon,
36:24 The sons of Zibeon: Aiah and *A*.
36:24 This is the *A* who discovered
36:25 The children of *A*: Dishon
36:25 and Oholibamah daughter of *A*.
36:29 Lotan, Shobal, Zibeon, *A*, Dishon,
1Ch 1:38 Lotan, Shobal, Zibeon, *A*, Dishon,
1:40 The sons of Zibeon: Aiah and *A*.
1:41 The son of *A*: Dishon.

ANAHARATH

Jos 19:19 Hapharaim, Shion, *A*, Rabbith,

ANAIAH

Ne 8: 4 *A*, Uriah, Hilkiah and Maaselah;
10:22 Pelatiah, Hanan, *A*, Hoshea,

ANAK (ANAKITES)

Nu 13:22 the descendants of *A*, lived.
13:28 even saw descendants of *A* there.
13:33 of *A* come from the Nephilim).
Jos 15:13 (Arba was the forefather of *A*.)
15:14 and Talmai—descendants of *A*.
21:11 (Arba was the forefather of *A*.)
Jdg 1:20 drove from it the three sons of *A*.

ANAKITES (ANAK)

Dt 1:28 We even saw the *A* there.' "
2:10 and numerous, and as tall as the *A*.
2:11 Like the *A*, they too were
2:21 and numerous, and as tall as the *A*.
9: 2 The people are strong and tall—*A*!
9: 2 "Who can stand up against the *A*?"
Jos 11:21 and destroyed the *A* from the hill
11:22 No *A* were left in Israelite territory
14:12 heard then that the *A* were there
14:15 the greatest man among the *A*.)
15:14 Caleb drove out the three *A*—

ANAMITES

Ge 10:13 *A*, Lehabites, Naphtuhites,
1Ch 1:11 *A*, Lehabites, Naphtuhites,

ANAMMELECH

2Ki 17:31 sacrifices to Adrammelech and *A*,

ANAN

Ne 10:26 Ahiah, Hanan, *A*, Malluch,

ANANI

1Ch 3:24 Johanan, Delaiah and *A*—

ANANIAH

Ne 3:23 the son of *A*, made repairs
11:32 in Anathoth, Nob and *A*, in Hazor,

ANANIAS

Ac 5: 1 Now a man named *A*, together
5: 3 "*A*, how is it that Satan has
5: 5 When *A* heard this, he fell down
5: 8 is this the price you and *A* got
9:10 there was a disciple named *A*.
9:10 "*A*!" "Yes, Lord," he answered.
9:12 he has seen a man named *A* come
9:13 *A* answered, "I have heard many
9:15 But the Lord said to *A*, "Go!
9:17 Then *A* went to the house
22:12 "A man named *A* came to see me.
23: 2 the high priest *A* ordered those
24: 1 days later the high priest *A* went

ANATH

Jdg 3:31 After Ehud came Shamgar son of *A*
5: 6 "In the days of Shamgar son of *A*,

ANATHOTH (ANATHOTHITE)

Jos 21:18 *A* and Almon, together
2Sa 23:27 from *A*, Mebunnai the Hushathite,
1Ki 2:26 "Go back to your fields in *A*.
1Ch 6:60 *A*, together with their pasturelands.
7: 8 Jeremoth, Abijah, *A* and Alemeth.
11:28 from *A*, Sibbecai the Hushathite,
Ezr 2:23 of Netophah 56 of *A* 128
Ne 7:27 of *A* 128 of Beth Azmaveth
10:19 Bezai, Hariph, *A*, Nebai, Magpiash
11:32 Bethel and its settlements, in *A*,
Isa 10:30 Poor *A*!
Jer 1: 1 of the priests at *A* in the territory
11:21 men of *A* who are seeking your life
11:23 disaster on the men of *A* in the year
29:27 not reprimanded Jeremiah from *A*,
32: 7 'Buy my field at *A*, because
32: 8 'Buy my field at *A* in the territory
32: 9 field at *A* from my cousin Hanamel

ANATHOTHITE (ANATHOTH)

1Ch 12: 3 Jehu the *A*, and Ishmaiah
27:12 was Abiezer the *A*, a Benjamite.

ANCESTOR (ANCESTORS ANCESTRAL ANCESTRY)

Ge 10: 21 Shem was the *a* of all the sons
Jos 17: 1 Makir was the *a* of the Gileadites,
Heb 7: 10 Levi was still in the body of his *a*.
Jas 2: 21 not our *a* Abraham considered

ANCESTORS (ANCESTOR)

Lev 26: 45 with their *a* whom I brought out
1Ki 19: 4 I am no better than my *a*."
Am 2: 4 the gods their *a* followed,
Ac 28: 17 or against the customs of our *a*,

ANCESTRAL (ANCESTOR)

Nu 1: 16 the leaders of their *a* tribes.
13: 2 From each *a* tribe send one
17: 2 the leader of each of their *a* tribes.
17: 3 staff for the head of each *a* tribe.
17: 6 the leader of each of their *a* tribes,
18: 2 from your *a* tribe to join you
26: 55 to the names for its *a* tribe.
33: 54 it according to your *a* tribes.
36: 3 taken from our *a* inheritance
Ne 11: 20 of Judah, each on his *a* property.

ANCESTRY (ANCESTOR)

Nu 1: 18 The people indicated their *a*
Eze 16: 3 Your *a* and birth were in the land
21: 30 in the land of your *a*,
29: 14 to Pathros, the land of their *a*.
Ro 9: 5 from them is traced the human *a*
Heb 7: 16 as to his *a* but on the basis

ANCHOR (ANCHORED ANCHORS)

Ac 27: 13 so they weighed *a* and sailed
27: 17 they lowered the sea *a*
Heb 6: 19 We have this hope as an *a*

ANCHORED (ANCHOR)

Mk 6: 53 landed at Gennesaret and *a* there.

ANCHORS (ANCHOR)

Ac 27: 29 they dropped four *a* from the stern
27: 30 to lower some *a* from the bow.
27: 40 Cutting loose the *a*, they left them

ANCIENT (ANCIENTS)

Ge 49: 26 the blessings of the *a* mountains,
Dt 33: 15 gifts of the *a* mountains
1Sa 27: 8 (From *a* times these peoples had
1Ch 4: 22 (These records are from *a* times.)
Ezr 4: 15 a place of rebellion from *a* times.
Ps 24: 7 be lifted up, you *a* doors,
24: 9 lift them up, you *a* doors,
68: 33 to him who rides the *a* skies above,
119: 52 I remember your *a* laws, O LORD,
Pr 22: 28 Do not move an *a* boundary stone
23: 10 Do not move an *a* boundary stone
Isa 19: 11 a disciple of the *a* kings"?
43: 13 Yes, and from *a* days I am he.
44: 7 since I established my *a* people,
46: 10 from *a* times, what is still to come.
58: 12 Your people will rebuild the *a* ruins
61: 4 They will rebuild the *a* ruins
64: 4 Since *a* times no one has heard,
Jer 5: 15 an *a* and enduring nation,
6: 16 ask for the *a* paths,
18: 15 and in the *a* paths.
Eze 25: 15 and with *a* hostility sought
26: 20 as in *a* ruins, with those who go
35: 5 you harbored an *a* hostility
36: 2 The *a* heights have become our
Da 7: 9 and the *A* of Days took his seat.
7: 13 He approached the *A* of Days
7: 22 until the *A* of Days came
Mic 5: 2 from *a* times."
Hab 3: 6 The *a* mountains crumbled
2Pe 2: 5 if he did not spare the *a* world
Rev 12: 9 that *a* serpent called the devil
20: 2 seized the dragon, that *a* serpent,

ANCIENTS (ANCIENT)

Heb 11: 2 is what the *a* were commended

ANDREW

Mt 4: 18 called Peter and his brother *A*.
10: 2 is called Peter) and his brother *A*;
Mk 1: 16 and his brother *A* casting a net
1: 29 John to the home of Simon and *A*.
3: 18 *A*, Philip, Bartholomew, Matthew,
13: 3 John and *A* asked him privately,
Lk 6: 14 his brother *A*, James, John, Philip,
Jn 1: 40 *A*, Simon Peter's brother, was one
1: 41 The first thing *A* did was
1: 44 like *A* and Peter, was
6: 8 Another of his disciples, *A*,
12: 22 Philip went to tell *A*; *A*
Ac 1: 13 James and *A*; Philip and Thomas,

ANDRONICUS

Ro 16: 7 Greet *A* and Junias, my relatives

ANEM

1Ch 6: 73 Daberath, Ramoth and *A*,

ANER

Ge 14: 13 a brother of Eshcol and *A*,
14: 24 the men who went with me—to *A*,
1Ch 6: 70 of Manasseh the Israelites gave *A*

ANGEL (ANGEL'S ANGELS ARCHANGEL)

Ge 16: 7 The *a* of the LORD found Hagar
16: 9 Then the *a* of the LORD told her,
16: 10 The *a* added, "I will
16: 11 The *a* of the LORD also said to her
21: 17 and the *a* of God called to Hagar
22: 11 But the *a* of the LORD called out
22: 15 The *a* of the LORD called
24: 7 he will send his *a* before you
24: 40 will send his *a* with you
31: 11 The *a* of God said to me
48: 16 the *A* who has delivered me
Ex 3: 2 There the *a* of the LORD appeared
14: 19 *a* of God, who had been traveling
23: 20 I am sending an *a* ahead of you
23: 23 My *a* will go ahead of you
32: 34 and my *a* will go before you.
33: 2 I will send an *a* before you
Nu 20: 16 and sent an *a* and brought us out
22: 22 and the *a* of the LORD stood
22: 23 When the donkey saw the *a*
22: 24 Then the *a* of the LORD stood
22: 25 When the donkey saw the *a*
22: 26 Then the *a* of the LORD moved
22: 27 When the donkey saw the *a*
22: 31 he saw the *a* of the LORD standing
22: 32 The *a* of the LORD asked him,
22: 34 Balaam said to the *a* of the LORD,
22: 35 The *a* of the LORD said to Balaam,
Jdg 2: 1 The *a* of the LORD went up
2: 4 When the *a* of the LORD had
5: 23 'Curse Meroz,' said the *a*
6: 11 The *a* of the LORD came
6: 12 When the *a* of the LORD appeared
6: 20 The *a* of God said
6: 21 the *a* of the LORD disappeared.
6: 21 *a* of the LORD touched the meat
6: 22 Gideon realized that it was the *a*
6: 22 I have seen the *a* of the LORD face
13: 3 The *a* of the LORD appeared
13: 6 He looked like an *a* of God,
13: 9 and the *a* of God came again
13: 13 The *a* of the LORD answered,
13: 15 Manoah said to the *a* of the LORD
13: 16 The *a* of the LORD replied,
13: 16 did not realize that it was the *a*
13: 17 inquired of the *a* of the LORD,
13: 20 the *a* of the LORD ascended
13: 21 Manoah realized that it was the *a*
13: 21 When the *a* of the LORD did not
1Sa 29: 9 pleasing in my eyes as an *a* of God;
2Sa 14: 17 for my lord the king is like an *a*
14: 20 lord has wisdom like that of an *a*
19: 27 My lord the king is like an *a* of God
24: 16 The *a* of the LORD was then
24: 16 When the *a* stretched out his hand
24: 16 and said to the *a* who was afflicting
24: 17 David saw the *a* who was striking
1Ki 13: 18 And an *a* said to me by the word
19: 5 All at once an *a* touched him
19: 7 The *a* of the LORD came back
2Ki 1: 3 But the *a* of the LORD said
1: 15 The *a* of the LORD said to Elijah,
19: 35 That night the *a* of the LORD went
1Ch 21: 12 with the *a* of the LORD ravaging
21: 15 God sent an *a* to destroy Jerusalem
21: 15 said to the *a* who was destroying
21: 15 *a* of the LORD was then standing
21: 15 *a* was doing so, the LORD saw it
21: 16 saw the *a* of the LORD standing
21: 18 the *a* of the LORD ordered Gad
21: 20 saw the *a*; his four sons who were
21: 27 Then the LORD spoke to the *a*,
21: 30 of the sword of the *a* of the LORD.
2Ch 32: 21 And the LORD sent an *a*,
Job 33: 23 "Yet if there is an *a* on his side
Ps 34: 7 The *a* of the LORD encamps
35: 5 with the *a* of the LORD driving
35: 6 with the *a* of the LORD pursuing
Isa 37: 36 Then the *a* of the LORD went out
63: 9 the *a* of his presence saved them.
Da 3: 28 who has sent his *a* and rescued his
6: 22 live forever! My God sent his *a*,
Hos 12: 4 He struggled with the *a*
Zec 1: 9 The *a* who was talking
1: 11 reported to the *a* of the LORD,
1: 12 Then the *a* of the LORD said,
1: 13 words to the *a* who talked
1: 14 the *a* who was speaking to me said,
1: 19 I asked the *a* who was speaking
2: 3 and another *a* came to meet him
2: 3 the *a* who was speaking to me left,
3: 1 before the *a* of the LORD,
3: 3 clothes as he stood before the *a*.
3: 4 *a* said to those who were standing
3: 5 while the *a* of the LORD stood by.
3: 6 *a* of the LORD gave this charge
4: 1 the *a* who talked with me returned
4: 4 I asked the *a* who talked with me,
4: 11 I asked the *a*, "What are these two
5: 5 Then the *a* who was speaking
5: 10 I asked the *a* who was speaking
6: 4 I asked the *a* who was speaking
6: 5 my lord?" The *a* answered me,
12: 8 like the *A* of the LORD going
Mt 1: 20 an *a* of the Lord appeared to him
1: 24 he did what the *a* of the Lord had
2: 13 an *a* of the Lord appeared
2: 19 an *a* of the Lord appeared
28: 2 for an *a* of the Lord came
28: 5 *a* said to the women, "Do not be
Lk 1: 11 an *a* of the Lord appeared to him,
1: 13 the *a* said to him: "Do not be afraid
1: 18 Zechariah asked the *a*, "How can I
1: 19 The *a* answered, "I am Gabriel.
1: 26 God sent the *a* Gabriel
1: 28 The *a* went to her and said,
1: 30 the *a* said to her, "Do not be afraid,
1: 34 Mary asked the *a*,
1: 35 I am a virgin?" The *a* answered,
1: 38 Then the *a* left her.
2: 9 An *a* of the Lord appeared to them,
2: 10 *a* said to them, "Do not be afraid.
2: 13 heavenly host appeared with the *a*,
2: 21 the name the *a* had given him
22: 43 An *a* from heaven appeared to him
Jn 12: 29 others said an *a* had spoken to him.
Ac 5: 19 But during the night an *a*
6: 15 his face was like the face of an *a*.
7: 30 an *a* appeared to Moses
7: 35 through the *a* who appeared to him
7: 38 and with the *a* who spoke to him
8: 26 Now an *a* of the Lord said to Philip
10: 3 He distinctly saw an *a* of God,
10: 4 The *a* answered, "Your prayers
10: 7 When the *a* who spoke
10: 22 holy *a* told him to have you come
11: 13 us how he had seen an *a* appear
12: 7 Suddenly an *a* of the Lord
12: 8 Then the *a* said to him, "Put
12: 8 and follow me," the *a* told him.
12: 9 idea that what the *a* was doing was
12: 10 one street, suddenly the *a* left him.
12: 11 a doubt that the Lord sent his *a*
12: 15 they said, "It must be his *a*."
12: 23 an *a* of the Lord struck him down,
23: 9 or an *a* has spoken to him?"
27: 23 Last night an *a* of the God whose I
1Co 10: 10 and were killed by the destroying *a*
2Co 11: 14 Satan himself masquerades as an *a*
Gal 1: 8 or an *a* from heaven should preach
4: 14 as if I were an *a* of God,
Rev 1: 1 by sending his *a* to his servant John

Rev 2: 1 "To the *a* of the church
2: 8 "To the *a* of the church
2: 12 "To the *a* of the church
2: 18 "To the *a* of the church
3: 1 "To the *a* of the church
3: 7 "To the *a* of the church
3: 14 "To the *a* of the church
5: 2 And I saw a mighty *a* proclaiming
7: 2 Then I saw another *a* coming up
8: 3 Another *a*, who had a golden
8: 5 Then the *a* took the censer,
8: 7 The first *a* sounded his trumpet,
8: 8 The second *a* sounded his trumpet,
8: 10 The third *a* sounded his trumpet,
8: 12 The fourth *a* sounded his trumpet,
9: 1 The fifth *a* sounded his trumpet,
9: 11 king over them the *a* of the Abyss,
9: 13 The sixth *a* blew his trumpet,
9: 14 to the sixth *a* who had the trumpet,
10: 1 I saw another mighty *a* coming
10: 5 the *a* I had seen standing on the sea
10: 7 days when the seventh *a* is about
10: 8 in the hand of the *a* who is standing
10: 9 So I went to the *a* and asked him
11: 15 The seventh *a* sounded his trumpet
14: 6 I saw another *a* flying in midair,
14: 8 A second *a* followed and said,
14: 9 A third *a* followed them
14: 15 another *a* came out of the temple
14: 17 Another *a* came out of the temple
14: 18 Still another *a*, who had charge
14: 19 The *a* swung his sickle on the earth
16: 2 The first *a* went and poured out his
16: 3 The second *a* poured out his bowl
16: 4 The third *a* poured out his bowl
16: 5 Then I heard the *a* in charge
16: 8 The fourth *a* poured out his bowl
16: 10 The fifth *a* poured out his bowl
16: 12 The sixth *a* poured out his bowl
16: 17 The seventh *a* poured out his bowl
17: 3 the *a* carried me away in the Spirit
17: 7 the *a* said to me: "Why are you
17: 15 *a* said to me, "The waters you saw,
18: 1 After this I saw another *a* coming
18: 21 a mighty *a* picked up a boulder
19: 9 Then the *a* said to me, "Write:
19: 17 And I saw an *a* standing in the sun,
20: 1 And I saw an *a* coming down out
21: 15 The *a* who talked with me had
21: 17 which the *a* was using.
22: 1 Then the *a* showed me the river
22: 6 The *a* said to me, "These words are
22: 6 sent his *a* to show his servants
22: 8 feet of the *a* who had been showing
22: 16 have sent my *a* to give you this

ANGEL'S (ANGEL)

Rev 8: 4 up before God from the *a* hand.
10: 10 the little scroll from the *a* hand

ANGELS (ANGEL)

Ge 19: 1 The two *a* arrived at Sodom
19: 15 the *a* urged Lot, saying, "Hurry!
28: 12 and the *a* of God were ascending
32: 1 and the *a* of God met him.
Job 1: 6 One day the *a* came
2: 1 On another day the *a* came
4: 18 if he charges his *a* with error,
38: 7 and all the *a* shouted for joy?
Ps 78: 25 Men ate the bread of *a*;
78: 49 a band of destroying *a*.
91: 11 command his *a* concerning you
103: 20 Praise the LORD, you his *a*,
148: 2 Praise him, all his *a*,
Mt 4: 6 command his *a* concerning you,
4: 11 and *a* came and attended him.
13: 39 of the age, and the harvesters are *a*.
13: 41 The Son of Man will send out his *a*,
13: 49 The *a* will come and separate
16: 27 in his Father's glory with his *a*,
18: 10 For I tell you that their *a*
22: 30 they will be like the *a* in heaven.
24: 31 And he will send his *a* with a loud
24: 36 not even the *a* in heaven,
25: 31 and all the *a* with him, he will sit
25: 41 prepared for the devil and his *a*.
26: 53 more than twelve legions of *a*?
Mk 1: 13 wild animals, and *a* attended him.
Mk 8: 38 in his Father's glory with the holy *a*
12: 25 they will be like the *a* in heaven.
13: 27 And he will send his *a*
13: 32 not even the *a* in heaven,
Lk 2: 15 When the *a* had left them
4: 10 command his *a* concerning you
9: 26 of the Father and of the holy *a*.
12: 8 him before the *a* of God.
12: 9 disowned before the *a* of God.
15: 10 in the presence of the *a* of God
16: 22 *a* carried him to Abraham's side.
20: 36 for they are like the *a*.
24: 23 us that they had seen a vision of *a*,
Jn 1: 51 and the *a* of God ascending
20: 12 look into the tomb and saw two *a*
Ac 7: 53 put into effect through *a*
23: 8 that there are neither *a* nor spirits,
Ro 8: 38 neither *a* nor demons, neither
1Co 4: 9 to the whole universe, to *a*
6: 3 you not know that we will judge *a*?
11: 10 this reason, and because of the *a*,
13: 1 in the tongues of men and of *a*,
Gal 3: 19 into effect through *a* by a mediator.
Col 2: 18 and the worship of *a* disqualify you
2Th 1: 7 in blazing fire with his powerful *a*.
1Ti 3: 16 was seen by *a*,
5: 21 and Christ Jesus and the elect *a*,
Heb 1: 4 as much superior to the *a*
1: 5 to which of the *a* did God ever say,
1: 6 "Let all God's *a* worship him."
1: 7 In speaking of the *a* he says,
1: 7 "He makes his *a* winds,
1: 13 To which of the *a* did God ever say
1: 14 Are not all *a* ministering spirits
2: 2 message spoken by *a* was binding,
2: 5 to *a* that he has subjected the world
2: 7 made him a little lower than the *a*;
2: 9 was made a little lower than the *a*,
2: 16 For surely it is not *a* he helps,
12: 22 thousands upon thousands of *a*
13: 2 some people have entertained *a*
1Pe 1: 12 Even *a* long to look
3: 22 with *a*, authorities and powers
2Pe 2: 4 For if God did not spare *a*
2: 11 even *a*, although they are stronger
Jude : 6 *a* who did not keep their positions
Rev 1: 20 The seven stars are the *a*
3: 5 name before my Father and his *a*.
5: 11 and heard the voice of many *a*,
7: 1 After this I saw four *a* standing
7: 2 to the four *a* who had been given
7: 11 All the *a* were standing
8: 2 And I saw the seven *a* who stand
8: 6 the seven *a* who had the seven
8: 13 to be sounded by the other three *a*
9: 14 "Release the four *a* who are bound
9: 15 the four *a* who had been kept ready
12: 7 his *a* fought against the dragon,
12: 7 the dragon and his *a* fought back.
12: 9 to the earth, and his *a* with him.
14: 10 sulfur in the presence of the holy *a*
15: 1 seven *a* with the seven last plagues
15: 6 Out of the temple came the seven *a*
15: 7 to the seven *a* seven golden bowls
15: 8 of the seven *a* were completed.
16: 1 the temple saying to the seven *a*,
17: 1 of the seven *a* who had the seven
21: 9 of the seven *a* who had the seven
21: 12 and with twelve *a* at the gates.

ANGER (ANGERED ANGERS ANGRY)

Ge 39: 19 treated me," he burned with *a*.
49: 6 for they have killed men in their *a*
49: 7 Cursed be their *a*, so fierce,
Ex 4: 14 Then the LORD's *a* burned
11: 8 Moses, hot with *a*, left Pharaoh.
15: 7 You unleashed your burning *a*;
22: 24 My *a* will be aroused, and I will kill
32: 10 alone so that my *a* may burn
32: 11 "why should your *a* burn
32: 12 Turn from your fierce *a*; relent
32: 19 his *a* burned and he threw
34: 6 slow to *a*, abounding in love
Lev 26: 28 then in my *a* I will be hostile
Nu 11: 1 he heard them his *a* was aroused.
11: 33 the *a* of the LORD burned
12: 9 The *a* of the LORD burned
14: 18 slow to *a*, abounding in love
Nu 24: 10 Balak's *a* burned against Balaam.
25: 3 the LORD's *a* burned against them
25: 4 the LORD's fierce *a* may turn
25: 11 has turned my *a* away
32: 10 LORD's *a* was aroused that day
32: 13 The LORD's *a* burned
Dt 4: 25 your God and provoking him to *a*,
6: 15 and his *a* will burn against you,
7: 4 and the LORD's *a* will burn
9: 7 the LORD your God to *a*
9: 18 and so provoking him to *a*.
9: 19 I feared the *a* and wrath
11: 17 Then the LORD's *a* will burn
13: 17 LORD will turn from his fierce *a*;
29: 23 the LORD overthrew in fierce *a*.
29: 24 Why this fierce, burning *a*?"
29: 27 Therefore the LORD's *a* burned
29: 28 In furious *a* and in great wrath
31: 29 to *a* by what your hands have made
Jos 7: 1 So the LORD's *a* burned
7: 26 the LORD turned from his fierce *a*
23: 16 the LORD's *a* will burn
Jdg 2: 12 They provoked the LORD to *a*
2: 14 In his *a* against Israel the LORD
3: 8 The *a* of the LORD burned
14: 19 Burning with *a*, he went up
1Sa 11: 6 in power, and he burned with *a*.
17: 28 he burned with *a* at him and asked,
20: 30 Saul's *a* flared up at Jonathan
20: 34 up from the table in fierce *a*;
2Sa 6: 7 The LORD's *a* burned
11: 20 the king's *a* may flare up,
12: 5 David burned with *a*
24: 1 Again the *a* of the LORD burned
1Ki 14: 9 you have provoked me to *a*
14: 15 to *a* by making Asherah poles.
14: 22 they stirred up his jealous *a* more
15: 30 the LORD, the God of Israel, to *a*.
16: 2 to provoke me to *a* by their sins.
16: 7 provoking him to *a*
16: 13 Israel to *a* by their worthless idols.
16: 26 to *a* by their worthless idols.
16: 33 to *a* than did all the kings of Israel
21: 22 you have provoked me to *a*
22: 53 to *a*, just as his father had done.
2Ki 13: 3 So the LORD's *a* burned
17: 11 that provoked the LORD to *a*.
17: 17 of the LORD, provoking him to *a*.
21: 6 of the LORD, provoking him to *a*.
21: 15 and have provoked me to *a*
22: 13 Great is the LORD's *a* that burns
22: 17 me to *a* by all the idols their hands
22: 17 my *a* will burn against this place
23: 19 that had provoked the LORD to *a*.
23: 26 away from the heat of his fierce *a*,
23: 26 done to provoke him to *a*.
24: 20 of the LORD's *a* that all this
1Ch 13: 10 The LORD's *a* burned
15: 13 the LORD our God broke out in *a*
2Ch 12: 12 the LORD's *a* turned from him,
24: 18 God's *a* came upon Judah
25: 15 The *a* of the LORD burned
28: 11 for the LORD's fierce *a* rests
28: 13 and his fierce *a* rests on Israel."
28: 25 the God of his fathers, to *a*.
29: 8 the *a* of the LORD has fallen
29: 10 so that his fierce *a* will turn away
30: 8 so that his fierce *a* will turn away
33: 6 of the LORD, provoking him to *a*.
34: 21 is the LORD's *a* that is poured
34: 25 me to *a* by all that their hands have
34: 25 my *a* will be poured out
Ezr 8: 22 but his great *a* is against all who
10: 14 until the fierce *a* of our God
Ne 9: 17 slow to *a* and abounding in love.
Est 1: 12 became furious and burned with *a*.
2: 1 when the *a* of King Xerxes had
Job 4: 9 at the blast of his *a* they perish.
9: 5 and overturns them in his *a*.
9: 13 God does not restrain his *a*;
10: 17 and increase your *a* toward me;
14: 13 conceal me till your *a* has passed!
16: 9 assails me and tears me in his *a*
18: 4 yourself to pieces in your *a*,
19: 11 His *a* burns against me;
20: 23 God will vent his burning *a*
21: 17 the fate God allots in his *a*?
32: 5 more to say, his *a* was aroused.

Job 35: 15 further, that his *a* never punishes
Ps 2: 5 Then he rebukes them in his *a*
4: 4 In your *a* do not sin;
6: 1 do not rebuke me in your *a*
7: 6 Arise, O LORD, in your *a;*
27: 9 do not turn your servant away in *a;*
30: 5 For his *a* lasts only a moment,
37: 8 Refrain from *a* and turn
38: 1 do not rebuke me in your *a*
55: 3 and revile me in their *a.*
56: 7 in your *a,* O God, bring
69: 24 let your fierce *a* overtake them.
74: 1 Why does your *a* smolder
77: 9 he in *a* withheld his compassion?"
78: 31 God's *a* rose against them;
78: 38 Time after time he restrained his *a*
78: 49 unleashed against them his hot *a,*
78: 50 He prepared a path for his *a;*
80: 4 how long will your *a* smolder
85: 3 and turned from your fierce *a.*
85: 5 Will you prolong your *a*
86: 15 slow to *a,* abounding in love
90: 7 We are consumed by your *a*
90: 11 Who knows the power of your *a?*
95: 11 So I declared on oath in my *a,*
103: 8 slow to *a,* abounding in love.
103: 9 nor will he harbor his *a* forever;
106: 29 LORD to *a* by their wicked deeds,
124: 3 when their *a* flared against us,
138: 7 hand against the *a* of my foes,
145: 8 slow to *a* and rich in love.
Pr 15: 1 but a harsh word stirs up *a.*
21: 14 A gift given in secret soothes *a,*
27: 4 *A* is cruel and fury overwhelming,
29: 8 but wise men turn away *a.*
29: 11 A fool gives full vent to his *a,*
30: 33 so stirring up *a* produces strife."
Ecc 5: 17 great frustration, affliction and *a.*
7: 9 for *a* resides in the lap of fools.
10: 4 If a ruler's *a* rises against you,
Isa 5: 25 Therefore the LORD's *a* burns
5: 25 for all this, his *a* is not turned away,
7: 4 because of the fierce *a* of Rezin
9: 12 for all this, his *a* is not turned away,
9: 17 for all this, his *a* is not turned away,
9: 21 for all this, his *a* is not turned away,
10: 4 for all this, his *a* is not turned away,
10: 5 to the Assyrian, the rod of my *a,*
10: 6 him against a people who *a* me,
10: 25 Very soon my *a* against you will
12: 1 your *a* has turned away
13: 9 a cruel day, with wrath and fierce
13: 13 in the day of his burning *a.*
14: 6 which in *a* struck down peoples
30: 27 with burning *a* and dense clouds
30: 30 with raging *a* and consuming fire,
42: 25 on them his burning *a,*
54: 8 In a surge of *a*
57: 17 him, and hid my face in *a,*
60: 10 Though in *a* I struck you,
63: 3 I trampled them in my *a*
63: 6 I trampled the nations in my *a;*
66: 15 he will bring down his *a* with fury,
Jer 4: 8 for the fierce *a* of the LORD
4: 26 before his fierce *a.*
7: 18 to other gods to provoke me to *a.*
7: 20 My *a* and my wrath will be poured
8: 19 me to *a* with their images,
10: 24 not in your *a,*
11: 17 me to *a* by burning incense
12: 13 because of the LORD's fierce *a.*"
15: 14 for my *a* will kindle a fire
17: 4 for you have kindled my *a,*
18: 23 with them in the time of your *a.*
21: 5 and a mighty arm in *a* and fury
23: 20 *a* of the LORD will not turn back
25: 6 do not provoke me to *a*
25: 37 of the fierce *a* of the LORD.
25: 38 because of the LORD's fierce *a.*
30: 24 fierce *a* of the LORD will not turn
32: 29 me to *a* by burning incense
32: 31 this city has so aroused my *a*
32: 37 I banish them in my furious *a*
33: 5 of the men I will slay in my *a*
36: 7 for the *a* and wrath pronounced
42: 18 'As my *a* and wrath have been
44: 3 me to *a* by burning incense
44: 6 my fierce *a* was poured out;
Jer 44: 8 Why provoke me to *a*
49: 37 even my fierce *a,*"
50: 13 of the LORD's *a* she will not be
51: 45 Run from the fierce *a* of the LORD
52: 3 of the LORD's *a* that all this
La 1: 12 me in the day of his fierce *a?*
2: 1 Zion with the cloud of his *a!*
2: 1 footstool in the day of his *a.*
2: 3 In fierce *a* he has cut off
2: 6 in his fierce *a* he has spurned
2: 21 them in the day of your *a;*
2: 22 In the day of the LORD's *a*
3: 43 "You have covered yourself with *a*
3: 66 Pursue them in *a* and destroy them
4: 11 he has poured out his fierce *a.*
Eze 3: 14 and in the *a* of my spirit,
5: 13 "Then my *a* will cease
5: 15 I inflict punishment on you in *a*
7: 3 I will unleash my *a* against you.
7: 8 and spend my *a* against you;
8: 17 and continually provoke me to *a?*
8: 18 Therefore I will deal with them in *a*
13: 13 and in my *a* hailstones
16: 26 me to *a* with your increasing
16: 38 of my wrath and jealous *a.*
16: 42 and my jealous *a* will turn away
20: 8 spend my *a* against them in Egypt.
20: 21 and spend my *a* against them
20: 28 offerings that provoked me to *a,*
21: 31 breathe out my fiery *a* against you;
22: 20 so will I gather you in my *a*
22: 31 and consume them with my fiery *a,*
23: 25 I will direct my jealous *a*
25: 14 Edom in accordance with my *a*
35: 11 you in accordance with the *a*
38: 18 my hot *a* will be aroused, declares
43: 8 So I destroyed them in my *a.*
Da 9: 16 turn away your *a* and your wrath
11: 20 he will be destroyed, yet not in *a*
Hos 8: 5 My *a* burns against them.
11: 9 I will not carry out my fierce *a,*
12: 14 has bitterly provoked him to *a;*
13: 11 So in my *a* I gave you a king,
14: 4 for my *a* has turned away
Joel 2: 13 slow to *a* and abounding in love,
Am 1: 11 because his *a* raged continually
Jnh 3: 9 compassion turn from his fierce *a*
4: 2 slow to *a* and abounding in love,
Mic 5: 15 I will take vengeance in *a*
Na 1: 3 The LORD is slow to *a*
1: 6 Who can endure his fierce *a?*
Hab 3: 12 and in *a* you threshed the nations.
Zep 2: 2 before the fierce *a*
2: 3 on the day of the LORD's *a.*
3: 8 all my fierce *a.*
3: 8 by the fire of my jealous *a.*
Zec 10: 3 My *a* burns against the shepherds,
Mt 18: 34 In *a* his master turned him
Mk 3: 5 He looked around at them in *a* and,
Ro 2: 8 evil, there will be wrath and *a.*
2Co 12: 20 outbursts of *a,* factions, slander,
Eph 4: 26 "In your *a* do not sin": Do not let
4: 31 rage and *a,* brawling and slander,
Col 3: 8 *a,* rage, malice, slander,
1Ti 2: 8 hands in prayer, without *a*
Heb 3: 11 So I declared on oath in my *a,*
4: 3 "So I declared on oath in my *a,*
11: 27 left Egypt, not fearing the king's *a;*
Jas 1: 20 for man's *a* does not bring about

ANGERED (ANGER)

Dt 32: 16 *a* him with their detestable idols.
32: 19 because he was *a* by his sons
32: 21 and *a* me with their worthless idols
Ezr 5: 12 our fathers *a* the God of heaven,
Ps 78: 58 They *a* him with their high places;
106: 32 of Meribah they *a* the LORD,
Pr 22: 24 do not associate with one easily *a,*
Zec 8: 14 pity when your fathers *a* me,"
1Co 13: 5 it is not easily *a,* it keeps no record

ANGERS (ANGER)

Pr 20: 2 he who *a* him forfeits his life.

ANGLE

2Ch 26: 9 and at the *a* of the wall,
Ne 3: 19 ascent to the armory as far as the *a.*
3: 20 from the *a* to the entrance
Ne 3: 24 from Azariah's house to the *a*
3: 25 son of Uzai worked opposite the *a*

ANGRY (ANGER)

Ge 4: 5 Cain was very *a,* and his face was
4: 6 "Why are you *a?* Why is your face
18: 30 "May the Lord not be *a,*
18: 32 "May the Lord not be *a,*
27: 45 When your brother is no longer *a*
30: 2 Jacob became *a* with her and said,
31: 35 said to her father, "Don't be *a,*
31: 36 Jacob was *a* and took Laban to task
40: 2 Pharaoh was *a* with his two
41: 10 Pharaoh was once *a*
44: 18 Do not be *a* with your servant,
45: 5 and do not be *a* with yourselves
Ex 16: 20 So Moses was *a* with them.
32: 22 "Do not be *a,* my lord," Aaron
Lev 10: 6 and the LORD will be *a*
10: 16 he was *a* with Eleazar and Ithamar,
Nu 11: 10 The LORD became exceedingly *a,*
16: 15 Then Moses became very *a*
16: 22 will you be *a* with the entire
22: 22 But God was very *a* when he went,
22: 27 he was *a* and beat her with his staff.
31: 14 Moses was *a* with the officers
32: 14 making the LORD even more *a*
Dt 1: 34 he was *a* and solemnly swore:
1: 37 of you the LORD became *a*
3: 26 of you the LORD was *a* with me
4: 21 The LORD was *a* with me
9: 8 wrath so that he was *a* enough
9: 19 for he was *a* enough with you
9: 20 And the LORD was *a* enough
9: 22 also made the LORD *a* at Taberah,
31: 17 On that day I will become *a*
32: 21 I will make them *a*
Jos 22: 18 tomorrow he will be *a*
Jdg 2: 20 Therefore the LORD was very *a*
6: 39 said to God, "Do not be *a* with me.
9: 30 son of Ebed said, he was very *a.*
10: 7 no longer served him, he became *a*
1Sa 18: 8 Saul was very *a;* this refrain galled
29: 4 the Philistine commanders were *a*
2Sa 3: 8 *a* because of what Ish-Bosheth
6: 8 David was *a* because the LORD's
19: 42 Why are you *a* about it? Have we
22: 8 they trembled because he was *a.*
1Ki 8: 46 and you become *a* with them
11: 9 The LORD became *a*
20: 43 and *a,* the king of Israel went
21: 4 *a* because Naboth the Jezreelite
2Ki 5: 11 But Naaman went away *a* and said,
13: 19 The man of God was *a* with him
17: 18 the LORD was very *a* with Israel
1Ch 13: 11 David was *a* because the LORD's
2Ch 6: 36 and you become *a* with them
16: 10 Asa was *a* with the seer
26: 19 ready to burn incense, became *a.*
28: 9 of your fathers, was *a* with Judah,
Ezr 9: 14 Would you not be *a* enough with us
Ne 4: 1 he became *a* and was greatly
4: 7 being closed, they were very *a.*
5: 6 and these charges, I was very *a.*
Est 2: 21 became *a* and conspired
Job 32: 2 became very *a* with Job
32: 3 also *a* with the three friends,
42: 7 "I am *a* with you and your two
Ps 2: 12 Kiss the Son, lest he be *a*
18: 7 they trembled because he was *a.*
60: 1 you have been *a*— now restore us!
76: 7 stand before you when you are *a?*
78: 21 LORD heard them, he was very *a;*
78: 59 God heard them, he was very *a;*
78: 62 he was very *a* with his inheritance.
79: 5 O LORD? Will you be *a* forever?
85: 5 Will you be *a* with us forever?
89: 38 you have been very *a*
95: 10 For forty years I was *a*
106: 40 Therefore the LORD was *a*
Pr 25: 23 so a sly tongue brings *a* looks.
29: 22 An *a* man stirs up dissension,
Ecc 5: 6 Why should God be *a*
SS 1: 6 My mother's sons were *a* with me
Isa 12: 1 Although you were *a* with me,
27: 4 I am not *a.*
34: 2 The LORD is *a* with all nations;
47: 6 I was *a* with my people

Isa 54: 9 So now I have sworn not to be *a*
57: 16 nor will I always be *a*,
64: 5 you were *a*.
64: 9 Do not be *a* beyond measure,
Jer 2: 35 he is not *a* with me.'
3: 5 will you always be *a?*
3: 12 'I will not be *a* forever.
10: 10 When he is *a*, the earth trembles;
37: 15 They were *a* with Jeremiah
La 5: 22 and are *a* with us beyond measure.
Eze 16: 42 I will be calm and no longer *a*.
Da 2: 12 This made the king so *a*
Jnh 4: 1 greatly displeased and became *a*.
4: 4 "Have you any right to be *a?*"
4: 9 a right to be *a* about the vine?"
4: 9 "I am *a* enough to die."
Mic 2: 7 "Is the Spirit of the LORD *a?*
7: 18 You do not stay *a* forever
Hab 3: 8 Were you *a* with the rivers,
Zec 1: 2 "The LORD was very *a*
1: 12 which you have been *a*
1: 15 I am very *a* with the nations that
1: 15 I was only a little *a*, but they added
7: 12 So the LORD Almighty was very *a*
Mt 5: 22 But I tell you that anyone who is *a*
Lk 14: 21 the owner of the house became *a*
15: 28 "The older brother became *a*
Jn 7: 23 why are you *a* with me
Ro 10: 19 I will make you *a* by a nation that
Eph 4: 26 go down while you are still *a*,
Heb 3: 10 That is why I was *a*
3: 17 with whom was he *a* for forty years
Jas 1: 19 slow to speak and slow to become *a*
Rev 11: 18 The nations were *a*,

ANGUISH (ANGUISHED)

Ex 15: 14 *a* will grip the people of Philistia.
Dt 2: 25 and be in *a* because of you."
1Sa 1: 16 been praying here out of my great *a*
Job 6: 2 "If only my *a* could be weighed
7: 11 I will speak out in the *a* of my spirit
15: 24 Distress and *a* fill him with terror;
26: 5 "The dead are in deep *a*,
Ps 6: 3 My soul is in *a*.
25: 17 free me from my *a*.
31: 7 and knew the *a* of my soul.
31: 10 My life is consumed by *a*
38: 8 I groan in *a* of heart.
39: 2 my *a* increased.
55: 4 My heart is in *a* within me;
116: 3 the *a* of the grave came upon me;
118: 5 In my *a* I cried to the LORD,
Pr 31: 6 wine to those who are in *a;*
Isa 13: 8 pain and *a* will grip them;
23: 5 they will be in *a* at the report
38: 15 because of this *a* of my soul.
38: 17 that I suffered such *a*.
65: 14 out from *a* of heart
Jer 4: 19 Oh, my *a*, my *a!*
6: 24 *A* has gripped us,
15: 8 *a* and terror.
49: 24 *a* and pain have seized her,
50: 43 *A* has gripped him,
La 1: 4 and she is in bitter *a*.
Eze 27: 31 weep over you with *a* of soul
30: 4 and *a* will come upon Cush.
30: 9 *A* will take hold of them on the day
Da 10: 16 "I am overcome with *a*
Joel 2: 6 of them, nations are in *a;*
Am 5: 16 cries of *a* in every public square.
Hab 3: 7 the dwellings of Midian in *a*.
Zep 1: 15 a day of distress and *a*,
Lk 21: 25 nations will be in *a* and perplexity
22: 44 in *a*, he prayed more earnestly,
Jn 16: 21 her baby is born she forgets the *a*
Ro 9: 2 and unceasing *a* in my heart.
2Co 2: 4 and *a* of heart and with many tears,

ANGUISHED (ANGUISH)

Jer 48: 5 *a* cries over the destruction are
Da 6: 20 he called to Daniel in an *a* voice,

ANIAM

1Ch 7: 19 Ahian, Shechem, Likhi and *A*.

ANIM

Jos 15: 50 Anab, Eshtemoh, *A*, Goshen,

ANIMAL (ANIMALS)

Ge 6: 20 of every kind of *a* and of every kind
7: 2 and two of every kind of unclean *a*,
7: 2 seven of every kind of clean *a*,
7: 14 with them every wild *a* according
9: 5 an accounting from every *a*.
37: 20 that a ferocious *a* devoured him.
37: 33 Some ferocious *a* has devoured
43: 16 slaughter an *a* and prepare dinner;
Ex 9: 4 so that no *a* belonging
9: 6 but not one *a* belonging
9: 19 and *a* that has not been brought in
11: 7 a dog will bark at any man or *a*.'
13: 2 belongs to me, whether man or *a*."
13: 15 firstborn in Egypt, both man and *a*.
19: 13 *a*, he shall not be permitted to live.'
21: 34 and the dead *a* will be his.
21: 35 the money and the dead *a* equally.
21: 36 and the dead *a* will be his.
21: 36 the owner must pay, *a* for *a*,
22: 4 "If the stolen *a* is found alive
22: 10 or any other *a* to his neighbor
22: 12 But if the *a* was stolen
22: 13 If it was torn to pieces by a wild *a*,
22: 13 required to pay for the torn *a*.
22: 14 "If a man borrows an *a*
22: 15 But if the owner is with the *a*,
22: 15 If the *a* was hired, the money paid
22: 19 with an *a* must be put to death.
22: 31 meat of an *a* torn by wild beasts;
Lev 1: 2 as your offering an *a* from
3: 1 and he offers an *a* from the herd,
3: 1 present before the LORD an *a*
3: 6 " 'If he offers an *a* from the flock
7: 21 or an unclean *a* or any unclean,
7: 24 The fat of an *a* found dead
7: 25 fat of an *a* from which an offering
7: 26 not eat the blood of any bird or *a*.
11: 3 You may eat any *a* that has a split
11: 26 " 'Every *a* that has a split hoof not
11: 39 " 'If an *a* that you are allowed
17: 13 living among you who hunts any *a*
18: 23 not have sexual relations with an *a*
18: 23 to an *a* to have sexual relations
20: 15 man has sexual relations with an *a*,
20: 15 to death, and you must kill the *a*.
20: 16 kill both the woman and the *a*.
20: 16 " 'If a woman approaches an *a*
20: 25 Do not defile yourselves by any *a*
22: 24 the LORD an *a* whose testicles are
24: 18 the life of someone's *a* must make
24: 21 Whoever kills an *a* must make
27: 9 he vowed is an *a* that is acceptable
27: 9 such an *a* given to the LORD
27: 10 if he should substitute one *a*
27: 11 is a ceremonially unclean *a*—
27: 11 the *a* must be presented
27: 13 the owner wishes to redeem the *a*,
27: 26 may dedicate the firstborn of an *a*,
27: 28 whether man or *a* or family land—
27: 32 every tenth *a* that passes
27: 33 both the *a* and its substitute
Nu 3: 13 in Israel, whether man or *a*.
8: 17 whether man or *a*, is mine.
18: 15 *a*, that is offered to the LORD is
Dt 4: 17 like any *a* on earth or any bird that
14: 6 You may eat any *a* that has a split
15: 21 If an *a* has a defect, is lame or blind
16: 2 to the LORD your God an *a*
27: 21 has sexual relations with any *a*."
Job 39: 15 that some wild *a* may trample them
Ps 50: 10 for every *a* of the forest is mine,
Pr 12: 10 for the needs of his *a*,
Ecc 3: 19 man has no advantage over the *a*.
3: 21 and if the spirit of the *a* goes
Jer 51: 62 so that neither man nor *a* will live
Eze 29: 11 of man or *a* will pass through it;
44: 31 or *a*, found dead or torn
Da 4: 16 let him be given the mind of an *a*,
5: 21 and given the mind of an *a;*
8: 4 No *a* could stand against him,
Hos 13: 8 a wild *a* will tear them apart.
Mal 1: 14 but then sacrifices a blemished *a*
Heb 12: 20 If even an *a* touches the mountain,
Jas 3: 3 obey us, we can turn the whole *a*.

ANIMALS (ANIMAL)

Ge 1: 24 wild *a*, each according to its kind."
1: 25 God made the wild *a* according
3: 1 of the wild *a* the LORD God had
3: 14 and all the wild *a!*
6: 7 and *a*, and creatures that move
7: 8 Pairs of clean and unclean *a*,
7: 16 The *a* going in were male
7: 21 wild *a*, all the creatures that swarm
7: 23 and *a* and the creatures that move
8: 1 Noah and all the wild *a*
8: 17 *a*, and all the creatures that move
8: 19 All the *a* and all the creatures that
8: 20 and, taking some of all the clean *a*
9: 10 the livestock and all the wild *a*,
30: 40 and dark-colored *a* that belonged
30: 40 did not put them with Laban's *a*.
30: 41 in front of the *a* so they would mate
30: 42 So the weak *a* went to Laban
30: 42 if the *a* were weak, he would not
31: 39 I did not bring you *a* torn
32: 17 who owns all these *a* in front of you
33: 13 hard just one day, all the *a* will die.
34: 23 and all their other *a* become ours?
36: 6 as his livestock and all his other *a*
45: 17 Load your *a* and return to the land
Ex 8: 17 gnats came upon men and *a*.
8: 18 And the gnats were on men and *a*.
9: 7 of the *a* of the Israelites had died.
9: 9 and *a* throughout the land."
9: 10 boils broke out on men and *a*.
9: 22 and *a* and on everything growing
9: 25 in the fields—both men and *a;*
12: 5 The *a* you choose must be year-old
12: 12 and *a*— and I will bring judgment
12: 21 and select the *a* for your families
20: 10 nor your *a*, nor the alien
23: 11 the wild *a* may eat what they leave.
23: 29 the wild *a* too numerous for you.
Lev 5: 2 the carcasses of unclean wild *a*
7: 24 or torn by wild *a* may be used
11: 2 'Of all the *a* that live on land,
11: 27 Of all the *a* that walk on all fours,
11: 29 " 'Of the *a* that move about
11: 46 are the regulations concerning *a*,
17: 15 by wild *a* must wash his clothes
19: 19 " 'Do not mate different kinds of *a*.
20: 25 unclean *a* and between unclean
22: 8 found dead or torn by wild *a*,
22: 25 and you must not accept such *a*
25: 7 and the wild *a* in your land.
26: 22 I will send wild *a* against you,
27: 27 If it is one of the unclean *a*,
Nu 7: 87 The total number of *a*
7: 88 number of *a* for the sacrifice
18: 15 every firstborn male of unclean *a*.
28: 31 Be sure the *a* are without defect.
31: 11 including the people and *a*,
31: 26 the people and *a* that were
31: 30 donkeys, sheep, goats or other *a*.
31: 47 out of every fifty persons and *a*,
Dt 5: 14 your donkey or any of your *a*,
7: 22 the wild *a* will multiply around you
12: 15 you may slaughter your *a* in any
12: 21 you may slaughter *a* from the herds
14: 4 These are the *a* you may eat: the ox
Jdg 20: 48 including the *a* and everything else
2Sa 21: 10 them by day or the wild *a* by night.
1Ki 4: 33 He also taught about *a* and birds,
18: 5 have to kill any of our *a*."
2Ki 3: 9 or for the *a* with them.
3: 17 and your other *a* will drink.
2Ch 29: 33 The *a* consecrated as sacrifices
35: 11 while the Levites skinned the *a*.
35: 13 They roasted the Passover *a*
Job 5: 23 the wild *a* will be at peace with you
12: 7 ask the *a*, and they will teach you,
37: 8 The *a* take cover;
40: 20 and all the wild *a* play nearby.
Ps 66: 15 I will sacrifice fat *a* to you
135: 8 the firstborn of men and *a*.
148: 10 wild *a* and all cattle,
Ecc 3: 18 may see that they are like the *a*.
3: 19 Man's fate is like that of the *a;*
Isa 1: 11 of rams and the fat of fattened *a;*
18: 6 and to the wild *a;*
18: 6 the wild *a* all winter.

Isa 30: 6 An oracle concerning the *a*
40: 16 nor its *a* enough for burnt offerings
43: 20 The wild *a* honor me,
Jer 9: 10 and the *a* are gone.
12: 4 the *a* and birds have perished.
21: 6 and *a*— and they will die
27: 5 its people and the *a* that are on it,
27: 6 even the wild *a* subject to him.
28: 14 give him control over the wild *a*.' "
31: 27 with the offspring of men and of *a*.
32: 43 without men or *a*,
33: 10 inhabited by neither men nor *a*,
33: 10 without men or *a*."
33: 12 desolate and without men or *a*—
36: 29 cut off both men and *a* from it?"
50: 3 both men and *a* will flee away.
Eze 4: 14 found dead or torn by wild *a*.
8: 10 and detestable *a* and all the idols
14: 13 and kill its men and their *a*,
14: 17 and I kill its men and their *a*,
14: 19 killing its men and their *a*,
14: 21 to kill its men and their *a*!
25: 13 and kill its men and their *a*.
29: 8 and kill your men and their *a*.
33: 27 give to the wild *a* to be devoured,
34: 3 and slaughter the choice *a*,
34: 5 they became food for all the wild *a*.
34: 8 has become food for all the wild *a*,
34: 28 nor will wild *a* devour them.
36: 11 number of men and *a* upon you,
39: 4 of carrion birds and to the wild *a*.
39: 17 kind of bird and all the wild *a*:
39: 18 all of them fattened *a* from Bashan.
44: 31 found dead or torn by wild *a*.
Da 4: 14 Let the *a* flee from under it
4: 15 live with the *a* among the plants
4: 23 let him live like wild *a*,
4: 25 and will live with the wild *a*;
4: 32 and will live with the wild *a*;
Hos 2: 12 and wild *a* will devour them.
Joel 1: 20 Even the wild *a* pant for you;
2: 22 Be not afraid, O wild *a*,
Hab 2: 17 of *a* will terrify you.
Zep 1: 3 "I will sweep away both men and *a*;
Zec 14: 15 and all the *a* in those camps.
Mal 1: 8 When you bring blind *a*
1: 8 sacrifice crippled or diseased *a*,
1: 13 crippled or diseased *a*
Mk 1: 13 He was with the wild *a*,
Ac 10: 12 all kinds of four-footed *a*,
11: 6 and saw four-footed *a* of the earth,
15: 20 from the meat of strangled *a*
15: 29 from the meat of strangled *a*
21: 25 from the meat of strangled *a*
Ro 1: 23 and birds and *a* and reptiles.
1Co 15: 39 kind of flesh, *a* have another,
Heb 13: 11 of *a* into the Most Holy Place
Jas 3: 7 All kinds of *a*, birds, reptiles
Jude : 10 like unreasoning *a*— these are

ANKLE (ANKLE-DEEP ANKLES)

Isa 3: 20 the headdresses and *a* chains

ANKLE-DEEP (ANKLE)

Eze 47: 3 me through water that was *a*.

ANKLES (ANKLE)

2Sa 22: 37 so that my *a* do not turn.
Ps 18: 36 so that my *a* do not turn.
Isa 3: 16 with ornaments jingling on their *a*.
Ac 3: 7 man's feet and *a* became strong.

ANNA

Lk 2: 36 *A*, the daughter of Phanuel,

ANNALS

1Ki 11: 41 in the book of the *a* of Solomon?
14: 19 in the book of the *a* of the kings
14: 29 in the book of the *a* of the kings
15: 7 in the book of the *a* of the kings
15: 23 in the book of the *a* of the kings
15: 31 in the book of the *a* of the kings
16: 5 in the book of the *a* of the kings
16: 14 in the book of the *a* of the kings
16: 20 in the book of the *a* of the kings
16: 27 in the book of the *a* of the kings
22: 39 in the book of the *a* of the kings
22: 45 in the book of the *a* of the kings
2Ki 1: 18 in the book of the *a* of the kings
8: 23 in the book of the *a* of the kings
10: 34 in the book of the *a* of the kings
12: 19 in the book of the *a* of the kings
13: 8 in the book of the *a* of the kings
13: 12 in the book of the *a* of the kings
14: 15 in the book of the *a* of the kings
14: 18 in the book of the *a* of the kings
14: 28 in the book of the *a* of the kings
15: 6 in the book of the *a* of the kings
15: 11 in the book of the *a* of the kings
15: 15 in the book of the *a* of the kings
15: 21 in the book of the *a* of the kings
15: 26 in the book of the *a* of the kings
15: 31 in the book of the *a* of the kings
15: 36 in the book of the *a* of the kings
16: 19 in the book of the *a* of the kings
20: 20 in the book of the *a* of the kings
21: 17 in the book of the *a* of the kings
21: 25 in the book of the *a* of the kings
23: 28 in the book of the *a* of the kings
24: 5 in the book of the *a* of the kings
1Ch 27: 24 in the book of the *a* of King David.
2Ch 20: 34 are written in the *a* of Jehu son
33: 18 are written in the *a* of the kings
Ne 12: 23 recorded in the book of the *a*.
Est 2: 23 in the book of the *a* in the presence
10: 2 in the book of the *a* of the kings

ANNAS

Lk 3: 2 during the high priesthood of *A*
Jn 18: 13 and brought him first to *A*,
18: 24 Then *A* sent him, still bound,
Ac 4: 6 *A* the high priest was there,

ANNIHILATE (ANNIHILATED ANNIHILATION)

Dt 9: 3 drive them out and *a* them quickly,
2Sa 21: 2 and Judah had tried to *a* them.)
2Ch 20: 23 Seir to destroy and *a* them.
Est 3: 13 kill and *a* all the Jews—young
8: 11 and *a* any armed force
Da 11: 44 rage to destroy and *a* many.

ANNIHILATED (ANNIHILATE)

2Ch 32: 21 who *a* all the fighting men

ANNIHILATION (ANNIHILATE)

Est 4: 8 of the text of the edict for their *a*,
7: 4 for destruction and slaughter and *a*

ANNIVERSARY

Dt 16: 6 on the *a* of your departure

ANNOTATIONS (NOTE)

2Ch 13: 22 are written in the *a*
24: 27 written in the *a* on the book

ANNOUNCE (ANNOUNCED ANNOUNCEMENT ANNOUNCES ANNOUNCING)

Jdg 7: 3 own strength has saved her, *a* now
Isa 42: 9 I *a* them to you."
48: 20 *A* this with shouts of joy
Jer 4: 5 "*A* in Judah and proclaim
5: 20 "*A* this to the house of Jacob
18: 7 If at any time I *a* that a nation
18: 9 if at another time I *a* that a nation
46: 14 "*A* this in Egypt, and proclaim it
48: 20 *A* by the Arnon
50: 2 *A* and proclaim among the nations,
51: 31 to *a* to the king of Babylon
Zec 9: 12 now I *a* that I will restore twice
Mt 6: 2 give to the needy, do not *a* it

ANNOUNCED (ANNOUNCE)

Ex 32: 5 an altar in front of the calf and *a*,
Lev 23: 44 So Moses *a* to the Israelites
Ru 4: 9 Then Boaz *a* to the elders
1Ki 20: 13 came to Ahab king of Israel and *a*,
Ps 68: 11 The Lord *a* the word,
Isa 48: 3 my mouth *a* them and I made them
48: 5 before they happened I *a* them
La 1: 21 May you bring the day you have *a*
Da 4: 17 " 'The decision is *a* by messengers;
Lk 23: 4 Then Pilate *a* to the chief priests
Gal 3: 8 and *a* the gospel in advance
Heb 2: 3 which was first *a* by the Lord,
Rev 10: 7 he *a* to his servants the prophets."

ANNOUNCEMENT (ANNOUNCE)

Isa 48: 16 "From the first *a* I have not spoken

ANNOUNCES (ANNOUNCE)

Dt 13: 1 and *a* to you a miraculous sign
Job 36: 33 His thunder *a* the coming storm;

ANNOUNCING (ANNOUNCE)

Jer 4: 15 A voice is *a* from Dan,

ANNOYANCE

Pr 12: 16 A fool shows his *a* at once,

ANNUAL (ANNUALLY)

Ex 30: 10 This *a* atonement must be made
Jdg 21: 19 there is the *a* festival of the LORD
1Sa 1: 21 family to offer the *a* sacrifice
2: 19 husband to offer the *a* sacrifice.
20: 6 an *a* sacrifice is being made there
2Ch 8: 13 New Moons and the three *a* feasts
Heb 10: 3 those sacrifices are an *a* reminder

ANNUALLY (ANNUAL)

2Ch 24: 5 and collect the money due *a*
Est 9: 21 them celebrate *a* the fourteenth

ANNULLED

Isa 28: 18 Your covenant with death will be *a*
Da 6: 8 and Persians, which cannot be *a*."
6: 12 and Persians, which cannot be *a*."

ANOINT (ANOINTED ANOINTING)

Ex 28: 41 and his sons, *a* and ordain them.
29: 7 *a* him by pouring it on his head.
29: 36 for it, and *a* it to consecrate it.
30: 26 use it to *a* the Tent of Meeting,
30: 30 "*A* Aaron and his sons
40: 9 anointing oil and *a* the tabernacle
40: 10 Then *a* the altar of burnt offering
40: 11 *A* the basin and its stand
40: 13 *a* him and consecrate him
40: 15 *A* them just as you anointed their
Jdg 9: 8 out to *a* a king for themselves.
9: 15 want to *a* me king over you,
1Sa 9: 16 *A* him leader over my people Israel
15: 1 to *a* you king over his people Israel;
16: 3 are to *a* for me the one I indicate."
16: 12 "Rise and *a* him; he is the one."
1Ki 1: 34 and Nathan the prophet *a* him king
19: 15 *a* Hazael king over Aram.
19: 16 Also, *a* Jehu son of Nimshi king
19: 16 *a* Elisha son of Shaphat
2Ki 9: 3 what the LORD says: I *a* you king
9: 6 'I *a* you king over the LORD's
9: 12 I *a* you king over Israel.' "
Ps 23: 5 You *a* my head with oil;
Ecc 9: 8 and always *a* your head with oil.
Da 9: 24 prophecy and to *a* the most holy.
Mk 16: 1 that they might go to *a* Jesus' body.
Jas 5: 14 and *a* him with oil in the name

ANOINTED (ANOINT)

Ge 31: 13 where you *a* a pillar and where you
Ex 29: 29 descendants so that they can be *a*
40: 15 them just as you *a* their father,
Lev 4: 3 " 'If the *a* priest sins, bringing guilt
4: 5 Then the *a* priest shall take some
4: 16 Then the *a* priest is to take some
6: 20 to the LORD on the day he is *a*:
6: 22 as *a* priest shall prepare it.
7: 36 the day they were *a*, the LORD
8: 10 anointing oil and *a* the tabernacle
8: 12 and *a* him to consecrate him.
16: 32 The priest who is *a* and ordained
Nu 3: 3 of Aaron's sons, the *a* priests,
7: 1 He also *a* and consecrated the altar
7: 1 he *a* it and consecrated it
7: 10 the altar was *a*, the leaders brought
7: 84 of the altar when it was *a*:
7: 88 of the altar after it was *a*.
35: 25 who was *a* with the holy oil.
1Sa 2: 10 and exalt the horn of his *a*."
2: 35 minister before my *a* one always.
10: 1 "Has not the LORD *a* you leader
12: 3 presence of the LORD and his *a*.
12: 5 and also his *a* is witness this day,

1Sa 15: 17 The LORD *a* you king over Israel.
16: 6 "Surely the LORD's *a* stands here
16: 13 and *a* him in the presence
24: 6 for he is the *a* of the LORD."
24: 6 the LORD's *a*, or lift my hand
24: 10 because he is the LORD's *a*.'
26: 9 can lay a hand on the LORD's *a*
26: 11 a hand on the LORD's *a*.
26: 16 guard your master, the LORD's *a*.
26: 23 a hand on the LORD's *a*.
2Sa 1: 14 hand to destroy the LORD's *a*?"
1: 16 you said, 'I killed the LORD's *a*.'"
2: 4 and there they *a* David king
2: 7 of Judah has *a* me king over them."
3: 39 though I am the *a* king, I am weak,
5: 3 and they *a* David king over Israel.
5: 17 heard that David had been *a* king
12: 7 says: 'I *a* you king over Israel,
19: 10 whom we *a* to rule over us,
19: 21 He cursed the LORD's *a*."
22: 51 shows unfailing kindness to his *a*,
23: 1 the man *a* by the God of Jacob,
1Ki 1: 39 the sacred tent and *a* Solomon.
1: 45 the prophet have *a* him king
5: 1 that Solomon had been *a* king
2Ki 11: 12 They *a* him, and the people
23: 30 *a* him and made him king in place
1Ch 11: 3 and they *a* David king over Israel,
14: 8 heard that David had been *a* king
16: 22 "Do not touch my *a* ones;
2Ch 6: 42 God, do not reject your *a* one.
22: 7 whom the LORD had *a*
23: 11 They *a* him and shouted, "Long
Ps 2: 2 and against his *A* One.
18: 50 shows unfailing kindness to his *a*,
20: 6 I know that the LORD saves his *a*;
28: 8 a fortress of salvation for his *a* one.
45: 2 your lips have been *a* with grace,
84: 9 look with favor on your *a* one.
89: 20 with my sacred oil I have *a* him.
89: 38 been very angry with your *a* one.
89: 51 mocked every step of your *a* one.
105: 15 "Do not touch my *a* ones;
132: 10 do not reject your *a* one.
132: 17 and set up a lamp for my *a* one.
Isa 45: 1 is what the LORD says to his *a*,
61: 1 because the LORD has *a* me
La 4: 20 The LORD's *a*, our very life breath
Eze 28: 14 You were *a* as a guardian cherub,
Da 9: 25 and rebuild Jerusalem until the *A*
9: 26 the *A* One will be cut off
Hab 3: 13 to save your *a* one.
Zec 4: 14 "These are the two who are *a*
Mk 6: 13 and *a* many sick people with oil
Lk 4: 18 because he has *a* me
Ac 4: 26 and against his *A* One.'
4: 27 holy servant Jesus, whom you *a*.
10: 38 how God *a* Jesus of Nazareth
2Co 1: 21 He *a* us, set his seal of ownership

ANOINTING (ANOINT)

Ex 25: 6 spices for the *a* oil
29: 7 Take the *a* oil and anoint him
29: 21 and some of the *a* oil and sprinkle it
30: 25 It will be the sacred *a* oil.
30: 25 Make these into a sacred *a* oil,
30: 31 is to be my sacred *a* oil
31: 11 and the *a* oil and fragrant incense
35: 8 spices for the *a* oil
35: 15 the *a* oil and the fragrant incense;
35: 28 for the *a* oil and for the fragrant
37: 29 made the sacred *a* oil and the pure,
39: 38 the *a* oil, the fragrant incense,
40: 9 "Take the *a* oil and anoint
40: 15 Their *a* will be to a priesthood that
Lev 8: 2 *a* oil, the bull for the sin offering,
8: 10 Then Moses took the *a* oil
8: 11 *a* the altar and all its utensils
8: 12 some of the *a* oil on Aaron's head
8: 30 Then Moses took some of the *a* oil
10: 7 because the LORD's *a* oil is on you
21: 10 who has had the *a* oil poured
21: 12 dedicated by the *a* oil of his God.
Nu 4: 16 regular grain offering and the *a* oil.
1Ch 29: 22 *a* him before the LORD to be ruler
Ps 45: 7 by *a* you with the oil of joy.
Heb 1: 9 by *a* you with the oil of joy."
1Jn 2: 20 you have an *a* from the Holy One,
1Jn 2: 27 about all things and as that *a* is real,
2: 27 as his *a* teaches you about all things
2: 27 the *a* you received

ANT (ANTS)

Pr 6: 6 Go to the *a*, you sluggard;

ANTELOPE

Dt 14: 5 the *a* and the mountain sheep.
Isa 13: 14 Like hunted *a*,
51: 20 like *a* caught in a net.

ANTHOTHIJAH

1Ch 8: 24 Zicri, Hanan, Hananiah, Elam, *A*,

ANTICHRIST (ANTICHRISTS)

1Jn 2: 18 have heard that the *a* is coming,
2: 22 a man is the *a*— he denies
4: 3 of the *a*, which you have heard is
2Jn : 7 person is the deceiver and the *a*.

ANTICHRISTS (ANTICHRIST)

1Jn 2: 18 even now many *a* have come.

ANTICIPATING

Ac 12: 11 the Jewish people were *a*."

ANTIOCH

Ac 6: 5 Parmenas, and Nicolas from *A*,
11: 19 *A*, telling the message only to Jews.
11: 20 went to *A* and began to speak
11: 22 and they sent Barnabas to *A*.
11: 26 he found him, he brought him to *A*.
11: 26 were first called Christians at *A*.
11: 27 came down from Jerusalem to *A*.
13: 1 church at *A* there were prophets
14: 19 Then some Jews came from *A*
14: 21 returned to Lystra, Iconium and *A*,
14: 26 From Attalia they sailed back to *A*,
15: 1 came down from Judea to *A*
15: 22 and send them to *A* with Paul
15: 23 To the Gentile believers in *A*,
15: 30 sent off and went down to *A*,
15: 35 Paul and Barnabas remained in *A*,
18: 22 church and then went down to *A*.
18: 23 After spending some time in *A*,
Gal 2: 11 came to *A*, I opposed him
2Ti 3: 11 of things happened to me in *A*,

ANTIPAS

Rev 2: 13 the days of *A*, my faithful witness,

ANTIPATRIS

Ac 23: 31 and brought him as far as *A*.

ANTS (ANT)

Pr 30: 25 *A* are creatures of little strength,

ANUB

1Ch 4: 8 who was the father of *A*

ANVIL

Isa 41: 7 spurs on him who strikes the *a*.

ANXIETIES (ANXIOUS)

Lk 21: 34 drunkenness and the *a* of life,

ANXIETY (ANXIOUS)

Ps 94: 19 When *a* was great within me,
Ecc 11: 10 So then, banish *a* from your heart
Eze 4: 16 people will eat rationed food in *a*
12: 19 They will eat their food in *a*
Php 2: 28 may be glad and I may have less *a*.
1Pe 5: 7 Cast all your *a* on him

ANXIOUS (ANXIETIES ANXIETY)

Dt 28: 65 the LORD will give you an *a* mind,
Ps 139: 23 test me and know my *a* thoughts.
Pr 12: 25 An *a* heart weighs a man down,
Ecc 2: 22 and *a* striving with which he labors
Php 4: 6 Do not be *a* about anything,

APARTMENT

Jer 36: 22 the king was sitting in the winter *a*,

APELLES

Ro 16: 10 Greet *A*, tested and approved

APES

1Ki 10: 22 silver and ivory, and *a* and baboons
2Ch 9: 21 silver and ivory, and *a* and baboons

APHEK

Jos 12: 18 one the king of *A* one the king
13: 4 Arah of the Sidonians as far as *A*,
19: 30 in the region of Aczib, Ummah, *A*
Jdg 1: 31 or Aczib or Helbah or *A* or Rehob,
1Sa 4: 1 Ebenezer, and the Philistines at *A*.
29: 1 gathered all their forces at *A*,
1Ki 20: 26 went up to *A* to fight against Israel.
20: 30 of them escaped to the city of *A*,
2Ki 13: 17 destroy the Arameans at *A*."

APHEKAH

Jos 15: 53 Janim, Beth Tappuah, *A*, Humtah,

APHIAH

1Sa 9: 1 the son of Becorath, the son of *A*

APOLLONIA

Ac 17: 1 passed through Amphipolis and *A*,

APOLLOS

Ac 18: 24 Meanwhile a Jew named *A*,
18: 27 When *A* wanted to go to Achaia,
19: 1 While *A* was at Corinth, Paul took
1Co 1: 12 another, "I follow *A*"; another,
3: 4 and another, "I follow *A*,"
3: 5 after all, is *A*? And what is Paul?
3: 6 I planted the seed, *A* watered it,
3: 22 whether Paul or *A* or Cephas
4: 6 to myself and *A* for your benefit,
16: 12 Now about our brother *A*:
Tit 3: 13 can to help Zenas the lawyer and *A*

APOLLYON

Rev 9: 11 is Abaddon, and in Greek, *A*.

APOSTLE (APOSTLES APOSTLES' APOSTLESHIP APOSTOLIC SUPER-APOSTLES)

Ro 1: 1 called to be an *a* and set apart
11: 13 as I am the *a* to the Gentiles,
1Co 1: 1 called to be an *a* of Christ Jesus
9: 1 Am I not an *a*? Have I not seen
9: 2 though I may not be an *a* to others,
15: 9 even deserve to be called an *a*,
2Co 1: 1 an *a* of Christ Jesus by the will
12: 12 The things that mark an *a*— signs,
Gal 1: 1 an *a*— sent not from men
2: 8 of Peter as an *a* to the Jews,
2: 8 work in my ministry as an *a*
Eph 1: 1 an *a* of Christ Jesus by the will
Col 1: 1 an *a* of Christ Jesus by the will
1Ti 1: 1 an *a* of Christ Jesus
2: 7 was appointed a herald and an *a*—
2Ti 1: 1 an *a* of Christ Jesus by the will
1: 11 I was appointed a herald and an *a*
Tit 1: 1 an *a* of Jesus Christ for the faith
Heb 3: 1 *a* and high priest whom we confess.
1Pe 1: 1 Peter, an *a* of Jesus Christ,
2Pe 1: 1 a servant and *a* of Jesus Christ,

APOSTLES (APOSTLE)

Mt 10: 2 are the names of the twelve *a*:
Mk 3: 14 twelve—designating them *a*—
6: 30 The *a* gathered around Jesus
Lk 6: 13 whom he also designated *a*:
9: 10 When the *a* returned, they
11: 49 'I will send them prophets and *a*,
17: 5 *a* said to the Lord, "Increase our
22: 14 Jesus and his *a* reclined at the table
24: 10 with them who told this to the *a*.
Ac 1: 2 Spirit to the *a* he had chosen.
1: 26 so he was added to the eleven *a*.
2: 37 and said to Peter and the other *a*,
2: 43 signs were done by the *a*.
4: 2 the *a* were teaching the people
4: 33 With great power the *a* continued
4: 36 whom the *a* called Barnabas
5: 12 The *a* performed many miraculous
5: 18 They arrested the *a* and put them
5: 21 and sent to the jail for the *a*.
5: 26 with his officers and brought the *a*.
5: 27 Having brought the *a*, they made
5: 29 Peter and the other *a* replied:

Ac 5:40 They called the *a* in and had them
5:41 The *a* left the Sanhedrin, rejoicing
6: 6 They presented these men to the *a*,
8: 1 except the *a* were scattered
8:14 When the *a* in Jerusalem heard
9:27 took him and brought him to the *a*.
11: 1 The *a* and the brothers
14: 4 with the Jews, others with the *a*.
14:14 But when the *a* Barnabas
15: 2 to go up to Jerusalem to see the *a*
15: 4 welcomed by the church and the *a*
15: 6 The *a* and elders met
15:22 the *a* and elders, with the whole
15:23 The *a* and elders, your brothers,
16: 4 the decisions reached by the *a*
Ro 16: 7 They are outstanding among the *a*,
1Co 4: 9 seems to me that God has put us *a*
9: 5 as do the other *a* and the Lord's
12:28 God has appointed first of all *a*,
12:29 Are all *a*? Are all prophets?
15: 7 to James, then to all the *a*,
15: 9 For I am the least of the *a*
2Co 11:13 are false *a*, deceitful workmen,
11:13 masquerading as *a* of Christ.
Gal 1:17 Jerusalem to see those who were *a*
1:19 I saw none of the other *a*—
Eph 2:20 built on the foundation of the *a*
3: 5 by the Spirit to God's holy *a*
4:11 It was he who gave some to be *a*,
1Th 2: 7 As *a* of Christ we could have been
2Pe 3: 2 and Savior through your *a*.
Jude :17 remember what the *a*
Rev 2: 2 have tested those who claim to be *a*
18:20 Rejoice, saints and *a* and prophets!
21:14 names of the twelve *a* of the Lamb.

APOSTLES' (APOSTLE)

Ac 2:42 themselves to the *a'* teaching
4:35 the sales and put it at the *a'* feet,
4:37 the money and put it at the *a'* feet.
5: 2 the rest and put it at the *a'* feet.
8:18 at the laying on of the *a'* hands,

APOSTLESHIP (APOSTLE)

Ro 1: 5 and *a* to call people from among all
1Co 9: 2 the seal of my *a* in the Lord.

APOSTOLIC (APOSTLE)

Ac 1:25 chosen to take over this *a* ministry,

APPAIM

1Ch 2:30 The sons of Nadab: Seled and *A*.
2:31 son of *A*: Ishi, who was the father

APPALLED

Lev 26:32 enemies who live there will be *a*.
1Ki 9: 8 all who pass by will be *a*
2Ch 7:21 all who pass by will be *a* and say,
Ezr 9: 3 and beard and sat down *a*.
9: 4 And I sat there *a* until the evening
Job 17: 8 Upright men are *a* at this;
18:20 Men of the west are *a* at his fate;
Ps 40:15 be *a* at their own shame.
Isa 52:14 as there were many who were *a*
59:16 he was *a* that there was no one
63: 5 I was *a* that no one gave support;
Jer 2:12 Be *a* at this, O heavens,
4: 9 and the prophets will be *a*."
18:16 all who pass by will be *a*
19: 8 all who pass by will be *a*
49:17 all who pass by will be *a*
Eze 4:17 They will be *a* at the sight
26:16 trembling every moment, *a* at you.
27:35 are *a* at you;
28:19 are *a* at you;
32:10 I will cause many peoples to be *a*
Da 8:27 I was *a* by the vision; it was

APPEAL (APPEALED APPEALING APPEALS)

Dt 15: 9 He may then *a* to the LORD
Job 5: 8 "But if it were I, I would *a* to God;
Ps 77:10 Then I thought, "To this I will *a*:
Ac 25:11 I *a* to Caesar!" After Festus had
25:21 When Paul made his *a* to be held
25:25 he made his *a* to the Emperor I
28:19 I was compelled to *a* to Caesar—
1Co 1:10 I *a* to you, brothers, in the name
2Co 5:20 God were making his *a* through us.
8:17 For Titus not only welcomed our *a*,
10: 1 gentleness of Christ, I *a* to you—
13:11 listen to my *a*, be of one mind,
1Th 2: 3 For the *a* we make does not spring
Phm : 9 yet I *a* to you on the basis of love.
:10 I *a* to you for my son Onesimus,
1Pe 5: 1 To the elders among you, I *a*

APPEALED (APPEAL)

Ex 5:15 the Israelite foremen went and *a*
Jos 10: 3 king of Jerusalem *a* to Hoham king
Est 2: 4 This advice *a* to the king,
Lk 23:20 Wanting to release Jesus, Pilate *a*
Ac 25:12 he declared: "You have *a* to Caesar
26:32 if he had not *a* to Caesar."
Ro 11: 2 how he *a* to God against Israel:

APPEALING (APPEAL)

2Pe 2:18 and, by *a* to the lustful desires

APPEALS (APPEAL)

2Sa 19:28 to make any more *a* to the king?"

APPEAR (APPEARANCE APPEARANCES APPEARED APPEARING APPEARS REAPPEARS)

Ge 1: 9 to one place, and let dry ground *a*."
27:12 I would *a* to be tricking him
Ex 4: 1 'The LORD did not *a* to you'?"
10:28 Make sure you do not *a*
10:29 "I will never *a* before you again."
22: 8 the owner of the house must *a*
23:15 is to *a* before me empty-handed.
23:17 to *a* before the Sovereign LORD.
34:20 is to *a* before me empty-handed.
34:23 to *a* before the Sovereign LORD,
34:24 to *a* before the LORD your God.
Lev 9: 4 For today the LORD will *a* to you
9: 6 glory of the LORD may *a* to you."
13: 4 but does not *a* to be more
13: 7 he must *a* before the priest again.
13:32 and it does not *a* to be more
14:37 or reddish depressions that *a*
16: 2 I *a* in the cloud over the atonement
Nu 16:16 to *a* before the LORD tomorrow—
Dt 16:16 man should *a* before the LORD
16:16 times a year all your men must *a*
31:11 when all Israel comes to *a*
1Sa 3:21 The LORD continued to *a*
2Sa 9: 2 They called him to *a* before David,
Ezr 10: 8 Anyone who failed to *a*
Job 19:18 when I *a*, they ridicule me.
Ps 102: 16 and *a* in his glory.
SS 2:12 Flowers *a* on the earth;
Isa 58: 8 and your healing will quickly *a*;
Eze 16:52 have made your sisters *a* righteous.
16:52 they *a* more righteous than you.
Da 7:23 is a fourth kingdom that will *a*
11: 2 Three more kings will *a* in Persia,
11: 3 Then a mighty king will *a*,
Hos 6: 3 he will *a*;
Zec 9:14 Then the LORD will *a* over them;
Mt 23:28 on the outside you *a* to people
24:11 and many false prophets will *a*
24:24 false prophets will *a* and perform
24:30 of the Son of Man will *a* in the sky,
Mk 13:22 false prophets will *a* and perform
Lk 19:11 of God was going to *a* at once.
Ac 5:27 they made them *a*
11:13 told us how he had seen an angel *a*
19:30 Paul wanted to *a* before the crowd,
2Co 5:10 we must all *a* before the judgment
Col 3: 4 also will *a* with him in glory.
Heb 9:24 now to *a* for us in God's presence.
9:28 and he will *a* a second time,

APPEARANCE (APPEAR)

Lev 13:55 if the mildew has not changed its *a*,
1Sa 16: 7 Do not consider his *a* or his height,
16: 7 Man looks at the outward *a*,
16:12 with a fine *a* and handsome
2Sa 14:25 praised for his handsome *a*
Ecc 8: 1 and changes its hard *a*.
SS 5:15 His *a* is like Lebanon,
Isa 52:14 his *a* was so disfigured beyond that
53: 2 in his *a* that we should desire him.
La 4: 7 their *a* like sapphires.
Eze 1: 5 In *a* their form was that of a man,
1:13 *a* of the living creatures was like
1:16 This was the *a* and structure
1:28 Like the *a* of a rainbow
1:28 This was the *a* of the likeness
8: 2 from there up his *a* was as bright
10:10 As for their *a*, the four
10:22 Their faces had the same *a*
40: 3 a man whose *a* was like bronze;
Da 1:13 Then compare our *a* with that
2:31 dazzling statue, awesome in *a*.
Joel 2: 4 They have the *a* of horses;
Mt 16: 3 how to interpret the *a* of the sky,
28: 3 His *a* was like lightning,
Lk 9:29 As he was praying, the *a*
12:56 how to interpret the *a* of the earth
Gal 2: 6 God does not judge by external *a*—
Php 2: 8 And being found in *a* as a man,
Col 2:23 Such regulations indeed have an *a*
Rev 4: 3 the one who sat there had the *a*

APPEARANCES (APPEAR)

Jn 7:24 Stop judging by mere *a*,

APPEARED (APPEAR)

Ge 2: 5 of the field had yet *a* on the earth
12: 7 but the LORD *a* to Abram and said
12: 7 to the LORD, who had *a* to him.
15:17 pot with a blazing torch *a*
17: 1 the LORD *a* to him and said,
18: 1 The LORD *a* to Abraham
26: 2 The LORD *a* to Isaac and said,
26:24 That night the LORD *a* to him
35: 1 who *a* to you when you were
35: 9 God *a* to him again and blessed
46:29 As soon as Joseph *a* before him,
48: 3 "God Almighty *a* to me at Luz
Ex 3: 2 of the LORD *a* to him in flames
3:16 Isaac and Jacob, *a* to me and said:
4: 5 the God of Jacob—has *a* to you."
6: 3 I *a* to Abraham, to Isaac
16:14 on the ground *a* on the desert floor.
Lev 9:23 of the LORD *a* to all the people.
Nu 14:10 glory of the LORD *a* at the Tent
16:19 glory of the LORD *a* to the entire
16:42 and the glory of the LORD *a*.
20: 6 the glory of the LORD *a* to them.
Dt 31:15 the LORD *a* at the Tent in a pillar
32:17 gods that recently *a*,
Jdg 6:12 angel of the LORD *a* to Gideon,
13: 3 The angel of the LORD *a* to her
13:10 The man who *a* to me the other day
14:11 When he *a*, he was given thirty
1Ki 3: 5 At Gibeon the LORD *a*
9: 2 as he had *a* to him at Gibeon.
9: 2 the LORD *a* to him a second time,
11: 9 of Israel, who had *a* to him twice.
2Ki 2:11 of fire *a* and separated the two
2Ch 1: 7 That night God *a* to Solomon
3: 1 where the LORD had *a*
7:12 the LORD *a* to him at night
Jer 31: 3 The LORD *a* to us in the past,
Eze 1:16 Each *a* to be made like a wheel
1:27 I saw that from what *a*
8: 2 From what *a* to be his waist
37: 8 and tendons and flesh *a* on them
Da 5: 5 the fingers of a human hand *a*
8: 1 after the one that had already *a*
11: 4 After he has *a*, his empire will be
Mt 1:20 an angel of the Lord *a* to him
2: 7 them the exact time the star had *a*.
2:13 an angel of the Lord *a* to Joseph
2:19 an angel of the Lord *a* in a dream
13:26 heads, then the weeds also *a*.
17: 3 then there *a* before them Moses
27:53 went into the holy city and *a*
Mk 9: 4 And there *a* before them Elijah
9: 7 a cloud *a* and enveloped them,
14:43 Judas, one of the Twelve, *a*.
16: 9 he *a* first to Mary Magdalene,
16:12 Afterward Jesus *a*
16:14 Later Jesus *a* to the Eleven
Lk 1:11 Then an angel of the Lord *a* to him,
1:80 desert until he *a* publicly to Israel.
2: 9 An angel of the Lord *a* to them,
2:13 of the heavenly host *a*
7:16 "A great prophet has *a* among us,"
9: 8 the dead, others that Elijah had *a*,

Lk 9: 31 and Elijah, *a* in glorious splendor,
9: 34 a cloud *a* and enveloped them,
22: 43 An angel from heaven *a* to him
24: 34 The Lord has risen and has *a*
Jn 8: 2 At dawn he *a* again
21: 1 Afterward Jesus *a* again
21: 14 This was now the third time Jesus *a*
Ac 1: 3 He *a* to them over a period
5: 36 Some time ago Theudas *a*,
5: 37 Judas the Galilean *a* in the days
7: 2 The God of glory *a*
7: 30 an angel *a* to Moses in the flames
7: 35 through the angel who *a* to him
8: 40 *a* at Azotus and traveled about,
9: 17 who *a* to you on the road
12: 7 Suddenly an angel of the Lord *a*
25: 2 and Jewish leaders *a* before him
25: 7 When Paul *a*, the Jews who had
26: 16 I have *a* to you to appoint you
27: 20 When neither sun nor stars *a*
1Co 15: 5 and that he *a* to Peter,
15: 6 he *a* to more than five hundred
15: 7 Then he *a* to James, then
15: 8 and last of all he *a* to me also,
1Ti 3: 16 He *a* in a body,
Tit 2: 11 of God that brings salvation has *a*
3: 4 and love of God our Savior *a*,
Heb 9: 26 now he has *a* once for all at the end
1Jn 1: 2 The life *a*; we have seen it
1: 2 with the Father and has *a* to us.
3: 5 But you know that he *a*
3: 8 The reason the Son of God *a* was
Rev 12: 1 and wondrous sign *a* in heaven:
12: 3 Then another sign *a* in heaven:

APPEARING (APPEAR)

Ex 16: 10 glory of the LORD *a* in the cloud.
Ps 21: 9 At the time of your *a*
Zec 5: 5 and see what this is that is *a*."
Jn 8: 13 "Here you are, *a* as your own
1Ti 6: 14 until the *a* of our Lord Jesus Christ,
2Ti 1: 10 through the *a* of our Savior,
4: 1 in view of his *a* and his kingdom,
4: 8 to all who have longed for his *a*.
Tit 2: 13 the glorious *a* of our great God

APPEARS (APPEAR)

Ge 9: 14 and the rainbow *a* in the clouds,
9: 16 Whenever the rainbow *a*
Lev 13: 3 and the sore *a* to be more
13: 14 But whenever raw flesh *a* on him,
13: 19 swelling or reddish-white spot *a*,
13: 20 if it *a* to be more than skin deep
13: 24 or white spot *a* in the raw flesh
13: 25 and it *a* to be more than skin deep,
13: 30 if it *a* to be more than skin deep
13: 34 and *a* to be no more than skin deep,
Dt 13: 1 *a* among you and announces
Ps 84: 7 till each *a* before God in Zion.
Pr 27: 25 hay is removed and new growth *a*
SS 6: 10 Who is this that *a* like the dawn,
Isa 16: 12 When Moab *a* at her high place,
60: 2 and his glory *a* over you.
Na 3: 17 but when the sun *a* they fly away,
Mal 3: 2 Who can stand when he *a*?
Col 3: 4 When Christ, who is your life, *a*,
Heb 7: 15 another priest like Melchizedek *a*,
Jas 4: 14 You are a mist that *a* for a little
1Pe 5: 4 And when the Chief Shepherd *a*,
1Jn 2: 28 when he *a* we may be confident
3: 2 But we know that when he *a*,

APPEASE

Pr 16: 14 but a wise man will *a* it.
Ac 16: 39 came to *a* them and escorted them

APPETITE (APPETITES)

Nu 11: 6 But now we have lost our *a*;
Pr 16: 26 The laborer's *a* works for him;
Ecc 6: 7 yet his *a* is never satisfied.
6: 9 sees than the roving of the *a*.
Isa 5: 14 Therefore the grave enlarges its *a*
Jer 50: 19 his *a* will be satisfied

APPETITES (APPETITE)

Isa 56: 11 They are dogs with mighty *a*;
Ro 16: 18 our Lord Christ, but their own *a*.

APPHIA

Phm : 2 and fellow worker, to *A* our sister,

APPIUS

Ac 28: 15 Forum of *A* and the Three Taverns

APPLE (APPLES)

Dt 32: 10 he guarded him as the *a* of his eye,
Ps 17: 8 Keep me as the *a* of your eye;
Pr 7: 2 guard my teachings as the *a*
SS 2: 3 Like an *a* tree
8: 5 Under the *a* tree I roused you;
Joel 1: 12 the palm and the *a* tree—
Zec 2: 8 whoever touches you touches the *a*

APPLES (APPLE)

Pr 25: 11 is like *a* of gold in settings of silver.
SS 2: 5 refresh me with *a*,
7: 8 the fragrance of your breath like *a*,

APPLIED (APPLY)

2Ki 20: 7 They did so and *a* it to the boil,
Pr 24: 32 I *a* my heart to what I observed
Ecc 1: 17 I *a* myself to the understanding
8: 9 as I *a* my mind to everything done
8: 16 When I *a* my mind
Da 4: 19 if only the dream *a* to your enemies
1Co 4: 6 I have *a* these things to myself

APPLIES (APPLY)

Ex 12: 49 The same law *a* to the native-born
21: 31 also *a* if the bull gores a son
Lev 7: 7 " 'The same law *a*
Nu 8: 24 to Moses, "This *a* to the Levites:
15: 29 same law *a* to everyone who sins
19: 14 "This is the law that *a*

APPLY (APPLIED APPLIES APPLYING)

Nu 5: 30 and is to *a* this entire law to her.
15: 16 and regulations will *a* both to you
Job 5: 27 So hear it and *a* it to yourself."
Pr 22: 17 *a* your heart to what I teach,
23: 12 *A* your heart to instruction
Isa 38: 21 a poultice of figs and *a* it to the boil,

APPLYING (APPLY)

Pr 2: 2 and *a* your heart to understanding,
Heb 9: 10 external regulations *a*

APPOINT (APPOINTED APPOINTING APPOINTMENT APPOINTS)

Ge 41: 34 Let Pharaoh *a* commissioners
Ex 18: 21 *a* them as officials over thousands,
Nu 1: 50 *a* the Levites to be in charge
3: 10 *A* Aaron and his sons to serve
27: 16 *a* a man over this community
34: 18 And *a* one leader from each tribe
Dt 16: 18 *A* judges and officials for each
17: 15 to *a* over you the king the LORD
20: 9 they shall *a* commanders over it.
Jos 18: 4 *A* three men from each tribe.
1Sa 2: 36 "*A* me to some priestly office
8: 5 walk in your ways; now *a* a king
2Ki 10: 5 We will not *a* anyone as king;
1Ch 15: 16 of the Levites to *a* their brothers
Ezr 7: 25 *a* magistrates and judges
Ne 7: 3 Also *a* residents of Jerusalem
Est 2: 3 Let the king *a* commissioners
Ps 61: 7 *a* your love and faithfulness
89: 27 I will also *a* him my firstborn,
109: 6 *A* an evil man to oppose him;
Jer 1: 10 today I *a* you over nations
23: 32 yet I did not send or *a* them.
49: 19 Who is the chosen one I will *a*
50: 44 Who is the chosen one I will *a*
51: 27 *A* a commander against her;
Da 6: 1 It pleased Darius to *a* 120 satraps
Hos 1: 11 and they will *a* one leader
Ac 26: 16 I have appeared to you to *a* you
1Co 6: 4 *a* as judges even men
1Th 5: 9 For God did not *a* us
Tit 1: 5 and *a* elders in every town,

APPOINTED (APPOINT)

Ge 18: 14 to you at the *a* time next year
Ex 5: 14 The Israelite foremen *a*
13: 10 at the *a* time year after year.
23: 15 Do this at the *a* time in the month
Ex 31: 6 I have *a* Oholiab son of Ahisamach
34: 18 Do this at the *a* time in the month
Lev 16: 21 in the care of a man *a* for the task.
23: 2 the *a* feasts of the LORD,
23: 2 These are my *a* feasts,
23: 4 are to proclaim at their *a* times:
23: 4 " 'These are the LORD's *a* feasts,
23: 37 (" 'These are the LORD's *a* feasts,
23: 44 to the Israelites the *a* feasts
Nu 1: 16 These were the men *a*
3: 32 He was *a* over those who were
3: 36 The Merarites were *a* to take care
9: 2 the Passover at the *a* time.
9: 3 it at the *a* time, at twilight
9: 7 the other Israelites at the *a* time?"
9: 13 the LORD's offering at the *a* time.
10: 10 your *a* feasts and New Moon
16: 2 leaders who had been *a* members
28: 2 present to me at the *a* time the food
29: 39 for the LORD at your *a* feasts:
Dt 1: 15 *a* them to have authority over you
Jos 4: 4 together the twelve men he had *a*
1Sa 8: 1 he *a* his sons as judges for Israel.
12: 6 "It is the LORD who *a* Moses
13: 14 and *a* him leader of his people,
25: 30 and has *a* him leader over Israel,
2Sa 6: 21 from his house when he *a* me ruler
7: 11 ever since the time I *a* leaders
15: 4 "If only I were *a* judge in the land!
17: 25 Absalom had *a* Amasa
18: 1 and *a* over them commanders
1Ki 1: 35 I have *a* him ruler over Israel
12: 31 *a* priests from all sorts of people,
13: 33 but once more *a* priests
2Ki 12: 11 to the men *a* to supervise the work
17: 32 also *a* all sorts of their own people
22: 5 to the men *a* to supervise the work
23: 5 away with the pagan priests *a*
25: 22 king of Babylon *a* Gedaliah son
25: 23 the king of Babylon had *a* Gedaliah
1Ch 15: 17 So the Levites *a* Heman son of Joel
16: 4 He *a* some of the Levites
17: 10 ever since the time I *a* leaders
22: 2 among them he *a* stonecutters
23: 31 Moon festivals and at *a* feasts.
24: 3 for their *a* order of ministering.
24: 19 This was their *a* order
26: 10 his father had *a* him the first),
2Ch 2: 4 at the *a* feasts of the LORD our
8: 14 also *a* the gatekeepers by divisions
8: 14 he *a* the divisions of the priests
11: 15 And he *a* his own priests
11: 22 Rehoboam *a* Abijah son of Maacah
19: 5 He *a* judges in the land, in each
19: 8 Jehoshaphat *a* some of the Levites,
20: 21 Jehoshaphat *a* men to sing
25: 16 "Have we *a* you an adviser
31: 3 New Moons and *a* feasts
32: 6 He *a* military officers
34: 10 to the men *a* to supervise the work
35: 2 He *a* the priests to their duties
36: 23 and he has *a* me to build a temple
Ezr 1: 2 and he has *a* me to build a temple
3: 5 for all the *a* feasts of the LORD,
5: 14 whom he had *a* governor,
Ne 5: 14 when I was *a* to be their governor
6: 7 even *a* prophets to make this
7: 1 the singers and the Levites were *a*.
9: 17 in their rebellion *a* a leader in order
10: 33 New Moon festivals and *a* feasts;
12: 44 At that time men were *a* to be
Est 8: 2 Esther *a* him over Haman's estate.
8: 12 The day *a* for the Jews to do this
9: 27 way prescribed and at the time *a*.
Job 20: 29 the heritage *a* for them by God."
30: 23 to the place *a* for all the living.
34: 13 Who *a* him over the earth?
Ps 75: 2 You say, "I choose the *a* time;
102: 13 the *a* time has come.
Pr 8: 23 I was *a* from eternity,
Isa 1: 14 Moon festivals and your *a* feasts
Jer 1: 5 I *a* you as a prophet to the nations
6: 17 I *a* watchmen over you and said,
8: 7 knows her *a* seasons,
14: 14 or *a* them or spoken to them.
29: 26 'The LORD has *a* you priest
33: 20 no longer come at their *a* time,
40: 5 of Babylon has *a* over the towns

Jer 40: 7 of Babylon had *a* Gedaliah son
40: 11 and had *a* Gedaliah son of Ahikam,
41: 2 whom the king of Babylon had *a*
41: 10 imperial guard had *a* Gedaliah son
41: 18 whom the king of Babylon had *a*
La 1: 4 for no one comes to her *a* feasts.
2: 6 her *a* feasts and her Sabbaths;
2: 7 as on the day of an *a* feast.
Eze 21: 11 " 'The sword is *a* to be polished,
36: 38 at Jerusalem during her *a* feasts.
44: 24 and my decrees for all my *a* feasts,
45: 17 at all the *a* feasts of the house
46: 9 before the LORD at the *a* feasts,
46: 11 " 'At the festivals and the *a* feasts,
Da 1: 11 guard whom the chief official had *a*
2: 24 whom the king had *a*
2: 49 request the king *a* Shadrach,
5: 11 *a* him chief of the magicians,
8: 19 the vision concerns the *a* time
11: 27 an end will still come at the *a* time.
11: 29 "At the *a* time he will invade
11: 35 for it will still come at the *a* time.
Hos 2: 11 her Sabbath days—all her *a* feasts.
6: 11 a harvest is *a*.
9: 5 do on the day of your *a* feasts,
12: 9 as in the days of your *a* feasts.
Mic 6: 9 Heed the rod and the One who *a* it.
Hab 1: 12 have *a* them to execute judgment;
2: 3 For the revelation awaits an *a* time;
Zep 2: 2 before the *a* time arrives
3: 18 "The sorrows for the *a* feasts
Mt 8: 29 to torture us before the *a* time?"
26: 18 'The Teacher says: My *a* time is
Mk 3: 14 He *a* twelve—designating them
3: 16 These are the twelve he *a*:
Lk 10: 1 this the Lord *a* seventy-two others
12: 14 who *a* me a judge or an arbiter
19: 12 country to have himself *a* king
Ac 3: 20 who has been *a* for you—
10: 42 that he is the one whom God *a*
12: 21 On the *a* day Herod, wearing his
13: 48 and all who were *a* for eternal life
14: 23 and Barnabas *a* elders for them
15: 2 So Paul and Barnabas were *a*,
17: 31 with justice by the man he has *a*.
Ro 9: 9 "At the *a* time I will return,
1Co 4: 5 judge nothing before the *a* time;
12: 28 And in the church God has *a* first
Eph 1: 22 *a* him to be head over everything
1Ti 2: 7 for this purpose I was *a* a herald
2Ti 1: 11 And of this gospel I was *a* a herald
Tit 1: 3 at his *a* season he brought his word
Heb 1: 2 whom he *a* heir of all things,
3: 2 faithful to the one who *a* him,
5: 1 and is *a* to represent them
7: 28 which came after the law, *a* the Son
8: 3 Every high priest is *a*

APPOINTING (APPOINT)

Ezr 3: 8 *a* Levites twenty years of age
1Ti 1: 12 he considered me faithful, *a* me

APPOINTMENT (APPOINT)

2Ch 31: 13 by *a* of King Hezekiah

APPOINTS (APPOINT)

Jer 31: 35 he who *a* the sun
Heb 7: 28 For the law *a* as high priests men

APPORTIONED

Dt 4: 19 things the LORD your God has *a*
Eph 4: 7 grace has been given as Christ *a* it.

APPRAISED

Job 28: 27 then he looked at wisdom and *a* it;

APPREHENSIVE

Lk 21: 26 *a* of what is coming on the world,

APPROACH (APPROACHED APPROACHES APPROACHING)

Ex 19: 22 Even the priests, who *a* the LORD,
24: 2 but Moses alone is to *a* the LORD;
28: 43 or *a* the altar to minister
30: 20 when they *a* the altar to minister
Lev 10: 3 " 'Among those who *a* me
18: 6 " 'No one is to *a* any close relative
18: 19 " 'Do not *a* a woman
Lev 21: 23 go near the curtain or *a* the altar,
1Sa 10: 5 As you *a* the town, you will meet
Job 31: 37 like a prince I would *a* him.)—
36: 33 even the cattle make known its *a*.
40: 19 yet his Maker can *a* him
41: 13 Who would *a* him with a bridle?
Ecc 12: 1 and the years *a* when you will say,
Isa 5: 19 Let it *a*,
41: 5 They *a* and come forward;
La 2: 3 hand at the *a* of the enemy.
Eze 42: 13 the priests who *a* the LORD will
Hos 7: 6 they *a* him with intrigue.
Eph 3: 12 in him we may *a* God with freedom
Heb 4: 16 Let us then *a* the throne of grace

APPROACHED (APPROACH)

Ge 18: 23 Then Abraham *a* him and said:
33: 3 seven times as he *a* his brother.
33: 6 their children *a* and bowed down.
Ex 14: 10 As Pharaoh *a*, the Israelites looked
20: 21 while Moses *a* the thick darkness
32: 19 When Moses *a* the camp
40: 32 the Tent of Meeting or *a* the altar,
Lev 16: 1 died when they *a* the LORD.
Nu 3: 38 Anyone else who *a* the sanctuary
27: 1 They *a* the entrance to the Tent
Dt 22: 14 this woman, but when I *a* her,
Jos 8: 11 *a* the city and arrived in front of it.
14: 6 men of Judah *a* Joshua at Gilgal,
21: 1 of the Levites *a* Eleazar the priest,
Jdg 3: 20 Ehud then *a* him while he was
9: 52 as he *a* the entrance to the tower
14: 5 As they *a* the vineyards of Timnah,
15: 14 As he *a* Lehi, the Philistines came
Ru 3: 7 Ruth *a* quietly, uncovered his feet
1Sa 9: 18 Saul *a* Samuel in the gateway
17: 40 sling in his hand, *a* the Philistine.
30: 21 and his men *a*, he greeted them.
2Sa 15: 5 whenever anyone *a* him to bow
16: 5 As King David *a* Bahurim,
2Ki 16: 12 he *a* it and presented offerings on it
1Ch 21: 21 *a*, and when Araunah looked
Est 5: 2 So Esther *a* and touched the tip
Jer 42: 1 the least to the greatest *a* Jeremiah
Da 3: 26 Nebuchadnezzar then *a*
7: 13 He *a* the Ancient of Days
7: 16 I *a* one of those standing there
Mt 14: 15 As evening *a*, the disciples came
17: 14 a man *a* Jesus and knelt before him.
21: 1 As they *a* Jerusalem and came
21: 34 the harvest time *a*, he sent his
27: 57 As evening *a*, there came a rich
Mk 11: 1 As they *a* Jerusalem and came
15: 42 as evening *a*, Joseph of Arimathea,
Lk 7: 12 As he *a* the town gate, a dead
9: 51 As the time *a* for him
18: 35 As Jesus *a* Jericho, a blind man was
19: 29 As he *a* Bethphage and Bethany
19: 41 As he *a* Jerusalem and saw the city,
22: 47 He *a* Jesus to kiss him,
24: 28 As they *a* the village

APPROACHES (APPROACH)

Lev 20: 16 " 'If a woman *a* an animal
Nu 3: 10 anyone else who *a* the sanctuary
Dt 23: 11 as evening *a* he is to wash himself,
2Ki 11: 8 Anyone who *a* your ranks must be
Est 4: 11 or woman who *a* the king

APPROACHING (APPROACH)

Ge 24: 63 as he looked up, he saw camels *a*.
Lev 18: 14 brother by *a* his wife to have sexual
2Ki 9: 17 in Jezreel saw Jehu's troops *a*,
Lk 22: 1 called the Passover, was *a*,
Jn 1: 47 When Jesus saw Nathanael *a*,
6: 19 they saw Jesus *a* the boat,
Ac 10: 9 day as they were *a* the city,
27: 27 the sailors sensed they were *a* land.
Heb 10: 25 all the more as you see the Day *a*.
1Jn 5: 14 is the assurance we have in *a* God:

APPROPRIATE

Ge 49: 28 giving each the blessing *a* to him.
1Ti 2: 10 *a* for women who profess

APPROVAL (APPROVE)

Jdg 18: 6 Your journey has the LORD's *a*."
Est 2: 17 and *a* more than any of the other
Hos 8: 4 they choose princes without my *a*.
Jn 6: 27 the Father has placed his seal of *a*."
Ac 8: 1 And Saul was there, giving *a*
22: 20 I stood there giving my *a*
1Co 11: 19 to show which of you have God's *a*
Gal 1: 10 trying to win the *a* of men,

APPROVE (APPROVAL APPROVED APPROVES)

1Sa 29: 6 but the rulers don't *a* of you.
Ps 49: 13 followers, who *a* their sayings.
Lk 11: 48 So you testify that you *a*
Ro 1: 32 also *a* of those who practice them.
2: 18 if you know his will and *a*
12: 2 and *a* what God's will is—
1Co 16: 3 of introduction to the men you *a*

APPROVED (APPROVE)

Ro 14: 18 pleasing to God and *a* by men.
16: 10 Greet Apelles, tested and *a*
2Co 10: 18 who commends himself who is *a*,
1Th 2: 4 as men *a* by God to be entrusted
2Ti 2: 15 to present yourself to God as one *a*,

APPROVES (APPROVE)

Ro 14: 22 not condemn himself by what he *a*.

APRONS

Ac 19: 12 *a* that had touched him were taken

APT (APTITUDE)

Pr 15: 23 A man finds joy in giving an *a* reply

APTITUDE (APT)

Da 1: 4 showing *a* for every kind

AQUEDUCT

2Ki 18: 17 stopped at the *a* of the Upper Pool,
Isa 7: 3 the end of the *a* of the Upper Pool,
36: 2 stopped at the *a* of the Upper Pool,

AQUILA

Ac 18: 2 There he met a Jew named *A*,
18: 18 accompanied by Priscilla and *A*.
18: 19 where Paul left Priscilla and *A*.
18: 26 When Priscilla and *A* heard him,
Ro 16: 3 and *A*, my fellow workers
1Co 16: 19 *A* and Priscilla greet you warmly
2Ti 4: 19 and *A* and the household

AR

Nu 21: 15 that lead to the site of *A*
21: 28 It consumed *A* of Moab,
Dt 2: 9 I have given *A* to the descendants
2: 18 to pass by the region of Moab at *A*.
2: 29 who live in *A*, did for us—
Isa 15: 1 *A* in Moab is ruined,

ARA

1Ch 7: 38 Jephunneh, Pispah and *A*.

ARAB (ARABIA ARABIAN ARABS)

Jos 15: 52 *A*, Dumah, Eshan, Janim,
Ne 2: 19 and Geshem the *A* heard about it,
6: 1 Geshem the *A* and the rest
Isa 13: 20 no *A* will pitch his tent there,

ARABAH

Dt 1: 1 that is, in the *A*— opposite Suph,
1: 7 the neighboring peoples in the *A*,
2: 8 We turned from the *A* road,
3: 17 border was the Jordan in the *A*,
3: 17 to the Sea of the *A* (the Salt Sea),
4: 49 and included all the *A* east
4: 49 the Sea of the *A*, below the slopes
11: 30 in the *A* in the vicinity of Gilgal.
Jos 3. 16 the Sea of the *A* (the Salt Sea) was
8: 14 at a certain place overlooking the *A*
11: 2 in the *A* south of Kinnereth,
11: 16 the *A* and the mountains of Israel
12: 1 all the eastern side of the *A*:
12: 3 over the eastern *A* from the Sea
12: 3 to the Sea of the *A* (the Salt Sea),
12: 8 the *A*, the mountain slopes,
18: 18 and on down into the *A*.
1Sa 23: 24 in the *A* south of Jeshimon.
2Sa 2: 29 his men marched through the *A*.
4: 7 traveled all night by way of the *A*.

2Ki 14: 25 Lebo Hamath to the Sea of the *A*,
25: 4 They fled toward the *A*,
Isa 33: 9 Sharon is like the *A*,
Jer 39: 4 and headed toward the *A*.
52: 7 They fled toward the *A*,
Eze 47: 8 region and goes down into the *A*,
Am 6: 14 to the valley of the *A*."
Zec 14: 10 Jerusalem, will become like the *A*.

ARABIA (ARAB)

2Ch 9: 14 Also all the kings of *A*
Isa 21: 13 An oracle concerning *A*:
21: 13 who camp in the thickets of *A*,
Jer 25: 24 all the kings of *A* and all the kings
Eze 27: 21 " '*A* and all the princes
30: 5 Cush and Put, Lydia and all *A*,
Gal 1: 17 but I went immediately into *A*
4: 25 Hagar stands for Mount Sinai in *A*

ARABIAN (ARAB)

1Ki 10: 15 traders and from all the *A* kings

ARABS (ARAB)

2Ch 17: 11 and the *A* brought him flocks:
21: 16 and of the *A* who lived
22: 1 who came with the *A* into the camp
26: 7 the *A* who lived in Gur Baal
Ne 4: 7 But when Sanballat, Tobiah, the *A*,
Ac 2: 11 to Judaism); Cretans and *A*—

ARAD

Nu 21: 1 When the Canaanite king of *A*,
33: 40 The Canaanite king of *A*, who lived
Jos 12: 14 one the king of *A* one the king
Jdg 1: 16 of Judah in the Negev near *A*
1Ch 8: 15 Jeremoth, Zebadiah, *A*, Eder,

ARAH

Jos 13: 4 from *A* of the Sidonians as far
1Ch 7: 39 The sons of Ulla: *A*, Hanniel
Ezr 2: 5 372 of *A* 775 of Pahath-Moab
Ne 6: 18 son-in-law to Shecaniah son of *A*,
7: 10 372 of *A* 652 of Pahath-Moab

ARAM (ARAMAIC ARAMAIC-SPEAKING ARAMEAN ARAMEANS)

Ge 10: 22 Asshur, Arphaxad, Lud and *A*.
10: 23 The sons of *A*: Uz, Hul, Gether
22: 21 Kemuel (the father of *A*), Kesed,
Nu 23: 7 "Balak brought me from *A*,
Jdg 3: 10 king of *A* into the hands of Othniel,
10: 6 the gods of *A*, the gods of Sidon,
2Sa 15: 8 servant was living at Geshur in *A*,
1Ki 11: 25 Rezon ruled in *A* and was hostile
15: 18 the king of *A*, who was ruling
19: 15 anoint Hazael king over *A*.
20: 1 king of *A* mustered his entire army.
20: 20 But Ben-Hadad king of *A* escaped
20: 22 king of *A* will attack you again."
20: 23 of the king of *A* advised him,
22: 1 years there was no war between *A*
22: 3 to retake it from the king of *A*?"
22: 31 of *A* had ordered his thirty-two
2Ki 5: 1 of the army of the king of *A*.
5: 1 the LORD had given victory to *A*.
5: 2 Now bands from *A* had gone out
5: 5 go," the king of *A* replied.
6: 8 the king of *A* was at war with Israel.
6: 11 This enraged the king of *A*.
6: 23 from *A* stopped raiding Israel's
6: 24 king of *A* mobilized his entire army
8: 7 and Ben-Hadad king of *A* was ill.
8: 9 Ben-Hadad king of *A* has sent me
8: 13 that you will become king of *A*,"
8: 28 against Hazael king of *A* at Ramoth
8: 29 in his battle with Hazael king of *A*.
9: 14 against Hazael king of *A*,
9: 15 in the battle with Hazael king of *A*.)
12: 17 this time Hazael king of *A* went up
12: 18 he sent them to Hazael king of *A*,
13: 3 the power of Hazael king of *A*
13: 4 the king of *A* was oppressing Israel.
13: 5 they escaped from the power of *A*.
13: 7 king of *A* had destroyed the rest
13: 17 the arrow of victory over *A*!"
13: 19 then you would have defeated *A*
13: 22 Hazael king of *A* oppressed Israel
13: 24 Hazael king of *A* died,
2Ki 15: 37 began to send Rezin king of *A*
16: 5 Rezin king of *A* and Pekah son
16: 6 king of *A* recovered Elath for *A*
16: 7 out of the hand of the king of *A*
1Ch 1: 17 Asshur, Arphaxad, Lud and *A*.
1: 17 The sons of *A*: Uz, Hul, Gether
2: 23 Geshur and *A* captured Havvoth
7: 34 Ahi, Rohgah, Hubbah and *A*.
2Ch 16: 2 and sent it to Ben-Hadad king of *A*,
16: 7 Because you relied on the king of *A*
16: 7 army of the king of *A* has escaped
18: 30 king of *A* had ordered his chariot
22: 5 against Hazael king of *A* at Ramoth
22: 6 in his battle with Hazael king of *A*.
24: 23 the army of *A* marched
28: 5 him over to the king of *A*.
28: 23 of the kings of *A* have helped them,
Isa 7: 1 King Rezin of *A* and Pekah son
7: 2 "*A* has allied itself with Ephraim";
7: 4 and *A* and of the son of Remaliah.
7: 5 *A*, Ephraim and Remaliah's son
7: 8 for the head of *A* is Damascus,
17: 3 the remnant of *A* will be
Eze 27: 16 " '*A* did business with you
Hos 12: 12 Jacob fled to the country of *A*;
Am 1: 5 The people of *A* will go into exile

ARAM MAACAH

1Ch 19: 6 from Aram Naharaim, *A*

ARAM NAHARAIM

Ge 24: 10 He set out for *A*
Dt 23: 4 son of Beor from Pethor in *A*
Jdg 3: 8 Cushan-Rishathaim king of *A*,
1Ch 19: 6 chariots and charioteers from *A*,

ARAMAIC (ARAM)

2Ki 18: 26 Please speak to your servants in *A*,
Ezr 4: 7 The letter was written in *A* script
4: 7 and in the *A* language.
Isa 36: 11 Please speak to your servants in *A*,
Da 2: 4 astrologers answered the king in *A*,
Jn 5: 2 which in *A* is called Bethesda
19: 13 (which in *A* is Gabbatha).
19: 17 (which in *A* is called Golgotha).
19: 20 and the sign was written in *A*,
20: 16 toward him and cried out in *A*,
Ac 21: 40 he said to them in *A*: "Brothers
22: 2 they heard him speak to them in *A*,
26: 14 I heard a voice saying to me in *A*,

ARAMAIC-SPEAKING (ARAM)

Ac 6: 1 against those of the *A* community

ARAMEAN (ARAM)

Ge 25: 20 Bethuel the *A* from Paddan Aram
25: 20 and sister of Laban the *A*.
28: 5 Laban son of Bethuel the *A*,
31: 20 Jacob deceived Laban the *A*
31: 24 came to Laban the *A* in a dream
Dt 26: 5 "My father was a wandering *A*,
2Sa 8: 6 in the *A* kingdom of Damascus,
10: 6 twenty thousand *A* foot soldiers
1Ki 20: 29 on the *A* foot soldiers in one day.
2Ki 5: 20 easy on Naaman, this *A*,
7: 10 "We went into the *A* camp
7: 14 the king sent them after the *A* army
24: 2 The LORD sent Babylonian, *A*,
1Ch 7: 14 through his *A* concubine.
18: 6 in the *A* kingdom of Damascus,
2Ch 24: 24 Although the *A* army had come
Jer 35: 11 the Babylonian and *A* armies.'

ARAMEANS (ARAM)

2Sa 8: 5 When the *A* of Damascus came
8: 6 and the *A* became subject to him
10: 8 while the *A* of Zobah and Rehob
10: 9 and deployed them against the *A*.
10: 11 "If the *A* are too strong for me,
10: 13 with him advanced to fight the *A*,
10: 14 saw that the *A* were fleeing,
10: 15 After the *A* saw that they had been
10: 16 Hadadezer had *A* brought
10: 17 The *A* formed their battle lines
10: 19 So the *A* were afraid to help
1Ki 10: 29 kings of the Hittites and of the *A*.
20: 20 the *A* fled, with the Israelites
20: 21 and inflicted heavy losses on the *A*.
1Ki 20: 26 spring Ben-Hadad mustered the *A*
20: 27 while the *A* covered
20: 28 'Because the *A* think the LORD is
22: 11 'With these you will gore the *A*
22: 35 up in his chariot facing the *A*.
2Ki 6: 9 because the *A* are going down there
7: 4 let's go over to the camp of the *A*
7: 5 and went to the camp of the *A*.
7: 6 for the Lord had caused the *A*
7: 12 I will tell you what the *A* have done
7: 15 equipment the *A* had thrown away
7: 16 and plundered the camp of the *A*.
8: 28 The *A* wounded Joram;
8: 29 the wounds the *A* had inflicted
9: 15 the wounds the *A* had inflicted
13: 17 You will completely destroy the *A*
1Ch 18: 5 When the *A* of Damascus came
18: 6 and the *A* became subject to him
19: 10 and deployed them against the *A*.
19: 12 "If the *A* are too strong for me,
19: 14 with him advanced to fight the *A*,
19: 15 saw that the *A* were fleeing,
19: 16 After the *A* saw that they had been
19: 16 *A* brought from beyond the River,
19: 17 lines to meet the *A* in battle,
19: 19 So the *A* were not willing
2Ch 1: 17 kings of the Hittites and of the *A*.
18: 10 'With these you will gore the *A*
18: 34 up in his chariot facing the *A*
22: 5 The *A* wounded Joram;
24: 25 When the *A* withdrew, they left
28: 5 The *A* defeated him and took many
Isa 9: 12 *A* from the east and Philistines
Am 9: 7 and the *A* from Kir?

ARAN

Ge 36: 28 The sons of Dishan: Uz and *A*.
1Ch 1: 42 The sons of Dishan: Uz and *A*.

ARARAT

Ge 8: 4 came to rest on the mountains of *A*.
2Ki 19: 37 and they escaped to the land of *A*.
Isa 37: 38 and they escaped to the land of *A*
Jer 51: 27 *A*, Minni and Ashkenaz.

ARAUNAH

2Sa 24: 16 threshing floor of *A* the Jebusite.
24: 18 floor of *A* the Jebusite."
24: 20 When *A* looked and saw the king
24: 21 *A* said, "Why has my lord the king
24: 22 *A* said to David, "Let my lord
24: 23 O king, *A* gives all this to the king."
24: 23 *A* also said to him, "May
24: 24 But the king replied to *A*, "No,
1Ch 21: 15 threshing floor of *A* the Jebusite.
21: 18 threshing floor of *A* the Jebusite.
21: 20 While *A* was threshing wheat,
21: 21 and when *A* looked and saw him,
21: 23 *A* said to David, "Take it!
21: 24 But King David replied to *A*, "No,
21: 25 David paid *A* six hundred shekels
21: 28 threshing floor of *A* the Jebusite,
2Ch 3: 1 threshing floor of *A* the Jebusite,

ARBA

Jos 14: 15 called Kiriath Arba after *A*,
15: 13 (*A* was the forefather of Anak.)
21: 11 (*A* was the forefather of Anak.)

ARBATHITE

2Sa 23: 31 Abi-Albon the *A*, Azmaveth
1Ch 11: 32 Abiel the *A*, Azmaveth

ARBITE

2Sa 23: 35 Hezro the Carmelite, Paarai the *A*,

ARBITER (ARBITRATE)

Lk 12: 14 who appointed me a judge or an *a*

ARBITRATE (ARBITER)

Job 9: 33 If only there were someone to *a*

ARCHANGEL (ANGEL)

1Th 4: 16 with the voice of the *a*
Jude : 9 *a* Michael, when he was disputing

ARCHELAUS

Mt 2: 22 when he heard that *A* was reigning

ARCHER (ARCHERS)

Ge 21:20 in the desert and became an *a*.
Pr 26:10 Like an *a* who wounds at random
Jer 51: 3 Let not the *a* string his bow,
Am 2:15 The *a* will not stand his ground,

ARCHERS (ARCHER)

Ge 49:23 With bitterness *a* attacked him;
1Sa 31: 3 and when the *a* overtook him,
2Sa 11:24 the *a* shot arrows at your servants
1Ch 10: 3 and when the *a* overtook him,
2Ch 35:23 *A* shot King Josiah, and he told his
Job 16:13 his *a* surround me.
Isa 66:19 and Lydians (famous as *a*),
Jer 4:29 At the sound of horsemen and *a*
50:29 "Summon *a* against Babylon,

ARCHIPPUS

Col 4:17 Tell *A*: "See to it that you complete
Phm : 2 to *A* our fellow soldier

ARCHITECT

Heb 11:10 whose *a* and builder is God.

ARCHIVES

Ezr 4:15 made in the *a* of your predecessors.
5:17 in the royal *a* of Babylon to see
6: 1 and they searched in the *a* stored

ARD (ARDITE)

Ge 46:21 Rosh, Muppim, Huppim and *A*.
Nu 26:40 The descendants of Bela through *A*
26:40 through *A*, the Ardite clan;

ARDENT

2Co 7: 7 your deep sorrow, your *a* concern

ARDITE (ARD)

Nu 26:40 the *A* clan; through Naaman,

ARDON

1Ch 2:18 her sons: Jesher, Shobab and *A*.

AREA (AREAS)

Ge 25:18 in the *a* from Havilah to Shur,
34: 2 the ruler of that *a*, saw her,
Ex 10:14 down in every *a* of the country
Lev 10:17 offering in the sanctuary *a*?
10:18 the goat in the sanctuary *a*,
13:33 except for the diseased *a*,
16: 3 is to enter the sanctuary *a*:
Nu 8: 2 they are to light the *a* in front
35: 5 will have this *a* as pastureland
Jos 13: 5 the region of the Amorites, the *a*
19:46 Rakkon, with the *a* facing Joppa.
Jdg 19: 1 in a remote *a* in the hill country
19:18 to a remote *a* in the hill country
1Sa 9: 4 and through the *a* around Shalisha,
14:14 men in an *a* of about half an acre.
23:23 I will go with you; if he is in the *a*,
27: 9 Whenever David attacked an *a*,
2Sa 5: 9 He built up the *a* around it,
1Ch 5: 8 They settled in the *a* from Aroer
Ne 12:29 and from the *a* of Geba
Eze 40: 5 surrounding the temple *a*.
41: 9 The open *a* between the side rooms
41:11 adjoining the open *a* was five
41:11 to the side rooms from the open *a*,
41:20 floor to the *a* above the entrance,
42:15 and measured the *a* all around:
42:15 was inside the temple *a*,
42:20 he measured the *a* on all four sides.
43:12 All the surrounding *a* on top
43:21 the temple *a* outside the sanctuary.
45: 1 wide; the entire *a* will be holy.
45: 5 An *a* 25,000 cubits long
45: 6 as its property an *a* 5,000
45: 7 side of the *a* formed by the sacred
48:15 The remaining *a*, 5,000 cubits wide
48:18 What remains of the *a*, bordering
48:21 on both sides of the *a* formed
48:22 in the center of the *a* that belongs
48:22 *a* belonging to the prince will lie
Mt 4:13 was by the lake in the *a* of Zebulun
21:12 Jesus entered the temple *a*
21:15 children shouting in the temple *a*,
Mk 5:10 again not to send them out of the *a*.
11:15 Jesus entered the temple *a*
Lk 4:37 throughout the surrounding *a*.
19:45 Then he entered the temple *a*
Jn 2:15 and drove all from the temple *a*,
8:20 while teaching in the temple *a*
10:23 was in the temple *a* walking
11:56 in the temple *a* they asked one
Ac 16: 3 of the Jews who lived in that *a*,
20: 2 He traveled through that *a*,
21:28 brought Greeks into the temple *a*
21:29 him into the temple *a*.)
2Co 10:15 our *a* of activity among you will

AREAS (AREA)

Jos 13: 1 there are still very large *a* of land
14: 1 Now these are the *a* the Israelites
Jdg 19:29 sent them into all the *a* of Israel.
1Ki 20:34 You may set up your own market *a*
2Ch 27: 4 forts and towers in the wooded *a*.
Eze 48:21 Both these *a* running the length

ARELI (ARELITE)

Ge 46:16 Shuni, Ezbon, Eri, Arodi and *A*.
Nu 26:17 through *A*, the Arelite clan.

ARELITE (ARELI)

Nu 26:17 through Areli, the *A* clan.

ARENA

1Co 4: 9 like men condemned to die in the *a*

AREOPAGUS

Ac 17:19 brought him to a meeting of the *A*,
17:22 up in the meeting of the *A*
17:34 of the *A*, also a woman named

ARETAS

2Co 11:32 governor under King *A* had the city

ARGOB

Dt 3: 4 region of *A*, Og's kingdom
3:13 region of *A* in Bashan used
3:14 took the whole region of *A* as far
1Ki 4:13 well as the district of *A* in Bashan
2Ki 15:25 Pekahiah, along with *A*

ARGUE (ARGUED ARGUING ARGUMENT ARGUMENTS)

Jdg 18:25 The Danites answered, "Don't *a*
Job 9:14 How can I find words to *a* with him
13: 3 and to *a* my case with God.
13: 8 Will you *a* the case for God?
15: 3 Would he *a* with useless words,
Pr 25: 9 If you *a* your case with a neighbor,
Isa 43:26 let us *a* the matter together;
Jn 6:52 to *a* sharply among themselves,
Ac 6: 9 began to *a* with Stephen,
Ro 3: 7 judge the world? Someone might *a*,

ARGUED (ARGUE)

1Ki 3:22 And so they *a* before the king.
Mk 9:34 the way they had *a* about who was
Ac 23: 9 stood up and *a* vigorously.

ARGUING (ARGUE)

2Sa 19: 9 the people were all *a*
Job 16: 3 What ails you that you keep on *a*?
Mk 9:14 the teachers of the law *a* with them
9:16 What are you *a* with them about?"
9:33 What were you *a* about on the road
Ac 19: 8 *a* persuasively about the kingdom
24:12 My accusers did not find me *a*
Php 2:14 without complaining or *a*,

ARGUMENT (ARGUE)

Job 13: 6 Hear now my *a*;
Lk 9:46 An *a* started among the disciples
Jn 3:25 An *a* developed between some
Ro 3: 5 on us? (I am using a human *a*.)
Heb 6:16 is said and puts an end to all *a*.

ARGUMENTS (ARGUE)

Job 6:25 But what do your *a* prove?
23: 4 and fill my mouth with *a*.
32:12 none of you has answered his *a*.
32:14 I will not answer him with your *a*.
Isa 41:21 "Set forth your *a*," says Jacob's
59: 4 rely on empty *a* and speak lies;
2Co 10: 5 We demolish *a* and every
Col 2: 4 you by fine-sounding *a*.
1Ti 6: 4 in controversies and *a* that result
2Ti 2:23 to do with foolish and stupid *a*,
Tit 3: 9 and *a* and quarrels about the law,

ARID

Mt 12:43 goes through *a* places seeking rest
Lk 11:24 goes through *a* places seeking rest

ARIDAI

Est 9: 9 Parmashta, Arisai, *A* and Vaizatha,

ARIDATHA

Est 9: 8 Poratha, Adalia, *A*, Parmashta,

ARIEH

2Ki 15:25 along with Argob and *A*,

ARIEL

Ezr 8:16 *A*, Shemaiah, Elnathan, Jarib,
Isa 29: 1 Woe to you, *A*, *A*,
29: 2 Yet I will besiege *A*;
29: 7 all the nations that fight against *A*,

ARIGHT (RIGHT)

Ps 90:12 Teach us to number our days *a*,

ARIMATHEA

Mt 27:57 there came a rich man from *A*,
Mk 15:43 evening approached, Joseph of *A*,
Lk 23:51 came from the Judean town of *A*
Jn 19:38 Joseph of *A* asked Pilate

ARIOCH

Ge 14: 1 king of Shinar, *A* king of Ellasar,
14: 9 of Shinar and *A* king of Ellasar—
Da 2:14 When *A*, the commander
2:15 *A* then explained the matter
2:24 to *A*, whom the king had appointed
2:25 *A* took Daniel to the king at once

ARISAI

Est 9: 9 Adalia, Aridatha, Parmashta, *A*,

ARISE (RISE)

Nu 23:18 "*A*, Balak, and listen;
Jdg 5:12 *A*, O Barak!
2Ch 6:41 "Now *a*, O LORD God,
Est 4:14 and deliverance for the Jews will *a*
Ps 3: 7 *A*, O LORD!
7: 6 *A*, O LORD, in your anger;
9:19 *A*, O LORD, let not man triumph;
10:12 *A*, LORD! Lift up your hand,
12: 5 I will now *a*," says the LORD.
35: 2 *a* and come to my aid.
59: 4 *A* to help me; look on my plight!
68: 1 May God *a*, may his enemies be
73:20 so when you *a*, O Lord,
102: 13 You will *a* and have compassion
132: 8 *a*, O LORD, and come
Pr 31:28 Her children *a* and call her blessed;
SS 2:10 "*A*, my darling,
2:13 *A*, come, my darling;
Isa 33:10 "Now will I *a*," says the LORD.
60: 1 "*A*, shine, for your light has come,
Jer 6: 4 *A*, let us attack at noon!
6: 5 So *a*, let us attack at night
30:21 their ruler will *a* from among them.
49:28 "*A*, and attack Kedar
49:31 "*A* and attack a nation at ease,
La 2:19 *A*, cry out in the night,
Da 7:24 After them another king will *a*,
8:23 a master of intrigue, will *a*.
11: 7 "One from her family line will *a*
12: 1 who protects your people, will *a*.
Hab 2: 7 Will not your debtors suddenly *a*?
Ac 20:30 from your own number men will *a*
Ro 15:12 one who will *a* to rule

ARISEN (RISE)

Dt 13:13 live in that wicked men have *a*

ARISES (RISE)

Ecc 10: 5 the sort of error that *a* from a ruler:

ARISTARCHUS

Ac 19:29 The people seized Gaius and *A*,
20: 4 *A* and Secundus from Thessalonica
27: 2 *A*, a Macedonian

Col 4: 10 My fellow prisoner *A* sends you his
Phm : 24 so do Mark, *A*, Demas and Luke,

ARISTOBULUS

Ro 16: 10 belong to the household of *A*.

ARK

Ge 6: 14 So make yourself an *a*
6: 15 The *a* is to be 450 feet long,
6: 16 Put a door in the side of the *a*
6: 16 and finish the *a* to within 18 inches
6: 18 and you will enter the *a*—
6: 19 are to bring into the *a* two
7: 1 "Go into the *a*, you and your whole
7: 7 and his sons' wives entered the *a*
7: 9 came to Noah and entered the *a*,
7: 13 of his three sons, entered the *a*.
7: 15 came to Noah and entered the *a*.
7: 17 increased they lifted the *a* high
7: 18 and the *a* floated on the surface
7: 23 and those with him in the *a*.
8: 1 that were with him in the *a*,
8: 4 of the seventh month the *a* came
8: 6 the window he had made in the *a*
8: 9 brought it back to himself in the *a*.
8: 9 so it returned to Noah in the *a*.
8: 10 again sent out the dove from the *a*.
8: 13 removed the covering from the *a*
8: 16 said to Noah, "Come out of the *a*,
8: 19 came out of the *a*, one kind
9: 10 out of the *a* with you—
9: 18 out of the *a* were Shem,
Ex 25: 15 are to remain in the rings of this *a*;
25: 16 Then put in the *a* the Testimony,
25: 21 Place the cover on top of the *a*
25: 21 and put in the *a* the Testimony,
25: 22 are over the *a* of the Testimony,
26: 33 and place the *a* of the Testimony
26: 34 cover on the *a* of the Testimony
30: 6 is before the *a* of the Testimony—
30: 26 the *a* of the Testimony, the table
31: 7 the *a* of the Testimony
35: 12 *a* with its poles and the atonement
37: 1 Bezalel made the *a* of acacia wood
37: 5 on the sides of the *a* to carry it.
39: 35 the *a* of the Testimony
40: 3 Place the *a* of the Testimony in it
40: 3 and shield the *a* with the curtain.
40: 5 in front of the *a* of the Testimony
40: 20 Testimony and placed it in the *a*,
40: 20 attached the poles to the *a*
40: 21 brought the *a* into the tabernacle
40: 21 shielded the *a* of the Testimony,
Lev 16: 2 of the atonement cover on the *a*,
Nu 3: 31 responsible for the care of the *a*,
4: 5 and cover the *a* of the Testimony
7: 89 cover on the *a* of the Testimony.
10: 33 The *a* of the covenant
10: 35 Whenever the *a* set out, Moses said
14: 44 *a* of the LORD's covenant moved
Dt 10: 3 So I made the *a* out of acacia wood
10: 5 put the tablets in the *a* I had made,
10: 8 Levi to carry the *a* of the covenant
31: 9 who carried the *a* of the covenant
31: 25 to the Levites who carried the *a*
31: 26 it beside the *a* of the covenant
Jos 3: 3 "When you see the *a*
3: 4 yards between you and the *a*;
3: 6 "Take up the *a* of the covenant
3: 8 Tell the priests who carry the *a*
3: 11 the *a* of the covenant of the Lord
3: 13 as the priests who carry the *a*
3: 14 the priests carrying the *a*
3: 15 who carried the *a* reached
3: 17 The priests who carried the *a*
4: 5 "Go over before the *a*
4: 7 cut off before the *a* of the covenant
4: 9 where the priests who carried the *a*
4: 10 carried the *a* remained standing
4: 11 the *a* of the LORD and the priests
4: 16 the priests carrying the *a*
4: 18 out of the river carrying the *a*
6: 4 of rams' horns in front of the *a*.
6: 6 "Take up the *a* of the covenant
6: 7 ahead of the *a* of the LORD."
6: 8 and the *a* of the LORD's covenant
6: 9 and the rear guard followed the *a*.
6: 11 he had the *a* of the LORD carried
Jos 6: 12 and the priests took up the *a*
6: 13 and the rear guard followed the *a*
6: 13 marching before the *a*
7: 6 ground before the *a* of the LORD,
8: 33 sides of the *a* of the covenant
Jdg 20: 27 In those days the *a* of the covenant
1Sa 3: 3 temple of the LORD, where the *a*
4: 3 Let us bring the *a* of the LORD's
4: 4 and they brought back the *a*
4: 4 there with the *a* of the covenant
4: 5 When the *a* of the LORD's
4: 6 When they learned that the *a*
4: 11 The *a* of God was captured,
4: 13 his heart feared for the *a* of God.
4: 17 and the *a* of God has been captured
4: 18 When he mentioned the *a* of God,
4: 19 she heard the news that the *a*
4: 21 of the capture of the *a* of God
4: 22 for the *a* of God has been captured
5: 1 the Philistines had captured the *a*
5: 2 carried the *a* into Dagon's temple
5: 3 ground before the *a* of the LORD!
5: 4 ground before the *a* of the LORD!
5: 7 *a* of the god of Israel must not stay
5: 8 So they moved the *a* of the God
5: 8 do with the *a* of the god of Israel?"
5: 8 "Have the *a* of the god
5: 10 As the *a* of God was entering
5: 10 So they sent the *a* of God to Ekron.
5: 10 They have brought the *a* of the god
5: 11 Send the *a* of the god of Israel away
6: 1 When the *a* of the LORD had been
6: 2 do with the *a* of the LORD?
6: 3 "If you return the *a* of the god
6: 8 Take the *a* of the LORD
6: 11 They placed the *a* of the LORD
6: 13 when they looked up and saw the *a*
6: 15 took down the *a* of the LORD,
6: 18 on which they set the *a*
6: 19 looked into the *a* of the LORD.
6: 20 To whom will the *a* go up
6: 21 The Philistines have returned the *a*
7: 1 and took up the *a* of the LORD.
7: 1 son to guard the *a* of the LORD.
7: 2 that the *a* remained at Kiriath
14: 18 to Ahijah, "Bring the *a* of God."
2Sa 6: 2 the cherubim that are on the *a*.
6: 2 to bring up from there the *a* of God
6: 3 They set the *a* of God on a new cart
6: 4 cart with the *a* of God on it,
6: 6 and took hold of the *a* of God,
6: 7 he died there beside the *a* of God.
6: 9 "How can the *a* of the LORD ever
6: 10 to take the *a* of the LORD to be
6: 11 The *a* of the LORD remained
6: 12 and brought up the *a* of God
6: 12 everything he has, because of the *a*
6: 13 those who were carrying the *a*
6: 15 house of Israel brought up the *a*
6: 16 As the *a* of the LORD was entering
6: 17 They brought the *a* of the LORD
7: 2 while the *a* of God remains
11: 11 *a* and Israel and Judah are staying
15: 24 They set down the *a* of God,
15: 24 were with him were carrying the *a*
15: 25 "Take the *a* of God back
15: 29 Abiathar took the *a* of God back
1Ki 2: 26 you carried the *a* of the Sovereign
3: 15 stood before the *a*
6: 19 temple to set the *a* of the covenant
8: 1 to bring up the *a* of the LORD's
8: 3 arrived, the priests took up the *a*,
8: 4 they brought up the *a* of the LORD
8: 5 about him were before the *a*,
8: 6 The priests then brought the *a*
8: 7 and overshadowed the *a* and its
8: 7 wings over the place of the *a*
8: 9 There was nothing in the *a*
8: 21 provided a place there for the *a*,
1Ch 6: 31 after the *a* came to rest there.
13: 3 Let us bring the *a* of our God back
13: 5 the *a* of God from Kiriath Jearim.
13: 6 from there the *a* of God the LORD
13: 6 the *a* that is called by the Name.
13: 7 They moved the *a* of God
13: 9 out his hand to steady the *a*,
13: 10 he had put his hand on the *a*.
13: 12 "How can I ever bring the *a* of God
1Ch 13: 13 He did not take the *a* to be
13: 14 The *a* of God remained
15: 1 he prepared a place for the *a*
15: 2 the Levites may carry the *a* of God
15: 2 them to carry the *a* of the LORD
15: 3 to bring up the *a* of the LORD
15: 12 and bring up the *a* of the LORD,
15: 14 to bring up the *a* of the LORD,
15: 15 the Levites carried the *a* of God
15: 23 were to be doorkeepers for the *a*.
15: 24 also to be doorkeepers for the *a*.
15: 24 trumpets before the *a* of God.
15: 25 to bring up the *a* of the covenant
15: 26 Levites who were carrying the *a*
15: 27 Levites who were carrying the *a*,
15: 28 So all Israel brought up the *a*
15: 29 As the *a* of the covenant
16: 1 They brought the *a* of God
16: 4 minister before the *a* of the LORD,
16: 6 before the *a* of the covenant
16: 37 before the *a* of the covenant
17: 1 while the *a* of the covenant
22: 19 so that you may bring the *a*
28: 2 of rest for the *a* of the covenant
28: 18 and shelter the *a* of the covenant
2Ch 1: 4 David had brought up the *a* of God
5: 2 to bring up the *a* of the LORD's
5: 4 arrived, the Levites took up the *a*,
5: 5 and they brought up the *a*
5: 6 about him were before the *a*,
5: 7 The priests then brought the *a*
5: 8 covered the *a* and its carrying poles
5: 8 wings over the place of the *a*
5: 9 from the *a*, could be seen
5: 10 There was nothing in the *a*
6: 11 There I have placed the *a*,
6: 41 you and the *a* of your might.
8: 11 the places the *a* of the LORD has
35: 3 "Put the sacred *a* in the temple that
Ps 78: 61 He sent the *a* of his might
132: 8 you and the *a* of your might.
Jer 3: 16 'The *a* of the covenant
Mt 24: 38 up to the day Noah entered the *a*;
Lk 17: 27 up to the day Noah entered the *a*.
Heb 9: 4 This *a* contained the gold jar
9: 4 the gold-covered *a* of the covenant
9: 5 Above the *a* were the cherubim
11: 7 in holy fear built an *a*
1Pe 3: 20 of Noah while the *a* was being built
Rev 11: 19 within his temple was seen the *a*

ARKITE (ARKITES)

2Sa 15: 32 Hushai the *A* was there
16: 16 Then Hushai the *A*, David's friend,
17: 5 "Summon also Hushai the *A*,
17: 14 of Hushai the *A* is better than that
1Ch 27: 33 Hushai the *A* was the king's friend.

ARKITES (ARKITE)

Ge 10: 17 Girgashites, Hivites, *A*, Sinites,
Jos 16: 2 to the territory of the *A* in Ataroth,
1Ch 1: 15 Girgashites, Hivites, *A*, Sinites,

ARM (ARMY)

Ex 6: 6 you with an outstretched *a*
15: 16 By the power of your *a*
Nu 11: 23 "Is the LORD's *a* too short?
20: 11 Then Moses raised his *a*
31: 3 "*A* some of your men to go to war
32: 17 But we are ready to *a* ourselves
32: 20 if you will *a* yourselves
Dt 4: 34 hand and an outstretched *a*,
5: 15 hand and an outstretched *a*.
7: 19 mighty hand and outstretched *a*,
9: 29 power and your outstretched *a*."
11: 2 his mighty hand, his outstretched *a*
26: 8 hand and an outstretched *a*,
33: 20 tearing at *a* or head.
2Sa 1: 10 on his *a* and have brought them
1Ki 8: 42 and your outstretched *a*—
2Ki 5: 18 leaning on my *a* and I bow there
7: 2 on whose *a* the king was leaning
7: 17 on whose *a* he leaned in charge
17: 36 mighty power and outstretched *a*,
2Ch 6: 32 and your outstretched *a*—
32: 8 With him is only the *a* of flesh,
Job 26: 2 you have saved the *a* that is feeble!
31: 22 then let my *a* fall from the shoulder

Job 35: 9 for relief from the *a* of the powerful
38: 15 and their upraised *a* is broken.
40: 9 Do you have an *a* like God's,
Ps 10: 15 Break the *a* of the wicked
44: 3 it was your right hand, your *a*,
44: 3 nor did their *a* bring them victory;
77: 15 With your mighty *a* you redeemed
79: 11 by the strength of your *a*
89: 10 with your strong *a* you scattered
89: 13 Your *a* is endued with power;
89: 21 surely my *a* will strengthen him.
98: 1 his right hand and his holy *a*
136: 12 a mighty hand and outstretched *a;*
SS 2: 6 His left *a* is under my head,
2: 6 and his right *a* embraces me.
8: 3 His left *a* is under my head
8: 3 and his right *a* embraces me.
8: 6 like a seal over your *a;*
Isa 17: 5 and harvests the grain with his *a*—
30: 30 will make them see his *a* coming
30: 32 in battle with the blows of his *a*.
40: 10 and his *a* rules for him.
44: 12 he forges it with the might of his *a*.
48: 14 *a* will be against the Babylonians.
50: 2 Was my *a* too short to ransom you?
51: 5 and my *a* will bring justice
51: 5 and wait in hope for my *a*.
51: 9 O *a* of the LORD;
52: 10 The LORD will lay bare his holy *a*
53: 1 and to whom has the *a*
59: 1 Surely the *a* of the LORD is not
59: 16 so his own *a* worked salvation
60: 4 your daughters are carried on the *a*
62: 8 and by his mighty *a:*
63: 5 so my own *a* worked salvation
63: 12 who sent his glorious *a* of power
66: 12 will nurse and be carried on her *a*
Jer 21: 5 and a mighty *a* in anger and fury
27: 5 outstretched *a* I made the earth
32: 17 great power and outstretched *a*.
32: 21 *a* and with great terror.
48: 25 her *a* is broken,''
Eze 4: 7 with bared *a* prophesy against her.
17: 9 It will not take a strong *a*
20: 33 *a* and with outpoured wrath.
20: 34 *a* and with outpoured wrath.
30: 21 I have broken the *a*
30: 22 good *a* as well as the broken one,
Zec 11: 17 May his *a* be completely withered,
11: 17 May the sword strike his *a*
Lk 1: 51 performed mighty deeds with his *a;*
Jn 12: 38 and to whom has the *a*
1Pe 4: 1 *a* yourselves also with the same

ARMAGEDDON

Rev 16: 16 that in Hebrew is called *A*.

ARMED (ARMY)

Ex 13: 18 out of Egypt *a* for battle.
Nu 31: 5 twelve thousand men *a* for battle,
32: 21 all of you will go *a* over the Jordan
32: 27 But your servants, every man *a*
32: 29 Reubenites, every man *a* for battle,
32: 30 if they do not cross over with you *a*
32: 32 before the LORD into Canaan *a*,
Dt 3: 18 But all your able-bodied men, *a*
Jos 1: 14 but all your fighting men, fully *a*,
4: 12 *a*, in front of the Israelites,
4: 13 About forty thousand *a*
6: 3 once with all the *a* men.
6: 7 with the *a* guard going ahead
6: 9 The *a* guard marched ahead
6: 13 The *a* men went ahead of them
Jdg 18: 11 *a* for battle, set out from Zorah
18: 16 The six hundred Danites, *a*
18: 17 and the six hundred *a* men stood
20: 2 four hundred thousand soldiers *a*
20: 25 all of them *a* with swords.
20: 35 Benjamites, all *a* with swords.
1Sa 2: 4 those who stumbled are *a*
2Sa 21: 16 was *a* with a new ⌊sword⌋,
22: 40 You *a* me with strength for battle;
2Ki 3: 25 but men *a* with slings surrounded it
1Ch 12: 2 they were *a* with bows
12: 23 of the men *a* for battle who came
12: 24 and spear—6,800 *a* for battle;
12: 37 *a* with every type of weapon—
20: 1 off to war, Joab led out the *a* forces.
2Ch 14: 8 *a* with small shields and with bows.
17: 17 men *a* with bows and shields;
17: 18 with 180,000 men *a* for battle.
Est 8: 11 and annihilate any *a* force
Ps 18: 39 You *a* me with strength for battle;
65: 6 having *a* yourself with strength,
78: 9 of Ephraim, though *a* with bows,
93: 1 and is *a* with strength.
Pr 6: 11 and scarcity like an *a* man.
24: 34 and scarcity like an *a* man.
Isa 15: 4 Therefore the *a* men
Jer 6: 23 They are *a* with bow and spear;
50: 42 They are *a* with bows and spears;
Eze 38: 4 your horses, your horsemen fully *a*,
Da 11: 31 "His *a* forces will rise up
Mt 26: 47 With him was a large crowd *a*
Mk 14: 43 With him was a crowd *a*
Lk 11: 21 fully *a*, guards his own house,

ARMIES (ARMY)

Ex 14: 20 coming between the *a* of Egypt
Jdg 8: 10 left of the *a* of the eastern peoples;
1Sa 17: 26 Philistine that he should defy the *a*
17: 36 because he has defied the *a*
17: 45 of the *a* of Israel, whom you have
1Ki 2: 5 the two commanders of Israel's *a*,
Ps 44: 9 you no longer go out with our *a*.
60: 10 and no longer go out with our *a?*
68: 12 "Kings and *a* flee in haste;
108: 11 and no longer go out with our *a?*
Isa 34: 2 his wrath is upon all their *a*.
Jer 35: 11 the Babylonian and Aramean *a*.'
Lk 21: 20 see Jerusalem surrounded by *a*,
Heb 11: 34 in battle and routed foreign *a*.
Rev 19: 14 *a* of heaven were following him,
19: 19 and their *a* gathered together

ARMLETS

Nu 31: 50 *a*, bracelets, signet rings, earrings

ARMONI

2Sa 21: 8 the king took *A* and Mephibosheth,

ARMOR (ARMY)

1Sa 14: 1 to the young man bearing his *a*,
17: 5 and wore a coat of scale *a*
17: 38 He put a coat of *a* on him
31: 9 off his head and stripped off his *a*,
31: 10 They put his *a* in the temple
1Ki 20: 11 on his *a* should not boast like one
22: 34 Israel between the sections of his *a*.
1Ch 10: 9 and took his head and his *a*,
10: 10 They put his *a* in the temple
2Ch 18: 33 Israel between the sections of his *a*.
26: 14 spears, helmets, coats of *a*,
Ne 4: 16 with spears, shields, bows and *a*.
Isa 45: 1 and to strip kings of their *a*,
Jer 46: 4 put on your *a!*
51: 3 nor let him put on his *a*.
Lk 11: 22 he takes away the *a*
Ro 13: 12 deeds of darkness and put on the *a*
Eph 6: 11 Put on the full *a* of God
6: 13 Therefore put on the full *a* of God,

ARMOR-BEARER (ARMY)

Jdg 9: 54 Hurriedly he called to his *a*,
1Sa 14: 6 Jonathan said to his young *a*,
14: 7 have in mind,'' his *a* said.
14: 12 Jonathan said to his *a*, "Climb up
14: 12 shouted to Jonathan and his *a*,
14: 13 and his *a* followed and killed
14: 13 with his *a* right behind him.
14: 14 and his *a* killed some twenty men
14: 17 and his *a* who were not there.
31: 4 But his *a* was terrified
31: 4 said to his *a*, "Draw your sword
31: 5 When the *a* saw that Saul was dead
31: 6 Saul and three of his sons and his *a*
2Sa 23: 37 the *a* of Joab son of Zeruiah,
1Ch 10: 4 But his *a* was terrified
10: 4 said to his *a*, "Draw your sword
10: 5 When the *a* saw that Saul was dead
11: 39 the *a* of Joab son of Zeruiah,

ARMOR-BEARERS (ARMY)

1Sa 16: 21 and David became one of his *a*.
2Sa 18: 15 of Joab's *a* surrounded Absalom,

ARMORY (ARMY)

2Ki 20: 13 his *a* and everything found
Ne 3: 19 a point facing the ascent to the *a*
Isa 39: 2 his entire *a* and everything found

ARMRESTS

1Ki 10: 19 On both sides of the seat were *a*,
2Ch 9: 18 On both sides of the seat were *a*,

ARMS (ARMY)

Ge 16: 5 I put my servant in your *a*,
24: 30 and the bracelets on his sister's *a*,
24: 47 and the bracelets on her *a*,
33: 4 he threw his *a* around his neck
45: 14 he threw his *a* around his brother
46: 29 he threw his *a* around his father
48: 14 the younger, and crossing his *a*,
49: 24 his strong *a* stayed limber,
Nu 11: 12 me to carry them in my *a*,
Dt 33: 27 underneath are the everlasting *a*.
Jdg 6: 35 calling them to *a*, and
10: 17 the Ammonites were called to *a*
15: 14 on his *a* became like charred flax,
16: 12 But he snapped the ropes off his *a*
2Sa 12: 3 from his cup and even slept in his *a*
12: 8 your master's wives into your *a*.
22: 33 It is God who *a* me with strength
22: 35 my *a* can bend a bow of bronze.
1Ki 17: 19 him from her *a*, carried him
2Ki 3: 21 who could bear *a* was called up
4: 16 "you will hold a son in your *a*."
Ps 18: 32 It is God who *a* me with strength
18: 34 my *a* can bend a bow of bronze.
129: 7 nor the one who gathers fill his *a*.
Pr 31: 17 her *a* are strong for her tasks.
31: 20 She opens her *a* to the poor
SS 5: 14 His *a* are rods of gold
Isa 40: 11 He gathers the lambs in his *a*
49: 22 they will bring your sons in their *a*
Jer 38: 12 and worn-out clothes under your *a*
La 2: 12 away in their mothers' *a*.
Eze 13: 20 and I will tear them from your *a;*
16: 11 I put bracelets on your *a*
23: 42 bracelets on the *a* of the woman
30: 22 will break both his *a*, the good arm
30: 24 I will strengthen the *a* of the king
30: 24 but I will break the *a* of Pharaoh,
30: 25 I will strengthen the *a* of the king
30: 25 but the *a* of Pharaoh will fall limp.
38: 8 many days you will be called to *a*.
Da 2: 32 its chest and *a* of silver, its belly
10: 6 his *a* and legs like the gleam
Hos 11: 3 taking them by the *a;*
Mk 9: 36 Taking him in his *a*, he said
10: 16 And he took the children in his *a*,
Lk 2: 28 Simeon took him in his *a*
15: 20 threw his *a* around him
Ac 20: 10 on the young man and put his *a*
Heb 12: 12 strengthen your feeble *a*

ARMY (ARM ARMED ARMIES ARMOR ARMOR-BEARER ARMOR-BEARERS ARMORY ARMS)

Ex 14: 4 through Pharaoh and all his *a*,
14: 6 chariot made ready and took his *a*
14: 17 through Pharaoh and all his *a*,
14: 19 traveling in front of Israel's *a*,
14: 24 and cloud at the Egyptian *a*
14: 28 the entire *a* of Pharaoh that had
15: 4 Pharaoh's chariots and his *a*
17: 13 Joshua overcame the Amalekite *a*
Nu 1: 3 more who are able to serve in the *a*.
1: 20 able to serve in the *a* were listed
1: 22 able to serve in the *a* were counted
1: 24 able to serve in the *a* were listed
1: 26 able to serve in the *a* were listed
1: 28 able to serve in the *a* were listed
1: 30 able to serve in the *a* were listed
1: 32 able to serve in the *a* were listed
1: 34 able to serve in the *a* were listed
1: 36 able to serve in the *a* were listed
1: 38 able to serve in the *a* were listed
1: 40 able to serve in the *a* were listed
1: 42 able to serve in the *a* were listed
1: 45 serve in Israel's *a* were counted
20: 20 them with a large and powerful *a*.
21: 23 He mustered his entire *a*

Nu 21: 33 and his whole *a* marched out
21: 34 with his whole *a* and his land.
21: 35 with his sons and his whole *a*,
26: 2 able to serve in the *a* of Israel.''
31: 14 angry with the officers of the *a*—
31: 48 were over the units of the *a*—
Dt 2: 32 and all his *a* came out to meet us
2: 33 with his sons and his whole *a*.
3: 1 with his whole *a* marched out
3: 2 him over to you with his whole *a*
3: 3 king of Bashan and all his *a*.
11: 4 what he did to the Egyptian *a*,
20: 1 and an *a* greater than yours,
20: 2 come forward and address the *a*.
20: 5 The officers shall say to the *a*:
20: 9 have finished speaking to the *a*,
Jos 5: 14 ''but as commander of the *a*
5: 15 of the LORD's *a* replied,
8: 1 Take the whole *a* with you,
8: 3 the whole *a* moved out to attack Ai
10: 7 up from Gilgal with his entire *a*,
10: 21 The whole *a* then returned safely
10: 24 said to the *a* commanders who had
10: 33 but Joshua defeated him and his *a*
11: 4 a huge *a*, as numerous
11: 7 *a* came against them suddenly
Jdg 4: 2 The commander of his *a* was Sisera
4: 7 the commander of Jabin's *a*,
4: 15 all his chariots and *a* by the sword,
4: 16 Barak pursued the chariots and *a*
7: 22 The *a* fled to Beth Shittah
8: 11 and fell upon the unsuspecting *a*.
8: 12 them, routing their entire *a*.
9: 29 'Call out your whole *a*!' ''
20: 10 Then, when the *a* arrives at Gibeah
20: 10 to get provisions for the *a*.
1Sa 4: 17 and the *a* has suffered heavy losses.
12: 9 the commander of the *a* of Hazor,
13: 6 and that their *a* was hard pressed,
14: 15 Then panic struck the whole *a*—
14: 16 Benjamin saw the *a* melting away
14: 25 The entire *a* entered the woods,
14: 28 ''Your father bound the *a*
14: 38 all you who are leaders of the *a*,
14: 50 of Saul's *a* was Abner son
15: 9 But Saul and the *a* spared Agag
17: 20 as the *a* was going out
17: 46 of the Philistine *a* to the birds
17: 55 commander of the *a*, ''Abner,
18: 5 Saul gave him a high rank in the *a*.
26: 5 of the *a*, had lain down.
26: 5 with the *a* encamped around him.
26: 7 and Abishai went to the *a* by night,
26: 14 out to the *a* and to Abner son
28: 1 men will accompany me in the *a*.''
28: 5 When Saul saw the Philistine *a*,
28: 19 also hand over the *a* of Israel
29: 6 to have you serve with me in the *a*.
31: 7 saw that the Israelite *a* had fled
2Sa 1: 12 and for the *a* of the LORD
2: 8 the commander of Saul's *a*,
5: 24 of you to strike the Philistine *a*.''
8: 9 David had defeated the entire *a*
8: 16 Joab son of Zeruiah was over the *a*;
10: 7 with the entire *a* of fighting men.
10: 16 of Hadadezer's *a* leading them.
10: 18 Shobach the commander of their *a*,
11: 1 men and the whole Israelite *a*.
11: 17 some of the men in David's *a* fell;
12: 29 So David mustered the entire *a*
12: 31 his entire *a* returned to Jerusalem.
17: 25 Amasa over the *a* in place of Joab.
18: 6 The *a* marched into the field
18: 7 There the *a* of Israel was defeated
19: 2 for the whole *a* the victory that day
19: 13 of my *a* in place of Joab.' ''
20: 23 Joab was over Israel's entire *a*;
24: 2 and the *a* commanders with him,
24: 4 Joab and the *a* commanders;
1Ki 1: 19 and Joab the commander of the *a*,
1: 25 the commanders of the *a*
2: 32 commander of Israel's *a*,
2: 32 commander of Judah's *a*—
2: 35 over the *a* in Joab's position
11: 15 Joab the commander of the *a*,
11: 21 Joab the commander of the *a* was
16: 15 The *a* was encamped
16: 16 Omri, the commander of the *a*,
1Ki 20: 1 king of Aram mustered his entire *a*.
20: 13 Do you see this vast *a*? I will give it
20: 19 of the city with the *a* behind them
20: 25 raise an *a* like the one you lost—
20: 28 I will deliver this vast *a*
22: 36 a cry spread through the *a*:
2Ki 3: 9 the *a* had no more water
4: 13 or the commander of the *a*?' ''
5: 1 commander of the *a* of the king
6: 15 an *a* with horses and chariots had
6: 24 king of Aram mobilized his entire *a*
7: 6 of chariots and horses and a great *a*
7: 14 them after the Aramean *a*.
8: 21 his *a*, however, fled back home.
9: 5 he found the *a* officers sitting
13: 7 left of the *a* of Jehoahaz
18: 17 his field commander with a large *a*,
25: 1 against Jerusalem with his whole *a*.
25: 4 and the whole *a* fled at night
25: 5 the Babylonian *a* pursued the king
25: 10 The whole Babylonian *a*,
25: 23 When all the *a* officers
25: 26 together with the *a* officers,
1Ch 10: 7 in the valley saw that the *a* had fled
12: 14 These Gadites were *a* commanders
12: 21 and they were commanders in his *a*
12: 22 until he had a great and mighty *a*.
14: 15 of you to strike the Philistine *a*.''
14: 16 they struck down the Philistine *a*,
18: 9 David had defeated the entire *a*
18: 15 Joab son of Zeruiah was over the *a*;
19: 8 with the entire *a* of fighting men.
19: 16 of Hadadezer's *a* leading them.
19: 18 the commander of their *a*.
20: 3 his entire *a* returned to Jerusalem.
25: 1 with the commanders of the *a*,
26: 26 and by the other *a* commanders.
27: 1 that concerned the *a* divisions that
27: 3 and chief of all the *a* officers
27: 5 The third *a* commander,
27: 34 was the commander of the royal *a*.
2Ch 13: 8 You are indeed a vast *a*
14: 8 Asa had an *a* of three hundred
14: 9 out against them with a vast *a*
14: 11 come against this vast *a*.
14: 13 and Asa and his *a* pursued them
16: 7 *a* of the king of Aram has escaped
16: 8 and Libyans a mighty *a*
20: 2 ''A vast *a* is coming against you
20: 12 to face this vast *a* that is attacking
20: 15 discouraged because of this vast *a*.
20: 21 they went out at the head of the *a*,
20: 24 and looked toward the vast *a*,
24: 23 the *a* of Aram marched
24: 24 Although the Aramean *a* had come
24: 24 into their hands a much larger *a*.
25: 11 and led his *a* to the Valley of Salt,
25: 12 The *a* of Judah also captured ten
26: 11 Uzziah had a well-trained *a*,
26: 13 Under their command was an *a*
26: 14 and slingstones for the entire *a*.
28: 9 out to meet the *a* when it returned
32: 7 of Assyria and the vast *a* with him,
33: 11 against them the *a* commanders
Ne 2: 9 The king had also sent *a* officers
4: 2 presence of his associates and the *a*
Ps 27: 3 Though an *a* besiege me,
33: 16 No king is saved by the size of his *a*
136: 15 swept Pharaoh and his *a*
Pr 30: 31 and a king with his *a* around him.
Isa 13: 4 an *a* for war.
36: 2 with a large *a* from Lachish
43: 17 the *a* and reinforcements together,
Jer 4: 16 'A besieging *a* is coming
6: 22 ''Look, an *a* is coming
32: 2 *a* of the king of Babylon was then
34: 1 and all his *a* and all the kingdoms
34: 7 while the *a* of the king
34: 21 to the *a* of the king of Babylon,
37: 5 Pharaoh's *a* had marched out
37: 7 'Pharaoh's *a*, which has marched
37: 10 the entire Babylonian *a* that is
37: 11 Jerusalem because of Pharaoh's *a*,
37: 11 the Babylonian *a* had withdrawn
38: 3 over to the *a* of the king of Babylon
39: 1 against Jerusalem with his whole *a*
39: 5 But the Babylonian *a* pursued them
40: 7 When all the *a* officers
Jer 40: 13 and all the *a* officers still
41: 11 and all the *a* officers who were
41: 13 the *a* officers who were with him,
41: 16 and all the *a* officers who were
42: 1 Then all the *a* officers, including
42: 8 and all the *a* officers who were
43: 4 son of Kareah and all the *a* officers
43: 5 and all the *a* officers led away all
46: 2 the *a* of Pharaoh Neco
50: 41 An *a* is coming from the north;
51: 3 completely destroy her *a*.
52: 4 against Jerusalem with his whole *a*.
52: 7 through, and the whole *a* fled.
52: 8 but the Babylonian *a* pursued King
52: 14 The whole Babylonian *a*
La 1: 15 he has summoned an *a* against me
Eze 1: 24 Almighty, like the tumult of an *a*.
17: 15 to Egypt to get horses and a large *a*
17: 17 Pharaoh with his mighty *a*
26: 7 with horsemen and a great *a*.
27: 10 served as soldiers in your *a*.
29: 18 and his *a* got no reward
29: 18 king of Babylon drove his *a*
29: 19 plunder the land as pay for his *a*.
29: 20 because he and his *a* did it for me,
30: 11 his *a*— the most ruthless of nations
32: 22 ''Assyria is there with her whole *a*;
32: 23 and her *a* lies around her grave.
32: 31 ''Pharaoh—he and all his *a*—
37: 10 stood up on their feet—a vast *a*.
38: 4 bring you out with your whole *a*—
38: 15 horses, a great horde, a mighty *a*.
Da 3: 20 soldiers in his *a* to tie up Shadrach,
11: 10 for war and assemble a great *a*,
11: 11 who will raise a large *a*,
11: 12 When the *a* is carried off, the king
11: 13 of the North will muster another *a*,
11: 13 with a huge *a* fully equipped.
11: 22 overwhelming *a* will be swept away
11: 25 with a large and very powerful *a*,
11: 25 ''With a large *a* he will stir up his
11: 26 his *a* will be swept away,
Joel 2: 2 a large and mighty *a* comes,
2: 5 like a mighty *a* drawn up for battle.
2: 11 thunders at the head of his *a*;
2: 20 ''I will drive the northern *a* far
2: 25 my great *a* that I sent among you.
Mt 22: 7 He sent his *a* and destroyed those
Rev 19: 19 the rider on the horse and his *a*.

ARNAN

1Ch 3: 21 of *A*, of Obadiah and of Shecaniah.

ARNON (ARNON'S)

Nu 21: 13 The *A* is the border of Moab,
21: 13 and camped alongside the *A*,
21: 14 the *A*
21: 24 land from the *A* to the Jabbok,
21: 26 from him all his land as far as the *A*.
22: 36 the Moabite town on the *A* border,
Dt 2: 24 Set out now and cross the *A* Gorge.
2: 36 From Aroer on the rim of the *A*
3: 8 from the *A* Gorge as far
3: 12 territory north of Aroer by the *A*
3: 16 down to the *A* Gorge (the middle
4: 48 Aroer on the rim of the *A* Gorge
Jos 12: 1 the *A* Gorge to Mount Hermon,
12: 2 from Aroer on the rim of the *A*
13: 9 from Aroer on the rim of the *A*
13: 16 from Aroer on the rim of the *A*
Jdg 11: 13 land from the *A* to the Jabbok,
11: 18 camped on the other side of the *A*.
11: 18 of Moab, for the *A* was its border.
11: 22 all of it from the *A* to the Jabbok
11: 26 and all the towns along the *A*.
2Ki 10: 33 by the *A* Gorge through Gilead
Isa 16: 2 Moab at the fords of the *A*.
Jer 48: 20 Announce by the *A*

ARNON'S (ARNON)

Nu 21: 28 the citizens of *A* heights.

ARODI (ARODITE)

Ge 46: 16 Shuni, Ezbon, Eri, *A* and Areli.
Nu 26: 17 through *A*, the Arodite clan;

ARODITE (ARODI)

Nu 26: 17 through Arodi, the *A* clan;

AROER (AROERITE)
Nu 32:34 built up Dibon, Ataroth, *A*,
Dt 2:36 From *A* on the rim of the Arnon
3:12 north of *A* by the Arnon
4:48 extended from *A* on the rim
Jos 12: 2 He ruled from *A* on the rim
13: 9 It extended from *A* on the rim
13:16 The territory from *A* on the rim
13:25 the Ammonite country as far as *A*,
Jdg 11:26 years Israel occupied Heshbon, *A*,
11:33 towns from *A* to the vicinity
1Sa 30:28 to those in *A*, Siphmoth, Eshtemoa
2Sa 24: 5 the Jordan, they camped near *A*,
2Ki 10:33 from *A* by the Arnon Gorge
1Ch 5: 8 settled in the area from *A* to Nebo
Isa 17: 2 The cities of *A* will be deserted
Jer 48:19 you who live in *A*.

AROERITE (AROER)
1Ch 11:44 and Jeiel the sons of Hotham the *A*,

AROMA (AROMATIC)
Ge 8:21 The LORD smelled the pleasing *a*
Ex 29:18 a pleasing *a*, an offering made
29:25 for a pleasing *a* to the LORD,
29:41 a pleasing *a*, an offering made
Lev 1: 9 an *a* pleasing to the LORD.
1:13 an *a* pleasing to the LORD.
1:17 an *a* pleasing to the LORD.
2: 2 an *a* pleasing to the LORD.
2: 9 an *a* pleasing to the LORD.
2:12 offered on the altar as a pleasing *a*.
3: 5 an *a* pleasing to the LORD.
3:16 made by fire, a pleasing *a*.
4:31 as an *a* pleasing to the LORD.
6:15 as an *a* pleasing to the LORD.
6:21 as an *a* pleasing to the LORD.
8:21 a pleasing *a*, an offering made
8:28 a pleasing *a*, an offering made
17: 6 as an *a* pleasing to the LORD.
23:13 to the LORD by fire, a pleasing *a*
23:18 an *a* pleasing to the LORD.
26:31 in the pleasing *a* of your offerings.
Nu 15: 3 as an *a* pleasing to the LORD—
15: 7 as an *a* pleasing to the LORD.
15:10 an *a* pleasing to the LORD.
15:13 as an *a* pleasing to the LORD.
15:14 as an *a* pleasing to the LORD,
15:24 as an *a* pleasing to the LORD,
18:17 an *a* pleasing to the LORD.
28: 2 by fire, as an *a* pleasing to me.'
28: 6 at Mount Sinai as a pleasing *a*,
28: 8 an *a* pleasing to the LORD.
28:13 is for a burnt offering, a pleasing *a*,
28:24 as an *a* pleasing to the LORD;
28:27 as an *a* pleasing to the LORD.
29: 2 As an *a* pleasing to the LORD,
29: 6 to the LORD by fire—a pleasing *a*
29: 8 an *a* pleasing to the LORD a burnt
29:13 as an *a* pleasing to the LORD,
29:36 as an *a* pleasing to the LORD,
Jer 48:11 and her *a* is unchanged.
2Co 2:15 For we are to God the *a* of Christ

AROMATIC (AROMA)
Ge 2:12 *a* resin and onyx are also there.)

AROSE (RISE)
Ge 13: 7 *a* between Abram's herdsmen
Jdg 5: 7 ceased until I, Deborah, *a*,
5: 7 *a* a mother in Israel.
1Sa 1:19 Early the next morning they *a*
Est 8: 4 and she *a* and stood before him.
SS 5: 5 I *a* to open for my lover,
Jnh 1: 4 such a violent storm *a* that the ship
Lk 22:24 Also a dispute *a* among them
Ac 6: 9 Opposition *a*, however,
19:23 that time there *a* a great
Gal 2: 4 ⌞This matter *a*⌟ because some false

AROUSE (ROUSE)
SS 2: 7 Do not *a* or awaken love
3: 5 Do not *a* or awaken love
8: 4 Do not *a* or awaken love
Ro 11:14 I may somehow *a* my own people
1Co 10:22 trying to *a* the Lord's jealousy?

AROUSED (ROUSE)
Ex 22:24 My anger will be *a*, and I will kill
Nu 11: 1 he heard them his anger was *a*.
32:10 The LORD's anger was *a* that day
Dt 9: 8 At Horeb you *a* the LORD's wrath
2Ch 21:16 The LORD *a* against Jehoram
36:16 the wrath of the LORD was *a*
Job 17: 8 the innocent are *a*
32: 5 more to say, his anger was *a*.
Ps 78:58 they *a* his jealousy with their idols.
Jer 32:31 this city has so *a* my anger
51:39 But while they are *a*,
Eze 38:18 anger will be *a*, declares
Hos 11: 8 all my compassion is *a*.
Ac 21:30 whole city was *a*, and the people
Ro 7: 5 the sinful passions *a*

AROUSES (ROUSE)
Pr 6:34 for jealousy *a* a husband's fury,

ARPAD
2Ki 18:34 the gods of Hamath and *A*?
19:13 the king of *A*, the king of the city
Isa 10: 9 Is not Hamath like *A*,
36:19 the gods of Hamath and *A*?
37:13 the king of *A*, the king of the city
Jer 49:23 "Hamath and *A* are dismayed,

ARPHAXAD
Ge 10:22 Elam, Asshur, *A*, Lud and Aram.
10:24 *A* was the father of Shelah,
11:10 he became the father of *A*.
11:11 after he became the father of *A*,
11:12 When *A* had lived 35 years,
11:13 *A* lived 403 years and had other
1Ch 1:17 Elam, Asshur, *A*, Lud and Aram.
1:18 *A* was the father of Shelah,
1:24 Shem, *A*, Shelah, Eber, Peleg, Reu,
Lk 3:36 the son of *A*, the son of Shem,

ARRANGE (ARRANGED ARRANGEMENT ARRANGEMENTS)
Lev 1: 7 on the altar and *a* wood on the fire.
1: 8 sons the priests shall *a* the pieces,
1:12 and the priest shall *a* them,
6:12 and *a* the burnt offering on the fire

ARRANGED (ARRANGE)
Ge 15:10 *a* the halves opposite each other;
22: 9 built an altar there and *a* the wood
Jdg 20:38 The men of Israel had *a*
2Sa 23: 5 *a* and secured in every part?
1Ki 18:33 He *a* the wood, cut the bull
2Ki 9:30 *a* her hair and looked out
2Ch 35:10 service was *a* and the priests stood
Mt 26:48 Now the betrayer had *a* a signal
Mk 14:44 Now the betrayer had *a* a signal
Ac 28:23 They *a* to meet Paul
1Co 12:18 But in fact God has *a* the parts
Heb 9: 6 everything had been *a* like this,

ARRANGEMENT (ARRANGE)
Eze 43:11 its *a*, its exits and entrances—
Ac 20:13 He had made this *a* because he was

ARRANGEMENTS (ARRANGE)
2Co 9: 5 finish the *a* for the generous gift

ARRAY (ARRAYED)
Ge 2: 1 were completed in all their vast *a*.
Dt 4:19 the stars—all the heavenly *a*—

ARRAYED (ARRAY)
Ps 110: 3 *A* in holy majesty,
Isa 61:10 and *a* me in a robe of righteousness

ARREST (ARRESTED ARRESTING)
Jer 36:26 of Abdeel to *a* Baruch the scribe
Mt 10:19 But when they *a* you, do not worry
21:46 They looked for a way to *a* him,
26: 4 and they plotted to *a* Jesus
26:48 "The one I kiss is the man; *a* him."
26:55 teaching, and you did not *a* me.
Mk 12:12 they looked for a way to *a* him
14: 1 looking for some sly way to *a* Jesus
14:44 *a* him and lead him away
14:49 courts, and you did not *a* me.
Lk 20:19 for a way to *a* him immediately,
Jn 7:32 sent temple guards to *a* him.
11:57 it so that they might *a* him.
18:36 fight to prevent my *a* by the Jews.
Ac 9:14 the chief priests to *a* all who call
2Co 11:32 guarded in order to *a* me.

ARRESTED (ARREST)
Jer 37:13 the son of Hananiah, *a* him
37:14 he *a* Jeremiah and brought him
Mt 14: 3 Now Herod had *a* John
26:50 forward, seized Jesus and *a* him.
26:57 Those who had *a* Jesus took him
Mk 6:17 had given orders to have John *a*,
13:11 Whenever you are *a* and brought
14:46 The men seized Jesus and *a* him.
Jn 18:12 and the Jewish officials *a* Jesus.
Ac 1:16 as guide for those who *a* Jesus—
5:18 They *a* the apostles and put them
12: 1 that King Herod *a* some who
21:33 commander came up and *a* him
28:17 I was *a* in Jerusalem and handed

ARRESTING (ARREST)
Ac 12: 4 After *a* him, he put him in prison,
22: 4 *a* both men and women

ARRIVAL (ARRIVE)
Ge 43:25 gifts for Joseph's *a* at noon,
Ezr 3: 8 after their *a* at the house of God
Jn 11:17 On his *a*, Jesus found that Lazarus

ARRIVE (ARRIVAL ARRIVED ARRIVES ARRIVING)
Ex 1:19 give birth before the midwives *a*."
Ne 2: 7 safe-conduct until I *a* in Judah?
Job 6:20 *a* there, only to be disappointed.
1Co 16: 3 Then, when I *a*, I will give letters

ARRIVED (ARRIVE)
Ge 12: 5 land of Canaan, and they *a* there.
19: 1 The two angels *a* at Sodom
33:18 he *a* safely at the city of Shechem
37:14 When Joseph *a* at Shechem,
42: 6 So when Joseph's brothers *a*,
46:28 When they *a* in the region
Nu 10:21 was to be set up before they *a*.
20: 1 the whole Israelite community *a*
Dt 9: 7 day you left Egypt until you *a* here,
11: 5 the desert until you *a* at this place,
Jos 8:11 approached the city and *a* in front
Jdg 3:27 When he *a* there, he blew
7:13 Gideon *a* just as a man was telling
Ru 1:19 When they *a* in Bethlehem,
2: 4 Just then Boaz *a* from Bethlehem
1Sa 4:13 When he *a*, there was Eli sitting
10:10 When they *a* at Gibeah,
13:10 Samuel *a*, and Saul went out
16: 4 When he *a* at Bethlehem,
16: 6 When they *a*, Samuel saw Eliab
25: 9 When David's men *a*, they gave
25:12 When they *a*, they reported every
26: 4 learned that Saul had definitely *a*.
30:26 When David *a* in Ziklag, he sent
2Sa 1: 2 On the third day a man *a*
2:32 and *a* at Hebron by daybreak.
3:23 and all the soldiers with him *a*,
4: 5 they *a* there in the heat of the day
11:22 and when he *a* he told David
15:32 When David *a* at the summit,
15:37 So David's friend Hushai *a*
16:14 with him *a* at their destination
18:31 Then the Cushite *a* and said,
19:30 lord the king has *a* home safely."
1Ki 1:22 the king, Nathan the prophet *a*.
1:42 son of Abiathar the priest *a*.
8: 3 When all the elders of Israel had *a*,
12:21 When Rehoboam *a* in Jerusalem,
22:15 When he *a*, the king asked him,
2Ki 6:32 but before he *a*, Elisha said
9: 5 When he *a*, he found the army
10: 7 When the letter *a*, these men took
10: 8 When the messenger *a*, he told
2Ch 5: 4 When all the elders of Israel had *a*,
11: 1 When Rehoboam *a* in Jerusalem,
18:14 When he *a*, the king asked him,
22: 7 When Ahaziah *a*, he went out
Ezr 2:68 When they *a* at the house
7: 8 Ezra *a* in Jerusalem

Ezr 7: 9 he *a* in Jerusalem on the first day
8: 32 we *a* in Jerusalem, where we rested
Est 6: 14 the king's eunuchs *a* and hurried
Isa 30: 4 and their envoys have *a* in Hanes,
Eze 7: 12 The time has come, the day has *a*.
23: 40 when they *a* you bathed yourself
33: 22 Now the evening before the man *a*,
47: 7 When I *a* there, I saw a great
Zec 6: 10 who have *a* from Babylon.
Mt 8: 28 When he *a* at the other side
17: 24 and his disciples *a* in Capernaum,
25: 10 to buy the oil, the bridegroom *a*.
26: 47 Judas, one of the Twelve, *a*.
Mk 3: 31 Then Jesus' mother and brothers *a*.
11: 27 They *a* again in Jerusalem,
14: 17 When evening came, Jesus *a*
Lk 8: 51 When he *a* at the house of Jairus,
Jn 4: 45 When he *a* in Galilee,
4: 47 this man heard that Jesus had *a*
12: 1 Jesus *a* at Bethany, where Lazarus
20: 6 *a* and went into the tomb.
Ac 1: 13 When they *a*, they went upstairs
5: 21 the high priest and his associates *a*,
8: 15 When they *a*, they prayed
9: 39 when he *a* he was taken upstairs
10: 24 The following day he *a* in Caesarea
11: 23 When he *a* and saw the evidence
13: 5 When they *a* at Salamis, they
18: 19 They *a* at Ephesus, where Paul left
19: 1 the road through the interior and *a*
20: 2 and finally *a* in Greece, where he
20: 15 on the following day *a* at Miletus.
20: 15 sail from there and *a* off Kios
20: 18 When they *a*, he said to them:
21: 17 When we *a* at Jerusalem,
23: 33 When the cavalry *a* in Caesarea,
25: 13 and Bernice *a* at Caesarea
28: 13 From there we set sail and *a*
1Co 16: 17 Fortunatus and Achaicus *a*,
Gal 2: 12 But when they *a*, he began

ARRIVES (ARRIVE)

Jdg 20: 10 Then, when the army *a* at Gibeah
1Sa 16: 11 we will not sit down until he *a*."
1Ki 14: 5 When she *a*, she will pretend
Hos 13: 13 when the time *a*,
Zep 2: 2 before the appointed time *a*
Mt 12: 44 When it *a*, it finds the house
Lk 11: 25 When it *a*, it finds the house swept
Heb 13: 23 If he *a* soon, I will come with him

ARRIVING (ARRIVE)

Ru 1: 22 *a* in Bethlehem as the barley
1Ki 10: 2 *A* at Jerusalem with a very great
2Ch 9: 1 *A* with a very great caravan—
28: 12 confronted those who were *a*
Ac 5: 22 on *a* at the jail, the officers did not
14: 27 On *a* there, they gathered
17: 10 On *a* there, they went
18: 27 On *a*, he was a great help
25: 1 Three days after *a* in the province,
27: 7 and had difficulty *a* off Cnidus.

ARROGANCE (ARROGANT)

Dt 1: 43 and in your *a* you marched up
1Sa 2: 3 or let your mouth speak such *a*,
15: 23 and *a* like the evil of idolatry.
Job 35: 12 because of the *a* of the wicked.
Ps 10: 2 In his *a* the wicked man hunts
17: 10 and their mouths speak with *a*.
73: 8 in their *a* they threaten oppression.
Pr 8: 13 I hate pride and *a*,
Isa 2: 17 The *a* of man will be brought low
9: 9 and *a* of heart,
13: 11 an end to the *a* of the haughty
Jer 48: 29 her pride and *a*
Eze 7: 10 rod has budded, *a* has blossomed!
Hos 5: 5 Israel's *a* testifies against them;
7: 10 Israel's *a* testifies against him,
Mk 7: 22 lewdness, envy, slander, *a* and folly
2Co 12: 20 slander, gossip, *a* and disorder.

ARROGANT (ARROGANCE)

2Ki 14: 10 defeated Edom and now you are *a*.
2Ch 25: 19 and now you are *a* and proud.
Ne 9: 16 became *a* and stiff-necked,
9: 29 they became *a* and disobeyed your
Ps 5: 5 The *a* cannot stand
73: 3 For I envied the *a*
75: 4 To the *a* I say, 'Boast no more,'
86: 14 The *a* are attacking me, O God;
94: 4 They pour out *a* words;
119: 21 You rebuke the *a*, who are cursed
119: 51 The *a* mock me without restraint,
119: 69 Though the *a* have smeared me
119: 78 May the *a* be put to shame
119: 85 The *a* dig pitfalls for me,
119:122 let not the *a* oppress me.
123: 4 much contempt from the *a*.
Pr 17: 7 *A* lips are unsuited to a fool—
21: 24 *a* man—"Mocker" is his name;
Isa 2: 11 eyes of the *a* man will be humbled
5: 15 the eyes of the *a* humbled.
33: 19 will see those *a* people no more,
Jer 13: 15 do not be *a*,
43: 2 and all the *a* men said to Jeremiah,
50: 31 "See, I am against you, O *a* one,"
50: 32 The *a* one will stumble and fall
Eze 16: 49 She and her daughters were *a*,
Da 5: 20 But when his heart became *a*
Hab 2: 5 he is *a* and never at rest.
Zep 3: 4 Her prophets are *a*;
Mal 3: 15 But now we call the *a* blessed.
4: 1 All the *a* and every evildoer will be
Ro 1: 30 God-haters, insolent, *a*
11: 20 Do not be *a*, but be afraid.
1Co 4: 18 Some of you have become *a*,
4: 19 only how these *a* people are
1Ti 6: 17 in this present world not to be *a*
2Pe 2: 10 and *a*, these men are not afraid

ARROW (ARROWS)

1Sa 20: 36 As the boy ran, he shot an *a*
20: 37 where Jonathan's *a* had fallen,
20: 37 "Isn't the *a* beyond you?"
20: 38 The boy picked up the *a*
2Ki 9: 24 The *a* pierced his heart
13: 17 the *a* of victory over Aram!"
13: 17 "The LORD's *a* of victory,
19: 32 or shoot an *a* here.
Job 20: 24 a bronze-tipped *a* pierces him.
34: 6 his *a* inflicts an incurable wound.'
Ps 91: 5 nor the *a* that flies by day,
Pr 7: 23 a noose till an *a* pierces his liver,
25: 18 Like a club or a sword or a sharp *a*
Isa 7: 24 Men will go there with bow and *a*,
37: 33 or shoot an *a* here.
49: 2 he made me into a polished *a*
Jer 9: 8 Their tongue is a deadly *a*;
Zec 9: 14 his *a* will flash like lightning

ARROWS (ARROW)

Ex 19: 13 surely be stoned or shot with *a*;
Nu 24: 8 with their *a* they pierce them.
Dt 32: 23 and spend my *a* against them.
32: 42 I will make my *a* drunk with blood,
1Sa 20: 20 I will shoot three *a* to the side of it,
20: 21 'Look, the *a* are on this side of you;
20: 21 send a boy and say, 'Go, find the *a*.'
20: 22 'Look, the *a* are beyond you,'
20: 36 "Run and find the *a* I shoot."
2Sa 11: 20 you know they would shoot *a*
11: 24 the archers shot *a* at your servants
22: 15 He shot *a* and scattered
2Ki 13: 15 and some *a*," and he did so.
13: 18 Then he said, "Take the *a*,"
1Ch 12: 2 and were able to shoot *a*
2Ch 26: 15 on the corner defenses to shoot *a*
Job 6: 4 The *a* of the Almighty are in me,
41: 28 *A* do not make him flee;
Ps 7: 13 he makes ready his flaming *a*.
11: 2 they set their *a* against the strings
18: 14 He shot his *a* and scattered
38: 2 For your *a* have pierced me,
45: 5 Let your sharp *a* pierce the hearts
57: 4 men whose teeth are spears and *a*,
58: 7 the bow, let their *a* be blunted.
64: 3 and aim their words like deadly *a*.
64: 7 But God will shoot them with *a*;
76: 3 There he broke the flashing *a*,
77: 17 your *a* flashed back and forth.
120: 4 you with a warrior's sharp *a*,
127: 4 Like *a* in the hands of a warrior
144: 6 shoot your *a* and rout them.
Pr 26: 18 firebrands or deadly *a*
Isa 5: 28 Their *a* are sharp,
Jer 50: 9 Their *a* will be like skilled warriors
50: 14 Shoot at her! Spare no *a*,
51: 11 "Sharpen the *a*,
La 3: 12 and made me the target for his *a*.
3: 13 with *a* from his quiver.
Eze 5: 16 and destructive *a* of famine,
21: 21 lots with *a*, he will consult his idols,
39: 3 make your *a* drop from your right
39: 9 the bows and *a*, the war clubs
Hab 3: 9 you called for many *a*.
3: 11 at the glint of your flying *a*,
Eph 6: 16 you can extinguish all the flaming *a*

ARSENAL

Jer 50: 25 The LORD has opened his *a*

ART (ARTISANS ARTISTIC ARTS)

2Ch 2: 7 experienced in the *a* of engraving,

ARTAXERXES

Ezr 4: 7 And in the days of *A* king of Persia,
4: 7 of his associates wrote a letter to *A*.
4: 8 against Jerusalem to *A* the king
4: 11 To King *A*, From your servants,
4: 23 letter of King *A* was read to Rehum
6: 14 Darius and *A*, kings of Persia.
7: 1 during the reign of *A* king of Persia,
7: 7 in the seventh year of King *A*.
7: 11 copy of the letter King *A* had given
7: 12 *A*, king of kings, To Ezra the priest,
7: 21 King *A*, order all the treasurers
8: 1 during the reign of King *A*:
Ne 2: 1 in the twentieth year of King *A*,
5: 14 from the twentieth year of King *A*,
13: 6 in the thirty-second year of *A* king

ARTEMAS

Tit 3: 12 as I send *A* or Tychicus to you,

ARTEMIS

Ac 19: 24 who made silver shrines of *A*,
19: 27 the great goddess *A* will be
19: 28 "Great is *A* of the Ephesians!"
19: 34 "Great is *A* of the Ephesians!"
19: 35 of the temple of the great *A*

ARTIFICIAL

Ne 3: 16 as the *a* pool and the House

ARTISANS (ART)

2Ki 24: 14 and all the craftsmen and *a*—
24: 16 and a thousand craftsmen and *a*.
Jer 24: 1 and the *a* of Judah were carried
29: 2 and the *a* had gone into exile

ARTISTIC (ART)

Ex 31: 4 to make *a* designs for work in gold,
35: 32 to make *a* designs for work in gold,
35: 33 in all kinds of *a* craftsmanship.

ARTS (ART)

Ex 7: 11 the same things by their secret *a*:
7: 22 the same things by their secret *a*,
8: 7 the same things by their secret *a*;
8: 18 to produce gnats by their secret *a*,
Rev 9: 21 their magic *a*, their sexual
21: 8 those who practice magic *a*,
22: 15 those who practice magic *a*,

ARUBBOTH

1Ki 4: 10 in *A* (Socoh and all the land

ARUMAH

Jdg 9: 41 Abimelech stayed in *A*,

ARVAD (ARVADITES)

Eze 27: 8 *A* were your oarsmen;
27: 11 Men of *A* and Helech

ARVADITES (ARVAD)

Ge 10: 18 Hivites, Arkites, Sinites, *A*,
1Ch 1: 16 Hivites, Arkites, Sinites, *A*,

ARZA

1Ki 16: 9 getting drunk in the home of *A*,

ASA (ASA'S)

1Ki 15: 8 And *A* his son succeeded him
15: 9 of Israel, *A* became king of Judah,

1Ki 15: 11 *A* did what was right in the eyes
15: 13 *A* cut the pole down and burned it
15: 16 There was war between *A*
15: 17 the territory of *A* king of Judah.
15: 18 *A* then took all the silver
15: 20 Ben-Hadad agreed with King *A*
15: 22 King *A* issued an order to all Judah
15: 22 With them King *A* built up Geba
15: 24 Then *A* rested with his fathers
15: 25 year of *A* king of Judah,
15: 28 in the third year of *A* king of Judah
15: 32 There was war between *A*
15: 33 In the third year of *A* king of Judah
16: 8 year of *A* king of Judah,
16: 10 year of *A* king of Judah.
16: 15 year of *A* king of Judah.
16: 23 year of *A* king of Judah,
16: 29 year of *A* king of Judah,
22: 41 Jehoshaphat son of *A* became king
22: 43 walked in the ways of his father *A*
22: 46 even after the reign of his father *A*.
1Ch 3: 10 *A* his son, Jehoshaphat his son,
9: 16 and Berekiah son of *A*, the son
2Ch 14: 1 *A* his son succeeded him as king,
14: 2 *A* did what was good and right
14: 8 *A* had an army of three hundred
14: 10 *A* went out to meet him,
14: 11 *A* called to the LORD his God
14: 12 struck down the Cushites before *A*
14: 13 and *A* and his army pursued them
15: 2 He went out to meet *A*
15: 2 *A* and all Judah and Benjamin.
15: 8 When *A* heard these words
15: 16 King *A* also deposed his
15: 16 *A* cut the pole down, broke it up
16: 1 the territory of *A* king of Judah.
16: 2 *A* then took the silver and gold out
16: 4 Ben-Hadad agreed with King *A*
16: 6 Then King *A* brought all the men
16: 7 came to *A* king of Judah
16: 10 *A* was angry with the seer
16: 10 the same time *A* brutally oppressed
16: 12 year of his reign *A* was afflicted
16: 13 year of his reign *A* died
17: 2 that his father *A* had captured.
20: 32 walked in the ways of his father *A*
21: 12 or of *A* king of Judah.
Jer 41: 9 was the one King *A* had made
Mt 1: 7 Abijah the father of *A*, *A* the father

ASA'S (ASA)

1Ki 15: 14 *A* heart was fully committed
15: 23 for all the other events of *A* reign,
2Ch 15: 10 of the fifteenth year of *A* reign.
15: 17 *A* heart was fully committed
15: 19 until the thirty-fifth year of *A* reign
16: 1 year of *A* reign Baasha king
16: 11 The events of *A* reign,

ASAHEL (ASAHEL'S)

2Sa 2: 18 Now *A* was as fleet-footed
2: 18 were there: Joab, Abishai and *A*.
2: 20 "Is that you, *A*?" "It is," he
2: 21 But *A* would not stop chasing him.
2: 22 Abner warned *A*, "Stop chasing
2: 23 But *A* refused to give up the pursuit
2: 23 to the place where *A* had fallen
2: 30 Besides *A*, nineteen
2: 32 They took *A* and buried him
3: 27 avenge the blood of his brother *A*,
3: 30 he had killed their brother *A*
23: 24 Among the Thirty were: *A*
1Ch 2: 16 sons were Abishai, Joab and *A*.
11: 26 mighty men were: *A* the brother
27: 7 was *A* the brother of Joab;
2Ch 17: 8 Zebadiah, *A*, Shemiramoth,
31: 13 Azaziah, Nahath, *A*, Jerimoth,
Ezr 10: 15 Only Jonathan son of *A*

ASAHEL'S (ASAHEL)

2Sa 2: 23 butt of his spear into *A* stomach,

ASAIAH

2Ki 22: 12 and *A* the king's attendant:
22: 14 *A* went to speak to the prophetess
1Ch 4: 36 Jaakobah, Jeshohaiah, *A*, Adiel,
6: 30 Haggiah his son and *A* his son.
9: 5 *A* the firstborn and his sons.
1Ch 15: 6 *A* the leader and 220 relatives;
15: 11 and Uriel, *A*, Joel, Shemaiah,
2Ch 34: 20 and *A* the king's attendant:

ASAPH (ASAPH'S)

2Ki 18: 18 son of *A* the recorder went out
18: 37 Joah son of *A* the recorder went
1Ch 6: 39 and Heman's associate *A*,
6: 39 at his right hand: *A* son of Berekiah
9: 15 the son of *A*; Obadiah son
15: 17 from his brothers, *A* son
15: 19 *A* and Ethan were
16: 5 *A* was to sound the cymbals,
16: 5 the God of Israel: *A* was the chief,
16: 7 day David first committed to *A*
16: 37 David left *A* and his associates
25: 1 set apart some of the sons of *A*,
25: 2 From the sons of *A*: Zaccur, Joseph
25: 2 The sons of *A* were
25: 2 were under the supervision of *A*,
25: 6 *A*, Jeduthun and Heman were
25: 9 which was for *A*, fell to Joseph,
26: 1 son of Kore, one of the sons of *A*.
2Ch 5: 12 Levites who were musicians—*A*,
20: 14 a Levite and descendant of *A*,
29: 13 from the descendants of *A*,
29: 30 words of David and of *A* the seer.
35: 15 *A*, Heman and Jeduthun the king's
35: 15 musicians, the descendants of *A*,
Ezr 2: 41 of *A* 128
3: 10 (the sons of *A*) with cymbals,
Ne 2: 8 And may I have a letter to *A*,
7: 44 of *A* 148
11: 17 the son of Zabdi, the son of *A*,
12: 35 the son of *A*, and his associates—
12: 46 in the days of David and *A*,
Isa 36: 3 son of *A* the recorder went out
36: 22 Joah son of *A* the recorder went

ASAPH'S (ASAPH)

Ne 11: 22 Uzzi was one of *A* descendants,

ASAREL

1Ch 4: 16 Ziph, Ziphah, Tiria and *A*.

ASARELAH

1Ch 25: 2 Zaccur, Joseph, Nethaniah and *A*.

ASCEND (ASCENDED ASCENDING ASCENT)

Dt 30: 12 "Who will *a* into heaven to get it
Ps 24: 3 Who may *a* the hill of the LORD?
Isa 14: 13 "I will *a* to heaven;
14: 14 I will *a* above the tops of the clouds
Jn 6: 62 of Man *a* to where he was before!
Ac 2: 34 For David did not *a* to heaven,
Ro 10: 6 'Who will *a* into heaven?' "

ASCENDED (ASCEND)

Jdg 13: 20 angel of the LORD *a* in the flame.
2Ki 19: 23 I have *a* the heights
Ps 47: 5 God has *a* amid shouts of joy,
68: 18 When you *a* on high,
Isa 37: 24 I have *a* the heights
Eph 4: 8 "When he *a* on high,
4: 9 (What does "he *a*" mean
4: 10 is the very one who *a* higher

ASCENDING (ASCEND)

Ge 28: 12 and the angels of God were *a*
Eze 41: 7 the temple was built in *a* stages,
Jn 1: 51 and the angels of God *a*

ASCENT (ASCEND)

Ne 3: 19 from a point facing the *a*
12: 37 City of David on the *a* to the wall

ASCRIBE

1Ch 16: 28 *A* to the LORD, O families
16: 28 *a* to the LORD glory and strength,
16: 29 *a* to the LORD the glory due his
Job 36: 3 I will *a* justice to my Maker.
Ps 29: 1 *A* to the LORD, O mighty ones,
29: 1 *a* to the LORD glory and strength.
29: 2 *A* to the LORD the glory due his
96: 7 *A* to the LORD, O families
96: 7 *a* to the LORD glory and strength.
96: 8 *A* to the LORD the glory due his

ASENATH

Ge 41: 45 gave him *A* daughter of Potiphera,
41: 50 born to Joseph by *A* daughter
46: 20 born to Joseph by *A* daughter

ASH (ASHES)

Lev 4: 12 burn it in a wood fire on the *a* heap.
1Sa 2: 8 and lifts the needy from the *a* heap;
Ps 113: 7 and lifts the needy from the *a* heap;
La 4: 5 now lie on *a* heaps.

ASHAMED (SHAME)

2Sa 19: 3 steal in who are *a* when they flee
2Ki 2: 17 until he was too *a* to refuse.
8: 11 with a fixed gaze until Hazael felt *a*
2Ch 30: 15 the Levites were *a* and consecrated
Ezr 8: 22 I was *a* to ask the king for soldiers
9: 6 I am too *a* and disgraced
Ps 6: 10 May all my enemies be *a*
83: 17 May they ever be *a* and dismayed;
Isa 1: 29 will be *a* because of the sacred
23: 4 Be *a*, O Sidon, and you, O fortress
24: 23 moon will be abashed, the sun *a*;
29: 22 "No longer will Jacob be *a*;
33: 9 Lebanon is *a* and withers;
41: 11 will surely be *a* and disgraced;
Jer 6: 15 Are they *a* of their loathsome
8: 12 Are they *a* of their loathsome
22: 22 Then you will be *a* and disgraced
31: 19 I was *a* and humiliated
48: 13 Then Moab will be *a* of Chemosh,
48: 13 as the house of Israel was *a*
50: 12 your mother will be greatly *a*;
Eze 16: 52 be *a* and bear your disgrace,
16: 54 and be *a* of all you have done
16: 61 be *a* when you receive your sisters,
16: 63 you will remember and be *a*
36: 32 Be *a* and disgraced
43: 10 that they may be *a* of their sins.
43: 11 if they are *a* of all they have done,
Hos 10: 6 Israel will be *a* of its wooden idols.
Mic 3: 7 The seers will be *a*
7: 16 Nations will see and be *a*,
Zec 13: 4 On that day every prophet will be *a*
Mk 8: 38 If anyone is *a* of me and my words
8: 38 the Son of Man will be *a* of him
Lk 9: 26 If anyone is *a* of me and my words,
9: 26 the Son of Man will be *a* of him
16: 3 enough to dig, and I'm *a* to beg—
Ro 1: 16 I am not *a* of the gospel,
6: 21 from the things you are now *a* of?
2Co 9: 4 would be *a* of having been
10: 8 you down, I will not be *a* of it.
Php 1: 20 and hope that I will in no way be *a*,
2Th 3: 14 in order that he may feel *a*.
2Ti 1: 8 So do not be *a* to testify about our
1: 8 to testify about our Lord, or *a*
1: 12 Yet I am not *a*, because I know
1: 16 and was not *a* of my chains.
2: 15 who does not need to be *a*
Tit 2: 8 those who oppose you may be *a*
Heb 2: 11 Jesus is not *a* to call them brothers.
11: 16 Therefore God is not *a*
1Pe 3: 16 in Christ may be *a* of their slander.
4: 16 do not be *a*, but praise God that

ASHAN

Jos 15: 42 Libnah, Ether, *A*, Iphtah, Ashnah,
19: 7 Ain, Rimmon, Ether and *A*—
1Ch 4: 32 Token and *A*— five towns—
6: 59 Eshtemoa, Hilen, Debir, *A*,

ASHBEL (ASHBELITE)

Ge 46: 21 Bela, Beker, *A*, Gera, Naaman, Ehi
Nu 26: 38 through *A*, the Ashbelite clan;
1Ch 8: 1 *A* the second son, Aharah the third

ASHBELITE (ASHBEL)

Nu 26: 38 through Ashbel, the *A* clan;

ASHDOD

Jos 11: 22 Gath and *A* did any survive.
13: 3 *A*, Ashkelon, Gath and Ekron—
15: 46 all that were in the vicinity of *A*,
15: 47 together with their villages; *A*,
1Sa 5: 1 they took it from Ebenezer to *A*.
5: 3 When the people of *A* rose
5: 5 temple at *A* step on the threshold.

1Sa 5: 6 heavy upon the people of *A*
5: 7 men of *A* saw what was happening,
6: 17 one each for *A*, Gaza, Ashkelon,
2Ch 26: 6 He then rebuilt towns near *A*
26: 6 the walls of Gath, Jabneh and *A*.
Ne 4: 7 the men of *A* heard that the repairs
13: 23 who had married women from *A*,
13: 24 children spoke the language of *A*
Isa 20: 1 came to *A* and attacked
Jer 25: 20 and the people left at *A*); Edom,
Am 1: 8 I will destroy the king of *A*
3: 9 Proclaim to the fortresses of *A*
Zep 2: 4 At midday *A* will be emptied
Zec 9: 6 Foreigners will occupy *A*,

ASHER (ASHER'S)

Ge 30: 13 So she named him *A*.
35: 26 maidservant Zilpah: Gad and *A*.
46: 17 The sons of *A*: Imnah, Ishvah,
Ex 1: 4 Dan and Naphtali; Gad and *A*.
Nu 1: 13 from *A*, Pagiel son of Ocran;
1: 40 From the descendants of *A*:
1: 41 from the tribe of *A* was 41,500.
2: 27 The tribe of *A* will camp next
2: 27 of the people of *A* is Pagiel son
7: 72 the leader of the people of *A*,
10: 26 over the division of the tribe of *A*,
13: 13 from the tribe of *A*, Sethur son
26: 44 The descendants of *A*
26: 46 (*A* had a daughter named Serah.)
26: 47 These were the clans of *A*;
34: 27 the leader from the tribe of *A*;
Dt 27: 13 Reuben, Gad, *A*, Zebulun,
33: 24 About *A* he said:
33: 24 "Most blessed of sons is *A*;
Jos 17: 7 from *A* to Micmethath east
17: 10 and bordered *A* on the north
17: 11 Within Issachar and *A*, Manasseh
19: 24 fifth lot came out for the tribe of *A*,
19: 31 the inheritance of the tribe of *A*,
19: 34 *A* on the west and the Jordan
21: 6 *A*, Naphtali and the half-tribe
21: 30 from the tribe of *A*, Mishal, Abdon,
Jdg 1: 31 Nor did *A* drive out those living
1: 32 of this the people of *A* lived
5: 17 *A* remained on the seacoast
6: 35 and also into *A*, Zebulun
7: 23 *A* and all Manasseh were called out
1Ki 4: 16 Baana son of Hushai—in *A*
1Ch 2: 2 Benjamin, Naphtali, Gad and *A*.
6: 62 towns from the tribes of Issachar, *A*
6: 74 tribe of *A* they received Mashal,
7: 30 The sons of *A*: Imnah, Ishvah,
7: 40 All these were descendants of *A*—
12: 36 of *A*, experienced soldiers prepared
2Ch 30: 11 Nevertheless, some men of *A*,
Eze 48: 2 "*A* will have one portion; it will
48: 3 the territory of *A* from east to west.
48: 34 the gate of *A* and the gate
Lk 2: 36 of Phanuel, of the tribe of *A*.
Rev 7: 6 from the tribe of *A* 12,000,

ASHER'S (ASHER)

Ge 49: 20 "*A* food will be rich;

ASHERAH (ASHERAHS)

Ex 34: 13 and cut down their *A* poles.
Dt 7: 5 cut down their *A* poles
12: 3 and burn their *A* poles in the fire;
16: 21 Do not set up any wooden *A* pole
Jdg 6: 25 and cut down the *A* pole beside it.
6: 26 the wood of the *A* pole that you cut
6: 28 with the *A* pole beside it cut down
6: 30 and cut down the *A* pole beside it."
1Ki 14: 15 LORD to anger by making *A* poles.
14: 23 and *A* poles on every high hill
15: 13 she had made a repulsive *A* pole.
16: 33 Ahab also made an *A* pole
18: 19 the four hundred prophets of *A*,
2Ki 13: 6 Also, the *A* pole remained standing
17: 10 and *A* poles on every high hill
17: 16 the shape of calves, and an *A* pole.
18: 4 and cut down the *A* poles.
21: 3 altars to Baal and made an *A* pole,
21: 7 He took the carved *A* pole he had
23: 4 and *A* and all the starry hosts.
23: 6 He took the *A* pole from the temple
23: 7 where women did weaving for *A*.
2Ki 23: 14 cut down the *A* poles and covered
23: 15 and burned the *A* pole also.
2Ch 14: 3 and cut down the *A* poles.
15: 16 she had made a repulsive *A* pole.
17: 6 and the *A* poles from Judah.
19: 3 you have rid the land of the *A* poles
24: 18 and worshiped *A* poles and idols.
31: 1 and cut down the *A* poles.
33: 3 to the Baals and made *A* poles.
33: 19 and set up *A* poles and idols
34: 3 *A* poles, carved idols and cast
34: 4 and smashed the *A* poles, the idols
34: 7 down the altars and the *A* poles
Isa 17: 8 will have no regard for the *A* poles
27: 9 no *A* poles or incense altars
Jer 17: 2 their altars and *A* poles
Mic 5: 14 from among you your *A* poles

ASHERAHS (ASHERAH)

Jdg 3: 7 and served the Baals and the *A*.

ASHES (ASH)

Ge 18: 27 though I am nothing but dust and *a*
Ex 27: 3 its pots to remove the *a*,
Lev 1: 16 side of the altar, where the *a* are.
4: 12 clean, where the *a* are thrown,
6: 10 and shall remove the *a*
6: 11 and carry the *a* outside the camp
Nu 4: 13 to remove the *a* from the bronze
19: 9 who is clean shall gather up the *a*
19: 10 The man who gathers up the *a*
19: 17 put some *a* from the burned
2Sa 13: 19 Tamar put *a* on her head
1Ki 13: 3 and the *a* on it will be poured out."
13: 5 and its *a* poured out according
2Ki 23: 4 of the Kidron Valley and took the *a*
Est 4: 1 put on sackcloth and *a*,
4: 3 Many lay on sackcloth and *a*.
Job 2: 8 with it as he sat among the *a*.
13: 12 Your maxims are proverbs of *a*;
30: 19 and I am reduced to dust and *a*.
42: 6 and repent in dust and *a*."
Ps 102: 9 For I eat *a* as my food
147: 16 and scatters the frost like *a*.
Isa 44: 20 on *a*, a deluded heart misleads him;
58: 5 and for lying on sackcloth and *a*?
61: 3 instead of *a*,
Jer 6: 26 and roll in *a*;
31: 40 dead bodies and *a* are thrown,
Eze 27: 30 and roll in *a*.
28: 18 I reduced you to *a* on the ground
Da 9: 3 in fasting, and in sackcloth and *a*.
Mal 4: 3 they will be *a* under the soles
Mt 11: 21 ago in sackcloth and *a*.
Lk 10: 13 sitting in sackcloth and *a*.
Heb 9: 13 and the *a* of a heifer sprinkled
2Pe 2: 6 Gomorrah by burning them to *a*,

ASHHUR

1Ch 2: 24 of Hezron bore him *A* the father
4: 5 *A* the father of Tekoa had two

ASHIMA

2Ki 17: 30 and the men from Hamath made *A*;

ASHKELON

Jos 13: 3 Ashdod, *A*, Gath and Ekron—
Jdg 1: 18 also took Gaza, *A* and Ekron—
14: 19 down to *A*, struck down thirty
1Sa 6: 17 Gaza, *A*, Gath and Ekron
2Sa 1: 20 proclaim it not in the streets of *A*,
Jer 25: 20 kings of the Philistines (those of *A*,
47: 5 *A* will be silenced.
47: 7 it to attack *A* and the seacoast?"
Am 1: 8 the one who holds the scepter in *A*.
Zep 2: 4 and *A* left in ruins.
2: 7 down in the houses of *A*.
Zec 9: 5 *A* will see it and fear;
9: 5 and *A* will be deserted.

ASHKENAZ

Ge 10: 3 *A*, Riphath and Togarmah.
1Ch 1: 6 *A*, Riphath and Togarmah.
Jer 51: 27 Ararat, Minni and *A*.

ASHNAH

Jos 15: 33 Eshtaol, Zorah, *A*, Zanoah,
15: 43 Ashan, Iphtah, *A*, Nezib, Keilah,

ASHORE (SHORE)

Lk 8: 27 When Jesus stepped *a*, he was met
Jn 21: 11 aboard and dragged the net *a*.

ASHPENAZ

Da 1: 3 Then the king ordered *A*, chief

ASHTAROTH

Dt 1: 4 king of Bashan, who reigned in *A*.
Jos 9: 10 king of Bashan, who reigned in *A*.
12: 4 who reigned in *A* and Edrei.
13: 12 who had reigned in *A* and Edrei
13: 31 *A* and Edrei (the royal cities of Og
1Ch 6: 71 Golan in Bashan and also *A*,

ASHTERATHITE

1Ch 11: 44 the Mithnite, Uzzia the *A*,

ASHTEROTH KARNAIM

Ge 14: 5 and defeated the Rephaites in *A*,

ASHTORETH (ASHTORETHS)

1Ki 11: 5 He followed *A* the goddess
11: 33 and worshiped *A* the goddess
2Ki 23: 13 built for *A* the vile goddess

ASHTORETHS (ASHTORETH)

Jdg 2: 13 and served Baal and the *A*.
10: 6 They served the Baals and the *A*,
1Sa 7: 3 and the *A* and commit yourselves
7: 4 put away their Baals and *A*,
12: 10 and served the Baals and the *A*.
31: 10 armor in the temple of the *A*

ASHURBANIPAL

Ezr 4: 10 and honorable *A* deported

ASHURI

2Sa 2: 9 He made him king over Gilead, *A*

ASHVATH

1Ch 7: 33 of Japhlet: Pasach, Bimhal and *A*.

ASIA

Ac 2: 9 Pontus and *A*, Phrygia
6: 9 as the provinces of Cilicia and *A*.
16: 6 the word in the province of *A*.
19: 10 in the province of *A* heard the word
19: 22 in the province of *A* a little longer.
19: 26 the whole province of *A*.
19: 27 throughout the province of *A*
20: 4 from the province of *A* Tychicus
20: 16 time in the province of *A*,
20: 18 came into the province of *A*.
21: 27 from the province of *A* saw Paul
24: 19 Jews from the province of *A*,
27: 2 along the coast of the province of *A*
Ro 16: 5 to Christ in the province of *A*.
1Co 16: 19 province of *A* send you greetings.
2Co 1: 8 suffered in the province of *A*.
2Ti 1: 15 the province of *A* has deserted me,
1Pe 1: 1 Cappadocia, *A* and Bithynia,
Rev 1: 4 churches in the province of *A*:

ASIEL

1Ch 4: 35 the son of *A*, also Elioenai,

ASLEEP (SLEEP)

Ge 41: 5 He fell *a* again and had a second
Jdg 4: 21 quietly to him while he lay fast *a*,
1Sa 26: 7 lying *a* inside the camp
1Ki 3: 20 side while I your servant was *a*.
19: 5 lay down under the tree and fell *a*.
Job 3: 13 I would be *a* and at rest
Mt 9: 24 The girl is not dead but *a*."
25: 5 they all became drowsy and fell *a*.
28: 13 stole him away while we were *a*.'
Mk 5: 39 The child is not dead but *a*."
14: 37 he said to Peter, "are you *a*?
Lk 8: 23 As they sailed, he fell *a*.
8: 52 "She is not dead but *a*."
22: 45 he found them *a*, exhausted
Jn 11: 11 "Our friend Lazarus has fallen *a*;
Ac 7: 60 When he had said this, he fell *a*.
13: 36 he fell *a*; he was buried
20: 9 When he was sound *a*, he fell
1Co 11: 30 and a number of you have fallen *a*.
15: 6 though some have fallen *a*.

1Co 15: 18 who have fallen *a* in Christ are lost.
15: 20 of those who have fallen *a*.
1Th 4: 13 be ignorant about those who fall *a*,
4: 14 with Jesus those who have fallen *a*
4: 15 precede those who have fallen *a*.
5: 6 who are *a*, but let us be alert
5: 10 whether we are awake or *a*,

ASNAH

Ezr 2: 50 Paseah, Besai, *A*, Meunim,

ASPATHA

Est 9: 7 Dalphon, *A*, Poratha, Adalia,

ASRIEL (ASRIELITE)

Nu 26: 31 through *A*, the Asrielite clan;
Jos 17: 2 *A*, Shechem, Hepher and Shemida.
1Ch 7: 14 *A* was his descendant

ASRIELITE (ASRIEL)

Nu 26: 31 through Asriel, the *A* clan;

ASSAIL (ASSAILANT ASSAILS)

Ps 17: 9 wings from the wicked who *a* me,
55: 4 the terrors of death *a* me.

ASSAILANT (ASSAIL)

Dt 25: 11 to rescue her husband from his *a*,

ASSAILS (ASSAIL)

Job 16: 9 God *a* me and tears me in his anger

ASSASSINATE (ASSASSINATED ASSASSINATION ASSASSINS)

Est 2: 21 and conspired to *a* King Xerxes.
6: 2 had conspired to *a* King Xerxes.

ASSASSINATED (ASSASSINATE)

2Ki 12: 20 and *a* him at Beth Millo,
15: 10 *a* him and succeeded him as king.
15: 14 *a* him and succeeded him as king.
15: 25 he *a* Pekahiah, along with Argob
15: 30 He attacked and *a* him,
21: 23 and *a* the king in his palace.
25: 25 came with ten men and *a* Gedaliah
2Ch 33: 24 against him and *a* him in his palace.
Jer 41: 16 after he had *a* Gedaliah son

ASSASSINATION (ASSASSINATE)

Jer 41: 4 The day after Gedaliah's *a*,

ASSASSINS (ASSASSINATE)

2Ki 14: 6 Yet he did not put the sons of the *a*

ASSAULT (ASSAULTS)

Dt 21: 5 to decide all cases of dispute and *a*.
Ps 62: 3 How long will you *a* a man?

ASSAULTS (ASSAULT)

Dt 17: 8 whether bloodshed, lawsuits or *a*—
19: 11 *a* and kills him, and then flees
Job 28: 9 Man's hand *a* the flinty rock

ASSEMBLE (ASSEMBLED ASSEMBLIES ASSEMBLING ASSEMBLY)

Ge 49: 2 "*A* and listen, sons of Jacob;
Ex 3: 16 *a* the elders of Israel and say
Nu 8: 9 *a* the whole Israelite community.
10: 3 the whole community is to *a*
10: 4 of Israel—are to *a* before you.
Dt 4: 10 "*A* the people before me
31: 12 *A* the people—men, women
31: 28 *A* before me all the elders
Jdg 21: 5 failed to *a* before the LORD
21: 5 failed to *a* before the LORD?"
21: 8 failed to *a* before the LORD
1Sa 7: 5 "*A* all Israel at Mizpah
2Sa 3: 21 *a* all Israel for my lord the king,
1Ch 22: 2 orders to *a* the aliens living
28: 1 officials of Israel to *a* at Jerusalem:
Ezr 10: 7 for all the exiles to *a* in Jerusalem.
Ne 7: 5 it into my heart to *a* the nobles,
Est 8: 11 the Jews in every city the right to *a*
Ps 47: 9 The nobles of the nations *a*
102: 22 *a* to worship the LORD.
Isa 4: 5 and over those who *a* there a cloud
11: 12 he will *a* the scattered people
43: 9 and the peoples *a*.
45: 20 *a*, you fugitives from the nations.
Isa 60: 4 All *a* and come to you;
Jer 49: 14 "*A* yourselves to attack it!
Eze 39: 17 '*A* and come together from all
Da 11: 10 prepare for war and *a* a great army,
Joel 3: 11 and *a* there.
Am 3: 9 "*A* yourselves on the mountains
Mic 4: 6 I will *a* the exiles
Zep 3: 8 I have decided to *a* the nations,
Ac 22: 30 and all the Sanhedrin to *a*.

ASSEMBLED (ASSEMBLE)

Ex 35: 1 Moses *a* the whole Israelite
Dt 33: 5 when the leaders of the people *a*,
33: 21 When the heads of the people *a*,
Jos 24: 1 Joshua *a* all the tribes of Israel
Jdg 9: 47 heard that they had *a* there,
10: 17 the Israelites *a* and camped
16: 23 Now the rulers of the Philistines *a*
20: 1 and *a* before the LORD in Mizpah.
1Sa 7: 6 When they had *a* at Mizpah,
7: 7 Philistines heard that Israel had *a*
13: 5 The Philistines *a* to fight Israel,
14: 20 all his men *a* and went to the battle.
17: 1 for war and *a* at Socoh in Judah.
17: 2 Saul and the Israelites *a*
25: 1 all Israel *a* and mourned for him;
28: 4 The Philistines *a* and came
2Sa 2: 30 pursuing Abner and *a* all his men.
1Ki 18: 20 *a* the prophets on Mount Carmel.
20: 15 Then he *a* the rest of the Israelites,
1Ch 13: 5 So David *a* all the Israelites,
15: 3 David *a* all Israel in Jerusalem
2Ch 12: 5 of Judah who had *a* in Jerusalem
15: 9 Then he *a* all Judah and Benjamin
15: 10 They *a* at Jerusalem
20: 26 On the fourth day they *a*
29: 4 *a* them in the square
29: 15 When they had *a* their brothers
30: 3 the people had not *a* in Jerusalem.
30: 13 crowd of people *a* in Jerusalem
30: 25 and all who had *a* from Israel,
32: 4 A large force of men *a*,
32: 6 *a* them before him in the square
Ezr 3: 1 the people *a* as one man
8: 15 I *a* them at the canal that flows
Ne 5: 16 All my men were *a* there
8: 1 all the people *a* as one man
Est 2: 19 the virgins were *a* a second time,
9: 2 The Jews *a* in their cities
9: 16 also *a* to protect themselves
9: 18 had *a* on the thirteenth
Ps 7: 7 Let the *a* peoples gather
Da 3: 3 all the other provincial officials *a*
Mt 26: 3 elders of the people *a* in the palace
26: 57 of the law and the elders had *a*.
Lk 1: 10 all the *a* worshipers were praying
24: 33 *a* together and saying, "It is true!
Ac 28: 17 When they had *a*, Paul said
1Co 5: 4 When you are *a* in the name

ASSEMBLIES (ASSEMBLE)

Lev 23: 2 are to proclaim as sacred *a*.
23: 4 the sacred *a* you are to proclaim
23: 37 as sacred *a* for bringing offerings
Isa 1: 13 I cannot bear your evil *a*.
Am 5: 21 I cannot stand your *a*.

ASSEMBLING (ASSEMBLE)

1Sa 13: 11 and that the Philistines were *a*

ASSEMBLY (ASSEMBLE)

Ge 49: 6 let me not join their *a*,
Ex 12: 16 On the first day hold a sacred *a*,
16: 3 to starve this entire *a* to death."
Lev 4: 14 the *a* must bring a young bull
8: 3 gather the entire *a* at the entrance
8: 4 and the *a* gathered at the entrance
8: 5 to the *a*, "This is what the LORD
9: 5 and the entire *a* came near
19: 2 "Speak to the entire *a* of Israel
23: 3 a Sabbath of rest, a day of sacred *a*.
23: 7 On the first day hold a sacred *a*
23: 8 on the seventh day hold a sacred *a*
23: 21 are to proclaim a sacred *a*
23: 24 a sacred *a* commemorated
23: 27 Hold a sacred *a* and deny
23: 35 The first day is a sacred *a*;
23: 36 It is the closing *a*; do no regular
Lev 23: 36 on the eighth day hold a sacred *a*
24: 14 and the entire *a* is to stone him.
24: 16 The entire *a* must stone him.
Nu 10: 7 To gather the *a*, blow the trumpets,
13: 26 to the whole *a* and showed them
14: 2 and the whole *a* said to them,
14: 5 whole Israelite *a* gathered there.
14: 7 and said to the entire Israelite *a*,
14: 10 whole *a* talked about stoning them.
15: 33 and Aaron and the whole *a*,
15: 35 The whole *a* must stone him
15: 36 So the *a* took him outside the camp
16: 3 yourselves above the LORD's *a*?"
16: 19 LORD appeared to the entire *a*.
16: 21 "Separate yourselves from this *a*
16: 22 with the entire *a* when only one
16: 24 "Say to the *a*, 'Move away
16: 26 He warned the *a*, "Move back
16: 42 when the *a* gathered in opposition
16: 45 "Get away from this *a*
16: 46 hurry to the *a* to make atonement
16: 47 and ran into the midst of the *a*.
20: 6 went from the *a* to the entrance
20: 8 Aaron gather the *a* together.
20: 10 and Aaron gathered the *a* together
25: 6 and the whole *a* of Israel
25: 7 the priest, saw this, he left the *a*,
27: 2 the leaders and the whole *a*,
27: 19 the entire *a* and commission him
27: 22 Eleazar the priest and the whole *a*.
28: 18 On the first day hold a sacred *a*
28: 25 On the seventh day hold a sacred *a*
28: 26 hold a sacred *a* and do no regular
29: 1 the seventh month hold a sacred *a*
29: 7 this seventh month hold a sacred *a*.
29: 12 hold a sacred *a* and do no regular
29: 35 " 'On the eighth day hold an *a*
31: 12 and the Israelite *a* at their camp
35: 12 before he stands trial before the *a*.
35: 24 the *a* must judge between him
35: 25 *a* must protect the one accused
Dt 5: 22 voice to your whole *a* there
9: 10 out of the fire, on the day of the *a*.
10: 4 out of the fire, on the day of the *a*.
16: 8 and on the seventh day hold an *a*
18: 16 on the day of the *a* when you said,
23: 1 or cutting may enter the *a*
23: 2 of his descendants may enter the *a*
23: 3 of his descendants may enter the *a*
23: 8 born to them may enter the *a*
31: 30 the hearing of the whole *a* of Israel:
33: 4 the possession of the *a* of Jacob.
Jos 8: 35 read to the whole *a* of Israel,
9: 15 and the leaders of the *a* ratified it
9: 18 The whole *a* grumbled
9: 18 leaders of the *a* had sworn an oath
18: 1 whole *a* of the Israelites gathered
20: 6 until he has stood trial before the *a*
20: 9 prior to standing trial before the *a*.
22: 12 the whole *a* of Israel gathered
22: 16 "The whole *a* of the LORD says:
Jdg 20: 2 in the *a* of the people of God,
21: 8 come to the camp for the *a*.
21: 10 the *a* sent twelve thousand fighting
21: 13 Then the *a* sent an offer of peace
21: 16 And the elders of the *a* said,
1Ki 8: 5 entire *a* of Israel that had gathered
8: 14 While the whole *a*
8: 22 in front of the whole *a* of Israel,
8: 55 and blessed the whole *a* of Israel
8: 65 and all Israel with him—a vast *a*,
12: 3 and the whole *a* of Israel went
12: 20 they sent and called him to the *a*
2Ki 10: 20 "Call an *a* in honor of Baal."
1Ch 13: 2 said to the whole *a* of Israel,
13: 4 The whole *a* agreed to do this,
28: 8 and of the *a* of the LORD,
29: 1 King David said to the whole *a*:
29: 10 in the presence of the whole *a*,
29: 20 Then David said to the whole *a*,
2Ch 1: 3 the whole *a* went to the high place
1: 5 and the *a* inquired of him there.
5: 6 entire *a* of Israel that had gathered
6: 3 While the whole *a*
6: 12 in front of the whole *a* of Israel
6: 13 down before the whole *a* of Israel
7: 8 and all Israel with him—a vast *a*,
7: 9 On the eighth day they held an *a*,

2Ch 20: 5 Jehoshaphat stood up in the *a*
20: 14 of Asaph, as he stood in the *a*.
23: 3 the whole *a* made a covenant
24: 6 and by the *a* of Israel for the Tent
28: 14 of the officials and all the *a*.
29: 23 brought before the king and the *a*,
29: 28 The whole *a* bowed in worship,
29: 31 So the *a* brought sacrifices
29: 32 burnt offerings the *a* brought was
30: 2 the whole *a* in Jerusalem decided
30: 4 both to the king and to the whole *a*.
30: 23 The whole *a* then agreed
30: 24 thousand sheep and goats for the *a*,
30: 25 The entire *a* of Judah rejoiced,
Ezr 10: 8 expelled from the *a* of the exiles.
10: 12 The whole *a* responded
10: 14 Let our officials act for the whole *a*
Ne 5: 13 At this the whole *a* said, "Amen,"
8: 2 brought the Law before the *a*,
8: 18 with the regulation, there was an *a*.
13: 1 should ever be admitted into the *a*
Job 30: 28 I stand up in the *a* and cry for help.
Ps 1: 5 nor sinners in the *a* of the righteous
22: 25 you comes my praise in the great *a*;
26: 5 I abhor the *a* of evildoers
26: 12 in the great *a* I will praise
35: 18 I will give you thanks in the great *a*
40: 9 righteousness in the great *a*;
40: 10 truth from the great *a*.
68: 26 praise the LORD in the *a* of Israel.
82: 1 God presides in the great *a*;
89: 5 in the *a* of the holy ones.
107: 32 in the *a* of the people
111: 1 council of the upright and in the *a*.
149: 1 his praise in the *a* of the saints.
Pr 5: 14 in the midst of the whole *a*."
24: 7 in the *a* at the gate he has nothing
26: 26 will be exposed in the *a*.
Isa 14: 13 enthroned on the mount of *a*,
Jer 26: 17 and said to the entire *a* of people,
44: 15 who were present—a large *a*—
La 1: 10 forbidden to enter your *a*.
Joel 1: 14 call a sacred *a*.
2: 15 call a sacred *a*.
2: 16 consecrate the *a*;
Mic 2: 5 in the *a* of the LORD
Lk 23: 1 Then the whole *a* rose
Ac 5: 21 the full *a* of the elders of Israel—
7: 38 He was in the *a* in the desert,
15: 12 The whole *a* became silent
19: 32 The *a* was in confusion: Some were
19: 39 it must be settled in a legal *a*.
19: 41 he had said this, he dismissed the *a*.
23: 7 Sadducees, and the *a* was divided.
Heb 12: 22 thousands of angels in joyful *a*,

ASSERTED (ASSERTING)

Lk 22: 59 About an hour later another *a*,

ASSERTING (ASSERTED)

Ac 24: 9 *a* that these things were true.

ASSESSMENTS

2Ki 23: 35 of the land according to their *a*.

ASSHUR (ASSHURITES)

Ge 2: 14 it runs along the east side of *A*
10: 22 Elam, *A*, Arphaxad, Lud and Aram
25: 18 of Egypt, as you go toward *A*.
Nu 24: 22 when *A* takes you captive."
24: 24 they will subdue *A* and Eber,
1Ch 1: 17 Elam, *A*, Arphaxad, Lud and Aram
Eze 27: 23 *A* and Kilmad traded with you.

ASSHURITES (ASSHUR)

Ge 25: 3 descendants of Dedan were the *A*,

ASSIGN (ASSIGNED ASSIGNMENT ASSIGNMENTS ASSIGNS REASSIGN)

Nu 4: 19 and *a* to each man his work
4: 27 You shall *a* to them as their
4: 32 *A* to each man the specific things
8: 26 are to *a* the responsibilities
34: 13 *A* this land by lot as an inheritance.
34: 17 are to *a* the land for you
34: 18 from each tribe to help *a* the land.
34: 29 commanded to *a* the inheritance
1Sa 8: 12 Some he will *a* to be commanders
Job 22: 24 and *a* your nuggets to the dust,
Mt 24: 51 *a* him a place with the hypocrites,
Lk 12: 46 *a* him a place with the unbelievers.

ASSIGNED (ASSIGN)

Ge 40: 4 of the guard *a* them to Joseph,
Nu 2: 9 All the men *a* to the camp of Judah
2: 16 All the men *a* to the camp
2: 24 All the men *a* to the camp
2: 31 All the men *a* to the camp
4: 49 each was *a* his work and told what
Jos 13: 8 of the LORD, had *a* it to them.
14: 2 Their inheritances were *a* by lot
19: 51 clans of Israel *a* by lot at Shiloh
21: 10 towns by name (these towns were *a*
24: 4 I *a* the hill country of Seir to Esau,
1Sa 15: 20 on the mission the LORD *a* me.
27: 5 let a place be *a* to me in one
29: 4 return to the place you *a* him.
1Ki 7: 14 and did all the work *a* to him.
14: 27 and *a* these to the commanders
2Ki 8: 6 Then he *a* an official to her case
1Ch 6: 48 Their fellow Levites were *a*
6: 54 as their territory (they were *a*
9: 22 The gatekeepers had been *a*
9: 29 Others were *a* to take care
26: 29 and his sons were *a* duties away
2Ch 2: 18 He *a* 70,000 of them to be carriers
12: 10 and *a* these to the commanders
23: 6 are to guard what the LORD has *a*
25: 5 *a* them according to their families
30: 22 seven days they ate their *a* portion
31: 2 Hezekiah *a* the priests
33: 8 of the Israelites leave the land I *a*
Ne 12: 31 *a* two large choirs to give thanks.
13: 10 also learned that the portions *a*
13: 30 *a* them duties, each to his own task.
Est 2: 9 He *a* to her seven maids selected
4: 5 one of the king's eunuchs *a*
Job 7: 3 nights of misery have been *a* to me.
Ps 16: 5 you have *a* me my portion
104: 8 to the place you *a* for them.
Isa 53: 9 He was *a* a grave with the wicked,
Eze 4: 5 I have *a* you the same number
4: 6 I have *a* you 40 days, a day
Da 1: 5 The king *a* them a daily amount
1: 10 who has *a* your food and drink.
Mk 13: 34 with his *a* task, and tells the one
Ac 22: 10 will be told all that you have been *a*
1Co 3: 5 as the Lord has *a* to each his task.
7: 17 place in life that the Lord *a* to him
2Co 10: 13 to the field God has *a* to us,

ASSIGNMENT (ASSIGN)

1Ch 23: 11 as one family with one *a*.

ASSIGNMENTS (ASSIGN)

2Ch 23: 18 to whom David had made *a*

ASSIGNS (ASSIGN)

Mic 2: 4 He *a* our fields to traitors.' "

ASSIR

Ex 6: 24 The sons of Korah were *A*,
1Ch 6: 22 *A* his son, Elkanah his son,
6: 23 Ebiasaph his son, *A* his son,
6: 37 the son of *A*, the son of Ebiasaph,

ASSIST (ASSISTANCE ASSISTANT ASSISTANTS ASSISTED)

Nu 1: 5 names of the men who are to *a* you:
3: 6 them to Aaron the priest to *a* him.
8: 26 They may *a* their brothers
18: 2 to join you and *a* you when you
2Ch 8: 14 and to *a* the priests according
13: 10 of Aaron, and the Levites *a* them.
Ezr 8: 20 had established to *a* the Levites.
Job 29: 12 fatherless who had none to *a* him.
Ro 15: 24 to have you *a* me on my journey

ASSISTANCE (ASSIST)

Ezr 8: 36 who then gave *a* to the people

ASSISTANT (ASSIST)

Dt 1: 38 But your *a*, Joshua son of Nun,
Ne 13: 13 the son of Mattaniah, their *a*,

ASSISTANTS (ASSIST)

Ne 5: 15 Their *a* also lorded it

ASSISTED (ASSIST)

2Ch 31: 15 and Shecaniah *a* him faithfully
Ezr 1: 6 All their neighbors *a* them
6: 22 so that he *a* them in the work

ASSOCIATE (ASSOCIATED ASSOCIATES)

Jos 23: 7 Do not *a* with these nations that
23: 12 with them and *a* with them,
1Ch 6: 39 of Israel; and Heman's *a* Asaph,
Pr 22: 24 do not *a* with one easily angered,
Jn 4: 9 (For Jews do not *a* with Samaritans
Ac 10: 28 law for a Jew to *a* with a Gentile
Ro 12: 16 but be willing to *a* with people
1Co 5: 9 to *a* with sexually immoral people
5: 11 am writing you that you must not *a*
2Th 3: 14 Do not *a* with him,

ASSOCIATED (ASSOCIATE)

Ne 13: 4 He was closely *a* with Tobiah,
Eze 37: 16 all the house of Israel *a* with him.'
37: 16 and the Israelites *a* with him.'
37: 19 of the Israelite tribes *a* with him,

ASSOCIATES (ASSOCIATE)

1Ch 6: 44 and from their *a*, the Merarites,
16: 7 his *a* this psalm of thanks
16: 37 his *a* before the ark of the covenant
16: 38 and his sixty-eight *a* to minister
Ezr 3: 2 and his *a* began to build the altar
4: 7 and the rest of his *a* wrote a letter
4: 9 together with the rest of their *a*—
4: 17 the rest of their *a* living in Samaria
4: 23 Shimshai the secretary and their *a*,
5: 3 Shethar-Bozenai and their *a* went
5: 6 and Shethar-Bozenai and their *a*,
6: 13 their *a* carried it out with diligence.
Ne 4: 2 and in the presence of his *a*
10: 10 and their *a*: Shebaniah, Hodiah,
11: 12 and their *a*, who carried on work
11: 13 his *a*, who were heads of families—
11: 14 and his *a*, who were brave warriors
11: 17 Bakbukiah, second among his *a*;
11: 19 Akkub, Talmon and their *a*,
12: 7 and their *a* in the days of Jeshua.
12: 8 who, together with his *a*,
12: 9 Bakbukiah and Unni, their *a*,
12: 24 Jeshua son of Kadmiel, and their *a*,
12: 36 and his *a*— Shemaiah, Azarel,
Job 34: 8 he *a* with wicked men.
Zec 3: 8 and your *a* seated before you,
Ac 5: 17 Then the high priest and all his *a*,
5: 21 the high priest and his *a* arrived,

ASSOS

Ac 20: 13 ahead to the ship and sailed for *A*,
20: 14 us at *A*, we took him aboard

ASSUME (ASSUMED)

Ne 10: 32 "We *a* the responsibility
10: 35 also *a* responsibility for bringing

ASSUMED (ASSUME)

1Sa 14: 47 After Saul had *a* rule over Israel,
Ac 21: 29 and *a* that Paul had brought him

ASSURANCE (ASSURE)

1Sa 17: 18 and bring back some *a* from them
Est 9: 30 words of good will and *a*—
Job 24: 22 become established, they have no *a*
1Ti 3: 13 great *a* in their faith in Christ Jesus.
Heb 10: 22 with a sincere heart in full *a* of faith
1Jn 5: 14 This is the *a* we have

ASSURE (ASSURANCE ASSURED ASSURES REASSURE REASSURED)

Lk 4: 25 I *a* you that there were many
Gal 1: 20 I *a* you before God that what I am

ASSURED (ASSURE)

Dt 9: 3 be *a* today that the LORD your
Jos 2: 14 lives for your lives!" the men *a* her.
1Sa 10: 16 "He *a* us that the donkeys had
Job 36: 4 Be *a* that my words are not false;
Jer 26: 15 Be *a*, however, that if you put me
Ac 2: 36 "Therefore let all Israel be *a* of this:

Col 4: 12 the will of God, mature and fully *a*.

ASSURES (ASSURE)

Jer 5: 24 who *a* us of the regular weeks

ASSYRIA (ASSYRIA'S ASSYRIAN ASSYRIANS)

Ge 10: 11 From that land he went to *A*,
2Ki 15: 19 Pul king of *A* invaded the land,
15: 20 So the king of *A* withdrew
15: 20 of silver to be given to the king of *A*
15: 29 Tiglath-Pileser king of *A* came
15: 29 and deported the people to *A*.
16: 7 to say to Tiglath-Pileser king of *A*,
16: 8 and sent it as a gift to the king of *A*.
16: 9 The king of *A* complied
16: 10 to meet Tiglath-Pileser king of *A*.
16: 18 in deference to the king of *A*.
17: 3 Shalmaneser king of *A* came up
17: 4 longer paid tribute to the king of *A*,
17: 4 of *A* discovered that Hoshea was
17: 5 king of *A* invaded the entire land,
17: 6 and deported the Israelites to *A*.
17: 6 the king of *A* captured Samaria
17: 23 from their homeland into exile in *A*
17: 24 The king of *A* brought people
17: 26 It was reported to the king of *A*:
17: 27 Then the king of *A* gave this order:
18: 7 He rebelled against the king of *A*
18: 9 Shalmaneser king of *A* marched
18: 11 The king of *A* deported Israel to *A*
18: 13 of *A* attacked all the fortified cities
18: 14 The king of *A* exacted
18: 14 to the king of *A* at Lachish:
18: 16 and gave it to the king of *A*.
18: 17 of *A* sent his supreme commander,
18: 19 what the great king, the king of *A*,
18: 23 of *A*: I will give you two thousand
18: 28 of *A*! This is what the king says:
18: 30 into the hand of the king of *A*.'
18: 31 This is what the king of *A* says:
18: 33 from the hand of the king of *A*?
19: 4 whom his master, the king of *A*,
19: 6 the king of *A* have blasphemed me.
19: 8 the king of *A* had left Lachish,
19: 10 handed over to the king of *A*.'
19: 11 of *A* have done to all the countries,
19: 20 concerning Sennacherib king of *A*.
19: 32 says concerning the king of *A*:
19: 36 Sennacherib king of *A* broke camp
20: 6 city from the hand of the king of *A*.
23: 29 to help the king of *A*.
1Ch 5: 6 king of *A* took into exile.
5: 26 Tiglath-Pileser king of *A*),
5: 26 the spirit of Pul king of *A* (that is,
2Ch 28: 16 sent to the king of *A* for help.
28: 20 Tiglath-Pileser king of *A* came
28: 21 presented them to the king of *A*,
30: 6 from the hand of the kings of *A*.
32: 1 Sennacherib king of *A* came
32: 4 "Why should the kings of *A* come
32: 7 because of the king of *A*
32: 9 when Sennacherib king of *A*
32: 10 is what Sennacherib king of *A* says:
32: 11 us from the hand of the king of *A*,'
32: 22 the hand of Sennacherib king of *A*
33: 11 army commanders of the king of *A*,
Ezr 4: 2 the time of Esarhaddon king of *A*,
6: 22 the attitude of the king of *A*,
Ne 9: 32 days of the kings of *A* until today.
Ps 83: 8 Even *A* has joined them
Isa 7: 17 he will bring the king of *A*."
7: 18 and for bees from the land of *A*.
7: 20 the king of *A*— to shave your head
8: 4 carried off by the king of *A*."
8: 7 the king of *A* with all his pomp.
10: 12 the king of *A* for the willful pride
11: 11 left of his people from *A*,
11: 16 that is left from *A*,
19: 23 to Egypt and the Egyptians to *A*.
19: 23 will be a highway from Egypt to *A*.
19: 24 and *A*, a blessing on the earth.
19: 25 my people, *A* my handiwork,
20: 1 king of *A*, came to Ashdod
20: 4 king of *A* will lead away stripped
20: 6 deliverance from the king of *A*!
27: 13 Those who were perishing in *A*
30: 31 of the LORD will shatter *A*;
31: 8 "*A* will fall by a sword that is not
36: 1 of *A* attacked all the fortified cities
36: 2 king of *A* sent his field commander
36: 4 what the great king, the king of *A*,
36: 8 of *A*: I will give you two thousand
36: 13 of *A*! This is what the king says:
36: 15 into the hand of the king of *A*.'
36: 16 This is what the king of *A* says:
36: 18 from the hand of the king of *A*?
37: 4 whom his master, the king of *A*,
37: 6 the king of *A* have blasphemed me.
37: 8 the king of *A* had left Lachish,
37: 10 handed over to the king of *A*.'
37: 11 of *A* have done to all the countries,
37: 21 concerning Sennacherib king of *A*,
37: 33 says concerning the king of *A*:
37: 37 Sennacherib king of *A* broke camp
38: 6 city from the hand of the king of *A*.
52: 4 lately, *A* has oppressed them.
Jer 2: 18 And why go to *A*
2: 36 as you were by *A*.
50: 17 was the king of *A*;
50: 18 as I punished the king of *A*.
La 5: 6 We submitted to Egypt and *A*
Eze 31: 3 Consider *A*, once a cedar
32: 22 "*A* is there with her whole army;
Hos 5: 13 then Ephraim turned to *A*,
7: 11 now turning to *A*.
8: 9 For they have gone up to *A*
9: 3 and eat unclean food in *A*.
10: 6 It will be carried to *A*
11: 5 and will not *A* rule over them
11: 11 like doves from *A*.
12: 1 He makes a treaty with *A*
14: 3 *A* cannot save us;
Mic 5: 6 of *A* with the sword,
7: 12 you from *A* and the cities of Egypt,
Na 3: 18 of *A*, your shepherds slumber;
Zep 2: 13 and destroy *A*,
Zec 10: 10 and gather them from *A*.

ASSYRIA'S (ASSYRIA)

Zec 10: 11 *A* pride will be brought down

ASSYRIAN (ASSYRIA)

2Ki 19: 17 that the *A* kings have laid waste
19: 35 thousand men in the *A* camp.
2Ch 32: 21 officers in the camp of the *A* king.
Isa 10: 5 Woe to the *A*, the rod of my anger,
14: 25 I will crush the *A* in my land;
37: 18 that the *A* kings have laid waste all
37: 36 thousand men in the *A* camp.
Mic 5: 5 When the *A* invades our land
5: 6 He will deliver us from the *A*

ASSYRIANS (ASSYRIA)

2Ki 18: 10 the end of three years the *A* took it.
Isa 10: 24 do not be afraid of the *A*,
19: 23 The *A* will go to Egypt
19: 23 and *A* will worship together.
23: 13 The *A* have made it
Eze 16: 28 in prostitution with the *A* too,
23: 5 the *A*— warriors clothed in blue,
23: 7 a prostitute to all the elite of the *A*
23: 9 the *A*, for whom she lusted.
23: 12 She too lusted after the *A*—
23: 23 and all the *A* with them, handsome

ASTIR

Ps 83: 2 See how your enemies are *a*,
Isa 14: 9 The grave below is all *a*

ASTONISHED (ASTONISHMENT)

Job 21: 5 Look at me and be *a*;
Mt 8: 10 was *a* and said to those following
12: 23 All the people were *a* and said,
19: 25 they were greatly *a* and asked,
22: 33 they were *a* at his teaching.
Mk 5: 42 At this they were completely *a*.
10: 32 and the disciples were *a*,
Lk 2: 48 his parents saw him, they were *a*.
5: 9 and all his companions were *a*
8: 56 Her parents were *a*, but he ordered
20: 26 *a* by his answer, they became silent
Jn 7: 21 I did one miracle, and you are all *a*.
Ac 3: 11 the people were *a* and came
4: 13 they were *a* and they took note
8: 13 *a* by the great signs and miracles he
9: 21 All those who heard him were *a*
10: 45 with Peter were *a* that the gift
12: 16 the door and saw him, they were *a*.
Gal 1: 6 I am *a* that you are
Rev 13: 3 The whole world was *a*
17: 6 When I saw her, I was greatly *a*.
17: 7 said to me: "Why are you *a*?
17: 8 the creation of the world will be *a*

ASTONISHING (ASTONISHMENT)

Da 12: 6 before these *a* things are fulfilled?"

ASTONISHMENT (ASTONISHED ASTONISHING)

Ge 43: 33 and they looked at each other in *a*.
Lk 1: 63 and to everyone's *a* he wrote,

ASTOUND (ASTOUNDED ASTOUNDING)

Isa 29: 14 once more I will *a* these people

ASTOUNDED (ASTOUND)

Ps 48: 5 they saw ⌞her⌟ and were *a*;

ASTOUNDING (ASTOUND)

La 1: 9 Her fall was *a*;
Da 8: 24 He will cause *a* devastation

ASTRAY

Nu 5: 12 'If a man's wife goes *a*
5: 19 have not gone *a* and become
5: 20 if you have gone *a* while married
5: 29 of jealousy when a woman goes *a*
Dt 13: 13 have led the people of their town *a*,
17: 17 wives, or his heart will be led *a*.
27: 18 is the man who leads the blind *a*
1Ki 11: 3 and his wives led him *a*.
2Ki 21: 9 Manasseh led them *a*,
2Ch 21: 11 themselves and had led Judah *a*.
33: 9 and the people of Jerusalem *a*,
Job 19: 4 If it is true that I have gone *a*,
Ps 58: 3 Even from birth the wicked go *a*;
95: 10 are a people whose hearts go *a*,
119: 67 Before I was afflicted I went *a*,
Pr 5: 23 led *a* by his own great folly.
7: 21 persuasive words she led him *a*;
10: 17 ignores correction leads others *a*.
12: 26 the way of the wicked leads them *a*
14: 22 Do not those who plot evil go *a*?
20: 1 whoever is led *a* by them is not
Isa 3: 12 my people, your guides lead you *a*;
9: 16 and those who are guided are led *a*.
19: 13 have led Egypt *a*.
30: 28 a bit that leads them *a*.
53: 6 We all, like sheep, have gone *a*,
Jer 4: 1 and no longer go *a*,
23: 13 and led my people Israel *a*.
23: 32 my people *a* with their reckless
50: 6 their shepherds have led them *a*
Eze 13: 10 " 'Because they lead my people *a*,
44: 10 far from me when Israel went *a*
44: 15 when the Israelites went *a* from me
48: 11 and did not go *a* as the Levites did
48: 11 did when the Israelites went *a*.
Hos 4: 12 spirit of prostitution leads them *a*;
Am 2: 4 they have been led *a* by false gods,
Mic 3: 5 who lead my people *a*,
Jn 16: 1 you so that you will not go *a*.
Ac 19: 26 led *a* large numbers of people here
1Co 12: 2 you were influenced and led *a*
2Co 11: 3 your minds may somehow be led *a*
Gal 2: 13 hypocrisy even Barnabas was led *a*.
Heb 3: 10 'Their hearts are always going *a*,
5: 2 who are ignorant and are going *a*,
1Pe 2: 25 For you were like sheep going *a*,
1Jn 2: 26 those who are trying to lead you *a*.
3: 7 do not let anyone lead you *a*.
Rev 12: 9 who leads the whole world *a*.
18: 23 spell all the nations were led *a*.

ASTROLOGER (ASTROLOGERS)

Da 2: 10 of any magician or enchanter or *a*.

ASTROLOGERS (ASTROLOGER)

Isa 47: 13 Let your *a* come forward,
Da 2: 2 *a* to tell him what he had dreamed.
2: 4 Then the *a* answered the king
2: 5 to the *a*, "This is what I have firmly
2: 10 *a* answered the king, "There is not

Da 3: 8 At this time some *a* came forward
4: 7 enchanters, *a* and diviners came,
5: 7 *a* and diviners to be brought
5: 11 enchanters, *a* and diviners.

ASUNDER

Ps 136: 13 to him who divided the Red Sea *a*
Isa 24: 19 the earth is split *a*,

ASWAN

Eze 29: 10 a desolate waste from Migdol to *A*,
30: 6 From Migdol to *A*

ASYNCRITUS

Ro 16: 14 Greet *A*, Phlegon, Hermes,

ATAD

Ge 50: 10 reached the threshing floor of *A*,
50: 11 at the threshing floor of *A*,

ATARAH

1Ch 2: 26 whose name was *A*; she was

ATAROTH

Nu 32: 3 and said, "*A*, Dibon, Jazer, Nimrah
32: 34 The Gadites built up Dibon, *A*,
Jos 16: 2 to the territory of the Arkites in *A*,
16: 7 it went down from Janoah to *A*

ATAROTH ADDAR

Jos 16: 5 of their inheritance went from *A*
18: 13 went down to *A* on the hill

ATE (EAT)

Ge 3: 6 who was with her, and he *a* it.
3: 6 wisdom, she took some and *a* it.
3: 12 fruit from the tree, and I *a* it."
3: 13 The serpent deceived me, and I *a*."
3: 17 and *a* from the tree about which I
18: 8 While they *a*, he stood near them
19: 3 bread without yeast, and they *a*.
24: 54 and the men who were with him *a*
25: 34 He *a* and drank, and then got up
26: 30 a feast for them, and they *a*
27: 25 Jacob brought it to him and he *a*;
27: 33 I *a* it just before you came
31: 46 and they *a* there by the heap
39: 6 with anything except the food he *a*.
41: 4 and gaunt *a* up the seven sleek,
41: 20 ugly cows *a* up the seven fat cows
41: 21 But even after they *a* them,
43: 32 and the Egyptians who *a* with him
Ex 16: 3 and *a* all the food we wanted,
16: 35 The Israelites *a* manna forty years,
16: 35 they *a* manna until they reached
24: 11 they saw God, and they *a*
Nu 11: 5 We remember the fish we *a*
25: 2 The people *a* and bowed
Dt 9: 9 I *a* no bread and drank no water.
9: 18 I *a* no bread and drank no water,
29: 6 You *a* no bread and drank no wine
32: 38 the gods who *a* the fat
Jos 5: 11 they *a* some of the produce
5: 12 after they *a* this food from the land;
5: 12 but that year they *a* of the produce
Jdg 14: 9 gave them some, and they too *a* it.
14: 9 out with his hands and *a*
19: 8 So the two of them *a* together.
Ru 2: 14 She *a* all she wanted and had some
1Sa 1: 18 she went her way and *a* something,
14: 32 them on the ground and *a* them.
28: 25 before Saul and his men, and they *a*
30: 12 He *a* and was revived,
2Sa 9: 11 Mephibosheth *a* at David's table
9: 13 he always *a* at the king's table,
11: 13 At David's invitation, he *a*
12: 20 they served him food, and he *a*.
1Ki 4: 20 they *a*, they drank and they were
13: 19 and *a* and drank in his house.
13: 22 You came back and *a* bread
19: 6 He *a* and drank and then lay
19: 8 So he got up and *a* and drank.
19: 21 gave it to the people, and they *a*.
2Ki 4: 44 and they *a* and had some left over,
6: 29 So we cooked my son and *a* him.
7: 8 They *a* and drank, and carried
9: 34 Jehu went in and *a* and drank.
23: 9 they *a* unleavened bread
2Ki 25: 29 the rest of his life *a* regularly
1Ch 29: 22 They *a* and drank with great joy
2Ch 30: 18 yet they *a* the Passover, contrary
30: 22 seven days they *a* their assigned
Ezr 6: 21 returned from the exile *a* it,
10: 6 he *a* no food and drank no water,
Ne 5: 14 nor my brothers *a* the food allotted
5: 17 and officials *a* at my table,
9: 25 They *a* to the full and were
Job 42: 11 and *a* with him in his house.
Ps 78: 25 Men *a* the bread of angels;
78: 29 They *a* till they had more
105: 35 they *a* up every green thing
105: 35 *a* up the produce of their soil.
106: 28 *a* sacrifices offered to lifeless gods;
Isa 44: 19 I roasted meat and I *a*.
Jer 15: 16 When your words came, I *a* them;
52: 33 the rest of his life *a* regularly
La 4: 5 Those who once *a* delicacies
Eze 3: 3 So I *a* it, and it tasted as sweet
Da 1: 15 young men who *a* the royal food.
4: 33 from people and *a* grass like cattle.
5: 21 the wild donkeys and *a* grass like
10: 3 I *a* no choice food; no meat
Mt 9: 10 and "sinners" came and *a* with him
12: 4 his companions *a* the consecrated
13: 4 and the birds came and *a* it up.
14: 20 They all *a* and were satisfied,
14: 21 of those who *a* was about five
15: 37 They all *a* and were satisfied.
15: 38 of those who *a* was four thousand,
Mk 1: 6 and he *a* locusts and wild honey.
2: 26 and *a* the consecrated bread,
4: 4 and the birds came and *a* it up.
6: 42 They all *a* and were satisfied,
8: 8 The people *a* and were satisfied.
Lk 4: 2 He *a* nothing during those days,
6: 4 he *a* what is lawful only for priests
8: 5 and the birds of the air *a* it up.
9: 17 They all *a* and were satisfied,
13: 26 'We *a* and drank with you,
24: 43 he took it and *a* it in their presence.
Jn 6: 26 but because you *a* the loaves
6: 31 Our forefathers *a* the manna
6: 49 Your forefathers *a* the manna
6: 58 Our forefathers *a* manna and died
Ac 2: 46 *a* together with glad and sincere
10: 41 by us who *a* and drank with him
11: 3 house of uncircumcised men and *a*
20: 11 again and broke bread and *a*.
27: 36 and *a* some food themselves.
1Co 10: 3 They all *a* the same spiritual food
Rev 10: 10 from the angel's hand and *a* it.

ATER

Ezr 2: 16 of *A* (through Hezekiah) 98
2: 42 the descendants of Shallum, *A*,
Ne 7: 21 of *A* (through Hezekiah) 98
7: 45 the descendants of Shallum, *A*,
10: 17 Bigvai, Adin, *A*, Hezekiah, Azzur,

ATHACH

1Sa 30: 30 to those in Hormah, Bor Ashan, *A*

ATHAIAH

Ne 11: 4 of Judah: *A* son of Uzziah,

ATHALIAH

2Ki 8: 26 His mother's name was *A*,
11: 1 When *A* the mother
11: 2 in a bedroom to hide him from *A*;
11: 3 for six years while *A* ruled the land.
11: 13 When *A* heard the noise made
11: 14 Then *A* tore her robes
11: 20 *A* had been slain with the sword
1Ch 8: 26 Shamsherai, Shehariah, *A*,
2Ch 22: 2 His mother's name was *A*,
22: 10 When *A* the mother
22: 11 she hid the child from *A*
22: 12 for six years while *A* ruled the land.
23: 12 When *A* heard the noise
23: 13 Then *A* tore her robes and shouted,
23: 21 *A* had been slain with the sword.
24: 7 that wicked woman *A* had broken
Ezr 8: 7 Jeshaiah son of *A*,

ATHARIM

Nu 21: 1 coming along the road to *A*,

ATHENIANS (ATHENS)

Ac 17: 21 (All the *A* and the foreigners who

ATHENS (ATHENIANS)

Ac 17: 15 Paul brought him to *A*
17: 16 Paul was waiting for them in *A*,
17: 22 "Men of *A*! I see that
18: 1 Paul left *A* and went to Corinth.
1Th 3: 1 best to be left by ourselves in *A*.

ATHLAI

Ezr 10: 28 Hananiah, Zabbai and *A*.

ATHLETE

2Ti 2: 5 if anyone competes as an *a*,

ATONE (ATONEMENT)

Ex 30: 15 to the LORD to *a* for your lives.
2Ch 29: 24 for a sin offering to *a* for all Israel,
Ps 79: 9 deliver us and *a* for our sins
Da 9: 24 an end to sin, to *a* for wickedness,

ATONED (ATONEMENT)

Dt 21: 8 And the bloodshed will be *a* for.
1Sa 3: 14 guilt of Eli's house will never be *a*
Ps 65: 3 you *a* for our transgressions.
78: 38 he *a* for their iniquities
Pr 16: 6 faithfulness sin is *a* for;
Isa 6: 7 guilt is taken away and your sin *a*
22: 14 your dying day this sin will not be *a*
27: 9 then, will Jacob's guilt be *a* for,

ATONEMENT (ATONE ATONED ATONING)

Ex 25: 17 "Make an *a* cover of pure gold—
26: 34 Put the *a* cover on the ark
29: 33 offerings by which *a* was made
29: 36 Purify the altar by making *a* for it,
29: 36 as a sin offering to make *a*.
29: 37 For seven days make *a* for the altar
30: 6 before the *a* cover that is
30: 10 Once a year Aaron shall make *a*
30: 10 This annual *a* must be made
30: 16 Receive the *a* money
30: 16 before the LORD, making *a*
31: 7 Testimony with the *a* cover on it,
32: 30 perhaps I can make *a* for your sin."
35: 12 ark with its poles and the *a* cover
37: 6 He made the *a* cover of pure gold
39: 35 with its poles and the *a* cover;
40: 20 and put the *a* cover over it.
Lev 1: 4 on his behalf to make *a* for him.
4: 20 In this way the priest will make *a*
4: 26 In this way the priest will make *a*
4: 31 In this way the priest will make *a*
4: 35 In this way the priest will make *a*
5: 6 and the priest shall make *a* for him
5: 10 make *a* for him for the sin he has
5: 13 In this way the priest will make *a*
5: 16 who will make *a* for him
5: 18 In this way the priest will make *a*
6: 7 In this way the priest will make *a*
6: 30 into the Tent of Meeting to make *a*
7: 7 belong to the priest who makes *a*
8: 15 he consecrated it to make *a* for it.
8: 34 by the LORD to make *a* for you.
9: 7 and your burnt offering and make *a*
9: 7 for the people and make *a* for them
10: 17 community by making *a* for them
12: 7 before the LORD to make *a* for her
12: 8 In this way the priest will make *a*
14: 18 make *a* for him before the LORD.
14: 19 make *a* for the one to be cleansed
14: 20 with the grain offering, and make *a*
14: 21 to be waved to make *a* for him,
14: 29 make *a* for him before the LORD.
14: 31 In this way the priest will make *a*
14: 53 In this way he will make *a*
15: 15 In this way he will make *a*
15: 30 In this way he will make *a* for her
16: 2 in front of the *a* cover on the ark,
16: 2 in the cloud over the *a* cover.
16: 6 offering to make *a* for himself
16: 10 used for making *a* by sending it
16: 11 offering to make *a* for himself
16: 13 the incense will conceal the *a* cover
16: 14 it on the front of the *a* cover;
16: 14 times before the *a* cover.

Lev 16: 15 He shall sprinkle it on the *a* cover
16: 16 In this way he will make *a*
16: 17 having made *a* for himself,
16: 17 to make *a* in the Most Holy Place
16: 18 before the LORD and make *a* for it
16: 20 When Aaron has finished making *a*
16: 24 to make *a* for himself
16: 27 the Most Holy Place to make *a*,
16: 30 on this day *a* will be made for you,
16: 32 as high priest is to make *a*.
16: 33 make *a* for the Most Holy Place,
16: 34 *A* is to be made once a year
17: 11 it is the blood that makes *a*
17: 11 it to you to make *a* for yourselves
19: 22 make *a* for him before the LORD
23: 27 this seventh month is the Day of *A*.
23: 28 because it is the Day of *A*,
23: 28 when *a* is made for you
25: 9 on the Day of *A* sound the trumpet
Nu 5: 8 ram with which *a* is made for him.
6: 11 a burnt offering to make *a* for him
7: 89 above the *a* cover on the ark
8: 12 to make *a* for the Levites.
8: 19 and to make *a* for them
8: 21 made *a* for them to purify them.
15: 25 The priest is to make *a*
15: 28 and when *a* has been made for him,
15: 28 is to make *a* before the LORD
16: 46 to the assembly to make *a* for them
16: 47 offered the incense and made *a*
25: 13 and made *a* for the Israelites."
28: 22 as a sin offering to make *a* for you.
28: 30 goat to make *a* for you.
29: 5 as a sin offering to make *a* for you.
29: 11 in addition to the sin offering for *a*
31: 50 to make *a* for ourselves
35: 33 and *a* cannot be made for the land
Dt 21: 8 Accept this *a* for your people Israel
32: 43 and make *a* for his land and people.
1Ch 6: 49 making *a* for Israel, in accordance
28: 11 its inner rooms and the place of *a*.
Ne 10: 33 offerings to make *a* for Israel;
Eze 16: 63 Then, when I make *a* for you
43: 20 so purify the altar and make *a* for it
43: 26 are to make *a* for the altar
45: 15 offerings to make *a* for the people,
45: 17 offerings to make *a* for the house
45: 20 so you are to make *a* for the temple
Ro 3: 25 presented him as a sacrifice of *a*,
Heb 2: 17 that he might make *a* for the sins
9: 5 overshadowing the place of *a*.

ATONING (ATONEMENT)

Ex 30: 10 with the blood of the *a* sin offering
1Jn 2: 2 He is the *a* sacrifice for our sins,
4: 10 as an *a* sacrifice for our sins.

ATROTH BETH JOAB

1Ch 2: 54 Bethlehem, the Netophathites, *A*,

ATROTH SHOPHAN

Nu 32: 35 Ataroth, Aroer, *A*, Jazer, Jogbehah, Beth

ATTACH (ATTACHED ATTACHING)

Ex 28: 14 and *a* the chains to the settings.
28: 26 *a* them to the other two corners
28: 27 and *a* them to the bottom
28: 37 cord to it to *a* it to the turban;
29: 6 *a* the sacred diadem to the turban.
39: 31 cord to it to *a* it to the turban,
Eze 37: 6 I will *a* tendons to you

ATTACHED (ATTACH)

Ge 29: 34 at last my husband will become *a*
32: 32 Israelites do not eat the tendon *a*
Ex 28: 7 is to have two shoulder pieces *a*
39: 4 which were *a* to two of its corners,
39: 19 *a* them to the other two corners
39: 20 and *a* them to the bottom
39: 25 and *a* them around the hem
40: 20 *a* the poles to the ark and put
1Ki 6: 10 they were *a* to the temple by beams
7: 28 They had side panels *a* to uprights.
7: 32 of the wheels were *a* to the stand.
7: 35 and panels were *a* to the top
2Ch 3: 16 hundred pomegranates and *a* them
9: 18 and a footstool of gold was *a* to it.
Eze 40: 43 were *a* to the wall all around.

ATTACHING (ATTACH)

Ex 28: 25 *a* them to the shoulder pieces
39: 18 *a* them to the shoulder pieces

ATTACK (ATTACKED ATTACKER ATTACKERS ATTACKING ATTACKS)

Ge 14: 15 Abram divided his men to *a* them
32: 11 I am afraid he will come and *a* me,
34: 30 forces against me and *a* me,
43: 18 He wants to *a* us and overpower us
49: 19 but he will *a* them at their heels.
Nu 13: 31 "We can't *a* those people;
20: 18 and *a* you with the sword."
Dt 20: 10 When you march up to *a* a city,
Jos 8: 1 army with you, and go up and *a* Ai.
8: 3 the whole army moved out to *a* Ai.
9: 18 But the Israelites did not *a* them,
10: 4 "Come up and help me *a* Gibeon,"
10: 19 *a* them from the rear and don't let
Jdg 7: 10 If you are afraid to *a*, go
7: 11 will be encouraged to *a* the camp."
9: 43 out of the city, he rose to *a* them.
9: 45 that day Abimelech pressed his *a*
10: 18 "Whoever will launch the *a*
18: 9 answered, "Come on, let's *a* them!
18: 25 some hot-tempered men will *a* you,
20: 34 Israel's finest men made a frontal *a*
1Sa 7: 7 the Philistines came up to *a* them.
14: 14 In that first *a* Jonathan
15: 3 *a* the Amalekites and totally
17: 48 Philistine moved closer to *a* him,
23: 2 Shall I go and *a* these Philistines?"
23: 2 *a* the Philistines and save Keilah."
24: 7 and did not allow them to *a* Saul.
2Sa 5: 6 to Jerusalem to *a* the Jebusites,
5: 19 "Shall I go and *a* the Philistines?
5: 23 *a* them in front of the balsam trees.
11: 25 Press the *a* against the city
17: 2 I would *a* him when he is weary
17: 9 If he should *a* your troops first,
17: 12 we will *a* him wherever he may be
1Ki 20: 12 So they prepared to *a* the city.
20: 12 he ordered his men: "Prepare to *a*
20: 22 the king of Aram will *a* you again."
22: 12 "*A* Ramoth Gilead and be
22: 15 or shall I refrain?" "*A* and be
22: 32 So they turned to *a* him,
2Ki 3: 8 "By what route shall we *a*?"
7: 6 and Egyptian kings to *a* us!"
12: 17 Then he turned to *a* Jerusalem.
17: 3 of Assyria came up to *a* Hoshea,
18: 25 come to *a* and destroy this place
1Ch 11: 6 "Whoever leads the *a*
14: 10 "Shall I go and *a* the Philistines?
14: 14 *a* them in front of the balsam trees.
2Ch 18: 2 and urged him to *a* Ramoth
18: 11 "*A* Ramoth Gilead and be
18: 14 or shall I refrain?" "*A* and be
18: 31 So they turned to *a* him,
Ne 4: 12 Wherever you turn, they will *a* us."
Est 8: 11 or province that might *a* them
9: 2 to *a* those seeking their destruction
Job 15: 21 all seems well, marauders *a* him.
15: 24 him, like a king poised to *a*,
19: 3 shamelessly you *a* me.
30: 21 of your hand you *a* me.
Ps 27: 2 my enemies and my foes *a* me,
56: 1 all day long they press their *a*.
59: 4 yet they are ready to *a* me.
109: 3 they *a* me without cause.
109: 28 when they *a* they will be put
Isa 21: 2 Elam, *a!* Media, lay siege!
29: 7 that *a* her and her fortress
36: 10 come to *a* and destroy this land
54: 15 If anyone does *a* you, it will not be
Jer 5: 6 a lion from the forest will *a* them,
6: 4 Arise, let us *a* at noon!
6: 5 So arise, let us *a* at night
6: 23 to *a* you, O Daughter of Zion."
12: 9 birds of prey surround and *a*?
18: 18 let's *a* him with our tongues
37: 8 will return and *a* this city;
37: 19 'The king of Babylon will not *a* you
43: 11 He will come and *a* Egypt,
46: 13 king of Babylon to *a* Egypt:
47: 7 it to *a* Ashkelon and the seacoast?"
Jer 49: 4 'Who will *a* me?'
49: 14 "Assemble yourselves to *a* it!
49: 28 "Arise, and *a* Kedar
49: 31 "Arise and *a* a nation at ease,
50: 3 A nation from the north will *a* her
50: 21 "*A* the land of Merathaim
50: 42 to *a* you, O Daughter of Babylon.
51: 48 destroyers will *a* her,"
Eze 38: 11 I will *a* a peaceful and unsuspecting
Da 8: 7 I saw him *a* the ram furiously,
11: 7 He will *a* the forces of the king
11: 39 He will *a* the mightiest fortresses
Hos 13: 8 I will *a* them and rip them open.
Joel 3: 9 the fighting men draw near and *a*.
Zec 12: 9 all the nations that *a* Jerusalem.
14: 13 and they will *a* each other.
Ac 16: 22 joined in the *a* against Paul
18: 10 no one is going to *a* and harm you,
18: 12 the Jews made a united *a* on Paul
2Ti 4: 18 will rescue me from every evil *a*
Rev 11: 7 up from the Abyss will *a* them,

ATTACKED (ATTACK)

Ge 4: 8 Cain *a* his brother Abel
34: 25 and *a* the unsuspecting city,
49: 19 "Gad will be *a* by a band of raiders,
49: 23 With bitterness archers *a* him;
Ex 17: 8 and *a* the Israelites at Rephidim.
Nu 14: 45 hill country came down and *a* them
21: 1 he *a* the Israelites and captured
Jos 8: 21 they turned around and *a* the men
10: 5 positions against Gibeon and *a* it.
10: 29 from Makkedah to Libnah and *a* it.
10: 31 took up positions against it and *a* it.
10: 34 took up positions against it and *a* it.
10: 36 up from Eglon to Hebron and *a* it.
10: 38 turned around and *a* Debir.
11: 7 the Waters of Merom and *a* them,
19: 47 so they went up and *a* Leshem,
Jdg 1: 4 When Judah *a*, the LORD gave
1: 8 The men of Judah *a* Jerusalem also
1: 17 *a* the Canaanites living in Zephath,
1: 22 Now the house of Joseph *a* Bethel,
3: 13 Eglon came and *a* Israel,
11: 12 us that you have *a* our country?"
15: 8 He *a* them viciously
18: 27 They *a* them with the sword
1Sa 13: 3 Jonathan *a* the Philistine outpost
13: 4 "Saul has *a* the Philistine outpost,
15: 7 Saul *a* the Amalekites all the way
27: 9 Whenever David *a* an area,
30: 1 They had *a* Ziklag and burned it,
2Sa 12: 29 and went to Rabbah, and *a*
1Ki 2: 32 of my father David he *a* two men
9: 16 (Pharaoh king of Egypt had *a*
14: 25 Shishak king of Egypt *a* Jerusalem.
20: 1 and besieged Samaria and *a* it.
2Ki 3: 25 with slings surrounded it and *a* it
12: 17 and *a* Gath and captured it.
14: 11 so Jehoash king of Israel *a*.
15: 10 He *a* him in front of the people,
15: 14 He *a* Shallum son of Jabesh
15: 16 *a* Tiphsah and everyone in the city
15: 30 He *a* and assassinated him,
18: 13 of Assyria *a* all the fortified cities
1Ch 4: 41 They *a* the Hamites
20: 1 Joab *a* Rabbah and left it in ruins.
2Ch 12: 2 Shishak king of Egypt *a* Jerusalem
12: 9 king of Egypt *a* Jerusalem,
13: 14 and saw that they were being *a*
14: 15 also *a* the camps of the herdsmen
21: 17 They *a* Judah, invaded it
25: 21 So Jehoash king of Israel *a*.
28: 17 *a* Judah and carried away prisoners
36: 6 king of Babylon *a* him
Est 8: 7 "Because Haman *a* the Jews,
Job 1: 15 the Sabeans *a* and carried them off.
Ps 53: 5 the bones of those who *a* you;
124: 2 side when men *a* us,
Isa 20: 1 came to Ashdod and *a*
36: 1 of Assyria *a* all the fortified cities
Jer 47: 1 Philistines before Pharaoh *a* Gaza:
49: 28 king of Babylon *a*:
Zec 14: 16 nations that have *a* Jerusalem will

ATTACKER (ATTACK)

Na 2: 1 An *a* advances against you,

ATTACKERS (ATTACK)
Ps 35:15 *a* gathered against me

ATTACKING (ATTACK)
1Ki 22:20 'Who will lure Ahab into *a*
2Ki 16:7 of the king of Israel, who are *a* me
16:9 Assyria complied by *a* Damascus
2Ch 18:19 king of Israel into *a* Ramoth Gilead
20:12 to face this vast army that is *a* us.
35:21 It is not you I am *a* at this time,
Ps 54:3 Strangers are *a* me;
56:2 many are *a* me in their pride.
86:14 The arrogant are *a* me, O God;
Jer 21:2 king of Babylon is *a* us.
32:24 to the Babylonians who are *a* it.
32:29 Babylonians who are *a* this city will
37:10 Babylonian army that is *a* you

ATTACKS (ATTACK)
Ge 32:8 "If Esau comes and *a* one group,
Ex 21:15 "Anyone who *a* his father
Dt 22:26 that of someone who *a*
Jos 15:16 in marriage to the man who *a*
Jdg 1:12 in marriage to the man who *a*
2Sa 22:44 from the *a* of my people;
Job 30:12 On my right the tribe *a*;
Ps 18:43 me from the *a* of the people;
55:20 My companion *a* his friends;
Pr 21:22 A wise man *a* the city
Isa 54:15 whoever *a* you will surrender
Eze 38:18 When Gog *a* the land of Israel,
Lk 11:22 But when someone stronger *a*
Jn 10:12 Then the wolf *a* the flock

ATTAI
1Ch 2:35 servant Jarha, and she bore him *A*.
2:36 *A* was the father of Nathan,
12:11 Jeremiah the fifth, *A* the sixth,
2Ch 11:20 who bore him Abijah, *A*, Ziza

ATTAIN (ATTAINED ATTAINING ATTAINS)
Ps 139:6 too lofty for me to *a*.
Pr 2:19 or *a* the paths of life.
Gal 3:3 are you now trying to *a* your goal
Php 3:11 to *a* to the resurrection

ATTAINED (ATTAIN)
Pr 16:31 it is *a* by a righteous life.
Ro 9:31 a law of righteousness, has not *a* it.
Php 3:16 up to what we have already *a*.
Heb 7:11 If perfection could have been *a*

ATTAINING (ATTAIN)
Pr 1:2 for *a* wisdom and discipline;
Eph 4:13 *a* to the whole measure

ATTAINS (ATTAIN)
Pr 11:19 The truly righteous man *a* life,

ATTALIA
Ac 14:25 in Perga, they went down to *A*.
14:26 From *A* they sailed back

ATTEMPT
Ac 27:30 In an *a* to escape from the ship,

ATTEND (ATTENDANCE ATTENDANT ATTENDANTS ATTENDED ATTENDING ATTENDS)
Ge 39:11 into the house to *a* to his duties,
1Ki 1:2 for a young virgin to *a* the king
Est 4:5 king's eunuchs assigned to *a* her,

ATTENDANCE (ATTEND)
SS 8:13 the gardens with friends in *a*,

ATTENDANT (ATTEND)
Ge 39:4 favor in his eyes and became his *a*.
1Ki 19:21 to follow Elijah and became his *a*.
2Ki 22:12 secretary and Asaiah the king's *a*:
2Ch 34:20 secretary and Asaiah the king's *a*:
Lk 4:20 gave it back to the *a* and sat down.
Ac 13:7 who was an *a* of the proconsul,

ATTENDANTS (ATTEND)
Ge 45:1 control himself before all his *a*,
Ex 2:5 and her *a* were walking
Jdg 3:19 "Quiet!" And all his *a* left him.
1Sa 8:14 olive groves and give them to his *a*.
8:15 and give it to his officials and *a*.
16:15 Saul's *a* said to him, "See,
16:17 to his *a*, "Find someone who plays
18:22 Then Saul ordered his *a*: "Speak
18:22 his *a* all like you; now become his
18:26 When the *a* told David these things
19:1 told his son Jonathan and all the *a*
28:7 to his *a*, "Find me a woman who is
2Ki 5:15 and all his *a* went back to the man
24:12 king of Judah, his mother, his *a*,
Ezr 8:17 so that they might bring *a* to us
Est 1:12 But when the *a* delivered the king's
2:2 the king's personal *a* proposed,
6:3 done for him," his *a* answered.
6:5 His *a* answered, "Haman is
Jer 25:19 Pharaoh king of Egypt, his *a*,
36:24 all his *a* who heard all these words
36:31 and his *a* for their wickedness;
37:2 nor his *a* nor the people
Mt 14:2 to his *a*, "This is John the Baptist;
22:13 "Then the king told the *a*,

ATTENDED (ATTEND)
Ge 40:4 them to Joseph, and he *a* them.
Jdg 14:20 given to the friend who had *a* him
1Sa 25:42 got on a donkey and, *a*
Da 7:10 Thousands upon thousands *a* him;
Mt 4:11 and angels came and *a* him.
Mk 1:13 the wild animals, and angels *a* him.

ATTENDING (ATTEND)
1Sa 4:20 women *a* her said, "Don't despair;
1Ki 1:15 the Shunammite was *a* him.
10:5 the *a* servants in their robes,
2Ch 9:4 the *a* servants in their robes,
22:8 who had been *a* Ahaziah,
Est 7:9 one of the eunuchs *a* the king, said,

ATTENDS (ATTEND)
Jn 3:29 friend who *a* the bridegroom waits

ATTENTION (ATTENTIVE)
Ge 39:23 The warden paid no *a* to anything
Ex 4:8 pay *a* to the first miraculous sign,
5:9 they keep working and pay no *a*
15:26 if you pay *a* to his commands
16:20 some of them paid no *a* to Moses;
23:21 Pay *a* to him and listen
Nu 5:15 a reminder offering to draw *a*
Dt 1:45 but he paid no *a* to your weeping
7:12 If you pay *a* to these laws
17:4 and this has been brought to your *a*
28:13 If you pay *a* to the commands
Jdg 11:28 paid no *a* to the message Jephthah
Ru 4:4 I should bring the matter to your *a*
1Sa 4:20 she did not respond or pay any *a*.
25:25 May my lord pay no *a*
1Ki 8:28 Yet give *a* to your servant's prayer
18:29 no one answered, no one paid *a*.
2Ch 6:19 Yet give *a* to your servant's prayer
33:10 and his people, but they paid no *a*.
Ne 8:13 the scribe to give *a* to the words
9:30 Yet they paid no *a*,
9:34 they did not pay *a*
Est 9:25 when the plot came to the king's *a*,
Job 7:17 that you give him so much *a*,
32:12 I gave you my full *a*
33:1 pay *a* to everything I say.
33:31 "Pay *a*, Job, and listen to me;
35:13 the Almighty pays no *a* to it.
Pr 4:1 pay *a* and gain understanding.
4:20 My son, pay *a* to what I say;
5:1 My son, pay *a* to my wisdom,
7:24 pay *a* to what I say.
17:4 a liar pays *a* to a malicious tongue.
22:17 Pay *a* and listen to the sayings
27:23 give careful *a* to your herds;
Ecc 7:21 Do not pay *a* to every word people
Isa 28:23 pay *a* and hear what I say.
34:1 pay *a*, you peoples!
42:20 many things, but have paid no *a*;
42:23 or pay close *a* in time to come?
48:18 If only you had paid *a*
Jer 7:24 But they did not listen or pay *a*;
7:26 they did not listen to me or pay *a*.
11:8 But they did not listen or pay *a*;
13:15 Hear and pay *a*,
17:23 Yet they did not listen or pay *a*;
18:18 and pay no *a* to anything he says."
25:4 you have not listened or paid any *a*
34:14 did not listen to me or pay *a* to me
35:15 But you have not paid *a* or listened
37:2 the people of the land paid any *a*
44:5 But they did not listen or pay *a*;
Eze 40:4 and pay *a* to everything I am going
44:5 Give *a* to the entrance
44:5 and give *a* to everything I tell you
Da 3:12 who pay no *a* to you, O king.
6:13 from Judah, pays no *a* to you,
9:13 and giving *a* to your truth.
11:18 he will turn his *a* to the coastlands
Hos 5:1 Pay *a*, you Israelites!
Zec 1:4 But they would not listen or pay *a*
7:11 "But they refused to pay *a*;
Mal 2:13 because he no longer pays *a*
Mt 7:3 and pay no *a* to the plank
22:5 "But they paid no *a* and went off—
22:16 you pay no *a* to who they are.
24:1 to him to call his *a* to its buildings.
Mk 12:14 you pay no *a* to who they are;
Lk 6:41 and pay no *a* to the plank
Ac 3:5 So the man gave them his *a*,
6:4 and will give our *a* to prayer
8:6 they all paid close *a* to what he said
8:10 gave him their *a* and exclaimed,
Tit 1:14 and will pay no *a* to Jewish myths
Heb 2:1 We must pay more careful *a*,
Jas 2:3 If you show special *a*
2Pe 1:19 and you will do well to pay *a* to it,
3Jn :10 I will call *a* to what he is doing,

ATTENTIVE (ATTENTION)
2Ch 6:40 your ears *a* to the prayers offered
7:15 my ears *a* to the prayers offered
Ne 1:6 let your ear be *a* and your eyes
1:11 let your ear be *a* to the prayer
Ps 34:15 and his ears are *a* to their cry;
130:2 Let your ears be *a*
1Pe 3:12 and his ears are *a* to their prayer,

ATTESTED
1Sa 3:20 recognized that Samuel was *a*

ATTITUDE (ATTITUDES)
Ge 31:2 And Jacob noticed that Laban's *a*
31:5 "I see that your father's *a*
1Ki 11:11 "Since this is your *a* and you have
Ezr 6:22 joy by changing the *a* of the king
Da 3:19 and his *a* toward them changed.
Eph 4:23 new in the *a* of your minds;
Php 2:5 Your *a* should be the same
1Pe 4:1 yourselves also with the same *a*,

ATTITUDES (ATTITUDE)
Heb 4:12 it judges the thoughts and *a*

ATTRACT (ATTRACTED ATTRACTIVE)
Isa 53:2 or majesty to *a* us to him,

ATTRACTED (ATTRACT)
Dt 21:11 a beautiful woman and are *a*
Est 2:17 Now the king was *a* to Esther more

ATTRACTIVE (ATTRACT)
Jdg 15:2 Isn't her younger sister more *a*?
Zec 9:17 How *a* and beautiful they will be!
Tit 2:10 teaching about God our Savior *a*.

AUDIENCE
1Ki 10:24 The whole world sought *a*
2Ch 9:23 of the earth sought *a* with Solomon
Pr 29:26 Many seek an *a* with a ruler,
Ac 12:20 joined together and sought an *a*
25:23 and entered the *a* room

AUGUSTUS
Lk 2:1 those days Caesar *A* issued

AUNT
Lev 18:14 have sexual relations; she is your *a*.
20:20 " 'If a man sleeps with his *a*,

AUTHOR
Ac 3:15 You killed the *a* of life,

Heb 2: 10 should make the *a*
12: 2 the *a* and perfecter of our faith,

AUTHORITIES (AUTHORITY)

Lk 12: 11 before synagogues, rulers and *a*,
Jn 7: 26 Have the *a* really concluded that
Ac 16: 19 into the marketplace to face the *a*.
Ro 13: 1 himself to the governing *a*,
13: 1 *a* that exist have been established
13: 5 it is necessary to submit to the *a*,
13: 6 for the *a* are God's servants,
Eph 3: 10 and *a* in the heavenly realms,
6: 12 but against the rulers, against the *a*,
Col 1: 16 thrones or powers or rulers or *a*;
2: 15 having disarmed the powers and *a*,
Tit 3: 1 people to be subject to rulers and *a*,
1Pe 3: 22 *a* and powers in submission to him.

AUTHORITY (AUTHORITIES AUTHORIZATION AUTHORIZED)

Ge 41: 35 the grain under the *a* of Pharaoh,
Nu 27: 20 Give him some of your *a*
Dt 1: 15 appointed them to have *a* over you
Ezr 7: 24 also to know that you have no *a*
Ne 3: 7 places under the *a* of the governor
Est 9: 29 with full *a* to confirm this second
Isa 22: 21 and hand your *a* over to him.
Jer 5: 31 the priests rule by their own *a*,
Da 4: 31 Your royal *a* has been taken
7: 6 had four heads, and it was given *a*
7: 12 beasts had been stripped of their *a*,
7: 14 He was given *a*, glory
Mt 7: 29 because he taught as one who had *a*
8: 9 For I myself am a man under *a*,
9: 6 the Son of Man has *a* on earth
9: 8 who had given such *a* to men.
10: 1 gave them *a* to drive out evil spirits
20: 25 and their high officials exercise *a*
21: 23 "And who gave you this *a*?"
21: 23 "By what *a* are you doing these
21: 24 by what *a* I am doing these things.
21: 27 by what *a* I am doing these things.
28: 18 "All *a* in heaven and on earth has
Mk 1: 22 he taught them as one who had *a*,
1: 27 A new teaching—and with *a*!
2: 10 the Son of Man has *a* on earth
3: 15 and to have *a* to drive out demons.
6: 7 and gave them *a* over evil spirits.
10: 42 and their high officials exercise *a*
11: 28 "And who gave you *a* to do this?"
11: 28 "By what *a* are you doing these
11: 29 by what *a* I am doing these things.
11: 33 by what *a* I am doing these things."
Lk 4: 6 "I will give you all their *a*
4: 32 because his message had *a*.
4: 36 With *a* and power he gives orders
5: 24 the Son of Man has *a* on earth
7: 8 For I myself am a man under *a*,
9: 1 and *a* to drive out all demons
10: 19 I have given you *a* to trample
20: 2 Who gave you this *a*?" He replied,
20: 2 us by what *a* you are doing these
20: 8 by what *a* I am doing these things."
20: 20 to the power and *a* of the governor.
22: 25 and those who exercise *a*
Jn 2: 18 us to prove your *a* to do all this?"
5: 27 And he has given him *a* to judge
10: 18 *a* to lay it down and *a*
17: 2 For you granted him *a*
Ac 1: 7 the Father has set by his own *a*.
9: 14 here with *a* from the chief priests
26: 10 On the *a* of the chief priests I put
26: 12 going to Damascus with the *a*
Ro 7: 1 that the law has *a* over a man only
13: 1 for there is no *a* except that which
13: 2 rebels against the *a* is rebelling
13: 3 to be free from fear of the one in *a*?
1Co 11: 10 to have a sign of *a* on her head.
15: 24 he has destroyed all dominion, *a*
2Co 10: 8 freely about the *a* the Lord gave
13: 10 have to be harsh in my use of *a*—
13: 10 the *a* the Lord gave me
Eph 1: 21 and *a*, power and dominion,
Col 2: 10 the head over every power and *a*.
1Th 4: 2 you by the *a* of the Lord Jesus.
1Ti 2: 2 for kings and all those in *a*,
2: 12 to teach or to have *a* over a man;
Tit 2: 15 Encourage and rebuke with all *a*.
Heb 13: 17 your leaders and submit to their *a*.
1Pe 2: 13 as the supreme *a*, or to governors,
2: 13 to every *a* instituted among men:
2Pe 2: 10 of the sinful nature and despise *a*.
Jude : 6 did not keep their positions of *a*
: 8 reject *a* and slander celestial beings
: 25 *a*, through Jesus Christ our Lord,
Rev 2: 26 I will give *a* over the nations—
2: 27 I have received *a* from my Father.
12: 10 and the *a* of his Christ.
13: 2 and his throne and great *a*.
13: 4 he had given *a* to the beast,
13: 5 his *a* for forty-two months.
13: 7 he was given *a* over every tribe,
13: 12 He exercised all the *a*
17: 12 but who for one hour will receive *a*
17: 13 and will give their power and *a*
18: 1 He had great *a*, and the earth was
20: 4 seated those who had been given *a*

AUTHORIZATION (AUTHORITY)

Ac 15: 24 out from us without our *a*

AUTHORIZED (AUTHORITY)

Ezr 3: 7 as *a* by Cyrus king of Persia.
5: 3 "Who *a* you to rebuild this temple
5: 9 "Who *a* you to rebuild this temple

AUTUMN

Dt 11: 14 both *a* and spring rains,
Ps 84: 6 the *a* rains also cover it with pools.
Jer 5: 24 who gives *a* and spring rains
Joel 2: 23 both *a* and spring rains, as before.
Jas 5: 7 and how patient he is for the *a*
Jude : 12 blown along by the wind; *a* trees,

AVAIL (AVAILABLE)

Isa 16: 12 it is to no *a*.
Da 11: 27 but to no *a*, because an end will still

AVAILABLE (AVAIL)

1Ki 7: 36 in every *a* space, with wreaths all

AVEN

Am 1: 5 the king who is in the Valley of *A*

AVENGE (VENGEANCE)

Lev 26: 25 sword upon you to *a* the breaking
Dt 32: 35 It is mine to *a*; I will repay.
32: 43 for he will *a* the blood
1Sa 24: 12 may the LORD *a* the wrongs you
2Sa 3: 27 to *a* the blood of his brother Asahel
2Ki 9: 7 I will *a* the blood of my servants
Est 8: 13 ready on that day to *a* themselves
Ps 79: 10 that you *a* the outpoured blood
Isa 1: 24 and *a* myself on my enemies.
Jer 5: 9 "Should I not *a* myself
5: 29 "Should I not *a* myself
9: 9 "Should I not *a* myself
15: 15 *A* me on my persecutors.
51: 36 and *a* you;
Ro 12: 19 "It is mine to *a*; I will repay,"
Heb 10: 30 "It is mine to *a*; I will repay,"
Rev 6: 10 of the earth and *a* our blood?"

AVENGED (VENGEANCE)

Ge 4: 24 If Cain is *a* seven times,
Jos 10: 13 till the nation *a* itself on its enemies
Jdg 9: 24 might be *a* on their brother
11: 36 now that the LORD has *a* you
1Sa 14: 24 before I have *a* myself
25: 31 or of having *a* himself.
2Sa 4: 8 day the LORD has *a* my lord
Ps 58: 10 will be glad when they are *a*,
Eze 5: 13 them will subside, and I will be *a*.
Ac 7: 24 and *a* him by killing the Egyptian.
Rev 19: 2 He has *a* on her the blood

AVENGER (VENGEANCE)

Nu 35: 12 places of refuge from the *a*,
35: 19 *a* of blood shall put the murderer
35: 21 *a* of blood shall put the murderer
35: 24 and the *a* of blood according
35: 25 of murder from the *a* of blood
35: 27 and the *a* of blood finds him
35: 27 the *a* of blood may kill the accused
Dt 19: 6 the *a* of blood might pursue him
19: 12 him over to the *a* of blood to die.
Jos 20: 3 find protection from the *a* of blood.
20: 5 If the *a* of blood pursues him,
20: 9 not be killed by the *a* of blood prior
2Sa 14: 11 God to prevent the *a* of blood
Ps 8: 2 to silence the foe and the *a*.

AVENGES (VENGEANCE)

2Sa 22: 48 He is the God who *a* me,
Ps 9: 12 For he who *a* blood remembers;
18: 47 He is the God who *a* me,
94: 1 O God who *a*, shine forth.
94: 1 O LORD, the God who *a*,

AVENGING (VENGEANCE)

1Sa 25: 26 and from *a* yourself with your own
25: 33 from *a* myself with my own hands.
Na 1: 2 The LORD is a jealous and *a* God;

AVERT

Jer 11: 15 consecrated meat *a* your

AVITH

Ge 36: 35 His city was named *A*.
1Ch 1: 46 His city was named *A*.

AVOID (AVOIDS)

Ne 5: 9 fear of our God to *a* the reproach
Ps 38: 11 My friends and companions *a* me
Pr 4: 15 *A* it, do not travel on it;
19: 7 much more do his friends *a* him!
20: 3 It is to a man's honor to *a* strife,
20: 19 so *a* a man who talks too much.
Ecc 7: 18 who fears God will *a* all extremes.
Eze 46: 20 to *a* bringing them
Zep 1: 9 all who *a* stepping on the threshold
Jn 18: 28 and to *a* ceremonial uncleanness
Ac 15: 29 You will do well to *a* these things.
20: 16 Ephesus to *a* spending time
2Co 8: 20 We want to *a* any criticism
Gal 6: 12 to *a* being persecuted for the cross
1Th 4: 3 you should *a* sexual immorality;
5: 22 *A* every kind of evil.
2Ti 2: 16 *A* godless chatter, because those
Tit 3: 9 But *a* foolish controversies

AVOIDS (AVOID)

Pr 16: 6 of the LORD a man *a* evil.
16: 17 The highway of the upright *a* evil;

AVVA

2Ki 17: 24 people from Babylon, Cuthah, *A*,

AVVIM

Jos 18: 23 Bethel, *A*, Parah, Ophrah,

AVVITES

Dt 2: 23 as for the *A* who lived in villages
Jos 13: 3 that of the *A*); from the south,
2Ki 17: 31 the *A* made Nibhaz and Tartak,

AWAIT (WAIT)

Isa 24: 17 Terror and pit and snare *a* you,
Jer 48: 43 Terror and pit and snare *a* you,
Hos 9: 8 yet snares *a* him on all his paths,
Gal 5: 5 But by faith we eagerly *a*
Php 3: 20 we eagerly *a* a Savior from there,

AWAITS (WAIT)

Job 17: 1 the grave *a* me.
Ps 65: 1 Praise *a* you, O God, in Zion;
Pr 15: 10 Stern discipline *a* him who leaves
28: 22 and is unaware that poverty *a* him.
Ecc 3: 19 the same fate *a* them both:
9: 1 knows whether love or hate *a* him.
Ob : 5 Oh, what a disaster *a* you—
Hab 2: 3 For the revelation *a* an appointed

AWAKE (WAKE)

Job 14: 12 are no more, men will not *a*
Ps 7: 6 *A*, my God; decree justice.
17: 15 when I *a*, I will be satisfied
35: 23 *A*, and rise to my defense!
44: 23 *A*, O Lord! Why do you sleep?
57: 8 *A*, harp and lyre!
57: 8 *A*, my soul!
102: 7 I lie *a*; I have become
108: 2 *A*, harp and lyre!
139: 18 When I *a*,

Pr 6: 22 when you *a*, they will speak to you.
20: 13 stay *a* and you will have food
SS 4: 16 *A*, north wind,
5: 2 I slept but my heart was *a*.
Isa 51: 9 *A*, *a*! Clothe yourself
51: 9 *a*, as in days gone by,
51: 17 *A*, *a*! Rise up,
52: 1 *A*, *a*, O Zion,
Jer 51: 39 then sleep forever and not *a*,''
51: 57 they will sleep forever and not *a*,''
Da 12: 2 sleep in the dust of the earth will *a*:
Zec 13: 7 ''*A*, O sword, against my shepherd,
Lk 9: 32 but when they became fully *a*,
1Th 5: 10 whether we are *a* or asleep,
Rev 16: 15 Blessed is he who stays *a*

AWAKEN (WAKE)

Ps 57: 8 I will *a* the dawn.
80: 2 *A* your might;
108: 2 I will *a* the dawn.
SS 2: 7 Do not arouse or *a* love
3: 5 Do not arouse or *a* love
8: 4 Do not arouse or *a* love

AWAKENED (WAKE)

1Ki 18: 27 Maybe he is sleeping and must be *a*
2Ki 4: 31 and told him, ''The boy has not *a*.''

AWAKENS (WAKE)

Isa 29: 8 but he *a* faint, with his thirst
29: 8 but he *a*, and his hunger remains;

AWAKES (WAKE)

Ps 73: 20 As a dream when one *a*,

AWARD

2Ti 4: 8 will *a* to me on that day—

AWARE

Ge 19: 33 He was not *a* of it when she lay
19: 35 Again he was not *a* of it
28: 16 in this place, and I was not *a* of it.''
Ex 34: 29 he was not *a* that his face was
Lev 4: 14 When they become *a*
4: 23 When he is made *a*
4: 28 When he is made *a*
Nu 15: 24 without the community being *a*
1Sa 14: 3 No one was *a* that Jonathan had
1Ki 8: 38 each one *a* of the afflictions
2Ch 6: 29 each one *a* of his afflictions
Ne 4: 15 our enemies heard that we were *a*
Mt 12: 15 *A* of this, Jesus withdrew
16: 8 *A* of their discussion, Jesus asked,
24: 50 and at an hour he is not *a* of.
26: 10 *A* of this, Jesus said to them,
Mk 8: 17 *A* of their discussion, Jesus asked
Lk 12: 46 and at an hour he is not *a* of.
Jn 6: 61 *A* that his disciples were grumbling
Ac 10: 28 ''You are well *a* that it is
Gal 4: 21 are you not *a* of what the law says?

AWE (AWESOME OVERAWED)

1Sa 12: 18 So all the people stood in *a*
1Ki 3: 28 they held the king in *a*,
Job 25: 2 ''Dominion and *a* belong to God;
Ps 119: 120 I stand in *a* of your laws.
Ecc 5: 7 Therefore stand in *a* of God.
Isa 29: 23 will stand in *a* of the God of Israel.
Jer 2: 19 and have no *a* of me,''
33: 9 they will be in *a* and will tremble
Hab 3: 2 I stand in *a* of your deeds,
Mal 2: 5 and stood in *a* of my name.
Mt 9: 8 they were filled with *a*;
Lk 1: 65 The neighbors were all filled with *a*
5: 26 They were filled with *a* and said,
7: 16 They were all filled with *a*
Ac 2: 43 Everyone was filled with *a*,
Heb 12: 28 acceptably with reverence and *a*,

AWESOME (AWE)

Ge 28: 17 and said, ''How *a* is this place!
Ex 15: 11 *a* in glory,
34: 10 among will see how *a* is the work
Dt 4: 34 or by great and *a* deeds,
7: 21 is among you, is a great and *a* God.
10: 17 the great God, mighty and *a*,
10: 21 and *a* wonders you saw
28: 58 revere this glorious and *a* name—
34: 12 performed the *a* deeds that Moses
Jdg 13: 6 like an angel of God, very *a*.
2Sa 7: 23 *a* wonders by driving out nations
1Ch 17: 21 *a* wonders by driving out nations
Ne 1: 5 of heaven, the great and *a* God
4: 14 and *a*, and fight for your brothers,
9: 32 the great, mighty and *a* God,
Job 10: 16 again display your *a* power
37: 22 God comes in *a* majesty.
Ps 45: 4 let your right hand display *a* deeds.
47: 2 How *a* is the LORD Most High,
65: 5 us with *a* deeds of righteousness,
66: 3 to God, ''How *a* are your deeds!
66: 5 how *a* his works in man's behalf!
68: 35 You are *a*, O God,
89: 7 he is more *a* than all who surround
99: 3 praise your great and *a* name
106: 22 and *a* deeds by the Red Sea.
111: 9 holy and *a* is his name.
145: 6 of the power of your *a* works,
Isa 64: 3 when you did *a* things that we did
Eze 1: 18 Their rims were high and *a*,
1: 22 expanse, sparkling like ice and *a*.
Da 2: 31 dazzling statue, *a* in appearance.
9: 4 ''O Lord, the great and *a* God,
Zep 2: 11 The LORD will be *a* to them

AWFUL

Jdg 20: 3 Tell us how this *a* thing happened.''
20: 12 ''What about this *a* crime that was
Ne 9: 18 they committed *a* blasphemies.
9: 26 they committed *a* blasphemies.
Jer 30: 7 How *a* that day will be!

AWL

Ex 21: 6 and pierce his ear with an *a*.
Dt 15: 17 then take an *a* and push it

AWNINGS

Eze 27: 7 your *a* were of blue and purple

AWOKE (WAKE)

Ge 9: 24 When Noah *a* from his wine
28: 16 When Jacob *a* from his sleep,
Jdg 16: 14 He *a* from his sleep and pulled up
16: 20 He *a* from his sleep and thought,
1Ki 3: 15 Solomon *a*— and he realized it had
Ps 78: 65 Then the Lord *a* as from sleep,
Jer 31: 26 At this I *a* and looked around.

AX

Dt 19: 5 and as he swings his *a* to fell a tree,
20: 19 trees by putting an *a* to them,
Jdg 9: 48 He took an *a* and cut
Ecc 10: 10 If the *a* is dull
Isa 10: 15 Does the *a* raise itself
10: 34 down the forest thickets with an *a*;
Mt 3: 10 The *a* is already at the root
Lk 3: 9 The *a* is already at the root

AXES (AX)

1Sa 13: 20 mattocks, *a* and sickles sharpened.
13: 21 and *a* and for repointing goads.
2Sa 12: 31 with saws and with iron picks and *a*
1Ch 20: 3 with saws and with iron picks and *a*
Ps 74: 5 They behaved like men wielding *a*
74: 6 with their *a* and hatchets.
Jer 46: 22 they will come against her with *a*,

AXHEAD (AX)

2Ki 6: 5 the iron *a* fell into the water.

AXLES

1Ki 7: 30 four bronze wheels with bronze *a*,
7: 32 the *a* of the wheels were attached
7: 33 made like chariot wheels; the *a*,

AYYAH

1Ch 7: 28 and its villages all the way to *A*

AZALIAH

2Ki 22: 3 Shaphan son of *A*, the son
2Ch 34: 8 he sent Shaphan son of *A*

AZANIAH

Ne 10: 9 The Levites: Jeshua son of *A*,

AZAREL

1Ch 12: 6 *A*, Joezer and Jashobeam
25: 18 12 the eleventh to *A*, his sons
27: 22 over Dan: *A* son of Jeroham.
Ezr 10: 41 Shashai, Sharai, *A*, Shelemiah,
Ne 11: 13 Amashsai son of *A*, the son
12: 36 Shemaiah, *A*, Milalai, Gilalai, Maai

AZARIAH (AZARIAH'S)

1Ki 4: 2 *A* son of Zadok—the priest;
4: 5 priests; *A* son of Nathan—
2Ki 14: 21 Then all the people of Judah took *A*
15: 1 *A* son of Amaziah king
15: 7 *A* rested with his fathers
15: 8 year of *A* king of Judah,
15: 17 year of *A* king of Judah,
15: 23 year of *A* king of Judah,
15: 27 year of *A* king of Judah,
1Ch 2: 8 The son of Ethan: *A*.
2: 39 father of *A*, *A* the father of Helez,
3: 12 Amaziah his son, *A* his son,
6: 9 of *A*, *A* the father of Johanan,
6: 10 father of *A* (it was he who served
6: 11 *A* the father of Amariah, Amariah
6: 14 father of *A*, *A* the father of Seraiah,
6: 36 the son of *A*, the son of Zephaniah,
9: 11 Jehoiarib; Jakin; *A* son of Hilkiah,
2Ch 15: 1 of God came upon *A* son of Oded.
15: 8 and the prophecy of *A* son
21: 2 were *A*, Jehiel, Zechariah,
23: 1 *A* son of Jeroham, Ishmael son
23: 1 son of Jehohanan, *A* son of Obed,
26: 17 *A* the priest with eighty other
26: 20 When *A* the chief priest
28: 12 in Ephraim—*A* son of Jehohanan,
29: 12 son of Abdi and *A* son of Jehallelel;
29: 12 son of Amasai and Joel son of *A*;
31: 10 *A* the chief priest, from the family
31: 13 and *A* the official in charge
Ezr 7: 1 the son of *A*, the son of Hilkiah,
7: 3 the son of *A*, the son of Meraioth,
Ne 3: 23 next to them, *A* son of Maaseiah,
7: 7 Jeshua, Nehemiah, *A*, Raamiah,
8: 7 Maaseiah, Kelita, *A*, Jozabad,
10: 2 Zedekiah, Seraiah, *A*, Jeremiah,
12: 33 along with *A*, Ezra, Meshullam,
Jer 43: 2 *A* son of Hoshaiah and Johanan
Da 1: 6 Daniel, Hananiah, Mishael and *A*.
1: 7 Meshach; and to *A*, Abednego.
1: 11 Hananiah, Mishael and *A*,
1: 19 Hananiah, Mishael and *A*;
2: 17 friends Hananiah, Mishael and *A*.

AZARIAH'S (AZARIAH)

2Ki 15: 6 As for the other events of *A* reign,
Ne 3: 24 from *A* house to the angle

AZARIAHU

2Ch 21: 2 *A*, Michael and Shephatiah.

AZAZ

1Ch 5: 8 Bela son of *A*, the son of Shema,

AZAZIAH

1Ch 15: 21 Jeiel and *A* were to play the harps,
27: 20 the Ephraimites: Hoshea son of *A*;
2Ch 31: 13 Jehiel, *A*, Nahath, Asahel,

AZBUK

Ne 3: 16 Beyond him, Nehemiah son of *A*,

AZEKAH

Jos 10: 10 and cut them down all the way to *A*
10: 11 road down from Beth Horon to *A*,
15: 35 Adullam, Socoh, *A*, Shaaraim,
1Sa 17: 1 between Socoh and *A*.
2Ch 11: 9 Ziph, Adoraim, Lachish, *A*, Zorah,
Ne 11: 30 and in *A* and its settlements.
Jer 34: 7 still holding out—Lachish and *A*.

AZEL

1Ch 8: 37 Eleasah his son and *A* his son.
8: 38 All these were the sons of *A*.
8: 38 *A* had six sons, and these were their
9: 43 Eleasah his son and *A* his son.
9: 44 These were the sons of *A*.
9: 44 *A* had six sons, and these were their
Zec 14: 5 for it will extend to *A*.

AZGAD
Ezr 2: 12 of Bani 642 of Bebai 623 of *A* 1,222
8: 12 the descendants of *A*, Johanan son
Ne 7: 17 648 of Bebai 628 of *A* 2,322
10: 15 Bani, Bunni, *A*, Bebai, Adonijah,

AZIEL
1Ch 15: 20 Zechariah, *A*, Shemiramoth, Jehiel

AZIZA
Ezr 10: 27 Mattaniah, Jeremoth, Zabad and *A*

AZMAVETH
2Sa 23: 31 the Arbathite, *A* the Barhumite,
1Ch 8: 36 was the father of Alemeth, *A*
9: 42 Jadah was the father of Alemeth, *A*
11: 33 the Arbathite, *A* the Baharumite,
12: 3 Jeziel and Pelet the sons of *A*;
27: 25 *A* son of Adiel was in charge
Ezr 2: 24 of Anathoth 128 of *A* 42 of Kiriath
Ne 12: 29 and from the area of Geba and *A*,

AZMON
Nu 34: 4 go to Hazar Addar and over to *A*,
Jos 15: 4 It then passed along to *A*

AZNOTH TABOR
Jos 19: 34 The boundary ran west through *A*

AZOR
Mt 1: 14 father of *A*, *A* the father of Zadok,

AZOTUS
Ac 8: 40 appeared at *A* and traveled about,

AZRIEL
1Ch 5: 24 Epher, Ishi, Eliel, *A*, Jeremiah,
27: 19 Jerimoth son of *A*;
Jer 36: 26 son of *A* and Shelemiah son

AZRIKAM
1Ch 3: 23 Elioenai, Hizkiah and *A*—
8: 38 *A*, Bokeru, Ishmael, Sheariah,
9: 14 the son of *A*, the son of Hashabiah,
9: 44 *A*, Bokeru, Ishmael, Sheariah,
2Ch 28: 7 *A* the officer in charge of the palace
Ne 11: 15 the son of *A*, the son of Hashabiah,

AZUBAH
1Ki 22: 42 His mother's name was *A* daughter
1Ch 2: 18 Hezron had children by his wife *A*
2: 19 When *A* died, Caleb married
2Ch 20: 31 His mother's name was *A* daughter

AZZAN
Nu 34: 26 Paltiel son of *A*, the leader

AZZUR
Ne 10: 17 Ater, Hezekiah, *A*, Hodiah,
Jer 28: 1 the prophet Hananiah son of *A*,
Eze 11: 1 among them Jaazaniah son of *A*

BAAL (BAAL'S BAALS)
Ex 14: 2 directly opposite *B* Zephon.
14: 9 Pi Hahiroth, opposite *B* Zephon.
Nu 25: 3 joined in worshiping the *B* of Peor.
25: 5 in worshiping the *B* of Peor."
33: 7 Hahiroth, to the east of *B* Zephon,
Dt 4: 3 you everyone who followed the *B*
Jdg 2: 13 and served *B* and the Ashtoreths.
6: 25 Tear down your father's altar to *B*
6: 31 by morning! If *B* really is a god,
6: 32 saying, "Let *B* contend with him,"
1Ki 16: 31 began to serve *B* and worship him.
16: 32 *B* in the temple of *B* that he built
18: 19 of *B* and the four hundred prophets
18: 21 follow him; but if *B* is God,
18: 22 but *B* has four hundred
18: 25 Elijah said to the prophets of *B*,
18: 26 on the name of *B* from morning
18: 26 "O *B*, answer us!" they shouted.
18: 40 them, "Seize the prophets of *B*.
19: 18 knees have not bowed down to *B*
22: 53 He served and worshiped *B*
2Ki 3: 2 of *B* that his father had made.
10: 18 "Ahab served *B* a little; Jehu will
10: 19 Now summon all the prophets of *B*
10: 19 order to destroy the ministers of *B*.
2Ki 10: 19 to hold a great sacrifice for *B*.
10: 20 "Call an assembly in honor of *B*."
10: 21 and all the ministers of *B* came;
10: 21 into the temple of *B* until it was full
10: 22 robes for all the ministers of *B*."
10: 23 Jehu said to the ministers of *B*,
10: 23 of Recab went into the temple of *B*.
10: 23 with you—only ministers of *B*."
10: 25 shrine of the temple of *B*.
10: 26 out of the temple of *B*
10: 27 and tore down the temple of *B*,
10: 27 demolished the sacred stone of *B*
10: 28 Jehu destroyed *B* worship in Israel.
11: 18 and killed Mattan the priest of *B*
11: 18 of the land went to the temple of *B*
17: 16 starry hosts, and they worshiped *B*.
21: 3 he also erected altars to *B*
23: 4 LORD all the articles made for *B*
23: 5 those who burned incense to *B*,
1Ch 5: 5 his son, Reaiah his son, *B* his son,
8: 30 Kish, *B*, Ner, Nadab, Gedor,
9: 36 Kish, *B*, Ner, Nadab, Gedor,
2Ch 23: 17 and killed Mattan the priest of *B*
23: 17 went to the temple of *B*
Ps 106: 28 They yoked themselves to the *B*
Jer 2: 8 The prophets prophesied by *B*,
7: 9 to *B* and follow other gods you
11: 13 incense to that shameful god *B* are
11: 17 to anger by burning incense to *B*.
12: 16 taught my people to swear by *B*—
19: 5 places of *B* to burn their sons
19: 5 sons in the fire as offerings to *B*—
23: 13 They prophesied by *B*
23: 27 name through *B* worship.
32: 29 burning incense on the roofs to *B*
32: 35 places for *B* in the Valley
Hos 2: 8 which they used for *B*.
13: 1 he became guilty of *B* worship
Zep 1: 4 from this place every remnant of *B*,
Ro 11: 4 have not bowed the knee to *B*."

BAAL GAD
Jos 11: 17 to *B* in the Valley of Lebanon
12: 7 from *B* in the Valley of Lebanon
13: 5 from *B* below Mount Hermon

BAAL HAMON
SS 8: 11 Solomon had a vineyard in *B*;

BAAL HAZOR
2Sa 13: 23 were at *B* near the border of

BAAL HERMON
Jdg 3: 3 from Mount *B* to Lebo Hamath.
1Ch 5: 23 in the land from Bashan to *B*,

BAAL MEON
Nu 32: 38 and *B* (these names were changed)
1Ch 5: 8 area from Aroer to Nebo and *B*.
Eze 25: 9 towns—Beth Jeshimoth, *B*

BAAL PEOR
Dt 4: 3 own eyes what the LORD did at *B*.
Hos 9: 10 But when they came to *B*,

BAAL PERAZIM
2Sa 5: 20 So David went to *B*,
5: 20 So that place was called *B*.
1Ch 14: 11 So David and his men went up to *B*
14: 11 So that place was called *B*.

BAAL SHALISHAH
2Ki 4: 42 A man came from *B*, bringing

BAAL TAMAR
Jdg 20: 33 and took up positions at *B*,

BAAL-BERITH
Jdg 8: 33 They set up *B* as their god
9: 4 shekels from the temple of *B*,

BAAL-HANAN
Ge 36: 38 *B* son of Acbor succeeded him
36: 39 When *B* son of Acbor died,
1Ch 1: 49 *B* son of Acbor succeeded him
1: 50 When *B* died, Hadad succeeded
27: 28 *B* the Gederite was in charge

BAAL-ZEBUB
2Ki 1: 2 and consult *B*, the god of Ekron,
1: 3 that you are going off to consult *B*,
1: 6 you are sending men to consult *B*,
1: 16 have sent messengers to consult *B*,

BAAL'S (BAAL)
Jdg 6: 28 there was *B* altar, demolished,
6: 30 he has broken down *B* altar
6: 31 "Are you going to plead *B* cause?
6: 32 because he broke down *B* altar.

BAALAH
Jos 15: 9 and went down toward *B* (that is,
15: 10 westward from *B* to Mount Seir,
15: 11 passed along to Mount *B*
15: 29 Beersheba, Biziothiah, *B*, Iim,
2Sa 6: 2 out from *B* of Judah to bring up
1Ch 13: 6 the Israelites with him went to *B*

BAALATH
Jos 19: 44 Eltekeh, Gibbethon, *B*, Jehud,
1Ki 9: 18 *B*, and Tadmor in the desert,
1Ch 4: 33 around these towns as far as *B*.
2Ch 8: 6 as well as *B* and all his store cities,

BAALATH BEER
Jos 19: 8 as far as *B* (Ramah in the Negev).

BAALIS
Jer 40: 14 "Don't you know that *B* king

BAALS (BAAL)
Jdg 2: 11 of the LORD and served the *B*.
3: 7 and served the *B* and the Asherahs.
8: 33 prostituted themselves to the *B*.
10: 6 They served the *B*
10: 10 our God and serving the *B*."
1Sa 7: 4 So the Israelites put away their *B*
12: 10 served the *B* and the Ashtoreths.
1Ki 18: 18 and have followed the *B*.
2Ch 17: 3 He did not consult the *B*
24: 7 even its sacred objects for the *B*.
28: 2 idols for worshiping the *B*.
33: 3 also erected altars to the *B*
34: 4 the altars of the *B* were torn down;
Jer 2: 23 I have not run after the *B*'?
9: 14 they have followed the *B*,
Hos 2: 13 she burned incense to the *B*;
2: 17 of the *B* from her lips;
11: 2 They sacrificed to the *B*

BAANA
1Ki 4: 12 *B* son of Ahilud—in Taanach
4: 16 *B* son of Hushai—in Asher
Ne 3: 4 and next to him Zadok son of *B*

BAANAH
2Sa 4: 2 One was named *B* and the other
4: 5 and *B*, the sons of Rimmon
4: 6 and his brother *B* slipped away.
4: 9 answered Recab and his brother *B*,
23: 29 Heled son of *B* the Netophathite,
1Ch 11: 30 Heled son of *B* the Netophathite,
Ezr 2: 2 Mispar, Bigvai, Rehum and *B*):
Ne 7: 7 Mispereth, Bigvai, Nehum and *B*):
10: 27 Anan, Malluch, Harim and *B*.

BAARA
1Ch 8: 8 divorced his wives Hushim and *B*.

BAASEIAH
1Ch 6: 40 the son of *B*, the son of Malkijah,

BAASHA (BAASHA'S)
1Ki 15: 16 *B* king of Israel throughout their
15: 17 *B* king of Israel went up
15: 19 treaty with *B* king of Israel
15: 21 When *B* heard this, he stopped
15: 22 and timber *B* had been using there.
15: 27 *B* son of Ahijah of the house
15: 28 *B* killed Nadab in the third year
15: 32 *B* king of Israel throughout their
15: 33 *B* son of Ahijah became king
16: 1 to Jehu son of Hanani against *B*:
16: 3 So I am about to consume *B*
16: 4 belonging to *B* who die in the city,
16: 6 *B* rested with his fathers

1Ki 16: 7 prophet Jehu son of Hanani to *B*
16: 8 Elah son of *B* became king of Israel
16: 12 against *B* through the prophet Jehu
16: 12 destroyed the whole family of *B*,
16: 13 because of all the sins *B*
21: 22 and that of *B* son of Ahijah,
2Ki 9: 9 like the house of *B* son of Ahijah.
2Ch 16: 1 year of Asa's reign *B* king
16: 3 treaty with *B* king of Israel
16: 5 When *B* heard this, he stopped
16: 6 and timber *B* had been using.
Jer 41: 9 defense against *B* king of Israel.

BAASHA'S (BAASHA)

1Ki 16: 5 As for the other events of *B* reign,
16: 11 he killed off *B* whole family.

BABBLER (BABBLING)

Ac 17: 18 "What is this *b* trying to say?"

BABBLING (BABBLER)

Mt 6: 7 do not keep on *b* like pagans,

BABEL (BABYLON)

Ge 11: 9 That is why it was called *B*—

BABIES (BABY)

Ge 25: 22 The *b* jostled each other within her
Ex 2: 6 "This is one of the Hebrew *b*."
Lk 18: 15 also bringing *b* to Jesus
Ac 7: 19 them to throw out their newborn *b*
1Pe 2: 2 Like newborn *b*, crave pure

BABOONS

1Ki 10: 22 silver and ivory, and apes and *b*.
2Ch 9: 21 silver and ivory, and apes and *b*.

BABY (BABIES BABY'S)

Ex 2: 6 She opened it and saw the *b*.
2: 7 women to nurse the *b* for you?"
2: 9 So the woman took the *b*
2: 9 "Take this *b* and nurse him for me,
1Ki 3: 17 I had a *b* while she was there
3: 18 was born, this woman also had a *b*.
3: 26 give her the living *b*! Don't kill him
3: 27 Give the living *b* to the first woman
Isa 49: 15 "Can a mother forget the *b*
Lk 1: 41 the *b* leaped in her womb,
1: 44 the *b* in my womb leaped for joy.
1: 57 time for Elizabeth to have her *b*,
2: 6 the time came for the *b* to be born,
2: 12 You will find a *b* wrapped in strips
2: 16 the *b*, who was lying in the manger.
Jn 16: 21 but when her *b* is born she forgets

BABY'S (BABY)

Ex 2: 8 the girl went and got the *b* mother.

BABYLON (BABEL BABYLON'S BABYLONIA BABYLONIAN BABYLONIANS BABYLONIANS')

Ge 10: 10 centers of his kingdom were *B*,
2Ki 17: 24 of Assyria brought people from *B*,
17: 30 *B* made Succoth Benoth,
20: 12 king of *B* sent Hezekiah letters
20: 14 "They came from *B*."
20: 17 this day, will be carried off to *B*.
20: 18 in the palace of the king of *B*."
24: 1 king of *B* invaded the land,
24: 7 of *B* had taken all his territory,
24: 10 king of *B* advanced on Jerusalem
24: 12 year of the reign of the king of *B*,
24: 15 Jerusalem to *B* the king's mother,
24: 15 took Jehoiachin captive to *B*.
24: 16 The king of *B* also deported
24: 16 also deported to *B* the entire force
24: 20 rebelled against the king of *B*.
25: 1 king of *B* marched
25: 6 taken to the king of *B* at Riblah,
25: 7 bronze shackles and took him to *B*.
25: 8 an official of the king of *B*,
25: 8 year of Nebuchadnezzar king of *B*,
25: 11 gone over to the king of *B*.
25: 13 and they carried the bronze to *B*.
25: 20 them to the king of *B* at Riblah.
25: 22 king of *B* appointed Gedaliah son
25: 23 king of *B* had appointed Gedaliah
25: 24 in the land and serve the king of *B*,
2Ki 25: 27 Evil-Merodach became king of *B*,
25: 28 kings who were with him in *B*.
1Ch 9: 1 of Judah were taken captive to *B*
2Ch 32: 31 envoys were sent by the rulers of *B*
33: 11 bronze shackles and took him to *B*.
36: 6 bronze shackles to take him to *B*.
36: 6 king of *B* attacked him
36: 7 took to *B* articles from the temple
36: 10 sent for him and brought him to *B*,
36: 18 He carried to *B* all the articles
36: 20 carried into exile to *B* the remnant,
Ezr 1: 11 up from *B* to Jerusalem.
2: 1 king of *B* had taken captive
2: 1 to *B* (they returned to Jerusalem
4: 9 Erech and *B*, the Elamites of Susa,
5: 12 and deported the people to *B*.
5: 12 the Chaldean, king of *B*,
5: 13 in the first year of Cyrus king of *B*,
5: 14 and brought to the temple in *B*.
5: 14 from the temple of *B* the gold
5: 17 in the royal archives of *B* to see
6: 1 stored in the treasury at *B*.
6: 5 in Jerusalem and brought to *B*,
7: 6 this Ezra came up from *B*.
7: 9 journey from *B* on the first day
7: 16 obtain from the province of *B*,
8: 1 up with me from *B* during the reign
Ne 7: 6 king of *B* had taken captive (they
13: 6 king of *B* I had returned
Est 2: 6 by Nebuchadnezzar king of *B*.
Ps 87: 4 "I will record Rahab and *B*
137: 1 By the rivers of *B* we sat and wept
137: 8 O Daughter of *B*, doomed
Isa 13: 1 oracle concerning *B* that Isaiah son
13: 19 *B*, the jewel of kingdoms,
14: 4 taunt against the king of *B*:
14: 22 "I will cut off from *B* her name
21: 9 '*B* has fallen, has fallen!
39: 1 king of *B* sent Hezekiah letters
39: 3 "They came to me from *B*."
39: 6 this day, will be carried off to *B*.
39: 7 in the palace of the king of *B*."
43: 14 "For your sake I will send to *B*
47: 1 Virgin Daughter of *B*;
48: 14 will carry out his purpose against *B*
48: 20 Leave *B*,
Jer 20: 4 Judah over to the king of *B*,
20: 4 who will carry them away to *B*
20: 5 as plunder and carry it off to *B*.
20: 6 in your house will go into exile to *B*
21: 2 king of *B* is attacking us.
21: 4 using to fight the king of *B*
21: 7 to Nebuchadnezzar king of *B*
21: 10 into the hands of the king of *B*,
22: 25 to Nebuchadnezzar king of *B*
24: 1 by Nebuchadnezzar king of *B*,
24: 1 exile from Jerusalem to *B*
25: 1 year of Nebuchadnezzar king of *B*.
25: 9 Nebuchadnezzar king of *B*,"
25: 11 the king of *B* seventy years.
25: 12 I will punish the king of *B*
27: 6 servant Nebuchadnezzar king of *B*;
27: 8 serve Nebuchadnezzar king of *B*
27: 9 'You will not serve the king of *B*.'
27: 11 under the yoke of the king of *B*
27: 12 under the yoke of the king of *B*,
27: 13 that will not serve the king of *B*?
27: 14 You will never serve the king of *B*,'
27: 16 house will be brought back from *B*.'
27: 17 the king of *B*, and you will live.
27: 18 and in Jerusalem not be taken to *B*.
27: 20 into exile from Jerusalem to *B*,
27: 20 king of *B* did not take away
27: 22 'They will be taken to *B*
28: 2 will break the yoke of the king of *B*.
28: 3 king of *B* removed from here
28: 3 removed from here and took to *B*.
28: 4 exiles from Judah who went to *B*,'
28: 4 the yoke of the king of *B*.' "
28: 6 back to this place from *B*.
28: 11 yoke of Nebuchadnezzar king of *B*
28: 14 serve Nebuchadnezzar king of *B*,
29: 1 into exile from Jerusalem to *B*.
29: 3 sent to King Nebuchadnezzar in *B*.
29: 4 into exile from Jerusalem to *B*:
29: 10 seventy years are completed for *B*,
29: 15 has raised up prophets for us in *B*,"
29: 20 away from Jerusalem to *B*.
Jer 29: 21 over to Nebuchadnezzar king of *B*,
29: 22 are in *B* will use this curse:
29: 22 whom the king of *B* burned
29: 28 He has sent this message to us in *B*:
32: 2 of *B* was then besieging Jerusalem,
32: 3 city over to the king of *B*,
32: 4 handed over to the king of *B*,
32: 5 He will take Zedekiah to *B*,
32: 28 and to Nebuchadnezzar king of *B*,
32: 36 handed over to the king of *B*';
34: 1 While Nebuchadnezzar king of *B*
34: 2 city over to the king of *B*,
34: 3 And you will go to *B*.
34: 3 the king of *B* with your own eyes,
34: 7 army of the king of *B* was fighting
34: 21 to the army of the king of *B*,
35: 11 king of *B* invaded this land,
36: 29 the king of *B* would certainly come
37: 1 by Nebuchadnezzar king of *B*;
37: 17 handed over to the king of *B*."
37: 19 'The king of *B* will not attack you
38: 3 over to the army of the king of *B*,
38: 17 to the officers of the king of *B*,
38: 18 to the officers of the king of *B*,
38: 22 out to the officials of the king of *B*.
38: 23 will be captured by the king of *B*;
39: 1 king of *B* marched
39: 3 the officials of the king of *B* came
39: 3 the other officials of the king of *B*.
39: 5 him to Nebuchadnezzar king of *B*
39: 6 the king of *B* slaughtered the sons
39: 7 bronze shackles to take him to *B*.
39: 9 exile to *B* the people who remained
39: 11 of *B* had given these orders about
39: 13 officers of the king of *B* sent
40: 1 were being carried into exile to *B*.
40: 4 Come with me to *B*, if you like,
40: 5 whom the king of *B* has appointed
40: 7 not been carried into exile to *B*,
40: 7 of *B* had appointed Gedaliah son
40: 9 in the land and serve the king of *B*,
40: 11 of *B* had left a remnant in Judah
41: 2 the king of *B* had appointed
41: 18 whom the king of *B* had appointed
42: 11 Do not be afraid of the king of *B*,
43: 3 or carry us into exile to *B*."
43: 10 servant Nebuchadnezzar king of *B*,
44: 30 over to Nebuchadnezzar king of *B*,
46: 2 by Nebuchadnezzar king of *B*
46: 13 king of *B* to attack Egypt:
46: 26 to Nebuchadnezzar king of *B*
49: 28 king of *B* attacked:
49: 30 king of *B* has plotted
50: 1 the prophet concerning *B*
50: 2 '*B* will be captured;
50: 8 "Flee out of *B*;
50: 9 I will stir up and bring against *B*
50: 13 All who pass *B* will be horrified
50: 14 "Take up your positions around *B*,
50: 16 Cut off from *B* the sower,
50: 17 was Nebuchadnezzar king of *B*."
50: 18 "I will punish the king of *B*
50: 23 How desolate is *B*
50: 24 I set a trap for you, O *B*,
50: 28 the fugitives and refugees from *B*
50: 29 "Summon archers against *B*,
50: 34 but unrest to those who live in *B*.
50: 35 "against those who live in *B*
50: 42 to attack you, O Daughter of *B*.
50: 43 of *B* has heard reports about them,
50: 44 I will chase *B* from its land
50: 45 the LORD has planned against *B*,
51: 1 a destroyer against *B*
51: 2 I will send foreigners to *B*
51: 4 They will fall down slain in *B*,
51: 6 "Flee from *B*!
51: 7 *B* was a gold cup in the LORD's
51: 8 *B* will suddenly fall and be broken.
51: 9 " 'We would have healed *B*,
51: 11 because his purpose is to destroy *B*.
51: 12 a banner against the walls of *B*!
51: 12 his decree against the people of *B*.
51: 24 "Before your eyes I will repay *B*
51: 29 purposes against *B* stand—
51: 29 to lay waste the land of *B*
51: 31 to announce to the king of *B*
51: 33 of *B* is like a threshing floor
51: 34 king of *B* has devoured us,

Jer 51:35 to our flesh be upon *B*,''
51:37 *B* will be a heap of ruins,
51:41 What a horror *B* will be
51:42 The sea will rise over *B*;
51:44 And the wall of *B* will fall.
51:44 I will punish Bel in *B*
51:47 when I will punish the idols of *B*;
51:48 will shout for joy over *B*,
51:49 *B* must fall because of Israel's slain,
51:49 have fallen because of *B*.
51:53 Even if *B* reaches the sky
51:54 "The sound of a cry comes from *B*,
51:55 The LORD will destroy *B*;
51:56 A destroyer will come against *B*;
51:59 went to *B* with Zedekiah king
51:60 had been recorded concerning *B*.
51:60 that would come upon *B*—
51:61 to Seraiah, "When you get to *B*,
51:64 'So will *B* sink to rise no more
52: 3 rebelled against the king of *B*.
52: 4 king of *B* marched
52: 9 taken to the king of *B* at Riblah
52:10 the king of *B* slaughtered the sons
52:11 bronze shackles and took him to *B*,
52:12 the king of *B*, came to Jerusalem.
52:12 year of Nebuchadnezzar king of *B*,
52:15 gone over to the king of *B*.
52:17 they carried all the bronze to *B*.
52:26 them to the king of *B* at Riblah.
52:31 Evil-Merodach became king of *B*,
52:32 kings who were with him in *B*.
52:34 king of *B* gave Jehoiachin a regular
Eze 17:12 bringing them back with him to *B*.
17:12 'The king of *B* went to Jerusalem
17:16 Sovereign LORD, he shall die in *B*,
17:20 him to *B* and execute judgment
19: 9 and brought him to the king of *B*.
21:19 the sword of the king of *B* to take,
21:21 For the king of *B* will stop
24: 2 because the king of *B* has laid siege
26: 7 Tyre Nebuchadnezzar king of *B*,
29:18 king of *B* drove his army
29:19 to Nebuchadnezzar king of *B*,
30:10 of Nebuchadnezzar king of *B*.
30:24 the arms of the king of *B*
30:25 into the hand of the king of *B*
30:25 the arms of the king of *B*,
32:11 " 'The sword of the king of *B*
Da 1: 1 Nebuchadnezzar king of *B* came
2:12 execution of all the wise men of *B*.
2:14 to put to death the wise men of *B*,
2:18 with the rest of the wise men of *B*.
2:24 Do not execute the wise men of *B*.
2:24 to execute the wise men of *B*,
2:48 ruler over the entire province of *B*
2:49 over the province of *B*,
3: 1 plain of Dura in the province of *B*.
3:12 over the affairs of the province of *B*
3:30 Abednego in the province of *B*.
4: 6 men of *B* be brought before me
4:29 on the roof of the royal palace of *B*,
4:30 "Is not this the great *B* I have built
5: 7 and said to these wise men of *B*,
7: 1 year of Belshazzar king of *B*,
Mic 4:10 You will go to *B*;
Zec 2: 7 you who live in the Daughter of *B*
6:10 Jedaiah, who have arrived from *B*.
Mt 1:11 at the time of the exile to *B*.
1:12 exile to *B*: Jeconiah was the father
1:17 from David to the exile to *B*,
Ac 7:43 into exile' beyond *B*.
1Pe 5:13 She who is in *B*, chosen together
Rev 14: 8 "Fallen! Fallen is *B* the Great,
16:19 God remembered *B* the Great
17: 5 MYSTERY *B* THE GREAT
18: 2 "Fallen! Fallen is *B* the Great!
18:10 O *B*, city of power!
18:21 the great city of *B* will be thrown

BABYLON'S (BABYLON)

Jer 50:46 of *B* capture the earth will tremble;
51:30 *B* warriors have stopped fighting;
51:58 "*B* thick wall will be leveled

BABYLONIA (BABYLON)

Jos 7:21 plunder a beautiful robe from *B*,
Isa 11:11 from Cush, from Elam, from *B*,
Jer 50:10 So *B* will be plundered;
51:24 in *B* for all the wrong they have
51:35 be on those who live in *B*,''
Eze 11:24 to the exiles in *B* in the vision given
12:13 I will bring him to *B*, the land
16:29 your promiscuity to include *B*,
Da 1: 2 off to the temple of his god in *B*
Zec 5:11 "To the country of *B*

BABYLONIAN (BABYLON)

2Ki 24: 2 The LORD sent *B*, Aramean,
25: 5 but the *B* army pursued the king
25:10 The whole *B* army,
25:24 Do not be afraid of the *B* officials,''
Jer 35:11 go to Jerusalem to escape the *B*
37:10 to defeat the entire *B* army that is
37:11 After the *B* army had withdrawn
39: 5 But the *B* army pursued them
41: 3 as the *B* soldiers who were there.
52: 8 the *B* army pursued King Zedekiah
52:14 The whole *B* army
Eze 23:15 them looked like *B* chariot officers,
Da 9: 1 ruler over the *B* kingdom—

BABYLONIANS (BABYLON)

2Ki 25: 4 the *B* were surrounding the city.
25:13 The *B* broke up the bronze pillars,
25:25 and the *B* who were with him
25:26 fled to Egypt for fear of the *B*.
2Ch 36:17 up against them the king of the *B*,
Isa 23:13 Look at the land of the *B*,
43:14 bring down as fugitives all the *B*,
47: 1 Daughter of the *B*.
47: 5 Daughter of the *B*;
48:14 his arm will be against the *B*.
48:20 flee from the *B*!
Jer 21: 4 and the *B* who are outside the wall
21: 9 to the *B* who are besieging you will
22:25 king of Babylon and to the *B*.
24: 5 from this place to the land of the *B*.
25:12 the land of the *B*, for their guilt,''
32: 4 out of the hands of the *B*
32: 5 against the *B*, you will not succeed
32:24 over to the *B* who are attacking it.
32:25 city will be handed over to the *B*,
32:28 to hand this city over to the *B*
32:29 *B* who are attacking this city will
32:43 it has been handed over to the *B*.'
33: 5 the sword in the fight with the *B*:
37: 5 when the *B* who were besieging
37: 8 Then the *B* will return
37: 9 'The *B* will surely leave us.'
37:13 "You are deserting to the *B*!''
37:14 "I am not deserting to the *B*.''
38: 2 goes over to the *B* will live.
38:18 city will be handed over to the *B*
38:19 Jews who have gone over to the *B*,
38:19 for the *B* may hand me
38:23 will be brought out to the *B*.
39: 8 The *B* set fire to the royal palace
40: 9 "Do not be afraid to serve the *B*,''
40:10 you before the *B* who come to us,
41:18 way to Egypt to escape the *B*.
43: 3 against us to hand us over to the *B*,
50: 1 Babylon and the land of the *B*:
50: 8 leave the land of the *B*,
50:25 do in the land of the *B*.
50:35 "A sword against the *B*!''
50:45 purposed against the land of the *B*:
51:54 destruction from the land of the *B*.
52: 7 the *B* were surrounding the city.
52:17 The *B* broke up the bronze pillars,
Eze 1: 3 River in the land of the *B*.
23:17 Then the *B* came to her, to the bed
23:23 the *B* and all the Chaldeans,
Da 1: 4 language and literature of the *B*.
5:30 night Belshazzar, king of the *B*,
Hab 1: 6 I am raising up the *B*,

BABYLONIANS' (BABYLON)

Isa 13:19 the glory of the *B*' pride,

BACA

Ps 84: 6 pass through the Valley of *B*,

BACKBONE

Lev 3: 9 entire fat tail cut off close to the *b*,

BACKGROUND

Est 2:10 her nationality and family *b*,
2:20 Esther had kept secret her family *b*

BACKS

Ex 23:27 make all your enemies turn their *b*
Jos 7:12 they turn their *b* and run
23:13 whips on your *b* and thorns
2Sa 22:41 You made my enemies turn their *b*
2Ch 29: 6 and turned their *b* on him.
Ne 9:26 they put your law behind their *b*.
9:29 Stubbornly they turned their *b*
Ps 18:40 You made my enemies turn their *b*
21:12 for you will make them turn their *b*
66:11 and laid burdens on our *b*.
69:23 and their *b* be bent forever.
Pr 19:29 and beatings for the *b* of fools.
26: 3 and a rod for the *b* of fools!
Isa 1: 4 and turned their *b* on him.
30: 6 carry their riches on donkeys' *b*,
59:13 turning our *b* on our God,
Jer 2:27 They have turned their *b* to me
32:33 They turned their *b* to me
Eze 8:16 With their *b* toward the temple
10:12 entire bodies, including their *b*,
29: 7 and their *b* were wrenched.
Zec 7:11 stubbornly they turned their *b*
Ro 11:10 and their *b* be bent forever.''
2Pe 2:21 and then to turn their *b*

BACKSLIDING (BACKSLIDINGS)

Jer 2:19 your *b* will rebuke you.
3:22 I will cure you of *b*.''
14: 7 For our *b* is great;
15: 6 "You keep on *b*.
Eze 37:23 them from all their sinful *b*,

BACKSLIDINGS (BACKSLIDING)

Jer 5: 6 and their *b* many.

BAFFLED

Da 5: 9 His nobles were *b*.
Ac 9:22 and *b* the Jews living in Damascus

BAG (BAGS)

Dt 25:13 two differing weights in your *b*—
1Sa 17:40 in the pouch of his shepherd's *b*
17:49 into his *b* and taking out a stone,
Job 14:17 My offenses will be sealed up in a *b*
Pr 16:11 in the *b* are of his making.
Mic 6:11 with a *b* of false weights?
Mt 10:10 take no *b* for the journey,
Mk 6: 8 no *b*, no money in your belts.
Lk 9: 3 no staff, no *b*, no bread, no money,
10: 4 Do not take a purse or *b* or sandals;
22:35 "When I sent you without purse, *b*
22:36 a *b*; and if you don't have a sword,
Jn 12: 6 as keeper of the money *b*, he used

BAGGAGE

1Sa 10:22 he has hidden himself among the *b*

BAGS (BAG)

Ge 42:25 orders to fill their *b* with grain,
43:11 products of the land in your *b*
2Ki 5:23 the two talents of silver in two *b*,
12:10 of the LORD and put it into *b*.
Isa 46: 6 Some pour out gold from their *b*

BAHARUMITE

1Ch 11:33 Azmaveth the *B*, Eliahba

BAHURIM

2Sa 3:16 behind her all the way to *B*.
16: 5 As King David approached *B*,
17:18 went to the house of a man in *B*.
19:16 son of Gera, the Benjamite from *B*,
1Ki 2: 8 son of Gera, the Benjamite from *B*,

BAKBAKKAR

1Ch 9:15 son of Hashabiah, a Merarite; *B*,

BAKBUK

Ezr 2:51 Meunim, Nephussim, *B*, Hakupha,
Ne 7:53 Meunim, Nephussim, *B*, Hakupha,

BAKBUKIAH

Ne 11:17 *B*, second among his associates;

Ne 12: 9 *B* and Unni, their associates,
12:25 Mattaniah, *B*, Obadiah,

BAKE (BAKED BAKER BAKERS BAKES BAKING)

Ge 11: 3 bricks and *b* them thoroughly."
18: 6 and knead it and *b* some bread."
Ex 16:23 So *b* what you want to *b*
Lev 24: 5 and *b* twelve loaves of bread,
26:26 able to *b* your bread in one oven,
Eze 4:12 *b* it in the sight of the people,
4:15 "I will let you *b* your bread
46:20 and the sin offering and *b* the grain

BAKED (BAKE)

Ge 40:17 kinds of *b* goods for Pharaoh,
Ex 12:39 they *b* cakes of unleavened bread.
Lev 2: 4 " 'If you bring a grain offering *b*
6:17 It must not be *b* with yeast;
7: 9 Every grain offering *b* in an oven
23:17 *b* with yeast, as a wave offering
1Sa 28:24 and *b* bread without yeast.
2Sa 13: 8 made the bread in his sight and *b* it.
1Ki 19: 6 a cake of bread *b* over hot coals,
2Ki 4:42 of barley bread *b* from the first ripe
Isa 44:19 I even *b* bread over its coals,
Da 2:33 partly of iron and partly of *b* clay.
2:41 and toes were partly of *b* clay
2:43 you saw the iron mixed with *b* clay,

BAKER (BAKE)

Ge 40: 1 the *b* of the king of Egypt offended
40: 2 the chief cupbearer and the chief *b*,
40: 5 and the *b* of the king of Egypt,
40:16 When the chief *b* saw that Joseph
40:20 and the chief *b* in the presence
40:22 but he hanged the chief *b*,
41:10 and the chief *b* in the house
Hos 7: 4 whose fire the *b* need not stir

BAKERS (BAKE)

1Sa 8:13 to be perfumers and cooks and *b*.
Jer 37:21 from the street of the *b* each day

BAKES (BAKE)

Isa 44:15 he kindles a fire and *b* bread.

BAKING (BAKE)

Ge 19: 3 for them, *b* bread without yeast,
1Ch 9:31 for *b* the offering bread.
23:29 the unleavened wafers, the *b*

BALAAM (BALAAM'S)

Nu 22: 5 to summon *B* son of Beor,
22: 7 to *B*, they told him what Balak had
22: 8 "Spend the night here," *B* said
22: 9 God came to *B* and asked,
22:10 men with you?" *B* said to God,
22:12 But God said to *B*, "Do not go
22:13 The next morning *B* got up
22:14 "*B* refused to come with us."
22:16 to *B* and said: "This is what Balak
22:18 But *B* answered them, "Even
22:20 That night God came to *B* and said
22:21 *B* got up in the morning, saddled
22:22 *B* was riding on his donkey,
22:23 *B* beat her to get her back
22:27 she lay down under *B*,
22:28 donkey's mouth, and she said to *B*,
22:29 *B* answered the donkey, "You
22:30 to *B*, "Am I not your own donkey,
22:34 *B* said to the angel of the LORD,
22:35 The angel of the LORD said to *B*,
22:35 *B* went with the princes of Balak.
22:36 Balak heard that *B* was coming,
22:37 to *B*, "Did I not send you an urgent
22:38 I have come to you now," *B* replied
22:39 Then *B* went with Balak to Kiriath
22:40 to *B* and the princes who were
22:41 The next morning Balak took *B* up
23: 1 *B* said, "Build me seven altars here,
23: 2 as *B* said, and the two
23: 3 Then *B* said to Balak, "Stay here
23: 4 God met with him, and *B* said,
23: 7 Then *B* uttered his oracle:
23:11 said to *B*, "What have you done
23:15 *B* said to Balak, "Stay here
23:16 The LORD met with *B*

Nu 23:25 said to *B*, "Neither curse them
23:26 nor bless them at all!" *B* answered,
23:27 Then Balak said to *B*, "Come,
23:28 Balak took *B* to the top of Peor,
23:29 *B* said, "Build me seven altars here,
23:30 Balak did as *B* had said,
24: 1 Now when *B* saw that it pleased
24: 2 When *B* looked out and saw Israel
24: 3 "The oracle of *B* son of Beor,
24:10 Balak's anger burned against *B*.
24:12 *B* answered Balak, "Did I not tell
24:15 "The oracle of *B* son of Beor,
24:20 *B* saw Amalek and uttered his
24:25 Then *B* got up and returned home
31: 8 killed *B* son of Beor with the sword
Dt 23: 4 and they hired *B* son of Beor
23: 5 your God would not listen to *B*
Jos 13:22 put to the sword *B* son of Beor,
24: 9 he sent for *B* son of Beor
24:10 But I would not listen to *B*,
Ne 13: 2 but had hired *B* to call a curse
Mic 6: 5 and what *B* son of Beor answered.
2Pe 2:15 to follow the way of *B* son of Beor,
Rev 2:14 hold to the teaching of *B*,

BALAAM'S (BALAAM)

Nu 22:25 crushing *B* foot against it.
22:31 Then the LORD opened *B* eyes,
23: 5 LORD put a message in *B* mouth
31:16 the ones who followed *B* advice
Jude :11 rushed for profit into *B* error;

BALADAN

2Ki 20:12 Merodach-Baladan son of *B* king
Isa 39: 1 Merodach-Baladan son of *B* king

BALAH

Jos 19: 3 Hazar Shual, *B*, Ezem, Eltolad,

BALAK (BALAK'S)

Nu 22: 2 *B* son of Zippor saw all that Israel
22: 4 So *B* son of Zippor, who was king
22: 5 *B* said: "A people has come out
22: 7 they told him what *B* had said.
22:10 said to God, "*B* son of Zippor,
22:14 the Moabite princes returned to *B*
22:15 Then *B* sent other princes,
22:16 "This is what *B* son of Zippor says:
22:18 "Even if *B* gave me his palace filled
22:35 Balaam went with the princes of *B*.
22:36 When *B* heard that Balaam was
22:37 *B* said to Balaam, "Did I not send
22:39 went with *B* to Kiriath Huzoth.
22:40 *B* sacrificed cattle and sheep,
22:41 next morning *B* took Balaam up
23: 2 *B* did as Balaam said, and the two
23: 3 Then Balaam said to *B*, "Stay here
23: 5 to *B* and give him this message."
23: 7 "*B* brought me from Aram,
23:11 *B* said to Balaam, "What have you
23:13 in my mouth?" Then *B* said to him,
23:15 Balaam said to *B*, "Stay here
23:16 to *B* and give him this message."
23:17 *B* asked him, "What did
23:18 "Arise, *B*, and listen;
23:25 *B* said to Balaam, "Neither curse
23:27 Then *B* said to Balaam, "Come,
23:28 *B* took Balaam to the top of Peor,
23:30 *B* did as Balaam had said,
24:12 Balaam answered *B*, "Did I not tell
24:13 'Even if *B* gave me his palace filled
24:25 returned home and *B* went his own
Jos 24: 9 When *B* son of Zippor, the king
Jdg 11:25 better than *B* son of Zippor,
Mic 6: 5 My people, remember what *B*
Rev 2:14 who taught *B* to entice

BALAK'S (BALAK)

Nu 22:13 got up and said to *B* princes,
24:10 *B* anger burned against Balaam.

BALANCE (BALANCES)

Lev 25:27 and refund the *b* to the man
Ps 62: 9 if weighed on a *b*, they are nothing;
Isa 40:12 and the hills in a *b*?

BALANCES (BALANCE)

Pr 16:11 *b* are from the LORD;

BALD (BALDHEAD BALDNESS)

Lev 13:40 a man has lost his hair and is *b*,
13:41 of his scalp and has a *b* forehead,
13:42 a reddish-white sore on his *b* head
Isa 3:17 the LORD will make their scalps *b*
Mic 1:16 make yourselves as *b* as the vulture

BALDHEAD (BALD)

2Ki 2:23 you *b*!" He turned around,
2:23 "Go on up, you *b*!" they said.

BALDNESS (BALD)

Isa 3:24 instead of well-dressed hair, *b*;

BALL

Isa 22:18 He will roll you up tightly like a *b*

BALM

Ge 37:25 camels were loaded with spices, *b*
43:11 a little *b* and a little honey,
2Ch 28:15 food and drink, and healing *b*.
Jer 8:22 Is there no *b* in Gilead?
46:11 "Go up to Gilead and get *b*,
51: 8 Get *b* for her pain;
Eze 27:17 honey, oil and *b* for your wares.

BALSAM

2Sa 5:23 attack them in front of the *b* trees.
5:24 marching in the tops of the *b* trees,
1Ch 14:14 attack them in front of the *b* trees.
14:15 marching in the tops of the *b* trees,

BAMAH

Eze 20:29 (It is called *B* to this day.)

BAMOTH

Nu 21:19 to Nahaliel, from Nahaliel to *B*,
21:20 and from *B* to the valley

BAMOTH BAAL

Nu 22:41 Balak took Balaam up to *B*,
Jos 13:17 the plateau, including Dibon, *B*,

BAN

1Ch 2: 7 violating the *b* on taking devoted

BAND (BANDED BANDS)

Ge 49:19 "Gad will be attacked by a *b*
Ex 39:23 and a *b* around this opening,
2Sa 1:10 on his head and the *b* on his arm
23:13 while a *b* of Philistines was
1Ki 7:35 there was a circular *b* half a cubit
11:24 became the leader of a *b* of rebels
2Ki 13:21 suddenly they saw a *b* of raiders;
19:31 out of Mount Zion a *b* of survivors.
1Ch 11:15 while a *b* of Philistines was
Ps 22:16 a *b* of evil men has encircled me,
78:49 a *b* of destroying angels.
86:14 a *b* of ruthless men seeks my life—
94:21 *b* together against the righteous
Isa 31: 4 and though a whole *b* of shepherds
37:32 out of Mount Zion a *b* of survivors.
Ac 5:37 and led a *b* of people in revolt.

BANDAGED

Isa 1: 6 not cleansed or *b*
Lk 10:34 He went to him and *b* his wounds,

BANDED (BAND)

Nu 14:35 which has *b* together against me.
16:11 all your followers have *b* together.
27: 3 who *b* together against the LORD,
2Sa 23:11 When the Philistines *b* together

BANDIT (BANDITS)

Pr 6:11 poverty will come on you like a *b*
23:28 Like a *b* she lies in wait,
24:34 poverty will come on you like a *b*

BANDITS (BANDIT)

Ezr 8:31 from enemies and *b* along the way.
Hos 7: 1 *b* rob in the streets;
2Co 11:26 in danger from *b*, in danger

BANDS (BAND)

Ex 27:10 and with silver hooks and *b*
27:11 and with silver hooks and *b*
27:17 the courtyard are to have silver *b*

Ex 36:38 of the posts and their *b* with gold
38:10 and with silver hooks and *b*
38:11 with silver hooks and *b*
38:12 with silver hooks and *b*
38:17 and *b* on the posts were silver,
38:17 posts of the courtyard had silver *b*.
38:19 Their hooks and *b* were silver,
38:28 of the posts, and to make their *b*.
2Sa 4:2 men who were leaders of raiding *b*.
2Ki 5:2 Now *b* from Aram had gone out
6:23 the *b* from Aram stopped raiding
1Ch 12:18 made them leaders of his raiding *b*.
12:21 helped David against raiding *b*,
Hos 6:9 so do *b* of priests;

BANGLES

Isa 3:18 the *b* and headbands and crescent

BANI

1Ch 6:46 the son of *B*, the son of Shemer,
9:4 the son of Imri, the son of *B*,
Ezr 2:10 of Zaccai 760 of *B* 642
8:10 descendants of *B*, Shelomith son
10:29 From the descendants of *B*:
10:34 From the descendants of *B*:
Ne 3:17 the Levites under Rehum son of *B*.
8:7 Jeshua, *B*, Sherebiah, Jamin,
9:4 Bunni, Sherebiah, *B* and Kenani—
9:4 Jeshua, *B*, Kadmiel, Shebaniah,
9:5 Jeshua, Kadmiel, *B*, Hashabneiah,
10:13 Shebaniah, Hodiah, *B* and Beninu.
10:14 Elam, Zattu, *B*, Bunni, Azgad,
11:22 in Jerusalem was Uzzi son of *B*,

BANISH (BANISHED BANISHMENT)

2Ki 13:23 or *b* them from his presence.
Ps 5:10 *B* them for their many sins,
125:5 the LORD will *b* with the evildoers
Ecc 11:10 So then, *b* anxiety from your heart
Jer 8:3 Wherever I *b* them, all
24:9 and cursing, wherever I *b* them.
25:10 I will *b* from them the sounds of joy
27:10 I will *b* you and you will perish.
27:15 I will *b* you and you will perish,
32:37 from all the lands where I *b* them
Zec 13:2 I will *b* the names of the idols

BANISHED (BANISH)

Ge 3:23 So the LORD God *b* him
Dt 30:4 Even if you have been *b*
2Sa 14:13 has not brought back his *b* son?
14:14 so that a *b* person may not remain
1Ch 12:1 while he was *b* from the presence
Job 18:18 and is *b* from the world.
20:8 *b* like a vision of the night.
30:5 They were *b* from their fellow men,
Isa 24:11 all gaiety is *b* from the earth.
Jer 16:15 countries where he had *b* them.'
23:8 countries where he had *b* them.'
23:12 they will be *b* to darkness
29:14 and places where I have *b* you,"
Jnh 2:4 I said, 'I have been *b*
Zec 5:3 every thief will be *b*, and according
5:3 who swears falsely will be *b*.

BANISHMENT (BANISH)

Ezr 7:26 *b*, confiscation of property,

BANK (BANKERS BANKS EMBANKMENT)

Ge 41:17 standing on the *b* of the Nile,
Ex 2:3 the reeds along the *b* of the Nile.
2:5 were walking along the river *b*.
7:15 Wait on the *b* of the Nile
Jos 13:23 of the Reubenites was the *b*
2Ki 2:13 and stood on the *b* of the Jordan.
Eze 47:6 he led me back to the *b* of the river.
Da 10:4 standing on the *b* of the great river,
12:5 and one on the opposite *b*.
12:5 one on this *b* of the river
Mt 8:32 down the steep *b* into the lake
Mk 5:13 down the steep *b* into the lake
Lk 8:33 down the steep *b* into the lake

BANKERS (BANK)

Mt 25:27 money on deposit with the *b*,

BANKS (BANK)

1Ch 12:15 when it was overflowing all its *b*,
Isa 8:7 run over all its *b*
Eze 47:12 grow on both *b* of the river.

BANNER (BANNERS)

Ex 17:15 and called it The LORD is my *B*.
Ps 60:4 who fear you, you have raised a *b*
SS 2:4 and his *b* over me is love.
Isa 5:26 He lifts up a *b* for the distant
11:10 the Root of Jesse will stand as a *b*
11:12 He will raise a *b* for the nations
13:2 Raise a *b* on a bare hilltop,
18:3 a *b* is raised on the mountains,
30:17 like a *b* on a hill."
49:22 I will lift up my *b* to the peoples;
62:10 Raise a *b* for the nations.
Jer 50:2 lift up a *b* and proclaim it;
51:12 Lift up a *b* against the walls
51:27 "Lift up a *b* in the land!
Eze 27:7 and served as your *b*;

BANNERS (BANNER)

Nu 2:2 standard with the *b* of his family."
Ps 20:5 will lift up our *b* in the name
SS 6:4 majestic as troops with *b*.

BANQUET (BANQUETS)

1Sa 25:36 in the house holding a *b* like that
Est 1:3 year of his reign he gave a *b*
1:5 king gave a *b*, lasting seven days,
1:9 also gave a *b* for the women
2:18 And the king gave a great *b*,
2:18 Esther's *b*, for all his nobles
5:4 come today to a *b* I have prepared
5:5 went to the *b* Esther had prepared.
5:8 tomorrow to the *b* I will prepare
5:12 the king to the *b* she gave.
6:14 away to the *b* Esther had prepared.
7:8 from the palace garden to the *b* hall
SS 2:4 He has taken me to the *b* hall,
Isa 25:6 a *b* of aged wine—
Da 5:1 King Belshazzar gave a great *b*
5:10 his nobles, came into the *b* hall.
Mt 22:2 a king who prepared a wedding *b*
22:3 to the *b* to tell them to come,
22:4 Come to the wedding *b*.'
22:8 servants, 'The wedding *b* is ready,
22:9 invite to the *b* anyone you find.'
25:10 went in with him to the wedding *b*.
Mk 6:21 On his birthday Herod gave a *b*
Lk 5:29 Then Levi held a great *b* for Jesus
12:36 master to return from a wedding *b*,
14:13 when you give a *b*, invite the poor,
14:16 man was preparing a great *b*
14:17 the time of the *b* he sent his servant
14:24 invited will get a taste of my *b*.'"
Jn 2:8 and take it to the master of the *b*."
2:9 of the *b* tasted the water that had

BANQUETS (BANQUET)

Isa 5:12 have harps and lyres at their *b*,
Mt 23:6 they love the place of honor at *b*
Mk 12:39 and the places of honor at *b*.
Lk 20:46 and the places of honor at *b*.

BAPTISM (BAPTIZE)

Mt 21:25 John's *b*— where did it come from?
Mk 1:4 and preaching a *b* of repentance
10:38 baptized with the *b* I am baptized
10:39 baptized with the *b* I am baptized
11:30 John's *b*— was it from heaven,
Lk 3:3 preaching a *b* of repentance
12:50 But I have a *b* to undergo,
20:4 John's *b*— was it from heaven,
Ac 1:22 beginning from John's *b*
10:37 after the *b* that John preached—
13:24 and *b* to all the people of Israel.
18:25 though he knew only the *b* of John.
19:3 did you receive?" "John's *b*,"
19:3 "Then what *b* did you receive?"
19:4 "John's *b* was a *b* of repentance.
Ro 6:4 with him through *b* into death
Eph 4:5 one Lord, one faith, one *b*;
Col 2:12 having been buried with him in *b*
1Pe 3:21 this water symbolizes *b* that now

BAPTISMS (BAPTIZE)

Heb 6:2 instruction about *b*, the laying

BAPTIST (BAPTIZE)

Mt 3:1 In those days John the *B* came,
11:11 anyone greater than John the *B*;
11:12 the days of John the *B* until now,
14:2 "This is John the *B*; he has risen
14:8 on a platter the head of John the *B*
16:14 say John the *B*; others say Elijah;
17:13 talking to them about John the *B*.
Mk 6:14 "John the *B* has been raised
6:24 "The head of John the *B*,"
6:25 head of John the *B* on a platter."
8:28 say John the *B*; others say Elijah;
Lk 7:20 "John the *B* sent us to you to ask,
7:33 For John the *B* came neither eating
9:19 say John the *B*; others say Elijah;

BAPTIZE (BAPTISM BAPTISMS BAPTIST BAPTIZED BAPTIZING)

Mt 3:11 He will *b* you with the Holy Spirit
3:11 "I *b* you with water for repentance.
Mk 1:8 I *b* you with water, but he will
1:8 he will *b* you with the Holy Spirit."
Lk 3:16 He will *b* you with the Holy Spirit
3:16 John answered them all, "I *b* you
Jn 1:25 "Why then do you *b*
1:26 nor the Prophet?" "I *b* with water,"
1:33 and remain is he who will *b*
1:33 me to *b* with water told me,
1Co 1:14 I am thankful that I did not *b* any
1:17 For Christ did not send me to *b*,

BAPTIZED (BAPTIZE)

Mt 3:6 they were *b* by him in the Jordan
3:13 to the Jordan to be *b* by John.
3:14 saying, "I need to be *b* by you,
3:16 as Jesus was *b*, he went up out
Mk 1:5 they were *b* by him in the Jordan
1:9 and was *b* by John in the Jordan.
10:38 or be *b* with the baptism I am
10:38 with the baptism I am *b* with?"
10:39 and be *b* with the baptism I am
10:39 with the baptism I am *b* with,
16:16 believes and is *b* will be saved,
Lk 3:7 to the crowds coming out to be *b*
3:12 Tax collectors also came to be *b*.
3:21 were being *b*, Jesus was *b* too.
7:29 because they had been *b* by John.
7:30 they had not been *b* by John.)
Jn 3:22 spent some time with them, and *b*.
3:23 were constantly coming to be *b*.
4:2 in fact it was not Jesus who *b*,
Ac 1:5 For John *b* with water,
1:5 but in a few days you will be *b*
2:38 Repent and be *b*, every one of you,
2:41 who accepted his message were *b*,
8:12 they were *b*, both men and women.
8:13 Simon himself believed and was *b*.
8:16 they had simply been *b*
8:36 Why shouldn't I be *b*?"
8:38 into the water and Philip *b* him.
9:18 was *b*, and after taking some food,
10:47 people from being *b* with water?
10:48 So he ordered that they be *b*
11:16 what the Lord had said, 'John *b*
11:16 you will be *b* with the Holy Spirit.'
16:15 members of her household were *b*,
16:33 he and all his family were *b*.
18:8 heard him believed and were *b*.
19:5 they were *b* into the name
22:16 be *b* and wash your sins away,
Ro 6:3 *b* into Christ Jesus were *b*
1Co 1:13 Were you *b* into the name of Paul?
1:15 so no one can say that you were *b*
1:16 I also *b* the household of Stephanas
1:16 I don't remember if I *b* anyone else
10:2 They were all *b* into Moses
12:13 For we were all *b* by one Spirit
15:29 what will those do who are *b*
15:29 why are people *b* for them?
Gal 3:27 all of you who were *b*

BAPTIZING (BAPTIZE)

Mt 3:7 coming to where he was *b*,
28:19 *b* them in the name of the Father
Mk 1:4 *b* in the desert region

Jn 1:28 of the Jordan, where John was *b*.
1:31 but the reason I came *b*
3:23 also was *b* at Aenon near Salim,
3:26 he is *b*, and everyone is going
4: 1 and *b* more disciples than John,
10:40 to the place where John had been *b*

BAR

Jdg 16: 3 and tore them loose, *b* and all.
Ne 7: 3 them shut the doors and *b* them.
Isa 9: 4 the *b* across their shoulders,

BAR-JESUS

Ac 13: 6 and false prophet named *B*,

BARABBAS

Mt 27:16 had a notorious prisoner, called *B*.
27:17 *B*, or Jesus who is called Christ?"
27:20 persuaded the crowd to ask for *B*
27:21 "*B*," they answered.
27:26 Then he released *B* to them.
Mk 15: 7 A man called *B* was in prison
15:11 to have Pilate release *B* instead.
15:15 Pilate released *B* to them.
Lk 23:18 with this man! Release *B* to us!"
23:19 (*B* had been thrown into prison
Jn 18:40 *B* had taken part in a rebellion.
18:40 "No, not him! Give us *B!*"

BARAK (BARAK'S)

Jdg 4: 6 She sent for *B* son of Abinoam
4: 8 *B* said to her, "If you go with me,
4: 9 So Deborah went with *B* to Kedesh
4:12 When they told Sisera that *B* son
4:14 So *B* went down Mount Tabor,
4:14 Then Deborah said to *B*, "Go!
4:16 But *B* pursued the chariots
4:22 *B* came by in pursuit of Sisera,
5: 1 *B* son of Abinoam sang this song:
5:12 Arise, O *B!*
5:15 yes, Issachar was with *B*,
1Sa 12:11 the LORD sent Jerub-Baal, *B*,
Heb 11:32 *B*, Samson, Jephthah, David,

BARAK'S (BARAK)

Jdg 4:15 At *B* advance, the LORD routed

BARAKEL

Job 32: 2 But Elihu son of *B* the Buzite,
32: 6 So Elihu son of *B* the Buzite said:

BARBARIAN

Col 3:11 circumcised or uncircumcised, *b*,

BARBER'S

Eze 5: 1 as a *b* razor to shave your head

BARBS

Nu 33:55 allow to remain will become *b*

BARE (BARED)

Jdg 14: 6 tore the lion apart with his *b* hands
2Sa 22:16 the foundations of the earth laid *b*
2Ki 9:13 them under him on the *b* steps.
Job 28: 9 lays *b* the roots of the mountains.
Ps 18:15 the foundations of the earth laid *b*
29: 9 and strips the forests *b*.
Isa 13: 2 Raise a banner on a *b* hilltop,
23:13 they stripped its fortresses *b*
27:10 they strip its branches *b*.
47: 2 Lift up your skirts, *b* your legs,
52:10 The LORD will lay *b* his holy arm
Jer 2:25 Do not run until your feet are *b*
49:10 But I will strip Esau *b*;
Eze 13:14 so that its foundation will be laid *b*.
16: 7 you who were naked and *b*.
16:22 when you were naked and *b*,
16:39 and leave you naked and *b*.
23:29 They will leave you naked and *b*,
24: 7 She poured it on the *b* rock;
24: 8 I put her blood on the *b* rock,
26: 4 her rubble and make her a *b* rock.
26:14 I will make you a *b* rock,
29:18 every head was rubbed *b*
Hos 2: 3 as *b* as on the day she was born;
Mic 1: 6 and lay *b* her foundations.
1Co 14:25 the secrets of his heart will be laid *b*
Heb 4:13 and laid *b* before the eyes of him
2Pe 3:10 and everything in it will be laid *b*.

BARED (BARE)

Isa 20: 4 with buttocks *b*—
Eze 4: 7 with *b* arm prophesy against her.

BAREFOOT

2Sa 15:30 his head was covered and he was *b*.
Isa 20: 2 going around stripped and *b*.
20: 3 Isaiah has gone stripped and *b*
20: 4 and *b* the Egyptian captives
Mic 1: 8 I will go about *b* and naked.

BARGAIN

2Ki 18:23 make a *b* with my master,
Isa 36: 8 make a *b* with my master,

BARHUMITE

2Sa 23:31 Azmaveth the *B*, Eliahba

BARIAH

1Ch 3:22 Igal, *B*, Neariah and Shaphat—

BARK

Ge 30:37 stripes on them by peeling the *b*
Ex 11: 7 the Israelites not a dog will *b*
Isa 56:10 they cannot *b*;
Joel 1: 7 It has stripped off their *b*

BARKOS

Ezr 2:53 Mehida, Harsha, *B*, Sisera, Temah,
Ne 7:55 Mehida, Harsha, *B*, Sisera, Temah,

BARLEY

Ex 9:31 since the *b* had headed
9:31 (The flax and *b* were destroyed,
Lev 27:16 of silver to a homer of *b* seed.
Nu 5:15 of an ephah of *b* flour on her behalf.
Dt 8: 8 a land with wheat and *b*, vines
Jdg 7:13 loaf of *b* bread came tumbling
Ru 1:22 as the *b* harvest was beginning.
2:17 Then she threshed the *b* she had
2:23 girls of Boaz to glean until the *b*
3: 2 Tonight he will be winnowing *b*
3:15 he poured into it six measures of *b*
3:17 He gave me these six measures of *b*
2Sa 14:30 next to mine, and he has *b* there.
17:28 They also brought wheat and *b*,
21: 9 just as the *b* harvest was beginning.
1Ki 4:28 the proper place their quotas of *b*
2Ki 4:42 twenty loaves of *b* bread baked
7: 1 and two seahs of *b* for a shekel
7:16 and two seahs of *b* sold for a shekel
7:18 and two seahs of *b* for a shekel
1Ch 11:13 where there was a field full of *b*,
2Ch 2:10 twenty thousand cors of *b*,
2:15 and *b* and the olive oil and wine he
27: 5 and ten thousand cors of *b*.
Job 31:40 and weeds instead of *b*."
Isa 28:25 *b* in its plot,
Jer 41: 8 We have wheat and *b*, oil
Eze 4: 9 "Take wheat and *b*, beans
4:12 Eat the food as you would a *b* cake;
13:19 people for a few handfuls of *b*
45:13 of an ephah from each homer of *b*.
Hos 3: 2 about a homer and a lethek of *b*.
Joel 1:11 grieve for the wheat and the *b*,
Jn 6: 9 a boy with five small *b* loaves
6:13 the pieces of the five *b* loaves left
Rev 6: 6 three quarts of *b* for a day's wages,

BARN (BARNS)

Hag 2:19 Is there yet any seed left in the *b?*
Mt 3:12 gathering the wheat into his *b*
13:30 the wheat and bring it into my *b*.' "
Lk 3:17 and to gather the wheat into his *b*,
12:24 they have no storeroom or *b*;

BARNABAS

Ac 4:36 the apostles called *B* (which means
9:27 But *B* took him and brought him
11:22 and they sent *B* to Antioch.
11:25 *B* went to Tarsus to look for Saul,
11:26 So for a whole year *B* and Saul met
11:30 sending their gift to the elders by *B*
12:25 When *B* and Saul had finished
13: 1 *B*, Simeon called Niger, Lucius
13: 2 "Set apart for me *B* and Saul
13: 7 for *B* and Saul because he wanted
13:42 and *B* were leaving the synagogue,
13:43 to Judaism followed Paul and *B*,
13:46 Paul and *B* answered them boldly:
13:50 persecution against Paul and *B*,
14: 1 At Iconium Paul and *B* went
14: 3 *B* spent considerable time there,
14:12 us in human form!" *B* they called
14:14 But when the apostles *B*
14:20 The next day he and *B* left
14:23 and *B* appointed elders for them
15: 2 So Paul and *B* were appointed,
15: 2 This brought Paul and *B*
15:12 listened to *B* and Paul telling about
15:22 them to Antioch with Paul and *B*.
15:25 to you with our dear friends *B*
15:35 Paul and *B* remained in Antioch,
15:36 Some time later Paul said to *B*,
15:37 *B* wanted to take John,
15:39 *B* took Mark and sailed for Cyprus,
1Co 9: 6 and *B* who must work for a living?
Gal 2: 1 to Jerusalem, this time with *B*.
2: 9 and *B* the right hand of fellowship
2:13 their hypocrisy even *B* was led
Col 4:10 as does Mark, the cousin of *B*.

BARNS (BARN)

Dt 28: 8 will send a blessing on your *b*
Ps 144:13 Our *b* will be filled
Pr 3:10 then your *b* will be filled
Mt 6:26 or reap or store away in *b*,
Lk 12:18 down my *b* and build bigger ones,

BARRACKS

Ac 21:34 that Paul be taken into the *b*.
21:37 about to take Paul into the *b*,
22:24 Paul to be taken into the *b*.
23:10 by force and bring him into the *b*.
23:16 he went into the *b* and told Paul.
23:32 while they returned to the *b*.

BARRED (BARS)

Pr 18:19 disputes are like the *b* gates
Isa 24:10 the entrance to every house is *b*.
La 3: 9 He has *b* my way with blocks
Jnh 2: 6 the earth beneath *b* me in forever.

BARREN

Ge 11:30 Sarai was *b*; she had no children.
25:21 of his wife, because she was *b*.
29:31 her womb, but Rachel was *b*.
Ex 23:26 and none will miscarry or be *b*
Nu 23: 3 Then he went off to a *b* height.
Dt 32:10 in a *b* and howling waste.
1Sa 2: 5 She who was *b* has borne seven
Job 3: 7 May that night be *b*;
15:34 of the godless will be *b*,
24:21 on the *b* and childless woman,
Ps 113: 9 He settles the *b* woman
Pr 30:16 the grave, the *b* womb,
Isa 41:18 I will make rivers flow on *b* heights
49: 9 and find pasture on every *b* hill.
49:21 I was bereaved and *b*;
54: 1 "Sing, O *b* woman,
Jer 2: 6 and led us through the *b* wilderness
3: 2 "Look up to the *b* heights and see.
3:21 A cry is heard on the *b* heights,
4:11 wind from the *b* heights
7:29 take up a lament on the *b* heights,
12:12 Over all the *b* heights in the desert
14: 6 donkeys stand on the *b* heights
Joel 2:20 it into a parched and *b* land,
Lk 1: 7 children, because Elizabeth was *b*;
1:36 said to be *b* is in her sixth month.
23:29 'Blessed are the *b* women,
Gal 4:27 "Be glad, O *b* woman,
Heb 11:11 and Sarah herself was *b*—

BARRIER (BARS)

Jer 5:22 an everlasting *b* it cannot cross.
Eph 2:14 two one and has destroyed the *b*,

BARS (BARRED BARRIER)

Lev 26:13 I broke the *b* of your yoke
Dt 3: 5 high walls and with gates and *b*,
1Sa 23: 7 by entering a town with gates and *b*
1Ki 4:13 cities with bronze gate *b*);
2Ch 8: 5 walls and with gates and *b*, as

2Ch 14: 7 with towers, gates and *b*.
Ne 3: 3 and put its doors and bolts and *b*
3: 6 and put its doors and bolts and *b*
3: 13 and put its doors and bolts and *b*
3: 14 and put its doors and bolts and *b*
3: 15 putting its doors and bolts and *b*
Job 38: 10 and set its doors and *b* in place,
Ps 68: 30 Humbled, may it bring *b* of silver.
107: 16 and cuts through *b* of iron.
147: 13 for he strengthens the *b*
Isa 45: 2 and cut through *b* of iron.
Jer 49: 31 nation that has neither gates nor *b;*
51: 30 the *b* of her gates are broken.
La 2: 9 their *b* he has broken
Eze 34: 27 when I break the *b* of their yoke
38: 11 and without gates and *b*.
Hos 11: 6 will destroy the *b* of their gates
Na 3: 13 fire has consumed their *b*.

BARSABBAS

Ac 1: 23 Joseph called *B* (also known
15: 22 They chose Judas (called *B)*

BARTER

Job 6: 27 and *b* away your friend.
41: 6 Will traders *b* for him?
La 1: 11 they *b* their treasures for food

BARTHOLOMEW

Mt 10: 3 and his brother John; Philip and *B;*
Mk 3: 18 Andrew, Philip, *B*, Matthew,
Lk 6: 14 John, Philip, *B*, Matthew, Thomas,
Ac 1: 13 and Thomas, *B* and Matthew;

BARTIMAEUS

Mk 10: 46 *B* (that is, the Son of Timaeus),

BARUCH

Ne 3: 20 *B* son of Zabbai zealously repaired
10: 6 Daniel, Ginnethon, *B*, Meshullam,
11: 5 and Maaseiah son of *B*, the son
Jer 32: 12 I gave this deed to *B* son of Neriah,
32: 13 I gave *B* these instructions:
32: 16 of purchase to *B* son of Neriah,
36: 4 So Jeremiah called *B* son of Neriah
36: 4 *B* wrote them on the scroll.
36: 5 Jeremiah told *B*, "I am restricted;
36: 8 *B* son of Neriah did everything
36: 10 *B* read to all the people
36: 13 everything he had heard *B* read
36: 14 So *B* son of Neriah went to them
36: 14 the son of Cushi, to say to *B*,
36: 15 So *B* read it to them.
36: 16 at each other in fear and said to *B*,
36: 17 Then they asked *B*, "Tell us,
36: 18 dictate it?" "Yes," *B* replied,
36: 19 Then the officials said to *B*,
36: 26 son of Abdeel to arrest *B* the scribe
36: 27 the words that *B* had written
36: 32 *B* wrote on it all the words
36: 32 it to the scribe *B* son of Neriah,
43: 3 But *B* son of Neriah is inciting you
43: 6 Jeremiah the prophet and *B* son
45: 1 Jeremiah the prophet told *B* son
45: 1 after *B* had written
45: 2 says to you, *B:* You said, 'Woe

BARZILLAI

2Sa 17: 27 and *B* the Gileadite from Rogelim
19: 31 *B* the Gileadite also came
19: 32 Now *B* was a very old man,
19: 33 The king said to *B*, "Cross
19: 34 *B* answered the king, "How many
19: 39 The king kissed *B* and gave him his
19: 39 and *B* returned to his home.
21: 8 to Adriel son of *B* the Meholathite.
1Ki 2: 7 kindness to the sons of *B* of Gilead
Ezr 2: 61 a daughter of *B* the Gileadite
2: 61 and *B* (a man who had married
Ne 7: 63 a daughter of *B* the Gileadite
7: 63 and *B* (a man who had married

BASE (BASED BASES BASIC BASING BASIS)

Ex 25: 31 *b* and shaft; its flowerlike cups,
29: 12 the rest of it at the *b* of the altar.
37: 17 *b* and shaft; its flowerlike cups,
38: 27 one talent for each *b*.
Lev 4: 7 out at the *b* of the altar
4: 18 out at the *b* of the altar
4: 25 of the blood at the *b* of the altar.
4: 30 of the blood at the *b* of the altar.
4: 34 of the blood at the *b* of the altar.
5: 9 out at the *b* of the altar.
8: 15 of the blood at the *b* of the altar.
9: 9 out at the *b* of the altar.
Nu 8: 4 from its *b* to its blossoms.
2Ki 16: 17 supported it and set it on a stone *b*.
Job 30: 8 A *b* and nameless brood,
SS 3: 10 its *b* of gold.
Isa 3: 5 the *b* against the honorable.
Eze 31: 4 all around its *b*
41: 8 that the temple had a raised *b* all
41: 11 *b* adjoining the open area was five
41: 22 its *b* and its sides were of wood.

BASED (BASE)

Lev 25: 50 is to be *b* on the rate paid
Nu 26: 53 as an inheritance *b* on the number
Ro 2: 2 those who do such things is *b*
10: 2 but their zeal is not *b* on knowledge
Gal 3: 12 The law is not *b* on faith;
Col 2: 22 they are *b* on human commands

BASEMATH

Ge 26: 34 also *B* daughter of Elon the Hittite.
36: 3 also *B* daughter of Ishmael
36: 4 Eliphaz to Esau, *B* bore Reuel,
36: 10 and Reuel, the son of Esau's wife *B*
36: 13 were grandsons of Esau's wife *B*.
36: 17 were grandsons of Esau's wife *B*.
1Ki 4: 15 (he had married *B* daughter

BASES (BASE)

Ex 26: 19 and make forty silver *b* to go
26: 19 two *b* for each frame, one
26: 21 twenty frames and forty silver *b*—
26: 25 eight frames and sixteen silver *b*—
26: 32 and standing on four silver *b*.
26: 37 And cast five bronze *b* for them.
27: 10 bronze *b* and with silver hooks
27: 11 bronze *b* and with silver hooks
27: 12 with ten posts and ten *b*.
27: 14 with three posts and three *b*,
27: 15 with three posts and three *b*.
27: 16 with four posts and four *b*.
27: 17 bands and hooks, and bronze *b*.
27: 18 five cubits high, and with bronze *b*.
35: 11 frames, crossbars, posts and *b;*
35: 17 the courtyard with its posts and *b*,
36: 24 and made forty silver *b* to go
36: 24 two *b* for each frame, one
36: 26 twenty frames and forty silver *b*—
36: 30 eight frames and sixteen silver *b*—
36: 36 and cast their four silver *b*.
36: 38 and made their five *b* of bronze.
38: 10 twenty posts and twenty bronze *b*,
38: 11 twenty posts and twenty bronze *b*,
38: 12 and ten *b*, with silver hooks
38: 14 with three posts and three *b*,
38: 15 with three posts and three *b*.
38: 17 The *b* for the posts were bronze.
38: 19 with four posts and four bronze *b*.
38: 27 100 *b* from the 100 talents,
38: 27 used to cast the *b* for the sanctuary
38: 30 it to make the *b* for the entrance
38: 31 *b* for the surrounding courtyard
39: 33 frames, crossbars, posts and *b;*
39: 40 the courtyard with its posts and *b*,
40: 18 he put the *b* in place, erected
Nu 3: 36 posts, *b*, all its equipment,
3: 37 courtyard with their *b*,
4: 31 its crossbars, posts and *b*,
4: 32 courtyard with their *b*,
SS 5: 15 set on *b* of pure gold.

BASEWORK

1Ki 7: 31 and with its *b* it measured a cubit

BASHAN

Nu 21: 33 of *B* and his whole army marched
21: 33 went up along the road toward *B*,
32: 33 and the kingdom of Og king of *B*—
Dt 1: 4 at Edrei had defeated Og king of *B*,
3: 1 of *B* with his whole army marched
3: 1 went up along the road toward *B*,
Dt 3: 3 gave into our hands Og king of *B*
3: 4 of Argob, Og's kingdom in *B*.
3: 10 and all *B* as far as Salecah
3: 10 towns of Og's kingdom in *B*.
3: 11 (Only Og king of *B* was left
3: 13 The rest of Gilead and also all of *B*,
3: 13 of Argob in *B* used to be known
3: 14 that to this day *B* is called Havvoth
4: 43 and Golan in *B*, for the Manassites.
4: 47 and the land of Og king of *B*,
29: 7 and Og king of *B* came out to fight
32: 14 with choice rams of *B*
33: 22 springing out of *B*."
Jos 9: 10 and Og king of *B*, who reigned
12: 4 And the territory of Og king of *B*,
12: 5 all of *B* to the border of the people
13: 11 and all *B* as far as Salecah—
13: 12 the whole kingdom of Og in *B*,
13: 30 Mahanaim and including all of *B*,
13: 30 all the settlements of Jair in *B*,
13: 30 the entire realm of Og king of *B*—
13: 31 Edrei (the royal cities of Og in *B)*.
17: 1 who had received Gilead and *B*
17: 5 land besides Gilead and *B* east
20: 8 and Golan in *B* in the tribe
21: 6 the half-tribe of Manasseh in *B*.
21: 27 Golan in *B* (a city of refuge
22: 7 Moses had given land in *B*,
1Ki 4: 13 as well as the district of Argob in *B*
4: 19 and the country of Og king of *B)*.
2Ki 10: 33 Gorge through Gilead to *B*.
1Ch 5: 11 Gadites lived next to them in *B*,
5: 12 then Janai and Shaphat, in *B*.
5: 16 in *B* and its outlying villages,
5: 23 in the land from *B* to Baal Hermon,
6: 62 of the tribe of Manasseh that is in *B*
6: 71 they received Golan in *B*
Ne 9: 22 and the country of Og king of *B*.
Ps 22: 12 strong bulls of *B* encircle me.
68: 15 of *B* are majestic mountains;
68: 15 rugged are the mountains of *B*.
68: 22 Lord says, "I will bring you from *B;*
135: 11 Og king of *B*
136: 20 and Og king of *B*—
Isa 2: 13 and all the oaks of *B*,
33: 9 and *B* and Carmel drop their leaves
Jer 22: 20 let your voice be heard in *B*,
50: 19 and he will graze on Carmel and *B;*
Eze 27: 6 Of oaks from *B*
39: 18 all of them fattened animals from *B*
Am 4: 1 you cows of *B* on Mount Samaria,
Mic 7: 14 Let them feed in *B* and Gilead
Na 1: 4 *B* and Carmel wither
Zec 11: 2 Wail, oaks of *B;*

BASIC (BASE)

Gal 4: 3 in slavery under the *b* principles
Col 2: 8 the *b* principles of this world rather
2: 20 died with Christ to the *b* principles

BASIN (BASINS)

Ex 12: 22 dip it into the blood in the *b*
30: 18 "Make a bronze *b*,
30: 28 and all its utensils, and the *b*
31: 9 the *b* with its stand—and
35: 16 the bronze *b* with its stand;
38: 8 They made the bronze *b*
39: 39 all its utensils; the *b* with its stand;
40: 7 place the *b* between the Tent
40: 11 Anoint the *b* and its stand
40: 30 He placed the *b* between the Tent
Lev 8: 11 and all its utensils and the *b*
1Ki 7: 30 and each had a *b* resting
7: 38 one *b* to go on each
Jn 13: 5 he poured water into a *b*

BASING (BASE)

2Ki 18: 19 On what are you *b* this confidence
2Ch 32: 10 On what are you *b* your confidence
Isa 36: 4 On what are you *b* this confidence

BASINS (BASIN)

1Ki 7: 38 He then made ten bronze *b*,
7: 40 He also made the *b* and shovels
7: 43 the ten stands with their ten *b;*
2Ki 12: 13 spent for making silver *b*,
16: 17 removed the *b* from the movable
2Ch 4: 6 He then made ten *b* for washing

2Ch 4: 14 the stands with their *b*; the Sea
Jer 52: 19 the imperial guard took away the *b*,

BASIS (BASE)

Lev 25: 15 on the *b* of the number
25: 15 sell to you on the *b* of the number
1Ki 20: 34 "On the *b* of a treaty I will set you
Eze 16: 61 but not on the *b* of my covenant
Da 6: 5 "We will never find any *b*
Lk 23: 4 "I find no *b* for a charge
23: 14 have found no *b* for your charges
Jn 8: 6 order to have a *b* for accusing him.
18: 38 I find no *b* for a charge against him.
19: 4 you to let you know that I find no *b*
19: 6 I find no *b* for a charge against him
Phm : 9 yet I appeal to you on the *b* of love.
Heb 7: 11 (for on the *b* of it the law was given
7: 16 but on the *b* of the power
7: 16 not on the *b* of a regulation

BASKET (BASKETFULS BASKETS)

Ge 40: 17 In the top *b* were all kinds
40: 17 out of the *b* on my head."
Ex 2: 3 she got a papyrus *b* for him
2: 5 She saw the *b* among the reeds
29: 3 Put them in a *b* and present them
29: 23 From the *b* of bread made
29: 32 and the bread that is in the *b*.
Lev 8: 2 and the *b* containing bread made
8: 26 Then from the *b* of bread made
8: 31 from the *b* of ordination offerings,
Nu 6: 15 a *b* of bread made without yeast—
6: 17 present the *b* of unleavened bread
6: 19 and a cake and a wafer from the *b*,
Dt 23: 24 but do not put any in your *b*.
26: 2 is giving you and put them in a *b*.
26: 4 The priest shall take the *b*
26: 10 Place the *b* before the LORD your
28: 5 Your *b* and your kneading trough
28: 17 Your *b* and your kneading trough
Jdg 6: 19 Putting the meat in a *b*
Ps 81: 6 their hands were set free from the *b*
Isa 40: 12 the dust of the earth in a *b*,
Jer 24: 2 One *b* had very good figs, like
24: 2 the other *b* had very poor figs,
Am 8: 1 Sovereign LORD showed me: a *b*
8: 2 "A *b* of ripe fruit," I answered
Zec 5: 6 He replied, "It is a measuring *b*."
5: 7 and there in the *b* sat a woman!
5: 8 and he pushed her back into the *b*
5: 9 and they lifted up the *b*
5: 10 "Where are they taking the *b*?"
5: 11 the *b* will be set there in its place."
Ac 9: 25 him in a *b* through an opening
2Co 11: 33 I was lowered in a *b* from a window

BASKETFULS (BASKET)

Mt 14: 20 the disciples picked up twelve *b*
15: 37 the disciples picked up seven *b*
16: 9 and how many *b* you gathered?
16: 10 and how many *b* you gathered?
Mk 6: 43 the disciples picked up twelve *b*
8: 8 the disciples picked up seven *b*
8: 19 how many *b* of pieces did you pick
8: 20 how many *b* of pieces did you pick
Lk 9: 17 the disciples picked up twelve *b*

BASKETS (BASKET)

Ge 40: 16 On my head were three *b* of bread.
40: 18 "The three *b* are three days.
2Ki 10: 7 They put their heads in *b*
Jer 24: 1 the LORD showed me two *b*
Mt 13: 48 and collected the good fish in *b*,
Jn 6: 13 and filled twelve *b* with the pieces

BAT (BATS)

Lev 11: 19 of heron, the hoopoe and the *b*.
Dt 14: 18 of heron, the hoopoe and the *b*.

BATCH

Ro 11: 16 then the whole *b* is holy;
1Co 5: 6 through the whole *b* of dough?
5: 7 old yeast that you may be a new *b*
Gal 5: 9 through the whole *b* of dough."

BATH (BATHE)

Isa 5: 10 vineyard will produce only a *b*
Eze 45: 10 accurate ephah and an accurate *b*.
45: 11 and the *b* are to be the same size,
45: 11 the *b* containing a tenth of a homer
45: 14 a tenth of a *b* from each cor (which
45: 14 portion of oil, measured by the *b*,
Jn 13: 10 person who has had a *b* needs only

BATH RABBIM

SS 7: 4 Heshbon by the gate of *B*.

BATHE (BATH BATHED BATHING BATHS)

Ex 2: 5 went down to the Nile to *b*,
Lev 14: 8 off all his hair and *b* with water;
14: 9 wash his clothes and *b* himself
15: 5 his bed must wash his clothes and *b*
15: 6 sat on must wash his clothes and *b*
15: 7 must wash his clothes and *b*
15: 8 person must wash his clothes and *b*
15: 10 things must wash his clothes and *b*
15: 11 water must wash his clothes and *b*
15: 13 and *b* himself with fresh water,
15: 16 he must *b* his whole body
15: 18 both must *b* with water,
15: 21 bed must wash his clothes and *b*
15: 22 sits on must wash his clothes and *b*
15: 27 he must wash his clothes and *b*
16: 4 so he must *b* himself with water
16: 24 He shall *b* himself with water
16: 26 wash his clothes and *b* himself
16: 28 wash his clothes and *b* himself
17: 15 must wash his clothes and *b*
17: 16 not wash his clothes and *b* himself,
Nu 19: 7 wash his clothes and *b* himself
19: 8 wash his clothes and *b* with water,
19: 19 must wash his clothes and *b*
Dt 33: 24 and let him *b* his feet in oil.
Ps 58: 10 when they *b* their feet in the blood

BATHED (BATHE)

Lev 22: 6 unless he has *b* himself with water.
1Ki 22: 38 in Samaria (where the prostitutes *b*
Isa 34: 6 sword of the LORD is *b* in blood,
Eze 16: 9 " 'I *b* you with water and washed
23: 40 when they arrived you *b* yourself

BATHING (BATHE)

2Sa 11: 2 From the roof he saw a woman *b*.
Job 36: 30 *b* the depths of the sea.

BATHS (BATHE)

1Ki 5: 11 addition to twenty thousand *b*
7: 26 It held two thousand *b*.
7: 38 each holding forty *b* and measuring
2Ch 2: 10 twenty thousand *b* of olive oil."
2: 10 twenty thousand *b* of wine
4: 5 It held three thousand *b*.
Ezr 7: 22 cors of wheat, a hundred *b* of wine,
7: 22 of wine, a hundred *b* of olive oil,
Eze 45: 14 each cor (which consists of ten *b*
45: 14 for ten *b* are equivalent to a homer

BATHSHEBA

2Sa 11: 3 The man said, "Isn't this *B*,
12: 24 Then David comforted his wife *B*,
1Ki 1: 11 Then Nathan asked *B*, Solomon's
1: 15 So *B* went to see the aged king
1: 16 *B* bowed low and knelt
1: 28 Then King David said, "Call in *B*."
1: 31 Then *B* bowed low with her face
2: 13 *B* asked him, "Do you come
2: 13 went to *B*, Solomon's mother.
2: 18 *B* replied, "I will speak to the king
2: 19 When *B* went to King Solomon
1Ch 3: 5 were by *B* daughter of Ammiel.

BATHSHUA

1Ch 2: 3 These three were born to him by *B*,

BATS (BAT)

Isa 2: 20 away to the rodents and *b*

BATTERED (BATTERING)

Isa 24: 12 its gate is *b* to pieces.

BATTERING (BATTERED)

2Sa 20: 15 While they were *b* the wall
Isa 22: 5 a day of *b* down walls
Eze 4: 2 against it and put *b* rams around it.
21: 22 to set *b* rams against the gates,
21: 22 where he is to set up *b* rams,
26: 9 of his *b* rams against your walls
Ac 27: 18 We took such a violent *b*

BATTLE (BATTLEMENTS BATTLES)

Ge 14: 8 drew up their *b* lines in the Valley
Ex 13: 18 out of Egypt armed for *b*.
Nu 10: 9 When you go into *b*
21: 33 out to meet them in *b* at Edrei.
31: 4 Send into *b* a thousand men
31: 5 twelve thousand men armed for *b*,
31: 6 Moses sent them into *b*, a thousand
31: 14 who returned from the *b*.
31: 21 to the soldiers who had gone into *b*
31: 27 the soldiers who took part in the *b*
31: 28 the soldiers who fought in the *b*,
31: 36 of those who fought in the *b* was:
32: 20 yourselves before the LORD for *b*,
32: 27 servants, every man armed for *b*,
32: 29 Reubenites, every man armed for *b*
Dt 2: 24 of it and engage him in *b*.
2: 32 out to meet us in *b* at Jahaz,
3: 1 out to meet us in *b* at Edrei.
3: 18 your able-bodied men, armed for *b*,
20: 2 When you are about to go into *b*,
20: 3 going into *b* against your enemies.
20: 5 die in *b* and someone else may
20: 6 die in *b* and someone else enjoy it.
20: 7 in *b* and someone else marry her."
20: 12 peace and they engage you in *b*,
Jos 4: 13 forty thousand armed for *b* crossed
8: 14 in the morning to meet Israel in *b*
11: 19 Israelites, who took them all in *b*.
13: 22 In addition to those slain in *b*,
14: 11 as vigorous to go out to *b* now
Jdg 3: 2 not had previous *b* experience):
8: 13 from the *b* by the Pass of Heres.
18: 11 armed for *b*, set out from Zorah
18: 16 six hundred Danites, armed for *b*,
20: 20 took up *b* positions against them
20: 23 again to *b* against the Benjamites,
20: 28 to *b* with Benjamin our brother,
20: 39 defeating them as in the first *b*."
20: 39 men of Israel would turn in the *b*.
20: 42 but they could not escape the *b*.
1Sa 4: 2 as the *b* spread, Israel was defeated
4: 12 day a Benjamite ran from the *b* line
4: 16 "I have just come from the *b* line;
7: 10 drew near to engage Israel in *b*.
13: 22 So on the day of the *b* not a soldier
14: 20 men assembled and went to the *b*.
14: 22 they joined the *b* in hot pursuit.
14: 23 *b* moved on beyond Beth Aven.
17: 2 and drew up their *b* line
17: 8 do you come out and line up for *b*?
17: 20 was going out to its *b* positions,
17: 22 ran to the *b* lines and greeted his
17: 28 came down only to watch the *b*."
17: 47 for the *b* is the LORD's,
17: 48 toward the *b* line to meet him.
18: 30 continued to go out to *b*,
23: 8 Saul called up all his forces for *b*,
26: 10 or he will go into *b* and perish.
29: 4 He must not go with us into *b*,
29: 9 'He must not go up with us into *b*.'
30: 24 of him who went down to the *b*.
2Sa 1: 4 He said, "The men fled from the *b*.
1: 25 "How the mighty have fallen in *b*!
2: 17 The *b* that day was very fierce,
3: 30 Asahel in the *b* at Gibeon.)
8: 10 on his victory in *b* over Hadadezer,
10: 8 and drew up in *b* formation
10: 9 Joab saw that there were *b* lines
10: 17 The Arameans formed their *b* lines
11: 18 sent David a full account of the *b*.
11: 19 the king this account of the *b*,
17: 11 you yourself leading them into *b*.
18: 6 and the *b* took place in the forest
18: 8 The *b* spread out over the whole
19: 3 ashamed when they flee from *b*.
19: 10 to rule over us, has died in *b*.
21: 15 Once again there was a *b*
21: 17 again will you go out with us to *b*,
21: 18 there was another *b*
21: 19 In another *b* with the Philistines
21: 20 In still another *b*, which took place
22: 35 He trains my hands for *b*;

2Sa 22: 40 You armed me with strength for *b;*
23: 9 gathered ⌞at Pas Dammim⌟ for *b.*
1Ki 2: 5 blood in peacetime as if in *b,*
20: 14 "And who will start the *b?"*
20: 29 the seventh day the *b* was joined.
20: 39 went into the thick of the *b,*
22: 30 disguised himself and went into *b.*
22: 30 "I will enter the *b* in disguise,
22: 35 All day long the *b* raged,
2Ki 3: 26 of Moab saw that the *b* had gone
8: 29 Ramoth in his *b* with Hazael king
9: 15 on him in the *b* with Hazael king
13: 25 in *b* from his father Jehoahaz.
14: 7 of Salt and captured Sela in *b,*
23: 29 marched out to meet him in *b,*
1Ch 5: 18 and who were trained for *b.*
5: 20 they cried out to him during the *b.*
5: 22 fell slain, because the *b* was God's.
7: 4 they had 36,000 men ready for *b,*
7: 40 The number of men ready for *b,*
11: 13 the Philistines gathered there for *b.*
12: 1 the warriors who helped him in *b;*
12: 8 ready for *b* and able
12: 23 armed for *b* who came to David
12: 24 6,800 armed for *b;* men of Simeon,
12: 25 warriors ready for *b*— 7,100;
12: 33 prepared for *b* with every type
12: 35 ready for *b*— 28,600; men of Asher
12: 36 experienced soldiers prepared for *b*
14: 15 to *b,* because that will mean God
18: 10 on his victory in *b* over Hadadezer,
19: 7 their towns and moved out for *b.*
19: 9 and drew up in *b* formation
19: 10 Joab saw that there were *b* lines
19: 17 formed his *b* lines opposite them.
19: 17 lines to meet the Arameans in *b,*
20: 5 In another *b* with the Philistines,
20: 6 In still another *b,* which took place
26: 27 taken in *b* they dedicated
2Ch 13: 3 Abijah went into *b* with a force
13: 3 and Jeroboam drew up a *b* line
13: 12 their trumpets will sound the *b* cry
13: 15 At the sound of their *b* cry,
13: 15 the men of Judah raised the *b* cry.
14: 10 and they took up *b* positions
17: 18 with 180,000 men armed for *b.*
18: 29 disguised himself and went into *b.*
18: 29 "I will enter the *b* in disguise,
18: 34 All day long the *b* raged,
20: 15 For the *b* is not yours, but God's.
20: 17 You will not have to fight this *b.*
22: 6 Ramoth in his *b* with Hazael king
25: 8 and fight courageously in *b,*
35: 20 marched out to meet him in *b.*
35: 22 himself to engage him in *b.*
Job 5: 20 in *b* from the stroke of the sword.
38: 23 for days of war and *b?*
39: 25 He catches the scent of *b* from afar,
39: 25 of commanders and the *b* cry.
Ps 18: 34 He trains my hands for *b;*
18: 39 You armed me with strength for *b;*
24: 8 the LORD mighty in *b.*
55: 18 from the *b* waged against me,
78: 9 turned back on the day of *b;*
89: 43 and have not supported him in *b.*
110: 3 on your day of *b.*
140: 7 shields my head in the day of *b*—
144: 1 my fingers for *b.*
Pr 21: 31 is made ready for the day of *b,*
Ecc 9: 11 or the *b* to the strong,
SS 3: 8 all experienced in *b,*
Isa 3: 25 your warriors in *b.*
8: 9 Prepare for *b,* and be shattered!
8: 9 Prepare for *b,* and be shattered!
9: 5 Every warrior's boot used in *b*
21: 15 and from the heat of *b.*
22: 2 nor did they die in *b.*
27: 4 I would march against them in *b;*
28: 6 to those who turn back the *b*
30: 32 he fights them in *b* with the blows
31: 4 down to do *b* on Mount Zion
31: 9 sight of the *b* standard their
42: 13 with a shout he will raise the *b* cry
Jer 4: 19 I have heard the *b* cry.
4: 21 How long must I see the *b* standard
6: 4 "Prepare for *b* against her!
6: 23 they come like men in *b* formation
8: 6 like a horse charging into *b.*
Jer 18: 21 young men slain by the sword in *b.*
20: 16 a *b* cry at noon.
46: 3 and march out for *b!*
48: 14 men valiant in *b'?*
49: 2 "when I will sound the *b* cry
49: 14 Rise up for *b!"*
50: 22 The noise of *b* is in the land,
50: 42 they come like men in *b* formation
51: 20 my weapon for *b*—
51: 27 Prepare the nations for *b*
51: 28 the nations for *b* against her—
Eze 7: 14 go into *b,* for my wrath is
13: 5 in the *b* on the day of the LORD.
21: 22 to sound the *b* cry,
Da 11: 10 carry the *b* as far as his fortress.
11: 20 destroyed, yet not in anger or in *b.*
11: 26 swept away, and many will fall in *b.*
11: 40 of the South will engage him in *b,*
Hos 1: 7 sword or *b,* or by horses
2: 18 Bow and sword and *b*
5: 8 Raise the *b* cry in Beth Aven;
10: 14 Beth Arbel on the day of *b,*
10: 14 the roar of *b* will rise
Joel 2: 5 like a mighty army drawn up for *b.*
Am 1: 14 amid war cries on the day of *b,*
Ob : 1 and let us go against her for *b'*'—
Mic 2: 8 like men returning from *b.*
Zep 1: 16 a day of trumpet and *b* cry
Zec 9: 10 and the *b* bow will be broken.
10: 3 make them like a proud horse in *b.*
10: 4 from him the *b* bow,
10: 5 trampling the muddy streets in *b.*
14: 3 as he fights in the day of *b.*
1Co 14: 8 who will get ready for *b?*
Heb 11: 34 and who became powerful in *b*
Jas 4: 1 from your desires that *b* within you
Rev 9: 7 looked like horses prepared for *b.*
9: 9 and chariots rushing into *b.*
16: 14 them for the *b* on the great day
20: 8 and Magog—to gather them for *b.*

BATTLEFIELD (FIELD)

Jdg 20: 21 Israelites on the *b* that day.
1Sa 4: 2 four thousand of them on the *b.*

BATTLEMENTS (BATTLE)

Isa 54: 12 I will make your *b* of rubies,

BATTLES (BATTLE)

1Sa 8: 20 to go out before us and fight our *b."*
18: 17 and fight the *b* of the LORD."
25: 28 because he fights the LORD's *b.*
2Ch 32: 8 God to help us and to fight our *b."*

BAY

Jos 15: 2 from the *b* at the southern end
15: 5 started from the *b* of the sea
18: 19 the northern *b* of the Salt Sea, at
Ac 27: 39 they saw a *b* with a sandy beach,

BAZLUTH

Ezr 2: 52 Hakupha, Harhur, *B,* Mehida,
Ne 7: 54 Hakupha, Harhur, *B,* Mehida,

BEACH

Ac 21: 5 and there on the *b* we knelt to pray.
27: 39 but they saw a bay with a sandy *b,*
27: 40 to the wind and made for the *b.*

BEAK

Ge 8: 11 in its *b* was a freshly plucked olive

BEALIAH

1Ch 12: 5 Gederathite, Eluzai, Jerimoth, *B,*

BEALOTH

Jos 15: 24 Ithnan, Ziph, Telem, *B,*

BEAM (BEAMS)

Ezr 6: 11 a *b* is to be pulled from his house

BEAMS (BEAM)

1Ki 6: 9 roofing it with *b* and cedar planks.
6: 10 to the temple by *b* of cedar.
6: 36 and one course of trimmed cedar *b.*
7: 2 supporting trimmed cedar *b.*
7: 3 forty-five *b,* fifteen to a row.
7: 3 with cedar above the *b* that rested
1Ki 7: 11 cut to size, and cedar *b.*
7: 12 and one course of trimmed cedar *b,*
2Ch 3: 7 overlaid the ceiling *b,* doorframes,
34: 11 *b* for the buildings that the kings
Ne 2: 8 timber to make *b* for the gates
3: 3 They laid its *b* and put its doors
3: 6 They laid its *b* and put its doors
Ps 104: 3 lays the *b* of his upper chambers
SS 1: 17 The *b* of our house are
Jer 22: 7 they will cut up your fine cedar *b*
Hab 2: 11 the *b* of the woodwork will echo it.
Zep 2: 14 the *b* of cedar will be exposed.

BEANS

2Sa 17: 28 and roasted grain, *b* and lentils,
Eze 4: 9 "Take wheat and barley, *b*

BEAR (BEARABLE BEARER BEARING BEARS BIRTH BIRTHDAY BIRTHRIGHT BORE BORN BORNE CHILDBEARING CHILDBIRTH HIGHBORN LOWBORN NATIVE-BORN NEWBORN REBIRTH STILLBORN UNBORN)

Ge 1: 11 on the land that *b* fruit with seed
4: 13 punishment is more than I can *b.*
17: 17 Will Sarah *b* a child at the age
17: 19 but your wife Sarah will *b* you a son
17: 21 whom Sarah will *b* to you
30: 3 so that she can *b* children for me
43: 9 I will *b* the blame before you all my
44: 32 I will *b* the blame before you,
Ex 16: 29 *B* in mind that the LORD has
28: 12 Aaron is to *b* the names
28: 29 he will *b* the names of the sons
28: 30 Aaron will always *b* the means
28: 38 and he will *b* the guilt involved
Lev 19: 18 or *b* a grudge against one
Nu 5: 31 the woman will *b* the consequences
9: 13 That man will *b* the consequences
18: 1 to *b* the responsibility for offenses
18: 1 to *b* the responsibility for offenses
18: 22 or they will *b* the consequences
18: 23 *b* the responsibility for offenses
Dt 1: 12 But how can I *b* your problems
21: 15 both *b* him sons but the firstborn is
Jdg 5: 14 those who *b* a commander's
10: 16 he could *b* Israel's misery no longer
1Sa 17: 34 When a lion or a *b* came
17: 36 has killed both the lion and the *b;*
17: 37 and the paw of the *b* will deliver me
2Sa 17: 8 fierce as a wild *b* robbed of her cubs
2Ki 3: 21 who could *b* arms was called up
19: 30 below and *b* fruit above.
Est 8: 6 For how can I *b* to see disaster fall
8: 6 How can I *b* to see the destruction
Job 9: 9 He is the Maker of the *B* and Orion
20: 13 though he cannot *b* to let it go
21: 3 *B* with me while I speak,
36: 2 "*B* with me a little longer
38: 32 or lead out the *B* with its cubs?
39: 2 you count the months till they *b?*
Ps 38: 4 like a burden too heavy to *b.*
89: 50 how I *b* in my heart the taunts
92: 14 They will still *b* fruit in old age,
Pr 17: 12 Better to meet a *b* robbed
18: 14 but a crushed spirit who can *b?*
28: 15 Like a roaring lion or a charging *b*
30: 21 under four it cannot *b* up:
Isa 1: 13 I cannot *b* your evil assemblies.
11: 1 from his roots a Branch will *b* fruit.
11: 7 The cow will feed with the *b,*
24: 6 its people must *b* their guilt.
37: 31 below and *b* fruit above.
53: 11 and he will *b* their iniquities.
65: 23 *b* children doomed to misfortune;
Jer 12: 2 they grow and *b* fruit.
12: 13 So *b* the shame of your harvest
14: 9 and we *b* your name;
15: 16 for I *b* your name,
17: 8 and never fails to *b* fruit."
30: 6 Can a man *b* children?
La 3: 10 Like a *b* lying in wait,
3: 27 It is good for a man to *b* the yoke
5: 7 and we *b* their punishment.
Eze 4: 4 You are to *b* their sin
4: 5 So for 390 days you will *b* the sin
4: 6 and *b* the sin of the house of Judah.
14: 10 They will *b* their guilt—

Eze 16: 52 *B* your disgrace, for you have
16: 52 be ashamed and *b* your disgrace,
16: 54 so that you may *b* your disgrace
16: 58 You will *b* the consequences
17: 8 *b* fruit and become a splendid vine
17: 23 it will produce branches and *b* fruit
23: 35 you must *b* the consequences
23: 49 *b* the consequences of your sins
32: 24 They *b* their shame
32: 25 they *b* their shame
32: 30 *b* their shame with those who go
34: 29 or *b* the scorn of the nations.
44: 10 idols must *b* the consequences
44: 12 that they must *b* the consequences
44: 13 they must *b* the shame
47: 12 Every month they will *b*,
Da 7: 5 beast, which looked like a *b*.
9: 19 and your people *b* your Name."
Hos 9: 16 Even if they *b* children,
10: 2 and now they must *b* their guilt.
13: 8 Like a *b* robbed of her cubs,
13: 16 of Samaria must *b* their guilt,
Am 5: 19 only to meet a *b*,
7: 10 The land cannot *b* all his words.
9: 12 and all the nations that *b* my name
Mic 6: 16 you will *b* the scorn of the nations
7: 9 I will *b* the LORD's wrath,
Na 1: 14 no descendants to *b* your name.
Mt 7: 18 A good tree cannot *b* bad fruit,
7: 18 and a bad tree cannot *b* good fruit.
7: 19 tree that does not *b* good fruit is cut
21: 19 "May you never *b* fruit again!"
Mk 4: 7 so that they did not *b* grain
Lk 1: 13 wife Elizabeth will *b* you a son,
1: 42 and blessed is the child you will *b!*
6: 43 nor does a bad tree *b* good fruit.
Jn 15: 2 branch that does *b* fruit he trims
15: 4 Neither can you *b* fruit
15: 4 No branch can *b* fruit by itself;
15: 5 he will *b* much fruit; apart
15: 8 glory, that you *b* much fruit,
15: 16 but I chose you to go and *b* fruit—
16: 12 more than you can now *b*.
Ac 15: 10 our fathers have been able to *b?*
15: 17 all the Gentiles who *b* my name,
Ro 7: 4 in order that we might *b* fruit
13: 4 for he does not *b* the sword
15: 1 ought to *b* with the failings
1Co 10: 13 tempted beyond what you can *b*.
15: 49 so shall we *b* the likeness
Gal 6: 17 for I *b* on my body the marks
Col 3: 13 *B* with each other and forgive
Heb 9: 28 appear a second time, not to *b* sin,
12: 20 because they could not *b* what was
13: 22 I urge you to *b* with my word
Jas 3: 12 tree *b* olives, or a grapevine *b* figs?
1Pe 4: 16 praise God that you *b* that name.
2Pe 3: 15 *B* in mind that our Lord's patience
Rev 13: 2 but had feet like those of a *b*

BEARABLE (BEAR)

Mt 10: 15 it will be more *b* for Sodom
11: 22 it will be more *b* for Tyre
11: 24 But I tell you that it will be more *b*
Lk 10: 12 it will be more *b* on that day
10: 14 But it will be more *b* for Tyre

BEARD (BEARDS)

Lev 14: 9 he must shave his head, his *b*,
19: 27 or clip off the edges of your *b*.
1Sa 21: 13 and letting saliva run down his *b*.
2Sa 10: 4 shaved off half of each man's *b*,
20: 9 Amasa by the *b* with his right hand
Ezr 9: 3 and *b* and sat down appalled.
Ps 133: 2 running down on Aaron's *b*,
133: 2 running down on the *b*,
Isa 15: 2 and every *b* cut off.
50: 6 to those who pulled out my *b*;
Jer 48: 37 and every *b* cut off;
Eze 5: 1 to shave your head and your *b*.

BEARDS (BEARD)

Lev 21: 5 or shave off the edges of their *b*
2Sa 10: 5 at Jericho till your *b* have grown,
1Ch 19: 5 at Jericho till your *b* have grown,
Isa 7: 20 and to take off your *b* also.
Jer 41: 5 men who had shaved off their *b*,

BEARER (BEAR)

1Sa 17: 7 His shield *b* went ahead of him.
17: 41 with his shield *b* in front of him,

BEARING (BEAR)

Ge 1: 12 and trees *b* fruit with seed
1: 12 plants *b* seed according
30: 1 she was not *b* Jacob any children,
Nu 13: 23 cut off a branch *b* a single cluster
Jdg 8: 18 "each one with the *b* of a prince."
1Sa 14: 1 said to the young man *b* his armor,
2Ch 12: 11 went with him, *b* the shields,
Pr 30: 29 four that move with stately *b*:
Isa 1: 14 I am weary of *b* them.
60: 6 *b* gold and incense
Jer 4: 31 a groan as of one *b* her first child—
Joel 2: 22 The trees are *b* their fruit;
Ro 2: 15 their consciences also *b* witness,
Eph 4: 2 *b* with one another in love.
Col 1: 10 *b* fruit in every good work,
Heb 13: 13 outside the camp, *b* the disgrace he
Rev 22: 2 *b* twelve crops of fruit, yielding its

BEARS (BEAR)

Ge 49: 21 that *b* beautiful fawns.
Ex 21: 4 and she *b* him sons or daughters,
Dt 25: 6 The first son she *b* shall carry
28: 57 her womb and the children she *b*.
1Ki 8: 43 house I have built *b* your Name.
2Ki 2: 24 Then two *b* came out of the woods
2Ch 6: 33 house I have built *b* your Name.
20: 9 this temple that *b* your Name
Job 39: 1 watch when the doe *b* her fawn?
Ps 68: 19 who daily *b* our burdens.
Isa 59: 11 We all growl like *b*;
Jer 7: 10 which *b* my Name, and say,
7: 11 Has this house, which *b* my Name,
7: 14 do to the house that *b* my Name,
7: 30 idols in the house that *b* my Name
25: 29 on the city that *b* my Name,
32: 34 idols in the house that *b* my Name
34: 15 me in the house that *b* my Name.
Da 9: 18 of the city that *b* your Name.
Mt 7: 17 every good tree *b* good fruit,
7: 17 fruit, but a bad tree *b* bad fruit.
Lk 6: 43 "No good tree *b* bad fruit,
13: 9 If it *b* fruit next year, fine! If not,
Jn 15: 2 branch in me that *b* no fruit,
Gal 4: 24 and *b* children who are to be slaves:
4: 27 who *b* no children;
1Pe 2: 19 if a man *b* up under the pain

BEAST (BEASTS)

2Ki 14: 9 a wild *b* in Lebanon came along
2Ch 25: 18 a wild *b* in Lebanon came along
Ps 36: 6 you preserve both man and *b*.
68: 30 Rebuke the *b* among the reeds,
73: 22 I was a brute *b* before you.
Isa 35: 9 nor will any ferocious *b* get up on it
Jer 7: 20 and *b*, on the trees of the field
Da 7: 5 there before me was a second *b*,
7: 6 This *b* had four heads,
7: 6 and there before me was another *b*,
7: 7 and there before me was a fourth *b*
7: 11 I kept looking until the *b* was slain
7: 19 the true meaning of the fourth *b*,
7: 19 the *b* that crushed and devoured its
7: 23 fourth *b* is a fourth kingdom that
Jnh 3: 7 Do not let any man or *b*, herd
3: 8 and *b* be covered with sackcloth.
Zec 8: 10 there were no wages for man or *b*.
2Pe 2: 16 by a donkey—a *b* without speech
Rev 11: 7 the *b* that comes up
13: 1 And I saw a *b* coming out of the sea
13: 2 The dragon gave the *b* his power
13: 2 The *b* I saw resembled a leopard,
13: 3 One of the heads of the *b* seemed
13: 3 was astonished and followed the *b*.
13: 4 also worshiped the *b* and asked,
13: 4 he had given authority to the *b*,
13: 4 "Who is like the *b?* Who can make
13: 5 The *b* was given a mouth
13: 8 of the earth will worship the *b*—
13: 11 Then I saw another *b*, coming out
13: 12 its inhabitants worship the first *b*,
13: 12 of the first *b* on his behalf,
13: 14 honor of the *b* who was wounded
Rev 13: 14 power to do on behalf of the first *b*,
13: 15 breath to the image of the first *b*,
13: 17 which is the name of the *b*
13: 18 him calculate the number of the *b*,
14: 9 "If anyone worships the *b*
14: 11 night for those who worship the *b*
15: 2 who had been victorious over the *b*
16: 2 people who had the mark of the *b*
16: 10 bowl on the throne of the *b*,
16: 13 out of the mouth of the *b*
17: 3 on a scarlet *b* that was covered
17: 7 of the woman and of the *b* she rides
17: 8 The *b*, which you saw, once was,
17: 8 astonished when they see the *b*,
17: 11 *b* who once was, and now is not,
17: 12 as kings along with the *b*.
17: 13 their power and authority to the *b*.
17: 16 *b* and the ten horns you saw will
17: 17 to give the *b* their power to rule,
19: 19 Then I saw the *b* and the kings
19: 20 But the *b* was captured,
19: 20 who had received the mark of the *b*
20: 4 They had not worshiped the *b*
20: 10 where the *b* and the false prophet

BEASTS (BEAST)

Ge 1: 30 And to all the *b* of the earth
2: 19 of the ground all the *b* of the field
2: 20 of the air and all the *b* of the field.
9: 2 fall upon all the *b* of the earth
31: 39 bring you animals torn by wild *b*;
Ex 22: 31 meat of an animal torn by wild *b*;
Lev 26: 6 I will remove savage *b*
Dt 28: 26 of the air and the *b* of the earth,
32: 24 against them the fangs of wild *b*,
1Sa 17: 44 of the air and the *b* of the field!"
17: 46 of the air and the *b* of the earth,
Job 5: 22 and need not fear the *b* of the earth
28: 8 Proud *b* do not set foot on it,
35: 11 to us than to the *b* of the earth
Ps 8: 7 and the *b* of the field,
49: 12 he is like the *b* that perish.
49: 20 is like the *b* that perish.
57: 4 I lie among ravenous *b*—
74: 19 over the life of your dove to wild *b*;
79: 2 of your saints to the *b* of the earth.
104: 11 to all the *b* of the field;
104: 20 and all the *b* of the forest prowl.
Pr 30: 30 a lion, mighty among *b*,
Isa 46: 1 their idols are borne by *b* of burden
56: 9 Come, all you *b* of the field,
56: 9 and devour, all you *b* of the forest!
Jer 7: 33 of the air and the *b* of the earth,
12: 9 Go and gather all the wild *b*;
15: 3 and the *b* of the earth to devour
16: 4 of the air and the *b* of the earth."
19: 7 of the air and the *b* of the earth.
34: 20 of the air and the *b* of the earth.
Eze 5: 17 I will send famine and wild *b*
14: 15 I send wild *b* through that country
14: 15 pass through it because of the *b*,
14: 21 famine and wild *b* and plague
29: 5 to the *b* of the earth and the birds
31: 6 all the *b* of the field
31: 13 and all the *b* of the field were
32: 4 and all the *b* of the earth gorge
34: 25 and rid the land of wild *b*
38: 20 birds of the air, the *b* of the field,
Da 2: 38 he has placed mankind and the *b*
4: 12 Under it the *b* of the field found
4: 21 giving shelter to the *b* of the field,
7: 3 Four great *b*, each different
7: 7 different from all the former *b*,
7: 12 (The other *b* had been stripped
7: 17 four great *b* are four kingdoms that
Hos 2: 18 with the *b* of the field and the birds
4: 3 the *b* of the field and the birds
Mic 5: 8 like a lion among the *b* of the forest
Zep 2: 15 a lair for wild *b!*
Ac 11: 6 wild *b*, reptiles, and birds of the air.
1Co 15: 32 If I fought wild *b* in Ephesus
2Pe 2: 12 They are like brute *b*, creatures
2: 12 and like *b* they too will perish.
Rev 6: 8 and by the wild *b* of the earth.

BEAT (BEATEN BEATING BEATINGS BEATS)

Ex 9: 25 it *b* down everything growing

Nu 14:45 and *b* them down all the way
22:23 Balaam *b* her to get her back
22:25 So he *b* her again.
22:27 and he was angry and *b* her
22:28 to make you *b* me these three times
Dt 1:44 *b* you down from Seir all the way
24:20 When you *b* the olives
2Sa 22:43 I *b* them as fine as the dust
Ne 13:25 I *b* some of the men and pulled out
Ps 18:42 I *b* them as fine as dust borne
78:66 He *b* back his enemies;
Pr 23:35 They *b* me, but I don't feel it!
SS 5:7 They *b* me, they bruised me;
Isa 2:4 They will *b* their swords
10:24 who *b* you with a rod
32:12 *B* your breasts for the pleasant
49:10 will the desert heat or the sun *b*
50:6 back to those who *b* me,
Jer 31:19 I *b* my breast.
Eze 21:12 Therefore *b* your breast.
Joel 3:10 *B* your plowshares into swords
Mic 4:3 They will *b* their swords
Na 2:7 and *b* upon their breasts.
Mt 7:25 and the winds blew and *b*
7:27 and the winds blew and *b*
21:35 they *b* one, killed another,
24:49 begins to *b* his fellow servants
Mk 12:3 *b* him and sent him away
12:5 of them they *b*, others they killed.
14:65 the guards took him and *b* him.
Lk 10:30 him of his clothes, *b* him
12:45 begins to *b* the menservants
18:13 but *b* his breast and said, 'God,
20:10 tenants *b* him and sent him away
20:11 also they *b* and treated shamefully
23:48 they *b* their breasts and went away.
Ac 16:37 "They *b* us publicly without a trial,
18:17 and *b* him in front of the court.
22:19 and *b* those who believe in you.
1Co 9:27 I *b* my body and make it my slave
Rev 7:16 The sun will not *b* upon them,

BEATEN (BEAT)

Ex 5:14 by Pharaoh's slave drivers were *b*
5:16 Your servants are being *b*,
Nu 22:32 "Why have you *b* your donkey
Dt 25:2 If the guilty man deserves to be *b*,
Jdg 20:36 Benjamites saw that they were *b*.
1Ki 6:32 and palm trees with *b* gold.
Isa 1:5 Why should you be *b* anymore?
17:6 as when an olive tree is *b*,
24:13 as when an olive tree is *b*,
28:18 you will be *b* down by it.
28:27 caraway is *b* out with a rod,
Jer 20:2 he had Jeremiah the prophet *b*
37:15 angry with Jeremiah and had him *b*
Lk 12:47 do what his master wants will be *b*
12:48 deserving punishment will be *b*
Ac 16:22 them to be stripped and *b*.
2Co 6:9 yet we live on; *b*, and yet not killed;
11:25 Three times I was *b* with rods,

BEATING (BEAT)

Ex 2:11 He saw an Egyptian *b* a Hebrew,
Pr 18:6 and his mouth invites a *b*.
Lk 22:63 Jesus began mocking and *b* him.
Ac 19:16 gave them such a *b* that they ran
21:32 his soldiers, they stopped *b* Paul.
1Co 9:26 I do not fight like a man *b* the air.
1Pe 2:20 if you receive a *b* for doing wrong

BEATINGS (BEAT)

Pr 19:29 and *b* for the backs of fools.
20:30 and *b* purge the inmost being.
2Co 6:5 in *b*, imprisonments and riots;

BEATS (BEAT)

Ex 21:20 "If a man *b* his male or female slave

BEAUTIFUL (BEAUTY)

Ge 6:2 that the daughters of men were *b*,
12:11 "I know what a *b* woman you are.
12:14 saw that she was a very *b* woman.
24:16 The girl was very *b*, a virgin;
26:7 of Rebekah, because she is *b*."
29:17 Rachel was lovely in form, and *b*.
49:21 that bears *b* fawns.
Nu 24:5 "How *b* are your tents, O Jacob,
Dt 21:11 among the captives a *b* woman
Jos 7:21 saw in the plunder a *b* robe
1Sa 25:3 was an intelligent and *b* woman,
2Sa 11:2 The woman was very *b*,
13:1 the *b* sister of Absalom son
14:27 and she became a *b* woman.
1Ki 1:3 throughout Israel for a *b* girl
1:4 The girl was very *b*; she took care
Est 2:2 for *b* young virgins for the king.
2:3 realm to bring all these *b* girls
Job 38:31 "Can you bind the *b* Pleiades?
42:15 land were there found women as *b*
Ps 48:2 It is *b* in its loftiness,
Pr 11:22 is a *b* woman who shows no
24:4 filled with rare and *b* treasures.
Ecc 3:11 He has made everything *b*
SS 1:8 If you do not know, most *b*
1:10 Your cheeks are *b* with earrings,
1:15 Oh, how *b*!
1:15 How *b* you are, my darling!
2:10 my *b* one, and come with me.
2:13 my *b* one, come with me."
4:1 How *b* you are, my darling!
4:1 Oh, how *b*!
4:7 All *b* you are, my darling;
5:9 most *b* of women?
6:1 most *b* of women?
6:4 You are *b*, my darling,
7:1 How *b* your sandaled feet,
7:6 How *b* you are and how pleasing,
Isa 4:2 of the LORD will be *b*
28:5 a *b* wreath
52:7 How *b* on the mountains
Jer 3:19 the most *b* inheritance
6:2 so *b* and delicate.
11:16 with fruit *b* in form.
46:20 "Egypt is a *b* heifer,
Eze 7:20 They were proud of their *b* jewelry
16:7 and became the most *b* of jewels.
16:12 and a *b* crown on your head.
16:13 You became very *b* and rose
20:6 and honey, the most *b* of all lands.
20:15 and honey, most *b* of all lands—
23:42 and *b* crowns on their heads.
27:24 traded with you *b* garments,
31:3 with *b* branches overshadowing
31:9 I made it *b*
33:32 who sings love songs with a *b* voice
Da 4:12 Its leaves were *b*, its fruit abundant
4:21 with *b* leaves and abundant fruit,
8:9 to the east and toward the *B* Land.
11:16 will establish himself in the *B* Land
11:41 He will also invade the *B* Land.
11:45 the seas at the *b* holy mountain.
Zec 9:17 How attractive and *b* they will be!
Mt 23:27 which look *b* on the outside
26:10 She has done a *b* thing to me.
Mk 14:6 She has done a *b* thing to me.
Lk 21:5 temple was adorned with *b* stones
Ac 3:2 carried to the temple gate called *B*,
3:10 at the temple gate called *B*,
Ro 10:15 "How *b* are the feet
1Pe 3:5 in God used to make themselves *b*.

BEAUTY (BEAUTIFUL)

Est 1:11 order to display her *b* to the people
2:3 let *b* treatments be given to them.
2:9 her with her *b* treatments
2:12 months of *b* treatments prescribed
Ps 27:4 to gaze upon the *b* of the LORD
37:20 LORD's enemies will be like the *b*
45:11 The king is enthralled by your *b*;
50:2 From Zion, perfect in *b*,
Pr 6:25 lust in your heart after her *b*
31:30 is deceptive, and *b* is fleeting;
Isa 3:24 instead of *b*, branding.
28:1 to the fading flower, his glorious *b*,
28:4 That fading flower, his glorious *b*,
33:17 Your eyes will see the king in his *b*
53:2 He had no *b* or majesty
61:3 to bestow on them a crown of *b*
La 2:15 the perfection of *b*,
Eze 16:14 had given you made your *b* perfect,
16:14 the nations on account of your *b*,
16:15 passed by and your *b* became his.
16:15 " 'But you trusted in your *b*
16:25 lofty shrines and degraded your *b*,
27:3 "I am perfect in *b*."
Eze 27:4 your builders brought your *b*
27:11 they brought your *b* to perfection.
28:7 draw their swords against your *b*
28:12 full of wisdom and perfect in *b*.
28:17 proud on account of your *b*,
31:7 It was majestic in *b*,
31:8 could match its *b*.
Jas 1:11 blossom falls and its *b* is destroyed.
1Pe 3:3 Your *b* should not come
3:4 the unfading *b* of a gentle

BEBAI

Ezr 2:11 of Bani 642 of *B* 623
8:11 Zechariah son of *B*,
8:11 descendants of *B*, Zechariah son
10:28 From the descendants of *B*:
Ne 7:16 of Binnui 648 of *B* 628
10:15 Bunni, Azgad, *B*, Adonijah, Bigvai,

BECKON

Isa 13:2 *b* to them
49:22 "See, I will *b* to the Gentiles,

BECORATH

1Sa 9:1 the son of *B*, the son of Aphiah

BED (BEDDING BEDS SICKBED)

Ge 19:4 Before they had gone to *b*,
39:7 "Come to *b* with me!"
39:10 he refused to go to *b* with her or
39:12 and said, "Come to *b* with me!"
48:2 his strength and sat up on the *b*.
49:4 up onto your father's *b*,
49:33 he drew his feet up into the *b*,
Ex 8:3 your bedroom and onto your *b*,
21:18 he does not die but is confined to *b*,
Lev 15:4 " 'Any *b* the man with a discharge
15:5 who touches his *b* must wash his
15:21 Whoever touches her *b* must wash
15:23 Whether it is the *b* or anything she
15:24 any *b* he lies on will be unclean.
15:26 is her *b* during her monthly period,
15:26 *b* she lies on while her discharge
Dt 3:11 His *b* was made of iron
22:30 he must not dishonor his father's *b*.
27:20 for he dishonors his father's *b*."
1Sa 19:13 took an idol and laid it on the *b*,
19:15 to me in his *b* so that I may kill him
19:16 there was the idol in the *b*,
2Sa 4:7 lying on the *b* in his bedroom.
4:11 in his own house and on his own *b*
11:2 evening David got up from his *b*
13:5 "Go to *b* and pretend to be ill,"
13:11 "Come to *b* with me, my sister."
1Ki 1:47 the king bowed in worship on his *b*
17:19 was staying, and laid him on his *b*.
21:4 He lay on his *b* sulking
2Ki 1:4 will not leave the *b* you are lying
1:6 will not leave the *b* you are lying
1:16 will never leave the *b* you are lying
4:10 and put in it a *b* and a table,
4:21 and laid him on the *b* of the man
4:34 Then he got on the *b* and lay
4:35 then got on the *b* and stretched out
1Ch 5:1 he defiled his father's marriage *b*,
2Ch 24:25 and they killed him in his *b*.
Job 7:13 When I think my *b* will comfort me
17:13 if I spread out my *b* in darkness,
33:19 Or a man may be chastened on a *b*
Ps 6:6 all night long I flood my *b*
36:4 Even on his *b* he plots evil;
41:3 restore him from his *b* of illness.
63:6 On my *b* I remember you;
132:3 or go to my *b*—
139:8 if I make my *b* in the depths,
Pr 7:16 I have covered my *b*
7:17 I have perfumed my *b*
22:27 your very *b* will be snatched
26:14 so a sluggard turns on his *b*.
31:22 She makes coverings for her *b*;
SS 1:16 And our *b* is verdant.
3:1 All night long on my *b*
Isa 28:20 The *b* is too short to stretch out on,
57:7 You have made your *b* on a high
57:8 me, you uncovered your *b*,
Eze 22:10 who dishonor their fathers' *b*;
23:17 came to her, to the *b* of love,
32:25 A *b* is made for her among the slain

Da 2:28 as you lay on your *b* are these:
4: 5 As I was lying in my *b*, the images
4:10 saw while lying in my *b*:
4:13 saw while lying in my *b*,
7: 1 his mind as he was lying on his *b*.
Mt 8:14 Peter's mother-in-law lying in *b*
Mk 1:30 Simon's mother-in-law was in *b*
4:21 lamp to put it under a bowl or a *b*?
7:30 and found her child lying on the *b*,
Lk 8:16 hides it in a jar or puts it under a *b*.
11: 7 and my children are with me in *b*.
17:34 night two people will be in one *b*;
Ac 28: 8 sick in *b*, suffering from fever
Heb 13: 4 and the marriage *b* kept pure,
Rev 2:22 So I will cast her on a *b* of suffering,

BEDAD

Ge 36:35 Husham died, Hadad son of *B*,
1Ch 1:46 Husham died, Hadad son of *B*,

BEDAN

1Ch 7:17 The son of Ulam: *B*.

BEDDING (BED)

2Sa 17:28 Gileadite from Rogelim brought *b*

BEDEIAH

Ezr 10:35 Benaiah, *B*, Keluhi, Vaniah,

BEDRIDDEN

Ac 9:33 a paralytic who had been *b*

BEDROOM (BEDROOMS)

Ex 8: 3 and your *b* and onto your bed,
2Sa 4: 7 lying on the bed in his *b*.
13:10 here into my *b* so I may eat
13:10 it to her brother Amnon in his *b*.
2Ki 6:12 very words you speak in your *b*."
11: 2 and his nurse in a *b* to hide him
2Ch 22:11 and put him and his nurse in a *b*.
Ecc 10:20 or curse the rich in your *b*,

BEDROOMS (BEDROOM)

Ps 105: 30 into the *b* of their rulers.

BEDS (BED)

Job 30: 6 to live in the dry stream *b*,
33:15 as they slumber in their *b*,
Ps 4: 4 when you are on your *b*,
149: 5 and sing for joy on their *b*.
SS 5:13 His cheeks are like *b* of spice
6: 2 to the *b* of spices,
Isa 57: 8 a pact with those whose *b* you love,
Hos 7:14 but wail upon their *b*.
Am 3:12 Samaria on the edge of their *b*
6: 4 You lie on *b* inlaid with ivory
Mic 2: 1 to those who plot evil on their *b*!
Ac 5:15 into the streets and laid them on *b*

BEELIADA

1Ch 14: 7 Japhia, Elishama, *B* and Eliphelet.

BEELZEBUB

Mt 10:25 of the house has been called *B*,
12:24 "It is only by *B*, the prince
12:27 And if I drive out demons by *B*,
Mk 3:22 possessed by *B*! By the prince
Lk 11:15 "By *B*, the prince of demons,
11:18 claim that I drive out demons by *B*.
11:19 Now if I drive out demons by *B*,

BEER

Nu 21:16 From there they continued on to *B*
Jdg 9:21 Then Jotham fled, escaping to *B*,
1Sa 1:15 I have not been drinking wine or *b*;
Pr 20: 1 Wine is a mocker and *b* a brawler;
31: 4 not for rulers to crave *b*,
31: 6 Give *b* to those who are perishing,
Isa 24: 9 the *b* is bitter to its drinkers.
28: 7 Priests and prophets stagger from *b*
28: 7 and reel from *b*:
28: 7 they reel from *b*,
29: 9 stagger, but not from *b*.
56:12 Let us drink our fill of *b*!
Mic 2:11 for you plenty of wine and *b*,'

BEER ELIM

Isa 15: 8 their lamentation as far as *B*.

BEER LAHAI ROI

Ge 16:14 That is why the well was called *B*;
24:62 Now Isaac had come from *B*,
25:11 son Isaac, who then lived near *B*.

BEERA

1Ch 7:37 Shamma, Shilshah, Ithran and *B*.

BEERAH

1Ch 5: 6 Baal his son, and *B* his son,
5: 6 *B* was a leader of the Reubenites.

BEERI

Ge 26:34 Judith daughter of *B* the Hittite,
Hos 1: 1 to Hosea son of *B* during the reigns

BEEROTH (BEEROTHITE)

Jos 9:17 Gibeon, Kephirah, *B*
18:25 Gibeon, Ramah, *B*, Mizpah,
2Sa 4: 2 *B* is considered part of Benjamin,
4: 3 the people of *B* fled to Gittaim
Ezr 2:25 Kephirah and *B* 743 of Ramah
Ne 7:29 Kephirah and *B* 743 of Ramah and

BEEROTHITE (BEEROTH)

2Sa 4: 2 of Rimmon the *B* from the tribe
4: 5 the sons of Rimmon the *B*,
4: 9 the sons of Rimmon the *B*,
23:37 the Ammonite, Naharai the *B*,

BEERSHEBA

Ge 21:14 and wandered in the desert of *B*.
21:31 So that place was called *B*,
21:32 the treaty had been made at *B*,
21:33 planted a tamarisk tree in *B*,
22:19 And Abraham stayed in *B*.
22:19 and they set off together for *B*.
26:23 From there he went up to *B*.
26:33 the name of the town has been *B*.
28:10 Jacob left *B* and set out for Haran.
46: 1 and when he reached *B*, he offered
46: 5 Jacob left *B*, and Israel's sons took
Jos 15:28 Hazar Shual, *B*, Biziothiah,
19: 2 It included: *B* (or Sheba), Moladah
Jdg 20: 1 all the Israelites from Dan to *B*
1Sa 3:20 to *B* recognized that Samuel was
8: 2 was Abijah, and they served at *B*.
2Sa 3:10 and Judah from Dan to *B*."
17:11 Let all Israel, from Dan to *B*—
24: 2 the tribes of Israel from Dan to *B*
24: 7 they went on to *B* in the Negev
24:15 of the people from Dan to *B* died.
1Ki 4:25 from Dan to *B*, lived in safety,
19: 3 When he came to *B* in Judah,
2Ki 12: 1 name was Zibiah; she was from *B*.
23: 8 to *B*, where the priests had burned
1Ch 4:28 They lived in *B*, Moladah,
21: 2 count the Israelites from *B* to Dan.
2Ch 19: 4 again among the people from *B*
24: 1 name was Zibiah; she was from *B*.
30: 5 throughout Israel, from *B* to Dan,
Ne 11:27 in *B* and its settlements,
11:30 from *B* to the Valley of Hinnom.
Am 5: 5 do not journey to *B*.
8:14 'As surely as the god of *B* lives'—

BEES

Dt 1:44 they chased you like a swarm of *b*
Jdg 14: 8 a swarm of *b* and some honey,
Ps 118: 12 They swarmed around me like *b*,
Isa 7:18 and for *b* from the land of Assyria.

BEFALL (BEFALLS)

Job 5:19 in seven no harm will *b* you.
Ps 91:10 then no harm will *b* you,

BEFALLS (BEFALL)

Pr 12:21 No harm *b* the righteous,

BEFUDDLED

Isa 28: 7 and are *b* with wine;

BEG (BEGGAR BEGGARS BEGGED BEGGING)

Jdg 13: 8 to the LORD: "O Lord, I *b* you,
1Sa 15:25 Now I *b* you, forgive my sin
2Sa 24:10 I *b* you, take away the guilt
2Ki 8: 3 went to the king to *b* for her house
8: 5 back to life came to *b* the king
1Ch 21: 8 Now, I *b* you, take away the guilt
Est 4: 8 go into the king's presence to *b*
7: 7 stayed behind to *b* Queen Esther
Job 19:16 though I *b* him with my own mouth
La 4: 4 the children *b* for bread,
Am 7: 5 "Sovereign LORD, I *b* you, stop!
Lk 8:28 I *b* you, don't torture me!"
9:38 Teacher, I *b* you to look at my son,
16: 3 ashamed to *b*—I know what I'll do
16:27 He answered, 'Then I *b* you, father,
Jn 9: 8 same man who used to sit and *b*?"
Ac 3: 2 day to *b* from those going
26: 3 I *b* you to listen to me patiently.
2Co 10: 2 I *b* you that when I come I may not

BEGGAR (BEG)

Lk 16:20 gate was laid a *b* named Lazarus,
16:22 "The time came when the *b* died
Ac 3:11 While the *b* held on to Peter

BEGGARS (BEG)

Ps 109: 10 May his children be wandering *b*;

BEGGED (BEG)

2Ki 1:13 he *b*, "please have respect
Est 8: 3 She *b* him to put an end
Hos 12: 4 he wept and *b* for his favor.
Mt 8:31 demons *b* Jesus, "If you drive us
14:36 and *b* him to let the sick just touch
18:26 'Be patient with me,' he *b*,
18:29 fell to his knees and *b* him,
18:32 debt of yours because you *b* me to.
Mk 1:40 to him and *b* him on his knees,
5:10 And he *b* Jesus again and again not
5:12 The demons *b* Jesus, "Send us
5:18 who had been demon-possessed *b*
6:56 They *b* him to let them touch
7:26 She *b* Jesus to drive the demon out
7:32 and they *b* him to place his hand
8:22 brought a blind man and *b* Jesus
Lk 5:12 face to the ground and *b* him,
8:31 And they *b* him repeatedly not
8:32 The demons *b* Jesus to let them go
8:38 whom the demons had gone out *b*
9:40 I *b* your disciples to drive it out,
Jn 4:47 he went to him and *b* him to come
Heb 12:19 those who heard it *b* that no further

BEGGING (BEG)

Job 41: 3 Will he keep *b* you for mercy?
Ps 37:25 or their children *b* bread.
Mk 10:46 was sitting by the roadside *b*.
Lk 18:35 sitting by the roadside *b*.
Jn 9: 8 had formerly seen him *b* asked,
Ac 3:10 to sit *b* at the temple gate called
16: 9 of Macedonia standing and *b* him,
19:31 sent him a message *b* him not

BEGINNING (BEGINNINGS)

Ge 1: 1 In the *b* God created the heavens
44:12 *b* with the oldest and ending
Lev 23:39 " 'So *b* with the fifteenth day
Dt 11:12 on it from the *b* of the year
31:24 the words of this law from *b* to end,
31:30 words of this song from *b* to end
Jdg 7:19 camp at the *b* of the middle watch,
Ru 1:22 as the barley harvest was *b*.
1Sa 3:12 against his family—from *b* to end.
2Sa 7:10 did at the *b* and have done ever
21: 9 just as the barley harvest was *b*.
21:10 From the *b* of the harvest
1Ch 17: 9 did at the *b* and have done ever
29:29 of King David's reign, from *b*
2Ch 9:29 of Solomon's reign, from *b* to end,
12:15 of Rehoboam's reign, from *b* to end
16:11 of Asa's reign, from *b* to end,
20:34 of Jehoshaphat's reign, from *b*
25:26 of Amaziah's reign, from *b* to end,
26:22 of Uzziah's reign, from *b* to end,
28:26 and all his ways, from *b* to end,
35:27 all the events, from *b* to end,
Ezr 4: 6 At the *b* of the reign of Xerxes,
Ps 102: 25 In the *b* you laid the foundations
111: 10 of the LORD is the *b* of wisdom;
Pr 1: 7 of the LORD is the *b* of knowledge
8:22 me at the *b* of his work,
8:23 from the *b*, before the world began.

Pr 9:10 of the LORD is the *b* of wisdom,
20:21 inheritance quickly gained at the *b*
Ecc 3:11 fathom what God has done from *b*
7:8 of a matter is better than its *b*,
10:13 At the *b* his words are folly;
Isa 1:26 your counselors as at the *b*.
40:21 Has it not been told you from the *b*
41:4 forth the generations from the *b*?
41:26 Who told of this from the *b*,
46:10 I make known the end from the *b*,
Jer 17:12 glorious throne, exalted from the *b*,
25:29 I am *b* to bring disaster
Eze 25:9 *b* at its frontier towns—
40:1 of our exile, at the *b* of the year,
42:12 There was a doorway at the *b*
48:30 *B* on the north side, which is 4,500
Da 12:1 from the *b* of nations until then.
Mic 1:13 You were the *b* of sin
Mt 14:30 he was afraid and, *b* to sink,
19:4 at the *b* the Creator 'made them
19:8 But it was not this way from the *b*.
20:8 *b* with the last ones hired
24:8 All these are the *b* of birth pains.
24:21 unequaled from the *b* of the world
Mk 1:1 *b* of the gospel about Jesus Christ,
10:6 at the *b* of creation God 'made
13:8 These are the *b* of birth pains.
13:19 of distress unequaled from the *b*,
Lk 1:3 investigated everything from the *b*,
11:50 shed since the *b* of the world,
24:27 *b* with Moses and all the Prophets,
24:47 name to all nations, *b* at Jerusalem.
Jn 1:1 In the *b* was the Word,
1:2 He was with God in the *b*.
6:64 Jesus had known from the *b* which
8:44 He was a murderer from the *b*,
15:27 been with me from the *b*.
Ac 1:22 *b* from John's baptism to the time
10:37 *b* in Galilee after the baptism that
11:15 as he had come on us at the *b*.
26:4 from the *b* of my life
2Co 3:1 Are we *b* to commend ourselves
8:6 since he had earlier made a *b*,
Gal 3:3 so foolish? After *b* with the Spirit,
Col 1:18 he is the *b* and the firstborn
2Th 2:13 because from the *b* God chose you
2Ti 1:9 in Christ Jesus before the *b* of time,
Tit 1:2 promised before the *b* of time,
Heb 1:10 "In the *b*, O Lord, you laid
7:3 without *b* of days or end of life,
2Pe 2:20 at the end than they were at the *b*.
3:4 as it has since the *b* of creation."
1Jn 1:1 That which was from the *b*,
2:7 which you have had since the *b*.
2:13 have known him who is from the *b*.
2:14 have known him who is from the *b*.
2:24 heard from the *b* remains in you.
3:8 devil has been sinning from the *b*.
3:11 the message you heard from the *b*:
2Jn :5 but one we have had from the *b*.
:6 As you have heard from the *b*,
Rev 21:6 and the Omega, the *B* and the End.
22:13 and the Last, the *B* and the End.

BEGINNINGS (BEGINNING)

Job 8:7 Your *b* will seem humble,

BEGOTTEN

Isa 45:10 'What have you *b*?'

BEGRUDGE

Dt 28:56 will *b* the husband she loves

BEHAVE (BEHAVED BEHAVES BEHAVIOR)

1Ki 1:6 "Why do you *b* as you do?"
Ro 13:13 Let us *b* decently, as in the daytime

BEHAVED (BEHAVE)

2Sa 15:6 Absalom *b* in this way
1Ki 21:26 He *b* in the vilest manner by going
Ps 74:5 They *b* like men wielding axes
Jer 2:23 See how you *b* in the valley;
16:12 But you have *b* more wickedly

BEHAVES (BEHAVE)

Pr 21:24 he *b* with overweening pride.

BEHAVIOR (BEHAVE)

Est 3:4 Mordecai's *b* would be tolerated,
Pr 8:13 evil *b* and perverse speech.
Col 1:21 your minds because of your evil *b*.
1Pe 3:1 without talk by the *b* of their wives,
3:16 maliciously against your good *b*

BEHEADED

Mt 14:10 and had John *b* in the prison.
Mk 6:16 he said, "John, the man I *b*,
6:27 The man went, *b* John in the prison
Lk 9:9 But Herod said, "I *b* John.
Rev 20:4 the souls of those who had been *b*

BEHEMOTH

Job 40:15 "Look at the *b*,

BEKA (BEKAS)

Ge 24:22 out a gold nose ring weighing a *b*
Ex 38:26 to the sanctuary shekel—one *b*

BEKAS (BEKA)

1Ki 10:16 six hundred *b* of gold went
2Ch 9:15 six hundred *b* of hammered gold
9:16 with three hundred *b* of gold

BEKER (BEKERITE)

Ge 46:21 Bela, *B*, Ashbel, Gera, Naaman,
Nu 26:35 through *B*, the Bekerite clan;
1Ch 7:6 Three sons of Benjamin: Bela, *B*
7:8 All these were the sons of *B*.
7:8 The sons of *B*: Zemirah, Joash,

BEKERITE (BEKER)

Nu 26:35 through Beker, the *B* clan;

BEL

Isa 46:1 *B* bows down, Nebo stoops low;
Jer 50:2 *B* will be put to shame,
51:44 I will punish *B* in Babylon

BELA (BELAITE)

Ge 14:2 and the king of *B* (that is, Zoar).
14:8 Zeboiim and the king of *B* (that is,
36:32 *B* son of Beor became king
36:33 When *B* died, Jobab son of Zerah
46:21 The sons of Benjamin: *B*, Beker,
Nu 26:38 through *B*, the Belaite clan;
26:40 The descendants of *B* through Ard
1Ch 1:43 *B* son of Beor, whose city was
1:44 When *B* died, Jobab son of Zerah
5:8 Zechariah, and *B* son of Azaz,
7:6 Three sons of Benjamin: *B*,
7:7 The sons of *B*: Ezbon, Uzzi, Uzziel,
8:1 was the father of *B* his firstborn,
8:3 The sons of *B* were: Addar, Gera,

BELAITE (BELA)

Nu 26:38 the *B* clan; through Ashbel,

BELIAL

2Co 6:15 there between Christ and *B*?

BELIEF (BELIEVE)

2Th 2:13 and through *b* in the truth.

BELIEFS (BELIEVE)

Job 11:4 You say to God, 'My *b* are flawless

BELIEVE (BELIEF BELIEFS BELIEVED BELIEVER BELIEVERS BELIEVES BELIEVING)

Ge 45:26 was stunned; he did not *b* them.
Ex 4:1 "What if they do not *b* me
4:5 so that they may *b* that the LORD,
4:8 sign, they may *b* the second.
4:8 "If they do not *b* you or pay
4:9 But if they do not *b* these two signs
Nu 14:11 How long will they refuse to *b*
1Ki 10:7 I did not *b* these things until I came
2Ch 9:6 But I did not *b* what they said
32:15 Do not *b* him, for no god
Job 9:16 I do not *b* he would give me
Ps 78:22 for they did not *b* in God
78:32 of his wonders, they did not *b*.
106:24 they did not *b* his promise.
119:66 for I *b* in your commands.
Pr 26:25 speech is charming, do not *b* him,
Isa 43:10 so that you may know and *b* me
Jer 29:31 to *b* a lie, this is what the LORD
40:14 son of Ahikam did not *b* them.
La 4:12 The kings of the earth did not *b*,
Hab 1:5 that you would not *b*,
Mt 9:28 Do you *b* that I am able to do this?"
18:6 one of these little ones who *b* in me
21:22 If you *b*, you will receive whatever
21:25 'Then why didn't you *b* him?'
21:32 and you did not *b* him,
21:32 you did not repent and *b* him.
24:23 or, 'There he is!' do not *b* it.
24:26 in the inner rooms,' do not *b* it.
27:42 from the cross, and we will *b* in him
Mk 1:15 Repent and *b* the good news!"
5:36 ruler, "Don't be afraid; just *b*."
9:24 "I do *b*; help me overcome my
9:42 one of these little ones who *b* in me
11:24 *b* that you have received it,
11:31 'Then why didn't you *b* him?'
13:21 or, 'Look, there he is!' do not *b* it.
15:32 the cross, that we may see and *b*."
16:11 she had seen him, they did not *b* it.
16:13 but they did not *b* them either.
16:14 to *b* those who had seen him
16:16 but whoever does not *b* will be
16:17 signs will accompany those who *b*:
Lk 1:20 because you did not *b* my words,
8:12 so that they cannot *b* and be saved.
8:13 They *b* for a while, but in the time
8:50 just *b*, and she will be healed."
20:5 'Why didn't you *b* him?'
22:67 you will not *b* me,
24:11 But they did not *b* the women,
24:25 to *b* all that the prophets have
24:41 And while they still did not *b* it
Jn 1:7 that through him all men might *b*.
1:50 You *b* because I told you I saw you
3:12 how then will you *b* if I speak
3:12 of earthly things and you do not *b*;
3:18 does not *b* stands condemned
4:21 Jesus declared, "*B* me, woman,
4:42 "We no longer *b* just
4:48 Jesus told him, "you will never *b*."
5:38 for you do not *b* the one he sent.
5:44 How can you *b* if you accept praise
5:46 believed Moses, you would *b* me,
5:47 how are you going to *b* what I say
5:47 since you do not *b* what he wrote,
6:29 to *b* in the one he has sent."
6:30 give that we may see it and *b* you?
6:36 seen me and still you do not *b*.
6:64 beginning which of them did not *b*
6:64 some of you who do not *b*."
6:69 We *b* and know that you are
7:5 his own brothers did not *b* in him.
8:24 if you do not *b* that I am the one I
8:45 I tell the truth, you do not *b* me!
8:46 the truth, why don't you *b* me?
9:18 The Jews still did not *b* that he had
9:35 "Do you *b* in the Son of Man?"
9:36 "Tell me so that I may *b* in him."
9:38 "Lord, I *b*," and he worshiped him.
10:25 "I did tell you, but you do not *b*.
10:26 you do not *b* because you are not
10:37 Do not *b* me unless I do what my
10:38 you do not *b* me, *b* the miracles,
11:15 so that you may *b*.
11:26 Do you *b* this?" "Yes, Lord,"
11:27 "I *b* that you are the Christ,
11:42 that they may *b* that you sent me."
11:48 on like this, everyone will *b* in him,
12:37 they still would not *b* in him.
12:39 For this reason they could not *b*,
12:44 in me, he does not *b* in me only,
13:19 does happen you will *b* that I am
14:10 Don't you *b* that I am in the Father
14:11 *B* me when I say that I am
14:11 or at least *b* on the evidence
14:29 when it does happen you will *b*.
16:9 because men do not *b* in me;
16:30 This makes us *b* that you came
16:31 "You *b* at last!" Jesus answered.
17:20 also for those who will *b* in me
17:21 that the world may *b* that you have
19:35 he testifies so that you also may *b*.
20:25 hand into his side, I will not *b* it."
20:27 Stop doubting and *b*."

Jn 20: 31 written that you may *b* that Jesus is
Ac 13: 41 that you would never *b*,
14: 2 refused to *b* stirred up the Gentiles
15: 7 the message of the gospel and *b*.
15: 11 We *b* it is through the grace
16: 31 They replied, ''*B* in the Lord Jesus,
16: 34 because they had come to *b* in God
19: 4 the people to *b* in the one coming
19: 9 refused to *b* and publicly maligned
22: 19 and beat those who *b* in you.
24: 14 I *b* everything that agrees
26: 27 Agrippa, do you *b* the prophets?
28: 24 he said, but others would not *b*.
Ro 3: 22 faith in Jesus Christ to all who *b*.
4: 11 he is the father of all who *b*
4: 24 for us who *b* in him who raised
6: 8 we *b* that we will also live with him.
10: 9 *b* in your heart that God raised him
10: 10 For it is with your heart that you *b*
10: 14 And how can they *b* in the one
14: 22 whatever you *b* about these things
16: 26 so that all nations might *b*
1Co 1: 21 preached to save those who *b*.
3: 5 through whom you came to *b*—
11: 18 and to some extent I *b* it.
2Co 4: 13 also *b* and therefore speak,
Gal 3: 5 or because you *b* what you heard?
3: 7 that those who *b* are children
3: 22 might be given to those who *b*.
Eph 1: 19 great power for us who *b*.
Php 1: 29 of Christ not only to *b* on him,
1Th 2: 13 which is at work in you who *b*.
4: 14 We *b* that Jesus died and rose again
4: 14 and so we *b* that God will bring
2Th 2: 11 delusion so that they will *b* the lie
1Ti 1: 16 for those who would *b* on him
4: 3 with thanksgiving by those who *b*
4: 10 and especially of those who *b*.
Tit 1: 6 a man whose children *b*
1: 15 who are corrupted and do not *b*,
Heb 10: 39 but of those who *b* and are saved.
11: 6 comes to him must *b* that he exists
Jas 1: 6 But when he asks, he must *b*
2: 19 Even the demons *b* that—
2: 19 You *b* that there is one God.
1Pe 1: 8 you *b* in him and are filled
1: 21 Through him you *b* in God,
2: 7 But to those who do not *b*,
2: 7 to you who *b*, this stone is precious
3: 1 if any of them do not *b* the word,
1Jn 3: 23 to *b* in the name of his Son,
4: 1 Dear friends, do not *b* every spirit,
5: 10 who does not *b* God has made
5: 13 things to you who *b* in the name
Jude : 5 later destroyed those who did not *b*

BELIEVED (BELIEVE)

Ge 15: 6 Abram *b* the LORD, and he
Ex 4: 31 signs before the people, and they *b*.
Job 29: 24 at them, they scarcely *b* it;
Ps 106: 12 Then they *b* his promises
116: 10 I *b*; therefore I said,
Isa 53: 1 Who has *b* our message
Jnh 3: 5 The Ninevites *b* God.
Mt 8: 13 will be done just as you *b* it would.''
Lk 1: 45 is she who has *b* that what the Lord
Jn 1: 12 to those who *b* in his name,
2: 22 Then they *b* the Scripture
2: 23 signs he was doing and *b*
3: 18 because he has not *b* in the name
4: 39 from that town *b* in him
4: 53 So he and all his household *b*.
5: 46 If you *b* Moses, you would believe
7: 39 whom those who *b*
7: 48 or of the Pharisees *b* in him?
8: 31 To the Jews who had *b* him,
10: 42 And in that place many *b* in Jesus.
11: 40 ''Did I not tell you that if you *b*,
12: 38 ''Lord, who has *b* our message
12: 42 even among the leaders *b* in him.
16: 27 and have *b* that I came from God.
17: 8 and they *b* that you sent me.
20: 8 He saw and *b*.
20: 29 who have not seen and yet have *b*.''
20: 29 you have seen me, you have *b*;
Ac 4: 4 But many who heard the message *b*
5: 14 and more men and women *b*
8: 12 But when they *b* Philip
8: 13 Simon himself *b* and was baptized.
9: 42 and many people *b* in the Lord.
11: 17 who *b* in the Lord Jesus Christ,
11: 21 and a great number of people *b*
13: 12 saw what had happened, he *b*,
13: 48 were appointed for eternal life *b*.
14: 1 number of Jews and Gentiles *b*.
17: 12 Many of the Jews *b*, as did
17: 34 became followers of Paul and *b*.
18: 8 his entire household *b* in the Lord;
18: 8 the Corinthians who heard him *b*
18: 27 help to those who by grace had *b*.
19: 2 the Holy Spirit when you *b*?''
19: 18 Many of those who *b* now came
21: 20 many thousands of Jews have *b*,
Ro 4: 3 Scripture say? ''Abraham *b* God,
4: 17 in the sight of God, in whom he *b*
4: 18 Abraham in hope *b*
10: 14 call on the one they have not *b* in?
10: 16 ''Lord, who has *b* our message?''
13: 11 now than when we first *b*.
1Co 15: 2 Otherwise, you have *b* in vain.
15: 11 we preach, and this is what you *b*.
2Co 4: 13 ''I *b*; therefore I have spoken.''
Gal 3: 6 Consider Abraham: ''He *b* God,
Eph 1: 13 Having *b*, you were marked in him
1Th 2: 10 were among you who *b*.
2Th 1: 10 at among all those who have *b*.
1: 10 you *b* our testimony to you.
2: 12 who have not *b* the truth
1Ti 3: 16 was *b* on in the world,
2Ti 1: 12 because I know whom I have *b*,
Heb 4: 3 Now we who have *b* enter that rest,
Jas 2: 23 that says, ''Abraham *b* God,
1Jn 5: 10 he has not *b* the testimony God has

BELIEVER (BELIEVE)

1Ki 18: 3 (Obadiah was a devout *b*
Ac 16: 1 whose mother was a Jewess and a *b*
16: 15 ''If you consider me a *b* in the Lord
1Co 7: 12 brother has a wife who is not a *b*
7: 13 has a husband who is not a *b*
2Co 6: 15 What does a *b* have in common
1Ti 5: 16 any woman who is a *b* has widows

BELIEVERS (BELIEVE)

Jn 4: 41 of his words many more became *b*.
Ac 1: 15 among the *b* (a group numbering
2: 44 All the *b* were together
4: 32 All the *b* were one in heart
5: 12 And all the *b* used to meet together
9: 41 he called the *b* and the widows
10: 45 The circumcised *b* who had come
11: 2 the circumcised *b* criticized him
15: 2 along with some other *b*,
15: 5 Then some of the *b* who belonged
15: 23 To the Gentile *b* in Antioch,
21: 25 for the Gentile *b*, we have written
1Co 6: 5 to judge a dispute between *b*?
14: 22 is for *b*, not for unbelievers;
14: 22 not for *b* but for unbelievers;
Gal 6: 10 who belong to the family of *b*.
1Th 1: 7 a model to all the *b* in Macedonia
1Ti 4: 12 set an example for the *b* in speech,
6: 2 benefit from their service are *b*,
Jas 2: 1 *b* in our glorious Lord Jesus Christ,
1Pe 2: 17 Love the brotherhood of *b*,

BELIEVES (BELIEVE)

Pr 14: 15 A simple man *b* anything,
Mk 9: 23 is possible for him who *b*.''
11: 23 *b* that what he says will happen,
16: 16 Whoever *b* and is baptized will be
Jn 3: 15 that everyone who *b*
3: 16 that whoever *b* in him shall not
3: 18 Whoever *b* in him is not
3: 36 Whoever *b* in the Son has eternal
5: 24 *b* him who sent me has eternal life
6: 35 and he who *b* in me will never be
6: 40 and *b* in him shall have eternal life,
6: 47 he who *b* has everlasting life.
7: 38 Whoever *b* in me, as the Scripture
11: 25 He who *b* in me will live, even
11: 26 and *b* in me will never die.
12: 44 Jesus cried out, ''When a man *b*
12: 46 so that no one who *b*
Ac 10: 43 about him that everyone who *b*
13: 39 him everyone who *b* is justified
Ro 1: 16 for the salvation of everyone who *b*
10: 4 righteousness for everyone who *b*.
1Jn 5: 1 Everyone who *b* that Jesus is
5: 5 Only he who *b* that Jesus is the Son
5: 10 Anyone who *b* in the Son

BELIEVING (BELIEVE)

Jn 20: 31 and that by *b* you may have life
Ac 9: 26 not *b* that he really was a disciple.
1Co 7: 14 sanctified through her *b* husband.
7: 15 A *b* man or woman is not bound
9: 5 right to take a *b* wife along with us,
Gal 3: 2 or by *b* what you heard? Are you
1Ti 6: 2 Those who have *b* masters are not

BELLOW (BELLOWS)

Job 6: 5 or an ox *b* when it has fodder?

BELLOWS (BELLOW)

Jer 6: 29 The *b* blow fiercely

BELLS

Ex 28: 33 with gold *b* between them.
28: 34 gold *b* and the pomegranates are
28: 35 The sound of the *b* will be heard
39: 25 And they made *b* of pure gold
39: 26 *b* and pomegranates alternated
Zec 14: 20 inscribed on the *b* of the horses,

BELLY

Ge 3: 14 You will crawl on your *b*
Lev 11: 42 whether it moves on its *b*
Jdg 3: 21 and plunged it into the king's *b*.
2Sa 20: 10 and Joab plunged it into his *b*,
Job 15: 2 or fill his *b* with the hot east wind?
20: 23 When he has filled his *b*,
40: 16 what power in the muscles of his *b*!
Da 2: 32 its *b* and thighs of bronze,
Mt 12: 40 three nights in the *b* of a huge fish,

BELONG (BELONGED BELONGING BELONGINGS BELONGS)

Ge 32: 17 'To whom do you *b*, and where are
32: 18 'They *b* to your servant Jacob.
40: 8 ''Do not interpretations *b* to God?
45: 11 and all who *b* to you will become
Ex 13: 12 of your livestock *b* to the LORD.
21: 4 her children shall *b* to her master,
29: 27 parts of the ordination ram that *b*
29: 29 ''Aaron's sacred garments will *b*
Lev 5: 13 of the offering will *b* to the priest,
7: 7 They *b* to the priest who makes
25: 30 the walled city shall *b* permanently
25: 55 for the Israelites *b* to me
Nu 5: 9 bring to a priest will *b* to him.
5: 10 to the priest will *b* to the priest.' ''
6: 20 they are holy and *b* to the priest,
Dt 10: 14 LORD your God *b* the heavens,
20: 15 and do not *b* to the nations nearby.
29: 29 The secret things *b*
29: 29 but the things revealed *b* to us
33: 8 ''Your Thummim and Urim *b*
Jos 2: 13 and sisters, and all who *b* to them,
6: 22 bring her out and all who *b* to her,
1Sa 25: 22 male of all who *b* to him!''
30: 13 ''To whom do you *b*, and where do
1Ki 8: 41 for the foreigner who does not *b*
2Ch 6: 32 for the foreigner who does not *b*
Ne 5: 5 and our vineyards *b* to others.''
Job 12: 13 ''To God *b* wisdom and power;
12: 16 To him *b* strength and victory;
25: 2 ''Dominion and awe *b* to God;
Ps 47: 9 for the kings of the earth *b* to God;
95: 4 and the mountain peaks *b* to him.
104: 18 The high mountains *b*
115: 16 The highest heavens *b*
Pr 16: 1 To man *b* the plans of the heart,
SS 7: 10 I *b* to my lover,
Isa 44: 5 One will say, 'I *b* to the LORD';
Jer 5: 10 for these people do not *b*
Eze 13: 9 They will not *b* to the council
18: 4 well as the son—both alike *b* to me
44: 29 to the LORD will *b* to them.
44: 30 and of all your special gifts will *b*
45: 5 cubits wide will *b* to the Levites,
45: 6 it will *b* to the whole house of Israel
46: 16 it will also *b* to his descendants;
48: 21 and the city property will *b*

Eze 48: 21 length of the tribal portions will *b*
Zep 2: 7 It will *b* to the remnant
Zec 9: 7 Those who are left will *b*
Mt 20: 23 These places *b* to those
Mk 9: 41 you *b* to Christ will certainly not
10: 40 These places *b* to those
13: 14 standing where it does not *b*—
Jn 8: 44 You *b* to your father, the devil,
8: 47 you do not hear is that you do not *b*
14: 24 they *b* to the Father who sent me.
15: 19 As it is, you do not *b* to the world,
Ac 5: 4 Didn't it *b* to you before it was sold
Ro 1: 6 called to *b* to Jesus Christ.
7: 4 that you might *b* to another,
8: 9 of Christ, he does not *b* to Christ.
14: 8 we live or die, we *b* to the Lord.
16: 10 Greet those who *b*
1Co 7: 4 The wife's body does not *b*
7: 4 the husband's body does not *b*
7: 39 but he must *b* to the Lord.
9: 19 Though I am free and *b* to no man,
12: 15 Because I am not a hand, I do not *b*
12: 16 Because I am not an eye, I do not *b*
15: 23 when he comes, those who *b*
2Co 10: 7 he should consider again that we *b*
Gal 3: 29 If you *b* to Christ, then you are
5: 24 Those who *b* to Christ Jesus have
6: 10 to those who *b* to the family
Php 4: 22 especially those who *b*
1Th 5: 5 We do not *b* to the night
5: 8 But since we *b* to the day, let us be
Jas 2: 7 name of him to whom you *b?*
1Jn 2: 19 but they did not really *b* to us.
3: 19 then is how we know that we *b*
Rev 19: 1 and glory and power *b* to our God,

BELONGED (BELONG)

Ge 30: 40 and dark-colored animals that *b*
31: 1 wealth from what *b* to our father."
Nu 3: 21 To Gershon *b* the clans
3: 27 To Kohath *b* the clans
3: 33 To Merari *b* the clans
27: 1 *b* to the clans of Manasseh son
Dt 11: 6 every living thing that *b* to them.
30: 5 to the land that *b* to your fathers,
Jos 6: 23 and brothers and all who *b* to her.
6: 25 with her family and all who *b* to her
14: 14 So Hebron has *b* to Caleb son
17: 6 The land of Gilead *b* to the rest
17: 8 of Manasseh, *b* to the Ephraimites
17: 10 On the south the land *b* to Ephraim
Jdg 6: 11 the oak in Ophrah that *b* to Joash
Ru 4: 3 piece of land that *b* to our brother
1Sa 27: 6 it has *b* to the kings of Judah ever
2Sa 8: 7 David took the gold shields that *b*
8: 8 towns that *b* to Hadadezer,
9: 7 restore to you all the land that *b*
9: 9 grandson everything that *b*
12: 4 he took the ewe lamb that *b*
16: 4 "All that *b* to Mephibosheth is now
1Ki 6: 22 overlaid with gold the altar that *b*
2Ki 8: 6 Give back everything that *b* to her,
9: 21 the plot of ground that had *b*
9: 25 him on the field that *b* to Naboth
11: 10 shields that had *b* to King David
12: 16 of the LORD; it *b* to the priests.
14: 28 Hamath, which had *b* to Yaudi,
1Ch 5: 2 of the firstborn *b* to Joseph)—
18: 8 towns that *b* to Hadadezer,
2Ch 23: 9 and small shields that had *b*
26: 23 a field for burial that *b* to the kings,
Eze 23: 41 placed the incense and oil that *b*
46: 19 which *b* to the priests,
Lk 1: 5 who *b* to the priestly division
2: 4 because he *b* to the house
5: 30 of the law who *b* to their sect
Jn 15: 19 If you *b* to the world, it would love
Ac 9: 2 that if he found any there who *b*
12: 1 King Herod arrested some who *b*
15: 5 of the believers who *b* to the party
27: 1 who *b* to the Imperial Regiment.
28: 7 an estate nearby that *b* to Publius,
Gal 2: 12 of those who *b* to the circumcision
Col 2: 20 why, as though you still *b* to it,
Heb 7: 13 He of whom these things are said *b*
1Jn 2: 19 going showed that none of them *b*
2: 19 if they had *b* to us, they would have
3: 12 who *b* to the evil one and murdered

BELONGING (BELONG)

Ge 14: 23 an oath that I will accept nothing *b*
50: 8 those *b* to his father's household.
Ex 9: 4 so that no animal *b*
9: 6 not one animal *b* to the Israelites
Lev 7: 20 meat of the fellowship offering *b*
7: 21 meat of the fellowship offering *b*
25: 34 pastureland *b* to their towns must
Nu 1: 50 all its furnishings and everything *b*
16: 26 Do not touch anything *b* to them,
17: 5 The staff *b* to the man I choose will
31: 42 The half *b* to the Israelites,
Dt 2: 19 of any land *b* to the Ammonites.
Jos 17: 9 There were towns *b*
Ru 2: 3 working in a field *b* to Boaz,
1Sa 6: 18 the number of Philistine towns *b*
9: 3 the donkeys *b* to Saul's father Kish
25: 34 not one male *b* to Nabal would
30: 14 and the territory *b* to Judah
1Ki 14: 11 Dogs will eat those *b*
14: 13 He is the only one *b*
16: 4 Dogs will eat those *b*
21: 1 an incident involving a vineyard *b*
21: 24 "Dogs will eat those *b*
1Ch 7: 5 relatives who were fighting men *b*
9: 18 These were the gatekeepers *b*
22: 19 and the sacred articles *b* to God
23: 7 *B* to the Gershonites: Ladan
26: 21 heads of families *b* to Ladan
28: 1 livestock *b* to the king and his sons,
2Ch 34: 33 idols from all the territory *b*
Ezr 1: 7 Cyrus brought out the articles *b*
Eze 37: 16 *b* to Joseph and all the house
37: 16 '*B* to Judah and the Israelites
48: 22 The area *b* to the prince will lie
Lk 5: 3 of the boats, the one *b* to Simon,
1Pe 2: 9 a holy nation, a people *b* to God,
Rev 13: 8 written in the book of life *b*

BELONGINGS (BELONG)

Ge 45: 20 Never mind about your *b*,
Jdg 14: 19 stripped them of their *b*
Jer 10: 17 Gather up your *b* to leave the land,
46: 19 Pack your *b* for exile,
Eze 12: 3 pack your *b* for exile
12: 4 bring out your *b* packed for exile.
12: 5 and take your *b* out through it.
12: 7 I took my *b* out at dusk, carrying

BELONGS (BELONG)

Ge 14: 24 share that *b* to the men who went
19: 12 else in the city who *b* to you?
23: 9 which *b* to him and is in the end
31: 16 away from our father *b* to us
31: 37 what have you found that *b*
47: 18 and our livestock *b* to you,
47: 26 a fifth of the produce *b* to Pharaoh.
49: 10 until he comes to whom it *b*
Ex 13: 2 among the Israelites *b* to me,
20: 17 or anything that *b* to your neighbor
34: 19 offspring of every womb *b* to me,
40: 4 in the table and set out what *b* on it.
Lev 2: 3 rest of the grain offering *b* to Aaron
2: 10 rest of the grain offering *b* to Aaron
7: 9 or on a griddle *b* to the priest who
7: 10 *b* equally to all the sons of Aaron.
7: 14 it *b* to the priest who sprinkles
7: 31 but the breast *b* to Aaron
14: 13 the guilt offering *b* to the priest;
24: 9 It *b* to Aaron and his sons,
27: 26 since the firstborn already *b*
27: 30 *b* to the LORD; it is holy
Nu 5: 8 the restitution *b* to the LORD
16: 5 the LORD will show who *b*
16: 30 with everything that *b* to them,
18: 9 that part *b* to you and your sons.
Dt 1: 17 of any man, for judgment *b* to God.
5: 21 or anything that *b* to your neighbor
21: 17 The right of the firstborn *b* to him.
Jos 7: 15 along with all that *b* to him.
1Sa 15: 3 totally destroy everything that *b*
1Ki 22: 3 Ramoth Gilead *b* to
1Ch 29: 16 from your hand, and all of it *b*
Job 41: 11 Everything under heaven *b* to me.
Ps 22: 28 for dominion *b* to the LORD
89: 18 Indeed, our shield *b* to the LORD,
111: 10 To him *b* eternal praise.
Jer 46: 10 But that day *b* to the LORD,
Eze 18: 4 For every living soul *b* to me,
21: 27 comes to whom it rightfully *b;*
46: 17 His inheritance *b* to his sons only;
48: 22 of the area that *b* to the prince.
Mt 19: 14 the kingdom of heaven *b* to such
25: 25 See, here is what *b* to you.'
Mk 10: 14 for the kingdom of God *b* to such
Lk 6: 30 and if anyone takes what *b* to you,
18: 16 for the kingdom of God *b* to such
Jn 3: 29 The bride *b* to the bridegroom.
3: 31 is from the earth *b* to the earth,
8: 35 place in the family, but a son *b*
8: 47 He who *b* to God hears what God
16: 15 All that *b* to the Father is mine.
Ac 1: 25 which Judas left to go where he *b*."
Ro 12: 5 each member *b* to all the others.
2Co 10: 7 If anyone is confident that he *b*
Col 3: 5 whatever *b* to your earthly nature:
Rev 7: 10 "Salvation *b* to our God,
17: 11 He *b* to the seven and is going

BELOVED (LOVE)

Dt 33: 12 "Let the *b* of the LORD rest secure
SS 5: 9 How is your *b* better than others,
5: 9 How is your *b* better
Jer 11: 15 "What is my *b* doing in my temple

BELSHAZZAR (BELSHAZZAR'S)

Da 5: 1 King *B* gave a great banquet
5: 2 While *B* was drinking his wine,
5: 9 King *B* became even more terrified
5: 22 O *B*, have not humbled yourself,
5: 30 That very night *B*, king
7: 1 year of *B* king of Babylon,

BELSHAZZAR'S (BELSHAZZAR)

Da 5: 29 at *B* command, Daniel was clothed
8: 1 In the third year of King *B* reign, I,

BELT (BELTS)

Ex 12: 11 with your cloak tucked into your *b*,
1Sa 18: 4 even his sword, his bow and his *b*.
2Sa 18: 11 shekels of silver and a warrior's *b*."
20: 8 it at his waist was a *b* with a dagger
1Ki 2: 5 and with that blood stained the *b*
18: 46 and, tucking his cloak into his *b*,
2Ki 1: 8 and a leather *b* around his waist."
4: 29 "Tuck your cloak into your *b*,
9: 1 "Tuck your cloak into your *b*,
Ps 109: 19 like a *b* tied forever around him.
Isa 5: 27 not a *b* is loosened at the waist,
11: 5 Righteousness will be his *b*
Jer 13: 1 "Go and buy a linen *b*
13: 2 I bought a *b*, as the LORD directed
13: 4 "Take the *b* you bought
13: 6 get the *b* I told you to hide there."
13: 7 I went to Perath and dug up the *b*
13: 10 be like this *b*— completely useless!
13: 11 a *b* is bound around a man's waist,
Da 10: 5 with a *b* of the finest gold
Mt 3: 4 he had a leather *b* around his waist.
Mk 1: 6 with a leather *b* around his waist,
Ac 21: 11 Coming over to us, he took Paul's *b*
21: 11 will bind the owner of this *b*
Eph 6: 14 with the *b* of truth buckled

BELTESHAZZAR

Da 1: 7 to Daniel, the name *B;*
2: 26 king asked Daniel (also called *B*),
4: 8 (He is called *B*, after the name
4: 9 I said, "*B*, chief of the magicians,
4: 18 Now, *B*, tell me what it means,
4: 19 *B* answered, "My lord,
4: 19 "*B*, do not let the dream
4: 19 called *B*) was greatly perplexed
5: 12 Daniel, whom the king called *B*,
10: 1 given to Daniel (who was called *B*).

BELTS (BELT)

Eze 23: 15 with *b* around their waists
Mt 10: 9 or silver or copper in your *b;*
Mk 6: 8 no bag, no money in your *b*.

BEN HINNOM (HINNOM)

Jos 15: 8 of *B* along the southern
18: 16 of the hill facing the Valley of *B*
2Ki 23: 10 which was in the Valley of *B*

2Ch 28: 3 in the Valley of *B*
33: 6 sons in the fire in the Valley of *B*
Jer 7: 31 in the Valley of *B*
7: 32 call it Topheth or the Valley of *B*
19: 2 and go out to the Valley of *B*
19: 6 place Topheth or the Valley of *B*
32: 35 Baal in the Valley of *B*

BEN-ABINADAB

1Ki 4: 11 all the land of Hepher were his); *B*

BEN-AMMI

Ge 19: 38 she named him *B*; he is the father

BEN-DEKER

1Ki 4: 9 in the hill country of Ephraim; *B*—

BEN-GEBER

1Ki 4: 13 *B*— in Ramoth Gilead

BEN-HADAD (BEN-HADAD'S)

1Ki 15: 18 sent them to *B* son of Tabrimmon,
15: 20 *B* agreed with King Asa
20: 1 *B* king of Aram mustered his entire
20: 2 saying, "This is what *B* says:
20: 5 and said, "This is what *B* says:
20: 9 and took the answer back to *B*.
20: 10 *B* sent another message to Ahab:
20: 12 *B* heard this message while he
20: 16 They set out at noon while *B*
20: 17 Now *B* had dispatched scouts,
20: 20 But *B* king of Aram escaped
20: 26 The next spring *B* mustered
20: 30 And *B* fled to the city and hid
20: 32 "Your servant *B* says: 'Please let
20: 33 When *B* came out, Ahab had him
20: 33 "Yes, your brother *B*!" they said.
20: 34 took from your father," *B* offered.
2Ki 6: 24 *B* king of Aram mobilized his
8: 7 and *B* king of Aram was ill.
8: 9 "Your son *B* king of Aram has sent
8: 14 When *B* asked, "What did Elisha
13: 3 king of Aram and *B* his son.
13: 24 and *B* his son succeeded him
13: 25 of Jehoahaz recaptured from *B* son
2Ch 16: 2 and sent it to *B* king of Aram,
16: 4 *B* agreed with King Asa
Jer 49: 27 it will consume the fortresses of *B*
Am 1: 4 will consume the fortresses of *B*.

BEN-HADAD'S (BEN-HADAD)

1Ki 20: 9 So he replied to *B* messengers,

BEN-HAIL

2Ch 17: 7 of his reign he sent his officials *B*,

BEN-HANAN

1Ch 4: 20 Amnon, Rinnah, *B* and Tilon.

BEN-HESED

1Ki 4: 10 *B*— in Arubboth (Socoh

BEN-HUR

1Ki 4: 8 These are their names: *B*—

BEN-ONI

Ge 35: 18 was dying—she named her son *B*.

BEN-ZOHETH

1Ch 4: 20 descendants of Ishi: Zoheth and *B*.

BENAIAH

2Sa 8: 18 *B* son of Jehoiada was
20: 23 *B* son of Jehoiada was
23: 20 *B* son of Jehoiada was a valiant
23: 21 *B* went against him with a club.
23: 22 the exploits of *B* son of Jehoiada;
23: 30 of Benjamin, *B* the Pirathonite,
1Ki 1: 8 Zadok the priest, *B* son of Jehoiada
1: 10 or *B* or the special guard
1: 26 and Zadok the priest, and *B* son
1: 32 Nathan the prophet and *B* son
1: 36 *B* son of Jehoiada answered
1: 38 Nathan the prophet, *B* son
1: 44 Nathan the prophet, *B* son
2: 25 orders to *B* son of Jehoiada,
2: 29 Then Solomon ordered *B* son
2: 30 So *B* entered the tent of the LORD
2: 30 *B* reported to the king, "This is
1Ki 2: 31 Then the king commanded *B*,
2: 34 So *B* son of Jehoiada went up
2: 35 The king put *B* son of Jehoiada
2: 46 the order to *B* son of Jehoiada,
4: 4 recorder; *B* son of Jehoiada—
1Ch 4: 36 Asaiah, Adiel, Jesimiel, *B*,
11: 22 *B* son of Jehoiada was a valiant
11: 23 *B* went against him with a club.
11: 24 the exploits of *B* son of Jehoiada;
11: 31 of Benjamin, *B* the Pirathonite,
15: 18 Unni, Eliab, *B*, Maaseiah,
15: 20 *B* were to play the lyres according
15: 24 *B* and Eliezer the priests were
16: 5 Jehiel, Mattithiah, Eliab, *B*,
16: 6 and *B* and Jahaziel the priests were
18: 17 *B* son of Jehoiada was
27: 5 was *B* son of Jehoiada the priest.
27: 6 This was the *B* who was a mighty
27: 14 was *B* the Pirathonite,
27: 34 succeeded by Jehoiada son of *B*
2Ch 20: 14 the son of *B*, the son of Jeiel,
31: 13 and *B* were supervisors
Ezr 10: 25 Mijamin, Eleazar, Malkijah and *B*.
10: 30 Adna, Kelal, *B*, Maaseiah,
10: 35 Amram and Uel, *B*, Bedeiah,
10: 43 Zabad, Zebina, Jaddai, Joel and *B*.
Eze 11: 1 son of Azzur and Pelatiah son of *B*,
11: 13 Pelatiah son of *B* died.

BENCHES

Mt 21: 12 and the *b* of those selling doves.
Mk 11: 15 and the *b* of those selling doves,

BEND (BENDING BENT)

Ge 49: 15 he will *b* his shoulder to the burden
2Sa 22: 35 my arms can *b* a bow of bronze.
Ps 7: 12 he will *b* and string his bow.
11: 2 For look, the wicked *b* their bows;
18: 34 my arms can *b* a bow of bronze.
37: 14 and *b* the bow
Isa 65: 12 will all *b* down for the slaughter;
Zec 9: 13 I will *b* Judah as I *b* my bow

BENDING (BEND)

Lk 24: 12 *B* over, he saw the strips

BENE BERAK

Jos 19: 45 Gibbethon, Baalath, Jehud, *B*,

BENE JAAKAN

Nu 33: 31 left Moseroth and camped at *B*.
33: 32 They left *B* and camped

BENEFACTORS

Lk 22: 25 over them call themselves *B*.

BENEFICIAL (BENEFIT)

1Co 6: 12 for me"—but not everything is *b*.
10: 23 but not everything is *b*.

BENEFIT (BENEFICIAL BENEFITED BENEFITS)

Job 22: 2 Can even a wise man *b* him?
22: 2 "Can a man be of *b* to God?
Ecc 5: 11 And what *b* are they to the owner
Isa 38: 17 Surely it was for my *b*
57: 12 and they will not *b* you.
Jer 23: 32 They do not *b* these people
Jn 11: 42 but I said this for the *b*
12: 30 This voice was for your *b*, not mine
Ro 6: 21 What *b* did you reap at that time
6: 22 the *b* you reap leads to holiness,
1Co 4: 6 to myself and Apollos for your *b*,
2Co 1: 15 first so that you might *b* twice.
4: 15 All this is for your *b*,
Eph 4: 29 that it may *b* those who listen.
1Ti 6: 2 those who *b* from their service are
Phm : 20 that I may have some *b* from you

BENEFITED (BENEFIT)

1Sa 19: 4 what he has done has *b* you greatly.

BENEFITS (BENEFIT)

Dt 18: 8 He is to share equally in their *b*,
Ps 103: 2 and forget not all his *b*.
Pr 11: 17 A kind man *b* himself,
Ecc 7: 11 and *b* those who see the sun.
Jn 4: 38 you have reaped the *b* of their labor

BENINU

Ne 10: 13 Shebaniah, Hodiah, Bani and *B*.

BENJAMIN (BENJAMIN'S BENJAMITE BENJAMITES)

Ge 35: 18 But his father named him *B*.
35: 24 The sons of Rachel: Joseph and *B*.
42: 4 did not send *B*, Joseph's brother,
42: 36 and now you want to take *B*.
43: 14 and *B* come back with you.
43: 15 double the amount of silver, and *B*
43: 16 When Joseph saw *B* with them,
43: 29 about and saw his brother *B*,
45: 12 and so can my brother *B*,
45: 14 and *B* embraced him, weeping.
45: 14 arms around his brother *B*
45: 22 to *B* he gave three hundred shekels
46: 19 Jacob's wife Rachel: Joseph and *B*.
46: 21 The sons of *B*: Bela, Beker, Ashbel,
49: 27 "*B* is a ravenous wolf;
Ex 1: 3 Zebulun and *B*; Dan and Naphtali;
Nu 1: 11 from *B*, Abidan son of Gideoni;
1: 36 From the descendants of *B*:
1: 37 from the tribe of *B* was 35,400.
2: 22 The tribe of *B* will be next.
2: 22 of the people of *B* is Abidan son
7: 60 the leader of the people of *B*,
10: 24 over the division of the tribe of *B*.
13: 9 from the tribe of *B*, Palti son
26: 38 The descendants of *B*
26: 41 These were the clans of *B*;
34: 21 from the tribe of *B*; Bukki son
Dt 27: 12 Judah, Issachar, Joseph and *B*.
33: 12 About *B* he said:
Jos 18: 11 The lot came up for the tribe of *B*,
18: 20 of the clans of *B* on all sides.
18: 21 The tribe of *B*, clan by clan,
18: 28 This was the inheritance of *B*
21: 4 the tribes of Judah, Simeon and *B*.
21: 17 tribe of *B* they gave them Gibeon,
Jdg 5: 14 *B* was with the people who
10: 9 *B* and the house of Ephraim;
19: 14 as they neared Gibeah in *B*.
20: 4 to Gibeah in *B* to spend the night.
20: 10 the army arrives at Gibeah in *B*,
20: 12 men throughout the tribe of *B*,
20: 17 from *B*, mustered four hundred
20: 24 drew near to *B* the second day.
20: 28 again to battle with *B* our brother,
20: 35 The LORD defeated *B*
20: 36 of Israel had given way before *B*,
20: 41 and the men of *B* were terrified,
20: 48 The men of Israel went back to *B*
21: 15 The people grieved for *B*,
21: 16 "With the women of *B* destroyed,
21: 21 of Shiloh and go to the land of *B*.
1Sa 9: 1 of Becorath, the son of Aphiah of *B*
9: 4 passed through the territory of *B*,
9: 16 a man from the land of *B*.
9: 21 of all the clans of the tribe of *B*?
10: 2 at Zelzah on the border of *B*.
10: 20 the tribe of *B* was chosen.
10: 21 he brought forward the tribe of *B*,
13: 2 were with Jonathan at Gibeah of *B*.
13: 15 and went up to Gibeah of *B*,
13: 16 them were staying in Geba of *B*,
14: 16 of *B* saw the army melting away
22: 7 said to them, "Listen, men of *B*!
2Sa 2: 9 also over Ephraim, *B* and all Israel
2: 15 men for *B* and Ish-Bosheth son
2: 25 the men of *B* rallied behind Abner.
3: 19 the whole house of *B* wanted to do.
4: 2 Beeroth is considered part of *B*,
4: 2 Beerothite from the tribe of *B*—
21: 14 in *B*, and did everything the king
23: 29 Ithai son of Ribai from Gibeah of *B*
1Ki 4: 18 of Ela—in *B*; Geber son of Uri—
12: 21 house of Judah and the tribe of *B*—
12: 23 to the whole house of Judah and *B*,
15: 22 them King Asa built up Geba in *B*,
1Ch 2: 2 Zebulun, Dan, Joseph, *B*, Naphtali
6: 60 tribe of *B* they were given Gibeon,
6: 65 and *B* they allotted the previously
7: 6 Three sons of *B*: Bela, Beker
7: 10 Jeush, *B*, Ehud, Kenaanah, Zethan
8: 1 *B* was the father of Bela his
8: 40 these were the descendants of *B*.

1Ch 9: 3 Those from Judah, from *B*,
9: 9 The people from *B*, as listed
11: 31 Ithai son of Ribai from Gibeah of *B*
12: 2 of Saul from the tribe of *B*):
12: 29 men of *B*, Saul's kinsmen—3,000,
21: 6 Joab did not include Levi and *B*
27: 21 over *B*: Jaasiel son of Abner;
2Ch 11: 1 the house of Judah and *B*—
11: 3 to all the Israelites in Judah and *B*,
11: 10 fortified cities in Judah and *B*.
11: 12 So Judah and *B* were his.
11: 23 the districts of Judah and *B*,
14: 8 and eighty thousand from *B*,
15: 2 to me, Asa and all Judah and *B*.
15: 8 the whole land of Judah and *B*
15: 9 Then he assembled all Judah and *B*
17: 17 From *B*: Eliada, a valiant soldier,
25: 5 of hundreds for all Judah and *B*.
31: 1 the altars throughout Judah and *B*
34: 9 *B* and the inhabitants of Jerusalem.
34: 32 and *B* pledge themselves to it;
Ezr 1: 5 the family heads of Judah and *B*,
4: 1 and *B* heard that the exiles were
10: 9 and *B* had gathered in Jerusalem.
10: 32 Malkijah, Shemaiah, Shimeon, *B*,
Ne 3: 23 *B* and Hasshub made repairs
11: 4 and *B* lived in Jerusalem):
11: 7 From the descendants of *B*:
11: 36 of the Levites of Judah settled in *B*.
12: 34 Meshullam, Judah, *B*, Shemaiah,
Est 2: 5 of Susa a Jew of the tribe of *B*,
Ps 68: 27 There is the little tribe of *B*,
80: 2 before Ephraim, *B* and Manasseh.
Jer 1: 1 at Anathoth in the territory of *B*.
6: 1 "Flee for safety, people of *B*!
17: 26 from the territory of *B*
20: 2 Gate of *B* at the LORD's temple.
32: 8 at Anathoth in the territory of *B*.
32: 44 and witnessed in the territory of *B*,
33: 13 in the territory of *B*, in the villages
37: 12 to the territory of *B* to get his share
37: 13 But when he reached the *B* Gate,
38: 7 While the king was sitting in the *B*
Eze 48: 22 of Judah and the border of *B*.
48: 23 rest of the tribes: *B* will have one
48: 24 the territory of *B* from east to west.
48: 32 the gate of *B* and the gate of Dan.
Hos 5: 8 lead on, O *B*.
Ob : 19 and *B* will possess Gilead.
Zec 14: 10 from the *B* Gate to the site
Ac 13: 21 tribe of *B*, who ruled forty years.
Ro 11: 1 of Abraham, from the tribe of *B*.
Php 3: 5 of the tribe of *B*, a Hebrew
Rev 7: 8 from the tribe of *B* 12,000.

BENJAMIN'S (BENJAMIN)

Ge 43: 34 *B* portion was five times as much
44: 12 And the cup was found in *B* sack.

BENJAMITE (BENJAMIN)

Jdg 3: 15 man, the son of Gera the *B*.
20: 46 thousand *B* swordsmen
21: 1 daughter in marriage to a *B*."
21: 17 The *B* survivors must have heirs,"
21: 18 be anyone who gives a wife to a *B*.'
1Sa 4: 12 That same day a *B* ran
9: 1 There was a *B*, a man of standing,
9: 21 am I not a *B*, from the smallest
2Sa 16: 11 then, this *B*! Leave him alone;
19: 16 son of Gera, the *B* from Bahurim,
20: 1 a *B*, happened to be there.
1Ki 2: 8 son of Gera, the *B* from Bahurim,
1Ch 27: 12 was Abiezer the Anathothite, a *B*.

BENJAMITES (BENJAMIN)

Jdg 1: 21 The *B*, however, failed
1: 21 the Jebusites live there with the *B*
19: 16 (the men of the place were *B*),
20: 3 *B* heard that the Israelites had
20: 13 But the *B* would not listen
20: 15 once the *B* mobilized twenty-six
20: 18 first to fight against the *B*?"
20: 20 of Israel went out to fight the *B*
20: 21 The *B* came out of Gibeah
20: 23 again to battle against the *B*,
20: 25 when the *B* came out from Gibeah
20: 30 up against the *B* on the third day
20: 31 The *B* came out to meet them
Jdg 20: 32 While the *B* were saying, "We are
20: 34 so heavy that the *B* did not realize
20: 35 Israelites struck down 25,100 *B*,
20: 36 the *B* saw that they were beaten.
20: 39 *B* had begun to inflict casualties
20: 40 the *B* turned and saw the smoke
20: 43 surrounded the *B*, chased them
20: 44 Eighteen thousand *B* fell, all
20: 45 They kept pressing after the *B*
21: 6 grieved for their brothers, the *B*.
21: 13 offer of peace to the *B* at the rock
21: 14 So the *B* returned at that time
21: 20 So they instructed the *B*, saying,
21: 23 So that is what the *B* did.
2Sa 2: 31 and sixty *B* who were with Abner.
3: 19 also spoke to the *B* in person.
19: 17 With him were a thousand *B*,
1Ch 9: 7 Of the *B*: Sallu son of Meshullam,
12: 16 Other *B* and some men from Judah
Ne 11: 31 of the *B* from Geba lived

BENO

1Ch 24: 26 The son of Jaaziah: *B*.
24: 27 from Jaaziah: *B*, Shoham,

BENT (BEND)

Ex 10: 10 children! Clearly you are *b* on evil.
1Sa 24: 9 'David is *b* on harming you'?
1Ki 18: 42 *b* down to the ground and put his
Ps 44: 16 of the enemy, who is *b* on revenge.
69: 23 and their backs be *b* forever.
106: 43 but they were *b* on rebellion
Pr 16: 30 he who purses his lips is *b* on evil.
17: 11 An evil man is *b* only on rebellion;
Isa 21: 15 from the *b* bow
51: 13 who is *b* on destruction?
Eze 22: 9 In you are slanderous men *b*
Da 11: 27 with their hearts *b* on evil,
Hos 11: 4 and *b* down to feed them.
Hab 1: 9 they all come *b* on violence.
Lk 4: 39 he *b* over her and rebuked the fever
13: 11 She was *b* over and could not
Jn 8: 6 Jesus *b* down and started to write
20: 5 He *b* over and looked
20: 11 she *b* over to look into the tomb
Ro 11: 10 and their backs be *b* forever."
Rev 6: 2 as a conqueror *b* on conquest.

BEON

Nu 32: 3 Elealeh, Sebam, Nebo and *B*—

BEOR

Ge 36: 32 Bela son of *B* became king
Nu 22: 5 to summon Balaam son of *B*,
24: 3 "The oracle of Balaam son of *B*,
24: 15 "The oracle of Balaam son of *B*,
31: 8 son of *B* with the sword.
Dt 23: 4 and they hired Balaam son of *B*
Jos 13: 22 put to the sword Balaam son of *B*,
24: 9 for Balaam son of *B* to put a curse
1Ch 1: 43 son of *B*, whose city was named
Mic 6: 5 what Balaam son of *B* answered.
2Pe 2: 15 the way of Balaam son of *B*,

BERA

Ge 14: 2 to war against *B* king of Sodom,

BERACAH

1Ch 12: 3 and Pelet the sons of Azmaveth; *B*,
2Ch 20: 26 assembled in the Valley of *B*,
20: 26 is why it is called the Valley of *B*

BERAIAH

1Ch 8: 21 *B* and Shimrath were the sons

BERAKIAH (BEREKIAH)

Mt 23: 35 to the blood of Zechariah son of *B*,

BEREA (BEREANS)

Ac 17: 10 sent Paul and Silas away to *B*.
17: 13 preaching the word of God at *B*,
17: 14 but Silas and Timothy stayed at *B*.
20: 4 by Sopater son of Pyrrhus from *B*,

BEREANS (BEREA)

Ac 17: 11 the *B* were of more noble character

BEREAVE (BEREAVED BEREAVEMENT BEREAVES)

Hos 9: 12 I will *b* them of every one.

BEREAVED (BEREAVE)

Ge 43: 14 As for me, if I am *b*, I am *b*."
Isa 49: 21 I was *b* and barren;

BEREAVEMENT (BEREAVE)

Isa 49: 20 The children born during your *b*
Jer 15: 7 I will bring *b* and destruction

BEREAVES (BEREAVE)

La 1: 20 Outside, the sword *b*;

BERED

Ge 16: 14 between Kadesh and *B*.
1Ch 7: 20 of Ephraim: Shuthelah, *B* his son,

BEREKIAH (BERAKIAH)

1Ch 3: 20 *B*, Hasadiah and Jushab-Hesed.
6: 39 Asaph son of *B*, the son of Shimea,
9: 16 son of Jeduthun; and *B* son of Asa,
15: 17 from his brothers, Asaph son of *B*;
15: 23 *B* and Elkanah were
2Ch 28: 12 son of Jehohanan, *B* son
Ne 3: 4 Next to him Meshullam son of *B*,
3: 30 Meshullam son of *B* made repairs
6: 18 daughter of Meshullam son of *B*.
Zec 1: 1 to the prophet Zechariah son of *B*,
1: 7 to the prophet Zechariah son of *B*,

BERI (BERITES)

1Ch 7: 36 Harnepher, Shual, *B*, Imrah, Bezer

BERIAH (BERIITE)

Ge 46: 17 Imnah, Ishvah, Ishvi and *B*.
46: 17 The sons of *B*: Heber and Malkiel.
Nu 26: 44 through *B*, the Beriite clan;
26: 45 and through the descendants of *B*:
1Ch 7: 23 He named him *B*, because there
7: 30 Imnah, Ishvah, Ishvi and *B*.
7: 31 The sons of *B*: Heber and Malkiel,
8: 13 its surrounding villages), and *B*
8: 16 Ishpah and Joha were the sons of *B*
23: 10 Jahath, Ziza, Jeush and *B*.
23: 11 and *B* did not have many sons;

BERIITE (BERIAH)

Nu 26: 44 through Beriah, the *B* clan;

BERITES (BERI)

2Sa 20: 14 through the entire region of the *B*,

BERNICE

Ac 25: 13 and *B* arrived at Caesarea
25: 23 and *B* came with great pomp
26: 30 and with him the governor and *B*

BEROTHAH

Eze 47: 16 *B* and Sibraim (which lies

BEROTHAI (BEROTHITE)

2Sa 8: 8 and *B*, towns that belonged

BEROTHITE (BEROTHAI)

1Ch 11: 39 the Ammonite, Naharai the *B*,

BERYL

Ex 28: 17 a *b*; in the second row a turquoise,
39: 10 a *b*; in the second row a turquoise,
Eze 28: 13 sapphire, turquoise and *b*.
Rev 21: 20 the eighth *b*, the ninth topaz,

BESAI

Ezr 2: 49 Uzza, Paseah, *B*, Asnah, Meunim,
Ne 7: 52 Uzza, Paseah, *B*, Meunim,

BESET

Ps 41: 8 "A vile disease has *b* him;
55: 5 Fear and trembling have *b* me;

BESIEGE (SIEGE)

Dt 20: 19 that you should *b* them? However,
28: 52 They will *b* all the cities
1Sa 23: 8 to go down to Keilah to *b* David
2Sa 12: 28 and *b* the city and capture it.
2Ch 6: 28 or when enemies *b* them in any
Ps 27: 3 Though an army *b* me,

Isa 29: 2 Yet I will *b* Ariel;
29: 7 and her fortress and *b* her,
Eze 4: 3 be under siege, and you shall *b* it.
Lk 11:53 and to *b* him with questions,

BESIEGED (SIEGE)

Jdg 9:50 went to Thebez and *b* it
1Sa 11: 1 Ammonite went up and *b* Jabesh
2Sa 11: 1 the Ammonites and *b* Rabbah.
20:15 *b* Sheba in Abel Beth Maacah.
1Ki 20: 1 he went up and *b* Samaria
2Ki 16: 5 against Jerusalem and *b* Ahaz,
1Ch 20: 1 and went to Rabbah and *b* it,
Ps 31:21 me when I was in a *b* city.
La 3: 5 He has *b* me and surrounded me
Da 1: 1 came to Jerusalem and *b* it.
Zec 12: 2 Judah will be *b* as well as Jerusalem

BESIEGES (SIEGE)

1Ki 8:37 or when an enemy *b* them in any

BESIEGING (SIEGE)

1Ki 15:27 while Nadab and all Israel were *b* it
2Ki 24:11 the city while his officers were *b* it.
Jer 4:16 'A *b* army is coming
21: 4 are outside the wall *b* you.
21: 9 the Babylonians who are *b* you will
32: 2 of Babylon was then *b* Jerusalem,
37: 5 who were *b* Jerusalem heard

BESODEIAH

Ne 3: 6 of Paseah and Meshullam son of *B*.

BESOR

1Sa 30: 9 men with him came to the *B*
30:21 and who were left behind at the *B*

BESTOW (BESTOWED BESTOWER BESTOWING BESTOWS)

Ps 31:19 which you *b* in the sight of men
Isa 45: 4 and *b* on you a title of honor,
61: 3 to *b* on them a crown of beauty
62: 2 that the mouth of the LORD will *b*.
Jer 23: 2 I will *b* punishment on you

BESTOWED (BESTOW)

1Ch 29:25 and *b* on him royal splendor such
Ps 21: 5 you have *b* on him splendor
89:19 "I have *b* strength on a warrior;
Jer 23: 2 and have not *b* care on them,

BESTOWER (BESTOW)

Isa 23: 8 the *b* of crowns,

BESTOWING (BESTOW)

Pr 8:21 *b* wealth on those who love me

BESTOWS (BESTOW)

Job 5:10 He *b* rain on the earth;
Ps 84:11 the LORD *b* favor and honor;
133: 3 For there the LORD *b* his blessing,

BETEN

Jos 19:25 Helkath, Hali, *B*, Acshaph,

BETH ANATH

Jos 19:38 Horem, *B* and Beth Shemesh.
Jdg 1:33 *B* became forced laborers for them.
1:33 those living in Beth Shemesh or *B*;

BETH ANOTH

Jos 15:59 Maarath, *B* and Eltekon—

BETH ARABAH

Jos 15: 6 continued north of *B* to the Stone
15:61 In the desert: *B*, Middin, Secacah,
18:18 to the northern slope of *B*
18:22 Beth Hoglah, Emek Keziz, *B*,

BETH ARBEL

Hos 10:14 as Shalman devastated *B*

BETH ASHBEA

1Ch 4:21 the clans of the linen workers at *B*,

BETH AVEN

Jos 7: 2 Ai, which is near *B*
18:12 coming out at the desert of *B*.
1Sa 13: 5 and camped at Micmash, east of *B*.
14:23 and the battle moved on beyond *B*.
Hos 4:15 do not go up to *B*.
5: 8 Raise the battle cry in *B*;
10: 5 for the calf-idol of *B*.

BETH AZMAVETH

Ne 7:28 of Anathoth 128 of *B* 42

BETH BAAL MEON

Jos 13:17 including Dibon, Bamoth Baal, *B*,

BETH BARAH

Jdg 7:24 ahead of them as far as *B*."
7:24 the waters of the Jordan as far as *B*.

BETH BIRI

1Ch 4:31 Hazar Susim, *B* and Shaaraim.

BETH CAR

1Sa 7:11 along the way to a point below *B*.

BETH DAGON

Jos 15:41 Lahmas, Kitlish, Gederoth, *B*,
19:27 It then turned east toward *B*,

BETH DIBLATHAIM

Jer 48:22 Nebo and *B*, to Kiriathaim,

BETH EDEN

Am 1: 5 the one who holds the scepter in *B*.

BETH EKED

2Ki 10:12 At *B* of the Shepherds, he met
10:14 slaughtered them by the well of *B*

BETH EMEK

Jos 19:27 went north to *B* and Neiel,

BETH EZEL

Mic 1:11 *B* is in mourning;

BETH GADER

1Ch 2:51 and Hareph the father of *B*.

BETH GAMUL

Jer 48:23 to Kiriathaim, *B* and Beth Meon,

BETH GILGAL

Ne 12:29 of the Netophathites, from *B*,

BETH HAGGAN

2Ki 9:27 happened, he fled up the road to *B*.

BETH HAKKEREM

Ne 3:14 of Recab, ruler of the district of *B*.
Jer 6: 1 Raise the signal over *B*!

BETH HARAM

Jos 13:27 and in the valley, *B*,

BETH HARAN

Nu 32:36 Beth Nimrah and *B* as fortified

BETH HOGLAH

Jos 15: 6 went up to *B* and continued north
18:19 went to the northern slope of *B*
18:21 had the following cities: Jericho, *B*,

BETH HORON

Jos 10:10 them along the road going up to *B*
10:11 the road down from *B* to Azekah,
16: 3 as far as the region of Lower *B*
16: 5 in the east to Upper *B*
18:13 on the hill south of Lower *B*.
18:14 From the hill facing *B*
21:22 Gezer, Kibzaim and *B*,
1Sa 13:18 of Shual, another toward *B*,
1Ki 9:17 He built up Lower *B*,
1Ch 6:68 *B*, Aijalon and Gath Rimmon,
7:24 who built Lower and Upper *B*
2Ch 8: 5 He rebuilt Upper *B*
8: 5 and Lower *B* as fortified cities,
25:13 towns from Samaria to *B*.

BETH JESHIMOTH

Nu 33:49 the Jordan from *B* to Abel Shittim.
Jos 12: 3 to *B*, and then southward below
13:20 the slopes of Pisgah, and *B*

Eze 25: 9 beginning at its frontier towns—*B*,

BETH LEBAOTH

Jos 19: 6 Beth Marcaboth, Hazar Susah, *B*

BETH MARCABOTH

Jos 19: 5 Bethul, Hormah, Ziklag, *B*,
1Ch 4:31 Bethuel, Hormah, Ziklag, *B*,

BETH MEON

Jer 48:23 Kiriathaim, Beth Gamul and *B*,

BETH MILLO

Jdg 9: 6 *B* gathered beside the great tree
9:20 citizens of Shechem and *B*,
9:20 citizens of Shechem and *B*,
2Ki 12:20 and assassinated him at *B*,

BETH NIMRAH

Nu 32:36 *B* and Beth Haran as fortified
Jos 13:27 and in the valley, Beth Haram, *B*,

BETH OPHRAH

Mic 1:10 In *B* roll in the dust.

BETH PAZZEZ

Jos 19:21 En Gannim, En Haddah and *B*.

BETH PELET

Jos 15:27 Hazar Gaddah, Heshmon, *B*,
Ne 11:26 in Moladah, in *B*, in Hazar Shual,

BETH PEOR

Dt 3:29 So we stayed in the valley near *B*.
4:46 and were in the valley near *B*
34: 6 in Moab, in the valley opposite *B*,
Jos 13:20 on the hill in the valley, *B*,

BETH RAPHA

1Ch 4:12 Eshton was the father of *B*,

BETH REHOB

Jdg 18:28 The city was in a valley near *B*.
2Sa 10: 6 Aramean foot soldiers from *B* and

BETH SHAN

Jos 17:11 and Asher, Manasseh also had *B*,
17:16 both those in *B* and its settlements
Jdg 1:27 did not drive out the people of *B*
1Sa 31:10 fastened his body to the wall of *B*.
31:12 and his sons from the wall of *B* and
31:12 journeyed through the night to *B*.
2Sa 21:12 from the public square at *B*,
1Ki 4:12 and in all of *B* next to Zarethan
4:12 from *B* to Abel Meholah
1Ch 7:29 the borders of Manasseh were *B*,

BETH SHEMESH

Jos 15:10 continued down to *B* and crossed
19:22 Tabor, Shahazumah and *B*,
19:38 Horem, Beth Anath and *B*.
21:16 Holon, Debir, Ain, Juttah and *B*,
Jdg 1:33 Naphtali drive out those living in *B*
1:33 those living in *B* and Beth Anath
1Sa 6: 9 up to its own territory, toward *B*,
6:12 the cows went straight up toward *B*
6:12 them as far as the border of *B*.
6:13 of *B* were harvesting their wheat in
6:14 came to the field of Joshua of *B*,
6:15 people of *B* offered burnt offerings
6:18 day in the field of Joshua of *B*.
6:19 struck down some of the men of *B*,
6:20 men of *B* asked, "Who can stand in
1Ki 4: 9 in Makaz, Shaalbim, *B*
2Ki 14:11 faced each other at *B* in Judah.
14:13 of Joash, the son of Ahaziah, at *B*.
1Ch 6:59 Hilen, Debir, Ashan, Juttah and *B*,
2Ch 25:21 king of Judah faced each other at *B*
25:23 of Joash, the son of Ahaziah, at *B*.
28:18 They captured and occupied *B*,

BETH SHITTAH

Jdg 7:22 The army fled to *B* toward Zererah

BETH TAPPUAH

Jos 15:53 Eshan, Janim, *B*, Aphekah,

BETH TOGARMAH

Eze 27:14 of *B* exchanged work horses,

Eze 38: 6 and *B* from the far north with

BETH ZUR

Jos 15:58 Halhul, *B*, Gedor, Maarath,
1Ch 2:45 and Maon was the father of *B*.
2Ch 11: 7 Bethlehem, Etam, Tekoa, *B*, Soco,
Ne 3:16 ruler of a half-district of *B*,

BETHANY

Mt 21:17 and went out of the city to *B*,
26: 6 While Jesus was in *B* in the home
Mk 11: 1 and *B* at the Mount of Olives,
11:11 he went out to *B* with the Twelve.
11:12 next day as they were leaving *B*,
14: 3 While he was in *B*, reclining
Lk 19:29 and *B* at the hill called the Mount
24:50 out to the vicinity of *B*,
Jn 1:28 This all happened at *B*
11: 1 He was from *B*, the village of Mary
11:18 *B* was less than two miles
12: 1 arrived at *B*, where Lazarus lived,

BETHEL

Ge 12: 8 went on toward the hills east of *B*
12: 8 with *B* on the west and Ai
13: 3 place to place until he came to *B*,
13: 3 to the place between *B*
28:19 He called that place *B*,
31:13 of *B*, where you anointed a pillar
35: 1 "Go up to *B* and settle there,
35: 3 Then come, let us go up to *B*,
35: 6 came to Luz (that is, *B)* in the land
35: 7 and he called the place El *B*,
35: 8 was buried under the oak below *B*.
35:15 where God had talked with him *B*.
35:16 Then they moved on from *B*.
Jos 7: 2 near Beth Aven to the east of *B*,
8: 9 and lay in wait between *B* and Ai,
8:12 and set them in ambush between *B*
8:17 or *B* who did not go after Israel.
12: 9 the king of Ai (near *B)* one the king
12:16 one the king of *B* one the king
16: 1 desert into the hill country of *B*.
16: 2 It went on from *B* (that is, Luz),
18:13 slope of Luz (that is, *B)*
18:22 Zemaraim, *B*, Avvim, Parah,
Jdg 1:22 the house of Joseph attacked *B*,
1:23 to spy out *B* (formerly called Luz),
4: 5 *B* in the hill country of Ephraim,
20:18 The Israelites went up to *B*
20:26 all the people, went up to *B*,
20:31 the one leading to *B* and the other
21: 2 went to *B*, where they sat
21:19 goes from *B* to Shechem,
21:19 to the north of *B*, and east
1Sa 7:16 went on a circuit from *B* to Gilgal
10: 3 up to God at *B* will meet you there.
13: 2 and in the hill country of *B*,
30:27 He sent it to those who were in *B*,
1Ki 12:29 One he set up in *B*, and the other
12:32 And at *B* he also installed priests
12:32 This he did in *B*, sacrificing
12:33 on the altar he had built at *B*.
13: 1 man of God came from Judah to *B*,
13: 4 out against the altar at *B*,
13:10 by the way he had come to *B*.
13:11 a certain old prophet living in *B*,
13:32 of the LORD against the altar in *B*
16:34 Hiel of *B* rebuilt Jericho.
2Ki 2: 2 So they went down to *B*.
2: 2 the LORD has sent me to *B*."
2: 3 of the prophets at *B* came out
2:23 From there Elisha went up to *B*.
10:29 worship of the golden calves at *B*
17:28 from Samaria came to live in *B*
23: 4 Valley and took the ashes to *B*.
23:15 the altar at *B*, the high place made
23:17 of *B* the very things you have done
23:19 he had done at *B*, Josiah removed
1Ch 7:28 and settlements included *B*
2Ch 13:19 and took from him the towns of *B*,
Ezr 2:28 Geba 621 of Micmash 122 of *B*
Ne 7:32 Geba 621 of Micmash 122 of *B*
11:31 Aija, *B* and its settlements,
Jer 48:13 ashamed when they trusted in *B*.
Hos 10:15 Thus will it happen to you, O *B*,
12: 4 He found him at *B*
Am 3:14 I will destroy the altars of *B*;
4: 4 "Go to *B* and sin;
5: 5 and *B* will be reduced to nothing."
5: 5 do not seek *B*,
5: 6 and *B* will have no one to quench it
7:10 the priest of *B* sent a message
7:13 Don't prophesy anymore at *B*,
Zec 7: 2 The people of *B* had sent Sharezer

BETHESDA

Jn 5: 2 which in Aramaic is called *B*

BETHLEHEM (BETHLEHEMITE)

Ge 35:19 on the way to Ephrath (that is, *B)*.
48: 7 the road to Ephrath" (that is, *B)*.
Jos 19:15 Nahalal, Shimron, Idalah and *B*.
Jdg 12: 8 After him, Ibzan of *B* led Israel.
12:10 Ibzan died, and was buried in *B*.
17: 7 A young Levite from *B* in Judah,
17: 9 "I'm a Levite from *B* in Judah,"
19: 1 Ephraim took a concubine from *B*
19: 2 back to her father's house in *B*,
19:18 I have been to *B* in Judah
19:18 We are on our way from *B* in Judah
Ru 1: 1 and a man from *B* in Judah,
1: 2 They were Ephrathites from *B*,
1:19 in *B*, the whole town was stirred
1:19 went on until they came to *B*.
1:22 in *B* as the barley harvest was
2: 4 Just then Boaz arrived from *B*
4:11 in Ephratah and be famous in *B*.
1Sa 16: 1 I am sending you to Jesse of *B*.
16: 4 When he arrived at *B*, the elders
16:18 a son of Jesse of *B* who knows how
17:12 who was from *B* in Judah.
17:15 Saul to tend his father's sheep at *B*.
17:58 the son of your servant Jesse of *B*."
20: 6 asked my permission to hurry to *B*,
20:28 me for permission to go to *B*.
2Sa 2:32 buried him in his father's tomb at *B*
23:14 and the Philistine garrison was at *B*
23:15 from the well near the gate of *B*!"
23:16 from the well near the gate of *B*
23:24 Elhanan son of Dodo from *B*,
1Ch 2:51 Salma the father of *B*,
2:54 The descendants of Salma: *B*,
4: 4 of Ephrathah and father of *B*.
11:16 and the Philistine garrison was at *B*
11:17 from the well near the gate of *B*!"
11:18 from the well near the gate of *B*
11:26 Elhanan son of Dodo from *B*,
2Ch 11: 6 *B*, Etam, Tekoa, Beth Zur, Soco,
Ezr 2:21 the men of *B* 123 of Netophah 56
Ne 7:26 the men of *B* and Netophah
Jer 41:17 at Geruth Kimham near *B*
Mic 5: 2 "But you, *B* Ephrathah,
Mt 2: 1 After Jesus was born in *B* in Judea,
2: 5 "In *B* in Judea," they replied,
2: 6 " 'But you, *B*, in the land of Judah,
2: 8 He sent them to *B* and said,
2:16 orders to kill all the boys in *B*
Lk 2: 4 to *B* the town of David,
2:15 go to *B* and see this thing that has
Jn 7:42 from David's family and from *B*,

BETHLEHEMITE (BETHLEHEM)

2Sa 21:19 Jaare-Oregim the *B* killed Goliath

BETHPHAGE

Mt 21: 1 came to *B* on the Mount of Olives,
Mk 11: 1 Jerusalem and came to *B*
Lk 19:29 As he approached *B* and Bethany

BETHSAIDA

Mt 11:21 to you, Korazin! Woe to you, *B*!
Mk 6:45 and go on ahead of him to *B*,
8:22 not understand?" They came to *B*,
Lk 9:10 by themselves to a town called *B*,
10:13 to you, Korazin! Woe to you, *B*!
Jn 1:44 and Peter, was from the town of *B*.
12:21 who was from *B* in Galilee,

BETHUEL

Ge 22:22 Hazo, Pildash, Jidlaph and *B*."
22:23 *B* became the father of Rebekah.
24:15 the daughter of *B* son of Milcah,
24:24 of *B*, the son that Milcah bore
24:47 'The daughter of *B* son of Nahor,
24:50 and *B* answered, "This is
25:20 *B* the Aramean from Paddan Aram
28: 2 house of your mother's father *B*.
28: 5 Laban son of *B* the Aramean,
1Ch 4:30 Ezem, Tolad, *B*, Hormah, Ziklag,

BETHUL

Jos 19: 4 Ezem, Eltolad, *B*, Hormah, Ziklag,

BETONIM

Jos 13:26 to Ramath Mizpah and *B*,

BETRAY (BETRAYED BETRAYER BETRAYING BETRAYS)

1Ch 12:17 come to *b* me to my enemies
Ps 89:33 nor will I ever *b* my faithfulness.
Pr 16:10 and his mouth should not *b* justice.
25: 9 do not *b* another man's confidence,
Isa 16: 3 do not *b* the refugees.
24:16 The treacherous *b*!
24:16 With treachery the treacherous *b*
Mt 10:21 "Brother will *b* brother to death,
24:10 and will *b* and hate each other,
26:21 the truth, one of you will *b* me."
26:23 into the bowl with me will *b* me.
26:25 the one who would *b* him, said,
Mk 13:12 "Brother will *b* brother to death,
14:10 priests to *b* Jesus to them.
14:18 one of you will *b* me—one who is
Lk 22: 4 with them how he might *b* Jesus.
22:21 going to *b* me is with mine
Jn 6:64 not believe and who would *b* him.
6:71 of the Twelve, was later to *b* him.)
12: 4 who was later to *b* him, objected,
13: 2 son of Simon, to *b* Jesus.
13:11 he knew who was going to *b* him,
13:21 one of you is going to *b* me."
21:20 "Lord, who is going to *b* you?")

BETRAYED (BETRAY)

2Sa 19:26 But Ziba my servant *b* me.
Ps 73:15 I would have *b* this generation
Isa 33: 1 you who have not been *b*!
33: 1 you will be *b*.
Jer 12: 6 even they have *b* you;
La 1: 2 All her friends have *b* her;
1:19 but they *b* me.
Mt 10: 4 and Judas Iscariot, who *b* him.
17:22 to be *b* into the hands of men.
20:18 of Man will be *b* to the chief priests
26:45 the Son of Man is *b* into the hands
27: 3 When Judas, who had *b* him,
27: 4 "for I have *b* innocent blood."
Mk 3:19 and Judas Iscariot, who *b* him.
9:31 to be *b* into the hands of men.
10:33 of Man will be *b* to the chief priests
14:41 the Son of Man is *b* into the hands
Lk 9:44 to be *b* into the hands of men."
21:16 You will be *b* by parents, brothers,
Jn 18: 2 who *b* him, knew the place,
Ac 7:52 now you have *b* and murdered him
1Co 11:23 on the night he was *b*, took bread,

BETRAYER (BETRAY)

Mt 26:46 Here comes my *b*!" While he was
26:48 Now the *b* had arranged a signal
Mk 14:42 Here comes my *b*!" Just
14:44 Now the *b* had arranged a signal

BETRAYING (BETRAY)

Isa 33: 1 when you stop *b*,
Lk 22:48 are you *b* the Son of Man

BETRAYS (BETRAY)

Pr 11:13 A gossip *b* a confidence,
20:19 A gossip *b* a confidence;
Isa 21: 2 The traitor *b*, the looter takes loot.
Hab 2: 5 indeed, wine *b* him;
Mt 26:24 to that man who *b* the Son of Man!
Mk 14:21 to that man who *b* the Son of Man!
Lk 22:22 but woe to that man who *b* him."

BETROTH (BETROTHED)

Hos 2:19 I will *b* you in righteousness
2:19 I will *b* you to me forever;
2:20 I will *b* you in faithfulness,

BETROTHED (BETROTH)

Dt 22:27 and though the *b* girl screamed,

Ge 1:22 and let the *b* increase on the earth
1:26 fish of the sea and the *b* of the air,
1:28 fish of the sea and the *b* of the air
1:30 of the earth and all the *b* of the air
2:19 of the field and all the *b* of the air.
2:20 the *b* of the air and all the beasts
6:7 along the ground, and *b* of the air—
7:8 of *b* and of all creatures that move
7:21 *b*, livestock, wild animals,
7:23 and the *b* of the air were wiped
8:17 *b*, the animals, and all the creatures
8:19 along the ground and all the *b*—
8:20 of all the clean animals and clean *b*,
9:2 of the earth and all the *b* of the air,
9:10 the *b*, the livestock and all the wild
15:10 the *b*, however, he did not cut
15:11 Then *b* of prey came
40:17 but the *b* were eating them out
40:19 And the *b* will eat away your flesh
Lev 1:14 the LORD is a burnt offering of *b*,
11:13 " 'These are the *b* you are to detest
11:46 regulations concerning animals, *b*,
14:4 shall order that two live clean *b*
14:5 of the *b* be killed over fresh water
14:49 purify the house he is to take two *b*
14:50 one of the *b* over fresh water
20:25 and between unclean and clean *b*.
Dt 28:26 food for all the *b* of the air
1Sa 17:44 I'll give your flesh to the *b* of the air
17:46 of the Philistine army to the *b*
2Sa 21:10 she did not let the *b*
1Ki 4:33 He also taught about animals and *b*
14:11 and the *b* of the air will feed
16:4 and the *b* of the air will feed
21:24 and the *b* of the air will feed
Job 12:7 *b* of the air, and they will tell you;
28:21 even from the *b* of the air.
35:11 makes us wiser than the *b* of the air
Ps 8:8 the *b* of the air,
78:27 flying *b* like sand on the seashore.
79:2 as food to the *b* of the air,
104:12 The *b* of the air nest by the waters;
104:17 There the *b* make their nests;
148:10 small creatures and flying *b*,
Pr 1:17 a net in full view of all the *b*!
Ecc 9:12 or *b* are taken in a snare,
12:4 when men rise up at the sound of *b*,
Isa 16:2 Like fluttering *b*
18:6 left to the mountain *b* of prey
18:6 the *b* will feed on them all summer,
31:5 Like *b* hovering overhead,
Jer 5:26 lie in wait like men who snare *b*
5:27 Like cages full of *b*,
7:33 food for the *b* of the air
9:10 The *b* of the air have fled
12:4 the animals and *b* have perished.
12:9 that other *b* of prey surround
15:3 to drag away and the *b* of the air
16:4 food for the *b* of the air
19:7 as food to the *b* of the air
34:20 food for the *b* of the air
Eze 13:20 the people that you ensnare like *b*.
13:20 which you ensnare people like *b*
17:23 *B* of every kind will nest in it;
29:5 of the earth and the *b* of the air.
31:6 All the *b* of the air
31:13 All the *b* of the air settled
32:4 I will let all the *b* of the air settle
38:20 The fish of the sea, the *b* of the air,
39:4 as food to all kinds of carrion *b*
Da 2:38 of the field and the *b* of the air.
4:12 the *b* of the air lived in its branches;
4:14 and the *b* from its branches.
4:21 in its branches for the *b* of the air—
Hos 2:18 of the field and the *b* of the air
4:3 of the field and the *b* of the air
7:12 down like *b* of the air.
11:11 like *b* from Egypt,
Zep 1:3 I will sweep away the *b* of the air
Mt 6:26 than clothes? Look at the *b*
8:20 and *b* of the air have nests,
13:4 and the *b* came and ate it up.
13:32 so that the *b* of the air come
Mk 4:4 and the *b* came and ate it up.
4:32 with such big branches that the *b*
Lk 8:5 and the *b* of the air ate it up.
9:58 and *b* of the air have nests,
12:24 more valuable you are than *b*!
Lk 13:19 and the *b* of the air perched
Ac 10:12 reptiles of the earth and *b* of the air
11:6 wild beasts, reptiles, and *b*
Ro 1:23 and *b* and animals and reptiles.
1Co 15:39 *b* another and fish another.
Jas 3:7 *b*, reptiles and creatures
Rev 19:17 voice to all the *b* flying in midair,
19:21 and all the *b* gorged themselves

BIRSHA

Ge 14:2 *B* king of Gomorrah, Shinab king

BIRTH (BEAR)

Ge 3:16 with pain you will give *b*
4:1 she conceived and gave *b* to Cain.
4:2 Later she gave *b* to his brother
4:17 she became pregnant and gave *b*
4:20 Adah gave *b* to Jabal; he was
4:25 and she gave *b* to a son
11:28 in the land of his *b*.
25:13 listed in the order of their *b*:
25:24 the time came for her to give *b*,
25:26 old when Rebekah gave *b* to them.
29:32 Leah became pregnant and gave *b*
29:33 when she gave *b* to a son she said,
29:34 when she gave *b* to a son she said,
29:35 when she gave *b* to a son she said,
30:21 Some time later she gave *b*
30:23 She became pregnant and gave *b*
30:25 After Rachel gave *b* to Joseph,
31:8 then all the flocks gave *b*
35:16 Rachel began to give *b*
38:3 she became pregnant and gave *b*
38:4 She conceived again and gave *b*
38:5 She gave *b* to still another son
38:5 at Kezib that she gave *b* to him.
38:27 the time came for her to give *b*,
38:28 As she was giving *b*, one
50:23 placed at *b* on Joseph's knees.
Ex 1:19 give *b* before the midwives arrive."
2:2 she became pregnant and gave *b*
2:22 Zipporah gave *b* to a son,
21:22 and she gives *b* prematurely
28:10 of Israel in the order of their *b*—
Lev 12:2 and gives *b* to a son will be
12:5 If she gives *b* to a daughter,
12:7 for the woman who gives *b* to a boy
Nu 11:12 these people? Did I give them *b*?
Dt 32:18 you forgot the God who gave you *b*
Jdg 13:5 a Nazirite, set apart to God from *b*,
13:5 you will conceive and give *b*
13:7 of God from *b* until the day
13:7 'You will conceive and give *b*
13:24 The woman gave *b* to a boy
16:17 a Nazirite set apart to God since *b*.
Ru 1:12 a husband tonight and then gave *b*
4:13 to conceive, and she gave *b* to a son
4:15 than seven sons, has given him *b*."
1Sa 1:20 time Hannah conceived and gave *b*
2:21 she conceived and gave *b*
4:19 she went into labor and gave *b*,
4:20 you have given *b* to a son."
2Sa 12:24 She gave *b* to a son, and they
1Ki 11:3 had seven hundred wives of royal *b*
2Ki 4:17 about that same time she gave *b*
19:3 children come to the point of *b*
1Ch 2:49 also gave *b* to Shaaph the father
4:9 saying, "I gave *b* to him in pain."
4:17 of Mered's wives gave *b* to Miriam,
4:18 (His Judean wife gave *b*
7:14 She gave *b* to Makir the father
7:16 Makir's wife Maacah gave *b*
7:18 His sister Hammoleketh gave *b*
7:23 she became pregnant and gave *b*
Job 3:1 and cursed the day of his *b*.
3:3 "May the day of my *b* perish,
3:11 "Why did I not perish at *b*,
15:35 They conceive trouble and give *b*
31:18 and from my *b* I guided the widow
38:29 Who gives *b* to the frost
39:1 when the mountain goats give *b*?
39:2 Do you know the time they give *b*?
Ps 7:14 conceives trouble gives *b*
22:10 From *b* I was cast upon you;
51:5 Surely I have been a sinner from *b*,
58:3 Even from *b* the wicked go astray;
71:6 From *b* I have relied on you;
Pr 8:24 were no oceans, I was given *b*,
Pr 8:25 before the hills, I was given *b*,
23:25 may she who gave you *b* rejoice!
Ecc 7:1 of death better than the day of *b*.
10:17 O land whose king is of noble *b*
SS 8:5 was in labor gave you *b*.
Isa 7:14 with child and will give *b* to a son,
8:3 she conceived and gave *b* to a son.
23:4 been in labor nor given *b*;
26:17 with child and about to give *b*
26:18 but we gave *b* to wind.
26:18 we have not given *b* to people
26:19 the earth will give *b* to her dead.
33:11 you give *b* to straw;
37:3 children come to the point of *b*
45:10 'What have you brought to *b*?'
46:3 and have carried since your *b*.
48:8 you were called a rebel from *b*.
49:1 from my *b* he has made mention
51:2 and to Sarah, who gave you *b*.
59:4 they conceive trouble and give *b*
66:7 she gives *b*;
66:8 than she gives *b* to her children.
66:9 Do I bring to the moment of *b*
Jer 2:14 Is Israel a servant, a slave by *b*?
2:27 and to stone, 'You gave me *b*.'
15:10 my mother, that you gave me *b*,
22:26 and the mother who gave you *b*
50:12 who gave you *b* will be disgraced.
Eze 16:3 and *b* were in the land
23:4 and gave *b* to sons and daughters.
31:6 gave *b* under its branches;
Hos 1:6 Gomer conceived again and gave *b*
5:7 they give *b* to illegitimate children.
9:11 no *b*, no pregnancy, no conception.
Mic 5:3 when she who is in labor gives *b*
Mt 1:18 This is how the *b* of Jesus Christ
1:21 She will give *b* to a son,
1:23 with child and will give *b* to a son,
1:25 with her until she gave *b* to a son.
24:8 these are the beginning of *b* pains.
Mk 13:8 These are the beginning of *b* pains.
Lk 1:14 many will rejoice because of his *b*,
1:15 with the Holy Spirit even from *b*.
1:31 be with child and give *b* to a son,
1:57 to have her baby, she gave *b*
2:7 and she gave *b* to her firstborn,
11:27 is the mother who gave you *b*
19:12 "A man of noble *b* went
Jn 3:6 Flesh gives *b* to flesh, but the Spirit
3:6 but the Spirit gives *b* to spirit.
9:1 he saw a man blind from *b*.
9:34 "You were steeped in sin at *b*;
16:21 A woman giving *b*
Ac 3:2 crippled from *b* was being carried
7:8 him eight days after his *b*.
14:8 lame from *b* and had never walked.
1Co 1:26 not many were of noble *b*.
Gal 1:15 who set me apart from *b*
2:15 "We who are Jews by *b*
Eph 2:11 you who are Gentiles by *b*
Jas 1:15 desire has conceived, it gives *b*
1:15 when it is full-grown, gives *b*
1:18 to give us *b* through the word
1Pe 1:3 great mercy he has given us new *b*
Rev 12:2 as she was about to give *b*.
12:4 woman who was about to give *b*,
12:5 She gave *b* to a son, a male child,
12:13 the woman who had given *b*

BIRTHDAY (BEAR)

Ge 40:20 Now the third day was Pharaoh's *b*
Mt 14:6 On Herod's *b* the daughter
Mk 6:21 On his *b* Herod gave a banquet

BIRTHRIGHT (BEAR)

Ge 25:31 Jacob replied, "First sell me your *b*
25:32 "What good is the *b* to me?"
25:33 oath to him, selling his *b* to Jacob.
25:34 So Esau despised his *b*.
27:36 He took my *b*, and now he's taken
1Ch 5:1 record in accordance with his *b*,

BIRZAITH

1Ch 7:31 Malkiel, who was the father of *B*.

BISHLAM

Ezr 4:7 of Artaxerxes king of Persia, *B*,

BIT (BITE BITES BITING BITS BITTEN)

Nu 21: 6 they *b* the people and many
2Ki 19: 28 and my *b* in your mouth,
Ps 32: 9 must be controlled by *b* and bridle
Isa 30: 28 a *b* that leads them astray.
37: 29 and my *b* in your mouth,

BITE (BIT)

Jer 8: 17 and they will *b* you,"
Am 5: 19 only to have a snake *b* him.
9: 3 command the serpent to *b* them.
Jn 6: 7 bread for each one to have a *b*!"

BITES (BIT)

Ge 49: 17 that *b* the horse's heels
Pr 23: 32 In the end it *b* like a snake
Ecc 10: 11 If a snake *b* before it is charmed,

BITHIAH

1Ch 4: 18 children of Pharaoh's daughter *B*,

BITHRON

2Sa 2: 29 continued through the whole *B*

BITHYNIA

Ac 16: 7 they tried to enter *B*, but the Spirit
1Pe 1: 1 Galatia, Cappadocia, Asia and *B*,

BITING (BIT)

Gal 5: 15 on *b* and devouring each other,

BITS (BIT)

Am 6: 11 and the small house into *b*.
Jas 3: 3 When we put *b* into the mouths

BITTEN (BIT)

Nu 21: 8 anyone who is *b* can look at it
21: 9 when anyone was *b* by a snake
Ecc 10: 8 through a wall may be *b* by a snake.

BITTER (BITTERNESS EMBITTER EMBITTERED)

Ge 27: 34 and *b* cry and said to his father,
Ex 1: 14 They made their lives *b*
12: 8 along with *b* herbs, and bread made
15: 23 drink its water because it was *b*.
Nu 5: 18 himself holds the *b* water that
5: 19 may this *b* water that brings a curse
5: 23 then wash them off into the *b* water
5: 24 the woman drink the *b* water that
5: 24 will enter her and cause *b* suffering.
5: 27 go into her and cause *b* suffering;
9: 11 with unleavened bread and *b* herbs
Dt 29: 18 you that produces such *b* poison.
Ru 1: 13 It is more *b* for me than for you,
1: 20 Almighty has made my life very *b*.
1Sa 14: 52 the days of Saul there was *b* war
30: 6 each one was *b* in spirit
1Ki 2: 8 who called down *b* curses
2Ki 4: 27 her alone! She is in *b* distress,
Job 3: 20 and life to the *b* of soul,
13: 26 write down *b* things against me
23: 2 "Even today my complaint is *b*;
Ps 71: 20 made me see troubles, many and *b*,
107: 12 So he subjected them to *b* labor;
Pr 5: 4 but in the end she is *b* as gall,
27: 7 what is *b* tastes sweet.
Ecc 7: 26 I find more *b* than death
Isa 5: 20 and sweet for *b*.
5: 20 who put *b* for sweet
24: 9 the beer is *b* to its drinkers.
Jer 2: 19 how evil and *b* it is for you
4: 18 How *b* it is!
6: 26 mourn with *b* wailing
9: 15 I will make this people eat *b* food
23: 15 "I will make them eat *b* food
La 1: 4 and she is in *b* anguish.
3: 15 He has filled me with *b* herbs
Eze 21: 6 them with broken heart and *b* grief.
27: 31 and with *b* mourning.
Am 8: 10 and the end of it like a *b* day.
Zep 1: 14 on the day of the LORD will be *b*,
Heb 12: 15 and that no *b* root grows up
Jas 3: 14 But if you harbor *b* envy
Rev 8: 11 A third of the waters turned *b*,
8: 11 from the waters that had become *b*.

BITTERNESS (BITTER)

Ge 49: 23 With *b* archers attacked him;
Dt 32: 32 and their clusters with *b*.
1Sa 1: 10 In *b* of soul Hannah wept much
15: 32 "Surely the *b* of death is past."
2Sa 2: 26 you realize that this will end in *b*?
Job 7: 11 I will complain in the *b* of my soul.
10: 1 and speak out in the *b* of my soul.
21: 25 Another man dies in *b* of soul,
27: 2 who has made me taste *b* of soul,
Pr 14: 10 Each heart knows its own *b*,
17: 25 and *b* to the one who bore him.
La 3: 5 with *b* and hardship.
3: 19 the *b* and the gall.
Eze 3: 14 and I went in *b* and in the anger
Am 5: 7 You who turn justice into *b*
6: 12 the fruit of righteousness into *b*—
Ac 8: 23 For I see that you are full of *b*
Ro 3: 14 full of cursing and *b*."
Eph 4: 31 Get rid of all *b*, rage and anger,

BIZIOTHIAH

Jos 15: 28 Beersheba, *B*, Baalah, Iim, Ezem,

BIZTHA

Est 1: 10 Mehuman, *B*, Harbona, Bigtha,

BLACK (BLACKENED BLACKER BLACKEST BLACKNESS)

Ex 10: 15 all the ground until it was *b*.
Lev 11: 13 the *b* vulture, the red kite,
11: 14 any kind of *b* kite, any kind
13: 31 and there is no *b* hair in it,
13: 37 is unchanged and *b* hair has grown
Dt 4: 11 with *b* clouds and deep darkness.
14: 12 the *b* vulture, the red kite,
14: 13 the *b* kite, any kind of falcon,
1Ki 18: 45 the sky grew *b* with clouds,
Job 30: 30 My skin grows *b* and peels;
SS 5: 11 and *b* as a raven.
Zec 6: 2 the second *b*, the third white,
6: 6 The one with the *b* horses is going
Mt 5: 36 make even one hair white or *b*.
Rev 6: 5 and there before me was a *b* horse!
6: 12 sun turned *b* like sackcloth made

BLACKENED (BLACK)

Job 30: 28 I go about *b*, but not by the sun;

BLACKER (BLACK)

La 4: 8 But now they are *b* than soot;

BLACKEST (BLACK)

Job 28: 3 recesses for ore in the *b* darkness.
2Pe 2: 17 *B* darkness is reserved for them.
Jude : 13 for whom *b* darkness has been

BLACKNESS (BLACK)

Job 3: 5 may *b* overwhelm its light.
Joel 2: 2 a day of clouds and *b*.
Am 5: 8 who turns *b* into dawn
Zep 1: 15 a day of clouds and *b*,

BLACKSMITH

1Sa 13: 19 Not a *b* could be found
Isa 44: 12 The *b* takes a tool
54: 16 "See, it is I who created the *b*

BLADE

Jdg 3: 22 Even the handle sank in after the *b*,
Eze 21: 16 wherever your *b* is turned.

BLAME

Ge 43: 9 I will bear the *b* before you all my
44: 10 the rest of you will be free from *b*."
44: 32 I will bear the *b* before you,
1Sa 25: 24 "My lord, let the *b* be on me alone.
2Sa 14: 9 let the *b* rest on me
Ro 9: 19 "Then why does God still *b* us?
1Ti 5: 7 so that no one may be open to *b*.
6: 14 or *b* until the appearing

BLAMELESS (BLAMELESSLY)

Ge 6: 9 *b* among the people of his time,
17: 1 walk before me and be *b*.
Dt 18: 13 You must be *b* before the LORD
2Sa 22: 24 I have been *b* before him
22: 26 to the *b* you show yourself *b*,
Job 1: 1 This man was *b* and upright;
1: 8 one on earth like him; he is *b*
2: 3 one on earth like him; he is *b*
4: 6 and your *b* ways your hope?
8: 20 God does not reject a *b* man
9: 20 if I were *b*, it would pronounce me
9: 21 "Although I am *b*,
9: 22 'He destroys both the *b*
12: 4 though righteous and *b*!
22: 3 gain if your ways were *b*?
31: 6 and he will know that I am *b*—
Ps 15: 2 He whose walk is *b*
18: 23 I have been *b* before him
18: 25 to the *b* you show yourself *b*,
19: 13 Then will I be *b*,
26: 1 for I have led a *b* life;
26: 11 But I lead a *b* life;
37: 18 The days of the *b* are known
37: 37 Consider the *b*, observe the upright
84: 11 from those whose walk is *b*.
101: 2 I will be careful to lead a *b* life—
101: 2 house with *b* heart.
101: 6 he whose walk is *b*
119: 1 Blessed are they whose ways are *b*,
119: 80 May my heart be *b*
Pr 2: 7 a shield to those whose walk is *b*,
2: 21 and the *b* will remain in it;
11: 5 of the *b* makes a straight way
11: 20 in those whose ways are *b*.
19: 1 Better a poor man whose walk is *b*
20: 7 The righteous man leads a *b* life;
28: 6 Better a poor man whose walk is *b*
28: 10 *b* will receive a good inheritance.
28: 18 He whose walk is *b* is kept safe,
Eze 28: 15 You were *b* in your ways
1Co 1: 8 so that you will be *b* on the day
Eph 1: 4 world to be holy and *b* in his sight.
5: 27 any other blemish, but holy and *b*.
Php 1: 10 and *b* until the day of Christ,
2: 15 so that you may become *b* and pure
1Th 2: 10 and *b* we were among you who
3: 13 hearts so that you will be *b*
5: 23 and body be kept *b* at the coming
Tit 1: 6 An elder must be *b*, the husband of
1: 7 he must be *b*— not overbearing,
Heb 7: 26 *b*, pure, set apart from sinners,
2Pe 3: 14 effort to be found spotless, *b*
Rev 14: 5 found in their mouths; they are *b*.

BLAMELESSLY (BLAMELESS)

Lk 1: 6 commandments and regulations *b*.

BLANKET (BLANKETS)

Isa 28: 20 the *b* too narrow to wrap

BLANKETS (BLANKET)

Jdg 5: 10 sitting on your saddle *b*,
Eze 27: 20 Dedan traded in saddle *b* with you.

BLASPHEME (BLASPHEMED BLASPHEMER BLASPHEMES BLASPHEMIES BLASPHEMING BLASPHEMOUS BLASPHEMY)

Ex 22: 28 "Do not *b* God or curse the ruler
Ac 26: 11 and I tried to force them to *b*.
1Ti 1: 20 over to Satan to be taught not to *b*.
2Pe 2: 12 these men *b* in matters they do not
Rev 13: 6 He opened his mouth to *b* God,

BLASPHEMED (BLASPHEME)

Lev 24: 11 of the Israelite woman *b* the name
2Ki 19: 6 of the king of Assyria have *b* me.
19: 22 Who is it you have insulted and *b*?
Isa 37: 6 of the king of Assyria have *b* me.
37: 23 Who is it you have insulted and *b*?
52: 5 my name is constantly *b*.
Eze 20: 27 your fathers *b* me by forsaking me:
Ac 19: 37 robbed temples nor *b* our goddess.
Ro 2: 24 name is *b* among the Gentiles

BLASPHEMER (BLASPHEME)

Lev 24: 14 "Take the *b* outside the camp.
24: 23 they took the *b* outside the camp
1Ti 1: 13 I was once a *b* and a persecutor

BLASPHEMES (BLASPHEME)

Lev 24: 16 anyone who *b* the name
24: 16 native-born, when he *b* the Name,

Nu 15: 30 native-born or alien, *b* the LORD,
Mk 3: 29 whoever *b* against the Holy Spirit
Lk 12: 10 but anyone who *b* against the Holy

BLASPHEMIES (BLASPHEME)

Ne 9: 18 or when they committed awful *b*.
9: 26 to you; they committed awful *b*.
Mk 3: 28 and *b* of men will be forgiven them.
Rev 13: 5 and *b* and to exercise his authority

BLASPHEMING (BLASPHEME)

Mt 9: 3 "This fellow is *b!*" Knowing their
Mk 2: 7 He's *b!* Who can forgive sins

BLASPHEMOUS (BLASPHEME)

Rev 13: 1 and on each head a *b* name.
17: 3 that was covered with *b* names.

BLASPHEMY (BLASPHEME)

Mt 12: 31 and *b* will be forgiven men,
12: 31 the *b* against the Spirit will not be
26: 65 Look, now you have heard the *b*.
26: 65 "He has spoken *b!* Why do we
Mk 14: 64 "You have heard the *b*.
Lk 5: 21 "Who is this fellow who speaks *b?*
Jn 10: 33 replied the Jews, "but for *b*,
10: 36 Why then do you accuse me of *b*
Ac 6: 11 words of *b* against Moses

BLAST (BLASTS)

Ex 15: 8 By the *b* of your nostrils
19: 13 horn sounds a long *b* may they go
19: 16 and a very loud trumpet *b*.
Nu 10: 5 When a trumpet *b* is sounded,
10: 6 At the sounding of a second *b*,
10: 6 The *b* will be the signal
10: 9 sound a *b* on the trumpets.
Jos 6: 5 you hear them sound a long *b*
6: 16 the priests sounded the trumpet *b*,
2Sa 22: 16 at the *b* of breath from his nostrils.
Job 4: 9 at the *b* of his anger they perish.
39: 25 At the *b* of the trumpet he snorts,
Ps 18: 15 the *b* of breath from your nostrils.
98: 6 and the *b* of the ram's horn—
147: 17 Who can withstand his icy *b?*
Isa 27: 8 with his fierce *b* he drives her out,
Eze 22: 20 a furnace to melt it with a fiery *b*,
Am 2: 2 tumult amid war cries and the *b*
Heb 12: 19 to a trumpet *b* or to such a voice

BLASTS (BLAST)

Lev 23: 24 commemorated with trumpet *b*.
Rev 8: 13 because of the trumpet *b* about

BLASTUS

Ac 12: 20 Having secured the support of *B*,

BLAZE (BLAZED BLAZES BLAZING)

Nu 21: 28 a *b* from the city of Sihon.
Jer 48: 45 a *b* from the midst of Sihon;

BLAZED (BLAZE)

Dt 4: 11 of the mountain while it *b* with fire
Jdg 13: 20 As the flame *b* up from the altar
2Sa 22: 9 burning coals *b* out of it.
22: 13 bolts of lightning *b* forth.
Ps 18: 8 burning coals *b* out of it.
106: 18 Fire *b* among their followers;
Jnh 4: 8 and the sun *b* on Jonah's head

BLAZES (BLAZE)

Hos 7: 6 in the morning it *b* like a flaming
Joel 2: 3 behind them a flame *b*.

BLAZING (BLAZE)

Ge 15: 17 pot with a *b* torch appeared
SS 8: 6 It burns like *b* fire,
Isa 10: 16 like a *b* flame.
34: 9 her land will become *b* pitch!
62: 1 her salvation like a *b* torch.
Eze 20: 47 The *b* flame will not be quenched,
Da 3: 6 be thrown into a *b* furnace."
3: 11 will be thrown into a *b* furnace.
3: 15 immediately into a *b* furnace.
3: 17 If we are thrown into the *b* furnace,
3: 20 and throw them into the *b* furnace.
3: 21 and thrown into the *b* furnace.
3: 23 firmly tied, fell into the *b* furnace.
Da 3: 26 the opening of the *b* furnace
7: 11 and thrown into the *b* fire.
Ac 26: 13 *b* around me and my companions.
2Th 1: 7 revealed from heaven in *b* fire
Rev 1: 14 and his eyes were like *b* fire.
2: 18 whose eyes are like *b* fire
4: 5 the throne, seven lamps were *b*.
8: 10 and a great star, *b* like a torch,
19: 12 His eyes are like *b* fire,

BLEACH

Mk 9: 3 anyone in the world could *b* them.

BLEAT (BLEATING)

Isa 34: 14 and wild goats will *b* to each other;

BLEATING (BLEAT)

1Sa 15: 14 "What then is this *b* of sheep

BLEEDING (BLOOD)

Lev 12: 4 days to be purified from her *b*.
12: 5 days to be purified from her *b*.
Mt 9: 20 to *b* for twelve years came up
Mk 5: 25 subject to *b* for twelve years.
5: 29 Immediately her *b* stopped
Lk 8: 43 subject to *b* for twelve years,
8: 44 and immediately her *b* stopped.
Ac 19: 16 out of the house naked and *b*.

BLEMISH (BLEMISHED BLEMISHES)

Lev 22: 21 be without defect or *b*
Nu 19: 2 or *b* and that has never been
2Sa 14: 25 of his foot there was no *b* in him.
Eph 5: 27 or wrinkle or any other *b*,
Col 1: 22 without *b* and free from accusation
1Pe 1: 19 a lamb without *b* or defect.

BLEMISHED (BLEMISH)

Mal 1: 14 but then sacrifices a *b* animal

BLEMISHES (BLEMISH)

2Pe 2: 13 and *b*, reveling in their pleasures
Jude : 12 These men are *b* at your love feasts

BLEND (BLENDED)

Ex 30: 25 a fragrant *b*, the work of a perfumer
30: 35 and make a fragrant *b* of incense,

BLENDED (BLEND)

2Ch 16: 14 with spices and various *b* perfumes
SS 7: 2 that never lacks *b* wine.

BLESS (BLESSED BLESSEDNESS BLESSES BLESSING BLESSINGS)

Ge 12: 2 and I will *b* you;
12: 3 I will *b* those who *b* you,
17: 16 I will *b* her and will surely give you
17: 16 I will *b* her so that she will be
17: 20 have heard you: I will surely *b* him;
22: 17 I will surely *b* you and make your
26: 3 I will be with you and will *b* you.
26: 24 I will *b* you and will increase
27: 29 and those who *b* you be blessed."
27: 34 "*B* me—me too, my father!"
27: 38 my father? *B* me too, my father!"
28: 3 May God Almighty *b* you
32: 26 not let you go unless you *b* me."
48: 9 "Bring them to me so I may *b* them
48: 16 —may he *b* these
Ex 12: 32 And also *b* me."
20: 24 I will come to you and *b* you.
Nu 6: 23 are to *b* the Israelites.
6: 24 Say to them: " ' "The LORD *b* you
6: 27 on the Israelites, and I will *b* them
22: 6 know that those you *b* are blessed,
23: 11 you have done nothing but *b* them
23: 20 I have received a command to *b;*
23: 25 them at all nor *b* them at all!"
24: 1 it pleased the LORD to *b* Israel,
24: 9 "May those who *b* you be blessed
Dt 1: 11 and *b* you as he has promised!
7: 13 He will love you and *b* you
7: 13 He will *b* the fruit of your womb,
14: 29 the LORD your God may *b* you
15: 4 inheritance, he will richly *b* you,
15: 6 the LORD your God will *b* you
15: 10 the LORD your God will *b* you
15: 18 the LORD your God will *b* you
Dt 16: 15 the LORD your God will *b* you
23: 20 the LORD your God may *b* you
24: 19 the LORD your God may *b* you
26: 15 and *b* your people Israel
27: 12 on Mount Gerizim to *b* the people:
28: 8 The LORD your God will *b* you
28: 12 and to *b* all the work of your hands.
30: 16 the LORD your God will *b* you
33: 11 *B* all his skills, O LORD,
33: 13 "May the LORD *b* his land
Jos 8: 33 to *b* the people of Israel.
Jdg 17: 2 "The LORD *b* you, my son!"
Ru 2: 4 LORD *b* you!" they called back.
2: 20 "The LORD *b* him!" Naomi said
3: 10 "The LORD *b* you, my daughter,"
1Sa 2: 20 Eli would *b* Elkanah and his wife,
9: 13 because he must *b* the sacrifice;
15: 13 Saul said, "The LORD *b* you!
23: 21 The LORD *b* you for your concern
2Sa 2: 5 LORD *b* you for
6: 20 home to *b* his household,
7: 29 Now be pleased to *b* the house
21: 3 that you will *b* the LORD's
1Ch 4: 10 that you would *b* me and enlarge
16: 43 returned home to *b* his family.
17: 27 have been pleased to *b* the house
2Ch 30: 27 the Levites stood to *b* the people,
Job 31: 20 and his heart did not *b* me
Ps 5: 12 O LORD, you *b* the righteous;
28: 9 people and *b* your inheritance;
41: 2 he will *b* him in the land
62: 4 With their mouths they *b*,
65: 10 and *b* its crops.
67: 1 God be gracious to us and *b* us
67: 6 and God, our God, will *b* us.
67: 7 God will *b* us,
72: 15 and *b* him all day long.
109: 28 They may curse, but you will *b;*
115: 12 He will *b* the house of Israel,
115: 12 he will *b* the house of Aaron,
115: 12 LORD remembers us and will *b* us:
115: 13 he will *b* those who fear the LORD
118: 26 of the LORD we *b* you.
128: 5 May the LORD *b* you from Zion
129: 8 we *b* you in the name of the LORD
132: 15 *b* her with abundant provisions;
134: 3 *b* you from Zion.
Pr 30: 11 and do not *b* their mothers;
Isa 19: 25 The LORD Almighty will *b* them,
Jer 31: 23 'The LORD *b* you, O righteous
Eze 34: 26 I will *b* them and the places
Hag 2: 19 " 'From this day on I will *b* you.' "
Zec 4: 7 God *b* it!' " Then the word
4: 7 the capstone to shouts of 'God *b* it!
Lk 6: 28 who hate you, *b* those who curse
Ac 3: 26 to you to *b* you by turning each
Ro 12: 14 Bless those who persecute you; *b*
12: 14 *B* those who persecute you;
1Co 4: 12 we *b;* when we are persecuted,
Heb 6: 14 "I will surely *b* you and give you

BLESSED (BLESS)

Ge 1: 22 God *b* them and said, "Be fruitful
1: 28 God *b* them and said to them,
2: 3 And God *b* the seventh day
5: 2 he *b* them and called them "man."
9: 1 Then God *b* Noah and his sons,
9: 26 *B* be the LORD, the God of Shem!
12: 3 will be *b* through you."
14: 19 God Most High, and he *b* Abram,
14: 19 "*B* be Abram by God Most High,
14: 20 And *b* be God Most High,
18: 18 on earth will be *b* through him.
22: 18 nations on earth will be *b*,
24: 1 the LORD had *b* him in every way.
24: 31 you who are *b* by the LORD,"
24: 35 The LORD has *b* my master
24: 60 they *b* Rebekah and said to her,
25: 11 Abraham's death, God *b* his son
26: 4 nations on earth will be *b*,
26: 12 because the LORD *b* him.
26: 29 And now you are *b* by the LORD."
27: 23 of his brother Esau; so he *b* him.
27: 27 that the LORD has *b*.
27: 27 the smell of his clothes, he *b* him
27: 29 and those who bless you be *b*."
27: 33 he will be *b!*" When Esau heard
27: 33 just before you came and I *b* him—

Ge 28: 1 and *b* him and commanded him:
28: 6 learned that Isaac had *b* Jacob
28: 6 when he *b* him he commanded him
28: 14 on earth will be *b* through you
30: 27 that the LORD has *b* me
30: 30 LORD has *b* you wherever I have
31: 55 and his daughters and *b* them.
32: 29 my name?" Then he *b* him there.
35: 9 appeared to him again and *b* him.
39: 5 the LORD *b* the household
47: 7 After Jacob *b* Pharaoh, Pharaoh
47: 10 Then Jacob *b* Pharaoh
48: 3 and there he *b* me and said to me,
48: 15 Then he *b* Joseph and said,
48: 20 He *b* them that day and said,
49: 28 said to them when he *b* them,
Ex 20: 11 the LORD *b* the Sabbath
32: 29 and he has *b* you this day."
39: 43 So Moses *b* them.
Lev 9: 22 toward the people and *b* them.
9: 23 they came out, they *b* the people;
Nu 22: 6 I know that those you bless are *b*,
22: 12 on those people, because they are *b*
23: 20 he has *b*, and I cannot change it.
24: 9 "May those who bless you be *b*
24: 10 you have *b* them these three times.
Dt 2: 7 The LORD your God has *b* you
7: 14 You will be *b* more
12: 7 the LORD your God has *b* you.
14: 24 and you have been *b* by the LORD
15: 14 as the LORD your God has *b* you.
16: 17 the LORD your God has *b* you.
28: 3 You will be *b* in the city
28: 3 in the city and *b* in the country.
28: 4 The fruit of your womb will be *b*,
28: 5 and your kneading trough will be *b*.
28: 6 You will be *b* when you come in
28: 6 come in and *b* when you go out.
33: 20 *B* is he who enlarges Gad's domain
33: 24 "Most *b* of sons is Asher;
33: 29 *B* are you, O Israel!
Jos 14: 13 Joshua *b* Caleb son of Jephunneh
17: 14 the LORD has *b* us abundantly."
22: 6 Joshua *b* them and sent them away
22: 7 Joshua sent them home, he *b* them,
24: 10 so he *b* you again and again,
Jdg 5: 24 most *b* of tent-dwelling women.
5: 24 "Most *b* of women be Jael,
13: 24 He grew and the LORD *b* him,
Ru 2: 19 *B* be the man who took notice
1Sa 25: 33 May you be *b* for your good
26: 25 "May you be *b*, my son David;
2Sa 6: 11 the LORD *b* him and his entire
6: 12 "The LORD has *b* the household
6: 18 he *b* the people in the name
7: 29 of your servant will be *b* forever."
14: 22 to pay him honor, and he *b* the king
1Ki 2: 45 But King Solomon will be *b*,
8: 14 the king turned around and *b* them.
8: 55 and *b* the whole assembly of Israel
8: 66 They *b* the king and then went
1Ch 13: 14 and the LORD *b* his household
16: 2 he *b* the people in the name
17: 27 have *b* it, and it will be *b* forever."
26: 5 (For God had *b* Obed-Edom.)
2Ch 6: 3 the king turned around and *b* them.
31: 8 the LORD and *b* his people Israel.
31: 10 the LORD has *b* his people,
Ne 9: 5 "*B* be your glorious name,
Job 1: 10 You have *b* the work of his hands,
5: 17 "*B* is the man whom God corrects;
29: 4 intimate friendship *b* my house,
29: 13 The man who was dying *b* me;
42: 12 The LORD *b* the latter part
Ps 1: 1 *B* is the man
2: 12 *B* are all who take refuge in him.
32: 1 *B* is he
32: 2 *B* is the man
33: 12 *B* is the nation whose God is
34: 8 *b* is the man who takes refuge
37: 26 their children will be *b*.
40: 4 *B* is the man
41: 1 *B* is he who has regard for the weak
45: 2 since God has *b* you forever.
49: 18 while he lived he counted himself *b*
65: 4 *B* is the man you choose
72: 17 All nations will be *b* through him,
72: 17 and they will call him *b*.
Ps 84: 4 *B* are those who dwell
84: 5 *B* are those whose strength is
84: 12 *b* is the man who trusts in you.
89: 15 *B* are those who have learned
94: 12 *B* is the man you discipline,
106: 3 *B* are they who maintain justice,
107: 38 he *b* them, and their numbers
112: 1 *B* is the man who fears the LORD,
112: 2 of the upright will be *b*.
115: 15 May you be *b* by the LORD,
118: 26 *B* is he who comes in the name
119: 1 *B* are they whose ways are
119: 2 *B* are they who keep his statutes
127: 5 *B* is the man
128: 1 *B* are all who fear the LORD,
128: 4 Thus is the man *b*
144: 15 *B* are the people of whom this is
144: 15 *b* are the people whose God is
146: 5 *B* is he whose help is the God
Pr 3: 13 *B* is the man who finds wisdom,
3: 18 those who lay hold of her will be *b*.
5: 18 May your fountain be *b*,
8: 32 *b* are those who keep my ways.
8: 34 *B* is the man who listens to me,
14: 21 but *b* is he who is kind to the needy
16: 20 and *b* is he who trusts in the LORD
20: 7 *b* are his children after him.
20: 21 will not be *b* at the end.
22: 9 A generous man will himself be *b*,
28: 14 *B* is the man who always fears
28: 20 A faithful man will be richly *b*,
29: 18 but *b* is he who keeps the law.
31: 28 Her children arise and call her *b*;
Ecc 10: 17 *B* are you, O land whose king is
SS 6: 9 maidens saw her and called her *b*;
Isa 19: 25 saying, "*B* be Egypt my people,
30: 18 *B* are all who wait for him!
32: 20 how *b* you will be,
51: 2 and I *b* him and made him many.
56: 2 *B* is the man who does this,
61: 9 are a people the LORD has *b*."
65: 23 for they will be a people *b*
Jer 4: 2 then the nations will be *b* by him
17: 7 *b* is the man who trusts
20: 14 day my mother bore me not be *b*!
Da 12: 12 *B* is the one who waits for
Mal 3: 12 Then all the nations will call you *b*,
3: 15 But now we call the arrogant *b*.
Mt 5: 3 saying: "*B* are the poor in spirit,
5: 4 *B* are those who mourn,
5: 5 *B* are the meek,
5: 6 *B* are those who hunger
5: 7 *B* are the merciful,
5: 8 *B* are the pure in heart,
5: 9 *B* are the peacemakers,
5: 10 *B* are those who are persecuted
5: 11 "*B* are you when people insult you,
11: 6 *B* is the man who does not fall
13: 16 *b* are your eyes because they see,
16: 17 "*B* are you, Simon son of Jonah,
21: 9 "*B* is he who comes in the name
23: 39 '*B* is he who comes in the name
25: 34 Come, you who are *b* by my Father
Mk 10: 16 put his hands on them and *b* them.
11: 9 "*B* is he who comes in the name
11: 10 "*B* is the coming kingdom
14: 61 the Son of the *B* One?" "I am,"
Lk 1: 42 and *b* is the child you will bear!
1: 42 "*B* are you among women,
1: 45 *B* is she who has believed that what
1: 48 on all generations will call me *b*,
2: 34 Simeon *b* them and said to Mary,
6: 20 "*B* are you who are poor,
6: 21 *B* are you who hunger now,
6: 21 *B* are you who weep now,
6: 22 *B* are you when men hate you,
7: 23 *B* is the man who does not fall
10: 23 "*B* are the eyes that see what you
11: 27 *B* is the mother who gave you birth
11: 28 "*B* rather are those who hear
13: 35 '*B* is he who comes in the name
14: 14 the blind, and you will be *b*.
14: 15 "*B* is the man who will eat
19: 38 "*B* is the king who comes
23: 29 you will say, '*B* are the barren
24: 50 he lifted up his hands and *b* them.
Jn 12: 13 "*B* is he who comes in the name
12: 13 "*B* is the King of Israel!"
Jn 13: 17 you will be *b* if you do them.
20: 29 *b* are those who have not seen
Ac 3: 25 peoples on earth will be *b*.'
20: 35 'It is more *b* to give than to receive
Ro 4: 7 apart from works: "*B* are they
4: 8 *B* is the man
14: 22 *B* is the man who does not
Gal 3: 8 All nations will be *b* through you."
3: 9 So those who have faith are *b*
Eph 1: 3 who has *b* us in the heavenly
1Ti 1: 11 to the glorious gospel of the *b* God,
6: 15 God, the *b* and only Ruler,
Tit 2: 13 while we wait for the *b* hope—
Heb 7: 1 the defeat of the kings and *b* him,
7: 6 and *b* him who had the promises.
7: 7 without doubt the lesser person is *b*
11: 20 By faith Isaac *b* Jacob
11: 21 when he was dying, *b* each
Jas 1: 12 *B* is the man who perseveres
1: 25 he will be *b* in what he does.
5: 11 we consider *b* those who have
1Pe 3: 14 suffer for what is right, you are *b*.
4: 14 you are *b*, for the Spirit of glory
Rev 1: 3 and *b* are those who hear it
1: 3 *B* is the one who reads the words
14: 13 *B* are the dead who die in the Lord
16: 15 *B* is he who stays awake
19: 9 '*B* are those who are invited
20: 6 *B* and holy are those who have part
22: 7 *B* is he who keeps the words
22: 14 "*B* are those who wash their robes,

BLESSEDNESS (BLESS)

Ro 4: 6 when he speaks of the *b* of the man
4: 9 Is this *b* only for the circumcised,

BLESSES (BLESS)

Ge 49: 25 of the Almighty, who *b* you
Ps 10: 3 he *b* the greedy and reviles
29: 11 the LORD *b* his people with peace.
37: 22 those the LORD *b* will inherit
147: 13 and *b* your people within you.
Pr 3: 33 but he *b* the home of the righteous.
27: 14 If a man loudly *b* his neighbor
Ro 10: 12 and richly *b* all who call on him,

BLESSING (BLESS)

Ge 12: 2 and you will be a *b*.
17: 18 Ishmael might live under your *b*!"
27: 4 so that I may give you my *b*
27: 7 so that I may give you my *b*
27: 10 so that he may give you his *b*
27: 12 a curse on myself rather than a *b*."
27: 19 so that you may give me your *b*."
27: 25 so that I may give you my *b*."
27: 30 After Isaac finished *b* him
27: 31 so that you may give me your *b*."
27: 35 came deceitfully and took your *b*."
27: 36 Haven't you reserved any *b* for me
27: 36 and now he's taken my *b*!"
27: 38 Do you have only one *b*, my father
27: 41 of the *b* his father had given him.
28: 4 and your descendants the *b*
39: 5 The *b* of the LORD was
48: 20 name will Israel pronounce this *b*:
49: 28 giving each the *b* appropriate
Ex 23: 25 and his *b* will be on your food
Lev 25: 21 I will send you such a *b*
Dt 11: 26 I am setting before you today a *b*
11: 27 the *b* if you obey the commands
12: 15 to the *b* the LORD your God gives
23: 5 turned the curse into a *b* for you,
28: 8 The LORD will send a *b*
29: 19 he invokes a *b* on himself and
33: 1 This is the *b* that Moses the man
33: 23 and is full of his *b*;
2Sa 7: 29 and with your *b* the house
13: 25 refused to go, but gave him his *b*.
19: 39 kissed Barzillai and gave him his *b*,
Ne 9: 5 and may it be exalted above all *b*
13: 2 however, turned the curse into a *b*.)
Ps 3: 8 May your *b* be on your people.
24: 5 He will receive *b* from the LORD
109: 17 he found no pleasure in *b*—
129: 8 "The *b* of the LORD be upon you;
133: 3 For there the LORD bestows his *b*,
Pr 10: 7 of the righteous will be a *b*,
10: 22 The *b* of the LORD brings wealth,

Pr 11: 11 Through the *b* of the upright a city
11: 26 *b* crowns him who is willing to sell.
24: 25 and rich *b* will come upon them.
Isa 19: 24 and Assyria, a *b* on the earth.
44: 3 and my *b* on your descendants.
65: 16 Whoever invokes a *b* in the land
Jer 16: 5 because I have withdrawn my *b*,
Eze 34: 26 there will be showers of *b*.
44: 30 meal so that a *b* may rest
Joel 2: 14 and leave behind a *b*—
Mic 2: 9 You take away my *b*
Zec 8: 13 will I save you, and you will be a *b*.
Mal 3: 10 so much *b* that you will not have
Lk 24: 51 While he was *b* them, he left them
Jn 1: 16 grace we have all received one *b*
Ac 15: 33 with the *b* of peace to return
Ro 15: 29 come in the full measure of the *b*
Gal 3: 14 us in order that the *b* given
Eph 1: 3 with every spiritual *b* in Christ.
Heb 6: 7 whom it is farmed receives the *b*
12: 17 though he sought the *b* with tears.
12: 17 when he wanted to inherit this *b*,
1Pe 3: 9 called so that you may inherit a *b*.
3: 9 or insult with insult, but with *b*,

BLESSINGS (BLESS)

Ge 49: 25 you with *b* of the heavens above,
49: 25 *b* of the breast and womb.
49: 25 *b* of the deep that lies below,
49: 26 Your father's *b* are greater
49: 26 greater than the *b* of the ancient
Dt 10: 8 and to pronounce *b* in his name,
11: 29 proclaim on Mount Gerizim the *b*,
16: 10 to the *b* the LORD your God has
21: 5 and to pronounce *b* in the name
28: 2 All these *b* will come upon you
30: 1 When all these *b* and curses I have
30: 19 set before you life and death, *b*
Jos 8: 34 all the words of the law—the *b*
1Ch 23: 13 to pronounce *b* in his name forever
Ps 21: 3 You welcomed him with rich *b*
21: 6 you have granted him eternal *b*
128: 2 *b* and prosperity will be yours.
Pr 10: 6 *B* crown the head of the righteous,
Hos 3: 5 and to his *b* in the last days.
Mal 2: 2 upon you, and I will curse your *b*.
Ac 13: 34 sure *b* promised to David.'
Ro 15: 27 shared in the Jews' spiritual *b*,
15: 27 to share with them their material *b*.
1Co 9: 23 the gospel, that I may share in its *b*.

BLEW (BLOW)

Ex 15: 10 But you *b* with your breath,
Jos 6: 9 of the priests who *b* the trumpets,
Jdg 3: 27 he *b* a trumpet in the hill country
6: 34 and he *b* a trumpet, summoning
7: 19 They *b* their trumpets
7: 20 three companies *b* the trumpets
2Sa 2: 28 So Joab *b* the trumpet,
2Ki 9: 13 Then they *b* the trumpet
2Ch 7: 6 the priests *b* their trumpets,
13: 14 The priests *b* their trumpets
Hag 1: 9 What you brought home, I *b* away.
Mt 7: 25 and the winds *b* and beat
7: 27 and the winds *b* and beat
Rev 9: 13 The sixth angel *b* his trumpet,

BLIGHT (BLIGHTED)

Dt 28: 22 and drought, with *b* and mildew,
1Ki 8: 37 or *b* or mildew, locusts
2Ch 6: 28 or *b* or mildew, locusts
Am 4: 9 I struck them with *b* and mildew.
Hag 2: 17 the work of your hands with *b*,

BLIGHTED (BLIGHT)

Ps 102: 4 My heart is *b* and withered like
Hos 9: 16 Ephraim is *b*,

BLIND (BLINDED BLINDFOLDS BLINDNESS BLINDS)

Ex 4: 11 gives him sight or makes him *b?*
Lev 19: 14 a stumbling block in front of the *b*,
21: 18 no man who is *b* or lame, disfigured
22: 22 Do not offer to the LORD the *b*,
Dt 15: 21 is lame or *b*, or has any serious flaw
27: 18 is the man who leads the *b* astray
28: 29 you will grope about like a *b* man
1Sa 2: 33 only to *b* your eyes with tears
2Sa 5: 6 the *b* and the lame can ward you
5: 8 and *b*' who are David's enemies."
5: 8 "The '*b* and lame' will not enter
Job 29: 15 I was eyes to the *b*
Ps 146: 8 the LORD gives sight to the *b*,
Isa 29: 9 *b* yourselves and be sightless;
29: 18 the eyes of the *b* will see.
35: 5 will the eyes of the *b* be opened
42: 7 to open eyes that are *b*,
42: 16 I will lead the *b* by ways they have
42: 18 look, you *b*, and see!
42: 19 Who is *b* but my servant,
42: 19 Who is *b* like the one committed
42: 19 *b* like the servant of the LORD?
43: 8 out those who have eyes but are *b*,
44: 9 would speak up for them are *b;*
56: 10 Israel's watchmen are *b*,
59: 10 Like the *b* we grope along the wall,
Jer 31: 8 Among them will be the *b*
La 4: 14 like men who are *b*.
Zep 1: 17 and they will walk like *b* men,
Zec 12: 4 I will *b* all the horses of the nations.
Mal 1: 8 When you bring *b* animals
Mt 9: 27 two *b* men followed him, calling
9: 28 had gone indoors, the *b* men came
11: 5 The *b* receive sight, the lame walk,
12: 22 a demon-possessed man who was *b*
15: 14 Leave them; they are *b* guides.
15: 14 a *b* man leads a *b* man, both will fall
15: 30 the lame, the *b*, the crippled,
15: 31 the lame walking and the *b* seeing.
20: 30 Two *b* men were sitting
21: 14 The *b* and the lame came to him
23: 16 "Woe to you, *b* guides! You say,
23: 17 You *b* fools! Which is greater:
23: 19 You *b* men! Which is greater:
23: 24 You *b* guides! You strain out a gnat
23: 26 *B* Pharisee! First clean the
Mk 8: 22 and some people brought a *b* man
8: 23 He took the *b* man by the hand
10: 46 a *b* man, Bartimaeus (that is,
10: 49 So they called to the *b* man,
10: 51 The *b* man said, "Rabbi, I want
Lk 4: 18 and recovery of sight for the *b*,
6: 39 "Can a *b* man lead a *b* man?
7: 21 and gave sight to many who were *b*
7: 22 The *b* receive sight, the lame walk,
14: 13 the crippled, the lame, the *b*,
14: 21 the crippled, the *b* and the lame.'
18: 35 a *b* man was sitting
Jn 5: 3 the *b*, the lame, the paralyzed.
9: 1 he saw a man *b* from birth.
9: 2 he was born *b?*" "Neither this man
9: 13 Pharisees the man who had been *b*.
9: 17 they turned again to the *b* man,
9: 18 did not believe that he had been *b*
9: 19 Is this the one you say was born *b?*
9: 20 "and we know he was born *b*.
9: 24 the man who had been *b*.
9: 25 I was *b* but now I see!"
9: 32 of opening the eyes of a man born *b*
9: 39 and those who see will become *b*."
9: 39 so that the *b* will see and those who
9: 40 "What? Are we *b* too?" Jesus said,
9: 41 Jesus said, "If you were *b*,
10: 21 Can a demon open the eyes of the *b*
11: 37 of the *b* man have kept this man
Ac 9: 9 For three days he was *b*,
13: 11 You are going to be *b*,
Ro 2: 19 that you are a guide for the *b*,
2Pe 1: 9 have them, he is nearsighted and *b*,
Rev 3: 17 pitiful, poor, *b* and naked.

BLINDED (BLIND)

Zec 11: 17 his right eye totally *b!*"
Jn 12: 40 elsewhere: "He has *b* their eyes
Ac 22: 11 the brilliance of the light had *b* me.
2Co 4: 4 The god of this age has *b* the minds
1Jn 2: 11 because the darkness has *b* him.

BLINDFOLDED

Mk 14: 65 they *b* him, struck him
Lk 22: 64 They *b* him and demanded,

BLINDFOLDS (BLIND)

Job 9: 24 he *b* its judges.

BLINDNESS (BLIND)

Ge 19: 11 with *b* so that they could not find
Dt 28: 28 will afflict you with madness, *b*
2Ki 6: 18 So he struck them with *b*,
6: 18 "Strike these people with *b*."

BLINDS (BLIND)

Ex 23: 8 for a bribe *b* those who see
Dt 16: 19 for a bribe *b* the eyes of the wise

BLOCK (BLOCKED BLOCKING BLOCKS)

Lev 19: 14 or put a stumbling *b* in front
Isa 44: 19 Shall I bow down to a *b* of wood?"
Eze 3: 20 and I put a stumbling *b* before him,
14: 4 and puts a wicked stumbling *b*
14: 7 and puts a wicked stumbling *b*
39: 11 It will *b* the way of travelers,
Hos 2: 6 Therefore I will *b* her path
Mt 16: 23 Satan! You are a stumbling *b* to me
Ro 11: 9 a stumbling *b* and a retribution
14: 13 not to put any stumbling *b*
1Co 1: 23 a stumbling *b* to Jews
8: 9 does not become a stumbling *b*
2Co 6: 3 We put no stumbling *b*

BLOCKED (BLOCK)

Lev 15: 3 flowing from his body or is *b*,
2Ch 32: 4 and they *b* all the springs
32: 30 was Hezekiah who *b* the upper
Job 19: 8 He has *b* my way so I cannot pass;
Pr 15: 19 of the sluggard is *b* with thorns,

BLOCKING (BLOCK)

2Ch 32: 3 military staff about *b* off the water

BLOCKS (BLOCK)

1Ki 5: 17 removed from the quarry large *b*
6: 7 only *b* dressed at the quarry were
7: 9 made of *b* of high-grade stone cut
La 3: 9 He has barred my way with *b*
Eze 14: 3 and put wicked stumbling *b*

BLOOD (BLEEDING BLOOD-STAINED BLOODSHED BLOODSHOT BLOODSTAINS BLOODTHIRSTY LIFEBLOOD)

Ge 4: 10 Your brother's *b* cries out to me
4: 11 mouth to receive your brother's *b*
9: 6 by man shall his *b* be shed;
9: 6 "Whoever sheds the *b* of man,
29: 14 "You are my own flesh and *b*."
37: 22 "Don't shed any *b*.
37: 26 kill our brother and cover up his *b?*
37: 27 our brother, our own flesh and *b*."
37: 31 and dipped the robe in the *b*.
42: 22 must give an accounting for his *b*."
49: 11 his robes in the *b* of grapes.
Ex 4: 9 take from the river will become *b*
4: 25 "Surely you are a bridegroom of *b*
4: 26 time she said "bridegroom of *b*,"
7: 17 and it will be changed into *b*.
7: 19 and they will turn to *b*.
7: 19 *B* will be everywhere in Egypt,
7: 20 all the water was changed into *b*.
7: 21 *B* was everywhere in Egypt.
12: 7 Then they are to take some of the *b*
12: 13 The *b* will be a sign for you
12: 13 and when I see the *b*, I will pass
12: 22 and put some of the *b* on the top
12: 22 dip it into the *b* in the basin
12: 23 he will see the *b* on the top
23: 18 "Do not offer the *b* of a sacrifice
24: 6 Moses took half of the *b*
24: 8 Moses then took the *b*, sprinkled it
24: 8 "This is the *b* of the covenant that
29: 12 Take some of the bull's *b*
29: 16 Slaughter it and take the *b*
29: 20 Then sprinkle *b* against the altar
29: 20 take some of its *b* and put it
29: 21 And take some of the *b* on the altar
30: 10 made with the *b* of the atoning sin
34: 25 "Do not offer the *b* of a sacrifice
Lev 1: 5 sons the priests shall bring the *b*
1: 11 sons the priests shall sprinkle its *b*
1: 15 its *b* shall be drained out
3: 2 sons the priests shall sprinkle the *b*
3: 8 Aaron's sons shall sprinkle its *b*
3: 13 Aaron's sons shall sprinkle its *b*

Lev 3: 17 You must not eat any fat or any *b*
4: 5 priest shall take some of the bull's *b*
4: 6 He is to dip his finger into the *b*
4: 7 of the *b* on the horns of the altar
4: 7 rest of the bull's *b* he shall pour out
4: 16 some of the bull's *b* into the Tent
4: 17 He shall dip his finger into the *b*
4: 18 The rest of the *b* he shall pour out
4: 18 is to put some of the *b* on the horns
4: 25 some of the *b* of the sin offering
4: 25 the rest of the *b* at the base
4: 30 some of the *b* with his finger
4: 30 the rest of the *b* at the base
4: 34 some of the *b* of the sin offering
4: 34 the rest of the *b* at the base
5: 9 rest of the *b* must be drained out
5: 9 some of the *b* of the sin offering
6: 27 and if any of the *b* is spattered
6: 30 any sin offering whose *b* is brought
7: 2 and its *b* is to be sprinkled
7: 14 to the priest who sprinkles the *b*
7: 26 you must not eat the *b* of any bird
7: 27 If anyone eats *b*, that person must
7: 33 The son of Aaron who offers the *b*
8: 15 rest of the *b* at the base of the altar.
8: 15 the bull and took some of the *b*,
8: 19 sprinkled the *b* against the altar
8: 23 the ram and took some of its *b*
8: 24 and put some of the *b* on the lobes
8: 24 he sprinkled *b* against the altar
8: 30 and some of the *b* from the altar
9: 9 His sons brought the *b* to him,
9: 9 and he dipped his finger into the *b*
9: 9 the rest of the *b* he poured out
9: 12 His sons handed him the *b*,
9: 18 His sons handed him the *b*,
10: 18 Since its *b* was not taken
12: 7 clean from her flow of *b*.
14: 6 into the *b* of the bird that was killed
14: 14 some of the *b* of the guilt offering
14: 17 on top of the *b* of the guilt offering.
14: 25 guilt offering and take some of its *b*
14: 28 put on the same places he put the *b*
14: 51 dip them into the *b* of the dead bird
14: 52 purify the house with the bird's *b*,
15: 19 a woman has her regular flow of *b*,
15: 25 a discharge of *b* for many days
16: 14 He is to take some of the bull's *b*
16: 15 and take its *b* behind the curtain
16: 15 do with it as he did with the bull's *b*
16: 18 He shall take some of the bull's *b*
16: 18 and some of the goat's *b* and put it
16: 19 He shall sprinkle some of the *b*
16: 27 whose *b* was brought
17: 4 he has shed *b* and must be cut
17: 6 is to sprinkle the *b* against the altar
17: 10 among them who eats any *b*—
17: 10 face against that person who eats *b*
17: 11 For the life of a creature is in the *b*,
17: 11 it is the *b* that makes atonement
17: 12 living among you eat *b*.''
17: 12 ''None of you may eat *b*,
17: 13 may be eaten must drain out the *b*
17: 14 the life of every creature is its *b*;
17: 14 the life of every creature is its *b*
17: 14 ''You must not eat the *b*
19: 26 meat with the *b* still in it.
20: 9 and his *b* will be on his own head.
20: 11 their *b* will be on their own heads.
20: 12 their *b* will be on their own heads.
20: 13 their *b* will be on their own heads.
20: 16 their *b* will be on their own heads.
20: 27 their *b* will be on their own heads
25: 49 or any *b* relative in his clan may
Nu 18: 17 Sprinkle their *b* on the altar
19: 4 is to take some of its *b* on his finger
19: 5 is to be burned—its hide, flesh, *b*
23: 24 and drinks the *b* of his victims.''
35: 19 avenger of *b* shall put the murderer
35: 21 avenger of *b* shall put the murderer
35: 24 and the avenger of *b* according
35: 25 of murder from the avenger of *b*
35: 27 and the avenger of *b* finds him
35: 27 avenger of *b* may kill the accused
35: 33 by the *b* of the one who shed it.
35: 33 the land on which *b* has been shed,
Dt 12: 16 But you must not eat the *b*;
12: 23 eat the *b*, because the *b* is the life,
Dt 12: 24 You must not eat the *b*; pour it out
12: 27 your God, both the meat and the *b*.
12: 27 *b* of your sacrifices must be poured
15: 23 But you must not eat the *b*;
19: 6 the avenger of *b* might pursue him
19: 10 so that innocent *b* will not be shed
19: 12 him over to the avenger of *b* to die.
19: 13 the guilt of shedding innocent *b*,
21: 7 ''Our hands did not shed this *b*,
21: 8 of the *b* of an innocent man.''
21: 9 the guilt of shedding innocent *b*,
32: 14 You drank the red *b* of the grape.
32: 42 the *b* of the slain and the captives,
32: 42 will make my arrows drunk with *b*,
32: 43 for he will avenge the *b*
Jos 2: 19 his *b* will be on his own head;
2: 19 his *b* will be on our head
20: 3 protection from the avenger of *b*.
20: 5 If the avenger of *b* pursues him,
20: 9 killed by the avenger of *b* prior
Jdg 9: 2 Remember, I am your flesh and *b*.''
9: 24 of their *b*, might be avenged
1Sa 14: 32 and ate them, together with the *b*.
14: 33 by eating meat that has *b* in it.''
14: 34 by eating meat with *b* still in it.' ''
26: 20 Now do not let my *b* fall
2Sa 1: 16 ''Your *b* be on your own head.
1: 22 From the *b* of the slain,
3: 27 to avenge the *b* of his brother
3: 28 before the LORD concerning the *b*
3: 29 May his *b* fall upon the head
4: 11 should I not now demand his *b*
5: 1 ''We are your own flesh and *b*.
14: 11 God to prevent the avenger of *b*
16: 7 you man of *b*, you scoundrel!
16: 8 to ruin because you are a man of *b*
16: 8 you for all the *b* you shed
19: 12 my brothers, my own flesh and *b*.
19: 13 'Are you not my own flesh and *b*?
20: 12 wallowing in his *b* in the middle
23: 17 ''Is it not the *b* of men who went
1Ki 2: 5 and with that *b* stained the belt
2: 5 shedding their *b* in peacetime
2: 9 head down to the grave in *b*.''
2: 31 of the innocent *b* that Joab shed.
2: 32 will repay him for the *b* he shed,
2: 33 the guilt of their *b* rest on the head
2: 37 your *b* will be on your own head.''
8: 19 who is your own flesh and *b*—
18: 28 until their *b* flowed.
21: 19 dogs will lick up your *b*—yes,
21: 19 where dogs licked up Naboth's *b*,
22: 35 The *b* from his wound ran
22: 38 and the dogs licked up his *b*,
2Ki 3: 22 the water looked red—like *b*.
3: 23 ''That's *b*!'' they said.
9: 7 and I will avenge the *b*
9: 7 *b* of all the LORD's servants shed
9: 26 of Naboth and the *b* of his sons,
9: 26 'Yesterday I saw the *b* of Naboth
9: 33 some of her *b* spattered the wall
16: 13 sprinkled the *b* of his fellowship
16: 15 Sprinkle on the altar all the *b*
20: 18 and *b*, that will be born to you,
21: 16 so much innocent *b* that he filled
24: 4 filled Jerusalem with innocent *b*,
24: 4 the shedding of innocent *b*.
25: 25 of Elishama, who was of royal *b*,
1Ch 11: 1 ''We are your own flesh and *b*.
11: 19 ''Should I drink the *b*
22: 8 'You have shed much *b*
22: 8 you have shed much *b* on the earth
28: 3 you are a warrior and have shed *b*.'
2Ch 6: 9 who is your own flesh and *b*—
29: 22 and sprinkled their *b* on the altar;
29: 22 and sprinkled their *b* on the altar.
29: 22 and the priests took the *b*
29: 24 and presented their *b* on the altar
30: 16 The priests sprinkled the *b* handed
35: 11 the priests sprinkled the *b* handed
Ne 5: 5 and *b* as our countrymen and
Job 16: 18 ''O earth, do not cover my *b*;
39: 30 His young ones feast on *b*,
Ps 9: 12 For he who avenges *b* remembers;
16: 4 will not pour out their libations of *b*
50: 13 or drink the *b* of goats?
58: 10 in the *b* of the wicked.
68: 23 feet in the *b* of your foes,
Ps 72: 14 for precious is their *b* in his sight.
78: 44 He turned their rivers to *b*;
79: 3 They have poured out *b* like water
79: 10 that you avenge the outpoured *b*
105: 29 He turned their waters into *b*,
106: 38 They shed innocent *b*,
106: 38 the land was desecrated by their *b*.
106: 38 the *b* of their sons and daughters,
Pr 1: 11 let's lie in wait for someone's *b*,
1: 16 they are swift to shed *b*.
1: 18 lie in wait for their own *b*;
6: 17 hands that shed innocent *b*,
12: 6 of the wicked lie in wait for *b*,
30: 33 and as twisting the nose produces *b*
Isa 1: 11 pleasure in the *b* of bulls and lambs
1: 15 Your hands are full of *b*;
9: 5 and every garment rolled in *b*
15: 9 Dimon's waters are full of *b*,
26: 21 The earth will disclose the *b* shed
34: 3 will be soaked with their *b*.
34: 6 sword of the LORD is bathed in *b*,
34: 6 the *b* of lambs and goats,
34: 7 Their land will be drenched with *b*,
39: 7 and *b* who will be born to you,
49: 26 they will be drunk on their own *b*,
58: 7 away from your own flesh and *b*?
59: 3 For your hands are stained with *b*,
59: 7 they are swift to shed innocent *b*.
63: 3 their *b* spattered my garments,
63: 6 and poured their *b* on the ground.''
66: 3 is like one who presents pig's *b*,
Jer 7: 6 do not shed innocent *b* in this place
19: 4 place with the *b* of the innocent.
22: 3 do not shed innocent *b* in this place
22: 17 on shedding innocent *b*
26: 15 guilt of innocent *b* on yourselves
41: 1 was of royal *b* and had been one
46: 10 till it has quenched its thirst with *b*.
51: 35 ''May our *b* be on those who live
La 4: 13 the *b* of the righteous.
4: 14 They are so defiled with *b*
Eze 3: 18 will hold you accountable for his *b*.
3: 20 will hold you accountable for his *b*.
11: 15 brothers who are your *b* relatives
16: 6 saw you kicking about in your *b*,
16: 6 you lay there in your *b* I said to you
16: 9 and washed the *b* from you
16: 22 and bare, kicking about in your *b*.
16: 36 you gave them your children's *b*,
16: 38 bring upon you the *b* vengeance
16: 38 commit adultery and who shed *b*;
18: 10 who sheds *b* or does any
18: 13 and his *b* will be on his own head.
21: 32 your *b* will be shed in your land,
22: 3 doom by shedding *b* in her midst
22: 4 because of the *b* you have shed
22: 6 are in you uses his power to shed *b*.
22: 9 men bent on shedding *b*;
22: 12 In you men accept bribes to shed *b*;
22: 13 and at the *b* you have shed
22: 27 they shed *b* and kill people
23: 37 have committed adultery and *b* is
23: 45 they are adulterous and *b* is
23: 45 who commit adultery and shed *b*,
24: 7 For the *b* she shed is in her midst:
24: 8 I put her *b* on the bare rock,
28: 23 and make *b* flow in her streets.
32: 6 the land with your flowing *b*
33: 4 his *b* will be on his own head.
33: 5 his *b* will be on his own head.
33: 6 watchman accountable for his *b*.'
33: 8 will hold you accountable for his *b*.
33: 25 and look to your idols and shed *b*,
33: 25 meat with the *b* still in it
36: 18 they had shed *b* in the land and
39: 17 There you will eat flesh and drink *b*
39: 18 and drink the *b* of the princes
39: 19 and drink *b* till you are drunk.
43: 18 and sprinkling *b* upon the altar
43: 20 You are to take some of its *b*
44: 7 and *b*, and you broke my covenant.
44: 15 me to offer sacrifices of fat and *b*,
45: 19 some of the *b* of the sin offering
Hos 6: 8 stained with footprints of *b*.
Joel 2: 30 *b* and fire and billows of smoke.
2: 31 and the moon to *b*
3: 19 in whose land they shed innocent *b*
Mic 7: 2 All men lie in wait to shed *b*;

Na 3: 1 Woe to the city of *b*,
Hab 2: 8 For you have shed man's *b*;
2: 17 For you have shed man's *b*;
Zep 1: 17 Their *b* will be poured out like dust
Zec 9: 7 I will take the *b* from their mouths,
9: 11 of the *b* of my covenant with you,
Mt 23: 30 in shedding the *b* of the prophets.'
23: 35 Abel to the *b* of Zechariah son
23: 35 all the righteous *b* that has been
23: 35 from the *b* of righteous Abel
26: 28 This is my *b* of the covenant,
27: 4 "for I have betrayed innocent *b*."
27: 6 since it is *b* money."
27: 8 it has been called the Field of *B*
27: 24 "I am innocent of this man's *b*,"
27: 25 "Let his *b* be on us
Mk 14: 24 "This is my *b* of the covenant,
Lk 11: 50 for the *b* of all the prophets that has
11: 51 from the *b* of Abel to the *b*
13: 1 the Galileans whose *b* Pilate had
22: 20 cup is the new covenant in my *b*,
22: 44 drops of *b* falling to the ground.
Jn 6: 53 of the Son of Man and drink his *b*,
6: 54 and drinks my *b* has eternal life,
6: 55 is real food and my *b* is real drink.
6: 56 and drinks my *b* remains in me,
19: 34 bringing a sudden flow of *b*
Ac 1: 19 Akeldama, that is, Field of *B*.)
2: 19 *b* and fire and billows of smoke.
2: 20 and the moon to *b*
5: 28 to make us guilty of this man's *b*."
15: 20 of strangled animals and from *b*.
15: 29 food sacrificed to idols, from *b*,
18: 6 "Your *b* be on your own heads!
20: 26 innocent of the *b* of all men.
20: 28 which he bought with his own *b*.
21: 25 from *b*, from the meat
22: 20 when the *b* of your martyr Stephen
Ro 3: 15 "Their feet are swift to shed *b*;
3: 25 of atonement, through faith in his *b*
5: 9 have now been justified by his *b*,
1Co 10: 16 give thanks a participation in the *b*
11: 25 cup is the new covenant in my *b*;
11: 27 against the body and *b* of the Lord.
15: 50 and *b* cannot inherit the kingdom
Eph 1: 7 we have redemption through his *b*,
2: 13 near through the *b* of Christ.
6: 12 not against flesh and *b*,
Col 1: 20 by making peace through his *b*,
Heb 2: 14 Since the children have flesh and *b*,
9: 7 once a year, and never without *b*,
9: 12 enter by means of the *b* of goats
9: 12 once for all by his own *b*,
9: 13 The *b* of goats and bulls
9: 14 How much more, then, will the *b*
9: 18 put into effect without *b*.
9: 19 he took the *b* of calves, together
9: 20 "This is the *b* of the covenant,
9: 21 with the *b* both the tabernacle
9: 22 everything be cleansed with *b*,
9: 22 of *b* there is no forgiveness.
9: 25 year with *b* that is not his own.
10: 4 it is impossible for the *b* of bulls
10: 19 enter the Most Holy Place by the *b*
10: 29 as an unholy thing the *b*
11: 28 Passover and the sprinkling of *b*,
12: 4 to the point of shedding your *b*.
12: 24 and to the sprinkled *b* that speaks
12: 24 word than the *b* of Abel.
13: 11 The high priest carries the *b*
13: 12 holy through his own *b*.
13: 20 who through the *b*
1Pe 1: 2 Christ and sprinkling by his *b*:
1: 19 but with the precious *b* of Christ,
1Jn 1: 7 and the *b* of Jesus, his Son,
5: 6 by water only, but by water and *b*.
5: 6 one who came by water and *b*—
5: 8 the Spirit, the water and the *b*;
Rev 1: 5 has freed us from our sins by his *b*,
5: 9 with your *b* you purchased men
6: 10 of the earth and avenge our *b*?"
6: 12 the whole moon turned *b* red,
7: 14 white in the *b* of the Lamb.
8: 7 came hail and fire mixed with *b*,
8: 8 A third of the sea turned into *b*,
11: 6 power to turn the waters into *b*
12: 11 him by the *b* of the Lamb
14: 20 and *b* flowed out of the press,
Rev 16: 3 and it turned into *b* like that
16: 4 of water, and they became *b*.
16: 6 and you have given them *b* to drink
16: 6 for they have shed the *b*
17: 6 drunk with the *b* of the saints,
17: 6 the *b* of those who bore testimony
18: 24 In her was found the *b* of prophets
19: 2 on her the *b* of his servants."
19: 13 He is dressed in a robe dipped in *b*,

BLOOD-STAINED (BLOOD)

2Sa 21: 1 on account of Saul and his *b* house;

BLOODGUILT (GUILT)

Ps 51: 14 Save me from *b*, O God,
Joel 3: 21 Their *b*, which I have not pardoned

BLOODSHED (BLOOD)

Ex 22: 2 the defender is not guilty of *b*;
22: 3 after sunrise, he is guilty of *b*.
Lev 17: 4 man shall be considered guilty of *b*;
Nu 35: 33 *B* pollutes the land, and atonement
Dt 17: 8 whether *b*, lawsuits or assaults—
19: 10 so that you will not be guilty of *b*.
21: 8 And the *b* will be atoned for.
22: 8 of *b* on your house if someone falls
1Sa 25: 26 from *b* and from avenging yourself
25: 31 the staggering burden of needless *b*
25: 33 and for keeping me from *b* this day
2Ch 19: 10 *b* or other concerns of the law,
Isa 5: 7 he looked for justice, but saw *b*;
Jer 48: 10 on him who keeps his sword from *b*
Eze 5: 17 and *b* will sweep through you,
7: 23 because the land is full of *b*
9: 9 full of *b* and the city is full
14: 19 wrath upon it through *b*,
22: 2 Will you judge this city of *b*?
24: 6 " 'Woe to the city of *b*,
24: 9 " 'Woe to the city of *b*!
35: 6 I will give you over to *b*
35: 6 did not hate *b*, *b* will pursue you.
38: 22 upon him with plague and *b*;
Hos 4: 2 and *b* follows *b*.
12: 14 leave upon him the guilt of his *b*
Mic 3: 10 who build Zion with *b*,
Hab 2: 12 to him who builds a city with *b*

BLOODSHOT (BLOOD)

Pr 23: 29 needless bruises? Who has *b* eyes?

BLOODSTAINS (BLOOD)

Isa 4: 4 he will cleanse the *b*

BLOODTHIRSTY (BLOOD)

Ps 5: 6 *b* and deceitful men
26: 9 or my life with *b* men,
55: 23 *b* and deceitful men
59: 2 and save me from *b* men.
139: 19 Away from me, you *b* men!
Pr 29: 10 *B* men hate a man of integrity

BLOOM

Ex 9: 31 had headed and the flax was in *b*.
SS 2: 15 our vineyards that are in *b*.
6: 11 or the pomegranates were in *b*.
7: 12 and if the pomegranates are in *b*—
Isa 35: 2 it will burst into *b*;

BLOSSOM (BLOSSOMED BLOSSOMING BLOSSOMS)

1Ki 7: 26 the rim of a cup, like a lily *b*.
2Ch 4: 5 the rim of a cup, like a lily *b*.
Isa 18: 5 when the *b* is gone
27: 6 Israel will bud and *b*
35: 1 the wilderness will rejoice and *b*.
Hos 14: 5 he will *b* like a lily.
14: 7 He will *b* like a vine,
Jas 1: 11 its *b* falls and its beauty is

BLOSSOMED (BLOSSOM)

Ge 40: 10 As soon as it budded, it *b*,
Nu 17: 8 but had budded, *b* and produced
Eze 7: 10 rod has budded, arrogance has *b*!

BLOSSOMING (BLOSSOM)

SS 2: 13 the *b* vines spread their fragrance.

BLOSSOMS (BLOSSOM)

Ex 25: 31 and *b* shall be of one piece with it.
25: 33 and *b* are to be on one branch,
25: 34 almond flowers with buds and *b*.
37: 17 and *b* were of one piece with it.
37: 19 and *b* were on one branch,
37: 20 almond flowers with buds and *b*.
Nu 8: 4 from its base to its *b*.
Job 15: 33 like an olive tree shedding its *b*.
Ecc 12: 5 when the almond tree *b*
SS 1: 14 to me a cluster of henna *b*
7: 12 if their *b* have opened,
Na 1: 4 and the *b* of Lebanon fade.

BLOT (BLOTS BLOTTED)

Ex 32: 32 then *b* me out of the book you have
32: 33 against me I will *b* out of my book.
Dt 9: 14 and *b* out their name
25: 19 you shall *b* out the memory
29: 20 and the LORD will *b* out his name
2Ki 14: 27 not said he would *b* out the name
Ne 4: 5 or *b* out their sins from your sight,
13: 14 and do not *b* out what I have
Ps 51: 1 *b* out my transgressions.
51: 9 and *b* out all my iniquity.
Jer 18: 23 or *b* out their sins from your sight.

BLOTS (BLOT)

Isa 43: 25 "I, even I, am he who *b* out
2Pe 2: 13 They are *b* and blemishes,

BLOTTED (BLOT)

Dt 25: 6 so that his name will not be *b* out
Ps 9: 5 you have *b* out their name for ever
69: 28 May they be *b* out of the book
109: 13 their names *b* out from the next
109: 14 of his mother never be *b* out.

BLOW (BLEW BLOWING BLOWN BLOWS WIND-BLOWN WINDBLOWN)

Ex 10: 13 the LORD made an east wind *b*
21: 19 one who struck the *b* will not be
Nu 10: 7 the assembly, *b* the trumpets,
10: 8 the priests, are to *b* the trumpets.
Jdg 7: 18 all who are with me *b* our trumpets,
7: 18 from all around the camp *b* yours
7: 20 hands the trumpets they were to *b*,
16: 28 and let me with one *b* get revenge
1Sa 6: 19 of the heavy *b* the LORD had dealt
1Ki 1: 34 *B* the trumpet and shout, 'Long
1Ch 15: 24 were to *b* trumpets before the ark
16: 6 were to *b* the trumpets regularly
2Ch 21: 14 that is yours, with a heavy *b*.
Ps 39: 10 by the *b* of your hand.
68: 2 may you *b* them away;
SS 4: 16 *B* on my garden,
Isa 5: 24 and their flowers *b* away like dust;
19: 7 will *b* away and be no more.
41: 16 and a gale will *b* them away.
57: 13 a mere breath will *b* them away.
Jer 6: 29 The bellows *b* fiercely
14: 17 a crushing *b*.
51: 27 *B* the trumpet among the nations!
Eze 7: 9 it is I the LORD who strikes the *b*.
7: 14 Though they *b* the trumpet
22: 21 I will *b* on you with my fiery wrath,
24: 16 with one *b* I am about to take away
33: 6 and does not *b* the trumpet
Joel 2: 1 *B* the trumpet in Zion;
2: 15 *B* the trumpet in Zion,
Ac 27: 13 a gentle south wind began to *b*,

BLOWING (BLOW)

Jos 6: 4 with the priests *b* the trumpets.
6: 8 *b* their trumpets, and the ark
6: 13 of the LORD and *b* the trumpets.
2Ki 11: 14 land were rejoicing and *b* trumpets.
2Ch 23: 13 land were rejoicing and *b* trumpets,
Hos 13: 15 *b* in from the desert;
Jn 6: 18 strong wind was *b* and the waters
Ac 2: 2 Suddenly a sound like the *b*
Rev 7: 1 wind from *b* on the land

BLOWN (BLOW)

1Sa 13: 3 Then Saul had the trumpet *b*
Ps 68: 2 As smoke is *b* away by the wind,
Isa 29: 5 the ruthless hordes like *b* chaff.
Eph 4: 14 and *b* here and there by every wind

Jas 1: 6 doubts is like a wave of the sea, *b*
Jude :12 without rain, *b* along by the wind;

BLOWS (BLOW)

Job 20: 23 and rain down his *b* upon him.
Ps 1: 4 that the wind *b* away.
103: 16 the wind *b* over it and it is gone,
Pr 6: 33 *B* and disgrace are his lot,
20: 30 *B* and wounds cleanse away evil,
Ecc 1: 6 The wind *b* to the south
Isa 14: 6 peoples with unceasing *b*,
27: 8 as on a day the east wind *b*.
30: 32 them in battle with the *b* of his arm.
40: 7 the breath of the LORD *b* on them.
40: 24 than he *b* on them and they wither,
Jer 4: 11 in the desert *b* toward my people,
Eze 26: 9 He will direct the *b*
33: 3 *b* the trumpet to warn the people,
Lk 12: 47 wants will be beaten with many *b*.
12: 48 will be beaten with few *b*.
12: 55 And when the south wind *b*,
Jn 3: 8 The wind *b* wherever it pleases.

BLUE

Ex 25: 4 gold, silver and bronze; *b*,
26: 1 of finely twisted linen and *b*,
26: 4 Make loops of *b* material
26: 31 "Make a curtain of *b*, purple
26: 36 to the tent make a curtain of *b*,
27: 16 a curtain twenty cubits long, of *b*,
28: 5 and *b*, purple and scarlet yarn,
28: 6 and of *b*, purple and scarlet yarn,
28: 8 and with *b*, purple and scarlet yarn,
28: 15 and of *b*, purple and scarlet yarn,
28: 28 the rings of the ephod with *b* cord,
28: 31 of the ephod entirely of *b* cloth,
28: 33 Make pomegranates of *b*, purple
28: 37 Fasten a *b* cord to it to attach it
35: 6 *b*, purple and scarlet yarn
35: 23 Everyone who had *b*, purple
35: 25 *b*, purple or scarlet yarn
35: 35 designers, embroiderers in *b*,
36: 8 of finely twisted linen and *b*,
36: 11 Then they made loops of *b* material
36: 35 They made the curtain of *b*,
36: 37 to the tent they made a curtain of *b*
38: 18 entrance to the courtyard was of *b*,
38: 23 and an embroiderer in *b*, purple
39: 1 From the *b*, purple and scarlet yarn
39: 2 and of *b*, purple and scarlet yarn,
39: 3 cut strands to be worked into the *b*,
39: 5 and with *b*, purple and scarlet yarn,
39: 8 and of *b*, purple and scarlet yarn,
39: 21 the rings of the ephod with *b* cord,
39: 22 of the ephod entirely of *b* cloth
39: 24 They made pomegranates of *b*,
39: 29 was of finely twisted linen and *b*,
39: 31 Then they fastened a *b* cord to it
Nu 4: 6 spread a cloth of solid *b* over that
4: 7 are to spread a *b* cloth
4: 9 "They are to take a *b* cloth
4: 11 are to spread a *b* cloth
4: 12 wrap them in a *b* cloth, cover that
15: 38 with a *b* cord on each tassel.
2Ch 2: 7 and in purple, crimson and *b* yarn,
2: 14 and with purple and *b* and crimson
3: 14 He made the curtain of *b*, purple
Est 1: 6 hangings of white and *b* linen,
8: 15 wearing royal garments of *b*
Jer 10: 9 is then dressed in *b* and purple—
Eze 23: 6 warriors clothed in *b*, governors
27: 7 your awnings were of *b* and purple
27: 24 you beautiful garments, *b* fabric,
Rev 9: 17 dark *b*, and yellow as sulfur.

BLUFF

Jdg 6: 26 God on the top of this *b*.

BLUNTED

Ps 58: 7 draw the bow, let their arrows be *b*.

BLURTS

Pr 12: 23 but the heart of fools *b* out folly.

BLUSH

Jer 3: 3 you refuse to *b* with shame.
6: 15 they do not even know how to *b*.
8: 12 they do not even know how to *b*.

BLUSTERING

Job 8: 2 Your words are a *b* wind.

BOANERGES

Mk 3: 17 John (to them he gave the name *B*,

BOARD (ABOARD BOARDED BOARDS)

Eze 27: 9 of Gebal were on *b*
27: 27 and everyone else on *b*
Ac 21: 2 over to Phoenicia, went on *b*
27: 6 sailing for Italy and put us on *b*.
27: 37 there were 276 of us on *b*.

BOARDED (BOARD)

Ac 27: 2 *b* a ship from Adramyttium about

BOARDS (BOARD)

Ex 27: 8 Make the altar hollow, out of *b*.
38: 7 They made it hollow, out of *b*.
1Ki 6: 15 lined its interior walls with cedar *b*,
6: 16 with cedar *b* from floor to ceiling

BOARS

Ps 80: 13 *B* from the forest ravage it

BOAST (BOASTED BOASTERS BOASTFUL BOASTING BOASTS)

Jdg 7: 2 In order that Israel may not *b*
1Ki 20: 11 armor should not *b* like one who
Ps 34: 2 My soul will *b* in the LORD;
44: 8 In God we make our *b* all day long,
49: 6 and *b* of their great riches?
52: 1 Why do you *b* all day long,
52: 1 Why do you *b* of evil, you mighty
75: 4 To the arrogant I say, '*B* no more,'
97: 7 those who *b* in idols—
Pr 27: 1 Do not *b* about tomorrow,
Isa 10: 15 the saw *b* against him who uses it?
28: 15 You *b*, "We have entered
61: 6 and in their riches you will *b*.
Jer 9: 23 or the rich man *b* of his riches,
9: 23 or the strong man *b* of his strength
9: 23 "Let not the wise man *b*
9: 24 but let him who boasts *b* about this:
49: 4 Why do you *b* of your valleys,
49: 4 *b* of your valleys so fruitful?
51: 41 the *b* of the whole earth seized!
Am 4: 5 *b* about them, you Israelites,
Ob :12 nor *b* so much
Ro 4: 2 he had something to *b* about—
11: 18 do not *b* over those branches.
1Co 1: 29 so that no one may *b* before him.
1: 31 Let him who boasts *b* in the Lord."
4: 7 why do you *b* as though you did
9: 15 have anyone deprive me of this *b*.
9: 16 I cannot *b*, for I am compelled
13: 4 it does not *b*, it is not proud.
2Co 1: 12 Now this is our *b*: Our conscience
1: 14 as we will *b* of you in the day
1: 14 to understand fully that you can *b*
10: 8 even if I *b* somewhat freely about
10: 13 will not *b* beyond proper limits,
10: 16 want to *b* about work already done
10: 17 Let him who boasts *b* in the Lord."
11: 12 with us in the things they *b* about.
11: 18 way the world does, I too will *b*.
11: 21 What anyone else dares to *b* about
11: 21 as a fool—I also dare to *b* about.
11: 30 I do not inwardly burn? If I must *b*,
11: 30 I will *b* of the things that show my
12: 5 I will *b* about a man like that,
12: 5 but I will not *b* about myself,
12: 6 Even if I should choose to *b*,
12: 9 Therefore I will *b* all the more
Gal 6: 13 that they may *b* about your flesh.
6: 14 May I never *b* except in the cross
Eph 2: 9 not by works, so that no one can *b*.
Php 2: 16 in order that I may *b* on the day
2Th 1: 4 God's churches we *b* about your
Heb 3: 6 and the hope of which we *b*.
Jas 3: 14 do not *b* about it or deny the truth.
4: 16 As it is, you *b* and brag.
Jude :16 they *b* about themselves

BOASTED (BOAST)

Ex 15: 9 "The enemy *b*,
Est 5: 11 Haman *b* to them about his vast
Isa 20: 5 and *b* in Egypt will be afraid
Jer 13: 20 the sheep of which you *b*?
Eze 35: 13 You *b* against me and spoke
Ac 8: 9 He *b* that he was someone great,
2Co 7: 14 I had *b* to him about you,

BOASTERS (BOAST)

Jer 48: 45 the skulls of the noisy *b*.

BOASTFUL (BOAST)

Ps 12: 3 and every *b* tongue
Da 7: 11 of the *b* words the horn was
Ro 1: 30 insolent, arrogant and *b*;
2Ti 3: 2 lovers of money, *b*, proud, abusive,
2Pe 2: 18 For they mouth empty, *b* words

BOASTING (BOAST)

Ps 94: 4 all the evildoers are full of *b*.
Ro 3: 27 Where, then, is *b*? It is excluded.
1Co 3: 21 So then, no more *b* about men!
5: 6 Your *b* is not good.
2Co 7: 14 so our *b* about you
9: 2 and I have been *b* about it
9: 3 in order that our *b* about you
10: 13 will confine our *b* to the field God
10: 14 We are not going too far in our *b*,
10: 15 limits by *b* of work done
11: 10 of Achaia will stop this *b* of mine.
11: 16 so that I may do a little *b*.
11: 17 In this self-confident *b* I am not
11: 18 Since many are *b* in the way
12: 1 I must go on *b*.
Jas 4: 16 All such *b* is evil.
1Jn 2: 16 the *b* of what he has and does—

BOASTS (BOAST)

1Sa 2: 1 My mouth *b* over my enemies,
Ps 10: 3 He *b* of the cravings of his heart;
Pr 20: 14 he goes and *b* about his purchase.
25: 14 is a man who *b* of gifts he does not
Isa 16: 6 but her *b* are empty.
Jer 9: 24 but let him who *b* boast about this:
48: 30 "and her *b* accomplish nothing.
Hos 12: 8 Ephraim *b*,
1Co 1: 31 "Let him who *b* boast in the Lord."
2Co 10: 17 "Let him who *b* boast in the Lord."
Jas 3: 5 of the body, but it makes great *b*.
Rev 18: 7 In her heart she *b*,

BOAT (BOATS LIFEBOAT)

Mt 4: 21 in a *b* with their father Zebedee,
4: 22 and immediately they left the *b*
8: 23 Then he got into the *b*
8: 24 so that the waves swept over the *b*.
9: 1 Jesus stepped into a *b*, crossed over
13: 2 around him that he got into a *b*
14: 13 he withdrew by *b* privately
14: 22 made the disciples get into the *b*
14: 24 the *b* was already a considerable
14: 29 Then Peter got down out of the *b*
14: 32 And when they climbed into the *b*,
14: 33 were in the *b* worshiped him,
15: 39 he got into the *b* and went
Mk 1: 19 and his brother John in a *b*,
1: 20 in the *b* with the hired men
3: 9 to have a small *b* ready for him,
4: 1 was so large that he got into a *b*
4: 36 him along, just as he was, in the *b*.
4: 37 and the waves broke over the *b*,
5: 2 When Jesus got out of the *b*,
5: 18 As Jesus was getting into the *b*,
5: 21 crossed over by *b* to the other side
6: 32 away by themselves in a *b*
6: 45 made his disciples get into the *b*
6: 47 the *b* was in the middle of the lake,
6: 51 he climbed into the *b* with them,
6: 54 As soon as they got out of the *b*,
8: 10 he got into the *b* with his disciples
8: 13 got back into the *b* and crossed
8: 14 had with them in the *b*.
Lk 5: 3 and taught the people from the *b*.
5: 7 partners in the other *b* to come
8: 22 So they got into a *b* and set out.
8: 23 so that the *b* was being swamped,
8: 37 So he got into the *b* and left.
Jn 6: 17 where they got into a *b*
6: 19 they saw Jesus approaching the *b*,
6: 21 and immediately the *b* reached
6: 21 willing to take him into the *b*,

Jn 6: 22 that only one *b* had been there,
21: 3 So they went out and got into the *b*
21: 6 net on the right side of the *b*
21: 8 other disciples followed in the *b*,

BOATS (BOAT)

Job 9: 26 They skim past like *b* of papyrus,
Isa 18: 2 sea in papyrus *b* over the water.
Mk 4: 36 There were also other *b* with him.
Lk 5: 2 he saw at the water's edge two *b*,
5: 3 into one of the *b*, the one belonging
5: 7 filled both *b* so full that they began
5: 11 So they pulled their *b* up on shore,
Jn 6: 23 Then some *b* from Tiberias landed
6: 24 they got into the *b* and went

BOAZ

Ru 2: 1 of standing, whose name was *B*.
2: 3 working in a field belonging to *B*,
2: 4 Just then *B* arrived
2: 5 *B* asked the foreman
2: 8 So *B* said to Ruth, "My daughter,
2: 11 me—a foreigner?" *B* replied,
2: 14 At mealtime *B* said to her,
2: 15 to glean, *B* gave orders to his men,
2: 19 the man I worked with today is *B*,"
2: 23 to the servant girls of *B* to glean
3: 2 Is not *B*, with whose servant girls
3: 7 When *B* had finished eating
3: 16 she told her everything *B* had done
4: 1 Meanwhile *B* went up
4: 1 *B* said, "Come over here, my
4: 2 *B* took ten of the elders of the town
4: 5 Then *B* said, "On the day you buy
4: 8 So the kinsman-redeemer said to *B*
4: 9 Then *B* announced to the elders
4: 13 So *B* took Ruth and she became his
4: 21 father of *B*, *B* the father of Obed,
1Ki 7: 21 and the one to the north *B*.
1Ch 2: 11 of Salmon, Salmon the father of *B*,
2: 12 *B* the father of Obed and Obed
2Ch 3: 17 and the one to the north *B*.
Mt 1: 5 mother was Rahab, *B* the father
1: 5 of *B*, whose mother was Rahab,
Lk 3: 32 the son of Obed, the son of *B*,

BODIES (BODY)

Ge 34: 27 of Jacob came upon the dead *b*
47: 18 left for our lord except our *b*
Ex 30: 32 Do not pour it on men's *b*
Lev 19: 28 " 'Do not cut your *b* for the dead
21: 5 edges of their beards or cut their *b*.
26: 30 and pile your dead *b* on the lifeless
Nu 8: 7 have them shave their whole *b*
14: 29 In this desert your *b* will fall—
14: 32 your *b* will fall in this desert.
14: 33 the last of your *b* lies in the desert.
1Sa 31: 12 They took down the *b* of Saul
2Sa 4: 12 hung the *b* by the pool in Hebron.
21: 10 down from the heavens on the *b*,
2Ki 10: 25 and officers threw the *b* out
19: 35 there were all the dead *b!*
1Ch 10: 12 and took the *b* of Saul and his sons
2Ch 20: 24 they saw only dead *b* lying
Ne 9: 37 They rule over our *b* and our cattle
Ps 44: 25 our *b* cling to the ground.
73: 4 their *b* are healthy and strong.
79: 2 They have given the dead *b*
Isa 5: 25 and the dead *b* are like refuse
26: 19 their *b* will rise.
34: 3 their dead *b* will send up a stench;
37: 36 there were all the dead *b!*
66: 24 and look upon the dead *b*
Jer 9: 22 " 'The dead *b* of men will lie
16: 4 and their dead *b* will become food
31: 40 The whole valley where dead *b*
33: 5 with the dead *b* of the men I will
34: 20 Their dead *b* will become food
41: 9 the cistern where he threw all the *b*
La 4: 7 their *b* more ruddy than rubies,
Eze 6: 5 I will lay the dead *b* of the Israelites
10: 12 Their entire *b*, including their
11: 7 The *b* you have thrown there are
Da 3: 27 the fire had not harmed their *b*,
Am 6: 10 is to burn the *b* comes
8: 3 Many, many *b*— flung everywhere
Na 2: 10 *b* tremble, every face grows pale.
3: 3 *b* without number,
Hab 2: 15 that he can gaze on their naked *b*.
Mt 24: 29 and the heavenly *b* will be shaken.'
27: 52 the *b* of many holy people who had
Mk 13: 25 and the heavenly *b* will be shaken.'
Lk 21: 26 for the heavenly *b* will be shaken.
Jn 19: 31 the Jews did not want the *b* left
19: 31 the legs broken and the *b* taken
Ac 7: 16 Their *b* were brought back
7: 42 to the worship of the heavenly *b*.
Ro 1: 24 of their *b* with one another.
7: 5 by the law were at work in our *b*,
8: 11 to your mortal *b* through his Spirit,
8: 23 as sons, the redemption of our *b*.
12: 1 to offer your *b* as living sacrifices,
1Co 6: 15 not know that your *b* are members
10: 5 their *b* were scattered
15: 40 heavenly *b* and there are earthly *b;*
15: 40 of the earthly *b* is another.
15: 40 of the heavenly *b* is one kind,
Eph 5: 28 to love their wives as their own *b*.
Php 3: 21 will transform our lowly *b*
Heb 3: 17 whose *b* fell in the desert?
10: 22 and having our *b* washed
13: 11 the *b* are burned outside the camp.
Jude : 8 these dreamers pollute their own *b*,
Rev 11: 8 Their *b* will lie in the street
11: 9 and nation will gaze on their *b*
18: 13 horses and carriages; and *b*

BODILY (BODY)

Lev 15: 2 'When any man has a *b* discharge,
22: 4 skin disease or a *b* discharge,
Lk 3: 22 on him in *b* form like a dove.
Col 2: 9 of the Deity lives in *b* form,

BODY (BODIES BODILY EMBODIMENT)

Ge 15: 4 from your own *b* will be your heir."
25: 25 and his whole *b* was like a hairy
35: 11 and kings will come from your *b*.
Ex 22: 27 the only covering he has for his *b*.
28: 42 as a covering for the *b*,
Lev 6: 10 linen undergarments next to his *b*,
13: 13 disease has covered his whole *b*,
15: 3 it continues flowing from his *b*
15: 16 he must bathe his whole *b*
16: 4 linen undergarments next to his *b;*
21: 11 a place where there is a dead *b*.
Nu 5: 2 unclean because of a dead *b*.
5: 22 that brings a curse enter your *b*
6: 6 he must not go near a dead *b*.
6: 11 being in the presence of the dead *b*.
9: 6 unclean on account of a dead *b*.
9: 7 unclean because of a dead *b*,
9: 10 because of a dead *b* or are away
19: 11 "Whoever touches the dead *b*
19: 13 Whoever touches the dead *b*
25: 8 and into the woman's *b*.
Dt 4: 8 as this *b* of laws I am setting
21: 2 from the *b* to the neighboring
21: 3 the town nearest the *b* shall take
21: 6 town nearest the *b* shall wash their
21: 22 and his *b* is hung on a tree,
21: 23 you must not leave his *b*
Jos 8: 29 them to take his *b* from the tree
1Sa 5: 4 the threshold; only his *b* remained.
31: 10 fastened his *b* to the wall of Beth
2Sa 7: 12 who will come from your own *b*,
1Ki 13: 22 Therefore your *b* will not be buried
13: 24 his *b* was thrown down on the road
13: 25 by saw the *b* thrown down there,
13: 25 with the lion standing beside the *b*,
13: 28 The lion had neither eaten the *b*
13: 28 and found the *b* thrown
13: 29 So the prophet picked up the *b*
13: 30 Then he laid the *b* in his own tomb,
2Ki 4: 34 upon him, the boy's *b* grew warm.
6: 30 he had sackcloth on his *b*.
9: 37 Jezebel's *b* will be like refuse
13: 21 When the *b* touched Elisha's bones
13: 21 so they threw the man's *b*
23: 30 Josiah's servants brought his *b*
Ezr 8: 20 a *b* that David and the officials had
Job 4: 15 and the hair on my *b* stood on end.
7: 5 My *b* is clothed with worms
7: 15 rather than this *b* of mine.
14: 22 He feels but the pain of his own *b*
21: 6 trembling seizes my *b*.
21: 24 his *b* well nourished,
Job 30: 30 my *b* burns with fever.
Ps 16: 9 my *b* also will rest secure,
31: 9 my soul and my *b* with grief.
38: 3 wrath there is no health in my *b;*
38: 7 there is no health in my *b*.
63: 1 my *b* longs for you,
109: 18 it entered into his *b* like water,
109: 24 my *b* is thin and gaunt.
139: 16 your eyes saw my unformed *b*.
Pr 3: 8 This will bring health to your *b*
4: 22 and health to a man's whole *b*.
5: 11 when your flesh and *b* are spent.
14: 30 A heart at peace gives life to the *b*,
Ecc 11: 5 or how the *b* is formed
11: 10 and cast off the troubles of your *b*,
12: 12 and much study wearies the *b*.
SS 5: 14 His *b* is like polished ivory
Isa 17: 4 the fat of his *b* will waste away.
20: 2 Take off the sackcloth from your *b*
21: 3 At this my *b* is racked with pain,
Jer 13: 22 and your *b* mistreated.
26: 23 his *b* thrown into the burial place
36: 30 his *b* will be thrown out
Eze 1: 11 and two wings covering its *b*.
1: 23 each had two wings covering its *b*.
16: 25 your *b* with increasing promiscuity
Da 4: 33 His *b* was drenched with the dew
5: 21 his *b* was drenched with the dew
7: 11 and its *b* destroyed and thrown
10: 6 His *b* was like chrysolite, his face
Mic 6: 7 the fruit of my *b* for the sin
Hag 2: 13 contact with a dead *b* touches one
Zec 13: 6 What are these wounds on your *b?'*
Mt 5: 29 of your *b* than for your whole *b*
5: 30 *b* than for your whole *b* to go
6: 22 your whole *b* will be full of light.
6: 22 "The eye is the lamp of the *b*.
6: 23 your whole *b* will be full
6: 25 or about your *b*, what you will wear
6: 25 the *b* more important than clothes?
10: 28 afraid of those who kill the *b*
10: 28 who can destroy both soul and *b*
14: 12 and took his *b* and buried it.
15: 17 the stomach and then out of the *b?*
26: 12 she poured this perfume on my *b*,
26: 26 saying, "Take and eat; this is my *b*
26: 41 spirit is willing, but the *b* is weak."
27: 58 to Pilate, he asked for Jesus' *b*,
27: 59 Joseph took the *b*, wrapped it
27: 64 disciples may come and steal the *b*
Mk 5: 29 she felt in her *b* that she was freed
6: 29 disciples came and took his *b*
7: 19 his stomach, and then out of his *b*."
14: 8 on my *b* beforehand to prepare
14: 22 saying, "Take it; this is my *b*."
14: 38 spirit is willing, but the *b* is weak."
15: 43 to Pilate and asked for Jesus' *b*.
15: 45 was so, he gave the *b* to Joseph.
15: 46 took down the *b*, wrapped it
16: 1 go to anoint Jesus' *b*.
Lk 11: 34 Your eye is the lamp of your *b*.
11: 34 your whole *b* also is full of light.
11: 34 your *b* also is full of darkness.
11: 36 if your whole *b* is full of light,
12: 4 afraid of those who kill the *b*
12: 5 after the killing of the *b*, has power
12: 22 or about your *b*, what you will wear
12: 23 and the *b* more than clothes.
17: 37 there is a dead *b*, there the vultures
22: 19 saying, "This is my *b* given for you;
23: 52 to Pilate, he asked for Jesus' *b*.
23: 55 and how his *b* was laid in it.
24: 3 they did not find the *b*
24: 23 this morning but didn't find his *b*.
Jn 2: 21 temple he had spoken of was his *b*.
13: 10 wash his feet; his whole *b* is clean.
19: 38 he came and took the *b*.
19: 38 of Arimathea asked Pilate for the *b*
19: 40 Taking Jesus' *b*, the two
20: 12 seated where Jesus' *b* had been,
Ac 1: 18 his *b* burst open and all his
2: 26 my *b* also will live in hope,
2: 31 the grave, nor did his *b* see decay.
5: 6 wrapped up his *b*, and carried him
9: 37 and her *b* was washed
13: 36 with his fathers and his *b* decayed.
Ro 4: 19 he faced the fact that his *b* was
6: 6 crucified with him so that the *b*

Ro 6: 12 in your mortal *b* so that you obey
6: 13 Do not offer the parts of your *b*
6: 13 and offer the parts of your *b* to him
6: 19 of your *b* in slavery to impurity
7: 4 to the law through the *b* of Christ,
7: 23 at work in the members of my *b*,
7: 24 me from this *b* of death?
8: 10 your *b* is dead because of sin,
8: 13 put to death the misdeeds of the *b*,
12: 4 us has one *b* with many members,
12: 5 we who are many form one *b*,
1Co 6: 13 The *b* is not meant
6: 13 for the Lord, and the Lord for the *b*
6: 16 a prostitute is one with her in *b*?
6: 18 a man commits are outside his *b*,
6: 18 sins against his own *b*.
6: 19 not know that your *b* is a temple
6: 20 Therefore honor God with your *b*.
7: 4 The wife's *b* does not belong
7: 4 the husband's *b* does not belong
7: 34 to be devoted to the Lord in both *b*
9: 27 I beat my *b* and make it my slave
10: 16 we break a participation in the *b*
10: 17 we, who are many, are one *b*,
11: 24 "This is my *b*, which is for you;
11: 27 guilty of sinning against the *b*
11: 29 drinks without recognizing the *b*
12: 12 The *b* is a unit, though it is made up
12: 12 its parts are many, they form one *b*.
12: 13 baptized by one Spirit into one *b*—
12: 14 the *b* is not made up of one part
12: 15 a hand, I do not belong to the *b*,"
12: 15 cease to be part of the *b*
12: 16 an eye, I do not belong to the *b*,"
12: 16 cease to be part of the *b*.
12: 17 If the whole *b* were an ear,
12: 17 If the whole *b* were an eye,
12: 18 has arranged the parts in the *b*,
12: 19 where would the *b* be? As it is,
12: 20 there are many parts, but one *b*.
12: 22 those parts of the *b* that seem
12: 24 has combined the members of the *b*
12: 25 should be no division in the *b*,
12: 27 Now you are the *b* of Christ,
13: 3 and surrender my *b* to the flames,
15: 35 With what kind of *b* will they come
15: 37 you do not plant the *b* that will be,
15: 38 But God gives it a *b* as he has
15: 38 kind of seed he gives its own *b*.
15: 42 The *b* that is sown is perishable,
15: 44 a natural *b*, it is raised a spiritual *b*.
15: 44 natural *b*, there is also a spiritual *b*.
2Co 4: 10 Jesus may also be revealed in our *b*.
4: 10 around in our *b* the death of Jesus,
4: 11 may be revealed in our mortal *b*.
5: 6 are at home in the *b* we are away
5: 8 would prefer to be away from the *b*
5: 9 whether we are at home in the *b*
5: 10 for the things done while in the *b*,
7: 1 everything that contaminates *b*
7: 5 came into Macedonia, this *b*
12: 2 Whether it was in the *b*
12: 2 or out of the *b* I do not know—
12: 3 in the *b* or apart from the *b* I do not
Gal 2: 20 The life I live in the *b*, I live by faith
6: 17 bear on my *b* the marks of Jesus.
Eph 1: 23 which is his *b*, the fullness
2: 11 in the *b* by the hands of men)—
2: 16 and in this one *b* to reconcile both
3: 6 members together of one *b*,
4: 4 There is one *b* and one Spirit—
4: 12 so that the *b* of Christ may be built
4: 16 From him the whole *b*, joined
4: 25 for we are all members of one *b*.
5: 23 his *b*, of which he is the Savior.
5: 29 no one ever hated his own *b*,
5: 30 for we are members of his *b*.
Php 1: 20 Christ will be exalted in my *b*,
1: 22 If I am to go on living in the *b*,
1: 24 for you that I remain in the *b*.
3: 21 that they will be like his glorious *b*.
Col 1: 18 And he is the head of the *b*,
1: 22 you by Christ's physical *b*
1: 24 sake of his *b*, which is the church.
2: 5 though I am absent from you in *b*,
2: 19 from whom the whole *b*, supported
2: 23 and their harsh treatment of the *b*,
3: 15 members of one *b* you were called
1Th 4: 4 learn to control his own *b*
5: 23 *b* be kept blameless at the coming
1Ti 3: 16 He appeared in a *b*,
4: 14 when the *b* of elders laid their
Heb 7: 10 still in the *b* of his ancestor.
10: 5 but a *b* you prepared for me;
10: 10 of the *b* of Jesus Christ once
10: 20 his *b*, and since we have a great
Jas 2: 26 As the *b* without the spirit is dead,
3: 2 able to keep his whole *b* in check.
3: 5 the tongue is a small part of the *b*,
3: 6 of evil among the parts of the *b*.
1Pe 2: 24 sins in his *b* on the tree,
3: 18 He was put to death in the *b*
3: 21 not the removal of dirt from the *b*
4: 1 since Christ suffered in his *b*,
4: 1 suffered in his *b* is done with sin.
4: 6 to men in regard to the *b*,
2Pe 1: 13 as long as I live in the tent of this *b*,
Jude : 9 with the devil about the *b* of Moses

BODYGUARD (GUARD)

1Sa 22: 14 of your *b* and highly respected
28: 2 I will make you my *b* for life."
2Sa 23: 23 David put him in charge of his *b*.
1Ch 11: 25 David put him in charge of his *b*.

BOHAN

Jos 15: 6 to the Stone of *B* son of Reuben.
18: 17 to the Stone of *B* son of Reuben.

BOIL (BOILED BOILING BOILS)

Ex 16: 23 to bake and *b* what you want to *b*.
Lev 13: 18 "When someone has a *b* on his skin
13: 19 and in the place where the *b* was,
13: 20 has broken out where the *b* was.
13: 23 it is only a scar from the *b*,
2Ki 20: 7 They did so and applied it to the *b*,
Isa 38: 21 of figs and apply it to the *b*,
64: 2 and causes water to *b*,
Eze 24: 5 bring it to a *b*

BOILED (BOIL)

Nu 6: 19 in his hands a *b* shoulder of the ram
1Sa 2: 13 and while the meat was being *b*,
2: 15 he won't accept *b* meat from you,
2Ch 35: 13 and *b* the holy offerings in pots,

BOILING (BOIL)

Job 41: 20 as from a *b* pot over a fire of reeds.
41: 31 the depths churn like a *b* caldron
Jer 1: 13 "I see a *b* pot, tilting away

BOILS (BOIL)

Ex 9: 9 festering *b* will break out on men
9: 10 and festering *b* broke out on men
9: 11 because of the *b* that were on them
Dt 28: 27 you with the *b* of Egypt
28: 35 with painful *b* that cannot be cured

BOKERU

1Ch 8: 38 Azrikam, *B*, Ishmael, Sheariah,
9: 44 Azrikam, *B*, Ishmael, Sheariah,

BOKIM

Jdg 2: 1 LORD went up from Gilgal to *B*
2: 5 and they called that place *B*.

BOLD (BOLDNESS EMBOLDENED)

Ge 18: 27 "Now that I have been so *b*
18: 31 "Now that I have been so *b*
Ps 138: 3 you made me *b* and stouthearted.
Pr 21: 29 A wicked man puts up a *b* front,
28: 1 but the righteous are as *b* as a lion.
2Co 3: 12 we have such a hope, we are very *b*.
10: 1 face with you, but "*b*" when away!
10: 2 I come I may not have to be as *b*
Phm : 8 although in Christ I could be *b*
2Pe 2: 10 *B* and arrogant, these men are not

BOLDNESS (BOLD)

Ac 4: 29 to speak your word with great *b*.

BOLT (BOLTED BOLTS)

2Sa 13: 17 of here and *b* the door after her."

BOLTED (BOLT)

2Sa 13: 18 servant put her out and *b* the door

BOLTS (BOLT)

Dt 33: 25 The *b* of your gates will be iron
2Sa 22: 13 *b* of lightning blazed forth.
22: 15 *b* of lightning and routed them.
Ne 3: 3 and put its doors and *b* and bars
3: 6 and put its doors and *b* and bars
3: 13 and put its doors and *b* and bars
3: 14 and put its doors and *b* and bars
3: 15 and putting its doors and *b*
Job 38: 35 Do you send the lightning *b*
Ps 18: 12 with hailstones and *b* of lightning.
18: 14 great *b* of lightning and routed
78: 48 their livestock to *b* of lightning.

BOND (BONDS)

Eze 20: 37 you into the *b* of the covenant.
Ac 17: 9 the others post *b* and let them go.
Eph 4: 3 of the Spirit through the *b* of peace.

BONDAGE

Ge 47: 19 and we with our land will be in *b*
47: 25 we will be in *b* to Pharaoh."
Ex 6: 9 their discouragement and cruel *b*.
Ezr 9: 8 our eyes and a little relief in our *b*.
9: 9 God has not deserted us in our *b*.
Isa 14: 3 suffering and turmoil and cruel *b*,
Jer 34: 9 was to hold a fellow Jew in *b*.
34: 10 and no longer hold them in *b*.
Ro 8: 21 liberated from its *b* to decay

BONDS (BOND)

Jer 2: 20 and tore off your *b*;
5: 5 and torn off the *b*.
30: 8 and will tear off their *b*;
Hos 10: 10 to put them in *b* for their double sin

BONE (BONES)

Ge 2: 23 "This is now *b* of my bones
Nu 19: 16 or anyone who touches a human *b*
19: 18 who has touched a human *b*
Pr 25: 15 and a gentle tongue can break a *b*.
Eze 37: 7 and the bones came together, *b* to *b*
39: 15 and one of them sees a human *b*,

BONES (BONE)

Ge 2: 23 "This is now bone of my *b*
50: 25 and then you must carry my *b* up
Ex 12: 46 Do not break any of the *b*.
13: 19 Moses took the *b* of Joseph
13: 19 and then you must carry my *b* up
Nu 9: 12 it till morning or break any of its *b*.
24: 8 and break their *b* in pieces;
Jos 24: 32 Joseph's *b*, which the Israelites had
1Sa 31: 13 Then they took their *b*
2Sa 21: 12 he went and took the *b* of Saul
21: 13 David brought the *b* of Saul
21: 13 the *b* of those who had been killed
21: 14 They buried the *b* of Saul
1Ki 13: 2 and human *b* will be burned on you
13: 31 is buried; lay my *b* beside his *b*.
2Ki 13: 21 When the body touched Elisha's *b*,
23: 14 covered the sites with human *b*.
23: 16 he had the *b* removed from them
23: 18 So they spared his *b* and those
23: 18 "Don't let anyone disturb his *b*."
23: 20 and burned human *b* on them.
1Ch 10: 12 Then they buried their *b*
2Ch 34: 5 He burned the *b* of the priests
Job 2: 5 hand and strike his flesh and *b*,
4: 14 and made all my *b* shake.
10: 11 knit me together with *b* and sinews
19: 20 I am nothing but skin and *b*;
20: 11 The youthful vigor that fills his *b*
21: 24 his *b* rich with marrow.
30: 17 Night pierces my *b*;
33: 19 pain with constant distress in his *b*,
33: 21 his *b*, once hidden, now stick out.
40: 18 His *b* are tubes of bronze,
Ps 6: 2 heal me, for my *b* are in agony.
22: 14 and all my *b* are out of joint.
22: 17 I can count all my *b*;
31: 10 and my *b* grow weak.
32: 3 my *b* wasted away
34: 20 he protects all his *b*,
38: 3 my *b* have no soundness
42: 10 My *b* suffer mortal agony
51: 8 let the *b* you have crushed rejoice.
53: 5 God scattered the *b*

Ps 102: 3 my *b* burn like glowing embers.
102: 5 I am reduced to skin and *b*.
109: 18 into his *b* like oil.
141: 7 so our *b* have been scattered
Pr 3: 8 and nourishment to your *b*.
12: 4 wife is like decay in his *b*.
14: 30 but envy rots the *b*.
15: 30 and good news gives health to the *b*
16: 24 to the soul and healing to the *b*.
17: 22 but a crushed spirit dries up the *b*.
Isa 38: 13 but like a lion he broke all my *b*;
Jer 8: 1 and the *b* of the people
8: 1 the *b* of the kings and officials
8: 1 the *b* of the priests and prophets,
20: 9 shut up in my *b*.
23: 9 all my *b* tremble.
50: 17 the last to crush his *b*
La 1: 13 sent it down into my *b*.
3: 4 and has broken my *b*.
4: 8 Their skin has shriveled on their *b*;
Eze 6: 5 and I will scatter your *b*
24: 4 Fill it with the best of these *b*;
24: 5 Pile wood beneath it for the *b*;
24: 5 and cook the *b* in it.
24: 10 and let the *b* be charred.
32: 27 for their sins rested on their *b*,
37: 1 middle of a valley; it was full of *b*.
37: 2 I saw a great many *b* on the floor
37: 2 of the valley, *b* that were very dry.
37: 3 "Son of man, can these *b* live?"
37: 4 Dry *b*, hear the word of the LORD
37: 4 "Prophesy to these *b* and say
37: 5 Sovereign LORD says to these *b*:
37: 7 sound, and the *b* came together,
37: 11 'Our *b* are dried up and our hope is
37: 11 these *b* are the whole house
Da 6: 24 them and crushed all their *b*.
Am 2: 1 the *b* of Edom's king,
3: 12 only two leg *b* or a piece of an ear,
Mic 3: 2 and the flesh from their *b*;
3: 3 and break their *b* in pieces;
Hab 3: 16 decay crept into my *b*,
Mt 23: 27 the inside are full of dead men's *b*
Lk 24: 39 a ghost does not have flesh and *b*,
Jn 19: 36 "Not one of his *b* will be broken,"
Heb 11: 22 and gave instructions about his *b*.

BOOK (BOOKS)

Ex 24: 7 he took the *B* of the Covenant
32: 32 out of the *b* you have written."
32: 33 against me I will blot out of my *b*.
Nu 21: 14 That is why the *B* of the Wars
Dt 28: 58 which are written in this *b*,
28: 61 recorded in this *B* of the Law
29: 20 written in this *b* will fall upon him,
29: 21 written in this *B* of the Law.
29: 27 on it all the curses written in this *b*.
30: 10 written in this *B* of the Law
31: 24 writing in a *b* the words of this law
31: 26 "Take this *B* of the Law
Jos 1: 8 Do not let this *B* of the Law depart
8: 31 in the *B* of the Law of Moses—
8: 34 as it is written in the *B* of the Law.
10: 13 as it is written in the *B* of Jashar.
23: 6 in the *B* of the Law of Moses,
24: 26 things in the *B* of the Law of God.
2Sa 1: 18 written in the *B* of Jashar):
1Ki 11: 41 in the *b* of the annals of Solomon?
14: 19 are written in the *b* of the annals
14: 29 written in the *b* of the annals
15: 7 written in the *b* of the annals
15: 23 written in the *b* of the annals
15: 31 written in the *b* of the annals
16: 5 written in the *b* of the annals
16: 14 written in the *b* of the annals
16: 20 written in the *b* of the annals
16: 27 written in the *b* of the annals
22: 39 written in the *b* of the annals
22: 45 written in the *b* of the annals
2Ki 1: 18 written in the *b* of the annals
8: 23 written in the *b* of the annals
10: 34 written in the *b* of the annals
12: 19 written in the *b* of the annals
13: 8 written in the *b* of the annals
13: 12 written in the *b* of the annals
14: 6 written in the *B* of the Law
14: 15 written in the *b* of the annals
14: 18 written in the *b* of the annals
2Ki 14: 28 written in the *b* of the annals
15: 6 written in the *b* of the annals
15: 11 in the *b* of the annals of the kings
15: 15 are written in the *b* of the annals
15: 21 written in the *b* of the annals
15: 26 are written in the *b* of the annals
15: 31 written in the *b* of the annals
15: 36 written in the *b* of the annals
16: 19 written in the *b* of the annals
20: 20 written in the *b* of the annals
21: 17 written in the *b* of the annals
21: 25 written in the *b* of the annals
22: 8 "I have found the *B* of the Law
22: 10 Hilkiah the priest has given me a *b*
22: 11 the words of the *B* of the Law,
22: 13 in this *b* that has been found.
22: 13 not obeyed the words of this *b*;
22: 16 everything written in the *b* the king
23: 2 words of the *B* of the Covenant,
23: 3 of the covenant written in this *b*.
23: 21 written in this *B* of the Covenant."
23: 24 in the *b* that Hilkiah the priest had
23: 28 written in the *b* of the annals
24: 5 written in the *b* of the annals
1Ch 9: 1 in the *b* of the kings of Israel.
27: 24 in the *b* of the annals of King David
2Ch 16: 11 are written in the *b* of the kings
17: 9 taking with them the *B* of the Law
20: 34 recorded in the *b* of the kings
24: 27 annotations on the *b* of the kings.
25: 4 in the *B* of Moses, where
25: 26 in the *b* of the kings of Judah
27: 7 are written in the *b* of the kings
28: 26 are written in the *b* of the kings
32: 32 son of Amoz in the *b* of the kings
34: 14 Hilkiah the priest found the *B*
34: 15 "I have found the *B* of the Law
34: 16 Shaphan took the *b* to the king
34: 18 Hilkiah the priest has given me a *b*
34: 21 in this *b* that has been found.
34: 21 with all that is written in this *b*."
34: 24 written in the *b* that has been read
34: 30 words of the *B* of the Covenant,
34: 31 of the covenant written in this *b*.
35: 12 as is written in the *B* of Moses.
35: 27 are written in the *b* of the kings
36: 8 are written in the *b* of the kings
Ezr 6: 18 to what is written in the *B* of Moses
Ne 8: 1 scribe to bring out the *B* of the Law
8: 3 attentively to the *B* of the Law.
8: 5 Ezra opened the *b*.
8: 8 They read from the *B* of the Law
8: 18 Ezra read from the *B* of the Law
9: 3 and read from the *B* of the Law
12: 23 recorded in the *b* of the annals.
13: 1 On that day the *B*
Est 2: 23 recorded in the *b* of the annals
6: 1 so he ordered the *b*
10: 2 written in the *b* of the annals
Ps 69: 28 May they be blotted out of the *b*
139: 16 were written in your *b*
Jer 25: 13 all that are written in this *b*
30: 2 in a *b* all the words I have spoken
Da 10: 21 tell you what is written in the *B*
12: 1 name is found written in the *b*—
Na 1: 1 The *b* of the vision
Mk 12: 26 have you not read in the *b*
Lk 3: 4 As is written in the *b* of the words
20: 42 declares in the *B* of Psalms:
Jn 20: 30 which are not recorded in this *b*.
Ac 1: 1 In my former *b*, Theophilus,
1: 20 "it is written in the *b* of Psalms,
7: 42 written in the *b* of the prophets:
8: 28 sitting in his chariot reading the *b*
Gal 3: 10 written in the *B* of the Law."
Php 4: 3 whose names are in the *b* of life.
Rev 3: 5 never erase his name from the *b*
13: 8 written in the *b* of life belonging
17: 8 in the *b* of life from the creation
20: 12 *b* was opened, which is the *b*
20: 15 was not found written in the *b*
21: 27 written in the Lamb's *b* of life.
22: 7 words of the prophecy in this *b*."
22: 9 of all who keep the words of this *b*.
22: 10 the words of the prophecy of this *b*,
22: 18 him the plagues described in this *b*.
22: 18 the words of the prophecy of this *b*:
22: 19 away from this *b* of prophecy,
Rev 22: 19 which are described in this *b*.

BOOKS (BOOK)

Ecc 12: 12 Of making many *b* there is no end,
Da 7: 10 and the *b* were opened.
Jn 21: 25 for the *b* that would be written.
Rev 20: 12 the throne, and *b* were opened.
20: 12 they had done as recorded in the *b*.

BOOSTING

Am 8: 5 *b* the price

BOOT

Isa 9: 5 Every warrior's *b* used in battle

BOOTH (BOOTHS)

Mt 9: 9 sitting at the tax collector's *b*.
Mk 2: 14 sitting at the tax collector's *b*.
Lk 5: 27 name of Levi sitting at his tax *b*.

BOOTHS (BOOTH)

Lev 23: 42 Israelites are to live in *b*
23: 42 in *b* for seven days: All native-born
23: 43 live in *b* when I brought them out
Ne 8: 14 were to live in *b* during the feast
8: 15 to make *b*"—as it is written.
8: 16 and built themselves *b*
8: 17 that had returned from exile built *b*

BOOTY

2Ch 14: 14 since there was much *b* there.
Jer 49: 32 and their large herds will be *b*.

BOR ASHAN

1Sa 30: 30 to those in Hormah, *B*, Athach and

BORDER (BORDERED BORDERING BORDERS)

Ge 25: 18 near the *b* of Egypt, as you go
49: 13 his *b* will extend toward Sidon.
Ex 16: 35 until they reached the *b* of Canaan.
Nu 20: 23 At Mount Hor, near the *b* of Edom
21: 13 The Arnon is the *b* of Moab,
21: 15 and lie along the *b* of Moab."
21: 24 because their *b* was fortified.
22: 36 the Moabite town on the Arnon *b*,
33: 37 at Mount Hor, on the *b* of Edom.
33: 44 at Iye Abarim, on the *b* of Moab.
34: 3 Desert of Zin along the *b* of Edom.
Dt 3: 14 as far as the *b* of the Geshurites
3: 16 middle of the gorge being the *b*)
3: 16 which is the *b* of the Ammonites.
3: 17 Its western *b* was the Jordan
Jos 4: 19 Gilgal on the eastern *b* of Jericho.
12: 2 which is the *b* of the Ammonites.
12: 5 all of Bashan to the *b* of the people
12: 5 of Gilead to the *b* of Sihon king
13: 10 out to the *b* of the Ammonites.
16: 8 From Tappuah the *b* went west
22: 11 altar on the *b* of Canaan at Geliloth
Jdg 7: 22 *b* of Abel Meholah near Tabbath.
11: 18 of Moab, for the Arnon was its *b*.
1Sa 6: 12 followed them as far as the *b*
10: 2 at Zelzah on the *b* of Benjamin.
2Sa 13: 23 Baal Hazor near the *b* of Ephraim,
1Ki 4: 21 of the Philistines, as far as the *b*
2Ki 3: 21 called up and stationed on the *b*.
2Ch 9: 26 of the Philistines, as far as the *b*
26: 8 and his fame spread as far as the *b*
Ps 78: 54 to the *b* of his holy land,
Isa 15: 8 echoes along the *b* of Moab;
19: 19 a monument to the LORD at its *b*.
Eze 29: 10 to Aswan, as far as the *b* of Cush.
45: 7 to the eastern *b* parallel to one
47: 16 lies on the *b* between Damascus
47: 16 which is on the *b* of Hauran.
47: 17 along the northern *b* of Damascus,
47: 17 with the *b* of Hamath to the north.
48: 1 northern *b* of Damascus next to
48: 1 part of its *b* from the east side
48: 2 it will *b* the territory of Dan
48: 3 it will *b* the territory of Asher
48: 4 it will *b* the territory of Naphtali
48: 5 it will *b* the territory of Manasseh
48: 6 it will *b* the territory of Ephraim
48: 7 it will *b* the territory of Reuben
48: 21 the 25,000 cubits to the western *b*.
48: 21 the sacred portion to the eastern *b*,

Eze 48: 22 lie between the *b* of Judah
48: 22 of Judah and the *b* of Benjamin.
48: 24 it will *b* the territory of Benjamin
48: 25 it will *b* the territory of Simeon
48: 26 it will *b* the territory of Issachar
48: 27 it will *b* the territory of Zebulun
Ob : 7 your allies will force you to the *b;*
Lk 17: 11 along the *b* between Samaria
Ac 16: 7 When they came to the *b* of Mysia,

BORDERED (BORDER)

Jos 17: 10 reached the sea and *b* Asher

BORDERING (BORDER)

Eze 45: 7 will have the land *b* each side
48: 8 "*B* the territory of Judah from east
48: 12 *b* the territory of the Levites.
48: 18 *b* on the sacred portion

BORDERLAND (LAND)

1Sa 13: 18 the third toward the *b* overlooking

BORDERS (BORDER)

Ge 10: 19 and the *b* of Canaan reached
23: 17 all the trees within the *b* of the field
Ex 13: 7 be seen anywhere within your *b.*
23: 31 "I will establish your *b*
1Ch 7: 29 Along the *b* of Manasseh
Ps 147: 14 He grants peace to your *b*
Isa 26: 15 you have extended all the *b*
60: 18 ruin or destruction within your *b,*
Eze 11: 10 judgment on you at the *b* of Israel.
11: 11 judgment on you at the *b* of Israel.
Am 1: 13 Gilead in order to extend his *b,*
Mic 5: 6 and marches into our *b.*
Zec 9: 2 upon Hamath too, which *b* on it,
Mal 1: 5 even beyond the *b* of Israel!'

BORE (BEAR)

Ge 16: 15 So Hagar *b* Abram a son,
16: 16 old when Hagar *b* him Ishmael.
21: 2 *b* a son to Abraham in his old age,
21: 3 Isaac to the son Sarah *b* him.
22: 23 Milcah *b* these eight sons
24: 24 the son that Milcah *b* to Nahor."
24: 47 of Nahor, whom Milcah *b* to him.'
25: 2 She *b* him Zimran, Jokshan,
25: 12 Hagar the Egyptian, *b* to Abraham.
30: 5 became pregnant and *b* him a son.
30: 7 conceived again and *b* Jacob
30: 10 Leah's servant Zilpah *b* Jacob a son
30: 12 Leah's servant Zilpah *b* Jacob
30: 17 became pregnant and *b* Jacob
30: 19 conceived again and *b* Jacob
30: 39 they *b* young that were streaked
31: 8 then all the flocks *b* streaked young
31: 39 by wild beasts; I *b* the loss myself.
36: 4 Adah *b* Eliphaz to Esau, Basemath
36: 4 Basemath *b* Reuel,
36: 5 and Oholibamah *b* Jeush, Jalam
36: 12 named Timna, who *b* him Amalek.
36: 14 whom she *b* to Esau: Jeush,
44: 27 know that my wife *b* me two sons.
46: 15 These were the sons Leah *b*
Ex 6: 20 who *b* him Aaron and Moses.
6: 23 and she *b* him Nadab and Abihu,
6: 25 of Putiel, and she *b* him Phinehas.
Nu 26: 59 To Amram she *b* Aaron, Moses
Jdg 8: 31 lived in Shechem, also *b* him a son,
11: 2 Gilead's wife also *b* him sons,
Ru 4: 12 whom Tamar *b* to Judah."
1Sa 20: 30 shame of the mother who *b* you?
2Sa 11: 27 became his wife and *b* him a son.
1Ki 11: 20 of Tahpenes *b* him a son named
14: 28 temple, the guards *b* the shields,
1Ch 2: 4 Judah's daughter-in-law, *b* him
2: 19 married Ephrath, who *b* him Hur.
2: 21 years old), and she *b* him Segub.
2: 24 of Hezron *b* him Ashhur the father
2: 29 who *b* him Ahban and Molid.
2: 35 servant Jarha, and she *b* him Attai.
4: 6 Naarah *b* him Ahuzzam, Hepher,
2Ch 11: 19 She *b* him sons: Jeush, Shemariah
11: 20 who *b* him Abijah, Attai, Ziza
Pr 17: 25 bitterness to the one who *b* him.
SS 6: 9 the favorite of the one who *b* her.
Isa 49: 21 'Who *b* me these?
51: 18 Of all the sons she *b*
Isa 53: 12 For he *b* the sin of many,
54: 1 you who never *b* a child;
Jer 20: 14 the day my mother *b* me not be
31: 19 I *b* the disgrace of my youth.'
Eze 16: 20 and daughters whom you *b* to me
23: 37 whom they *b* to me, as food
Hos 1: 3 and she conceived and *b* him a son.
Lk 23: 29 the wombs that never *b*
Ro 7: 5 so that we *b* fruit for death.
9: 22 *b* with great patience the objects
Heb 13: 13 camp, bearing the disgrace he *b.*
1Pe 2: 24 He himself *b* our sins in his body
Rev 17: 6 of those who *b* testimony to Jesus.

BORED (BORE)

2Ki 12: 9 the priest took a chest and *b* a hole

BORN (BEAR)

Ge 4: 18 To Enoch was *b* Irad, and Irad was
5: 4 After Seth was *b,* Adam lived 800
5: 30 After Noah was *b,* Lamech lived
6: 1 and daughters were *b* to them,
10: 21 Sons were also *b* to Shem,
10: 25 Two sons were *b* to Eber: One was
14: 14 he called out the 318 trained men *b*
17: 12 those *b* in your household
17: 13 Whether *b* in your household
17: 17 "Will a son be *b* to a man
17: 23 and all those *b* in his household
17: 27 including those *b* in his household
21: 5 when his son Isaac was *b* to him.
35: 26 *b* to him in Paddan Aram.
36: 5 who were *b* to him in Canaan.
37: 3 he had been *b* to him in his old age;
41: 50 two sons were *b* to Joseph
44: 20 and there is a young son *b* to him
46: 18 These were the children *b* to Jacob
46: 20 and Ephraim were *b* to Joseph
46: 22 of Rachel who were *b* to Jacob—
46: 25 These were the sons *b* to Jacob
46: 27 With the two sons who had been *b*
48: 5 your two sons *b* to you in Egypt
48: 6 Any children *b* to you
Ex 1: 22 Every boy that is *b* you must throw
12: 48 then he may take part like one *b*
23: 12 and the slave *b* in your household,
Lev 18: 9 she was *b* in the same home
18: 11 *b* to your father; she is your sister.
22: 11 or if a slave is *b* in his household,
22: 27 When a cow, a sheep or a goat is *b,*
25: 45 of their clans *b* in your country,
Nu 26: 59 who was *b* to the Levites in Egypt.
Dt 23: 2 No one *b* of a forbidden marriage
23: 8 The third generation of children *b*
Jos 5: 5 but all the people *b* in the desert
Jdg 13: 8 to bring up the boy who is to be *b.*"
18: 29 their forefather Dan, who was *b*
2Sa 3: 2 Sons were *b* to David in Hebron:
3: 5 These were *b* to David in Hebron.
5: 13 and daughters were *b* to him.
5: 14 of the children *b* to him there:
12: 14 show utter contempt, the son *b*
14: 27 and a daughter were *b* to Absalom.
1Ki 1: 6 and was *b* next after Absalom.)
3: 18 The third day after my child was *b,*
13: 2 'A son named Josiah will be *b*
2Ki 20: 18 that will be *b* to you, will be taken
1Ch 1: 19 Two sons were *b* to Eber: One was
1: 32 The sons *b* to Keturah, Abraham's
2: 3 These three were *b* to him
2: 9 The sons *b* to Hezron were:
3: 1 sons of David *b* to him in Hebron:
3: 4 These six were *b* to David
3: 5 and these were the children *b*
8: 8 Sons were *b* to Shaharaim in Moab
14: 4 of the children *b* to him there:
Job 3: 3 the night it was said, 'A boy is *b!*'
5: 7 Yet man is *b* to trouble
8: 9 for we were *b* only yesterday
11: 12 wild donkey's colt can be *b* a man.
14: 1 "Man *b* of woman
15: 7 "Are you the first man ever *b?*
15: 14 one *b* of woman, that he could be
25: 4 How can one *b* of woman be pure?
38: 21 for you were already *b!*
Ps 78: 6 even the children yet to be *b,*
87: 4 'This one was *b* in Zion.'"
87: 5 This one and that one were *b* in her
Ps 87: 6 "This one was *b* in Zion."
90: 2 Before the mountains were *b*
127: 4 are sons *b* in one's youth.
Pr 17: 17 and a brother is *b* for adversity.
Ecc 2: 7 and had other slaves who were *b*
3: 2 a time to be *b* and a time to die,
4: 14 or he may have been *b* in poverty
Isa 9: 6 For to us a child is *b,*
39: 7 and blood who will be *b* to you,
49: 1 Before I was *b* the LORD called
49: 20 *b* during your bereavement
66: 8 Can a country be *b* in a day
Jer 1: 5 before you were *b* I set you apart;
16: 3 and daughters *b* in this land
20: 14 Cursed be the day I was *b!*
20: 15 "A child is *b* to you—a son!"
22: 26 where neither of you was *b,*
Eze 16: 4 the day you were *b* your cord was
16: 5 day you were *b* you were despised.
Hos 2: 3 as bare as on the day she was *b;*
Zec 13: 3 to whom he was *b,* will say to him,
Mt 1: 16 of whom was *b* Jesus, who is called
2: 1 After Jesus was *b* in Bethlehem
2: 2 is the one who has been *b* king
2: 4 them where the Christ was to be *b.*
11: 11 Among those *b* of women there has
19: 12 because they were *b* that way;
26: 24 for him if he had not been *b.*"
Mk 7: 26 The woman was a Greek, *b*
14: 21 for him if he had not been *b.*"
Lk 1: 35 one to be *b* will be called the Son
2: 6 the time came for the baby to be *b,*
2: 11 of David a Savior has been *b* to you
7: 28 among those *b* of women there is
Jn 1: 13 children *b* not of natural descent,
1: 13 or a husband's will, but *b* of God.
3: 3 a man is *b* again, he cannot see
3: 4 How can a man be *b* when he is old
3: 4 into his mother's womb to be *b!*"
3: 5 unless a man is *b* of water
3: 7 at my saying, 'You must be *b* again
3: 8 It is with everyone *b* of the Spirit."
8: 58 "before Abraham was *b,* I am!"
9: 2 his parents, that he was *b* blind?"
9: 19 Is this the one you say was *b* blind?
9: 20 "and we know he was *b* blind.
9: 32 opening the eyes of a man *b* blind
16: 21 because of her joy that a child is *b*
16: 21 but when her baby is *b* she forgets
18: 37 In fact, for this reason I was *b,*
Ac 7: 20 "At that time Moses was *b,*
22: 3 "I am a Jew, *b* in Tarsus of Cilicia,
22: 28 But I was *b* a citizen," Paul replied.
Ro 9: 11 before the twins were *b*
1Co 11: 12 so also man is *b* of woman.
15: 8 also, as to one abnormally *b.*
Gal 4: 4 *b* of a woman, *b* under law,
4: 23 his son by the free woman was *b*
4: 23 son by the slave woman was *b*
4: 29 At that time the son *b*
4: 29 ordinary way persecuted the son *b*
Heb 11: 23 for three months after he was *b,*
1Pe 1: 23 For you have been *b* again,
2Pe 2: 12 *b* only to be caught and destroyed,
1Jn 2: 29 who does what is right has been *b*
3: 9 No one who is *b* of God will
3: 9 because he has been *b* of God.
4: 7 Everyone who loves has been *b*
5: 1 believes that Jesus is the Christ is *b*
5: 4 for everyone *b* of God overcomes
5: 18 We know that anyone *b*
5: 18 the one who was *b*
Rev 12: 4 her child the moment it was *b.*

BORNE (BEAR)

Ge 16: 1 Abram's wife, had *b* him no
16: 15 Ishmael to the son she had *b.*
21: 7 Yet I have *b* him a son
21: 9 whom Hagar the Egyptian had *b*
22: 20 she has *b* sons to your brother
24: 36 master's wife Sarah has *b* him a son
29: 34 because I have *b* him three sons."
30: 20 because I have *b* him six sons."
31: 43 or about the children they have *b?*
34: 1 the daughter Leah had *b* to Jacob,
1Sa 2: 5 was barren has *b* seven children,
2Sa 12: 15 the child that Uriah's wife had *b*
21: 8 daughter Rizpah, whom she had *b*

2Sa 21: 8 whom she had *b* to Adriel son
1Ki 3: 21 I saw that it wasn't the son I had *b*
Ps 18: 42 fine as dust *b* on the wind;
Isa 46: 1 their idols are *b* by beasts of burden
49: 15 compassion on the child she has *b?*
Hag 2: 19 and the olive tree have not *b* fruit.
Mt 20: 12 equal to us who have *b* the burden
1Co 15: 49 as we have *b* the likeness

BORROW (BORROWED BORROWER BORROWS)

Dt 15: 6 lend to many nations but will *b*
28: 12 lend to many nations but will *b*
Ne 5: 4 "We have had to *b* money
Ps 37: 21 The wicked *b* and do not repay,
Mt 5: 42 away from the one who wants to *b*

BORROWED (BORROW)

2Ki 6: 5 "it was *b!*" The man of God asked,
Jer 15: 10 I have neither lent nor *b*,

BORROWER (BORROW)

Ex 22: 15 the *b* will not have to pay.
Pr 22: 7 and the *b* is servant to the lender.
Isa 24: 2 for *b* as for lender,

BORROWS (BORROW)

Ex 22: 14 "If a man *b* an animal

BOSOM (BOSOMS)

Pr 5: 20 Why embrace the *b*
Eze 23: 8 caressed her virgin *b* and poured
23: 21 when in Egypt your *b* was caressed

BOSOMS (BOSOM)

Eze 23: 3 and their virgin *b* caressed.

BOTHER (BOTHERING)

2Sa 14: 10 and he will not *b* you again."
Mk 5: 35 "Why *b* the teacher any more?"
Lk 8: 49 "Don't *b* the teacher any more."
11: 7 one inside answers, 'Don't *b* me.

BOTHERING (BOTHER)

Mt 26: 10 "Why are you *b* this woman?
Mk 14: 6 "Why are you *b* her? She has done
Lk 18: 5 yet because this widow keeps *b* me,

BOTTLED-UP

Job 32: 19 inside I am like *b* wine,

BOTTLES

Isa 3: 20 the perfume *b* and charms,

BOUGHS

Ps 80: 11 It sent out its *b* to the Sea,
118: 27 With *b* in hand, join
Isa 10: 33 will lop off the *b* with great power.
17: 6 four or five on the fruitful *b*,"
Eze 17: 6 branches and put out leafy *b*.
31: 5 its *b* increased
31: 6 nested in its *b*,
31: 7 with its spreading *b*,
31: 8 equal its *b*,
31: 12 Its *b* fell on the mountains

BOUGHT (BUY)

Ge 17: 12 *b* with money from a foreigner—
17: 13 born in your household or *b*
17: 23 born in his household or *b*
17: 27 born in his household or *b*
25: 10 the field Abraham had *b*
33: 19 he *b* from the sons of Hamor,
39: 1 *b* him from the Ishmaelites who
47: 20 So Joseph *b* all the land in Egypt
47: 23 "Now that I have *b* you
49: 30 which Abraham *b* as a burial place
49: 32 cave in it were *b* from the Hittites."
50: 13 which Abraham had *b*
Ex 12: 44 Any slave you have *b* may eat of it
15: 16 until the people you *b* pass by.
Lev 27: 22 to the LORD a field he has *b*,
27: 24 to the person from whom he *b* it,
Jos 24: 32 the tract of land that Jacob *b*
Ru 4: 9 you are witnesses that I have *b*
2Sa 12: 3 one little ewe lamb he had *b*.
24: 24 So David *b* the threshing floor
1Ki 16: 24 He *b* the hill of Samaria
Ne 5: 8 we have *b* back our Jewish brothers
Job 28: 15 It cannot be *b* with the finest gold,
28: 16 It cannot be *b* with the gold
28: 19 it cannot be *b* with pure gold.
Ecc 2: 7 I *b* male and female slaves
Isa 43: 24 You have not *b* any fragrant
Jer 13: 2 So I *b* a belt, as the LORD directed
13: 4 the belt you *b* and are wearing
32: 9 so I *b* the field at Anathoth
32: 15 and vineyards will again be *b*
32: 43 Once more fields will be *b*
32: 44 Fields will be *b* for silver,
Eze 27: 19 from Uzal *b* your merchandise;
Hos 3: 2 I *b* her for fifteen shekels of silver
Mt 13: 44 and sold all he had and *b* that field.
13: 46 sold everything he had and *b* it.
Mk 15: 46 So Joseph *b* some linen cloth,
16: 1 Salome *b* spices so that they might
Lk 14: 18 The first said, 'I have just *b* a field,
14: 19 'I have just *b* five yoke of oxen,
Ac 1: 18 Judas *b* a field; there he fell
7: 16 in the tomb that Abraham had *b*
20: 28 which he *b* with his own blood.
1Co 6: 20 You are not your own; you were *b*
7: 23 You were *b* at a price; do not
2Pe 2: 1 the sovereign Lord who *b* them—

BOULDER

Rev 18: 21 mighty angel picked up a *b* the size

BOUND (BIND)

Ge 22: 9 He *b* his son Isaac and laid him
42: 24 from them and *b* before their eyes.
44: 30 whose life is closely *b* up
Jdg 15: 13 So they *b* him with two new ropes
1Sa 14: 24 because Saul had *b* the people
14: 27 that his father had *b* the people
14: 28 "Your father *b* the army
25: 29 life of my master will be *b* securely
2Sa 3: 34 Your hands were not *b*,
2Ki 25: 7 *b* him with bronze shackles
2Ch 33: 11 *b* him with bronze shackles
36: 6 and *b* him with bronze shackles
Job 16: 8 You have *b* me—and it has
36: 8 But if men are *b* in chains,
Pr 22: 15 Folly is *b* up in the heart of a child,
Isa 16: 14 servant *b* by contract would count
21: 16 servant *b* by contract would count
24: 22 like prisoners *b* in a dungeon;
Jer 13: 11 as a belt is *b* around a man's waist,
13: 11 so I *b* the whole house of Israel
39: 7 and *b* him with bronze shackles
40: 1 He had found Jeremiah *b* in chains
52: 11 *b* him with bronze shackles
La 1: 14 "My sins have been *b* into a yoke;
Eze 3: 25 you will be *b* so that you cannot go
30: 21 It has not been *b* up for healing
34: 4 healed the sick or *b* up the injured.
Da 3: 21 were *b* and thrown
4: 15 its roots, *b* with iron and bronze,
4: 23 but leave the stump, *b* with iron
Jnh 1: 3 where he found a ship *b*
Mt 14: 3 Herod had arrested John and *b* him
16: 19 bind on earth will be *b* in heaven,
18: 18 bind on earth will be *b* in heaven,
23: 16 of the temple, he is *b* by his oath.'
23: 18 by the gift on it, he is *b* by his oath.'
27: 2 They *b* him, led him away
Mk 6: 17 and he had him *b* and put in prison.
15: 1 They *b* Jesus, led him away
Lk 13: 16 day from what *b* her?"
13: 16 whom Satan has kept *b*
17: 1 people to sin are *b* to come,
Jn 18: 12 They *b* him and brought him first
18: 24 Then Annas sent him, still *b*,
Ac 12: 6 sleeping between two soldiers, *b*
21: 13 I am ready not only to be *b*,
21: 33 him to be *b* with two chains.
23: 12 and *b* themselves with an oath not
28: 20 of Israel that I am *b* with this chain
Ro 7: 2 by law a married woman is *b*
7: 6 by dying to what once *b* us,
11: 32 For God has *b* all men
1Co 7: 15 is not *b* in such circumstances;
7: 39 A woman is *b* to her husband
Jude : 6 *b* with everlasting chains
Rev 9: 14 "Release the four angels who are *b*
20: 2 and *b* him for a thousand years.

BOUNDARIES (BOUNDARY)

Nu 34: 2 as an inheritance will have these *b:*
34: 12 with its *b* on every side.' "
Dt 32: 8 he set up *b* for the peoples
Jos 15: 12 These are the *b* around the people
18: 20 These were the *b* that marked out
2Ki 14: 25 He was the one who restored the *b*
Ps 74: 17 It was you who set all the *b*
Pr 15: 25 but he keeps the widow's *b* intact.
Isa 10: 13 I removed the *b* of nations,
Eze 47: 13 "These are the *b* by which you are
Mic 7: 11 the day for extending your *b*.

BOUNDARY (BOUNDARIES BOUNDLESS BOUNDS)

Nu 34: 3 your southern *b* will start
34: 6 This will be your *b* on the west.
34: 6 " 'Your western *b* will be the coast
34: 7 " 'For your northern *b*, run a line
34: 8 Then the *b* will go to Zedad,
34: 9 This will be your *b* on the north.
34: 10 " 'For your eastern *b*, run a line
34: 11 The *b* will go down from Shepham
34: 12 *b* will go down along the Jordan
Dt 19: 14 move your neighbor's *b* stone set
27: 17 who moves his neighbor's *b* stone."
Jos 13: 23 *b* of the Reubenites was the bank
15: 2 Their southern *b* started
15: 4 This is their southern *b*.
15: 5 The eastern *b* is the Salt Sea as far
15: 5 The northern *b* started
15: 7 The *b* then went up to Debir
15: 9 From the hilltop the *b* headed
15: 11 The *b* ended at the sea.
15: 12 The western *b* is the coastline
15: 21 Negev toward the *b* of Edom were:
16: 5 The *b* of their inheritance went
17: 7 The *b* ran southward from there
17: 8 on the *b* of Manasseh,
17: 9 Then the *b* continued south
17: 9 *b* of Manasseh was the northern
18: 12 On the north side their *b* began
18: 14 on the south the *b* turned south
18: 15 the *b* came out at the spring of
18: 16 The *b* went down to the foot
18: 19 This was the southern *b*.
18: 20 The Jordan formed the *b*
19: 10 The *b* of their inheritance went
19: 14 the *b* went around on the north
19: 22 The *b* touched Tabor, Shahazumah
19: 26 On the west the *b* touched Carmel
19: 29 The *b* then turned back
19: 33 Their *b* went from Heleph
19: 34 The *b* ran west through
22: 25 LORD has made the Jordan a *b*
Jdg 1: 36 The *b* of the Amorites was
Job 24: 2 Men move *b* stones;
26: 10 for a *b* between light and darkness.
Ps 16: 6 The *b* lines have fallen for me
104: 9 You set a *b* they cannot cross;
Pr 8: 29 when he gave the sea its *b*
22: 28 Do not move an ancient *b* stone
23: 10 Do not move an ancient *b* stone
Jer 5: 22 I made the sand a *b* for the sea,
Eze 47: 15 "This is to be the *b* of the land:
47: 17 The *b* will extend from the sea
47: 17 This will be the north *b*.
47: 18 This will be the east *b*.
47: 18 "On the east side the *b* will run
47: 19 This will be the south *b*.
47: 20 This will be the west *b*.
47: 20 the Great Sea will be the *b*
48: 28 southern *b* of Gad will run south
Hos 5: 10 who move *b* stones.

BOUNDING

SS 2: 8 *b* over the hills.

BOUNDLESS (BOUNDARY)

Ps 119: 96 but your commands are *b*.
Na 3: 9 Egypt were her *b* strength;

BOUNDS (BOUNDARY)

Hos 4: 2 they break all *b*,
2Co 7: 4 all our troubles my joy knows no *b*.

BOUNTY

Ge 49: 26 than the *b* of the age-old hills.

Dt 28: 12 heavens, the storehouse of his *b*,
1Ki 10: 13 he had given her out of his royal *b*.
Ps 65: 11 You crown the year with your *b*,
68: 10 from your *b*, O God, you provided
Jer 31: 12 rejoice in the *b* of the LORD—
31: 14 my people will be filled with my *b*

BOW (BOWED BOWING BOWMEN BOWS BOWSHOT)

Ge 27: 3 weapons—your quiver and *b*—
27: 29 and peoples *b* down to you.
27: 29 sons of your mother *b* down to you.
37: 10 *b* down to the ground before you?"
48: 22 with my sword and my *b*."
49: 8 your father's sons will *b*
49: 24 But his *b* remained steady,
Ex 20: 5 You shall not *b* down to them
23: 24 Do not *b* down before their gods
Lev 26: 1 in your land to *b* down before it.
Dt 5: 9 You shall not *b* down to them
8: 19 and worship and *b* down to them,
11: 16 and worship other gods and *b*
26: 10 before the LORD your God and *b*
30: 17 away to *b* down to other gods
33: 3 At your feet they all *b* down,
Jos 23: 7 You must not serve them or *b*
23: 16 and serve other gods and *b*
24: 12 it with your own sword and *b*.
1Sa 2: 36 and *b* down before him for a piece
18: 4 even his sword, his *b* and his belt
2Sa 1: 18 of the *b* (it is written in the Book
1: 22 the *b* of Jonathan did not turn back
15: 5 him to *b* down before him,
16: 4 "I humbly *b*," Ziba said.
22: 35 my arms can bend a *b* of bronze.
22: 40 you made my adversaries *b*
1Ki 22: 34 But someone drew his *b* at random
2Ki 5: 18 also—when I *b* down in the temple
5: 18 leaning on my arm and I *b* there
5: 18 the temple of Rimmon to *b* down
6: 22 with your own sword or *b*?
9: 24 Jehu drew his *b* and shot Joram
13: 15 "Get a *b* and some arrows,"
13: 16 "Take the *b* in your hands,"
17: 35 Do not worship any other gods or *b*
17: 36 To him you shall *b* down
1Ch 5: 18 who could use a *b*, and who were
8: 40 warriors who could handle the *b*.
2Ch 18: 33 But someone drew his *b* at random
Job 29: 20 the *b* ever new in my hand.'
30: 11 that God has unstrung my *b*
Ps 5: 7 in reverence will I *b* down
7: 12 he will bend and string his *b*.
18: 34 my arms can bend a *b* of bronze.
18: 39 you made my adversaries *b*
21: 12 aim at them with drawn *b*.
22: 27 will *b* down before him,
37: 14 and bend the *b*
44: 6 I do not trust in my *b*,
46: 9 he breaks the *b* and shatters
58: 7 they draw the *b*, let their arrows
60: 4 to be unfurled against the *b*.
72: 9 The desert tribes will *b* before him
72: 11 All kings will *b* down to him
78: 57 as unreliable as a faulty *b*.
81: 9 you shall not *b* down to an alien
95: 6 Come, let us *b* down in worship,
138: 2 I will *b* down toward your holy
Pr 14: 19 men will *b* down in the presence
Isa 2: 8 they *b* down to the work
7: 24 Men will go there with *b* and arrow
21: 15 from the bent *b*
22: 3 without using the *b*.
41: 2 to windblown chaff with his *b*.
44: 19 Shall I *b* down to a block of wood?"
45: 14 They will *b* down before you
45: 23 Before me every knee will *b*;
46: 2 They stoop and *b* down together;
46: 6 and they *b* down and worship it.
49: 7 princes will see and *b* down,
49: 23 They will *b* down before you
60: 14 all who despise you will *b*
66: 23 all mankind will come and *b*
Jer 6: 23 They are armed with *b* and spear;
9: 3 like a *b*, to shoot lies;
27: 8 or *b* its neck under his yoke,
27: 11 But if any nation will *b* its neck
27: 12 "*B* your neck under the yoke
Jer 46: 9 men of Lydia who draw the *b*.
49: 35 "See, I will break the *b* of Elam,
50: 14 all you who draw the *b*.
50: 29 all those who draw the *b*.
51: 3 Let not the archer string his *b*,
La 2: 4 Like an enemy he has strung his *b*;
3: 12 He drew his *b*
Eze 39: 3 Then I will strike your *b*
Hos 1: 5 In that day I will break Israel's *b*
1: 7 and I will save them—not by *b*,
2: 18 *B* and sword and battle
7: 16 they are like a faulty *b*.
Mic 5: 13 you will no longer *b* down
6: 6 and *b* down before the exalted God
Hab 3: 9 You uncovered your *b*,
Zep 1: 5 those who *b* down and swear
1: 5 who *b* down on the housetops
Zec 9: 10 and the battle *b* will be broken.
9: 13 I will bend Judah as I bend my *b*
10: 4 from him the battle *b*,
Mt 4: 9 if you will *b* down and worship me
Ac 27: 30 to lower some anchors from the *b*.
27: 41 *b* stuck fast and would not move,
Ro 14: 11 'Every knee will *b* before me;
Php 2: 10 name of Jesus every knee should *b*,
Rev 6: 2 Its rider held a *b*, and he was given

BOWED (BOW)

Ge 18: 2 tent to meet them and *b* low
19: 1 *b* down with his face to the ground.
23: 7 and *b* down before the people
23: 12 Again Abraham *b*
24: 26 Then the man *b* down
24: 48 and I *b* down and worshiped
24: 52 he *b* down to the ground
33: 3 *b* down to the ground seven times
33: 6 their children approached and *b*
33: 7 and Rachel, and they too *b* down.
33: 7 and her children came and *b* down.
37: 7 around mine and *b* down to it."
42: 6 they *b* down to him with their faces
43: 26 and they *b* down before him
43: 28 And they *b* low to pay him honor
48: 12 *b* down with his face to the ground.
Ex 4: 31 they *b* down and worshiped.
12: 27 Then the people *b* down
18: 7 and *b* down and kissed him.
32: 8 They have *b* down to it
34: 8 Moses *b* to the ground at once
Nu 22: 31 So he *b* low and fell facedown.
25: 2 and *b* down before these gods.
Dt 29: 26 and worshiped other gods and *b*
Ru 2: 10 she *b* down with her face
1Sa 20: 41 and *b* down before Jonathan three
24: 8 David *b* down and prostrated
25: 23 *b* down before David with her face
25: 41 She *b* down with her face
28: 14 he *b* down and prostrated himself
2Sa 9: 6 he *b* down to pay him honor.
9: 8 Mephibosheth *b* down and said,
14: 33 *b* down with his face to the ground
18: 21 The Cushite *b* down before Joab
18: 28 He *b* down before the king
24: 20 and *b* down before the king
1Ki 1: 16 Bathsheba *b* low and knelt
1: 23 and *b* with his face to the ground.
1: 31 Bathsheba *b* low with her face
1: 47 the king *b* in worship on his bed
1: 53 and *b* down to King Solomon,
2: 19 *b* down to her and sat
18: 7 Obadiah recognized him, *b*
19: 18 all whose knees have not *b*
2Ki 2: 15 and *b* to the ground before him.
4: 37 fell at his feet and *b* to the ground.
17: 16 They *b* down to all the starry hosts,
21: 3 He *b* down to all the starry hosts
21: 21 his father had worshiped, and *b*
1Ch 21: 21 *b* down before David with his face
29: 20 they *b* low and fell prostrate
2Ch 20: 18 Jehoshaphat *b* with his face
25: 14 *b* down to them and burned
29: 28 The whole assembly *b* in worship,
29: 30 and *b* their heads and worshiped.
33: 3 He *b* down to all the starry hosts
Ne 8: 6 Then they *b* down and worshiped
Ps 35: 14 I *b* my head in grief
38: 6 I am *b* down and brought very low;
57: 6 I was *b* down in distress.
Ps 145: 14 and lifts up all who are *b* down.
146: 8 the LORD lifts up those who are *b*
La 2: 10 have *b* their heads to the ground.
Da 10: 15 I *b* with my face toward the ground
Mt 2: 11 they *b* down and worshiped him.
Lk 24: 5 In their fright the women *b*
Jn 19: 30 he *b* his head and gave up his spirit.
Ro 11: 4 thousand who have not *b* the knee

BOWELS

2Ch 21: 15 ill with a lingering disease of the *b*,
21: 15 until the disease causes your *b*
21: 18 with an incurable disease of the *b*.
21: 19 *b* came out because of the disease,

BOWING (BOW)

Ge 37: 9 eleven stars were *b* down to me."
Ex 11: 8 *b* down before me and saying, 'Go,
Dt 4: 19 enticed into *b* down to them
17: 3 *b* down to them or to the sun
Isa 58: 5 only for *b* one's head like a reed
60: 14 of your oppressors will come *b*
Eze 8: 16 they were *b* down to the sun

BOWL (BOWL-SHAPED BOWLFUL BOWLS)

Nu 7: 13 silver sprinkling *b* weighing
7: 19 silver sprinkling *b* weighing
7: 25 silver sprinkling *b* weighing
7: 31 silver sprinkling *b* weighing
7: 37 silver sprinkling *b* weighing
7: 43 silver sprinkling *b* weighing
7: 49 silver sprinkling *b* weighing
7: 55 silver sprinkling *b* weighing
7: 61 silver sprinkling *b* weighing
7: 67 silver sprinkling *b* weighing
7: 73 silver sprinkling *b* weighing
7: 79 silver sprinkling *b* weighing
7: 85 each sprinkling *b* seventy shekels.
Jdg 5: 25 in a *b* fit for nobles she brought him
2Ki 2: 20 "Bring me a new *b*," he said,
Ecc 12: 6 or the golden *b* is broken;
Zec 4: 2 lampstand with a *b* at the top
4: 3 one on the right of the *b*
9: 15 they will be full like a *b*
Mt 5: 15 light a lamp and put it under a *b*.
26: 23 into the *b* with me will betray me.
Mk 4: 21 bring in a lamp to put it under a *b*
14: 20 bread into the *b* with me.
Lk 11: 33 it will be hidden, or under a *b*.
Rev 16: 2 and poured out his *b* on the land,
16: 3 The second angel poured out his *b*
16: 4 The third angel poured out his *b*
16: 8 The fourth angel poured out his *b*
16: 10 The fifth angel poured out his *b*
16: 12 The sixth angel poured out his *b*
16: 17 The seventh angel poured out his *b*

BOWL-SHAPED (BOWL)

1Ki 7: 20 above the *b* part next
7: 41 decorating the two *b* capitals
7: 41 the two *b* capitals on top
7: 42 decorating the *b* capitals on top
2Ch 4: 12 decorating the two *b* capitals
4: 12 the two *b* capitals on top
4: 13 decorating the *b* capitals on top

BOWLFUL (BOWL)

Jdg 6: 38 wrung out the dew—a *b* of water.
Ps 80: 5 made them drink tears by the *b*.
Am 6: 6 You drink wine by the *b*

BOWLS (BOWL)

Ex 24: 6 half of the blood and put it in *b*,
25: 29 *b* for the pouring out of offerings.
27: 3 and its shovels, sprinkling *b*,
37: 16 its plates and ladles and *b*
38: 3 its pots, shovels, sprinkling *b*,
Nu 4: 7 *b*, and the jars for drink offerings;
4: 14 forks, shovels and sprinkling *b*.
7: 84 twelve silver sprinkling *b*
2Sa 17: 28 and *b* and articles of pottery.
1Ki 7: 40 and shovels and sprinkling *b*.
7: 45 the pots, shovels and sprinkling *b*.
7: 50 wick trimmers, sprinkling *b*,
2Ki 12: 13 wick trimmers, sprinkling *b*,
25: 15 the censers and sprinkling *b*—
1Ch 28: 17 gold for the forks, sprinkling *b*

2Ch 4: 8 made a hundred gold sprinkling *b*.
4: 11 and shovels and sprinkling *b*.
4: 22 sprinkling *b*, ladles and censers;
Ezr 1: 10 matching silver *b* 410
1: 10 gold *b* 30
8: 27 *b* of gold valued at 1,000
Ne 7: 70 gold, 50 *b* and 530 garments
Pr 23: 30 who go to sample *b* of mixed wine.
Isa 22: 24 from the *b* to all the jars.
65: 11 and fill *b* of mixed wine for Destiny
Jer 35: 5 Then I set *b* full of wine
52: 18 wick trimmers, sprinkling *b*,
52: 19 and *b* used for drink offerings—
52: 19 censers, sprinkling *b*, pots,
Zec 14: 20 house will be like the sacred *b*
Rev 5: 8 and they were holding golden *b* full
15: 7 seven angels seven golden *b* filled
16: 1 pour out the seven *b*
17: 1 angels who had the seven *b* came
21: 9 angels who had the seven *b* full

BOWMEN (BOW)

Isa 21: 17 The survivors of the *b*, the warriors

BOWS (BOW)

1Sa 2: 4 "The *b* of the warriors are broken,
1Ch 12: 2 they were armed with *b*
2Ch 14: 8 with small shields and with *b*.
17: 17 men armed with *b* and shields; next
26: 14 *b* and slingstones for the entire
Ne 4: 13 with their swords, spears and *b*.
4: 16 equipped with spears, shields, *b*
Ps 11: 2 For look, the wicked bend their *b*;
37: 15 and their *b* will be broken.
66: 4 All the earth *b* down to you;
78: 9 of Ephraim, though armed with *b*,
Isa 5: 28 all their *b* are strung;
13: 18 Their *b* will strike down the young
44: 15 he makes an idol and *b* down to it.
44: 17 he *b* down to it and worships.
46: 1 Bel *b* down, Nebo stoops low;
Jer 50: 42 They are armed with *b* and spears;
51: 56 and their *b* will be broken.
Eze 39: 9 and large shields, the *b* and arrows,

BOWSHOT (BOW)

Ge 21: 16 about a *b* away, for she thought,

BOZEZ

1Sa 14: 4 one was called *B*, and the other

BOZKATH

Jos 15: 39 Joktheel, Lachish, *B*, Eglon,
2Ki 22: 1 of Adaiah; she was from *B*.

BOZRAH

Ge 36: 33 of Zerah from *B* succeeded him
1Ch 1: 44 of Zerah from *B* succeeded him
Isa 34: 6 For the LORD has a sacrifice in *B*
63: 1 from *B*, with his garments stained
Jer 48: 24 Beth Meon, to Kerioth and *B*—
49: 13 "that *B* will become a ruin
49: 22 spreading its wings over *B*.
Am 1: 12 will consume the fortresses of *B*."

BRACE (BRACING)

Job 38: 3 *B* yourself like a man;
40: 7 out of the storm: "*B* yourself like
Na 2: 1 *b* yourselves,

BRACELETS

Ge 24: 22 two gold *b* weighing ten shekels.
24: 30 and the *b* on his sister's arms,
24: 47 in her nose and the *b* on her arms,
Nu 31: 50 *b*, signet rings, earrings
Isa 3: 19 the earrings and *b* and veils,
Eze 16: 11 I put *b* on your arms and a necklace
23: 42 and they put *b* on the arms

BRACING (BRACE)

Jdg 16: 29 *B* himself against them, his right

BRAG

Am 4: 5 and *b* about your freewill offerings
Ro 2: 17 *b* about your relationship to God;
2: 23 temples? You who *b* about the law,
Jas 4: 16 As it is, you boast and *b*.

BRAIDED (BRAIDS)

Ex 28: 14 and two *b* chains of pure gold,
28: 22 "For the breastpiece make *b* chains
39: 15 the breastpiece they made *b* chains
1Ti 2: 9 not with *b* hair or gold or pearls
1Pe 3: 3 as *b* hair and the wearing

BRAIDS (BRAIDED)

Jdg 16: 13 Delilah took the seven *b*
16: 13 "If you weave the seven *b*
16: 19 to shave off the seven *b* of his hair,

BRAMBLES

Isa 34: 13 nettles and *b* her strongholds.

BRANCH (BRANCHES)

Ge 49: 11 his colt to the choicest *b*;
Ex 25: 33 and blossoms are to be on one *b*,
25: 33 three on the next *b*, and the same
37: 19 and blossoms were on one *b*,
37: 19 three on the next *b* and the same
Nu 4: 2 of the Kohathite *b* of the Levites
13: 23 cut off a *b* bearing a single cluster
Isa 4: 2 In that day the *B* of the LORD will
9: 14 both palm *b* and reed
11: 1 from his roots a *B* will bear fruit.
14: 19 like a rejected *b*;
19: 15 head or tail, palm *b* or reed.
Jer 1: 11 "I see the *b* of an almond tree,"
23: 5 up to David a righteous *B*,
33: 15 I will make a righteous *B* sprout
Eze 8: 17 at them putting the *b* to their nose!
15: 2 than that of a *b* on any of the trees
19: 14 No strong *b* is left on it
Zec 3: 8 going to bring my servant, the *B*.
6: 12 and he will *b* out from his place
6: 12 is the man whose name is the *B*,
Mal 4: 1 or a *b* will be left to them.
Jn 15: 2 He cuts off every *b*
15: 2 while every *b* that does bear fruit
15: 4 No *b* can bear fruit by itself;
15: 6 he is like a *b* that is thrown away

BRANCHES (BRANCH)

Ge 30: 37 the white inner wood of the *b*.
30: 37 took fresh-cut *b* from poplar,
30: 38 Then he placed the peeled *b*
30: 39 they mated in front of the *b*.
30: 41 Jacob would place the *b*
30: 41 so they would mate near the *b*,
40: 10 and on the vine were three *b*.
40: 12 "The three *b* are three days.
49: 22 whose *b* climb over a wall.
Ex 25: 32 Six *b* are to extend from the sides
25: 33 and the same for all six *b* extending
25: 35 of *b* extending from the lampstand,
25: 35 under the third pair—six *b* in all.
25: 36 and *b* shall all be of one piece
37: 18 Six *b* extended from the sides
37: 19 and the same for all six *b* extending
37: 21 of *b* extending from the lampstand,
37: 21 under the third pair—six *b* in all.
37: 22 and the *b* were all of one piece
Lev 23: 40 palm fronds, leafy *b* and poplars,
Dt 24: 20 do not go over the *b* a second time.
Jdg 9: 48 He took an ax and cut off some *b*,
9: 49 the men cut *b* and followed
2Sa 18: 9 under the thick *b* of a large oak,
Ne 8: 15 and bring back *b* from olive
8: 16 went out and brought back *b*
Job 15: 32 and his *b* will not flourish.
18: 16 and his *b* wither above.
29: 19 the dew will lie all night on my *b*.
Ps 80: 10 the mighty cedars with its *b*.
104: 12 they sing among the *b*.
Isa 17: 6 or three olives on the topmost *b*,
18: 5 and take away the spreading *b*.
27: 10 they strip its *b* bare.
Jer 5: 10 Strip off her *b*,
6: 9 pass your hand over the *b* again,
11: 16 and its *b* will be broken.
48: 32 Your *b* spread as far as the sea;
Eze 17: 6 Its *b* turned toward him,
17: 6 and produced *b* and put out leafy
17: 7 stretched out its *b* to him for water.
17: 8 water so that it would produce *b*,
17: 23 it will produce *b* and bear fruit
17: 23 shelter in the shade of its *b*.
19: 10 it was fruitful and full of *b*
19: 11 Its *b* were strong,
19: 11 and for its many *b*.
19: 12 its strong *b* withered
19: 14 Fire spread from one of its main *b*
21: 19 Make a signpost where the road *b*
31: 3 with beautiful *b* overshadowing
31: 5 and its *b* grew long,
31: 6 gave birth under its *b*;
31: 8 compare with its *b*—
31: 9 beautiful with abundant *b*,
31: 12 its *b* lay broken in all the ravines
31: 13 beasts of the field were among its *b*.
36: 8 will produce *b* and fruit
Da 4: 12 and the birds of the air lived in its *b*
4: 14 Cut down the tree and trim off its *b*
4: 14 under it and the birds from its *b*.
4: 21 places in its *b* for the birds
Joel 1: 7 leaving their *b* white.
Zec 4: 12 "What are these two olive *b*
Mt 13: 32 of the air come and perch in its *b*."
21: 8 while others cut *b* from the trees
Mk 4: 32 with such big *b* that the birds
11: 8 while others spread *b* they had cut
Lk 13: 19 the birds of the air perched in its *b*
Jn 12: 13 They took palm *b* and went out
15: 5 "I am the vine; you are the *b*.
15: 6 such *b* are picked up, thrown
Ro 11: 16 if the root is holy, so are the *b*.
11: 17 If some of the *b* have been broken
11: 18 do not boast over those *b*.
11: 19 "*B* were broken off so that I could
11: 21 if God did not spare the natural *b*,
11: 24 the natural *b*, be grafted
Heb 9: 19 scarlet wool and *b* of hyssop,
Rev 7: 9 were holding palm *b* in their hands.

BRANDING

Isa 3: 24 instead of beauty, *b*.

BRANDISH (BRANDISHED BRANDISHES BRANDISHING)

Ps 35: 3 *B* spear and javelin
Isa 10: 15 or a club *b* him who is not wood!
Eze 32: 10 when I *b* my sword before them.

BRANDISHED (BRANDISH)

Na 2: 3 the spears of pine are *b*.

BRANDISHES (BRANDISH)

Eze 30: 25 the king of Babylon and he *b* it

BRANDISHING (BRANDISH)

Eze 38: 4 all of them *b* their swords.

BRAVE (BRAVEST)

1Sa 14: 52 Saul saw a mighty or *b* man,
16: 18 He is a *b* man and a warrior.
2Sa 2: 7 Now then, be strong and *b*,
13: 28 you this order? Be strong and *b*."
17: 10 and that those with him are *b*.
1Ch 5: 24 They were *b* warriors, famous men,
7: 40 *b* warriors and outstanding leaders.
8: 40 of Ulam were *b* warriors who could
12: 8 They were *b* warriors, ready
12: 21 for all of them were *b* warriors,
12: 28 men, and Zadok, a *b* young warrior
12: 30 men of Ephraim, *b* warriors,
28: 1 mighty men and all the *b* warriors.
2Ch 14: 8 All these were *b* fighting men.
Ne 11: 6 in Jerusalem totaled 468 *b* men.
11: 14 who were *b* warriors—128 men.
Isa 33: 7 their *b* men cry aloud in the streets;

BRAVEST (BRAVE)

2Sa 17: 10 the *b* soldier, whose heart is like
Am 2: 16 Even the *b* warriors

BRAWLER (BRAWLERS BRAWLING)

Pr 20: 1 Wine is a mocker and beer a *b*;

BRAWLERS (BRAWLER)

Isa 5: 14 masses with all their *b* and revelers.

BRAWLING (BRAWLER)

Eph 4: 31 rage and anger, *b* and slander,

BRAY (BRAYED)
Job 6: 5 Does a wild donkey *b*

BRAYED (BRAY)
Job 30: 7 They *b* among the bushes

BRAZEN
Pr 7: 13 and with a *b* face she said:
Jer 3: 3 Yet you have the *b* look
Eze 16: 30 things, acting like a *b* prostitute!

BREACH (BREAK)
Job 30: 14 through a gaping *b*;
Ps 106: 23 stood in the *b* before him

BREACHES (BREAK)
Isa 22: 9 had many *b* in its defenses;

BREACHING (BREAK)
Ps 144: 14 There will be no *b* of walls,
Pr 17: 14 Starting a quarrel is like *b* a dam;

BREAD
Ge 14: 18 king of Salem brought out *b*
18: 6 and knead it and bake some *b*.''
19: 3 baking *b* without yeast,
25: 34 Then Jacob gave Esau some *b*
27: 17 tasty food and the *b* she had made.
40: 16 my head were three baskets of *b*.
45: 23 and *b* and other provisions
Ex 12: 8 and *b* made without yeast.
12: 15 are to eat *b* made without yeast.
12: 17 the Feast of Unleavened *B*,
12: 18 are to eat *b* made without yeast,
12: 20 you must eat unleavened *b*.''
12: 39 they baked cakes of unleavened *b*.
13: 6 For seven days eat *b* made
13: 7 unleavened *b* during those seven
16: 4 ''I will rain down *b* from heaven
16: 8 all the *b* you want in the morning,
16: 12 morning you will be filled with *b*.
16: 15 It is the *b* the LORD has given you
16: 29 why on the sixth day he gives you *b*
16: 31 people of Israel called the *b* manna.
16: 32 so they can see the *b* I gave you
18: 12 to eat *b* with Moses' father-in-law
23: 15 for seven days eat *b* made
23: 15 the Feast of Unleavened *B*;
25: 30 Put the *b* of the Presence
29: 2 make *b*, and cakes mixed with oil,
29: 23 the basket of *b* made without yeast,
29: 32 and the *b* that is in the basket.
29: 34 or any *b* is left over till morning,
34: 18 For seven days eat *b* made
34: 18 the Feast of Unleavened *B*,
34: 28 and forty nights without eating *b*
35: 13 and all its articles and the *b*
39: 36 table with all its articles and the *b*
40: 23 out the *b* on it before the LORD,
Lev 7: 12 cakes of *b* made without yeast
7: 13 with cakes of *b* made with yeast
8: 2 and the basket containing *b* made
8: 26 he took a cake of *b*, and one made
8: 26 the basket of *b* made without yeast,
8: 31 there with the *b* from the basket
8: 32 the rest of the meat and the *b*.
23: 6 Feast of Unleavened *B* begins;
23: 6 for seven days you must eat *b* made
23: 14 You must not eat any *b*, or roasted
23: 18 with this *b* seven male lambs,
23: 20 together with the *b* of the firstfruits
24: 5 and bake twelve loaves of *b*,
24: 7 portion to represent the *b*
24: 8 This *b* is to be set out
26: 26 When I cut off your supply of *b*,
26: 26 able to bake your *b* in one oven,
26: 26 they will dole out the *b* by weight.
Nu 4: 7 the *b* that is continually there is
6: 15 a basket of *b* made without yeast—
6: 17 present the basket of unleavened *b*
9: 11 together with unleavened *b*
21: 5 There is no *b*! There is no water!
28: 17 for seven days eat *b* made
Dt 8: 3 that man does not live on *b* alone
8: 9 a land where *b* will not be scarce
9: 9 I ate no *b* and drank no water.
9: 18 I ate no *b* and drank no water,
16: 3 it with *b* made with yeast,
Dt 16: 3 seven days eat unleavened *b*, the *b*
16: 8 For six days eat unleavened *b*
16: 16 at the Feast of Unleavened *B*,
23: 4 come to meet you with *b*
29: 6 You ate no *b* and drank no wine
Jos 5: 11 unleavened *b* and roasted grain.
9: 5 All the *b* of their food supply was
9: 12 This *b* of ours was warm
Jdg 6: 19 of flour he made *b* without yeast.
6: 20 the meat and the unleavened *b*,
6: 21 consuming the meat and the *b*.
6: 21 the meat and the unleavened *b*.
7: 13 loaf of barley *b* came tumbling
8: 5 my troops some *b*; they are worn
8: 6 Why should we give *b*
8: 15 Why should we give *b*
19: 19 and fodder for our donkeys and *b*
Ru 2: 14 Have some *b* and dip it
1Sa 2: 36 and a crust of *b* and plead,
10: 3 another three loaves of *b*,
10: 4 and offer you two loaves of *b*,
16: 20 Jesse took a donkey loaded with *b*,
17: 17 loaves of *b* for your brothers
21: 3 Give me five loaves of *b*,
21: 4 there is some consecrated *b* here—
21: 4 ''I don't have any ordinary *b*
21: 6 by hot *b* on the day it was taken
21: 6 priest gave him the consecrated *b*,
21: 6 since there was no *b* there
21: 6 the *b* of the Presence that had been
22: 13 giving him *b* and a sword
25: 11 Why should I take my *b* and water,
25: 18 She took two hundred loaves of *b*,
28: 24 and baked *b* without yeast.
2Sa 3: 35 if I taste *b* or anything else
6: 19 he gave a loaf of *b*, a cake of dates
13: 6 make some special *b* in my sight,
13: 8 made the *b* in his sight and baked it
13: 9 took the pan and served him the *b*,
13: 10 Tamar took the *b* she had prepared
16: 1 with two hundred loaves of *b*,
16: 2 the *b* and fruit are for the men
1Ki 7: 48 on which was the *b* of the Presence
13: 8 would I eat *b* or drink water here.
13: 9 'You must not eat *b* or drink water
13: 16 can I eat *b* or drink water with you
13: 17 'You must not eat *b* or drink water
13: 18 to your house so that he may eat *b*
13: 22 You came back and ate *b*
14: 3 Take ten loaves of *b* with you,
17: 6 The ravens brought him *b*
17: 6 and meat in the morning and *b*
17: 11 And bring me, please, a piece of *b*.''
17: 12 she replied, ''I don't have any *b*—
17: 13 first make a small cake of *b* for me
19: 6 a cake of *b* baked over hot coals,
22: 27 and give him nothing but *b*
2Ki 4: 42 twenty loaves of barley *b* baked
18: 32 a land of *b* and vineyards, a land
23: 9 they ate unleavened *b*
1Ch 9: 31 for baking the offering *b*
9: 32 for every Sabbath the *b* set out
16: 3 he gave a loaf of *b*, a cake of dates
23: 29 were in charge of the *b* set out
28: 16 for each table for consecrated *b*;
2Ch 2: 4 out the consecrated *b* regularly,
4: 19 on which was the *b* of the Presence
8: 13 the Feast of Unleavened *B*,
13: 11 They set out the *b*
18: 26 and give him nothing but *b*
29: 18 for setting out the consecrated *b*,
30: 13 of Unleavened *B* in the second
30: 21 of Unleavened *B* for seven days
35: 17 of Unleavened *B* for seven days.
Ezr 6: 22 with joy the Feast of Unleavened *B*
Ne 9: 15 In their hunger you gave them *b*
10: 33 for the *b* set out on the table;
Job 23: 12 of his mouth more than my daily *b*.
31: 17 if I have kept my *b* to myself,
Ps 14: 4 devour my people as men eat *b*
37: 25 or their children begging *b*.
41: 9 he who shared my *b*,
53: 4 devour my people as men eat *b*
78: 25 Men ate the *b* of angels;
80: 5 them with the *b* of tears;
104: 15 and *b* that sustains his heart.
105: 40 satisfied them with the *b* of heaven.
Pr 4: 17 They eat the *b* of wickedness
Pr 6: 26 reduces you to a loaf of *b*,
28: 21 man will do wrong for a piece of *b*.
30: 8 but give me only my daily *b*.
31: 27 and does not eat the *b* of idleness.
Ecc 11: 1 Cast your *b* upon the waters,
Isa 28: 28 Grain must be ground to make *b*;
30: 20 Although the Lord gives you the *b*
33: 16 His *b* will be supplied,
36: 17 a land of *b* and vineyards.
44: 15 he kindles a fire and bakes *b*.
44: 19 I even baked *b* over its coals,
51: 14 nor will they lack *b*.
55: 2 Why spend money on what is not *b*
55: 10 for the sower and *b* for the eater,
Jer 7: 18 and make cakes of *b* for the Queen
37: 21 and given *b* from the street
37: 21 until all the *b* in the city was gone.
38: 9 when there is no longer any *b*
42: 14 hear the trumpet or be hungry for *b*
La 1: 11 as they search for *b*;
2: 12 ''Where is *b* and wine?''
4: 4 the children beg for *b*,
5: 6 to get enough *b*.
5: 9 We get our *b* at the risk of our lives
Eze 4: 9 use them to make *b* for yourself.
4: 15 ''I will let you bake your *b*
13: 19 handfuls of barley and scraps of *b*.
45: 21 during which you shall eat *b* made
Hos 9: 4 be to them like the *b* of mourners;
Am 4: 5 Burn leavened *b* as a thank offering
4: 6 and lack of *b* in every town,
7: 12 Earn your *b* there and do your
Ob : 7 those who eat your *b* will set a trap
Hag 2: 12 that fold touches some *b* or stew,
Mt 4: 3 tell these stones to become *b*.''
4: 4 'Man does not live on *b* alone,
6: 11 Give us today our daily *b*.
7: 9 asks for *b*, will give him a stone?
12: 4 ate the consecrated *b*—
14: 17 ''We have here only five loaves of *b*
15: 26 right to take the children's *b*
15: 33 ''Where could we get enough *b*
16: 5 the disciples forgot to take *b*.
16: 7 ''It is because we didn't bring any *b*
16: 8 yourselves about having no *b*?
16: 11 I was not talking to you about *b*?
16: 12 to guard against the yeast used in *b*
26: 17 day of the Feast of Unleavened *B*,
26: 26 Jesus took *b*, gave thanks
Mk 2: 26 and ate the consecrated *b*,
6: 8 no *b*, no bag, no money
6: 37 spend that much on *b* and give it
6: 43 basketfuls of broken pieces of *b*
7: 27 right to take the children's *b*
8: 4 place can anyone get enough *b*
8: 14 disciples had forgotten to bring *b*,
8: 16 ''It is because we have no *b*.''
8: 17 are you talking about having no *b*?
14: 1 of Unleavened *B* were only two
14: 12 day of the Feast of Unleavened *B*,
14: 20 ''one who dips *b* into the bowl
14: 22 Jesus took *b*, gave thanks
Lk 4: 3 tell this stone to become *b*.''
4: 4 'Man does not live on *b* alone.' ''
6: 4 and taking the consecrated *b*,
7: 33 the Baptist came neither eating *b*
9: 3 no staff, no bag, no *b*, no money,
9: 13 ''We have only five loaves of *b*
11: 3 Give us each day our daily *b*.
11: 5 'Friend, lend me three loaves of *b*,
11: 8 and give him the *b* because he is his
22: 1 Now the Feast of Unleavened *B*,
22: 7 came the day of Unleavened *B*
22: 19 And he took *b*, gave thanks
24: 30 at the table with them, he took *b*,
24: 35 by them when he broke the *b*.
Jn 6: 5 ''Where shall we buy *b*
6: 7 wages would not buy enough *b*
6: 23 where the people had eaten the *b*
6: 31 He gave them *b* from heaven to eat
6: 32 my Father who gives you the true *b*
6: 32 not Moses who has given you the *b*
6: 33 For the *b* of God is he who comes
6: 34 ''from now on give us this *b*.''
6: 35 Jesus declared, ''I am the *b* of life.
6: 41 ''I am the *b* that came
6: 48 I am the *b* of life.
6: 50 But here is the *b* that comes

SS 8: 1 who was nursed at my mother's *b!*
8: 8 and her *b* are not yet grown.
8: 10 and my *b* are like towers.
Isa 32: 12 Beat your *b* for the pleasant fields,
60: 16 and be nursed at royal *b*.
66: 11 satisfied at her comforting *b;*
La 4: 3 Even jackals offer their *b*
Eze 16: 7 Your *b* were formed and your hair
23: 3 In that land their *b* were fondled
23: 21 and your young *b* fondled.
23: 34 and tear your *b*.
Hos 2: 2 unfaithfulness from between her *b*.
9: 14 and *b* that are dry.
Na 2: 7 and beat upon their *b*.
Lk 23: 29 and the *b* that never nursed!'
23: 48 they beat their *b* and went away.

BREATH (BREATHE BREATHED BREATHES BREATHING GOD-BREATHED)

Ge 1: 30 everything that has the *b* of life in it
2: 7 into his nostrils the *b* of life,
6: 17 every creature that has the *b* of life
7: 15 of all creatures that have the *b*
7: 22 on dry land that had the *b* of life
Ex 15: 10 But you blew with your *b*,
2Sa 22: 16 at the blast of *b* from his nostrils.
Job 4: 9 At the *b* of God they are destroyed
7: 7 O God, that my life is but a *b;*
9: 18 He would not let me regain my *b*
12: 10 and the *b* of all mankind.
15: 30 *b* of God's mouth will carry him
19: 17 My *b* is offensive to my wife;
26: 13 By his *b* the skies became fair;
27: 3 the *b* of God in my nostrils,
32: 8 *b* of the Almighty, that gives him
33: 4 the *b* of the Almighty gives me life.
34: 14 and he withdrew his spirit and *b*,
37: 10 The *b* of God produces ice,
41: 21 His *b* sets coals ablaze,
Ps 18: 15 at the blast of *b* from your nostrils.
33: 6 by the *b* of his mouth.
39: 5 Each man's life is but a *b*.
39: 11 each man is but a *b*.
62: 9 Lowborn men are but a *b*,
62: 9 together they are only a *b*.
104: 29 when you take away their *b*,
135: 17 nor is there *b* in their mouths.
144: 4 Man is like a *b;*
150: 6 everything that has *b* praise
Ecc 3: 19 All have the same *b;* man has no
SS 7: 8 the fragrance of your *b* like apples,
Isa 2: 22 who has but a *b* in his nostrils.
11: 4 with the *b* of his lips he will slay
25: 4 For the *b* of the ruthless
30: 28 His *b* is like a rushing torrent,
30: 33 the *b* of the LORD,
33: 11 your *b* is a fire that consumes you.
40: 7 the *b* of the LORD blows on them.
42: 5 who gives *b* to its people,
57: 13 a mere *b* will blow them away.
57: 16 the *b* of man that I have created.
59: 19 that the *b* of the LORD drives
Jer 4: 31 the Daughter of Zion gasping for *b*,
10: 14 they have no *b* in them.
38: 16 LORD lives, who has given us *b*,
51: 17 they have no *b* in them.
La 4: 20 LORD's anointed, our very life *b*,
Eze 37: 5 I will make *b* enter you,
37: 6 I will put *b* in you, and you will
37: 8 but there was no *b* in them.
37: 9 O *b*, and breathe into these slain,
37: 9 "Prophesy to the *b;* prophesy,
37: 10 me, and *b* entered them;
Hab 2: 19 there is no *b* in it.
Ac 17: 25 and *b* and everything else.
2Co 1: 17 manner so that in the same *b* I say,
2Th 2: 8 overthrow with the *b* of his mouth
Rev 11: 11 and a half days a *b* of life
13: 15 power to give *b* to the image

BREATHE (BREATH)

Jer 15: 9 and *b* her last.
Eze 21: 31 *b* out my fiery anger against you;
37: 9 O breath, and *b* into these slain,
Da 10: 17 is gone and I can hardly *b*."

BREATHED (BREATH)

Ge 2: 7 *b* into his nostrils the breath of life,
25: 8 Then Abraham *b* his last
25: 17 He *b* his last and died,
35: 18 As she *b* her last—
35: 29 Then he *b* his last and died
49: 33 *b* his last and was gathered
Jos 10: 40 He totally destroyed all who *b*,
11: 11 not sparing anything that *b*,
11: 14 not sparing anyone that *b*.
1Ki 15: 29 not leave Jeroboam anyone that *b*,
Mk 15: 37 With a loud cry, Jesus *b* his last.
Lk 23: 46 When he had said this, he *b* his last.
Jn 20: 22 And with that he *b* on them

BREATHES (BREATH)

Dt 20: 16 do not leave alive anything that *b*.
Job 14: 10 he *b* his last and is no more.

BREATHING (BREATH)

1Ki 17: 17 and worse, and finally stopped *b*.
Ps 27: 12 *b* out violence.
Ac 9: 1 Saul was still *b* out murderous

BRED (BREED)

Est 8: 10 who rode fast horses especially *b*

BREED (BRED BREEDING BREEDS)

Job 21: 10 Their bulls never fail to *b;*

BREEDING (BREED)

Ge 31: 10 "In *b* season I once had a dream

BREEDS (BREED)

Pr 13: 10 Pride only *b* quarrels,

BREEZE (BREEZES)

Ps 78: 39 a passing *b* that does not return.

BREEZES (BREEZE)

Ps 147: 18 he stirs up his *b*, and the waters

BRIBE (BRIBERY BRIBES BRIBING)

Ex 23: 8 for a *b* blinds those who see
23: 8 "Do not accept a *b*,
Dt 16: 19 Do not accept a *b*,
16: 19 for a *b* blinds the eyes of the wise
27: 25 "Cursed is the man who accepts a *b*
1Sa 12: 3 whose hand have I accepted a *b*
Job 36: 18 do not let a large *b* turn you aside.
Ps 15: 5 and does not accept a *b*
Pr 6: 35 will refuse the *b*, however great it
17: 8 *b* is a charm to the one who gives it;
17: 23 A wicked man accepts a *b* in secret
21: 14 *b* concealed in the cloak pacifies
Ecc 7: 7 and a *b* corrupts the heart.
Isa 5: 23 who acquit the guilty for a *b*,
Mic 3: 11 Her leaders judge for a *b*,
Ac 24: 26 that Paul would offer him a *b*,

BRIBERY (BRIBE)

2Ch 19: 7 is no injustice or partiality or *b*."

BRIBES (BRIBE)

Dt 10: 17 no partiality and accepts no *b*.
1Sa 8: 3 accepted *b* and perverted justice.
Job 15: 34 of those who love *b*.
Ps 26: 10 whose right hands are full of *b*.
Pr 15: 27 but he who hates *b* will live.
29: 4 for *b* tears it down.
Isa 1: 23 they all love *b*
33: 15 keeps his hand from accepting *b*,
Eze 22: 12 In you men accept *b* to shed blood;
Am 5: 12 oppress the righteous and take *b*
Mic 7: 3 the judge accepts *b*,

BRIBING (BRIBE)

Eze 16: 33 *b* them to come to you

BRICK (BRICKMAKING BRICKS BRICKWORK)

Ge 11: 3 They used *b* instead of stone,
Ex 1: 14 bitter with hard labor in *b*
Isa 65: 3 and burning incense on altars of *b;*
Jer 43: 9 them in clay in the *b* pavement

BRICKMAKING (BRICK)

2Sa 12: 31 and he made them work at *b*.

BRICKS (BRICK)

Ge 11: 3 let's make *b* and bake them
Ex 5: 7 the people with straw for making *b;*
5: 8 to make the same number of *b*
5: 14 you met your quota of *b* yesterday
5: 16 yet we are told, 'Make *b!*'
5: 18 must produce your full quota of *b*."
5: 19 the number of *b* required of you
Isa 9: 10 "The *b* have fallen down,

BRICKWORK (BRICK)

Na 3: 14 repair the *b!*

BRIDAL (BRIDE)

Ge 29: 27 Finish out this daughter's *b* week;

BRIDE (BRIDAL)

Ge 34: 12 Make the price for the *b*
1Sa 18: 25 for the *b* than a hundred Philistine
Ps 45: 9 at your right hand is the royal *b*
SS 4: 8 with me from Lebanon, my *b*,
4: 9 stolen my heart, my sister, my *b;*
4: 10 is your love, my sister, my *b!*
4: 11 as the honeycomb, my *b;*
4: 12 garden locked up, my sister, my *b;*
5: 1 into my garden, my sister, my *b;*
Isa 49: 18 you will put them on, like a *b*.
61: 10 a *b* adorns herself with her jewels.
62: 5 as a bridegroom rejoices over his *b*,
Jer 2: 2 how as a *b* you loved me
2: 32 a *b* her wedding ornaments?
7: 34 and gladness and to the voices of *b*
16: 9 to the voices of *b* and bridegroom
25: 10 the voices of *b* and bridegroom,
33: 11 the voices of *b* and bridegroom,
Joel 2: 16 and the *b* her chamber.
Jn 3: 29 The *b* belongs to the bridegroom.
Rev 18: 23 The voice of bridegroom and *b*
19: 7 and his *b* has made herself ready.
21: 2 as a *b* beautifully dressed
21: 9 I will show you the *b*, the wife
22: 17 The Spirit and the *b* say, "Come!"

BRIDE-PRICE

Ex 22: 16 he must pay the *b*, and she shall be
22: 17 he must still pay the *b* for virgins.

BRIDEGROOM (BRIDEGROOM'S BRIDEGROOMS)

Ex 4: 25 Surely you are a *b* of blood to me,"
4: 26 (At that time she said "*b* of blood,"
Ps 19: 5 which is like a *b* coming forth
Isa 61: 10 as a *b* adorns his head like a priest,
62: 5 as a *b* rejoices over his bride,
Jer 7: 34 and *b* in the towns of Judah
16: 9 voices of bride and *b* in this place.
25: 10 and *b*, the sound of millstones
33: 11 the voices of bride and *b*,
Joel 2: 16 Let the *b* leave his room
Mt 9: 15 guests of the *b* mourn while he is
9: 15 when the *b* will be taken from them
25: 1 and went out to meet the *b*.
25: 5 The *b* was a long time in coming,
25: 6 'Here's the *b!* Come out
25: 10 way to buy the oil, the *b* arrived.
Mk 2: 19 the guests of the *b* fast while he is
2: 20 when the *b* will be taken from them
Lk 5: 34 of the *b* fast while he is with them?
5: 35 when the *b* will be taken from them
Jn 2: 9 Then he called the *b* aside and said,
3: 29 The bride belongs to the *b*.
3: 29 The friend who attends the *b* waits
Rev 18: 23 The voice of *b* and bride

BRIDEGROOM'S (BRIDEGROOM)

Jn 3: 29 of joy when he hears the *b* voice.

BRIDEGROOMS (BRIDEGROOM)

Jdg 14: 10 feast there, as was customary for *b*.

BRIDLE (BRIDLES)

Job 41: 13 Who would approach him with a *b*
Ps 32: 9 but must be controlled by bit and *b*

BRIDLES (BRIDLE)

Rev 14: 20 the horses' *b* for a distance of 1,600

BRIEF

Ezr 9: 8 "But now, for a *b* moment,
Job 20: 5 that the mirth of the wicked is *b*,
Isa 54: 7 "For a *b* moment I abandoned you,

BRIER (BRIERS)

Mic 7: 4 The best of them is like a *b*,

BRIERS (BRIER)

Jdg 8: 7 flesh with desert thorns and *b*."
8: 16 them with desert thorns and *b*.
Job 31: 40 then let *b* come up instead of wheat
Isa 5: 6 and *b* and thorns will grow there.
7: 23 there will be only *b* and thorns.
7: 24 for the land will be covered with *b*
7: 25 no longer go there for fear of the *b*
9: 18 it consumes *b* and thorns,
10: 17 his thorns and his *b*.
27: 4 only there were *b* and thorns
32: 13 overgrown with thorns and *b*—
55: 13 instead of *b* the myrtle will grow.
Eze 2: 6 *b* and thorns are all around you
28: 24 neighbors who are painful *b*
Hos 9: 6 of silver will be taken over by *b*,
Lk 6: 44 from thornbushes, or grapes from *b*

BRIGHT (BRIGHTENED BRIGHTENS BRIGHTER BRIGHTNESS)

Lev 13: 2 *b* spot on his skin that may become
14: 56 and for a swelling, a rash or a *b* spot
Job 25: 5 If even the moon is not *b*
37: 21 *b* as it is in the skies
SS 6: 10 fair as the moon, *b* as the sun,
Eze 1: 13 it was *b*, and lightning flashed out
8: 2 there up his appearance was as *b*
Mt 17: 5 a *b* cloud enveloped them,
Lk 9: 29 and his clothes became as *b*
Ac 22: 6 a *b* light from heaven flashed
Rev 19: 8 Fine linen, *b* and clean,
22: 16 of David, and the *b* Morning Star."

BRIGHTENED (BRIGHT)

1Sa 14: 27 hand to his mouth, and his eyes *b*.
14: 29 See how my eyes *b*

BRIGHTENS (BRIGHT)

Pr 16: 15 When a king's face *b*, it means life;
Ecc 8: 1 Wisdom *b* a man's face

BRIGHTER (BRIGHT)

Job 11: 17 Life will be *b* than noonday,
Pr 4: 18 shining ever *b* till the full light
Isa 30: 26 the sunlight will be seven times *b*,
La 4: 7 Their princes were *b* than snow
Ac 26: 13 a light from heaven, *b* than the sun,

BRIGHTNESS (BRIGHT)

2Sa 22: 13 Out of the *b* of his presence
23: 4 like the *b* after rain
Ps 18: 12 of the *b* of his presence clouds
Isa 59: 9 for *b*, but we walk in deep shadows.
60: 3 and kings to the *b* of your dawn.
60: 19 will the *b* of the moon shine on you
Da 12: 3 who are wise will shine like the *b*
Am 5: 20 pitch-dark, without a ray of *b?*

BRILLIANCE (BRILLIANT)

Ac 22: 11 the *b* of the light had blinded me.
Rev 1: 16 was like the sun shining in all its *b*.
21: 11 its *b* was like that of a very precious

BRILLIANT (BRILLIANCE)

Ecc 9: 11 or wealth to the *b*
Eze 1: 4 and surrounded by *b* light.
1: 27 and *b* light surrounded him.

BRIM

Pr 3: 10 your vats will *b* over with new wine
Jn 2: 7 so they filled them to the *b*.

BRINK

Pr 5: 14 I have come to the *b* of utter ruin

BRITTLE

Da 2: 42 will be partly strong and partly *b*.

BROAD (BROADEN)

Nu 25: 4 and expose them in *b* daylight
2Sa 12: 11 lie with your wives in *b* daylight.
12: 12 in *b* daylight before all Israel.' "
Ne 3: 8 Jerusalem as far as the *B* Wall.
12: 38 Tower of the Ovens to the *B* Wall,
Job 37: 10 and the *b* waters become frozen.
Isa 30: 23 cattle will graze in *b* meadows.
33: 21 It will be like a place of *b* rivers
Am 8: 9 and darken the earth in *b* daylight.
Mt 7: 13 and *b* is the road that leads
2Pe 2: 13 is to carouse in *b* daylight.

BROADEN (BROAD)

2Sa 22: 37 You *b* the path beneath me,
Ps 18: 36 You *b* the path beneath me,

BROILED

Lk 24: 42 They gave him a piece of *b* fish,

BROKE (BREAK)

Ex 9: 10 and festering boils *b* out on men
34: 1 on the first tablets, which you *b*.
Lev 24: 10 and a fight *b* out in the camp
26: 13 I *b* the bars of your yoke
Dt 10: 2 on the first tablets, which you *b*.
32: 51 because both of you *b* faith with me
Jos 3: 14 So when the people *b* camp
Jdg 6: 32 because he *b* down Baal's altar.
7: 19 *b* the jars that were in their hands.
1Sa 11: 11 of the night they *b* into the camp
19: 8 Once more war *b* out,
23: 28 Saul *b* off his pursuit of David
2Sa 23: 16 So the three mighty men *b*
2Ki 8: 21 he rose up and *b* through by night;
14: 13 and *b* down the wall of Jerusalem
18: 4 He *b* into pieces the bronze snake
19: 36 king of Assyria *b* camp
23: 8 He *b* down the shrines at the gates
25: 10 *b* down the walls around Jerusalem
25: 13 The Babylonians *b* up the bronze
1Ch 11: 18 the Three *b* through the Philistine
15: 13 time that the LORD our God *b* out
20: 4 war *b* out with the Philistines,
2Ch 15: 16 *b* it up and burned it
21: 9 he rose up and *b* through by night.
25: 23 and *b* down the wall of Jerusalem
26: 6 and *b* down the walls of Gath,
26: 19 leprosy *b* out on his forehead.
34: 4 These he *b* to pieces and scattered
36: 19 and *b* down the wall of Jerusalem;
Job 22: 9 and *b* the strength of the fatherless.
29: 17 I *b* the fangs of the wicked
Ps 74: 13 you *b* the heads of the monster
76: 3 There he *b* the flashing arrows,
78: 21 his fire *b* out against Jacob,
102: 23 of my life he *b* my strength;
106: 29 and a plague *b* out among them.
107: 14 and *b* away their chains.
Isa 7: 17 since Ephraim *b* away from Judah
37: 37 king of Assyria *b* camp
38: 13 but like a lion he *b* all my bones;
Jer 2: 20 "Long ago you *b* off your yoke
28: 10 of the prophet Jeremiah and *b* it,
31: 32 because they *b* my covenant,
39: 8 and *b* down the walls of Jerusalem.
52: 14 commander of the imperial guard *b*
52: 17 The Babylonians *b* up the bronze
Eze 17: 4 he *b* off its topmost shoot
17: 16 he despised and whose treaty he *b*.
17: 19 and my covenant that he *b*.
19: 7 He *b* down their strongholds
29: 7 you *b* and their backs were
44: 7 and blood, and you *b* my covenant.
Da 2: 45 a rock that *b* the iron, the bronze,
Zec 11: 10 took my staff called Favor and *b* it,
11: 14 I *b* my second staff called Union,
Mt 14: 19 he gave thanks and *b* the loaves.
15: 36 he *b* them and gave them
26: 26 took bread, gave thanks and *b* it,
27: 52 The tombs *b* open and the bodies
Mk 4: 37 and the waves *b* over the boat,
5: 4 and *b* the irons on his feet.
6: 41 he gave thanks and *b* the loaves.
8: 6 he *b* them and gave them
8: 19 When I *b* the five loaves
8: 20 "And when I *b* the seven loaves
14: 3 She *b* the jar and poured
14: 22 took bread, gave thanks and *b* it,
14: 72 And he *b* down and wept.
Lk 9: 16 he gave thanks and *b* them.
22: 19 and *b* it, and gave it to them,
24: 30 *b* it and began to give it to them.
24: 35 by them when he *b* the bread.
Jn 19: 32 *b* the legs of the first man who had
Ac 2: 46 They *b* bread in their homes
8: 1 that day a great persecution *b* out
20: 11 he went upstairs again and *b* bread
23: 7 *b* out between the Pharisees
27: 35 Then he *b* it and began to eat.
1Co 11: 24 when he had given thanks, he *b* it
Rev 16: 2 and painful sores *b* out

BROKEN (BREAK)

Ge 17: 14 his people; he has *b* my covenant."
38: 29 "So this is how you have *b* out!"
Ex 21: 8 because he has *b* faith with her.
Lev 6: 21 and present the grain offering *b*
6: 28 the meat is cooked in must be *b;*
11: 35 or cooking pot must be *b* up.
13: 20 skin disease that has *b* out where
13: 25 an infectious disease that has *b* out
13: 39 it is a harmless rash that has *b* out
15: 12 that the man touches must be *b*,
Nu 15: 31 word and *b* his commands,
Dt 21: 6 over the heifer whose neck was *b*
Jdg 6: 30 because he has *b* down Baal's altar
1Sa 2: 4 "The bows of the warriors are *b*,
4: 18 His neck was *b* and he died,
5: 4 His head and hands had been *b* off
14: 33 "You have *b* faith," he said.
2Sa 5: 20 the LORD has *b* out
6: 8 the LORD's wrath had *b* out
1Ki 19: 10 have rejected your covenant, *b*
19: 14 have rejected your covenant, *b*
2Ki 25: 4 Then the city wall was *b* through,
1Ch 13: 11 the LORD's wrath had *b* out
14: 11 God has *b* out against my enemies
2Ch 24: 7 that wicked woman Athaliah had *b*
32: 5 hard repairing all the *b* sections
Ne 1: 3 The wall of Jerusalem is *b* down,
2: 13 which had been *b* down,
Job 2: 8 Then Job took a piece of *b* pottery
4: 10 yet the teeth of the great lions are *b*
4: 20 and dusk they are *b* to pieces;
7: 5 my skin is *b* and festering.
17: 1 My spirit is *b*,
24: 20 but are *b* like a tree.
30: 24 no one lays a hand on a *b* man
31: 22 let it be *b* off at the joint.
31: 39 or *b* the spirit of its tenants,
38: 15 and their upraised arm is *b*.
Ps 3: 7 you have *b* the teeth of the wicked.
31: 12 I have become like *b* pottery.
34: 20 not one of them will be *b*.
37: 15 and their bows will be *b*.
37: 17 the power of the wicked will be *b*,
51: 17 The sacrifices of God are a *b* spirit;
51: 17 a *b* and contrite heart,
69: 20 Scorn has *b* my heart
80: 12 Why have you *b* down its walls
89: 40 You have *b* through all his walls
119:126 your law is being *b*.
124: 7 the snare has been *b*,
Pr 25: 28 Like a city whose walls are *b* down
Ecc 4: 12 of three strands is not quickly *b*.
12: 6 or the golden bowl is *b;*
12: 6 or the wheel *b* at the well,
Isa 1: 28 sinners will both be *b* together,
5: 27 not a sandal thong is *b*.
8: 15 they will fall and be *b*,
10: 27 the yoke will be *b*
14: 5 The LORD has *b* the rod
14: 29 that the rod that struck you is *b;*
24: 5 and *b* the everlasting covenant.
24: 19 The earth is *b* up,
27: 11 When its twigs are dry, they are *b*
33: 8 The treaty is *b*,
33: 20 nor any of its ropes *b*.
58: 12 will be called Repairer of *B* Walls,
59: 5 when one is *b*, an adder is hatched.
Jer 2: 13 *b* cisterns that cannot hold water.
5: 5 But with one accord they too had *b*
11: 10 of Judah have *b* the covenant I
11: 16 and its branches will be *b*.
22: 28 man Jehoiachin a despised, *b* pot,
23: 9 My heart is *b* within me;
28: 12 prophet Hananiah had *b* the yoke

Jer 28: 13 You have *b* a wooden yoke,
33: 21 can be *b* and David will no longer
39: 2 the city wall was *b* through.
48: 4 Moab will be *b;*
48: 17 how *b* the glorious staff!'
48: 17 say, 'How *b* is the mighty scepter,
48: 25 her arm is *b,"*
48: 38 for I have *b* Moab
50: 23 How *b* and shattered
51: 8 Babylon will suddenly fall and be *b*
51: 30 the bars of her gates are *b.*
51: 56 and their bows will be *b.*
52: 7 Then the city wall was *b* through,
La 2: 9 their bars he has *b* and destroyed.
3: 4 and has *b* my bones.
3: 16 He has *b* my teeth with gravel;
Eze 6: 6 your incense altars *b* down,
21: 6 Groan before them with *b* heart
26: 2 'Aha! The gate to the nations is *b,*
26: 10 a city whose walls have been *b*
30: 21 I have *b* the arm of Pharaoh king
30: 22 the good arm as well as the *b* one,
31: 12 its branches lay *b* in all the ravines
32: 28 will be *b* and will lie
Da 2: 35 and the gold were *b* to pieces
8: 8 of his power his large horn was *b*
8: 22 that replaced the one that was *b*
11: 4 his empire will be *b* up
12: 7 the holy people has been finally *b,*
Hos 6: 7 they have *b* the covenant—
8: 1 the people have *b* my covenant
8: 6 It will be *b* in pieces,
Joel 1: 17 the granaries have been *b* down,
Am 9: 11 I will repair its *b* places,
Mic 1: 7 All her idols will be *b* to pieces;
Zec 9: 10 and the battle bow will be *b.*
Mal 2: 11 with one another? Judah has *b* faith
2: 14 because you have *b* faith with her,
Mt 14: 20 of *b* pieces that were left over.
15: 37 of *b* pieces that were left over.
21: 44 on this stone will be *b* to pieces,
24: 43 would not have let his house be *b*
Mk 6: 43 basketfuls of *b* pieces of bread
8: 8 of *b* pieces that were left over.
Lk 8: 29 he had *b* his chains and had been
9: 17 of *b* pieces that were left over.
12: 39 would not have let his house be *b*
20: 18 on that stone will be *b* to pieces,
Jn 7: 23 the law of Moses may not be *b,*
10: 35 and the Scripture cannot be *b*—
19: 31 they asked Pilate to have the legs *b*
19: 36 "Not one of his bones will be *b,"*
Ac 27: 41 and the stern was *b* to pieces
Ro 11: 17 of the branches have been *b* off,
11: 19 "Branches were *b*
11: 20 they were *b* off because of unbelief,
1Ti 5: 12 they have *b* their first pledge.

BROKENHEARTED (HEART)

Ps 34: 18 The LORD is close to the *b*
109: 16 and the needy and the *b.*
147: 3 He heals the *b*
Isa 61: 1 He has sent me to bind up the *b,*

BROKENNESS (BREAK)

Isa 65: 14 and wail in *b* of spirit.

BRONZE (BRONZE-TIPPED)

Ge 4: 22 forged all kinds of tools out of *b*
Ex 25: 3 silver and *b;* blue, purple
26: 11 Then make fifty *b* clasps
26: 37 And cast five *b* bases for them.
27: 2 and overlay the altar with *b.*
27: 3 Make all its utensils of *b*—
27: 4 Make a grating for it, a *b* network,
27: 4 and make a *b* ring at each
27: 6 the altar and overlay them with *b.*
27: 10 twenty posts and twenty *b* bases
27: 11 twenty posts and twenty *b* bases
27: 17 bands and hooks, and *b* bases.
27: 18 five cubits high, and with *b* bases.
27: 19 for the courtyard, are to be of *b.*
30: 18 "Make a *b* basin, with its *b* stand,
31: 4 silver and *b,* to cut and set stones,
35: 5 silver and *b;* blue, purple
35: 16 and all its utensils; the *b* basin
35: 16 of burnt offering with its *b* grating,
35: 24 an offering of silver or *b* brought it
Ex 35: 32 silver and *b,* to cut and set stones,
36: 18 They made fifty *b* clasps
36: 38 and made their five bases of *b.*
38: 2 and they overlaid the altar with *b.*
38: 3 They made all its utensils of *b*—
38: 4 a *b* network, to be under its ledge,
38: 5 They cast *b* rings to hold the poles
38: 5 for the four corners of the *b* grating
38: 6 wood and overlaid them with *b.*
38: 8 They made the *b* basin
38: 8 and its *b* stand from the mirrors
38: 10 twenty posts and twenty *b* bases,
38: 11 twenty posts and twenty *b* bases,
38: 17 The bases for the posts were *b.*
38: 19 with four posts and four *b* bases.
38: 20 the surrounding courtyard were *b.*
38: 29 *b* from the wave offering was 70
38: 30 the *b* altar with its *b* grating
39: 39 the *b* altar with its *b* grating,
Lev 6: 28 but if it is cooked in a *b* pot,
26: 19 and the ground beneath you like *b.*
Nu 4: 13 remove the ashes from the *b* altar
16: 39 collected the *b* censers brought
21: 9 So Moses made a *b* snake
21: 9 and looked at the *b* snake,
31: 22 LORD gave Moses: Gold, silver, *b,*
Dt 28: 23 The sky over your head will be *b,*
33: 25 of your gates will be iron and *b,*
Jos 6: 19 and gold and the articles of *b*
6: 24 and gold and the articles of *b*
22: 8 with silver, gold, *b* and iron,
Jdg 16: 21 Binding him with *b* shackles,
1Sa 17: 5 He had a *b* helmet on his head
17: 5 armor of *b* weighing five thousand
17: 6 a *b* javelin was slung on his back.
17: 6 on his legs he wore *b* greaves,
17: 38 and a *b* helmet on his head.
2Sa 8: 8 David took a great quantity of *b.*
8: 10 articles of silver and gold and *b.*
21: 16 whose *b* spearhead weighed three
22: 35 my arms can bend a bow of *b.*
1Ki 4: 13 walled cities with *b* gate bars),
7: 14 a man of Tyre and a craftsman in *b*
7: 14 experienced in all kinds of *b* work.
7: 15 He cast two *b* pillars, each eighteen
7: 16 made two capitals of cast *b* to set
7: 27 also made ten movable stands of *b;*
7: 30 had four *b* wheels with *b* axles,
7: 38 He then made ten *b* basins,
7: 45 of the LORD were of burnished *b.*
7: 47 of the *b* was not determined.
8: 64 *b* altar before the LORD was too
14: 27 So King Rehoboam made *b* shields
2Ki 16: 14 The *b* altar that stood
16: 15 But I will use the *b* altar
16: 17 from the *b* bulls that supported it
18: 4 into pieces the *b* snake Moses had
25: 7 bound him with *b* shackles
25: 13 Babylonians broke up the *b* pillars,
25: 13 and they carried the *b* to Babylon.
25: 13 the *b* Sea that were at the temple
25: 14 and all the *b* articles used
25: 16 The *b* from the two pillars,
25: 17 The *b* capital on top
25: 17 and pomegranates of *b* all around.
1Ch 15: 19 Ethan were to sound the *b* cymbals
18: 8 David took a great quantity of *b.*
18: 8 the pillars and various *b* articles.
18: 8 used to make the *b* Sea,
18: 10 of articles of gold and silver and *b,*
22: 3 and more *b* than could be weighed.
22: 14 quantities of *b* and iron too great
22: 16 *b* and iron—craftsmen
29: 2 silver for the silver, *b* for the *b,*
29: 7 eighteen thousand talents of *b*
2Ch 1: 5 the *b* altar that Bezalel son of Uri,
1: 6 up to the *b* altar before the LORD
2: 7 skilled to work in gold and silver, *b*
2: 14 *b* and iron, stone and wood,
4: 1 He made a *b* altar twenty cubits
4: 9 and overlaid the doors with *b.*
4: 16 of the LORD were of polished *b.*
4: 18 of the *b* was not determined.
6: 13 Now he had made a *b* platform,
7: 7 *b* altar he had made could not hold
12: 10 So King Rehoboam made *b* shields
24: 12 and *b* to repair the temple.
33: 11 bound him with *b* shackles
2Ch 36: 6 and bound him with *b* shackles
Ezr 8: 27 and two fine articles of polished *b,*
Job 6: 12 Is my flesh *b?*
37: 18 hard as a mirror of cast *b?*
40: 18 His bones are tubes of *b,*
41: 27 and *b* like rotten wood.
Ps 18: 34 my arms can bend a bow of *b.*
107: 16 for he breaks down gates of *b*
Isa 45: 2 I will break down gates of *b*
48: 4 your forehead was *b.*
60: 17 Instead of wood I will bring you *b,*
60: 17 Instead of *b* I will bring you gold,
Jer 1: 18 a *b* wall to stand against the whole
6: 28 They are *b* and iron;
15: 12 iron from the north—or *b?*
15: 20 a fortified wall of *b;*
39: 7 and bound him with *b* shackles
52: 11 bound him with *b* shackles
52: 17 Babylonians broke up the *b* pillars,
52: 17 the *b* Sea that were at the temple
52: 17 they carried all the *b* to Babylon.
52: 18 and all the *b* articles used
52: 20 The *b* from the two pillars,
52: 20 and the twelve *b* bulls under it,
52: 22 The *b* capital on top
52: 22 and pomegranates of *b* all around.
Eze 1: 7 and gleamed like burnished *b.*
9: 2 and stood beside the *b* altar.
27: 13 and articles of *b* for your wares.
40: 3 man whose appearance was like *b;*
Da 2: 32 and thighs of *b,* its legs of iron,
2: 35 Then the iron, the clay, the *b,*
2: 39 Next, a third kingdom, one of *b,*
2: 45 a rock that broke the iron, the *b,*
4: 15 and *b,* remain in the ground,
4: 23 and *b,* in the grass of the field,
5: 4 of *b,* iron, wood and stone.
5: 23 of *b,* iron, wood and stone,
7: 19 with its iron teeth and *b* claws—
10: 6 legs like the gleam of burnished *b.*
Mic 4: 13 I will give you hoofs of *b*
Zec 6: 1 of *b!* The first chariot had red
Rev 1: 15 His feet were like *b* glowing
2: 18 whose feet are like burnished *b.*
9: 20 silver, *b,* stone and wood—
18: 12 costly wood, *b,* iron and marble;

BRONZE-TIPPED (BRONZE)

Job 20: 24 a *b* arrow pierces him.

BROOCHES

Ex 35: 22 *b,* earrings, rings and ornaments.

BROOD

Nu 32: 14 "And here you are, a *b* of sinners,
Job 30: 8 A base and nameless *b,*
Isa 1: 4 a *b* of evildoers,
57: 4 Are you not a *b* of rebels,
Mt 3: 7 he said to them: "You *b* of vipers!
12: 34 You *b* of vipers, how can you who
23: 33 "You snakes! You *b* of vipers!
Lk 3: 7 "You *b* of vipers! Who warned you
2Pe 2: 14 experts in greed—an accursed *b!*

BROOK

2Sa 17: 20 "They crossed over the *b."*
1Ki 17: 4 You will drink from the *b,*
17: 6 evening, and he drank from the *b.*
17: 7 Some time later the *b* dried up
Ps 110: 7 from a *b* beside the way;
Pr 18: 4 of wisdom is a bubbling *b.*
Jer 15: 18 be to me like a deceptive *b,*

BROOM

1Ki 19: 4 He came to a *b* tree, sat
Job 30: 4 their food was the root of the *b* tree
Ps 120: 4 with burning coals of the *b* tree.
Isa 14: 23 her with the *b* of destruction,"

BROTH

Jdg 6: 19 meat in a basket and its *b* in a pot,
6: 20 on this rock, and pour out the *b."*
Isa 65: 4 whose pots hold *b* of unclean meat;

BROTHER (BROTHER-IN-LAW BROTHER'S BROTHERHOOD BROTHERLY BROTHERS)

Ge 4: 2 Later she gave birth to his *b* Abel.

Ge 4: 8 Cain attacked his *b* Abel
4: 8 Now Cain said to his *b* Abel,
4: 9 "Where is your *b* Abel?" "I don't
10: 21 whose older *b* was Japheth;
10: 25 was divided; his *b* was named
14: 13 a *b* of Eshcol and Aner, all
20: 5 and didn't she also say, 'He is my *b*
20: 13 say of me, "He is my *b*." ' "
20: 16 am giving your *b* a thousand
22: 20 she has borne sons to your *b* Nahor
22: 21 Uz the firstborn, Buz his *b*,
22: 23 sons to Abraham's *b* Nahor.
24: 15 the wife of Abraham's *b* Nahor.
24: 29 Rebekah had a *b* named Laban,
24: 48 of my master's *b* for his son.
24: 53 also gave costly gifts to her *b*
24: 55 But her *b* and her mother replied,
25: 26 After this, his *b* came out,
27: 6 your father say to your *b* Esau,
27: 11 "But my *b* Esau is a hairy man,
27: 23 were hairy like those of his *b* Esau;
27: 30 his *b* Esau came in from hunting.
27: 35 "Your *b* came deceitfully
27: 40 and you will serve your *b*.
27: 41 then I will kill my *b* Jacob."
27: 42 "Your *b* Esau is consoling himself
27: 43 at once to my *b* Laban in Haran.
27: 45 When your *b* is no longer angry
28: 2 of Laban, your mother's *b*.
28: 5 of Bethuel the Aramean, the *b* of
29: 10 his mother's *b*, and Laban's sheep,
32: 3 of him to his *b* Esau in the land
32: 6 they said, "We went to your *b* Esau
32: 11 I pray, from the hand of my *b* Esau,
32: 13 he selected a gift for his *b* Esau:
32: 17 "When my *b* Esau meets you
33: 3 seven times as he approached his *b*.
33: 9 "I already have plenty, my *b*.
35: 1 fleeing from your *b* Esau."
35: 7 when he was fleeing from his *b*.
36: 6 some distance from his *b* Jacob.
37: 26 "What will we gain if we kill our *b*
37: 27 he is our *b*, our own flesh and blood
38: 8 to produce offspring for your *b*."
38: 9 from producing offspring for his *b*.
38: 29 his *b* came out, and she said,
38: 30 his *b*, who had the scarlet thread
42: 4 Joseph's *b*, with the others,
42: 15 unless your youngest *b* comes here.
42: 16 one of your number to get your *b*;
42: 20 you must bring your youngest *b*
42: 21 being punished because of our *b*.
42: 34 But bring your youngest *b* to me
42: 34 Then I will give your *b* back to you,
42: 38 his *b* is dead and he is the only one
43: 3 see my face again unless your *b* is
43: 4 If you will send our *b* along with us,
43: 5 see my face again unless your *b* is
43: 6 the man you had another *b*?"
43: 7 'Bring your *b* down here'?"
43: 7 you have another *b*?' We simply
43: 13 Take your *b* also and go back
43: 14 man so that he will let your other *b*
43: 29 about and saw his *b* Benjamin,
43: 29 he asked, "Is this your youngest *b*,
43: 30 Deeply moved at the sight of his *b*,
44: 19 'Do you have a father or a *b*?'
44: 20 His *b* is dead, and he is the only
44: 23 'Unless your youngest *b* comes
44: 26 Only if our youngest *b* is
44: 26 unless our youngest *b* is with us.'
45: 4 he said, "I am your *b* Joseph,
45: 12 and so can my *b* Benjamin,
45: 14 arms around his *b* Benjamin
48: 19 his younger *b* will be greater
Ex 4: 14 "What about your *b*, Aaron
7: 1 your *b* Aaron will be your prophet.
7: 2 and your *b* Aaron is to tell Pharaoh
28: 1 Have Aaron your *b* brought to you
28: 2 sacred garments for your *b* Aaron,
28: 4 sacred garments for your *b* Aaron
28: 41 put these clothes on your *b* Aaron
32: 27 each killing his *b* and friend
Lev 16: 2 "Tell your *b* Aaron not
18: 14 " 'Do not dishonor your father's *b*
18: 16 that would dishonor your *b*.
19: 17 " 'Do not hate your *b* in your heart.
20: 21 impurity; he has dishonored his *b*.
Lev 21: 2 or father, his son or daughter, his *b*,
Nu 6: 7 or mother or *b* or sister dies,
20: 8 your *b* Aaron gather the assembly
20: 14 "This is what your *b* Israel says:
27: 13 your people, as your *b* Aaron was,
36: 2 inheritance of our *b* Zelophehad
Dt 1: 16 the case is between *b* Israelites
3: 18 over ahead of your *b* Israelites.
13: 6 If your very own *b*, or your son
15: 2 from his fellow Israelite or *b*,
15: 3 cancel any debt your *b* owes you.
15: 7 or tightfisted toward your poor *b*.
15: 9 will toward your needy *b*
17: 15 one who is not a *b* Israelite.
19: 18 giving false testimony against his *b*,
19: 19 as he intended to do to his *b*.
22: 2 If the *b* does not live near you
23: 7 abhor an Edomite, for he is your *b*.
23: 19 Do not charge your *b* interest,
23: 20 interest, but not a *b* Israelite,
24: 7 kidnapping one of his *b* Israelites
24: 14 whether he is a *b* Israelite
25: 3 your *b* will be degraded
25: 5 Her husband's *b* shall take her
25: 6 carry on the name of the dead *b*
25: 7 "My husband's *b* refuses to carry
28: 54 have no compassion on his own *b*
32: 50 your *b* Aaron died on Mount Hor
Jos 15: 17 Othniel son of Kenaz, Caleb's *b*,
Jdg 1: 13 Caleb's younger *b*, took it;
3: 9 Caleb's younger *b*, who saved them
9: 3 for they said, "He is our *b*."
9: 18 of Shechem because he is your *b*)—
9: 21 he was afraid of his *b* Abimelech.
9: 24 avenged on their *b* Abimelech
20: 28 to battle with Benjamin our *b*,
Ru 4: 3 belonged to our *b* Elimelech.
1Sa 14: 3 a son of Ichabod's *b* Ahitub son
17: 28 When Eliab, David's oldest *b*,
20: 29 my *b* has ordered me to be there.
26: 6 Joab's *b*, "Who will go
2Sa 1: 26 I grieve for you, Jonathan my *b*;
2: 22 How could I look your *b* Joab
3: 27 to avenge the blood of his *b* Asahel
3: 30 and his *b* Abishai murdered Abner
3: 30 he had killed their *b* Asahel
4: 6 and his *b* Baanah slipped away.
4: 9 answered Recab and his *b* Baanah,
10: 10 the command of Abishai his *b*
13: 3 son of Shimeah, David's *b*.
13: 4 with Tamar, my *b* Absalom's sister
13: 7 "Go to the house of your *b* Amnon
13: 8 went to the house of her *b* Amnon,
13: 10 and brought it to her *b* Amnon
13: 12 "Don't, my *b*!" she said to him.
13: 20 Her *b* Absalom said to her,
13: 20 lived in her *b* Absalom's house,
13: 20 quiet now, my sister; he is your *b*.
13: 20 "Has that Amnon, your *b*,
13: 26 please let my *b* Amnon come
13: 32 Jonadab son of Shimeah, David's *b*
14: 7 for the life of his *b* whom he killed;
14: 7 over the one who struck his *b* down
18: 2 a third under Joab's *b* Abishai son
20: 9 to Amasa, "How are you, my *b*?"
20: 10 his *b* Abishai pursued Sheba son
21: 21 son of Shimeah, David's *b*,
23: 18 Abishai the *b* of Joab son
23: 24 the Thirty were: Asahel the *b*
1Ki 1: 10 the special guard or his *b* Solomon.
2: 7 when I fled from your *b* Absalom.
2: 15 and the kingdom has gone to my *b*;
2: 21 in marriage to your *b* Adonijah."
2: 22 after all, he is my older *b*— yes,
9: 13 these you have given me, my *b*?"
13: 30 "Oh, my *b*!" After burying him,
20: 32 "Is he still alive? He is my *b*."
20: 33 Yes, your *b* Ben-Hadad!" they said
1Ch 1: 19 was divided; his *b* was named
2: 32 Shammai's *b*: Jether and Jonathan.
2: 42 sons of Caleb the *b* of Jerahmeel:
4: 11 Shuhah's *b*, was the father
7: 16 His *b* was named Sheresh,
7: 35 The sons of his *b* Helem: Zophah,
8: 39 of his *b* Eshek: Ulam his firstborn,
11: 20 Abishai the *b* of Joab was chief
11: 26 mighty men were: Asahel the *b*
11: 38 son of Ezbai, Joel the *b* of Nathan,
1Ch 11: 45 son of Shimri, his *b* Joha the Tizite,
19: 11 the command of Abishai his *b*,
19: 15 they too fled before his *b* Abishai
20: 5 son of Jair killed Lahmi the *b*
20: 7 Jonathan son of Shimea, David's *b*,
24: 25 The *b* of Micah: Isshiah;
24: 31 of the oldest *b* were treated
26: 22 of Jehieli, Zetham and his *b* Joel.
27: 7 the fourth month, was Asahel the *b*
27: 18 over Judah: Elihu, a *b* of David;
2Ch 31: 12 and his *b* Shimei was next in rank.
31: 13 under Conaniah and Shimei his *b*,
36: 4 Neco took Eliakim's *b* Jehoahaz
36: 4 king of Egypt made Eliakim, a *b*
Ezr 7: 18 your *b* Jews may then do whatever
Ne 7: 2 charge of Jerusalem my *b* Hanani,
Job 30: 29 I have become a *b* of jackals,
Ps 35: 14 as though for my friend or *b*.
50: 20 speak continually against your *b*
Pr 17: 17 and a *b* is born for adversity.
18: 9 is *b* to one who destroys.
18: 19 An offended *b* is more unyielding
18: 24 a friend who sticks closer than a *b*.
27: 10 neighbor nearby than a *b* far away.
Ecc 4: 8 he had neither son nor *b*.
SS 8: 1 If only you were to me like a *b*,
Isa 9: 19 no one will spare his *b*.
19: 2 *b* will fight against *b*,
41: 6 and says to his *b*, "Be strong!"
Jer 9: 4 For every *b* is a deceiver,
22: 18 'Alas, my *b*! Alas, my sister!'
31: 34 or a man his *b*, saying, 'Know
Eze 18: 18 robbed his *b* and did what was
38: 21 man's sword will be against his *b*.
44: 25 or daughter, *b* or unmarried sister,
Am 1: 11 Because he pursued his *b*
Ob : 10 the violence against your *b* Jacob,
: 12 should not look down on your *b*
Mic 7: 2 each hunts his *b* with a net.
Hag 2: 22 each by the sword of his *b*.
Mal 1: 2 "Was not Esau Jacob's *b*?"
Mt 4: 18 called Peter and his *b* Andrew.
4: 21 son of Zebedee and his *b* John.
5: 22 angry with his *b* will be subject
5: 22 anyone who says to his *b*, 'Raca,'
5: 23 that your *b* has something
5: 24 and be reconciled to your *b*;
7: 4 How can you say to your *b*,
10: 2 and his *b* John; Philip
10: 2 is called Peter) and his *b* Andrew;
10: 21 "Brother will betray *b* to death,
10: 21 "*B* will betray brother to death,
12: 50 will of my Father in heaven is my *b*
14: 3 his *b* Philip's wife,
17: 1 James and John the *b* of James,
18: 15 you have won your *b* over.
18: 15 "If your *b* sins against you,
18: 21 many times shall I forgive my *b*
18: 35 you forgive your *b* from your heart
22: 24 his *b* must marry the widow
22: 25 no children, he left his wife to his *b*.
22: 26 to the second and third *b*,
Mk 1: 16 and his *b* Andrew casting a net
1: 19 of Zebedee and his *b* John in a boat
3: 17 and his *b* John (to them he gave
3: 35 Whoever does God's will is my *b*
5: 37 James and John the *b* of James.
6: 3 Isn't this Mary's son and the *b*
6: 17 his *b* Philip's wife, whom he had
12: 19 and have children for his *b*.
12: 19 wrote for us that if a man's *b* dies
13: 12 "*B* will betray *b* to death,
Lk 3: 1 his *b* Philip tetrarch of Iturea
6: 14 his *b* Andrew, James, John, Philip,
6: 42 How can you say to your *b*, '*B*,
12: 13 tell my *b* to divide the inheritance
15: 27 'Your *b* has come,' he replied,
15: 28 "The older *b* became angry
15: 32 because this *b* of yours was dead
17: 3 "If your *b* sins, rebuke him,
20: 28 and have children for his *b*.
20: 28 wrote for us that if a man's *b* dies
Jn 1: 40 Andrew, Simon Peter's *b*,
1: 41 was to find his *b* Simon
6: 8 Andrew, Simon Peter's *b*, spoke up
11: 2 whose *b* Lazarus now lay sick,
11: 19 them in the loss of their *b*.
11: 21 my *b* would not have died.

Jn 11: 23 to her, "Your *b* will rise again."
11: 32 my *b* would not have died."
Ac 9: 17 he said, "*B* Saul, the Lord—Jesus,
12: 2 He had James, the *b* of John,
21: 20 Then they said to Paul: "You see, *b*
22: 13 '*B* Saul, receive your sight!'
Ro 14: 10 then, why do you judge your *b*?
14: 10 why do you look down on your *b*?
14: 15 If your *b* is distressed
14: 15 not by your eating destroy your *b*
14: 21 anything else that will cause your *b*
16: 23 and our *b* Quartus send you their
1Co 1: 1 and our *b* Sosthenes, To the church
5: 11 with anyone who calls himself a *b*
6: 6 one *b* goes to law against another—
7: 12 If any *b* has a wife who is not
8: 11 this weak *b*, for whom Christ died,
8: 13 if what I eat causes my *b* to fall
16: 12 Now about our *b* Apollos:
2Co 1: 1 and Timothy our *b*, To the church
2: 13 I did not find my *b* Titus there.
8: 18 along with him the *b* who is praised
8: 22 with them our *b* who has often
12: 18 go to you and I sent our *b* with him.
Gal 1: 19 only James, the Lord's *b*.
Eph 6: 21 the dear *b* and faithful servant
Php 2: 25 my *b*, fellow worker and fellow
Col 1: 1 and Timothy our *b*, To the holy
4: 7 He is a dear *b*, a faithful minister
4: 9 and dear *b*, who is one of you.
1Th 3: 2 who is our *b* and God's fellow
4: 6 matter no one should wrong his *b*
2Th 3: 6 away from every *b* who is idle
3: 15 as an enemy, but warn him as a *b*.
Phm : 1 of Christ Jesus, and Timothy our *b*,
: 7 *b*, have refreshed the hearts
: 16 as a man and as a *b* in the Lord.
: 16 but better than a slave, as a dear *b*.
: 20 *b*, that I may have some benefit
Heb 8: 11 or a man his *b*, saying, 'Know
13: 23 know that our *b* Timothy has been
Jas 1: 9 *b* in humble circumstances ought
2: 15 Suppose a *b* or sister is
4: 11 Anyone who speaks against his *b*
1Pe 5: 12 whom I regard as a faithful *b*,
2Pe 3: 15 just as our dear *b* Paul
1Jn 2: 9 hates his *b* is still in the darkness.
2: 10 Whoever loves his *b* lives
2: 11 But whoever hates his *b* is
3: 10 is anyone who does not love his *b*.
3: 12 to the evil one and murdered his *b*.
3: 15 who hates his *b* is a murderer,
3: 17 material possessions and sees his *b*
4: 20 For anyone who does not love his *b*
4: 20 yet hates his *b*, he is a liar.
4: 21 loves God must also love his *b*.
5: 16 If anyone sees his *b* commit a sin
Jude : 1 of Jesus Christ and a *b* of James,
Rev 1: 9 your *b* and companion

BROTHER-IN-LAW (BROTHER)

Ge 38: 8 as a *b* to produce offspring
Dt 25: 5 and fulfill the duty of a *b* to her.
25: 7 He will not fulfill the duty of a *b*
Jdg 4: 11 descendants of Hobab, Moses' *b*,

BROTHER'S (BROTHER)

Ge 4: 9 "Am I my *b* keeper?" The LORD
4: 10 Your *b* blood cries out to me
4: 11 mouth to receive your *b* blood
4: 21 His *b* name was Jubal; he was
27: 44 a while until your *b* fury subsides.
38: 8 with your *b* wife and fulfill your
38: 9 so whenever he lay with his *b* wife,
Lev 18: 16 sexual relations with your *b* wife;
20: 21 " 'If a man marries his *b* wife,
Dt 22: 1 If you see your *b* ox or sheep
22: 3 the same if you find your *b* donkey
22: 4 If you see your *b* donkey
25: 7 to carry on his *b* name in Israel.
25: 7 want to marry his *b* wife,
25: 9 his *b* widow shall go up to him
25: 9 will not build up his *b* family line."
Job 1: 13 drinking wine at the oldest *b* house
1: 18 drinking wine at the oldest *b* house
Pr 27: 10 and do not go to your *b* house
Hos 12: 3 In the womb he grasped his *b* heel;
Mt 7: 3 the speck of sawdust in your *b* eye
7: 5 remove the speck from your *b* eye.
Mk 6: 18 lawful for you to have your *b* wife."
Lk 3: 19 his *b* wife, and all the other evil
6: 41 the speck of sawdust in your *b* eye
6: 42 remove the speck from your *b* eye.
Ro 14: 13 or obstacle in your *b* way.
1Jn 3: 12 were evil and his *b* were righteous.

BROTHERHOOD (BROTHER)

Am 1: 9 disregarding a treaty of *b*,
Zec 11: 14 breaking the *b* between Judah
1Pe 2: 17 Love the *b* of believers, fear God,

BROTHERLY (BROTHER)

Ro 12: 10 devoted to one another in *b* love.
1Th 4: 9 Now about *b* love we do not need
2Pe 1: 7 and to godliness, *b* kindness;
1: 7 kindness; and to *b* kindness,

BROTHERS (BROTHER)

Ge 9: 22 and told his two *b* outside.
9: 25 will he be to his *b*."
13: 8 herdsmen and mine, for we are *b*.
16: 12 hostility toward all his *b*."
25: 18 lived in hostility toward all their *b*.
27: 29 Be lord over your *b*,
29: 4 "My *b*, where are you from?"
34: 11 said to Dinah's father and *b*,
34: 25 Simeon and Levi, Dinah's *b*,
37: 2 was tending the flocks with his *b*,
37: 4 When his *b* saw that their father
37: 5 and when he told it to his *b*,
37: 8 His *b* said to him, "Do you intend
37: 9 dream, and he told it to his *b*.
37: 10 and I and your *b* actually come
37: 10 he told his father as well as his *b*,
37: 11 His *b* were jealous of him,
37: 12 Now his *b* had gone to graze their
37: 13 your *b* are grazing the flocks
37: 14 and see if all is well with your *b*
37: 16 He replied, "I'm looking for my *b*.
37: 17 So Joseph went after his *b*
37: 23 So when Joseph came to his *b*,
37: 26 said to his *b*, "What will we gain
37: 27 His *b* agreed.
37: 28 his *b* pulled Joseph up out
37: 30 He went back to his *b* and said,
38: 1 Judah left his *b* and went
38: 11 "He may die too, just like his *b*."
42: 3 Then ten of Joseph's *b* went
42: 6 So when Joseph's *b* arrived,
42: 7 As soon as Joseph saw his *b*,
42: 8 Although Joseph recognized his *b*,
42: 13 "Your servants were twelve *b*,
42: 19 let one of your *b* stay here in prison
42: 28 been returned," he said to his *b*.
42: 32 We were twelve *b*, sons
42: 33 Leave one of your *b* here with me,
43: 32 by himself, the *b* by themselves,
44: 14 when Judah and his *b* came in,
44: 33 and let the boy return with his *b*.
45: 1 he made himself known to his *b*.
45: 3 Joseph said to his *b*, "I am Joseph!
45: 3 his *b* were not able to answer him,
45: 4 Then Joseph said to his *b*,
45: 15 Afterward his *b* talked with him.
45: 15 And he kissed all his *b* and wept
45: 16 palace that Joseph's *b* had come,
45: 17 said to Joseph, "Tell your *b*,
45: 24 Then he sent his *b* away, and
46: 31 Then Joseph said to his *b*
46: 31 'My *b* and my father's household,
47: 1 told Pharaoh, "My father and *b*,
47: 2 five of his *b* and presented them
47: 3 Pharaoh asked the *b*, "What is
47: 5 and your *b* have come to you,
47: 6 your *b* in the best part of the land.
47: 11 Joseph settled his father and his *b*
47: 12 also provided his father and his *b*
48: 6 under the names of their *b*.
48: 22 as one who is over your *b*,
49: 5 "Simeon and Levi are *b*—
49: 8 "Judah, your *b* will praise you;
49: 26 the brow of the prince among his *b*.
50: 8 and his *b* and those belonging
50: 14 with his *b* and all the others who
50: 15 When Joseph's *b* saw that their
50: 17 I ask you to forgive your *b* the sins
Ge 50: 18 His *b* then came and threw
50: 24 Then Joseph said to his *b*,
Ex 1: 6 Now Joseph and all his *b*
32: 29 were against your own sons and *b*,
Lev 21: 10 the one among his *b* who has had
Nu 8: 26 They may assist their *b*
20: 3 died when our *b* fell dead
27: 9 give his inheritance to his *b*.
27: 10 If he has no *b*, give his inheritance
27: 10 give his inheritance to his father's *b*
27: 11 father had no *b*, give his
Dt 1: 16 Hear the disputes between your *b*
1: 28 Our *b* have made us lose heart.
2: 4 of your *b* the descendants of Esau,
2: 8 went on past our *b* the descendants
3: 20 the LORD gives rest to your *b*
10: 9 or inheritance among their *b*;
15: 7 among your *b* in any of the towns
15: 11 to be openhanded toward your *b*
17: 15 be from among your own *b*.
17: 20 consider himself better than his *b*
18: 2 have no inheritance among their *b*;
18: 15 me from among your own *b*.
18: 18 you from among their *b*;
20: 8 home so that his *b* will not become
25: 5 If *b* are living together
33: 9 He did not recognize his *b*
33: 16 the brow of the prince among his *b*.
33: 24 let him be favored by his *b*,
Jos 1: 14 You are to help your *b*
1: 14 must cross over ahead of your *b*.
2: 13 my *b* and sisters, and all who
2: 18 your *b* and all your family
6: 23 her father and mother and *b*
14: 8 but my *b* who went up
17: 4 along with the *b* of their father,
17: 4 us an inheritance among our *b*."
22: 3 you have not deserted your *b*
22: 4 your God has given your *b* rest
22: 7 side of the Jordan with their *b*.)
22: 8 and divide with your *b* the plunder
Jdg 1: 3 said to the Simeonites their *b*,
1: 17 went with the Simeonites their *b*
8: 19 Gideon replied, "Those were my *b*,
9: 1 went to his mother's *b* in Shechem
9: 3 When the *b* repeated all this
9: 5 one stone murdered his seventy *b*,
9: 24 who had helped him murder his *b*.
9: 26 moved with his *b* into Shechem,
9: 31 and his *b* have come to Shechem
9: 41 and Zebul drove Gaal and his *b* out
9: 56 father by murdering his seventy *b*.
11: 3 So Jephthah fled from his *b*
16: 31 his *b* and his father's whole family
18: 8 their *b* asked them, "How did you
18: 14 the land of Laish said to their *b*,
20: 23 our *b*?" The LORD answered,
21: 6 the Israelites grieved for their *b*,
21: 22 When their fathers or *b* complain
1Sa 16: 13 him in the presence of his *b*,
17: 17 these ten loaves of bread for your *b*
17: 18 See how your *b* are and bring back
17: 22 to the battle lines and greeted his *b*.
20: 29 let me get away to see my *b*.'
22: 1 When his *b* and his father's
30: 23 David replied, "No, my *b*,
2Sa 2: 26 men to stop pursuing their *b*?"
2: 27 pursuit of their *b* until morning."
19: 12 You are my *b*, my own flesh
19: 41 "Why did our *b*, the men of Judah,
1Ki 1: 9 He invited all his *b*, the king's sons,
12: 24 Do not go up to fight against your *b*
1Ch 4: 9 was more honorable than his *b*.
4: 27 his *b* did not have many children;
5: 2 Judah was the strongest of his *b*
9: 17 Talmon, Ahiman and their *b*,
9: 25 Their *b* in their villages had
9: 32 of their Kohathite *b* were in charge
13: 2 of our *b* throughout the territories
15: 16 of the Levites to appoint their *b*
15: 17 and from their *b* the Merarites,
15: 17 from his *b*, Asaph son of Berekiah;
15: 18 and with them their *b* next in rank:
23: 32 and, under their *b* the descendants
24: 31 as their *b* the descendants
28: 2 Listen to me, my *b* and my people.
2Ch 11: 4 Do not go up to fight against your *b*
11: 22 to be the chief prince among his *b*,

2Ch 19:10 come on you and your *b*.
21: 2 Jehoram's *b*, the sons
21: 4 he put all his *b* to the sword
21:13 also murdered your own *b*,
29:15 When they had assembled their *b*
30: 7 Do not be like your fathers and *b*,
30: 9 then your *b* and your children will
35: 9 his *b*, and Hashabiah, Jeiel
Ezr 3: 8 and the rest of their *b* (the priests
3: 9 and his sons and *b* and Kadmiel
3: 9 of Henadad and their sons and *b*—
6:20 for their *b* the priests
8:18 and Sherebiah's sons and *b*,
8:19 and his *b* and nephews, 20 men.
8:24 Hashabiah and ten of their *b*,
10:18 and his *b*: Maaseiah, Eliezer,
Ne 1: 2 one of my *b*, came from Judah
4:14 and fight for your *b*, your sons
4:23 Neither I nor my *b* nor my men
5: 1 outcry against their Jewish *b*.
5: 8 Now you are selling your *b*,
5: 8 back our Jewish *b* who were sold
5:10 I and my *b* and my men are
5:14 nor my *b* ate the food allotted
10:29 all these now join their *b* the nobles
13:13 distributing the supplies to their *b*.
Job 6:15 But my *b* are as undependable
19:13 "He has alienated my *b* from me;
19:17 I am loathsome to my own *b*.
22: 6 security from your *b* for no reason;
42:11 All his *b* and sisters and everyone
42:15 an inheritance along with their *b*.
Ps 22:22 I will declare your name to my *b*;
69: 8 I am a stranger to my *b*,
122: 8 For the sake of my *b* and friends,
133: 1 is when *b* live together in unity!
Pr 6:19 who stirs up dissension among *b*.
17: 2 the inheritance as one of the *b*.
Isa 3: 6 A man will seize one of his *b*
66: 5 "Your *b* who hate you,
66:20 And they will bring all your *b*,
Jer 7:15 as I did all your *b*, the people
9: 4 do not trust your *b*.
12: 6 Your *b*, your own family—
35: 3 and his *b* and all his sons—
Eze 11:15 came to me: "Son of man, your *b*—
11:15 your *b* who are your blood relatives
Hos 2: 1 "Say of your *b*, 'My people,'
13:15 even though he thrives among his *b*
Mic 5: 3 and the rest of his *b* return
Mt 1: 2 Jacob the father of Judah and his *b*,
1:11 and his *b* at the time of the exile
4:18 he saw two *b*, Simon called Peter
4:21 on from there, he saw two other *b*,
5:47 And if you greet only your *b*,
12:46 his mother and *b* stood outside,
12:47 and *b* are standing outside,
12:48 and who are my *b*?" Pointing
12:49 "Here are my mother and my *b*.
13:55 and aren't his *b* James, Joseph,
19:29 everyone who has left houses or *b*
20:24 they were indignant with the two *b*
22:25 Now there were seven *b* among us.
23: 8 only one Master and you are all *b*.
25:40 one of the least of these *b* of mine,
28:10 Go and tell my *b* to go to Galilee;
Mk 3:31 Then Jesus' mother and *b* arrived.
3:32 and *b* are outside looking for you."
3:33 "Who are my mother and my *b*?"
3:34 "Here are my mother and my *b*!
10:29 or *b* or sisters or mother or father
10:30 *b*, sisters, mothers, children
12:20 Now there were seven *b*.
Lk 8:19 Now Jesus' mother and *b* came
8:20 and *b* are standing outside,
8:21 *b* are those who hear God's word
14:12 do not invite your friends, your *b*
14:26 and children, his *b* and sisters—
16:28 my father's house, for I have five *b*.
18:29 one who has left home or wife or *b*
20:29 Now there were seven *b*.
21:16 You will be betrayed by parents, *b*,
22:32 turned back, strengthen your *b*."
Jn 2:12 Capernaum with his mother and *b*
7: 3 was near, Jesus' *b* said to him,
7: 5 his own *b* did not believe in him.
7:10 after his *b* had left for the Feast,
20:17 Go instead to my *b* and tell them,
Jn 21:23 among the *b* that this disciple
Ac 1:14 the mother of Jesus, and his *b*.
1:16 hundred and twenty) and said, "*B*,
2:29 "*B*, I can tell you confidently that
2:37 *B*, what shall we do?" Peter replied
3:17 "Now, *b*, I know that you acted
6: 3 *B*, choose seven men
7: 2 To this he replied: "*B* and fathers,
7:13 Joseph told his *b* who he was,
7:26 you are *b*; why do you want
9:30 When the *b* learned of this,
10:23 and some of the *b* from Joppa went
11: 1 the *b* throughout Judea heard that
11:12 These six *b* also went with me,
11:29 help for the *b* living in Judea.
12:17 "Tell James and the *b* about this,"
13:15 word to them, saying, "*B*,
13:26 "*B*, children of Abraham,
13:38 my *b*, I want you to know that
14: 2 poisoned their minds against the *b*.
15: 1 to Antioch and were teaching the *b*
15: 3 This news made all the *b* very glad.
15: 7 got up and addressed them: "*B*,
15:13 James spoke up: "*B*, listen to me.
15:22 who were leaders among the *b*.
15:23 The apostles and elders, your *b*,
15:32 to encourage and strengthen the *b*.
15:33 sent off by the *b* with the blessing
15:36 visit the *b* in all the towns where
15:40 commended by the *b* to the grace
16: 2 *b* at Lystra and Iconium spoke well
16:40 where they met with the *b*
17: 6 and some other *b* before the city
17:10 the *b* sent Paul and Silas away
17:14 The *b* immediately sent Paul
18:18 he left the *b* and sailed for Syria,
18:27 the *b* encouraged him
21: 7 where we greeted the *b*
21:17 the *b* received us warmly.
22: 1 he said to them in Aramaic: "*B*
22: 5 from them to their *b* in Damascus,
23: 1 at the Sanhedrin and said, "My *b*,
23: 5 high priest?" Paul replied, "*B*,
23: 6 called out in the Sanhedrin, "My *b*,
28:14 we found some *b* who invited us
28:15 The *b* there had heard that we were
28:17 Paul said to them: "My *b*,
28:21 and none of the *b* who has come
Ro 1:13 I do not want you to be unaware, *b*,
7: 1 *b*— for I am speaking
7: 4 So, my *b*, you also died to the law
8:12 Therefore, *b*, we have an obligation
8:29 be the firstborn among many *b*.
9: 3 off from Christ for the sake of my *b*
10: 1 *B*, my heart's desire and prayer
11:25 *b*, so that you may not be conceited
12: 1 *b*, in view of God's mercy,
15:14 I myself am convinced, my *b*,
15:30 *b*, by our Lord Jesus Christ
16:14 Hermas and the *b* with them.
16:17 *b*, to watch out for those who cause
1Co 1:10 *b*, in the name of our Lord Jesus
1:11 *b*, some from Chloe's household
1:26 *B*, think of what you were
2: 1 *b*, I did not come with eloquence
3: 1 *B*, I could not address you
4: 6 Now, *b*, I have applied these things
6: 8 do wrong, and you do this to your *b*
7:24 *B*, each man, as responsible to God
7:29 *b*, is that the time is short.
8:12 sin against your *b* in this way
9: 5 and the Lord's *b* and Cephas?
10: 1 you to be ignorant of the fact, *b*,
11:33 my *b*, when you come together
12: 1 Now about spiritual gifts, *b*,
14: 6 Now, *b*, if I come to you and speak
14:20 *B*, stop thinking like children.
14:26 *b*? When you come together,
14:39 my *b*, be eager to prophesy,
15: 1 Now, *b*, I want to remind you
15: 6 hundred of the *b* at the same time,
15:31 I die every day—I mean that, *b*—
15:50 *b*, that flesh and blood cannot
15:58 Therefore, my dear *b*, stand firm.
16:11 am expecting him along with the *b*.
16:12 him to go to you with the *b*.
16:15 *b*, to submit to such as these
16:20 All the *b* here send you greetings.
2Co 1: 8 you to be uninformed, *b*,
8: 1 *b*, we want you to know about
8:23 for our *b*, they are representatives
9: 3 But I am sending the *b*
9: 5 necessary to urge the *b* to visit you
11: 9 for the *b* who came
11:26 and in danger from false *b*.
13:11 Finally, *b*, good-by.
Gal 1: 2 all the *b* with me, To the churches
1:11 *b*, that the gospel I preached is not
2: 4 some false *b* had infiltrated our
3:15 *B*, let me take an example
4:12 I plead with you, *b*, become like me
4:28 *b*, like Isaac, are children
4:31 *b*, we are not children
5:11 *B*, if I am still preaching
5:13 You, my *b*, were called to be free.
6: 1 *B*, if someone is caught in a sin,
6:18 be with your spirit, *b*.
Eph 6:23 Peace to the *b*, and love with faith
Php 1:12 Now I want you to know, *b*,
1:14 most of the *b* in the Lord have been
3: 1 Finally, my *b*, rejoice in the Lord!
3:13 *B*, I do not consider myself yet
3:17 others in following my example, *b*,
4: 1 my *b*, you whom I love and long for
4: 8 Finally, *b*, whatever is true,
4:21 *b* who are with me send greetings.
Col 1: 2 and faithful *b* in Christ at Colosse:
4:15 greetings to the *b* at Laodicea,
1Th 1: 4 *B* loved by God, we know that he
2: 1 *b*, that our visit to you was not
2: 9 Surely you remember, *b*, our toil
2:14 *b*, became imitators
2:17 But, *b*, when we were torn away
3: 7 *b*, in all our distress
4: 1 *b*, we instructed you how to live
4:10 you do love all the *b*
4:10 *b*, to do so more and more.
4:13 *B*, we do not want you
5: 1 *b*, about times and dates we do not
5: 4 *b*, are not in darkness
5:12 *b*, to respect those who work hard
5:14 *b*, warn those who are idle,
5:25 *B*, pray for us.
5:26 Greet all the *b* with a holy kiss.
5:27 to have this letter read to all the *b*.
2Th 1: 3 always to thank God for you, *b*,
2: 1 *b*, not to become easily unsettled
2:13 God for you, *b* loved by the Lord,
2:15 *b*, stand firm and hold
3: 1 *b*, pray for us that the message
3: 6 Jesus Christ, we command you, *b*,
3:13 *b*, never tire of doing what is right.
1Ti 4: 6 you point these things out to the *b*,
5: 1 younger men as *b*, older women
6: 2 for them because they are *b*.
2Ti 4:21 Linus, Claudia and all the *b*.
Heb 2:11 Jesus is not ashamed to call them *b*.
2:12 "I will declare your name to my *b*;
2:17 to be made like his *b* in every way,
3: 1 holy *b*, who share in the heavenly
3:12 *b*, that none of you has a sinful,
7: 5 even though their *b* are descended
7: 5 their *b*— even though their
10:19 *b*, since we have confidence
13: 1 Keep on loving each other as *b*.
13:22 *B*, I urge you to bear with my word
Jas 1: 2 Consider it pure joy, my *b*,
1:16 Don't be deceived, my dear *b*.
1:19 My dear *b*, take note of this:
2: 1 My *b*, as believers
2: 5 evil thoughts? Listen, my dear *b*:
2:14 judgment! What good is it, my *b*,
3: 1 presume to be teachers, my *b*,
3:10 My *b*, this should not be.
3:12 My *b*, can a fig tree bear olives,
4:11 *B*, do not slander one another.
5: 7 then, *b*, until the Lord's coming.
5: 9 grumble against each other, *b*,
5:10 Judge is standing at the door! *B*,
5:12 Above all, my *b*, do not swear—
5:19 My *b*, if one of you should wander
1Pe 1:22 you have sincere love for your *b*,
3: 8 be sympathetic, love as *b*,
5: 9 because you know that your *b*
2Pe 1:10 my *b*, be all the more eager
1Jn 3:13 Do not be surprised, my *b*,

1Jn 3: 14 death to life, because we love our *b*.
3: 16 to lay down our lives for our *b*.
3Jn : 3 joy to have some *b* come
: 5 in what you are doing for the *b*,
: 10 he refuses to welcome the *b*.
Rev 6: 11 and *b* who were to be killed
12: 10 For the accuser of our *b*,
19: 10 and with your *b* who hold
22: 9 and with your *b* the prophets

BROW

Ge 3: 19 By the sweat of your *b*
49: 26 on the *b* of the prince
Dt 33: 16 on the *b* of the prince
Job 16: 15 and buried my *b* in the dust.
Lk 4: 29 and took him to the *b* of the hill

BROWN

Zec 1: 8 Behind him were red, *b*

BROWSE (BROWSES)

SS 4: 5 that *b* among the lilies.
6: 2 to *b* in the gardens

BROWSES (BROWSE)

SS 2: 16 he *b* among the lilies.
6: 3 he *b* among the lilies.

BRUISE (BRUISED BRUISES)

Ex 21: 25 wound for wound, *b* for *b*.

BRUISED (BRUISE)

Lev 22: 24 an animal whose testicles are *b*,
Ps 105: 18 They *b* his feet with shackles,
SS 5: 7 They beat me, they *b* me;
Isa 42: 3 A *b* reed he will not break,
Mt 12: 20 A *b* reed he will not break,

BRUISES (BRUISE)

Pr 23: 29 Who has needless *b*? Who has
Isa 30: 26 when the LORD binds up the *b*

BRUSH (BRUSHING)

Job 30: 4 In the *b* they gathered salt herbs,

BRUSHING (BRUSH)

Eze 3: 13 the wings of the living creatures *b*

BRUSHWOOD (WOOD)

Ac 28: 3 Paul gathered a pile of *b* and,

BRUTAL (BRUTE)

Eze 21: 31 I will hand you over to *b* men,
2Ti 3: 3 slanderous, without self-control, *b*,

BRUTE (BRUTAL BRUTES)

Ps 73: 22 I was a *b* beast before you.
2Pe 2: 12 They are like *b* beasts, creatures

BRUTES (BRUTE)

Tit 1: 12 "Cretans are always liars, evil *b*,

BUBASTIS

Eze 30: 17 men of Heliopolis and *B*

BUBBLING

Pr 18: 4 the fountain of wisdom is a *b* brook
Isa 35: 7 the thirsty ground *b* springs.

BUCKET (BUCKETS)

Isa 40: 15 the nations are like a drop in a *b*;

BUCKETS (BUCKET)

Ex 7: 19 in the wooden *b* and stone jars."
Nu 24: 7 Water will flow from their *b*;

BUCKLED (BUCKLER)

Eph 6: 14 belt of truth *b* around your waist,

BUCKLER (BUCKLED)

Ps 35: 2 Take up shield and *b*;

BUD (BUDDED BUDS)

Ex 25: 35 One *b* shall be under the first pair
25: 35 a second *b* under the second pair,
25: 35 and a third *b* under the third pair—
37: 21 One *b* was under the first pair
37: 21 a second *b* under the second pair,
37: 21 and a third *b* under the third pair—
Job 14: 9 yet at the scent of water it will *b*
Isa 17: 11 plant them, you bring them to *b*,
27: 6 Israel will *b* and blossom
55: 10 and making it *b* and flourish,
Hab 3: 17 Though the fig tree does not *b*

BUDDED (BUD)

Ge 40: 10 As soon as it *b*, it blossomed,
Nu 17: 8 had not only sprouted but had *b*,
SS 6: 11 to see if the vines had *b*
7: 12 vineyards to see if the vines have *b*,
Eze 7: 10 the rod has *b*, arrogance has
Heb 9: 4 Aaron's rod that had *b*,

BUDS (BUD)

Ex 25: 31 *b* and blossoms shall be
25: 33 shaped like almond flowers with *b*
25: 34 shaped like almond flowers with *b*
25: 36 The *b* and branches shall all be
37: 17 *b* and blossoms were of one piece
37: 19 shaped like almond flowers with *b*
37: 20 shaped like almond flowers with *b*
37: 22 The *b* and the branches were all

BUFFETED

Mt 14: 24 *b* by the waves because the wind

BUILD (BUILDER BUILDERS BUILDING BUILDINGS BUILDS BUILT REBUILD REBUILDING REBUILT WELL-BUILT)

Ge 6: 15 This is how you are to *b* it.
11: 4 "Come, let us *b* ourselves a city,
16: 2 perhaps I can *b* a family
30: 3 through her I too can *b* a family."
35: 1 and *b* an altar there to God,
35: 3 where I will *b* an altar to God,
Ex 20: 25 do not *b* it with dressed stones,
27: 1 "*B* an altar of acacia wood,
Nu 23: 1 Balaam said, "*B* me seven altars
23: 29 Balaam said, "*B* me seven altars
32: 16 "We would like to *b* pens here
32: 24 *B* cities for your women
Dt 6: 10 flourishing cities you did not *b*,
8: 12 when you *b* fine houses
16: 21 pole beside the altar you *b*
19: 3 *B* roads to them and divide
20: 20 and use them to *b* siege works
22: 8 When you *b* a new house, make
25: 9 man who will not *b* up his brother's
27: 5 *B* there an altar to the LORD your
27: 6 *B* the altar of the LORD your God
28: 30 You will *b* a house, but you will not
Jos 22: 16 *b* yourselves an altar in rebellion
22: 26 'Let us get ready and *b* an altar—
24: 13 did not toil and cities you did not *b*,
Jdg 6: 26 Then *b* a proper kind of altar
2Sa 7: 5 Are you the one to *b* me a house
7: 13 He is the one who will *b* a house
7: 27 saying, 'I will *b* a house for you.'
24: 18 and *b* an altar to the LORD
24: 21 "so I can *b* an altar to the LORD,
1Ki 2: 36 "*B* yourself a house in Jerusalem
5: 3 he could not *b* a temple
5: 5 in your place will *b* the temple
5: 5 to *b* a temple for the Name
6: 1 he began to *b* the temple
8: 17 it in his heart to *b* a temple
8: 18 was in your heart to *b* a temple
8: 19 he is the one who will *b* the temple
8: 19 you are not the one to *b* the temple,
9: 15 to *b* the LORD's temple,
9: 19 whatever he desired to *b*
11: 38 I will *b* you a dynasty as enduring
2Ki 6: 2 let us *b* a place there for us to live."
19: 32 or *b* a siege ramp against it.
1Ch 14: 1 carpenters to *b* a palace for him.
17: 4 the one to *b* me a house to dwell
17: 10 you that the LORD will *b* a house
17: 12 He is the one who will *b* a house
17: 25 servant that you will *b* a house
21: 18 and *b* an altar to the LORD
21: 22 so I can *b* an altar to the LORD,
22: 6 and charged him to *b* a house
22: 7 it in my heart to *b* a house
22: 8 You are not to *b* a house
22: 10 He is the one who will *b* a house
22: 11 and *b* the house of the LORD your
22: 19 Begin to *b* the sanctuary
1Ch 28: 2 I had it in my heart to *b* a house
28: 2 of our God, and I made plans to *b* it
28: 3 'You are not to *b* a house
28: 6 son is the one who will *b* my house
28: 10 has chosen you to *b* a temple
29: 19 to *b* the palatial structure
2Ch 2: 1 Solomon gave orders to *b* a temple
2: 3 cedar to *b* a palace to live in.
2: 4 Now I am about to *b* a temple
2: 5 I am going to *b* will be great,
2: 6 I to *b* a temple for him,
2: 6 who is able to *b* a temple for him,
2: 9 the temple I *b* must be large
2: 12 who will *b* a temple for the LORD
3: 1 Solomon began to *b* the temple
6: 7 it in his heart to *b* a temple
6: 8 was in your heart to *b* a temple
6: 9 he is the one who will *b* the temple
6: 9 you are not the one to *b* the temple,
8: 6 whatever he desired to *b*
14: 7 "Let us *b* up these towns,"
36: 23 me to *b* a temple for him
Ezr 1: 2 me to *b* a temple for him
1: 3 and *b* the temple of the LORD,
1: 5 and *b* the house of the LORD
3: 2 his associates began to *b* the altar
4: 2 Let us help you *b* because, like you,
4: 3 We alone will *b* it for the LORD,
6: 14 elders of the Jews continued to *b*
Job 19: 12 they *b* a siege ramp against me
20: 19 he has seized houses he did not *b*.
30: 12 they *b* their siege ramps against me
39: 27 and *b* his nest on high?
Ps 28: 5 and never *b* them up again
51: 18 *b* up the walls of Jerusalem.
Pr 24: 27 after that, *b* your house.
Ecc 3: 3 a time to tear down and a time to *b*,
SS 8: 9 we will *b* towers of silver on her.
Isa 37: 33 or *b* a siege ramp against it.
54: 11 I will *b* you with stones
57: 14 "*B* up, *b* up, prepare the road!
62: 10 *B* up, *b* up the highway!
65: 21 They will *b* houses and dwell
65: 22 No longer will they *b* houses
66: 1 Where is the house you will *b*
Jer 1: 10 and overthrow, to *b* and to plant."
6: 6 *b* siege ramps against Jerusalem.
22: 14 'I will *b* myself a great palace
24: 6 I will *b* them up and not tear them
29: 5 "*B* houses and settle down;
29: 28 Therefore *b* houses and settle
31: 4 I will *b* you up again
31: 28 so I will watch over them to *b*
35: 7 Also you must never *b* houses,
42: 10 I will *b* you up and not tear you
49: 16 Though you *b* your nest as high
Eze 4: 2 works against it, *b* a ramp up
11: 3 Will it not soon be time to *b* houses
21: 22 to *b* a ramp and to erect siege
22: 30 them who would *b* up the wall
26: 8 *b* a ramp up to your walls
28: 26 will *b* houses and plant vineyards;
Da 11: 15 will come and *b* up siege ramps
Am 9: 11 and *b* it as it used to be,
Mic 3: 10 who *b* Zion with bloodshed,
Hab 1: 10 they *b* earthen ramps and capture
Zep 1: 13 They will *b* houses
Hag 1: 8 bring down timber and *b* the house,
Zec 5: 11 of Babylonia to *b* a house for it.
6: 12 and *b* the temple of the LORD.
6: 13 It is he who will *b* the temple
6: 15 help to *b* the temple of the LORD,
Mal 1: 4 "They may *b*, but I will demolish.
Mt 16: 18 and on this rock I will *b* my church,
23: 29 You *b* tombs for the prophets
27: 40 going to destroy the temple and *b* it
Mk 14: 58 and in three days will *b* another,
15: 29 going to destroy the temple and *b* it
Lk 11: 47 you *b* tombs for the prophets,
11: 48 prophets, and you *b* their tombs.
12: 18 down my barns and *b* bigger ones,
14: 28 one of you wants to *b* a tower.
14: 30 'This fellow began to *b*
19: 43 enemies will *b* an embankment
Jn 2: 20 forty-six years to *b* this temple,
Ac 7: 49 of house will you *b* for me?
20: 32 which can *b* you up and give you
Ro 15: 2 neighbor for his good, to *b* him up.

1Co 14: 12 excel in gifts that *b* up the church.
1Th 5: 11 one another and *b* each other up,
Heb 8: 5 about to *b* the tabernacle:
Jude : 20 *b* yourselves up in your most holy

BUILDER (BUILD)

1Co 3: 10 I laid a foundation as an expert *b*,
Heb 3: 3 the *b* of a house has greater honor
3: 4 but God is the *b* of everything.
11: 10 whose architect and *b* is God.

BUILDERS (BUILD)

2Ki 12: 11 the carpenters and *b*, the masons
22: 6 carpenters, the *b* and the masons.
2Ch 34: 11 and *b* to purchase dressed stone,
Ezr 3: 10 When the *b* laid the foundation
Ne 4: 5 insults in the face of the *b*.
4: 18 and each of the *b* wore his sword
Ps 118: 22 The stone the *b* rejected
127: 1 its *b* labor in vain.
Eze 27: 4 your *b* brought your beauty
Mt 21: 42 " 'The stone the *b* rejected
Mk 12: 10 " 'The stone the *b* rejected
Lk 20: 17 " 'The stone the *b* rejected
Ac 4: 11 " 'the stone you *b* rejected,
1Pe 2: 7 "The stone the *b* rejected

BUILDING (BUILD)

Ge 4: 17 Cain was then *b* a city,
11: 5 and the tower that the men were *b*.
11: 8 and they stopped *b* the city.
Jos 22: 19 or against us by *b* an altar
22: 29 away from him today by *b* an altar
1Ki 3: 1 David until he finished *b* his palace
5: 18 and stone for the *b* of the temple.
6: 5 he built a structure around the *b*,
6: 7 In *b* the temple, only blocks
6: 12 "As for this temple you are *b*,
6: 38 He had spent seven years *b* it.
9: 1 Solomon had finished *b* the temple
15: 21 he stopped *b* Ramah and withdrew
2Ki 25: 9 Every important *b* he burned down
1Ch 22: 2 stone for *b* the house of God.
29: 16 provided for *b* you a temple
2Ch 3: 2 He began *b* on the second day
3: 3 Solomon laid for *b* the temple
3: 4 long across the width of the *b*
16: 5 he stopped *b* Ramah
32: 5 of the wall and *b* towers on it.
Ezr 3: 8 to supervise the *b* of the house
4: 1 that the exiles were *b* a temple
4: 3 with us in *b* a temple to our God.
4: 4 and make them afraid to go on *b*.
5: 4 of the men constructing this *b*?"
5: 8 The people are *b* it
6: 14 They finished *b* the temple
Ne 3: 1 *b* as far as the Tower
4: 3 "What they are *b*—
4: 17 of Judah who were *b* the wall.
6: 6 and therefore you are *b* the wall.
Jer 52: 13 Every important *b* he burned down
Eze 41: 12 The *b* facing the temple courtyard
41: 12 of the *b* was five cubits thick all
41: 13 and the *b* with its walls were
41: 15 length of the *b* facing the courtyard
42: 2 The *b* whose door faced north was
42: 5 and middle floors of the *b*.
Mic 7: 11 The day for *b* your walls will come,
Lk 6: 48 He is like a man *b* a house,
17: 28 buying and selling, planting and *b*.
Ro 15: 20 so that I would not be *b*
1Co 3: 9 you are God's field, God's *b*.
3: 10 and someone else is *b* on it.
2Co 5: 1 we have a *b* from God, an eternal
10: 8 us for *b* you up rather
13: 10 the Lord gave me for *b* you up,
Eph 2: 21 him the whole *b* is joined together
4: 29 helpful for *b* others up according

BUILDINGS (BUILD)

1Ki 9: 10 which Solomon built these two *b*—
1Ch 15: 1 After David had constructed *b*
28: 11 its *b*, its storerooms, its upper parts
29: 4 the overlaying of the walls of the *b*,
2Ch 32: 28 made *b* to store the harvest of grain
34: 11 and beams for the *b* that the kings
Isa 22: 10 You counted the *b* in Jerusalem
Jer 22: 23 who are nestled in cedar *b*,
Eze 40: 2 side were some *b* that looked like
Mt 24: 1 to him to call his attention to its *b*.
Mk 13: 1 stones! What magnificent *b*!"
13: 2 "Do you see all these great *b*?"

BUILDS (BUILD)

Job 27: 18 house he *b* is like a moth's cocoon,
Ps 127: 1 Unless the LORD *b* the house,
147: 2 The LORD *b* up Jerusalem;
Pr 14: 1 The wise woman *b* her house,
17: 19 he who *b* a high gate invites
Jer 22: 13 "Woe to him who *b* his palace
Am 9: 6 he who *b* his lofty palace
Hab 2: 9 "Woe to him who *b* his realm
2: 12 "Woe to him who *b* a city
1Co 3: 10 one should be careful how he *b*.
3: 12 If any man *b* on this foundation
8: 1 Knowledge puffs up, but love *b* up.
Eph 4: 16 grows and *b* itself up in love,

BUILT (BUILD)

Ge 8: 20 Then Noah *b* an altar to the LORD
10: 11 where he *b* Nineveh, Rehoboth Ir,
12: 7 So he *b* an altar there to the LORD
12: 8 There he *b* an altar to the LORD
13: 4 and where he had first *b* an altar.
13: 18 where he *b* an altar to the LORD.
22: 9 Abraham *b* an altar there
26: 25 Isaac *b* an altar there and called
33: 17 where he *b* a place for himself
35: 7 There he *b* an altar, and he called
Ex 1: 11 and they *b* Pithom and Rameses
17: 15 Moses *b* an altar and called it
24: 4 and *b* an altar at the foot
32: 5 he *b* an altar in front of the calf
38: 1 They *b* the altar of burnt offering
Nu 13: 22 (Hebron had been *b* seven years
23: 14 and there he *b* seven altars
32: 34 The Gadites *b* up Dibon, Ataroth,
32: 36 and *b* pens for their flocks.
Dt 20: 5 "Has anyone *b* a new house
Jos 8: 30 Joshua *b* on Mount Ebal an altar
8: 31 He *b* it according to what is written
11: 13 of the cities *b* on their mounds—
19: 50 he *b* up the town and settled there.
22: 10 of Manasseh *b* an imposing altar
22: 11 heard that they had *b* the altar
22: 23 If we have *b* our own altar
22: 28 which our fathers *b*, not
Jdg 1: 26 where he *b* a city and called it Luz,
6: 24 So Gideon *b* an altar to the LORD
6: 28 sacrificed on the newly *b* altar!
21: 4 the next day the people *b* an altar
Ru 4: 11 who together *b* up the house
1Sa 7: 17 he *b* an altar there to the LORD.
14: 35 Then Saul *b* an altar to the LORD;
2Sa 5: 9 He *b* up the area around it,
5: 11 and they *b* a palace for David.
7: 7 "Why have you not *b* me a house
20: 15 They *b* a siege ramp up to the city,
24: 25 David *b* an altar to the LORD
1Ki 3: 2 a temple had not yet been *b*
6: 2 The temple that King Solomon *b*
6: 5 inner sanctuary he *b* a structure
6: 7 site while it was being *b*.
6: 9 he *b* the temple and completed it,
6: 10 And he *b* the side rooms all
6: 14 So Solomon *b* the temple
6: 36 And he *b* the inner courtyard
7: 2 He *b* the Palace of the Forest
7: 7 He *b* the throne hall, the Hall
8: 13 I have indeed *b* a magnificent
8: 16 to have a temple *b* for my Name
8: 20 I have *b* the temple for the Name
8: 27 How much less this temple I have *b*
8: 43 house I have *b* bears your Name.
8: 44 the temple I have *b* for your Name,
8: 48 the temple I have *b* for your Name;
9: 3 which you have *b*,
9: 10 during which Solomon *b* these two
9: 17 He *b* up Lower Beth Horon,
9: 24 David to the palace Solomon had *b*
9: 25 on the altar he had *b* for the LORD
9: 26 King Solomon also *b* ships
10: 4 Solomon and the palace he had *b*,
11: 7 Solomon *b* a high place
11: 27 Solomon had *b* the supporting
11: 38 enduring as the one I *b* for David
1Ki 12: 25 there he went out and *b* up Peniel.
12: 31 Jeroboam *b* shrines on high places
12: 33 on the altar he had *b* at Bethel.
15: 22 With them King Asa *b* up Geba
15: 23 all he did and the cities he *b*,
16: 24 of silver and *b* a city on the hill,
16: 32 of Baal that he *b* in Samaria.
18: 32 With the stones he *b* an altar
22: 39 the palace he *b* and inlaid
22: 48 Now Jehoshaphat *b* a fleet
2Ki 16: 11 So Uriah the priest *b* an altar
16: 18 Sabbath canopy that had been *b*
17: 9 city they *b* themselves high
21: 4 He *b* altars in the temple
21: 5 he *b* altars to all the starry hosts.
23: 12 and the altars Manasseh had *b*
23: 13 king of Israel had *b* for Ashtoreth
23: 19 kings of Israel had *b* in the towns
25: 1 and *b* siege works all around it.
1Ch 6: 10 as priest in the temple Solomon *b*
6: 32 until Solomon *b* the temple
7: 24 *b* Lower and Upper Beth Horon
8: 12 Shemed (who *b* Ono and Lod
11: 8 He *b* up the city around it,
17: 6 "Why have you not *b* me a house
21: 26 David *b* an altar to the LORD
22: 5 to be *b* for the LORD should be
22: 19 God into the temple that will be *b*
2Ch 3: 8 He *b* the Most Holy Place,
6: 2 I have *b* a magnificent temple
6: 5 to have a temple *b* for my Name
6: 10 I have *b* the temple for the Name
6: 18 How much less this temple I have *b*
6: 33 house I have *b* bears your Name.
6: 34 the temple I have *b* for your Name,
6: 38 and toward the temple I have *b*
8: 1 which Solomon *b* the temple
8: 4 He also *b* up Tadmor in the desert
8: 4 and all the store cities he had *b*
8: 11 to the palace he had *b* for her,
8: 12 of the LORD that he had *b* in front
9: 3 as well as the palace he had *b*,
11: 5 *b* up towns for defense in Judah:
14: 6 He *b* up the fortified cities of Judah
14: 7 So they *b* and prospered.
16: 6 With them he *b* up Geba
17: 12 he *b* forts and store cities in Judah
20: 8 and have *b* in it a sanctuary
20: 36 these were *b* at Ezion Geber,
21: 11 *b* high places on the hills of Judah
26: 9 Uzziah *b* towers in Jerusalem
26: 10 He also *b* towers in the desert
27: 4 He *b* towns in the Judean hills
28: 25 town in Judah he *b* high places
32: 5 He *b* another wall outside that one
32: 29 He *b* villages and acquired great
33: 4 He *b* altars in the temple
33: 5 he *b* altars to all the starry hosts.
33: 15 as all the altars he had *b*
33: 19 the sites where he *b* high places
35: 3 son of David king of Israel *b*.
Ezr 3: 3 they *b* the altar on its foundation
4: 13 should know that if this city is *b*
4: 16 inform the king that if this city is *b*
5: 11 one that a great king of Israel *b*
5: 11 temple that was *b* many years ago,
Ne 3: 2 Zaccur son of Imri *b* next to them.
3: 2 of Jericho *b* the adjoining section,
8: 4 stood on a high wooden platform *b*
8: 16 and *b* themselves booths
8: 17 returned from exile *b* booths
12: 29 for the singers had *b* villages
Est 5: 14 Haman, and he had the gallows *b*.
5: 14 a gallows *b*, seventy-five feet
Job 3: 14 who *b* for themselves places now
Ps 78: 69 He *b* his sanctuary like the high
122: 3 Jerusalem is *b* like a city
Pr 9: 1 Wisdom has *b* her house;
24: 3 By wisdom a house is *b*,
Ecc 2: 4 I *b* houses for myself and planted
9: 14 and *b* huge siegeworks against it.
SS 4: 4 *b* with elegance;
Isa 5: 2 He *b* a watchtower in it
22: 11 You *b* a reservoir between the two
44: 26 towns of Judah, 'They shall be *b*,'
Jer 7: 31 They have *b* the high places
18: 9 kingdom is to be *b* up and planted,
18: 15 and on roads not *b* up.

Jer 19: 5 They have *b* the high places of Baal
32: 24 "See how the siege ramps are *b* up
32: 31 From the day it was *b* until now,
32: 35 They *b* high places for Baal
35: 9 have ever drunk wine or *b* houses
45: 4 I will overthrow what I have *b*
52: 4 and *b* siege works all around it.
Eze 13: 10 a flimsy wall is *b*, they cover it
16: 24 you *b* a mound for yourself
16: 25 every street you *b* your lofty
16: 31 When you *b* your mounds
17: 17 when ramps are *b* and siege works
41: 7 surrounding the temple was *b*
43: 18 blood upon the altar when it is *b*:
46: 23 with places for fire *b* all
Da 4: 30 not this the great Babylon I have *b*
Hos 8: 11 "Though Ephraim *b* many altars
8: 14 and *b* palaces;
10: 1 he *b* more altars;
Am 5: 11 though you have *b* stone mansions,
7: 7 by a wall that had been *b* true
Hag 1: 2 for the LORD's house to be *b*.' "
Zec 8: 9 strong so that the temple may be *b*.
9: 3 Tyre has *b* herself a stronghold;
Mt 7: 24 is like a wise man who *b* his house
7: 26 like a foolish man who *b* his house
21: 33 winepress in it and *b* a watchtower.
Mk 12: 1 the winepress and *b* a watchtower.
Lk 4: 29 of the hill on which the town was *b*,
6: 48 not shake it, because it was well *b*.
6: 49 is like a man who *b* a house
7: 5 and has *b* our synagogue."
Ac 7: 47 it was Solomon who *b* the house
17: 24 does not live in temples *b* by hands.
28: 2 They *b* a fire and welcomed us all
1Co 3: 14 If what he has *b* survives, he will
2Co 5: 1 in heaven, not *b* by human hands.
Eph 2: 20 *b* on the foundation of the apostles
2: 22 in him you too are being *b* together
4: 12 the body of Christ may be *b* up
Col 2: 7 live in him, rooted and *b* up in him,
Heb 3: 4 For every house is *b* by someone,
11: 7 in holy fear *b* an ark
1Pe 2: 5 are being *b* into a spiritual house
3: 20 of Noah while the ark was being *b*.

BUKKI

Nu 34: 22 tribe of Benjamin; *B* son of Jogli,
1Ch 6: 5 father of *B*, *B* the father of Uzzi,
6: 51 Abishua his son, *B* his son,
Ezr 7: 4 the son of *B*, the son of Abishua,

BUKKIAH

1Ch 25: 4 from his sons: *B*, Mattaniah, Uzziel
25: 13 12 the sixth to *B*, his sons

BUL

1Ki 6: 38 year in the month of *B*,

BULGES (BULGING)

Job 15: 27 and his waist *b* with flesh,

BULGING (BULGES)

Isa 30: 13 like a high wall, cracked and *b*,

BULL (BULL'S BULLS)

Ex 21: 28 of the *b* will not be held responsible
21: 28 the *b* must be stoned to death,
21: 28 "If a *b* gores a man or a woman
21: 29 the *b* has had the habit of goring
21: 29 the *b* must be stoned and the owner
21: 31 also applies if the *b* gores a son
21: 32 If the *b* gores a male or female
21: 32 the slave, and the *b* must be stoned.
21: 35 If a man's *b* injures the *b* of another
21: 36 the *b* had the habit of goring,
29: 1 a young *b* and two rams without
29: 3 along with the *b* and the two rams.
29: 10 Bring the *b* to the front of the Tent
29: 36 Sacrifice a *b* each day as a sin
Lev 1: 5 is to slaughter the young *b*
4: 3 bring to the LORD a young *b*
4: 4 is to present the *b* at the entrance
4: 8 fat from the *b* of the sin offering—
4: 11 the hide of the *b* and all its flesh,
4: 12 that is, all the rest of the *b*—
4: 14 the assembly must bring a young *b*
4: 15 and the *b* shall be slaughtered
Lev 4: 20 and do with this *b* just
4: 20 did with the *b* for the sin offering.
4: 21 Then he shall take the *b*
4: 21 and burn it as he burned the first *b*.
8: 2 the anointing oil, the *b*
8: 14 He then presented the *b*
8: 15 Moses slaughtered the *b*
8: 17 But the *b* with its hide and its flesh
9: 2 "Take a *b* calf for your sin offering
16: 3 with a young *b* for a sin offering
16: 6 "Aaron is to offer the *b*
16: 11 and he is to slaughter the *b*
16: 11 "Aaron shall bring the *b*
16: 27 The *b* and the goat
23: 18 one young *b* and two rams.
Nu 7: 15 filled with incense; one young *b*,
7: 21 filled with incense; one young *b*,
7: 27 filled with incense; one young *b*,
7: 33 filled with incense; one young *b*,
7: 39 filled with incense; one young *b*,
7: 45 filled with incense; one young *b*,
7: 51 filled with incense; one young *b*,
7: 57 filled with incense; one young *b*,
7: 63 filled with incense; one young *b*,
7: 69 filled with incense; one young *b*,
7: 75 filled with incense; one young *b*,
7: 81 filled with incense; one young *b*,
8: 8 Have them take a young *b*
8: 8 are to take a second young *b*
15: 8 " 'When you prepare a young *b*
15: 9 bring with the *b* a grain offering
15: 11 Each *b* or ram, each lamb
15: 24 is to offer a young *b* for a burnt
23: 2 and the two of them offered a *b*
23: 4 and on each altar I have offered a *b*
23: 14 offered a *b* and a ram on each altar.
23: 30 offered a *b* and a ram on each altar.
28: 12 With each *b* there is
28: 14 With each *b* there is
28: 20 With each *b* prepare a grain
28: 28 With each *b* there is
29: 2 a burnt offering of one young *b*,
29: 3 With the *b* prepare a grain offering
29: 8 a burnt offering of one young *b*,
29: 9 With the *b* prepare a grain offering
29: 36 a burnt offering of one *b*, one ram
29: 37 With the *b*, the ram and the lambs,
Dt 18: 3 from the people who sacrifice a *b*
33: 17 In majesty he is like a firstborn *b*;
Jdg 6: 25 "Take the second *b*
6: 26 offer the second *b* as a burnt
6: 28 and the second *b* sacrificed
1Sa 1: 24 along with a three-year-old *b*,
1: 25 When they had slaughtered the *b*,
2Sa 6: 13 he sacrificed a *b* and a fattened calf
1Ki 18: 23 I will prepare the other *b*
18: 26 So they took the *b* given them
18: 33 cut the *b* into pieces and laid it
2Ch 13: 9 consecrate himself with a young *b*
Ps 50: 9 need of a *b* from your stall
69: 31 more than a *b* with its horns
106: 20 of a *b*, which eats grass.
Isa 34: 7 the *b* calves and the great bulls.
66: 3 But whoever sacrifices a *b*
Eze 43: 19 You are to give a young *b*
43: 21 are to take the *b* for the sin offering
43: 22 as it was purified with the *b*.
43: 23 you are to offer a young *b*
43: 25 also to provide a young *b* and a ram
45: 18 to take a young *b* without defect
45: 22 that day the prince is to provide a *b*
45: 24 a grain offering an ephah for each *b*
46: 6 is to offer a young *b*,
46: 7 offering one ephah with the *b*,
46: 11 is to be an ephah with a *b*,

BULL'S (BULL)

Ex 29: 12 Take some of the *b* blood
29: 14 But burn the *b* flesh and its hide
Lev 4: 5 shall take some of the *b* blood
4: 7 rest of the *b* blood he shall pour out
4: 15 on the *b* head before the LORD,
4: 16 some of the *b* blood into the Tent
16: 14 He is to take some of the *b* blood
16: 15 as he did with the *b* blood:
16: 18 He shall take some of the *b* blood

BULLS (BULL)

Ge 32: 15 ten *b*, and twenty female donkeys
Ex 24: 5 sacrificed young *b* as fellowship
Nu 7: 87 came to twelve young *b*,
8: 12 hands on the heads of the *b*,
23: 1 prepare seven *b* and seven rams
23: 29 prepare seven *b* and seven rams
28: 11 a burnt offering of two young *b*,
28: 19 a burnt offering of two young *b*,
28: 27 a burnt offering of two young *b*,
29: 13 a burnt offering of thirteen young *b*
29: 14 of the thirteen *b* prepare a grain
29: 17 day prepare twelve young *b*,
29: 18 With the *b*, rams and lambs,
29: 20 On the third day prepare eleven *b*,
29: 21 With the *b*, rams and lambs,
29: 23 " 'On the fourth day prepare ten *b*,
29: 24 With the *b*, rams and lambs,
29: 26 " 'On the fifth day prepare nine *b*,
29: 27 With the *b*, rams and lambs,
29: 29 " 'On the sixth day prepare eight *b*,
29: 30 With the *b*, rams and lambs,
29: 32 the seventh day prepare seven *b*,
29: 33 With the *b*, rams and lambs,
1Ki 7: 25 The Sea stood on twelve *b*,
7: 29 between the uprights were lions, *b*
7: 29 *b* were wreaths of hammered work.
7: 44 the Sea and the twelve *b* under it;
18: 23 Get two *b* for us.
18: 25 one of the *b* and prepare it first,
2Ki 16: 17 from the bronze *b* that supported it
1Ch 15: 26 seven *b* and seven rams were
29: 21 a thousand *b*, a thousand rams
2Ch 4: 3 The *b* were cast in two rows
4: 3 figures of *b* encircled it—
4: 4 The Sea stood on twelve *b*,
4: 15 the Sea and the twelve *b* under it;
29: 21 They brought seven *b*, seven rams,
29: 22 So they slaughtered the *b*,
29: 32 assembly brought was seventy *b*,
29: 33 amounted to six hundred *b*
30: 24 of Judah provided a thousand *b*
30: 24 them with a thousand *b*
Ezr 6: 9 Whatever is needed—young *b*,
6: 17 of God they offered a hundred *b*,
7: 17 With this money be sure to buy *b*,
8: 35 twelve *b* for all Israel, ninety-six
Job 21: 10 Their *b* never fail to breed;
42: 8 now take seven *b* and seven rams
Ps 22: 12 Many *b* surround me;
22: 12 strong *b* of Bashan encircle me.
50: 13 Do I eat the flesh of *b*
51: 19 then *b* will be offered on your altar.
66: 15 I will offer *b* and goats.
68: 30 the herd of *b* among the calves
Isa 1: 11 in the blood of *b* and lambs
34: 7 the bull calves and the great *b*.
Jer 50: 27 Kill all her young *b*;
52: 20 and the twelve bronze *b* under it,
Eze 39: 18 *b*—all of them fattened animals
45: 23 is to provide seven *b*
Hos 12: 11 Do they sacrifice *b* in Gilgal?
Ac 14: 13 brought *b* and wreaths
Heb 9: 13 The blood of goats and *b*
10: 4 it is impossible for the blood of *b*

BUNAH

1Ch 2: 25 Ram his firstborn, *B*, Oren,

BUNCH

Ex 12: 22 Take a *b* of hyssop, dip it

BUNDLE (BUNDLES)

1Sa 25: 29 securely in the *b* of the living

BUNDLES (BUNDLE)

Ru 2: 16 out some stalks for her from the *b*
Mt 13: 30 and tie them in *b* to be burned,

BUNNI

Ne 9: 4 Kadmiel, Shebaniah, *B*, Sherebiah,
10: 15 Elam, Zattu, Bani, *B*, Azgad, Bebai
11: 15 the son of *B*; Shabbethai

BURDEN (BURDENED BURDENS BURDENSOME)

Ge 49: 15 he will bend his shoulder to the *b*
Nu 11: 11 to displease you that you put the *b*

Nu 11: 14 by myself; the *b* is too heavy for me
11: 17 They will help you carry the *b*
Dt 1: 9 "You are too heavy a *b* for me
1Sa 25: 31 on his conscience the staggering *b*
2Sa 13: 25 we would only be a *b* to you."
15: 33 go with me, you will be a *b* to me.
19: 35 should your servant be an added *b*
Ne 5: 15 placed a heavy *b* on the people
Job 7: 20 Have I become a *b* to you?
Ps 38: 4 like a *b* too heavy to bear.
81: 6 the *b* from their shoulders;
Pr 27: 3 Stone is heavy and sand a *b*,
Ecc 1: 13 What a heavy *b* God has laid
3: 10 I have seen the *b* God has laid
Isa 1: 14 They have become a *b* to me;
10: 27 In that day their *b* will be lifted
14: 25 his *b* removed from their shoulders
46: 1 a *b* for the weary.
46: 1 their idols are borne by beasts of *b*.
46: 2 unable to rescue the *b*,
Zep 3: 18 they are a *b* and a reproach to you.
Mal 1: 13 'What a *b*!' and you sniff
Mt 11: 30 my yoke is easy and my *b* is light."
20: 12 equal to us who have borne the *b*
Ac 15: 28 to us not to *b* you with anything
2Co 11: 9 from being a *b* to you in any way,
11: 9 needed something, I was not a *b*
12: 13 except that I was never a *b* to you?
12: 14 and I will not be a *b* to you,
12: 16 I have not been a *b* to you.
1Th 2: 7 of Christ we could have been a *b*
2: 9 day in order not to be a *b* to anyone
2Th 3: 8 so that we would not be a *b* to any
Heb 13: 17 not a *b*, for that would be
Rev 2: 24 (I will not impose any other *b*

BURDENED (BURDEN)

Isa 43: 23 have not *b* you with grain offerings
43: 24 But you have *b* me with your sins
Mic 6: 3 How have I *b* you? Answer me.
Mt 11: 28 all you who are weary and *b*,
2Co 5: 4 are in this tent, we groan and are *b*,
Gal 5: 1 do not let yourselves be *b* again
1Ti 5: 16 not let the church be *b* with them,

BURDENS (BURDEN)

Nu 4: 24 as they work and carry *b*:
Dt 1: 12 and your *b* and your disputes all
Ps 66: 11 and laid *b* on our backs.
68: 19 who daily bears our *b*.
73: 5 from the *b* common to man;
Isa 9: 4 the yoke that *b* them,
Lk 11: 46 down with *b* they can hardly carry,
Gal 6: 2 Carry each other's *b*,

BURDENSOME (BURDEN)

Isa 46: 1 images that are carried about are *b*,
1Jn 5: 3 And his commands are not *b*,

BURIAL (BURY)

Ge 23: 4 me some property for a *b* site here
23: 9 me for the full price as a *b* site
23: 20 Abraham by the Hittites as a *b* site.
49: 30 a *b* place from Ephron the Hittite,
50: 13 a *b* place from Ephron the Hittite,
2Ch 26: 23 them in a field for *b* that belonged
Ecc 6: 3 and does not receive proper *b*,
Isa 14: 20 you will not join them in *b*,
Jer 22: 19 He will have the *b* of a donkey—
26: 23 his body thrown into the *b* place
Eze 39: 11 that day I will give Gog a *b* place
Mt 26: 12 she did it to prepare me for *b*.
27: 7 as a *b* place for foreigners.
Mk 14: 8 beforehand to prepare for my *b*.
Jn 12: 7 perfume for the day of my *b*.
19: 40 accordance with Jewish *b* customs.
20: 7 as the *b* cloth that had been
Rev 11: 9 on their bodies and refuse them *b*.

BURIED (BURY)

Ge 15: 15 and be *b* at a good old age.
23: 19 Afterward Abraham *b* his wife
25: 9 and Ishmael *b* him in the cave
25: 10 There Abraham was *b*
35: 4 and Jacob *b* them under the oak
35: 8 was *b* under the oak below Bethel.
35: 19 was *b* on the way to Ephrath (that
35: 29 And his sons Esau and Jacob *b* him
Ge 47: 30 and bury me where they are *b*."
48: 7 So I *b* her there beside the road
49: 31 and his wife Sarah were *b*,
49: 31 were *b*, and there I *b* Leah.
50: 13 and *b* him in the cave in the field
Nu 11: 34 there they *b* the people who had
20: 1 There Miriam died and was *b*.
Dt 10: 6 There Aaron died and was *b*,
34: 6 He *b* him in Moab, in the valley
Jos 24: 30 And they *b* him in the land
24: 32 were *b* at Shechem in the tract
24: 33 of Aaron died and was *b* at Gibeah,
Jdg 2: 9 And they *b* him in the land
8: 32 and was *b* in the tomb of his father
10: 2 then he died, and was *b* in Shamir.
10: 5 When Jair died, he was *b* in Kamon
12: 7 and was *b* in a town in Gilead.
12: 10 Then Ibzan died, and was *b*
12: 12 and was *b* in Aijalon in the land
12: 15 and was *b* at Pirathon in Ephraim,
16: 31 They brought him back and *b* him
Ru 1: 17 die I will die, and there I will be *b*.
1Sa 25: 1 they *b* him at his home in Ramah.
28: 3 *b* him in his own town of Ramah.
31: 13 and *b* them under a tamarisk tree
2Sa 2: 4 Jabesh Gilead who had *b* Saul,
2: 32 and *b* him in his father's tomb
3: 32 They *b* Abner in Hebron,
4: 12 *b* it in Abner's tomb at Hebron.
17: 23 and was *b* in his father's tomb.
21: 14 They *b* the bones of Saul
1Ki 2: 10 and was *b* in the City of David.
2: 34 and he was *b* on his own land
11: 43 was *b* in the city of David his father
13: 22 Therefore your body will not be *b*
13: 31 grave where the man of God is *b*;
14: 13 to Jeroboam who will be *b*,
14: 18 They *b* him, and all Israel mourned
14: 31 and was *b* with them in the City
15: 8 and was *b* in the City of David.
15: 24 and was *b* with them in the city
16: 6 with his fathers and was *b* in Tirzah
16: 28 rested with his fathers and was *b*
22: 37 to Samaria, and they *b* him there.
22: 50 and was *b* with them in the city
2Ki 8: 24 and was *b* with them in the City
9: 28 *b* him with his fathers in his tomb
10: 35 rested with his fathers and was *b*
12: 21 was *b* with his fathers in the City
13: 9 rested with his fathers and was *b*
13: 13 Jehoash was *b* in Samaria
13: 20 Elisha died and was *b*.
14: 16 was *b* in Samaria with the kings
14: 20 was *b* in Jerusalem with his fathers,
15: 7 and was *b* near them in the City
15: 38 and was *b* with them in the City
16: 20 and was *b* with them in the City
21: 18 and was *b* in his palace garden,
21: 26 He was *b* in his grave in the garden
22: 20 and you will be *b* in peace.
23: 30 and *b* him in his own tomb.
1Ch 10: 12 Then they *b* their bones
2Ch 9: 31 was *b* in the city of David his father
12: 16 and was *b* in the City of David.
14: 1 and was *b* in the City of David.
16: 14 They *b* him in the tomb that he had
21: 1 and was *b* with them in the City
21: 20 and was *b* in the City of David,
22: 9 They *b* him, for they said,
24: 16 He was *b* with the kings in the City
24: 25 and was *b* in the City of David,
25: 28 was *b* with his fathers in the City
26: 23 and was *b* near them in a field
27: 9 and was *b* in the City of David.
28: 27 and was *b* in the city of Jerusalem,
32: 33 was *b* on the hill where the tombs
33: 20 rested with his fathers and was *b*
34: 28 and you will be *b* in peace.
35: 24 He was *b* in the tombs of his fathers
Ne 2: 3 the city where my fathers are *b* lies
2: 5 in Judah where my fathers are *b*
Job 16: 15 and *b* my brow in the dust.
Ps 106: 17 it *b* the company of Abiram.
Ecc 8: 10 Then too, I saw the wicked *b*—
Jer 8: 2 They will not be gathered up or *b*,
16: 4 They will not be mourned or *b*
16: 6 They will not be *b* or mourned,
20: 6 There you will die and be *b*,
Jer 25: 33 be mourned or gathered up or *b*,
43: 10 over these stones I have *b* here;
Eze 39: 11 and all his hordes will be *b* there.
39: 15 it until the gravediggers have *b* it
Mt 14: 12 and took his body and *b* it.
Lk 16: 22 The rich man also died and was *b*.
Ac 2: 29 patriarch David died and was *b*,
5: 6 and carried him out and *b* him.
5: 9 of the men who *b* your husband are
5: 10 and *b* her beside her husband.
8: 2 Godly men *b* Stephen
13: 36 he was *b* with his fathers
Ro 6: 4 *b* with him through baptism
1Co 15: 4 that he was *b*, that he was raised
Col 2: 12 having been *b* with him in baptism

BURIES (BURY)

Pr 19: 24 The sluggard *b* his hand in the dish;
26: 15 The sluggard *b* his hand in the dish;

BURN (BURNED BURNED-OUT BURNING BURNS BURNT)

Ex 3: 2 the bush was on fire it did not *b* up.
3: 3 why the bush does not *b* up."
12: 10 left till morning, you must *b* it.
21: 25 *b* for *b*, wound for wound,
29: 13 the fat around them, and *b* them
29: 14 But *b* the bull's flesh and its hide
29: 18 Then *b* the entire ram on the altar.
29: 25 and *b* them on the altar
29: 34 left over till morning, *b* it up.
30: 7 "Aaron must *b* fragrant incense
30: 8 He must *b* incense again
30: 8 twilight so incense will *b* regularly
32: 10 alone so that my anger may *b*
32: 11 "why should your anger *b*
Lev 1: 9 the priest is to *b* all of it on the altar
1: 13 to bring all of it and *b* it on the altar
1: 15 off the head and *b* it on the altar;
1: 17 and then the priest shall *b* it
2: 2 and *b* this as a memorial portion
2: 9 *b* it on the altar as an offering made
2: 11 for you are not to *b* any yeast
2: 16 priest shall *b* the memorial portion
3: 5 Aaron's sons are to *b* it on the altar
3: 11 The priest shall *b* them on the altar
3: 16 The priest shall *b* them on the altar
4: 10 the priest shall *b* them on the altar
4: 12 *b* it in a wood fire on the ash heap.
4: 19 the fat from it and *b* it on the altar,
4: 21 and *b* it as he burned the first bull.
4: 26 He shall *b* all the fat on the altar
4: 31 and the priest shall *b* it on the altar
4: 35 and the priest shall *b* it on the altar
5: 12 and *b* it on the altar on top
6: 12 *b* the fat of the fellowship offerings
6: 15 *b* the memorial portion on the altar
7: 5 The priest shall *b* them on the altar
7: 31 The priest shall *b* the fat
8: 32 Then *b* up the rest of the meat
13: 24 appears in the raw flesh of the *b*,
13: 24 "When someone has a *b* on his skin
13: 25 that has broken out in the *b*.
13: 28 it is a swelling from the *b*,
13: 28 it is only a scar from the *b*.
13: 52 He must *b* up the clothing,
13: 55 *B* it with fire, whether the mildew
16: 25 also *b* the fat of the sin offering
17: 6 and *b* the fat as an aroma pleasing
Nu 5: 26 as a memorial offering and *b* it
16: 40 to *b* incense before the LORD,
18: 17 blood on the altar and *b* their fat
Dt 6: 15 and his anger will *b* against you,
7: 4 and the LORD's anger will *b*
7: 5 and *b* their idols in the fire.
7: 25 of their gods you are to *b* in the fire
11: 17 Then the LORD's anger will *b*
12: 3 *b* their Asherah poles in the fire;
12: 31 They even *b* their sons
13: 16 and completely *b* the town
29: 20 and zeal will *b* against that man.
Jos 11: 6 their horses and *b* their chariots."
11: 13 Yet Israel did not *b* any
23: 16 the LORD's anger will *b*
Jdg 12: 1 We're going to *b* down your house
14: 15 or we will *b* you and your father's
1Sa 2: 28 to go up to my altar, to *b* incense,
1Ki 14: 10 I will *b* up the house of Jeroboam

1Ki 22:43 offer sacrifices and *b* incense there.
2Ki 12: 3 offer sacrifices and *b* incense there.
14: 4 offer sacrifices and *b* incense there.
15: 4 offer sacrifices and *b* incense there.
15:35 offer sacrifices and *b* incense there.
22:17 my anger will *b* against this place
23: 5 the kings of Judah to *b* incense
1Ch 14:12 and David gave orders to *b* them
2Ch 2: 6 as a place to *b* sacrifices before him
4:20 to *b* in front of the inner sanctuary
26:16 temple of the LORD to *b* incense
26:18 Uzziah, to *b* incense to the LORD.
26:18 been consecrated to *b* incense.
26:19 in his hand ready to *b* incense,
28:25 places to *b* sacrifices to other gods
29: 7 They did not *b* incense
29:11 before him and to *b* incense."
32:12 before one altar and *b* sacrifices
Ne 10:34 of wood to *b* on the altar
Ps 79: 5 long will your jealousy *b* like fire?
89:46 long will your wrath *b* like fire?
102: 3 my bones *b* like glowing embers.
Isa 1:31 both will *b* together,
10:17 in a single day it will *b*
47:14 the fire will *b* them up.
57: 5 You *b* with lust among the oaks
Jer 4: 4 wrath will break out and *b* like fire
4: 4 *b* with no one to quench it.
6:29 to *b* away the lead with fire,
7: 9 *b* incense to Baal and follow other
7:20 and it will *b* and not be quenched.
7:31 of Ben Hinnom to *b* their sons
11:12 to the gods to whom they *b* incense
11:13 altars you have set up to *b* incense
15:14 that will *b* against you."
17: 4 and it will *b* forever."
18:15 they *b* incense to worthless idols,
19: 5 of Baal to *b* their sons in the fire
21:12 wrath will break out and *b* like fire
21:12 *b* with no one to quench it.
32:29 set it on fire; they will *b* it down,
33:18 to *b* grain offerings
34: 2 of Babylon, and he will *b* it down.
34:22 against it, take it and *b* it down.
36:25 urged the king not to *b* the scroll,
37: 8 they will capture it and *b* it down.'
37:10 would come out and *b* this city
38:18 the Babylonians and they will *b* it
43:12 he will *b* their temples
43:13 will *b* down the temples of the gods
44:17 We will *b* incense to the Queen
44:25 out the vows we made to *b* incense
48:35 and *b* incense to their gods,"
Eze 5: 2 *b* a third of the hair with fire
5: 4 them into the fire and *b* them up.
16:41 They will *b* down your houses
23:47 daughters and *b* down their houses.
39: 9 weapons for fuel and *b* them up—
43:21 and *b* it in the designated part
Hos 4:13 and *b* offerings on the hills,
Am 4: 5 *B* leavened bread as a thank
6:10 is to *b* the bodies comes
Na 2:13 "I will *b* up your chariots in smoke,
Mal 4: 1 is coming; it will *b* like a furnace.
Lk 1: 9 temple of the Lord and *b* incense.
3:17 but he will *b* up the chaff
1Co 7: 9 to marry than to *b* with passion.
2Co 11:29 I do not inwardly *b*? If I must boast
Rev 17:16 they will eat her flesh and *b* her

BURNED (BURN)

Ge 38:24 "Bring her out and have her *b*
39:19 is how your slave treated me," he *b*
Ex 4:14 the LORD's anger *b* against Moses
32:19 his anger *b* and he threw the tablets
32:20 the calf they had made and *b* it
40:27 and *b* fragrant incense on it,
Lev 4:21 and burn it as he *b* the first bull.
4:26 as he *b* the fat of the fellowship
6:22 and is to be *b* completely.
6:23 of a priest shall be *b* completely;
6:30 must not be eaten; it must be *b*.
7:17 over till the third day must be *b* up.
7:19 must not be eaten; it must be *b* up.
8:16 and their fat, and *b* it on the altar.
8:17 its offal he *b* up outside the camp,
8:20 the ram into pieces and *b* the head,
8:21 and *b* the whole ram on the altar
Lev 8:28 and *b* them on the altar on top
9:10 On the altar he *b* the fat,
9:11 the hide he *b* up outside the camp.
9:13 and he *b* them on the altar.
9:14 *b* them on top of the burnt offering
9:17 and *b* it on the altar in addition
9:20 then Aaron *b* the fat on the altar.
10:16 and found that it had been *b* up,
13:52 the article must be *b* up.
13:57 whatever has the mildew must be *b*
16:27 flesh and offal are to be *b* up.
19: 6 until the third day must be *b* up.
20:14 and they must be *b* in the fire,
21: 9 disgraces her father; she must be *b*
Nu 11: 1 fire from the LORD *b* among them
11: 3 from the LORD had *b* among them
11:33 of the LORD *b* against the people,
12: 9 anger of the LORD *b* against them,
16:39 by those who had been *b* up,
19: 5 the heifer is to be *b*— its hide, flesh
19:17 from the *b* purification offering
24:10 Balak's anger *b* against Balaam.
25: 3 the LORD's anger *b* against them.
31:10 They *b* all the towns where
32:13 The LORD's anger *b* against Israel
Dt 9:21 the calf you had made, and *b* it
29:27 Therefore the LORD's anger *b*
Jos 6:24 Then they *b* the whole city
7: 1 the LORD's anger *b* against Israel.
7:25 had stoned the rest, they *b* them.
8:28 So Joshua *b* Ai and made it
11: 9 their horses and *b* their chariots.
11:11 breathed, and he *b* up Hazor itself.
11:13 except Hazor, which Joshua *b*.
Jdg 3: 8 anger of the LORD *b* against Israel
15: 5 He *b* up the shocks and standing
15: 6 the Philistines went up and *b* her
18:27 them with the sword and *b*
1Sa 2:15 But even before the fat was *b*,
2:16 "Let the fat be *b* up first,
11: 6 him in power, and he *b* with anger.
17:28 he *b* with anger at him and asked,
30: 1 They had attacked Ziklag and *b* it,
30:14 And we *b* Ziklag."
31:12 went to Jabesh, where they *b* them.
2Sa 6: 7 The LORD's anger *b*
12: 5 David *b* with anger
23: 7 they are *b* up where they lie."
24: 1 of the LORD *b* against Israel,
1Ki 3: 3 and *b* incense on the high places.
11: 8 who *b* incense and offered
13: 2 and human bones will be *b* on you
15:13 and *b* it in the Kidron Valley.
18:38 LORD fell and *b* up the sacrifice,
19:21 He *b* the plowing equipment
2Ki 10:26 out of the temple of Baal and *b* it.
13: 3 the LORD's anger *b* against Israel,
16: 4 and *b* incense at the high places,
17:11 At every high place they *b* incense,
17:31 the Sepharvites *b* their children
22:17 and *b* incense to other gods
23: 4 He *b* them outside Jerusalem
23: 5 those who *b* incense to Baal,
23: 6 outside Jerusalem and *b* it there
23: 8 where the priests had *b* incense.
23:11 Josiah then *b* the chariots
23:15 He *b* the high place and ground it
23:15 and *b* the Asherah pole also.
23:16 and *b* on the altar to defile it,
23:20 and *b* human bones on them.
23:26 which *b* against Judah
25: 9 Every important building he *b*
1Ch 13:10 The LORD's anger *b*
2Ch 15:16 and *b* it in the Kidron Valley.
25:14 to them and *b* sacrifices to them.
25:15 of the LORD *b* against Amaziah,
28: 3 He *b* sacrifices in the Valley
28: 4 and *b* incense at the high places,
34: 5 He *b* the bones of the priests
34:25 and *b* incense to other gods
36:19 they *b* all the palaces
Ne 1: 3 and its gates have been *b* with fire."
2:17 and its gates have been *b* with fire.
4: 2 *b* as they are?" Tobiah
Est 1:12 the king became furious and *b*
Job 1:16 *b* up the sheep and the servants,
Ps 39: 3 and as I meditated, the fire *b*;
74: 7 They *b* your sanctuary
Ps 74: 8 They *b* every place where God was
80:16 down, it is *b* with fire;
Pr 6:27 lap without his clothes being *b*?
Isa 1: 7 your cities *b* with fire;
24: 6 earth's inhabitants are *b* up,
33:12 The peoples will be *b* as if to lime;
43: 2 you will not be *b*;
64:11 has been *b* with fire,
65: 7 "Because they *b* sacrifices
Jer 2:15 his towns are *b* and deserted.
19: 4 they have *b* sacrifices in it
19:13 all the houses where they *b* incense
29:22 the king of Babylon *b* in the fire.'
36:23 until the entire scroll was *b*
36:27 After the king *b* the scroll
36:28 Jehoiakim king of Judah *b* up.
36:29 You *b* that scroll and said,
36:32 king of Judah had *b* in the fire.
38:17 and this city will not be *b* down;
38:23 and this city will be *b* down."
44:19 "When we *b* incense to the Queen
44:21 and think about the incense *b*
44:23 Because you have *b* incense
52:13 Every important building he *b*
La 2: 3 He has *b* in Jacob like a flaming fire
Eze 15: 5 useful when the fire has *b* it
24:11 and its deposit *b* away.
Da 11:33 or be *b* or captured or plundered.
Hos 2:13 she *b* incense to the Baals;
11: 2 and they *b* incense to images.
Joel 1:19 and flames have *b* up all the trees
Am 2: 1 Because he *b*, as if to lime,
Mic 1: 7 all her temple gifts will be *b*
Mt 13:30 and tie them in bundles to be *b*,
13:40 "As the weeds are pulled up and *b*
22: 7 those murderers and *b* their city.
Jn 5:35 John was a lamp that *b*
15: 6 thrown into the fire and *b*.
Ac 19:19 together and *b* them publicly.
1Co 3:15 If it is *b* up, he will suffer loss;
Heb 6: 8 In the end it will be *b*.
13:11 the bodies are *b* outside the camp.
Rev 8: 7 A third of the earth was *b* up,
8: 7 a third of the trees were *b* up,
8: 7 and all the green grass was *b* up.

BURNED-OUT (BURN)

Jer 51:25 and make you a *b* mountain.

BURNING (BURN)

Ge 19:24 rained down *b* sulfur on Sodom
Ex 15: 7 You unleashed your *b* anger;
27:20 so that the lamps may be kept *b*.
27:21 are to keep the lamps *b*
30: 1 altar of acacia wood for *b* incense.
Lev 1: 8 on the *b* wood that is on the altar.
1:12 on the *b* wood that is on the altar.
3: 5 offering that is on the *b* wood,
6: 9 the fire must be kept *b* on the altar.
6:12 The fire on the altar must be kept *b*
6:13 The fire must be kept *b*
16:12 full of *b* coals from the altar
24: 2 lamps may be kept *b* continually.
Nu 19: 6 and throw them onto the *b* heifer.
Dt 29:23 The whole land will be a *b* waste
29:24 Why this fierce, *b* anger?"
33:16 of him who dwelt in the *b* bush.
Jdg 14:19 *B* with anger, he went up
2Sa 14: 7 put out the only *b* coal I have left,
22: 9 *b* coals blazed out of it.
1Ki 9:25 *b* incense before the LORD
2Ki 18: 4 the Israelites had been *b* incense
2Ch 2: 4 it to him for *b* fragrant incense
Job 18: 5 the flame of his fire stops *b*.
18:15 *b* sulfur is scattered
20:23 God will vent his *b* anger
Ps 11: 6 fiery coals and *b* sulfur;
18: 8 *b* coals blazed out of it.
18:28 You, O LORD, keep my lamp *b*;
118: 12 they died out as quickly as *b* thorns
120: 4 with *b* coals of the broom tree.
140: 10 Let *b* coals fall upon them;
Pr 25:22 you will heap *b* coals on his head,
Isa 9: 5 will be destined for *b*,
13:13 in the day of his *b* anger.
30:27 with *b* anger and dense clouds
30:33 like a stream of *b* sulfur,
33:14 of us can dwell with everlasting *b*

Isa 34: 9 her dust into *b* sulfur;
35: 7 The *b* sand will become a pool,
42: 25 he poured out on them his *b* anger,
44: 15 It is man's fuel for *b;*
65: 3 and *b* incense on altars of brick;
65: 5 a fire that keeps *b* all day.
Jer 1: 16 in *b* incense to other gods
11: 17 me to anger by *b* incense to Baal.
20: 9 his word is in my heart like a *b* fire,
32: 29 to anger by *b* incense on the roofs
36: 22 with a fire *b* in the firepot in front
44: 3 me to anger by *b* incense
44: 5 or stop *b* incense to other gods.
44: 8 *b* incense to other gods in Egypt,
44: 15 that their wives were *b* incense
44: 18 ever since we stopped *b* incense
Eze 1: 13 the living creatures was like *b* coals
10: 2 Fill your hands with *b* coals
36: 5 In my *b* zeal I have spoken
38: 22 hailstones and *b* sulfur on him
Hos 7: 4 *b* like an oven
13: 5 in the land of *b* heat.
Am 4: 11 You were like a *b* stick snatched
Zec 3: 2 Is not this man a *b* stick snatched
8: 2 I am *b* with jealousy for her."
Mt 3: 12 *b* up the chaff with unquenchable
Lk 1: 10 the time for the *b* of incense came,
12: 35 for service and keep your lamps *b,*
24: 32 "Were not our hearts *b* within us
Jn 21: 9 a fire of *b* coals there with fish
Ac 7: 30 the flames of a *b* bush in the desert
Ro 12: 20 you will heap *b* coals on his head."
Heb 12: 18 that can be touched and that is *b*
2Pe 2: 6 and Gomorrah by *b* them to ashes,
Rev 14: 10 with *b* sulfur in the presence
18: 9 her luxury see the smoke of her *b,*
18: 18 When they see the smoke of her *b,*
19: 20 alive into the fiery lake of *b* sulfur.
20: 10 was thrown into the lake of *b* sulfur
21: 8 be in the fiery lake of *b* sulfur.

BURNISHED

1Ki 7: 45 of the LORD were of *b* bronze.
Eze 1: 7 and gleamed like *b* bronze.
Da 10: 6 and legs like the gleam of *b* bronze,
Rev 2: 18 and whose feet are like *b* bronze.

BURNS (BURN)

Ex 22: 6 so that it *b* shocks of grain
Lev 16: 28 man who *b* them must wash his
Nu 19: 8 The man who *b* it must
Dt 32: 22 one that *b* to the realm of death
1Ki 14: 10 house of Jeroboam as one *b* dung,
2Ki 22: 13 Great is the LORD's anger that *b*
Job 19: 11 His anger *b* against me;
30: 30 my body *b* with fever.
31: 12 It is a fire that *b* to Destruction;
Ps 46: 9 he *b* the shields with fire.
SS 8: 6 It *b* like blazing fire,
Isa 5: 25 Therefore the LORD's anger *b*
9: 18 Surely wickedness *b* like a fire;
44: 16 Half of the wood he *b* in the fire;
66: 3 and whoever *b* memorial incense,
Jer 48: 45 it *b* the foreheads of Moab,
Eze 15: 4 as fuel and the fire *b* both ends
Hos 8: 5 My anger *b* against them.
Hab 1: 16 and *b* incense to his dragnet,
Zec 10: 3 My anger *b* against the shepherds,

BURNT (BURN)

Ge 8: 20 he sacrificed *b* offerings on it.
22: 2 as a *b* offering on one
22: 3 cut enough wood for the *b* offering,
22: 6 took the wood for the *b* offering
22: 7 where is the lamb for the *b* offering
22: 8 provide the lamb for the *b* offering,
22: 13 as a *b* offering instead of his son.
Ex 10: 25 and *b* offerings to present
18: 12 brought a *b* offering and other
20: 24 and sacrifice on it your *b* offerings
24: 5 and they offered *b* offerings
29: 18 It is a *b* offering to the LORD,
29: 25 the altar along with the *b* offering
29: 42 to come this *b* offering is
30: 9 or any *b* offering or grain offering,
30: 28 of *b* offering and all its utensils,
31: 9 of *b* offering and all its utensils,
32: 6 and sacrificed *b* offerings
Ex 35: 16 the altar of *b* offering
38: 1 altar of *b* offering of acacia wood,
40: 6 Place the altar of *b* offering in front
40: 10 Then anoint the altar of *b* offering
40: 29 altar of *b* offering near the entrance
40: 29 and offered on it *b* offerings
Lev 1: 3 " 'If the offering is a *b* offering
1: 4 hand on the head of the *b* offering,
1: 6 He is to skin the *b* offering
1: 9 It is a *b* offering, an offering made
1: 10 " 'If the offering is a *b* offering
1: 13 It is a *b* offering, an offering made
1: 14 to the LORD is a *b* offering of birds
1: 17 It is a *b* offering, an offering made
3: 5 altar on top of the *b* offering that is
4: 7 the base of the altar of *b* offering
4: 10 them on the altar of *b* offering.
4: 18 the base of the altar of *b* offering
4: 24 the place where the *b* offering is
4: 25 the horns of the altar of *b* offering
4: 29 it at the place of the *b* offering.
4: 30 the horns of the altar of *b* offering
4: 33 the place where the *b* offering is
4: 34 the horns of the altar of *b* offering
5: 7 and the other for a *b* offering.
5: 10 a *b* offering in the prescribed way
6: 9 The *b* offering is to remain
6: 9 the regulations for the *b* offering:
6: 10 of the *b* offering that the fire has
6: 12 arrange the *b* offering on the fire
6: 25 the place the *b* offering is
7: 2 the place where the *b* offering is
7: 8 The priest who offers a *b* offering
7: 37 the regulations for the *b* offering,
8: 18 the ram for the *b* offering,
8: 21 ram on the altar as a *b* offering,
8: 28 on the altar on top of the *b* offering
9: 2 and a ram for your *b* offering,
9: 3 without defect—for a *b* offering,
9: 7 sin offering and your *b* offering
9: 12 Then he slaughtered the *b* offering.
9: 13 handed him the *b* offering piece
9: 14 on top of the *b* offering on the altar.
9: 16 He brought the *b* offering
9: 17 to the morning's *b* offering.
9: 22 the *b* offering and the fellowship
9: 24 and consumed the *b* offering
10: 19 their *b* offering before the LORD,
12: 6 a year-old lamb for a *b* offering
12: 8 one for a *b* offering and the other
14: 13 and the *b* offering are slaughtered.
14: 19 priest shall slaughter the *b* offering
14: 22 and the other for a *b* offering.
14: 31 and the other as a *b* offering,
15: 15 and the other for a *b* offering.
15: 30 and the other for a *b* offering.
16: 3 offering and a ram for a *b* offering.
16: 5 offering and a ram for a *b* offering.
16: 24 and the *b* offering for the people,
16: 24 sacrifice the *b* offering for himself
17: 8 them who offers a *b* offering
22: 18 a gift for a *b* offering to the LORD,
23: 12 as a *b* offering to the LORD a lamb
23: 18 They will be a *b* offering
23: 37 the *b* offerings and grain offerings,
Nu 6: 11 as a *b* offering to make atonement
6: 14 without defect for a *b* offering,
6: 16 the sin offering and the *b* offering.
7: 15 lamb a year old, for a *b* offering;
7: 21 lamb a year old, for a *b* offering;
7: 27 lamb a year old, for a *b* offering;
7: 33 lamb a year old, for a *b* offering;
7: 39 lamb a year old, for a *b* offering;
7: 45 lamb a year old, for a *b* offering;
7: 51 lamb a year old, for a *b* offering;
7: 57 lamb a year old, for a *b* offering;
7: 63 lamb a year old, for a *b* offering;
7: 69 lamb a year old, for a *b* offering;
7: 75 lamb a year old, for a *b* offering;
7: 81 lamb a year old, for a *b* offering;
7: 87 of animals for the *b* offering came
8: 12 and the other for a *b* offering,
10: 10 the trumpets over your *b* offerings
15: 3 whether *b* offerings or sacrifices,
15: 5 With each lamb for the *b* offering
15: 8 as a *b* offering or sacrifice,
15: 24 to offer a young bull for a *b* offering
28: 3 as a regular *b* offering each day.
Nu 28: 6 is the regular *b* offering instituted
28: 10 This is the *b* offering
28: 10 in addition to the regular *b* offering
28: 11 present to the LORD a *b* offering
28: 13 is for a *b* offering, a pleasing aroma,
28: 14 This is the monthly *b* offering
28: 15 Besides the regular *b* offering
28: 19 a *b* offering of two young bulls,
28: 23 to the regular morning *b* offering.
28: 24 in addition to the regular *b* offering
28: 27 Present a *b* offering
28: 31 in addition to the regular *b* offering
29: 2 prepare a *b* offering
29: 6 daily *b* offerings with their grain
29: 8 pleasing to the LORD a *b* offering
29: 11 and the regular *b* offering
29: 13 a *b* offering of thirteen young bulls,
29: 16 in addition to the regular *b* offering
29: 19 in addition to the regular *b* offering
29: 22 in addition to the regular *b* offering
29: 25 in addition to the regular *b* offering
29: 28 in addition to the regular *b* offering
29: 31 in addition to the regular *b* offering
29: 34 in addition to the regular *b* offering
29: 36 a *b* offering of one bull, one ram
29: 38 in addition to the regular *b* offering
29: 39 your *b* offerings, grain offerings,
Dt 12: 6 there bring your *b* offerings
12: 11 your *b* offerings and sacrifices,
12: 13 sacrifice your *b* offerings anywhere
12: 27 Present your *b* offerings
13: 16 as a whole *b* offering
27: 6 and offer *b* offerings on it
33: 10 and whole *b* offerings on your altar
Jos 8: 31 offered to the LORD *b* offerings
22: 23 and to offer *b* offerings and grain
22: 26 but not for *b* offerings or sacrifices
22: 27 sanctuary with our *b* offerings,
22: 28 not for *b* offerings and sacrifices,
22: 29 by building an altar for *b* offerings,
Jdg 6: 26 offer the second bull as a *b* offering
11: 31 and I will sacrifice it as a *b* offering
13: 16 But if you prepare a *b* offering,
13: 23 not have accepted a *b* offering
20: 26 and presented *b* offerings
21: 4 and presented *b* offerings
1Sa 6: 14 as a *b* offering to the LORD.
6: 15 Beth Shemesh offered *b* offerings
7: 9 as a whole *b* offering to the LORD.
7: 10 was sacrificing the *b* offering,
10: 8 down to you to sacrifice *b* offerings
13: 9 And Saul offered up the *b* offering.
13: 9 "Bring me the *b* offering
13: 12 compelled to offer the *b* offering."
15: 22 the LORD delight in *b* offerings
2Sa 6: 17 and David sacrificed *b* offerings
6: 18 finished sacrificing the *b* offerings
24: 22 Here are oxen for the *b* offering,
24: 24 the LORD my God *b* offerings that
24: 25 and sacrificed *b* offerings
1Ki 3: 4 offered a thousand *b* offerings
3: 15 and sacrificed *b* offerings
8: 64 and there he offered *b* offerings,
8: 64 small to hold the *b* offerings,
9: 25 year Solomon sacrificed *b* offerings
10: 5 and the *b* offerings he made
2Ki 5: 17 will never again make *b* offerings
10: 24 to make sacrifices and *b* offerings.
10: 25 had finished making the *b* offering,
16: 13 He offered up his *b* offering
16: 15 altar all the blood of the *b* offerings
16: 15 and the *b* offering of all the people
16: 15 offer the morning *b* offering
16: 15 the king's *b* offering and his grain
1Ch 6: 49 offerings on the altar of *b* offering
16: 1 and they presented *b* offerings
16: 2 finished sacrificing the *b* offerings
16: 40 in Gibeon to present *b* offerings
16: 40 on the altar of *b* offering regularly,
21: 23 the oxen for the *b* offerings,
21: 24 sacrifice a *b* offering that costs me
21: 26 and sacrificed *b* offerings
21: 26 heaven on the altar of *b* offering.
21: 29 and the altar of *b* offering were
22: 1 also the altar of *b* offering for Israel
23: 31 and whenever *b* offerings were
29: 21 and presented *b* offerings to him:
2Ch 1: 6 offered a thousand *b* offerings on it

2Ch 2: 4 and for making *b* offerings every
4: 6 for the *b* offerings were rinsed,
7: 1 and consumed the *b* offering
7: 7 and there he offered *b* offerings
7: 7 could not hold the *b* offerings,
8: 12 Solomon sacrificed *b* offerings
9: 4 and the *b* offerings he made
13: 11 evening they present *b* offerings
23: 18 to present the *b* offerings
24: 14 and for the *b* offerings,
24: 14 *b* offerings were presented
29: 7 or present any *b* offerings
29: 18 the altar of *b* offering
29: 24 the king had ordered the *b* offering
29: 27 the order to sacrifice the *b* offering
29: 28 of the *b* offering was completed.
29: 31 were willing brought *b* offerings.
29: 32 all of them for *b* offerings
29: 32 of *b* offerings the assembly brought
29: 34 few to skin all the *b* offerings;
29: 35 There were *b* offerings
29: 35 that accompanied the *b* offerings.
30: 15 brought *b* offerings to the temple
31: 2 to offer *b* offerings and fellowship
31: 3 and evening *b* offerings
31: 3 for the *b* offerings on the Sabbaths,
35: 12 They set aside the *b* offerings
35: 14 were sacrificing the *b* offerings
35: 16 and the offering of *b* offerings
Ezr 3: 2 Israel to sacrifice *b* offerings on it,
3: 3 and sacrificed *b* offerings on it
3: 4 number of *b* offerings prescribed
3: 5 presented the regular *b* offerings,
3: 6 to offer *b* offerings to the LORD,
6: 9 male lambs for *b* offerings
8: 35 All this was a *b* offering
8: 35 captivity sacrificed *b* offerings
Ne 10: 33 grain offerings and *b* offerings;
Job 1: 5 he would sacrifice a *b* offering
42: 8 sacrifice a *b* offering for yourselves
Ps 20: 3 and accept your *b* offerings.
40: 6 *b* offerings and sin offerings
50: 8 your *b* offerings, which are ever
51: 16 do not take pleasure in *b* offerings.
51: 19 whole *b* offerings to delight you;
66: 13 to your temple with *b* offerings
Isa 1: 11 more than enough of *b* offerings,
40: 16 its animals enough for *b* offerings.
43: 23 brought me sheep for *b* offerings,
56: 7 Their *b* offerings and sacrifices
Jer 6: 20 Your *b* offerings are not acceptable
7: 21 add your *b* offerings
7: 22 them commands about *b* offerings
14: 12 though they offer *b* offerings
17: 26 bringing *b* offerings and sacrifices,
33: 18 continually to offer *b* offerings,
Eze 40: 38 where the *b* offerings were washed.
40: 39 on which the *b* offerings, sin
40: 42 for slaughtering the *b* offerings
40: 42 of dressed stone for the *b* offerings,
43: 18 for sacrificing *b* offerings
43: 24 as a *b* offering to the LORD.
43: 27 are to present your *b* offerings
44: 11 they may slaughter the *b* offerings
45: 15 *b* offerings and fellowship offerings
45: 17 prince to provide the *b* offerings,
45: 17 *b* offerings and fellowship offerings
45: 23 as a *b* offering to the LORD,
45: 25 *b* offerings, grain offerings and oil.
46: 2 are to sacrifice his *b* offering
46: 4 The *b* offering the prince brings
46: 12 He shall offer his *b* offering
46: 12 a *b* offering or fellowship offerings
46: 13 lamb without defect for a *b* offering
46: 15 by morning for a regular *b* offering.
Hos 6: 6 of God rather than *b* offerings.
Am 5: 22 you bring me *b* offerings
Mic 6: 6 come before him with *b* offerings,
Mk 12: 33 important than all *b* offerings
Heb 10: 6 with *b* offerings and sin offerings
10: 8 *b* offerings and sin offerings you

BURST (BURSTS)

Ge 7: 11 springs of the great deep *b* forth,
27: 34 he *b* out with a loud and bitter cry
Job 26: 8 yet the clouds do not *b*
32: 19 like new wineskins ready to *b*.
38: 8 when it *b* forth from the womb,
Ps 60: 1 O God, and *b* forth upon us;
98: 4 *b* into jubilant song with music;
Isa 35: 2 it will *b* into bloom;
44: 23 *B* into song, you mountains,
49: 13 *b* into song, O mountains!
52: 9 *B* into songs of joy together,
54: 1 *b* into song, shout for joy,
55: 12 will *b* into song before you,
Jer 23: 19 will *b* out in wrath,
30: 23 will *b* out in wrath,
Eze 7: 10 It has come! Doom has *b* forth,
13: 11 and violent winds will *b* forth.
Mt 9: 17 If they do, the skins will *b*,
Mk 2: 22 If he does, the wine will *b* the skins,
Lk 5: 37 the new wine will *b* the skins,
Ac 1: 18 his body *b* open and all his

BURSTS (BURST)

Job 16: 14 Again and again he *b* upon me;

BURY (BURIAL BURIED BURIES BURYING)

Ge 23: 4 here so I can *b* my dead."
23: 6 *B* your dead in the choicest
23: 8 willing to let me *b* my dead,
23: 11 *B* your dead."
23: 13 from me so I can *b* my dead there."
23: 15 between me and you? *B* your dead
47: 29 Do not *b* me in Egypt,
47: 30 and *b* me where they are buried."
49: 29 *B* me with my fathers in the cave
50: 5 Now let me go up and *b* my father;
50: 5 *b* me in the tomb I dug for myself
50: 6 "Go up and *b* your father,
50: 7 So Joseph went up to *b* his father.
50: 14 gone with him to *b* his father.
Dt 21: 23 Be sure to *b* him that same day,
1Ki 2: 31 Strike him down and *b* him,
11: 15 who had gone up to *b* the dead,
13: 29 city to mourn for him and *b* him.
13: 31 *b* me in the grave where the man
14: 13 mourn for him and *b* him.
2Ki 9: 10 at Jezreel, and no one will *b* her.' "
9: 34 *b* her, for she was a king's daughter
9: 35 But when they went out to *b* her,
Job 27: 15 plague will *b* those who survive
40: 13 *B* them all in the dust together;
Ps 79: 3 and there is no one to *b* the dead.
Jer 7: 32 for they will *b* the dead in Topheth
14: 16 There will be no one to *b* them
19: 11 They will *b* the dead in Topheth
43: 9 and *b* them in clay in the brick
La 3: 29 Let him *b* his face in the dust—
Eze 39: 13 the people of the land will *b* them,
39: 14 others will *b* those that remain
Hos 9: 6 and Memphis will *b* them.
Mt 8: 21 first let me go and *b* my father."
8: 22 and let the dead *b* their own dead."
Lk 9: 59 first let me go and *b* my father."
9: 60 "Let the dead *b* their own dead,

BURYING (BURY)

Ge 23: 6 you his tomb for *b* your dead."
50: 14 After *b* his father, Joseph returned
Nu 33: 4 who were *b* all their firstborn,
2Sa 2: 5 to Saul your master by *b* him
1Ki 13: 31 "Oh, my brother!" After *b* him,
2Ki 13: 21 while some Israelites were *b* a man,
Eze 39: 12 of Israel will be *b* them in order

BUSH (BUSHES)

Ex 3: 2 in flames of fire from within a *b*.
3: 2 the *b* was on fire it did not burn up.
3: 3 why the *b* does not burn up."
3: 4 called to him from within the *b*,
Dt 33: 16 of him who dwelt in the burning *b*.
Jer 17: 6 will be like a *b* in the wastelands;
48: 6 become like a *b* in the desert.
Mk 12: 26 the account of the *b*, how God said
Lk 20: 37 But in the account of the *b*,
Ac 7: 30 flames of a burning *b* in the desert
7: 35 who appeared to him in the *b*.

BUSHELS

Lk 16: 7 A thousand *b* of wheat,' he replied.

BUSHES (BUSH)

Ge 21: 15 she put the boy under one of the *b*.
Job 30: 7 They brayed among the *b*

BUSINESS

1Sa 21: 8 because the king's *b* was urgent."
Est 3: 9 for the men who carry out this *b*."
Ecc 4: 8 a miserable *b*!
Eze 27: 12 " 'Tarshish did *b* with you
27: 16 " 'Aram did *b* with you
27: 18 did *b* with you in wine
27: 21 they did *b* with you in lambs,
Da 8: 27 and went about the king's *b*.
Zec 8: 10 No one could go about his *b* safely
Mt 22: 5 one to his field, another to his *b*.
Jn 15: 15 does not know his master's *b*.
Ac 19: 24 in no little *b* for the craftsmen.
19: 25 receive a good income from this *b*.
1Co 5: 12 What *b* is it of mine to judge those
1Th 4: 11 to mind your own *b* and to work
Jas 1: 11 even while he goes about his *b*.
4: 13 carry on *b* and make money."

BUSTLES

Ps 39: 6 He *b* about, but only in vain;

BUSY

1Ki 18: 27 Perhaps he is deep in thought, or *b*,
20: 40 While your servant was *b* here
Isa 32: 6 his mind is *b* with evil:
Hag 1: 9 of you is *b* with his own house.
2Th 3: 11 They are not *b*; they are
Tit 2: 5 to be *b* at home, to be kind,

BUSYBODIES

2Th 3: 11 They are not busy; they are *b*.
1Ti 5: 13 *b*, saying things they ought not to.

BUTCHERED

1Sa 14: 32 they *b* them on the ground
28: 24 at the house, which she *b* at once.
Jer 12: 3 Drag them off like sheep to be *b*!
Mt 22: 4 and fattened cattle have been *b*,

BUTT (BUTTING)

2Sa 2: 23 so Abner thrust the *b* of his spear

BUTTER

Ps 55: 21 His speech is smooth as *b*,
Pr 30: 33 as churning the milk produces *b*,

BUTTING (BUTT)

Eze 34: 21 *b* all the weak sheep

BUTTOCKS

2Sa 10: 4 garments in the middle at the *b*,
1Ch 19: 4 garments in the middle at the *b*,
Isa 20: 4 young and old, with *b* bared—

BUY (BOUGHT BUYER BUYERS BUYING BUYS)

Ge 41: 57 to Egypt to *b* grain from Joseph,
42: 2 Go down there and *b* some for us,
42: 3 went down to *b* grain from Egypt.
42: 5 among those who went to *b* grain,
42: 7 Canaan," they replied, "to *b* food."
42: 10 Your servants have come to *b* food.
43: 2 Go back and *b* us a little more food
43: 4 we will go down and *b* food for you
43: 20 down here the first time to *b* food.
43: 22 additional silver with us to *b* food.
44: 25 'Go back and *b* a little more food.'
47: 19 *B* us and our land in exchange
47: 22 he did not *b* the land of the priests,
Ex 21: 2 "If you *b* a Hebrew servant,
Lev 25: 14 one of your countrymen or *b* any
25: 15 are to *b* from your countryman
25: 44 from them you may *b* slaves.
25: 45 *b* some of the temporary residents
27: 27 he may *b* it back at its set value,
Dt 14: 26 the silver to *b* whatever you like:
28: 68 female slaves, but no one will *b* you
Ru 4: 4 and suggest that you *b* it
4: 5 "On the day you *b* the land
4: 8 said to Boaz, "*B* it yourself."
2Sa 24: 21 "To *b* your threshing floor,"
Ezr 7: 17 With this money be sure to *b* bulls,
Ne 10: 31 we will not *b* from them
Pr 23: 23 *B* the truth and do not sell it;
Isa 55: 1 Come, *b* wine and milk

Isa 55: 1 come, *b* and eat!
Jer 13: 1 "Go and *b* a linen belt
19: 1 "Go and *b* a clay jar from a potter.
32: 7 and say, '*B* my field at Anathoth,
32: 7 it is your right and duty to *b* it.'
32: 8 and possess it, *b* it for yourself.'
32: 8 '*B* my field at Anathoth
32: 25 '*B* the field with silver
La 5: 4 We must *b* the water we drink;
Mt 14: 15 and *b* themselves some food."
25: 9 and *b* some for yourselves.'
25: 10 were on their way to *b* the oil,
27: 7 the money to *b* the potter's field
27: 10 them to *b* the potter's field,
Mk 6: 36 *b* themselves something to eat."
Lk 9: 13 we go and *b* food for all this crowd
22: 36 a sword, sell your cloak and *b* one.
Jn 4: 8 gone into the town to *b* food.)
6: 5 "Where shall we *b* bread
6: 7 wages would not *b* enough bread
13: 29 to *b* what was needed for the Feast,
Ac 8: 20 you thought you could *b* the gift
1Co 7: 30 were not; those who *b* something,
Rev 3: 18 you to *b* from me gold refined
13: 17 so that no one could *b* or sell

BUYER (BUY)

Lev 25: 28 possession of the *b* until the Year
25: 30 shall belong permanently to the *b*
25: 50 and his *b* are to count the time
Pr 20: 14 no good, it's no good!" says the *b;*
Isa 24: 2 for seller as for *b,*
Eze 7: 12 Let not the *b* rejoice nor the seller

BUYERS (BUY)

Zec 11: 5 Their *b* slaughter them

BUYING (BUY)

Ge 47: 14 payment for the grain they were *b,*
Am 8: 6 *b* the poor with silver
Mt 21: 12 and drove out all who were *b*
Mk 11: 15 driving out those who were *b*
Lk 17: 28 and drinking, *b* and selling,

BUYS (BUY)

Lev 22: 11 But if a priest *b* a slave with money,
Pr 31: 16 She considers a field and *b* it;
Rev 18: 11 no one *b* their cargoes any more—

BUZ (BUZITE)

Ge 22: 21 Uz the firstborn, *B* his brother,
1Ch 5: 14 the son of Jahdo, the son of *B.*
Jer 25: 23 *B* and all who are in distant places;

BUZI

Eze 1: 3 the son of *B,* by the Kebar River

BUZITE (BUZ)

Job 32: 2 But Elihu son of Barakel the *B,*
32: 6 So Elihu son of Barakel the *B* said:

BYPATHS (PATH)

Jer 18: 15 They made them walk in *b*

BYWORD (WORD)

1Ki 9: 7 Israel will then become a *b*
2Ch 7: 20 I will make it a *b* and an object
Job 17: 6 God has made me a *b* to everyone,
30: 9 I have become a *b* among them.
Ps 44: 14 You have made us a *b*
Jer 24: 9 and a *b,* an object of ridicule
Eze 14: 8 and make him an example and a *b.*
23: 10 She became a *b* among women,
Joel 2: 17 a *b* among the nations.

CAB

2Ki 6: 25 and a fourth of a *c* of seed pods

CABBON

Jos 15: 40 Bozkath, Eglon, *C,* Lahmas,

CABUL

Jos 19: 27 and Neiel, passing *C* on the left.
1Ki 9: 13 And he called them the Land of *C,*

CAESAR (CAESAR'S)

Mt 22: 17 Is it right to pay taxes to *C* or not?"
22: 21 "Give to *C* what is Caesar's,
Mk 12: 14 Is it right to pay taxes to *C* or not?
12: 17 "Give to *C* what is Caesar's
Lk 2: 1 In those days *C* Augustus issued
3: 1 year of the reign of Tiberius *C*—
20: 22 Is it right for us to pay taxes to *C*
20: 25 "Then give to *C* what is Caesar's,
23: 2 He opposes payment of taxes to *C*
Jn 19: 12 claims to be a king opposes *C.*"
19: 12 this man go, you are no friend of *C.*
19: 15 "We have no king but *C,*"
Ac 25: 8 or against the temple or against *C.*"
25: 11 to *C!*" After Festus had conferred
25: 12 To *C* you will go!" A few days later
25: 12 "You have appealed to *C.*
25: 21 held until I could send him to *C.*"
26: 32 if he had not appealed to *C.*"
27: 24 You must stand trial before *C;*
28: 19 I was compelled to appeal to *C*—

CAESAR'S (CAESAR)

Mt 22: 21 And whose inscription?" "*C,*"
22: 21 "Give to Caesar what is *C,*
Mk 12: 16 And whose inscription?" "*C,*"
12: 17 "Give to Caesar what is *C*
Lk 20: 25 and inscription are on it?" "*C,*"
20: 25 "Then give to Caesar what is *C,*
Ac 17: 7 They are all defying *C* decrees,
25: 10 "I am now standing before *C* court,
Php 4: 22 those who belong to *C* household.

CAESAREA

Ac 8: 40 in all the towns until he reached *C.*
9: 30 they took him down to *C*
10: 1 At *C* there was a man named
10: 24 The following day he arrived in *C.*
11: 11 sent to me from *C* stopped
12: 19 Then Herod went from Judea to *C*
18: 22 When he landed at *C,* he went up
21: 8 we reached *C* and stayed
21: 16 disciples from *C* accompanied us
23: 23 to go to *C* at nine tonight.
23: 33 When the cavalry arrived in *C,*
24: 1 down to *C* with some of the elders
25: 1 up from *C* to Jerusalem,
25: 4 answered, "Paul is being held at *C,*
25: 6 with them, he went down to *C,*
25: 13 and Bernice arrived at *C*
25: 24 him in Jerusalem and here in *C,*

CAESAREA PHILIPPI

Mt 16: 13 came to the region of *C,*
Mk 8: 27 went on to the villages around *C.*

CAGE (CAGES)

Eze 19: 9 hooks they pulled him into a *c*

CAGES (CAGE)

Jer 5: 27 Like *c* full of birds,

CAIAPHAS

Mt 26: 3 whose name was *C,* and they
26: 57 had arrested Jesus took him to *C,*
Lk 3: 2 high priesthood of Annas and *C,*
Jn 11: 49 Then one of them, named *C,*
18: 13 who was the father-in-law of *C,*
18: 14 *C* was the one who had advised
18: 24 still bound, to *C* the high priest.
18: 28 Jesus from *C* to the palace
Ac 4: 6 priest was there, and so were *C,*

CAIN

Ge 4: 1 she conceived and gave birth to *C.*
4: 2 kept flocks, and *C* worked the soil.
4: 3 the course of time *C* brought some
4: 5 but on *C* and his offering he did not
4: 5 *C* was very angry, and his face was
4: 6 Then the LORD said to *C,*
4: 8 Now *C* said to his brother Abel,
4: 8 *C* attacked his brother Abel
4: 9 Then the LORD said to *C,*
4: 13 *C* said to the LORD, "My
4: 15 Then the LORD put a mark on *C*
4: 15 "Not so; if anyone kills *C,*
4: 16 So *C* went out from the LORD's
4: 17 *C* lay with his wife, and she became
4: 17 *C* was then building a city,
4: 24 If *C* is avenged seven times,
4: 25 in place of Abel, since *C* killed him
Heb 11: 4 God a better sacrifice than *C* did.
1Jn 3: 12 Do not be like *C,* who belonged
Jude : 11 They have taken the way of *C;*

CAINAN

Lk 3: 36 the son of *C,*
3: 37 the son of *C,*

CAKE (CAKES RAISIN-CAKES)

Ex 29: 23 take a loaf, and a *c* made with oil,
Lev 8: 26 he took a *c* of bread, and one made
Nu 6: 19 and a *c* and a wafer from the basket
15: 20 Present a *c* from the first
1Sa 30: 12 part of a *c* of pressed figs
2Sa 6: 19 a *c* of dates and a *c* of raisins
1Ki 17: 13 first make a small *c* of bread for me
19: 6 by his head was a *c* of bread baked
1Ch 16: 3 a *c* of dates and a *c* of raisins
Eze 4: 12 the food as you would a barley *c;*
Hos 7: 8 Ephraim is a flat *c* not turned over.

CAKES (CAKE)

Ex 12: 39 they baked *c* of unleavened bread.
29: 2 make bread, and *c* mixed with oil,
Lev 2: 4 *c* made without yeast and mixed
7: 12 and *c* of fine flour well-kneaded
7: 12 is to offer *c* of bread made
7: 13 an offering with *c* of bread made
Nu 6: 15 *c* made of fine flour mixed with oil,
11: 8 it in a pot or made it into *c.*
1Sa 25: 18 a hundred *c* of raisins and two
25: 18 and two hundred *c* of pressed figs,
30: 12 of pressed figs and two *c* of raisins.
2Sa 16: 1 a hundred *c* of figs and a skin
16: 1 a hundred *c* of raisins, a hundred
1Ki 14: 3 some *c* and a jar of honey,
1Ch 12: 40 fig *c,* raisin *c,*
Isa 16: 7 for the raisin *c* of Kir Hareseth.
Jer 7: 18 and make *c* of bread for the Queen
44: 19 we were making *c* like her image

CALAH

Ge 10: 11 he built Nineveh, Rehoboth Ir, *C*
10: 12 is between Nineveh and *C;* that

CALAMITIES (CALAMITY)

Dt 29: 22 lands will see the *c* that have fallen
32: 23 "I will heap *c* upon them
1Sa 10: 19 who saves you out of all your *c*
2Sa 19: 7 you than all the *c* that have come
Job 5: 19 From six *c* he will rescue you;
Pr 24: 22 who knows what *c* they can bring?
Isa 51: 19 These double *c* have come
La 3: 38 that both *c* and good things come?

CALAMITY (CALAMITIES)

2Sa 12: 11 going to bring *c* upon you.
24: 16 was grieved because of the *c*
1Ch 21: 15 and was grieved because of the *c*
2Ch 20: 9 saying, 'If *c* comes upon us,
Ne 13: 18 so that our God brought all this *c*
Job 18: 12 *C* is hungry for him;
21: 17 How often does *c* come upon them,
21: 30 man is spared from the day of *c,*
Ps 107: 39 by oppression, *c* and sorrow;
Pr 1: 26 I will mock when *c* overtakes you
1: 27 when *c* overtakes you like a storm,
14: 32 When *c* comes, the wicked are
21: 23 keeps himself from *c.*
24: 16 the wicked are brought down by *c.*
Isa 47: 11 A *c* will fall upon you
Jer 14: 16 out on them the *c* they deserve.
32: 42 As I have brought all this great *c*
48: 16 her *c* will come quickly.
Eze 6: 10 in vain to bring this *c* on them.
7: 26 *C* upon *c* will come,
35: 5 to the sword at the time of their *c,*
Joel 2: 13 and he relents from sending *c.*
Ob : 13 nor look down on them in their *c*
Jnh 1: 7 out who is responsible for this *c.*"
4: 2 a God who relents from sending *c.*
Mic 2: 3 for it will be a time of *c.*
Hab 3: 16 I will wait patiently for the day of *c*
Zec 1: 15 angry, but they added to the *c.*'

CALAMUS

SS 4: 14 *c* and cinnamon,
Isa 43: 24 You have not bought any fragrant *c*
Jer 6: 20 or sweet *c* from a distant land?

Eze 27: 19 cassia and *c* for your wares.

CALCOL

1Ki 4: 31 wiser than Heman, *C* and Darda,
1Ch 2: 6 Ethan, Heman, *C* and Darda

CALCULATE (CALCULATED)

Rev 13: 18 let him *c* the number of the beast,

CALCULATED (CALCULATE)

Ac 19: 19 When they *c* the value

CALDRON (CALDRONS)

1Sa 2: 14 it into the pan or kettle or *c*
Job 41: 31 the depths churn like a boiling *c*

CALDRONS (CALDRON)

2Ch 35: 13 *c* and pans and served them

CALEB (CALEB'S CALEBITE)

Nu 13: 6 tribe of Judah, *C* son of Jephunneh;
13: 30 *C* silenced the people before Moses
14: 6 of Nun and *C* son of Jephunneh,
14: 24 my servant *C* has a different spirit
14: 30 except *C* son of Jephunneh
14: 38 and *C* son of Jephunneh survived.
26: 65 one of them was left except *C* son
32: 12 *C* son of Jephunneh the Kenizzite
34: 19 These are their names: *C* son
Dt 1: 36 except *C* son of Jephunneh.
Jos 14: 6 *C* son of Jephunneh the Kenizzite
14: 13 Joshua blessed *C* son of Jephunneh
14: 14 So Hebron has belonged to *C* son
15: 13 Joshua gave to *C* son
15: 14 From Hebron *C* drove out
15: 16 *C* said, "I will give my daughter
15: 17 so *C* gave his daughter Acsah
15: 18 got off the donkey, *C* asked her,
15: 19 So *C* gave her the upper
21: 12 given to *C* son of Jephunneh
Jdg 1: 12 *C* said, "I will give my daughter
1: 13 so *C* gave his daughter Acsah
1: 14 got off her donkey, *C* asked her,
1: 15 Then *C* gave her the upper
1: 20 promised, Hebron was given to *C*,
1Sa 30: 14 to Judah and the Negev of *C*.
1Ch 2: 9 were: Jerahmeel, Ram and *C*.
2: 18 *C* son of Hezron had children
2: 19 Azubah died, *C* married Ephrath,
2: 42 The sons of *C* the brother
2: 50 These were the descendants of *C*:
4: 15 The sons of *C* son of Jephunneh:
6: 56 given to *C* son of Jephunneh.

CALEB EPHRATHAH

1Ch 2: 24 After Hezron died in *C*,

CALEB'S (CALEB)

Jos 15: 17 Othniel son of Kenaz, *C* brother,
Jdg 1: 13 son of Kenaz, *C* younger brother,
3: 9 son of Kenaz, *C* younger brother,
1Ch 2: 46 *C* concubine Ephah was
2: 48 *C* concubine Maacah was
2: 49 *C* daughter was Acsah.

CALEBITE (CALEB)

1Sa 25: 3 a *C*, was surly and mean

CALF (CALVE CALVED CALVES)

Ge 18: 7 tender *c* and gave it to a servant,
18: 8 and the *c* that had been prepared,
Ex 32: 4 into an idol cast in the shape of a *c*,
32: 5 he built an altar in front of the *c*
32: 8 cast in the shape of a *c*.
32: 19 and saw the *c* and the dancing,
32: 20 And he took the *c* they had made
32: 24 into the fire, and out came this *c*!"
32: 35 did with the *c* Aaron had made.
Lev 9: 2 "Take a bull *c* for your sin offering
9: 3 goat for a sin offering, a *c*
9: 8 slaughtered the *c* as a sin offering
Dt 9: 16 cast in the shape of a *c*.
9: 21 thing of yours, the *c* you had made,
1Sa 28: 24 The woman had a fattened *c*
2Sa 6: 13 he sacrificed a bull and a fattened *c*
2Ch 11: 15 and for the goat and *c* idols he had
Ne 9: 18 cast for themselves an image of a *c*
Ps 29: 6 He makes Lebanon skip like a *c*,
Ps 106: 19 At Horeb they made a *c*
Pr 15: 17 than a fattened *c* with hatred.
Isa 11: 6 the *c* and the lion and the yearling
Jer 31: 18 You disciplined me like an unruly *c*
34: 18 I will treat like the *c* they cut in two
34: 19 walked between the pieces of the *c*,
Eze 1: 7 their feet were like those of a *c*
Hos 8: 6 This *c*— a craftsman has made it;
8: 6 that *c* of Samaria.
Lk 15: 23 Bring the fattened *c* and kill it.
15: 27 your father has killed the fattened *c*
15: 30 you kill the fattened *c* for him!'
Ac 7: 41 made an idol in the form of a *c*.

CALF-IDOL (IDOL)

Hos 8: 5 Throw out your *c*, O Samaria!
10: 5 for the *c* of Beth Aven.

CALF-IDOLS (IDOL)

Hos 13: 2 and kiss the *c*."

CALL (CALLED CALLING CALLS SO-CALLED)

Ge 4: 26 At that time men began to *c*
17: 15 you are no longer to *c* her Sarai;
17: 19 you a son, and you will *c* him Isaac.
24: 57 "Let's *c* the girl and ask her about it
30: 13 The women will *c* me happy."
Dt 3: 9 Sidonians; the Amorites *c* it Senir.)
4: 26 I *c* heaven and earth as witnesses
18: 19 I myself will *c* him to account.
30: 19 This day I *c* heaven and earth
31: 14 *C* Joshua and present yourselves
31: 28 and *c* heaven and earth to testify
Jos 22: 23 may the LORD himself *c* us
Jdg 8: 1 Why didn't you *c* us
9: 29 '*C* out your whole army!' "
Ru 1: 20 be Naomi?" "Don't *c* me Naomi,"
1: 20 "*C* me Mara,
1: 21 Why *c* me Naomi? The LORD has
1Sa 3: 5 "I did not *c*; go back and lie down."
3: 6 "I did not *c*; go back and lie down."
12: 17 I will *c* upon the LORD
20: 16 May the LORD *c* David's enemies
23: 28 *c* this place Sela Hammahlekoth.
2Sa 15: 2 Absalom would *c* out to him,
22: 4 I *c* to the LORD, who is worthy
1Ki 1: 28 King David said, "*C* in Bathsheba
1: 32 King David said, "*C*
18: 24 I will *c* on the name of the LORD.
18: 24 you *c* on the name of your god,
18: 25 *C* on the name of your god,
2Ki 4: 12 servant Gehazi, "*C*
4: 15 Then Elisha said, "*C* her."
4: 36 and said, "*C* the Shunammite."
5: 11 *c* on the name of the LORD his
10: 20 "*C* an assembly in honor of Baal."
1Ch 16: 8 to the LORD, *c* on his name;
2Ch 24: 22 "May the LORD see this and *c* you
Ne 13: 2 but had hired Balaam to *c* a curse
Job 5: 1 "*C* if you will, but who will answer
14: 15 You will *c* and I will answer you;
19: 7 I *c* for help, there is no justice.
27: 10 Will he *c* upon God at all times?
Ps 4: 1 Answer me when I *c* to you,
4: 3 the LORD will hear when I *c*
10: 13 "He won't *c* me to account"?
10: 15 *c* him to account for his
14: 4 and who do not *c* on the LORD?
17: 6 I *c* on you, O God,
18: 3 I *c* to the LORD, who is worthy
20: 9 Answer us when we *c*!
27: 7 Hear my voice when I *c*, O LORD;
28: 1 To you I *c*, O LORD my Rock;
28: 2 as I *c* to you for help,
50: 15 and *c* upon me in the day of trouble
53: 4 and who do not *c* on God?
55: 16 But I *c* to God,
56: 9 back when I *c* for help.
61: 2 I *c* as my heart grows faint;
61: 2 the ends of the earth I *c* to you,
65: 8 you *c* forth songs of joy.
72: 17 and they will *c* him blessed.
79: 6 that do not *c* on your name;
80: 18 and we will *c* on your name.
86: 3 for I *c* to you all day long.
86: 5 in love to all who *c* to you.
86: 7 of my trouble I will *c* to you,
Ps 88: 9 I *c* to you, O LORD, every day;
89: 26 He will *c* out to me, 'You are my
91: 15 He will *c* upon me, and I will
102: 2 when I *c*, answer me quickly.
105: 1 to the LORD, *c* on his name;
116: 2 I will *c* on him as long as I live.
116: 13 and *c* on the name of the LORD.
116: 17 and *c* on the name of the LORD.
119: 145 I *c* with all my heart; answer me,
119: 146 I *c* out to you; save me
120: 1 I *c* on the LORD in my distress,
141: 1 Hear my voice when I *c* to you.
141: 1 I *c* to you; come quickly to me.
145: 18 near to all who *c* on him,
145: 18 to all who *c* on him in truth.
147: 9 for the young ravens when they *c*.
Pr 1: 28 "Then they will *c* to me
2: 3 and if you *c* out for insight
7: 4 and *c* understanding your kinsman;
8: 1 Does not wisdom *c* out?
8: 4 "To you, O men, I *c* out;
31: 28 children arise and *c* her blessed;
Ecc 3: 15 and God will *c* the past to account.
Isa 5: 20 Woe to those who *c* evil good
7: 14 to a son, and will *c* him Immanuel.
8: 2 And I will *c* in Uriah the priest
8: 12 He said: "Do not *c* conspiracy
8: 12 that these people *c* conspiracy;
12: 4 to the LORD, *c* on his name;
30: 7 Therefore I *c* her
44: 5 another will *c* himself by the name
45: 4 I *c* you by name
48: 2 you who *c* yourselves citizens
54: 6 The LORD will *c* you back
55: 6 *c* on him while he is near.
58: 5 Is that what you *c* a fast,
58: 9 you will *c*, and the LORD will
58: 13 if you *c* the Sabbath a delight
60: 14 will *c* you The City of the LORD,
60: 18 but you will *c* your walls Salvation
62: 4 No longer will they *c* you Deserted
62: 6 You who *c* on the LORD,
65: 1 To a nation that did not *c*
65: 24 Before they *c* I will answer;
Jer 3: 17 time they will *c* Jerusalem
3: 19 I thought you would *c* me 'Father'
7: 27 when you *c* to them, they will not
7: 32 people will no longer *c* it Topheth
9: 17 *C* for the wailing women to come;
10: 25 on the peoples who do not *c*
11: 14 listen when they *c* to me in the time
19: 6 will no longer *c* this place Topheth
29: 12 Then you will *c* upon me and come
33: 3 '*C* to me and I will answer you
La 3: 8 Even when I *c* out or cry for help,
3: 21 Yet this I *c* to mind
Eze 9: 1 I heard him *c* out in a loud voice,
36: 29 I will *c* for the grain and make it
39: 17 *C* out to every kind of bird
Da 5: 12 *C* for Daniel, and he will tell you
Hos 1: 4 said to Hosea, "*C* him Jezreel,
1: 6 to Hosea, "*C* her Lo-Ruhamah,
1: 9 the LORD said, "*C* him Lo-Ammi,
2: 16 you will no longer *c* me 'my master
2: 16 "you will *c* me 'my husband';
11: 7 Even if they *c* to the Most High,
Joel 1: 14 *c* a sacred assembly.
1: 19 To you, O LORD, I *c*,
2: 15 *c* a sacred assembly,
Jnh 1: 6 Get up and *c* on your god!
3: 8 Let everyone *c* urgently on God.
Hab 1: 2 O LORD, must I *c* for help,
Zep 3: 9 that all of them may *c* on the name
Zec 13: 9 They will *c* on my name
Mal 3: 12 all the nations will *c* you blessed,
3: 15 But now we *c* the arrogant blessed.
Mt 1: 23 and they will *c* him Immanuel"—
9: 13 come to *c* the righteous,
20: 8 '*C* the workers and pay them their
23: 7 and to have men *c* them 'Rabbi.'
23: 9 do not *c* anyone on earth 'father,'
24: 1 up to him to *c* his attention
24: 31 angels with a loud trumpet *c*,
26: 53 Do you think I cannot *c*
26: 74 Then he began to *c* down curses
Mk 2: 17 I have not come to *c* the righteous,
3: 31 they sent someone in to *c* him.
10: 18 "Why do you *c* me good?"

Mk 10: 49 Jesus stopped and said, "*C* him."
14: 71 He began to *c* down curses
15: 12 with the one you *c* the king
15: 18 And they began to *c* out to him,
Lk 1: 48 on all generations will *c* me blessed
5: 32 I have not come to *c* the righteous,
6: 46 "Why do you *c* me, 'Lord, Lord,'
9: 54 us to *c* fire down from heaven
18: 19 "Why do you *c* me good?"
22: 25 authority over them *c* themselves
Jn 4: 16 Go, *c* your husband and come back
9: 11 man they *c* Jesus made some mud
13: 13 "You *c* me 'Teacher' and 'Lord,'
15: 15 I no longer *c* you servants,
Ac 2: 39 all whom the Lord our God will *c*."
9: 14 to arrest all who *c* on your name."
9: 21 among those who *c* on this name?
10: 15 "Do not *c* anything impure that
10: 28 that I should not *c* any man impure
11: 9 'Do not *c* anything impure that
24: 14 of the Way, which they *c* a sect.
Ro 1: 5 and apostleship to *c* people
2: 17 Now you, if you *c* yourself a Jew;
9: 25 I will *c* her 'my loved one' who is
9: 25 "I will *c* them 'my people' who are
10: 12 and richly blesses all who *c* on him,
10: 14 can they *c* on the one they have not
11: 29 gifts and his *c* are irrevocable.
1Co 1: 2 with all those everywhere who *c*
14: 8 trumpet does not sound a clear *c*,
2Co 1: 23 I *c* God as my witness that it was
Eph 2: 11 by those who *c* themselves
1Th 4: 7 For God did not *c* us to be impure,
4: 16 and with the trumpet *c* of God,
2Ti 2: 22 along with those who *c*
Heb 2: 11 ashamed to *c* them brothers.
Jas 5: 14 He should *c* the elders
1Pe 1: 17 Since you *c* on a Father who judges
3Jn : 10 I will *c* attention to what he is
Rev 8: 13 in midair *c* out in a loud voice:

CALLED (CALL)

Ge 1: 5 God *c* the light "day"
1: 5 and the darkness he *c* "night."
1: 8 God *c* the expanse "sky."
1: 10 God *c* the dry ground "land,"
1: 10 and the gathered waters he *c* "seas
2: 19 and whatever the man *c* each living
2: 23 she shall be *c* 'woman,'
3: 9 But the LORD God *c* to the man,
5: 2 he blessed them and *c* them "man
11: 9 That is why it was *c* Babel—
12: 8 and *c* on the name of the LORD.
13: 4 There Abram *c* on the name
14: 14 he *c* out the 318 trained men born
16: 14 the well was *c* Beer Lahai Roi;
17: 5 No longer will you be *c* Abram;
19: 5 They *c* to Lot, "Where are the men
19: 22 (That is why the town was *c* Zoar.)
20: 9 Then Abimelech *c* Abraham in
21: 17 and the angel of God *c* to Hagar
21: 31 So that place was *c* Beersheba,
21: 33 and there he *c* upon the name
22: 11 the angel of the LORD *c* out to him
22: 14 Abraham *c* that place "The LORD
22: 15 angel of the LORD *c* to Abraham
24: 58 So they *c* Rebekah and asked her,
25: 30 (That is why he was also *c* Edom.)
26: 25 and *c* on the name of the LORD.
26: 33 found water!" He *c* it Shibah,
27: 1 he *c* for Esau his older son
28: 1 Isaac *c* for Jacob and blessed him
28: 19 He *c* that place Bethel,
28: 19 though the city used to be *c* Luz.
31: 47 *c* it Jegar Sahadutha, and Jacob *c* it
31: 48 That is why it was *c* Galeed.
31: 49 also *c* Mizpah, because he said,
32: 30 So Jacob *c* the place Peniel, saying,
33: 17 That is why the place is *c* Succoth.
33: 20 up an altar and *c* it El Elohe Israel.
35: 7 and he *c* the place El Bethel,
35: 10 but you will no longer be *c* Jacob;
39: 14 she *c* her household servants.
47: 29 he *c* for his son Joseph
48: 16 May they be *c* by my name
49: 1 Then Jacob *c* for his sons and said:
50: 11 place near the Jordan is *c* Abel
Ex 3: 4 God *c* to him from within the bush,
Ex 15: 23 (That is why the place is *c* Marah.)
16: 31 people of Israel *c* the bread manna.
17: 7 And he *c* the place Massah
17: 15 and *c* it The LORD is my Banner.
19: 3 and the LORD *c* to him
19: 20 *c* Moses to the top of the mountain.
24: 16 on the seventh day the LORD *c*
34: 31 But Moses *c* to them; so Aaron
Lev 1: 1 The LORD *c* to Moses
Nu 1: 18 and they *c* the whole community
11: 3 So that place was *c* Taberah,
13: 24 That place was *c* the Valley
32: 41 and *c* them Havvoth Jair.
32: 42 and *c* it Nobah after himself.
Dt 2: 11 but the Moabites *c* them Emites.
2: 20 Ammonites *c* them Zamzummites.
3: 9 (Hermon is *c* Sirion
3: 14 to this day Bashan is *c* Havvoth
28: 10 on earth will see that you are *c*
Jos 3: 16 at a town *c* Adam in the vicinity
4: 4 Joshua *c* together the twelve men
5: 9 So the place has been *c* Gilgal
6: 6 So Joshua son of Nun *c* the priests
7: 26 that place has been *c* the Valley
8: 16 men of Ai were *c* to pursue them,
14: 15 (Hebron used to be *c* Kiriath Arba
15: 15 Debir (formerly *c* Kiriath Sepher).
Jdg 1: 10 Hebron (formerly *c* Kiriath Arba)
1: 11 Debir (formerly *c* Kiriath Sepher).
1: 17 Therefore it was *c* Hormah.
1: 23 to spy out Bethel (formerly *c* Luz),
1: 26 where he built a city and *c* it Luz,
2: 5 and they *c* that place Bokim.
6: 24 and *c* it "The LORD is Peace."
6: 32 day they *c* Gideon "Jerub-Baal,"
7: 15 to the camp of Israel and *c* out,
7: 23 Asher and all Manasseh were *c* out
7: 24 all the men of Ephraim were *c* out
9: 54 Hurriedly he *c* to his armor-bearer,
10: 4 to this day are *c* Havvoth Jair.
10: 17 When the Ammonites were *c*
12: 1 men of Ephraim *c* out their forces,
12: 2 I *c*, you didn't save me out
12: 4 Jephthah then *c* together the men
15: 17 and the place was *c* Ramath Lehi.
15: 19 So the spring was *c* En Hakkore,
16: 9 hidden in the room, she *c* to him,
16: 12 hidden in the room, she *c* to him,
16: 14 Again she *c* to him, "Samson,
16: 19 she *c* a man to shave
16: 20 she *c*, "Samson, the Philistines are
16: 25 So they *c* Samson out of the prison,
18: 12 is *c* Mahaneh Dan to this day.
18: 22 lived near Micah were *c* together
18: 23 with you that you *c* out your men
18: 29 though the city used to be *c* Laish.
Ru 2: 4 The LORD bless you!" they *c* back
1Sa 1: 2 one was *c* Hannah and the other
3: 4 Then the LORD *c* Samuel.
3: 5 and said, "Here I am; you *c* me."
3: 6 Again the LORD *c*, "Samuel!"
3: 6 and said, "Here I am; you *c* me."
3: 8 The LORD *c* Samuel a third time,
3: 8 and said, "Here I am; you *c* me."
3: 16 but Eli *c* him and said, "Samuel,
5: 8 So they *c* together all the rulers
5: 11 So they *c* together all the rulers
6: 2 the Philistines *c* for the priests
9: 9 of today used to be *c* a seer.)
9: 26 and Samuel *c* to Saul on the roof,
12: 18 Then Samuel *c* upon the LORD,
14: 4 one was *c* Bozez, and the other
16: 8 Then Jesse *c* Abinadab
19: 7 So Jonathan *c* David and told him
20: 37 Jonathan *c* out after him, "Isn't
23: 8 Saul *c* up all his forces for battle,
24: 8 out of the cave and *c* out to Saul,
26: 14 He *c* out to the army
28: 15 So I have *c* on you to tell me what
29: 6 So Achish *c* David and said to him,
2Sa 1: 7 and saw me, he *c* out to me,
1: 15 Then David *c* one of his men
2: 16 that place in Gibeon was *c* Helkath
2: 26 Abner *c* out to Joab, "Must
5: 9 in the fortress and *c* it the City
5: 20 So that place was *c* Baal Perazim.
6: 2 which is *c* by the Name, the name
6: 8 that place is *c* Perez Uzzah.
2Sa 9: 2 They *c* him to appear before David,
13: 17 He *c* his personal servant and said,
18: 18 and it is *c* Absalom's Monument
18: 25 The watchman *c* out to the king
18: 26 and he *c* down to the gatekeeper,
18: 28 Then Ahimaaz *c* out to the king,
20: 16 a wise woman *c* from the city,
22: 7 I *c* out to my God.
22: 7 In my distress I *c* to the LORD;
1Ki 2: 8 who *c* down bitter curses
9: 13 And he *c* them the Land of Cabul,
12: 20 they sent and *c* him
17: 10 He *c* to her and asked, "Would you
17: 11 he *c*, "And bring me, please,
18: 26 Then they *c* on the name of Baal
20: 39 by, the prophet *c* out to him,
22: 9 So the king of Israel *c* one
2Ki 2: 24 and *c* down a curse on them
3: 10 "Has the LORD *c* us three kings
3: 13 the LORD who *c* us three kings
3: 21 who could bear arms was *c* up
4: 12 he *c* her, and she stood before him.
4: 15 So he *c* her, and she stood
4: 22 She *c* her husband and said,
7: 10 and *c* out to the city gatekeepers
9: 17 he *c* out, "I see some troops
9: 32 up at the window and *c* out,
11: 14 Athaliah tore her robes and *c* out,
18: 4 (It was *c* Nehushtan.)
18: 18 They *c* for the king; and Eliakim
18: 28 the commander stood and *c* out
20: 11 Then the prophet Isaiah *c*
23: 1 the king *c* together all the elders
1Ch 4: 14 It was *c* this because its people
9: 23 the LORD—the house *c* the Tent.
11: 7 and so it was *c* the City of David.
13: 6 the ark that is *c* by the Name.
13: 11 day that place is *c* Perez Uzzah.
14: 11 So that place was *c* Baal Perazim.
15: 4 He *c* together the descendants
21: 26 He *c* on the LORD, and the LORD
22: 6 Then he *c* for his son Solomon
2Ch 7: 14 if my people, who are *c*
14: 11 Then Asa *c* to the LORD his God
18: 8 So the king of Israel *c* one
20: 26 This is why it is *c* the Valley
24: 5 He *c* together the priests
25: 5 Amaziah *c* the people
32: 18 they *c* out in Hebrew to the people
34: 29 the king *c* together all the elders
Ezr 2: 61 of Barzillai the Gileadite and was *c*
Ne 5: 7 I *c* together a large meeting to deal
7: 63 of Barzillai the Gileadite and was *c*
9: 4 who *c* with loud voices
13: 11 Then I *c* them together
13: 25 and *c* curses down on them.
Est 4: 11 since I was *c* to go to the king."
9: 26 Therefore these days were *c* Purim,
Job 12: 4 I *c* upon God and he answered—
31: 14 answer when *c* to account?
Ps 18: 6 In my distress I *c* to the LORD;
30: 2 O LORD my God, I *c* to you
30: 8 To you, O LORD, I *c*;
31: 22 mercy when I *c* to you for help.
34: 6 This poor man *c*, and the LORD
81: 7 In your distress you *c* and I rescued
99: 6 among those who *c* on his name;
99: 6 they *c* on the LORD
105: 16 He *c* down famine on the land
116: 4 Then I *c* on the name of the LORD
138: 3 When I *c*, you answered me;
Pr 1: 24 But since you rejected me when I *c*
16: 21 The wise in heart are *c* discerning,
SS 5: 6 I *c* him but he did not answer.
6: 9 maidens saw her and *c* her blessed;
Isa 1: 26 Afterward you will be *c*
4: 1 only let us be *c* by your name.
4: 3 remain in Jerusalem, will be *c* holy,
9: 6 And he will be *c*
19: 18 One of them will be *c* the City
22: 12 *c* you on that day
31: 4 is *c* together against him,
32: 5 No longer will the fool be *c* noble
34: 12 to be *c* a kingdom,
35: 8 it will be *c* the Way of Holiness.
36: 13 the commander stood and *c* out
41: 9 from its farthest corners I *c* you.
42: 6 have *c* you in righteousness;

Isa 43: 1 I have *c* you by name; you are mine
43: 7 everyone who is *c* by my name,
43: 22 "Yet you have not *c* upon me,
47: 1 No more will you be *c*
47: 5 no more will you be *c*
48: 1 you who are *c* by the name of Israel
48: 8 you were *c* a rebel from birth.
48: 12 Israel, whom I have *c*:
48: 15 yes, I have *c* him.
49: 1 Before I was born the LORD *c* me;
50: 2 When I *c*, why was there no one
51: 2 When I *c* him he was but one,
54: 5 he is *c* the God of all the earth.
56: 7 for my house will be *c*
58: 12 you will be *c* Repairer
61: 3 They will be *c* oaks
61: 6 you will be *c* priests of the LORD,
62: 2 you will be *c* by a new name
62: 4 But you will be *c* Hephzibah,
62: 12 They will be *c* The Holy People,
62: 12 and you will be *c* Sought After,
63: 19 they have not been *c* by your name.
65: 12 for I *c* but you did not answer,
66: 4 For when I *c*, no one answered,
Jer 3: 4 Have you not just *c* to me:
6: 30 They are *c* rejected silver,
7: 13 but you did not listen; I *c* you,
11: 16 LORD *c* you a thriving olive tree
23: 6 the name by which he will be *c*:
30: 17 'because you are *c* an outcast,
33: 16 the name by which it will be *c*:
35: 17 but they did not listen; I *c* to them,
36: 4 Jeremiah *c* Baruch son of Neriah,
42: 8 So he *c* together Johanan son
La 1: 19 "I *c* to my allies
2: 15 "Is this the city that was *c*
3: 55 I *c* on your name, O LORD,
3: 57 You came near when I *c* you,
Eze 9: 3 the LORD *c* to the man clothed
10: 13 the wheels being *c* "the whirling
20: 29 (It is *c* Bamah to this day.)
38: 8 After many days you will be *c*
39: 11 *c* the Valley of Hamon Gog.
39: 16 a town *c* Hamonah will be there.)
Da 2: 26 asked Daniel (also *c* Belteshazzar),
4: 8 (He is *c* Belteshazzar,
4: 14 He *c* in a loud voice: 'Cut
4: 19 (also *c* Belteshazzar) was greatly
5: 7 The king *c* out for the enchanters,
5: 12 whom the king *c* Belteshazzar,
6: 20 he *c* to Daniel in an anguished
10: 1 to Daniel (who was *c* Belteshazzar
Hos 1: 10 they will be *c* 'sons
2: 23 I will say to those *c* 'Not my people
2: 23 to the one I *c* 'Not my loved one.'
11: 1 and out of Egypt I *c* my son.
11: 2 But the more I *c* Israel,
Jnh 2: 2 the depths of the grave I *c* for help,
2: 2 "In my distress I *c* to the LORD,
Hab 3: 9 you *c* for many arrows.
Hag 1: 11 I *c* for a drought on the fields
Zec 6: 8 he *c* to me, "Look, those going
7: 13 so when they *c*, I would not listen,'
7: 13 " 'When I *c*, they did not listen;
8: 3 Almighty will be *c* The Holy
8: 3 Then Jerusalem will be *c* The City
11: 7 I took two staffs and *c* one Favor
11: 10 I took my staff *c* Favor and broke it
11: 14 I broke my second staff *c* Union,
Mal 1: 4 They will be *c* The Wicked Land,
2: 5 this *c* for reverence and he revered
Mt 1: 16 was born Jesus, who is *c* Christ.
2: 4 When he had *c* together all
2: 7 Then Herod *c* the Magi secretly
2: 15 "Out of Egypt I *c* my son."
2: 23 and lived in a town *c* Nazareth.
2: 23 "He will be *c* a Nazarene."
4: 18 Simon *c* Peter and his brother
4: 21 Jesus *c* them, and immediately
5: 9 for they will be *c* sons of God.
5: 19 others to do the same will be *c* least
5: 19 these commands will be *c* great
10: 1 He *c* his twelve disciples to him
10: 2 Simon (who is *c* Peter)
10: 25 of the house has been *c* Beelzebub,
15: 10 Jesus *c* the crowd to him and said,
15: 32 Jesus *c* his disciples to him and said
18: 2 He *c* a little child and had him

Mt 18: 32 "Then the master *c* the servant in.
20: 25 Jesus *c* them together and said,
20: 32 Jesus stopped and *c* them.
21: 13 " 'My house will be *c* a house
23: 8 "But you are not to be *c* 'Rabbi,'
23: 10 Nor are you to be *c* 'teacher,'
25: 14 who *c* his servants and entrusted
26: 14 the one *c* Judas Iscariot—
26: 36 disciples to a place *c* Gethsemane,
27: 8 That is why it has been *c* the Field
27: 16 a notorious prisoner, *c* Barabbas.
27: 17 Barabbas, or Jesus who is *c* Christ
27: 22 with Jesus who is *c* Christ?"
27: 33 came to a place *c* Golgotha (which
Mk 1: 20 Without delay he *c* them,
3: 13 and *c* to him those he wanted,
3: 23 So Jesus *c* them and spoke to them
7: 14 Again Jesus *c* the crowd to him
8: 1 Jesus *c* his disciples to him and said
8: 34 Then he *c* the crowd to him
9: 35 Jesus *c* the Twelve and said,
10: 42 Jesus *c* them together and said,
10: 49 So they *c* to the blind man,
11: 17 " 'My house will be *c*
14: 32 went to a place *c* Gethsemane,
15: 7 A man *c* Barabbas was in prison
15: 16 and *c* together the whole company
15: 22 to the place *c* Golgotha (which
Lk 1: 32 will be *c* the Son of the Most High.
1: 35 to be born will be *c* the Son of God.
1: 60 and said, "No! He is to be *c* John."
1: 76 will be *c* a prophet
2: 25 a man in Jerusalem *c* Simeon,
6: 13 he *c* his disciples to him
6: 15 Simon who was *c* the Zealot,
7: 11 Jesus went to a town *c* Nain,
8: 2 Mary (*c* Magdalene)
8: 8 When he said this, he *c* out,
9: 1 When Jesus had *c* the Twelve
9: 10 themselves to a town *c* Bethsaida,
9: 38 A man in the crowd *c* out,
10: 39 She had a sister *c* Mary, who sat
11: 27 a woman in the crowd *c* out,
13: 12 he *c* her forward and said to her,
15: 19 no longer worthy to be *c* your son;
15: 21 no longer worthy to be *c* your son.'
15: 26 So he *c* one of the servants
16: 2 So he *c* him in and asked him,
16: 5 "So he *c* in each one of his master's
16: 24 So he *c* to him, 'Father Abraham,
17: 13 stood at a distance and *c* out
18: 16 But Jesus *c* the children to him
18: 38 He *c* out, "Jesus, Son of David,
19: 13 So he *c* ten of his servants
19: 29 Bethany at the hill *c* the Mount
21: 37 on the hill *c* the Mount of Olives,
22: 1 *c* the Passover, was approaching,
22: 3 Satan entered Judas, *c* Iscariot,
22: 47 and the man who was *c* Judas,
23: 13 Pilate *c* together the chief priests,
23: 33 came to the place *c* The Skull,
23: 46 Jesus *c* out with a loud voice,
24: 13 going to a village *c* Emmaus,
Jn 1: 42 You will be *c* Cephas" (which,
1: 48 tree before Philip *c* you."
2: 9 Then he *c* the bridegroom aside
4: 5 to a town in Samaria *c* Sychar,
4: 25 know that Messiah" (*c* Christ) "is
5: 2 which in Aramaic is *c* Bethesda
10: 35 you are gods'? If he *c* them 'gods,'
11: 16 Then Thomas (*c* Didymus) said
11: 28 and *c* her sister Mary aside.
11: 43 Jesus *c* in a loud voice, "Lazarus,
11: 47 and the Pharisees *c* a meeting
11: 54 to a village *c* Ephraim, where he
12: 17 the word that he had *c* Lazarus
15: 15 Instead, I have *c* you friends,
19: 17 (which in Aramaic is *c* Golgotha).
20: 24 Now Thomas (*c* Didymus),
21: 2 Simon Peter, Thomas (*c* Didymus),
21: 5 He *c* out to them, "Friends,
Ac 1: 12 from the hill *c* the Mount of Olives,
1: 19 so they *c* that field
1: 23 Joseph *c* Barsabbas (also known
3: 2 to the temple gate *c* Beautiful,
3: 10 at the temple gate *c* Beautiful,
3: 11 the place *c* Solomon's Colonnade.
4: 9 If we are being *c* to account today

Ac 4: 18 Then they *c* them in again
4: 36 the apostles *c* Barnabas (which
5: 21 they *c* together the Sanhedrin—
5: 40 They *c* the apostles
6: 9 of the Freedmen (as it was *c*)—
9: 10 The Lord *c* to him in a vision,
9: 41 Then he *c* the believers
10: 5 a man named Simon who is *c* Peter.
10: 7 Cornelius *c* two of his servants
10: 18 They *c* out, asking
10: 24 and had *c* together his relatives
10: 32 to Joppa for Simon who is *c* Peter.
11: 13 to Joppa for Simon who is *c* Peter.
11: 26 disciples were first *c* Christians
12: 12 *c* Mark, where many people had
12: 25 taking with them John, also *c* Mark
13: 1 Barnabas, Simeon *c* Niger,
13: 2 for the work to which I have *c* them
13: 9 Then Saul, who was also *c* Paul,
14: 10 faith to be healed and *c* out,
14: 12 and Paul they *c* Hermes
14: 12 form!" Barnabas they *c* Zeus,
15: 22 They chose Judas (*c* Barsabbas)
15: 37 wanted to take John, also *c* Mark,
16: 10 concluding that God had *c* us
16: 29 We are all here!" The jailer *c*
17: 7 there is another king, one *c* Jesus."
19: 25 He *c* them together,
23: 6 *c* out in the Sanhedrin, "My
23: 17 Then Paul *c* one of the centurions
23: 23 Then he *c* two of his centurions
24: 2 Paul was *c* in, Tertullus presented
27: 8 and came to a place *c* Fair
27: 14 hurricane force, *c*
27: 16 to the lee of a small island *c* Cauda,
28: 1 out that the island was *c* Malta.
28: 17 days later he *c* together the leaders
Ro 1: 1 *c* to be an apostle and set apart
1: 6 among those who are *c* to belong
1: 7 loved by God and *c* to be saints:
7: 3 is still alive, she is *c* an adulteress.
8: 28 who have been *c* according
8: 30 And those he predestined, he also *c*
8: 30 those he *c*, he also justified;
9: 24 also *c*, not only from the Jews
9: 26 they will be *c* 'sons
1Co 1: 1 *c* to be an apostle of Christ Jesus
1: 2 in Christ Jesus and *c* to be holy,
1: 9 who has *c* you into fellowship
1: 24 but to those whom God has *c*,
1: 26 of what you were when you were *c*.
7: 15 God has *c* us to live in peace.
7: 17 and to which God has *c* him.
7: 18 circumcised when he was *c*?
7: 18 uncircumcised when he was *c*?
7: 20 was in when God *c* him.
7: 21 Were you a slave when you were *c*?
7: 22 slave when he was *c* by the Lord is
7: 22 when he was *c* is Christ's slave.
7: 24 in the situation God *c* him to.
15: 9 even deserve to be *c* an apostle,
Gal 1: 6 deserting the one who *c* you
1: 15 from birth and *c* me by his grace,
5: 13 You, my brothers, were *c* to be free
Eph 1: 18 the hope to which he has *c* you,
2: 11 and *c* "uncircumcised"
4: 4 as you were *c* to one hope
4: 4 to one hope when you were *c*
Php 3: 14 which God has *c* me heavenward
Col 3: 15 of one body you were *c* to peace.
4: 11 who is *c* Justus, also sends
2Th 2: 4 over everything that is *c* God
2: 14 He *c* you to this through our gospel
1Ti 6: 12 life to which you were *c*
6: 20 of what is falsely *c* knowledge,
2Ti 1: 9 who has saved us and *c* us
Heb 3: 13 daily, as long as it is *c* Today,
5: 4 he must be *c* by God, just
9: 2 bread; this was *c* the Holy Place.
9: 3 was a room *c* the Most Holy
9: 15 that those who are *c* may receive
11: 8 when *c* to go to a place he would
11: 16 is not ashamed to be *c* their God,
Jas 2: 23 and he was *c* God's friend.
1Pe 1: 15 But just as he who *c* you is holy,
2: 9 of him who *c* you out of darkness
2: 21 this you were *c*, because Christ
3: 6 obeyed Abraham and *c* him her

1Pe 3: 9 to this you were *c* so that you may
5: 10 who *c* you to his eternal glory
2Pe 1: 3 of him who *c* us by his own glory
1Jn 3: 1 that we should be *c* children
Jude : 1 To those who have been *c*,
Rev 6: 10 They *c* out in a loud voice,
6: 16 They *c* to the mountains
7: 2 He *c* out in a loud voice
11: 8 which is figuratively *c* Sodom
12: 9 that ancient serpent *c* the devil
14: 15 *c* in a loud voice to him who was
14: 18 *c* in a loud voice to him who had
16: 16 that in Hebrew is *c* Armageddon.
17: 14 and with him will be his *c*,
19: 11 whose rider is *c* Faithful and True.

CALLING (CALL)

Ex 33: 7 some distance away, *c* it the "tent
Nu 10: 2 them for *c* the community together
Jdg 6: 35 throughout Manasseh, *c* them
12: 1 fight the Ammonites without *c* us
1Sa 3: 8 that the LORD was *c* the boy.
3: 10 stood there, *c* as at the other times,
1Ki 16: 24 *c* it Samaria, after Shemer,
2Ki 9: 23 *c* out to Ahaziah, "Treachery,
14: 7 *c* it Joktheel, the name it has
2Ch 30: 5 *c* the people to come to Jerusalem
Est 5: 10 *C* together his friends and Zeresh,
Ps 69: 3 I am worn out *c* for help;
Pr 9: 15 *c* out to those who pass by,
Isa 6: 3 And they were *c* to one another:
40: 3 A voice of one *c*:
41: 2 *c* him in righteousness
41: 4 *c* forth the generations
Jer 25: 29 for I am *c* down a sword
Da 8: 16 a man's voice from the Ulai *c*,
Hos 7: 11 now *c* to Egypt,
Am 7: 4 The Sovereign LORD was *c*
Mic 6: 9 The LORD is *c* to the city—
Mt 3: 3 "A voice of one *c* in the desert,
9: 27 two blind men followed him, *c* out,
11: 16 in the marketplaces and *c* out
27: 47 they said, "He's *c* Elijah."
Mk 1: 3 "a voice of one *c* in the desert,
6: 7 *C* the Twelve to him, he sent them
10: 49 Cheer up! On your feet! He's *c* you
12: 43 *C* his disciples to him, Jesus said,
15: 35 they said, "Listen, he's *c* Elijah."
Lk 3: 4 "A voice of one *c* in the desert,
7: 18 *C* two of them, he sent them
7: 32 sitting in the marketplace and *c* out
Jn 1: 23 I am the voice of one *c* in the desert
5: 18 he was even *c* God his own Father,
Ac 22: 16 wash your sins away, *c* on his name
Eph 4: 1 worthy of the *c* you have received.
2Th 1: 11 may count you worthy of his *c*,
Heb 3: 1 who share in the heavenly *c*,
4: 7 again set a certain day, *c* it Today,
8: 13 By *c* this covenant "new,"
2Pe 1: 10 all the more eager to make your *c*

CALLOUS (CALLOUSED)

Ps 17: 10 They close up their *c* hearts,
73: 7 From their *c* hearts comes iniquity;
119: 70 Their hearts are *c* and unfeeling,

CALLOUSED (CALLOUS)

Isa 6: 10 Make the heart of this people *c*;
Mt 13: 15 this people's heart has become *c*;
Ac 28: 27 this people's heart has become *c*;

CALLS (CALL)

Ge 46: 33 When Pharaoh *c* you in and asks,
1Sa 3: 9 and if he *c* you, say, 'Speak, LORD
26: 14 "Who are you who *c* to the king?"
Ps 42: 7 Deep *c* to deep
147: 4 and *c* them each by name.
Pr 1: 20 Wisdom *c* aloud in the street,
9: 3 has sent out her maids, and she *c*
Isa 21: 11 Someone *c* to me from Seir,
40: 26 and *c* them each by name.
41: 25 from the rising sun who *c*
45: 3 God of Israel, who *c* you by name.
59: 4 No one *c* for justice;
64: 7 No one *c* on your name
Hos 7: 7 and none of them *c* on me.
Joel 2: 32 And everyone who *c*
2: 32 whom the LORD *c*.
Am 5: 8 who *c* for the waters of the sea
9: 6 who *c* for the waters of the sea
Zep 2: 14 *c* will echo through the windows,
Mt 22: 43 speaking by the Spirit, *c* him 'Lord
22: 45 If then David *c* him 'Lord,'
Mk 12: 37 David himself *c* him 'Lord.'
Lk 15: 6 Then he *c* his friends and neighbors
15: 9 she *c* her friends and neighbors
20: 37 for he *c* the Lord 'the God
20: 44 David *c* him 'Lord.'
Jn 10: 3 He *c* his own sheep by name
Ac 2: 21 And everyone who *c*
Ro 4: 17 and *c* things that are not as
9: 12 not by works but by him who *c*—
10: 13 "Everyone who *c* on the name
1Co 5: 11 with anyone who *c* himself
Gal 4: 6 the Spirit who *c* out, "*Abba*, Father
5: 8 come from the one who *c* you.
1Th 2: 12 who *c* you into his kingdom
5: 24 The one who *c* you is faithful
Rev 2: 20 who *c* herself a prophetess.
13: 10 This *c* for patient endurance
13: 18 This *c* for wisdom.
14: 12 This *c* for patient endurance
17: 9 "This *c* for a mind with wisdom.

CALM (CALMED CALMNESS CALMS)

Ps 107: 30 They were glad when it grew *c*,
Isa 7: 4 keep *c* and don't be afraid.
Eze 16: 42 I will be *c* and no longer angry.
Jnh 1: 11 to make the sea *c* down for us?"
1: 12 he replied, "and it will become *c*.
1: 15 and the raging sea grew *c*.
Mt 8: 26 the waves, and it was completely *c*.
Mk 4: 39 died down and it was completely *c*.
Lk 8: 24 the storm subsided, and all was *c*.

CALMED (CALM)

Ne 8: 11 The Levites *c* all the people, saying

CALMNESS (CALM)

Ecc 10: 4 *c* can lay great errors to rest.

CALMS (CALM)

Pr 15: 18 but a patient man *c* a quarrel.

CALNEH

Ge 10: 10 Erech, Akkad and *C*, in Shinar.
Am 6: 2 Go to *C* and look at it;

CALNO

Isa 10: 9 'Has not *C* fared like Carchemish?

CALVE (CALF)

Job 21: 10 their cows *c* and do not miscarry.

CALVED (CALF)

1Sa 6: 7 with two cows that have *c*

CALVES (CALF)

Dt 7: 13 the *c* of your herds and the lambs
28: 4 the *c* of your herds and the lambs
28: 18 and the *c* of your herds
28: 51 nor any *c* of your herds
1Sa 6: 7 take their *c* away and pen them up.
6: 10 to the cart and penned up their *c*.
14: 32 and, taking sheep, cattle and *c*,
15: 9 fat *c* and lambs—everything that
1Ki 1: 9 fattened *c* at the Stone of Zoheleth
1: 19 numbers of cattle, fattened *c*,
1: 25 numbers of cattle, fattened *c*,
12: 28 the king made two golden *c*.
12: 32 sacrificing to the *c* he had made.
2Ki 10: 29 worship of the golden *c* at Bethel
17: 16 two idols cast in the shape of *c*,
2Ch 13: 8 you the golden *c* that Jeroboam
Ps 68: 30 of bulls among the *c* of the nations.
Isa 27: 10 there the *c* graze,
34: 7 the bull *c* and the great bulls.
Jer 46: 21 are like fattened *c*.
Am 6: 4 and fattened *c*.
Mic 6: 6 with *c* a year old?
Mal 4: 2 leap like *c* released from the stall.
Heb 9: 12 means of the blood of goats and *c*;
9: 19 the blood of *c*, together with water,

CAMEL (CAMEL'S CAMELS CAMELS' SHE-CAMEL)

Ge 24: 64 She got down from her *c*
Lev 11: 4 The *c*, though it chews the cud,
Dt 14: 7 divided you may not eat the *c*,
Mt 19: 24 it is easier for a *c* to go
23: 24 strain out a gnat but swallow a *c*.
Mk 10: 25 It is easier for a *c* to go
Lk 18: 25 it is easier for a *c* to go

CAMEL-LOADS (LOAD)

2Ki 8: 9 a gift forty *c* of all the finest wares

CAMEL'S (CAMEL)

Ge 31: 34 and put them inside her *c* saddle
Mt 3: 4 John's clothes were made of *c* hair,
Mk 1: 6 John wore clothing made of *c* hair,

CAMELS (CAMEL)

Ge 12: 16 and maidservants, and *c*.
24: 10 servant took ten of his master's *c*
24: 11 He had the *c* kneel
24: 14 'Drink, and I'll water your *c* too'—
24: 19 "I'll draw water for your *c* too,
24: 20 and drew enough for all his *c*.
24: 22 When the *c* had finished drinking,
24: 30 standing by the *c* near the spring.
24: 31 the house and a place for the *c*."
24: 32 and fodder were brought for the *c*,
24: 32 house, and the *c* were unloaded.
24: 35 maidservants, and *c* and donkeys.
24: 44 and I'll draw water for your *c* too,"
24: 46 and she watered the *c* also.
24: 46 'Drink, and I'll water your *c* too.'
24: 61 and mounted their *c* and went back
24: 63 he looked up, he saw *c* approaching
30: 43 menservants, and *c* and donkeys.
31: 17 put his children and his wives on *c*,
32: 7 the flocks and herds and *c* as well.
32: 15 thirty female *c* with their young,
37: 25 Their *c* were loaded with spices,
Ex 9: 3 donkeys and *c* and on your cattle
Jdg 6: 5 to count the men and their *c*;
7: 12 Their *c* could no more be counted
1Sa 15: 3 cattle and sheep, *c* and donkeys.' "
27: 9 donkeys and *c*, and clothes.
30: 17 young men who rode off on *c*
1Ki 10: 2 with *c* carrying spices, large
1Ch 5: 21 of the Hagrites—fifty thousand *c*,
12: 40 came bringing food on donkeys, *c*,
27: 30 Ishmaelite was in charge of the *c*.
2Ch 9: 1 with *c* carrying spices, large
14: 15 off droves of sheep and goats and *c*.
Ezr 2: 67 mules, 435 *c* and 6,720
Ne 7: 69 mules, 435 *c* and 6,720
Job 1: 3 thousand sheep, three thousand *c*,
1: 17 and swept down on your *c*
42: 12 thousand sheep, six thousand *c*,
Isa 21: 7 or riders on *c*,
30: 6 their treasures on the humps of *c*,
60: 6 Herds of *c* will cover your land,
60: 6 young *c* of Midian and Ephah.
66: 20 on mules and *c*," says the LORD.
Jer 49: 29 off with all their goods and *c*.
49: 32 Their *c* will become plunder,
Eze 25: 5 Rabbah into a pasture for *c*
Zec 14: 15 *c* and donkeys, and all the animals

CAMELS' (CAMEL)

Jdg 8: 21 the ornaments off their *c'* necks.
8: 26 chains that were on their *c'* necks.

CAMP (CAMPED CAMPING CAMPS ENCAMP ENCAMPED ENCAMPS)

Ge 32: 2 he said, "This is the *c* of God!"
32: 21 he himself spent the night in the *c*.
Ex 16: 13 a layer of dew around the *c*.
16: 13 quail came and covered the *c*,
19: 16 Everyone in the *c* trembled.
19: 17 out of the *c* to meet with God,
29: 14 its hide and its offal outside the *c*.
32: 17 There is the sound of war in the *c*."
32: 19 When Moses approached the *c*
32: 26 So he stood at the entrance to the *c*
32: 27 forth through the *c* from one end
33: 7 outside the *c* some distance away,
33: 7 to the tent of meeting outside the *c*.
33: 11 Then Moses would return to the *c*,

Ex 36: 6 sent this word throughout the *c*:
Lev 4: 12 he must take outside the *c*
4: 21 he shall take the bull outside the *c*
6: 11 and carry the ashes outside the *c*
8: 17 its offal he burned up outside the *c*
9: 11 the hide he burned up outside the *c*
10: 4 carry your cousins outside the *c*,
10: 5 outside the *c*, as Moses ordered.
13: 46 he must live outside the *c*.
14: 3 The priest is to go outside the *c*
14: 8 After this he may come into the *c*,
16: 26 afterward he may come into the *c*.
16: 27 must be taken outside the *c*;
16: 28 afterward he may come into the *c*.
17: 3 a lamb or a goat in the *c*
24: 10 out in the *c* between him
24: 14 Take the blasphemer outside the *c*.
24: 23 took the blasphemer outside the *c*
Nu 1: 52 man in his own *c* under his own
2: 2 are to *c* around the Tent
2: 3 the divisions of the *c* of Judah are
2: 5 of Issachar will *c* next to them.
2: 9 All the men assigned to the *c*
2: 10 the divisions of the *c* of Reuben
2: 12 tribe of Simeon will *c* next to them.
2: 16 assigned to the *c* of Reuben,
2: 17 and the *c* of the Levites will set out
2: 18 the divisions of the *c* of Ephraim
2: 24 assigned to the *c* of Ephraim,
2: 25 north will be the divisions of the *c*
2: 27 tribe of Asher will *c* next to them.
2: 31 to the *c* of Dan number 157,600.
3: 23 The Gershonite clans were to *c*
3: 29 were to *c* on the south side
3: 35 they were to *c* on the north side
3: 38 and his sons were to *c* to the east
4: 5 When the *c* is to move, Aaron
4: 15 and when the *c* is ready to move,
5: 2 away from the *c* anyone who has
5: 3 the *c* so they will not defile their *c*,
5: 4 they sent them outside the *c*.
9: 18 the tabernacle, they remained in *c*.
9: 22 the Israelites would remain in *c*
10: 14 The divisions of the *c*
10: 18 The divisions of the *c*
10: 22 The divisions of the *c*
10: 25 the divisions of the *c* of Dan set out
10: 31 You know where we should *c*
10: 34 day when they set out from the *c*.
11: 1 some of the outskirts of the *c*.
11: 9 When the dew settled on the *c*
11: 26 and Medad, had remained in the *c*.
11: 26 and they prophesied in the *c*.
11: 27 Medad are prophesying in the *c*."
11: 30 elders of Israel returned to the *c*.
11: 31 them down all around the *c*
11: 32 spread them out all around the *c*.
12: 14 her outside the *c* for seven days;
12: 15 outside the *c* for seven days,
14: 44 covenant moved from the *c*.
15: 35 must stone him outside the *c*."
15: 36 assembly took him outside the *c*
19: 3 it is to be taken outside the *c*
19: 7 He may then come into the *c*,
19: 9 clean place outside the *c*.
31: 12 assembly at their *c* on the plains
31: 13 went to meet them outside the *c*.
31: 19 stay outside the *c* seven days.
31: 24 Then you may come into the *c*."
Dt 1: 7 Break *c* and advance
1: 33 to search out places for you to *c*
2: 14 men had perished from the *c*,
2: 15 eliminated them from the *c*.
23: 10 he is to go outside the *c*
23: 11 at sunset he may return to the *c*.
23: 12 outside the *c* where you can go
23: 14 Your *c* must be holy,
23: 14 about in your *c* to protect you
Jos 1: 11 through the *c* and tell the people,
3: 2 the officers went throughout the *c*,
3: 14 So when the people broke *c*
4: 8 them over with them to their *c*,
5: 8 were in *c* until they were healed.
6: 11 Then the people returned to *c*
6: 14 the city once and returned to the *c*.
6: 18 Otherwise you will make the *c*
6: 23 in a place outside the *c* of Israel.
8: 11 They set up *c* north of Ai,
Jos 8: 13 all those in the *c* to the north
9: 6 went to Joshua in the *c* at Gilgal
10: 6 word to Joshua in the *c* at Gilgal:
10: 15 with all Israel to the *c* at Gilgal.
10: 21 to Joshua in the *c* at Makkedah
10: 43 with all Israel to the *c* at Gilgal.
11: 5 and made *c* together at the Waters
18: 9 to Joshua in the *c* at Shiloh.
Jdg 7: 1 The *c* of Midian was north of them
7: 8 Now the *c* of Midian lay below him
7: 9 "Get up, go down against the *c*,
7: 10 to the *c* with your servant Purah
7: 11 went down to the outposts of the *c*.
7: 11 will be encouraged to attack the *c*."
7: 13 tumbling into the Midianite *c*.
7: 14 and the whole *c* into his hands."
7: 15 He returned to the *c* of Israel
7: 15 LORD has given the Midianite *c*
7: 17 When I get to the edge of the *c*,
7: 18 from all around the *c* blow yours
7: 19 the edge of the *c* at the beginning
7: 21 man held his position around the *c*,
7: 22 the men throughout the *c* to turn
18: 12 On their way they set up *c*
20: 19 and pitched *c* near Gibeah.
21: 8 come to the *c* for the assembly.
21: 12 them to the *c* at Shiloh in Canaan.
1Sa 4: 3 When the soldiers returned to *c*,
4: 5 LORD's covenant came into the *c*,
4: 6 of the LORD had come into the *c*,
4: 6 shouting in the Hebrew *c*?"
4: 7 "A god has come into the *c*,"
11: 11 broke into the *c* of the Ammonites
13: 17 out from the Philistine *c*
14: 15 the whole army—those in the *c*
14: 19 in the Philistine *c* increased more
14: 21 up with them to their *c* went
17: 1 They pitched *c* at Ephes Dammim,
17: 4 came out of the Philistine *c*.
17: 17 your brothers and hurry to their *c*.
17: 20 He reached the *c* as the army was
17: 53 Philistines, they plundered their *c*.
26: 3 Saul made his *c* beside the road
26: 5 Saul was lying inside the *c*,
26: 6 down into the *c* with me to Saul?"
26: 7 lying asleep inside the *c*
28: 4 all the Israelites and set up *c*
28: 4 and came and set up *c* at Shunem,
2Sa 1: 2 day a man arrived from Saul's *c*,
1: 3 "I have escaped from the Israelite *c*
1Ki 16: 16 Israel that very day there in the *c*.
16: 16 in the *c* heard that Zimri had
2Ki 3: 24 when the Moabites came to the *c*
6: 8 "I will set up my *c* in such
7: 4 go over to the *c* of the Arameans
7: 5 and went to the *c* of the Arameans.
7: 5 they reached the edge of the *c*,
7: 7 They left the *c* as it was
7: 8 leprosy reached the edge of the *c*
7: 10 "We went into the Aramean *c*
7: 12 so they have left the *c* to hide
7: 16 plundered the *c* of the Arameans.
19: 35 thousand men in the Assyrian *c*.
19: 36 king of Assyria broke *c*
1Ch 9: 18 belonging to the *c* of the Levites.
2Ch 22: 1 who came with the Arabs into the *c*
32: 21 in the *c* of the Assyrian king.
Ps 78: 28 down inside their *c*,
106: 16 In the *c* they grew envious
Isa 10: 29 "We will *c* overnight at Geba."
21: 13 who *c* in the thickets of Arabia,
37: 36 thousand men in the Assyrian *c*.
37: 37 king of Assyria broke *c*
Mic 4: 10 the city to *c* in the open field.
Heb 13: 11 the bodies are burned outside the *c*.
13: 13 outside the *c*, bearing the disgrace
Rev 20: 9 surrounded the *c* of God's people,

CAMPAIGN (CAMPAIGNS)

Jos 10: 42 lands Joshua conquered in one *c*,
Eze 29: 18 army in a hard *c* against Tyre;
29: 18 from the *c* he led against Tyre.

CAMPAIGNS (CAMPAIGN)

1Sa 18: 13 and David led the troops in their *c*.
18: 16 because he led them in their *c*.
2Sa 5: 2 Israel on their military *c*.
1Ch 11: 2 Israel on their military *c*.

CAMPED (CAMP)

Ge 31: 25 Laban and his relatives *c* there too.
33: 18 and *c* within sight of the city.
Ex 13: 20 After leaving Succoth they *c*
14: 9 they *c* by the sea near Pi Hahiroth,
15: 27 and they *c* there near the water.
17: 1 They *c* at Rephidim, but there was
18: 5 where he was *c* near the mountain
19: 2 Israel *c* there in the desert in front
Nu 21: 10 moved on and *c* at Oboth.
21: 11 from Oboth and *c* in Iye Abarim,
21: 12 on and *c* in the Zered Valley.
21: 13 and *c* alongside the Arnon,
22: 1 and *c* along the Jordan
33: 5 The Israelites left Rameses and *c*
33: 6 They left Succoth and *c* at Etham,
33: 7 Baal Zephon, and *c* near Migdol.
33: 8 Desert of Etham, they *c* at Marah.
33: 9 palm trees, and they *c* there.
33: 10 They left Elim and *c* by the Red
33: 11 They left the Red Sea and *c*
33: 12 Desert of Sin and *c* at Dophkah.
33: 13 They left Dophkah and *c* at Alush.
33: 14 They left Alush and *c* at Rephidim,
33: 15 and *c* in the Desert of Sinai.
33: 16 the Desert of Sinai and *c* at Kibroth
33: 17 They left Kibroth Hattaavah and *c*
33: 18 They left Hazeroth and *c*
33: 19 They left Rithmah and *c*
33: 20 Rimmon Perez and *c* at Libnah.
33: 21 They left Libnah and *c* at Rissah.
33: 22 They left Rissah and *c*
33: 23 They left Kehelathah and *c*
33: 24 They left Mount Shepher and *c*
33: 25 They left Haradah and *c*
33: 26 They left Makheloth and *c*
33: 27 They left Tahath and *c* at Terah.
33: 28 They left Terah and *c* at Mithcah.
33: 29 They left Mithcah and *c*
33: 30 They left Hashmonah and *c*
33: 31 Moseroth and *c* at Bene Jaakan.
33: 32 They left Bene Jaakan and *c*
33: 33 They left Hor Haggidgad and *c*
33: 34 They left Jotbathah and *c*
33: 35 They left Abronah and *c*
33: 36 left Ezion Geber and *c* at Kadesh,
33: 37 They left Kadesh and *c*
33: 41 They left Mount Hor and *c*
33: 42 They left Zalmonah and *c* at Punon
33: 43 They left Punon and *c* at Oboth.
33: 44 left Oboth and *c* at Iye Abarim,
33: 45 left Iyim and *c* at Dibon Gad.
33: 46 They left Dibon Gad and *c*
33: 47 and *c* in the mountains of Abarim,
33: 48 and *c* on the plains of Moab
33: 49 of Moab they *c* along the Jordan
Jos 3: 1 where they *c* before crossing over.
4: 19 *c* at Gilgal on the eastern border
5: 10 while *c* at Gilgal on the plains
Jdg 6: 4 They *c* on the land and ruined
6: 33 and *c* in the Valley of Jezreel.
7: 1 all his men *c* at the spring of Harod.
10: 17 called to arms and *c* in Gilead,
10: 17 the Israelites assembled and *c*
11: 18 *c* on the other side of the Arnon.
15: 9 The Philistines went up and *c*
1Sa 4: 1 The Israelites *c* at Ebenezer,
13: 5 They went up and *c* at Micmash,
13: 16 while the Philistines *c* at Micmash.
17: 2 and *c* in the Valley of Elah
26: 5 went to the place where Saul had *c*.
29: 1 and Israel *c* by the spring in Jezreel
2Sa 11: 11 and my lord's men are *c*
17: 26 Absalom *c* in the land of Gilead.
24: 5 After crossing the Jordan, they *c*
1Ki 20: 27 Israelites *c* opposite them like two
20: 29 For seven days they *c*
1Ch 19: 7 who came and *c* near Medeba,
Ezr 8: 15 and we *c* there three days.
Jer 52: 4 They *c* outside the city

CAMPFIRES (FIRE)

Jdg 5: 16 Why did you stay among the *c*
Ps 68: 13 Even while you sleep among the *c*,

CAMPING (CAMP)

Nu 10: 5 the tribes *c* on the east are

CAMPS (CAMP)

Ge 25: 16 to their settlements and c.
Nu 2: 17 out in the middle of the c.
2: 32 All those in the c, by their divisions
10: 2 and for having the c set out.
10: 6 the c on the south are to set out.
31: 10 had settled, as well as all their c.
Dt 29: 11 in your c who chop your wood
2Ch 14: 15 also attacked the c of the herdsmen
Ps 68: 12 in the c men divide the plunder.
Eze 4: 2 set up c against it and put battering
25: 4 They will set up their c
Am 4: 10 nostrils with the stench of your c,
Zec 14: 15 and all the animals in those c.

CANA

Jn 2: 1 third day a wedding took place at C
2: 11 Jesus performed in C of Galilee.
4: 46 Once more he visited C in Galilee,
21: 2 Nathanael from C in Galilee,

CANAAN (CANAANITE CANAANITES)

Ge 9: 18 (Ham was the father of C.)
9: 22 of C, saw his father's nakedness
9: 25 "Cursed be C!
9: 26 May C be the slave of Shem.
9: 27 and may C be his slave."
10: 6 Cush, Mizraim, Put and C.
10: 15 C was the father of Sidon his
10: 19 and the borders of C reached
11: 31 Ur of the Chaldeans to go to C.
12: 5 and they set out for the land of C,
13: 12 Abram lived in the land of C,
16: 3 had been living in C ten years,
17: 8 of C, where you are now an alien,
23: 2 (that is, Hebron) in the land of C,
23: 19 is at Hebron) in the land of C.
31: 18 to his father Isaac in the land of C.
33: 18 at the city of Shechem in C and
35: 6 (that is, Bethel) in the land of C.
36: 2 wives from the women of C:
36: 5 who were born to him in C.
36: 6 all the goods he had acquired in C,
37: 1 his father had stayed, the land of C.
42: 5 for the famine was in the land of C
42: 7 "From the land of C," they replied,
42: 13 who lives in the land of C.
42: 29 their father Jacob in the land of C,
42: 32 now with our father in C.'
44: 8 the land of C the silver we found
45: 17 and return to the land of C,
45: 25 their father Jacob in the land of C.
46: 6 possessions they had acquired in C,
46: 12 Onan had died in the land of C).
46: 31 who were living in the land of C,
47: 1 have come from the land of C
47: 4 because the famine is severe in C
47: 13 both Egypt and C wasted away
47: 14 C in payment for the grain they
47: 15 people of Egypt and C was gone,
48: 3 to me at Luz in the land of C,
48: 7 in the land of C while we were still
49: 30 of Machpelah, near Mamre in C,
50: 5 dug for myself in the land of C."
50: 13 They carried him to the land of C
Ex 6: 4 them to give them the land of C,
15: 15 the people of C will melt away;
16: 35 until they reached the border of C.
Lev 14: 34 "When you enter the land of C,
18: 3 as they do in the land of C,
25: 38 of Egypt to give you the land of C
Nu 13: 2 men to explore the land of C,
13: 17 Moses sent them to explore C,
26: 19 sons of Judah, but they died in C.
32: 30 their possession with you in C."
32: 32 before the LORD into C armed,
33: 40 who lived in the Negev of C,
33: 51 'When you cross the Jordan into C,
34: 2 say to them: 'When you enter C,
34: 29 to the Israelites in the land of C.
35: 10 'When you cross the Jordan into C,
35: 14 and three in C as cities of refuge.
Dt 32: 49 across from Jericho, and view C,
Jos 5: 12 ate of the produce of C.
14: 1 as an inheritance in the land of C,
21: 2 families of Israel at Shiloh in C
22: 9 at Shiloh in C to return to Gilead,
Jos 22: 10 near the Jordan in the land of C,
22: 11 altar on the border of C at Geliloth
22: 32 returned to C from their meeting
24: 3 throughout C and gave him many
Jdg 3: 1 of the wars in C (he did this only
4: 2 a king of C, who reigned in Hazor.
5: 19 the kings of C fought
21: 12 them to the camp at Shiloh in C.
1Ch 1: 8 Cush, Mizraim, Put and C.
1: 13 C was the father of Sidon his
16: 18 "To you I will give the land of C
Ps 105: 11 "To you I will give the land of C
106: 38 they sacrificed to the idols of C,
135: 11 and all the kings of C—
Isa 19: 18 Egypt will speak the language of C
Ob : 20 of Israelite exiles who are in C
Zep 2: 5 O C, land of the Philistines.
Ac 7: 11 a famine struck all Egypt and C,
13: 19 He overthrew seven nations in C

CANAANITE (CANAAN)

Ge 10: 18 Later the C clans scattered
28: 1 "Do not marry a C woman.
28: 6 "Do not marry a C woman,"
28: 8 how displeasing the C women were
38: 2 daughter of a C man named Shua.
46: 10 and Shaul the son of a C woman.
Ex 6: 15 and Shaul the son of a C woman.
Nu 21: 1 When the C king of Arad,
33: 40 The C king of Arad, who lived
Jos 5: 1 all the C kings along the seacoast
13: 3 as C (the territory of the five
Jdg 1: 32 lived among the C inhabitants
1: 33 lived among the C inhabitants
4: 23 the C king, before the Israelites.
4: 24 C king, until they destroyed him.
1Ki 9: 16 He killed its C inhabitants
1Ch 2: 3 to him by Bathshua, a C woman.
Zec 14: 21 that day there will no longer be a C
Mt 15: 22 C woman from that vicinity came

CANAANITES (CANAAN)

Ge 12: 6 The C were then in the land.
13: 7 The C and Perizzites were
15: 21 Perizzites, Rephaites, Amorites, C,
24: 3 son from the daughters of the C,
24: 37 son from the daughters of the C,
34: 30 me by making me a stench to the C
50: 11 When the C who lived there saw
Ex 3: 8 the home of the C, Hittites,
3: 17 in Egypt into the land of the C,
13: 5 you into the land of the C,
13: 11 you into the land of the C
23: 23 Perizzites, C, Hivites and Jebusites
23: 28 C and Hittites out of your way.
33: 2 before you and drive out the C,
34: 11 C, Hittites, Perizzites, Hivites
Nu 13: 29 and the C live near the sea
14: 25 and C are living in the valleys,
14: 43 the Amalekites and C will face you
14: 45 and C who lived in that hill country
21: 3 and gave the C over to them.
Dt 1: 7 to the land of the C and to Lebanon
7: 1 Girgashites, Amorites, C,
11: 30 of those C living in the Arabah
20: 17 Hittites, Amorites, C, Perizzites,
Jos 3: 10 drive out before you the C,
7: 9 The C and the other people
9: 1 C, Perizzites, Hivites and Jebusites
11: 3 the C in the east and west; to
12: 8 C, Perizzites, Hivites and Jebusites
13: 4 from the south, all the land of the C
16: 10 They did not dislodge the C living
16: 10 to this day the C live
17: 12 for the C were determined to live
17: 13 they subjected the C
17: 16 all the C who live in the plain have
17: 18 though the C have iron chariots
24: 11 Perizzites, C, Hittites, Girgashites,
Jdg 1: 1 and fight for us against the C?"
1: 3 to us, to fight against the C.
1: 4 the LORD gave the C
1: 5 putting to rout the C and Perizzites
1: 9 down to fight against the C living
1: 10 They advanced against the C living
1: 17 attacked the C living in Zephath,
1: 27 for the C were determined to live
1: 28 they pressed the C
Jdg 1: 29 but the C continued to live there
1: 29 did Ephraim drive out the C living
1: 30 did Zebulun drive out the C living
3: 3 rulers of the Philistines, all the C,
3: 5 The Israelites lived among the C,
2Sa 24: 7 all the towns of the Hivites and C.
Ezr 9: 1 like those of the C, Hittites,
Ne 9: 8 to his descendants the land of the C
9: 24 You subdued before them the C,
9: 24 you handed the C over to them,
Eze 16: 3 and birth were in the land of the C;

CANAL (CANALS)

Ezr 8: 15 at the c that flows toward Ahava,
8: 21 by the Ahava C, I proclaimed a fast
8: 31 out from the Ahava C to go
Da 8: 2 in the vision I was beside the Ulai C
8: 3 beside the c, and the horns were
8: 6 I had seen standing beside the c

CANALS (CANAL)

Ex 7: 19 over the streams and c,
8: 5 staff over the streams and c
Isa 19: 6 The c will stink;

CANCEL (CANCELED CANCELING)

Dt 15: 1 seven years you must c debts.
15: 2 Every creditor shall c the loan he
15: 3 you must c any debt your brother
Ne 10: 31 the land and will c all debts.

CANCELED (CANCEL)

Mt 18: 27 pity on him, c the debt
18: 32 'I c all that debt of yours
Lk 7: 42 so he c the debts of both.
7: 43 the one who had the bigger debt c."
Col 2: 14 having c the written code,

CANCELING (CANCEL)

Dt 15: 2 for c debts has been proclaimed.
15: 9 the year for c debts, is near,"
31: 10 in the year for c debts,

CANDACE

Ac 8: 27 in charge of all the treasury of C,

CANE

Ex 30: 23 shekels of fragrant c, 500 shekels
Zec 8: 4 each with c in hand

CANNEH

Eze 27: 23 C and Eden and merchants

CANOPY

2Sa 22: 12 He made darkness his c
2Ki 16: 18 away the Sabbath c that had been
Ps 18: 11 made darkness his covering, his c
Isa 4: 5 over all the glory will be a c.
40: 22 stretches out the heavens like a c,
Jer 43: 10 he will spread his royal c

CAPABLE

Ex 18: 21 select c men from all the people—
18: 25 He chose c men from all Israel
1Ch 26: 6 because they were very c men.
26: 8 and their relatives were c men
26: 31 c men among the Hebronites were
Ezr 8: 18 they brought us Sherebiah, a c man

CAPERNAUM

Mt 4: 13 Nazareth, he went and lived in C,
8: 5 When Jesus had entered C,
11: 23 C, will you be lifted up to the skies?
17: 24 and his disciples arrived in C,
Mk 1: 21 to C, and when the Sabbath came,
2: 1 when Jesus again entered C,
9: 33 They came to C.
Lk 4: 23 we have heard that you did in C.' "
4: 31 Then he went down to C, a town
7: 1 of the people, he entered C.
10: 15 C, will you be lifted up to the skies?
Jn 2: 12 went down to C with his mother
4: 46 official whose son lay sick at C.
6: 17 and set off across the lake for C.
6: 24 and went to C in search of Jesus.
6: 59 teaching in the synagogue in C.

CAPES

Isa 3: 22 the fine robes and the *c* and cloaks,

CAPHTOR (CAPHTORITES)

Dt 2: 23 out from *C* destroyed them
Jer 47: 4 the remnant from the coasts of *C*.
Am 9: 7 the Philistines from *C*

CAPHTORITES (CAPHTOR)

Ge 10: 14 whom the Philistines came) and *C*.
Dt 2: 23 the *C* coming out from Caphtor
1Ch 1: 12 whom the Philistines came) and *C*.

CAPITAL (CAPITALS)

Dt 21: 22 guilty of a *c* offense is put to death
1Ki 7: 16 each *c* was five cubits high.
7: 17 top of the pillars, seven for each *c*.
7: 18 He did the same for each *c*.
2Ki 25: 17 The bronze *c* on top
2Ch 3: 15 each with a *c* on top measuring five
Jer 52: 22 The bronze *c* on top

CAPITALS (CAPITAL)

1Ki 7: 16 made two *c* of cast bronze to set
7: 17 interwoven chains festooned the *c*
7: 18 network to decorate the *c* on top
7: 19 The *c* on top of the pillars
7: 20 On the *c* of both pillars,
7: 22 The *c* on top were in the shape
7: 41 decorating the two bowl-shaped *c*
7: 41 the two bowl-shaped *c* on top
7: 42 decorating the bowl-shaped *c*
2Ch 4: 12 decorating the two bowl-shaped *c*
4: 12 the two bowl-shaped *c* on top
4: 13 decorating the bowl-shaped *c*

CAPPADOCIA

Ac 2: 9 Judea and *C*, Pontus and Asia,
1Pe 1: 1 Galatia, *C*, Asia and Bithynia,

CAPSTONE (STONE)

Ps 118: 22 has become the *c*;
Zec 4: 7 he will bring out the *c* to shouts
Mt 21: 42 has become the *c*;
Mk 12: 10 has become the *c*;
Lk 20: 17 has become the *c*'?
Ac 4: 11 which has become the *c*.'
1Pe 2: 7 has become the *c*,"

CAPTAIN (CAPTAINS)

Ge 37: 36 one of Pharaoh's officials, the *c*
39: 1 one of Pharaoh's officials, the *c*
40: 3 in the house of the *c* of the guard,
40: 4 The *c* of the guard assigned them
41: 10 in the house of the *c* of the guard.
41: 12 a servant of the *c* of the guard.
1Sa 22: 14 *c* of your bodyguard and highly
2Ki 1: 9 sent to Elijah a *c* with his company
1: 9 *c* went up to Elijah, who was sitting
1: 10 and consumed the *c* and his men.
1: 10 down!' " Elijah answered the *c*,
1: 11 The *c* said to him, "Man of God,
1: 11 sent to Elijah another *c*
1: 13 So the king sent a third *c*
1: 13 This third *c* went up and fell
Isa 3: 3 the *c* of fifty and man of rank,
Jer 37: 13 reached the Benjamin Gate, the *c*
Jnh 1: 6 The *c* went to him and said,
Ac 4: 1 and the *c* of the temple guard
5: 24 the *c* of the temple guard
5: 26 the *c* went with his officers
Rev 18: 17 "Every sea *c*, and all who travel

CAPTAINS (CAPTAIN)

Jdg 5: 14 From Makir *c* came down,
1Ki 9: 22 officials, his officers, his *c*,
2Ki 1: 14 and consumed the first two *c*
2Ch 8: 9 of his *c*, and commanders

CAPTIVATE (CAPTURE)

Pr 6: 25 or let her *c* you with her eyes,

CAPTIVATED (CAPTURE)

Pr 5: 19 may you ever be *c* by her love.
5: 20 Why be *c*, my son, by an adulteress

CAPTIVE (CAPTURE)

Ge 14: 14 that his relative had been taken *c*,
Nu 24: 22 when Asshur takes you *c*."
Dt 1: 39 that you said would be taken *c*,
Jdg 5: 12 Take *c* your captives, O son
1Sa 30: 2 and had taken *c* the women
30: 3 and sons and daughters taken *c*
1Ki 8: 46 who takes them *c* to his own land,
8: 47 in the land where they are held *c*,
8: 48 of their enemies who took them *c*,
20: 39 and someone came to me with a *c*
2Ki 5: 2 had taken *c* a young girl from Israel
17: 27 one of the priests you took *c*
24: 15 Nebuchadnezzar took Jehoiachin *c*
1Ch 3: 17 descendants of Jehoiachin the *c*:
5: 21 one hundred thousand people *c*,
9: 1 of Judah were taken *c* to Babylon
2Ch 6: 36 who takes them *c* to a land far away
6: 37 in the land where they are held *c*,
28: 8 The Israelites took *c*
Ezr 2: 1 king of Babylon had taken *c*
Ne 7: 6 had taken *c* (they returned
Est 2: 6 among those taken *c*
Ps 69: 33 and does not despise his *c* people.
106: 46 by all who held them *c*.
SS 7: 5 the king is held *c* by its tresses.
Isa 52: 2 O *c* Daughter of Zion.
Jer 13: 17 the LORD's flock will be taken *c*.
22: 12 place where they have led him *c*;
41: 10 son of Nethaniah took them *c*
41: 14 All the people Ishmael had taken *c*
43: 12 their temples and take their gods *c*.
48: 7 you too will be taken *c*,
La 1: 5 *c* before the foe.
Eze 6: 9 where they have been carried *c*,
21: 23 them of their guilt and take them *c*.
21: 24 have done this, you will be taken *c*.
Am 1: 6 she took *c* whole communities
Na 3: 10 Yet she was taken *c*
Hab 2: 5 and takes *c* all the peoples.
Ac 8: 23 full of bitterness and *c* to sin."
2Co 10: 5 and we take *c* every thought
Col 2: 8 See to it that no one takes you *c*
2Ti 2: 26 who has taken them *c* to do his will.

CAPTIVES (CAPTURE)

Ge 31: 26 off my daughters like *c* in war.
Nu 21: 29 and his daughters as *c*
31: 12 and animals, and brought the *c*,
31: 19 must purify yourselves and your *c*.
Dt 21: 10 into your hands and you take *c*,
21: 11 among the *c* a beautiful woman
32: 42 the blood of the slain and the *c*,
Jdg 5: 12 Take captive your *c*, O son
Job 3: 18 *C* also enjoy their ease;
Ps 68: 18 you led *c* in your train;
126: 1 the LORD brought back the *c*
Isa 10: 4 but to cringe among the *c*
14: 2 They will make *c* of their captors
14: 17 and would not let his *c* go home?"
20: 4 and barefoot the Egyptian *c*
42: 7 to free *c* from prison
49: 9 to say to the *c*, 'Come out,'
49: 24 or *c* rescued from the fierce?
49: 25 "Yes, *c* will be taken from warriors,
61: 1 to proclaim freedom for the *c*
Jer 40: 1 among all the *c* from Jerusalem
41: 10 Ishmael made *c* of all the rest
Eze 12: 11 They will go into exile as *c*.
Am 1: 9 she sold whole communities of *c*
Eph 4: 8 he led *c* in his train

CAPTIVITY (CAPTURE)

Dt 28: 41 because they will go into *c*.
Jdg 18: 30 until the time of the *c* of the land.
2Ki 25: 21 So Judah went into *c*, away
2Ch 6: 37 plead with you in the land of their *c*
6: 38 of their *c* where they were taken,
29: 9 daughters and our wives are in *c*.
Ezr 2: 1 up from the *c* of the exiles,
3: 8 from the *c* to Jerusalem) began
8: 35 from *c* sacrificed burnt offerings
9: 7 subjected to the sword and *c*,
Ne 4: 4 them over as plunder in a land of *c*.
7: 6 up from the *c* of the exiles whom
Ps 78: 61 He sent ⌞the ark of⌟ his might into *c*,
144: 14 no going into *c*,
Isa 46: 2 they themselves go off into *c*.
Jer 15: 2 those for *c*, to *c*.'
29: 14 "and will bring you back from *c*.
Jer 30: 3 Israel and Judah back from *c*
31: 23 "When I bring them back from *c*,
33: 7 back from *c* and will rebuild them
43: 11 *c* to those destined for *c*,
48: 46 and your daughters into *c*.
52: 27 So Judah went into *c*, away
La 2: 14 sin to ward off your *c*.
Eze 29: 14 I will bring them back from *c*
30: 17 the cities themselves will go into *c*.
30: 18 and her villages will go into *c*.
39: 25 I will now bring Jacob back from *c*
Rev 13: 10 If anyone is to go into *c*,
13: 10 into *c* he will go.

CAPTORS (CAPTURE)

2Ch 30: 9 be shown compassion by their *c*
Ps 137: 3 for there our *c* asked us for songs,
Isa 14: 2 They will make captives of their *c*
Jer 50: 33 All their *c* hold them fast,

CAPTURE (CAPTIVATE CAPTIVATED CAPTIVE CAPTIVES CAPTIVITY CAPTORS CAPTURED CAPTURES CAPTURING RECAPTURE RECAPTURED)

Dt 20: 19 it to *c* it, do not destroy its trees
1Sa 4: 21 because of the *c* of the ark of God
19: 14 When Saul sent the men to *c* David
19: 20 at Ramah"; so he sent men to *c* him
23: 26 in on David and his men to *c* them,
2Sa 12: 28 and besiege the city and *c* it.
2Ki 6: 13 "so I can send men and *c* him."
2Ch 32: 18 afraid in order to *c* the city.
Job 40: 24 Can anyone *c* him by the eyes,
Jer 18: 22 for they have dug a pit to *c* me
32: 3 king of Babylon, and he will *c* it.
32: 28 king of Babylon, who will *c* it.
37: 8 they will *c* it and burn it down.'
38: 3 of the king of Babylon, who will *c* it
50: 46 of Babylon's *c* the earth will
Da 11: 15 ramps and will *c* a fortified city.
Hab 1: 10 build earthen ramps and *c* them.
Mt 26: 55 out with swords and clubs to *c* me?
Mk 14: 48 out with swords and clubs to *c* me?

CAPTURED (CAPTURE)

Nu 21: 1 attacked the Israelites and *c* some
21: 25 Israel *c* all the cities
21: 32 the Israelites *c* its surrounding
31: 9 Israelites *c* the Midianite women
31: 26 the people and animals that were *c*.
32: 39 *c* it and drove out the Amorites
32: 41 *c* their settlements and called them
32: 42 And Nobah *c* Kenath and its
Dt 2: 35 from the towns we had *c* we carried
21: 13 clothes she was wearing when *c*.
Jos 8: 19 They entered the city and *c* it
10: 35 They *c* it that same day
11: 10 Joshua turned back and *c* Hazor
11: 17 He *c* all their kings and struck them
Jdg 7: 25 also *c* two of the Midianite leaders,
8: 12 but he pursued them and *c* them,
9: 45 against the city until he had *c* it
9: 50 to Thebez and besieged it and *c* it.
12: 5 The Gileadites *c* the fords
1Sa 4: 11 The ark of God was *c*,
4: 17 and the ark of God has been *c*."
4: 19 the ark of God had been *c*
4: 22 for the ark of God has been *c*."
5: 1 After the Philistines had *c* the ark
7: 14 to Gath that the Philistines had *c*
30: 5 David's two wives had been *c*—
2Sa 5: 7 David *c* the fortress of Zion,
8: 4 David *c* a thousand of his chariots,
12: 26 the Ammonites and *c* the royal
12: 29 to Rabbah, and attacked and *c* it.
1Ki 9: 16 of Egypt had attacked and *c* Gezer.
2Ki 6: 22 "Would you kill men you have *c*
12: 17 and attacked Gath and *c* it.
14: 7 Valley of Salt and *c* Sela in battle,
14: 13 king of Israel *c* Amaziah king
17: 6 the king of Assyria *c* Samaria
18: 10 Samaria was *c* in Hezekiah's sixth
18: 13 cities of Judah and *c* them.
25: 6 and scattered, and he was *c*.
1Ch 2: 23 (But Geshur and Aram *c* Havvoth
11: 5 David *c* the fortress of Zion,
18: 4 David *c* a thousand of his chariots,

2Ch 8: 3 went to Hamath Zobah and *c* it.
12: 4 he *c* the fortified cities of Judah
15: 8 from the towns he had *c* in the hills
17: 2 Ephraim that his father Asa had *c*.
22: 9 his men *c* him while he was hiding
25: 12 also *c* ten thousand men alive,
25: 23 king of Israel *c* Amaziah king
28: 18 *c* and occupied Beth Shemesh,
Ne 9: 25 They *c* fortified cities and fertile
Isa 8: 15 they will be snared and *c*."
13: 15 Whoever is *c* will be thrust through
20: 1 to Ashdod and attacked and *c* it—
22: 3 they have been *c* without using
28: 13 be injured and snared and *c*.
36: 1 cities of Judah and *c* them.
Jer 10: 18 them so that they may be *c*."
34: 3 but will surely be *c* and handed
38: 23 will be *c* by the king of Babylon;
38: 28 until the day Jerusalem was *c*.
39: 5 They *c* him and took him
48: 1 Kiriathaim will be disgraced and *c*;
48: 41 The cities will be *c*
50: 2 'Babylon will be *c*;
50: 9 and from the north she will be *c*.
50: 24 you were found and *c*
51: 31 that his entire city is *c*,
51: 41 "How Sheshach will be *c*,
51: 56 her warriors will be *c*,
52: 9 and scattered, and he was *c*.
Da 11: 33 or be burned or *c* or plundered.
Am 4: 10 along with your *c* horses.
Zec 14: 2 the city will be *c*, the houses
Rev 19: 20 beast was *c*, and with him the false

CAPTURES (CAPTURE)

Jos 15: 16 who attacks and *c* Kiriath Sepher."
Jdg 1: 12 attacks and *c* Kiriath Sepher."

CAPTURING (CAPTURE)

Jdg 11: 22 *c* all of it from the Arnon
2Ki 16: 9 by attacking Damascus and *c* it.

CARAVAN (CARAVANS)

Ge 37: 25 and saw a *c* of Ishmaelites coming
1Ki 10: 2 at Jerusalem with a very great *c*—
2Ch 9: 1 Arriving with a very great *c*—

CARAVANS (CARAVAN)

Job 6: 18 *C* turn aside from their routes;
6: 19 The *c* of Tema look for water,
Isa 21: 13 You *c* of Dedanites,

CARAWAY

Isa 28: 25 he not sow *c* and scatter cummin?
28: 27 *C* is not threshed with a sledge,
28: 27 *c* is beaten out with a rod,

CARCAS

Est 1: 10 Bigtha, Abagtha, Zethar and *C*—

CARCASS (CARCASSES)

Lev 11: 26 whoever touches ⌞the *c* of⌟ any
11: 37 If a *c* falls on any seeds that are
11: 38 put on the seed and a *c* falls on it,
11: 39 who touches the *c* will be unclean
11: 40 of the *c* must wash his clothes,
11: 40 who picks up the *c* must wash his
Jdg 14: 8 turned aside to look at the lion's *c*.
14: 9 taken the honey from the lion's *c*.
Mt 24: 28 there is a *c*, there the vultures

CARCASSES (CARCASS)

Ge 15: 11 birds of prey came down on the *c*,
Lev 5: 2 the *c* of unclean wild animals
11: 8 not eat their meat or touch their *c*;
11: 11 and you must detest their *c*.
11: 24 whoever touches their *c* will be
11: 25 of their *c* must wash his clothes,
11: 27 whoever touches their *c* will be
11: 28 who picks up their *c* must wash his
11: 35 of their *c* falls on becomes unclean;
11: 36 one of these *c* is unclean.
Dt 14: 8 to eat their meat or touch their *c*.
28: 26 Your *c* will be food for all the birds
1Sa 17: 46 Today I will give the *c*
Jer 7: 33 *c* of this people will become food
19: 7 and I will give their *c* as food

CARCHEMISH

2Ch 35: 20 up to fight at *C* on the Euphrates,
Isa 10: 9 'Has not Calno fared like *C*?
Jer 46: 2 was defeated at *C* on

CARE (CARED CAREFUL CARES CARING)

Ge 2: 15 of Eden to work it and take *c* of it.
30: 29 livestock has fared under my *c*.
30: 35 he placed them in the *c* of his sons.
32: 16 He put them in the *c* of his servants
33: 13 and that I must *c* for the ewes
39: 4 to his *c* everything he owned.
39: 6 in Joseph's *c* everything he had;
39: 8 he owns he has entrusted to my *c*.
39: 23 to anything under Joseph's *c*,
42: 37 to my *c*, and I will bring him back."
Ex 12: 6 Take *c* of them until the fourteenth
Lev 6: 2 entrusted to him or left in his *c*
16: 21 desert in the *c* of a man appointed
Nu 1: 50 they are to take *c* of it and encamp
1: 53 for the *c* of the tabernacle
3: 8 They are to take *c*
3: 25 for the *c* of the tabernacle
3: 28 for the *c* of the sanctuary.
3: 31 responsible for the *c* of the ark,
3: 32 for the *c* of the sanctuary.
3: 36 appointed to take *c* of the frames
3: 38 for the *c* of the sanctuary
4: 4 the *c* of the most holy things.
18: 4 be responsible for the *c* of the Tent
18: 5 for the *c* of the sanctuary
31: 30 for the *c* of the LORD's tabernacle
31: 47 for the *c* of the LORD's tabernacle.
Dt 7: 11 take *c* to follow the commands,
2Sa 15: 16 concubines to take *c* of the palace.
16: 21 left to take *c* of the palace.
18: 3 Even if half of us die, they won't *c*;
18: 3 to flee, they won't *c* about us.
19: 24 He had not taken *c* of his feet
20: 3 left to take *c* of the palace
1Ki 1: 2 to attend the king and take *c* of him
1: 4 she took *c* of the king and waited
2Ki 9: 34 "Take *c* of that cursed woman,"
1Ch 9: 29 to take *c* of the furnishings
9: 30 But some of the priests took *c*
26: 28 were in the *c* of Shelomith
27: 32 son of Hacmoni took *c*
2Ch 25: 24 been in the *c* of Obed-Edom,
32: 22 He took *c* of them on every side.
Ezr 10: 13 this matter cannot be taken *c*
Est 2: 3 placed under the *c* of Hegai,
2: 8 and put under the *c* of Hegai.
2: 14 of the harem to the *c* of Shaashgaz,
Job 3: 4 may God above not *c* about it;
21: 21 what does he *c* about the family
Ps 8: 4 the son of man that you *c* for him?
65: 9 You *c* for the land and water it;
88: 5 who are cut off from your *c*.
95: 7 the flock under his *c*.
144: 3 what is man that you *c* for him,
Pr 29: 7 The righteous *c* about justice
SS 1: 6 made me take *c* of the vineyards;
Isa 13: 17 who do not *c* for silver
34: 15 *c* for her young under the shadow
Jer 6: 20 What do I *c* about incense
15: 15 remember me and *c* for me.
23: 2 and have not bestowed *c* on them,
30: 14 they *c* nothing for you.
Eze 34: 2 Should not shepherds take *c*
34: 2 shepherds of Israel who only take *c*
34: 3 but you do not take *c* of the flock.
Hos 14: 8 I will answer him and *c* for him.
Am 7: 14 I also took *c* of sycamore-fig trees.
Mic 2: 8 from those who pass by without a *c*
Zep 2: 7 The LORD their God will *c*
Zec 10: 3 for the LORD Almighty will *c*
11: 16 over the land who will not *c*
Mt 27: 55 from Galilee to *c* for his needs.
Mk 4: 38 Teacher, don't you *c* if we drown?"
5: 26 deal under the *c* of many doctors
Lk 10: 34 him to an inn and took *c* of him.
10: 40 don't you *c* that my sister has left
13: 7 said to the man who took *c*
18: 4 I don't fear God or *c* about men,
Jn 21: 16 Jesus said, "Take *c* of my sheep."
Ac 9: 34 Get up and take *c* of your mat."
Ac 13: 40 Take *c* that what the prophets have
24: 23 friends to take *c* of his needs.
1Co 4: 3 I *c* very little if I am judged by you
Php 2: 25 sent to take *c* of my needs.
1Ti 3: 5 how can he take *c* of God's church
6: 20 what has been entrusted to your *c*.
Heb 2: 6 the son of man that you *c* for him?
1Pe 1: 10 and with the greatest *c*,
5: 2 of God's flock that is under your *c*,
Rev 12: 6 where she might be taken *c*
12: 14 where she would be taken *c*

CARED (CARE)

Dt 32: 10 He shielded him and *c* for him;
Ru 4: 16 laid him in her lap and *c* for him.
La 2: 20 the children they have *c* for?
2: 22 those I *c* for and reared,
Eze 34: 8 but *c* for themselves rather
Hos 12: 13 by a prophet he *c* for him.
13: 5 I *c* for you in the desert,
Mk 15: 41 women had followed him and *c*
Lk 18: 2 feared God nor *c* about men.
Jn 12: 6 because he *c* about the poor but
Ac 7: 20 For three months he was *c*

CAREFREE

Ps 73: 12 always *c*, they increase in wealth.
Eze 23: 42 "The noise of a *c* crowd was
Zep 2: 15 This is the *c* city

CAREFUL (CARE)

Ge 31: 24 "Be *c* not to say anything to Jacob,
31: 29 'Be *c* not to say anything to Jacob,
Ex 19: 12 'Be *c* that you do not go up
23: 13 "Be *c* to do everything I have said
34: 12 Be *c* not to make a treaty
34: 15 "Be *c* not to make a treaty
Lev 18: 4 and be *c* to follow my decrees.
25: 18 " 'Follow my decrees and be *c*
26: 3 and are *c* to obey my commands,
Dt 2: 4 afraid of you, but be very *c*.
4: 9 before you today? Only be *c*,
4: 23 Be *c* not to forget the covenant
5: 32 So be *c* to do what the LORD your
6: 3 be *c* to obey so that it may go well
6: 12 be *c* that you do not forget
6: 25 And if we are *c* to obey all this law
7: 12 attention to these laws and are *c*
8: 1 Be *c* to follow every command I am
8: 11 Be *c* that you do not forget
11: 16 Be *c*, or you will be enticed
12: 1 and laws you must be *c* to follow
12: 13 Be *c* not to sacrifice your burnt
12: 19 Be *c* not to neglect the Levites
12: 28 Be *c* to obey all these regulations I
12: 30 be *c* not to be ensnared
15: 5 are *c* to follow all these commands
15: 9 Be *c* not to harbor this wicked
17: 10 Be *c* to do everything they direct
24: 8 cases of leprous diseases be very *c*
Jos 1: 7 Be *c* to obey all the law my servant
1: 8 so that you may be *c*
22: 5 But be very *c* to keep
23: 6 be *c* to obey all that is written
23: 11 be very *c* to love the LORD your
1Ki 8: 25 if only your sons are *c* in all they do
2Ki 10: 31 Yet Jehu was not *c* to keep the law
17: 37 You must always be *c*
21: 8 if only they will be *c*
1Ch 22: 13 if you are *c* to observe the decrees
28: 8 Be *c* to follow all the commands
2Ch 6: 16 if only your sons are *c* in all they do
33: 8 if only they will be *c*
Ezr 4: 22 Be *c* not to neglect this matter.
Job 36: 18 Be *c* that no one entices you
Ps 101: 2 I will be *c* to lead a blameless life—
Pr 13: 24 he who loves him is *c*
27: 23 give *c* attention to your herds;
Isa 7: 4 Be *c*, keep calm and don't be afraid.
Jer 17: 21 Be *c* not to carry a load
17: 24 But if you are *c* to obey me,
22: 4 For if you are *c* to carry out these
Eze 11: 20 will follow my decrees and be *c*
18: 19 has been *c* to keep all my decrees,
20: 19 follow my decrees and be *c*
20: 21 they were not *c* to keep my laws—
36: 27 you to follow my decrees and be *c*
37: 24 and be *c* to keep my decrees.

Mic 7: 5 be c of your words.
Hag 1: 5 "Give c thought to your ways.
1: 7 "Give c thought to your ways.
2: 15 give c thought to this from this day
2: 18 Give c thought: Is there yet any
2: 18 give c thought to the day
Mt 2: 8 and make a c search for the child.
6: 1 "Be c not to do your 'acts
16: 6 "Be c," Jesus said to them.
Mk 8: 15 "Be c," Jesus warned them.
Lk 21: 34 Be c, or your hearts will be weighed
Ro 12: 17 Be c to do what is right in the eyes
1Co 3: 10 each one should be c how he builds
8: 9 Be c, however, that the exercise
10: 12 standing firm, be c that you don't
Eph 5: 15 Be very c, then, how you live—
2Ti 4: 2 great patience and c instruction.
Tit 3: 8 may be c to devote themselves
Heb 2: 1 We must pay more c attention,
4: 1 let us be c that none

CARELESS

Mt 12: 36 for every c word they have spoken.

CARES (CARE)

Dt 11: 12 It is a land the LORD your God c
Job 39: 16 she c not that her labor was in vain,
Ps 55: 22 Cast your c on the LORD
142: 4 no one c for my life.
Pr 12: 10 A righteous man c for the needs
Ecc 5: 3 when there are many c,
Jer 12: 11 because there is no one who c.
30: 17 Zion for whom no one c.'
Na 1: 7 He c for those who trust in him,
Jn 10: 13 and c nothing for the sheep.
Eph 5: 29 but he feeds and c for it, just
1Pe 5: 7 on him because he c for you.

CARESSED (CARESSING)

Eze 23: 3 fondled and their virgin bosoms c.
23: 8 c her virgin bosom and poured out
23: 21 when in Egypt your bosom was c

CARESSING (CARESSED)

Ge 26: 8 and saw Isaac c his wife Rebekah.

CARGO (CARGOES)

Eze 27: 25 You are filled with heavy c
Jnh 1: 5 And they threw the c into the sea
Ac 21: 3 where our ship was to unload its c.
27: 10 and bring great loss to ship and c,
27: 18 began to throw the c overboard.

CARGOES (CARGO)

1Ki 10: 11 from there they brought great c
Rev 18: 11 no one buys their c any more—
18: 12 c of gold, silver, precious stones
18: 13 iron and marble; c of cinnamon

CARING (CARE)

1Th 2: 7 like a mother c for her little
1Ti 5: 4 practice by c for their own family

CARITES

2Ki 11: 4 the C and the guards and had them
11: 19 commanders of hundreds, the C,

CARMEL (CARMELITE)

Jos 12: 22 king of Jokneam in C one the king
15: 55 Maon, C, Ziph, Juttah, Jezreel,
19: 26 the west the boundary touched C
1Sa 15: 12 he was told, "Saul has gone to C.
25: 2 which he was shearing in C.
25: 2 who had property there at C,
25: 5 Go up to Nabal at C and greet him
25: 7 at C nothing of theirs was missing.
25: 40 His servants went to C
27: 3 of Jezreel and Abigail of C,
30: 5 Abigail, the widow of Nabal of C.
2Sa 2: 2 Abigail, the widow of Nabal of C.
3: 3 of Abigail the widow of Nabal of C;
1Ki 18: 19 over Israel to meet me on Mount C
18: 20 the prophets on Mount C.
18: 42 but Elijah climbed to the top of C,
2Ki 2: 25 And he went on to Mount C
4: 25 to the man of God at Mount C.
1Ch 3: 1 Daniel the son of Abigail of C;
SS 7: 5 head crowns you like Mount C.
Isa 33: 9 and Bashan and C drop their leaves
35: 2 the splendor of C and Sharon;
Jer 46: 18 like C by the sea.
50: 19 and he will graze on C and Bashan;
Am 1: 2 and the top of C withers."
9: 3 hide themselves on the top of C,
Na 1: 4 Bashan and C wither

CARMELITE (CARMEL)

2Sa 23: 35 Hezro the C, Paarai the Arbite,
1Ch 11: 37 Hezro the C, Naarai son of Ezbai,

CARMI (CARMITE)

Ge 46: 9 Hanoch, Pallu, Hezron and C.
Ex 6: 14 Hanoch and Pallu, Hezron and C.
Nu 26: 6 through C, the Carmite clan.
Jos 7: 1 Achan son of C, the son of Zimri,
7: 18 Achan son of C, the son of Zimri,
1Ch 2: 7 of C: Achar, who brought disaster
4: 1 Perez, Hezron, C, Hur and Shobal.
5: 3 Hanoch, Pallu, Hezron and C.

CARMITE (CARMI)

Nu 26: 6 through Carmi, the C clan.

CARNELIAN

Rev 4: 3 had the appearance of jasper and c.
21: 20 the sixth c, the seventh chrysolite,

CAROUSE (CAROUSING)

2Pe 2: 13 of pleasure is to c in broad daylight.

CAROUSING (CAROUSE)

1Pe 4: 3 orgies, c and detestable idolatry.

CARPENTER (CARPENTER'S CARPENTERS)

Isa 44: 13 The c measures with a line
Mk 6: 3 does miracles! Isn't this the c?

CARPENTER'S (CARPENTER)

Mt 13: 55 "Isn't this the c son? Isn't his

CARPENTERS (CARPENTER)

2Sa 5: 11 along with cedar logs and c
2Ki 12: 11 the c and builders, the masons
22: 6 the c, the builders and the masons.
1Ch 14: 1 and c to build a palace for him.
22: 15 stonecutters, masons and c,
2Ch 24: 12 c to restore the LORD's temple,
34: 11 They also gave money to the c
Ezr 3: 7 money to the masons and c,

CARPUS

2Ti 4: 13 bring the cloak that I left with C

CARRIAGE (CARRIAGES)

SS 3: 7 Look! It is Solomon's c,
3: 9 Solomon made for himself the c;

CARRIAGES (CARRIAGE)

Rev 18: 13 cattle and sheep; horses and c;

CARRIED (CARRY)

Ge 14: 12 also c off Abram's nephew Lot
22: 6 and he himself c the fire
31: 26 and you've c off my daughters like
34: 29 They c off all their wealth
40: 15 For I was forcibly c
50: 13 They c him to the land of Canaan
Ex 10: 19 caught up the locusts and c them
12: 34 and c it on their shoulders
19: 4 and how I c you on eagles' wings
27: 7 on two sides of the altar when it is c
34: 4 and he c the two stone tablets
Lev 10: 5 and c them, still in their tunics,
Nu 10: 17 and Merarites, who c it,
13: 23 Two of them c it on a pole
Dt 1: 31 how the LORD your God c you,
2: 35 the towns we had captured we c
3: 7 the plunder from their cities we c
31: 9 who c the ark of the covenant
31: 25 to the Levites who c the ark
33: 21 he c out the LORD's righteous will
Jos 3: 15 as the priests who c the ark reached
3: 17 The priests who c the ark
4: 8 and they c them over with them
4: 9 where the priests who c the ark
4: 10 the priests who c the ark remained
6: 11 ark of the LORD c around the city,
8: 33 facing those who c it—the priests,
11: 14 Israelites c off for themselves all
22: 3 have c out the mission the LORD
Jdg 3: 18 on their way the men who had c it.
5: 19 but they c off no silver, no plunder.
16: 3 c them to the top of the hill that
21: 23 and c her off to be his wife.
Ru 2: 18 She c it back to town, and her
1Sa 5: 2 they c the ark into Dagon's temple
15: 11 and has not c out my instructions."
15: 13 I have c out the LORD's
17: 34 and c off a sheep from the flock,
23: 5 fought the Philistines and c
30: 2 but c them off as they went
2Sa 5: 21 and David and his men c them off.
23: 16 the gate of Bethlehem and c it back
1Ki 2: 26 you c the ark of the Sovereign
8: 4 The priests and Levites c them up,
14: 26 He c off the treasures of the temple
15: 22 and they c away from Ramah
16: 20 and the rebellion he c out,
17: 19 c him to the upper room where he
17: 23 and c him down from the room
2Ki 4: 20 servant had lifted him up and c him
5: 23 and they c them ahead of Gehazi.
7: 8 and drank, and c away silver,
18: 12 to the commands nor c them out.
20: 17 up until this day, will be c
23: 34 But he took Jehoahaz and c him
24: 14 He c into exile all Jerusalem:
25: 11 the commander of the guard c
25: 13 and they c the bronze to Babylon.
1Ch 11: 18 the gate of Bethlehem and c it back
15: 15 And the Levites c the ark of God
18: 7 David took the gold shields c
23: 32 And so the Levites c out their
2Ch 5: 5 who were Levites, c them up;
8: 16 All Solomon's work was c out,
12: 9 he c off the treasures of the temple
14: 13 The men of Judah c
14: 15 and c off droves of sheep and goats
16: 6 and they c away from Ramah
21: 17 and c off all the goods found
24: 12 it to the men who c out the work
25: 13 c off great quantities of plunder.
28: 8 which they c back to Samaria.
28: 17 Judah and c away prisoners,
29: 16 and c it out to the Kidron Valley.
35: 3 to be c about on your shoulders.
35: 16 service of the LORD was c out
36: 4 brother Jehoahaz and c him
36: 18 He c to Babylon all the articles
36: 20 He c into exile to Babylon
Ezr 1: 7 Nebuchadnezzar had c away
5: 8 The work is being c
6: 12 Let it be c out with diligence.
6: 13 and their associates c it out
Ne 3: 17 c out repairs for his district.
4: 17 Those who c materials did their
11: 12 who c on work for the temple—
Est 2: 6 who had been c into exile
4: 17 c out all of Esther's instructions.
9: 1 by the king was to be c out.
Job 1: 15 the Sabeans attacked and c them
1: 17 on your camels and c them off.
10: 19 had been c straight from the womb
15: 12 Why has your heart c you away,
21: 32 He is c to the grave,
22: 16 They were c off before their time,
Ecc 8: 11 for a crime is not quickly c out,
Isa 8: 4 of Samaria will be c off by the king
39: 6 up until this day, will be c
41: 4 Who has done this and c it through,
46: 1 The images that are c about are
46: 3 and have c since your birth.
53: 4 and c our sorrows,
60: 4 your daughters are c on the arm.
63: 9 he lifted them up and c them
66: 12 you will nurse and be c on her arm
Jer 10: 5 they must be c
13: 19 All Judah will be c into exile,
13: 19 c completely away.
24: 1 artisans of Judah were c into exile
27: 20 away when he c Jehoiachin son
29: 1 people Nebuchadnezzar had c
29: 4 says to all those I c into exile
29: 7 to which I have c you into exile.

Jer 29:14 from which I *c* you into exile."
35:16 of Recab have *c* out the command
39:9 of the imperial guard *c* into exile
40:1 Judah who were being *c* into exile
40:7 and who had not been *c* into exile
49:29 their shelters will be *c* off
52:15 of the guard *c* into exile some
52:17 they *c* all the bronze to Babylon.
52:28 of the people Nebuchadnezzar *c*
Eze 6:9 where they have been *c* captive,
16:16 where you *c* on your prostitution.
17:4 *c* it away to a land of merchants,
17:12 and *c* off her king and her nobles,
17:13 *c* away the leading men of the land,
23:14 she *c* her prostitution still further.
23:18 When she *c* on her prostitution
30:4 her wealth will be *c* away
44:15 and who faithfully *c* out the duties
Da 1:2 These he *c* off to the temple
11:12 When the army is *c* off, the king
Hos 10:6 It will be *c* to Assyria
Joel 3:5 and *c* off my finest treasures
Ob :11 while strangers *c* off his wealth
Na 2:7 be exiled and *c* away.
Mal 2:3 and you will be *c* off with it.
Mt 8:17 and *c* our diseases."
14:11 to the girl, who *c* it to her mother.
Mk 2:3 to him a paralytic, *c* by four
6:55 *c* the sick on mats to wherever they
Lk 7:12 a dead person was being *c* out—
16:22 the angels *c* him to Abraham's side.
Jn 20:15 "Sir, if you have *c* him away,
Ac 3:2 crippled from birth was being *c*
5:6 and *c* him out and buried him.
5:10 *c* her out and buried her
13:29 When they had *c* out all that was
21:35 had to be *c* by the soldiers.
23:30 of a plot to be *c* out against the man
Heb 13:9 Do not be *c* away by all kinds
2Pe 1:21 as they were *c* along by the Holy
3:17 so that you may not be *c* away
Rev 17:3 the angel *c* me away in the Spirit
21:10 And he *c* me away in the Spirit

CARRIERS (CARRY)

Jos 9:21 water *c* for the entire community."
9:23 water *c* for the house of my God."
9:27 and water *c* for the community
1Ki 5:15 Solomon had seventy thousand *c*
2Ch 2:2 as *c* and eighty thousand
2:18 of them to be *c* and 80,000
Eze 27:25 as *c* for your wares.

CARRIES (CARRY)

Nu 11:12 as a nurse *c* an infant,
Dt 1:31 as a father *c* his son, all the way you
32:11 and *c* them on its pinions.
Job 23:14 He *c* out his decree against me,
27:21 The east wind *c* him off,
Isa 40:11 and *c* them close to his heart;
44:26 who *c* out the words of his servants
Hag 2:12 If a person *c* consecrated meat
Heb 13:11 The high priest *c* the blood

CARRION

Eze 39:4 as food to all kinds of *c* birds

CARRY (CARRIED CARRIERS CARRIES CARRYING)

Ge 44:1 as much food as they can *c*,
45:27 Joseph had sent to *c* him back,
47:30 *c* me out of Egypt and bury me
50:25 and then you must *c* my bones up
Ex 13:19 and then you must *c* my bones up
25:14 on the sides of the chest to *c* it.
25:28 with gold and *c* the table with them
30:4 to hold the poles used to *c* it.
36:1 to know how to *c* out all the work
36:3 to *c* out the work of constructing
37:5 rings on the sides of the ark to *c* it.
37:27 to hold the poles used to *c* it.
Lev 4:5 and *c* it into the Tent of Meeting.
6:11 and *c* the ashes outside the camp
10:4 *c* your cousins outside the camp,
16:22 goat will *c* on itself all their sins
26:14 and *c* out all these commands,
26:15 and fail to *c* out all my commands
Nu 1:50 They are to *c* the tabernacle
4:15 are to *c* those things that are
4:19 man his work and what he is to *c*.
4:24 as they work and *c* burdens:
4:25 They are to *c* the curtains
4:27 their responsibility all they are to *c*.
4:31 to *c* the frames of the tabernacle,
4:32 man the specific things he is to *c*.
4:49 his work and told what to *c*.
7:9 to *c* on their shoulders the holy
11:12 me to *c* them in my arms,
11:14 I cannot *c* all these people
11:17 They will help you *c* the burden
11:17 that you will not have to *c* it alone.
31:3 to *c* out the LORD's vengeance
Dt 1:9 heavy a burden for me to *c* alone.
10:8 of Levi to *c* the ark of the covenant
14:24 your God and cannot *c* your tithe
25:6 The first son she bears shall *c*
25:7 refuses to *c* on his brother's name
29:11 chop your wood and *c* your water.
Jos 3:8 Tell the priests who *c* the ark
3:13 as the priests who *c* the ark
4:3 and to *c* them over with you
6:4 Have seven priests *c* trumpets
6:6 and have seven priests *c* trumpets
8:2 that you may *c* off their plunder
8:27 But Israel did *c* off for themselves
1Sa 3:12 At that time I will *c* out
20:40 "Go, *c* them back to town."
21:15 here to *c* on like this in front
28:18 or *c* out his fierce wrath
2Sa 18:18 "I have no son to *c* on the memory
24:12 of them for me to *c* out against you
1Ki 1:30 I will surely *c* out today what I
3:7 how to *c* out my duties.
6:12 *c* out my regulations and keep all
18:12 the Spirit of the LORD may *c* you
20:6 you value and *c* it away.' "
2Ki 4:19 His father told a servant, "*C* him
5:17 much earth as a pair of mules can *c*,
1Ch 15:2 the Levites may *c* the ark of God,
15:2 the LORD chose them to *c* the ark
21:10 of them for me to *c* out against you
23:26 need to *c* the tabernacle
2Ch 20:25 his men went to *c* off their plunder,
24:11 and empty the chest and *c* it back
30:12 of mind to *c* out what the king
Est 3:9 for the men who *c* out this business
9:13 to *c* out this day's edict tomorrow
Job 12:6 those who *c* their god
15:30 of God's mouth will *c* him away.
20:28 A flood will *c* off his house,
24:10 they *c* the sheaves, but still go
Ps 28:9 their shepherd and *c* them forever.
37:7 when they *c* out their wicked
149:9 to *c* out the sentence written
Ecc 5:15 that he can *c* in his hand.
10:20 a bird of the air may *c* your words,
Isa 5:29 and *c* it off with no one to rescue.
10:23 the LORD Almighty, will *c* out
13:3 warriors to *c* out my wrath—
15:7 they *c* away over the Ravine
28:19 as it comes it will *c* you away;
30:1 "to those who *c* out plans that are
30:6 the envoys *c* their riches
33:23 even the lame will *c* off plunder.
45:20 are those who *c* about idols
46:4 I have made you and I will *c* you;
46:7 to their shoulders and *c* it;
48:14 will *c* out his purpose
49:22 *c* your daughters on their shoulders
52:11 you who *c* the vessels of the LORD
57:13 The wind will *c* all of them off,
Jer 17:21 Be careful not to *c* a load
20:4 who will *c* them away to Babylon
20:5 as plunder and *c* it off to Babylon.
22:4 careful to *c* out these commands,
43:3 or *c* us into exile to Babylon."
44:25 'We will certainly *c* out the vows
46:9 men of Cush and Put who *c* shields,
51:12 The LORD will *c* out his purpose,
Eze 12:6 they are watching and *c* them out
25:17 I will *c* out great vengeance
29:19 and he will *c* off its wealth.
38:13 hordes to loot, to *c* off silver
Da 11:8 and gold and *c* them off to Egypt.
11:10 *c* the battle as far as his fortress.
Hos 5:14 I will *c* them off, with no one
Hos 11:9 I will not *c* out my fierce anger,
Am 6:10 comes to *c* them out of the house
Mic 2:1 At morning's light they *c* it out
Mt 3:11 whose sandals I am not fit to *c*.
12:29 enter a strong man's house and *c*
27:32 and they forced him to *c* the cross.
Mk 3:27 enter a strong man's house and *c*
11:16 not allow anyone to *c* merchandise
15:21 and they forced him to *c* the cross.
Lk 11:46 with burdens they can hardly *c*,
14:27 anyone who does not *c* his cross
23:26 and made him *c* it behind Jesus.
Jn 5:10 the law forbids you to *c* your mat."
8:44 want to *c* out your father's desire.
Ac 5:9 and they will *c* you out also."
9:15 to *c* my name before the Gentiles
Ro 7:18 what is good, but I cannot *c* it out.
9:28 For the Lord will *c* out
2Co 4:10 We always *c* around in our body
8:19 accompany us as we *c* the offering,
Gal 6:2 *C* each other's burdens,
6:5 for each one should *c* his own load.
Php 1:6 in you will *c* it on to completion
Heb 9:6 room to *c* on their ministry.
Jas 4:13 *c* on business and make money."

CARRYING (CARRY)

Ex 25:27 to hold the poles used in *c* the table
37:14 to hold the poles used in *c* the table
37:15 The poles for *c* the table were made
38:7 be on the sides of the altar for *c* it.
Nu 4:10 of sea cows and put it on a *c* frame.
4:12 and put them on a *c* frame.
4:15 are to come to do the *c*.
4:27 whether *c* or doing other work,
4:47 *c* the Tent of Meeting numbered
10:21 the Kohathites set out, *c* the holy
Dt 27:26 words of this law by *c* them out."
Jos 3:3 the priests, who are Levites, *c* it,
3:14 the priests *c* the ark
4:16 "Command the priests *c* the ark
4:18 out of the river *c* the ark
6:8 seven priests *c* the seven trumpets
6:13 seven priests *c* the seven trumpets
1Sa 10:3 One will be *c* three young goats,
2Sa 6:13 When those who were *c* the ark
15:24 were with him were *c* the ark
1Ki 8:7 the ark and its *c* poles.
10:2 with camels *c* spices, large
10:22 three years it returned *c* gold,
1Ch 12:24 men of Judah, *c* shield and spear—
12:34 together with 37,000 men *c* shields
15:26 the Levites who were *c* the ark
15:27 all the Levites who were *c* the ark,
28:7 unswerving in *c* out my commands
2Ch 5:8 and covered the ark and its *c* poles.
7:11 had succeeded in *c* out all he had
9:1 with camels *c* spices, large
9:21 three years it returned, *c* gold,
Ne 6:3 "I am *c* on a great project
10:32 for *c* out the commands
Ps 126:6 *c* seed to sow,
126:6 *c* sheaves with him.
Jer 17:27 Sabbath day holy by not *c* any load
Eze 12:7 *c* them on my shoulders
44:8 Instead of *c* out your duty in regard
Mal 3:14 gain by *c* out his requirements
Mk 14:13 a man *c* a jar of water will meet you
Lk 5:18 Some men came *c* a paralytic
7:14 the coffin, and those *c* it stood still.
22:10 a man *c* a jar of water will meet you
Jn 18:3 They were *c* torches, lanterns
19:17 *C* his own cross, he went out
Ac 23:31 So the soldiers, *c* out their orders,
27:43 kept them from *c* out their plan.
1Co 16:10 for he is *c* on the work of the Lord,
1Jn 5:2 loving God and *c* out his

CARSHENA

Est 1:14 *C*, Shethar, Admatha, Tarshish,

CART (CARTS)

Nu 7:3 an ox from each leader and a *c*
1Sa 6:7 Hitch the cows to the *c*,
6:7 "Now then, get a new *c* ready,
6:8 of the LORD and put it on the *c*,
6:10 to the *c* and penned up their calves.
6:11 the ark of the LORD on the *c*

1Sa 6: 14 The *c* came to the field of Joshua
6: 14 chopped up the wood of the *c*
2Sa 6: 3 They set the ark of God on a new *c*
6: 3 were guiding the new *c* with the ark
1Ch 13: 7 from Abinadab's house on a new *c*,
Isa 5: 18 and wickedness as with *c* ropes,
28: 28 wheels of his threshing *c* over it,
Am 2: 13 a *c* crushes when loaded with grain.

CARTS (CART)

Ge 45: 19 Take some *c* from Egypt
45: 21 Joseph gave them *c*, as Pharaoh
45: 27 when he saw the *c* Joseph had sent
46: 5 in the *c* that Pharaoh had sent
Nu 7: 3 before the LORD six covered *c*
7: 6 So Moses took the *c* and oxen
7: 7 He gave two *c* and four oxen
7: 8 and he gave four *c* and eight oxen
Ps 65: 11 your *c* overflow with abundance.

CARTWHEEL

Isa 28: 27 nor is a *c* rolled over cummin;

CARVED (CARVES CARVINGS)

Lev 26: 1 do not place a *c* stone in your land
Nu 33: 52 Destroy all their *c* images
Jdg 17: 3 for my son to make a *c* image
18: 14 other household gods, a *c* image
18: 17 went inside and took the *c* image,
18: 18 house and took the *c* image,
18: 20 household gods and the *c* image
1Ki 6: 18 *c* with gourds and open flowers.
6: 29 he *c* cherubim, palm trees
6: 32 olive wood doors he *c* cherubim,
6: 35 He *c* cherubim, palm trees
2Ki 21: 7 He took the *c* Asherah pole he had
2Ch 3: 7 and he *c* cherubim on the walls.
33: 7 He took the *c* image he had made
34: 3 Asherah poles, *c* idols
Ps 74: 6 They smashed all the *c* paneling
144: 12 *c* to adorn a palace.
Eze 41: 18 outer sanctuary were *c* cherubim
41: 19 They were *c* all around the whole
41: 20 and palm trees were *c* on the wall
41: 25 outer sanctuary were *c* cherubim
41: 25 palm trees like those *c* on the walls,
41: 26 with palm trees *c* on each side.
Mic 5: 13 I will destroy your *c* images
Na 1: 14 I will destroy the *c* images
Hab 2: 18 since a man has *c* it?

CARVES (CARVED)

Dt 27: 15 "Cursed is the man who *c* an image

CARVINGS (CARVED)

1Ki 6: 35 gold hammered evenly over the *c*.

CASE (CASES)

Ex 18: 22 have them bring every difficult *c*
Lev 5: 4 in any *c* when he learns
5: 13 as in the *c* of the grain offering.' "
Nu 27: 5 So Moses brought their *c*
Dt 1: 16 the *c* is between brother Israelites
1: 17 Bring me any *c* too hard for you,
6: 24 and be kept alive, as is the *c* today.
22: 26 This *c* is like that of someone who
25: 1 and the judges will decide the *c*,
Jos 20: 4 and state his *c* before the elders
2Sa 15: 4 has a complaint or *c* could come
20: 21 or destroy! That is not the *c*.
1Ki 15: 5 except in the *c* of Uriah the Hittite.
2Ki 8: 6 he assigned an official to her *c*
2Ch 19: 10 In every *c* that comes before you
Job 13: 3 and to argue my *c* with God.
13: 8 Will you argue the *c* for God?
13: 18 Now that I have prepared my *c*,
23: 4 I would state my *c* before him
23: 7 an upright man could present his *c*
29: 16 I took up the *c* of the stranger.
35: 14 that your *c* is before him
37: 19 we cannot draw up our *c*
Pr 18: 17 to present his *c* seems right,
22: 23 for the LORD will take up their *c*
23: 11 he will take up their *c* against you.
25: 9 If you argue your *c* with a neighbor
Isa 1: 17 plead the *c* of the widow.
1: 23 the widow's *c* does not come
41: 21 "Present your *c*," says the LORD.
43: 26 state the *c* for your innocence.
59: 4 no one pleads his *c* with integrity.
Jer 5: 28 they do not plead the *c*
12: 1 when I bring a *c* before you.
La 3: 58 O Lord, you took up my *c*;
Mic 6: 1 plead your *c* before the mountains;
6: 2 For the LORD has a *c*
7: 9 until he pleads my *c*
Lk 13: 33 In any *c*, I must keep going today
Ac 5: 38 in the present *c* I advise you:
19: 40 In that *c* we would not be able
23: 15 accurate information about his *c*.
23: 30 present to you their *c* against him.
23: 35 "I will hear your *c*
24: 2 Tertullus presented his *c*
24: 22 he said, "I will decide your *c*."
25: 14 Festus discussed Paul's *c*
25: 17 here with me, I did not delay the *c*,
1Co 5: 10 In that *c* you would have
14: 7 in the *c* of lifeless things that make
2Co 10: 14 would be the *c* if we had not come
Gal 3: 15 duly established, so it is in this *c*.
5: 11 In that *c* the offense
2Ti 3: 9 as in the *c* of those men, their folly
Heb 6: 9 of better things in your *c*—
7: 8 In the one *c*, the tenth is collected
7: 8 but in the other *c*, by him who is
9: 16 In the *c* of a will, it is necessary

CASES (CASE)

Ex 18: 22 the simple *c* they can decide
18: 26 The difficult *c* they brought
22: 9 In all *c* of illegal possession of an ox
22: 9 to bring their *c* before the judges.
Dt 17: 8 If *c* come before your courts that
21: 5 and to decide all *c* of dispute
24: 8 In *c* of leprous diseases be very
Ezr 10: 16 sat down to investigate the *c*,
1Co 6: 2 not competent to judge trivial *c*?

CASIPHIA

Ezr 8: 17 I sent them to Iddo, the leader in *C*.
8: 17 the temple servants in *C*,

CASLUHITES

Ge 10: 14 *C* (from whom the Philistines came
1Ch 1: 12 *C* (from whom the Philistines came

CASSIA

Ex 30: 24 shekels of *c*— all according
Ps 45: 8 with myrrh and aloes and *c*;
Eze 27: 19 *c* and calamus for your wares.

CAST (CASTING CASTS OUTCAST)

Ex 25: 12 *C* four gold rings for it
26: 37 And *c* five bronze bases for them.
32: 4 made it into an idol *c* in the shape
32: 8 have made themselves an idol *c*
34: 17 "Do not make *c* idols.
36: 36 and *c* their four silver bases.
37: 3 He *c* four gold rings for it
37: 13 They *c* four gold rings for the table
38: 5 They *c* bronze rings
38: 27 of silver were used to *c* the bases
Lev 16: 8 He is to *c* lots for the two goats—
19: 4 or make gods of *c* metal.
Nu 33: 52 carved images and their *c* idols,
Dt 9: 12 have made a *c* idol for themselves."
9: 16 made for yourselves an idol *c*
Jos 18: 6 I will *c* lots for you in the presence
18: 8 I will *c* lots for you here at Shiloh
18: 10 Joshua then *c* lots for them
Jdg 17: 3 to make a carved image and a *c* idol
18: 14 a carved image and a *c* idol?
18: 17 and the *c* idol while the priest
18: 18 household gods and the *c* idol,
1Sa 14: 42 "*C* the lot between me
2Sa 23: 6 all to be *c* aside like thorns,
1Ki 7: 15 He *c* two bronze pillars, each
7: 16 also made two capitals of *c* bronze
7: 23 He made the Sea of *c* metal,
7: 24 The gourds were *c* in two rows
7: 30 *c* with wreaths on each side.
7: 33 spokes and hubs were all of *c* metal
7: 37 They were all *c* in the same molds
7: 46 The king had them *c* in clay molds
2Ki 17: 16 made for themselves two idols *c*
1Ch 24: 31 also *c* lots, just as their brothers
1Ch 25: 8 as student, *c* lots for their duties.
26: 13 Lots were *c* for each gate,
26: 14 lots were *c* for his son Zechariah,
2Ch 4: 2 He made the Sea of *c* metal,
4: 3 The bulls were *c* in two rows
4: 17 The king had them *c* in clay molds
28: 2 also made *c* idols for worshiping
34: 3 carved idols and *c* images.
Ne 9: 18 even when they *c* for themselves
10: 34 have *c* lots to determine when each
11: 1 and the rest of the people *c* lots
Est 3: 7 of Nisan, they *c* the *pur* (that is,
9: 24 them and had *c* the *pur* (that
Job 6: 27 even *c* lots for the fatherless
37: 18 hard as a mirror of *c* bronze?
Ps 22: 10 From birth I was *c* upon you;
22: 18 and *c* lots for my clothing.
50: 17 and *c* my words behind you.
51: 11 Do not *c* me from your presence
55: 22 *C* your cares on the LORD
71: 9 Do not *c* me away when I am old;
73: 18 you *c* them down to ruin.
89: 44 and *c* his throne to the ground.
106: 19 and worshiped an idol *c* from metal
Pr 16: 33 The lot is *c* into the lap,
23: 5 *C* but a glance at riches,
29: 18 there is no revelation, the people *c*
Ecc 11: 1 *C* your bread upon the waters,
11: 10 and *c* off the troubles of your body,
Isa 14: 12 You have been *c* down to the earth,
14: 19 But you are *c* out of your tomb
19: 8 all who *c* hooks into the Nile;
38: 8 I will make the shadow *c*
57: 20 whose waves *c* up mire and mud.
Jer 22: 28 *c* into a land they do not know?
23: 39 and *c* you out of my presence
La 3: 31 For men are not *c* off
Eze 21: 21 He will *c* lots with arrows,
31: 11 I *c* it aside, and the most ruthless
32: 3 I will *c* my net over you,
Joel 3: 3 They *c* lots for my people
Am 4: 3 you will be *c* out toward Harmon,"
5: 7 and *c* righteousness to the ground
Ob : 11 and *c* lots for Jerusalem,
Jnh 1: 7 They *c* lots and the lot fell
1: 7 let us *c* lots to find out who is
Mic 5: 12 and you will no longer *c* spells.
Na 1: 14 the carved images and *c* idols
3: 10 Lots were *c* for her nobles,
Mal 3: 11 in your fields will not *c* their fruit,"
Mk 15: 24 they *c* lots to see what each would
Jn 19: 24 and *c* lots for my clothing."
Ac 26: 10 to death, I *c* my vote against them.
1Pe 5: 7 *C* all your anxiety on him
Rev 2: 22 So I will *c* her on a bed of suffering,

CASTING (CAST)

Pr 18: 18 *C* the lot settles disputes
Eze 24: 6 piece without *c* lots for them.
26: 3 like the sea *c* up its waves.
Mt 4: 18 They were *c* a net into the lake,
27: 35 divided up his clothes by *c* lots.
Mk 1: 16 and his brother Andrew *c* a net
Lk 23: 34 divided up his clothes by *c* lots.

CASTOR

Ac 28: 11 the figurehead of the twin gods *C*

CASTS (CAST)

Dt 18: 11 engages in witchcraft, or *c* spells,
27: 15 who carves an image or *c* an idol—
Ps 15: 3 and *c* no slur on his fellow man,
147: 6 but *c* the wicked to the ground.
Isa 26: 5 and *c* it down to the dust.
40: 19 As for an idol, a craftsman *c* it,
44: 10 Who shapes a god and *c* an idol,

CASUALTIES

Jdg 20: 31 began to inflict *c* on the Israelites
20: 39 begun to inflict *c* on the men
2Sa 18: 7 and the *c* that day were great—
1Ki 20: 29 inflicted a hundred thousand *c*
2Ch 13: 17 there were five hundred thousand *c*
28: 5 who inflicted heavy *c* on him.
Na 3: 3 Many *c*,

CATASTROPHE

Ge 19: 29 of the *c* that overthrew the cities

Isa 47: 11 a *c* you cannot foresee

CATCH (CATCHES CAUGHT)

Ge 44: 4 and when you *c* up with them,
Dt 32: 11 that spreads its wings to *c* them
Jos 2: 5 You may *c* up with them."
Job 23: 9 to the south, I *c* no glimpse of him.
Ps 10: 9 he lies in wait to *c* the helpless;
SS 2: 15 *C* for us the foxes,
Jer 2: 34 you did not *c* them breaking in.
5: 26 like those who set traps to *c* men.
16: 16 the LORD, "and they will *c* them.
Hos 2: 7 after her lovers but not *c* them;
7: 12 I will *c* them.
Am 3: 5 earth when there is nothing to *c*?
Mt 17: 27 the first fish you *c*; open its mouth
Mk 12: 13 and Herodians to Jesus to *c* him
Lk 5: 4 and let down the nets for a *c*."
5: 9 at the *c* of fish they had taken,
5: 10 from now on you will *c* men."
11: 54 to *c* him in something he might say.
20: 20 They hoped to *c* Jesus

CATCHES (CATCH)

Job 5: 13 He *c* the wise in their craftiness,
39: 25 He *c* the scent of battle from afar,
Ps 10: 9 he *c* the helpless and drags them
Hab 1: 15 he *c* them in his net,
1Co 3: 19 "He *c* the wise in their craftiness";

CATTLE

Ge 12: 16 and Abram acquired sheep and *c*,
20: 14 Abimelech brought sheep and *c*
21: 27 So Abraham brought sheep and *c*
24: 35 He has given him sheep and *c*,
32: 5 I have *c* and donkeys, sheep
47: 17 and goats, their *c* and donkeys.
Ex 9: 3 camels and on your *c* and sheep
11: 5 and all the firstborn of the *c* as well.
20: 24 your sheep and goats and your *c*.
22: 1 he must pay back five head of *c*
22: 30 Do the same with your *c*
Lev 7: 23 'Do not eat any of the fat of *c*,
22: 19 a male without defect from the *c*,
26: 22 destroy your *c* and make you
Nu 22: 40 Balak sacrificed *c* and sheep,
31: 28 whether persons, *c*, donkeys,
31: 30 whether persons, *c*, donkeys, sheep
31: 33 *c*, 61,000 donkeys and 32,000
31: 38 *c*, of which the tribute
31: 44 was 337,500 sheep, 36,000 *c*,
35: 3 and pasturelands for their *c*,
Dt 11: 15 grass in the fields for your *c*,
14: 26 *c*, sheep, wine or other fermented
Jos 6: 21 young and old, *c*, sheep
7: 24 his sons and daughters, his *c*,
Jdg 6: 4 neither sheep nor *c* nor donkeys.
1Sa 8: 16 maidservants and the best of your *c*
14: 32 and, taking sheep, *c* and calves,
14: 34 'Each of you bring me your *c*
15: 3 children and infants, *c* and sheep,
15: 9 and the best of the sheep and *c*,
15: 14 What is this lowing of *c* that I hear
15: 15 *c* to sacrifice to the LORD your
15: 21 The soldiers took sheep and *c*
22: 19 and its *c*, donkeys and sheep.
27: 9 but took sheep and *c*, donkeys
2Sa 12: 2 a very large number of sheep and *c*,
12: 4 or *c* to prepare a meal
1Ki 1: 9 *c* and fattened calves at the Stone
1: 19 has sacrificed great numbers of *c*,
1: 25 and sacrificed great numbers of *c*,
4: 23 ten head of stall-fed *c*, twenty
4: 23 twenty of pasture-fed *c*
8: 5 *c* that they could not be recorded
8: 63 twenty-two thousand *c*
2Ki 3: 17 your *c* and your other animals will
1Ch 12: 40 raisin cakes, wine, oil, *c* and sheep,
2Ch 5: 6 *c* that they could not be recorded
7: 5 of twenty-two thousand head of *c*
15: 11 LORD seven hundred head of *c*
18: 2 slaughtered many sheep and *c*
32: 28 he made stalls for various kinds of *c*
35: 7 and also three thousand *c*—
35: 8 offerings and three hundred *c*.
35: 9 head of *c* for the Levites.
35: 12 They did the same with the *c*.
Ne 9: 37 They rule over our bodies and our *c*
10: 36 firstborn of our sons and of our *c*,
Job 18: 3 Why are we regarded as *c*
36: 33 the *c* make known its approach.
Ps 50: 10 and the *c* on a thousand hills.
78: 48 He gave over their *c* to the hail,
104: 14 He makes grass grow for the *c*,
147: 9 He provides food for the *c*
148: 10 wild animals and all *c*,
Isa 7: 25 become places where *c* are turned
22: 13 slaughtering of *c* and killing
30: 23 In that day your *c* will graze
63: 14 like *c* that go down to the plain,
Jer 9: 10 and the lowing of *c* is not heard.
Eze 32: 13 I will destroy all her *c*
32: 13 or muddied by the hoofs of *c*.
Da 4: 25 you will eat grass like *c*
4: 32 animals; you will eat grass like *c*.
4: 33 from people and ate grass like *c*.
5: 21 wild donkeys and ate grass like *c*;
Joel 1: 18 How the *c* moan!
Jnh 4: 11 hand from their left, and many *c*
Hab 3: 17 and no *c* in the stalls,
Hag 1: 11 *c*, and on the labor of your hands."
Mt 22: 4 fattened *c* have been butchered,
Jn 2: 14 courts he found men selling *c*,
2: 15 the temple area, both sheep and *c*;
Rev 18: 13 of fine flour and wheat; *c* and sheep

CAUDA

Ac 27: 16 to the lee of a small island called *C*,

CAUGHT (CATCH)

Ge 22: 13 there in a thicket he saw a ram *c*
27: 27 When Isaac *c* the smell
31: 23 *c* up with him in the hill country
39: 12 She *c* him by his cloak and said,
44: 6 When he *c* up with them, he
Ex 10: 19 which *c* up the locusts
21: 16 when he is *c* must be put to death.
22: 2 "If a thief is *c* breaking in
22: 7 if he is *c*, must pay back double.
Nu 5: 13 and she has not been *c* in the act),
11: 22 fish in the sea were *c* for them?"
Dt 24: 7 If a man is *c* kidnapping one
Jos 7: 15 He who is *c* with the devoted
8: 22 so that they were *c* in the middle,
Jdg 1: 6 but they chased him and *c* him,
8: 14 He *c* a young man of Succoth
15: 4 and *c* three hundred foxes
21: 23 each man *c* one and carried her
1Sa 9: 17 When Samuel *c* sight of Saul,
15: 27 Saul *c* hold of the edge of his robe,
2Sa 18: 9 Absalom's head got *c* in the tree.
Job 4: 12 my ears *c* a whisper of it.
Ps 9: 15 their feet are *c* in the net they have
10: 2 who are *c* in the schemes he
59: 12 let them be *c* in their pride.
Pr 6: 31 if he is *c*, he must pay sevenfold,
30: 28 a lizard can be *c* with the hand,
Ecc 9: 12 As fish are *c* in a cruel net,
Isa 13: 15 all who are *c* will fall by the sword.
22: 3 you who were *c* were taken
24: 18 will be *c* in a snare.
51: 20 like antelope *c* in a net.
Jer 2: 26 As a thief is disgraced when he is *c*,
6: 11 both husband and wife will be *c*
41: 12 They *c* up with him
48: 27 Was she *c* among thieves,
48: 44 will be *c* in a snare;
50: 24 and you were *c* before you knew it;
La 4: 20 was *c* in their traps.
Eze 12: 13 and he will be *c* in my snare;
17: 20 and he will be *c* in my snare.
Am 3: 4 den when he has *c* nothing?
Mt 13: 47 into the lake and *c* all kinds of fish.
14: 31 reached out his hand and *c* him.
Lk 5: 5 all night and haven't *c* anything.
5: 6 they *c* such a large number
Jn 8: 3 brought in a woman *c* in adultery.
8: 4 this woman was *c* in the act
21: 3 but that night they *c* nothing.
21: 10 some of the fish you have just *c*."
Ac 27: 15 The ship was *c* by the storm
2Co 12: 2 who fourteen years ago was *c* up
12: 4 God knows—was *c* up to Paradise.
12: 16 crafty fellow that I am, I *c* you
Gal 6: 1 Brothers, if someone is *c* in a sin,
1Th 4: 17 and are left will be *c* up with them
2Pe 2: 12 born only to be *c* and destroyed,

CAULK

Eze 27: 9 as shipwrights to *c* your seams.

CAUSE (CAUSED CAUSES CAUSING)

Ex 20: 24 Wherever I *c* my name
23: 33 or they will *c* you to sin against me,
33: 19 "I will *c* all my goodness to pass
Nu 5: 21 "may the LORD *c* your people
5: 24 will enter her and *c* bitter suffering.
5: 27 go into her and *c* bitter suffering;
16: 5 The man he chooses he will *c*
32: 15 will be the *c* of their destruction."
Dt 3: 28 will *c* them to inherit the land that
10: 18 He defends the *c* of the fatherless
28: 25 The LORD will *c* you
33: 7 his own hands he defends his *c*.
Jos 22: 25 So your descendants might *c* ours
Jdg 6: 31 "Are you going to plead Baal's *c*?
1Sa 24: 15 May he consider my *c*
25: 39 who has upheld my *c* against Nabal
1Ki 8: 45 and their plea, and uphold their *c*.
8: 49 and their plea, and uphold their *c*.
8: 50 and *c* their conquerors
8: 59 that he may uphold the *c*
8: 59 the *c* of his people Israel according
2Ki 2: 21 Never again will it *c* death
14: 10 ask for trouble and *c* your own
2Ch 6: 35 and their plea, and uphold their *c*.
6: 39 and their pleas, and uphold their *c*.
20: 27 for the LORD had given them *c*
25: 19 ask for trouble and *c* your own
Job 5: 8 I would lay my *c* before him.
Ps 7: 4 or without *c* have robbed my foe—
9: 4 have upheld my right and my *c*;
35: 7 and without *c* dug a pit for me,
35: 7 they hid their net for me without *c*
35: 19 who are my enemies without *c*;
37: 6 of your *c* like the noonday sun.
43: 1 and plead my *c* against an ungodly
69: 4 many are my enemies without *c*,
74: 22 Rise up, O God, and defend your *c*;
82: 3 Defend the *c* of the weak
109: 3 they attack me without *c*.
119: 78 for wronging me without *c*;
119: 86 for men persecute me without *c*.
119:154 Defend my *c* and redeem me;
119:161 Rulers persecute me without *c*,
140: 12 and upholds the *c* of the needy.
146: 7 He upholds the *c* of the oppressed
Pr 24: 28 against your neighbor without *c*,
Ecc 8: 3 Do not stand up for a bad *c*,
Isa 1: 17 Defend the *c* of the fatherless,
1: 23 They do not defend the *c*
16: 5 and speeds the *c* of righteousness.
30: 30 The LORD will *c* men
34: 8 of retribution, to uphold Zion's *c*.
40: 27 my *c* is disregarded by my God"?
47: 12 perhaps you will *c* terror.
53: 10 to crush him and *c* him to suffer,
58: 14 I will *c* you to ride on the heights
64: 2 *c* the nations to quake before you!
Jer 11: 20 for to you I have committed my *c*.
20: 12 for to you I have committed my *c*.
22: 16 He defended the *c* of the poor
30: 13 There is no one to plead your *c*,
40: 15 and *c* all the Jews who are gathered
50: 34 He will vigorously defend their *c*
51: 36 "See, I will defend your *c*
La 3: 52 who were my enemies without *c*
3: 59 Uphold my *c*!
Eze 14: 23 I have done nothing in it without *c*,
32: 10 I will *c* many peoples to be appalled
32: 12 I will *c* your hordes to fall
33: 12 of the wicked man will not *c* him
36: 12 I will *c* people, my people Israel,
36: 15 of the peoples or *c* your nation
Da 8: 24 He will *c* astounding devastation
8: 25 He will *c* deceit to prosper,
Mt 18: 7 of the things that *c* people to sin!
Lk 2: 34 child is destined to *c* the falling
17: 1 "Things that *c* people
17: 2 neck than for him to *c* one
Ro 14: 21 else that will *c* your brother
16: 17 out for those who *c* divisions
1Co 8: 13 so that I will not *c* him to fall.
10: 32 Do not *c* anyone to stumble,

2Co 4:15 more people may *c* thanksgiving
Gal 6:17 Finally, let no one *c* me trouble,
Php 4:3 at my side in the *c* of the gospel,
Heb 12:15 no bitter root grows up to *c* trouble
Rev 13:15 and *c* all who refused to worship

CAUSED (CAUSE)

Ge 2:21 the LORD God *c* the man to fall
5:29 and painful toil of our hands *c*
Jdg 7:22 the LORD *c* the men
1Ki 11:25 adding to the trouble *c* by Hadad.
14:16 and has *c* Israel to commit."
15:26 which he had *c* Israel to commit.
15:30 and had *c* Israel to commit,
15:34 which he had *c* Israel to commit.
16:2 and *c* my people Israel to sin
16:13 and had *c* Israel to commit,
16:19 and had *c* Israel to commit.
16:26 which he had *c* Israel to commit,
21:22 to anger and have *c* Israel to sin.'
22:52 son of Nebat, who *c* Israel to sin.
2Ki 3:3 which he had *c* Israel to commit;
7:6 for the Lord had *c* the Arameans
10:29 which he had *c* Israel to commit—
10:31 which he had *c* Israel to commit.
13:2 which he had *c* Israel to commit,
13:6 which he had *c* Israel to commit;
13:11 which he had *c* Israel to commit;
14:24 which he had *c* Israel to commit.
15:9 which he had *c* Israel to commit.
15:18 which he had *c* Israel to commit.
15:24 which he had *c* Israel to commit.
15:28 which he had *c* Israel to commit.
17:21 and *c* them to commit a great sin.
21:16 besides the sin that he had *c* Judah
23:15 of Nebat, who had *c* Israel to sin—
2Ch 21:11 and had *c* the people of Jerusalem
Ezr 6:12 who has *c* his Name to dwell there,
Job 34:28 They *c* the cry of the poor to come
Ps 106:46 He *c* them to be pitied
111:4 He has *c* his wonders
140:9 with the trouble their lips have *c*.
Isa 21:2 to an end all the groaning she *c*.
Jer 50:6 *c* them to roam on the mountains.
Eze 32:30 slain in disgrace despite the terror *c*
Da 1:9 Now God had *c* the official
Am 3:6 has not the LORD *c* it?
Mal 2:8 and by your teaching have *c* many
2:9 "So I have *c* you to be despised
Ac 10:40 the dead on the third day and *c* him
17:6 "These men who have *c* trouble all
2Co 2:5 If anyone has *c* grief, he has not
7:8 Even if I *c* you sorrow by my letter,
Jas 4:5 without reason that the spirit he *c*
2Pe 1:4 in the world *c* by evil desires.

CAUSES (CAUSE)

Nu 5:21 you when he *c* your thigh
2Ch 21:15 until the disease *c* your bowels
Ps 7:16 The trouble he *c* recoils on himself;
Pr 10:10 He who winks maliciously *c* grief,
Isa 8:14 a stone that *c* men to stumble
61:11 and a garden *c* seeds to grow,
64:2 and *c* water to boil,
Da 8:13 the rebellion that *c* desolation,
9:27 one who *c* desolation will place
11:31 the abomination that *c* desolation.
12:11 abomination that *c* desolation is set
Mt 5:29 If your right eye *c* you to sin,
5:30 And if your right hand *c* you to sin,
5:32 for marital unfaithfulness, *c* her
5:45 He *c* his sun to rise on the evil
13:41 his kingdom everything that *c* sin
18:6 if anyone *c* one of these little ones
18:8 or your foot *c* you to sin,
18:9 And if your eye *c* you to sin,
24:15 'the abomination that *c* desolation,'
Mk 9:42 if anyone *c* one of these little ones
9:43 If your hand *c* you to sin, cut it off.
9:45 And if your foot *c* you to sin,
9:47 And if your eye *c* you to sin,
13:14 'the abomination that *c* desolation'
Ro 9:33 lay in Zion a stone that *c* men
14:20 to eat anything that *c* someone else
1Co 8:13 if what I eat *c* my brother to fall
Col 2:19 grows as God *c* it to grow.
Jas 4:1 What *c* fights and quarrels
1Pe 2:8 "A stone that *c* men to stumble

CAUSING (CAUSE)

Dt 8:3 *c* you to hunger and then feeding
1Ki 17:20 staying with, by *c* her son to die?"
Ps 105:29 *c* their fish to die.
Rev 13:13 *c* fire to come down from heaven

CAUTIONED (CAUTIOUS)

Ac 23:22 the young man and *c* him,

CAUTIOUS (CAUTIONED)

Pr 12:26 A righteous man is *c* in friendship,

CAVALRY

Ne 2:9 sent army officers and *c* with me.
Da 11:40 and *c* and a great fleet of ships.
Joel 2:4 they gallop along like *c*.
Na 3:3 Charging *c*,
Hab 1:8 Their *c* gallops headlong;
Ac 23:32 The next day they let the *c* go
23:33 When the *c* arrived in Caesarea,

CAVE (CAVERNS CAVES)

Ge 19:30 and his two daughters lived in a *c*.
23:9 behalf so he will sell me the *c*
23:11 and I give you the *c* that is in it.
23:17 both the field and the *c* in it,
23:19 in the *c* in the field of Machpelah
23:20 the *c* in it were deeded to Abraham
25:9 in the *c* of Machpelah near Mamre,
49:29 with my fathers in the *c* in the field
49:30 the *c* in the field of Machpelah,
49:32 and the *c* in it were bought
50:13 and buried him in the *c* in the field
Jos 10:16 and hidden in the *c* at Makkedah.
10:17 hiding in the *c* at Makkedah,
10:18 up to the mouth of the *c*,
10:22 "Open the mouth of the *c*
10:23 the five kings out of the *c*—
10:27 into the *c* where they had been
10:27 of the *c* they placed large rocks,
Jdg 15:8 stayed in a *c* in the rock of Etam.
15:11 down to the *c* in the rock of Etam
1Sa 22:1 and escaped to the *c* of Adullam.
24:3 a *c* was there, and Saul went
24:3 and his men were far back in the *c*.
24:7 Saul left the *c* and went his way.
24:8 Then David went out of the *c*
24:10 you into my hands in the *c*.
2Sa 17:9 hidden in a *c* or some other place.
23:13 down to David at the *c* of Adullam,
1Ki 19:9 There he went into a *c*
19:13 and stood at the mouth of the *c*.
1Ch 11:15 to the rock at the *c* of Adullam,
Jer 48:28 nest at the mouth of a *c*.
Jn 11:38 It was a *c* with a stone laid

CAVERNS (CAVE)

Isa 2:21 They will flee to *c* in the rocks

CAVES (CAVE)

Jdg 6:2 for themselves in mountain clefts, *c*
1Sa 13:6 they hid in *c* and thickets,
1Ki 18:4 and hidden them in two *c*,
18:13 of the LORD's prophets in two *c*,
Isa 2:19 Men will flee to *c* in the rocks
Jer 49:8 Turn and flee, hide in deep *c*,
49:30 Stay in deep *c*, you who live
Eze 33:27 those in strongholds and *c* will die
Heb 11:38 and in *c* and holes in the ground.
Rev 6:15 and every free man hid in *c*

CEASE (CEASED CEASING)

Ge 8:22 will never *c*."
Jos 9:23 You will never *c* to serve
2Ki 18:6 and did not *c* to follow him;
Ne 9:19 of cloud did not *c* to guide them
Est 9:28 days of Purim should never *c*
Job 3:17 There the wicked *c* from turmoil,
6:17 but that *c* to flow in the dry season,
Ps 46:9 He makes wars *c* to the ends
Ecc 12:3 when the grinders *c* because they
Isa 16:4 and destruction will *c*;
Jer 18:14 ever *c* to flow?
31:36 the descendants of Israel ever *c*
47:6 *c* and be still.'
Eze 5:13 "Then my anger will *c*
1Co 12:15 not for that reason *c* to be part
12:16 not for that reason *c* to be part
1Co 13:8 they will *c*; where there are tongues

CEASED (CEASE)

Jdg 5:7 Village life in Israel *c*,
5:7 *c* until I, Deborah, arose,
Ps 36:3 he has *c* to be wise and to do good.

CEASING (CEASE)

Ps 35:15 They slandered me without *c*.
Jer 14:17 night and day without *c*;

CEDAR (CEDARS)

Lev 14:4 live clean birds and some *c* wood,
14:6 with the *c* wood, the scarlet yarn
14:49 to take two birds and some *c* wood,
14:51 Then he is to take the *c* wood,
14:52 water, the live bird, the *c* wood,
Nu 19:6 The priest is to take some *c* wood,
2Sa 5:11 along with *c* logs and carpenters
7:2 "Here I am, living in a palace of *c*,
7:7 you not built me a house of *c*?"'
1Ki 4:33 from the *c* of Lebanon
5:8 do all you want in providing the *c*
5:10 Solomon supplied with all the *c*
6:9 roofing it with beams and *c* planks.
6:10 to the temple by beams of *c*.
6:15 its interior walls with *c* boards,
6:16 the temple with *c* boards from floor
6:18 Everything was *c*; no stone was
6:18 The inside of the temple was *c*,
6:20 and he also overlaid the altar of *c*.
6:36 one course of trimmed *c* beams.
7:2 of *c* columns supporting trimmed
7:2 supporting trimmed *c* beams.
7:3 It was roofed with *c*
7:7 and he covered it with *c* from floor
7:11 cut to size, and *c* beams.
7:12 one course of trimmed *c* beams,
9:11 had supplied him with all the *c*
10:27 *c* as plentiful as sycamore-fig trees
2Ki 14:9 in Lebanon sent a message to a *c*
1Ch 14:1 along with *c* logs, stonemasons
17:1 "Here I am, living in a palace of *c*,
17:6 you not built me a house of *c*?"'
22:4 also provided more *c* logs
2Ch 1:15 *c* as plentiful as sycamore-fig trees
2:3 David when you sent him *c*
2:3 "Send me *c* logs as you did
2:8 also *c*, pine and algum logs
9:27 *c* as plentiful as sycamore-fig trees
25:18 in Lebanon sent a message to a *c*
Ezr 3:7 so that they would bring *c* logs
Job 40:17 His tail sways like a *c*;
Ps 92:12 they will grow like a *c* of Lebanon;
SS 8:9 we will enclose her with panels of *c*
Isa 41:19 the *c* and the acacia, the myrtle
Jer 22:7 they will cut up your fine *c* beams
22:14 panels it with *c*
22:15 a king to have more and more *c*?
22:23 who are nestled in *c* buildings,
Eze 17:3 Taking hold of the top of a *c*,
17:22 a shoot from the very top of a *c*
17:23 bear fruit and become a splendid *c*.
27:5 they took a *c* from Lebanon
31:3 Consider Assyria, once a *c*
Hos 14:5 Like a *c* of Lebanon
14:6 his fragrance like a *c* of Lebanon.
Zep 2:14 the beams of *c* will be exposed.
Zec 11:2 O pine tree, for the *c* has fallen;

CEDARS (CEDAR)

Nu 24:6 like *c* beside the waters.
Jdg 9:15 and consume the *c* of Lebanon!'
1Ki 5:6 give orders that *c* of Lebanon be
2Ki 19:23 I have cut down its tallest *c*,
Ps 29:5 in pieces the *c* of Lebanon.
29:5 of the LORD breaks the *c*;
80:10 the mighty *c* with its branches.
104:16 the *c* of Lebanon that he planted.
148:9 fruit trees and all *c*,
SS 1:17 The beams of our house are *c*
5:15 choice as its *c*.
Isa 2:13 for all the *c* of Lebanon, tall
9:10 but we will replace them with *c*."
14:8 Even the pine trees and the *c*
37:24 I have cut down its tallest *c*,
44:14 He cut down *c*,
Eze 31:8 The *c* in the garden of God

Am 2: 9 though he was tall as the *c*
Zec 11: 1 so that fire may devour your *c!*

CEILING

1Ki 6: 15 the floor of the temple to the *c,*
6: 16 boards from floor to *c* to form
7: 7 it with cedar from floor to *c.*
2Ch 3: 7 overlaid the *c* beams, doorframes,

CELEBRATE (CELEBRATED CELEBRATING CELEBRATION CELEBRATIONS)

Ex 10: 9 we are to *c* a festival to the LORD
12: 14 generations to come you shall *c* it
12: 17 *C* this day as a lasting ordinance
12: 17 "*C* the Feast of Unleavened Bread,
12: 47 community of Israel must *c* it.
12: 48 to *c* the LORD's Passover must
23: 14 are to *c* a festival to me.
23: 15 "*C* the Feast of Unleavened Bread;
23: 16 "*C* the Feast of Harvest
23: 16 "*C* the Feast of Ingathering
34: 18 "*C* the Feast of Unleavened Bread.
34: 22 "*C* the Feast of Weeks
Lev 23: 39 *c* the festival to the LORD
23: 41 *C* this as a festival to the LORD
23: 41 for the generations to come; *c* it
Nu 9: 2 "Have the Israelites *c* the Passover
9: 3 *C* it at the appointed time,
9: 4 told the Israelites to *c* the Passover,
9: 6 of them could not *c* the Passover
9: 10 they may still *c* the LORD's
9: 11 are to *c* it on the fourteenth day
9: 12 When they *c* the Passover,
9: 13 on a journey fails to *c* the Passover,
9: 14 to *c* the LORD's Passover must do
29: 12 *C* a festival to the LORD
Dt 16: 1 *c* the Passover of the LORD your
16: 10 Then *c* the Feast of Weeks
16: 13 *C* the Feast of Tabernacles
16: 15 For seven days *c* the Feast
Jdg 16: 23 to Dagon their god and to *c,*
2Sa 6: 21 the LORD's people Israel—I will *c*
2Ki 23: 21 "*C* the Passover to the LORD your
2Ch 30: 1 and *c* the Passover to the LORD,
30: 2 decided to *c* the Passover
30: 3 able to *c* it at the regular time
30: 5 and *c* the Passover to the LORD,
30: 13 in Jerusalem to *c* the Feast
30: 23 to *c* the festival seven more days;
Ne 8: 12 of food and to *c* with great joy,
12: 27 to *c* joyfully the dedication
Est 9: 21 to have them *c* annually
Ps 145: 7 They will *c* your abundant
Isa 30: 29 as on the night you *c* a holy festival
Na 1: 15 *C* your festivals, O Judah,
Zec 14: 16 and to *c* the Feast of Tabernacles.
14: 18 up to *c* the Feast of Tabernacles.
14: 19 up to *c* the Feast of Tabernacles.
Mt 26: 18 I am going to *c* the Passover
Lk 15: 23 Let's have a feast and *c.*
15: 24 So they began to *c.*
15: 29 goat so I could *c* with my friends.
15: 32 But we had to *c* and be glad,
Rev 11: 10 will *c* by sending each other gifts,

CELEBRATED (CELEBRATE)

Jos 5: 10 the Israelites *c* the Passover.
1Ki 8: 65 They *c* it before the LORD our
2Ki 23: 23 this Passover was *c* to the LORD
2Ch 7: 9 for they had *c* the dedication
30: 5 It had not been *c* in large numbers
30: 21 present in Jerusalem *c* the Feast
30: 23 another seven days they *c* joyfully.
35: 1 Josiah *c* the Passover to the LORD
35: 17 who were present *c* the Passover
35: 18 of Israel had ever *c* such a Passover
35: 19 This Passover was *c*
Ezr 3: 4 they *c* the Feast of Tabernacles
6: 16 *c* the dedication of the house
6: 19 month, the exiles *c* the Passover.
6: 22 For seven days they *c*
Ne 8: 17 the Israelites had not *c* it like this.
8: 18 They *c* the feast for seven days,
Est 9: 28 cease to be *c* by the Jews,

CELEBRATING (CELEBRATE)

Ex 31: 16 *c* it for the generations to come
2Sa 6: 5 of Israel were *c* with all their might
1Ch 13: 8 and all the Israelites were *c*
15: 29 she saw King David dancing and *c,*
Est 8: 17 with feasting and *c.*

CELEBRATION (CELEBRATE)

1Sa 11: 15 and all the Israelites held a great *c.*
2Ch 35: 16 out for the *c* of the Passover
Est 8: 15 And the city of Susa held a joyous *c*
9: 22 and their mourning into a day of *c.*
9: 23 to continue the *c* they had begun,
Ac 7: 41 and held a *c* in honor of what their
Col 2: 16 a New Moon *c* or a Sabbath day.

CELEBRATIONS (CELEBRATE)

Hos 2: 11 I will stop all her *c:*

CELESTIAL

2Pe 2: 10 afraid to slander *c* beings;
Jude : 8 authority and slander *c* beings.

CELL

Jer 37: 16 put into a vaulted *c* in a dungeon,
Ac 12: 7 appeared and a light shone in the *c.*
16: 24 he put them in the inner *c*

CENCHREA

Ac 18: 18 he had his hair cut off at *C*
Ro 16: 1 a servant of the church in *C.*

CENSER (CENSERS)

Lev 16: 12 is to take a *c* full of burning coals
Nu 16: 17 Each man is to take his *c*
16: 18 So each man took his *c,* put fire
16: 46 "Take your *c* and put incense in it,
2Ch 26: 19 who had a *c* in his hand ready
Eze 8: 11 Each had a *c* in his hand,
Rev 8: 3 Another angel, who had a golden *c,*
8: 5 Then the angel took the *c,*

CENSERS (CENSER)

Lev 10: 1 sons Nadab and Abihu took their *c,*
Nu 16: 6 Take *c* and tomorrow put fire
16: 17 Aaron are to present your *c* also."
16: 17 it—250 *c* in all—and present
16: 37 for the *c* are holy—the *c*
16: 37 to take the *c* out of the smoldering
16: 38 Hammer the *c* into sheets
16: 39 collected the bronze *c* brought
1Ki 7: 50 sprinkling bowls, ladles and *c;*
2Ki 25: 15 the imperial guard took away the *c*
2Ch 4: 22 sprinkling bowls, ladles and *c;*
Jer 52: 19 *c,* sprinkling bowls, pots,

CENSUS

Ex 30: 12 When you take a *c* of the Israelites
38: 25 counted in the *c* was 100 talents
Nu 1: 2 "Take a *c* of the whole Israelite
1: 49 or include them in the *c*
4: 2 "Take a *c* of the Kohathite branch
4: 22 "Take a *c* also of the Gershonites
14: 29 or more who was counted in the *c*
26: 2 "Take a *c* of the whole Israelite
26: 4 "Take a *c* of the men twenty years
2Ki 12: 4 the money collected in the *c,*
1Ch 21: 1 incited David to take a *c* of Israel.
2Ch 2: 17 Solomon took a *c* of all the aliens
2: 17 after the *c* his father David had
Lk 2: 1 a decree that a *c* should be taken
2: 2 (This was the first *c* that took place
Ac 5: 37 appeared in the days of the *c*

CENTER (CENTERS)

Ex 26: 28 The *c* crossbar is to extend
28: 32 an opening for the head in its *c.*
36: 33 They made the *c* crossbar
39: 23 with an opening in the *c*
Nu 35: 5 on the north, with the town in the *c*
Jdg 9: 37 down from the *c* of the land,
1Ki 7: 25 hindquarters were toward the *c.*
2Ch 4: 4 hindquarters were toward the *c.*
6: 13 it in the *c* of the outer court.
Eze 1: 4 *c* of the fire looked like glowing
5: 5 set in the *c* of the nations,
38: 12 living at the *c* of the land."
48: 8 the sanctuary will be in the *c* of it.
Eze 48: 10 In the *c* of it will be the sanctuary
48: 15 The city will be in the *c* of it
48: 21 temple sanctuary will be in the *c*
48: 22 lie in the *c* of the area that belongs
Rev 4: 6 In the *c,* around the throne,
5: 6 standing in the *c* of the throne,
7: 17 For the Lamb at the *c*

CENTERS (CENTER)

Ge 10: 10 The first *c* of his kingdom were

CENTRAL

Jdg 16: 29 reached toward the two *c* pillars

CENTURION (CENTURION'S CENTURIONS)

Mt 8: 5 had entered Capernaum, a *c* came
8: 8 *c* replied, "Lord, I do not deserve
8: 13 Then Jesus said to the *c,* "Go!
27: 54 When the *c* and those
Mk 15: 39 And when the *c,* who stood there
15: 44 Summoning the *c,* he asked him
15: 45 learned from the *c* that it was so,
Lk 7: 3 The *c* heard of Jesus and sent some
7: 6 when the *c* sent friends to say
23: 47 The *c,* seeing what had happened,
Ac 10: 1 a *c* in what was known
10: 22 come from Cornelius the *c.*
22: 25 Paul said to the *c* standing there,
22: 26 When the *c* heard this, he went
23: 18 The *c* said, "Paul, the prisoner,
24: 23 He ordered the *c* to keep Paul
27: 1 handed over to a *c* named Julius,
27: 6 There the *c* found an Alexandrian
27: 11 But the *c,* instead of listening
27: 31 Paul said to the *c* and the soldiers,
27: 43 the *c* wanted to spare Paul's life

CENTURION'S (CENTURION)

Lk 7: 2 There a *c* servant, whom his master

CENTURIONS (CENTURION)

Ac 23: 17 Paul called one of the *c* and said,
23: 23 two of his *c* and ordered them,

CEPHAS

Jn 1: 42 You will be called *C*" (which,
1Co 1: 12 another, "I follow *C*"; still another,
3: 22 Paul or Apollos or *C* or the world
9: 5 and the Lord's brothers and *C?*

CEREMONIAL (CEREMONY)

Lev 14: 2 at the time of his *c* cleansing,
15: 13 off seven days for his *c* cleansing;
Mk 7: 3 they give their hands a *c* washing,
Jn 2: 6 used by the Jews for *c* washing,
3: 25 Jew over the matter of *c* washing.
11: 55 to Jerusalem for their *c* cleansing
18: 28 to avoid *c* uncleanness the Jews did
Heb 9: 10 drink and various *c* washings—
13: 9 not by *c* foods, which are

CEREMONIALLY (CEREMONY)

Lev 4: 12 outside the camp to a place *c* clean,
5: 2 touches anything *c* unclean—
6: 11 the camp to a place that is *c* clean.
7: 19 anyone *c* clean may eat it.
7: 19 touches anything *c* unclean must
10: 14 Eat them in a *c* clean place;
11: 4 not have a split hoof; it is *c* unclean
12: 2 birth to a son will be *c* unclean
12: 7 and then she will be *c* clean
13: 3 he shall pronounce him *c* unclean.
14: 8 with water; then he will be *c* clean.
15: 28 and after that she will be *c* clean.
15: 33 lies with a woman who is *c* unclean.
21: 1 must not make himself *c* unclean
22: 3 of your descendants is *c* unclean
27: 11 he vowed is a *c* unclean animal—
Nu 5: 2 who is *c* unclean because of a dead
6: 7 must not make himself *c* unclean
8: 6 Israelites and make them *c* clean.
9: 6 they were *c* unclean on account
9: 13 But if a man who is *c* clean
18: 11 household who is *c* clean may eat
18: 13 household who is *c* clean may eat
19: 7 but he will be *c* unclean till evening
19: 9 and put them in a *c* clean place

Nu 19:18 Then a man who is *c* clean is
Dt 12:15 Both the *c* unclean and the clean
12:22 Both the *c* unclean and the clean
14: 7 they are *c* unclean for you.
15:22 Both the *c* unclean and the clean
1Sa 20:26 to David to make him *c* unclean—
2Ch 13:11 the bread on the *c* clean table
30:17 for all those who were not *c* clean
Ezr 6:20 themselves and were all *c* clean.
Ne 12:30 Levites had purified themselves *c*,
Isa 66:20 of the LORD in *c* clean vessels.
Eze 22:10 period when they are *c* unclean.
Mk 7: 2 that is, *c* unwashed—hands.
Ac 24:18 I was *c* clean when they found me
Heb 9:13 those who are *c* unclean sanctify

CEREMONIES (CEREMONY)

Heb 9:21 and everything used in its *c*.

CEREMONY (CEREMONIAL CEREMONIALLY CEREMONIES)

Ge 50:11 Egyptians are holding a solemn *c*
Ex 12:25 as he promised, observe this *c*.
12:26 'What does this *c* mean to you?'
13: 5 are to observe this *c* in this month:

CERTAIN (CERTAINTY)

Ge 15:13 for *c* that your descendants will be
28:11 When he reached a *c* place,
Nu 16: 1 and *c* Reubenites—Dathan
Jos 8:14 at a *c* place overlooking the Arabah
Jdg 13: 2 A *c* man of Zorah, named Manoah,
1Sa 1: 1 There was a *c* man
21: 2 king charged me with a *c* matter
21: 2 them to meet me at a *c* place.
25: 2 *c* man in Maon, who had property
2Sa 12: 1 "There were two men in a *c* town,
1Ki 13:11 there was a *c* old prophet living
2Ki 19: 7 that when he hears a *c* report,
2Ch 17: 8 With them were *c* Levites—
Ne 7:73 along with *c* of the people
Est 3: 8 "There is a *c* people dispersed
Isa 37: 7 so that when he hears a *c* report,
Da 2: 8 "I am *c* that you are trying
Hos 5: 9 I proclaim what is *c*.
Mt 26:18 "Go into the city to a *c* man
Mk 15:21 A *c* man from Cyrene, Simon,
Lk 7:41 money to a *c* moneylender.
11: 1 day Jesus was praying in a *c* place.
12:16 of a *c* rich man produced a good
14:16 "A *c* man was preparing a great
18: 2 "In a *c* town there was a judge who
18:18 *c* ruler asked him, "Good teacher,
Jn 3:25 and a *c* Jew over the matter
4:46 there was a *c* royal official whose
Ac 7:16 at Shechem for a *c* sum of money.
28:23 arranged to meet Paul on a *c* day,
Gal 2:12 Before *c* men came from James,
1Ti 1: 3 that you may command *c* men not
4: 3 order them to abstain from *c* foods,
Heb 4: 7 Therefore God again set a *c* day,
11: 1 and *c* of what we do not see.
2Pe 1:19 word of the prophets made more *c*,
Jude : 4 For *c* men whose condemnation

CERTAINTY (CERTAIN)

Lk 1: 4 so that you may know the *c*
Jn 17: 8 They knew with *c* that I came

CERTIFICATE (CERTIFIED)

Dt 24: 1 and he writes her a *c* of divorce,
24: 3 and writes her a *c* of divorce,
Isa 50: 1 "Where is your mother's *c*
Jer 3: 8 I gave faithless Israel her *c*
Mt 5:31 divorces his wife must give her a *c*
19: 7 that a man give his wife a *c*
Mk 10: 4 a man to write a *c* of divorce

CERTIFIED (CERTIFICATE)

Jn 3:33 has accepted it has *c* that God is

CHAFF

Job 13:25 Will you chase after dry *c*?
21:18 like *c* swept away by a gale?
41:28 slingstones are like *c* to him.
Ps 1: 4 They are like *c*
35: 5 May they be like *c* before the wind,
83:13 like *c* before the wind.
Isa 17:13 before the wind like *c* on the hills,
29: 5 the ruthless hordes like blown *c*.
33:11 You conceive *c*,
40:24 sweeps them away like *c*.
41: 2 to windblown *c* with his bow.
41:15 and reduce the hills to *c*.
Jer 13:24 "I will scatter you like *c*
Da 2:35 became like *c* on a threshing floor
Hos 13: 3 like *c* swirling from a threshing
Zep 2: 2 and that day sweeps on like *c*,
Mt 3:12 up the *c* with unquenchable fire."
Lk 3:17 but he will burn up the *c*

CHAIN (CHAINED CHAINS)

Ge 41:42 and put a gold *c* around his neck.
2Ch 3: 5 it with palm tree and *c* designs.
Pr 1: 9 and a *c* to adorn your neck.
Da 5: 7 and have a gold *c* placed
5:16 and have a gold *c* placed
5:29 a gold *c* was placed around his neck
Mk 5: 3 him any more, not even with a *c*.
Ac 28:20 of Israel that I am bound with this *c*
Rev 20: 1 and holding in his hand a great *c*.

CHAINED (CHAIN)

Mk 5: 4 For he had often been *c* hand
Lk 8:29 and though he was *c* hand and foot
2Ti 2: 9 But God's word is not *c*.
2: 9 the point of being *c* like a criminal.
Heb 11:36 while still others were *c*

CHAINS (CHAIN)

Ex 28:14 and attach the *c* to the settings.
28:14 and two braided *c* of pure gold,
28:22 For the breastpiece make braided *c*
28:24 Fasten the two gold *c* to the rings
28:25 ends of the *c* to the two settings,
39:15 breastpiece they made braided *c*
39:17 They fastened the two gold *c*
39:18 ends of the *c* to the two settings,
Jdg 8:26 *c* that were on their camels' necks.
1Ki 6:21 he extended gold *c* across the front
7:17 network of interwoven *c* festooned
2Ki 23:33 Pharaoh Neco put him in *c*
2Ch 3:16 He made interwoven *c*
3:16 and attached them to the *c*.
Job 36: 8 But if men are bound in *c*,
Ps 2: 3 "Let us break their *c*," they say,
107:10 prisoners suffering in iron *c*,
107:14 and broke away their *c*.
116:16 you have freed me from my *c*.
Ecc 7:26 and whose hands are *c*.
Isa 3:20 the headdresses and ankle *c*
28:22 or your *c* will become heavier;
40:19 and fashions silver *c* for it.
45:14 coming over to you in *c*.
52: 2 yourself from the *c* on your neck,
58: 6 to loose the *c* of injustice
Jer 40: 1 bound in *c* among all the captives
40: 4 you from the *c* on your wrists.
La 3: 7 he has weighed me down with *c*.
Eze 7:23 "Prepare *c*, because the land is full
Na 3:10 and all her great men were put in *c*.
Mk 5: 4 but he tore the *c* apart
Lk 8:29 he had broken his *c* and had been
Ac 12: 6 with two *c*, and sentries stood
12: 7 and the *c* fell off Peter's wrists.
16:26 and everybody's *c* came loose.
21:33 him to be bound with two *c*.
22:29 had put Paul, a Roman citizen, in *c*.
26:29 what I am, except for these *c*."
Eph 6:20 for which I am an ambassador in *c*.
Php 1: 7 for whether I am in *c* or defending
1:13 and to everyone else that I am in *c*
1:14 Because of my *c*, most
1:17 trouble for me while I am in *c*.
Col 4: 3 of Christ, for which I am in *c*.
4:18 Remember my *c*.
2Ti 1:16 and was not ashamed of my *c*.
Phm :10 became my son while I was in *c*.
:13 me while I am in *c* for the gospel.
Jude : 6 with everlasting *c* for judgment

CHAIR

1Sa 1: 9 sitting on a *c* by the doorpost
4:13 sitting on his *c* by the side
4:18 backward off his *c* by the side
2Ki 4:10 and a table, a *c* and a lamp for him.

CHALCEDONY

Rev 21:19 the third *c*, the fourth emerald,

CHALDEA (CHALDEAN CHALDEANS)

Eze 23:15 chariot officers, natives of *C*.
23:16 and sent messengers to them in *C*.

CHALDEAN (CHALDEA)

Ezr 5:12 over to Nebuchadnezzar the *C*,

CHALDEANS (CHALDEA)

Ge 11:28 Haran died in Ur of the *C*,
11:31 from Ur of the *C* to go to Canaan.
15: 7 of Ur of the *C* to give you this land
Ne 9: 7 and brought him out of Ur of the *C*
Job 1:17 The *C* formed three raiding parties
Eze 12:13 land of the *C*, but he will not see it,
23:14 figures of *C* portrayed in red,
23:23 the Babylonians and all the *C*,
Ac 7: 4 "So he left the land of the *C*

CHALK

Isa 27: 9 to be like *c* stones crushed to pieces

CHALLENGE (CHALLENGED)

2Ki 14: 8 king of Israel, with the *c*: "Come,
2Ch 25:17 he sent this *c* to Jehoash son
Jer 49:19 Who is like me and who can *c* me?
50:44 Who is like me and who can *c* me?
Mal 3:15 and even those who *c* God escape

CHALLENGED (CHALLENGE)

Jn 8:13 The Pharisees *c* him, "Here you are
18:26 whose ear Peter had cut off, *c* him,

CHAMBER (CHAMBERS)

Job 37: 9 The tempest comes out from its *c*,
Ps 45:13 is the princess within her *c*;
Joel 2:16 and the bride her *c*.

CHAMBERS (CHAMBER)

Ezr 8:29 in the *c* of the house of the LORD
Ps 104: 3 of his upper *c* on their waters.
104:13 the mountains from his upper *c*;
Pr 7:27 leading down to the *c* of death.
SS 1: 4 The king has brought me into his *c*.

CHAMELEON

Lev 11:30 the wall lizard, the skink and the *c*

CHAMPION (CHAMPIONS)

1Sa 17: 4 A *c* named Goliath, who was
17:23 Goliath, the Philistine *c* from Gath
Ps 19: 5 like a *c* rejoicing to run his course.

CHAMPIONS (CHAMPION)

Isa 5:22 and *c* at mixing drinks,

CHANCE

Jos 8:20 but they had no *c* to escape
1Sa 6: 9 and that it happened to us by *c*."
19: 2 "My father Saul is looking for a *c*
Ecc 9:11 but time and *c* happen to them all.
Mk 6:31 that they did not even have a *c*

CHANGE (CHANGED CHANGERS CHANGES CHANGING)

Ge 35: 2 yourselves and *c* your clothes.
Ex 13:17 they might *c* their minds
Lev 13:16 Should the raw flesh *c*
Nu 23:19 of man, that he should *c* his mind.
23:20 he has blessed, and I cannot *c* it.
1Sa 15:29 of Israel does not lie or *c* his mind;
15:29 that he should *c* his mind."
2Sa 14:20 this to *c* the present situation.
1Ki 8:47 and if they have a *c* of heart
13:33 Jeroboam did not *c* his evil ways,
2Ch 6:37 and if they have a *c* of heart
Ezr 6:12 who lifts a hand to *c* this decree
Job 9:27 I will *c* my expression, and smile,'
14:20 you *c* his countenance
Ps 55:19 men who never *c* their ways
102:26 Like clothing you will *c* them
110: 4 and will not *c* his mind:
Jer 7: 5 If you really *c* your ways
13:16 and *c* it to deep gloom.
13:23 Can the Ethiopian *c* his skin
Da 2: 9 hoping the situation will *c*.

Da 7:25 his saints and try to *c* the set times
Mal 3: 6 "I the LORD do not *c*.
Mt 18: 3 unless you *c* and become like little
Ac 6:14 and *c* the customs Moses handed
Gal 4:20 be with you now and *c* my tone,
Heb 7:12 there must also be a *c* of the law.
7:12 when there is a *c* of the priesthood,
7:21 and will not *c* his mind:
12:17 He could bring about no *c* of mind,
Jas 1:17 who does not *c* like shifting
4: 9 *C* your laughter to mourning
Jude : 4 who *c* the grace of our God

CHANGED (CHANGE)

Ge 31:41 and you *c* my wages ten times.
41:14 he had shaved and *c* his clothes,
Ex 7:15 in your hand the staff that was *c*
7:17 and it will be *c* into blood.
7:20 and all the water was *c* into blood.
10:19 And the LORD *c* the wind
14: 5 and his officials *c* their minds about
Lev 13:55 mildew has not *c* its appearance,
Nu 32:38 Baal Meon (these names were *c*)
Jdg 7:19 just after they had *c* the guard.
1Sa 10: 6 you will be *c* into a different person
10: 9 to leave Samuel, God *c* Saul's heart
2Sa 12:20 put on lotions and *c* his clothes,
1Ki 2:15 things *c*, and the kingdom has gone
2Ki 23:34 *c* Eliakim's name to Jehoiakim.
24: 1 But then he *c* his mind
24:17 and *c* his name to Zedekiah.
2Ch 36: 4 *c* Eliakim's name to Jehoiakim.
Jer 2:11 Has a nation ever *c* its gods?
15: 7 for they have not *c* their ways.
34:11 But afterward they *c* their minds
Da 3:19 and his attitude toward them *c*.
4:16 Let his mind be *c* from that
6:15 edict that the king issues can be *c*."
6:17 Daniel's situation might not be *c*.
Hos 11: 8 My heart is *c* within me;
Mt 21:29 but later he *c* his mind and went.
Lk 9:29 the appearance of his face *c*,
Ac 28: 6 they *c* their minds and said he was
1Co 15:51 but we will all be *c*— in a flash,
15:52 imperishable, and we will be *c*.
Heb 1:12 like a garment they will be *c*.

CHANGERS (CHANGE)

Mt 21:12 the tables of the money *c*
Mk 11:15 the tables of the money *c*
Jn 2:15 scattered the coins of the money *c*

CHANGES (CHANGE)

Ezr 6:11 I decree that if anyone *c* this edict,
Ecc 8: 1 and *c* its hard appearance.
Da 2:21 He *c* times and seasons;

CHANGING (CHANGE)

Ge 31: 7 me by *c* my wages ten times.
Ezr 6:22 them with joy by *c* the attitude
Jer 2:36 *c* your ways?

CHANNEL (CHANNELED CHANNELS)

Job 38:25 Who cuts a *c* for the torrents of rain

CHANNELED (CHANNEL)

2Ch 32:30 *c* the water down to the west side

CHANNELS (CHANNEL)

Job 6:17 and in the heat vanish from their *c*.
Isa 8: 7 It will overflow all its *c*,
Eze 31: 4 and sent their *c*
Zec 4: 2 on it, with seven *c* to the lights.

CHANT

Eze 32:16 and all her hordes they will *c* it,
32:16 daughters of the nations will *c* it;
32:16 "This is the lament they will *c*

CHAOS

Isa 34:11 the measuring line of *c*

CHARACTER (CHARACTERS)

Ru 3:11 that you are a woman of noble *c*.
Pr 12: 4 of noble *c* is her husband's crown,
31:10 A wife of noble *c* who can find?
Ac 17:11 noble *c* than the Thessalonians,
Ro 5: 4 perseverance, *c*; and *c*, hope.
1Co 15:33 "Bad company corrupts good *c*."

CHARACTERS (CHARACTER)

Ac 17: 5 so they rounded up some bad *c*

CHARCOAL

Pr 26:21 As *c* to embers and as wood to fire,

CHARGE (CHARGED CHARGES CHARGING)

Ge 24: 2 the one in *c* of all that he had,
39: 4 him in *c* of his household,
39: 5 him in *c* of his household
39: 6 he had; with Joseph in *c*,
39: 8 "With me in *c*," he told her,
39:22 Joseph in *c* of all those held
41:33 put him in *c* of the land of Egypt.
41:40 You shall be in *c* of my palace,
41:41 you in *c* of the whole land
41:43 him in *c* of the whole land
47: 6 put them in *c* of my own livestock
Ex 5: 6 and foremen in *c* of the people:
22:25 like a moneylender; *c* him no
23: 7 Have nothing to do with a false *c*
Lev 5: 1 when he hears a public *c* to testify
Nu 1:50 Levites to be in *c* of the tabernacle
4:16 is to be in *c* of the entire tabernacle
4:16 is to have *c* of the oil for the light,
7: 2 in *c* of those who were counted,
18: 8 you in *c* of the offerings presented
Dt 22:20 the *c* is true and no proof
23:19 Do not *c* your brother interest,
23:20 You may *c* a foreigner interest,
2Sa 20:24 Adoniram was in *c* of forced labor;
23:23 him in *c* of his bodyguard.
1Ki 2: 1 he gave a *c* to Solomon his son.
4: 5 in *c* of the district officers;
4: 6 Ahishar—in *c* of the palace;
4: 6 son of Abda—in *c* of forced labor.
5:14 Adoniram was in *c*
9:23 in *c* of Solomon's projects—
11:28 him in *c* of the whole labor force
12:18 who was in *c* of forced labor,
16: 9 the man in *c* of the palace at Tirzah
18: 3 who was in *c* of his palace.
2Ki 7:17 officer on whose arm he leaned in *c*
11:15 who were in *c* of the troops:
15: 5 Jotham the king's son had *c*
25:19 in *c* of conscripting the people
25:19 the officer in *c* of the fighting men
1Ch 6:31 put in *c* of the music in the house
9:11 the official in *c* of the house of God
9:20 was in *c* of the gatekeepers,
9:23 and their descendants were in *c*
9:27 and they had *c* of the key
9:28 were in *c* of the articles used
9:32 their Kohathite brothers were in *c*
11:25 him in *c* of his bodyguard.
15:22 was in *c* of the singing;
15:27 who was in *c* of the singing
23:28 to be in *c* of the courtyards,
23:29 They were in *c* of the bread set out
26:20 were in *c* of the treasuries
26:22 They were in *c* of the treasuries
26:24 was the officer in *c* of the treasuries
26:26 and his relatives were in *c*
26:32 them in *c* of the Reubenites,
27: 2 In *c* of the first division,
27: 4 In *c* of the division
27: 6 was in *c* of his division.
27:25 was in *c* of the royal storehouses.
27:25 was in *c* of the storehouses
27:26 Ezri son of Kelub was in *c*
27:27 was in *c* of the produce
27:27 was in *c* of the vineyards.
27:28 Baal-Hanan the Gederite was in *c*
27:28 Joash was in *c* of the supplies
27:29 son of Adlai was in *c* of the herds
27:29 was in *c* of the herds grazing
27:30 was in *c* of the camels.
27:30 was in *c* of the donkeys.
27:31 Jaziz the Hagrite was in *c*
27:31 in *c* of King David's property.
28: 1 the officials in *c* of all the property
28: 8 now I *c* you in the sight of all Israel
29: 6 in *c* of the king's work gave
2Ch 10:18 who was in *c* of forced labor,
23:14 who were in *c* of the troops,
24:13 men in *c* of the work were diligent,
26:21 Jotham his son had *c* of the palace
28: 7 Azrikam the officer in *c*
31:12 a Levite, was in *c* of these things,
31:13 and Azariah the official in *c*
31:14 in *c* of the freewill offerings given
34:13 had *c* of the laborers
Ne 7: 2 put in *c* of Jerusalem my brother
11:16 who had *c* of the outside work
11:21 Ziha and Gishpa were in *c* of them.
12: 8 was in *c* of the songs
12:44 to be in *c* of the storerooms
13: 4 in *c* of the storerooms of the house
13:13 Pedaiah in *c* of the storerooms
Est 2: 3 is in *c* of the women;
2: 8 to Hegai, who had *c* of the harem.
2:14 was in *c* of the concubines.
2:15 the king's eunuch who was in *c*
Job 34:13 him in *c* of the whole world?
Ps 69:27 *C* them with crime upon crime;
SS 2: 7 Daughters of Jerusalem, I *c* you
3: 5 Daughters of Jerusalem, I *c* you
5: 8 O daughters of Jerusalem, I *c* you
5: 9 that you *c* us so?
8: 4 Daughters of Jerusalem, I *c* you:
Isa 3: 6 take *c* of this heap of ruins!"
22:15 to Shebna, who is in *c* of the palace:
33:18 the officer in *c* of the towers?"
Jer 15:13 I will give as plunder, without *c*,
29:26 of Jehoiada to be in *c* of the house
40: 7 and had put him in *c* of the men,
46: 9 *C*, O horses!
52:25 in *c* of conscripting the people
52:25 the officer in *c* of the fighting men,
Eze 40:45 is for the priests who have *c*
40:46 is for the priests who have *c*
44: 8 you put others in *c* of my sanctuary
44:11 having *c* of the gates of the temple
44:14 Yet I will put them in *c*
Da 2:48 placed him in *c* of all its wise men.
Hos 4: 1 because the LORD has a *c* to bring
4: 4 "But let no man bring a *c*,
12: 2 The LORD has a *c* to bring
Joel 2: 7 They *c* like warriors;
Mic 6: 2 he is lodging a *c* against Israel.
Zec 3: 6 of the LORD gave this *c* to Joshua:
3: 7 will govern my house and have *c*
Mt 24:45 put in *c* of the servants
24:47 him in *c* of all his possessions.
25:21 I will put you in *c* of many things.
25:23 I will put you in *c* of many things.
26:63 "I *c* you under oath
27:14 even to a single *c*— to the great
27:37 his head they placed the written *c*
Mk 3:21 they went to take *c* of him,
13:34 house in *c* of his servants,
15:26 notice of the *c* against him read:
Lk 12:42 puts in *c* of his servants
12:44 him in *c* of all his possessions.
19:17 in a very small matter, take *c*
19:19 "His master answered, 'You take *c*
23: 4 basis for a *c* against this man."
Jn 13:29 Since Judas had *c* of the money,
18:38 "I find no basis for a *c* against him.
19: 4 basis for a *c* against him."
19: 6 I find no basis for a *c* against him."
19:16 So the soldiers took *c* of Jesus.
Ac 8:27 an important official in *c*
23:29 but there was no *c* against him that
25:18 they did not *c* him with any
28:19 not that I had any *c* to bring
Ro 3: 9 have already made the *c* that Jews
8:33 Who will bring any *c*
1Co 9:18 the gospel I may offer it free of *c*,
2Co 11: 7 the gospel of God to you free of *c*?
Gal 3:24 So the law was put in *c* to lead us
1Th 5:27 I *c* you before the Lord
1Ti 5:21 I *c* you, in the sight of God
6:13 I *c* you to keep this commandment
2Ti 4: 1 I give you this *c*: Preach the Word;
Tit 1: 6 are not open to the *c* of being wild
Phm : 18 or owes you anything, *c* it to me.
Rev 14:18 Still another angel, who had *c*
16: 5 the angel in *c* of the waters say:

CHARGED (CHARGE)

Dt 1:16 And I *c* your judges at that time:
Jos 6:20 so every man *c* straight in,

Jdg 20: 33 and the Israelite ambush c out
1Sa 21: 2 The king c me with a certain matter
1Ch 22: 6 and c him to build a house
Eze 18: 20 of the wicked will be c against him.
Da 8: 4 I watched the ram as he c
8: 6 beside the canal and c at him
Ac 18: 13 they c, "is persuading the people
19: 40 are in danger of being c with rioting

CHARGES (CHARGE)

1Ki 21: 13 and brought c against Naboth
Ne 5: 6 I heard their outcry and these c,
Job 4: 18 if he c his angels with error,
10: 2 tell me what c you have against me.
13: 19 Can anyone bring c against me?
22: 4 and brings c against you?
23: 6 he would not press c against me.
24: 12 But God c no one with wrongdoing
39: 21 and c into the fray.
Isa 50: 8 Who then will bring c against me?
Jer 2: 9 will bring c against your children's
2: 9 "Therefore I bring c
2: 29 "Why do you bring c against me?
25: 31 for the LORD will bring c
Da 6: 4 to find grounds for c against Daniel
6: 5 basis for c against this man Daniel
Hos 4: 4 who bring c against a priest.
Lk 23: 14 basis for your c against him.
Jn 18: 29 "What c are you bringing
Ac 7: 1 "Are these c true?" To this he
19: 38 They can press c.
24: 1 they brought their c against Paul
24: 8 about all these c we are bringing
24: 13 to you the c they are now making
24: 19 and bring c if they have anything
25: 2 and presented the c against Paul.
25: 5 and press c against the man there,
25: 7 bringing many serious c
25: 9 trial before me there on these c?"
25: 11 But if the c brought against me
25: 15 of the Jews brought c against him
25: 16 to defend himself against their c.
25: 20 and stand trial there on these c.
25: 27 a prisoner without specifying the c

CHARGING (CHARGE)

Ne 5: 11 and also the usury you are c them
Job 1: 22 sin by c God with wrongdoing.
15: 26 defiantly c against him
Pr 28: 15 Like a roaring lion or a c bear
Jer 8: 6 like a horse c into battle.
Na 3: 3 C cavalry,

CHARIOT (CHARIOTEERS CHARIOTS)

Ge 41: 43 He had him ride in a c
46: 29 Joseph had his c made ready
Ex 14: 6 So he had his c made ready
Jdg 4: 15 and Sisera abandoned his c
5: 28 'Why is his c so long in coming?
2Sa 8: 4 but a hundred of the c horses.
15: 1 Absalom provided himself with a c
1Ki 4: 26 four thousand stalls for c horses,
4: 28 straw for the c horses and the other
7: 33 wheels were made like c wheels;
10: 26 which he kept in the c cities and
10: 29 They imported a c from Egypt
12: 18 managed to get into his c
18: 44 'Hitch up your c and go
20: 25 horse for horse and c for c—
20: 33 Ahab had him come up into his c
22: 31 his thirty-two c commanders,
22: 32 When the c commanders saw
22: 33 c commanders saw that he was not
22: 34 The king told his c driver,
22: 35 ran onto the floor of the c,
22: 35 up in his c facing the Arameans.
22: 38 They washed the c at a pool
2Ki 2: 11 suddenly a c of fire and horses
5: 21 got down from the c to meet him.
5: 26 got down from his c to meet you?
8: 21 him and his c commanders,
9: 16 he got into his c and rode to Jezreel
9: 21 each in his own c, to meet Jehu.
9: 21 "Hitch up my c," Joram ordered.
9: 24 and he slumped down in his c.
9: 25 Jehu said to Bidkar, his c officer,
9: 27 him in his c on the way up
9: 28 His servants took him by c
2Ki 10: 15 and Jehu helped him up into the c.
10: 16 Then he had him ride along in his c
23: 30 in a c from Megiddo to Jerusalem
1Ch 18: 4 but a hundred of the c horses.
28: 18 He also gave him the plan for the c,
2Ch 1: 14 which he kept in the c cities and
1: 17 They imported a c from Egypt
9: 25 which he kept in the c cities and
10: 18 managed to get into his c
18: 30 had ordered his c commanders,
18: 31 When the c commanders saw
18: 32 when the c commanders saw that
18: 33 The king told the c driver,
18: 34 up in his c facing the Arameans
21: 9 him and his c commanders,
35: 24 So they took him out of his c,
35: 24 put him in the other c he had
Ps 76: 6 both horse and c lie still.
104: 3 He makes the clouds his c
Isa 5: 28 their c wheels like a whirlwind.
21: 9 Look, here comes a man in a c
Jer 51: 21 with you I shatter c and driver,
Eze 23: 15 looked like Babylonian c officers,
23: 23 c officers and men of high rank,
Mic 1: 13 harness the team to the c.
Zec 6: 2 The first c had red horses,
Ac 8: 28 sitting in his c reading the book
8: 29 "Go to that c and stay near it."
8: 30 Then Philip ran up to the c
8: 38 And he ordered the c to stop.

CHARIOTEERS (CHARIOT)

1Sa 13: 5 thousand chariots, six thousand c,
2Sa 8: 4 seven thousand c and twenty
10: 18 killed seven hundred of their c
1Ki 9: 22 commanders of his chariots and c.
1Ch 18: 4 seven thousand c and twenty
19: 6 to hire chariots and c from Aram
19: 7 thirty-two thousand chariots and c,
19: 18 killed seven thousand of their c
2Ch 8: 9 commanders of his chariots and c.
Isa 22: 6 with her c and horses,
Jer 46: 9 Drive furiously, O c!

CHARIOTS (CHARIOT)

Ge 50: 9 C and horsemen also went up
Ex 14: 7 He took six hundred of the best c,
14: 7 along with all the other c of Egypt,
14: 9 all Pharaoh's horses and c,
14: 17 through his c and his horsemen.
14: 18 glory through Pharaoh, his c
14: 23 and all Pharaoh's horses and c
14: 25 made the wheels of their c come
14: 26 and their c and horsemen."
14: 28 and covered the c and horsemen—
15: 4 Pharaoh's c and his army
15: 19 c and horsemen went into the sea,
Dt 11: 4 to its horses and c,
20: 1 c and an army greater than yours,
Jos 11: 4 a large number of horses and c—
11: 6 their horses and burn their c."
11: 9 their horses and burned their c.
17: 16 live in the plain have iron c,
17: 18 the Canaanites have iron c and
24: 6 the Egyptians pursued them with c
Jdg 1: 19 the plains, because they had iron c.
4: 3 he had nine hundred iron c
4: 7 with his c and his troops
4: 13 together his nine hundred iron c
4: 15 all his c and army by the sword,
4: 16 But Barak pursued the c and army
5: 28 Why is the clatter of his c delayed?'
1Sa 8: 11 and make them serve with his c
8: 11 and they will run in front of his c.
8: 12 of war and equipment for his c.
13: 5 three thousand c, six thousand
2Sa 1: 6 with the c and riders almost
8: 4 David captured a thousand of his c,
1Ki 1: 5 So he got c and horses ready,
9: 19 and the towns for his c
9: 22 and the commanders of his c
10: 26 Solomon accumulated c and horses
10: 26 he had fourteen hundred c
16: 9 who had command of half his c,
20: 1 kings with their horses and c,
20: 21 and overpowered the horses and c
2Ki 2: 12 The c and horsemen of Israel!"
5: 9 Naaman went with his horses and c
2Ki 6: 14 Then he sent horses and c
6: 15 and c had surrounded the city.
6: 17 and c of fire all around Elisha.
7: 6 Arameans to hear the sound of c
7: 14 So they selected two c
8: 21 Jehoram went to Zair with all his c.
9: 25 in c behind Ahab his father
10: 2 and you have c and horses,
13: 7 ten c and ten thousand foot
13: 14 "The c and horsemen of Israel!"
18: 24 you are depending on Egypt for c
19: 23 "With my many c
23: 11 Josiah then burned the c dedicated
1Ch 18: 4 David captured a thousand of his c,
19: 6 a thousand talents of silver to hire c
19: 7 They hired thirty-two thousand c
2Ch 1: 14 Solomon accumulated c and horses
1: 14 he had fourteen hundred c
8: 6 cities for his c and for his horses—
8: 9 of his c and charioteers.
9: 25 thousand stalls for horses and c,
12: 3 With twelve hundred c
14: 9 a vast army and three hundred c,
16: 8 army with great numbers of c
21: 9 there with his officers and all his c.
Ps 20: 7 Some trust in c and some in horses,
68: 17 The c of God are tens of thousands
SS 1: 9 to one of the c of Pharaoh.
6: 12 among the royal c of my people.
Isa 2: 7 there is no end to their c.
21: 7 When he sees c
22: 7 Your choicest valleys are full of c,
22: 18 there your splendid c will remain—
31: 1 who trust in the multitude of their c
36: 9 you are depending on Egypt for c
37: 24 'With my many c
43: 17 who drew out the c and horses,
66: 15 and his c are like a whirlwind;
66: 20 on horses, in c and wagons,
Jer 4: 13 his c come like a whirlwind,
17: 25 their officials will come riding in c
22: 4 in c and on horses, accompanied
47: 3 at the noise of enemy c
50: 37 A sword against her horses and c
Eze 23: 24 c and wagons and with a throng
26: 7 king of kings, with horses and c,
26: 10 and c when he enters your gates
Da 11: 40 out against him with c
Joel 2: 5 With a noise like that of c
Mic 5: 10 and demolish your c.
Na 2: 3 The metal on the c flashes
2: 4 The c storm through the streets,
2: 13 "I will burn up your c in smoke,
3: 2 and jolting c!
Hab 3: 8 and your victorious c?
Hag 2: 22 I will overthrow c and their drivers;
Zec 6: 1 before me were four c coming out
9: 10 I will take away the c
Rev 9: 9 of many horses and c rushing

CHARM (CHARMED CHARMER CHARMING CHARMS)

Pr 17: 8 bribe is a c to the one who gives it;
31: 30 C is deceptive, and beauty is

CHARMED (CHARM)

Ecc 10: 11 If a snake bites before it is c,
Jer 8: 17 vipers that cannot be c,

CHARMER (CHARM)

Ps 58: 5 that will not heed the tune of the c,
Ecc 10: 11 there is no profit for the c.

CHARMING (CHARM)

Pr 26: 25 his speech is c, do not believe
SS 1: 16 Oh, how c!

CHARMS (CHARM)

Isa 3: 20 the perfume bottles and c,
Eze 13: 18 to the women who sew magic c
13: 20 I am against your magic c

CHARRED (CHARS)

Jdg 15: 14 on his arms became like c flax,
Eze 15: 5 the fire has burned it and it is c?
24: 10 and let the bones be c.

CHARS (CHARRED)

Eze 15: 4 burns both ends and *c* the middle,

CHASE (CHASED CHASES CHASING)

Lev 26: 8 Five of you will *c* a hundred,
26: 8 hundred of you will *c* ten thousand,
Dt 32: 30 How could one man *c* a thousand,
Job 13: 25 Will you *c* after dry chaff?
Isa 1: 23 and *c* after gifts.
Jer 49: 19 I will *c* Edom from its land
50: 44 I will *c* Babylon from its land
Hos 2: 7 She will *c* after her lovers

CHASED (CHASE)

Dt 1: 44 they *c* you like a swarm of bees
Jos 7: 5 They *c* the Israelites
8: 24 the desert where they had *c* them,
Jdg 1: 6 but they *c* him and caught him,
9: 40 Abimelech *c* him, and many fell
20: 43 *c* them and easily overran them
2Sa 2: 19 He *c* Abner, turning neither
2Ki 9: 27 Jehu *c* him, shouting, "Kill him too
Jer 50: 17 that lions have *c* away.
La 4: 19 they *c* us over the mountains

CHASES (CHASE)

Pr 12: 11 he who *c* fantasies lacks judgment.
28: 19 one who *c* fantasies will have his

CHASING (CHASE)

1Sa 17: 53 returned from *c* the Philistines,
2Sa 2: 21 But Asahel would not stop *c* him.
2: 22 Abner warned Asahel, "Stop *c* me!
Ecc 1: 14 all of them are meaningless, a *c*
1: 17 but I learned that this, too, is a *c*
2: 11 everything was meaningless, a *c*
2: 17 All of it is meaningless, a *c*
2: 26 This too is meaningless, a *c*
4: 4 This too is meaningless, a *c*
4: 6 and *c* after the wind.
4: 16 This too is meaningless, a *c*
6: 9 a *c* after the wind.

CHASM

Lk 16: 26 and you a great *c* has been fixed,

CHASTENED

Job 33: 19 Or a man may be *c* on a bed of pain
Ps 118: 18 The LORD has *c* me severely,

CHATTER (CHATTERING)

1Ti 6: 20 Turn away from godless *c*
2Ti 2: 16 Avoid godless *c*, because those

CHATTERING (CHATTER)

Pr 10: 8 but a *c* fool comes to ruin.
10: 10 and a *c* fool comes to ruin.

CHEAPER

Jn 2: 10 and then the *c* wine after the guests

CHEAT (CHEATED CHEATING CHEATS)

Mal 1: 14 "Cursed is the *c* who has
1Co 6: 8 you yourselves *c* and do wrong,

CHEATED (CHEAT)

Ge 31: 7 yet your father has *c* me
1Sa 12: 3 Whom have I *c*? Whom have I
12: 4 "You have not *c* or oppressed us,"
Lk 19: 8 if I have *c* anybody out of anything,
1Co 6: 7 Why not rather be *c*? Instead,

CHEATING (CHEAT)

Am 8: 5 and *c* with dishonest scales,

CHEATS (CHEAT)

Lev 6: 2 or if he *c* him, or if he finds lost

CHECK (CHECKED)

Ge 30: 33 whenever you *c* on the wages you
Jas 3: 2 able to keep his whole body in *c*.

CHECKED (CHECK)

2Ki 6: 10 So the king of Israel *c*
Ezr 8: 15 When I *c* among the people
Ps 106: 30 and the plague was *c*.

CHEEK (CHEEKS)

Job 16: 10 they strike my *c* in scorn
La 3: 30 Let him offer his *c*
Mic 5: 1 ruler on the *c* with a rod.
Mt 5: 39 someone strikes you on the right *c*,
Lk 6: 29 If someone strikes you on one *c*,

CHEEKS (CHEEK)

SS 1: 10 Your *c* are beautiful with earrings,
5: 13 His *c* are like beds of spice
Isa 50: 6 my *c* to those who pulled out my
La 1: 2 tears are upon her *c*.

CHEER (CHEERED CHEERFUL CHEERING CHEERS)

1Ki 21: 7 over Israel? Get up and eat! *C* up.
Mk 10: 49 they called to the blind man, "*C* up

CHEERED (CHEER)

Php 2: 19 also may be *c* when I receive news

CHEERFUL (CHEER)

Pr 15: 13 A happy heart makes the face *c*,
15: 15 but the *c* heart has a continual feast
15: 30 A *c* look brings joy to the heart,
17: 22 A *c* heart is good medicine,
2Co 9: 7 for God loves a *c* giver.

CHEERING (CHEER)

1Ki 1: 45 From there they have gone up *c*,
2Ch 23: 12 the people running and *c* the king,
Ecc 2: 3 I tried *c* myself with wine,

CHEERS (CHEER)

Jdg 9: 13 which *c* both gods and men,
Pr 12: 25 but a kind word *c* him up.

CHEESE (CHEESES)

2Sa 17: 29 and *c* from cows' milk for David
Job 10: 10 and curdle me like *c*,

CHEESES (CHEESE)

1Sa 17: 18 these ten *c* to the commander

CHEMOSH

Nu 21: 29 You are destroyed, O people of *C!*
Jdg 11: 24 take what your god *C* gives you?
1Ki 11: 7 for *C* the detestable god of Moab,
11: 33 *C* the god of the Moabites,
2Ki 23: 13 for *C* the vile god of Moab,
Jer 48: 7 and *C* will go into exile
48: 13 Then Moab will be ashamed of *C*,
48: 46 The people of *C* are destroyed;

CHERISH (CHERISHED CHERISHES)

Ps 17: 14 You still the hunger of those you *c*;
83: 3 they plot against those you *c*.

CHERISHED (CHERISH)

Ps 66: 18 If I had *c* sin in my heart,
Hos 9: 16 I will slay their *c* offspring."

CHERISHES (CHERISH)

Pr 19: 8 he who *c* understanding prospers.

CHERUB (CHERUBIM)

Ex 25: 19 Make one *c* on one end
25: 19 and the second *c* on the other;
37: 8 He made one *c* on one end
37: 8 and the second *c* on the other;
1Ki 6: 24 of the first *c* was five cubits long,
6: 25 second *c* also measured ten cubits,
6: 26 The height of each *c* was ten cubits.
6: 27 The wing of one *c* touched one wall
2Ch 3: 11 of the first *c* was five cubits long
3: 11 touched the wing of the other *c*.
3: 12 of the second *c* was five cubits long
3: 12 touched the wing of the first *c*.
Eze 10: 14 that of a *c*, the second the face
28: 14 You were anointed as a guardian *c*,
28: 16 and I expelled you, O guardian *c*,
41: 18 Each *c* had two faces: the face

CHERUBIM (CHERUB)

Ge 3: 24 side of the Garden of Eden *c*
Ex 25: 18 make two *c* out of hammered gold
25: 19 make the *c* of one piece
25: 20 The *c* are to face each other,
25: 20 *c* are to have their wings spread
25: 22 cover between the two *c* that are
26: 1 with *c* worked into them
26: 31 with *c* worked into it
36: 8 with *c* worked into them
36: 35 with *c* worked into it
37: 7 Then he made two *c* out
37: 9 The *c* faced each other, looking
37: 9 *c* had their wings spread upward,
Nu 7: 89 him from between the two *c*
1Sa 4: 4 who is enthroned between the *c*.
2Sa 6: 2 enthroned between the *c* that are
22: 11 He mounted the *c* and flew;
1Ki 6: 23 a pair of *c* of olive wood,
6: 25 for the two *c* were identical in size
6: 27 placed the *c* inside the innermost
6: 28 He overlaid the *c* with gold.
6: 29 he carved *c*, palm trees
6: 32 and overlaid the *c* and palm trees
6: 32 two olive wood doors he carved *c*,
6: 35 He carved *c*, palm trees
7: 29 bulls and *c*— and on the uprights
7: 36 He engraved *c*, lions and palm
8: 6 put it beneath the wings of the *c*.
8: 7 The *c* spread their wings
2Ki 19: 15 of Israel, enthroned between the *c*,
1Ch 13: 6 who is enthroned between the *c*—
28: 18 *c* of gold that spread their wings
2Ch 3: 7 and he carved *c* on the walls.
3: 10 he made a pair of sculptured *c*
3: 11 of the *c* was twenty cubits.
3: 13 of these *c* extended twenty cubits.
3: 14 fine linen, with *c* worked into it.
5: 7 put it beneath the wings of the *c*.
5: 8 The *c* spread their wings
Ps 18: 10 He mounted the *c* and flew;
80: 1 who sit enthroned between the *c*,
99: 1 he sits enthroned between the *c*,
Isa 37: 16 of Israel, enthroned between the *c*,
Eze 9: 3 of Israel went up from above the *c*,
10: 1 was over the heads of the *c*.
10: 2 burning coals from among the *c*
10: 2 in among the wheels beneath the *c*.
10: 3 Now the *c* were standing
10: 4 of the LORD rose from above the *c*
10: 5 of the wings of the *c* could be heard
10: 6 from among the *c*,"
10: 7 one of the *c* reached out his hand
10: 8 of the *c* could be seen what looked
10: 9 and I saw beside the *c* four wheels,
10: 9 of the *c*; the wheels sparkled like
10: 11 The *c* went in whatever direction
10: 11 did not turn about as the *c* went.
10: 11 of the four directions the *c* faced;
10: 14 Each of the *c* had four faces:
10: 15 Then the *c* rose upward.
10: 16 When the *c* moved, the wheels
10: 16 and when the *c* spread their wings
10: 17 When the *c* stood still, they
10: 17 and when the *c* rose, they rose
10: 18 temple and stopped above the *c*.
10: 19 the *c* spread their wings
10: 20 and I realized that they were *c*.
11: 22 the *c*, with the wheels beside them,
41: 18 Palm trees alternated with *c*.
41: 18 and outer sanctuary were carved *c*
41: 20 *c* and palm trees were carved
41: 25 the outer sanctuary were carved *c*
Heb 9: 5 Above the ark were the *c*

CHEST (CHESTS)

Ex 25: 10 "Have them make a *c*
25: 14 on the sides of the *c* to carry it.
Dt 10: 1 Also make a wooden *c*.
10: 2 Then you are to put them in the *c*."
1Sa 6: 8 in a *c* beside it put the gold objects
6: 11 with it the *c* containing the gold
6: 15 with the *c* containing the gold
2Ki 12: 9 Jehoiada the priest took a *c*
12: 9 into the *c* all the money that was
12: 10 amount of money in the *c*,
2Ch 24: 8 a *c* was made and placed outside,
24: 10 dropping them into the *c*
24: 11 Whenever the *c* was brought
24: 11 and empty the *c* and carry it back
Job 41: 24 His *c* is hard as rock,
Da 2: 32 its *c* and arms of silver, its belly
Rev 1: 13 with a golden sash around his *c*.

CHESTS (CHEST)

Rev 15: 6 wore golden sashes around their *c*.

CHEW (CHEWED CHEWS)

Lev 11: 4 There are some that only *c* the cud
11: 7 does not *c* the cud; it is unclean
11: 26 that does not *c* the cud is unclean
Dt 14: 7 Although they *c* the cud, they do
14: 7 of those that *c* the cud
14: 8 a split hoof, it does not *c* the cud.

CHEWED (CHEW)

Jnh 4: 7 which *c* the vine so that it withered

CHEWS (CHEW)

Lev 11: 3 divided and that *c* the cud.
11: 4 The camel, though it *c* the cud,
11: 5 The coney, though it *c* the cud,
11: 6 The rabbit, though it *c* the cud,
Dt 14: 6 divided in two and that *c* the cud.

CHICKS

Mt 23: 37 a hen gathers her *c* under her wings
Lk 13: 34 a hen gathers her *c* under her wings

CHIEF (CHIEFS)

Ge 24: 2 He said to the *c* servant
40: 2 the *c* cupbearer and the *c* baker,
40: 9 *c* cupbearer told Joseph his dream.
40: 16 When the *c* baker saw that Joseph
40: 20 and the *c* baker in the presence
40: 20 the heads of the *c* cupbearer
40: 21 He restored the *c* cupbearer
40: 22 but he hanged the *c* baker,
40: 23 The *c* cupbearer, however,
41: 9 the *c* cupbearer said to Pharaoh,
41: 10 and the *c* baker in the house
Nu 3: 32 *c* leader of the Levites was Eleazar
25: 15 a tribal *c* of a Midianite family.
Dt 29: 10 your leaders and *c* men, your
Jos 22: 14 him they sent ten of the *c* men,
2Sa 23: 8 a Tahkemonite, was *c* of the Three;
23: 13 three of the thirty *c* men came
23: 18 son of Zeruiah was *c* of the Three.
1Ki 4: 2 And these were his *c* officials:
4: 4 commander in *c*; Zadok
9: 23 also the *c* officials in charge
2Ki 10: 11 as all his *c* men, his close friends
15: 25 One of his *c* officers, Pekah son
18: 17 his *c* officer and his field
25: 18 as prisoners Seraiah the *c* priest,
25: 19 the secretary who was *c* officer
1Ch 5: 7 Jeiel the *c*, Zechariah,
5: 12 Joel was the *c*, Shapham
9: 17 Shallum their *c* being stationed
11: 11 a Hacmonite, was *c* of the officers;
11: 20 brother of Joab was *c* of the Three.
11: 42 who was *c* of the Reubenites,
12: 3 Ahiezer their *c* and Joash the sons
12: 9 Ezer was the *c*, Obadiah
12: 18 came upon Amasai, *c* of the Thirty,
16: 5 Asaph was the *c*, Zechariah second
18: 17 and David's sons were *c* officials
26: 12 through their *c* men,
26: 31 Jeriah was their *c* according
27: 3 and *c* of all the army officers
27: 5 He was *c* and there were 24,000
2Ch 8: 10 also King Solomon's *c* officials—
11: 22 be the *c* prince among his brothers,
19: 11 "Amariah the *c* priest will be
24: 6 summoned Jehoiada the *c* priest
24: 11 officer of the *c* priest would come
26: 20 When Azariah the *c* priest
31: 10 and Azariah the *c* priest,
Ezr 7: 5 the son of Aaron the *c* priest—
Ne 11: 9 Joel son of Zicri was their *c* officer,
11: 14 Their *c* officer was Zabdiel son
11: 22 The *c* officer of the Levites
Job 29: 9 the *c* men refrained from speaking
29: 25 the way for them and sat as their *c*;
Isa 2: 2 as *c* among the mountains;
33: 18 "Where is that *c* officer?
Jer 20: 1 the *c* officer in the temple
39: 3 Nebo-Sarsekim a *c* officer,
39: 13 the guard, Nebushazban a *c* officer,
52: 24 as prisoners Seraiah the *c* priest,
52: 25 the secretary who was *c* officer
Eze 38: 2 the *c* prince of Meshech and Tubal;
38: 3 *c* prince of Meshech and Tubal.
39: 1 *c* prince of Meshech and Tubal.
Da 1: 3 Then the king ordered Ashpenaz, *c*
1: 7 *c* official gave them new names:
1: 8 and he asked the *c* official
1: 11 the guard whom the *c* official had
1: 18 the *c* official presented them
4: 9 "Belteshazzar, *c* of the magicians,
5: 11 appointed him *c* of the magicians,
10: 13 Then Michael, one of the *c* princes,
Mic 4: 1 as *c* among the mountains;
Mt 2: 4 together all the people's *c* priests
16: 21 *c* priests and teachers of the law,
20: 18 will be betrayed to the *c* priests
21: 15 But when the *c* priests
21: 23 the *c* priests and the elders
21: 45 When the *c* priests
26: 3 Then the *c* priests and the elders
26: 14 went to the *c* priests and asked,
26: 47 sent from the *c* priests
26: 59 *c* priests and the whole Sanhedrin
27: 1 all the *c* priests and the elders
27: 3 thirty silver coins to the *c* priests
27: 6 The *c* priests picked up the coins
27: 12 he was accused by the *c* priests
27: 20 *c* priests and the elders persuaded
27: 41 In the same way the *c* priests,
27: 62 *c* priests and the Pharisees went
28: 11 to the *c* priests everything that had
28: 12 When the *c* priests had met
Mk 8: 31 *c* priests and teachers of the law,
10: 33 will be betrayed to the *c* priests
11: 18 The *c* priests and the teachers
11: 27 in the temple courts, the *c* priests,
14: 1 and the *c* priests and the teachers
14: 10 went to the *c* priests to betray Jesus
14: 43 sent from the *c* priests, the teachers
14: 53 and all the *c* priests, elders
14: 55 *c* priests and the whole Sanhedrin
15: 1 the *c* priests, with the elders,
15: 3 The *c* priests accused him
15: 10 envy that the *c* priests had handed
15: 11 the *c* priests stirred up the crowd
15: 31 In the same way the *c* priests
Lk 9: 22 *c* priests and teachers of the law,
19: 2 he was a *c* tax collector
19: 47 But the *c* priests, the teachers
20: 1 the *c* priests and the teachers
20: 19 and the *c* priests looked for a way
22: 2 and the *c* priests and the teachers
22: 4 And Judas went to the *c* priests
22: 52 Then Jesus said to the *c* priests,
22: 66 both the *c* priests and teachers
23: 4 Pilate announced to the *c* priests
23: 10 The *c* priests and the teachers
23: 13 Pilate called together the *c* priests,
24: 20 *c* priests and our rulers handed him
Jn 7: 32 the *c* priests and the Pharisees sent
7: 45 guards went back to the *c* priests
11: 47 *c* priests and the Pharisees called
11: 57 *c* priests and Pharisees had given
12: 10 So the *c* priests made plans
18: 3 some officials from the *c* priests
18: 35 and your *c* priests who handed you
19: 6 As soon as the *c* priests
19: 15 Caesar," the *c* priests answered.
19: 21 The *c* priests of the Jews protested
Ac 4: 23 and reported all that the *c* priests
5: 24 and the *c* priests were puzzled,
9: 14 with authority from the *c* priests
9: 21 as prisoners to the *c* priests?"
14: 12 because he was the *c* speaker.
19: 14 a Jewish *c* priest, were doing this.
22: 30 him and ordered the *c* priests
23: 14 They went to the *c* priests
25: 2 where the *c* priests and Jewish
25: 15 the *c* priests and elders
26: 10 of the *c* priests I put many
26: 12 and commission of the *c* priests.
28: 7 the *c* official of the island.
Eph 2: 20 Jesus himself as the *c* cornerstone.
1Pe 5: 4 And when the *C* Shepherd appears,

CHIEFS (CHIEF)

Ge 36: 15 *C* Teman, Omar, Zepho, Kenaz,
36: 15 the *c* among Esau's descendants:
36: 16 These were the *c* descended
36: 17 These were the *c* descended
36: 17 *C* Nahath, Zerah, Shammah
36: 18 These were the *c* descended
36: 18 *C* Jeush, Jalam and Korah.
36: 19 Edom), and these were their *c*.
36: 21 sons of Seir in Edom were Horite *c*.
36: 29 These were the Horite *c*: Lotan,
36: 30 These were the Horite *c*, according
36: 40 These were the *c* descended
36: 43 These were the *c* of Edom,
Ex 15: 15 The *c* of Edom will be terrified,
Jos 13: 21 defeated him and the Midianite *c*,
1Ki 8: 1 and the *c* of the Israelite families,
1Ch 1: 51 The *c* of Edom were: Timna, Alvah
1: 54 These were the *c* of Edom.
7: 3 All five of them were *c*.
8: 28 *c* as listed in their genealogy,
9: 34 *c* as listed in their genealogy,
11: 10 These were the *c* of David's mighty
11: 15 Three of the thirty *c* came
12: 32 do—200 *c*, with all their relatives
2Ch 5: 2 and the *c* of the Israelite families,

CHILD (CHILD'S CHILDHOOD CHILDISH CHILDREN CHILDREN'S GRANDCHILDREN)

Ge 4: 25 "God has granted me another *c*
16: 11 "You are now with *c*
17: 17 Will Sarah bear a *c* at the age
18: 13 I really have a *c*, now that I am
21: 8 The *c* grew and was weaned,
Ex 2: 2 When she saw that he was a fine *c*,
2: 3 Then she placed the *c* in it
2: 10 When the *c* grew older, she took
Jdg 11: 34 of tambourines! She was an only *c*.
Ru 4: 16 Then Naomi took the *c*, laid him
1Sa 1: 27 for this *c*, and the LORD has
2Sa 12: 15 the LORD struck the *c* that Uriah's
12: 16 David pleaded with God for the *c*.
12: 18 How can we tell him the *c* is dead?
12: 18 On the seventh day the *c* died.
12: 18 to tell him that the *c* was dead,
12: 18 "While the *c* was still living,
12: 19 and he realized the *c* was dead.
12: 19 "Is the *c* dead?" he asked.
12: 21 While the *c* was alive, you fasted
12: 21 but now that the *c* is dead,
12: 22 gracious to me and let the *c* live.'
12: 22 "While the *c* was still alive,
1Ki 3: 7 But I am only a little *c*
3: 18 The third day after my *c* was born,
3: 25 "Cut the living *c* in two
17: 23 picked up the *c* and carried him
2Ki 4: 18 *c* grew, and one day he went out
4: 26 Is your *c* all right?' " "Everything is
2Ch 22: 11 she hid the *c* from Athaliah
Job 3: 16 in the ground like a stillborn *c*,
24: 9 The fatherless *c* is snatched
Ps 58: 8 like a stillborn *c*, may they not see
131: 2 like a weaned *c* is my soul
131: 2 like a weaned *c* with its mother,
Pr 4: 3 and an only *c* of my mother,
20: 11 Even a *c* is known by his actions,
22: 6 Train a *c* in the way he should go,
22: 15 Folly is bound up in the heart of a *c*
23: 13 not withhold discipline from a *c*;
29: 15 *c* left to itself disgraces his mother.
Ecc 6: 3 I say that a stillborn *c* is better
Isa 7: 14 The virgin will be with *c*
9: 6 For to us a *c* is born,
10: 19 that a *c* could write them down
11: 6 and a little *c* will lead them.
11: 8 the young *c* put his hand
26: 17 As a woman with *c* and about
26: 18 We were with *c*, we writhed in pain
49: 15 compassion on the *c* she has borne?
54: 1 you who never bore a *c*;
66: 13 As a mother comforts her *c*,
Jer 1: 6 how to speak; I am only a *c*."
1: 7 "Do not say, 'I am only a *c*.'
4: 31 a groan as of one bearing her first *c*
20: 15 "A *c* is born to you—a son!"
31: 20 the *c* in whom I delight?
Hos 11: 1 "When Israel was a *c*, I loved him,
13: 13 but he is a *c* without wisdom;
Zec 12: 10 as one mourns for an only *c*,
Mt 1: 18 to be with *c* through the Holy Spirit
1: 23 "The virgin will be with *c*
2: 8 and make a careful search for the *c*.

Mt 2: 9 over the place where the *c* was.
2: 11 they saw the *c* with his mother
2: 13 to search for the *c* to kill him."
2: 13 "take the *c* and his mother
2: 14 took the *c* and his mother
2: 20 take the *c* and his mother
2: 21 took the *c* and his mother
10: 21 brother to death, and a father his *c;*
18: 2 He called a little *c* and had him
18: 4 himself like this *c* is the greatest
18: 5 welcomes a little *c* like this
Mk 5: 39 The *c* is not dead but asleep."
5: 40 and went in where the *c* was.
7: 30 and found her *c* lying on the bed,
9: 36 He took a little *c* and had him stand
10: 15 God like a little *c* will never enter
12: 21 but he also died, leaving no *c.*
13: 12 brother to death, and a father his *c.*
Lk 1: 31 You will be with *c* and give birth
1: 36 going to have a *c* in her old age,
1: 42 and blessed is the *c* you will bear!
1: 59 came to circumcise the *c,*
1: 62 what he would like to name the *c.*
1: 66 "What then is this *c* going to be?"
1: 76 my *c,* will be called a prophet
1: 80 And the *c* grew and became strong
2: 5 to him and was expecting a *c.*
2: 17 had been told them about this *c,*
2: 27 in the *c* Jesus to do
2: 34 "This *c* is destined
2: 38 spoke about the *c* to all who were
2: 40 And the *c* grew and became strong;
8: 54 My *c,* get up!" Her spirit returned,
9: 38 look at my son, for he is my only *c.*
9: 47 took a little *c* and had him stand
9: 48 "Whoever welcomes this little *c*
18: 17 God like a little *c* will never enter
Jn 4: 49 "Sir, come down before my *c* dies."
7: 22 you circumcise a *c* on the Sabbath.
7: 23 Now if a *c* can be circumcised
16: 21 because of her joy that a *c* is born
16: 21 woman giving birth to a *c* has pain
Ac 7: 5 at that time Abraham had no *c.*
7: 20 born, and he was no ordinary *c.*
13: 10 "You are a *c* of the devil
26: 4 I have lived ever since I was a *c,*
1Co 13: 11 When I was a *c,* I talked like a *c,*
13: 11 thought like a *c,* I reasoned like a *c.*
Gal 4: 1 is that as long as the heir is a *c,*
Heb 11: 23 they saw he was no ordinary *c,*
1Jn 3: 10 does not do what is right is not a *c*
5: 1 who loves the father loves his *c*
Rev 12: 4 might devour her *c* the moment it
12: 5 And her *c* was snatched up to God
12: 5 She gave birth to a son, a male *c,*
12: 13 who had given birth to the male *c.*

CHILD'S (CHILD)

2Ki 4: 30 But the *c* mother said, "As surely
Job 33: 25 then his flesh is renewed like a *c;*
Mt 2: 20 trying to take the *c* life are dead."
Mk 5: 40 he took the *c* father and mother
Lk 2: 33 The *c* father and mother marveled
8: 51 and the *c* father and mother.

CHILDBEARING (BEAR)

Ge 3: 16 greatly increase your pains in *c;*
18: 11 and Sarah was past the age of *c.*

CHILDBIRTH (BEAR)

Ge 35: 17 she was having great difficulty in *c,*
Ex 1: 16 you help the Hebrew women in *c*
Isa 42: 14 But now, like a woman in *c,*
Hos 13: 13 as of a woman in *c* come to him,
Ro 8: 22 as in the pains of *c* right up
Gal 4: 19 the pains of *c* until Christ is formed
1Ti 2: 15 women will be kept safe through *c,*

CHILDHOOD (CHILD)

Ge 8: 21 of his heart is evil from *c.*
Isa 47: 12 which you have labored at since *c.*
47: 15 and trafficked with since *c.*
Mk 9: 21 has he been like this?" "From *c,*"

CHILDISH (CHILD)

1Co 13: 11 When I became a man, I put *c* ways

CHILDLESS

Ge 15: 2 can you give me since I remain *c*
Lev 20: 20 be held responsible; they will die *c.*
20: 21 They will be *c.*
Dt 7: 14 of your men or women will be *c,*
32: 25 street the sword will make them *c;*
Jdg 13: 2 who was sterile and remained *c.*
13: 3 "You are sterile and *c,*
1Sa 15: 33 As your sword has made women *c,*
15: 33 so will your mother be *c*
Job 24: 21 on the barren and *c* woman,
Jer 18: 21 Let their wives be made *c*
22: 30 "Record this man as if *c,*
Eze 5: 17 you, and they will leave you *c.*
14: 15 that country and they leave it *c*
36: 14 devour men or make your nation *c,*
Lk 20: 29 one married a woman and died *c.*

CHILDREN (CHILD)

Ge 3: 16 with pain you will give birth to *c.*
6: 4 of men and had *c* by them.
11: 30 Now Sarai was barren; she had no *c*
15: 3 "You have given me no *c;*
16: 1 Abram's wife, had borne him no *c.*
16: 2 LORD has kept me from having *c.*
18: 19 so that he will direct his *c*
20: 17 girls so they could have *c* again,
21: 7 that Sarah would nurse *c?*
21: 23 or my *c* or my descendants.
29: 35 Then she stopped having *c.*
30: 1 So she said to Jacob, "Give me *c,*
30: 1 she was not bearing Jacob any *c,*
30: 2 who has kept you from having *c?*"
30: 3 her so that she can bear *c* for me
30: 9 saw that she had stopped having *c,*
30: 26 and *c,* for whom I have served you,
31: 16 our father belongs to us and our *c.*
31: 17 Then Jacob put his *c* and his wives
31: 43 or about the *c* they have borne?
31: 43 *c* are my *c,* and the flocks are my
32: 11 and also the mothers with their *c.*
33: 1 so he divided the *c* among Leah,
33: 2 Leah and her *c* next, and Rachel
33: 2 put the maidservants and their *c*
33: 5 and saw the women and *c.*
33: 5 "They are the *c* God has graciously
33: 6 and their *c* approached
33: 7 and her *c* came and bowed down.
33: 13 lord knows that the *c* are tender
33: 14 droves before me and that of the *c,*
34: 29 and all their women and *c,*
36: 25 The *c* of Anah: Dishon
42: 36 "You have deprived me of my *c.*
43: 8 you and our *c* may live and not die.
45: 10 you, your *c* and grandchildren,
45: 19 carts from Egypt for your *c*
46: 5 took their father Jacob and their *c*
46: 18 These were the *c* born to Jacob
47: 12 according to the number of their *c.*
47: 24 and your households and your *c.*"
48: 6 Any *c* born to you
48: 11 me to see your *c* too."
50: 8 Only their *c* and their flocks
50: 21 I will provide for you and your *c.*"
50: 23 Also the *c* of Makir son
50: 23 third generation of Ephraim's *c.*
Ex 10: 2 them that you may tell your *c*
10: 10 along with your women and *c!*
10: 24 Even your women and *c* may go
12: 26 And when your *c* ask you,
12: 37 men on foot, besides women and *c.*
17: 3 our *c* and livestock die of thirst?"
20: 5 punishing the *c* for the sin
21: 4 her *c* shall belong to her master,
21: 5 and *c* and do not want to go free,'
22: 24 widows and your *c* fatherless
34: 7 and their *c* for the sin of the fathers
34: 7 he punishes the *c* and their
Lev 10: 14 have been given to you and your *c*
10: 15 share for you and your *c,*
18: 21 of your *c* to be sacrificed to Molech
20: 2 any of his *c* to Molech must be put
20: 3 for by giving his *c* to Molech,
20: 4 one of his *c* to Molech
22: 13 yet has no *c,* and she returns to live
25: 41 Then he and his *c* are to be released
25: 46 You can will them to your *c*
Lev 25: 54 his *c* are to be released in the Year
26: 22 and they will rob you of your *c,*
Nu 5: 28 of guilt and will be able to have *c.*
14: 3 Our wives and *c* will be taken
14: 18 he punishes the *c* for the sin
14: 31 for your *c* that you said would be
14: 33 Your *c* will be shepherds here
16: 27 *c* and little ones at the entrances
31: 9 *c* and took all the Midianite herds,
32: 16 and cities for our women and *c.*
32: 17 and *c* will live in fortified cities,
32: 24 Build cities for your women and *c,*
32: 26 Our *c* and wives, our flocks
Dt 1: 39 your *c* who do not yet know good
2: 34 them—men, women and *c.*
3: 6 every city—men, women and *c.*
3: 19 your *c* and your livestock (I know
4: 9 Teach them to your *c*
4: 9 and to their *c* after them.
4: 10 and may teach them to their *c.*"
4: 25 you have had *c* and grandchildren
4: 40 well with you and your *c* after you
5: 9 punishing the *c* for the sin
5: 29 well with them and their *c* forever!
6: 2 your *c* and their *c* after them may
6: 7 Impress them on your *c.*
11: 2 today that your *c* were not
11: 5 It was not your *c* who saw what he
11: 19 them to your *c,* talking about them
11: 21 the days of your *c* may be many
12: 25 well with you and your *c* after you,
12: 28 well with you and your *c* after you,
14: 1 You are the *c* of the LORD your
20: 14 *c,* the livestock and everything else
23: 8 The third generation of *c* born
24: 16 nor *c* put to death for their fathers;
24: 16 put to death for their *c,*
28: 54 the wife he loves or his surviving *c,*
28: 55 of the flesh of his *c* that he is eating.
28: 57 from her womb and the *c* she bears.
29: 11 with your *c* and your wives,
29: 22 Your *c* who follow you
29: 29 belong to us and to our *c* forever,
30: 2 your *c* return to the LORD your
30: 19 so that you and your *c* may live
31: 12 the people—men, women and *c,*
31: 13 Their *c,* who do not know this law,
32: 5 shame they are no longer his *c,*
32: 20 *c* who are unfaithful.
32: 46 so that you may command your *c*
33: 9 or acknowledge his own *c,*
Jos 1: 14 your *c* and your livestock may stay
4: 6 In the future, when your *c* ask you,
8: 35 including the women and *c,*
14: 9 and that of your *c* forever,
Jdg 18: 21 Putting their little *c,* their livestock
21: 10 including the women and *c.*
1Sa 1: 2 Peninnah had *c,* but Hannah had
2: 5 who was barren has borne seven *c,*
2: 20 "May the LORD give you *c*
15: 3 *c* and infants, cattle and sheep,
22: 19 its *c* and infants, and its cattle,
30: 22 each man may take his wife and *c*
2Sa 5: 14 names of the *c* born to him there:
6: 23 of Saul had no *c* to the day
12: 3 and it grew up with him and his *c.*
1Ki 11: 20 lived with Pharaoh's own *c.*
20: 3 of your wives and *c* are mine.' "
20: 5 and gold, your wives and your *c.*
20: 7 sent for my wives and my *c,*
2Ki 8: 12 dash their little *c* to the ground,
10: 1 and to the guardians of Ahab's *c.*
14: 6 nor *c* put to death for their fathers;
14: 6 put to death for their *c,*
17: 31 and the Sepharvites burned their *c*
17: 41 this day their *c* and grandchildren
19: 3 when *c* come to the point of birth
1Ch 2: 18 son of Hezron had *c* by his wife
2: 30 Seled died without *c.*
2: 32 Jether died without *c.*
3: 5 these were the *c* born to him there:
4: 18 were the *c* of Pharaoh's daughter
4: 27 his brothers did not have many *c;*
6: 3 The *c* of Amram: Aaron, Moses
7: 4 for they had many wives and *c.*
14: 4 names of the *c* born to him there:
2Ch 20: 13 with their wives and *c*
25: 4 nor *c* put to death for their fathers;

2Ch 25: 4 put to death for their *c*,
30: 9 your *c* will be shown compassion
Ezr 8: 21 for a safe journey for us and our *c*,
9: 12 it to your *c* as an everlasting
10: 1 and *c*— gathered around him.
10: 3 away all these women and their *c*,
10: 44 some of them had *c* by these wives.
Ne 12: 43 The women and *c* also rejoiced.
13: 24 Half of their *c* spoke the language
Est 3: 13 and little *c*— on a single day,
8: 11 them and their women and *c*;
Job 1: 5 "Perhaps my *c* have sinned
5: 4 His *c* are far from safety,
5: 25 will know that your *c* will be many,
8: 4 When your *c* sinned against him,
17: 5 the eyes of his *c* will fail.
20: 10 His *c* must make amends
21: 8 They see their *c* established
21: 11 They send forth their *c* as a flock;
24: 5 wasteland provides food for their *c*.
27: 14 However many his *c*, their fate is
29: 5 and my *c* were around me,
42: 16 he saw his *c* and their *c*
Ps 8: 2 From the lips of *c* and infants
17: 14 and they store up wealth for their *c*.
34: 11 Come, my *c*, listen to me;
37: 25 or their *c* begging bread.
37: 26 their *c* will be blessed.
69: 36 the *c* of his servants will inherit it,
72: 4 and save the *c* of the needy;
73: 15 betrayed this generation of your *c*.
78: 4 We will not hide them from their *c*;
78: 5 forefathers to teach their *c*,
78: 6 and they in turn would tell their *c*.
78: 6 even the *c* yet to be born,
90: 16 your splendor to their *c*.
102: 28 The *c* of your servants will live
103: 13 As a father has compassion on his *c*
103: 17 with their children's *c*—
109: 9 May his *c* be fatherless
109: 10 May his *c* be wandering beggars;
109: 12 or take pity on his fatherless *c*.
112: 2 His *c* will be mighty in the land;
113: 9 as a happy mother of *c*.
115: 14 both you and your *c*.
127: 3 *c* a reward from him.
128: 6 live to see your children's *c*.
148: 12 old men and *c*.
Pr 13: 22 for his children's *c*,
14: 26 and for his *c* it will be a refuge.
17: 6 Children's *c* are a crown
17: 6 and parents are the pride of their *c*.
20: 7 blessed are his *c* after him.
31: 28 Her *c* arise and call her blessed;
Ecc 6: 3 A man may have a hundred *c*
Isa 1: 2 "I reared *c* and brought them up,
1: 4 *c* given to corruption.
3: 4 mere *c* will govern them.
8: 18 and the *c* the LORD has given me.
13: 18 look with compassion on *c*.
28: 9 To *c* weaned from their milk,
29: 23 When they see among them their *c*,
30: 1 "Woe to the obstinate *c*,"
30: 9 are rebellious people, deceitful *c*,
30: 9 *c* unwilling to listen
37: 3 when *c* come to the point of birth
38: 19 fathers tell their *c*
43: 5 I will bring your *c* from the east
45: 11 do you question me about my *c*,
47: 8 or suffer the loss of *c*.'
47: 9 loss of *c* and widowhood.
48: 19 your *c* like its numberless grains;
49: 20 *c* born during your bereavement
49: 25 and your *c* I will save.
54: 1 more are the *c* of the desolate
57: 5 you sacrifice your *c* in the ravines
59: 21 or from the mouths of your *c*,
65: 23 or bear *c* doomed to misfortune;
66: 8 labor than she gives birth to her *c*.
Jer 2: 9 against your children's *c*.
4: 22 They are senseless *c*;
5: 7 Your *c* have forsaken me
6: 11 "Pour it out on the *c* in the street
7: 18 *c* gather wood, the fathers light
9: 21 it has cut off the *c* from the streets
17: 2 Even their *c* remember
18: 21 So give their *c* over to famine;
22: 28 Why will he and his *c* be hurled out

Jer 30: 6 Can a man bear *c*?
30: 20 Their *c* will be as in days of old,
31: 15 Rachel weeping for her *c*
31: 15 because her *c* are no more."
31: 17 Your *c* will return to their own land
32: 18 into the laps of their *c* after them.
32: 39 and the good of their *c* after them.
36: 31 I will punish him and his *c*
38: 23 and *c* will be brought out
40: 7 *c* who were the poorest in the land
41: 16 *c* and court officials he had brought
43: 6 *c* and the king's daughters whom
44: 7 the *c* and infants, and so leave
47: 3 Fathers will not turn to help their *c*;
49: 10 His *c*, relatives and neighbors will
La 1: 5 Her *c* have gone into exile,
1: 16 My *c* are destitute
2: 11 because *c* and infants faint
2: 19 him for the lives of your *c*,
2: 20 the *c* they have cared for?
3: 33 or grief to the *c* of men.
4: 4 the *c* beg for bread,
4: 10 have cooked their own *c*,
Eze 5: 10 and *c* will eat their fathers.
5: 10 in your midst fathers will eat their *c*
9: 6 and maidens, women and *c*,
16: 21 You slaughtered my *c*
16: 45 despised her husband and her *c*;
16: 45 their husbands and their *c*.
20: 18 I said to their *c* in the desert,
20: 21 " 'But the *c* rebelled against me:
23: 37 they even sacrificed their *c*,
23: 39 the very day they sacrificed their *c*
36: 12 never again deprive them of their *c*.
36: 13 and deprive your nation of its *c*,"
37: 25 their *c* and their children's *c* will
47: 22 settled among you and who have *c*.
Da 6: 24 along with their wives and *c*.
Hos 1: 2 to yourself an adulterous wife and *c*
2: 4 I will not show my love to her *c*,
2: 4 because they are the *c* of adultery.
4: 6 I also will ignore your *c*.
5: 7 they give birth to illegitimate *c*.
9: 12 Even if they rear *c*,
9: 13 their *c* to the slayer."
9: 16 Even if they bear *c*,
10: 14 dashed to the ground with their *c*.
11: 10 his *c* will come trembling
Joel 1: 3 Tell it to your *c*,
1: 3 and let your *c* tell it to their *c*,
1: 3 and their *c* to the next generation.
2: 16 gather the *c*,
Mic 1: 16 for the *c* in whom you delight;
2: 9 blessing from their *c* forever.
Zec 10: 7 Their *c* will see it and be joyful;
10: 9 They and their *c* will survive,
Mal 4: 6 the hearts of the fathers to their *c*,
4: 6 the hearts of the *c* to their fathers;
Mt 2: 18 Rachel weeping for her *c*
3: 9 of these stones God can raise up *c*
7: 11 how to give good gifts to your *c*,
10: 21 *c* will rebel against their parents
11: 16 They are like *c* sitting
11: 25 and revealed them to little *c*.
14: 21 besides women and *c*.
15: 38 besides women and *c*.
18: 3 you change and become like little *c*
18: 25 that he and his wife and his *c*
19: 13 Then little *c* were brought to Jesus
19: 14 "Let the little *c* come to me,
19: 29 or sisters or father or mother or *c*
21: 15 the *c* shouting in the temple area,
21: 16 you hear what these *c* are saying?"
21: 16 " 'From the lips of *c* and infants
22: 24 must marry the widow and have *c*
22: 24 that if a man dies without having *c*,
22: 25 since he had no *c*, he left his wife
23: 37 longed to gather your *c* together,
27: 25 Let his blood be on us and on our *c*
Mk 7: 27 "First let the *c* eat all they want,"
9: 37 one of these little *c* in my name
10: 13 People were bringing little *c*
10: 14 "Let the little *c* come to me,
10: 16 And he took the *c* in his arms,
10: 24 "*C*, how hard it is to enter
10: 29 or father or *c* or fields for me
10: 30 sisters, mothers, *c* and fields—
12: 19 and have *c* for his brother.

Mk 12: 19 dies and leaves a wife but no *c*,
12: 20 and died without leaving any *c*.
12: 22 In fact, none of the seven left any *c*.
13: 12 *C* will rebel against their parents
Lk 1: 7 they had no *c*, because Elizabeth
1: 17 the hearts of the fathers to their *c*
3: 8 of these stones God can raise up *c*
7: 32 They are like *c* sitting
7: 35 wisdom is proved right by all her *c*
10: 21 and revealed them to little *c*.
11: 7 and my *c* are with me in bed.
11: 13 how to give good gifts to your *c*,
13: 34 longed to gather your *c* together,
14: 26 his wife and *c*, his brothers
18: 16 But Jesus called the *c* to him
18: 16 "Let the little *c* come to me,
18: 29 or *c* for the sake of the kingdom
19: 44 you and the *c* within your walls.
20: 28 and have *c* for his brother.
20: 28 dies and leaves a wife but no *c*,
20: 31 way the seven died, leaving no *c*.
20: 36 They are God's *c*, since they are
20: 36 since they are *c* of the resurrection.
23: 28 weep for yourselves and for your *c*.
Jn 1: 12 the right to become *c* of God—
1: 13 *c* born not of natural descent,
8: 39 "If you were Abraham's *c*,"
8: 41 "We are not illegitimate *c*,"
11: 52 but also for the scattered *c* of God,
13: 33 "My *c*, I will be with you only
Ac 2: 39 The promise is for you and your *c*
13: 26 *c* of Abraham, and you
13: 33 their *c*, by raising up Jesus.
21: 5 *c* accompanied us out of the city,
21: 21 not to circumcise their *c*
Ro 8: 16 with our spirit that we are God's *c*.
8: 17 Now if we are *c*, then we are heirs
8: 21 into the glorious freedom of the *c*
9: 7 are they all Abraham's *c*.
9: 8 it is the *c* of the promise who are
9: 8 not the natural *c* who are God's *c*,
9: 10 but Rebecca's *c* had one
1Co 4: 14 but to warn you, as my dear *c*.
7: 14 Otherwise your *c* would be unclean
14: 20 Brothers, stop thinking like *c*.
2Co 6: 13 as to my *c*— open wide your hearts
12: 14 parents, but parents for their *c*.
12: 14 *c* should not have to save up
Gal 3: 7 that those who believe are *c*
4: 3 when we were *c*, we were in slavery
4: 19 My dear *c*, for whom I am again
4: 24 and bears *c* who are to be slaves:
4: 25 because she is in slavery with her *c*.
4: 27 more are the *c* of the desolate
4: 27 who bears no *c*;
4: 28 like Isaac, are *c* of promise.
4: 31 we are not *c* of the slave woman,
Eph 5: 1 dearly loved *c* and live a life of love
5: 8 as *c* of light (for the fruit
6: 1 *C*, obey your parents in the Lord,
6: 4 do not exasperate your *c*; instead,
Php 2: 15 *c* of God without fault in a crooked
Col 3: 20 *C*, obey your parents in everything,
3: 21 Fathers, do not embitter your *c*,
1Th 2: 7 like a mother caring for her little *c*.
2: 11 as a father deals with his own *c*,
1Ti 3: 4 and see that his *c* obey him
3: 12 and must manage his *c* and his
5: 4 if a widow has *c* or grandchildren,
5: 10 bringing up *c*, showing hospitality
5: 14 widows to marry, to have *c*,
Tit 1: 6 a man whose *c* believe
2: 4 to love their husbands and *c*,
Heb 2: 13 and the *c* God has given me."
2: 14 Since the *c* have flesh and blood,
12: 8 then you are illegitimate *c*
1Pe 1: 14 As obedient *c*, do not conform
1Jn 2: 1 My dear *c*, I write this to you
2: 12 I write to you, dear *c*,
2: 13 I write to you, dear *c*,
2: 18 Dear *c*, this is the last hour;
2: 28 And now, dear *c*, continue in him,
3: 1 that we should be called *c* of God!
3: 2 Dear friends, now we are *c* of God,
3: 7 Dear *c*, do not let anyone lead you
3: 10 This is how we know who the *c*
3: 10 and who the *c* of the devil are:
3: 18 the love of God be in him? Dear *c*,

1Jn 4: 4 dear *c*, are from God and have
5: 2 is how we know that we love the *c*
5: 19 We know that we are *c* of God,
5: 21 Dear *c*, keep yourselves from idols.
2Jn : 1 To the chosen lady and her *c*,
: 4 some of your *c* walking in the truth,
: 13 *c* of your chosen sister send their
3Jn : 4 than to hear that my *c* are walking
Rev 2: 23 I will strike her *c* dead.

CHILDREN'S (CHILD)

Ps 103: 17 with their *c* children—
128: 6 may you live to see your *c* children.
Pr 13: 22 an inheritance for his *c* children,
17: 6 *C* children are a crown to the aged,
Isa 54: 13 and great will be your *c* peace.
Jer 2: 9 against your *c* children.
31: 29 and the *c* teeth are set on edge.'
Eze 16: 36 you gave them your *c* blood,
18: 2 and the *c* teeth are set on edge'?
37: 25 and their *c* children will live there
Mt 15: 26 "It is not right to take the *c* bread
Mk 7: 27 for it is not right to take the *c* bread
7: 28 under the table eat the *c* crumbs."

CHIN

Lev 13: 29 a sore on the head or on the *c*,
13: 30 infectious disease of the head or *c*.

CHIRP

Isa 10: 14 or opened its mouth to *c*.' "

CHISEL (CHISELED CHISELING CHISELS)

Ex 34: 1 "*C* out two stone tablets like
Dt 10: 1 "*C* out two stone tablets like
1Ki 6: 7 *c* or any other iron tool was heard
Jer 10: 3 and a craftsman shapes it with his *c*

CHISELED (CHISEL)

Ex 34: 4 Moses *c* out two stone tablets like
Dt 10: 3 *c* out two stone tablets like the first

CHISELING (CHISEL)

Isa 22: 16 and *c* your resting place in the rock

CHISELS (CHISEL)

Isa 44: 13 he roughs it out with *c*

CHLOE'S

1Co 1: 11 from *C* household have informed

CHOICE (CHOICEST CHOOSE CHOOSES CHOOSING CHOSE CHOSEN)

Ge 18: 7 he ran to the herd and selected a *c*,
27: 9 and bring me two *c* young goats,
Lev 23: 40 are to take *c* fruit from the trees,
Dt 12: 11 and all the *c* possessions you have
32: 14 with *c* rams of Bashan
1Sa 2: 29 fattening yourselves on the *c* parts
1Ki 4: 23 gazelles, roebucks and *c* fowl.
1Ch 7: 40 *c* men, brave warriors
21: 11 'Take your *c*: three years of famine,
Ne 5: 18 six *c* sheep and some poultry were
8: 10 and enjoy *c* food and sweet drinks,
Job 36: 16 of your table laden with *c* food.
Pr 8: 10 knowledge rather than *c* gold,
8: 19 what I yield surpasses *c* silver.
10: 20 of the righteous is *c* silver,
18: 8 of a gossip are like *c* morsels;
21: 20 of the wise are stores of *c* food
26: 22 of a gossip are like *c* morsels;
SS 4: 13 pomegranates with *c* fruits,
4: 16 and taste its *c* fruits.
5: 15 *c* as its cedars.
Isa 1: 22 your *c* wine is diluted with water.
Jer 2: 21 I had planted you like a *c* vine
Eze 20: 40 your offerings and your *c* gifts,
24: 4 all the *c* pieces—the leg
34: 3 and slaughter the *c* animals,
Da 1: 16 So the guard took away their *c* food
10: 3 I ate no *c* food; no meat
Am 5: 22 you bring *c* fellowship offerings,
6: 4 You dine on *c* lambs
Zec 11: 16 but will eat the meat of the *c* sheep,
Jn 2: 10 brings out the *c* wine first
Ac 15: 7 that some time ago God made a *c*
Ro 8: 20 not by its own *c*, but by the will

CHOICEST (CHOICE)

Ge 23: 6 dead in the *c* of our tombs.
49: 11 his colt to the *c* branch;
Dt 33: 15 with the *c* gifts of the ancient
2Ki 19: 23 the *c* of its pines.
Job 22: 25 the *c* silver for you.
33: 20 and his soul loathes the *c* meal.
Isa 5: 2 and planted it with the *c* vines.
16: 8 have trampled down the *c* vines,
22: 7 Your *c* valleys are full of chariots,
37: 24 the *c* of its pines.
Eze 31: 16 the *c* and best of Lebanon,
Hab 1: 16 and enjoys the *c* food.

CHOIR (CHOIRS)

Ne 12: 38 The second *c* proceeded in

CHOIRS (CHOIR)

1Ch 15: 27 in charge of the singing of the *c*.
Ne 12: 31 assigned two large *c* to give thanks.
12: 40 two *c* that gave thanks then took
12: 42 The *c* sang under the direction

CHOKE (CHOKED)

Mt 13: 22 and the deceitfulness of wealth *c* it,
18: 28 He grabbed him and began to *c* him
Mk 4: 19 come in and *c* the word,

CHOKED (CHOKE)

Mt 13: 7 which grew up and *c* the plants.
Mk 4: 7 which grew up and *c* the plants,
Lk 8: 7 up with it and *c* the plants.
8: 14 go on their way they are *c*

CHOOSE (CHOICE)

Ex 12: 5 The animals you *c* must be year-old
17: 9 "*C* some of our men and go out
34: 16 when you *c* some of their daughters
Nu 14: 4 "We should *c* a leader
17: 5 to the man I *c* will sprout,
Dt 1: 13 *C* some wise, understanding
7: 7 and *c* you because you were more
12: 5 place the LORD your God will *c*
12: 11 place the LORD your God will *c*
12: 14 at the place the LORD will *c* in one
12: 18 place the LORD your God will *c*—
12: 26 go to the place the LORD will *c*.
14: 23 God at the place he will *c*
14: 24 the place where the LORD will *c*
14: 25 place the LORD your God will *c*.
15: 20 God at the place he will *c*.
16: 2 herd at the place the LORD will *c*
16: 6 in the place he will *c* as a dwelling
16: 7 place the LORD your God will *c*.
16: 11 God at the place he will *c*
16: 15 God at the place the LORD will *c*.
16: 16 God at the place he will *c*:
17: 8 place the LORD your God will *c*.
17: 10 you at the place the LORD will *c*.
18: 6 to the place the LORD will *c*,
26: 2 place the LORD your God will *c*
30: 19 Now *c* life, so that you
31: 11 God at the place he will *c*,
Jos 3: 12 *c* twelve men from the tribes
4: 2 "*C* twelve men
9: 27 at the place the LORD would *c*.
24: 15 then *c* for yourselves this day
1Sa 17: 8 *C* a man and have him come
2Sa 17: 1 "I would *c* twelve thousand men
24: 12 *C* one of them for me to carry out
1Ki 18: 23 Let them *c* one for themselves,
18: 25 "*C* one of the bulls and prepare it
2Ki 10: 3 *c* the best and most worthy
18: 32 *C* life and not death! "Do not listen
1Ch 21: 10 *C* one of them for me to carry out
Ps 65: 4 Blessed is the man you *c*
75: 2 You say, "I *c* the appointed time;
78: 67 he did not *c* the tribe of Ephraim;
Pr 1: 29 and did not *c* to fear the LORD,
3: 31 or *c* any of his ways,
8: 10 *C* my instruction instead of silver,
16: 16 to *c* understanding rather
Isa 7: 15 to reject the wrong and *c* the right.
7: 16 to reject the wrong and *c* the right,
14: 1 once again he will *c* Israel
56: 4 who *c* what pleases me
66: 4 also will *c* harsh treatment for them
Jer 3: 14 I will *c* one of you from every town
33: 26 and will not *c* one of his sons to rule
Eze 33: 2 of the land *c* one of their men
Hos 8: 4 they *c* princes without my approval
Zec 1: 17 comfort Zion and *c* Jerusalem.' "
2: 12 and will again *c* Jerusalem.
Jn 15: 16 You did not *c* me, but I chose you
Ac 1: 21 Therefore it is necessary to *c* one
6: 3 *c* seven men from among you who
15: 22 decided to *c* some of their own men
15: 25 So we all agreed to *c* some men
2Co 12: 6 Even if I should *c* to boast,
Php 1: 22 Yet what shall I *c*? I do not know!
1Pe 4: 3 in the past doing what pagans *c*

CHOOSES (CHOICE)

Lev 16: 2 not to come whenever he *c*
Nu 16: 5 The man he *c* he will cause to come
16: 7 man the LORD *c* will be the one
Dt 12: 21 place where the LORD your God *c*
17: 15 the king the LORD your God *c*.
23: 16 and in whatever town he *c*.
2Sa 15: 15 to do whatever our lord the king *c*
Ps 68: 16 at the mountain where God *c*
Isa 41: 24 he who *c* you is detestable.
Mt 11: 27 to whom the Son *c* to reveal him.
Lk 10: 22 to whom the Son *c* to reveal him."
Jn 7: 17 If any one *c* to do God's will,
Jas 4: 4 Anyone who *c* to be a friend

CHOOSING (CHOICE)

1Ki 12: 33 of his own *c*, he offered sacrifices
Ro 9: 22 *c* to show his wrath and make his

CHOP (CHOPPED)

Dt 29: 11 in your camps who *c* your wood
Jer 46: 23 They will *c* down her forest,"
Mic 3: 3 who *c* them up like meat

CHOPPED (CHOP)

1Sa 6: 14 The people *c* up the wood

CHOSE (CHOICE)

Ge 6: 2 they married any of them they *c*.
13: 11 So Lot *c* for himself the whole plain
47: 2 He *c* five of his brothers
Ex 18: 25 He *c* capable men from all Israel
Dt 4: 37 and *c* their descendants after them,
10: 15 and he *c* you, their descendants,
33: 21 He *c* the best land for himself;
Jos 8: 3 He *c* thirty thousand
Jdg 5: 8 When they *c* new gods,
1Sa 2: 28 I *c* your father out of all the tribes
13: 2 Saul *c* three thousand men
17: 40 *c* five smooth stones
2Sa 6: 21 who *c* me rather than your father
1Ki 11: 34 whom I *c* and who observed my
11: 36 the city where I *c* to put my Name.
2Ki 23: 27 the city I *c*, and this temple,
1Ch 15: 2 the LORD *c* them to carry the ark
28: 4 He *c* Judah as leader,
28: 4 the house of Judah he *c* my family,
28: 4 *c* me from my whole family
2Ch 24: 3 Jehoiada *c* two wives for him,
Ne 9: 7 who *c* Abram and brought him out
Job 29: 25 I *c* the way for them and sat
Ps 33: 12 the people he *c* for his inheritance.
47: 4 He *c* our inheritance for us,
78: 68 but he *c* the tribe of Judah,
78: 70 He *c* David his servant
Isa 65: 12 and *c* what displeases me."
66: 4 and *c* what displeases me."
Jer 33: 24 rejected the two kingdoms he *c*'?
Eze 20: 5 LORD says: On the day I *c* Israel,
Lk 6: 13 to him and *c* twelve of them,
Jn 5: 35 you *c* for a time to enjoy his light.
15: 16 but I *c* you to go and bear fruit—
Ac 6: 5 They *c* Stephen, a man full of faith
13: 17 of the people of Israel *c* our fathers
15: 22 They *c* Judas (called Barsabbas)
15: 40 sailed for Cyprus, but Paul *c* Silas
1Co 1: 27 But God *c* the foolish things
1: 27 God *c* the weak things of the world
1: 28 He *c* the lowly things of this world
Eph 1: 4 he *c* us in him before the creation
2Th 2: 13 from the beginning God *c* you
Heb 11: 25 He *c* to be mistreated
Jas 1: 18 He *c* to give us birth

CHOSEN (CHOICE)

Ge 18: 19 For I have *c* him, so that he will
24: 14 let her be the one you have *c*
24: 44 let her be the one the LORD has *c*
Ex 31: 2 "See, I have *c* Bezalel son of Uri,
35: 30 the LORD has *c* Bezalel son of Uri,
Lev 16: 10 goat *c* by lot as the scapegoat shall
Dt 7: 6 LORD your God has *c* you out
14: 2 the LORD has *c* you
18: 5 the LORD your God has *c* them
21: 5 the LORD your God has *c* them
Jos 24: 22 against yourselves that you have *c*
Jdg 10: 14 and cry out to the gods you have *c*.
20: 15 addition to seven hundred *c* men
20: 16 were seven hundred *c* men who
1Sa 8: 18 for relief from the king you have *c*,
10: 20 the tribe of Benjamin was *c*.
10: 21 Finally Saul son of Kish was *c*.
10: 21 clan by clan, and Matri's clan was *c*
10: 24 you see the man the LORD has *c?*
12: 13 Now here is the king you have *c*,
16: 1 I have *c* one of his sons to be king."
16: 8 "The LORD has not *c* this one
16: 9 "Nor has the LORD *c* this one."
16: 10 "The LORD has not *c* these."
24: 2 So Saul took three thousand *c* men
26: 2 with his three thousand *c* men
2Sa 6: 1 together out of Israel *c* men,
16: 18 "No, the one *c* by the LORD,
21: 6 of Saul—the Lord's *c* one."
1Ki 3: 8 here among the people you have *c*,
8: 16 I have not *c* a city in any tribe
8: 16 I have *c* David to rule my people
8: 44 LORD toward the city you have *c*
8: 48 toward the city you have *c*
11: 13 sake of Jerusalem, which I have *c*."
11: 32 which I have *c* out of all the tribes
14: 21 the city the LORD had *c* out
2Ki 21: 7 which I have *c* out of all the tribes
1Ch 9: 22 those *c* to be gatekeepers
16: 13 O sons of Jacob, his *c* ones.
16: 41 Jeduthun and the rest of those *c*
28: 5 he has *c* my son Solomon to sit
28: 6 for I have *c* him to be my son,
28: 10 for the LORD has *c* you
29: 1 the one whom God has *c*, is young
2Ch 6: 5 I have not *c* a city in any tribe
6: 5 have I *c* anyone to be the leader
6: 6 But now I have *c* Jerusalem
6: 6 I have *c* David to rule my people
6: 34 to you toward this city you have *c*
6: 38 toward the city you have *c*
7: 12 and have *c* this place for myself
7: 16 I have *c* and consecrated this
12: 13 the city the LORD had *c* out
29: 11 for the LORD has *c* you to stand
33: 7 which I have *c* out of all the tribes
Ne 1: 9 bring them to the place I have *c*
Ps 25: 12 in the way *c* for him.
89: 3 made a covenant with my *c* one,
105: 6 O sons of Jacob, his *c* ones.
105: 26 and Aaron, whom he had *c*.
105: 43 his *c* ones with shouts of joy;
106: 5 enjoy the prosperity of your *c* ones,
106: 23 had not Moses, his *c* one,
119: 30 I have *c* the way of truth;
119:173 for I have *c* your precepts.
132: 13 For the LORD has *c* Zion,
135: 4 For the LORD has *c* Jacob
Isa 1: 29 that you have *c*.
41: 8 Jacob, whom I have *c*,
41: 9 I have *c* you and have not rejected
42: 1 my *c* one in whom I delight;
43: 10 "and my servant whom I have *c*,
43: 20 to give drink to my people, my *c*,
44: 1 Israel, whom I have *c*.
44: 2 Jeshurun, whom I have *c*.
45: 4 of Israel my *c*,
48: 14 The LORD's *c* ally
49: 7 One of Israel, who has *c* you."
58: 5 Is this the kind of fast I have *c*,
58: 6 the kind of fasting I have *c*:
65: 9 my *c* people will inherit them,
65: 15 name to my *c* ones as a curse;
65: 22 my *c* ones will long enjoy
66: 3 They have *c* their own ways,
Jer 49: 19 Who is the *c* one I will appoint
Jer 50: 44 Who is the *c* one I will appoint
Am 3: 2 out of Egypt: "You only have I *c*
Hag 2: 23 for I have *c* you,' declares
Zec 3: 2 who has *c* Jerusalem, rebuke you!
Mt 12: 18 Here is my servant whom I have *c*,
22: 14 For many are invited, but few are *c*
27: 15 to release a prisoner *c* by the crowd
Mk 13: 20 whom he has *c*, he has shortened
Lk 1: 9 he was *c* by lot, according
9: 35 whom I have *c*; listen to him."
10: 42 Mary has *c* what is better,
18: 7 bring about justice for his *c* ones,
23: 35 the Christ of God, the *C* One."
Jn 6: 70 "Have I not *c* you, the Twelve?
13: 18 to all of you; I know those I have *c*.
15: 19 but I have *c* you out of the world.
Ac 1: 2 Spirit to the apostles he had *c*.
1: 24 of these two you have *c* to take
9: 15 This man is my *c* instrument
10: 41 whom God had already *c*—
22: 14 'The God of our fathers has *c* you
Ro 8: 33 against those whom God has *c?*
11: 5 present time there is a remnant *c*
16: 13 Greet Rufus, *c* in the Lord,
2Co 8: 19 he was *c* by the churches
Eph 1: 11 also *c*, having been predestined
Col 1: 27 To them God has *c* to make known
3: 12 Therefore, as God's *c* people,
1Th 1: 4 we know that he has *c* you,
Jas 2: 5 Has not God *c* those who are poor
1Pe 1: 2 who have been *c* according
1: 20 He was *c* before the creation
2: 4 rejected by men but *c* by God
2: 6 a *c* and precious cornerstone,
2: 9 But you are a *c* people, a royal
5: 13 is in Babylon, *c* together with you,
2Jn : 1 To the *c* lady and her children,
: 13 of your *c* sister send their greetings.
Rev 17: 14 and with him will be his called, *c*

CHRIST (CHRIST'S CHRISTIAN CHRISTIANS CHRISTS)

Mt 1: 1 of Jesus *C* the son of David,
1: 16 was born Jesus, who is called *C*.
1: 17 fourteen from the exile to the *C*.
1: 18 the birth of Jesus *C* came about.
2: 4 he asked them where the *C* was
11: 2 heard in prison what *C* was doing,
16: 16 Peter answered, "You are the *C*,
16: 20 to tell anyone that he was the *C*.
22: 42 "What do you think about the *C?*
23: 10 for you have one Teacher, the *C*.
24: 5 I am the *C*,' and will deceive many.
24: 23 here is the *C!*' or, 'There he is!'
26: 63 if you are the *C*, the Son of God."
26: 68 and said, "Prophesy to us, *C*.
27: 17 Barabbas, or Jesus who is called *C*
27: 22 with Jesus who is called *C?*"
Mk 1: 1 of the gospel about Jesus *C*,
8: 29 Peter answered, "You are the *C*."
9: 41 to *C* will certainly not lose his
12: 35 of the law say that the *C* is the son
13: 21 'Look, here is the *C!*' or, 'Look,
14: 61 "Are you the *C*, the Son
15: 32 Let this *C*, this King of Israel,
Lk 2: 11 born to you; he is *C* the Lord.
2: 26 before he had seen the Lord's *C*.
3: 15 if John might possibly be the *C*.
4: 41 because they knew he was the *C*.
9: 20 Peter answered, "The *C* of God."
20: 41 is it that they say the *C* is the Son
22: 67 If you are the *C*," they said, "tell us
23: 2 taxes to Caesar and claims to be *C*,
23: 35 himself if he is the *C* of God,
23: 39 "Aren't you the *C?* Save yourself
24: 26 Did not the *C* have
24: 46 The *C* will suffer and rise
Jn 1: 17 and truth came through Jesus *C*.
1: 20 confessed freely, "I am not the *C*."
1: 25 baptize if you are not the *C*,
1: 41 found the Messiah" (that is, the *C*).
3: 28 'I am not the *C* but am sent ahead
4: 25 Messiah" (called *C*) "is coming.
4: 29 this be the *C?*" They came out
7: 26 really concluded that he is the *C?*
7: 27 when the *C* comes, no one will
7: 31 They said, "When the *C* comes,
7: 41 How can the *C* come from Galilee?
Jn 7: 41 Others said, "He is the *C*."
7: 42 Scripture say that the *C* will come
9: 22 that Jesus was the *C* would be put
10: 24 If you are the *C*, tell us plainly."
11: 27 "I believe that you are the *C*,
12: 34 Law that the *C* will remain forever,
17: 3 and Jesus *C*, whom you have sent.
20: 31 you may believe that Jesus is the *C*,
Ac 2: 31 spoke of the resurrection of the *C*,
2: 36 you crucified, both Lord and *C*."
2: 38 in the name of Jesus *C*
3: 6 In the name of Jesus *C* of Nazareth
3: 18 saying that his *C* would suffer.
3: 20 and that he may send the *C*,
4: 10 by the name of Jesus *C* of Nazareth
5: 42 the good news that Jesus is the *C*.
8: 5 and proclaimed the *C* there.
8: 12 of God and the name of Jesus *C*,
9: 22 by proving that Jesus is the *C*.
9: 34 said to him, "Jesus *C* heals you.
10: 36 news of peace through Jesus *C*,
10: 48 baptized in the name of Jesus *C*.
11: 17 who believed in the Lord Jesus *C*,
15: 26 for the name of our Lord Jesus *C*.
16: 18 name of Jesus *C* I command you
17: 3 I am proclaiming to you is the *C*,"
17: 3 proving that the *C* had to suffer
18: 5 to the Jews that Jesus was the *C*.
18: 28 the Scriptures that Jesus was the *C*.
24: 24 as he spoke about faith in *C* Jesus.
26: 23 that the *C* would suffer and,
28: 31 and taught about the Lord Jesus *C*.
Ro 1: 1 Paul, a servant of *C* Jesus,
1: 4 from the dead: Jesus *C* our Lord.
1: 6 called to belong to Jesus *C*.
1: 7 and from the Lord Jesus *C*.
1: 8 God through Jesus *C* for all of you,
2: 16 men's secrets through Jesus *C*,
3: 22 comes through faith in Jesus *C*
3: 24 redemption that came by *C* Jesus.
5: 1 God through our Lord Jesus *C*,
5: 6 we were still powerless, *C* died
5: 8 While we were still sinners, *C* died
5: 11 in God through our Lord Jesus *C*,
5: 15 Jesus *C*, overflow to the many!
5: 17 life through the one man, Jesus *C*.
5: 21 life through Jesus *C* our Lord.
6: 3 into *C* Jesus were baptized
6: 4 as *C* was raised from the dead
6: 8 died with *C*, we believe that we will
6: 9 that since *C* was raised
6: 11 but alive to God in *C* Jesus.
6: 23 life in *C* Jesus our Lord.
7: 4 to the law through the body of *C*,
7: 25 through Jesus *C* our Lord! So then,
8: 1 for those who are in *C* Jesus,
8: 2 because through *C* Jesus the law
8: 9 Spirit of *C*, he does not belong to *C*.
8: 10 But if *C* is in you, your body is dead
8: 11 he who raised *C* from the dead will
8: 17 heirs of God and co-heirs with *C*,
8: 34 Who is he that condemns? *C* Jesus,
8: 35 us from the love of *C?*
8: 39 of God that is in *C* Jesus our Lord.
9: 1 the truth in *C*—I am not lying,
9: 3 and cut off from *C* for the sake
9: 5 is traced the human ancestry of *C*,
10: 4 *C* is the end of the law
10: 6 to bring *C* down) "or 'Who will
10: 7 that is, to bring *C* up from the dead
10: 17 heard through the word of *C*.
12: 5 so in *C* we who are many form one
13: 14 yourselves with the Lord Jesus *C*,
14: 9 *C* died and returned to life
14: 15 your brother for whom *C* died.
14: 18 because anyone who serves *C*
15: 3 For even *C* did not please himself
15: 5 yourselves as you follow *C* Jesus,
15: 6 and Father of our Lord Jesus *C*.
15: 7 then, just as *C* accepted you,
15: 8 I tell you that *C* has become
15: 16 minister of *C* Jesus to the Gentiles
15: 17 Therefore I glory in *C* Jesus
15: 18 except what *C* has accomplished
15: 19 fully proclaimed the gospel of *C*.
15: 20 the gospel where *C* was not known,
15: 29 measure of the blessing of *C*.
15: 30 by our Lord Jesus *C*

Ro 16: 3 my fellow workers in *C* Jesus.
16: 5 to *C* in the province of Asia.
16: 7 and they were in *C* before I was.
16: 9 our fellow worker in *C*,
16: 10 Apelles, tested and approved in *C*.
16: 16 the churches of *C* send greetings.
16: 18 people are not serving our Lord *C*,
16: 25 and the proclamation of Jesus *C*,
16: 27 be glory forever through Jesus *C!*
1Co 1: 1 an apostle of *C* Jesus by the will
1: 2 on the name of our Lord Jesus *C*—
1: 2 to those sanctified in *C* Jesus
1: 3 our Father and the Lord Jesus *C*.
1: 4 of his grace given you in *C* Jesus.
1: 6 testimony about *C* was confirmed
1: 7 for our Lord Jesus *C* to be revealed.
1: 8 on the day of our Lord Jesus *C*.
1: 9 with his Son Jesus *C* our Lord,
1: 10 in the name of our Lord Jesus *C*,
1: 12 still another, "I follow *C*."
1: 13 Is *C* divided? Was Paul crucified
1: 17 For *C* did not send me to baptize,
1: 17 lest the cross of *C* be emptied
1: 23 but we preach *C* crucified:
1: 24 *C* the power of God
1: 30 of him that you are in *C* Jesus,
2: 2 except Jesus *C* and him crucified.
2: 16 But we have the mind of *C*.
3: 1 but as worldly—mere infants in *C*.
3: 11 one already laid, which is Jesus *C*.
3: 23 and you are of *C*, and *C* is of God.
4: 1 ought to regard us as servants of *C*
4: 10 We are fools for *C*, but you are
4: 10 you are so wise in *C!* We are weak,
4: 15 for in *C* Jesus I became your father
4: 15 have ten thousand guardians in *C*,
4: 17 you of my way of life in *C* Jesus,
5: 7 For *C*, our Passover lamb,
6: 11 in the name of the Lord Jesus *C*
6: 15 Shall I then take the members of *C*
6: 15 bodies are members of *C* himself?
8: 6 and there is but one Lord, Jesus *C*,
8: 11 this weak brother, for whom *C* died
8: 12 conscience, you sin against *C*.
9: 12 rather than hinder the gospel of *C*.
10: 4 them, and that rock was *C*.
10: 16 a participation in the blood of *C?*
10: 16 a participation in the body of *C?*
11: 1 as I follow the example of *C*.
11: 3 is man, and the head of *C* is God.
11: 3 the head of every man is *C*,
12: 12 So it is with *C*.
12: 27 Now you are the body of *C*,
15: 3 that *C* died for our sins according
15: 12 is preached that *C* has been raised
15: 13 then not even *C* has been raised.
15: 14 And if *C* has not been raised,
15: 15 about God that he raised *C*
15: 16 then *C* has not been raised either.
15: 17 And if *C* has not been raised,
15: 18 who have fallen asleep in *C* are lost
15: 19 only for this life we have hope in *C*,
15: 20 But *C* has indeed been raised
15: 22 so in *C* all will be made alive.
15: 23 But each in his own turn: *C*,
15: 27 who put everything under *C*.
15: 31 glory over you in *C* Jesus our Lord.
15: 57 victory through our Lord Jesus *C*.
16: 24 My love to all of you in *C* Jesus.
2Co 1: 1 an apostle of *C* Jesus by the will
1: 2 our Father and the Lord Jesus *C*.
1: 3 and Father of our Lord Jesus *C*,
1: 5 as the sufferings of *C* flow
1: 5 through *C* our comfort overflows.
1: 19 For the Son of God, Jesus *C*,
1: 20 has made, they are "Yes" in *C*.
1: 21 both us and you stand firm in *C*.
2: 10 in the sight of *C* for your sake,
2: 12 to Troas to preach the gospel of *C*
2: 14 us in triumphal procession in *C*
2: 15 are to God the aroma of *C*
2: 17 in *C* we speak before God
3: 3 show that you are a letter from *C*,
3: 4 this is ours through *C* before God.
3: 14 because only in *C* is it taken away.
4: 4 light of the gospel of the glory of *C*,
4: 5 not preach ourselves, but Jesus *C*
4: 6 of the glory of God in the face of *C*.
2Co 5: 10 before the judgment seat of *C*,
5: 16 Though we once regarded *C*
5: 17 Therefore, if anyone is in *C*,
5: 18 us to himself through *C*
5: 19 the world to himself in *C*,
6: 15 What harmony is there between *C*
8: 9 the grace of our Lord Jesus *C*,
8: 23 of the churches and an honor to *C*.
9: 13 confession of the gospel of *C*,
10: 1 the meekness and gentleness of *C*,
10: 5 thought to make it obedient to *C*.
10: 7 again that we belong to *C* just
10: 7 is confident that he belongs to *C*,
10: 14 as far as you with the gospel of *C*.
11: 2 you to one husband, to *C*,
11: 3 sincere and pure devotion to *C*.
11: 10 As surely as the truth of *C* is in me,
11: 13 masquerading as apostles of *C*.
11: 23 Are they servants of *C?* (I am out
12: 2 in *C* who fourteen years ago was
12: 19 in the sight of God as those in *C;*
13: 3 demanding proof that *C* is speaking
13: 5 Do you not realize that *C* Jesus is
13: 14 May the grace of the Lord Jesus *C*,
Gal 1: 1 but by Jesus *C* and God the Father,
1: 3 our Father and the Lord Jesus *C*,
1: 6 who called you by the grace of *C*
1: 7 are trying to pervert the gospel of *C*
1: 10 I would not be a servant of *C*.
1: 12 it by revelation from Jesus *C*.
1: 22 the churches of Judea that are in *C*.
2: 4 on the freedom we have in *C* Jesus
2: 16 but by faith in Jesus *C*.
2: 16 in *C* Jesus that we may be justified
2: 16 we may be justified by faith in *C*
2: 17 If, while we seek to be justified in *C*
2: 17 does that mean that *C* promotes sin
2: 20 I have been crucified with *C*
2: 20 I no longer live, but *C* lives in me.
2: 21 *C* died for nothing!" You foolish
3: 1 very eyes Jesus *C* was clearly
3: 13 *C* redeemed us from the curse
3: 14 to the Gentiles through *C* Jesus,
3: 16 meaning one person, who is *C*.
3: 22 given through faith in Jesus *C*,
3: 24 us to *C* that we might be justified
3: 26 of God through faith in *C* Jesus,
3: 27 have clothed yourselves with *C*.
3: 27 into *C* have clothed yourselves
3: 28 for you are all one in *C* Jesus.
3: 29 to *C*, then you are Abraham's seed,
4: 14 as if I were *C* Jesus himself.
4: 19 of childbirth until *C* is formed
5: 1 for freedom that *C* has set us free.
5: 2 *C* will be of no value to you at all.
5: 4 by law have been alienated from *C;*
5: 6 For in *C* Jesus neither circumcision
5: 24 to *C* Jesus have crucified the sinful
6: 2 way you will fulfill the law of *C*.
6: 12 being persecuted for the cross of *C*.
6: 14 in the cross of our Lord Jesus *C*,
6: 18 The grace of our Lord Jesus *C* be
Eph 1: 1 an apostle of *C* Jesus by the will
1: 1 in Ephesus, the faithful in *C* Jesus:
1: 2 our Father and the Lord Jesus *C*.
1: 3 and Father of our Lord Jesus *C*,
1: 3 with every spiritual blessing in *C*.
1: 5 as his sons through Jesus *C*,
1: 9 which he purposed in *C*, to be put
1: 10 together under one head, even *C*.
1: 12 who were the first to hope in *C*,
1: 13 also were included in *C*
1: 17 the God of our Lord Jesus *C*,
1: 20 which he exerted in *C*
2: 5 made us alive with *C*
2: 6 And God raised us up with *C*
2: 6 in the heavenly realms in *C* Jesus,
2: 7 in his kindness to us in *C* Jesus.
2: 10 created in *C* Jesus
2: 12 time you were separate from *C*,
2: 13 in *C* Jesus you who once were far
2: 13 near through the blood of *C*.
2: 20 with *C* Jesus himself as the chief
3: 1 the prisoner of *C* Jesus for the sake
3: 4 insight into the mystery of *C*,
3: 6 together in the promise in *C* Jesus.
3: 8 the unsearchable riches of *C*,
3: 11 accomplished in *C* Jesus our Lord.
Eph 3: 17 so that *C* may dwell in your hearts
3: 18 and high and deep is the love of *C*,
3: 21 *C* Jesus throughout all generations,
4: 7 has been given as *C* apportioned it.
4: 12 the body of *C* may be built up
4: 13 measure of the fullness of *C*.
4: 15 into him who is the Head, that is, *C*
4: 20 did not come to know *C* that way.
4: 32 just as in *C* God forgave you.
5: 2 as *C* loved us and gave himself up
5: 5 inheritance in the kingdom of *C*
5: 14 and *C* will shine on you."
5: 20 in the name of our Lord Jesus *C*.
5: 21 out of reverence for *C*.
5: 23 as *C* is the head of the church,
5: 24 Now as the church submits to *C*,
5: 25 just as *C* loved the church
5: 29 just as *C* does the church—
5: 32 am talking about *C* and the church.
6: 5 of heart, just as you would obey *C*.
6: 6 but like slaves of *C*, doing the will
6: 23 the Father and the Lord Jesus *C*.
6: 24 to all who love our Lord Jesus *C*
Php 1: 1 and Timothy, servants of *C* Jesus,
1: 1 the saints in *C* Jesus at Philippi,
1: 2 our Father and the Lord Jesus *C*.
1: 6 until the day of *C* Jesus.
1: 8 of you with the affection of *C* Jesus
1: 10 and blameless until the day of *C*,
1: 11 comes through Jesus *C*—
1: 13 else that I am in chains for *C*.
1: 15 It is true that some preach *C* out
1: 17 The former preach *C* out
1: 18 motives or true, *C* is preached.
1: 19 given by the Spirit of Jesus *C*,
1: 20 as always *C* will be exalted
1: 21 to live is *C* and to die is gain.
1: 23 I desire to depart and be with *C*,
1: 26 in *C* Jesus will overflow on account
1: 27 worthy of the gospel of *C*.
1: 29 on behalf of *C* not only to believe
2: 1 from being united with *C*,
2: 5 be the same as that of *C* Jesus:
2: 11 confess that Jesus *C* is Lord,
2: 16 on the day of *C* that I did not run
2: 21 own interests, not those of Jesus *C*.
2: 30 he almost died for the work of *C*,
3: 3 glory in *C* Jesus, and who put no
3: 7 now consider loss for the sake of *C*.
3: 8 of knowing *C* Jesus my Lord,
3: 8 that I may gain *C* and be found
3: 9 but that which is through faith in *C*
3: 10 I want to know *C* and the power
3: 12 of that for which *C* Jesus took hold
3: 14 called me heavenward in *C* Jesus.
3: 18 as enemies of the cross of *C*.
3: 20 from there, the Lord Jesus *C*,
4: 7 and your minds in *C* Jesus.
4: 19 to his glorious riches in *C* Jesus.
4: 21 Greet all the saints in *C* Jesus.
4: 23 The grace of the Lord Jesus *C* be
Col 1: 1 an apostle of *C* Jesus by the will
1: 2 faithful brothers in *C* at Colosse:
1: 3 the Father of our Lord Jesus *C*,
1: 4 heard of your faith in *C* Jesus
1: 7 minister of *C* on our behalf,
1: 27 which is *C* in you, the hope of glory
1: 28 may present everyone perfect in *C*.
2: 2 the mystery of God, namely, *C*,
2: 5 and how firm your faith in *C* is.
2: 6 as you received *C* Jesus as Lord,
2: 8 of this world rather than on *C*.
2: 9 For in *C* all the fullness
2: 10 you have been given fullness in *C*,
2: 11 with the circumcision done by *C*,
2: 13 God made you alive with *C*.
2: 17 the reality, however, is found in *C*.
2: 20 Since you died with *C*
3: 1 then, you have been raised with *C*,
3: 1 where *C* is seated at the right hand
3: 3 and your life is now hidden with *C*
3: 4 When *C*, who is your life, appears,
3: 11 Scythian, slave or free, but *C* is all,
3: 15 Let the peace of *C* rule
3: 16 Let the word of *C* dwell
3: 24 It is the Lord *C* you are serving.
4: 3 we may proclaim the mystery of *C*,
4: 12 one of you and a servant of *C* Jesus,

1Th 1: 1 the Father and the Lord Jesus *C:*
1: 3 by hope in our Lord Jesus *C.*
2: 7 of *C* we could have been a burden
2: 14 in Judea, which are in *C* Jesus:
3: 2 in spreading the gospel of *C,*
4: 16 and the dead in *C* will rise first.
5: 9 through our Lord Jesus *C.*
5: 18 will for you in *C* Jesus.
5: 23 at the coming of our Lord Jesus *C.*
5: 28 of our Lord Jesus *C* be with you.
2Th 1: 1 our Father and the Lord Jesus *C:*
1: 2 the Father and the Lord Jesus *C.*
1: 12 of our God and the Lord Jesus *C.*
2: 1 the coming of our Lord Jesus *C*
2: 14 in the glory of our Lord Jesus *C.*
2: 16 May our Lord Jesus *C* himself
3: 6 In the name of the Lord Jesus *C,*
3: 12 in the Lord Jesus *C* to settle down
3: 18 of our Lord Jesus *C* be with you all.
1Ti 1: 1 an apostle of *C* Jesus
1: 1 and of *C* Jesus our hope,
1: 2 the Father and *C* Jesus our Lord.
1: 12 I thank *C* Jesus our Lord, who has
1: 14 and love that are in *C* Jesus.
1: 15 *C* Jesus came into the world
1: 16 *C* Jesus might display his unlimited
2: 5 the man *C* Jesus, who gave himself
3: 13 assurance in their faith in *C* Jesus.
4: 6 will be a good minister of *C* Jesus,
5: 11 overcome their dedication to *C,*
5: 21 and *C* Jesus and the elect angels,
6: 3 instruction of our Lord Jesus *C*
6: 13 life to everything, and of *C* Jesus,
6: 14 the appearing of our Lord Jesus *C,*
2Ti 1: 1 an apostle of *C* Jesus by the will
1: 1 promise of life that is in *C* Jesus,
1: 2 the Father and *C* Jesus our Lord.
1: 9 us in *C* Jesus before the beginning
1: 10 appearing of our Savior, *C* Jesus,
1: 13 with faith and love in *C* Jesus.
2: 1 in the grace that is in *C* Jesus.
2: 3 us like a good soldier of *C* Jesus.
2: 8 Remember Jesus *C,* raised
2: 10 the salvation that is in *C* Jesus,
3: 12 life in *C* Jesus will be persecuted,
3: 15 salvation through faith in *C* Jesus.
4: 1 presence of God and of *C* Jesus,
Tit 1: 1 an apostle of Jesus *C* for the faith
1: 4 the Father and *C* Jesus our Savior.
2: 13 our great God and Savior, Jesus *C,*
3: 6 through Jesus *C* our Savior,
Phm : 1 Paul, a prisoner of *C* Jesus,
: 3 our Father and the Lord Jesus *C.*
: 6 of every good thing we have in *C.*
: 8 although in *C* I could be bold
: 9 now also a prisoner of *C* Jesus—
: 20 in the Lord; refresh my heart in *C.*
: 23 my fellow prisoner for *C* Jesus,
: 25 The grace of the Lord Jesus *C* be
Heb 3: 6 But *C* is faithful as a son
3: 14 to share in *C* if we hold firmly
5: 5 So *C* also did not take
6: 1 the elementary teachings about *C*
9: 11 When *C* came as high priest
9: 14 more, then, will the blood of *C,*
9: 15 For this reason *C* is the mediator
9: 24 For *C* did not enter a man-made
9: 26 Then *C* would have had
9: 28 so *C* was sacrificed once
10: 5 when *C* came into the world,
10: 10 of the body of Jesus *C* once for all.
11: 26 regarded disgrace for the sake of *C*
13: 8 Jesus *C* is the same yesterday
13: 21 through Jesus *C,* to whom be glory
Jas 1: 1 of God and of the Lord Jesus *C,*
2: 1 in our glorious Lord Jesus *C,*
1Pe 1: 1 apostle of Jesus *C,* To God's elect,
1: 2 for obedience to Jesus *C*
1: 3 and Father of our Lord Jesus *C!*
1: 3 of Jesus *C* from the dead,
1: 7 honor when Jesus *C* is revealed.
1: 11 he predicted the sufferings of *C*
1: 11 the Spirit of *C* in them was pointing
1: 13 you when Jesus *C* is revealed.
1: 19 but with the precious blood of *C,*
2: 5 acceptable to God through Jesus *C.*
2: 21 because *C* suffered for you,
3: 15 in your hearts set apart *C* as Lord.
1Pe 3: 16 behavior in *C* may be ashamed
3: 18 For *C* died for sins once for all,
3: 21 you by the resurrection of Jesus *C,*
4: 1 since *C* suffered in his body,
4: 11 may be praised through Jesus *C.*
4: 13 participate in the sufferings of *C,*
4: 14 insulted because of the name of *C,*
5: 10 you to his eternal glory in *C,*
5: 14 Peace to all of you who are in *C.*
2Pe 1: 1 a servant and apostle of Jesus *C,*
1: 1 and Savior Jesus *C* have received
1: 8 knowledge of our Lord Jesus *C.*
1: 11 of our Lord and Savior Jesus *C.*
1: 14 as our Lord Jesus *C* has made clear
1: 16 and coming of our Lord Jesus *C,*
2: 20 and Savior Jesus *C* and are again
3: 18 of our Lord and Savior Jesus *C.*
1Jn 1: 3 and with his Son, Jesus *C.*
2: 1 Jesus *C,* the Righteous One.
2: 22 man who denies that Jesus is the *C.*
3: 16 Jesus *C* laid down his life for us.
3: 23 in the name of his Son, Jesus *C,*
4: 2 that Jesus *C* has come
5: 1 believes that Jesus is the *C* is born
5: 6 by water and blood—Jesus *C.*
5: 20 even in his Son Jesus *C.*
2Jn : 3 God the Father and from Jesus *C,*
: 7 who do not acknowledge Jesus *C*
: 9 teaching of *C* does not have God;
Jude : 1 a servant of Jesus *C* and a brother
: 1 the Father and kept by Jesus *C:*
: 4 deny Jesus *C* our only Sovereign
: 17 of our Lord Jesus *C* foretold.
: 21 of our Lord Jesus *C* to bring you
: 25 through Jesus *C* our Lord,
Rev 1: 1 The revelation of Jesus *C,*
1: 2 and the testimony of Jesus *C.*
1: 5 from Jesus *C,* who is the faithful
11: 15 kingdom of our Lord and of his *C,*
12: 10 and the authority of his *C.*
20: 4 reigned with *C* a thousand years.
20: 6 they will be priests of God and of *C*

CHRIST'S (CHRIST)

1Co 7: 22 man when he was called is *C* slave.
9: 21 from God's law but am under *C* law
2Co 5: 14 For *C* love compels us,
5: 20 We are therefore *C* ambassadors,
5: 20 We implore you on *C* behalf:
12: 9 so that *C* power may rest on me.
12: 10 for *C* sake, I delight in weaknesses,
Col 1: 22 by *C* physical body through death
1: 24 lacking in regard to *C* afflictions,
2Th 3: 5 God's love and *C* perseverance.
1Pe 5: 1 a witness of *C* sufferings

CHRISTIAN (CHRIST)

Ac 26: 28 you can persuade me to be a *C?"*
1Pe 4: 16 as a *C,* do not be ashamed,

CHRISTIANS (CHRIST)

Ac 11: 26 The disciples were first called *C*

CHRISTS (CHRIST)

Mt 24: 24 For false *C* and false prophets will
Mk 13: 22 For false *C* and false prophets will

CHRONIC

Lev 13: 11 it is a *c* skin disease and the priest

CHRONICLES

Est 6: 1 so he ordered the book of the *c,*

CHRYSOLITE

Ex 28: 20 in the fourth row a *c,* an onyx
39: 13 in the fourth row a *c,* an onyx
SS 5: 14 set with *c.*
Eze 1: 16 They sparkled like *c,* and all four
10: 9 the wheels sparkled like *c.*
28: 13 *c,* onyx and jasper,
Da 10: 6 His body was like *c,* his face like
Rev 21: 20 the seventh *c,* the eighth beryl,

CHRYSOPRASE

Rev 21: 20 the tenth *c,* the eleventh jacinth,

CHURCH (CHURCHES)

Mt 16: 18 and on this rock I will build my *c,*
Mt 18: 17 if he refuses to listen even to the *c,*
18: 17 tell it to the *c;* and if he refuses
Ac 5: 11 Great fear seized the whole *c*
8: 1 out against the *c* at Jerusalem,
8: 3 But Saul began to destroy the *c*
9: 31 Then the *c* throughout Judea,
11: 22 the ears of the *c* at Jerusalem,
11: 26 met with the *c* and taught great
12: 1 some who belonged to the *c,*
12: 5 the *c* was earnestly praying to God
13: 1 In the *c* at Antioch there were
14: 23 elders for them in each *c*
14: 27 they gathered the *c* together
15: 3 The *c* sent them on their way,
15: 4 they were welcomed by the *c*
15: 22 and elders, with the whole *c,*
15: 30 where they gathered the *c* together
18: 22 he went up and greeted the *c*
20: 17 to Ephesus for the elders of the *c.*
20: 28 Be shepherds of the *c* of God,
Ro 16: 1 a servant of the *c* in Cenchrea.
16: 5 also the *c* that meets at their house.
16: 23 and the whole *c* here enjoy,
1Co 1: 2 To the *c* of God in Corinth,
4: 17 I teach everywhere in every *c.*
5: 12 of mine to judge those outside the *c*
6: 4 even men of little account in the *c!*
10: 32 Jews, Greeks or the *c* of God—
11: 18 when you come together as a *c,*
11: 22 Or do you despise the *c* of God
12: 28 in the *c* God has appointed first
14: 4 but he who prophesies edifies the *c.*
14: 5 so that the *c* may be edified.
14: 12 to excel in gifts that build up the *c.*
14: 19 in the *c* I would rather speak five
14: 23 So if the whole *c* comes together
14: 26 done for the strengthening of the *c.*
14: 28 speaker should keep quiet in the *c*
14: 35 for a woman to speak in the *c.*
15: 9 because I persecuted the *c* of God.
16: 19 and so does the *c* that meets
2Co 1: 1 To the *c* of God in Corinth,
Gal 1: 13 how intensely I persecuted the *c*
Eph 1: 22 to be head over everything for the *c*
3: 10 intent was that now, through the *c,*
3: 21 to him be glory in the *c*
5: 23 as Christ is the head of the *c,*
5: 24 Now as the *c* submits to Christ,
5: 25 just as Christ loved the *c*
5: 27 her to himself as a radiant *c,*
5: 29 just as Christ does the *c*—
5: 32 I am talking about Christ and the *c.*
Php 3: 6 *c;* as for legalistic righteousness,
4: 15 not one *c* shared with me
Col 1: 18 he is the head of the body, the *c;*
1: 24 the sake of his body, which is the *c.*
4: 15 to Nympha and the *c* in her house.
4: 16 also read in the *c* of the Laodiceans
1Th 1: 1 To the *c* of the Thessalonians
2Th 1: 1 To the *c* of the Thessalonians
1Ti 3: 5 how can he take care of God's *c?)*
3: 15 which is the *c* of the living God,
5: 16 not let the *c* be burdened with them
5: 16 so that the *c* can help those widows
5: 17 the affairs of the *c* well are worthy
Phm : 2 to the *c* that meets in your home:
Heb 12: 23 to the *c* of the firstborn, whose
Jas 5: 14 the elders of the *c* to pray over him
3Jn : 6 have told the *c* about your love.
: 9 I wrote to the *c,* but Diotrephes,
: 10 and puts them out of the *c.*
Rev 2: 1 the angel of the *c* in Ephesus write:
2: 8 the angel of the *c* in Smyrna write:
2: 12 angel of the *c* in Pergamum write:
2: 18 the angel of the *c* in Thyatira write:
3: 1 To the angel of the *c* in Sardis write
3: 7 angel of the *c* in Philadelphia write:
3: 14 angel of the *c* in Laodicea write:

CHURCHES (CHURCH)

Ac 15: 41 and Cilicia, strengthening the *c.*
16: 5 the *c* were strengthened in the faith
Ro 16: 4 all the *c* of the Gentiles are grateful
16: 16 All the *c* of Christ send greetings.
1Co 7: 17 is the rule I lay down in all the *c.*
11: 16 no other practice—nor do the *c*
14: 34 should remain silent in the *c.*
16: 1 Do what I told the Galatian *c* to do.

1Co 16: 19 The *c* in the province
2Co 8: 1 God has given the Macedonian *c*.
8: 18 praised by all the *c* for his service
8: 19 chosen by the *c* to accompany us
8: 23 they are representatives of the *c*
8: 24 pride in you, so that the *c* can see it.
11: 8 other *c* by receiving support
11: 28 of my concern for all the *c*.
12: 13 were you inferior to the other *c*,
Gal 1: 2 with me, To the *c* in Galatia:
1: 22 unknown to the *c* of Judea that are
1Th 2: 14 imitators of God's *c* in Judea,
2: 14 the same things those *c* suffered
2Th 1: 4 among God's *c* we boast about
Rev 1: 4 To the seven *c* in the province
1: 11 you see and send it to the seven *c*:
1: 20 seven lampstands are the seven *c*.
1: 20 stars are the angels of the seven *c*,
2: 7 hear what the Spirit says to the *c*.
2: 11 hear what the Spirit says to the *c*.
2: 17 hear what the Spirit says to the *c*.
2: 23 all the *c* will know that I am he who
2: 29 hear what the Spirit says to the *c*.
3: 6 hear what the Spirit says to the *c*.
3: 13 hear what the Spirit says to the *c*.
3: 22 hear what the Spirit says to the *c*."
22: 16 to give you this testimony for the *c*.

CHURN (CHURNED CHURNING CHURNS)
Job 41: 31 makes the depths *c* like a boiling

CHURNED (CHURN)
Job 26: 12 By his power he *c* up the sea;

CHURNING (CHURN)
Job 30: 27 The *c* inside me never stops;
Pr 30: 33 For as *c* the milk produces butter,
Eze 32: 2 *c* the water with your feet
Da 7: 2 winds of heaven *c* up the great sea.
Hab 3: 15 *c* the great waters.

CHURNS (CHURN)
Isa 51: 15 who *c* up the sea so that its waves

CILICIA
Ac 6: 9 well as the provinces of *C* and Asia.
15: 23 believers in Antioch, Syria and *C*:
15: 41 He went through Syria and *C*,
21: 39 from Tarsus in *C*, a citizen
22: 3 born in Tarsus of *C*, but brought up
23: 34 Learning that he was from *C*,
27: 5 the open sea off the coast of *C*
Gal 1: 21 Later I went to Syria and *C*.

CINNAMON
Ex 30: 23 shekels) of fragrant *c*,
Pr 7: 17 with myrrh, aloes and *c*.
SS 4: 14 calamus and *c*,
Rev 18: 13 cargoes of *c* and spice, of incense,

CIRCLE (CIRCLED CIRCLING CIRCULAR ENCIRCLE ENCIRCLED ENCIRCLING)
2Sa 5: 23 but *c* around behind them
1Ch 14: 14 but *c* around them and attack them
Isa 40: 22 enthroned above the *c* of the earth,
Mk 3: 34 at those seated in a *c* around him

CIRCLED (CIRCLE)
Jos 6: 15 on that day they *c* the city seven

CIRCLING (CIRCLE)
Jos 6: 11 carried around the city, *c* it once.

CIRCUIT
1Sa 7: 16 went on a *c* from Bethel to Gilgal
Ps 19: 6 and makes its *c* to the other;

CIRCULAR (CIRCLE)
1Ki 7: 23 the Sea of cast metal, *c* in shape,
7: 31 that had a *c* frame one cubit
7: 35 the stand there was a *c* band half
2Ch 4: 2 the Sea of cast metal, *c* in shape,

CIRCULATED
Mt 28: 15 And this story has been widely *c*

CIRCUMCISE (CIRCUMCISED CIRCUMCISING CIRCUMCISION)
Dt 10: 16 *C* your hearts, therefore,
30: 6 LORD your God will *c* your hearts
Jos 5: 2 and *c* the Israelites again."
Jer 4: 4 *C* yourselves to the LORD,
4: 4 *c* your hearts,
Lk 1: 59 day they came to *c* the child,
2: 21 when it was time to *c* him,
Jn 7: 22 you *c* a child on the Sabbath.
Ac 21: 21 telling them not to *c* their children

CIRCUMCISED (CIRCUMCISE)
Ge 17: 10 Every male among you shall be *c*.
17: 12 who is eight days old must be *c*,
17: 13 with your money, they must be *c*.
17: 14 who has not been *c* in the flesh,
17: 23 and *c* them, as God told him.
17: 24 years old when he was *c*,
17: 26 and his son Ishmael were both *c*
17: 27 from a foreigner, was *c* with him.
21: 4 Abraham *c* him, as God
34: 14 sister to a man who is not *c*.
34: 17 But if you will not agree to be *c*,
34: 22 the condition that our males be *c*,
34: 24 and every male in the city was *c*.
Ex 12: 44 eat of it after you have *c* him,
12: 48 the males in his household *c*;
Lev 12: 3 On the eighth day the boy is to be *c*
Jos 5: 3 and *c* the Israelites at Gibeath
5: 5 people that came out had been *c*,
5: 7 and these were the ones Joshua *c*.
5: 7 they had not been *c* on the way.
5: 8 after the whole nation had been *c*,
Jer 9: 25 I will punish all who are *c* only
Jn 7: 23 if a child can be *c* on the Sabbath
Ac 7: 8 and *c* him eight days after his birth.
10: 45 The *c* believers who had come
11: 2 the *c* believers criticized him
15: 1 "Unless you are *c*, according
15: 5 "The Gentiles must be *c*
16: 3 so he *c* him because of the Jews
Ro 2: 25 as though you had not been *c*.
2: 26 be regarded as though they were *c*?
2: 26 those who are not *c* keep the law's
2: 27 The one who is not *c* physically
3: 30 who will justify the *c* by faith
4: 9 Is this blessedness only for the *c*,
4: 10 Was it after he was *c*, or before?
4: 11 all who believe but have not been *c*,
4: 12 Abraham had before he was *c*.
4: 12 father of the *c* who not only are *c*
1Co 7: 18 Was a man already *c*
7: 18 he was called? He should not be *c*.
Gal 2: 3 was compelled to be *c*, even
5: 2 that if you let yourselves be *c*,
5: 3 who lets himself be *c* that he is
6: 12 trying to compel you to be *c*.
6: 13 even those who are *c* obey the law,
6: 13 to be *c* that they may boast about
Php 3: 5 I have more: *c* on the eighth day,
Col 2: 11 *c*, in the putting off of the sinful
3: 11 *c* or uncircumcised, barbarian,

CIRCUMCISING (CIRCUMCISE)
Ge 34: 15 us by *c* all your males.

CIRCUMCISION (CIRCUMCISE)
Ge 17: 11 to undergo *c*, and it will be the sign
Ex 4: 26 of blood," referring to *c*.)
Jn 7: 22 because Moses gave you *c*
Ac 7: 8 he gave Abraham the covenant of *c*
Ro 2: 25 *C* has value if you observe the law,
2: 27 you have the written code and *c*,
2: 28 nor is *c* merely outward
2: 29 and *c* is *c* of the heart, by the Spirit,
3: 1 or what value is there in *c*?
4: 11 And he received the sign of *c*,
1Co 7: 19 *C* is nothing and uncircumcision is
Gal 2: 12 those who belonged to the *c* group.
5: 6 For in Christ Jesus neither *c*
5: 11 Brothers, if I am still preaching *c*,
6: 15 Neither *c* nor uncircumcision
Eph 2: 11 call themselves "the *c*" (that done
Php 3: 3 we who are the *c*, we who worship
Col 2: 11 but with the *c* done by Christ,
2: 11 not with a *c* done by the hands
Tit 1: 10 especially those of the *c* group.

CIRCUMFERENCE
Jer 52: 21 cubits high and twelve cubits in *c*;

CIRCUMSTANCES
1Ch 29: 30 and the *c* that surrounded him
Ro 4: 10 Under what *c* was it credited?
1Co 7: 15 or woman is not bound in such *c*;
Php 4: 11 to be content whatever the *c*.
Col 4: 8 that you may know about our *c*
1Th 5: 18 continually; give thanks in all *c*,
Jas 1: 9 The brother in humble *c* ought
1Pe 1: 11 and *c* to which the Spirit of Christ

CISTERN (CISTERNS)
Ge 37: 22 Throw him into this *c* here
37: 24 took him and threw him into the *c*.
37: 24 *c* was empty; there was no water
37: 28 pulled Joseph up out of the *c*
37: 29 When Reuben returned to the *c*
Lev 11: 36 or a *c* for collecting water remains
1Sa 19: 22 and went to the great *c* at Secu.
2Ki 18: 31 and drink water from his own *c*,
Pr 5: 15 Drink water from your own *c*,
Isa 30: 14 or scooping water out of a *c*."
36: 16 and drink water from his own *c*,
Jer 38: 6 Jeremiah by ropes into the *c*;
38: 6 and put him into the *c* of Malkijah,
38: 7 they had put Jeremiah into the *c*.
38: 9 They have thrown him into a *c*,
38: 10 out of the *c* before he dies."
38: 11 with ropes to Jeremiah in the *c*.
38: 13 and lifted him out of the *c*.
41: 7 them and threw them into a *c*.
41: 9 the *c* where he threw all the bodies

CISTERNS (CISTERN)
Ge 37: 20 and throw him into one of these *c*
1Sa 13: 6 among the rocks, and in pits and *c*.
2Ch 26: 10 in the desert and dug many *c*,
Jer 2: 13 and have dug their own *c*,
2: 13 broken *c* that cannot hold water.
14: 3 they go to the *c*

CITADEL (CITADELS)
2Sa 12: 26 and captured the royal *c*.
1Ki 16: 18 went into the *c* of the royal palace
2Ki 15: 25 in the *c* of the royal palace
Ezr 6: 2 in the *c* of Ecbatana in the province
Ne 1: 1 while I was in the *c* of Susa, Hanani
2: 8 for the gates of the *c* by the temple
7: 2 Hananiah the commander of the *c*,
Est 1: 2 from his royal throne in the *c*
1: 5 who were in the *c* of Susa.
2: 3 into the harem at the *c* of Susa.
2: 5 there was in the *c* of Susa a Jew
2: 8 many girls were brought to the *c*
3: 15 the edict was issued in the *c* of Susa
8: 14 also issued in the *c* of Susa.
9: 6 In the *c* of Susa, the Jews killed
9: 11 slain in the *c* of Susa was reported
9: 12 sons of Haman in the *c* of Susa.
Pr 18: 19 are like the barred gates of a *c*.
Isa 32: 14 *c* and watchtower will become
Da 8: 2 in the *c* of Susa in the province

CITADELS (CITADEL)
Ps 48: 3 God is in her *c*;
48: 13 view her *c*,
122: 7 and security within your *c*."
Isa 34: 13 Thorns will overrun her *c*,

CITIES (CITY)
Ge 13: 12 lived among the *c* of the plain
19: 25 Thus he overthrew those *c*
19: 25 including all those living in the *c*—
19: 29 So when God destroyed the *c*
19: 29 that overthrew the *c* where Lot had
22: 17 of the *c* of their enemies,
41: 35 to be kept in the *c* for food.
41: 48 in Egypt and stored it in the *c*.
Ex 1: 11 Rameses as store *c* for Pharaoh.
Lev 26: 25 When you withdraw into your *c*,
26: 31 I will turn your *c* into ruins
26: 33 and your *c* will lie in ruins.
Nu 13: 28 the *c* are fortified and very large.
21: 2 we will totally destroy their *c*."

Nu 21: 25 Israel captured all the *c*
32: 16 and *c* for our women and children.
32: 17 and children will live in fortified *c*,
32: 24 Build *c* for your women
32: 26 and herds will remain here in the *c*
32: 33 the whole land with its *c*
32: 36 and Beth Haran as fortified *c*,
32: 38 names to the *c* they rebuilt.
35: 6 towns you give the Levites will be *c*
35: 11 towns to be your *c* of refuge,
35: 13 six towns you give will be your *c*
35: 14 and three in Canaan as *c* of refuge.
Dt 1: 28 the *c* are large, with walls up
3: 4 At that time we took all his *c*.
3: 4 of the sixty *c* that we did not take
3: 5 All these *c* were fortified
3: 7 the plunder from their *c* we carried
4: 41 Then Moses set aside three *c* east
4: 42 He could flee into one of these *c*
4: 43 The *c* were these: Bezer
6: 10 flourishing *c* you did not build,
9: 1 with large *c* that have walls up
19: 2 yourselves three *c* centrally
19: 5 That man may flee to one of these *c*
19: 7 to set aside for yourselves three *c*.
19: 9 are to set aside three more *c*.
19: 11 and then flees to one of these *c*,
20: 15 are to treat all the *c* that are
20: 16 in the *c* of the nations the LORD
28: 52 They will besiege all the *c*
28: 52 to all the *c* throughout your land
28: 55 on you during the siege of all your *c*
28: 57 enemy will inflict on you in your *c*.
Jos 9: 17 on the third day came to their *c*:
10: 2 like one of the royal *c*; it was larger
10: 19 and don't let them reach their *c*,
10: 20 were left reached their fortified *c*.
11: 12 Joshua took all these royal *c*
11: 13 of the *c* built on their mounds—
11: 14 plunder and livestock of these *c*,
13: 31 Edrei (the royal *c* of Og in Bashan).
14: 12 and their *c* were large and fortified,
18: 21 had the following *c*: Jericho,
19: 35 The fortified *c* were Ziddim, Zer,
20: 2 to designate the *c* of refuge,
20: 4 "When he flees to one of these *c*,
20: 9 flee to these designated *c*
24: 13 did not toil and *c* you did not build;
2Sa 10: 12 for our people and the *c* of our God
20: 6 he will find fortified *c* and escape
1Ki 4: 13 and its sixty large walled *c*
8: 37 besieges them in any of their *c*,
9: 19 as well as all his store *c*
10: 26 which he kept in the chariot *c* and
15: 23 all he did and the *c* he built,
20: 34 "I will return the *c* my father took
22: 39 with ivory, and the *c* he fortified,
2Ki 18: 13 Assyria attacked all the fortified *c*
19: 25 that you have turned fortified *c*
1Ch 19: 13 for our people and the *c* of our God
2Ch 1: 14 which he kept in the chariot *c* and
6: 28 besiege them in any of their *c*,
8: 4 and all the store *c* he had built
8: 5 Lower Beth Horon as fortified *c*,
8: 6 and all the *c* for his chariots
8: 6 as well as Baalath and all his store *c*
9: 25 which he kept in the chariot *c* and
11: 10 These were fortified *c* in Judah
11: 12 put shields and spears in all the *c*,
11: 23 Benjamin, and to all the fortified *c*.
12: 4 he captured the fortified *c* of Judah
14: 6 He built up the fortified *c* of Judah,
16: 4 and all the store *c* of Naphtali.
17: 2 troops in all the fortified *c* of Judah
17: 12 he built forts and store *c* in Judah
17: 19 in the fortified *c* throughout Judah.
19: 5 in each of the fortified *c* of Judah.
19: 10 countrymen who live in the *c*—
21: 3 as well as fortified *c* in Judah,
32: 1 He laid siege to the fortified *c*,
33: 14 in all the fortified *c* in Judah.
Ne 9: 25 They captured fortified *c*
Est 9: 2 in their *c* in all the provinces
Ps 9: 6 you have uprooted their *c*;
69: 35 and rebuild the *c* of Judah.
Isa 1: 7 your *c* burned with fire;
6: 11 "Until the *c* lie ruined
14: 17 who overthrew its *c*
14: 21 and cover the earth with their *c*.
17: 2 The *c* of Aroer will be deserted
17: 9 day their strong *c*, which they left
19: 18 In that day five *c* in Egypt will
25: 3 *c* of ruthless nations will revere you
36: 1 Assyria attacked all the fortified *c*
37: 26 that you have turned fortified *c*
54: 3 and settle in their desolate *c*.
61: 4 they will renew the ruined *c*
64: 10 Your sacred *c* have become
Jer 4: 5 Let us flee to the fortified *c*!'
4: 16 cry against the *c* of Judah.
5: 17 the fortified *c* in which you trust.
8: 14 Let us flee to the fortified *c*
13: 19 The *c* in the Negev will be shut up,
14: 2 her *c* languish;
34: 7 These were the only fortified *c* left
34: 7 the other *c* of Judah that were still
46: 8 I will destroy *c* and their people.'
48: 18 and ruin your fortified *c*.
48: 41 The *c* will be captured
Eze 26: 19 like *c* no longer inhabited,
29: 12 forty years among ruined *c*.
29: 12 her *c* will lie desolate forty years
30: 7 and their *c* will lie
30: 7 lie among ruined *c*.
30: 17 and the *c* themselves will go
36: 35 the *c* that were lying in ruins,
36: 38 So will the ruined *c* be filled
Hos 8: 14 But I will send fire upon their *c*
11: 6 Swords will flash in their *c*,
Am 9: 14 they will rebuild the ruined *c*
Mic 5: 11 I will destroy the *c* of your land
5: 14 and demolish your *c*.
7: 12 from Assyria and the *c* of Egypt,
Hab 1: 10 They laugh at all fortified *c*;
2: 8 and *c* and everyone in them.
2: 17 and *c* and everyone in them.
Zep 1: 16 cry against the fortified *c*
3: 6 Their *c* are destroyed,
Zec 8: 20 of many *c* will yet come,
Mt 10: 23 going through the *c* of Israel
11: 20 to denounce the *c* in which most
Lk 19: 17 small matter, take charge of ten *c*.'
19: 19 'You take charge of five *c*.'
Ac 14: 6 fled to the Lycaonian *c* of Lystra
26: 11 went to foreign *c* to persecute them
2Pe 2: 6 if he condemned the *c* of Sodom
Rev 16: 19 and the *c* of the nations collapsed.

CITIZEN (CITIZENS CITIZENSHIP)

Lk 15: 15 out to a *c* of that country,
Ac 21: 39 in Cilicia, a *c* of no ordinary city.
22: 25 you to flog a Roman *c* who hasn't
22: 26 "This man is a Roman *c*."
22: 27 are you a Roman *c*?" "Yes, I am,"
22: 28 "But I was born a *c*," Paul replied.
22: 29 that he had put Paul, a Roman *c*,
23: 27 I had learned that he is a Roman *c*.

CITIZENS (CITIZEN)

Nu 21: 28 the *c* of Arnon's heights.
Jos 8: 33 All Israel, aliens and *c* alike,
24: 11 The *c* of Jericho fought against you
Jdg 9: 2 "Ask all the *c* of Shechem,
9: 3 this to the *c* of Shechem,
9: 6 Then all the *c* of Shechem
9: 7 "Listen to me, *c* of Shechem,
9: 18 king over the *c* of Shechem
9: 20 and consume you, *c* of Shechem
9: 20 from you, *c* of Shechem and
9: 23 spirit between Abimelech and the *c*
9: 24 and on the *c* of Shechem,
9: 25 to him these *c* of Shechem set men
9: 26 its *c* put their confidence in him.
9: 39 So Gaal led out the *c* of Shechem
9: 46 the *c* in the tower of Shechem went
1Sa 23: 11 Will the *c* of Keilah surrender me
23: 12 "Will the *c* of Keilah surrender me
2Sa 21: 12 from the *c* of Jabesh Gilead.
Isa 48: 2 you who call yourselves *c*
Eze 26: 17 you and your *c*;
Ac 16: 37 even though we are Roman *c*,
16: 38 that Paul and Silas were Roman *c*,
Eph 2: 19 but fellow *c* with God's people

CITIZENSHIP (CITIZEN)

Ac 22: 28 "I had to pay a big price for my *c*."
Eph 2: 12 excluded from *c* in Israel
Php 3: 20 But our *c* is in heaven.

CITRON

Rev 18: 12 scarlet cloth; every sort of *c* wood,

CITY (CITIES CITY'S)

Ge 4: 17 Cain was then building a *c*,
10: 12 and Calah; that is the great *c*.
11: 4 "Come, let us build ourselves a *c*,
11: 5 the LORD came down to see the *c*
11: 8 and they stopped building the *c*.
18: 24 are fifty righteous people in the *c*?
18: 26 people in the *c* of Sodom,
18: 28 Will you destroy the whole *c*
19: 1 sitting in the gateway of the *c*.
19: 4 from every part of the *c* of Sodom
19: 12 or anyone else in the *c* who belongs
19: 14 the LORD is about to destroy the *c*
19: 15 away when the *c* is punished."
19: 16 and led them safely out of the *c*,
23: 10 come to the gate of his *c*.
23: 18 come to the gate of the *c*.
28: 19 though the *c* used to be called Luz.
33: 18 and camped within sight of the *c*.
33: 18 at the *c* of Shechem in Canaan
34: 20 went to the gate of their *c* to speak
34: 24 male in the *c* was circumcised.
34: 24 of the *c* gate agreed with Hamor
34: 25 and attacked the unsuspecting *c*,
34: 27 looted the *c* where their sister had
34: 28 everything else of theirs in the *c*
36: 32 His *c* was named Dinhabah.
36: 35 His *c* was named Avith.
36: 39 His *c* was named Pau,
41: 48 In each *c* he put the food grown
44: 4 far from the *c* when Joseph said
44: 13 donkeys and returned to the *c*.
Ex 9: 29 "When I have gone out of the *c*,
9: 33 left Pharaoh and went out of the *c*.
Lev 25: 29 If a man sells a house in a walled *c*,
25: 30 house in the walled *c* shall belong
Nu 21: 26 Heshbon was the *c* of Sihon king
21: 27 let Sihon's *c* be restored.
21: 28 a blaze from the *c* of Sihon.
24: 19 and destroy the survivors of the *c*."
35: 25 send him back to the *c* of refuge
35: 26 outside the limits of the *c* of refuge
35: 27 of blood finds him outside the *c*,
35: 28 in his *c* of refuge until the death
35: 32 for anyone who has fled to a *c*
Dt 3: 6 destroying every *c*— men,
17: 5 done this evil deed to your *c* gate
19: 12 bring him back from the *c*,
20: 10 When you march up to attack a *c*,
20: 12 you in battle, lay siege to that *c*.
20: 14 and everything else in the *c*,
20: 19 siege to a *c* for a long time,
20: 20 until the *c* at war with you falls.
28: 3 You will be blessed in the *c*
28: 16 You will be cursed in the *c*
34: 3 the *C* of Palms, as far as Zoar.
Jos 2: 5 when it was time to close the *c* gate
2: 15 lived in was part of the *c* wall.
6: 3 March around the *c* once
6: 4 march around the *c* seven times,
6: 5 then the wall of the *c* will collapse
6: 7 "Advance! March around the *c*,
6: 11 of the LORD carried around the *c*,
6: 14 marched around the *c* once
6: 15 day they circled the *c* seven times.
6: 15 marched around the *c* seven times
6: 16 For the LORD has given you the *c*
6: 17 The *c* and all that is in it are
6: 20 straight in, and they took the *c*.
6: 21 They devoted the *c* to the LORD
6: 24 Then they burned the whole *c*
6: 26 who undertakes to rebuild this *c*,
7: 5 the Israelites from the *c* gate
8: 1 his people, his *c* and his land.
8: 2 Set an ambush behind the *c*."
8: 4 are to set an ambush behind the *c*.
8: 5 with me will advance on the *c*,
8: 6 have lured them away from the *c*,
8: 7 up from ambush and take the *c*.
8: 8 When you have taken the *c*,
8: 11 and approached the *c* and arrived
8: 11 the valley between them and the *c*.

Jos 8: 12 and Ai, to the west of the *c*.
8: 13 in the camp to the north of the *c*
8: 14 and all the men of the *c* hurried out
8: 14 set against him behind the *c*.
8: 16 and were lured away from the *c*.
8: 17 They left the *c* open and went
8: 18 into your hand I will deliver the *c*.''
8: 19 They entered the *c* and captured it
8: 20 of the *c* rising against the sky,
8: 21 that smoke was going up from the *c*
8: 21 that the ambush had taken the *c*
8: 22 also came out of the *c* against them,
8: 27 the livestock and plunder of this *c*,
8: 29 down at the entrance of the *c* gate.
10: 2 because Gibeon was an important *c*
10: 28 He put the *c* and its king
10: 30 The LORD also gave that *c*
10: 30 The *c* and everyone in it Joshua put
10: 32 The *c* and everyone in it he put
10: 37 They took the *c* and put it
10: 39 They took the *c*, its king
11: 19 not one *c* made a treaty of peace
15: 8 slope of the Jebusite *c* (that is,
15: 62 Nibshan, the *C* of Salt
18: 16 the southern slope of the Jebusite *c*
18: 28 Haeleph, the Jebusite *c* (that is,
19: 29 and went to the fortified *c* of Tyre,
20: 4 case before the elders of that *c*.
20: 4 stand in the entrance of the *c* gate
20: 4 they are to admit him into their *c*
20: 6 stay in that *c* until he has stood trial
21: 12 around the *c* they had given
21: 13 the priest they gave Hebron (a *c*
21: 21 they were given Shechem (a *c*
21: 27 Golan in Bashan (a *c* of refuge
21: 32 Kedesh in Galilee (a *c* of refuge
21: 38 Ramoth in Gilead (a *c* of refuge
Jdg 1: 8 They put the *c* to the sword
1: 16 went up from the *C* of Palms
1: 17 and they totally destroyed the *c*.
1: 18 Ekron—each *c* with its territory.
1: 24 spies saw a man coming out of the *c*
1: 24 "Show us how to get into the *c*
1: 25 and they put the *c* to the sword
1: 26 where he built a *c* and called it Luz,
3: 13 and they took possession of the *C*
5: 8 war came to the *c* gates,
5: 11 went down to the *c* gates.
9: 30 of the *c* heard what Gaal son
9: 31 are stirring up the *c* against you.
9: 33 at sunrise, advance against the *c*.
9: 35 at the entrance to the *c* gate just
9: 43 saw the people coming out of the *c*,
9: 44 at the entrance to the *c* gate.
9: 45 Then he destroyed the *c*
9: 45 against the *c* until he had captured
9: 51 Inside the *c*, however, was a strong
9: 51 all the people of the *c*— fled.
16: 2 wait for him all night at the *c* gate.
16: 3 took hold of the doors of the *c* gate,
18: 27 the sword and burned down their *c*.
18: 28 The Danites rebuilt the *c*
18: 28 The *c* was in a valley
18: 29 the *c* used to be called Laish.
19: 11 let's stop at this *c* of the Jebusites
19: 12 We won't go into an alien *c*,
19: 15 They went and sat in the *c* square,
19: 17 saw the traveler in the *c* square,
19: 22 men of the *c* surrounded the house.
20: 11 united as one man against the *c*.
20: 31 and were drawn away from the *c*.
20: 32 away from the *c* to the roads."
20: 37 and put the whole *c* to the sword.
20: 38 cloud of smoke from the *c*,
20: 40 of smoke began to rise from the *c*,
20: 40 of the whole *c* going up into the sky
1Sa 5: 9 He afflicted the people of the *c*,
5: 9 LORD's hand was against that *c*,
5: 11 For death had filled the *c*
5: 12 and the outcry of the *c* went up
15: 5 Saul went to the *c* of Amalek
27: 5 live in the royal *c* with you?"
2Sa 5: 7 fortress of Zion, the *C* of David.
5: 9 and called it the *C* of David.
6: 10 to be with him in the *C* of David.
6: 12 of Obed-Edom to the *C* of David
6: 16 of the LORD was entering the *C*
10: 3 them to you to explore the *c*

2Sa 10: 8 at the entrance to their *c* gate,
10: 14 Abishai and went inside the *c*.
11: 16 So while Joab had the *c* under siege
11: 17 When the men of the *c* came out
11: 20 get so close to the *c* to fight?
11: 23 back to the entrance to the *c* gate.
11: 25 Press the attack against the *c*
12: 28 Otherwise I will take the *c*,
12: 28 and besiege the *c* and capture it.
12: 30 quantity of plunder from the *c*
15: 2 of the road leading to the *c* gate.
15: 14 and put the *c* to the sword."
15: 24 people had finished leaving the *c*.
15: 25 Take the ark of God back into the *c*
15: 27 Go back to the *c* in peace,
15: 34 return to the *c* and say to Absalom,
15: 37 as Absalom was entering the *c*.
17: 13 all Israel will bring ropes to that *c*,
17: 13 into a *c*, then all Israel will bring
17: 17 not risk being seen entering the *c*.
18: 3 you to give us support from the *c*."
19: 3 The men stole into the *c* that day
20: 15 They built a siege ramp up to the *c*,
20: 16 a wise woman called from the *c*,
20: 19 to destroy a *c* that is a mother
20: 21 and I'll withdraw from the *c*."
20: 22 and his men dispersed from the *c*,
1Ki 1: 41 meaning of all the noise in the *c*?"
1: 45 and the *c* resounds with it.
2: 10 and was buried in the *C* of David.
3: 1 He brought her to the *C* of David
8: 1 from Zion, the *C* of David.
8: 16 I have not chosen a *c* in any tribe
8: 44 toward the *c* you have chosen
8: 48 toward the *c* you have chosen
9: 24 up from the *C* of David
11: 27 wall of the *c* of David his father.
11: 32 sake of my servant David and the *c*
11: 36 the *c* where I chose
11: 43 and was buried in the *c*
13: 25 in the *c* where the old prophet lived
13: 29 back to his own *c* to mourn for him
14: 11 to Jeroboam who die in the *c*,
14: 12 When you set foot in your *c*,
14: 21 the *c* the LORD had chosen out
14: 31 buried with them in the *C* of David.
15: 8 and was buried in the *C* of David.
15: 24 buried with them in the *c*
16: 4 to Baasha who die in the *c*,
16: 18 Zimri saw that the *c* was taken,
16: 24 of silver and built a *c* on the hill,
20: 2 messengers into the *c* to Ahab king
20: 12 So they prepared to attack the *c*.
20: 19 of the *c* with the army behind them
20: 30 And Ben-Hadad fled to the *c*
20: 30 of them escaped to the *c* of Aphek,
21: 8 lived in Naboth's *c* with him.
21: 11 nobles who lived in Naboth's *c* did
21: 13 So they took him outside the *c*
21: 24 belonging to Ahab who die in the *c*,
22: 26 back to Amon the ruler of the *c*
22: 50 buried with them in the *c*
2Ki 2: 19 The men of the *c* said to Elisha,
3: 19 will overthrow every fortified *c*
3: 27 as a sacrifice on the *c* wall.
6: 14 by night and surrounded the *c*.
6: 15 and chariots had surrounded the *c*.
6: 19 is not the road and this is not the *c*.
6: 20 they entered the *c*, Elisha said,
6: 25 There was a great famine in the *c*;
7: 3 at the entrance of the *c* gate.
7: 4 go into the *c*'— the famine is there,
7: 10 and called out to the *c* gatekeepers
7: 12 them alive and get into the *c*.' "
7: 13 of the horses that are left in the *c*.
8: 24 buried with them in the *C* of David.
9: 15 don't let anyone slip out of the *c*
9: 28 in his tomb in the *C* of David.
10: 2 horses, a fortified *c* and weapons,
10: 5 administrator, the *c* governor,
10: 6 were with the leading men of the *c*,
10: 8 of the *c* gate until morning."
11: 20 *c* was quiet, because Athaliah had
12: 21 with his fathers in the *C* of David.
14: 20 with his fathers, in the *C* of David.
15: 7 buried near them in the *C* of David.
15: 16 everyone in the *c* and its vicinity,
15: 38 City of David, the *c* of his father.

2Ki 15: 38 buried with them in the *C* of David,
16: 20 buried with them in the *C* of David.
17: 9 to fortified *c* they built themselves
18: 8 From watchtower to fortified *c*,
18: 30 this *c* will not be given
19: 13 the king of the *c* of Sepharvaim,
19: 32 "He will not enter this *c*
19: 33 not enter this *c*, declares
19: 34 I will defend this *c* and save it,
20: 6 I will defend this *c* for my sake
20: 6 and this *c* from the hand of the king
20: 20 which he brought water into the *c*,
23: 8 the Gate of Joshua, the *c* governor,
23: 8 which is on the left of the *c* gate.
23: 17 I see?" The men of the *c* said,
23: 27 the *c* I chose, and this temple,
24: 11 himself came up to the *c*
25: 1 He encamped outside the *c*
25: 2 The *c* was kept under siege
25: 3 the famine in the *c* had become
25: 4 the *c* wall was broken through,
25: 4 were surrounding the *c*.
25: 11 the people who remained in the *c*,
25: 19 of his men who were found in the *c*.
25: 19 still in the *c*, he took the officer
1Ch 1: 43 whose *c* was named Dinhabah.
1: 46 His *c* was named Avith.
1: 50 His *c* was named Pau,
6: 56 villages around the *c* were given
6: 57 of Aaron were given Hebron (a *c*
6: 67 they were given Shechem (a *c*
11: 5 fortress of Zion, the *C* of David.
11: 7 and so it was called the *C* of David.
11: 8 He built up the *c* around it,
11: 8 while Joab restored the rest of the *c*
13: 13 to be with him in the *C* of David.
15: 1 for himself in the *C* of David,
15: 29 of the LORD was entering the *C*
19: 9 at the entrance to their *c*,
19: 15 Abishai and went inside the *c*.
20: 2 quantity of plunder from the *c*
2Ch 5: 2 from Zion, the *C* of David.
6: 5 I have not chosen a *c* in any tribe
6: 34 you toward this *c* you have chosen
6: 38 toward the *c* you have chosen
8: 11 up from the *C* of David
9: 31 and was buried in the *c*
12: 13 the *c* the LORD had chosen out
12: 16 and was buried in the *C* of David.
14: 1 and was buried in the *C* of David.
15: 6 by another and one *c* by another,
16: 14 out for himself in the *C* of David.
18: 25 back to Amon the ruler of the *c*
21: 1 buried with them in the *C* of David.
21: 20 and was buried in the *C* of David,
23: 21 *c* was quiet, because Athaliah had
24: 16 with the kings in the *C* of David,
24: 25 and was buried in the *C* of David,
25: 28 with his fathers in the *C* of Judah.
27: 9 and was buried in the *C* of David.
28: 15 the *C* of Palms, and returned
28: 27 was buried in the *c* of Jerusalem,
29: 20 gathered the *c* officials together
32: 3 from the springs outside the *c*,
32: 5 terraces of the *C* of David.
32: 6 him in the square at the *c* gate
32: 18 afraid in order to capture the *c*.
32: 30 to the west side of the *C* of David.
33: 14 wall of the *C* of David,
33: 15 and he threw them out of the *c*.
34: 8 and Maaseiah the ruler of the *c*,
Ezr 4: 10 and settled in the *c* of Samaria
4: 12 that rebellious and wicked *c*.
4: 13 should know that if this *c* is built
4: 15 That is why this *c* was destroyed.
4: 15 will find that this *c* is a rebellious *c*,
4: 16 inform the king that if this *c* is built
4: 19 was found that this *c* has a long
4: 21 so that this *c* will not be rebuilt
Ne 2: 3 when the *c* where my fathers are
2: 5 let him send me to the *c*
2: 8 for the *c* wall and for the residence
3: 15 going down from the *C* of David.
7: 4 Now the *c* was large and spacious,
11: 1 holy *c*, while the remaining nine
11: 9 over the Second District of the *c*.
11: 18 Levites in the holy *c* totaled 284.
12: 37 of the *C* of David on the ascent

Ne 13: 18 calamity upon us and upon this *c?*
Est 3: 15 but the *c* of Susa was bewildered.
4: 1 went out into the *c*, wailing loudly
4: 6 in the open square of the *c* in front
6: 9 on the horse through the *c* streets,
6: 11 on horseback through the *c* streets,
8: 11 in every *c* the right to assemble
8: 15 *c* of Susa held a joyous celebration.
8: 17 In every province and in every *c*,
9: 28 in every province and in every *c*.
Job 24: 12 of the dying rise from the *c*,
29: 7 "When I went to the gate of the *c*
Ps 31: 21 me when I was in a besieged *c*.
46: 4 whose streams make glad the *c*
48: 1 in the *c* of our God, his holy
48: 2 the *c* of the Great King.
48: 8 in the *c* of our God:
48: 8 in the *c* of the LORD Almighty,
55: 9 for I see violence and strife in the *c*.
55: 11 forces are at work in the *c;*
59: 6 and prowl about the *c*.
59: 14 and prowl about the *c*.
60: 9 Who will bring me to the fortified *c*
87: 3 O *c* of God: *Selah*
101: 8 evildoer from the *c* of the LORD.
107: 4 to a *c* where they could settle.
107: 7 to a *c* where they could settle.
107: 36 they founded a *c* where they could
108: 10 Who will bring me to the fortified *c*
122: 3 Jerusalem is built like a *c*
127: 1 the LORD watches over the *c*,
Pr 1: 21 of the *c* she makes her speech:
8: 3 beside the gates leading into the *c*,
9: 3 from the highest point of the *c*.
9: 14 a seat at the highest point of the *c*,
10: 15 of the rich is their fortified *c*,
11: 10 righteous prosper, the *c* rejoices;
11: 11 of the upright a *c* is exalted,
16: 32 than one who takes a *c*.
18: 11 of the rich is their fortified *c;*
18: 19 more unyielding than a fortified *c*,
21: 22 A wise man attacks the *c*
25: 28 Like a *c* whose walls are broken
29: 8 Mockers stir up a *c*,
31: 23 husband is respected at the *c* gate,
31: 31 works bring her praise at the *c* gate.
Ecc 7: 19 than ten rulers in a *c*.
8: 10 praise in the *c* where they did this.
9: 14 There was once a small *c*
9: 15 and he saved the *c* by his wisdom.
9: 15 there lived in that *c* a man poor
SS 3: 2 I will get up now and go about the *c*
3: 3 as they made their rounds in the *c*.
5: 7 as they made their rounds in the *c*.
Isa 1: 8 like a *c* under siege.
1: 21 See how the faithful *c* has become
1: 26 The Faithful *C*."
1: 26 The *C* of Righteousness,
14: 31 Wail, O gate! Howl, O *c!*
17: 1 Damascus will no longer be a *c*
17: 3 The fortified *c* will disappear
19: 2 *c* against *c*,
19: 18 One of them will be called the *C*
22: 2 O *c* of tumult and revelry?
22: 7 horsemen are posted at the *c* gates;
22: 9 you saw that the *C* of David
23: 7 Is this your *c* of revelry,
23: 7 the old, old *c*,
23: 16 Take up a harp, walk through the *c*,
24: 10 The ruined *c* lies desolate;
24: 12 The *c* is left in ruins,
25: 2 You have made the *c* a heap
25: 2 foreigners' stronghold a *c* no more;
26: 1 We have a strong *c;*
26: 5 he lays the lofty *c* low;
27: 10 The fortified *c* stands desolate,
28: 1 to that *c*, the pride of those laid low
29: 1 the *c* where David settled!
32: 13 and for this *c* of revelry.
32: 14 the noisy *c* deserted;
32: 19 and the *c* is leveled completely,
33: 20 upon Zion, the *c* of our festivals;
36: 15 this *c* will not be given
37: 13 the king of the *c* of Sepharvaim,
37: 33 "He will not enter this *c*
37: 34 he will not enter this *c*,"
37: 35 "I will defend this *c* and save it,
38: 6 I will defend this *c*.
Isa 38: 6 and this *c* from the hand of the king
45: 13 He will rebuild my *c*
48: 2 yourselves citizens of the holy *c*
52: 1 O Jerusalem, the holy *c*.
54: 11 "O afflicted *c*, lashed by storms
60: 14 will call you The *C* of the LORD,
62: 12 The *C* No Longer Deserted.
66: 6 Hear that uproar from the *c*,
Jer 1: 18 Today I have made you a fortified *c*
5: 1 I will forgive this *c*.
6: 6 This *c* must be punished;
8: 16 the *c* and all who live there."
14: 18 if I go into the *c*,
15: 7 at the *c* gates of the land.
17: 24 the gates of this *c* on the Sabbath,
17: 25 and this *c* will be inhabited forever.
17: 25 gates of this *c* with their officials.
19: 8 I will devastate this *c* and make it
19: 11 smash this nation and this *c* just
19: 12 I will make this *c* like Topheth.
19: 15 I am going to bring on this *c*
20: 5 enemies all the wealth of this *c*—
21: 4 And I will gather them inside this *c*
21: 6 down those who live in this *c*—
21: 7 in this *c* who survive the plague,
21: 9 Whoever stays in this *c* will die
21: 10 have determined to do this *c* harm
22: 8 done such a thing to this great *c?'*
22: 8 many nations will pass by this *c*
23: 39 along with the *c* I gave to you
25: 29 on the *c* that bears my Name,
26: 6 and this *c* an object of cursing
26: 9 this *c* will be desolate and deserted
26: 11 he has prophesied against this *c*.
26: 12 this *c* all the things you have heard.
26: 15 on this *c* and on those who live in it
26: 20 the same things against this *c*
27: 17 Why should this *c* become a ruin?
27: 19 furnishings that are left in this *c*,
29: 7 and prosperity of the *c*
29: 16 all the people who remain in this *c*,
30: 18 the *c* will be rebuilt on her ruins,
31: 38 "when this *c* will be rebuilt for me
31: 40 The *c* will never again be uprooted
32: 3 to hand this *c* over to the king
32: 24 ramps are built up to take the *c*.
32: 24 the *c* will be handed
32: 25 And though the *c* will be handed
32: 28 hand this *c* over to the Babylonians
32: 29 who are attacking this *c* will come
32: 31 this *c* has so aroused my anger
32: 36 "You are saying about this *c*,
33: 4 says about the houses in this *c*
33: 5 I will hide my face from this *c*
33: 9 Then this *c* will bring me renown,
34: 2 to hand this *c* over to the king
34: 22 and I will bring them back to this *c*.
37: 8 will return and attack this *c;*
37: 10 would come out and burn this *c*
37: 12 started to leave the *c* to go
37: 21 until all the bread in the *c* was gone
38: 2 'Whoever stays in this *c* will die
38: 3 'This *c* will certainly be handed
38: 4 the soldiers who are left in this *c*,
38: 9 is no longer any bread in the *c*."
38: 17 and this *c* will not be burned down;
38: 18 this *c* will be handed
38: 23 and this *c* will be burned down."
39: 2 the *c* wall was broken through.
39: 4 they left the *c* at night by way
39: 9 the people who remained in the *c*,
39: 16 against this *c* through disaster,
41: 7 When they went into the *c*,
49: 25 Why has the *c* of renown not been
51: 31 that his entire *c* is captured,
52: 4 They camped outside the *c*
52: 5 The *c* was kept under siege
52: 6 the famine in the *c* had become
52: 7 They left the *c* at night
52: 7 the *c* wall was broken through,
52: 7 were surrounding the *c*.
52: 15 and those who remained in the *c*,
52: 25 of his men who were found in the *c*.
52: 25 still in the *c*, he took the officer
La 1: 1 How deserted lies the *c*,
1: 19 perished in the *c*
2: 11 faint in the streets of the *c*.
2: 12 men in the streets of the *c*,
La 2: 15 "Is this the *c* that was called
3: 51 because of all the women of my *c*.
5: 14 The elders are gone from the *c* gate
Eze 4: 1 and draw the *c* of Jerusalem on it.
4: 3 the *c* and turn your face toward it.
5: 2 it with the sword all around the *c*.
5: 2 of the hair with fire inside the *c*.
7: 15 and those in the *c* will be devoured
7: 23 and the *c* is full of violence.
9: 1 "Bring the guards of the *c* here,
9: 4 "Go throughout the *c* of Jerusalem
9: 5 "Follow him through the *c* and kill,
9: 7 and began killing throughout the *c*.
9: 9 and the *c* is full of injustice.
10: 2 and scatter them over the *c*."
11: 2 and giving wicked advice in this *c*.
11: 3 This *c* is a cooking pot,
11: 6 have killed many people in this *c*
11: 7 are the meat and this *c* is the pot,
11: 9 I will drive you out of the *c*
11: 11 This *c* will not be a pot for you,
11: 23 LORD went up from within the *c*
17: 4 where he planted it in a *c* of traders
21: 19 the road branches off to the *c*.
22: 2 Will you judge this *c* of bloodshed?
22: 3 O *c* that brings on herself doom
22: 5 O infamous *c*, full of turmoil.
22: 20 put you inside the *c* and melt you.
24: 6 " 'Woe to the *c* of bloodshed,
24: 9 " 'Woe to the *c* of bloodshed!
26: 10 as men enter a *c* whose walls have
26: 17 " 'How you are destroyed, O *c*
26: 19 When I make you a desolate *c*,
33: 21 The *c* has fallen!" Now the evening
40: 1 year after the fall of the *c*—
40: 2 some buildings that looked like a *c*.
43: 3 seen when he came to destroy the *c*
45: 6 " 'You are to give the *c*
45: 7 district and the property of the *c*.
48: 15 The *c* will be in the center of it
48: 15 will be for the common use of the *c*,
48: 17 for the *c* will be 250 cubits
48: 18 food for the workers of the *c*.
48: 19 from the *c* who farm it will come
48: 20 along with the property of the *c*.
48: 21 and the *c* property will belong
48: 22 and the property of the *c* will lie
48: 30 "These will be the exits of the *c:*
48: 31 the gates of the *c* will be named
48: 35 the name of the *c* from that time
Da 9: 16 your wrath from Jerusalem, your *c*,
9: 18 of the *c* that bears your Name.
9: 19 your *c* and your people bear your
9: 24 your holy *c* to finish transgression,
9: 26 who will come will destroy the *c*
11: 15 and will capture a fortified *c*.
Hos 6: 8 Gilead is a *c* of wicked men,
Joel 2: 9 They rush upon the *c;*
Am 3: 6 When a trumpet sounds in a *c*,
3: 6 When disaster comes to a *c*,
4: 6 you empty stomachs in every *c*
5: 3 *c* that marches out a thousand
5: 9 and brings the fortified *c* to ruin),
6: 8 I will deliver up the *c*
7: 17 will become a prostitute in the *c*,
Jnh 1: 2 "Go to the great *c* of Nineveh
3: 2 "Go to the great *c* of Nineveh
3: 3 Now Nineveh was a very large *c;*
3: 4 into the *c*, going a day's journey,
4: 5 sat down at a place east of the *c*.
4: 5 to see what would happen to the *c*.
4: 11 be concerned about that great *c?"*
Mic 4: 10 for now you must leave the *c*
5: 1 Marshal your troops, O *c* of troops,
6: 9 The LORD is calling to the *c*—
Na 2: 5 They dash to the *c* wall;
2: 7 It is decreed that the *c*
3: 1 Woe to the *c* of blood,
Hab 2: 12 "Woe to him who builds a *c*
Zep 2: 15 This is the carefree *c*
3: 1 Woe to the *c* of oppressors,
3: 7 I said to the *c*,
3: 11 because I will remove from this *c*
Zec 2: 4 'Jerusalem will be a *c* without walls
8: 3 Jerusalem will be called The *C*
8: 5 The *c* streets will be filled
8: 21 and the inhabitants of one *c* will go
14: 2 Half of the *c* will go into exile,

Zec 14: 2 people will not be taken from the *c*.
14: 2 the *c* will be captured, the houses
Mt 4: 5 the devil took him to the holy *c*
5: 14 A *c* on a hill cannot be hidden.
5: 35 for it is the *c* of the Great King.
12: 25 and every *c* or household divided
21: 10 the whole *c* was stirred and asked,
21: 17 and went out of the *c* to Bethany,
21: 18 as he was on his way back to the *c*,
22: 7 murderers and burned their *c*.
26: 18 "Go into the *c* to a certain man
27: 53 they went into the holy *c*
28: 11 some of the guards went into the *c*
Mk 10: 46 were leaving the *c*, a blind man,
11: 19 came, they went out of the *c*.
14: 13 telling them, "Go into the *c*,
14: 16 into the *c* and found things just
Lk 19: 41 Jerusalem and saw the *c*,
21: 21 in the country not enter the *c*.
21: 21 let those in the *c* get out,
22: 10 He replied, "As you enter the *c*,
23: 19 prison for an insurrection in the *c*,
24: 49 in the *c* until you have been clothed
Jn 19: 20 Jesus was crucified was near the *c*,
Ac 1: 12 a Sabbath day's walk from the *c*.
4: 27 people of Israel in this *c* to conspire
7: 58 dragged him out of the *c*
8: 5 Philip went down to a *c* in Samaria
8: 8 So there was great joy in that *c*.
8: 9 had practiced sorcery in the *c*
9: 6 "Now get up and go into the *c*,
9: 24 on the *c* gates in order to kill him.
10: 9 as they were approaching the *c*,
11: 5 "I was in the *c* of Joppa praying,
12: 10 to the iron gate leading to the *c*.
13: 44 almost the whole *c* gathered
13: 50 and the leading men of the *c*.
14: 4 The people of the *c* were divided;
14: 13 whose temple was just outside the *c*
14: 13 wreaths to the *c* gates because he
14: 19 and dragged him outside the *c*,
14: 20 he got up and went back into the *c*.
14: 21 preached the good news in that *c*
15: 21 in every *c* from the earliest times
16: 12 and the leading *c* of that district
16: 13 went outside the *c* gate to the river,
16: 14 cloth from the *c* of Thyatira,
16: 20 are throwing our *c* into an uproar
16: 39 requesting them to leave the *c*.
17: 5 a mob and started a riot in the *c*.
17: 6 brothers before the *c* officials,
17: 8 and the *c* officials were thrown
17: 16 to see that the *c* was full of idols.
18: 10 I have many people in this *c*."
19: 29 Soon the whole *c* was in an uproar.
19: 35 The *c* clerk quieted the crowd
19: 35 all the world know that the *c*
20: 23 in every *c* the Holy Spirit warns me
21: 5 accompanied us out of the *c*,
21: 29 Trophimus the Ephesian in the *c*
21: 30 The whole *c* was aroused,
21: 31 the Roman troops that the whole *c*
21: 39 in Cilicia, a citizen of no ordinary *c*
22: 3 of Cilicia, but brought up in this *c*.
24: 12 or anywhere else in the *c*.
25: 23 and the leading men of the *c*.
2Co 11: 26 in danger in the *c*, in danger
11: 32 under King Aretas had the *c*
Gal 4: 25 to the present *c* of Jerusalem,
Heb 11: 10 forward to the *c* with foundations,
11: 16 for he has prepared a *c* for them.
12: 22 to the heavenly Jerusalem, the *c*
13: 12 also suffered outside the *c* gate
13: 14 here we do not have an enduring *c*,
13: 14 looking for the *c* that is to come.
Jas 4: 13 we will go to this or that *c*,
Rev 2: 13 who was put to death in your *c*
3: 12 and the name of the *c* of my God,
11: 2 on the holy *c* for 42 months.
11: 8 lie in the street of the great *c*,
11: 13 and a tenth of the *c* collapsed.
14: 20 in the winepress outside the *c*,
16: 19 The great *c* split into three parts,
17: 18 you saw is the great *c* that rules
18: 10 O Babylon, *c* of power!
18: 10 " 'Woe! Woe, O great *c*,
18: 16 " 'Woe! Woe, O great *c*,
18: 18 'Was there ever a *c* like this great *c*
Rev 18: 19 " 'Woe! Woe, O great *c*,
18: 21 great *c* of Babylon will be thrown
20: 9 of God's people, the *c* he loves.
21: 2 saw the Holy *C*, the new
21: 10 and showed me the Holy *C*,
21: 14 of the *c* had twelve foundations,
21: 15 rod of gold to measure the *c*,
21: 16 He measured the *c* with the rod
21: 16 The *c* was laid out like a square,
21: 18 and the *c* of pure gold, as pure
21: 19 of the *c* walls were decorated
21: 21 The street of the *c* was of pure gold,
21: 22 I did not see a temple in the *c*,
21: 23 The *c* does not need the sun
22: 2 middle of the great street of the *c*.
22: 3 and of the Lamb will be in the *c*,
22: 14 may go through the gates into the *c*
22: 19 in the tree of life and in the holy *c*,

CITY'S (CITY)

Ro 16: 23 who is the *c* director

CIVILIAN

2Ti 2: 4 a soldier gets involved in *c* affairs—

CLAD

Na 2: 3 the warriors are *c* in scarlet.
Zep 1: 8 and all those *c*

CLAIM (CLAIMED CLAIMING CLAIMS RECLAIM RECLAIMED)

2Sa 19: 43 we have a greater *c* on David
Ne 2: 20 or any *c* or historic right to it."
Job 3: 5 and deep shadow *c* it once more;
41: 11 Who has a *c* against me that I must
Ps 73: 9 Their mouths lay *c* to heaven,
Pr 25: 6 do not *c* a place among great men;
Jer 23: 38 Although you *c*, 'This is the oracle
23: 38 I told you that you must not *c*,
Lk 11: 18 you *c* that I drive out demons
Jn 4: 20 you Jews *c* that the place where we
8: 24 do not believe that I am ⌊the one I *c*
8: 54 My Father, whom you *c*⌋
9: 41 but now that you *c* you can see,
10: 33 a mere man, *c* to be God."
Ro 3: 8 saying and as some *c* that we say—
2Co 3: 5 to *c* anything for ourselves,
Tit 1: 16 They *c* to know God,
1Jn 1: 6 If we *c* to have fellowship
1: 8 If we *c* to be without sin, we
1: 10 If we *c* we have not sinned,
Rev 2: 2 that you have tested those who *c*
3: 9 who *c* to be Jews though they are

CLAIMED (CLAIM)

2Sa 18: 8 and the forest *c* more lives that day
1Ki 18: 10 or kingdom *c* you were not there,
Mk 6: 15 And still others *c*, "He is a prophet,
Jn 9: 9 and beg?" Some *c* that he was.
19: 7 because he *c* to be the Son of God."
19: 21 but that this man *c* to be king
Ac 4: 32 No one *c* that any
25: 19 named Jesus who Paul *c* was alive.
Ro 1: 22 Although they *c* to be wise,

CLAIMING (CLAIM)

Mt 24: 5 For many will come in my name, *c*,
Mk 13: 6 Many will come in my name, *c*,
Lk 21: 8 For many will come in my name, *c*,
Jn 8: 25 "Just what I have been *c* all along,"
Ac 5: 36 time ago Theudas appeared, *c*

CLAIMS (CLAIM)

2Sa 15: 3 "Look, your *c* are valid and proper,
Pr 20: 6 Many a man *c* to have unfailing
Ecc 8: 17 Even if a wise man *c* he knows,
Jer 23: 34 or a priest or anyone else *c*,
Lk 23: 2 taxes to Caesar and *c* to be Christ,
Jn 19: 12 Anyone who *c* to be a king opposes
Jas 2: 14 if a man *c* to have faith
1Jn 2: 6 Whoever *c* to live in him must walk
2: 9 Anyone who *c* to be in the light

CLAMOR

Ps 74: 23 Do not ignore the *c*
Isa 31: 4 or disturbed by their *c*—

CLAN (CLANS)

Ge 24: 38 father's family and to my own *c*,
24: 40 a wife for my son from my own *c*
24: 41 Then, when you go to my *c*,
Ex 6: 25 heads of the Levite families, *c* by *c*.
Lev 25: 10 property and each to his own *c*.
25: 41 and he will go back to his own *c*
25: 47 or to a member of the alien's *c*,
25: 49 relative in his *c* may redeem him.
Nu 2: 34 each with his *c* and family.
26: 5 the Hanochite *c*; through Pallu,
26: 5 the Palluite *c*; through Hezron,
26: 6 the Hezronite *c*; through Carmi,
26: 6 through Carmi, the Carmite *c*.
26: 12 the Jakinite *c*; through Zerah,
26: 12 the Jaminite *c*; through Jakin,
26: 12 the Nemuelite *c*; through Jamin,
26: 13 the Zerahite *c*; through Shaul,
26: 13 through Shaul, the Shaulite *c*.
26: 15 the Haggite *c*; through Shuni,
26: 15 the Shunite *c*; through Ozni,
26: 15 the Zephonite *c*; through Haggi,
26: 16 the Erite *c*; through Arodi,
26: 16 the Oznite *c*; through Eri,
26: 17 the Arodite *c*; through Areli,
26: 17 through Areli, the Arelite *c*.
26: 20 the Perezite *c*; through Zerah,
26: 20 the Shelanite *c*; through Perez,
26: 20 through Zerah, the Zerahite *c*.
26: 21 the Hezronite *c*; through Hamul,
26: 21 through Hamul, the Hamulite *c*.
26: 23 the Puite *c*; through Jashub,
26: 23 the Tolaite *c*; through Puah,
26: 24 the Jashubite *c*; through Shimron,
26: 24 through Shimron, the Shimronite *c*
26: 26 the Elonite *c*; through Jahleel,
26: 26 the Seredite *c*; through Elon,
26: 26 through Jahleel, the Jahleelite *c*.
26: 29 Makirite *c* (Makir was the father
26: 29 through Gilead, the Gileadite *c*.
26: 30 the Helekite *c*; through Asriel,
26: 30 the Iezerite *c*; through Helek,
26: 31 the Asrielite *c*; through Shechem,
26: 31 the Shechemite *c*;
26: 32 the Shemidaite *c*; through Hepher,
26: 32 through Hepher, the Hepherite *c*.
26: 35 the Bekerite *c*; through Tahan,
26: 35 the Shuthelahite *c*; through Beker,
26: 35 through Tahan, the Tahanite *c*.
26: 36 through Eran, the Eranite *c*.
26: 38 the Ahiramite *c*; through Shupham
26: 38 the Ashbelite *c*; through Ahiram,
26: 38 the Belaite *c*; through Ashbel,
26: 39 the Shuphamite *c*;
26: 39 through Hupham, the Huphamite *c*
26: 40 the Ardite *c*; through Naaman,
26: 40 through Naaman, the Naamite *c*.
26: 42 through Shuham, the Shuhamite *c*.
26: 44 the Imnite *c*; through Ishvi,
26: 44 the Ishvite *c*; through Beriah,
26: 44 through Beriah, the Beriite *c*;
26: 45 the Heberite *c*; through Malkiel,
26: 45 through Malkiel, the Malkielite *c*.
26: 48 the Gunite *c*; through Jezer,
26: 48 the Jahzeelite *c*; through Guni,
26: 49 the Jezerite *c*; through Shillem,
26: 49 through Shillem, the Shillemite *c*.
26: 57 the Gershonite *c*; through Kohath,
26: 57 the Kohathite *c*; through Merari,
26: 57 through Merari, the Merarite *c*.
26: 58 the Korahite *c*.
26: 58 the Libnite *c*, the Hebronite *c*,
26: 58 the Mahlite *c*, the Mushite *c*,
27: 4 father's name disappear from his *c*
27: 11 to the nearest relative in his *c*,
36: 1 heads of the *c* of Gilead son
36: 6 within the tribal *c* of their father.
36: 8 someone in her father's tribal *c*,
36: 12 remained in their father's *c*
Dt 29: 18 *c* or tribe among you today whose
Jos 7: 14 takes shall come forward *c* by *c*;
7: 14 *c* that the LORD takes shall come
7: 17 He had the *c* of the Zerahites come
13: 15 given to the tribe of Reuben, *c* by *c*:
13: 23 of the Reubenites, *c* by *c*.
13: 24 *c* by *c*: The territory of Jazer,
13: 28 inheritance of the Gadites, *c* by *c*.

Jos 13:29 descendants of Manasseh, *c* by *c:*
13:31 for half of the sons of Makir, *c* by *c*.
15:1 for the tribe of Judah, *c* by *c*,
15:20 of the tribe of Judah, *c* by *c:*
16:5 the territory of Ephraim, *c* by *c:*
16:8 the tribe of the Ephraimites, *c* by *c*.
18:11 up for the tribe of Benjamin, *c* by *c*.
18:21 The tribe of Benjamin, *c* by *c*,
19:1 out for the tribe of Simeon, *c* by *c*.
19:8 the tribe of the Simeonites, *c* by *c*.
19:10 up for Zebulun, *c* by *c:*
19:16 the inheritance of Zebulun, *c* by *c*.
19:17 out for Issachar, *c* by *c*.
19:23 of the tribe of Issachar, *c* by *c*.
19:24 out for the tribe of Asher, *c* by *c*.
19:31 of the tribe of Asher, *c* by *c*.
19:32 out for Naphtali, *c* by *c:*
19:39 of the tribe of Naphtali, *c* by *c*.
19:40 out for the tribe of Dan, *c* by *c*.
19:48 of the tribe of Dan, *c* by *c*.
21:4 out for the Kohathites, *c* by *c*.
21:7 The descendants of Merari, *c* by *c*,
Jdg 4:17 and the *c* of Heber the Kenite.
6:15 My *c* is the weakest in Manasseh,
9:1 to them and to all his mother's *c*,
12:9 as wives from outside his *c*.
12:9 in marriage to those outside his *c*,
13:2 from the *c* of the Danites,
17:7 living within the *c* of Judah,
18:11 men from the *c* of the Danites,
18:19 it better that you serve a tribe and *c*
Ru 2:1 from the *c* of Elimelech, a man
2:3 who was from the *c* of Elimelech.
1Sa 9:21 is not my *c* the least of all the clans
10:21 *c* by *c*, and Matri's *c* was chosen.
18:18 or my father's *c* in Israel,
20:6 being made there for his whole *c*.'
2Sa 14:7 Now the whole *c* has risen up
16:5 a man from the same *c*
1Ch 4:27 so their entire *c* did not become
6:54 were from the Kohathite *c*,
6:62 descendants of Gershon, *c* by *c*,
6:63 The descendants of Merari, *c* by *c*,
6:71 From the *c* of the half-tribe
Jer 3:14 and two from every *c* and bring you
Zec 12:12 The land will mourn, each *c*
12:12 the *c* of the house of David
12:12 the *c* of the house of Nathan
12:13 the *c* of Shimei and their wives,
12:13 the *c* of the house of Levi

CLANGING

1Co 13:1 a resounding gong or a *c* cymbal.

CLANS (CLAN)

Ge 10:5 by their *c* within their nations,
10:18 Later the Canaanite *c* scattered
10:20 the descendants of Ham by their *c*
10:31 the sons of Shem by their *c*
10:32 These are the *c* of Noah's sons,
36:40 according to their *c* and regions:
Ex 6:14 These were the *c* of Reuben.
6:15 These were the *c* of Simeon.
6:17 by *c*, were Libni and Shimei.
6:19 These were the *c* of Levi according
6:24 These were the Korahite *c*.
Lev 25:45 and members of their *c* born
Nu 1:2 Israelite community by their *c*
1:16 They were the heads of the *c*
1:18 indicated their ancestry by their *c*
1:20 according to the records of their *c*
1:22 according to the records of their *c*
1:24 according to the records of their *c*
1:26 according to the records of their *c*
1:28 according to the records of their *c*
1:30 according to the records of their *c*
1:32 according to the records of their *c*
1:34 according to the records of their *c*
1:36 according to the records of their *c*
1:38 according to the records of their *c*
1:40 according to the records of their *c*
1:42 according to the records of their *c*
3:15 the Levites by their families and *c*.
3:18 the names of the Gershonite *c:*
3:19 The Kohathite *c:* Amram, Izhar,
3:20 The Merarite *c:* Mahli and Mushi.
3:20 These were the Levite *c*, according
3:21 To Gershon belonged the *c*
Nu 3:21 these were the Gershonite *c*.
3:23 The Gershonite *c* were to camp
3:27 To Kohath belonged the *c*
3:27 these were the Kohathite *c*.
3:29 The Kohathite *c* were to camp
3:30 of the Kohathite *c* was Elizaphan
3:33 To Merari belonged the *c*
3:33 these were the Merarite *c*.
3:35 of the Merarite *c* was Zuriel son
3:39 and Aaron according to their *c*,
4:2 branch of the Levites by their *c*
4:18 the Kohathite tribal *c* are not cut
4:22 by their families and *c*.
4:24 the service of the Gershonite *c*
4:28 of the Gershonite *c* at the Tent
4:29 "Count the Merarites by their *c*
4:33 This is the service of the Merarite *c*
4:34 counted the Kohathites by their *c*
4:36 the Tent of Meeting, counted by *c*,
4:37 in the Kohathite *c* who served
4:38 were counted by their *c*
4:40 counted by their *c* and families,
4:41 in the Gershonite *c* who served
4:42 Merarites were counted by their *c*
4:44 counted by their *c*, were 3,200.
4:45 the total of those in the Merarite *c*.
4:46 counted all the Levites by their *c*
10:4 the heads of the *c* of Israel—
26:7 These were the *c* of Reuben;
26:12 of Simeon by their *c* were:
26:14 These were the *c* of Simeon;
26:15 of Gad by their *c* were:
26:18 These were the *c* of Gad; those
26:20 of Judah by their *c* were:
26:22 These were the *c* of Judah;
26:23 of Issachar by their *c* were:
26:25 These were the *c* of Issachar;
26:26 of Zebulun by their *c* were:
26:27 These were the *c* of Zebulun;
26:28 by their *c* through Manasseh
26:34 These were the *c* of Manasseh;
26:35 descendants of Ephraim by their *c:*
26:37 These were the *c* of Ephraim;
26:37 descendants of Joseph by their *c*.
26:38 of Benjamin by their *c* were:
26:41 These were the *c* of Benjamin;
26:42 These were the *c* of Dan: All
26:42 the descendants of Dan by their *c:*
26:43 All of them were Shuhamite *c*;
26:44 of Asher by their *c* were:
26:47 These were the *c* of Asher;
26:48 of Naphtali by their *c* were:
26:50 These were the *c* of Naphtali;
26:57 who were counted by their *c*:
26:58 also were Levite *c:* the Libnite clan,
27:1 belonged to the *c* of Manasseh son
31:5 were supplied from the *c* of Israel.
33:54 the land by lot, according to your *c*.
36:1 were from the *c* of the descendants
36:12 within the *c* of the descendants
Jos 7:17 The *c* of Judah came forward,
14:1 of the tribal *c* of Israel allotted
15:12 the people of Judah by their *c*.
17:2 son of Joseph by their *c*.
17:2 the *c* of Abiezer, Helek, Asriel,
18:20 of the *c* of Benjamin on all sides.
18:28 inheritance of Benjamin for its *c*.
19:51 of the tribal *c* of Israel assigned
21:5 from the *c* of the tribes of Ephraim,
21:6 from the *c* of the tribes of Issachar
21:10 from the Kohathite *c* of the Levites
21:20 The rest of the Kohathite *c*
21:26 given to the rest of the Kohathite *c*.
21:27 Levite *c* of the Gershonites were
21:33 of the Gershonite *c* were thirteen,
21:34 The Merarite *c* (the rest
21:40 towns allotted to the Merarite *c*,
22:14 division among the Israelite *c*.
22:21 to the heads of the *c* of Israel:
22:30 the heads of the *c* of the Israelites
Jdg 18:2 These men represented all their *c*.
21:24 went home to their tribes and *c*,
1Sa 9:21 of all the *c* of the tribe of Benjamin?
10:19 the LORD by your tribes and *c*."
23:23 down among all the *c* of Judah."
1Ch 2:53 half the Manahathites, and the *c*
2:55 the *c* of scribes who lived at Jabez.
4:2 These were the *c* of the Zorathites.
1Ch 4:8 of the *c* of Aharhel son of Harum.
4:21 the *c* of the linen workers
4:38 by name were leaders of their *c*.
5:7 relatives by *c*, listed according
6:19 These are the *c* of the Levites listed
6:60 distributed among the Kohathite *c*,
6:61 towns from the *c* of half the tribe
6:66 of the Kohathite *c* were given
6:70 to the rest of the Kohathite *c*.
7:5 belonging to all the *c* of Issachar,
12:30 famous in their own *c*— 20,800;
Job 31:34 so dreaded the contempt of the *c*
Jer 2:4 all you *c* of the house of Israel.
31:1 the God of all the *c* of Israel,
Mic 5:2 you are small among the *c* of Judah
Zec 12:14 all the rest of the *c* and their wives.

CLAP (CLAPPED CLAPS)

Job 21:5 *c* your hand over your mouth.
Ps 47:1 *C* your hands, all you nations;
98:8 Let the rivers *c* their hands,
Pr 30:32 *c* your hand over your mouth!
Isa 55:12 will *c* their hands.
La 2:15 *c* their hands at you;

CLAPPED (CLAP)

2Ki 11:12 and the people *c* their hands
Eze 25:6 Because you have *c* your hands

CLAPS (CLAP)

Job 27:23 It *c* its hands in derision
34:37 scornfully he *c* his hands among us
Na 3:19 *c* his hands at your fall,

CLASH

Ps 150:5 praise him with the *c* of cymbals,

CLASP (CLASPED CLASPS)

Isa 2:6 and *c* hands with pagans.

CLASPED (CLASP)

Mt 28:9 *c* his feet and worshiped him.

CLASPS (CLASP)

Ex 26:6 Then make fifty gold *c*
26:11 Then make fifty bronze *c*
26:33 Hang the curtain from the *c*
35:11 *c*, frames, crossbars, posts
36:13 Then they made fifty gold *c*
36:18 They made fifty bronze *c*
39:33 its *c*, frames, crossbars, posts

CLASSIFY

2Co 10:12 dare to *c* or compare ourselves

CLATTER

Jdg 5:28 Why is the *c* of his chariots delayed
Na 3:2 the *c* of wheels,

CLAUDIA

2Ti 4:21 Linus, *C* and all the brothers.

CLAUDIUS

Ac 11:28 happened during the reign of *C*.)
18:2 because *C* had ordered all the Jews
23:26 *C* Lysias, To His Excellency,

CLAWS

Da 4:33 and his nails like the *c* of a bird.
7:19 with its iron teeth and bronze *c*

CLAY

Lev 6:28 The *c* pot the meat is cooked
11:33 If one of them falls into a *c* pot,
14:5 killed over fresh water in a *c* pot.
14:42 take new *c* and plaster the house.
14:50 birds over fresh water in a *c* pot.
15:12 *c* pot that the man touches must be
Nu 5:17 shall take some holy water in a *c* jar
1Ki 7:46 cast in *c* molds in the plain
2Ch 4:17 cast in *c* molds in the plain
Job 4:19 more those who live in houses of *c*,
10:9 that you molded me like *c*.
13:12 your defenses are defenses of *c*.
27:16 and clothes like piles of *c*,
33:6 I too have been taken from *c*.
38:14 The earth takes shape like *c*
Ps 12:6 like silver refined in a furnace of *c*,
Isa 29:16 were thought to be like the *c*!

Isa 41: 25 as if he were a potter treading the *c*.
45: 9 Does the *c* say to the potter,
64: 8 We are the *c*, you are the potter;
Jer 18: 4 from the *c* was marred in his hands;
18: 6 "Like *c* in the hand of the potter,
19: 1 "Go and buy a *c* jar from a potter.
32: 14 and put them in a *c* jar
43: 9 them in *c* in the brick pavement
La 4: 2 are now considered as pots of *c*,
Eze 4: 1 "Now, son of man, take a *c* tablet,
Da 2: 33 partly of iron and partly of baked *c*.
2: 34 the statue on its feet of iron and *c*
2: 35 Then the iron, the *c*, the bronze,
2: 41 and toes were partly of baked *c*
2: 41 even as you saw iron mixed with *c*.
2: 42 toes were partly iron and partly *c*,
2: 43 any more than iron mixes with *c*.
2: 43 saw the iron mixed with baked *c*,
2: 45 the *c*, the silver and the gold
Na 3: 14 Work the *c*,
Ro 9: 21 of the same lump of *c* some pottery
2Co 4: 7 we have this treasure in jars of *c*
2Ti 2: 20 and *c*; some are for noble purposes

CLEAN (CLEANNESS CLEANSE CLEANSED CLEANSES CLEANSING)

Ge 7: 2 seven of every kind of *c* animal,
7: 8 Pairs of *c* and unclean animals,
8: 20 of all the *c* animals and *c* birds,
20: 5 a clear conscience and *c* hands."
Lev 4: 12 the camp to a place ceremonially *c*,
6: 11 to a place that is ceremonially *c*.
7: 19 anyone ceremonially *c* may eat it.
10: 10 between the unclean and the *c*,
10: 14 Eat them in a ceremonially *c* place;
11: 32 till evening, and then it will be *c*.
11: 36 for collecting water remains *c*,
11: 37 are to be planted, they remain *c*.
11: 47 between the unclean and the *c*,
12: 7 and then she will be ceremonially *c*
12: 8 for her, and she will be *c*.' "
13: 6 the priest shall pronounce him *c*;
13: 6 wash his clothes, and he will be *c*.
13: 7 to the priest to be pronounced *c*,
13: 13 Since it has all turned white, he is *c*.
13: 13 he shall pronounce that person *c*.
13: 17 infected person *c*; then he will be *c*.
13: 23 the priest shall pronounce him *c*.
13: 28 the priest shall pronounce him *c*;
13: 34 the priest shall pronounce him *c*.
13: 34 wash his clothes, and he will be *c*.
13: 35 in the skin after he is pronounced *c*,
13: 37 He is *c*, and the priest shall
13: 37 the priest shall pronounce him *c*.
13: 39 out on the skin; that person is *c*.
13: 40 has lost his hair and is bald, he is *c*.
13: 41 and has a bald forehead, he is *c*.
13: 58 be washed again, and it will be *c*."
13: 59 for pronouncing them *c* or unclean.
14: 4 shall order that two live *c* birds
14: 7 disease and pronounce him *c*.
14: 8 then he will be ceremonially *c*.
14: 9 with water, and he will be *c*.
14: 11 pronounces him *c* shall present
14: 20 for him, and he will be *c*.
14: 48 he shall pronounce the house *c*,
14: 53 for the house, and it will be *c*."
14: 57 to determine when something is *c*
15: 8 spits on someone who is *c*,
15: 13 with fresh water, and he will be *c*.
15: 28 after that she will be ceremonially *c*
16: 30 you will be *c* from all your sins.
17: 15 till evening; then he will be *c*.
20: 25 and between unclean and *c* birds.
20: 25 make a distinction between *c*
22: 7 goes down, he will be *c*,
Nu 8: 6 and make them ceremonially *c*.
9: 13 But if a man who is ceremonially *c*
18: 11 who is ceremonially *c* may eat it.
18: 13 who is ceremonially *c* may eat it.
19: 9 them in a ceremonially *c* place
19: 9 "A man who is *c* shall gather up
19: 12 and seventh days, he will not be *c*.
19: 12 the seventh day; then he will be *c*.
19: 18 a man who is ceremonially *c* is
19: 19 The man who is *c* is
19: 19 and that evening he will be *c*.
31: 23 the fire, and then it will be *c*.
Nu 31: 24 your clothes and you will be *c*.
Dt 12: 15 unclean and the *c* may eat it.
12: 22 unclean and the *c* may eat.
14: 11 You may eat any *c* bird.
14: 20 creature that is *c* you may eat.
15: 22 unclean and the *c* may eat it,
2Ki 5: 14 became *c* like that of a young boy.
2Ch 13: 11 bread on the ceremonially *c* table
30: 17 those who were not ceremonially *c*
30: 19 if he is not *c* according to the rules
Ezr 6: 20 and were all ceremonially *c*.
Job 17: 9 with *c* hands will grow stronger.
33: 9 I am *c* and free from guilt.
37: 21 after the wind has swept them *c*.
Ps 24: 4 He who has *c* hands and a pure
51: 7 with hyssop, and I will be *c*;
Pr 20: 9 I am *c* and without sin"?
Ecc 9: 2 and the bad, the *c* and the unclean,
Isa 1: 16 wash and make yourselves *c*.
66: 20 LORD in ceremonially *c* vessels.
Eze 16: 4 washed with water to make you *c*,
22: 26 between the unclean and the *c*;
24: 13 you will not be *c* again
36: 25 I will sprinkle *c* water on you,
36: 25 water on you, and you will be *c*;
44: 23 between the unclean and the *c*.
Am 7: 2 When they had stripped the land *c*,
Zec 3: 5 So they put a *c* turban on his head
3: 5 "Put a *c* turban on his head."
Mt 8: 2 are willing, you can make me *c*."
8: 3 "Be *c*!" Immediately he was cured
12: 44 the house unoccupied, swept *c*
23: 25 You *c* the outside of the cup
23: 26 First *c* the inside of the cup
23: 26 and then the outside also will be *c*.
27: 59 wrapped it in a *c* linen cloth,
Mk 1: 40 are willing, you can make me *c*."
1: 41 "Be *c*!" Immediately the leprosy
7: 19 Jesus declared all foods "*c*.")
Lk 5: 12 are willing, you can make me *c*."
5: 13 "Be *c*!" And immediately
11: 25 it finds the house swept *c*
11: 39 you Pharisees *c* the
11: 41 and everything will be *c* for you.
Jn 13: 10 to wash his feet; his whole body is *c*
13: 10 you are *c*, though not every one
13: 11 why he said not every one was *c*.
15: 2 that does bear fruit he trims *c*
15: 3 are already *c* because of the word
Ac 10: 15 impure that God has made *c*."
11: 9 impure that God has made *c*.'
24: 18 I was ceremonially *c*
Ro 14: 20 All food is *c*, but it is wrong
Heb 9: 13 them so that they are outwardly *c*.
Rev 15: 6 were dressed in *c*, shining linen
19: 8 Fine linen, bright and *c*,
19: 14 dressed in fine linen, white and *c*.

CLEANNESS (CLEAN)

2Sa 22: 21 according to the *c*
22: 25 according to my *c* in his sight.
Job 22: 30 through the *c* of your hands."
Ps 18: 20 according to the *c*
18: 24 according to the *c* of my hands

CLEANSE (CLEAN)

Lev 16: 19 it with his finger seven times to *c* it
16: 30 will be made for you, to *c* you.
Ps 51: 2 and *c* me from my sin.
51: 7 *C* me with hyssop, and I will be
Pr 20: 30 Blows and wounds *c* away evil,
Isa 4: 4 he will *c* the bloodstains
Jer 4: 11 *c*; a wind too strong for that comes
33: 8 I will *c* them from all the sin they
Eze 24: 13 Because I tried to *c* you
36: 25 I will *c* you from all your impurities
36: 33 On the day I *c* you
37: 23 backsliding, and I will *c* them.
39: 12 them in order to *c* the land.
39: 14 regularly employed to *c* the land.
39: 16 And so they will *c* the land.'
43: 26 atonement for the altar and *c* it;
Zec 13: 1 to *c* them from sin and impurity.
Mt 10: 8 *c* those who have leprosy,
Heb 9: 14 *c* our consciences from acts that
10: 22 having our hearts sprinkled to *c* us

CLEANSED (CLEAN)

Lev 14: 4 brought for the one to be *c*.
14: 7 one to be *c* of the infectious disease
14: 8 to be *c* must wash his clothes,
14: 11 shall present both the one to be *c*
14: 14 of the right ear of the one to be *c*,
14: 17 of the right ear of the one to be *c*,
14: 18 put on the head of the one to be *c*
14: 19 one to be *c* from his uncleanness.
14: 25 of the right ear of the one to be *c*,
14: 28 of the right ear of the one to be *c*,
14: 29 put on the head of the one to be *c*,
14: 31 on behalf of the one to be *c*."
15: 13 When a man is *c* from his discharge
15: 28 When she is *c* from her discharge,
22: 4 the sacred offerings until he is *c*.
Nu 19: 19 The person being *c* must wash his
Jos 22: 17 very day we have not *c* ourselves
2Ki 5: 10 will be restored and you will be *c*."
5: 12 Couldn't I wash in them and be *c*?"
5: 13 when he tells you, 'Wash and be *c*
Pr 30: 12 and yet are not *c* of their filth;
Isa 1: 6 not *c* or bandaged
Eze 24: 13 but you would not be *c*
44: 26 After he is *c*, he must wait seven
Lk 4: 27 yet not one of them was *c*—
17: 14 And as they went, they were *c*.
17: 17 "Were not all ten *c*? Where are
Heb 9: 22 requires that nearly everything be *c*
10: 2 worshipers would have been *c* once
2Pe 1: 9 has forgotten that he has been *c*

CLEANSES (CLEAN)

2Ti 2: 21 If a man *c* himself from the latter,

CLEANSING (CLEAN)

Lev 14: 2 at the time of his ceremonial *c*,
14: 23 them for his *c* to the priest
14: 32 the regular offerings for his *c*.
15: 13 off seven days for his ceremonial *c*;
Nu 6: 9 head on the day of his *c*—
8: 7 Sprinkle the water of *c* on them;
19: 9 for use in the water of *c*;
19: 13 water of *c* has not been sprinkled
19: 20 water of *c* has not been sprinkled
19: 21 of *c* will be unclean till evening.
19: 21 who sprinkles the water of *c* must
31: 23 also be purified with the water of *c*.
Mk 1: 44 that Moses commanded for your *c*,
Lk 5: 14 that Moses commanded for your *c*,
Jn 11: 55 Jerusalem for their ceremonial *c*
Eph 5: 26 *c* her by the washing with water

CLEFT (CLEFTS)

Ex 33: 22 I will put you in a *c* in the rock

CLEFTS (CLEFT)

Jdg 6: 2 for themselves in mountain *c*,
SS 2: 14 My dove in the *c* of the rock,
Jer 49: 16 you who live in the *c* of the rocks,
Ob : 3 you who live in the *c* of the rocks

CLEMENT

Php 4: 3 along with *C* and the rest

CLEOPAS

Lk 24: 18 One of them, named *C*, asked him,

CLERESTORY

1Ki 6: 4 He made narrow *c* windows

CLERK

Ac 19: 35 The city *c* quieted the crowd

CLEVER (CLEVERNESS)

Isa 3: 3 skilled craftsman and *c* enchanter.
5: 21 and *c* in their own sight.

CLEVERNESS (CLEVER)

Isa 25: 11 despite the *c* of their hands.

CLIFF (CLIFFS)

1Sa 14: 4 the Philistine outpost was a *c*;
14: 5 One *c* stood to the north
2Ch 25: 12 took them to the top of a *c*
Job 39: 28 He dwells on a *c* and stays there
Lk 4: 29 in order to throw him down the *c*.

CLIFFS (CLIFF)
Ps 141: 6 will be thrown down from the *c*,
Jer 51: 25 roll you off the *c*,
Eze 38: 20 *c* will crumble and every wall will

CLIMAX
Eze 21: 25 of punishment has reached its *c*,
21: 29 of punishment has reached its *c*.
35: 5 their punishment reached its *c*,

CLIMB (CLIMBED CLIMBING CLIMBS)
Ge 49: 22 whose branches *c* over a wall.
1Sa 14: 10 'Come up to us,' we will *c* up,
14: 12 to his armor-bearer, "*C* up after me
SS 7: 8 I said, "I will *c* the palm tree;
Jer 4: 29 some *c* up among the rocks.
Joel 2: 9 They *c* into the houses;
Am 9: 2 Though they *c* up to the heavens,

CLIMBED (CLIMB)
Dt 32: 50 that you have *c* you will die
34: 1 Then Moses *c* Mount Nebo
Jos 15: 8 From there it *c* to the top
Jdg 9: 7 *c* up on the top of Mount Gerizim
9: 51 and *c* up on the tower roof.
1Sa 14: 13 Jonathan *c* up, using his hands
2Sa 17: 18 a well in his courtyard, and they *c*
17: 21 the two *c* out of the well
1Ki 18: 42 but Elijah *c* to the top of Carmel,
Ne 4: 3 if even a fox *c* up on it,
Isa 57: 8 you *c* into it and opened it wide;
Jer 9: 21 has *c* in through our windows
Eze 40: 6 He *c* its steps and measured
Mt 14: 32 And when they *c* into the boat,
Mk 6: 51 Then he *c* into the boat with them,
Lk 19: 4 *c* a sycamore-fig tree to see him,
Jn 21: 11 Simon Peter *c* aboard

CLIMBING (CLIMB)
2Ch 20: 16 They will be *c* up by the Pass of Ziz

CLIMBS (CLIMB)
Isa 24: 18 whoever *c* out of the pit
Jer 48: 44 whoever *c* out of the pit
Jn 10: 1 but *c* in by some other way,

CLING (CLINGING CLINGS CLUNG)
Dt 28: 60 that you dreaded, and they will *c*
2Ki 5: 27 Naaman's leprosy will *c* to you
Job 41: 17 they *c* together and cannot be
Ps 31: 6 I hate those who *c*
44: 25 our bodies *c* to the ground.
101: 3 they will not *c* to me.
137: 6 May my tongue *c* to the roof
Jer 8: 5 They *c* to deceit;
Jnh 2: 8 "Those who *c* to worthless idols
Ro 12: 9 Hate what is evil; *c* to what is good.

CLINGING (CLING)
1Ki 1: 51 and is *c* to the horns of the altar.

CLINGS (CLING)
Job 8: 15 he *c* to it, but it does not hold.

CLIP
Lev 19: 27 or *c* off the edges of your beard.

CLOAK (CLOAKS)
Ge 39: 12 But he left his *c* in her hand
39: 12 She caught him by his *c* and said,
39: 13 When she saw that he had left his *c*
39: 15 he left his *c* beside me
39: 16 She kept his *c* beside her
39: 18 he left his *c* beside me
Ex 4: 6 So Moses put his hand into his *c*,
4: 6 "Put your hand inside your *c*."
4: 7 Moses put his hand back into his *c*,
4: 7 "Now put it back into your *c*,"
12: 11 with your *c* tucked into your belt,
22: 26 If you take your neighbor's *c*
22: 27 his *c* is the only covering he has
Dt 22: 3 or his *c* or anything he loses.
22: 12 the four corners of the *c* you wear.
24: 13 Return his *c* to him by sunset
24: 17 or take the *c* of the widow
1Ki 11: 29 him on the way, wearing a new *c*.
11: 30 hold of the new *c* he was wearing
18: 46 and, tucking his *c* into his belt,
1Ki 19: 13 he pulled his *c* over his face
19: 19 and threw his *c* around him.
2Ki 2: 8 Elijah took his *c*, rolled it up
2: 13 He picked up the *c* that had fallen
2: 14 Then he took the *c* that had fallen
4: 29 "Tuck your *c* into your belt,
4: 39 gourds and filled the fold of his *c*.
9: 1 "Tuck your *c* into your belt,
Ezr 9: 3 I heard this, I tore my tunic and *c*,
9: 5 with my tunic and *c* torn,
Ps 109: 19 it be like a *c* wrapped about him,
109: 29 and wrapped in shame as in a *c*.
Pr 21: 14 in the *c* pacifies great wrath.
30: 4 has wrapped up the waters in his *c*?
SS 5: 7 they took away my *c*,
Isa 3: 6 "You have a *c*, you be our leader;
59: 17 wrapped himself in zeal as in a *c*.
Mt 5: 40 let him have your *c* as well.
9: 20 and touched the edge of his *c*.
9: 21 If I only touch his *c*, I will be healed
14: 36 the sick just touch the edge of his *c*,
24: 18 one in the field go back to get his *c*.
Mk 5: 27 in the crowd and touched his *c*,
6: 56 them touch even the edge of his *c*,
10: 50 Throwing his *c* aside, he jumped
13: 16 one in the field go back to get his *c*.
Lk 6: 29 someone takes your *c*, do not stop
8: 44 and touched the edge of his *c*,
22: 36 you don't have a sword, sell your *c*
Ac 12: 8 "Wrap your *c* around you
2Ti 4: 13 bring the *c* that I left with Carpus

CLOAKS (CLOAK)
2Ki 9: 13 They hurried and took their *c*
Isa 3: 22 the fine robes and the capes and *c*,
Mt 21: 7 placed their *c* on them,
21: 8 A very large crowd spread their *c*
Mk 11: 7 to Jesus and threw their *c* over it,
11: 8 Many people spread their *c*
Lk 19: 35 threw their *c* on the colt
19: 36 people spread their *c* on the road.
Ac 22: 23 off their *c* and flinging dust

CLODS
Job 38: 38 and the *c* of earth stick together?
Joel 1: 17 shriveled beneath the *c*.

CLOPAS
Jn 19: 25 Mary the wife of *C*, and Mary

CLOSE (CLOSED CLOSER CLOSES CLOSING ENCLOSE ENCLOSED)
Ge 27: 22 Jacob went *c* to his father Isaac,
45: 4 to his brothers, "Come *c* to me."
46: 4 Joseph's own hand will *c* your eyes
48: 10 So Joseph brought his sons *c* to him
48: 13 and brought them *c* to him.
Ex 25: 27 The rings are to be *c* to the rim
28: 27 *c* to the seam just
37: 14 The rings were put *c* to the rim
39: 20 *c* to the seam just
Lev 3: 9 cut off *c* to the backbone,
14: 38 and at the entrance *c* up the house
18: 6 is to approach any *c* relative
18: 12 she is your father's *c* relative.
18: 13 she is your mother's *c* relative.
18: 17 daughter; they are her *c* relatives.
20: 4 of the community *c* their eyes
20: 19 for that would dishonor a *c* relative
21: 2 except for a *c* relative, such
Nu 5: 8 But if that person has no *c* relative
22: 25 she pressed *c* to the wall, crushing
Jos 2: 5 when it was time to *c* the city gate,
Jdg 16: 9 snaps when it comes *c* to a flame.
Ru 2: 20 "That man is our *c* relative;
2: 23 Ruth stayed *c* to the servant girls
2Sa 11: 20 'Why did you get so *c* to the city
11: 21 Why did you get so *c* to the wall?'
12: 11 give them to one who is *c* to you,
1Ki 21: 1 *c* to the palace of Ahab king
21: 2 since it is *c* to my palace.
2Ki 10: 11 his *c* friends and his priests,
11: 8 Stay *c* to the king wherever he goes
2Ch 23: 7 Stay *c* to the king wherever he goes
Ne 6: 10 and let us *c* the temple doors,
Job 13: 27 you keep *c* watch on all my paths
33: 11 he keeps *c* watch on all my paths.'
41: 16 each is so *c* to the next
Ps 17: 10 They *c* up their callous hearts,
34: 18 LORD is *c* to the brokenhearted
41: 9 Even my *c* friend, whom I trusted,
55: 13 my companion, my *c* friend,
63: 8 I stay *c* to you;
69: 15 or the pit *c* its mouth over me.
88: 15 youth I have been afflicted and *c*
148: 14 of Israel, the people *c* to his heart.
Pr 16: 28 and a gossip separates *c* friends.
17: 9 the matter separates *c* friends.
Isa 6: 10 and *c* their eyes.
40: 11 and carries them *c* to his heart;
42: 23 or pay *c* attention in time to come?
56: 1 for my salvation is *c* at hand
66: 9 "Do I *c* up the womb
Jer 30: 21 him near and he will come *c* to me,
30: 21 himself to be *c* to me?'
La 3: 56 heard my plea: "Do not *c* your ears
Eze 22: 4 You have brought your days to a *c*,
Da 12: 4 *c* up and seal the words of the scroll
Joel 2: 1 It is *c* at hand—
Zec 13: 7 against the man who is *c* to me!"
Mt 6: 6 *c* the door and pray to your Father,
Lk 20: 20 Keeping a *c* watch on him,
21: 34 day will *c* on you unexpectedly
Jn 4: 47 heal his son, who was *c* to death.
Ac 8: 6 they all paid *c* attention
9: 24 and night they kept *c* watch
10: 24 together his relatives and *c* friends.
Rev 6: 8 Hades was following *c* behind him.

CLOSE-KNIT (KNIT)
Job 40: 17 the sinews of his thighs are *c*.

CLOSED (CLOSE)
Ge 2: 21 and *c* up the place with flesh.
8: 2 of the heavens had been *c*,
20: 18 the LORD had *c* up every womb
Lev 14: 46 while it is *c* up will be unclean
Nu 16: 33 everything they owned; the earth *c*
Jdg 3: 22 not pull the sword out, and the fat *c*
1Sa 1: 5 and the LORD had *c* her womb.
1: 6 the LORD had *c* her womb,
Ne 4: 7 and that the gaps were being *c*,
Job 17: 4 You have *c* their minds
Ecc 12: 4 when the doors to the street are *c*
Isa 32: 3 of those who see will no longer be *c*
44: 18 and their minds *c* so they cannot
Jer 6: 10 Their ears are *c*
La 3: 54 the waters *c* over my head,
Da 12: 9 because the words are *c* up
Mt 13: 15 and they have *c* their eyes.
Ac 28: 27 and they have *c* their eyes.

CLOSER (CLOSE)
Ex 3: 5 "Do not come any *c*," God said.
1Sa 17: 41 of him, kept coming *c* to David.
17: 48 As the Philistine moved *c*
2Sa 18: 25 And the man came *c* and *c*.
Pr 18: 24 there is a friend who sticks *c*

CLOSES (CLOSE)
Pr 28: 27 he who *c* his eyes to them receives
Lk 13: 25 of the house gets up and *c* the door,

CLOSING (CLOSE)
Lev 23: 36 It is the *c* assembly; do no regular
1Sa 23: 26 and his forces were *c* in on David
Ps 77: 4 You kept my eyes from *c*;
Eze 21: 14 *c* in on them from every side.

CLOTH (CLOTHS)
Ex 28: 31 robe of the ephod entirely of blue *c*,
39: 22 of the ephod entirely of blue *c*—
Lev 11: 32 whether it is made of wood, *c*,
Nu 4: 6 spread a *c* of solid blue over that
4: 7 Presence they are to spread a blue *c*
4: 8 are to spread a scarlet *c*,
4: 9 "They are to take a blue *c*
4: 11 altar they are to spread a blue *c*
4: 12 in a blue *c*, cover that with hides
4: 13 and spread a purple *c* over it.
Dt 22: 17 Then her parents shall display the *c*
1Sa 21: 9 wrapped in a *c* behind the ephod.
2Ki 8: 15 But the next day he took a thick *c*,
Isa 19: 10 The workers in *c* will be dejected,
30: 22 them away like a menstrual *c*
Eze 16: 4 rubbed with salt or wrapped in *c*.

Eze 16: 13 costly fabric and embroidered *c*.
Mt 9: 16 of unshrunk *c* on an old garment,
27: 59 wrapped it in a clean linen *c*,
Mk 2: 21 of unshrunk *c* on an old garment.
15: 46 So Joseph bought some linen *c*,
Lk 2: 12 find a baby wrapped in strips of *c*
19: 20 kept it laid away in a piece of *c*.
23: 53 wrapped it in linen *c* and placed it
Jn 11: 44 of linen, and a *c* around his face.
20: 7 The *c* was folded up by itself,
20: 7 as the burial *c* that had been
Ac 16: 14 a dealer in purple *c* from the city
Rev 18: 12 scarlet *c*; every sort of citron wood,

CLOTHE (CLOTHED CLOTHES CLOTHING)

Job 10: 11 *c* me with skin and flesh
39: 19 or *c* his neck with a flowing mane?
40: 10 and *c* yourself in honor
Ps 45: 3 *c* yourself with splendor
73: 6 they *c* themselves with violence.
132: 16 I will *c* her priests with salvation,
132: 18 I will *c* his enemies with shame,
Isa 22: 21 I will *c* him with your robe
50: 3 I *c* the sky with darkness
51: 9 awake! *C* yourself with strength,
52: 1 *c* yourself with strength.
58: 7 when you see the naked, to *c* him,
Eze 34: 3 *c* yourselves with the wool
Mt 6: 30 will he not much more *c* you,
25: 38 or needing clothes and *c* you?
25: 43 clothes and you did not *c* me,
Lk 12: 28 how much more will he *c* you,
Ro 13: 14 *c* yourselves with the Lord Jesus
1Co 15: 53 For the perishable must *c* itself
Col 3: 12 *c* yourselves with compassion,
1Pe 5: 5 *C* yourselves with humility

CLOTHED (CLOTHE)

Ge 3: 21 for Adam and his wife and *c* them.
Lev 8: 7 *c* him with the robe and put
2Sa 1: 24 who *c* you in scarlet and finery,
1Ch 15: 27 David was *c* in a robe of fine linen,
21: 16 *c* in sackcloth, fell facedown.
2Ch 6: 41 O LORD God, be *c* with salvation,
28: 15 the plunder they *c* all who were
Est 4: 2 no one *c* in sackcloth was allowed
Job 7: 5 My body is *c* with worms and scabs
8: 22 Your enemies will be *c* in shame,
Ps 30: 11 removed my sackcloth and *c* me
35: 26 be *c* with shame and disgrace.
65: 12 the hills are *c* with gladness.
104: 1 you are *c* with splendor
109: 29 My accusers will be *c* with disgrace
132: 9 May your priests be *c*
Pr 31: 21 for all of them are *c* in scarlet.
31: 22 she is *c* in fine linen and purple.
31: 25 She is *c* with strength and dignity;
Ecc 9: 8 Always be *c* in white,
Isa 61: 10 For he has *c* me with garments
Eze 7: 18 on sackcloth and be *c* with terror.
7: 27 the prince will be *c* with despair,
9: 2 With them was a man *c*
9: 3 the LORD called to the man *c*
10: 2 said to the man *c* in linen,
16: 10 I *c* you with an embroidered dress
23: 6 the Assyrians—warriors *c* in blue,
26: 16 *C* with terror, they will sit
31: 15 of it I *c* Lebanon with gloom,
Da 5: 7 and tells me what it means will be *c*
5: 16 you will be *c* in purple
5: 29 command, Daniel was *c*
12: 6 of them said to the man *c* in linen,
12: 7 The man *c* in linen, who was
Zec 3: 5 turban on his head and *c* him,
6: 13 and he will be *c* with majesty
Mt 25: 36 I needed clothes and you *c* me,
Lk 24: 49 until you have been *c* with power
Jn 19: 2 They *c* him in a purple robe
1Co 15: 54 When the perishable has been *c*
2Co 5: 2 to be *c* with our heavenly dwelling,
5: 3 when we are *c*, we will not be found
5: 4 to be *c* with our heavenly dwelling,
Gal 3: 27 into Christ have *c* yourselves
Rev 11: 3 for 1,260 days, *c* in sackcloth."
12: 1 in heaven: a woman *c* with the sun,

CLOTHES (CLOTHE)

Ge 27: 15 Then Rebekah took the best *c*
27: 27 Isaac caught the smell of his *c*,
28: 20 and *c* to wear so that I return safely
35: 2 yourselves and change your *c*.
37: 29 Joseph was not there, he tore his *c*.
37: 34 Jacob tore his *c*, put on sackcloth
38: 14 she took off her widow's *c*,
38: 19 and put on her widow's *c* again.
41: 14 he had shaved and changed his *c*,
44: 13 At this, they tore their *c*.
45: 22 shekels of silver and five sets of *c*.
Ex 19: 10 Have them wash their *c*
19: 14 them, and they washed their *c*.
28: 41 After you put these *c*
Lev 6: 10 priest shall then put on his linen *c*,
6: 11 Then he is to take off these *c*
10: 6 unkempt, and do not tear your *c*,
11: 25 of their carcasses must wash his *c*,
11: 28 up their carcasses must wash his *c*,
11: 40 of the carcass must wash his *c*,
11: 40 up the carcass must wash his *c*,
13: 6 The man must wash his *c*,
13: 34 He must wash his *c*, and he will be
13: 45 disease must wear torn *c*,
14: 8 to be cleansed must wash his *c*,
14: 9 must wash his *c* and bathe himself
14: 47 eats in the house must wash his *c*.
15: 5 touches his bed must wash his *c*
15: 6 sat on must wash his *c*
15: 7 has a discharge must wash his *c*
15: 8 that person must wash his *c*
15: 10 up those things must wash his *c*
15: 11 hands with water must wash his *c*
15: 13 must wash his *c* and bathe himself
15: 21 touches her bed must wash his *c*
15: 22 sits on must wash his *c*
15: 27 he must wash his *c* and bathe
16: 26 as a scapegoat must wash his *c*
16: 28 who burns them must wash his *c*
17: 15 by wild animals must wash his *c*
17: 16 But if he does not wash his *c*
21: 10 hair become unkempt or tear his *c*.
Nu 8: 7 whole bodies and wash their *c*,
8: 21 themselves and washed their *c*.
14: 6 tore their *c* and said
19: 7 the priest must wash his *c*
19: 8 wash his *c* and bathe with water,
19: 10 of the heifer must also wash his *c*,
19: 19 being cleansed must wash his *c*
19: 21 of cleansing must also wash his *c*,
31: 24 On the seventh day wash your *c*
Dt 8: 4 Your *c* did not wear out
21: 13 and put aside the *c* she was wearing
22: 11 Do not wear *c* of wool
29: 5 your *c* did not wear out,
Jos 7: 6 Then Joshua tore his *c*
9: 5 on their feet and wore old *c*.
9: 13 And our *c* and sandals are worn out
Jdg 11: 35 he tore his *c* and cried, "Oh!
14: 12 linen garments and thirty sets of *c*.
14: 13 garments and thirty sets of *c*."
14: 19 and gave their *c* to those who had
17: 10 shekels of silver a year, your *c*
Ru 3: 3 yourself, and put on your best *c*.
1Sa 4: 12 his *c* torn and dust on his head.
27: 9 donkeys and camels, and *c*.
28: 8 himself, putting on other *c*,
2Sa 1: 2 with his *c* torn and with dust
1: 11 men with him took hold of their *c*
3: 31 "Tear your *c* and put on sackcloth
12: 20 put on lotions and changed his *c*,
13: 31 his *c* and lay down on the ground;
13: 31 stood by with their *c* torn.
14: 2 in mourning *c*, and don't use any
19: 24 washed his *c* from the day the king
1Ki 21: 27 he tore his *c*, put on sackcloth
2Ki 2: 12 Then he took hold of his own *c*
5: 26 or to accept *c*, olive groves,
7: 8 and carried away silver, gold and *c*,
18: 37 with their *c* torn, and told him what
19: 1 he tore his *c* and put on sackcloth
25: 29 So Jehoiachin put aside his prison *c*
2Ch 28: 15 They provided them with *c*
Ne 4: 23 the guards with me took off our *c*;
9: 21 their *c* did not wear out
Est 4: 1 he tore his *c*, put on sackcloth
Est 4: 4 She sent *c* for him to put on instead
Job 9: 31 so that even my *c* would detest me.
24: 7 Lacking *c*, they spend the night
24: 10 Lacking *c*, they go about naked;
27: 16 and *c* like piles of clay,
37: 17 You who swelter in your *c*
Pr 6: 27 lap without his *c* being burned?
23: 21 and drowsiness *c* them in rags.
Isa 4: 1 and provide our own *c*;
23: 18 for abundant food and fine *c*.
32: 11 Strip off your *c*,
36: 22 with their *c* torn, and told him what
37: 1 he tore his *c* and put on sackcloth
Jer 2: 34 On your *c* men find
36: 24 no fear, nor did they tear their *c*.
38: 11 and worn-out *c* from there
38: 12 and worn-out *c* under your arms
41: 5 torn their *c* and cut themselves
52: 33 So Jehoiachin put aside his prison *c*
Eze 16: 13 your *c* were of fine linen
16: 18 And you took your embroidered *c*
16: 39 They will strip you of your *c*
23: 26 of your *c* and take your fine jewelry
42: 14 are to put on other *c* before they go
44: 17 court, they are to wear linen *c*;
44: 19 put on other *c*, so that they do not
44: 19 take off the *c* they have been
Da 3: 21 trousers, turbans and other *c*,
Zep 1: 8 clad in foreign *c*.
Hag 1: 6 You put on *c*, but are not warm.
Zec 3: 3 Now Joshua was dressed in filthy *c*
3: 4 before him, "Take off his filthy *c*."
Mt 3: 4 John's *c* were made of camel's hair,
6: 25 the body more important than *c*?
6: 28 "And why do you worry about *c*?
6: 30 If that is how God *c* the grass
11: 8 A man dressed in fine *c*? No,
11: 8 those who wear fine *c* are
17: 2 and his *c* became as white
22: 11 who was not wearing wedding *c*.
22: 12 get in here without wedding *c*?'
25: 36 I needed *c* and you clothed me,
25: 38 or needing *c* and clothe you?
25: 43 I needed *c* and you did not clothe
25: 44 or a stranger or needing *c* or sick
26: 65 the high priest tore his *c* and said,
27: 31 took off the robe and put his own *c*
27: 35 they divided up his *c* by casting lots
28: 3 and his *c* were white as snow.
Mk 5: 28 If I just touch his *c*, I will be healed
5: 30 "Who touched my *c*?" "You see
9: 3 His *c* became dazzling white,
14: 63 The high priest tore his *c*.
15: 20 the purple robe and put his own *c*
15: 24 Dividing up his *c*, they cast lots
Lk 7: 25 A man dressed in fine *c*? No,
7: 25 those who wear expensive *c*
8: 27 long time this man had not worn *c*
9: 29 and his *c* became as bright
10: 30 They stripped him of his *c*,
12: 23 and the body more than *c*.
12: 28 If that is how God *c* the grass
23: 34 they divided up his *c* by casting lots
24: 4 in *c* that gleamed like lightning
Jn 11: 44 Take off the grave *c* and let him go
13: 12 he put on his *c* and returned
19: 23 they took his *c*, dividing them
Ac 7: 58 the witnesses laid their *c* at the feet
10: 30 a man in shining *c* stood before me
12: 8 "Put on your *c* and sandals."
14: 14 they tore their *c* and rushed out
18: 6 he shook out his *c* in protest
22: 20 guarding the *c* of those who were
1Ti 2: 9 or gold or pearls or expensive *c*,
Jas 2: 2 and a poor man in shabby *c*
2: 2 wearing a gold ring and fine *c*,
2: 3 attention to the man wearing fine *c*
2: 15 sister is without *c* and daily food.
5: 2 and moths have eaten your *c*.
1Pe 3: 3 wearing of gold jewelry and fine *c*.
Rev 3: 4 Sardis who have not soiled their *c*.
3: 18 you can become rich; and white *c*
16: 15 he who stays awake and keeps his *c*

CLOTHING (CLOTHE)

Ge 24: 53 and silver jewelry and articles of *c*
45: 22 To each of them he gave new *c*,
Ex 3: 22 articles of silver and gold and for *c*,

Ex 12: 34 in kneading troughs wrapped in *c*.
12: 35 articles of silver and gold and for *c*.
21: 10 deprive the first one of her food, *c*
Lev 13: 47 any woolen or linen *c*, any woven
13: 47 "If any *c* is contaminated
13: 49 and if the contamination in the *c*,
13: 51 if the mildew has spread in the *c*,
13: 52 He must burn up the *c*,
13: 53 the mildew has not spread in the *c*,
13: 56 the contaminated part out of the *c*,
13: 57 But if it reappears in the *c*,
13: 58 *c*, or the woven or knitted material,
13: 59 by mildew in woolen or linen *c*,
14: 55 for mildew in *c* or in a house,
15: 17 Any *c* or leather that has semen
19: 19 Do not wear *c* woven of two kinds
Dt 10: 18 the alien, giving him food and *c*.
22: 5 A woman must not wear men's *c*,
22: 5 nor a man wear women's *c*,
Jos 22: 8 and a great quantity of *c*—
Jdg 3: 16 to his right thigh under his *c*.
2Ki 5: 5 shekels of gold and ten sets of *c*.
5: 22 talent of silver and two sets of *c*.' "
5: 23 in two bags, with two sets of *c*.
7: 15 the whole road strewn with the *c*
2Ch 20: 25 and *c* and also articles of value—
Job 22: 6 you stripped men of their *c*,
29: 14 I put on righteousness as my *c*;
30: 18 great power ⌊God⌋ becomes like *c*
31: 19 seen anyone perishing for lack of *c*,
Ps 22: 18 and cast lots for my *c*.
102: 26 Like *c* you will change them
Pr 27: 26 the lambs will provide you with *c*,
Isa 3: 7 I have no food or *c* in my house;
3: 24 instead of fine *c*, sackcloth;
59: 6 Their cobwebs are useless for *c*;
63: 3 and I stained all my *c*.
Eze 18: 7 and provides *c* for the naked.
18: 16 and provides *c* for the naked.
Da 7: 9 His *c* was as white as snow;
Zec 14: 14 quantities of gold and silver and *c*.
Mt 7: 15 They come to you in sheep's *c*,
Mk 1: 6 John wore *c* made of camel's hair,
Jn 13: 4 off his outer *c*, and wrapped a towel
19: 24 and cast lots for my *c*."
Ac 9: 39 and other *c* that Dorcas had made
20: 33 anyone's silver or gold or *c*.
1Ti 6: 8 But if we have food and *c*,
Jude : 23 the *c* stained by corrupted flesh.

CLOTHS (CLOTH)

Lk 2: 7 him in *c* and placed him

CLOUD (CLOUDBURST CLOUDS THUNDERCLOUD)

Ex 13: 21 them in a pillar of *c* to guide them
13: 22 Neither the pillar of *c* by day
14: 19 The pillar of *c* also moved
14: 20 the night the *c* brought darkness
14: 24 and *c* at the Egyptian army
16: 10 of the LORD appearing in the *c*.
19: 9 going to come to you in a dense *c*,
19: 16 with a thick *c* over the mountain,
24: 15 on the mountain, the *c* covered it,
24: 16 called to Moses from within the *c*.
24: 16 six days the *c* covered
24: 18 Then Moses entered the *c*
33: 9 the pillar of *c* would come down
33: 10 pillar of *c* standing at the entrance
34: 5 the LORD came down in the *c*
40: 34 the *c* covered the Tent of Meeting,
40: 35 because the *c* had settled upon it,
40: 36 whenever the *c* lifted
40: 37 but if the *c* did not lift,
40: 38 So the *c* of the LORD was
40: 38 and fire was in the *c* by night,
Lev 16: 2 in the *c* over the atonement cover.
Nu 9: 15 From evening till morning the *c*
9: 15 was set up, the *c* covered it.
9: 16 continued to be; the *c* covered it,
9: 17 Whenever the *c* lifted
9: 17 wherever the *c* settled,
9: 18 as the *c* stayed over the tabernacle,
9: 19 When the *c* remained
9: 20 Sometimes the *c* was
9: 21 Sometimes the *c* stayed only
9: 21 whenever the *c* lifted, they set out.
9: 22 Whether the *c* stayed
Nu 10: 11 *c* lifted from above the tabernacle
10: 12 to place until the *c* came to rest
10: 34 The *c* of the LORD was over them
11: 25 the LORD came down in the *c*
12: 5 came down in a pillar of *c*;
12: 10 the *c* lifted from above the Tent,
14: 14 before them in a pillar of *c* by day
14: 14 that your *c* stays over them,
16: 42 suddenly the *c* covered it
Dt 1: 33 in fire by night and in a *c* by day,
5: 22 the *c* and the deep darkness;
31: 15 and the *c* stood over the entrance
31: 15 appeared at the Tent in a pillar of *c*,
Jdg 20: 38 that they should send up a great *c*
1Ki 8: 10 the *c* filled the temple
8: 11 their service because of the *c*,
8: 12 that he would dwell in a dark *c*;
18: 44 *c* as small as a man's hand is rising
2Ch 5: 13 of the LORD was filled with a *c*,
5: 14 their service because of the *c*,
6: 1 that he would dwell in a dark *c*;
Ne 9: 12 day you led them with a pillar of *c*,
9: 19 By day the pillar of *c* did not cease
Job 3: 5 may a *c* settle over it;
7: 9 As a *c* vanishes and is gone,
30: 15 my safety vanishes like a *c*.
Ps 78: 14 He guided them with the *c* by day
99: 7 to them from the pillar of *c*;
105: 39 He spread out a *c* as a covering,
Pr 16: 15 his favor is like a rain *c* in spring
Isa 4: 5 over those who assemble there a *c*
14: 31 A *c* of smoke comes from the north
18: 4 like a *c* of dew in the heat
19: 1 See, the LORD rides on a swift *c*
25: 5 reduced by the shadow of a *c*,
44: 22 swept away your offenses like a *c*,
La 2: 1 Zion with the *c* of his anger!
3: 44 You have covered yourself with a *c*
Eze 1: 4 immense *c* with flashing lightning
8: 11 a fragrant *c* of incense was rising.
10: 3 and a *c* filled the inner court.
10: 4 The *c* filled the temple,
32: 7 I will cover the sun with a *c*,
38: 9 will be like a *c* covering the land.
38: 16 people Israel like a *c* that covers
Mt 17: 5 a bright *c* enveloped them,
17: 5 and a voice from the *c* said,
Mk 9: 7 a *c* appeared and enveloped them,
9: 7 and a voice came from the *c*:
Lk 9: 34 a *c* appeared and enveloped them,
9: 34 were afraid as they entered the *c*.
9: 35 A voice came from the *c*, saying,
12: 54 When you see a *c* rising in the west,
21: 27 of Man coming in a *c* with power
Ac 1: 9 and a *c* hid him from their sight
1Co 10: 1 our forefathers were all under the *c*
10: 2 baptized into Moses in the *c*
Heb 12: 1 by such a great *c* of witnesses,
Rev 10: 1 He was robed in a *c*, with a rainbow
11: 12 And they went up to heaven in a *c*,
14: 14 and there before me was a white *c*,
14: 14 seated on the *c* was one "like a son
14: 15 to him who was sitting on the *c*,
14: 16 seated on the *c* swung his sickle

CLOUDBURST (CLOUD)

Isa 30: 30 with *c*, thunderstorm and hail.

CLOUDLESS

2Sa 23: 4 sunrise on a *c* morning,

CLOUDS (CLOUD)

Ge 9: 13 I have set my rainbow in the *c*,
9: 14 Whenever I bring *c* over the earth
9: 14 and the rainbow appears in the *c*,
9: 16 the rainbow appears in the *c*,
Dt 4: 11 with black *c* and deep darkness.
33: 26 and on the *c* in his majesty.
Jdg 5: 4 the *c* poured down water.
2Sa 22: 10 dark *c* were under his feet.
22: 12 the dark rain *c* of the sky.
1Ki 18: 45 the sky grew black with *c*,
Job 20: 6 and his head touches the *c*,
22: 14 Thick *c* veil him, so he does not see
26: 8 He wraps up the waters in his *c*,
26: 8 yet the *c* do not burst
26: 9 spreading his *c* over it.
35: 5 gaze at the *c* so high above you.
Job 36: 28 the *c* pour down their moisture
36: 29 how he spreads out the *c*,
37: 11 He loads the *c* with moisture;
37: 13 He brings the *c* to punish men,
37: 15 you know how God controls the *c*
37: 16 you know how the *c* hang poised,
38: 9 when I made the *c* its garment
38: 34 "Can you raise your voice to the *c*
38: 37 Who has the wisdom to count the *c*
Ps 18: 9 dark *c* were under his feet.
18: 11 the dark rain *c* of the sky.
18: 12 of his presence *c* advanced,
68: 4 extol him who rides on the *c*—
77: 17 The *c* poured down water,
97: 2 *C* and thick darkness surround him
104: 3 He makes the *c* his chariot
135: 7 He makes *c* rise from the ends
147: 8 He covers the sky with *c*;
148: 8 lightning and hail, snow and *c*,
Pr 3: 20 and the *c* let drop the dew.
8: 28 when he established the *c* above
25: 14 Like *c* and wind without rain
Ecc 11: 3 If *c* are full of water,
11: 4 whoever looks at the *c* will not reap
12: 2 and the *c* return after the rain;
Isa 5: 6 I will command the *c*
5: 30 the light will be darkened by the *c*.
14: 14 I will ascend above the tops of the *c*
30: 27 with burning anger and dense *c*
45: 8 let the *c* shower it down.
60: 8 Who are these that fly along like *c*,
Jer 4: 13 Look! He advances like the *c*,
10: 13 he makes *c* rise from the ends
51: 9 it rises as high as the *c*.
51: 16 he makes *c* rise from the ends
Eze 1: 28 of a rainbow in the *c* on a rainy day,
30: 3 a day of *c*,
30: 18 She will be covered with *c*,
34: 12 they were scattered on a day of *c*
Da 7: 13 coming with the *c* of heaven.
Joel 2: 2 a day of *c* and blackness.
Na 1: 3 and *c* are the dust of his feet.
Zep 1: 15 a day of *c* and blackness,
Zec 10: 1 the LORD who makes the storm *c*.
Mt 24: 30 of Man coming on the *c* of the sky,
26: 64 and coming on the *c* of heaven."
Mk 13: 26 coming in *c* with great power
14: 62 and coming on the *c* of heaven."
1Th 4: 17 with them in the *c* to meet the Lord
Jude : 12 They are *c* without rain, blown
Rev 1: 7 Look, he is coming with the *c*,

CLUB (CLUBS)

2Sa 23: 21 Benaiah went against him with a *c*
1Ch 11: 23 Benaiah went against him with a *c*.
Job 41: 29 A *c* seems to him but a piece
Pr 25: 18 Like a *c* or a sword or a sharp arrow
Isa 10: 5 in whose hand is the *c* of my wrath!
10: 15 a *c* brandish him who is not wood!
10: 24 and lift up a *c* against you,
Jer 51: 20 "You are my war *c*,

CLUBS (CLUB)

Eze 39: 9 and arrows, the war *c* and spears.
Mt 26: 47 armed with swords and *c*,
26: 55 with swords and *c* to capture me?
Mk 14: 43 armed with swords and *c*,
14: 48 with swords and *c* to capture me?
Lk 22: 52 come with swords and *c*?

CLUNG (CLING)

Ru 1: 14 mother-in-law good-by, but Ruth *c*
2Ki 3: 3 Nevertheless he *c* to the sins
La 1: 9 Her filthiness *c* to her skirts;

CLUSTER (CLUSTERS)

Nu 13: 23 cut off a branch bearing a single *c*
13: 24 of the *c* of grapes the Israelites cut
SS 1: 14 to me a *c* of henna blossoms
Isa 65: 8 "As when juice is still found in a *c*
Mic 7: 1 there is no *c* of grapes to eat,

CLUSTERS (CLUSTER)

Ge 40: 10 and its *c* ripened into grapes.
Dt 32: 32 and their *c* with bitterness.
SS 7: 7 and your breasts like *c* of fruit.
7: 8 May your breasts be like the *c*
Rev 14: 18 and gather the *c* of grapes

CLUTCHES

Job 5: 15 from the *c* of the powerful.
6: 23 me from the *c* of the ruthless'?
16: 11 thrown me into the *c* of the wicked.
Hab 2: 9 to escape the *c* of ruin!
Ac 12: 11 and rescued me from Herod's *c*

CNIDUS

Ac 27: 7 and had difficulty arriving off *C*.

CO-HEIRS (INHERIT)

Ro 8: 17 heirs of God and *c* with Christ,

COAL (COALS)

2Sa 14: 7 out the only burning *c* I have left,
Isa 6: 6 flew to me with a live *c* in his hand,

COALS (COAL)

Lev 16: 12 full of burning *c* from the altar
Nu 16: 37 scatter the *c* some distance away,
2Sa 22: 9 burning *c* blazed out of it.
1Ki 19: 6 a cake of bread baked over hot *c*,
Job 41: 21 His breath sets *c* ablaze,
Ps 11: 6 fiery *c* and burning sulfur;
18: 8 burning *c* blazed out of it.
120: 4 with burning *c* of the broom tree.
140: 10 Let burning *c* fall upon them;
Pr 6: 28 Can a man walk on hot *c*
25: 22 you will heap burning *c* on his head
Isa 30: 14 found for taking *c* from a hearth
44: 12 and works with it in the *c*;
44: 19 I even baked bread over its *c*,
47: 14 Here are no *c* to warm anyone;
54: 16 who fans the *c* into flame
Eze 1: 13 living creatures was like burning *c*
10: 2 *c* from among the cherubim
24: 11 Then set the empty pot on the *c*
Jn 21: 9 of burning *c* there with fish on it,
Ro 12: 20 you will heap burning *c* on his head

COARSE

Eph 5: 4 or *c* joking, which are out of place,

COAST (COASTLANDS COASTLINE COASTS SEACOAST)

Nu 34: 6 western boundary will be the *c*
Jos 9: 1 along the entire *c* of the Great Sea
Isa 20: 6 people who live on this *c* will say,
Ac 17: 14 immediately sent Paul to the *c*,
27: 2 ports along the *c* of the province
27: 5 sailed across the open sea off the *c*
27: 8 moved along the *c* with difficulty

COASTLANDS (COAST)

Jer 25: 22 the kings of the *c* across the sea;
31: 10 proclaim it in distant *c*:
Eze 26: 15 Will not the *c* tremble at the sound
26: 18 Now the *c* tremble
27: 15 and many *c* were your customers;
27: 35 All who live in the *c*
39: 6 on those who live in safety in the *c*,
Da 11: 18 he will turn his attention to the *c*
11: 30 of the western *c* will oppose him,

COASTLINE (COAST)

Jos 15: 12 The western boundary is the *c*
15: 47 of Egypt and the *c* of the Great

COASTS (COAST)

Jer 2: 10 Cross over to the *c* of Kittim
47: 4 the remnant from the *c* of Caphtor.
Eze 27: 3 merchant of peoples on many *c*,
27: 6 wood from the *c* of Cyprus
27: 7 and purple from the *c* of Elishah.

COAT (COATED COATING COATS)

Ge 6: 14 in it and *c* it with pitch inside
Dt 27: 2 up some large stones and *c* them
27: 4 I command you today, and *c* them
1Sa 17: 5 and wore a *c* of scale armor
17: 38 He put a *c* of armor on him
Job 41: 13 Who can strip off his outer *c*?

COATED (COAT)

Ex 2: 3 and *c* it with tar and pitch.

COATING (COAT)

Pr 26: 23 Like a *c* of glaze over earthenware

COATS (COAT)

2Ch 26: 14 spears, helmets, *c* of armor,

COAX

Jdg 14: 15 "*C* your husband into explaining

COBRA (COBRAS)

Ps 58: 4 that of a *c* that has stopped its ears,
91: 13 upon the lion and the *c*;
Isa 11: 8 near the hole of the *c*,

COBRAS (COBRA)

Dt 32: 33 the deadly poison of *c*.

COBWEBS (WEB)

Isa 59: 6 Their *c* are useless for clothing;

COCOON

Job 27: 18 house he builds is like a moth's *c*,

CODE

Ro 2: 27 even though you have the written *c*
2: 29 by the Spirit, not by the written *c*.
7: 6 not in the old way of the written *c*.
Col 2: 14 having canceled the written *c*,

COFFIN

Ge 50: 26 he was placed in a *c* in Egypt.
Lk 7: 14 Then he went up and touched the *c*

COHORTS

Job 9: 13 the *c* of Rahab cowered at his feet.

COILED (COILING)

2Sa 22: 6 The cords of the grave *c* around me
Ps 18: 5 The cords of the grave *c* around me

COILING (COILED)

Isa 27: 1 Leviathan the *c* serpent;

COIN (COINS)

Mt 17: 27 and you will find a four-drachma *c*.
22: 19 Show me the *c* used
Mk 12: 16 They brought the *c*, and he asked
Lk 15: 9 with me; I have found my lost *c*.'

COINS (COIN)

Mt 26: 15 out for him thirty silver *c*.
27: 3 and returned the thirty silver *c*
27: 6 The chief priests picked up the *c*
27: 9 "They took the thirty silver *c*,
Mk 12: 42 and put in two very small copper *c*,
Lk 10: 35 next day he took out two silver *c*
15: 8 suppose a woman has ten silver *c*
21: 2 put in two very small copper *c*.
Jn 2: 15 he scattered the *c* of the money

COL-HOZEH

Ne 3: 15 repaired by Shallun son of *C*,
11: 5 the son of *C*, the son of Hazaiah,

COLD

Ge 8: 22 *c* and heat,
31: 40 in the daytime and the *c* at night,
Job 24: 7 to cover themselves in the *c*.
37: 9 the *c* from the driving winds.
Pr 25: 20 takes away a garment on a *c* day,
25: 25 Like *c* water to a weary soul
Na 3: 17 that settle in the walls on a *c* day—
Zec 14: 6 that day there will be no light, no *c*
Mt 10: 42 if anyone gives a cup of *c* water
24: 12 the love of most will grow *c*,
Jn 18: 18 It was *c*, and the servants
Ac 28: 2 us all because it was raining and *c*.
2Co 11: 27 gone without food; I have been *c*
Rev 3: 15 that you are neither *c* nor hot.
3: 16 lukewarm—neither hot nor *c*—

COLLAPSE (COLLAPSED COLLAPSES)

Jos 6: 5 then the wall of the city will *c*
Ps 10: 10 His victims are crushed, they *c*;
Eze 26: 18 are terrified at your *c*.'
Mt 15: 32 or they may *c* on the way."
Mk 8: 3 them home hungry, they will *c*

COLLAPSED (COLLAPSE)

Jos 6: 20 the wall *c*; so every man charged
Jdg 7: 13 that the tent overturned and *c*."
1Ki 20: 30 wall *c* on twenty-seven thousand
Job 1: 19 It *c* on them and they are dead,
Hab 3: 6 and the age-old hills *c*.
Lk 6: 49 it *c* and its destruction was
Rev 11: 13 and a tenth of the city *c*.
16: 19 and the cities of the nations *c*.

COLLAPSES (COLLAPSE)

Isa 30: 13 that *c* suddenly, in an instant.
Eze 13: 12 When the wall *c*, will people not
Na 2: 6 and the palace *c*.

COLLAR

Ex 28: 32 There shall be a woven edge like a *c*
39: 23 of the robe like the opening of a *c*,
Ps 133: 2 down upon the *c* of his robes.

COLLECT (COLLECTED COLLECTING COLLECTION COLLECTIONS COLLECTOR COLLECTOR'S COLLECTORS COLLECTS)

Ge 41: 35 They should *c* all the food
Nu 3: 47 *c* five shekels for each one,
2Ki 12: 4 "*C* all the money that is brought
12: 8 they would not *c* any more money
2Ch 20: 25 that it took three days to *c* it.
24: 5 and *c* the money due annually
Ne 10: 37 for it is the Levites who *c* the tithes
Mt 13: 30 First *c* the weeds and tie them
17: 25 the kings of the earth *c* duty
21: 34 to the tenants to *c* his fruit.
Mk 12: 2 to the tenants to *c* from them some
Lk 3: 13 "Don't *c* any more
Heb 7: 5 to *c* a tenth from the people—

COLLECTED (COLLECT)

Ge 41: 48 Joseph *c* all the food produced
47: 14 Joseph *c* all the money that was
Nu 3: 49 So Moses *c* the redemption money
3: 50 the Israelites he *c* silver weighing
16: 39 So Eleazar the priest *c* the bronze
2Ki 12: 4 the money *c* in the census,
22: 4 which the doorkeepers have *c*
2Ch 24: 11 and *c* a great amount of money.
34: 9 who were the doorkeepers had *c*
Ecc 12: 11 their *c* sayings like firmly
Zec 14: 14 the surrounding nations will be *c*—
Mt 13: 48 and *c* the good fish in baskets,
Lk 19: 23 I could have *c* it with interest?'
Heb 7: 6 yet he *c* a tenth from Abraham
7: 8 the tenth is *c* by men who die;

COLLECTING (COLLECT)

Lev 11: 36 a cistern for *c* water remains clean,

COLLECTION (COLLECT)

Isa 57: 13 let your *c* ⌊of idols⌋ save you!
1Co 16: 1 Now about the *c* for God's people:

COLLECTIONS (COLLECT)

1Co 16: 2 that when I come no *c* will have

COLLECTOR (COLLECT)

Da 11: 20 "His successor will send out a tax *c*
Mt 10: 3 Thomas and Matthew the tax *c*;
18: 17 as you would a pagan or a tax *c*.
Lk 5: 27 and saw a tax *c* by the name
18: 10 one a Pharisee and the other a tax *c*
18: 11 adulterers—or even like this tax *c*.
18: 13 "But the tax *c* stood at a distance.
19: 2 was a chief tax *c* and was wealthy.

COLLECTOR'S (COLLECT)

Mt 9: 9 sitting at the tax *c* booth.
Mk 2: 14 sitting at the tax *c* booth.

COLLECTORS (COLLECT)

Mt 5: 46 Are not even the tax *c* doing that?
9: 10 many tax *c* and "sinners" came
9: 11 does your teacher eat with tax *c*
11: 19 a friend of tax *c* and "sinners." '
17: 24 the *c* of the two-drachma tax came
21: 31 the tax *c* and the prostitutes are
21: 32 but the tax *c* and the prostitutes did
Mk 2: 15 many tax *c* and "sinners" were
2: 16 eating with the "sinners" and tax *c*,
2: 16 "Why does he eat with tax *c*
Lk 3: 12 Tax *c* also came to be baptized.

Lk 5: 29 and a large crowd of tax *c*
5: 30 and drink with tax *c* and 'sinners'?"
7: 29 the tax *c*, when they heard Jesus'
7: 34 a friend of tax *c* and "sinners." '
15: 1 the tax *c* and "sinners" were all

COLLECTS (COLLECT)

Heb 7: 9 even say that Levi, who *c* the tenth,

COLONNADE (COLUMN)

1Ki 7: 6 He made a *c* fifty cubits long
Jn 10: 23 area walking in Solomon's *C*.
Ac 3: 11 in the place called Solomon's *C*.
5: 12 to meet together in Solomon's *C*.

COLONNADES (COLUMN)

Jn 5: 2 is surrounded by five covered *c*.

COLONY

Ac 16: 12 a Roman *c* and the leading city

COLORED (COLORFUL COLORS)

Pr 7: 16 bed with *c* linens from Egypt.

COLORFUL (COLORED)

Jdg 5: 30 *c* garments as plunder for Sisera,
5: 30 *c* garments embroidered,

COLORS (COLORED)

1Ch 29: 2 turquoise, stones of various *c*,
Eze 17: 3 of varied *c* came to Lebanon.

COLOSSE

Col 1: 2 and faithful brothers in Christ at *C*:

COLT

Ge 49: 11 his *c* to the choicest branch;
Job 11: 12 than a wild donkey's *c* can be born
Zec 9: 9 on a *c*, the foal of a donkey.
Mt 21: 2 find a donkey tied there, with her *c*
21: 5 on a *c*, the foal of a donkey.' "
21: 7 They brought the donkey and the *c*
Mk 11: 2 you will find a *c* tied there,
11: 4 and found a *c* outside in the street,
11: 5 What are you doing, untying that *c*
11: 7 When they brought the *c* to Jesus
Lk 19: 30 you will find a *c* tied there,
19: 33 As they were untying the *c*,
19: 33 "Why are you untying the *c*?"
19: 35 threw their cloaks on the *c*
Jn 12: 15 seated on a donkey's *c*."

COLUMN (COLONNADE COLONNADES COLUMNS)

Jdg 20: 40 when the *c* of smoke began to rise
SS 3: 6 like a *c* of smoke,
Isa 9: 18 so that it rolls upward in a *c*

COLUMNS (COLUMN)

1Ki 7: 2 of cedar *c* supporting trimmed
7: 3 the beams that rested on the *c*—
Jer 36: 23 Jehudi had read three or four *c*
Joel 2: 20 with its front *c* going
Zep 2: 14 will roost on her *c*.

COMB (COMBED)

Ps 19: 10 than honey from the *c*.
Pr 24: 13 honey from the *c* is sweet

COMBED (COMB)

Isa 19: 9 with *c* flax will despair,

COMBINE (COMBINED)

Heb 4: 2 those who heard did not *c* it

COMBINED (COMBINE)

1Co 12: 24 God has *c* the members of the body

COMFORT (COMFORTED COMFORTER COMFORTERS COMFORTING COMFORTS)

Ge 5: 29 "He will *c* us in the labor
37: 35 and daughters came to *c* him,
Ru 2: 13 "You have given me *c*
1Ch 7: 22 and his relatives came to *c* him.
Job 2: 11 sympathize with him and *c* him.
7: 13 When I think my bed will *c* me
16: 5 *c* from my lips would bring you
36: 16 to the *c* of your table laden
Ps 23: 4 rod and your staff, they *c* me.
71: 21 and *c* me once again.
119: 50 My *c* in my suffering is this:
119: 52 and I find *c* in them.
119: 76 May your unfailing love be my *c*,
119: 82 I say, "When will you *c* me?"
Isa 40: 1 *C*, *c* my people,
51: 3 The LORD will surely *c* Zion
51: 19 who can *c* you?—
57: 18 I will guide him and restore *c*
61: 2 to *c* all who mourn,
66: 13 so will I *c* you;
Jer 16: 7 food to *c* those who mourn
31: 13 I will give them *c* and joy instead
La 1: 2 there is none to *c* her.
1: 9 there was none to *c* her.
1: 16 No one is near to *c* me,
1: 17 but there is no one to *c* her.
1: 21 but there is no one to *c* me.
2: 13 that I may *c* you,
Eze 16: 54 all you have done in giving them *c*.
Na 3: 7 Where can I find anyone to *c* you?"
Zec 1: 17 and the LORD will again *c* Zion
10: 2 they give *c* in vain.
Lk 6: 24 you have already received your *c*.
Jn 11: 19 and Mary to *c* them in the loss
1Co 14: 3 encouragement and *c*.
2Co 1: 3 of compassion and the God of all *c*,
1: 4 so that we can *c* those
1: 4 with the *c* we ourselves have
1: 5 through Christ our *c* overflows.
1: 6 if we are comforted, it is for your *c*,
1: 6 it is for your *c* and salvation;
1: 7 so also you share in our *c*.
2: 7 you ought to forgive and *c* him,
7: 7 also by the *c* you had given him.
Php 2: 1 if any *c* from his love,
Col 4: 11 and they have proved a *c* to me.

COMFORTED (COMFORT)

Ge 24: 67 Isaac was *c* after his mother's death
37: 35 comfort him, but he refused to be *c*.
2Sa 12: 24 Then David *c* his wife Bathsheba,
Job 42: 11 They *c* and consoled him
Ps 77: 2 and my soul refused to be *c*.
86: 17 have helped me and *c* me.
Isa 12: 1 and you have *c* me.
52: 9 for the LORD has *c* his people,
54: 11 lashed by storms and not *c*,
66: 13 and you will be *c* over Jerusalem."
Jer 31: 15 and refusing to be *c*,
Mt 2: 18 and refusing to be *c*,
5: 4 for they will be *c*.
Lk 16: 25 but now he is *c* here and you are
Ac 20: 12 man home alive and were greatly *c*.
2Co 1: 6 if we are *c*, it is for your comfort,
7: 6 *c* us by the coming of Titus,

COMFORTER (COMFORT)

Ecc 4: 1 and they have no *c*;
4: 1 and they have no *c*.
Jer 8: 18 O my *C* in sorrow,

COMFORTERS (COMFORT)

Job 16: 2 miserable *c* are you all!
Ps 69: 20 for *c*, but I found none.

COMFORTING (COMFORT)

Isa 66: 11 satisfied at her *c* breasts;
Zec 1: 13 *c* words to the angel who talked
Jn 11: 31 *c* her, noticed how quickly she got
1Th 2: 12 *c* and urging you to live lives

COMFORTS (COMFORT)

Job 29: 25 I was like one who *c* mourners.
Isa 49: 13 For the LORD *c* his people
51: 12 "I, even I, am he who *c* you.
66: 13 As a mother *c* her child,
2Co 1: 4 who *c* us in all our troubles,
7: 6 But God, who *c* the downcast,

COMMAND (COMMANDED COMMANDER COMMANDER-IN-CHIEF COMMANDER'S COMMANDERS COMMANDING COMMANDMENT COMMANDMENTS COMMANDS SECOND-IN-COMMAND)

Ex 7: 2 You are to say everything I *c* you,
27: 20 "*C* the Israelites to bring you clear
34: 11 Obey what I *c* you today.
38: 21 recorded at Moses' *c* by the Levites
Lev 6: 9 "Give Aaron and his sons this *c*:
10: 1 before the LORD, contrary to his *c*
24: 2 "*C* the Israelites to bring you clear
Nu 3: 39 counted at the LORD's *c* by Moses
4: 37 to the LORD's *c* through Moses.
4: 41 them according to the LORD's *c*.
4: 45 to the LORD's *c* through Moses.
4: 49 At the LORD's *c* through Moses,
5: 2 "*C* the Israelites to send away
9: 18 At the LORD's *c* the Israelites set
9: 18 and at his *c* they encamped.
9: 20 and then at his *c* they would set out
9: 20 at the LORD's *c* they would
9: 23 At the LORD's *c* they encamped,
9: 23 and at the LORD's *c* they set out.
9: 23 with his *c* through Moses.
10: 13 at the LORD's *c* through Moses.
10: 14 son of Amminadab was in *c*.
10: 18 Elizur son of Shedeur was in *c*.
10: 22 Elishama son of Ammihud was in *c*
10: 25 son of Ammishaddai was in *c*.
13: 3 at the LORD's *c* Moses sent them
14: 41 are you disobeying the LORD's *c*?
20: 24 rebelled against my *c* at the waters
22: 18 or small to go beyond the *c*
23: 20 I have received a *c* to bless;
24: 13 to go beyond the *c* of the LORD—
27: 14 of you disobeyed my *c* to honor me
27: 21 At his *c* he and the entire
27: 21 and at his *c* they will come in."
28: 2 "Give this *c* to the Israelites
31: 49 counted the soldiers under our *c*,
33: 2 At the LORD's *c* Moses recorded
33: 38 At the LORD's *c* Aaron the priest
34: 2 "*C* the Israelites and say to them:
35: 2 "*C* the Israelites to give the Levites
36: 5 at the LORD's *c* Moses gave this
Dt 1: 26 you rebelled against the *c*
1: 43 You rebelled against the LORD's *c*
2: 37 But in accordance with the *c*
4: 2 Do not add to what I *c* you
8: 1 to follow every *c* I am giving you
9: 23 But you rebelled against the *c*
11: 28 from the way that I *c* you today
12: 11 are to bring everything I *c* you:
12: 14 there observe everything I *c* you.
12: 32 See that you do all I *c* you;
15: 11 I *c* you to be openhanded
15: 15 That is why I give you this *c* today.
17: 3 to my *c* has worshiped other gods,
18: 18 he will tell them everything I *c* him
19: 7 This is why I *c* you to set
19: 9 all these laws I *c* you today—
24: 18 That is why I *c* you to do this.
24: 22 That is why I *c* you to do this.
27: 4 as I *c* you today, and coat them
30: 2 to everything I *c* you today,
30: 16 For I *c* you today to love
31: 23 The LORD gave this *c*
31: 25 he gave this *c* to the Levites who
32: 46 so that you may *c* your children
Jos 1: 13 "Remember the *c* that Moses
1: 18 whatever you may *c* them,
4: 16 "*C* the priests carrying the ark
15: 13 with the LORD's *c* to him,
17: 4 according to the LORD's *c*.
22: 9 with the *c* of the LORD
Jdg 9: 29 If only this people were under my *c*
1Sa 13: 13 not kept the *c* the LORD your
13: 14 you have not kept the LORD's *c*."
15: 24 I violated the LORD's *c*
16: 16 Let our lord *c* his servants here
18: 13 gave him *c* over a thousand men,
2Sa 10: 10 under the *c* of Abishai his brother
18: 2 a third under the *c* of Joab,
20: 7 out under the *c* of Abishai.
1Ki 2: 43 and obey the *c* I gave you?"
5: 17 At the king's *c* they removed
9: 4 do all I *c* and observe my decrees
11: 10 did not keep the LORD's *c*.
11: 38 If you do whatever I *c* you
13: 21 not kept the *c* the LORD your
16: 9 who had *c* of half his chariots,
18: 36 have done all these things at your *c*
2Ki 24: 3 Judah according to the LORD's *c*,

1Ch 11: 6 and so he received the *c*.
12: 9 the second in *c*, Eliab the third,
12: 32 with all their relatives under their *c*
19: 11 under the *c* of Abishai his brother,
21: 6 the king's *c* was repulsive to him.
21: 7 This *c* was also evil in the sight
22: 12 when he puts you in *c* over Israel,
28: 21 the people will obey your every *c*.''
2Ch 7: 13 or *c* locusts to devour the land
7: 17 do all I *c*, and observe my decrees
24: 8 At the king's *c*, a chest was made
26: 13 Under their *c* was an army
30: 6 At the king's *c*, couriers went
35: 22 to what Neco had said at God's *c*
Ezr 6: 14 to the *c* of the God of Israel
Est 1: 8 By the king's *c* each guest was
1: 12 attendants delivered the king's *c*,
1: 15 ''She has not obeyed the *c*
3: 3 Why do you disobey the king's *c*?''
3: 15 Spurred on by the king's *c*,
8: 14 spurred on by the king's *c*.
Job 39: 27 Does the eagle soar at your *c*
Ps 71: 3 give the *c* to save me,
78: 23 Yet he gave a *c* to the skies above
91: 11 For he will *c* his angels concerning
147: 15 He sends his *c* to the earth;
Pr 8: 29 waters would not overstep his *c*,
13: 13 but he who respects a *c* is rewarded
Ecc 8: 2 Obey the king's *c*, I say,
8: 5 Whoever obeys his *c* will come
Isa 5: 6 I will *c* the clouds
Jer 1: 7 you to and say whatever I *c* you.
1: 17 and say to them whatever I *c* you.
7: 23 Walk in all the ways I *c* you,
7: 23 but I gave them this *c*: Obey me,
7: 31 something I did not *c* nor did it
11: 4 Obey me and do everything I *c* you
19: 5 something I did not *c* or mention,
26: 2 Tell them everything I *c* you;
35: 6 son of Recab gave us this *c*:
35: 14 they obey their forefather's *c*.
35: 14 wine and this *c* has been kept.
35: 16 carried out the *c* their forefather
35: 18 'You have obeyed the *c*
43: 4 people disobeyed the LORD's *c*
La 1: 18 yet I rebelled against his *c*.
Eze 21: 22 to give the *c* to slaughter,
38: 7 gathered about you, and take *c*
Da 3: 22 The king's *c* was so urgent
3: 28 in him and defied the king's *c*
4: 26 The *c* to leave the stump of the tree
5: 29 Then at Belshazzar's *c*, Daniel was
6: 24 At the king's *c*, the men who had
Joel 2: 11 mighty are those who obey his *c*.
Am 6: 11 For the LORD has given the *c*,
9: 3 there I will *c* the serpent
9: 4 there I will *c* the sword
9: 9 ''For I will give the *c*,
Na 1: 14 has given a *c* concerning you,
Mt 4: 6 He will *c* his angels concerning you
15: 3 why do you break the *c* of God
19: 7 ''did Moses *c* that a man give his
Mk 9: 25 and dumb spirit,'' he said, ''I *c* you,
10: 3 What did Moses *c* you?'' he replied
Lk 4: 10 '' 'He will *c* his angels concerning
Jn 10: 18 This *c* I received from my Father.''
12: 50 I know that his *c* leads
14: 15 love me, you will obey what I *c*.
15: 12 My *c* is this: Love each other
15: 14 friends if you do what I *c*.
15: 17 This is my *c*: Love each other.
Ac 1: 4 he gave them this *c*: ''Do not leave
16: 18 of Jesus Christ I *c* you to come out
19: 13 whom Paul preaches, I *c* you
25: 23 At the *c* of Festus, Paul was
Ro 5: 14 who did not sin by breaking a *c*,
16: 26 by the *c* of the eternal God,
1Co 7: 6 I say this as a concession, not as a *c*
7: 10 To the married I give this *c* (not I,
7: 25 I have no *c* from the Lord,
14: 37 writing to you is the Lord's *c*.
Gal 5: 14 law is summed up in a single *c*:
1Th 4: 16 down from heaven, with a loud *c*,
2Th 3: 4 will continue to do the things we *c*.
3: 6 of the Lord Jesus Christ, we *c* you,
3: 12 Such people we *c* and urge
1Ti 1: 1 Jesus by the *c* of God our Savior
1: 3 so that you may *c* certain men not
1Ti 1: 5 goal of this *c* is love, which comes
4: 11 *C* and teach these things.
6: 17 *C* those who are rich
6: 18 *C* them to do good, to be rich
Tit 1: 3 to me by the *c* of God our Savior,
Heb 11: 3 universe was formed at God's *c*,
2Pe 3: 2 and the *c* given by our Lord
1Jn 2: 7 I am not writing you a new *c*
2: 7 This old *c* is the message you have
2: 8 Yet I am writing you a new *c*;
3: 23 this is his *c*: to believe in the name
4: 21 And he has given us this *c*:
2Jn : 5 I am not writing you a new *c*
: 6 his *c* is that you walk in love.
Rev 3: 10 Since you have kept my *c*

COMMANDED (COMMAND)

Ge 2: 16 And the LORD God *c* the man,
3: 11 from the tree that I *c* you not to eat
3: 17 from the tree about which I *c* you,
6: 22 did everything just as God *c* him.
7: 5 Noah did all that the LORD *c* him.
7: 9 the ark, as God had *c* Noah.
7: 16 living thing, as God had *c* Noah.
21: 4 circumcised him, as God *c* him.
28: 1 and blessed him and *c* him:
28: 6 that when he blessed him he *c* him,
45: 21 gave them carts, as Pharaoh had *c*,
50: 12 Jacob's sons did as he had *c* them:
Ex 4: 28 the miraculous signs he had *c* him
6: 13 he *c* them to bring the Israelites out
7: 6 did just as the LORD *c* them.
7: 10 and did just as the LORD *c*.
7: 20 Aaron did just as the LORD had *c*.
12: 28 did just what the LORD *c* Moses
12: 50 just what the LORD had *c* Moses
16: 16 This is what the LORD has *c*:
16: 23 ''This is what the LORD *c*:
16: 24 it until morning, as Moses *c*,
16: 32 ''This is what the LORD has *c*:
16: 34 As the LORD *c* Moses, Aaron put
17: 1 from place to place as the LORD *c*.
19: 7 all the words the LORD had *c* him
23: 15 made without yeast, as I *c* you.
29: 35 his sons everything I have *c* you,
31: 6 to make everything I have *c* you:
31: 11 are to make them just as I *c* you.''
32: 8 to turn away from what I *c* them
32: 28 The Levites did as Moses *c*,
34: 4 as the LORD had *c* him;
34: 18 made without yeast, as I *c* you.
34: 34 the Israelites what he had been *c*,
35: 1 are the things the LORD has *c* you
35: 4 ''This is what the LORD has *c*:
35: 10 make everything the LORD has *c*:
35: 29 through Moses had *c* them to do.
36: 1 the work just as the LORD has *c*.''
36: 5 for doing the work the LORD *c*
38: 22 everything the LORD *c* Moses;
39: 1 for Aaron, as the LORD *c* Moses.
39: 5 linen, as the LORD *c* Moses.
39: 7 of Israel, as the LORD *c* Moses.
39: 21 ephod—as the LORD *c* Moses.
39: 26 ministering, as the LORD *c* Moses.
39: 29 as the LORD *c* Moses.
39: 31 the turban, as the LORD *c* Moses.
39: 32 just as the LORD *c* Moses.
39: 42 as the LORD had *c* Moses.
39: 43 done it just as the LORD had *c*.
40: 16 just as the LORD *c* him.
40: 19 over the tent, as the LORD *c* him.
40: 21 Testimony, as the LORD *c* him.
40: 23 the LORD, as the LORD *c* him.
40: 25 the LORD, as the LORD *c* him.
40: 27 incense on it, as the LORD *c* him.
40: 29 grain offerings, as the LORD *c* him
40: 32 the altar, as the LORD *c* Moses.
Lev 7: 36 the LORD *c* that the Israelites give
7: 38 Sinai on the day he *c* the Israelites
8: 4 Moses did as the LORD *c* him,
8: 5 ''This is what the LORD has *c*
8: 9 front of it, as the LORD *c* Moses.
8: 13 on them, as the LORD *c* Moses.
8: 17 the camp, as the LORD *c* Moses.
8: 21 by fire, as the LORD *c* Moses.
8: 29 offering, as the LORD *c* Moses.
8: 31 I *c*, saying, 'Aaron and his sons are
8: 34 What has been done today was *c*
Lev 8: 35 for that is what I have been *c*.''
8: 36 sons did everything the LORD *c*
9: 5 They took the things Moses *c*
9: 6 ''This is what the LORD has *c* you
9: 7 for them, as the LORD has *c*.''
9: 10 as the LORD *c* Moses; the flesh
9: 21 as a wave offering, as Moses *c*.
10: 13 LORD by fire; for so I have been *c*.
10: 15 your children, as the LORD has *c*
10: 18 goat in the sanctuary area, as I *c*.''
16: 34 it was done, as the LORD *c* Moses.
17: 2 'This is what the LORD has *c*:
24: 23 did as the LORD *c* Moses.
Nu 1: 19 one by one, as the LORD *c* Moses.
1: 54 all this just as the LORD *c* Moses.
2: 33 Israelites, as the LORD *c* Moses.
2: 34 did everything the LORD *c* Moses;
3: 16 he was *c* by the word of the LORD.
3: 42 the Israelites, as the LORD *c* him.
3: 51 he was *c* by the word of the LORD.
4: 49 counted, as the LORD *c* Moses.
8: 3 just as the LORD *c* Moses.
8: 20 Levites just as the LORD *c* Moses.
8: 22 Levites just as the LORD *c* Moses.
9: 5 just as the LORD *c* Moses.
15: 36 to death, as the LORD *c* Moses.
17: 11 Moses did just as the LORD *c* him.
19: 2 of the law that the LORD has *c*:
20: 9 LORD's presence, just as he *c* him.
20: 27 Moses did as the LORD *c*:
26: 4 or more, as the LORD *c* Moses.''
27: 11 as the LORD *c* Moses.' ''
27: 22 Moses did as the LORD *c* him.
29: 40 Israelites all that the LORD *c* him.
31: 7 as the LORD *c* Moses,
31: 31 priest did as the LORD *c* Moses.
31: 41 part, as the LORD *c* Moses.
31: 47 as the LORD *c* him, and gave them
34: 13 Moses *c* the Israelites: ''Assign this
34: 29 These are the men the LORD *c*
36: 2 ''When the LORD *c* my lord
36: 10 did as the LORD *c* Moses.
Dt 1: 3 the LORD had *c* him concerning
1: 19 Then, as the LORD our God *c* us,
1: 41 as the LORD our God *c* us.''
3: 18 I *c* you at that time: ''The LORD
3: 21 At that time I *c* Joshua: ''You have
4: 5 laws as the LORD my God *c* me,
4: 13 which he *c* you to follow
5: 12 as the LORD your God has *c* you.
5: 15 the LORD your God has *c* you
5: 16 as the LORD your God has *c* you,
5: 32 the LORD your God has *c* you;
5: 33 the LORD your God has *c* you,
6: 20 laws the LORD our God has *c* you
6: 24 The LORD *c* us to obey all these
6: 25 as he has *c* us, that will be our
9: 12 quickly from what I *c* them
9: 16 the way that the LORD had *c* you.
10: 5 the LORD *c* me, and they are there
12: 21 as I have *c* you, and in your own
13: 5 the way the LORD your God *c* you
18: 20 my name anything I have not *c* him
20: 17 as the LORD your God has *c* you.
24: 8 carefully what I have *c* them.
26: 13 the widow, according to all you *c*.
26: 14 I have done everything you *c* me.
27: 1 the elders of Israel *c* the people:
27: 11 the same day Moses *c* the people:
29: 1 the covenant the LORD *c* Moses
31: 5 do to them all that I have *c* you.
31: 10 Then Moses *c* them: ''At the end
31: 29 to turn from the way I have *c* you.
34: 9 did what the LORD had *c* Moses.
Jos 1: 9 Have I not *c* you? Be strong
1: 16 Whatever you have *c* us we will do,
4: 8 the Israelites did as Joshua *c* them.
4: 10 the LORD had *c* Joshua was done
4: 17 Joshua *c* the priests, ''Come up out
6: 10 But Joshua had *c* the people,
6: 16 Joshua *c* the people, ''Shout!
7: 11 my covenant, which I *c* them
8: 8 Do what the LORD has *c*.
8: 31 of the LORD had *c* the Israelites.
8: 33 of the LORD had formerly *c*
8: 35 that Moses had *c* that Joshua did
9: 24 your God had *c* his servant Moses
10: 40 the LORD, the God of Israel, had *c*

Jos 11:12 the servant of the LORD had *c*.
11:15 As the LORD *c* his servant Moses,
11:15 of all that the LORD *c* Moses.
11:15 so Moses *c* Joshua, and Joshua did
11:20 as the LORD had *c* Moses.
14:2 as the LORD had *c* through Moses
14:5 just as the LORD had *c* Moses.
17:4 "The LORD *c* Moses
19:50 among them, as the LORD had *c*.
21:2 LORD *c* through Moses that you
21:3 LORD had *c*, the Israelites gave
21:8 as the LORD had *c* through Moses
22:2 Moses the servant of the LORD *c*,
22:2 have obeyed me in everything I *c*.
23:16 LORD your God, which he *c* you,
Jdg 13:14 must do everything I have *c* her."
2Sa 5:25 So David did as the LORD *c* him,
7:7 any of their rulers whom I *c*
18:5 The king *c* Joab, Abishai and Ittai,
18:12 In our hearing the king *c* you
21:14 and did everything the king *c*.
24:19 as the LORD had *c* through Gad.
1Ki 2:31 Then the king *c* Benaiah, "Do
11:11 and my decrees, which I *c* you,
13:9 For I was *c* by the word
17:9 I have *c* a widow in that place
18:40 he is God!" Then Elijah *c* them,
2Ki 7:14 He *c* the drivers, "Go and find out
11:5 He *c* them, saying, "This is what
14:6 Law of Moses where the LORD *c*:
17:13 the entire Law that I *c* your fathers
17:35 with the Israelites, he *c* them:
18:12 Moses the servant of the LORD *c*.
18:36 king had *c*, "Do not answer him.
21:8 careful to do everything I *c* them
1Ch 6:49 Moses the servant of God had *c*.
14:16 So David did as God *c* him,
15:15 as Moses had *c* in accordance
16:15 the word he *c*, for a thousand
17:6 any of their leaders whom I *c*
24:19 the God of Israel, had *c* him.
2Ch 8:13 for offerings *c* by Moses
8:18 And Hiram sent him ships *c*
14:4 He *c* Judah to seek the LORD,
25:4 of Moses, where the LORD *c*:
29:21 king *c* the priests, the descendants
29:25 this was *c* by the LORD
33:8 do everything I *c* them concerning
35:6 doing what the LORD *c*
Ezr 4:3 King Cyrus, the king of Persia, *c* us
Ne 8:1 which the LORD had *c* for Israel.
8:14 which the LORD had *c*
13:22 I *c* the Levites to purify themselves
Est 1:10 he *c* the seven eunuchs who served
1:17 'King Xerxes *c* Queen Vashti
3:2 the king had *c* this concerning him.
6:10 "Go at once," the king *c* Haman.
9:1 the edict *c* by the king was
9:14 So the king *c* that this be done.
Ps 33:9 he *c*, and it stood firm.
78:5 which he *c* our forefathers
105:8 the word he *c*, for a thousand
106:34 as the LORD had *c* them,
148:5 for he *c* and they were created.
Isa 13:3 I have *c* my holy ones;
36:21 king had *c*, "Do not answer him."
Jer 11:4 the terms I *c* your forefathers
11:8 curses of the covenant I had *c* them
17:22 day holy, as I *c* your forefathers.
26:8 everything the LORD had *c* him
32:23 they did not do what you *c* them
32:35 I never *c*, nor did it enter my mind,
35:8 Jonadab son of Recab *c* us.
35:10 our forefather Jonadab *c* us.
36:26 Instead, the king *c* Jerahmeel,
38:10 king *c* Ebed-Melech the Cushite,
47:7 rest when the LORD has *c* it,
50:21 "Do everything I have *c* you.
Eze 9:11 saying, "I have done as you *c*."
10:6 When the LORD *c* the man
12:7 So I did as I was *c*.
24:18 next morning I did as I had been *c*.
37:7 So I prophesied as I was *c*.
37:10 So I prophesied as he *c* me,
Da 3:4 "This is what you are *c* to do,
3:20 and *c* some of the strongest soldiers
4:6 So I *c* that all the wise men
Am 2:12 and *c* the prophets not to prophesy.
Jnh 2:10 And the LORD *c* the fish,
Zec 1:6 which I *c* my servants the prophets,
Mt 1:24 the angel of the Lord had *c* him
8:4 and offer the gift Moses *c*,
27:10 potter's field, as the Lord *c* me."
28:20 to obey everything I have *c* you.
Mk 1:44 offer the sacrifices that Moses *c*
7:36 Jesus *c* them not to tell anyone.
Lk 5:14 offer the sacrifices that Moses *c*
8:29 For Jesus had *c* the evil spirit
Jn 8:5 In the Law Moses *c* us
12:49 the Father who sent me *c* me what
14:31 exactly what my Father has *c* me.
18:11 Jesus *c* Peter, "Put your sword
Ac 4:18 in again and *c* them not to speak
10:33 to everything the Lord has *c* you
10:42 He *c* us to preach to the people
13:47 For this is what the Lord has *c* us:
16:23 and the jailer was *c* to guard them
1Co 9:14 Lord has *c* that those who preach
Heb 9:20 which God has *c* you to keep."
12:20 they could not bear what was *c*:
1Jn 3:23 and to love one another as he *c* us.
2Jn :4 in the truth, just as the Father *c* us.

COMMANDER (COMMAND)

Ge 21:22 and Phicol the *c* of his forces said
21:32 Phicol the *c* of his forces returned
26:26 and Phicol the *c* of his forces.
Jos 5:14 *c* of the army of the LORD I have
5:15 The *c* of the LORD's army replied,
Jdg 4:2 The *c* of his army was Sisera,
4:7 I will lure Sisera, the *c*
11:6 "Come," they said, "be our *c*,
11:11 the people made him head and *c*
1Sa 12:9 the *c* of the army of Hazor,
14:50 The name of the *c*
17:18 cheeses to the *c* of their unit.
17:55 he said to Abner, *c* of the army,
26:5 the *c* of the army, had lain down.
2Sa 2:8 son of Ner, the *c* of Saul's army,
10:16 with Shobach the *c*
10:18 down Shobach the *c* of their army,
19:13 on you are not the *c* of my army
23:19 He became their *c*, even
1Ki 1:19 and Joab the *c* of the army,
2:32 son of Jether, *c* of Judah's army—
2:32 son of Ner, *c* of Israel's army,
4:4 son of Jehoiada—*c* in chief;
11:15 with Edom, Joab the *c* of the army,
11:21 and that Joab the *c* of the army was
16:16 they proclaimed Omri, the *c*
2Ki 4:13 to the king or the *c* of the army?' "
5:1 Now Naaman was *c* of the army
9:5 "For you, *c*," he replied.
9:5 "I have a message for you, *c*,"
18:17 and his field *c* with a large army,
18:17 king of Assyria sent his supreme *c*,
18:19 The field *c* said to them, "Tell
18:26 Shebna and Joah said to the field *c*,
18:27 But the *c* replied, "Was it only
18:28 Then the *c* stood and called out
18:37 told him what the field *c* had said.
19:4 will hear all the words of the field *c*,
19:8 When the field *c* heard that
25:8 Nebuzaradan *c* of the imperial
25:10 under the *c* of the imperial guard,
25:11 Nebuzaradan the *c*
25:12 But the *c* left behind some
25:15 *c* of the imperial guard took away
25:18 The *c* of the guard took
25:20 Nebuzaradan the *c* took them all
1Ch 11:21 the Three and became their *c*,
19:16 with Shophach the *c*
19:18 killed Shophach the *c* of their army
27:5 third army *c*, for the third month,
27:8 was the *c* Shamhuth the Izrahite.
27:34 Joab was the *c* of the royal army.
2Ch 17:14 Adnah the *c*, with 300,000
17:15 Jehohanan the *c*, with 280,000;
Ne 7:2 with Hananiah the *c* of the citadel,
Pr 6:7 It has no *c*,
Isa 20:1 In the year that the supreme *c*,
36:2 When the *c* stopped
36:2 the king of Assyria sent his field *c*
36:4 The field *c* said to them, "Tell
36:11 Shebna and Joah said to the field *c*,
36:12 But the *c* replied, "Was it only
Isa 36:13 Then the *c* stood and called out
36:22 told him what the field *c* had said.
37:4 will hear the words of the field *c*,
37:8 When the field *c* heard that
55:4 a leader and *c* of the peoples.
Jer 39:9 Nebuzaradan *c* of the imperial
39:10 Nebuzaradan the *c* of the guard left
39:11 Jeremiah through Nebuzaradan *c*
39:13 So Nebuzaradan the *c* of the guard,
40:1 the LORD after Nebuzaradan *c*
40:2 When the *c* of the guard found
40:5 Then the *c* gave him provisions
41:10 over whom Nebuzaradan *c*
43:6 daughters whom Nebuzaradan *c*
51:27 Appoint a *c* against her;
52:12 Nebuzaradan *c* of the imperial
52:14 under the *c* of the imperial guard
52:15 Nebuzaradan the *c*
52:19 *c* of the imperial guard took away
52:24 The *c* of the guard took
52:26 Nebuzaradan the *c* took them all
52:30 exile by Nebuzaradan the *c*
Da 2:14 When Arioch, the *c*
11:18 a *c* will put an end to his insolence
Jn 18:12 detachment of soldiers with its *c*
Ac 21:31 news reached the *c*
21:32 When the rioters saw the *c*
21:33 The *c* came up and arrested him
21:34 and since the *c* could not get
21:37 he asked the *c*, "May I say
22:24 the *c* ordered Paul to be taken
22:26 he went to the *c* and reported it.
22:27 The *c* went to Paul and asked,
22:28 the *c* said, "I had to pay a big price
22:29 The *c* himself was alarmed
22:30 since the *c* wanted
23:10 so violent that the *c* was afraid Paul
23:15 and the Sanhedrin petition the *c*
23:17 "Take this young man to the *c*;
23:18 So he took him to the *c*.
23:19 The *c* took the young man
23:22 The *c* dismissed the young man
24:22 When Lysias the *c* comes," he said,

COMMANDER-IN-CHIEF (COMMAND)

1Ch 11:6 on the Jebusites will become *c*."

COMMANDER'S (COMMAND)

Jdg 5:14 Zebulun those who bear a *c* staff.
Ac 21:40 Having received the *c* permission,

COMMANDERS (COMMAND)

Nu 31:14 the *c* of thousands and *c*
31:48 the *c* of thousands and *c*
31:52 and *c* of hundreds that Moses
31:52 the gold from the *c* of thousands
31:54 and *c* of hundreds and brought it
31:54 the gold from the *c* of thousands
Dt 1:15 as *c* of thousands, of hundreds,
20:9 they shall appoint *c* over it.
Jos 10:24 said to the army *c* who had come
1Sa 8:12 assign to be *c* of thousands
8:12 of thousands and *c* of fifties,
18:30 The Philistine *c* continued
22:7 all of you *c* of thousands
22:7 of thousands and *c* of hundreds?
29:3 The *c* of the Philistines asked,
29:4 But the Philistine *c* were angry
29:9 the Philistine *c* have said,
2Sa 18:1 of thousands and *c* of hundreds.
18:1 over them *c* of thousands
18:5 Absalom to each of the *c*.
19:6 have made it clear today that the *c*
24:2 to Joab and the army *c* with him,
24:4 overruled Joab and the army *c*;
1Ki 1:25 the *c* of the army and Abiathar
2:5 did to the two *c* of Israel's armies,
9:22 and the *c* of his chariots
14:27 assigned these to the *c* of the guard
15:20 and sent the *c* of his forces
20:14 of the provincial *c* will do it.' "
20:15 officers of the provincial *c*,
20:17 of the provincial *c* went out first.
20:19 of the provincial *c* marched out
22:31 ordered his thirty-two chariot *c*,
22:32 the chariot *c* saw Jehoshaphat,
22:33 the chariot *c* saw that he was not
2Ki 8:21 surrounded him and his chariot *c*,

2Ki 11: 4 sent for the *c* of units of a hundred,
11: 9 The *c* of units of a hundred did just
11: 10 Then he gave the *c* the spears
11: 15 Jehoiada the priest ordered the *c*
11: 19 He took with him the *c* of hundreds
1Ch 12: 14 These Gadites were army *c;*
12: 21 and they were *c* in his army.
13: 1 the *c* of thousands and *c*
15: 25 the *c* of units of a thousand went
21: 2 said to Joab and the *c* of the troops,
25: 1 together with the *c* of the army,
26: 26 and by the other army *c*.
26: 26 heads of families who were the *c*
26: 26 of thousands and *c* of hundreds,
27: 1 *c* of thousands and *c* of hundreds,
28: 1 the *c* of the divisions in the service
28: 1 the *c* of thousands and *c*
29: 6 the *c* of thousands and *c*
2Ch 1: 2 of thousands and *c* of hundreds,
1: 2 to the *c* of thousands
8: 9 they were his fighting men, *c*
8: 9 *c* of his chariots and charioteers.
11: 11 their defenses and put *c*
12: 10 assigned these to the *c* of the guard
16: 4 and sent the *c* of his forces
17: 14 From Judah, *c* of units of 1,000:
18: 30 of Aram had ordered his chariot *c*,
18: 31 the chariot *c* saw Jehoshaphat,
18: 32 when the chariot *c* saw that he was
21: 9 surrounded him and his chariot *c*,
23: 1 with the *c* of units of a hundred:
23: 9 Then he gave the *c* of units
23: 14 Jehoiada the priest sent out the *c*
23: 20 He took with him the *c* of hundreds
25: 5 and *c* of hundreds for all Judah
25: 5 to their families to *c* of thousands
33: 11 against them the army *c* of the king
33: 14 He stationed military *c*
Job 39: 25 the shout of *c* and the battle cry.
Isa 10: 8 'Are not my *c* all kings?' he says.
31: 9 battle standard their *c* will panic,"
Eze 23: 6 clothed in blue, governors and *c*,
23: 12 and *c*, warriors in full dress,
23: 23 all of them governors and *c*,
Da 11: 5 but one of his *c* will become
Mk 6: 21 and military *c* and the leading men

COMMANDING (COMMAND)

Dt 30: 11 what I am *c* you today is not too
Ezr 4: 8 Rehum the *c* officer and Shimshai
4: 9 Rehum the *c* officer and Shimshai
4: 17 this reply: To Rehum the *c* officer,
Ac 23: 3 the law by *c* that I be struck!"
2Co 8: 8 I am not *c* you, but I want
2Ti 2: 4 he wants to please his *c* officer.

COMMANDMENT (COMMAND)

Jos 22: 5 But be very careful to keep the *c*
Mt 22: 36 which is the greatest *c* in the Law?"
22: 38 This is the first and greatest *c*.
Mk 12: 31 There is no *c* greater than these."
Lk 23: 56 the Sabbath in obedience to the *c*.
Jn 13: 34 "A new *c* I give you: Love one
Ro 7: 8 the opportunity afforded by the *c*,
7: 9 when the *c* came, sin sprang to life
7: 10 that the very *c* that was intended
7: 11 and through the *c* put me to death.
7: 11 the opportunity afforded by the *c*,
7: 12 and the *c* is holy, righteous
7: 13 through the *c* sin might become
13: 9 and whatever other *c* there may be,
Eph 6: 2 which is the first *c* with a promise
1Ti 6: 14 you to keep this *c* without spot
Heb 9: 19 Moses had proclaimed every *c*
2Pe 2: 21 on the sacred *c* that was passed

COMMANDMENTS (COMMAND)

Ex 20: 6 who love me and keep my *c*.
34: 28 of the covenant—the Ten *C*.
Dt 4: 13 to you his covenant, the Ten *C*,
5: 10 who love me and keep my *c*.
5: 22 These are the *c* the LORD
6: 6 These *c* that I give you today are
9: 10 were all the *c* the LORD
10: 4 The Ten *C* he had proclaimed
Ps 119: 47 for I delight in your *c*
119: 48 I reach out my hands for your *c*,
119:176 for I have not forgotten your *c*.

Ecc 12: 13 Fear God and keep his *c*,
Mt 5: 19 one of the least of these *c*
19: 17 If you want to enter life, obey the *c*
22: 40 the Prophets hang on these two *c*."
Mk 10: 19 You know the *c:* 'Do not murder,
12: 28 "Of all the *c*, which is the most
Lk 1: 6 observing all the Lord's *c*
18: 20 You know the *c:* 'Do not commit
Ro 13: 9 The *c*, "Do not commit adultery,"
Eph 2: 15 in his flesh the law with its *c*
Rev 12: 17 those who obey God's *c*
14: 12 part of the saints who obey God's *c*

COMMANDS (COMMAND)

Ge 26: 5 my *c*, my decrees and my laws."
Ex 8: 27 to the LORD our God, as he *c* us."
15: 26 if you pay attention to his *c*
16: 28 long will you refuse to keep my *c*
18: 23 If you do this and God so *c*,
24: 12 and *c* I have written for their
25: 22 give you all my *c* for the Israelites.
34: 32 gave them all the *c* the LORD had
Lev 4: 2 in any of the LORD's *c*—
4: 13 forbidden in any of the LORD's *c*,
4: 22 any of the *c* of the LORD his God,
4: 27 forbidden in any of the LORD's *c*,
5: 17 forbidden in any of the LORD's *c*,
22: 31 "Keep my *c* and follow them.
26: 3 and are careful to obey my *c*,
26: 14 to me and carry out all these *c*,
26: 15 and fail to carry out all my *c*
27: 34 These are the *c* the LORD gave
Nu 9: 8 the LORD *c* concerning you."
15: 22 of these *c* the LORD gave Moses—
15: 23 any of the LORD's *c* to you
15: 31 LORD's word and broken his *c*,
15: 39 and so you will remember all the *c*
15: 40 you will remember to obey all my *c*
30: 1 "This is what the LORD *c:*
32: 25 your servants will do as our lord *c*.
36: 6 This is what the LORD *c*
36: 13 These are the *c* and regulations
Dt 4: 2 keep the *c* of the LORD your God
4: 40 and *c*, which I am giving you today,
5: 29 to fear me and keep all my *c* always
5: 31 me so that I may give you all the *c*,
6: 1 These are the *c*, decrees
6: 2 all his decrees and *c* that I give you,
6: 17 Be sure to keep the *c*
7: 9 those who love him and keep his *c*.
7: 11 Therefore, take care to follow the *c*
8: 2 or not you would keep his *c*.
8: 6 Observe the *c* of the LORD your
8: 11 failing to observe his *c*, his laws
10: 13 and to observe the LORD's *c*
11: 1 decrees, his laws and his *c* always.
11: 8 all the *c* I am giving you today,
11: 13 faithfully obey the *c* I am giving
11: 22 observe all these *c* I am giving
11: 27 the blessing if you obey the *c*
11: 28 the curse if you disobey the *c*
13: 4 Keep his *c* and obey him; serve him
13: 18 keeping all his *c* that I am giving
15: 5 to follow all these *c* I am giving you
26: 13 I have not turned aside from your *c*
26: 16 LORD your God *c* you this day
26: 17 that you will keep his decrees, *c*
26: 18 and that you are to keep all his *c*.
27: 1 "Keep all these *c* that I give you
27: 10 follow his *c* and decrees that I give
28: 1 carefully follow all his *c* I give you
28: 9 if you keep the *c* of the LORD your
28: 13 If you pay attention to the *c*
28: 14 from any of the *c* I give you today,
28: 15 and do not carefully follow all his *c*
28: 45 observe the *c* and decrees he gave
30: 8 and follow all his *c* I am giving you
30: 10 LORD your God and keep his *c*
30: 16 and to keep his *c*, decrees and laws;
Jos 22: 5 to walk in all his ways, to obey his *c*
Jdg 2: 17 way of obedience to the LORD's *c*.
3: 4 they would obey the LORD's *c*,
4: 6 the God of Israel, *c* you: 'Go,
1Sa 12: 14 and do not rebel against his *c*,
12: 15 and if you rebel against his *c*,
2Sa 9: 11 my lord the king *c* his servant
1Ki 2: 3 and keep his decrees and *c*,
3: 14 and obey my statutes and *c*

1Ki 6: 12 and keep all my *c* and obey them,
8: 58 in all his ways and to keep the *c*,
8: 61 to live by his decrees and obey his *c*
9: 6 do not observe the *c* and decrees I
11: 34 who observed my *c* and statutes.
11: 38 eyes by keeping my statutes and *c*,
14: 8 who kept my *c* and followed me
15: 5 any of the LORD's *c* all the days
18: 18 have abandoned the LORD's *c*
20: 24 Remove all the kings from their *c*
2Ki 17: 13 Observe my *c* and decrees,
17: 16 They forsook all the *c*
17: 19 and even Judah did not keep the *c*
17: 34 and *c* that the LORD gave
17: 37 the laws and *c* he wrote for you.
18: 6 he kept the *c* the LORD had given
18: 12 They neither listened to the *c*
23: 3 to follow the LORD and keep his *c*,
1Ch 28: 7 unswerving in carrying out my *c*
28: 8 to follow all the *c* of the LORD
29: 19 devotion to keep your *c*,
2Ch 7: 19 the decrees and *c* I have given
8: 15 from the king's *c* to the priests
14: 4 and to obey his laws and *c*.
17: 4 and followed his *c* rather
19: 10 *c*, decrees or ordinances—
24: 20 Why do you disobey the LORD's *c*
31: 21 in obedience to the law and the *c*,
34: 31 to follow the LORD and keep his *c*,
Ezr 7: 11 learned in matters concerning the *c*
9: 10 we have disregarded the *c* you gave
9: 14 Shall we again break your *c*
10: 3 of those who fear the *c* of our God.
Ne 1: 5 those who love him and obey his *c*,
1: 7 We have not obeyed the *c*,
1: 9 if you return to me and obey my *c*,
9: 13 and decrees and *c* that are good.
9: 14 holy Sabbath and gave them *c*,
9: 16 and did not obey your *c*.
9: 29 arrogant and disobeyed your *c*.
9: 34 they did not pay attention to your *c*
10: 29 and to obey carefully all the *c*,
10: 32 for carrying out the *c* to give a third
12: 45 according to the *c* of David
Job 23: 12 from the *c* of his lips;
36: 10 and *c* them to repent of their evil.
36: 32 and *c* it to strike its mark.
37: 12 earth to do whatever he *c* them.
Ps 19: 8 The *c* of the LORD are radiant,
78: 7 but would keep his *c*.
89: 31 and fail to keep my *c*,
112: 1 who finds great delight in his *c*.
119: 6 shame when I consider all your *c*.
119: 10 do not let me stray from your *c*.
119: 19 do not hide your *c* from me.
119: 21 and who stray from your *c*.
119: 32 I run in the path of your *c*,
119: 35 Direct me in the path of your *c*,
119: 60 to obey your *c*.
119: 66 for I believe in your *c*.
119: 73 me understanding to learn your *c*.
119: 86 All your *c* are trustworthy;
119: 96 but your *c* are boundless.
119: 98 Your *c* make me wiser
119:115 that I may keep the *c* of my God!
119:127 Because I love your *c*
119:131 longing for your *c*.
119:143 but your *c* are my delight.
119:151 and all your *c* are true.
119:166 and I follow your *c*.
119:172 for all your *c* are righteous.
Pr 2: 1 and store up my *c* within you,
3: 1 but keep my *c* in your heart,
4: 4 keep my *c* and you will live.
6: 20 My son, keep your father's *c*
6: 23 For these *c* are a lamp,
7: 1 and store up my *c* within you.
7: 2 Keep my *c* and you will live;
10: 8 The wise in heart accept *c*,
Isa 48: 18 you had paid attention to my *c*,
58: 2 has not forsaken the *c* of its God.
Jer 7: 22 just give them *c* about burnt
22: 4 careful to carry out these *c*,
22: 5 But if you do not obey these *c*,
Da 9: 4 all who love him and obey his *c*,
9: 5 we have turned away from your *c*
Zep 2: 3 you who do what he *c*.
Mt 5: 19 teaches these *c* will be called great

Mk 7: 8 You have let go of the *c* of God
7: 9 way of setting aside the *c* of God
Lk 8: 25 He *c* even the winds and the water,
Jn 14: 21 Whoever has my *c* and obeys them,
15: 10 If you obey my *c*, you will remain
15: 10 as I have obeyed my Father's *c*
Ac 17: 30 but now he *c* all people everywhere
1Co 7: 19 Keeping God's *c* is what counts.
Col 2: 22 because they are based on human *c*
Tit 1: 14 or to the *c* of those who reject
1Jn 2: 3 come to know him if we obey his *c*.
2: 4 but does not do what he *c* is a liar,
3: 22 we obey his *c* and do what pleases
3: 24 Those who obey his *c* live in him,
5: 2 loving God and carrying out his *c*.
5: 3 And his *c* are not burdensome,
5: 3 This is love for God: to obey his *c*.
2Jn : 6 that we walk in obedience to his *c*.

COMMEMORATE (COMMEMORATED)

Ex 12: 14 "This is a day you are to *c*;
13: 3 said to the people, "*C* this day,
Jdg 11: 40 out for four days to *c* the daughter
2Ch 35: 25 and women singers *c* Josiah

COMMEMORATED (COMMEMORATE)

Lev 23: 24 a sacred assembly *c*

COMMEND (COMMENDABLE COMMENDED COMMENDS)

Ps 145: 4 One generation will *c* your works
Ecc 8: 15 So I *c* the enjoyment of life,
Ro 13: 3 do what is right and he will *c* you.
16: 1 I *c* to you our sister Phoebe,
2Co 3: 1 beginning to *c* ourselves again?
4: 2 the truth plainly we *c* ourselves
5: 12 trying to *c* ourselves to you again,
6: 4 as servants of God we *c* ourselves
10: 12 with some who *c* themselves.
1Pe 2: 14 and to *c* those who do right.

COMMENDABLE (COMMEND)

1Pe 2: 19 For it is *c* if a man bears up
2: 20 you endure it, this is *c* before God.

COMMENDED (COMMEND)

Ne 11: 2 The people *c* all the men who
Job 29: 11 and those who saw me *c* me,
Lk 16: 8 master *c* the dishonest manager
Ac 15: 40 *c* by the brothers to the grace
2Co 12: 11 I ought to have been *c* by you,
Heb 11: 2 This is what the ancients were *c* for
11: 4 By faith he was *c* as a righteous
11: 5 he was *c* as one who pleased God.
11: 39 These were all *c* for their faith,

COMMENDS (COMMEND)

Pr 15: 2 of the wise *c* knowledge,
2Co 10: 18 but the one whom the Lord *c*.
10: 18 not the one who *c* himself who is

COMMISSION (COMMISSIONED COMMISSIONERS)

Nu 27: 19 and *c* him in their presence.
Dt 3: 28 But *c* Joshua, and encourage
31: 14 of Meeting, where I will *c* him."
Ac 26: 12 Damascus with the authority and *c*
Col 1: 25 by the *c* God gave me to present

COMMISSIONED (COMMISSION)

Nu 27: 23 he laid his hands on him and *c* him,

COMMISSIONERS (COMMISSION)

Ge 41: 34 Let Pharaoh appoint *c*
Est 2: 3 Let the king appoint *c*

COMMIT (COMMITS COMMITTED COMMITTING)

Ex 20: 14 "You shall not *c* adultery.
Dt 5: 18 "You shall not *c* adultery.
1Sa 7: 3 and *c* yourselves to the LORD
1Ki 14: 16 and has caused Israel to *c*."
15: 26 which he had caused Israel to *c*.
15: 30 and had caused Israel to *c*,
15: 34 which he had caused Israel to *c*.
16: 13 and had caused Israel to *c*,
16: 19 and had caused Israel to *c*.
16: 26 which he had caused Israel to *c*,
1Ki 16: 31 trivial to *c* the sins of Jeroboam son
2Ki 3: 3 which he had caused Israel to *c*;
10: 29 which he had caused Israel to *c*—
10: 31 which he had caused Israel to *c*.
13: 2 which he had caused Israel to *c*,
13: 6 which he had caused Israel to *c*;
13: 11 which he had caused Israel to *c*;
14: 24 which he had caused Israel to *c*.
15: 9 which he had caused Israel to *c*.
15: 18 which he had caused Israel to *c*.
15: 24 which he had caused Israel to *c*.
15: 28 which he had caused Israel to *c*.
17: 21 and caused them to *c* a great sin.
21: 16 sin that he had caused Judah to *c*,
Ezr 9: 14 the peoples who *c* such detestable
Ne 6: 13 so that I would *c* a sin by doing this,
Ps 31: 5 Into your hands I *c* my spirit;
37: 5 *C* your way to the LORD;
Pr 16: 3 *C* to the LORD whatever you do,
Jer 7: 9 murder, *c* adultery and perjury,
23: 14 They *c* adultery and live a lie.
Eze 16: 38 of women who *c* adultery
16: 51 Samaria did not *c* half the sins you
18: 7 He does not *c* robbery
18: 16 He does not *c* robbery
22: 9 mountain shrines and *c* lewd acts.
22: 29 practice extortion and *c* robbery;
23: 45 of women who *c* adultery
Hos 4: 14 when they *c* adultery,
4: 15 "Though you *c* adultery, O Israel,
Mt 5: 27 that it was said, 'Do not *c* adultery.'
5: 32 causes her to *c* adultery,
19: 18 do not *c* adultery, do not steal,
Mk 10: 19 do not *c* adultery, do not steal,
Lk 18: 20 'Do not *c* adultery, do not murder,
23: 46 into your hands I *c* my spirit."
Ac 20: 32 I *c* you to God and to the word
Ro 2: 22 do you *c* adultery? You who abhor
2: 22 that people should not *c* adultery,
13: 9 "Do not *c* adultery,"
1Co 10: 8 We should not *c* sexual immorality,
Jas 2: 11 do not *c* adultery but do *c* murder,
2: 11 "Do not *c* adultery," also said,
1Pe 4: 19 to God's will should *c* themselves
1Jn 5: 16 anyone sees his brother *c* a sin that
Rev 2: 22 I will make those who *c* adultery

COMMITS (COMMIT)

Lev 5: 15 "When a person *c* a violation
6: 3 if he *c* any such sin that people may
20: 10 " 'If a man *c* adultery
Ps 10: 14 The victim *c* himself to you;
36: 4 he *c* himself to a sinful course
Pr 6: 32 man who *c* adultery lacks
29: 22 a hot-tempered one *c* many sins.
Ecc 8: 12 a wicked man *c* a hundred crimes
Eze 18: 12 He *c* robbery.
18: 14 who sees all the sins his father *c*,
18: 24 from his righteousness and *c* sin
18: 26 from his righteousness and *c* sin,
22: 11 you one man *c* a detestable offense
Mt 5: 32 a woman so divorced *c* adultery.
19: 9 marries another woman *c* adultery
Mk 10: 11 marries another woman *c* adultery
10: 12 another man, she *c* adultery."
Lk 16: 18 a divorced woman *c* adultery.
16: 18 marries another woman *c* adultery,
1Co 6: 18 All other sins a man *c* are

COMMITTED (COMMIT)

Ge 31: 36 What sin have I *c* that you hunt me
50: 17 the wrongs they *c* in treating you
Ex 32: 30 the people, "You have *c* a great sin.
32: 31 a great sin these people have *c*!
Lev 4: 3 as a sin offering for the sin he has *c*.
4: 14 become aware of the sin they *c*,
4: 23 he is made aware of the sin he *c*,
4: 28 for the sin he *c* a female goat
4: 28 he is made aware of the sin he *c*,
4: 35 for him for the sin he has *c*,
5: 6 as a penalty for the sin he has *c*,
5: 10 for him for the sin he has *c*,
5: 13 him for any of these sins he has *c*,
5: 18 the wrong he has *c* unintentionally,
19: 22 the LORD for the sin he has *c*,
Nu 5: 7 and must confess the sin he has *c*.
12: 11 us the sin we have so foolishly *c*.
Dt 9: 18 because of all the sin you had *c*,
Dt 19: 15 or offense he may have *c*.
22: 26 she has *c* no sin deserving death.
Jdg 20: 6 because they *c* this lewd
20: 12 about this awful crime that was *c*
1Sa 14: 38 find out what sin has been *c* today.
1Ki 8: 50 forgive all the offenses they have *c*
8: 61 But your hearts must be fully *c*
14: 16 because of the sins Jeroboam has *c*
14: 22 By the sins they *c* they stirred up
15: 3 He *c* all the sins his father had done
15: 14 Asa's heart was fully *c*
15: 30 because of the sins Jeroboam had *c*
16: 13 his son Elah had *c* and had caused
16: 19 because of the sins he had *c*,
16: 19 the sin he had *c* and had caused
2Ki 21: 11 of Judah has *c* these detestable sins
21: 17 all he did, including the sin he *c*,
1Ch 16: 7 That day David first *c* to Asaph
2Ch 15: 17 Asa's heart was fully *c*
16: 9 those whose hearts are fully *c*
34: 16 doing everything that has been *c*
Ne 1: 6 and my father's house, have *c*
9: 18 or when they *c* awful blasphemies.
9: 26 they *c* awful blasphemies.
Job 13: 23 many wrongs and sins have I *c*?
Isa 42: 19 Who is blind like the one *c* to me,
Jer 2: 13 "My people have *c* two sins:
3: 6 tree and has *c* adultery there.
3: 8 she also went out and *c* adultery.
3: 9 she defiled the land and *c* adultery
5: 7 yet they *c* adultery
11: 20 for to you I have *c* my cause.
16: 10 What sin have we *c*
20: 12 for to you I have *c* my cause.
29: 23 they have *c* adultery
33: 8 them from all the sin they have *c*
37: 18 "What crime have I *c* against you
41: 11 son of Nethaniah had *c*,
44: 9 and the wickedness *c* by you
44: 9 you forgotten the wickedness *c*
Eze 18: 21 away from all the sins he has *c*
18: 22 the offenses he has *c* will be
18: 24 and because of the sins he has *c*,
18: 26 of the sin he has *c* he will die.
18: 27 away from the wickedness he has *c*
18: 28 considers all the offenses he has *c*
18: 31 of all the offenses you have *c*,
23: 37 They *c* adultery with their idols;
23: 37 for they have *c* adultery
33: 16 sins he has *c* will be remembered
Mal 2: 11 A detestable thing has been *c*
Mt 5: 28 lustfully has already *c* adultery
11: 27 "All things have been *c* to me
27: 23 What crime has he *c*?" asked Pilate
Mk 15: 7 insurrectionists who had *c* murder
15: 14 What crime has he *c*?" asked Pilate
Lk 10: 22 "All things have been *c* to me
23: 22 "Why? What crime has this man *c*?
Ac 14: 23 *c* them to the Lord
14: 26 where they had been *c* to the grace
Ro 1: 27 Men *c* indecent acts
3: 25 the sins *c* beforehand
1Co 9: 17 I am simply discharging the trust *c*
2Co 5: 19 And he has *c* to us the message
Heb 9: 7 and for the sins the people had *c*
9: 15 free from the sins *c* under the first
1Pe 2: 22 "He *c* no sin,
Rev 17: 2 the kings of the earth *c* adultery
18: 3 of the earth *c* adultery with her,
18: 9 kings of the earth who *c* adultery

COMMITTING (COMMIT)

Hos 6: 9 *c* shameful crimes.
Rev 2: 14 and by *c* sexual immorality.

COMMON

Ge 11: 1 had one language and a *c* speech.
2Sa 16: 10 "What do you and I have in *c*,
19: 22 "What do you and I have in *c*,
1Ki 10: 27 as *c* in Jerusalem as stones,
2Ki 23: 6 over the graves of the *c* people.
2Ch 1: 15 gold as *c* in Jerusalem as stones,
9: 27 as *c* in Jerusalem as stones,
Ne 7: 5 and the *c* people for registration
Ps 73: 5 from the burdens *c* to man;
Pr 1: 14 and we will share a *c* purse"—
22: 2 Rich and poor have this in *c*:
29: 13 the oppressor have this in *c*:

Ecc 9: 2 All share a *c* destiny—
Jer 26: 23 into the burial place of the *c* people
Eze 22: 26 between the holy and the *c;*
42: 20 to separate the holy from the *c.*
44: 23 and the *c* and show them how
48: 15 will be for the *c* use of the city,
Ac 2: 44 together and had everything in *c.*
Ro 9: 21 noble purposes and some for *c* use?
1Co 10: 13 has seized you except what is *c*
12: 7 of the Spirit is given for the *c* good.
2Co 6: 14 and wickedness have in *c?*
6: 15 have in *c* with an unbeliever?
Tit 1: 4 To Titus, my true son in our *c* faith:

COMMOTION

Job 39: 7 He laughs at the *c* in the town;
Isa 22: 2 O town full of *c,*
Jer 3: 23 Surely the ⌊idolatrous⌋ *c* on the hills
10: 22 a great *c* from the land of the north
Mk 5: 38 Jesus saw a *c,* with people crying
5: 39 "Why all this *c* and wailing?
Ac 12: 18 there was a great *c*
19: 40 able to account for this *c,*

COMMUNITIES (COMMUNITY)

Am 1: 6 Because she took captive whole *c*
1: 9 Because she sold whole *c*

COMMUNITY (COMMUNITIES COMMUNITY'S)

Ge 28: 3 until you become a *c* of peoples.
35: 11 a *c* of nations will come from you,
48: 4 I will make you a *c* of peoples,
Ex 12: 3 Tell the whole *c* of Israel that
12: 6 of the *c* of Israel must slaughter
12: 19 cut off from the *c* of Israel,
12: 47 whole *c* of Israel must celebrate it.
16: 1 The whole Israelite *c* set out
16: 2 In the desert the whole *c* grumbled
16: 9 "Say to the entire Israelite *c,*
16: 10 speaking to the whole Israelite *c,*
16: 22 and the leaders of the *c* came
17: 1 The whole Israelite *c* set out
34: 31 leaders of the *c* came back to him,
35: 1 assembled the whole Israelite *c*
35: 4 Moses said to the whole Israelite *c,*
35: 20 the whole Israelite *c* withdrew
38: 25 those of the *c* who were counted
Lev 4: 13 the whole Israelite *c* sins
4: 13 the *c* is unaware of the matter,
4: 15 The elders of the *c* are
4: 21 This is the sin offering for the *c.*
4: 27 of the *c* sins unintentionally
10: 6 will be angry with the whole *c.*
10: 17 guilt of the *c* by making atonement
16: 5 From the Israelite *c* he is
16: 17 his household and the whole *c*
16: 33 and all the people of the *c.*
20: 2 The people of the *c* are
20: 4 the people of the *c* close their eyes
Nu 1: 2 a census of the whole Israelite *c*
1: 16 the men appointed from the *c,*
1: 18 they called the whole *c* together
1: 53 wrath will not fall on the Israelite *c.*
3: 7 and for the whole *c* at the Tent
4: 34 of the *c* counted the Kohathites
8: 9 and assemble the whole Israelite *c.*
8: 20 and the whole Israelite *c* did
10: 2 use them for calling the *c* together
10: 3 the whole *c* is to assemble
13: 26 and the whole Israelite *c* at Kadesh
14: 1 people of the *c* raised their voices
14: 27 long will this wicked *c* grumble
14: 35 things to this whole wicked *c,*
14: 36 and made the whole *c* grumble
15: 15 The *c* is to have the same rules
15: 24 then the whole *c* is
15: 24 without the *c* being aware of it,
15: 25 for the whole Israelite *c,*
15: 26 The whole Israelite *c* and the aliens
16: 2 well-known *c* leaders who had
16: 3 The whole *c* is holy, every one
16: 9 to stand before the *c* and minister
16: 9 you from the rest of the Israelite *c*
16: 33 perished and were gone from the *c.*
16: 41 day the whole Israelite *c* grumbled
19: 9 kept by the Israelite *c* for use
19: 20 he must be cut off from the *c,*
Nu 20: 1 month the whole Israelite *c* arrived
20: 2 Now there was no water for the *c,*
20: 4 Why did you bring the LORD's *c*
20: 8 out of the rock for the *c* so they
20: 11 and the *c* and their livestock drank.
20: 12 you will not bring this *c*
20: 22 The whole Israelite *c* set out
20: 27 Hor in the sight of the whole *c.*
20: 29 and when the whole *c* learned that
26: 2 of the whole Israelite *c* by families
26: 9 Abiram were the *c* officials who
27: 14 for when the *c* rebelled
27: 16 appoint a man over this *c* to go out
27: 20 the whole Israelite *c* will obey him.
27: 21 entire *c* of the Israelites will go out,
31: 13 leaders of the *c* went to meet them
31: 26 and the family heads of the *c* are
31: 27 in the battle and the rest of the *c.*
32: 2 and to the leaders of the *c,*
Jos 9: 21 and water carriers for the entire *c.*"
9: 27 and water carriers for the *c*
22: 17 a plague fell on the *c* of the LORD!
22: 18 angry with the whole *c* of Israel.
22: 20 come upon the whole *c* of Israel?
22: 30 the priest and the leaders of the *c*—
2Ch 31: 18 and daughters of the whole *c* listed
Jer 30: 20 and their *c* will be established
Ac 6: 1 those of the Aramaic-speaking *c*
25: 24 whole Jewish *c* has petitioned me

COMMUNITY'S (COMMUNITY)

Nu 31: 43 the *c* half—was 337,500 sheep,

COMPACT (COMPACTED)

2Sa 3: 21 so that they may make a *c* with you
5: 3 the king made a *c* with them
1Ch 11: 3 he made a *c* with them at Hebron

COMPACTED (COMPACT)

Ps 122: 3 that is closely *c* together.

COMPANIES (COMPANY)

Jdg 7: 16 the three hundred men into three *c,*
7: 20 The three *c* blew the trumpets
9: 34 positions near Shechem in four *c.*
9: 43 divided them into three *c*
9: 44 Then two *c* rushed upon those
9: 44 and the *c* with him rushed forward
2Ki 11: 5 are in the three *c* that are going
11: 7 in the other two *c* that normally go

COMPANION (COMPANIONS)

1Ki 20: 35 sons of the prophets said to his *c,*
Job 30: 29 a *c* of owls.
Ps 55: 13 my *c,* my close friend,
55: 20 My *c* attacks his friends;
Pr 13: 20 but a *c* of fools suffers harm.
28: 7 a *c* of gluttons disgraces his father.
29: 3 *c* of prostitutes squanders his
Rev 1: 9 your brother and *c* in the suffering

COMPANIONS (COMPANION)

Jdg 14: 11 he appeared, he was given thirty *c.*
2Ki 9: 2 get him away from his *c*
Ps 38: 11 My friends and *c* avoid me
45: 7 your God, has set you above your *c*
45: 14 her virgin *c* follow her
88: 18 have taken my *c* and loved ones
Pr 18: 24 A man of many *c* may come to ruin
Isa 1: 23 *c* of thieves;
Mt 12: 3 when he and his *c* were hungry?
12: 4 his *c* ate the consecrated bread—
26: 51 one of Jesus' *c* reached
Mk 1: 36 and his *c* went to look for him,
2: 25 and his *c* were hungry and in need?
2: 26 And he also gave some to his *c.*"
Lk 5: 9 and all his *c* were astonished
6: 3 when he and his *c* were hungry?
6: 4 And he also gave some to his *c.*"
9: 32 Peter and his *c* were very sleepy,
24: 24 some of our *c* went to the tomb
Ac 13: 13 his *c* sailed to Perga in Pamphylia,
16: 6 *c* traveled throughout the region
19: 29 Paul's traveling *c* from Macedonia,
20: 34 own needs and the needs of my *c.*
22: 9 My *c* saw the light, but they did not
22: 11 My *c* led me by the hand
26: 13 blazing around me and my *c.*
Heb 1: 9 your God, has set you above your *c*

COMPANY (COMPANIES)

Ge 13: 9 land before you? Let's part *c.*
13: 11 two men parted *c:* Abram lived
50: 9 It was a very large *c.*
Jdg 9: 37 a *c* is coming from the direction
2Ki 1: 9 a captain with his *c* of fifty men.
2: 3 The *c* of the prophets
2: 5 The *c* of the prophets
2: 7 men of the *c* of the prophets went
2: 15 The *c* of the prophets from Jericho,
4: 1 The wife of a man from the *c*
4: 38 While the *c* of the prophets was
5: 22 'Two young men from the *c*
6: 1 The *c* of the prophets said to Elisha
9: 1 a man from the *c* of the prophets
Ezr 2: 2 in *c* with Zerubbabel, Jeshua,
2: 64 The whole *c* numbered 42,360,
Ne 7: 7 in *c* with Zerubbabel, Jeshua,
7: 66 The whole *c* numbered 42,360,
8: 17 The whole *c* that had returned
Job 15: 34 For the *c* of the godless will be
34: 8 He keeps *c* with evildoers;
Ps 14: 5 present in the *c* of the righteous.
68: 11 and great was the *c* of those who
106: 17 it buried the *c* of Abiram.
Pr 21: 16 comes to rest in the *c* of the dead.
24: 1 do not desire their *c;*
Jer 15: 17 I never sat in the *c* of revelers,
Eze 27: 34 your wares and all your *c*
Ob : 20 This *c* of Israelite exiles who are
Mt 27: 27 gathered the whole *c* of soldiers
Mk 15: 16 and called together the whole *c*
Lk 2: 13 Suddenly a great *c*
2: 44 Thinking he was in their *c,*
Ac 15: 39 disagreement that they parted *c.*
Ro 15: 24 after I have enjoyed your *c* for
1Co 15: 33 "Bad *c* corrupts good character."

COMPARE (COMPARED COMPARING COMPARISON)

Job 28: 17 Neither gold nor crystal can *c*
28: 19 The topaz of Cush cannot *c* with it;
39: 13 but they cannot *c* with the pinions
Ps 86: 8 no deeds can *c* with yours.
89: 6 skies above can *c* with the LORD?
Pr 3: 15 nothing you desire can *c* with her.
8: 11 nothing you desire can *c* with her.
Isa 40: 18 To whom, then, will you *c* God?
40: 18 What image will you *c* him to?
40: 25 "To whom will you *c* me?
46: 5 "To whom will you *c* me
La 2: 13 With what can I *c* you,
Eze 31: 8 *c* with its branches—
Da 1: 13 Then *c* our appearance with that
Mt 11: 16 "To what can I *c* this generation?
Lk 7: 31 I *c* the people of this generation?
13: 18 What shall I *c* it to? It is like
13: 20 What shall I *c* the kingdom of God
2Co 10: 12 and *c* themselves with themselves,
10: 12 or *c* ourselves with some who

COMPARED (COMPARE)

Jdg 8: 2 What have I accomplished *c* to you
8: 3 What was I able to do *c* to you?"
Isa 46: 5 you liken me that we may be *c?*
Eze 31: 2 Who can be *c* with you in majesty?
31: 18 the trees of Eden can be *c* with you
Php 3: 8 I consider everything a loss *c*

COMPARING (COMPARE)

Ro 8: 18 present sufferings are not worth *c*
2Co 8: 8 the sincerity of your love by *c* it
Gal 6: 4 without *c* himself to somebody else

COMPARISON (COMPARE)

2Co 3: 10 now in *c* with the surpassing glory.

COMPASSES

Isa 44: 13 and marks it with *c.*

COMPASSION (COMPASSIONATE COMPASSIONS)

Ex 33: 19 I will have *c* on whom I will have *c.*
Dt 13: 17 he will show you mercy, have *c*
28: 54 man among you will have no *c*
30: 3 restore your fortunes and have *c*

Dt 32: 36 and have *c* on his servants
Jdg 2: 18 for the LORD had *c* on them
1Ki 3: 26 son was alive was filled with *c*
2Ki 13: 23 and had *c* and showed concern
2Ch 30: 9 and your children will be shown *c*
Ne 9: 19 of your great *c* you did not
9: 27 and in your great *c* you gave them
9: 28 in your *c* you delivered them time
Ps 51: 1 according to your great *c*
77: 9 Has he in anger withheld his *c*?"
90: 13 Have *c* on your servants.
102: 13 You will arise and have *c* on Zion,
103: 4 and crowns me with love and *c*.
103: 13 As a father has *c* on his children,
103: 13 so the LORD has *c*
116: 5 our God is full of *c*.
119: 77 Let your *c* come to me that I may
119:156 Your *c* is great, O LORD;
135: 14 and have *c* on his servants.
145: 9 he has *c* on all he has made.
Isa 13: 18 will they look with *c* on children.
14: 1 The LORD will have *c* on Jacob;
27: 11 so their Maker has no *c* on them,
30: 18 he rises to show you *c*.
49: 10 He who has *c* on them will guide
49: 13 and will have *c* on his afflicted ones
49: 15 and have no *c* on the child she has
51: 3 and will look with *c* on all her ruins
54: 7 with deep *c* I will bring you back.
54: 8 I will have *c* on you,"
54: 10 says the LORD, who has *c* on you.
60: 10 in favor I will show you *c*.
63: 7 to his *c* and many kindnesses.
63: 15 and *c* are withheld from us.
Jer 12: 15 I will again have *c* and will bring
13: 14 *c* to keep me from destroying them
15: 6 I can no longer show *c*
21: 7 show them no mercy or pity or *c*.'
30: 18 and have *c* on his dwellings;
31: 20 I have great *c* for him,"
33: 26 restore their fortunes and have *c*
42: 12 I will show you *c* so that he will
42: 12 so that he will have *c* on you
La 3: 32 he brings grief, he will show *c*,
Eze 9: 5 without showing pity or *c*.
16: 5 or had *c* enough to do any
39: 25 and will have *c* on all the people
Hos 2: 19 in love and *c*.
11: 8 all my *c* is aroused.
13: 14 "I will have no *c*,
14: 3 for in you the fatherless find *c*."
Am 1: 11 stifling all *c*,
Jnh 3: 9 with *c* turn from his fierce anger
3: 10 he had *c* and did not bring
Mic 7: 19 You will again have *c* on us;
Zec 7: 9 show mercy and *c* to one another.
10: 6 because I have *c* on them.
Mal 3: 17 as in *c* a man spares his son who
Mt 9: 36 When he saw the crowds, he had *c*
14: 14 he had *c* on them and healed their
15: 32 "I have *c* for these people;
20: 34 Jesus had *c* on them and touched
Mk 1: 41 with *c*, Jesus reached out his hand
6: 34 and saw a large crowd, he had *c*
8: 2 "I have *c* for these people;
Lk 15: 20 and was filled with *c* for him;
Ro 9: 15 and I will have *c* on whom I have *c*
2Co 1: 3 the Father of *c* and the God
Php 2: 1 and *c*, then make my joy complete
Col 3: 12 clothe yourselves with *c*, kindness,
Jas 5: 11 The Lord is full of *c* and mercy.

COMPASSIONATE (COMPASSION)
Ex 22: 27 out to me, I will hear, for I am *c*.
34: 6 the LORD, the *c* and gracious God
2Ch 30: 9 LORD your God is gracious and *c*.
Ne 9: 17 gracious and *c*, slow to anger
Ps 86: 15 O Lord, are a *c* and gracious God,
103: 8 The LORD is *c* and gracious,
111: 4 the LORD is gracious and *c*.
112: 4 the gracious and *c* and righteous
145: 8 The LORD is gracious and *c*,
La 4: 10 With their own hands *c* women
Joel 2: 13 for he is gracious and *c*,
Jnh 4: 2 that you are a gracious and *c* God,
Eph 4: 32 Be kind and *c* to one another,
1Pe 3: 8 love as brothers, be *c* and humble.

COMPASSIONS (COMPASSION)
La 3: 22 for his *c* never fail.

COMPEL (COMPELLED COMPELS COMPULSION)
Gal 6: 12 trying to *c* you to be circumcised.

COMPELLED (COMPEL)
1Sa 13: 12 So I felt *c* to offer the burnt offering
Ezr 4: 23 and *c* them by force to stop.
Ac 20: 22 "And now, *c* by the Spirit,
28: 19 I was *c* to appeal to Caesar—
1Co 9: 16 I cannot boast, for I am *c* to preach.
Gal 2: 3 with me, was *c* to be circumcised,

COMPELS (COMPEL)
Ex 3: 19 you go unless a mighty hand *c* him.
Job 32: 18 and the spirit within me *c* me;
2Co 5: 14 For Christ's love *c* us, because we

COMPENSATE (COMPENSATION)
Ex 21: 26 he must let the servant go free to *c*
21: 27 he must let the servant go free to *c*

COMPENSATION (COMPENSATE)
Pr 6: 35 He will not accept any *c*;

COMPETE (COMPETES)
Jer 12: 5 how can you *c* with horses?

COMPETENCE (COMPETENT)
2Co 3: 5 but our *c* comes from God.

COMPETENT (COMPETENCE)
Ro 15: 14 and *c* to instruct one another.
1Co 6: 2 are you not *c* to judge trivial cases?
2Co 3: 5 Not that we are *c* to claim anything
3: 6 He has made us *c* as ministers

COMPETES (COMPETE)
1Co 9: 25 Everyone who *c* in the games goes
2Ti 2: 5 Similarly, if anyone *c* as an athlete,
2: 5 unless he *c* according to the rules.

COMPLACENCY (COMPLACENT)
Pr 1: 32 and the *c* of fools will destroy them
Eze 30: 9 ships to frighten Cush out of her *c*.

COMPLACENT (COMPLACENCY)
Isa 32: 9 You women who are so *c*,
32: 11 Tremble, you *c* women;
Am 6: 1 Woe to you who are *c* in Zion,
Zep 1: 12 and punish those who are *c*,

COMPLAIN (COMPLAINED COMPLAINING COMPLAINT COMPLAINTS)
Jdg 21: 22 When their fathers or brothers *c*
Job 7: 11 I will *c* in the bitterness of my soul.
33: 13 Why do you *c* to him
Isa 29: 24 those who *c* will accept instruction
40: 27 and *c*, O Israel,
56: 3 And let not any eunuch *c*,
La 3: 39 Why should any living man *c*

COMPLAINED (COMPLAIN)
Ge 21: 25 Abraham *c* to Abimelech about
Nu 11: 1 the people *c* about their hardships
Lk 5: 30 to their sect *c* to his disciples,
Ac 6: 1 Jews among them *c* against those

COMPLAINING (COMPLAIN)
Php 2: 14 Do everything without *c* or arguing

COMPLAINT (COMPLAIN)
2Sa 15: 2 came with a *c* to be placed
15: 4 Then everyone who has a *c*
Job 7: 13 and my couch will ease my *c*,
9: 27 If I say, 'I will forget my *c*,
10: 1 I will give free rein to my *c*
21: 4 "Is my *c* directed to man?
23: 2 "Even today my *c* is bitter;
Ps 64: 1 Hear me, O God, as I voice my *c*;
142: 2 I pour out my *c* before him;
Hab 2: 1 what answer I am to give to this *c*.
Ac 18: 14 were making a *c* about some

COMPLAINTS (COMPLAIN)
Nu 14: 27 heard the *c* of these grumbling
Pr 23: 29 Who has strife? Who has *c*?

COMPLETE (COMPLETED COMPLETING COMPLETION)
Ex 5: 13 "*C* the work required of you
Dt 16: 15 your hands, and your joy will be *c*.
1Ki 7: 1 to *c* the construction of his palace.
2Ki 12: 15 because they acted with *c* honesty.
Est 2: 12 she had to *c* twelve months
Zec 4: 9 this temple; his hands will also *c* it.
Lk 6: 49 and its destruction was *c*."
14: 28 see if he has enough money to *c* it?
Jn 3: 29 That joy is mine, and it is now *c*.
15: 11 and that your joy may be *c*.
16: 24 will receive, and your joy will be *c*.
17: 23 May they be brought to *c* unity
Ac 3: 16 him that has given this *c* healing
20: 24 *c* the task the Lord Jesus has given
Ro 15: 14 *c* in knowledge and competent
2Co 7: 16 I am glad I can have *c* confidence
8: 7 in *c* earnestness and in your love
10: 6 once your obedience is *c*.
Php 2: 2 then make my joy *c*
Col 2: 2 riches of *c* understanding,
4: 17 to it that you *c* the work you have
Jas 1: 4 so that you may be mature and *c*,
2: 22 his faith was made *c* by what he did
1Jn 1: 4 We write this to make our joy *c*.
2: 5 God's love is truly made *c* in him.
4: 12 and his love is made *c* in us.
4: 17 Love is made *c* among us
2Jn : 12 to face, so that our joy may be *c*.
Rev 3: 2 for I have not found your deeds *c*

COMPLETED (COMPLETE)
Ge 2: 1 earth were *c* in all their vast array.
29: 21 My time is *c*, and I want to lie
Ex 39: 32 the Tent of Meeting, was *c*.
Lev 8: 33 the days of your ordination are *c*,
Jos 3: 17 the whole nation had *c* the crossing
1Ki 6: 9 So he built the temple and *c* it,
6: 14 Solomon built the temple and *c* it.
7: 22 so the work on the pillars was *c*.
2Ch 29: 28 of the burnt offering was *c*.
36: 21 until the seventy years were *c*
Ezr 6: 15 The temple was *c* on the third day
Ne 6: 9 for the work, and it will not be *c*."
6: 15 the wall was *c* on the twenty-fifth
Isa 40: 2 that her hard service has been *c*,
Jer 29: 10 "When seventy years are *c*
Da 11: 36 until the time of wrath is *c*,
12: 7 broken, all these things will be *c*."
Lk 1: 23 When his time of service was *c*,
2: 22 to the Law of Moses had been *c*,
12: 50 and how distressed I am until it is *c*
Jn 19: 28 Later, knowing that all was now *c*,
Ac 14: 26 God for the work they had now *c*.
Ro 15: 28 So after I have *c* this task
Rev 6: 11 to be killed as they had been was *c*.
15: 1 because with them God's wrath is *c*
15: 8 plagues of the seven angels were *c*.

COMPLETING (COMPLETE)
Jn 17: 4 on earth by *c* the work you gave me
Ac 13: 25 As John was *c* his work, he said:

COMPLETION (COMPLETE)
2Ch 8: 16 of the LORD was laid until its *c*.
2Co 8: 6 to *c* this act of grace on your part.
8: 11 to do it may be matched by your *c*
Php 1: 6 on to *c* until the day of Christ Jesus

COMPLIED (COMPLY)
2Ki 16: 9 Assyria *c* by attacking Damascus

COMPLIMENTS
Pr 23: 8 and will have wasted your *c*.

COMPLY (COMPLIED)
Est 3: 4 spoke to him but he refused to *c*.

COMPOSED
2Ch 35: 25 Jeremiah *c* laments for Josiah,

COMPREHEND (COMPREHENDED)

Job 28: 13 Man does not *c* its worth;
Ecc 8: 17 No one can *c* what goes
8: 17 he knows, he cannot really *c* it.

COMPREHENDED (COMPREHEND)

Job 38: 18 Have you *c* the vast expanses

COMPULSION (COMPEL)

1Co 7: 37 who is under no *c* but has control
2Co 9: 7 not reluctantly or under *c*,

COMPUTE

Lev 25: 52 he is to *c* that and pay

CONANIAH

2Ch 31: 12 *C*, a Levite, was in charge
31: 13 Benaiah were supervisors under *C*
35: 9 Also *C* along with Shemaiah

CONCEAL (CONCEALED CONCEALS)

Lev 16: 13 the incense will *c* the atonement
Job 14: 13 and *c* me till your anger has passed!
27: 11 ways of the Almighty I will not *c*.
40: 22 The lotuses *c* him in their shadow;
Ps 40: 10 I do not *c* your love and your truth
Pr 25: 2 It is the glory of God to *c* a matter;
Isa 26: 21 she will *c* her slain no longer.
Jer 49: 10 so that he cannot *c* himself.

CONCEALED (CONCEAL)

Jdg 9: 34 took up *c* positions near Shechem
Job 10: 13 But this is what you *c* in your heart,
24: 15 and he keeps his face *c*.
28: 21 *c* even from the birds of the air.
31: 33 if I have *c* my sin as men do,
Pr 21: 14 bribe *c* in the cloak pacifies great
26: 26 His malice may be *c* by deception,
Isa 49: 2 and *c* me in his quiver.
Jer 16: 17 nor is their sin *c* from my eyes.
Mt 10: 26 There is nothing *c* that will not be
Mk 4: 22 and whatever is *c* is meant
Lk 8: 17 nothing *c* that will not be known
12: 2 There is nothing *c* that will not be

CONCEALS (CONCEAL)

Pr 10: 18 He who *c* his hatred has lying lips,
28: 13 He who *c* his sins does not prosper,

CONCEDE (CONCESSION)

Dt 32: 31 as even our enemies *c*.

CONCEIT (CONCEITED CONCEITS)

Isa 16: 6 her overweening pride and *c*,
Jer 48: 29 her overweening pride and *c*,
Php 2: 3 out of selfish ambition or vain *c*,

CONCEITED (CONCEIT)

1Sa 17: 28 I know how *c* you are and how
Ro 11: 25 brothers, so that you may not be *c*:
12: 16 Do not be *c*.
2Co 12: 7 To keep me from becoming *c*
Gal 5: 26 Let us not become *c*, provoking
1Ti 3: 6 or he may become *c* and fall
6: 4 he is *c* and understands nothing.
2Ti 3: 4 of the good, treacherous, rash, *c*,

CONCEITS (CONCEIT)

Ps 73: 7 evil *c* of their minds know no

CONCEIVE (CONCEIVED CONCEIVES CONCEPTION)

Nu 11: 12 Did I *c* all these people? Did I give
Jdg 13: 3 you are going to *c* and have a son.
13: 5 you will *c* and give birth to a son.
13: 7 'You will *c* and give birth to a son.
Ru 4: 13 And the LORD enabled her to *c*,
Job 15: 35 They *c* trouble and give birth
Isa 33: 11 You *c* chaff,
59: 4 they *c* trouble and give birth to evil.

CONCEIVED (CONCEIVE)

Ge 4: 1 and she *c* and gave birth to Cain.
16: 4 He slept with Hagar, and she *c*.
29: 33 She *c* again, and when she gave
29: 34 Again she *c*, and when she gave
29: 35 She *c* again, and when she gave
30: 7 Rachel's servant Bilhah *c* again
30: 19 Leah *c* again and bore Jacob a sixth
38: 4 She *c* again and gave birth to a son
1Sa 1: 20 So in the course of time Hannah *c*
2: 21 she *c* and gave birth to three sons
2Sa 11: 5 The woman *c* and sent word
Ps 51: 5 from the time my mother *c* me.
SS 3: 4 to the room of the one who *c* me.
8: 5 there your mother *c* you,
Isa 8: 3 and she *c* and gave birth to a son.
46: 3 I have upheld since you were *c*,
59: 13 uttering lies our hearts have *c*.
Hos 1: 3 and she *c* and bore him a son.
1: 6 Gomer *c* again and gave birth
2: 5 and has *c* them in disgrace.
Mt 1: 20 what is *c* in her is from the Holy
Lk 2: 21 him before he had been *c*.
1Co 2: 9 no mind has *c*
Jas 1: 15 after desire has *c*, it gives birth

CONCEIVES (CONCEIVE)

Ps 7: 14 *c* trouble gives birth

CONCEPTION (CONCEIVE)

Hos 9: 11 no birth, no pregnancy, no *c*.

CONCERN (CONCERNED CONCERNS)

Ge 39: 6 he did not *c* himself with anything
39: 8 "my master does not *c* himself
1Sa 23: 21 "The LORD bless you for your *c*
2Ki 13: 23 and had compassion and showed *c*
Job 9: 21 I have no *c* for myself;
19: 4 my error remains my *c* alone.
Ps 131: 1 I do not *c* myself with great matters
Pr 29: 7 but the wicked have no such *c*.
Eze 36: 21 I had *c* for my holy name, which
Ac 15: 14 God at first showed his *c* by taking
18: 17 But Gallio showed no *c* whatever.
1Co 7: 32 I would like you to be free from *c*.
12: 25 that its parts should have equal *c*
2Co 7: 7 your deep sorrow, your ardent *c*
7: 11 what alarm, what longing, what *c*,
8: 16 of Titus the same *c* I have for you.
11: 28 of my *c* for all the churches.
Php 4: 10 at last you have renewed your *c*

CONCERNED (CONCERN)

Ge 21: 11 greatly because it *c* his son.
Ex 2: 25 Israelites and was *c* about them.
3: 7 and I am *c* about their suffering.
4: 31 that the LORD was *c* about them
1Sa 22: 8 None of you is *c* about me
2Sa 13: 33 should not be *c* about the report
1Ch 27: 1 in all that *c* the army divisions that
Ps 142: 4 no one is *c* for me.
Eze 36: 9 I am *c* for you and will look on you
Da 10: 1 was true and it *c* a great war.
Jnh 4: 10 "You have been *c* about this vine,
4: 11 Should I not be *c* about that great
Ro 11: 28 as election is *c*, they are loved
11: 28 as the gospel is *c*, they are enemies
1Co 7: 32 An unmarried man is *c* about
7: 33 a married man is *c* about the affairs
7: 34 But a married woman is *c* about
7: 34 virgin is *c* about the Lord's affairs:
9: 9 Is it about oxen that God is *c*?
Php 4: 10 you have been *c*, but you had no
2Ti 3: 8 as far as the faith is *c*, are rejected.

CONCERNS (CONCERN)

2Ch 19: 10 bloodshed or other *c* of the law,
Eze 12: 10 This oracle *c* the prince
Da 8: 17 that the vision *c* the time
8: 19 the vision *c* the appointed time
8: 26 for it *c* the distant future."
10: 14 for the vision *c* a time yet to come

CONCESSION (CONCEDE)

1Co 7: 6 I say this as a *c*, not as a command.

CONCLUDE (CONCLUDED CONCLUDES CONCLUDING CONCLUSION)

Ro 3: 9 What shall we *c* then? Are we any

CONCLUDED (CONCLUDE)

Ecc 9: 1 on all this and *c* that the righteous
Jn 7: 26 the authorities really *c* that he is

CONCLUDES (CONCLUDE)

Ps 72: 20 This *c* the prayers of David son

CONCLUDING (CONCLUDE)

Ac 16: 10 *c* that God had called us

CONCLUSION (CONCLUDE)

Ecc 12: 13 here is the *c* of the matter:

CONCUBINE (CONCUBINES)

Ge 22: 24 His *c*, whose name was Reumah,
35: 22 and slept with his father's *c* Bilhah,
36: 12 also had a *c* named Timna,
Jdg 8: 31 His *c*, who lived in Shechem,
19: 1 country of Ephraim took a *c*
19: 9 with his *c* and his servant,
19: 10 his two saddled donkeys and his *c*.
19: 24 is my virgin daughter, and his *c*.
19: 25 So the man took his *c* and sent her
19: 27 there lay his *c*, fallen
19: 29 he took a knife and cut up his *c*,
20: 4 my *c* came to Gibeah in Benjamin
20: 5 They raped my *c*, and she died.
20: 6 I took my *c*, cut her into pieces
2Sa 3: 7 had had a *c* named Rizpah
3: 7 sleep with my father's *c*?"
21: 11 Aiah's daughter Rizpah, Saul's *c*,
1Ch 1: 32 Abraham's *c*: Zimran, Jokshan,
2: 46 Caleb's *c* Ephah was the mother
2: 48 Caleb's *c* Maacah was the mother
7: 14 through his Aramean *c*.

CONCUBINES (CONCUBINE)

Ge 25: 6 he gave gifts to the sons of his *c*
2Sa 5: 13 David took more *c* and wives
15: 16 but he left ten *c* to take care
16: 21 with your father's *c* whom he left
16: 22 lay with his father's *c* in the sight
19: 5 and the lives of your wives and *c*.
20: 3 he took the ten *c* he had left
1Ki 11: 3 of royal birth and three hundred *c*,
1Ch 3: 9 of David, besides his sons by his *c*.
2Ch 11: 21 he had eighteen wives and sixty *c*,
11: 21 than any of his other wives and *c*.
Est 2: 14 eunuch who was in charge of the *c*.
SS 6: 8 and eighty *c*,
6: 9 the queens and *c* praised her.
Da 5: 2 and his *c* might drink from them.
5: 3 and his *c* drank from them.
5: 23 and your *c* drank wine from them.

CONDEMN (CONDEMNATION CONDEMNED CONDEMNING CONDEMNS SELF-CONDEMNED)

Job 9: 20 innocent, my mouth would *c* me;
10: 2 I will say to God: Do not *c* me,
34: 17 Will you *c* the just and mighty One
34: 29 if he remains silent, who can *c* him?
40: 8 Would you *c* me to justify yourself?
Ps 94: 21 and *c* the innocent to death.
109: 7 and may his prayers *c* him.
109: 31 from those who *c* him.
Isa 50: 9 Who is he that will *c* me?
Mt 12: 41 with this generation and *c* it;
12: 42 with this generation and *c* it;
20: 18 They will *c* him to death
Mk 10: 33 They will *c* him to death
Lk 6: 37 Do not *c*, and you will not be
11: 31 men of this generation and *c* them,
11: 32 with this generation and *c* it,
Jn 3: 17 Son into the world to *c* the world,
7: 51 "Does our law *c* a man
8: 11 "Then neither do I *c* you,"
12: 48 very word which I spoke will *c* him
Ro 2: 27 yet obeys the law will *c* you who,
14: 3 everything must not *c* the man who
14: 22 is the man who does not *c* himself
2Co 7: 3 this to *c* you; I have said
1Jn 3: 20 presence whenever our hearts *c* us.
3: 21 if our hearts do not *c* us,

CONDEMNATION (CONDEMN)

Jer 42: 18 of *c* and reproach; you will never
44: 12 and horror, of *c* and reproach.
Ro 3: 8 may result"? Their *c* is deserved.
5: 16 followed one sin and brought *c*,
5: 18 of one trespass was *c* for all men,
8: 1 there is now no *c* for those who are

2Pe 2: 3 Their *c* has long been hanging
Jude : 4 certain men whose *c* was written

CONDEMNED (CONDEMN)

Dt 13: 17 of those *c* things shall be found
Job 32: 3 to refute Job, and yet had *c* him.
Ps 34: 21 the foes of the righteous will be *c*.
34: 22 who takes refuge in him will be *c*.
37: 33 let them be *c* when brought to trial.
79: 11 preserve those *c* to die.
102: 20 and release those *c* to death."
Mt 12: 7 you would not have *c* the innocent.
12: 37 and by your words you will be *c*."
23: 33 How will you escape being *c* to hell
27: 3 betrayed him, saw that Jesus was *c*,
Mk 14: 64 They all *c* him as worthy of death.
16: 16 whoever does not believe will be *c*.
Lk 6: 37 condemn, and you will not be *c*.
Jn 3: 18 Whoever believes in him is not *c*,
3: 18 does not believe stands *c* already
5: 24 has eternal life and will not be *c*;
5: 29 who have done evil will rise to be *c*.
8: 10 Has no one *c* you?" "No one, sir,"
16: 11 prince of this world now stands *c*.
Ac 25: 15 against him and asked that he be *c*.
Ro 3: 7 why am I still *c* as a sinner?"
8: 3 And so he *c* sin in sinful man,
14: 23 But the man who has doubts is *c*
1Co 4: 9 like men *c* to die in the arena.
11: 32 disciplined so that we will not be *c*
Gal 1: 8 let him be eternally *c*! As we have
1: 9 let him be eternally *c*! Am I now
2Th 2: 12 that all will be *c* who have not
Tit 2: 8 of speech that cannot be *c*,
Heb 11: 7 By his faith he *c* the world
Jas 5: 6 You have *c* and murdered innocent
5: 12 and your "No," no, or you will be *c*
2Pe 2: 6 if he *c* the cities of Sodom
Rev 19: 2 He has *c* the great prostitute

CONDEMNING (CONDEMN)

Dt 25: 1 the innocent and *c* the guilty.
1Ki 8: 32 *c* the guilty and bringing
Pr 17: 15 the guilty and *c* the innocent—
Ac 13: 27 yet in *c* him they fulfilled the words
Ro 2: 1 judge the other, you are *c* yourself,

CONDEMNS (CONDEMN)

Job 15: 6 Your own mouth *c* you, not mine;
Pr 12: 2 but the LORD *c* a crafty man.
Ro 8: 34 Who is he that *c*? Christ Jesus,
2Co 3: 9 the ministry that *c* men is glorious,

CONDITION (CONDITIONS)

Ge 34: 15 consent to you on one *c* only:
34: 22 only on the *c* that our males be
1Sa 11: 2 on the *c* that I gouge out the right
Pr 27: 23 Be sure you know the *c*
Mt 12: 45 And the final *c* of that man is worse
Lk 11: 26 And the final *c* of that man is worse
Jn 5: 6 been in this *c* for a long time,

CONDITIONS (CONDITION)

Jer 32: 11 copy containing the terms and *c*,

CONDUCT (CONDUCTED CONDUCTS SAFE-CONDUCT)

Est 1: 17 For the queen's *c* will become
1: 18 about the queen's *c* will respond
Job 34: 31 Who denounces his *c* to his face?
34: 11 upon him what his *c* deserves.
Pr 10: 23 A fool finds pleasure in evil *c*,
20: 11 by whether his *c* is pure and right.
21: 8 but the *c* of the innocent is upright.
Ecc 6: 8 how to *c* himself before others?
Jer 4: 18 "Your own *c* and actions
6: 15 ashamed of their loathsome *c*?
8: 12 ashamed of their loathsome *c*?
17: 10 to reward a man according to his *c*,
32: 19 reward everyone according to his *c*
Eze 7: 3 I will judge you according to your *c*
7: 4 I will surely repay you for your *c*
7: 8 I will judge you according to your *c*
7: 9 you in accordance with your *c*
7: 27 with them according to their *c*,
14: 22 you see their *c* and their actions,
14: 23 consoled when you see their *c*
16: 27 who were shocked by your lewd *c*.
Eze 20: 43 There you will remember your *c*
24: 14 will be judged according to your *c*
36: 17 Their *c* was like a woman's
36: 17 they defiled it by their *c*
36: 19 I judged them according to their *c*
36: 32 ashamed and disgraced for your *c*,
Da 6: 4 in his *c* of government affairs,
Ac 13: 18 and endured their *c* forty years
Php 1: 27 *c* yourselves in a manner worthy
1Ti 3: 15 to *c* themselves in God's household

CONDUCTED (CONDUCT)

2Co 1: 12 testifies that we have *c* ourselves

CONDUCTS (CONDUCT)

Ps 112: 5 who *c* his affairs with justice.

CONEY (CONEYS CONIES)

Lev 11: 5 The *c*, though it chews the cud,
Dt 14: 7 eat the camel, the rabbit or the *c*.

CONEYS (CONEY)

Ps 104: 18 the crags are a refuge for the *c*.

CONFECTIONS

Eze 27: 17 wheat from Minnith and *c*,

CONFER (CONFERRED CONFERRING)

Ne 6: 7 so come, let us *c* together."
Lk 22: 29 And I *c* on you a kingdom,

CONFERRED (CONFER)

2Sa 3: 17 Abner *c* with the elders of Israel
1Ki 1: 7 Adonijah *c* with Joab son
1Ch 13: 1 David *c* with each of his officers,
Lk 22: 29 just as my Father *c* one on me,
Ac 4: 15 the Sanhedrin and then *c* together.
25: 12 After Festus had *c* with his council,

CONFERRING (CONFER)

2Ki 6: 8 After *c* with his officers, he said,

CONFESS (CONFESSED CONFESSES CONFESSING CONFESSION)

Lev 5: 5 he must *c* in what way he has
16: 21 and *c* over it all the wickedness
26: 40 " 'But if they will *c* their sins
Nu 5: 7 must *c* the sin he has committed.
1Ki 8: 33 back to you and *c* your name,
8: 35 toward this place and *c* your name
2Ch 6: 24 they turn back and *c* your name,
6: 26 toward this place and *c* your name
Ne 1: 6 I *c* the sins we Israelites, including
Ps 32: 5 I said, "I will *c*
38: 18 I *c* my iniquity;
Jn 1: 20 fail to *c*, but confessed freely,
12: 42 they would not *c* their faith
Ro 10: 9 That if you *c* with your mouth,
10: 10 it is with your mouth that you *c*
14: 11 every tongue will *c* to God.' "
Php 2: 11 every tongue *c* that Jesus Christ is
Heb 3: 1 and high priest whom we *c*.
13: 15 the fruit of lips that *c* his name.
Jas 5: 16 Therefore *c* your sins to each other
1Jn 1: 9 If we *c* our sins, he is faithful

CONFESSED (CONFESS)

1Sa 7: 6 day they fasted and there they *c*,
Ne 9: 2 in their places and *c* their sins
Da 9: 4 to the LORD my God and *c*:
Jn 1: 20 but *c* freely, "I am not the Christ."
Ac 19: 18 and openly *c* their evil deeds.

CONFESSES (CONFESS)

Pr 28: 13 whoever *c* and renounces them
2Ti 2: 19 and, "Everyone who *c* the name

CONFESSING (CONFESS)

Ezr 10: 1 While Ezra was praying and *c*,
Da 9: 20 *c* my sin and the sin
Mt 3: 6 *C* their sins, they were baptized
Mk 1: 5 *C* their sins, they were baptized

CONFESSION (CONFESS)

Ezr 10: 11 Now make *c* to the LORD,
Ne 9: 3 and spent another fourth in *c*
2Co 9: 13 obedience that accompanies your *c*
1Ti 6: 12 called when you made your good *c*
6: 13 Pontius Pilate made the good *c*,

CONFIDE (CONFIDES CONFIDING)

Jdg 16: 15 I love you,' when you won't *c* in me

CONFIDENCE (CONFIDENT SELF-CONFIDENCE SELF-CONFIDENT)

Jdg 9: 26 and its citizens put their *c* in him.
2Ki 18: 19 On what are you basing this *c*
2Ch 32: 8 And the people gained *c*
32: 10 On what are you basing your *c*,
Job 4: 6 Should not your piety be your *c*
Ps 71: 5 my *c* since my youth.
Pr 3: 26 for the LORD will be your *c*
3: 32 but takes the upright into his *c*.
11: 13 A gossip betrays a *c*,
20: 19 A gossip betrays a *c*;
25: 9 do not betray another man's *c*,
31: 11 Her husband has full *c* in her
Isa 32: 17 will be quietness and *c* forever.
36: 4 On what are you basing this *c*
Jer 17: 7 whose *c* is in him.
49: 31 which lives in *c*,"
Eze 29: 16 a source of *c* for the people of Israel
Mic 7: 5 put no *c* in a friend.
2Co 2: 3 I had *c* in all of you, that you would
3: 4 Such *c* as this is ours
7: 4 I have great *c* in you; I take great
7: 16 I am glad I can have complete *c*
8: 22 so because of his great *c* in you.
Eph 3: 12 God with freedom and *c*.
Php 3: 3 and who put no *c* in the flesh—
3: 4 I myself have reasons for such *c*.
3: 4 reasons to put *c* in the flesh,
2Th 3: 4 We have *c* in the Lord that you are
Heb 3: 14 till the end the *c* we had at first.
4: 16 the throne of grace with *c*,
10: 19 since we have *c* to enter the Most
10: 35 So do not throw away your *c*;
13: 6 So we say with *c*,
1Jn 3: 21 we have *c* before God and receive
4: 17 us so that we will have *c* on the day

CONFIDENT (CONFIDENCE)

Job 6: 20 because they had been *c*;
Ps 27: 3 even then will I be *c*.
27: 13 I am still *c* of this:
Lk 18: 9 To some who were *c*
2Co 1: 15 Because I was *c* of this, I planned
5: 6 Therefore we are always *c*
5: 8 We are *c*, I say, and would prefer
9: 4 ashamed of having been so *c*.
10: 7 If anyone is *c* that he belongs
Gal 5: 10 I am *c* in the Lord that you will
Php 1: 6 day until now, being *c* of this,
2: 24 I am *c* in the Lord that I myself will
Phm : 21 *C* of your obedience, I write to you,
Heb 6: 9 we are *c* of better things
1Jn 2: 28 that when he appears we may be *c*

CONFIDES (CONFIDE)

Ps 25: 14 The LORD *c* in those who fear him

CONFIDING (CONFIDE)

1Sa 20: 2 great or small, without *c* in me.

CONFINE (CONFINED CONFINEMENT CONFINES)

Nu 12: 14 *C* her outside the camp
2Co 10: 13 but will *c* our boasting

CONFINED (CONFINE)

Ge 39: 20 where the king's prisoners were *c*.
40: 3 same prison where Joseph was *c*.
Ex 21: 18 and he does not die but is *c* to bed,
Nu 12: 15 So Miriam was *c* outside the camp
Jdg 1: 34 The Amorites *c* the Danites
Ps 88: 8 I am *c* and cannot escape;
Jer 32: 2 and Jeremiah the prophet was *c*
33: 1 While Jeremiah was still *c*
39: 15 While Jeremiah had been *c*

CONFINEMENT (CONFINE)

2Sa 20: 3 They were kept in *c* till the day

CONFINES (CONFINE)

Job 11: 10 comes along and *c* you in prison

CONFIRM (CONFIRMED CONFIRMING CONFIRMS)

Ge 17: 2 I will *c* my covenant between me
26: 3 and will *c* the oath I swore
Nu 30: 13 Her husband may *c* or nullify any
Dt 29: 13 to *c* you this day as his people,
1Ki 1: 14 and *c* what you have said."
Est 9: 29 to *c* this second letter concerning
Da 9: 27 He will *c* a covenant with many
Ac 15: 27 to *c* by word of mouth what we are
Ro 15: 8 to *c* the promises made

CONFIRMED (CONFIRM)

Dt 4: 31 which he *c* to them by oath.
1Sa 11: 15 went to Gilgal and *c* Saul
1Ch 16: 17 He *c* it to Jacob as a decree,
2Ch 1: 9 promise to my father David be *c*,
Est 9: 32 Esther's decree *c* these regulations
Job 28: 27 he *c* it and tested it.
Ps 105: 10 He *c* it to Jacob as a decree,
119: 106 I have taken an oath and *c* it,
Mk 16: 20 and *c* his word by the signs that
Ac 14: 3 who *c* the message of his grace
1Co 1: 6 our testimony about Christ was *c*
Heb 2: 3 was *c* to us by those who heard him
6: 17 heirs of what was promised, he *c* it

CONFIRMING (CONFIRM)

2Ki 23: 3 *c* the words of the covenant written
Php 1: 7 or defending and *c* the gospel,

CONFIRMS (CONFIRM)

Nu 30: 14 He *c* them by saying nothing to her
30: 14 then he *c* all her vows
Dt 8: 18 so *c* his covenant, which he swore
Ro 9: 1 my conscience *c* it
Heb 6: 16 and the oath *c* what is said

CONFISCATION

Ezr 7: 26 banishment, *c* of property,
Heb 10: 34 and joyfully accepted the *c*

CONFLICT (CONFLICTS)

Hab 1: 3 there is strife, and *c* abounds.
Gal 5: 17 They are in *c* with each other,

CONFLICTS (CONFLICT)

2Co 7: 5 *c* on the outside, fears within.

CONFORM (CONFORMED CONFORMITY CONFORMS)

Ro 12: 2 Do not *c* any longer to the pattern
1Pe 1: 14 do not *c* to the evil desires you had

CONFORMED (CONFORM)

Eze 5: 7 *c* to the standards of the nations
11: 12 but have *c* to the standards
Ro 8: 29 predestined to be *c* to the likeness

CONFORMITY (CONFORM)

Eph 1: 11 in *c* with the purpose of his will,

CONFORMS (CONFORM)

1Ti 1: 11 to the sound doctrine that *c*

CONFOUND

Ps 55: 9 the wicked, O Lord, *c* their speech,

CONFRONT (CONFRONTED CONFRONTING CONFRONTS)

Ex 8: 20 early in the morning and *c* Pharaoh
9: 13 *c* Pharaoh and say to him,
Jdg 14: 4 an occasion to *c* the Philistines;
1Sa 12: 7 I am going to *c* you with evidence
Job 9: 32 that we might *c* each other in court.
30: 27 days of suffering *c* me.
33: 5 prepare yourself and *c* me.
Ps 17: 13 Rise up, O LORD, *c* them,
Isa 50: 8 Let him *c* me!
Eze 16: 2 *c* Jerusalem with her detestable
20: 4 Then *c* them with the detestable
22: 2 Then *c* her with all her detestable
23: 36 Then *c* them with their detestable

CONFRONTED (CONFRONT)

2Sa 22: 6 the snares of death *c* me.
22: 19 They *c* me in the day of my disaster
2Ch 26: 18 They *c* him and said, "It is not right
28: 12 *c* those who were arriving
Ps 18: 5 the snares of death *c* me.
18: 18 They *c* me in the day of my disaster

CONFRONTING (CONFRONT)

Isa 27: 4 there were briers and thorns *c* me!
30: 11 and stop *c* us

CONFRONTS (CONFRONT)

Job 31: 14 what will I do when God *c* me?

CONFUSE (CONFUSED CONFUSING CONFUSION)

Ge 11: 7 *c* their language so they will not
Ps 55: 9 *C* the wicked, O Lord, confound

CONFUSED (CONFUSE)

Ge 11: 9 there the LORD *c* the language

CONFUSING (CONFUSE)

Pr 23: 33 and your mind imagine *c* things.

CONFUSION (CONFUSE)

Ex 14: 3 wandering around the land in *c*,
14: 24 Egyptian army and threw it into *c*.
23: 27 into *c* every nation you encounter.
Dt 7: 23 throwing them into great *c*
28: 20 *c* and rebuke in everything you put
28: 28 you with madness, blindness and *c*
Jos 10: 10 them into *c* before Israel,
1Sa 14: 20 found the Philistines in total *c*,
2Sa 18: 29 I saw great *c* just as Joab was about
Ps 35: 26 be put to shame and *c*;
40: 14 be put to shame and *c*;
70: 2 be put to shame and *c*;
71: 24 have been put to shame and *c*.
Isa 41: 29 their images are but wind and *c*.
Jer 51: 34 he has thrown us into *c*,
Mic 7: 4 Now is the time of their *c*.
Ac 19: 32 in *c*: Some were shouting one thing
Gal 1: 7 people are throwing you into *c*
5: 10 you into *c* will pay the penalty,

CONGEALED

Ex 15: 8 the deep waters *c* in the heart

CONGRATULATE

2Sa 8: 10 and *c* him on his victory in battle
1Ki 1: 47 come to *c* our lord King David,
1Ch 18: 10 and *c* him on his victory in battle

CONGREGATION (CONGREGATIONS)

Ps 22: 22 in the *c* I will praise you.
68: 26 Praise God in the great *c*;
Ac 13: 43 When the *c* was dismissed,
Heb 2: 12 of the *c* I will sing your praises."

CONGREGATIONS (CONGREGATION)

1Co 14: 33 As in all the *c* of the saints,

CONIES (CONEY)

Pr 30: 26 *c* are creatures of little power,

CONJURE

Isa 47: 11 you will not know how to *c* it away.

CONNECTED (CONNECTING CONNECTION)

Lev 3: 3 that covers the inner parts or is *c*
3: 9 that covers the inner parts or is *c*
3: 14 that covers the inner parts or is *c*
4: 8 that covers the inner parts or is *c*

CONNECTING (CONNECTED)

Ex 28: 28 *c* it to the waistband,
39: 21 *c* it to the waistband

CONNECTION (CONNECTED)

Nu 18: 7 as priests in *c* with everything
1Ch 6: 49 incense in *c* with all that was done
Ac 11: 19 in *c* with Stephen traveled
Col 2: 19 He has lost *c* with the Head,

CONQUER (CONQUERED CONQUEROR CONQUERORS CONQUERS CONQUEST)

Dt 2: 31 begin to *c* and possess his land."
2Ch 32: 1 thinking to *c* them for himself.
Rev 13: 7 against the saints and to *c* them.

CONQUERED (CONQUER)

Ge 14: 7 they *c* the whole territory of
Nu 24: 18 Edom will be *c*;
24: 18 Seir, his enemy, will be *c*,
Jos 10: 42 and their lands Joshua *c*
12: 6 LORD, and the Israelites *c* them.
12: 7 and the Israelites *c* on the west side
23: 4 nations I *c*— between the Jordan
1Ki 15: 20 He *c* Ijon, Dan, Abel Bethmaacah
2Ch 16: 4 They *c* Ijon, Dan, Abel Maim
27: 5 king of the Ammonites and *c* them.
Heb 11: 33 who through faith *c* kingdoms,

CONQUEROR (CONQUER)

Mic 1: 15 I will bring a *c* against you
Rev 6: 2 he rode out as a *c* bent on conquest.

CONQUERORS (CONQUER)

1Ki 8: 47 plead with you in the land of their *c*
8: 50 cause their *c* to show them mercy;
Ro 8: 37 than *c* through him who loved us.

CONQUERS (CONQUER)

2Sa 5: 8 "Anyone who *c* the Jebusites will

CONQUEST (CONQUER)

Am 6: 13 rejoice in the *c* of Lo Debar
Rev 6: 2 as a conqueror bent on *c*.

CONSCIENCE (CONSCIENCE-STRICKEN CONSCIENCES CONSCIENTIOUS)

Ge 20: 5 I have done this with a clear *c*
20: 6 I know you did this with a clear *c*,
1Sa 25: 31 have on his *c* the staggering burden
Job 27: 6 my *c* will not reproach me as long
Ac 23: 1 to God in all good *c* to this day."
24: 16 to keep my *c* clear before God
Ro 9: 1 my *c* confirms it in the Holy Spirit
13: 5 punishment but also because of *c*.
1Co 4: 4 My *c* is clear, but that does not
8: 7 since their *c* is weak, it is defiled.
8: 10 with a weak *c* sees you who have
8: 12 in this way and wound their weak *c*
10: 25 without raising questions of *c*,
10: 27 you without raising questions of *c*.
10: 28 man who told you and for *c*' sake—
10: 29 freedom be judged by another's *c*?
10: 29 the other man's *c*, I mean,
2Co 1: 12 Our *c* testifies that we have
4: 2 to every man's *c* in the sight of God
5: 11 and I hope it is also plain to your *c*.
1Ti 1: 5 and a good *c* and a sincere faith.
1: 19 holding on to faith and a good *c*.
3: 9 truths of the faith with a clear *c*.
2Ti 1: 3 as my forefathers did, with a clear *c*
Heb 9: 9 able to clear the *c* of the worshiper.
10: 22 to cleanse us from a guilty *c*
13: 18 We are sure that we have a clear *c*
1Pe 3: 16 and respect, keeping a clear *c*,
3: 21 the pledge of a good *c* toward God.

CONSCIENCE-STRICKEN (CONSCIENCE)

1Sa 24: 5 David was *c* for having cut
2Sa 24: 10 David was *c* after he had counted

CONSCIENCES (CONSCIENCE)

Ro 2: 15 their *c* also bearing witness,
1Ti 4: 2 whose *c* have been seared
Tit 1: 15 their minds and *c* are corrupted.
Heb 9: 14 cleanse our *c* from acts that lead

CONSCIENTIOUS (CONSCIENCE)

2Ch 29: 34 for the Levites had been more *c*

CONSCIOUS

Ro 3: 20 through the law we become *c* of sin
1Pe 2: 19 of unjust suffering because he is *c*

CONSCRIPTED (CONSCRIPTING)

1Ki 5: 13 King Solomon *c* laborers
9: 15 of the forced labor King Solomon *c*
9: 21 these Solomon *c* for his slave labor
2Ch 2: 2 He *c* seventy thousand men
8: 8 these Solomon *c* for his slave labor

CONSCRIPTING (CONSCRIPTED)

2Ki 25: 19 in charge of *c* the people of the land
Jer 52: 25 in charge of *c* the people of the land

CONSECRATE (CONSECRATED CONSECRATING CONSECRATION RECONSECRATED)

Ex 13: 2 "*C* to me every firstborn male
19: 10 and *c* them today and tomorrow.
19: 22 the LORD, must *c* themselves,
28: 38 in the sacred gifts the Israelites *c*,
28: 41 *C* them so they may serve me
29: 1 This is what you are to do to *c* them
29: 27 "*C* those parts of the ordination
29: 36 for it, and anoint it to *c* it.
29: 37 atonement for the altar and *c* it.
29: 44 and the altar and will *c* Aaron
29: 44 "So I will *c* the Tent of Meeting
30: 29 You shall *c* them so they will be
30: 30 and *c* them so they may serve me
40: 9 *c* it and all its furnishings,
40: 10 *c* the altar, and it will be most holy.
40: 11 the basin and its stand and *c* them.
40: 13 and *c* him so he may serve me
Lev 8: 11 the basin with its stand, to *c* them.
8: 12 and anointed him to *c* him.
11: 44 the LORD your God; *c* yourselves
16: 19 and to *c* it from the uncleanness
20: 7 " '*C* yourselves and be holy,
22: 2 the sacred offerings the Israelites *c*
22: 3 sacred offerings that the Israelites *c*
25: 10 *C* the fiftieth year and proclaim
Nu 6: 11 That same day he is to *c* his head.
11: 18 '*C* yourselves in preparation
Jos 3: 5 told the people, "*C* yourselves,
7: 13 '*C* yourselves in preparation
7: 13 "Go, *c* the people.
Jdg 17: 3 "I solemnly *c* my silver
1Sa 16: 5 *C* yourselves and come
1Ch 15: 12 fellow Levites are to *c* yourselves
23: 13 to *c* the most holy things,
29: 5 who is willing to *c* himself today
2Ch 13: 9 Whoever comes to *c* himself
29: 5 and *c* the temple of the LORD,
29: 5 *C* yourselves now and consecrate
30: 17 and could not *c* ⌞their lambs⌟
35: 6 *c* yourselves and prepare
Isa 66: 17 Those who *c* and purify themselves
Eze 44: 19 so that they do not *c* the people
Joel 2: 16 *c* the assembly;

CONSECRATED (CONSECRATE)

Ex 19: 14 he *c* them, and they washed their
29: 21 and their garments will be *c*.
29: 43 and the place will be *c* by my glory.
Lev 8: 10 and everything in it, and so *c* them.
8: 15 So he *c* it to make atonement for it.
8: 30 So he *c* Aaron and his garments
Nu 6: 8 the period of his separation he is *c*
7: 1 He also anointed and *c* the altar
7: 1 and *c* it and all its furnishings.
15: 40 all my commands and will be *c*
Dt 12: 26 But take your *c* things
1Sa 7: 1 *c* Eleazar his son to guard the ark
16: 5 Then he *c* Jesse and his sons
21: 4 there is some *c* bread here
21: 6 So the priest gave him the *c* bread,
1Ki 8: 64 same day the king *c* the middle part
9: 3 I have *c* this temple, which you
9: 7 and will reject this temple I have *c*
13: 33 wanted to become a priest he *c*
1Ch 15: 14 and Levites *c* themselves in order
28: 16 of gold for each table for *c* bread;
2Ch 2: 4 for setting out the *c* bread regularly
5: 11 who were there had *c* themselves,
7: 7 Solomon *c* the middle part
7: 16 *c* this temple so that my Name may
7: 20 and will reject this temple I have *c*
23: 6 they may enter because they are *c*,
26: 18 who have been *c* to burn incense.
29: 15 their brothers and *c* themselves,
29: 17 eight more days they *c* the temple
29: 18 the table for setting out the *c* bread,
29: 19 *c* all the articles that King Ahaz
29: 33 animals *c* as sacrifices amounted
29: 34 and until other priests had been *c*,
30: 3 enough priests had *c* themselves
30: 8 sanctuary, which he has *c* forever.
30: 15 were ashamed and *c* themselves
30: 17 in the crowd had not *c* themselves,
30: 24 number of priests *c* themselves.
2Ch 31: 14 to the LORD and also the *c* gifts.
35: 3 and who had been *c* to the LORD:
36: 14 which he had *c* in Jerusalem.
Ezr 8: 28 these articles are *c* to the LORD.
Ps 50: 5 "Gather to me my *c* ones,
106: 16 of Aaron, who was *c* to the LORD.
Jer 11: 15 Can *c* meat avert ⌞your
Eze 48: 11 This will be for the *c* priests,
Hos 9: 10 they *c* themselves
Zep 1: 7 he has *c* those he has invited.
Hag 2: 12 If a person carries *c* meat
2: 12 does it become *c*?' " The priests
Mt 12: 4 his companions ate the *c* bread—
Mk 2: 26 house of God and ate the *c* bread,
Lk 2: 23 is to be *c* to the Lord"),
6: 4 of God, and taking the *c* bread,
1Ti 4: 5 because it is *c* by the word of God
Heb 9: 2 *c* bread; this was called the Holy

CONSECRATING (CONSECRATE)

2Ch 29: 34 in *c* themselves than the priests had
31: 18 they were faithful in *c* themselves.
Eze 46: 20 the outer court and *c* the people."

CONSECRATION (CONSECRATE)

Ex 28: 3 for his *c*, so he may serve me
29: 33 made for their ordination and *c*.
2Ch 29: 17 They began the *c* on the first day

CONSENT (CONSENTED)

Ge 34: 15 We will give our *c* to you
34: 22 But the men will *c* to live with us
34: 23 So let us give our *c* to them,
Job 39: 9 "Will the wild ox *c* to serve you?
Hos 8: 4 They set up kings without my *c*;
Ac 23: 21 waiting for your *c* to their request."
1Co 7: 5 except by mutual *c* and for a time,
Phm : 14 to do anything without your *c*,

CONSENTED (CONSENT)

Mt 3: 15 Then John *c*.
Lk 22: 6 He *c*, and watched
23: 51 who had not *c* to their decision

CONSEQUENCES

Nu 5: 31 the woman will bear the *c* of her sin
9: 13 That man will bear the *c* of his sin.
18: 22 or they will bear the *c* of their sin
Eze 16: 58 You will bear the *c*
23: 35 you must bear the *c*
23: 49 bear the *c* of your sins of idolatry.
44: 10 me after their idols must bear the *c*
44: 12 hand that they must bear the *c*

CONSIDER (CONSIDERABLE CONSIDERATE CONSIDERED CONSIDERS RECONSIDER)

Ex 30: 32 is sacred, and you are to *c* it sacred.
30: 37 formula for yourselves; *c* it holy
Lev 19: 23 years you are to *c* it forbidden;
21: 8 *C* them holy, because I the LORD,
Nu 23: 9 and do not *c* themselves one
Dt 15: 18 Do not *c* it a hardship
17: 20 and not *c* himself better
32: 7 *c* the generations long past.
Jdg 5: 10 who walk along the road, *c*
19: 30 Think about it! *C* it! Tell us what
1Sa 12: 24 *c* what great things he has done
16: 7 "Do not *c* his appearance
24: 15 May he *c* my cause and uphold it;
1Ki 2: 9 But now, do not *c* him innocent.
1Ch 28: 10 *C* now, for the LORD has chosen
2Ch 19: 6 "*C* carefully what you do,
Job 4: 7 "*C* now: Who, being innocent,
13: 24 and *c* me your enemy?
23: 5 and *c* what he would say.
37: 14 stop and *c* God's wonders.
Ps 5: 1 *c* my sighing.
8: 3 When I *c* your heavens,
10: 14 you *c* it to take it in hand.
37: 37 *C* the blameless, observe
45: 10 Listen, O daughter, *c* and give ear:
48: 13 *c* well her ramparts,
50: 22 "*C* this, you who forget God,
77: 12 and *c* all your mighty deeds.
107: 43 and *c* the great love of the LORD.
119: 6 when I *c* all your commands.
119: 15 and *c* your ways.
Ps 119: 128 because I *c* all your precepts right,
137: 6 if I do not *c* Jerusalem
143: 5 and *c* what your hands have done.
Pr 6: 6 *c* its ways and be wise!
20: 25 and only later to *c* his vows.
Ecc 2: 12 I turned my thoughts to *c* wisdom,
7: 13 *C* what God has done:
7: 14 but when times are bad, *c*:
Isa 41: 20 may *c* and understand,
41: 22 so that we may *c* them
47: 7 But you did not *c* these things
Jer 2: 19 *C* then and realize
2: 23 *c* what you have done.
2: 31 "You of this generation, *c* the word
5: 1 look around and *c*,
9: 17 *C* now! Call for the wailing women
La 1: 9 she did not *c* her future.
1: 11 "Look, O LORD, and *c*,
2: 20 "Look, O LORD, and *c*:
Eze 31: 3 *C* Assyria, once a cedar in Lebanon
43: 10 Let them *c* the plan,
47: 22 to *c* them as native-born Israelites;
Da 8: 25 and he will *c* himself superior.
9: 23 *c* the message and understand
10: 11 *c* carefully the words I am about
Hag 2: 15 *c* how things were
Mk 4: 24 "*C* carefully what you hear,"
Lk 7: 7 *c* myself worthy to come to you.
8: 18 Therefore *c* carefully how you
12: 24 *C* the ravens: They do not sow
12: 27 about the rest? "*C* how the lilies
14: 31 Will he not first sit down and *c*
Ac 4: 29 *c* their threats and enable your
5: 35 *c* carefully what you intend to do
13: 46 and do not *c* yourselves worthy
15: 6 and elders met to *c* this question.
16: 15 If you *c* me a believer in the Lord,"
20: 24 I *c* my life worth nothing to me,
26: 2 I *c* myself fortunate to stand
26: 8 any of you *c* it incredible that God
Ro 8: 18 I *c* that our present sufferings are
11: 18 *c* this: You do not support the root,
11: 22 *C* therefore the kindness
14: 16 Do not allow what you *c* good
1Co 10: 18 *C* the people of Israel: Do not those
2Co 10: 7 he should *c* again that we belong
Gal 3: 6 *C* Abraham: "He believed God,
Php 2: 3 but in humility *c* others better
2: 6 not *c* equality with God something
3: 7 was to my profit I now *c* loss
3: 8 I *c* everything a loss compared
3: 8 I *c* them rubbish, that I may gain
3: 13 I do not *c* myself yet
1Ti 6: 1 of slavery should *c* their masters
Phm : 17 if you *c* me a partner, welcome him
Heb 10: 24 And let us *c* how we may spur one
12: 3 *C* him who endured such
13: 7 *C* the outcome of their way of life
Jas 1: 2 *C* it pure joy, my brothers,
3: 5 *C* what a great forest is set on fire
5: 11 we *c* blessed those who have

CONSIDERABLE (CONSIDER)

Mt 14: 24 the boat was already a *c* distance
Ac 14: 3 and Barnabas spent *c* time there,

CONSIDERATE (CONSIDER)

Tit 3: 2 to be peaceable and *c*,
Jas 3: 17 then peace-loving, *c*, submissive,
1Pe 2: 18 only to those who are good and *c*,
3: 7 in the same way be *c* as you live

CONSIDERED (CONSIDER)

Ge 30: 33 not dark-colored will be *c* stolen."
Lev 17: 4 that man shall be *c* guilty
25: 31 walls around them are to be *c*
Dt 2: 11 they too were *c* Rephaites,
2: 20 (That too was *c* a land
1Sa 26: 21 Because you *c* my life precious
2Sa 4: 2 Beeroth is *c* part of Benjamin,
1Ki 10: 21 because silver was *c* of little value
16: 31 He not only *c* it trivial
2Ch 9: 20 because silver was *c* of little value
Ne 13: 13 these men were *c* trustworthy.
Job 1: 8 "Have you *c* my servant Job?
2: 3 "Have you *c* my servant Job?
18: 3 and *c* stupid in your sight?
34: 6 I am *c* a liar;

Ps 44: 22 we are *c* as sheep to be slaughtered.
119: 59 I have *c* my ways
Isa 53: 4 yet we *c* him stricken by God,
65: 20 will be *c* accursed.
La 4: 2 are now *c* as pots of clay,
Hos 9: 7 the prophet is *c* a fool,
Mt 1: 20 But after he had *c* this, an angel
14: 5 because they *c* him a prophet.
Lk 20: 35 But those who are *c* worthy
22: 24 which of them was *c* to be greatest.
Ro 8: 36 we are *c* as sheep to be slaughtered
2Co 11: 12 opportunity to be *c* equal with us
1Ti 1: 12 me strength, that he *c* me faithful,
Heb 11: 11 he *c* him faithful who had made
Jas 2: 21 our ancestor Abraham *c* righteous
2: 25 Rahab the prostitute *c* righteous

CONSIDERS (CONSIDER)

Job 33: 10 he *c* me his enemy.
Ps 33: 15 who *c* everything they do.
Pr 31: 16 She *c* a field and buys it;
Eze 18: 28 Because he *c* all the offenses he has
Ro 14: 5 One man *c* one day more sacred
14: 5 another man *c* every day alike.
Jas 1: 26 If anyone *c* himself religious

CONSIGN (CONSIGNING)

Isa 43: 28 and I will *c* Jacob to destruction
Eze 32: 18 and *c* to the earth below both her

CONSIGNING (CONSIGN)

2Sa 12: 31 *c* them to labor with saws
1Ch 20: 3 *c* them to labor with saws

CONSIST (CONSISTED CONSISTING CONSISTS)

Lev 2: 4 it is to *c* of fine flour: cakes made
Eze 45: 12 The shekel is to *c* of twenty gerahs.
Lk 12: 15 a man's life does not *c*

CONSISTED (CONSIST)

Jos 17: 5 Manasseh's share *c* of ten tracts
1Ch 27: 1 Each division *c* of 24,000 men.

CONSISTING (CONSIST)

Eze 46: 14 *c* of a sixth of an ephah with a third

CONSISTS (CONSIST)

Eze 45: 14 from each cor (which *c* of ten baths
Eph 5: 9 fruit of the light *c* in all goodness,

CONSOLATION (CONSOLE)

Job 6: 10 Then I would still have this *c*—
21: 2 let this be the *c* you give me.
Ps 94: 19 your *c* brought joy to my soul.
Lk 2: 25 He was waiting for the *c* of Israel,

CONSOLATIONS (CONSOLE)

Job 15: 11 Are God's *c* not enough for you,

CONSOLE (CONSOLATION CONSOLATIONS CONSOLED CONSOLING)

Job 21: 34 "So how can you *c* me
Isa 22: 4 Do not try to *c* me
51: 19 who can *c* you?
Jer 16: 7 give them a drink to *c* them.
48: 17 *C* her, all who live around her,

CONSOLED (CONSOLE)

2Sa 13: 39 for he was *c* concerning Amnon's
Job 42: 11 and *c* him over all the trouble
Eze 14: 22 you will be *c* regarding the disaster
14: 23 You will be *c* when you see their
31: 16 that were well-watered, were *c*
32: 31 he will be *c* for all his hordes that

CONSOLING (CONSOLE)

Ge 27: 42 "Your brother Esau is *c* himself

CONSORT

Ps 26: 4 nor do I *c* with hypocrites;
Hos 4: 14 the men themselves *c* with harlots

CONSPICUOUS

Eze 19: 11 *c* for its height

CONSPIRACY (CONSPIRE)

2Sa 15: 12 And so the *c* gained strength,
2Ki 15: 15 of Shallum's reign, and the *c* he led,
Ps 64: 2 Hide me from the *c* of the wicked,
Isa 8: 12 He said: "Do not call *c*
8: 12 everything that these people call *c*;
Jer 11: 9 "There is a *c* among the people
Eze 22: 25 There is a *c* of her princes
Am 7: 10 "Amos is raising a *c* against you
Ac 23: 12 next morning the Jews formed a *c*

CONSPIRATORS (CONSPIRE)

2Sa 15: 31 is among the *c* with Absalom."

CONSPIRE (CONSPIRACY CONSPIRATORS CONSPIRED)

Ps 31: 13 they *c* against me
56: 6 They *c*, they lurk,
59: 3 Fierce men *c* against me
71: 10 to kill me *c* together.
83: 3 With cunning they *c*
105: 25 to *c* against his servants.
Mic 7: 3 they all *c* together.
Ac 4: 27 to *c* against your holy servant Jesus

CONSPIRED (CONSPIRE)

1Sa 22: 8 Is that why you have all *c*
22: 13 "Why have you *c* against me,
1Ki 2: 28 who had *c* with Adonijah
2Ki 9: 14 the son of Nimshi, *c* against Joram.
10: 9 It was I who *c* against my master
12: 20 His officials *c* against him
14: 19 They *c* against him in Jerusalem,
15: 10 son of Jabesh *c* against Zechariah.
15: 25 son of Remaliah, *c* against him.
15: 30 son of Elah *c* against Pekah son
21: 23 Amon's officials *c* against him
2Ch 24: 25 His officials *c* against him
24: 26 Those who *c* against him were
25: 27 they *c* against him in Jerusalem
33: 24 Amon's officials *c* against him
Est 2: 21 and *c* to assassinate King Xerxes.
6: 2 and who had *c* to assassinate King
Da 2: 9 You have *c* to tell me misleading
Ac 9: 23 gone by, the Jews *c* to kill him,

CONSTANT

Nu 17: 5 of this *c* grumbling against you
Dt 28: 66 You will live in *c* suspense,
Job 33: 19 pain with *c* distress in his bones,
Pr 19: 13 wife is like a *c* dripping.
27: 15 a *c* dripping on a rainy day;
Isa 51: 13 that you live in *c* terror every day
Eze 30: 16 Memphis will be in *c* distress.
Ac 27: 33 "you have been in *c* suspense
1Ti 6: 5 and *c* friction between men
Heb 5: 14 by *c* use have trained themselves

CONSTELLATIONS

2Ki 23: 5 to the *c* and to all the starry hosts.
Job 9: 9 the Pleiades and the *c* of the south.
38: 32 Can you bring forth the *c*
Isa 13: 10 The stars of heaven and their *c*

CONSTRUCT (CONSTRUCTED CONSTRUCTING CONSTRUCTION CONSTRUCTIVE)

2Ch 20: 36 He agreed with him to *c* a fleet

CONSTRUCTED (CONSTRUCT)

1Ki 9: 24 he *c* the supporting terraces.
1Ch 15: 1 After David had *c* buildings
Eze 40: 17 and a pavement that had been *c* all

CONSTRUCTING (CONSTRUCT)

Ex 36: 1 the work of *c* the sanctuary are
36: 3 the work of *c* the sanctuary.
Ezr 5: 4 names of the men *c* this building?"

CONSTRUCTION (CONSTRUCT)

1Ki 7: 1 to complete the *c* of his palace.
2Ki 16: 10 with detailed plans for its *c*.
Ezr 5: 16 to the present it has been under *c*
6: 8 of the Jews in the *c* of this house

CONSTRUCTIVE (CONSTRUCT)

1Co 10: 23 but not everything is *c*.

CONSULT (CONSULTATION CONSULTED CONSULTING CONSULTS)

1Sa 28: 8 "*C* a spirit for me," he said,
28: 16 Samuel said, "Why do you *c* me,
2Ki 1: 2 to them, "Go and *c* Baal-Zebub,
1: 3 going off to *c* Baal-Zebub,
1: 6 are sending men to *c* Baal-Zebub,
1: 16 sent messengers to *c* Baal-Zebub,
1: 16 to *c* that you have sent messengers
8: 8 *C* the LORD through him; ask him
2Ch 17: 3 He did not *c* the Baals
25: 15 "Why do you *c* this people's gods,
Est 1: 13 for the king to *c* experts in matters
Pr 15: 12 he will not *c* the wise.
Isa 8: 19 When men tell you to *c* mediums
8: 19 Why *c* the dead on behalf
19: 3 they will *c* the idols and the spirits
40: 14 Whom did the LORD *c*
Eze 21: 21 he will *c* his idols, he will examine
Hos 4: 12 They *c* a wooden idol
Gal 1: 16 I did not *c* any man, nor did I go up

CONSULTATION (CONSULT)

1Ch 12: 19 after *c*, their rulers sent him away.

CONSULTED (CONSULT)

1Ki 12: 6 King Rehoboam *c* the elders who
12: 8 *c* the young men who had grown
2Ki 21: 6 and *c* mediums and spiritists.
1Ch 10: 13 and even *c* a medium for guidance,
2Ch 10: 6 King Rehoboam *c* the elders who
10: 8 *c* the young men who had grown
25: 17 king of Judah *c* his advisers,
32: 3 he *c* with his officials and military
33: 6 and *c* mediums and spiritists.
Jer 8: 2 which they have followed and *c*

CONSULTING (CONSULT)

2Ch 20: 21 After *c* the people, Jehoshaphat
Isa 30: 2 Egypt without *c* me;

CONSULTS (CONSULT)

Dt 18: 11 or spiritist or who *c* the dead.
Eze 14: 10 as guilty as the one who *c* him.

CONSUME (CONSUMED CONSUMES CONSUMING)

Dt 5: 25 we die? This great fire will *c* us,
Jdg 9: 15 and *c* the cedars of Lebanon!'
9: 20 out from Abimelech and *c* you,
9: 20 *c* Abimelech!" Then Jotham fled,
1Ki 16: 3 So I am about to *c* Baasha
21: 21 I will *c* your descendants
2Ki 1: 10 and *c* you and your fifty men!"
1: 12 and *c* you and your fifty men!"
Job 5: 5 The hungry *c* his harvest,
15: 34 fire will *c* the tents
20: 26 A fire unfanned will *c* him
Ps 21: 9 and his fire will *c* them.
39: 11 you *c* their wealth like a moth—
59: 13 *c* them in wrath,
59: 13 *c* them till they are no more.
Ecc 5: 11 so do those who *c* them.
Isa 10: 17 in a single day it will burn and *c*
26: 11 reserved for your enemies *c* them.
Jer 17: 27 that will *c* her fortresses.' "
21: 14 that will *c* everything around you
49: 27 it will *c* the fortresses
50: 32 that will *c* all who are around her."
Eze 15: 7 of the fire, the fire will yet *c* them.
20: 47 it will *c* all your trees, both green
21: 28 polished to *c*
22: 31 and *c* them with my fiery anger,
Hos 8: 14 that will *c* their fortresses."
Am 1: 4 that will *c* the fortresses
1: 7 that will *c* her fortresses.
1: 10 that will *c* her fortresses."
1: 12 that will *c* the fortresses of Bozrah
1: 14 that will *c* her fortresses
2: 2 that will *c* the fortresses of Kerioth.
2: 5 that will *c* the fortresses
Ob : 18 and they will set it on fire and *c* it.
Na 3: 15 and, like grasshoppers, *c* you.
Zec 12: 6 They will *c* right and left all
Jn 2: 17 "Zeal for your house will *c* me."
Heb 10: 27 raging fire that will *c* the enemies

CONSUMED (CONSUME)

Ge 31: 40 The heat *c* me in the daytime
Ex 15: 7 it *c* them like stubble.
Lev 6: 10 the burnt offering that the fire has *c*
9: 24 the LORD and *c* the burnt offering
10: 2 presence of the LORD and *c* them,
Nu 11: 1 *c* some of the outskirts of the camp.
11: 33 and before it could be *c*,
16: 35 *c* the 250 men who were offering
21: 28 It *c* Ar of Moab,
2Ki 1: 10 fell from heaven and *c* the captain
1: 12 and *c* him and his fifty men.
1: 14 and *c* the first two captains
2Ch 7: 1 down from heaven and *c* the burnt
Ps 31: 10 My life is *c* by anguish
78: 63 Fire *c* their young men,
90: 7 We are *c* by your anger
106: 18 a flame *c* the wicked.
119: 20 My soul is *c* with longing
Ecc 10: 12 but a fool is *c* by his own lips.
Isa 42: 25 it *c* them, but they did not take it
Jer 3: 24 our youth shameful gods have *c*
La 3: 22 LORD's great love we are not *c*,
4: 11 that *c* her foundations.
Eze 19: 12 and fire *c* them.
19: 14 and *c* its fruit.
23: 25 of you who are left will be *c* by fire.
28: 18 and it *c* you,
Na 1: 10 they will be *c* like dry stubble.
3: 13 fire has *c* their bars.
Zep 1: 18 the whole world will be *c*,
3: 8 The whole world will be *c*
Zec 9: 4 and she will be *c* by fire.
Rev 18: 8 She will be *c* by fire,

CONSUMES (CONSUME)

Ps 69: 9 for zeal for your house *c* me,
83: 14 As fire *c* the forest
97. 3 and *c* his foes on every side.
Isa 9: 18 it *c* briers and thorns,
24: 6 Therefore a curse *c* the earth;
33: 11 your breath is a fire that *c* you.
Jer 5: 14 and these people the wood it *c*.
La 2: 3 that *c* everything around it.

CONSUMING (CONSUME)

Ex 24: 17 of the LORD looked like a *c* fire
Dt 4: 24 For the LORD your God is a *c* fire,
32: 24 *c* pestilence and deadly plague;
Jdg 6: 21 flared from the rock, *c* the meat
2Sa 22: 9 *c* fire came from his mouth,
Ps 18: 8 *c* fire came from his mouth,
Isa 30: 27 and his tongue is a *c* fire.
30: 30 down with raging anger and *c* fire,
33: 14 Who of us can dwell with the *c* fire?
Joel 2: 5 like a crackling fire *c* stubble,
Heb 12: 29 and awe, for our God is a *c* fire.

CONTACT

Hag 2: 13 "If a person defiled by *c*

CONTAIN (CONTAINED CONTAINER CONTAINING CONTAINS)

1Ki 8: 27 the highest heaven, cannot *c* you.
2Ch 2: 6 the highest heavens, cannot *c* him?
6: 18 the highest heavens, cannot *c* you.
Ecc 8: 8 power over the wind to *c* it;
2Pe 3: 16 His letters *c* some things that are

CONTAINED (CONTAIN)

Ac 10: 12 It *c* all kinds of four-footed animals
Heb 9: 4 This ark *c* the gold jar of manna,

CONTAINER (CONTAIN)

Nu 19: 15 every open *c* without a lid fastened

CONTAINING (CONTAIN)

Ex 13: 3 Eat nothing *c* yeast.
23: 18 to me along with anything *c* yeast.
34: 25 to me along with anything *c* yeast,
Lev 8: 2 and the basket *c* bread made
1Sa 6: 11 with it the chest *c* the gold rats
6: 15 with the chest *c* the gold objects,
Jer 32: 11 the sealed copy *c* the terms
36: 27 burned the scroll *c* the words that
Eze 45: 11 the bath *c* a tenth of a homer

CONTAINS (CONTAIN)

Job 28: 6 and its dust *c* nuggets of gold.
Pr 15: 6 of the righteous *c* great treasure,

CONTAMINATED (CONTAMINATES CONTAMINATION)

Lev 13: 47 "If any clothing is *c* with mildew—
13: 54 order that the *c* article be washed.
13: 56 he is to tear the *c* part out
14: 40 is to order that the *c* stones be torn

CONTAMINATES (CONTAMINATED)

2Co 7: 1 from everything that *c* body

CONTAMINATION (CONTAMINATED)

Lev 13: 49 and if the *c* in the clothing,
13: 52 or any leather article that has the *c*
13: 59 are the regulations concerning *c*

CONTEMPLATING

Isa 33: 15 and shuts his eyes against *c* evil—

CONTEMPT (CONTEMPTIBLE CONTEMPTUOUS)

Lev 22: 9 and die for treating them with *c*.
Nu 14: 11 will these people treat me with *c*?
14: 23 me with *c* will ever see it.
16: 30 have treated the LORD with *c*."
Dt 17: 12 The man who shows *c* for the judge
1Sa 2: 17 the LORD's offering with *c*.
25: 39 Nabal for treating me with *c*.
2Sa 12: 14 of the LORD show utter *c*,
19: 43 So why do you treat us with *c*?
Job 12: 5 Men at ease have *c* for misfortune
12: 21 He pours *c* on nobles
31: 34 and so dreaded the *c* of the clans
Ps 31: 11 I am the utter *c* of my neighbors;
31: 18 for with pride and *c*
107: 40 he who pours *c* on nobles
119: 22 Remove from me scorn and *c*,
123: 3 for we have endured much *c*.
123: 4 much *c* from the arrogant.
Pr 14: 31 He who oppresses the poor shows *c*
17: 5 He who mocks the poor shows *c*
18: 3 When wickedness comes, so does *c*
27: 11 anyone who treats me with *c*.
Eze 22: 7 treated father and mother with *c*;
Da 12: 2 others to shame and everlasting *c*.
Hos 12: 14 and will repay him for his *c*.
Na 3: 6 I will treat you with *c*
Ro 2: 4 Or do you show *c* for the riches
Gal 4: 14 you did not treat me with *c*
1Th 5: 20 do not treat prophecies with *c*.

CONTEMPTIBLE (CONTEMPT)

1Sa 3: 13 his sons made themselves *c*,
Eze 35: 12 heard all the *c* things you have
Da 11: 21 by a *c* person who has not been
Mal 1: 7 saying that the LORD's table is *c*.
1: 12 It is defiled,' and of its food, 'It is *c*.'

CONTEMPTUOUS (CONTEMPT)

Dt 17: 13 be afraid, and will not be *c* again.
Pr 19: 16 but he who is *c* of his ways will die.

CONTEND (CONTENDED CONTENDING CONTENDS CONTENTION CONTENTIOUS)

Ge 6: 3 "My Spirit will not *c*
Jdg 6: 32 saying, "Let Baal *c* with him,"
Ps 35: 1 *C*, O LORD, with those who
35: 1 with those who *c* with me;
35: 23 *C* for me, my God and Lord.
127: 5 when they *c* with their enemies
Ecc 6: 10 no man can *c*
Isa 27: 8 By warfare and exile you *c* with her
49: 25 I will *c* with those who *c* with you,
Jude : 3 you to *c* for the faith that was once

CONTENDED (CONTEND)

Dt 33: 8 you *c* with him at the waters
Php 4: 3 help these women who have *c*

CONTENDING (CONTEND)

Php 1: 27 *c* as one man for the faith

CONTENDS (CONTEND)

Job 40: 2 "Will the one who *c*
Jer 15: 10 whom the whole land strives and *c*!

CONTENT (CONTENTED CONTENTMENT)

Jos 7: 7 If only we had been *c* to stay
Pr 13: 25 The righteous eat to their hearts' *c*,
19: 23 one rests *c*, untouched by trouble.
Ecc 4: 8 yet his eyes were not *c*
Lk 3: 14 don't accuse people falsely—be *c*
Php 4: 11 to be *c* whatever the circumstances
4: 12 I have learned the secret of being *c*
1Ti 6: 8 and clothing, we will be *c* with that.
Heb 13: 5 and be *c* with what you have,

CONTENTED (CONTENT)

Da 4: 4 was at home in my palace, *c*

CONTENTION (CONTEND)

Ps 80: 6 of *c* to our neighbors,

CONTENTIOUS (CONTEND)

1Co 11: 16 If anyone wants to be *c* about this,

CONTENTMENT (CONTENT)

Job 36: 11 and their years in *c*.
SS 8: 10 like one bringing *c*.
1Ti 6: 6 But godliness with *c* is great gain.

CONTENTS

Lev 1. 16 He is to remove the crop with its *c*

CONTEST

Heb 10: 32 in a great *c* in the face of suffering.

CONTINUAL (CONTINUE)

1Ki 14: 30 There was *c* warfare
2Ch 12: 15 There was *c* warfare
Pr 15: 15 but the cheerful heart has a *c* feast.
Eph 4: 19 of impurity, with a *c* lust for more.

CONTINUE (CONTINUAL CONTINUED CONTINUES CONTINUING)

Ex 9: 2 refuse to let them go and *c*
33: 13 and *c* to find favor with you
40: 15 be to a priesthood that will *c*
Lev 25: 22 and will *c* to eat from it
25: 35 so he can *c* to live among you.
25: 36 so that your countryman may *c*
26: 5 Your threshing will *c*
26: 5 and the grape harvest will *c*
26: 23 but *c* to be hostile toward me,
26: 27 but *c* to be hostile toward me,
Nu 34: 4 *c* on to Zin and go south
34: 9 *c* to Ziphron and end at Hazar
34. 11 *c* along the slopes east of the Sea
Dt 22: 19 She shall *c* to be his wife; he must
Jos 13: 13 they *c* to live among the Israelites
Jdg 19: 27 and stepped out to *c* on his way,
Ru 2: 13 "May I *c* to find favor in your eyes,
2Sa 7: 29 that it may *c* forever in your sight;
1Ki 8: 23 servants who *c* wholeheartedly
2Ki 17: 41 and grandchildren *c* to do as their
1Ch 17: 27 that it may *c* forever in your sight;
2Ch 6: 14 servants who *c* wholeheartedly
Est 9: 23 to *c* the celebration they had begun
Ps 36: 10 *C* your love to those who know you
72: 17 may it *c* as long as the sun.
89: 36 that his line will *c* forever
Isa 47: 7 You said, 'I will *c* forever—
Jer 3: 5 Will your wrath *c* forever?'
18: 12 We will *c* with our own plans;
23: 26 How long will this *c* in the hearts
Eze 20: 31 you *c* to defile yourselves
Da 4: 27 that then your prosperity will *c*."
9: 26 War will *c* until the end,
12: 10 but the wicked will *c* to be wicked.
Hos 4: 18 they *c* their prostitution;
Mal 2: 4 covenant with Levi may *c*,"
Jn 17: 26 and will *c* to make you known
Ac 13: 43 urged them to *c* in the grace of God
Ro 1: 32 they not only *c* to do these very
11: 22 provided that you *c* in his kindness.
2Co 1: 10 we have set our hope that he will *c*
11: 9 you in any way, and will *c* to do so.
Gal 2: 10 they asked was that we should *c*
3: 10 Cursed is everyone who does not *c*
Php 1: 18 Yes, and I will *c* to rejoice,
1: 25 and I will *c* with all of you

Php 2: 12 *c* to work out your salvation
Col 1: 23 if you *c* in your faith, established
2: 6 received Christ Jesus as Lord, *c*
2Th 2: 7 one who now holds it back will *c*
3: 4 will *c* to do the things we command
1Ti 2: 15 if they *c* in faith, love and holiness
2Ti 3: 14 *c* in what you have learned
Heb 6: 10 as you have helped his people and *c*
1Pe 4: 19 to their faithful Creator and *c*
1Jn 2: 28 And now, dear children, *c* in him,
3: 9 born of God will *c* to sin,
5: 18 born of God does not *c* to sin;
2Jn : 9 and does not *c* in the teaching
3Jn : 3 and how you *c* to walk in the truth.
Rev 22: 11 Let him who does wrong *c*
22: 11 and let him who is holy *c* to be holy
22: 11 let him who does right *c* to do right;
22: 11 let him who is vile *c* to be vile;

CONTINUED (CONTINUE)

Ge 8: 5 The waters *c* to recede
12: 9 Then Abram set out and *c*
26: 13 and his wealth *c* to grow
29: 1 Then Jacob *c* on his journey
30: 36 while Jacob *c* to tend the rest
42: 2 He *c*, "I have heard that there is
Ex 36: 3 people *c* to bring freewill offerings
Nu 9: 16 That is how it *c* to be; the cloud
21: 16 From there they *c* on to Beer,
Jos 9: 21 They *c*, "Let them live,
15: 3 *c* on to Zin and went
15: 6 and *c* north of Beth Arabah
15: 7 It *c* along to the Waters
15: 10 *c* down to Beth Shemesh
16: 6 Upper Beth Horon and *c* to the sea.
17: 9 Then the boundary *c* south
18: 16 It *c* down the Hinnom Valley
18: 17 went to En Shemesh, *c* to Geliloth,
18: 18 It *c* to the northern slope
19: 13 Then it *c* eastward to Gath Hepher
Jdg 1: 29 but the Canaanites *c* to live there
14: 17 because she *c* to press him.
18: 31 They *c* to use the idols Micah had
1Sa 2: 26 the boy Samuel *c* to grow in stature
3: 21 The LORD *c* to appear at Shiloh,
7: 15 Samuel *c* as judge over Israel all
18: 30 The Philistine commanders *c*
30: 10 four hundred men *c* the pursuit.
2Sa 2: 27 the men would have *c* the pursuit
2: 29 *c* through the whole Bithron
15: 30 David *c* up the Mount of Olives,
16: 13 and his men *c* along the road
20: 18 She *c*, "Long ago they used to say,
1Ki 2: 17 So he *c*, "Please ask King Solomon
3: 6 You have *c* this great kindness
5: 11 Solomon *c* to do this
18: 29 they *c* their frantic prophesying
22: 19 but only bad?" Micaiah *c*,
22: 43 and the people *c* to offer sacrifices
2Ki 12: 3 the people *c* to offer sacrifices
13: 6 Israel to commit; they *c* in them.
13: 11 Israel to commit; he *c* in them.
14: 4 the people *c* to offer sacrifices
15: 4 the people *c* to offer sacrifices
15: 35 the people *c* to offer sacrifices
2Ch 12: 13 firmly in Jerusalem and *c*
18: 18 but only bad?" Micaiah *c*,
27: 2 however, *c* their corrupt practices.
29: 28 All this *c* until the sacrifice
33: 17 *c* to sacrifice at the high places,
Ezr 6: 14 So the elders of the Jews *c* to build
10: 6 *c* to mourn over the unfaithfulness
Ne 4: 21 So we *c* the work with half the men
5: 9 So I *c*, "What you are doing is not
12: 37 Fountain Gate they *c* directly up
Est 2: 20 for she *c* to follow Mordecai's
Job 27: 1 And Job *c* his discourse: "As surely
29: 1 Job *c* his discourse: "How I long
36: 1 Elihu *c*: "Bear with me a little
Ps 78: 17 But they *c* to sin against him,
Isa 64: 5 But when we *c* to sin against them,
Jer 32: 20 and have *c* them to this day,
Da 7: 11 I *c* to watch because of the boastful
10: 12 Then he *c*, "Do not be afraid,
Mk 4: 24 carefully what you hear," he *c*.
Lk 4: 24 "I tell you the truth," he *c*,
15: 11 Jesus *c*: "There was a man who had
Jn 8: 23 But he *c*, "You are from below;
Jn 12: 17 the crowd that was with him had *c*
Ac 2: 46 Every day they *c* to meet together
4: 33 With great power the apostles *c*
12: 24 But the word of God *c* to increase
14: 7 where they *c* to preach the good
15: 38 had not *c* with them in the work.
21: 5 when our time was up, we left and *c*
21: 7 We *c* our voyage from Tyre
27: 20 many days and the storm *c* raging,

CONTINUES (CONTINUE)

Lev 15: 3 Whether it *c* flowing from his body
15: 25 or has a discharge that *c*
15: 26 on while her discharge *c* will be
Ps 100: 5 *c* through all generations.
119: 90 Your faithfulness *c*
2Co 10: 15 Our hope is that, as your faith *c*
1Ti 5: 5 and *c* night and day to pray
Jas 1: 25 *c* to do this, not forgetting what he
1Jn 3: 6 No one who *c* to sin has
2Jn : 9 whoever *c* in the teaching has both

CONTINUING (CONTINUE)

Ex 28: 29 as a *c* memorial before the LORD.
Nu 15: 23 *c* through the generations to come
Ro 13: 8 the *c* debt to love one another,
Heb 7: 23 since death prevented them from *c*
2Pe 2: 9 while *c* their punishment.

CONTRACT

Isa 16: 14 bound by *c* would count them,
21: 16 a servant bound by *c* would count it

CONTRADICT

Lk 21: 15 will be able to resist or *c*.

CONTRARY

Lev 10: 1 fire before the LORD, *c*
Dt 17: 3 *c* to my command has worshiped
Jos 22: 27 On the *c*, it is to be a witness
2Ch 30: 18 yet they ate the Passover, *c*
Ps 119: 85 *c* to your law.
Ac 18: 13 God in ways *c* to the law."
Ro 9: 7 On the *c*, "It is through Isaac that
11: 24 and *c* to nature were grafted
12: 20 On the *c*: "If your enemy
16: 17 obstacles in your way that are *c*
1Co 9: 12 On the *c*, we put up
12: 22 "I don't need you!" On the *c*,
2Co 2: 17 On the *c*, in Christ we speak
4: 2 On the *c*, by setting forth the truth
10: 4 On the *c*, they have divine power
Gal 2: 7 On the *c*, they saw that I had been
3: 12 law is not based on faith; on the *c*,
5: 17 and the Spirit what is *c*
5: 17 the sinful nature desires what is *c*
1Th 2: 4 On the *c*, we speak as men
2Th 3: 8 On the *c*, we worked night and day,
1Ti 1: 10 and for whatever else is *c*
2Ti 1: 17 On the *c*, when he was in Rome,

CONTRIBUTE (CONTRIBUTED CONTRIBUTING CONTRIBUTION CONTRIBUTIONS)

2Ki 15: 20 had to *c* fifty shekels of silver

CONTRIBUTED (CONTRIBUTE)

2Ch 31: 3 king *c* from his own possessions
35: 8 also *c* voluntarily to the people
Ne 7: 70 heads of the families *c* to the work.
12: 47 all Israel *c* the daily portions

CONTRIBUTING (CONTRIBUTE)

Ro 12: 8 if it is *c* to the needs of others,

CONTRIBUTION (CONTRIBUTE)

Ex 29: 28 It is the *c* the Israelites are to make
Lev 7: 14 as an offering, a *c* to the LORD;
7: 32 offerings to the priest as a *c*.
Ne 10: 34 at set times each year a *c* of wood
Ro 15: 26 pleased to make a *c* for the poor

CONTRIBUTIONS (CONTRIBUTE)

Lev 22: 12 she may not eat any of the sacred *c*.
Nu 5: 9 All the sacred *c* the Israelites bring
2Ch 24: 10 all the people brought their *c* gladly
31: 10 began to bring their *c* to the temple
31: 12 they faithfully brought in the *c*,
2Ch 31: 14 distributing the *c* made
Ne 10: 39 are to bring their *c* of grain,
12: 44 charge of the storerooms for the *c*,
13: 5 as well as the *c* for the priests.
13: 31 also made provision for *c* of wood

CONTRITE

Ps 51: 17 a broken and *c* heart,
Isa 57: 15 also with him who is *c* and lowly
57: 15 and to revive the heart of the *c*.
66: 2 he who is humble and *c* in spirit,

CONTROL (CONTROLLED CONTROLLING CONTROLS SELF-CONTROL SELF-CONTROLLED)

Ge 45: 1 Joseph could no longer *c* himself
Ex 32: 25 Aaron had let them get out of *c*
Jos 18: 1 country was brought under their *c*,
2Sa 8: 1 from the *c* of the Philistines.
8: 3 to restore his *c* along the Euphrates
1Ki 11: 24 where they settled and took *c*.
1Ch 18: 1 from the *c* of the Philistines.
18: 3 establish his *c* along the Euphrates
2Ch 17: 5 the kingdom under his *c*;
25: 3 the kingdom was firmly in his *c*,
Pr 29: 11 a wise man keeps himself under *c*.
Ecc 2: 19 Yet he will have *c* over all the work
Jer 28: 14 give him *c* over the wild animals.' "
Da 11: 43 He will gain *c* of the treasures
Ro 6: 20 free from the *c* of righteousness.
1Co 7: 9 But if they cannot *c* themselves,
7: 37 but has *c* over his own will,
14: 32 subject to the *c* of prophets.
Php 3: 21 to bring everything under his *c*,
1Th 4: 4 you should learn to *c* his own body
2Ti 3: 6 gain *c* over weak-willed women,
1Jn 5: 19 is under the *c* of the evil one.
Rev 16: 9 who had *c* over these plagues,

CONTROLLED (CONTROL)

Jdg 10: 4 They *c* thirty towns in Gilead,
1Ch 2: 22 who *c* twenty-three towns
Ps 32: 9 but must be *c* by bit and bridle
Ro 7: 5 For when we were *c*
8: 6 but the mind *c* by the Spirit is life
8: 8 Those *c* by the sinful nature cannot
8: 9 are *c* not by the sinful nature

CONTROLLING (CONTROL)

Ge 43: 31 he came out and, *c* himself, said,

CONTROLS (CONTROL)

Job 37: 15 you know how God *c* the clouds
Pr 16: 32 a man who *c* his temper

CONTROVERSIES

Ac 26: 3 with all the Jewish customs and *c*.
1Ti 1: 4 These promote *c* rather
6: 4 He has an unhealthy interest in *c*
Tit 3: 9 But avoid foolish *c* and genealogies

CONVENED (CONVENES)

Ac 25: 6 and the next day he *c* the court
25: 17 but *c* the court the next day

CONVENES (CONVENED)

Job 11: 10 and *c* a court, who can oppose him?

CONVENIENT

Ac 24: 25 When I find it *c*, I will send for you

CONVERSATION

1Sa 19: 7 David and told him the whole *c*.
Jer 38: 24 not let anyone know about this *c*.
38: 27 for no one had heard his *c*
Col 4: 6 Let your *c* be always full of grace,

CONVERT (CONVERTED CONVERTS)

Mt 23: 15 over land and sea to win a single *c*,
Ac 6: 5 from Antioch, a *c* to Judaism.
Ro 16: 5 who was the first *c* to Christ
1Ti 3: 6 He must not be a recent *c*,

CONVERTED (CONVERT)

Ac 15: 3 told how the Gentiles had been *c*.

CONVERTS (CONVERT)

Ac 2: 11 from Rome (both Jews and *c*
13: 43 devout *c* to Judaism followed Paul

1Co 16: 15 of Stephanas were the first *c*

CONVICT (CONVICTED CONVICTION CONVICTIONS)

Dt 19: 15 enough to *c* a man accused
2Sa 14: 13 says this, does he not *c* himself,
Pr 24: 25 with those who *c* the guilty,
Jn 16: 8 he will *c* the world of guilt in regard
Jude : 15 and to *c* all the ungodly

CONVICTED (CONVICT)

Jas 2: 9 you sin and are *c* by the law

CONVICTION (CONVICT)

1Th 1: 5 the Holy Spirit and with deep *c*.

CONVICTIONS (CONVICT)

Jos 14: 7 back a report according to my *c*,

CONVINCE (CONVINCED CONVINCING)

Ac 28: 23 and tried to *c* them about Jesus

CONVINCED (CONVINCE)

Ge 45: 28 "I'm *c!* My son Joseph is still alive.
Lk 16: 31 will not be *c* even if someone rises
Ac 19: 26 and hear how this fellow Paul has *c*
26: 9 "I too was *c* that I ought
26: 26 I am *c* that none of this has escaped
28: 24 Some were *c* by what he said,
Ro 2: 19 if you are *c* that you are a guide
8: 38 For I am *c* that neither death
14: 5 Each one should be fully *c*
14: 14 I am fully *c* that no food is unclean
15: 14 I myself am *c*, my brothers,
1Co 14: 24 he will be *c* by all that he is a sinner
2Co 5: 14 we are *c* that one died for all,
Php 1: 25 *C* of this, I know that I will remain,
2Ti 1: 12 and am *c* that he is able
3: 14 have learned and have become *c*

CONVINCING (CONVINCE)

Ac 1: 3 and gave many *c* proofs that he was

CONVOCATIONS

Isa 1: 13 New Moons, Sabbaths and *c*—

CONVULSED

Ps 77: 16 the very depths were *c*.
Mk 9: 26 *c* him violently and came out.

CONVULSION

Mk 9: 20 immediately threw the boy into a *c*.
Lk 9: 42 him to the ground in a *c*.

CONVULSIONS

Lk 9: 39 it throws him into *c*

COOING

SS 2: 12 the *c* of doves

COOK (COOKED COOKING COOKS)

Ex 23: 19 "Do not *c* a young goat
29: 31 and *c* the meat in a sacred place.
34: 26 "Do not *c* a young goat
Lev 8: 31 "*C* the meat at the entrance
Dt 14: 21 Do not *c* a young goat
1Sa 9: 23 said to the *c*, "Bring the piece
9: 24 the *c* took up the leg with what was
1Ki 19: 21 plowing equipment to *c* the meat
2Ki 4: 38 and *c* some stew for these men."
Eze 24: 5 and *c* the bones in it.
24: 10 *C* the meat well,
46: 20 the priests will *c* the guilt offering
46: 24 at the temple will *c* the sacrifices
Zec 14: 21 some of the pots and *c* in them.

COOKED (COOK)

Ex 12: 9 Do not eat the meat raw or *c*
Lev 2: 7 If your grain offering is *c* in a pan,
6: 28 The clay pot the meat is *c*
6: 28 but if it is *c* in a bronze pot,
7: 9 baked in an oven or *c* in a pan
Nu 11: 8 They *c* it in a pot or made it
2Ki 6: 29 So we *c* my son and ate him.
La 4: 10 have *c* their own children,

COOKING (COOK)

Ge 25: 29 Once when Jacob was *c* some stew,
Lev 11: 35 an oven or *c* pot must be broken up.
Eze 11: 3 This city is a *c* pot, and we are
24: 3 " 'Put on the *c* pot; put it on
Zec 14: 20 *c* pots in the LORD's house will be

COOKS (COOK)

1Sa 8: 13 daughters to be perfumers and *c*

COOL (COOLNESS)

Ge 3: 8 in the garden in the *c* of the day,
Jer 18: 14 its *c* waters from distant sources
Lk 16: 24 finger in water and *c* my tongue,

COOLNESS (COOL)

Pr 25: 13 Like the *c* of snow at harvest time

COPIED (COPY)

Jos 8: 32 Joshua *c* on stones the law
Pr 25: 1 *c* by the men of Hezekiah king
Eze 16: 47 and *c* their detestable practices,

COPIES (COPY)

Jer 32: 14 unsealed *c* of the deed of purchase,
Heb 9: 23 for the *c* of the heavenly things

COPPER

Dt 8: 9 and you can dig *c* out of the hills.
Job 28: 2 and *c* is smelted from ore.
Eze 22: 18 all of them are the *c*, tin, iron
22: 20 As men gather silver, *c*, iron,
24: 11 till it becomes hot and its *c* glows
Mt 10: 9 or silver or *c* in your belts;
Mk 12: 42 and put in two very small *c* coins,
Lk 21: 2 put in two very small *c* coins.

COPY (COPIED COPIES)

Dt 17: 18 for himself on a scroll a *c* of this law
2Ki 11: 12 him with a *c* of the covenant
2Ch 23: 11 him with a *c* of the covenant
Ezr 4: 11 (This is a *c* of the letter they sent
4: 23 *c* of the letter of King Artaxerxes
5: 6 This is a *c* of the letter that Tattenai
7: 11 This is a *c* of the letter King
Est 3: 14 A *c* of the text of the edict was
4: 8 gave him a *c* of the text of the edict
8: 13 A *c* of the text of the edict was
Jer 32: 11 as well as the unsealed *c*—
32: 11 the sealed *c* containing the terms
Heb 8: 5 They serve at a sanctuary that is a *c*
9: 24 sanctuary that was only a *c*

COR (CORS)

Eze 45: 14 a bath from each *c* (which consists

CORAL

Job 28: 18 *C* and jasper are not worthy
Eze 27: 16 *c* and rubies for your merchandise.

CORBAN

Mk 7: 11 received from me is *C*' (that is,

CORD (CORDS)

Ge 38: 18 its *c*, and the staff in your hand,"
38: 25 if you recognize whose seal and *c*
Ex 28: 28 the rings of the ephod with blue *c*,
28: 37 Fasten a blue *c* to it to attach it
39: 21 the rings of the ephod with blue *c*,
39: 31 Then they fastened a blue *c* to it
Nu 15: 38 with a blue *c* on each tassel.
Jos 2: 18 you have tied this scarlet *c*
2: 21 she tied the scarlet *c* in the window
2Sa 8: 2 them off with a length of *c*.
Job 41: 2 Can you put a *c* through his nose
Ecc 4: 12 *c* of three strands is not quickly
12: 6 before the silver *c* is severed,
Eze 16: 4 you were born your *c* was not cut,
40: 3 in the gateway with a linen *c*

CORDIAL

Ezr 5: 7 To King Darius: *C* greetings.

CORDS (CORD)

2Sa 22: 6 The *c* of the grave coiled
Est 1: 6 fastened with *c* of white linen
Job 4: 21 Are not the *c* of their tent pulled up
36: 8 held fast by *c* of affliction,
38: 31 Can you loose the *c* of Orion?
Ps 18: 4 The *c* of death entangled me;
18: 5 The *c* of the grave coiled
116: 3 The *c* of death entangled me,
129: 4 from the *c* of the wicked.
140: 5 they have spread out the *c*
Pr 5: 22 the *c* of his sin hold him fast.
Isa 5: 18 sin along with *c* of deceit,
54: 2 lengthen your *c*,
58: 6 and untie the *c* of the yoke,
Eze 27: 24 multicolored rugs with *c* twisted
Hos 11: 4 them with *c* of human kindness,
Jn 2: 15 So he made a whip out of *c*,

CORIANDER

Ex 16: 31 It was white like *c* seed
Nu 11: 7 The manna was like *c* seed

CORINTH (CORINTHIANS)

Ac 18: 1 Paul left Athens and went to *C*.
18: 18 Paul stayed on in *C* for some time.
19: 1 was at *C*, Paul took the road
1Co 1: 2 To the church of God in *C*,
2Co 1: 1 To the church of God in *C*,
1: 23 spare you that I did not return to *C*.
2Ti 4: 20 in *C*, and I left Trophimus sick

CORINTHIANS (CORINTH)

Ac 18: 8 of the *C* who heard him believed
2Co 6: 11 We have spoken freely to you, *C*,

CORMORANT

Lev 11: 17 the little owl, the *c*, the great owl,
Dt 14: 17 the osprey, the *c*, the stork,

CORNELIUS

Ac 10: 1 there was a man named *C*,
10: 4 "*C!*" *C* stared at him in fear.
10: 7 *C* called two of his servants
10: 17 sent by *C* found out where Simon's
10: 22 come from *C* the centurion.
10: 24 *C* was expecting them
10: 25 *C* met him and fell at his feet
10: 30 sent for me?" *C* answered:
10: 31 stood before me and said, '*C*,

CORNER (CORNERS)

Ru 3: 9 "Spread the *c* of your garment
1Sa 24: 4 and cut off a *c* of Saul's robe.
24: 5 for having cut off a *c* of his robe.
24: 11 I cut off the *c* of your robe
1Ki 7: 34 one on each *c*, projecting
7: 39 at the southeast *c* of the temple.
2Ki 14: 13 the Ephraim Gate to the *C* Gate—
2Ch 4: 10 on the south side, at the southeast *c*
25: 23 the Ephraim Gate to the *C* Gate—
26: 9 towers in Jerusalem at the *C* Gate,
26: 15 on the *c* defenses to shoot arrows
28: 24 at every street *c* in Jerusalem.
Ne 3: 24 house to the angle and the *c*,
3: 31 and as far as the room above the *c*;
3: 32 and between the room above the *c*
Pr 7: 8 going down the street near her *c*,
7: 12 at every *c* she lurks.)
21: 9 Better to live on a *c* of the roof
25: 24 Better to live on a *c* of the roof
Jer 31: 38 Tower of Hananel to the *C* Gate.
31: 40 as far as the *c* of the Horse Gate,
Eze 16: 8 I spread the *c* of my garment
46: 21 and I saw in each *c* another court.
Am 3: 12 and on the *c* of their couches."
Zep 1: 16 and against the *c* towers.
Zec 14: 10 to the *C* Gate, and from the Tower
Ac 26: 26 because it was not done in a *c*.

CORNERS (CORNER)

Ex 25: 26 and fasten them to the four *c*,
26: 23 frames for the *c* at the far end.
26: 24 At these two *c* they must be double
27: 2 Make a horn at each of the four *c*,
27: 4 at each of the four *c* of the network.
28: 7 pieces attached to two of its *c*,
28: 23 them to two *c* of the breastpiece.
28: 24 the rings at the *c* of the breastpiece,
28: 26 the other two *c* of the breastpiece
36: 28 made for the *c* of the tabernacle
36: 29 At these two *c* the frames were
37: 13 and fastened them to the four *c*,
38: 2 a horn at each of the four *c*,
38: 5 for the four *c* of the bronze grating.
39: 4 which were attached to two of its *c*,
39: 16 to two of the *c* of the breastpiece.

Ex 39: 17 the rings at the *c* of the breastpiece,
39: 19 the other two *c* of the breastpiece
Nu 15: 38 tassels on the *c* of your garments,
Dt 22: 12 Make tassels on the four *c*
Job 1: 19 and struck the four *c* of the house.
Isa 41: 9 from its farthest *c* I called you.
Eze 7: 2 come upon the four *c* of the land.
41: 22 its *c*, its base and its sides were
43: 20 and on the four *c* of the upper ledge
45: 19 on the four *c* of the upper ledge
46: 21 and led me around to its four *c*,
46: 22 In the four *c* of the outer court
46: 22 in the four *c* was the same size.
Zec 9: 15 used for sprinkling the *c* of the altar
Mt 6: 5 on the street *c* to be seen by men.
22: 9 Go to the street *c* and invite
Ac 10: 11 let down to earth by its four *c*.
11: 5 let down from heaven by its four *c*,
Rev 7: 1 standing at the four *c* of the earth,
20: 8 nations in the four *c* of the earth—

CORNERSTONE (STONE)

Job 38: 6 or who laid its *c*—
Isa 28: 16 a precious *c* for a sure foundation;
Jer 51: 26 rock will be taken from you for a *c*,
Zec 10: 4 From Judah will come the *c*,
Eph 2: 20 Christ Jesus himself as the chief *c*.
1Pe 2: 6 a chosen and precious *c*,

CORNERSTONES (STONE)

Isa 19: 13 the *c* of her peoples

CORPSE (CORPSES)

Lev 22: 4 touches something defiled by a *c*
Isa 14: 19 Like a *c* trampled underfoot,
Mk 9: 26 so much like a *c* that many said,

CORPSES (CORPSE)

Na 3: 3 people stumbling over the *c*—

CORRECT (CORRECTED CORRECTING CORRECTION CORRECTIONS CORRECTS)

Job 6: 26 Do you mean to *c* what I say,
40: 2 contends with the Almighty *c* him?
Jer 10: 24 *C* me, LORD, but only with justice
2Ti 4: 2 *c*, rebuke and encourage—

CORRECTED (CORRECT)

Pr 29: 19 A servant cannot be *c*

CORRECTING (CORRECT)

2Ti 3: 16 *c* and training in righteousness,

CORRECTION (CORRECT)

Lev 26: 23 things you do not accept my *c*
Job 36: 10 He makes them listen to *c*
Pr 5: 12 How my heart spurned *c!*
10: 17 whoever ignores *c* leads others
12: 1 but he who hates *c* is stupid.
13: 18 but whoever heeds *c* is honored.
15: 5 whoever heeds *c* shows prudence.
15: 10 he who hates *c* will die.
15: 12 A mocker resents *c;*
15: 32 whoever heeds *c* gains
29: 15 The rod of *c* imparts wisdom,
Jer 2: 30 they did not respond to *c*.
5: 3 crushed them, but they refused *c*.
7: 28 LORD its God or responded to *c*.
Zep 3: 2 she accepts no *c*.
3: 7 and accept *c!'*

CORRECTIONS (CORRECT)

Pr 6: 23 and the *c* of discipline

CORRECTS (CORRECT)

Job 5: 17 "Blessed is the man whom God *c;*
Pr 9: 7 Whoever *c* a mocker invites insult;

CORRESPONDING (CORRESPONDS)

1Ch 23: 6 into groups *c* to the sons of Levi:
2Ch 3: 8 its length *c* to the width
Eze 42: 12 to the *c* wall extending eastward,

CORRESPONDS (CORRESPONDING)

Gal 4: 25 *c* to the present city of Jerusalem,

CORRODED (CORROSION)

Jas 5: 3 Your gold and silver are *c*.

CORROSION (CORRODED)

Jas 5: 3 Their *c* will testify against you

CORRUPT (CORRUPTED CORRUPTION CORRUPTS)

Ge 6: 11 Now the earth was *c* in God's sight
6: 12 God saw how *c* the earth had
Ex 32: 7 out of Egypt, have become *c*.
Dt 4: 16 so that you do not become *c*
4: 25 if you then become *c* and make any
9: 12 out of Egypt have become *c*.
31: 29 sure to become utterly *c*
Jdg 2: 19 more *c* than those of their fathers,
2Ch 27: 2 continued their *c* practices.
Job 15: 16 much less man, who is vile and *c*,
Ps 14: 1 They are *c*, their deeds are vile;
14: 3 they have together become *c;*
53: 1 They are *c*, and their ways are vile;
53: 3 they have together become *c;*
94: 20 Can a *c* throne be allied with you—
Pr 4: 24 keep *c* talk far from your lips.
6: 12 who goes about with a *c* mouth,
19: 28 A *c* witness mocks at justice,
Jer 2: 21 me into a *c*, wild vine?
Eze 20: 44 evil ways and your *c* practices,
Da 6: 4 and neither *c* nor negligent.
11: 32 flattery he will *c* those who have
Hos 5: 3 Israel is *c*.
Ac 2: 40 yourselves from this *c* generation."
1Ti 6: 5 friction between men of *c* mind,
2Pe 2: 10 of those who follow the *c* desire

CORRUPTED (CORRUPT)

Ge 6: 12 people on earth had *c* their ways.
Eze 28: 17 and you *c* your wisdom
2Co 7: 2 wronged no one, we have *c* no one,
Eph 4: 22 which is being *c* by its deceitful
Tit 1: 15 but to those who are *c* and do not
1: 15 their minds and consciences are *c*.
Jude : 23 the clothing stained by *c* flesh.
Rev 19: 2 who *c* the earth by her adulteries.

CORRUPTION (CORRUPT)

2Ki 23: 13 on the south of the Hill of *C*—
Ezr 9: 11 polluted by the *c* of its peoples.
Job 17: 14 if I say to *c*, 'You are my father,'
Ps 55: 23 the wicked into the pit of *c;*
Isa 1: 4 children given to *c*.
Da 6: 4 They could find no *c* in him,
Hos 9: 9 They have sunk deep into *c*,
2Pe 1: 4 escape the *c* in the world caused
2: 20 If they have escaped the *c*

CORRUPTS (CORRUPT)

Ecc 7: 7 and a bribe *c* the heart.
1Co 15: 33 "Bad company *c* good character."
Jas 3: 6 It *c* the whole person, sets

CORS (COR)

1Ki 4: 22 daily provisions were thirty *c*
4: 22 of fine flour and sixty *c* of meal,
5: 11 gave Hiram twenty thousand *c*
2Ch 2: 10 twenty thousand *c* of barley,
2: 10 twenty thousand *c* of ground wheat
27: 5 and ten thousand *c* of barley.
27: 5 ten thousand *c* of wheat
Ezr 7: 22 a hundred *c* of wheat, a hundred

COS

Ac 21: 1 out to sea and sailed straight to *C*.

COSAM

Lk 3: 28 the son of Addi, the son of *C*,

COSMETIC (COSMETICS)

2Sa 14: 2 and don't use any *c* lotions.

COSMETICS (COSMETIC)

Est 2: 12 and six with perfumes and *c*.

COST (COSTLY COSTS)

Nu 11: 5 ate in Egypt at no *c*—
16: 38 sinned at the *c* of their lives.
Jos 6: 26 at the *c* of his youngest
6: 26 "At the *c* of his firstborn son
2Sa 24: 24 burnt offerings that *c* me nothing."
1Ki 16: 34 at the *c* of his firstborn son Abiram,
16: 34 at the *c* of his youngest son Segub,
1Ch 12: 19 "It will *c* us our heads if he deserts
Pr 4: 7 Though it *c* all you have, get
7: 23 little knowing it will *c* him his life.
23: 7 who is always thinking about the *c*.
Isa 55: 1 milk without money and without *c*.
Lk 14: 28 and estimate the *c* to see
Rev 21: 6 to drink without *c* from the spring

COSTLY (COST)

Ge 24: 53 he also gave *c* gifts to her brother
Est 1: 6 mother-of-pearl and other *c* stones.
Ps 49: 8 the ransom for a life is *c*,
Eze 16: 10 and covered you with *c* garments.
16: 13 *c* fabric and embroidered cloth.
Da 11: 38 with precious stones and *c* gifts.
1Co 3: 12 silver, *c* stones, wood, hay or straw,
Rev 18: 12 *c* wood, bronze, iron and marble;

COSTS (COST)

1Ch 21: 24 a burnt offering that *c* me nothing."
Ezr 6: 4 The *c* are to be paid
Pr 6: 31 it *c* him all the wealth of his house.

COUCH (COUCHES)

Ge 49: 4 onto my *c* and defiled it.
1Sa 28: 23 from the ground and sat on the *c*.
2Ki 4: 32 was the boy lying dead on his *c*.
Est 7: 8 falling on the *c* where Esther was
Job 7: 13 and my *c* will ease my complaint,
Ps 6: 6 and drench my *c* with tears.
Eze 23: 41 on an elegant *c*, with a table spread

COUCHES (COUCH)

Est 1: 6 There were *c* of gold and silver
Am 3: 12 and on the corner of their *c*."
6: 4 and lounge on your *c*.

COUNCIL (COUNCILS)

Ge 49: 6 Let me not enter their *c*,
Nu 16: 2 been appointed members of the *c*.
Job 15: 8 Do you listen in on God's *c?*
Ps 89: 7 In the *c* of the holy ones God is
107: 32 and praise him in the *c* of the elders
111: 1 heart in the *c* of the upright
Jer 23: 18 stood in the *c* of the LORD
23: 22 But if they had stood in my *c*,
Eze 13: 9 belong to the *c* of my people
Mk 15: 43 a prominent member of the *C*,
Lk 22: 66 At daybreak the *c* of the elders
23: 50 a member of the *C*, a good
Jn 3: 1 a member of the Jewish ruling *c*.
Ac 17: 33 At that, Paul left the *C*.
22: 5 high priest and all the *c* can testify.
25: 12 Festus had conferred with his *c*,

COUNCILS (COUNCIL)

Mt 10: 17 will hand you over to the local *c*
Mk 13: 9 will be handed over to the local *c*

COUNSEL (COUNSELED COUNSELOR COUNSELORS COUNSELS)

2Sa 15: 31 turn Ahithophel's *c*
1Ki 22: 5 "First seek the *c* of the LORD."
2Ch 18: 4 "First seek the *c* of the LORD."
22: 5 also followed their *c* when he went
25: 16 and have not listened to my *c*."
Ezr 10: 3 in accordance with the *c* of my lord
Job 12: 13 *c* and understanding are his.
21: 16 aloof from the *c* of the wicked.
22: 18 aloof from the *c* of the wicked.
29: 21 waiting in silence for my *c*.
38: 2 "Who is this that darkens my *c*
42: 3 'Who is this that obscures my *c*
Ps 1: 1 walk in the *c* of the wicked
32: 8 I will *c* you and watch over you.
73: 24 You guide me with your *c*,
106: 13 and did not wait for his *c*.
107: 11 despised the *c* of the Most High.
Pr 8: 14 *C* and sound judgment are mine;
15: 22 Plans fail for lack of *c*,
22: 20 sayings of *c* and knowledge,
27: 9 from his earnest *c*.
Isa 11: 2 the Spirit of *c* and of power,
16: 3 "Give us *c*,
28: 29 wonderful in *c* and magnificent
41: 28 no one among them to give *c*,
45: 21 let them take *c* together.
47: 13 All the *c* you have received has

Jer 18: 18 nor will *c* from the wise,
38: 15 I did give you *c*, you would not
49: 7 Has *c* perished from the prudent?
Eze 7: 26 as will the *c* of the elders.
1Ti 5: 14 So I *c* younger widows to marry,
Rev 3: 18 I *c* you to buy from me gold refined

COUNSELED (COUNSEL)

Mic 6: 5 king of Moab *c*

COUNSELOR (COUNSEL)

2Sa 15: 12 David's *c*, to come from Giloh,
1Ch 26: 14 cast for his son Zechariah, a wise *c*,
27: 32 Jonathan, David's uncle, was a *c*,
27: 33 Ahithophel was the king's *c*.
Isa 3: 3 the *c*, skilled craftsman
9: 6 Wonderful *C*, Mighty God,
40: 13 or instructed him as his *c*?
Mic 4: 9 Has your *c* perished,
Jn 14: 16 he will give you another *C* to be
14: 26 But the *C*, the Holy Spirit,
15: 26 "When the *C* comes, whom I will
16: 7 the *C* will not come to you;
Ro 11: 34 Or who has been his *c*?"

COUNSELORS (COUNSEL)

Ezr 4: 5 They hired *c* to work against them
Job 3: 14 rest with kings and *c* of the earth,
12: 17 He leads *c* away stripped
Ps 119: 24 they are my *c*.
Isa 1: 26 your *c* as at the beginning.
19: 11 wise *c* of Pharaoh give senseless

COUNSELS (COUNSEL)

Ps 16: 7 I will praise the LORD, who *c* me;
Na 1: 11 and *c* wickedness.

COUNT (COUNTED COUNTING COUNTS)

Ge 13: 16 so that if anyone could *c* the dust,
15: 5 if indeed you can *c* them."
15: 5 up at the heavens and *c* the stars—
16: 10 they will be too numerous to *c*."
Ex 30: 12 a census of the Israelites to *c* them,
Lev 15: 13 he is to *c* off seven days
15: 28 she must *c* off seven days,
23: 15 the sheaf of the wave offering, *c*
23: 16 *C* off fifty days up to the day
25: 8 " '*C* off seven sabbaths of years—
25: 50 and his buyer are to *c* the time
Nu 1: 49 "You must not *c* the tribe of Levi
3: 15 *C* every male a month old or more
3: 15 "*C* the Levites by their families
3: 40 "*C* all the firstborn Israelite males
4: 3 *C* all the men from thirty
4: 23 *C* all the men from thirty
4: 29 "*C* the Merarites by their clans
4: 30 *C* all the men from thirty
6: 12 The previous days do not *c*,
23: 10 Who can *c* the dust of Jacob
31: 26 community are to *c* all the people
Dt 16: 9 *C* off seven weeks
Jdg 6: 5 It was impossible to *c* the men
2Sa 24: 1 saying, "Go and *c* Israel and Judah
1Ki 3: 8 too numerous to *c* or number.
1Ch 21: 2 and *c* the Israelites from Beersheba
27: 24 son of Zeruiah began to *c* the men
Job 14: 16 Surely then you will *c* my steps
19: 15 my maidservants *c* me a stranger;
31: 4 and *c* my every step?
38: 37 has the wisdom to *c* the clouds?
39: 2 Do you *c* the months till they bear?
Ps 22: 17 I can *c* all my bones;
32: 2 whose sin the LORD does not *c*
48: 12 *c* her towers,
139: 18 Were I to *c* them,
139: 22 I *c* them my enemies.
Isa 16: 14 bound by contract would *c* them,
21: 16 bound by contract would *c* it,
46: 5 you compare me or *c* me equal?
Ro 4: 8 whose sin the Lord will never *c*
6: 11 *c* yourselves dead to sin
2Th 1: 11 that our God may *c* you worthy
Rev 7: 9 multitude that no one could *c*,
11: 1 and *c* the worshipers there.

COUNTED (COUNT)

Ge 13: 16 then your offspring could be *c*.
32: 12 of the sea, which cannot be *c*.' "
Ex 30: 12 for his life at the time he is *c*.
30: 13 crosses over to those already *c* is
38: 25 of the community who were *c*
38: 26 who had crossed over to those *c*,
Nu 1: 19 so he *c* them in the Desert of Sinai:
1: 22 able to serve in the army were *c*
1: 44 These were the men *c* by Moses
1: 45 in Israel's army were *c* according
1: 47 were not *c* along with the others.
2: 32 *c* according to their families.
2: 33 were not *c* along with the other
3: 16 So Moses *c* them, as he was
3: 22 or more who were *c* was 7,500.
3: 34 or more who were *c* was 6,200.
3: 39 number of Levites *c* at the LORD's
3: 42 So Moses *c* all the firstborn
4: 34 of the community *c* the Kohathites
4: 36 in the Tent of Meeting, *c* by clans,
4: 37 and Aaron *c* them according
4: 38 The Gershonites were *c*
4: 40 *c* by their clans and families,
4: 41 and Aaron *c* them according
4: 42 The Merarites were *c* by their clans
4: 44 *c* by their clans, were 3,200.
4: 45 and Aaron *c* them according
4: 46 leaders of Israel *c* all the Levites
4: 49 Thus they were *c*, as the LORD
7: 2 in charge of those who were *c*,
14: 29 or more who was *c* in the census
26: 57 These were the Levites who were *c*
26: 62 were not *c* along with the other
26: 63 These are the ones *c* by Moses
26: 63 the priest when they *c* the Israelites
26: 64 the priest when they *c* the Israelites
26: 64 was among those *c* by Moses
31: 49 "Your servants have *c* the soldiers
Jos 13: 3 of it *c* as Canaanite (the territory
Jdg 7: 12 Their camels could no more be *c*
21: 9 For when they *c* the people,
1Sa 13: 15 Saul *c* the men who were with him.
2Sa 2: 15 So they stood up and were *c* off—
24: 10 after he had *c* the fighting men,
1Ki 8: 5 they could not be recorded or *c*.
2Ki 12: 10 *c* the money that had been brought
1Ch 9: 28 they *c* them when they were
21: 17 ordered the fighting men to be *c*?
22: 4 more cedar logs than could be *c*,
23: 3 thirty years old or more were *c*,
23: 11 so they were *c* as one family
23: 14 of Moses the man of God were *c*
23: 24 their names and *c* individually,
23: 27 the Levites were *c*
2Ch 5: 6 they could not be recorded or *c*.
Ezr 1: 8 who *c* them out to Sheshbazzar
Job 5: 9 miracles that cannot be *c*.
Ps 49: 18 while he lived he *c* himself blessed
88: 4 I am *c* among those who go
Ecc 1: 15 what is lacking cannot be *c*.
Isa 22: 10 You *c* the buildings in Jerusalem
Jer 46: 23 they cannot be *c*.
Hos 1: 10 which cannot be measured or *c*.
Mt 26: 15 So they *c* out for him thirty silver
Ac 5: 41 because they had been *c* worthy
2Th 1: 5 and as a result you will be *c* worthy

COUNTENANCE

Job 14: 20 you change his *c* and send him

COUNTERFEIT

2Th 2: 9 displayed in all kinds of *c* miracles,
1Jn 2: 27 not *c*—just as it has taught you,

COUNTING (COUNT)

Ge 46: 26 not *c* his sons' wives—numbered
Dt 24: 15 because he is poor and is *c* on it.
Jdg 8: 26 shekels, not *c* the ornaments,
2Co 5: 19 not *c* men's sins against them.

COUNTLESS

Nu 10: 36 to the *c* thousands of Israel."
Job 21: 33 and a *c* throng goes before him.
Jer 33: 22 as *c* as the stars of the sky
Heb 11: 12 as *c* as the sand on the seashore.

COUNTRIES (COUNTRY)

Ge 41: 57 all the *c* came to Egypt to buy grain
Dt 29: 16 through the *c* on the way here.
1Ki 4: 21 These *c* brought tribute
2Ki 18: 35 the gods of these *c* has been able
19: 11 of Assyria have done to all the *c*,
2Ch 9: 28 from Egypt and from all other *c*.
20: 29 upon all the kingdoms of the *c*
Isa 10: 14 so I gathered all the *c*;
36: 20 the gods of these *c* has been able
37: 11 of Assyria have done to all the *c*,
Jer 16: 15 of all the *c* where he had banished
23: 3 out of all the *c* where I have driven
23: 8 of all the *c* where he had banished
27: 6 Now I will hand all your *c*
28: 8 and plague against many *c*
40: 11 all the other *c* heard that the king
40: 12 from all the *c* where they had been
51: 28 and all the *c* they rule.
Eze 5: 5 of the nations, with *c* all around her
5: 6 than the nations and *c* around her.
11: 16 and scattered them among the *c*,
11: 16 in the *c* where they have gone.'
11: 17 from the *c* where you have been
12: 15 and scatter them through the *c*.
20: 23 and scatter them through the *c*,
20: 34 from the *c* where you have been
20: 41 from the *c* where you have been
22: 4 and a laughingstock to all the *c*.
22: 15 and scatter you through the *c*;
25: 7 and exterminate you from the *c*.
29: 12 and scatter them through the *c*.
30: 23 and scatter them through the *c*.
30: 26 and scatter them through the *c*.
34: 13 and gather them from the *c*,
35: 10 two nations and *c* will be ours
36: 19 they were scattered through the *c*;
36: 24 I will gather you from all the *c*
39: 27 them from the *c* of their enemies,
Da 9: 7 in all the *c* where you have
11: 40 He will invade many *c*
11: 41 Many *c* will fall, but Edom,
11: 42 will extend his power over many *c*;
Zec 8: 7 people from the *c* of the east

COUNTRY (COUNTRIES COUNTRYSIDE)

Ge 10: 30 toward Sephar, in the eastern hill *c*.
12: 1 said to Abram, "Leave your *c*,
14: 6 and the Horites in the hill *c* of Seir,
15: 13 strangers in a *c* not their own,
21: 23 and the *c* where you are living
24: 4 go to my *c* and my own relatives
24: 5 back to the *c* you came from?"
25: 27 a man of the open *c*,
25: 29 Esau came in from the open *c*,
27: 3 and go out to the open *c*
27: 5 left for the open *c* to hunt game
31: 21 he headed for the hill *c* of Gilead.
31: 23 up with him in the hill *c* of Gilead.
31: 25 tent in the hill *c* of Gilead
31: 54 offered a sacrifice there in the hill *c*
32: 3 in the land of Seir, the *c* of Edom.
32: 9 back to your *c* and your relatives,
36: 8 Edom) settled in the hill *c* of Seir.
36: 9 of the Edomites in the hill *c* of Seir.
36: 35 who defeated Midian in the *c*
41: 36 held in reserve for the *c*,
41: 36 so that the *c* may not be ruined
41: 56 had spread over the whole *c*,
Ex 1: 10 fight against us and leave the *c*."
6: 1 he will drive them out of his *c*."
6: 11 to let the Israelites go out of his *c*."
7: 2 to let the Israelites go out of his *c*.
8: 2 I will plague your whole *c*
10: 4 locusts into your *c* tomorrow.
10: 14 area of the *c* in great numbers.
11: 10 not let the Israelites go out of his *c*.
12: 33 the people to hurry and leave the *c*.
13: 17 on the road through the Philistine *c*
18: 27 and he returned to his own *c*.
Lev 25: 24 Throughout the *c* that you hold
25: 31 are to be considered as open *c*.
25: 45 of their clans born in your *c*,
26: 6 sword will not pass through your *c*.
26: 34 you are in the *c* of your enemies;
Nu 13: 17 the Negev and on into the hill *c*.
13: 29 and Amorites live in the hill *c*;
14: 40 up toward the high hill *c*.
14: 44 up toward the high hill *c*,
14: 45 lived in that hill *c* came down
20: 17 Please let us pass through your *c*.
21: 22 "Let us pass through your *c*.

Nu 22: 6 and drive them out of the *c*.
22: 13 "Go back to your own *c*,
Dt 1: 7 into the hill *c* of the Amorites;
1: 19 toward the hill *c* of the Amorites
1: 20 "You have reached the hill *c*
1: 24 They left and went up into the hill *c*
1: 41 easy to go up into the hill *c*.
1: 43 you marched up into the hill *c*.
2: 1 way around the hill *c* of Seir.
2: 3 way around this hill *c* long enough;
2: 5 I have given Esau the hill *c* of Seir
2: 24 king of Heshbon, and his *c*.
2: 27 "Let us pass through your *c*.
2: 31 begun to deliver Sihon and his *c*
3: 12 including half the hill *c* of Gilead,
3: 25 that fine hill *c* and Lebanon."
9: 28 *c* from which you brought us will
11: 3 king of Egypt and to his whole *c*;
22: 25 But if out in the *c* a man happens
22: 27 the man found the girl out in the *c*,
23: 7 you lived as an alien in his *c*.
28: 3 in the city and blessed in the *c*.
28: 16 in the city and cursed in the *c*.
28: 24 the rain of your *c* into dust
28: 40 trees throughout your *c*
Jos 1: 4 the Euphrates—all the Hittite *c*—
2: 9 live in this *c* are melting in fear
7: 9 people of the *c* will hear about this
9: 1 in the hill *c*, in the western foothills
9: 6 "We have come from a distant *c*;
9: 9 come from a very distant *c*
9: 11 all those living in our *c* said to us,
10: 6 from the hill *c* have joined forces
10: 40 including the hill *c*, the Negev,
11: 3 Perizzites and Jebusites in the hill *c*
11: 16 took this entire land: the hill *c*,
11: 21 and from all the hill *c* of Israel.
11: 21 from all the hill *c* of Judah,
11: 21 the Anakites from the hill *c*:
12: 8 the hill *c*, the western foothills,
13: 21 with Sihon—who lived in that *c*.
13: 25 and half the Ammonite *c* as far
14: 12 give me this hill *c* that the LORD
15: 48 In the hill *c*: Shamir, Jattir, Socoh,
16: 1 the desert into the hill *c* of Bethel.
17: 15 if the hill *c* of Ephraim is too small
17: 16 "The hill *c* is not enough for us,
17: 18 but the forested hill *c* as well.
18: 1 The *c* was brought
18: 12 and headed west into the hill *c*,
19: 50 in the hill *c* of Ephraim.
20: 7 Hebron) in the hill *c* of Judah.
20: 7 Shechem in the hill *c* of Ephraim,
20: 7 in Galilee in the hill *c* of Naphtali,
21: 11 in the hill *c* of Judah.
21: 21 In the hill *c* of Ephraim they were
22: 33 them to devastate the *c* where
24: 4 I assigned the hill *c* of Seir to Esau,
24: 30 in the hill *c* of Ephraim,
24: 33 Phinehas in the hill *c* of Ephraim.
Jdg 1: 9 the Canaanites living in the hill *c*,
1: 19 They took possession of the hill *c*,
1: 34 confined the Danites to the hill *c*,
2: 9 in the hill *c* of Ephraim,
3: 27 a trumpet in the hill *c* of Ephraim,
4: 5 and Bethel in the hill *c* of Ephraim,
6: 3 other eastern peoples invaded the *c*
7: 24 throughout the hill *c* of Ephraim,
10: 1 in Shamir, in the hill *c* of Ephraim.
11: 12 us that you have attacked our *c*?"
11: 17 permission to go through your *c*,'
11: 18 along the eastern side of the *c*
11: 19 through your *c* to our own place.'
11: 21 of the Amorites who lived in that *c*,
12: 15 in the hill *c* of the Amalekites.
17: 1 from the hill *c* of Ephraim said
17: 8 house in the hill *c* of Ephraim.
18: 2 The men entered the hill *c*
18: 13 went on to the hill *c* of Ephraim
19: 1 area in the hill *c* of Ephraim took
19: 16 man from the hill *c* of Ephraim,
19: 18 in the hill *c* of Ephraim where I live
Ru 1: 1 to live for a while in the *c* of Moab.
1Sa 1: 1 Zuphite from the hill *c* of Ephraim,
6: 5 of the rats that are destroying the *c*,
6: 18 towns with their *c* villages.
9: 4 through the hill *c* of Ephraim
13: 2 and in the hill *c* of Bethel,
1Sa 14: 22 in the hill *c* of Ephraim heard that
14: 29 father has made trouble for the *c*.
27: 5 to me in one of the *c* towns,
2Sa 10: 8 were by themselves in the open *c*.
19: 9 But now he has fled the *c*
20: 21 from the hill *c* of Ephraim,
1Ki 4: 8 in the hill *c* of Ephraim; Ben-Deker
4: 19 and the *c* of Og king of Bashan).
4: 19 in Gilead (the *c* of Sihon king
10: 6 heard in my own *c* about your
10: 13 with her retinue to her own *c*.
11: 21 that I may return to my own *c*."
11: 22 want to go back to your own *c*?"
11: 29 of them were alone out in the *c*,
12: 25 Shechem in the hill *c* of Ephraim
14: 11 feed on those who die in the *c*.
16: 4 feed on those who die in the *c*."
21: 24 feed on those who die in the *c*."
2Ki 5: 22 to me from the hill *c* of Ephraim.
8: 6 land from the day she left the *c*
13: 20 used to enter the *c* every spring.
17: 26 what the god of that *c* requires.
18: 25 me to march against this *c*
19: 7 he will return to his own *c*,
24: 7 out from his own *c* again,
1Ch 1: 46 who defeated Midian in the *c*
4: 42 of Ishi, invaded the hill *c* of Seir.
6: 67 In the hill *c* of Ephraim they were
19: 3 spy out the *c* and overthrow it?"
19: 9 were by themselves in the open *c*.
2Ch 9: 5 heard in my own *c* about your
9: 12 with her retinue to her own *c*.
13: 4 in the hill *c* of Ephraim, and said,
14: 1 and in his days the *c* was at peace
19: 4 Beersheba to the hill *c* of Ephraim
Ne 8: 15 "Go out into the hill *c*
9: 22 They took over the *c* of Sihon king
9: 22 and the *c* of Og king of Bashan.
Ps 78: 54 to the hill *c* his right hand had
105: 31 and gnats throughout their *c*.
105: 33 and shattered the trees of their *c*.
Pr 28: 2 When a *c* is rebellious, it has many
29: 4 By justice a king gives a *c* stability,
Isa 1: 7 Your *c* is desolate,
13: 5 to destroy the whole *c*.
22: 18 and throw you into a large *c*.
36: 10 me to march against this *c*
37: 7 he will return to his own *c*,
63: 13 Like a horse in open *c*,
66: 8 Can a *c* be born in a day
Jer 12: 5 If you stumble in safe *c*,
12: 15 his own inheritance and his own *c*.
14: 18 If I go into the *c*,
15: 13 sins throughout your *c*.
17: 3 because of sin throughout your *c*.
17: 26 from the hill *c* and the Negev,
22: 26 who gave you birth into another *c*,
25: 11 This whole *c* will become
32: 44 and in the towns of the hill *c*,
33: 13 of the hill *c*, of the western foothills
40: 4 Look, the whole *c* lies before you;
40: 7 in the open *c* heard that the king
40: 13 still in the open *c* came to Gedaliah
Eze 7: 15 those in the *c* will die by the sword,
14: 13 if a *c* sins against me
14: 15 if I send wild beasts through that *c*
14: 17 "Or if I bring a sword against that *c*
21: 19 both starting from the same *c*.
33: 27 those out in the *c* I will give
Da 11: 9 but will retreat to his own *c*.
11: 19 toward the fortresses of his own *c*
11: 28 and then return to his own *c*.
11: 28 to his own *c* with great wealth,
Hos 12: 12 Jacob fled to the *c* of Aram;
Am 7: 17 you yourself will die in a pagan *c*.
Jnh 1: 8 What is your *c*? From what people
Zec 5: 11 "To the *c* of Babylonia
6: 6 going toward the north *c*,
6: 8 toward the north *c* have given my
Mt 2: 12 to their *c* by another route.
14: 35 word to all the surrounding *c*.
Mk 15: 21 passing by on his way in from the *c*,
16: 12 while they were walking in the *c*.
Lk 1: 39 to a town in the hill *c* of Judah,
1: 65 and throughout the hill *c*
3: 3 into all the *c* around the Jordan,
7: 17 Judea and the surrounding *c*.
14: 23 'Go out to the roads and *c* lanes
Lk 15: 4 leave the ninety-nine in the open *c*
15: 13 off for a distant *c* and there
15: 14 a severe famine in that whole *c*,
15: 15 out to a citizen of that *c*,
19: 12 went to a distant *c* to have himself
21: 21 let those in the *c* not enter the city.
23: 26 who was on his way in from the *c*,
Jn 4: 44 prophet has no honor in his own *c*.)
11: 55 up from the *c* to Jerusalem
Ac 7: 3 'Leave your *c* and your people,'
7: 6 strangers in a *c* not their own,
7: 7 they will come out of that *c*
9: 32 As Peter traveled about the *c*,
10: 39 did in the *c* of the Jews
12: 20 on the king's *c* for their food supply
13: 17 power he led them out of that *c*
14: 6 Derbe and to the surrounding *c*,
26: 4 beginning of my life in my own *c*,
2Co 11: 26 in danger in the *c*, in danger at sea;
Heb 11: 9 land like a stranger in a foreign *c*;
11: 14 looking for a *c* of their own.
11: 15 thinking of the *c* they had left,
11: 16 they were longing for a better *c*—

COUNTRYMAN (COUNTRYMEN)

Lev 25: 15 are to buy from your *c* on the basis
25: 25 and redeem what his *c* has sold.
25: 36 so that your *c* may continue to live

COUNTRYMEN (COUNTRYMAN)

Lev 25: 14 " 'If you sell land to one of your *c*
25: 25 " 'If one of your *c* becomes poor
25: 35 " 'If one of your *c* becomes poor
25: 39 " 'If one of your *c* becomes poor
25: 47 and one of your *c* becomes poor
Nu 32: 6 "Shall your *c* go to war
2Sa 15: 20 going? Go back, and take your *c*.
2Ch 19: 10 you from your fellow *c* who live
28: 11 back your fellow *c* you have taken
28: 15 back to their fellow *c* at Jericho,
35: 5 of the families of your fellow *c*,
35: 6 the lambs, for your fellow *c*,
Ne 3: 18 made by their *c* under Binnui son
5: 5 as our *c* and though our sons are
5: 7 usury from your own *c*!"
Jer 22: 13 making his *c* work for nothing,
29: 16 your *c* who did not go with you
34: 15 of you proclaimed freedom to his *c*.
34: 17 freedom for your fellow *c*.
Eze 3: 11 Go now to your *c* in exile
33: 2 speak to your *c* and say to them:
33: 12 son of man, say to your *c*,
33: 17 "Yet your *c* say, 'The way
33: 30 your *c* are talking together about
37: 18 "When your *c* ask you, 'Won't you
2Co 11: 26 danger from my own *c*, in danger
1Th 2: 14 from your own *c* the same things

COUNTRYSIDE (COUNTRY)

1Sa 30: 16 scattered over the *c*, eating,
2Sa 15: 23 The whole *c* wept aloud
18: 8 battle spread out over the whole *c*,
1Ki 20: 27 while the Arameans covered the *c*.
2Ki 7: 12 have left the camp to hide in the *c*,
Job 5: 10 he sends water upon the *c*.
SS 7: 11 Come, my lover, let us go to the *c*,
Mk 1: 5 whole Judean *c* and all the people
5: 14 and reported this in the town and *c*,
6: 36 so they can go to the surrounding *c*
6: 56 into villages, towns or *c*—
Lk 4: 14 spread through the whole *c*.
8: 34 and reported this in the town and *c*,
9: 12 and *c* and find food and lodging,
Jn 3: 22 went out into the Judean *c*,

COUNTS (COUNT)

Job 19: 11 he *c* me among his enemies.
Jer 33: 13 the hand of the one who *c* them,'
Jn 6: 63 The Spirit gives life; the flesh *c*
1Co 7: 19 God's commands is what *c*.
Gal 5: 6 only thing that *c* is faith expressing
6: 15 means anything; what *c* is a new

COURAGE (COURAGEOUS)

Jos 2: 11 everyone's *c* failed because of you,
5: 1 and they no longer had the *c*
2Sa 4: 1 he lost *c*, and all Israel became
7: 27 So your servant has found *c*

1Ch 17: 25 So your servant has found *c* to pray
2Ch 15: 8 son of Oded the prophet, he took *c*.
19: 11 Act with *c*, and may the LORD be
Ezr 7: 28 I took *c* and gathered leading men
10: 4 We will support you, so take *c*
Ps 107: 26 in their peril their *c* melted away.
Eze 22: 14 Will your *c* endure or your hands
Da 11: 25 and *c* against the king of the South.
Mt 14: 27 said to them: "Take *c!*
Mk 6: 50 spoke to them and said, "Take *c!*
Ac 4: 13 When they saw the *c* of Peter
23: 11 "Take *c!* As you have testified
27: 22 now I urge you to keep up your *c*,
27: 25 So keep up your *c*, men,
1Co 16: 13 stand firm in the faith; be men of *c;*
Php 1: 20 will have sufficient *c* so that now
Heb 3: 6 if we hold on to our *c* and the hope

COURAGEOUS (COURAGE)

Dt 31: 6 Be strong and *c*.
31: 7 of all Israel, "Be strong and *c*,
31: 23 son of Nun: "Be strong and *c*,
Jos 1: 6 and *c*, because you will lead these
1: 7 Be strong and very *c*.
1: 9 commanded you? Be strong and *c*.
1: 18 Only be strong and *c!*"
10: 25 Be strong and *c*.
1Ch 22: 13 Be strong and *c*.
28: 20 "Be strong and *c*, and do the work.
2Ch 26: 17 priest with eighty other *c* priests
32: 7 with these words: "Be strong and *c*.

COURIER (COURIERS)

Jer 51: 31 One *c* follows another

COURIERS (COURIER)

2Ch 30: 6 *c* went throughout Israel
30: 10 The *c* went from town to town
Est 3: 13 Dispatches were sent by *c*
3: 15 king's command, the *c* went out,
8: 10 and sent them by mounted *c*,
8: 14 The *c*, riding the royal horses,

COURSE (COURSES)

Ge 4: 3 In the *c* of time Cain brought some
Dt 2: 37 the land along the *c* of the Jabbok
1Sa 1: 20 in the *c* of time Hannah conceived
22: 15 inquired of God for him? Of *c* not!
2Sa 2: 1 In the *c* of time, David inquired
8: 1 In the *c* of time, David defeated
10: 1 In the *c* of time, the king
13: 1 In the *c* of time, Amnon son
15: 1 In the *c* of time, Absalom provided
21: 18 In the *c* of time, there was another
1Ki 6: 36 and one *c* of trimmed cedar beams.
7: 12 and one *c* of trimmed cedar beams,
1Ch 18: 1 In the *c* of time, David defeated
19: 1 In the *c* of time, Nahash king
20: 4 In the *c* of time, war broke out
2Ch 21: 19 In the *c* of time, at the end
Job 1: 5 a period of feasting had run its *c*,
Ps 19: 5 a champion rejoicing to run his *c*.
36: 4 he commits himself to a sinful *c*
102: 23 In the *c* of my life he broke my
Pr 2: 8 for he guards the *c* of the just
15: 21 of understanding keeps a straight *c*.
16: 9 In his heart a man plans his *c*,
17: 23 to pervert the *c* of justice.
Ecc 1: 6 ever returning on its *c*.
Jer 8: 6 Each pursues his own *c*
23: 10 The [prophets] follow an evil *c*
Joel 2: 7 not swerving from their *c*.
Ac 27: 7 wind did not allow us to hold our *c*,
Ro 10: 18 Did they not hear? Of *c* they did:
2Co 12: 18 same spirit and follow the same *c?*
13: 5 unless, of *c*, you fail the test?
Jas 3: 6 sets the whole *c* of his life on fire,

COURSES (COURSE)

Jdg 5: 20 from their *c* they fought
1Ki 6: 36 of three *c* of dressed stone
7: 12 by a wall of three *c* of dressed stone
Ezr 6: 4 with three *c* of large stones

COURT (COURTS)

Ge 50: 4 Joseph said to Pharaoh's *c*,
50: 7 the dignitaries of his *c*
Ex 21: 22 husband demands and the *c* allows.
Dt 25: 1 it to *c* and the judges will decide
Jdg 4: 5 She held *c* under the Palm
1Ki 3: 15 Then he gave a feast for all his *c*.
2Ki 20: 4 Before Isaiah had left the middle *c*,
23: 11 They were in the *c* near the room
1Ch 26: 18 As for the *c* to the west, there were
26: 18 at the road and two at the *c* itself.
2Ch 4: 9 the large *c* and the doors for the *c*,
6: 13 it in the center of the outer *c*.
Ne 3: 25 palace near the *c* of the guard.
Est 4: 11 inner *c* without being summoned
5: 1 stood in the inner *c* of the palace,
5: 2 Queen Esther standing in the *c*,
6: 4 Haman had just entered the outer *c*
6: 4 The king said, "Who is in the *c?*"
6: 5 "Haman is standing in the *c*."
Job 5: 4 crushed in *c* without a defender.
9: 32 we might confront each other in *c*.
11: 10 convenes a *c*, who can oppose him?
11: 19 and many will *c* your favor.
31: 21 knowing that I had influence in *c*,
Pr 22: 22 and do not crush the needy in *c*,
25: 8 do not bring hastily to *c*,
29: 9 If a wise man goes to *c* with a fool,
Isa 3: 13 The LORD takes his place in *c;*
29: 21 who ensnare the defender in *c*
Jer 19: 14 in the *c* of the LORD's temple
29: 2 the *c* officials and the leaders
34: 19 and Jerusalem, the *c* officials,
41: 16 and *c* officials he had brought
Eze 8: 3 to the north gate of the inner *c*,
8: 7 me to the entrance to the *c*.
8: 16 me into the inner *c* of the house
10: 3 and a cloud filled the inner *c*.
10: 4 and the *c* was full of the radiance
10: 5 as far away as the outer *c*,
40: 17 been constructed all around the *c;*
40: 17 he brought me into the outer *c*.
40: 19 to the outside of the inner *c;*
40: 20 north, leading into the outer *c*.
40: 23 to the inner *c* facing the north gate,
40: 27 inner *c* also had a gate facing south,
40: 28 into the inner *c* through the south
40: 30 the inner *c* were twenty-five
40: 31 Its portico faced the outer *c;*
40: 32 me to the inner *c* on the east side,
40: 34 Its portico faced the outer *c;*
40: 37 Its portico faced the outer *c;*
40: 44 within the inner *c*, were two rooms,
40: 47 he measured the *c:* It was square—
41: 15 and the portico facing the *c*,
42: 1 led me northward into the outer *c*
42: 3 the pavement of the outer *c*,
42: 3 twenty cubits from the inner *c*
42: 7 to the rooms and the outer *c;*
42: 8 to the outer *c* was fifty cubits long,
42: 9 one enters them from the outer *c*.
42: 10 the length of the wall of the outer *c*,
42: 14 go into the outer *c* until they leave
43: 5 and brought me into the inner *c*,
44: 17 at the gates of the inner *c*
44: 17 they enter the gates of the inner *c*,
44: 19 into the outer *c* where the people
44: 21 wine when he enters the inner *c*.
44: 27 into the inner *c* of the sanctuary
45: 19 and on the gateposts of the inner *c*.
46: 1 gate of the inner *c* facing east is
46: 20 bringing them into the outer *c*
46: 21 He then brought me to the outer *c*
46: 21 and I saw in each corner another *c*.
46: 22 of the outer *c* were enclosed courts,
Da 1: 3 Ashpenaz, chief of his *c* officials,
2: 49 himself remained at the royal *c*.
7: 10 The *c* was seated,
7: 26 the *c* will sit, and his power will be
Am 5: 10 you hate the one who reproves in *c*
Mt 5: 25 adversary who is taking you to *c*.
Ac 18: 12 on Paul and brought him into *c*.
18: 16 So he had them ejected from the *c*.
18: 17 and beat him in front of the *c*.
25: 6 and the next day he convened the *c*
25: 10 am now standing before Caesar's *c*,
25: 17 but convened the *c* the next day
1Co 4: 3 judged by you or by any human *c;*
Jas 2: 6 ones who are dragging you into *c?*
Rev 11: 2 But exclude the outer *c;* do not

COURTS (COURT)

Dt 17: 8 before your *c* that are too difficult
2Ki 21: 5 In both *c* of the temple
23: 12 built in the two *c* of the temple
1Ch 28: 6 who will build my house and my *c*,
28: 12 in his mind for the *c* of the temple
2Ch 33: 5 In both *c* of the temple
Ne 8: 16 in the *c* of the house of God
13: 7 room in the *c* of the house of God.
Ps 65: 4 and bring near to live in your *c!*
84: 2 even faints for the *c* of the LORD;
84: 10 Better is one day in your *c*
92: 13 flourish in the *c* of our God.
96: 8 an offering and come into his *c*.
100: 4 and his *c* with praise;
116: 19 in the *c* of the house of the LORD
135: 2 in the *c* of the house of our God.
Isa 1: 12 this trampling of my *c?*
62: 9 it in the *c* of my sanctuary."
Eze 9: 7 and fill the *c* with the slain.
42: 6 floor had no pillars, as the *c* had;
46: 22 of the outer court were enclosed *c*,
46: 22 of the *c* in the four corners was
46: 23 of each of the four *c* was a ledge
Am 5: 12 deprive the poor of justice in the *c*.
5: 15 maintain justice in the *c*.
Zec 3: 7 my house and have charge of my *c*,
8: 16 and sound judgment in your *c;*
Mt 21: 23 Jesus entered the temple *c*, and,
26: 55 sat in the temple *c* teaching,
Mk 11: 16 merchandise through the temple *c*.
11: 27 Jesus was walking in the temple *c*,
12: 35 Jesus was teaching in the temple *c*,
14: 49 teaching in the temple *c*,
Lk 2: 27 he went into the temple *c*.
2: 46 they found him in the temple *c*,
20: 1 teaching the people in the temple *c*
22: 53 was with you in the temple *c*,
Jn 2: 14 In the temple *c* he found men
7: 14 did Jesus go up to the temple *c*
7: 28 still teaching in the temple *c*,
8: 2 he appeared again in the temple *c*,
Ac 2: 46 to meet together in the temple *c*.
3: 2 from those going into the temple *c*.
3: 8 went with them into the temple *c*,
5: 20 Go, stand in the temple *c*," he said,
5: 21 they entered the temple *c*,
5: 25 in the temple *c* teaching the people
5: 42 in the temple *c* and from house
19: 38 the *c* are open and there are
24: 18 me in the temple *c* doing this.
26: 21 the Jews seized me in the temple *c*

COURTYARD (COURTYARDS)

Ex 27: 9 "Make a *c* for the tabernacle.
27: 12 of the *c* shall be fifty cubits wide
27: 13 the *c* shall also be fifty cubits wide.
27: 16 "For the entrance to the *c*,
27: 17 All the posts around the *c* are
27: 18 *c* shall be a hundred cubits long
27: 19 pegs for it and those for the *c*,
35: 17 the curtain for the entrance to the *c*
35: 17 the curtains of the *c* with its posts
35: 18 for the tabernacle and for the *c*,
38: 9 Next they made the *c*.
38: 15 side of the entrance to the *c*,
38: 16 All the curtains around the *c* were
38: 17 the posts of the *c* had silver bands.
38: 18 curtains of the *c*, five cubits high,
38: 18 for the entrance to the *c* was of blue
38: 20 of the surrounding *c* were bronze.
38: 31 and those for the surrounding *c*.
38: 31 the bases for the surrounding *c*
39: 40 the curtain for the entrance to the *c*
39: 40 the curtains of the *c* with its posts
39: 40 the ropes and tent pegs for the *c;*
40: 8 Set up the *c* around it and put
40: 8 the curtain at the entrance to the *c*.
40: 33 Then Moses set up the *c*
40: 33 the curtain at the entrance to the *c*.
Lev 6: 16 are to eat it in the *c* of the Tent
6: 26 in the *c* of the Tent of Meeting.
Nu 3: 26 the curtains of the *c*, the curtain
3: 26 to the *c* surrounding the tabernacle
3: 37 as the posts of the surrounding *c*
4: 26 of the *c* surrounding the tabernacle
4: 32 as the posts of the surrounding *c*

2Sa 17: 18 a well in his *c*, and they climbed
1Ki 6: 36 he built the inner *c* of three courses
7: 9 from the outside to the great *c*
7: 12 The great *c* was surrounded
7: 12 as was the inner *c* of the temple
8: 64 part of the *c* in front of the temple
2Ch 4: 9 He made the *c* of the priests,
7: 7 part of the *c* in front of the temple
20: 5 the LORD in the front of the new *c*
24: 21 in the *c* of the LORD's temple.
29: 16 They brought out to the *c*
Est 2: 11 and forth near the *c* of the harem
Jer 26: 2 in the *c* of the LORD's house
32: 2 confined in the *c* of the guard
32: 8 came to me in the *c* of the guard
32: 12 sitting in the *c* of the guard.
33: 1 confined in the *c* of the guard,
36: 10 was in the upper *c* at the entrance
36: 20 they went to the king in the *c*
37: 21 remained in the *c* of the guard.
37: 21 to be placed in the *c* of the guard
38: 6 which was in the *c* of the guard.
38: 13 remained in the *c* of the guard.
38: 28 remained in the *c* of the guard
39: 14 out of the *c* of the guard.
39: 15 confined in the *c* of the guard,
Eze 40: 14 up to the portico facing the *c*.
41: 12 The building facing the temple *c*
41: 13 and the temple *c* and the building
41: 14 width of the temple *c* on the east,
41: 15 length of the building facing the *c*
42: 1 to the rooms opposite the temple *c*
42: 10 adjoining the temple *c*
42: 13 facing the temple *c* are the priests'
Mt 26: 58 right up to the *c* of the high priest.
26: 69 Now Peter was sitting out in the *c*,
Mk 14: 54 right into the *c* of the high priest.
14: 66 While Peter was below in the *c*,
Lk 22: 55 a fire in the middle of the *c*
Jn 18: 15 with Jesus into the high priest's *c*,

COURTYARDS (COURTYARD)

Ex 8: 13 died in the houses, in the *c*
1Ch 23: 28 in charge of the *c*, the side rooms,
2Ch 23: 5 are to be in the *c* of the temple
Ne 8: 16 on their own roofs, in their *c*,

COUSIN (COUSINS)

Lev 25: 49 or a *c* or any blood relative
Est 2: 7 Mordecai had a *c* named Hadassah
Jer 32: 8 my *c* Hanamel came to me
32: 9 at Anathoth from my *c* Hanamel
32: 12 in the presence of my *c* Hanamel
Col 4: 10 as does Mark, the *c* of Barnabas.

COUSINS (COUSIN)

Lev 10: 4 carry your *c* outside the camp,
Nu 36: 11 married their *c* on their father's
1Ch 23: 22 Their *c*, the sons of Kish, married

COVENANT (COVENANTED COVENANTS)

Ge 6: 18 But I will establish my *c* with you,
9: 9 "I now establish my *c* with you
9: 11 I establish my *c* with you: Never
9: 12 a *c* for all generations to come:
9: 12 of the *c* I am making between me
9: 13 the sign of the *c* between me
9: 15 I will remember my *c* between me
9: 16 and remember the everlasting *c*
9: 17 the sign of the *c* I have established
15: 18 On that day the LORD made a *c*
17: 2 I will confirm my *c* between me
17: 4 "As for me, this is my *c* with you:
17: 7 as an everlasting *c* between me
17: 7 will establish my *c* as an everlasting
17: 9 "As for you, you must keep my *c*,
17: 10 This is my *c* with you and your
17: 10 the *c* you are to keep: Every male
17: 11 the sign of the *c* between me
17: 13 My *c* in your flesh is
17: 13 is to be an everlasting *c*.
17: 14 his people; he has broken my *c*."
17: 19 I will establish my *c* with him
17: 19 an everlasting *c* for his descendants
17: 21 But my *c* I will establish with Isaac,
31: 44 Come now, let's make a *c*,
Ex 2: 24 and he remembered his *c*
Ex 6: 4 also established my *c* with them
6: 5 and I have remembered my *c*.
19: 5 if you obey me fully and keep my *c*,
23: 32 Do not make a *c* with them
24: 7 Then he took the Book of the *C*
24: 8 of the *c* that the LORD has made
31: 16 generations to come as a lasting *c*.
34: 10 "I am making a *c* with you.
34: 27 with these words I have made a *c*
34: 28 on the tablets the words of the *c*—
Lev 2: 13 the salt of the *c* of your God out
24: 8 of the Israelites, as a lasting *c*.
26: 9 and I will keep my *c* with you.
26: 15 my commands and so violate my *c*,
26: 25 you to avenge the breaking of the *c*.
26: 42 and my *c* with Isaac and my *c*
26: 42 with Isaac and my *c* with Abraham,
26: 44 them completely, breaking my *c*
26: 45 for their sake I will remember the *c*
Nu 10: 33 The ark of the *c* of the LORD went
14: 44 nor the ark of the LORD's *c* moved
18: 19 It is an everlasting *c* of salt
25: 12 tell him I am making my *c*
25: 13 and his descendants will have a *c*
Dt 4: 13 declared to you his *c*, the Ten
4: 23 Be careful not to forget the *c*
4: 31 forget the *c* with your forefathers,
5: 2 The LORD our God made a *c*
5: 3 fathers that the LORD made this *c*,
7: 9 keeping his *c* of love
7: 12 LORD your God will keep his *c*
8: 18 so confirms his *c*, which he swore
9: 9 of the *c* that the LORD had made
9: 11 stone tablets, the tablets of the *c*.
9: 15 tablets of the *c* were in my hands.
10: 8 the ark of the *c* of the LORD,
17: 2 God in violation of his *c*,
29: 1 in addition to the *c* he had made
29: 1 of the *c* the LORD commanded
29: 9 Carefully follow the terms of this *c*,
29: 12 a *c* the LORD is making
29: 12 into a *c* with the LORD your God,
29: 14 I am making this *c*, with its oath,
29: 21 curses of the *c* written in this Book
29: 25 the *c* he made with them
29: 25 this people abandoned the *c*
31: 9 the ark of the *c* of the LORD,
31: 16 and break the *c* I made with them.
31: 20 rejecting me and breaking my *c*.
31: 25 the ark of the *c* of the LORD:
31: 26 it beside the ark of the *c*
33: 9 and guarded your *c*.
Jos 3: 3 of the *c* of the LORD your God,
3: 6 "Take up the ark of the *c*
3: 8 priests who carry the ark of the *c*:
3: 11 the ark of the *c* of the Lord
3: 14 ark of the *c* went ahead of them.
3: 17 of the *c* of the LORD stood firm
4: 7 the ark of the *c* of the LORD.
4: 9 the ark of the *c* had stood.
4: 18 the ark of the *c* of the LORD.
6: 6 the ark of the *c* of the LORD
6: 8 of the LORD's *c* followed them.
7: 11 have violated my *c*, which I
7: 15 He has violated the *c* of the LORD
8: 33 of the ark of the *c* of the LORD,
23: 16 If you violate the *c*
24: 25 On that day Joshua made a *c*
Jdg 2: 1 'I will never break my *c* with you,
2: 2 and you shall not make a *c*
2: 20 nation has violated the *c* that I laid
20: 27 the ark of the *c* of God was there,
1Sa 4: 3 ark of the LORD's *c* from Shiloh,
4: 4 of the *c* of the LORD Almighty,
4: 4 there with the ark of the *c* of God.
4: 5 the ark of the LORD's *c* came
18: 3 And Jonathan made a *c* with David
20: 8 into a *c* with you before the LORD.
20: 16 Jonathan made a *c* with the house
22: 8 me when my son makes a *c*
23: 18 of them made a *c* before the LORD
2Sa 15: 24 him were carrying the ark of the *c*
23: 5 made with me an everlasting *c*,
1Ki 3: 15 stood before the ark of the Lord's *c*
6: 19 the ark of the *c* of the LORD there.
8: 1 the ark of the LORD's *c* from Zion,
8: 6 the ark of the LORD's *c* to its place
8: 9 where the LORD made a *c*
1Ki 8: 21 in which is the *c* of the LORD that
8: 23 you who keep your *c* of love
11: 11 and you have not kept my *c*
19: 10 The Israelites have rejected your *c*,
19: 14 The Israelites have rejected your *c*,
2Ki 11: 4 He made a *c* with them
11: 12 him with a copy of the *c*
11: 17 He also made a *c* between the king
11: 17 Jehoiada then made a *c*
13: 23 because of his *c* with Abraham,
17: 15 and the *c* he had made
17: 35 When the LORD made a *c*
17: 38 Do not forget the *c* I have made
18: 12 had violated his *c*— all that Moses
23: 2 the words of the Book of the *C*,
23: 3 and renewed the *c* in the presence
23: 3 people pledged themselves to the *c*.
23: 3 words of the *c* written in this book.
23: 21 as it is written in this Book of the *C*
1Ch 15: 25 the ark of the *c* of the LORD
15: 26 the ark of the *c* of the LORD,
15: 28 of the *c* of the LORD with shouts,
15: 29 As the ark of the *c*
16: 6 before the ark of the *c* of God.
16: 15 He remembers his *c* forever,
16: 16 the *c* he made with Abraham,
16: 17 to Israel as an everlasting *c*:
16: 37 the ark of the *c* of the LORD
17: 1 the ark of the *c* of the LORD is
22: 19 the ark of the *c* of the LORD
28: 2 for the ark of the *c* of the LORD,
28: 18 the ark of the *c* of the LORD.
2Ch 5: 2 the ark of the LORD's *c* from Zion,
5: 7 the ark of the LORD's *c* to its place
5: 10 where the LORD made a *c*
6: 11 in which is the *c* of the LORD that
6: 14 you who keep your *c* of love
13: 5 and his descendants forever by a *c*
15: 12 They entered into a *c*
21: 7 of the *c* the LORD had made
23: 1 He made a *c* with the commanders
23: 3 the whole assembly made a *c*
23: 11 him with a copy of the *c*
23: 16 Jehoiada then made a *c* that he
29: 10 intend to make a *c* with the LORD,
34: 30 the words of the Book of the *C*,
34: 31 and renewed the *c* in the presence
34: 31 words of the *c* written in this book.
34: 32 in accordance with the *c* of God,
Ezr 10: 3 let us make a *c* before our God
Ne 1: 5 who keeps his *c* of love
9: 8 and you made a *c* with him to give
9: 32 and awesome God, who keeps his *c*
13: 29 and the *c* of the priesthood
Job 5: 23 For you will have a *c*
31: 1 "I made a *c* with my eyes
Ps 25: 10 who keep the demands of his *c*.
25: 14 he makes his *c* known to them.
44: 17 or been false to your *c*.
50: 5 who made a *c* with me by sacrifice
50: 16 or take my *c* on your lips?
55: 20 he violates his *c*.
74: 20 Have regard for your *c*,
78: 10 they did not keep God's *c*
78: 37 they were not faithful to his *c*.
89: 3 "I have made a *c* with my chosen
89: 28 and my *c* with him will never fail.
89: 34 I will not violate my *c*
89: 39 You have renounced the *c*
103: 18 with those who keep his *c*
105: 8 He remembers his *c* forever,
105: 9 the *c* he made with Abraham,
105: 10 to Israel as an everlasting *c*:
106: 45 for their sake he remembered his *c*
111: 5 he remembers his *c* forever.
111: 9 he ordained his *c* forever—
132: 12 if your sons keep my *c*
Pr 2: 17 ignored the *c* she made before God
Isa 24: 5 and broken the everlasting *c*.
28: 15 into a *c* with death,
28: 18 Your *c* with death will be annulled;
42: 6 you to be a *c* for the people
49: 8 you to be a *c* for the people,
54: 10 nor my *c* of peace be removed,"
55: 3 I will make an everlasting *c*
56: 4 and hold fast to my *c*—
56: 6 and who hold fast to my *c*—
59: 21 this is my *c* with them," says

Isa 61: 8 make an everlasting *c* with them.
Jer 3: 16 'The ark of the *c* of the LORD.'
11: 2 "Listen to the terms of this *c*
11: 3 does not obey the terms of this *c*—
11: 6 'Listen to the terms of this *c*
11: 8 of the *c* I had commanded them
11: 10 of Judah have broken the *c* I made
14: 21 Remember your *c* with us
22: 9 'Because they have forsaken the *c*
31: 31 "when I will make a new *c*
31: 32 It will not be like the *c*
31: 32 because they broke my *c*,
31: 33 "This is the *c* I will make
32: 40 I will make an everlasting *c*
33: 20 *c* with the day and my *c*
33: 21 and my *c* with the Levites who are
33: 21 then my *c* with David my servant
33: 25 'If I have not established my *c*
34: 8 after King Zedekiah had made a *c*
34: 10 into this *c* agreed that they would
34: 13 I made a *c* with your forefathers
34: 15 even made a *c* before me
34: 18 The men who have violated my *c*
34: 18 of the *c* they made before me,
50: 5 the LORD in an everlasting *c*
Eze 16: 8 and entered into a *c* with you,
16: 59 my oath by breaking the *c*.
16: 60 Yet I will remember the *c* I made
16: 60 and I will establish an everlasting *c*
16: 61 not on the basis of my *c* with you.
16: 62 So I will establish my *c* with you,
17: 18 the oath by breaking the *c*.
17: 19 despised and my *c* that he broke.
20: 37 you into the bond of the *c*.
30: 5 and the people of the *c* land will fall
34: 25 I will make a *c* of peace with them
37: 26 I will make a *c* of peace with them;
37: 26 them; it will be an everlasting *c*.
44: 7 fat and blood, and you broke my *c*.
Da 9: 4 who keeps his *c* of love
9: 27 He will confirm a *c* with many
11: 22 a prince of the *c* will be destroyed.
11: 28 set against the holy *c*.
11: 30 and vent his fury against the holy *c*.
11: 30 to those who forsake the holy *c*.
11: 32 those who have violated the *c*,
Hos 2: 18 In that day I will make a *c* for them
6: 7 Like Adam, they have broken the *c*
8: 1 the people have broken my *c*
Zec 9: 11 of the blood of my *c* with you,
11: 10 revoking the *c* I had made
Mal 2: 4 so that my *c* with Levi may
2: 5 "My *c* was with him, a *c* of life
2: 8 you have violated the *c* with Levi,"
2: 10 Why do we profane the *c*
2: 14 the wife of your marriage *c*.
3: 1 of the *c*, whom you desire,
Mt 26: 28 blood of the *c*, which is poured out
Mk 14: 24 "This is my blood of the *c*,
Lk 1: 72 and to remember his holy *c*,
22: 20 "This cup is the new *c* in my blood,
Ac 3: 25 and of the *c* God made
7: 8 Then he gave Abraham the *c*
Ro 11: 27 And this is my *c* with them
1Co 11: 25 "This cup is the new *c* in my blood;
2Co 3: 6 as ministers of a new *c*—
3: 14 remains when the old *c* is read.
Gal 3: 15 to a human *c* that has been duly
3: 17 aside the *c* previously established
4: 24 One *c* is from Mount Sinai
Heb 7: 22 become the guarantee of a better *c*.
8: 6 as the *c* of which he is mediator is
8: 7 nothing wrong with that first *c*,
8: 8 when I will make a new *c*
8: 9 It will not be like the *c*
8: 9 they did not remain faithful to my *c*
8: 10 This is the *c* I will make
8: 13 By calling this *c* "new," he has
9: 1 Now the first *c* had regulations
9: 4 and the gold-covered ark of the *c*.
9: 4 and the stone tablets of the *c*.
9: 15 Christ is the mediator of a new *c*,
9: 15 sins committed under the first *c*.
9: 18 the first *c* was not put into effect
9: 20 "This is the blood of the *c*,
10: 16 "This is the *c* I will make with them
10: 29 blood of the *c* that sanctified him,
12: 24 to Jesus the mediator of a new *c*,
Heb 13: 20 blood of the eternal *c* brought back
Rev 11: 19 his temple was seen the ark of his *c*.

COVENANTED (COVENANT)

2Ch 7: 18 as I *c* with David your father
Hag 2: 5 'This is what I *c* with you

COVENANTS (COVENANT)

Ro 9: 4 theirs the divine glory, the *c*,
Gal 4: 24 for the women represent two *c*.
Eph 2: 12 foreigners to the *c* of the promise,

COVER (COVER-UP COVERED COVERING COVERINGS COVERS GOLD-COVERED)

Ge 20: 16 This is to *c* the offense against you
37: 26 kill our brother and *c* up his blood?
Ex 10: 5 They will *c* the face of the ground
21: 33 digs one and fails to *c* it and an ox
25: 17 "Make an atonement *c* of pure gold
25: 18 gold at the ends of the *c*.
25: 19 cherubim of one piece with the *c*,
25: 20 each other, looking toward the *c*.
25: 20 overshadowing the *c* with them.
25: 21 Place the *c* on top of the ark
25: 22 above the *c* between the two
26: 13 sides of the tabernacle so as to *c* it.
26: 34 Put the atonement *c* on the ark
30: 6 before the atonement *c* that is
31: 7 with the atonement *c* on it,
33: 22 and *c* you with my hand
35: 12 atonement *c* and the curtain that
37: 6 He made the atonement *c*
37: 7 gold at the ends of the *c*.
37: 8 them of one piece with the *c*.
37: 9 each other, looking toward the *c*.
37: 9 overshadowing the *c* with them.
39: 35 with its poles and the atonement *c*;
40: 20 and put the atonement *c* over it.
Lev 13: 45 *c* the lower part of his face
16: 2 front of the atonement *c* on the ark,
16: 2 in the cloud over the atonement *c*.
16: 13 will conceal the atonement *c*
16: 14 it on the front of the atonement *c*;
16: 14 times before the atonement *c*.
16: 15 it on the atonement *c*
17: 13 must drain out the blood and *c* it
Nu 4: 5 *c* the ark of the Testimony with it.
4: 6 Then they are to *c* this with hides
4: 8 *c* that with hides of sea cows
4: 9 *c* the lampstand that is for light,
4: 11 and *c* that with hides of sea cows
4: 12 *c* that with hides of sea cows
7: 89 above the atonement *c* on the ark
22: 5 they *c* the face of the land
Dt 23: 13 dig a hole and *c* up your excrement
Jdg 9: 31 Under *c* he sent messengers
1Ki 18: 6 divided the land they were to *c*,
Ne 4: 5 Do not *c* up their guilt
Job 14: 17 you will *c* over my sin.
16: 18 "O earth, do not *c* my blood,
21: 26 and worms *c* them both.
24: 7 they have nothing to *c* themselves
37: 8 The animals take *c*;
38: 34 and *c* yourself with a flood of water
Ps 10: 9 He lies in wait like a lion in *c*;
17: 12 like a great lion crouching in *c*.
32: 5 and did not *c* up my iniquity.
83: 16 *C* their faces with shame
84: 6 the autumn rains also *c* it
91: 4 He will *c* you with his feathers,
104: 9 never again will they *c* the earth.
Isa 8: 8 outspread wings will *c* the breadth
10: 31 the people of Gebim take *c*.
11: 9 as the waters *c* the sea.
14: 11 and worms *c* you.
14: 21 and *c* the earth with their cities.
54: 9 would never again *c* the earth.
59: 6 they cannot *c* themselves
60: 6 Herds of camels will *c* your land,
Jer 3: 25 and let our disgrace *c* us.
14: 3 they *c* their heads.
14: 4 and *c* their heads.
46: 8 She says, 'I will rise and *c* the earth;
51: 42 its roaring waves will *c* her.
Eze 12: 6 *C* your face so that you cannot see
12: 12 He will *c* his face so that he cannot
13: 10 when a flimsy wall is built, they *c* it
Eze 13: 11 those who *c* it with whitewash that
24: 7 where the dust would *c* it.
24: 17 do not *c* the lower part of your face
24: 22 You will not *c* the lower part
26: 10 be so many that they will *c* you
26: 19 over you and its vast waters *c* you,
32: 7 I snuff you out, I will *c* the heavens
32: 7 I will *c* the sun with a cloud,
37: 6 upon you and *c* you with skin;
Hos 2: 9 intended to *c* her nakedness.
10: 8 and *c* their altars.
10: 8 say to the mountains, "*C* us!"
Mic 3: 7 They will all *c* their faces
Hab 2: 14 as the waters *c* the sea.
2: 16 and disgrace will *c* your glory.
Zec 5: 7 Then the *c* of lead was raised,
5: 8 the lead *c* down over its mouth.
Lk 23: 30 and to the hills, "*C* us!" '
1Co 11: 6 If a woman does not *c* her head,
11: 6 shaved off, she should *c* her head.
11: 7 A man ought not to *c* his head,
1Th 2: 5 did we put on a mask to *c* up greed
Jas 5: 20 and *c* over a multitude of sins.
Rev 3: 18 so you can *c* your shameful

COVER-UP (COVER)

1Pe 2: 16 but do not use your freedom as a *c*

COVERED (COVER)

Ge 7: 19 under the entire heavens were *c*.
7: 20 *c* the mountains to a depth of more
9: 23 and *c* their father's nakedness.
24: 65 So she took her veil and *c* herself.
27: 16 *c* his hands and the smooth part
38: 14 *c* herself with a veil
38: 15 for she had *c* her face.
Ex 8: 6 the frogs came up and *c* the land.
10: 15 They *c* all the ground
10: 22 and total darkness *c* all Egypt
14: 28 and *c* the chariots and horsemen—
15: 5 The deep waters have *c* them;
15: 10 and the sea *c* them.
16: 13 evening quail came and *c* the camp,
19: 18 Mount Sinai was *c* with smoke,
24: 15 up on the mountain, the cloud *c* it,
24: 16 six days the cloud *c* the mountain,
40: 34 the cloud *c* the Tent of Meeting,
Lev 13: 13 if the disease has *c* his whole body,
Nu 7: 3 gifts before the LORD six *c* carts
9: 15 was set up, the cloud *c* it.
9: 16 the cloud *c* it, and at night it looked
16: 42 suddenly the cloud *c* it
Jos 24: 7 the sea over them and *c* them.
Jdg 4: 19 gave him a drink, and *c* him up.
6: 39 and the ground *c* with dew."
6: 40 all the ground was *c* with dew.
2Sa 15: 30 his head was *c* and he was barefoot.
15: 30 people with him *c* their heads too
19: 4 The king *c* his face and cried aloud,
1Ki 6: 15 and *c* the floor of the temple
6: 21 Solomon *c* the inside of the temple
6: 30 also *c* the floors of both the inner
7: 7 and he *c* it with cedar from floor
20: 27 the Arameans *c* the countryside.
2Ki 3: 25 on every good field until it was *c*.
18: 16 gold with which he had *c* the doors
23: 14 and *c* the sites with human bones.
2Ch 3: 5 with pine and *c* it with fine gold
5: 8 and *c* the ark and its carrying poles.
16: 14 him on a bier *c* with spices
Est 6: 12 with his head *c* in grief,
7: 8 king's mouth, they *c* Haman's face.
Job 15: 27 "Though his face is *c* with fat
29: 9 *c* their mouths with their hands;
Ps 32: 1 whose sins are *c*.
34: 5 their faces are never *c* with shame.
44: 15 and my face is *c* with shame
44: 19 and *c* us over with deep darkness.
65: 13 The meadows are *c* with flocks
71: 13 be *c* with scorn and disgrace.
80: 10 The mountains were *c*
85: 2 and *c* all their sins.
89: 45 you have *c* him with a mantle
104: 6 You *c* it with the deep
106: 11 The waters *c* their adversaries;
140: 9 be *c* with the trouble their lips have
Pr 7: 16 I have *c* my bed
24: 31 the ground was *c* with weeds,

CRAFTSMEN (CRAFT)

Ex 31: 6 Also I have given skill to all the *c*
35: 35 all of them master *c* and designers.
35: 35 skill to do all kinds of work as *c*,
36: 4 all the skilled *c* who were doing all
1Ki 5: 18 The *c* of Solomon and Hiram
2Ki 24: 14 and all the *c* and artisans—
24: 16 and a thousand *c* and artisans.
1Ch 4: 14 this because its people were *c*.
22: 16 and iron—*c* beyond number.
29: 5 for all the work to be done by the *c*.
2Ch 2: 7 and Jerusalem with my skilled *c*,
2: 14 He will work with your *c*
Ne 11: 35 and in the Valley of the *C*.
Isa 44: 11 *c* are nothing but men.
Jer 24: 1 the *c* and the artisans
29: 2 the *c* and the artisans had gone
52: 15 along with the rest of the *c*
Eze 27: 9 Veteran *c* of Gebal were on board
Hos 13: 2 all of them the work of *c*.
Zec 1: 20 Then the LORD showed me four *c*.
1: 21 but the *c* have come to terrify them
Ac 19: 24 in no little business for the *c*.
19: 38 and his fellow *c* have a grievance

CRAFTY (CRAFT)

Ge 3: 1 the serpent was more *c* than any
1Sa 23: 22 They tell me he is very *c*.
Job 5: 12 He thwarts the plans of the *c*,
15: 5 you adopt the tongue of the *c*.
Pr 7: 10 like a prostitute and with *c* intent.
12: 2 but the LORD condemns a *c* man.
14: 17 and a *c* man is hated.
2Co 12: 16 *c* fellow that I am, I caught you

CRAG (CRAGS)

Dt 32: 13 and with oil from the flinty *c*,
Job 39: 28 a rocky *c* is his stronghold.
Ps 78: 16 he brought streams out of a rocky *c*

CRAGS (CRAG)

1Sa 24: 2 and his men near the *C*
Ps 104: 18 the *c* are a refuge for the coneys.
Pr 30: 26 yet they make their home in the *c*;
Isa 2: 21 and to the overhanging *c*
57: 5 and under the overhanging *c*.
Am 6: 12 Do horses run on the rocky *c*?

CRASH

Zep 1: 10 and a loud *c* from the hills.
Mt 7: 27 house, and it fell with a great *c*."

CRAVE (CRAVED CRAVES CRAVING CRAVINGS)

Nu 11: 4 with them began to *c* other food,
Dt 12: 20 you *c* meat and say, "I would like
Pr 23: 3 Do not *c* his delicacies,
23: 6 do not *c* his delicacies;
31: 4 not for rulers to *c* beer,
Mic 7: 1 none of the early figs that I *c*.
1Pe 2: 2 newborn babies, *c* pure spiritual

CRAVED (CRAVE)

Nu 11: 34 the people who had *c* other food.
Ps 78: 18 by demanding the food they *c*.
78: 29 for he had given them what they *c*.
78: 30 turned from the food they *c*,

CRAVES (CRAVE)

Pr 13: 4 The sluggard *c* and gets nothing,
21: 10 The wicked man *c* evil;
21: 26 All day long he *c* for more,

CRAVING (CRAVE)

Job 20: 20 he will have no respite from his *c*;
Ps 106: 14 In the desert they gave in to their *c*;
Pr 10: 3 but he thwarts the *c* of the wicked.
13: 2 the unfaithful have a *c* for violence.
21: 25 The sluggard's *c* will be the death
Jer 2: 24 sniffing the wind in her *c*—

CRAVINGS (CRAVE)

Ps 10: 3 He boasts of the *c* of his heart;
Eph 2: 3 gratifying the *c* of our sinful nature
1Jn 2: 16 in the world—the *c* of sinful man,

CRAWL (CRAWLING)

Ge 3: 14 You will *c* on your belly
Mic 7: 17 like creatures that *c* on the ground.

CRAWLING (CRAWL)

Lev 22: 5 he touches any *c* thing that makes
1Sa 14: 11 "The Hebrews are *c* out
Eze 8: 10 over the walls all kinds of *c* things

CREAM

Job 20: 17 the rivers flowing with honey and *c*
29: 6 when my path was drenched with *c*

CREATE (CREATED CREATES CREATING CREATION CREATOR)

Ps 51: 10 *C* in me a pure heart, O God,
Isa 4: 5 Then the LORD will *c* over all
45: 7 I bring prosperity and *c* disaster;
45: 7 I form the light and *c* darkness,
45: 18 he did not *c* it to be empty,
65: 17 "Behold, I will *c*
65: 18 for I will *c* Jerusalem to be a delight
65: 18 forever in what I will *c*,
Jer 31: 22 The LORD will *c* a new thing
Mal 2: 10 one Father? Did not one God *c* us?
Eph 2: 15 His purpose was to *c*

CREATED (CREATE)

Ge 1: 1 In the beginning God *c* the heavens
1: 21 God *c* the great creatures of the sea
1: 27 So God *c* man in his own image,
1: 27 in the image of God he *c* him;
1: 27 male and female he *c* them.
2: 4 and the earth when they were *c*.
5: 1 When God *c* man, he made him
5: 2 He *c* them male and female;
5: 2 time they were *c*, he blessed them
6: 7 whom I have *c*, from the face
Dt 4: 32 from the day God *c* man
Ps 89: 12 You *c* the north and the south;
89: 47 what futility you have *c* all men!
102: 18 a people not yet *c* may praise
104: 30 they are *c*,
139: 13 For you *c* my inmost being;
148: 5 for he commanded and they were *c*
Isa 40: 26 Who *c* all these?
41: 20 that the Holy One of Israel has *c* it.
42: 5 he who *c* the heavens and stretched
43: 1 he who *c* you, O Jacob,
43: 7 whom I *c* for my glory,
45: 8 I, the LORD, have *c* it.
45: 12 and *c* mankind upon it.
45: 18 he who *c* the heavens,
48: 7 They are *c* now, and not long ago;
54: 16 And it is I who have *c* the destroyer
54: 16 "See, it is I who *c* the blacksmith
57: 16 the breath of man that I have *c*.
Eze 21: 30 In the place where you were *c*,
28: 13 the day you were *c* they were
28: 15 ways from the day you were *c*
Mk 13: 19 when God *c* the world, until now—
Ro 1: 25 and served *c* things rather
1Co 11: 9 neither was man *c* for woman,
Eph 2: 10 *c* in Christ Jesus to do good works,
3: 9 hidden in God, who *c* all things.
4: 24 *c* to be like God in true
Col 1: 16 For by him all things were *c*:
1: 16 all things were *c* by him
1Ti 4: 3 which God *c* to be received
4: 4 For everything God *c* is good,
Heb 12: 27 *c* things—so that what cannot be
Jas 1: 18 a kind of firstfruits of all he *c*.
Rev 4: 11 and by your will they were *c*
4: 11 for you *c* all things,
10: 6 who *c* the heavens and all that is

CREATES (CREATE)

Am 4: 13 *c* the wind,

CREATING (CREATE)

Ge 2: 3 the work of *c* that he had done.
Isa 57: 19 *c* praise on the lips of the mourners

CREATION (CREATE)

Hab 2: 18 he who makes it trusts in his own *c*;
Mt 13: 35 hidden since the *c* of the world."
25: 34 for you since the *c* of the world.
Mk 10: 6 of *c* God 'made them male
16: 15 and preach the good news to all *c*.
Jn 17: 24 me before the *c* of the world.
Ro 1: 20 For since the *c* of the world God's
8: 19 The *c* waits in eager expectation
8: 20 For the *c* was subjected
8: 21 in hope that the *c* itself will be
8: 22 that the whole *c* has been groaning
8: 39 depth, nor anything else in all *c*,
2Co 5: 17 he is a new *c*; the old has gone,
Gal 6: 15 anything; what counts is a new *c*.
Eph 1: 4 us in him before the *c* of the world
Col 1: 15 God, the firstborn over all *c*.
Heb 4: 3 finished since the *c* of the world.
4: 13 Nothing in all *c* is hidden
9: 11 that is to say, not a part of this *c*.
9: 26 times since the *c* of the world.
1Pe 1: 20 chosen before the *c* of the world,
2Pe 3: 4 as it has since the beginning of *c*."
Rev 3: 14 true witness, the ruler of God's *c*.
13: 8 slain from the *c* of the world.
17: 8 life from the *c* of the world will be

CREATOR (CREATE)

Ge 14: 19 *C* of heaven and earth.
14: 22 God Most High, *C* of heaven
Dt 32: 6 Is he not your Father, your *C*,
Ecc 12: 1 Remember your *C*
Isa 27: 11 and their *C* shows them no favor.
40: 28 the *C* of the ends of the earth.
43: 15 Israel's *C*, your King."
Mt 19: 4 the beginning the *C* 'made them
Ro 1: 25 created things rather than the *C*
Col 3: 10 in knowledge in the image of its *C*.
1Pe 4: 19 themselves to their faithful *C*

CREATURE (CREATURES)

Ge 1: 28 and over every living *c* that moves
2: 19 the man called each living *c*,
6: 17 every *c* that has the breath of life
6: 20 and of every kind of *c* that moves
7: 4 earth every living *c* I have made."
7: 14 every *c* that moves
8: 17 kind of living *c* that is with you—
9: 2 upon every *c* that moves
9: 10 and with every living *c* that was
9: 10 with you—every living *c* on earth.
9: 12 you and every living *c* with you,
Lev 11: 41 " 'Every *c* that moves about
11: 42 not to eat any *c* that moves about
11: 44 unclean by any *c* that moves about
11: 46 and every *c* that moves about
17: 11 For the life of a *c* is in the blood,
17: 14 You must not eat the blood of any *c*
17: 14 the life of every *c* is its blood
17: 14 the life of every *c* is its blood;
Dt 4: 18 or like any *c* that moves
14: 20 any winged *c* that is clean you may
Job 12: 10 In his hand is the life of every *c*
14: 15 for the *c* your hands have made.
41: 33 a *c* without fear.
Ps 136: 25 and who gives food to every *c*.
145: 21 Let every *c* praise his holy name
Isa 47: 8 "Now then, listen, you wanton *c*,
Eze 1: 11 one touching the wing of another *c*
1: 15 beside each *c* with its four faces.
38: 20 every *c* that moves
Da 4: 12 from it every *c* was fed.
Col 1: 23 to every *c* under heaven,
Rev 4: 7 The first living *c* was like a lion,
5: 13 Then I heard every *c* in heaven
6: 3 I heard the second living *c* say,
6: 5 I heard the third living *c* say,
6: 7 the voice of the fourth living *c* say,

CREATURES (CREATURE)

Ge 1: 20 "Let the water teem with living *c*,
1: 21 God created the great *c* of the sea
1: 24 the land produce living *c* according
1: 24 *c* that move along the ground,
1: 25 and all the *c* that move
1: 26 and over all the *c* that move
1: 30 all the *c* that move on the ground—
6: 7 and *c* that move along the ground,
6: 19 bring into the ark two of all living *c*,
7: 8 of all *c* that move along the ground,
7: 15 Pairs of all *c* that have the breath
7: 21 all the *c* that swarm over the earth,
7: 23 the *c* that move along the ground
8: 17 and all the *c* that move
8: 19 and all the *c* that move

Ge 8:21 again will I destroy all living *c*,
9:15 you and all living *c* of every kind.
9:16 and all living *c* of every kind
Lev 5:2 or of unclean *c* that move
11:9 " 'Of all the *c* living in the water
11:10 all *c* in the seas or streams that do
11:10 or among all the other living *c*
11:21 some winged *c* that walk
11:23 all other winged *c* that have four
11:43 defile yourselves by any of these *c*.
11:47 between living *c* that may be eaten
Dt 14:9 Of all the *c* living in the water,
Ps 50:11 and the *c* of the field are mine.
74:14 food to the *c* of the desert.
80:13 and the *c* of the field feed on it.
104:24 the earth is full of your *c*.
104:25 teeming with *c* beyond number—
148:7 you great sea *c* and all ocean
148:10 small *c* and flying birds,
Pr 30:25 Ants are *c* of little strength,
30:26 conies are *c* of little power,
Isa 13:21 But desert *c* will lie there,
23:13 a place for desert *c*;
34:14 Desert *c* will meet with hyenas,
34:14 there the night *c* will also repose
Jer 50:39 desert *c* and hyenas will live there,
Eze 1:5 was what looked like four living *c*.
1:13 moved back and forth among the *c*;
1:13 of the living *c* was like burning
1:14 *c* sped back and forth like flashes
1:15 As I looked at the living *c*,
1:17 did not turn about as the *c* went.
1:17 of the four directions the *c* faced;
1:19 When the living *c* moved,
1:19 and when the living *c* rose
1:20 of the living *c* was in the wheels.
1:21 When the *c* moved, they
1:21 also moved; when the *c* stood still,
1:21 of the living *c* was in the wheels.
1:21 when the *c* rose from the ground,
1:22 of the living *c* was what looked like
1:24 When the *c* moved, I heard
3:13 the wings of the living *c* brushing
10:15 These were the living *c* I had seen
10:17 the spirit of the living *c* was in them
10:20 These were the living *c* I had seen
47:9 of living *c* will live wherever
Hos 2:18 the *c* that move along the ground.
Mic 7:17 like *c* that crawl on the ground.
Hab 1:14 like sea *c* that have no ruler.
Zep 2:14 *c* of every kind.
Jas 3:7 and *c* of the sea are being tamed
2Pe 2:12 They are like brute beasts, *c*
Rev 4:6 the throne, were four living *c*,
4:8 of the four living *c* had six wings
4:9 Whenever the living *c* give glory,
5:6 encircled by the four living *c*
5:8 four living *c* and the twenty-four
5:11 and the living *c* and the elders.
5:14 The four living *c* said, "Amen,"
6:1 one of the four living *c* say
6:6 a voice among the four living *c*,
7:11 the elders and the four living *c*.
8:9 a third of the living *c* in the sea died
14:3 and before the four living *c*
15:7 Then one of the four living *c* gave
19:4 and the four living *c* fell down

CREDIT (ACCREDITED CREDITED CREDITOR CREDITORS CREDITS)

Est 2:22 it to the king, giving *c* to Mordecai.
Lk 6:32 those who love you, what *c* is that
6:33 what *c* is that to you? Even
6:34 what *c* is that to you? Even
Ro 4:24 to whom God will *c* righteousness
1Pe 2:20 it to your *c* if you receive a beating

CREDITED (CREDIT)

Ge 15:6 and he *c* it to him as righteousness.
Lev 7:18 It will not be *c* to the one who
1Sa 18:8 "They have *c* David with tens
Ps 106:31 This was *c* to him as righteousness
Eze 18:20 of the righteous man will be *c*
Ro 4:3 and it was *c* to him as righteousness
4:4 his wages are not *c* to him as a gift,
4:5 his faith is *c* as righteousness.
4:9 saying that Abraham's faith was *c*
4:10 Under what circumstances was it *c*
Ro 4:11 order that righteousness might be *c*
4:22 This is why "it was *c* to him
4:23 The words "it was *c*
Gal 3:6 and it was *c* to him as righteousness
Php 4:17 for what may be *c* to your account.
Jas 2:23 and it was *c* to him as righteousness

CREDITOR (CREDIT)

Dt 15:2 Every *c* shall cancel the loan he has
2Ki 4:1 But now his *c* is coming
Ps 109:11 May a *c* seize all he has;
Isa 24:2 for debtor as for *c*.

CREDITORS (CREDIT)

Isa 50:1 Or to which of my *c*

CREDITS (CREDIT)

Ro 4:6 whom God *c* righteousness apart

CREPT

1Sa 24:4 Then David *c* up unnoticed
Hab 3:16 decay *c* into my bones,

CRESCENS

2Ti 4:10 *C* has gone to Galatia,

CRESCENT

Isa 3:18 and headbands and *c* necklaces,

CREST

Est 6:8 one with a royal *c* placed
SS 4:8 Descend from the *c* of Amana,

CRETANS (CRETE)

Ac 2:11 converts to Judaism); *C* and Arabs
Tit 1:12 "*C* are always liars, evil brutes,

CRETE (CRETANS)

Ac 27:7 to the lee of *C*, opposite Salmone.
27:12 harbor in *C*, facing both southwest
27:13 and sailed along the shore of *C*.
27:21 taken my advice not to sail from *C*;
Tit 1:5 in *C* was that you might straighten

CREVICE (CREVICES)

Jer 13:4 hide it there in a *c* in the rocks."

CREVICES (CREVICE)

Isa 7:19 and in the *c* in the rocks,
Jer 16:16 and hill and from the *c* of the rocks.

CRICKET

Lev 11:22 katydid, *c* or grasshopper.

CRIED (CRY)

Ge 41:55 the people *c* to Pharaoh for food.
45:1 he *c* out, "Have everyone leave my
Ex 2:23 groaned in their slavery and *c* out,
8:12 Moses *c* out to the LORD about
14:10 They were terrified and *c* out
15:25 Then Moses *c* out to the LORD,
17:4 Then Moses *c* out to the LORD,
Nu 11:2 When the people *c* out to Moses,
12:13 So Moses *c* out to the LORD,
16:22 and Aaron fell facedown and *c* out,
20:16 but when we *c* out to the LORD,
Dt 26:7 Then we *c* out to the LORD,
Jos 24:7 But they *c* to the LORD for help,
Jdg 3:9 But when they *c* out to the LORD,
3:15 Again the Israelites *c* out
4:3 they *c* to the LORD for help.
5:28 behind the lattice she *c* out,
6:6 the Israelites that they *c* out
6:7 When the Israelites *c* to the LORD
10:10 the Israelites *c* out to the LORD,
10:12 Maonites oppressed you and you *c*
11:35 he tore his clothes and *c*, "Oh!
14:17 She *c* the whole seven days
15:18 he was very thirsty, he *c* out
21:3 the God of Israel," they *c*,
1Sa 5:10 the people of Ekron *c* out,
7:9 He *c* out to the LORD
12:8 they *c* to the LORD for help,
12:10 They *c* out to the LORD and said,
15:11 he *c* out to the LORD all that night
28:12 she *c* out at the top of her voice
2Sa 19:4 king covered his face and *c* aloud,
22:42 They *c* for help, but there was no
1Ki 13:2 He *c* out against the altar
1Ki 13:4 man of God *c* out against the altar
13:21 He *c* out to the man
17:20 Then he *c* out to the LORD,
17:21 out on the boy three times and *c*
18:39 fell prostrate and *c*, "The LORD—
22:32 but when Jehoshaphat *c* out,
2Ki 2:12 saw this and *c* out, "My father!
4:1 of the prophets *c* out to Elisha,
4:40 they *c* out, "O man of God,
6:5 he *c* out, "it was borrowed!"
6:26 a woman *c* to him, "Help me,
13:14 "My father! My father!" he *c*.
1Ch 4:10 Jabez *c* out to the God of Israel,
5:20 they *c* out to him during the battle.
2Ch 13:14 Then they *c* out to the LORD.
18:31 but Jehoshaphat *c* out,
32:20 son of Amoz *c* out in prayer
Ne 9:27 they were oppressed they *c* out
9:28 And when they *c* out to you again,
Job 29:12 I rescued the poor who *c* for help,
Ps 18:6 I *c* to my God for help.
18:41 They *c* for help, but there was no
22:5 They *c* to you and were saved;
30:8 to the Lord I *c* for mercy:
31:17 for I have *c* out to you;
66:17 I *c* out to him with my mouth;
77:1 I *c* out to God for help;
77:1 I *c* out to God to hear me.
107:6 they *c* out to the LORD
107:13 they *c* to the LORD
107:19 they *c* to the LORD
107:28 they *c* out to the LORD
118:5 In my anguish I *c* to the LORD,
137:7 "Tear it down," they *c*,
Isa 6:5 "Woe to me!" I *c*.
38:14 I *c* like a swift or thrush,
Eze 11:13 Then I fell facedown and *c* out
Am 7:2 I *c* out, "Sovereign LORD, forgive
7:5 Then I *c* out, "Sovereign LORD,
Jnh 1:5 and each *c* out to his own god.
1:14 Then they *c* to the LORD,
Mt 14:26 they said, and *c* out in fear.
14:30 beginning to sink, *c* out, "Lord,
27:46 About the ninth hour Jesus *c* out
27:50 And when Jesus had *c* out again
Mk 1:23 possessed by an evil spirit *c* out,
3:11 they fell down before him and *c* out
6:49 They *c* out, because they all saw
15:34 And at the ninth hour Jesus *c* out
Lk 4:33 He *c* out at the top of his voice,
8:28 he *c* out and fell at his feet,
23:18 With one voice they *c* out,
Jn 7:28 *c* out, "Yes, you know me,
12:44 Jesus *c* out, "When a man believes
20:16 toward him and *c* out in Aramaic,
Ac 7:60 Then he fell on his knees and *c* out,
Rev 7:10 And they *c* out in a loud voice:
12:2 She was pregnant and *c* out in pain
19:4 And they *c*:
19:17 who *c* in a loud voice

CRIES (CRY)

Ge 4:10 Your brother's blood *c* out to me
Ex 22:27 When he *c* out to me, I will hear,
Nu 16:34 At their *c*, all the Israelites
Job 30:24 when he *c* for help in his distress.
31:38 "if my land *c* out against me
Ps 47:1 shout to God with *c* of joy.
Pr 1:21 head of the noisy streets she *c* out,
8:3 at the entrances, she *c* aloud:
Isa 5:7 for righteousness, but heard *c*
15:5 My heart *c* out over Moab;
26:17 writhes and *c* out in her pain,
46:7 Though one *c* out to it, it does not
56:12 each one *c*, "let me get wine!
Jer 30:5 " '*C* of fear are heard—
46:12 your *c* will fill the earth.
48:3 Listen to the *c* from Horonaim,
48:3 *c* of great havoc and destruction.
48:5 anguished *c* over the destruction
Hos 8:2 Israel *c* out to me,
Am 1:14 amid war *c* on the day of battle,
2:2 tumult amid war *c* and the blast
5:16 *c* of anguish in every public square.
Jn 1:15 He *c* out, saying, "This was he
Ro 9:27 Isaiah *c* out concerning Israel:
Heb 5:7 prayers and petitions with loud *c*
Jas 5:4 *c* of the harvesters have reached

CRIME (CRIMES CRIMINAL CRIMINALS)

Ge 31:36 "What is my *c?*" he asked Laban.
Dt 19:15 to convict a man accused of any *c*
19:16 the stand to accuse a man of a *c,*
25: 2 the number of lashes his *c* deserves,
Jdg 9:24 this in order that the *c*
20:12 about this awful *c* that was
1Sa 20: 1 What is my *c?* How have I
Ezr 6:11 And for this *c* his house is
Ps 69:27 Charge them with *c* upon *c;*
Ecc 8:11 for a *c* is not quickly carried out,
Jer 37:18 "What *c* have I committed
Hab 2:12 and establishes a town by *c!*
Mt 27:23 "Why? What *c* has he committed?"
Mk 15:14 "Why? What *c* has he committed?"
Lk 23:22 What *c* has this man committed?
Ac 18:14 some misdemeanor or serious *c,*
24:20 should state what *c* they found
28:18 guilty of any *c* deserving death.

CRIMES (CRIME)

Ecc 8:12 a wicked man commits a hundred *c*
Jer 18:23 Do not forgive their *c*
41:11 heard about all the *c* Ishmael son
Hos 6: 9 committing shameful *c.*
7: 1 and the *c* of Samaria revealed.
Ac 25:18 with any of the *c* I had expected.
Rev 18: 5 and God has remembered her *c.*

CRIMINAL (CRIME)

Lk 23:40 But the other *c* rebuked him.
Jn 18:30 "If he were not a *c,*" they replied,
2Ti 2: 9 the point of being chained like a *c.*
1Pe 4:15 or thief or any other kind of *c,*

CRIMINALS (CRIME)

1Ki 1:21 son Solomon will be treated as *c.*"
Lk 23:32 both *c,* were also led out with him
23:33 along with the *c*— one on his right,
23:39 One of the *c* who hung there hurled

CRIMSON

2Ch 2: 7 and in purple, *c* and blue yarn,
2:14 and blue and *c* yarn and fine linen.
3:14 purple and *c* yarn and fine linen,
Isa 1:18 though they are red as *c,*
63: 1 with his garments stained *c?*

CRINGE (CRINGING)

Ps 18:44 foreigners *c* before me.
66: 3 that your enemies *c* before you.
81:15 who hate the LORD would *c*
Isa 10: 4 but to *c* among the captives

CRINGING (CRINGE)

2Sa 22:45 and foreigners come *c* to me;

CRIPPLE (CRIPPLED CRIPPLES)

Ac 4: 9 for an act of kindness shown to a *c*

CRIPPLED (CRIPPLE)

Lev 21:19 no man with a *c* foot or hand,
2Sa 4: 4 to leave, he fell and became *c.*
9: 3 of Jonathan; he is *c* in both feet."
9:13 ate at the king's table, and he was *c*
Mal 1: 8 When you sacrifice *c* or diseased
1:13 *c* or diseased animals and offer
Mt 15:30 the *c,* the dumb and many others,
15:31 the *c* made well, the lame walking
18: 8 or *c* than to have two hands
Mk 9:45 better for you to enter life *c*
Lk 13:11 a woman was there who had been *c*
14:13 invite the poor, the *c,* the lame,
14:21 the *c,* the blind and the lame.'
Ac 3: 2 man *c* from birth was being carried
14: 8 In Lystra there sat a man *c*

CRIPPLES (CRIPPLE)

Ac 8: 7 many paralytics and *c* were healed.

CRISIS

1Co 7:26 of the present *c,* I think that it is

CRISPUS

Ac 18: 8 *C,* the synagogue ruler,
1Co 1:14 did not baptize any of you except *C*

CRITICAL (CRITICISM)

1Sa 13: 6 Israel saw that their situation was *c*

CRITICISM (CRITICAL CRITICIZED)

2Co 8:20 We want to avoid any *c*

CRITICIZED (CRITICISM)

Jdg 8: 1 Midian?" And they *c* him sharply.
Ac 11: 2 the circumcised believers *c* him

CROCUS

Isa 35: 1 Like the *c,*

CROOKED

Dt 32: 5 but a warped and *c* generation.
2Sa 22:27 to the *c* you show yourself shrewd.
Ps 18:26 to the *c* you show yourself shrewd.
125: 5 But those who turn to *c* ways
Pr 2:15 whose paths are *c*
5: 6 her paths are *c,* but she knows it
8: 8 none of them is *c* or perverse.
10: 9 he who takes *c* paths will be found
Ecc 7:13 what he has made *c?*
Isa 59: 8 have turned them into *c* roads;
La 3: 9 he has made my paths *c.*
Lk 3: 5 The *c* roads shall become straight,
Php 2:15 children of God without fault in a *c*

CROP (CROPS)

Ge 47:24 when the *c* comes in, give a fifth
Lev 1:16 is to remove the *c* with its contents
25:22 you will eat from the old *c*
Isa 5: 2 he looked for a *c* of good grapes,
Am 7: 1 just as the second *c* was coming up.
Hab 3:17 though the olive *c* fails
Mt 13: 8 where it produced a *c*— a hundred,
13:23 He produces a *c,* yielding
21:41 share of the *c* at harvest time."
Mk 4: 8 produced a *c,* multiplying thirty,
4:20 accept it, and produce a *c*— thirty,
Lk 8: 8 It came up and yielded a *c,*
8:15 and by persevering produce a *c.*
12:16 rich man produced a good *c.*
Jn 4:36 even now he harvests the *c*
Heb 6: 7 that produces a *c* useful to those
Jas 5: 7 for the land to yield its valuable *c*

CROPS (CROP)

Ge 4:12 it will no longer yield its *c* for you.
26:12 Isaac planted *c* in that land
Ex 23:10 to sow your fields and harvest the *c*
23:16 gather in your *c* from the field.
23:16 with the firstfruits of the *c* you sow
Lev 23:39 after you have gathered the *c*
25: 3 your vineyards and gather their *c.*
25:15 of years left for harvesting *c.*
25:16 selling you is the number of *c.*
25:20 if we do not plant or harvest our *c*
26: 4 and the ground will yield its *c*
26:20 because your soil will not yield its *c*
Dt 7:13 the *c* of your land—your grain,
22: 9 not only the *c* you plant but
28: 4 the *c* of your land and the young
28:11 and the *c* of your ground—
28:18 womb will be cursed, and the *c*
28:42 take over all your trees and the *c*
28:51 and the *c* of your land until you are
30: 9 young of your livestock and the *c*
Jdg 6: 3 the Israelites planted their *c,*
6: 4 ruined the *c* all the way to Gaza
2Sa 9:10 the land for him and bring in the *c,*
Ne 10:35 each year the firstfruits of our *c*
10:37 a tithe of our *c* to the Levites,
Job 31: 8 and may my *c* be uprooted.
Ps 65:10 and bless its *c.*
78:46 He gave their *c* to the grasshopper,
Pr 3: 9 with the firstfruits of all your *c;*
10: 5 He who gathers *c* in summer is
28: 3 like a driving rain that leaves no *c.*
Jer 35: 9 or had vineyards, fields or *c.*
Eze 34:27 and the ground will yield its *c;*
34:29 for them a land renowned for its *c,*
36:30 of the trees and the *c* of the field,
Hag 1:10 their dew and the earth its *c.*
Zec 8:12 the ground will produce its *c,*
Mal 3:11 pests from devouring your *c,*
Lk 12:17 I have no place to store my *c.*'
Ac 14:17 from heaven and *c* in their seasons;
2Ti 2: 6 the first to receive a share of the *c.*
Jas 5:18 and the earth produced its *c.*
Rev 22: 2 bearing twelve *c* of fruit, yielding

CROSS (CROSSED CROSSES CROSSING CROSSINGS)

Ex 30:14 All who *c* over, those twenty years
Nu 32: 5 Do not make us *c* the Jordan."
32:27 will *c* over to fight
32:29 *c* over the Jordan with you
32:30 they do not *c* over with you armed,
32:32 We will *c* over before the LORD
33:51 'When you *c* the Jordan
34: 4 the end of the Salt Sea, *c* south
35:10 'When you *c* the Jordan
Dt 2:13 Now get up and *c* the Zered Valley
2:24 "Set out now and *c* the Arnon
2:29 until we *c* the Jordan
3:18 must *c* over ahead
3:27 you are not going to *c* this Jordan.
4:21 swore that I would not *c* the Jordan
4:22 but you are about to *c* over
4:22 in this land; I will not *c* the Jordan;
9: 1 about to *c* the Jordan to go
11:31 You are about to *c* the Jordan
12:10 But you will *c* the Jordan
30:13 "Who will *c* the sea to get it
31: 2 'You shall not *c* the Jordan.'
31: 3 also will *c* over ahead of you,
31: 3 LORD your God himself will *c*
34: 4 but you will not *c* over into it."
Jos 1: 2 get ready to *c* the Jordan River
1:11 now you will *c* the Jordan here
1:14 must *c* over ahead of your brothers.
3: 6 and *c* over ahead of the people."
3:14 people broke camp to *c* the Jordan,
Jdg 3:28 they allowed no one to *c* over.
12: 5 "Let me *c* over," the men
1Sa 14: 4 pass that Jonathan intended to *c*
14: 8 we will *c* over toward the men
30:10 were too exhausted to *c* the ravine.
2Sa 17:16 in the desert; *c* over without fail,
17:21 "Set out and *c* the river at once;
19:31 down from Rogelim to *c* the Jordan
19:33 "*C* over with me and stay with me
19:36 Your servant will *c* over the Jordan
19:37 Let him *c* over with my lord
19:38 "Kimham shall *c* over with me,
1Ki 2:37 you leave and *c* the Kidron Valley,
Ps 104: 9 You set a boundary they cannot *c;*
Isa 11:15 so that men can *c* over in sandals.
23: 6 *C* over to Tarshish;
23:12 "Up, *c* over to Cyprus;
51:10 so that the redeemed might *c* over?
Jer 2:10 *C* over to the coasts of Kittim
5:22 an everlasting barrier it cannot *c.*
5:22 they may roar, but they cannot *c* it.
9:12 like a desert that no one can *c?*
41:10 set out to *c* over to the Ammonites.
Eze 33:28 desolate so that no one will *c* them.
47: 5 a river that no one could *c.*
47: 5 now it was a river that I could not *c*
Mt 8:18 he gave orders to *c* to the other side
10:38 and anyone who does not take his *c*
16:24 and take up his *c* and follow me.
27:32 and they forced him to carry the *c.*
27:40 yourself! Come down from the *c,*
27:42 come down now from the *c,*
Mk 8:34 and take up his *c* and follow me.
15:21 and they forced him to carry the *c.*
15:30 come down from the *c*
15:32 come down now from the *c,*
Lk 9:23 take up his *c* daily and follow me.
14:27 anyone who does not carry his *c*
16:26 can anyone *c* over from there to us
23:26 and put the *c* on him and made him
Jn 19:17 Carrying his own *c,* he went out
19:19 prepared and fastened to the *c.*
19:25 Near the *c* of Jesus stood his
Ac 2:23 to death by nailing him to the *c.*
1Co 1:17 lest the *c* of Christ be emptied
1:18 the message of the *c* is foolishness
Gal 5:11 offense of the *c* has been abolished.
6:12 persecuted for the *c* of Christ.
6:14 in the *c* of our Lord Jesus Christ,
Eph 2:16 both of them to God through the *c,*
Php 2: 8 even death on a *c!*
3:18 as enemies of the *c* of Christ.

Col 1:20 through his blood, shed on the *c*.
2:14 he took it away, nailing it to the *c*.
2:15 triumphing over them by the *c*.
Heb 12:2 set before him endured the *c*,

CROSS-EXAMINED (EXAMINE)

Ac 12:19 he *c* the guards and ordered that

CROSSBAR (CROSSBARS)

Ex 26:28 The center *c* is to extend from end
36:33 They made the center *c*

CROSSBARS (CROSSBAR)

Ex 26:26 "Also make *c* of acacia wood:
26:29 Also overlay the *c* with gold.
26:29 and make gold rings to hold the *c*.
35:11 clasps, frames, *c*, posts and bases;
36:31 They also made *c* of acacia wood:
36:34 They also overlaid the *c* with gold.
36:34 and made gold rings to hold the *c*.
39:33 frames, *c*, posts and bases;
40:18 inserted the *c* and set up the posts.
Nu 3:36 its *c*, posts, bases, all its equipment,
4:31 the frames of the tabernacle, its *c*,
Jer 27:2 and *c* and put it on your neck.

CROSSED (CROSS)

Ge 32:10 staff when I *c* this Jordan,
32:22 and *c* the ford of the Jabbok.
Ex 38:26 from everyone who had *c*
Dt 2:13 So we *c* the valley.
2:14 Barnea until we *c* the Zered Valley.
27:2 When you have *c* the Jordan
27:3 words of this law when you have *c*
27:4 And when you have *c* the Jordan,
27:12 When you have *c* the Jordan,
Jos 3:16 the people *c* over opposite Jericho.
4:7 When it *c* the Jordan, the waters
4:11 and as soon as all of them had *c*,
4:12 the half-tribe of Manasseh *c* over,
4:13 for battle *c* over before the LORD
4:22 'Israel *c* the Jordan on dry ground.'
4:23 before you until you had *c* over.
4:23 up before us until we had *c* over.
5:1 the Israelites until we had *c* over,
15:3 end of the Salt Sea, *c* south
15:10 to Beth Shemesh and *c* to Timnah.
16:2 *c* over to the territory
18:13 From there it *c* to the south slope
24:11 " 'Then you *c* the Jordan
Jdg 6:33 eastern peoples joined forces and *c*
8:4 came to the Jordan and *c* it.
10:9 *c* the Jordan to fight against Judah,
11:29 He *c* Gilead and Manasseh,
12:1 *c* over to Zaphon and said
12:3 and *c* over to fight the Ammonites,
1Sa 13:7 *c* the Jordan to the land of Gad
26:13 Then David *c* over to the other side
2Sa 2:29 They *c* the Jordan, continued
10:17 *c* the Jordan and went to Helam.
15:23 The king also *c* the Kidron Valley,
17:20 woman answered them, "They *c*
17:22 was left who had not *c* the Jordan.
17:22 with him set out and *c* the Jordan.
17:24 and Absalom *c* the Jordan
19:18 They *c* at the ford to take the king's
19:18 son of Gera *c* the Jordan,
19:39 So all the people *c* the Jordan,
19:39 the Jordan, and then the king *c*
19:40 When the king *c* over to Gilgal,
19:40 over to Gilgal, Kimham *c* with him.
2Ki 2:8 two of them *c* over on dry ground.
2:9 When they had *c*, Elijah said
2:14 and to the left, and he *c* over.
1Ch 12:15 It was they who *c* the Jordan
19:17 all Israel and *c* the Jordan;
Mt 9:1 *c* over and came to his own town.
14:34 When they had *c* over, they landed
Mk 5:21 When Jesus had again *c*
6:53 When they had *c* over, they landed
8:13 into the boat and *c* to the other side
Jn 5:24 he has *c* over from death to life.
6:1 Jesus *c* to the far shore of the Sea
18:1 his disciples and *c* the Kidron
Ac 20:15 day after that we *c* over to Samos,

CROSSES (CROSS)

Ex 30:13 one who *c* over to those already
Jn 19:31 left on the *c* during the Sabbath,

CROSSING (CROSS)

Ge 31:21 with all he had, and *c* the River,
48:14 he was the younger, and *c* his arms,
Dt 4:14 the land that you are *c* the Jordan
4:26 the land that you are *c* the Jordan
6:1 the land that you are *c* the Jordan
11:8 the land that you are *c* the Jordan
11:11 But the land you are *c* the Jordan
30:18 in the land you are *c* the Jordan
31:13 live in the land you are *c* the Jordan
32:47 in the land you are *c* the Jordan
Jos 3:1 where they camped before *c* over.
3:17 whole nation had completed the *c*
4:1 nation had finished *c* the Jordan,
2Sa 24:5 After *c* the Jordan, they camped
Da 8:5 *c* the whole earth without touching
Ac 21:2 found a ship *c* over to Phoenicia,

CROSSINGS (CROSS)

Jer 51:32 the river *c* seized,

CROSSROADS (ROAD)

Jer 6:16 "Stand at the *c* and look;
Ob :14 You should not wait at the *c*

CROUCH (CROUCHES CROUCHING)

Nu 24:9 Like a lion they *c* and lie down,
Job 38:40 the lions when they *c* in their dens
39:3 They *c* down and bring forth their

CROUCHES (CROUCH)

Ge 49:9 Like a lion he *c* and lies down,

CROUCHING (CROUCH)

Ge 4:7 sin is *c* at your door; it desires
Ps 17:12 like a great lion *c* in cover.

CROW (CROWED CROWS)

Jn 18:27 at that moment a rooster began to *c*

CROWD (CROWDED CROWDING CROWDS)

Ex 23:2 Do not follow the *c* in doing wrong.
23:2 justice by siding with the *c*,
Jdg 6:31 replied to the hostile *c* around him,
2Sa 6:19 person in the whole *c* of Israelites,
2Ch 30:13 A very large *c* of people assembled
30:17 many in the *c* had not consecrated
Ezr 10:1 a large *c* of Israelites—men,
Job 31:34 because I so feared the *c*
Ps 64:2 from that noisy *c* of evildoers,
Jer 9:2 a *c* of unfaithful people.
Eze 7:11 none of that *c*— no wealth,
7:12 for wrath is upon the whole *c*.
7:13 concerning the whole *c* will not be
7:14 for my wrath is upon the whole *c*.
23:42 of a carefree *c* was around her;
Mt 8:18 When Jesus saw the *c* around him,
9:8 When the *c* saw this, they were
9:23 the flute players and the noisy *c*,
9:25 After the *c* had been put outside,
9:33 The *c* was amazed and said,
11:7 began to speak to the *c* about John:
12:46 Jesus was still talking to the *c*,
13:34 things to the *c* in parables;
13:36 Then he left the *c* and went
14:14 Jesus landed and saw a large *c*,
14:22 while he dismissed the *c*.
15:10 Jesus called the *c* to him and said,
15:33 in this remote place to feed such a *c*
15:35 He told the *c* to sit
15:39 After Jesus had sent the *c* away,
17:14 to the *c*, a man approached Jesus
20:29 Jericho, a large *c* followed him.
20:31 The *c* rebuked them and told them
21:8 A very large *c* spread their cloaks
21:46 but they were afraid of the *c*
26:47 With him was a large *c* armed
26:55 At that time Jesus said to the *c*,
27:15 release a prisoner chosen by the *c*.
27:17 So when the *c* had gathered,
27:20 the elders persuaded the *c* to ask
27:24 washed his hands in front of the *c*.
Mk 2:4 him to Jesus because of the *c*,
2:13 A large *c* came to him,
3:7 and a large *c* from Galilee followed
Mk 3:9 of the *c* he told his disciples
3:20 a house, and again a *c* gathered,
3:32 A *c* was sitting around him,
4:1 The *c* that gathered
4:36 Leaving the *c* behind, they took
5:21 a large *c* gathered around him.
5:24 A large *c* followed and pressed
5:27 she came up behind him in the *c*
5:30 He turned around in the *c*
6:34 Jesus landed and saw a large *c*,
6:45 while he dismissed the *c*.
7:14 Again Jesus called the *c* to him
7:17 After he had left the *c*
7:33 him aside, away from the *c*,
8:1 days another large *c* gathered.
8:6 He told the *c* to sit
8:34 Then he called the *c* to him
9:14 they saw a large *c* around them
9:17 A man in the *c* answered, "Teacher
9:25 Jesus saw that a *c* was running
10:46 with a large *c*, were leaving the city
11:18 because the whole *c* was amazed
12:12 But they were afraid of the *c*;
12:37 The large *c* listened to him
12:41 watched the *c* putting their money
14:43 With him was a *c* armed
15:8 The *c* came up and asked Pilate
15:11 But the chief priests stirred up the *c*
15:15 to satisfy the *c*, Pilate released
Lk 3:10 should we do then?" the *c* asked.
4:30 But he walked right through the *c*
5:19 a way to do this because of the *c*,
5:19 the tiles into the middle of the *c*,
5:29 and a large *c* of tax collectors
6:17 A large *c* of his disciples was there
7:9 and turning to the *c* following him,
7:11 and a large *c* went along with him.
7:12 And a large *c* from the town was
7:24 began to speak to the *c* about John:
8:4 While a large *c* was gathering
8:19 to get near him because of the *c*.
8:40 Jesus returned, a *c* welcomed him,
9:12 "Send the *c* away so they can go
9:13 we go and buy food for all this *c*."
9:37 the mountain, a large *c* met him.
9:38 man in the *c* called out, "Teacher,
11:14 spoke, and the *c* was amazed.
11:27 a woman in the *c* called out,
12:1 when a *c* of many thousands had
12:13 Someone in the *c* said to him,
12:54 to the *c*: "When you see a cloud
18:36 When he heard the *c* going by,
19:3 man he could not, because of the *c*.
19:37 whole *c* of disciples began joyfully
19:39 in the *c* said to Jesus,
22:6 to them when no *c* was present.
22:47 he was still speaking a *c* came up,
23:4 to the chief priests and the *c*,
Jn 5:13 away into the *c* that was there.
6:2 a great *c* of people followed him
6:5 saw a great *c* coming toward him,
6:22 The next day the *c* that had stayed
6:24 Once the *c* realized that neither
7:20 the *c* answered.
7:31 many in the *c* put their faith in him.
7:32 heard the *c* whispering such
12:9 Meanwhile a large *c*
12:12 next day the great *c* that had come
12:17 *c* that was with him had continued
12:29 *c* that was there and heard it said it
12:34 The *c* spoke up, "We have heard
Ac 2:6 a *c* came together in bewilderment,
2:14 his voice and addressed the *c*:
14:11 When the *c* saw what Paul had
14:13 and the *c* wanted to offer sacrifices
14:14 clothes and rushed out into the *c*,
14:18 they had difficulty keeping the *c*
14:19 and Iconium and won the *c* over.
16:22 The *c* joined in the attack
17:5 in order to bring them out to the *c*.
17:8 *c* and the city officials were thrown
19:30 Paul wanted to appear before the *c*,
19:33 some of the *c* shouted instructions
19:35 The city clerk quieted the *c*
21:27 They stirred up the whole *c*
21:32 and soldiers and ran down to the *c*.
21:34 Some in the *c* shouted one thing
21:36 The *c* that followed kept shouting,

Ac 21:40 on the steps and motioned to the *c*.
22:22 The *c* listened to Paul
24:12 or stirring up a *c* in the synagogues
24:18 There was no *c* with me,

CROWDED (CROWD)

Jdg 16:27 Now the temple was *c* with men
2Ki 10:21 They *c* into the temple of Baal
Jer 26: 9 all the people *c* around Jeremiah
Da 3:27 and royal advisers *c* around them.

CROWDING (CROWD)

Mk 3: 9 to keep the people from *c* him.
5:31 You see the people *c* against you,"
Lk 5: 1 with the people *c* around him
8:45 the people are *c* and pressing

CROWDS (CROWD)

Mt 4:25 Large *c* from Galilee,
5: 1 when he saw the *c*, he went up
7:28 the *c* were amazed at his teaching,
8: 1 the mountainside, large *c* followed
9:36 he saw the *c*, he had compassion
13: 2 Such large *c* gathered
14:13 the *c* followed him on foot
14:15 Send the *c* away, so they can go
15:30 Great *c* came to him, bringing
19: 2 Large *c* followed him,
21: 9 The *c* that went ahead of him
21:11 "Who is this?" The *c* answered,
22:33 When the *c* heard this, they were
23: 1 said to the *c* and to his disciples:
Mk 10: 1 Again *c* of people came to him,
Lk 3: 7 John said to the *c* coming out
5:15 so that *c* of people came
8:42 the *c* almost crushed him.
9:11 but the *c* learned about it
9:18 "Who do the *c* say I am?" They
11:29 As the *c* increased, Jesus said,
14:25 Large *c* were traveling with Jesus,
Jn 7:12 Among the *c* there was widespread
Ac 5:16 *C* gathered also from the towns
8: 6 When the *c* heard Philip
13:45 the Jews saw the *c*, they were filled
17:13 agitating the *c* and stirring them up

CROWED (CROW)

Mt 26:74 the man!" Immediately a rooster *c*.
Mk 14:72 the rooster *c* the second
Lk 22:60 as he was speaking, the rooster *c*.

CROWN (CROWNED CROWNS)

Jdg 9: 6 in Shechem to *c* Abimelech king.
2Sa 1:10 I took the *c* that was on his head
12:30 He took the *c* from the head
2Ki 11:12 out the king's son and put the *c*
1Ch 20: 2 David took the *c* from the head
2Ch 23:11 out the king's son and put the *c*
Est 1:11 Queen Vashti, wearing her royal *c*,
2:17 So he set a royal *c* on her head
8:15 a large *c* of gold and a purple robe
Job 19: 9 and removed the *c* from my head.
31:36 I would put it on like a *c*.
Ps 21: 3 placed a *c* of pure gold on his head.
65:11 You *c* the year with your bounty,
89:39 and have defiled his *c* in the dust.
132:18 *c* on his head will be resplendent."
Pr 4: 9 present you with a *c* of splendor."
10: 6 Blessings *c* the head
12: 4 noble character is her husband's *c*,
14:24 The wealth of the wise is their *c*,
16:31 Gray hair is a *c* of splendor;
17: 6 Children's children are a *c*
27:24 a *c* is not secure for all generations.
SS 3:11 at King Solomon wearing the *c*,
3:11 *c* with which his mother crowned
Isa 28: 5 will be a glorious *c*,
35:10 everlasting joy will *c* their heads.
51:11 everlasting joy will *c* their heads.
61: 3 to bestow on them a *c* of beauty
62: 3 You will be a *c* of splendor
Jer 2:16 have shaved the *c* of your head.
La 5:16 The *c* has fallen from our head.
Eze 16:12 and a beautiful *c* on your head.
21:26 Take off the turban, remove the *c*.
Zec 6:11 the silver and gold and make a *c*,
6:14 The *c* will be given to Heldai,
9:16 like jewels in a *c*.
Mt 27:29 and then wove a *c* of thorns
Mk 15:17 then wove a *c* of thorns
Jn 19: 2 The soldiers twisted together a *c*
19: 5 When Jesus came out wearing the *c*
1Co 9:25 it to get a *c* that will last forever.
9:25 it to get a *c* that will not last;
Php 4: 1 and long for, my joy and *c*,
1Th 2:19 or the *c* in which we will glory
2Ti 2: 5 he does not receive the victor's *c*
4: 8 store for me the *c* of righteousness,
Jas 1:12 he will receive the *c*
1Pe 5: 4 you will receive the *c*
Rev 2:10 and I will give you the *c* of life.
3:11 so that no one will take your *c*.
6: 2 held a bow, and he was given a *c*,
12: 1 and a *c* of twelve stars on her head.
14:14 a son of man" with a *c* of gold

CROWNED (CROWN)

Ps 8: 5 and *c* him with glory and honor.
Pr 14:18 the prudent are *c* with knowledge.
SS 3:11 crown with which his mother *c* him
Heb 2: 7 you *c* him with glory and honor
2: 9 now *c* with glory and honor

CROWNS (CROWN)

Ps 68:21 the hairy *c* of those who go
103: 4 and *c* me with love and compassion
149: 4 he *c* the humble with salvation.
Pr 11:26 blessing *c* him who is willing to sell.
SS 7: 5 Your head *c* you like Mount
Isa 23: 8 the bestower of *c*,
Jer 13:18 for your glorious *c*
Eze 23:42 and beautiful *c* on their heads.
Rev 4: 4 and had *c* of gold on their heads.
4:10 They lay their *c* before the throne
9: 7 heads they wore something like *c*
12: 3 ten horns and seven *c* on his heads.
13: 1 with ten *c* on his horns,
19:12 and on his head are many *c*.

CROWS (CROW)

Mt 26:34 this very night, before the rooster *c*
26:75 "Before the rooster *c*, you will
Mk 13:35 or when the rooster *c*, or at dawn.
14:30 before the rooster *c* twice you
14:72 "Before the rooster *c* twice you will
Lk 22:34 Peter, before the rooster *c* today,
22:61 "Before the rooster *c* today,
Jn 13:38 before the rooster *c*, you will

CRUCIBLE

Pr 17: 3 The *c* for silver and the furnace
27:21 The *c* for silver and the furnace

CRUCIFIED (CRUCIFY)

Mt 20:19 to be mocked and flogged and *c*.
26: 2 of Man will be handed over to be *c*
27:26 and handed him over to be *c*.
27:35 When they had *c* him, they divided
27:38 Two robbers were *c* with him,
27:44 same way the robbers who were *c*
28: 5 looking for Jesus, who was *c*.
Mk 15:15 and handed him over to be *c*.
15:24 And they *c* him.
15:25 the third hour when they *c* him.
15:27 They *c* two robbers with him,
15:32 Those *c* with him also heaped
16: 6 for Jesus the Nazarene, who was *c*.
Lk 23:23 insistently demanded that he be *c*,
23:33 *c* him, along with the criminals—
24: 7 be *c* and on the third day be raised
24:20 sentenced to death, and they *c* him;
Jn 19:16 him over to them to be *c*.
19:18 Here they *c* him, and with him two
19:20 for the place where Jesus was *c* was
19:23 When the soldiers *c* Jesus,
19:32 of the first man who had been *c*
19:41 At the place where Jesus was *c*,
Ac 2:36 whom you *c*, both Lord and Christ
4:10 whom you *c* but whom God raised
Ro 6: 6 For we know that our old self was *c*
1Co 1:13 Is Christ divided? Was Paul *c*
1:23 but we preach Christ *c*: a stumbling
2: 2 except Jesus Christ and him *c*.
2: 8 they would not have *c* the Lord
2Co 13: 4 to be sure, he was *c* in weakness,
Gal 2:20 I have been *c* with Christ
Gal 3: 1 Christ was clearly portrayed as *c*.
5:24 Christ Jesus have *c* the sinful
6:14 which the world has been *c*
Rev 11: 8 where also their Lord was *c*.

CRUCIFY (CRUCIFIED CRUCIFYING)

Mt 23:34 Some of them you will kill and *c*;
27:22 They all answered, "*C* him!" "Why
27:23 they shouted all the louder, "*C* him
27:31 Then they led him away to *c* him.
Mk 15:13 "*C* him!" they shouted.
15:14 they shouted all the louder, "*C* him
15:20 Then they led him out to *c* him.
Lk 23:21 they kept shouting, "*C* him! *C* him
Jn 19: 6 they shouted, "*C*! *C*!"
19: 6 "You take him and *c* him.
19:10 either to free you or to *c* you?"
19:15 Crucify him!" "Shall I *c* your king
19:15 away! Take him away! *C* him!"

CRUCIFYING (CRUCIFY)

Heb 6: 6 to their loss they are *c* the Son

CRUEL (CRUELTY)

Ge 49: 7 and their fury, so *c*!
Ex 6: 9 discouragement and *c* bondage.
Dt 28:33 but *c* oppression all your days.
Ps 71: 4 from the grasp of evil and *c* men.
Pr 5: 9 and your years to one who is *c*,
11:17 but a *c* man brings himself harm.
12:10 the kindest acts of the wicked are *c*.
27: 4 Anger is *c* and fury overwhelming,
Ecc 9:12 As fish are caught in a *c* net,
Isa 13: 9 a *c* day, with wrath and fierce
14: 3 and turmoil and *c* bondage,
19: 4 over to the power of a *c* master,
Jer 6:23 they are *c* and show no mercy.
15:21 redeem you from the grasp of the *c*
30:14 and punished you as would the *c*,
50:42 they are *c* and without mercy.

CRUELTY (CRUEL)

Na 3:19 your endless *c*?

CRUMBLE (CRUMBLED CRUMBLES CRUMBLING)

Lev 2: 6 *C* it and pour oil on it; it is a grain
Eze 38:20 cliffs will *c* and every wall will fall

CRUMBLED (CRUMBLE)

Hab 3: 6 The ancient mountains *c*

CRUMBLES (CRUMBLE)

Job 14:18 "But as a mountain erodes and *c*

CRUMBLING (CRUMBLE)

Job 15:28 houses *c* to rubble.

CRUMBS

Mt 15:27 even the dogs eat the *c* that fall
Mk 7:28 under the table eat the children's *c*

CRUSH (CRUSHED CRUSHES CRUSHING)

Ge 3:15 he will *c* your head,
Nu 24:17 He will *c* the foreheads of Moab,
Job 6: 9 that God would be willing to *c* me,
9:17 He would *c* me with a storm
19: 2 and *c* me with words?
24:11 They *c* olives among the terraces;
39:15 unmindful that a foot may *c* them,
40:12 *c* the wicked where they stand.
Ps 68:21 Surely God will *c* the heads
72: 4 he will *c* the oppressor.
74: 8 "We will *c* them completely!"
89:23 I will *c* his foes before him
94: 5 They *c* your people, O LORD;
110: 5 he will *c* kings on the day
Pr 22:22 and do not *c* the needy in court,
Isa 14:25 I will *c* the Assyrian in my land;
41:15 thresh the mountains and *c* them,
53:10 it was the LORD's will to *c* him
Jer 50:17 the last to *c* his bones
La 1:15 me to *c* my young men.
3:34 To *c* underfoot
Da 2:40 so it will *c* and break all the others.
2:44 It will *c* all those kingdoms
Am 2:13 "Now then, I will *c* you

Am 4: 1 oppress the poor and *c* the needy
Mic 6: 15 you will *c* grapes but not drink
Ro 16: 20 The God of peace will soon *c* Satan

CRUSHED (CRUSH)

Lev 2: 14 offer *c* heads of new grain roasted
2: 16 the memorial portion of the *c* grain
22: 24 whose testicles are bruised, *c,*
Nu 11: 8 it in a handmill or *c* it in a mortar.
Dt 9: 21 Then I *c* it and ground it to powder
Jdg 5: 26 She struck Sisera, she *c* his head,
10: 8 who that year shattered and *c* them
2Sa 22: 38 "I pursued my enemies and *c* them;
22: 39 I *c* them completely, and they
2Ch 14: 13 they were *c* before the LORD
15: 6 One nation was being *c* by another
34: 7 the Asherah poles and *c* the idols
Job 4: 19 who are *c* more readily than a moth
5: 4 *c* in court without a defender.
16: 12 he seized me by the neck and *c* me.
34: 25 in the night and they are *c.*
Ps 10: 10 His victims are *c,* they collapse;
18: 38 I *c* them so that they could not rise;
34: 18 and saves those who are *c* in spirit.
38: 8 I am feeble and utterly *c;*
44: 2 you *c* the peoples
44: 19 you *c* us and made us a haunt
51: 8 let the bones you have *c* rejoice.
74: 14 It was you who *c* the heads
89: 10 You *c* Rahab like one of the slain;
Pr 17: 22 but a *c* spirit dries up the bones.
18: 14 but a *c* spirit who can bear?
Isa 21: 10 O my people, *c* on the threshing
23: 12 O Virgin Daughter of Sidon, now *c*
27: 9 to be like chalk stones *c* to pieces,
53: 5 he was *c* for our iniquities;
Jer 5: 3 you *c* them, but they refused
8: 21 Since my people are *c,* I am *c;*
22: 20 for all your allies are *c.*
Eze 30: 8 and all her helpers are *c.*
Da 6: 24 overpowered them and *c* all their
7: 7 it *c* and devoured its victims
7: 19 the beast that *c* and devoured its
Hab 3: 13 You *c* the leader of the land
Mal 1: 4 we have been *c,* we will rebuild
Mt 21: 44 but he on whom it falls will be *c.*"
Lk 8: 42 his way, the crowds almost *c* him.
20: 18 but he on whom it falls will be *c.*"
2Co 4: 8 not *c;* perplexed, but not in despair;

CRUSHES (CRUSH)

Ps 143: 3 he *c* me to the ground;
Pr 15: 4 but a deceitful tongue *c* the spirit.
15: 13 but heartache *c* the spirit.
Am 2: 13 as a cart *c* when loaded with grain.

CRUSHING (CRUSH)

Nu 22: 25 close to the wall, *c* Balaam's foot
Dt 23: 1 one who has been emasculated by *c*
Ps 110: 6 and *c* the rulers of the whole earth.
Isa 3: 15 What do you mean by *c* my people
Jer 14: 17 a *c* blow.
Da 7: 23 trampling it down and *c* it.

CRUST (ENCRUSTED)

1Sa 2: 36 and a *c* of bread and plead,
Pr 17: 1 Better a dry *c* with peace and quiet

CRUTCH

2Sa 3: 29 or leprosy or who leans on a *c*

CRY (CRIED CRIES CRYING)

Ge 27: 34 and bitter *c* and said to his father,
Ex 2: 23 *c* for help because of their slavery
3: 9 And now the *c* of the Israelites has
22: 23 I will certainly hear their *c.*
22: 23 If you do and they *c* out to me,
Lev 13: 45 part of his face and *c* out,
Nu 20: 16 he heard our *c* and sent an angel
Dt 24: 15 Otherwise he may *c* to the LORD
33: 7 "Hear, O LORD, the *c* of Judah;
Jos 6: 10 not give a war *c,* do not raise your
Jdg 10: 14 *c* out to the gods you have chosen.
1Sa 4: 13 the whole town sent up a *c.*
8: 18 you will *c* out for relief
9: 16 for their *c* has reached me."
17: 20 battle positions, shouting the war *c.*
2Sa 22: 7 my *c* came to his ears.
1Ki 8: 28 Hear the *c* and the prayer that your
8: 52 to them whenever they *c* out to you
17: 22 The LORD heard Elijah's *c,*
22: 36 a *c* spread through the army:
1Ch 16: 35 *C* out, "Save us, O God our Savior;
2Ch 6: 19 Hear the *c* and the prayer that your
13: 12 trumpets will sound the battle *c*
13: 15 At the sound of their battle *c,*
13: 15 the men of Judah raised the battle *c*
20: 9 and will *c* out to you in our distress,
Ne 9: 9 you heard their *c* at the Red Sea.
Job 16: 18 may my *c* never be laid to rest!
19: 7 "Though I *c,* 'I've been wronged!'
24: 12 of the wounded *c* out for help.
27: 9 Does God listen to his *c*
30: 20 "I *c* out to you, O God,
30: 28 in the assembly and *c* for help.
34: 28 They caused the *c* of the poor
34: 28 so that he heard the *c* of the needy.
35: 9 "Men *c* out under a load
35: 12 does not answer when men *c* out
36: 13 when he fetters them, they do not *c*
38: 41 raven when its young *c* out to God
39: 25 of commanders and the battle *c.*
Ps 3: 4 To the LORD I *c* aloud,
5: 2 Listen to my *c* for help,
6: 9 The LORD has heard my *c*
9: 12 he does not ignore the *c*
10: 17 them, and you listen to their *c,*
17: 1 listen to my *c.*
18: 6 my *c* came before him, into his ears
22: 2 O my God, I *c* out by day,
22: 24 but has listened to his *c* for help.
28: 2 Hear my *c* for mercy
28: 6 for he has heard my *c* for mercy.
29: 9 And in his temple all *c,* "Glory!"
31: 22 Yet you heard my *c* for mercy
34: 15 and his ears are attentive to their *c;*
34: 17 righteous *c* out, and the LORD
39: 12 listen to my *c* for help;
40: 1 he turned to me and heard my *c.*
55: 17 I *c* out in distress,
57: 2 I *c* out to God Most High,
61: 1 Hear my *c,* O God;
72: 12 he will deliver the needy who *c* out,
84: 2 my heart and my flesh *c* out
86: 6 listen to my *c* for mercy.
88: 1 day and night I *c* out before you.
88: 2 turn your ear to my *c.*
88: 13 But I *c* to you for help, O LORD;
102: 1 let my *c* for help come to you.
106: 44 distress when he heard their *c;*
116: 1 he heard my *c* for mercy.
119:147 I rise before dawn and *c* for help;
119:169 May my *c* come before you,
130: 1 Out of the depths I *c* to you,
130: 2 attentive to my *c* for mercy.
140: 6 Hear, O LORD, my *c* for mercy.
142: 1 I *c* aloud to the LORD;
142: 5 I *c* to you, O LORD;
142: 6 Listen to my *c,*
143: 1 listen to my *c* for mercy;
144: 14 no *c* of distress in our streets.
145: 19 he hears their *c* and saves them.
Pr 2: 3 and *c* aloud for understanding,
21: 13 he too will *c* out and not be
21: 13 to the *c* of the poor,
30: 15 'Give! Give!' they *c.*
Isa 3: 7 But in that day he will *c* out,
8: 9 Raise the war *c,* you nations,
10: 30 *C* out, O Daughter of Gallim!
15: 4 Heshbon and Elealeh *c* out,
15: 4 the armed men of Moab *c* out,
19: 20 When they *c* out to the LORD
24: 11 In the streets they *c* out for wine;
30: 19 be when you *c* for help!
33: 7 their brave men *c* aloud
40: 6 A voice says, "*C* out."
40: 6 And I said, "What shall I *c?*"
42: 2 He will not shout or *c* out,
42: 13 a shout he will raise the battle *c*
42: 14 I *c* out, I gasp and pant.
57: 13 When you *c* out for help,
58: 9 you will *c* for help, and he will say:
65: 14 but you will *c* out
Jer 3: 21 A *c* is heard on the barren heights,
4: 5 *C* aloud and say:
4: 16 raising a war *c* against the cities
Jer 4: 19 I have heard the battle *c.*
4: 31 I hear a *c* as of a woman in labor,
4: 31 the *c* of the Daughter
8: 19 Listen to the *c* of my people
11: 11 Although they *c* out to me,
11: 12 and *c* out to the gods to whom they
12: 6 they have raised a loud *c*
14: 2 and a *c* goes up from Jerusalem.
14: 12 I will not listen to their *c;*
18: 22 Let a *c* be heard from their houses
20: 8 Whenever I speak, I *c* out
20: 16 a battle *c* at noon.
22: 20 *c* out from Abarim,
22: 20 "Go up to Lebanon and *c* out,
25: 36 Hear the *c* of the shepherds,
30: 15 Why do you *c* out over your wound
31: 6 a day when watchmen *c* out
47: 2 The people will *c* out;
47: 6 sword of the LORD,' you *c,*
48: 4 her little ones will *c* out.
48: 20 Wail and *c* out!
48: 31 for all Moab I *c* out,
48: 34 "The sound of their *c* rises
49: 2 "when I will sound the battle *c*
49: 3 *C* out, O inhabitants of Rabbah!
49: 21 their *c* will resound to the Red Sea.
50: 46 *c* will resound among the nations.
51: 54 sound of a *c* comes from Babylon,
La 2: 18 *c* out to the Lord.
2: 19 Arise, *c* out in the night,
3: 8 Even when I call out or *c* for help,
3: 56 to my *c* for relief."
4: 15 You are unclean!" men *c* to them.
Eze 6: 11 stamp your feet and *c* out "Alas!"
21: 12 *C* out and wail, son of man,
21: 22 to sound the battle *c,*
27: 28 when your seamen *c* out.
27: 30 and *c* bitterly over you;
Hos 5: 8 Raise the battle *c* in Beth Aven;
7: 14 They do not *c* out to me
Joel 1: 14 and *c* out to the LORD.
Jnh 2: 2 and you listened to my *c.*
Mic 3: 4 Then they will *c* out to the LORD,
4: 9 Why do you now *c* aloud—
Na 2: 8 "Stop! Stop!" they *c,*
Hab 1: 2 Or *c* out to you, "Violence!"
2: 11 The stones of the wall will *c* out,
Zep 1: 10 "a *c* will go up from the Fish Gate,
1: 14 *c* on the day of the LORD will be
1: 16 a day of trumpet and battle *c*
Mt 12: 19 He will not quarrel or *c* out;
25: 6 "At midnight the *c* rang out:
Mk 5: 5 and in the hills he would *c* out
15: 37 With a loud *c,* Jesus breathed his
15: 39 heard his *c* and saw how he died,
Lk 7: 13 out to her and he said, "Don't *c.*"
7: 32 and you did not *c.*'
18: 7 who *c* out to him day and night?
19: 40 keep quiet, the stones will *c* out."
Ro 8: 15 And by him we *c,* "*Abba,* Father."
Gal 4: 27 break forth and *c* aloud,
Rev 18: 10 they will stand far off and *c:*
18: 16 will weep and mourn and *c* out:
18: 19 with weeping and mourning *c* out:

CRYING (CRY)

Ge 21: 17 God has heard the boy *c*
21: 17 God heard the boy *c,* and the angel
Ex 2: 6 He was *c,* and she felt sorry for him
3: 7 I have heard them *c* out
5: 8 are lazy; that is why they are *c* out,
14: 15 "Why are you *c* out to me?
Jdg 7: 21 all the Midianites ran, *c* out
1Sa 7: 8 "Do not stop *c* out
Isa 22: 5 and of *c* out to the mountains.
65: 19 the sound of weeping and of *c*
Eze 9: 8 I fell facedown, *c* out, "Ah,
Mt 15: 22 *c* out, "Lord, Son of David,
15: 23 for she keeps *c* out after us."
Mk 5: 38 with people *c* and wailing loudly.
Jn 20: 11 but Mary stood outside the tomb *c.*
20: 13 "Woman, why are you *c?*"
20: 15 Woman," he said, "why are you *c?*
Ac 9: 39 *c* and showing him the robes
Jas 5: 4 who mowed your fields are *c* out
Rev 21: 4 or mourning or *c* or pain,

CRYSTAL

Job 28: 17 *c* can compare with it,
Rev 4: 6 a sea of glass, clear as *c*.
21: 11 jewel, like a jasper, clear as *c*.
22: 1 of the water of life, as clear as *c*,

CUB (CUBS)

Ge 49: 9 You are a lion's *c*, O Judah;
Dt 33: 22 "Dan is a lion's *c*,

CUBIT (CUBITS)

Ex 25: 10 a half wide, and a *c* and a half high.
25: 10 half cubits long, a *c* and a half wide,
25: 17 and a half cubits long and a *c*
25: 23 a *c* wide and a *c* and a half high.
26: 13 The tent curtains will be a *c* longer
26: 16 is to be ten cubits long and a *c*
30: 2 *c* long and a *c* wide,
36: 21 frame was ten cubits long and a *c*
37: 1 a half wide, and a *c* and a half high.
37: 1 half cubits long, a *c* and a half wide,
37: 6 and a half cubits long and a *c*
37: 10 a *c* wide, and a *c* and a half high.
37: 25 *c* long and a *c* wide,
1Ki 7: 24 gourds encircled it—ten to a *c*.
7: 31 had a circular frame one *c* deep.
7: 31 with its basework it measured a *c*
7: 32 The diameter of each wheel was a *c*
7: 35 was a circular band half a *c* deep
2Ch 3: 3 and twenty cubits wide (using the *c*
4: 3 of bulls encircled it—ten to a *c*.
Eze 40: 5 of which was a *c* and a handbreadth
40: 12 each alcove was a wall one *c* high,
40: 42 a *c* and a half wide and a *c* high.
40: 42 for the burnt offerings, each a *c*
43: 13 Its gutter is a *c* deep and a *c* wide,
43: 13 that *c* being a *c* and a handbreadth:
43: 14 it is four cubits high and a *c* wide.
43: 14 it is two cubits high and a *c* wide,
43: 17 and a gutter of a *c* all around.
43: 17 with a rim of half a *c* and a gutter

CUBITS (CUBIT)

Ex 25: 10 two and a half *c* long, a cubit
25: 17 two and a half *c* long and a cubit
25: 23 table of acacia wood—two *c* long,
26: 2 twenty-eight *c* long and four *c* wide
26: 8 thirty *c* long and four *c* wide.
26: 16 Each frame is to be ten *c* long
27: 1 five *c* long and five *c* wide.
27: 1 three *c* high; it is to be square,
27: 9 south side shall be a hundred *c* long
27: 11 also be a hundred *c* long and is
27: 12 the courtyard shall be fifty *c* wide
27: 13 courtyard shall also be fifty *c* wide.
27: 14 Curtains fifteen *c* long are to be
27: 15 and curtains fifteen *c* long are to be
27: 16 provide a curtain twenty *c* long,
27: 18 a hundred *c* long and fifty *c* wide,
27: 18 of finely twisted linen five *c* high,
30: 2 two *c* high—its horns of one piece
36: 9 twenty-eight *c* long and four *c* wide
36: 15 thirty *c* long and four *c* wide.
36: 21 Each frame was ten *c* long
37: 1 two and a half *c* long, a cubit
37: 6 two and a half *c* long and a cubit
37: 10 table of acacia wood—two *c* long,
37: 25 two *c* high—its horns of one piece
38: 1 five *c* long and five *c* wide.
38: 1 three *c* high; it was square,
38: 9 south side was a hundred *c* long
38: 11 a hundred *c* long and had twenty
38: 12 The west end was fifty *c* wide
38: 13 the sunrise, was also fifty *c* wide.
38: 14 Curtains fifteen *c* long were
38: 15 and curtains fifteen *c* long were
38: 18 It was twenty *c* long and, like
38: 18 of the courtyard, five *c* high,
1Ki 6: 2 for the LORD was sixty *c* long,
6: 3 and projected ten *c* from the front
6: 3 that is twenty *c*, and projected ten
6: 6 The lowest floor was five *c* wide,
6: 6 the middle floor six *c* and the third
6: 10 The height of each was five *c*,
6: 16 partitioned off twenty *c* at the rear
6: 17 front of this room was forty *c* long.
6: 20 inner sanctuary was twenty *c* long,
1Ki 6: 23 of olive wood, each ten *c* high.
6: 24 and the other wing five *c*—
6: 24 of the first cherub was five *c* long,
6: 24 ten *c* from wing tip to wing tip.
6: 25 second cherub also measured ten *c*,
6: 26 height of each cherub was ten *c*.
7: 2 of Lebanon a hundred *c* long,
7: 6 He made a colonnade fifty *c* long
7: 10 some measuring ten *c* and some
7: 15 each eighteen *c* high and twelve *c*
7: 16 each capital was five *c* high.
7: 19 in the shape of lilies, four *c* high.
7: 23 from rim to rim and five *c* high.
7: 23 measuring ten *c* from rim to rim
7: 23 of thirty *c* to measure around it.
7: 27 each was four *c* long, four wide
7: 38 and measuring four *c* across,
2Ch 3: 3 and twenty *c* wide (using the cubit
3: 3 the temple of God was sixty *c* long
3: 4 of the building and twenty *c* high.
3: 4 of the temple was twenty *c* long
3: 8 twenty *c* long and twenty *c* wide.
3: 11 its other wing, also five *c* long,
3: 11 of the cherubim was twenty *c*.
3: 11 of the first cherub was five *c* long
3: 12 and its other wing, also five *c* long,
3: 12 the second cherub was five *c* long
3: 13 these cherubim extended twenty *c*.
3: 15 a capital on top measuring five *c*.
3: 15 ⌊together⌋ were thirty-five *c* long,
4: 1 made a bronze altar twenty *c* long,
4: 1 twenty *c* wide and ten *c* high.
4: 2 from rim to rim and five *c* high.
4: 2 measuring ten *c* from rim to rim
4: 2 of thirty *c* to measure around it.
6: 13 a bronze platform, five *c* long,
6: 13 five *c* wide and three *c* high,
Jer 52: 21 and twelve *c* in circumference;
52: 21 of the pillars was eighteen *c* high
52: 22 top of the one pillar was five *c* high
Eze 40: 5 in the man's hand was six long *c*,
40: 7 the alcoves were five *c* thick.
40: 9 and its jambs were two *c* thick.
40: 9 it was eight *c* deep and its jambs
40: 11 and its length was thirteen *c*.
40: 11 it was ten *c* and its length was
40: 12 and the alcoves were six *c* square.
40: 13 the distance was twenty-five *c*
40: 14 the inside of the gateway—sixty *c*.
40: 15 end of its portico was fifty *c*.
40: 19 it was a hundred *c* on the east side
40: 21 fifty *c* long and twenty-five *c* wide.
40: 23 opposite one; it was a hundred *c*.
40: 25 fifty *c* long and twenty-five *c* wide.
40: 27 the south side; it was a hundred *c*.
40: 29 fifty *c* long and twenty-five *c* wide.
40: 30 twenty-five *c* wide and five *c* deep.)
40: 33 fifty *c* long and twenty-five *c* wide.
40: 36 fifty *c* long and twenty-five *c* wide.
40: 47 *c* long and a hundred *c* wide.
40: 48 of the entrance was fourteen *c*
40: 48 projecting walls were three *c* wide
40: 48 they were five *c* wide on either side
40: 49 The portico was twenty *c* wide,
40: 49 and twelve *c* from front to back.
41: 1 of the jambs was six *c* on each side.
41: 2 The entrance was ten *c* wide,
41: 2 on each side of it were five *c* wide.
41: 2 was forty *c* long and twenty *c* wide.
41: 3 The entrance was six *c* wide,
41: 3 of the entrance was seven *c*.
41: 3 the entrance; each was two *c* wide.
41: 4 and its width was twenty *c*
41: 4 inner sanctuary; it was twenty *c*,
41: 5 around the temple was four *c* wide.
41: 5 of the temple; it was six *c* thick,
41: 8 the length of the rod, six long *c*.
41: 9 of the side rooms was five *c* thick.
41: 10 rooms was twenty *c* wide all
41: 11 the open area was five *c* wide all
41: 12 and its length was ninety *c*.
41: 12 of the building was five *c* thick all
41: 12 on the west side was seventy *c* wide
41: 13 the temple; it was a hundred *c* long,
41: 13 walls were also a hundred *c* long.
41: 14 of the temple, was a hundred *c*.
41: 15 on each side; it was a hundred *c*.
41: 22 altar three *c* high and two *c* square;
Eze 42: 2 a hundred *c* long and fifty *c* wide.
42: 3 Both in the section twenty *c*
42: 4 ten *c* wide and a hundred *c* long.
42: 7 in front of the rooms for fifty *c*.
42: 8 sanctuary was a hundred *c* long.
42: 8 to the outer court was fifty *c* long,
42: 16 rod; it was five hundred *c*.
42: 17 it was five hundred *c*
42: 18 it was five hundred *c*
42: 19 it was five hundred *c*
42: 20 five hundred *c* long and five
42: 20 long and five hundred *c* wide,
43: 13 of the altar in long *c*,
43: 14 to the larger ledge it is four *c* high
43: 14 to the lower ledge it is two *c* high
43: 15 The altar hearth is four *c* high,
43: 16 twelve *c* long and twelve *c* wide.
43: 17 fourteen *c* long and fourteen *c* wide
45: 1 25,000 *c* long and 20,000 *c* wide;
45: 2 a section 500 *c* square is to be
45: 2 with 50 *c* around it for open land.
45: 3 25,000 *c* long and 10,000 *c* wide.
45: 5 An area 25,000 *c* long and 10,000
45: 5 *c* wide will belong to the Levites,
45: 6 *c* wide and 25,000 *c* long, adjoining
46: 22 forty *c* long and thirty *c* wide;
47: 3 he measured off a thousand *c*
47: 4 measured off another thousand *c*
48: 8 *c* wide, and its length from east
48: 9 be 25,000 *c* long and 10,000 *c* wide.
48: 10 It will be 25,000 *c* long
48: 10 10,000 *c* wide on the west side,
48: 10 25,000 *c* long on the south side.
48: 10 *c* wide on the east side and 25,000
48: 13 25,000 *c* long and 10,000 *c* wide.
48: 13 be 25,000 *c* and its width 10,000 *c*.
48: 15 5,000 *c* wide and 25,000 *c* long,
48: 16 north side 4,500 *c*, the south side
48: 16 the south side 4,500 *c*, the east side
48: 16 *c*, and the west side 4,500 *c*.
48: 17 250 *c* on the south, 250 *c*
48: 17 for the city will be 250 *c*
48: 17 on the east, and 250 *c* on the west.
48: 18 and 10,000 *c* on the west side.
48: 18 *c* on the east side and 10,000
48: 20 portion will be a square, 25,000 *c*
48: 21 and westward from the 25,000 *c*
48: 21 *c* of the sacred portion
48: 30 north side, which is 4,500 *c* long,
48: 32 *c* long, will be three gates:
48: 33 which measures 4,500 *c*, will be
48: 34 *c* long, will be three gates:
48: 35 all around will be 18,000 *c*.
Rev 21: 17 its wall and it was 144 *c* thick,

CUBS (CUB)

2Sa 17: 8 fierce as a wild bear robbed of her *c*
Job 4: 11 the *c* of the lioness are scattered.
38: 32 or lead out the Bear with its *c*?
Pr 17: 12 to meet a bear robbed of her *c*
Jer 51: 38 they growl like lion *c*.
Eze 19: 2 and reared her *c*.
19: 3 She brought up one of her *c*,
19: 5 she took another of her *c*
Hos 13: 8 Like a bear robbed of her *c*,
Na 2: 11 and the *c*, with nothing to fear?
2: 12 The lion killed enough for his *c*

CUCUMBERS

Nu 11: 5 also the *c*, melons, leeks, onions

CUD

Lev 11: 3 divided and that chews the *c*.
11: 4 The camel, though it chews the *c*,
11: 4 are some that only chew the *c*
11: 5 The coney, though it chews the *c*,
11: 6 The rabbit, though it chews the *c*,
11: 7 does not chew the *c*; it is unclean
11: 26 that does not chew the *c* is unclean
Dt 14: 6 in two and that chews the *c*.
14: 7 Although they chew the *c*,
14: 7 of those that chew the *c*
14: 8 a split hoof, it does not chew the *c*.

CULTIVATE (CULTIVATED)

Dt 28: 39 will plant vineyards and *c* them
Ps 104: 14 and plants for man to *c*—

CULTIVATED (CULTIVATE)
Isa 5: 6 neither pruned nor *c*,
7: 25 As for all the hills once *c* by the hoe
Jer 13: 21 those you *c* as your special allies?
Eze 36: 34 The desolate land will be *c* instead
Ro 11: 24 were grafted into a *c* olive tree,

CUMMIN
Isa 28: 25 he not sow caraway and scatter *c?*
28: 27 and *c* with a stick.
28: 27 nor is a cartwheel rolled over *c;*
Mt 23: 23 of your spices—mint, dill and *c*.

CUN
1Ch 18: 8 and *C*, towns that belonged

CUNNING
Ps 64: 6 the mind and heart of man are *c*.
83: 3 With *c* they conspire
2Co 11: 3 deceived by the serpent's *c*,
Eph 4: 14 and by the *c* and craftiness of men

CUP (CUPS)
Ge 40: 11 Pharaoh's *c* was in my hand,
40: 11 and put the *c* in his hand.''
40: 11 squeezed them into Pharaoh's *c*
40: 13 you will put Pharaoh's *c* in his hand
40: 21 so that he once again put the *c*
44: 2 Then put my *c*, the silver one,
44: 5 Isn't this the *c* my master drinks
44: 12 the *c* was found in Benjamin's sack.
44: 16 one who was found to have the *c*.''
44: 17 to have the *c* will become my slave.
2Sa 12: 3 drank from his *c* and even slept
1Ki 7: 26 and its rim was like the rim of a *c*,
2Ch 4: 5 and its rim was like the rim of a *c*,
Ps 16: 5 assigned me my portion and my *c;*
23: 5 my *c* overflows.
75: 8 In the hand of the LORD is a *c*
116: 13 I will lift up the *c* of salvation
Pr 23: 31 when it sparkles in the *c*,
Isa 51: 17 the *c* of his wrath,
51: 22 from that *c*, the goblet of my wrath,
51: 22 the *c* that made you stagger;
Jer 25: 15 ''Take from my hand this *c* filled
25: 17 I took the *c* from the LORD's hand
25: 28 refuse to take the *c* from your hand
49: 12 to drink the *c* must drink it,
51: 7 Babylon was a gold *c*
La 4: 21 But to you also the *c* will be passed;
Eze 23: 31 so I will put her *c* into your hand.
23: 32 a *c* large and deep;
23: 32 ''You will drink your sister's *c*,
23: 33 the *c* of ruin and desolation,
23: 33 the *c* of your sister Samaria.
Hab 2: 16 *c* from the LORD's right hand is
Zec 12: 2 make Jerusalem a *c* that sends all
Mt 10: 42 if anyone gives a *c* of cold water
20: 22 ''Can you drink the *c* I am going
20: 23 ''You will indeed drink from my *c*,
23: 25 You clean the outside of the *c*
23: 26 First clean the inside of the *c*
26: 27 Then he took the *c*, gave thanks
26: 39 may this *c* be taken from me.
26: 42 possible for this *c* to be taken away
Mk 9: 41 anyone who gives you a *c* of water
10: 38 ''Can you drink the *c* I drink
10: 39 ''You will drink the *c* I drink
14: 23 Then he took the *c*, gave thanks
14: 36 Take this *c* from me.
Lk 11: 39 Pharisees clean the outside of the *c*
22: 17 After taking the *c*, he gave thanks
22: 20 after the supper he took the *c*,
22: 20 ''This *c* is the new covenant
22: 42 if you are willing, take this *c*
Jn 18: 11 I not drink the *c* the Father has
1Co 10: 16 Is not the *c* of thanksgiving
10: 21 the *c* of the Lord and the *c*
11: 25 after supper he took the *c*, saying,
11: 25 ''This *c* is the new covenant
11: 26 you eat this bread and drink this *c*,
11: 27 or drinks the *c* of the Lord
11: 28 of the bread and drinks of the *c*.
Rev 14: 10 strength into the *c* of his wrath.
16: 19 gave her the *c* filled with the wine
17: 4 She held a golden *c* in her hand,
18: 6 a double portion from her own *c*.

CUPBEARER (CUPBEARERS)
Ge 40: 1 the *c* and the baker of the king
40: 2 the chief *c* and the chief baker,
40: 5 the *c* and the baker of the king
40: 9 the chief *c* told Joseph his dream.
40: 13 you used to do when you were his *c*
40: 20 He lifted up the heads of the chief *c*
40: 21 He restored the chief *c*
40: 23 The chief *c*, however, did not
41: 9 Then the chief *c* said to Pharaoh,
Ne 1: 11 I was *c* to the king.

CUPBEARERS (CUPBEARER)
1Ki 10: 5 servants in their robes, his *c*,
2Ch 9: 4 the *c* in their robes and the burnt

CUPS (CUP)
Ex 25: 31 base and shaft; its flowerlike *c*,
25: 33 Three *c* shaped like almond flowers
25: 34 are to be four *c* shaped like almond
37: 17 base and shaft; its flowerlike *c*,
37: 19 Three *c* shaped like almond flowers
37: 20 lampstand were four *c* shaped like
Jer 35: 5 and some *c* before the men
Mk 7: 4 as the washing of *c*, pitchers

CURDLE (CURDS)
Job 10: 10 and *c* me like cheese,

CURDLED (CURDS)
Jdg 5: 25 for nobles she brought him *c* milk.

CURDS (CURDLE CURDLED)
Ge 18: 8 He then brought some *c* and milk
Dt 32: 14 with *c* and milk from herd
2Sa 17: 29 beans and lentils, honey and *c*,
Isa 7: 15 He will eat *c* and honey
7: 22 of the milk they give, he will have *c*
7: 22 remain in the land will eat *c*
Eze 34: 3 You eat the *c*, clothe yourselves

CURE (CURED)
2Ki 5: 3 He would *c* him of his leprosy.''
5: 6 you so that you may *c* him
5: 11 hand over the spot and *c* me
Jer 3: 22 I will *c* you of backsliding.''
17: 9 and beyond *c*.
30: 15 your pain that has no *c?*
Hos 5: 13 But he is not able to *c* you,
Lk 9: 1 out all demons and to *c* diseases,

CURED (CURE)
Dt 28: 27 from which you cannot be *c*.
28: 35 with painful boils that cannot be *c*,
2Ki 5: 7 to me to be *c* of his leprosy?
Mt 8: 3 Immediately he was *c*
11: 5 those who have leprosy are *c*,
Mk 1: 42 the leprosy left him and he was *c*.
Lk 6: 18 troubled by evil spirits were *c*,
7: 21 very time Jesus *c* many who had
7: 22 those who have leprosy are *c*,
8: 2 also some women who had been *c*
8: 36 demon-possessed man had been *c*.
Jn 5: 9 once the man was *c;* he picked up
Ac 19: 12 and their illnesses were *c*
28: 9 sick on the island came and were *c*.

CURRENT (CURRENTS)
Ge 23: 16 the weight *c* among the merchants.

CURRENTS (CURRENT)
Jnh 2: 3 and the *c* swirled about me;

CURRY
Pr 19: 6 Many *c* favor with a ruler,

CURSE (ACCURSED CURSED CURSES CURSING)
Ge 4: 11 Now you are under a *c*
8: 21 ''Never again will I *c* the ground
12: 3 and whoever curses you I will *c;*
27: 12 bring down a *c* on myself rather
27: 13 ''My son, let the *c* fall on me.
27: 29 May those who *c* you be cursed
Ex 22: 28 or *c* the ruler of your people.
Lev 19: 14 '' 'Do not *c* the deaf or put
24: 11 the name of the LORD with a *c;*
Nu 5: 18 the bitter water that brings a *c*.
Nu 5: 19 water that brings a *c* not harm you.
5: 21 the LORD cause your people to *c*
5: 21 woman under this *c* of the oath—
5: 22 that brings a *c* enter your body
5: 24 the bitter water that brings a *c*,
5: 27 to drink the water that brings a *c*,
22: 6 and those you *c* are cursed.''
22: 6 come and put a *c* on these people,
22: 11 come and put a *c* on them for me.
22: 12 You must not put a *c*
22: 17 put a *c* on these people for me.''
23: 7 'Come,' he said, '*c* Jacob for me;
23: 8 How can I *c*
23: 11 I brought you to *c* my enemies,
23: 13 And from there, *c* them for me.''
23: 25 ''Neither *c* them at all
23: 27 to let you *c* them for me from there
24: 9 and those who *c* you be cursed!''
24: 10 ''I summoned you to *c* my enemies,
Dt 11: 26 before you today a blessing and a *c*
11: 28 the *c* if you disobey the commands
21: 23 hung on a tree is under God's *c*.
23: 4 to pronounce a *c* on you.
23: 5 turned the *c* into a blessing for you,
Jos 9: 23 near us? You are now under a *c:*
24: 9 son of Beor to put a *c* on you.
Jdg 5: 23 '*C* Meroz,' said the angel
5: 23 '*C* its people bitterly,
9: 57 The *c* of Jotham son
17: 2 about which I heard you utter a *c*—
2Sa 16: 9 should this dead dog *c* my lord
16: 10 '*C* David,' who can ask, 'Why do
16: 11 Leave him alone; let him *c*,
2Ki 2: 24 and called down a *c* on them
Ne 10: 29 and bind themselves with a *c*
13: 2 Balaam to call a *c* down on them.
13: 2 turned the *c* into a blessing.)
Job 1: 11 he will surely *c* you to your face.''
2: 5 he will surely *c* you to your face.''
2: 9 *C* God and die!'' He replied,
3: 8 May those who *c* days *c* that day,
31: 30 by invoking a *c* against his life—
Ps 62: 4 but in their hearts they *c*.
102: 8 against me use my name as a *c*.
109: 17 He loved to pronounce a *c*—
109: 28 They may *c*, but you will bless;
Pr 3: 33 The LORD's *c* is on the house
11: 26 People *c* the man who hoards grain
24: 24 peoples will *c* him and nations
26: 2 an undeserved *c* does not come
27: 14 it will be taken as a *c*.
30: 10 he will *c* you, and you will pay for it
30: 11 are those who *c* their fathers
Ecc 10: 20 or *c* the rich in your bedroom,
Isa 8: 21 will *c* their king and their God.
24: 6 Therefore a *c* consumes the earth;
65: 15 name to my chosen ones as a *c;*
Jer 23: 10 of the *c* the land lies parched
29: 22 are in Babylon will use this *c:*
48: 10 A *c* on him who keeps his sword
48: 10 ''A *c* on him who is lax
La 3: 65 and may your *c* be on them!
Zec 5: 3 ''This is the *c* that is going out
Mal 2: 2 and I will *c* your blessings.
2: 2 LORD Almighty, ''I will send a *c*
3: 9 are under a *c*— the whole nation
4: 6 and strike the land with a *c*.''
Lk 6: 28 bless those who *c* you, pray
Jn 7: 49 of the law—there is a *c* on them.''
Ro 12: 14 persecute you; bless and do not *c*.
1Co 16: 22 does not love the Lord—a *c* be
Gal 3: 10 on observing the law are under a *c*,
3: 13 of the law by becoming a *c* for us,
3: 13 us from the *c* of the law
Jas 3: 9 with it we *c* men, who have been
Rev 22: 3 No longer will there be any *c*.

CURSED (CURSE)
Ge 3: 14 ''*C* are you above all the livestock
3: 17 ''*C* is the ground because of you;
5: 29 by the ground the LORD has *c*.''
9: 25 ''*C* be Canaan!
27: 29 May those who curse you be *c*
49: 7 *C* be their anger, so fierce,
Lev 20: 9 He has *c* his father or his mother,
Nu 22: 6 and those you curse are *c*.''
23: 8 those whom God has not *c?*
24: 9 and those who curse you be *c!*''

Dt 27:15 "*C* is the man who carves an image
27:16 "*C* is the man who dishonors his
27:17 "*C* is the man who moves his
27:18 "*C* is the man who leads the blind
27:19 "*C* is the man who withholds justice
27:20 "*C* is the man who sleeps
27:21 "*C* is the man who has sexual
27:22 "*C* is the man who sleeps
27:23 "*C* is the man who sleeps
27:24 "*C* is the man who kills his
27:25 "*C* is the man who accepts a bribe
27:26 "*C* is the man who does not uphold
28:16 You will be *c* in the city
28:16 in the city and *c* in the country.
28:17 and your kneading trough will be *c*.
28:18 The fruit of your womb will be *c*,
28:19 You will be *c* when you come in
28:19 come in and *c* when you go out.
Jos 6:26 "*C* before the LORD is the man
Jdg 9:27 and drinking, they *c* Abimelech.
21:18 '*C* be anyone who gives a wife
1Sa 14:24 "*C* be any man who eats food
14:28 '*C* be any man who eats food today
17:43 the Philistine *c* David by his gods.
26:19 may they be *c* before the LORD!
2Sa 16:5 was Shimei son of Gera, and he *c*
16:7 As he *c*, Shimei said, "Get out,
19:21 He *c* the LORD's anointed."
1Ki 21:10 them testify that he has *c* both God
21:13 "Naboth has *c* both God
2Ki 9:34 "Take care of that *c* woman,"
Job 1:5 and *c* God in their hearts."
3:1 opened his mouth and *c* the day
5:3 but suddenly his house was *c*.
24:18 their portion of the land is *c*,
Ps 119:21 You rebuke the arrogant, who are *c*
Ecc 7:22 times you yourself have *c* others.
Jer 11:3 '*C* is the man who does not obey
17:5 "*C* is the one who trusts in man,
20:14 *C* be the day I was born!
20:15 *C* be the man who brought my
Mal 1:14 "*C* is the cheat who has
2:2 Yes, I have already *c* them,
Mt 25:41 'Depart from me, you who are *c*,
Mk 11:21 The fig tree you *c* has withered!"
Ro 9:3 I could wish that I myself were *c*
1Co 4:12 When we are *c*, we bless;
12:3 "Jesus be *c*," and no one can say,
Gal 3:10 "*C* is everyone who does not
3:13 *C* is everyone who is hung on a tree
Heb 6:8 and is in danger of being *c*.
Rev 16:9 and they *c* the name of God,
16:11 in agony and *c* the God of heaven
16:21 And they *c* God on account

CURSES (CURSE)

Ge 12:3 and whoever *c* you I will curse;
Ex 21:17 "Anyone who *c* his father
Lev 20:9 " 'If anyone *c* his father or mother,
24:15 the Israelites: 'If anyone *c* his God,
Nu 5:23 is to write these *c* on a scroll
Dt 11:29 and on Mount Ebal the *c*.
27:13 on Mount Ebal to pronounce *c*:
28:15 all these *c* will come upon you
28:20 The LORD will send on you *c*,
28:45 All these *c* will come upon you.
29:20 All the *c* written in this book will
29:21 according to all the *c*
29:27 on it all the *c* written in this book.
30:1 and *c* I have set before you come
30:7 your God will put all these *c*
30:19 and death, blessings and *c*.
Jos 8:34 the blessings and the *c*— just
1Ki 2:8 who called down bitter *c*
2Ch 34:24 all the *c* written in the book that
Ne 13:25 and called *c* down on them.
Ps 10:7 His mouth is full of *c* and lies
37:22 but those he *c* will be cut off.
59:12 For the *c* and lies they utter,
Pr 20:20 If a man *c* his father or mother,
28:27 to them receives many *c*.
Jer 11:8 So I brought on them all the *c*
15:10 yet everyone *c* me.
Da 9:11 "Therefore the *c* and sworn
Mt 15:4 and 'Anyone who *c* his father
26:74 he began to call down *c* on himself
Mk 7:10 and, 'Anyone who *c* his father
14:71 He began to call down *c* on himself,

CURSING (CURSE)

2Sa 16:10 If he is *c* because the LORD said
16:12 for the *c* I am receiving today."
16:13 *c* as he went and throwing stones
Ps 109:18 He wore *c* as his garment;
Ecc 7:21 or you may hear your servant *c* you
Jer 24:9 an object of ridicule and *c*,
25:18 an object of horror and scorn and *c*,
26:6 an object of *c* among all the nations
29:18 and an object of *c* and horror,
42:18 You will be an object of *c*
44:8 and make yourselves an object of *c*
44:12 They will become an object of *c*
44:22 your land became an object of *c*
49:13 and of *c*; and all its towns will be
Hos 4:2 There is only *c*, lying and murder,
Zec 8:13 an object of *c* among the nations,
Ro 3:14 "Their mouths are full of *c*
Jas 3:10 the same mouth come praise and *c*.

CURTAIN (CURTAINS)

Ex 26:4 the edge of the end *c* in one set,
26:4 with the end *c* in the other set.
26:5 Make fifty loops on one *c*
26:5 loops on the end *c* of the other set,
26:9 Fold the sixth *c* double at the front
26:10 edge of the end *c* in the other set.
26:10 the edge of the end *c* in one set
26:12 the half *c* that is left over is to hang
26:31 "Make a *c* of blue, purple
26:33 Hang the *c* from the clasps
26:33 The *c* will separate the Holy Place
26:33 ark of the Testimony behind the *c*.
26:35 outside the *c* on the north side
26:36 to the tent make a *c* of blue,
26:37 Make gold hooks for this *c*
27:16 provide a *c* twenty cubits long,
27:21 outside the *c* that is in front
30:6 the altar in front of the *c* that is
35:12 cover and the *c* that shields it;
35:15 the *c* for the doorway
35:17 and the *c* for the entrance
36:11 the edge of the end *c* in one set,
36:11 with the end *c* in the other set.
36:12 They also made fifty loops on one *c*
36:12 loops on the end *c* of the other set,
36:17 edge of the end *c* in the other set.
36:17 the edge of the end *c* in one set
36:35 They made the *c* of blue, purple
36:37 to the tent they made a *c* of blue,
38:18 The *c* for the entrance
38:27 for the sanctuary and for the *c*—
39:34 of sea cows and the shielding *c*;
39:38 the *c* for the entrance to the tent;
39:40 and the *c* for the entrance
40:3 and shield the ark with the *c*.
40:5 and put the *c* at the entrance
40:8 and put the *c* at the entrance
40:21 hung the shielding *c* and shielded
40:22 side of the tabernacle outside the *c*
40:26 Tent of Meeting in front of the *c*
40:28 he put up the *c* at the entrance
40:33 and put up the *c* at the entrance
Lev 4:6 in front of the *c* of the sanctuary.
4:17 seven times in front of the *c*.
16:2 Place behind the *c* in front
16:12 and take them behind the *c*.
16:15 and take its blood behind the *c*
21:23 he must not go near the *c*
24:3 Outside the *c* of the Testimony
Nu 3:25 the *c* at the entrance to the Tent
3:26 the *c* at the entrance
3:31 the *c*, and everything related
4:5 and take down the shielding *c*
4:26 and altar, the *c* for the entrance,
18:7 at the altar and inside the *c*.
2Ch 3:14 He made the *c* of blue, purple
Mt 27:51 At that moment the *c*
Mk 15:38 The *c* of the temple was torn in two
Lk 23:45 the *c* of the temple was torn in two.
Heb 6:19 the inner sanctuary behind the *c*,
9:3 Behind the second *c* was a room
10:20 opened for us through the *c*,

CURTAINS (CURTAIN)

Ex 26:1 with ten *c* of finely twisted linen
26:2 All the *c* are to be the same size—
26:3 Join five of the *c* together,
26:6 use them to fasten the *c* together
26:7 "Make *c* of goat hair for the tent
26:8 All eleven *c* are to be the same size
26:9 Join five of the *c* together
26:12 the additional length of the tent *c*,
26:13 The tent *c* will be a cubit longer
27:9 is to have *c* of finely twisted linen,
27:11 cubits long and is to have *c*,
27:12 be fifty cubits wide and have *c*,
27:14 *C* fifteen cubits long are to be
27:15 and *c* fifteen cubits long are to be
27:18 with *c* of finely twisted linen five
35:17 the *c* of the courtyard with its posts
36:8 with ten *c* of finely twisted linen
36:9 All the *c* were the same size—
36:10 They joined five of the *c* together
36:13 to fasten the two sets of *c* together
36:14 They made *c* of goat hair
36:15 All eleven *c* were the same size—
36:16 five of the *c* into one set
38:9 and had *c* of finely twisted linen,
38:12 end was fifty cubits wide and had *c*,
38:14 *C* fifteen cubits long were
38:15 and *c* fifteen cubits long were
38:16 All the *c* around the courtyard
38:18 and, like the *c* of the courtyard,
39:40 the *c* of the courtyard with its posts
Nu 3:26 of Meeting, the *c* of the courtyard,
4:25 are to carry the *c* of the tabernacle,
4:25 the *c* for the entrance to the Tent
4:26 the *c* of the courtyard surrounding
SS 1:5 like the tent *c* of Solomon.
Isa 54:2 stretch your tent *c* wide,

CURVED

Jos 15:3 to Addar and *c* around to Karka.
15:10 Then it *c* westward from Baalah
16:6 on the north it *c* eastward
18:17 then *c* north, went to En Shemesh,

CUSH (CUSHITE CUSHITES)

Ge 2:13 winds through the entire land of *C*.
10:6 The sons of Ham: *C*, Mizraim,
10:7 The sons of *C*: Seba, Havilah,
10:8 *C* was the father of Nimrod,
1Ch 1:8 The sons of Ham: *C*, Mizraim,
1:9 The sons of *C*: Seba, Havilah, Sabta
1:10 *C* was the father of Nimrod,
Est 1:1 stretching from India to *C*:
8:9 stretching from India to *C*.
Job 28:19 The topaz of *C* cannot compare
Ps 68:31 *C* will submit herself to God.
87:4 too, and Tyre, along with *C*—
Isa 11:11 from Upper Egypt, from *C*,
18:1 wings along the rivers of *C*,
20:3 and portent against Egypt and *C*,
20:5 Those who trusted in *C*
43:3 *C* and Seba in your stead.
45:14 and the merchandise of *C*,
Jer 46:9 men of *C* and Put who carry shields
Eze 29:10 to Aswan, as far as the border of *C*.
30:4 and anguish will come upon *C*.
30:5 *C* and Put, Lydia and all Arabia,
30:9 me in ships to frighten *C* out
38:5 Persia, *C* and Put will be with them
Na 3:9 *C* and Egypt were her boundless
Zep 3:10 From beyond the rivers of *C*

CUSHAN

Hab 3:7 I saw the tents of *C* in distress,

CUSHAN-RISHATHAIM

Jdg 3:8 *C* king of Aram Naharaim,
3:10 The LORD gave *C* king of Aram

CUSHI

Jer 36:14 the son of *C*, to say to Baruch,
Zep 1:1 came to Zephaniah son of *C*,

CUSHION

Mk 4:38 was in the stern, sleeping on a *c*.

CUSHITE (CUSH)

Nu 12:1 Moses because of his *C* wife,
12:1 for he had married a *C*.
2Sa 18:21 The *C* bowed down before Joab
18:21 Then Joab said to a *C*, "Go,

2Sa 18: 22 please let me run behind the *C*."
18: 23 way of the plain and outran the *C*.
18: 31 Then the *C* arrived and said,
18: 32 king asked the *C*, "Is the young
18: 32 man Absalom safe?" The *C* replied,
2Ki 19: 9 a report that Tirhakah, the *C* king
2Ch 14: 9 Zerah the *C* marched out
Isa 20: 4 the Egyptian captives and *C* exiles,
37: 9 a report that Tirhakah, the *C* king
Jer 38: 7 a *C*, an official in the royal palace,
38: 10 commanded Ebed-Melech the *C*,
38: 12 Ebed-Melech the *C* said
39: 16 "Go and tell Ebed-Melech the *C*,

CUSHITES (CUSH)

2Ch 12: 3 *C* that came with him from Egypt,
14: 12 The *C* fled, and Asa and his army
14: 12 struck down the *C* before Asa
14: 13 of *C* fell that they could not
16: 8 Were not the *C* and Libyans
21: 16 of the Arabs who lived near the *C*.
Am 9: 7 the same to me as the *C*?"
Zep 2: 12 "You too, O *C*,

CUSTODY

Ge 40: 3 and put them in *c* in the house
40: 4 been in *c* for some time,
40: 7 in *c* with him in his master's house,
42: 17 he put them all in *c* for three days.
Lev 24: 12 They put him in *c* until the will
Nu 15: 34 and they kept him in *c*,
1Ch 29: 8 in the *c* of Jehiel the Gershonite.

CUSTOM (ACCUSTOMED CUSTOMS)

Ge 19: 31 as is the *c* all over the earth.
29: 26 "It is not our *c* here
Jdg 8: 24 (It was the *c* of the Ishmaelites
11: 39 comes the Israelite *c* that each year
1Ki 18: 28 was their *c*, until their blood flowed
2Ki 11: 14 standing by the pillar, as the *c* was.
Est 9: 27 to establish the *c* that they
Job 1: 5 This was Job's regular *c*.
Mt 27: 15 it was the governor's *c* at the Feast
Mk 10: 1 and as was his *c*, he taught them.
15: 6 Now it was the *c* at the Feast
Lk 1: 9 according to the *c*
2: 27 for him what the *c*
2: 42 up to the Feast, according to the *c*.
4: 16 into the synagogue, as was his *c*.
Jn 18: 39 But it is your *c* for me to release
Ac 15: 1 according to the *c* taught by Moses
17: 2 As his *c* was, Paul went
25: 16 told them that it is not the Roman *c*

CUSTOMERS

Eze 27: 15 and many coastlands were your *c*;
27: 21 all the princes of Kedar were your *c*

CUSTOMS (CUSTOM)

Lev 18: 30 any of the detestable *c* that were
20: 23 to the *c* of the nations I am going
2Ki 17: 33 with the *c* of the nations
Est 3: 8 Their *c* are different from those
Ps 106: 35 and adopted their *c*.
Jer 10: 3 For the *c* of the peoples are
Jn 19: 40 in accordance with Jewish burial *c*.
Ac 6: 14 and change the *c* Moses handed
16: 21 an uproar by advocating *c* unlawful
21: 21 or live according to our *c*.
26: 3 acquainted with all the Jewish *c*
28: 17 or against the *c* of our ancestors,
Gal 2: 14 Gentiles to follow Jewish *c*?

CUT (CUTS CUTTER CUTTING)

Ge 9: 11 Never again will all life be *c*
15: 10 however, he did not *c* in half.
15: 10 *c* them in two and arranged
17: 14 will be *c* off from his people;
22: 3 When he had *c* enough wood
Ex 4: 25 *c* off her son's foreskin
12: 15 day through the seventh must be *c*
12: 19 must be *c* off from the community
29: 17 *C* the ram into pieces and wash
30: 33 other than a priest must be *c*
30: 38 it to enjoy its fragrance must be *c*
31: 5 and bronze, to *c* and set stones,
31: 14 work on that day must be *c*
34: 13 and *c* down their Asherah poles.
Ex 35: 33 and bronze, to *c* and set stones,
39: 3 *c* strands to be worked into the blue
Lev 1: 6 is to skin the burnt offering and *c* it
1: 12 He is to *c* it into pieces,
3: 9 the entire fat tail *c* off close
7: 20 that person must be *c*
7: 21 that person must be *c*
7: 25 made to the LORD must be *c*
7: 27 that person must be *c*
8: 20 He *c* the ram into pieces
17: 4 and must be *c* off from his people.
17: 9 that man must be *c*
17: 10 and will *c* him off from his people.
17: 14 anyone who eats it must be *c* off."
18: 29 such persons must be *c*
19: 8 that person must be *c*
19: 27 " 'Do not *c* the hair at the sides
19: 28 Do not *c* your bodies for the dead
20: 3 and I will *c* him off from his people;
20: 5 will *c* off from their people both
20: 6 and I will *c* him off from his people.
20: 17 They must be *c* off before the eyes
20: 18 must be *c* off from their people.
21: 5 of their beards or *c* their bodies.
22: 3 that person must be *c*
22: 24 are bruised, crushed, torn or *c*.
23: 29 himself on that day must be *c*
26: 26 When I *c* off your supply of bread,
26: 30 *c* down your incense altars
Nu 4: 18 the Kohathite tribal clans are not *c*
9: 13 that person must be *c*
13: 23 they *c* off a branch bearing a single
13: 24 of grapes the Israelites *c* off there.
15: 30 and that person must be *c*
15: 31 that person must surely be *c* off;
19: 13 That person must be *c*
19: 20 must be *c* off from the community,
Dt 7: 5 *c* down their Asherah poles
12: 3 *c* down the idols of their gods
12: 29 The LORD your God will *c*
14: 1 Do not *c* yourselves or shave
19: 5 forest with his neighbor to *c* wood,
20: 19 Do not *c* them down.
20: 20 you may *c* down trees that you
25: 12 him by his private parts, you shall *c*
25: 18 *c* off all who were lagging behind;
Jos 3: 13 water flowing downstream will be *c*
3: 16 (the Salt Sea) was completely *c*
4: 7 the flow of the Jordan was *c*
4: 7 the waters of the Jordan were *c* off.
8: 22 Israel *c* them down, leaving them
10: 10 *c* them down all the way to Azekah
Jdg 1: 6 and *c* off his thumbs and big toes.
1: 7 big toes *c* off have picked up scraps
6: 25 *c* down the Asherah pole beside it.
6: 26 of the Asherah pole that you *c*
6: 28 with the Asherah pole beside it *c*
6: 30 *c* down the Asherah pole beside it
9: 48 He took an ax and *c*
9: 49 So all the men *c* branches
19: 29 a knife and *c* up his concubine,
20: 6 *c* her into pieces and sent one piece
20: 21 and *c* down twenty-two thousand
20: 25 they *c* down another eighteen
20: 42 of the towns *c* them down there.
20: 45 the Israelites *c* down five thousand
21: 6 Today one tribe is *c* off from Israel
1Sa 2: 31 when I will *c* short your strength
2: 33 Every one of you that I do not *c*
11: 7 a pair of oxen, *c* them into pieces,
17: 46 you down and *c* off your head.
17: 51 he *c* off his head with the sword.
20: 15 and do not ever *c* off your kindness
20: 15 even when the LORD has *c*
24: 4 and *c* off a corner of Saul's robe.
24: 5 for having *c* off a corner
24: 11 I *c* off the corner of your robe
24: 21 by the LORD that you will not *c*
28: 9 He has *c* off the mediums
31: 9 They *c* off his head and stripped
2Sa 4: 7 and killed him, they *c* off his head.
4: 12 They *c* off their hands and feet
7: 9 and I have *c* off all your enemies
10: 4 *c* off their garments in the middle
14: 16 hand of the man who is trying to *c*
14: 26 Whenever he *c* the hair of his head
14: 26 he used to *c* his hair from time
16: 9 Let me go over and *c* off his head."
2Sa 20: 22 they *c* off the head of Sheba son
1Ki 3: 25 "*C* the living child in two
3: 26 *C* him in two!" Then the king gave
5: 6 cedars of Lebanon be *c* for me.
5: 18 of Gebal *c* and prepared the timber
7: 9 blocks of high-grade stone *c* to size
7: 11 Above were high-grade stones, *c*
9: 7 then I will *c* off Israel
14: 10 I will *c* off from Jeroboam every
14: 14 over Israel who will *c* off the family
15: 13 Asa *c* the pole down and burned it
18: 23 and let them *c* it into pieces
18: 33 *c* the bull into pieces and laid it
21: 21 *c* off from Ahab every last male
2Ki 3: 19 You will *c* down every good tree,
3: 25 and *c* down every good tree.
4: 39 he *c* them up into the pot of stew,
6: 4 and began to *c* down trees.
6: 6 Elisha *c* a stick and threw it there,
6: 32 murderer is sending someone to *c*
9: 8 I will *c* off from Ahab every last
10: 25 they *c* them down with the sword.
18: 4 and *c* down the Asherah poles.
19: 7 and there I will have him *c*
19: 23 I have *c* down its tallest cedars,
19: 37 *c* him down with the sword,
23: 14 and *c* down the Asherah poles
1Ch 17: 8 and I have *c* off all your enemies
19: 4 *c* off their garments in the middle
2Ch 2: 10 the woodsmen who *c* the timber,
2: 16 and we will *c* all the logs
14: 3 and *c* down the Asherah poles.
15: 16 Asa *c* the pole down, broke it up
16: 14 him in the tomb that he had *c* out
31: 1 and *c* down the Asherah poles.
32: 21 some of his sons *c* him
34: 4 he *c* to pieces the incense altars
34: 7 and *c* to pieces all the incense altars
Job 6: 9 to let loose his hand and *c* me off!
14: 7 If it is *c* down, it will sprout again,
17: 1 my days are *c* short,
24: 24 they are *c* off like heads of grain.
26: 12 by his wisdom he *c* Rahab to pieces
27: 8 hope has the godless when he is *c*
Ps 12: 3 May the LORD *c* off all flattering
31: 22 "I am *c* off from your sight!"
34: 16 to *c* off the memory of them
37: 9 For evil men will be *c* off,
37: 22 but those he curses will be *c* off.
37: 28 of the wicked will be *c* off;
37: 34 when the wicked are *c* off,
37: 38 of the wicked will be *c* off.
74: 5 to *c* through a thicket of trees.
75: 10 I will *c* off the horns
80: 16 Your vine is *c* down, it is burned
88: 5 who are *c* off from your care.
89: 45 You have *c* short the days
101: 8 I will *c* off every evildoer
102: 23 he *c* short my days.
109: 13 May his descendants be *c* off,
109: 15 that he may *c* off the memory
118: 10 of the LORD I *c* them off.
118: 11 of the LORD I *c* them off.
118: 12 name of the LORD I *c* them off.
129: 4 he has *c* me free from the cords
Pr 2: 22 but the wicked will be *c*
10: 27 the years of the wicked are *c* short.
10: 31 but a perverse tongue will be *c* out.
23: 18 and your hope will not be *c* off.
24: 14 and your hope will not be *c* off.
Isa 5: 2 and *c* out a winepress as well.
6: 13 leave stumps when they are *c* down
9: 14 LORD will *c* off from Israel both
10: 34 He will *c* down the forest thickets
11: 13 and Judah's enemies will be *c* off;
14: 8 no woodsman comes to *c* us down
14: 22 "I will *c* off from Babylon her name
15: 2 and every beard *c* off.
18: 5 and *c* down and take away
18: 5 he will *c* off the shoots
22: 16 to *c* out a grave for yourself here,
22: 25 hanging on it will be *c* down."
29: 20 an eye for evil will be *c* down—
33: 12 like *c* thornbushes they will be set
37: 7 and there I will have him *c*
37: 24 I have *c* down its tallest cedars,
37: 38 *c* him down with the sword,
38: 12 and he has *c* me off from the loom;

Isa 44: 14 He *c* down cedars,
45: 2 and *c* through bars of iron.
48: 9 so as not to *c* you off.
48: 19 their name would never be *c* off
51: 1 to the rock from which you were *c*
51: 9 Was it not you who *c* Rahab
53: 8 For he was *c* off from the land
56: 5 that will not be *c* off.
Jer 6: 6 "*C* down the trees
7: 29 *C* off your hair and throw it away;
9: 21 it has *c* off the children
9: 22 like *c* grain behind the reaper,
10: 3 they *c* a tree out of the forest,
11: 19 let us *c* him off from the land
16: 6 and no one will *c* himself
22: 7 and they will *c* up your fine cedar
34: 18 I will treat like the calf they *c*
36: 23 king *c* them off with a scribe's knife
36: 29 and destroy this land and *c*
41: 5 *c* themselves came from Shechem,
46: 22 like men who *c* down trees.
47: 4 and to *c* off all survivors
47: 5 how long will you *c* yourselves?
48: 25 Moab's horn is *c* off;
48: 37 and every beard *c* off;
50: 16 *C* off from Babylon the sower,
51: 13 the time for you to be *c* off.
La 2: 3 In fierce anger he has *c* off
3: 54 I thought I was about to be *c* off.
Eze 4: 16 I will *c* off the supply of food
5: 16 and *c* off your supply of food.
14: 8 I will *c* him off from my people.
14: 13 against it to *c* off its food supply
16: 4 you were born your cord was not *c*,
21: 3 *c* off from you both the righteous
21: 4 going to *c* off the righteous
23: 25 They will *c* off your noses
23: 47 *c* them down with their swords;
25: 7 I will *c* you off from the nations
25: 16 and I will *c* off the Kerethites
30: 15 and *c* off the hordes of Thebes.
31: 12 of foreign nations *c* it down
35: 7 *c* off from it all who come and go.
37: 11 and our hope is gone; we are *c* off.'
39: 10 wood from the fields or *c* it
Da 2: 5 I will have you *c* into pieces
2: 34 a rock was *c* out, but not
2: 45 of the rock *c* out of a mountain,
3: 29 and Abednego be *c* into pieces
4: 14 '*C* down the tree and trim
4: 23 '*C* down the tree and destroy it,
9: 26 the Anointed One will be *c* off
Hos 6: 5 Therefore I *c* you in pieces
Joel 1: 9 are *c* off from the house
1: 16 Has not the food been *c* off
Am 3: 14 the horns of the altar will be *c* off
9: 1 "*C* off the heads of all the people—
Ob : 9 will be *c* down in the slaughter.
: 14 to *c* down their fugitives,
Na 1: 12 they will be *c* down and pass away.
3: 15 the sword will *c* you down
Zep 1: 3 when I *c* off man from the face
1: 4 I will *c* off from this place every
3: 6 "I have *c* off nations;
3: 7 her dwelling would not be *c* off,
Zec 9: 6 I will *c* off the pride
11: 2 the dense forest has been *c* down!
Mal 2: 12 may the LORD *c* him
Mt 3: 10 not produce good fruit will be *c*
5: 30 right hand causes you to sin, *c* it
7: 19 that does not bear good fruit is *c*
18: 8 your foot causes you to sin, *c* it off
21: 8 while others *c* branches
24: 22 If those days had not been *c* short,
24: 51 He will *c* him to pieces
27: 60 his own new tomb that he had *c* out
Mk 5: 5 hills he would cry out and *c* himself
9: 43 If your hand causes you to sin, *c* it
9: 45 if your foot causes you to sin, *c* it
11: 8 others spread branches they had *c*
13: 20 Lord had not *c* short those days,
15: 46 placed it in a tomb *c* out of rock.
Lk 3: 9 not produce good fruit will be *c*
12: 46 He will *c* him to pieces
13: 7 *C* it down! Why should it use up
13: 9 fine! If not, then *c* it down.' "
23: 53 placed it in a tomb *c* in the rock,
Jn 18: 26 of the man whose ear Peter had *c*
Ac 2: 37 they were *c* to the heart
3: 23 to him will be completely *c* off
18: 18 he had his hair *c* off at Cenchrea
27: 32 So the soldiers *c* the ropes that held
Ro 9: 3 and *c* off from Christ for the sake
11: 22 Otherwise, you also will be *c* off.
11: 24 if you were *c* out of an olive tree
1Co 11: 6 for a woman to have her hair *c*
11: 6 she should have her hair *c* off;
2Co 11: 12 doing in order to *c* the ground
Gal 5: 7 Who *c* in on you and kept you

CUTHAH

2Ki 17: 24 brought people from Babylon, *C*,
17: 30 the men from *C* made Nergal,

CUTS (CUT)

Job 28: 4 where people dwell he *c* a shaft,
38: 25 Who *c* a channel for the torrents
Ps 107: 16 and *c* through bars of iron.
Jn 15: 2 He *c* off every branch

CUTTER (CUT)

Ex 28: 11 the way a gem *c* engraves a seal.

CUTTING (CUT)

Dt 23: 1 or *c* may enter the assembly
2Ki 6: 5 As one of them was *c* down a tree,
2Ch 2: 8 men are skilled in *c* timber there.
Ps 78: 31 *c* down the young men of Israel.
Pr 26: 6 Like *c* off one's feet or drinking
Jer 44: 7 disaster on yourselves by *c*
Mt 26: 51 of the high priest, *c* off his ear.
Mk 14: 47 of the high priest, *c* off his ear.
Lk 22: 50 of the high priest, *c* off his right ear.
Jn 18: 10 struck the high priest's servant, *c*
Ac 27: 40 *C* loose the anchors, they left them

CUZA

Lk 8: 3 Joanna the wife of *C*, the manager

CYCLE

Isa 29: 1 and let your *c* of festivals go on.

CYMBAL (CYMBALS)

1Co 13: 1 a resounding gong or a clanging *c*.

CYMBALS (CYMBAL)

2Sa 6: 5 lyres, tambourines, sistrums and *c*.
1Ch 13: 8 lyres, tambourines, *c* and trumpets.
15: 16 instruments: lyres, harps and *c*.
15: 19 Ethan were to sound the bronze *c*;
15: 28 and of *c*, and the playing of lyres
16: 5 Asaph was to sound the *c*,
16: 42 the sounding of the trumpets and *c*
25: 1 accompanied by harps, lyres and *c*.
25: 6 with *c*, lyres and harps,
2Ch 5: 12 dressed in fine linen and playing *c*,
5: 13 Accompanied by trumpets, *c*
29: 25 in the temple of the LORD with *c*,
Ezr 3: 10 Levites (the sons of Asaph) with *c*,
Ne 12: 27 and with the music of *c*,
Ps 150: 5 praise him with resounding *c*.
150: 5 praise him with the clash of *c*,

CYPRESS

Ge 6: 14 So make yourself an ark of *c* wood;
Isa 41: 19 the fir and the *c* together,
44: 14 or perhaps took a *c* or oak.
60: 13 the pine, the fir and the *c* together,
Eze 27: 6 of *c* wood from the coasts

CYPRUS

Isa 23: 1 From the land of *C*
23: 12 "Up, cross over to *C*;
Eze 27: 6 wood from the coasts of *C*
Ac 4: 36 from *C*, whom the apostles called
11: 19 *C* and Antioch, telling the message
11: 20 however, men from *C* and Cyrene,
13: 4 and sailed from there to *C*.
15: 39 took Mark and sailed for *C*,
21: 3 After sighting *C* and passing
21: 16 He was a man from *C* and one of
27: 4 the lee of *C* because the winds were

CYRENE

Mt 27: 32 a man from *C*, named Simon,
Mk 15: 21 A certain man from *C*, Simon,
Lk 23: 26 they seized Simon from *C*,
Ac 2: 10 and the parts of Libya near *C*;
6: 9 Jews of *C* and Alexandria as well
11: 20 however, men from Cyprus and *C*,
13: 1 Simeon called Niger, Lucius of *C*,

CYRUS

2Ch 36: 22 In the first year of *C* king of Persia,
36: 22 the heart of *C* king of Persia
36: 23 "This is what *C* king of Persia says:
Ezr 1: 1 In the first year of *C* king of Persia,
1: 1 the heart of *C* king of Persia
1: 2 "This is what *C* king of Persia says:
1: 7 King *C* brought out the articles
1: 8 *C* king of Persia had them brought
3: 7 as authorized by *C* king of Persia.
4: 3 as King *C*, the king of Persia,
4: 5 reign of *C* king of Persia
5: 13 King *C* issued a decree
5: 13 year of *C* king of Babylon,
5: 14 "Then King *C* gave them
5: 17 of Babylon to see if King *C* did
6: 3 In the first year of King *C*,
6: 14 God of Israel and the decrees of *C*,
Isa 44: 28 who says of *C*, 'He is my shepherd
45: 1 to *C*, whose right hand I take hold
45: 13 will raise up *C* in my righteousness:
Da 1: 21 there until the first year of King *C*.
6: 28 and the reign of *C* the Persian.
10: 1 In the third year of *C* king of Persia

DABBESHETH

Jos 19: 11 ran to Maralah, touched *D*,

DABERATH

Jos 19: 12 and went on to *D* and up to Japhia.
21: 28 Kishion, *D*, Jarmuth
1Ch 6: 72 *D*, Ramoth and Anem, together

DAGGER

2Sa 2: 16 thrust his *d* into his opponent's side
20: 8 a belt with a *d* in its sheath.
20: 10 guard against the *d* in Joab's hand,

DAGON (DAGON'S)

Jdg 16: 23 offer a great sacrifice to *D* their god
1Sa 5: 2 Dagon's temple and set it beside *D*.
5: 3 They took *D* and put him back
5: 3 early the next day, there was *D*,
5: 4 when they rose, there was *D*,
5: 5 to this day neither the priests of *D*
5: 7 upon us and upon *D* our god."
1Ch 10: 10 hung up his head in the temple of *D*

DAGON'S (DAGON)

1Sa 5: 2 they carried the ark into *D* temple
5: 5 nor any others who enter *D* temple

DALMANUTHA

Mk 8: 10 and went to the region of *D*.

DALMATIA

2Ti 4: 10 gone to Galatia, and Titus to *D*.

DALPHON

Est 9: 7 *D*, Aspatha, Poratha, Adalia,

DAM

Pr 17: 14 a quarrel is like breaching a *d*;

DAMAGE (DAMAGED)

2Ki 12: 5 used to repair whatever *d* is found
12: 7 aren't you repairing the *d* done
Ac 27: 21 have spared yourselves this *d*
Rev 6: 6 and do not *d* the oil and the wine!"

DAMAGED (DAMAGE)

Lev 21: 20 or running sores or *d* testicles.

DAMARIS

Ac 17: 34 also a woman named *D*,

DAMASCENES (DAMASCUS)

2Co 11: 32 the city of the *D* guarded in order

DAMASCUS (DAMASCENES)

Ge 14: 15 as far as Hobah, north of *D*.
15: 2 inherit my estate is Eliezer of *D*?"
2Sa 8: 5 When the Arameans of *D* came

2Sa 8: 6 in the Aramean kingdom of *D*,
1Ki 11: 24 went to *D*, where they settled
15: 18 king of Aram, who was ruling in *D*.
19: 15 and go to the Desert of *D*.
20: 34 set up your own market areas in *D*,
2Ki 5: 12 and Pharpar, the rivers of *D*,
8: 7 went to *D*, and Ben-Hadad king
8: 9 of all the finest wares of *D*.
14: 28 how he recovered for Israel both *D*
16: 9 of Assyria complied by attacking *D*
16: 10 He saw an altar in *D* and sent
16: 10 Then King Ahaz went to *D*
16: 11 that King Ahaz had sent from *D*
16: 12 When the king came back from *D*
1Ch 18: 5 When the Arameans of *D* came
18: 6 in the Aramean kingdom of *D*,
2Ch 16: 2 king of Aram, who was ruling in *D*.
24: 23 all the plunder to their king in *D*.
28: 5 prisoners and brought them to *D*.
28: 23 offered sacrifices to the gods of *D*,
SS 7: 4 looking toward *D*.
Isa 7: 8 and the head of *D* is only Rezin.
7: 8 for the head of Aram is *D*,
8: 4 the wealth of *D* and the plunder
10: 9 and Samaria like *D*?
17: 1 An oracle concerning *D*:
17: 1 "See, *D* will no longer be a city
17: 3 and royal power from *D*;
Jer 49: 23 Concerning *D*:
49: 24 *D* has become feeble,
49: 27 "I will set fire to the walls of *D*;
Eze 27: 18 *D*, because of your many products
47: 16 lies on the border between *D*
47: 17 along the northern border of *D*,
47: 18 run between Hauran and *D*,
48: 1 and the northern border of *D* next
Am 1: 3 "For three sins of *D*,
1: 5 I will break down the gate of *D*;
5: 27 into exile beyond *D*,"
Zec 9: 1 and will rest upon *D*—
Ac 9: 2 for letters to the synagogues in *D*,
9: 3 As he neared *D* on his journey,
9: 8 So they led him by the hand into *D*.
9: 10 In *D* there was a disciple named
9: 19 days with the disciples in *D*.
9: 22 and baffled the Jews living in *D*
9: 27 in *D* he had preached fearlessly
22: 5 from them to their brothers in *D*,
22: 6 "About noon as I came near *D*,
22: 10 the Lord said, 'and go into *D*.
22: 11 me by the hand into *D*,
26: 12 going to *D* with the authority
26: 20 First to those in *D*, then to those
2Co 11: 32 In *D* the governor
Gal 1: 17 into Arabia and later returned to *D*

DAMPNESS

SS 5: 2 my hair with the *d* of the night."

DAN (DANITE DANITES)

Ge 14: 14 and went in pursuit as far as *D*.
30: 6 Because of this she named him *D*.
35: 25 of Rachel's maidservant Bilhah: *D*
46: 23 The son of *D*: Hushim.
49: 16 "*D* will provide justice
49: 17 *D* will be a serpent by the roadside,
Ex 1: 4 and Benjamin; *D* and Naphtali;
31: 6 of the tribe of *D*, to help him.
35: 34 of the tribe of *D*, the ability
38: 23 of the tribe of *D*— a craftsman
Nu 1: 12 from *D*, Ahiezer son
1: 38 From the descendants of *D*:
1: 39 from the tribe of *D* was 62,700.
2: 25 be the divisions of the camp of *D*,
2: 25 of the people of *D* is Ahiezer son
2: 31 to the camp of *D* number 157,600.
7: 66 the leader of the people of *D*,
10: 25 divisions of the camp of *D* set out,
13: 12 from the tribe of *D*, Ammiel son
26: 42 These were the clans of *D*:
26: 42 descendants of *D* by their clans:
34: 22 the leader from the tribe of *D*;
Dt 27: 13 Asher, Zebulun, *D* and Naphtali.
33: 22 About *D* he said:
33: 22 "*D* is a lion's cub,
34: 1 from Gilead to *D*, all of Naphtali,
Jos 19: 40 lot came out for the tribe of *D*,
19: 47 named it *D* after their forefather.)
Jos 19: 48 the inheritance of the tribe of *D*,
21: 5 clans of the tribes of Ephraim, *D*
21: 23 tribe of *D* they received Eltekeh,
Jdg 5: 17 *D*, why did he linger by the ships?
18: 29 *D* after their forefather *D*,
18: 30 for the tribe of *D* until the time
20: 1 the Israelites from *D* to Beersheba
1Sa 3: 20 from *D* to Beersheba recognized
2Sa 3: 10 and Judah from *D* to Beersheba."
17: 11 Let all Israel, from *D* to Beersheba
24: 2 of Israel from *D* to Beersheba
24: 15 people from *D* to Beersheba died.
1Ki 4: 25 from *D* to Beersheba, lived
12: 29 up in Bethel, and the other in *D*.
12: 30 as far as *D* to worship the one there
15: 20 He conquered Ijon, *D*,
2Ki 10: 29 the golden calves at Bethel and *D*.
1Ch 2: 2 Issachar, Zebulun, *D*, Joseph,
12: 35 men of *D*, ready for battle—
21: 2 the Israelites from Beersheba to *D*.
27: 22 over *D*: Azarel son of Jeroham.
2Ch 2: 14 whose mother was from *D*
16: 4 They conquered Ijon, *D*,
30: 5 from Beersheba to *D*,
Jer 4: 15 A voice is announcing from *D*,
8: 16 is heard from *D*;
Eze 48: 1 the northern frontier, *D* will have
48: 2 the territory of *D* from east to west.
48: 32 gate of Benjamin and the gate of *D*.
Am 8: 14 'As surely as your god lives, O *D*,'

DAN JAAN

2Sa 24: 6 on to *D* and around toward Sidon.

DANCE (DANCED DANCES DANCING)

Job 21: 11 their little ones *d* about.
Ecc 3: 4 a time to mourn and a time to *d*,
SS 6: 13 as on the *d* of Mahanaim?
Jer 31: 4 and go out to *d* with the joyful.
31: 13 Then maidens will *d* and be glad,
Mt 11: 17 and you did not *d*;
Lk 7: 32 and you did not *d*;

DANCED (DANCE)

1Sa 18: 7 As they *d*, they sang:
2Sa 6: 14 *d* before the LORD
1Ki 18: 26 they *d* around the altar they had
Mt 14: 6 daughter of Herodias *d* for them
Mk 6: 22 of Herodias came in and *d*,

DANCES (DANCE)

1Sa 21: 11 the one they sing about in their *d*:
29: 5 David they sang about in their *d*:

DANCING (DANCE)

Ex 15: 20 with tambourines and *d*.
32: 19 and saw the calf and the *d*,
Jdg 11: 34 *d* to the sound of tambourines!
21: 21 of Shiloh come out to join in the *d*,
21: 23 the girls were *d*, each man caught
1Sa 18: 6 Saul with singing and *d*,
2Sa 6: 16 she saw King David leaping and *d*
1Ch 15: 29 And when she saw King David *d*
Ps 30: 11 You turned my wailing into *d*;
149: 3 Let them praise his name with *d*
150: 4 praise him with tambourine and *d*,
La 5: 15 our *d* has turned to mourning.
Lk 15: 25 the house, he heard music and *d*.

DANDLED

Isa 66: 12 and *d* on her knees.

DANGER (DANGEROUS DANGERS ENDANGER ENDANGERED ENDANGERS)

1Sa 20: 21 you are safe; there is no *d*.
Pr 22: 3 A prudent man sees *d*
27: 12 The prudent see *d* and take refuge,
Mt 5: 22 will be in *d* of the fire of hell.
Lk 8: 23 swamped, and they were in great *d*.
Ac 19: 27 There is *d* not only that our trade
19: 40 we are in *d* of being charged
Ro 8: 35 famine or nakedness or *d* or sword?
2Co 11: 26 I have been in *d* from rivers,
11: 26 and in *d* from false brothers.
11: 26 from Gentiles; in *d* in the city,
11: 26 from rivers, in *d* from bandits,
11: 26 in *d* from Gentiles;
2Co 11: 26 in *d* from my own countrymen,
11: 26 in *d* in the country, in *d* at sea;
Heb 6: 8 and is in *d* of being cursed.

DANGEROUS (DANGER)

Ac 27: 9 and sailing had already become *d*

DANGERS (DANGER)

Ecc 12: 5 and of *d* in the streets;

DANGLES

Job 28: 4 far from men he *d* and sways.

DANIEL (DANIEL'S)

1Ch 3: 1 *D* the son of Abigail of Carmel;
Ezr 8: 2 of the descendants of Ithamar, *D*;
Ne 10: 6 Obadiah, *D*, Ginnethon,
Eze 14: 14 Noah, *D* and Job—were in it,
14: 20 even if Noah, *D* and Job were in it,
28: 3 Are you wiser than *D*?
Da 1: 6 *D*, Hananiah, Mishael and Azariah
1: 7 to *D*, the name Belteshazzar;
1: 8 *D* resolved not to defile himself
1: 9 to show favor and sympathy to *D*,
1: 10 but the official told *D*, "I am afraid
1: 11 chief official had appointed over *D*,
1: 11 *D* then said to the guard whom
1: 17 And *D* could understand visions
1: 19 and he found none equal to *D*,
1: 21 *D* remained there until the first
2: 13 and men were sent to look for *D*
2: 14 *D* spoke to him with wisdom
2: 15 then explained the matter to *D*.
2: 16 *D* went in to the king and asked
2: 17 Then *D* returned to his house
2: 19 Then *D* praised the God of heaven
2: 19 the mystery was revealed to *D*
2: 24 *D* went to Arioch, whom the king
2: 25 Arioch took *D* to the king at once
2: 26 The king asked *D* (also called
2: 27 *D* replied, "No wise man,
2: 46 fell prostrate before *D*
2: 47 to *D*, "Surely your God is the God
2: 48 the king placed *D* in a high position
2: 49 while *D* himself remained
4: 8 *D* came into my presence
4: 19 *D* (also called Belteshazzar) was
5: 12 Call for *D*, and he will tell you what
5: 12 This man *D*, whom the king called
5: 13 So *D* was brought before the king,
5: 13 the king said to him, "Are you *D*,
5: 17 Then *D* answered the king,
5: 29 Belshazzar's command, *D* was
6: 2 over them, one of whom was *D*.
6: 3 Now *D* so distinguished himself
6: 4 grounds for charges against *D*
6: 5 for charges against this man *D*
6: 10 when *D* learned that the decree
6: 11 as a group and found *D* praying
6: 13 Then they said to the king, "*D*,
6: 14 he was determined to rescue *D*
6: 16 and they brought *D* and threw him
6: 16 said to *D*, "May your God,
6: 20 called to *D* in an anguished voice,
6: 20 "*D*, servant of the living God,
6: 21 *D* answered, "O king, live forever!
6: 23 gave orders to lift *D* out of the den.
6: 23 when *D* was lifted from the den,
6: 24 falsely accused *D* were brought
6: 26 and reverence the God of *D*.
6: 27 He has rescued *D*
6: 28 So *D* prospered during the reign
7: 1 king of Babylon, *D* had a dream,
7: 2 *D* said: "In my vision
7: 15 "I, *D*, was troubled in spirit,
7: 28 *D*, was deeply troubled
8: 1 of King Belshazzar's reign, I, *D*,
8: 15 *D*, was watching the vision
8: 27 *D*, was exhausted and lay ill
9: 2 *D*, understood from the Scriptures,
9: 22 instructed me and said to me, "*D*,
10: 1 to *D* (who was called Belteshazzar
10: 2 *D*, mourned for three weeks.
10: 7 *D*, was the only one who saw
10: 11 "*D*, you who are highly esteemed,
10: 12 he continued, "Do not be afraid, *D*.
12: 4 *D*, close up and seal the words
12: 5 *D*, looked, and there

Da 12: 9 He replied, "Go your way, *D*,
Mt 24: 15 spoken of through the prophet *D*—

DANIEL'S (DANIEL)

Da 2: 49 at *D* request the king appointed
6: 17 so that *D* situation might not be

DANITE (DAN)

Lev 24: 11 the daughter of Dibri the *D*.)

DANITES (DAN)

Jos 19: 47 *D* had difficulty taking possession
Jdg 1: 34 The Amorites confined the *D*
13: 2 from the clan of the *D*,
18: 1 tribe of the *D* was seeking a place
18: 2 the *D* sent five warriors from Zorah
18: 11 men from the clan of the *D*,
18: 16 The six hundred *D*, armed
18: 22 together and overtook the *D*.
18: 23 the *D* turned and said to Micah,
18: 25 The *D* answered, "Don't argue
18: 26 So the *D* went their way,
18: 28 *D* rebuilt the city and settled there.
18: 30 There the *D* set up
Eze 27: 19 " '*D* and Greeks from Uzal bought

DANNAH

Jos 15: 49 Jattir, Socoh, *D*, Kiriath Sannah

DAPPLED

Zec 6: 3 the fourth *d*— all of them powerful.
6: 6 and the one with the *d* horses

DARDA

1Ki 4: 31 Calcol and *D*, the sons of Mahol.
1Ch 2: 6 Heman, Calcol and *D*— five in all.

DARE (DARED DARES DARING)

2Sa 3: 11 Ish-Bosheth did not *d*
Job 13: 16 for no godless man would *d* come
Pr 29: 24 under oath and *d* not testify.
Jn 2: 16 How *d* you turn my Father's house
9: 34 in sin at birth; how *d* you lecture us
Ac 7: 32 with fear and did not *d* to look.
23: 4 You *d* to insult God's high priest?"
Ro 5: 7 man someone might possibly *d*
1Co 6: 1 *d* he take it before the ungodly
2Co 10: 12 We do not *d* to classify
11: 21 as a fool—I also *d* to boast about.
Jude : 9 did not *d* to bring a slanderous

DARED (DARE)

Est 7: 5 Where is the man who has *d*
Mt 22: 46 and from that day on no one *d*
Mk 12: 34 then on no one *d* ask him any more
Lk 20: 40 And no one *d* to ask him any more
Jn 21: 12 None of the disciples *d* ask him,
Ac 5: 13 No one else *d* join them, even
1Th 2: 2 help of our God we *d* to tell you his

DARES (DARE)

Ge 49: 9 like a lioness—who *d* to rouse him
Nu 24: 9 like a lioness—who *d*
Job 41: 14 Who *d* open the doors of his mouth
La 4: 14 that no one *d* to touch their
2Co 11: 21 What anyone else *d* to boast about

DARICS

1Ch 29: 7 and ten thousand *d* of gold,
Ezr 8: 27 bowls of gold valued at 1,000 *d*,

DARING (DARE)

Job 32: 6 not *d* to tell you what I know.

DARIUS

Ezr 4: 5 to the reign of *D* king of Persia.
4: 24 of the reign of *D* king of Persia.
5: 5 until a report could go to *D*
5: 6 of Trans-Euphrates, sent to King *D*
5: 7 To King *D*: Cordial greetings.
6: 1 King *D* then issued an order,
6: 12 I *D* have decreed it.
6: 13 of the decree King *D* had sent,
6: 14 *D* and Artaxerxes, kings of Persia.
6: 15 year of the reign of King *D*.
Ne 12: 22 in the reign of *D* the Persian.
Da 5: 31 *D* the Mede took over the kingdom
6: 1 It pleased *D* to appoint 120 satraps
Da 6: 6 "O King *D*, live forever! The royal
6: 9 So King *D* put the decree in writing
6: 25 King *D* wrote to all the peoples,
6: 28 prospered during the reign of *D*
9: 1 In the first year of *D* son
11: 1 And in the first year of *D* the Mede
Hag 1: 1 In the second year of King *D*,
1: 15 in the second year of King *D*.
2: 10 in the second year of *D*, the word
Zec 1: 1 month of the second year of *D*,
1: 7 of Shebat, in the second year of *D*,
7: 1 In the fourth year of King *D*,

DARK (DARKEN DARKENED DARKENING DARKENS DARKER DARKEST DARKNESS PITCH-DARK)

Dt 28: 29 about like a blind man in the *d*.
2Sa 22: 10 *d* clouds were under his feet.
22: 12 the *d* rain clouds of the sky.
1Ki 8: 12 that he would dwell in a *d* cloud;
2Ch 6: 1 that he would dwell in a *d* cloud;
Job 3: 9 May its morning stars become *d*;
18: 6 The light in his tent becomes *d*;
22: 11 why it is so *d* you cannot see,
24: 16 In the *d*, men break into houses,
34: 22 There is no *d* place, no deep
Ps 18: 9 *d* clouds were under his feet.
18: 11 the *d* rain clouds of the sky.
35: 6 may their path be *d* and slippery,
74: 20 of violence fill the *d* places
105: 28 darkness and made the land *d*—
139: 12 the darkness will not be *d* to you;
Pr 2: 13 paths to walk in *d* ways,
7: 9 as the *d* of night set in.
31: 15 She gets up while it is still *d*;
Ecc 12: 2 and the moon and the stars grow *d*,
SS 1: 5 *D* am I, yet lovely,
1: 5 *d* like the tents of Kedar,
1: 6 Do not stare at me because I am *d*,
Isa 50: 10 Let him who walks in the *d*,
Jer 4: 28 and the heavens above grow *d*,
Eze 30: 18 *D* will be the day at Tahpanhes
Mic 3: 6 and the day will go *d* for them.
Mt 10: 27 you in the *d*, speak in the daylight;
Mk 1: 35 while it was still *d*, Jesus got up,
Lk 11: 36 of it *d*, it will be completely lighted,
12: 3 said in the *d* will be heard
Jn 6: 17 By now it was *d*, and Jesus had not
12: 35 in the *d* does not know where he is
20: 1 day of the week, while it was still *d*,
Ro 2: 19 a light for those who are in the *d*,
Eph 6: 12 against the powers of this *d* world
2Pe 1: 19 as to a light shining in a *d* place,
Rev 8: 12 so that a third of them turned *d*.
9: 17 breastplates were fiery red, *d* blue,

DARK-COLORED

Ge 30: 32 every *d* lamb and every spotted
30: 33 that is not *d* will be considered
30: 35 white on them) and all the *d* lambs,
30: 40 *d* animals that belonged to Laban.

DARKEN (DARK)

Eze 32: 7 and *d* their stars;
32: 8 I will *d* over you;
Am 8: 9 and *d* the earth in broad daylight.

DARKENED (DARK)

Job 6: 16 overflow when *d* by thawing ice
Ps 69: 23 May their eyes be *d*
SS 1: 6 because I am *d* by the sun.
Isa 5: 30 the light will be *d* by the clouds.
13: 10 The rising sun will be *d*
Joel 2: 10 the sun and moon are *d*,
3: 15 The sun and moon will be *d*,
Mt 24: 29 " 'the sun will be *d*,
Mk 13: 24 " 'the sun will be *d*,
Ro 1: 21 and their foolish hearts were *d*.
11: 10 May their eyes be *d*
Eph 4: 18 They are *d* in their understanding
Rev 9: 2 and sky were *d* by the smoke

DARKENING (DARK)

Jer 13: 16 stumble on the *d* hills.

DARKENS (DARK)

Job 38: 2 "Who is this that *d* my counsel
Am 5: 8 and *d* day into night,

DARKER (DARK)

Ge 49: 12 His eyes will be *d* than wine,

DARKEST (DARK)

Ps 88: 6 in the *d* depths.

DARKNESS (DARK)

Ge 1: 2 *d* was over the surface of the deep,
1: 4 he separated the light from the *d*.
1: 5 and the *d* he called "night."
1: 18 and to separate light from *d*.
15: 12 and dreadful *d* came over him.
15: 17 the sun had set and *d* had fallen,
Ex 10: 21 over Egypt—*d* that can be felt."
10: 21 so that *d* will spread over Egypt—
10: 22 and total *d* covered all Egypt
14: 20 the night the cloud brought *d*
20: 21 approached the thick *d* where God
Dt 4: 11 with black clouds and deep *d*.
5: 22 the cloud and the deep *d*;
5: 23 you heard the voice out of the *d*,
Jos 24: 7 and he put *d* between you
1Sa 2: 9 but the wicked will be silenced in *d*.
2Sa 22: 12 He made *d* his canopy around him
22: 29 the LORD turns my *d* into light.
Job 3: 4 That day—may it turn to *d*;
3: 5 May *d* and deep shadow claim it
3: 6 That night—may thick *d* seize it;
5: 14 *D* comes upon them in the daytime
10: 22 where even the light is like *d*."
11: 17 and *d* will become like morning.
12: 22 He reveals the deep things of *d*
12: 25 They grope in *d* with no light;
15: 22 He despairs of escaping the *d*;
15: 23 he knows the day of *d* is at hand.
15: 30 He will not escape the *d*;
17: 12 in the face of *d* they say, 'Light is
17: 13 if I spread out my bed in *d*,
18: 18 He is driven from light into *d*
19: 8 he has shrouded my paths in *d*.
20: 26 total *d* lies in wait for his treasures.
22: 13 Does he judge through such *d*?
23: 17 Yet I am not silenced by the *d*,
23: 17 by the thick *d* that covers my face.
24: 17 of them, deep *d* is their morning;
24: 17 with the terrors of *d*.
26: 10 for a boundary between light and *d*.
28: 3 Man puts an end to the *d*;
28: 3 recesses for ore in the blackest *d*.
29: 3 and by his light I walked through *d*
30: 26 looked for light, then came *d*.
37: 19 draw up our case because of our *d*.
38: 9 and wrapped it in thick *d*,
38: 19 And where does *d* reside?
Ps 18: 11 He made *d* his covering, his
18: 28 my God turns my *d* into light.
44: 19 and covered us over with deep *d*.
82: 5 They walk about in *d*;
88: 12 wonders known in the place of *d*,
88: 18 the *d* is my closest friend.
91: 6 the pestilence that stalks in the *d*,
97: 2 Clouds and thick *d* surround him;
104: 20 You bring *d*, it becomes night,
105: 28 He sent *d* and made the land dark
107: 10 sat in *d* and the deepest gloom,
107: 14 He brought them out of *d*
112: 4 Even in *d* light dawns
139: 11 If I say, "Surely the *d* will hide me
139: 12 even the *d* will not be dark to you,
139: 12 for *d* is as light to you.
143: 3 he makes me dwell in *d*
Pr 4: 19 the way of the wicked is like deep *d*
20: 20 lamp will be snuffed out in pitch *d*.
Ecc 2: 13 just as light is better than *d*.
2: 14 while the fool walks in the *d*;
5: 17 All his days he eats in *d*,
6: 4 and in *d* its name is shrouded.
6: 4 without meaning, it departs in *d*,
11: 8 But let him remember the days of *d*
Isa 5: 20 and light for *d*,
5: 20 who put *d* for light
5: 30 he will see *d* and distress;
8: 22 and see only distress and *d*
8: 22 and they will be thrust into utter *d*.
9: 2 Jordan—The people walking in *d*
29: 15 who do their work in *d* and think,
29: 18 and out of gloom and *d*

Isa 42: 7 the dungeon those who sit in *d*.
42: 16 I will turn the *d* into light
45: 3 I will give you the treasures of *d*,
45: 7 I form the light and create *d*,
45: 19 from somewhere in a land of *d*;
47: 5 "Sit in silence, go into *d*,
49: 9 and to those in *d*, 'Be free!'
50: 3 I clothe the sky with *d*
58: 10 then your light will rise in the *d*,
59: 9 We look for light, but all is *d*;
60: 2 See, *d* covers the earth
60: 2 and thick *d* is over the peoples,
Jer 2: 6 a land of drought and *d*,
2: 31 or a land of great *d*?
13: 16 God before he brings the *d*,
13: 16 but he will turn it to thick *d*
23: 12 they will be banished to *d*
La 3: 2 walk in *d* rather than light;
3: 6 He has made me dwell in *d*
Eze 8: 12 house of Israel are doing in the *d*,
32: 8 I will bring *d* over your land,
34: 12 scattered on a day of clouds and *d*.
Da 2: 22 he knows what lies in *d*,
Joel 2: 2 a day of *d* and gloom,
2: 31 The sun will be turned to *d*
Am 4: 13 he who turns dawn to *d*,
5: 18 That day will be *d*, not light.
5: 20 Will not the day of the LORD be *d*,
Mic 3: 6 and *d*, without divination.
7: 8 Though I sit in *d*,
Na 1: 8 he will pursue his foes into *d*.
Zep 1: 15 a day of *d* and gloom,
Mt 4: 16 the people living in *d*
6: 23 If then the light within you is *d*,
6: 23 how great is that *d*! "No one can
6: 23 your whole body will be full of *d*.
8: 12 into the *d*, where there will be
22: 13 and throw him outside, into the *d*,
25: 30 servant outside, into the *d*,
27: 45 hour until the ninth hour *d* came
Mk 15: 33 At the sixth hour *d* came
Lk 1: 79 heaven to shine on those living in *d*
11: 34 are bad, your body also is full of *d*.
11: 35 that the light within you is not *d*.
22: 53 this is your hour—when *d* reigns."
23: 44 and *d* came over the whole land
Jn 1: 5 The light shines in the *d*,
1: 5 but the *d* has not understood it.
3: 19 but men loved *d* instead of light
8: 12 follows me will never walk in *d*,
12: 35 before *d* overtakes you.
12: 46 believes in me should stay in *d*.
Ac 2: 20 The sun will be turned to *d*
13: 11 Immediately mist and *d* came
26: 18 and turn them from *d* to light,
Ro 13: 12 So let us put aside the deeds of *d*
1Co 4: 5 bring to light what is hidden in *d*
2Co 4: 6 who said, "Let light shine out of *d*
6: 14 fellowship can light have with *d*?
Eph 5: 8 For you were once *d*, but now you
5: 11 to do with the fruitless deeds of *d*,
Col 1: 13 us from the dominion of *d*
1Th 5: 4 in *d* so that this day should surprise
5: 5 belong to the night or to the *d*.
Heb 12: 18 to *d*, gloom and storm;
1Pe 2: 9 out of *d* into his wonderful light.
2Pe 2: 17 Blackest *d* is reserved for them.
1Jn 1: 5 in him there is no *d* at all.
1: 6 with him yet walk in the *d*,
2: 8 because the *d* is passing
2: 9 but hates his brother is still in the *d*.
2: 11 and walks around in the *d*;
2: 11 because the *d* has blinded him.
2: 11 hates his brother is in the *d*
Jude : 6 in *d*, bound with everlasting chains
: 13 for whom blackest *d* has been
Rev 16: 10 his kingdom was plunged into *d*.

DARKON

Ezr 2: 56 Jaala, *D*, Giddel, Shephatiah,
Ne 7: 58 Jaala, *D*, Giddel, Shephatiah,

DARLING

SS 1: 9 I liken you, my *d*, to a mare
1: 15 How beautiful you are, my *d*
2: 2 is my *d* among the maidens.
2: 10 "Arise, my *d*,
2: 13 Arise, come, my *d*;
SS 4: 1 How beautiful you are, my *d*!
4: 7 All beautiful you are, my *d*;
5: 2 "Open to me, my sister, my *d*,
6: 4 You are beautiful, my *d*,

DART (DARTING)

Job 41: 21 and flames *d* from his mouth.
41: 26 does the spear or the *d*
Na 2: 4 they *d* about like lightning.

DARTING (DART)

Pr 7: 23 like a bird *d* into a snare,
26: 2 a fluttering sparrow or a *d* swallow,
Isa 14: 29 fruit will be a *d*, venomous serpent.
30: 6 of adders and *d* snakes,

DASH (DASHED DASHES)

Jdg 20: 37 been in ambush made a sudden *d*
2Ki 8: 12 *d* their little children to the ground,
Ps 2: 9 you will *d* them to pieces like
Eze 23: 34 you will *d* it to pieces
Na 2: 5 They *d* to the city wall;
Lk 19: 44 They will *d* you to the ground,
Rev 2: 27 he will *d* them to pieces like

DASHED (DASH)

2Ch 25: 12 down so that all were *d* to pieces.
Ps 119:116 do not let my hopes be *d*.
Isa 13: 16 Their infants will be *d* to pieces
Hos 10: 14 when mothers were *d*
13: 16 their little ones will be *d*
Na 3: 10 Her infants were *d* to pieces
Ac 27: 29 Fearing that we would be *d*

DASHES (DASH)

Ps 137: 9 and *d* them against the rocks.

DATE (DATES)

Eze 24: 2 of man, record this *d*, this very *d*,
Ac 21: 26 notice of the *d* when the days

DATES (DATE)

2Sa 6: 19 a cake of *d* and a cake of raisins
1Ch 16: 3 a cake of *d* and a cake of raisins
Ac 1: 7 or *d* the Father has set
1Th 5: 1 *d* we do not need to write to you,

DATHAN

Nu 16: 1 and certain Reubenites—*D*
16: 12 Moses summoned *D* and Abiram,
16: 24 away from the tents of Korah, *D*
16: 25 and went to *D* and Abiram,
16: 27 away from the tents of Korah, *D*
16: 27 *D* and Abiram had come out
26: 9 The same *D* and Abiram were
26: 9 the sons of Eliab were Nemuel, *D*
Dt 11: 6 and what he did to *D* and Abiram,
Ps 106: 17 earth opened up and swallowed *D*;

DAUGHTER (DAUGHTERS GRANDDAUGHTER GRANDDAUGHTERS)

2Ki 19: 21 The *D* of Jerusalem
19: 21 " 'The Virgin *D* of Zion
Ps 9: 14 praises in the gates of the *D* of Zion
45: 12 The *D* of Tyre will come with a gift,
137: 8 O *D* of Babylon, doomed
Isa 1: 8 The *D* of Zion is left
10: 30 Cry out, O *D* of Gallim!
10: 32 fist at the mount of the *D* of Zion,
16: 1 to the mount of the *D* of Zion.
23: 10 the *D* of Tarshish, like the Nile,
23: 12 O Virgin *D* of Sidon, now crushed!
37: 22 The *D* of Jerusalem
37: 22 "The Virgin *D* of Zion
47: 1 Virgin *D* of Babylon;
47: 1 *D* of the Babylonians.
47: 5 *D* of the Babylonians;
52: 2 O captive *D* of Zion.
62: 11 "Say to the *D* of Zion,
Jer 4: 31 the cry of the *D* of Zion gasping
6: 2 I will destroy the *D* of Zion,
6: 23 to attack you, O *D* of Zion."
46: 11 O Virgin *D* of Egypt.
46: 24 The *D* of Egypt will be put
48: 18 O inhabitants of the *D* of Dibon,
50: 42 to attack you, O *D* of Babylon.
51: 33 *D* of Babylon is like a threshing
La 1: 6 from the *D* of Zion.
1: 15 the Virgin *D* of Judah.
2: 1 How the Lord has covered the *D*
2: 2 the strongholds of the *D* of Judah.
2: 4 fire on the tent of the *D* of Zion.
2: 5 lamentation for the *D* of Judah.
2: 8 the wall around the *D* of Zion.
2: 10 The elders of the *D* of Zion
2: 13 O Virgin *D* of Zion?
2: 13 O *D* of Jerusalem?
2: 15 heads at the *D* of Jerusalem:
2: 18 O wall of the *D* of Zion,
4: 21 Rejoice and be glad, O *D* of Edom,
4: 22 O *D* of Edom, he will punish your
4: 22 O *D* of Zion, your punishment will
Mic 1: 13 sin to the *D* of Zion,
4: 8 O stronghold of the *D* of Zion,
4: 8 come to the *D* of Jerusalem."
4: 10 Writhe in agony, O *D* of Zion,
4: 13 "Rise and thresh, O *D* of Zion,
Zep 3: 14 O *D* of Jerusalem!
3: 14 Sing, O *D* of Zion;
Zec 2: 7 you who live in the *D* of Babylon!"
2: 10 "Shout and be glad, O *D* of Zion.
9: 9 Rejoice greatly, O *D* of Zion!
9: 9 Shout, *D* of Jerusalem!
Mt 21: 5 through the prophet: "Say to the *D*
Mk 5: 34 "*D*, your faith has healed you.
Lk 8: 48 "*D*, your faith has healed you.
Jn 12: 15 "Do not be afraid, O *D* of Zion;

DAUGHTERS (DAUGHTER)

Ps 45: 9 *D* of kings are among your honored
SS 2: 7 *D* of Jerusalem, I charge you
3: 5 *D* of Jerusalem, I charge you
8: 4 *D* of Jerusalem, I charge you:
Lk 23: 28 and said to them, "*D* of Jerusalem,

DAVID (DAVID'S)

Ru 4: 17 the father of Jesse, the father of *D*.
4: 22 of Jesse, and Jesse the father of *D*.
1Sa 16: 13 Spirit of the LORD came upon *D*
16: 19 "Send me your son *D*, who is
16: 20 sent them with his son *D* to Saul.
16: 21 *D* became one of his armor-bearers
16: 21 *D* came to Saul and entered his
16: 22 "Allow *D* to remain in my service,
16: 23 *D* would take his harp and play.
17: 12 *D* was the son of an Ephrathite
17: 14 *D* was the youngest.
17: 15 *D* went back and forth from Saul
17: 17 Now Jesse said to his son *D*,
17: 20 in the morning *D* left the flock
17: 22 *D* left his things with the keeper
17: 23 his usual defiance, and *D* heard it.
17: 26 *D* asked the men standing near him
17: 29 "Now what have I done?" said *D*.
17: 31 What *D* said was overheard
17: 32 *D* said to Saul, "Let no one lose
17: 34 *D* said to Saul, "Your servant has
17: 37 said to *D*, "Go, and the LORD be
17: 38 Saul dressed *D* in his own tunic.
17: 39 *D* fastened on his sword
17: 41 of him, kept coming closer to *D*.
17: 42 He looked *D* over and saw that he
17: 43 He said to *D*, "Am I a dog,
17: 43 the Philistine cursed *D* by his gods.
17: 45 *D* said to the Philistine, "You come
17: 48 *D* ran quickly toward the battle
17: 50 So *D* triumphed over the Philistine
17: 51 *D* ran and stood over him.
17: 54 *D* took the Philistine's head
17: 55 As Saul watched *D* going out
17: 57 as *D* returned from killing
17: 57 with *D* still holding the Philistine's
17: 58 *D* said, "I am the son
18: 1 After *D* had finished talking
18: 1 became one in spirit with *D*,
18: 2 From that day Saul kept *D*
18: 3 Jonathan made a covenant with *D*
18: 4 he was wearing and gave it to *D*,
18: 5 *D* did it so successfully that Saul
18: 6 after *D* had killed the Philistine,
18: 7 and *D* his tens of thousands."
18: 8 "They have credited *D* with tens
18: 9 on Saul kept a jealous eye on *D*.
18: 10 while *D* was playing the harp,
18: 11 But *D* eluded him twice.

2Sa 5:11 king of Tyre sent messengers to *D*,
5:12 And *D* knew that the LORD had
5:13 *D* took more concubines
5:17 Philistines heard that *D* had been
5:17 but *D* heard about it and went
5:19 so *D* inquired of the LORD,
5:20 So *D* went to Baal Perazim,
5:21 and *D* and his men carried them off
5:23 so *D* inquired of the LORD,
5:25 *D* did as the LORD commanded
6: 1 *D* again brought together out
6: 5 *D* and the whole house
6: 8 *D* was angry because the LORD's
6: 9 *D* was afraid of the LORD that day
6:10 to be with him in the City of *D*.
6:12 King *D* was told, "The LORD has
6:12 So *D* went down and brought up
6:12 to the City of *D* with rejoicing.
6:14 *D*, wearing a linen ephod, danced
6:16 And when she saw King *D* leaping
6:16 LORD was entering the City of *D*,
6:17 and *D* sacrificed burnt offerings
6:17 inside the tent that *D* had pitched
6:20 When *D* returned home
6:21 *D* said to Michal, "It was
7: 5 saying: "Go and tell my servant *D*,
7: 8 "Now then, tell my servant *D*,
7:17 Nathan reported to *D* all the words
7:18 Then King *D* went in and sat
7:20 "What more can *D* say to you?
7:26 the house of your servant *D* will be
8: 1 *D* defeated the Philistines
8: 2 *D* also defeated the Moabites.
8: 2 the Moabites became subject to *D*
8: 3 *D* fought Hadadezer son of Rehob,
8: 4 *D* captured a thousand
8: 5 *D* struck down twenty-two
8: 6 LORD gave *D* victory everywhere
8: 7 *D* took the gold shields that
8: 8 King *D* took a great quantity
8: 9 Hamath heard that *D* had defeated
8:10 Joram to King *D* to greet him
8:11 King *D* dedicated these articles
8:13 *D* became famous after he returned
8:14 LORD gave *D* victory everywhere
8:14 the Edomites became subject to *D*.
8:15 *D* reigned over all Israel, doing
9: 1 *D* asked, "Is there anyone still left
9: 2 They called him to appear before *D*
9: 5 So King *D* had him brought
9: 6 *D* said, "Mephibosheth!" "Your
9: 6 the son of Saul, came to *D*,
9: 7 "Don't be afraid," *D* said to him,
10: 2 So *D* sent a delegation
10: 2 *D* thought, "I will show kindness
10: 3 Hasn't *D* sent them to you
10: 3 "Do you think *D* is honoring your
10: 5 When *D* was told about this,
10: 7 *D* sent Joab out with the entire
10:17 When *D* was told of this, he
10:17 formed their battle lines to meet *D*
10:18 and *D* killed seven hundred
11: 1 But *D* remained in Jerusalem.
11: 1 *D* sent Joab out with the king's
11: 2 One evening *D* got up from his bed
11: 3 *D* sent someone to find out about
11: 4 Then *D* sent messengers to get her.
11: 5 conceived and sent word to *D*,
11: 6 And Joab sent him to *D*.
11: 6 So *D* sent this word to Joab:
11: 7 *D* asked him how Joab was,
11: 8 Then *D* said to Uriah, "Go
11:10 When *D* was told, "Uriah did not
11:11 you go home?" Uriah said to *D*,
11:12 not do such a thing!" Then *D* said
11:13 with him, and *D* made him drunk.
11:14 In the morning *D* wrote a letter
11:18 Joab sent *D* a full account
11:22 arrived he told *D* everything Joab
11:23 to *D*, "The men overpowered us
11:25 *D* told the messenger, "Say this
11:27 *D* had her brought to his house,
11:27 the thing *D* had done displeased
12: 1 The LORD sent Nathan to *D*.
12: 5 *D* burned with anger
12: 7 said to *D*, "You are the man!
12:13 *D* said to Nathan, "I have sinned
12:15 that Uriah's wife had borne to *D*,

2Sa 12:16 *D* pleaded with God for the child.
12:18 spoke to *D* but he would not listen
12:19 *D* noticed that his servants were
12:20 Then *D* got up from the ground.
12:24 *D* comforted his wife Bathsheba,
12:27 Joab then sent messengers to *D*,
12:29 So *D* mustered the entire army
12:31 *D* and his entire army returned
13: 1 Amnon son of *D* fell in love
13: 1 sister of Absalom son of *D*.
13: 7 *D* sent word to Tamar at the palace
13:21 When King *D* heard all this,
13:30 came to *D*: "Absalom has struck
13:37 King *D* mourned for his son every
15:13 A messenger came and told *D*,
15:14 *D* said to all his officials who were
15:22 *D* said to Ittai, "Go ahead,
15:30 But *D* continued up the Mount
15:31 So *D* prayed, "O LORD, turn
15:31 *D* had been told, "Ahithophel is
15:32 When *D* arrived at the summit,
15:33 *D* said to him, "If you go with me,
16: 1 When *D* had gone a short distance
16: 5 As King *D* approached Bahurim,
16: 6 He pelted *D* and all the king's
16:10 'Curse *D*,' who can ask, 'Why do
16:11 *D* then said to Abishai
16:13 So *D* and his men continued
16:23 was how both *D* and Absalom
17: 1 and set out tonight in pursuit of *D*.
17:16 a message immediately and tell *D*,
17:17 and they were to go and tell King *D*
17:21 and went to inform King *D*.
17:22 So *D* and all the people
17:24 *D* went to Mahanaim,
17:27 When *D* came to Mahanaim,
17:29 and cheese from cows' milk for *D*
18: 1 *D* mustered the men who were
18: 2 *D* sent the troops out—a third
18:24 While *D* was sitting
19:11 King *D* sent this message to Zadok
19:16 the men of Judah to meet King *D*.
19:22 *D* replied, "What do you
19:43 claim on *D* than you have.
20: 1 "We have no share in *D*,
20: 2 the men of Israel deserted *D*
20: 3 When *D* returned to his palace
20: 6 *D* said to Abishai, "Now Sheba son
20:11 is for *D*, let him follow Joab!"
20:21 hand against the king, against *D*.
21: 1 so *D* sought the face of the LORD.
21: 1 the reign of *D*, there was a famine
21: 3 *D* asked the Gibeonites, "What
21: 4 me to do for you?" *D* asked.
21: 7 oath before the LORD between *D*
21:11 When *D* was told what Aiah's
21:13 *D* brought the bones of Saul
21:15 *D* went down with his men to fight
21:16 said he would kill *D*.
21:22 and they fell at the hands of *D*
22: 1 *D* sang to the LORD the words
22:51 to *D* and his descendants forever."
23: 1 These are the last words of *D*:
23: 1 "The oracle of *D* son of Jesse,
23: 9 was with *D* when they taunted
23:13 down to *D* at the cave of Adullam,
23:14 At that time *D* was
23:15 *D* longed for water and said, "Oh,
23:16 and carried it back to *D*.
23:17 And *D* would not drink it.
23:23 And *D* put him in charge
24: 1 and he incited *D* against them,
24:10 *D* was conscience-stricken
24:11 Before *D* got up the next morning,
24:12 David's seer: "Go and tell *D*,
24:13 So Gad went to *D* and said to him,
24:14 *D* said to Gad, "I am
24:17 When *D* saw the angel who was
24:18 On that day Gad went to *D*
24:19 So *D* went up, as the LORD had
24:21 your threshing floor," *D* answered,
24:22 to *D*, "Let my lord the king take
24:24 So *D* bought the threshing floor
24:25 *D* built an altar to the LORD there
1Ki 1: 1 When King *D* was old
1:13 Go in to King *D* and say to him,
1:28 King *D* said, "Call in Bathsheba."
1:31 May my lord King *D* live forever!"

1Ki 1:32 King *D* said, "Call
1:37 than the throne of my lord King *D*
1:43 "Our lord King *D* has made
1:47 to congratulate our lord King *D*,
2: 1 When the time drew near for *D*
2:10 Then *D* rested with his fathers
2:10 and was buried in the City of *D*.
2:12 sat on the throne of his father *D*,
2:24 on the throne of my father *D*
2:26 LORD before my father *D*
2:32 of my father *D* he attacked two
2:33 But on *D* and his descendants,
2:44 the wrong you did to my father *D*.
3: 1 of *D* until he finished building his
3: 3 to the statutes of his father *D*,
3: 6 to your servant, my father *D*,
3: 7 king in place of my father *D*.
3:14 commands as *D* your father did,
5: 1 been on friendly terms with *D*.
5: 1 king to succeed his father *D*,
5: 3 against my father *D* from all sides,
5: 5 as the LORD told my father *D*,
5: 7 for he has given *D* a wise son
6:12 promise I gave to *D* your father.
7:51 his father *D* had dedicated—
8: 1 covenant from Zion, the City of *D*.
8:15 with his own mouth to my father *D*
8:16 I have chosen *D* to rule my people
8:17 "My father *D* had it in his heart
8:18 But the LORD said to my father *D*,
8:20 I have succeeded *D* my father
8:24 to your servant *D* my father;
8:25 keep for your servant *D* my father
8:26 promised your servant *D* my father
8:66 LORD had done for his servant *D*
9: 4 uprightness, as *D* your father did,
9: 5 as I promised *D* your father
9:24 up from the City of *D*
11: 4 the heart of *D* his father had been.
11: 6 as *D* his father had done.
11:12 for the sake of *D* your father,
11:13 tribe for the sake of *D* my servant
11:15 Earlier when *D* was fighting
11:21 Hadad heard that *D* rested
11:24 rebels when *D* destroyed the forces
11:27 the wall of the city of *D* his father.
11:32 But for the sake of my servant *D*
11:33 nor kept my statutes and laws as *D*,
11:34 life for the sake of *D* my servant,
11:36 so that *D* my servant may always
11:38 as *D* my servant did, I will be
11:38 built for *D* and will give Israel
11:43 buried in the city of *D* his father.
12:16 Look after your own house, O *D*!"
12:16 "What share do we have in *D*,
12:19 against the house of *D* to this day.
12:20 remained loyal to the house of *D*.
12:26 now likely revert to the house of *D*.
13: 2 will be born to the house of *D*.
14: 8 away from the house of *D*
14: 8 have not been like my servant *D*,
14:31 buried with them in the City of *D*.
15: 3 heart of *D* his forefather had been.
15: 5 For *D* had done what was right
15: 8 and was buried in the City of *D*.
15:11 as his father *D* had done.
15:24 them in the city of his father *D*.
22:50 them in the city of *D* his father.
2Ki 8:19 for the sake of his servant *D*,
8:19 promised to maintain a lamp for *D*
8:24 buried with them in the City of *D*.
9:28 fathers in his tomb in the City of *D*.
11:10 that had belonged to King *D*
12:21 with his fathers in the City of *D*.
14: 3 but not as his father *D* had done.
14:20 with his fathers, in the City of *D*.
15: 7 buried near them in the City of *D*.
15:38 buried with them in the City of *D*,
16: 2 Unlike *D* his father, he did not do
16:20 buried with them in the City of *D*.
17:21 away from the house of *D*,
18: 3 just as his father *D* had done.
19:34 for the sake of *D* my servant."
20: 5 the God of your father *D*, says:
20: 6 and for the sake of my servant *D*.' "
21: 7 of which the LORD had said to *D*
22: 2 in all the ways of his father *D*,
1Ch 2:15 the sixth Ozem and the seventh *D*.

1Ch 3: 1 These were the sons of *D* born
3: 4 These six were born to *D*
3: 4 *D* reigned in Jerusalem thirty-three
3: 9 All these were the sons of *D*,
4: 31 towns until the reign of *D*.
6: 31 These are the men *D* put in charge
7: 2 the reign of *D*, the descendants
9: 22 to their positions of trust by *D*
10: 14 the kingdom over to *D* son of Jesse.
11: 1 All Israel came together to *D*
11: 3 come to King *D* at Hebron,
11: 3 they anointed *D* king over Israel,
11: 4 *D* and all the Israelites marched
11: 5 Jebusites who lived there said to *D*,
11: 5 *D* captured the fortress of Zion,
11: 5 the fortress of Zion, the City of *D*.
11: 6 *D* had said, "Whoever leads
11: 7 and so it was called the City of *D*.
11: 7 *D* then took up residence
11: 9 *D* became more and more powerful
11: 13 He was with *D* at Pas Dammim
11: 15 down to *D* to the rock at the cave
11: 16 At that time *D* was
11: 17 *D* longed for water and said, "Oh,
11: 18 and carried it back to *D*.
11: 19 to bring it back, *D* would not drink
11: 25 And *D* put him in charge
12: 1 were the men who came to *D*
12: 8 defected to *D* at his stronghold
12: 16 also came to *D* in his stronghold.
12: 17 *D* went out to meet them
12: 18 *D* received them and made them
12: 18 "We are yours, O *D*!
12: 19 defected to *D* when he went
12: 20 When *D* went to Ziklag, these were
12: 21 helped *D* against raiding bands,
12: 22 Day after day men came to help *D*,
12: 23 for battle who came to *D* at Hebron
12: 31 by name to come and make *D* king
12: 33 to help *D* with undivided loyalty—
12: 38 also of one mind to make *D* king.
12: 38 to make *D* king over all Israel.
12: 39 men spent three days there with *D*,
13: 1 *D* conferred with each
13: 5 So *D* assembled all the Israelites,
13: 6 *D* and all the Israelites
13: 8 *D* and all the Israelites were
13: 11 *D* was angry because the LORD's
13: 12 *D* was afraid of God that day
13: 13 ark to be with him in the City of *D*.
14: 1 king of Tyre sent messengers to *D*,
14: 2 And *D* knew that the LORD had
14: 3 In Jerusalem *D* took more wives
14: 8 Philistines heard that *D* had been
14: 8 but *D* heard about it and went out
14: 10 so *D* inquired of God: "Shall I go
14: 11 So *D* and his men went up to Baal
14: 12 and *D* gave orders to burn them
14: 14 so *D* inquired of God again,
14: 16 So *D* did as God commanded him,
15: 1 After *D* had constructed buildings
15: 1 for himself in the City of *D*,
15: 2 Then *D* said, "No one
15: 3 *D* assembled all Israel in Jerusalem
15: 11 Then *D* summoned Zadok
15: 16 *D* told the leaders of the Levites
15: 25 So *D* and the elders of Israel
15: 27 Now *D* was clothed in a robe
15: 27 *D* also wore a linen ephod.
15: 29 And when she saw King *D* dancing
15: 29 LORD was entering the City of *D*,
16: 1 it inside the tent that *D* had pitched
16: 2 After *D* had finished sacrificing
16: 7 That day *D* first committed
16: 37 *D* left Asaph and his associates
16: 39 *D* left Zadok the priest
16: 43 and *D* returned home to bless his
17: 1 After *D* was settled in his palace,
17: 2 replied to *D*, "Whatever you have
17: 4 saying: "Go and tell my servant *D*,
17: 7 "Now then, tell my servant *D*,
17: 15 Nathan reported to *D* all the words
17: 16 Then King *D* went in and sat
17: 18 "What more can *D* say to you
17: 24 the house of your servant *D* will be
18: 1 *D* defeated the Philistines
18: 2 *D* also defeated the Moabites,
18: 3 *D* fought Hadadezer king of Zobah

1Ch 18: 4 *D* captured a thousand
18: 5 *D* struck down twenty-two
18: 6 LORD gave *D* victory everywhere
18: 7 *D* took the gold shields carried
18: 8 *D* took a great quantity of bronze,
18: 9 Hamath heard that *D* had defeated
18: 10 Hadoram to King *D* to greet him
18: 11 King *D* dedicated these articles
18: 13 LORD gave *D* victory everywhere
18: 13 the Edomites became subject to *D*.
18: 14 *D* reigned over all Israel, doing
19: 2 So *D* sent a delegation
19: 2 *D* thought, "I will show kindness
19: 3 "Do you think *D* is honoring your
19: 5 and told *D* about the men,
19: 8 *D* sent Joab out with the entire
19: 17 When *D* was told of this, he
19: 17 *D* formed his lines
19: 18 and *D* killed seven thousand
19: 19 they made peace with *D*
20: 1 but *D* remained in Jerusalem.
20: 2 *D* took the crown from the head
20: 3 *D* and his entire army returned
20: 3 *D* did this to all the Ammonite
20: 8 and they fell at the hands of *D*
21: 1 incited *D* to take a census of Israel.
21: 2 So *D* said to Joab
21: 5 number of the fighting men to *D*:
21: 8 Then *D* said to God, "I have sinned
21: 10 David's seer, "Go and tell *D*,
21: 11 So Gad went to *D* and said to him,
21: 13 *D* said to Gad, "I am
21: 16 Then *D* and the elders, clothed
21: 16 *D* looked up and saw the angel
21: 17 *D* said to God, "Was it not I who
21: 18 of the LORD ordered Gad to tell *D*
21: 19 So *D* went up in obedience
21: 21 bowed down before *D* with his face
21: 21 *D* approached, and when Araunah
21: 22 *D* said to him, "Let me have
21: 23 Araunah said to *D*, "Take it!
21: 24 But King *D* replied to Araunah,
21: 25 So *D* paid Araunah six hundred
21: 26 *D* built an altar to the LORD there
21: 28 when *D* saw that the LORD had
21: 30 *D* could not go before it to inquire
22: 1 Then *D* said, "The house
22: 2 So *D* gave orders to assemble
22: 4 large numbers of them to *D*.
22: 5 So *D* made extensive preparations
22: 5 *D* said, "My son Solomon is young
22: 7 *D* said to Solomon: "My son,
22: 17 *D* ordered all the leaders of Israel
23: 1 When *D* was old and full of years,
23: 4 *D* said, "Of these, twenty-four
23: 6 *D* divided the Levites
23: 25 For *D* had said, "Since the LORD,
23: 27 to the last instructions of *D*,
24: 3 *D* separated them into divisions
24: 31 in the presence of King *D*
25: 1 *D*, together with the commanders
26: 26 for the things dedicated by King *D*,
26: 32 and King *D* put them in charge
27: 18 Elihu, a brother of *D*; over Issachar
27: 23 *D* did not take the number
27: 24 in the book of the annals of King *D*.
28: 1 *D* summoned all the officials
28: 2 King *D* rose to his feet and said:
28: 11 *D* gave his son Solomon the plans
28: 19 "All this is in writing," *D* said,
28: 20 *D* also said to Solomon his son,
29: 1 King *D* said to the whole assembly:
29: 9 *D* the king also rejoiced greatly.
29: 10 *D* praised the LORD
29: 20 Then *D* said to the whole assembly,
29: 22 acknowledged Solomon son of *D*
29: 23 as king in place of his father *D*.
29: 26 *D* son of Jesse was king
2Ch 1: 1 son of *D* established himself firmly
1: 4 *D* had brought up the ark of God
1: 8 great kindness to *D* my father
1: 9 to my father *D* be confirmed,
2: 3 as you did for my father *D*
2: 7 whom my father *D* provided.
2: 12 He has given King *D* a wise son,
2: 14 those of my lord, *D* your father.
2: 17 the census his father *D* had taken;
3: 1 Jebusite, the place provided by *D*.

2Ch 3: 1 had appeared to his father *D*.
5: 1 his father *D* had dedicated—
5: 2 covenant from Zion, the City of *D*.
6: 4 with his mouth to my father *D*.
6: 6 I have chosen *D* to rule my people
6: 7 "My father *D* had it in his heart
6: 8 But the LORD said to my father *D*,
6: 10 I have succeeded *D* my father
6: 15 to your servant *D* my father;
6: 16 keep for your servant *D* my father
6: 17 your servant *D* come true.
6: 42 to *D* your servant."
7: 6 which King *D* had made
7: 10 things the LORD had done for *D*
7: 17 before me as *D* your father did,
7: 18 as I covenanted with *D* your father
8: 11 in the palace of *D* king of Israel,
8: 11 up from the City of *D*
8: 14 because this was what *D* the man
8: 14 the ordinance of his father *D*,
9: 31 buried in the city of *D* his father.
10: 16 Look after your own house, O *D*!"
10: 16 "What share do we have in *D*,
10: 19 against the house of *D* to this day.
11: 17 walking in the ways of *D*
12: 16 and was buried in the City of *D*.
13: 5 given the kingship of Israel to *D*
13: 6 an official of Solomon son of *D*,
14: 1 and was buried in the City of *D*.
16: 14 out for himself in the City of *D*.
17: 3 the ways his father *D* had followed.
21: 1 buried with them in the City of *D*.
21: 7 promised to maintain a lamp for *D*
21: 7 willing to destroy the house of *D*.
21: 12 the God of your father *D*, says:
21: 20 and was buried in the City of *D*.
23: 3 concerning the descendants of *D*.
23: 9 that had belonged to King *D*
23: 18 and singing, as *D* had ordered.
23: 18 to whom *D* had made assignments
24: 16 with the kings in the City of *D*,
24: 25 and was buried in the City of *D*.
27: 9 and was buried in the City of *D*.
28: 1 Unlike *D* his father, he did not do
29: 2 just as his father *D* had done.
29: 25 lyres in the way prescribed by *D*
29: 27 the instruments of *D* king of Israel.
29: 30 the LORD with the words of *D*
30: 26 the days of Solomon son of *D* king
32: 5 terraces of the City of *D*.
32: 30 to the west side of the City of *D*.
33: 7 of which God had said to *D*
33: 14 the outer wall of the City of *D*,
34: 2 walked in the ways of his father *D*,
34: 3 to seek the God of his father *D*.
35: 3 son of *D* king of Israel built.
35: 4 written by *D* king of Israel
35: 15 were in the places prescribed by *D*,
Ezr 3: 10 as prescribed by *D* king of Israel.
8: 2 Daniel; of the descendants of *D*,
8: 20 a body that *D* and the officials had
Ne 3: 15 going down from the City of *D*.
3: 16 a point opposite the tombs of *D*, as
12: 24 as prescribed by *D* the man of God.
12: 36 prescribed by *D* the man of God.
12: 37 and passed above the house of *D*
12: 37 steps of the City of *D* on the ascent
12: 45 according to the commands of *D*
12: 46 in the days of *D* and Asaph,
Ps 18: 50 to *D* and his descendants forever.
72: 20 concludes the prayers of *D* son
78: 70 He chose *D* his servant
78: 72 *D* shepherded them with integrity
89: 3 I have sworn to *D* my servant,
89: 20 I have found *D* my servant;
89: 35 and I will not lie to *D*—
89: 49 in your faithfulness you swore to *D*
122: 5 the thrones of the house of *D*.
132: 1 O LORD, remember *D*
132: 10 For the sake of *D* your servant,
132: 11 The LORD swore an oath to *D*,
132: 17 I will make a horn grow for *D*
144: 10 who delivers his servant *D*
Pr 1: 1 The proverbs of Solomon son of *D*,
Ecc 1: 1 son of *D*, king in Jerusalem:
SS 4: 4 Your neck is like the tower of *D*,
Isa 7: 2 Now the house of *D* was told,
7: 13 "Hear now, you house of *D*!

Isa 16: 5 one from the house of *D*—
22: 9 you saw that the City of *D*
22: 22 shoulder the key to the house of *D*;
29: 1 the city where *D* settled!
37: 35 for the sake of *D* my servant!''
38: 5 the God of your father *D*, says:
55: 3 my faithful love promised to *D*.
Jer 21: 12 of *D*, this is what the LORD says:
22: 30 none will sit on the throne of *D*
23: 5 up to *D* a righteous Branch,
30: 9 and *D* their king,
33: 17 '*D* will never fail to have a man
33: 21 covenant with *D* my servant—
33: 21 *D* will no longer have a descendant
33: 22 the descendants of *D* my servant
33: 26 of Jacob and *D* my servant
36: 30 one to sit on the throne of *D*;
Eze 34: 23 my servant *D*, and he will tend
34: 24 and my servant *D* will be prince
37: 24 '' 'My servant *D* will be king
37: 25 *D* my servant will be their prince
Hos 3: 5 LORD their God and *D* their king.
Am 6: 5 on your harps like *D*
Zec 12: 7 so that the honor of the house of *D*
12: 8 and the house of *D* will be like God
12: 8 feeblest among them will be like *D*,
12: 10 I will pour out on the house of *D*
12: 12 the clan of the house of *D*
13: 1 will be opened to the house of *D*
Mt 1: 1 of Jesus Christ the son of *D*,
1: 6 and Jesse the father of King *D*.
1: 6 *D* was the father of Solomon,
1: 17 fourteen from *D* to the exile
1: 17 in all from Abraham to *D*,
1: 20 ''Joseph son of *D*, do not be afraid
9: 27 of *D*!'' When he had gone indoors,
12: 3 ''Haven't you read what *D* did
12: 23 ''Could this be the Son of *D*?''
15: 22 Lord, Son of *D*, have mercy on me!
20: 30 ''Lord, Son of *D*, have mercy on us
20: 31 ''Lord, Son of *D*, have mercy on us
21: 9 ''Hosanna to the Son of *D*!''
21: 15 ''Hosanna to the Son of *D*,''
22: 42 ''The son of *D*,'' they replied.
22: 43 ''How is it then that *D*, speaking
22: 45 If then *D* calls him 'Lord,'
Mk 2: 25 ''Have you never read what *D* did
10: 47 Jesus, Son of *D*, have mercy on me
10: 48 ''Son of *D*, have mercy on me!''
11: 10 coming kingdom of our father *D*!''
12: 35 say that the Christ is the son of *D*?
12: 36 *D* himself, speaking
12: 37 *D* himself calls him 'Lord.'
Lk 1: 27 named Joseph, a descendant of *D*.
1: 32 give him the throne of his father *D*,
1: 69 us in the house of his servant *D*
2: 4 to Bethlehem the town of *D*,
2: 4 to the house and line of *D*.
2: 11 town of *D* a Savior has been born
3: 31 the son of *D*,
6: 3 ''Have you never read what *D* did
18: 38 Jesus, Son of *D*, have mercy on me
18: 39 ''Son of *D*, have mercy on me!''
20: 41 they say the Christ is the Son of *D*?
20: 42 *D* himself declares in the Book
20: 44 *D* calls him 'Lord.'
Jn 7: 42 the town where *D* lived?'' Thus
Ac 1: 16 the mouth of *D* concerning Judas,
2: 25 *D* said about him:
2: 29 that the patriarch *D* died
2: 34 For *D* did not ascend to heaven,
4: 25 of your servant, our father *D*:
7: 45 in the land until the time of *D*,
13: 22 Saul, he made *D* their king.
13: 22 'I have found *D* son of Jesse a man
13: 34 sure blessings promised to *D*.'
13: 36 when *D* had served God's purpose
Ro 1: 3 nature was a descendant of *D*,
4: 6 *D* says the same thing
11: 9 And *D* says:
2Ti 2: 8 from the dead, descended from *D*.
Heb 4: 7 long time later he spoke through *D*,
11: 32 Barak, Samson, Jephthah, *D*,
Rev 3: 7 and true, who holds the key of *D*.
5: 5 the Root of *D*, has triumphed.
22: 16 the Root and the Offspring of *D*,

DAVID'S (DAVID)

1Sa 17: 28 When Eliab, *D* oldest brother,
19: 11 But Michal, *D* wife, warned him,
19: 11 Saul sent men to *D* house
20: 15 cut off every one of *D* enemies
20: 16 ''May the LORD call *D* enemies
20: 25 to Saul, but *D* place was empty.
20: 27 of the month, *D* place was empty
23: 3 But *D* men said to him, ''Here
25: 9 Nabal this message in *D* name.
25: 9 When *D* men arrived, they gave
25: 10 Nabal answered *D* servants,
25: 12 *D* men turned around and went
25: 42 went with *D* messengers
25: 44 *D* wife, to Paltiel son of Laish,
26: 17 Saul recognized *D* voice and said,
30: 5 *D* two wives had been captured—
30: 20 saying, ''This is *D* plunder.''
30: 22 among *D* followers said,
2Sa 2: 13 son of Zeruiah and *D* men went out
2: 17 of Israel were defeated by *D* men.
2: 30 of *D* men were found missing.
2: 31 *D* men had killed three hundred
3: 5 Ithream the son of *D* wife Eglah.
3: 10 and establish *D* throne over Israel
3: 22 Just then *D* men and Joab returned
5: 8 and blind' who are *D* enemies.''
8: 18 and *D* sons were royal advisers.
9: 11 ate at *D* table like one
10: 2 When *D* men came to the land
10: 4 So Hanun seized *D* men, shaved
10: 6 had become a stench in *D* nostrils,
11: 13 At *D* invitation, he ate
11: 17 some of the men in *D* army fell;
12: 18 *D* servants were afraid
12: 30 and it was placed on *D* head.
13: 3 son of Shimeah, *D* brother.
13: 32 Jonadab son of Shimeah, *D* brother
15: 12 *D* counselor, to come from Giloh,
15: 37 So *D* friend Hushai arrived
16: 6 the special guard were on *D* right
16: 16 Then Hushai the Arkite, *D* friend,
18: 7 of Israel was defeated by *D* men,
18: 9 Absalom happened to meet *D* men.
20: 26 and Ira the Jairite was *D* priest.
21: 17 Then *D* men swore to him, saying,
21: 17 son of Zeruiah came to *D* rescue;
21: 21 son of Shimeah, *D* brother,
23: 8 are the names of *D* mighty men:
24: 11 *D* seer: ''Go and tell David,
1Ki 1: 8 and *D* special guard did not join
1: 11 without our lord *D* knowing it?
1: 38 and put Solomon on King *D* mule
2: 45 and *D* throne will remain secure
11: 39 I will humble *D* descendants
15: 4 for *D* sake the LORD his God gave
1Ch 11: 10 the chiefs of *D* mighty men—
11: 11 this is the list of *D* mighty men:
14: 17 *D* fame spread throughout every
18: 17 and *D* sons were chief officials
19: 2 When *D* men came to Hanun
19: 4 Hanun seized *D* men, shaved them
19: 6 had become a stench in *D* nostrils,
20: 2 and it was placed on *D* head.
20: 7 Jonathan son of Shimea, *D* brother,
21: 9 The LORD said to Gad, *D* seer,
26: 31 year of *D* reign a search was made
27: 31 in charge of King *D* property.
27: 32 Jonathan, *D* uncle, was a counselor
29: 24 as well as all of King *D* sons,
29: 29 As for the events of King *D* reign,
2Ch 11: 18 the daughter of *D* son Jerimoth
13: 8 is in the hands of *D* descendants.
29: 26 ready with *D* instruments,
32: 33 the tombs of *D* descendants are.
Isa 9: 7 He will reign on *D* throne
Jer 13: 13 the kings who sit on *D* throne,
17: 25 sit on *D* throne will come
22: 2 you who sit on *D* throne—you,
22: 4 sit on *D* throne will come
29: 16 the king who sits on *D* throne
33: 15 Branch sprout from *D* line;
Am 9: 11 *D* fallen tent.
Jn 7: 42 the Christ will come from *D* family
Ac 15: 16 and rebuild *D* fallen tent.

DAWN (DAWNED DAWNS)

Ge 19: 15 coming of *d*, the angels urged Lot,
Jdg 16: 2 saying, ''At *d* we'll kill him.''
19: 25 and at *d* they let her go.
1Sa 14: 36 by night and plunder them till *d*,
Ne 4: 21 from the first light of *d*
Job 3: 9 and not see the first rays of *d*,
4: 20 Between *d* and dusk they are
7: 4 The night drags on, and I toss till *d*.
38: 12 or shown the *d* its place,
41: 18 his eyes are like the rays of *d*.
Ps 37: 6 your righteousness shine like the *d*,
57: 8 I will awaken the *d*.
108: 2 I will awaken the *d*.
110: 3 from the womb of the *d*
119: 147 I rise before *d* and cry for help;
139: 9 If I rise on the wings of the *d*,
Pr 4: 18 is like the first gleam of *d*,
SS 6: 10 Who is this that appears like the *d*,
Isa 8: 20 to this word, they have no light of *d*
14: 12 O morning star, son of the *d*!
38: 13 I waited patiently till *d*,
58: 8 your light will break forth like the *d*
60: 3 kings to the brightness of your *d*.
62: 1 righteousness shines out like the *d*,
Da 6: 19 light of *d*, the king got up
Joel 2: 2 *d* spreading across the mountains
Am 4: 13 he who turns *d* to darkness,
5: 8 who turns blackness into *d*
Jnh 4: 7 But at *d* the next day God provided
Mt 28: 1 at *d* on the first day of the week,
Mk 13: 35 or when the rooster crows, or at *d*.
Jn 8: 2 At *d* he appeared again
Ac 27: 33 Just before *d* Paul urged them all

DAWNED (DAWN)

Ge 44: 3 As morning *d*, the men were sent
Dt 33: 2 and *d* over them from Seir;
Isa 9: 2 a light has *d*.
Mt 4: 16 a light has *d*.''
Ac 12: 12 When this had *d* on him, he went

DAWNS (DAWN)

Ps 65: 8 where morning *d* and evening
112: 4 in darkness light *d* for the upright,
Hos 10: 15 When that day *d*,
2Pe 1: 19 until the day *d* and the morning

DAY (DAY'S DAYS DAYTIME MIDDAY SEVEN-DAY THREE-DAY)

Ge 1: 5 God called the light ''*d*''
1: 5 and there was morning—the first *d*
1: 8 there was morning—the second *d*.
1: 13 there was morning—the third *d*.
1: 14 to separate the *d* from the night,
1: 16 the greater light to govern the *d*
1: 18 to govern the *d* and the night,
1: 19 there was morning—the fourth *d*.
1: 23 there was morning—the fifth *d*.
1: 31 there was morning—the sixth *d*.
2: 2 By the seventh *d* God had finished
2: 2 so on the seventh *d* he rested
2: 3 And God blessed the seventh *d*
3: 8 in the garden in the cool of the *d*,
7: 11 on that *d* all the springs
7: 11 on the seventeenth *d*
7: 13 On that very *d* Noah and his sons,
8: 4 and on the seventeenth *d*
8: 5 on the first *d* of the tenth month
8: 13 By the first *d* of the first month
8: 14 By the twenty-seventh *d*
8: 22 *d* and night
15: 18 On that *d* the LORD made
17: 23 On that very *d* Abraham took his
17: 26 both circumcised on that same *d*.
18: 1 to his tent in the heat of the *d*.
19: 31 One *d* the older daughter said
19: 34 The next *d* the older daughter said
21: 8 and on the *d* Isaac was weaned
22: 4 On the third *d* Abraham looked up
22: 14 And to this *d* it is said, ''On
26: 32 That *d* Isaac's servants came
26: 33 and to this *d* the name
27: 2 and don't know the *d* of my death.
27: 45 should I lose both of you in one *d*?''
30: 35 That same *d* he removed all
31: 22 On the third *d* Laban was told that

Ge 31:39 me for whatever was stolen by *d*
32:32 to this *d* the Israelites do not eat
33:13 If they are driven hard just one *d*,
33:16 that *d* Esau started on his way back
35: 3 me in the *d* of my distress
35:20 to this *d* that pillar marks Rachel's
39:10 she spoke to Joseph *d* after *d*,
39:11 One *d* he went into the house
40:20 the third *d* was Pharaoh's birthday,
42:18 On the third *d*, Joseph said to them
48:15 all my life to this *d*,
48:20 He blessed them that *d* and said,
Ex 2:11 One *d*, after Moses had grown up,
2:13 The next *d* he went out
5: 6 That same *d* Pharaoh gave this
5:13 work required of you for each *d*,
5:19 of bricks required of you for each *d*
8:22 on that *d* I will deal differently
9: 6 And the next *d* the LORD did it:
9:18 from the *d* it was founded till now.
10: 6 from the *d* they settled in this land
10:13 blow across the land all that *d*
10:28 The *d* you see my face you will die
12: 3 of Israel that on the tenth *d*
12: 6 until the fourteenth *d* of the month,
12:14 "This is a *d* you are
12:15 On the first *d* remove the yeast
12:15 yeast in it from the first *d*
12:16 On the first *d* hold a sacred
12:16 and another one on the seventh *d*.
12:17 Celebrate this *d* as a lasting
12:17 on this very *d* that I brought your
12:18 the evening of the fourteenth *d*
12:18 the evening of the twenty-first *d*.
12:41 to the very *d*, all the LORD's
12:51 on that very *d* the LORD brought
13: 3 "Commemorate this *d*, the *d* you
13: 6 and on the seventh *d* hold a festival
13: 8 On that *d* tell your son, 'I do this
13:21 By *d* the LORD went ahead
13:21 so that they could travel by *d*
13:22 Neither the pillar of cloud by *d*
14:30 That *d* the LORD saved Israel
16: 1 on the fifteenth *d* of the second
16: 4 The people are to go out each *d*
16: 4 and gather enough for that *d*.
16: 5 On the sixth *d* they are
16:22 On the sixth *d*, they gathered twice
16:23 'Tomorrow is to be a *d* of rest,
16:26 but on the seventh *d*, the Sabbath,
16:27 out on the seventh *d* to gather it,
16:29 on the sixth *d* he gives you bread
16:29 to stay where he is on the seventh *d*
16:30 the people rested on the seventh *d*.
18:13 The next *d* Moses took his seat
19: 1 on the very *d*— they came
19:11 and be ready by the third *d*,
19:11 on that *d* the LORD will come
19:15 "Prepare yourselves for the third *d*.
19:16 of the third *d* there was thunder
20: 8 "Remember the Sabbath *d*
20:10 but the seventh *d* is a Sabbath
20:11 but he rested on the seventh *d*.
20:11 the LORD blessed the Sabbath *d*
21:21 if the slave gets up after a *d*
22:30 but give them to me on the eighth *d*
23:12 but on the seventh *d* do not work,
24:16 on the seventh *d* the LORD called
29:36 Sacrifice a bull each *d*
29:38 offer on the altar regularly each *d*:
31:14 work on that *d* must be cut
31:15 the seventh *d* is a Sabbath of rest,
31:15 work on the Sabbath *d* must be put
31:17 and on the seventh *d* he abstained
32: 6 So the next *d* the people rose early
32:28 and that *d* about three thousand
32:29 and he has blessed you this *d*."
32:30 The next *d* Moses said
34:21 but on the seventh *d* you shall rest;
35: 2 the seventh *d* shall be your holy *d*,
35: 3 of your dwellings on the Sabbath *d*
40: 2 on the first *d* of the first month.
40:17 up on the first *d* of the first month
40:37 until the *d* it lifted.
40:38 was over the tabernacle by *d*,
Lev 6: 5 owner on the *d* he presents his guilt
6:20 the LORD on the *d* he is anointed:
7:15 eaten on the *d* it is offered;
Lev 7:16 eaten on the *d* he offers it,
7:16 over may be eaten on the next *d*.
7:17 till the third *d* must be burned up.
7:18 offering is eaten on the third *d*,
7:35 gone on the *d* they were presented
7:36 On the *d* they were anointed,
7:38 Sinai on the *d* he commanded
8:35 entrance to the Tent of Meeting *d*
9: 1 On the eighth *d* Moses summoned
12: 3 On the eighth *d* the boy is
13: 5 On the seventh *d* the priest is
13: 6 On the seventh *d* the priest is
13:27 On the seventh *d* the priest is
13:32 On the seventh *d* the priest is
13:34 On the seventh *d* the priest is
13:51 On the seventh *d* he is
14: 9 On the seventh *d* he must shave
14:10 "On the eighth *d* he must bring two
14:23 "On the eighth *d* he must bring
14:39 On the seventh *d* the priest shall
15:14 On the eighth *d* he must take two
15:29 On the eighth *d* she must take two
16:29 On the tenth *d* of the seventh
16:30 on this *d* atonement will be made
19: 6 eaten on the *d* you sacrifice it
19: 6 until the third *d* must be burned up.
19: 6 you sacrifice it or on the next *d*;
19: 7 If any of it is eaten on the third *d*,
22:27 From the eighth *d*
22:28 and its young on the same *d*.
22:30 It must be eaten that same *d*;
23: 3 of rest, a *d* of sacred assembly.
23: 3 the seventh *d* is a Sabbath of rest,
23: 5 twilight on the fourteenth *d*
23: 6 On the fifteenth *d*
23: 7 On the first *d* hold a sacred
23: 8 And on the seventh *d* hold a sacred
23:11 it on the *d* after the Sabbath.
23:12 On the *d* you wave the sheaf,
23:14 until the very *d* you bring this
23:15 the *d* you brought the sheaf
23:15 " 'From the *d* after the Sabbath,
23:16 to the *d* after the seventh Sabbath,
23:21 On that same *d* you are
23:24 are to have a *d* of rest,
23:24 'On the first *d* of the seventh
23:27 day of this seventh month is the *D*
23:27 tenth *d* of this seventh month is
23:28 Do no work on that *d*,
23:28 because it is the *D* of Atonement,
23:29 himself on that *d* must be cut
23:30 who does any work on that *d*.
23:32 evening of the ninth *d* of the month
23:34 'On the fifteenth *d*
23:35 The first *d* is a sacred assembly;
23:36 and on the eighth *d* hold a sacred
23:37 drink offerings required for each *d*.
23:39 and the eighth *d* also is a *d* of rest.
23:39 the first *d* is a *d* of rest.
23:39 " 'So beginning with the fifteenth *d*
23:40 On the first *d* you are
25: 9 on the *D* of Atonement sound
25: 9 on the tenth *d* of the seventh
27:23 man must pay its value on that *d*
Nu 1: 1 on the first *d* of the second month
1:18 on the first *d* of the second month.
6: 9 head on the *d* of his cleansing—
6: 9 of his cleansing—the seventh *d*.
6:10 on the eighth *d* he must bring two
6:11 That same *d* he is to consecrate his
7:11 "Each *d* one leader is
7:12 on the first *d* was Nahshon son
7:18 On the second *d* Nethanel son
7:24 On the third *d*, Eliab son of Helon,
7:30 On the fourth *d* Elizur son
7:36 On the fifth *d* Shelumiel son
7:42 On the sixth *d* Eliasaph son
7:48 On the seventh *d* Elishama son
7:54 On the eighth *d* Gamaliel son
7:60 On the ninth *d* Abidan son
7:66 On the tenth *d* Ahiezer son
7:72 On the eleventh *d* Pagiel son
7:78 On the twelfth *d* Ahira son of Enan
9: 3 on the fourteenth *d* of this month,
9: 5 twilight on the fourteenth *d*
9: 6 and Aaron that same *d* and said
9: 6 celebrate the Passover on that *d*
9:11 it on the fourteenth *d*
Nu 9:15 On the *d* the tabernacle, the Tent
9:21 Whether by *d* or by night,
10:11 On the twentieth *d*
10:34 over them by *d* when they set out
11:10 You will not eat it for just one *d*,
11:32 All that *d* and night and all the next
11:32 all the next *d* the people went out
14:14 before them in a pillar of cloud by *d*
15:23 from the *d* the LORD gave them
15:32 gathering wood on the Sabbath *d*.
16:41 The next *d* the whole Israelite
17: 8 The next *d* Moses entered the Tent
19:12 on the third *d* and on the seventh *d*;
19:19 on the seventh *d* he is to purify him
22:30 you have always ridden, to this *d*?
28: 3 as a regular burnt offering each *d*.
28: 9 On the Sabbath *d*, make an offering
28:16 " 'On the fourteenth *d*
28:17 On the fifteenth *d*
28:18 On the first *d* hold a sacred
28:24 made by fire every *d* for seven days
28:25 On the seventh *d* hold a sacred
28:26 " 'On the *d* of firstfruits,
29: 1 It is a *d* for you to sound
29: 1 " 'On the first *d* of the seventh
29: 7 " 'On the tenth *d* of this seventh
29:12 " 'On the fifteenth *d*
29:17 " 'On the second *d* prepare twelve
29:20 On the third *d* prepare eleven bulls,
29:23 On the fourth *d* prepare ten bulls,
29:26 " 'On the fifth *d* prepare nine bulls,
29:29 On the sixth *d* prepare eight bulls,
29:32 " 'On the seventh *d* prepare seven
29:35 On the eighth *d* hold an assembly
30:14 nothing to her about it from *d* to *d*,
31:24 On the seventh *d* wash your
32:10 LORD's anger was aroused that *d*
33: 3 *d* of the first month, the *d*
33:38 on the first *d* of the fifth month
Dt 1: 3 on the first *d* of the eleventh month
1:33 in fire by night and in a cloud by *d*,
2:22 have lived in their place to this *d*.
2:25 This very *d* I will begin
3:14 to this *d* Bashan is called Havvoth
4:10 Remember the *d* you stood
4:15 of any kind the *d* the LORD spoke
4:26 against you this *d* that you will
4:32 from the *d* God created man
4:39 to heart this *d* that the LORD is
5:12 "Observe the Sabbath *d*
5:14 but the seventh *d* is a Sabbath
5:15 you to observe the Sabbath *d*.
8:11 decrees that I am giving you this *d*.
9: 7 From the *d* you left Egypt
9:10 of the fire, on the *d* of the assembly
10: 4 of the fire, on the *d* of the assembly
16: 4 of the first *d* remain until morning.
16: 8 on the seventh *d* hold an assembly
18:16 at Horeb on the *d* of the assembly
21:23 Be sure to bury him that same *d*,
24:15 Pay him his wages each *d*
26:16 your God commands you this *d*
26:17 have declared this *d* that
26:18 has declared this *d* that you are
27:11 On the same *d* Moses commanded
28:13 your God that I give you this *d*
28:29 *d* after *d* you will be oppressed
28:32 watching for them *d* after *d*,
28:66 filled with dread both night and *d*,
29: 4 to this *d* the LORD has not given
29:12 LORD is making with you this *d*
29:13 to confirm you this *d* as his people,
30:18 to you this *d* that you will certainly
30:19 This *d* I call heaven and earth
31:14 "Now the *d* of your death is near.
31:17 On that *d* I will become angry
31:17 and on that *d* they will ask,
31:18 certainly hide my face on that *d*
31:22 Moses wrote down this song that *d*
32:35 their *d* of disaster is near
32:46 solemnly declared to you this *d*,
32:48 On that same *d* the LORD told
33:12 for he shields him all *d* long,
34: 6 to this *d* no one knows where his
Jos 1: 8 meditate on it *d* and night,
4: 9 And they are there to this *d*.
4:14 That *d* the LORD exalted Joshua
4:19 On the tenth *d* of the first month

Jos 5: 9 has been called Gilgal to this *d*.
5: 10 of the fourteenth *d* of the month,
5: 11 *d* after the Passover, that very *d*,
5: 12 The manna stopped the *d*
6: 4 On the seventh *d*, march
6: 10 word until the *d* I tell you to shout.
6: 14 So on the second *d* they marched
6: 15 On the seventh *d*, they got up
6: 15 that on that *d* they circled the city
6: 25 lives among the Israelites to this *d*.
7: 26 of rocks, which remains to this *d*.
8: 25 men and women fell that *d*—
8: 28 of ruins, a desolate place to this *d*.
8: 29 over it, which remains to this *d*.
9: 12 it at home on the *d* we left to come
9: 17 on the third *d* came to their cities:
9: 27 And that is what they are to this *d*.
9: 27 That *d* he made the Gibeonites
10: 12 On the *d* the LORD gave
10: 13 delayed going down about a full *d*.
10: 14 There has never been a *d* like it
10: 14 a *d* when the LORD listened
10: 27 rocks, which are there to this *d*.
10: 28 That *d* Joshua took Makkedah.
10: 32 and Joshua took it on the second *d*.
10: 35 They captured it that same *d*
13: 13 live among the Israelites to this *d*.
14: 9 So on that *d* Moses swore to me,
14: 11 as the *d* Moses sent me out;
14: 12 the LORD promised me that *d*.
15: 18 One *d* when she came to Othniel,
15: 63 to this *d* the Jebusites live there
16: 10 to this *d* the Canaanites live
22: 3 a long time now—to this very *d*—
22: 17 to this very *d* we have not cleansed
22: 22 the LORD, do not spare us this *d*.
22: 24 fear that some *d* your descendants
23: 9 to this *d* no one has been able
24: 15 for yourselves this *d* whom you will
24: 25 On that *d* Joshua made a covenant
Jdg 1: 14 One *d* when she came to Othniel,
1: 21 to this *d* the Jebusites live there
1: 26 which is its name to this *d*.
3: 30 That *d* Moab was made subject
4: 14 This is the *d* the LORD has given
4: 23 On that *d* God subdued Jabin,
5: 1 On that *d* Deborah and Barak son
6: 24 To this *d* it stands in Ophrah
6: 32 So that *d* they called Gideon
6: 38 Gideon rose early the next *d*;
9: 8 One *d* the trees went out
9: 42 The next *d* the people
9: 45 All that *d* Abimelech pressed his
10: 4 to this *d* are called Havvoth Jair.
11: 27 decide the dispute this *d*
13: 7 from birth until the *d* of his death
13: 10 appeared to me the other *d*!"
14: 15 On the fourth *d*, they said
14: 17 on the seventh *d* he finally told her,
14: 18 sunset on the seventh *d* the men
16: 1 One *d* Samson went to Gaza,
16: 16 after *d* until he was tired to death.
16: 16 such nagging she prodded him *d*
18: 12 is called Mahaneh Dan to this *d*.
19: 5 On the fourth *d* they got up early
19: 8 On the morning of the fifth *d*,
19: 9 the night here; the *d* is nearly
19: 11 and the *d* was almost gone,
19: 30 since the *d* the Israelites came up
20: 21 Israelites on the battlefield that *d*.
20: 22 stationed themselves the first *d*.
20: 24 near to Benjamin the second *d*.
20: 26 They fasted that *d* until evening
20: 30 the Benjamites on the third *d*
20: 35 and on that *d* the Israelites struck
20: 46 On that *d* twenty-five thousand
21: 4 Early the next *d* the people built
Ru 3: 1 One *d* Naomi her mother-in-law
4: 5 "On the *d* you buy the land
4: 14 who this *d* has not left you
1Sa 1: 4 Whenever the *d* came for Elkanah
2: 34 they will both die on the same *d*.
4: 12 That same *d* a Benjamite ran
4: 16 fled from it this very *d*."
5: 3 of Ashdod rose early the next *d*,
5: 5 why to this *d* neither the priests
6: 15 On that *d* the people
6: 16 then returned that same *d* to Ekron

1Sa 6: 18 is a witness to this *d* in the field
7: 6 On that *d* they fasted and there
7: 10 But that *d* the LORD thundered
8: 8 from the *d* I brought them up out
8: 8 out of Egypt until this *d*,
8: 18 When that *d* comes, you will cry
8: 18 will not answer you in that *d*."
9: 15 Now the *d* before Saul came,
9: 24 And Saul dined with Samuel that *d*
10: 9 all these signs were fulfilled that *d*.
11: 11 The next *d* Saul separated his men
11: 11 them until the heat of the *d*.
11: 13 for this *d* the LORD has rescued
12: 2 leader from my youth until this *d*.
12: 5 also his anointed is witness this *d*,
12: 18 and that same *d* the LORD sent
13: 22 on the *d* of the battle not a soldier
14: 1 One *d* Jonathan son of Saul said
14: 23 So the LORD rescued Israel that *d*,
14: 24 of Israel were in distress that *d*,
14: 31 have been even greater?" That *d*,
14: 37 But God did not answer him that *d*.
15: 35 Until the *d* Samuel died, he did not
16: 13 and from that *d* on the Spirit
17: 10 "This *d* I defy the ranks of Israel!
17: 46 This *d* the LORD will hand you
18: 2 From that *d* Saul kept David
18: 10 The next *d* an evil spirit
19: 24 He lay that way all that *d* and night
20: 5 evening of the *d* after tomorrow.
20: 12 by this time the *d* after tomorrow!
20: 19 The *d* after tomorrow,
20: 26 Saul said nothing that *d*,
20: 27 But the next *d*, the second *d*
20: 34 on that second *d* of the month he
21: 6 bread on the *d* it was taken away.
21: 7 of Saul's servants was there that *d*,
21: 10 That *d* David fled from Saul
22: 15 Was that *d* the first time I inquired
22: 18 That *d* he killed eighty-five men
22: 22 David said to Abiathar: "That *d*,
23: 14 *D* after *d* Saul searched for him,
24: 4 This is the very *d* the LORD spoke
24: 10 This *d* you have seen
25: 16 and *d* they were a wall
25: 33 me from bloodshed this *d*
27: 6 on that *d* Achish gave him Ziklag,
28: 20 for he had eaten nothing all that *d*
29: 3 from the *d* he left Saul until now,
29: 6 From the *d* you came to me
29: 8 servant from the *d* I came to you
30: 1 men reached Ziklag on the third *d*.
30: 17 until the evening of the next *d*,
30: 25 for Israel from that *d* to this.
31: 6 his men died together that same *d*.
31: 8 next *d*, when the Philistines came
2Sa 1: 2 On the third *d* a man arrived
2: 17 The battle that *d* was very fierce,
3: 8 This very *d* I am loyal to the house
3: 35 to eat something while it was still *d*
3: 37 So on that *d* all the people
3: 38 man has fallen in Israel this *d*?
4: 3 have lived there as aliens to this *d*.
4: 5 there in the heat of the *d*
4: 8 This *d* the LORD has avenged my
5: 8 On that *d*, David said, "Anyone
6: 8 that place is called Perez Uzzah.
6: 9 afraid of the LORD that *d*
6: 23 children to the *d* of her death.
7: 6 from the *d* I brought the Israelites
7: 6 out of Egypt to this *d*.
11: 12 Uriah remained in Jerusalem that *d*
11: 12 "Stay here one more *d*,
12: 18 On the seventh *d* the child died.
13: 32 since the *d* Amnon raped his sister
13: 37 mourned for his son every *d*.
18: 7 and the casualties that *d* were great
18: 8 the forest claimed more lives that *d*
18: 18 Absalom's Monument to this *d*.
19: 2 army the victory that *d* was turned
19: 2 on that *d* the troops heard it said,
19: 3 The men stole into the city that *d*
19: 19 on the *d* my lord the king left
19: 22 This *d* you have become my
19: 24 clothes from the *d* the king left
19: 24 left until the *d* he returned safely.
20: 3 till the *d* of their death,
21: 10 the birds of the air touch them by *d*

2Sa 22: 19 in the *d* of my disaster,
23: 10 about a great victory that *d*.
23: 20 went down into a pit on a snowy *d*
24: 18 On that *d* Gad went to David
1Ki 2: 8 on me the *d* I went to Mahanaim.
2: 37 *d* you leave and cross the Kidron
2: 42 'On the *d* you leave
3: 6 son to sit on his throne this very *d*.
3: 18 The third *d* after my child was born
8: 16 'Since the *d* I brought my people
8: 28 praying in your presence this *d*.
8: 29 toward this temple night and *d*,
8: 59 be near to the LORD our God *d*
8: 64 On that same *d* the king
8: 66 On the following *d* he sent
9: 13 a name they have to this *d*.
9: 21 slave labor force, as it is to this *d*.
10: 12 imported or seen since that *d*.)
12: 19 against the house of David to this *d*
12: 32 on the fifteenth *d* of the eighth
12: 33 On the fifteenth *d*
13: 3 That same *d* the man
13: 11 man of God had done there that *d*.
14: 14 This is the *d*! What? Yes, even now
16: 16 king over Israel that very *d* there
17: 14 until the *d* the LORD gives rain
17: 15 there was food every *d* for Elijah
20: 29 and on the seventh *d* the battle was
20: 29 the Aramean foot soldiers in one *d*.
21: 9 "Proclaim a *d* of fasting
21: 29 I will not bring this disaster in his *d*
22: 25 out on the *d* you go to hide
22: 35 All *d* long the battle raged,
2Ki 2: 22 has remained wholesome to this *d*,
4: 8 One *d* Elisha went to Shunem.
4: 11 One *d* when Elisha came, he went
4: 18 and one *d* he went out to his father,
6: 29 next *d* I said to her, 'Give up your
7: 9 This is a *d* of good news
8: 6 land from the *d* she left the country
8: 15 But the next *d* he took a thick cloth
8: 22 To this *d* Edom has been
10: 27 it for a latrine to this *d*.
13: 23 To this *d* he has been unwilling
14: 7 Joktheel, the name it has to this *d*.
15: 5 with leprosy until the *d* he died,
16: 6 and have lived there to this *d*.
17: 34 To this *d* they persist
17: 41 To this *d* their children
19: 3 This *d* is a *d* of distress and rebuke
19: 37 One *d*, while he was worshiping
20: 5 On the third *d* from now you will
20: 8 LORD on the third *d* from now?"
20: 17 fathers have stored up until this *d*,
21: 15 from the *d* their forefathers came
21: 15 out of Egypt until this *d*."
25: 1 on the tenth *d* of the tenth month,
25: 3 By the ninth *d* of the ⌊fourth⌋
25: 8 On the seventh *d* of the fifth month
25: 27 prison on the twenty-seventh *d*
25: 30 *D* by *d* the king gave Jehoiachin
1Ch 4: 41 them, as is evident to this *d*.
4: 43 and they have lived there to this *d*.
5: 26 of Gozan, where they are to this *d*.
9: 33 were responsible for the work *d*
10: 8 next *d*, when the Philistines came
11: 22 went down into a pit on a snowy *d*
12: 22 *D* after *d* men came
13: 11 *d* that place is called Perez Uzzah.
13: 12 David was afraid of God that *d*
16: 7 That *d* David first committed
16: 23 proclaim his salvation *d* after *d*.
17: 5 from the *d* I brought Israel up out
17: 5 out of Egypt to this *d*.
26: 17 There were six Levites a *d*
26: 17 four a *d* on the south and two
26: 17 on the east, four a *d* on the north,
29: 21 The next *d* they made sacrifices
29: 22 in the presence of the LORD that *d*
2Ch 3: 2 on the second *d* of the second
6: 5 'Since the *d* I brought my people
6: 20 open toward this temple *d*
7: 9 On the eighth *d* they held
7: 10 On the twenty-third *d*
8: 8 slave labor force, as it is to this *d*.
8: 16 from the *d* the foundation
9: 20 of little value in Solomon's *d*.
10: 19 against the house of David to this *d*

2Ch 18: 24 out on the *d* you go to hide
18: 34 All *d* long the battle raged,
20: 26 On the fourth *d* they assembled
20: 26 the Valley of Beracah to this *d.*
21: 10 To this *d* Edom has been
26: 21 leprosy until the *d* he died.
28: 6 In one *d* Pekah son
29: 17 by the eighth *d* of the month they
29: 17 finishing on the sixteenth *d*
29: 17 on the first *d* of the first month,
30: 15 lamb on the fourteenth *d*
30: 21 priests sang to the LORD every *d,*
35: 1 slaughtered on the fourteenth *d*
35: 25 and to this *d* all the men
Ezr 3: 4 offerings prescribed for each *d.*
3: 6 On the first *d* of the seventh month
5: 16 From that *d* to the present it has
6: 15 on the third *d* of the month Adar,
6: 19 On the fourteenth *d*
7: 9 on the first *d* of the fifth month,
7: 9 on the first *d* of the first month,
8: 31 On the twelfth *d* of the first month
8: 33 On the fourth *d,* in the house
9: 15 We are left this *d* as a remnant.
10: 9 And on the twentieth *d*
10: 13 cannot be taken care of in a *d*
10: 16 On the first *d* of the tenth month
10: 17 and by the first *d* of the first month
Ne 1: 6 servant is praying before you *d*
4: 2 sacrifices? Will they finish in a *d?*
4: 9 and posted a guard *d* and night
4: 16 From that *d* on, half
4: 22 guards by night and workmen by *d*
5: 18 Each *d* one ox, six choice sheep
6: 10 One *d* I went to the house
8: 2 on the first *d* of the seventh month
8: 9 "This *d* is sacred to the LORD
8: 10 This *d* is sacred to our Lord.
8: 11 "Be still, for this is a sacred *d.*
8: 13 On the second *d* of the month,
8: 17 of Joshua son of Nun until that *d,*
8: 18 *D* after *d,* from the first *d*
8: 18 and on the eighth *d,* in accordance
9: 1 On the twenty-fourth *d*
9: 3 God for a fourth of the *d,*
9: 10 yourself, which remains to this *d.*
9: 12 By *d* you led them with a pillar
9: 19 By *d* the pillar of cloud did not
10: 31 on the Sabbath or on any holy *d.*
12: 43 And on that *d* they offered great
13: 1 On that *d* the Book
13: 15 them against selling food on that *d.*
13: 17 desecrating the Sabbath *d?*
13: 19 brought in on the Sabbath *d.*
13: 22 in order to keep the Sabbath *d* holy
Est 1: 10 the seventh *d,* when King Xerxes
1: 18 This very *d* the Persian
2: 11 Every *d* he walked back
3: 4 *D* after *d* they spoke to him
3: 7 the presence of Haman to select a *d*
3: 12 Then on the thirteenth *d*
3: 13 and little children—on a single *d,*
3: 13 thirteenth *d* of the twelfth month,
3: 14 so they would be ready for that *d.*
4: 16 or drink for three days, night or *d.*
5: 1 On the third *d* Esther put
5: 9 Haman went out that *d* happy
7: 2 drinking wine on that second *d,*
8: 1 That same *d* King Xerxes gave
8: 9 on the twenty-third *d*
8: 12 King Xerxes was the thirteenth *d*
8: 12 The *d* appointed for the Jews
8: 13 on that *d* to avenge themselves
9: 1 On the thirteenth *d*
9: 1 On this *d* the enemies
9: 11 reported to the king that same *d.*
9: 15 on the fourteenth *d* of the month
9: 17 and made it a *d* of feasting and joy.
9: 17 on the thirteenth *d* of the month
9: 18 and made it a *d* of feasting and joy.
9: 19 a *d* for giving presents
9: 19 as a *d* of joy and feasting,
9: 22 mourning into a *d* of celebration.
Job 1: 6 One *d* the angels came
1: 13 One *d* when Job's sons
2: 1 On another *d* the angels came
3: 1 and cursed the *d* of his birth.
3: 3 "May the *d* of my birth perish,

Job 3: 4 That *d*— may it turn to darkness;
3: 8 those who curse days curse that *d,*
3: 16 who never saw the light of *d?*
15: 23 he knows the *d* of darkness is
17: 12 These men turn night into *d;*
20: 28 on the *d* of God's wrath.
21: 30 delivered from the *d* of wrath?
21: 30 spared from the *d* of calamity,
24: 16 but by *d* they shut themselves in;
Ps 1: 2 on his law he meditates *d* and night
7: 11 who expresses his wrath every *d.*
13: 2 every *d* have sorrow in my heart?
18: 18 in the *d* of my disaster,
19: 2 *D* after *d* they pour forth speech;
22: 2 out by *d,* but you do not answer,
25: 5 and my hope is in you all *d* long.
27: 5 For in the *d* of trouble
32: 3 through my groaning all *d* long.
32: 4 For *d* and night
35: 28 and of your praises all *d* long.
37: 13 for he knows their *d* is coming.
38: 6 all *d* long I go about mourning.
38: 12 all *d* long they plot deception.
42: 3 while men say to me all *d* long,
42: 3 *d* and night,
42: 8 By *d* the LORD directs his love,
42: 10 saying to me all *d* long,
44: 8 God we make our boast all *d* long,
44: 15 My disgrace is before me all *d* long,
44: 22 your sake we face death all *d* long;
46: 5 God will help her at break of *d.*
50: 15 and call upon me in the *d* of trouble
52: 1 Why do you boast all *d* long,
55: 10 *D* and night they prowl about
56: 1 all *d* long they press their attack.
56: 2 My slanderers pursue me all *d* long
56: 5 All *d* long they twist my words;
61: 8 and fulfill my vows *d* after *d.*
71: 8 declaring your splendor all *d* long.
71: 15 of your salvation all *d* long,
71: 17 to this *d* I declare your marvelous
71: 24 all *d* long,
72: 15 and bless him all *d* long.
73: 14 All *d* long I have been plagued;
74: 16 The *d* is yours, and yours
74: 22 how fools mock you all *d* long.
78: 9 turned back on the *d* of battle;
78: 14 with the cloud by *d*
78: 42 the *d* he redeemed them
78: 43 *d* he displayed his miraculous signs
81: 3 on the *d* of our Feast;
84: 10 Better is one *d* in your courts
86: 3 for I call to you all *d* long.
86: 7 In the *d* of my trouble I will call
88: 1 *d* and night I cry out before you.
88: 9 I call to you, O LORD, every *d;*
88: 17 All *d* long they surround me like
89: 16 in your name all *d* long;
90: 4 are like a *d* that has just gone by,
91: 5 nor the arrow that flies by *d,*
95: 8 as you did that *d* at Massah
96: 2 proclaim his salvation *d* after *d.*
102: 8 All *d* long my enemies taunt me;
110: 3 on your *d* of battle.
110: 5 on the *d* of his wrath.
118: 24 This is the *d* the LORD has made;
119: 91 Your laws endure to this *d,*
119: 97 I meditate on it all *d* long.
119:164 Seven times a *d* I praise you
121: 6 the sun will not harm you by *d,*
136: 8 the sun to govern the *d,*
137: 7 on the *d* Jerusalem fell.
139: 12 the night will shine like the *d,*
140: 2 and stir up war every *d.*
140: 7 head in the *d* of battle—
145: 2 Every *d* I will praise you
146: 4 on that very *d* their plans come
Pr 4: 18 till the full light of *d.*
7: 9 at twilight, as the *d* was fading,
8: 30 I was filled with delight *d* after *d,*
11: 4 Wealth is worthless in the *d*
16: 4 even the wicked for a *d* of disaster.
21: 26 All *d* long he craves for more,
21: 31 for the *d* of battle,
25: 20 takes away a garment on a cold *d,*
27: 1 not know what a *d* may bring forth.
27: 15 a constant dripping on a rainy *d;*
Ecc 7: 1 *d* of death better than the *d* of birth

Ecc 8: 8 power over the *d* of his death.
8: 16 his eyes not seeing sleep *d* or night
SS 2: 17 Until the *d* breaks
3: 11 him on the *d* of his wedding,
3: 11 the *d* his heart rejoiced.
4: 6 Until the *d* breaks
8: 8 sister for the *d* she is spoken for?
Isa 2: 11 alone will be exalted in that *d.*
2: 12 The LORD Almighty has a *d*
2: 17 alone will be exalted in that *d,*
2: 20 In that *d* men will throw away
3: 7 But in that *d* he will cry out,
3: 18 In that *d* the Lord will snatch away
4: 1 In that *d* seven women
4: 2 In that *d* the Branch
4: 5 there a cloud of smoke by *d*
4: 6 and shade from the heat of the *d,*
5: 30 In that *d* they will roar over it
7: 18 In that *d* the LORD will whistle
7: 20 In that *d* the Lord will use a razor
7: 21 In that *d,* a man will keep alive
7: 23 In that *d,* in every place where
9: 4 For as in the *d* of Midian's defeat,
9: 14 palm branch and reed in a single *d;*
10: 3 do on the *d* of reckoning,
10: 17 in a single *d* it will burn
10: 20 In that *d* the remnant of Israel,
10: 27 In that *d* their burden will be lifted
10: 32 This *d* they will halt at Nob;
11: 10 In that *d* the Root
11: 11 In that *d* the Lord will reach out his
12: 1 In that *d* you will say:
12: 4 In that *d* you will say:
13: 6 Wail, for the *d* of the LORD is near
13: 9 See, the *d* of the LORD is coming
13: 9 a cruel *d,* with wrath and fierce
13: 13 in the *d* of his burning anger.
14: 3 On the *d* the LORD gives you
17: 4 "In that *d* the glory
17: 7 In that *d* men will look
17: 9 In that *d* their strong cities,
17: 11 in the *d* of disease and incurable
17: 11 though on the *d* you set them out,
19: 16 In that *d* the Egyptians will be like
19: 18 In that *d* five cities
19: 19 In that *d* there will be an altar
19: 21 in that *d* they will acknowledge
19: 23 In that *d* there will be a highway
19: 24 In that *d* Israel will be the third,
20: 6 In that *d* the people who live
21: 8 "Day after *d,* my lord, I stand
21: 8 "*D* after day, my lord, I stand
22: 5 a *d* of battering down walls
22: 5 the LORD Almighty, has a *d*
22: 8 And you looked in that *d*
22: 12 called you on that *d*
22: 14 "Till your dying *d* this sin will not
22: 20 In that *d* I will summon my servant
22: 25 "In that *d,*" declares the LORD
24: 21 In that *d* the LORD will punish
25: 9 In that *d* they will say,
26: 1 In that *d* this song will be sung
27: 1 In that *d,*
27: 2 In that *d*—
27: 3 I guard it *d* and night
27: 8 as on a *d* the east wind blows.
27: 12 In that *d* the LORD will thresh
27: 13 in that *d* a great trumpet will sound
28: 5 In that *d* the LORD Almighty
28: 19 morning after morning, by *d*
29: 18 In that *d* the deaf will hear
30: 23 In that *d* your cattle will graze
30: 25 In the *d* of great slaughter,
31: 7 For in that *d* every one
34: 8 For the LORD has a *d*
34: 10 It will not be quenched night and *d;*
37: 3 This *d* is a *d* of distress and rebuke
37: 38 One *d,* while he was worshiping
38: 12 *d* and night you made an end of me
38: 13 *d* and night you made an end of me
39: 6 fathers have stored up until this *d,*
47: 9 you in a moment, on a single *d:*
49: 8 in the *d* of salvation I will help you;
51: 13 live in constant terror every *d*
52: 5 "And all *d* long
52: 6 therefore in that *d* they will know
58: 2 For *d* after *d* they seek me out;
58: 3 "Yet on the *d* of your fasting,

Isa 58: 5 a *d* acceptable to the LORD?
58: 5 only a *d* for a man
58: 13 and the LORD's holy *d* honorable,
58: 13 as you please on my holy *d*,
60: 11 they will never be shut, *d* or night,
60: 19 sun will no more be your light by *d*,
61: 2 and the *d* of vengeance of our God,
62: 6 they will never be silent *d* or night.
63: 4 For the *d* of vengeance was
65: 2 All *d* long I have held out my
65: 5 a fire that keeps burning all *d*.
66: 8 Can a country be born in a *d*
Jer 3: 25 from our youth till this *d*
4: 9 "In that *d*," declares the LORD,
7: 25 Egypt until now, *d* after *d*,
9: 1 I would weep *d* and night
12: 3 apart for the *d* of slaughter!
14: 17 night and *d* without ceasing;
15: 9 Her sun will set while it is still *d*;
16: 13 there you will serve other gods *d*
17: 16 you know I have not desired the *d*
17: 17 in the *d* of disaster.
17: 18 Bring on them the *d* of disaster;
17: 21 not to carry a load on the Sabbath *d*
17: 22 but keep the Sabbath *d* holy,
17: 24 but keep the Sabbath *d* holy
17: 27 me to keep the Sabbath *d* holy
17: 27 of Jerusalem on the Sabbath *d*,
18: 17 face in the *d* of their disaster."
20: 3 next *d*, when Pashhur released him
20: 7 I am ridiculed all *d* long;
20: 8 insult and reproach all *d* long.
20: 14 Cursed be the *d* I was born!
20: 14 May the *d* my mother bore me not
25: 3 king of Judah until this very *d*—
27: 22 until the *d* I come for them,'
30: 7 How awful that *d* will be!
30: 8 " 'In that *d*,' declares the LORD
31: 6 will be a *d* when watchmen cry
31: 35 the sun to shine by *d*,
32: 20 and have continued them to this *d*,
32: 31 From the *d* it was built until now,
33: 20 can break my covenant with the *d*
33: 20 so that *d* and night no longer come
33: 25 established my covenant with *d*
35: 14 To this *d* they do not drink wine,
36: 6 of the LORD on a *d* of fasting
36: 30 and exposed to the heat by *d*
37: 21 the street of the bakers each *d*
38: 28 until the *d* Jerusalem was captured.
39: 2 on the ninth *d* of the fourth month
39: 17 But I will rescue you on that *d*,
41: 4 *d* after Gedaliah's assassination,
44: 10 To this *d* they have not humbled
46: 10 But that *d* belongs to the LORD,
46: 10 a *d* of vengeance, for vengeance
46: 21 for the *d* of disaster is coming
47: 4 For the *d* has come
48: 41 In that *d* the hearts
49: 22 In that *d* the hearts
49: 26 soldiers will be silenced in that *d*,"
50: 27 Woe to them! For their *d* has come
50: 30 soldiers will be silenced in that *d*,"
50: 31 "for your *d* has come,
51: 2 side in the *d* of her disaster.
52: 4 on the tenth *d* of the tenth month,
52: 6 By the ninth *d* of the fourth month
52: 11 him in prison till the *d* of his death.
52: 12 On the tenth *d* of the fifth month,
52: 31 prison on the twenty-fifth *d*
52: 34 *D* by *d* the king
52: 34 as he lived, till the *d* of his death.
La 1: 12 me in the *d* of his fierce anger?
1: 13 faint all the *d* long.
1: 21 you bring the *d* you have
2: 1 footstool in the *d* of his anger.
2: 7 as on the *d* of an appointed feast.
2: 16 This is the *d* we have waited for;
2: 18 *d* and night;
2: 21 them in the *d* of your anger;
2: 22 In the *d* of the LORD's anger
2: 22 "As you summon to a feast *d*,
3: 3 again and again, all *d* long.
3: 14 they mock me in song all *d* long.
3: 62 and mutter against me all *d* long.
Eze 1: 1 in the fourth month on the fifth *d*,
1: 28 rainbow in the clouds on a rainy *d*,
2: 3 in revolt against me to this very *d*.
Eze 4: 6 I have assigned you 40 days, a *d*
4: 10 shekels of food to eat each *d*
7: 7 The time has come, the *d* is near;
7: 10 "The *d* is here! It has come!
7: 12 time has come, the *d* has arrived.
7: 19 in the *d* of the LORD's wrath.
8: 1 in the sixth month on the fifth *d*,
12: 7 During the *d* I brought out my
13: 5 in the battle on the *d* of the LORD.
16: 4 On the *d* you were born your cord
16: 5 on the *d* you were born you were
16: 56 Sodom in the *d* of your pride,
20: 1 in the fifth month on the tenth *d*,
20: 5 says: On the *d* I chose Israel,
20: 6 On that *d* I swore to them that I
20: 29 (It is called Bamah to this *d*.)
20: 31 with all your idols to this *d*.
21: 25 prince of Israel, whose *d* has come,
21: 29 whose *d* has come,
22: 14 strong in the *d* I deal with you?
22: 24 or showers in the *d* of wrath.'
23: 39 On the very *d* they sacrificed their
24: 1 in the tenth month on the tenth *d*,
24: 2 siege to Jerusalem this very *d*.
24: 25 on the *d* I take away their
24: 26 on that *d* a fugitive will come
26: 1 on the first *d* of the month,
26: 18 tremble on the *d* of your fall;
27: 27 the sea on the *d* of your shipwreck.
28: 13 on the *d* you were created they
28: 15 ways from the *d* you were created
29: 1 in the tenth month on the twelfth *d*
29: 17 in the first month on the first *d*,
29: 21 "On that *d* I will make a horn grow
30: 2 "Alas for that *d*!"
30: 3 For the *d* is near,
30: 3 a *d* of clouds,
30: 3 the *d* of the LORD is near—
30: 9 of them on the *d* of Egypt's doom,
30: 9 " 'On that *d* messengers will go out
30: 18 Dark will be the *d* at Tahpanhes
30: 20 in the first month on the seventh *d*,
31: 1 in the third month on the first *d*,
31: 15 On the *d* it was brought
32: 1 in the twelfth month on the first *d*,
32: 10 On the *d* of your downfall
32: 17 on the fifteenth *d* of the month,
33: 21 in the tenth month on the fifth *d*,
34: 12 where they were scattered on a *d*
36: 33 On the *d* I cleanse you
38: 10 On that *d* thoughts will come
38: 14 In that *d*, when my people Israel
38: 18 This is what will happen in that *d*:
39: 8 This is the *d* I have spoken of.
39: 11 " 'On that *d* I will give Gog a burial
39: 13 am glorified will be a memorable *d*
39: 13 and the *d* I am glorified will be
39: 22 From that *d* forward the house
40: 1 on that very *d* the hand
43: 22 "On the second *d* you are
43: 27 of these days, from the eighth *d* on,
44: 27 On the *d* he goes into the inner
45: 18 month on the first *d* you are
45: 20 on the seventh *d* of the month
45: 21 month on the fourteenth *d* you are
45: 22 On that *d* the prince is
45: 23 Every *d* during the seven days
45: 25 month on the fifteenth *d*,
46: 1 but on the Sabbath *d* and on the *d*
46: 4 to the LORD on the Sabbath *d* is
46: 6 On the *d* of the New Moon he is
46: 12 as he does on the Sabbath *d*.
46: 13 " 'Every *d* you are
Da 6: 10 Three times a *d* he got
6: 13 He still prays three times a *d*."
9: 7 this *d* we are covered with shame—
9: 15 a name that endures to this *d*,
10: 4 On the twenty-fourth *d*
10: 12 Since the first *d* that you set your
Hos 1: 5 In that *d* I will break Israel's bow
1: 11 for great will be the *d* of Jezreel.
2: 3 as bare as on the *d* she was born;
2: 15 in the *d* she came up out of Egypt.
2: 16 "In that *d*," declares the LORD,
2: 18 In that *d* I will make a covenant
2: 21 "In that *d* I will respond,"
4: 5 You stumble *d* and night,
5: 9 on the *d* of reckoning.
Hos 6: 2 on the third *d* he will restore us,
7: 5 On the *d* of the festival of our king
9: 5 on the *d* of your appointed feasts,
10: 14 Beth Arbel on the *d* of battle,
10: 15 When that *d* dawns,
12: 1 he pursues the east wind all *d*
Joel 1: 15 For the *d* of the LORD is near;
1: 15 What a dreadful *d*!
2: 1 for the *d* of the LORD is coming.
2: 2 a *d* of clouds and blackness.
2: 2 a *d* of darkness and gloom,
2: 11 The *d* of the LORD is great;
2: 31 and dreadful *d* of the LORD.
3: 14 For the *d* of the LORD is near
3: 18 "In that *d* the mountains will drip
Am 1: 14 amid violent winds on a stormy *d*.
1: 14 amid war cries on the *d* of battle,
2: 16 will flee naked on that *d*,"
3: 14 On the *d* I punish Israel for her sins
5: 8 and darkens *d* into night,
5: 18 That *d* will be darkness, not light.
5: 18 long for the *d* of the LORD?
5: 18 long for the *d* of the LORD!
5: 20 Will not the *d* of the LORD be
6: 3 You put off the evil *d*
8: 3 "In that *d*," declares the Sovereign
8: 9 "In that *d*," declares the Sovereign
8: 10 and the end of it like a bitter *d*.
8: 13 "In that *d*
9: 11 "In that *d* I will restore
Ob : 8 "In that *d*," declares the LORD,
: 11 On the *d* you stood aloof
: 12 Judah in the *d* of their destruction,
: 12 brother in the *d* of his misfortune,
: 12 much in the *d* of their trouble.
: 13 calamity in the *d* of their disaster,
: 13 people in the *d* of their disaster,
: 13 wealth in the *d* of their disaster.
: 14 survivors in the *d* of their trouble.
: 15 "The *d* of the LORD is near
Jnh 4: 7 at dawn the next *d* God provided
Mic 2: 4 In that *d* men will ridicule you;
3: 6 and the *d* will go dark for them.
4: 6 "In that *d*," declares the LORD,
4: 7 Zion from that *d* and forever.
5: 10 "In that *d*," declares the LORD,
7: 4 The *d* of your watchmen has come,
7: 4 the *d* God visits you.
7: 11 *d* for building your walls will come,
7: 11 *d* for extending your boundaries.
7: 12 In that *d* people will come to you
Na 2: 3 on the *d* they are made ready;
3: 17 that settle in the walls on a cold *d*
Hab 3: 2 Renew them in our *d*,
3: 16 patiently for the *d* of calamity
Zep 1: 7 for the *d* of the LORD is near.
1: 8 On the *d* of the LORD's sacrifice
1: 9 On that *d* I will punish
1: 10 "On that *d*," declares the LORD,
1: 14 The great *d* of the LORD is near—
1: 14 on the *d* of the LORD will be bitter
1: 15 That *d* will be a *d* of wrath,
1: 15 a *d* of clouds and blackness,
1: 15 a *d* of darkness and gloom,
1: 15 a *d* of distress and anguish,
1: 15 a *d* of trouble and ruin,
1: 16 a *d* of trumpet and battle cry
1: 18 on the *d* of the LORD's wrath.
2: 2 and that *d* sweeps on like chaff,
2: 2 before the *d* of the LORD's wrath
2: 3 on the *d* of the LORD's anger.
3: 5 and every new *d* he does not fail,
3: 8 "for the *d* I will stand up to testify.
3: 11 On that *d* you will not be put
3: 16 On that *d* they will say
Hag 1: 1 on the first *d* of the sixth month,
1: 15 on the twenty-fourth *d*
2: 1 On the twenty-first *d*
2: 10 On the twenty-fourth *d*
2: 15 thought to this from this *d* on—
2: 18 from this twenty-fourth *d*
2: 18 this *d* on, from this twenty-fourth
2: 18 to the *d* when the foundation
2: 19 " 'From this *d* on I will bless you.' "
2: 20 time on the twenty-fourth *d*
2: 23 " 'On that *d*,' declares the LORD
Zec 1: 7 On the twenty-fourth *d*
2: 11 joined with the LORD in that *d*

Zec 3: 9 the sin of this land in a single *d*.
3: 10 " 'In that *d* each of you will invite
4: 10 Who despises the *d* of small things?
6: 10 Go the same *d* to the house
7: 1 on the fourth *d* of the ninth month,
9: 16 their God will save them on that *d*
11: 11 It was revoked on that *d*,
12: 3 On that *d*, when all the nations
12: 4 On that *d* I will strike every horse
12: 6 "On that *d* I will make the leaders
12: 8 On that *d* the LORD will shield
12: 9 On that *d* I will set out
12: 11 On that *d* the weeping
13: 1 On that *d* a fountain will be opened
13: 2 "On that *d*, I will banish the names
13: 4 "On that *d* every prophet will be
14: 1 A *d* of the LORD is coming
14: 3 as he fights in the *d* of battle.
14: 4 On that *d* his feet will stand
14: 6 On that *d* there will be no light,
14: 7 It will be a unique *d*,
14: 7 or nighttime—a *d* known
14: 8 On that *d* living water will flow out
14: 9 On that *d* there will be one LORD,
14: 13 On that *d* men will be stricken
14: 20 that *d* HOLY TO THE LORD
14: 21 on that *d* there will no longer be
Mal 3: 2 who can endure the *d* of his coming
3: 17 "in the *d* when I make up my
4: 1 that *d* that is coming will set them
4: 1 "Surely the *d* is coming; it will burn
4: 3 the soles of your feet on the *d*
4: 5 dreadful *d* of the LORD comes.
Mt 6: 34 Each *d* has enough trouble
7: 22 Many will say to me on that *d*,
10: 15 Gomorrah on the *d* of judgment
11: 22 and Sidon on the *d* of judgment
11: 23 it would have remained to this *d*.
11: 24 for Sodom on the *d* of judgment
12: 5 in the temple desecrate the *d*
12: 36 account on the *d* of judgment
13: 1 That same *d* Jesus went out
16: 21 and on the third *d* be raised to life.
17: 23 and on the third *d* he will be raised
20: 2 to pay them a denarius for the *d*
20: 6 standing here all *d* long doing
20: 12 of the work and the heat of the *d*.'
20: 19 On the third *d* he will be raised
22: 23 That same *d* the Sadducees,
22: 46 and from that *d* on no one dared
24: 36 No one knows about that *d* or hour
24: 38 up to the *d* Noah entered the ark;
24: 42 on what *d* your Lord will come.
24: 50 on a *d* when he does not expect
25: 13 you do not know the *d* or the hour.
26: 17 On the first *d* of the Feast
26: 29 the vine from now on until that *d*
26: 55 Every *d* I sat in the temple courts
27: 8 called the Field of Blood to this *d*.
27: 62 The next *d*, the one
27: 62 the one after Preparation *D*,
27: 64 to be made secure until the third *d*.
28: 1 at dawn on the first *d* of the week,
28: 15 among the Jews to this very *d*.
Mk 2: 20 and on that *d* they will fast.
4: 27 Night and *d*, whether he sleeps
4: 35 That *d* when evening came,
5: 5 Night and *d* among the tombs
6: 35 By this time it was late in the *d*,
11: 12 The next *d* as they were leaving
13: 32 No one knows about that *d* or hour
14: 12 On the first *d* of the Feast
14: 25 the fruit of the vine until that *d*
14: 49 Every *d* I was with you, teaching
15: 42 It was Preparation *D* (that is,
15: 42 the *d* before the Sabbath).
16: 2 early on the first *d* of the week,
16: 9 early on the first *d* of the week,
Lk 1: 20 to speak until the *d* this happens,
1: 59 On the eighth *d* they came
2: 21 On the eighth *d*, when it was time
2: 37 but worshiped night and *d*,
2: 44 company, they traveled on for a *d*.
4: 16 and on the Sabbath *d* he went
5: 1 One *d* as Jesus was standing
5: 17 One *d* as he was teaching,
6: 23 "Rejoice in that *d* and leap for joy,
8: 22 One *d* Jesus said to his disciples,

Lk 9: 22 and on the third *d* be raised to life."
9: 37 The next *d*, when they came
10: 12 bearable on that *d* for Sodom
10: 35 next *d* he took out two silver coins
11: 1 One *d* Jesus was praying
11: 3 Give us each *d* our daily bread.
12: 46 on a *d* when he does not expect
13: 16 on the Sabbath *d* from what bound
13: 32 on the third *d* I will reach my goal.'
13: 33 and tomorrow and the next *d*—
14: 5 falls into a well on the Sabbath *d*,
16: 19 and lived in luxury every *d*.
17: 4 sins against you seven times in a *d*,
17: 24 in his *d* will be like the lightning,
17: 27 up to the *d* Noah entered the ark.
17: 29 But the *d* Lot left Sodom, fire
17: 30 on the *d* the Son of Man is revealed
17: 31 On that *d* no one who is on the roof
18: 7 who cry out to him *d* and night?
18: 33 On the third *d* he will rise again."
19: 42 on this *d* what would bring you
19: 47 Every *d* he was teaching
20: 1 One *d* as he was teaching
21: 34 *d* will close on you unexpectedly
21: 37 Each *d* Jesus was teaching
22: 7 came the *d* of Unleavened Bread
22: 53 Every *d* I was with you
23: 12 That *d* Herod and Pilate became
23: 54 It was Preparation *D*,
24: 1 On the first *d* of the week,
24: 7 on the third *d* be raised again.' "
24: 13 Now that same *d* two of them were
24: 21 it is the third *d* since all this took
24: 29 it is nearly evening; the *d* is almost
24: 46 rise from the dead on the third *d*,
Jn 1: 29 The next *d* John saw Jesus coming
1: 35 The next *d* John was there again
1: 39 and spent that *d* with him.
1: 43 The next *d* Jesus decided to leave
2: 1 On the third *d* a wedding took
5: 9 The *d* on which this took place was
5: 17 always at his work to this very *d*,
6: 22 next *d* the crowd that had stayed
6: 39 but raise them up at the last *d*.
6: 40 and I will raise him up at the last *d*
6: 44 and I will raise him up at the last *d*.
6: 54 and I will raise him up at the last *d*.
7: 37 and greatest *d* of the Feast,
8: 56 at the thought of seeing my *d*;
9: 4 as it is *d*, we must do the work
9: 14 the *d* on which Jesus had made
11: 9 walks by *d* will not stumble,
11: 24 in the resurrection at the last *d*."
11: 53 So from that *d* on they plotted
12: 7 perfume for the *d* of my burial.
12: 12 next *d* the great crowd that had
12: 48 will condemn him at the last *d*.
14: 20 On that *d* you will realize that I am
16: 23 In that *d* you will no longer ask me
16: 26 In that *d* you will ask in my name.
19: 14 It was the *d* of Preparation
19: 31 Now it was the *d* of Preparation,
19: 31 next *d* was to be a special Sabbath.
19: 42 Because it was the Jewish *d*
20: 1 Early on the first *d* of the week,
20: 19 evening of that first *d* of the week,
Ac 1: 2 to teach until the *d* he was taken up
2: 1 When the *d* of Pentecost came,
2: 20 and glorious *d* of the Lord.
2: 29 and his tomb is here to this *d*.
2: 41 added to their number that *d*.
2: 46 Every *d* they continued
3: 1 One *d* Peter and John were going
3: 2 where he was put every *d* to beg
4: 3 them in jail until the next *d*.
4: 5 The next *d* the rulers, elders
5: 42 *D* after *d*, in the temple courts
7: 26 The next *d* Moses came
8: 1 On that *d* a great persecution broke
9: 24 *D* and night they kept close watch
10: 3 One *d* at about three
10: 9 About noon the following *d*
10: 23 The next *d* Peter started out
10: 24 The following *d* he arrived
10: 40 him from the dead on the third *d*
12: 21 On the appointed *d* Herod,
14: 20 The next *d* he and Barnabas left
16: 11 and the next *d* on to Neapolis.

Ac 17: 11 examined the Scriptures every *d*
17: 17 as in the marketplace *d* by *d*
17: 31 he has set a *d* when he will judge
20: 7 On the first *d* of the week we came
20: 7 he intended to leave the next *d*,
20: 15 The next *d* we set sail from there
20: 15 The *d* after that we crossed
20: 15 and on the following *d* arrived
20: 16 if possible, by the *d* of Pentecost.
20: 18 from the first *d* I came
20: 31 each of you night and *d* with tears.
21: 1 The next *d* we went to Rhodes
21: 7 and stayed with them for a *d*.
21: 8 Leaving the next *d*, we reached
21: 18 The next *d* Paul and the rest
21: 26 The next *d* Paul took the men
22: 30 The next *d*, since the commander
23: 1 in all good conscience to this *d*."
23: 32 The next *d* they let the cavalry go
25: 6 the next *d* he convened the court
25: 17 but convened the court the next *d*
25: 23 next *d* Agrippa and Bernice came
26: 7 as they earnestly serve God *d*
26: 22 I have had God's help to this very *d*
27: 3 The next *d* we landed at Sidon;
27: 18 storm that the next *d* they began
27: 19 On the third *d*, they threw
28: 13 The next *d* the south wind came up
28: 13 and on the following *d* we reached
28: 23 to meet Paul on a certain *d*,
Ro 2: 5 yourself for the *d* of God's wrath,
2: 16 This will take place on the *d*
8: 36 your sake we face death all *d* long;
10: 21 "All *d* long I have held out my
11: 8 to this very *d*."
13: 12 nearly over; the *d* is almost here.
14: 5 man considers every *d* alike.
14: 5 man considers one *d* more sacred
14: 6 He who regards one *d* as special,
1Co 1: 8 on the *d* of our Lord Jesus Christ.
3: 13 because the *D* will bring it to light.
5: 5 his spirit saved on the *d* of the Lord
10: 8 in one *d* twenty-three thousand
15: 4 raised on the third *d* according
15: 31 I die every *d*—I mean that,
16: 2 On the first *d* of every week,
2Co 1: 14 of you in the *d* of the Lord Jesus.
3: 14 for to this *d* the same veil remains
3: 15 Even to this *d* when Moses is read,
4: 16 we are being renewed *d* by *d*.
6: 2 in the *d* of salvation I helped you."
6: 2 time of God's favor, now is the *d*
11: 25 I spent a night and a *d*
Eph 4: 30 sealed for the *d* of redemption.
6: 13 so that when the *d* of evil comes,
Php 1: 5 gospel from the first *d* until now,
1: 6 until the *d* of Christ Jesus.
1: 10 and blameless until the *d* of Christ,
2: 16 on the *d* of Christ that I did not run
3: 5 circumcised on the eighth *d*,
Col 1: 6 among you since the *d* you heard it
1: 9 since the *d* we heard about you,
2: 16 Moon celebration or a Sabbath *d*.
1Th 2: 9 and *d* in order not to be a burden
3: 10 *d* we pray most earnestly that we
5: 2 for you know very well that the *d*
5: 4 so that this *d* should surprise you
5: 5 sons of the light and sons of the *d*.
5: 8 But since we belong to the *d*,
2Th 1: 10 of his power on the *d* he comes
2: 2 saying that the *d* of the Lord has
2: 3 for that *d* will not come,
3: 8 contrary, we worked night and *d*,
1Ti 5: 5 and continues night and *d* to pray
2Ti 1: 3 and *d* I constantly remember you
1: 12 I have entrusted to him for that *d*.
1: 18 mercy from the Lord on that *d*!
4: 8 will award to me on that *d*—
Heb 4: 4 he has spoken about the seventh *d*
4: 4 "And on the seventh *d* God rested
4: 7 Therefore God again set a certain *d*
4: 8 have spoken later about another *d*.
7: 27 need to offer sacrifices *d* after *d*,
10: 11 *D* after *d* every priest stands
10: 25 as you see the *D* approaching.
Jas 5: 5 yourselves in the *d* of slaughter.
1Pe 2: 12 glorify God on the *d* he visits us.
2Pe 1: 19 until the *d* dawns and the morning

2Pe 2: 8 living among them *d* after *d*,
2: 9 unrighteous for the *d* of judgment,
3: 7 being kept for the *d* of judgment
3: 8 With the Lord a *d* is like
3: 8 and a thousand years are like a *d*.
3: 10 *d* of the Lord will come like a thief.
3: 12 That *d* will bring about
3: 12 as you look forward to the *d* of God
1Jn 4: 17 confidence on the *d* of judgment,
Jude : 6 chains for judgment on the great *D*.
Rev 1: 10 On the Lord's *D* I was in the Spirit,
4: 8 *D* and night they never stop saying:
6: 17 For the great *d* of their wrath has
7: 15 serve him *d* and night in his temple
8: 12 A third of the *d* was without light,
9: 15 and *d* and month and year were
12: 10 accuses them before our God *d*
14: 11 There is no rest *d* or night
16: 14 on the great *d* of God Almighty.
18: 8 in one *d* her plagues will overtake
20: 10 They will be tormented *d*
21: 25 On no *d* will its gates ever be shut,

DAY'S (DAY)

Nu 11: 31 as far as a *d* walk in any direction.
1Ki 8: 59 Israel according to each *d* need,
19: 4 while he himself went a *d* journey
1Ch 16: 37 according to each *d* requirements.
2Ch 8: 14 according to each *d* requirement.
Est 9: 13 to carry out this *d* edict tomorrow
Jnh 3: 4 going a *d* journey, and he
Ac 1: 12 a Sabbath *d* walk from the city.
Rev 6: 6 three quarts of barley for a *d* wages,
6: 6 "A quart of wheat for a *d* wages,

DAYBREAK

Ge 32: 24 and a man wrestled with him till *d*.
32: 26 the man said, "Let me go, for it is *d*
Ex 14: 27 at *d* the sea went back to its place.
Jos 6: 15 they got up at *d* and marched
Jdg 19: 26 At *d* the woman went back
1Sa 9: 26 They rose about *d* and Samuel
25: 34 would have been left alive by *d*."
25: 36 So she told him nothing until *d*.
2Sa 2: 32 and arrived at Hebron by *d*.
17: 22 By *d*, no one was left who had not
Ne 8: 3 He read it aloud from *d* till noon
Lk 4: 42 At *d* Jesus went out
22: 66 At *d* the council of the elders
Ac 5: 21 At *d* they entered the temple

DAYLIGHT

Nu 25: 4 them in broad *d* before the LORD,
Jdg 19: 26 at the door and lay there until *d*.
2Sa 12: 11 lie with your wives in broad *d*.
12: 12 thing in broad *d* before all Israel.' "
2Ki 7: 9 until *d*, punishment will overtake
Job 3: 9 may it wait for *d* in vain
24: 14 When *d* is gone, the murderer rises
Jer 6: 4 But, alas, the *d* is fading,
Am 8: 9 and darken the earth in broad *d*.
Mt 10: 27 speak in the *d*; what is whispered
Lk 12: 3 in the dark will be heard in the *d*,
Jn 11: 9 "Are there not twelve hours of *d*?
Ac 16: 35 When it was *d*, the magistrates sent
20: 11 After talking until *d*, he left.
27: 29 from the stern and prayed for *d*.
27: 39 When *d* came, they did not
2Pe 2: 13 of pleasure is to carouse in broad *d*.

DAYS (DAY)

Ge 1: 14 as signs to mark seasons and *d*
3: 14 all the *d* of your life.
3: 17 all the *d* of your life.
6: 3 his *d* will be a hundred
6: 4 were on the earth in those *d*—
7: 4 Seven *d* from now I will send rain
7: 4 rain on the earth for forty *d*
7: 10 after the seven *d* the floodwaters
7: 12 And rain fell on the earth forty *d*
7: 17 For forty *d* the flood kept coming
7: 24 the earth for a hundred and fifty *d*.
8: 3 fifty *d* the water had gone down,
8: 6 After forty *d* Noah opened
8: 10 He waited seven more *d*
8: 12 He waited seven more *d*
17: 12 you who is eight *d* old must be
21: 4 When his son Isaac was eight *d* old,
24: 55 "Let the girl remain with us ten *d*
27: 41 "The *d* of mourning
29: 20 but they seemed like only a few *d*
31: 23 he pursued Jacob for seven *d*
34: 25 Three *d* later, while all
37: 34 and mourned for his son many *d*.
40: 12 "The three branches are three *d*.
40: 13 Within three *d* Pharaoh will lift up
40: 18 "The three baskets are three *d*.
40: 19 Within three *d* Pharaoh will lift
42: 17 all in custody for three *d*.
49: 1 happen to you in *d* to come.
50: 3 mourned for him seventy *d*.
50: 3 taking a full forty *d*,
50: 4 When the *d* of mourning had
Ex 7: 25 Seven *d* passed after the LORD
10: 22 covered all Egypt for three *d*.
10: 23 or leave his place for three *d*.
12: 15 For seven *d* you are
12: 16 Do no work at all on these *d*,
12: 19 For seven *d* no yeast is to be found
13: 6 For seven *d* eat bread made
13: 7 bread during those seven *d*;
13: 14 "In *d* to come, when your son asks
15: 22 For three *d* they traveled
16: 5 much as they gather on the other *d*
16: 26 Six *d* you are to gather it,
16: 29 day he gives you bread for two *d*.
20: 9 Six *d* you shall labor and do all
20: 11 For in six *d* the LORD made
22: 30 stay with their mothers for seven *d*,
23: 12 "Six *d* do your work,
23: 15 for seven *d* eat bread made
24: 16 For six *d* the cloud covered
24: 18 he stayed on the mountain forty *d*
29: 30 is to wear them seven *d*.
29: 35 taking seven *d* to ordain them.
29: 37 For seven *d* make atonement
31: 15 For six *d* work is to be done,
31: 17 for in six *d* the LORD made
34: 18 For seven *d* eat bread made
34: 21 "Six *d* you shall labor,
34: 28 there with the LORD forty *d*
35: 2 For six *d*, work is to be done,
Lev 8: 33 to the Tent of Meeting for seven *d*,
8: 33 until the *d* of your ordination are
8: 33 your ordination will last seven *d*.
8: 35 for seven *d* and do what the LORD
12: 2 ceremonially unclean for seven *d*,
12: 4 until the *d* of her purification are
12: 4 woman must wait thirty-three *d*
12: 5 Then she must wait sixty-six *d*
12: 6 " 'When the *d* of her purification
13: 4 person in isolation for seven *d*.
13: 5 him in isolation another seven *d*.
13: 21 to put him in isolation for seven *d*.
13: 26 to put him in isolation for seven *d*.
13: 31 person in isolation for seven *d*.
13: 33 him in isolation another seven *d*.
13: 50 the affected article for seven *d*.
13: 54 is to isolate it for another seven *d*.
14: 8 stay outside his tent for seven *d*.
14: 38 close up the house for seven *d*.
15: 13 is to count off seven *d*
15: 19 monthly period will last seven *d*,
15: 24 he will be unclean for seven *d*;
15: 25 just as in the *d* of her period.
15: 25 of blood for many *d* at a time other
15: 28 she must count off seven *d*,
22: 27 remain with its mother for seven *d*.
23: 3 " 'There are six *d* when you may
23: 6 for seven *d* you must eat bread
23: 8 For seven *d* present an offering
23: 16 Count off fifty *d* up to the day
23: 34 begins, and it lasts for seven *d*.
23: 36 For seven *d* present offerings made
23: 39 festival to the LORD for seven *d*;
23: 40 the LORD your God for seven *d*.
23: 41 to the LORD for seven *d* each year
23: 42 Live in booths for seven *d*:
Nu 6: 12 The previous *d* do not count,
9: 20 over the tabernacle only a few *d*;
9: 22 over the tabernacle for two *d*
10: 33 before them during those three *d*
10: 33 LORD and traveled for three *d*.
11: 19 or two *d*, or five, ten or twenty *d*,
12: 14 been in disgrace for seven *d*?
12: 14 her outside the camp for seven *d*;
Nu 12: 15 outside the camp for seven *d*,
13: 25 At the end of forty *d* they returned
14: 34 of the forty *d* you explored the land
19: 11 anyone will be unclean for seven *d*.
19: 12 himself on the third and seventh *d*,
19: 14 is in it will be unclean for seven *d*,
19: 16 will be unclean for seven *d*.
19: 19 person on the third and seventh *d*,
20: 29 of Israel mourned for him thirty *d*.
24: 14 do to your people in *d* to come."
28: 17 for seven *d* eat bread made
28: 24 made by fire every day for seven *d*
29: 12 a festival to the LORD for seven *d*.
31: 19 and seventh *d* you must purify
31: 19 stay outside the camp seven *d*.
33: 8 for three *d* in the Desert of Etham,
Dt 1: 2 (It takes eleven *d* to go from Horeb
1: 46 so you stayed in Kadesh many *d*—
4: 30 then in later *d* you will return
4: 32 Ask now about the former *d*,
5: 13 Six *d* you shall labor and do all
5: 33 prolong your *d* in the land that you
9: 9 I stayed on the mountain forty *d*
9: 11 At the end of the forty *d*
9: 18 before the LORD for forty *d*
9: 25 before the LORD those forty *d*
10: 10 stayed on the mountain forty *d*
11: 21 as the *d* that the heavens are
11: 21 so that your *d* and the *d*
16: 3 for seven *d* eat unleavened bread,
16: 3 so that all the *d* of your life you
16: 4 in all your land for seven *d*.
16: 8 For six *d* eat unleavened bread
16: 13 Feast of Tabernacles for seven *d*
16: 15 For seven *d* celebrate the Feast
17: 19 he is to read it all the *d* of his life
28: 33 but cruel oppression all your *d*.
31: 29 In *d* to come, disaster will fall
32: 7 Remember the *d* of old;
33: 25 and your strength will equal your *d*
34: 8 in the plains of Moab thirty *d*,
Jos 1: 5 up against you all the *d* of your life.
1: 11 Three *d* from now you will cross
2: 16 Hide yourselves there three *d*
2: 22 the hills and stayed there three *d*,
3: 2 After three *d* the officers went
4: 14 they revered him all the *d* of his life
6: 3 Do this for six *d*.
6: 14 They did this for six *d*.
9: 16 Three *d* after they made the treaty
Jdg 5: 6 in the *d* of Jael, the roads were
5: 6 "In the *d* of Shamgar son of Anath,
11: 40 out for four *d* to commemorate
14: 12 within the seven *d* of the feast,
14: 14 For three *d* they could not give
14: 17 She cried the whole seven *d*
15: 20 years in the *d* of the Philistines.
17: 6 In those *d* Israel had no king;
18: 1 And in those *d* the tribe
18: 1 In those *d* Israel had no king.
19: 1 In those *d* Israel had no king.
19: 4 so he remained with him three *d*,
20: 27 (In those *d* the ark of the covenant
21: 25 In those *d* Israel had no king;
Ru 1: 1 In the *d* when the judges ruled,
1Sa 1: 11 to the LORD for all the *d* of his life
3: 1 In those *d* the word
7: 15 judge over Israel all the *d* of his life.
9: 20 the donkeys you lost three *d* ago,
10: 8 you must wait seven *d* until I come
11: 3 "Give us seven *d* so we can send
13: 8 He waited seven *d*, the time set
14: 52 All the *d* of Saul there was bitter
17: 16 For forty *d* the Philistine came
18: 29 his enemy the rest of his *d*.
25: 10 away from their masters these *d*.
25: 38 About ten *d* later, the LORD
27: 1 "One of these *d* I will be destroyed
28: 1 In those *d* the Philistines gathered
30: 12 or drunk any water for three *d*
30: 13 me when I became ill three *d* ago.
31: 13 at Jabesh, and they fasted seven *d*.
2Sa 1: 1 and stayed in Ziklag two *d*.
7: 12 When your *d* are over
14: 2 who has spent many *d* grieving
16: 23 in those *d* the advice Ahithophel
20: 4 to come to me within three *d*,
21: 9 during the first *d* of the harvest,

2Sa 24: 8 end of nine months and twenty *d*.
24: 13 Or three *d* of plague in your land?
1Ki 8: 65 and seven *d* more, fourteen *d* in all.
8: 65 the LORD our God for seven *d*
10: 21 of little value in Solomon's *d*.
11: 34 I have made him ruler all the *d*
12: 5 for three *d* and then come back
12: 12 Three *d* later Jeroboam
12: 12 "Come back to me in three *d*."
15: 5 of the LORD's commands all the *d*
16: 15 Zimri reigned in Tirzah seven *d*.
19: 8 he traveled forty *d* and forty nights
20: 29 For seven *d* they camped
21: 29 it on his house in the *d* of his son."
2Ki 2: 17 who searched for three *d*
3: 9 a roundabout march of seven *d*,
10: 32 In those *d* the LORD began
15: 37 (In those *d* the LORD began
19: 25 In *d* of old I planned it;
20: 1 In those *d* Hezekiah became ill
23: 22 nor throughout the *d* of the kings
23: 22 since the *d* of the judges who led
1Ch 4: 41 in the *d* of Hezekiah king of Judah.
7: 22 mourned for them many *d*,
10: 12 in Jabesh, and they fasted seven *d*.
12: 39 The men spent three *d* there
17: 11 When your *d* are over
21: 12 sword of the LORD—*d* of plague
21: 12 three *d* of the sword of the LORD
29: 15 Our *d* on earth are like a shadow,
2Ch 7: 8 the festival at that time for seven *d*,
7: 9 and the festival for seven *d* more.
7: 9 dedication of the altar for seven *d*
10: 5 "Come back to me in three *d*."
10: 12 Three *d* later Jeroboam
10: 12 "Come back to me in three *d*."
14: 1 in his *d* the country was at peace
15: 5 In those *d* it was not safe
20: 25 much plunder that it took three *d*
26: 5 God during the *d* of Zechariah,
29: 17 For eight more *d* they consecrated
30: 21 for seven *d* with great rejoicing,
30: 22 For the seven *d* they ate their
30: 23 celebrate the festival seven more *d*;
30: 23 for another seven *d* they celebrated
30: 26 for since the *d* of Solomon son
32: 24 In those *d* Hezekiah became ill
32: 26 them during the *d* of Hezekiah.
35: 17 of Unleavened Bread for seven *d*.
35: 18 this in Israel since the *d*
36: 9 Jerusalem three months and ten *d*.
Ezr 4: 7 And in the *d* of Artaxerxes king
6: 22 For seven *d* they celebrated
8: 15 and we camped there three *d*.
8: 32 where we rested three *d*.
9: 7 From the *d* of our forefathers
10: 8 within three *d* would forfeit all his
10: 9 Within the three *d*, all the men
Ne 1: 4 For some *d* I mourned and fasted
2: 11 after staying there three *d* I set out
5: 18 every ten *d* an abundant supply
6: 15 twenty-fifth of Elul, in fifty-two *d*.
6: 17 Also, in those *d* the nobles
8: 17 From the *d* of Joshua son of Nun
8: 18 celebrated the feast for seven *d*,
9: 32 from the *d* of the kings of Assyria
12: 7 their associates in the *d* of Jeshua.
12: 12 In the *d* of Joiakim, these were
12: 22 of the Levites in the *d* of Eliashib,
12: 26 They served in the *d* of Joiakim son
12: 26 in the *d* of Nehemiah the governor
12: 46 in the *d* of David and Asaph,
12: 47 So in the *d* of Zerubbabel
13: 15 In those *d* I saw men
13: 23 in those *d* I saw men
Est 1: 4 For a full 180 *d* he displayed
1: 5 When these *d* were
1: 5 gave a banquet, lasting seven *d*,
4: 11 But thirty *d* have passed
4: 16 Do not eat or drink for three *d*,
9: 21 fifteenth *d* of the month of Adar
9: 22 to observe the *d* as *d* of feasting
9: 26 these *d* were called Purim,
9: 27 fail observe these two *d* every year,
9: 28 And these *d* of Purim should never
9: 28 These *d* should be remembered
9: 31 to establish these *d* of Purim
Job 2: 13 on the ground with him for seven *d*

Job 3: 6 included among the *d* of the year
3: 8 those who curse *d* curse that day,
7: 1 Are not his *d* like those
7: 6 "My *d* are swifter than a weaver's
7: 16 me alone; my *d* have no meaning
8: 9 and our *d* on earth are
9: 25 "My *d* are swifter than a runner;
10: 5 Are your *d* like those of a mortal
10: 20 Are not my few *d* almost over?
14: 1 is of few *d* and full of trouble.
14: 5 Man's *d* are determined;
14: 14 All the *d* of my hard service
15: 20 All his *d* the wicked man suffers
17: 1 my *d* are cut short,
17: 11 My *d* have passed, my plans are
24: 1 look in vain for such *d*?
29: 2 for the *d* when God watched
29: 4 for the *d* when I was in my prime,
29: 18 my *d* as numerous as the grains
30: 16 *d* of suffering grip me.
30: 27 *d* of suffering confront me.
33: 25 it is restored as in the *d* of his youth
36: 11 the rest of their *d* in prosperity
38: 23 for *d* of war and battle?
Ps 21: 4 length of *d*, for ever and ever.
23: 6 all the *d* of my life,
25: 13 He will spend his *d* in prosperity,
27: 4 all the *d* of my life,
34: 12 and desires to see many good *d*,
37: 18 The *d* of the blameless are known
37: 19 in *d* of famine they will enjoy
39: 4 and the number of my *d*;
39: 5 have made my *d* a mere
44: 1 in *d* long ago.
44: 1 what you did in their *d*,
49: 5 fear when evil *d* come,
55: 23 will not live out half their *d*.
61: 6 Increase the *d* of the king's life,
72: 7 In his *d* the righteous will flourish;
77: 5 I thought about the former *d*,
78: 33 So he ended their *d* in futility
89: 45 You have cut short the *d*
90: 9 All our *d* pass away
90: 10 The length of our *d* is seventy years
90: 12 Teach us to number our *d* aright,
90: 14 for joy and be glad all our *d*.
90: 15 many *d* as you have afflicted us,
93: 5 house for endless *d*, O LORD.
94: 13 you grant him relief from *d*
102: 3 For my *d* vanish like smoke;
102: 11 My *d* are like the evening shadow;
102: 23 he cut short my *d*.
102: 24 O my God, in the midst of my *d*;
103: 15 As for man, his *d* are like grass,
109: 8 May his *d* be few;
128: 5 all the *d* of your life;
139: 16 All the *d* ordained for me
143: 5 I remember the *d* of long ago;
144: 4 his *d* are like a fleeting shadow.
Pr 9: 11 through me your *d* will be many,
15: 15 All the *d* of the oppressed are
31: 12 all the *d* of her life.
31: 25 she can laugh at the *d* to come.
Ecc 2: 3 during the few *d* of their lives.
2: 16 in *d* to come both will be forgotten.
2: 23 All his *d* his work is pain and grief;
5: 17 All his *d* he eats in darkness,
5: 18 under the sun during the few *d*
5: 20 reflects on the *d* of his life,
6: 12 and meaningless *d* he passes
7: 10 "Why were the old *d* better
8: 13 and their *d* will not lengthen like
8: 15 him in his work all the *d*
9: 9 all the *d* of this meaningless life
9: 9 the sun—all your meaningless *d*.
11: 1 after many *d* you will find it again.
11: 8 let him remember the *d* of darkness
11: 9 in the *d* of your youth.
12: 1 Creator in the *d* of your youth,
12: 1 before the *d* of trouble come
Isa 1: 26 I will restore your judges as in *d*
2: 2 and Jerusalem: In the last *d*
13: 22 and her *d* will not be prolonged.
24: 22 and be punished after many *d*.
27: 6 In *d* to come Jacob will take root,
30: 8 that for the *d* to come
30: 26 like the light of seven full *d*,
37: 26 In *d* of old I planned it;

Isa 38: 1 In those *d* Hezekiah became ill
38: 20 all the *d* of our lives
43: 13 Yes, and from ancient *d* I am he.
51: 9 awake, as in *d* gone by,
53: 10 see his offspring and prolong his *d*,
54: 9 "To me this is like the *d* of Noah,
60: 20 and your *d* of sorrow will end.
63: 9 all the *d* of old.
63: 11 his people recalled the *d* of old,
63: 11 the *d* of Moses and his people—
65: 20 an infant that lives but a few *d*,
65: 22 For as the *d* of a tree,
65: 22 so will be the *d* of my people;
Jer 2: 32 *d* without number.
3: 16 In those *d*, when your numbers
3: 18 In those *d* the house
5: 18 in those *d*," declares the LORD,
7: 32 So beware, the *d* are coming,
9: 25 "The *d* are coming," declares
13: 6 Many *d* later the LORD said to me
16: 9 and in your *d* I will bring an end
16: 14 "However, the *d* are coming,"
19: 6 So beware, the *d* are coming,
20: 18 and to end my *d* in shame?
23: 5 "The *d* are coming," declares
23: 6 In his *d* Judah will be saved
23: 7 "So then, the *d* are coming,"
23: 20 In *d* to come
26: 18 in the *d* of Hezekiah king
30: 3 *d* are coming,' declares the LORD,
30: 20 Their children will be as in *d* of old,
30: 24 In *d* to come
31: 27 "The *d* are coming," declares
31: 29 In those *d* people will no longer say
31: 38 "The *d* are coming," declares
33: 14 *d* are coming,' declares the LORD,
33: 15 " 'In those *d* and at that time
33: 16 In those *d* Judah will be saved
42: 7 Ten *d* later the word
48: 12 But *d* are coming,"
48: 47 Moab in *d* to come,"
49: 2 But the *d* are coming,"
49: 39 Elam in *d* to come,"
50: 4 "In those *d*, at that time,"
50: 20 In those *d*, at that time,"
51: 52 *d* are coming," declares the LORD
La 1: 7 In the *d* of her affliction
1: 7 that were hers in *d* of old.
4: 18 was near, our *d* were numbered,
5: 21 renew our *d* as of old
Eze 3: 15 I sat among them for seven *d*—
3: 16 At the end of seven *d* the word
4: 4 sin for the number of *d* you lie
4: 5 So for 390 *d* you will bear the sin
4: 5 assigned you the same number of *d*
4: 6 I have assigned you 40 *d*, a day
4: 8 other until you have finished the *d*
4: 9 it during the 390 *d* you lie
5: 2 When the *d* of your siege come
12: 22 *d* go by and every vision comes
12: 23 *d* are near when every vision will
12: 25 For in your *d*, you rebellious house,
16: 22 you did not remember the *d*
16: 43 you did not remember the *d*
16: 60 with you in the *d* of your youth,
22: 4 You have brought your *d* to a close,
23: 19 as she recalled the *d* of her youth,
38: 8 After many *d* you will be called
38: 16 In *d* to come, O Gog, I will bring
38: 17 of in former *d* by my servants
43: 25 "For seven *d* you are
43: 26 For seven *d* they are
43: 27 end of these *d*, from the eighth day
44: 26 is cleansed, he must wait seven *d*.
45: 21 a feast lasting seven *d*,
45: 23 Every day during the seven *d*
45: 25 " 'During the seven *d* of the Feast,
46: 1 is to be shut on the six working *d*,
Da 1: 12 "Please test your servants for ten *d*:
1: 14 to this and tested them for ten *d*.
1: 15 of the ten *d* they looked healthier
2: 28 what will happen in *d*
5: 26 God has numbered the *d*
6: 7 or man during the next thirty *d*,
6: 12 the next thirty *d* anyone who prays
7: 9 and the Ancient of *D* took his seat.
7: 13 He approached the Ancient of *D*
7: 22 until the Ancient of *D* came

Da 8:27 exhausted and lay ill for several *d*.
10:13 kingdom resisted me twenty-one *d*.
11:6 In those *d* she will be handed over,
12:11 is set up, there will be 1,290 *d*.
12:12 and reaches the end of the 1,335 *d*.
12:13 at the end of the *d* you will rise
Hos 2:11 her Sabbath *d*— all her appointed
2:13 I will punish her for the *d*
2:15 as in the *d* of her youth,
3:3 "You are to live with me many *d;*
3:4 For the Israelites will live many *d*
3:5 and to his blessings in the last *d*.
6:2 After two *d* he will revive us;
9:5 on the festival *d* of the LORD?
9:7 The *d* of punishment are coming,
9:7 the *d* of reckoning are at hand.
9:9 as in the *d* of Gibeah.
10:9 "Since the *d* of Gibeah, you have
12:9 as in the *d* of your appointed feasts.
Joel 1:2 like this ever happened in your *d*
1:2 or in the *d* of your forefathers?
2:29 I will pour out my Spirit in those *d*.
3:1 "In those *d* and at that time,
Am 8:11 "The *d* are coming," declares
9:13 "The *d* are coming," declares
Jnh 1:17 Jonah was inside the fish three *d*
3:3 it took three *d* to go all through it.
3:4 "Forty more *d* and Nineveh will be
Mic 4:1 In the last *d*
7:14 as in *d* long ago.
7:15 "As in the *d* when you came out
7:20 fathers in *d* long ago.
Hab 1:5 going to do something in your *d*
Zec 8:23 "In those *d* ten men
14:5 earthquake in the *d* of Uzziah king
Mal 3:4 as in *d* gone by, as in former years.
Mt 3:1 In those *d* John the Baptist came,
4:2 After fasting forty *d* and forty
11:12 From the *d* of John the Baptist
12:40 For as Jonah was three *d*
12:40 so the Son of Man will be three *d*
15:32 have already been with me three *d*
17:1 After six *d* Jesus took
23:30 lived in the *d* of our forefathers,
24:19 be in those *d* for pregnant women
24:22 If those *d* had not been cut short,
24:22 the elect those *d* will be shortened.
24:29 after the distress of those *d*
24:37 As it was in the *d* of Noah,
24:38 For in the *d* before the flood,
26:2 the Passover is two *d* away—
26:61 and rebuild it in three *d*.' "
27:40 the temple and build it in three *d*,
27:63 'After three *d* I will rise again.'
Mk 1:13 and he was in the desert forty *d*,
2:1 A few *d* later, when Jesus again
2:26 In the *d* of Abiathar the high priest,
8:1 During those *d* another large
8:2 have already been with me three *d*
8:31 and after three *d* rise again.
9:2 After six *d* Jesus took Peter,
9:31 and after three *d* he will rise."
10:34 Three *d* later he will rise."
13:17 be in those *d* for pregnant women
13:19 will be *d* of distress unequaled
13:20 the Lord had not cut short those *d*,
13:24 in those *d*, following that distress,
14:1 Bread were only two *d* away,
14:58 and in three *d* will build another,
15:29 the temple and build it in three *d*,
Lk 1:25 "In these *d* he has shown his favor
1:75 righteousness before him all our *d*.
2:1 In those *d* Caesar Augustus issued
2:46 After three *d* they found him
4:2 He ate nothing during those *d*,
4:2 where for forty *d* he was tempted
5:35 from them; in those *d* they will fast
6:12 One of those *d* Jesus went out
9:28 About eight *d* after Jesus said this,
13:14 So come and be healed on those *d*,
13:14 "There are six *d* for work.
17:22 long to see one of the *d* of the Son
17:26 will it be in the *d* of the Son of Man
17:26 "Just as it was in the *d* of Noah,
17:28 "It was the same in the *d* of Lot.
19:43 The *d* will come upon you
21:23 be in those *d* for pregnant women
24:18 have happened there in these *d?*"
Jn 2:12 There they stayed for a few *d*.
2:19 and I will raise it again in three *d*."
2:20 you are going to raise it in three *d*
4:40 with them, and he stayed two *d*.
4:43 After the two *d* he left for Galilee.
10:40 had been baptizing in the early *d*.
11:6 he stayed where he was two more *d*
11:17 been in the tomb for four *d*.
11:39 for he has been there four *d*."
12:1 Six *d* before the Passover,
Ac 1:3 to them over a period of forty *d*
1:5 but in a few *d* you will be baptized
1:15 In those *d* Peter stood up
2:17 by the prophet Joel: " 'In the last *d*,
2:18 I will pour out my Spirit in those *d*,
3:24 have spoken, have foretold these *d*.
5:37 appeared in the *d* of the census
6:1 In those *d* when the number
7:8 and circumcised him eight *d*
9:9 For three *d* he was blind,
9:19 Saul spent several *d*
9:23 After many *d* had gone by,
10:30 "Four *d* ago I was in my house
10:48 Peter to stay with them for a few *d*.
13:31 and for many *d* he was seen
13:41 going to do something in your *d*
16:12 And we stayed there several *d*.
16:18 She kept this up for many *d*.
17:2 on three Sabbath *d* he reasoned
20:6 and five *d* later joined the others
20:6 at Troas, where we stayed seven *d*.
21:4 we stayed with them seven *d*.
21:10 we had been there a number of *d*,
21:26 when the *d* of purification would
21:27 When the seven *d* were nearly over
24:1 Five *d* later the high priest Ananias
24:11 more than twelve *d* ago I went up
24:24 Several *d* later Felix came
25:1 Three *d* after arriving
25:6 After spending eight or ten *d*
25:13 A few *d* later King Agrippa
25:14 they were spending many *d* there,
27:7 made slow headway for many *d*
27:20 nor stars appeared for many *d*
27:33 "For the last fourteen *d*," he said,
28:7 and for three *d* entertained us
28:12 Syracuse and stayed there three *d*.
28:17 Three *d* later he called together
Gal 1:18 and stayed with him fifteen *d*.
4:10 You are observing special *d*
Eph 5:16 opportunity, because the *d* are evil.
Php 4:15 in the early *d* of your acquaintance
2Ti 3:1 will be terrible times in the last *d*.
Heb 1:2 in these last *d* he has spoken to us
5:7 During the *d* of Jesus' life on earth,
7:3 without beginning of *d*
10:32 Remember those earlier *d*
11:30 marched around them for seven *d*.
Jas 5:3 have hoarded wealth in the last *d*.
1Pe 3:10 and see good *d*
3:20 when God waited patiently in the *d*
2Pe 3:3 that in the last *d* scoffers will come,
Rev 2:10 will suffer persecution for ten *d*.
2:13 in the *d* of Antipas, my faithful
9:6 During those *d* men will seek death
10:7 in the *d* when the seventh angel is
11:3 and they will prophesy for 1,260 *d*,
11:9 a half *d* men from every people,
11:11 and a half *d* a breath of life
12:6 might be taken care of for 1,260 *d*.

DAYTIME (DAY)

Ge 31:40 The heat consumed me in the *d*
Jdg 6:27 it at night rather than in the *d*.
Job 5:14 upon them in the *d;*
Eze 12:3 belongings for exile and in the *d*,
12:4 During the *d*, while they watch,
Zec 14:7 It will be a unique day, without *d*
Ro 13:13 as in the *d*, not in orgies

DAZZLING

Da 2:31 *d* statue, awesome in appearance.
Mk 9:3 His clothes became *d* white,

DEACON (DEACONS)

1Ti 3:12 A *d* must be the husband of

DEACONS (DEACON)

Php 1:1 together with the overseers and *d:*
1Ti 3:8 *D*, likewise, are to be men worthy
3:10 against them, let them serve as *d*.

DEAD (DIE)

Ge 20:3 *d* because of the woman you have
23:3 rose from beside his *d* wife
23:4 here so I can bury my *d*."
23:6 Bury your *d* in the choicest
23:6 tomb for burying your *d*."
23:8 willing to let me bury my *d*,
23:11 Bury your *d*."
23:13 from me so I can bury my *d* there."
23:15 between me and you? Bury your *d*
34:27 of Jacob came upon the *d* bodies
42:38 his brother is *d* and he is the only
44:20 His brother is *d*, and he is the only
50:15 saw that their father was *d*,
Ex 4:19 men who wanted to kill you are *d*."
12:30 a house without someone *d*.
14:30 Israel saw the Egyptians lying *d*
21:34 and the *d* animal will be his.
21:35 money and the *d* animal equally.
21:36 and the *d* animal will be his.
Lev 7:24 The fat of an animal found *d*
11:31 when they are *d* will be unclean
14:51 them into the blood of the *d* bird
17:15 who eats anything found *d*
19:28 " 'Do not cut your bodies for the *d*
21:11 a place where there is a *d* body.
22:8 He must not eat anything found *d*
26:30 pile your *d* bodies on the lifeless
Nu 3:4 fell *d* before the LORD
5:2 unclean because of a *d* body.
6:6 he must not go near a *d* body.
6:11 being in the presence of the *d* body.
9:6 unclean on account of a *d* body.
9:7 unclean because of a *d* body,
9:10 are unclean because of a *d* body
16:48 stood between the living and the *d*,
19:11 "Whoever touches the *d* body
19:13 Whoever touches the *d* body
20:3 died when our brothers fell *d*
Dt 14:1 the front of your heads for the *d*,
14:21 eat anything you find already *d*.
18:11 or spiritist or who consults the *d*.
25:6 carry on the name of the *d* brother
26:14 nor have I offered any of it to the *d*.
Jos 1:2 aide: "Moses my servant is *d*.
Jdg 3:25 saw their lord fallen to the floor, *d*.
4:22 peg through his temple—*d*.
5:27 where he sank, there he fell—*d*.
9:55 saw that Abimelech was *d*,
Ru 1:8 as you have shown to your *d*
2:20 kindness to the living and the *d*."
4:5 name of the *d* with his property."
4:5 you acquire the *d* man's widow,
4:10 name of the *d* with his property,
1Sa 4:17 Hophni and Phinehas, are *d*,
4:19 and her husband were *d*,
17:51 saw that their hero was *d*,
17:52 Their *d* were strewn
24:14 Whom are you pursuing? A *d* dog?
25:39 David heard that Nabal was *d*,
28:3 Samuel was *d*, and all Israel had
31:5 armor-bearer saw that Saul was *d*,
31:8 the Philistines came to strip the *d*,
2Sa 1:4 Saul and his son Jonathan are *d*."
1:5 and his son Jonathan are *d?*"
2:7 brave, for Saul your master is *d*,
4:10 when a man told me, 'Saul is *d*,'
9:8 should notice a *d* dog like me?"
11:17 moreover, Uriah the Hittite was *d*.
11:21 your servant Uriah the Hittite is *d*
11:24 your servant Uriah the Hittite is *d*
11:26 wife heard that her husband was *d*,
12:18 How can we tell him the child is *d?*
12:18 to tell him that the child was *d*,
12:19 and he realized the child was *d*.
12:19 "Is the child *d?*" he asked.
12:19 "Yes," they replied, "he is *d*."
12:21 but now that the child is *d*,
12:23 now that he is *d*, why should I fast?
13:32 all the princes; only Amnon is *d*.
13:33 Only Amnon is *d*."
13:33 report that all the king's sons are *d*.

2Sa 14: 2 spent many days grieving for the *d*.
14: 5 indeed a widow; my husband is *d*.
16: 9 "Why should this *d* dog curse my
18: 20 because the king's son is *d*."
19: 6 alive today and all of us were *d*.
23: 10 to Eleazar, but only to strip the *d*.
1Ki 3: 20 and put her *d* son by my breast.
3: 21 to nurse my son—and he was *d!*
3: 22 insisted, "No! The *d* one is yours;
3: 22 one is my son; the *d* one is yours."
3: 23 No! Your son is *d* and mine is alive
3: 23 'My son is alive and your son is *d*,'
11: 15 who had gone up to bury the *d*,
11: 21 commander of the army was also *d*.
21: 14 "Naboth has been stoned and is *d*."
21: 15 He is no longer alive, but *d*."
21: 16 Ahab heard that Naboth was *d*,
2Ki 4: 1 "Your servant my husband is *d*,
4: 32 there was the boy lying *d*
8: 5 king how Elisha had restored the *d*
11: 1 of Ahaziah saw that her son was *d*,
19: 35 there were all the *d* bodies!
1Ch 10: 5 armor-bearer saw that Saul was *d*,
10: 8 the Philistines came to strip the *d*,
21: 14 thousand men of Israel fell *d*.
2Ch 20: 24 they saw only *d* bodies lying
22: 10 of Ahaziah saw that her son was *d*,
Job 1: 19 It collapsed on them and they are *d*
26: 5 "The *d* are in deep anguish,
Ps 6: 5 one remembers you when he is *d*.
31: 12 by them as though I were *d*;
79: 2 They have given the *d* bodies
79: 3 and there is no one to bury the *d*.
88: 5 I am set apart with the *d*,
88: 10 Do those who are *d* rise up
88: 10 you show your wonders to the *d?*
110: 6 judge the nations, heaping up the *d*
115: 17 It is not the *d* who praise
143: 3 like those long *d*.
Pr 2: 18 and her paths to the spirits of the *d*.
9: 18 do they know that the *d* are there,
21: 16 to rest in the company of the *d*.
Ecc 4: 2 And I declared that the *d*,
9: 3 and afterward they join the *d*.
9: 4 a live dog is better off than a *d* lion!
9: 5 but the *d* know nothing;
10: 1 As *d* flies give perfume a bad smell,
Isa 5: 25 and the *d* bodies are like refuse
8: 19 Why consult the *d* on behalf
19: 3 the idols and the spirits of the *d*,
26: 14 They are now *d*, they live no more;
26: 19 But your *d* will live;
26: 19 the earth will give birth to her *d*.
34: 3 their *d* bodies will send up a stench;
37: 36 there were all the *d* bodies!
59: 10 among the strong, we are like the *d*.
66: 24 and look upon the *d* bodies
Jer 7: 32 for they will bury the *d* in Topheth
9: 22 " 'The *d* bodies of men will lie
16: 4 their *d* bodies will become food
16: 7 those who mourn for the *d*—
19: 11 They will bury the *d* in Topheth
22: 10 Do not weep for the *d* king
31: 40 The whole valley where *d* bodies
33: 5 will be filled with the *d* bodies
34: 20 Their *d* bodies will become food
41: 9 of Nethaniah filled it with the *d*.
La 3: 6 like those long *d*.
Eze 4: 14 have never eaten anything found *d*
6: 5 I will lay the *d* bodies
11: 6 and filled its streets with the *d*.
24: 17 quietly; do not mourn for the *d*.
44: 25 himself by going near a *d* person;
44: 25 if the *d* person was his father
44: 31 found *d* or torn by wild animals.
Am 1: 8 till the last of the Philistines is *d*,"
Na 3: 3 piles of *d*,
Hag 2: 13 contact with a *d* body touches one
Mt 2: 20 trying to take the child's life are *d*."
8: 22 and let the *d* bury their own *d*."
9: 24 The girl is not *d* but asleep."
10: 8 raise the *d*, cleanse those who have
11: 5 the deaf hear, the *d* are raised,
14: 2 Baptist; he has risen from the *d!*
17: 9 of Man has been raised from the *d*
22: 31 But about the resurrection of the *d*
22: 32 He is not the God of the *d*
23: 27 the inside are full of *d* men's bones
Mt 27: 64 that he has been raised from the *d*.
28: 4 they shook and became like *d* men.
28: 7 'He has risen from the *d*
Mk 5: 35 "Your daughter is *d*," they said.
5: 39 The child is not *d* but asleep."
6: 14 Baptist has been raised from the *d*,
6: 16 has been raised from the *d!*"
9: 9 Son of Man had risen from the *d*.
9: 10 "rising from the *d*" meant.
9: 26 a corpse that many said, "He's *d*."
12: 25 When the *d* rise, they will neither
12: 26 about the *d* rising—have you not
12: 27 He is not the God of the *d*,
15: 44 to hear that he was already *d*.
Lk 7: 12 a *d* person was being carried out—
7: 15 The *d* man sat up and began to talk,
7: 22 the deaf hear, the *d* are raised,
8: 49 "Your daughter is *d*," he said.
8: 52 "She is not *d* but asleep."
8: 53 at him, knowing that she was *d*.
9: 7 John had been raised from the *d*,
9: 60 "Let the *d* bury their own *d*,
10: 30 and went away, leaving him half *d*.
15: 24 For this son of mine was *d*
15: 32 because this brother of yours was *d*
16: 30 if someone from the *d* goes to them
16: 31 even if someone rises from the *d*.' "
17: 37 replied, "Where there is a *d* body,
20: 35 from the *d* will neither marry
20: 37 even Moses showed that the *d* rise,
20: 38 He is not the God of the *d*,
24: 5 look for the living among the *d?*
24: 46 rise from the *d* on the third day,
Jn 2: 22 After he was raised from the *d*,
5: 21 as the Father raises the *d*
5: 25 when the *d* will hear the voice
11: 14 he told them plainly, "Lazarus is *d*,
11: 39 said Martha, the sister of the *d* man
11: 44 come out!" The *d* man came out,
12: 1 whom Jesus had raised from the *d*.
12: 9 whom he had raised from the *d*.
12: 17 the tomb, raising him from the *d*.
19: 33 and found that he was already *d*,
20: 9 had to rise from the *d*.)
21: 14 after he was raised from the *d*.
Ac 2: 24 But God raised him from the *d*,
3: 15 but God raised him from the *d*.
4: 2 in Jesus the resurrection of the *d*.
4: 10 but whom God raised from the *d*,
5: 10 came in and, finding her *d*,
5: 30 fathers raised Jesus from the *d*—
9: 40 Turning toward the *d* woman,
10: 40 him from the *d* on the third day
10: 41 with him after he rose from the *d*.
10: 42 as judge of the living and the *d*.
13: 30 But God raised him from the *d*,
13: 34 that God raised him from the *d*,
13: 37 raised from the *d* did not see decay.
14: 19 outside the city, thinking he was *d*.
17: 3 had to suffer and rise from the *d*.
17: 31 men by raising him from the *d*."
17: 32 about the resurrection of the *d*,
20: 9 third story and was picked up *d*.
23: 6 hope in the resurrection of the *d*."
24: 21 of the *d* that I am on trial
25: 19 about a *d* man named Jesus who
26: 8 it incredible that God raises the *d?*
26: 23 and, as the first to rise from the *d*,
28: 6 to swell up or suddenly fall over *d*,
Ro 1: 4 God by his resurrection from the *d*:
4: 17 the God who gives life to the *d*
4: 19 and that Sarah's womb was also *d*.
4: 19 that his body was as good as *d*—
4: 24 raised Jesus our Lord from the *d*.
6: 4 raised from the *d* through the glory
6: 9 since Christ was raised from the *d*,
6: 11 count yourselves *d* to sin
7: 4 to him who was raised from the *d*,
7: 8 For apart from law, sin is *d*.
8: 10 your body is *d* because of sin,
8: 11 Jesus from the *d* is living in you,
8: 11 who raised Christ from the *d* will
10: 7 to bring Christ up from the *d*).
10: 9 that God raised him from the *d*,
11: 15 acceptance be but life from the *d?*
14: 9 he might be the Lord of both the *d*
1Co 6: 14 God raised the Lord from the *d*,
15: 12 Christ has been raised from the *d*,
1Co 15: 12 there is no resurrection of the *d?*
15: 13 If there is no resurrection of the *d*,
15: 15 him if in fact the *d* are not raised.
15: 15 that he raised Christ from the *d*.
15: 16 For if the *d* are not raised,
15: 20 has indeed been raised from the *d*,
15: 21 the resurrection of the *d* comes
15: 29 If the *d* are not raised at all,
15: 29 do who are baptized for the *d?*
15: 32 I gained? If the *d* are not raised,
15: 35 may ask, "How are the *d* raised?
15: 42 be with the resurrection of the *d*.
15: 52 the *d* will be raised imperishable,
2Co 1: 9 but on God, who raises the *d*.
4: 14 the Lord Jesus from the *d* will
Gal 1: 1 who raised him from the *d*—
Eph 1: 20 when he raised him from the *d*
2: 1 you were *d* in your transgressions
2: 5 when we were *d* in transgressions
5: 14 rise from the *d*,
Php 3: 11 to the resurrection from the *d*.
Col 1: 18 the firstborn from among the *d*,
2: 12 who raised him from the *d*.
2: 13 When you were *d* in your sins
1Th 1: 10 whom he raised from the *d*—Jesus
4: 16 and the *d* in Christ will rise first.
1Ti 5: 6 widow who lives for pleasure is *d*
2Ti 2: 8 raised from the *d*, descended
4: 1 who will judge the living and the *d*,
Heb 6: 2 the resurrection of the *d*,
11: 4 he still speaks, even though he is *d*.
11: 12 this one man, and he as good as *d*,
11: 19 that God could raise the *d*,
11: 35 Women received back their *d*,
13: 20 back from the *d* our Lord Jesus,
Jas 2: 17 is not accompanied by action, is *d*.
2: 26 As the body without the spirit is *d*,
2: 26 so faith without deeds is *d*.
1Pe 1: 3 of Jesus Christ from the *d*,
1: 21 who raised him from the *d*
4: 5 ready to judge the living and the *d*.
4: 6 even to those who are now *d*,
Jude : 12 fruit and uprooted—twice *d*.
Rev 1: 5 witness, the firstborn from the *d*,
1: 17 I fell at his feet as though *d*.
1: 18 I am the Living One; I was *d*,
2: 23 I will strike her children *d*.
3: 1 of being alive, but you are *d*.
11: 18 time has come for judging the *d*,
14: 13 Blessed are the *d* who die
16: 3 into blood like that of a *d* man,
20: 5 (The rest of the *d* did not come
20: 12 And I saw the *d*, great and small,
20: 12 The *d* were judged according
20: 13 The sea gave up the *d* that were
20: 13 and Hades gave up the *d* that were

DEADENED (DIE)

Jn 12: 40 and *d* their hearts,

DEADLY (DIE)

Ex 10: 17 to take this *d* plague away from me
Dt 32: 24 consuming pestilence and *d* plague
32: 33 the *d* poison of cobras.
Ps 7: 13 He has prepared his *d* weapons;
64: 3 and aim their words like *d* arrows.
91: 3 and from the *d* pestilence.
144: 10 servant David from the *d* sword.
Pr 21: 6 is a fleeting vapor and a *d* snare.
26: 18 firebrands or *d* arrows
Jer 9: 8 Their tongue is a *d* arrow;
16: 4 "They will die of *d* diseases.
Eze 5: 16 When I shoot at you with my *d*
9: 2 each with a *d* weapon in his hand.
Mk 16: 18 and when they drink *d* poison,
2Co 1: 10 us from such a *d* peril,
Jas 3: 8 It is a restless evil, full of *d* poison.

DEAF

Ex 4: 11 Who makes him *d* or dumb?
Lev 19: 14 " 'Do not curse the *d* or put
Dt 1: 45 to your weeping and turned a *d* ear
Ps 28: 1 do not turn a *d* ear to me.
38: 13 I am like a *d* man, who cannot hear,
39: 12 be not *d* to my weeping.
Pr 28: 9 If anyone turns a *d* ear to the law,
Isa 29: 18 In that day the *d* will hear
35: 5 and the ears of the *d* unstopped.

Isa 42: 18 "Hear, you *d;*
42: 19 and *d* like the messenger I send?
43: 8 who have ears but are *d.*
Mic 7: 16 and their ears will become *d.*
Mt 11: 5 the *d* hear, the dead are raised,
Mk 7: 32 brought a man to him who was *d*
7: 37 "He even makes the *d* hear
9: 25 "You *d* and dumb spirit," he said,
Lk 7: 22 the *d* hear, the dead are raised,

DEAL (DEALER DEALING DEALINGS DEALS DEALT)

Ge 21: 23 God that you will not *d* falsely
Ex 1: 10 we must *d* shrewdly with them
8: 22 on that day I will *d* differently
Ru 1: 17 May the Lord *d* with me,
1Sa 3: 17 May God *d* with you, be it ever
14: 44 Saul said, "May God *d* with me,
20: 13 may the Lord *d* with me,
24: 4 into your hands for you to *d* with
25: 22 May God *d* with David, be it ever
2Sa 3: 9 May God *d* with Abner, be it ever
3: 22 with them a great *d* of plunder.
3: 35 saying, "May God *d* with me,
19: 13 May God *d* with me, be it ever
1Ki 2: 6 *D* with him according
2: 23 "May God *d* with me, be it ever
8: 39 *d* with each man according
19: 2 "May the gods *d* with me,
20: 10 "May the gods *d* with me,
2Ki 6: 31 He said, "May God *d* with me,
2Ch 6: 30 and *d* with each man according
12: 15 and of Iddo the seer that *d*
28: 8 They also took a great *d* of plunder,
Ne 5: 7 called together a large meeting to *d*
9: 24 to *d* with them as they pleased.
Job 42: 8 and not *d* with you according
Ps 109: 21 *d* well with me for your name's
119:124 *D* with your servant according
Isa 10: 11 shall I not *d* with Jerusalem
23: 17 the Lord will *d* with Tyre.
Jer 2: 8 Those who *d* with the law did not
7: 5 and *d* with each other justly,
18: 23 *d* with them in the time
24: 8 'so will I *d* with Zedekiah king
32: 5 remain until I *d* with him,
La 1: 22 *d* with them
Eze 7: 27 I will *d* with them according
8: 18 Therefore I will *d* with them
16: 59 I will *d* with you as you deserve,
20: 44 when I *d* with you
22: 14 strong in the day I *d* with you?
23: 25 and they will *d* with you in fury.
23: 29 They will *d* with you in hatred
25: 14 and they will *d* with Edom
31: 11 for him to *d* with according
Zep 3: 19 At that time I will *d*
Zec 8: 11 now I will not *d* with the remnant
Mt 27: 19 for I have suffered a great *d* today
Mk 5: 26 She had suffered a great *d*
Ac 16: 16 She earned a great *d* of money
2Ti 4: 14 the metalworker did me a great *d*
Heb 5: 2 He is able to *d* gently

DEALER (DEAL)

Ac 16: 14 a *d* in purple cloth from the city

DEALING (DEAL)

2Sa 7: 19 Is this your usual way of *d*
Ezr 10: 17 of the first month they finished *d*
Lk 16: 8 shrewd in *d* with their own kind
2Co 13: 3 He is not weak in *d* with you,

DEALINGS (DEAL)

1Sa 25: 3 was surly and mean in his *d.*

DEALS (DEAL)

Dt 25: 16 anyone who *d* dishonestly.
Jer 5: 1 who *d* honestly and seeks the truth,
1Th 2: 11 as a father *d* with his own children,

DEALT (DEAL)

Ex 10: 2 and grandchildren how I *d* harshly
1Sa 6: 19 heavy blow the Lord had *d* them,
2Sa 22: 21 "The Lord has *d*
Ps 18: 20 Lord has *d* with me according
Isa 10: 11 as I *d* with Samaria and her idols
La 1: 22 as you have *d* with me
Eze 39: 24 I *d* with them according
Ac 7: 19 He *d* treacherously with our people
1Th 2: 11 For you know that we *d* with each

DEAR (DEARER)

2Sa 1: 26 you were very *d* to me.
Ps 102: 14 For her stones are *d*
Jer 31: 20 Is not Ephraim my *d* son,
Jn 2: 4 "*D* woman, why do you involve me
19: 26 he said to his mother, "*D* woman,
Ac 15: 25 to you with our *d* friends Barnabas
Ro 16: 5 Greet my *d* friend Epenetus,
16: 9 in Christ, and my *d* friend Stachys.
16: 12 Greet my *d* friend Persis, another
1Co 4: 14 but to warn you, as my *d* children.
10: 14 my *d* friends, flee from idolatry.
15: 58 Therefore, my *d* brothers,
2Co 7: 1 we have these promises, *d* friends,
12: 19 and everything we do, *d* friends,
Gal 4: 19 My *d* children, for whom I am
Eph 6: 21 the *d* brother and faithful servant
Php 2: 12 my *d* friends, as you have always
4: 1 firm in the Lord, *d* friends!
Col 1: 7 Epaphras, our *d* fellow servant,
4: 7 He is a *d* brother, a faithful
4: 9 our faithful and *d* brother,
4: 14 Our *d* friend Luke, the doctor,
1Th 2: 8 because you had become so *d* to us.
1Ti 6: 2 their service are believers, and *d*
2Ti 1: 2 To Timothy, my *d* son: Grace,
Phm : 1 To Philemon our *d* friend
: 16 He is very *d* to me but
: 16 better than a slave, as a *d* brother.
Heb 6: 9 we speak like this, *d* friends,
Jas 1: 16 Don't be deceived, my *d* brothers.
1: 19 My *d* brothers, take note of this:
2: 5 thoughts? Listen, my *d* brothers:
1Pe 2: 11 *D* friends, I urge you, as aliens
4: 12 *D* friends, do not be surprised
2Pe 3: 1 *D* friends, this is now my second
3: 8 not forget this one thing, *d* friends:
3: 14 *d* friends, since you are looking
3: 15 just as our *d* brother Paul
3: 17 *d* friends, since you already know
1Jn 2: 1 My *d* children, I write this to you
2: 7 *D* friends, I am not writing you
2: 12 I write to you, *d* children,
2: 13 I write to you, *d* children,
2: 18 *D* children, this is the last hour;
2: 28 *d* children, continue in him,
3: 2 *D* friends, now we are children
3: 7 *D* children, do not let anyone lead
3: 18 love of God be in him? *D* children,
3: 21 *D* friends, if our hearts do not
4: 1 *D* friends, do not believe every
4: 4 *d* children, are from God
4: 7 *D* friends, let us love one another,
4: 11 *D* friends, since God so loved us,
5: 21 *D* children, keep yourselves
2Jn : 5 *d* lady, I am not writing you a new
3Jn : 1 The elder, To my *d* friend Gaius,
: 2 *D* friend, I pray that you may enjoy
: 5 *D* friend, you are faithful
: 11 *D* friend, do not imitate what is evil
Jude : 3 *D* friends, although I was very
: 17 But, *d* friends, remember what
: 20 *d* friends, build yourselves up

DEARER (DEAR)

Phm : 16 dear to me but even *d* to you,

DEATH (DIE)

Ge 24: 67 comforted after his mother's *d.*
25: 11 After Abraham's *d,* God blessed
26: 11 or his wife shall surely be put to *d.*"
27: 2 and don't know the day of my *d.*
38: 7 so the Lord put him to *d.*
38: 10 Lord's sight; so he put him to *d*
38: 24 and have her burned to *d!*"
42: 37 sons to *d* if I do not bring him back
Ex 16: 3 to starve this entire assembly to *d.*"
19: 12 mountain shall surely be put to *d.*
21: 12 kills him shall surely be put to *d.*
21: 14 from my altar and put him to *d.*
21: 15 or his mother must be put to *d.*
21: 16 when he is caught must be put to *d.*
21: 17 or mother must be put to *d.*
21: 28 a bull gores a man or a woman to *d,*
Ex 21: 28 the bull must be stoned to *d,*
21: 29 the owner also must be put to *d.*
22: 19 with an animal must be put to *d.*
23: 7 an innocent or honest person to *d,*
31: 14 who desecrates it must be put to *d;*
31: 15 the Sabbath day must be put to *d.*
35: 2 work on it must be put to *d.*
Lev 16: 1 to Moses after the *d* of the two sons
19: 20 Yet they are not to be put to *d,*
20: 2 to Molech must be put to *d.*
20: 4 and they fail to put him to *d,*
20: 9 or mother, he must be put to *d.*
20: 10 and the adulteress must be put to *d.*
20: 11 and the woman must be put to *d;*
20: 12 both of them must be put to *d.*
20: 13 put to *d;* their blood will be
20: 15 to *d,* and you must kill the animal.
20: 16 put to *d;* their blood will be
20: 27 among you must be put to *d.*
24: 16 of the Lord must be put to *d.*
24: 16 the Name, he must be put to *d.*
24: 17 a human being, he must be put to *d.*
24: 21 kills a man must be put to *d.*
27: 29 be ransomed; he must be put to *d.*
Nu 1: 51 goes near it shall be put to *d.*
3: 10 the sanctuary must be put to *d.*"
3: 38 the sanctuary was to be put to *d.*
11: 15 put me to *d* right now—
14: 15 people to *d* all at one time,
15: 36 the camp and stoned him to *d,*
16: 29 If these men die a natural *d*
18: 7 near the sanctuary must be put to *d*
19: 16 someone who has died a natural *d,*
19: 18 someone who has died a natural *d.*
23: 10 Let me die the *d* of the righteous,
25: 5 "Each of you must put to *d* those
25: 15 put to *d* was Cozbi daughter of Zur,
35: 16 the murderer shall be put to *d.*
35: 17 the murderer shall be put to *d.*
35: 18 the murderer shall be put to *d.*
35: 19 he meets him, he shall put him to *d.*
35: 19 of blood shall put the murderer to *d*
35: 21 murderer to *d* when he meets him.
35: 21 that person shall be put to *d;*
35: 25 there until the *d* of the high priest,
35: 28 after the *d* of the high priest may he
35: 28 city of refuge until the *d*
35: 30 is to be put to *d* on the testimony
35: 30 who kills a person is to be put to *d*
35: 31 He must surely be put to *d.*
35: 32 land before the *d* of the high priest.
Dt 9: 28 out to put them to *d* in the desert.'
13: 5 or dreamer must be put to *d,*
13: 9 You must certainly put him to *d.*
13: 9 the first in putting him to *d,*
13: 10 Stone him to *d,* because he tried
17: 5 and stone that person to *d.*
17: 6 put to *d* on the testimony
17: 6 witnesses a man shall be put to *d,*
17: 7 the first in putting him to *d,*
17: 12 Lord your God must be put to *d.*
18: 20 of other gods, must be put to *d.*"
19: 6 though he is not deserving of *d,*
21: 21 of his town shall stone him to *d.*
21: 22 guilty of a capital offense is put to *d*
22: 21 of her town shall stone her to *d.*
22: 24 of that town and stone them to *d*—
22: 26 has committed no sin deserving *d.*
24: 16 children put to *d* for their fathers;
24: 16 put to *d* for their children.
30: 15 and prosperity, *d* and destruction.
30: 19 set before you life and *d,*
31: 14 "Now the day of your *d* is near.
31: 29 that after my *d* you are sure
32: 22 to the realm of *d* below.
32: 39 I put to *d* and I bring to life,
33: 1 on the Israelites before his *d.*
Jos 1: 1 After the *d* of Moses the servant
1: 18 command them, will be put to *d.*
2: 13 and that you will save us from *d.*"
11: 17 them down, putting them to *d.*
20: 6 until the *d* of the high priest who is
Jdg 1: 1 After the *d* of Joshua, the Israelites
6: 31 fights for him shall be put to *d*
13: 7 from birth until the day of his *d.*'"
14: 15 and your father's household to *d.*
15: 6 and burned her and her father to *d.*
16: 16 after day until he was tired to *d.*

Jdg 20: 13 so that we may put them to *d*
21: 5 should certainly be put to *d*.
Ru 1: 17 if anything but *d* separates you
2: 11 since the *d* of your husband—
1Sa 2: 6 LORD brings *d* and makes alive;
2: 25 the LORD's will to put them to *d*.
5: 11 For *d* had filled the city with panic;
6: 19 putting seventy of them to *d*
11: 12 and we will put them to *d*.''
11: 13 ''No one shall be put to *d* today,
14: 45 Jonathan, and he was not put to *d*.
15: 3 Do not spare them; put to *d* men
15: 32 ''Surely the bitterness of *d* is past.''
15: 33 Agag to *d* before the LORD
19: 6 David will not be put to *d*.''
20: 3 a step between me and *d*.''
20: 32 ''Why should he be put to *d*?
22: 22 I am responsible for the *d*
28: 9 for my life to bring about my *d*?''
2Sa 1: 1 After the *d* of Saul, David returned
1: 9 I am in the throes of *d*,
1: 23 and in *d* they were not parted.
4: 10 and put him to *d* in Ziklag.
6: 23 children to the day of her *d*.
8: 2 lengths of them were put to *d*,
13: 39 consoled concerning Amnon's *d*.
14: 7 so that we may put him to *d*
14: 32 of anything, let him put me to *d*.''
15: 21 whether it means life or *d*,
17: 3 *d* of the man you seek will mean
19: 21 ''Shouldn't Shimei be put to *d*
19: 22 put to *d* in Israel today?
19: 28 but *d* from my lord the king,
20: 3 confinement till the day of their *d*,
21: 1 he put the Gibeonites to *d*.''
21: 4 right to put anyone in Israel to *d*.''
21: 9 they were put to *d*
22: 5 ''The waves of *d* swirled about me;
22: 6 the snares of *d* confronted me.
1Ki 1: 51 servant to *d* with the sword.' ''
2: 8 'I will not put you to *d* by the sword
2: 24 Adonijah shall be put to *d* today!''
2: 26 but I will not put you to *d* now,
3: 11 asked for the *d* of your enemies
11: 40 and stayed there until Solomon's *d*.
12: 18 but all Israel stoned him to *d*.
18: 9 over to Ahab to be put to *d*?
19: 10 prophets to *d* with the sword.
19: 14 prophets to *d* with the sword.
19: 17 put to *d* any who escape the sword
19: 17 put to *d* any who escape the sword
21: 10 take him out and stone him to *d*.''
21: 13 the city and stoned him to *d*.
21: 15 that Naboth had been stoned to *d*,
22: 20 and going to his *d* there?'
2Ki 1: 1 After Ahab's *d*, Moab rebelled
2: 21 Never again will it cause *d*
4: 40 O man of God, there is *d* in the pot
11: 8 your ranks must be put to *d*
11: 15 ''She must not be put to *d*
11: 16 and there she was put to *d*.
14: 6 children put to *d* for their fathers;
14: 6 put to *d* for their children,
14: 6 the sons of the assassins to *d*,
14: 17 years after the *d* of Jehoash son
16: 9 to Kir and put Rezin to *d*.
18: 32 not *d*! ''Do not listen to Hezekiah,
19: 35 put to *d* a hundred and eighty-five
20: 1 ill and was at the point of *d*.
1Ch 2: 3 so the LORD put him to *d*.
10: 14 So the LORD put him to *d*
22: 5 preparations before his *d*.
2Ch 1: 11 nor for the *d* of your enemies,
10: 18 but the Israelites stoned him to *d*.
15: 13 were to be put to *d*, whether small
18: 19 and going to his *d* there?'
22: 4 after his father's *d* they became his
22: 9 brought to Jehu and put to *d*.
23: 7 enters the temple must be put to *d*.
23: 14 ''Do not put her to *d* at the temple
23: 15 and there they put her to *d*.
24: 17 After the *d* of Jehoiada,
24: 21 him to *d* in the courtyard
25: 4 Yet he did not put their sons to *d*,
25: 4 children put to *d* for their fathers;
25: 4 put to *d* for their children,
25: 25 years after the *d* of Jehoash son
32: 24 ill and was at the point of *d*.

Ezr 7: 26 king must surely be punished by *d*,
Est 4: 11 but one law: that he be put to *d*.
9: 15 to *d* in Susa three hundred men,
Job 3: 21 long for *d* that does not come,
5: 20 famine he will ransom you from *d*
7: 15 so that I prefer strangling and *d*,
9: 23 When a scourge brings sudden *d*,
17: 16 Will it go down to the gates of *d*?
26: 6 *D* is naked before God;
28: 22 Destruction and *D* say,
30: 23 I know you will bring me down to *d*
33: 22 and his life to the messengers of *d*.
38: 17 Have the gates of *d* been shown
38: 17 the gates of the shadow of *d*?
Ps 9: 13 and lift me up from the gates of *d*,
13: 3 light to my eyes, or I will sleep in *d*;
18: 4 The cords of *d* entangled me;
18: 5 the snares of *d* confronted me.
22: 15 you lay me in the dust of *d*.
23: 4 the valley of the shadow of *d*,
33: 19 to deliver them from *d*
44: 22 for your sake we face *d* all day long
49: 14 and *d* will feed on them.
55: 4 the terrors of *d* assail me.
55: 15 Let *d* take my enemies by surprise;
56: 13 you have delivered my soul from *d*
68: 20 LORD comes escape from *d*.
72: 13 and save the needy from *d*.
78: 31 he put to *d* the sturdiest
78: 50 he did not spare them from *d*
88: 15 I have been afflicted and close to *d*;
89: 48 What man can live and not see *d*,
90: 5 sweep men away in the sleep of *d*;
94: 17 dwelt in the silence of *d*.
94: 21 and condemn the innocent to *d*.
102: 20 and release those condemned to *d*
107: 18 and drew near the gates of *d*.
109: 16 but hounded to *d* the poor
116: 3 The cords of *d* entangled me,
116: 8 have delivered my soul from *d*,
116: 15 is the *d* of his saints.
118: 18 but he has not given me over to *d*.
141: 8 refuge—do not give me over to *d*.
Pr 2: 18 For her house leads down to *d*
5: 5 Her feet go down to *d*;
7: 27 leading down to the chambers of *d*.
8: 36 all who hate me love *d*.''
10: 2 but righteousness delivers from *d*.
11: 4 but righteousness delivers from *d*.
11: 19 he who pursues evil goes to his *d*.
13: 14 turning a man from the snares of *d*.
14: 12 but in the end it leads to *d*.
14: 27 turning a man from the snares of *d*.
14: 32 in *d* the righteous have a refuge.
15: 11 *D* and Destruction lie open
16: 14 A king's wrath is a messenger of *d*,
16: 25 but in the end it leads to *d*.
18: 21 tongue has the power of life and *d*,
19: 18 do not be a willing party to his *d*
21: 25 The sluggard's craving will be the *d*
23: 14 and save his soul from *d*.
24: 11 Rescue those being led away to *d*;
27: 20 *D* and Destruction are never
28: 17 will be a fugitive till *d*;
Ecc 7: 1 and the day of *d* better than the day
7: 2 for *d* is the destiny of every man;
7: 26 I find more bitter than *d*
8: 8 power over the day of his *d*.
SS 8: 6 for love is as strong as *d*,
Isa 9: 2 in the land of the shadow of *d*
25: 8 he will swallow up *d* forever.
28: 15 into a covenant with *d*,
28: 18 with *d* will be annulled;
37: 36 went out and put to *d* a hundred
38: 1 ill and was at the point of *d*.
38: 10 must I go through the gates of *d*
38: 18 *d* cannot sing your praise;
53: 9 and with the rich in his *d*,
53: 12 he poured out his life unto *d*,
57: 2 they find rest as they lie in *d*.
65: 15 Sovereign LORD will put you to *d*,
Jer 8: 3 of this evil nation will prefer *d*
9: 21 *D* has climbed in through our
15: 2 '' 'Those destined for *d*, to *d*;
18: 21 let their men be put to *d*,
21: 8 the way of life and the way of *d*.
26: 11 This man should be sentenced to *d*
26: 15 however, that if you put me to *d*,

Jer 26: 16 man should not be sentenced to *d*!
26: 19 anyone else in Judah put him to *d*?
26: 21 the king sought to put him to *d*.
26: 24 over to the people to be put to *d*.
29: 21 them to *d* before your very eyes
38: 4 ''This man should be put to *d*.
38: 9 where he will starve to *d*
43: 11 bringing *d* to those destined for *d*,
52: 11 him in prison till the day of his *d*.
52: 34 long as he lived, till the day of his *d*
La 1: 20 inside, there is only *d*.
Eze 18: 13 he will surely be put to *d*
18: 23 pleasure in the *d* of the wicked?
18: 32 pleasure in the *d* of anyone,
28: 8 and you will die a violent *d*
28: 10 will die the *d* of the uncircumcised
31: 14 they are all destined for *d*,
33: 11 pleasure in the *d* of the wicked,
Da 2: 13 and his friends to put them to *d*.
2: 13 issued to put the wise men to *d*,
2: 14 to put to *d* the wise men of Babylon
5: 19 Those the king wanted to put to *d*,
5: 19 he put to *d*; those he wanted
Hos 13: 14 I will redeem them from *d*.
13: 14 Where, O *d*, are your plagues?
Hab 2: 5 and like *d* is never satisfied,
Mt 2: 15 stayed until the *d* of Herod.
4: 16 in the land of the shadow of *d*
10: 21 parents and have them put to *d*.
10: 21 ''Brother will betray brother to *d*,
15: 4 or mother must be put to *d*.'
16: 28 are standing here will not taste *d*
20: 18 They will condemn him to *d*
24: 9 over to be persecuted and put to *d*,
26: 38 with sorrow to the point of *d*.
26: 59 so that they could put him to *d*.
26: 66 He is worthy of *d*,'' they answered.
27: 1 to the decision to put Jesus to *d*.
Mk 7: 10 or mother must be put to *d*.'
9: 1 are standing here will not taste *d*
10: 33 They will condemn him to *d*
13: 12 parents and have them put to *d*.
13: 12 ''Brother will betray brother to *d*,
14: 34 with sorrow to the point of *d*,''
14: 55 so that they could put him to *d*,
14: 64 all condemned him as worthy of *d*.
Lk 1: 79 and in the shadow of *d*,
9: 27 are standing here will not taste *d*
15: 17 and here I am starving to *d*!
21: 16 and they will put some of you to *d*.
22: 33 to go with you to prison and to *d*.''
23: 15 he has done nothing to deserve *d*.
23: 22 in him no grounds for the *d* penalty
24: 20 him over to be sentenced to *d*,
Jn 4: 47 heal his son, who was close to *d*.
5: 24 he has crossed over from *d* to life.
8: 51 my word, he will never see *d*.''
8: 52 your word, he will never taste *d*.
11: 4 ''This sickness will not end in *d*
11: 13 Jesus had been speaking of his *d*,
12: 33 to show the kind of *d* he was going
18: 32 of *d* he was going to die would be
21: 19 this to indicate the kind of *d*
Ac 2: 23 put him to *d* by nailing him
2: 24 because it was impossible for *d*
2: 24 freeing him from the agony of *d*,
5: 33 and wanted to put them to *d*.
7: 4 After the *d* of his father, God sent
8: 1 was there, giving approval to his *d*.
12: 2 of John, put to *d* with the sword.
13: 28 no proper ground for a *d* sentence,
22: 4 the followers of this Way to their *d*,
23: 29 charge against him that deserved *d*
25: 11 of doing anything deserving *d*,
25: 25 had done nothing deserving of *d*,
26: 10 and when they were put to *d*,
26: 31 not doing anything that deserves *d*
28: 18 guilty of any crime deserving *d*.
Ro 1: 32 who do such things deserve *d*,
4: 25 delivered over to *d* for our sins
5: 10 to him through the *d* of his Son,
5: 12 and in this way *d* came to all men,
5: 12 the world through one man, and *d*
5: 14 *d* reigned from the time of Adam
5: 17 *d* reigned through that one man,
5: 21 so that, just as sin reigned in *d*,
6: 3 Jesus were baptized into his *d*?
6: 4 him through baptism into *d*

Ro 6: 5 have been united with him in his *d*,
6: 9 *d* no longer has mastery over him.
6: 10 The *d* he died, he died to sin once
6: 13 who have been brought from *d*
6: 16 which leads to *d*, or to obedience,
6: 21 Those things result in *d*!
6: 23 For the wages of sin is *d*,
7: 5 so that we bore fruit for *d*.
7: 10 to bring life actually brought *d*.
7: 11 the commandment put me to *d*.
7: 13 become *d* to me? By no means!
7: 13 it produced *d* in me
7: 24 me from this body of *d*?
8: 2 free from the law of sin and *d*.
8: 6 The mind of sinful man is *d*,
8: 13 put to *d* the misdeeds of the body,
8: 36 your sake we face *d* all day long;
8: 38 For I am convinced that neither *d*
1Co 3: 22 the world or life or *d* or the present
11: 26 you proclaim the Lord's *d*
15: 21 For since *d* came through a man,
15: 26 The last enemy to be destroyed is *d*
15: 54 *D* has been swallowed up in victory
15: 55 Where, O *d*, is your sting?"
15: 55 "Where, O *d*, is your victory?
15: 56 The sting of *d* is sin, and the power
2Co 1: 9 our hearts we felt the sentence of *d*.
2: 16 To the one we are the smell of *d*;
3: 7 Now if the ministry that brought *d*,
4: 10 around in our body the *d* of Jesus,
4: 11 given over to *d* for Jesus' sake,
4: 12 So then, *d* is at work in us,
7: 10 but worldly sorrow brings *d*.
11: 23 been exposed to *d* again and again.
Eph 2: 16 by which he put to *d* their hostility.
Php 1: 20 in my body, whether by life or by *d*.
2: 8 and became obedient to *d*—
2: 8 even *d* on a cross!
3: 10 becoming like him in his *d*, and so,
Col 1: 22 body through *d* to present you holy
3: 5 to *d*, therefore, whatever belongs
2Ti 1: 10 who has destroyed *d* and has
Heb 2: 9 and honor because he suffered *d*,
2: 9 the grace of God he might taste *d*
2: 14 by his *d* he might destroy him who
2: 14 him who holds the power of *d*—
2: 15 held in slavery by their fear of *d*.
5: 7 one who could save him from *d*,
6: 1 repentance from acts that lead to *d*,
7: 23 since *d* prevented them
9: 14 from acts that lead to *d*,
9: 16 it is necessary to prove the *d*
11: 5 so that he did not experience *d*;
11: 19 he did receive Isaac back from *d*.
11: 37 they were put to *d* by the sword.
Jas 1: 15 it is full-grown, gives birth to *d*.
5: 20 of his way will save him from *d*
1Pe 3: 18 He was put to *d* in the body
1Jn 3: 14 know that we have passed from *d*
3: 14 who does not love remains in *d*.
5: 16 There is a sin that leads to *d*.
5: 16 a sin that does not lead to *d*,
5: 16 those whose sin does not lead to *d*.
5: 17 there is sin that does not lead to *d*.
Rev 1: 18 And I hold the keys of *d* and Hades
2: 10 Be faithful, even to the point of *d*,
2: 11 hurt at all by the second *d*.
2: 13 who was put to *d* in your city—
6: 8 Its rider was named *D*,
9: 6 During those days men will seek *d*,
9: 6 long to die, but *d* will elude them.
12: 11 as to shrink from *d*.
18: 8 *d*, mourning and famine.
20: 6 The second *d* has no power
20: 13 *d* and Hades gave up the dead that
20: 14 The lake of fire is the second *d*.
20: 14 Then *d* and Hades were thrown
21: 4 There will be no more *d*
21: 8 This is the second *d*."

DEATH'S (DIE)

Job 18: 13 *d* firstborn devours his limbs.

DEATHLY (DIE)

Jer 30: 6 every face turned *d* pale?
Da 10: 8 my face turned *d* pale and I was

DEATHS (DIE)

1Sa 4: 21 and the *d* of her father-in-law

DEBATE (DEBATED DEBATING)

Ac 15: 2 into sharp dispute and *d* with them.
18: 28 refuted the Jews in public *d*,

DEBATED (DEBATE)

Ac 9: 29 and *d* with the Grecian Jews,

DEBATING (DEBATE)

Mk 12: 28 of the law came and heard them *d*.

DEBAUCHERY

Ro 13: 13 not in sexual immorality and *d*,
2Co 12: 21 and *d* in which they have indulged.
Gal 5: 19 impurity and *d*; idolatry
Eph 5: 18 drunk on wine, which leads to *d*.
1Pe 4: 3 living in *d*, lust, drunkenness,

DEBIR

Jos 10: 3 of Lachish and *D* king of Eglon.
10: 38 turned around and attacked *D*.
10: 39 They did to *D* and its king
11: 21 from Hebron, *D* and Anab,
12: 13 one the king of *D* one the king
13: 26 Mahanaim to the territory of *D*;
15: 7 up to *D* from the Valley of Achor
15: 15 *D* (formerly called Kiriath Sepher).
15: 49 *D*), Anab, Eshtemoh, Anim,
21: 15 Jattir, Eshtemoa, Holon, *D*, Ain,
Jdg 1: 11 *D* (formerly called Kiriath Sepher).
1Ch 6: 58 Jattir, Eshtemoa, Hilen, *D*, Ashan,

DEBORAH

Ge 35: 8 Now *D*, Rebekah's nurse,
Jdg 4: 4 *D*, a prophetess, the wife
4: 5 the Palm of *D* between Ramah
4: 9 So *D* went with Barak to Kedesh,
4: 9 *D* said, "I will go with you.
4: 10 and *D* also went with him.
4: 14 Then *D* said to Barak, "Go!
5: 1 On that day *D* and Barak son
5: 7 ceased until I, *D*, arose,
5: 12 "Wake up, wake up, *D*!
5: 15 princes of Issachar were with *D*;

DEBT (DEBTOR DEBTORS DEBTS)

Dt 15: 3 must cancel any *d* your brother
24: 6 the upper one—as security for a *d*,
1Sa 22: 2 or in *d* or discontented gathered
Job 24: 9 of the poor is seized for a *d*.
Mt 18: 25 that he had be sold to repay the *d*.
18: 27 canceled the *d* and let him go.
18: 30 into prison until he could pay the *d*.
18: 32 'I canceled all that *d* of yours
Lk 7: 43 who had the bigger *d* canceled."
Ro 13: 8 Let no *d* remain outstanding,
13: 8 continuing *d* to love one another,

DEBTOR (DEBT)

Isa 24: 2 for *d* as for creditor.

DEBTORS (DEBT)

Hab 2: 7 Will not your *d* suddenly arise?
Mt 6: 12 as we also have forgiven our *d*.
Lk 16: 5 called in each one of his master's *d*.

DEBTS (DEBT)

Dt 15: 1 seven years you must cancel *d*.
15: 2 time for canceling *d* has been
15: 9 the year for canceling *d*, is near,"
31: 10 in the year for canceling *d*,
2Ki 4: 7 "Go, sell the oil and pay your *d*.
Ne 10: 31 the land and will cancel all *d*.
Pr 22: 26 or puts up security for *d*;
Mt 6: 12 Forgive us our *d*,
Lk 7: 42 so he canceled the *d* of both.

DECAPOLIS

Mt 4: 25 Large crowds from Galilee, the *D*,
Mk 5: 20 in the *D* how much Jesus had done
7: 31 and into the region of the *D*.

DECAY (DECAYED)

Ps 16: 10 will you let your Holy One see *d*.
49: 9 and not see *d*.
49: 14 their forms will *d* in the grave,
Pr 12: 4 a disgraceful wife is like *d*
Isa 5: 24 so their roots will *d*
Hab 3: 16 *d* crept into my bones,
Ac 2: 27 will you let your Holy One see *d*.
2: 31 to the grave, nor did his body see *d*.
13: 34 never to *d*, is stated in these words:
13: 35 will not let your Holy One see *d*.'
13: 37 raised from the dead did not see *d*.
Ro 8: 21 liberated from its bondage to *d*

DECAYED (DECAY)

Jer 49: 7 Has their wisdom *d*?
Ac 13: 36 with his fathers and his body *d*.

DECEIT (DECEIVE)

Job 15: 35 their womb fashions *d*."
27: 4 and my tongue will utter no *d*.
31: 5 or my foot has hurried after *d*—
Ps 5: 9 with their tongue they speak *d*.
32: 2 and in whose spirit is no *d*.
50: 19 and harness your tongue to *d*.
52: 2 you who practice *d*.
101: 7 No one who practices *d*
Pr 6: 14 who plots evil with *d* in his heart—
12: 20 There is *d* in the hearts
26: 24 but in his heart he harbors *d*.
Isa 5: 18 sin along with cords of *d*,
30: 12 and depended on *d*,
53: 9 nor was any *d* in his mouth.
Jer 5: 27 their houses are full of *d*;
6: 13 all practice *d*.
8: 5 They cling to *d*;
8: 10 all practice *d*.
9: 6 in their *d* they refuse
9: 8 it speaks with *d*.
Da 8: 25 He will cause *d* to prosper,
Hos 7: 1 They practice *d*,
11: 12 the house of Israel with *d*.
Zep 1: 9 gods with violence and *d*.
3: 13 nor will *d* be found in their mouths.
Zec 10: 2 The idols speak *d*,
Mk 7: 22 greed, malice, *d*, lewdness, envy,
Ac 13: 10 You are full of all kinds of *d*
Ro 1: 29 murder, strife, *d* and malice.
3: 13 their tongues practice *d*."
1Pe 2: 1 yourselves of all malice and all *d*,
2: 22 and no *d* was found in his mouth."

DECEITFUL (DECEIVE)

Job 11: 11 Surely he recognizes *d* men;
Ps 5: 6 bloodthirsty and *d* men
17: 1 it does not rise from *d* lips.
26: 4 I do not sit with *d* men,
36: 3 of his mouth are wicked and *d*;
43: 1 rescue me from *d* and wicked men.
52: 4 O you *d* tongue!
55: 23 bloodthirsty and *d* men
109: 2 for wicked and *d* men
119: 29 Keep me from *d* ways;
120: 2 and from *d* tongues.
120: 3 and what more besides, O *d* tongue
144: 8 whose right hands are *d*.
144: 11 whose right hands are *d*.
Pr 12: 5 but the advice of the wicked is *d*.
14: 25 but a false witness is *d*.
15: 4 but a *d* tongue crushes the spirit.
17: 20 he whose tongue is *d* falls
Isa 30: 9 are rebellious people, *d* children,
Jer 17: 9 The heart is *d* above all things
Hos 10: 2 Their heart is *d*,
2Co 11: 13 men are false apostles, *d* workmen,
Eph 4: 14 of men in their *d* scheming.
4: 22 is being corrupted by its *d* desires;
1Pe 3: 10 and his lips from *d* speech.
Rev 21: 27 who does what is shameful or *d*,

DECEITFULNESS (DECEIVE)

Ps 119: 118 for their *d* is in vain.
Mt 13: 22 and the *d* of wealth choke it,
Mk 4: 19 the *d* of wealth and the desires
Heb 3: 13 of you may be hardened by sin's *d*.

DECEIVE (DECEIT DECEITFUL DECEITFULNESS DECEIVED DECEIVER DECEIVERS DECEIVES DECEIVING DECEPTION DECEPTIVE)

Ge 31: 27 run off secretly and *d* me?
Lev 19: 11 " 'Do not *d* one another.

Jos 9:22 "Why did you *d* us by saying,
1Sa 19:17 "Why did you *d* me like this
2Sa 3:25 came to *d* you and observe your
2Ki 18:29 Do not let Hezekiah *d* you.
19:10 depend on *d* you when he says,
2Ch 32:15 Now do not let Hezekiah *d* you
Job 13: 9 you *d* him as you might *d* men?
15:31 Let him not *d* himself
Pr 14: 5 A truthful witness does not *d*,
24:28 or use your lips to *d*.
Isa 36:14 Do not let Hezekiah *d* you.
37:10 depend on *d* you when he says,
Jer 29: 8 and diviners among you *d* you.
37: 9 Do not *d* yourselves, thinking,
Ob : 7 your friends will *d* and overpower
Zec 13: 4 garment of hair in order to *d*.
Mt 24: 5 'I am the Christ,' and will *d* many.
24:11 will appear and *d* many people.
24:24 and miracles to *d* even the elect—
Mk 13: 6 'I am he,' and will *d* many.
13:22 and miracles to *d* the elect—
Ro 16:18 and flattery they *d* the minds
1Co 3:18 Do not *d* yourselves.
Eph 5: 6 Let no one *d* you with empty words
Col 2: 4 this so that no one may *d* you
2Th 2: 3 Don't let anyone *d* you in any way,
Jas 1:22 to the word, and so *d* yourselves.
1Jn 1: 8 we *d* ourselves and the truth is not
Rev 20: 8 and will go out to *d* the nations

DECEIVED (DECEIVE)

Ge 3:13 "The serpent *d* me, and I ate."
27:36 He has *d* me these two times:
29:25 Why have you *d* me?" Laban
31:20 Jacob *d* Laban the Aramean
31:26 What have you done? You've *d* me,
Nu 25:18 as enemies when they *d* you
1Sa 28:12 "Why have you *d* me? You are Saul
Job 12:16 both *d* and deceiver are his.
Isa 19:13 the leaders of Memphis are *d*;
Jer 4:10 completely you have *d* this people
20: 7 O LORD, you *d* me, and I was *d*;
20:10 "Perhaps he will be *d*;
49:16 the pride of your heart have *d* you,
Hos 7:11 easily *d* and senseless—
Ob : 3 The pride of your heart has *d* you,
Lk 21: 8 "Watch out that you are not *d*.
Jn 7:47 "You mean he has *d* you also?"
Ro 7:11 by the commandment, *d* me,
1Co 6: 9 the kingdom of God? Do not be *d*:
2Co 11: 3 Eve was *d* by the serpent's cunning
Gal 6: 7 Do not be *d*: God cannot be
1Ti 2:14 And Adam was not the one *d*;
2:14 it was the woman who was *d*
2Ti 3:13 to worse, deceiving and being *d*.
Tit 3: 3 *d* and enslaved by all kinds
Jas 1:16 Don't be *d*, my dear brothers.
Rev 13:14 he *d* the inhabitants of the earth.
20:10 And the devil, who *d* them,

DECEIVER (DECEIVE)

Job 12:16 both deceived and *d* are his.
Jer 9: 4 For every brother is a *d*,
Mic 2:11 If a liar and *d* comes and says,
Mt 27:63 while he was still alive that *d* said,
2Jn : 7 Any such person is the *d*

DECEIVERS (DECEIVE)

Ps 49: 5 when wicked *d* surround me—
Tit 1:10 and *d*, especially those
2Jn : 7 Many *d*, who do not acknowledge

DECEIVES (DECEIVE)

Pr 26:19 is a man who *d* his neighbor
Jer 9: 5 Friend *d* friend,
Mt 24: 4 "Watch out that no one *d* you.
Mk 13: 5 "Watch out that no one *d* you.
Jn 7:12 replied, "No, he *d* the people."
Gal 6: 3 when he is nothing, he *d* himself.
2Th 2:10 sort of evil that *d* those who are
Jas 1:26 he *d* himself and his religion is

DECEIVING (DECEIVE)

Lev 6: 2 by *d* his neighbor about something
1Ti 4: 1 follow *d* spirits and things taught
2Ti 3:13 go from bad to worse, *d*
Rev 20: 3 him from *d* the nations any more

DECENCY (DECENTLY)

1Ti 2: 9 women to dress modestly, with *d*

DECENTLY (DECENCY)

Ro 13:13 Let us behave *d*, as in the daytime,

DECEPTION (DECEIVE)

Ps 12: 2 their flattering lips speak with *d*.
38:12 all day long they plot *d*.
Pr 14: 8 but the folly of fools is *d*.
26:26 His malice may be concealed by *d*,
Jer 3:23 and mountains is a *d*;
9: 6 You live in the midst of *d*;
Hos 10:13 you have eaten the fruit of *d*.
Mt 27:64 This last *d* will be worse
2Co 4: 2 we do not use *d*, nor do we distort

DECEPTIVE (DECEIVE)

Pr 11:18 The wicked man earns *d* wages,
23: 3 for that food is *d*.
31:30 Charm is *d*, and beauty is fleeting;
Jer 7: 4 Do not trust in *d* words and say,
7: 8 in *d* words that are worthless.
15:18 Will you be to me like a *d* brook,
Mic 1:14 The town of Aczib will prove *d*
Col 2: 8 through hollow and *d* philosophy,

DECIDE (DECIDED DECISION DECISIONS)

Ex 18:16 and I *d* between the parties
18:22 cases they can *d* themselves.
33: 5 and I will *d* what to do with you.'"
Dt 21: 5 to *d* all cases of dispute and assault.
25: 1 and the judges will *d* the case,
Jdg 11:27 *d* the dispute this day
1Sa 24:15 May the LORD be our judge and *d*
2Sa 24:13 *d* how I should answer the one who
1Ch 21:12 *d* how I should answer the one who
Job 22:28 What you *d* on will be done,
34:33 You must *d*, not I;
Isa 11: 3 or *d* by what he hears with his ears;
Eze 44:24 *d* it according to my ordinances.
Jn 19:24 "Let's *d* by lot who will get it."
Ac 4:21 They could not *d* how
24:22 he said, "I will *d* your case."

DECIDED (DECIDE)

Ge 41:32 is that the matter has been firmly *d*
Ex 18:26 the simple ones they *d* themselves.
Jdg 4: 5 to her to have their disputes *d*.
2Ch 24: 4 Some time later Joash *d*
30: 2 in Jerusalem *d* to celebrate
30: 5 They *d* to send a proclamation
Est 7: 7 that the king had already *d* his fate,
Jer 4:28 I have *d* and will not turn back."
Da 2: 5 "This is what I have firmly *d*:
2: 8 that this is what I have firmly *d*:
Zep 3: 8 I have *d* to assemble the nations,
Mt 27: 7 So they *d* to use the money
Lk 23:24 So Pilate *d* to grant their demand.
Jn 1:43 The next day Jesus *d* to leave
9:22 the Jews had *d* that anyone who
Ac 3:13 though he had *d* to let him go.
4:28 and will had *d* beforehand should
7:23 he *d* to visit his fellow Israelites.
11:29 *d* to provide help for the brothers
15:22 *d* to choose some of their own men
19:21 Paul *d* to go to Jerusalem,
20: 3 he *d* to go back through Macedonia
20:16 Paul had *d* to sail past Ephesus
25:25 to the Emperor I *d* to send him
27: 1 When it was *d* that we would sail
27:12 the majority *d* that we should sail
27:39 where they *d* to run the ship
2Co 9: 7 man should give what he has *d*
Tit 3:12 because I have *d* to winter there.

DECIMATED

2Sa 21: 5 against us so that we have been *d*

DECISION (DECIDE)

Ex 28:29 heart on the breastpiece of *d*
2Sa 15: 2 to be placed before the king for a *d*,
Ezr 5:17 Then let the king send us his *d*
10: 8 with the *d* of the officials
Pr 16:33 but its every *d* is from the LORD.
Isa 16: 3 render a *d*.
Da 4:17 The *d* is announced by messengers;
Joel 3:14 multitudes in the valley of *d*!
3:14 near in the valley of *d*.
Mt 27: 1 came to the *d* to put Jesus to death.
Mk 15: 1 the whole Sanhedrin, reached a *d*.
Lk 23:51 who had not consented to their *d*
Jn 1:13 nor of human *d* or a husband's will,
Ac 21:25 to them our *d* that they should
25:21 to be held over for the Emperor's *d*

DECISIONS (DECIDE)

Ex 28:15 Fashion a breastpiece for making *d*
28:30 of making *d* for the Israelites
Nu 27:21 who will obtain *d* for him
Dt 17:10 according to the *d* they give you
17:11 teach you and the *d* they give you.
Isa 11: 4 with justice he will give *d*
28: 7 they stumble when rendering *d*.
58: 2 They ask me for just *d*
Jn 8:16 But if I do judge, my *d* are right,
Ac 16: 4 they delivered the *d* reached

DECK (DECKED DECKS)

Eze 27: 6 they made your *d*, inlaid with ivory
Jnh 1: 5 But Jonah had gone below *d*,

DECKED (DECK)

Hos 2:13 she *d* herself with rings and jewelry

DECKS (DECK)

Ge 6:16 make lower, middle and upper *d*.

DECLARE (DECLARED DECLARES DECLARING)

Ex 22: 9 whom the judges *d* guilty must pay
Dt 5: 1 and laws I *d* in your hearing today.
5: 5 and you to *d* to you the word
21: 7 they shall *d*: "Our hands did not
26: 3 "I *d* today to the LORD your God
26: 5 you shall *d* before the LORD your
30:18 I *d* to you this day that you will
32:40 I lift my hand to heaven and *d*:
1Ki 1:36 the God of my lord the king, so *d* it.
8:32 *D* the innocent not guilty,
2Ki 9: 3 and pour the oil on his head and *d*,
1Ch 16:24 *D* his glory among the nations,
17:10 " 'I *d* to you that the LORD will
2Ch 6:23 *D* the innocent not guilty
Job 34:34 "Men of understanding *d*,
Ps 5:10 *D* them guilty, O God!
9:14 that I may *d* your praises
19: 1 The heavens *d* the glory of God,
22:22 I will *d* your name to my brothers;
40: 5 they would be too many to *d*.
51:15 and my mouth will *d* your praise.
71:17 this day I *d* your marvelous deeds.
71:18 till I *d* your power
75: 9 As for me, I will *d* this forever;
89: 2 I will *d* that your love stands firm
96: 3 *D* his glory among the nations,
106: 2 or fully *d* his praise?
Isa 41:22 Or *d* to us the things to come,
42: 9 and new things I *d*;
44: 7 Let him *d* and lay out before me
45:19 I *d* what is right.
45:21 *D* what is to be, present it—
58: 1 *D* to my people their rebellion
Jer 23:31 wag their own tongues and yet *d*,
Eze 38:19 and fiery wrath I *d* that
Da 4:17 the holy ones *d* the verdict,
Joel 1:14 *D* a holy fast;
2:15 *d* a holy fast,
Mic 3: 8 to *d* to Jacob his transgression,
Ac 20:26 I *d* to you today that I am innocent
1Co 15:50 I *d* to you, brothers, that flesh
Gal 5: 3 Again I *d* to every man who lets
Eph 6:20 Pray that I may *d* it fearlessly,
Heb 2:12 "I will *d* your name to my brothers;
1Pe 2: 9 that you may *d* the praises
1Jn 1: 5 heard from him and *d* to you:

DECLARED (DECLARE)

Nu 14:17 as you have *d*: 'The LORD is slow
Dt 4:13 He *d* to you his covenant, the Ten
26:17 You have *d* this day that
26:18 LORD has *d* this day that you are
26:19 He has *d* that he will set you
32:46 all the words I have solemnly *d*
1Ki 1:24 *d* that Adonijah shall be king

1Ki 8: 53 you *d* through your servant Moses
13: 3 "This is the sign the LORD has *d:*
13: 32 For the message he *d* by the word
22: 11 had made iron horns and he *d,*
22: 28 Micaiah *d,* "If you ever return
22: 38 as the word of the LORD had *d.*
2Ki 9: 6 the oil on Jehu's head and *d,*
13: 17 of victory over Aram!" Elisha *d.*
24: 13 the LORD had *d,* Nebuchadnezzar
2Ch 18: 10 he *d,* "This is what the LORD says:
18: 27 Micaiah *d,* "If you ever return
Job 15: 18 what wise men have *d,*
Ps 88: 11 Is your love *d* in the grave,
95: 11 So I *d* on oath in my anger,
102: 21 of the LORD will be *d* in Zion
Pr 30: 1 This man *d* to Ithiel,
Ecc 4: 2 And I *d* that the dead,
Isa 5: 9 The LORD Almighty has *d*
45: 21 who *d* it from the distant past?
Jnh 3: 5 They *d* a fast, and all of them,
Mt 26: 35 But Peter *d,* "Even if I have to die
26: 61 Finally two came forward and *d,*
Mk 7: 19 Jesus *d* all foods "clean.")
10: 20 he *d,* "all these I have kept
12: 36 speaking by the Holy Spirit, *d:*
14: 29 Peter *d,* "Even if all fall away,
Jn 1: 49 Then Nathanael *d,* "Rabbi,
3: 3 In reply Jesus *d,* "I tell you
4: 21 Jesus *d,* "Believe me, woman,
4: 26 Jesus *d,* "I who speak to you am he
6: 35 Jesus *d,* "I am the bread of life.
7: 46 way this man does," the guards *d.*
8: 11 neither do I condemn you," Jesus *d*
20: 25 that they had seen the Lord, he *d,*
Ac 20: 21 I have *d* to both Jews and Greeks
25: 12 he *d:* "You have appealed
28: 23 and *d* to them the kingdom of God
Ro 1: 4 Spirit of holiness was *d* with power
2: 13 the law who will be *d* righteous.
3: 20 no one will be *d* righteous
Heb 3: 11 So I *d* on oath in my anger,
4: 3 "So I *d* on oath in my anger,
7: 8 by him who is *d* to be living.
7: 17 For it is *d:*

DECLARES (DECLARE)

Ge 22: 16 "I swear by myself, *d* the LORD,
Ex 21: 5 if the servant *d,* 'I love my master
Nu 14: 28 'As surely as I live, *d* the LORD,
1Sa 2: 30 But now the LORD *d:* 'Far be it
2: 30 the LORD, the God of Israel, *d:*
2Sa 7: 11 LORD *d* to you that the LORD
2Ki 9: 26 on this plot of ground, *d* the LORD
9: 26 the blood of his sons, *d* the LORD,
19: 33 not enter this city, *d* the LORD.
22: 19 I have heard you, *d* the LORD.
2Ch 34: 27 I have heard you, *d* the LORD.
Isa 1: 24 the Mighty One of Israel, *d:*
3: 15 *d* the Lord, the LORD Almighty.
14: 22 *d* the LORD Almighty.
14: 22 *d* the LORD.
14: 23 *d* the LORD Almighty.
17: 3 *d* the LORD Almighty.
17: 6 *d* the LORD, the God of Israel.
19: 4 *d* the Lord, the LORD Almighty.
22: 25 "In that day," *d* the LORD
30: 1 *d* the LORD,
31: 9 *d* the LORD,
37: 34 *d* the LORD.
41: 14 will help you," *d* the LORD,
43: 10 are my witnesses," *d* the LORD,
43: 12 are my witnesses," *d* the LORD,
49: 18 As surely as I live," *d* the LORD,
52: 5 do I have here?" *d* the LORD.
52: 5 *d* the LORD.
54: 17 *d* the LORD.
55: 8 *d* the LORD.
56: 8 The Sovereign LORD *d*—
59: 20 *d* the LORD.
66: 2 *d* the LORD.
66: 17 their end together," *d* the LORD.
66: 22 *d* the LORD, "so will your name
Jer 1: 8 and will rescue you," *d* the LORD.
1: 15 northern kingdoms," *d* the LORD.
1: 19 and will rescue you," *d* the LORD.
2: 3 *d* the LORD.
2: 9 *d* the LORD.
2: 12 *d* the LORD.

Jer 2: 19 *d* the Lord, the LORD Almighty.
2: 22 *d* the Sovereign LORD.
2: 29 *d* the LORD.
3: 1 *d* the LORD.
3: 10 but only in pretense," *d* the LORD
3: 12 faithless Israel,' *d* the LORD,
3: 12 for I am merciful,' *d* the LORD,
3: 13 *d* the LORD.
3: 14 faithless people," *d* the LORD,
3: 16 *d* the LORD, "men will no longer
3: 20 *d* the LORD.
4: 1 *d* the LORD.
4: 9 "In that day," *d* the LORD,
4: 17 *d* the LORD.
5: 9 *d* the LORD.
5: 11 *d* the LORD.
5: 15 O house of Israel," *d* the LORD,
5: 18 even in those days," *d* the LORD,
5: 22 you not fear me?" *d* the LORD.
5: 29 *d* the LORD.
6: 12 *d* the LORD.
7: 11 I have been watching! *d* the LORD
7: 13 all these things, *d* the LORD,
7: 19 they are provoking? *d* the LORD.
7: 30 evil in my eyes, *d* the LORD.
7: 32 the days are coming, *d* the LORD,
8: 1 " 'At that time, *d* the LORD,
8: 3 to life, *d* the LORD Almighty.'
8: 13 away their harvest, *d* the LORD.
8: 17 *d* the LORD.
9: 3 *d* the LORD.
9: 6 *d* the LORD.
9: 9 *d* the LORD.
9: 22 Say, "This is what the LORD *d:*
9: 24 *d* the LORD.
9: 25 days are coming," *d* the LORD,
12: 17 and destroy it," *d* the LORD.
13: 11 *d* the LORD, 'to be my people
13: 14 fathers and sons alike, *d* the LORD
13: 25 *d* the LORD,
15: 3 against them," *d* the LORD,
15: 6 have rejected me," *d* the LORD.
15: 9 *d* the LORD.
15: 20 *d* the LORD.
16: 5 from this people," *d* the LORD.
16: 11 fathers forsook me,' *d* the LORD,
16: 14 the days are coming," *d* the LORD
16: 16 *d* the LORD, "and they will catch
17: 24 careful to obey me, *d* the LORD,
18: 6 as this potter does?" *d* the LORD.
19: 6 the days are coming, *d* the LORD,
19: 12 those who live here, *d* the LORD.
21: 7 *d* the LORD, I will hand
21: 10 and not good, *d* the LORD.
21: 13 *d* the LORD—
21: 14 *d* the LORD.
22: 5 these commands, *d* the LORD,
22: 16 *d* the LORD.
22: 24 "As surely as I live," *d* the LORD,
23: 1 of my pasture!" *d* the LORD.
23: 2 evil you have done," *d* the LORD.
23: 4 will any be missing," *d* the LORD.
23: 5 days are coming," *d* the LORD,
23: 7 the days are coming," *d* the LORD
23: 11 *d* the LORD.
23: 12 *d* the LORD.
23: 23 *d* the LORD,
23: 24 *d* the LORD.
23: 24 *d* the LORD.
23: 28 to do with grain?" *d* the LORD.
23: 29 my word like fire," *d* the LORD,
23: 30 "Therefore," *d* the LORD,
23: 31 and yet declare, 'The LORD *d.*'
23: 31 *d* the LORD, "I am
23: 32 false dreams," *d* the LORD.
23: 32 people in the least," *d* the LORD.
23: 33 I will forsake you, *d* the LORD.'
25: 7 listen to me," *d* the LORD,
25: 9 king of Babylon," *d* the LORD,
25: 12 for their guilt," *d* the LORD,
25: 29 live on the earth, *d* the LORD
25: 31 *d* the LORD.
27: 8 famine and plague, *d* the LORD,
27: 11 and to live there, *d* the LORD." ' "
27: 15 I have not sent them,' *d* the LORD
27: 22 come for them,' *d* the LORD.
28: 4 *d* the LORD, 'for I will break
29: 9 have not sent them," *d* the LORD.

Jer 29: 11 have for you," *d* the LORD,
29: 14 found by you," *d* the LORD,
29: 14 have banished you," *d* the LORD,
29: 19 to my words," *d* the LORD,
29: 19 not listened either," *d* the LORD.
29: 23 am a witness to it," *d* the LORD.
29: 32 *d* the LORD, because he has
30: 3 The days are coming,' *d* the LORD
30: 8 In that day,' *d* the LORD
30: 10 *d* the LORD.
30: 11 *d* the LORD.
30: 17 *d* the LORD,
30: 21 *d* the LORD.
31: 1 "At that time," *d* the LORD,
31: 14 *d* the LORD.
31: 16 *d* the LORD.
31: 17 *d* the LORD.
31: 20 *d* the LORD.
31: 27 days are coming," *d* the LORD,
31: 28 and to plant," *d* the LORD.
31: 31 The time is coming," *d* the LORD,
31: 32 *d* the LORD.
31: 33 after that time," *d* the LORD.
31: 34 *d* the LORD.
31: 36 *d* the LORD,
31: 37 *d* the LORD.
31: 38 days are coming," *d* the LORD,
32: 5 until I deal with him, *d* the LORD.
32: 30 hands have made, *d* the LORD.
32: 44 their fortunes, *d* the LORD."
33: 14 The days are coming,' *d* the LORD
34: 5 make this promise, *d* the LORD.' "
34: 17 for you, *d* the LORD—
34: 22 to give the order, *d* the LORD,
35: 13 and obey my words?' *d* the LORD.
39: 17 you on that day, *d* the LORD;
39: 18 you trust in me, *d* the LORD.' "
42: 11 afraid of him, *d* the LORD,
44: 29 you in this place,' *d* the LORD,
45: 5 on all people, *d* the LORD,
46: 5 *d* the LORD.
46: 18 "As surely as I live," *d* the King,
46: 23 *d* the LORD,
46: 26 as in times past," *d* the LORD.
46: 28 for I am with you," *d* the LORD.
48: 12 *d* the LORD,
48: 15 *d* the King, whose name is
48: 25 *d* the LORD.
48: 30 *d* the LORD,
48: 35 *d* the LORD.
48: 38 *d* the LORD.
48: 43 *d* the LORD.
48: 44 *d* the LORD.
48: 47 *d* the LORD.
49: 2 *d* the LORD,
49: 5 *d* the Lord, the LORD Almighty.
49: 6 *d* the LORD.
49: 13 I swear by myself," *d* the LORD,
49: 16 *d* the LORD.
49: 26 *d* the LORD Almighty.
49: 30 *d* the LORD.
49: 31 *d* the LORD,
49: 32 *d* the LORD.
49: 37 *d* the LORD.
49: 38 *d* the LORD.
49: 39 *d* the LORD.
50: 4 *d* the LORD,
50: 10 *d* the LORD.
50: 20 *d* the LORD,
50: 21 *d* the LORD.
50: 30 *d* the LORD.
50: 31 *d* the Lord, the LORD Almighty,
50: 35 *d* the LORD—
50: 40 *d* the LORD,
51: 24 done in Zion," *d* the LORD.
51: 25 *d* the LORD.
51: 26 *d* the LORD.
51: 39 *d* the LORD.
51: 48 *d* the LORD.
51: 52 days are coming," *d* the LORD,
51: 53 *d* the LORD.
51: 57 *d* the King, whose name is
Eze 5: 11 as I live, *d* the Sovereign LORD,
11: 8 bring against you, *d* the Sovereign
11: 21 they have done, *d* the Sovereign
12: 25 *d* the Sovereign LORD.' "
12: 28 *d* the Sovereign LORD.' "
13: 6 They say, "The LORD *d,*"

Eze 13: 7 "The LORD *d*," though I have not
13: 8 am against you, *d* the Sovereign
13: 16 *d* the Sovereign LORD." '
14: 11 *d* the Sovereign LORD.' "
14: 14 their righteousness, *d*
14: 16 as I live, *d* the Sovereign LORD,
14: 18 as I live, *d* the Sovereign LORD,
14: 20 as I live, *d* the Sovereign LORD,
14: 23 it without cause, *d* the Sovereign
15: 8 been unfaithful, *d* the Sovereign
16: 8 *d* the Sovereign LORD,
16: 14 beauty perfect, *d* the Sovereign
16: 19 is what happened, *d* the Sovereign
16: 23 to you, *d* the Sovereign LORD.
16: 30 you are, *d* the Sovereign
16: 43 you have done, *d* the Sovereign
16: 48 as I live, *d* the Sovereign LORD,
16: 58 detestable practices, *d* the LORD.
16: 63 *d* the Sovereign LORD.' "
17: 16 as I live, *d* the Sovereign LORD,
18: 3 as I live, *d* the Sovereign LORD,
18: 9 *d* the Sovereign LORD.
18: 23 of the wicked? *d* the Sovereign
18: 30 to his ways, *d* the Sovereign
18: 32 of anyone, *d* the Sovereign LORD.
20: 3 of me, *d* the Sovereign LORD.'
20: 31 as I live, *d* the Sovereign LORD,
20: 33 as I live, *d* the Sovereign LORD,
20: 36 will judge you, *d* the Sovereign
20: 40 of Israel, *d* the Sovereign LORD,
20: 44 *d* the Sovereign LORD.' "
21: 7 surely take place, *d* the Sovereign
21: 13 will not succeed! *d* the Sovereign
22: 12 have forgotten me, *d* the Sovereign
22: 31 they have done, *d* the Sovereign
23: 34 I have spoken, *d* the Sovereign
24: 14 *d* the Sovereign LORD.' "
25: 14 *d* the Sovereign LORD.' "
26: 5 I have spoken, *d* the Sovereign
26: 14 have spoken, *d* the Sovereign
26: 21 again be found, *d* the Sovereign
28: 10 *d* the Sovereign LORD.' "
29: 20 it for me, *d* the Sovereign LORD.
30: 6 *d* the Sovereign LORD.
31: 18 *d* the Sovereign LORD.' "
32: 8 *d* the Sovereign LORD.
32: 14 *d* the Sovereign LORD.
32: 16 will chant it, *d* the Sovereign
32: 31 by the sword, *d* the Sovereign
32: 32 by the sword, *d* the Sovereign
33: 11 as I live, *d* the Sovereign LORD,
34: 8 as I live, *d* the Sovereign LORD,
34: 15 lie down, *d* the Sovereign LORD.
34: 30 are my people, *d* the Sovereign
34: 31 *d* the Sovereign LORD.' "
35: 6 as I live, *d* the Sovereign LORD,
35: 11 as I live, *d* the Sovereign LORD,
36: 14 nation childless, *d* the Sovereign
36: 15 *d* the Sovereign LORD.' "
36: 23 am the LORD, *d* the Sovereign
36: 32 this for your sake, *d* the Sovereign
37: 14 and I have done it, *d* the LORD.' "
38: 18 will be aroused, *d* the Sovereign
38: 21 all my mountains, *d* the Sovereign
39: 5 I have spoken, *d* the Sovereign
39: 8 surely take place, *d* the Sovereign
39: 10 who looted them, *d* the Sovereign
39: 13 for them, *d* the Sovereign LORD.
39: 20 of every kind,' *d* the Sovereign
39: 29 of Israel, *d* the Sovereign LORD."
43: 19 before me, *d* the Sovereign LORD.
43: 27 will accept you, *d* the Sovereign
44: 12 of their sin, *d* the Sovereign LORD
44: 15 and blood, *d* the Sovereign LORD.
44: 27 for himself, *d* the Sovereign LORD
45: 9 my people, *d* the Sovereign
45: 15 for the people, *d* the Sovereign
47: 23 his inheritance," *d* the Sovereign
48: 29 be their portions," *d* the Sovereign
Hos 2: 13 *d* the LORD.
2: 16 "In that day," *d* the LORD,
2: 21 *d* the LORD—
11: 11 *d* the LORD.
Joel 2: 12 "Even now," *d* the LORD,
Am 2: 11 *d* the LORD.
2: 16 *d* the LORD.
3: 10 to do right," *d* the LORD,
3: 13 *d* the Lord, the LORD God
Am 3: 15 *d* the LORD.
4: 3 *d* the LORD.
4: 5 *d* the Sovereign LORD.
4: 6 *d* the LORD.
4: 8 *d* the LORD.
4: 9 *d* the LORD.
4: 10 *d* the LORD.
4: 11 *d* the LORD.
6: 8 the LORD God Almighty *d*:
6: 14 For the LORD God Almighty *d*,
8: 3 "In that day," *d* the Sovereign
8: 9 "In that day," *d* the Sovereign
8: 11 days are coming," *d* the Sovereign
9: 7 *d* the LORD.
9: 8 *d* the LORD.
9: 12 *d* the LORD, who will do these
9: 13 days are coming," *d* the LORD,
Ob : 4 *d* the LORD.
: 8 "In that day," *d* the LORD,
Mic 4: 6 "In that day," *d* the LORD,
5: 10 "In that day," *d* the LORD,
Na 2: 13 *d* the LORD Almighty.
3: 5 am against you," *d* the LORD
Zep 1: 2 *d* the LORD.
1: 3 *d* the LORD.
1: 10 "On that day," *d* the LORD,
2: 9 *d* the LORD Almighty, the God
3: 8 for me," *d* the LORD,
Hag 1: 9 Why?" *d* the LORD Almighty.
1: 13 "I am with you," *d* the LORD.
2: 4 O Zerubbabel,' *d* the LORD.
2: 4 people of the land,' *d* the LORD,
2: 4 with you,' *d* the LORD Almighty.
2: 8 and the gold is mine,' *d* the LORD
2: 9 will grant peace,' *d* the LORD
2: 14 nation in my sight,' *d* the LORD.
2: 17 turn to me,' *d* the LORD.
2: 23 have chosen you,' *d* the LORD
2: 23 son of Shealtiel,' *d* the LORD,
2: 23 " 'On that day,' *d* the LORD
Zec 1: 3 to me,' *d* the LORD Almighty,
1: 4 pay attention to me,' *d* the LORD.
1: 16 out over Jerusalem,' *d* the LORD
2: 5 *d* the LORD, 'and I will be its glory
2: 6 land of the north," *d* the LORD,
2: 6 winds of heaven," *d* the LORD.
2: 10 live among you," *d* the LORD.
3: 10 fig tree,' *d* the LORD Almighty."
5: 4 LORD Almighty *d*, 'I will send it
8: 6 to me?" *d* the LORD Almighty.
8: 11 did in the past," *d* the LORD
8: 17 I hate all this," *d* the LORD.
10: 12 *d* the LORD.
11: 6 people of the land," *d* the LORD.
12: 1 the spirit of man within him, *d*:
12: 4 rider with madness," *d* the LORD.
13: 2 no more," *d* the LORD
13: 7 *d* the LORD Almighty.
13: 8 In the whole land," *d* the LORD,
Lk 20: 42 David himself *d* in the Book
Ro 2: 16 Jesus Christ, as my gospel *d*.
Gal 3: 22 Scripture *d* that the whole world is
Heb 8: 8 "The time is coming,' *d* the Lord,
8: 9 away from them, *d* the Lord.
8: 10 after that time, *d* the Lord.

DECLARING (DECLARE)

Ps 71: 8 *d* your splendor all day long.
Jer 50: 28 *d* in Zion
Ac 2: 11 we hear them *d* the wonders

DECLINED

Ac 18: 20 to spend more time with them, he *d*

DECORATE (DECORATED DECORATES DECORATING DECORATIONS)

1Ki 7: 18 network to *d* the capitals on top
Mt 23: 29 and *d* the graves of the righteous.

DECORATED (DECORATE)

2Ki 25: 17 and a half feet high and was *d*
2Ch 3: 5 it with fine gold and *d* it
SS 5: 14 *d* with sapphires.
Jer 52: 22 and was *d* with a network
Eze 40: 16 faces of the projecting walls were *d*
40: 31 outer court; palm trees *d* its jambs,
40: 34 palm trees *d* the jambs on
40: 37 palm trees *d* the jambs on
Rev 21: 19 foundations of the city walls were *d*

DECORATES (DECORATE)

Jer 22: 14 and *d* it in red.

DECORATING (DECORATE)

1Ki 7: 41 of network *d* the two bowl-shaped
7: 42 *d* the bowl-shaped capitals on top
2Ch 4: 12 of network *d* the two bowl-shaped
4: 13 *d* the bowl-shaped capitals on top

DECORATIONS (DECORATE)

Eze 40: 22 and its palm tree *d* had the same
40: 26 it had palm tree *d* on the faces

DECREASE (DECREASED)

Lev 25: 16 are few, you are to *d* the price,
Jer 29: 6 Increase in number there; do not *d*.

DECREASED (DECREASE)

Ps 107: 39 Then their numbers *d*,
Jer 30: 19 and they will not be *d*;

DECREE (DECREED DECREES)

Ex 15: 25 There the LORD made a *d*
1Ch 16: 17 He confirmed it to Jacob as a *d*,
Ezr 5: 13 King Cyrus issued a *d*
5: 17 did in fact issue a *d* to rebuild this
6: 3 the king issued a *d* concerning
6: 8 I hereby *d* what you are to do
6: 11 I *d* that if anyone changes this edict
6: 12 who lifts a hand to change this *d*
6: 13 of the *d* King Darius had sent,
7: 13 Now I *d* that any of the Israelites
Est 1: 19 let him issue a royal *d* and let it be
3: 9 let a *d* be issued to destroy them,
8: 8 write another *d* in the king's name
9: 32 Esther's *d* confirmed these
Job 23: 14 He carries out his *d* against me,
28: 26 when he made a *d* for the rain
Ps 2: 7 I will proclaim the *d* of the LORD:
7: 6 Awake, my God; *d* justice.
81: 4 this is a *d* for Israel,
105: 10 He confirmed it to Jacob as a *d*,
148: 6 he gave a *d* that will never pass
Jer 51: 12 his *d* against the people of Babylon.
Da 2: 13 *d* was issued to put the wise men
2: 15 did the king issue such a harsh *d*?"
3: 10 You have issued a *d*, O king,
3: 29 Therefore I *d* that the people
4: 24 and this is the *d* the Most High has
6: 7 and enforce the *d* that anyone who
6: 8 issue the *d* and put it in writing
6: 9 So King Darius put the *d* in writing
6: 10 learned that the *d* had been
6: 12 The king answered, "The *d* stands
6: 12 and spoke to him about his royal *d*:
6: 12 "Did you not publish a *d* that
6: 13 or to the *d* you put in writing.
6: 15 Persians no *d* or edict that the king
6: 26 "I issue a *d* that in every part
9: 25 From the issuing of the *d* to restore
Jnh 3: 7 By the *d* of the king and his nobles:
Lk 2: 1 Augustus issued a *d* that a census
Ro 1: 32 know God's righteous *d* that those

DECREED (DECREE)

1Ki 22: 23 The LORD has *d* disaster for you."
2Ki 8: 1 because the LORD has *d* a famine
2Ch 18: 22 The LORD has *d* disaster for you."
Ezr 6: 12 I Darius have *d* it.
Est 2: 1 and what he had *d* about her.
9: 31 and Queen Esther had *d* for them,
Job 14: 5 you have *d* the number
Ps 78: 5 He *d* statutes for Jacob
Isa 10: 22 Destruction has been *d*,
10: 23 destruction *d* upon the whole land.
28: 22 me of the destruction *d*
Jer 11: 17 who planted you, has *d* disaster
13: 25 the portion I have *d* for you,"
16: 10 'Why has the LORD *d* such a great
40: 2 LORD your God *d* this disaster
La 1: 17 The LORD has *d* for Jacob
2: 17 which he *d* long ago.
3: 37 happen if the Lord has not *d* it?
Da 4: 31 "This is what is *d* for you, King
9: 24 "Seventy 'sevens' are *d*
9: 26 and desolations have been *d*.

Da 9:27 until the end that is *d* is poured out
Na 2: 7 It is *d* that ⌊the city⌋
Lk 22:22 Son of Man will go as it has been *d*.

DECREES (DECREE)

Ge 26: 5 my commands, my *d* and my laws
Ex 15:26 to his commands and keep all his *d*,
18:16 inform them of God's *d* and laws."
18:20 Teach them the *d* and laws,
Lev 10:11 Israelites all the *d* the LORD has
18: 4 and be careful to follow my *d*.
18: 5 Keep my *d* and laws,
18:26 you must keep my *d* and my laws.
19:19 " 'Keep my *d*.
19:37 " 'Keep all my *d* and all my laws
20: 8 Keep my *d* and follow them.
20:22 " 'Keep all my *d* and laws
25:18 " 'Follow my *d* and be careful
26: 3 If you follow my *d* and are careful
26:15 if you reject my *d* and abhor my
26:43 my laws and abhorred my *d*.
26:46 These are the *d*, the laws
Dt 4: 1 the *d* and laws I am about
4: 5 I have taught you *d* and laws
4: 6 who will hear about all these *d*
4: 8 to have such righteous *d* and laws
4:14 me at that time to teach you the *d*
4:40 Keep his *d* and commands,
4:45 *d* and laws Moses gave them
5: 1 the *d* and laws I declare
5:31 *d* and laws you are to teach them
6: 1 *d* and laws the LORD your God
6: 2 as you live by keeping all his *d*
6:17 the stipulations and *d* he has given
6:20 *d* and laws the LORD our God has
6:24 us to obey all these *d*
7:11 *d* and laws I give you today.
8:11 his *d* that I am giving you this day.
10:13 and *d* that I am giving you today
11: 1 his *d*, his laws and his commands
11:32 be sure that you obey all the *d*
12: 1 These are the *d* and laws you must
16:12 and follow carefully these *d*.
17:19 these *d* and not consider himself
26:16 you this day to follow these *d*
26:17 that you will keep his *d*, commands
27:10 and *d* that I give you today."
28:15 and *d* I am giving you today,
28:45 the commands and *d* he gave you.
30:10 and *d* that are written in this Book
30:16 to keep his commands, *d* and laws;
Jos 24:25 at Shechem he drew up for them *d*
2Sa 22:23 I have not turned away from his *d*.
1Ki 2: 3 and keep his *d* and commands,
6:12 if you follow my *d*,
8:58 *d* and regulations he gave our
8:61 by his *d* and obey his commands,
9: 4 and observe my *d* and laws,
9: 6 the commands and *d* I have given
11:11 not kept my covenant and my *d*,
2Ki 17:13 Observe my commands and *d*,
17:15 They rejected his *d*
17:34 nor adhere to the *d* and ordinances,
17:37 always be careful to keep the *d*
23: 3 regulations and *d* with all his heart
1Ch 22:13 if you are careful to observe the *d*
29:19 and *d* and to do everything
2Ch 7:17 and observe my *d* and laws,
7:19 forsake the *d* and commands I have
19:10 commands, *d* or ordinances—
33: 8 *d* and ordinances given
34:31 regulations and *d* with all his heart
Ezr 6:14 God of Israel and the *d* of Cyrus,
7:10 to teaching its *d* and laws in Israel.
7:11 and *d* of the LORD for Israel:
Ne 1: 7 *d* and laws you gave your servant
9:13 and *d* and commands that are good
9:14 *d* and laws through your servant
10:29 and *d* of the LORD our God.
Ps 18:22 I have not turned away from his *d*.
44: 4 who *d* victories for Jacob.
89:31 if they violate my *d*
94:20 one that brings on misery by its *d?*
99: 7 his statutes and the *d* he gave them.
119: 5 steadfast in obeying your *d!*
119: 8 I will obey your *d;*
119: 12 teach me your *d*.
119: 16 I delight in your *d;*
Ps 119: 23 servant will meditate on your *d*.
119: 26 teach me your *d*.
119: 33 O LORD, to follow your *d;*
119: 48 and I meditate on your *d*.
119: 54 Your *d* are the theme of my song
119: 64 teach me your *d*.
119: 68 teach me your *d*.
119: 71 so that I might learn your *d*.
119: 80 heart be blameless toward your *d*,
119: 83 I do not forget your *d*.
119:112 My heart is set on keeping your *d*
119:117 I will always have regard for your *d*
119:118 reject all who stray from your *d*,
119:124 and teach me your *d*.
119:135 and teach me your *d*.
119:145 and I will obey your *d*.
119:155 for they do not seek out your *d*.
119:171 for you teach me your *d*.
147: 19 his laws and *d* to Israel.
Pr 31: 5 drink and forget what the law *d*,
Isa 10: 1 to those who issue oppressive *d*,
Jer 31:35 who *d* the moon and stars
31:36 "Only if these *d* vanish
44:10 followed my law and the *d* I set
44:23 or his *d* or his stipulations,
Eze 5: 6 and has not followed my *d*.
5: 6 and *d* more than the nations
5: 7 and have not followed my *d*
11:12 for you have not followed my *d*
11:20 Then they will follow my *d*
18: 9 He follows my *d*
18:17 keeps my laws and follows my *d*.
18:19 has been careful to keep all my *d*,
18:21 keeps all my *d* and does what is just
20:11 I gave them my *d* and made known
20:13 They did not follow my *d*
20:16 not follow my *d* and desecrated my
20:19 follow my *d* and be careful
20:21 They did not follow my *d*,
20:24 had rejected my *d* and desecrated
33:15 follows the *d* that give life,
36:27 and move you to follow my *d*
37:24 and be careful to keep my *d*.
44:24 my *d* for all my appointed feasts,
Am 2: 4 and have not kept his *d*,
Zec 1: 6 But did not my words and my *d*,
Mal 3: 7 you have turned away from my *d*
4: 4 the *d* and laws I gave him at Horeb
Ac 17: 7 They are all defying Caesar's *d*,

DEDAN (DEDANITES)

Ge 10: 7 The sons of Raamah: Sheba and *D*.
25: 3 of *D* were the Asshurites,
25: 3 was the father of Sheba and *D;*
1Ch 1: 9 The sons of Raamah: Sheba and *D*.
1:32 The sons of Jokshan: Sheba and *D*.
Jer 25:23 of the coastlands across the sea; *D*,
49: 8 you who live in *D*,
Eze 25:13 and from Teman to *D* they will fall
27:20 " '*D* traded in saddle blankets
38:13 *D* and the merchants of Tarshish

DEDANITES (DEDAN)

Isa 21:13 You caravans of *D*,

DEDICATE (DEDICATED DEDICATES DEDICATION)

Lev 27: 2 vow to *d* persons to the LORD
27:26 may *d* the firstborn of an animal,
Nu 6:12 He must *d* himself to the LORD
Dt 20: 5 and someone else may *d* it.
2Ch 2: 4 to *d* it to him for burning fragrant
Pr 20:25 for a man to *d* something rashly
Eze 43:26 and cleanse it; thus they will *d* it.

DEDICATED (DEDICATE)

Lev 21:12 he has been *d* by the anointing oil
Nu 6: 9 thus defiling the hair he has *d*,
6:18 shave off the hair that he *d*.
18: 6 *d* to the LORD to do the work
Dt 20: 5 built a new house and not *d* it?
2Sa 8:11 King David *d* these articles
8:12 also *d* the plunder taken
1Ki 7:51 in the things his father David had *d*
8:63 and all the Israelites *d* the temple
15:15 that he and his father had *d*.
2Ki 12:18 Judah took all the sacred objects *d*
12:18 and the gifts he himself had *d*
2Ki 23:11 Josiah then burned the chariots *d*
23:11 the kings of Judah had *d* to the sun.
1Ch 18:11 King David *d* these articles
26:20 and the treasuries for the *d* things.
26:26 for the things *d* by King David,
26:27 taken in battle they *d* for the repair
26:28 and all the other *d* things were
26:28 everything *d* by Samuel the seer
28:12 for the treasuries for the *d* things.
2Ch 5: 1 in the things his father David had *d*
7: 5 all the people *d* the temple of God.
15:18 that he and his father had *d*.
29:31 "You have now *d* yourselves
31: 6 and a tithe of the holy things *d*
31:12 contributions, tithes and *d* gifts.
Ne 3: 1 They *d* it and set its doors in place,
3: 1 which they *d*, and as far
Lk 21: 5 and with gifts *d* to God.

DEDICATES (DEDICATE)

Lev 27:14 " 'If a man *d* his house
27:15 the man who *d* his house redeems
27:16 " 'If a man *d* to the LORD part
27:17 If he *d* his field during the Year
27:18 But if he *d* his field after the Jubilee
27:19 If the man who *d* the field wishes
27:22 " 'If a man *d* to the LORD a field

DEDICATION (DEDICATE)

Nu 6:19 shaved off the hair of his *d*,
7:10 brought their offerings for its *d*
7:11 offering for the *d* of the altar."
7:84 leaders for the *d* of the altar
7:88 the offerings for the *d* of the altar
2Ch 7: 9 for they had celebrated the *d*
Ezr 6:16 celebrated the *d* of the house
6:17 For the *d* of this house
Ne 12:27 At the *d* of the wall of Jerusalem,
12:27 to celebrate joyfully the *d*
Da 3: 2 to the *d* of the image he had set up.
3: 3 officials assembled for the *d*
Jn 10:22 came the Feast of *D* at Jerusalem.
1Ti 5:11 sensual desires overcome their *d*

DEED (DEEDED DEEDS)

Dt 17: 5 or woman who has done this evil *d*
Ecc 3:17 a time for every *d*."
12:14 For God will bring every *d*
Jer 32:10 and sealed the *d*, had it witnessed,
32:11 I took the *d* of purchase—
32:12 and I gave this *d* to Baruch son
32:12 the witnesses who had signed the *d*
32:14 copies of the *d* of purchase,
32:16 After I had given the *d* of purchase
Lk 24:19 powerful in word and *d* before God
Col 3:17 you do, whether in word or *d*,
2Th 2:17 and strengthen you in every good *d*

DEEDED (DEED)

Ge 23:17 was *d* to Abraham as his property
23:20 the cave in it were *d* to Abraham

DEEDS (DEED)

Dt 3:24 or on earth who can do the *d*
4:34 or by great and awesome *d*,
34:12 the awesome *d* that Moses
1Sa 2: 3 and by him *d* are weighed.
2:23 all the people about these wicked *d*
24:13 'From evildoers come evil *d*,'
2Sa 3:39 evildoer according to his evil *d!*"
1Ch 16:24 his marvelous *d* among all peoples.
Ezr 9:13 to us is a result of our evil *d*
Ne 6:19 kept reporting to me his good *d*
Job 34:25 Because he takes note of their *d*,
Ps 14: 1 They are corrupt, their *d* are vile;
17: 4 As for the *d* of men—
26: 7 and telling of all your wonderful *d*.
28: 4 Repay them for their *d*
45: 4 right hand display awesome *d*.
65: 5 with awesome *d* of righteousness,
66: 3 "How awesome are your *d!*
71:17 day I declare your marvelous *d*.
72:18 who alone does marvelous *d*.
73:28 I will tell of all your *d*.
75: 1 men tell of your wonderful *d*.
77:11 I will remember the *d* of the LORD
77:12 and consider all your mighty *d*.
78: 4 the praiseworthy *d* of the LORD,

Ps 78: 7 and would not forget his *d*
86: 8 no *d* can compare with yours.
86: 10 you are great and do marvelous *d;*
88: 12 or your righteous *d* in the land
90: 16 May your *d* be shown
92: 4 For you make me glad by your *d,*
96: 3 his marvelous *d* among all peoples.
101: 3 The *d* of faithless men I hate;
103: 7 his *d* to the people of Israel:
106: 22 and awesome *d* by the Red Sea.
106: 29 LORD to anger by their wicked *d,*
106: 39 by their *d* they prostituted
107: 8 and his wonderful *d* for men,
107: 15 and his wonderful *d* for men,
107: 21 and his wonderful *d* for men.
107: 24 his wonderful *d* in the deep.
107: 31 and his wonderful *d* for men.
111: 3 Glorious and majestic are his *d,*
141: 4 to take part in wicked *d*
141: 5 ever against the *d* of evildoers;
145: 6 and I will proclaim your great *d.*
Pr 5: 22 evil *d* of a wicked man ensnare
8: 22 before his *d* of old;
Isa 1: 16 Take your evil *d*
3: 8 and *d* are against the LORD,
3: 10 they will enjoy the fruit of their *d.*
5: 12 regard for the *d* of the LORD,
32: 8 and by noble *d* he stands.
41: 29 Their *d* amount to nothing;
59: 6 Their *d* are evil *d,*
63: 7 the *d* for which he is to be praised,
65: 7 the full payment for their former *d*
Jer 5: 28 Their evil *d* have no limit;
17: 10 according to what his *d* deserve."
21: 14 I will punish you as your *d* deserve,
23: 22 and from their evil *d.*
25: 14 repay them according to their *d*
32: 19 purposes and mighty are your *d.*
32: 19 to his conduct and as his *d* deserve.
32: 44 for silver, and *d* will be signed,
48: 7 Since you trust in your *d* and riches
50: 29 Repay her for her *d;*
Eze 22: 28 Her prophets whitewash these *d*
36: 31 your evil ways and wicked *d,*
Hos 4: 9 and repay them for their *d.*
5: 4 "Their *d* do not permit them
7: 2 that I remember all their evil *d.*
9: 15 Because of their sinful *d,*
12: 2 and repay him according to his *d.*
Ob : 15 your *d* will return upon your own
Mic 7: 13 as the result of their *d.*
Hab 3: 2 I stand in awe of your *d,* O LORD.
Mt 5: 16 that they may see your good *d*
Lk 1: 51 He has performed mighty *d*
23: 41 we are getting what our *d* deserve.
Jn 3: 19 of light because their *d* were evil.
3: 20 for fear that his *d* will be exposed.
Ac 19: 18 and openly confessed their evil *d.*
26: 20 prove their repentance by their *d.*
Ro 13: 12 So let us put aside the *d* of darkness
Eph 5: 11 do with the fruitless *d* of darkness,
1Ti 2: 10 but with good *d,* appropriate
5: 10 and is well known for her good *d,*
5: 10 herself to all kinds of good *d.*
5: 25 the same way, good *d* are obvious,
6: 18 rich in good *d,* and to be generous
Heb 10: 24 on toward love and good *d.*
Jas 2: 14 claims to have faith but has no *d?*
2: 18 Show me your faith without *d,*
2: 18 "You have faith; I have *d.*"
2: 20 faith without *d* is useless?
2: 26 so faith without *d* is dead.
3: 13 by *d* done in the humility that
1Pe 2: 12 they may see your good *d*
2Pe 2: 8 soul by the lawless *d* he saw
Rev 2: 2 I know your *d,* your hard work
2: 19 I know your *d,* your love and faith,
2: 23 each of you according to your *d.*
3: 1 I know your *d;* you have
3: 2 I have not found your *d* complete
3: 8 I know your *d.*
3: 15 I know your *d,* that you are neither
14: 13 for their *d* will follow them."
15: 3 "Great and marvelous are your *d,*

DEEP (DEEPER DEEPEST DEEPS DEPTH DEPTHS)

Ge 1: 2 was over the surface of the *d,*
2: 21 the man to fall into a *d* sleep;
7: 11 springs of the great *d* burst forth,
8: 2 Now the springs of the *d*
15: 12 setting, Abram fell into a *d* sleep,
49: 25 blessings of the *d* that lies below,
Ex 15: 5 The *d* waters have covered them;
15: 8 the *d* waters congealed in the heart
Lev 13: 3 appears to be more than skin *d,*
13: 4 appear to be more than skin *d*
13: 20 if it appears to be more than skin *d*
13: 21 and it is not more than skin *d*
13: 25 it appears to be more than skin *d,*
13: 26 and if it is not more than skin *d*
13: 30 if it appears to be more than skin *d*
13: 31 seem to be more than skin *d*
13: 32 appear to be more than skin *d,*
13: 34 appears to be no more than skin *d,*
Dt 4: 11 with black clouds and *d* darkness.
5: 22 the cloud and the *d* darkness;
33: 13 and with the *d* waters that lie below
1Sa 26: 12 LORD had put them into a *d* sleep.
2Sa 22: 17 he drew me out of *d* waters.
24: 14 said to Gad, "I am in *d* distress.
1Ki 7: 31 had a circular frame one cubit *d.*
7: 35 was a circular band half a cubit *d.*
18: 27 Perhaps he is *d* in thought, or busy,
1Ch 21: 13 said to Gad, "I am in *d* distress.
Job 3: 5 and *d* shadow claim it once more;
4: 13 when *d* sleep falls on men,
7: 12 I the sea, or the monster of the *d,*
10: 21 to the land of gloom and *d* shadow,
10: 22 of *d* shadow and disorder,
12: 22 He reveals the *d* things of darkness
12: 22 and brings *d* shadows into the light.
16: 16 *d* shadows ring my eyes;
24: 17 *d* darkness is their morning;
26: 5 "The dead are in *d* anguish,
28: 14 The *d* says, 'It is not in me';
33: 15 when *d* sleep falls on men
34: 22 is no dark place, no *d* shadow,
38: 16 or walked in the recesses of the *d?*
38: 30 when the surface of the *d* is frozen?
41: 32 would think the *d* had white hair.
Ps 18: 16 he drew me out of *d* waters.
33: 7 he puts the *d* into storehouses.
36: 6 your justice like the great *d.*
42: 7 *D* calls to *d*
44: 19 covered us over with *d* darkness.
69: 2 I have come into the *d* waters;
69: 14 from the *d* waters.
104: 6 You covered it with the *d*
107: 24 his wonderful deeds in the *d.*
Pr 4: 19 of the wicked is like *d* darkness;
7: 18 let's drink *d* of love till morning,
8: 27 the horizon on the face of the *d,*
8: 28 securely the fountains of the *d,*
18: 4 of a man's mouth are *d* waters,
19: 15 Laziness brings on *d* sleep,
20: 5 of a man's heart are *d* waters,
22: 14 mouth of an adulteress is a *d* pit;
23: 27 for a prostitute is a *d* pit
25: 3 heavens are high and the earth is *d,*
Isa 29: 10 brought over you a *d* sleep:
30: 33 Its fire pit has been made *d*
44: 27 who says to the watery *d,* 'Be dry,
51: 10 the waters of the great *d,*
54: 7 with *d* compassion I will bring you
59: 9 but we walk in *d* shadows.
Jer 13: 16 and change it to *d* gloom.
49: 8 Turn and flee, hide in *d* caves,
49: 30 Stay in *d* caves, you who live
La 2: 13 Your wound is as *d* as the sea.
Eze 23: 32 a cup large and *d;*
31: 4 *d* springs made it grow tall;
31: 15 to the grave I covered the *d* springs
40: 6 of the gate; it was one rod *d.*
40: 7 facing the temple was one rod *d.*
40: 9 it was eight cubits *d* and its jambs
40: 30 cubits wide and five cubits *d.)*
43: 13 gutter is a cubit *d* and a cubit wide,
47: 5 and was *d* enough to swim in—
Da 2: 22 He reveals *d* and hidden things;
8: 18 I was in a *d* sleep, with my face
10: 9 I fell into a *d* sleep, my face
Hos 5: 2 The rebels are *d* in slaughter.
9: 9 They have sunk *d* into corruption,
Am 7: 4 dried up the great *d* and devoured
Jnh 1: 5 lay down and fell into a *d* sleep.
2: 3 You hurled me into the *d,*
2: 5 the *d* surrounded me;
Hab 3: 10 the *d* roared
Mk 7: 34 and with a *d* sigh said to him,
Lk 5: 4 to Simon, "Put out into *d* water,
6: 48 down *d* and laid the foundation
Jn 4: 11 to draw with and the well is *d.*
Ac 20: 9 who was sinking into a *d* sleep
27: 28 and found it was ninety feet *d.*
27: 28 was a hundred and twenty feet *d.*
Ro 10: 7 'Who will descend into the *d?*' "
1Co 2: 10 all things, even the *d* things
2Co 7: 7 your *d* sorrow, your ardent
Eph 3: 18 and high and *d* is the love of Christ,
1Th 1: 5 and with *d* conviction.
1Ti 3: 9 hold of the *d* truths of the faith
Rev 2: 24 Satan's so-called *d* secrets (I

DEEPER (DEEP)

Lev 14: 37 appear to be *d* than the surface
Job 11: 8 They are *d* than the depths

DEEPEST (DEEP)

Job 10: 22 to the land of *d* night,
Ps 107: 10 sat in darkness and the *d* gloom,
107: 14 of darkness and the *d* gloom
Isa 7: 11 whether in the *d* depths

DEEPS (DEEP)

Pr 3: 20 his knowledge the *d* were divided,

DEER

Dt 12: 15 or *d,* according to the blessing
12: 22 Eat them as you would gazelle or *d.*
14: 5 the gazelle, the roe *d,* the wild goat,
14: 5 the goat, the *d,* the gazelle,
15: 22 as if it were gazelle or *d.*
2Sa 22: 34 makes my feet like the feet of a *d;*
1Ki 4: 23 as well as *d,* gazelles, roebucks
Ps 18: 33 makes my feet like the feet of a *d;*
42: 1 As the *d* pants for streams of water,
Pr 5: 19 A loving doe, a graceful *d*—
7: 22 like a *d* stepping into a noose
Isa 35: 6 Then will the lame leap like a *d,*
La 1: 6 Her princes are like *d*
Hab 3: 19 makes my feet like the feet of a *d,*

DEFAMED

Isa 48: 11 How can I let myself be *d?*

DEFEAT (DEFEATED DEFEATING)

Ex 32: 18 it is not the sound of *d;*
Nu 22: 6 then I will be able to *d* them
Jdg 2: 15 was against them to *d* them,
1Sa 4: 3 "Why did the LORD bring *d*
2Ki 13: 19 now you will *d* it only three times."
Ps 92: 11 My eyes have seen the *d*
Isa 9: 4 For as in the day of Midian's *d,*
Jer 37: 10 to *d* the entire Babylonian army
Heb 7: 1 returning from the *d* of the kings

DEFEATED (DEFEAT)

Ge 14: 5 and *d* the Rephaites in Ashteroth
36: 35 who *d* Midian in the country
Lev 26: 17 you so that you will be *d*
Nu 14: 42 You will be *d* by your enemies,
Dt 1: 4 This was after he had *d* Sihon king
1: 4 at Edrei had *d* Og king of Bashan,
1: 42 You will be *d* by your enemies.' "
4: 46 was *d* by Moses and the Israelites
7: 2 over to you and you have *d* them,
28: 7 up against you will be *d* before you.
28: 25 you to be *d* before your enemies.
29: 7 to fight against us, but we *d* them.
Jos 10: 10 who *d* them in a great victory
10: 33 but Joshua *d* him and his army—
11: 8 They *d* them and pursued them all
12: 1 the land whom the Israelites had *d*
13: 12 Moses had *d* them and taken
13: 21 Moses had *d* him
Jdg 1: 10 called Kiriath Arba) and *d* Sheshai,
11: 21 Israel's hands, and they *d* them.
20: 35 The LORD *d* Benjamin
1Sa 4: 2 Israel was *d* by the Philistines,
4: 10 and the Israelites were *d*
14: 48 valiantly and *d* the Amalekites,
2Sa 2: 17 of Israel were *d* by David's men.
5: 20 and there he *d* them.

2Sa 8: 1 David *d* the Philistines
8: 2 David also *d* the Moabites.
8: 9 that David had *d* the entire army
10: 19 saw that they had been *d*
18: 7 of Israel was *d* by David's men,
1Ki 8: 33 your people Israel have been *d*
2Ki 13: 19 then you would have *d* Aram
13: 25 Three times Jehoash *d* him,
14: 7 the one who *d* ten thousand
14: 10 You have indeed *d* Edom
18: 8 to fortified city, he *d* the Philistines
1Ch 1: 46 who *d* Midian in the country
5: 10 who were *d* at their hands;
14: 11 and there he *d* them.
18: 1 David *d* the Philistines
18: 2 David also *d* the Moabites,
18: 9 that David had *d* the entire army
19: 19 saw that they had been *d*
2Ch 6: 24 your people Israel have been *d*
20: 22 invading Judah, and they were *d*.
25: 19 to yourself that you have *d* Edom,
28: 5 Arameans *d* him and took many
28: 23 who had *d* him; for he thought,
Jer 46: 2 was *d* at Carchemish on
46: 5 their warriors are *d*.
Da 11: 11 raise a large army, but it will be *d*.
1Co 6: 7 have been completely *d* already.

DEFEATING (DEFEAT)

Ge 14: 17 returned from *d* Kedorlaomer
Jdg 20: 32 "We are *d* them as before,"
20: 39 "We are *d* them as in the first battle
2Sa 1: 1 returned from *d* the Amalekites
Da 7: 21 war against the saints and *d* them,

DEFECT (DEFECTED DEFECTS)

Ex 12: 5 must be year-old males without *d*,
29: 1 young bull and two rams without *d*.
Lev 1: 3 he is to offer a male without *d*.
1: 10 he is to offer a male without *d*.
3: 1 the LORD an animal without *d*.
3: 6 to offer a male or female without *d*.
4: 3 the LORD a young bull without *d*
4: 23 his offering a male goat without *d*.
4: 28 a female goat without *d*.
4: 32 he is to bring a female without *d*.
5: 15 without *d* and of the proper value
5: 18 without *d* and of the proper value.
6: 6 without *d* and of the proper value.
9: 2 both without *d*, and present them
9: 3 both a year old and without *d*—
14: 10 without *d*, along with three-tenths
21: 17 descendants who has a *d* may come
21: 18 No man who has any *d* may come
21: 20 or who has any eye *d*, or who has
21: 21 Aaron the priest who has any *d* is
21: 21 He has a *d*; he must not come
21: 23 the holy food; yet because of his *d*,
22: 19 a male without *d* from the cattle,
22: 20 Do not bring anything with a *d*,
22: 21 it must be without *d* or blemish
23: 12 LORD a lamb a year old without *d*,
23: 18 each a year old and without *d*,
Nu 6: 14 lamb without *d* for a burnt offering,
6: 14 lamb without *d* for a sin offering,
6: 14 without *d* for a fellowship offering,
19: 2 to bring you a red heifer without *d*
28: 3 two lambs a year old without *d*,
28: 9 of two lambs a year old without *d*,
28: 11 lambs a year old, all without *d*.
28: 19 lambs a year old, all without *d*.
28: 31 Be sure the animals are without *d*.
29: 2 lambs a year old, all without *d*.
29: 8 lambs a year old, all without *d*.
29: 13 lambs a year old, all without *d*.
29: 17 lambs a year old, all without *d*.
29: 20 lambs a year old, all without *d*.
29: 23 lambs a year old, all without *d*.
29: 26 lambs a year old, all without *d*.
29: 29 lambs a year old, all without *d*.
29: 32 lambs a year old, all without *d*.
29: 36 lambs a year old, all without *d*.
Dt 15: 21 If an animal has a *d*, is lame
17: 1 a sheep that has any *d* or flaw in it,
Eze 43: 22 goat without *d* for a sin offering,
43: 23 ram from the flock, both without *d*.
43: 25 ram from the flock, both without *d*.
45: 18 are to take a young bull without *d*
Eze 45: 23 rams without *d* as a burnt offering
46: 4 lambs and a ram, all without *d*.
46: 6 six lambs and a ram, all without *d*.
46: 13 lamb without *d* for a burnt offering
Da 1: 4 young men without any physical *d*,
1Pe 1: 19 a lamb without blemish or *d*.

DEFECTED (DEFECT)

1Ch 12: 8 Some Gadites *d* to David
12: 19 of the men of Manasseh *d* to David
12: 20 men of Manasseh who *d* to him:

DEFECTS (DEFECT)

Lev 22: 25 they are deformed and have *d*.' "

DEFEND (DEFENDED DEFENDER DEFENDERS DEFENDING DEFENDS DEFENSE DEFENSES)

Jdg 6: 31 *d* himself when someone breaks
2Ki 19: 34 I will *d* this city and save it,
20: 6 I will *d* this city for my sake
Job 13: 15 I will surely *d* my ways to his face.
Ps 72: 4 He will *d* the afflicted
74: 22 Rise up, O God, and *d* your cause;
82: 2 "How long will you *d* the unjust
82: 3 *D* the cause of the weak
119:154 *D* my cause and redeem me;
Pr 31: 9 *d* the rights of the poor and needy
Ecc 4: 12 two can *d* themselves.
Isa 1: 17 *D* the cause of the fatherless,
1: 23 They do not *d* the cause
37: 35 "I will *d* this city and save it,
38: 6 I will *d* this city.
Jer 5: 28 they do not *d* the rights of the poor.
50: 34 He will vigorously *d* their cause
51: 36 "See, I will *d* your cause
Da 3: 16 need to *d* ourselves before you
Zec 9: 8 But I will *d* my house
Lk 12: 11 about how you will *d* yourselves
21: 14 how you will *d* yourselves.
Ac 25: 16 to *d* himself against their charges.

DEFENDED (DEFEND)

2Sa 23: 12 He *d* it and struck the Philistines
1Ch 11: 14 They *d* it and struck the Philistines
Jer 22: 16 He *d* the cause of the poor

DEFENDER (DEFEND)

Ex 22: 2 the *d* is not guilty of bloodshed;
Job 5: 4 crushed in court without a *d*.
Ps 68: 5 to the fatherless, a *d* of widows,
Pr 23: 11 for their *D* is strong;
Isa 19: 20 he will send them a savior and *d*,
29: 21 who ensnare the *d* in court

DEFENDERS (DEFEND)

2Sa 11: 16 he knew the strongest *d* were.

DEFENDING (DEFEND)

2Ki 9: 14 Israel had been *d* Ramoth Gilead
Ps 10: 18 *d* the fatherless and the oppressed,
Ro 2: 15 now accusing, now even *d* them.)
2Co 12: 19 that we have been *d* ourselves
Php 1: 7 or *d* and confirming the gospel,

DEFENDS (DEFEND)

Dt 10: 18 He *d* the cause of the fatherless
33: 7 With his own hands he *d* his cause.
Isa 51: 22 your God, who *d* his people:

DEFENSE (DEFEND)

2Ch 11: 5 and built up towns for *d* in Judah:
Job 31: 35 I sign now my *d*— let the Almighty
Ps 35: 23 Awake, and rise to my *d*!
Jer 41: 9 as part of his *d* against Baasha king
Na 3: 8 The river was her *d*,
Ac 7: 24 went to his *d* and avenged him
19: 33 to make a *d* before the people.
22: 1 and fathers, listen now to my *d*."
24: 10 so I gladly make my *d*.
25: 8 Paul made his *d*: "I have done
26: 1 with his hand and began his *d*:
26: 2 as I make my *d* against all
26: 24 point Festus interrupted Paul's *d*.
1Co 9: 3 This is my *d* to those who sit
Php 1: 16 here for the *d* of the gospel.
2Ti 4: 16 At my first *d*, no one came
1Jn 2: 1 speaks to the Father in our *d*—

DEFENSES (DEFEND)

2Ch 11: 11 He strengthened their *d*
26: 15 on the corner *d* to shoot arrows
Job 13: 12 your *d* are *d* of clay.
Isa 22: 8 the *d* of Judah are stripped away.
22: 9 had many breaches in its *d*;
Joel 2: 8 They plunge through *d*
Na 3: 14 strengthen your *d*!

DEFERENCE (DEFERRED)

2Ki 16: 18 in *d* to the king of Assyria.

DEFERRED (DEFERENCE)

Pr 13: 12 Hope *d* makes the heart sick,

DEFIANCE (DEFY)

1Sa 17: 23 his lines and shouted his usual *d*,

DEFIANT (DEFY)

Pr 7: 11 (She is loud and *d*,

DEFIANTLY (DEFY)

Nu 15: 30 who sins *d*, whether native-born
Job 15: 26 *d* charging against him

DEFIED (DEFY)

1Sa 17: 36 because he has *d* the armies
17: 45 armies of Israel, whom you have *d*.
1Ki 13: 21 'You have *d* the word of the LORD
13: 26 the man of God who *d* the word
Isa 65: 7 and *d* me on the hills,
Jer 48: 26 for she has *d* the LORD.
48: 42 because she *d* the LORD.
50: 29 For she has *d* the LORD,
Da 3: 28 and *d* the king's command

DEFIES (DEFY)

Pr 18: 1 he *d* all sound judgment.

DEFILE (DEFILED DEFILEMENT DEFILES DEFILING)

Ex 20: 25 for you will *d* it if you use a tool
Lev 11: 43 Do not *d* yourselves by any
18: 20 your neighbor's wife and *d* yourself
18: 23 with an animal and *d* yourself
18: 24 " 'Do not *d* yourselves in any
18: 28 if you *d* the land, it will vomit you
18: 30 and do not *d* yourselves with them.
20: 25 Do not *d* yourselves by any animal
21: 4 him by marriage, and so *d* himself.
21: 15 so he will not *d* his offspring
Nu 5: 3 camp so they will not *d* their camp,
18: 32 you will not *d* the holy offerings
35: 34 Do not *d* the land where you live
2Ki 23: 16 and burned on the altar to *d* it,
Isa 30: 22 Then you will *d* your idols overlaid
Eze 7: 21 of the earth, and they will *d* it.
9: 7 "*D* the temple and fill the courts
14: 11 will they *d* themselves anymore
18: 6 He does not *d* his neighbor's wife
18: 15 He does not *d* his neighbor's wife.
20: 7 do not *d* yourselves with the idols
20: 18 or *d* yourselves with their idols.
20: 30 Will you *d* yourselves the way your
20: 31 you continue to *d* yourselves
37: 23 They will no longer *d* themselves
43: 7 will never again *d* my holy name—
44: 25 sister, then he may *d* himself.
44: 25 " 'A priest must not *d* himself
Da 1: 8 Daniel resolved not to *d* himself
1: 8 not to *d* himself this way.
Heb 12: 15 up to cause trouble and *d* many.
Rev 14: 4 are those who did not *d* themselves

DEFILED (DEFILE)

Ge 34: 5 his daughter Dinah had been *d*,
34: 13 their sister Dinah had been *d*,
34: 27 city where their sister had been *d*.
49: 4 onto my couch and *d* it.
Lev 18: 24 to drive out before you became *d*.
18: 25 Even the land was *d*;
18: 27 before you, and the land became *d*.
19: 31 for you will be *d* by them.
20: 3 he has *d* my sanctuary
21: 7 " 'They must not marry women *d*
21: 14 or a woman *d* by prostitution,
22: 4 unclean if he touches something *d*
Nu 5: 20 you have *d* yourself by sleeping

Nu 5: 27 If she has *d* herself and been
5: 28 the woman has not *d* herself
6: 12 he became *d* during his separation.
19: 20 because he has *d* the sanctuary
Dt 22: 9 the fruit of the vineyard will be *d*.
24: 4 again after she has been *d*.
Jos 22: 19 If the land you possess is *d*,
2Sa 1: 21 the shield of the mighty was *d*,
2Ki 23: 19 *d* all the shrines at the high places
1Ch 5: 1 when he *d* his father's marriage bed
Ne 13: 29 because they *d* the priestly office
Job 31: 7 or if my hands have been *d*,
Ps 74: 7 they *d* the dwelling place
79: 1 they have *d* your holy temple,
89: 39 and have *d* his crown in the dust.
106: 39 They *d* themselves
Isa 24: 5 The earth is *d* by its people;
52: 1 The uncircumcised and *d*
Jer 2: 7 But you came and *d* my land
2: 23 "How can you say, 'I am not *d*;
3: 1 not the land be completely *d*?
3: 2 You have *d* the land
3: 9 she *d* the land and committed
7: 30 that bears my Name and have *d* it.
16: 18 because they have *d* my land
19: 13 of Judah will be *d* like this place,
32: 34 house that bears my Name and *d* it.
La 4: 14 They are so *d* with blood
Eze 4: 13 the people of Israel will eat *d* food
4: 14 LORD! I have never *d* myself.
5: 11 because you have *d* my sanctuary
20: 26 I let them become *d*
20: 43 by which you have *d* yourselves,
22: 4 have become *d* by the idols you
22: 16 When you have been *d* in the eyes
23: 7 and *d* herself with all the idols
23: 13 I saw that she too *d* herself;
23: 17 After she had been *d* by them,
23: 17 and in their lust they *d* her.
23: 30 and *d* yourself with their idols.
23: 38 same time they *d* my sanctuary
36: 17 they *d* it by their conduct
36: 18 they had *d* it with their idols.
43: 8 they *d* my holy name
Hos 6: 10 and Israel is *d*.
Mic 2: 10 because it is *d*,
4: 11 They say, "Let her be *d*,
Zep 3: 1 rebellious and *d*!
Hag 2: 13 does it become *d*?" "Yes,"
2: 13 the priests replied, "it becomes *d*."
2: 13 "If a person *d* by contact
2: 14 and whatever they offer there is *d*.
Mal 1: 7 But you ask, 'How have we *d* you?'
1: 7 "You place *d* food on my altar.
1: 12 'It is *d*,' and of its food, 'It is
Ac 21: 28 temple area and *d* this holy place."
1Co 8: 7 their conscience is weak, it is *d*.

DEFILEMENT (DEFILE)

2Ch 29: 5 Remove all *d* from the sanctuary.

DEFILES (DEFILE)

Lev 21: 9 " 'If a priest's daughter *d* herself
Nu 5: 29 and *d* herself while married
19: 13 to purify himself *d* the LORD's
Eze 18: 11 He *d* his neighbor's wife.
22: 3 and *d* herself by making idols,
22: 11 another shamefully *d* his
33: 26 each of you *d* his neighbor's wife.

DEFILING (DEFILE)

Lev 15: 31 for *d* my dwelling place,
Nu 6: 9 thus *d* the hair he has dedicated,
2Ch 36: 14 and *d* the temple of the LORD,

DEFINITE

1Sa 23: 23 back to me with *d* information.
Ac 25: 26 But I have nothing *d* to write

DEFORMED

Lev 21: 18 or *d*; no man with a crippled foot
22: 23 or a sheep that is *d* or stunted,
22: 25 they are *d* and have defects.' "

DEFRAUD

Lev 19: 13 Do not *d* your neighbor or rob him.
Hos 12: 7 he loves to *d*.
Mic 2: 2 They *d* a man of his home,
Mal 3: 5 against those who *d* laborers
Mk 10: 19 do not *d*, honor your father

DEFY (DEFIANCE DEFIANT DEFIANTLY DEFIED DEFIES DEFYING)

1Sa 17: 10 "This day I *d* the ranks of Israel!
17: 25 out? He comes out to *d* Israel.
17: 26 that he should *d* the armies

DEFYING (DEFY)

Isa 3: 8 *d* his glorious presence.
Ac 17: 7 They are all *d* Caesar's decrees,

DEGRADE (DEGRADED DEGRADING)

Lev 19: 29 " 'Do not *d* your daughter

DEGRADED (DEGRADE)

Dt 25: 3 your brother will be *d* in your eyes.
Eze 16: 25 lofty shrines and *d* your beauty,

DEGRADING (DEGRADE)

Ro 1: 24 impurity for the *d* of their bodies

DEITY

Col 2: 9 of the *D* lives in bodily form,

DEJECTED

Ge 40: 6 morning, he saw that they were *d*.
Isa 19: 10 The workers in cloth will be *d*,

DELAIAH

1Ch 3: 24 Akkub, Johanan, *D* and Anani—
24: 18 to *D* and the twenty-fourth
Ezr 2: 60 The descendants of *D*, Tobiah
Ne 6: 10 to the house of Shemaiah son of *D*,
7: 62 the descendants of *D*, Tobiah
Jer 36: 12 Elishama the secretary, *D* son
36: 25 *D* and Gemariah urged the king

DELAY (DELAYED)

Ge 45: 9 Come down to me; don't *d*.
2Ki 9: 3 don't *d*!" So the young man,
Ps 40: 17 O my God, do not *d*.
70: 5 O LORD, do not *d*.
119: 60 I will hasten and not *d*
Ecc 5: 4 vow to God, do not *d* in fulfilling it.
Isa 48: 9 my own name's sake I *d* my wrath;
Jer 4: 6 Flee for safety without *d*!
Eze 12: 25 and it shall be fulfilled without *d*.
Da 9: 19 For your sake, O my God, do not *d*
Hab 2: 3 it will certainly come and will not *d*
Mk 1: 20 Without *d* he called them,
Ac 25: 17 here with me, I did not *d* the case,
Heb 10: 37 is coming will come and will not *d*.
Rev 10: 6 and said, "There will be no more *d*!

DELAYED (DELAY)

Ge 43: 10 if we had not *d*, we could have gone
Jos 10: 13 and *d* going down about a full day.
Jdg 5: 28 Why is the clatter of his chariots *d*
Isa 46: 13 and my salvation will not be *d*.
Eze 12: 28 of my words will be *d* any longer;
1Ti 3: 15 these instructions so that, if I am *d*,

DELEGATION

Jos 9: 4 as a *d* whose donkeys were loaded
2Sa 10: 2 So David sent a *d* to express his
1Ch 19: 2 So David sent a *d* to express his
Lk 14: 32 he will send a *d* while the other is
19: 14 and sent a *d* after him to say,

DELICACIES (DELICATE)

Ge 49: 20 he will provide *d* fit for a king.
Ps 141: 4 let me not eat of their *d*.
Pr 23: 3 Do not crave his *d*,
23: 6 do not crave his *d*;
Jer 51: 34 and filled his stomach with our *d*,
La 4: 5 Those who once ate *d*

DELICACY (DELICATE)

SS 7: 13 and at our door is every *d*,

DELICATE (DELICACIES DELICACY)

Isa 47: 1 tender or *d*.
Jer 6: 2 so beautiful and *d*.

DELICIOUS

Pr 9: 17 food eaten in secret is *d*!"

DELIGHT (DELIGHTED DELIGHTFUL DELIGHTING DELIGHTS)

Lev 26: 31 and I will take no *d* in the pleasing
Dt 30: 9 The LORD will again *d* in you
1Sa 2: 1 for I *d* in your deliverance.
15: 22 "Does the LORD *d*
Ne 1: 11 the prayer of your servants who *d*
Job 22: 26 Surely then you will find *d*
27: 10 Will he find *d* in the Almighty?
Ps 1: 2 But his *d* is in the law of the LORD
16: 3 in whom is all my *d*.
35: 9 and *d* in his salvation.
35: 27 those who *d* in my vindication
37: 4 *D* yourself in the LORD
43: 4 to God, my joy and my *d*.
51: 16 You do not *d* in sacrifice,
51: 19 whole burnt offerings to *d* you;
62: 4 they take *d* in lies.
68: 30 Scatter the nations who *d* in war.
111: 2 by all who *d* in them.
112: 1 who finds great *d* in his commands.
119: 16 I *d* in your decrees;
119: 24 Your statutes are my *d*;
119: 35 for there I find *d*.
119: 47 for I *d* in your commandments
119: 70 but I *d* in your law.
119: 77 for your law is my *d*.
119: 92 If your law had not been my *d*,
119:143 but your commands are my *d*.
119:174 and your law is my *d*.
147: 10 nor his *d* in the legs of a man;
149: 4 For the LORD takes *d*
Pr 1: 22 How long will mockers *d*
2: 14 who *d* in doing wrong
8: 30 I was filled with *d* day after day,
11: 1 but accurate weights are his *d*.
29: 17 he will bring *d* to your soul.
Ecc 2: 10 My heart took *d* in all my work,
SS 1: 4 We rejoice and *d* in you;
2: 3 I *d* to sit in his shade,
Isa 5: 7 are the garden of his *d*.
11: 3 he will *d* in the fear of the LORD.
13: 17 and have no *d* in gold.
32: 14 the *d* of donkeys, a pasture
42: 1 my chosen one in whom I *d*;
55: 2 and your soul will *d* in the richest
58: 13 if you call the Sabbath a *d*
61: 10 I *d* greatly in the LORD;
62: 4 for the LORD will take *d* in you,
65: 18 for I will create Jerusalem to be a *d*
65: 19 and take *d* in my people;
66: 3 their souls *d* in their abominations;
66: 11 *d* in her overflowing abundance."
Jer 9: 24 for in these I *d*,"
15: 16 they were my joy and my heart's *d*,
31: 20 the child in whom I *d*?
49: 25 the town in which I *d*?
Eze 24: 16 away from you the *d* of your eyes.
24: 21 in which you take pride, the *d*
24: 25 and glory, the *d* of their eyes,
Hos 7: 3 *d* the king with their wickedness,
Mic 1: 16 for the children in whom you *d*;
7: 18 but *d* to show mercy.
Zep 3: 17 He will take great *d* in you,
Mt 12: 18 the one I love, in whom I *d*;
Mk 12: 37 large crowd listened to him with *d*.
Lk 1: 14 He will be a joy and *d* to you,
Ro 7: 22 in my inner being I *d* in God's law;
1Co 13: 6 Love does not *d* in evil
2Co 12: 10 for Christ's sake, I *d* in weaknesses,
Col 2: 5 and *d* to see how orderly you are

DELIGHTED (DELIGHT)

Ge 34: 19 he was *d* with Jacob's daughter.
Ex 18: 9 Jethro was *d* to hear about all
Dt 30: 9 just as he *d* in your fathers,
2Sa 22: 20 he rescued me because he *d* in me.
1Ki 10: 9 who has *d* in you and placed you
2Ch 9: 8 who has *d* in you and placed you
Est 5: 14 This suggestion *d* Haman,
Ps 18: 19 he rescued me because he *d* in me.
Isa 1: 29 oaks in which you have *d*;
Mk 14: 11 They were *d* to hear this
Lk 13: 17 but the people were *d* with all
22: 5 They were *d* and agreed
2Co 7: 13 we were especially *d*
1Th 2: 8 so much that we were *d* to share

2Th 2: 12 but have *d* in wickedness.

DELIGHTFUL (DELIGHT)

Ps 16: 6 surely I have a *d* inheritance.
SS 1: 2 for your love is more *d* than wine.
4: 10 How *d* is your love, my sister,
Mal 3: 12 for yours will be a *d* land,''

DELIGHTING (DELIGHT)

Pr 8: 31 and *d* in mankind.

DELIGHTS (DELIGHT)

Est 6: 6 for the man the king *d* to honor?''
6: 7 ''For the man the king *d* to honor,
6: 9 Let them robe the man the king *d*
6: 9 for the man the king *d* to honor!' ''
6: 11 for the man the king *d* to honor!''
Ps 22: 8 since he *d* in him.''
35: 27 who *d* in the well-being
36: 8 from your river of *d*.
37: 23 The LORD *d* in the way of the man
147: 11 the LORD *d* in those who fear him,
Pr 3: 12 as a father the son he *d* in.
10: 23 of understanding *d* in wisdom.
11: 20 he *d* in those whose ways are
12: 22 but he *d* in men who are truthful.
14: 35 A king *d* in a wise servant,
15: 21 Folly *d* a man who lacks judgment,
18: 2 but *d* in airing his own opinions.
23: 24 he who has a wise son *d* in him.
Ecc 2: 8 as well—the *d* of the heart of man.
SS 7: 6 O love, with your *d!*
Col 2: 18 Do not let anyone who *d*

DELILAH

Jdg 16: 4 of Sorek whose name was *D*.
16: 6 So *D* said to Samson, ''Tell me
16: 10 *D* said to Samson, ''You have made
16: 12 So *D* took new ropes and tied him
16: 13 *D* then said to Samson, ''Until now,
16: 13 *D* took the seven braids of his head,
16: 18 When *D* saw that he had told her

DELIVER (DELIVERANCE DELIVERED DELIVERER DELIVERERS DELIVERING DELIVERS DELIVERY)

Nu 21: 2 ''If you will *d* these people
Dt 1: 27 out of Egypt to *d* us into the hands
2: 31 I have begun to *d* Sihon
7: 23 the LORD your God will *d* them
23: 14 and to *d* your enemies to you.
31: 5 The LORD will *d* them to you,
32: 39 and no one can *d* from my hand.
Jos 7: 7 people across the Jordan to *d* us
8: 18 for into your hand I will *d* the city
Jdg 7: 2 for me to *d* Midian into their hands
1Sa 4: 8 Who will *d* us from the hand
7: 3 and he will *d* you out of the hand
9: 16 he will *d* my people from the hand
12: 10 But now *d* us from the hands
17: 37 of the bear will *d* me from the hand
26: 24 and *d* me from all trouble.''
2Sa 14: 16 to *d* his servant from the hand
1Ki 20: 28 I will *d* this vast army
2Ki 17: 39 it is he who will *d* you
18: 29 He cannot *d* you from my hand.
18: 30 'The LORD will surely *d* us;
18: 32 when he says, 'The LORD will *d* us
18: 35 then can the LORD *d* Jerusalem
19: 3 and there is no strength to *d* them.
19: 12 by my forefathers *d* them:
19: 19 Now, O LORD our God, *d* us
20: 6 And I will *d* you and this city
1Ch 16: 35 gather us and *d* us from the nations
2Ch 32: 13 able to *d* their land from my hand?
32: 14 How then can your god *d* you
32: 15 How much less will your god *d* you
32: 15 has been able to *d* his people
Ezr 7: 19 *D* to the God of Jerusalem all
Job 6: 23 *d* me from the hand of the enemy,
22: 30 He will *d* even one who is not
Ps 3: 2 ''God will not *d* him.''
3: 7 *D* me, O my God!
6: 4 Turn, O LORD, and *d* me;
7: 1 and *d* me from all who pursue me,
22: 8 Let him *d* him,
22: 20 *D* my life from the sword,
31: 1 *d* me in your righteousness.
Ps 31: 15 *d* me from my enemies
33: 19 to *d* them from death
50: 15 I will *d* you, and you will honor me
59: 1 *D* me from my enemies, O God;
59: 2 *D* me from evildoers
69: 14 *d* me from those who hate me,
71: 2 *d* me in your righteousness;
71: 4 *D* me, O my God, from the hand
72: 12 For he will *d* the needy who cry out
79: 9 *d* us and atone for our sins
82: 4 *d* them from the hand
91: 15 I will *d* him and honor him.
109: 21 of the goodness of your love, *d* me.
119:153 Look upon my suffering and *d* me,
119:170 *d* me according to your promise.
144: 7 *d* me and rescue me
144: 11 *D* me and rescue me
Pr 20: 22 for the LORD, and he will *d* you.
Isa 31: 5 he will shield it and *d* it,
36: 14 He cannot *d* you! Do not let
36: 15 'The LORD will surely *d* us;
36: 18 when he says, 'The LORD will *d* us
36: 20 then can the LORD *d* Jerusalem
37: 3 and there is no strength to *d* them.
37: 12 by my forefathers *d* them—
37: 20 Now, O LORD our God, *d* us
38: 6 And I will *d* you and this city
43: 13 No one can *d* out of my hand.
Jer 15: 11 ''Surely I will *d* you
42: 11 and will save you and *d* you
Am 6: 8 I will *d* up the city
Mic 5: 6 He will *d* us from the Assyrian
Hab 3: 13 You came out to *d* your people,
Mt 6: 13 but *d* us from the evil one.'
Lk 21: 12 They will *d* you to synagogues
2Co 1: 10 a deadly peril, and he will *d* us.
1: 10 hope that he will continue to *d* us,

DELIVERANCE (DELIVER)

Ge 45: 7 and to save your lives by a great *d*.
49: 18 ''I look for your *d*, O LORD.
Ex 14: 13 you will see the *d* the LORD will
Jdg 13: 5 and he will begin the *d* of Israel
1Sa 2: 1 for I delight in your *d*.
14: 45 who has brought about this great *d*
2Ch 12: 7 but will soon give them *d*.
20: 17 see the *d* the LORD will give you,
Est 4: 14 and *d* for the Jews will arise
Job 13: 16 this might turn out for my *d*,
Ps 3: 8 From the LORD comes *d*.
32: 7 and surround me with songs of *d*.
33: 17 A horse is a vain hope for *d;*
78: 22 or trust in his *d*.
Isa 20: 6 and *d* from the king of Assyria!
59: 11 for *d*, but it is far away.
Joel 2: 32 there will be *d*,
Ob : 17 But on Mount Zion will be *d;*
Php 1: 19 to me will turn out for my *d*.

DELIVERED (DELIVER)

Ge 14: 20 who *d* your enemies into your hand
48: 16 the Angel who has *d* me
Dt 2: 33 the LORD our God *d* him
7: 2 the LORD your God has *d* them
Jos 6: 2 I have *d* Jericho into your hands,
8: 1 For I have *d* into your hands
24: 10 and I *d* you out of his hand.
Jdg 13: 1 so the LORD *d* them
16: 23 Our god has *d* Samson, our enemy,
16: 24 ''Our god has *d* our enemy
1Sa 7: 14 Israel *d* the neighboring territory
10: 18 I *d* you from the power of Egypt
11: 9 is hot tomorrow, you will be *d*.' ''
12: 11 and he *d* you from the hands
17: 37 The LORD who *d* me
24: 10 own eyes how the LORD *d* you
24: 18 the LORD *d* me into your hands,
26: 8 ''Today God has *d* your enemy
26: 23 The LORD *d* you
2Sa 4: 9 who has *d* me out of all trouble,
12: 7 and I *d* you from the hand of Saul.
18: 19 the king that the LORD has *d* him
18: 28 He has *d* up the men who lifted
18: 31 The LORD has *d* you today
19: 9 ''The king *d* us from the hand
22: 1 song when the LORD *d* him
22: 44 ''You have *d* me from the attacks
1Ki 1: 29 who has *d* me out of every trouble,
1Ki 9: 28 which they *d* to King Solomon.
2Ki 17: 13 that I *d* to you through my servants
18: 33 god of any nation ever *d* his land
19: 11 And will you be *d?* Did the gods
2Ch 8: 18 which they *d* to King Solomon.
13: 16 and God *d* them into their hands.
16: 8 he *d* them into your hand.
24: 24 LORD *d* into their hands a much
Ezr 8: 36 also *d* the king's orders
Ne 9: 28 your compassion you *d* them time
Est 1: 12 when the attendants *d* the king's
Job 21: 30 that he is *d* from the day of wrath?
22: 30 will be *d* through the cleanness
23: 7 I would be *d* forever from my judge
Ps 18: 43 You have *d* me from the attacks
22: 4 they trusted and you *d* them.
34: 4 he *d* me from all my fears.
54: 7 For he has *d* me from all my
56: 13 For you have *d* my soul from death
60: 5 that those you love may be *d*.
86: 13 you have *d* my soul
106: 43 Many times he *d* them,
107: 6 and he *d* them from their distress.
108: 6 that those you love may be *d*.
116: 8 have *d* my soul from death,
119:117 Uphold me, and I will be *d;*
Isa 36: 18 god of any nation ever *d* his land
37: 11 And will you be *d?* Did the gods
Eze 35: 5 *d* the Israelites over to the sword
Da 1: 2 And the Lord *d* Jehoiakim king
11: 41 of Ammon will be *d* from his hand.
12: 1 written in the book—will be *d*.
Lk 24: 7 of Man must be *d* into the hands
Ac 12: 21 *d* a public address to the people.
15: 30 church together and *d* the letter.
16: 4 they *d* the decisions reached
23: 33 they *d* the letter to the governor
Ro 4: 25 He was *d* over to death for our sins
2Co 1: 10 He has *d* us from such a deadly
2Th 3: 2 pray that we may be *d* from wicked
2Ti 4: 17 And I was *d* from the lion's mouth.
Jude : 5 you that the Lord *d* his people out

DELIVERER (DELIVER)

Jdg 3: 9 for them a *d*, Othniel son of Kenaz,
3: 15 and he gave them a *d*— Ehud,
2Sa 22: 2 is my rock, my fortress and my *d;*
2Ki 13: 5 The LORD provided a *d* for Israel,
Ps 18: 2 is my rock, my fortress and my *d;*
40: 17 You are my help and my *d;*
70: 5 You are my help and my *d;*
140: 7 O Sovereign LORD, my strong *d*,
144: 2 my stronghold and my *d*,
Ac 7: 35 sent to be their ruler and *d*
Ro 11: 26 ''The *d* will come from Zion;

DELIVERERS (DELIVER)

Ne 9: 27 great compassion you gave them *d*,
Ob : 21 *D* will go up on Mount Zion

DELIVERING (DELIVER)

1Sa 14: 48 *d* Israel from the hands
24: 15 me by *d* me from your hand.''

DELIVERS (DELIVER)

Dt 20: 13 When the LORD your God *d* it
21: 10 and the LORD your God *d* them
Job 36: 15 those who suffer he *d*
Ps 34: 7 and he *d* them.
34: 17 he *d* them from all their troubles.
34: 19 but the LORD *d* him from them all
37: 40 The LORD helps them and *d* them
37: 40 he *d* them from the wicked
41: 1 the LORD *d* him in times
97: 10 and *d* them from the hand
144: 10 who *d* his servant David
Pr 10: 2 but righteousness *d* from death.
11: 4 but righteousness *d* from death.
11: 6 of the upright *d* them,
Isa 66: 7 she *d* a son.

DELIVERY (DELIVER)

Ex 1: 16 and observe them on the *d* stool,
1Sa 4: 19 and near the time of *d*.
Isa 66: 9 and not give *d?*'' says the LORD.
66: 9 when I bring to *d?*'' says your God.

DELUDED (DELUSION)
Isa 44:20 on ashes, a *d* heart misleads him;
Rev 19:20 these signs he had *d* those who had

DELUGED
2Pe 3: 6 also the world of that time was *d*

DELUSION (DELUDED DELUSIONS)
2Th 2:11 God sends them a powerful *d*

DELUSIONS (DELUSION)
Ps 4: 2 How long will you love *d*
Jer 14:14 and the *d* of their own minds.
23:26 who prophesy the *d*

DEMAND (DEMANDED DEMANDING DEMANDS)
Ge 9: 5 I will surely *d* an accounting.
9: 5 I will *d* an accounting
9: 5 I will *d* an accounting for the life
Dt 23:21 LORD your God will certainly *d* it
2Sa 3:13 I *d* one thing of you: Do not come
4:11 should I not now *d* his blood
21: 4 "We have no right to *d* silver
1Ki 20: 5 'I sent to *d* your silver and gold,
20: 9 but this *d* I cannot meet.' "
2Ki 18:14 I will pay whatever you *d* of me."
Ne 5:12 "And we will not *d* anything more
Job 17: 3 Give me, O God, the pledge you *d*.
Lk 6:30 belongs to you, do not *d* it back.
23:24 So Pilate decided to grant their *d*.
1Co 1:22 Jews *d* miraculous signs

DEMANDED (DEMAND)
Ge 31:39 And you *d* payment from me
Ex 21:30 However, if payment is *d* of him,
21:30 life by paying whatever is *d*.
Jdg 6:30 The men of the town *d* of Joash,
1Ki 20: 9 will do all you *d* the first time,
2Ki 6:11 He summoned his officers and *d*
23:35 the silver and gold he *d*.
Ne 5:18 I never *d* the food allotted
Job 22: 6 You *d* security from your brothers
Ps 137: 3 our tormentors *d* songs of joy;
Mt 18:28 'Pay back what you owe me!' he *d*.
Lk 12:20 This very night your life will be *d*
12:48 been given much, much will be *d*;
22:64 They blindfolded him and *d*,
23:23 shouts they insistently *d* that he be
Jn 2:18 Jews *d* of him, "What miraculous
9:10 were your eyes opened?" they *d*.
18:22 to answer the high priest?" he *d*.

DEMANDING (DEMAND)
2Sa 3:14 *d*, "Give me my wife Michal,
Ps 78:18 by *d* the food they craved.
2Co 13: 3 since you are *d* proof that Christ is

DEMANDS (DEMAND)
Ex 21:22 whatever the woman's husband *d*
1Ki 20: 8 Don't listen to him or agree to his *d*
Ne 5:18 the *d* were heavy on these people.
Ps 25:10 for those who keep the *d*
Isa 43:23 nor wearied you with *d* for incense.
Mic 7: 3 the ruler *d* gifts,

DEMAS
Col 4:14 the doctor, and *D* send greetings.
2Ti 4:10 for *D*, because he loved this world,
Phm :24 And so do Mark, Aristarchus, *D*

DEMETRIUS
Ac 19:24 A silversmith named *D*, who made
19:38 *D* and his fellow craftsmen have
3Jn :12 *D* is well spoken of by everyone—

DEMOLISH (DEMOLISHED)
Ex 23:24 You must *d* them and break their
Nu 33:52 and *d* all their high places.
Jer 43:13 in Egypt he will *d* the sacred pillars
Eze 26: 9 *d* your towers with his weapons.
26:12 your walls and *d* your fine houses
Hos 10: 2 The LORD will *d* their altars
Mic 5:10 and *d* your chariots.
5:14 and *d* your cities.
Mal 1: 4 "They may build, but I will *d*.
2Co 10: 4 divine power to *d* strongholds.
10: 5 We *d* arguments and every

DEMOLISHED (DEMOLISH)
Nu 21:30 We have *d* them as far as Nophah,
Jdg 6:28 got up, there was Baal's altar, *d*,
2Ki 10:27 They *d* the sacred stone of Baal
23:15 even that altar and high place he *d*.
2Ch 33: 3 places his father Hezekiah had *d*;
Jer 31:40 will never again be uprooted or *d*."
Eze 6: 4 altars will be *d* and your incense
6: 6 be laid waste and the high places *d*,
Am 3:15 and the mansions will be *d*,"
Zep 1:13 their houses *d*.
3: 6 their strongholds are *d*.

DEMON (DEMON-POSSESSED DEMON-POSSESSION DEMONS)
Mt 9:33 And when the *d* was driven out,
11:18 and they say, 'He has a *d*.'
17:18 Jesus rebuked the *d*, and it came
Mk 7:26 to drive the *d* out of her daughter.
7:29 the *d* has left your daughter."
7:30 lying on the bed, and the *d* gone.
Lk 4:33 there was a man possessed by a *d*,
4:35 Then the *d* threw the man
7:33 wine, and you say, 'He has a *d*.'
8:29 driven by the *d* into solitary places.
9:42 the *d* threw him to the ground
11:14 When the *d* left, the man who had
11:14 was driving out a *d* that was mute.
Jn 8:49 "I am not possessed by a *d*,"
10:21 Can a *d* open the eyes of the blind
10:21 sayings of a man possessed by a *d*.

DEMON-POSSESSED (DEMON DEMON-POSSESSION)
Mt 4:24 those suffering severe pain, the *d*,
8:16 many who were *d* were brought
8:28 two *d* men coming
8:33 what had happened to the *d* men.
9:32 man who was *d* and could not talk
12:22 they brought him a *d* man who was
Mk 1:32 brought to Jesus all the sick and *d*.
5:16 what had happened to the *d* man—
5:18 the man who had been *d* begged
Lk 8:27 met by a *d* man from the town.
8:36 the people how the *d* man had been
Jn 7:20 "You are *d*," the crowd answered.
8:48 that you are a Samaritan and *d*?"
8:52 "Now we know that you are *d*!
10:20 Many of them said, "He is *d*
Ac 19:13 Jesus over those who were *d*.

DEMON-POSSESSION (DEMON DEMON-POSSESSED)
Mt 15:22 is suffering terribly from *d*."

DEMONS (DEMON)
Dt 32:17 to *d*, which are not God—
Ps 106:37 and their daughters to *d*.
Mt 7:22 and in your name drive out *d*
8:31 *d* begged Jesus, "If you drive us
9:34 prince of *d* that he drives out *d*."
10: 8 who have leprosy, drive out *d*.
12:24 of *d*, that this fellow drives out
12:24 that this fellow drives out *d*."
12:27 And if I drive out *d* by Beelzebub,
12:28 if I drive out *d* by the Spirit of God,
Mk 1:34 He also drove out many *d*,
1:34 but he would not let the *d* speak
1:39 their synagogues and driving out *d*.
3:15 to have authority to drive out *d*.
3:22 the prince of *d* he is driving out *d*."
5:12 The *d* begged Jesus, "Send us
5:15 possessed by the legion of *d*,
6:13 They drove out many *d*
9:38 "we saw a man driving out *d*
16: 9 out of whom he had driven seven *d*
16:17 In my name they will drive out *d*;
Lk 4:41 *d* came out of many people,
8: 2 from whom seven *d* had come out;
8:30 because many *d* had gone into him.
8:32 The *d* begged Jesus to let them go
8:33 When the *d* came out of the man,
8:35 from whom the *d* had gone out,
8:38 from whom the *d* had gone out
9: 1 and authority to drive out all *d*
9:49 "we saw a man driving out *d*
10:17 the *d* submit to us in your name."
11:15 the prince of *d*, he is driving out *d*."
11:18 you claim that I drive out *d*
Lk 11:19 Now if I drive out *d* by Beelzebub,
11:20 if I drive out *d* by the finger of God,
13:32 'I will drive out *d* and heal people
Ro 8:38 neither angels nor *d*, neither
1Co 10:20 of pagans are offered to *d*,
10:20 you to be participants with *d*.
10:21 of the Lord and the cup of *d* too;
10:21 the Lord's table and the table of *d*.
1Ti 4: 1 spirits and things taught by *d*.
Jas 2:19 Good! Even the *d* believe that—
Rev 9:20 they did not stop worshiping *d*,
16:14 of *d* performing miraculous signs,
18: 2 She has become a home for *d*

DEMONSTRATE (DEMONSTRATES DEMONSTRATION)
Ro 3:25 He did this to *d* his justice,
3:26 he did it to *d* his justice

DEMONSTRATES (DEMONSTRATE)
Ro 5: 8 God *d* his own love for us in this:

DEMONSTRATION (DEMONSTRATE)
1Co 2: 4 but with a *d* of the Spirit's power,

DEN (DENS)
Jer 7:11 become a *d* of robbers to you?
Da 6: 7 shall be thrown into the lions' *d*.
6:12 would be thrown into the lions' *d*?"
6:16 and threw him into the lions' *d*.
6:17 and placed over the mouth of the *d*,
6:19 and hurried to the lions' *d*.
6:20 When he came near the *d*,
6:23 orders to lift Daniel out of the *d*.
6:23 when Daniel was lifted from the *d*,
6:24 and thrown into the lions' *d*,
6:24 they reached the floor of the *d*,
Am 3: 4 Does he growl in his *d*
Na 2:11 Where now is the lions' *d*,
Mt 21:13 you are making it a '*d* of robbers.' "
Mk 11:17 you have made it 'a *d* of robbers.' "
Lk 19:46 but you have made it 'a *d* of robbers

DENARII (DENARIUS)
Mt 18:28 who owed him a hundred *d*.
Lk 7:41 One owed him five hundred *d*,

DENARIUS (DENARII)
Mt 20: 2 agreed to pay them a *d* for the day
20: 9 hour came and each received a *d*.
20:10 each one of them also received a *d*.
20:13 Didn't you agree to work for a *d*?
22:19 They brought him a *d*,
Mk 12:15 Bring me a *d* and let me look at it."
Lk 20:24 and said to them, "Show me a *d*.

DENIED (DENY)
Job 6:10 that I had not *d* the words
27: 2 as God lives, who has *d* me justice,
31:13 "If I have *d* justice
31:16 "If I have *d* the desires of the poor
38:15 The wicked are *d* their light,
Ecc 2:10 I *d* myself nothing my eyes desired;
Mt 26:70 But he *d* it before them all.
26:72 He *d* it again, with an oath:
Mk 14:68 But he *d* it.
14:70 Again he *d* it.
Lk 8:45 When they all *d* it, Peter said,
22:57 But he *d* it.
Jn 18:25 He *d* it, saying, "I am not."
18:27 Peter *d* it, and at that moment
1Ti 5: 8 he has *d* the faith and is worse
Rev 3: 8 my word and have not *d* my name.

DENIES (DENY)
Job 34: 5 but God *d* me justice.
1Jn 2:22 It is the man who *d* that Jesus is
2:22 he *d* the Father and the Son.
2:23 No one who *d* the Son has

DENOUNCE (DENOUNCED DENOUNCES)
Nu 5:21 *d* you when he causes your thigh
23: 7 come, *d* Israel.'
23: 8 How can I *d*
Pr 24:24 will curse him and nations *d* him.
Mt 11:20 Then Jesus began to *d* the cities

DENOUNCED (DENOUNCE)
Nu 23: 8 those whom the LORD has not *d*?
Da 3: 8 came forward and *d* the Jews.
1Co 10: 30 why am I *d* because of something I

DENOUNCES (DENOUNCE)
Job 17: 5 If a man *d* his friends for reward,
21: 31 Who *d* his conduct to his face?

DENS (DEN)
Job 37: 8 they remain in their *d*.
38: 40 lions when they crouch in their *d*
Ps 104: 22 they return and lie down in their *d*.
SS 4: 8 from the lions' *d*
Mic 7: 17 will come trembling out of their *d*;
Na 2: 12 and his *d* with the prey.

DENSE
Ge 19: 28 and he saw *d* smoke rising
Ex 8: 24 *D* swarms of flies poured
19: 9 going to come to you in a *d* cloud,
Isa 30: 27 with burning anger and *d* clouds
Jer 46: 23 "*d* though it be.
Zec 11: 2 the *d* forest has been cut down!

DENY (DENIED DENIES DENYING)
Ex 23: 6 "Do not *d* justice to your poor
Lev 16: 29 month you must *d* yourselves
16: 31 and you must *d* yourselves;
23: 27 sacred assembly and *d* yourselves,
23: 29 Anyone who does not *d* himself
23: 32 and you must *d* yourselves.
Nu 29: 7 You must *d* yourselves
30: 13 or any sworn pledge to *d* herself.
Job 27: 5 till I die, I will not *d* my integrity.
Isa 5: 23 but *d* justice to the innocent.
La 3: 35 to *d* a man his rights
Am 2: 7 and *d* justice to the oppressed.
Mt 16: 24 he must *d* himself and take up his
Mk 8: 34 he must *d* himself and take up his
Lk 9: 23 he must *d* himself and take up his
22: 34 you will *d* three times that you
Ac 4: 16 miracle, and we cannot *d* it.
Tit 1: 16 but by their actions they *d* him.
Jas 3: 14 do not boast about it or *d* the truth.
Jude : 4 *d* Jesus Christ our only Sovereign

DENYING (DENY)
Eze 22: 29 mistreat the alien, *d* them justice.
2Ti 3: 5 a form of godliness but *d* its power.
2Pe 2: 1 *d* the sovereign Lord who bought

DEPART (DEPARTED DEPARTING DEPARTS DEPARTURE)
Ge 49: 10 The scepter will not *d* from Judah,
Jos 1: 8 of the Law *d* from your mouth;
2Sa 12: 10 therefore, the sword will never *d*
Job 1: 21 and naked I will *d*.
Ps 39: 13 before I *d* and am no more."
Isa 49: 17 those who laid you waste *d*
52: 11 *D*, *d*, go out from there!
59: 21 put in your mouth will not *d*
Jer 43: 12 and *d* from there unscathed.
Mt 25: 41 '*D* from me, you who are cursed,
Php 1: 23 I desire to *d* and be with Christ,

DEPARTED (DEPART)
Jos 2: 21 So she sent them away and they *d*.
1Sa 4: 21 "The glory has *d* from Israel"—
4: 22 "The glory has *d* from Israel,
16: 14 of the LORD had *d* from Saul,
Job 23: 12 I have not *d* from the commands
Ps 119: 102 I have not *d* from your laws,
Isa 14: 9 the spirits of the *d* to greet you—
26: 14 those *d* spirits do not rise.
La 1: 6 All the splendor has *d*
Eze 10: 18 LORD *d* from over the threshold
Jn 4: 50 man took Jesus at his word and *d*.

DEPARTING (DEPART)
Hos 1: 2 adultery in *d* from the LORD."

DEPARTS (DEPART)
Ps 146: 4 When their spirit *d*, they return
Ecc 5: 15 and as he comes, so he *d*.
5: 16 As a man comes, so he *d*,
6: 4 without meaning, it *d* in darkness,

DEPARTURE (DEPART)
Dt 16: 3 the time of your *d* from Egypt.
16: 6 anniversary of your *d* from Egypt.
Lk 9: 31 spoke about his *d*, which he was
2Ti 4: 6 and the time has come for my *d*.
2Pe 1: 15 after my *d* you will always be able

DEPEND (DEPENDED DEPENDENT DEPENDING DEPENDS)
2Ki 18: 21 king of Egypt to all who *d* on him.
19: 10 Do not let the god you *d*
Ps 62: 7 My salvation and my honor *d*
Isa 36: 6 king of Egypt to all who *d* on him.
37: 10 Do not let the god you *d*
Ro 9: 16 *d* on man's desire or effort,

DEPENDED (DEPEND)
Isa 30: 12 and *d* on deceit,
Hos 10: 13 Because you have *d*
Ac 12: 20 they *d* on the king's country

DEPENDENT (DEPEND)
Lev 21: 3 or an unmarried sister who is *d*
1Th 4: 12 and so that you will not be *d*

DEPENDING (DEPEND)
2Ki 18: 20 On whom are you *d*, that you rebel
18: 21 Look now, you are *d* on Egypt,
18: 22 "We are *d* on the LORD our God
18: 24 you are *d* on Egypt for chariots
Isa 36: 5 On whom are you *d*, that you rebel
36: 6 Look now, you are *d* on Egypt,
36: 7 "We are *d* on the LORD our God
36: 9 you are *d* on Egypt for chariots

DEPENDS (DEPEND)
Jer 17: 5 who *d* on flesh for his strength
Ro 12: 18 as it *d* on you, live at peace
Gal 3: 18 For if the inheritance *d* on the law,
3: 18 then it no longer *d* on a promise;
Col 2: 8 which *d* on human tradition

DEPLOYED
1Sa 4: 2 The Philistines *d* their forces
2Sa 10: 9 and *d* them against the Arameans.
10: 10 *d* them against the Ammonites.
1Ch 19: 10 and *d* them against the Arameans.
19: 11 were *d* against the Ammonites.

DEPORTED
2Ki 15: 29 and *d* the people to Assyria.
16: 9 He *d* its inhabitants to Kir
17: 6 and *d* the Israelites to Assyria.
17: 26 "The people you *d* and resettled
18: 11 king of Assyria *d* Israel to Assyria
24: 16 also *d* to Babylon the entire force
1Ch 6: 15 Jehozadak was *d* when the LORD
8: 6 in Geba and were *d* to Manahath:
8: 7 who *d* them and who was the father
Ezr 4: 10 and honorable Ashurbanipal *d*
5: 12 and *d* the people to Babylon.

DEPOSE (DEPOSED DEPOSES)
Isa 22: 19 I will *d* you from your office,

DEPOSED (DEPOSE)
1Ki 15: 13 even *d* his grandmother Maacah
2Ch 15: 16 also *d* his grandmother Maacah
Da 5: 20 he was *d* from his royal throne

DEPOSES (DEPOSE)
Da 2: 21 he sets up kings and *d* them.

DEPOSIT (DEPOSITED)
Ezr 5: 15 *d* them in the temple in Jerusalem.
Eze 24: 6 whose *d* will not go away!
24: 11 and its *d* burned away.
24: 12 its heavy *d* has not been removed,
Mt 25: 27 money on *d* with the bankers,
Lk 19: 23 didn't you put my money on *d*,
2Co 1: 22 put his Spirit in our hearts as a *d*,
5: 5 and has given us the Spirit as a *d*,
Eph 1: 14 who is a *d* guaranteeing our
2Ti 1: 14 Guard the good *d* that was

DEPOSITED (DEPOSIT)
1Sa 10: 25 and *d* it before the LORD.
Ezr 6: 5 they are to be *d* in the house

DEPRAVED (DEPRAVITY)
Eze 16: 47 ways you soon became more *d*
23: 11 and prostitution she was more *d*
Ro 1: 28 he gave them over to a *d* mind,
Php 2: 15 fault in a crooked and *d* generation,
2Ti 3: 8 oppose the truth—men of *d* minds,

DEPRAVITY (DEPRAVED)
Ro 1: 29 of wickedness, evil, greed and *d*.
2Pe 2: 19 they themselves are slaves of *d*—

DEPRESSIONS
Lev 14: 37 reddish *d* that appear to be deeper

DEPRIVE (DEPRIVED DEPRIVES DEPRIVING)
Ex 21: 10 he must not *d* the first one
Dt 24: 17 Do not *d* the alien or the fatherless
Pr 18: 5 or to *d* the innocent of justice.
31: 5 *d* all the oppressed of their rights.
Isa 10: 2 to *d* the poor of their rights
29: 21 with false testimony *d* the innocent
La 3: 36 to *d* a man of justice—
Eze 36: 12 you will never again *d* them
36: 13 and *d* your nation of its children,"
Am 5: 12 and you *d* the poor of justice
Mal 3: 5 and the fatherless, and *d* aliens
1Co 7: 5 Do not *d* each other
9: 15 die than have anyone *d* me

DEPRIVED (DEPRIVE)
Ge 42: 36 "You have *d* me of my children.
Jer 5: 25 your sins have *d* you of good.
La 3: 17 I have been *d* of peace;
Mic 7: 16 *d* of all their power.
Ac 8: 33 In his humiliation he was *d*

DEPRIVES (DEPRIVE)
Job 12: 24 He *d* the leaders of the earth

DEPRIVING (DEPRIVE)
Ecc 4: 8 why am I *d* myself of enjoyment?"

DEPTH (DEEP)
Ge 7: 20 and covered the mountains to a *d*
La 3: 60 You have seen the *d*
Ro 8: 39 any powers, neither height nor *d*,
11: 33 the *d* of the riches of the wisdom
2Co 2: 4 to let you know the *d* of my love
Php 1: 9 more in knowledge and *d* of insight

DEPTHS (DEEP)
Ex 15: 5 they sank to the *d* like a stone.
Ne 9: 11 you hurled their pursuers into the *d*
Job 11: 8 deeper than the *d* of the grave—
36: 30 bathing the *d* of the sea.
41: 31 He makes the *d* churn like a boiling
Ps 30: 1 for you lifted me out of the *d*
63: 9 down to the *d* of the earth.
68: 22 you from the *d* of the sea,
69: 2 I sink in the miry *d*,
69: 15 or the *d* swallow me up
71: 20 from the *d* of the earth
77: 16 the very *d* were convulsed.
86: 13 from the *d* of the grave.
88: 6 in the darkest *d*.
95: 4 In his hand are the *d* of the earth,
106: 9 he led them through the *d*
107: 26 heavens and went down to the *d*;
130: 1 Out of the *d* I cry to you, O LORD;
135: 6 in the seas and all their *d*.
139: 8 bed in the *d*, you are there.
139: 15 in the *d* of the earth,
148: 7 great sea creatures and all ocean *d*,
Pr 9: 18 are in the *d* of the grave.
Isa 7: 11 whether in the deepest *d*
14: 15 to the *d* of the pit.
29: 15 Woe to those who go to great *d*
51: 10 who made a road in the *d* of the sea
63: 13 who led them through the *d*?
La 3: 55 from the *d* of the pit.
Eze 26: 19 when I bring the ocean *d* over you
27: 34 the sea in the *d* of the waters;
32: 23 Their graves are in the *d* of the pit
Am 9: 2 down to the *d* of the grave,
Jnh 2: 2 From the *d* of the grave I called
Mic 7: 19 iniquities into the *d* of the sea.
Zec 10: 11 and all the *d* of the Nile will dry up.

Mt 11:23 No, you will go down to the *d*.
18: 6 to be drowned in the *d* of the sea.
Lk 10:15 No, you will go down to the *d*.

DEPUTY

Jdg 9:28 isn't Zebul his *d*? Serve the men
1Ki 22:47 king in Edom; a *d* ruled.

DERBE

Ac 14: 6 *D* and to the surrounding country,
14:20 day he and Barnabas left for *D*.
16: 1 He came to *D* and then to Lystra,
20: 4 Gaius from *D*, Timothy also,

DERIDE (DERIDES DERISION)

Hab 1:10 They *d* kings

DERIDES (DERIDE)

Pr 11:12 who lacks judgment *d* his neighbor,

DERISION (DERIDE)

Job 27:23 It claps its hands in *d*
Ps 44:13 the scorn and *d* of those around us.
79: 4 of scorn and *d* to those around us.
Eze 23:32 it will bring scorn and *d*,
Mic 6:16 and your people to *d*;

DERIVES

Eph 3:15 in heaven and on earth *d* its name.

DESCEND (DESCENDED DESCENDING DESCENDS DESCENT)

Dt 32: 2 and my words *d* like dew,
Job 17:16 Will we *d* together into the dust?"
Ps 49:17 his splendor will not *d* with him.
SS 4: 8 *D* from the crest of Amana,
Isa 5:14 into it will *d* their nobles
14:19 those who *d* to the stones of the pit.
Ro 10: 7 "or 'Who will *d* into the deep?' "

DESCENDED (DESCEND)

Ge 36:16 These were the chiefs *d*
36:17 These were the chiefs *d* from Reuel
36:18 These were the chiefs *d*
36:40 These were the chiefs *d* from Esau,
Ex 19:18 because the LORD *d* on it in fire.
19:20 The LORD *d* to the top
Jos 16: 3 *d* westward to the territory
2Sa 21:20 He also was *d* from Rapha.
1Ki 18:31 for each of the tribes *d* from Jacob,
1Ch 2:53 From these *d* the Zorathites
20: 6 He also was *d* from Rapha.
2Ch 34:12 Levites *d* from Merari,
34:12 and Meshullam, *d* from Kohath.
Ezr 2:59 not show that their families were *d*
Ne 7:61 not show that their families were *d*
10:38 A priest *d* from Aaron is
Isa 57: 9 you *d* to the grave itself!
Lk 3:22 and the Holy Spirit *d* on him
Ro 9: 6 For not all who are *d*
Eph 4: 9 except that he also *d* to the lower,
4:10 He who *d* is the very one who
2Ti 2: 8 raised from the dead, *d* from David
Heb 7: 5 their brothers are *d* from Abraham.
7:14 For it is clear that our Lord *d*

DESCENDING (DESCEND)

Ge 28:12 of God were ascending and *d* on it.
1Sa 25:20 and his men *d* toward her,
SS 4: 1 *d* from Mount Gilead.
6: 5 *d* from Gilead.
Mt 3:16 the Spirit of God *d* like a dove
Mk 1:10 and the Spirit *d* on him like a dove.
Jn 1:51 and *d* on the Son of Man."

DESCENDS (DESCEND)

Isa 34: 5 see, it *d* in judgment on Edom,

DESCENT (DESCEND)

Ge 10:32 according to their lines of *d*,
Ne 9: 2 Those of Israelite *d* had separated
13: 3 Israel all who were of foreign *d*.
Eze 44:22 marry only virgins of Israelite *d*
Da 9: 1 son of Xerxes (a Mede by *d*),
Jn 1:13 children born not of natural *d*,
Heb 7: 6 did not trace his *d* from Levi,

DESCRIBE (DESCRIBED DESCRIBES DESCRIPTION DESCRIPTIONS)

Eze 43:10 *d* the temple to the people of Israel,
Mk 4:30 or what parable shall we use to *d* it?

DESCRIBED (DESCRIBE)

1Ki 4:33 He *d* plant life, from the cedar
Ac 12:17 *d* how the Lord had brought him
15:14 Simon has *d* to us how God
Rev 22:18 to him the plagues *d* in this book.
22:19 and in the holy city, which are *d*

DESCRIBES (DESCRIBE)

Ro 10: 5 Moses *d* in this way

DESCRIPTION (DESCRIBE)

Jos 18: 4 of the land and to write a *d* of it,
18: 8 of the land and write a *d* of it.
18: 9 They wrote its *d* on a scroll,

DESCRIPTIONS (DESCRIBE)

Jos 18: 6 After you have written *d*

DESECRATE (DESECRATED DESECRATES DESECRATING)

Lev 21:12 the sanctuary of his God or *d* it,
21:23 and so *d* my sanctuary.
22:15 The priests must not *d* the sacred
Dt 21:23 You must not *d* the land
Eze 7:22 and they will *d* my treasured place;
7:22 robbers will enter it and *d* it.
24:21 I am about to *d* my sanctuary—
Da 11:31 up to *d* the temple fortress
Mt 12: 5 the priests in the temple *d* the day
Ac 24: 6 and even tried to *d* the temple;

DESECRATED (DESECRATE)

Lev 19: 8 he has *d* what is holy to the LORD;
2Ki 23: 8 of Judah and *d* the high places,
23:10 He *d* Topheth, which was
23:13 *d* the high places that were east
Ps 106:38 and the land was *d* by their blood.
Isa 47: 6 and *d* my inheritance;
Eze 7:24 and their sanctuaries will be *d*.
20:13 and they utterly *d* my Sabbaths.
20:16 my decrees and *d* my Sabbaths.
20:21 by them—and they *d* my Sabbaths
20:24 my decrees and *d* my Sabbaths,
22: 8 my holy things and *d* my Sabbaths
23:38 my sanctuary and *d* my Sabbaths.
23:39 they entered my sanctuary and *d* it.
25: 3 over my sanctuary when it was *d*
28:18 you have *d* your sanctuaries.
Mal 2:11 Judah has *d* the sanctuary

DESECRATES (DESECRATE)

Ex 31:14 Anyone who *d* it must be put

DESECRATING (DESECRATE)

Ne 13:17 you are doing—*d* the Sabbath day?
13:18 against Israel by *d* the Sabbath."
Isa 56: 2 who keeps the Sabbath without *d* it
56: 6 who keep the Sabbath without *d* it
Eze 44: 7 *d* my temple while you offered me

DESERT (DESERTED DESERTING DESERTS)

Ge 14: 6 far as El Paran near the *d*.
16: 7 Hagar near a spring in the *d*;
21:14 wandered in the *d* of Beersheba.
21:20 in the *d* and became an archer.
21:21 While he was living in the *D*
36:24 in the *d* while he was grazing
37:22 him into this cistern here in the *d*,
Ex 3: 1 the flock to the far side of the *d*
3:18 into the *d* to offer sacrifices
4:27 "Go into the *d* to meet Moses."
5: 1 hold a festival to me in the *d*.' "
5: 3 into the *d* to offer sacrifices
7:16 that they may worship me in the *d*.
8:27 into the *d* to offer sacrifices
8:28 to the LORD your God in the *d*,
13:18 the people around by the *d* road
13:20 at Etham on the edge of the *d*.
14: 3 in confusion, hemmed in by the *d*.'
14:11 Egypt that you brought us to the *d*
14:12 the Egyptians than to die in the *d*!"
15:22 and they went into the *D* of Shur.
15:22 in the *d* without finding water.
16: 1 from Elim and came to the *D* of Sin
16: 2 In the *d* the whole community
16: 3 out into this *d* to starve this entire
16:10 they looked toward the *d*,
16:14 the ground appeared on the *d* floor.
16:32 eat in the *d* when I brought you out
17: 1 out from the *D* of Sin,
18: 5 him in the *d*, where he was camped
19: 1 they came to the *D* of Sinai.
19: 2 and Israel camped there in the *d*
19: 2 they entered the *D* of Sinai,
23:31 and from the *d* to the River.
Lev 7:38 to the LORD, in the *D* of Sinai.
11:18 the white owl, the *d* owl, the osprey
16:10 atonement by sending it into the *d*
16:21 away into the *d* in the care
16:22 and the man shall release it in the *d*
Nu 1: 1 Tent of Meeting in the *D* of Sinai
1:19 And so he counted them in the *D*
3: 4 fire before him in the *D* of Sinai.
3:14 said to Moses in the *D* of Sinai,
9: 1 spoke to Moses in the *D* of Sinai
9: 5 did so in the *D* of Sinai at twilight
10:12 came to rest in the *D* of Paran.
10:12 out from the *D* of Sinai
10:31 where we should camp in the *d*,
12:16 and encamped in the *D* of Paran.
13: 3 out from the *D* of Paran.
13:21 and explored the land from the *D*
13:26 at Kadesh in the *D* of Paran.
14: 2 died in Egypt! Or in this *d*!
14:16 so he slaughtered them in the *d*.'
14:22 and in the *d* but who disobeyed me
14:25 out toward the *d* along the route
14:29 In this *d* your bodies will fall—
14:32 your bodies will fall in this *d*.
14:33 the last of your bodies lies in the *d*.
14:35 They will meet their end in this *d*;
15:32 While the Israelites were in the *d*,
16:13 and honey to kill us in the *d*?
20: 1 community arrived at the *D*
20: 4 LORD's community into this *d*,
21: 5 out of Egypt to die in the *d*?
21:11 Abarim, in the *d* that faces Moab
21:13 which is in the *d* extending
21:18 they went from the *d* to Mattanah,
21:23 out into the *d* against Israel.
24: 1 but turned his face toward the *d*.
26:64 they counted the Israelites in the *D*
26:65 they would surely die in the *d*,
27: 3 and said, "Our father died in the *d*.
27:14 at the waters in the *D* of Zin,
27:14 in Kadesh, in the *D* of Zin.)
32:13 wander in the *d* forty years,
32:15 again leave all this people in the *d*,
33: 6 at Etham, on the edge of the *d*.
33: 8 for three days in the *D* of Etham,
33: 8 passed through the sea into the *d*,
33:11 and camped in the *D* of Sin.
33:12 They left the *D* of Sin and camped
33:15 and camped in the *D* of Sinai.
33:16 They left the *D* of Sinai
33:36 camped at Kadesh, in the *D* of Zin.
34: 3 of the *D* of Zin along the border
Dt 1: 1 Israel in the *d* east of the Jordan—
1:19 and dreadful *d* that you have seen,
1:31 before your very eyes, and in the *d*.
1:40 out toward the *d* along the route
2: 1 out toward the *d* along the route
2: 7 journey through this vast *d*.
2: 8 traveled along the *d* road of Moab.
2:26 From the *d* of Kedemoth I sent
4:43 Bezer in the *d* plateau,
8: 2 the way in the *d* these forty years,
8:15 through the vast and dreadful *d*,
8:16 He gave you manna to eat in the *d*,
9: 7 LORD your God to anger in the *d*.
9:28 out to put them to death in the *d*.'
11: 5 for you in the *d* until you arrived
11:24 from the *d* to Lebanon,
14:17 the white owl, the *d* owl, the osprey
29: 5 years that I led you through the *d*,
32:10 In a *d* land he found him,
32:51 Meribah Kadesh in the *D* of Zin
Jos 1: 4 territory will extend from the *d*
5: 4 died in the *d* on the way
5: 5 born in the *d* during the journey

Jos 5: 6 about in the *d* forty years
8: 15 and they fled toward the *d*.
8: 20 toward the *d* had turned back
8: 24 and in the *d* where they had chased
12: 8 the mountain slopes, the *d*
14: 10 while Israel moved about in the *d*.
15: 1 to the *D* of Zin in the extreme
15: 61 In the *d:* Beth Arabah, Middin,
16: 1 up from there through the *d*
18: 12 coming out at the *d* of Beth Aven.
20: 8 in the *d* on the plateau in the tribe
24: 7 you lived in the *d* for a long time.
Jdg 1: 16 among the people of the *D* of Judah
8: 7 I will tear your flesh with *d* thorns
8: 16 by punishing them with *d* thorns
11: 16 Israel went through the *d*
11: 18 "Next they traveled through the *d*,
11: 22 and from the *d* to the Jordan.
20: 42 Israelites in the direction of the *d*,
20: 45 and fled toward the *d* to the rock
20: 47 and fled into the *d* to the rock
1Sa 4: 8 with all kinds of plagues in the *d*.
13: 18 the Valley of Zeboim facing the *d*.
17: 28 you leave those few sheep in the *d?*
23: 14 David stayed in the *d* strongholds
23: 14 and in the hills of the *D* of Ziph.
23: 15 was at Horesh in the *D* of Ziph,
23: 24 his men were in the *D* of Maon,
23: 25 and stayed in the *D* of Maon.
23: 25 he went into the *D* of Maon
24: 1 "David is in the *D* of En Gedi."
25: 1 moved down into the *D* of Maon.
25: 4 While David was in the *d*,
25: 14 "David sent messengers from the *d*
25: 21 property in the *d* so that nothing
26: 2 So Saul went down to the *D* of Ziph
26: 3 but David stayed in the *d*.
2Sa 15: 23 the people moved on toward the *d*.
15: 28 the fords in the *d* until word comes
16: 2 who become exhausted in the *d*."
17: 16 the night at the fords in the *d;*
17: 29 and tired and thirsty in the *d*."
1Ki 2: 34 buried on his own land in the *d*.
9: 18 Tadmor in the *d*, within his land,
19: 4 went a day's journey into the *d*.
19: 15 and go to the *D* of Damascus.
2Ki 3: 8 "Through the *D* of Edom,"
1Ch 5: 9 up to the edge of the *d* that extends
6: 78 they received Bezer in the *d*,
12: 8 to David at his stronghold in the *d*.
21: 29 which Moses had made in the *d*,
2Ch 1: 3 servant had made in the *d*.
8: 4 He also built up Tadmor in the *d*
20: 16 end of the gorge in the *D* of Jeruel.
20: 20 left for the *D* of Tekoa.
20: 24 to the place that overlooks the *d*
24: 9 God had required of Israel in the *d*.
26: 10 in the *d* and dug many cisterns,
Ne 9: 17 Therefore you did not *d* them,
9: 19 you did not abandon them in the *d*.
9: 21 years you sustained them in the *d;*
Job 1: 19 a mighty wind swept in from the *d*
24: 5 Like wild donkeys in the *d*,
38: 26 a *d* with no one in it,
Ps 29: 8 of the LORD shakes the *d;*
29: 8 the LORD shakes the *D* of Kadesh.
55: 7 and stay in the *d; Selah*
65: 12 The grasslands of the *d* overflow;
72: 9 The *d* tribes will bow before him
74: 14 food to the creatures of the *d*.
75: 6 or from the *d* can exalt a man.
78: 15 He split the rocks in the *d*
78: 17 in the *d* against the Most High.
78: 19 "Can God spread a table in the *d?*
78: 40 rebelled against him in the *d*
78: 52 led them like sheep through the *d*.
95: 8 you did that day at Massah in the *d*
102: 6 I am like a *d* owl,
105: 41 like a river it flowed in the *d*.
106: 9 through the depths as through a *d*.
106: 14 In the *d* they gave
106: 26 he would make them fall in the *d*,
107: 4 Some wandered in *d* wastelands,
107: 33 He turned rivers into a *d*,
107: 35 He turned the *d* into pools of water
136: 16 who led his people through the *d*,
Pr 21: 19 Better to live in a *d*
SS 3: 6 Who is this coming up from the *d*
SS 8: 5 Who is this coming up from the *d*
Isa 13: 21 But *d* creatures will lie there,
14: 17 the man who made the world a *d*,
16: 1 from Sela, across the *d*,
16: 8 and spread toward the *d*.
21: 1 An oracle concerning the *D*
21: 1 an invader comes from the *d*,
23: 13 a place for *d* creatures;
25: 5 and like the heat of the *d*.
27: 10 settlement, forsaken like the *d;*
32: 2 like streams of water in the *d*
32: 15 and the *d* becomes a fertile field,
32: 16 Justice will dwell in the *d*
34: 11 *d* owl and screech owl will possess
34: 14 *D* creatures will meet with hyenas,
35: 1 *d* and the parched land will be glad;
35: 6 and streams in the *d*.
40: 3 "In the *d* prepare
41: 18 I will turn the *d* into pools of water,
41: 19 I will put in the *d*
42: 11 Let the *d* and its towns raise their
43: 19 I am making a way in the *d*
43: 20 because I provide water in the *d*
49: 10 will the *d* heat or the sun beat
50: 2 I turn rivers into a *d;*
64: 10 Your sacred cities have become a *d*
64: 10 Zion is a *d*, Jerusalem a desolation.
Jer 2: 2 and followed me through the *d*,
2: 24 a wild donkey accustomed to the *d*,
2: 31 "Have I been a *d* to Israel
3: 2 sat like a nomad in the *d*.
4: 11 in the *d* blows toward my people,
4: 26 and the fruitful land was a *d;*
5: 6 a wolf from the *d* will ravage them,
9: 2 Oh, that I had in the *d*
9: 10 lament concerning the *d* pastures.
9: 12 laid waste like a *d* that no one can
9: 26 live in the *d* in distant places.
12: 12 Over all the barren heights in the *d*
13: 24 driven by the *d* wind.
17: 6 in the parched places of the *d*,
17: 11 his life is half gone, they will *d* him,
22: 6 I will surely make you like a *d*,
23: 10 the pastures in the *d* are withered.
25: 24 foreign people who live in the *d;*
31: 2 will find favor in the *d;*
48: 6 become like a bush in the *d*.
50: 12 a wilderness, a dry land, a *d*.
50: 39 *d* creatures and hyenas will live
51: 43 a dry and *d* land,
La 4: 3 like ostriches in the *d*.
4: 19 and lay in wait for us in the *d*.
5: 9 because of the sword in the *d*.
Eze 6: 14 waste from the *d* to Diblah—
19: 13 Now it is planted in the *d*,
20: 10 and brought them into the *d*.
20: 13 and destroy them in the *d*.
20: 13 rebelled against me in the *d*.
20: 15 in the *d* that I would not bring
20: 17 or put an end to them in the *d*.
20: 18 I said to their children in the *d*,
20: 21 anger against them in the *d*.
20: 23 in the *d* that I would disperse them
20: 35 you into the *d* of the nations
20: 36 in the *d* of the land of Egypt,
23: 42 brought from the *d* along with men
29: 5 I will leave you in the *d*,
34: 25 beasts so that they may live in the *d*
Hos 2: 3 I will make her like a *d*,
2: 14 I will lead her into the *d*
9: 10 it was like finding grapes in the *d;*
13: 5 I cared for you in the *d*,
13: 15 blowing in from the *d;*
Joel 2: 3 behind them, a *d* waste—
3: 19 Edom a *d* waste,
Am 2: 10 and I led you forty years in the *d*
5: 25 forty years in the *d*, O house
Hab 1: 9 Their hordes advance like a *d* wind
Zep 2: 13 and dry as the *d*.
2: 14 The *d* owl and the screech owl
Mal 1: 3 left his inheritance to the *d* jackals
Mt 3: 1 preaching in the *D* of Judea
3: 3 "A voice of one calling in the *d*,
4: 1 the Spirit into the *d* to be tempted
11: 7 "What did you go out into the *d*
24: 26 out in the *d*,' do not go out; or,
Mk 1: 3 "a voice of one calling in the *d*,
1: 4 baptizing in the *d* region
Mk 1: 12 the Spirit sent him out into the *d*,
1: 13 and he was in the *d* forty days,
Lk 1: 80 in the *d* until he appeared publicly
3: 2 to John son of Zechariah in the *d*.
3: 4 "A voice of one calling in the *d*,
4: 1 and was led by the Spirit in the *d*,
7: 24 "What did you go out into the *d*
Jn 1: 23 the voice of one calling in the *d*,
3: 14 Moses lifted up the snake in the *d*,
6: 31 forefathers ate the manna in the *d;*
6: 49 forefathers ate the manna in the *d*,
11: 54 withdrew to a region near the *d*,
Ac 7: 30 bush in the *d* near Mount Sinai.
7: 36 and for forty years in the *d*.
7: 38 He was in the assembly in the *d*,
7: 42 forty years in the *d*, O house
7: 44 of Testimony with them in the *d*.
8: 26 "Go south to the road—the *d* road
13: 18 their conduct forty years in the *d*.
21: 38 out into the *d* some time ago?"
1Co 10: 5 bodies were scattered over the *d*.
Heb 3: 8 during the time of testing in the *d*,
3: 17 whose bodies fell in the *d?*
Rev 12: 6 fled into the *d* to a place prepared
12: 14 the place prepared for her in the *d*,
17: 3 away in the Spirit into a *d*.

DESERTED (DESERT)

Lev 26: 22 in number that your roads will be *d*
26: 43 For the land will be *d* by them
Dt 32: 18 You *d* the Rock, who fathered you;
Jos 22: 3 you have not *d* your brothers
2Sa 20: 2 So all the men of Israel *d* David
Ezr 9: 9 our God has not *d* us
Ps 69: 25 May their place be *d;*
Isa 6: 11 until the houses are left *d*
17: 2 The cities of Aroer will be *d*
32: 14 the noisy city *d;*
33: 8 The highways are *d*,
54: 6 if you were a wife *d* and distressed
62: 4 No longer will they call you *D*,
62: 12 The City No Longer *D*.
Jer 2: 15 his towns are burned and *d*.
4: 29 All the towns are *d;*
26: 9 this city will be desolate and *d?*"
33: 10 the streets of Jerusalem that are *d*,
38: 22 your friends have *d* you.'
44: 2 Today they lie *d* and in ruins
La 1: 1 How *d* lies the city,
Eze 14: 5 who have all *d* me for their idols.'
36: 4 *d* towns that have been plundered
Hos 4: 10 because they have *d* the LORD
Am 5: 2 *d* in her own land,
Zep 3: 6 I have left their streets *d*,
Zec 9: 5 and Ashkelon will be *d*.
Mt 26: 56 all the disciples *d* him and fled.
Mk 14: 50 Then everyone *d* him and fled.
Ac 1: 20 " 'May his place be *d;*
15: 38 he had *d* them in Pamphylia
2Ti 1: 15 in the province of Asia has *d* me,
4: 10 has *d* me and has gone
4: 16 to my support, but everyone *d* me.

DESERTING (DESERT)

Jer 37: 13 "You are *d* to the Babylonians!"
37: 14 "I am not *d* to the Babylonians."
Gal 1: 6 are so quickly *d* the one who called

DESERTS (DESERT)

1Ch 12: 19 heads if he *d* to his master Saul.")
Pr 19: 4 but a poor man's friend *d* him.
Isa 48: 21 when he led them through the *d;*
51: 3 he will make her *d* like Eden,
Jer 2: 6 through a land of *d* and rifts,
14: 5 *d* her newborn fawn
Zec 11: 17 who *d* the flock!
Heb 11: 38 They wandered in *d* and mountains

DESERVE (DESERVED DESERVES DESERVING)

Ge 40: 15 to *d* being put in a dungeon."
Lev 26: 21 times over, as your sins *d*.
Jdg 20: 10 it can give them what they *d*
1Sa 26: 16 you and your men *d* to die,
1Ki 2: 26 You *d* to die, but I will not put you
Ps 28: 4 bring back upon them what they *d*.
94: 2 pay back to the proud what they *d*.
103: 10 he does not treat us as our sins *d*

Pr 3: 27 from those who *d* it,
Ecc 8: 14 men who get what the righteous *d*.
8: 14 men who get what the wicked *d*,
Isa 66: 6 repaying his enemies all they *d*.
Jer 14: 16 out on them the calamity they *d*.
17: 10 according to what his deeds *d*."
21: 14 I will punish you as your deeds *d*,
32: 19 to his conduct and as his deeds *d*.
49: 12 "If those who do not *d*
La 3: 64 Pay them back what they *d*,
Eze 16: 59 I will deal with you as you *d*,
Zec 1: 6 to us what our ways and practices *d*
Mt 8: 8 I do not *d* to have you come
22: 8 those I invited did not *d* to come.
Lk 7: 6 for I do not *d* to have you come
23: 15 he has done nothing to *d* death.
23: 41 for we are getting what our deeds *d*
Ro 1: 32 those who do such things *d* death,
1Co 15: 9 even *d* to be called an apostle,
16: 18 Such men *d* recognition.
2Co 11: 15 end will be what their actions *d*.
Rev 16: 6 blood to drink as they *d*."

DESERVED (DESERVE)

2Sa 19: 28 descendants *d* nothing
Ezr 9: 13 less than our sins have *d*
Job 33: 27 but I did not get what I *d*.
Ac 23: 29 charge against him that *d* death
Ro 3: 8 result"? Their condemnation is *d*.

DESERVES (DESERVE)

Nu 35: 31 the life of a murderer, who *d* to die.
Dt 25: 2 If the guilty man *d* to be beaten,
25: 2 the number of lashes his crime *d*,
Jdg 9: 16 and if you have treated him as he *d*
2Sa 12: 5 the man who did this *d* to die!
Job 34: 11 upon him what his conduct *d*.
Jer 51: 6 he will pay her what she *d*.
Lk 7: 4 "This man *d* to have you do this,
10: 7 for the worker *d* his wages.
Ac 26: 31 is not doing anything that *d* death
1Ti 1: 15 saying that *d* full acceptance:
4: 9 saying that *d* full acceptance
5: 18 and "The worker *d* his wages."
Heb 10: 29 severely do you think a man *d*

DESERVING (DESERVE)

Dt 19: 6 even though he is not *d* of death,
22: 26 she has committed no sin *d* death.
Mt 10: 13 If the home is *d*, let your peace rest
Lk 12: 48 does things *d* punishment will be
Ac 25: 11 guilty of doing anything *d* death,
25: 25 I found he had done nothing *d*
28: 18 guilty of any crime *d* death.

DESIGN (DESIGNED DESIGNER DESIGNERS DESIGNS)

1Ki 7: 8 set farther back, was similar in *d*.
2Ch 2: 14 can execute any *d* given to him.
24: 13 of God according to its original *d*
Eze 43: 11 its whole *d* and all its regulations
43: 11 so that they may be faithful to its *d*
43: 11 to them the *d* of the temple—
Ac 17: 29 an image made by man's *d* and skill

DESIGNATE (DESIGNATED DESIGNATING)

Ex 21: 13 he is to flee to a place I will *d*.
Dt 23: 12 *D* a place outside the camp where
Jos 20: 2 "Tell the Israelites to *d* the cities

DESIGNATED (DESIGNATE)

Jos 20: 8 the Jordan of Jericho they *d* Bezer
20: 9 could flee to these *d* cities
2Sa 24: 15 until the end of the time *d*,
1Ch 12: 31 *d* by name to come and make
16: 41 and *d* by name to give thanks
28: 14 He *d* the weight of gold
2Ch 28: 15 men *d* by name took the prisoners,
31: 19 men were *d* by name
Ezr 10: 16 and all of them *d* by name.
Ne 13: 31 contributions of wood at *d* times,
Est 9: 31 days of Purim at their *d* times,
Eze 43: 21 and burn it in the *d* part
Lk 6: 13 also *d* apostles: Simon (whom he
Heb 5: 10 and was *d* by God to be high priest

DESIGNATING (DESIGNATE)

Mk 3: 14 appointed twelve—*d* them

DESIGNED (DESIGN)

2Ch 26: 15 In Jerusalem he made machines *d*

DESIGNER (DESIGN)

Ex 38: 23 and *d*, and an embroiderer in blue,

DESIGNERS (DESIGN)

Ex 35: 35 all of them master craftsmen and *d*.
35: 35 *d*, embroiderers in blue, purple

DESIGNS (DESIGN)

Ex 31: 4 to make artistic *d* for work in gold,
35: 32 to make artistic *d* for work in gold,
2Ch 3: 5 it with palm tree and chain *d*.

DESIRABLE (DESIRE)

Ge 3: 6 and also *d* for gaining wisdom,
Pr 22: 1 A good name is more *d*
Jer 3: 19 and give you a *d* land,

DESIRE (DESIRABLE DESIRED DESIRES)

Ge 3: 16 Your *d* will be for your husband,
Dt 5: 21 You shall not set your *d*
1Sa 9: 20 to whom is all the *d* of Israel turned
2Sa 19: 38 anything you *d* from me I will do
23: 5 and grant me my every *d*?
1Ch 29: 18 keep this *d* in the hearts
2Ch 1: 11 "Since this is your heart's *d*
9: 8 and his *d* to uphold them forever,
Job 13: 3 But I *d* to speak to the Almighty
21: 14 We have no *d* to know your ways.
Ps 10: 17 O LORD, the *d* of the afflicted;
20: 4 May he give you the *d*
21: 2 You have granted him the *d*
27: 12 me over to the *d* of my foes,
40: 6 Sacrifice and offering you did not *d*
40: 8 I *d* to do your will, O my God;
40: 14 may all who *d* my ruin
41: 2 him to the *d* of his foes.
51: 6 Surely you *d* truth
70: 2 may all who *d* my ruin
73: 25 with you, I *d* nothing on earth.
Pr 3: 15 nothing you *d* can compare
8: 11 and nothing you *d* can compare
10: 24 what the righteous *d* will be
11: 23 The *d* of the righteous ends only
12: 12 The wicked *d* the plunder
17: 16 since he has no *d* to get wisdom?
24: 1 do not *d* their company;
Ecc 12: 5 and *d* no longer is stirred.
SS 6: 12 my *d* set me among the royal
7: 10 and his *d* is for me.
Isa 26: 8 are the *d* of our hearts.
53: 2 appearance that we should *d* him.
55: 11 but will accomplish what I *d*
Eze 24: 25 delight of their eyes, their heart's *d*,
Hos 6: 6 For I *d* mercy, not sacrifice,
Mic 7: 3 the powerful dictate what they *d*—
Mal 3: 1 whom you *d*, will come," says
Mt 9: 13 learn what this means: 'I *d* mercy,
12: 7 what these words mean, 'I *d* mercy,
Jn 8: 44 want to carry out your father's *d*.
Ro 7: 8 in me every kind of covetous *d*
7: 18 For I have the *d* to do what is good,
9: 16 depend on man's *d* or effort,
10: 1 my heart's *d* and prayer to God
1Co 12: 31 But eagerly *d* the greater gifts.
14: 1 and eagerly *d* spiritual gifts,
2Co 8: 10 but also to have the *d* to do so.
8: 13 Our *d* is not that others might be
Php 1: 23 I *d* to depart and be with Christ,
Heb 10: 5 Sacrifice and offering you did not *d*
10: 8 and sin offerings you did not *d*,
13: 18 *d* to live honorably in every way.
Jas 1: 14 by his own evil *d*, he is dragged
1: 15 Then, after *d* has conceived,
2Pe 2: 10 of those who follow the corrupt *d*

DESIRED (DESIRE)

1Ki 9: 1 and had achieved all he had *d* to do
9: 19 whatever he *d* to build in Jerusalem
10: 13 gave the queen of Sheba all she *d*
2Ch 8: 6 whatever he *d* to build in Jerusalem
9: 12 gave the queen of Sheba all she *d*
Ps 107: 30 he guided them to their *d* haven.
Ps 132: 13 he has *d* it for his dwelling:
132: 14 will sit enthroned, for I have *d* it—
Ecc 2: 10 I denied myself nothing my eyes *d*;
Jer 17: 16 you know I have not *d* the day
Da 11: 37 or for the one *d* by women,
Hag 2: 7 and the *d* of all nations will come,
Lk 22: 15 "I have eagerly *d* to eat this

DESIRES (DESIRE)

Ge 4: 7 at your door; it *d* to have you,
41: 16 will give Pharaoh the answer he *d*."
2Sa 3: 21 rule over all that your heart *d*."
1Ki 11: 37 rule over all that your heart *d*;
Job 17: 11 and so are the *d* of my heart.
31: 16 "If I have denied the *d* of the poor
Ps 34: 12 and *d* to see many good days,
37: 4 he will give you the *d* of your heart.
103: 5 He satisfies my *d* with good things,
140: 8 do not grant the wicked their *d*,
145: 16 satisfy the *d* of every living thing.
145: 19 He fulfills the *d* of those who fear
Pr 11: 6 the unfaithful are trapped by evil *d*.
13: 4 *d* of the diligent are fully satisfied.
19: 22 What a man *d* is unfailing love;
Ecc 6: 2 so that he lacks nothing his heart *d*,
SS 2: 7 love until it so *d*.
3: 5 love until it so *d*.
8: 4 love until it so *d*.
Hab 2: 4 his *d* are not upright—
Mk 4: 19 and the *d* for other things come in
Ro 1: 24 over in the sinful *d* of their hearts
6: 12 body so that you obey its evil *d*.
8: 5 set on what that nature *d*;
8: 5 set on what the Spirit *d*.
13: 14 to gratify the *d* of the sinful nature.
Gal 5: 16 and you will not gratify the *d*
5: 17 the sinful nature *d* what is contrary
5: 24 nature with its passions and *d*.
Eph 2: 3 and following its *d* and thoughts.
4: 22 being corrupted by its deceitful *d*;
Col 3: 5 impurity, lust, evil *d* and greed,
1Ti 3: 1 an overseer, he *d* a noble task.
5: 11 their sensual *d* overcome their
6: 9 and harmful *d* that plunge men
2Ti 2: 22 Flee the evil *d* of youth,
3: 6 are swayed by all kinds of evil *d*,
4: 3 Instead, to suit their own *d*,
Jas 1: 20 about the righteous life that God *d*.
4: 1 from your *d* that battle within you?
1Pe 1: 14 conform to the evil *d* you had
2: 11 to abstain from sinful *d*, which war
4: 2 of his earthly life for evil human *d*,
2Pe 1: 4 in the world caused by evil *d*.
2: 18 to the lustful *d* of sinful human
3: 3 and following their own evil *d*.
1Jn 2: 17 The world and its *d* pass away,
Jude : 16 they follow their own evil *d*;
: 18 will follow their own ungodly *d*."

DESOLATE (DESOLATION DESOLATIONS)

Ge 47: 19 that the land may not become *d*."
Ex 23: 29 because the land would become *d*
Lev 26: 34 years all the time that it lies *d*
26: 35 time that it lies *d*, the land will have
26: 43 while it lies *d* without them.
Jos 8: 28 heap of ruins, a *d* place to this day.
2Sa 13: 20 Absalom's house, a *d* woman.
Job 30: 3 land in *d* wastelands at night.
38: 27 to satisfy a *d* wasteland
Isa 1: 7 Your country is *d*,
5: 9 the great houses will become *d*,
13: 9 to make the land *d*
24: 10 The ruined city lies *d*;
27: 10 The fortified city stands *d*,
34: 10 to generation it will lie *d*;
49: 8 and to reassign its *d* inheritances,
49: 19 you were ruined and made *d*
54: 1 are the children of the *d* woman
54: 3 and settle in their *d* cities.
62: 4 or name your land *D*.
Jer 6: 8 and make your land *d*
7: 34 for the land will become *d*.
9: 10 They are *d* and untraveled,
10: 22 It will make the towns of Judah *d*,
12: 10 field into a *d* wasteland.
12: 11 parched and *d* before me;
25: 11 country will become a *d* wasteland,

Jer 25: 12 "and will make it *d* forever.
25: 38 and their land will become *d*
26: 9 this city will be *d* and deserted?"
32: 43 'It is a *d* waste, without men
33: 10 "It is a *d* waste, without men
33: 12 *d* and without men or animals—
44: 6 and made them the *d* ruins they are
44: 22 and a *d* waste without inhabitants,
48: 9 her towns will become *d*,
49: 33 a *d* place forever.
50: 13 but will be completely *d*.
50: 23 How *d* is Babylon
51: 26 for you will be *d* forever,"
51: 43 Her towns will be *d*,
51: 62 live in it; it will be *d* forever.'
La 1: 4 All her gateways are *d*,
1: 13 He made me *d*,
5: 18 dim for Mount Zion, which lies *d*,
Eze 6: 14 and make the land a *d* waste
12: 20 be laid waste and the land will be *d*.
14: 15 and it becomes *d* so that no one can
14: 16 be saved, but the land would be *d*.
15: 8 make the land *d* because they have
26: 19 When I make you a *d* city,
29: 9 Egypt will become a *d* wasteland.
29: 10 a *d* waste from Migdol to Aswan,
29: 12 and her cities will lie *d* forty years
29: 12 of Egypt *d* among devastated lands
30: 7 *d* among *d* lands,
32: 15 When I make Egypt *d*
33: 28 I will make the land a *d* waste,
33: 28 mountains of Israel will become *d*
33: 29 I have made the land a *d* waste
35: 3 you and make you a *d* waste.
35: 4 towns into ruins and you will be *d*.
35: 7 I will make Mount Seir a *d* waste
35: 9 will make you *d* forever; your
35: 14 earth rejoices, I will make you *d*.
35: 15 You will be *d*, O Mount Seir,
35: 15 of the house of Israel became *d*,
36: 4 to the *d* ruins and the deserted
36: 34 instead of lying *d* in the sight
36: 34 *d* land will be cultivated instead
36: 35 the cities that were lying in ruins, *d*
36: 36 and have replanted what was *d*.
38: 8 of Israel, which had long been *d*.
Da 9: 17 with favor on your *d* sanctuary.
Joel 3: 19 But Egypt will be *d*,
Mic 7: 13 The earth will become *d*
Zep 2: 13 leaving Nineveh utterly *d*
Zec 7: 14 The land was left so *d*
7: 14 they made the pleasant land *d*.' "
Mt 23: 38 Look, your house is left to you *d*.
Lk 13: 35 Look, your house is left to you *d*.
Gal 4: 27 are the children of the *d* woman

DESOLATION (DESOLATE)

2Ch 36: 21 all the time of its *d* it rested,
Isa 17: 9 And all will be *d*.
34: 11 and the plumb line of *d*.
64: 10 even Zion is a desert, Jerusalem a *d*
Eze 23: 33 the cup of ruin and *d*,
Da 8: 13 the rebellion that causes *d*,
9: 2 that the *d* of Jerusalem would last
9: 18 see the *d* of the city that bears your
9: 27 And one who causes *d* will place
11: 31 up the abomination that causes *d*.
12: 11 abomination that causes *d* is set up,
Mt 24: 15 'the abomination that causes *d*,'
Mk 13: 14 that causes *d*' standing where
Lk 21: 20 you will know that its *d* is near.

DESOLATIONS (DESOLATE)

Ps 46: 8 the *d* he has brought on the earth.
Da 9: 26 the end, and *d* have been decreed.

DESPAIR (DESPAIRED DESPAIRING DESPAIRS)

1Sa 4: 20 attending her said, "Don't *d*;
Job 9: 23 he mocks the *d* of the innocent.
Ps 88: 15 suffered your terrors and am in *d*.
Ecc 2: 20 So my heart began to *d*
Isa 19: 9 with combed flax will *d*,
61: 3 instead of a spirit of *d*.
Jer 17: 16 I have not desired the day of *d*.
Eze 4: 16 and drink rationed water in *d*,
7: 27 the prince will be clothed with *d*,
12: 19 and drink their water in *d*,
Joel 1: 11 *D*, you farmers,
2Co 4: 8 perplexed, but not in *d*; persecuted,

DESPAIRED (DESPAIR)

2Co 1: 8 ability to endure, so that we *d*

DESPAIRING (DESPAIR)

Dt 28: 65 weary with longing, and a *d* heart.
Job 6: 14 A *d* man should have the devotion
6: 26 treat the words of a *d* man as wind?
Jer 14: 3 dismayed and *d*,

DESPAIRS (DESPAIR)

Job 15: 22 He *d* of escaping the darkness;

DESPERATE

2Sa 12: 18 He may do something *d*."
Ps 60: 3 have shown your people *d* times;
79: 8 for we are in *d* need.
142: 6 for I am in *d* need;

DESPISE (DESPISED DESPISES)

Ge 16: 4 she began to *d* her mistress.
1Sa 2: 30 those who *d* me will be disdained.
2Sa 12: 9 Why did you *d* the word
Est 1: 17 and so they will *d* their husbands
Job 5: 17 so do not *d* the discipline
7: 16 I *d* my life; I would not live forever.
9: 21 I *d* my own life.
36: 5 God is mighty, but does not *d* men;
42: 6 Therefore I *d* myself
Ps 51: 17 O God, you will not *d*.
69: 33 and does not *d* his captive people.
73: 20 you will *d* them as fantasies.
102: 17 he will not *d* their plea.
Pr 1: 7 but fools *d* wisdom and discipline.
3: 11 do not *d* the LORD's discipline
6: 30 Men do not *d* a thief if he steals
23: 22 do not *d* your mother
SS 8: 1 and no one would *d* me.
Isa 60: 14 all who *d* you will bow
Jer 4: 30 Your lovers *d* you;
14: 19 Do you *d* Zion?
14: 21 of your name do not *d* us;
23: 17 to those who *d* me,
33: 24 So they *d* my people and no longer
La 1: 8 All who honored her *d* her,
Eze 16: 57 all those around you who *d* you.
Am 5: 10 and *d* him who tells the truth.
5: 21 "I hate, I *d* your religious feasts;
Mic 3: 9 who *d* justice
Mal 1: 6 O priests, who *d* my name.
Mt 6: 24 devoted to the one and *d* the other.
Lk 16: 13 devoted to the one and *d* the other.
1Co 11: 22 Or do you *d* the church of God
Tit 2: 15 Do not let anyone *d* you.
2Pe 2: 10 of the sinful nature and *d* authority.

DESPISED (DESPISE)

Ge 25: 34 So Esau *d* his birthright.
Nu 15: 31 Because he has *d* the LORD's
1Sa 10: 27 They *d* him and brought him no
15: 9 but everything that was *d*
17: 42 ruddy and handsome, and he *d* him
2Sa 6: 16 before the LORD, she *d* him
12: 10 you *d* me and took the wife
1Ch 15: 29 celebrating, she *d* him in her heart.
2Ch 36: 16 *d* his words and scoffed
Ne 4: 4 Hear us, O our God, for we are *d*.
Ps 22: 6 by men and *d* by the people.
22: 24 For he has not *d* or disdained
53: 5 them to shame, for God *d* them.
106: 24 Then they *d* the pleasant land;
107: 11 and *d* the counsel of the Most High
119:141 Though I am lowly and *d*,
Pr 12: 8 but men with warped minds are *d*.
Ecc 9: 16 But the poor man's wisdom is *d*,
Isa 16: 14 and all her many people will be *d*,
33: 8 its witnesses are *d*,
49: 7 to him who was *d* and abhorred
53: 3 He was *d* and rejected by men,
53: 3 he was *d*, and we esteemed him not
Jer 22: 28 Is this man Jehoiachin a *d*,
49: 15 *d* among men.
La 1: 11 for I am *d*."
Eze 16: 5 the day you were born you were *d*.
16: 45 who *d* her husband and her
16: 45 who *d* their husbands and their
Eze 16: 59 because you have *d* my oath
17: 16 whose oath he *d* and whose treaty
17: 18 He *d* the oath by breaking
17: 19 on his head my oath that he *d*
21: 10 have *d* the rod and all advice.
21: 13 Why is it that you have *d* the rod?
22: 8 You have *d* my holy things
Ob : 2 you will be utterly *d*.
Mal 1: 6 'How have we *d* your name?'
2: 9 "So I have caused you to be *d*
1Co 1: 28 of this world and the *d* things—

DESPISES (DESPISE)

Ge 16: 5 knows she is pregnant, she *d* me.
2Ki 19: 21 *d* you and mocks you.
Ps 15: 4 who *d* a vile man
Pr 14: 2 he whose ways are devious *d* him.
14: 21 He who *d* his neighbor sins,
15: 20 but a foolish man *d* his mother.
15: 32 who ignores discipline *d* himself,
Isa 37: 22 *d* and mocks you.
Zec 4: 10 "Who *d* the day of small things?

DESPOIL (SPOIL)

Jer 30: 16 all who make spoil of you I will *d*.

DESTINATION

2Sa 16: 14 arrived at their *d* exhausted.

DESTINE (DESTINED DESTINY PREDESTINED)

Isa 65: 12 I will *d* you for the sword,

DESTINED (DESTINE)

Ps 49: 14 Like sheep they are *d* for the grave,
Isa 9: 5 will be *d* for burning,
Jer 15: 2 " 'Those *d* for death, to death;
43: 11 bringing death to those *d* for death,
43: 11 captivity to those *d* for captivity,
43: 11 the sword to those *d* for the sword.
Eze 31: 14 they are all *d* for death,
Lk 2: 34 "This child is *d* to cause the falling
1Co 2: 7 and that God *d* for our glory
Col 2: 22 These are all *d* to perish with use,
1Th 3: 3 know quite well that we were *d*
Heb 9: 27 Just as man is *d* to die once,
1Pe 2: 8 which is also what they were *d* for.

DESTINY (DESTINE)

Job 8: 13 Such is the *d* of all who forget God;
Ps 73: 17 then I understood their final *d*.
Ecc 7: 2 for death is the *d* of every man;
9: 2 share a common *d*— the righteous
9: 3 the sun: The same *d* overtakes all.
Isa 65: 11 and fill bowls of mixed wine for *D*,
Php 3: 19 Their *d* is destruction, their god is

DESTITUTE

Ge 45: 11 belong to you will become *d*.'
Job 20: 19 oppressed the poor and left them *d*;
Ps 102: 17 to the prayer of the *d*;
Pr 31: 8 for the rights of all who are *d*.
Isa 3: 26 *d*, she will sit on the ground.
La 1: 16 My children are *d*
4: 5 are *d* in the streets.
Heb 11: 37 *d*, persecuted and mistreated—

DESTROY (DESTROYED DESTROYER DESTROYERS DESTROYING DESTROYS DESTRUCTION DESTRUCTIVE)

Ge 6: 13 I am surely going to *d* both them
6: 17 floodwaters on the earth to *d* all life
8: 21 again will I *d* all living creatures,
9: 11 will there be a flood to *d* the earth."
9: 15 waters become a flood to *d* all life.
18: 28 Will you *d* the whole city
18: 28 there," he said, "I will not *d* it."
18: 31 the sake of twenty, I will not *d* it."
18: 32 "For the sake of ten, I will not *d* it."
19: 13 because we are going to *d* this place
19: 13 so great that he has sent us to *d* it."
19: 14 the LORD is about to *d* the city!"
20: 4 Lord, will you *d* an innocent nation
Ex 15: 9 and my hand will *d* them.'
32: 10 against them and that I may *d* them
33: 3 and I might *d* you on the way."
33: 5 even for a moment, I might *d* you.
Lev 23: 30 I will *d* from among his people

Lev 26: 16 and fever that will *d* your sight
26: 22 *d* your cattle and make you so few
26: 30 I will *d* your high places, cut
26: 44 as to *d* them completely,
Nu 14: 12 down with a plague and *d* them,
21: 2 we will totally *d* their cities."
24: 19 and *d* the survivors of the city."
33: 52 *D* all their carved images
Dt 1: 27 the hands of the Amorites to *d* us.
4: 31 he will not abandon or *d* you
6: 15 and he will *d* you from the face
7: 2 then you must *d* them totally.
7: 4 against you and will quickly *d* you.
7: 16 You must *d* all the peoples
7: 24 up against you; you will *d* them.
9: 3 He will *d* them; he will subdue
9: 8 that he was angry enough to *d* you
9: 14 so that I may *d* them and blot out
9: 19 enough with you to *d* you.
9: 20 enough with Aaron to *d* him,
9: 25 LORD had said he would *d* you.
9: 26 LORD, do not *d* your people,
10: 10 It was not his will to *d* you.
12: 2 *D* completely all the places
13: 15 *D* it completely, both its people
20: 17 Completely *d* them—the Hittites,
20: 19 do not *d* its trees by putting an ax
28: 63 it will please him to ruin and *d* you.
31: 3 He will *d* these nations before you,
33: 27 saying, '*D* him!'
Jos 7: 7 the hands of the Amorites to *d* us?
7: 12 you *d* whatever among you is
11: 20 so that he might *d* them totally,
1Sa 15: 3 totally *d* everything that belongs
15: 6 Amalekites so that I do not *d* you
15: 9 were unwilling to *d* completely,
15: 18 completely *d* those wicked people,
23: 10 and *d* the town on account of me.
26: 9 said to Abishai, "Don't *d* him!
26: 15 came to *d* your lord the king.
2Sa 1: 14 hand to *d* the LORD's anointed?"
11: 25 the attack against the city and *d* it.'
20: 19 trying to *d* a city that is a mother
20: 20 it from me to swallow up or *d*!
24: 16 out his hand to *d* Jerusalem,
2Ki 8: 19 LORD was not willing to *d* Judah.
9: 7 You are to *d* the house
10: 19 in order to *d* the ministers of Baal.
11: 1 to *d* the whole royal family
13: 17 will completely *d* the Arameans
13: 23 he has been unwilling to *d* them
18: 25 against this country and *d* it.' "
18: 25 and *d* this place without word
24: 2 them to *d* Judah, in accordance
1Ch 21: 15 God sent an angel to *d* Jerusalem.
2Ch 12: 7 I will not *d* them but will soon give
20: 10 from them and did not *d* them.
20: 23 the men from Mount Seir to *d*
20: 23 they helped to *d* one another.
20: 37 the LORD will *d* what you have
21: 7 willing to *d* the house of David.
22: 7 anointed to *d* the house of Ahab.
22: 10 to *d* the whole royal family
25: 16 that God has determined to *d* you,
35: 21 who is with me, or he will *d* you."
Ezr 6: 12 or to *d* this temple in Jerusalem.
9: 14 be angry enough with us to *d* us,
Est 3: 6 a way to *d* all Mordecai's people,
3: 9 let a decree be issued to *d* them,
3: 13 provinces with the order to *d*,
8: 5 and wrote to *d* the Jews
8: 11 and protect themselves; to *d*,
9: 24 plotted against the Jews to *d* them
Job 10: 8 Will you now turn and *d* me?
14: 19 so you *d* man's hope.
Ps 5: 6 You *d* those who tell lies;
21: 10 You will *d* their descendants
54: 5 in your faithfulness *d* them.
69: 4 those who seek to *d* me.
73: 27 you *d* all who are unfaithful to you.
74: 11 folds of your garment and *d* them!
78: 38 and did not *d* them.
83: 4 they say, "let us *d* them as a nation,
94: 23 and *d* them for their wickedness;
94: 23 the LORD our God will *d* them.
106: 23 So he said he would *d* them—
106: 34 They did not *d* the peoples
119: 95 The wicked are waiting to *d* me,
Ps 143: 12 *d* all my foes,
145: 20 but all the wicked he will *d*.
Pr 1: 32 complacency of fools will *d* them;
Ecc 5: 6 and *d* the work of your hands?
7: 16 why *d* yourself?
Isa 10: 7 his purpose is to *d*,
10: 18 it will completely *d*,
11: 9 They will neither harm nor *d*
13: 5 to *d* the whole country.
13: 9 and *d* the sinners within it.
14: 30 But your root I will *d* by famine;
25: 7 On this mountain he will *d*
32: 7 schemes to *d* the poor with lies,
34: 2 He will totally *d* them,
36: 10 against this country and *d* it.' "
36: 10 and *d* this land without the LORD?
65: 8 I will not *d* them all.
65: 8 and men say, 'Don't *d* it,
65: 25 They will neither harm nor *d*
Jer 1: 10 to *d* and overthrow, to build
4: 27 though I will not *d* it completely.
5: 10 but do not *d* them completely.
5: 17 With the sword they will *d*
5: 18 "I will not *d* you completely.
6: 2 I will *d* the Daughter of Zion,
6: 5 and *d* her fortresses!"
11: 19 "Let us *d* the tree and its fruit;
12: 17 I will completely uproot and *d* it,"
14: 12 I will *d* them with the sword,
15: 3 beasts of the earth to devour and *d*.
15: 6 I will lay hands on you and *d* you;
17: 18 *d* them with double destruction.
21: 10 the king of Babylon, and he will *d* it
25: 9 I will completely *d* them
27: 8 until I *d* it by his hand.
30: 11 I will not completely *d* you.
30: 11 'Though I completely *d* all
31: 28 to overthrow, *d* and bring disaster,
36: 29 *d* this land and cut off both men
44: 8 You will *d* yourselves and make
44: 11 disaster on you and to *d* all Judah.
46: 8 I will *d* cities and their people.'
46: 28 I will not completely *d* you.
46: 28 "Though I completely *d* all
47: 4 about to *d* the Philistines,
47: 4 come to *d* all the Philistines
49: 20 he will completely *d* their pasture
49: 28 and *d* the people of the East.
49: 38 and *d* her king and officials,"
50: 21 kill and completely *d* them,"
50: 26 Completely *d* her
50: 45 he will completely *d* their pasture
51: 3 completely *d* her army.
51: 11 because his purpose is to *d* Babylon
51: 20 with you I *d* kingdoms,
51: 25 you who *d* the whole earth,"
51: 55 The LORD will *d* Babylon;
51: 62 you have said you will *d* this place,
La 3: 66 Pursue them in anger and *d* them
Eze 5: 16 of famine, I will shoot to *d* you.
6: 3 and I will *d* your high places.
9: 8 going to *d* the entire remnant
11: 13 Will you completely *d* the remnant
14: 9 and *d* him from among my people
16: 39 your mounds and *d* your lofty
17: 17 siege works erected to *d* many lives
20: 13 on them and *d* them in the desert.
20: 17 them with pity and did not *d* them
22: 30 the land so I would not have to *d* it,
25: 7 I will *d* you, and you will know that
25: 15 ancient hostility sought to *d* Judah,
25: 16 and *d* those remaining
26: 4 They will *d* the walls of Tyre
30: 11 will be brought in to *d* the land.
30: 13 " 'I will *d* the idols
32: 13 I will *d* all her cattle
34: 16 but the sleek and the strong I will *d*
43: 3 seen when he came to *d* the city
Da 4: 23 'Cut down the tree and *d* it,
8: 24 He will *d* the mighty men
8: 25 he will *d* many and take his stand
9: 26 ruler who will come will *d* the city
11: 16 and will have the power to *d* it.
11: 26 king's provisions will try to *d* him;
11: 44 he will set out in a great rage to *d*
Hos 4: 5 So I will *d* your mother—
10: 2 and *d* their sacred stones.
11: 6 will *d* the bars of their gates
Hos 13: 9 "I will *d* you, O Israel,
Am 1: 5 I will *d* the king who is
1: 8 I will *d* the king of Ashdod
2: 3 I will *d* her ruler
3: 14 I will *d* the altars of Bethel;
9: 8 I will *d* it
9: 8 yet I will not totally *d*
Ob : 8 "will I not *d* the wise men of Edom,
Mic 1: 7 I will *d* all her images.
5: 10 "I will *d* your horses
5: 11 I will *d* the cities of your land
5: 12 I will *d* your witchcraft
5: 13 I will *d* your carved images
6: 13 Therefore, I have begun to *d* you,
Na 1: 14 I will *d* the carved images
Zep 2: 5 "I will *d* you,
2: 13 and *d* Assyria,
Zec 5: 4 It will remain in his house and *d* it,
9: 4 and *d* her power on the sea,
9: 15 They will *d*
12: 9 out to *d* all the nations that attack
Mt 6: 19 where moth and rust *d*,
6: 20 where moth and rust do not *d*,
10: 28 of the one who can *d* both soul
26: 61 'I am able to *d* the temple of God
27: 40 You who are going to *d* the temple
Mk 1: 24 to *d* us? I know who you are—
14: 58 'I will *d* this man-made temple
15: 29 You who are going to *d* the temple
Lk 4: 34 to *d* us? I know who you are—
6: 9 or to *d* it?" He looked
9: 54 fire down from heaven to *d* them?"
Jn 2: 19 answered them, "*D* this temple,
10: 10 only to steal and kill and *d*;
Ac 6: 14 Jesus of Nazareth will *d* this place
8: 3 But Saul began to *d* the church.
Ro 14: 15 not by your eating *d* your brother
14: 20 Do not *d* the work of God
1Co 1: 19 "I will *d* the wisdom of the wise;
3: 17 God will *d* him; for God's temple is
6: 13 but God will *d* them both.
Gal 1: 13 the church of God and tried to *d* it.
1: 23 the faith he once tried to *d*."
2Th 2: 8 *d* by the splendor of his coming.
2Ti 2: 18 and they *d* the faith of some.
Heb 2: 14 death he might *d* him who holds
Jas 4: 12 the one who is able to save and *d*.
1Jn 3: 8 was to *d* the devil's work.
Jude : 10 are the very things that *d* them.
Rev 11: 18 destroying those who *d* the earth."

DESTROYED (DESTROY)

Ge 13: 10 was before the LORD *d* Sodom
19: 29 when God *d* the cities of the plain,
34: 30 I and my household will be *d*."
Ex 9: 31 (The flax and barley were *d*,
9: 32 were not *d*, because they ripen
22: 20 other than the LORD must be *d*.
Lev 10: 6 for those the LORD has *d* by fire.
Nu 21: 3 They completely *d* them
21: 29 You are *d*, O people of Chemosh!
21: 30 Heshbon is *d* all the way to Dibon.
24: 22 yet you Kenites will be *d*
Dt 2: 12 They *d* the Horites
2: 21 The LORD *d* them
2: 22 when he *d* the Horites
2: 23 out from Caphtor *d* them
2: 34 his towns and completely *d* them—
3: 6 We completely *d* them,
4: 3 The LORD your God *d*
4: 26 there long but will certainly be *d*.
7: 23 great confusion until they are *d*.
8: 19 you today that you will surely be *d*.
8: 20 Like the nations the LORD *d*
8: 20 so you will be *d* for not obeying
12: 30 after they have been *d* before you,
19: 1 your God has *d* the nations whose
28: 20 until you are *d* and come
28: 21 with diseases until he has *d* you
28: 45 and overtake you until you are *d*,
28: 48 on your neck until he has *d* you.
28: 51 crops of your land until you are *d*.
28: 61 Book of the Law until you are *d*.
30: 18 day that you will certainly be *d*.
31: 4 whom he *d* along with their land.
31: 17 face from them, and they will be *d*.
Jos 2: 10 Jordan, whom you completely *d*.
6: 21 *d* with the sword every living thing

Jos 7: 15 with the devoted things shall be *d*
8: 26 until he had *d* all who lived in Ai.
10: 1 had taken Ai and totally *d* it,
10: 20 the Israelites *d* them completely
10: 28 and totally *d* everyone in it.
10: 35 and totally *d* everyone in it,
10: 37 they totally *d* it and everyone in it.
10: 39 Everyone in it they totally *d*.
10: 40 He totally *d* all who breathed,
11: 11 They totally *d* them, not sparing
11: 12 He totally *d* them, as Moses
11: 14 until they completely *d* them,
11: 21 Joshua totally *d* them and their
11: 21 and *d* the Anakites from the hill
23: 15 until he has *d* you from this good
24: 8 I *d* them from before you,
Jdg 1: 17 and they totally *d* the city.
4: 24 Canaanite king, until they *d* him.
9: 45 he *d* the city and scattered salt
21: 16 "With the women of Benjamin *d*,
1Sa 15: 8 and all his people he totally *d*
15: 9 despised and weak they totally *d*.
15: 15 God, but we totally *d* the rest."
15: 20 I completely *d* the Amalekites
27: 1 of these days I will be *d* by the hand
30: 3 they found it *d* by fire and their
2Sa 11: 1 They *d* the Ammonites
14: 11 so that my son will not be *d*."
21: 5 "As for the man who *d* us
22: 38 I did not turn back till they were *d*.
22: 41 and I *d* my foes.
1Ki 11: 16 until they had *d* all the men
11: 24 of rebels when David *d* the forces
15: 29 that breathed, but *d* them all,
16: 7 and also because he *d* it.
16: 12 Zimri *d* the whole family of Baasha
22: 11 the Arameans until they are *d*.' "
2Ki 3: 25 They *d* the towns, and each man
10: 17 there of Ahab's family; he *d* them,
10: 28 So Jehu *d* Baal worship in Israel.
13: 7 for the king of Aram had *d* the rest
13: 19 Aram and completely *d* it.
19: 12 the gods of the nations that were *d*
19: 18 gods into the fire and *d* them,
21: 3 places his father Hezekiah had *d*;
21: 9 than the nations the LORD had *d*
1Ch 4: 41 were there and completely *d* them,
5: 25 whom God had *d* before them.
2Ch 8: 8 whom the Israelites had not *d*—
12: 12 from him, and he was not totally *d*.
14: 14 They *d* all the villages
18: 10 the Arameans until they are *d*.' "
31: 1 After they had *d* all of them,
31: 1 They *d* the high places
32: 14 that my fathers *d* has been able
33: 9 than the nations the LORD had *d*
36: 19 and *d* everything of value there.
Ezr 4: 15 That is why this city was *d*.
5: 12 who *d* this temple and deported
Ne 2: 3 and its gates have been *d* by fire?"
2: 13 its gates, which had been *d* by fire.
Est 9: 6 the Jews killed and *d* five hundred
Job 4: 7 Where were the upright ever *d*?
4: 9 At the breath of God they are *d*;
19: 26 And after my skin has been *d*,
22: 20 'Surely our foes are *d*,
Ps 2: 12 and you be *d* in your way,
9: 5 the nations and *d* the wicked;
11: 3 When the foundations are being *d*,
18: 37 I did not turn back till they were *d*.
18: 40 and I *d* my foes.
37: 38 But all sinners will be *d*;
48: 7 You *d* them like ships of Tarshish
63: 9 They who seek my life will be *d*;
73: 19 How suddenly are they *d*,
78: 47 He *d* their vines with hail
79: 7 and *d* his homeland.
88: 16 your terrors have *d* me.
92: 7 they will be forever *d*.
105: 16 and *d* all their supplies of food;
Pr 6: 15 he will suddenly be *d*—
11: 3 the unfaithful are *d*
11: 11 by the mouth of the wicked it is *d*.
14: 11 The house of the wicked will be *d*,
21: 28 listens to him will be *d* forever.
22: 8 and the rod of his fury will be *d*.
29: 1 will suddenly be *d*—
Isa 5: 5 and it will be *d*;
14: 20 for you have *d* your land
15: 1 *d* in a night!
15: 1 *d* in a night!
23: 1 For Tyre is *d*
23: 11 that her fortresses be *d*.
23: 14 your fortress is *d*!
33: 1 you who have not been *d*!
33: 1 you will be *d*;
34: 5 the people I have totally *d*.
37: 12 the gods of the nations that were *d*
37: 19 gods into the fire and *d* them,
48: 19 nor *d* from before me."
55: 13 which will not be *d*."
Jer 4: 20 In an instant my tents are *d*,
9: 16 with the sword until I have *d* them
10: 20 My tent is *d*;
10: 25 and *d* his homeland.
18: 7 and *d*, and if that nation I warned
24: 10 against them until they are *d*
44: 27 and famine until they are all *d*.
48: 8 and the plateau *d*,
48: 15 Moab will be *d* and her towns
48: 20 that Moab is *d*.
48: 42 Moab will be *d* as a nation
48: 46 The people of Chemosh are *d*;
49: 3 "Wail, O Heshbon, for Ai is *d*!
51: 6 Do not be *d* because of her sins.
La 2: 5 and *d* her strongholds.
2: 6 he has *d* his place of meeting.
2: 9 their bars he has broken and *d*.
2: 11 because my people are *d*,
2: 22 my enemy has *d*."
3: 48 because my people are *d*.
4: 10 food when my people were *d*.
Eze 13: 14 When it falls, you will be *d* in it;
26: 17 How you are *d*, O city of renown,
36: 35 desolate and *d*, are now fortified
36: 36 the LORD have rebuilt what was *d*
43: 8 So I *d* them in my anger.
Da 2: 44 up a kingdom that will never be *d*,
6: 26 his kingdom will not be *d*,
7: 11 and its body *d* and thrown
7: 14 kingdom is one that will never be *d*.
7: 26 away and completely *d* forever.
8: 25 Yet he will be *d*, but not
11: 20 he will be *d*, yet not in anger
11: 22 a prince of the covenant will be *d*.
Hos 4: 6 my people are *d* from lack
10: 8 of wickedness will be *d*—
10: 15 king of Israel will be completely *d*.
Joel 1: 10 the grain is *d*,
1: 11 because the harvest of the field is *d*.
Am 2: 9 I *d* his fruit above
2: 9 "I *d* the Amorite before them,
3: 15 adorned with ivory will be *d*
7: 9 "The high places of Isaac will be *d*
Ob : 10 you will be *d* forever.
Jnh 3: 4 more days and Nineveh will be *d*."
Mic 5: 9 and all your foes will be *d*.
Na 1: 15 they will be completely *d*.
Hab 2: 8 you have *d* lands and cities
2: 17 you have *d* lands and cities
Zep 3: 6 Their cities are *d*;
Zec 11: 3 their rich pastures are *d*!
14: 11 inhabited; never again will it be *d*.
Mal 3: 6 O descendants of Jacob, are not *d*.
Mt 22: 7 his army and *d* those murderers
Lk 17: 27 Then the flood came and *d* them all
17: 29 down from heaven and *d* them all.
Ac 27: 22 will be lost; only the ship will be *d*.
1Co 5: 5 so that the sinful nature may be *d*
8: 11 for whom Christ died, is *d*
15: 24 Father after he has *d* all dominion,
15: 26 The last enemy to be *d* is death.
2Co 4: 9 abandoned; struck down, but not *d*.
5: 1 if the earthly tent we live in is *d*,
Gal 2: 18 not! If I rebuild what I *d*,
5: 15 or you will be *d* by each other.
Eph 2: 14 the two one and has *d* the barrier,
Php 1: 28 a sign to them that they will be *d*,
2Ti 1: 10 who has *d* death and has brought
Heb 10: 39 of those who shrink back and are *d*,
Jas 1: 11 its blossom falls and its beauty is *d*.
2Pe 2: 12 born only to be caught and *d*,
3: 6 of that time was deluged and *d*.
3: 10 the elements will be *d* by fire,
3: 11 Since everything will be *d*
Jude : 5 later *d* those who did not believe.
Jude : 11 have been *d* in Korah's rebellion.
Rev 8: 9 and a third of the ships were *d*.

DESTROYER (DESTROY)

Ex 12: 23 and he will not permit the *d*
Isa 16: 4 be their shelter from the *d*."
33: 1 Woe to you, O *d*,
54: 16 And it is I who have created the *d*
Jer 4: 7 a *d* of nations has set out.
6: 26 for suddenly the *d*
15: 8 At midday I will bring a *d*
48: 8 The *d* will come against every town
48: 32 The *d* has fallen
51: 1 "See, I will stir up the spirit of a *d*
51: 56 A *d* will come against Babylon;
Heb 11: 28 so that the *d* of the firstborn would

DESTROYERS (DESTROY)

Jer 12: 12 *d* will swarm,
15: 3 kinds of *d* against them,"
22: 7 I will send *d* against you,
51: 48 *d* will attack her,"
51: 53 I will send *d* against her,"
Na 2: 2 though *d* have laid them waste

DESTROYING (DESTROY)

Dt 3: 6 *d* every city—men, women
1Sa 6: 5 of the rats that are *d* the country,
2Ki 19: 11 the countries, *d* them completely.
1Ch 21: 15 to the angel who was *d* the people,
Est 9: 5 with the sword, killing and *d* them,
Job 30: 13 they succeed in *d* me—
Ps 52: 7 and grew strong by *d* others!"
78: 49 a band of *d* angels.
106: 23 him to keep his wrath from *d* them.
Isa 33: 1 When you stop *d*,
37: 11 the countries, *d* them completely.
Jer 13: 14 to keep me from *d* them.' "
23: 1 "Woe to the shepherds who are *d*
25: 36 for the LORD is *d* their pasture.
51: 25 "I am against you, O *d* mountain,
La 2: 8 did not withhold his hand from *d*.
Hab 1: 17 *d* nations without mercy?
Lk 9: 39 ever leaves him and is *d* him.
1Co 10: 10 and were killed by the *d* angel.
Rev 11: 18 for *d* those who destroy the earth."

DESTROYS (DESTROY)

Ex 21: 26 or maidservant in the eye and *d* it,
Job 9: 22 'He *d* both the blameless
12: 23 makes nations great, and *d* them;
Ps 91: 6 nor the plague that *d* at midday.
Pr 6: 32 whoever does so *d* himself.
11: 9 mouth the godless *d* his neighbor,
18: 9 is brother to one who *d*.
28: 24 he is partner to him who *d*.
Ecc 9: 18 but one sinner *d* much good.
Jer 48: 18 for he who *d* Moab
Zep 2: 11 when he *d* all the gods of the land.
Lk 12: 33 comes near and no moth *d*.
1Co 3: 17 If anyone *d* God's temple,

DESTRUCTION (DESTROY)

Lev 27: 29 devoted to *d* may be ransomed;
Nu 32: 15 and you will be the cause of their *d*
Dt 7: 10 him he will repay to their face by *d*;
7: 26 and detest it, for it is set apart for *d*.
7: 26 like it, will be set apart for *d*.
29: 23 It will be like the *d* of Sodom
30: 15 and prosperity, death and *d*.
Jos 6: 18 the camp of Israel liable to *d*
6: 18 will not bring about your own *d*
7: 12 among you is devoted to *d*.
7: 12 they have been made liable to *d*.
2Sa 14: 11 of blood from adding to the *d*,
22: 5 the torrents of *d* overwhelmed me.
1Ki 13: 34 to its *d* from the face of the earth.
Est 4: 7 treasury for the *d* of the Jews.
7: 4 and my people have been sold for *d*
8: 6 bear to see the *d* of my family?"
9: 2 to attack those seeking their *d*.
9: 24 the lot) for their ruin and *d*.
Job 5: 21 and need not fear when *d* comes.
5: 22 You will laugh at *d* and famine
21: 20 Let his own eyes see his *d*;
26: 6 *D* lies uncovered.
28: 22 *D* and Death say,
31: 12 It is a fire that burns to *D*;

Job 31: 23 For I dreaded *d* from God,
Ps 5: 9 their heart is filled with *d*.
18: 4 the torrents of *d* overwhelmed me.
30: 9 "What gain is there in my *d*,
52: 2 Your tongue plots *d*;
74: 3 all this *d* the enemy has brought
88: 11 your faithfulness in *D*?
137: 8 of Babylon, doomed to *d*,
Pr 15: 11 and *D* lie open before the LORD—
16: 18 Pride goes before *d*,
17: 19 he who builds a high gate invites *d*.
24: 22 for those two will send sudden *d*
27: 20 Death and *D* are never satisfied,
Isa 10: 22 *D* has been decreed,
10: 23 the *d* decreed upon the whole land.
10: 25 my wrath will be directed to their *d*
13: 6 come like *d* from the Almighty
14: 23 her with the broom of *d*,"
15: 5 they lament their *d*.
16: 4 and *d* will cease;
19: 18 of them will be called the City of *D*.
22: 4 me over the *d* of my people."
28: 22 of the *d* decreed against the whole
30: 28 shakes the nations in the sieve of *d*;
38: 17 me from the pit of *d*;
43: 28 and I will consign Jacob to *d*
51: 13 who is bent on *d*?
51: 19 ruin and *d*, famine and sword—
59: 7 ruin and *d* mark their ways.
60: 18 nor ruin or *d* within your borders,
Jer 4: 6 even terrible *d*."
6: 1 even terrible *d*.
6: 7 Violence and *d* resound in her;
15: 7 I will bring bereavement and *d*
17: 18 destroy them with double *d*.
20: 8 proclaiming violence and *d*.
48: 3 cries of great havoc and *d*.
48: 5 cries over the *d* are heard.
50: 22 the noise of great *d*!
51: 54 the sound of great *d*
La 1: 7 and laughed at her *d*.
3: 47 ruin and *d*."
Eze 21: 31 men skilled in *d*.
32: 9 peoples when I bring about your *d*
Hos 7: 13 *D* to them,
8: 4 themselves to their own *d*.
9: 6 Even if they escape from *d*,
13: 14 Where, O grave, is your *d*?
Joel 1: 15 come like *d* from the Almighty.
Am 5: 9 he flashes *d* on the stronghold
Ob : 12 Judah in the day of their *d*,
Jnh 3: 10 upon them the *d* he had threatened
Hab 1: 3 *D* and violence are before me;
2: 17 your *d* of animals will terrify you.
Mt 7: 13 broad is the road that leads to *d*,
Lk 6: 49 it collapsed and its *d* was complete
Jn 17: 12 except the one doomed to *d*
Ro 9: 22 of his wrath—prepared for *d*?
Gal 6: 8 from that nature will reap *d*;
Php 3: 19 Their destiny is *d*, their god is their
1Th 5: 3 *d* will come on them suddenly,
2Th 1: 9 punished with everlasting *d*
2: 3 is revealed, the man doomed to *d*.
1Ti 6: 9 that plunge men into ruin and *d*.
2Pe 2: 1 bringing swift *d* on themselves.
2: 3 and their *d* has not been sleeping.
3: 7 of judgment and *d* of ungodly men.
3: 12 That day will bring about the *d*
3: 16 other Scriptures, to their own *d*.
Rev 17: 8 out of the Abyss and go to his *d*.
17: 11 to the seven and is going to his *d*.

DESTRUCTIVE (DESTROY)

Ex 12: 13 No *d* plague will touch you
Lev 13: 51 it is a *d* mildew; the article is
13: 52 the mildew is *d*; the article must be
14: 44 it is a *d* mildew; the house is
Ps 55: 11 *D* forces are at work in the city;
Isa 28: 2 Like a hailstorm and a *d* wind,
Eze 5: 16 you with my deadly and *d* arrows
13: 13 torrents of rain will fall with *d* fury.
2Pe 2: 1 will secretly introduce *d* heresies,

DETACHMENT (DETACHMENTS)

1Sa 13: 23 Now a *d* of Philistines had gone out
Jn 18: 3 guiding a *d* of soldiers
18: 12 *d* of soldiers with its commander
Ac 23: 23 "Get ready a *d* of two hundred

DETACHMENTS (DETACHMENT)

1Sa 13: 17 from the Philistine camp in three *d*.

DETAIL (DETAILED DETAILS)

Ac 21: 19 reported in *d* what God had done
Col 2: 18 into great *d* about what he has seen
Heb 9: 5 discuss these things in *d* now.

DETAILED (DETAIL)

2Ki 16: 10 with *d* plans for its construction.

DETAILS (DETAIL)

1Ki 6: 38 finished in all its *d* according
1Ch 28: 19 in all the *d* of the plan."
29: 30 together with the *d* of his reign

DETAIN (DETAINED)

Ge 24: 56 But he said to them, "Do not *d* me,
Jdg 13: 16 replied, "Even though you *d* me,

DETAINED (DETAIN)

1Sa 21: 7 *d* before the LORD; he was Doeg
Da 10: 13 because I was *d* there with the king

DETECT

Job 39: 29 his eyes *d* it from afar.
Ps 36: 2 too much to *d* or hate his sin.
Ob : 7 but you will not *d* it.

DETER

Mt 3: 14 But John tried to *d* him, saying,

DETERMINE (DETERMINED DETERMINES)

Ex 12: 4 You are to *d* the amount
22: 8 appear before the judges to *d*
Lev 14: 57 to *d* when something is clean
25: 27 he is to *d* the value for the years
27: 18 priest will *d* the value according
27: 23 the priest will *d* its value up
Ne 10: 34 have cast lots to *d* when each
Da 11: 17 He will *d* to come with the might

DETERMINED (DETERMINE)

Jos 17: 12 for the Canaanites were *d* to live
Jdg 1: 27 for the Canaanites were *d* to live
1: 35 And the Amorites were *d*
Ru 1: 18 Naomi realized that Ruth was *d*
1Sa 20: 7 you can be sure that he is *d*
20: 9 least inkling that my father was *d*
2Sa 17: 14 For the LORD had *d*
1Ki 7: 47 the weight of the bronze was not *d*.
20: 42 set free a man I had *d* should die.
2Ki 12: 11 When the amount had been *d*,
1Ch 12: 38 to Hebron fully *d* to make David
2Ch 4: 18 the weight of the bronze was not *d*.
25: 16 "I know that God has *d*
Job 14: 5 Man's days are *d*;
Ecc 7: 23 "I am *d* to be wise"—
Isa 14: 26 This is the plan *d* for the whole
Jer 21: 10 I have *d* to do this city harm
42: 15 'If you are *d* to go to Egypt
42: 17 all who are *d* to go to Egypt
44: 11 I am *d* to bring disaster on you
44: 12 of Judah who were *d* to go to Egypt
La 2: 8 The LORD *d* to tear down
Da 6: 14 he was *d* to rescue Daniel
11: 36 for what has been *d* must take place
Hos 11: 7 My people are *d* to turn from me.
Hab 2: 13 Has not the LORD Almighty *d*
Zec 1: 6 practices deserve, just as he *d* to do
8: 14 I had *d* to bring disaster upon you
8: 15 "so now I have *d* to do good again
Jn 8: 40 As it is, you are *d* to kill me,
Ac 5: 28 and are *d* to make us guilty
17: 26 and he *d* the times set for them
1Co 15: 38 But God gives it a body as he has *d*,

DETERMINES (DETERMINE)

Ps 147: 4 He *d* the number of the stars
Pr 16: 9 but the LORD *d* his steps.
1Co 12: 11 them to each one, just as he *d*.

DETEST (DETESTABLE DETESTED DETESTS)

Lev 11: 10 in the water—you are to *d*.
11: 11 And since you are to *d* them,
11: 11 and you must *d* their carcasses.
11: 13 " 'These are the birds you are to *d*
11: 23 that have four legs you are to *d*.
Nu 21: 5 And we *d* this miserable food!"
Dt 7: 26 and *d* it, for it is set apart
Job 9: 31 even my clothes would *d* me.
19: 19 All my intimate friends *d* me;
30: 10 They *d* me and keep their distance;
Pr 8: 7 for my lips *d* wickedness.
13: 19 but fools *d* turning from evil.
16: 12 Kings *d* wrongdoing,
24: 9 and men *d* a mocker.
29: 27 The righteous *d* the dishonest;
29: 27 the wicked *d* the upright.
Am 6: 8 and *d* his fortresses;

DETESTABLE (DETEST)

Ge 43: 32 for that is *d* to Egyptians.
46: 34 for all shepherds are *d*
Ex 8: 26 And if we offer sacrifices that are *d*
8: 26 the LORD our God would be *d*
Lev 7: 21 or any unclean, *d* thing—
11: 12 and scales is to be *d* to you.
11: 13 and not eat because they are *d*:
11: 20 walk on all fours are to be *d* to you.
11: 41 about on the ground is *d*;
11: 42 on all fours or on many feet; it is *d*.
18: 22 as one lies with a woman; that is *d*.
18: 26 must not do any of these *d* things,
18: 29 any of these *d* things—
18: 30 any of the *d* customs that were
20: 13 both of them have done what is *d*.
Dt 7: 25 for it is *d* to the LORD your God.
7: 26 Do not bring a *d* thing
12: 31 kinds of *d* things the LORD hates.
13: 14 proved that this *d* thing has been
14: 3 Do not eat any *d* thing.
17: 1 for that would be *d* to him.
17: 4 proved that this *d* thing has been
18: 9 learn to imitate the *d* ways
18: 12 Anyone who does these things is *d*
18: 12 of these *d* practices the LORD
20: 18 to follow all the *d* things they do
24: 4 That would be *d* in the eyes
27: 15 a thing *d* to the LORD, the work
29: 17 saw among them their *d* images
32: 16 and angered him with their *d* idols.
1Ki 11: 5 the *d* god of the Ammonites.
11: 7 and for Molech the *d* god
11: 7 for Chemosh the *d* god of Moab,
14: 24 engaged in all the *d* practices
2Ki 16: 3 following the *d* ways
21: 2 following the *d* practices
21: 11 Judah has committed these *d* sins.
23: 13 for Molech the *d* god of the people
23: 24 all the other *d* things seen in Judah
2Ch 15: 8 He removed the *d* idols
28: 3 following the *d* ways
33: 2 following the *d* practices
34: 33 Josiah removed all the *d* idols
36: 8 the *d* things he did and all that was
36: 14 following all the *d* practices
Ezr 9: 1 peoples with their *d* practices,
9: 11 By their *d* practices they have filled
9: 14 who commit such *d* practices?
Pr 6: 16 seven that are *d* to him:
21: 27 The sacrifice of the wicked is *d*—
28: 9 even his prayers are *d*.
Isa 1: 13 Your incense is *d* to me.
41: 24 he who chooses you is *d*.
44: 19 Shall I make a *d* thing
Jer 2: 7 and made my inheritance *d*.
4: 1 "If you put your *d* idols out
7: 10 safe to do all these *d* things?
7: 30 They have set up their *d* idols
13: 27 I have seen your *d* acts
16: 18 inheritance with their *d* idols."
32: 35 that they should do such a *d* thing
44: 4 'Do not do this *d* thing that I hate!'
44: 22 actions and the *d* things you did,
Eze 5: 9 Because of all your *d* idols,
5: 11 your vile images and *d* practices,
6: 9 and for all their *d* practices.
6: 11 *d* practices of the house of Israel,
7: 3 repay you for all your *d* practices.
7: 4 and the *d* practices among you.
7: 8 repay you for all your *d* practices.
7: 9 and the *d* practices among you.
7: 20 and used it to make their *d* idols

Eze 8: 6 see things that are even more *d*."
8: 6 the utterly *d* things the house
8: 9 and *d* things they are doing here."
8: 10 and *d* animals and all the idols
8: 13 doing things that are even more *d*."
8: 15 will see things that are even more *d*
8: 17 to do the *d* things they are doing
9: 4 over all the *d* things that are done
11: 18 all its vile images and *d* idols.
11: 21 to their vile images and *d* idols,
12: 16 acknowledge all their *d* practices.
14: 6 and renounce all your *d* practices!
16: 2 Jerusalem with her *d* practices
16: 22 In all your *d* practices
16: 36 and because of all your *d* idols,
16: 43 to all your other *d* practices?
16: 47 and copied their *d* practices,
16: 50 and did *d* things before me.
16: 51 You have done more *d* things
16: 58 lewdness and your *d* practices,
18: 12 He does *d* things.
18: 13 he has done all these *d* things,
18: 24 does the same *d* things the wicked
20: 4 confront them with the *d* practices
22: 2 her with all her *d* practices
22: 11 you one man commits a *d* offense
23: 36 them with their *d* practices,
33: 26 on your sword, you do *d* things,
33: 29 of all the *d* things they have done.'
36: 31 for your sins and *d* practices.
43: 8 name by their *d* practices.
44: 6 Enough of your *d* practices,
44: 7 to all your other *d* practices,
44: 13 the shame of their *d* practices.
Mal 2: 11 A *d* thing has been committed
Lk 16: 15 among men is *d* in God's sight.
Tit 1: 16 They are *d*, disobedient
1Pe 4: 3 orgies, carousing and *d* idolatry.
Rev 18: 2 haunt for every unclean and *d* bird.

DETESTED (DETEST)
Zec 11: 8 The flock *d* me, and I grew weary

DETESTS (DETEST)
Dt 22: 5 LORD your God *d* anyone who
23: 18 the LORD your God *d* them both.
25: 16 LORD your God *d* anyone who
Pr 3: 32 for the LORD *d* a perverse man
11: 20 The LORD *d* men
12: 22 The LORD *d* lying lips,
15: 8 The LORD *d* the sacrifice
15: 9 The LORD *d* the way
15: 26 The LORD *d* the thoughts
16: 5 The LORD *d* all the proud of heart
17: 15 the LORD *d* them both.
20: 10 the LORD *d* them both.
20: 23 The LORD *d* differing weights,

DETHRONED
2Ch 36: 3 king of Egypt *d* him in Jerusalem

DETRIMENT
Ezr 4: 22 to the *d* of the royal interests?

DEUEL
Nu 1: 14 Eliasaph son of *D*; from Naphtali,
2: 14 people of Gad is Eliasaph son of *D*.
7: 42 On the sixth day Eliasaph son of *D*,
7: 47 the offering of Eliasaph son of *D*.
10: 20 and Eliasaph son of *D* was

DEVASTATE (DEVASTATED DEVASTATION)
Jos 22: 33 them to *d* the country where
Job 12: 15 he lets them loose, they *d* the land.
Isa 24: 1 and *d* it;
Jer 19: 8 I will *d* this city and make it
51: 2 to winnow her and to *d* her land;
Hos 11: 9 nor *d* Ephraim again.

DEVASTATED (DEVASTATE)
Jdg 11: 33 He *d* twenty towns from Aroer
Job 16: 7 you have *d* my entire household.
Ps 78: 45 and frogs that *d* them.
Isa 61: 4 and restore the places long *d*;
61: 4 that have been *d* for generations.
Jer 4: 30 What are you doing, O *d* one?
Eze 6: 6 your altars will be laid waste and *d*,
Eze 19: 7 and *d* their towns.
29: 12 of Egypt desolate among *d* lands,
Hos 10: 14 as Shalman *d* Beth Arbel
10: 14 so that all your fortresses will be *d*

DEVASTATION (DEVASTATE)
1Sa 5: 6 he brought *d* upon them
Da 8: 24 He will cause astounding *d*

DEVELOPED (DEVELOPS)
Eze 16: 7 *d* and became the most beautiful
Jn 3: 25 An argument *d* between some

DEVELOPS (DEVELOPED)
Jas 1: 3 of your faith *d* perseverance.

DEVIATE
2Ch 8: 15 They did not *d* from the king's

DEVICES (DEVISE)
Ps 81: 12 to follow their own *d*.

DEVIL (DEVIL'S)
Mt 4: 1 the desert to be tempted by the *d*.
4: 5 the *d* took him to the holy city
4: 8 *d* took him to a very high mountain
4: 11 the *d* left him, and angels came
13: 39 the enemy who sows them is the *d*.
25: 41 the eternal fire prepared for the *d*
Lk 4: 2 forty days he was tempted by the *d*.
4: 3 *d* said to him, "If you are the Son
4: 5 The *d* led him up to a high place
4: 9 The *d* led him to Jerusalem
4: 13 When the *d* had finished all this
8: 12 then the *d* comes and takes away
Jn 6: 70 of you is a *d*!" (He meant Judas,
8: 44 You belong to your father, the *d*,
13: 2 the *d* had already prompted Judas
Ac 10: 38 were under the power of the *d*,
13: 10 "You are a child of the *d*
Eph 4: 27 and do not give the *d* a foothold.
1Ti 3: 6 under the same judgment as the *d*.
2Ti 2: 26 and escape from the trap of the *d*,
Heb 2: 14 the *d*— and free those who all their
Jas 3: 15 but is earthly, unspiritual, of the *d*.
4: 7 Resist the *d*, and he will flee
1Pe 5: 8 Your enemy the *d* prowls
1Jn 3: 8 because the *d* has been sinning
3: 8 who does what is sinful is of the *d*,
3: 10 and who the children of the *d* are:
Jude : 9 with the *d* about the body of Moses
Rev 2: 10 the *d* will put some of you in prison
12: 9 that ancient serpent called the *d*
12: 12 the *d* has gone down to you!
20: 2 that ancient serpent, who is the *d*,
20: 10 And the *d*, who deceived them,

DEVIL'S (DEVIL)
Eph 6: 11 stand against the *d* schemes.
1Ti 3: 7 into disgrace and into the *d* trap.
1Jn 3: 8 was to destroy the *d* work.

DEVIOUS
Pr 2: 15 and who are *d* in their ways.
14: 2 he whose ways are *d* despises him.
21: 8 The way of the guilty is *d*,

DEVISE (DEVICES DEVISED DEVISES DEVISING)
Ps 21: 11 and *d* wicked schemes, they cannot
35: 20 but *d* false accusations
58: 2 No, in your heart you *d* injustice,
119:150 Those who *d* wicked schemes are
140: 2 who *d* evil plans in their hearts
Isa 8: 10 *D* your strategy, but it will be
Eze 38: 10 and you will *d* an evil scheme.

DEVISED (DEVISE)
2Sa 14: 13 "Why then have you *d* a thing like
Est 8: 3 which he had *d* against the Jews.
8: 5 *d* and wrote to destroy the Jews
9: 25 that the evil scheme Haman had *d*
Ps 64: 6 "We have *d* a perfect plan!"
Jer 49: 30 he has *d* a plan against you.
Da 11: 25 because of the plots *d* against him.
Mt 28: 12 met with the elders and *d* a plan,

DEVISES (DEVISE)
2Sa 14: 14 he *d* ways so that a banished
Ps 10: 2 who are caught in the schemes he *d*
Pr 6: 18 a heart that *d* wicked schemes,

DEVISING (DEVISE)
Jer 18: 11 for you and *d* a plan against you.

DEVOTE (DEVOTED DEVOTES DEVOTING DEVOTION DEVOUT)
1Ch 22: 19 Now *d* your heart and soul
2Ch 31: 4 Levites so they could *d* themselves
Job 11: 13 "Yet if you *d* your heart to him
Jer 30: 21 for who is he who will *d* himself
Mic 4: 13 You will *d* their ill-gotten gains
1Co 7: 5 so that you may *d* yourselves
Col 4: 2 *D* yourselves to prayer, being
1Ti 1: 4 nor to *d* themselves to myths
4: 13 *d* yourself to the public reading
Tit 3: 8 may be careful to *d* themselves
3: 14 people must learn to *d* themselves

DEVOTED (DEVOTE)
Lev 27: 21 like a field *d* to the LORD;
27: 28 everything so *d* is most holy
27: 29 " 'No person *d* to destruction may
Nu 18: 14 "Everything in Israel that is *d*
Jos 6: 17 is in it are to be *d* to the LORD.
6: 18 But keep away from the *d* things,
6: 21 They *d* the city to the LORD
7: 1 in regard to the *d* things;
7: 11 have taken some of the *d* things;
7: 12 among you is *d* to destruction.
7: 13 says: That which is *d* is among you,
7: 15 with the *d* things shall be destroyed
22: 20 unfaithfully regarding the *d* things,
1Sa 15: 21 the best of what was *d* to God,
1Ki 11: 4 and his heart was not fully *d*
15: 3 his heart was not fully *d*
1Ch 2: 7 the ban on taking *d* things.
2Ch 17: 6 His heart was *d* to the ways
Ezr 7: 10 For Ezra had *d* himself to the study
Ne 5: 16 I *d* myself to the work on this wall.
Ps 86: 2 Guard my life, for I am *d* to you.
Ecc 1: 13 I *d* myself to study and to explore
Eze 11: 21 But as for those whose hearts are *d*
20: 16 For their hearts were *d*
44: 29 and everything in Israel *d*
Mt 6: 24 or he will be *d* to the one
15: 5 from me is a gift *d* to God,'
Mk 7: 11 from me is Corban' (that is, a gift *d*
Lk 16: 13 or he will be *d* to the one
Ac 2: 42 They *d* themselves
18: 5 Paul *d* himself exclusively
Ro 12: 10 Be *d* to one another
1Co 7: 34 Her aim is to be *d* to the Lord
16: 15 and they have *d* themselves
2Co 7: 12 for yourselves how *d* to us you are.

DEVOTES (DEVOTE)
Lev 27: 28 nothing that a man owns and *d*

DEVOTING (DEVOTE)
1Ti 5: 10 *d* herself to all kinds of good deeds.

DEVOTION (DEVOTE)
2Ki 20: 3 and with wholehearted *d* and have
1Ch 28: 9 and serve him with wholehearted *d*
29: 3 in my *d* to the temple
29: 19 son Solomon the wholehearted *d*
2Ch 32: 32 and his acts of *d* are written
35: 26 of Josiah's reign and his acts of *d*,
Job 6: 14 despairing man should have the *d*
15: 4 and hinder *d* to God.
Isa 38: 3 and with wholehearted *d* and have
Jer 2: 2 " 'I remember the *d* of your youth,
Eze 33: 31 With their mouths they express *d*,
1Co 7: 35 way in undivided *d* to the Lord.
2Co 11: 3 from your sincere and pure *d*

DEVOUR (DEVOURED DEVOURING DEVOURS)
Ex 10: 5 They will *d* what little you have left
10: 12 *d* everything growing in the fields,
Lev 26: 38 the land of your enemies will *d* you
Nu 24: 8 They *d* hostile nations
Dt 28: 38 little, because locusts will *d* it.
28: 51 They will *d* the young

Dt 32: 22 It will *d* the earth and its harvests
2Sa 2: 26 "Must the sword *d* forever?
1Ki 21: 23 'Dogs will *d* Jezebel by the wall
2Ki 9: 10 dogs will *d* her on the plot
9: 36 Jezreel dogs will *d* Jezebel's flesh.
2Ch 7: 13 or command locusts to *d* the land
Job 20: 21 Nothing is left for him to *d;*
20: 26 and *d* what is left in his tent.
Ps 14: 4 those who *d* my people
27: 2 me to *d* my flesh,
53: 4 those who *d* my people
Pr 30: 14 knives to *d* the poor from the earth,
Isa 9: 20 On the right they will *d,*
31: 8 not of mortals, will *d* them.
51: 8 the worm will *d* them like wool.
56: 9 and *d,* all you beasts of the forest!
Jer 5: 17 They will *d* your harvests and food,
5: 17 they will *d* your flocks and herds,
5: 17 *d* your sons and daughters;
5: 17 *d* your vines and fig trees.
8: 16 They have come to *d*
12: 9 bring them to *d.*
12: 12 for the sword of the LORD will *d*
15: 3 and the beasts of the earth to *d*
30: 16 But all who *d* you will be devoured
46: 10 The sword will *d* till it is satisfied,
50: 17 The first to *d* him
Eze 22: 25 they *d* people, take treasures
34: 28 nor will wild animals *d* them.
35: 12 have been given over to us to *d.*"
36: 13 "You *d* men and deprive your
36: 14 therefore you will no longer *d* men
Da 7: 23 and will *d* the whole earth,
Hos 2: 12 and wild animals will *d* them
5: 7 will *d* them and their fields.
7: 7 they *d* their rulers.
13: 8 Like a lion I will *d* them;
Am 5: 6 it will *d,*
Na 2: 13 the sword will *d* your young lions.
3: 15 There the fire will *d* you;
Hab 1: 8 fly like a vulture swooping to *d;*
3: 14 gloating as though about to *d*
Zec 11: 1 so that fire may *d* your cedars!
Mk 12: 40 They *d* widows' houses
Lk 20: 47 They *d* widows' houses
1Pe 5: 8 lion looking for someone to *d.*
Rev 12: 4 so that he might *d* her child

DEVOURED (DEVOUR)

Ge 37: 20 say that a ferocious animal *d* him.
37: 33 Some ferocious animal has *d* him.
Ex 10: 15 They *d* all that was left
Nu 26: 10 died when the fire *d* the 250 men.
Job 31: 39 if I have *d* its yield
Ps 44: 11 You gave us up to be *d* like sheep
78: 45 He sent swarms of flies that *d* them
79: 7 for they have *d* Jacob
Isa 1: 20 you will be *d* by the sword."
9: 12 have *d* Israel with open mouth,
49: 19 those who *d* you will be far away.
Jer 2: 3 all who *d* her were held guilty,
2: 30 Your sword has *d* your prophets
10: 25 For they have *d* Jacob;
10: 25 they have *d* him completely
30: 16 But all who devour you will be *d;*
50: 7 Whoever found them *d* them;
51: 34 king of Babylon has *d* us,
Eze 7: 15 those in the city will be *d* by famine
19: 3 and he *d* men.
19: 6 and he *d* men.
33: 27 give to the wild animals to be *d,*
Da 7: 7 it crushed and *d* its victims
7: 19 beast that crushed and *d* its victims
Joel 1: 19 for fire has *d* the open pastures
1: 20 and fire has *d* the open pastures.
Am 4: 9 Locusts *d* your fig and olive trees,
7: 4 up the great deep and *d* the land.
Rev 20: 9 down from heaven and *d* them.

DEVOURING (DEVOUR)

Dt 9: 3 across ahead of you like a *d* fire.
Isa 29: 6 and tempest and flames of a *d* fire.
Mal 3: 11 pests from *d* your crops,
Gal 5: 15 keep on biting and *d* each other,

DEVOURS (DEVOUR)

Ge 49: 27 in the morning he *d* the prey,
Nu 13: 32 land we explored *d* those living
Nu 23: 24 that does not rest till he *d* his prey
Dt 32: 42 while my sword *d* flesh:
2Sa 11: 25 the sword *d* one as well as another.
Job 18: 13 death's firstborn *d* his limbs.
22: 20 and fire *d* their wealth.'
Ps 50: 3 a fire *d* before him,
Pr 21: 20 but a foolish man *d* all he has.
Jer 46: 14 for the sword *d* those around you.'
Joel 2: 3 Before them fire *d,*
Rev 11: 5 their mouths and *d* their enemies.

DEVOUT (DEVOTE)

1Ki 18: 3 (Obadiah was a *d* believer
Isa 57: 1 *d* men are taken away,
Lk 2: 25 Simeon, who was righteous and *d.*
Ac 10: 2 his family were *d* and God-fearing;
10: 7 one of his soldiers who was a *d* man
13: 43 and *d* converts to Judaism followed
22: 12 He was a *d* observer of the law

DEW

Ge 27: 28 May God give you of heaven's *d*
27: 39 away from the *d* of heaven above.
Ex 16: 13 a layer of *d* around the camp.
16: 14 When the *d* was gone, thin flakes
Nu 11: 9 When the *d* settled on the camp
Dt 32: 2 and my words descend like *d,*
33: 13 with the precious *d* from heaven
33: 28 where the heavens drop *d.*
Jdg 6: 37 If there is *d* only on the fleece
6: 38 the fleece and wrung out the *d*—
6: 39 and the ground covered with *d.*"
6: 40 all the ground was covered with *d.*
2Sa 1: 21 may you have neither *d* nor rain,
17: 12 as *d* settles on the ground.
1Ki 17: 1 there will be neither *d*
Job 29: 19 the *d* will lie all night
38: 28 Who fathers the drops of *d?*
Ps 110: 3 you will receive the *d* of your youth
133: 3 It is as if the *d* of Hermon
Pr 3: 20 and the clouds let drop the *d.*
19: 12 but his favor is like *d* on the grass.
SS 5: 2 My head is drenched with *d,*
Isa 18: 4 like a cloud of *d* in the heat
26: 19 Your *d* is like the *d* of the morning;
Da 4: 15 drenched with the *d* of heaven,
4: 23 drenched with the *d* of heaven;
4: 25 be drenched with the *d* of heaven.
4: 33 drenched with the *d* of heaven
5: 21 drenched with the *d* of heaven,
Hos 6: 4 like the early *d* that disappears.
13: 3 like the early *d* that disappears,
14: 5 I will be like the *d* to Israel;
Mic 5: 7 like *d* from the LORD,
Hag 1: 10 the heavens have withheld their *d*
Zec 8: 12 and the heavens will drop their *d.*

DIADEM

Ex 29: 6 attach the sacred *d* to the turban.
39: 30 They made the plate, the sacred *d,*
Lev 8: 9 the sacred *d,* on the front of it,
Isa 62: 3 a royal *d* in the hand of your God.

DIAMETER

1Ki 7: 32 The *d* of each wheel was a cubit

DIBLAH

Eze 6: 14 waste from the desert to *D*—

DIBLAIM

Hos 1: 3 he married Gomer daughter of *D,*

DIBON

Nu 21: 30 is destroyed all the way to *D.*
32: 3 "Ataroth, *D,* Jazer, Nimrah,
32: 34 The Gadites built up *D,* Ataroth,
Jos 13: 9 plateau of Medeba as far as *D,*
13: 17 including *D,* Bamoth Baal,
Ne 11: 25 in *D* and its settlements,
Isa 15: 2 *D* goes up to its temple,
Jer 48: 18 O inhabitants of the Daughter of *D*
48: 22 Jahzah and Mephaath, to *D,*

DIBON GAD

Nu 33: 45 They left Iyim and camped at *D.*
33: 46 They left *D* and camped

DIBRI

Lev 24: 11 the daughter of *D* the Danite.)

DICTATE (DICTATED DICTATING DICTATION)

Jer 36: 17 Did Jeremiah *d* it?" "Yes,"
Mic 7: 3 the powerful *d* what they desire—

DICTATED (DICTATE)

Jer 36: 4 and while Jeremiah *d* all the words
36: 6 of the LORD that you wrote as I *d.*
36: 18 "he *d* all these words to me,
36: 32 son of Neriah, and as Jeremiah *d,*

DICTATING (DICTATE)

Jer 45: 1 the words Jeremiah was then *d:*

DICTATION (DICTATE)

Jer 36: 27 had written at Jeremiah's *d,*

DIDYMUS

Jn 11: 16 Thomas (called *D*) said to the rest
20: 24 Now Thomas (called *D*), one
21: 2 Simon Peter, Thomas (called *D*),

DIE (DEAD DEADENED DEADLY DEATH DEATH'S DEATHLY DEATHS DIED DIES DYING)

Ge 2: 17 when you eat of it you will surely *d*
3: 3 you must not touch it, or you will *d*
3: 4 will not surely *d,*" the serpent said
19: 19 will overtake me, and I'll *d.*
20: 7 sure that you and all yours will *d.*"
21: 16 "I cannot watch the boy *d.*"
25: 32 "Look, I am about to *d,*" Esau said.
27: 4 give you my blessing before I *d.*"
27: 7 presence of the LORD before I *d.*'
30: 1 "Give me children, or I'll *d!*"
33: 13 just one day, all the animals will *d.*
38: 11 For he thought, "He may *d* too,
42: 2 so that we may live and not *d.*"
42: 20 verified and that you may not *d.*"
43: 8 our children may live and not *d.*
44: 9 he will *d;* and the rest
44: 22 if he leaves him, his father will *d.*'
44: 31 that the boy isn't there, he will *d.*
45: 28 I will go and see him before I *d.*"
46: 30 to Joseph, "Now I am ready to *d,*
47: 15 Why should we *d* before your eyes?
47: 19 seed so that we may live and not *d,*
47: 29 drew near for Israel to *d,*
48: 21 said to Joseph, "I am about to *d,*
50: 5 and said, "I am about to *d;*
50: 24 to his brothers, "I am about to *d.*
Ex 7: 18 The fish in the Nile will *d,*
9: 4 belonging to the Israelites will *d.*' "
9: 19 out in the field, and they will *d.*' "
10: 28 The day you see my face you will *d*
11: 5 Every firstborn son in Egypt will *d,*
12: 33 they said, "we will all *d!*"
14: 11 us to the desert to *d?*
14: 12 Egyptians than to *d* in the desert!"
17: 3 and our children and livestock *d*
20: 19 speak to us or we will *d.*"
21: 18 he does not *d* but is confined to bed
28: 35 so that he will not *d.*
28: 43 that they will not incur guilt and *d.*
30: 20 with water so that they will not *d.*
30: 21 and feet so that they will not *d.*
Lev 8: 35 so you will not *d;* for that is what I
10: 6 or you will *d* and the LORD will be
10: 7 the Tent of Meeting or you will *d,*
10: 9 the Tent of Meeting, or you will *d.*
15: 31 they will not *d* in their uncleanness
16: 2 or else he will *d,* because I appear
16: 13 so that he will not *d.*
20: 20 responsible; they will *d* childless.
21: 1 for any of his people who *d,*
22: 9 *d* for treating them with contempt.
Nu 4: 15 the holy things or they will *d.*
4: 19 and not *d* when they come
4: 20 even for a moment, or they will *d.*"
14: 35 in this desert; here they will *d.*"
15: 35 said to Moses, "The man must *d.*
16: 29 If these men *d* a natural death
17: 10 against me, so that they will not *d.*"
17: 12 said to Moses, "We will *d!*
17: 13 going to *d?*" The LORD said

Nu 17:13 the tabernacle of the LORD will *d*.
18: 3 or both they and you will *d*.
18:22 of their sin and will *d*.
18:32 of the Israelites, and you will not *d*
20: 4 and our livestock should *d* here?
20:26 to his people; he will *d* there.''
21: 5 out of Egypt to *d* in the desert?
23:10 Let me *d* the death of the righteous
26:11 of Korah, however, did not *d* out.
26:65 those Israelites they would surely *d*
35:12 accused of murder may not *d*
35:31 of a murderer, who deserves to *d*.
Dt 4:22 I will *d* in this land; I will not cross
5:25 But now, why should we *d?*
5:25 and we will *d* if we hear the voice
18:16 great fire anymore, or we will *d*.''
19:12 over to the avenger of blood to *d*.
20: 5 or he may *d* in battle and someone
20: 6 or he may *d* in battle and someone
20: 7 or he may *d* in battle and someone
22:22 with her and the woman must *d*.
22:25 the man who has done this shall *d*.
24: 7 or sells him, the kidnapper must *d*.
24:16 each is to *d* for his own sin.
31:27 much more will you rebel after I *d!*
32:50 that you have climbed you will *d*
33: 6 ''Let Reuben live and not *d*,
Jdg 6:23 You are not going to *d*.''
6:30 He must *d*, because he has broken
13:22 ''We are doomed to *d!*'' he said
15:18 Must I now *d* of thirst
16:30 ''Let me *d* with the Philistines!''
Ru 1:17 Where you *d* I will *d*, and there I
1Sa 2:33 and all your descendants will *d*
2:34 they will both *d* on the same day.
5:12 Those who did not *d* were afflicted
12:19 servants so that we will not *d*,
14:39 with my son Jonathan, he must *d*.''
14:43 And now must I *d?*'' Saul said,
14:44 if you do not *d*, Jonathan.''
14:45 said to Saul, ''Should Jonathan *d*—
20: 2 ''You are not going to *d!* Look,
20:31 for he must *d!*'' ''Why should he be
22:16 ''You will surely *d*, Ahimelech,
26:10 his time will come and he will *d*,
26:16 you and your men deserve to *d*,
2Sa 3:33 Abner have died as the lawless *d?*
11:15 so he will be struck down and *d*.''
12: 5 the man who did this deserves to *d*
12:13 You are not going to *d*.
12:14 the son born to you will *d*.''
14:14 cannot be recovered, so we must *d*.
18: 3 Even if half of us *d*, they won't care
19:23 said to Shimei, ''You shall not *d*.''
19:37 that I may *d* in my own town
1Ki 1:52 but if evil is found in him, he will *d*
2: 1 drew near for David to *d*,
2:26 deserve to *d*, but I will not put you
2:30 But he answered, ''No, I will *d* here
2:37 you can be sure you will *d;*
2:42 you can be sure you will *d'?*
13:31 he said to his sons, ''When I *d*,
14:11 feed on those who *d* in the country.
14:11 to Jeroboam who *d* in the city,
14:12 foot in your city, the boy will *d*.
16: 4 on those who *d* in the country.''
16: 4 to Baasha who *d* in the city,
17:12 that we may eat it—and *d*.''
17:20 by causing her son to *d?*''
19: 4 and prayed that he might *d*.
20:42 a man I had determined should *d*.
21:24 on those who *d* in the country.''
21:24 to Ahab who *d* in the city,
2Ki 1: 4 You will certainly *d!*'' ''
1: 6 You will certainly *d!*'' ' '' The king
1:16 You will certainly *d!*'' So he died,
7: 3 Why stay here until we *d?* If we say
7: 4 And if we stay here, we will *d*.
7: 4 the famine is there, and we will *d*.
7: 4 we live; if they kill us, then we *d*.''
8:10 to me that he will in fact *d*.''
14: 6 each is to *d* for his own sins.''
20: 1 you will *d;* you will not recover.''
2Ch 25: 4 each is to *d* for his own sins.''
32:11 to let you *d* of hunger and thirst.
Est 9:28 *d* out among their descendants.
Job 2: 9 Curse God and *d!*'' He replied,
3:11 and *d* as I came from the womb?
Job 4:21 so that they *d* without wisdom?'
12: 2 and wisdom will *d* with you!
13:19 If so, I will be silent and *d*.
14: 8 and its stump *d* in the soil,
27: 5 till I *d*, I will not deny my integrity.
29:18 I thought, 'I will *d* in my own house
34:20 They *d* in an instant, in the middle
36:12 and *d* without knowledge.
36:14 They *d* in their youth,
Ps 37: 2 green plants they will soon *d* away.
41: 5 When will he *d* and his name perish
49:10 For all can see that wise men *d;*
79:11 preserve those condemned to *d*.
82: 7 But you will *d* like mere men;
104: 29 they *d* and return to the dust.
105: 29 causing their fish to *d*.
118: 17 I will not *d* but live,
Pr 5:23 He will *d* for lack of discipline,
10:21 but fools *d* for lack of judgment.
15:10 he who hates correction will *d*.
19:16 is contemptuous of his ways will *d*.
23:13 with the rod, he will not *d*.
30: 7 do not refuse me before I *d:*
Ecc 2:16 the fool, the wise man too must *d!*
3: 2 a time to be born and a time to *d*,
7:17 why *d* before your time?
9: 5 For the living know that they will *d*
Isa 5:13 their men of rank will *d* of hunger
22: 2 nor did they *d* in battle.
22:13 ''for tomorrow we *d!*''
22:18 There you will *d*
38: 1 because you are going to *d;*
50: 2 and *d* of thirst.
51: 6 and its inhabitants *d* like flies.
51:14 they will not *d* in their dungeon,
59: 5 Whoever eats their eggs will *d*,
66:24 their worm will not *d*, nor will their
Jer 11:21 or you will *d* by our hands'—
11:22 Their young men will *d*
16: 4 ''They will *d* of deadly diseases.
16: 6 and low will *d* in this land.
20: 6 There you will *d* and be buried,
21: 6 and they will *d* of a terrible plague.
21: 9 in this city will *d* by the sword,
22:12 He will *d* in the place where they
22:26 born, and there you both will *d*.
26: 8 seized him and said, ''You must *d!*
27:13 and your people *d* by the sword,
28:16 This very year you are going to *d*,
31:30 everyone will *d* for his own sin;
34: 4 You will not *d* by the sword;
34: 5 by the sword; you will *d* peacefully.
37:20 the secretary, or I will *d* there.''
38: 2 in this city will *d* by the sword,
38:24 this conversation, or you may *d*.
38:26 to Jonathan's house to *d* there.' ''
42:16 into Egypt, and there you will *d*.
42:17 to settle there will *d* by the sword,
42:22 of this: You will *d* by the sword,
44:12 fall by the sword or *d* from famine.
44:12 they will *d* by sword or famine.
La 4: 9 off than those who *d* of famine;
Eze 3:18 that wicked man will *d* for his sin,
3:18 to a wicked man, 'You will surely *d*
3:19 he will *d* for his sin; but you will
3:20 block before him, he will *d*.
3:20 you did not warn him, he will *d*
5:12 of your people will *d* of the plague
6:12 He that is far away will *d*
6:12 and is spared will *d* of famine.
7:15 in the country will *d* by the sword,
12:13 will not see it, and there he will *d*.
17:16 the Sovereign LORD, he shall *d*
18: 4 soul who sins is the one who will *d*.
18:17 He will not *d* for his father's sin;
18:18 But his father will *d* for his own sin,
18:20 soul who sins is the one who will *d*.
18:21 he will surely live; he will not *d*.
18:24 sins he has committed, he will *d*.
18:26 he will *d* for it; because of the sin he
18:26 the sin he has committed he will *d*.
18:28 he will surely live; he will not *d*.
18:31 Why will you *d*, O house of Israel?
28: 8 and you will *d* a violent death
28:10 You will *d* the death
33: 8 'O wicked man, you will surely *d*,'
33: 8 that wicked man will *d* for his sin,
33: 9 he will *d* for his sin, but you will
Eze 33:11 Why will you *d*, O house of Israel?'
33:13 he will *d* for the evil he has done.
33:14 wicked man, 'You will surely *d*,'
33:15 he will surely live; he will not *d*.
33:18 and does evil, he will *d* for it.
33:27 and caves will *d* of a plague.
Am 6: 9 left in one house, they too will *d*.
7:11 '' 'Jeroboam will *d* by the sword,
7:17 and you yourself will *d*
9:10 will *d* by the sword,
Jnh 1:14 please do not let us *d*
4: 3 better for me to *d* than to live.''
4: 8 better for me to *d* than to live.''
4: 8 to *d*, and said, ''It would be better
4: 9 ''I am angry enough to *d*.''
Hab 1:12 my Holy One, we will not *d*.
Zec 11: 9 Let the dying *d*, and the perishing
13: 3 will say to him, 'You must *d*,
Mt 26:35 ''Even if I have to *d* with you,
26:52 ''for all who draw the sword will *d*
Mk 9:48 '' 'their worm does not *d*,
14:31 ''Even if I have to *d* with you,
Lk 2:26 the Holy Spirit that he would not *d*
7: 2 highly, was sick and about to *d*.
13:33 for surely no prophet can *d*
20:36 and they can no longer *d;*
Jn 6:50 which a man may eat and not *d*.
8:21 and you will *d* in your sin.
8:24 I told you that you would *d*
8:24 you will indeed *d* in your sins.''
11:16 also go, that we may *d* with him.''
11:26 and believes in me will never *d*.
11:50 better for you that one man *d*
11:51 he prophesied that Jesus would *d*
12:33 the kind of death he was going to *d*.
18:32 going to *d* would be fulfilled.
19: 7 according to that law he must *d*,
21:23 did not say that he would not *d;*
21:23 that this disciple would not *d*.
Ac 7:19 babies so that they would *d*.
21:13 also to *d* in Jerusalem for the name
25:11 death, I do not refuse to *d*.
Ro 5: 7 Very rarely will anyone *d*
5: 7 someone might possibly dare to *d*.
6: 9 he cannot *d* again; death no longer
8:13 to the sinful nature, you will *d;*
14: 8 and if we *d*, we *d* to the Lord.
14: 8 we live or *d*, we belong to the Lord.
1Co 4: 9 like men condemned to *d*
9:15 I would rather *d* than have anyone
15:22 in Adam all *d*, so in Christ all will
15:31 I *d* every day—I mean that,
15:32 for tomorrow we *d*.''
2Co 7: 3 our hearts that we would live or *d*
Php 1:21 to live is Christ and to *d* is gain.
Heb 7: 8 the tenth is collected by men who *d*
9:27 Just as man is destined to *d* once,
1Pe 2:24 so that we might *d* to sins
Rev 3: 2 what remains and is about to *d*,
9: 6 to *d*, but death will elude them.
11: 5 wants to harm them must *d*.
14:13 Blessed are the dead who *d*

DIED (DIE)

Ge 5: 5 lived 930 years, and then he *d*.
5: 8 Seth lived 912 years, and then he *d*.
5:11 lived 905 years, and then he *d*.
5:14 lived 910 years, and then he *d*.
5:17 lived 895 years, and then he *d*.
5:20 lived 962 years, and then he *d*.
5:27 lived 969 years, and then he *d*.
5:31 lived 777 years, and then he *d*.
7:22 the breath of life in its nostrils *d*.
9:29 lived 950 years, and then he *d*.
11:28 Haran *d* in Ur of the Chaldeans,
11:32 Terah lived 205 years, and he *d*
23: 2 She *d* at Kiriath Arba
25: 8 Abraham breathed his last and *d*
25:17 He breathed his last and *d*,
26:18 had stopped up after Abraham *d*,
35: 8 *d* and was buried under the oak
35:19 So Rachel *d* and was buried
35:29 Then he breathed his last and *d*
36:33 When Bela *d*, Jobab son of Zerah
36:34 When Jobab *d*, Husham
36:35 When Husham *d*, Hadad son
36:36 When Hadad *d*, Samlah
36:37 When Samlah *d*, Shaul

Ge 36: 38 When Shaul *d*, Baal-Hanan son
36: 39 When Baal-Hanan son of Acbor *d*,
38: 12 wife, the daughter of Shua, *d*.
46: 12 Onan had *d* in the land of Canaan).
48: 7 to my sorrow Rachel *d* in the land
50: 16 left these instructions before he *d*:
50: 26 So Joseph *d* at the age of a hundred
Ex 1: 6 brothers and all that generation *d*,
2: 23 long period, the king of Egypt *d*.
7: 21 The fish in the Nile *d*,
8: 13 The frogs *d* in the houses,
9: 6 All the livestock of the Egyptians *d*
9: 6 belonging to the Israelites *d*.
9: 7 the animals of the Israelites had *d*.
16: 3 "If only we had *d* by the LORD's
32: 28 three thousand of the people *d*.
Lev 10: 2 and they *d* before the LORD.
16: 1 who *d* when they approached
Nu 11: 2 to the LORD and the fire *d* down.
14: 2 "If only we had *d* in Egypt!
14: 37 *d* of a plague before the LORD.
16: 49 But 14,700 people *d* from the plague,
16: 49 in addition to those who had *d*
19: 16 someone who has *d* a natural death
19: 18 someone who has *d* a natural death
20: 1 There Miriam *d* and was buried.
20: 3 only we had *d* when our brothers
20: 28 And Aaron *d* there on top
20: 29 learned that Aaron had *d*,
21: 6 the people and many Israelites *d*.
25: 9 but those who *d* in the plague
26: 10 whose followers *d*
26: 19 of Judah, but they *d* in Canaan.
26: 61 and Abihu *d* when they made
27: 3 but he *d* for his own sin
27: 3 "Our father *d* in the desert.
33: 38 where he *d* on the first day
33: 39 old when he *d* on Mount Hor.
Dt 2: 16 men among the people had *d*,
10: 6 There Aaron *d* and was buried,
32: 50 as your brother Aaron *d*
34: 5 of the LORD *d* there in Moab,
34: 7 and twenty years old when he *d*,
Jos 5: 4 *d* in the desert on the way
5: 6 age when they left Egypt had *d*,
10: 11 more of them *d* from the hailstones
22: 20 He was not the only one who *d*
24: 29 *d* at the age of a hundred and ten.
24: 33 And Eleazar son of Aaron *d*
Jdg 1: 7 him to Jerusalem, and he *d* there.
2: 8 *d* at the age of a hundred and ten.
2: 19 But when the judge *d*, the people
2: 21 the nations Joshua left when he *d*.
3: 11 until Othniel son of Kenaz *d*.
4: 1 After Ehud *d*, the Israelites once
4: 21 temple into the ground, and he *d*.
8: 32 Gideon son of Joash *d*
8: 33 No sooner had Gideon *d*
9: 49 thousand men and women, also *d*.
9: 54 him through, and he *d*.
10: 2 then he *d*, and was buried
10: 5 When Jair *d*, he was buried
12: 7 Then Jephthah the Gileadite *d*,
12: 10 Then Ibzan *d*, and was buried
12: 12 Elon *d*, and was buried in Aijalon
12: 15 Then Abdon son of Hillel *d*,
16: 30 when he *d* than while he lived.
20: 5 raped my concubine, and she *d*.
Ru 1: 3 Elimelech, Naomi's husband, *d*,
1: 5 both Mahlon and Kilion also *d*,
1Sa 4: 11 two sons, Hophni and Phinehas, *d*.
4: 18 His neck was broken and he *d*,
15: 35 Until the day Samuel *d*, he did not
25: 1 Samuel *d*, and all Israel assembled
25: 38 the LORD struck Nabal and he *d*.
31: 5 fell on his sword and *d* with him.
31: 6 all his men *d* together that same
31: 7 and that Saul and his sons had *d*,
2Sa 1: 4 Many of them fell and *d*.
1: 15 So he struck him down, and he *d*.
2: 23 He fell there and *d* on the spot.
2: 23 where Asahel had fallen and *d*.
3: 27 him in the stomach, and he *d*.
3: 33 "Should Abner have *d*
4: 1 son of Saul heard that Abner had *d*
6: 7 he *d* there beside the ark of God.
10: 1 the king of the Ammonites *d*,
10: 18 of their army, and he *d* there.
2Sa 11: 21 so that he *d* in Thebez? Why did
11: 24 and some of the king's men *d*.
12: 18 On the seventh day the child *d*.
17: 23 So he *d* and was buried
18: 33 If only I had *d* instead of you—
19: 10 to rule over us, has *d* in battle.
20: 10 being stabbed again, Amasa *d*.
24: 15 people from Dan to Beersheba *d*.
1Ki 2: 25 he struck down Adonijah and he *d*.
3: 19 the night this woman's son *d*
14: 17 threshold of the house, the boy *d*.
16: 18 So he *d*, because of the sins he had
16: 22 So Tibni *d* and Omri became king.
22: 35 the chariot, and that evening he *d*.
22: 37 So the king *d* and was brought
2Ki 1: 17 You will certainly die!" So he *d*,
3: 5 But after Ahab *d*, the king
4: 20 on her lap until noon, and then he *d*
7: 17 him in the gateway, and he *d*,
7: 20 him in the gateway, and he *d*.
8: 15 it over the king's face, so that he *d*.
9: 27 he escaped to Megiddo and *d* there
12: 21 He *d* and was buried
13: 14 from the illness from which he *d*.
13: 20 Elisha *d* and was buried.
13: 24 Hazael king of Aram *d*,
15: 5 with leprosy until the day he *d*,
23: 34 him off to Egypt, and there he *d*.
1Ch 1: 44 When Bela *d*, Jobab son of Zerah
1: 45 When Jobab *d*, Husham
1: 46 When Husham *d*, Hadad son
1: 47 When Hadad *d*, Samlah
1: 48 When Samlah *d*, Shaul
1: 49 When Shaul *d*, Baal-Hanan son
1: 50 When Baal-Hanan *d*, Hadad
1: 51 Hadad also *d*.
2: 19 When Azubah *d*, Caleb married
2: 24 Hezron *d* in Caleb Ephrathah,
2: 30 Seled *d* without children.
2: 32 Jether *d* without children.
10: 5 he too fell on his sword and *d*.
10: 6 So Saul and three of his sons *d*,
10: 6 and all his house *d* together.
10: 7 and that Saul and his sons had *d*,
10: 13 Saul *d* because he was unfaithful
13: 10 So he *d* there before God.
19: 1 Nahash king of the Ammonites *d*,
23: 22 Eleazar *d* without having sons:
24: 2 Abihu *d* before their father did,
29: 28 He *d* at a good old age, having
2Ch 13: 20 LORD struck him down and he *d*.
16: 13 forty-first year of his reign Asa *d*
18: 34 Then at sunset he *d*.
21: 19 because of the disease, and he *d*
24: 15 and he *d* at the age of a hundred
24: 25 So he *d* and was buried in the City
26: 21 leprosy until the day he *d*.
32: 33 Jerusalem honored him when he *d*.
35: 24 him to Jerusalem, where he *d*.
Est 2: 7 when her father and mother *d*.
Job 10: 18 I wish I had *d* before any eye saw
42: 17 And so he *d*, old and full of years.
Ps 118: 12 but they *d* out as quickly
Ecc 4: 2 who had already *d*,
Isa 6: 1 In the year that King Uzziah *d*,
14: 28 came in the year King Ahaz *d*:
Jer 28: 17 year, Hananiah the prophet *d*.
Eze 11: 13 Pelatiah son of Benaiah *d*.
13: 19 killed those who should not have *d*
24: 18 and in the evening my wife *d*.
Hos 13: 1 of Baal worship and *d*.
Jnh 4: 10 up overnight and *d* overnight.
Mt 2: 19 After Herod *d*, an angel
8: 32 into the lake and *d* in the water.
9: 18 and said, "My daughter has just *d*.
14: 32 into the boat, the wind *d* down.
22: 25 The first one married and *d*,
22: 27 Finally, the woman *d*.
27: 52 holy people who had *d* were raised
Mk 4: 39 Then the wind *d* down
6: 51 with them, and the wind *d* down.
12: 20 and *d* without leaving any children.
12: 21 but he also *d*, leaving no child.
12: 22 Last of all, the woman *d* too.
15: 39 heard his cry and saw how he *d*,
15: 44 he asked him if Jesus had already *d*
Lk 13: 4 Or those eighteen who *d*
16: 22 The rich man also *d* and was buried
Lk 16: 22 "The time came when the beggar *d*
20: 29 married a woman and *d* childless.
20: 31 and in the same way the seven *d*,
20: 32 Finally, the woman *d* too.
Jn 6: 49 the manna in the desert, yet they *d*.
6: 58 Our forefathers ate ⌊manna⌋ and *d*,
8: 52 Abraham *d* and so did the prophets
8: 53 He *d*, and so did the prophets.
11: 21 my brother would not have *d*.
11: 32 my brother would not have *d*."
18: 14 good if one man *d* for the people.
Ac 2: 29 that the patriarch David *d*
5: 5 heard this, he fell down and *d*.
5: 10 fell down at his feet and *d*.
7: 15 where he and our fathers *d*.
9: 37 that time she became sick and *d*,
12: 23 and he was eaten by worms and *d*
Ro 5: 6 we were still powerless, Christ *d*
5: 8 we were still sinners, Christ *d*
5: 15 For if the many *d* by the trespass
6: 2 By no means! We *d* to sin;
6: 7 anyone who has *d* has been freed
6: 8 if we *d* with Christ, we believe that
6: 10 The death he *d*, he *d* to sin once
7: 4 also *d* to the law through the body
7: 9 came, sin sprang to life and I *d*.
8: 34 Christ Jesus, who *d*— more
14: 9 Christ *d* and returned to life
14: 15 brother for whom Christ *d*.
1Co 8: 11 for whom Christ *d*, is destroyed
10: 8 twenty-three thousand of them *d*.
15: 3 that Christ *d* for our sins according
2Co 5: 14 *d* for all, and therefore all *d*.
5: 15 but for him who *d* for them
5: 15 he *d* for all, that those who live
Gal 2: 19 For through the law I *d* to the law
2: 21 Christ *d* for nothing!" You foolish
Php 2: 27 Indeed he was ill, and almost *d*.
2: 30 he almost *d* for the work of Christ,
Col 2: 20 Since you *d* with Christ
3: 3 For you *d*, and your life is now
1Th 4: 14 We believe that Jesus *d*
5: 10 He *d* for us so that, whether we are
2Ti 2: 11 If we *d* with him,
Heb 9: 15 now that he has *d* as a ransom
9: 17 in force only when somebody has *d*
10: 28 the law of Moses *d* without mercy
11: 13 living by faith when they *d*.
1Pe 3: 18 For Christ *d* for sins once for all,
2Pe 3: 4 Ever since our fathers *d*,
Rev 2: 8 who *d* and came to life again.
8: 9 of the living creatures in the sea *d*,
8: 11 and many people *d* from the waters
16: 3 and every living thing in the sea *d*.

DIES (DIE)

Ge 27: 10 give you his blessing before he *d*."
Ex 21: 20 and the slave *d* as a direct result,
21: 35 the bull of another and it *d*,
22: 2 in and is struck so that he *d*,
22: 10 neighbor for safekeeping and it *d*
22: 14 or *d* while the owner is not present,
Lev 11: 32 When one of them *d* and falls
11: 39 that you are allowed to eat *d*,
Nu 6: 7 or mother or brother or sister *d*,
6: 9 " 'If someone *d* suddenly
19: 14 applies when a person *d* in a tent:
27: 8 'If a man *d* and leaves no son,
35: 16 with an iron object so that he *d*,
35: 17 and he strikes someone so that he *d*
35: 18 and he hits someone so that he *d*,
35: 20 at him intentionally so that he *d*
35: 21 him with his fist so that he *d*,
35: 23 on him that could kill him, and he *d*
Dt 24: 3 or if he *d*, then her first husband,
25: 5 and one of them *d* without a son,
Job 14: 10 But man *d* and is laid low;
14: 14 If a man *d*, will he live again?
21: 23 One man *d* in full vigor,
21: 25 Another man *d* in bitterness of soul
Ps 49: 17 nothing with him when he *d*,
Pr 11: 7 a wicked man *d*, his hope perishes;
26: 20 without gossip a quarrel *d* down.
Ecc 3: 19 both: As one *d*, so *d* the other.
Isa 65: 20 he who *d* at a hundred
Jer 38: 10 out of the cistern before he *d*."
Mt 22: 24 if a man *d* without having children,
Mk 12: 19 for us that if a man's brother *d*

Lk 20: 28 for us that if a man's brother *d*
Jn 4: 49 Sir, come down before my child *d*."
11: 25 in me will live, even though he *d*;
12: 24 But if it *d*, it produces many seeds.
12: 24 of wheat falls to the ground and *d*,
Ro 7: 2 but if her husband *d*, she is released
7: 3 if her husband *d*, she is released
14: 7 and none of us *d* to himself alone.
1Co 7: 39 But if her husband *d*, she is free
15: 36 does not come to life unless it *d*.

DIFFERENCE (DIFFERENT)

2Sa 19: 35 Can I tell the *d* between what is
2Ch 12: 8 so that they may learn the *d*
Eze 22: 26 they teach that there is no *d*
44: 23 are to teach my people the *d*
Ro 3: 22 There is no *d*, for all have sinned
10: 12 For there is no *d* between Jew
Gal 2: 6 whatever they were makes no *d*

DIFFERENCES (DIFFERENT)

1Co 11: 19 to be *d* among you to show which

DIFFERENT (DIFFERENCE DIFFERENCES DIFFERING DIFFERS)

Lev 19: 19 " 'Do not mate *d* kinds of animals.
Nu 14: 24 my servant Caleb has a *d* spirit
1Sa 10: 6 you will be changed into a *d* person
Est 1: 7 each one *d* from the other,
3: 8 Their customs are *d* from those
Da 7: 3 Four great beasts, each *d*
7: 7 It was *d* from all the former beasts,
7: 19 which was *d* from all the others
7: 23 It will be *d* from all the other
7: 24 them another king will arise, *d*
11: 29 but this time the outcome will be *d*
Mk 16: 12 Jesus appeared in a *d* form
Ro 12: 6 We have *d* gifts, according
1Co 4: 7 For who makes you *d*
12: 4 There are *d* kinds of gifts,
12: 5 There are *d* kinds of service,
12: 6 There are *d* kinds of working,
12: 10 to speak in *d* kinds of tongues,
12: 28 and those speaking in *d* kinds
2Co 11: 4 or a *d* gospel from the one you
11: 4 or if you receive a *d* spirit
Gal 1: 6 and are turning to a *d* gospel—
4: 1 he is no *d* from a slave,
Heb 7: 13 are said belonged to a *d* tribe,
Jas 2: 25 and sent them off in a *d* direction?

DIFFERING (DIFFERENT)

Dt 25: 13 Do not have two *d* weights
25: 14 Do not have two *d* measures
Pr 20: 10 Differing weights and *d* measures
20: 10 *D* weights and differing measures
20: 23 The LORD detests *d* weights,

DIFFERS (DIFFERENT)

1Co 15: 41 and star *d* from star in splendor.

DIFFICULT (DIFFICULTIES DIFFICULTY)

Ge 47: 9 My years have been few and *d*,
Ex 18: 22 but have them bring every *d* case
18: 26 The *d* cases they brought to Moses,
Dt 17: 8 before your courts that are too *d*
30: 11 commanding you today is not too *d*
2Ki 2: 10 "You have asked a *d* thing,"
Eze 3: 5 of obscure speech and *d* language,
3: 6 of obscure speech and *d* language,
Da 2: 11 What the king asks is too *d*.
4: 9 and no mystery is too *d* for you.
5: 12 riddles and solve *d* problems.
5: 16 and to solve *d* problems.
Ac 15: 19 that we should not make it *d*

DIFFICULTIES (DIFFICULT)

Dt 31: 17 and *d* will come upon them,
31: 21 when many disasters and *d* come
2Co 12: 10 in hardships, in persecutions, in *d*.

DIFFICULTY (DIFFICULT)

Ge 35: 16 began to give birth and had great *d*.
35: 17 she was having great *d* in childbirth
Ex 14: 25 come off so that they had *d* driving.
Jos 19: 47 Danites had *d* taking possession
Ac 14: 18 they had *d* keeping the crowd

Ac 27: 7 and had *d* arriving off Cnidus.
27: 8 We moved along the coast with *d*

DIG (DIGGING DIGS DUG GRAVEDIGGERS)

Dt 6: 11 wells you did not *d*, and vineyards
8: 9 you can *d* copper out of the hills.
23: 13 equipment have something to *d*
23: 13 *d* a hole and cover up your
Ps 119: 85 The arrogant *d* pitfalls for me,
Eze 8: 8 "Son of man, now *d* into the wall."
12: 5 *d* through the wall and take your
Am 9: 2 Though they *d* down to the depths
Lk 13: 8 and I'll *d* around it and fertilize it.
16: 3 I'm not strong enough to *d*,

DIGGING (DIG)

Mk 2: 4 above Jesus and, after *d* through it,

DIGNITARIES (DIGNITY)

Ge 50: 7 the *d* of his court and all the *d*
Isa 43: 28 I will disgrace the *d* of your temple,

DIGNITY (DIGNITARIES)

Ex 28: 2 your brother Aaron, to give him *d*
28: 40 to give them *d* and honor.
Job 30: 15 my *d* is driven away as by the wind,
Pr 31: 25 She is clothed with strength and *d*;

DIGS (DIG)

Ex 21: 33 or *d* one and fails to cover it
Ps 7: 15 He who *d* a hole and scoops it out
Pr 26: 27 If a man *d* a pit, he will fall into it;
Ecc 10: 8 Whoever *d* a pit may fall into it;

DIKLAH

Ge 10: 27 Hadoram, Uzal, *D*, Obal, Abimael,
1Ch 1: 21 Hadoram, Uzal, *D*, Obal, Abimael,

DILEAN

Jos 15: 38 Migdal Gad, *D*, Mizpah, Joktheel,

DILIGENCE (DILIGENT)

Ezr 5: 8 The work is being carried on with *d*
6: 12 Let it be carried out with *d*.
6: 13 associates carried it out with *d*.
7: 21 with *d* whatever Ezra the priest,
7: 23 let it be done with *d* for the temple
Heb 6: 11 to show this same *d* to the very end

DILIGENT (DILIGENCE)

2Ch 24: 13 men in charge of the work were *d*,
Pr 10: 4 but *d* hands bring wealth.
12: 24 *D* hands will rule,
12: 27 the *d* man prizes his possessions.
13: 4 of the *d* are fully satisfied.
21: 5 The plans of the *d* lead to profit
1Ti 4: 15 Be *d* in these matters; give yourself

DILL

Mt 23: 23 a tenth of your spices—mint, *d*

DILUTED

Isa 1: 22 your choice wine is *d* with water.

DIM

Job 17: 7 My eyes have grown *d* with grief;
Ps 88: 9 my eyes are *d* with grief.
Ecc 12: 3 through the windows grow *d*;
La 5: 17 of these things our eyes grow *d*

DIMENSIONS

Job 38: 5 marked off its *d*? Surely you know!
Eze 42: 11 and width, with similar exits and *d*.

DIMINISH

Ps 107: 38 and he did not let their herds *d*.

DIMNAH

Jos 21: 35 Jokneam, Kartah, *D* and Nahalal,

DIMON (DIMON'S)

Isa 15: 9 but I will bring still more upon *D*—

DIMON'S (DIMON)

Isa 15: 9 *D* waters are full of blood,

DIMONAH

Jos 15: 22 Jagur, Kinah, *D*, Adadah, Kedesh,

DIN

Jer 51: 55 he will silence her noisy *d*.

DINAH (DINAH'S)

Ge 30: 21 to a daughter and named her *D*.
34: 1 *D*, the daughter Leah had borne
34: 3 drawn to *D* daughter of Jacob,
34: 5 that his daughter *D* had been
34: 13 Because their sister *D* had been
34: 26 and took *D* from Shechem's house
46: 15 besides his daughter *D*.

DINAH'S (DINAH)

Ge 34: 11 Then Shechem said to *D* father
34: 25 Simeon and Levi, *D* brothers,

DINE (DINED DINNER)

1Sa 20: 5 I am supposed to *d* with the king;
Est 7: 1 went to *d* with Queen Esther,
Pr 23: 1 When you sit to *d* with a ruler,
Am 6: 4 You *d* on choice lambs

DINED (DINE)

1Sa 9: 24 And Saul *d* with Samuel that day.

DINHABAH

Ge 36: 32 His city was named *D*.
1Ch 1: 43 of Beor, whose city was named *D*.

DINNER (DINE)

Ge 43: 16 slaughter an animal and prepare *d*;
Est 5: 14 Then go with the king to the *d*
Mt 9: 10 While Jesus was having *d*
14: 9 of his oaths and his *d* guests,
22: 4 invited that I have prepared my *d*:
Mk 2: 15 While Jesus was having *d*
6: 22 she pleased Herod and his *d* guests.
6: 26 of his oaths and his *d* guests,
Lk 7: 36 Jesus to have *d* with him,
14: 12 "When you give a luncheon or *d*,
Jn 12: 2 Here a *d* was given in Jesus' honor.

DIONYSIUS

Ac 17: 34 Among them was *D*, a member

DIOTREPHES

3Jn : 9 but *D*, who loves to be first,

DIP (DIPPED DIPPING DIPS)

Ex 12: 22 *d* it into the blood in the basin
Lev 4: 6 He is to *d* his finger into the blood
4: 17 He shall *d* his finger into the blood
14: 6 then to take the live bird and *d* it,
14: 16 *d* his right forefinger into the oil
14: 51 *d* them into the blood
Nu 19: 18 *d* it in the water and sprinkle
Ru 2: 14 and *d* it in the wine vinegar."
Lk 16: 24 and send Lazarus to *d* the tip

DIPPED (DIP)

Ge 37: 31 and *d* the robe in the blood.
Lev 9: 9 and he *d* his finger into the blood
1Sa 14: 27 and *d* it into the honeycomb.
2Ki 5: 14 *d* himself in the Jordan seven times
Mt 26: 23 "The one who has *d* his hand
Jn 13: 26 bread when I have *d* it in the dish."
Rev 19: 13 He is dressed in a robe *d* in blood,

DIPPING (DIP)

Jn 13: 26 Then, *d* the piece of bread,

DIPS (DIP)

Mk 14: 20 "one who *d* bread into the bowl

DIRE

Dt 28: 48 in nakedness and *d* poverty,
Isa 21: 2 A *d* vision has been shown to me:

DIRECT (DIRECTED DIRECTING DIRECTION DIRECTIONS DIRECTIVES DIRECTOR DIRECTORS DIRECTS)

Ge 18: 19 so that he will *d* his children
46: 26 those who were his *d* descendants,
Ex 21: 20 and the slave dies as a *d* result,
Dt 17: 10 to do everything they *d* you to do.
2Ch 34: 12 Over them to *d* them were Jahath
Ps 119: 35 *D* me in the path of your
119:133 *D* my footsteps according

Jer 10: 23 it is not for man to *d* his steps.
Eze 23: 25 I will *d* my jealous anger
26: 9 He will *d* the blows
2Th 3: 5 May the Lord *d* your hearts
1Ti 5: 17 The elders who *d* the affairs

DIRECTED (DIRECT)

Ge 24: 51 master's son, as the LORD has *d*.''
45: 19 You are also *d* to tell them, 'Do this
47: 11 district of Rameses, as Pharaoh *d*.
50: 2 Then Joseph *d* the physicians
Nu 16: 40 as the LORD *d* him through Moses
Dt 2: 1 Sea, as the LORD had *d* me.
4: 14 And the LORD *d* me at that time
6: 1 laws the LORD your God *d* me
Jos 4: 10 just as Moses had *d* Joshua.
4: 12 Israelites, as Moses had *d* them.
11: 9 did to them as the LORD had *d*:
11: 23 just as the LORD had *d* Moses,
1Sa 17: 20 and set out, as Jesse had *d*.
1Ki 5: 16 the project and *d* the workmen.
21: 11 as Jezebel *d* in the letters she had
Job 21: 4 ''Is my complaint *d* to man?
Pr 20: 24 A man's steps are *d* by the LORD.
Isa 10: 25 my wrath will be *d*
Jer 13: 2 as the LORD *d*, and put it
Mt 14: 19 And he *d* the people to sit
26: 19 as Jesus had *d* them and prepared
Mk 6: 39 Jesus *d* them to have all the people
Ac 7: 44 It had been made as God *d* Moses,
22: 24 He *d* that he be flogged
Tit 1: 5 elders in every town, as I *d* you.

DIRECTING (DIRECT)

1Ch 15: 21 were to play the harps, *d* according

DIRECTION (DIRECT)

Ex 38: 21 Levites under the *d* of Ithamar son
Nu 4: 27 is to be done under the *d* of Aaron
4: 28 to be under the *d* of Ithamar son
4: 33 under the *d* of Ithamar son
7: 8 all under the *d* of Ithamar son
11: 31 as far as a day's walk in any *d*
Dt 28: 7 They will come at you from one *d*
28: 25 You will come at them from one *d*
Jos 8: 20 chance to escape in any *d*,
Jdg 9: 37 from the *d* of the soothsayers' tree
20: 42 the Israelites in the *d* of the desert,
2Sa 13: 34 ''I see men in the *d* of Horonaim,
1Ki 18: 6 Ahab going in one *d* and Obadiah
2Ki 3: 20 water flowing from the *d* of Edom!
2Ch 26: 11 officer under the *d* of Hananiah,
34: 4 Under his *d* the altars
Ezr 5: 8 rapid progress under their *d*.
Ne 12: 38 choir proceeded in the opposite *d*.
12: 42 sang under the *d* of Jezrahiah.
Job 37: 12 At his *d* they swirl around
Pr 7: 8 walking along in the *d* of her house
Eze 9: 2 from the *d* of the upper gate,
10: 11 went in whatever *d* the head faced,
Jas 2: 25 and sent them off in a different *d*?

DIRECTIONS (DIRECT)

Ge 46: 28 of him to Joseph to get *d* to Goshen
1Sa 14: 16 saw the army melting away in all *d*.
2Ch 35: 4 according to the *d* written
Eze 1: 17 of the four *d* the creatures faced;
10: 11 of the four *d* the cherubim faced;
Ac 21: 30 the people came running from all *d*.
1Co 11: 34 when I come I will give further *d*

DIRECTIVES (DIRECT)

1Co 11: 17 In the following *d* I have no praise

DIRECTOR (DIRECT)

Ne 11: 17 the *d* who led in thanksgiving
Hab 3: 19 For the *d* of music.
Ro 16: 23 who is the city's *d* of public works,

DIRECTORS (DIRECT)

Ne 12: 46 there had been *d* for the singers

DIRECTS (DIRECT)

Jdg 20: 9 We'll go up against it as the lot *d*.
Ps 42: 8 By day the LORD *d* his love,
Pr 21: 1 he *d* it like a watercourse wherever
Isa 48: 17 who *d* you in the way you should

DIRGE

Mt 11: 17 we sang a *d*,
Lk 7: 32 we sang a *d*,

DIRT

2Sa 16: 13 and showering him with *d*.
Zec 9: 3 and gold like the *d* of the streets.
1Pe 3: 21 not the removal of *d* from the body

DISABLED

Jn 5: 3 number of *d* people used to lie—
Heb 12: 13 so that the lame may not be *d*,

DISAGREED (DISAGREEMENT)

Ac 28: 25 They *d* among themselves

DISAGREEMENT (DISAGREED)

Ac 15: 39 had such a sharp *d* that they parted

DISAPPEAR (DISAPPEARED DISAPPEARS)

Nu 27: 4 Why should our father's name *d*
Ru 4: 10 so that his name will not *d*
Isa 2: 18 and the idols will totally *d*.
17: 3 The fortified city will *d*
29: 20 the mockers will *d*,
Mt 5: 18 and earth *d*, not the smallest letter,
5: 18 will by any means *d* from the Law
Lk 16: 17 earth to *d* than for the least stroke
Heb 8: 13 is obsolete and aging will soon *d*.
2Pe 3: 10 The heavens will *d* with a roar;

DISAPPEARED (DISAPPEAR)

Jdg 6: 21 And the angel of the LORD *d*.
1Ki 20: 40 busy here and there, the man *d*.''
Lk 24: 31 and they recognized him, and he *d*

DISAPPEARS (DISAPPEAR)

Job 14: 11 As water *d* from the sea
Hos 6: 4 like the early dew that *d*.
13: 3 like the early dew that *d*,
1Co 13: 10 perfection comes, the imperfect *d*.

DISAPPOINT (DISAPPOINTED)

Ro 5: 5 And hope does not *d* us,

DISAPPOINTED (DISAPPOINT)

Job 6: 20 they arrive there, only to be *d*.
Ps 22: 5 in you they trusted and were not *d*.
Isa 49: 23 those who hope in me will not be *d*
Jer 2: 36 You will be *d* by Egypt

DISAPPROVE

Pr 24: 18 or the LORD will see and *d*

DISARMED (DISARMS)

Col 2: 15 And having *d* the powers

DISARMS (DISARMED)

Job 12: 21 and *d* the mighty.

DISASTER (DISASTERS DISASTROUS)

Ge 19: 19 this *d* will overtake me, and I'll die.
Ex 32: 12 and do not bring *d* on your people.
32: 14 his people the *d* he had threatened.
Dt 28: 61 and *d* not recorded in this Book
29: 19 This will bring *d* on the watered
29: 21 from all the tribes of Israel for *d*,
31: 29 *d* will fall upon you because you
32: 35 their day of *d* is near
Jos 6: 18 to destruction and bring *d* on it.
7: 25 The LORD will bring *d*
7: 25 Why have you brought this *d* on us
24: 20 he will turn and bring *d* on you
Jdg 20: 34 did not realize how near *d* was.
20: 41 they realized that *d* had come
1Sa 6: 9 the LORD has brought this great *d*
25: 17 *d* is hanging over our master
2Sa 17: 14 in order to bring *d* on Absalom.
22: 19 in the day of my *d*,
1Ki 5: 4 and there is no adversary or *d*.
8: 37 whatever *d* or disease may come,
9: 9 is why the LORD brought all this *d*
14: 10 I am going to bring *d* on the house
21: 21 'I am going to bring *d* on you.
21: 29 I will not bring this *d* in his day,
22: 23 The LORD has decreed *d* for you.''
2Ki 6: 33 ''This *d* is from the LORD.
21: 12 going to bring such *d* on Jerusalem
22: 16 I am going to bring *d* on this place
22: 20 will not see all the *d* I am going
1Ch 2: 7 who brought *d* on Israel
2Ch 6: 28 whatever *d* or disease may come,
7: 22 that is why he brought all this *d*
18: 22 The LORD has decreed *d* for you.''
34: 24 I am going to bring *d* on this place
34: 28 will not see all the *d* I am going
Est 8: 6 bear to see *d* fall on my people?
Job 18: 12 *d* is ready for him when he falls.
31: 3 *d* for those who do wrong?
Ps 18: 18 in the day of my *d*,
37: 19 In times of *d* they will not wither;
57: 1 wings until the *d* has passed.
91: 10 no *d* will come near your tent.
140: 11 may *d* hunt down men of violence.
Pr 1: 26 I in turn will laugh at your *d*;
1: 27 when *d* sweeps over you like
3: 25 Have no fear of sudden *d*
6: 15 Therefore *d* will overtake him
16: 4 even the wicked for a day of *d*.
17: 5 over *d* will not go unpunished.
27: 10 house when *d* strikes you—
Ecc 11: 2 you do not know what *d* may come
Isa 3: 9 They have brought *d*
3: 11 *D* is upon them!
10: 3 when *d* comes from afar?
31: 2 Yet he too is wise and can bring *d*;
45: 7 I bring prosperity and create *d*;
47: 11 *D* will come upon you,
Jer 1: 14 ''From the north *d* will be poured
2: 3 and *d* overtook them,' ''
4: 6 For I am bringing *d* from the north,
4: 15 proclaiming *d* from the hills
4: 20 *D* follows *d*,
6: 1 For *d* looms out of the north,
6: 19 I am bringing *d* on this people,
11: 11 on them a *d* they cannot escape.
11: 12 them at all when *d* strikes.
11: 17 who planted you, has decreed *d*
11: 23 because I will bring *d* on the men
15: 11 in times of *d* and times of distress.
16: 10 the LORD decreed such a great *d*
17: 17 you are my refuge in the day of *d*.
17: 18 Bring on them the day of *d*;
18: 8 not inflict on it the *d* I had planned.
18: 11 I am preparing a *d* for you
18: 17 face in the day of their *d*.''
19: 3 I am going to bring a *d*
19: 15 around it every *d* I pronounced
23: 12 I will bring *d* on them
25: 29 I am beginning to bring *d*
25: 32 ''Look! *D* is spreading
26: 3 bring on them the *d* I was planning
26: 13 not bring the *d* he has pronounced
26: 19 did not bring the *d* he pronounced
26: 19 to bring a terrible *d* on ourselves!''
28: 8 *d* and plague against many
31: 28 to overthrow, destroy and bring *d*,
32: 23 you brought all this *d* upon them.
35: 17 in Jerusalem every *d* I pronounced
36: 3 of Judah hear about every *d* I plan
36: 31 of Judah every *d* I pronounced
39: 16 words against this city through *d*,
40: 2 LORD your God decreed this *d*
42: 10 over the *d* I have inflicted on you.
42: 17 escape the *d* I will bring on them.'
44: 2 You saw the great *d* I brought
44: 7 Why bring such great *d*
44: 11 I am determined to bring *d* on you
44: 23 this *d* has come upon you,
45: 5 For I will bring *d* on all people,
46: 21 for the day of *d* is coming
49: 8 for I will bring *d* on Esau
49: 32 and will bring *d* on them
49: 37 I will bring *d* upon them,
51: 2 side in the day of her *d*.
51: 64 of the *d* I will bring upon her.
Eze 7: 5 An unheard-of *d* is coming.
7: 5 *D*! An unheard-of disaster is
14: 22 every *d* I have brought upon it.
14: 22 regarding the *d* I have brought
Da 9: 12 rulers by bringing upon us great *d*.
9: 13 all this *d* has come upon us,
9: 14 hesitate to bring the *d* upon us,
Am 3: 6 When *d* comes to a city,
9: 10 '*D* will not overtake or meet us.'

Ob : 5 Oh, what a *d* awaits you—
: 13 calamity in the day of their *d*,
: 13 people in the day of their *d*,
: 13 wealth in the day of their *d*.
Mic 1: 12 *d* has come from the LORD,
2: 3 I am planning *d* against this people,
3: 11 No *d* will come upon us."
Zec 8: 14 determined to bring *d* upon you

DISASTERS (DISASTER)

Dt 28: 59 harsh and prolonged *d*, and severe
31: 17 Many *d* and difficulties will come
31: 17 'Have not these *d* come upon us
31: 21 when many *d* and difficulties come
Jer 51: 60 about all the *d* that would come

DISASTROUS (DISASTER)

Ac 27: 10 see that our voyage is going to be *d*

DISCARD (DISCARDED)

Ps 119:119 of the earth you *d* like dross;

DISCARDED (DISCARD)

Ps 102: 26 and they will be *d*.

DISCERN (DISCERNED DISCERNING DISCERNMENT)

Dt 32: 29 and *d* what their end will be!
Job 6: 30 Can my mouth not *d* malice?
34: 4 Let us *d* for ourselves what is right;
Ps 19: 12 Who can *d* his errors?
139: 3 You *d* my going out and my lying
Php 1: 10 you may be able to *d* what is best

DISCERNED (DISCERN)

1Co 2: 14 because they are spiritually *d*.

DISCERNING (DISCERN)

Ge 41: 33 "And now let Pharaoh look for a *d*
41: 39 there is no one so *d* and wise as you
2Sa 14: 17 is like an angel of God in *d* good
1Ki 3: 9 So give your servant a *d* heart
3: 12 I will give you a wise and *d* heart,
Pr 1: 5 and let the *d* get guidance—
8: 9 To the *d* all of them are right;
10: 13 on the lips of the *d*,
14: 6 knowledge comes easily to the *d*.
14: 33 in the heart of the *d*
15: 14 The *d* heart seeks knowledge,
16: 21 The wise in heart are called *d*,
17: 24 A *d* man keeps wisdom in view,
17: 28 and *d* if he holds his tongue.
18: 15 heart of the *d* acquires knowledge;
19: 25 rebuke a *d* man, and he will gain
28: 7 He who keeps the law is a *d* son,
Da 2: 21 and knowledge to the *d*.
Hos 14: 9 Who is *d*? He will understand them

DISCERNMENT (DISCERN)

Dt 32: 28 there is no *d* in them.
1Ki 3: 11 but for *d* in administering justice,
2Ch 2: 12 endowed with intelligence and *d*,
Job 12: 20 and takes away the *d* of elders.
Ps 119:125 I am your servant; give me *d*
Pr 3: 21 preserve sound judgment and *d*,
17: 10 A rebuke impresses a man of *d*
28: 11 a poor man who has *d* sees

DISCHARGE (DISCHARGED DISCHARGING)

Lev 15: 2 has a bodily *d*, the *d* is unclean.
15: 3 This is how his *d* will bring about
15: 4 with a *d* lies on will be unclean,
15: 6 man with a *d* sat on must wash his
15: 7 the man who has a *d* must wash his
15: 8 " 'If the man with the *d* spits
15: 11 Anyone the man with a *d* touches
15: 13 When a man is cleansed from his *d*,
15: 15 for the man because of his *d*.
15: 25 be unclean as long as she has the *d*,
15: 25 or has a *d* that continues
15: 25 " 'When a woman has a *d* of blood
15: 26 on while her *d* continues will be
15: 28 " 'When she is cleansed from her *d*,
15: 30 for the uncleanness of her *d*.
15: 32 the regulations for a man with a *d*,
15: 33 for a man or a woman with a *d*,
22: 4 skin disease or a bodily *d*,
Nu 5: 2 has an infectious skin disease or a *d*
2Ti 4: 5 *d* all the duties of your ministry.

DISCHARGED (DISCHARGE)

Ecc 8: 8 As no one is *d* in time of war,

DISCHARGING (DISCHARGE)

1Co 9: 17 I am simply *d* the trust committed

DISCIPLE (DISCIPLES DISCIPLES')

Isa 19: 11 a *d* of the ancient kings"?
Mt 10: 42 these little ones because he is my *d*,
27: 57 who had himself become a *d*
Lk 14: 26 his own life—he cannot be my *d*.
14: 27 and follow me cannot be my *d*.
14: 33 everything he has cannot be my *d*.
Jn 9: 28 are this fellow's *d*! We are disciples
13: 23 of them, the *d* whom Jesus loved,
13: 24 Simon Peter motioned to this *d*
18: 15 Because this *d* was known
18: 15 another *d* were following Jesus.
18: 16 The other *d*, who was known
19: 26 and the *d* whom he loved standing
19: 27 and to the *d*, "Here is your mother
19: 27 this *d* took her into his home.
19: 38 Now Joseph was a *d* of Jesus,
20: 2 Simon Peter and the other *d*,
20: 3 the other *d* started for the tomb.
20: 4 but the other *d* outran Peter
20: 8 Finally the other *d*, who had
21: 7 Then the *d* whom Jesus loved said
21: 20 saw that the *d* whom Jesus loved
21: 23 brothers that this *d* would not die.
21: 24 This is the *d* who testifies
Ac 9: 10 there was a *d* named Ananias.
9: 26 not believing that he really was a *d*.
9: 36 there was a *d* named Tabitha
16: 1 where a *d* named Timothy lived,

DISCIPLES (DISCIPLE)

Isa 8: 16 and seal up the law among my *d*.
Mt 5: 1 His *d* came to him, and he began
8: 21 one of his *d*, said to him, "Lord,
8: 23 the boat and his *d* followed him.
8: 25 The *d* went and woke him, saying,
9: 10 and ate with him and his *d*.
9: 11 saw this, they asked his *d*,
9: 14 Then John's *d* came and asked him
9: 14 but your *d* do not fast?" Jesus
9: 19 went with him, and so did his *d*.
9: 37 to his *d*, "The harvest is plentiful
10: 1 He called his twelve *d* to him
11: 1 finished instructing his twelve *d*,
11: 2 he sent his *d* to ask him, "Are you
11: 7 As John's *d* were leaving, Jesus
12: 1 His *d* were hungry and began
12: 2 Your *d* are doing what is unlawful
12: 49 my brothers?" Pointing to his *d*,
13: 10 The *d* came to him and asked,
13: 36 His *d* came to him and said,
14: 12 John's *d* came and took his body
14: 15 the *d* came to him and said,
14: 19 Then he gave them to the *d*,
14: 19 and the *d* gave them to the people.
14: 20 the *d* picked up twelve basketfuls
14: 22 Immediately Jesus made the *d* get
14: 26 When the *d* saw him walking
15: 2 "Why do your *d* break the tradition
15: 12 Then the *d* came to him and asked,
15: 23 his *d* came to him and urged him,
15: 32 Jesus called his *d* to him and said,
15: 33 His *d* answered, "Where could we
15: 36 broke them and gave them to the *d*,
15: 37 Afterward the *d* picked up seven
16: 5 the *d* forgot to take bread.
16: 13 he asked his *d*, "Who do people say
16: 20 Then he warned his *d* not
16: 21 to explain to his *d* that he must go
16: 24 to his *d*, "If anyone would come
17: 6 to him!" When the *d* heard this,
17: 10 The *d* asked him, "Why then do
17: 13 *d* understood that he was talking
17: 16 I brought him to your *d*,
17: 19 Then the *d* came to Jesus in private
17: 23 And the *d* were filled with grief.
17: 24 and his *d* arrived in Capernaum,
18: 1 At that time the *d* came to Jesus
19: 10 The *d* said to him, "If this is
Mt 19: 13 the *d* rebuked those who brought
19: 23 said to his *d*, "I tell you the truth,
19: 25 When the *d* heard this, they were
20: 17 he took the twelve *d* aside
20: 29 and his *d* were leaving Jericho,
21: 1 Jesus sent two *d*, saying to them,
21: 6 The *d* went and did as Jesus had
21: 20 When the *d* saw this, they were
22: 16 They sent their *d* to him
23: 1 said to the crowds and to his *d*:
24: 1 away when his *d* came up to him
24: 3 the *d* came to him privately.
26: 1 he said to his *d*, "As you know,
26: 8 When the *d* saw this, they were
26: 17 the *d* came to Jesus and asked,
26: 18 with my *d* at your house.' "
26: 19 *d* did as Jesus had directed them
26: 26 and gave it to his *d*, saying,
26: 35 And all the other *d* said the same.
26: 36 Then Jesus went with his *d*
26: 40 to his *d* and found them sleeping.
26: 45 Then he returned to the *d* and said
26: 56 Then all the *d* deserted him
27: 64 his *d* may come and steal the body
28: 7 Then go quickly and tell his *d*:
28: 8 filled with joy, and ran to tell his *d*.
28: 13 'His *d* came during the night
28: 16 Then the eleven *d* went to Galilee,
28: 19 Therefore go and make *d*
Mk 2: 15 eating with him and his *d*,
2: 16 they asked his *d*: "Why does he eat
2: 18 John's *d* and the Pharisees were
2: 18 the *d* of the Pharisees are fasting,
2: 18 "How is it that John's *d*
2: 23 and as his *d* walked along,
3: 7 withdrew with his *d* to the lake,
3: 9 Because of the crowd he told his *d*
3: 20 so that he and his *d* were not
4: 34 when he was alone with his own *d*,
4: 35 he said to his *d*, "Let us go
4: 38 The *d* woke him and said to him,
4: 40 He said to his *d*, "Why are you
5: 31 his *d* answered, "and yet you can
5: 40 and the *d* who were with him,
6: 1 home town, accompanied by his *d*.
6: 29 John's *d* came and took his body
6: 35 in the day, so his *d* came to him.
6: 41 Then he gave them to his *d* to set
6: 43 the *d* picked up twelve basketfuls
6: 45 Immediately Jesus made his *d* get
6: 48 He saw the *d* straining at the oars,
7: 2 and saw some of his *d* eating food
7: 5 "Why don't your *d* live according
7: 17 his *d* asked him about this parable.
8: 1 Jesus called his *d* to him and said,
8: 4 His *d* answered, "But where
8: 6 and gave them to his *d* to set
8: 7 and told the *d* to distribute them.
8: 8 Afterward the *d* picked up seven
8: 10 he got into the boat with his *d*
8: 14 The *d* had forgotten to bring bread,
8: 27 and his *d* went on to the villages
8: 33 Jesus turned and looked at his *d*,
8: 34 the crowd to him along with his *d*
9: 14 When they came to the other *d*,
9: 18 I asked your *d* to drive out
9: 28 gone indoors, his *d* asked him
9: 31 because he was teaching his *d*.
10: 10 the *d* asked Jesus about this.
10: 13 them, but the *d* rebuked them.
10: 23 looked around and said to his *d*,
10: 24 The *d* were amazed at his words.
10: 26 The *d* were even more amazed,
10: 32 and the *d* were astonished,
10: 46 his *d*, together with a large crowd,
11: 1 two of his *d*, saying to them,
11: 14 And his *d* heard him say it.
12: 43 Calling his *d* to him, Jesus said,
13: 1 one of his *d* said to him, "Look,
14: 12 Passover lamb, Jesus' *d* asked him,
14: 13 So he sent two of his *d*, telling them
14: 14 I may eat the Passover with my *d*?'
14: 16 The *d* left, went into the city
14: 22 and gave it to his *d*, saying,
14: 32 and Jesus said to his *d*, "Sit here
14: 37 to his *d* and found them sleeping.
16: 7 But go, tell his *d* and Peter,
16: 20 Then the *d* went out and preached

Lk 5: 30 to their sect complained to his *d*,
5: 33 and so do the *d* of the Pharisees,
5: 33 "John's *d* often fast and pray,
6: 1 and his *d* began to pick some heads
6: 13 he called his *d* to him and chose
6: 17 A large crowd of his *d* was there
6: 20 Looking at his *d*, he said:
7: 11 and his *d* and a large crowd went
7: 18 John's *d* told him about all these
8: 9 His *d* asked him what this parable
8: 22 One day Jesus said to his *d*,
8: 24 The *d* went and woke him, saying,
8: 25 is your faith?" he asked his *d*.
9: 14 But he said to his *d*, "Have them sit
9: 15 The *d* did so, and everybody sat
9: 16 Then he gave them to the *d* to set
9: 17 the *d* picked up twelve basketfuls
9: 18 in private and his *d* were with him,
9: 36 The *d* kept this to themselves,
9: 40 I begged your *d* to drive it out,
9: 43 he said to his *d*, "Listen carefully
9: 46 An argument started among the *d*
9: 54 When the *d* James and John saw
10: 23 turned to his *d* and said privately,
10: 38 and his *d* were on their way,
11: 1 just as John taught his *d*."
11: 1 one of his *d* said to him, "Lord,
12: 1 Jesus began to speak first to his *d*,
12: 22 said to his *d*: "Therefore I tell you,
16: 1 Jesus told his *d*: "There was a rich
17: 1 to his *d*: "Things that cause people
17: 22 said to his *d*, "The time is coming
18: 1 Then Jesus told his *d* a parable
18: 15 When the *d* saw this, they rebuked
18: 34 The *d* did not understand any
19: 29 he sent two of his *d*, saying to them
19: 37 of *d* began joyfully
19: 39 "Teacher, rebuke your *d*!"
20: 45 Jesus said to his *d*, "Beware
21: 5 of his *d* were remarking about how
22: 11 I may eat the Passover with my *d*?'
22: 38 *d* said, "See, Lord, here are two
22: 39 of Olives, and his *d* followed him.
22: 45 from prayer and went back to the *d*
Jn 1: 35 was there again with two of his *d*.
1: 37 When the two *d* heard him say this,
2: 2 and Jesus and his *d* had
2: 11 and his *d* put their faith in him.
2: 12 his mother and brothers and his *d*.
2: 17 His *d* remembered that it is written
2: 22 his *d* recalled what he had said.
3: 22 and his *d* went out into the Judean
3: 25 between some of John's *d*
4: 1 and baptizing more *d* than John,
4: 2 not Jesus who baptized, but his *d*.
4: 8 (His *d* had gone into the town
4: 27 Just then his *d* returned
4: 31 Meanwhile his *d* urged him,
4: 33 Then his *d* said to each other,
6: 3 hillside and sat down with his *d*.
6: 8 Another of his *d*, Andrew,
6: 12 to his *d*, "Gather the pieces that
6: 16 his *d* went down to the lake,
6: 22 Jesus had not entered it with his *d*,
6: 24 neither Jesus nor his *d* were there,
6: 60 On hearing it, many of his *d* said,
6: 61 Aware that his *d* were grumbling
6: 66 many of his *d* turned back
7: 3 so that your *d* may see the miracles
8: 31 to my teaching, you are really my *d*
9: 2 His *d* asked him, "Rabbi, who
9: 27 Do you want to become his *d*, too
9: 28 are this fellow's disciple! We are *d*
11: 7 he said to his *d*, "Let us go back
11: 12 His *d* replied, "Lord, if he sleeps,
11: 13 but his *d* thought he meant natural
11: 16 said to the rest of the *d*,
11: 54 where he stayed with his *d*.
12: 4 But one of his *d*, Judas Iscariot,
12: 16 At first his *d* did not understand all
13: 22 His *d* stared at one another,
13: 35 men will know that you are my *d*
15: 8 showing yourselves to be my *d*.
16: 17 Some of his *d* said to one another,
16: 29 Then Jesus' *d* said, "Now you are
18: 1 and he and his *d* went into it.
18: 1 with his *d* and crossed the Kidron
18: 2 had often met there with his *d*.
Jn 18: 17 are not another of this man's *d*?"
18: 19 priest questioned Jesus about his *d*
18: 25 Surely you are not another of his *d*
20: 10 the *d* went back to their homes,
20: 18 went to the *d* with the news:
20: 19 when the *d* were together,
20: 20 The *d* were overjoyed
20: 24 not with the *d* when Jesus came.
20: 25 When the other *d* told him that
20: 26 A week later his *d* were
20: 30 signs in the presence of his *d*,
21: 1 to his *d* by the Sea of Tiberias.
21: 2 and two other *d* were together.
21: 4 *d* did not realize that it was Jesus.
21: 8 The other *d* followed in the boat,
21: 12 None of the *d* dared ask him,
21: 14 to his *d* after he was raised
Ac 6: 1 the number of *d* was increasing,
6: 2 Twelve gathered all the *d* together
6: 7 of *d* in Jerusalem increased rapidly,
9: 1 threats against the Lord's *d*.
9: 19 days with the *d* in Damascus.
9: 26 tried to join the *d*, but they were all
9: 38 so when the *d* heard that Peter was
11: 26 The *d* were first called Christians
11: 29 The *d*, each according to his ability
13: 52 And the *d* were filled with joy
14: 20 But after the *d* had gathered
14: 21 and won a large number of *d*.
14: 22 strengthening the *d*
14: 28 stayed there a long time with the *d*.
15: 10 of the *d* a yoke that neither we
18: 23 Phrygia, strengthening all the *d*.
18: 27 and wrote to the *d* there
19: 1 There he found some *d*
19: 9 He took the *d* with him
19: 30 but the *d* would not let him.
20: 1 Paul sent for the *d*
20: 30 in order to draw away *d* after them.
21: 4 Finding the *d* there, we stayed
21: 5 All the *d* and their wives
21: 16 from Cyprus and one of the early *d*.
21: 16 the *d* from Caesarea accompanied

DISCIPLES' (DISCIPLE)

Jn 13: 5 and began to wash his *d'* feet,

DISCIPLINE (DISCIPLINED DISCIPLINES SELF-DISCIPLINE)

Dt 4: 36 made you hear his voice to *d* you.
11: 2 and experienced the *d*
21: 18 listen to them when they *d* him,
Job 5: 17 so do not despise the *d*
Ps 6: 1 or *d* me in your wrath.
38: 1 or *d* me in your wrath.
39: 11 You rebuke and *d* men for their sin;
94: 12 Blessed is the man you *d*, O LORD
105: 22 to *d* his princes as he pleased
Pr 1: 2 for attaining wisdom and *d*;
1: 7 but fools despise wisdom and *d*.
3: 11 do not despise the LORD's *d*
5: 12 You will say, "How I hated *d*!
5: 23 He will die for lack of *d*,
6: 23 and the corrections of *d*
10: 17 He who heeds *d* shows the way
12: 1 Whoever loves *d* loves knowledge,
13: 18 He who ignores *d* comes to poverty
13: 24 who loves him is careful to *d* him.
15: 5 A fool spurns his father's *d*,
15: 10 Stern *d* awaits him who leaves
15: 32 He who ignores *d* despises himself,
19: 18 *D* your son, for in that there is hope
22: 15 the rod of *d* will drive it far
23: 13 Do not withhold *d* from a child;
23: 23 get wisdom, *d* and understanding.
29: 17 *D* your son, and he will give you
Jer 17: 23 would not listen or respond to *d*.
30: 11 I will *d* you but only with justice;
32: 33 would not listen or respond to *d*.
46: 28 I will *d* you but only with justice;
Hos 5: 2 I will *d* all of them.
Heb 12: 5 do not make light of the Lord's *d*,
12: 7 as *d*; God is treating you
12: 8 (and everyone undergoes *d*),
12: 11 No *d* seems pleasant at the time,
Rev 3: 19 Those whom I love I rebuke and *d*.

DISCIPLINED (DISCIPLINE)

Pr 1: 3 for acquiring a *d* and prudent life,
Isa 26: 16 when you *d* them,
Jer 31: 18 and I have been *d*.
31: 18 'You *d* me like an unruly calf,
1Co 11: 32 we are being *d* so that we will not
Tit 1: 8 upright, holy and *d*.
Heb 12: 7 For what son is not *d* by his father?
12: 8 you are not *d* (and everyone
12: 9 all had human fathers who *d* us
12: 10 Our fathers *d* us for a little while

DISCIPLINES (DISCIPLINE)

Dt 8: 5 so the LORD your God *d* you.
8: 5 your heart that as a man *d* his son,
Ps 94: 10 Does he who *d* nations not punish?
Pr 3: 12 the LORD *d* those he loves,
Heb 12: 6 because the Lord *d* those he loves,
12: 10 but God *d* us for our good,

DISCLOSE (DISCLOSED)

Job 11: 6 and *d* to you the secrets of wisdom,
Isa 26: 21 The earth will *d* the blood shed

DISCLOSED (DISCLOSE)

Mt 10: 26 concealed that will not be *d*,
Mk 4: 22 is hidden is meant to be *d*,
Lk 8: 17 is nothing hidden that will not be *d*,
12: 2 concealed that will not be *d*,
Col 1: 26 and generations, but is now *d*
Heb 9: 8 Holy Place had not yet been *d*

DISCOMFORT

Jnh 4: 6 shade for his head to ease his *d*,

DISCONTENTED

1Sa 22: 2 in debt or *d* gathered around him,

DISCORD

Est 1: 18 end of disrespect and *d*.
Gal 5: 20 idolatry and witchcraft; hatred, *d*,

DISCOURAGE (DISCOURAGED DISCOURAGEMENT DISCOURAGING)

Nu 32: 7 Why do you *d* the Israelites
Ezr 4: 4 out to *d* the people of Judah

DISCOURAGED (DISCOURAGE)

Nu 32: 9 they *d* the Israelites
Dt 1: 21 Do not be afraid; do not be *d*."
31: 8 Do not be afraid; do not be *d*."
Jos 1: 9 Do not be terrified; do not be *d*,
8: 1 "Do not be afraid; do not be *d*.
10: 25 "Do not be afraid; do not be *d*.
1Ch 22: 13 Do not be afraid or *d*.
28: 20 or *d*, for the LORD God,
2Ch 20: 15 or *d* because of this vast army.
20: 17 Do not be afraid; do not be *d*.
32: 7 or *d* because of the king of Assyria
Job 4: 5 to you, and you are *d*;
Isa 42: 4 he will not falter or be *d*
Eph 3: 13 to be *d* because of my sufferings
Col 3: 21 children, or they will become *d*.

DISCOURAGEMENT (DISCOURAGE)

Ex 6: 9 of their *d* and cruel bondage.

DISCOURAGING (DISCOURAGE)

Jer 38: 4 He is *d* the soldiers who are left

DISCOURSE (DISCOURSED)

Job 27: 1 Job continued his *d*: "As surely
29: 1 Job continued his *d*: "How I long

DISCOURSED (DISCOURSE)

Ac 24: 25 As Paul *d* on righteousness,

DISCOVER (DISCOVERED)

Ecc 7: 14 Therefore, a man cannot *d*
7: 24 who can *d* it?
7: 27 thing to another to *d* the scheme
8: 17 man cannot *d* its meaning.
2Co 13: 6 trust that you will *d* that we have

DISCOVERED (DISCOVER)

Ge 26: 19 and *d* a well of fresh water there.
36: 24 is the Anah who *d* the hot springs
Dt 22: 28 and rapes her and they are *d*,

Jdg 16: 9 the secret of his strength was not *d*.
21: 8 They *d* that no one
Ru 3: 8 and *d* a woman lying at his feet.
1Sa 22: 6 that David and his men had been *d*.
2Ki 17: 4 king of Assyria *d* that Hoshea was
23: 24 book that Hilkiah the priest had *d*
Ps 44: 21 would not God have *d* it,
Ecc 7: 27 the Teacher, "this is what I have *d*:
Ro 4: 1 our forefather, *d* in this matter? If,

DISCREDIT (DISCREDITED)

Ne 6: 13 would give me a bad name to *d* me.
Job 40: 8 "Would you *d* my justice?

DISCREDITED (DISCREDIT)

Ac 19: 27 great goddess Artemis will be *d*,
2Co 6: 3 so that our ministry will not be *d*.

DISCRETION

1Ch 22: 12 May the LORD give you *d*
Pr 1: 4 knowledge and *d* to the young—
2: 11 *D* will protect you,
5: 2 that you may maintain *d*
8: 12 I possess knowledge and *d*.
11: 22 a beautiful woman who shows no *d*.

DISCRIMINATED

Jas 2: 4 have you not *d* among yourselves

DISCUSS (DISCUSSED DISCUSSING DISCUSSION DISCUSSIONS)

Lk 6: 11 to *d* with one another what they
Heb 9: 5 But we cannot *d* these things

DISCUSSED (DISCUSS)

1Sa 20: 23 And about the matter you and I *d*
Mt 16: 7 They *d* this among themselves
21: 25 They *d* it among themselves
Mk 8: 16 They *d* this with one another
11: 31 They *d* it among themselves
Lk 20: 5 They *d* it among themselves
22: 4 *d* with them how he might betray
24: 15 and *d* these things with each other,
Ac 25: 14 Festus *d* Paul's case with the king.

DISCUSSING (DISCUSS)

Mk 9: 10 *d* what "rising from the dead"
Lk 24: 17 "What are you *d* together

DISCUSSION (DISCUSS)

Mt 16: 8 Aware of their *d*, Jesus asked,
Mk 8: 17 Aware of their *d*, Jesus asked them:
Ac 15: 7 After much *d*, Peter got up

DISCUSSIONS (DISCUSS)

Ac 19: 9 and had *d* daily in the lecture hall

DISDAINED (DISDAINFUL)

1Sa 2: 30 but those who despise me will be *d*.
Job 30: 1 whose fathers I would have *d*
Ps 22: 24 For he has not despised or *d*
Jer 30: 19 and they will not be *d*.

DISDAINFUL (DISDAINED)

Pr 30: 13 whose glances are so *d*;

DISEASE (DISEASED DISEASES)

Lev 13: 2 may become an infectious skin *d*,
13: 3 skin deep, it is an infectious skin *d*.
13: 8 him unclean; it is an infectious *d*.
13: 9 anyone has an infectious skin *d*,
13: 11 is a chronic skin *d* and the priest
13: 12 "If the *d* breaks out all over his skin
13: 13 if the *d* has covered his whole body
13: 15 is unclean; he has an infectious *d*.
13: 20 an infectious skin *d* that has broken
13: 25 it is an infectious *d* that has broken
13: 25 unclean; it is an infectious skin *d*.
13: 27 unclean; it is an infectious skin *d*.
13: 30 an infectious *d* of the head or chin.
13: 42 it is an infectious *d* breaking out
13: 43 like an infectious skin *d*,
13: 45 such an infectious *d* must wear torn
14: 3 healed of his infectious skin *d*,
14: 7 to be cleansed of the infectious *d*
14: 32 who has an infectious skin *d*
14: 54 for any infectious skin *d*,
22: 4 of Aaron has an infectious skin *d*
Nu 5: 2 who has an infectious skin *d*
Dt 7: 15 will keep you free from every *d*.
28: 22 will strike you with wasting *d*,
1Ki 8: 37 whatever disaster or *d* may come,
2Ch 6: 28 whatever disaster or *d* may come,
16: 12 Though his *d* was severe,
16: 12 afflicted with a *d* in his feet.
21: 15 ill with a lingering *d* of the bowels,
21: 15 until the *d* causes your bowels
21: 18 with an incurable *d* of the bowels.
21: 19 bowels came out because of the *d*,
Ps 41: 8 "A vile *d* has beset him;
106: 15 but sent a wasting *d* upon them.
Isa 10: 16 will send a wasting *d*
17: 11 in the day of *d* and incurable pain.
Mt 4: 23 and healing every *d* and sickness
9: 35 and healing every *d* and sickness.
10: 1 and to heal every *d* and sickness.

DISEASED (DISEASE)

Lev 13: 33 be shaved except for the *d* area,
13: 44 the man is *d* and is unclean.
14: 2 for the *d* person at the time
1Ki 15: 23 however, his feet became *d*.
Mal 1: 8 you sacrifice crippled or *d* animals,
1: 13 or *d* animals and offer them

DISEASES (DISEASE)

Ge 12: 17 But the LORD inflicted serious *d*
Ex 15: 26 bring on you any of the *d* I brought
Lev 14: 57 the regulations for infectious skin *d*
26: 16 wasting *d* and fever that will
Dt 7: 15 on you the horrible *d* you knew
24: 8 cases of leprous *d* be very careful
28: 21 with *d* until he has destroyed you
28: 60 bring upon you all the *d*
29: 22 the *d* with which the LORD has
Ps 103: 3 and heals all my *d*;
Jer 16: 4 "They will die of deadly *d*.
Mt 4: 24 him all who were ill with various *d*,
8: 17 and carried our *d*."
Mk 1: 34 healed many who had various *d*.
3: 10 those with *d* were pushing forward
Lk 6: 18 and to be healed of their *d*.
7: 21 time Jesus cured many who had *d*,
8: 2 cured of evil spirits and *d*:
9: 1 drive out all demons and to cure *d*,

DISFIGURE (DISFIGURED)

Mt 6: 16 for they *d* their faces

DISFIGURED (DISFIGURE)

Lev 21: 18 no man who is blind or lame, *d*
Isa 52: 14 his appearance was so *d*

DISGRACE (DISGRACED DISGRACEFUL DISGRACES)

Ge 30: 23 "God has taken away my *d*."
34: 14 That would be a *d* to us.
Lev 20: 17 they have sexual relations, it is a *d*.
Nu 12: 14 been in *d* for seven days?
1Sa 11: 2 and so bring *d* on all Israel."
17: 26 and removes this *d* from Israel?
2Sa 13: 13 Where could I get rid of my *d*?
2Ki 19: 3 a day of distress and rebuke and *d*,
2Ch 32: 21 he withdrew to his own land in *d*.
Ne 1: 3 are in great trouble and *d*.
2: 17 and we will no longer be in *d*."
Ps 6: 10 may they turn back in sudden *d*.
35: 26 be clothed with shame and *d*.
40: 14 be turned back in *d*.
44: 15 My *d* is before me all day long,
52: 1 you who are a *d* in the eyes of God?
70: 2 be turned back in *d*.
71: 13 be covered with scorn and *d*.
74: 21 not let the oppressed retreat in *d*;
83: 17 may they perish in *d*.
109: 29 My accusers will be clothed with *d*
119: 39 Take away the *d* I dread,
Pr 6: 33 Blows and *d* are his lot,
11: 2 When pride comes, then comes *d*,
13: 5 but the wicked bring shame and *d*.
14: 34 but sin is a *d* to any people.
18: 3 and with shame comes *d*.
19: 26 is a son who brings shame and *d*.
Isa 4: 1 Take away our *d*!"
22: 18 you *d* to your master's house!
25: 8 he will remove the *d* of his people
Isa 30: 3 Egypt's shade will bring you *d*.
30: 5 but only shame and *d*."
37: 3 a day of distress and rebuke and *d*,
43: 28 So I will *d* the dignitaries
45: 16 they will go off into *d* together.
54: 4 Do not fear *d*; you will not be
61: 7 and instead of *d*
Jer 3: 25 and let our *d* cover us.
23: 40 I will bring upon you everlasting *d*
31: 19 because I bore the *d* of my youth.'
La 3: 30 and let him be filled with *d*.
5: 1 look, and see our *d*.
Eze 16: 52 Bear your *d*, for you have furnished
16: 52 be ashamed and bear your *d*,
16: 54 so that you may bear your *d*
28: 16 So I drove you in *d* from the mount
32: 30 slain in *d* despite the terror caused
36: 30 so that you will no longer suffer *d*
Hos 2: 5 and has conceived them in *d*.
Mic 2: 6 *d* will not overtake us."
Hab 2: 16 and *d* will cover your glory.
Mt 1: 19 want to expose her to public *d*,
Lk 1: 25 taken away my *d* among the people
Ac 5: 41 of suffering *d* for the Name.
1Co 11: 6 and if it is a *d* for a woman
11: 14 it is a *d* to him, but that
1Ti 3: 7 so that he will not fall into *d*
Heb 6: 6 and subjecting him to public *d*.
11: 26 He regarded *d* for the sake
13: 13 the camp, bearing the *d* he bore.

DISGRACED (DISGRACE)

2Sa 13: 22 because he had *d* his sister Tamar.
Ezr 9: 6 and *d* to lift up my face to you,
Ps 35: 4 be *d* and put to shame;
69: 6 not be *d* because of me,
69: 19 You know how I am scorned, *d*
Isa 1: 29 will be *d* because of the gardens
41: 11 will surely be ashamed and *d*;
45: 16 of idols will be put to shame and *d*;
45: 17 you will never be put to shame or *d*,
50: 7 I will not be *d*.
Jer 2: 26 so the house of Israel is *d*—
2: 26 "As a thief is *d* when he is caught,
15: 9 she will be *d* and humiliated.
20: 11 They will fail and be thoroughly *d*;
22: 22 Then you will be ashamed and *d*
48: 1 Kiriathaim will be *d* and captured;
48: 1 the stronghold will be *d*
48: 20 Moab is *d* for she is shattered.
50: 12 she who gave you birth will be *d*.
51: 47 her whole land will be *d*
51: 51 "We are *d*,
Eze 36: 32 Be ashamed and *d*
Hos 10: 6 Ephraim will be *d*;
Mic 3: 7 and the diviners *d*.

DISGRACEFUL (DISGRACE)

Ge 34: 7 Shechem had done a *d* thing
Dt 22: 21 She has done a *d* thing in Israel
Jos 7: 15 and has done a *d* thing in Israel!' "
Jdg 19: 23 is my guest, don't do this *d* thing.
19: 24 to this man, don't do such a *d* thing
20: 6 they committed this lewd and *d* act
Pr 10: 5 during harvest is a *d* son.
12: 4 a *d* wife is like decay in his bones.
17: 2 wise servant will rule over a *d* son,
Hos 4: 7 their Glory for something *d*.
1Co 14: 35 for it is *d* for a woman to speak

DISGRACES (DISGRACE)

Lev 21: 9 she *d* her father; she must be
Pr 28: 7 of gluttons *d* his father.
29: 15 but a child left to itself *d* his mother

DISGUISE (DISGUISED DISGUISES)

Ge 38: 14 herself with a veil to *d* herself,
1Ki 14: 2 said to his wife, "Go, *d* yourself,
22: 30 "I will enter the battle in *d*,
2Ch 18: 29 "I will enter the battle in *d*,

DISGUISED (DISGUISE)

1Sa 28: 8 So Saul *d* himself, putting
1Ki 20: 38 He *d* himself with his headband
22: 30 So the king of Israel *d* himself
2Ch 18: 29 So the king of Israel *d* himself
35: 22 *d* himself to engage him in battle.

DISGUISES (DISGUISE)
Pr 26: 24 A malicious man *d* himself

DISGUST (DISGUSTED)
Eze 23: 17 she turned away from them in *d.*
23: 18 I turned away from her in *d,*
23: 22 those you turned away from in *d,*
23: 28 to those you turned away from in *d*

DISGUSTED (DISGUST)
Ge 27: 46 *d* with living because of these

DISH (DISHES)
2Ki 21: 13 out Jerusalem as one wipes a *d,*
1Ch 28: 17 the weight of gold for each gold *d;*
28: 17 the weight of silver for each silver *d*
Pr 19: 24 sluggard buries his hand in the *d;*
26: 15 sluggard buries his hand in the *d;*
Mt 23: 25 the outside of the cup and *d,*
23: 26 the inside of the cup and *d,*
Lk 11: 39 the outside of the cup and *d,*
11: 41 is inside the *d* to the poor,
Jn 13: 26 when I have dipped it in the *d.*"

DISHAN
Ge 36: 21 Zibeon, Anah, Dishon, Ezer and *D*
36: 28 The sons of *D:* Uz and Aran.
36: 30 Zibeon, Anah, Dishon, Ezer and *D*
1Ch 1: 38 Zibeon, Anah, Dishon, Ezer and *D*
1: 42 The sons of *D:* Uz and Aran.

DISHEARTENED (HEART)
Dt 20: 8 brothers will not become *d* too."
Jer 49: 23 They are *d,*
Eze 13: 22 Because you *d* the righteous

DISHES (DISH)
Nu 7: 85 silver *d* weighed two thousand four
1Ki 7: 50 the pure gold *d,* wick trimmers,
Ezr 1: 9 inventory: gold *d* 30 silver *d* 1,000

DISHON
Ge 36: 21 Zibeon, Anah, *D,* Ezer and Dishan.
36: 25 *D* and Oholibamah daughter
36: 26 The sons of *D:* Hemdan, Eshban,
36: 30 Zibeon, Anah, *D,* Ezer and Dishan.
1Ch 1: 38 Zibeon, Anah, *D,* Ezer and Dishan.
1: 41 The son of Anah: *D.*
1: 41 The sons of *D:* Hemdan, Eshban,

DISHONEST
Ex 18: 21 trustworthy men who hate *d* gain
Lev 19: 35 " 'Do not use *d* standards
1Sa 8: 3 They turned aside after *d* gain
Pr 11: 1 The LORD abhors *d* scales,
13: 11 *D* money dwindles away,
20: 23 and *d* scales do not please him.
29: 27 The righteous detest the *d;*
Jer 22: 17 are set only on *d* gain,
Eze 28: 18 By your many sins and *d* trade
Hos 12: 7 The merchant uses *d* scales;
Am 8: 5 and cheating with *d* scales,
Mic 6: 11 Shall I acquit a man with *d* scales,
Lk 16: 8 master commended the *d* manager
16: 10 whoever is *d* with very little will
16: 10 with very little will also be *d*
1Ti 3: 8 wine, and not pursuing *d* gain.
Tit 1: 7 not violent, not pursuing *d* gain.
1: 11 and that for the sake of *d* gain

DISHONOR (DISHONORED DISHONORS)
Lev 18: 7 " 'Do not *d* your father
18: 8 wife; that would *d* your father.
18: 10 daughter; that would *d* you.
18: 14 " 'Do not *d* your father's brother
18: 16 that would *d* your brother.
20: 19 for that would *d* a close relative;
Dt 22: 30 he must not *d* his father's bed.
Pr 30: 9 and so *d* the name of my God.
Jer 14: 21 do not *d* your glorious throne.
20: 11 their *d* will never be forgotten.
La 2: 2 princes down to the ground in *d.*
Eze 22: 10 are those who *d* their fathers' bed;
Jn 8: 49 I honor my Father and you *d* me.
Ro 2: 23 do you *d* God by breaking the law?
1Co 15: 43 it is sown in *d,* it is raised in glory;
2Co 6: 8 through glory and *d,* bad report

DISHONORED (DISHONOR)
Lev 20: 11 father's wife, he has *d* his father.
20: 17 He has *d* his sister and will be held
20: 20 with his aunt, he has *d* his uncle.
20: 21 of impurity; he has *d* his brother.
Dt 21: 14 as a slave, since you have *d* her.
Ezr 4: 14 proper for us to see the king *d,*
1Co 4: 10 You are honored, we are *d!*

DISHONORS (DISHONOR)
Dt 27: 16 Cursed is the man who *d* his father
27: 20 for he *d* his father's bed."
Job 20: 3 I hear a rebuke that *d* me,
Mic 7: 6 For a son *d* his father,
1Co 11: 4 with his head covered *d* his head.
11: 5 her head uncovered *d* her head—

DISILLUSIONMENT
Ps 7: 14 conceives trouble gives birth to *d.*

DISLIKES
Dt 22: 13 *d* her and slanders her
22: 16 marriage to this man, but he *d* her.
24: 3 and her second husband *d* her

DISLODGE
Jos 15: 63 Judah could not *d* the Jebusites,
16: 10 They did not *d* the Canaanites
Jdg 1: 21 however, failed to *d* the Jebusites,

DISLOYAL
Ps 78: 57 Like their fathers they were *d*

DISMAY (DISMAYED)
Job 41: 22 *d* goes before him.
Ps 35: 4 be turned back in *d.*
116: 11 And in my *d* I said,

DISMAYED (DISMAY)
1Sa 17: 11 and all the Israelites were *d*
2Ki 19: 26 are *d* and put to shame.
Job 4: 5 it strikes you, and you are *d.*
32: 15 They are *d* and have no more to say
Ps 6: 10 all my enemies be ashamed and *d;*
30: 7 I was *d.*
83: 17 May they ever be ashamed and *d;*
143: 4 my heart within me is *d.*
Isa 28: 16 the one who trusts will never be *d.*
37: 27 are *d* and put to shame.
41: 10 do not be *d,* for I am your God.
41: 23 so that we will be *d* and filled
Jer 8: 9 they will be *d* and trapped.
14: 3 *d* and despairing,
14: 4 the farmers are *d*
30: 10 do not be *d,* O Israel,'
46: 27 do not be *d,* O Israel.
49: 23 "Hamath and Arpad are *d,*

DISMISS (DISMISSED)
Lk 2: 29 you now *d* your servant in peace.

DISMISSED (DISMISS)
Jdg 2: 6 After Joshua had *d* the Israelites,
1Sa 10: 25 Then Samuel *d* the people.
2Ch 25: 10 So Amaziah *d* the troops who had
Mt 14: 22 while he *d* the crowd.
14: 23 After he had *d* them, he went up
Mk 6: 45 to Bethsaida, while he *d* the crowd.
Ac 13: 43 When the congregation was *d,*
19: 41 he had said this, he *d* the assembly.
23: 22 The commander *d* the young man

DISOBEDIENCE (DISOBEY)
Jos 22: 22 in rebellion or *d* to the LORD,
Jer 43: 7 So they entered Egypt in *d*
Ro 5: 19 as through the *d* of the one man
11: 30 mercy as a result of their *d,*
11: 32 to *d* so that he may have mercy
2Co 10: 6 ready to punish every act of *d,*
Heb 2: 2 and *d* received its just punishment,
4: 6 go in, because of their *d.*
4: 11 fall by following their example of *d.*

DISOBEDIENT (DISOBEY)
Ne 9: 26 "But they were *d* and rebelled
Lk 1: 17 and the *d* to the wisdom
Ac 26: 19 I was not *d* to the vision
Ro 10: 21 hands to a *d* and obstinate people."
Ro 11: 30 as you who were at one time *d*
11: 31 so they too have now become *d*
Eph 2: 2 now at work in those who are *d.*
5: 6 comes on those who are *d.*
5: 12 to mention what the *d* do in secret.
2Ti 3: 2 proud, abusive, *d* to their parents,
Tit 1: 6 to the charge of being wild and *d.*
1: 16 *d* and unfit for doing anything
3: 3 At one time we too were foolish, *d,*
Heb 11: 31 killed with those who were *d.*

DISOBEY (DISOBEDIENCE DISOBEDIENT DISOBEYED DISOBEYING DISOBEYS)
Dt 11: 28 the curse if you *d* the commands
2Ch 24: 20 'Why do you *d* the LORD's
Est 3: 3 Why do you *d* the king's command
Jer 42: 13 and so *d* the LORD your God,
Ro 1: 30 they *d* their parents; they are
1Pe 2: 8 because they *d* the message—

DISOBEYED (DISOBEY)
Nu 14: 22 and in the desert but who *d* me
27: 14 both of you *d* my command
Jdg 2: 2 Yet you have *d* me.
Ne 9: 29 arrogant and *d* your commands.
Isa 24: 5 they have *d* the laws,
Jer 43: 4 and all the people *d* the LORD's
Lk 15: 29 for you and never *d* your orders.
Heb 3: 18 rest if not to those who *d?*
1Pe 3: 20 the spirits in prison who *d* long ago

DISOBEYING (DISOBEY)
Nu 14: 41 "Why are you *d* the LORD's

DISOBEYS (DISOBEY)
Eze 33: 12 man will not save him when he *d.*

DISORDER
Job 10: 22 of deep shadow and *d,*
1Co 14: 33 For God is not a God of *d*
2Co 12: 20 slander, gossip, arrogance and *d.*
Jas 3: 16 there you find *d* and every evil

DISOWN (DISOWNED DISOWNS)
Pr 30: 9 I may have too much and *d* you
Mt 10: 33 I will *d* him before my Father
26: 34 you will *d* me three times."
26: 35 to die with you, I will never *d* you."
26: 75 you will *d* me three times."
Mk 14: 30 you yourself will *d* me three
14: 31 to die with you, I will never *d* you."
14: 72 twice you will *d* me three times."
Lk 22: 61 you will *d* me three times."
Jn 13: 38 you will *d* me three times!
2Ti 2: 12 If we *d* him,
2: 12 he will also *d* us;
2: 13 for he cannot *d* himself.

DISOWNED (DISOWN)
Lk 12: 9 me before men will be *d*
Ac 3: 13 and you *d* him before Pilate,
3: 14 You *d* the Holy and Righteous One

DISOWNS (DISOWN)
Job 8: 18 that place *d* it and says, 'I never
Mt 10: 33 But whoever *d* me before men,
Lk 12: 9 he who *d* me before men will be

DISPATCH (DISPATCHED DISPATCHES)
Isa 10: 6 I *d* him against a people who anger

DISPATCHED (DISPATCH)
1Ki 20: 17 Now Ben-Hadad had *d* scouts,

DISPATCHES (DISPATCH)
Est 1: 22 He sent *d* to all parts
3: 13 *D* were sent by couriers
8: 5 overruling the *d* that Haman
8: 10 sealed the *d* with the king's signet

DISPENSES
Zep 3: 5 by morning he *d* his justice,

DISPERSE (DISPERSED DISPERSES DISPERSING)
Ge 49: 7 and *d* them in Israel.
Eze 12: 15 when I *d* them among the nations
20: 23 in the desert that I would *d* them

Eze 22: 15 I will *d* you among the nations
29: 12 And I will *d* the Egyptians
30: 23 I will *d* the Egyptians
30: 26 I will *d* the Egyptians

DISPERSED (DISPERSE)

2Sa 20: 22 and his men *d* from the city,
1Ki 1: 49 guests rose in alarm and *d*.
Est 3: 8 "There is a certain people *d*
Job 38: 24 the place where the lightning is *d*,
Eze 36: 19 I *d* them among the nations,
Ac 5: 36 all his followers were *d*,

DISPERSES (DISPERSE)

Dt 30: 1 the LORD your God *d* you
Job 12: 23 he enlarges nations, and *d* them.

DISPERSING (DISPERSE)

2Ch 11: 23 *d* some of his sons

DISPLACES

Pr 30: 23 a maidservant who *d* her mistress.

DISPLAY (DISPLAYED DISPLAYS)

Dt 22: 17 Then her parents shall *d* the cloth
Est 1: 11 in order to *d* her beauty
Job 10: 16 again *d* your awesome power
Ps 19: 2 night after night they *d* knowledge.
45: 4 your right hand *d* awesome deeds.
77: 14 *d* your power among the peoples.
Isa 49: 3 in whom I will *d* my splendor."
60: 21 for the *d* of my splendor.
61: 3 LORD for the *d* of his splendor.
Eze 39: 21 I will *d* my glory among the nations
Ro 9: 17 that I might *d* my power in you
1Co 4: 9 on *d* at the end of the procession,
1Ti 1: 16 Christ Jesus might *d* his unlimited

DISPLAYED (DISPLAY)

Ex 14: 31 saw the great power the LORD *d*
Nu 14: 17 Now may the Lord's strength be *d*,
1Ki 11: 41 all he did and the wisdom he *d*—
Est 1: 4 a full 180 days he *d* the vast wealth
Job 26: 3 And what great insight you have *d!*
Ps 78: 43 the day he *d* his miraculous signs
Jn 9: 3 work of God might be *d* in his life.
2Th 2: 9 the work of Satan *d* in all kinds

DISPLAYS (DISPLAY)

Pr 14: 29 but a quick-tempered man *d* folly.
Isa 44: 23 he *d* his glory in Israel.

DISPLEASE (DISPLEASED DISPLEASES DISPLEASING DISPLEASURE)

Nu 11: 11 to *d* you that you put the burden
1Sa 29: 7 do nothing to *d* the Philistine rulers
1Th 2: 15 They *d* God and are hostile

DISPLEASED (DISPLEASE)

Ge 48: 17 hand on Ephraim's head he was *d;*
Nu 22: 34 Now if you are *d*, I will go back."
1Sa 8: 6 this *d* Samuel; so he prayed
2Sa 11: 27 David had done *d* the LORD.
Ne 13: 8 I was greatly *d* and threw all
Isa 59: 15 The LORD looked and was *d*
Jnh 4: 1 Jonah was greatly *d* and became

DISPLEASES (DISPLEASE)

Isa 65: 12 and chose what *d* me."
66: 4 and chose what *d* me."

DISPLEASING (DISPLEASE)

Ge 28: 8 then realized how *d* the Canaanite
Dt 24: 1 marries a woman who becomes *d*

DISPLEASURE (DISPLEASE)

Ps 85: 4 and put away your *d* toward us.

DISPOSAL (DISPOSED)

Mt 26: 53 at my *d* more than twelve legions
Ac 5: 4 wasn't the money at your *d?*

DISPOSED (DISPOSAL)

Ex 3: 21 make the Egyptians favorably *d*
11: 3 made the Egyptians favorably *d*
12: 36 made the Egyptians favorably *d*
Dt 31: 21 I know what they are *d* to do,
1Sa 20: 12 If he is favorably *d* toward you,

DISPOSSESS (DISPOSSESSING)

Dt 9: 1 and *d* nations greater and stronger
11: 23 and you will *d* nations larger
12: 29 you are about to invade and *d*.
18: 14 The nations you will *d* listen
Isa 54: 3 your descendants will *d* nations

DISPOSSESSING (DISPOSSESS)

Dt 12: 2 the nations you are *d* worship their
Eze 45: 9 Stop *d* my people, declares

DISPUTABLE (DISPUTE)

Ro 14: 1 passing judgment on *d* matters.

DISPUTE (DISPUTABLE DISPUTED DISPUTES DISPUTING)

Ex 18: 16 they have a *d*, it is brought
24: 14 and anyone involved in a *d* can go
Dt 19: 17 in the *d* must stand in the presence
21: 5 to decide all cases of *d* and assault.
25: 1 When men have a *d*, they are
Jdg 11: 27 decide the *d* this day
Job 9: 3 Though one wished to *d* with him,
9: 14 "How then can I *d* with him?
Pr 17: 14 before a *d* breaks out.
Eze 44: 24 " 'In any *d*, the priests are to serve
Lk 22: 24 Also a *d* arose among them
Ac 15: 2 and Barnabas into sharp *d*
17: 18 and Stoic philosophers began to *d*
23: 7 *d* broke out between the Pharisees
23: 10 The *d* became so violent that
25: 19 they had some points of *d*
1Co 6: 1 If any of you has a *d* with another,
6: 5 to judge a *d* between believers?

DISPUTED (DISPUTE)

Ge 26: 20 the well Esek, because they *d*

DISPUTES (DISPUTE)

Ex 18: 19 before God and bring their *d*
Dt 1: 12 and your burdens and your *d* all
1: 16 Hear the *d* between your brothers
Jdg 4: 5 to her to have their *d* decided.
2Ch 19: 8 law of the LORD and to settle *d*.
Pr 18: 18 Casting the lot settles *d*
18: 19 *d* are like the barred gates
Isa 2: 4 and will settle *d* for many peoples.
Mic 4: 3 will settle *d* for strong nations far
1Co 6: 4 if you have *d* about such matters,

DISPUTING (DISPUTE)

1Ti 2: 8 in prayer, without anger or *d*.
Jude : 9 when he was *d* with the devil about

DISQUALIFIED (DISQUALIFY)

1Co 9: 27 I myself will not be *d* for the prize.

DISQUALIFY (DISQUALIFIED)

Col 2: 18 and the worship of angels *d* you

DISQUIETING

Job 4: 13 Amid *d* dreams in the night,

DISREGARDED (DISREGARDING)

Ezr 9: 10 For we have *d* the commands you
Isa 40: 27 my cause is *d* by my God"?

DISREGARDING (DISREGARDED)

Am 1: 9 *d* a treaty of brotherhood,

DISREPUTE

2Pe 2: 2 will bring the way of truth into *d*.

DISRESPECT

Est 1: 18 There will be no end of *d*

DISROBING

2Sa 6: 20 *d* in the sight of the slave girls

DISSENSION (DISSENSIONS)

Pr 6: 14 he always stirs up *d*.
6: 19 and a man who stirs up *d*
10: 12 Hatred stirs up *d*,
15: 18 A hot-tempered man stirs up *d*,
16: 28 A perverse man stirs up *d*,
28: 25 A greedy man stirs up *d*,
29: 22 An angry man stirs up *d*,
Ro 13: 13 debauchery, not in *d* and jealousy.

DISSENSIONS (DISSENSION)

Gal 5: 20 selfish ambition, *d*, factions

DISSIPATION

Lk 21: 34 will be weighed down with *d*,
1Pe 4: 4 with them into the same flood of *d*,

DISSOLVED

Isa 34: 4 the stars of the heavens will be *d*

DISSUADE (DISSUADED)

Eze 3: 18 or speak out to *d* him
33: 8 out to *d* him from his ways,

DISSUADED (DISSUADE)

Ac 21: 14 he would not be *d*, we gave up

DISTAFF

Pr 31: 19 In her hand she holds the *d*

DISTILL

Job 36: 27 which *d* as rain to the streams;

DISTINCTION

Ex 8: 23 I will make a *d* between my people
9: 4 But the LORD will make a *d*
11: 7 know that the LORD makes a *d*
Lev 20: 25 therefore make a *d* between clean
Mal 3: 18 And you will again see the *d*
Ac 15: 9 He made no *d* between us
1Co 14: 7 unless there is a *d* in the notes?

DISTINGUISH (DISTINGUISHED DISTINGUISHING)

Ex 33: 16 What else will *d* me and your
Lev 10: 10 You must *d* between the holy
11: 47 You must *d* between the unclean
1Ki 3: 9 and to *d* between right and wrong.
Ezr 3: 13 No one could *d* the sound
Eze 22: 26 they do not *d* between the holy
44: 23 how to *d* between the unclean
1Co 12: 10 the ability to *d* between spirits,
Heb 5: 14 themselves to *d* good from evil.

DISTINGUISHED (DISTINGUISH)

Nu 22: 15 more numerous and more *d*
2Sa 6: 20 king of Israel has *d* himself today,
Da 6: 3 Now Daniel so *d* himself
Lk 14: 8 for a person more *d*

DISTINGUISHING (DISTINGUISH)

2Th 3: 17 which is the *d* mark

DISTORT (DISTORTED)

Jer 23: 36 and so you *d* the words
Mic 3: 9 and *d* all that is right;
Ac 20: 30 and *d* the truth in order
2Co 4: 2 nor do we *d* the word of God.
2Pe 3: 16 ignorant and unstable people *d*,

DISTORTED (DISTORT)

Eze 27: 35 and their faces are *d* with fear.

DISTRACTED

Lk 10: 40 But Martha was *d* by all

DISTRAUGHT

Ps 55: 2 My thoughts trouble me and I am *d*

DISTRESS (DISTRESSED DISTRESSES DISTRESSING)

Ge 32: 7 *d* Jacob divided the people who
35: 3 me in the day of my *d*
42: 21 that's why this *d* has come upon us
Dt 4: 30 are in *d* and all these things have
28: 57 in the *d* that your enemy will inflict
Jdg 2: 15 They were in great *d*.
10: 9 Ephraim; and Israel was in great *d*.
1Sa 2: 32 and you will see *d* in my dwelling.
14: 24 the men of Israel were in *d* that day
22: 2 All those who were in *d* or in debt
28: 15 "I am in great *d*," Saul said.
2Sa 16: 12 be that the LORD will see my *d*
22: 7 In my *d* I called to the LORD;
24: 14 David said to Gad, "I am in deep *d*.
2Ki 4: 27 "Leave her alone! She is in bitter *d*,
19: 3 This day is a day of *d* and rebuke
1Ch 21: 13 David said to Gad, "I am in deep *d*.

2Ch 15: 4 in their *d* they turned to the LORD
15: 6 them with every kind of *d*.
20: 9 and will cry out to you in our *d*,
33: 12 In his *d* he sought the favor
Ne 9: 37 We are in great *d*.
Est 4: 4 about Mordecai, she was in great *d*.
7: 4 no such *d* would justify disturbing
Job 15: 24 *D* and anguish fill him with terror;
20: 22 of his plenty, *d* will overtake him;
27: 9 cry when *d* comes upon him?
30: 24 when he cries for help in his *d*.
33: 19 pain with constant *d* in his bones,
36: 16 you from the jaws of *d*
36: 19 you so you would not be in *d*?
Ps 4: 1 Give me relief from my *d*;
18: 6 In my *d* I called to the LORD;
20: 1 when you are in *d*;
25: 18 Look upon my affliction and my *d*
31: 9 to me, O LORD, for I am in *d*;
35: 26 May all who gloat over my *d*
55: 17 I cry out in *d*,
57: 6 I was bowed down in *d*.
69: 29 I am in pain and *d*;
77: 2 When I was in *d*, I sought the Lord;
81: 7 In your *d* you called and I rescued
102: 2 when I am in *d*.
106: 44 But he took note of their *d*
107: 6 and he delivered them from their *d*.
107: 13 and he saved them from their *d*.
107: 19 and he saved them from their *d*.
107: 28 and he brought them out of their *d*.
119:143 Trouble and *d* have come upon me,
120: 1 I call on the LORD in my *d*,
144: 14 no cry of *d* in our streets.
Pr 1: 27 when *d* and troubles overwhelm
Isa 5: 7 righteousness, but heard cries of *d*.
5: 30 he will see darkness and *d*;
8: 22 and see only *d* and darkness
9: 1 gloom for those who were in *d*.
25: 4 a refuge for the needy in his *d*,
26: 16 they came to you in their *d*;
30: 6 Through a land of hardship and *d*,
33: 2 our salvation in time of *d*.
37: 3 This day is a day of *d* and rebuke
63: 9 In all their *d* he too was distressed,
Jer 10: 18 I will bring *d* on them
11: 14 call to me in the time of their *d*.
14: 8 its Savior in times of *d*,
15: 11 in times of disaster and times of *d*.
16: 19 my refuge in time of *d*,
La 1: 3 her in the midst of her *d*.
1: 21 All my enemies have heard of my *d*
Eze 30: 16 Memphis will be in constant *d*.
Da 12: 1 There will be a time of *d* such
Jnh 2: 2 "In my *d* I called to the LORD,
Hab 3: 7 I saw the tents of Cushan in *d*,
Zep 1: 15 a day of *d* and anguish,
1: 17 I will bring *d* on the people
Mt 24: 21 For then there will be great *d*,
24: 29 "Immediately after the *d*
Mk 13: 19 of *d* unequaled from the beginning,
13: 24 But in those days, following that *d*,
Lk 21: 23 There will be great *d* in the land
Ro 2: 9 *d* for every human being who does
2Co 2: 4 For I wrote you out of great *d*
1Th 3: 7 in all our *d* and persecution we
Jas 1: 27 after orphans and widows in their *d*

DISTRESSED (DISTRESS)

Ge 21: 11 The matter *d* Abraham greatly
21: 12 "Do not be so *d* about the boy
42: 21 We saw how *d* he was
45: 5 do not be *d* and do not be angry
1Sa 30: 6 David was greatly *d*
Ezr 10: 9 greatly *d* by the occasion and
Job 6: 20 They are *d*, because they had been
Isa 8: 21 *D* and hungry, they will roam
54: 6 as if you were a wife deserted and *d*
63: 9 In all their distress he too was *d*,
La 1: 20 "See, O LORD, how *d* I am!
Da 6: 14 king heard this, he was greatly *d*;
Mt 14: 9 The king was *d*, but
18: 31 they were greatly *d* and went
Mk 3: 5 deeply *d* at their stubborn hearts,
6: 26 The king was greatly *d*, but
14: 33 and he began to be deeply *d*
Lk 12: 50 how *d* I am until it is completed!
Ac 17: 16 he was greatly *d* to see that the city

Ro 14: 15 If your brother is *d*
2Co 1: 6 If we are *d*, it is for your comfort
2: 3 that when I came I should not be *d*
Php 2: 26 is *d* because you heard he was ill.
2Pe 2: 7 who was *d* by the filthy lives

DISTRESSES (DISTRESS)

1Sa 10: 19 out of all your calamities and *d*.
2Co 6: 4 hardships and *d*; in beatings,

DISTRESSING (DISTRESS)

Ex 33: 4 the people heard these *d* words,

DISTRIBUTE (DISTRIBUTED DISTRIBUTES DISTRIBUTING DISTRIBUTION)

Nu 33: 54 *D* it according to your ancestral
33: 54 *D* the land by lot, according
2Ch 31: 19 designated by name to *d* portions
Eze 47: 21 "You are to *d* this land
Da 11: 24 He will *d* plunder, loot
11: 39 and will *d* the land at a price.
Mk 8: 7 and told the disciples to *d* them.

DISTRIBUTED (DISTRIBUTE)

Nu 26: 55 Be sure that the land is *d* by lot.
26: 56 Each inheritance is to be *d* by lot
Jos 18: 10 and there he *d* the land
1Ch 6: 60 which were *d* among the Kohathite
2Ch 31: 16 they *d* to the males three years old
31: 17 And they *d* to the priests enrolled
Est 2: 18 and *d* gifts with royal liberality.
Jn 6: 11 and *d* to those who were seated
Ac 4: 35 and it was *d* to anyone
Heb 2: 4 gifts of the Holy Spirit *d* according

DISTRIBUTES (DISTRIBUTE)

Isa 34: 17 his hand *d* them by measure.

DISTRIBUTING (DISTRIBUTE)

2Ch 31: 14 *d* the contributions made
31: 15 *d* to their fellow priests according
Ne 13: 13 made responsible for *d* the supplies

DISTRIBUTION (DISTRIBUTE)

Ac 6: 1 overlooked in the daily *d* of food.

DISTRICT (DISTRICTS HALF-DISTRICT)

Ge 47: 11 *d* of Rameses, as Pharaoh directed.
1Sa 9: 4 They went on into the *d* of Shaalim
9: 5 When they reached the *d* of Zuph,
1Ki 4: 5 in charge of the *d* officers;
4: 7 also had twelve *d* governors
4: 13 as well as the *d* of Argob in Bashan
4: 19 was the only governor over the *d*.
4: 27 The *d* officers, each in his month,
2Ki 22: 14 in Jerusalem, in the Second *D*.
2Ch 34: 22 in Jerusalem, in the Second *D*.
Ezr 5: 8 should know that we went to the *d*
Ne 3: 14 son of Recab, ruler of the *d* of Beth
3: 15 ruler of the *d* of Mizpah.
3: 17 carried out repairs for his *d*.
3: 17 ruler of half the *d* of Keilah,
11: 9 was over the Second *D* of the city.
Ecc 5: 8 If you see the poor oppressed in a *d*
Eze 45: 1 a portion of the land as a sacred *d*,
45: 3 In the sacred *d*, measure
45: 7 of the area formed by the sacred *d*
Zep 1: 11 Wail, you who live in the market *d*;
Mt 2: 22 he withdrew to the *d* of Galilee,
Ac 16: 12 city of that *d* of Macedonia.

DISTRICTS (DISTRICT)

Jdg 5: 15 In the *d* of Reuben
5: 16 In the *d* of Reuben
1Ch 27: 25 of the storehouses in the outlying *d*
2Ch 11: 13 from all their *d* sided with him.
11: 23 sons throughout the *d* of Judah

DISTURB (DISTURBANCE DISTURBED DISTURBING)

2Ki 23: 18 "Don't let anyone *d* his bones."

DISTURBANCE (DISTURB)

Ac 19: 23 arose a great *d* about the Way.
24: 18 nor was I involved in any *d*.

DISTURBED (DISTURB)

1Sa 28: 15 "Why have you *d* me
2Sa 7: 10 of their own and no longer be *d*.
1Ch 17: 9 of their own and no longer be *d*.
Ne 2: 10 were very much *d* that someone
Job 20: 2 because I am greatly *d*.
Ps 42: 5 Why so *d* within me?
42: 11 Why so *d* within me?
43: 5 Why so *d* within me?
Isa 31: 4 or *d* by their clamor—
La 1: 20 and in my heart I am *d*,
Da 7: 15 passed through my mind *d* me.
Mt 2: 3 King Herod heard this he was *d*,
Ac 4: 2 They were greatly *d*
15: 24 our authorization and *d* you,

DISTURBING (DISTURB)

Est 7: 4 distress would justify *d* the king."

DITCHES

2Ki 3: 16 says: Make this valley full of *d*.

DIVIDE (DIVIDED DIVIDES DIVIDING DIVISION DIVISIONS DIVISIVE SUBDIVISION SUBDIVISIONS)

Ex 14: 16 hand over the sea to *d* the water
15: 9 I will *d* the spoils;
21: 35 the live one and *d* both the money
Nu 31: 27 *D* the spoils between the soldiers
Dt 19: 3 and *d* into three parts the land
31: 7 and you must *d* it among them
Jos 13: 7 and *d* it as an inheritance
18: 5 You are to *d* the land
22: 8 *d* with your brothers the plunder
2Sa 19: 29 I order you and Ziba to *d* the fields
Job 27: 17 and the innocent will *d* his silver.
41: 6 Will they *d* him up
Ps 22: 18 They *d* my garments among them
68: 12 in the camps men *d* the plunder.
Isa 7: 6 let us tear it apart and *d* it
53: 12 he will *d* the spoils with the strong,
Eze 5: 1 a set of scales and *d* up the hair.
47: 13 by which you are to *d* the land
47: 14 You are to *d* it equally among them
Mic 2: 5 to *d* the land by lot.
Lk 12: 13 tell my brother to *d* the inheritance
22: 17 "Take this and *d* it among you.
Jude : 19 These are the men who *d* you,

DIVIDED (DIVIDE)

Ge 2: 10 and from there it *d*; it had four
10: 25 because in his time the earth was *d*;
14: 15 During the night Abram *d* his men
32: 7 distress Jacob *d* the people who
33: 1 so he *d* the children among Leah,
Ex 14: 21 waters were *d*, and the Israelites
Lev 11: 3 that has a split hoof completely *d*
11: 7 it has a split hoof completely *d*,
11: 26 has a split hoof not completely *d*
Dt 14: 6 any animal that has a split hoof *d*
14: 7 a split hoof completely *d* you may
32: 8 when he *d* all mankind,
Jos 14: 5 So the Israelites *d* the land,
Jdg 9: 43 *d* them into three companies
1Ki 18: 6 they *d* the land they were to cover,
2Ki 2: 8 The water *d* to the right
2: 14 it *d* to the right and to the left,
1Ch 1: 19 because in his time the earth was *d*;
23: 6 David *d* the Levites
24: 4 and they were *d* accordingly:
24: 5 They *d* them impartially
Ne 9: 11 You *d* the sea before them,
Ps 78: 13 He *d* the sea and led them through;
136: 13 to him who *d* the Red Sea asunder
Pr 3: 20 by his knowledge the deeps were *d*,
Isa 18: 2 whose land is *d* by rivers.
18: 7 whose land is *d* by rivers—
33: 23 an abundance of spoils will be *d*
63: 12 who *d* the waters before them,
Eze 37: 22 or be *d* into two kingdoms.
Da 2: 41 so this will be a *d* kingdom;
5: 28 Your kingdom is *d* and given
Joel 3: 2 and *d* up my land.
Am 7: 17 land will be measured and *d* up,
Mic 2: 4 my people's possession is *d* up.
Zec 14: 1 when your plunder will be *d*
Mt 12: 25 household *d* against itself will not
12: 25 "Every kingdom *d*

Mt 12: 26 If Satan drives out Satan, he is *d*
27: 35 they *d* up his clothes by casting lots
Mk 3: 24 If a kingdom is *d* against itself,
3: 25 If a house is *d* against itself,
3: 26 if Satan opposes himself and is *d*,
6: 41 also *d* the two fish among them all.
Lk 11: 17 and a house *d* against itself will fall.
11: 17 "Any kingdom *d* against itself will
11: 18 If Satan is *d* against himself,
12: 52 in one family *d* against each other,
12: 53 They will be *d*, father against son
15: 12 So he *d* his property between them.
23: 34 they *d* up his clothes by casting lots
Jn 7: 43 Thus the people were *d*
9: 16 miraculous signs?" So they were *d*.
10: 19 these words the Jews were again *d*.
19: 24 "They *d* my garments among them
Ac 14: 4 The people of the city were *d;*
23: 7 and the assembly was *d*.
1Co 1: 13 Is Christ *d?* Was Paul crucified
7: 34 his wife—and his interests are *d*.

DIVIDES (DIVIDE)

Ge 49: 27 in the evening he *d* the plunder."
Lk 11: 22 the man trusted and *d* up the spoils.

DIVIDING (DIVIDE)

Jos 19: 49 When they had finished *d* the land
19: 51 And so they finished *d* the land.
Jdg 5: 30 they not finding and *d* the spoils:
7: 16 *D* the three hundred men
Isa 9: 3 rejoice when *d* the plunder.
Mk 15: 24 *D* up his clothes, they cast lots
Jn 19: 23 they took his clothes, *d* them
Eph 2: 14 destroyed the barrier, the *d* wall
Heb 4: 12 it penetrates even to *d* soul

DIVINATION (DIVINATIONS DIVINE DIVINER DIVINERS)

Ge 30: 27 by *d* that the LORD has blessed
44: 5 drinks from and also uses for *d?*
44: 15 like me can find things out by *d?"*
Lev 19: 26 " 'Do not practice *d* or sorcery.
Nu 22: 7 taking with them the fee for *d*.
23: 23 no *d* against Israel.
Dt 18: 10 who practices *d* or sorcery,
18: 14 to those who practice sorcery or *d*.
Jos 13: 22 son of Beor, who practiced *d*.
1Sa 15: 23 For rebellion is like the sin of *d*,
2Ki 17: 17 They practiced *d* and sorcery
21: 6 practiced sorcery and *d*,
2Ch 33: 6 practiced sorcery, *d* and witchcraft
Isa 2: 6 they practice *d* like the Philistines
Eze 13: 23 see false visions or practice *d*.
Mic 3: 6 and darkness, without *d*.

DIVINATIONS (DIVINATION)

Jer 14: 14 prophesying to you false visions, *d*,
Eze 12: 24 or flattering *d* among the people
13: 6 visions are false and their *d* a lie.
13: 7 and uttered lying *d* when you say,
13: 9 see false visions and utter lying *d*.
21: 29 and lying *d* about you,
22: 28 them by false visions and lying *d*.

DIVINE (DIVINATION)

Isa 35: 4 with *d* retribution
Ac 8: 10 "This man is the *d* power known
17: 29 not think that the *d* being is like
19: 27 will be robbed of her *d* majesty."
Ro 1: 20 his eternal power and *d* nature—
9: 4 theirs the *d* glory, the covenants,
2Co 10: 4 they have *d* power
2Pe 1: 3 His *d* power has given us
1: 4 you may participate in the *d* nature

DIVINER (DIVINATION)

Da 2: 27 or *d* can explain to the king

DIVINERS (DIVINATION)

1Sa 6: 2 called for the priests and the *d*
Isa 44: 25 and makes fools of *d*,
Jer 27: 9 your *d*, your interpreters of dreams
29: 8 and *d* among you deceive you.
Da 4: 7 enchanters, astrologers and *d* came
5: 7 astrologers and *d* to be brought
5: 11 enchanters, astrologers and *d*.
Mic 3: 7 and the *d* disgraced.

Zec 10: 2 *d* see visions that lie;

DIVISION (DIVIDE)

Nu 2: 4 His *d* numbers 74,600.
2: 6 His *d* numbers 54,400.
2: 8 His *d* numbers 57,400.
2: 11 His *d* numbers 46,500.
2: 13 His *d* numbers 59,300.
2: 15 His *d* numbers 45,650.
2: 19 His *d* numbers 40,500.
2: 21 His *d* numbers 32,200.
2: 23 His *d* numbers 35,400.
2: 26 His *d* numbers 62,700.
2: 28 His *d* numbers 41,500.
2: 30 His *d* numbers 53,400.
10: 15 of Zuar was over the *d* of the tribe
10: 16 of Helon was over the *d* of the tribe
10: 19 was over the *d* of the tribe
10: 20 of Deuel was over the *d* of the tribe
10: 23 was over the *d* of the tribe
10: 24 was over the *d* of the tribe
10: 26 of Ocran was over the *d* of the tribe
10: 27 of Enan was over the *d* of the tribe
Jos 22: 14 of a family *d* among the Israelite
1Ch 27: 1 Each *d* consisted of 24,000 men.
27: 2 There were 24,000 men in his *d*.
27: 2 of the first *d*, for the first month,
27: 4 Mikloth was the leader of his *d*.
27: 4 There were 24,000 men in his *d*.
27: 4 of the *d* for the second month was
27: 5 there were 24,000 men in his *d*.
27: 6 Ammizabad was in charge of his *d*.
27: 7 There were 24,000 men in his *d*.
27: 8 There were 24,000 men in his *d*.
27: 9 There were 24,000 men in his *d*.
27: 10 There were 24,000 men in his *d*.
27: 11 There were 24,000 men in his *d*.
27: 12 There were 24,000 men in his *d*.
27: 13 There were 24,000 men in his *d*.
27: 14 There were 24,000 men in his *d*.
27: 15 There were 24,000 men in his *d*.
Ezr 10: 16 one from each family *d*,
Lk 1: 5 to the priestly *d* of Abijah;
1: 8 Once when Zechariah's *d* was
12: 51 on earth? No, I tell you, but *d*.
1Co 12: 25 so that there should be no *d*

DIVISIONS (DIVIDE)

Ge 36: 30 according to their *d*, in the land
Ex 6: 26 out of Egypt by their *d*."
7: 4 of judgment I will bring out my *d*,
12: 17 very day that I brought your *d* out
12: 41 all the LORD's *d* left Egypt.
12: 51 out of Egypt by their *d*.
Nu 1: 3 to number by their *d* all the men
1: 52 are to set up their tents by *d*,
2: 3 the *d* of the camp of Judah are
2: 9 to their *d*, number 186,400.
2: 10 On the south will be the *d*
2: 16 to their *d*, number 151,450.
2: 18 On the west will be the *d*
2: 24 to their *d*, number 108,100.
2: 25 On the north will be the *d*
2: 32 by their *d*, number 603,550.
10: 14 The *d* of the camp
10: 18 The *d* of the camp
10: 22 The *d* of the camp
10: 25 the *d* of the camp of Dan set out,
10: 28 order of march for the Israelite *d*
33: 1 of Egypt by *d* under the leadership
Jos 11: 23 to Israel according to their tribal *d*.
12: 7 of Israel according to their tribal *d*
18: 10 according to their tribal *d*.
1Sa 11: 11 separated his men into three *d;*
1Ch 24: 1 These were the *d* of the sons
24: 3 David separated them into *d*
26: 1 The *d* of the gatekeepers:
26: 12 These *d* of the gatekeepers,
26: 19 were the *d* of the gatekeepers
27: 1 concerned the army *d* that were
28: 1 commanders of the *d* in the service
28: 13 instructions for the *d* of the priests
28: 21 The *d* of the priests and Levites are
2Ch 5: 11 themselves, regardless of their *d*.
8: 14 appointed the gatekeepers by *d*
8: 14 he appointed the *d* of the priests
23: 8 had not released any of the *d*.
26: 11 ready to go out by *d* according

2Ch 31: 2 the priests and Levites to *d*—
31: 15 fellow priests according to their *d*,
31: 16 to their responsibilities and their *d*.
31: 17 to their responsibilities and their *d*.
35: 4 yourselves by families in your *d*,
35: 10 places with the Levites in their *d*
Ezr 6: 18 they installed the priests in their *d*
Ne 11: 36 Some of the *d* of the Levites
Ro 16: 17 to watch out for those who cause *d*
1Co 1: 10 another so that there may be no *d*
11: 18 there are *d* among you,

DIVISIVE (DIVIDE)

Tit 3: 10 Warn a *d* person once,

DIVORCE (DIVORCED DIVORCES)

Dt 22: 19 he must not *d* her as long as he lives
22: 29 He can never *d* her as long
24: 1 and he writes her a certificate of *d*,
24: 3 and writes her a certificate of *d*,
Isa 50: 1 is your mother's certificate of *d*
Jer 3: 8 faithless Israel her certificate of *d*
Mal 2: 16 "I hate *d*," says the LORD God
Mt 1: 19 he had in mind to *d* her quietly.
5: 31 must give her a certificate of *d*.'
19: 3 for a man to *d* his wife for any
19: 7 man give his wife a certificate of *d*
19: 8 permitted you to *d* your wives
Mk 10: 2 Is it lawful for a man to *d* his wife?"
10: 4 a man to write a certificate of *d*
1Co 7: 11 And a husband must not *d* his wife.
7: 12 to live with him, he must not *d* her.
7: 13 to live with her, she must not *d* him
7: 27 Are you married? Do not seek a *d*.

DIVORCED (DIVORCE)

Lev 21: 7 or *d* from their husbands,
21: 14 not marry a widow, a *d* woman,
22: 13 daughter becomes a widow or is *d*,
Nu 30: 9 or *d* woman will be binding on her.
Dt 24: 4 then her first husband, who *d* her,
1Ch 8: 8 after he had *d* his wives Hushim
Eze 44: 22 not marry widows or *d* women;
Mt 5: 32 a woman so *d* commits adultery.
Lk 16: 18 who marries a *d* woman commits

DIVORCES (DIVORCE)

Jer 3: 1 "If a man *d* his wife
Mt 5: 31 'Anyone who *d* his wife must give
5: 32 tell you that anyone who *d* his wife,
19: 9 tell you that anyone who *d* his wife,
Mk 10: 11 "Anyone who *d* his wife
10: 12 And if she *d* her husband
Lk 16: 18 "Anyone who *d* his wife

DIZAHAB

Dt 1: 1 Tophel, Laban, Hazeroth and *D*.

DIZZINESS

Isa 19: 14 a spirit of *d;*

DO-NOTHING

Isa 30: 7 Rahab the *D*.

DOCTOR (DOCTORS)

Mt 9: 12 "It is not the healthy who need a *d*,
Mk 2: 17 "It is not the healthy who need a *d*,
Lk 5: 31 "It is not the healthy who need a *d*,
Col 4: 14 the *d*, and Demas send greetings.

DOCTORS (DOCTOR)

Mk 5: 26 deal under the care of many *d*

DOCTRINE (DOCTRINES)

1Ti 1: 10 to the sound *d* that conforms
4: 16 Watch your life and *d* closely.
2Ti 4: 3 men will not put up with sound *d*.
Tit 1: 9 can encourage others by sound *d*
2: 1 is in accord with sound *d*.

DOCTRINES (DOCTRINE)

1Ti 1: 3 not to teach false *d* any longer
6: 3 If anyone teaches false *d*

DOCUMENT (DOCUMENTS)

Est 8: 8 for no *d* written in the king's name

DOCUMENTS (DOCUMENT)

Jer 32: 14 God of Israel, says: Take these *d*,

DODAI
2Sa 23: 9 was Eleazar son of *D* the Ahohite.
1Ch 11: 12 was Eleazar son of *D* the Ahohite,
27: 4 second month was *D* the Ahohite;

DODAVAHU
2Ch 20: 37 Eliezer son of *D*

DODO
Jdg 10: 1 the son of *D*, rose to save Israel.
2Sa 23: 24 Elhanan son of *D* from Bethlehem,
1Ch 11: 26 Elhanan son of *D* from Bethlehem,

DOE
Ge 49: 21 "Naphtali is a *d* set free
Job 39: 1 watch when the *d* bears her fawn?
Pr 5: 19 A loving *d*, a graceful deer—
Jer 14: 5 Even the *d* in the field

DOEG
1Sa 21: 7 he was *D* the Edomite, Saul's head
22: 9 *D* the Edomite, who was standing
22: 18 So *D* the Edomite turned
22: 18 king then ordered *D*, "You turn
22: 22 when *D* the Edomite was there,

DOG (DOG'S DOGS)
Ex 11: 7 the Israelites not a *d* will bark
Jdg 7: 5 water with their tongues like a *d*
1Sa 17: 43 He said to David, "Am I a *d*,
24: 14 Whom are you pursuing? A dead *d*
2Sa 9: 8 should notice a dead *d* like me?"
16: 9 should this dead *d* curse my lord
2Ki 8: 13 a mere *d*, accomplish such a feat?"
Job 18: 11 and *d* his every step.
Pr 26: 11 As a *d* returns to its vomit,
26: 17 Like one who seizes a *d* by the ears
Ecc 9: 4 a live *d* is better off than a dead lion
2Pe 2: 22 "A *d* returns to its vomit," and,

DOG'S (DOG)
2Sa 3: 8 "Am I a *d* head—on Judah's side?
Isa 66: 3 like one who breaks a *d* neck;

DOGS (DOG)
Ex 22: 31 by wild beasts; throw it to the *d*.
1Ki 14: 11 *D* will eat those belonging
16: 4 *D* will eat those belonging
21: 19 the place where *d* licked up
21: 19 *d* will lick up your blood—yes,
21: 23 '*D* will devour Jezebel by the wall
21: 24 "*D* will eat those belonging
22: 38 and the *d* licked up his blood,
2Ki 9: 10 *d* will devour her on the plot
9: 36 at Jezreel *d* will devour Jezebel's
Job 30: 1 disdained to put with my sheep *d*.
Ps 22: 16 *D* have surrounded me;
22: 20 from the power of the *d*.
59: 6 snarling like *d*,
59: 14 snarling like *d*,
68: 23 of your *d* have their share."
Isa 56: 10 they are all mute *d*,
56: 11 They are *d* with mighty appetites;
Jer 15: 3 to kill and the *d* to drag away
Mt 7: 6 "Do not give *d* what is sacred;
15: 26 bread and toss it to their *d*."
15: 27 even the *d* eat the crumbs that fall
Mk 7: 27 bread and toss it to their *d*."
7: 28 *d* under the table eat the children's
Lk 16: 21 Even the *d* came and licked his
Php 3: 2 for those *d*, those men who do evil,
Rev 22: 15 Outside are the *d*, those who

DOLE
Lev 26: 26 they will *d* out the bread by weight.

DOMAIN (DOMINION)
Dt 33: 20 Blessed is he who enlarges Gad's *d*
Eze 27: 4 Your *d* was on the high seas;

DOMINION (DOMAIN)
Job 25: 2 "*D* and awe belong to God;
38: 33 Can you set up ⌞God's⌟ *d*
Ps 22: 28 for *d* belongs to the LORD
103: 22 everywhere in his *d*.
114: 2 Israel his *d*.
145: 13 *d* endures through all generations.
Da 2: 37 The God of heaven has given you *d*
4: 3 his *d* endures from generation
4: 22 and your *d* extends to distant parts
4: 34 His *d* is an eternal *d*;
6: 26 his *d* will never end.
7: 14 His *d* is an everlasting *d* that will
Mic 4: 8 the former *d* will be restored to you
1Co 15: 24 Father after he has destroyed all *d*,
Eph 1: 21 *d*, and every title that can be given,
Col 1: 13 us from the *d* of darkness

DONATED
Ezr 8: 25 and all Israel present there had *d*

DONKEY (DONKEY'S DONKEYS DONKEYS')
Ge 16: 12 He will be a wild *d* of a man;
22: 3 Abraham got up and saddled his *d*.
22: 5 "Stay here with the *d* while I
42: 27 sack to get feed for his *d*,
49: 11 He will tether his *d* to a vine,
49: 14 "Issachar is a rawboned *d*
Ex 4: 20 put them on a *d* and started back
13: 13 with a lamb every firstborn *d*,
20: 17 or *d*, or anything that belongs
21: 33 and an ox or a *d* falls into it,
22: 4 whether ox or *d* or sheep—
22: 9 of illegal possession of an ox, a *d*,
22: 10 "If a man gives a *d*, an ox, a sheep
23: 4 your enemy's ox or *d* wandering
23: 5 If you see the *d* of someone who
23: 12 so that your ox and your *d* may rest
34: 20 Redeem the firstborn *d* with a lamb
Nu 16: 15 taken so much as a *d* from them,
22: 21 saddled his *d* and went
22: 22 Balaam was riding on his *d*,
22: 23 When the *d* saw the angel
22: 25 When the *d* saw the angel
22: 27 When the *d* saw the angel
22: 29 Balaam answered the *d*, "You have
22: 30 I not your own *d*, which you have
22: 30 *d* said to Balaam, "Am I not your
22: 32 you beaten your *d* these three
22: 33 The *d* saw me and turned away
Dt 5: 14 your *d* or any of your animals,
5: 21 or maidservant, his ox or *d*,
22: 3 same if you find your brother's *d*
22: 4 If you see your brother's *d*
22: 10 with an ox and a *d* yoked together.
28: 31 Your *d* will be forcibly taken
Jos 15: 18 got off the *d*, Caleb asked her,
Jdg 1: 14 got off her *d*, Caleb asked her,
15: 15 Finding a fresh jawbone of a *d*,
19: 28 Then the man put her on his *d*
1Sa 12: 3 I taken? Whose *d* have I taken?
16: 20 So Jesse took a *d* loaded with bread
25: 20 As she came riding her *d*
25: 23 she quickly got off her *d*
25: 42 Abigail quickly got on a *d* and,
2Sa 17: 23 he saddled his *d* and set out
19: 26 'I will have my *d* saddled
1Ki 2: 40 he saddled his *d* and went
13: 13 And when they had saddled the *d*
13: 13 to his sons, "Saddle the *d* for me."
13: 23 had brought him back saddled his *d*
13: 24 with both the *d* and the lion
13: 27 "Saddle the *d* for me,"
13: 28 eaten the body nor mauled the *d*.
13: 28 with the *d* and the lion standing
13: 29 laid it on the *d*, and brought it back
2Ki 4: 22 and a *d* so I can go to the man
4: 24 She saddled the *d* and said
Job 6: 5 Does a wild *d* bray
24: 3 They drive away the orphan's *d*
39: 5 "Who let the wild *d* go free?
Pr 26: 3 for the horse, a halter for the *d*,
Isa 1: 3 the *d* his owner's manger,
Jer 2: 24 a wild *d* accustomed to the desert,
22: 19 He will have the burial of a *d*—
Hos 8: 9 like a wild *d* wandering alone.
Zec 9: 9 gentle and riding on a *d*,
9: 9 on a colt, the foal of a *d*.
Mt 21: 2 at once you will find a *d* tied there,
21: 5 gentle and riding on a *d*,
21: 5 on a colt, the foal of a *d*.' "
21: 7 They brought the *d* and the colt,
Lk 10: 34 Then he put the man on his own *d*,
13: 15 on the Sabbath untie his ox or *d*
Jn 12: 14 Jesus found a young *d*
2Pe 2: 16 for his wrongdoing by a *d*—

DONKEY'S (DONKEY)
Nu 22: 28 the LORD opened the *d* mouth,
Jdg 15: 16 With a *d* jawbone
15: 16 "With a *d* jawbone
2Ki 6: 25 lasted so long that a *d* head sold
Job 11: 12 wise than a wild *d* colt can be born
Jn 12: 15 seated on a *d* colt."

DONKEYS (DONKEY)
Ge 12: 16 male and female *d*, menservants
24: 35 maidservants, and camels and *d*.
30: 43 menservants, and camels and *d*.
32: 5 I have cattle and *d*, sheep and goats
32: 15 twenty female *d* and ten male *d*.
34: 28 seized their flocks and herds and *d*
36: 24 desert while he was grazing the *d*
42: 26 they loaded their grain on their *d*
43: 18 seize us as slaves and take our *d*."
43: 24 and provided fodder for their *d*.
44: 3 sent on their way with their *d*.
44: 13 Then they all loaded their *d*
45: 23 and ten female *d* loaded with grain
45: 23 ten *d* loaded with the best things
47: 17 and goats, their cattle and *d*.
Ex 9: 3 on your horses and *d* and camels
Nu 31: 28 whether persons, cattle, *d*,
31: 30 whether persons, cattle, *d*, sheep,
31: 34 cattle, 61,000 *d* and 32,000
31: 39 *d*, of which the tribute
31: 45 cattle, 30,500 *d* and 16,000
Jos 6: 21 young and old, cattle, sheep and *d*.
7: 24 daughters, his cattle, *d* and sheep,
9: 4 a delegation whose *d* were loaded
Jdg 5: 10 "You who ride on white *d*,
6: 4 neither sheep nor cattle nor *d*.
10: 4 had thirty sons, who rode thirty *d*.
12: 14 grandsons, who rode on seventy *d*.
15: 16 I have made *d* of them.
19: 3 with him his servant and two *d*.
19: 10 with his two saddled *d*
19: 19 and fodder for our *d* and bread
19: 21 him into his house and fed his *d*.
1Sa 8: 16 and *d* he will take for his own use.
9: 3 and go and look for the *d*."
9: 3 *d* belonging to Saul's father Kish
9: 4 Shaalim, but the *d* were not there.
9: 5 will stop thinking about the *d*
9: 20 As for the *d* you lost three days ago
10: 2 'The *d* you set out to look
10: 14 "Looking for the *d*," he said.
10: 16 us that the *d* had been found."
15: 3 cattle and sheep, camels and *d*.' "
22: 19 and its cattle, *d* and sheep.
25: 18 pressed figs, and loaded them on *d*.
27: 9 *d* and camels, and clothes.
2Sa 16: 1 He had a string of *d* saddled
16: 2 "The *d* are for the king's household
2Ki 7: 7 their tents and their horses and *d*.
7: 10 only tethered horses and *d*,
1Ch 5: 21 sheep and two thousand *d*.
12: 40 Naphtali came bringing food on *d*,
27: 30 was in charge of the *d*.
2Ch 28: 15 who were weak they put on *d*.
Ezr 2: 67 mules, 435 camels and 6,720 *d*
Ne 7: 69 mules, 435 camels and 6,720 *d*
13: 15 in grain and loading it on *d*,
Job 1: 3 yoke of oxen and five hundred *d*,
1: 14 and the *d* were grazing nearby,
24: 5 Like wild *d* in the desert,
42: 12 yoke of oxen and a thousand *d*.
Ps 104: 11 the wild *d* quench their thirst.
Isa 21: 7 riders on *d*
30: 24 *d* that work the soil will eat fodder
32: 14 the delight of *d*, a pasture for flocks
32: 20 letting your oxen and *d* range free.
Jer 14: 6 Wild *d* stand on the barren heights
Eze 23: 20 whose genitals were like those of *d*
Da 5: 21 he lived with the wild *d*
Zec 14: 15 and *d*, and all the animals

DONKEYS' (DONKEY)
Isa 30: 6 carry their riches on *d'* backs,

DOOM (DOOMED)
Dt 32: 35 and their *d* rushes upon them."
Eze 7: 7 It has come! *D* has come upon you

Eze 7: 10 It has come! *D* has burst forth,
22: 3 on herself *d* by shedding blood
30: 3 a time of *d* for the nations.
30: 9 of them on the day of Egypt's *d*,
Rev 18: 10 In one hour your *d* has come!'

DOOMED (DOOM)

Jdg 13: 22 We are *d* to die!'' he said to his wife
2Ki 7: 13 like all these Israelites who are *d*.
Ps 137: 8 of Babylon, *d* to destruction,
Isa 65: 23 or bear children *d* to misfortune;
Jer 8: 14 For the LORD our God has *d* us
Jn 17: 12 except the one *d* to destruction
2Th 2: 3 lawlessness is revealed, the man *d*

DOOR (DOORS)

Ge 4: 7 sin is crouching at your *d;*
6: 16 Put a *d* in the side of the ark
19: 6 and shut the *d* behind him and said,
19: 9 forward to break down the *d*.
19: 10 back into the house and shut the *d*.
19: 11 so that they could not find the *d*.
19: 11 were at the *d* of the house,
Ex 12: 22 one of you shall go out the *d*
21: 6 He shall take him to the *d*
Dt 15: 17 it through his ear lobe into the *d*,
22: 21 to the *d* of her father's house
Jdg 11: 31 out of the *d* of my house
19: 22 Pounding on the *d*, they shouted
19: 26 fell down at the *d* and lay there
19: 27 and opened the *d* of the house
2Sa 13: 17 of here and bolt the *d* after her.''
13: 18 put her out and bolted the *d*
1Ki 14: 6 the sound of her footsteps at the *d*,
2Ki 4: 4 go inside and shut the *d* behind you
4: 5 afterward shut the *d* behind her
4: 21 then shut the *d* and went out.
4: 33 shut the *d* on the two of them
5: 9 stopped at the *d* of Elisha's house.
6: 32 shut the *d* and hold it shut
9: 3 open the *d* and run; don't delay!''
9: 10 Then he opened the *d* and ran.
Job 31: 9 if I have lurked at my neighbor's *d*,
31: 32 for my *d* was always open
Ps 141: 3 keep watch over the *d* of my lips.
Pr 5: 8 do not go near the *d* of her house,
9: 14 She sits at the *d* of her house,
26: 14 As a *d* turns on its hinges,
SS 7: 13 and at our *d* is every delicacy,
8: 9 If she is a *d*,
Eze 41: 24 Each *d* had two leaves—two
41: 24 two hinged leaves for each *d*.
42: 2 building whose *d* faced north was
Hos 2: 15 of Achor a *d* of hope.
Mt 6: 6 close the *d* and pray to your Father
7: 7 and the *d* will be opened to you.
7: 8 who knocks, the *d* will be opened.
24: 33 is near, right at the *d*.
25: 10 And the *d* was shut.
25: 11 Open the *d* for us!' ''But he replied,
Mk 1: 33 The whole town gathered at the *d*,
2: 2 not even outside the *d*,
13: 29 is near, right at the *d*.
13: 34 tells the one at the *d* to keep watch.
Lk 11: 7 The *d* is already locked,
11: 9 and the *d* will be opened to you.
11: 10 who knocks, the *d* will be opened.
12: 36 they can immediately open the *d*
13: 24 to enter through the narrow *d*,
13: 25 pleading, 'Sir, open the *d* for us.'
13: 25 the house gets up and closes the *d*,
Jn 18: 16 Peter had to wait outside at the *d*.
18: 17 the girl at the *d* asked Peter.
Ac 5: 9 buried your husband are at the *d*,
12: 13 Rhoda came to answer the *d*.
12: 14 ''Peter is at the *d!*'' ''You're out
12: 16 and when they opened the *d*
14: 27 how he had opened the *d* of faith
18: 7 went next *d* to the house of Titius
1Co 16: 9 a great *d* for effective work has
2Co 2: 12 found that the Lord had opened a *d*
Col 4: 3 that God may open a *d*
Jas 5: 9 The Judge is standing at the *d!*
Rev 3: 8 before you an open *d* that no one
3: 20 I stand at the *d* and knock.
3: 20 hears my voice and opens the *d*,
4: 1 before me was a *d* standing open

DOORFRAME (DOORFRAMES)

Ex 12: 22 and on both sides of the *d*.
12: 23 and sides of the *d* and will pass
Eze 41: 21 sanctuary had a rectangular *d*,

DOORFRAMES (DOORFRAME)

Ex 12: 7 of the *d* of the houses where they
Dt 6: 9 Write them on the *d* of your houses
11: 20 Write them on the *d* of your houses
2Ch 3: 7 He overlaid the ceiling beams, *d*,

DOORKEEPER (DOORKEEPERS)

Ps 84: 10 I would rather be a *d* in the house
Jer 35: 4 of Maaseiah son of Shallum the *d*.

DOORKEEPERS (DOORKEEPER)

2Ki 22: 4 which the *d* have collected
23: 4 the *d* to remove from the temple
25: 18 next in rank and the three *d*.
1Ch 15: 23 Elkanah were to be *d* for the ark.
15: 24 Jehiah were also to be *d* for the ark.
2Ch 23: 19 also stationed *d* at the gates
34: 9 who were the *d* had collected
34: 13 were secretaries, scribes and *d*.
Jer 52: 24 next in rank and the three *d*.

DOORPOST (DOORPOSTS)

Ex 21: 6 the *d* and pierce his ear with an awl
1Sa 1: 9 by the *d* of the LORD's temple.

DOORPOSTS (DOORPOST)

2Ki 18: 16 and *d* of the temple of the LORD,
Isa 6: 4 At the sound of their voices the *d*
57: 8 Behind your doors and your *d*
Eze 43: 8 threshold and their *d* beside my *d*,
45: 19 and put it on the *d* of the temple,

DOORS (DOOR)

Jdg 3: 23 he shut the *d* of the upper room
3: 24 and found the *d* of the upper room
3: 25 but when he did not open the *d*
16: 3 took hold of the *d* of the city gate,
1Sa 3: 15 and then opened the *d* of the house
21: 13 making marks on the *d* of the gate
1Ki 6: 31 of the inner sanctuary he made *d*
6: 32 the two olive wood *d* he carved
6: 34 made two pine *d*, each having two
7: 50 and also for the *d* of the main hall
7: 50 for the *d* of the innermost room,
2Ki 18: 16 with which he had covered the *d*
1Ch 22: 3 nails for the *d* of the gateways
2Ch 3: 7 walls and *d* of the temple with gold,
4: 9 and overlaid the *d* with bronze.
4: 9 and the large court and the *d*
4: 22 and the gold *d* of the temple:
4: 22 and the *d* of the main hall.
4: 22 the inner *d* to the Most Holy Place
23: 4 are to keep watch at the *d*,
28: 24 He shut the *d* of the LORD's
29: 3 he opened the *d* of the temple
29: 7 They also shut the *d* of the portico
Ne 3: 1 They dedicated it and set its *d*
3: 3 put its *d* and bolts and bars in place.
3: 6 put its *d* and bolts and bars in place.
3: 13 They rebuilt it and put its *d*
3: 14 He rebuilt it and put its *d* and bolts
3: 15 roofing it over and putting its *d*
6: 1 up to that time I had not set the *d*
6: 10 and let us close the temple *d*,
7: 1 and I had set the *d* in place,
7: 3 have them shut the *d* and bar them.
13: 19 I ordered the *d* to be shut
Job 3: 10 for it did not shut the *d*
38: 8 ''Who shut up the sea behind *d*
38: 10 and set its *d* and bars in place,
41: 14 Who dares open the *d* of his mouth
Ps 24: 7 be lifted up, you ancient *d*,
24: 9 lift them up, you ancient *d*,
78: 23 and opened the *d* of the heavens;
Pr 8: 34 watching daily at my *d*,
Ecc 12: 4 when the *d* to the street are closed
Isa 26: 20 and shut the *d* behind you;
45: 1 to open *d* before him
57: 8 Behind your *d* and your doorposts
Eze 26: 2 and its *d* have swung open to me;
33: 30 and at the *d* of the houses,
41: 23 the Most Holy Place had double *d*.
41: 25 on the *d* of the outer sanctuary
42: 4 Their *d* were on the north.
Zec 11: 1 Open your *d*, O Lebanon,
Mal 1: 10 of you would shut the temple *d*,
Jn 20: 19 with the *d* locked for fear
20: 26 Though the *d* were locked,
Ac 5: 19 of the Lord opened the *d* of the jail
5: 23 with the guards standing at the *d;*
16: 26 At once all the prison *d* flew open,
16: 27 and when he saw the prison *d* open,

DOORWAY (DOORWAYS)

Ex 12: 23 and will pass over that *d*,
35: 15 the curtain for the *d* at the entrance
Jdg 4: 20 ''Stand in the *d* of the tent,''
19: 27 fallen in the *d* of the house,
2Ki 4: 15 called her, and she stood in the *d*.
Est 2: 21 king's officers who guarded the *d*,
6: 2 who guarded the *d* and who had
Pr 8: 34 waiting at my *d*.
Eze 8: 8 dug into the wall and saw a *d* there.
40: 38 A room with a *d* was by the portico
42: 12 There was a *d* at the beginning
Mk 11: 4 outside in the street, tied at a *d*.

DOORWAYS (DOORWAY)

1Ki 7: 5 All the *d* had rectangular frames;
Eze 42: 12 the *d* on the north were the *d*
Zep 2: 14 rubble will be in the *d*,

DOPHKAH

Nu 33: 12 the Desert of Sin and camped at *D*.
33: 13 They left *D* and camped at Alush.

DOR

Jos 12: 23 in Carmel one the king of *D*
17: 11 Ibleam and the people of *D*, Endor,
Jdg 1: 27 or Taanach or *D* or Ibleam
1Ch 7: 29 Taanach, Megiddo and *D*,

DORCAS

Ac 9: 36 is *D)*, who was always doing good
9: 39 other clothing that *D* had made

DOTHAN

Ge 37: 17 I heard them say, 'Let's go to *D*.' ''
37: 17 brothers and found them near *D*.
2Ki 6: 13 The report came back: ''He is in *D*

DOUBLE

Ge 43: 12 Take *d* the amount of silver
43: 15 and *d* the amount of silver,
Ex 22: 4 or sheep—he must pay back *d*.
22: 7 if he is caught, must pay back *d*.
22: 9 declare guilty must pay back *d*
26: 9 Fold the sixth curtain *d* at the front
26: 24 these two corners they must be *d*
28: 16 and a span wide—and folded *d*.
36: 29 two corners the frames were *d*
39: 9 and a span wide—and folded *d*.
Dt 21: 17 by giving him a *d* share of all he has
1Sa 1: 5 But to Hannah he gave a *d* portion
2Ki 2: 9 ''Let me inherit a *d* portion
Isa 40: 2 *d* for all her sins.
51: 19 These *d* calamities have come
61: 7 and so they will inherit a *d* portion
61: 7 my people will receive a *d* portion,
Jer 16: 18 I will repay them *d*
17: 18 destroy them with *d* destruction.
Eze 41: 23 the Most Holy Place had *d* doors.
Hos 10: 10 to put them in bonds for their *d* sin.
1Ti 5: 17 church well are worthy of *d* honor,
Rev 18: 6 Mix her a *d* portion
18: 6 pay her back *d* for what she has

DOUBLE-EDGED (EDGE)

Jdg 3: 16 Ehud had made a *d* sword about
Ps 149: 6 and a *d* sword in their hands,
Pr 5: 4 sharp as a *d* sword.
Heb 4: 12 Sharper than any *d* sword,
Rev 1: 16 of his mouth came a sharp *d* sword.
2: 12 of him who has the sharp, *d* sword.

DOUBLE-MINDED (MIND)

Ps 119:113 I hate *d* men,
Jas 1: 8 he is a *d* man, unstable
4: 8 and purify your hearts, you *d*.

DOUBLE-PRONGED

Eze 40: 43 *d* hooks, each a handbreadth long,

DOUBT (DOUBTED DOUBTING DOUBTS)

Mt 14: 31 he said, "why did you *d?*"
21: 21 if you have faith and do not *d*,
Mk 11: 23 and does not *d* in his heart
Ac 12: 11 without a *d* that the Lord sent his
1Co 11: 19 No *d* there have to be differences
Heb 7: 7 And without *d* the lesser person is
Jas 1: 6 he must believe and not *d*,
Jude : 22 Be merciful to those who *d*;

DOUBTED (DOUBT)

Mt 28: 17 they worshiped him; but some *d*.

DOUBTING (DOUBT)

Jn 20: 27 Stop *d* and believe."

DOUBTS (DOUBT)

Lk 24: 38 and why do *d* rise in your minds?
Ro 14: 23 the man who has *d* is condemned
Jas 1: 6 he who *d* is like a wave of the sea,

DOUGH

Ex 12: 34 So the people took their *d*
12: 39 The *d* was without yeast
12: 39 With the *d* they had brought
2Sa 13: 8 She took some *d*, kneaded it,
Jer 7: 18 and the women knead the *d*
Hos 7: 4 the kneading of the *d* till it rises.
Mt 13: 33 until it worked all through the *d*."
Lk 13: 21 until it worked all through the *d*."
Ro 11: 16 If the part of the *d* offered
1Co 5: 6 through the whole batch of *d?*
Gal 5: 9 through the whole batch of *d*."

DOVE (DOVES)

Ge 8: 8 Then he sent out a *d* to see
8: 9 But the *d* could find no place
8: 9 out his hand and took the *d*
8: 10 again sent out the *d* from the ark.
8: 11 When the *d* returned to him
8: 12 more days and sent the *d* out again,
15: 9 along with a *d* and a young pigeon
Lev 1: 14 he is to offer a *d* or a young pigeon.
12: 6 and a young pigeon or a *d*
Ps 55: 6 "Oh, that I had the wings of a *d!*
68: 13 the wings of ⌊my⌋ *d* are sheathed
74: 19 of your *d* to wild beasts;
SS 2: 14 My *d* in the clefts of the rock
5: 2 my *d*, my flawless one.
6: 9 but my *d*, my perfect one, is unique
Isa 38: 14 I moaned like a mourning *d*.
Jer 8: 7 and the *d*, the swift and the thrush
48: 28 Be like a *d* that makes its nest
Hos 7: 11 "Ephraim is like a *d*,
Mt 3: 16 Spirit of God descending like a *d*
Mk 1: 10 Spirit descending on him like a *d*.
Lk 3: 22 on him in bodily form like a *d*.
Jn 1: 32 as a *d* and remain on him.

DOVES (DOVE)

Lev 5: 7 is to bring two *d* or two young
5: 11 he cannot afford two *d*
12: 8 is to bring two *d* or two young
14: 22 and two *d* or two young pigeons,
14: 30 Then he shall sacrifice the *d*
15: 14 the eighth day he must take two *d*
15: 29 the eighth day she must take two *d*
Nu 6: 10 the eighth day he must bring two *d*
SS 1: 15 Your eyes are *d*.
2: 12 the cooing of *d*
4: 1 Your eyes behind your veil are *d*.
5: 12 His eyes are like *d*
Isa 59: 11 we moan mournfully like *d*.
60: 8 like *d* to their nests?
Eze 7: 16 moaning like *d* of the valleys,
Hos 11: 11 like *d* from Assyria.
Na 2: 7 Its slave girls moan like *d*
Mt 10: 16 as snakes and as innocent as *d*.
21: 12 and the benches of those selling *d*.
Mk 11: 15 and the benches of those selling *d*,
Lk 2: 24 "a pair of *d* or two young pigeons."
Jn 2: 14 and *d*, and others sitting
2: 16 To those who sold *d* he said,

DOWNCAST

Ge 4: 5 was very angry, and his face was *d*.
4: 6 Why is your face *d?* If you do what
1Sa 1: 18 and her face was no longer *d*.
Job 22: 29 then he will save the *d*.
Ps 42: 5 Why are you *d*, O my soul?
42: 6 My soul is *d* within me;
42: 11 Why are you *d*, O my soul?
43: 5 Why are you *d*, O my soul?
La 3: 20 and my soul is *d* within me.
Lk 24: 17 They stood still, their faces *d*.
2Co 7: 6 But God, who comforts the *d*,

DOWNFALL

1Ki 13: 34 house of Jeroboam that led to its *d*
2Ki 14: 10 cause your own *d* and that of Judah
2Ch 22: 7 God brought about Ahaziah's *d*.
25: 19 cause your own *d* and that of Judah
26: 16 powerful, his pride led to his *d*.
28: 23 But they were his *d* and the *d*
Est 6: 13 before whom your *d* has started,
Ps 5: 10 Let their intrigues be their *d*.
Pr 18: 12 Before his *d* a man's heart is proud,
29: 16 but the righteous will see their *d*.
Jer 48: 2 in Heshbon men will plot her *d*:
Eze 18: 30 then sin will not be your *d*.
32: 10 On the day of your *d*
Hos 14: 1 Your sins have been your *d!*
Mic 7: 10 My eyes will see her *d*;

DOWNHEARTED (HEART)

1Sa 1: 8 Why don't you eat? Why are you *d*

DOWNPOUR (POUR)

Job 37: 6 to the rain shower, 'Be a mighty *d*.'
Isa 28: 2 like a driving rain and a flooding *d*,

DOWNSTAIRS (STAIRS)

Ac 10: 20 So get up and go *d*.

DOWNSTREAM (STREAM)

Jos 3: 13 the water flowing *d* will be cut off

DRACHMAS (FOUR-DRACHMA TWO-DRACHMA)

Ezr 2: 69 *d* of gold, 5,000 minas of silver
Ne 7: 70 to the treasury 1,000 *d* of gold,
7: 71 *d* of gold and 2,200 minas of silver.
7: 72 of the people was 20,000 *d* of gold,
Ac 19: 19 the total came to fifty thousand *d*.

DRAG (DRAGGED DRAGGING DRAGS)

2Sa 17: 13 and we will *d* it down to the valley
Job 36: 20 to *d* people away from their homes.
Ps 28: 3 Do not *d* me away with the wicked,
Pr 21: 7 of the wicked will *d* them away,
Jer 12: 3 *D* them off like sheep
15: 3 the dogs to *d* away and the birds
Eze 39: 2 you around and *d* you along.
Lk 12: 58 or he may *d* you off to the judge,

DRAGGED (DRAG)

2Sa 20: 12 he *d* him from the road into a field
Jer 22: 19 *d* away and thrown
49: 20 young of the flock will be *d* away;
50: 45 young of the flock will be *d* away;
La 3: 11 he *d* me from the path
Eze 32: 20 let her be *d* off with all her hordes.
Jn 21: 11 climbed aboard and *d* the net
Ac 7: 58 *d* him out of the city and began
8: 3 he *d* off men and women
14: 19 and *d* him outside the city,
16: 19 and *d* them into the marketplace
17: 6 they *d* Jason and some other
21: 30 they *d* him from the temple,
Jas 1: 14 by his own evil desire, he is *d* away

DRAGGING (DRAG)

Jas 2: 6 they not the ones who are *d* you

DRAGNET (NET)

Hab 1: 15 he gathers them up in his *d*;
1: 16 and burns incense to his *d*,

DRAGON

Rev 12: 3 an enormous red *d*
12: 4 The *d* stood in front
12: 7 and his angels fought against the *d*,
Rev 12: 7 the *d* and his angels fought back.
12: 9 The great *d* was hurled down—
12: 13 When the *d* saw that he had been
12: 16 the river that the *d* had spewed out
12: 17 the *d* was enraged at the woman
13: 1 the *d* stood on the shore of the sea.
13: 2 The *d* gave the beast his power
13: 4 Men worshiped the *d* because he
13: 11 like a lamb, but he spoke like a *d*.
16: 13 out of the mouth of the *d*,
20: 2 He seized the *d*, that ancient

DRAGS (DRAG)

Job 7: 4 The night *d* on, and I toss till dawn.
24: 22 God *d* away the mighty
Ps 10: 9 he catches the helpless and *d* them
Ecc 12: 5 the grasshopper *d* himself along

DRAIN (DRAINED DRAINING)

Lev 17: 13 may be eaten must *d* out the blood
26: 16 your sight and *d* away your life.
Eze 23: 34 You will drink it and *d* it dry;

DRAINED (DRAIN)

Lev 1: 15 its blood shall be *d* out on the side
5: 9 the rest of the blood must be *d* out
2Ki 19: 26 Their people, *d* of power,
Isa 37: 27 Their people, *d* of power,
51: 17 you who have *d* to its dregs

DRAINING (DRAIN)

Na 2: 8 and its water is *d* away.

DRANK (DRINK)

Ge 9: 21 When he *d* some of its wine,
24: 46 So I *d*, and she watered the camels
24: 54 and *d* and spent the night there.
25: 34 He ate and *d*, and then got up
26: 30 feast for them, and they ate and *d*.
27: 25 and he brought some wine and he *d*
43: 34 they feasted and *d* freely with him.
Ex 24: 11 they saw God, and they ate and *d*.
Nu 20: 11 community and their livestock *d*.
Dt 9: 9 I ate no bread and *d* no water.
9: 18 I ate no bread and *d* no water,
29: 6 You ate no bread and *d* no wine
32: 14 You *d* the red blood of the grape.
32: 38 *d* the wine of their drink offerings?
Jdg 15: 19 When Samson *d*, his strength
2Sa 11: 13 At David's invitation, he ate and *d*
12: 3 *d* from his cup and even slept
1Ki 4: 20 they *d* and they were happy.
13: 19 and ate and *d* in his house.
13: 22 *d* water in the place where he told
17: 6 and meat in the evening, and he *d*
19: 6 and *d* and then lay down again.
19: 8 So he got up and ate and *d*.
2Ki 7: 8 and *d*, and carried away silver,
9: 34 Jehu went in and ate and *d*.
1Ch 29: 22 and *d* with great joy in the presence
Ezr 10: 6 he ate no food and *d* no water,
Job 29: 23 *d* in my words as the spring rain.
Jer 51: 7 The nations *d* her wine;
Da 5: 1 of his nobles and *d* wine with them.
5: 3 and his concubines *d* from them.
5: 4 As they *d* the wine, they praised
5: 23 your concubines *d* wine from them.
Ob : 16 Just as you *d* on my holy hill,
Mk 14: 23 it to them, and they all *d* from it.
Lk 13: 26 "Then you will say, 'We ate and *d*
Jn 4: 12 who gave us the well and *d*
Ac 10: 41 and *d* with him after he rose
1Co 10: 4 and *d* the same spiritual drink;
10: 4 for they *d* from the spiritual rock

DRAW (DRAWING DRAWN DRAWS DREW)

Ge 24: 11 time the women go out to *d* water.
24: 13 are coming out to *d* water.
24: 19 "I'll *d* water for your camels too,
24: 20 back to the well to *d* more water,
24: 43 if a maiden comes out to *d* water
24: 44 and I'll *d* water for your camels too
Ex 2: 16 and they came to *d* water
15: 9 I will *d* my sword
Lev 26: 33 will *d* out my sword and pursue
Nu 5: 15 offering to *d* attention to guilt.
Jos 8: 26 For Joshua did not *d* back the hand

Jdg 8: 20 But Jether did not *d* his sword,
9: 54 "*D* your sword and kill me,
20: 32 and *d* them away from the city
1Sa 9: 11 some girls coming out to *d* water,
31: 4 *D* your sword and run me through,
1Ch 10: 4 *D* your sword and run me through,
Job 37: 19 we cannot *d* up our case
Ps 37: 14 The wicked *d* the sword
58: 7 when they *d* the bow, let their
144: 14 our oxen will *d* heavy loads.
Isa 5: 18 Woe to those who *d* sin
12: 3 With joy you will *d* water
Jer 46: 9 men of Lydia who *d* the bow.
50: 14 all you who *d* the bow.
50: 29 all those who *d* the bow.
Eze 4: 1 and *d* the city of Jerusalem on it.
21: 3 I will *d* my sword from its scabbard
28: 7 they will *d* their swords
30: 11 They will *d* their swords
40: 46 are the only Levites who may *d*
45: 4 and who *d* near to minister
Joel 3: 9 Let all the fighting men *d* near
Na 3: 14 *D* water for the siege,
Zep 3: 2 she does not *d* near to her God.
Hag 2: 16 to a wine vat to *d* fifty measures,
Mt 26: 52 "for all who *d* the sword will die
Lk 1: 1 undertaken to *d* up an account
Jn 2: 8 "Now *d* some out and take it
4: 7 Samaritan woman came to *d* water,
4: 11 "you have nothing to *d* with
4: 15 to keep coming here to *d* water."
12: 32 up from the earth, will *d* all men
Ac 20: 30 truth in order to *d* away disciples
Gal 2: 12 to *d* back and separate himself
Heb 7: 19 by which we *d* near to God.
10: 1 make perfect those who *d*
10: 22 let us *d* near to God

DRAWING (DRAW)

1Sa 17: 21 the Philistines were *d* up their lines
1Ch 24: 5 divided them impartially by *d* lots,
Lk 21: 28 because your redemption is *d* near

DRAWN (DRAW)

Ge 34: 3 His heart was *d* to Dinah daughter
Nu 22: 23 the road with a *d* sword in his hand,
22: 31 in the road with his sword *d*.
Dt 30: 17 and if you are *d* away to bow
Jos 5: 13 of him with a *d* sword in his hand.
Jdg 20: 31 and were *d* away from the city.
1Ch 21: 16 with a *d* sword in his hand
Job 19: 6 and *d* his net around me.
Ps 3: 6 *d* up against me on every side.
21: 12 when you aim at them with *d* bow.
55: 21 yet they are *d* swords.
141: 4 Let not my heart be *d*
Isa 21: 15 from the *d* sword,
50: 5 I have not *d* back.
Jer 31: 3 I have *d* you with loving-kindness.
Eze 5: 2 I will pursue them with *d* sword.
5: 12 the winds and pursue with *d* sword.
12: 14 I will pursue them with *d* sword.
21: 5 that I the LORD have *d* my sword
21: 28 *d* for the slaughter,
32: 20 The sword is *d*; let her be dragged
Joel 2: 5 like a mighty army *d* up for battle.
Mic 5: 6 the land of Nimrod with *d* sword.
Jn 2: 9 the servants who had *d* the water

DRAWS (DRAW)

Job 33: 22 His soul *d* near to the pit,
36: 27 "He *d* up the drops of water,
Ps 88: 3 and my life *d* near the grave.
Pr 20: 5 a man of understanding *d* them out
Isa 51: 5 My righteousness *d* near speedily,
Jn 4: 36 Even now the reaper *d* his wages,
6: 44 the Father who sent me *d* him,

DREAD (DREADED DREADFUL DREADS)

Ge 9: 2 *d* of you will fall upon all the beasts
Ex 1: 12 Egyptians came to *d* the Israelites
15: 16 terror and *d* will fall upon them.
Nu 22: 3 Moab was filled with *d*
Dt 28: 66 filled with *d* both night and day,
2Ch 29: 8 he has made them an object of *d*
Job 9: 28 I still *d* all my sufferings,
13: 11 Would not the *d* of him fall on you?
Ps 14: 5 they are, overwhelmed with *d*,
31: 11 I am a *d* to my friends—
53: 5 they were, overwhelmed with *d*,
53: 5 where there was nothing to *d*.
105: 38 *d* of Israel had fallen on them.
119: 39 Take away the disgrace I *d*,
Isa 2: 10 the ground from *d* of the LORD
2: 19 the ground from *d* of the LORD
2: 21 crags from *d* of the LORD
7: 16 the two kings you *d* will be laid
8: 12 and do not *d* it.
8: 13 he is the one you are to *d*,
66: 4 will bring upon them what they *d*.
Jer 42: 16 the famine you *d* will follow you

DREADED (DREAD)

Dt 28: 60 the diseases of Egypt that you *d*,
32: 27 but I *d* the taunt of the enemy,
Job 3: 25 what I *d* has happened to me.
31: 23 For I *d* destruction from God,
31: 34 and so *d* the contempt of the clans
Isa 57: 11 "Whom have you so *d* and feared
Da 5: 19 and men of every language *d*
Hab 1: 7 They are a feared and *d* people;

DREADFUL (DREAD)

Ge 15: 12 and *d* darkness came over him.
Dt 1: 19 and *d* desert that you have seen,
8: 15 you through the vast and *d* desert,
Job 6: 21 you see something *d* and are afraid.
Eze 14: 21 Jerusalem my four *d* judgments—
Joel 1: 15 What a *d* day!
2: 11 it is *d*.
2: 31 the coming of the great and *d* day
Mal 4: 5 and *d* day of the LORD comes.
Mt 24: 19 How *d* it will be in those days
Mk 13: 17 How *d* it will be in those days
Lk 21: 23 How *d* it will be in those days
Heb 10: 31 It is a *d* thing to fall into the hands

DREADS (DREAD)

Pr 10: 24 What the wicked *d* will overtake

DREAM (DREAMED DREAMER DREAMERS DREAMING DREAMS)

Ge 20: 3 came to Abimelech in a *d* one night
20: 6 Then God said to him in the *d*,
28: 12 He had a *d* in which he saw
31: 10 "In breeding season I once had a *d*
31: 11 angel of God said to me in the *d*,
31: 24 came to Laban the Aramean in a *d*
37: 5 Joseph had a *d*, and when he told it
37: 6 to them, "Listen to this *d* I had:
37: 8 of his *d* and what he had said.
37: 9 Then he had another *d*,
37: 9 "Listen," he said, "I had another *d*,
37: 10 and said, "What is this *d* you had?
40: 5 each *d* had a meaning of its own.
40: 5 in prison—had a *d* the same night,
40: 9 In my *d* I saw a vine in front of me,
40: 9 chief cupbearer told Joseph his *d*.
40: 16 he said to Joseph, "I too had a *d*:
41: 1 Pharaoh had a *d*: He was standing
41: 5 asleep again and had a second *d*:
41: 7 Pharaoh woke up; it had been a *d*.
41: 11 Each of us had a *d* the same night,
41: 11 each *d* had a meaning of its own.
41: 12 man the interpretation of his *d*.
41: 15 you hear a *d* you can interpret
41: 15 "I had a *d*, and no one can interpret
41: 17 In my *d* I was standing on the bank
41: 26 years; it is one and the same *d*.
41: 32 The reason the *d* was given
Jdg 7: 13 as a man was telling a friend his *d*.
7: 13 "I had a *d*," he was saying.
7: 15 When Gideon heard the *d*
1Ki 3: 5 to Solomon during the night in a *d*,
3: 15 and he realized it had been a *d*.
Job 20: 8 Like a *d* he flies away, no more
33: 15 In a *d*, in a vision of the night,
Ps 73: 20 As a *d* when one awakes,
Ecc 5: 3 As a *d* comes when there are many
Isa 29: 7 will be as it is with a *d*,
56: 10 they lie around and *d*,
Jer 23: 25 They say, 'I had a *d*! I had a *d*!'
23: 28 the prophet who has a *d* tell his *d*,
Da 2: 3 "I have had a *d* that troubles me
2: 4 Tell your servants the *d*,
2: 5 you do not tell me what my *d* was
Da 2: 6 if you tell me the *d* and explain it,
2: 6 tell me the *d* and interpret it for me
2: 7 Let the king tell his servants the *d*,
2: 9 If you do not tell me the *d*,
2: 9 tell me the *d*, and I will know that
2: 16 so that he might interpret the *d*
2: 23 known to us the *d* of the king."
2: 24 and I will interpret his *d* for him."
2: 25 can tell the king what his *d* means."
2: 26 able to tell me what I saw in my *d*
2: 28 Your *d* and the visions that passed
2: 36 "This was the *d*, and now we will
2: 45 *d* is true and the interpretation is
4: 5 I had a *d* that made me afraid.
4: 6 before me to interpret the *d* for me.
4: 7 diviners came, I told them the *d*,
4: 8 my presence and I told him the *d*.
4: 9 Here is my *d*; interpret it for me.
4: 18 "This is the *d* that I, King
4: 19 do not let the *d* or its meaning
4: 19 if only the *d* applied
7: 1 king of Babylon, Daniel had a *d*,
7: 1 wrote down the substance of his *d*.
Joel 2: 28 your old men will *d* dreams,
Mt 1: 20 of the Lord appeared to him in a *d*
2: 12 warned in a *d* not to go back
2: 13 the Lord appeared to Joseph in a *d*.
2: 19 appeared in a *d* to Joseph in Egypt
2: 22 Having been warned in a *d*,
27: 19 suffered a great deal today in a *d*
Ac 2: 17 your old men will *d* dreams.

DREAMED (DREAM)

Ps 126: 1 we were like men who *d*.
Da 2: 2 to tell him what he had *d*.

DREAMER (DREAM)

Ge 37: 19 "Here comes that *d*!" they said
Dt 13: 3 to the words of that prophet or *d*.
13: 5 or *d* must be put to death,

DREAMERS (DREAM)

Jude : 8 these *d* pollute their own bodies,

DREAMING (DREAM)

Ecc 5: 7 Much *d* and many words are

DREAMS (DREAM)

Ge 37: 20 Then we'll see what comes of his *d*
40: 8 belong to God? Tell me your *d*."
40: 8 "We both had *d*," they answered,
41: 8 Pharaoh told them his *d*,
41: 12 told him our *d*, and he interpreted
41: 22 "In my *d* I also saw seven heads
41: 25 "The *d* of Pharaoh are one
42: 9 he remembered his *d* about them
Nu 12: 6 I speak to him in *d*.
Dt 13: 1 or one who foretells by *d*,
1Sa 28: 6 the LORD did not answer him by *d*
28: 15 either by prophets or by *d*.
Job 4: 13 Amid disquieting *d* in the night,
7: 14 even then you frighten me with *d*
Isa 29: 8 as when a hungry man *d* that he is
29: 8 as when a thirsty man *d* that he is
Jer 23: 27 They think the *d* they tell one
23: 32 against those who prophesy false *d*
27: 9 diviners, your interpreters of *d*,
29: 8 listen to the *d* you encourage them
Da 1: 17 could understand visions and *d*
2: 1 his reign, Nebuchadnezzar had *d*;
5: 12 and also the ability to interpret *d*,
Joel 2: 28 your old men will dream *d*,
Zec 10: 2 they tell *d* that are false,
Ac 2: 17 your old men will dream *d*.

DREGS

Ps 75: 8 drink it down to its very *d*.
Isa 51: 17 you who have drained to its *d*
Jer 48: 11 like wine left on its *d*,
Zep 1: 12 who are like wine left on its *d*,

DRENCH (DRENCHED)

Ps 6: 6 and *d* my couch with tears.
65: 10 You *d* its furrows
Isa 16: 9 I *d* you with tears!
Eze 32: 6 I will *d* the land with your flowing

DRENCHED (DRENCH)

Job 24: 8 They are *d* by mountain rains
29: 6 when my path was *d* with cream
SS 5: 2 My head is *d* with dew,
Isa 34: 7 Their land will be *d* with blood,
Da 4: 15 " 'Let him be *d* with the dew
4: 23 Let him be *d* with the dew
4: 25 and be *d* with the dew of heaven.
4: 33 His body was *d* with the dew
5: 21 and his body was *d* with the dew

DRESS (DRESSED DRESSING WELL-DRESSED)

Ex 29: 5 and *d* Aaron with the tunic,
29: 8 Bring his sons and *d* them in tunics
40: 13 *d* Aaron in the sacred garments,
40: 14 Bring his sons and *d* them in tunics.
2Sa 14: 2 *D* in mourning clothes,
Jer 4: 30 Why *d* yourself in scarlet
6: 14 They *d* the wound of my people
8: 11 They *d* the wound of my people
Eze 16: 10 you with an embroidered *d*
23: 12 in full *d*, mounted horsemen,
Lk 12: 37 tell you the truth, he will *d* himself
Jn 21: 18 and someone else will *d* you
1Ti 2: 9 I also want women to *d* modestly,

DRESSED (DRESS)

Ge 41: 42 He *d* him in robes of fine linen
Ex 20: 25 do not build it with *d* stones,
1Sa 17: 38 Then Saul *d* David in his own tunic
25: 18 two skins of wine, five *d* sheep,
1Ki 5: 17 of *d* stone for the temple.
6: 7 only blocks *d* at the quarry were
6: 36 of three courses of *d* stone
7: 12 by a wall of three courses of *d* stone
22: 10 *D* in their royal robes, the king
2Ki 12: 12 *d* stone for the repair of the temple
22: 6 and *d* stone to repair the temple.
1Ch 22: 2 stonecutters to prepare *d* stone
2Ch 5: 12 *d* in fine linen and playing cymbals,
18: 9 *D* in their royal robes, the king
34: 11 and builders to purchase *d* stone,
Pr 7: 10 *d* like a prostitute and with crafty
Isa 9: 10 but we will rebuild with *d* stone;
Jer 10: 9 is then *d* in blue and purple—
Eze 16: 10 I *d* you in fine linen and covered
40: 42 also four tables of *d* stone
Da 10: 5 before me was a man *d* in linen,
Zec 3: 3 Now Joshua was *d* in filthy clothes
Mt 6: 29 in all his splendor was *d* like one
11: 8 A man *d* in fine clothes? No,
Mk 5: 15 sitting there, *d* and in his right
16: 5 they saw a young man *d*
Lk 7: 25 A man *d* in fine clothes? No,
8: 35 sitting at Jesus' feet, *d*
12: 27 in all his splendor was *d* like one
12: 35 "Be *d* ready for service
16: 19 "There was a rich man who was *d*
Jn 21: 18 you were younger you *d* yourself
Ac 1: 10 when suddenly two men *d*
Rev 1: 13 *d* in a robe reaching
3: 4 They will walk with me, *d* in white,
3: 5 overcomes will, like them, be *d*
4: 4 They were *d* in white and had
15: 6 They were *d* in clean, shining linen
17: 4 The woman was *d* in purple
18: 16 *d* in fine linen, purple and scarlet,
19: 13 He is *d* in a robe dipped in blood,
19: 14 on white horses and *d* in fine linen,
21: 2 as a bride beautifully *d*

DRESSING (DRESS)

Lk 23: 11 *D* him in an elegant robe, they sent

DREW (DRAW)

Ge 14: 8 *d* up their battle lines in the Valley
24: 20 and *d* enough for all his camels.
24: 45 down to the spring and *d* water,
38: 29 But when he *d* back his hand,
47: 29 When the time *d* near for Israel
49: 33 he *d* his feet up into the bed,
Ex 2: 10 saying, "I *d* him out of the water."
2: 19 He even *d* water for us
Jos 24: 25 and there at Shechem he *d* up
Jdg 3: 21 *d* the sword from his right thigh
20: 24 the Israelites *d* near to Benjamin
1Sa 7: 6 they *d* water and poured it out
1Sa 7: 10 Philistines *d* near to engage Israel
17: 2 and *d* up their battle line
17: 51 and *d* it from the scabbard.
2Sa 10: 8 and *d* up in battle formation
22: 17 he *d* me out of deep waters.
23: 16 *d* water from the well near the gate
1Ki 2: 1 When the time *d* near for David
22: 34 But someone *d* his bow at random
2Ki 9: 24 Jehu *d* his bow and shot Joram
1Ch 11: 18 *d* water from the well near the gate
19: 9 and *d* up in battle formation
2Ch 13: 3 and Jeroboam *d* up a battle line
18: 31 God *d* them away from him,
18: 33 But someone *d* his bow at random
Ps 18: 16 he *d* me out of deep waters.
107: 18 and *d* near the gates of death.
Isa 43: 17 who *d* out the chariots and horses,
La 3: 12 He *d* his bow
Mt 26: 51 *d* it out and struck the servant
Mk 14: 47 of those standing near *d* his sword
Jn 18: 6 they *d* back and fell to the ground.
18: 10 *d* it and struck the high priest's
Ac 1: 26 Then they *d* lots, and the lot fell
7: 17 "As the time *d* near for God
16: 27 he *d* his sword and was about
23: 19 man by the hand, *d* him aside

DRIED (DRY)

Ge 8: 7 and forth until the water had *d* up
8: 13 the water had *d* up from the earth
Jos 2: 10 how the LORD *d* up the water
4: 23 Sea when he *d* it up before us
4: 23 LORD your God *d* up the Jordan
5: 1 the LORD had *d* up the Jordan
Jdg 16: 7 fresh thongs that have not been *d*,
16: 8 fresh thongs that had not been *d*,
1Ki 17: 7 Some time later the brook *d* up
2Ki 19: 24 I have *d* up all the streams of Egypt
Ps 22: 15 My strength is *d* up like a potsherd,
74: 15 you *d* up the ever flowing rivers.
106: 9 rebuked the Red Sea, and it *d* up;
Isa 15: 6 The waters of Nimrim are *d* up
37: 25 I have *d* up all the streams of Egypt
51: 10 Was it not you who *d* up the sea,
Jer 48: 34 the waters of Nimrim are *d* up.
Eze 37: 11 'Our bones are *d* up and our hope is
Joel 1: 10 the ground is *d* up;
1: 10 the new wine is *d* up,
1: 12 The vine is *d* up
1: 12 all the trees of the field—are *d* up.
1: 17 for the grain has *d* up.
1: 20 the streams of water have *d* up
Am 4: 7 another had none and *d* up.
7: 4 it *d* up the great deep and devoured
Rev 16: 12 and its water was *d* up to prepare

DRIES (DRY)

Pr 17: 22 but a crushed spirit *d* up the bones.
Isa 24: 4 The earth *d* up and withers,
24: 7 new wine *d* up and the vine
Na 1: 4 He rebukes the sea and *d* it up;

DRIFT

Heb 2: 1 so that we do not *d* away.

DRINK (DRANK DRINKERS DRINKING DRINKS DRUNK DRUNKARD DRUNKARD'S DRUNKARDS DRUNKEN DRUNKENNESS)

Ge 19: 32 Let's get our father to *d* wine
19: 33 they got their father to *d* wine,
19: 34 him to *d* wine again tonight,
19: 35 father to *d* wine that night
21: 19 with water and gave the boy a *d*.
24: 14 down your jar that I may have a *d*,'
24: 14 '*D*, and I'll water your camels too
24: 18 jar to her hands and gave him a *d*.
24: 18 "*D*, my lord," she said,
24: 19 After she had given him a *d*,
24: 43 "Please let me *d* a little water
24: 44 "*D*, and I'll draw water
24: 45 I said to her, 'Please give me a *d*.'
24: 46 '*D*, and I'll water your camels too.'
30: 38 of the flocks when they came to *d*.
30: 38 were in heat and came to *d*,
35: 14 and he poured out a *d* offering on it
Ex 7: 18 will not be able to *d* its water.' "
7: 21 the Egyptians could not *d* its water.
Ex 7: 24 because they could not *d* the water
15: 23 they could not *d* its water
15: 24 saying, "What are we to *d*?"
17: 1 water for the people to *d*.
17: 2 and said, "Give us water to *d*."
17: 6 out of it for the people to *d*."
29: 40 of a hin of wine as a *d* offering.
29: 41 its *d* offering as in the morning—
30: 9 and do not pour a *d* offering on it.
32: 6 sat down to eat and *d*
32: 20 and made the Israelites *d* it.
37: 16 for the pouring out of *d* offerings.
Lev 10: 9 and your sons are not to *d* wine
10: 9 other fermented *d* whenever you
23: 13 its *d* offering of a fourth of a hin
23: 18 grain offerings and *d* offerings—
23: 37 *d* offerings required for each day.
Nu 4: 7 and the jars for *d* offerings;
5: 24 have the woman *d* the bitter water
5: 26 is to have the woman *d* the water.
5: 27 to *d* the water that brings a curse,
6: 3 He must not *d* grape juice
6: 3 from wine and other fermented *d*
6: 3 must not *d* vinegar made from wine
6: 3 or from other fermented *d*.
6: 15 grain offerings and *d* offerings,
6: 17 its grain offering and *d* offering.
6: 20 After that, the Nazirite may *d* wine
15: 5 of a hin of wine as a *d* offering.
15: 7 of a hin of wine as a *d* offering.
15: 10 a hin of wine as a *d* offering.
15: 24 grain offering and *d* offering,
20: 5 And there is no water to *d*!"
20: 8 and their livestock can *d*."
20: 17 vineyard, or *d* water from any well
20: 19 our livestock *d* any of your water,
21: 22 vineyard, or *d* water from any well.
28: 7 Pour out the *d* offering
28: 7 The accompanying *d* offering is
28: 7 hin of fermented *d* with each lamb.
28: 8 and *d* offering that you prepare
28: 9 together with its *d* offering
28: 10 burnt offering and its *d* offering.
28: 14 is to be a *d* offering of half a hin
28: 15 offering with its *d* offering.
28: 24 burnt offering and its *d* offering.
28: 31 together with their *d* offerings.
29: 6 and *d* offerings as specified.
29: 11 offering, and their *d* offerings.
29: 16 its grain offering and *d* offering.
29: 18 and *d* offerings according
29: 19 offering, and their *d* offerings
29: 21 and *d* offerings according
29: 22 its grain offering and *d* offering.
29: 24 and *d* offerings according
29: 25 its grain offering and *d* offering.
29: 27 and *d* offerings according
29: 28 its grain offering and *d* offering.
29: 30 and *d* offerings according
29: 31 its grain offering and *d* offering.
29: 33 and *d* offerings according
29: 34 its grain offering and *d* offering.
29: 37 and *d* offerings according
29: 38 its grain offering and *d* offering.
29: 39 *d* offerings and fellowship offerings
33: 14 water for the people to *d*.
Dt 2: 6 you eat and the water you *d*.' "
2: 28 water to *d* for their price in silver.
14: 26 wine or other fermented *d*,
28: 39 but you will not *d* the wine
29: 6 no wine or other fermented *d*.
32: 38 drank the wine of their *d* offerings?
Jdg 4: 19 gave him a *d*, and covered him up.
7: 5 from those who kneel down to *d*."
7: 6 got down on their knees to *d*.
13: 4 Now see to it that you *d* no wine
13: 4 other fermented *d* and that you do
13: 7 *d* no wine or other fermented *d*
13: 14 nor *d* any wine or other fermented
13: 14 other fermented *d* nor eat anything
19: 6 sat down to eat and *d* together.
19: 21 they had something to eat and *d*.
Ru 2: 9 get a *d* from the water jars the men
1Sa 30: 11 They gave him water to *d*
2Sa 11: 11 and *d* and lie with my wife?
23: 15 that someone would get me a *d*
23: 16 But he refused to *d* it; instead,
23: 17 And David would not *d* it.

1Ki 13: 8 would I eat bread or *d* water here.
13: 9 'You must not eat bread or *d* water
13: 16 or *d* water with you in this place.
13: 17 must not eat bread or *d* water there
13: 18 he may eat bread and *d* water.' "
13: 22 where he told you not to eat or *d*.
17: 4 You will *d* from the brook,
17: 10 water in a jar so I may have a *d?"*
18: 41 Elijah said to Ahab, "Go, eat and *d*
18: 42 So Ahab went off to eat and *d*,
2Ki 3: 17 and your other animals will *d*.
6: 22 *d* and then go back to their master
16: 13 offering, poured out his *d* offering,
16: 15 grain offering and their *d* offering.
18: 27 own filth and *d* their own urine?"
18: 31 and *d* water from his own cistern,
1Ch 11: 17 that someone would get me a *d*
11: 18 But he refused to *d* it; instead,
11: 19 bring it back, David would not *d* it.
11: 19 "Should I *d* the blood
29: 21 together with their *d* offerings,
2Ch 28: 15 food and *d*, and healing balm.
29: 35 the *d* offerings that accompanied
Ezr 3: 7 and *d* and oil to the people of Sidon
7: 17 grain offerings and *d* offerings,
Ne 8: 12 the people went away to eat and *d*,
Est 1: 8 allowed to *d* in his own way,
3: 15 The king and Haman sat down to *d*
4: 16 Do not eat or *d* for three days,
Job 1: 4 sisters to eat and *d* with them.
21: 20 let him *d* of the wrath
Ps 36: 8 you give them *d* from your river
50: 13 or *d* the blood of goats?
73: 10 and *d* up waters in abundance.
75: 8 *d* it down to its very dregs.
78: 44 they could not *d* from their streams
80: 5 you have made them *d* tears
102: 9 and mingle my *d* with tears
110: 7 He will *d* from a brook
Pr 4: 17 and *d* the wine of violence.
5: 15 *D* water from your own cistern,
7: 18 let's *d* deep of love till morning;
9: 5 and *d* the wine I have mixed.
23: 7 "Eat and *d*," he says to you,
23: 20 join those who *d* too much wine
23: 35 up so I can find another *d?"*
25: 21 if he is thirsty, give him water to *d*.
31: 4 not for kings to *d* wine,
31: 5 lest they *d* and forget what the law
31: 7 let them *d* and forget their poverty
Ecc 2: 24 *d* and find satisfaction in his work.
3: 13 That every man may eat and *d*,
5: 18 and proper for a man to eat and *d*,
8: 15 under the sun than to eat and *d*
9: 7 and *d* your wine with a joyful heart,
SS 5: 1 Eat, O friends, and *d;*
5: 1 *d* your fill, O lovers.
8: 2 I would give you spiced wine to *d*,
Isa 21: 5 they eat, they *d!*
22: 13 "Let us eat and *d*," you say,
24: 9 No longer do they *d* wine
36: 12 own filth and *d* their own urine?"
36: 16 and *d* water from his own cistern,
43: 20 to give *d* to my people, my chosen,
51: 22 you will never *d* again.
56: 12 Let us *d* our fill of beer!
57: 6 you have poured out *d* offerings
60: 16 You will *d* the milk of nations
62: 8 again will foreigners *d* the new
62: 9 who gather the grapes will *d* it
65: 13 my servants will *d*,
66: 11 you will *d* deeply
Jer 2: 18 Assyria to *d* water from the River?
2: 18 Egypt to *d* water from the Shihor?
7: 18 They pour out *d* offerings
8: 14 and given us poisoned water to *d*,
9: 15 bitter food and *d* poisoned water.
16: 7 nor will anyone give them a *d*
16: 8 and sit down to eat and *d*.
19: 13 and poured out *d* offerings
22: 15 not your father have food and *d?*
23: 15 and *d* poisoned water,
25: 15 nations to whom I send you *d* it.
25: 16 When they *d* it, they will stagger
25: 17 nations to whom he sent me *d* it:
25: 26 the king of Sheshach will *d* it too.
25: 27 says: *D*, get drunk and vomit,
25: 28 Almighty says: You must *d* it!
Jer 25: 28 the cup from your hand and *d*,
32: 29 and by pouring out *d* offerings
35: 2 LORD and give them wine to *d*."
35: 5 and said to them, "*D* some wine."
35: 6 they replied, "We do not *d* wine,
35: 6 your descendants must ever *d* wine
35: 14 To this day they do not *d* wine,
35: 14 ordered his sons not to *d* wine
44: 17 will pour out *d* offerings to her just
44: 18 and pouring out *d* offerings to her,
44: 19 and poured out *d* offerings to her,
44: 19 pouring out *d* offerings to her?"
44: 25 pour out *d* offerings to the Queen
49: 12 deserve to *d* the cup must *d* it,
49: 12 not go unpunished, but must *d* it.
52: 19 and bowls used for *d* offerings—
La 5: 4 We must buy the water we *d;*
Eze 4: 11 a hin of water and *d* it at set times.
4: 16 and *d* rationed water in despair,
12: 18 shudder in fear as you *d* your water
12: 19 and *d* their water in despair,
20: 28 and poured out their *d* offerings.
23: 32 "You will *d* your sister's cup,
23: 34 You will *d* it and drain it dry;
25: •4 will eat your fruit and *d* your milk.
34: 18 enough for you to *d* clear water?
34: 19 and *d* what you have muddied
39: 17 you will eat flesh and *d* blood.
39: 18 and *d* the blood of the princes
39: 19 and *d* blood till you are drunk.
44: 21 No priest is to *d* wine
45: 17 and *d* offerings at the festivals,
Da 1: 10 who has assigned your food and *d*.
1: 12 vegetables to eat and water to *d*.
1: 16 and the wine they were to *d*
5: 2 his concubines might *d* from them.
Hos 2: 5 and my linen, my oil and my *d*.'
Joel 1: 9 Grain offerings and *d* offerings
1: 13 the grain offerings and *d* offerings
2: 14 grain offerings and *d* offerings
3: 3 that they might *d*.
Am 2: 8 they *d* wine taken as fines.
2: 12 you made the Nazirites *d* wine
4: 8 but did not get enough to *d*,
5: 11 you will not *d* their wine.
6: 6 You *d* wine by the bowlful
9: 14 plant vineyards and *d* their wine;
Ob : 16 so all the nations will *d* continually;
: 16 they will *d* and *d*
Jnh 3: 7 anything; do not let them eat or *d*.
Mic 6: 15 crush grapes but not *d* the wine.
Hab 2: 15 to him who gives *d* to his neighbors
2: 16 it is your turn! *D* and be exposed!
Zep 1: 13 but not *d* the wine.
Hag 1: 6 You *d*, but never have your fill.
Zec 9: 15 They will *d* and roar as with wine;
Mt 6: 25 or *d;* or about your body,
6: 31 'What shall we *d?*' or 'What shall
20: 22 "Can you *d* the cup I am going to *d*
20: 23 "You will indeed *d* from my cup,
24: 49 and to eat and *d* with drunkards.
25: 35 and you gave me something to *d*,
25: 37 thirsty and give you something to *d*
25: 42 and you gave me nothing to *d*,
26: 27 saying, "*D* from it, all of you.
26: 29 I will not *d* of this fruit of the vine
26: 29 day when I *d* it anew with you
26: 42 cup to be taken away unless I *d* it,
27: 34 There they offered him wine to *d*,
27: 34 after tasting it, he refused to *d* it.
27: 48 and offered it to Jesus to *d*.
Mk 10: 38 "Can you *d* the cup I *d*
10: 39 "You will *d* the cup I *d*
14: 25 I will not *d* again of the fruit
14: 25 vine until that day when I *d* it anew
15: 36 and offered it to Jesus to *d*.
16: 18 and when they *d* deadly poison,
Lk 1: 15 to take wine or other fermented *d*,
5: 30 "Why do you eat and *d*
12: 19 Take life easy; eat, *d* and be merry
12: 29 heart on what you will eat or *d;*
12: 45 and to eat and *d* and get drunk.
17: 8 after that you may eat and *d*'?
17: 8 and wait on me while I eat and *d;*
22: 18 For I tell you I will not *d* again
22: 30 and *d* at my table in my kingdom
Jn 2: 10 the guests have had too much to *d;*
4: 7 to her, "Will you give me a *d?"*
Jn 4: 9 How can you ask me for a *d?"*
4: 10 and who it is that asks you for a *d*,
6: 53 of the Son of Man and *d* his blood,
6: 55 is real food and my blood is real *d*
7: 37 let him come to me and *d*.
18: 11 Shall I not *d* the cup the Father has
19: 30 When he had received the *d*,
Ac 9: 9 and did not eat or *d* anything.
23: 12 or *d* until they had killed Paul.
23: 21 or *d* until they have killed him.
Ro 12: 20 is thirsty, give him something to *d*.
14: 21 not to eat meat or *d* wine
1Co 9: 4 we have the right to food and *d?*
9: 7 and does not *d* of the milk?
10: 4 and drank the same spiritual *d;*
10: 7 "The people sat down to eat and *d*
10: 21 You cannot *d* the cup of the Lord
10: 31 you eat or *d* or whatever you do,
11: 22 Don't you have homes to eat and *d*
11: 25 do this, whenever you *d* it,
11: 26 you eat this bread and *d* this cup,
12: 13 were all given the one Spirit to *d*.
15: 32 "Let us eat and *d*,
Php 2: 17 being poured out like a *d* offering
Col 2: 16 you by what you eat or *d*,
2Ti 4: 6 being poured out like a *d* offering,
Heb 9: 10 *d* and various ceremonial washings
Rev 14: 8 all the nations *d* the maddening
14: 10 too, will *d* of the wine of God's fury
16: 6 you have given them blood to *d*
21: 6 to *d* without cost from the spring

DRINKERS (DRINK)

Isa 24: 9 the beer is bitter to its *d*.
Joel 1: 5 Wail, all you *d* of wine;

DRINKING (DRINK)

Ge 24: 19 until they have finished *d*."
24: 22 When the camels had finished *d*,
Ex 7: 24 dug along the Nile to get *d* water,
34: 28 without eating bread or *d* water.
Jdg 9: 27 While they were eating and *d*,
19: 4 eating and *d*, and sleeping there.
Ru 3: 3 until he has finished eating and *d*.
3: 7 and *d* and was in good spirits,
1Sa 1: 9 they had finished eating and *d*
1: 15 I have not been *d* wine or beer;
30: 16 *d* and reveling because of the great
2Sa 13: 28 is in high spirits from *d* wine
1Ki 1: 25 and *d* with him and saying,
13: 23 of God had finished eating and *d*,
20: 12 and the kings were *d* in their tents,
2Ki 6: 23 after they had finished eating and *d*
1Ch 12: 39 *d*, for their families had supplied
Est 5: 6 As they were *d* wine, the king
7: 2 as they were *d* wine on that second
Job 1: 13 *d* wine at the oldest brother's house
1: 18 *d* wine at the oldest brother's house
Pr 26: 6 off one's feet or *d* violence
Isa 5: 22 to those who are heroes at *d* wine
22: 13 eating of meat and *d* of wine!
29: 8 a thirsty man dreams that he is *d*,
Da 5: 2 While Belshazzar was *d* his wine,
Zec 7: 6 And when you were eating and *d*,
Mt 11: 18 For John came neither eating nor *d*
11: 19 The Son of Man came eating and *d*,
24: 38 people were eating and *d*, marrying
Lk 5: 33 but yours go on eating and *d*."
5: 39 one after *d* old wine wants the new,
7: 33 neither eating bread nor *d* wine,
7: 34 The Son of Man came eating and *d*,
10: 7 and *d* whatever they give you,
17: 27 *d*, marrying and being given
17: 28 People were eating and *d*,
Ro 14: 17 God is not a matter of eating and *d*,
1Ti 5: 23 Stop *d* only water, and use a little

DRINKS (DRINK)

Ge 44: 5 Isn't this the cup my master *d* from
Nu 23: 24 and *d* the blood of his victims."
Dt 11: 11 valleys that *d* rain from heaven.
2Sa 19: 35 servant taste what he eats and *d?*
Ne 8: 10 and enjoy choice food and sweet *d*,
Job 6: 4 my spirit *d* in their poison;
15: 16 who *d* up evil like water!
34: 7 who *d* scorn like water?
Isa 5: 11 the morning to run after their *d*,
5: 22 and champions at mixing *d*,

Isa 44: 12 he *d* no water and grows faint.
Hos 4: 18 Even when their *d* are gone,
Am 4: 1 to your husbands, "Bring us some *d*
Jn 4: 13 "Everyone who *d* this water will be
4: 14 whoever *d* the water I give him will
6: 54 and *d* my blood has eternal life,
6: 56 and *d* my blood remains in me,
1Co 11: 27 or *d* the cup of the Lord
11: 28 eats of the bread and *d* of the cup.
11: 29 and *d* judgment on himself.
11: 29 *d* without recognizing the body
Heb 6: 7 Land that *d* in the rain often falling

DRIP (DRIPPED DRIPPING)

Pr 5: 3 the lips of an adulteress *d* honey,
Joel 3: 18 day the mountains will *d* new wine,
Am 9: 13 wine will *d* from the mountains

DRIPPED (DRIP)

SS 5: 5 and my hands *d* with myrrh,

DRIPPING (DRIP)

Pr 19: 13 wife is like a constant *d*.
27: 15 a constant *d* on a rainy day;
SS 5: 13 *d* with myrrh.

DRIVE (DRIVEN DRIVER DRIVER'S DRIVERS DRIVES DRIVING DROVE)

Ex 6: 1 my mighty hand he will *d* them out
11: 1 he will *d* you out completely.
23: 28 ahead of you to *d* the Hivites,
23: 29 But I will not *d* them out
23: 30 Little by little I will *d* them out
23: 31 and you will *d* them out before you.
33: 2 an angel before you and *d* out
34: 11 I will *d* out before you
34: 24 I will *d* out nations before you
Lev 18: 24 to *d* out before you became defiled.
20: 23 going to *d* out before you.
Nu 22: 6 and *d* them out of the country.
22: 11 to fight them and *d* them away.' "
33: 52 *d* out all the inhabitants of the land
33: 55 if you do not *d* out the inhabitants
Dt 4: 27 to which the LORD will *d* you.
4: 38 to *d* out before you nations greater
7: 17 How can we *d* them out?"
7: 22 your God will *d* out those nations
9: 3 And you will *d* them out
9: 4 going to *d* them out before you.
9: 5 LORD your God will *d* them out
11: 23 then the LORD will *d* out all these
18: 12 your God will *d* out those nations
28: 34 The sights you see will *d* you mad.
28: 36 The LORD will *d* you
28: 37 where the LORD will *d* you.
33: 27 He will *d* out your enemy
Jos 3: 10 and that he will certainly *d* out
13: 6 myself will *d* them out before
13: 13 Israelites did not *d* out the people
14: 12 I will *d* them out just as he said."
17: 13 but did not *d* them out completely.
17: 18 they are strong, you can *d* them out
23: 5 your God himself will *d* them out
23: 13 will no longer *d* out these nations
Jdg 1: 19 they were unable to *d* the people
1: 27 Manasseh did not *d* out the people
1: 29 Nor did Ephraim *d* out
1: 30 Neither did Zebulun *d* out
1: 31 Nor did Asher *d* out those living
1: 33 Neither did Naphtali *d* out those
2: 3 I tell you that I will not *d* them out
2: 21 I will no longer *d* out
2: 23 he did not *d* them out at once
11: 7 and *d* me from my father's house?
2Ch 13: 9 But didn't you *d* out the priests
20: 7 did you not *d* out the inhabitants
20: 11 us by coming to *d* us out
Job 24: 3 They *d* away the orphan's donkey
30: 22 You snatch me up and *d* me
Ps 36: 11 the hand of the wicked *d* me away.
Pr 22: 10 *D* out the mocker, and out goes
22: 15 of discipline will *d* it far from him.
Isa 22: 23 I will *d* him like a peg
Jer 22: 22 wind will *d* all your shepherds
29: 18 all the nations where I *d* them.
46: 9 *D* furiously, O charioteers!
49: 2 Then Israel will *d* out
Eze 4: 13 the nations where I will *d* them."
Eze 8: 6 things that will *d* me far
11: 7 city is the pot, but I will *d* you out
11: 9 I will *d* you out of the city
Hos 9: 15 I will *d* them out of my house.
10: 11 I will *d* Ephraim,
Joel 2: 20 "I will *d* the northern army far
Mic 2: 9 You *d* the women of my people
Mt 7: 22 and in your name *d* out demons
8: 31 begged Jesus, "If you *d* us out,
10: 1 authority to *d* out evil spirits
10: 8 who have leprosy, *d* out demons.
12: 27 if I *d* out demons by Beelzebub,
12: 27 whom do your people *d* them out?
12: 28 But if I *d* out demons by the Spirit
17: 19 "Why couldn't we *d* it out?"
Mk 3: 15 to have authority to *d* out demons.
3: 23 "How can Satan *d* out Satan?
7: 26 Jesus to *d* the demon out
9: 18 your disciples to *d* out the spirit,
9: 28 "Why couldn't we *d* it out?"
16: 17 In my name they will *d* out demons
Lk 9: 1 and authority to *d* out all demons
9: 40 I begged your disciples to *d* it out,
11: 18 you claim that I *d* out demons
11: 19 do your followers *d* them out?
11: 19 if I *d* out demons by Beelzebub,
11: 20 But if I *d* out demons by the finger
13: 32 'I will *d* out demons and heal
Jn 6: 37 comes to me I will never *d* away.

DRIVEN (DRIVE)

Ge 4: 11 are under a curse and *d*
33: 13 If they are *d* hard just one day,
Ex 10: 11 were *d* out of Pharaoh's presence.
12: 39 they had been *d* out of Egypt
Nu 32: 21 until he has *d* his enemies out
Dt 9: 4 LORD your God has *d* them out
12: 29 But when you have *d* them out
19: 1 and when you have *d* them out
Jos 8: 15 all Israel let themselves be *d* back
23: 9 "The LORD has *d* out
Jdg 11: 23 has *d* the Amorites out
1Sa 26: 19 They have now *d* me
1Ki 14: 24 of the nations the LORD had *d* out
2Ki 16: 3 of the nations the LORD had *d* out
17: 8 of the nations the LORD had *d* out
17: 11 whom the LORD had *d* out
21: 2 of the nations the LORD had *d* out
2Ch 28: 3 of the nations the LORD had *d* out
33: 2 of the nations the LORD had *d* out
Job 6: 13 now that success has been *d*
18: 18 He is *d* from light into darkness
30: 8 they were *d* out of the land.
30: 15 my dignity is *d* away as by the wind
Ps 109: 10 may they be *d* from their ruined
Isa 17: 13 *d* before the wind like chaff
22: 25 peg *d* into the firm place will give
59: 14 So justice is *d* back,
Jer 13: 24 *d* by the desert wind.
23: 2 my flock and *d* them away
23: 3 the countries where I have *d* them
49: 5 "Every one of you will be *d* away,
La 3: 2 He has *d* me away and made me
Eze 34: 21 horns until you have *d* them away,
Da 4: 25 You will be *d* away from people
4: 32 You will be *d* away from people
4: 33 He was *d* away from people
5: 21 He was *d* away from people
Am 9: 4 Though they are *d* into exile
Mic 4: 7 those *d* away a strong nation.
Mt 9: 33 And when the demon was *d* out,
Mk 16: 9 of whom he had *d* seven demons.
Lk 8: 29 and had been *d* by the demon
Jn 12: 31 prince of this world will be *d* out.
Ac 27: 15 way to it and were *d* along.
27: 17 and let the ship be *d* along.
27: 27 night we were still being *d*
28: 3 it on the fire, a viper, *d* out
Jas 3: 4 and are *d* by strong winds,
2Pe 2: 17 springs without water and mists *d*

DRIVER (DRIVE)

1Ki 22: 34 The king told his chariot *d*,
2Ch 18: 33 The king told the chariot *d*,
Jer 51: 21 with you I shatter chariot and *d*,

DRIVER'S (DRIVE)

Job 3: 18 no longer hear the slave *d* shout.
Job 39: 7 he does not hear a *d* shout.

DRIVERS (DRIVE)

Ex 3: 7 crying out because of their slave *d*,
5: 6 gave this order to the slave *d*
5: 10 slave *d* and the foremen went out
5: 13 The slave *d* kept pressing them,
5: 14 by Pharaoh's slave *d* were beaten
2Ki 7: 14 He commanded the *d*, "Go
Hag 2: 22 will overthrow chariots and their *d*;

DRIVES (DRIVE)

Dt 7: 1 *d* out before you many nations—
2Ki 9: 20 of Nimshi—he *d* like a madman."
Pr 16: 26 his hunger *d* him on.
19: 26 robs his father and *d* out his mother
20: 26 he *d* the threshing wheel over them
Isa 27: 8 with his fierce blast he *d* her out,
28: 28 Though he *d* the wheels
59: 19 the breath of the LORD *d* along.
Mt 9: 34 of demons that he *d* out demons."
12: 24 that this fellow *d* out demons."
12: 26 If Satan *d* out Satan, he is divided
1Jn 4: 18 But perfect love *d* out fear,

DRIVING (DRIVE)

Ge 4: 14 Today you are *d* me from the land,
Ex 14: 25 off so that they had difficulty *d*.
2Sa 7: 23 awesome wonders by *d* out nations
1Ki 19: 19 he himself was *d* the twelfth pair.
2Ki 9: 20 The *d* is like that of Jehu son
16: 6 Elath for Aram by *d* out the men
1Ch 17: 21 awesome wonders by *d* out nations
Job 37: 9 the cold from the *d* winds.
Ps 35: 5 angel of the LORD *d* them away;
Pr 28: 3 is like a *d* rain that leaves no crops.
Isa 25: 4 is like a storm *d* against a wall
28: 2 like a *d* rain and a flooding
Jer 30: 23 a *d* wind swirling down
Eze 46: 18 inheritance of the people, *d* them
Mk 1: 39 synagogues and *d* out demons.
3: 22 of demons he is *d* out demons."
9: 38 "we saw a man *d* out demons
11: 15 began *d* out those who were buying
Lk 9: 49 "we saw a man *d* out demons
11: 14 Jesus was *d* out a demon that was
11: 15 of demons, he is *d* out demons."
19: 45 began *d* out those who were selling.
Ac 19: 13 went around *d* out evil spirits tried
26: 24 Your great learning is *d* you insane

DROP (DROPPED DROPPING DROPS)

Dt 28: 40 because the olives will *d* off.
33: 28 where the heavens *d* dew.
Pr 3: 20 and the clouds let *d* the dew.
17: 14 so *d* the matter before a dispute
SS 4: 11 Your lips *d* sweetness
Isa 33: 9 Bashan and Carmel *d* their leaves.
40: 15 Surely the nations are like a *d*
Eze 39: 3 and make your arrows *d*
Zec 8: 12 and the heavens will *d* their dew.
Lk 16: 17 stroke of a pen to *d* out of the Law.
Rev 6: 13 as late figs *d* from a fig tree

DROPPED (DROP)

Jdg 9: 53 a woman *d* an upper millstone
15: 14 and the bindings *d* from his hands.
2Sa 20: 8 As he stepped forward, it *d* out
Ac 27: 29 they *d* four anchors from the stern

DROPPING (DROP)

2Ch 24: 10 *d* them into the chest

DROPS (DROP)

Nu 35: 23 *d* a stone on him that could kill him
Job 36: 27 "He draws up the *d* of water,
38: 28 Who fathers the *d* of dew?
Lk 22: 44 his sweat was like *d* of blood falling

DROPSY

Lk 14: 2 of him was a man suffering from *d*.

DROSS

Ps 119: 119 of the earth you discard like *d*;
Pr 25: 4 Remove the *d* from the silver,
Isa 1: 22 Your silver has become *d*,
1: 25 will thoroughly purge away your *d*
Eze 22: 18 They are but the *d* of silver.

Eze 22: 18 house of Israel has become *d* to me;
22: 19 'Because you have all become *d*,

DROUGHT

Dt 28: 22 with scorching heat and *d*,
Job 12: 15 he holds back the waters, there is *d;*
24: 19 *d* snatch away the melted snow,
Jer 2: 6 a land of *d* and darkness,
14: 1 to Jeremiah concerning the *d:*
17: 8 It has no worries in a year of *d*
50: 38 A *d* on her waters!
Hag 1: 11 I called for a *d* on the fields

DROVE (DRIVE DROVES)

Ge 3: 24 After he *d* the man out, he placed
15: 11 carcasses, but Abram *d* them away.
31: 18 he *d* all his livestock ahead of him,
Ex 2: 17 came along and *d* them away,
14: 21 night the LORD *d* the sea back
Nu 11: 31 and *d* quail in from the sea.
21: 32 *d* out the Amorites who were there
25: 8 He *d* the spear through both
32: 39 *d* out the Amorites who were there
Dt 2: 12 descendants of Esau *d* them out.
2: 21 who *d* them out and settled
2: 22 They *d* them out and have lived
Jos 15: 14 Caleb *d* out the three Anakites—
24: 12 which *d* them out before you—
24: 18 And the LORD *d* out before us all
Jdg 1: 20 who *d* from it the three sons
1: 28 but never *d* them out completely.
4: 21 She *d* the peg through his temple
6: 9 I *d* them from before you
9: 41 Zebul *d* Gaal and his brothers out
11: 2 grown up, they *d* Jephthah away.
1Sa 19: 10 as Saul *d* the spear into the wall.
30: 20 and his men *d* them ahead
2Sa 11: 23 but we *d* them back to the entrance
1Ki 21: 26 like the Amorites the LORD *d* out
1Ch 8: 13 who *d* out the inhabitants of Gath.
Ne 13: 28 And I *d* him away from me.
Ps 44: 2 your hand you *d* out the nations
78: 55 He *d* out nations before them
80: 8 you *d* out the nations and planted it
Jer 49: 2 those who *d* her out,"
Eze 28: 16 I *d* you in disgrace from the mount
29: 18 king of Babylon *d* his army
Mt 8: 16 and he *d* out the spirits with a word
21: 12 and *d* out all who were buying
Mk 1: 34 He also *d* out many demons,
6: 13 They *d* out many demons
Lk 4: 29 They got up, *d* him out of the town,
Jn 2: 15 and *d* all from the temple area,
Ac 7: 45 land from the nations God *d* out
2Co 12: 11 a fool of myself, but you *d* me to it.
1Th 2: 15 and the prophets and also *d* us out.

DROVES (DROVE)

Ge 33: 8 mean by all these *d* I met?"
33: 14 at the pace of the *d* before me
Ex 12: 38 as well as large *d* of livestock,
2Ch 14: 15 and carried off *d* of sheep and goats

DROWN (DROWNED)

Mt 8: 25 We're going to *d!*" He replied,
Mk 4: 38 don't you care if we *d?*" He got up,
Lk 8: 24 Master, Master, we're going to *d!*"

DROWNED (DROWN)

Ex 15: 4 are *d* in the Red Sea.
Job 10: 15 and *d* in my affliction.
Mt 18: 6 and to be *d* in the depths of the sea.
Mk 5: 13 bank into the lake and were *d*.
Lk 8: 33 bank into the lake and was *d*.
Heb 11: 29 tried to do so, they were *d*.

DROWSINESS (DROWSY)

Pr 23: 21 and *d* clothes them in rags.

DROWSY (DROWSINESS)

Mt 25: 5 they all became *d* and fell asleep.

DRUNK (DRINK)

Ge 9: 21 he became *d* and lay uncovered
Lev 11: 34 and any liquid that could be *d*
Dt 32: 42 I will make my arrows *d* with blood
1Sa 1: 13 Eli thought she was *d* and said
1: 14 long will you keep on getting *d?*
25: 36 He was in high spirits and very *d*.
30: 12 or *d* any water for three days
2Sa 11: 13 with him, and David made him *d*.
1Ki 16: 9 getting *d* in the home of Arza,
20: 16 were in their tents getting *d*.
2Ki 19: 24 and *d* the water there.
SS 5: 1 I have *d* my wine and my milk.
Isa 29: 9 be *d*, but not from wine,
34: 5 My sword has *d* its fill
37: 25 and *d* the water there.
49: 26 they will be *d* on their own blood,
51: 17 you who have *d* from the hand
51: 21 made *d*, but not with wine.
63: 6 in my wrath I made them *d*
Jer 25: 27 says: Drink, get *d* and vomit,
35: 8 and daughters have ever *d* wine
48: 26 "Make her *d*,
51: 7 she made the whole earth *d*.
51: 39 and make them *d*,
51: 57 make her officials and wise men *d*,
La 4: 21 you will be *d* and stripped naked.
Eze 39: 19 and drink blood till you are *d*.
Na 1: 10 and *d* from their wine;
3: 11 You too will become *d;*
Hab 2: 15 it from the wineskin till they are *d*,
Lk 12: 45 and to eat and drink and get *d*.
Ac 2: 15 men are not *d*, as you suppose.
1Co 11: 21 remains hungry, another gets *d*.
Eph 5: 18 Do not get *d* on wine, which leads
1Th 5: 7 and those who get *d*, get *d* at night.
Rev 17: 6 I saw that the woman was *d*
18: 3 For all the nations have *d*

DRUNKARD (DRINK)

Dt 21: 20 He is a profligate and a *d*."
Isa 19: 14 as a *d* staggers around in his vomit.
24: 20 The earth reels like a *d*,
Mt 11: 19 and a *d*, a friend of tax collectors
Lk 7: 34 and a *d*, a friend of tax collectors
1Co 5: 11 or a slanderer, a *d* or a swindler.

DRUNKARD'S (DRINK)

Pr 26: 9 Like a thornbush in a *d* hand

DRUNKARDS (DRINK)

Job 12: 25 he makes them stagger like *d*.
Ps 69: 12 and I am the song of the *d*.
Pr 23: 21 for *d* and gluttons become poor,
Isa 28: 1 wreath, the pride of Ephraim's *d*,
28: 3 wreath, the pride of Ephraim's *d*,
Joel 1: 5 Wake up, you *d*, and weep!
Mt 24: 49 and to eat and drink with *d*.
1Co 6: 10 nor the greedy nor *d* nor slanderers

DRUNKEN (DRINK)

Ps 107: 27 reeled and staggered like *d* men;
Jer 23: 9 I am like a *d* man,

DRUNKENNESS (DRINK)

Ecc 10: 17 for strength and not for *d*.
Jer 13: 13 I am going to fill with *d* all who live
Eze 23: 33 You will be filled with *d*
Lk 21: 34 weighed down with dissipation, *d*
Ro 13: 13 and *d*, not in sexual immorality
Gal 5: 21 factions and envy; *d*, orgies,
1Pe 4: 3 living in debauchery, lust, *d*, orgies,

DRUSILLA

Ac 24: 24 later Felix came with his wife *D*,

DRY (DRIED DRIES DRYING)

Ge 1: 9 place, and let *d* ground appear."
1: 10 God called the *d* ground "land,"
7: 22 on *d* land that had the breath
8: 13 the surface of the ground was *d*.
8: 14 month the earth was completely *d*.
Ex 4: 9 and pour it on the *d* ground.
14: 16 go through the sea on *d* ground.
14: 21 east wind and turned it into *d* land.
14: 22 went through the sea on *d* ground,
14: 29 went through the sea on *d* ground,
15: 19 through the sea on *d* ground.
Lev 7: 10 whether mixed with oil or *d*,
Dt 29: 19 on the watered land as well as the *d*
Jos 3: 17 firm on *d* ground in the middle
3: 17 the crossing on *d* ground.
4: 18 on the *d* ground than the waters
4: 22 crossed the Jordan on *d* ground.'
9: 5 bread of their food supply was *d*
9: 12 But now see how *d* and moldy it is.
Jdg 6: 37 on the fleece and all the ground is *d*
6: 39 This time make the fleece *d*
6: 40 the fleece was *d;* all the ground
1Ki 17: 14 and the jug of oil will not run *d*
17: 16 and the jug of oil did not run *d*,
2Ki 2: 8 of them crossed over on *d* ground.
Ne 9: 11 passed through it on *d* ground,
Job 6: 17 that cease to flow in the *d* season,
13: 25 Will you chase after *d* chaff?
14: 11 a riverbed becomes parched and *d*,
18: 16 His roots *d* up below
30: 6 to live in the *d* stream beds,
Ps 58: 9 whether they be green or *d*—
63: 1 in a *d* and weary land
66: 6 He turned the sea into *d* land,
90: 6 by evening it is *d* and withered.
95: 5 and his hands formed the *d* land.
Pr 17: 1 Better a *d* crust with peace
Isa 5: 24 as *d* grass sinks down in the flames,
11: 15 The LORD will *d* up
19: 5 The waters of the river will *d* up,
19: 5 the riverbed will be parched and *d*.
19: 6 of Egypt will dwindle and *d* up.
27: 11 its twigs are *d*, they are broken
42: 15 and *d* up all their vegetation;
42: 15 and *d* up the pools.
44: 3 and streams on the *d* ground;
44: 27 and I will *d* up your streams,'
44: 27 who says to the watery deep, 'Be *d*,
50: 2 By a mere rebuke I *d* up the sea,
53: 2 and like a root out of *d* ground.
56: 3 "I am only a *d* tree."
Jer 2: 25 and your throat is *d*.
50: 12 a wilderness, a *d* land, a desert.
50: 38 They will *d* up.
51: 36 I will *d* up her sea
51: 36 and make her springs *d*.
51: 43 a *d* and desert land,
La 4: 8 it has become as *d* as a stick.
Eze 17: 24 I *d* up the green tree and make
17: 24 and make the *d* tree flourish.
19: 13 in a *d* and thirsty land.
20: 47 all your trees, both green and *d*.
23: 34 You will drink it and drain it *d;*
30: 12 I will *d* up the streams of the Nile
37: 2 the valley, bones that were very *d*.
37: 4 '*D* bones, hear the word
Hos 9: 14 and breasts that are *d*.
13: 15 and his well *d* up.
Am 1: 2 the pastures of the shepherds *d* up,
Jnh 2: 10 and it vomited Jonah onto *d* land.
Na 1: 4 he makes all the rivers run *d*.
1: 10 will be consumed like *d* stubble.
Zep 2: 13 and *d* as the desert.
Hag 2: 6 the earth, the sea and the *d* land.
Zec 10: 11 all the depths of the Nile will *d* up.
Lk 23: 31 what will happen when it is *d?*"
Heb 11: 29 through the Red Sea as on *d* land;

DRYING (DRY)

Jn 13: 5 *d* them with the towel that was

DUE

Lev 19: 20 there must be *d* punishment.
Dt 18: 3 This is the share *d* the priests
32: 35 In *d* time their foot will slip;
1Ch 16: 29 to the LORD the glory *d* his name.
2Ch 24: 5 and collect the money *d* annually
31: 4 to give the portion *d* the priests
Job 36: 17 with the judgment *d* the wicked;
Ps 29: 2 to the LORD the glory *d* his name;
90: 11 great as the fear that is *d* you.
96: 8 to the LORD the glory *d* his name;
Pr 11: 31 If the righteous receive their *d*
Isa 49: 4 Yet what is *d* me is
59: 18 he will repay the islands their *d*.
Jer 10: 7 This is your *d*.
Mal 1: 6 where is the honor *d* me? If I am
1: 6 where is the respect *d* me?"
Ro 1: 27 in themselves the *d* penalty
2Co 5: 10 each one may receive what is *d* him
Eph 4: 18 is in them *d* to the hardening
1Pe 5: 6 that he may lift you up in *d* time.

DUG (DIG)

Ge 21: 30 as a witness that I *d* this well."

Ge 26: 15 that his father's servants had *d*
26: 18 reopened the wells that had been *d*
26: 19 Isaac's servants *d* in the valley
26: 21 Then they *d* another well,
26: 22 on from there and *d* another well,
26: 25 and there his servants *d* a well.
26: 32 told him about the well they had *d*.
50: 5 me in the tomb I *d* for myself
Ex 7: 24 all the Egyptians *d* along the Nile
Nu 21: 18 about the well that the princes *d*,
1Ki 18: 32 and he *d* a trench around it large
2Ki 19: 24 I have *d* wells in foreign lands
2Ch 26: 10 in the desert and *d* many cisterns,
Ne 9: 25 wells already *d*, vineyards,
Ps 9: 15 into the pit they have *d*;
35: 7 and without cause *d* a pit for me,
57: 6 They *d* a pit in my path—
94: 13 till a pit is *d* for the wicked.
Isa 5: 2 He *d* it up and cleared it of stones
37: 25 I have *d* wells in foreign lands
Jer 2: 13 and have *d* their own cisterns,
13: 7 I went to Perath and *d* up the belt
18: 20 Yet they have *d* a pit for me.
18: 22 for they have *d* a pit to capture me
Eze 8: 8 I *d* into the wall and saw a doorway
12: 7 in the evening I *d* through the wall
12: 12 a hole will be *d* in the wall for him
Mt 21: 33 *d* a winepress in it and built
25: 18 *d* a hole in the ground
Mk 12: 1 *d* a pit for the winepress
Lk 6: 48 who *d* down deep and laid

DULL
Lev 13: 39 and if the spots are *d* white,
Ecc 10: 10 If the ax is *d*
Isa 6: 10 make their ears *d*
59: 1 nor his ear too *d* to hear.
La 4: 1 the fine gold become *d*!
Mt 15: 16 still so *d*?" Jesus asked them.
Mk 7: 18 "Are you so *d*?" he asked.
2Co 3: 14 But their minds were made *d*,

DUMAH
Ge 25: 14 Mibsam, Mishma, *D*, Massa,
Jos 15: 52 Arab, *D*, Eshan, Janim,
1Ch 1: 30 Mibsam, Mishma, *D*, Massa,
Isa 21: 11 An oracle concerning *D*:

DUMB
Ex 4: 11 Who makes him deaf or *d*?
Isa 35: 6 the tongue of the *d* shout for joy.
Mt 9: 33 the man who had been *d* spoke.
15: 30 crippled, the *d* and many others,
15: 31 when they saw the *d* speaking,
Mk 7: 37 the deaf hear and the *d* speak."
9: 25 "You deaf and *d* spirit," he said,
Lk 11: 14 the man who had been *d* spoke,
1Co 12: 2 and led astray to *d* idols.

DUMPED
Lev 14: 41 scraped off *d* into an unclean place

DUNG
1Ki 14: 10 house of Jeroboam as one burns *d*,
Ne 2: 13 the Jackal Well and the *D* Gate,
3: 13 of the wall as far as the *D* Gate.
3: 14 The *D* Gate was repaired
12: 31 to the right, toward the *D* Gate.
Job 20: 7 will perish forever, like his own *d*;

DUNGEON (DUNGEONS)
Ge 40: 15 to deserve being put in a *d*."
41: 14 he was quickly brought from the *d*.
Ex 12: 29 who was in the *d*, and the firstborn
Isa 24: 22 like prisoners bound in a *d*;
42: 7 to release from the *d* those who sit
51: 14 they will not die in their *d*,
Jer 37: 16 put into a vaulted cell in a *d*,

DUNGEONS (DUNGEON)
2Pe 2: 4 them into gloomy *d* to be held

DUPLICITY
Pr 11: 3 unfaithful are destroyed by their *d*.
Lk 20: 23 He saw through their *d*

DURA
Da 3: 1 up on the plain of *D* in the province

DUSK
Jos 2: 5 At *d*, when it was time
1Sa 30: 17 them from *d* until the evening
2Ki 7: 5 At *d* they got up and went
7: 7 in the *d* and abandoned their tents
Job 4: 20 and *d* they are broken to pieces;
24: 15 eye of the adulterer watches for *d*;
Eze 12: 6 watching and carry them out at *d*.
12: 7 I took my belongings out at *d*,
12: 12 things on his shoulder at *d*
Hab 1: 8 fiercer than wolves at *d*.

DUST
Ge 2: 7 man from the *d* of the ground
3: 14 and you will eat *d*
3: 19 and to *d* you will return."
3: 19 for *d* you are
13: 16 so that if anyone could count the *d*,
13: 16 will make your offspring like the *d*
18: 27 I am nothing but *d* and ashes,
28: 14 Your descendants will be like the *d*
Ex 8: 16 and strike the *d* of the ground,'
8: 16 of Egypt the *d* will become gnats."
8: 17 All the *d* throughout the land
8: 17 and struck the *d* of the ground,
9: 9 It will become fine *d*
Nu 5: 17 and put some *d* from the tabernacle
23: 10 Who can count the *d* of Jacob
Dt 9: 21 and ground it to powder as fine as *d*
9: 21 and threw the *d* into a stream that
28: 24 the rain of your country into *d*
32: 24 venom of vipers that glide in the *d*.
Jos 7: 6 and sprinkled *d* on their heads
1Sa 2: 8 He raises the poor from the *d*
4: 12 his clothes torn and *d* on his head.
2Sa 1: 2 and with *d* on his head.
15: 32 his robe torn and *d* on his head.
22: 43 fine as the *d* of the earth;
1Ki 16: 2 "I lifted you up from the *d*
20: 10 if enough *d* remains in Samaria
2Ki 13: 7 and made them like the *d*
23: 6 and scattered the *d* over the graves
2Ch 1: 9 as numerous as the *d* of the earth.
Ne 9: 1 and having *d* on their heads.
Job 2: 12 and sprinkled *d* on their heads.
4: 19 whose foundations are in the *d*,
7: 21 For I will soon lie down in the *d*;
10: 9 Will you now turn me to *d* again?
16: 15 and buried my brow in the *d*.
17: 16 we descend together into the *d*?"
20: 11 will lie with him in the *d*.
21: 26 Side by side they lie in the *d*,
22: 24 and assign your nuggets to the *d*,
27: 16 Though he heaps up silver like *d*
28: 6 and its *d* contains nuggets of gold.
30: 19 and I am reduced to *d* and ashes.
34: 15 and man would return to the *d*.
38: 38 heavens when the *d* becomes hard
40: 13 Bury them all in the *d* together;
42: 6 and repent in *d* and ashes."
Ps 7: 5 and make me sleep in the *d*.
18: 42 fine as *d* borne on the wind;
22: 15 you lay me in the *d* of death.
22: 29 down to the *d* will kneel before him
30: 9 Will the *d* praise you?
44: 25 We are brought down to the *d*;
72: 9 and his enemies will lick the *d*.
78: 27 down on them like *d*,
89: 39 and have defiled his crown in the *d*.
90: 3 You turn men back to *d*,
90: 3 "Return to *d*, O sons of men."
102: 14 her very *d* moves them to pity.
103: 14 he remembers that we are *d*.
104: 29 they die and return to the *d*.
113: 7 He raises the poor from the *d*
119: 25 I am laid low in the *d*;
Pr 8: 26 or any of the *d* of the world.
Ecc 3: 20 all come from *d*, and to *d* all return.
12: 7 the *d* returns to the ground it came
Isa 5: 24 and their flowers blow away like *d*;
25: 12 to the very *d*.
26: 5 and casts it down to the *d*.
26: 19 You who dwell in the *d*,
29: 4 of the *d* your speech will whisper.
29: 4 speech will mumble out of the *d*.
29: 5 enemies will become like fine *d*,
34: 7 and the *d* will be soaked with fat.
Isa 34: 9 her *d* into burning sulfur;
40: 12 Who has held the *d* of the earth
40: 15 as though they were fine *d*.
40: 15 they are regarded as *d* on the scales
41: 2 He turns them to *d* with his sword,
47: 1 "Go down, sit in the *d*,
49: 23 they will lick the *d* at your feet.
52: 2 Shake off your *d*;
65: 25 but *d* will be the serpent's food.
Jer 17: 13 from you will be written in the *d*
25: 34 roll in the *d*, you leaders
La 2: 10 they have sprinkled *d*
2: 21 together in the *d* of the streets;
3: 16 he has trampled me in the *d*.
3: 29 Let him bury his face in the *d*—
Eze 24: 7 where the *d* would cover it.
26: 10 that they will cover you with *d*.
27: 30 they will sprinkle *d* on their heads
Da 12: 2 Multitudes who sleep in the *d*
Am 2: 7 as upon the *d* of the ground
Jnh 3: 6 sackcloth and sat down in the *d*.
Mic 1: 10 roll in the *d*.
7: 17 They will lick *d* like a snake,
Na 1: 3 and clouds are the *d* of his feet.
Zep 1: 17 blood will be poured out like *d*
Zec 9: 3 she has heaped up silver like *d*,
Mt 10: 14 shake the *d* off your feet
Mk 6: 11 shake the *d* off your feet
Lk 9: 5 shake the *d* off your feet
10: 11 Even the *d* of your town that sticks
Ac 13: 51 So they shook the *d* from their feet
22: 23 off their cloaks and flinging *d*
1Co 15: 47 was of the *d* of the earth,
Rev 18: 19 They will throw *d* on their heads,

DUTIES (DUTY)
Ge 39: 11 into the house to attend to his *d*,
Ex 18: 20 and the *d* they are to perform.
Nu 3: 7 They are to perform *d* for him
4: 28 *d* are to be under the direction
8: 26 in performing their *d* at the Tent
18: 3 are to perform all the *d* of the Tent,
1Ki 3: 7 do not know how to carry out my *d*
1Ch 6: 32 They performed their *d* according
6: 48 to all the other *d* of the tabernacle,
9: 25 share their *d* for seven-day periods.
9: 33 and were exempt from other *d*
23: 28 of other *d* at the house
25: 8 well as student, cast lots for their *d*.
26: 12 had *d* for ministering in the temple
26: 29 and his sons were assigned *d* away
2Ch 8: 14 divisions of the priests for their *d*,
31: 2 each of them according to their *d*
31: 16 the LORD to perform the daily *d*
35: 2 He appointed the priests to their *d*
Ne 10: 33 and for all the *d* of the house
13: 30 and assigned them *d*, each
Eze 44: 14 in charge of the *d* of the temple
44: 15 and who faithfully carried out the *d*
2Ti 4: 5 discharge all the *d* of your ministry
Heb 10: 11 and performs his religious *d*;

DUTY (DUTIES)
Ge 38: 8 brother's wife and fulfill your *d*
Nu 4: 31 This is their *d* as they perform
Dt 24: 5 or have any other *d* laid on him.
25: 5 and fulfill the *d* of a brother-in-law
25: 7 He will not fulfill the *d*
1Ki 14: 27 of the guard on *d* at the entrance
2Ki 11: 5 going on *d* on the Sabbath—
11: 7 go off Sabbath *d* are all
11: 9 and those who were going off *d*—
11: 9 going on *d* on the Sabbath
1Ch 23: 28 The *d* of the Levites was
27: 1 were on *d* month by month
2Ch 12: 10 of the guard on *d* at the entrance
23: 4 going on *d* on the Sabbath are
23: 6 except the priests and Levites on *d*;
23: 8 and those who were going off *d*—
23: 8 going on *d* on the Sabbath
Ezr 4: 13 taxes, tribute or *d* will be paid,
4: 20 tribute and *d* were paid to them.
7: 24 tribute or *d* on any of the priests,
Ne 7: 3 While the gatekeepers are still on *d*
Ecc 12: 13 for this is the whole *d* of man.
Jer 32: 7 relative it is your right and *d*
Eze 44: 8 of carrying out your *d* in regard
45: 17 It will be the *d* of the prince

Mt 17: 25 the kings of the earth collect *d*
Lk 1: 8 Zechariah's division was on *d*
17: 10 we have only done our *d*.' "
Jn 18: 16 spoke to the girl on *d* there
Ac 23: 1 I have fulfilled my *d* to God
Ro 15: 16 the Gentiles with the priestly *d*
1Co 7: 3 husband should fulfill his marital *d*

DWARFED

Lev 21: 20 or who is hunchbacked or *d*,

DWELL (DWELLERS DWELLING DWELLINGS DWELLS DWELT TENT-DWELLING)

Ex 25: 8 for me, and I will *d* among them.
29: 45 Then I will *d* among the Israelites
29: 46 so that I might *d* among them.
Nu 5: 3 not defile their camp, where I *d*
35: 34 land where you live and where I *d*,
35: 34 the LORD, *d* among the Israelites
2Sa 7: 5 the one to build me a house to *d* in?
1Ki 8: 12 LORD has said that he would *d*
8: 13 a place for you to *d* forever."
8: 27 "But will God really *d* on earth?
1Ch 17: 4 the one to build me a house to *d* in.
23: 25 has come to *d* in Jerusalem forever,
2Ch 6: 1 LORD has said that he would *d*
6: 2 a place for you to *d* forever."
6: 18 "But will God really *d* on earth
Ezr 6: 12 has caused his Name to *d* there,
Job 11: 14 and allow no evil to *d* in your tent,
17: 2 my eyes must *d* on their hostility.
28: 4 from where people *d* he cuts a shaft
28: 12 Where does understanding *d*?
28: 20 Where does understanding *d*?
Ps 4: 8 make me *d* in safety.
5: 4 with you the wicked cannot *d*.
15: 1 who may *d* in your sanctuary?
23: 6 I will *d* in the house of the LORD
27: 4 that I may *d* in the house
37: 3 *d* in the land and enjoy safe pasture
37: 29 and *d* in it forever.
39: 12 For I *d* with you as an alien,
43: 3 to the place where you *d*.
61: 4 I long to *d* in your tent forever
68: 16 the LORD himself will *d* forever?
68: 18 O LORD God, might *d* there.
69: 25 let there be no one to *d*
69: 36 who love his name will *d* there.
84: 4 Blessed are those who *d*
84: 10 than *d* in the tents of the wicked.
85: 9 that his glory may *d* in our land.
101: 6 that they may *d* with me;
101: 7 will *d* in my house;
120: 5 Woe to me that I *d* in Meshech,
143: 3 he makes me *d* in darkness
Pr 8: 12 wisdom, *d* together with prudence;
SS 8: 13 You who *d* in the gardens
Isa 1: 21 righteousness used to *d* in her—
13: 21 there the owls will *d*,
26: 5 He humbles those who *d* on high,
26: 19 You who *d* in the dust,
32: 16 Justice will *d* in the desert
33: 14 of us can *d* with the consuming fire
33: 14 us can *d* with everlasting burning?"
33: 16 this is the man who will *d*
33: 24 of those who *d* there will be
34: 17 and *d* there from generation
38: 11 with those who now *d* in this world
43: 18 do not *d* on the past.
44: 13 that it may *d* in a shrine.
65: 21 They will build houses and *d*
Jer 17: 6 He will *d* in the parched places
47: 2 all who *d* in the land will wail
48: 28 Abandon your towns and *d*
49: 18 no man will *d* in it.
49: 33 no man will *d* in it."
50: 39 and there the owl will *d*.
50: 40 no man will *d* in it.
La 3: 6 He has made me *d* in darkness
Eze 7: 7 upon you—you who *d* in the land.
26: 20 I will make you *d* in the earth
Hos 14: 7 Men will *d* again in his shade.
Joel 3: 17 *d* in Zion, my holy hill.
Zep 2: 6 by the sea, where the Kerethites *d*,
Zec 8: 3 return to Zion and *d* in Jerusalem.
Jn 5: 38 nor does his word *d* in you,
Ac 1: 20 let there be no one to *d* in it,'
Eph 3: 17 so that Christ may *d* in your hearts
Col 1: 19 to have all his fullness *d* in him,
3: 16 the word of Christ *d* in you richly
Rev 12: 12 and you who *d* in them!

DWELLERS (DWELL)

Isa 5: 3 "Now you *d* in Jerusalem

DWELLING (DWELL)

Ge 27: 39 "Your *d* will be
Ex 15: 13 them to your holy *d*.
15: 17 O LORD, you made for your *d*,
Lev 15: 31 for defiling my *d* place,
26: 11 I will put my *d* place among you,
Nu 24: 5 your *d* places, O Israel!
24: 21 "Your *d* place is secure,
Dt 12: 5 to put his Name there for his *d*.
12: 11 LORD your God will choose as a *d*
14: 23 at the place he will choose as a *d*
16: 2 place the LORD will choose as a *d*
16: 6 in the place he will choose as a *d*
16: 11 at the place he will choose as a *d*
26: 2 LORD your God will choose as a *d*
26: 15 from heaven, your holy *d* place,
1Sa 2: 29 offering that I prescribed for my *d*?
2: 32 and you will see distress in my *d*.
2Sa 7: 6 place to place with a tent as my *d*.
15: 25 let me see it and his *d* place again.
1Ki 8: 30 Hear from heaven, your *d* place,
8: 39 hear from heaven, your *d* place.
8: 43 hear from heaven, your *d* place,
8: 49 then from heaven, your *d* place,
1Ch 9: 19 the entrance to the *d* of the LORD.
16: 27 strength and joy in his *d* place.
17: 5 from one *d* place to another.
2Ch 6: 21 Hear from heaven, your *d* place;
6: 30 hear from heaven, your *d* place.
6: 33 hear from heaven, your *d* place.
6: 39 then from heaven, your *d* place,
29: 6 away from the LORD's *d* place
30: 27 reached heaven, his holy *d* place.
31: 2 at the gates of the LORD's *d*.
36: 15 on his people and on his *d* place.
Ezr 7: 15 whose *d* is in Jerusalem, together
Ne 1: 9 to the place I have chosen as a *d*
Job 18: 15 sulfur is scattered over his *d*.
18: 21 Surely such is the *d* of an evil man;
23: 3 if only I could go to his *d*!
Ps 27: 5 he will keep me safe in his *d*;
31: 20 in your *d* you keep them safe
33: 14 from his *d* place he watches
68: 5 is God in his holy *d*.
74: 7 they defiled the *d* place
76: 2 his *d* place in Zion.
84: 1 How lovely is your *d* place,
90: 1 Lord, you have been our *d* place
91: 9 If you make the Most High your *d*
132: 5 a *d* for the Mighty One of Jacob."
132: 7 "Let us go to his *d* place;
132: 13 he has desired it for his *d*:
Pr 24: 15 do not raid his *d* place;
Isa 18: 4 and will look on from my *d* place,
26: 21 the LORD is coming out of his *d*
32: 18 live in peaceful *d* places,
Jer 7: 12 in Shiloh where I first made a *d*
25: 30 he will lift his voice from his holy *d*
31: 23 O righteous *d*, O sacred mountain.'
La 2: 6 has laid waste his *d* like a garden;
Eze 3: 12 LORD be praised in his *d* place!—
37: 27 My *d* place will be with them;
Mic 1: 3 LORD is coming from his *d* place;
Hab 1: 6 to seize *d* places not their own.
Zep 3: 7 Then her *d* would not be cut off,
Zec 2: 13 roused himself from his holy *d*."
Ac 7: 46 that he might provide a *d* place
2Co 5: 2 to be clothed with our heavenly *d*,
5: 4 to be clothed with our heavenly *d*,
Eph 2: 22 to become a *d* in which God lives
Rev 13: 6 to slander his name and his *d* place
21: 3 "Now the *d* of God is with men,

DWELLINGS (DWELL)

Ex 35: 3 in any of your *d* on the Sabbath day
1Ch 4: 41 attacked the Hamites in their *d*
5: 10 they occupied the *d* of the Hagrites
Job 38: 20 Do you know the paths to their *d*?
Ps 49: 11 their *d* for endless generations,
87: 2 more than all the *d* of Jacob.
Isa 58: 12 Restorer of Streets with *D*.
Jer 30: 18 and have compassion on his *d*;
51: 30 Her *d* are set on fire;
La 2: 2 all the *d* of Jacob;
Hab 3: 7 the *d* of Midian in anguish.
Zec 12: 7 "The LORD will save the *d*
Lk 16: 9 will be welcomed into eternal *d*.

DWELLS (DWELL)

Job 28: 23 and he alone knows where it *d*,
39: 28 He *d* on a cliff and stays there
Ps 26: 8 the place where your glory *d*.
46: 4 holy place where the Most High *d*.
91: 1 He who *d* in the shelter
135: 21 to him who *d* in Jerusalem.
Isa 8: 18 from the LORD Almighty, who *d*
33: 5 The LORD is exalted, for he *d*
La 1: 3 She *d* among the nations;
Da 2: 22 and light *d* with him.
Joel 3: 21 The LORD *d* in Zion! The words
Mt 23: 21 and by the one who *d* in it.

DWELT (DWELL)

Dt 33: 16 of him who *d* in the burning bush.
2Sa 7: 6 I have not *d* in a house
1Ch 17: 5 I have not *d* in a house
Job 29: 25 I *d* as a king among his troops;
Ps 74: 2 Mount Zion, where you *d*.
94: 17 I would soon have *d* in the silence

DWINDLE (DWINDLES)

Isa 19: 6 the streams of Egypt will *d*

DWINDLES (DWINDLE)

Pr 13: 11 Dishonest money *d* away,

DYED

Ex 25: 5 ram skins *d* red and hides
26: 14 a covering of ram skins *d* red,
35: 7 ram skins *d* red and hides
35: 23 ram skins *d* red or hides
36: 19 a covering of ram skins *d* red,
39: 34 the covering of ram skins *d* red,

DYING (DIE)

Ge 35: 18 for she was *d*— she named her son
1Sa 4: 20 As she was *d*, the women attending
2Ch 24: 22 he lay *d*, "May the LORD see this
Job 11: 20 their hope will become a *d* gasp."
24: 12 The groans of the *d* rise
29: 13 The man who was *d* blessed me;
Isa 22: 14 "Till your *d* day this sin will not be
Hos 4: 3 and the fish of the sea are *d*.
Zec 11: 9 Let the *d* die, and the perishing
Mk 5: 23 with him, "My little daughter is *d*.
Lk 8: 42 a girl of about twelve, was *d*.
Jn 11: 37 man have kept this man from *d*?"
Ro 7: 6 by *d* to what once bound us,
2Co 6: 9 yet regarded as unknown; *d*,
Heb 11: 21 when he was *d*, blessed each

DYNASTY

1Sa 25: 28 will certainly make a lasting *d*
1Ki 2: 24 and has founded a *d* for me
11: 38 I will build you a *d* as enduring

DYSENTERY

Ac 28: 8 suffering from fever and *d*.

EAGER (EAGERNESS)

2Ch 26: 20 Indeed, he himself was *e* to leave,
Ps 56: 6 *e* to take my life.
Pr 28: 20 one *e* to get rich will not go
28: 22 A stingy man is *e* to get rich
31: 13 and works with *e* hands.
Isa 58: 2 seem *e* for God to come near them.
58: 2 they seem *e* to know my ways,
Zep 3: 7 But they were still *e*
Ro 1: 15 am so *e* to preach the gospel
8: 19 The creation waits in *e* expectation
1Co 14: 12 Since you are *e* to have spiritual
14: 39 my brothers, be *e* to prophesy,
2Co 8: 11 so that your *e* willingness
Gal 2: 10 the very thing I was *e* to do.
Php 2: 28 Therefore I am all the more *e*
1Ti 6: 10 Some people, *e* for money,
Tit 2: 14 a people that are his very own, *e*
1Pe 3: 13 to harm you if you are *e* to do good

1Pe 5: 2 greedy for money, but *e* to serve;
2Pe 1: 10 be all the more *e* to make your
Jude : 3 although I was very *e* to write

EAGERNESS (EAGER)

Ac 17: 11 received the message with great *e*
2Co 7: 11 what *e* to clear yourselves,
8: 19 and to show our *e* to help.
9: 2 For I know your *e* to help,

EAGLE (EAGLE'S EAGLES EAGLES')

Lev 11: 13 the *e*, the vulture, the black vulture,
Dt 14: 12 the *e*, the vulture, the black vulture,
28: 49 of the earth, like an *e* swooping
32: 11 like an *e* that stirs up its nest
Job 39: 27 Does the *e* soar at your command
Pr 23: 5 and fly off to the sky like an *e*.
30: 19 the way of an *e* in the sky,
Jer 48: 40 "Look! An *e* is swooping down,
49: 22 An *e* will soar and swoop down,
Eze 1: 10 each also had the face of an *e*.
10: 14 and the fourth the face of an *e*.
17: 3 A great *e* with powerful wings,
17: 7 " 'But there was another great *e*
Da 4: 33 hair grew like the feathers of an *e*
7: 4 and it had the wings of an *e*.
Hos 8: 1 An *e* is over the house
Ob : 4 Though you soar like the *e*
Rev 4: 7 the fourth was like a flying *e*.
8: 13 I heard an *e* that was flying
12: 14 given the two wings of a great *e*,

EAGLE'S (EAGLE)

Ps 103: 5 my youth is renewed like the *e*.
Jer 49: 16 you build your nest as high as the *e*,

EAGLES (EAGLE)

2Sa 1: 23 They were swifter than *e*,
Job 9: 26 like *e* swooping down on their prey
Isa 40: 31 They will soar on wings like *e*;
Jer 4: 13 his horses are swifter than *e*.
La 4: 19 swifter than *e* in the sky;

EAGLES' (EAGLE)

Ex 19: 4 and how I carried you on *e'* wings

EAR (EARS)

Ex 21: 6 and pierce his *e* with an awl.
Lev 8: 23 put it on the lobe of Aaron's right *e*,
14: 14 on the lobe of the right *e* of the one
14: 17 on the lobe of the right *e* of the one
14: 25 on the lobe of the right *e* of the one
14: 28 on the lobe of the right *e* of the one
Dt 1: 45 and turned a deaf *e* to you.
15: 17 and push it through his *e* lobe
2Ki 19: 16 Give *e*, O LORD, and hear;
Ne 1: 6 let your *e* be attentive and your
1: 11 let your *e* be attentive to the prayer
Job 12: 11 Does not the *e* test words
34: 3 For the *e* tests words
Ps 5: 1 Give *e* to my words, O LORD,
17: 1 Give *e* to my prayer—
17: 6 give *e* to me and hear my prayer.
28: 1 do not turn a deaf *e* to me.
31: 2 Turn your *e* to me,
45: 10 O daughter, consider and give *e*:
49: 4 I will turn my *e* to a proverb;
71: 2 turn your *e* to me and save me.
88: 2 turn your *e* to my cry.
94: 9 he who implanted the *e* not hear?
102: 2 Turn your *e* to me;
116: 2 Because he turned his *e* to me,
Pr 2: 2 turning your *e* to wisdom
25: 12 a wise man's rebuke to a listening *e*.
28: 9 If anyone turns a deaf *e* to the law,
Ecc 1: 8 or the *e* its fill of hearing.
Isa 37: 17 Give *e*, O LORD, and hear;
48: 8 of old your *e* has not been open.
50: 4 wakens my *e* to listen like one
55: 3 Give *e* and come to me;
59: 1 nor his *e* too dull to hear.
64: 4 no *e* has perceived,
Da 9: 18 Give *e*, O God, and hear; open
Am 3: 12 two leg bones or a piece of an *e*,
Mt 10: 27 what is whispered in your *e*,
26: 51 of the high priest, cutting off his *e*.
Mk 14: 47 of the high priest, cutting off his *e*.
Lk 12: 3 what you have whispered in the *e*
Lk 22: 50 high priest, cutting off his right *e*.
22: 51 And he touched the man's *e*
Jn 18: 10 servant, cutting off his right *e*.
18: 26 of the man whose *e* Peter had cut
1Co 2: 9 no *e* has heard,
12: 16 if the *e* should say, "Because I am
12: 17 If the whole body were an *e*,
Rev 2: 7 He who has an *e*, let him hear what
2: 11 He who has an *e*, let him hear what
2: 17 He who has an *e*, let him hear what
2: 29 He who has an *e*, let him hear what
3: 6 He who has an *e*, let him hear what
3: 13 He who has an *e*, let him hear what
3: 22 He who has an *e*, let him hear what
13: 9 He who has an *e*, let him hear.

EARN (EARNED EARNERS EARNINGS EARNS)

Dt 23: 19 anything else that may *e* interest.
Am 7: 12 *E* your bread there and do your
Hag 1: 6 You *e* wages, only to put them
2Th 3: 12 down and *e* the bread they eat.
Rev 18: 17 all who *e* their living from the sea,

EARNED (EARN)

Pr 31: 31 Give her the reward she has *e*,
Lk 19: 16 'Sir, your mina has *e* ten more.'
19: 18 'Sir, your mina has *e* five more.'
Ac 16: 16 She *e* a great deal of money

EARNERS (EARN)

Isa 19: 10 all the wage *e* will be sick at heart.

EARNEST (EARNESTNESS)

Pr 27: 9 from his *e* counsel.
Rev 3: 19 So be *e*, and repent.

EARNESTNESS (EARNEST)

Dt 18: 6 in all *e* to the place the LORD will
2Co 7: 11 what *e*, what eagerness
8: 7 in complete *e* and in your love
8: 8 by comparing it with the *e* of others

EARNINGS (EARN)

Dt 23: 18 You must not bring the *e*
Pr 31: 16 out of her *e* she plants a vineyard.
Isa 23: 18 and her *e* will be set apart

EARNS (EARN)

Pr 11: 18 The wicked man *e* deceptive wages

EARRING (EARRINGS)

Jdg 8: 24 each of you give me an *e*
Pr 25: 12 Like an *e* of gold or an ornament

EARRINGS (EARRING)

Ex 32: 2 Take off the gold *e* that your wives,
32: 3 So all the people took off their *e*
35: 22 brooches, *e*, rings and ornaments.
Nu 31: 50 signet rings, *e* and necklaces—
Jdg 8: 24 of the Ishmaelites to wear gold *e*.)
SS 1: 10 Your cheeks are beautiful with *e*,
1: 11 We will make you *e* of gold,
Isa 3: 19 the *e* and bracelets and veils,
Eze 16: 12 *e* on your ears and a beautiful

EARS (EAR)

Ge 35: 4 they had and the rings in their *e*,
Ex 29: 20 on the lobes of the right *e* of Aaron
Lev 8: 24 blood on the lobes of their right *e*,
Dt 29: 4 or eyes that see or *e* that hear.
1Sa 3: 11 in Israel that will make the *e*
15: 14 is this bleating of sheep in my *e*?
2Sa 7: 22 as we have heard with our own *e*.
22: 7 my cry came to his *e*.
2Ki 19: 28 your insolence has reached my *e*,
21: 12 Judah that the *e* of everyone who
1Ch 17: 20 as we have heard with our own *e*.
2Ch 6: 40 and your *e* attentive to the prayers
7: 15 and my *e* attentive to the prayers
Job 4: 12 my *e* caught a whisper of it.
13: 1 my *e* have heard and understood it.
13: 17 let your *e* take in what I say.
15: 21 Terrifying sounds fill his *e*;
28: 22 of it has reached our *e*.'
29: 22 my words fell gently on their *e*.
33: 16 he may speak in their *e*
42: 5 My *e* had heard of you
Ps 18: 6 my cry came before him, into his *e*.
34: 15 and his *e* are attentive to their cry;
40: 6 but my *e* you have pierced;
44: 1 We have heard with our *e*, O God;
58: 4 of a cobra that has stopped its *e*,
92: 11 my *e* have heard the rout
115: 6 they have *e*, but cannot hear,
130: 2 Let your *e* be attentive
135: 17 they have *e*, but cannot hear,
Pr 18: 15 the *e* of the wise seek it out.
20: 12 *E* that hear and eyes that see—
21: 13 If a man shuts his *e* to the cry
23: 12 and your *e* to words of knowledge.
26: 17 Like one who seizes a dog by the *e*
Isa 6: 10 hear with their *e*,
6: 10 make their *e* dull
11: 3 decide by what he hears with his *e*;
30: 21 your *e* will hear a voice behind you,
32: 3 the *e* of those who hear will listen.
33: 15 who stops his *e* against plots
35: 5 and the *e* of the deaf unstopped.
37: 29 your insolence has reached my *e*,
42: 20 your *e* are open, but you hear
43: 8 who have *e* but are deaf.
50: 5 LORD has opened my *e*,
Jer 5: 21 who have *e* but do not hear:
6: 10 Their *e* are closed
9: 20 open your *e* to the words
19: 3 on this place that will make the *e*
26: 11 You have heard it with your own *e*
La 3: 56 my plea: "Do not close your *e*
Eze 8: 18 Although they shout in my *e*,
12: 2 but do not see and *e* to hear
16: 12 on your *e* and a beautiful crown
23: 25 cut off your noses and your *e*,
40: 4 your eyes and hear with your *e*
Mic 7: 16 and their *e* will become deaf.
Zec 7: 11 their backs and stopped up their *e*.
Mt 11: 15 He who has *e*, let him hear.
13: 9 He who has *e*, let him hear."
13: 15 hear with their *e*,
13: 15 they hardly hear with their *e*,
13: 16 and your *e* because they hear.
13: 43 He who has *e*, let him hear.
Mk 4: 9 "He who has *e* to hear, let him hear
4: 23 If anyone has *e* to hear, let him
7: 33 put his fingers into the man's *e*.
7: 35 At this, the man's *e* were opened,
8: 18 *e* but fail to hear? And don't you
Lk 1: 44 of your greeting reached my *e*,
8: 8 "He who has *e* to hear, let him hear
14: 35 "He who has *e* to hear, let him hear
Ac 7: 51 with uncircumcised hearts and *e*!
7: 57 At this they covered their *e* and,
11: 22 of this reached the *e* of the church
17: 20 some strange ideas to our *e*,
28: 27 hear with their *e*,
28: 27 they hardly hear with their *e*,
Ro 11: 8 and *e* so that they could not hear,
2Ti 4: 3 to say what their itching *e* want
4: 4 They will turn their *e* away
Jas 5: 4 the harvesters have reached the *e*
1Pe 3: 12 his *e* are attentive to their prayer,

EARTH (EARTH'S EARTHEN EARTHLY)

Ge 1: 1 God created the heavens and the *e*.
1: 2 Now the *e* was formless and empty,
1: 15 of the sky to give light on the *e*."
1: 17 of the sky to give light on the *e*,
1: 20 fly above the *e* across the expanse
1: 22 and let the birds increase on the *e*."
1: 26 over the livestock, over all the *e*,
1: 28 and increase in number; fill the *e*
1: 29 plant on the face of the whole *e*
1: 30 And to all the beasts of the *e*
2: 1 and the *e* were completed
2: 4 When the LORD God made the *e*
2: 4 and the *e* when they were created.
2: 5 God had not sent rain on the *e*
2: 5 the field had yet appeared on the *e*
2: 6 but streams came up from the *e*
4: 12 be a restless wanderer on the *e*."
4: 14 will be a restless wanderer on the *e*,
6: 1 to increase in number on the *e*
6: 4 were on the *e* in those days—
6: 5 wickedness on the *e* had become,
6: 6 that he had made man on the *e*,
6: 7 from the face of the *e*— men

Ge 6: 11 the *e* was corrupt in God's sight
6: 12 on *e* had corrupted their ways.
6: 12 saw how corrupt the *e* had become,
6: 13 for the *e* is filled with violence
6: 13 to destroy both them and the *e*.
6: 17 Everything on *e* will perish.
6: 17 on the *e* to destroy all life
7: 3 kinds alive throughout the *e*.
7: 4 of the *e* every living creature I have
7: 4 rain on the *e* for forty days
7: 6 the floodwaters came on the *e*.
7: 10 the floodwaters came on the *e*.
7: 12 And rain fell on the *e* forty days
7: 17 the flood kept coming on the *e*,
7: 17 they lifted the ark high above the *e*.
7: 18 and increased greatly on the *e*,
7: 19 They rose greatly on the *e*,
7: 21 creatures that swarm over the *e*,
7: 21 moved on the *e* perished—
7: 23 of the air were wiped from the *e*.
7: 23 on the face of the *e* was wiped out;
7: 24 The waters flooded the *e*
8: 1 and he sent a wind over the *e*
8: 3 water receded steadily from the *e*.
8: 7 the water had dried up from the *e*.
8: 9 water over all the surface of the *e;*
8: 11 the water had receded from the *e*.
8: 13 the water had dried up from the *e*.
8: 14 month the *e* was completely
8: 17 so they can multiply on the *e*
8: 19 everything that moves on the *e*—
8: 22 "As long as the *e* endures,
9: 1 increase in number and fill the *e*.
9: 2 fall upon all the beasts of the *e*
9: 7 multiply on the *e* and increase
9: 10 every living creature on *e*.
9: 11 there be a flood to destroy the *e*."
9: 13 covenant between me and the *e*.
9: 14 Whenever I bring clouds over the *e*
9: 16 creatures of every kind on the *e*."
9: 17 between me and all life on the *e*."
9: 19 who were scattered over the *e*.
10: 8 to be a mighty warrior on the *e*.
10: 25 in his time the *e* was divided;
10: 32 out over the *e* after the flood.
11: 4 over the face of the whole *e*."
11: 8 them from there over all the *e*,
11: 9 them over the face of the whole *e*.
12: 3 and all peoples on *e*
13: 16 your offspring like the dust of the *e*,
14: 19 Creator of heaven and *e*.
14: 22 High, Creator of heaven and *e*,
18: 18 and all nations on *e* will be blessed
18: 25 the Judge of all the *e* do right?"
19: 31 as is the custom all over the *e*.
22: 18 nations on *e* will be blessed,
24: 3 God of heaven and the God of *e*,
26: 4 nations on *e* will be blessed,
26: 15 stopped up, filling them with *e*.
28: 12 he saw a stairway resting on the *e*,
28: 14 All peoples on *e* will be blessed
28: 14 will be like the dust of the *e*,
45: 7 to preserve for you a remnant on *e*
48: 16 greatly upon the *e*."
Ex 9: 14 there is no one like me in all the *e*.
9: 15 would have wiped you off the *e*.
9: 16 might be proclaimed in all the *e*.
9: 29 know that the *e* is the LORD's.
15: 12 and the *e* swallowed them.
19: 5 Although the whole *e* is mine,
20: 4 or on the *e* beneath or in the waters
20: 11 made the heavens and the *e*,
20: 24 " 'Make an altar of *e* for me
31: 17 made the heavens and the *e*,
32: 12 to wipe them off the face of the *e*'?
33: 16 people on the face of the *e*?"
Lev 17: 13 out the blood and cover it with *e*,
Nu 12: 3 else on the face of the *e*.)
14: 21 of the LORD fills the whole *e*,
16: 30 and the *e* opens its mouth
16: 32 and the *e* opened its mouth
16: 33 they owned; the *e* closed
16: 34 "The *e* is going to swallow us too!"
26: 10 The *e* opened its mouth
Dt 3: 24 or on *e* who can do the deeds
4: 17 or like any animal on *e*
4: 26 *e* as witnesses against you this day
4: 32 the day God created man on the *e;*
Dt 4: 36 On *e* he showed you his great fire,
4: 39 in heaven above and on the *e* below
5: 8 or on the *e* beneath or in the waters
7: 6 on the face of the *e* to be his people,
10: 14 even the highest heavens, the *e*
11: 6 when the *e* opened its mouth right
11: 21 that the heavens are above the *e*.
14: 2 the peoples on the face of the *e*,
28: 1 high above all the nations on *e*.
28: 10 on *e* will see that you are called
28: 25 of horror to all the kingdoms on *e*.
28: 26 of the air and the beasts of the *e*,
28: 49 of the *e*, like an eagle swooping
28: 64 from one end of the *e* to the other.
30: 19 This day I call heaven and *e*
31: 28 and *e* to testify against them.
32: 1 hear, O *e*, the words of my mouth.
32: 22 It will devour the *e* and its harvests
33: 16 with the best gifts of the *e*
33: 17 even those at the ends of the *e*.
Jos 2: 11 in heaven above and on the *e* below
3: 11 of the Lord of all the *e* will go
3: 13 the Lord of all the *e*— set foot
4: 24 of the *e* might know that the hand
7: 9 and wipe out our name from the *e*.
23: 14 I am about to go the way of all the *e*
Jdg 5: 4 the *e* shook, the heavens poured,
1Sa 2: 8 of the *e* are the LORD's;
2: 10 LORD will judge the ends of the *e*.
17: 46 of the air and the beasts of the *e*,
20: 15 enemies from the face of the *e*."
20: 31 as the son of Jesse lives on this *e*,
2Sa 4: 11 from your hand and rid the *e* of you
7: 9 names of the greatest men of the *e*.
7: 23 nation on *e* that God went out
14: 7 descendant on the face of the *e*."
22: 8 "The *e* trembled and quaked,
22: 16 the foundations of the *e* laid bare
22: 43 fine as the dust of the *e;*
23: 4 that brings the grass from the *e*.'
1Ki 2: 2 I am about to go the way of all the *e*
8: 23 in heaven above or on *e* below—
8: 27 "But will God really dwell on *e*?
8: 43 of the *e* may know your name
8: 60 of the *e* may know that the LORD
10: 23 than all the other kings of the *e*.
13: 34 destruction from the face of the *e*.
2Ki 5: 17 much *e* as a pair of mules can carry,
19: 15 God over all the kingdoms of the *e*.
19: 15 You have made heaven and *e*.
19: 19 on *e* may know that you alone,
1Ch 1: 10 grew to be a mighty warrior on *e*.
1: 19 in his time the *e* was divided;
16: 14 his judgments are in all the *e*.
16: 23 Sing to the LORD, all the *e;*
16: 30 Tremble before him, all the *e!*
16: 31 heavens rejoice, let the *e* be glad;
16: 33 for he comes to judge the *e*.
17: 8 names of the greatest men of the *e*.
17: 21 nation on *e* whose God went out
21: 16 standing between heaven and *e*,
22: 8 blood on the *e* in my sight.
29: 11 in heaven and *e* is yours.
29: 15 Our days on *e* are like a shadow,
2Ch 1: 9 as numerous as the dust of the *e*.
2: 12 of Israel, who made heaven and *e!*
6: 14 you in heaven or on *e*—
6: 18 "But will God really dwell on *e*
6: 33 of the *e* may know your name
9: 22 than all the other kings of the *e*.
9: 23 the kings of the *e* sought audience
16: 9 the LORD range throughout the *e*
36: 23 given me all the kingdoms of the *e*
Ezr 1: 2 given me all the kingdoms of the *e*
5: 11 of the God of heaven and *e*,
Ne 9: 6 and all their starry host, the *e*
Job 1: 7 "From roaming through the *e*
1: 8 There is no one on *e* like him;
2: 2 "From roaming through the *e*
2: 3 There is no one on *e* like him;
3: 14 with kings and counselors of the *e*,
5: 10 He bestows rain on the *e;*
5: 22 need not fear the beasts of the *e*.
5: 25 descendants like the grass of the *e*.
7: 1 not man have hard service on *e*?
8: 9 and our days on *e* are but a shadow.
9: 6 He shakes the *e* from its place
11: 9 Their measure is longer than the *e*
Job 12: 8 speak to the *e*, and it will teach you,
12: 24 of the *e* of their reason;
16: 18 "O *e*, do not cover my blood;
18: 4 is the *e* to be abandoned
18: 17 of him perishes from the *e;*
19: 25 in the end he will stand upon the *e*.
20: 4 ever since man was placed on the *e*,
20: 27 the *e* will rise up against him.
26: 7 he suspends the *e* over nothing.
28: 2 Iron is taken from the *e*,
28: 5 The *e*, from which food comes,
28: 24 for he views the ends of the *e*
34: 13 Who appointed him over the *e*?
35: 11 to us than to the beasts of the *e*
37: 3 and sends it to the ends of the *e*.
37: 6 He says to the snow, 'Fall on the *e*,'
37: 12 around over the face of the whole *e*
37: 13 or to water his *e* and show his love.
38: 13 that it might take the *e* by the edges
38: 14 The *e* takes shape like clay
38: 18 the vast expanses of the *e*?
38: 24 east winds are scattered over the *e*?
38: 33 ⌊God's⌋ dominion over the *e*?
38: 38 and the clods of *e* stick together?
41: 33 Nothing on *e* is his equal—
Ps 2: 2 The kings of the *e* take their stand
2: 8 the ends of the *e* your possession.
2: 10 be warned, you rulers of the *e*.
8: 1 majestic is your name in all the *e!*
8: 9 majestic is your name in all the *e!*
10: 18 who is of the *e*, may terrify no more
18: 7 The *e* trembled and quaked,
18: 15 the foundations of the *e* laid bare
19: 4 Their voice goes out into all the *e*,
21: 10 their descendants from the *e*,
22: 27 All the ends of the *e*
22: 29 All the rich of the *e* will feast
24: 1 *e* is the LORD's, and everything
33: 5 the *e* is full of his unfailing love.
33: 8 Let all the *e* fear the LORD;
33: 14 all who live on *e*—
34: 16 off the memory of them from the *e*.
46: 2 will not fear, though the *e* give way
46: 6 he lifts his voice, the *e* melts.
46: 8 he has brought on the *e*.
46: 9 cease to the ends of the *e;*
46: 10 I will be exalted in the *e*."
47: 2 the great King over all the *e!*
47: 7 For God is the King of all the *e;*
47: 9 for the kings of the *e* belong to God
48: 2 the joy of the whole *e*.
48: 10 reaches to the ends of the *e;*
50: 1 speaks and summons the *e*
50: 4 the *e*, that he may judge his people:
57: 5 let your glory be over all the *e*.
57: 11 let your glory be over all the *e*.
58: 2 hands mete out violence on the *e*.
58: 11 there is a God who judges the *e*."
59: 13 it will be known to the ends of the *e*
61: 2 From the ends of the *e* I call to you,
63: 9 down to the depths of the *e*.
65: 5 the hope of all the ends of the *e*
66: 1 Shout with joy to God, all the *e!*
66: 4 All the *e* bows down to you;
67: 2 may your ways be known on *e*,
67: 4 and guide the nations of the *e*.
67: 7 all the ends of the *e* will fear him.
68: 8 the *e* shook,
68: 32 Sing to God, O kingdoms of the *e*,
69: 34 Let heaven and *e* praise him,
71: 20 from the depths of the *e*
72: 6 like showers watering the *e*.
72: 8 from the River to the ends of the *e*.
72: 19 may the whole *e* be filled
73: 9 tongues take possession of the *e*.
73: 25 with you, I desire nothing on *e*.
74: 12 you bring salvation upon the *e*.
74: 17 who set all the boundaries of the *e;*
75: 3 When the *e* and all its people quake
75: 8 and all the wicked of the *e*
76: 12 he is feared by the kings of the *e*.
77: 18 the *e* trembled and quaked.
78: 69 like the *e* that he established
79: 2 of your saints to the beasts of the *e*.
82: 5 the foundations of the *e* are shaken.
82: 8 Rise up, O God, judge the *e*,
83: 18 are the Most High over all the *e*.
85: 11 springs forth from the *e*,

Ps 89:11 are yours, and yours also the *e;*
89:27 of the kings of the *e.*
90: 2 or you brought forth the *e*
94: 2 Rise up, O Judge of the *e;*
95: 4 In his hand are the depths of the *e,*
96: 1 sing to the LORD, all the *e.*
96: 9 tremble before him, all the *e.*
96:11 heavens rejoice, let the *e* be glad;
96:13 he comes to judge the *e.*
97: 1 The LORD reigns, let the *e* be glad;
97: 4 the *e* sees and trembles.
97: 5 before the Lord of all the *e.*
97: 9 are the Most High over all the *e;*
98: 3 all the ends of the *e* have seen
98: 4 for joy to the LORD, all the *e,*
98: 9 for he comes to judge the *e.*
99: 1 let the *e* shake.
100: 1 for joy to the LORD, all the *e.*
102: 15 of the *e* will revere your glory.
102: 19 from heaven he viewed the *e,*
102: 25 you laid the foundations of the *e,*
103: 11 high as the heavens are above the *e,*
104: 5 He set the *e* on its foundations;
104: 9 never again will they cover the *e.*
104: 13 the *e* is satisfied by the fruit
104: 14 bringing forth food from the *e:*
104: 24 the *e* is full of your creatures.
104: 30 and you renew the face of the *e.*
104: 32 He looks at the *e,* and it trembles;
104: 35 But may sinners vanish from the *e*
105: 7 his judgments are in all the *e.*
106: 17 *e* opened up and swallowed
108: 5 and let your glory be over all the *e.*
109: 15 off the memory of them from the *e.*
110: 6 crushing the rulers of the whole *e.*
113: 6 look on the heavens and the *e?*
114: 7 O *e,* at the presence of the Lord,
115: 15 the Maker of heaven and *e.*
115: 16 but the *e* he has given to man.
119: 19 I am a stranger on *e;*
119: 64 The *e* is filled with your love,
119: 87 They almost wiped me from the *e,*
119: 90 you established the *e,* and it
119:119 of the *e* you discard like dross;
121: 2 the Maker of heaven and *e.*
124: 8 the Maker of heaven and *e.*
134: 3 the Maker of heaven and *e,*
135: 6 in the heavens and on the *e,*
135: 7 rise from the ends of the *e;*
136: 6 who spread out the *e*
138: 4 of the *e* praise you,
139: 15 in the depths of the *e,*
141: 7 "As one plows and breaks up the *e,*
146: 6 the Maker of heaven and *e,*
147: 8 he supplies the *e* with rain
147: 15 He sends his command to the *e;*
148: 7 Praise the LORD from the *e,*
148: 11 kings of the *e* and all nations,
148: 11 you princes and all rulers on *e,*
148: 13 his splendor is above the *e*
Pr 8:16 and all nobles who rule on *e.*
8:26 before he made the *e* or its fields
8:29 out the foundations of the *e.*
11:31 righteous receive their due on *e,*
17:24 to the ends of the *e.*
25: 3 heavens are high and the *e* is deep,
30: 4 established all the ends of the *e?*
30:14 to devour the poor from the *e,*
30:21 "Under three things the *e* trembles,
30:24 "Four things on *e* are small,
Ecc 1: 4 but the *e* remains forever.
3:21 of the animal goes down into the *e*
5: 2 and you are on *e,*
7:20 There is not a righteous man on *e*
8:14 else meaningless that occurs on *e:*
8:16 and to observe man's labor on *e—*
11: 3 they pour rain upon the *e.*
SS 2:12 Flowers appear on the *e;*
Isa 1: 2 Hear, O heavens! Listen, O *e!*
2:19 when he rises to shake the *e.*
2:21 when he rises to shake the *e.*
5:26 for those at the ends of the *e.*
6: 3 the whole *e* is full of his glory."
8:22 Then they will look toward the *e*
11: 4 He will strike the *e* with the rod
11: 4 decisions for the poor of the *e.*
11: 9 for the *e* will be full
11:12 from the four quarters of the *e.*
13:13 and the *e* will shake from its place
14:12 You have been cast down to the *e,*
14:16 "Is this the man who shook the *e*
14:21 and cover the *e* with their cities.
18: 3 you who live on the *e,*
19:24 and Assyria, a blessing on the *e.*
23: 8 traders are renowned in the *e?*
23: 9 all who are renowned on the *e.*
23:17 the kingdoms on the face of the *e.*
24: 1 LORD is going to lay waste the *e*
24: 3 The *e* will be completely laid waste
24: 4 The *e* dries up and withers,
24: 4 the exalted of the *e* languish.
24: 5 The *e* is defiled by its people;
24: 6 Therefore a curse consumes the *e;*
24:11 all gaiety is banished from the *e.*
24:13 So will it be on the *e*
24:16 of the *e* we hear singing:
24:17 O people of the *e.*
24:18 the foundations of the *e* shake.
24:19 The *e* is broken up,
24:19 the *e* is split asunder,
24:19 the *e* is thoroughly shaken.
24:20 The *e* reels like a drunkard,
24:21 and the kings on the *e* below.
25: 8 people from all the *e.*
26: 9 your judgments come upon the *e,*
26:18 have not brought salvation to the *e;*
26:19 the *e* will give birth to her dead.
26:21 The *e* will disclose the blood shed
26:21 of the *e* for their sins.
29: 4 will come ghostlike from the *e;*
34: 1 Let the *e* hear, and all that is in it,
37:16 God over all the kingdoms of the *e.*
37:16 You have made heaven and *e.*
37:20 on *e* may know that you alone,
40:12 the dust of the *e* in a basket,
40:21 since the *e* was founded?
40:22 enthroned above the circle of the *e,*
40:28 the Creator of the ends of the *e.*
41: 5 the ends of the *e* tremble.
41: 9 I took you from the ends of the *e,*
42: 4 till he establishes justice on *e.*
42: 5 who spread out the *e* and all that
42:10 his praise from the ends of the *e,*
43: 6 daughters from the ends of the *e—*
44:23 shout aloud, O *e* beneath.
44:24 who spread out the *e* by myself,
45: 8 Let the *e* open wide,
45:12 It is I who made the *e*
45:18 he who fashioned and made the *e,*
45:22 all you ends of the *e;*
48:13 hand laid the foundations of the *e,*
48:20 Send it out to the ends of the *e;*
49: 6 salvation to the ends of the *e.*"
49:13 rejoice, O *e;*
51: 6 look at the *e* beneath;
51: 6 the *e* will wear out like a garment
51:13 and laid the foundations of the *e,*
51:16 who laid the foundations of the *e,*
52:10 and all the ends of the *e* will see
54: 5 he is called the God of all the *e.*
54: 9 would never again cover the *e.*
55: 9 the heavens are higher than the *e,*
55:10 it without watering the *e*
60: 2 See, darkness covers the *e*
62: 7 and makes her the praise of the *e.*
62:11 proclamation to the ends of the *e:*
65:17 new heavens and a new *e.*
66: 1 and the *e* is my footstool.
66:22 the new *e* that I make will endure
Jer 4:23 I looked at the *e,*
4:28 Therefore the *e* will mourn
6:19 Hear, O *e:*
6:22 up from the ends of the *e.*
7:33 of the air and the beasts of the *e,*
9:24 justice and righteousness on *e,*
10:10 When he is angry, the *e* trembles;
10:11 not make the heavens and the *e,*
10:11 will perish from the *e* and
10:12 But God made the *e* by his power;
10:13 from the ends of the *e.*
15: 3 and the beasts of the *e* to devour
15: 4 to all the kingdoms of the *e*
16: 4 of the air and the beasts of the *e.*"
16:19 from the ends of the *e* and say,
19: 7 of the air and the beasts of the *e.*
23:24 "Do not I fill heaven and *e?*"
24: 9 offense to all the kingdoms of the *e,*
25:26 the kingdoms on the face of the *e.*
25:29 a sword upon all who live on the *e,*
25:30 shout against all who live on the *e.*
25:31 resound to the ends of the *e,*
25:32 rising from the ends of the *e.*"
25:33 from one end of the *e* to the other.
26: 6 among all the nations of the *e.*' "
27: 5 and outstretched arm I made the *e*
28:16 you from the face of the *e.*
29:18 to all the kingdoms of the *e*
31: 8 gather them from the ends of the *e.*
31:22 will create a new thing on *e—*
31:37 and the foundations of the *e*
32:17 and the *e* by your great power
33: 2 he who made the *e,* the LORD who
33: 9 before all nations on *e* that hear
33:25 and the fixed laws of heaven and *e,*
34:17 to all the kingdoms of the *e.*
34:20 of the air and the beasts of the *e.*
44: 8 among all the nations on *e.*
46: 8 'I will rise and cover the *e;*
46:12 your cries will fill the *e.*
49:21 of their fall the *e* will tremble;
50:23 is the hammer of the whole *e!*
50:41 up from the ends of the *e.*
50:46 capture the *e* will tremble;
51: 7 she made the whole *e* drunk.
51:15 "He made the *e* by his power;
51:16 from the ends of the *e.*
51:25 you who destroy the whole *e,*"
51:41 the boast of the whole *e* seized!
51:48 heaven and *e* and all that is in them
51:49 just as the slain in all the *e*
La 2: 1 Israel from heaven to *e;*
2:15 the joy of the whole *e?*"
4:12 The kings of the *e* did not believe,
Eze 7:21 and as loot to the wicked of the *e,*
8: 3 The Spirit lifted me up between *e*
26:20 I will make you dwell in the *e*
27:33 you enriched the kings of the *e.*
28:17 So I threw you to the *e;*
29: 5 to the beasts of the *e* and the birds
31:12 All the nations of the *e* came out
31:14 for the *e* below, among mortal men,
31:16 were consoled in the *e* below.
31:18 the trees of Eden to the *e* below;
32: 4 of the *e* gorge themselves on you.
32:18 and consign to the *e* below both her
32:24 down uncircumcised to the *e* below
34: 6 were scattered over the whole *e,*
35:14 While the whole *e* rejoices,
38:20 on the face of the *e* will tremble
39:18 the blood of the princes of the *e*
Da 2:10 on *e* who can do what the king asks
2:35 mountain and filled the whole *e.*
2:39 will rule over the whole *e.*
4:11 it was visible to the ends of the *e.*
4:15 animals among the plants of the *e.*
4:20 the whole *e,* with beautiful leaves
4:22 extends to distant parts of the *e.*
4:35 All the peoples of the *e*
4:35 and the peoples of the *e.*
6:27 in the heavens and on the *e.*
7:17 kingdoms that will rise from the *e.*
7:23 and will devour the whole *e,*
7:23 kingdom that will appear on *e.*
8: 5 crossing the whole *e*
8:10 of the starry host down to the *e*
12: 2 in the dust of the *e* will awake:
Hos 2:21 and they will respond to the *e;*
2:22 and the *e* will respond to the grain,
6: 3 the spring rains that water the *e.*"
Joel 2:10 Before them the *e* shakes,
2:30 and on the *e,*
3:16 the *e* and the sky will tremble.
Am 3: 2 chosen of all the families of the *e:*
3: 5 Does a trap spring up from the *e*
4:13 and treads the high places of the *e*
8: 9 and darken the *e* in broad daylight.
9: 5 he who touches the *e* and it melts,
9: 6 and sets its foundation on the *e,*
9: 8 it from the face of the *e—*
Jnh 2: 6 the *e* beneath barred me in forever.
Mic 1: 2 listen, O *e* and all who are in it,
1: 3 treads the high places of the *e.*
4:13 their wealth to the Lord of all the *e.*
5: 4 will reach to the ends of the *e.*

Mic 6: 2 everlasting foundations of the *e*.
7: 13 The *e* will become desolate
Na 1: 5 The *e* trembles at his presence,
2: 13 I will leave you no prey on the *e*.
Hab 1: 6 who sweep across the whole *e*
2: 14 For the *e* will be filled
2: 20 let all the *e* be silent before him."
3: 3 and his praise filled the *e*.
3: 6 He stood, and shook the *e*;
3: 9 You split the *e* with rivers;
3: 12 In wrath you strode through the *e*
Zep 1: 2 everything from the face of the *e*,"
1: 3 cut off man from the face of the *e*,"
1: 18 end of all who live in the *e*."
3: 20 among all the peoples of the *e*
Hag 1: 10 their dew and the *e* its crops.
2: 6 more shake the heavens and the *e*,
2: 21 I will shake the heavens and the *e*.
Zec 1: 10 sent to go throughout the *e*."
1: 11 "We have gone throughout the *e*
4: 10 which range throughout the *e*.)"
4: 14 to serve the LORD of all the *e*."
5: 9 the basket between heaven and *e*.
6: 7 And he said, "Go throughout the *e*
6: 7 So they went throughout the *e*.
6: 7 straining to go throughout the *e*.
9: 10 from the River to the ends of the *e*.
12: 1 who lays the foundation of the *e*,
12: 3 of the *e* are gathered against her,
14: 9 will be king over the whole *e*.
14: 17 of the peoples of the *e* do not go up
Mt 5: 5 for they will inherit the *e*.
5: 13 "You are the salt of the *e*.
5: 18 until heaven and *e* disappear,
5: 35 or by the *e*, for it is his footstool;
6: 10 done on *e* as it is in heaven.
6: 19 up for yourselves treasures on *e*,
9: 6 authority on *e* to forgive sins..
10: 34 come to bring peace to the *e*.
11: 25 Father, Lord of heaven and *e*,
12: 40 three nights in the heart of the *e*.
12: 42 from the ends of the *e* to listen
16: 19 bind on *e* will be bound
16: 19 loose on *e* will be loosed
17: 25 the kings of the *e* collect duty
18: 18 bind on *e* will be bound
18: 18 loose on *e* will be loosed
18: 19 on *e* agree about anything you ask
23: 9 And do not call anyone on *e* 'father
23: 35 blood that has been shed on *e*,
24: 30 all the nations of the *e* will mourn.
24: 35 Heaven and *e* will pass away,
27: 51 The *e* shook and the rocks split.
28: 18 and on *e* has been given to me.
Mk 2: 10 authority on *e* to forgive sins
13: 27 from the ends of the *e* to the ends
13: 31 Heaven and *e* will pass away,
Lk 2: 14 on *e* peace to men
5: 24 authority on *e* to forgive sins..
10: 21 Father, Lord of heaven and *e*,
11: 31 from the ends of the *e* to listen
12: 49 "I have come to bring fire on the *e*,
12: 51 came to bring peace on *e*?
12: 56 to interpret the appearance of the *e*
16: 17 and *e* to disappear than for the least
18: 8 will he find faith on the *e*?"
21: 25 On the *e*, nations will be in anguish
21: 33 Heaven and *e* will pass away,
21: 35 live on the face of the whole *e*.
Jn 3: 31 and speaks as one from the *e*.
3: 31 is from the *e* belongs to the *e*,
12: 32 when I am lifted up from the *e*,
17: 4 I have brought you glory on *e*
Ac 1: 8 Samaria, and to the ends of the *e*."
2: 19 and signs on the *e* below,
3: 25 peoples on *e* will be blessed.'
4: 24 "you made the heaven and the *e*
4: 26 The kings of the *e* take their stand
7: 49 and the *e* is my footstool.
8: 33 For his life was taken from the *e*."
10: 11 let down to *e* by its four corners.
10: 12 as well as reptiles of the *e*
11: 6 saw four-footed animals of the *e*,
13: 47 salvation to the ends of the *e*.' "
14: 15 who made heaven and *e* and sea
17: 24 in it is the Lord of heaven and *e*
17: 26 they should inhabit the whole *e*;
22: 22 Rid the *e* of him! He's not fit to live

Ro 9: 17 might be proclaimed in all the *e*."
9: 28 his sentence on *e* with speed
10: 18 voice has gone out into all the *e*,
1Co 4: 13 we have become the scum of the *e*,
8: 5 whether in heaven or on *e*
10: 26 The *e* is the Lord's, and everything
15: 47 was of the dust of the *e*,
15: 48 so are those who are of the *e*;
Eph 1: 10 and on *e* together under one head,
3: 15 in heaven and on *e* derives its name
6: 3 you may enjoy long life on the *e*."
Php 2: 10 in heaven and on *e* and under the *e*,
Col 1: 16 things in heaven and on *e*,
1: 20 things on *e* or things in heaven,
Heb 1: 10 you laid the foundations of the *e*,
5: 7 During the days of Jesus' life on *e*,
8: 4 were on *e*, he would not be a priest,
11: 13 they were aliens and strangers on *e*.
12: 25 him who warned them on *e*,
12: 26 At that time his voice shook the *e*,
12: 26 more I will shake not only the *e*
Jas 5: 5 You have lived on *e* in luxury
5: 12 or by *e* or by anything else.
5: 18 and the *e* produced its crops.
2Pe 3: 5 and the *e* was formed out of water
3: 7 and *e* are reserved for fire,
3: 10 and the *e* and everything
3: 13 to a new heaven and a new *e*,
Rev 1: 5 and the ruler of the kings of the *e*.
1: 7 all the peoples of the *e* will mourn
3: 10 to test those who live on the *e*.
5: 3 But no one in heaven or on *e*
5: 3 or under the *e* could open the scroll
5: 6 of God sent out into all the *e*.
5: 10 and they will reign on the *e* "
5: 13 and under the *e* and on the sea,
5: 13 creature in heaven and on *e*
6: 4 power to take peace from the *e*
6: 8 a fourth of the *e* to kill by sword,
6: 8 and by the wild beasts of the *e*.
6: 10 you judge the inhabitants of the *e*
6: 13 and the stars in the sky fell to *e*,
6: 15 Then the kings of the *e*, the princes,
7: 1 at the four corners of the *e*,
7: 1 winds of the *e* to prevent any wind
8: 5 and hurled it on the *e*;
8: 7 A third of the *e* was burned up,
8: 7 and it was hurled down upon the *e*.
8: 13 Woe to the inhabitants of the *e*,
9: 1 fallen from the sky to the *e*.
9: 3 locusts came down upon the *e*
9: 3 that of scorpions of the *e*.
9: 4 not to harm the grass of the *e*
10: 6 and all that is in them, the *e*
11: 4 stand before the Lord of the *e*.
11: 6 and to strike the *e* with every kind
11: 10 The inhabitants of the *e* will gloat
11: 10 tormented those who live on the *e*.
11: 18 those who destroy the *e*."
12: 4 of the sky and flung them to the *e*.
12: 9 He was hurled to the *e*,
12: 12 But woe to the *e* and the sea,
12: 13 that he had been hurled to the *e*,
12: 16 But the *e* helped the woman
13: 8 of the *e* will worship the beast—
13: 11 another beast, coming out of the *e*.
13: 12 and made the *e* and its inhabitants
13: 13 down from heaven to *e* in full view
13: 14 he deceived the inhabitants of the *e*
14: 3 who had been redeemed from the *e*
14: 6 to those who live on the *e*—
14: 7 him who made the heavens, the *e*,
14: 15 for the harvest of the *e* is ripe."
14: 16 over the *e*, and the *e* was harvested.
14: 19 The angel swung his sickle on the *e*,
16: 1 bowls of God's wrath on the *e*."
16: 18 occurred since man has been on *e*,
17: 2 kings of the *e* committed adultery
17: 2 of the *e* were intoxicated
17: 5 ABOMINATIONS OF THE *E*.
17: 8 of the *e* whose names have not
17: 18 rules over the kings of the *e*."
18: 1 and the *e* was illuminated
18: 3 kings of the *e* committed adultery
18: 3 the merchants of the *e* grew rich
18: 9 of the *e* who committed adultery
18: 11 "The merchants of the *e* will weep
18: 24 of all who have been killed on the *e*

Rev 19: 2 who corrupted the *e*
19: 19 saw the beast and the kings of the *e*
20: 8 in the four corners of the *e*—
20: 9 across the breadth of the *e*
20: 11 *E* and sky fled from his presence,
21: 1 I saw a new heaven and a new *e*,
21: 1 and the first *e* had passed away,
21: 24 of the *e* will bring their splendor

EARTH'S (EARTH)

Ge 27: 28 and of *e* richness—
27: 39 away from the *e* richness,
Job 38: 4 when I laid the *e* foundation?
Pr 3: 19 the LORD laid the *e* foundations,
Isa 24: 6 Therefore *e* inhabitants are burned
Rev 14: 18 clusters of grapes from the *e* vine,

EARTHEN (EARTH)

Hab 1: 10 they build *e* ramps and capture

EARTHENWARE

Pr 26: 23 Like a coating of glaze over *e*

EARTHLY (EARTH)

Jn 3: 12 I have spoken to you of *e* things
1Co 15: 40 bodies and there are *e* bodies;
15: 40 splendor of the *e* bodies is another.
15: 48 As was the *e* man,
15: 49 borne the likeness of the *e* man,
2Co 5: 1 we know that if the *e* tent we live
Eph 4: 9 descended to the lower, *e* regions?
6: 5 obey your *e* masters with respect
Php 3: 19 Their mind is on *e* things.
Col 3: 2 on things above, not on *e* things.
3: 5 whatever belongs to your *e* nature:
3: 22 obey your *e* masters in everything;
Heb 9: 1 for worship and also an *e* sanctuary
Jas 3: 15 come down from heaven but is *e*,
1Pe 4: 2 of his *e* life for evil human desires,

EARTHQUAKE (QUAKE)

1Ki 19: 11 After the wind there was an *e*,
19: 11 but the LORD was not in the *e*.
19: 12 After the *e* came a fire,
Isa 29: 6 with thunder and *e* and great noise,
Eze 38: 19 at that time there shall be a great *e*
Am 1: 1 Israel two years before the *e*,
Zec 14: 5 as you fled from the *e* in the days
Mt 27: 54 who were guarding Jesus saw the *e*
28: 2 There was a violent *e*, for an angel
Ac 16: 26 such a violent *e* that
Rev 6: 12 There was a great *e*.
8: 5 flashes of lightning and an *e*.
11: 13 people were killed in the *e*,
11: 13 that very hour there was a severe *e*
11: 19 an *e* and a great hailstorm.
16: 18 No *e* like it has ever occurred
16: 18 peals of thunder and a severe *e*.

EARTHQUAKES (QUAKE)

Mt 24: 7 There will be famines and *e*
Mk 13: 8 There will be *e* in various places,
Lk 21: 11 There will be great *e*, famines

EASE

Job 3: 18 Captives also enjoy their *e*;
7: 13 and my couch will *e* my complaint,
12: 5 Men at *e* have contempt
21: 23 completely secure and at *e*,
Pr 1: 33 and be at *e*, without fear of harm."
Jer 12: 1 Why do all the faithless live at *e*?
49: 31 "Arise and attack a nation at *e*,
La 1: 5 her enemies are at *e*.
Jnh 4: 6 for his head to *e* his discomfort,

EASIER (EASY)

Mt 9: 5 Which is *e*: to say, 'Your sins are
19: 24 it is *e* for a camel to go
Mk 2: 9 Which is *e*: to say to the paralytic,
10: 25 It is *e* for a camel to go
Lk 5: 23 Which is *e*: to say, 'Your sins are
16: 17 It is *e* for heaven and earth
18: 25 it is *e* for a camel to go

EAST (EASTERN EASTWARD NORTHEASTER SOUTHEAST)

Ge 2: 8 God had planted a garden in the *e*,
2: 14 it runs along the *e* side of Asshur.

Ge 3:24 he placed on the *e* side
4:16 lived in the land of Nod, *e* of Eden.
12: 8 Bethel on the west and Ai on the *e*.
12: 8 went on toward the hills *e* of Bethel
13:11 Jordan and set out toward the *e*.
13:14 look north and south, *e* and west.
25: 6 Isaac to the land of the *e*.
28:14 out to the west and to the *e*,
41: 6 thin and scorched by the *e* wind.
41:23 thin and scorched by the *e* wind.
41:27 of grain scorched by the *e* wind:
Ex 10:13 the LORD made an *e* wind blow
14:21 back with a strong *e* wind
27:13 On the *e* end, toward the sunrise,
38:13 The *e* end, toward the sunrise,
Lev 1:16 throw it to the *e* side of the altar,
Nu 2: 3 On the *e*, toward the sunrise,
3:38 to camp to the *e* of the tabernacle,
10: 5 camping on the *e* are to set out.
32:19 to us on the *e* side of the Jordan."
33: 7 to the *e* of Baal Zephon,
34: 3 On the *e*, your southern boundary
34:11 along the slopes *e* of the Sea
34:11 to Riblah on the *e* side of Ain
34:15 on the *e* side of the Jordan
35: 5 three thousand feet on the *e* side,
Dt 1: 1 in the desert *e* of the Jordan—
1: 5 *E* of the Jordan in the territory
3: 8 of the Amorites the territory *e*
3:27 and north and south and *e*.
4:41 aside three cities *e* of the Jordan,
4:46 near Beth Peor *e* of the Jordan,
4:47 the two Amorite kings *e*
4:49 and included all the Arabah *e*
Jos 1:14 in the land that Moses gave you *e*
1:15 servant of the LORD gave you *e*
2:10 of the Amorites *e* of the Jordan,
7: 2 near Beth Aven to the *e* of Bethel,
9:10 of the Amorites *e* of the Jordan—
11: 3 to the Canaanites in the *e* and west;
11: 8 to the Valley of Mizpah on the *e*,
12: 1 took over *e* of the Jordan,
13: 3 on the *e* of Egypt to the territory
13: 5 Lebanon to the *e*, from Baal Gad
13: 8 that Moses had given them *e*
13:27 king of Heshbon (the *e* side
13:32 across the Jordan *e* of Jericho.
14: 3 tribes their inheritance *e*
16: 1 Jordan of Jericho, *e* of the waters
16: 5 in the *e* to Upper Beth Horon
16: 6 passing by it to Janoah on the *e*.
17: 5 and Bashan *e* of the Jordan,
17: 7 to Micmethath *e* of Shechem.
17:10 on the north and Issachar on the *e*.
18: 7 on the *e* side of the Jordan.
19:12 It turned *e* from Sarid
19:27 turned *e* toward Beth
19:34 on the west and the Jordan on the *e*
20: 8 On the *e* side of the Jordan
24: 8 land of the Amorites who lived *e*
Jdg 8:11 the route of the nomads *e* of Nobah
10: 8 on the *e* side of the Jordan
20:43 in the vicinity of Gibeah on the *e*.
21:19 *e* of the road that goes from Bethel
1Sa 13: 5 and camped at Micmash, *e* of Beth
15: 7 Havilah to Shur, to the *e* of Egypt.
1Ki 4:30 the wisdom of all the men of the *E*,
7:25 facing south and three facing *e*.
11: 7 On a hill *e* of Jerusalem, Solomon
17: 3 and hide in the Kerith Ravine, *e*
17: 5 went to the Kerith Ravine, *e*
2Ki 10:33 throughout their territory *e*
13:17 "Open the *e* window," he said,
23:13 the high places that were *e*
1Ch 4:39 of Gedor to the *e* of the valley
5: 9 To the *e* they occupied the land up
5:10 throughout the entire region *e*
6:78 tribe of Reuben across the Jordan *e*
7:28 Naaran to the *e*, Gezer
9:18 at the King's Gate on the *e*,
9:24 were on the four sides: *e*,
12:15 living in the valleys, to the *e*
12:37 and from *e* of the Jordan,
26:14 The lot for the *E* Gate fell
26:17 were six Levites a day on the *e*,
2Ch 4: 4 facing south and three facing *e*.
5:12 stood on the *e* side of the altar,
29: 4 them in the square on the *e* side
2Ch 31:14 the Levite, keeper of the *E* Gate,
Ne 3:26 the Water Gate toward the *e*
3:29 guard at the *E* Gate, made repairs.
12:37 David to the Water Gate on the *e*.
Job 1: 3 man among all the people of the *E*.
15: 2 or fill his belly with the hot *e* wind?
18:20 men of the *e* are seized with horror.
23: 8 "But if I go to the *e*, he is not there;
27:21 The *e* wind carries him off,
38:24 or the place where the *e* winds are
Ps 48: 7 shattered by an *e* wind.
75: 6 No one from the *e* or the west
78:26 He let loose the *e* wind
103:12 as far as the *e* is from the west,
107: 3 from *e* and west, from north
Isa 2: 6 full of superstitions from the *E*;
9:12 from the *e* and Philistines
11:14 will plunder the people to the *e*.
24:15 Therefore in the *e* give glory
27: 8 as on a day the *e* wind blows.
41: 2 Who has stirred up one from the *e*,
43: 5 will bring your children from the *e*
46:11 From the *e* I summon a bird of prey
Jer 18:17 Like a wind from the *e*,
31:40 out to the Kidron Valley on the *e*
49:28 and destroy the people of the *E*.
Eze 8:16 and their faces toward the *e*,
8:16 bowing down to the sun in the *e*.
10:19 at the entrance to the *e* gate
11: 1 house of the LORD that faces *e*.
11:23 stopped above the mountain *e* of it.
17:10 when the *e* wind strikes it—
19:12 The *e* wind made it shrivel,
25: 4 to give you to the people of the *E*
25:10 Ammonites to the people of the *E*
27:26 the *e* wind will break you to pieces
39:11 the valley of those who travel *e*
40: 6 Then he went to the gate facing *e*.
40:10 Inside the *e* gate were three alcoves
40:19 was a hundred cubits on the *e* side
40:22 as those of the gate facing *e*.
40:23 gate, just as there was on the *e*
40:32 me to the inner court on the *e* side,
41:14 of the temple courtyard on the *e*,
42: 9 had an entrance on the *e* side
42:15 he led me out by the *e* gate
42:16 He measured the *e* side
43: 1 me to the gate facing *e*,
43: 2 God of Israel coming from the *e*.
43: 4 temple through the gate facing *e*.
43:17 The steps of the altar face *e*."
44: 1 the one facing *e*, and it was shut.
45: 7 and eastward from the *e* side,
46: 1 gate of the inner court facing *e* is
46:12 the gate facing *e* is to be opened
47: 1 toward the *e* (for the temple faced *e*
47: 2 outside to the outer gate facing *e*,
47:18 On the *e* side the boundary will run
47:18 This will be the *e* boundary.
48: 1 part of its border from the *e* side
48: 2 the territory of Dan from *e* to west.
48: 3 territory of Asher from *e* to west.
48: 4 of Naphtali from *e* to west.
48: 5 of Manasseh from *e* to west.
48: 6 of Ephraim from *e* to west.
48: 7 territory of Reuben from *e* to west.
48: 8 length from *e* to west will equal one
48: 8 the territory of Judah from *e*
48:10 cubits wide on the *e* side
48:16 cubits, the *e* side 4,500 cubits,
48:17 250 cubits on the *e*, and 250 cubits
48:18 cubits on the *e* side and 10,000
48:23 it will extend from the *e* side
48:24 of Benjamin from *e* to west.
48:25 territory of Simeon from *e* to west.
48:26 territory of Issachar from *e* to west.
48:27 territory of Zebulun from *e* to west.
48:32 "On the *e* side, which is 4,500
Da 8: 9 to the *e* and toward the Beautiful
11:44 But reports from the *e*
Hos 12: 1 he pursues the *e* wind all day
13:15 *e* wind from the LORD will come,
Am 8:12 and wander from north to *e*,
Jnh 4: 5 sat down at a place *e* of the city.
4: 8 God provided a scorching *e* wind,
Zec 8: 7 people from the countries of the *e*
14: 4 Mount of Olives, *e* of Jerusalem,
14: 4 split in two from *e* to west,
Mt 2: 1 Magi from the *e* came to Jerusalem
2: 2 We saw his star in the *e*
2: 9 seen in the *e* went ahead of them
8:11 you that many will come from the *e*
24:27 as the lightning comes from the *e*
Lk 13:29 People will come from *e* and west
Rev 7: 2 angel coming up from the *e*,
16:12 the way for the kings from the *E*.
21:13 There were three gates on the *e*,

EASTERN (EAST)

Ge 10:30 toward Sephar, in the *e* hill country
29: 1 came to the land of the *e* peoples.
Nu 23: 7 of Moab from the *e* mountains.
34:10 " 'For your *e* boundary, run a line
Jos 4:19 at Gilgal on the *e* border of Jericho.
12: 1 including all the *e* side
12: 3 also ruled over the *e* Arabah
15: 5 The *e* boundary is the Salt Sea
18:20 formed the boundary on the *e* side.
Jdg 6: 3 and other *e* peoples invaded
6:33 and other *e* peoples joined forces
7:12 all the other *e* peoples had settled
8:10 left of the armies of the *e* peoples;
11:18 passed along the *e* side
Eze 45: 7 to the *e* border parallel to one
47: 8 flows toward the *e* region
47:18 to the *e* sea and as far as Tamar.
48:21 the sacred portion to the *e* border,
Joel 2:20 front columns going into the *e* sea
Zec 14: 8 half to the *e* sea and half

EASTWARD (EAST)

Ge 11: 2 As men moved *e*, they found
Jos 16: 6 it curved *e* to Taanath Shiloh,
19:13 it continued *e* to Gath Hepher
1Ki 17: 3 turn *e* and hide in the Kerith
Eze 42:12 corresponding wall extending *e*,
45: 7 westward from the west side and *e*
47: 3 As the man went *e*
48:21 It will extend *e* from the 25,000

EASY (EASIER)

Dt 1:41 thinking it *e* to go up
2Ki 3:18 This is an *e* thing in the eyes
5:20 "My master was too *e* on Naaman,
Mt 11:30 For my yoke is *e* and my burden is
Lk 12:19 Take life *e*; eat, drink and be merry

EAT (ATE EATEN EATER EATING EATS)

Ge 2:16 "You are free to *e* from any tree
2:17 but you must not *e* from the tree
2:17 when you *e* of it you will surely die
3: 1 'You must not *e* from any tree
3: 2 "We may *e* fruit from the trees
3: 3 'You must not *e* fruit
3: 5 "For God knows that when you *e*
3:11 tree that I commanded you not to *e*
3:14 and you will *e* dust
3:17 I commanded you, 'You must not *e*
3:17 through painful toil you will *e* of it
3:18 and you will *e* the plants of the field
3:19 you will *e* your food
3:22 take also from the tree of life and *e*,
9: 4 you must not *e* meat that has its
18: 5 Let me get you something to *e*,
24:33 "I will not *e* until I have told you
27: 4 food I like and bring it to me to *e*,
27: 7 prepare me some tasty food to *e*,
27:10 Then take it to your father to *e*,
27:19 and *e* some of my game
27:25 bring me some of your game to *e*,
27:31 sit up and *e* some of my game,
28:20 food to *e* and clothes to wear
32:32 the Israelites do not *e* the tendon
37:25 As they sat down to *e* their meal,
40:19 the birds will *e* away your flesh."
43:16 they are to *e* with me at noon."
43:25 had heard that they were to *e* there.
43:32 because Egyptians could not *e*
Ex 2:20 Invite him to have something to *e*."
12: 4 with what each person will *e*.
12: 7 the houses where they *e* the lambs.
12: 8 are to *e* the meat roasted
12: 9 Do not *e* the meat raw
12:11 This is how you are to *e* it:
12:11 *E* it in haste; it is the LORD's
12:15 are to *e* bread made without yeast.

Ex 12: 16 to prepare food for everyone to *e*—
12: 18 are to *e* bread made without yeast,
12: 20 *E* nothing made with yeast.
12: 20 you must *e* unleavened bread.''
12: 43 the Passover: ''No foreigner is to *e*
12: 44 Any slave you have bought may *e*
12: 45 and a hired worker may not *e* of it.
12: 48 No uncircumcised male may *e* of it.
13: 3 *E* nothing containing yeast.
13: 6 For seven days *e* bread made
13: 7 *E* unleavened bread
16: 8 meat to *e* in the evening
16: 12 'At twilight you will *e* meat,
16: 15 the LORD has given you to *e*.
16: 25 ''*E* it today,'' Moses said,
16: 32 to *e* in the desert when I brought
18: 12 the elders of Israel to *e* bread
22: 31 do not *e* the meat of an animal torn
23: 11 the wild animals may *e* what they
23: 15 for seven days *e* bread made
29: 32 and his sons are to *e* the meat
29: 33 But no one else may *e* them,
29: 33 They are to *e* these offerings
32: 6 Afterward they sat down to *e*
34: 15 and you will *e* their sacrifices.
34: 18 For seven days *e* bread made
Lev 3: 17 You must not *e* any fat
6: 16 and his sons shall *e* the rest of it,
6: 16 they are to *e* it in the courtyard
6: 18 descendant of Aaron may *e* it.
6: 26 The priest who offers it shall *e* it;
6: 29 male in a priest's family may *e* it;
7: 6 male in a priest's family may *e* it,
7: 19 anyone ceremonially clean may *e* it
7: 23 'Do not *e* any of the fat of cattle,
7: 24 purpose, but you must not *e* it.
7: 26 you must not *e* the blood
8: 31 'Aaron and his sons are to *e* it.'
8: 31 and *e* it there with the bread
10: 12 and *e* it prepared without yeast
10: 13 *E* it in a holy place, because it is
10: 14 *E* them in a ceremonially clean
10: 14 your daughters may *e* the breast
10: 17 ''Why didn't you *e* the sin offering
11: 2 these are the ones you may *e*:
11: 3 You may *e* any animal that has
11: 4 split hoof, but you must not *e* them.
11: 8 You must not *e* their meat
11: 9 you may *e* any that have fins
11: 11 you must not *e* their meat
11: 13 not *e* because they are detestable:
11: 21 walk on all fours that you may *e*:
11: 22 Of these you may *e* any kind
11: 39 that you are allowed to *e* dies,
11: 42 to *e* any creature that moves about
17: 12 living among you *e* blood.''
17: 12 ''None of you may *e* blood,
17: 14 ''You must not *e* the blood
19: 25 in the fifth year you may *e* its fruit.
19: 26 '' 'Do not *e* any meat
21: 22 He may *e* the most holy food
22: 4 he may not *e* the sacred offerings
22: 6 He must not *e* any
22: 7 that he may *e* the sacred offerings,
22: 8 He must not *e* anything found dead
22: 10 a priest's family may *e* the sacred
22: 10 of a priest or his hired worker *e* it.
22: 11 that slave may *e* his food.
22: 12 she may not *e* any
22: 13 person, however, may *e* any
22: 13 she may *e* of her father's food.
22: 16 them to *e* the sacred offerings
23: 6 seven days you must *e* bread made
23: 14 You must not *e* any bread,
24: 9 who are to *e* it in a holy place,
25: 12 *e* only what is taken directly
25: 19 and you will *e* your fill
25: 20 ''What will we *e* in the seventh year
25: 22 and will continue to *e* from it
25: 22 you will *e* from the old crop
26: 5 and you will *e* all the food you want
26: 16 because your enemies will *e* it.
26: 26 You will *e*, but you will not be
26: 29 You will *e* the flesh of your sons
Nu 6: 3 not drink grape juice or *e* grapes
6: 4 he must not *e* anything that comes
9: 11 They are to *e* the lamb, together
11: 4 ''If only we had meat to *e*!
Nu 11: 13 meat to *e*!' I cannot carry all these
11: 18 give you meat, and you will *e* it.
11: 18 when you will *e* meat.
11: 18 ''If only we had meat to *e*!
11: 19 You will not *e* it for just one day,
11: 21 meat to *e* for a whole month!'
15: 19 and you *e* the food of the land,
18: 10 *E* it as something most holy;
18: 10 most holy; every male shall *e* it.
18: 11 who is ceremonially clean may *e* it.
18: 13 who is ceremonially clean may *e* it.
18: 31 and your households may *e* the rest
28: 17 for seven days *e* bread made
Dt 2: 6 them in silver for the food you *e*
2: 28 Sell us food to *e* and water to drink
4: 28 which cannot see or hear or *e*
6: 11 then when you *e* and are satisfied,
8: 12 when you *e* and are satisfied,
8: 16 He gave you manna to *e*
11: 15 and you will *e* and be satisfied.
12: 7 you and your families shall *e*
12: 15 unclean and the clean may *e* it.
12: 15 *e* as much of the meat as you want,
12: 16 But you must not *e* the blood;
12: 17 You must not *e* in your own towns
12: 18 you are to *e* them in the presence
12: 20 then you may *e* as much of it
12: 21 and in your own towns you may *e*
12: 22 *E* them as you would gazelle
12: 22 unclean and the clean may *e*.
12: 23 But be sure you do not *e* the blood,
12: 23 and you must not *e* the life
12: 24 You must not *e* the blood;
12: 25 Do not *e* it, so that it may go well
12: 27 your God, but you may *e* the meat.
14: 3 Do not *e* any detestable thing.
14: 4 These are the animals you may *e*:
14: 6 You may *e* any animal that has
14: 7 divided you may not *e* the camel,
14: 8 You are not to *e* their meat
14: 9 you may *e* any that has fins
14: 10 have fins and scales you may not *e*;
14: 11 You may *e* any clean bird.
14: 12 But these you may not *e*: the eagle,
14: 19 unclean to you; do not *e* them.
14: 20 creature that is clean you may *e*.
14: 21 Do not *e* anything you find already
14: 21 and he may *e* it, or you may sell it
14: 23 *E* the tithe of your grain, new wine
14: 26 and your household shall *e* there
14: 29 live in your towns may come and *e*
15: 20 and your family are to *e* them
15: 22 You are to *e* it in your own towns.
15: 22 unclean and the clean may *e* it,
15: 23 But you must not *e* the blood;
16: 3 Do not *e* it with bread made
16: 3 for seven days *e* unleavened bread,
16: 7 *e* it at the place the LORD your
16: 8 For six days *e* unleavened bread
20: 19 because you can *e* their fruit.
23: 24 you may *e* all the grapes you want,
26: 12 so that they may *e* in your towns
28: 31 your eyes, but you will *e* none
28: 33 do not know will *e* what your land
28: 39 because worms will *e* them.
28: 53 you will *e* the fruit of the womb,
28: 57 For she intends to *e* them secretly
31: 20 and when they *e* their fill
Jos 24: 13 live in them and *e* from vineyards
Jdg 13: 4 that you do not *e* anything unclean,
13: 7 and do not *e* anything unclean,
13: 14 She must not *e* anything that
13: 14 drink nor *e* anything unclean.
13: 16 I will not *e* any of your food.
14: 14 ''Out of the eater, something to *e*;
19: 5 yourself with something to *e*;
19: 6 So the two of them sat down to *e*
19: 21 they had something to *e* and drink.
1Sa 1: 7 her till she wept and would not *e*.
1: 8 Why don't you *e*? Why are you
2: 36 office so I can have food to *e*.'' ' ''
9: 13 those who are invited will *e*.
9: 13 up to the high place to *e*.
9: 19 for today you are to *e* with me,
9: 24 *E*, because it was set aside for you
14: 34 slaughter them here and *e* them.
20: 24 came, the king sat down to *e*.
20: 34 day of the month he did not *e*,
1Sa 28: 22 give you some food so you may *e*
28: 23 He refused and said, ''I will not *e*.''
30: 11 water to drink and food to *e*—
2Sa 3: 35 and urged David to *e* something
9: 7 and you will always *e* at my table.''
9: 10 will always *e* at my table.''
11: 11 How could I go to my house to *e*
12: 17 he would not *e* any food with them.
12: 21 you get up and *e*!'' He answered,
13: 5 and give me something to *e*.
13: 5 and then *e* it from her hand.' ''
13: 6 so I may *e* from her hand.''
13: 9 him the bread, but he refused to *e*.
13: 10 so I may *e* from your hand.''
13: 11 But when she took it to him to *e*,
16: 2 and fruit are for the men to *e*,
17: 29 milk for David and his people to *e*.
1Ki 2: 7 among those who *e* at your table.
13: 7 with me and have something to *e*,
13: 8 would I *e* bread or drink water here
13: 9 'You must not *e* bread
13: 15 ''Come home with me and *e*.''
13: 16 nor can I *e* bread or drink water
13: 17 'You must not *e* bread
13: 18 house so that he may *e* bread
13: 22 the place where he told you not to *e*
14: 11 Dogs will *e* those belonging
16: 4 Dogs will *e* those belonging
17: 12 that we may *e* it—and die.''
18: 19 of Asherah, who *e* at Jezebel's table
18: 41 And Elijah said to Ahab, ''Go, *e*
18: 42 So Ahab went off to *e* and drink,
19: 5 him and said, ''Get up and *e*.''
19: 7 and *e*, for the journey is too much
21: 4 on his bed sulking and refused to *e*.
21: 5 Why won't you *e*?'' He answered
21: 7 as king over Israel? Get up and *e*!
21: 24 ''Dogs will *e* those belonging
2Ki 4: 8 came by, he stopped there to *e*.
4: 40 as they began to *e* it, they cried out,
4: 40 in the pot!'' And they could not *e* it
4: 41 ''Serve it to the people to *e*.''
4: 42 ''Give it to the people to *e*,''
4: 43 They will *e* and have some left over
4: 43 ''Give it to the people to *e*.
6: 22 before them so that they may *e*
6: 28 and tomorrow we'll *e* my son.'
6: 28 son so we may *e* him today,
6: 29 Give up your son so we may *e* him,'
7: 2 ''but you will not *e* any of it!''
7: 19 but you will not *e* any of it!''
18: 27 will have to *e* their own filth
18: 31 one of you will *e* from his own vine
19: 29 This year you will *e* what grows
19: 29 plant vineyards and *e* their fruit.
25: 3 food for the people to *e*.
2Ch 31: 10 we have had enough to *e*
Ezr 2: 63 ordered them not to *e* any
9: 12 and *e* the good things of the land
Ne 5: 2 in order for us to *e* and stay alive,
7: 65 ordered them not to *e* any
8: 12 Then all the people went away to *e*
9: 36 forefathers so they could *e* its fruit
Est 4: 16 Do not *e* or drink for three days,
Job 1: 4 would invite their three sisters to *e*
27: 14 will never have enough to *e*.
31: 8 then may others *e* what I have
Ps 14: 4 devour my people as men *e* bread
22: 26 The poor will *e* and be satisfied;
50: 13 Do I *e* the flesh of bulls
53: 4 devour my people as men *e* bread
78: 24 down manna for the people to *e*,
78: 25 sent them all the food they could *e*.
102: 4 I forget to *e* my food.
102: 9 For I *e* ashes as my food
127: 2 toiling for food to *e*—
128: 2 You will *e* the fruit of your labor;
141: 4 let me not *e* of their delicacies.
Pr 1: 31 they will *e* the fruit of their ways
4: 17 They *e* the bread of wickedness
9: 5 ''Come, *e* my food
13: 25 righteous *e* to their hearts' content,
18: 21 and those who love it will *e* its fruit.
23: 6 Do not *e* the food of a stingy man,
23: 7 ''*E* and drink,'' he says to you,
24: 13 *E* honey, my son, for it is good;
25: 16 If you find honey, *e* just enough—
25: 21 is hungry, give him food to *e*;

Pr 25:27 It is not good to *e* too much honey,
27:18 who tends a fig tree will *e* its fruit,
31:27 and does not *e* the bread of idleness
Ecc 2:24 can do nothing better than to *e*
2:25 who can *e* or find enjoyment?
3:13 That every man may *e* and drink,
5:18 proper for a man to *e* and drink,
8:15 for a man under the sun than to *e*
9:7 Go, *e* your food with gladness,
10:17 whose princes *e* at a proper time—
SS 5:1 *E*, O friends, and drink;
Isa 1:19 you will *e* the best from the land;
4:1 and say, "We will *e* our own food
7:15 He will *e* curds and honey
7:22 remain in the land will *e* curds
7:22 they give, he will have curds to *e*.
9:20 on the left they will *e*,
11:7 and the lion will *e* straw like the ox.
21:5 they *e*, they drink!
22:13 "Let us *e* and drink," you say,
30:24 that work the soil will *e* fodder
36:12 will have to *e* their own filth
36:16 one of you will *e* from his own vine
37:30 plant vineyards and *e* their fruit.
37:30 "This year you will *e* what grows
49:26 make your oppressors *e* their own
50:9 the moths will *e* them up.
51:8 For the moth will *e* them up like
55:1 come, buy and *e*!
55:2 listen to me, and *e* what is good,
62:9 but those who harvest it will *e* it
65:4 who *e* the flesh of pigs,
65:13 "My servants will *e*,
65:21 plant vineyards and *e* their fruit
65:22 or plant and others *e*.
65:25 and the lion will *e* straw like the ox,
66:17 of those who *e* the flesh of pigs
Jer 2:7 land to *e* its fruit and rich produce.
7:21 and *e* the meat yourselves!
9:15 I will make this people *e* bitter food
16:8 and sit down to *e* and drink.
19:9 I will make them *e* the flesh
19:9 and they will *e* one another's flesh
23:15 "I will make them *e* bitter food
29:5 plant gardens and *e* what they
29:28 and *e* what they produce.' "
52:6 food for the people to *e*.
La 2:20 Should women *e* their offspring,
Eze 2:8 open your mouth and *e* what I give
3:1 *e* what is before you, *e* this scroll;
3:2 and he gave me the scroll to *e*.
3:3 *e* this scroll I am giving you
4:9 to *e* it during the 390 days you lie
4:10 to *e* each day and *e* it at set times.
4:12 *E* the food as you would a barley
4:13 people of Israel will *e* defiled food
4:16 The people will *e* rationed food
5:10 and children will *e* their fathers.
5:10 midst fathers will *e* their children,
12:18 tremble as you *e* your food,
12:19 They will *e* their food in anxiety
16:19 olive oil and honey I gave you to *e*
18:2 " 'The fathers *e* sour grapes,
18:6 He does not *e* at the mountain
18:15 "He does not *e* at the mountain
22:9 in you are those who *e*
24:17 *e* the customary food of mourners
24:22 *e* the customary food of mourners
25:4 they will *e* your fruit and drink
33:25 Since you *e* meat with the blood
34:3 care of the flock? You *e* the curds,
39:17 There you will *e* flesh and drink
39:18 You will *e* the flesh of mighty men
39:19 you will *e* fat till you are glutted
39:20 At my table you will *e* your fill
42:13 the LORD will *e* the most holy
44:3 the gateway to *e* in the presence
44:29 They will *e* the grain offerings,
44:31 The priests must not *e* anything,
45:21 which you shall *e* bread made
Da 1:12 vegetables to *e* and water to drink.
1:13 young men who *e* the royal food,
4:25 you will *e* grass like cattle
4:32 you will *e* grass like cattle.
7:5 'Get up and *e* your fill of flesh!'
11:26 Those who *e* from the king's
Hos 4:10 "They will *e* but not have enough;
8:13 and they *e* the meat,
Hos 9:3 and *e* unclean food in Assyria.
9:4 all who *e* them will be unclean.
Joel 2:26 plenty to *e*, until you are full,
Am 9:14 will make gardens and *e* their fruit.
Ob :7 those who *e* your bread will set
Jnh 3:7 do not let them *e* or drink.
Mic 3:3 who *e* my people's flesh,
6:14 You will *e* but not be satisfied;
7:1 there is no cluster of grapes to *e*,
Zep 3:13 They will *e* and lie down
Hag 1:6 You *e*, but never have enough.
Zec 11:9 who are left *e* one another's flesh."
11:16 will *e* the meat of the choice sheep,
Mt 6:25 what you will *e* or drink;
6:31 saying, 'What shall we *e*?'
9:11 "Why does your teacher *e*
12:1 heads of grain and *e* them.
14:16 You give them something to *e*."
15:2 wash their hands before they *e*!"
15:27 even the dogs *e* the crumbs that fall
15:32 three days and have nothing to *e*.
24:49 and to *e* and drink with drunkards.
25:35 and you gave me something to *e*,
25:42 and you gave me nothing to *e*,
26:17 for you to *e* the Passover?"
26:26 "Take and *e*; this is my body."
Mk 2:16 "Why does he *e* with tax collectors
2:26 which is lawful only for priests to *e*.
3:20 his disciples were not even able to *e*
5:43 them to give her something to *e*.
6:31 did not even have a chance to *e*,
6:36 buy themselves something to *e*."
6:37 on bread and give it to them to *e*?"
6:37 "You give them something to *e*."
7:3 Pharisees and all the Jews do not *e*
7:4 from the marketplace they do not *e*
7:27 First let the children *e* all they want
7:28 under the table *e* the children's
8:1 Since they had nothing to *e*,
8:2 three days and have nothing to *e*.
11:14 "May no one ever *e* fruit
14:12 for you to *e* the Passover?"
14:14 where I may *e* the Passover
Lk 5:30 "Why do you *e* and drink
6:1 in their hands and *e* the kernels.
6:4 what is lawful only for priests to *e*.
8:55 them to give her something to *e*.
9:13 "You give them something to *e*."
10:8 and are welcomed, *e* what is set
11:37 a Pharisee invited him to *e*
12:19 Take life easy; *e*, drink
12:22 what you will *e*, or about your body
12:29 heart on what you will *e*
12:45 womenservants and to *e* and drink
14:1 when Jesus went to *e* in the house
14:15 "Blessed is the man who will *e*
16:21 and longing to *e* what fell
17:7 'Come along now and sit down to *e*
17:8 after that you may *e* and drink'?
17:8 and wait on me while I *e* and drink;
22:8 for us to *e* the Passover."
22:11 where I may *e* the Passover
22:15 desired to *e* this Passover with you
22:16 I will not *e* it again
22:30 so that you may *e* and drink
24:41 "Do you have anything here to *e*?"
Jn 4:31 urged him, "Rabbi, *e* something."
4:32 to *e* that you know nothing about."
6:5 bread for these people to *e*?"
6:12 When they had all had enough to *e*,
6:31 bread from heaven to *e*.' "
6:50 which a man may *e* and not die.
6:52 can this man give us his flesh to *e*?"
6:53 you *e* the flesh of the Son of Man
18:28 wanted to be able to *e* the Passover.
Ac 9:9 and did not *e* or drink anything.
10:10 and wanted something to *e*,
10:13 Kill and *e*."
11:7 Kill and *e*.'
23:12 themselves with an oath not to *e*
23:14 to *e* anything until we have killed
23:21 They have taken an oath not to *e*
27:33 dawn Paul urged them all to *e*.
27:35 Then he broke it and began to *e*.
Ro 14:2 faith allows him to *e* everything,
14:3 who does not *e* everything must
14:15 is distressed because of what you *e*,
14:20 to *e* anything that causes someone
Ro 14:21 It is better not to *e* meat
1Co 5:11 With such a man do not even *e*.
8:7 when they *e* such food they think
8:8 we are no worse if we do not *e*,
8:10 to *e* what has been sacrificed
8:13 I will never *e* meat again,
8:13 if what I *e* causes my brother to fall
9:7 and does not *e* of its grapes?
10:7 The people sat down to *e* and drink
10:18 not those who *e* the sacrifices
10:25 *E* anything sold in the meat market
10:27 *e* whatever is put before you
10:28 in sacrifice," then do not *e* it,
10:31 So whether you *e* or drink
11:20 it is not the Lord's Supper you *e*,
11:21 as you *e*, each of you goes ahead
11:22 Don't you have homes to *e*
11:26 For whenever you *e* this bread
11:33 when you come together to *e*,
11:34 If anyone is hungry, he should *e*
15:32 "Let us *e* and drink,
Gal 2:12 he used to *e* with the Gentiles.
Col 2:16 let anyone judge you by what you *e*
2Th 3:8 nor did we *e* anyone's food
3:10 man will not work, he shall not *e*."
3:12 down and earn the bread they *e*.
Heb 13:9 of no value to those who *e* them.
13:10 at the tabernacle have no right to *e*.
Jas 5:3 against you and *e* your flesh like
Rev 2:7 the right to *e* from the tree of life,
3:20 I will come in and *e* with him,
10:9 He said to me, "Take it and *e* it.
17:16 they will *e* her flesh and burn her
19:18 so that you may *e* the flesh of kings,

EATEN (EAT)

Ge 3:11 Have you *e* from the tree that I
6:21 kind of food that is to be *e*
14:24 nothing but what my men have *e*
31:38 nor have I *e* rams from your flocks.
31:54 After they had *e*, they spent
43:2 when they had *e* all the grain they
Ex 12:46 "It must be *e* inside one house;
21:28 and its meat must not be *e*.
29:34 It must not be *e*, because it is
Lev 6:16 but it is to be *e* without yeast
6:23 completely; it must not be *e*."
6:26 it is to be *e* in a holy place,
6:30 in the Holy Place must not be *e*;
7:6 but it must be *e* in a holy place;
7:15 offering of thanksgiving must be *e*
7:16 left over may be *e* on the next day.
7:16 the sacrifice shall be *e*
7:18 meat of the fellowship offering is *e*
7:19 unclean must not be *e*;
10:18 you should have *e* the goat
10:19 if I had *e* the sin offering today?"
11:34 Any food that could be *e*
11:41 is detestable; it is not to be *e*.
11:47 and those that may not be *e*.' "
11:47 living creatures that may be *e*
17:13 bird that may be *e* must drain out
19:6 It shall be *e* on the day you sacrifice
19:7 If any of it is *e* on the third day,
19:23 it forbidden; it must not be *e*.
22:30 It must be *e* that same day;
25:7 the land produces may be *e*.
Nu 12:12 womb with its flesh half *e* away."
Dt 8:10 When you have *e* and are satisfied,
26:14 I have not *e* any of the sacred
Ru 2:18 left over after she had *e* enough.
1Sa 14:30 been if the men had *e* today some
28:20 for he had *e* nothing all that day
30:12 for he had not *e* any food
2Sa 19:42 Have we *e* any of the king's
1Ki 13:28 The lion had neither *e* the body
Job 6:6 Is tasteless food *e* without salt,
13:28 like a garment *e* by moths.
Pr 9:17 food *e* in secret is delicious!"
23:8 will vomit up the little you have *e*
30:17 will be *e* by the vultures.
SS 5:1 I have *e* my honeycomb
Jer 24:2 so bad they could not be *e*.
24:3 are so bad they cannot be *e*."
24:8 which are so bad they cannot be *e*,'
29:17 are so bad they cannot be *e*.
31:29 'The fathers have *e* sour grapes,
Eze 4:14 I have never *e* anything found dead

Hos 10: 13 you have *e* the fruit of deception.
Joel 1: 4 other locusts have *e*.
1: 4 the great locusts have *e;*
1: 4 the young locusts have *e;*
2: 25 for the years the locusts have *e*—
Mk 6: 44 men who had *e* was five thousand.
Jn 6: 13 left over by those who had *e*.
6: 23 where the people had *e* the bread
Ac 10: 14 "I have never *e* anything impure
12: 23 and he was *e* by worms and died.
27: 33 food—you haven't *e* anything.
27: 38 When they had *e* as much
Jas 5: 2 and moths have *e* your clothes.
Rev 10: 10 when I had *e* it, my stomach turned

EATER (EAT)

Jdg 14: 14 "Out of the *e*, something to eat;
Isa 55: 10 for the sower and bread for the *e*,
Na 3: 12 the figs fall into the mouth of the *e*.

EATING (EAT)

Ge 40: 17 but the birds were *e* them out
Ex 34: 28 and forty nights without *e* bread
Lev 26: 10 will still be *e* last year's harvest
Dt 27: 7 *e* them and rejoicing
28: 55 the flesh of his children that he is *e*.
Jdg 9: 27 While they were *e* and drinking,
19: 4 *e* and drinking, and sleeping there.
Ru 3: 3 there until he has finished *e*
3: 7 When Boaz had finished *e*
1Sa 1: 9 Once when they had finished *e*
9: 13 The people will not begin *e*
14: 33 LORD by *e* meat that has blood
14: 34 sin against the LORD by *e* meat
30: 16 scattered over the countryside, *e*,
1Ki 1: 25 Right now they are *e* and drinking
13: 23 the man of God had finished *e*
2Ki 6: 23 and after they had finished *e*
1Ch 12: 39 three days there with David, *e*
Isa 22: 13 *e* of meat and drinking of wine!
29: 8 a hungry man dreams that he is *e*,
Jer 41: 1 While they were *e* together there,
Da 6: 18 and spent the night without *e*
Zec 7: 6 And when you were *e* and drinking
Mt 11: 18 For John came neither *e*
11: 19 The Son of Man came *e*
15: 20 *e* with unwashed hands does not
24: 38 people were *e* and drinking,
26: 21 And while they were *e*, he said,
26: 26 While they were *e*, Jesus took
Mk 2: 15 and "sinners" were *e* with him
2: 16 law who were Pharisees saw him *e*
7: 2 some of his disciples *e* food
7: 5 of the elders instead of *e* their food
14: 18 they were reclining at the table *e*,
14: 18 you will betray me—one who is *e*
14: 22 While they were *e*, Jesus took
16: 14 to the Eleven as they were *e;*
Lk 5: 29 and others were *e* with them.
5: 33 but yours go on *e* and drinking."
7: 33 the Baptist came neither *e* bread
7: 34 The Son of Man came *e*
7: 37 that town learned that Jesus was *e*
10: 7 *e* and drinking whatever they give
15: 16 with the pods that the pigs were *e*,
17: 27 People were *e*, drinking, marrying
17: 28 People were *e* and drinking,
Jn 21: 15 When they had finished *e*,
Ac 1: 4 while he was *e* with them,
Ro 14: 15 not by your *e* destroy your brother
14: 17 kingdom of God is not a matter of *e*
14: 23 because his *e* is not from faith;
1Co 8: 4 about *e* food sacrificed to idols:
8: 10 you who have this knowledge *e*
Jude : 12 *e* with you without the slightest
Rev 2: 14 to sin by *e* food sacrificed to idols
2: 20 and the *e* of food sacrificed to idols.

EATS (EAT)

Ex 12: 15 for whoever *e* anything with yeast
12: 19 whoever *e* anything with yeast
Lev 7: 18 the person who *e* any
7: 20 anyone who is unclean *e* any meat
7: 21 and then *e* any of the meat
7: 25 Anyone who *e* the fat of an animal
7: 27 If anyone *e* blood, that person must
11: 40 Anyone who *e* some
14: 47 or *e* in the house must wash his
Lev 17: 10 against that person who *e* blood
17: 10 among them who *e* any blood—
17: 14 anyone who *e* it must be cut off."
17: 15 who *e* anything found dead
19: 8 Whoever *e* it will be held
22: 14 " 'If anyone *e* a sacred offering
1Sa 14: 24 "Cursed be any man who *e* food
14: 28 be any man who *e* food today!'
2Sa 19: 35 Can your servant taste what he *e*
Job 18: 13 It *e* away parts of his skin;
39: 24 frenzied excitement he *e* up
Ps 106: 20 for an image of a bull, which *e* grass
Pr 30: 20 She *e* and wipes her mouth
Ecc 5: 12 whether he *e* little or much,
5: 17 All his days he *e* in darkness,
Isa 44: 16 he roasts his meat and *e* his fill.
59: 5 Whoever *e* their eggs will die,
Jer 31: 30 own sin; whoever *e* sour grapes—
Eze 18: 11 "He *e* at the mountain shrines.
Lk 15: 2 "This man welcomes sinners and *e*
Jn 6: 51 If a man *e* of this bread, he will live
6: 54 Whoever *e* my flesh and drinks my
6: 56 Whoever *e* my flesh and drinks my
Ro 14: 2 faith is weak, *e* only vegetables.
14: 3 man who *e* everything must not
14: 6 He who *e* meat, *e* to the Lord,
14: 23 has doubts is condemned if he *e*,
1Co 11: 27 whoever *e* the bread or drinks
11: 28 himself before he *e* of the bread
11: 29 For anyone who *e* and drinks
11: 29 recognizing the body of the Lord *e*

EAVES

1Ki 7: 9 and from foundation to *e*,

EBAL

Ge 36: 23 Manahath, *E*, Shepho and Onam.
Dt 11: 29 and on Mount *E* the curses.
27: 4 set up these stones on Mount *E*,
27: 13 on Mount *E* to pronounce curses:
Jos 8: 30 Joshua built on Mount *E* an altar
8: 33 half of them in front of Mount *E*,
1Ch 1: 40 Manahath, *E*, Shepho and Onam.

EBB (EBBED EBBING EBBS)

La 2: 12 as their lives *e* away

EBBED (EBB)

Ps 107: 5 and their lives *e* away.

EBBING (EBB)

Jnh 2: 7 "When my life was *e* away,

EBBS (EBB)

Job 30: 16 "And now my life *e* away;

EBED

Jdg 9: 26 Now Gaal son of *E* moved
9: 28 son of *E* said, "Who is Abimelech,
9: 30 city heard what Gaal son of *E* said,
9: 31 of *E* and his brothers have come
9: 35 Now Gaal son of *E* had gone out
Ezr 8: 6 of Adin, *E* son of Jonathan,

EBED-MELECH

Jer 38: 7 But *E*, a Cushite, an official
38: 8 *E* went out of the palace
38: 10 the king commanded *E* the Cushite
38: 11 So *E* took the men with him
38: 12 *E* the Cushite said to Jeremiah,
39: 16 "Go and tell *E* the Cushite,

EBENEZER

1Sa 4: 1 The Israelites camped at *E*,
5: 1 they took it from *E* to Ashdod.
7: 12 He named it *E*, saying, "Thus far

EBER

Ge 10: 21 the ancestor of all the sons of *E*.
10: 24 and Shelah the father of *E*.
10: 25 born to *E:* One was named Peleg,
11: 14 he became the father of *E*.
11: 15 after he became the father of *E*,
11: 16 When *E* had lived 34 years,
11: 17 *E* lived 430 years and had other
Nu 24: 24 they will subdue Asshur and *E*,
1Ch 1: 18 and Shelah the father of *E*.
1: 19 born to *E:* One was named Peleg,
1Ch 1: 25 Arphaxad, Shelah, *E*, Peleg, Reu,
5: 13 Jacan, Zia and *E*— seven in all.
8: 12 The sons of Elpaal: *E*, Misham,
8: 22 Ishpan, *E*, Eliel, Abdon, Zicri,
Ne 12: 20 Kallai; of Amok's, *E;* of Hilkiah's,
Lk 3: 35 the son of Peleg, the son of *E*,

EBEZ

Jos 19: 20 Rabbith, Kishion, *E*, Remeth,

EBIASAPH

1Ch 6: 23 Elkanah his son, *E* his son,
6: 37 the son of *E*, the son of Korah,
9: 19 the son of *E*, the son of Korah,

EBONY

Eze 27: 15 you with ivory tusks and *e*.

ECBATANA

Ezr 6: 2 in the citadel of *E* in the province

ECHO (ECHOES)

Hab 2: 11 the beams of the woodwork will *e* it
Zep 2: 14 calls will *e* through the windows,

ECHOES (ECHO)

Isa 15: 8 Their outcry *e* along the border

EDEN

Ge 2: 8 in *E;* and there he put the man he
2: 10 the garden flowed from *E*,
2: 15 him in the Garden of *E* to work it
3: 23 him from the Garden of *E*
3: 24 side of the Garden of *E* cherubim
4: 16 lived in the land of Nod, east of *E*.
2Ki 19: 12 people of *E* who were in Tel Assar?
2Ch 29: 12 son of Zimmah and *E* son of Joah;
31: 15 *E*, Miniamin, Jeshua, Shemaiah,
Isa 37: 12 Rezeph and the people of *E*
51: 3 he will make her deserts like *E*,
Eze 27: 23 and *E* and merchants of Sheba,
28: 13 You were in *E*,
31: 9 the envy of all the trees of *E*
31: 16 Then all the trees of *E*, the choicest
31: 18 of the trees of *E* can be compared
31: 18 with the trees of *E* to the earth
36: 35 has become like the garden of *E;*
Joel 2: 3 the land is like the garden of *E*,

EDER

Jos 15: 21 *E*, Jagur, Kinah, Dimonah,
1Ch 8: 15 Zebadiah, Arad, *E*, Michael,
23: 23 The sons of Mushi: Mahli, *E*
24: 30 And the sons of Mushi: Mahli, *E*

EDGE (DOUBLE-EDGED EDGES)

Ex 13: 20 at Etham on the *e* of the desert.
26: 4 along the *e* of the end curtain
26: 10 also along the *e* of the end curtain
26: 10 loops along the *e* of the end curtain
28: 26 on the inside *e* next to the ephod.
28: 32 shall be a woven *e* like a collar
36: 11 along the *e* of the end curtain
36: 17 also along the *e* of the end curtain
36: 17 loops along the *e* of the end curtain
39: 19 on the inside *e* next to the ephod.
Nu 20: 16 a town on the *e* of your territory.
22: 36 at the *e* of his territory.
33: 6 at Etham, on the *e* of the desert.
Jos 3: 8 'When you reach the *e*
3: 15 their feet touched the water's *e*,
Jdg 7: 17 When I get to the *e* of the camp,
7: 19 with him reached the *e* of the camp
1Sa 9: 27 going down to the *e* of the town,
15: 27 Saul caught hold of the *e* of his robe
2Ki 7: 5 When they reached the *e*
7: 8 men who had leprosy reached the *e*
1Ch 5: 9 to the *e* of the desert that extends
Ps 89: 43 You have turned back the *e*
Ecc 10: 10 and its *e* unsharpened,
Jer 31: 29 and the children's teeth are set on *e*
31: 30 his own teeth will be set on *e*.
Eze 18: 2 and the children's teeth are set on *e*
43: 13 with a rim of one span around the *e*
Am 3: 12 Samaria on the *e* of their beds
Zec 8: 23 hold of one Jew by the *e* of his robe
Mt 9: 20 and touched the *e* of his cloak.
14: 36 him to let the sick just touch the *e*

Mk 4: 1 along the shore at the water's *e*.
6: 56 him to let them touch even the *e*
Lk 5: 2 he saw at the water's *e* two boats,
8: 44 and touched the *e* of his cloak,
Heb 11: 34 and escaped the *e* of the sword;

EDGES (EDGE)

Lev 19: 9 reap to the very *e* of your field
19: 27 or clip off the *e* of your beard.
21: 5 or shave off the *e* of their beards
23: 22 reap to the very *e* of your field
Job 38: 13 that it might take the earth by the *e*

EDICT

Ezr 6: 11 that if anyone changes this *e*,
Est 1: 20 when the king's *e* is proclaimed
2: 8 and *e* had been proclaimed,
3: 14 of the text of the *e* was to be issued
3: 15 and the *e* was issued in the citadel
4: 3 In every province to which the *e*
4: 8 text of the *e* for their annihilation,
8: 11 The king's *e* granted the Jews
8: 13 of the text of the *e* was to be issued
8: 14 the *e* was also issued in the citadel
8: 17 wherever the *e* of the king went,
9: 1 the *e* commanded by the king was
9: 13 to carry out this day's *e* tomorrow
9: 14 An *e* was issued in Susa,
Da 6: 7 that the king should issue an *e*
6: 15 or *e* that the king issues can be
Heb 11: 23 they were not afraid of the king's *e*.

EDIFICATION (EDIFIED EDIFIES)

Ro 14: 19 leads to peace and to mutual *e*.

EDIFIED (EDIFICATION)

1Co 14: 5 so that the church may be *e*.
14: 17 but the other man is not *e*.

EDIFIES (EDIFICATION)

1Co 14: 4 but he who prophesies *e* the church
14: 4 speaks in a tongue *e* himself,

EDOM (EDOM'S EDOMITE EDOMITES)

Ge 25: 30 (That is why he was also called *E*.)
32: 3 in the land of Seir, the country of *E*
36: 1 the account of Esau (that is, *E*).
36: 8 *E*) settled in the hill country of Seir
36: 16 descended from Eliphaz in *E*;
36: 17 chiefs descended from Reuel in *E*;
36: 19 *E*), and these were their chiefs.
36: 21 of Seir in *E* were Horite chiefs.
36: 31 in *E* before any Israelite king
36: 32 Bela son of Beor became king of *E*.
36: 43 These were the chiefs of *E*,
Ex 15: 15 The chiefs of *E* will be terrified,
Nu 20: 14 from Kadesh to the king of *E*,
20: 18 *E* answered: "You may not pass
20: 20 Then *E* came out against them
20: 21 Since *E* refused to let them go
20: 23 near the border of *E*,
21: 4 to the Red Sea, to go around *E*.
24: 18 *E* will be conquered;
33: 37 at Mount Hor, on the border of *E*.
34: 3 of Zin along the border of *E*.
Jos 15: 1 down to the territory of *E*,
15: 21 toward the boundary of *E* were:
Jdg 5: 4 marched from the land of *E*,
11: 17 but the king of *E* would not listen.
11: 17 sent messengers to the king of *E*,
11: 18 skirted the lands of *E* and Moab,
1Sa 14: 47 Moab, the Ammonites, *E*,
2Sa 8: 12 *E* and Moab, the Ammonites
8: 14 He put garrisons throughout *E*,
1Ki 9: 26 is near Elath in *E*, on the shore
11: 14 from the royal line of *E*.
11: 15 had struck down all the men in *E*.
11: 15 when David was fighting with *E*,
11: 16 had destroyed all the men in *E*.
22: 47 There was then no king in *E*;
2Ki 3: 8 "Through the Desert of *E*,"
3: 9 the king of Judah and the king of *E*.
3: 12 the king of *E* went down to him.
3: 20 flowing from the direction of *E*!
3: 26 to break through to the king of *E*,
8: 20 *E* rebelled against Judah
8: 22 To this day *E* has been in rebellion
14: 10 You have indeed defeated *E*
1Ch 1: 43 in *E* before any Israelite king
1: 51 The chiefs of *E* were: Timna, Alvah
1: 54 These were the chiefs of *E*.
18: 11 *E* and Moab, the Ammonites
18: 13 He put garrisons in *E*,
2Ch 8: 17 and Elath on the seacoast of *E*.
20: 2 coming against you from *E*,
21: 8 *E* rebelled against Judah
21: 10 To this day *E* has been in rebellion
25: 19 yourself that you have defeated *E*,
25: 20 because they sought the gods of *E*.
Ps 60: 8 upon *E* I toss my sandal;
60: 9 Who will lead me to *E*?
83: 6 the tents of *E* and the Ishmaelites,
108: 9 upon *E* I toss my sandal;
108: 10 Who will lead me to *E*?
Isa 11: 14 They will lay hands on *E* and Moab
34: 5 see, it descends in judgment on *E*,
34: 6 and a great slaughter in *E*.
34: 11 God will stretch out over *E*
63: 1 Who is this coming from *E*,
Jer 9: 26 Egypt, Judah, *E*, Ammon,
25: 21 and the people left at Ashdod); *E*,
27: 3 Then send word to the kings of *E*,
40: 11 *E* and all the other countries heard
49: 7 Concerning *E*: This is what
49: 17 "*E* will become an object of horror;
49: 19 I will chase *E* from its land
49: 20 the LORD has planned against *E*,
La 4: 21 be glad, O Daughter of *E*,
4: 22 of *E*, he will punish your sin
Eze 16: 57 scorned by the daughters of *E*
25: 12 'Because *E* took revenge
25: 13 I will stretch out my hand against *E*
25: 14 I will take vengeance on *E*
25: 14 they will deal with *E* in accordance
32: 29 "*E* is there, her kings and all her
35: 15 O Mount Seir, you and all of *E*.
36: 5 of the nations, and against all *E*,
Da 11: 41 Many countries will fall, but *E*,
Joel 3: 19 *E* a desert waste,
Am 1: 6 and sold them to *E*,
1: 9 communities of captives to *E*,
1: 11 "For three sins of *E*,
9: 12 they may possess the remnant of *E*
Ob : 1 Sovereign LORD says about *E*—
: 8 will I not destroy the wise men of *E*
Mal 1: 4 *E* may say, "Though we have been

EDOM'S (EDOM)

Isa 34: 9 *E* streams will be turned into pitch,
Jer 49: 22 In that day the hearts of *E* warriors
Am 2: 1 the bones of *E* king,

EDOMITE (EDOM)

Dt 23: 7 Do not abhor an *E*,
1Sa 21: 7 was Doeg the *E*, Saul's head
22: 9 But Doeg the *E*, who was standing
22: 18 Doeg the *E* turned and struck them
22: 22 when Doeg the *E* was there,
1Ki 11: 14 Hadad the *E*, from the royal line
11: 17 with some *E* officials who had

EDOMITES (EDOM)

Ge 36: 9 father of the *E* in the hill country
36: 43 This was Esau, the father of the *E*.
2Sa 8: 13 striking down eighteen thousand *E*
8: 14 all the *E* became subject to David.
1Ki 11: 1 Moabites, Ammonites, *E*,
2Ki 8: 21 The *E* surrounded him
14: 7 one who defeated ten thousand *E*
16: 6 *E* then moved into Elath
1Ch 18: 12 struck down eighteen thousand *E*
18: 13 all the *E* became subject to David.
2Ch 21: 9 The *E* surrounded him
25: 14 returned from slaughtering the *E*,
28: 17 The *E* had again come
Ps 137: 7 O LORD, what the *E* did

EDREI

Nu 21: 33 out to meet them in battle at *E*.
Dt 1: 4 and at *E* had defeated Og king
3: 1 out to meet us in battle at *E*.
3: 10 all Bashan as far as Salecah and *E*,
Jos 12: 4 who reigned in Ashtaroth and *E*.
13: 12 reigned in Ashtaroth and *E*
13: 31 *E* (the royal cities of Og in Bashan
19: 37 Ramah, Hazor, Kedesh, *E*,

EDUCATED

Ac 7: 22 Moses was *e* in all the wisdom

EFFECT (EFFECTIVE EFFECTS)

Job 41: 26 sword that reaches him has no *e*,
Isa 32: 17 *e* of righteousness will be quietness
Ac 7: 53 put into *e* through angels
1Co 15: 10 his grace to me was not without *e*.
Gal 3: 19 put into *e* through angels
Eph 1: 10 put into *e* when the times will have
Heb 9: 17 it never takes *e* while the one who
9: 18 put into *e* without blood.

EFFECTIVE (EFFECT)

1Co 16: 9 a great door for *e* work has opened
Jas 5: 16 a righteous man is powerful and *e*.

EFFECTS (EFFECT)

Ac 28: 5 off into the fire and suffered no ill *e*

EFFORT (EFFORTS)

Ecc 2: 19 into which I have poured my *e*
Da 6: 14 and made every *e* until sundown
Lk 13: 24 "Make every *e* to enter
Jn 5: 44 yet make no *e* to obtain the praise
Ro 9: 16 depend on man's desire or *e*,
14: 19 make every *e* to do what leads
Gal 3: 3 to attain your goal by human *e*?
Eph 4: 3 Make every *e* to keep the unity
1Th 2: 16 to all men in their *e* to keep us
2: 17 intense longing we made every *e*
Heb 4: 11 make every *e* to enter that rest,
12: 14 Make every *e* to live in peace
2Pe 1: 5 make every *e* to add
1: 15 And I will make every *e* to see that
3: 14 make every *e* to be found spotless,

EFFORTS (EFFORT)

Job 36: 19 or even all your mighty *e*
Ecc 6: 7 All man's *e* are for his mouth,
8: 17 Despite all his *e* to search it out,
Eze 24: 12 It has frustrated all *e*;
29: 20 as a reward for his *e* because he
Gal 4: 11 that somehow I have wasted my *e*
1Th 3: 5 and our *e* might have been useless

EGG (EGGS)

Job 6: 6 is there flavor in the white of an *e*?
Lk 11: 12 for an *e*, will give him a scorpion?

EGGS (EGG)

Dt 22: 6 sitting on the young or on the *e*,
Job 39: 14 She lays her *e* on the ground
Isa 10: 14 as men gather abandoned *e*,
34: 15 The owl will nest there and lay *e*,
59: 5 They hatch the *e* of vipers
59: 5 Whoever eats their *e* will die,
Jer 17: 11 a partridge that hatches *e* it did not

EGLAH

2Sa 3: 5 Ithream the son of David's wife *E*.
1Ch 3: 3 the sixth, Ithream, by his wife *E*.

EGLAIM

Isa 15: 8 their wailing reaches as far as *E*,

EGLATH SHELISHIYAH

Isa 15: 5 as far as *E*.
Jer 48: 34 as far as Horonaim and *E*,

EGLON

Jos 10: 3 of Lachish and Debir king of *E*.
10: 5 Lachish and *E*—joined forces.
10: 23 Hebron, Jarmuth, Lachish and *E*.
10: 34 moved on from Lachish to *E*;
10: 36 up from *E* to Hebron
10: 37 as at *E*, they totally destroyed it
12: 12 one the king of *E* one the king
15: 39 Lachish, Bozkath, *E*, Cabbon,
Jdg 3: 12 did this evil the LORD gave *E* king
3: 13 *E* came and attacked Israel,
3: 14 subject to *E* king of Moab
3: 15 him with tribute to *E* king of Moab.
3: 17 the tribute to *E* king of Moab,

EGYPT (EGYPT'S EGYPTIAN EGYPTIAN'S EGYPTIANS)

Ge 12: 10 went down to *E* to live there

Ge 12: 11 As he was about to enter *E*,
12: 14 to *E*, the Egyptians saw that she
13: 1 up from *E* to the Negev,
13: 10 like the land of *E*, toward Zoar.
15: 18 from the river of *E*
21: 21 mother got a wife for him from *E*.
25: 18 near the border of *E*, as you go
26: 2 "Do not go down to *E*; live
37: 25 way to take them down to *E*.
37: 28 Ishmaelites, who took him to *E*.
37: 36 the Midianites sold Joseph in *E*
39: 1 Joseph had been taken down to *E*.
40: 1 king of *E* offended their master,
40: 1 their master, the king of *E*.
40: 5 and the baker of the king of *E*,
41: 8 the magicians and wise men of *E*.
41: 19 cows in all the land of *E*.
41: 29 coming throughout the land of *E*,
41: 30 abundance in *E* will be forgotten,
41: 33 put him in charge of the land of *E*.
41: 34 a fifth of the harvest of *E*
41: 36 of famine that will come upon *E*,
41: 41 in charge of the whole land of *E*."
41: 43 in charge of the whole land of *E*.
41: 44 one will lift hand or foot in all *E*."
41: 45 went throughout the land of *E*.
41: 46 and traveled throughout *E*.
41: 46 the service of Pharaoh king of *E*.
41: 48 years of abundance in *E*
41: 53 of abundance in *E* came to an end,
41: 54 land of *E* there was food.
41: 55 When all *E* began to feel
41: 56 famine was severe throughout *E*.
41: 57 And all the countries came to *E*
42: 1 learned that there was grain in *E*,
42: 2 I have heard that there is grain in *E*
42: 3 went down to buy grain from *E*.
43: 2 the grain they had brought from *E*,
43: 15 They hurried down to *E*
45: 4 the one you sold into *E*! And now,
45: 8 entire household and ruler of all *E*.
45: 9 God has made me lord of all *E*.
45: 13 all the honor accorded me in *E*
45: 18 give you the best of the land of *E*
45: 19 carts from *E* for your children
45: 20 the best of all *E* will be yours.' "
45: 23 loaded with the best things of *E*,
45: 25 So they went up out of *E*
45: 26 In fact, he is ruler of all *E*."
46: 3 "Do not be afraid to go down to *E*,
46: 4 I will go down to *E* with you,
46: 6 and all his offspring went to *E*.
46: 7 He took with him to *E* his sons
46: 8 his descendants) who went to *E*:
46: 20 In *E*, Manasseh and Ephraim were
46: 26 All those who went to *E* with Jacob
46: 27 which went to *E*, were seventy
46: 27 who had been born to Joseph in *E*,
47: 6 and the land of *E* is before you;
47: 11 his father and his brothers in *E*
47: 13 both *E* and Canaan wasted away
47: 14 money that was to be found in *E*
47: 15 When the money of the people of *E*
47: 15 all *E* came to Joseph and said,
47: 20 So Joseph bought all the land in *E*
47: 21 from one end of *E* to the other.
47: 26 as a law concerning land in *E*—
47: 27 Now the Israelites settled in *E*
47: 28 Jacob lived in *E* seventeen years,
47: 29 me in *E*, but when I rest
47: 30 of *E* and bury me where they are
48: 5 born to you in *E* before I came
50: 7 and all the dignitaries of *E*—
50: 14 his father, Joseph returned to *E*,
50: 22 Joseph stayed in *E*,
50: 26 he was placed in a coffin in *E*.
Ex 1: 1 of Israel who entered *E* with Jacob,
1: 5 in all; Joseph was already in *E*.
1: 8 about Joseph, came to power in *E*.
1: 15 The king of *E* said
1: 17 the king of *E* had told them to do;
1: 18 king of *E* summoned the midwives
2: 23 that long period, the king of *E* died.
3: 7 the misery of my people in *E*.
3: 10 my people the Israelites out of *E*."
3: 11 and bring the Israelites out of *E*?"
3: 12 have brought the people out of *E*,
3: 16 what has been done to you in *E*.
Ex 3: 17 of your misery in *E* into the land
3: 18 the elders are to go to the king of *E*
3: 19 the king of *E* will not let you go
4: 18 to my own people in *E* to see if any
4: 19 to *E*, for all the men who wanted
4: 20 on a donkey and started back to *E*.
4: 21 to Moses, "When you return to *E*,
5: 4 But the king of *E* said, "Moses
5: 12 all over *E* to gather stubble
6: 11 tell Pharaoh king of *E*
6: 13 Israelites and Pharaoh king of *E*,
6: 13 to bring the Israelites out of *E*.
6: 26 out of *E* by their divisions."
6: 27 bringing the Israelites out of *E*.
6: 27 of *E* about bringing the Israelites
6: 28 the LORD spoke to Moses in *E*,
6: 29 king of *E* everything I tell you."
7: 3 miraculous signs and wonders in *E*,
7: 4 Then I will lay my hand on *E*
7: 5 I stretch out my hand against *E*
7: 19 Blood will be everywhere in *E*,
7: 19 hand over the waters of *E*—
7: 21 Blood was everywhere in *E*.
8: 5 up on the land of *E*.' "
8: 6 hand over the waters of *E*,
8: 7 frogs come up on the land of *E*.
8: 16 of *E* the dust will become gnats."
8: 17 the land of *E* became gnats.
8: 24 throughout *E* the land was ruined
9: 4 the livestock of Israel and that of *E*,
9: 9 dust over the whole land of *E*,
9: 18 hailstorm that has ever fallen on *E*,
9: 22 growing in the fields of *E*."
9: 22 sky so that hail will fall all over *E*—
9: 23 LORD rained hail on the land of *E*;
9: 24 storm in all the land of *E*
9: 25 Throughout *E* hail struck
10: 7 not yet realize that *E* is ruined?"
10: 12 "Stretch out your hand over *E*
10: 13 stretched out his staff over *E*,
10: 14 they invaded all *E* and settled
10: 15 or plant in all the land of *E*.
10: 19 Not a locust was left anywhere in *E*
10: 21 so that darkness will spread over *E*
10: 22 and total darkness covered all *E*
11: 1 plague on Pharaoh and on *E*.
11: 3 in *E* by Pharaoh's officials
11: 4 midnight I will go throughout *E*.
11: 5 Every firstborn son in *E* will die,
11: 6 be loud wailing throughout *E*—
11: 7 makes a distinction between *E*
11: 9 wonders may be multiplied in *E*."
12: 1 said to Moses and Aaron in *E*,
12: 12 judgment on all the gods of *E*.
12: 12 same night I will pass through *E*
12: 13 will touch you when I strike *E*.
12: 17 I brought your divisions out of *E*.
12: 27 the houses of the Israelites in *E*
12: 29 struck down all the firstborn in *E*,
12: 30 and there was loud wailing in *E*,
12: 39 dough they had brought from *E*,
12: 39 they had been driven out of *E*
12: 40 lived in *E* was 430 years.
12: 41 all the LORD's divisions left *E*.
12: 42 night to bring them out of *E*,
12: 51 out of *E* by their divisions.
13: 3 the day you came out of *E*,
13: 8 did for me when I came out of *E*.'
13: 9 out of *E* with his mighty hand.
13: 14 the LORD brought us out of *E*,
13: 15 LORD killed every firstborn in *E*,
13: 16 out of *E* with his mighty hand."
13: 17 their minds and return to *E*."
13: 18 out of *E* armed for battle.
14: 5 of *E* was told that the people had
14: 7 with all the other chariots of *E*,
14: 8 the heart of Pharaoh king of *E*,
14: 11 done to us by bringing us out of *E*?
14: 11 graves in *E* that you brought us
14: 12 Didn't we say to you in *E*,
14: 20 coming between the armies of *E*
14: 25 fighting for them against *E*."
16: 1 after they had come out of *E*.
16: 3 died by the LORD's hand in *E*!
16: 6 LORD who brought you out of *E*,
16: 32 when I brought you out of *E*.' "
17: 3 "Why did you bring us up out of *E*
18: 1 LORD had brought Israel out of *E*.
Ex 19: 1 month after the Israelites left *E*—
19: 4 have seen what I did to *E*,
20: 2 who brought you out of *E*,
22: 21 for you were aliens in *E*.
23: 9 because you were aliens in *E*.
23: 15 in that month you came out of *E*.
29: 46 who brought them out of *E*
32: 1 Moses who brought us up out of *E*,
32: 4 who brought you up out of *E*."
32: 7 whom you brought up out of *E*,
32: 8 who brought you up out of *E*.'
32: 11 out of *E* with great power
32: 23 Moses who brought us up out of *E*,
33: 1 the people you brought up out of *E*,
34: 18 in that month you came out of *E*.
Lev 11: 45 out of *E* to be your God;
18: 3 You must not do as they do in *E*,
19: 34 yourself, for you were aliens in *E*.
19: 36 who brought you out of *E*.
22: 33 out of *E* to be your God.
23: 43 when I brought them out of *E*.
25: 38 who brought you out of *E*
25: 42 out of *E*, they must not be sold
25: 55 servants, whom I brought out of *E*.
26: 13 who brought you out of *E*
26: 45 out of *E* in the sight of the nations
Nu 1: 1 after the Israelites came out of *E*.
3: 13 struck down all the firstborn in *E*,
8: 17 struck down all the firstborn in *E*,
9: 1 year after they came out of *E*.
11: 5 We remember the fish we ate in *E*
11: 18 We were better off in *E*!"
11: 20 "Why did we ever leave *E*?" ' "
13: 22 years before Zoan in *E*.)
14: 2 "If only we had died in *E*!
14: 3 better for us to go back to *E*?"
14: 4 choose a leader and go back to *E*."
14: 19 from the time they left *E* until now
14: 22 miraculous signs I performed in *E*
15: 41 out of *E* to be your God.
20: 5 out of *E* to this terrible place?
20: 15 Our forefathers went down into *E*,
20: 16 an angel and brought us out of *E*.
21: 5 out of *E* to die in the desert?
22: 5 "A people has come out of *E*;
22: 11 out of *E* covers the face of the land.
23: 22 God brought them out of *E*;
24: 8 "God brought them out of *E*;
26: 4 the Israelites who came out of *E*:
26: 59 who was born to the Levites in *E*.
32: 11 of *E* will see the land I promised
33: 1 Israelites when they came out of *E*
33: 38 after the Israelites came out of *E*.
34: 5 join the Wadi of *E* and end
Dt 1: 27 so he brought us out of *E*
1: 30 for you in *E*, before your very eyes,
4: 20 out of *E*, to be the people
4: 34 for you in *E* before your very eyes?
4: 37 out of *E* by his Presence
4: 45 them when they came out of *E*
4: 46 the Israelites as they came out of *E*.
5: 6 who brought you out of *E*,
5: 15 that you were slaves in *E*
6: 12 who brought you out of *E*,
6: 21 out of *E* with a mighty hand.
6: 21 "We were slaves of Pharaoh in *E*,
6: 22 upon *E* and Pharaoh and his whole
7: 8 the power of Pharaoh king of *E*.
7: 15 horrible diseases you knew in *E*,
7: 18 did to Pharaoh and to all *E*.
8: 14 who brought you out of *E*,
9: 7 From the day you left *E*
9: 12 out of *E* have become corrupt.
9: 26 out of *E* with a mighty hand.
10: 19 for you yourselves were aliens in *E*.
10: 22 down into *E* were seventy in all,
11: 3 both to Pharaoh king of *E*
11: 3 the things he did in the heart of *E*,
11: 10 to take over is not like the land of *E*
13: 5 who brought you out of *E*
13: 10 who brought you out of *E*,
15: 15 that you were slaves in *E*
16: 1 of Abib he brought you out of *E*
16: 3 because you left *E* in haste—
16: 3 the time of your departure from *E*.
16: 6 of your departure from *E*.
16: 12 that you were slaves in *E*,
17: 16 or make the people return to *E*

Dt 20: 1 who brought you up out of *E*,
23: 4 way when you came out of *E*,
24: 9 the way after you came out of *E*.
24: 18 that you were slaves in *E*
24: 22 that you were slaves in *E*.
25: 17 the way when you came out of *E*.
26: 5 and he went down into *E*
26: 8 out of *E* with a mighty hand
28: 27 you with the boils of *E*
28: 60 the diseases of *E* that you dreaded,
28: 68 will send you back in ships to *E*
29: 2 seen all that the LORD did in *E*
29: 16 yourselves know how we lived in *E*
29: 25 when he brought them out of *E*.
34: 11 the LORD sent him to do in *E*—
Jos 2: 10 for you when you came out of *E*,
5: 4 All those who came out of *E*—
5: 4 desert on the way after leaving *E*.
5: 5 during the journey from *E* had not.
5: 6 age when they left *E* had died,
5: 9 have rolled away the reproach of *E*
9: 9 reports of him: all that he did in *E*,
13: 3 on the east of *E* to the territory
15: 4 to Azmon and joined the Wadi of *E*
15: 47 as far as the Wadi of *E*
24: 4 Jacob and his sons went down to *E*.
24: 6 I brought your fathers out of *E*,
24: 14 beyond the River and in *E*,
24: 17 and our forefathers up out of *E*,
24: 32 Israelites had brought up from *E*,
Jdg 2: 1 "I brought you up out of *E*
2: 12 who had brought them out of *E*.
6: 8 I brought you up out of *E*,
6: 9 I snatched you from the power of *E*
6: 13 the LORD bring us up out of *E*?'
11: 13 "When Israel came up out of *E*,
11: 16 But when they came up out of *E*,
19: 30 day the Israelites came up out of *E*.
1Sa 2: 27 were in *E* under Pharaoh?
8: 8 out of *E* until this day,
10: 18 says: 'I brought Israel up out of *E*,
10: 18 you from the power of *E*
12: 6 your forefathers up out of *E*.
12: 8 brought your forefathers out of *E*
12: 8 "After Jacob entered *E*, they cried
15: 2 them as they came up from *E*.
15: 6 when they came up out of *E*."
15: 7 Havilah to Shur, to the east of *E*.
27: 8 in the land extending to Shur and *E*
2Sa 7: 6 I brought the Israelites up out of *E*
7: 23 whom you redeemed from *E*?
1Ki 3: 1 an alliance with Pharaoh king of *E*
4: 21 as far as the border of *E*.
4: 30 greater than all the wisdom of *E*.
6: 1 the Israelites had come out of *E*,
8: 9 Israelites after they came out of *E*.
8: 16 I brought my people Israel out of *E*,
8: 21 when he brought them out of *E*."
8: 51 whom you brought out of *E*,
8: 53 brought our fathers out of *E*."
8: 65 Lebo Hamath to the Wadi of *E*.
9: 9 who brought their fathers out of *E*,
9: 16 (Pharaoh king of *E* had attacked
10: 28 horses were imported from *E*
10: 29 from *E* for six hundred shekels
11: 17 to *E* with some Edomite officials
11: 18 went to *E*, to Pharaoh king of *E*,
11: 21 was in *E*, Hadad heard that David
11: 40 but Jeroboam fled to *E*,
12: 2 Nebat heard this (he was still in *E*,
12: 2 Solomon), he returned from *E*.
12: 28 who brought you up out of *E*."
14: 25 king of *E* attacked Jerusalem.
2Ki 17: 4 he had sent envoys to So king of *E*,
17: 7 out of *E* from under the power
17: 7 the power of Pharaoh king of *E*.
17: 36 out of *E* with mighty power
18: 21 Look now, you are depending on *E*
18: 21 king of *E* to all who depend
18: 24 though you are depending on *E*
19: 9 king of *E*, was marching out
19: 24 I have dried up all the streams of *E*
21: 15 out of *E* until this day."
23: 29 Pharaoh Neco king of *E* went up
23: 34 Jehoahaz and carried him off to *E*,
24: 7 The king of *E* did not march out
24: 7 from the Wadi of *E*
25: 26 to *E* for fear of the Babylonians.

1Ch 13: 5 from the Shihor River in *E*
17: 5 the day I brought Israel up out of *E*
17: 21 whom you redeemed from *E*?
2Ch 1: 16 horses were imported from *E*
1: 17 from *E* for six hundred shekels
5: 10 Israelites after they came out of *E*.
6: 5 day I brought my people out of *E*,
7: 8 Lebo Hamath to the Wadi of *E*.
7: 22 who brought them out of *E*,
9: 26 as far as the border of *E*.
9: 28 horses were imported from *E*
10: 2 Solomon), he returned from *E*.
10: 2 of Nebat heard this (he was in *E*,
12: 2 king of *E* attacked Jerusalem
12: 3 that came with him from *E*,
12: 9 king of *E* attacked Jerusalem,
20: 10 to invade when they came from *E*;
26: 8 spread as far as the border of *E*,
35: 20 Neco king of *E* went up to fight
36: 3 The king of *E* dethroned him
36: 4 Jehoahaz and carried him off to *E*.
36: 4 The king of *E* made Eliakim,
Ne 9: 9 suffering of our forefathers in *E*;
9: 18 who brought you up out of *E*,'
Ps 68: 31 Envoys will come from *E*;
78: 12 in the land of *E*, in the region
78: 43 his miraculous signs in *E*,
78: 51 down all the firstborn of *E*,
80: 8 You brought a vine out of *E*;
81: 5 when he went out against *E*,
81: 10 who brought you up out of *E*.
105: 23 Then Israel entered *E*;
105: 38 *E* was glad when they left,
106: 7 When our fathers were in *E*,
106: 21 who had done great things in *E*,
114: 1 When Israel came out of *E*,
135: 8 He struck down the firstborn of *E*,
135: 9 wonders into your midst, O *E*,
136: 10 down the firstborn of *E*
Pr 7: 16 bed with colored linens from *E*.
Isa 7: 18 flies from the distant streams of *E*
10: 24 lift up a club against you, as *E* did.
10: 26 as he did in *E*.
11: 11 from Lower *E*, from Upper *E*,
11: 16 Israel when they came up from *E*.
19: 1 An oracle concerning *E*:
19: 1 The idols of *E* tremble before him,
19: 1 and is coming to *E*.
19: 6 the streams of *E* will dwindle
19: 12 has planned against *E*.
19: 13 have led *E* astray.
19: 14 they make *E* stagger
19: 15 There is nothing *E* can do—
19: 18 cities in *E* will speak the language
19: 19 to the LORD in the heart of *E*,
19: 20 LORD Almighty in the land of *E*.
19: 22 The LORD will strike *E*
19: 23 The Assyrians will go to *E*
19: 23 a highway from *E* to Assyria.
19: 24 along with *E* and Assyria,
19: 25 saying, "Blessed be *E* my people,
20: 3 and portent against *E* and Cush,
20: 5 and boasted in *E* will be afraid
23: 5 When word comes to *E*,
27: 12 Euphrates to the Wadi of *E*,
27: 13 who were exiled in *E* will come
30: 2 who go down to *E*
30: 7 to *E*, whose help is utterly useless.
31: 1 to those who go down to *E* for help,
36: 6 Look now, you are depending on *E*
36: 6 king of *E* to all who depend
36: 9 though you are depending on *E*
37: 9 king of *E*, was marching out
37: 25 I have dried up all the streams of *E*
43: 3 I give *E* for your ransom,
45: 14 products of *E* and the merchandise
52: 4 At first my people went down to *E*
Jer 2: 6 who brought us up out of *E*
2: 18 Now why go to *E*
2: 36 You will be disappointed by *E*
7: 22 I brought your forefathers out of *E*
7: 25 the time your forefathers left *E*
9: 26 *E*, Judah, Edom, Ammon,
11: 4 when I brought them out of *E*,
11: 7 up from *E* until today,
16: 14 brought the Israelites up out of *E*,'
23: 7 brought the Israelites up out of *E*,'
24: 8 they remain in this land or live in *E*

Jer 25: 19 Pharaoh king of *E*, his attendants,
26: 21 heard of it and fled in fear to *E*.
26: 22 sent Elnathan son of Acbor to *E*,
26: 23 They brought Uriah out of *E*
31: 32 the hand to lead them out of *E*,
32: 20 miraculous signs and wonders in *E*
32: 21 brought your people Israel out of *E*
34: 13 when I brought them out of *E*,
37: 5 army had marched out of *E*,
37: 7 will go back to its own land, to *E*.
41: 17 to *E* to escape the Babylonians.
42: 14 'No, we will go and live in *E*,
42: 15 'If you are determined to go to *E*
42: 16 you dread will follow you into *E*,
42: 17 to go to *E* to settle there will die
42: 18 out on you when you go to *E*.
42: 19 has told you, 'Do not go to *E*.'
43: 2 go to *E* to settle there.'
43: 7 So they entered *E* in disobedience
43: 11 He will come and attack *E*,
43: 12 fire to the temples of the gods of *E*;
43: 12 so will he wrap *E* around himself
43: 13 down the temples of the gods of *E*
43: 13 in *E* he will demolish the sacred
44: 1 all the Jews living in Lower *E*—
44: 1 and Memphis—and in Upper *E*:
44: 8 burning incense to other gods in *E*,
44: 12 to go to *E* to settle there.
44: 12 will all perish in *E*; they will fall
44: 13 live in *E* with the sword,
44: 14 gone to live in *E* will escape
44: 15 living in Lower and Upper *E*,
44: 24 all you people of Judah in *E*.
44: 26 all Jews living in *E*: 'I swear
44: 26 in *E* will ever again invoke my
44: 27 the Jews in *E* will perish by sword
44: 28 live in *E* will know whose word will
44: 28 of Judah from *E* will be very few.
44: 30 to hand Pharaoh Hophra king of *E*
46: 2 Concerning *E*: This is the message
46: 2 Pharaoh Neco king of *E*,
46: 8 *E* rises like the Nile,
46: 11 O Virgin Daughter of *E*.
46: 13 king of Babylon to attack *E*:
46: 14 this in *E*, and proclaim it
46: 17 king of *E* is only a loud noise;
46: 19 you who live in *E*,
46: 20 "*E* is a beautiful heifer,
46: 22 *E* will hiss like a fleeing serpent
46: 24 The Daughter of *E* will be put
46: 25 on *E* and her gods and her kings,
46: 26 *E* will be inhabited as in times past
La 5: 6 We submitted to *E* and Assyria
Eze 17: 15 him by sending his envoys to *E*
19: 4 hooks to the land of *E*.
20: 5 and revealed myself to them in *E*.
20: 6 of *E* into a land I had searched out
20: 7 yourselves with the idols of *E*.
20: 8 nor did they forsake the idols of *E*.
20: 8 spend my anger against them in *E*.
20: 9 by bringing them out of *E*.
20: 10 Therefore I led them out of *E*
20: 36 in the desert of the land of *E*,
23: 3 They became prostitutes in *E*,
23: 8 up the prostitution she began in *E*,
23: 19 when she was a prostitute in *E*.
23: 21 in *E* your bosom was caressed
23: 27 and prostitution you began in *E*.
23: 27 or remember *E* anymore.
27: 7 linen from *E* was your sail
29: 2 against him and against all *E*.
29: 2 face against Pharaoh king of *E*
29: 3 am against you, Pharaoh king of *E*,
29: 6 in *E* will know that I am the LORD
29: 9 *E* will become a desolate wasteland
29: 10 and I will make the land of *E* a ruin
29: 12 *E* desolate among devastated
29: 16 *E* will no longer be a source
29: 19 to give *E* to Nebuchadnezzar king
29: 20 I have given him *E* as a reward
30: 4 A sword will come against *E*,
30: 4 When the slain fall in *E*,
30: 5 fall by the sword along with *E*.
30: 6 " 'The allies of *E* will fall
30: 8 when I set fire to *E*
30: 10 will put an end to the hordes of *E*
30: 11 will draw their swords against *E*
30: 13 longer will there be a prince in *E*,

Eze 30: 15 the stronghold of *E*,
30: 16 I will set fire to *E*;
30: 18 when I break the yoke of *E*;
30: 19 So I will inflict punishment on *E*,
30: 21 the arm of Pharaoh king of *E*.
30: 22 I am against Pharaoh king of *E*.
30: 25 and he brandishes it against *E*.
31: 2 say to Pharaoh king of *E*
32: 2 concerning Pharaoh king of *E*
32: 12 They will shatter the pride of *E*,
32: 15 When I make *E* desolate
32: 16 for *E* and all her hordes they will
32: 18 wail for the hordes of *E*
32: 21 the mighty leaders will say of *E*
47: 19 along the Wadi ⌞of *E*⌟ to the Great
48: 28 along the Wadi ⌞of *E*⌟ to the Great
Da 9: 15 out of *E* with a mighty hand
11: 8 and gold and carry them off to *E*.
11: 42 over many countries; *E* will not
11: 43 and silver and all the riches of *E*,
Hos 2: 15 as in the day she came up out of *E*.
7: 11 now calling to *E*,
7: 16 ridiculed in the land of *E*.
8: 13 They will return to *E*.
9: 3 Ephraim will return to *E*
9: 6 *E* will gather them,
11: 1 and out of *E* I called my son.
11: 5 "Will they not return to *E*
11: 11 like birds from *E*,
12: 1 and sends olive oil to *E*.
12: 9 ⌞who brought you⌟ out of *E*;
12: 13 to bring Israel up from *E*,
13: 4 ⌞who brought you⌟ out of *E*.
Joel 3: 19 But *E* will be desolate,
Am 2: 10 "I brought you up out of *E*,
3: 1 whole family I brought up out of *E*:
3: 9 and to the fortresses of *E*:
4: 10 as I did to *E*.
8: 8 like the river of *E*.
9: 5 then sinks like the river of *E*—
9: 7 "Did I not bring Israel up from *E*,
Mic 6: 4 I brought you up out of *E*
7: 12 even from *E* to the Euphrates
7: 12 from Assyria and the cities of *E*,
7: 15 in the days when you came out of *E*
Na 3: 9 *E* were her boundless strength;
Hag 2: 5 with you when you came out of *E*.
Zec 10: 10 I will bring them back from *E*
14: 19 This will be the punishment of *E*
Mt 2: 13 and his mother and escape to *E*.
2: 14 during the night and left for *E*,
2: 15 "Out of *E* I called my son."
2: 19 appeared in a dream to Joseph in *E*
Ac 2: 10 *E* and the parts of Libya
7: 9 they sold him as a slave into *E*.
7: 10 so he made him ruler over *E*
7: 10 the goodwill of Pharaoh king of *E*;
7: 11 a famine struck all *E* and Canaan,
7: 12 heard that there was grain in *E*,
7: 15 Then Jacob went down to *E*,
7: 17 of our people in *E* greatly increased
7: 18 about Joseph, became ruler of *E*.
7: 34 I will send you back to *E*.'
7: 34 the oppression of my people in *E*.
7: 36 and miraculous signs in *E*,
7: 36 out of *E* and did wonders
7: 39 in their hearts turned back to *E*.
7: 40 fellow Moses who led us out of *E*—
13: 17 prosper during their stay in *E*.
Heb 3: 16 not all those Moses led out of *E*?
8: 9 the hand to lead them out of *E*,
11: 22 the exodus of the Israelites from *E*
11: 26 value than the treasures of *E*,
11: 27 By faith he left *E*, not fearing
Jude : 5 Lord delivered his people out of *E*,
Rev 11: 8 is figuratively called Sodom and *E*,

EGYPT'S (EGYPT)

Isa 20: 4 with buttocks bared—to *E* shame.
30: 2 to *E* shade for refuge.
30: 3 *E* shade will bring you disgrace.
Eze 30: 9 hold of them on the day of *E* doom,
Zec 10: 11 and *E* scepter will pass away.

EGYPTIAN (EGYPT)

Ge 16: 1 she had an *E* maidservant named
16: 3 wife took her *E* maidservant Hagar
21: 9 son whom Hagar the *E* had borne
25: 12 Hagar the *E*, bore to Abraham.
39: 1 an *E* who was one
39: 2 lived in the house of his *E* master.
39: 5 blessed the household of the *E*
Ex 1: 19 women are not like *E* women;
2: 11 He saw an *E* beating a Hebrew,
2: 12 he killed the *E* and hid him
2: 14 of killing me as you killed the *E*?"
2: 19 *E* rescued us from the shepherds.
7: 11 the *E* magicians also did the same
7: 22 *E* magicians did the same things
14: 24 cloud at the *E* army and threw it
Lev 24: 10 and an *E* father went out
Dt 11: 4 what he did to the *E* army,
23: 7 not abhor an *E*, because you lived
1Sa 30: 11 They found an *E* in a field
30: 13 "I am an *E*, the slave
2Sa 23: 21 Although the *E* had a spear
23: 21 And he struck down a huge *E*.
2Ki 7: 6 has hired the Hittite and *E* kings
1Ch 2: 34 He had an *E* servant named Jarha.
11: 23 Although the *E* had a spear like
11: 23 struck down an *E* who was seven
Isa 11: 15 the gulf of the *E* sea;
19: 2 "I will stir up *E* against *E*—
20: 4 and barefoot the *E* captives
Zec 14: 18 If the *E* people do not go up
Ac 7: 24 and avenged him by killing the *E*.
7: 24 of them being mistreated by an *E*,
7: 28 as you killed the *E* yesterday?'
21: 38 "Aren't you the *E* who started

EGYPTIAN'S (EGYPT)

2Sa 23: 21 snatched the spear from the *E* hand
1Ch 11: 23 snatched the spear from the *E* hand

EGYPTIANS (EGYPT)

Ge 12: 12 When the *E* see you, they will say,
12: 14 *E* saw that she was a very beautiful
41: 55 Then Pharaoh told all the *E*,
41: 56 and sold grain to the *E*,
43: 32 and the *E* who ate with him
43: 32 *E* could not eat with Hebrews,
43: 32 for that is detestable to *E*.
45: 2 so loudly that the *E* heard him,
46: 34 shepherds are detestable to the *E*."
47: 20 The *E*, one and all, sold their fields,
50: 3 *E* mourned for him seventy days.
50: 11 *E* are holding a solemn ceremony
Ex 1: 12 so the *E* came to dread
1: 14 hard labor the *E* used them
3: 8 them from the hand of the *E*
3: 9 the way the *E* are oppressing them.
3: 20 strike the *E* with all the wonders
3: 21 will make the *E* favorably disposed
3: 22 And so you will plunder the *E*."
6: 5 whom the *E* are enslaving,
6: 6 out from under the yoke of the *E*.
6: 7 out from under the yoke of the *E*.
7: 5 *E* will know that I am the LORD
7: 18 the *E* will not be able
7: 21 so bad that the *E* could not drink
7: 24 And all the *E* dug along the Nile
8: 21 The houses of the *E* will be full
8: 26 God would be detestable to the *E*.
9: 6 All the livestock of the *E* died,
9: 11 were on them and on all the *E*.
10: 2 how I dealt harshly with the *E*
10: 6 of all your officials and all the *E*—
11: 3 made the *E* favorably disposed
12: 23 the land to strike down the *E*,
12: 27 when he struck down the *E*.' "
12: 30 all the *E* got up during the night,
12: 33 The *E* urged the people to hurry
12: 35 asked the *E* for articles of silver
12: 36 asked for; so they plundered the *E*.
12: 36 had made the *E* favorably disposed
14: 4 *E* will know that I am the LORD."
14: 9 The *E*— all Pharaoh's horses
14: 10 and there were the *E*, marching
14: 12 for us to serve the *E* than to die
14: 12 'Leave us alone; let us serve the *E*'?
14: 13 *E* you see today you will never see
14: 17 hearts of the *E* so that they will go
14: 18 *E* will know that I am the LORD
14: 23 *E* pursued them, and all Pharaoh's
14: 25 And the *E* said, "Let's get away
14: 26 waters may flow back over the *E*
Ex 14: 27 The *E* were fleeing toward it,
14: 30 Israel from the hands of the *E*,
14: 30 and Israel saw the *E* lying dead
14: 31 the LORD displayed against the *E*,
15: 26 of the diseases I brought on the *E*,
18: 8 done to Pharaoh and the *E*
18: 9 them from the hand of the *E*.
18: 10 the people from the hand of the *E*.
18: 10 you from the hand of the *E*
32: 12 Why should the *E* say, 'It was
Lev 26: 13 would no longer be slaves to the *E*;
Nu 14: 13 "Then the *E* will hear about it!
20: 15 *E* mistreated us and our fathers,
33: 3 boldly in full view of all the *E*,
Dt 26: 6 But the *E* mistreated us
Jos 24: 5 I afflicted the *E* by what I did there
24: 6 the *E* pursued them with chariots
24: 7 darkness between you and the *E*;
24: 7 your own eyes what I did to the *E*.
Jdg 10: 11 "When the *E*, the Amorites,
1Sa 4: 8 They are the gods who struck the *E*
6: 6 as the *E* and Pharaoh did?
Ezr 9: 1 Moabites, *E* and Amorites.
Ne 9: 10 how arrogantly the *E* treated them.
Isa 19: 1 hearts of the *E* melt within them.
19: 3 The *E* will lose heart,
19: 4 I will hand the *E* over
19: 16 In that day the *E* will be like
19: 17 of Judah will bring terror to the *E*;
19: 21 will make himself known to the *E*,
19: 23 The *E* and Assyrians will worship
19: 23 go to Egypt and the *E* to Assyria.
31: 3 But the *E* are men and not God;
Eze 16: 26 engaged in prostitution with the *E*,
29: 12 And I will disperse the *E*
29: 13 of forty years I will gather the *E*
30: 23 I will disperse the *E*
30: 26 I will disperse the *E*
Ac 7: 22 educated in all the wisdom of the *E*
Heb 11: 29 but when the *E* tried to do so,

EHI

Ge 46: 21 Gera, Naaman, *E*, Rosh, Muppim,

EHUD

Jdg 3: 15 and he gave them a deliverer—*E*,
3: 16 *E* had made a double-edged sword
3: 18 After *E* had presented the tribute,
3: 20 *E* then approached him
3: 21 *E* reached with his left hand,
3: 22 *E* did not pull the sword out,
3: 23 Then *E* went out to the porch;
3: 26 While they waited, *E* got away.
3: 31 After *E* came Shamgar son
4: 1 After *E* died, the Israelites once
1Ch 7: 10 Jeush, Benjamin, *E*, Kenaanah,
8: 6 These were the descendants of *E*,

EJECTED

Ac 18: 16 So he had them *e* from the court.

EKER

1Ch 2: 27 of Jerahmeel: Maaz, Jamin and *E*.

EKRON

Jos 13: 3 Ashdod, Ashkelon, Gath and *E*—
13: 3 to the territory of *E* on the north,
15: 11 It went to the northern slope of *E*,
15: 45 *E*, with its surrounding settlements
15: 46 settlements and villages; west of *E*,
19: 43 Elon, Timnah, *E*, Eltekeh,
Jdg 1: 18 and *E*— each city with its territory.
1Sa 5: 10 So they sent the ark of God to *E*.
5: 10 *E*, the people of *E* cried out,
6: 16 then returned that same day to *E*.
6: 17 Gaza, Ashkelon, Gath and *E*.
7: 14 The towns from *E*
17: 52 of Gath and to the gates of *E*.
17: 52 the Shaaraim road to Gath and *E*.
2Ki 1: 2 consult Baal-Zebub, the god of *E*,
1: 3 god of *E*?' Therefore this is what
1: 6 of *E*? Therefore you will not leave
1: 16 of *E*? Because you have done this,
Jer 25: 20 *E*, and the people left at Ashdod);
Am 1: 8 I will turn my hand against *E*
Zep 2: 4 and *E* uprooted.
Zec 9: 5 and *E* too, for her hope will wither.
9: 7 and *E* will be like the Jebusites.

EL BETHEL
Ge 35: 7 and he called the place *E*

EL ELOHE
Ge 33: 20 and called it *E* Israel

EL PARAN
Ge 14: 6 as far as *E* near the desert.

EL-BERITH
Jdg 9: 46 the stronghold of the temple of *E*.

ELA
1Ki 4: 18 Shimei son of *E*— in Benjamin;

ELAH (ELAH'S)
Ge 36: 41 Jetheth, Oholibamah, *E*, Pinon,
1Sa 17: 2 and camped in the Valley of *E*
17: 19 the men of Israel in the Valley of *E*,
21: 9 whom you killed in the Valley of *E*,
1Ki 16: 6 And *E* his son succeeded him
16: 8 *E* son of Baasha became king
16: 9 *E* was in Tirzah at the time,
16: 13 and his son *E* had committed
2Ki 15: 30 Then Hoshea son of *E* conspired
17: 1 Hoshea son of *E* became king
18: 1 of Hoshea son of *E* king of Israel,
18: 9 of Hoshea son of *E* king of Israel,
1Ch 1: 52 Jetheth, Oholibamah, *E*, Pinon,
4: 15 The son of *E*: Kenaz.
4: 15 of Caleb son of Jephunneh: Iru, *E*
9: 8 son of Jeroham; *E* son of Uzzi,

ELAH'S (ELAH)
1Ki 16: 14 As for the other events of *E* reign,

ELAM (ELAM'S ELAMITES)
Ge 10: 22 The sons of Shem: *E*, Asshur,
14: 1 Kedorlaomer king of *E*
14: 9 against Kedorlaomer king of *E*,
1Ch 1: 17 The sons of Shem: *E*, Asshur,
8: 24 Hanan, Hananiah, *E*, Anthothijah,
26: 3 Jathniel the fourth, *E* the fifth,
Ezr 2: 7 of *E* 1,254 of Zattu 945
2: 31 of the other *E* 1,254
8: 7 the descendants of *E*, Jeshaiah son
10: 2 one of the descendants of *E*,
10: 26 From the descendants of *E*:
Ne 7: 12 of *E* 1,254 of Zattu 845
7: 34 of the other *E* 1,254
10: 14 Parosh, Pahath-Moab, *E*, Zattu,
12: 42 Jehohanan, Malkijah, *E* and Ezer.
Isa 11: 11 from Cush, from *E*, from Babylonia
21: 2 *E*, attack! Media, lay siege!
22: 6 *E* takes up the quiver,
Jer 25: 25 all the kings of Zimri, *E* and Media;
49: 34 the prophet concerning *E*,
49: 35 "See, I will break the bow of *E*,
49: 36 I will bring against *E* the four winds
49: 37 I will shatter *E* before their foes,
49: 38 I will set my throne in *E*
49: 39 "Yet I will restore the fortunes of *E*
Eze 32: 24 "*E* is there, with all her hordes
Da 8: 2 citadel of Susa in the province of *E*,

ELAM'S (ELAM)
Jer 49: 36 where *E* exiles do not go.

ELAMITES (ELAM)
Ezr 4: 9 Erech and Babylon, the *E* of Susa,
Ac 2: 9 and *E*, residents of Mesopotamia,

ELAPSED
1Sa 18: 26 So before the allotted time *e*,

ELASAH
Ezr 10: 22 Ishmael, Nethanel, Jozabad and *E*.
Jer 29: 3 the letter to *E* son of Shaphan

ELATED (ELATION)
1Sa 11: 9 to the men of Jabesh, they were *e*.

ELATH
Dt 2: 8 which comes up from *E* and Ezion
1Ki 9: 26 which is near *E* in Edom,
2Ki 14: 22 He was the one who rebuilt *E*
16: 6 Edomites then moved into *E*
16: 6 of Aram recovered *E* for Aram
2Ch 8: 17 and *E* on the seacoast of Edom.
2Ch 26: 2 He was the one who rebuilt *E*

ELATION (ELATED)
Pr 28: 12 righteous triumph, there is great *e*;

ELDAAH
Ge 25: 4 Epher, Hanoch, Abida and *E*.
1Ch 1: 33 Epher, Hanoch, Abida and *E*.

ELDAD
Nu 11: 26 whose names were *E* and Medad,
11: 27 "*E* and Medad are prophesying

ELDER (ELDERLY ELDERS)
Isa 3: 2 the soothsayer and *e*,
1Ti 5: 19 an accusation against an *e*
Tit 1: 6 *e* must be blameless, the husband
1Pe 5: 1 among you, I appeal as a fellow *e*,
2Jn : 1 The *e*, To the chosen lady
3Jn : 1 The *e*, To my dear friend Gaius,

ELDERLY (ELDER)
Lev 19: 32 show respect for the *e*

ELDERS (ELDER)
Ex 3: 16 assemble the *e* of Israel
3: 18 the *e* are to go to the king of Egypt
3: 18 "The *e* of Israel will listen to you.
4: 29 Aaron brought together all the *e*
12: 21 Moses summoned all the *e* of Israel
17: 5 with you some of the *e* of Israel
17: 6 this in the sight of the *e* of Israel.
18: 12 Aaron came with all the *e* of Israel
19: 7 and summoned the *e* of the people
24: 1 and seventy of the *e* of Israel.
24: 9 and the seventy *e* of Israel went up
24: 14 He said to the *e*, "Wait here for us
Lev 4: 15 The *e* of the community are
9: 1 and his sons and the *e* of Israel.
Nu 11: 16 seventy of Israel's *e* who are known
11: 24 brought together seventy of their *e*
11: 25 and put the Spirit on the seventy *e*.
11: 26 They were listed among the *e*,
11: 30 the *e* of Israel returned to the camp
16: 25 and the *e* of Israel followed him.
22: 4 said to the *e* of Midian,
22: 7 The *e* of Moab and Midian left,
Dt 5: 23 men of your tribes and your *e* came
19: 12 the *e* of his town shall send for him,
21: 2 your *e* and judges shall go out
21: 3 *e* of the town nearest the body shall
21: 6 Then all the *e* of the town nearest
21: 19 and bring him to the *e* at the gate
21: 20 They shall say to the *e*, "This son
22: 15 a virgin to the town *e* at the gate.
22: 16 The girl's father will say to the *e*,
22: 17 the cloth before the *e* of the town,
22: 18 and the *e* shall take the man
25: 7 go to the *e* at the town gate
25: 8 the *e* of his town shall summon him
25: 9 up to him in the presence of the *e*,
27: 1 *e* of Israel commanded the people:
29: 10 and chief men, your *e* and officials,
31: 9 and to all the *e* of Israel.
31: 28 before me all the *e* of your tribes
32: 7 your *e*, and they will explain to you
Jos 7: 6 The *e* of Israel did the same,
8: 33 with their *e*, officials and judges,
9: 11 And our *e* and all those living
20: 4 case before the *e* of that city,
23: 2 summoned all Israel—their *e*,
24: 1 He summoned the *e*, leaders,
24: 31 and of the *e* who outlived him
Jdg 2: 7 and of the *e* who outlived him
8: 14 of Succoth, the *e* of the town.
8: 16 He took the *e* of the town
11: 5 the *e* of Gilead went
11: 8 The *e* of Gilead said to him,
11: 10 will I really be your head?" The *e*
11: 11 Jephthah went with the *e* of Gilead
21: 16 And the *e* of the assembly said,
Ru 4: 2 Boaz took ten of the *e* of the town
4: 4 the presence of the *e* of my people.
4: 9 Then Boaz announced to the *e*
4: 11 the *e* and all those at the gate said,
1Sa 4: 3 to camp, the *e* of Israel asked,
8: 4 all the *e* of Israel gathered together
11: 3 The *e* of Jabesh said to him,
1Sa 15: 30 me before the *e* of my people
16: 4 the *e* of the town trembled
30: 26 of the plunder to the *e* of Judah,
2Sa 3: 17 conferred with the *e* of Israel
5: 3 When all the *e* of Israel had come
12: 17 The *e* of his household stood
17: 4 to Absalom and to all the *e* of Israel
17: 15 and the *e* of Israel to do such
19: 11 the priests: "Ask the *e* of Judah,
1Ki 8: 1 at Jerusalem the *e* of Israel,
8: 3 When all the *e* of Israel had arrived
12: 6 consulted the *e* who had
12: 8 rejected the advice the *e* gave him
12: 13 the advice given him by the *e*,
20: 7 king of Israel summoned all the *e*
20: 8 The *e* and the people all answered,
21: 8 and sent them to the *e*
21: 11 So the *e* and nobles who lived
2Ki 6: 32 and the *e* were sitting with him.
6: 32 he arrived, Elisha said to the *e*,
10: 1 to the *e* and to the guardians
10: 5 the *e* and the guardians sent this
23: 1 the king called together all the *e*
1Ch 11: 3 When all the *e* of Israel had come
15: 25 So David and the *e* of Israel
21: 16 and the *e*, clothed in sackcloth,
2Ch 5: 2 to Jerusalem the *e* of Israel,
5: 4 When all the *e* of Israel had arrived
10: 6 consulted the *e* who had
10: 8 rejected the advice the *e* gave him
10: 13 Rejecting the advice of the *e*,
34: 29 the king called together all the *e*
Ezr 5: 5 watching over the *e* of the Jews,
5: 9 We questioned the *e* and asked
6: 7 and the Jewish *e* rebuild this house
6: 8 are to do for these *e* of the Jews
6: 14 the *e* of the Jews continued to build
10: 8 the decision of the officials and *e*,
10: 14 along with the *e* and judges
Job 12: 20 takes away the discernment of *e*.
Ps 105: 22 and teach his *e* wisdom.
107: 32 praise him in the council of the *e*.
119: 100 more understanding than the *e*,
Pr 31: 23 among the *e* of the land.
Isa 3: 14 judgment against the *e* and leaders
9: 15 *e* and prominent men are the head,
24: 23 and before its *e*, gloriously.
Jer 19: 1 along some of the *e* of the people
26: 17 of the *e* of the land stepped forward
29: 1 to the surviving *e* among the exiles
La 1: 19 My priests and my *e*
2: 10 The *e* of the Daughter of Zion
4: 16 the *e* no favor.
5: 12 *e* are shown no respect.
5: 14 The *e* are gone from the city gate;
Eze 7: 26 as will the counsel of the *e*.
8: 1 and the *e* of Judah were sitting
8: 11 front of them stood seventy *e*
8: 12 have you seen what the *e*
9: 6 So they began with the *e* who were
14: 1 Some of the *e* of Israel came to me
20: 1 some of the *e* of Israel came
20: 3 speak to the *e* of Israel
Joel 1: 2 Hear this, you *e*;
1: 14 Summon the *e*
2: 16 bring together the *e*,
Mt 15: 2 break the tradition of the *e*?
16: 21 things at the hands of the *e*,
21: 23 the *e* of the people came to him.
26: 3 and the *e* of the people assembled
26: 47 sent from the chief priests and the *e*
26: 57 of the law and the *e* had assembled.
27: 1 and the *e* of the people came
27: 3 coins to the chief priests and the *e*.
27: 12 by the chief priests and the *e*,
27: 20 the *e* persuaded the crowd to ask
27: 41 of the law and the *e* mocked him.
28: 12 the chief priests had met with the *e*
Mk 7: 3 holding to the tradition of the *e*.
7: 5 to the tradition of the *e* instead
8: 31 things and be rejected by the *e*,
11: 27 of the law and the *e* came to him.
14: 43 the teachers of the law, and the *e*.
14: 53 *e* and teachers of the law came
15: 1 the chief priests, with the *e*,
Lk 7: 3 and sent some *e* of the Jews to him,
9: 22 things and be rejected by the *e*,
20: 1 together with the *e*, came up to him

Lk 22: 52 and the *e*, who had come for him,
22: 66 the council of the *e* of the people,
Ac 4: 5 *e* and teachers of the law met
4: 8 Rulers and *e* of the people!
4: 23 that the chief priests and *e* had said
5: 21 the full assembly of the *e* of Israel
6: 12 the *e* and the teachers of the law.
11: 30 gift to the *e* by Barnabas
14: 23 and Barnabas appointed *e* for them
15: 2 the apostles and *e* about this
15: 4 the church and the apostles and *e*,
15: 6 and *e* met to consider this question.
15: 22 and *e*, with the whole church,
15: 23 The apostles and *e*, your brothers,
16: 4 and *e* in Jerusalem for the people
20: 17 to Ephesus for the *e* of the church.
21: 18 and all the *e* were present.
23: 14 They went to the chief priests and *e*
24: 1 to Caesarea with some of the *e*
25: 15 and *e* of the Jews brought charges
1Ti 4: 14 when the body of *e* laid their hands
5: 17 The *e* who direct the affairs
Tit 1: 5 and appoint *e* in every town,
Jas 5: 14 He should call the *e* of the church
1Pe 5: 1 To the *e* among you, I appeal
Rev 4: 4 seated on them were twenty-four *e*.
4: 10 the twenty-four *e* fall
5: 5 Then one of the *e* said to me,
5: 6 the four living creatures and the *e*.
5: 8 and the twenty-four *e* fell
5: 11 and the living creatures and the *e*.
5: 14 and the *e* fell down and worshiped.
7: 11 around the *e* and the four living
7: 13 Then one of the *e* asked me,
11: 16 the twenty-four *e*, who were seated
14: 3 the four living creatures and the *e*.
19: 4 twenty-four *e* and the four living

ELEAD
1Ch 7: 21 *E* were killed by the native-born

ELEADAH
1Ch 7: 20 Tahath his son, *E* his son, Tahath

ELEALEH
Nu 32: 3 Jazer, Nimrah, Heshbon, *E*, Sebam
32: 37 the Reubenites rebuilt Heshbon, *E*
Isa 15: 4 Heshbon and *E* cry out,
16: 9 O Heshbon, O *E*,
Jer 48: 34 rises from Heshbon to *E* and Jahaz,

ELEASAH
1Ch 2: 40 father of *E*, *E* the father of Sismai,
8: 37 *E* his son and Azel his son.
9: 43 *E* his son and Azel his son.

ELEAZAR (ELEAZAR'S)
Ex 6: 23 and Abihu, *E* and Ithamar.
6: 25 *E* son of Aaron married one
28: 1 and Abihu, *E* and Ithamar,
Lev 10: 6 and his sons *E* and Ithamar,
10: 12 his remaining sons, *E* and Ithamar,
10: 16 he was angry with *E* and Ithamar,
Nu 3: 2 and Abihu, *E* and Ithamar.
3: 4 so only *E* and Ithamar served
3: 32 of the Levites was *E* son of Aaron,
4: 16 "*E* son of Aaron, the priest,
16: 37 "Tell *E* son of Aaron, the priest,
16: 39 *E* the priest collected the bronze
19: 3 Give it to *E* the priest; it is
19: 4 Then *E* the priest is to take some
20: 25 Get Aaron and his son *E*
20: 26 and put them on his son *E*,
20: 28 and put them on his son *E*.
20: 28 *E* came down from the mountain,
25: 7 When Phinehas son of *E*, the son
25: 11 "Phinehas son of *E*, the son
26: 1 said to Moses and *E* son of Aaron,
26: 3 and *E* the priest spoke with them
26: 60 and Abihu, *E* and Ithamar.
26: 63 *E* the priest when they counted
27: 2 *E* the priest, the leaders
27: 19 Have him stand before *E* the priest
27: 21 He is to stand before *E* the priest,
27: 22 had him stand before *E* the priest
31: 6 along with Phinehas son of *E*,
31: 12 plunder to Moses and *E* the priest
31: 13 *E* the priest and all the leaders
Nu 31: 21 *E* the priest said to the soldiers who
31: 26 "You and *E* the priest
31: 29 to *E* the priest as the LORD's part.
31: 31 So Moses and *E* the priest did
31: 41 gave the tribute to *E* the priest
31: 51 and *E* the priest accepted
31: 52 that Moses and *E* presented
31: 54 and *E* the priest accepted the gold
32: 2 came to Moses and *E* the priest
32: 28 orders about them to *E* the priest
34: 17 *E* the priest and Joshua son of Nun.
Dt 10: 6 and *E* his son succeeded him
Jos 14: 1 land of Canaan, which *E* the priest,
17: 4 They went to *E* the priest,
19: 51 are the territories that *E* the priest,
21: 1 Levites approached *E* the priest,
22: 13 Israelites sent Phinehas son of *E*,
22: 31 And Phinehas son of *E*, the priest,
22: 32 Then Phinehas son of *E*, the priest,
24: 33 And *E* son of Aaron died
Jdg 20: 28 with Phinehas son of *E*, the son
1Sa 7: 1 and consecrated *E* his son
2Sa 23: 9 Next to him was *E* son
23: 10 The troops returned to *E*,
1Ch 6: 3 Nadab, Abihu, *E* and Ithamar.
6: 4 *E* was the father of Phinehas,
6: 50 *E* his son, Phinehas his son,
9: 20 son of *E* was in charge
11: 12 Next to him was *E* son
23: 21 The sons of Mahli: *E* and Kish.
23: 22 *E* died without having sons:
24: 1 of Aaron were Nadab, Abihu, *E*
24: 2 so *E* and Ithamar served
24: 3 help of Zadok a descendant of *E*
24: 5 among the descendants of both *E*
24: 6 one family being taken from *E*
24: 28 From Mahli: *E*, who had no sons.
Ezr 7: 5 the son of Phinehas, the son of *E*,
8: 33 *E* son of Phinehas was with him,
10: 25 Izziah, Malkijah, Mijamin, *E*,
Ne 12: 42 Shemaiah, *E*, Uzzi, Jehohanan,
Mt 1: 15 of *E*, *E* the father of Matthan,

ELEAZAR'S (ELEAZAR)
1Ch 24: 4 found among *E* descendants
24: 4 of families from *E* descendants

ELECT (ELECTION)
Mt 24: 22 the sake of the *e* those days will be
24: 24 miracles to deceive even the *e*—
24: 31 and they will gather his *e*
Mk 13: 20 sake of the *e*, whom he has chosen,
13: 22 and miracles to deceive the *e*—
13: 27 gather his *e* from the four winds,
Ro 11: 7 it did not obtain, but the *e* did.
1Ti 5: 21 and Christ Jesus and the *e* angels,
2Ti 2: 10 everything for the sake of the *e*,
Tit 1: 1 Christ for the faith of God's *e*
1Pe 1: 1 To God's *e*, strangers in the world,

ELECTION (ELECT)
Ro 9: 11 God's purpose in *e* might stand:
11: 28 but as far as *e* is concerned,
2Pe 1: 10 to make your calling and *e* sure.

ELEGANCE (ELEGANT)
SS 4: 4 built with *e*;

ELEGANT (ELEGANCE)
Eze 23: 41 You sat on an *e* couch,
Lk 23: 11 Dressing him in an *e* robe,

ELEMENTARY (ELEMENTS)
Heb 5: 12 someone to teach you the *e* truths
6: 1 us leave the *e* teachings about

ELEMENTS (ELEMENTARY)
2Pe 3: 10 the *e* will be destroyed by fire,
3: 12 and the *e* will melt in the heat.

ELEVATE (ELEVATED ELEVATING)
2Co 11: 7 to *e* you by preaching the gospel

ELEVATED (ELEVATE)
Est 5: 11 how he had *e* him above the other

ELEVATING (ELEVATE)
Est 3: 1 *e* him and giving him a seat

ELHANAN
2Sa 21: 19 *E* son of Jaare-Oregim
23: 24 *E* son of Dodo from Bethlehem,
1Ch 11: 26 *E* son of Dodo from Bethlehem,
20: 5 *E* son of Jair killed Lahmi

ELI (ELI'S)
1Sa 1: 3 the two sons of *E*, were priests
1: 9 *E* the priest was sitting on a chair
1: 12 to the LORD, *E* observed her
1: 13 *E* thought she was drunk
1: 17 *E* answered, "Go in peace,
1: 25 they brought the boy to *E*,
2: 11 the LORD under *E* the priest.
2: 20 *E* would bless Elkanah and his wife
2: 22 Now *E*, who was very old,
2: 27 Now a man of God came to *E*
3: 1 before the LORD under *E*.
3: 2 One night *E*, whose eyes were
3: 5 But *E* said, "I did not call;
3: 5 he ran to *E* and said, "Here I am;
3: 6 And Samuel got up and went to *E*
3: 6 "My son," *E* said, "I did not call;
3: 8 and Samuel got up and went to *E*
3: 8 *E* realized that the LORD was
3: 9 So *E* told Samuel, "Go
3: 12 out against *E* everything I spoke
3: 14 I swore to the house of *E*,
3: 15 He was afraid to tell *E* the vision,
3: 16 but *E* called him and said, "Samuel
3: 17 was it he said to you?" *E* asked.
3: 18 Then *E* said, "He is the LORD;
4: 13 there was *E* sitting on his chair
4: 14 The man hurried over to *E*,
4: 14 *E* heard the outcry and asked,
4: 16 He told *E*, "I have just come
4: 16 *E* asked, "What happened, my son
4: 18 *E* fell backward off his chair
14: 3 the son of *E*, the LORD's priest
1Ki 2: 27 at Shiloh about the house of *E*.

ELI'S (ELI)
1Sa 2: 12 *E* sons were wicked men; they had
3: 14 of *E* house will never be atoned
4: 4 And *E* two sons, Hophni
4: 11 and *E* two sons, Hophni

ELIAB
Nu 1: 9 from Zebulun, *E* son of Helon;
2: 7 of Zebulun is *E* son of Helon.
7: 24 On the third day, *E* son of Helon,
7: 29 the offering of *E* son of Helon.
10: 16 and *E* son of Helon was
16: 1 Dathan and Abiram, sons of *E*,
16: 12 and Abiram, the sons of *E*.
26: 8 The son of Pallu was *E*,
26: 9 and the sons of *E* were Nemuel,
Dt 11: 6 Abiram, sons of *E* the Reubenite,
1Sa 16: 6 Samuel saw *E* and thought,
17: 13 The firstborn was *E*; the second,
17: 28 When *E*, David's oldest brother,
1Ch 2: 13 was the father of *E* his firstborn;
6: 27 Nahath his son, *E* his son,
12: 9 second in command, *E* the third,
15: 18 Jehiel, Unni, *E*, Benaiah, Maaseiah
15: 20 Shemiramoth, Jehiel, Unni, *E*,
16: 5 Jehiel, Mattithiah, *E*, Benaiah,
2Ch 11: 18 the daughter of Jesse's son *E*.

ELIADA
2Sa 5: 16 Japhia, Elishama, *E* and Eliphelet.
1Ki 11: 23 Rezon son of *E*, who had fled
1Ch 3: 8 Japhia, Elishama, *E* and Eliphelet
2Ch 17: 17 From Benjamin: *E*, a valiant

ELIAHBA
2Sa 23: 32 the Barhumite, *E* the Shaalbonite,
1Ch 11: 33 the Baharumite, *E* the Shaalbonite,

ELIAKIM (ELIAKIM'S)
2Ki 18: 18 and *E* son of Hilkiah the palace
18: 26 Then *E* son of Hilkiah, and Shebna
18: 37 Then *E* son of Hilkiah the palace
19: 2 He sent *E* the palace administrator,
23: 34 Pharaoh Neco made *E* son
2Ch 36: 4 The king of Egypt made *E*,
Ne 12: 41 *E*, Maaseiah, Mijamin, Micaiah,
Isa 22: 20 I will summon my servant, *E* son

Isa 36: 3 *E* son of Hilkiah the palace
36: 11 Then *E*, Shebna and Joah said
36: 22 Then *E* son of Hilkiah the palace
37: 2 He sent *E* the palace administrator,
Mt 1: 13 father of *E*, *E* the father of Azor,
Lk 3: 30 the son of Jonam, the son of *E*,

ELIAKIM'S (ELIAKIM)

2Ki 23: 34 and changed *E* name to Jehoiakim.
2Ch 36: 4 But Neco took *E* brother Jehoahaz
36: 4 and changed *E* name to Jehoiakim.

ELIAM

2Sa 11: 3 the daughter of *E* and the wife
23: 34 *E* son of Ahithophel the Gilonite,

ELIASAPH

Nu 1: 14 from Gad, *E* son of Deuel;
2: 14 people of Gad is *E* son of Deuel.
3: 24 of the Gershonites was *E* son
7: 42 On the sixth day *E* son of Deuel,
7: 47 the offering of *E* son of Deuel.
10: 20 and *E* son of Deuel was

ELIASHIB (ELIASHIB'S)

1Ch 3: 24 Hodaviah, *E*, Pelaiah, Akkub,
24: 12 the eleventh to *E*, the twelfth
Ezr 10: 6 to the room of Jehohanan son of *E*.
10: 24 From the singers: *E*.
10: 27 Elioenai, *E*, Mattaniah, Jeremoth,
10: 36 Vaniah, Meremoth, *E*, Mattaniah,
Ne 3: 1 *E* the high priest and his fellow
3: 20 of the house of *E* the high priest.
12: 10 father of *E*, *E* the father of Joiada,
12: 22 of the Levites in the days of *E*.
12: 23 of Johanan son of *E* were recorded
13: 4 *E* the priest had been put in charge
13: 7 about the evil thing *E* had done
13: 28 of *E* the high priest was son-in-law

ELIASHIB'S (ELIASHIB)

Ne 3: 21 from the entrance of *E* house

ELIATHAH

1Ch 25: 4 *E*, Giddalti and Romamti-Ezer;
25: 27 the twentieth to *E*, his sons

ELIDAD

Nu 34: 21 tribe of Simeon; *E* son of Kislon,

ELIEHOENAI

1Ch 26: 3 the sixth and *E* the seventh.
Ezr 8: 4 of Pahath-Moab, *E* son of Zerahiah

ELIEL

1Ch 5: 24 Epher, Ishi, *E*, Azriel, Jeremiah,
6: 34 the son of *E*, the son of Toah,
8: 20 Zabdi, Elienai, Zillethai, *E*, Adaiah
8: 22 Ishpan, Eber, *E*, Abdon, Zicri,
11: 46 Joha the Tizite, *E* the Mahavite,
11: 47 *E*, Obed and Jaasiel the Mezobaite.
12: 11 Attai the sixth, *E* the seventh,
15: 9 *E* the leader and 80 relatives;
15: 11 *E* and Amminadab the Levites.
2Ch 31: 13 Jerimoth, Jozabad, *E*, Ismakiah,

ELIENAI

1Ch 8: 20 Zicri, Zabdi, *E*, Zillethai, Eliel,

ELIEZER

Ge 15: 2 one who will inherit my estate is *E*
Ex 18: 4 and the other was named *E*,
1Ch 7: 8 Zemirah, Joash, *E*, Elioenai, Omri,
15: 24 *E* the priests were to blow trumpets
23: 15 sons of Moses: Gershom and *E*.
23: 17 *E* had no other sons, but the sons
23: 17 of *E*: Rehabiah was the first.
26: 25 through *E*: Rehabiah his son,
27: 16 over the Reubenites: *E* son of Zicri;
2Ch 20: 37 *E* son of Dodavahu
Ezr 8: 16 So I summoned *E*, Ariel, Shemaiah
10: 18 Maaseiah, *E*, Jarib and Gedaliah.
10: 23 is Kelita), Pethahiah, Judah and *E*.
10: 31 *E*, Ishijah, Malkijah, Shemaiah,
Lk 3: 29 the son of Joshua, the son of *E*,

ELIHOREPH

1Ki 4: 3 *E* and Ahijah, sons of Shisha—

ELIHU

1Sa 1: 1 the son of *E*, the son of Tohu,
1Ch 12: 20 Michael, Jozabad, *E* and Zillethai,
26: 7 his relatives *E* and Semakiah were
27: 18 over Judah: *E*, a brother of David;
Job 32: 2 But *E* son of Barakel the Buzite,
32: 4 Now *E* had waited before speaking
32: 6 So *E* son of Barakel the Buzite said:
34: 1 Then *E* said: "Hear my words,
35: 1 *E* said: "Do you think this is just?
36: 1 *E* continued: "Bear

ELIJAH (ELIJAH'S)

1Ki 17: 1 Now *E* the Tishbite, from Tishbe
17: 2 the word of the LORD came to *E*:
17: 13 *E* said to her, "Don't be afraid.
17: 15 So there was food every day for *E*
17: 15 away and did as *E* had told her.
17: 16 word of the LORD spoken by *E*.
17: 18 She said to *E*, "What do you have
17: 19 "Give me your son," *E* replied.
17: 23 *E* picked up the child and carried
17: 24 Then the woman said to *E*,
18: 1 the word of the LORD came to *E*:
18: 2 *E* went to present himself to Ahab.
18: 7 my lord *E*?" "Yes," he replied.
18: 7 was walking along, *E* met him.
18: 8 "Go tell your master, '*E* is here.' "
18: 11 to my master and say, '*E* is here.'
18: 14 to my master and say, '*E* is here.'
18: 15 *E* said, "As the LORD Almighty
18: 16 and Ahab went to meet *E*.
18: 17 When he saw *E*, he said to him,
18: 18 trouble for Israel," *E* replied.
18: 21 *E* went before the people and said,
18: 22 *E* said to them, "I am the only one
18: 25 *E* said to the prophets of Baal,
18: 27 At noon *E* began to taunt them.
18: 30 Then *E* said to all the people,
18: 31 *E* took twelve stones, one for each
18: 36 the prophet *E* stepped forward
18: 40 Then *E* commanded them,
18: 40 and *E* had them brought
18: 41 And *E* said to Ahab, "Go,
18: 42 but *E* climbed to the top of Carmel,
18: 43 Seven times *E* said, "Go back."
18: 44 So *E* said, "Go and tell Ahab,
18: 46 power of the LORD came upon *E*
19: 1 told Jezebel everything *E* had done
19: 2 So Jezebel sent a messenger to *E*
19: 3 *E* was afraid and ran for his life.
19: 9 "What are you doing here, *E*?"
19: 13 When *E* heard it, he pulled his
19: 13 "What are you doing here, *E*?"
19: 19 So *E* went from there and found
19: 19 *E* went up to him and threw his
19: 20 then left his oxen and ran after *E*.
19: 20 "Go back," *E* replied.
19: 21 out to follow *E* and became his
21: 17 the LORD came to *E* the Tishbite:
21: 20 yes, yours!' " Ahab said to *E*,
21: 28 the LORD came to *E* the Tishbite:
2Ki 1: 3 of the LORD said to *E* the Tishbite
1: 4 will certainly die!' " So *E* went.
1: 8 "That was *E* the Tishbite."
1: 9 The captain went up to *E*,
1: 9 Then he sent to *E* a captain
1: 10 down!' " *E* answered the captain,
1: 11 sent to *E* another captain
1: 12 "If I am a man of God," *E* replied,
1: 13 and fell on his knees before *E*.
1: 15 The angel of the LORD said to *E*,
1: 15 *E* got up and went down with him
1: 17 of the LORD that *E* had spoken.
2: 1 about to take *E* up to heaven
2: 1 *E* and Elisha were on their way
2: 2 *E* said to Elisha, "Stay here;
2: 4 Then *E* said to him, "Stay here,
2: 6 Then *E* said to him, "Stay here;
2: 7 facing the place where *E*
2: 8 *E* took his cloak, rolled it up
2: 9 When they had crossed, *E* said
2: 10 asked a difficult thing," *E* said,
2: 11 *E* went up to heaven in a whirlwind
2: 13 up the cloak that had fallen from *E*
2: 14 now is the LORD, the God of *E*?"
2: 15 "The spirit of *E* is resting on Elisha
2Ki 3: 11 to pour water on the hands of *E*."
9: 36 through his servant *E* the Tishbite:
10: 10 promised through his servant *E*."
10: 17 word of the LORD spoken to *E*.
1Ch 8: 27 *E* and Zicri were the sons
2Ch 21: 12 a letter from *E* the prophet,
Ezr 10: 21 *E*, Shemaiah, Jehiel and Uzziah.
10: 26 Jehiel, Abdi, Jeremoth and *E*.
Mal 4: 5 I will send you the prophet *E*
Mt 11: 14 he is the *E* who was to come.
16: 14 others say *E*; and still others,
17: 3 before them Moses and *E*,
17: 4 one for Moses and one for *E*."
17: 10 law say that *E* must come first?"
17: 11 *E* comes and will restore all things.
17: 12 But I tell you, *E* has already come,
27: 47 they said, "He's calling *E*."
27: 49 Let's see if *E* comes to save him."
Mk 6: 15 Others said, "He is *E*."
8: 28 others say *E*; and still others,
9: 4 And there appeared before them *E*
9: 5 one for Moses and one for *E*."
9: 11 law say that *E* must come first?"
9: 12 "To be sure, *E* does come first,
9: 13 But I tell you, *E* has come,
15: 35 they said, "Listen, he's calling *E*."
15: 36 Let's see if *E* comes to take him
Lk 1: 17 in the spirit and power of *E*,
4: 26 Yet *E* was not sent to any of them,
9: 8 others that *E* had appeared,
9: 19 others say *E*; and still others,
9: 30 *E*, appeared in glorious splendor,
9: 33 one for Moses and one for *E*."
Jn 1: 21 Are you *E*?" He said, "I am not."
1: 25 nor *E*, nor the Prophet?" "I baptize
Ro 11: 2 says in the passage about *E*—
Jas 5: 17 *E* was a man just like us.

ELIJAH'S (ELIJAH)

1Ki 17: 22 The LORD heard *E* cry,
Lk 4: 25 widows in Israel in *E* time,

ELIKA

2Sa 23: 25 the Harodite, *E* the Harodite,

ELIM

Ex 15: 27 to *E*, where there were twelve
16: 1 Israelite community set out from *E*
16: 1 which is between *E* and Sinai,
Nu 33: 9 They left Marah and went to *E*,
33: 10 They left *E* and camped by the Red

ELIMELECH

Ru 1: 2 man's name was *E*, his wife's name
1: 3 Now *E*, Naomi's husband, died,
2: 1 from the clan of *E*, a man
2: 3 who was from the clan of *E*.
4: 3 that belonged to our brother *E*.
4: 9 from Naomi all the property of *E*,

ELIMINATE (ELIMINATED)

Dt 7: 22 allowed to *e* them all at once,

ELIMINATED (ELIMINATE)

Dt 2: 15 until he had completely *e* them

ELIOENAI

1Ch 3: 23 *E*, Hizkiah and Azrikam—
3: 24 The sons of *E*: Hodaviah, Eliashib,
4: 36 also *E*, Jaakobah, Jeshohaiah,
7: 8 Joash, Eliezer, *E*, Omri, Jeremoth,
Ezr 10: 22 *E*, Maaseiah, Ishmael, Nethanel,
10: 27 *E*, Eliashib, Mattaniah, Jeremoth,
Ne 12: 41 Maaseiah, Mijamin, Micaiah, *E*,

ELIPHAL

1Ch 11: 35 of Sacar the Hararite, *E* son of Ur,

ELIPHAZ

Ge 36: 4 Adah bore *E* to Esau, Basemath
36: 10 *E*, the son of Esau's wife Adah,
36: 11 The sons of *E*: Teman, Omar,
36: 12 Esau's son *E* also had a concubine
36: 15 The sons of *E* the firstborn of Esau:
36: 16 were the chiefs descended from *E*
1Ch 1: 35 The sons of Esau: *E*, Reuel, Jeush,
1: 36 The sons of *E*: Teman, Omar,
Job 2: 11 three friends, *E* the Temanite,

Job 4: 1 Then *E* the Temanite replied:
15: 1 Then *E* the Temanite replied:
22: 1 Then *E* the Temanite replied:
42: 7 he said to *E* the Temanite,
42: 9 *E* the Temanite, Bildad the Shuhite

ELIPHELEHU

1Ch 15: 18 Mattithiah, *E*, Mikneiah,
15: 21 and Mattithiah, *E*, Mikneiah,

ELIPHELET

2Sa 5: 16 Japhia, Elishama, Eliada and *E*.
23: 34 *E* son of Ahasbai the Maacathite,
1Ch 3: 6 Elishua, *E*, Nogah, Nepheg, Japhia
3: 8 Elishama, Eliada and *E*—
8: 39 the second son and *E* the third.
14: 7 Japhia, Elishama, Beeliada and *E*.
Ezr 8: 13 whose names were *E*, Jeuel
10: 33 Mattattah, Zabad, *E*, Jeremai,

ELISHA (ELISHA'S)

1Ki 19: 16 anoint *E* son of Shaphat
19: 17 *E* will put to death any who escape
19: 19 and found *E* son of Shaphat.
19: 20 *E* then left his oxen and ran
19: 21 So *E* left him and went back.
2Ki 2: 1 *E* were on their way from Gilgal.
2: 2 But *E* said, "As surely
2: 2 Elijah said to *E*, "Stay here;
2: 3 *E* replied, "but do not speak of it."
2: 3 prophets at Bethel came out to *E*
2: 4 Elijah said to him, "Stay here, *E*;
2: 5 prophets at Jericho went up to *E*
2: 7 and *E* had stopped at the Jordan.
2: 9 Elijah said to *E*, "Tell me,
2: 9 portion of your spirit," *E* replied.
2: 12 *E* saw this and cried out, "My
2: 12 of Israel!" And *E* saw him no more
2: 15 The spirit of Elijah is resting on *E*."
2: 16 No," *E* replied, "do not send them
2: 18 When they returned to *E*,
2: 19 The men of the city said to *E*,
2: 22 to the word *E* had spoken.
2: 23 From there *E* went up to Bethel.
3: 11 "*E* son of Shaphat is here.
3: 13 *E* said to the king of Israel,
3: 14 *E* said, "As surely as the LORD
3: 15 hand of the LORD came upon *E*
4: 1 of the prophets cried out to *E*,
4: 2 *E* replied to her, "How can I help
4: 3 *E* said, "Go around and ask all
4: 8 One day *E* went to Shunem.
4: 11 One day when *E* came, he went up
4: 13 *E* said to him, "Tell her, 'You have
4: 14 done for her?" *E* asked.
4: 15 Then *E* said, "Call her."
4: 16 About this time next year," *E* said,
4: 17 to a son, just as *E* had told her.
4: 29 'Don't raise my hopes'?" *E* said
4: 31 So Gehazi went back to meet *E*
4: 32 When *E* reached the house,
4: 35 *E* turned away and walked back
4: 36 *E* summoned Gehazi and said,
4: 38 *E* returned to Gilgal and there was
4: 41 *E* said, "Get some flour."
4: 42 Give it to the people to eat," *E* said
4: 43 *E* answered, "Give it to the people
5: 8 When *E* the man of God heard that
5: 10 *E* sent a messenger to say to him,
5: 19 "Go in peace," *E* said.
5: 20 the servant of *E* the man of God,
5: 25 and stood before his master *E*.
5: 25 have you been, Gehazi?" *E* asked.
5: 26 *E* said to him, "Was not my spirit
6: 1 company of the prophets said to *E*,
6: 3 your servants?" "I will," *E* replied.
6: 6 *E* cut a stick and threw it there,
6: 10 Time and again *E* warned the king,
6: 12 said one of his officers, "but *E*,
6: 17 And *E* prayed, "O LORD,
6: 17 and chariots of fire all around *E*.
6: 18 came down toward him, *E* prayed
6: 18 with blindness, as *E* had asked.
6: 19 *E* told them, "This is not the road
6: 20 After they entered the city, *E* said,
6: 21 he asked *E*, "Shall I kill them,
6: 31 if the head of *E* son
6: 32 Now *E* was sitting in his house,
2Ki 6: 32 but before he arrived, *E* said
7: 1 *E* said, "Hear the word
7: 2 answered *E*, "but you will not eat
8: 1 *E* had said to the woman whose
8: 4 all the great things *E* has done."
8: 5 telling the king how *E* had restored
8: 5 this is her son whom *E* restored
8: 5 woman whose son *E* had brought
8: 7 *E* went to Damascus,
8: 9 illness?' " Hazael went to meet *E*,
8: 10 from this illness?' " *E* answered,
8: 13 king of Aram," answered *E*.
8: 14 Then Hazael left *E* and returned
8: 14 asked, "What did *E* say
9: 1 The prophet *E* summoned a man
13: 14 *E* was suffering from the illness
13: 15 and horsemen of Israel!" *E* said,
13: 16 *E* put his hands on the king's hands
13: 17 of victory over Aram!" *E* declared.
13: 17 "Shoot!" *E* said, and he shot.
13: 18 *E* told him, "Strike the ground."
13: 20 *E* died and was buried.
Lk 4: 27 in the time of *E* the prophet,

ELISHA'S (ELISHA)

2Ki 5: 9 and stopped at the door of *E* house.
5: 27 Gehazi went from *E* presence
13: 21 When the body touched *E* bones,
13: 21 threw the man's body into *E* tomb.

ELISHAH

Ge 10: 4 The sons of Javan: *E*, Tarshish,
1Ch 1: 7 The sons of Javan: *E*, Tarshish,
Eze 27: 7 and purple from the coasts of *E*.

ELISHAMA

Nu 1: 10 from Ephraim, *E* son of Ammihud;
2: 18 of Ephraim is *E* son of Ammihud.
7: 48 On the seventh day *E* son
7: 53 the offering of *E* son of Ammihud.
10: 22 *E* son of Ammihud was
2Sa 5: 16 Elishua, Nepheg, Japhia, *E*,
2Ki 25: 25 the son of *E*, who was
1Ch 2: 41 and Jekamiah the father of *E*.
3: 8 Nogah, Nepheg, Japhia, *E*,
7: 26 Ammihud his son, *E* his son,
14: 7 Nogah, Nepheg, Japhia, *E*,
2Ch 17: 8 and the priests *E* and Jehoram.
Jer 36: 12 were sitting: *E* the secretary,
36: 20 in the room of *E* the secretary,
36: 21 it from the room of *E* the secretary
41: 1 son of Nethaniah, the son of *E*,

ELISHAPHAT

2Ch 23: 1 son of Adaiah, and *E* son of Zicri.

ELISHEBA

Ex 6: 23 Aaron married *E*, daughter

ELISHUA

2Sa 5: 15 Solomon, Ibhar, *E*, Nepheg, Japhia
1Ch 3: 6 *E*, Eliphelet, Nogah, Nepheg,
14: 5 Solomon, Ibhar, *E*, Elpelet, Nogah,

ELITE

Eze 23: 7 to all the *e* of the Assyrians

ELIUD

Mt 1: 15 father of *E*, *E* the father of Eleazar,

ELIZABETH

Lk 1: 5 his wife *E* was also a descendant
1: 7 no children, because *E* was barren;
1: 13 Your wife *E* will bear you a son,
1: 24 this his wife *E* became pregnant
1: 36 Even *E* your relative is going
1: 40 Zechariah's home and greeted *E*.
1: 41 When *E* heard Mary's greeting,
1: 41 *E* was filled with the Holy Spirit.
1: 56 Mary stayed with *E*
1: 57 time for *E* to have her baby,

ELIZAPHAN

Nu 3: 30 of the Kohathite clans was *E* son
34: 25 son of Joseph; *E* son of Parnach,
1Ch 15: 8 from the descendants of *E*,
2Ch 29: 13 from the descendants of *E*,

ELIZUR

Nu 1: 5 from Reuben, *E* son of Shedeur;
2: 10 of Reuben is *E* son of Shedeur.
7: 30 On the fourth day *E* son of Shedeur
7: 35 the offering of *E* son of Shedeur.
10: 18 *E* son of Shedeur was in command.

ELKANAH

Ex 6: 24 The sons of Korah were Assir, *E*
1Sa 1: 1 whose name was *E* son of Jeroham,
1: 4 Whenever the day came for *E*
1: 8 *E* her husband would say to her,
1: 19 *E* lay with Hannah his wife,
1: 21 When the man *E* went up
1: 23 to you," *E* her husband told her.
2: 11 Then *E* went home to Ramah,
2: 20 Eli would bless *E* and his wife,
1Ch 6: 23 *E* his son, Ebiasaph his son,
6: 25 The descendants of *E*: Amasai,
6: 26 Amasai, Ahimoth, *E* his son,
6: 27 *E* his son and Samuel his son.
6: 34 the son of *E*, the son of Jeroham,
6: 35 the son of *E*, the son of Mahath,
6: 36 the son of *E*, the son of Joel,
9: 16 Berekiah son of Asa, the son of *E*,
12: 6 and Shephatiah the Haruphite; *E*,
15: 23 and *E* were to be doorkeepers
2Ch 28: 7 and *E*, second to the king.

ELKOSHITE

Na 1: 1 book of the vision of Nahum the *E*.

ELLASAR

Ge 14: 1 king of Shinar, Arioch king of *E*,
14: 9 of Shinar and Arioch king of *E*—

ELMADAM

Lk 3: 28 the son of *E*, the son of Er,

ELNAAM

1Ch 11: 46 Jeribai and Joshaviah the sons of *E*,

ELNATHAN

2Ki 24: 8 name was Nehushta daughter of *E*;
Ezr 8: 16 Shemaiah, *E*, Jarib, *E*, Nathan,
8: 16 and *E*, who were men of learning,
Jer 26: 22 sent *E* son of Acbor to Egypt,
36: 12 son of Shemaiah, *E* son of Acbor,
36: 25 Even though *E*, Delaiah

ELOI

Mt 27: 46 "*E*, *E*, *lama sabachthani?*"—
Mk 15: 34 "*E*, *E*, *lama sabachthani?*"—

ELON (ELONITE)

Ge 26: 34 Basemath daughter of *E* the Hittite
36: 2 Adah daughter of *E* the Hittite,
46: 14 The sons of Zebulun: Sered, *E*
Nu 26: 26 through *E*, the Elonite clan;
Jos 19: 43 Ithlah, *E*, Timnah, Ekron, Eltekeh,
Jdg 12: 11 *E* the Zebulunite led Israel ten
12: 12 *E* died, and was buried in Aijalon

ELON BETHHANAN

1Ki 4: 9 Shaalbim, Beth Shemesh and *E*;

ELONITE (ELON)

Nu 26: 26 the *E* clan; through Jahleel,

ELOQUENCE (ELOQUENT)

1Co 2: 1 come with *e* or superior wisdom

ELOQUENT (ELOQUENCE)

Ex 4: 10 "O Lord, I have never been *e*,

ELPAAL

1Ch 8: 11 By Hushim he had Abitub and *E*.
8: 12 The sons of *E*: Eber, Misham,
8: 18 Izliah and Jobab were the sons of *E*

ELPELET

1Ch 14: 5 Ibhar, Elishua, *E*, Nogah, Nepheg,

ELTEKEH

Jos 19: 44 Timnah, Ekron, *E*, Gibbethon,

Jos 21: 23 the tribe of Dan they received *E*,

ELTEKON

Jos 15: 59 Beth Anoth and *E*— six towns

ELTOLAD

Jos 15: 30 Iim, Ezem, *E*, Kesil, Hormah,
19: 4 Balah, Ezem, *E*, Bethul, Hormah,

ELUDE (ELUDED)

Job 11: 20 and escape will *e* them;
Rev 9: 6 long to die, but death will *e* them.

ELUDED (ELUDE)

1Sa 18: 11 But David *e* him twice.
19: 10 but David *e* him as Saul drove

ELUL

Ne 6: 15 completed on the twenty-fifth of *E*,

ELUZAI

1Ch 12: 5 Jozabad the Gederathite, *E*,

ELYMAS

Ac 13: 8 *E* the sorcerer (for that is what his
13: 9 looked straight at *E* and said,

ELZABAD

1Ch 12: 12 Johanan the eighth, *E* the ninth,
26: 7 Othni, Rephael, Obed and *E*;

ELZAPHAN

Ex 6: 22 The sons of Uzziel were Mishael, *E*
Lev 10: 4 Moses summoned Mishael and *E*,

EMASCULATE (EMASCULATED)

Gal 5: 12 the whole way and *e* themselves!

EMASCULATED (EMASCULATE)

Dt 23: 1 No one who has been *e* by crushing

EMBALM (EMBALMED EMBALMING)

Ge 50: 2 in his service to *e* his father Israel.

EMBALMED (EMBALM)

Ge 50: 2 physicians *e* him, taking a full forty
50: 26 after they *e* him, he was placed

EMBALMING (EMBALM)

Ge 50: 3 for that was the time required for *e*.

EMBANKMENT (BANK)

Lk 19: 43 when your enemies will build an *e*

EMBARRASS (EMBARRASSED EMBARRASSMENT)

Ru 2: 15 among the sheaves, don't *e* her

EMBARRASSED (EMBARRASS)

2Co 7: 14 about you, and you have not *e* me.

EMBARRASSMENT (EMBARRASS)

Jdg 3: 25 They waited to the point of *e*,

EMBEDDED

Ecc 12: 11 sayings like firmly *e* nails—

EMBERS

Ps 102: 3 my bones burn like glowing *e*.
Pr 26: 21 As charcoal to *e* and as wood to fire

EMBITTER (BITTER)

Col 3: 21 Fathers, do not *e* your children,

EMBITTERED (BITTER)

Ps 73: 21 and my spirit *e*,

EMBODIMENT (BODY)

Ro 2: 20 have in the law the *e* of knowledge

EMBOLDENED (BOLD)

1Co 8: 10 won't he be *e* to eat what has been

EMBRACE (EMBRACED EMBRACES EMBRACING)

Pr 3: 18 of life to those who *e* her;
4: 8 *e* her, and she will honor you.
5: 20 Why *e* the bosom of another man's
Ecc 3: 5 a time to *e* and a time to refrain,
Mic 7: 5 Even with her who lies in your *e*

EMBRACED (EMBRACE)

Ge 29: 13 He *e* him and kissed him
33: 4 Esau ran to meet Jacob and *e* him;
45: 14 and Benjamin *e* him, weeping.
48: 10 his father kissed them and *e* them.
1Ki 9: 9 and have *e* other gods, worshiping
2Ch 7: 22 and have *e* other gods, worshiping
Ac 20: 37 as they *e* him and kissed him.

EMBRACES (EMBRACE)

SS 2: 6 and his right arm *e* me.
8: 3 and his right arm *e* me.

EMBRACING (EMBRACE)

Ecc 2: 3 myself with wine, and *e* folly—

EMBROIDERED (EMBROIDERER EMBROIDERERS)

Jdg 5: 30 colorful garments *e*,
5: 30 highly *e* garments for my neck—
Ps 45: 14 In *e* garments she is led to the king;
Eze 16: 10 I clothed you with an *e* dress
16: 13 and costly fabric and *e* cloth.
16: 18 And you took your *e* clothes to put
26: 16 and take off their *e* garments.
27: 7 Fine *e* linen from Egypt was your
27: 16 purple fabric, *e* work, fine linen,
27: 24 *e* work and multicolored rugs

EMBROIDERER (EMBROIDERED)

Ex 26: 36 twisted linen—the work of an *e*.
27: 16 the work of an *e*— with four posts
28: 39 The sash is to be the work of an *e*.
36: 37 of an *e*; and they made five posts
38: 18 twisted linen—the work of an *e*.
38: 23 and designer, and an *e* in blue,
39: 29 the work of an *e*— as the LORD

EMBROIDERERS (EMBROIDERED)

Ex 35: 35 *e* in blue, purple and scarlet yarn

EMEK KEZIZ

Jos 18: 21 Jericho, Beth Hoglah, *E*,

EMERALD

Ex 28: 18 and an *e*; in the third row a jacinth,
39: 11 and an *e*; in the third row a jacinth,
Eze 28: 13 ruby, topaz and *e*,
Rev 4: 3 resembling an *e*, encircled
21: 19 the fourth *e*, the fifth sardonyx,

EMERGE

Da 8: 22 represent four kingdoms that will *e*

EMISSION

Lev 15: 16 " 'When a man has an *e* of semen,
15: 18 and there is an *e* of semen,
15: 32 for anyone made unclean by an *e*
22: 4 by anyone who has an *e* of semen,
Dt 23: 10 is unclean because of a nocturnal *e*,
Eze 23: 20 and whose *e* was like that of horses.

EMITES

Ge 14: 5 the *E* in Shaveh Kiriathaim
Dt 2: 10 (The *E* used to live there—
2: 11 but the Moabites called them *E*.

EMMAUS

Lk 24: 13 going to a village called *E*,

EMPEROR (EMPIRE)

Ac 25: 25 to the *E* I decided to send him

EMPEROR'S (EMPIRE)

Ac 25: 21 to be held over for the *E* decision,

EMPIRE (EMPEROR EMPEROR'S IMPERIAL)

Est 10: 1 imposed tribute throughout the *e*,
Jer 34: 1 in the *e* he ruled were fighting
Da 11: 4 because his *e* will be uprooted
11: 4 his *e* will be broken up

EMPLOYED

Eze 39: 14 " 'Men will be regularly *e*

EMPTIED (EMPTY)

Ge 24: 20 she quickly *e* her jar into the trough
Lev 14: 36 the house to be *e* before he goes
Ne 5: 13 such a man be shaken out and *e*!"
Zep 2: 4 At midday Ashdod will be *e*
1Co 1: 17 the cross of Christ be *e* of its power.

EMPTIES (EMPTY)

Eze 47: 8 When it *e* into the Sea, the water

EMPTY (EMPTIED EMPTIES EMPTYING)

Ge 1: 2 Now the earth was formless and *e*,
37: 24 cistern was *e*; there was no water
Jdg 7: 16 *e* jars in the hands of all of them,
Ru 1: 21 the LORD has brought me back *e*.
1Sa 6: 3 do not send it away *e*,
20: 18 because your seat will be *e*.
20: 25 to Saul, but David's place was *e*.
20: 27 David's place was *e* again.
2Ki 4: 3 ask all your neighbors for *e* jars.
18: 20 but you speak only *e* words.
2Ch 24: 11 priest would come and *e* the chest
Job 15: 2 a wise man answer with *e* notions
26: 7 the northern ⌊skies⌋ over *e* space;
35: 13 God does not listen to their *e* plea;
35: 16 So Job opens his mouth with *e* talk;
Pr 14: 4 there are no oxen, the manger is *e*,
Isa 16: 6 but her boasts are *e*.
32: 6 the hungry he leaves *e*
36: 5 but you speak only *e* words.
45: 18 he did not create it to be *e*,
55: 11 It will not return to me *e*,
59: 4 They rely on *e* arguments
Jer 4: 23 and it was formless and *e*;
48: 12 they will *e* her jars
51: 34 he has made us an *e* jar.
Eze 24: 6 *E* it piece by piece
24: 11 Then set the *e* pot on the coals
Am 4: 6 "I gave you *e* stomachs
Mic 6: 14 your stomach will still be *e*.
Lk 1: 53 but has sent the rich away *e*.
Eph 5: 6 no one deceive you with *e* words,
1Pe 1: 18 from the *e* way of life handed
2Pe 2: 18 For they mouth *e*, boastful words

EMPTY-HANDED

Ge 31: 42 would surely have sent me away *e*.
Ex 3: 21 when you leave you will not go *e*.
23: 15 "No one is to appear before me *e*.
34: 20 "No one is to appear before me *e*.
Dt 15: 13 him, do not send him away *e*.
16: 16 appear before the LORD *e*:
Ru 3: 17 back to your mother-in-law *e*.' "
Job 22: 9 And you sent widows away *e*
Jer 50: 9 who do not return *e*.
Mk 12: 3 beat him and sent him away *e*.
Lk 20: 10 beat him and sent him away *e*.
20: 11 treated shamefully and sent away *e*

EMPTYING (EMPTY)

Ge 42: 35 As they were *e* their sacks,
Hab 1: 17 Is he to keep on *e* his net,

EN EGLAIM

Eze 47: 10 from En Gedi to *E*

EN GANNIM

Jos 15: 34 Ashnah, Zanoah, *E*, Tappuah,
19: 21 Rabbith, Kishion, Ebez, Remeth, *E*
21: 29 Kishion, Daberath, Jarmuth and *E*,

EN GEDI

Jos 15: 62 the City of Salt and *E*—
1Sa 23: 29 and lived in the strongholds of *E*.
24: 1 "David is in the Desert of *E*."
2Ch 20: 2 in Hazazon Tamar" (that is, *E*).
SS 1: 14 from the vineyards of *E*.
Eze 47: 10 from *E* to En Eglaim

EN HADDAH

Jos 19: 21 Remeth, En Gannim, *E*

EN HAKKORE

Jdg 15: 19 So the spring was called *E*,

EN HAZOR

Jos 19: 37 Hazor, Kedesh, Edrei, *E*, Iron,

EN MISHPAT
Ge 14: 7 and went to *E* (that is, Kadesh),

EN RIMMON
Ne 11: 29 in *E*, in Zorah, in Jarmuth, Zanoah,

EN ROGEL
Jos 15: 7 and came out at *E*.
18: 16 of the Jebusite city and so to *E*.
2Sa 17: 17 and Ahimaaz were staying at *E*.
1Ki 1: 9 at the Stone of Zoheleth near *E*.

EN SHEMESH
Jos 15: 7 continued along to the Waters of *E*
18: 17 went to *E*, continued to Geliloth,

EN TAPPUAH
Jos 17: 7 to include the people living at *E*.

ENABLE (ABLE)
Ecc 6: 2 God does not *e* him to enjoy them,
Lk 1: 74 to *e* us to serve him without fear
Ac 4: 29 *e* your servants to speak your word

ENABLED (ABLE)
Lev 26: 13 *e* you to walk with heads held high.
Ru 4: 13 And the LORD *e* her to conceive,
Jn 6: 65 unless the Father has *e* him."
Ac 2: 4 other tongues as the Spirit *e* them.
7: 10 and *e* him to gain the goodwill
Heb 11: 11 was *e* to become a father

ENABLES (ABLE)
2Sa 22: 34 he *e* me to stand on the heights.
Ps 18: 33 he *e* me to stand on the heights.
Ecc 5: 19 and possessions, and *e* him
Hab 3: 19 he *e* me to go on the heights.
Php 3: 21 by the power that *e* him

ENABLING (ABLE)
Ac 14: 3 the message of his grace by *e* them

ENAIM
Ge 38: 14 then sat down at the entrance to *E*,
38: 21 was beside the road at *E*?"

ENAM
Jos 15: 34 Tappuah, *E*, Jarmuth, Adullam,

ENAN
Nu 1: 15 from Naphtali, Ahira son of *E*."
2: 29 of Naphtali is Ahira son of *E*.
7: 78 On the twelfth day Ahira son of *E*,
7: 83 was the offering of Ahira son of *E*.
10: 27 and Ahira son of *E* was

ENCAMP (CAMP)
Ex 14: 2 They are to *e* by the sea, directly
14: 2 turn back and *e* near Pi Hahiroth,
Nu 1: 50 to take care of it and *e* around it.
2: 3 are to *e* under their standard.
2: 17 out in the same order as they *e*,
9: 20 LORD's command they would *e*,
Job 19: 12 and *e* around my tent.
Isa 29: 3 I will *e* against you all around;
Jer 50: 29 *E* all around her;

ENCAMPED (CAMP)
Ge 26: 17 and *e* in the Valley of Gerar
Nu 2: 34 that is the way they *e*
9: 17 the cloud settled, the Israelites *e*.
9: 18 and at his command they *e*.
9: 23 At the LORD's command they *e*,
12: 16 and *e* in the Desert of Paran.
24: 2 and saw Israel *e* tribe by tribe,
Dt 23: 9 you are *e* against your enemies,
Jdg 11: 20 He mustered all his men and *e*
1Sa 26: 5 with the army *e* around him.
2Sa 23: 13 of Philistines was *e* in the Valley
1Ki 16: 15 The army was *e* near Gibbethon,
2Ki 25: 1 He *e* outside the city and built siege
1Ch 11: 15 of Philistines was *e* in the Valley

ENCAMPS (CAMP)
Ps 34: 7 The angel of the LORD *e*

ENCHANTER (ENCHANTERS)
Ps 58: 5 however skillful the *e* may be.
Isa 3: 3 skilled craftsman and clever *e*,
Da 2: 10 a thing of any magician or *e*
2: 27 Daniel replied, "No wise man, *e*,

ENCHANTERS (ENCHANTER)
Da 1: 20 and *e* in his whole kingdom.
2: 2 king summoned the magicians, *e*,
4: 7 *e*, astrologers and diviners came,
5: 7 The king called out for the *e*,
5: 11 *e*, astrologers and diviners.
5: 15 and *e* were brought before me

ENCIRCLE (CIRCLE)
Ps 22: 12 strong bulls of Bashan *e* me.
Isa 29: 3 I will *e* you with towers
Lk 19: 43 *e* you and hem you in on every side

ENCIRCLED (CIRCLE)
1Ki 7: 24 Below the rim, gourds *e* it—
2Ch 4: 3 figures of bulls *e* it—ten to a cubit.
Ps 22: 16 a band of evil men has *e* me,
SS 7: 2 *e* by lilies.
Rev 4: 3 an emerald, *e* the throne.
5: 6 *e* by the four living creatures
5: 11 They *e* the throne and the living

ENCIRCLING (CIRCLE)
1Ki 7: 18 in two rows *e* each network
2Ch 33: 14 of the Fish Gate and *e* the hill

ENCLOSE (CLOSE)
SS 8: 9 we will *e* her with panels of cedar.

ENCLOSED (CLOSE)
Est 1: 5 in the *e* garden of the king's palace,
SS 4: 12 you are a spring *e*, a sealed fountain
Eze 46: 22 of the outer court were *e* courts,

ENCOUNTER
Ex 23: 27 into confusion every nation you *e*.
2Sa 23: 8 men, whom he killed in one *e*.
1Ch 11: 11 men, whom he killed in one *e*.

ENCOURAGE (ENCOURAGED ENCOURAGEMENT ENCOURAGES ENCOURAGING)
Dt 1: 38 *E* him, because he will lead Israel
3: 28 and *e* and strengthen him,
2Sa 11: 25 Say this to *e* Joab."
19: 7 Now go out and *e* your men.
Job 16: 5 But my mouth would *e* you;
Ps 10: 17 you *e* them, and you listen
64: 5 They *e* each other in evil plans,
Isa 1: 17 *e* the oppressed.
Jer 29: 8 to the dreams you *e* them to have.
Ac 15: 32 to *e* and strengthen the brothers.
Ro 12: 8 if it is encouraging, let him *e*;
Eph 6: 22 how we are, and that he may *e* you.
Col 4: 8 and that he may *e* your hearts.
1Th 3: 2 to strengthen and *e* you
4: 18 Therefore *e* each other
5: 11 Therefore *e* one another
5: 14 those who are idle, *e* the timid,
2Th 2: 17 *e* your hearts and strengthen you
2Ti 4: 2 rebuke and *e*— with great patience
Tit 1: 9 so that he can *e* others
2: 6 *e* the young men to be
2: 15 *E* and rebuke with all authority.
Heb 3: 13 But *e* one another daily, as long
10: 25 but let us *e* one another—

ENCOURAGED (ENCOURAGE)
Jdg 7: 11 you will be *e* to attack the camp."
20: 22 But the men of Israel *e* one another
2Ch 22: 3 for his mother *e* him
32: 6 and *e* them with these words:
35: 2 and *e* them in the service
Eze 13: 22 you *e* the wicked not to turn
Ac 9: 31 It was strengthened; and *e*
11: 23 and *e* them all to remain true
16: 40 met with the brothers and *e* them.
18: 27 the brothers *e* him and wrote
27: 36 They were all *e* and ate some food
28: 15 men Paul thanked God and was *e*.
Ro 1: 12 and I may be mutually *e*
1Co 14: 31 everyone may be instructed and *e*.
2Co 7: 4 I am greatly *e*; in all our troubles
7: 13 By all this we are *e*.
Php 1: 14 brothers in the Lord have been *e*
Col 2: 2 My purpose is that they may be *e*
1Th 3: 7 persecution we were *e* about you
Heb 6: 18 offered to us may be greatly *e*.

ENCOURAGEMENT (ENCOURAGE)
Ac 4: 36 Barnabas (which means Son of *E*),
13: 15 a message of *e* for the people,
20: 2 speaking many words of *e*
Ro 15: 4 *e* of the Scriptures we might have
15: 5 and *e* give you a spirit of unity
1Co 14: 3 to men for their strengthening, *e*
2Co 7: 13 to our own *e*, we were especially
Php 2: 1 If you have any *e* from being united
2Th 2: 16 and by his grace gave us eternal *e*
Phm : 7 love has given me great joy and *e*,
Heb 12: 5 word of *e* that addresses you

ENCOURAGES (ENCOURAGE)
Isa 41: 7 The craftsman *e* the goldsmith,

ENCOURAGING (ENCOURAGE)
Ac 14: 22 *e* them to remain true to the faith.
15: 31 and were glad for its *e* message.
20: 1 for the disciples and, after *e* them,
Ro 12: 8 if it is *e*, let him encourage;
1Th 2: 12 *e*, comforting and urging you
1Pe 5: 12 *e* you and testifying that this is

ENCROACH
Dt 2: 37 you did not *e* on any of the land
Pr 23: 10 or *e* on the fields of the fatherless,

ENCRUSTED (CRUST)
Eze 24: 6 to the pot now *e*,

END (ENDED ENDING ENDS)
Ge 6: 13 I am going to put an *e* to all people,
8: 3 At the *e* of the hundred
23: 9 to him and is in the *e* of his field.
41: 53 of abundance in Egypt came to an *e*
47: 21 from one *e* of Egypt to the other.
Ex 12: 41 At the *e* of the 430 years,
23: 16 of Ingathering at the *e* of the year,
25: 19 Make one cherub on one *e*
26: 4 and do the same with the *e* curtain
26: 4 the edge of the *e* curtain in one set,
26: 5 and fifty loops on the *e* curtain
26: 10 also along the edge of the *e* curtain
26: 10 the edge of the *e* curtain in one set
26: 22 Make six frames for the far *e*,
26: 22 that is, the west *e* of the tabernacle,
26: 23 frames for the corners at the far *e*.
26: 27 at the far *e* of the tabernacle.
26: 28 to extend from *e* to *e* at the middle
27: 12 west *e* of the courtyard shall be
27: 13 On the east *e*, toward the sunrise,
32: 27 the camp from one *e* to the other,
36: 11 the edge of the *e* curtain in one set,
36: 11 with the *e* curtain in the other set.
36: 12 and fifty loops on the *e* curtain
36: 17 also along the edge of the *e* curtain
36: 17 the edge of the *e* curtain in one set
36: 27 They made six frames for the far *e*,
36: 27 that is, the west *e* of the tabernacle,
36: 28 of the tabernacle at the far *e*.
36: 32 at the far *e* of the tabernacle.
36: 33 extended from *e* to *e* at the middle
37: 8 He made one cherub on one *e*
38: 12 The west *e* was fifty cubits wide
38: 13 The east *e*, toward the sunrise,
Nu 13: 25 At the *e* of forty days they returned
14: 35 They will meet their *e* in this desert
16: 21 so I can put an *e* to them at once."
16: 45 so I can put an *e* to them at once."
17: 10 will put an *e* to their grumbling
23: 10 and may my *e* be like theirs!"
25: 11 that in my zeal I did not put an *e*
34: 3 start from the *e* of the Salt Sea,
34: 5 the Wadi of Egypt and *e* at the Sea.
34: 9 to Ziphron and *e* at Hazar Enan.
34: 12 down along the Jordan and *e*
Dt 4: 32 ask from one *e* of the heavens
8: 16 you so that in the *e* it might go well
9: 11 At the *e* of the forty days
11: 12 the beginning of the year to its *e*.

Dt 13: 7 from one *e* of the land to the other),
14: 28 At the *e* of every three years,
15: 1 At the *e* of every seven years you
28: 64 from one *e* of the earth to the other.
31: 10 "At the *e* of every seven years,
31: 24 of this law from beginning to *e*,
31: 30 from beginning to *e* in the hearing
32: 20 "and see what their *e* will be;
32: 29 and discern what their *e* will be!
Jos 13: 27 the territory up to the *e* of the Sea
15: 2 at the southern *e* of the Salt Sea,
15: 8 at the northern *e* of the Valley
24: 20 on you and make an *e* of you,
Ru 3: 7 down at the far *e* of the grain pile.
1Sa 3: 12 from beginning to *e*.
14: 27 so he reached out the *e*
14: 43 honey with the *e* of my staff.
2Sa 2: 26 Don't you realize that this will *e*
15: 7 At the *e* of four years, Absalom
24: 8 Jerusalem at the *e* of nine months
24: 15 until the *e* of the time designated,
1Ki 9: 10 At the *e* of twenty years,
10: 20 one at either *e* of each step.
2Ki 8: 3 At the *e* of the seven years she
10: 21 full from one *e* to the other.
18: 10 At the *e* of three years
21: 16 he filled Jerusalem from *e* to *e*—
24: 20 and in the *e* he thrust them
1Ch 29: 29 beginning to *e*, they are written
2Ch 8: 1 At the *e* of twenty years,
9: 19 one at either *e* of each step.
9: 29 from beginning to *e*,
12: 15 from beginning to *e*,
16: 11 of Asa's reign, from beginning to *e*,
20: 16 them at the *e* of the gorge
20: 34 from beginning to *e*,
21: 19 at the *e* of the second year,
25: 26 from beginning to *e*,
26: 22 from beginning to *e*,
28: 26 from beginning to *e*, are written
35: 27 all the events, from beginning to *e*,
Ezr 9: 11 impurity from one *e* to the other.
Ne 3: 21 of Eliashib's house to the *e* of it.
4: 11 and will kill them and put an *e*
9: 31 great mercy you did not put an *e*
Est 1: 18 There will be no *e* of disrespect
8: 3 him to put an *e* to the evil plan
Job 4: 15 and the hair on my body stood on *e*
7: 6 they come to an *e* without hope.
16: 3 long-winded speeches never *e*?
18: 2 "When will you *e* these speeches?
19: 25 and that in the *e* he will stand
21: 21 his allotted months come to an *e*?
28: 3 Man puts an *e* to the darkness;
Ps 7: 9 bring to an *e* the violence
19: 6 It rises at one *e* of the heavens
39: 4 "Show me, O LORD, my life's *e*
48: 14 he will be our guide even to the *e*.
89: 44 You have put an *e* to his splendor
102: 27 and your years will never *e*.
107: 27 they were at their wits' *e*.
112: 8 in the *e* he will look in triumph
119: 33 then I will keep them to the *e*.
119:112 to the very *e*.
Pr 1: 19 Such is the *e* of all who go
5: 4 but in the *e* she is bitter as gall,
5: 11 At the *e* of your life you will groan,
14: 12 but in the *e* it leads to death.
14: 13 and joy may *e* in grief.
16: 25 but in the *e* it leads to death.
19: 20 and in the *e* you will be wise.
20: 21 will not be blessed at the *e*.
23: 32 In the *e* it bites like a snake
25: 8 for what will you do in the *e*
28: 23 in the *e* gain more favor
29: 21 he will bring grief in the *e*.
Ecc 3: 11 done from beginning to *e*.
4: 8 There was no *e* to his toil,
4: 16 There was no *e* to all the people
7: 8 The *e* of a matter is better
10: 13 at the *e* they are wicked madness—
12: 12 making many books there is no *e*,
Isa 2: 7 there is no *e* to their chariots.
2: 7 there is no *e* to their treasures.
7: 3 Ahaz at the *e* of the aqueduct
9: 7 there will be no *e*.
10: 7 to put an *e* to many nations.
10: 25 soon my anger against you will *e*
Isa 13: 11 I will put an *e* to the arrogance
14: 4 the oppressor has come to an *e*!
16: 4 The oppressor will come to an *e*,
16: 10 for I have put an *e* to the shouting.
21: 2 to an *e* all the groaning she caused.
21: 16 pomp of Kedar will come to an *e*.
23: 15 But at the *e* of these seventy years,
23: 17 At the *e* of seventy years,
38: 12 day and night you made an *e* of me.
38: 13 day and night you made an *e* of me.
46: 10 I make known the *e*
60: 20 and your days of sorrow will *e*.
66: 17 they will meet their *e* together,"
Jer 5: 31 But what will you do in the *e*?
7: 34 I will bring an *e* to the sounds of joy
12: 12 from one *e* of the land to the other;
16: 9 and in your days I will bring an *e*
17: 11 in the *e* he will prove to be a fool.
20: 18 and to *e* my days in shame?
25: 33 from one *e* of the earth to the other.
48: 2 let us put an *e* to that nation.'
48: 35 In Moab I will put an *e*
49: 37 until I have made an *e* of them.
51: 13 your *e* has come,
51: 64 The words of Jeremiah *e* here.
52: 3 and in the *e* he thrust them
La 3: 53 They tried to *e* my life in a pit
4: 18 Our *e* was near, our days were
4: 18 for our *e* had come.
4: 22 of Zion, your punishment will *e*;
Eze 3: 16 At the *e* of seven days the word
5: 2 the days of your siege come to an *e*,
7: 2 The *e*! The *e* has come
7: 3 The *e* is now upon you
7: 6 The *e* has come! The *e* has come!
7: 24 I will put an *e* to the pride
12: 23 going to put an *e* to this proverb,
20: 17 or put an *e* to them in the desert.
22: 4 and the *e* of your years has come.
22: 15 I will put an *e* to your uncleanness.
23: 48 "So I will put an *e* to lewdness
26: 13 I will put an *e* to your noisy songs,
26: 21 I will bring you to a horrible *e*
27: 36 you have come to a horrible *e*
28: 19 you have come to a horrible *e*
29: 13 At the *e* of forty years I will gather
30: 10 " 'I will put an *e* to the hordes
30: 13 put an *e* to the images in Memphis.
30: 18 proud strength will come to an *e*.
33: 28 proud strength will come to an *e*,
39: 14 At the *e* of the seven months they
40: 15 entrance of the gateway to the far *e*
41: 4 across the *e* of the outer sanctuary.
43: 27 At the *e* of these days,
46: 19 showed me a place at the western *e*.
Da 1: 15 At the *e* of the ten days they looked
1: 18 At the *e* of the time set by the king
2: 44 kingdoms and bring them to an *e*,
4: 34 At the *e* of that time, I,
5: 26 of your reign and brought it to an *e*.
6: 26 his dominion will never *e*.
7: 28 "This is the *e* of the matter.
8: 17 vision concerns the time of the *e*."
8: 19 the appointed time of the *e*.
9: 24 to put an *e* to sin, to atone
9: 26 The *e* will come like a flood:
9: 26 War will continue until the *e*,
9: 27 of that 'seven' he will put an *e*
9: 27 until the *e* that is decreed is poured
11: 18 but a commander will put an *e*
11: 27 because an *e* will still come
11: 35 spotless until the time of the *e*,
11: 40 "At the time of the *e* the king
11: 45 Yet he will come to his *e*,
12: 4 of the scroll until the time of the *e*.
12: 9 and sealed until the time of the *e*.
12: 12 and reaches the *e* of the 1,335
12: 13 at the *e* of the days you will rise
12: 13 "As for you, go your way till the *e*.
Hos 1: 4 and I will put an *e* to the kingdom
11: 6 and put an *e* to their plans.
Am 6: 7 your feasting and lounging will *e*.
8: 10 and the *e* of it like a bitter day.
Na 1: 8 he will make an *e* of ⌞Nineveh⌟;
1: 9 he will bring to an *e*;
Hab 2: 3 it speaks of the *e*
Zep 1: 18 for he will make a sudden *e*
Mt 10: 22 firm to the *e* will be saved.
Mt 13: 39 The harvest is the *e* of the age,
13: 40 so it will be at the *e* of the age.
13: 49 be at the *e* of the age.
21: 41 those wretches to a wretched *e*,"
24: 3 and of the *e* of the age?"
24: 6 must happen, but the *e* is still
24: 13 firm to the *e* will be saved.
24: 14 nations, and then the *e* will come.
24: 31 from one *e* of the heavens
28: 20 to the very *e* of the age."
Mk 3: 26 he cannot stand; his *e* has come.
13: 7 must happen, but the *e* is still
13: 13 firm to the *e* will be saved.
Lk 1: 33 his kingdom will never *e*."
4: 2 and at the *e* of them he was hungry.
17: 24 the sky from one *e* to the other.
21: 9 but the *e* will not come right away
Jn 11: 4 "This sickness will not *e* in death.
Ac 21: 26 the days of purification would *e*
Ro 10: 4 Christ is the *e* of the law
1Co 1: 8 He will keep you strong to the *e*,
4: 9 display at the *e* of the procession,
15: 24 the *e* will come, when he hands
2Co 11: 15 Their *e* will be what their actions
Col 1: 29 To this *e* I labor, struggling
Heb 1: 12 and your years will never *e*."
3: 14 till the *e* the confidence we had
6: 8 In the *e* it will be burned.
6: 11 this same diligence to the very *e*,
6: 16 and puts an *e* to all argument.
7: 3 beginning of days or *e* of life,
9: 26 once for all at the *e* of the ages
11: 22 when his *e* was near,
1Pe 4: 7 The *e* of all things is near.
2Pe 2: 20 worse off at the *e* than they were
Rev 2: 26 and does my will to the *e*,
21: 6 Omega, the Beginning and the *E*.
22: 13 the Last, the Beginning and the *E*.

ENDANGER (DANGER)

Ru 4: 6 because I might *e* my own estate.
1Co 15: 30 why do we *e* ourselves every hour?

ENDANGERED (DANGER)

Ecc 10: 9 whoever splits logs may be *e*

ENDANGERS (DANGER)

Lev 19: 16 do anything that *e* your neighbor's

ENDED (END)

Jos 15: 11 The boundary *e* at the sea.
16: 8 west to the Kanah Ravine and *e*
17: 9 side of the ravine and *e* at the sea.
19: 14 and *e* at the Valley of Iphtah
19: 22 and *e* at the Jordan.
2Ch 31: 1 all this had *e*, the Israelites who
Job 31: 40 The words of Job are *e*.
39: 3 their labor pains are *e*.
Ps 78: 33 So he *e* their days in futility
Pr 22: 10 quarrels and insults are *e*.
Isa 14: 4 How his fury has *e*!
Jer 8: 20 the summer has *e*,
Am 8: 5 and the Sabbath be *e*
Ac 20: 1 When the uproar had *e*, Paul sent
Rev 20: 3 until the thousand years were *e*.
20: 5 until the thousand years were *e*.)

ENDING (END)

Ge 44: 12 beginning with the oldest and *e*
Jos 15: 4 the Wadi of Egypt, *e* at the sea.
16: 3 and on to Gezer, *e* at the sea.
19: 33 to Lakkum and *e* at the Jordan.

ENDLESS

Job 22: 5 Are not your sins *e*?
Ps 9: 6 *E* ruin has overtaken the enemy,
49: 11 their dwellings for *e* generations,
93: 5 house for *e* days, O LORD.
106: 31 for *e* generations to come.
Na 2: 9 The supply is *e*,
3: 19 your *e* cruelty?
1Ti 1: 4 to myths and *e* genealogies.

ENDOR

Jos 17: 11 *E*, Taanach and Megiddo,
1Sa 28: 7 "There is one in *E*," they said.
Ps 83: 10 who perished at *E*

ENDOW (ENDOWED)

Job 39: 17 for God did not *e* her with wisdom
Ps 72: 1 *E* the king with your justice,

ENDOWED (ENDOW)

2Ch 2: 12 *e* with intelligence
Job 38: 36 Who *e* the heart with wisdom
Isa 55: 5 for he has *e* you with splendor."
60: 9 for he has *e* you with splendor.

ENDS (END)

Ex 25: 18 gold at the *e* of the cover.
25: 19 piece with the cover, at the two *e*.
28: 25 and the other *e* of the chains
37: 7 gold at the *e* of the cover.
37: 8 at the two *e* he made them
39: 18 and the other *e* of the chains
Dt 28: 49 from the *e* of the earth, like
33: 17 even those at the *e* of the earth.
1Sa 2: 10 the LORD will judge the *e*
1Ki 8: 8 so long that their *e* could be seen
2Ch 5: 9 were so long that their *e*,
Job 28: 24 for he views the *e* of the earth
37: 3 and sends it to the *e* of the earth.
Ps 2: 8 the *e* of the earth your possession.
19: 4 their words to the *e* of the world.
22: 27 All the *e* of the earth
46: 9 cease to the *e* of the earth;
48: 10 reaches to the *e* of the earth;
59: 13 known to the *e* of the earth
61: 2 From the *e* of the earth I call to you
65: 5 the hope of all the *e* of the earth
67: 7 all the *e* of the earth will fear him.
72: 8 from the River to the *e* of the earth.
98: 3 all the *e* of the earth have seen
135: 7 rise from the *e* of the earth;
Pr 11: 23 of the righteous *e* only in good,
12: 24 but laziness *e* in slave labor.
16: 4 out everything for his own *e*—
17: 24 to the *e* of the earth.
18: 1 unfriendly man pursues selfish *e*;
20: 17 he *e* up with a mouth full of gravel.
30: 4 Who has established all the *e*
Isa 5: 26 for those at the *e* of the earth.
13: 5 from the *e* of the heavens—
24: 16 From the *e* of the earth we hear
40: 28 the Creator of the *e* of the earth.
41: 5 the *e* of the earth tremble.
41: 9 I took you from the *e* of the earth,
42: 10 his praise from the *e* of the earth,
43: 6 daughters from the *e* of the earth—
45: 22 all you *e* of the earth;
48: 20 Send it out to the *e* of the earth;
49: 6 salvation to the *e* of the earth."
52: 10 and all the *e* of the earth will see
58: 4 Your fasting *e* in quarreling
62: 11 proclamation to the *e* of the earth:
Jer 6: 22 up from the *e* of the earth.
10: 13 from the *e* of the earth.
16: 19 from the *e* of the earth and say,
25: 31 resound to the *e* of the earth,
25: 32 rising from the *e* of the earth."
31: 8 gather them from the *e* of the earth.
48: 47 Here *e* the judgment on Moab.
50: 41 up from the *e* of the earth.
51: 16 from the *e* of the earth.
Eze 15: 4 and the fire burns both *e* and chars
Da 4: 11 it was visible to the *e* of the earth.
Mic 5: 4 will reach to the *e* of the earth.
Zec 9: 10 from the River to the *e* of the earth.
Mt 12: 42 for she came from the *e* of the earth
Mk 13: 27 from the *e* of the earth to the *e*
Lk 11: 31 for she came from the *e* of the earth
Ac 1: 8 Samaria, and to the *e* of the earth."
13: 47 salvation to the *e* of the earth.' "
Ro 10: 18 their words to the *e* of the world."

ENDUED

Ps 89: 13 Your arm is *e* with power;

ENDURANCE (ENDURE)

Ro 15: 4 through *e* and the encouragement
15: 5 May the God who gives *e*
2Co 1: 6 which produces in you patient *e*
6: 4 in great *e*; in troubles, hardships
Col 1: 11 might so that you may have great *e*
1Th 1: 3 and your *e* inspired by hope
1Ti 6: 11 faith, love, *e* and gentleness.
2Ti 3: 10 patience, love, *e*, persecutions,
Tit 2: 2 and sound in faith, in love and in *e*.
Rev 1: 9 and patient *e* that are ours in Jesus,
13: 10 This calls for patient *e*
14: 12 This calls for patient *e* on the part

ENDURE (ENDURANCE ENDURED ENDURES ENDURING)

1Sa 13: 14 But now your kingdom will not *e*;
2Sa 7: 16 and your kingdom will *e* forever
Job 14: 2 a fleeting shadow, he does not *e*.
15: 29 be rich and his wealth will not *e*,
20: 21 his prosperity will not *e*.
Ps 37: 18 and their inheritance will *e* forever.
49: 12 despite his riches, does not *e*;
55: 12 I could *e* it;
69: 7 For I *e* scorn for your sake,
69: 10 I must *e* scorn;
72: 5 He will *e* as long as the sun,
72: 17 May his name *e* forever;
89: 29 his throne as long as the heavens *e*.
89: 36 his throne *e* before me like the sun;
101: 5 him will I not *e*.
104: 31 of the LORD *e* forever;
119: 91 Your laws *e* to this day,
Pr 12: 19 Truthful lips *e* forever,
27: 24 for riches do not *e* forever,
Ecc 3: 14 everything God does will *e* forever;
Isa 66: 22 the new earth that I make will *e*
66: 22 will your name and descendants *e*.
Jer 10: 10 the nations cannot *e* his wrath.
10: 19 This is my sickness, and I must *e* it
44: 22 could no longer *e* your wicked
Eze 22: 14 Will your courage *e* or your hands
Da 2: 44 to an end, but it will itself *e* forever.
Joel 2: 11 Who can *e* it?
Na 1: 6 Who can *e* his fierce anger?
Mal 3: 2 who can *e* the day of his coming?
1Co 4: 12 when we are persecuted, we *e* it;
2Co 1: 8 far beyond our ability to *e*,
2Ti 2: 3 *E* hardship with us like a good
2: 10 Therefore I *e* everything
2: 12 if we *e*,
4: 5 head in all situations, *e* hardship,
Heb 12: 7 *E* hardship as discipline; God is
1Pe 2: 20 a beating for doing wrong and *e* it?
2: 20 suffer for doing good and you *e* it,
Rev 3: 10 kept my command to *e* patiently,

ENDURED (ENDURE)

Ps 123: 3 for we have *e* much contempt.
123: 4 We have *e* much ridicule
132: 1 and all the hardships he *e*.
Ac 13: 18 and *e* their conduct forty years
2Ti 3: 11 and Lystra, the persecutions I *e*.
Heb 12: 2 set before him *e* the cross,
12: 3 him who *e* such opposition
Rev 2: 3 and have *e* hardships for my name,

ENDURES (ENDURE)

Ge 8: 22 "As long as the earth *e*,
1Ch 16: 34 his love *e* forever.
16: 41 "for his love *e* forever."
2Ch 5: 13 his love *e* forever."
7: 3 his love *e* forever."
7: 6 saying, "His love *e* forever."
20: 21 for his love *e* forever."
Ezr 3: 11 his love to Israel *e* forever."
Ps 100: 5 is good and his love *e* forever;
102: 12 renown *e* through all generations.
106: 1 his love *e* forever.
107: 1 his love *e* forever.
111: 3 and his righteousness *e* forever.
112: 3 and his righteousness *e* forever.
112: 9 his righteousness *e* forever;
117: 2 of the LORD *e* forever.
118: 1 his love *e* forever.
118: 2 "His love *e* forever."
118: 3 "His love *e* forever."
118: 4 "His love *e* forever."
118: 29 his love *e* forever.
119: 90 you established the earth, and it *e*.
125: 1 cannot be shaken but *e* forever.
135: 13 Your name, O LORD, *e* forever,
136: 1 *His love e forever.*
136: 2 *His love e forever.*
136: 3 *His love e forever.*
136: 4 *His love e forever.*
Ps 136: 5 *His love e forever.*
136: 6 *His love e forever.*
136: 7 *His love e forever.*
136: 8 *His love e forever.*
136: 9 *His love e forever.*
136: 10 *His love e forever.*
136: 11 *His love e forever.*
136: 12 *His love e forever.*
136: 13 *His love e forever.*
136: 14 *His love e forever.*
136: 15 *His love e forever.*
136: 16 *His love e forever.*
136: 17 *His love e forever.*
136: 18 *His love e forever.*
136: 19 *His love e forever.*
136: 20 *His love e forever.*
136: 21 *His love e forever.*
136: 22 *His love e forever.*
136: 23 *His love e forever.*
136: 24 *His love e forever.*
136: 25 *His love e forever.*
136: 26 *His love e forever.*
138: 8 your love, O LORD, *e* forever—
145: 13 *e* through all generations.
Jer 33: 11 his love *e* forever."
La 5: 19 your throne *e* from generation
Da 4: 3 his dominion *e* from generation
4: 34 his kingdom *e* from generation
6: 26 and he *e* forever;
9: 15 made for yourself a name that *e*
Jn 6: 27 but for food that *e* to eternal life,
2Co 9: 9 his righteousness *e* forever."

ENDURING (ENDURE)

1Ki 11: 38 I will build you a dynasty as *e*
Ps 19: 9 *e* forever.
Pr 8: 18 *e* wealth and prosperity.
Jer 5: 15 an ancient and *e* nation,
2Th 1: 4 persecutions and trials you are *e*.
Heb 13: 14 For here we do not have an *e* city,
1Pe 1: 23 through the living and *e* word

ENEMIES (ENEMY)

Ge 14: 20 who delivered your *e*
22: 17 possession of the cities of their *e*,
24: 60 the gates of their *e*."
49: 8 be on the neck of your *e*;
Ex 1: 10 if war breaks out, will join our *e*,
23: 22 I will be an enemy to your *e*
23: 27 make all your *e* turn their backs
32: 25 become a laughingstock to their *e*.
Lev 26: 7 You will pursue your *e*,
26: 8 and your *e* will fall by the sword
26: 16 in vain, because your *e* will eat it.
26: 17 that you will be defeated by your *e*;
26: 32 so that your *e* who live there will be
26: 34 you are in the country of your *e*;
26: 36 the lands of their *e* that the sound
26: 37 able to stand before your *e*.
26: 38 the land of your *e* will devour you.
26: 39 away in the lands of their *e*
26: 41 them into the land of their *e*—
26: 44 when they are in the land of their *e*,
Nu 10: 9 your God and rescued from your *e*.
10: 35 May your *e* be scattered;
14: 42 You will be defeated by your *e*,
23: 11 I brought you to curse my *e*,
24: 10 "I summoned you to curse my *e*,
25: 17 "Treat the Midianites as *e*
25: 18 as *e* when they deceived you
32: 21 LORD until he has driven his *e* out
Dt 1: 42 You will be defeated by your *e*.' "
6: 19 thrusting out all your *e* before you,
12: 10 rest from all your *e* around you
20: 1 When you go to war against your *e*
20: 3 going into battle against your *e*.
20: 4 fight for you against your *e*
20: 14 your God gives you from your *e*.
21: 10 When you go to war against your *e*
23: 9 you are encamped against your *e*,
23: 14 and to deliver your *e* to you.
25: 19 rest from all the *e* around you
28: 7 will grant that the *e* who rise up
28: 25 you to be defeated before your *e*.
28: 31 Your sheep will be given to your *e*,
28: 48 will serve the *e* the LORD sends
28: 68 offer yourselves for sale to your *e*
30: 7 curses on your *e* who hate

Dt 32:31 as even our *e* concede.
32:43 he will take vengeance on his *e*
33:29 Your *e* will cower before you,
Jos 5:13 "Are you for us or for our *e?*"
7: 8 that Israel has been routed by its *e?*
7:12 cannot stand against their *e;*
7:13 against your *e* until you remove it.
10:13 till the nation avenged itself on its *e*
10:19 But don't stop! Pursue your *e,*
10:25 to all the *e* you are going to fight."
21:44 Not one of their *e* withstood them;
21:44 the LORD handed all their *e*
22: 8 brothers the plunder from your *e.*"
23: 1 rest from all their *e* around them,
Jdg 2:14 He sold them to their *e* all around,
2:18 out of the hands of their *e*
5:31 So may all your *e* perish, O LORD!
8:34 hands of all their *e* on every side.
11:36 LORD has avenged you of your *e,*
1Sa 2: 1 My mouth boasts over my *e,*
4: 3 save us from the hand of our *e.*"
12:10 us from the hands of our *e,*
12:11 the hands of your *e* on every side,
14:24 I have avenged myself on my *e!*"
14:30 the plunder they took from their *e.*
14:47 fought against their *e* on every side:
18:25 to take revenge on his *e.*' "
20:15 one of David's *e* from the face
20:16 "May the LORD call David's *e*
25:26 may your *e* and all who intend
25:29 the lives of your *e* he will hurl away
29: 8 against the *e* of my lord the king?"
30:26 from the plunder of the LORD's *e*
2Sa 3:18 and from the hand of all their *e.*' "
5: 8 and blind' who are David's *e.*"
5:20 out against my *e* before me."
7: 1 rest from all his *e* around him,
7: 9 cut off all your *e* from before you.
7:11 also give you rest from all your *e.*
12:14 by doing this you have made the *e*
18:19 him from the hand of his *e.*"
18:32 "May the *e* of my lord the king
19: 9 us from the hand of our *e;*
22: 1 him from the hand of all his *e*
22: 4 and I am saved from my *e.*
22:15 shot arrows and scattered ⌞the *e*⌟,
22:38 "I pursued my *e* and crushed them;
22:41 You made my *e* turn their backs
22:49 who sets me free from my *e.*
24:13 months of fleeing from your *e*
1Ki 3:11 have asked for the death of your *e*
5: 3 God until the LORD put his *e*
8:44 go to war against their *e,*
8:48 of their *e* who took them captive,
2Ki 17:39 you from the hand of all your *e.*"
21:14 and hand them over to their *e.*
1Ch 12:17 come to betray me to my *e*
14:11 out against my *e* by my hand."
17: 8 cut off all your *e* from before you.
17:10 I will also subdue all your *e.*
21:12 of being swept away before your *e,*
22: 9 rest from all his *e* on every side.
2Ch 1:11 nor for the death of your *e,*
6:28 or when *e* besiege them in any
6:34 go to war against their *e,*
20:27 cause to rejoice over their *e.*
20:29 fought against the *e* of Israel.
26:13 to support the king against his *e.*
Ezr 4: 1 When the *e* of Judah and Benjamin
8:22 to protect us from *e* on the road,
8:31 and he protected us from *e*
Ne 4:11 our *e* said, "Before they know it
4:15 When our *e* heard that we were
5: 9 the reproach of our Gentile *e?*
6: 1 of our *e* that I had rebuilt the wall
6:16 When all our *e* heard about this
6:16 our *e* lost their self-confidence,
9:27 So you handed them over to their *e*
9:27 them from the hand of their *e.*
9:28 hand of their *e* so that they ruled
Est 8:11 to plunder the property of their *e.*
8:13 to avenge themselves on their *e.*
9: 1 On this day the *e* of the Jews had
9: 5 down all their *e* with the sword,
9:16 and get relief from their *e.*
9:22 the Jews got relief from their *e,*
Job 8:22 Your *e* will be clothed in shame,
19:11 he counts me among his *e.*

Job 27: 7 "May my *e* be like the wicked,
Ps 3: 7 For you have struck all my *e*
5: 8 because of my *e*—
6:10 May all my *e* be ashamed
7: 6 rise up against the rage of my *e.*
8: 2 because of your *e,*
9: 3 My *e* turn back;
9:13 see how my *e* persecute me!
10: 5 he sneers at all his *e.*
17: 9 from my mortal *e* who surround me
18: 3 and I am saved from my *e.*
18:14 his arrows and scattered ⌞the *e*⌟,
18:37 I pursued my *e* and overtook them;
18:40 You made my *e* turn their backs
18:48 who saves me from my *e.*
21: 8 hand will lay hold on all your *e;*
23: 5 in the presence of my *e.*
25: 2 nor let my *e* triumph over me.
25:19 See how my *e* have increased
27: 2 when my *e* and my foes attack me,
27: 6 above the *e* who surround me;
30: 1 and did not let my *e* gloat over me.
31:11 Because of all my *e,*
31:15 deliver me from my *e*
35:19 who are my *e* without cause;
37:20 LORD's *e* will be like the beauty
38:19 are those who are my vigorous *e;*
41: 5 My *e* say of me in malice,
41: 7 All my *e* whisper together
44: 5 Through you we push back our *e;*
44: 7 but you give us victory over our *e,*
45: 5 pierce the hearts of the king's *e;*
55:15 Let death take my *e* by surprise;
56: 9 Then my *e* will turn back
59: 1 Deliver me from my *e,* O God;
60:12 and he will trample down our *e.*
66: 3 that your *e* cringe before you.
68: 1 God arise, may his *e* be scattered;
68:21 God will crush the heads of his *e,*
69: 4 many are my *e* without cause,
69:19 all my *e* are before you.
71:10 For my *e* speak against me;
72: 9 and his *e* will lick the dust.
74:23 of your *e,* which rises continually.
78:53 but the sea engulfed their *e.*
78:66 He beat back his *e;*
80: 6 and our *e* mock us.
81:14 how quickly would I subdue their *e*
83: 2 See how your *e* are astir,
86:17 that my *e* may see it and be put
89:10 strong arm you scattered your *e.*
89:42 you have made all his *e* rejoice.
89:51 with which your *e* have mocked,
92: 9 For surely your *e,* O LORD,
92: 9 surely your *e* will perish;
102: 8 All day long my *e* taunt me;
106: 42 Their *e* oppressed them
108: 13 and he will trample down our *e.*
110: 1 hand until I make your *e*
110: 2 you will rule in the midst of your *e.*
118: 7 I will look in triumph on my *e.*
119: 98 make me wiser than my *e,*
119:139 for my *e* ignore your words.
127: 5 contend with their *e* in the gate.
132: 18 I will clothe his *e* with shame,
136: 24 and freed us from our *e,*
139: 22 I count them my *e,*
143: 9 Rescue me from my *e,* O LORD,
143: 12 In your unfailing love, silence my *e*
144: 6 forth lightning and scatter ⌞the *e*⌟;
Pr 16: 7 his *e* live at peace with him.
Isa 1:24 and avenge myself on my *e.*
9:11 and has spurred their *e* on.
11:13 and Judah's *e* will be cut off;
26:11 reserved for your *e* consume them.
29: 5 your many *e* will become like fine
41:12 Though you search for your *e,*
42:13 and will triumph over his *e.*
59:18 wrath to his *e*
62: 8 as food for your *e,*
63:18 now our *e* have trampled
64: 2 make your name known to your *e*
66: 6 repaying his *e* all they deserve.
Jer 12: 7 love into the hands of her *e.*
15: 9 the sword before their *e,*"
15:11 surely I will make your *e* plead
15:14 I will enslave you to your *e*
17: 4 I will enslave you to your *e*

Jer 18:17 I will scatter them before their *e;*
19: 7 fall by the sword before their *e,*
19: 9 them by the *e* who seek their lives.'
20: 4 fall by the sword of their *e.*
20: 5 hand over to their *e* all the wealth
21: 7 and to their *e* who seek their lives.
30:16 all your *e* will go into exile.
34:20 over to their *e* who seek their lives.
34:21 over to their *e* who seek their lives,
44:30 over to his *e* who seek his life,
50: 7 their *e* said, 'We are not guilty,
51:55 ⌞of *e*⌟ will rage like great waters;
La 1: 2 they have become her *e.*
1: 5 her *e* are at ease.
1: 7 Her *e* looked at her
1:21 All my *e* have heard of my distress;
2:16 All your *e* open their mouths
3:46 "All our *e* have opened their
3:52 Those who were my *e*
3:62 what my *e* whisper and mutter
4:12 that *e* and foes could enter
Eze 16:27 you over to the greed of your *e,*
39:23 and handed them over to their *e,*
39:27 them from the countries of their *e,*
Da 4:19 if only the dream applied to your *e*
Am 9: 4 into exile by their *e,*
Mic 4:10 out of the hand of your *e.*
5: 9 in triumph over your *e,*
7: 6 a man's *e* are the members
Na 1: 2 maintains his wrath against his *e.*
3:13 are wide open to your *e;*
Mt 5:44 Love your *e* and pray
10:36 a man's *e* will be the members
22:44 hand until I put your *e*
Mk 12:36 hand until I put your *e*
Lk 1:71 of long ago), salvation from our *e*
1:74 to rescue us from the hand of our *e,*
6:27 Love your *e,* do good
6:35 But love your *e,* do good to them,
19:27 those *e* of mine who did not want
19:43 you when your *e* will build
20:43 hand until I make your *e*
23:12 before this they had been *e.*
Ac 2:35 hand until I make your *e*
Ro 5:10 For if, when we were God's *e,*
11:28 they are *e* on your account;
1Co 15:25 reign until he has put all his *e*
Php 3:18 many live as *e* of the cross of Christ
Col 1:21 from God and were *e* in your minds
Heb 1:13 hand until I make your *e*
10:13 for his *e* to be made his footstool,
10:27 raging fire that will consume the *e*
Rev 11: 5 their mouths and devours their *e.*
11:12 in a cloud, while their *e* looked on.

ENEMY (ENEMIES ENEMY'S ENMITY)

Ex 15: 6 shattered the *e.*
15: 9 "The *e* boasted,
23:22 I will be an *e* to your enemies
Lev 26:25 and you will be given into *e* hands.
Nu 10: 9 against an *e* who is oppressing you,
24:18 Seir, his *e,* will be conquered,
35:23 then since he was not his *e*
Dt 28:53 the suffering that your *e* will inflict
28:55 of the suffering your *e* will inflict
28:57 the distress that your *e* will inflict
32:27 but I dreaded the taunt of the *e,*
32:42 the heads of the *e* leaders."
33:27 He will drive out your *e* before you,
Jdg 3:28 the LORD has given Moab, your *e,*
16:23 god has delivered Samson, our *e,*
16:24 "Our god has delivered our *e*
1Sa 18:29 and he remained his *e* the rest
19:17 send my *e* away so that he escaped
24: 4 'I will give your *e* into your hands
24:19 a man finds his *e,* does he let him
26: 8 "Today God has delivered your *e*
28:16 from you and become your *e?*
2Sa 4: 8 your *e,* who tried to take your life.
22:18 He rescued me from my powerful *e*
1Ki 8:33 Israel have been defeated by an *e*
8:37 or when an *e* besieges them in any
8:46 and give them over to the *e,*
21:20 my *e!*" "I have found you,"
2Ki 6:18 As the *e* came down toward him,
2Ch 6:24 Israel have been defeated by an *e*
6:36 and give them over to the *e,*
25: 8 will overthrow you before the *e,*

Ge 4:18 To *E* was born Irad, and Irad was
5:18 he became the father of *E*.
5:19 after he became the father of *E*,
5:21 When *E* had lived 65 years,
5:22 *E* walked with God 300 years
5:23 Altogether, *E* lived 365 years.
5:24 *E* walked with God; then he was no
1Ch 1:3 Mahalalel, Jared, *E*, Methuselah,
Lk 3:37 the son of Methuselah, the son of *E*
Heb 11:5 By faith *E* was taken from this life,
Jude :14 *E*, the seventh from Adam,

ENORMOUS

Da 2:31 an *e*, dazzling statue, awesome
4:10 Its height was *e*.
Rev 12:3 an *e* red dragon with seven heads

ENOS

Lk 3:38 the son of *E*,

ENOSH

Ge 4:26 had a son, and he named him *E*.
5:6 he became the father of *E*.
5:7 after he became the father of *E*,
5:9 When *E* had lived 90 years,
5:10 *E* lived 815 years and had other
5:11 Altogether, *E* lived 905 years,
1Ch 1:1 Adam, Seth, *E*, Kenan, Mahalalel,

ENRAGED (RAGE)

2Ki 6:11 This *e* the king of Aram.
2Ch 16:10 he was so *e* that he put him
Est 3:5 or pay him honor, he was *e*.
Isa 8:21 they will become *e* and, looking
57:17 I was *e* by his sinful greed;
Eze 16:43 but *e* me with all these things,
Mt 22:7 The king was *e*.
Rev 12:17 the dragon was *e* at the woman

ENRICH (RICH)

Ps 65:9 you *e* it abundantly.
Pr 5:10 your toil *e* another man's house.

ENRICHED (RICH)

Isa 23:2 whom the seafarers have *e*.
Eze 27:33 you *e* the kings of the earth.
1Co 1:5 For in him you have been *e*

ENROLL (ENROLLED ENROLLMENT)

2Sa 24:2 to Beersheba and *e* the fighting
24:4 of the king to *e* the fighting men

ENROLLED (ENROLL)

2Ch 31:17 to the priests *e* by their families

ENROLLMENT (ENROLL)

2Ch 17:14 Their *e* by families was as follows:

ENSLAVE (SLAVE)

Jer 15:14 I will *e* you to your enemies
17:4 I will *e* you to your enemies
30:8 no longer will foreigners *e* them.

ENSLAVED (SLAVE)

Ge 15:13 they will be *e* and mistreated four
Ne 5:5 our daughters have already been *e*,
Jer 25:14 They themselves will be *e*
34:11 they had freed and *e* them again.
Eze 34:27 the hands of those who *e* them.
Na 3:4 who *e* nations by her prostitution
Ac 7:6 they will be *e* and mistreated four
Gal 4:9 Do you wish to be *e* by them all
Tit 3:3 and *e* by all kinds of passions

ENSLAVES (SLAVE)

2Co 11:20 even put up with anyone who *e* you

ENSLAVING (SLAVE)

Ex 6:5 whom the Egyptians are *e*,

ENSNARE (SNARE)

Pr 5:22 of a wicked man *e* him;
Ecc 7:26 but the sinner she will *e*.
Isa 29:21 who *e* the defender in court
Eze 13:18 Will you *e* the lives of my people
13:18 for their heads in order to *e* people.
13:20 the people that you *e* like birds.
13:20 with which you *e* people like birds

ENSNARED (SNARE)

Dt 7:25 for yourselves, or you will be *e* by it
12:30 be careful not to be *e*
Ps 9:16 the wicked are *e* by the work
Pr 6:2 *e* by the words of your mouth,
22:25 and get yourself *e*.

ENSURE

Ps 119:122 *E* your servant's well-being;

ENTANGLE (ENTANGLED ENTANGLES)

Ps 35:8 may the net they hid *e* them,

ENTANGLED (ENTANGLE)

Ps 18:4 The cords of death *e* me;
116:3 The cords of death *e* me,
Na 1:10 They will be *e* among thorns
2Pe 2:20 and are again *e* in it and overcome,

ENTANGLES (ENTANGLE)

Heb 12:1 and the sin that so easily *e*,

ENTER (ENTERED ENTERING ENTERS ENTRANCE ENTRANCES ENTRYWAY REENTERED)

Ge 6:18 with you, and you will *e* the ark—
12:11 As he was about to *e* Egypt,
49:6 Let me not *e* their council,
Ex 12:23 the destroyer to *e* your houses
12:25 When you *e* the land that
28:43 them whenever they *e* the Tent
30:20 Whenever they *e* the Tent
40:35 Moses could not *e* the Tent
Lev 14:34 "When you *e* the land of Canaan,
16:3 is to *e* the sanctuary area:
19:23 " 'When you *e* the land
21:11 He must not *e* a place where there
23:10 'When you *e* the land I am going
25:2 'When you *e* the land I am going
Nu 5:22 that brings a curse *e* your body
5:24 and this water will *e* her
14:30 one of you will *e* the land I swore
15:2 'After you *e* the land I am giving
15:18 'When you *e* the land
20:24 He will not *e* the land I give
34:2 say to them: 'When you *e* Canaan,
Dt 1:37 "You shall not *e* it, either.
1:38 Joshua son of Nun, will *e* it.
1:39 from bad—they will *e* the land.
4:21 *e* the good land the LORD your
8:1 may live and increase and may *e*
10:11 so that they may *e* and possess
11:31 about to cross the Jordan to *e*
17:14 When you *e* the land the LORD
18:9 When you *e* the land the LORD
23:1 or cutting may *e* the assembly
23:2 descendants may *e* the assembly
23:3 descendants may *e* the assembly
23:8 born to them may *e* the assembly
23:24 If you *e* your neighbor's vineyard,
23:25 If you *e* your neighbor's grainfield,
27:3 to *e* the land the LORD your God
29:12 here in order to *e* into a covenant
30:18 you are crossing the Jordan to *e*
32:52 you will not *e* the land I am giving
Jos 2:18 on us unless, when we *e* the land,
Jdg 11:18 They did not *e* the territory
1Sa 5:5 any others who *e* Dagon's temple
9:13 As soon as you *e* the town,
2Sa 5:8 and lame' will not *e* the palace."
1Ki 22:30 "I will *e* the battle in disguise,
2Ki 11:16 where the horses *e* the palace
13:20 used to *e* the country every spring.
19:32 "He will not *e* this city
19:33 he will not *e* this city, declares
2Ch 7:2 The priests could not *e* the temple
18:29 "I will *e* the battle in disguise,
23:6 No one is to *e* the temple
23:6 they may *e* because they are
23:19 was in any way unclean might *e*.
27:2 unlike him he did not *e* the temple
31:16 all who would *e* the temple
Ne 9:23 land that you told their fathers to *e*
Est 1:19 to *e* the presence of King Xerxes.
4:2 in sackcloth was allowed to *e* it.
Ps 45:15 they *e* the palace of the king.
95:11 "They shall never *e* my rest."
100:4 *E* his gates with thanksgiving
Ps 118:19 I will *e* and give thanks
118:20 through which the righteous may *e*.
132:3 "I will not *e* my house
Pr 2:10 For wisdom will *e* your heart,
Isa 10:28 They *e* Aiath;
13:2 them to *e* the gates of the nobles.
26:2 that the righteous nation may *e*,
26:20 Go, my people, *e* your rooms
35:10 They will *e* Zion with singing;
37:33 "He will not *e* this city
37:34 he will not *e* this city,"
51:11 They will *e* Zion with singing;
52:1 will not *e* you again.
57:2 *e* into peace;
59:14 honesty cannot *e*.
Jer 3:16 It will never *e* their minds
7:31 not command nor did it *e* my mind.
16:5 "Do not *e* a house where there is
16:8 do not *e* a house where there is
19:5 or mention, nor did it *e* my mind.
21:13 Who can *e* our refuge?"
32:35 commanded, nor did it *e* my mind,
La 1:10 forbidden to *e* your assembly.
1:10 *e* her sanctuary—
4:12 that enemies and foes could *e*
Eze 7:22 robbers will *e* it and desecrate it.
13:9 nor will they *e* the land of Israel.
20:38 yet they will not *e* the land of Israel
26:10 men *e* a city whose walls have been
37:5 I will make breath *e* you,
42:14 Once the priests *e* the holy
44:2 must not be opened; no one may *e*
44:3 He is to *e* by way of the portico
44:9 and flesh is to *e* my sanctuary,
44:16 They alone are to *e* my sanctuary;
44:17 " 'When they *e* the gates
46:2 The prince is to *e* from the
Da 1:5 were to *e* the king's service.
11:7 king of the North and *e* his fortress;
Joel 2:9 like thieves they *e*
3:2 There I will *e* into judgment
Zec 5:4 and it will *e* the house of the thief
Mt 5:20 will certainly not *e* the kingdom
7:13 leads to destruction, and many *e*
7:13 "*E* through the narrow gate.
7:21 Lord,' will *e* the kingdom of heaven
10:5 or *e* any town of the Samaritans.
10:11 "Whatever town or village you *e*,
10:12 As you *e* the home, give it your
12:29 how can anyone *e* a strong man's
18:3 you will never *e* the kingdom
18:8 It is better for you to *e* life maimed
18:9 better for you to *e* life with one eye
19:17 to *e* life, obey the commandments
19:23 man to *e* the kingdom of heaven.
19:24 man to *e* the kingdom of God."
23:13 You yourselves do not *e*,
23:13 will you let those *e* who are trying
Mk 1:45 could no longer *e* a town openly
3:27 no one can *e* a strong man's house
6:10 Whenever you *e* a house, stay there
9:25 out of him and never *e* him again."
9:43 It is better for you to *e* life maimed
9:45 It is better for you to *e* life crippled
9:47 for you to *e* the kingdom of God
10:15 like a little child will never *e* it."
10:23 is for the rich to *e* the kingdom
10:24 is to *e* the kingdom of God!
10:25 man to *e* the kingdom of God."
11:2 as you *e* it, you will find a colt tied
13:15 or *e* the house to take anything out.
Lk 9:4 Whatever house you *e*, stay there
10:5 "When you *e* a house, first say,
10:8 "When you *e* a town and are
10:10 But when you *e* a town
13:24 will try to *e* and will not be able to.
13:24 "Make every effort to *e*
18:17 like a little child will never *e* it."
18:24 is for the rich to *e* the kingdom
18:25 man to *e* the kingdom of God."
19:30 as you *e* it, you will find a colt tied
21:21 those in the country not *e* the city.
22:10 He replied, "As you *e* the city,
24:26 these things and then *e* his glory?"
Jn 3:4 "Surely he cannot *e* a second time
3:5 he cannot *e* the kingdom of God.
10:1 man who does not *e* the sheep pen
18:28 the Jews did not *e* the palace;

Ac 3: 3 he saw Peter and John about to *e*,
14: 22 many hardships to *e* the kingdom
16: 7 of Mysia, they tried to *e* Bithynia,
Heb 3: 11 'They shall never *e* my rest.' "
3: 18 that they would never *e* his rest
3: 19 we see that they were not able to *e*,
4: 3 'They shall never *e* my rest.' "
4: 3 we who have believed *e* that rest,
4: 5 "They shall never *e* my rest."
4: 6 remains that some will *e* that rest,
4: 11 make every effort to *e* that rest,
9: 12 He did not *e* by means of the blood
9: 24 Christ did not *e* a man-made
9: 25 Nor did he *e* heaven
10: 19 to *e* the Most Holy Place
Rev 15: 8 and no one could *e* the temple
21: 27 Nothing impure will ever *e* it,

ENTERED (ENTER)

Ge 7: 7 and his sons' wives *e* the ark
7: 9 came to Noah and *e* the ark,
7: 13 wives of his three sons, *e* the ark.
7: 15 came to Noah and *e* the ark.
19: 3 go with him and *e* his house.
31: 33 of Leah's tent, he *e* Rachel's tent.
41: 46 old when he *e* the service
Ex 1: 1 of Israel who *e* Egypt with Jacob,
19: 2 they *e* the Desert of Sinai,
24: 18 Then Moses *e* the cloud
33: 8 watching Moses until he *e* the tent.
34: 34 But whenever he *e* the LORD's
40: 32 washed whenever they *e* the Tent
Lev 16: 23 on before he *e* the Most Holy Place
Nu 7: 89 When Moses *e* the Tent of Meeting
17: 8 The next day Moses *e* the Tent
Dt 26: 1 When you have *e* the land
Jos 2: 1 *e* the house of a prostitute named
2: 3 came to you and *e* your house,
8: 19 They *e* the city and captured it
Jdg 4: 18 So he *e* her tent, and she put
18: 2 The men *e* the hill country
1Sa 4: 13 When the man *e* the town
12: 8 "After Jacob *e* Egypt, they cried
14: 25 The entire army *e* the woods,
16: 21 came to Saul and *e* his service.
19: 16 when the men *e*, there was the idol
1Ki 2: 30 So Benaiah *e* the tent of the LORD
2Ki 6: 20 After they *e* the city, Elisha said,
7: 8 They returned and *e* another tent
7: 8 of the camp and *e* one of the tents.
9: 31 As Jehu *e* the gate, she asked,
10: 25 and then *e* the inner shrine
1Ch 5: 17 All these were *e* in the genealogical
24: 19 ministering when they *e* the temple
27: 24 the number was not *e* in the book
2Ch 8: 11 ark of the LORD has *e* are holy."
15: 12 They *e* into a covenant
20: 28 They *e* Jerusalem and went
26: 16 and *e* the temple of the LORD
Est 6: 4 Haman had just *e* the outer court
6: 6 When Haman *e*, the king asked
Job 3: 6 nor be *e* in any of the months.
38: 22 "Have you *e* the storehouses
Ps 73: 17 me till I *e* the sanctuary of God;
105: 23 Then Israel *e* Egypt;
109: 18 it *e* into his body like water,
Isa 28: 15 "We have *e* into a covenant
Jer 9: 21 and has *e* our fortresses;
34: 10 people who *e* into this covenant
43: 7 So they *e* Egypt in disobedience
51: 51 because foreigners have *e*
Eze 4: 14 meat has ever *e* my mouth."
16: 8 and *e* into a covenant with you,
23: 39 they *e* my sanctuary
37: 10 me, and breath *e* them;
43: 4 glory of the LORD *e* the temple
44: 2 the God of Israel, has *e* through it.
46: 9 through the gate by which he *e*,
Da 1: 19 so they *e* the king's service.
Am 5: 19 as though he *e* his house
Ob : 11 and foreigners *e* his gates
Mt 8: 5 When Jesus had *e* Capernaum,
9: 23 When Jesus *e* the ruler's house
12: 4 He *e* the house of God, and he
21: 10 When Jesus *e* Jerusalem, the whole
21: 12 Jesus *e* the temple area
21: 23 Jesus *e* the temple courts, and,
24: 38 up to the day Noah *e* the ark;
Mt 26: 58 He *e* and sat down with the guards
Mk 2: 1 when Jesus again *e* Capernaum,
2: 26 he *e* the house of God and ate
3: 20 Jesus *e* a house, and again a crowd
7: 17 had left the crowd and *e* the house,
7: 24 He *e* a house and did not want
11: 11 Jesus *e* Jerusalem and went
11: 15 Jesus *e* the temple area
16: 5 As they *e* the tomb, they saw
Lk 1: 40 where she *e* Zechariah's home
6: 4 He *e* the house of God,
7: 1 of the people, he *e* Capernaum.
7: 45 from the time I *e*, has not stopped
9: 34 they were afraid as they *e* the cloud
11: 52 You yourselves have not *e*,
17: 27 up to the day Noah *e* the ark.
19: 1 Jesus *e* Jericho and was passing
19: 45 Then he *e* the temple area
22: 3 Then Satan *e* Judas, called Iscariot,
24: 3 but when they *e*, they did not find
Jn 6: 22 and that Jesus had not *e* it
11: 30 Now Jesus had not yet *e* the village
13: 27 as Judas took the bread, Satan *e*
16: 28 from the Father and *e* the world;
Ac 5: 21 At daybreak they *e* the temple
9: 17 Ananias went to the house and *e* it.
10: 25 As Peter *e* the house, Cornelius
11: 8 or unclean has ever *e* my mouth.'
11: 12 and we *e* the man's house.
13: 14 the Sabbath they *e* the synagogue
19: 8 Paul *e* the synagogue and spoke
25: 23 and *e* the audience room
Ro 5: 12 as sin *e* the world through one man,
Heb 6: 20 went before us, has *e* on our behalf.
9: 6 the priests *e* regularly
9: 7 the high priest *e* the inner room,
9: 12 but he *e* the Most Holy Place once
9: 24 he *e* heaven itself, now to appear
Rev 11: 11 a breath of life from God *e* them,

ENTERING (ENTER)

Nu 32: 9 from *e* the land the LORD had
Dt 4: 5 them in the land you are *e*
7: 1 into the land you are *e* to possess
11: 10 The land you are *e* to take
11: 29 into the land you are *e* to possess,
23: 20 to in the land you are *e* to possess.
28: 21 from the land you are *e* to possess.
28: 63 from the land you are *e* to possess.
30: 16 you in the land you are *e* to possess.
31: 16 gods of the land they are *e*.
1Sa 5: 10 As the ark of God was *e* Ekron,
9: 14 as they were *e* it, there was Samuel,
23: 7 himself by *e* a town with gates
2Sa 6: 16 the ark of the LORD was *e* the City
15: 37 as Absalom was *e* the city.
17: 17 could not risk being seen *e* the city.
1Ki 15: 17 *e* the territory of Asa king of Judah.
2Ki 11: 19 *e* by way of the gate of the guards.
1Ch 15: 29 of the LORD was *e* the City
2Ch 16: 1 *e* the territory of Asa king of Judah.
Ezr 9: 11 'The land you are *e*
Mt 21: 31 the prostitutes are *e* the kingdom
Lk 11: 52 have hindered those who were *e*."
Heb 4: 1 the promise of *e* his rest still stands,

ENTERS (ENTER)

Ex 28: 29 Whenever Aaron *e* the Holy Place,
28: 30 heart whenever he *e* the presence
28: 35 heard when he *e* the Holy Place
Nu 19: 14 Anyone who *e* the tent
2Ki 5: 18 When my master *e* the temple
12: 9 as one *e* the temple of the LORD.
2Ch 23: 7 Anyone who *e* the temple must be
Isa 3: 14 The LORD *e* into judgment
Eze 26: 10 and chariots when he *e* your gates
42: 9 as one *e* them from the outer court.
42: 12 by which one *e* the rooms.
44: 21 wine when he *e* the inner court.
46: 8 When the prince *e*, he is to go
46: 9 and whoever *e* by the south gate is
46: 9 whoever *e* by the north gate
47: 8 into the Arabah, where it *e* the Sea.
Mt 15: 17 see that whatever *e* the mouth goes
Mk 7: 18 you see that nothing that *e* a man
14: 14 Say to the owner of the house he *e*,
Lk 22: 10 Follow him to the house that he *e*,
Jn 10: 2 The man who *e* by the gate is
Jn 10: 9 whoever *e* through me will be
Heb 4: 10 for anyone who *e* God's rest
6: 19 It *e* the inner sanctuary
9: 25 the high priest *e* the Most Holy

ENTERTAIN (ENTERTAINED ENTERTAINMENT)

Jdg 16: 25 "Bring out Samson to *e* us."
Mt 9: 4 "Why do you *e* evil thoughts
1Ti 5: 19 Do not *e* an accusation
Heb 13: 2 Do not forget to *e* strangers,

ENTERTAINED (ENTERTAIN)

Ac 28: 7 and for three days *e* us hospitably.
Heb 13: 2 so doing some people have *e* angels

ENTERTAINMENT (ENTERTAIN)

Da 6: 18 without any *e* being brought to him

ENTHRALLED

Ps 45: 11 The king is *e* by your beauty;

ENTHRONED (THRONE)

1Sa 4: 4 who is *e* between the cherubim.
2Sa 6: 2 who is *e* between the cherubim that
2Ki 19: 15 of Israel, *e* between the cherubim,
1Ch 13: 6 who is *e* between the cherubim—
Ps 2: 4 The One *e* in heaven laughs;
9: 11 to the LORD, *e* in Zion;
22: 3 Yet you are *e* as the Holy One;
29: 10 The LORD sits *e* over the flood;
29: 10 the LORD is *e* as King forever.
55: 19 God, who is *e* forever,
61: 7 May he be *e* in God's presence
80: 1 who sit *e* between the cherubim,
99: 1 he sits *e* between the cherubim,
102: 12 But you, O LORD, sit *e* forever;
113: 5 the One who sits *e* on high,
132: 14 here I will sit *e*, for I have desired it
Isa 14: 13 I will sit *e* on the mount
37: 16 of Israel, *e* between the cherubim,
40: 22 He sits *e* above the circle
52: 2 rise up, sit *e*, O Jerusalem.

ENTHRONES (THRONE)

Job 36: 7 he *e* them with kings

ENTHUSIASM

2Co 8: 17 he is coming to you with much *e*
9: 2 and your *e* has stirred most of them

ENTICE (ENTICED ENTICES)

Pr 1: 10 My son, if sinners *e* you,
2Pe 2: 18 they *e* people who are just escaping
Rev 2: 14 who taught Balak to *e* the Israelites

ENTICED (ENTICE)

Dt 4: 19 do not be *e* into bowing
11: 16 or you will be *e* to turn away
2Ki 17: 21 Jeroboam *e* Israel away
Job 31: 9 If my heart has been *e* by a woman,
31: 27 so that my heart was secretly *e*
Jas 1: 14 desire, he is dragged away and *e*.

ENTICES (ENTICE)

Dt 13: 6 your closest friend secretly *e* you,
Job 36: 18 Be careful that no one *e* you
Pr 16: 29 A violent man *e* his neighbor

ENTIRE

Ge 2: 11 through the *e* land of Havilah,
2: 13 it winds through the *e* land of Cush.
7: 19 under the *e* heavens were covered.
19: 25 those cities and the *e* plain,
45: 8 lord of his *e* household
Ex 14: 28 the *e* army of Pharaoh that had
16: 3 to starve this *e* assembly to death."
16: 9 "Say to the *e* Israelite community,
29: 18 Then burn the *e* ram on the altar.
Lev 3: 9 the *e* fat tail cut off close
8: 3 and gather the *e* assembly
9: 5 and the *e* assembly came near
19: 2 "Speak to the *e* assembly of Israel
24: 14 and the *e* assembly is to stone him.
24: 16 The *e* assembly must stone him.
27: 32 The *e* tithe of the herd and flock—
Nu 4: 16 to be in charge of the *e* tabernacle
5: 30 and is to apply this *e* law to her.

Nu 6: 5 " 'During the *e* period of his vow
14: 7 and said to the *e* Israelite assembly,
16: 19 LORD appeared to the *e* assembly.
16: 22 angry with the *e* assembly
20: 29 the *e* house of Israel mourned
21: 23 He mustered his *e* army
27: 19 *e* assembly and commission him
27: 21 *e* community of the Israelites will
Dt 2: 14 that *e* generation of fighting men
Jos 6: 23 They brought out her *e* family
8: 11 The *e* force that was
9: 1 along the *e* coast of the Great Sea
9: 21 water carriers for the *e* community
10: 7 up from Gilgal with his *e* army,
11: 16 So Joshua took this *e* land:
11: 23 So Joshua took the *e* land,
13: 21 and the *e* realm of Sihon king
13: 30 the *e* realm of Og king of Bashan—
24: 17 He protected us on our *e* journey
Jdg 8: 12 them, routing their *e* army.
1Sa 14: 25 The *e* army entered the woods,
2Sa 6: 11 blessed him and his *e* household.
6: 15 *e* house of Israel brought up the ark
7: 17 the words of this *e* revelation.
8: 9 that David had defeated the *e* army
10: 7 with the *e* army of fighting men.
12: 29 So David mustered the *e* army
12: 31 his *e* army returned to Jerusalem.
15: 16 with his *e* household following him
20: 14 through the *e* region of the Berites,
20: 23 Joab was over Israel's *e* army;
24: 8 gone through the *e* land,
1Ki 8: 5 the *e* assembly of Israel that had
20: 1 king of Aram mustered his *e* army.
2Ki 6: 24 king of Aram mobilized his *e* army
15: 18 During his *e* reign he did not turn
17: 5 king of Assyria invaded the *e* land,
17: 13 with the *e* Law that I commanded
24: 16 deported to Babylon the *e* force
1Ch 4: 27 so their *e* clan did not become
5: 10 throughout the *e* region east
17: 15 the words of this *e* revelation.
18: 9 that David had defeated the *e* army
19: 8 with the *e* army of fighting men.
20: 3 his *e* army returned to Jerusalem.
2Ch 5: 6 the *e* assembly of Israel that had
26: 14 and slingstones for the *e* army.
29: 18 "We have purified the *e* temple
30: 25 The *e* assembly of Judah rejoiced,
34: 9 and the *e* remnant of Israel
35: 16 So at that time the *e* service
Ezr 4: 5 during the *e* reign of Cyrus king
8: 34 and the *e* weight was recorded
Job 16: 7 have devastated my *e* household.
Isa 39: 2 his *e* armory and everything found
Jer 26: 17 said to the *e* assembly of people,
36: 23 until the *e* scroll was burned
37: 10 to defeat the *e* Babylonian army
42: 2 God for this *e* remnant.
51: 31 that his *e* city is captured,
Eze 9: 8 to destroy the *e* remnant of Israel
10: 12 Their *e* bodies, including their
20: 40 there in the land the *e* house
45: 1 cubits wide; the *e* area will be holy.
48: 20 The *e* portion will be a square,
Da 2: 48 over the *e* province of Babylon
11: 17 with the might of his *e* kingdom
Lk 2: 1 taken of the *e* Roman world.
Ac 11: 28 spread over the *e* Roman world.
18: 8 and his *e* household believed
Gal 5: 14 The *e* law is summed up

ENTRAILS

Zep 1: 17 and their *e* like filth.

ENTRANCE (ENTER)

Ge 18: 1 Mamre while he was sitting at the *e*
18: 2 he hurried from the *e* of his tent
18: 10 listening at the *e* to the tent,
38: 14 then sat down at the *e* to Enaim,
43: 19 spoke to him at the *e* to the house.
Ex 26: 36 For the *e* to the tent make a curtain
27: 14 are to be on one side of the *e*,
27: 16 "For the *e* to the courtyard,
29: 4 and his sons to the *e* to the Tent
29: 11 at the *e* to the Tent of Meeting.
29: 32 At the *e* to the Tent of Meeting,
29: 42 at the *e* to the Tent of Meeting
Ex 32: 26 So he stood at the *e* to the camp
33: 9 come down and stay at the *e*,
33: 10 standing at the *e* to the tent,
33: 10 worshiped, each at the *e* to his tent.
35: 15 doorway at the *e* to the tabernacle;
35: 17 curtain for the *e* to the courtyard;
36: 37 For the *e* to the tent they made
38: 8 at the *e* to the Tent of Meeting.
38: 14 were on one side of the *e*,
38: 15 side of the *e* to the courtyard,
38: 18 The curtain for the *e*
38: 30 for the *e* to the Tent of Meeting,
38: 31 those for its *e* and all the tent pegs
39: 38 and the curtain for the *e* to the tent;
39: 40 curtain for the *e* to the courtyard;
40: 5 curtain at the *e* to the tabernacle.
40: 6 in front of the *e* to the tabernacle,
40: 8 curtain at the *e* to the courtyard.
40: 12 and his sons to the *e* to the Tent
40: 28 curtain at the *e* to the tabernacle.
40: 29 near the *e* to the tabernacle,
40: 33 curtain at the *e* to the courtyard.
Lev 1: 3 it at the *e* to the Tent of Meeting
1: 5 altar on all sides at the *e* to the Tent
3: 2 and slaughter it at the *e* to the Tent
4: 4 bull at the *e* to the Tent of Meeting
4: 7 offering at the *e* to the Tent
4: 18 offering at the *e* to the Tent
8: 3 at the *e* to the Tent of Meeting."
8: 4 gathered at the *e* to the Tent
8: 31 "Cook the meat at the *e* to the Tent
8: 33 Do not leave the *e* to the Tent
8: 35 You must stay at the *e* to the Tent
10: 7 Do not leave the *e* to the Tent
12: 6 to the priest at the *e* to the Tent
14: 11 the LORD at the *e* to the Tent
14: 23 to the priest at the *e* to the Tent
14: 38 and at the *e* close up the house
15: 14 the LORD to the *e* to the Tent
15: 29 to the priest at the *e* to the Tent
16: 7 the LORD at the *e* to the Tent
17: 4 of bringing it to the *e* to the Tent
17: 5 at the *e* to the Tent of Meeting
17: 6 of the LORD at the *e* to the Tent
17: 9 it to the *e* to the Tent of Meeting
19: 21 ram to the *e* to the Tent of Meeting
Nu 3: 25 the curtain at the *e* to the Tent
3: 26 the curtain at the *e*
4: 25 the curtains for the *e* to the Tent
4: 26 the curtain for the *e*, the ropes
6: 10 to the priest at the *e* to the Tent
6: 13 is to be brought to the *e* to the Tent
6: 18 at the *e* to the Tent of Meeting,
10: 3 before you at the *e* to the Tent
11: 10 each at the *e* to his tent.
12: 5 he stood at the *e* to the Tent
16: 18 and Aaron at the *e* to the Tent
16: 19 to them at the *e* to the Tent
16: 50 to Moses at the *e* to the Tent
20: 6 the assembly to the *e* to the Tent
25: 6 at the *e* to the Tent of Meeting.
27: 2 They approached the *e* to the Tent
Dt 31: 15 stood over the *e* to the Tent.
Jos 8: 29 it down at the *e* of the city gate.
19: 51 of the LORD at the *e* to the Tent
20: 4 is to stand in the *e* of the city gate
Jdg 9: 35 and was standing at the *e*
9: 40 all the way to the *e* to the gate.
9: 44 to a position at the *e* to the city gate
9: 52 as he approached the *e* to the tower
18: 16 for battle, stood at the *e* to the gate.
18: 17 stood at the *e* to the gate.
1Sa 2: 22 at the *e* to the Tent of Meeting.
17: 52 and pursued the Philistines to the *e*
2Sa 10: 8 formation at the *e* to their city gate,
11: 9 Uriah slept at the *e* to the palace
11: 23 back to the *e* to the city gate.
1Ki 6: 8 The *e* to the lowest floor was
6: 31 For the *e* of the inner sanctuary he
6: 33 wood for the *e* to the main hall.
14: 27 on duty at the *e* to the royal palace.
22: 10 by the *e* of the gate of Samaria,
2Ki 7: 3 with leprosy at the *e* of the city gate
10: 8 in two piles at the *e* of the city gate
12: 9 The priests who guarded the *e* put
23: 8 at the *e* to the Gate of Joshua,
23: 11 removed from the *e* to the temple
1Ch 9: 19 for guarding the *e* to the dwelling
1Ch 9: 21 at the *e* to the Tent of Meeting.
19: 9 formation at the *e* to their city,
2Ch 12: 10 on duty at the *e* to the royal palace.
18: 9 by the *e* to the gate of Samaria,
23: 13 standing by his pillar at the *e*.
23: 15 as she reached the *e* of the Horse
33: 14 as far as the *e* of the Fish Gate
Ne 3: 20 from the angle to the *e* of the house
3: 21 from the *e* of Eliashib's house
Est 5: 1 throne in the hall, facing the *e*.
Ps 119: 130 The *e* of your words gives light;
Isa 24: 10 the *e* to every house is barred.
Jer 1: 15 in the *e* of the gates of Jerusalem;
19: 2 near the *e* of the Potsherd Gate.
26: 10 places at the *e* of the New Gate
36: 10 courtyard at the *e* of the New Gate
38: 14 brought to the third *e* to the temple
43: 9 at the *e* to Pharaoh's palace
Eze 8: 3 to the *e* to the north gate
8: 5 and in the *e* north of the gate
8: 7 he brought me to the *e* to the court.
8: 14 me to the *e* to the north gate
8: 16 and there at the *e* to the temple,
10: 19 They stopped at the *e*
11: 1 There at the *e* to the gate were
40: 11 the width of the *e* to the gateway;
40: 15 distance from the *e* of the gateway
40: 40 near the steps at the *e*
40: 48 width of the *e* was fourteen cubits
41: 2 The *e* was ten cubits wide,
41: 3 The *e* was six cubits wide,
41: 3 and measured the jambs of the *e*;
41: 3 sidewalls of the *e* was seven cubits.
41: 17 of the *e* to the inner sanctuary
41: 20 the floor to the area above the *e*,
42: 9 The lower rooms had an *e*
44: 5 attention to the *e* of the temple
46: 3 the LORD at the *e* to that gateway.
46: 19 me through the *e* at the side
47: 1 back to the *e* to the temple,
Mt 27: 60 stone in front of the *e* to the tomb
Mk 15: 46 a stone against the *e* of the tomb.
16: 3 away from the *e* of the tomb?"
Jn 11: 38 cave with a stone laid across the *e*.
20: 1 had been removed from the *e*.
Ac 12: 6 and sentries stood guard at the *e*.
12: 13 Peter knocked at the outer *e*,

ENTRANCES (ENTER)

Ex 33: 8 and stood at the *e* to their tents,
Nu 16: 27 little ones at the *e* to their tents.
Pr 8: 3 at the *e*, she cries aloud:
Eze 41: 11 There were *e* to the side rooms
43: 11 its arrangement, its exits and *e*—

ENTREAT (ENTREATY)

Zec 7: 2 to *e* the LORD by asking
8: 21 'Let us go at once to *e* the LORD
8: 22 LORD Almighty and to *e* him."

ENTREATY (ENTREAT)

2Ch 33: 13 the LORD was moved by his *e*
33: 19 and how God was moved by his *e*,

ENTRUST (TRUST)

Ge 42: 37 *E* him to my care, and I will bring
2Ki 22: 5 Have them *e* it to the men
Jn 2: 24 Jesus would not *e* himself to them,
2Ti 2: 2 the presence of many witnesses *e*

ENTRUSTED (TRUST)

Ge 39: 4 and he *e* to his care everything he
39: 8 everything he owns he has *e*
Lev 6: 2 his neighbor about something *e*
6: 4 or what was *e* to him, or the lost
1Ki 15: 18 He *e* it to his officials and sent
2Ki 22: 7 account for the money *e* to them,
22: 9 and have *e* it to the workers
1Ch 9: 26 were *e* with the responsibility
9: 31 was *e* with the responsibility
2Ch 34: 10 they *e* it to the men appointed
34: 17 and have *e* it to the supervisors
Ezr 7: 19 God of Jerusalem all the articles *e*
Est 2: 8 to the king's palace and *e* to Hegai,
6: 9 horse be *e* to one of the king's most
Jer 13: 20 Where is the flock that was *e* to you
29: 3 He *e* the letter to Elasah son
Mt 25: 14 and *e* his property to them.

Mt 25: 20 he said, 'you *e* me with five talents.
25: 22 he said, 'you *e* me with two talents;
Lk 12: 48 and from the one who has been *e*
Jn 5: 22 but has *e* all judgment to the Son,
Ro 3: 2 they have been *e* with the very
6: 17 of teaching to which you were *e*.
1Co 4: 1 as those *e* with the secret things
1Th 2: 4 by God to be *e* with the gospel.
1Ti 1: 11 of the blessed God, which he *e*
6: 20 guard what has been *e* to your care.
2Ti 1: 12 able to guard what I have *e* to him
1: 14 Guard the good deposit that was *e*
Tit 1: 3 light through the preaching *e* to me
1: 7 Since an overseer is *e*
1Pe 2: 23 he *e* himself to him who judges
5: 3 not lording it over those *e* to you,
Jude : 3 once for all *e* to the saints.

ENTRYWAY (ENTER)

2Ki 16: 18 and removed the royal *e*
Mk 14: 68 he said, and went out into the *e*.

ENTWINES

Job 8: 17 it *e* its roots around a pile of rocks

ENVELOPED

Isa 42: 25 It *e* them in flames, yet they did not
Mt 17: 5 speaking, a bright cloud *e* them,
Mk 9: 7 Then a cloud appeared and *e* them,
Lk 9: 34 a cloud appeared and *e* them,

ENVIED (ENVY)

Ge 26: 14 servants that the Philistines *e* him.
Ps 73: 3 For I *e* the arrogant

ENVIOUS (ENVY)

Dt 32: 21 I will make them *e*
Ps 37: 1 or be *e* of those who do wrong;
106: 16 In the camp they grew *e* of Moses
Pr 24: 19 or be *e* of the wicked,
Mt 20: 15 Or are you *e* because I am generous
Ro 10: 19 "I will make you *e*
11: 11 to the Gentiles to make Israel *e*.

ENVOY (ENVOYS)

Pr 13: 17 but a trustworthy *e* brings healing.
Jer 49: 14 An *e* was sent to the nations to say,
Ob : 1 An *e* was sent to the nations to say,

ENVOYS (ENVOY)

1Ki 5: 1 he sent his *e* to Solomon,
2Ki 17: 4 for he had sent *e* to So king
2Ch 32: 31 But when *e* were sent by the rulers
Ps 68: 31 *E* will come from Egypt;
Isa 14: 32 given to the *e* of that nation?
18: 2 which sends *e* by sea
30: 4 and their *e* have arrived in Hanes,
30: 6 the *e* carry their riches
33: 7 the *e* of peace weep bitterly.
39: 2 Hezekiah received the *e* gladly
Jer 27: 3 through the *e* who have come
Eze 17: 15 him by sending his *e* to Egypt

ENVY (ENVIED ENVIOUS ENVYING)

Job 5: 2 and *e* slays the simple.
Ps 68: 16 gaze in *e*, O rugged mountains,
Pr 3: 31 Do not *e* a violent man
14: 30 but *e* rots the bones.
23: 17 Do not let your heart *e* sinners,
24: 1 Do not *e* wicked men,
Ecc 4: 4 from man's *e* of his neighbor.
Eze 31: 9 the *e* of all the trees of Eden
Mt 27: 18 out of *e* that they had handed Jesus
Mk 7: 22 malice, deceit, lewdness, *e*, slander
15: 10 out of *e* that the chief priests had
Ro 1: 29 They are full of *e*, murder, strife,
11: 14 arouse my own people to *e*
1Co 13: 4 It does not *e*, it does not boast,
Gal 5: 21 factions and *e*; drunkenness, orgies
Php 1: 15 that some preach Christ out of *e*
1Ti 6: 4 and arguments that result in *e*,
Tit 3: 3 lived in malice and *e*, being hated
Jas 3: 14 But if you harbor bitter *e*
3: 16 where you have *e* and selfish
4: 5 caused to live in us tends toward *e*,
1Pe 2: 1 *e*, and slander of every kind.

ENVYING (ENVY)

Gal 5: 26 provoking and *e* each other.

EPAPHRAS

Col 1: 7 it from *E*, our dear fellow servant,
4: 12 *E*, who is one of you and a servant
Phm : 23 *E*, my fellow prisoner

EPAPHRODITUS

Php 2: 25 necessary to send back to you *E*,
4: 18 received from *E* the gifts you sent.

EPENETUS

Ro 16: 5 Greet my dear friend *E*, who was

EPHAH

Ge 25: 4 The sons of Midian were *E*, Epher,
Ex 16: 36 (An omer is one tenth of an *e*.)
29: 40 a tenth of an *e* of fine flour mixed
Lev 5: 11 a tenth of an *e* of fine flour
6: 20 a tenth of an *e* of fine flour
14: 10 along with three-tenths of an *e*
14: 21 a tenth of an *e* of fine flour mixed
19: 36 an honest *e* and an honest hin.
23: 13 offering of two-tenths of an *e*
23: 17 of two-tenths of an *e* of fine flour,
24: 5 two-tenths of an *e* for each loaf.
Nu 5: 15 of a tenth of an *e* of barley flour
15: 4 of a tenth of an *e* of fine flour mixed
15: 6 offering of two-tenths of an *e*
15: 9 offering of three-tenths of an *e*
28: 5 of a tenth of an *e* of fine flour mixed
28: 9 offering of two-tenths of an *e*
28: 12 offering of three-tenths of an *e*
28: 12 offering of two-tenths of an *e*
28: 13 of a tenth of an *e* of fine flour mixed
28: 20 offering of three-tenths of an *e*
28: 28 offering of three-tenths of an *e*
29: 3 offering of three-tenths of an *e*
29: 9 offering of three-tenths of an *e*
29: 14 offering of three-tenths of an *e*
Jdg 6: 19 from an *e* of flour he made bread
Ru 2: 17 and it amounted to about an *e*.
1Sa 1: 24 an *e* of flour and a skin of wine,
17: 17 "Take this *e* of roasted grain
1Ch 1: 33 The sons of Midian: *E*, Epher,
2: 46 Caleb's concubine *E* was
2: 47 Geshan, Pelet, *E* and Shaaph.
Isa 5: 10 a homer of seed only an *e* of grain."
60: 6 young camels of Midian and *E*.
Eze 45: 10 an accurate *e* and an accurate bath.
45: 11 The *e* and the bath are
45: 11 and the *e* a tenth of a homer;
45: 13 a sixth of an *e* from each homer
45: 13 and a sixth of an *e* from each homer
45: 24 along with a hin of oil for each *e*.
45: 24 as a grain offering an *e* for each bull
45: 24 for each bull and an *e* for each ram,
46: 5 along with a hin of oil for each *e*.
46: 5 given with the ram is to be an *e*,
46: 7 a grain offering one *e* with the bull,
46: 7 along with a hin of oil with each *e*.
46: 7 with the bull, one *e* with the ram,
46: 11 along with a hin of oil for each *e*.
46: 11 an *e* with a bull, an *e* with a ram,
46: 14 of a sixth of an *e* with a third
Mic 6: 10 and the short *e*, which is accursed?

EPHAI

Jer 40: 8 the sons of *E* the Netophathite,

EPHER

Ge 25: 4 *E*, Hanoch, Abida and Eldaah.
1Ch 1: 33 *E*, Hanoch, Abida and Eldaah.
4: 17 Jether, Mered, *E* and Jalon.
5: 24 *E*, Ishi, Eliel, Azriel, Jeremiah,

EPHES DAMMIM

1Sa 17: 1 camp at *E*, between Socoh and

EPHESIAN (EPHESUS)

Ac 21: 29 previously seen Trophimus the *E*

EPHESIANS (EPHESUS)

Ac 19: 28 "Great is Artemis of the *E*!"
19: 34 "Great is Artemis of the *E*!"

EPHESUS (EPHESIAN EPHESIANS)

Ac 18: 19 at *E*, where Paul left Priscilla
18: 21 Then he set sail from *E*.
18: 24 a native of Alexandria, came to *E*.
19: 1 the interior and arrived at *E*.
19: 17 to the Jews and Greeks living in *E*,
19: 26 numbers of people here in *E*
19: 35 of *E* is the guardian of the temple
19: 35 the crowd and said: "Men of *E*,
20: 16 to sail past *E* to avoid spending
20: 17 Paul sent to *E* for the elders
1Co 15: 32 in *E* for merely human reasons,
16: 8 I will stay on at *E* until Pentecost,
Eph 1: 1 To the saints in *E*, the faithful
1Ti 1: 3 in *E* so that you may command
2Ti 1: 18 how many ways he helped me in *E*.
4: 12 I sent Tychicus to *E*.
Rev 1: 11 to *E*, Smyrna, Pergamum, Thyatira
2: 1 the angel of the church in *E* write:

EPHLAL

1Ch 2: 37 father of *E*, *E* the father of Obed,

EPHOD

Ex 25: 7 other gems to be mounted on the *e*
28: 4 a breastpiece, an *e*, a robe,
28: 6 "Make the *e* of gold, and of blue,
28: 8 of one piece with the *e*
28: 12 on the shoulder pieces of the *e*
28: 15 Make it like the *e*: of gold,
28: 25 pieces of the *e* at the front.
28: 26 on the inside edge next to the *e*.
28: 27 just above the waistband of the *e*.
28: 27 pieces on the front of the *e*,
28: 28 to the rings of the *e* with blue cord,
28: 28 will not swing out from the *e*.
28: 31 robe of the *e* entirely of blue cloth,
29: 5 Fasten the *e* on him
29: 5 the robe of the *e*, the *e* itself
35: 9 other gems to be mounted on the *e*
35: 27 other gems to be mounted on the *e*
39: 2 They made the *e* of gold,
39: 4 made shoulder pieces for the *e*,
39: 5 of one piece with the *e*
39: 7 on the shoulder pieces of the *e*
39: 8 They made it like the *e*: of gold,
39: 18 pieces of the *e* at the front.
39: 19 on the inside edge next to the *e*.
39: 20 just above the waistband of the *e*.
39: 20 pieces on the front of the *e*,
39: 21 to the rings of the *e* with blue cord,
39: 21 would not swing out from the *e*—
39: 22 of the *e* entirely of blue cloth—
Lev 8: 7 tied the *e* to him by its skillfully
8: 7 with the robe and put the *e* on him.
Nu 34: 23 the tribe of Dan; Hanniel son of *E*,
Jdg 8: 27 Gideon made the gold into an *e*,
17: 5 and he made an *e* and some idols
18: 14 one of these houses has an *e*,
18: 17 and took the carved image, the *e*,
18: 18 the *e*, the other household gods
18: 20 He took the *e*, the other household
1Sa 2: 18 LORD—a boy wearing a linen *e*.
2: 28 and to wear an *e* in my presence.
14: 3 was Ahijah, who was wearing an *e*.
21: 9 it is wrapped in a cloth behind the *e*
22: 18 men who wore the linen *e*.
23: 6 of Ahimelech had brought the *e*
23: 9 to Abiathar the priest, "Bring the *e*
30: 7 of Ahimelech, "Bring me the *e*."
2Sa 6: 14 wearing a linen *e*, danced
1Ch 15: 27 David also wore a linen *e*.
Hos 3: 4 or sacred stones, without *e* or idol.

EPHPHATHA

Mk 7: 34 *E*!" (which means, "Be opened!").

EPHRAIM (EPHRAIM'S EPHRAIMITE EPHRAIMITES)

Ge 41: 52 The second son he named *E*
46: 20 and *E* were born to Joseph
48: 1 took his two sons Manasseh and *E*
48: 5 *E* and Manasseh will be mine,
48: 13 *E* on his right toward Israel's left
48: 20 So he put *E* ahead of Manasseh.
48: 20 'May God make you like *E*
Nu 1: 10 from *E*, Elishama son of Ammihud
1: 32 From the descendants of *E*:

Nu 1: 33 from the tribe of *E* was 40,500.
2: 18 camp of *E* under their standard.
2: 18 of the people of *E* is Elishama son
2: 24 the men assigned to the camp of *E*,
7: 48 the leader of the people of *E*
10: 22 of the camp of *E* went next,
13: 8 from the tribe of *E*, Hoshea son
26: 28 through Manasseh and *E* were:
26: 35 the descendants of *E* by their clans:
26: 37 These were the clans of *E*;
34: 24 from the tribe of *E* son of Joseph;
Dt 33: 17 Such are the ten thousands of *E*;
34: 2 the territory of *E* and Manasseh,
Jos 14: 4 two tribes—Manasseh and *E*.
16: 4 and *E*, the descendants of Joseph,
16: 5 This was the territory of *E*,
16: 10 live among the people of *E*
17: 9 to *E* lying among the towns
17: 10 the south the land belonged to *E*,
17: 15 if the hill country of *E* is too small
17: 17 to *E* and Manasseh—"You are
19: 50 in the hill country of *E*.
20: 7 Shechem in the hill country of *E*,
21: 5 from the clans of the tribes of *E*,
21: 20 towns from the tribe of *E*:
21: 21 of *E* they were given Shechem
24: 30 in the hill country of *E*,
24: 33 Phinehas in the hill country of *E*.
Jdg 1: 29 Nor did *E* drive out the Canaanites
2: 9 in the hill country of *E*,
3: 27 a trumpet in the hill country of *E*,
4: 5 and Bethel in the hill country of *E*,
5: 14 from *E*, whose roots were
7: 24 So all the men of *E* were called out
7: 24 throughout the hill country of *E*,
10: 1 in Shamir, in the hill country of *E*.
10: 9 Benjamin and the house of *E*;
12: 1 men of *E* called out their forces,
12: 4 Gileadites are renegades from *E*
12: 4 of Gilead and fought against *E*.
12: 5 and whenever a survivor of *E* said,
12: 5 fords of the Jordan leading to *E*,
12: 15 and was buried at Pirathon in *E*,
17: 1 country of *E* said to his mother,
17: 8 house in the hill country of *E*.
18: 2 men entered the hill country of *E*
18: 13 went on to the hill country of *E*
19: 1 country of *E* took a concubine
19: 16 man from the hill country of *E*,
19: 18 in the hill country of *E* where I live.
1Sa 1: 1 Zuphite from the hill country of *E*,
9: 4 through the hill country of *E*
14: 22 of *E* heard that the Philistines were
2Sa 2: 9 and also over *E*, Benjamin
13: 23 Baal Hazor near the border of *E*,
18: 6 battle took place in the forest of *E*.
20: 21 from the hill country of *E*,
1Ki 4: 8 in the hill country of *E*; Ben-Deker
12: 25 Shechem in the hill country of *E*
2Ki 5: 22 to me from the hill country of *E*.
14: 13 wall of Jerusalem from the *E* Gate
1Ch 6: 66 towns from the tribe of *E*.
6: 67 of *E* they were given Shechem
7: 20 The descendants of *E*: Shuthelah,
7: 22 Their father *E* mourned
9: 3 from *E* and Manasseh who lived
12: 30 men of *E*, brave warriors, famous
2Ch 13: 4 in the hill country of *E*, and said,
15: 8 he had captured in the hills of *E*.
15: 9 Benjamin and the people from *E*,
17: 2 towns of *E* that his father Asa had
19: 4 Beersheba to the hill country of *E*
25: 7 not with any of the people of *E*.
25: 10 who had come to him from *E*
25: 23 wall of Jerusalem from the *E* Gate
28: 12 Then some of the leaders in *E*—
30: 1 wrote letters to *E* and Manasseh,
30: 10 went from town to town in *E*
30: 18 the many people who came from *E*,
31: 1 Benjamin and in *E* and Manasseh.
34: 6 In the towns of Manasseh, *E*
34: 9 *E* and the entire remnant of Israel
Ne 8: 16 and the one by the Gate of *E*.
12: 39 over the Gate of *E*, the Jeshanah
Ps 60: 7 *E* is my helmet,
78: 9 The men of *E*, though armed
78: 67 he did not choose the tribe of *E*;
80: 2 before *E*, Benjamin and Manasseh.
Ps 108: 8 *E* is my helmet,
Isa 7: 2 "Aram has allied itself with *E*";
7: 5 *E* and Remaliah's son have plotted
7: 8 *E* will be too shattered
7: 9 The head of *E* is Samaria,
7: 17 since *E* broke away from Judah—
9: 9 *E* and the inhabitants of Samaria—
9: 21 feed on *E*, and *E* on Manasseh;
11: 13 *E* will not be jealous of Judah,
11: 13 nor Judah hostile toward *E*.
17: 3 fortified city will disappear from *E*,
Jer 4: 15 disaster from the hills of *E*.
7: 15 all your brothers, the people of *E*.'
31: 6 out on the hills of *E*,
31: 9 and *E* is my firstborn son.
31: 20 Is not *E* my dear son,
50: 19 on the hills of *E* and Gilead.
Eze 48: 5 "*E* will have one portion; it will
48: 6 the territory of *E* from east to west.
Hos 4: 17 *E* is joined to idols;
5: 3 I know all about *E*;
5: 3 *E*, you have now turned
5: 5 even *E*, stumble in their sin;
5: 9 *E* will be laid waste
5: 11 *E* is oppressed,
5: 12 I am like a moth to *E*,
5: 13 then *E* turned to Assyria,
5: 13 "When *E* saw his sickness,
5: 14 For I will be like a lion to *E*,
6: 4 "What can I do with you, *E*?
6: 10 There *E* is given to prostitution
7: 1 the sins of *E* are exposed
7: 8 *E* is a flat cake not turned over.
7: 8 "*E* mixes with the nations;
7: 11 "*E* is like a dove,
8: 9 *E* has sold herself to lovers.
8: 11 "Though *E* built many altars
9: 3 *E* will return to Egypt
9: 8 is the watchman over *E*,
9: 13 But *E* will bring out
9: 13 I have seen *E*, like Tyre,
9: 16 *E* is blighted,
10: 6 *E* will be disgraced;
10: 11 I will drive *E*,
10: 11 *E* is a trained heifer
11: 3 It was I who taught *E* to walk,
11: 8 "How can I give you up, *E*?
11: 9 nor devastate *E* again.
11: 12 *E* has surrounded me with lies,
12: 1 *E* feeds on the wind;
12: 8 *E* boasts,
12: 14 But *E* has bitterly provoked him
13: 1 When *E* spoke, men trembled;
13: 12 The guilt of *E* is stored up,
14: 8 O *E*, what more have I to do
Ob : 19 They will occupy the fields of *E*
Zec 9: 10 will take away the chariots from *E*
9: 13 and fill it with *E*.
Jn 11: 54 a village called *E*, where he stayed

EPHRAIM'S (EPHRAIM)

Ge 48: 14 his right hand and put it on *E* head,
48: 17 hand on *E* head he was displeased;
48: 17 hand to move it from *E* head
50: 23 the third generation of *E* children.
Jdg 8: 2 the gleanings of *E* grapes better
Isa 11: 13 *E* jealousy will vanish,
28: 1 wreath, the pride of *E* drunkards,
28: 3 wreath, the pride of *E* drunkards,
Jer 31: 18 "I have surely heard *E* moaning:
Eze 37: 16 of wood, and write on it, '*E* stick,
37: 19 which is in *E* hand—
Hos 9: 11 *E* glory will fly away like a bird—

EPHRAIMITE (EPHRAIM)

Jdg 12: 5 "Are you an *E*?" If he replied, "No
1Sa 1: 1 son of Tohu, the son of Zuph, an *E*.
1Ki 11: 26 one of Solomon's officials, an *E*
1Ch 27: 10 was Helez the Pelonite, an *E*.
27: 14 was Benaiah the Pirathonite, an *E*.
2Ch 28: 7 an *E* warrior, killed Maaseiah

EPHRAIMITES (EPHRAIM)

Jos 16: 8 inheritance of the tribe of the *E*,
16: 9 for the *E* within the inheritance
17: 8 of Manasseh, belonged to the *E*.)
Jdg 8: 1 Now the *E* asked Gideon,
12: 4 them down because the *E* had said,
Jdg 12: 6 Forty-two thousand *E* were killed
1Ch 27: 20 over the *E*: Hoshea son of Azaziah;
Zec 10: 7 The *E* will become like mighty men

EPHRATAH

Ru 4: 11 May you have standing in *E*

EPHRATH (EPHRATHITE EPHRATHITES)

Ge 35: 16 were still some distance from *E*,
35: 19 was buried on the way to *E* (that is,
48: 7 on the way, a little distance from *E*.
48: 7 there beside the road to *E*" (that is,
1Ch 2: 19 Caleb married *E*, who bore him

EPHRATHAH

1Ch 2: 50 The sons of Hur the firstborn of *E*:
4: 4 the firstborn of *E* and father
Ps 132: 6 We heard it in *E*,
Mic 5: 2 "But you, Bethlehem *E*,

EPHRATHITE (EPHRATH)

1Sa 17: 12 the son of an *E* named Jesse,

EPHRATHITES (EPHRATH)

Ru 1: 2 They were *E* from Bethlehem,

EPHRON (EPHRON'S)

Ge 23: 8 and intercede with *E* son of Zohar
23: 10 *E* the Hittite was sitting
23: 13 and he said to *E* in their hearing,
23: 14 *E* answered Abraham, "Listen
25: 9 in the field of *E* son
49: 29 cave in the field of *E* the Hittite,
49: 30 as a burial place from *E* the Hittite,
50: 13 as a burial place from *E* the Hittite,
Jos 15: 9 came out at the towns of Mount *E*
2Ch 13: 19 *E*, with their surrounding villages.

EPHRON'S (EPHRON)

Ge 23: 16 Abraham agreed to *E* terms
23: 17 *E* field in Machpelah near Mamre

EPICUREAN

Ac 17: 18 of *E* and Stoic philosophers began

EPILEPTIC (EPILEPTICS)

Mt 17: 15 "He is an *e* and is suffering greatly.

EPILEPTICS (EPILEPTIC)

Mt 4: 24 the demon-possessed, the *e*

EQUAL (EQUALED EQUALITY EQUITY)

Ge 44: 18 you are *e* to Pharaoh himself.
47: 9 and they do not *e* the years
Ex 30: 34 pure frankincense, all in *e* amounts,
Dt 33: 25 and your strength will *e* your days.
1Sa 9: 2 without *e* among the Israelites—
1Ki 3: 13 in your lifetime you will have no *e*
Job 41: 33 Nothing on earth is his *e*—
Isa 40: 25 who is my *e*?" says the Holy One.
46: 5 you compare me or count me *e*?
Eze 31: 8 *e* its boughs,
45: 12 plus fifteen shekels *e* one mina.
48: 8 length from east to west will *e* one
Da 1: 19 and he found none *e* to Daniel,
Mt 20: 12 'and you have made them *e*
Jn 5: 18 making himself *e* with God.
1Co 12: 25 that its parts should have *e* concern
2Co 2: 16 And who is *e* to such a task?
11: 12 to be considered *e* with us

EQUALED (EQUAL)

Mt 24: 21 until now—and never to be *e* again
Mk 13: 19 until now—and never to be *e* again

EQUALITY (EQUAL)

2Co 8: 13 pressed, but that there might be *e*.
8: 14 Then there will be *e*, as it is written:
Php 2: 6 did not consider *e*

EQUIP (EQUIPMENT EQUIPPED)

Heb 13: 21 *e* you with everything good

EQUIPMENT (EQUIP)

Nu 3: 36 its crossbars, posts, bases, all its *e*,
4: 26 and all the *e* used in its service.
4: 32 all their *e* and everything related
Dt 23: 13 As part of your *e* have something

1Sa 8: 12 of war and e for his chariots.
1Ki 19: 21 He burned the plowing e
2Ki 7: 15 e the Arameans had thrown away
2Ch 20: 25 among them a great amount of e
Ne 13: 9 into them the e of the house of God
Zec 11: 15 "Take again the e of a foolish

EQUIPPED (EQUIP)

2Ch 14: 8 e with large shields and with spears
Ne 4: 16 while the other half were e
Da 11: 13 advance with a huge army fully e.
2Ti 3: 17 man of God may be thoroughly e

EQUITY (EQUAL)

Ps 96: 10 he will judge the peoples with e.
98: 9 and the peoples with e.
99: 4 you have established e;

EQUIVALENT

Lev 27: 2 to the LORD by giving e values,
Eze 45: 14 for ten baths are e to a homer).

ER

Ge 38: 3 birth to a son, who was named E.
38: 6 Judah got a wife for E, his firstborn
38: 7 E, Judah's firstborn, was wicked
46: 12 Perez and Zerah (but E
46: 12 The sons of Judah: E, Onan,
Nu 26: 19 E and Onan were sons of Judah,
1Ch 2: 3 The sons of Judah: E, Onan
2: 3 E, Judah's firstborn, was wicked
4: 21 son of Judah: E the father of Lecah,
Lk 3: 28 the son of Elmadam, the son of E,

ERAN (ERANITE)

Nu 26: 36 through E, the Eranite clan.

ERANITE (ERAN)

Nu 26: 36 through Eran, the E clan.

ERASE

Ex 17: 14 I will completely e the memory
Dt 32: 26 and e their memory from mankind,
Rev 3: 5 I will never e his name

ERASTUS

Ac 19: 22 Timothy and E, to Macedonia,
Ro 16: 23 E, who is the city's director
2Ti 4: 20 E stayed in Corinth, and I left

ERECH

Ge 10: 10 E, Akkad and Calneh, in Shinar.
Ezr 4: 9 E and Babylon, the Elamites

ERECT (ERECTED)

Dt 16: 22 and do not e a sacred stone,
Eze 4: 2 Then lay siege to it: E siege works
21: 22 build a ramp and to e siege works.

ERECTED (ERECT)

Ex 40: 18 the bases in place, e the frames,
2Sa 18: 18 and e it in the King's Valley
1Ki 7: 21 He e the pillars at the portico
2Ki 21: 3 he also e altars to Baal
23: 12 the kings of Judah had e on the roof
2Ch 3: 17 He e the pillars in the front
33: 3 he also e altars to the Baals
Est 6: 4 on the gallows he had e for him.
Eze 17: 17 siege works e to destroy many lives

ERI (ERITE)

Ge 46: 16 Shuni, Ezbon, E, Arodi and Areli.
Nu 26: 16 the Oznite clan; through E,

ERITE (ERI)

Nu 26: 16 the E clan; through Arodi,

ERODES

Job 14: 18 "But as a mountain e and crumbles

ERRED

Nu 15: 28 who e by sinning unintentionally,
1Sa 26: 21 like a fool and have e greatly."

ERROR

Job 4: 18 if he charges his angels with e,
19: 4 my e remains my concern alone.
Ecc 10: 5 the sort of e that arises from a ruler:
Isa 32: 6 spreads e concerning the LORD;
Isa 47: 15 Each of them goes on in his e;
Mt 22: 29 are in e because you do not know
Mk 12: 24 not in e because you do not know
1Th 2: 3 we make does not spring from e
Jas 5: 20 Whoever turns a sinner from the e
2Pe 2: 18 escaping from those who live in e.
3: 17 away by the e of lawless men
Jude : 11 rushed for profit into Balaam's e;

ERRORS

Ps 19: 12 Who can discern his e?
Ecc 10: 4 calmness can lay great e to rest.

ESARHADDON

2Ki 19: 37 And E his son succeeded him
Ezr 4: 2 since the time of E king of Assyria,
Isa 37: 38 And E his son succeeded him

ESAU (ESAU'S)

Ge 25: 25 so they named him E.
25: 27 and E became a skillful hunter,
25: 28 loved E, but Rebekah loved Jacob.
25: 29 E came in from the open country,
25: 32 "Look, I am about to die," E said.
25: 34 So E despised his birthright.
25: 34 Then Jacob gave E some bread
26: 34 When E was forty years old,
27: 1 he called for E his older son
27: 5 When E left for the open country
27: 5 as Isaac spoke to his son E.
27: 6 say to your brother E,
27: 11 "But my brother E is a hairy man,
27: 15 clothes of E her older son,
27: 19 to his father, "I am E your firstborn
27: 21 you really are my son E or not."
27: 22 but the hands are the hands of E."
27: 23 hairy like those of his brother E;
27: 24 "Are you really my son E?"
27: 30 his brother E came in from hunting
27: 32 he answered, "your firstborn, E."
27: 34 When E heard his father's words,
27: 36 E said, "Isn't he rightly named
27: 37 for me?" Isaac answered E,
27: 38 my father!" Then E wept aloud.
27: 38 my son?" E said to his father,
27: 41 E held a grudge against Jacob
27: 42 told what her older son E had said,
27: 42 "Your brother E is consoling
28: 5 who was the mother of Jacob and E
28: 6 E learned that Isaac had blessed
28: 8 E then realized how displeasing
32: 3 of him to his brother E in the land
32: 4 are to say to my master E:
32: 6 "We went to your brother E,
32: 8 "If E comes and attacks one group,
32: 11 from the hand of my brother E,
32: 13 he selected a gift for his brother E:
32: 17 "When my brother E meets you
32: 18 They are a gift sent to my lord E,
32: 19 thing to E when you meet him.
33: 1 Jacob looked up and there was E,
33: 4 But E ran to meet Jacob
33: 5 E looked up and saw the women
33: 8 E asked, "What do you mean
33: 9 But E said, "I already have plenty,
33: 11 Jacob insisted, E accepted it.
33: 12 Then E said, "Let us be on our way
33: 15 E said, "Then let me leave some
33: 16 that day E started on his way back
35: 1 fleeing from your brother E."
35: 29 his sons E and Jacob buried him.
36: 1 This is the account of E (that is,
36: 2 E took his wives from the women
36: 4 to E, Basemath bore Reuel,
36: 5 the sons of E, who were born
36: 6 E took his wives and sons
36: 8 So E (that is, Edom) settled
36: 9 This is the account of E the father
36: 14 whom she bore to E: Jeush,
36: 15 sons of Eliphaz the firstborn of E:
36: 19 These were the sons of E (that is,
36: 40 were the chiefs descended from E,
36: 43 This was E, the father
Dt 2: 4 brothers the descendants of E,
2: 5 I have given E the hill country
2: 8 our brothers the descendants of E,
2: 12 descendants of E drove them out.
2: 22 the same for the descendants of E,
Dt 2: 29 as the descendants of E, who live
Jos 24: 4 and to Isaac I gave Jacob and E.
24: 4 the hill country of Seir to E,
1Ch 1: 34 The sons of Isaac: E and Israel.
1: 35 The sons of E: Eliphaz, Reuel,
Jer 49: 8 for I will bring disaster on E
49: 10 But I will strip E bare;
Ob : 6 But how E will be ransacked,
: 8 in the mountains of E?
: 18 survivors from the house of E."
: 18 the house of E will be stubble,
: 19 the mountains of E,
: 21 to govern the mountains of E.
Mal 1: 2 "Was not E Jacob's brother?"
1: 3 loved Jacob, but E I have hated,
Ro 9: 13 "Jacob I loved, but E I hated."
Heb 11: 20 and E in regard to their future.
12: 16 immoral, or is godless like E,

ESAU'S (ESAU)

Ge 25: 26 with his hand grasping E heel;
36: 10 Eliphaz, the son of E wife Adah,
36: 10 These are the names of E sons:
36: 10 the son of E wife Basemath.
36: 12 E son Eliphaz also had a concubine
36: 12 were grandsons of E wife Adah.
36: 13 grandsons of E wife Basemath.
36: 14 of E wife Oholibamah daughter
36: 15 the chiefs among E descendants:
36: 17 grandsons of E wife Basemath.
36: 17 of E son Reuel: Chiefs Nahath,
36: 18 The sons of E wife Oholibamah:
36: 18 from E wife Oholibamah daughter
Ob : 9 and everyone in E mountains

ESCAPE (ESCAPED ESCAPES ESCAPING)

Ge 7: 7 the ark to e the waters of the flood.
32: 8 the group that is left may e."
Jos 8: 20 chance to e in any direction,
Jdg 20: 42 but they could not e the battle.
1Sa 19: 10 That night David made good his e.
19: 18 David had fled and made his e,
27: 1 is to e to the land of the Philistines.
2Sa 15: 14 or none of us will e from Absalom.
20: 6 or he will find fortified cities and e
1Ki 12: 18 into his chariot and e to Jerusalem.
19: 17 put to death any who e the sword
19: 17 put to death any who e the sword
2Ki 10: 24 men I am placing in your hands e,
10: 25 "Go in and kill them; let no one e."
2Ch 10: 18 into his chariot and e to Jerusalem.
Est 4: 13 alone of all the Jews will e.
Job 11: 20 and e will elude them;
15: 30 He will not e the darkness;
Ps 56: 7 On no account let them e;
68: 20 from the Sovereign LORD comes e
88: 8 I am confined and cannot e;
Pr 11: 9 through knowledge the righteous e.
Ecc 7: 26 man who pleases God will e her,
Isa 20: 6 then can we e?' " An oracle
Jer 11: 11 on them a disaster they cannot e.
21: 9 are besieging you will live; he will e
25: 35 of the flock no place to e.
32: 4 of Judah will not e out of the hands
34: 3 You will not e from his grasp
35: 11 to Jerusalem to e the Babylonian
38: 2 He will e with his life; he will live.'
38: 18 you yourself will not e
38: 23 You yourself will not e
39: 18 fall by the sword but will e
41: 18 way to Egypt to e the Babylonians.
42: 17 e the disaster I will bring on them.'
44: 14 gone to live in Egypt will e
44: 28 Those who e the sword
45: 5 but wherever you go I will let you e
46: 6 nor the strong e.
48: 8 and not a town will e.
50: 29 let no one e.
La 3: 7 He has walled me in so I cannot e;
Eze 6: 8 for some of you will e the sword
6: 9 those who e will remember me—
7: 16 and e will be in the mountains,
17: 15 Will he break the treaty and yet e?
17: 15 Will he who does such things e?
17: 18 did all these things, he shall not e.
Da 11: 42 many countries; Egypt will not e.
Hos 9: 6 Even if they e from destruction,
Am 2: 14 The swift will not e,

Am 9: 1 none will *e*.
Hab 2: 9 to *e* the clutches of ruin!
Zec 2: 7 *E*, you who live in the Daughter
Mal 3:15 even those who challenge God *e*.' "
Mt 2:13 and his mother and *e* to Egypt.
23:33 How will you *e* being condemned
Lk 21:36 able to *e* all that is about to happen,
Ac 27:30 In an attempt to *e* from the ship,
Ro 2: 3 think you will *e* God's judgment?
1Th 5: 3 woman, and they will not *e*.
2Ti 2:26 and *e* from the trap of the devil,
Heb 2: 3 how shall we *e* if we ignore such
12:25 If they did not *e* when they refused
2Pe 1: 4 and *e* the corruption in the world

ESCAPED (ESCAPE)

Ge 14:13 One who had *e* came and reported
Jdg 3:26 passed by the idols and *e* to Seirah.
3:29 all vigorous and strong; not a man *e*
9: 5 son of Jerub-Baal, *e* by hiding.
1Sa 19:12 a window, and he fled and *e*.
19:17 send my enemy away so that he *e*
22: 1 and *e* to the cave of Adullam.
22:20 son of Ahimelech son of Ahitub, *e*
23:13 Saul was told that David had *e*
2Sa 1: 3 "I have *e* from the Israelite camp."
1Ki 20:20 king of Aram *e* on horseback
20:30 The rest of them *e* to the city
2Ki 9:27 but he *e* to Megiddo and died there
13: 5 and they *e* from the power of Aram
19:37 and they *e* to the land of Ararat.
1Ch 4:43 remaining Amalekites who had *e*,
2Ch 16: 7 king of Aram has *e* from your hand.
20:24 lying on the ground; no one had *e*.
30: 6 who have *e* from the hand
36:20 to Babylon the remnant, who *e*
Job 1:15 and I am the only one who has *e*
1:16 and I am the only one who has *e*
1:17 and I am the only one who has *e*
1:19 and I am the only one who has *e*
19:20 I have *e* with only the skin
Ps 124: 7 We have *e* like a bird
124: 7 and we have *e*.
Isa 37:38 and they *e* to the land of Ararat.
Jer 41:15 eight of his men *e* from Johanan
51:50 You who have *e* the sword,
La 2:22 no one *e* or survived;
Eze 33:21 who had *e* from Jerusalem came
Jn 10:39 to seize him, but he *e* their grasp.
Ac 16:27 he thought the prisoners had *e*.
26:26 none of this has *e* his notice,
28: 4 for though he *e* from the sea,
Heb 11:34 and *e* the edge of the sword;
2Pe 2:20 If they have *e* the corruption

ESCAPES (ESCAPE)

Ps 33:16 no warrior *e* by his great strength.
Pr 12:13 but a righteous man *e* trouble.
Joel 2: 3 nothing *e* them.

ESCAPING (ESCAPE)

Jdg 9:21 Then Jotham fled, *e* to Beer,
Job 15:22 He despairs of *e* the darkness;
Jer 48:19 the man fleeing and the woman *e*,
Hos 13: 3 like smoke *e* through a window.
Ac 27:42 them from swimming away and *e*.
1Co 3:15 only as one *e* through the flames.
2Pe 2:18 they entice people who are just *e*

ESCORT (ESCORTED)

Da 11: 6 together with her royal *e*
Ac 16:37 come themselves and *e* us out.''

ESCORTED (ESCORT)

1Ki 1:38 on King David's mule and *e* him
SS 3: 7 *e* by sixty warriors,
Ac 16:39 and *e* them from the prison,

ESEK

Ge 26:20 So he named the well *E*,

ESH-BAAL

1Ch 8:33 Malki-Shua, Abinadab and *E*.
9:39 Malki-Shua, Abinadab and *E*.

ESHAN

Jos 15:52 Arab, Dumah, *E*, Janim,

ESHBAN

Ge 36:26 Hemdan, *E*, Ithran and Keran.
1Ch 1:41 Hemdan, *E*, Ithran and Keran.

ESHCOL

Ge 14:13 a brother of *E* and Aner, all
14:24 went with me—to Aner, *E*
Nu 13:23 When they reached the Valley of *E*
13:24 place was called the Valley of *E*
32: 9 they went up to the Valley of *E*
Dt 1:24 and came to the Valley of *E*

ESHEK

1Ch 8:39 of his brother *E*: Ulam his firstborn

ESHTAOL (ESHTAOLITES)

Jos 15:33 *E*, Zorah, Ashnah, Zanoah,
19:41 Zorah, *E*, Ir Shemesh, Shaalabbin,
Jdg 13:25 between Zorah and *E*.
16:31 *E* in the tomb of Manoah his father
18: 2 warriors from Zorah and *E*
18: 8 they returned to Zorah and *E*,
18:11 set out from Zorah and *E*.

ESHTAOLITES (ESHTAOL)

1Ch 2:53 descended the Zorathites and *E*.

ESHTARAH

Jos 21:27 accused of murder) and Be *E*,

ESHTEMOA

Jos 21:14 Libnah, Jattir, *E*, Holon, Debir,
1Sa 30:28 to those in Aroer, Siphmoth, *E*
1Ch 4:17 and Ishbah the father of *E*.
4:19 Garmite, and *E* the Maacathite.
6:57 and Libnah, Jattir, *E*, Hilen, Debir,

ESHTEMOH

Jos 15:50 Anab, *E*, Anim, Goshen, Holon

ESHTON

1Ch 4:11 of Mehir, who was the father of *E*.
4:12 *E* was the father of Beth Rapha,

ESLI

Lk 3:25 the son of Nahum, the son of *E*,

ESTABLISH (ESTABLISHED ESTABLISHES ESTABLISHING REESTABLISHED)

Ge 6:18 But I will *e* my covenant with you,
9: 9 "I now *e* my covenant with you
9:11 I *e* my covenant with you:
17: 7 I will *e* my covenant
17:19 I will *e* my covenant with him
17:21 But my covenant I will *e* with Isaac
Ex 23:31 "I will *e* your borders
Dt 28: 9 The LORD will *e* you
1Sa 2:35 I will firmly *e* his house,
2Sa 3:10 and *e* David's throne over Israel
7:11 the LORD himself will *e* a house
7:12 own body, and I will *e* his kingdom.
7:13 I will *e* the throne of his kingdom
1Ki 8:32 and so *e* his innocence.
9: 5 I will *e* your royal throne
1Ch 17:11 own sons, and I will *e* his kingdom.
17:12 and I will *e* his throne forever.
18: 3 when he went to *e* his control
22:10 I will *e* the throne of his kingdom
28: 7 I will *e* his kingdom forever
2Ch 6:23 and so *e* his innocence.
7:18 and laws, I will *e* your royal throne,
Est 9:27 to *e* the custom that they
9:31 to *e* these days of Purim
Ps 87: 5 the Most High himself will *e* her."
89: 4 'I will *e* your line forever
89:29 I will *e* his line forever,
90:17 yes, *e* the work of our hands.
90:17 *e* the work of our hands for us—
Isa 26:12 LORD, you *e* peace for us;
Eze 16:60 and I will *e* an everlasting covenant
16:62 So I will *e* my covenant with you,
37:26 I will *e* them and increase their
Da 11:16 He will *e* himself in the Beautiful
Ro 10: 3 God and sought to *e* their own,
16:25 able to *e* you by my gospel
Heb 10: 9 sets aside the first to *e* the second.

ESTABLISHED (ESTABLISH)

Ge 9:17 the sign of the covenant I have *e*
47:26 Joseph *e* it as a law concerning land
Ex 6: 4 also *e* my covenant with them
15:17 sanctuary, O Lord, your hands *e*.
Lev 26:46 the regulations that the LORD *e*
Dt 19:15 A matter must be *e*
1Sa 13:13 he would have *e* your kingdom
20:31 nor your kingdom will be *e*.
24:20 of Israel will be *e* in your hands.
2Sa 5:12 knew that the LORD had *e* him
7:16 your throne will be *e* forever.' "
7:24 You have *e* your people Israel
7:26 of your servant David will be *e*
1Ki 2:12 David, and his rule was firmly *e*.
2:24 he who has *e* me securely
2:46 The kingdom was now firmly *e*
1Ch 14: 2 knew that the LORD had *e* him
16:30 world is firmly *e*; it cannot be
17:14 his throne will be *e* forever.' "
17:23 and his house be *e* forever.
17:24 of your servant David will be *e*
17:24 that it will be *e* and that your name
2Ch 1: 1 son of David *e* himself firmly
12: 1 as king was *e* and he had become
12:13 King Rehoboam *e* himself firmly
17: 5 The LORD *e* the kingdom
21: 4 When Jehoram *e* himself firmly
Ezr 8:20 officials had *e* to assist the Levites.
Est 9:31 and as they had *e* for themselves
Job 12:19 and overthrows men long *e*.
21: 8 They see their children *e*
24:22 they become *e*, they have no
28:25 When he *e* the force of the wind
Ps 9: 7 he has *e* his throne for judgment.
24: 2 and *e* it upon the waters.
74:16 you *e* the sun and moon.
78: 5 and *e* the law in Israel,
78:69 like the earth that he *e* forever.
81: 5 He *e* it as a statute for Joseph
89: 2 that you *e* your faithfulness
89:37 it will be *e* forever like the moon,
93: 1 The world is firmly *e*;
93: 2 Your throne was *e* long ago;
96:10 The world is firmly *e*, it cannot be
99: 4 you have *e* equity,
102:28 their descendants will be *e*
103:19 The LORD has *e* his throne
119:90 you *e* the earth, and it endures.
119:152 that you *e* them to last forever.
140:11 Let slanderers not be *e* in the land;
Pr 8:28 when he *e* the clouds above
12: 3 A man cannot be *e*
16:12 a throne is *e* through righteousness.
24: 3 and through understanding it is *e*;
25: 5 and his throne will be *e*
30: 4 Who has *e* all the ends of the earth?
Isa 2: 2 of the LORD's temple will be *e*
14:32 "The LORD has *e* Zion,
16: 5 In love a throne will be *e*;
44: 7 since I *e* my ancient people,
54:14 In righteousness you will be *e*:
Jer 12:16 then they will be *e*
30:20 and their community will be *e*
33: 2 the LORD who formed it and *e* it
33:25 'If I have not *e* my covenant
Mic 4: 1 of the LORD's temple will be *e*
Mt 18:16 so that 'every matter may be *e*
Ro 13: 1 authorities that exist have been *e*
13: 1 except that which God has *e*.
2Co 13: 1 "Every matter must be *e*
Gal 3:15 covenant that has been duly *e*,
3:17 set aside the covenant previously *e*
Eph 3:17 being rooted and *e* in love,
Col 1:23 if you continue in your faith, *e*
2Pe 1:12 are firmly *e* in the truth you now

ESTABLISHES (ESTABLISH)

Job 25: 2 he *e* order in the heights of heaven.
Isa 42: 4 till he *e* justice on earth.
62: 7 give him no rest till he *e* Jerusalem
Mic 7: 9 and *e* my right.
Hab 2:12 and *e* a town by crime!

ESTABLISHING (ESTABLISH)

Isa 9: 7 *e* and upholding it

ESTATE

Ge 15: 2 one who will inherit my *e* is Eliezer
31: 14 in the inheritance of our father's *e?*
Ru 4: 6 I might endanger my own *e*.
Est 8: 1 Xerxes gave Queen Esther the *e*
8: 2 appointed him over Haman's *e*.
8: 7 I have given his *e* to Esther,
Ps 136: 23 who remembered us in our low *e*
Lk 15: 12 'Father, give me my share of the *e*.'
Ac 28: 7 was an *e* nearby that belonged
Gal 4: 1 although he owns the whole *e*.

ESTEEM (ESTEEMED)

Est 10: 3 in high *e* by his many fellow Jews,
Pr 4: 8 *E* her, and she will exalt you;
Isa 66: 2 "This is the one I *e:*

ESTEEMED (ESTEEM)

Pr 22: 1 to be *e* is better than silver or gold.
Isa 53: 3 he was despised, and we *e* him not.
Da 9: 23 to tell you, for you are highly *e*.
10: 11 "Daniel, you who are highly *e*,
10: 19 Do not be afraid, O man highly *e*,"

ESTHER (ESTHER'S)

Est 2: 7 who was also known as *E*,
2: 8 *E* also was taken to the king's
2: 10 *E* had not revealed her nationality
2: 11 of the harem to find out how *E* was
2: 15 *E* won the favor of everyone who
2: 15 *E* (the girl Mordecai had adopted,
2: 17 attracted to *E* more than to any
2: 20 But *E* had kept secret her family
2: 22 about the plot and told Queen *E*,
4: 5 Then *E* summoned Hathach,
4: 8 to show to *E* and explain it to her,
4: 9 to *E* what Mordecai had said.
4: 15 Then *E* sent this reply to Mordecai
5: 1 On the third day *E* put
5: 2 When he saw Queen *E* standing
5: 2 *E* approached and touched the tip
5: 3 Queen *E?* What is your request?
5: 4 "If it pleases the king," replied *E*,
5: 5 to the banquet *E* had prepared.
5: 5 "so that we may do what *E* asks."
5: 6 the king again asked *E*,
5: 7 *E* replied, "My petition
5: 12 the only person Queen *E* invited
6: 14 to the banquet *E* had prepared.
7: 1 Haman went to dine with Queen *E*,
7: 2 "Queen *E*, what is your petition?
7: 3 Then Queen *E* answered, "If I have
7: 5 King Xerxes asked Queen *E*,
7: 6 *E* said, "The adversary
7: 7 behind to beg Queen *E* for his life.
7: 8 on the couch where *E* was reclining
8: 1 Xerxes gave Queen *E* the estate
8: 1 for *E* had told how he was related
8: 2 *E* appointed him over Haman's
8: 3 *E* again pleaded with the king,
8: 4 king extended the gold scepter to *E*
8: 7 I have given his estate to *E*,
8: 7 King Xerxes replied to Queen *E*
9: 12 The king said to Queen *E*,
9: 13 If it pleases the king," *E* answered,
9: 29 So Queen *E*, daughter of Abihail,
9: 31 Queen *E* had decreed for them,

ESTHER'S (ESTHER)

Est 2: 18 gave a great banquet, *E* banquet,
4: 4 When *E* maids and eunuchs came
4: 12 When *E* words were reported
4: 17 carried out all of *E* instructions.
9: 32 *E* decree confirmed these

ESTIMATE

Lk 14: 28 *e* the cost to see if he has enough

ESTRANGED

2Sa 14: 14 banished person may not remain *e*
Job 19: 13 my acquaintances are completely *e*

ETAM

Jdg 15: 8 stayed in a cave in the rock of *E*.
15: 11 down to the cave in the rock of *E*
1Ch 4: 3 These were the sons of *E:* Jezreel,
4: 32 Their surrounding villages were *E*,
2Ch 11: 6 Bethlehem, *E*, Tekoa, Beth Zur,

ETERNAL (ETERNALLY ETERNITY)

Ge 21: 33 the name of the LORD, the *E* God.
Dt 33: 27 The *e* God is your refuge,
1Ki 10: 9 of the LORD's *e* love for Israel,
Ps 16: 11 with *e* pleasures at your right hand.
21: 6 you have granted him *e* blessings
111: 10 To him belongs *e* praise.
119: 89 Your word, O LORD, is *e;*
119:160 all your righteous laws are *e*.
Ecc 12: 5 Then man goes to his *e* home
Isa 26: 4 LORD, the LORD, is the Rock *e*.
47: 7 the *e* queen!'
Jer 10: 10 he is the living God, the *e* King.
Da 4: 3 His kingdom is an *e* kingdom;
4: 34 His dominion is an *e* dominion;
Hab 3: 6 His ways are *e*.
Mt 18: 8 two feet and be thrown into *e* fire.
19: 16 good thing must I do to get *e* life?"
19: 29 as much and will inherit *e* life.
25: 41 into the *e* fire prepared for the devil
25: 46 but the righteous to *e* life."
25: 46 they will go away to *e* punishment,
Mk 3: 29 be forgiven; he is guilty of an *e* sin."
10: 17 "what must I do to inherit *e* life?"
10: 30 and in the age to come, *e* life.
Lk 10: 25 "what must I do to inherit *e* life?"
16: 9 will be welcomed into *e* dwellings.
18: 18 what must I do to inherit *e* life?"
18: 30 and, in the age to come, *e* life."
Jn 3: 15 believes in him may have *e* life.
3: 16 him shall not perish but have *e* life.
3: 36 believes in the Son has *e* life,
4: 14 spring of water welling up to *e* life."
4: 36 now he harvests the crop for *e* life,
5: 24 believes him who sent me has *e* life
5: 39 that by them you possess *e* life.
6: 27 but for food that endures to *e* life,
6: 40 believes in him shall have *e* life,
6: 54 and drinks my blood has *e* life,
6: 68 You have the words of *e* life.
10: 28 I give them *e* life, and they shall
12: 25 in this world will keep it for *e* life.
12: 50 that his command leads to *e* life.
17: 2 all people that he might give *e* life
17: 3 this is *e* life: that they may know
Ac 13: 46 yourselves worthy of *e* life,
13: 48 were appointed for *e* life believed.
Ro 1: 20 his *e* power and divine nature—
2: 7 and immortality, he will give *e* life.
5: 21 righteousness to bring *e* life
6: 22 to holiness, and the result is *e* life.
6: 23 but the gift of God is *e* life
16: 26 by the command of the *e* God,
2Co 4: 17 for us an *e* glory that far outweighs
4: 18 temporary, but what is unseen is *e*.
5: 1 from God, an *e* house in heaven,
Gal 6: 8 from the Spirit will reap *e* life.
Eph 3: 11 to his *e* purpose which he
2Th 2: 16 his grace gave us *e* encouragement
1Ti 1: 16 believe on him and receive *e* life.
1: 17 Now to the King *e*, immortal,
6: 12 Take hold of the *e* life
2Ti 2: 10 is in Christ Jesus, with *e* glory.
Tit 1: 2 resting on the hope of *e* life,
3: 7 heirs having the hope of *e* life.
Heb 5: 9 he became the source of *e* salvation
6: 2 of the dead, and *e* judgment.
9: 12 having obtained *e* redemption.
9: 14 through the *e* Spirit offered himself
9: 15 the promised *e* inheritance—
13: 20 of the *e* covenant brought back
1Pe 5: 10 you to his *e* glory in Christ,
2Pe 1: 11 into the *e* kingdom of our Lord
1Jn 1: 2 and we proclaim to you the *e* life,
2: 25 what he promised us—even *e* life.
3: 15 know that no murderer has *e* life
5: 11 God has given us *e* life,
5: 13 you may know that you have *e* life.
5: 20 He is the true God and *e* life.
Jude : 7 who suffer the punishment of *e* fire.
: 21 Christ to bring you to *e* life.
Rev 14: 6 and he had the *e* gospel to proclaim

ETERNALLY (ETERNAL)

Gal 1: 8 let him be *e* condemned! As we
1: 9 let him be *e* condemned! Am I now

ETERNITY (ETERNAL)

Ps 93: 2 you are from all *e*.
Pr 8: 23 I was appointed from *e*,
Ecc 3: 11 also set *e* in the hearts of men;

ETH KAZIN

Jos 19: 13 eastward to Gath Hepher and *E;*

ETHAM

Ex 13: 20 leaving Succoth they camped at *E*
Nu 33: 6 They left Succoth and camped at *E*
33: 7 left *E*, turned back to Pi Hahiroth,
33: 8 for three days in the Desert of *E*,

ETHAN

1Ki 4: 31 including *E* the Ezrahite—
1Ch 2: 6 *E*, Heman, Calcol and Darda—
2: 8 The son of *E:* Azariah.
6: 42 the son of *E*, the son of Zimmah,
6: 44 at his left hand: *E* son of Kishi,
15: 17 their brothers the Merarites, *E* son
15: 19 and *E* were to sound the bronze

ETHANIM

1Ki 8: 2 of the festival in the month of *E*,

ETHBAAL

1Ki 16: 31 married Jezebel daughter of *E* king

ETHER

Jos 15: 42 Libnah, *E*, Ashan, Iphtah, Ashnah,
19: 7 Ain, Rimmon, *E* and Ashan—

ETHIOPIAN (ETHIOPIANS)

Jer 13: 23 Can the *E* change his skin
Ac 8: 27 and on his way he met an *E* eunuch

ETHIOPIANS (ETHIOPIAN)

Ac 8: 27 of Candace, queen of the *E*.

ETHNAN

1Ch 4: 7 Zereth, Zohar, *E*, and Koz,

ETHNI

1Ch 6: 41 the son of *E*, the son of Zerah,

EUBULUS

2Ti 4: 21 *E* greets you, and so do Pudens,

EUNICE

2Ti 1: 5 and in your mother *E* and,

EUNUCH (EUNUCHS)

Est 2: 3 the king's *e*, who is in charge
2: 14 the king's *e* who was in charge
2: 15 the king's *e* who was in charge
Isa 56: 3 And let not any *e* complain,
Ac 8: 27 on his way he met an Ethiopian *e*,
8: 32 The *e* was reading this passage
8: 34 The *e* asked Philip, "Tell me,
8: 36 came to some water and the *e* said,
8: 38 and the *e* went down into the water
8: 39 and the *e* did not see him again,

EUNUCHS (EUNUCH)

2Ki 9: 32 Two or three *e* looked down at him
20: 18 they will become *e* in the palace
Est 1: 10 the seven *e* who served
1: 15 King Xerxes that the *e* have taken
4: 4 When Esther's maids and *e* came
4: 5 one of the king's *e* assigned
6: 14 king's *e* arrived and hurried Haman
7: 9 one of the *e* attending the king, said
Isa 39: 7 they will become *e* in the palace
56: 4 "To the *e* who keep my Sabbaths,
Mt 19: 12 For some are *e* because they were

EUODIA

Php 4: 2 I plead with *E* and I plead

EUPHRATES (TRANS-EUPHRATES)

Ge 2: 14 And the fourth river is the *E*.
15: 18 the *E*— the land of the Kenites,
Dt 1: 7 as far as the great river, the *E*.
11: 24 from the *E* River to the western sea
Jos 1: 4 the *E*— all the Hittite country—
2Sa 8: 3 control along the *E* River.
2Ki 23: 29 to the *E* River to help the king of

2Ki 24: 7 the Wadi of Egypt to the *E* River.
1Ch 5: 9 desert that extends to the *E* River,
18: 3 control along the *E* River.
2Ch 35: 20 up to fight at Carchemish on the *E*,
Isa 11: 15 hand over the *E* River
27: 12 from the flowing *E* to the Wadi
Jer 46: 2 at Carchemish on the *E* River
46: 6 In the north by the River *E*
46: 10 land of the north by the River *E*.
51: 63 a stone to it and throw it into the *E*.
Mic 7: 12 even from Egypt to the *E*
Rev 9: 14 bound at the great river *E*.''
16: 12 bowl on the great river *E*,

EUTYCHUS

Ac 20: 9 was a young man named *E*,

EVANGELIST (EVANGELISTS)

Ac 21: 8 stayed at the house of Philip the *e*,
2Ti 4: 5 hardship, do the work of an *e*,

EVANGELISTS (EVANGELIST)

Eph 4: 11 some to be prophets, some to be *e*,

EVE

Ge 3: 20 Adam named his wife *E*,
4: 1 Adam lay with his wife *E*,
2Co 11: 3 as *E* was deceived by the serpent's
1Ti 2: 13 For Adam was formed first, then *E*

EVEN-TEMPERED (TEMPER)

Pr 17: 27 and a man of understanding is *e*.

EVENING (EVENINGS)

Ge 1: 5 there was *e*, and there was morning
1: 8 there was *e*, and there was morning
1: 13 there was *e*, and there was morning
1: 19 there was *e*, and there was morning
1: 23 there was *e*, and there was morning
1: 31 there was *e*, and there was morning
8: 11 the dove returned to him in the *e*,
19: 1 arrived at Sodom in the *e*,
24: 11 toward *e*, the time the women go
24: 63 out to the field one *e* to meditate,
29: 23 when *e* came, he took his daughter
30: 16 came in from the fields that *e*,
49: 27 in the *e* he divides the plunder.''
Ex 12: 18 from the *e* of the fourteenth day
12: 18 until the *e* of the twenty-first day.
16: 6 ''In the *e* you will know that it was
16: 8 he gives you meat to eat in the *e*
16: 13 That *e* quail came and covered
18: 13 around him from morning till *e*.
18: 14 around you from morning till *e*?''
27: 21 the LORD from *e* till morning.
Lev 6: 20 it in the morning and half in the *e*.
11: 24 carcasses will be unclean till *e*.
11: 25 and he will be unclean till *e*.
11: 27 carcasses will be unclean till *e*.
11: 28 and he will be unclean till *e*.
11: 31 they are dead will be unclean till *e*.
11: 32 it will be unclean till *e*,
11: 39 the carcass will be unclean till *e*.
11: 40 and he will be unclean till *e*.
11: 40 and he will be unclean till *e*.
14: 46 it is closed up will be unclean till *e*.
15: 5 and he will be unclean till *e*.
15: 6 and he will be unclean till *e*.
15: 7 and he will be unclean till *e*.
15: 8 and he will be unclean till *e*.
15: 10 and he will be unclean till *e*.
15: 10 under him will be unclean till *e*;
15: 11 and he will be unclean till *e*.
15: 16 and he will be unclean till *e*.
15: 17 and it will be unclean till *e*.
15: 18 and they will be unclean till *e*.
15: 19 touches her will be unclean till *e*.
15: 21 and he will be unclean till *e*.
15: 22 and he will be unclean till *e*.
15: 23 touches it, he will be unclean till *e*.
15: 27 and he will be unclean till *e*.
17: 15 and he will be unclean till *e*;
22: 6 such thing will be unclean till *e*.
23: 32 From the *e* of the ninth day
23: 32 month until the following *e* you are
24: 3 the LORD from *e* till morning,
Nu 9: 15 From *e* till morning the cloud
9: 21 only from *e* till morning,
19: 7 will be ceremonially unclean till *e*.
19: 8 and he too will be unclean till *e*.
19: 10 and he too will be unclean till *e*.
19: 19 and that *e* he will be clean
19: 21 of cleansing will be unclean till *e*.
19: 22 touches it becomes unclean till *e*.''
Dt 16: 4 on the *e* of the first day remain
16: 6 must sacrifice the Passover in the *e*,
23: 11 *e* approaches he is to wash himself,
28: 67 in the *e*, ''If only it were morning
28: 67 ''If only it were *e*!''
Jos 5: 10 On the *e* of the fourteenth day
7: 6 of the LORD, remaining there till *e*
8: 29 on a tree and left him there until *e*.
10: 26 hanging on the trees until *e*.
Jdg 19: 9 said, ''Now look, it's almost *e*.
19: 16 That *e* an old man
20: 23 and wept before the LORD until *e*,
20: 26 They fasted that day until *e*
21: 2 where they sat before God until *e*,
Ru 2: 17 So Ruth gleaned in the field until *e*.
1Sa 14: 24 man who eats food before *e* comes,
17: 16 came forward every morning and *e*
20: 5 in the field until the *e* of the day
20: 19 The day after tomorrow, toward *e*,
30: 17 them from dusk until the *e*
2Sa 1: 12 and wept and fasted till *e* for Saul
11: 2 One *e* David got up from his bed
11: 13 But in the *e* Uriah went out to sleep
1Ki 17: 6 and bread and meat in the *e*,
18: 29 until the time for the *e* sacrifice.
22: 35 of the chariot, and that *e* he died.
2Ki 16: 15 offering and the *e* grain offering,
1Ch 16: 40 *e*, in accordance with everything
23: 30 They were to do the same in the *e*
2Ch 2: 4 *e* and on Sabbaths and New Moons
13: 11 and *e* they present burnt offerings
13: 11 on the gold lampstand every *e*.
18: 34 facing the Arameans until *e*.
31: 3 *e* burnt offerings and for the burnt
Ezr 3: 3 both the morning and *e* sacrifices.
9: 4 appalled until the *e* sacrifice.
9: 5 Then, at the *e* sacrifice, I rose
Ne 13: 19 When *e* shadows fell on the gates
Est 2: 14 In the *e* she would go there
Job 7: 2 longing for the *e* shadows,
Ps 55: 17 *E*, morning and noon
59: 6 They return at *e*,
59: 14 They return at *e*,
65: 8 where morning dawns and *e* fades
90: 6 by *e* it is dry and withered.
102: 11 My days are like the *e* shadow;
104: 23 to his labor until *e*.
109: 23 I fade away like an *e* shadow;
141: 2 of my hands be like the *e* sacrifice.
Ecc 11: 6 and at *e* let not your hands be idle,
Isa 17: 14 In the *e*, sudden terror!
Jer 6: 4 and the shadows of *e* grow long.
Eze 12: 4 in the *e*, while they are watching,
12: 7 in the *e* I dug through the wall
24: 18 and in the *e* my wife died.
33: 22 Now the *e* before the man arrived,
46: 2 but the gate will not be shut until *e*.
Da 9: 21 about the time of the *e* sacrifice.
Zep 2: 7 In the *e* they will lie down
3: 3 her rulers are *e* wolves,
Zec 14: 7 When *e* comes, there will be light.
Mt 8: 16 When *e* came, many who were
14: 15 As *e* approached, the disciples
14: 23 When *e* came, he was there alone,
16: 2 He replied, ''When *e* comes,
20: 8 ''When *e* came, the owner
26: 20 When *e* came, Jesus was reclining
27: 57 As *e* approached, there came a rich
Mk 1: 32 That *e* after sunset the people
4: 35 That day when *e* came, he said
6: 47 When *e* came, the boat was
11: 19 When *e* came, they went out
13: 35 whether in the *e*, or at midnight,
14: 17 When *e* came, Jesus arrived
15: 42 *e* approached, Joseph of Arimathea
Lk 21: 37 and each *e* he went out
24: 29 for it is nearly *e*; the day is almost
Jn 6: 16 When *e* came, his disciples went
13: 2 The *e* meal was being served,
20: 19 On the *e* of that first day
Ac 4: 3 and John, and because it was *e*,
28: 23 From morning till *e* he explained

EVENINGS (EVENING)

Da 8: 14 ''It will take 2,300 *e* and mornings;
8: 26 of the *e* and mornings that has been

EVER (EVERLASTING FOREVER FOREVERMORE)

Ge 24: 16 a virgin; no man had *e* lain with her
Ex 5: 23 *E* since I went to Pharaoh to speak
9: 18 worst hailstorm that has *e* fallen
10: 6 nor your forefathers have *e* seen
10: 14 of locusts, nor will there *e* be again.
11: 6 there has *e* been or *e* will be again.
15: 18 LORD will reign for *e* and *e*.''
Nu 11: 20 saying, ''Why did we *e* leave Egypt
14: 23 me with contempt will *e* see it.
14: 23 one of them will *e* see the land I
35: 26 '' 'But if the accused *e* goes
Dt 4: 32 has anything like it *e* been heard of
4: 32 so great as this *e* happened,
4: 34 Has any god *e* tried to take
5: 26 mortal man has *e* heard the voice
8: 19 If you *e* forget the LORD your
9: 24 rebellious against the LORD *e*
34: 12 For no one has *e* shown the mighty
Jos 7: 7 why did you *e* bring this people
7: 26 been called the Valley of Achor *e*
14: 14 of Jephunneh the Kenizzite *e* since,
22: 28 we said, 'If they *e* say this to us,
Jdg 11: 25 Did he *e* quarrel with Israel
16: 17 ''No razor has *e* been used
Ru 1: 17 deal with me, be it *e* so severely,
1Sa 1: 11 no razor will *e* be used on his head
3: 17 deal with you, be it *e* so severely,
14: 44 deal with me, be it *e* so severely,
20: 13 deal with me, be it *e* so severely,
20: 15 and do not *e* cut off your kindness
25: 22 deal with David, be it *e* so severely,
27: 6 to the kings of Judah *e* since.
2Sa 3: 9 deal with Abner, be it *e* so severely,
3: 35 deal with me, be it *e* so severely,
6: 9 ark of the LORD *e* come to me?''
7: 7 did I *e* say to any of their rulers
7: 11 and have done *e* since the time I
13: 32 Absalom's expressed intention *e*
19: 13 deal with me, be it *e* so severely,
1Ki 2: 23 deal with me, be it *e* so severely,
3: 12 anyone like you, nor will there *e* be.
10: 20 Nothing like it had *e* been made
19: 2 deal with me, be it *e* so severely,
20: 10 deal with me, be it *e* so severely,
22: 28 declared, ''If you *e* return safely,
2Ki 6: 31 deal with me, be it *e* so severely,
18: 33 of any nation *e* delivered his land
1Ch 13: 12 ''How can I *e* bring the ark of God
17: 6 did I *e* say to any of their leaders
17: 10 and have done *e* since the time I
29: 25 as no king over Israel *e* had before.
2Ch 1: 12 no king who was before you *e* had
9: 11 Nothing like them had *e* been seen
9: 19 Nothing like it had *e* been made
18: 27 declared, ''If you *e* return safely,
32: 13 the gods of those nations *e* able
35: 18 of Israel had *e* celebrated such
Ne 13: 1 or Moabite should *e* be admitted
Job 4: 7 being innocent, has *e* perished?
4: 7 were the upright *e* destroyed?
6: 22 Have I *e* said, 'Give something
15: 7 ''Are you the first man *e* born?
20: 4 *e* since man was placed
29: 20 the bow *e* new in my hand.'
38: 12 ''Have you *e* given orders
Ps 5: 11 let them *e* sing for joy.
9: 5 blotted out their name for *e* and *e*.
9: 18 the hope of the afflicted *e* perish.
10: 16 The LORD is King for *e* and *e*;
21: 4 length of days, for *e* and *e*.
25: 3 will *e* be put to shame,
25: 15 My eyes are *e* on the LORD,
26: 3 for your love is *e* before me,
38: 17 and my pain is *e* with me.
45: 6 O God, will last for *e* and *e*;
45: 17 nations will praise you for *e* and *e*.
46: 1 an *e* present help in trouble.
48: 14 For this God is our God for *e* and *e*;
49: 8 no payment is *e* enough—
50: 8 your burnt offerings, which are *e*
52: 8 God's unfailing love for *e* and *e*.

Ps 61: 8 will I *e* sing praise to your name
71: 6 I will *e* praise you.
72: 15 May people *e* pray for him
74: 15 you dried up the *e* flowing rivers.
83: 17 May they *e* be ashamed
84: 4 they are *e* praising you.
89: 33 nor will I *e* betray my faithfulness.
111: 8 They are steadfast for *e* and *e*,
119: 44 your law, for *e* and *e*.
119: 98 for they are *e* with me.
132: 12 sit on your throne for *e* and *e*."
132: 14 This is my resting place for *e* and *e*;
132: 16 and her saints will *e* sing for joy.
141: 5 Yet my prayer is *e*
145: 1 I will praise your name for *e* and *e*.
145: 2 and extol your name for *e* and *e*.
145: 21 his holy name for *e* and *e*.
148: 6 He set them in place for *e* and *e*;
Pr 4: 18 shining *e* brighter till the full light
5: 19 may you *e* be captivated
30: 13 those whose eyes are *e* so haughty,
Ecc 1: 6 *e* returning on its course.
Isa 6: 9 be *e* seeing, but never perceiving.'
6: 9 " 'Be *e* hearing, but never
34: 10 no one will *e* pass through it again.
36: 18 of any nation *e* delivered his land
49: 16 your walls are *e* before me.
59: 12 Our offenses are *e* with us,
66: 8 Who has *e* heard of such a thing?
66: 8 Who has *e* seen such things?
Jer 2: 10 see if there has *e* been anything like
2: 11 Has a nation *e* changed its gods?
6: 7 and wounds are *e* before me.
7: 7 I gave your forefathers for *e* and *e*.
18: 13 Who has *e* heard anything like this?
18: 14 *e* cease to flow?
18: 14 *e* vanish from its rocky slopes?
19: 4 nor the kings of Judah *e* knew,
20: 18 Why did I *e* come out of the womb
25: 5 and your fathers for *e* and *e*.
31: 36 the descendants of Israel *e* cease
33: 18 *e* fail to have a man to stand
35: 6 descendants must *e* drink wine.
35: 8 and daughters have *e* drunk wine
44: 3 nor you nor your fathers *e* knew.
44: 18 *e* since we stopped burning incense
44: 26 in Egypt will *e* again invoke my
La 2: 20 Whom have you *e* treated like this?
Eze 4: 14 unclean meat has *e* entered my
15: 3 Is wood *e* taken from it
16: 16 happen, nor should they *e* occur.
27: 32 "Who was *e* silenced like Tyre,
31: 14 trees by the waters are *e*
31: 14 trees so well-watered are *e*
Da 2: 10 has *e* asked such a thing
2: 20 be to the name of God for *e* and *e*;
6: 22 Nor have I *e* done any wrong
7: 18 it forever—yes, for *e* and *e*.'
9: 12 heaven nothing has *e* been done
12: 3 like the stars for *e* and *e*.
Joel 1: 2 Has anything like this *e* happened
2: 2 nor *e* will be in ages to come.
Mic 4: 5 our God for *e* and *e*.
Mal 3: 7 *E* since the time of your forefathers
Mt 9: 33 "Nothing like this has *e* been seen
13: 14 you will be *e* seeing but never
13: 14 " 'You will be *e* hearing
Mk 4: 12 *e* hearing but never understanding;
4: 12 " 'they may be *e* seeing
11: 2 which no one has *e* ridden.
11: 14 "May no one *e* eat fruit
Lk 9: 39 It scarcely *e* leaves him
19: 30 which no one has *e* ridden.
Jn 1: 18 No one has *e* seen God,
3: 13 No one has *e* gone into heaven
4: 29 who told me everything I *e* did.
4: 39 "He told me everything I *e* did."
7: 46 "No one *e* spoke the way this man
9: 32 Nobody has *e* heard
10: 8 All who *e* came before me were
19: 41 in which no one had *e* been laid.
Ac 7: 52 Was there *e* a prophet your fathers
11: 8 unclean has *e* entered my mouth.'
20: 25 the kingdom will *e* see me again.
26: 4 all know the way I have lived *e*
28: 26 you will be *e* seeing but never
28: 26 "You will be *e* hearing
Ro 11: 35 "Who has *e* given to God,
2Co 7: 7 so that my joy was greater than *e*.
Gal 1: 5 to whom be glory for *e* and *e*.
Eph 1: 15 *e* since I heard about your faith
3: 21 all generations, for *e* and *e*!
5: 29 no one *e* hated his own body,
Php 4: 20 and Father be glory for *e* and *e*.
1Ti 1: 17 be honor and glory for *e* and *e*.
2Ti 4: 18 To him be glory for *e* and *e*.
Heb 1: 5 which of the angels did God *e* say,
1: 8 O God, will last for *e* and *e*,
1: 13 which of the angels did God *e* say,
7: 13 one from that tribe has *e* served
13: 21 to whom be glory for *e* and *e*.
1Pe 4: 11 the glory and the power for *e* and *e*.
5: 11 To him be the power for *e* and *e*.
2Pe 3: 4 is this 'coming' he promised? *E*
1Jn 4: 12 No one has *e* seen God;
Rev 1: 6 him be glory and power for *e* and *e*!
1: 18 and behold I am alive for *e* and *e*!
4: 9 throne and who lives for *e* and *e*,
4: 10 worship him who lives for *e* and *e*.
5: 13 for *e* and *e*!" The four living
7: 12 be to our God for *e* and *e*.
10: 6 swore by him who lives for *e* and *e*,
11: 15 and he will reign for *e* and *e*."
14: 11 of their torment rises for *e* and *e*.
15: 7 wrath of God, who lives for *e* and *e*.
16: 18 earthquake like it has *e* occurred
18: 18 'Was there *e* a city like this great
18: 22 will *e* be found in you again.
19: 3 from her goes up for *e* and *e*."
20: 10 day and night for *e* and *e*.
21: 25 On no day will its gates *e* be shut,
21: 27 Nothing impure will *e* enter it,
22: 5 And they will reign for *e* and *e*.

EVER-INCREASING (INCREASE)

Ro 6: 19 to impurity and to *e* wickedness,
2Co 3: 18 into his likeness with *e* glory,

EVERLASTING (EVER)

Ge 9: 16 and remember the *e* covenant
17: 7 an *e* covenant between me and you
17: 8 I will give as an *e* possession to you
17: 13 in your flesh is to be an *e* covenant.
17: 19 an *e* covenant for his descendants
48: 4 *e* possession to your descendants
Nu 18: 19 It is an *e* covenant of salt
Dt 33: 15 and the fruitfulness of the *e* hills;
33: 27 and underneath are the *e* arms.
2Sa 23: 5 made with me an *e* covenant,
1Ch 16: 17 to Israel as an *e* covenant:
16: 36 from *e* to *e*.
29: 10 from *e* to *e*.
Ezr 9: 12 to your children as an *e* inheritance
Ne 9: 5 your God, who is from *e* to *e*."
Ps 41: 13 from *e* to *e*.
52: 5 God will bring you down to *e* ruin:
74: 3 through these *e* ruins,
78: 66 he put them to *e* shame.
90: 2 from *e* to *e* you are God.
103: 17 But from *e* to *e*
105: 10 to Israel as an *e* covenant:
106: 48 from *e* to *e*.
119: 142 Your righteousness is *e*
139: 24 and lead me in the way *e*.
145: 13 Your kingdom is an *e* kingdom,
Isa 9: 6 *E* Father, Prince of Peace.
24: 5 and broken the *e* covenant.
30: 8 it may be an *e* witness.
33: 14 Who of us can dwell with *e* burning
35: 10 *e* joy will crown their heads.
40: 28 The LORD is the *e* God,
45: 17 the LORD with an *e* salvation;
45: 17 to ages *e*.
51: 11 *e* joy will crown their heads.
54: 8 but with *e* kindness
55: 3 I will make an *e* covenant with you,
55: 13 for an *e* sign,
56: 5 I will give them an *e* name
60: 15 I will make you the *e* pride
60: 19 for the LORD will be your *e* light,
60: 20 the LORD will be your *e* light,
61: 7 and *e* joy will be theirs.
61: 8 and make an *e* covenant with them.
63: 12 to gain for himself *e* renown,
Jer 5: 22 an *e* barrier it cannot cross.
23: 40 I will bring upon you *e* disgrace—
Jer 23: 40 *e* shame that will not be forgotten."
25: 9 of horror and scorn, and an *e* ruin.
31: 3 "I have loved you with an *e* love;
32: 40 I will make an *e* covenant
50: 5 the LORD in an *e* covenant
Eze 16: 60 and I will establish an *e* covenant
37: 26 with them; it will be an *e* covenant.
Da 7: 14 dominion is an *e* dominion that will
7: 27 His kingdom will be an *e* kingdom,
9: 24 to bring in *e* righteousness,
12: 2 others to shame and *e* contempt.
12: 2 some to *e* life, others to shame
Mic 6: 2 you *e* foundations of the earth.
Hab 1: 12 O LORD, are you not from *e*?
Jn 6: 47 the truth, he who believes has *e* life.
2Th 1: 9 punished with *e* destruction
Jude : 6 bound with *e* chains for judgment

EVI

Nu 31: 8 Among their victims were *E*,
Jos 13: 21 *E*, Rekem, Zur, Hur and Reba—

EVIDENCE (EVIDENT)

Ex 22: 13 he shall bring in the remains as *e*
1Sa 12: 7 you with *e* before the LORD
Mt 26: 59 looking for false *e* against Jesus
Mk 14: 55 looking for *e* against Jesus
Jn 14: 11 on the *e* of the miracles themselves.
Ac 11: 23 and saw the *e* of the grace of God,
2Th 1: 5 All this is *e* that God's judgment is
Jas 2: 20 do you want *e* that faith

EVIDENT (EVIDENCE)

1Ch 4: 41 completely destroyed them, as is *e*
Gal 2: 17 it becomes *e* that we ourselves are
Php 4: 5 Let your gentleness be *e* to all.

EVIL (EVILDOER EVILDOERS EVILS)

Ge 2: 9 of the knowledge of good and *e*.
2: 17 of the knowledge of good and *e*,
3: 5 be like God, knowing good and *e*."
3: 22 one of us, knowing good and *e*.
6: 5 of his heart was only *e* all the time.
8: 21 of his heart is *e* from childhood.
44: 4 'Why have you repaid good with *e*?
Ex 10: 10 children! Clearly you are bent on *e*.
32: 12 with *e* intent that he brought them
32: 22 how prone these people are to *e*.
Lev 5: 4 or *e*— in any matter one might
Nu 32: 13 generation of those who had done *e*
Dt 1: 35 a man of this *e* generation shall see
4: 25 doing *e* in the eyes
9: 18 doing what was *e* in the LORD's
13: 5 You must purge the *e*
13: 11 you will do such an *e* thing again.
17: 2 LORD gives you is found doing *e*
17: 5 or woman who has done this *e* deed
17: 7 You must purge the *e*
17: 12 You must purge the *e* from Israel.
19: 19 You must purge the *e*
19: 20 again will such an *e* thing be done
21: 21 You must purge the *e*
22: 21 You must purge the *e*
22: 22 You must purge the *e* from Israel.
22: 24 You must purge the *e*
24: 7 You must purge the *e*
28: 20 because of the *e* you have done
31: 29 because you will do *e* in the sight
Jos 23: 15 on you all the *e* he has threatened,
Jdg 2: 11 Then the Israelites did *e* in the eyes
2: 19 refused to give up their *e* practices
3: 7 The Israelites did *e* in the eyes
3: 12 Once again the Israelites did *e*
3: 12 they did this *e* the LORD gave
4: 1 the Israelites once again did *e*
6: 1 Again the Israelites did *e*
9: 23 God sent an *e* spirit
10: 6 Again the Israelites did *e*
13: 1 Again the Israelites did *e*
20: 13 and purge the *e* from Israel."
1Sa 12: 17 will realize what an *e* thing you did
12: 19 to all our other sins the *e* of asking
12: 20 "You have done all this *e*;
12: 25 Yet if you persist in doing *e*,
15: 19 do *e* in the eyes of the LORD?"
15: 23 and arrogance like the *e* of idolatry.
16: 14 *e* spirit from the LORD tormented
16: 15 an *e* spirit from God is tormenting

1Sa 16: 16 when the *e* spirit from God comes
16: 23 and the *e* spirit would leave him.
18: 10 The next day an *e* spirit
19: 9 an *e* spirit from the LORD came
24: 13 'From evildoers come *e* deeds,'
25: 21 He has paid me back *e* for good.
30: 22 all the *e* men and troublemakers
2Sa 3: 39 evildoer according to his *e* deeds!"
12: 9 by doing what is *e* in his eyes?
14: 17 of God in discerning good and *e*.
22: 22 I have not done *e* by turning
23: 6 But *e* men are all to be cast
1Ki 1: 52 but if *e* is found in him, he will die."
11: 6 So Solomon did *e* in the eyes
13: 33 did not change his *e* ways,
14: 9 You have done more *e*
14: 22 Judah did *e* in the eyes
15: 26 He did *e* in the eyes of the LORD,
15: 34 He did *e* in the eyes of the LORD,
16: 7 of all the *e* he had done in the eyes
16: 19 doing *e* in the eyes of the LORD
16: 25 But Omri did *e* in the eyes
16: 30 son of Omri did more *e* in the eyes
21: 20 yourself to do *e* in the eyes
21: 25 who sold himself to do *e* in the eyes
22: 52 He did *e* in the eyes of the LORD,
2Ki 3: 2 He did *e* in the eyes of the LORD,
8: 18 He did *e* in the eyes of the LORD.
8: 27 and did *e* in the eyes of the LORD,
13: 2 He did *e* in the eyes of the LORD
13: 11 He did *e* in the eyes of the LORD
14: 24 He did *e* in the eyes of the LORD
15: 9 He did *e* in the eyes of the LORD,
15: 18 He did *e* in the eyes of the LORD.
15: 24 Pekahiah did *e* in the eyes
15: 28 He did *e* in the eyes of the LORD.
17: 2 He did *e* in the eyes of the LORD,
17: 13 and seers: "Turn from your *e* ways.
17: 17 sold themselves to do *e* in the eyes
21: 2 He did *e* in the eyes of the LORD,
21: 6 He did much *e* in the eyes
21: 9 so that they did more *e*
21: 11 He has done more *e*
21: 15 they have done *e* in my eyes
21: 16 so that they did *e* in the eyes
21: 20 He did *e* in the eyes of the LORD,
23: 32 He did *e* in the eyes of the LORD,
23: 37 he did *e* in the eyes of the LORD,
24: 9 He did *e* in the eyes of the LORD,
24: 19 He did *e* in the eyes of the LORD,
1Ch 21: 7 This command was also *e*
2Ch 12: 14 He did *e* because he had not set his
21: 6 He did *e* in the eyes of the LORD.
22: 4 He did *e* in the eyes of the LORD,
29: 6 they did *e* in the eyes
33: 2 He did *e* in the eyes of the LORD,
33: 6 He did much *e* in the eyes
33: 9 so that they did more *e*
33: 22 He did *e* in the eyes of the LORD,
36: 5 He did *e* in the eyes
36: 9 He did *e* in the eyes of the LORD.
36: 12 He did *e* in the eyes
Ezr 9: 13 to us is a result of our *e* deeds
Ne 9: 28 they again did what was *e*
9: 35 or turn from their *e* ways.
13: 7 learned about the *e* thing Eliashib
Est 8: 3 to the *e* plan of Haman the Agagite,
9: 25 orders that the *e* scheme Haman
Job 1: 1 he feared God and shunned *e*.
1: 8 a man who fears God and shuns *e*."
2: 3 a man who fears God and shuns *e*.
4: 8 I have observed, those who plow *e*
11: 11 when he sees *e*, does he not take
11: 14 and allow no *e* to dwell in your tent
15: 16 who drinks up *e* like water!
15: 35 trouble and give birth to *e*;
16: 11 God has turned me over to *e* men
18: 21 such is the dwelling of an *e* man;
20: 12 "Though *e* is sweet in his mouth
21: 30 that the *e* man is spared
22: 15 that *e* men have trod?
24: 20 *e* men are no longer remembered
28: 28 and to shun *e* is understanding.' "
30: 26 Yet when I hoped for good, *e* came;
34: 10 Far be it from God to do *e*,
36: 10 to repent of their *e*.
36: 21 Beware of turning to *e*,
Ps 5: 4 not a God who takes pleasure in *e*;
Ps 6: 8 Away from me, all you who do *e*,
7: 4 if I have done *e* to him who is
7: 14 He who is pregnant with *e*
10: 7 trouble and *e* are under his tongue.
10: 15 the arm of the wicked and *e* man;
18: 21 I have not done *e* by turning
21: 11 Though they plot *e* against you
22: 16 a band of *e* men has encircled me,
23: 4 I will fear no *e*,
27: 2 When *e* men advance against me
28: 3 with those who do *e*,
28: 4 and for their *e* work;
34: 13 keep your tongue from *e*
34: 14 Turn from *e* and do good;
34: 16 is against those who do *e*,
34: 21 *E* will slay the wicked;
35: 12 They repay me *e* for good
36: 4 Even on his bed he plots *e*;
37: 1 Do not fret because of *e* men
37: 8 do not fret—it leads only to *e*.
37: 9 For *e* men will be cut off,
37: 27 Turn from *e* and do good;
38: 20 Those who repay my good with *e*
49: 5 fear when *e* days come,
50: 19 You use your mouth for *e*
51: 4 and done what is *e* in your sight,
52: 1 boast of *e*, you mighty man?
52: 3 You love *e* rather than good,
54: 5 Let *e* recoil on those who slander
55: 15 for *e* finds lodging among them.
64: 5 encourage each other in *e* plans,
71: 4 from the grasp of *e* and cruel men.
73: 7 *e* conceits of their minds know no
97: 10 those who love the LORD hate *e*,
101: 4 I will have nothing to do with *e*.
109: 5 They repay me *e* for good,
109: 6 Appoint an *e* man to oppose him;
109: 20 to those who speak *e* of me.
119:101 kept my feet from every *e* path
125: 3 their hands to do *e*.
139: 20 They speak of you with *e* intent;
140: 1 Rescue me, O LORD, from *e* men,
140: 2 who devise *e* plans in their hearts
141: 4 not my heart be drawn to what is *e*,
Pr 2: 14 and rejoice in the perverseness of *e*,
3: 7 fear the LORD and shun *e*.
4: 14 or walk in the way of *e* men.
4: 16 For they cannot sleep till they do *e*;
4: 27 keep your foot from *e*.
5: 22 *e* deeds of a wicked man ensnare
6: 14 who plots *e* with deceit in his heart
6: 18 feet that are quick to rush into *e*,
8: 13 To fear the LORD is to hate *e*;
8: 13 *e* behavior and perverse speech.
10: 23 A fool finds pleasure in *e* conduct,
10: 29 but it is the ruin of those who do *e*.
11: 6 unfaithful are trapped by *e* desires.
11: 19 he who pursues *e* goes to his death.
11: 27 *e* comes to him who searches for it.
12: 12 wicked desire the plunder of *e* men,
12: 13 An *e* man is trapped
12: 20 in the hearts of those who plot *e*,
13: 19 but fools detest turning from *e*.
14: 16 man fears the LORD and shuns *e*,
14: 19 *E* men will bow
14: 22 Do not those who plot *e* go astray?
15: 28 the mouth of the wicked gushes *e*.
16: 6 of the LORD a man avoids *e*.
16: 17 highway of the upright avoids *e*;
16: 27 A scoundrel plots *e*,
16: 30 he who purses his lips is bent on *e*.
17: 4 A wicked man listens to *e* lips;
17: 11 An *e* man is bent only on rebellion;
17: 13 If a man pays back *e* for good,
17: 13 *e* will never leave his house.
19: 28 of the wicked gulps down *e*.
20: 8 he winnows out all *e* with his eyes.
20: 30 Blows and wounds cleanse away *e*,
21: 10 The wicked man craves *e*;
21: 27 so when brought with *e* intent!
24: 8 He who plots *e*
24: 19 Do not fret because of *e* men
24: 20 for the *e* man has no future hope,
26: 23 are fervent lips with an *e* heart.
28: 5 *E* men do not understand justice,
28: 10 leads the upright along an *e* path
29: 6 An *e* man is snared by his own sin,
30: 32 or if you have planned *e*,
Ecc 4: 3 who has not seen the *e*
5: 13 I have seen a grievous *e*
5: 16 This too is a grievous *e*:
6: 1 I have seen another *e* under the sun
6: 2 This is meaningless, a grievous *e*.
9: 3 This is the *e* in everything that
9: 3 are full of *e* and there is madness
9: 12 so men are trapped by *e* times
10: 5 There is an *e* I have seen
12: 14 whether it is good or *e*.
Isa 1: 13 I cannot bear your *e* assemblies.
1: 16 Take your *e* deeds
5: 20 Woe to those who call *e* good
5: 20 and good *e*,
13: 11 I will punish the world for its *e*,
26: 10 of uprightness they go on doing *e*
29: 20 an eye for *e* will be cut down—
32: 6 his mind is busy with *e*:
32: 7 he makes up *e* schemes
33: 15 eyes against contemplating *e*—
55: 7 and the *e* man his thoughts.
56: 2 keeps his hand from doing any *e*."
57: 1 away to be spared from *e*.
59: 4 trouble and give birth to *e*.
59: 6 Their deeds are *e* deeds,
59: 7 Their thoughts are *e* thoughts;
59: 15 whoever shuns *e* becomes a prey.
65: 12 You did *e* in my sight
66: 4 They did *e* in my sight
Jer 2: 19 how *e* and bitter it is for you
3: 5 but you do all the *e* you can."
3: 17 the stubbornness of their *e* hearts.
4: 4 because of the *e* you have done—
4: 14 wash the *e* from your heart
4: 22 They are skilled in doing *e*;
5: 28 Their *e* deeds have no limit;
7: 24 inclinations of their *e* hearts.
7: 26 did more *e* than their forefathers.'
7: 30 of Judah have done *e* in my eyes,
8: 3 of this *e* nation will prefer death
11: 8 the stubbornness of their *e* hearts.
11: 15 as she works out her *e* schemes
11: 17 and the house of Judah have done *e*
13: 23 who are accustomed to doing *e*.
16: 12 of his *e* heart instead of obeying me
18: 8 nation I warned repents of its *e*,
18: 10 and if it does *e* in my sight
18: 11 So turn from your *e* ways,
18: 12 the stubbornness of his *e* heart.' "
18: 20 Should good be repaid with *e*?
21: 12 because of the *e* you have done—
23: 2 on you for the *e* you have done,"
23: 10 The prophets follow an *e* course
23: 22 and from their *e* deeds.
23: 22 turned them from their *e* ways
25: 5 your *e* ways and your *e* practices,
26: 3 and each will turn from his *e* way.
26: 3 because of the *e* they have done.
32: 30 but *e* in my sight from their youth;
32: 32 me by all the *e* they have done—
44: 3 because of the *e* they have done.
52: 2 He did *e* in the eyes of the LORD,
Eze 3: 18 him from his *e* ways in order
3: 19 his wickedness or from his *e* ways,
3: 20 from his righteousness and does *e*,
6: 9 for the *e* they have done
11: 2 are the men who are plotting *e*
13: 22 not to turn from their *e* ways
20: 43 for all the *e* you have done.
20: 44 and not according to your *e* ways
30: 12 and sell the land to *e* men;
33: 11 Turn! Turn from your *e* ways!
33: 13 he will die for the *e* he has done.
33: 13 in his righteousness and does *e*,
33: 15 and does no *e*, he will surely live;
33: 18 from his righteousness and does *e*,
36: 31 you will remember your *e* ways
38: 10 and you will devise an *e* scheme.
Da 11: 27 with their hearts bent on *e*,
Hos 7: 2 that I remember all their *e* deeds.
7: 15 but they plot *e* against me.
10: 13 you have reaped *e*,
Am 5: 13 for the times are *e*.
5: 14 Seek good, not *e*,
5: 15 Hate *e*, love good;
6: 3 You put off the *e* day
9: 4 them for *e* and not for good."
Jnh 3: 8 Let them give up their *e* ways

Jnh 3:10 how they turned from their *e* ways,
Mic 2: 1 to those who plot *e* on their beds!
3: 2 you who hate good and love *e;*
3: 4 because of the *e* they have done.
7: 3 Both hands are skilled in doing *e;*
Na 1:11 who plots *e* against the LORD
Hab 1:13 Your eyes are too pure to look on *e;*
Zec 1: 4 your *e* ways and your *e* practices.
7:10 In your hearts do not think *e*
8:17 do not plot *e* against your neighbor,
Mal 2:17 "All who do *e* are good in the eyes
Mt 5:11 falsely say all kinds of *e* against you
5:37 beyond this comes from the *e* one.
5:39 I tell you, Do not resist an *e* person.
5:45 He causes his sun to rise on the *e*
6:13 but deliver us from the *e* one.'
7:11 If you, then, though you are *e,*
9: 4 "Why do you entertain *e* thoughts
10: 1 authority to drive out *e* spirits
12:34 you who are *e* say anything good?
12:35 and the *e* man brings *e* things out
12:35 out of the *e* stored up in him.
12:43 "When an *e* spirit comes out
13:19 the *e* one comes and snatches away
13:38 The weeds are the sons of the *e* one
13:41 that causes sin and all who do *e.*
15:19 out of the heart come *e* thoughts,
22:18 knowing their *e* intent, said,
Mk 1:23 possessed by an *e* spirit cried out,
1:26 *e* spirit shook the man violently
1:27 He even gives orders to *e* spirits
3: 4 to do good or to do *e,* to save life
3:11 Whenever the *e* spirits saw him,
3:30 were saying, "He has an *e* spirit."
5: 2 a man with an *e* spirit came
5: 8 you *e* spirit!" Then Jesus asked him
5:13 and the *e* spirits came out
6: 7 gave them authority over *e* spirits.
7:21 come *e* thoughts, sexual
7:25 possessed by an *e* spirit came
9:25 to the scene, he rebuked the *e* spirit
Lk 3:19 all the other *e* things he had done,
4:33 possessed by a demon, an *e* spirit.
4:36 power he gives orders to *e* spirits
6: 9 to do good or to do *e,* to save life
6:18 troubled by *e* spirits were cured,
6:22 and reject your name as *e,*
6:45 and the *e* man brings *e* things out
6:45 out of the *e* stored up in his heart.
7:21 sicknesses and *e* spirits,
8: 2 who had been cured of *e* spirits
8:29 Jesus had commanded the *e* spirit
9:42 But Jesus rebuked the *e* spirit,
11:13 If you then, though you are *e,*
11:24 "When an *e* spirit comes out
Jn 3:19 of light because their deeds were *e.*
3:20 Everyone who does *e* hates
5:29 and those who have done *e* will rise
7: 7 I testify that what it does is *e.*
17:15 you protect them from the *e* one.
Ac 5:16 and those tormented by *e* spirits,
8: 7 *e* spirits came out of many,
19:12 cured and the *e* spirits left them.
19:13 around driving out *e* spirits tried
19:15 The *e* spirit answered them,
19:16 man who had the *e* spirit jumped
19:18 and openly confessed their *e* deeds.
23: 5 'Do not speak *e* about the ruler
Ro 1:29 with every kind of wickedness, *e,*
1:30 they invent ways of doing *e;*
2: 8 who reject the truth and follow *e,*
2: 9 for every human being who does *e:*
3: 8 "Let us do *e* that good may result"?
6:12 body so that you obey its *e* desires.
7:19 no, the *e* I do not want to do—
7:21 to do good, *e* is right there with me.
12: 9 Hate what is *e;* cling
12:17 Do not repay anyone *e* for *e.*
12:21 Do not be overcome by *e,*
12:21 but overcome *e* with good.
14:16 good to be spoken of as *e.*
16:19 and innocent about what is *e.*
1Co 10: 6 from setting our hearts on *e* things
13: 6 Love does not delight in *e*
14:20 In regard to *e* be infants,
Gal 1: 4 to rescue us from the present *e* age,
Eph 5:16 because the days are *e.*
6:12 forces of *e* in the heavenly realms.
Eph 6:13 so that when the day of *e* comes,
6:16 all the flaming arrows of the *e* one.
Php 3: 2 men who do *e,* those mutilators
Col 1:21 because of your *e* behavior.
3: 5 impurity, lust, *e* desires and greed,
1Th 5:22 Avoid every kind of *e.*
2Th 2:10 of *e* that deceives those who are
3: 2 delivered from wicked and *e* men,
3: 3 and protect you from the *e* one.
1Ti 6: 4 *e* suspicions and constant friction
6:10 of money is a root of all kinds of *e.*
2Ti 2:22 Flee the *e* desires of youth,
3: 6 are swayed by all kinds of *e* desires,
3:13 while *e* men and impostors will go
4:18 me from every *e* attack
Tit 1:12 "Cretans are always liars, *e* brutes,
Heb 5:14 to distinguish good from *e.*
Jas 1:13 For God cannot be tempted by *e,*
1:14 by his own *e* desire, he is dragged
1:21 and the *e* that is so prevalent,
2: 4 become judges with *e* thoughts?
3: 6 a world of *e* among the parts
3: 8 It is a restless *e,* full
3:16 find disorder and every *e* practice.
4:16 All such boasting is *e.*
1Pe 1:14 conform to the *e* desires you had
2:16 your freedom as a cover-up for *e;*
3: 9 Do not repay *e* with *e* or insult
3:10 must keep his tongue from *e*
3:11 He must turn from *e* and do good;
3:12 is against those who do *e."*
3:17 for doing good than for doing *e.*
4: 2 life for *e* human desires,
2Pe 1: 4 in the world caused by *e* desires.
3: 3 and following their own *e* desires.
1Jn 2:13 you have overcome the *e* one.
2:14 and you have overcome the *e* one.
3:12 Because his own actions were *e*
3:12 who belonged to the *e* one
5:18 and the *e* one does not touch him.
5:19 is under the control of the *e* one.
3Jn :11 do not imitate what is *e*
:11 who does what is *e* has not seen
Jude :16 they follow their own *e* desires;
Rev 16:13 I saw three *e* spirits that looked like
18: 2 and a haunt for every *e* spirit,

EVIL-MERODACH

2Ki 25:27 in the year *E* became king
Jer 52:31 in the year *E* became king

EVILDOER (EVIL)

2Sa 3:39 the LORD repay the *e* according
Ps 101: 8 I will cut off every *e*
Mal 4: 1 and every *e* will be stubble,

EVILDOERS (EVIL)

1Sa 24:13 saying goes, 'From *e* come evil
Job 8:20 or strengthen the hands of *e.*
34: 8 He keeps company with *e;*
34:22 where *e* can hide.
Ps 14: 4 Will *e* never learn—
14: 6 You *e* frustrate the plans
26: 5 I abhor the assembly of *e*
36:12 See how the *e* lie fallen—
53: 4 Will the *e* never learn—
59: 2 Deliver me from *e*
64: 2 from that noisy crowd of *e,*
92: 7 and all *e* flourish,
92: 9 all *e* will be scattered.
94: 4 all the *e* are full of boasting.
94:16 will take a stand for me against *e?*
119:115 Away from me, you *e,*
125: 5 the LORD will banish with the *e.*
141: 4 deeds with men who are *e;*
141: 5 ever against the deeds of *e;*
141: 9 from the traps set by *e.*
Pr 21:15 but terror to *e.*
Isa 1: 4 a brood of *e,*
31: 2 against those who help *e.*
Jer 23:14 They strengthen the hands of *e,*
Hos 10: 9 the *e* in Gibeah?
Mal 3:15 Certainly the *e* prosper, and
Mt 7:23 you *e!"* "Therefore everyone who
Lk 13:27 Away from me, all you *e!"*
18:11 *e,* adulterers—or even like this tax

EVILS (EVIL)

Mk 7:23 All these *e* come from inside

EWE (EWES)

Ge 21:28 Abraham set apart seven *e* lambs
21:29 of these seven *e* lambs you have set
Lev 14:10 male lambs and one *e* lamb a year
Nu 6:14 a year-old *e* lamb without defect
2Sa 12: 3 one little *e* lamb he had bought.
12: 4 he took the *e* lamb that belonged

EWES (EWE)

Ge 32:14 two hundred *e* and twenty rams,
33:13 and that I must care for the *e*

EXACT (EXACTED EXACTING)

Ge 43:21 the *e* weight—in the mouth
Est 4: 7 including the *e* amount
Mt 2: 7 from them the *e* time the star had
Jn 4:53 realized that this was the *e* time
Ac 17:26 the *e* places where they should live.
Heb 1: 3 the *e* representation of his being,

EXACTED (EXACT)

2Ki 15:20 Menahem *e* this money from Israel
18:14 of Assyria *e* from Hezekiah king
23:35 he taxed the land and *e* the silver

EXACTING (EXACT)

Ne 5: 7 "You are *e* usury from your own
5:10 But let the *e* of usury stop!

EXALT (EXALTED EXALTS)

Ex 15: 2 my father's God, and I will *e* him.
Jos 3: 7 begin to *e* you in the eyes
1Sa 2:10 and *e* the horn of his anointed."
1Ch 25: 5 the promises of God to *e* him.
29:12 power to *e* and give strength to all.
Job 19: 5 If indeed you would *e* yourselves
Ps 30: 1 I will *e* you, O LORD,
34: 3 let us *e* his name together.
35:26 may all who *e* themselves over me
37:34 He will *e* you to possess the land;
38:16 *e* themselves over me
75: 6 or from the desert can *e* a man.
89:17 and by your favor you *e* our horn.
99: 5 *E* the LORD our God
99: 9 *E* the LORD our God
107: 32 Let them *e* him in the assembly
118: 28 you are my God, and I will *e* you.
145: 1 I will *e* you, my God the King;
Pr 4: 8 Esteem her, and she will *e* you;
25: 6 Do not *e* yourself in the king's
Isa 24:15 *e* the name of the LORD, the God
25: 1 I will *e* you and praise your name,
Eze 29:15 and will never again *e* itself
Da 4:37 *e* and glorify the King of heaven,
11:36 He will *e* and magnify himself
11:37 but will *e* himself above them all.
Hos 11: 7 he will by no means *e* them.

EXALTED (EXALT)

Ex 15: 1 for he is highly *e.*
15:21 for he is highly *e.*
Nu 24: 7 their kingdom will be *e.*
Jos 4:14 That day the LORD *e* Joshua
2Sa 5:12 and had *e* his kingdom for the sake
22:47 *E* be God, the Rock, my Savior!
22:49 You *e* me above my foes;
23: 1 of the man *e* by the Most High,
1Ch 14: 2 that his kingdom had been highly *e*
17:17 as though I were the most *e* of men,
29:11 you are *e* as head over all.
29:25 The LORD highly *e* Solomon
Ne 9: 5 and may it be *e* above all blessing
Job 24:24 For a little while they are *e,*
36:22 "God is *e* in his power.
37:23 beyond our reach and *e* in power;
Ps 18:46 *E* be God my Savior!
18:48 You *e* me above my foes;
21:13 Be *e,* O LORD, in your strength;
27: 6 Then my head will be *e*
35:27 they always say, "The LORD be *e,*
40:16 "The LORD be *e!"*
46:10 I will be *e* among the nations,
46:10 I will be *e* in the earth."
47: 9 he is greatly *e.*
57: 5 Be *e,* O God, above the heavens;

Ps 57: 11 Be *e*, O God, above the heavens;
70: 4 "Let God be *e*!"
89: 13 hand is strong, your right hand *e*.
89: 19 I have *e* a young man
89: 24 through my name his horn will be *e*
89: 27 the most *e* of the kings of the earth.
89: 42 You have *e* the right hand
92: 8 But you, O LORD, are *e* forever.
92: 10 You have *e* my horn like that
97: 9 you are *e* far above all gods.
99: 2 he is *e* over all the nations.
108: 5 Be *e*, O God, above the heavens,
113: 4 The LORD is *e* over all the nations
138: 2 for you have *e* above all things
148: 13 for his name alone is *e*;
Pr 11: 11 of the upright a city is *e*,
30: 32 have played the fool and *e* yourself,
Isa 2: 11 the LORD alone will be *e*
2: 12 for all that is *e*
2: 17 the LORD alone will be *e*
5: 16 the LORD Almighty will be *e*
6: 1 *e*, and the train of his robe filled
12: 4 and proclaim that his name is *e*.
24: 4 the *e* of the earth languish.
33: 5 The LORD is *e*, for he dwells
33: 10 "Now will I be *e*;
52: 13 be raised and lifted up and highly *e*.
Jer 17: 12 A glorious throne, *e*
La 2: 17 he has *e* the horn of your foes.
Eze 21: 26 The lowly will be *e* and the *e* will be
Hos 13: 1 he was *e* in Israel.
Mic 6: 6 and bow down before the *e* God?
Mt 23: 12 whoever humbles himself will be *e*.
Lk 14: 11 he who humbles himself will be *e*."
18: 14 he who humbles himself will be *e*."
Ac 2: 33 *E* to the right hand of God,
5: 31 God *e* him to his own right hand
Php 1: 20 always Christ will be *e* in my body,
2: 9 Therefore God *e* him
Heb 7: 26 from sinners, *e* above the heavens.

EXALTS (EXALT)

1Sa 2: 7 he humbles and he *e*.
Job 36: 7 and *e* them forever.
Ps 75: 7 He brings one down, he *e* another.
Pr 14: 34 Righteousness *e* a nation,
Mt 23: 12 For whoever *e* himself will be
Lk 14: 11 For everyone who *e* himself will be
18: 14 For everyone who *e* himself will be
2Th 2: 4 *e* himself over everything that is

EXAMINE (CROSS-EXAMINED EXAMINED EXAMINES EXAMINING)

Ge 37: 32 *E* it to see whether it is your son's
Lev 13: 3 The priest is to *e* the sore
13: 5 seventh day the priest is to *e* him,
13: 6 day the priest is to *e* him again,
13: 8 The priest is to *e* him,
13: 10 The priest is to *e* him,
13: 13 the priest is to *e* him,
13: 17 The priest is to *e* him,
13: 20 The priest is to *e* it, and if it appears
13: 25 the priest is to *e* the spot,
13: 27 seventh day the priest is to *e* him,
13: 30 the chin, the priest is to *e* the sore,
13: 32 day the priest is to *e* the sore,
13: 34 day the priest is to *e* the itch
13: 36 the priest is to *e* him,
13: 39 the priest is to *e* them,
13: 43 The priest is to *e* him and,
13: 50 The priest is to *e* the mildew
13: 51 On the seventh day he is to *e* it,
13: 55 the priest is to *e* it,
14: 3 to go outside the camp and *e* him.
14: 36 before he goes in to *e* the mildew,
14: 37 He is to *e* the mildew on the walls,
14: 44 the priest is to go and *e* it and,
14: 48 "But if the priest comes to *e* it
Job 7: 18 that you *e* him every morning
34: 23 God has no need to *e* men further,
Ps 11: 4 his eyes *e* them.
17: 3 you probe my heart and *e* me
26: 2 *e* my heart and my mind;
Jer 17: 10 and *e* the mind,
20: 12 Almighty, you who *e* the righteous
La 3: 40 Let us *e* our ways and test them,
Eze 21: 21 consult his idols, he will *e* the liver.
1Co 11: 28 A man ought to *e* himself
2Co 13: 5 *E* yourselves to see whether you

EXAMINED (EXAMINE)

Job 5: 27 "We have *e* this, and it is true.
13: 9 Would it turn out well if he *e* you?
Lk 23: 14 I have *e* him in your presence
Ac 17: 11 *e* the Scriptures every day to see
28: 18 They *e* me and wanted

EXAMINES (EXAMINE)

Lev 13: 3 When the priest *e* him, he shall
13: 21 But if, when the priest *e* it,
13: 26 But if the priest *e* it and there is no
13: 31 when the priest *e* this kind of sore,
13: 53 "But if, when the priest *e* it,
13: 56 when the priest *e* it, the mildew has
Ps 11: 5 The LORD *e* the righteous,
Pr 5: 21 and he *e* all his paths.

EXAMINING (EXAMINE)

Ne 2: 13 *e* the walls of Jerusalem, which had
2: 15 the valley by night, *e* the wall.
Ac 24: 8 By *e* him yourself you will be able

EXAMPLE (EXAMPLES)

2Ki 14: 3 In everything he followed the *e*
Ecc 9: 13 also saw under the sun this *e*
Eze 14: 8 and make him an *e* and a byword.
Jn 13: 15 have set you an *e* that you should
Ro 7: 2 as long as he lives? For *e*,
1Co 11: 1 Follow my *e*, as I follow
11: 1 as I follow the *e* of Christ.
Gal 3: 15 let me take an *e* from everyday life.
Php 3: 17 Join with others in following my *e*,
2Th 3: 7 how you ought to follow our *e*.
1Ti 1: 16 as an *e* for those who would believe
4: 12 set an *e* for the believers in speech,
Tit 2: 7 In everything set them an *e*
Heb 4: 11 fall by following their *e*
Jas 3: 4 Or take ships as an *e*.
5: 10 as an *e* of patience in the face
1Pe 2: 21 leaving you an *e*, that you should
2Pe 2: 6 made them an *e* of what is going
Jude : 7 as an *e* of those who suffer

EXAMPLES (EXAMPLE)

1Co 10: 6 Now these things occurred as *e*,
10: 11 as *e* and were written down
1Pe 5: 3 to you, but being *e* to the flock.

EXASPERATE

Eph 6: 4 Fathers, do not *e* your children;

EXCEED (EXCEEDED EXCESSIVE)

Nu 3: 46 Israelites who *e* the number
Job 14: 5 and have set limits he cannot *e*.

EXCEEDED (EXCEED)

Nu 3: 49 from those who *e* the number
1Ki 10: 7 wealth you have far *e* the report I
2Ch 9: 6 you have far *e* the report I heard.

EXCEL (EXCELLED EXCELLENCY EXCELLENT EXCELLING)

Ge 49: 4 as the waters, you will no longer *e*,
1Co 14: 12 to *e* in gifts that build up the church
2Co 8: 7 But just as you *e* in everything
8: 7 also *e* in this grace of giving.

EXCELLED (EXCEL)

Isa 10: 10 kingdoms whose images *e* those

EXCELLENCY (EXCEL)

Ac 23: 26 Lysias, To His *E*, Governor Felix:

EXCELLENT (EXCEL)

Ps 45: 2 You are the most *e* of men
Lk 1: 3 for you, most *e* Theophilus,
Ac 24: 3 and in every way, most *e* Felix,
26: 25 most *e* Festus," Paul replied.
1Co 12: 31 now I will show you the most *e* way
Php 4: 8 if anything is *e* or praiseworthy—
1Ti 3: 13 have served well gain an *e* standing
Tit 3: 8 These things are *e* and profitable

EXCELLING (EXCEL)

Ge 49: 3 *e* in honor, *e* in power.

EXCEPTION (EXCEPTIONAL)

Est 4: 11 The only *e* to this is for the king

EXCEPTIONAL (EXCEPTION)

Da 6: 3 by his *e* qualities that the king

EXCESSIVE (EXCEED)

Eze 18: 8 or take *e* interest.
18: 13 lends at usury and takes *e* interest.
18: 17 and takes no usury or *e* interest.
22: 12 you take usury and *e* interest
2Co 2: 7 not be overwhelmed by *e* sorrow.
Rev 18: 3 rich from her *e* luxuries."

EXCHANGE (EXCHANGED EXCHANGING)

Ge 47: 16 food in *e* for your livestock,
47: 17 food in *e* for their horses,
47: 17 with food in *e* for all their livestock.
47: 19 Buy us and our land in *e* for food,
Lev 27: 10 He must not *e* it or substitute
Dt 14: 25 then *e* your tithe for silver,
1Ki 21: 2 In *e* I will give you a better
Isa 43: 4 I will give men in *e* for you,
43: 4 and people in *e* for your life.
Eze 48: 14 They must not sell or *e* any of it.
Mt 16: 26 Or what can a man give in *e*
Mk 8: 37 Or what can a man give in *e*
2Co 6: 13 As a fair *e*—I speak

EXCHANGED (EXCHANGE)

Ps 106: 20 They *e* their Glory
Jer 2: 11 But my people have *e* their Glory
Eze 27: 12 they *e* silver, iron, tin and lead
27: 13 they *e* slaves and articles of bronze
27: 14 Beth Togarmah *e* work horses,
27: 16 they *e* turquoise, purple fabric,
27: 17 they *e* wheat from Minnith
27: 19 they *e* wrought iron, cassia
27: 22 your merchandise they *e* the finest
Hos 4: 7 they *e* their Glory
Ro 1: 23 *e* the glory of the immortal God
1: 25 They *e* the truth of God for a lie,
1: 26 their women *e* natural relations

EXCHANGING (EXCHANGE)

Jn 2: 14 and others sitting at tables *e* money

EXCITEMENT

Job 39: 24 In frenzied *e* he eats up the ground;

EXCLAIM (EXCLAIMED EXCLAIMING)

Ps 35: 10 My whole being will *e*,
Jer 46: 17 There they will *e*,
Rev 18: 18 they will *e*, 'Was there ever a city

EXCLAIMED (EXCLAIM)

Jdg 6: 22 he *e*, "Ah, Sovereign LORD!
Ru 1: 19 the women *e*, "Can this be Naomi
2: 10 She *e*, "Why have I found such
2Ki 3: 10 "What!" *e* the king of Israel.
Est 7: 8 The king *e*, "Will he even molest
Mt 27: 54 they were terrified, and *e*,
Mk 1: 37 they *e*: "Everyone is looking
9: 24 Immediately the boy's father *e*,
Lk 1: 42 a loud voice she *e*: "Blessed are you
Jn 8: 52 At this the Jews *e*, "Now we know
Ac 8: 10 gave him their attention and *e*,
12: 14 back without opening it and *e*,

EXCLAIMING (EXCLAIM)

1Co 14: 25 *e*, "God is really among you!"

EXCLUDE (EXCLUDED)

Isa 56: 3 "The LORD will surely *e* me
66: 5 and *e* you because of my name,
Lk 6: 22 when they *e* you and insult you
Rev 11: 2 *e* the outer court; do not measure it

EXCLUDED (EXCLUDE)

2Ch 26: 21 and *e* from the temple of the
Ezr 2: 62 and so were *e* from the priesthood
Ne 7: 64 and so were *e* from the priesthood
13: 3 they *e* from Israel all who were
Ro 3: 27 Where, then, is boasting? It is *e*.
Eph 2: 12 *e* from citizenship in Israel

EXCREMENT

Dt 23: 13 dig a hole and cover up your *e*.
Eze 4: 12 sight of the people, using human *e*
4: 15 cow manure instead of human *e*.''

EXCUSE (EXCUSES)

Ps 25: 3 who are treacherous without *e*.
Lk 14: 18 Please *e* me.'
14: 19 Please *e* me.'
Jn 15: 22 they have no *e* for their sin.
Ro 1: 20 so that men are without *e*.
2: 1 You, therefore, have no *e*,

EXCUSES (EXCUSE)

Lk 14: 18 ''But they all alike began to make *e*.

EXECUTE (EXECUTED EXECUTING EXECUTION EXECUTIONER)

2Ch 2: 14 and can *e* any design given to him.
Isa 66: 16 the LORD will *e* judgment
Eze 11: 10 and I will *e* judgment on you
11: 11 I will *e* judgment on you
17: 20 and *e* judgment upon him there
20: 35 I will *e* judgment upon you.
38: 22 I will *e* judgment upon him
Da 2: 24 Do not *e* the wise men of Babylon.
2: 24 to *e* the wise men of Babylon,
Hab 1: 12 appointed them to *e* judgment;
Jn 18: 31 But we have no right to *e* anyone,''

EXECUTED (EXECUTE)

2Ki 14: 5 he *e* the officials who had
25: 21 of Hamath, the king had them *e*.
2Ch 24: 24 of their fathers, judgment was *e*
25: 3 he *e* the officials who had
Jer 52: 27 of Hamath, the king had them *e*.
Da 2: 18 and his friends might not be *e*
Mt 27: 20 for Barabbas and to have Jesus *e*.
Lk 23: 32 were also led out with him to be *e*.
Ac 12: 19 and ordered that they be *e*.
13: 28 they asked Pilate to have him *e*.

EXECUTING (EXECUTE)

2Ch 22: 8 While Jehu was *e* judgment

EXECUTION (EXECUTE)

Da 2: 12 and furious that he ordered the *e*

EXECUTIONER (EXECUTE)

Mk 6: 27 So he immediately sent an *e*

EXEMPT

1Sa 17: 25 will *e* his father's family from taxes
1Ki 15: 22 order to all Judah—no one was *e*—
1Ch 9: 33 and were *e* from other duties
Mt 17: 26 the sons are *e*,'' Jesus said to him.

EXERCISE (EXERCISED EXERCISES EXERTED)

Mt 20: 25 and their high officials *e* authority
Mk 10: 42 and their high officials *e* authority
Lk 22: 25 and those who *e* authority
1Co 8: 9 that the *e* of your freedom does not
Rev 13: 5 *e* his authority for forty-two

EXERCISED (EXERCISE)

Da 11: 4 nor will it have the power he *e*,
Rev 13: 12 He *e* all the authority

EXERCISES (EXERCISE)

Jer 9: 24 I am the LORD, who *e* kindness,

EXERTED (EXERCISE)

Eph 1: 20 which he *e* in Christ

EXHAUST (EXHAUSTED)

Jer 51: 58 the peoples *e* themselves
Hab 2: 13 that the nations *e* themselves

EXHAUSTED (EXHAUST)

Jdg 4: 21 to him while he lay fast asleep, *e*.
8: 4 *e* yet keeping up the pursuit,
8: 15 we give bread to your *e* men?' ''
1Sa 14: 31 Micmash to Aijalon, they were *e*.
30: 10 for two hundred men were too *e*
30: 21 hundred men who had been too *e*
2Sa 16: 2 is to refresh those who become *e*
16: 14 arrived at their destination *e*.
2Sa 21: 15 the Philistines, and he became *e*.
Jer 51: 30 Their strength is *e*;
Da 8: 27 was *e* and lay ill for several days.
Lk 12: 33 in heaven that will not be *e*,
22: 45 he found them asleep, *e*

EXHORT (EXHORTATION EXHORTED)

1Ti 5: 1 but *e* him as if he were your father.

EXHORTATION (EXHORT)

Heb 13: 22 you to bear with my word of *e*,

EXHORTED (EXHORT)

Lk 3: 18 other words John *e* the people

EXILE (EXILED EXILES)

2Sa 15: 19 an *e* from your homeland.
2Ki 17: 23 taken from their homeland into *e*
24: 14 He carried into *e* all Jerusalem:
25: 11 into *e* the people who remained
25: 27 of the *e* of Jehoiachin king of Judah
1Ch 5: 6 king of Assyria took into *e*.
5: 22 they occupied the land until the *e*.
5: 26 the half-tribe of Manasseh into *e*.
6: 15 and Jerusalem into *e* by the hand
2Ch 36: 20 into *e* to Babylon the remnant,
Ezr 6: 21 who had returned from the *e* ate it,
Ne 1: 2 Jewish remnant that survived the *e*,
1: 3 ''Those who survived the *e*
8: 17 returned from *e* built booths
Est 2: 6 carried into *e* from Jerusalem
Isa 5: 13 Therefore my people will go into *e*
27: 8 and *e* you contend with her—
Jer 1: 3 people of Jerusalem went into *e*.
13: 19 All Judah will be carried into *e*,
20: 6 live in your house will go into *e*
22: 22 and your allies will go into *e*.
24: 1 into *e* from Jerusalem to Babylon
27: 20 of Judah into *e* from Jerusalem
29: 1 into *e* from Jerusalem to Babylon.
29: 2 gone into *e* from Jerusalem.)
29: 4 into *e* from Jerusalem to Babylon:
29: 7 to which I have carried you into *e*.
29: 14 from which I carried you into *e*.''
29: 16 who did not go with you into *e*—
30: 10 from the land of their *e*.
30: 16 all your enemies will go into *e*.
39: 9 of the imperial guard carried into *e*
40: 1 who were being carried into *e*
40: 7 who had not been carried into *e*
43: 3 or carry us into *e* to Babylon.''
46: 19 Pack your belongings for *e*,
46: 27 from the land of their *e*.
48: 7 and Chemosh will go into *e*
48: 11 she has not gone into *e*.
48: 46 your sons are taken into *e*
49: 3 for Molech will go into *e*,
52: 15 of the guard carried into *e* some
52: 28 Nebuchadnezzar carried into *e*:
52: 30 745 Jews taken into *e*
52: 31 of the *e* of Jehoiachin king of Judah
La 1: 3 Judah has gone into *e*.
1: 5 Her children have gone into *e*,
1: 18 have gone into *e*.
4: 22 he will not prolong your *e*.
Eze 1: 2 year of the *e* of King Jehoiachin—
3: 11 Go now to your countrymen in *e*
12: 3 pack your belongings for *e*
12: 4 go out like those who go into *e*.
12: 4 out your belongings packed for *e*.
12: 7 out my things packed for *e*.
12: 11 They will go into *e* as captives.
25: 3 of Judah when they went into *e*,
33: 21 In the twelfth year of our *e*,
39: 23 of Israel went into *e* for their sin,
39: 28 them into *e* among the nations,
40: 1 In the twenty-fifth year of our *e*,
Hos 10: 5 because it is taken from them into *e*
Am 1: 5 of Aram will go into *e* to Kir,''
1: 15 Her king will go into *e*,
5: 5 For Gilgal will surely go into *e*,
5: 27 into *e* beyond Damascus,''
6: 7 among the first to go into *e*;
7: 11 and Israel will surely go into *e*,
7: 17 And Israel will certainly go into *e*,
9: 4 into *e* by their enemies,
Mic 1: 16 for they will go from you into *e*.
Na 3: 10 and went into *e*.
Zec 14: 2 Half of the city will go into *e*,
Mt 1: 11 at the time of the *e* to Babylon.
1: 12 After the *e* to Babylon: Jeconiah
1: 17 fourteen from the *e* to the Christ.
1: 17 from David to the *e* to Babylon,
Ac 7: 43 into *e*' beyond Babylon.

EXILED (EXILE)

2Ki 17: 28 one of the priests who had been *e*
Ne 1: 9 even if your *e* people are
Isa 27: 13 and those who were *e* in Egypt will
49: 21 I was *e* and rejected.
Jer 22: 10 weep bitterly for him who is *e*,
La 2: 9 her princes are *e* among the nations
Am 9: 14 I will bring back my *e* people Israel;
Na 2: 7 be *e* and carried away.

EXILES (EXILE)

Ezr 1: 11 these along when the *e* came up
2: 1 up from the captivity of the *e*,
4: 1 heard that the *e* were building
6: 16 the Levites and the rest of the *e*—
6: 19 the *e* celebrated the Passover.
6: 20 the Passover lamb for all the *e*,
8: 35 Then the *e* who had returned
9: 4 of this unfaithfulness of the *e*.
10: 6 over the unfaithfulness of the *e*.
10: 7 Jerusalem for all the *e* to assemble
10: 8 from the assembly of the *e*.
10: 16 So the *e* did as was proposed.
Ne 7: 6 of the *e* whom Nebuchadnezzar
Ps 147: 2 he gathers the *e* of Israel.
Isa 11: 12 and gather the *e* of Israel;
20: 4 Egyptian captives and Cushite *e*,
45: 13 and set my *e* free,
56: 8 he who gathers the *e* of Israel:
Jer 24: 5 I regard as good the *e* from Judah,
28: 4 and all the other *e* from Judah who
28: 6 and all the *e* back to this place
29: 1 to the surviving elders among the *e*
29: 19 And you *e* have not listened either
29: 20 all you *e* whom I have sent away
29: 22 all the *e* from Judah who are
29: 31 ''Send this message to all the *e*:
49: 36 where Elam's *e* do not go.
Eze 1: 1 among the *e* by the Kebar River,
3: 15 the *e* who lived at Tel Aviv
11: 24 brought me to the *e* in Babylonia
11: 25 I told the *e* everything the LORD
Da 2: 25 ''I have found a man among the *e*
5: 13 of the *e* my father the king brought
6: 13 who is one of the *e* from Judah,
Ob : 20 company of Israelite *e* who are
: 20 the *e* from Jerusalem who are
Mic 4: 6 I will assemble the *e*
Zec 6: 10 and gold from the *e* Heldai,

EXIST (EXISTED EXISTS)

Ro 13: 1 The authorities that *e* have been

EXISTED (EXIST)

2Pe 3: 5 ago by God's word the heavens *e*

EXISTS (EXIST)

Ecc 6: 10 Whatever *e* has already been
Heb 2: 10 and through whom everything *e*,
11: 6 to him must believe that he *e*

EXITS

Eze 42: 11 with similar *e* and dimensions.
43: 11 its arrangement, its *e* and entrances
44: 5 and all the *e* of the sanctuary.
48: 30 ''These will be the *e* of the city:

EXODUS

Heb 11: 22 spoke about the *e* of the Israelites

EXORBITANT

Pr 28: 8 increases his wealth by *e* interest

EXPAND (EXPANSE)

2Co 10: 15 of activity among you will greatly *e*

EXPANSE (EXPAND EXPANSES)

Ge 1: 6 there be an *e* between the waters
1: 7 So God made the *e* and separated
1: 7 water under the *e* from the water
1: 8 God called the *e* ''sky.''

Ge 1:14 "Let there be lights in the *e*
1:15 let them be lights in the *e* of the sky
1:17 God set them in the *e* of the sky
1:20 the earth across the *e* of the sky."
Eze 1:22 was what looked like an *e*,
1:23 Under the *e* their wings were
1:25 from above the *e* over their heads
1:26 Above the *e* over their heads was
10:1 of sapphire above the *e* that was

EXPANSES (EXPANSE)

Job 38:18 Have you comprehended the vast *e*

EXPECT (EXPECTANT EXPECTANTLY EXPECTATION EXPECTED EXPECTING)

Isa 58:4 *e* your voice to be heard on high.
64:3 awesome things that we did not *e*,
Eze 13:6 yet they *e* their words to be fulfilled
Mt 11:3 or should we *e* someone else?"
24:44 at an hour when you do not *e* him.
24:50 on a day when he does not *e* him
Lk 6:34 from whom you *e* repayment,
7:19 or should we *e* someone else?"
7:20 or should we *e* someone else?' "
12:40 at an hour when you do not *e* him."
12:46 on a day when he does not *e* him
2Co 10:2 I *e* to be toward some people who
Php 1:20 I eagerly *e* and hope that I will

EXPECTANT (EXPECT)

Jer 31:8 *e* mothers and women in labor;

EXPECTANTLY (EXPECT)

Job 29:21 "Men listened to me *e*,
Lk 3:15 The people were waiting *e*

EXPECTATION (EXPECT)

Ps 5:3 and wait in *e*.
Eze 19:5 her *e* gone,
Ro 8:19 waits in eager *e* for the sons
Heb 10:27 but only a fearful *e* of judgment

EXPECTED (EXPECT)

Ge 48:11 "I never *e* to see your face again,
Pr 11:7 all he *e* from his power comes
Hag 1:9 "You *e* much, but see, it turned out
Mt 20:10 came who were hired first, they *e*
Ac 16:13 where we *e* to find a place of prayer
25:18 him with any of the crimes I had *e*.
28:6 The people *e* him to swell up
2Co 8:5 And they did not do as we *e*,

EXPECTING (EXPECT)

Lk 2:5 married to him and was *e* a child.
6:34 lend to 'sinners,' *e* to be repaid
6:35 and lend to them without *e*
8:40 for they were all *e* him.
Ac 3:5 *e* to get something from them.
10:24 Cornelius was *e* them and had
1Co 16:11 I am *e* him along with the brothers.

EXPEL

1Co 5:13 *E* the wicked man from among you

EXPELLED (EXPEL)

1Sa 28:3 Saul had *e* the mediums
1Ki 15:12 He *e* the male shrine prostitutes
Ezr 10:8 and would himself be *e*
Eze 28:16 and I *e* you, O guardian cherub,
Ac 13:50 and *e* them from their region.

EXPEND

2Co 12:15 you everything I have and *e* myself

EXPENSE (EXPENSES EXPENSIVE)

Lk 10:35 you for any extra *e* you may have.'
1Co 9:7 Who serves as a soldier at his own *e*

EXPENSES (EXPENSE)

2Ki 12:12 and met all the other *e*
Ezr 6:8 The *e* of these men are
Ac 21:24 purification rites and pay their *e*,

EXPENSIVE (EXPENSE)

Mt 26:7 jar of very *e* perfume,
Mk 14:3 jar of very *e* perfume,
Lk 7:25 those who wear *e* clothes
Jn 12:3 a pint of pure nard, an *e* perfume;
1Ti 2:9 or gold or pearls or *e* clothes,

EXPERIENCE (EXPERIENCED)

Nu 16:29 and *e* only what usually happens
Jdg 3:2 who had not had previous battle *e*):
Heb 11:5 so that he did not *e* death;

EXPERIENCED (EXPERIENCE)

Dt 11:2 *e* the discipline of the LORD your
Jos 24:31 who had *e* everything the LORD
Jdg 3:1 those Israelites who had not *e* any
2Sa 17:8 Besides, your father is an *e* fighter;
1Ki 7:14 and *e* in all kinds of bronze work.
1Ch 12:33 *e* soldiers prepared for battle
12:36 *e* soldiers prepared for battle—
2Ch 2:7 and *e* in the art of engraving,
2:14 He is *e* in all kinds of engraving
17:13 kept *e* fighting men in Jerusalem.
Ecc 1:16 I have *e* much of wisdom
SS 3:8 all *e* in battle,
Ro 11:25 Israel has *e* a hardening in part

EXPERT (EXPERTS)

Mt 22:35 One of them, an *e* in the law,
Lk 10:25 On one occasion an *e*
10:37 *e* in the law replied, "The one who
1Co 3:10 I laid a foundation as an *e* builder,

EXPERTS (EXPERT)

Est 1:13 king to consult *e* in matters of law
Lk 7:30 *e* in the law rejected God's purpose
11:45 of the *e* in the law answered him,
11:46 Jesus replied, "And you *e*
11:52 "Woe to you *e* in the law,
14:3 Jesus asked the Pharisees and *e*
2Pe 2:14 they are *e* in greed—an accursed

EXPLAIN (EXPLAINED EXPLAINING EXPLAINS EXPLANATION)

Ge 41:24 but none could *e* it to me."
Dt 32:7 your elders, and they will *e* to you.
Jdg 14:16 "so why should I *e* it to you?"
1Ki 10:3 hard for the king to *e* to her.
2Ch 9:2 hard for him to *e* to her.
Est 4:8 to show to Esther and *e* it to her,
Job 15:17 "Listen to me and I will *e* to you;
Jer 9:12 by the LORD and can *e* it?
Da 2:6 if you tell me the dream and *e* it,
2:27 or diviner can *e* to the king
5:12 *e* riddles and solve difficult
5:15 it means, but they could not *e* it.
10:14 come to *e* to you what will happen
Mt 13:36 "*E* to us the parable of the weeds
15:15 Peter said, "*E* the parable to us."
16:21 From that time on Jesus began to *e*
Jn 4:25 he will *e* everything to us."
Ac 2:14 let me *e* this to you; listen carefully
Heb 5:11 it is hard to *e* because you are slow
Rev 17:7 I will *e* to you the mystery

EXPLAINED (EXPLAIN)

Jdg 14:16 "I haven't even *e* it to my father
14:17 She in turn *e* the riddle
14:19 to those who had *e* the riddle.
1Sa 10:25 Samuel *e* to the people
Da 2:15 Arioch then *e* the matter to Daniel.
2:17 and *e* the matter to his friends
Zec 1:10 standing among the myrtle trees *e*,
Mk 4:34 his own disciples, he *e* everything.
Lk 24:27 he *e* to them what was said
Ac 11:4 and *e* everything to them precisely
18:26 and *e* to him the way of God more
28:23 From morning till evening he *e*

EXPLAINING (EXPLAIN)

Jdg 14:15 your husband into *e* the riddle
Isa 28:9 To whom is he *e* his message?
Ac 17:3 *e* and proving that the Christ had

EXPLAINS (EXPLAIN)

Ac 8:31 he said, "unless someone *e* it to me

EXPLANATION (EXPLAIN)

Ecc 8:1 Who knows the *e* of things?
Da 7:23 gave me this *e*: 'The fourth beast

EXPLOIT (EXPLOITED EXPLOITING EXPLOITS)

Pr 22:22 Do not *e* the poor because they are
Isa 58:3 and *e* all your workers.
2Co 12:17 Did I *e* you through any
12:18 Titus did not *e* you, did he?
2Pe 2:3 greed these teachers will *e* you

EXPLOITED (EXPLOIT)

2Co 7:2 no one, we have *e* no one.

EXPLOITING (EXPLOIT)

Jas 2:6 Is it not the rich who are *e* you?

EXPLOITS (EXPLOIT)

2Sa 23:17 Such were the *e* of the three mighty
23:20 Kabzeel, who performed great *e*.
23:22 Such were the *e* of Benaiah son
1Ki 22:45 he achieved and his military *e*,
1Ch 11:19 Such were the *e* of the three mighty
11:22 Kabzeel, who performed great *e*.
11:24 Such were the *e* of Benaiah son
2Co 11:20 or *e* you or takes advantage of you

EXPLORE (EXPLORED EXPLORING)

Nu 13:2 "Send some men to *e* the land
13:16 of the men Moses sent to *e* the land
13:17 Moses sent them to *e* Canaan,
14:36 men Moses had sent to *e* the land,
14:38 Of the men who went to *e* the land,
Jos 14:7 from Kadesh Barnea to *e* the land.
Jdg 18:2 Eshtaol to spy out the land and *e* it.
18:2 They told them, "Go, *e* the land."
2Sa 10:3 them to you to *e* the city
1Ch 19:3 Haven't his men come to you to *e*
Ecc 1:13 and to *e* by wisdom all that is done

EXPLORED (EXPLORE)

Nu 13:21 *e* the land from the Desert of Zin
13:32 The land we *e* devours those living
13:32 report about the land they had *e*.
14:6 among those who had *e* the land,
14:7 and *e* is exceedingly good.
14:34 of the forty days you *e* the land—
Dt 1:24 to the Valley of Eshcol and *e* it.

EXPLORING (EXPLORE)

Nu 13:25 days they returned from *e* the land.

EXPORTED

1Ki 10:29 also *e* them to all the kings
2Ch 1:17 also *e* them to all the kings

EXPOSE (EXPOSED EXPOSES EXPOSING)

Nu 25:4 and *e* them in broad daylight
Job 20:27 The heavens will *e* his guilt;
Isa 57:12 I will *e* your righteousness
La 2:14 they did not *e* your sin
4:22 and *e* your wickedness.
Eze 25:9 therefore I will *e* the flank of Moab,
Hos 2:10 So now I will *e* her lewdness
Mt 1:19 and did not want to *e* her
1Co 4:5 will *e* the motives of men's hearts.
Eph 5:11 of darkness, but rather *e* them.

EXPOSED (EXPOSE)

Ex 20:26 lest your nakedness be *e* on it.'
Lev 20:18 he has *e* the source of her flow,
2Sa 21:6 and *e* before the LORD at Gibeah
21:9 *e* them on a hill before the LORD.
21:13 been killed and *e* were gathered up.
22:16 The valleys of the sea were *e*
Ne 4:13 points of the wall at the *e* places,
Est 6:2 that Mordecai had *e* Bigthana
Ps 18:15 The valleys of the sea were *e*
Pr 26:26 his wickedness will be *e*
Isa 47:3 Your nakedness will be *e*
Jer 8:2 They will be *e* to the sun
36:30 his body will be thrown out and *e*
Eze 16:36 and *e* your nakedness in your
23:18 openly and *e* her nakedness,
23:29 of your prostitution will be *e*.
Hos 7:1 the sins of Ephraim are *e*
Hab 2:16 Now it is your turn! Drink and be *e*
Zep 2:14 the beams of cedar will be *e*.
Jn 3:20 for fear that his deeds will be *e*.
2Co 11:23 and been *e* to death again and again
Eph 5:13 everything *e* by the light becomes
Heb 10:33 Sometimes you were publicly *e*
Rev 16:15 not go naked and be shamefully *e*."

EXPOSES (EXPOSE)

Pr 13: 16 but a fool e his folly.

EXPOSING (EXPOSE)

Ge 30: 37 and e the white inner wood

EXPOUND

Dt 1: 5 Moses began to e this law, saying:
Ps 49: 4 with the harp I will e my riddle:

EXPRESS (EXPRESSED EXPRESSES EXPRESSING EXPRESSION EXPRESSIONS)

2Sa 10: 2 sent a delegation to e his sympathy
10: 3 men to you to e sympathy?
1Ch 19: 2 Ammonites to e sympathy to him,
19: 2 sent a delegation to e his sympathy
19: 3 men to you to e sympathy?
Eze 33: 31 With their mouths they e devotion,
Ro 8: 26 us with groans that words cannot e.
Col 4: 8 you for the e purpose that you may

EXPRESSED (EXPRESS)

2Sa 13: 32 been Absalom's e intention ever
Eph 2: 7 e in his kindness to us

EXPRESSES (EXPRESS)

Ps 7: 11 a God who e his wrath every day.

EXPRESSING (EXPRESS)

1Co 2: 13 e spiritual truths in spiritual words.
Gal 5: 6 thing that counts is faith e itself

EXPRESSION (EXPRESS)

Lev 7: 12 " 'If he offers it as an e
Job 9: 27 I will change my e, and smile,'

EXPRESSIONS (EXPRESS)

2Co 9: 12 overflowing in many e of thanks

EXTEND (EXTENDED EXTENDING EXTENDS EXTENSIVE EXTENT)

Ge 9: 27 May God e the territory of Japheth
49: 13 his border will e toward Sidon.
Ex 25: 32 Six branches are to e from the sides
26: 28 is to e from end to end
Nu 35: 4 the Levites will e out fifteen
Jos 1: 4 Your territory will e
1Ch 11: 10 support to e it over the whole land,
Est 4: 11 is for the king to e the gold scepter
Ps 109: 12 May no one e kindness to him
110: 2 LORD will e your mighty scepter
Isa 66: 12 "I will e peace to her like a river,
Eze 45: 7 It will e westward from the west
47: 17 The boundary will e from the sea
48: 21 It will e eastward from the 25,000
48: 23 it will e from the east side
Da 11: 42 He will e his power
Am 1: 13 Gilead in order to e his borders,
Zec 9: 10 His rule will e from sea to sea
14: 5 for it will e to Azel.

EXTENDED (EXTEND)

Ex 36: 33 so that it e from end to end
37: 18 Six branches e from the sides
Dt 4: 48 This land e from Aroer on the rim
Jos 13: 9 It e from Aroer on the rim
15: 1 e down to the territory of Edom,
17: 7 territory of Manasseh e from Asher
19: 11 and e to the ravine near Jokneam.
1Ki 6: 3 hall of the temple e the width
6: 21 he e gold chains across the front
1Ch 5: 16 of Sharon as far as they e.
21: 16 sword in his hand e over Jerusalem.
2Ch 3: 13 of these cherubim e twenty cubits.
Ezr 7: 28 and who has e his good favor to me
Est 8: 4 Then the king e the gold scepter
Isa 26: 15 you have e all the borders
Eze 42: 7 it e in front of the rooms

EXTENDING (EXTEND)

Ex 25: 33 and the same for all six branches e
25: 35 of branches e from the lampstand,
37: 19 and the same for all six branches e
37: 21 of branches e from the lampstand,
Nu 21: 13 the desert e into Amorite territory.
Dt 3: 16 the Gadites I gave the territory e
Jos 13: 30 The territory e from Mahanaim
1Sa 27: 8 lived in the land e to Shur
2Ch 5: 9 were so long that their ends, e
Eze 42: 12 the corresponding wall e eastward,
Mic 7: 11 the day for e your boundaries.

EXTENDS (EXTEND)

Nu 21: 30 which e to Medeba."
1Ch 5: 9 the edge of the desert that e
Pr 31: 20 and e her hands to the needy.
Da 4: 22 your dominion e to distant parts
Lk 1: 50 His mercy e to those who fear him,

EXTENSIVE (EXTEND)

1Ch 22: 5 So David made e preparations
2Ch 27: 3 did e work on the wall at the hill
Ne 4: 19 "The work is e and spread out,

EXTENT (EXTEND)

Jn 13: 1 he now showed them the full e
1Co 11: 18 and to some e I believe it.
2Co 2: 5 to some e— not to put it too

EXTERMINATE (EXTERMINATING)

1Ki 9: 21 whom the Israelites could not e—
Eze 25: 7 and e you from the countries.

EXTERMINATING (EXTERMINATE)

Jos 11: 20 might destroy them totally, e them

EXTERNAL

Gal 2: 6 judge by e appearance—
Heb 9: 10 e regulations applying

EXTINGUISH (EXTINGUISHED)

Eph 6: 16 which you can e all the flaming

EXTINGUISHED (EXTINGUISH)

2Sa 21: 17 the lamp of Israel will not be e."
Isa 43: 17 e, snuffed out like a wick:

EXTOL

Job 36: 24 Remember to e his work,
Ps 34: 1 I will e the LORD at all times;
68: 4 e him who rides on the clouds—
95: 2 and e him with music and song.
109: 30 mouth I will greatly e the LORD;
111: 1 I will e the LORD with all my heart
115: 18 it is we who e the LORD,
117: 1 e him, all you peoples.
145: 2 and e your name for ever and ever.
145: 10 your saints will e you.
147: 12 E the LORD, O Jerusalem;

EXTORT (EXTORTION)

Lk 3: 14 "Don't e money and don't accuse

EXTORTION (EXTORT)

Lev 6: 4 what he has stolen or taken by e,
Ps 62: 10 Do not trust in e
Ecc 7: 7 E turns a wise man into a fool,
Isa 33: 15 who rejects gain from e
Jer 22: 17 and on oppression and e."
Eze 18: 18 he practiced e, robbed his brother
22: 12 gain from your neighbors by e.
22: 29 The people of the land practice e
Hab 2: 6 and makes himself wealthy by e!

EXTRA

Mt 10: 10 or e tunic, or sandals or a staff;
Mk 6: 9 Wear sandals but not an e tunic.
Lk 9: 3 no bread, no money, no e tunic.
10: 35 for any e expense you may have.'

EXTRAORDINARY

Ac 19: 11 God did e miracles through Paul.

EXTREME (EXTREMES)

Jos 15: 1 to the Desert of Zin in the e south.
2Co 8: 2 and their e poverty welled up

EXTREMES (EXTREME)

Ecc 7: 18 who fears God will avoid all e.

EXULT

Ps 89: 16 they e in your righteousness.
Isa 14: 8 e over you and say,
45: 25 will be found righteous and will e.

EYE (EYEBROWS EYED EYELIDS EYES EYESIGHT)

Ge 2: 9 trees that were pleasing to the e
3: 6 good for food and pleasing to the e,
Ex 21: 24 you are to take life for life, e for e,
21: 26 free to compensate for the e.
21: 26 in the e and destroys it,
Lev 21: 20 dwarfed, or who has any e defect,
24: 20 fracture for fracture, e for e,
Nu 24: 3 oracle of one whose e sees clearly,
24: 15 oracle of one whose e sees clearly,
Dt 19: 21 life for life, e for e, tooth for tooth,
32: 10 he guarded him as the apple of his e
1Sa 11: 2 that I gouge out the right e
18: 9 on Saul kept a jealous e on David.
Ezr 5: 5 the e of their God was watching
Job 7: 8 e that now sees me will see me no
10: 18 before any e saw me.
14: 3 Do you fix your e on such a one?
20: 9 e that saw him will not see him
24: 15 The e of the adulterer watches
24: 15 he thinks, 'No e will see me,'
28: 7 no falcon's e has seen it.
Ps 17: 8 Keep me as the apple of your e;
35: 19 maliciously wink the e.
94: 9 Does he who formed the e not see?
Pr 6: 13 who winks with his e,
7: 2 my teachings as the apple of your e.
16: 30 with his e is plotting perversity;
30: 17 "The e that mocks a father,
Ecc 1: 8 The e never has enough of seeing,
6: 9 Better what the e sees
Isa 29: 20 all who have an e for evil will be cut
64: 4 no e has seen any God besides you,
La 2: 4 all who were pleasing to the e;
Zec 2: 8 you touches the apple of his e—
11: 17 his right e totally blinded!"
11: 17 strike his arm and his right e!
12: 4 "I will keep a watchful e
Mt 5: 29 If your right e causes you to sin,
5: 38 'E for e, and tooth for tooth.'
6: 22 "The e is the lamp of the body.
7: 3 of sawdust in your brother's e
7: 3 to the plank in your own e?
7: 4 Let me take the speck out of your e
7: 4 time there is a plank in your own e?
7: 5 take the plank out of your own e,
7: 5 the speck from your brother's e.
18: 9 And if your e causes you to sin,
18: 9 you to enter life with one e
19: 24 to go through the e of a needle
Mk 9: 47 And if your e causes you to sin,
9: 47 the kingdom of God with one e
10: 25 to go through the e of a needle
Lk 6: 41 of sawdust in your brother's e
6: 41 to the plank in your own e?
6: 42 fail to see the plank in your own e?
6: 42 first take the plank out of your e,
6: 42 let me take the speck out of your e,'
6: 42 the speck from your brother's e.
11: 34 Your e is the lamp of your body.
18: 25 to go through the e of a needle
1Co 2: 9 "No e has seen,
12: 16 I am not an e, I do not belong
12: 17 If the whole body were an e,
12: 21 The e cannot say to the hand,
15: 52 of an e, at the last trumpet.
Eph 6: 6 favor when their e is on you,
Col 3: 22 not only when their e is on you
Rev 1: 7 and every e will see him,

EYEBROWS (EYE)

Lev 14: 9 his e and the rest of his hair.

EYED (EYE)

Ecc 5: 8 for one official is e by a higher one,

EYELIDS (EYE)

Ps 132: 4 no slumber to my e,
Pr 6: 4 no slumber to your e.
Jer 9: 18 and water streams from our e.

EYES (EYE)

Ge 3: 5 eat of it your e will be opened,
3: 7 the e of both of them were opened,
6: 8 favor in the e of the LORD.
13: 14 "Lift up your e from where you are
18: 3 "If I have found favor in your e,

Ge 19: 19 servant has found favor in your *e*,
21: 19 Then God opened her *e*
27: 1 his *e* were so weak that he could no
29: 17 Leah had weak *e*, but Rachel was
30: 27 "If I have found favor in your *e*,
31: 40 at night, and sleep fled from my *e*.
32: 5 that I may find favor in your *e*.' "
33: 8 "To find favor in your *e*, my lord,"
33: 10 "If I have found favor in your *e*,
33: 15 favor in the *e* of my lord."
34: 11 "Let me find favor in your *e*,
39: 4 Joseph found favor in his *e*
39: 21 favor in the *e* of the prison warden.
42: 24 from them and bound before their *e*
46: 4 Joseph's own hand will close your *e*
47: 15 Why should we die before your *e*?
47: 19 should we perish before your *e*—
47: 25 favor in the *e* of our lord;
47: 29 "If I have found favor in your *e*,
48: 10 Now Israel's *e* were failing
49: 12 His *e* will be darker than wine,
50: 4 "If I have found favor in your *e*,
Ex 8: 26 that are detestable in their *e*.
15: 26 and do what is right in his *e*,
33: 13 If I have found favor in your *e*,
34: 9 if I have found favor in your *e*,"
Lev 20: 4 of the community close their *e*
20: 17 cut off before the *e* of their people.
Nu 10: 31 in the desert, and you can be our *e*.
11: 15 if I have found favor in your *e*—
13: 33 like grasshoppers in our own *e*,
15: 39 the lusts of your own hearts and *e*.
16: 14 Will you gouge out the *e*
20: 8 Speak to that rock before their *e*
22: 31 the LORD opened Balaam's *e*,
24: 4 prostrate, and whose *e* are opened:
24: 16 prostrate, and whose *e* are opened:
25: 6 right before the *e* of Moses
27: 14 to honor me as holy before their *e*."
32: 5 If we have found favor in your *e*,"
33: 55 remain will become barbs in your *e*
Dt 1: 30 before your very *e*,
3: 21 with your own *e* all that the LORD
3: 27 Look at the land with your own *e*,
4: 3 with your own *e* what the LORD
4: 9 forget the things your *e* have seen
4: 25 in the *e* of the LORD your God
4: 34 for you in Egypt before your very *e*
6: 22 Before our *e* the LORD sent
7: 19 with your own *e* the great trials,
9: 17 them to pieces before your *e*.
10: 21 wonders you saw with your own *e*.
11: 7 it was your own *e* that saw all these
11: 12 the *e* of the LORD your God are
12: 25 right in the *e* of the LORD.
12: 28 in the *e* of the LORD your God.
13: 18 and doing what is right in his *e*.
16: 19 for a bribe blinds the *e* of the wise
17: 2 in the *e* of the LORD your God
21: 7 blood, nor did our *e* see it done.
21: 9 right in the *e* of the LORD.
24: 4 detestable in the *e* of the LORD.
25: 3 brother will be degraded in your *e*.
28: 31 will be slaughtered before your *e*,
28: 32 you will wear out your *e* watching
28: 65 *e* weary with longing,
28: 67 and the sights that your *e* will see.
29: 2 Your *e* have seen all that
29: 3 With your own *e* you saw those
29: 4 or *e* that see or ears that hear.
34: 4 I have let you see it with your *e*,
34: 7 yet his *e* were not weak
Jos 3: 7 to exalt you in the *e* of all Israel,
23: 13 on your backs and thorns in your *e*,
24: 7 saw with your own *e* what I did
24: 17 those great signs before our *e*.
Jdg 2: 11 evil in the *e* of the LORD
3: 7 evil in the *e* of the LORD;
3: 12 evil in the *e* of the LORD,
4: 1 evil in the *e* of the LORD.
6: 1 evil in the *e* of the LORD,
6: 17 If now I have found favor in your *e*,
10: 6 evil in the *e* of the LORD.
13: 1 evil in the *e* of the LORD,
16: 21 gouged out his *e* and took him
16: 28 on the Philistines for my two *e*."
Ru 2: 2 anyone in whose *e* I find favor."
2: 10 in your *e* that you notice me—

Ru 2: 13 continue to find favor in your *e*,
1Sa 1: 18 your servant find favor in your *e*."
2: 33 only to blind your *e* with tears
3: 2 whose *e* were becoming
3: 18 let him do what is good in his *e*."
4: 15 whose *e* were set so that he could
12: 3 a bribe to make me shut my *e*?
12: 16 about to do before your *e*!
12: 17 did in the *e* of the LORD
14: 27 to his mouth, and his *e* brightened.
14: 29 See how my *e* brightened
15: 17 you were once small in your own *e*,
15: 19 and do evil in the *e* of the LORD?"
20: 3 that I have found favor in your *e*,
20: 29 If I have found favor in your *e*,
24: 10 with your own *e* how the LORD
27: 5 "If I have found favor in your *e*,
29: 9 pleasing in my *e* as an angel of God
2Sa 6: 22 I will be humiliated in my own *e*.
12: 9 by doing what is evil in his *e*?
12: 11 Before your very *e* I will take your
14: 22 that he has found favor in your *e*,
15: 25 If I find favor in the LORD's *e*,
16: 4 "May I find favor in your *e*,
22: 28 your *e* are on the haughty
24: 3 may the *e* of my lord the king see it.
1Ki 1: 20 the *e* of all Israel are on you,
1: 48 who has allowed my *e*
8: 29 May your *e* be open
8: 52 "May your *e* be open
9: 3 My *e* and my heart will always be
10: 7 I came and saw with my own *e*.
11: 6 evil in the *e* of the LORD;
11: 33 nor done what is right in my *e*,
11: 38 in my *e* by keeping my statutes
14: 8 doing only what was right in my *e*.
14: 22 evil in the *e* of the LORD.
15: 5 right in the *e* of the LORD
15: 11 right in the *e* of the LORD,
15: 26 He did evil in the *e* of the LORD,
15: 34 He did evil in the *e* of the LORD,
16: 7 done in the *e* of the LORD,
16: 19 doing evil in the *e* of the LORD
16: 25 Omri did evil in the *e* of the LORD
16: 30 evil in the *e* of the LORD than any
20: 38 with his headband down over his *e*.
20: 41 removed the headband from his *e*,
21: 20 to do evil in the *e* of the LORD.
21: 25 to do evil in the *e* of the LORD,
22: 43 right in the *e* of the LORD.
22: 52 He did evil in the *e* of the LORD,
2Ki 3: 2 He did evil in the *e* of the LORD,
3: 18 thing in the *e* of the LORD;
4: 34 mouth to mouth, *e* to *e*, hands
4: 35 seven times and opened his *e*.
6: 17 O LORD, open his *e* so he may see
6: 17 the LORD opened the servant's *e*,
6: 20 Then the LORD opened their *e*
6: 20 open the *e* of these men
7: 2 "You will see it with your own *e*,"
7: 19 "You will see it with your own *e*,
8: 18 He did evil in the *e* of the LORD.
8: 27 and did evil in the *e* of the LORD,
9: 30 heard about it, she painted her *e*,
10: 30 accomplishing what is right in my *e*
12: 2 Joash did what was right in the *e*
13: 2 He did evil in the *e* of the LORD
13: 11 He did evil in the *e* of the LORD
14: 3 right in the *e* of the LORD,
14: 24 He did evil in the *e* of the LORD
15: 3 right in the *e* of the LORD,
15: 9 He did evil in the *e* of the LORD,
15: 18 He did evil in the *e* of the LORD.
15: 24 evil in the *e* of the LORD.
15: 28 He did evil in the *e* of the LORD.
15: 34 right in the *e* of the LORD,
16: 2 in the *e* of the LORD his God.
17: 2 He did evil in the *e* of the LORD,
17: 17 to do evil in the *e* of the LORD,
18: 3 right in the *e* of the LORD,
19: 16 and hear; open your *e*, O LORD,
19: 22 and lifted your *e* in pride?
20: 3 have done what is good in your *e*."
21: 2 He did evil in the *e* of the LORD,
21: 6 evil in the *e* of the LORD,
21: 15 they have done evil in my *e*
21: 16 evil in the *e* of the LORD.
21: 20 He did evil in the *e* of the LORD,

2Ki 22: 2 right in the *e* of the LORD
22: 20 Your *e* will not see all the disaster I
23: 32 He did evil in the *e* of the LORD,
23: 37 he did evil in the *e* of the LORD,
24: 9 He did evil in the *e* of the LORD,
24: 19 He did evil in the *e* of the LORD,
25: 7 Then they put out his *e*, bound him
25: 7 the sons of Zedekiah before his *e*.
2Ch 6: 20 May your *e* be open
6: 40 may your *e* be open and your ears
7: 15 Now my *e* will be open
7: 16 My *e* and my heart will always be
9: 6 I came and saw with my own *e*.
14: 2 right in the *e* of the LORD his God
16: 9 For the *e* of the LORD range
20: 12 to do, but our *e* are upon you."
20: 32 right in the *e* of the LORD.
21: 6 He did evil in the *e* of the LORD.
22: 4 He did evil in the *e* of the LORD,
24: 2 in the *e* of the LORD all the years
25: 2 right in the *e* of the LORD,
26: 4 right in the *e* of the LORD,
27: 2 right in the *e* of the LORD,
28: 1 right in the *e* of the LORD.
29: 2 right in the *e* of the LORD,
29: 6 they did evil in the *e*
29: 8 as you can see with your own *e*.
33: 2 He did evil in the *e* of the LORD,
33: 6 evil in the *e* of the LORD,
33: 22 He did evil in the *e* of the LORD,
34: 2 right in the *e* of the LORD
34: 28 Your *e* will not see all the disaster I
36: 5 He did evil in the *e*
36: 9 He did evil in the *e* of the LORD.
36: 12 He did evil in the *e*
Ezr 9: 8 and so our God gives light to our *e*
Ne 1: 6 your *e* open to hear the prayer your
9: 32 hardship seem trifling in your *e*—
Job 3: 10 me to hide trouble from my *e*.
4: 16 A form stood before my *e*,
7: 7 my *e* will never see happiness again
10: 4 Do you have *e* of flesh?
11: 20 But the *e* of the wicked will fail,
13: 1 "My *e* have seen all this,
15: 12 and why do your *e* flash,
15: 15 the heavens are not pure in his *e*,
16: 9 fastens on me his piercing *e*.
16: 16 deep shadows ring my *e*;
16: 20 as my *e* pour out tears to God;
17: 2 my *e* must dwell on their hostility.
17: 5 the *e* of his children will fail.
17: 7 My *e* have grown dim with grief;
19: 27 with my own *e*—I, and not another
21: 8 their offspring before their *e*.
21: 20 Let his own *e* see his destruction;
24: 23 but his *e* are on their ways.
25: 5 and the stars are not pure in his *e*,
27: 19 when he opens his *e*, all is gone.
28: 10 his *e* see all its treasures.
28: 21 from the *e* of every living thing,
29: 15 I was *e* to the blind
31: 1 "I made a covenant with my *e*
31: 7 if my heart has been led by my *e*,
31: 16 let the *e* of the widow grow weary,
32: 1 he was righteous in his own *e*.
34: 21 "His *e* are on the ways of men;
36: 7 He does not take his *e*
39: 29 his *e* detect it from afar.
40: 24 Can anyone capture him by the *e*,
41: 18 his *e* are like the rays of dawn.
42: 5 but now my *e* have seen you.
Ps 6: 7 My *e* grow weak with sorrow;
11: 4 his *e* examine them.
13: 3 Give light to my *e*, or I will sleep
17: 2 may your *e* see what is right.
17: 11 with *e* alert, to throw me
18: 27 low those whose *e* are haughty.
19: 8 giving light to the *e*.
25: 15 My *e* are ever on the LORD,
31: 9 my *e* grow weak with sorrow,
33: 18 But the *e* of the LORD are
34: 15 The *e* of the LORD are
35: 21 With our own *e* we have seen it."
36: 1 God before his *e*.
36: 2 For in his own *e* he flatters himself
38: 10 even the light has gone from my *e*.
52: 1 you who are a disgrace in the *e*
54: 7 my *e* have looked in triumph

Ps 66: 7 his *e* watch the nations—
69: 3 My *e* fail,
69: 23 May their *e* be darkened
77: 4 You kept my *e* from closing;
79: 10 Before our *e*, make known
88: 9 my *e* are dim with grief.
91: 8 You will only observe with your *e*
92: 11 My *e* have seen the defeat
101: 3 I will set before my *e*
101: 5 whoever has haughty *e*
101: 6 My *e* will be on the faithful
115: 5 *e*, but they cannot see;
116: 8 my *e* from tears,
118: 23 and it is marvelous in our *e*.
119: 18 Open my *e* that I may see
119: 37 my *e* away from worthless things;
119: 82 My *e* fail, looking for your promise;
119:123 *e* fail, looking for your salvation,
119:136 Streams of tears flow from my *e*,
119:148 *e* stay open through the watches
121: 1 I lift up my *e* to the hills—
123: 1 I lift up my *e* to you,
123: 2 As the *e* of slaves look to the hand
123: 2 as the *e* of a maid look to the hand
123: 2 so our *e* look to the LORD our
131: 1 my *e* are not haughty;
132: 4 I will allow no sleep to my *e*,
135: 16 *e*, but they cannot see;
139: 16 your *e* saw my unformed body.
141: 8 But my *e* are fixed on you,
145: 15 The *e* of all look to you,
Pr 3: 7 Do not be wise in your own *e*;
4: 25 Let your *e* look straight ahead,
6: 4 Allow no sleep to your *e*,
6: 17 haughty *e*,
6: 25 or let her captivate you with her *e*,
10: 26 to the teeth and smoke to the *e*,
15: 3 The *e* of the LORD are everywhere
17: 24 a fool's *e* wander to the ends
20: 8 he winnows out all evil with his *e*.
20: 12 Ears that hear and *e* that see—
21: 4 Haughty *e* and a proud heart,
22: 12 The *e* of the LORD keep watch
23: 26 and let your *e* keep to my ways,
23: 29 bruises? Who has bloodshot *e*?
23: 33 Your *e* will see strange sights
25: 8 What you have seen with your *e*
26: 5 or he will be wise in his own *e*.
26: 12 Do you see a man wise in his own *e*
26: 16 The sluggard is wiser in his own *e*
27: 20 and neither are the *e* of man.
28: 11 rich man may be wise in his own *e*,
28: 27 he who closes his *e*
29: 13 The LORD gives sight to the *e*
30: 12 those who are pure in their own *e*
30: 13 those whose *e* are ever so haughty,
Ecc 2: 10 myself nothing my *e* desired;
2: 14 The wise man has *e* in his head,
4: 8 yet his *e* were not content
5: 11 except to feast his *e* on them?
8: 16 his *e* not seeing sleep day or night
11: 7 and it pleases the *e* to see the sun.
11: 9 and whatever your *e* see,
SS 1: 15 Your *e* are doves.
4: 1 Your *e* behind your veil are doves.
4: 9 heart with one glance of your *e*,
5: 12 His *e* are like doves
6: 5 Turn your *e* from me;
7: 4 Your *e* are the pools of Heshbon
8: 10 Thus I have become in his *e*
Isa 1: 15 I will hide my *e* from you;
2: 11 The *e* of the arrogant man will be
3: 16 flirting with their *e*,
5: 15 the *e* of the arrogant humbled.
5: 21 those who are wise in their own *e*
6: 5 and my *e* have seen the King,
6: 10 and close their *e*.
6: 10 they might see with their *e*,
10: 12 and the haughty look in his *e*.
11: 3 judge by what he sees with his *e*,
13: 16 to pieces before their *e*;
17: 7 turn their *e* to the Holy One
29: 10 He has sealed your *e* (the prophets
29: 18 the *e* of the blind will see.
30: 20 with your own *e* you will see them.
32: 3 *e* of those who see will no longer be
33: 15 his *e* against contemplating evil—
33: 17 Your *e* will see the king
Isa 33: 20 your *e* will see Jerusalem,
35: 5 will the *e* of the blind be opened
37: 17 and hear; open your *e*, O LORD,
37: 23 and lifted your *e* in pride?
38: 3 have done what is good in your *e*.''
38: 14 My *e* grew weak as I looked
40: 26 Lift your *e* and look to the heavens:
42: 7 to open *e* that are blind,
43: 8 Lead out those who have *e*
44: 18 their *e* are plastered
49: 5 honored in the *e* of the LORD
49: 18 Lift up your *e* and look around;
51: 6 Lift up your *e* to the heavens,
52: 8 they will see it with their own *e*.
59: 10 feeling our way like men without *e*.
60: 4 ''Lift up your *e* and look about you:
65: 16 and hidden from my *e*.
Jer 4: 30 Why shade your *e* with paint?
5: 3 do not your *e* look for truth?
5: 21 who have *e* but do not see,
7: 30 of Judah have done evil in my *e*,
9: 1 and my *e* a fountain of tears!
9: 18 us till our *e* overflow with tears
13: 17 my *e* will weep bitterly,
13: 20 Lift up your *e* and see
14: 17 '' 'Let my *e* overflow with tears
16: 9 Before your *e* and in your days I
16: 17 My *e* are on all their ways;
16: 17 is their sin concealed from my *e*.
20: 4 with your own *e* you will see them
22: 17 ''But your *e* and your heart
24: 6 My *e* will watch over them
29: 21 them to death before your very *e*.
31: 16 and your *e* from tears,
32: 4 and see him with his own *e*.
32: 19 Your *e* are open to all the ways
34: 3 king of Babylon with your own *e*,
39: 6 the sons of Zedekiah before his *e*
39: 7 Then he put out Zedekiah's *e*
39: 16 they will be fulfilled before your *e*.
51: 24 ''Before your *e* I will repay Babylon
52: 2 He did evil in the *e* of the LORD,
52: 10 the sons of Zedekiah before his *e*;
52: 11 Then he put out Zedekiah's *e*,
La 1: 16 and my *e* overflow with tears.
2: 11 My *e* fail from weeping,
2: 18 your *e* no rest.
3: 48 Streams of tears flow from my *e*
3: 49 My *e* will flow unceasingly,
4: 17 Moreover, our *e* failed,
5: 17 of these things our *e* grow dim
Eze 1: 18 and all four rims were full of *e* all
6: 9 and by their *e*, which have lusted
10: 12 were completely full of *e*,
12: 2 They have *e* to see but do not see
20: 7 the vile images you have set your *e*
20: 8 the vile images they had set their *e*
20: 9 it from being profaned in the *e*
20: 14 profaned in the *e* of the nations
20: 22 profaned in the *e* of the nations
20: 24 their *e* ⌊lusted⌋ after their fathers'
22: 16 defiled in the *e* of the nations,
22: 26 and they shut their *e* to the keeping
23: 40 painted your *e* and put
24: 16 from you the delight of your *e*.
24: 21 the delight of your *e*, the object
24: 25 of their *e*, their heart's desire,
36: 23 holy through you before their *e*.
37: 20 before their *e* the sticks you have
38: 16 holy through you before their *e*.
40: 4 look with your *e* and hear
Da 4: 34 raised my *e* toward heaven,
7: 8 This horn had *e* like the *e* of a man
7: 20 that had *e* and a mouth that spoke
8: 5 between his *e* came from the west,
8: 21 horn between his *e* is the first king.
9: 18 open your *e* and see the desolation
10: 6 like lightning, his *e* like flaming
Hos 2: 10 lewdness before the *e* of her lovers;
Joel 1: 16 off before our very *e*—
Am 9: 4 I will fix my *e* upon them
9: 8 ''Surely the *e* of the Sovereign
Mic 4: 11 let our *e* gloat over Zion!''
7: 10 My *e* will see her downfall;
Hab 1: 13 Your *e* are too pure to look on evil;
Zep 3: 20 fortunes before your very *e*,''
Zec 3: 9 There are seven *e* on that one stone
4: 10 These seven are the *e* of the LORD
Zec 9: 1 for the *e* of men and all the tribes
14: 12 their *e* will rot in their sockets,
Mal 1: 5 You will see it with your own *e*
2: 17 good in the *e* of the LORD,
Mt 6: 22 If your *e* are good, your whole
6: 23 if your *e* are bad, your whole body
9: 29 Then he touched their *e* and said,
13: 15 and they have closed their *e*.
13: 15 they might see with their *e*,
13: 16 blessed are your *e* because they see,
18: 9 life with one eye than to have two *e*
20: 34 on them and touched their *e*.
21: 42 and it is marvelous in our *e*'?
26: 43 because their *e* were heavy.
Mk 8: 18 Do you have *e* but fail to see,
8: 23 When he had spit on the man's *e*
8: 25 Jesus put his hands on the man's *e*.
8: 25 his *e* were opened, his sight was
9: 47 with one eye than to have two *e*
12: 11 and it is marvelous in our *e*'?''
14: 40 because their *e* were heavy.
Lk 2: 30 For my *e* have seen your salvation,
4: 20 The *e* of everyone
10: 23 ''Blessed are the *e* that see what
11: 34 When your *e* are good, your whole
16: 15 ones who justify yourselves in the *e*
19: 42 but now it is hidden from your *e*.
24: 31 Then their *e* were opened
Jn 4: 35 open your *e* and look at the fields!
9: 6 saliva, and put it on the man's *e*.
9: 10 ''How then were your *e* opened?''
9: 11 made some mud and put it on my *e*.
9: 14 opened the man's *e* was a Sabbath.
9: 15 mud on my *e*,'' the man replied,
9: 17 him? It was your *e* he opened.''
9: 21 who opened his *e*, we don't know.
9: 26 How did he open your *e*?''
9: 30 comes from, yet he opened my *e*.
9: 32 of opening the *e* of a man born
10: 21 Can a demon open the *e*
11: 37 ''Could not he who opened the *e*
12: 40 elsewhere: ''He has blinded their *e*
12: 40 so they can neither see with their *e*,
Ac 1: 9 he was taken up before their very *e*,
9: 8 when he opened his *e* he could see
9: 18 like scales fell from Saul's *e*,
9: 40 She opened her *e*, and seeing Peter
26: 18 I am sending you to open their *e*
28: 27 and they have closed their *e*.
28: 27 they might see with their *e*,
Ro 3: 18 fear of God before their *e*.''
11: 8 *e* so that they could not see
11: 10 May their *e* be darkened
12: 17 right in the *e* of everybody.
2Co 4: 18 So we fix our *e* not on what is seen,
8: 21 not only in the *e* of the Lord but
8: 21 of the Lord but also in the *e* of men.
Gal 3: 1 Before your very *e* Jesus Christ was
4: 15 you would have torn out your *e*
Eph 1: 18 also that the *e* of your heart may be
Heb 4: 13 and laid bare before the *e* of him
12: 2 Let us fix our *e* on Jesus, the author
Jas 2: 5 poor in the *e* of the world to be rich
1Pe 3: 12 For the *e* of the Lord are
2Pe 2: 14 With *e* full of adultery, they never
1Jn 1: 1 which we have seen with our *e*,
2: 16 the lust of his *e* and the boasting
Rev 1: 14 and his *e* were like blazing fire.
2: 18 whose *e* are like blazing fire
3: 18 and salve to put on your *e*,
4: 6 and they were covered with *e*,
4: 8 and was covered with *e* all around,
5: 6 He had seven horns and seven *e*,
7: 17 wipe away every tear from their *e*.''
19: 12 His *e* are like blazing fire,
21: 4 He will wipe every tear from their *e*

EYESIGHT (EYE)

Jer 14: 6 their *e* fails

EYEWITNESSES (WITNESS)

Lk 1: 2 by those who from the first were *e*
2Pe 1: 16 but we were *e* of his majesty.

EZBAI

1Ch 11: 37 Naarai son of *E*, Joel the brother

EZBON
Ge 46: 16 Zephon, Haggi, Shuni, *E*, Eri,
1Ch 7: 7 The sons of Bela: *E*, Uzzi, Uzziel,

EZEKIEL
Eze 1: 3 of the LORD came to *E* the priest,
24: 24 *E* will be a sign to you; you will do

EZEL
1Sa 20: 19 began, and wait by the stone *E*.

EZEM
Jos 15: 29 Baalah, Iim, *E*, Eltolad, Kesil,
19: 3 Hazar Shual, Balah, *E*, Eltolad,
1Ch 4: 29 Bilhah, *E*, Tolad, Bethuel,

EZER
Ge 36: 21 Anah, Dishon, *E* and Dishan.
36: 27 The sons of *E*: Bilhan, Zaavan
36: 30 Anah, Dishon, *E* and Dishan.
1Ch 1: 38 Anah, Dishon, *E* and Dishan.
1: 42 The sons of *E*: Bilhan, Zaavan
4: 4 and *E* the father of Hushah.
7: 21 *E* and Elead were killed
12: 9 *E* was the chief, Obadiah
Ne 3: 19 Next to him, *E* son of Jeshua,
12: 42 Jehohanan, Malkijah, Elam and *E*.

EZION GEBER
Nu 33: 35 left Abronah and camped at *E*.
33: 36 They left *E* and camped at Kadesh,
Dt 2: 8 which comes up from Elath and *E*,
1Ki 9: 26 King Solomon also built ships at *E*,
22: 48 set sail—they were wrecked at *E*.
2Ch 8: 17 Then Solomon went to *E* and
20: 36 After these were built at *E*,

EZRA (EZRA'S)
Ezr 7: 1 *E* son of Seraiah, the son
7: 6 this *E* came up from Babylon.
7: 8 *E* arrived in Jerusalem
7: 10 For *E* had devoted himself
7: 11 had given to *E* the priest
7: 12 king of kings, To *E* the priest,
7: 21 diligence whatever *E* the priest,
7: 25 *E*, in accordance with the wisdom
10: 1 While *E* was praying
10: 2 the descendants of Elam, said to *E*,
10: 5 So *E* rose up and put the leading
10: 6 *E* withdrew from before the house
10: 10 Then *E* the priest stood up
10: 16 *E* the priest selected men who were
Ne 8: 1 They told *E* the scribe
8: 2 the seventh month *E* the priest
8: 4 *E* the scribe stood
8: 5 *E* opened the book.
8: 6 *E* praised the LORD, the great
8: 9 the governor, *E* the priest
8: 13 gathered around *E* the scribe
8: 18 *E* read from the Book of the Law
12: 1 Seraiah, Jeremiah, *E*, Amariah,
12: 26 and of *E* the priest and scribe.
12: 33 along with Azariah, *E*, Meshullam,
12: 36 *E* the scribe led the procession.

EZRA'S (EZRA)
Ne 12: 13 Hananiah; of *E*, Meshullam;

EZRAH
1Ch 4: 17 The sons of *E*: Jether, Mered,

EZRAHITE
1Ki 4: 31 including Ethan the *E*— wiser

EZRI
1Ch 27: 26 *E* son of Kelub was in charge

FABRIC
Jdg 16: 13 seven braids of my head into the *f*
16: 13 them into the *f* and tightened it
16: 14 up the pin and the loom, with the *f*.
Eze 16: 13 costly *f* and embroidered cloth.
27: 16 purple *f*, embroidered work,
27: 24 with you beautiful garments, blue *f*,

FACE (FACED FACEDOWN FACES FACING STERN-FACED)
Ge 1: 29 plant on the *f* of the whole earth
4: 5 very angry, and his *f* was downcast.
4: 6 angry? Why is your *f* downcast?
6: 7 from the *f* of the earth—
7: 4 and I will wipe from the *f*
7: 23 Every living thing on the *f*
11: 4 over the *f* of the whole earth."
11: 9 them over the *f* of the whole earth.
19: 1 down with his *f* to the ground.
30: 40 but made the rest *f* the streaked
32: 30 "It is because I saw God *f* to *f*,
33: 10 For to see your *f* is like seeing the *f*
38: 15 for she had covered her *f*.
43: 3 'You will not see my *f* again
43: 5 'You will not see my *f* again
43: 31 After he had washed his *f*,
44: 23 you will not see my *f* again.'
44: 26 We cannot see the man's *f*
48: 11 I never expected to see your *f* again
48: 12 down with his *f* to the ground.
Ex 3: 6 Moses hid his *f*, because he was
10: 5 They will cover the *f* of the ground
10: 28 The day you see my *f* you will die."
13: 17 For God said, "If they *f* war,
25: 20 The cherubim are to *f* each other,
32: 12 to wipe them off the *f* of the earth'?
33: 11 would speak to Moses *f* to *f*,
33: 16 people on the *f* of the earth?"
33: 20 But," he said, "you cannot see my *f*
33: 23 but my *f* must not be seen."
34: 29 was not aware that his *f* was radiant
34: 30 saw Moses, his *f* was radiant,
34: 33 to them, he put a veil over his *f*.
34: 35 over his *f* until he went in to speak
34: 35 they saw that his *f* was radiant.
Lev 13: 45 cover the lower part of his *f*
17: 10 I will set my *f* against that person
20: 3 I will set my *f* against that man
20: 5 I will set my *f* against that man
20: 6 " 'I will set my *f* against the person
26: 17 I will set my *f* against you
Nu 6: 25 the LORD make his *f* shine
6: 26 the LORD turn his *f* toward you
11: 15 and do not let me *f* my own ruin."
12: 3 else on the *f* of the earth.)
12: 8 With him I speak *f* to *f*,
12: 14 "If her father had spit in her *f*,
14: 14 O LORD, have been seen *f* to *f*,
14: 43 and Canaanites will *f* you there.
22: 5 they cover the *f* of the land
22: 11 of Egypt covers the *f* of the land.
24: 1 but turned his *f* toward the desert.
Dt 5: 4 The LORD spoke to you *f* to *f* out
6: 15 you from the *f* of the land.
7: 6 the peoples on the *f* of the earth
7: 10 repay to their *f* by destruction;
7: 10 to their *f* those who hate him.
14: 2 the peoples on the *f* of the earth,
25: 9 off one of his sandals, spit in his *f*
31: 17 I will hide my *f* from them,
31: 18 And I will certainly hide my *f*
32: 20 I will hide my *f* from them," he said
34: 10 whom the LORD knew *f* to *f*,
Jos 5: 1 had the courage to *f* the Israelites.
7: 10 What are you doing down on your *f*
Jdg 6: 22 the angel of the LORD *f* to *f*!"
Ru 2: 10 down with her *f* to the ground.
1Sa 1: 18 and her *f* was no longer downcast.
5: 3 fallen on his *f* on the ground
5: 4 fallen on his *f* on the ground
20: 15 enemies from the *f* of the earth."
20: 41 with his *f* to the ground.
24: 8 himself with his *f* to the ground.
25: 23 David with her *f* to the ground.
25: 41 down with her *f* to the ground
28: 14 himself with his *f* to the ground.
2Sa 2: 22 I look your brother Joab in the *f*?"
14: 4 she fell with her *f* to the ground
14: 7 descendant on the *f* of the earth."
14: 22 Joab fell with his *f* to the ground
14: 24 and did not see the *f* of the king.
14: 24 own house; he must not see my *f*."
14: 28 without seeing the king's *f*.
14: 32 I want to see the king's *f*,
14: 33 down with his *f* to the ground
2Sa 18: 28 the king with his *f* to the ground
19: 4 The king covered his *f*
21: 1 so David sought the *f* of the LORD
24: 20 the king with his *f* to the ground.
1Ki 1: 23 and bowed with his *f* to the ground
1: 31 low with her *f* to the ground
13: 34 destruction from the *f* of the earth.
18: 42 and put his *f* between his knees.
19: 13 he pulled his cloak over his *f*
22: 24 and slapped Micaiah in the *f*.
2Ki 4: 29 Lay my staff on the boy's *f*."
4: 31 and laid the staff on the boy's *f*,
8: 15 and spread it over the king's *f*,
14: 8 challenge: "Come, meet me *f* to *f*."
20: 2 Hezekiah turned his *f* to the wall
1Ch 16: 11 seek his *f* always.
21: 21 David with his *f* to the ground.
2Ch 7: 14 and seek my *f* and turn
18: 23 and slapped Micaiah in the *f*.
20: 12 to *f* this vast army that is attacking
20: 17 Go out to *f* them tomorrow,
20: 18 bowed with his *f* to the ground,
25: 17 of Israel: "Come, meet me *f* to *f*."
30: 9 He will not turn his *f* from you
Ezr 9: 6 and disgraced to lift up my *f* to you,
Ne 2: 2 "Why does your *f* look so sad
2: 3 Why should my *f* not look sad
4: 5 insults in the *f* of the builders.
Est 7: 8 mouth, they covered Haman's *f*.
Job 1: 11 he will surely curse you to your *f*."
2: 5 he will surely curse you to your *f*."
4: 15 A spirit glided past my *f*,
6: 28 Would I lie to your *f*?
11: 15 then you will lift up your *f*
13: 15 will surely defend my ways to his *f*.
13: 24 Why do you hide your *f*
15: 27 "Though his *f* is covered with fat
16: 16 My *f* is red with weeping,
17: 6 a man in whose *f* people spit.
17: 12 in the *f* of darkness they say,
21: 31 denounces his conduct to his *f*?
22: 26 and will lift up your *f* to God.
23: 17 thick darkness that covers my *f*.
24: 15 and he keeps his *f* concealed.
26: 9 He covers the *f* of the full moon,
26: 10 on the *f* of the waters
29: 24 the light of my *f* was precious
30: 10 they do not hesitate to spit in my *f*.
33: 26 he sees God's *f* and shouts for joy;
34: 29 If he hides his *f*, who can see him?
37: 12 over the *f* of the whole earth
Ps 4: 6 Let the light of your *f* shine upon us
10: 11 he covers his *f* and never sees."
11: 7 upright men will see his *f*.
13: 1 How long will you hide your *f*
17: 15 in righteousness I will see your *f*;
22: 24 he has not hidden his *f* from him
24: 6 who seek your *f*, O God of Jacob.
27: 8 My heart says of you, "Seek his *f*!"
27: 8 Your *f*, LORD, I will seek.
27: 9 Do not hide your *f* from me,
30: 7 but when you hid your *f*,
31: 16 Let your *f* shine on your servant;
34: 16 the *f* of the LORD is
44: 3 and the light of your *f*,
44: 15 and my *f* is covered with shame
44: 22 Yet for your sake we *f* death all day
44: 24 Why do you hide your *f*
50: 21 and accuse you to your *f*
51: 9 Hide your *f* from my sins
67: 1 and make his *f* shine upon us; *Selah*
69: 7 and shame covers my *f*.
69: 17 Do not hide your *f*
80: 3 make your *f* shine upon us,
80: 7 make your *f* shine upon us,
80: 19 make your *f* shine upon us,
88: 14 and hide your *f* from me?
102: 2 Do not hide your *f* from me
104: 15 oil to make his *f* shine,
104: 29 When you hide your *f*,
104: 30 and you renew the *f* of the earth.
105: 4 seek his *f* always.
119: 58 I have sought your *f*
119: 135 Make your *f* shine
143: 7 Do not hide your *f* from me
Pr 7: 13 and with a brazen *f* she said:
8: 27 the horizon on the *f* of the deep,
15: 13 A happy heart makes the *f* cheerful

Pr 16: 15 When a king's *f* brightens,
27: 19 As water reflects a *f*,
Ecc 7: 3 because a sad *f* is good for the heart
8: 1 Wisdom brightens a man's *f*
SS 2: 14 and your *f* is lovely.
2: 14 show me your *f*,
Isa 8: 17 who is hiding his *f* from the house
23: 17 the kingdoms on the *f* of the earth.
24: 1 he will ruin its *f*
38: 2 Hezekiah turned his *f* to the wall
50: 6 I did not hide my *f*
50: 7 Therefore have I set my *f* like flint,
50: 8 Let us *f* each other!
54: 8 I hid my *f* from you for a moment,
57: 17 I punished him, and hid my *f*
59: 2 your sins have hidden his *f*
64: 7 for you have hidden your *f* from us
65: 3 me to my very *f*,
Jer 13: 26 I will pull up your skirts over your *f*
18: 17 show them my back and not my *f*
25: 26 the kingdoms on the *f* of the earth.
28: 16 you from the *f* of the earth.
30: 6 every *f* turned deathly pale?
32: 4 and will speak with him *f* to *f*
33: 5 I will hide my *f* from this city
34: 3 and he will speak with you *f* to *f*.
La 3: 29 Let him bury his *f* in the dust—
Eze 1: 10 Each of the four had the *f* of a man,
1: 10 and on the left the *f* of an ox;
1: 10 and on the right side each had the *f*
1: 10 each also had the *f* of an eagle.
4: 3 the city and turn your *f* toward it.
4: 7 Turn your *f* toward the siege
6: 2 set your *f* against the mountains
7: 22 I will turn my *f* away from them,
10: 14 One *f* was that of a cherub,
10: 14 and the fourth the *f* of an eagle.
10: 14 of a man, the third the *f* of a lion,
10: 14 that of a cherub, the second the *f*
12: 6 Cover your *f* so that you cannot see
12: 12 He will cover his *f*
13: 17 set your *f* against the daughters
14: 4 wicked stumbling block before his *f*
14: 7 wicked stumbling block before his *f*
14: 8 I will set my *f* against that man
15: 7 And when I set my *f* against them,
15: 7 I will set my *f* against them.
20: 35 *f* to *f*, I will execute judgment
20: 46 set your *f* toward the south;
20: 47 and every *f* from south
21: 2 set your *f* against Jerusalem
24: 17 not cover the lower part of your *f*
24: 22 not cover the lower part of your *f*
25: 2 set your *f* against the Ammonites
28: 21 of man, set your *f* against Sidon;
29: 2 set your *f* against Pharaoh king
35: 2 set your *f* against Mount Seir;
38: 2 Son of man, set your *f* against Gog,
38: 20 and all the people on the *f*
39: 23 So I hid my *f* from them
39: 24 and I hid my *f* from them.
39: 29 I will no longer hide my *f*
41: 19 the *f* of a lion toward the palm tree
41: 19 the *f* of a man toward the palm tree
43: 17 The steps of the altar *f* east."
Da 5: 6 His *f* turned pale and he was
5: 9 terrified and his *f* grew more pale.
7: 28 my thoughts, and my *f* turned pale,
8: 18 with my *f* to the ground.
10: 6 like chrysolite, his *f* like lightning,
10: 8 my *f* turned deathly pale
10: 9 fell into a deep sleep, my *f*
10: 15 with my *f* toward the ground
Hos 2: 2 the adulterous look from her *f*
5: 15 And they will seek my *f*;
Joel 2: 6 every *f* turns pale.
Am 5: 8 out over the *f* of the land—
9: 6 out over the *f* of the land—
9: 8 it from the *f* of the earth—
Mic 3: 4 At that time he will hide his *f*
Na 2: 10 bodies tremble, every *f* grows pale.
3: 5 "I will lift your skirts over your *f*.
Zep 1: 2 everything from the *f* of the earth,"
1: 3 off man from the *f* of the earth,"
Mt 6: 17 oil on your head and wash your *f*,
17: 2 His *f* shone like the sun,
18: 10 angels in heaven always see the *f*
26: 39 he fell with his *f* to the ground
Mt 26: 67 they spit in his *f* and struck him
Mk 10: 22 At this the man's *f* fell.
Lk 5: 12 he fell with his *f* to the ground
9: 29 the appearance of his *f* changed,
21: 35 live on the *f* of the whole earth.
Jn 11: 44 of linen, and a cloth around his *f*.
18: 22 officials nearby struck him in the *f*.
19: 3 And they struck him in the *f*.
Ac 6: 15 they saw that his *f* was like the *f*
16: 19 marketplace to *f* the authorities.
20: 38 they would never see his *f* again.
Ro 8: 36 "For your sake we *f* death all day
1Co 7: 28 who marry will *f* many troubles
13: 12 reflection; then we shall see *f* to *f*.
2Co 3: 7 could not look steadily at the *f*
3: 13 veil over his *f* to keep the Israelites
4: 6 the glory of God in the *f* of Christ.
10: 1 who am "timid" when *f* to *f*
11: 20 forward or slaps you in the *f*.
11: 28 I *f* daily the pressure of my concern
Gal 2: 11 I opposed him to his *f*,
Heb 9: 27 and after that to *f* judgment,
10: 32 contest in the *f* of suffering.
Jas 1: 2 whenever you *f* trials
1: 23 says is like a man who looks at his *f*
5: 10 of patience in the *f* of suffering,
1Pe 3: 12 but the *f* of the Lord is
2Jn : 12 to visit you and talk with you *f* to *f*,
3Jn : 14 see you soon, and we will talk *f* to *f*.
Rev 1: 16 His *f* was like the sun shining
4: 7 the third had a *f* like a man,
6: 16 hide us from the *f* of him who sits
10: 1 above his head; his *f* was like
22: 4 They will see his *f*, and his name

FACED (FACE)

Ex 37: 9 The cherubim *f* each other,
Nu 8: 3 the lamps so that they *f* forward
2Ki 14: 11 king of Judah *f* each other
23: 29 but Neco *f* him and killed him
2Ch 25: 21 king of Judah *f* each other
Ne 8: 3 as he *f* the square before the Water
Eze 1: 17 the four directions the creatures *f*;
10: 11 in whatever direction the head *f*,
10: 11 the four directions the cherubim *f*;
40: 9 of the gateway *f* the temple.
40: 16 the openings all around *f* inward.
40: 31 Its portico *f* the outer court;
40: 34 Its portico *f* the outer court;
40: 37 Its portico *f* the outer court;
42: 2 building whose door *f* north was
42: 3 gallery *f* gallery at the three levels.
47: 1 the east (for the temple *f* east).
Ac 25: 16 man before he has *f* his accusers
Ro 4: 19 he *f* the fact that his body was
Heb 11: 36 Some *f* jeers and flogging,

FACEDOWN (FACE)

Ge 17: 3 Abram fell *f*, and God said to him,
17: 17 Abraham fell *f*; he laughed
Lev 9: 24 they shouted for joy and fell *f*.
Nu 14: 5 and Aaron fell *f* in front
16: 4 When Moses heard this, he fell *f*.
16: 22 and Aaron fell *f* and cried out,
16: 45 And they fell *f*.
20: 6 to the Tent of Meeting and fell *f*,
22: 31 So he bowed low and fell *f*.
Jos 5: 14 Then Joshua fell *f* to the ground
7: 6 fell *f* to the ground before the ark
1Sa 17: 49 and he fell *f* on the ground.
1Ch 21: 16 clothed in sackcloth, fell *f*.
Eze 1: 28 I fell *f*, and I heard the voice
3: 23 by the Kebar River, and I fell *f*.
9: 8 I fell *f*, crying out, "Ah, Sovereign
11: 13 I fell *f* and cried out in a loud voice,
43: 3 by the Kebar River, and I fell *f*.
44: 4 temple of the LORD, and I fell *f*.
Mt 17: 6 they fell *f* to the ground, terrified.

FACES (FACE)

Ge 9: 23 Their *f* were turned the other way
40: 7 "Why are your *f* so sad today?"
42: 6 to him with their *f* to the ground.
Nu 21: 11 in the desert that *f* Moab
Jos 15: 7 *f* the Pass of Adummim south
18: 17 *f* the Pass of Adummim, and
Jdg 13: 20 fell with their *f* to the ground.
16: 3 to the top of the hill that *f* Hebron.
1Sa 26: 1 hill of Hakilah, which *f* Jeshimon?"
1Ki 7: 9 a saw on their inner and outer *f*.
1Ch 12: 8 Their *f* were the *f* of lions,
2Ch 7: 3 with their *f* to the ground,
29: 6 They turned their *f* away
Ne 8: 6 LORD with their *f* to the ground.
Job 40: 13 shroud their *f* in the grave.
Ps 34: 5 their *f* are never covered
83: 16 Cover their *f* with shame
Isa 3: 9 on their *f* testifies against them;
3: 15 and grinding the *f* of the poor?"
6: 2 two wings they covered their *f*,
13: 8 their *f* aflame.
25: 8 the tears from all *f*;
29: 22 no longer will their *f* grow pale.
49: 23 you with their *f* to the ground;
53: 3 one from whom men hide their *f*
Jer 2: 27 and not their *f*;
5: 3 They made their *f* harder
32: 33 backs to me and not their *f*;
50: 5 and turn their *f* toward it.
51: 51 and shame covers our *f*,
Eze 1: 6 but each of them had four *f*
1: 8 All four of them had *f* and wings,
1: 10 Their *f* looked like this: Each
1: 11 Such were their *f*.
1: 15 beside each creature with its four *f*.
7: 18 Their *f* will be covered with shame
8: 16 and their *f* toward the east,
9: 2 which *f* north, each
10: 14 Each of the cherubim had four *f*:
10: 21 Each had four *f* and four wings,
10: 22 Their *f* had the same appearance
11: 1 the house of the LORD that *f* east.
14: 3 stumbling blocks before their *f*.
27: 35 and their *f* are distorted with fear.
40: 10 and the *f* of the projecting walls
40: 14 He measured along the *f*
40: 16 The *f* of the projecting walls were
40: 26 on the *f* of the projecting walls
41: 18 Each cherub had two *f*: the face
Mic 3: 7 They will all cover their *f*
Mal 2: 3 I will spread on your *f* the offal
Mt 6: 16 for they disfigure their *f*
23: 13 the kingdom of heaven in men's *f*.
Lk 24: 5 down with their *f* to the ground,
24: 17 They stood still, their *f* downcast.
2Co 3: 18 who with unveiled *f* all reflect
Rev 7: 11 down on their *f* before the throne
9: 7 and their *f* resembled human *f*.
11: 16 fell on their *f* and worshiped God,

FACING (FACE)

Jos 8: 33 *f* those who carried it—the priests,
18: 14 From the hill *f* Beth Horon
18: 16 foot of the hill *f* the Valley of Ben
19: 46 and Rakkon, with the area *f* Joppa.
1Sa 13: 18 the Valley of Zeboim *f* the desert.
17: 21 drawing up their lines *f* each other.
26: 3 on the hill of Hakilah *f* Jeshimon,
1Ki 7: 4 high in sets of three, *f* each other.
7: 5 part in sets of three, *f* each other.
7: 25 three *f* north, three *f* west,
7: 25 three *f* south and three *f* east.
22: 35 up in his chariot *f* the Arameans.
2Ki 2: 7 *f* the place where Elijah
2Ch 3: 13 stood on their feet, *f* the main hall.
4: 4 three *f* north, three *f* west,
4: 4 three *f* south and three *f* east.
18: 34 up in his chariot *f* the Arameans
Ne 3: 19 from a point *f* the ascent
Est 5: 1 throne in the hall, *f* the entrance.
Eze 40: 6 Then he went to the gate *f* east.
40: 7 to the portico *f* the temple was one
40: 14 up to the portico *f* the courtyard.
40: 20 and width of the gate *f* north,
40: 22 as those of the gate *f* east.
40: 23 to the inner court *f* the north gate,
40: 24 south side and I saw a gate *f* south.
40: 27 inner court also had a gate *f* south,
40: 44 side of the north gate and *f* south,
40: 44 side of the south gate and *f* north.
40: 45 "The room *f* south is
40: 46 and the room *f* north is
41: 12 building *f* the temple courtyard
41: 15 and the portico *f* the court,
41: 15 of the building *f* the courtyard
42: 13 south rooms *f* the temple courtyard

Eze 43: 1 man brought me to the gate *f* east,
43: 4 the temple through the gate *f* east.
44: 1 the one *f* east, and it was shut.
46: 1 of the inner court *f* east is to be shut
46: 12 the gate *f* east is to be opened
46: 19 gate to the sacred rooms *f* north,
47: 2 the outside to the outer gate *f* east,
Ac 20: 23 that prison and hardships are *f* me.
27: 12 *f* both southwest and northwest.

FACT (FACTS)

Ge 45: 26 In *f*, he is ruler of all Egypt.''
47: 18 hide from our lord the *f* that
2Sa 13: 15 In *f*, he hated her more
2Ki 8: 10 to me that he will in *f* die.''
Ezr 5: 17 if King Cyrus did in *f* issue a decree
Mk 3: 27 In *f*, no one can enter a strong
7: 25 In *f*, as soon as she heard about him
12: 22 In *f*, none of the seven left any
Jn 4: 2 in *f* it was not Jesus who baptized,
4: 18 *f* is, you have had five husbands,
9: 37 ''You have now seen him; in *f*,
10: 5 will never follow a stranger; in *f*,
16: 2 out of the synagogue; in *f*,
18: 37 In *f*, for this reason I was born,
Ac 2: 32 and we are all witnesses of the *f*.
13: 34 The *f* that God raised him
Ro 4: 2 in *f*, Abraham was justified
4: 19 he faced the *f* that his body was
1Co 6: 7 The very *f* that you have lawsuits
10: 1 you to be ignorant of the *f*,
12: 18 But in *f* God has arranged the parts
15: 15 him if in *f* the dead are not raised.
2Co 11: 20 fools since you are so wise! In *f*,
1Th 3: 4 In *f*, when we were with you,
4: 1 to please God, as in *f* you are living
4: 10 in *f*, you do love all the brothers
5: 11 as in *f* you are doing.
1Ti 5: 15 have in *f* already turned away
2Ti 3: 12 In *f*, everyone who wants
Tit 1: 15 In *f*, both their minds
Heb 5: 12 In *f*, though by this time you ought
9: 22 In *f*, the law requires that nearly
1Jn 3: 4 who sins breaks the law; in *f*,

FACTIONS

1Ki 16: 21 of Israel were split into two *f*;
2Co 12: 20 outbursts of anger, *f*, slander,
Gal 5: 20 selfish ambition, dissensions, *f*

FACTS (FACT)

Ac 19: 36 since these *f* are undeniable,

FADE (FADED FADES FADING)

Ps 109: 23 I *f* away like an evening shadow;
Isa 17: 4 In that day the glory of Jacob will *f*;
Na 1: 4 and the blossoms of Lebanon *f*.
Jas 1: 11 the rich man will *f* away
1Pe 1: 4 spoil or *f*—kept in heaven for you,
5: 4 of glory that will never *f* away.

FADED (FADE)

Lev 13: 6 if the sore has *f* and has not spread
13: 21 more than skin deep and has *f*,
13: 26 more than skin deep and has *f*,
13: 28 has not spread in the skin but has *f*,
13: 56 mildew has *f* after the article has

FADES (FADE)

Ps 65: 8 morning dawns and evening *f*
Ecc 12: 4 and the sound of grinding *f*;

FADING (FADE)

Pr 7: 9 house at twilight, as the day was *f*,
Isa 1: 30 will be like an oak with *f* leaves,
28: 1 to the *f* flower, his glorious beauty,
28: 4 That *f* flower, his glorious beauty,
Jer 6: 4 But, alas, the daylight is *f*,
2Co 3: 7 *f* though it was, will not
3: 11 if what was *f* away came with glory,
3: 13 at it while the radiance was *f* away.

FAIL (FAILED FAILING FAILINGS FAILS FAILURE)

Lev 20: 4 and they *f* to put him to death,
26: 15 and *f* to carry out all my commands
Nu 15: 22 if you unintentionally *f* to keep any
32: 23 ''But if you *f* to do this, you will be
9: 13 and not on a journey *f* to celebrate
19: 13 and *f* to purify himself defiles
2Sa 17: 16 cross over without *f*, or the king
1Ki 2: 4 you will never *f* to have a man
8: 25 'You shall never *f* to have a man
9: 5 'You shall never *f* to have a man
2Ki 10: 10 against the house of Ahab will *f*.
1Ch 28: 20 He will not *f* you or forsake you
2Ch 6: 16 'You shall never *f* to have a man
7: 18 'You shall never *f* to have a man
34: 33 they did not *f* to follow the LORD,
Ezr 6: 9 must be given them daily without *f*,
Est 9: 27 without *f* observe these two days
Job 11: 20 But the eyes of the wicked will *f*,
14: 7 and its new shoots will not *f*.
17: 5 the eyes of his children will *f*.
21: 10 Their bulls never *f* to breed;
41: 12 ''I will not *f* to speak of his limbs,
Ps 6: 7 they *f* because of all my foes.
69: 3 My eyes *f*,
73: 26 My flesh and my heart may *f*,
89: 28 my covenant with him will never *f*.
89: 31 and *f* to keep my commands,
119: 82 My eyes *f*, looking
119: 123 My eyes *f*, looking
Pr 15: 22 Plans *f* for lack of counsel,
Isa 32: 10 the grape harvest will *f*,
33: 16 and water will not *f* him.
51: 6 my righteousness will never *f*.
58: 11 like a spring whose waters never *f*.
Jer 20: 11 They will *f* and be thoroughly
33: 17 'David will never *f* to have a man
33: 18 ever *f* to have a man to stand
35: 19 of Recab will never *f* to have a man
La 2: 11 My eyes *f* from weeping,
3: 22 for his compassions never *f*.
Eze 2: 5 whether they listen or *f* to listen—
2: 7 whether they listen or *f* to listen,
3: 11 whether they listen or *f* to listen.''
30: 6 and her proud strength will *f*.
47: 12 will not wither, nor will their fruit *f*.
Hos 9: 2 the new wine will *f* them.
13: 15 his spring will *f*
Zep 3: 5 and every new day he does not *f*,
Mk 8: 18 Do you have eyes but *f* to see,
8: 18 and ears but *f* to hear?
10: 30 gospel will *f* to receive a hundred
Lk 6: 42 when you yourself *f*
18: 30 of God will *f* to receive many times
22: 32 Simon, that your faith may not *f*.
Jn 1: 20 He did not *f* to confess,
Ac 5: 38 activity is of human origin, it will *f*.
2Co 13: 5 unless, of course, you *f* the test?

FAILED (FAIL)

Lev 5: 16 for what he has *f* to do in regard
Jos 2: 11 and everyone's courage *f*
21: 45 promises to the house of Israel *f*;
23: 14 has been fulfilled; not one has *f*.
23: 14 LORD your God gave you has *f*.
Jdg 1: 21 *f* to dislodge the Jebusites,
8: 35 *f* to show gratitude to the family
21: 5 a solemn oath that anyone who *f*
21: 5 the tribes of Israel has *f* to assemble
21: 8 of the tribes of Israel *f* to assemble
1Sa 3: 13 themselves contemptible, and he *f*
25: 37 his heart *f* him and he became like
1Ki 8: 56 Not one word has *f*
15: 5 and had not *f* to keep any
2Ki 3: 26 to the king of Edom, but they *f*.
Ezr 10: 8 Anyone who *f* to appear
Ne 9: 17 *f* to remember the miracles you
Job 32: 15 words have *f* them.
Ps 77: 8 Has his promise *f* for all time?
La 4: 17 Moreover, our eyes *f*,
Ro 9: 6 as though God's word had *f*.
2Co 13: 6 discover that we have not *f* the test.
13: 7 though we may seem to have *f*.
Jas 5: 4 wages you *f* to pay the workmen

FAILING (FAIL)

Ge 48: 10 Now Israel's eyes were *f*
Dt 8: 11 *f* to observe his commands,
1Sa 12: 23 sin against the LORD by *f* to pray

FAILINGS (FAIL)

Ro 15: 1 ought to bear with the *f* of the weak

FAILS (FAIL)

Ex 21: 33 digs one and *f* to cover it and an ox
Nu 9: 13 and not on a journey *f* to celebrate
19: 13 and *f* to purify himself defiles
2Ki 10: 19 Anyone who *f* to come will no
Ps 31: 10 strength *f* because of my affliction,
38: 10 My heart pounds, my strength *f* me
40: 12 and my heart *f* within me.
Pr 8: 36 whoever *f* to find me harms himself
Ecc 6: 6 but *f* to enjoy his prosperity.
Isa 65: 20 he who *f* to reach a hundred
Jer 14: 6 their eyesight *f*
15: 18 like a spring that *f*?
17: 8 and never *f* to bear fruit.''
Joel 1: 10 the oil *f*.
Hab 3: 17 though the olive crop *f*
1Co 13: 8 Love never *f*.

FAILURE (FAIL)

1Th 2: 1 that our visit to you was not a *f*.

FAINT (FAINTED FAINTING FAINTS)

1Sa 14: 28 That is why the men are *f*.''
Job 23: 16 God has made my heart *f*;
26: 14 how *f* the whisper we hear of him!
Ps 6: 2 to me, LORD, for I am *f*;
61: 2 I call as my heart grows *f*;
77: 3 I mused, and my spirit grew *f*.
142: 3 When my spirit grows *f* within me,
143: 4 So my spirit grows *f* within me;
Ecc 12: 4 but all their songs grow *f*;
SS 2: 5 for I am *f* with love.
5: 8 Tell him I am *f* with love.
Isa 15: 4 and their hearts are *f*.
29: 8 but he awakens *f*, with his thirst
40: 31 they will walk and not be *f*.
44: 12 he drinks no water and grows *f*.
57: 10 and so you did not *f*.
57: 16 of man would grow *f* before me—
Jer 8: 18 my heart is *f* within me.
15: 9 The mother of seven will grow *f*
31: 25 the weary and satisfy the *f*.''
La 1: 13 *f* all the day long.
1: 22 and my heart is *f*.''
2: 11 because children and infants *f*
2: 12 as they *f* like wounded men
2: 19 who *f* from hunger
5: 17 Because of this our hearts are *f*,
Eze 21: 7 every spirit will become *f*
Am 8: 13 will *f* because of thirst.
Jnh 4: 8 on Jonah's head so that he grew *f*.
Lk 21: 26 will *f* from terror, apprehensive

FAINT-HEARTED (HEART)

Dt 20: 3 Do not be *f* or afraid; do not be
20: 8 shall add, ''Is any man afraid or *f*?

FAINTED (FAINT)

Isa 51: 20 Your sons have *f*;

FAINTING (FAINT)

Jer 4: 31 ''Alas! I am *f*;

FAINTS (FAINT)

Ps 84: 2 My soul yearns, even *f*
119: 81 My soul *f* with longing
143: 7 my spirit *f* with longing.

FAIR (FAIRNESS)

Jdg 9: 16 if you have been *f* to Jerub-Baal
Job 26: 13 By his breath the skies became *f*;
Pr 1: 3 doing what is right and just and *f*;
2: 9 and *f*—every good path.
SS 6: 10 *f* as the moon, bright as the sun,
Hos 10: 11 a yoke on her *f* neck.
Mt 16: 2 you say, 'It will be *f* weather,
2Co 6: 13 As a *f* exchange—I speak
Col 4: 1 slaves with what is right and *f*,

FAIR HAVENS

Ac 27: 8 and came to a place called *F*,

FAIRNESS (FAIR)

Pr 29: 14 If a king judges the poor with *f*,

FAITH (FAITHFUL FAITHFULLY FAITHFULNESS FAITHLESS)

Ex 21: 8 because he has broken *f* with her.
Dt 32: 51 both of you broke *f* with me
Jos 22: 16 'How could you break *f*

Jdg 9:16 and in good *f* when you made
9:19 and in good *f* toward Jerub-Baal
1Sa 14:33 "You have broken *f*," he said.
2Ch 20:20 Have *f* in the LORD your God
20:20 have *f* in his prophets and you will
Isa 7:9 If you do not stand firm in your *f*,
26:2 the nation that keeps *f*.
Hab 2:4 but the righteous will live by his *f*—
Mal 2:10 by breaking *f* with one another?
2:11 one another? Judah has broken *f*.
2:14 because you have broken *f* with her
2:15 and do not break *f* with the wife
2:16 in your spirit, and do not break *f*.
Mt 6:30 O you of little *f*? So do not worry,
8:10 anyone in Israel with such great *f*.
8:26 He replied, "You of little *f*,
9:2 When Jesus saw their *f*, he said
9:22 he said, "your *f* has healed you."
9:29 According to your *f* will it be done
13:58 there because of their lack of *f*.
14:31 of little *f*," he said, "why did you
15:28 "Woman, you have great *f*!
16:8 Jesus asked, "You of little *f*,
17:20 if you have *f* as small as a mustard
17:20 "Because you have so little *f*.
21:21 if you have *f* and do not doubt,
24:10 many will turn away from the *f*
Mk 2:5 When Jesus saw their *f*, he said
4:40 still have no *f*?" They were
5:34 "Daughter, your *f* has healed you.
6:6 he was amazed at their lack of *f*.
10:52 said Jesus, "your *f* has healed you."
11:22 "Have *f* in God," Jesus answered.
16:14 he rebuked them for their lack of *f*
Lk 5:20 When Jesus saw their *f*, he said,
7:9 I have not found such great *f*
7:50 the woman, "Your *f* has saved you;
8:25 "Where is your *f*?" he asked his
8:48 "Daughter, your *f* has healed you.
12:28 will he clothe you, O you of little *f*!
17:5 "Increase our *f*!" He replied,
17:6 "If you have *f* as small
17:19 your *f* has made you well."
18:8 will he find *f* on the earth?"
18:42 your sight; your *f* has healed you."
22:32 Simon, that your *f* may not fail.
Jn 2:11 and his disciples put their *f* in him.
7:31 in the crowd put their *f* in him.
8:30 he spoke, many put their *f* in him.
11:45 had seen what Jesus did, put their *f*
12:11 to Jesus and putting their *f* in him.
12:42 they would not confess their *f*
14:12 anyone who has *f* in me will do
Ac 3:16 By *f* in the name of Jesus, this man
3:16 *f* that comes through him that has
6:5 full of *f* and of the Holy Spirit;
6:7 of priests became obedient to the *f*.
11:24 full of the Holy Spirit and *f*,
13:8 to turn the proconsul from the *f*.
14:9 saw that he had *f* to be healed
14:22 them to remain true to the *f*.
14:27 the door of *f* to the Gentiles.
15:9 for he purified their hearts by *f*.
16:5 were strengthened in the *f*
20:21 and have *f* in our Lord Jesus.
24:24 as he spoke about *f* in Christ Jesus.
26:18 those who are sanctified by *f*
27:25 for I have *f* in God that it will
Ro 1:5 to the obedience that comes from *f*.
1:8 because your *f* is being reported all
1:12 encouraged by each other's *f*.
1:17 is by *f* from first to last,
1:17 "The righteous will live by *f*."
3:3 What if some did not have *f*?
3:3 lack of *f* nullify God's faithfulness?
3:22 comes through *f* in Jesus Christ
3:25 a sacrifice of atonement, through *f*
3:26 one who justifies the man who has *f*
3:27 the law? No, but on that of *f*.
3:28 by *f* apart from observing the law.
3:30 through that same *f*.
3:30 will justify the circumcised by *f*
3:31 nullify the law by this *f*? Not at all!
4:5 his *f* is credited as righteousness.
4:9 that Abraham's *f* was credited
4:11 had by *f* while he was still
4:12 of the *f* that our father Abraham
4:13 the righteousness that comes by *f*.
Ro 4:14 *f* has no value and the promise is
4:16 Therefore, the promise comes by *f*,
4:16 are of the *f* of Abraham.
4:19 Without weakening in his *f*,
4:20 but was strengthened in his *f*
5:1 we have been justified through *f*,
5:2 access by *f* into this grace
9:30 a righteousness that is by *f*;
9:32 Because they pursued it not by *f*
10:6 the righteousness that is by *f* says:
10:8 the word of *f* we are proclaiming:
10:17 *f* comes from hearing the message,
11:20 of unbelief, and you stand by *f*.
12:3 measure of *f* God has given you.
12:6 let him use it in proportion to his *f*.
14:1 Accept him whose *f* is weak,
14:2 One man's *f* allows him
14:2 but another man, whose *f* is weak,
14:23 because his eating is not from *f*;
14:23 that does not come from *f* is sin.
1Co 2:5 so that your *f* might not rest
12:9 to another *f* by the same Spirit,
13:2 and if I have a *f* that can move
13:13 And now these three remain: *f*,
15:14 is useless and so is your *f*.
15:17 has not been raised, your *f* is futile;
16:13 stand firm in the *f*; be men
2Co 1:24 Not that we lord it over your *f*,
1:24 because it is by *f* you stand firm.
4:13 With that same spirit of *f* we
5:7 We live by *f*, not by sight.
8:7 in *f*, in speech, in knowledge,
10:15 as your *f* continues to grow,
13:5 to see whether you are in the *f*;
Gal 1:23 now preaching the *f* he once tried
2:16 Jesus that we may be justified by *f*
2:16 but by *f* in Jesus Christ.
2:16 have put our *f* in Christ Jesus that
2:20 I live by *f* in the Son of God,
3:8 would justify the Gentiles by *f*,
3:9 So those who have *f* are blessed
3:9 along with Abraham, the man of *f*.
3:11 "The righteous will live by *f*."
3:12 based on *f*; on the contrary,
3:14 by *f* we might receive the promise
3:22 being given through *f*
3:23 Before this *f* came, we were held
3:23 up until *f* should be revealed.
3:24 that we might be justified by *f*.
3:25 that *f* has come, we are no longer
3:26 of God through *f* in Christ Jesus,
5:5 But by *f* we eagerly await
5:6 that counts is *f* expressing itself
Eph 1:15 ever since I heard about your *f*
2:8 through *f*—and this not
3:12 through *f* in him we may approach
3:17 dwell in your hearts through *f*.
4:5 one Lord, one *f*, one baptism;
4:13 up until we all reach unity in the *f*
6:16 to all this, take up the shield of *f*,
6:23 love with *f* from God the Father
Php 1:25 for your progress and joy in the *f*,
1:27 as one man for the *f* of the gospel
2:17 and service coming from your *f*,
3:9 comes from God and is by *f*.
3:9 that which is through *f* in Christ—
Col 1:4 heard of your *f* in Christ Jesus
1:5 the *f* and love that spring
1:23 continue in your *f*, established
2:5 and how firm your *f* in Christ is.
2:7 in the *f* as you were taught,
2:12 him through your *f* in the power
1Th 1:3 Father your work produced by *f*,
1:8 your *f* in God has become known
3:2 and encourage you in your *f*,
3:5 I sent to find out about your *f*.
3:6 brought good news about your *f*
3:7 about you because of your *f*.
3:10 supply what is lacking in your *f*.
5:8 on *f* and love as a breastplate,
2Th 1:3 because your *f* is growing more
1:4 and *f* in all the persecutions
1:11 and every act prompted by your *f*.
3:2 evil men, for not everyone has *f*.
1Ti 1:2 To Timothy my true son in the *f*:
1:4 than God's work—which is by *f*.
1:5 a good conscience and a sincere *f*.
1:14 along with the *f* and love that are
1Ti 1:19 and so have shipwrecked their *f*.
1:19 on to *f* and a good conscience.
2:7 of the true *f* to the Gentiles.
2:15 if they continue in *f*, love
3:9 of the *f* with a clear conscience.
3:13 assurance in their *f* in Christ Jesus.
4:1 later times some will abandon the *f*
4:6 brought up in the truths of the *f*
4:12 in life, in love, in *f* and in purity.
5:8 he has denied the *f* and is worse
6:10 have wandered from the *f*
6:11 pursue righteousness, godliness, *f*,
6:12 Fight the good fight of the *f*.
6:21 so doing have wandered from the *f*.
2Ti 1:5 been reminded of your sincere *f*,
1:13 with *f* and love in Christ Jesus.
2:18 and they destroy the *f* of some.
2:22 and pursue righteousness, *f*,
3:8 as far as the *f* is concerned,
3:10 my purpose, *f*, patience, love,
3:15 wise for salvation through *f*
4:7 finished the race, I have kept the *f*.
Tit 1:1 Christ for the *f* of God's elect
1:2 a *f* and knowledge resting
1:4 my true son in our common *f*:
1:13 so that they will be sound in the *f*
2:2 self-controlled, and sound in *f*,
3:15 Greet those who love us in the *f*.
Phm :5 because I hear about your *f*
:6 may be active in sharing your *f*,
Heb 4:2 heard did not combine it with *f*.
4:14 firmly to the *f* we profess.
6:1 and of *f* in God, instruction about
6:12 but to imitate those who through *f*
10:22 heart in full assurance of *f*,
10:38 But my righteous one will live by *f*.
11:1 *f* is being sure of what we hope for
11:3 By *f* we understand that
11:4 And by *f* he still speaks, even
11:4 By *f* Abel offered God a better
11:4 By *f* he was commended
11:5 By *f* Enoch was taken from this life
11:6 And without *f* it is impossible
11:7 By his *f* he condemned the world
11:7 By *f* Noah, when warned about
11:7 the righteousness that comes by *f*.
11:8 By *f* Abraham, when called to go
11:9 By *f* he made his home
11:11 By *f* Abraham, even though he was
11:13 living by *f* when they died.
11:17 By *f* Abraham, when God tested
11:20 By *f* Isaac blessed Jacob
11:21 By *f* Jacob, when he was dying,
11:22 By *f* Joseph, when his end was near
11:23 By *f* Moses' parents hid him
11:24 By *f* Moses, when he had grown up
11:27 By *f* he left Egypt, not fearing
11:28 By *f* he kept the Passover
11:29 By *f* the people passed
11:30 By *f* the walls of Jericho fell,
11:31 By *f* the prostitute Rahab,
11:33 through *f* conquered kingdoms,
11:39 were all commended for their *f*,
12:2 the author and perfecter of our *f*,
13:7 way of life and imitate their *f*.
Jas 1:3 of your *f* develops perseverance.
2:5 the eyes of the world to be rich in *f*
2:14 has no deeds? Can such *f* save him?
2:14 if a man claims to have *f*
2:17 In the same way, *f* by itself,
2:18 I will show you my *f* by what I do.
2:18 Show me your *f* without deeds,
2:18 "You have *f*; I have deeds."
2:20 do you want evidence that *f*
2:22 You see that his *f* and his actions
2:22 and his *f* was made complete
2:24 by what he does and not by *f* alone.
2:26 so *f* without deeds is dead.
5:15 in *f* will make the sick person well;
1Pe 1:5 who through *f* are shielded
1:7 These have come so that your *f*—
1:9 you are receiving the goal of your *f*,
1:21 and so your *f* and hope are in God.
5:9 Resist him, standing firm in the *f*,
2Pe 1:1 Jesus Christ have received a *f*
1:5 effort to add to your *f* goodness;
1Jn 5:4 overcome the world, even our *f*.
Jude :3 to contend for the *f* that was once

Jude :20 up in your most holy *f*
Rev 2:13 You did not renounce your *f* in me,
2:19 your love and *f*, your service

FAITHFUL (FAITH)

Nu 12: 7 he is *f* in all my house.
Dt 7: 9 your God is God; he is the *f* God,
32: 4 A *f* God who does no wrong,
1Sa 2:35 I will raise up for myself a *f* priest,
2Sa 20:19 We are the peaceful and *f* in Israel.
22:26 "To the *f* you show yourself *f*,
1Ki 3: 6 because he was *f* to you
2Ch 31:18 were *f* in consecrating themselves.
31:20 and *f* before the LORD his God.
Ne 9: 8 You found his heart *f* to you,
Ps 12: 1 the *f* have vanished
18:25 To the *f* you show yourself *f*,
25:10 of the LORD are loving and *f*
31:23 The LORD preserves the *f*,
33: 4 he is *f* in all he does.
37:28 and will not forsake his *f* ones.
78: 8 whose spirits were not *f* to him.
78:37 they were not *f* to his covenant.
89:19 to your *f* people you said:
89:24 My *f* love will be with him,
89:37 the *f* witness in the sky."
97:10 for he guards the lives of his *f* ones
101: 6 My eyes will be on the *f* in the land,
111: 7 The works of his hands are *f*
145: 13 The LORD is *f* to all his promises
146: 6 the LORD, who remains *f* forever.
Pr 2: 8 and protects the way of his *f* ones.
20: 6 but a *f* man who can find?
27: 6 but *f* are the wounds of a friend.
28:20 A *f* man will be richly blessed,
31:26 and *f* instruction is on her tongue.
Isa 1:21 See how the *f* city has become
1:26 The *F* City."
49: 7 because of the LORD, who is *f*,
55: 3 my *f* love promised to David.
Jer 42: 5 *f* witness against us if we do not act
Eze 43:11 so that they may be *f* to its design
48:11 who were *f* in serving me
Hos 11:12 even against the *f* Holy One.
Zec 8: 8 I will be *f* and righteous to them
Mt 24:45 Who then is the *f* and wise servant,
25:21 'Well done, good and *f* servant!
25:21 You have been *f* with a few things;
25:23 You have been *f* with a few things;
25:23 'Well done, good and *f* servant!
Lk 12:42 then is the *f* and wise manager,
Ro 12:12 patient in affliction, *f* in prayer.
1Co 1: 9 his Son Jesus Christ our Lord, is *f*.
4: 2 been given a trust must prove *f*.
4:17 my son whom I love, who is *f*
10:13 And God is *f*; he will not let you be
2Co 1:18 no"? But as surely as God is *f*,
Eph 1: 1 in Ephesus, the *f* in Christ Jesus:
6:21 the dear brother and *f* servant
Col 1: 2 and *f* brothers in Christ at Colosse:
1: 7 who is a *f* minister of Christ
4: 7 a *f* minister and fellow servant
4: 9 He is coming with Onesimus, our *f*
1Th 5:24 The one who calls you is *f*
2Th 3: 3 the Lord is *f*, and he will strengthen
1Ti 1:12 he considered me *f*, appointing me
5: 9 has been *f* to her husband,
2Ti 2:13 he will remain *f*,
Heb 2:17 and *f* high priest in service to God,
3: 2 He was *f* to the one who appointed
3: 2 as Moses was *f* in all God's house.
3: 5 Moses was *f* as a servant
3: 6 But Christ is *f* as a son
8: 9 because they did not remain *f*
10:23 for he who promised is *f*.
11:11 he considered him *f* who had made
1Pe 4:19 themselves to their *f* Creator
5:12 whom I regard as a *f* brother,
1Jn 1: 9 he is *f* and just and will forgive us
3Jn : 5 you are *f* in what you are doing
Rev 1: 5 who is the *f* witness, the firstborn
2:10 Be *f*, even to the point of death,
2:13 the days of Antipas, my *f* witness,
3:14 the words of the Amen, the *f*
14:12 commandments and remain *f*
17:14 his called, chosen and *f* followers."
19:11 whose rider is called *F* and True.

FAITHFULLY (FAITH)

Dt 11:13 if you *f* obey the commands I am
Jos 2:14 *f* when the LORD gives us the land
1Sa 12:24 and serve him *f* with all your heart;
1Ki 2: 4 and if they walk *f* before me
2Ki 20: 3 how I have walked before you *f*
22: 7 because they are acting *f*."
2Ch 19: 9 must serve *f* and wholeheartedly
31:12 they *f* brought in the contributions,
31:15 and Shecaniah assisted him *f*
32: 1 all that Hezekiah had so *f* done,
34:12 The men did the work *f*.
Ne 9:33 you have acted *f*, while we did
13:14 so *f* done for the house of my God
Isa 38: 3 how I have walked before you *f*
Jer 23:28 one who has my word speak it *f*.
Eze 18: 9 and *f* keeps my laws.
44:15 and who *f* carried out the duties
1Pe 4:10 *f* administering God's grace

FAITHFULNESS (FAITH)

Ge 24:27 not abandoned his kindness and *f*
24:49 if you will show kindness and *f*
32:10 and *f* you have shown your servant.
47:29 you will show me kindness and *f*.
Ex 34: 6 *f*, maintaining love to thousands,
Jos 24:14 the LORD and serve him with all *f*.
1Sa 26:23 man for his righteousness and *f*.
2Sa 2: 6 now show you kindness and *f*,
15:20 May kindness and *f* be with you."
Ps 30: 9 Will it proclaim your *f*?
36: 5 your *f* to the skies.
40:10 I speak of your *f* and salvation.
54: 5 in your *f* destroy them.
57: 3 God sends his love and his *f*.
57:10 your *f* reaches to the skies.
61: 7 appoint your love and *f*
71:22 the harp for your *f*, O my God;
85:10 Love and *f* meet together;
85:11 *F* springs forth from the earth,
86:15 to anger, abounding in love and *f*.
88:11 your *f* in Destruction?
89: 1 mouth I will make your *f* known
89: 2 that you established your *f*
89: 5 your *f* too, in the assembly
89: 8 and your *f* surrounds you.
89:14 love and *f* go before you.
89:33 nor will I ever betray my *f*.
89:49 which in your *f* you swore to David
91: 4 his *f* will be your shield
92: 2 and your *f* at night,
98: 3 and his *f* to the house of Israel;
100: 5 *f* continues through all
108: 4 your *f* reaches to the skies.
111: 8 done in *f* and uprightness.
115: 1 because of your love and *f*.
117: 2 the *f* of the LORD endures forever.
119: 75 and in *f* you have afflicted me.
119: 90 *f* continues through all
138: 2 name for your love and your *f*,
143: 1 in your *f* and righteousness
Pr 3: 3 Let love and *f* never leave you;
14:22 plan what is good find love and *f*.
16: 6 Through love and *f* sin is atoned for
20:28 Love and *f* keep a king safe;
Isa 11: 5 and *f* the sash around his waist.
16: 5 in *f* a man will sit on it—
25: 1 for in perfect *f*
38:18 cannot hope for your *f*.
38:19 about your *f*.
42: 3 In *f* he will bring forth justice;
61: 8 In my *f* I will reward them
La 3:23 great is your *f*.
Hos 2:20 I will betroth you in *f*,
4: 1 "There is no *f*, no love,
Mt 23:23 of the law—justice, mercy and *f*.
Ro 3: 3 lack of faith nullify God's *f*?
Gal 5:22 patience, kindness, goodness, *f*,
3Jn : 3 and tell about your *f* to the truth
Rev 13:10 and *f* on the part of the saints.

FAITHLESS (FAITH)

Ps 78:57 fathers they were disloyal and *f*,
101: 3 The deeds of *f* men I hate;
119:158 I look on the *f* with loathing,
Pr 14:14 The *f* will be fully repaid
Jer 3: 6 you seen what *f* Israel has done?
3: 8 I gave *f* Israel her certificate
3:11 "*F* Israel is more righteous
3:12 *f* Israel,' declares the LORD,
3:14 *f* people," declares the LORD,
3:22 "Return, *f* people;
12: 1 Why do all the *f* live at ease?
Ro 1:31 they are senseless, *f*, heartless,
2Ti 2:13 if we are *f*,

FALCON (FALCON'S FALCONS)

Dt 14:13 any kind of *f*, any kind of raven,

FALCON'S (FALCON)

Job 28: 7 no *f* eye has seen it.

FALCONS (FALCON)

Isa 34:15 there also the *f* will gather,

FALL (FALLEN FALLING FALLS FELL FELLED FELLING)

Ge 2:21 the man to *f* into a deep sleep;
9: 2 and dread of you will *f*
27:13 "My son, let the curse *f* on me.
Ex 9:19 the hail will *f* on every man
9:22 so that hail will *f* all over Egypt—
15:16 terror and dread will *f* upon them.
Lev 26: 7 they will *f* by the sword before you.
26: 8 your enemies will *f* by the sword
26:36 they will *f*, even though no one is
Nu 1:53 Testimony so that wrath will not *f*
14: 3 only to let us *f* by the sword?
14:29 In this desert your bodies will *f*—
14:32 your bodies will *f* in this desert.
14:43 and you will *f* by the sword."
18: 5 so that wrath will not *f*
Dt 28:52 walls in which you trust *f* down.
29:20 in this book will *f* upon him,
31:29 disaster will *f* upon you
32: 2 Let my teaching *f* like rain
Jos 9:20 so that wrath will not *f* on us
Jdg 15:18 and *f* into the hands
1Sa 3:19 none of his words *f* to the ground.
14:45 hair of his head will *f* to the ground,
18:25 was to have David *f* by the hands
26:20 Now do not let my blood *f*
2Sa 3:29 May his blood *f* upon the head
14:11 hair of your son's head will *f*
17:12 and we will *f* on him as dew settles
24:14 Let us *f* into the hands
24:14 but do not let me *f* into the hands
24:17 Let your hand *f* upon me
1Ki 1:52 hair of his head will *f* to the ground;
2Ki 6: 6 "Where did it *f*?" When he showed
9:18 "*F* in behind me."
9:19 to do with peace? *F* in behind me."
1Ch 21:13 Let me *f* into the hands
21:13 but do not let me *f* into the hands
21:17 let your hand *f* upon me
2Ch 34:11 of Judah had allowed to *f* into ruin.
Est 8: 6 bear to see disaster *f* on my people?
Job 13:11 Would not the dread of him *f*
31:22 let my arm *f* from the shoulder,
36:28 abundant showers *f* on mankind.
37: 6 to the snow, '*F* on the earth,'
Ps 10:10 they *f* under his strength.
13: 4 and my foes will rejoice when I *f*.
20: 8 to their knees and *f*,
27: 2 they will stumble and *f*.
35: 8 may they *f* into the pit, to their ruin
37:24 though he stumble, he will not *f*,
38:17 For I am about to *f*,
45: 5 let the nations *f* beneath your feet.
46: 2 and the mountains *f* into the heart
46: 5 God is within her, she will not *f*;
46: 6 Nations are in uproar, kingdoms *f*;
55:22 he will never let the righteous *f*.
69: 9 of those who insult you *f* on me.
82: 7 you will *f* like every other ruler."
91: 7 A thousand may *f* at your side,
106: 26 that he would make them *f*
106: 27 make their descendants *f*
118: 13 I was pushed back and about to *f*,
140: 10 Let burning coals *f* upon them;
141: 10 Let the wicked *f* into their own
145: 14 The LORD upholds all those who *f*
Pr 4:16 till they make someone *f*.
11:28 Whoever trusts in his riches will *f*,
16:18 a haughty spirit before a *f*.

Pr 22:14 is under the LORD's wrath will f
26:27 If a man digs a pit, he will f into it;
28:10 will f into his own trap,
28:18 ways are perverse will suddenly f.
Ecc 9:12 that f unexpectedly upon them.
10:8 Whoever digs a pit may f into it;
Isa 3:25 Your men will f by the sword,
8:14 and a rock that makes them f.
8:15 they will f and be broken,
9:8 it will f on Israel.
10:4 or f among the slain.
10:34 Lebanon will f before the Mighty
13:15 all who are caught will f
22:25 it will be sheared off and will f,
24:18 will f into a pit;
28:13 so that they will go and f backward,
30:25 when the towers f,
31:3 he who is helped will f;
31:8 Assyria will f by a sword that is not
31:9 Their stronghold will f
34:4 all the starry host will f
34:7 And the wild oxen will f with them,
40:7 The grass withers and the flowers f,
40:8 The grass withers and the flowers f,
40:30 and young men stumble and f;
47:11 A calamity will f upon you
51:23 'F prostrate that we may walk
Jer 6:15 So they will f among the fallen;
8:4 " 'When men f down, do they not
8:12 So they will f among the fallen;
13:18 will f from your heads."
19:7 I will make them f by the sword
20:4 your own eyes you will see them f
23:12 and there they will f.
25:27 and f to rise no more
25:34 you will f and be shattered like fine
34:17 'freedom' to f by the sword,
39:18 you will not f by the sword
44:12 they will f by the sword
46:6 they stumble and f.
46:12 both will f down together."
46:16 they will f over each other.
48:16 "The f of Moab is at hand;
48:44 will f into a pit,
49:21 of their f the earth will tremble;
49:26 her young men will f in the streets;
50:15 She surrenders, her towers f,
50:30 her young men will f in the streets;
50:32 arrogant one will stumble and f
51:4 They will f down slain in Babylon,
51:8 Babylon will suddenly f
51:44 And the wall of Babylon will f.
51:49 must f because of Israel's slain,
51:64 And her people will f.' "
La 1:9 Her f was astounding;
Eze 5:12 a third will f by the sword
6:7 Your people will f slain among you,
6:11 for they will f by the sword,
6:12 he that is near will f by the sword,
11:10 You will f by the sword,
13:11 with whitewash that it is going to f.
13:13 of rain will f with destructive fury.
13:21 and they will no longer f prey
17:21 All his fleeing troops will f
23:25 and those of you who are left will f
24:21 left behind will f by the sword.
25:13 to Dedan they will f by the sword.
26:11 and your strong pillars will f
26:15 tremble at the sound of your f,
26:18 tremble on the day of your f;
28:23 The slain will f within her,
29:5 You will f on the open field
30:4 When the slain f in Egypt,
30:5 people of the covenant land will f
30:6 they will f by the sword within her,
30:6 " 'The allies of Egypt will f
30:17 will f by the sword,
30:22 make the sword f from his hand.
30:25 but the arms of Pharaoh will f limp.
31:16 the sound of its f when I brought it
32:12 I will cause your hordes to f
32:20 They will f among those killed
33:12 him to f when he turns from it.
33:27 left in the ruins will f by the sword,
35:8 by the sword will f on your hills
36:15 or cause your nation to f,
38:20 and every wall will f to the ground.
39:4 the mountains of Israel you will f,
Eze 39:5 You will f in the open field,
40:1 year after the f of the city—
44:12 made the house of Israel f into sin,
Da 3:5 you must f down and worship
3:6 Whoever does not f down
3:10 and all kinds of music must f down
3:11 and that whoever does not f down
3:15 if you are ready to f down
11:19 own country but will stumble and f,
11:26 will be swept away, and many will f
11:33 for a time they will f by the sword
11:34 When they f, they will receive
11:41 Many countries will f, but Edom,
Hos 7:7 All their kings f,
7:16 Their leaders will f by the sword
10:8 and to the hills, "F on us!"
13:16 They will f by the sword;
Am 3:5 Does a bird f into a trap
3:14 and f to the ground.
7:17 and daughters will f by the sword.
8:14 they will f,
9:9 but not a kernel will f to the ground
Na 3:12 the figs f into the mouth
3:19 claps his hands at your f,
Hag 2:22 horses and their riders will f,
Mt 7:25 yet it did not f, because it had its
10:29 of them will f to the ground apart
11:6 is the man who does not f away
15:14 man leads a blind man, both will f
15:27 even the dogs eat the crumbs that f
24:29 the stars will f from the sky,
26:31 "This very night you will all f away
26:33 "Even if all f away on account
26:41 and pray so that you will not f
Mk 4:17 of the word, they quickly f away.
13:25 the stars will f from the sky,
14:27 "You will all f away," Jesus told
14:29 "Even if all f away, I will not."
14:38 and pray so that you will not f
Lk 6:39 Will they not both f into a pit?
7:23 is the man who does not f away
8:13 in the time of testing they f away.
10:18 "I saw Satan f like lightning
11:17 a house divided against itself will f.
21:24 They will f by the sword
22:40 "Pray that you will not f
22:46 and pray so that you will not f
23:30 say to the mountains, "F on us!"
Ac 5:15 that at least Peter's shadow might f
27:32 held the lifeboat and let it f away.
28:6 to swell up or suddenly f over dead,
Ro 3:23 and f short of the glory of God,
9:33 and a rock that makes them f,
11:11 as to f beyond recovery?
14:21 that will cause your brother to f.
1Co 8:13 if what I eat causes my brother to f
8:13 so that I will not cause him to f.
10:12 be careful that you don't f!
14:25 So he will f down and worship God
1Th 4:13 ignorant about those who f asleep,
1Ti 3:6 and f under the same judgment
3:7 so that he will not f into disgrace
6:9 want to get rich f into temptation
Heb 4:11 so that no one will f
6:6 if they f away, to be brought back
10:31 thing to f into the hands
1Pe 1:24 the grass withers and the flowers f,
2:8 and a rock that makes them f."
2Pe 1:10 do these things, you will never f,
3:17 and f from your secure position.
Rev 3:9 I will make them come and f
4:10 the twenty-four elders f
6:16 "F on us and hide us from the face

FALLEN (FALL)

Ge 15:17 the sun had set and darkness had f,
Ex 9:18 the worst hailstorm that has ever f
23:5 of someone who hates you f
Lev 19:10 or pick up the grapes that have f.
Dt 22:4 your brother's donkey or his ox f
29:22 will see the calamities that have f
Jos 2:9 that a great fear of you has f on us,
Jdg 3:25 There they saw their lord f
8:10 twenty thousand swordsmen had f.
19:27 f in the doorway of the house,
1Sa 5:3 f on his face on the ground
5:4 f on his face on the ground
20:37 where Jonathan's arrow had f,
1Sa 31:8 his three sons f on Mount Gilboa.
2Sa 1:10 after he had f he could not survive.
1:12 because they had f by the sword.
1:19 How the mighty have f!
1:25 "How the mighty have f in battle!
1:27 "How the mighty have f!
2:23 to the place where Asahel had f
3:38 a great man has f in Israel this day?
2Ki 1:2 Ahaziah had f through the lattice
1:14 fire has f from heaven
2:13 He picked up the cloak that had f
2:14 Then he took the cloak that had f
1Ch 10:8 and his sons f on Mount Gilboa.
2Ch 14:14 of the LORD had f upon them.
29:8 anger of the LORD has f on Judah
29:9 This is why our fathers have f
Ps 9:15 The nations have f
16:6 The boundary lines have f for me
36:12 See how the evildoers lie f—
57:6 but they have f into it themselves.
68:14 it was like snow f on Zalmon.
105:38 dread of Israel had f on them.
Pr 6:3 you have f into your neighbor's
Isa 9:10 "The bricks have f down,
14:12 How you have f from heaven,
21:9 'Babylon has f, has f!
Jer 3:3 and no spring rains have f.
6:15 So they will fall among the f;
8:12 So they will fall among the f;
48:32 The destroyer has f
51:47 and her slain will all lie f within her
51:49 have f because of Babylon.
La 2:21 have f by the sword.
5:16 The crown has f from our head.
Eze 21:15 and the f be many,
31:13 birds of the air settled on the f tree,
32:22 all who have f by the sword.
32:23 the land of the living are slain, f
32:24 of them are slain, f by the sword.
32:27 warriors who have f,
33:21 "The city has f!" Now the evening
Am 5:2 up concerning you: "F is Virgin
9:11 David's f tent.
Mic 7:8 Though I have f, I will rise.
Zec 11:2 O pine tree, for the cedar has f;
Jn 11:11 "Our friend Lazarus has f asleep;
Ac 15:16 and rebuild David's f tent.
Ro 15:3 of those who insult you have f
1Co 11:30 and a number of you have f asleep.
15:6 though some have f asleep.
15:18 who have f asleep in Christ are lost.
15:20 of those who have f asleep.
Gal 5:4 you have f away from grace.
1Th 4:14 with Jesus those who have f asleep
4:15 precede those who have f asleep.
Heb 4:1 of you be found to have f short of it.
Rev 2:5 the height from which you have f!
9:1 I saw a star that had f from the sky
14:8 "F! F is Babylon the Great,
17:10 Five have f, one is, the other has
18:2 "F! F is Babylon the Great!

FALLING (FALL)

Ge 8:2 the rain had stopped f from the sky.
Est 7:8 Haman was f on the couch where
8:3 pleaded with the king, f at his feet
Ps 72:6 He will be like rain f
133:3 were f on Mount Zion.
Isa 3:8 Judah is f;
Mk 15:19 F on their knees, they worshiped
Lk 2:34 This child is destined to cause the f
22:44 drops of blood f to the ground.
Heb 6:7 drinks in the rain often f on it
Jude :24 able to keep you from f

FALLS (FALL)

Ex 21:33 and an ox or a donkey f into it,
Lev 11:32 of them dies and f on something,
11:33 If one of them f into a clay pot,
11:35 one of their carcasses f
11:37 If a carcass f on any seeds that are
11:38 on the seed and a carcass f on it,
16:9 shall bring the goat whose lot f
Nu 24:4 who f prostrate, and whose eyes
24:16 who f prostrate, and whose eyes
33:54 Whatever f to them
Dt 20:20 until the city at war with you f.
22:8 house if someone f from the roof.

2Sa 3: 29 on a crutch or who *f* by the sword
3: 34 one *f* before wicked men.''
Job 4: 13 when deep sleep *f* on men,
9: 24 When a land *f* into the hands
18: 12 disaster is ready for him when he *f*.
33: 15 when deep sleep *f* on men
Ps 7: 15 *f* into the pit he has made.
Pr 11: 14 For lack of guidance a nation *f*,
13: 17 A wicked messenger *f* into trouble,
17: 20 he whose tongue is deceitful *f*
24: 16 a righteous man *f* seven times,
24: 17 Do not gloat when your enemy *f*;
28: 14 he who hardens his heart *f*
Ecc 4: 10 But pity the man who *f*
4: 10 If one *f* down,
11: 3 Whether a tree *f* to the south
11: 3 the place where it *f*, there will it lie.
Isa 24: 20 that it *f*— never to rise again.
Eze 13: 14 When it *f*, you will be destroyed
Mt 12: 11 and it *f* into a pit on the Sabbath,
13: 21 of the word, he quickly *f* away.
17: 15 He often *f* into the fire
21: 44 He who *f* on this stone will be
21: 44 but he on whom it *f* will be crushed
Lk 14: 5 or an ox that *f* into a well
20: 18 Everyone who *f* on that stone will
20: 18 but he on whom it *f* will be crushed
Jn 12: 24 a kernel of wheat *f* to the ground
Ro 14: 4 To his own master he stands or *f*.
Jas 1: 11 its blossom *f* and its beauty is

FALSE (FALSEHOOD FALSELY)

Ex 20: 16 ''You shall not give *f* testimony
23: 1 ''Do not spread *f* reports.
23: 7 Have nothing to do with a *f* charge
Dt 5: 20 ''You shall not give *f* testimony
19: 18 giving *f* testimony
Job 24: 25 not so, who can prove me *f*
36: 4 Be assured that my words are not *f*;
41: 9 Any hope of subduing him is *f*;
Ps 4: 2 you love delusions and seek *f* gods?
24: 4 or swear by what is *f*.
27: 12 for *f* witnesses rise up against me,
35: 20 but devise *f* accusations
40: 4 to those who turn aside to *f* gods.
44: 17 or been *f* to your covenant.
Pr 6: 19 a *f* witness who pours out lies
12: 17 but a *f* witness tells lies.
13: 5 The righteous hate what is *f*,
14: 5 but a *f* witness pours out lies.
14: 25 but a *f* witness is deceitful.
19: 5 A *f* witness will not go unpunished,
19: 9 A *f* witness will not go unpunished,
21: 28 A *f* witness will perish,
25: 18 is the man who gives *f* testimony
Isa 29: 21 and with *f* testimony deprive
41: 29 See, they are all *f*!
44: 25 who foils the signs of *f* prophets
57: 11 that you have been *f* to me,
63: 8 sons who will not be *f* to me'';
Jer 13: 25 and trusted in *f* gods.
14: 14 are prophesying to you *f* visions,
16: 19 possessed nothing but *f* gods,
23: 16 they fill you with *f* hopes.
23: 32 those who prophesy *f* dreams,''
50: 36 A sword against her *f* prophets!
La 2: 14 were *f* and misleading.
2: 14 were *f* and worthless;
Eze 12: 24 For there will be no more *f* visions
13: 6 Their visions are *f* and their
13: 7 Have you not seen *f* visions
13: 8 Because of your *f* words
13: 9 the prophets who see *f* visions
13: 23 you will no longer see *f* visions
21: 23 It will seem like a *f* omen
21: 29 Despite *f* visions concerning you
22: 28 deeds for them by *f* visions
Hos 10: 4 take *f* oaths
Am 2: 4 they have been led astray by *f* gods,
Mic 6: 11 with a bag of *f* weights?
Hab 2: 3 and will not prove *f*.
Zec 10: 2 they tell dreams that are *f*,
Mal 2: 6 and nothing *f* was found on his lips.
Mt 7: 15 ''Watch out for *f* prophets.
15: 19 theft, *f* testimony, slander.
19: 18 not steal, do not give *f* testimony,
24: 11 and many *f* prophets will appear
24: 24 For *f* Christs and *f* prophets will
26: 59 looking for *f* evidence against Jesus
26: 60 many *f* witnesses came forward.
Mk 10: 19 do not give *f* testimony, do not
13: 22 For *f* Christs and *f* prophets will
14: 57 gave this *f* testimony against him:
Lk 6: 26 their fathers treated the *f* prophets.
18: 20 not steal, do not give *f* testimony,
Jn 1: 47 in whom there is nothing *f*.''
7: 18 there is nothing *f* about him.
Ac 6: 13 They produced *f* witnesses,
13: 6 and *f* prophet named Bar-Jesus,
1Co 15: 15 found to be *f* witnesses about God,
2Co 11: 13 For such men are *f* apostles,
11: 26 and in danger from *f* brothers.
Gal 2: 4 some *f* brothers had infiltrated our
Php 1: 18 whether from *f* motives or true,
Col 2: 18 anyone who delights in *f* humility
2: 23 their *f* humility and their harsh
1Ti 1: 3 not to teach *f* doctrines any longer
6: 3 If anyone teaches *f* doctrines
2Pe 2: 1 also *f* prophets among the people,
2: 1 there will be *f* teachers among you.
1Jn 4: 1 many *f* prophets have gone out
Rev 2: 2 but are not, and have found them *f*.
16: 13 out of the mouth of the *f* prophet.
19: 20 with him the *f* prophet who had
20: 10 and the *f* prophet had been thrown.

FALSEHOOD (FALSE)

Job 21: 34 left of your answers but *f*!''
31: 5 ''If I have walked in *f*
Ps 52: 3 *f* rather than speaking the truth.
119: 163 I hate and abhor *f*
Pr 30: 8 Keep *f* and lies far from me;
Isa 28: 15 and *f* our hiding place.''
Ro 3: 7 ''If my *f* enhances God's
Eph 4: 25 each of you must put off *f*
1Jn 4: 6 Spirit of truth and the spirit of *f*.
Rev 22: 15 everyone who loves and practices *f*

FALSELY (FALSE)

Ge 21: 23 before God that you will not deal *f*
Lev 6: 3 if he swears *f*, or if he commits any
6: 5 or whatever it was he swore *f* about
19: 12 '' 'Do not swear *f* by my name
Ps 41: 6 he speaks *f*, while his heart gathers
101: 7 no one who speaks *f*
Jer 5: 2 still they are swearing *f*.''
8: 8 has handled it *f*?
Da 6: 24 the men who had *f* accused Daniel
Zec 5: 3 everyone who swears *f* will be
5: 4 of him who swears *f* by my name.
8: 17 and do not love to swear *f*.
Mt 5: 11 *f* say all kinds of evil against you
Mk 14: 56 Many testified *f* against him,
Lk 3: 14 and don't accuse people *f*—
1Ti 6: 20 ideas of what is *f* called knowledge,

FALTER (FALTERED FALTERING FALTERS)

Pr 24: 10 If you *f* in times of trouble,
Isa 42: 4 he will not *f* or be discouraged

FALTERED (FALTER)

Ps 105: 37 from among their tribes no one *f*.

FALTERING (FALTER)

Ex 6: 12 to me, since I speak with *f* lips?''
6: 30 with *f* lips, why would Pharaoh
Job 4: 4 you have strengthened *f* knees.

FALTERS (FALTER)

Isa 21: 4 My heart *f*,

FAME (FAMOUS)

Dt 26: 19 *f* and honor high above all
Jos 6: 27 his *f* spread throughout the land.
9: 9 of the *f* of the LORD your God.
1Ki 4: 31 his *f* spread to all the surrounding
10: 1 queen of Sheba heard about the *f*
1Ch 14: 17 *f* spread throughout every land,
22: 5 and *f* and splendor in the sight
2Ch 9: 1 of Sheba heard of Solomon's *f*,
26: 8 and his *f* spread as far as the border
26: 15 His *f* spread far and wide,
Isa 66: 19 islands that have not heard of my *f*
Jer 48: 17 all who know her *f*;
Eze 16: 14 your *f* spread among the nations
16: 15 used your *f* to become a prostitute.
Hos 14: 7 and his *f* will be like the wine
Hab 3: 2 LORD, I have heard of your *f*;

FAMILIAR

Ps 139: 3 you are *f* with all my ways.
Isa 53: 3 of sorrows, and *f* with suffering.
Ac 26: 26 The king is *f* with these things,

FAMILIES (FAMILY)

Ge 45: 18 bring your father and your *f* back
Ex 1: 21 he gave them *f* of their own.
6: 14 These were the heads of their *f*:
6: 25 were the heads of the Levite *f*,
12: 21 and select the animals for your *f*
Nu 1: 2 community by their clans and *f*,
1: 18 ancestry by their clans and *f*,
1: 20 to the records of their clans and *f*.
1: 22 to the records of their clans and *f*.
1: 24 to the records of their clans and *f*.
1: 26 to the records of their clans and *f*.
1: 28 to the records of their clans and *f*.
1: 30 to the records of their clans and *f*.
1: 32 to the records of their clans and *f*.
1: 34 to the records of their clans and *f*.
1: 36 to the records of their clans and *f*.
1: 38 to the records of their clans and *f*.
1: 40 to the records of their clans and *f*.
1: 42 to the records of their clans and *f*.
1: 45 were counted according to their *f*.
1: 47 The *f* of the tribe of Levi, however,
2: 32 counted according to their *f*.
3: 15 ''Count the Levites by their *f*
3: 20 Levite clans, according to their *f*.
3: 24 The leader of the *f*
3: 30 The leader of the *f*
3: 35 The leader of the *f*
4: 2 of the Levites by their clans and *f*.
4: 22 also of the Gershonites by their *f*
4: 29 the Merarites by their clans and *f*.
4: 34 the Kohathites by their clans and *f*.
4: 38 counted by their clans and *f*.
4: 40 counted by their clans and *f*,
4: 42 counted by their clans and *f*.
4: 46 the Levites by their clans and *f*.
7: 2 of *f* who were the tribal leaders
26: 2 whole Israelite community by *f*—
34: 14 because the *f* of the tribe of Reuben
36: 1 the heads of the Israelite *f*.
Dt 12: 7 you and your *f* shall eat
Jos 7: 17 of the Zerahites come forward by *f*.
21: 1 heads of the other tribal *f* of Israel
2Sa 15: 22 and the *f* that were with him.
1Ki 8: 1 and the chiefs of the Israelite *f*,
2Ki 10: 13 down to greet the *f* of the king
1Ch 4: 38 Their *f* increased greatly,
5: 13 Their relatives, by *f*, were: Michael
5: 24 These were the heads of their *f*:
5: 24 famous men, and heads of their *f*.
7: 2 and Samuel—heads of their *f*.
7: 7 Jerimoth and Iri, heads of *f*—
7: 9 record listed the heads of *f*
7: 11 sons of Jediael were heads of *f*.
7: 40 of *f*, choice men, brave warriors
8: 6 who were heads of *f* of those living
8: 10 These were his sons, heads of *f*.
8: 13 who were heads of *f* of those living
8: 28 All these were heads of *f*, chiefs
9: 9 All these men were heads of their *f*.
9: 13 heads of *f*, numbered 1,760.
9: 33 were musicians, heads of Levite *f*,
9: 34 All these were heads of Levite *f*,
12: 39 for their *f* had supplied provisions
15: 12 You are the heads of the Levitical *f*
16: 28 to the LORD, O *f* of nations,
23: 9 These were the heads of the *f*
23: 24 descendants of Levi by their *f*—
23: 24 heads of *f* as they were registered
24: 4 of *f* from Eleazar's descendants
24: 4 of *f* from Ithamar's descendants.
24: 6 and the heads of *f* of the priests
24: 30 the Levites, according to their *f*.
24: 31 and the heads of *f* of the priests
24: 31 *f* of the oldest brother were treated
26: 13 according to their *f*, young
26: 21 and who were heads of *f* belonging
26: 26 of *f* who were the commanders
26: 31 the genealogical records of their *f*.

1Ch 26: 32 who were able men and heads of f,
27: 1 heads of f, commanders
29: 6 Then the leaders of f, the officers
2Ch 1: 2 leaders in Israel, the heads of f—
5: 2 and the chiefs of the Israelite f,
17: 14 Their enrollment by f was
19: 8 and heads of Israelite f
23: 2 and the heads of Israelite f
25: 5 according to their f to commanders
31: 17 by their f in the genealogical
35: 4 Prepare yourselves by f
35: 5 of the f of your fellow countrymen,
35: 12 subdivisions of the f of the people
Ezr 2: 59 show that their f were descended
2: 68 of the f gave freewill offerings
4: 2 and to the heads of the f and said,
4: 3 heads of the f of Israel answered,
Ne 4: 13 posting them by f,
7: 5 people for registration by f.
7: 61 show that their f were descended
7: 70 of the f contributed to the work.
7: 71 heads of the f gave to the treasury
8: 13 of all the f, along with the priests
10: 34 when each of our f is to bring
11: 13 who were heads of f—242 men;
12: 12 were the heads of the priestly f:
Ps 22: 27 and all the f of the nations
68: 6 God sets the lonely in f,
96: 7 to the LORD, O f of nations,
107: 41 and increased their f like flocks.
Am 3: 2 chosen of all the f of the earth;

FAMILY (FAMILIES)

Ge 7: 1 into the ark, you and your whole f,
16: 2 perhaps I can build a f through her
19: 32 and preserve our f line
19: 34 him so we can preserve our f line
24: 38 but go to my father's f
24: 40 and from my father's f.
30: 3 that through her I too can build a f
43: 7 closely about ourselves and our f.
46: 27 members of Jacob's f, which went
50: 22 along with all his father's f.
Ex 1: 1 each with his f: Reuben, Simeon,
12: 3 is to take a lamb for his f,
Lev 6: 29 Any male in a priest's f may eat it;
7: 6 Any male in a priest's f may eat it,
20: 5 f and will cut off from their people
22: 10 one outside a priest's f may eat
25: 10 of you is to return to his f property
27: 16 to the LORD part of his f land,
27: 22 which is not part of his f land,
27: 28 whether man or animal or f land—
Nu 1: 4 each the head of his f, is to help you
1: 44 each one representing his f.
2: 2 standard with the banners of his f."
2: 34 each with his clan and f.
3: 1 This is the account of the f
11: 10 the people of every f wailing,
18: 1 and your father's f are to bear
25: 6 to his f a Midianite woman right
25: 14 the leader of a Simeonite f.
25: 15 a tribal chief of a Midianite f.
31: 26 the f heads of the community are
32: 28 to the f heads of the Israelite tribes.
36: 1 The f heads of the clan
Dt 15: 16 because he loves you and your f
15: 20 and your f are to eat them
18: 8 from the sale of f possessions.
25: 5 must not marry outside the f.
25: 9 not build up his brother's f line."
25: 10 as The F of the Unsandaled.
Jos 2: 12 you will show kindness to my f,
2: 18 and all your f into your house.
6: 23 They brought out her entire f
6: 25 with her f and all who belonged
7: 14 takes shall come forward f by f;
7: 14 f that the LORD takes shall come
7: 18 Joshua had his f come forward man
13: 29 to half the f of the descendants
21: 1 f heads of the Levites approached
22: 14 each the head of a f division
Jdg 1: 25 but spared the man and his whole f.
6: 15 and I am the least in my f."
6: 27 But because he was afraid of his f
8: 27 a snare to Gideon and his f.
8: 35 to the f of Jerub-Baal (that is,
9: 16 fair to Jerub-Baal and his f,
Jdg 9: 18 revolted against my father's f,
9: 19 toward Jerub-Baal and his f today,
11: 2 to get any inheritance in our f,"
16: 31 and his father's whole f went
18: 25 you and your f will lose your lives."
Ru 4: 10 will not disappear from among his f
4: 12 may your f be like that of Perez,
4: 18 This, then, is the f line of Perez:
1Sa 1: 21 up with all his f to offer the annual
2: 31 will not be an old man in your f line
2: 32 in your f line there will never be
2: 36 left in your f line will come
3: 12 everything I spoke against his f—
3: 13 him that I would judge his f forever
9: 20 if not to you and all your father's f
17: 25 and will exempt his father's f
18: 18 what is my f or my father's clan
20: 15 cut off your kindness from my f—
20: 29 our f is observing a sacrifice
22: 11 of Ahitub and his father's whole f,
22: 15 your servant or any of his father's f,
22: 16 you and your father's whole f."
22: 22 the death of your father's whole f.
24: 21 name from my father's f."
27: 3 Each man had his f with him,
2Sa 2: 3 each with his f, and they settled
3: 8 of your father Saul and to his f
7: 18 LORD, and what is my f,
9: 9 that belonged to Saul and his f.
14: 9 rest on me and on my father's f,
16: 5 as Saul's f came out from there.
21: 4 or gold from Saul or his f,
24: 17 fall upon me and my f."
1Ki 14: 14 cut off the f of Jeroboam.
15: 29 he killed Jeroboam's whole f.
16: 11 he killed off Baasha's whole f.
16: 12 So Zimri destroyed the whole f
17: 15 and for the woman and her f.
18: 18 "But you and your father's f have.
2Ki 8: 1 "Go away with your f
8: 2 She and her f went away
8: 27 related by marriage to Ahab's f.
10: 17 all who were left there of Ahab's f;
11: 1 to destroy the whole royal f.
1Ch 5: 15 the son of Guni, was head of their f.
7: 4 According to their f genealogy,
7: 23 there had been misfortune in his f.
9: 19 from his f (the Korahites) were
12: 27 leader of the f of Aaron, with 3,700
12: 28 with 22 officers from his f;
13: 14 remained with the f of Obed-Edom
16: 43 David returned home to bless his f.
17: 16 O LORD God, and what is my f,
21: 17 fall upon me and my f,
23: 11 as one f with one assignment.
24: 6 one f being taken from Eleazar
26: 6 who were leaders in their father's f
27: 15 from the f of Othniel.
28: 4 me from my whole f to be king
28: 4 the house of Judah he chose my f,
2Ch 22: 10 to destroy the whole royal f
26: 12 The total number of f leaders
31: 10 from the f of Zadok, answered,
Ezr 1: 5 Then the f heads of Judah
2: 36 (through the f of Jeshua) 973
2: 62 These searched for their f records,
3: 12 priests and Levites and f heads,
8: 1 These are the f heads and those
8: 29 the Levites and the f heads of Israel
10: 16 one from each f division,
10: 16 selected men who were f heads,
Ne 7: 39 (through the f of Jeshua) 973
7: 64 These searched for their f records,
12: 12 of Seraiah's f, Meraiah;
12: 22 The f heads of the Levites
12: 23 f heads among the descendants
Est 2: 10 her nationality and f background,
2: 20 had kept secret her f background
4: 14 you and your father's f will perish.
8: 6 to see the destruction of my f?"
9: 28 in every generation by every f,
Job 21: 21 does he care about the f he leaves
32: 2 son of Barakel the Buzite, of the f
Pr 11: 29 on his f will inherit only wind,
15: 27 greedy man brings trouble to his f,
27: 27 milk to feed you and your f
31: 15 she provides food for her f
Isa 22: 24 the glory of his f will hang on him:
Jer 12: 6 Your brothers, your own f—
35: 2 to the Recabite f and invite them
35: 3 the whole f of the Recabites.
35: 5 before the men of the Recabite f
35: 18 said to the f of the Recabites,
38: 17 down; you and your f will live.
Eze 17: 13 he took a member of the royal f
43: 19 who are Levites, of the f of Zadok,
Da 1: 3 of the Israelites from the royal f
11: 7 "One from her f line will arise
Am 3: 1 against the whole f I brought up out
Mk 3: 21 When his f heard about this,
5: 19 to your f and tell them how much
Lk 9: 61 go back and say good-by to my f."
12: 52 in one f divided against each other,
Jn 7: 42 the Christ will come from David's f
8: 35 has no permanent place in the f,
Ac 4: 6 the other men of the high priest's f.
7: 13 Pharaoh learned about Joseph's f.
7: 14 for his father Jacob and his whole f,
10: 2 He and all his f were devout
16: 33 and all his f were baptized.
16: 34 and the whole f was filled with joy,
Gal 6: 10 belong to the f of believers.
Eph 3: 15 from whom his whole f in heaven
1Ti 3: 4 He must manage his own f well
3: 5 how to manage his own f,
5: 4 practice by caring for their own f
5: 8 and especially for his immediate f,
5: 16 is a believer has widows in her f,
Heb 2: 11 are made holy are of the same f.
11: 7 in holy fear built an ark to save his f
1Pe 4: 17 to begin with the f of God;

FAMINE (FAMINES)

Ge 12: 10 Now there was a f in the land,
12: 10 for a while because the f was severe
26: 1 Now there was a f in the land—
26: 1 besides the earlier f
41: 27 wind: They are seven years of f.
41: 30 and the f will ravage the land.
41: 30 seven years of f will follow them.
41: 31 the f that follows it will be so severe
41: 36 may not be ruined by the f."
41: 36 years of f that will come
41: 50 Before the years of f came,
41: 54 There was f in all the other lands,
41: 54 and the seven years of f began,
41: 55 When all Egypt began to feel the f,
41: 56 When the f had spread
41: 56 for the f was severe
41: 57 the f was severe in all the world.
42: 5 for the f was in the land of Canaan
43: 1 the f was still severe in the land.
45: 6 For two years now there has been f
45: 11 five years of f are still to come.
47: 4 because the f is severe in Canaan
47: 13 region because the f was severe;
47: 13 wasted away because of the f.
47: 20 the f was too severe for them.
Dt 32: 24 I will send wasting f against them,
Ru 1: 1 the judges ruled, there was a f
2Sa 21: 1 there was a f for three successive
24: 13 come upon you three years of f
1Ki 8: 37 When f or plague comes to the land
18: 2 Now the f was severe in Samaria,
2Ki 4: 38 and there was a f in that region.
6: 25 There was a great f in the city;
7: 4 go into the city'—the f is there,
8: 1 because the LORD has decreed a f
25: 3 day of the ⌊fourth⌋ month the f
1Ch 21: 12 'Take your choice: three years of f,
2Ch 6: 28 When f or plague comes to the land
20: 9 sword of judgment, or plague or f,
Ne 5: 3 our homes to get grain during the f
Job 5: 20 In f he will ransom you from death,
5: 22 You will laugh at destruction and f
Ps 33: 19 and keep them alive in f.
37: 19 in days of f they will enjoy plenty.
105: 16 He called down f on the land
Isa 14: 30 But your root I will destroy by f;
51: 19 ruin and destruction, f and sword
Jer 5: 12 we will never see sword or f.
11: 22 their sons and daughters by f.
14: 12 will destroy them with the sword, f
14: 13 will not see the sword or suffer f.
14: 15 'No sword or f will touch this land.'
14: 15 will perish by sword and f.

Jer 14: 16 of Jerusalem because of the *f*
14: 18 I see the ravages of *f*.
16: 4 They will perish by sword and *f*,
18: 21 So give their children over to *f*;
21: 7 and *f*, to Nebuchadnezzar king
21: 9 in this city will die by the sword, *f*
24: 10 *f* and plague against them
27: 8 *f* and plague, declares the LORD,
27: 13 *f* and plague with which the LORD
29: 17 *f* and plague against them
29: 18 *f* and plague and will make them
32: 24 Because of the sword, *f* and plague,
32: 36 *f* and plague it will be handed
34: 17 to fall by the sword, plague and *f*.
38: 2 in this city will die by the sword, *f*
42: 16 and the *f* you dread will follow you
42: 17 settle there will die by the sword, *f*
42: 22 *f* and plague in the place where you
44: 12 fall by the sword or die from *f*.
44: 12 they will die by sword or *f*.
44: 13 *f* and plague, as I punished
44: 18 have been perishing by sword and *f*
44: 27 and *f* until they are all destroyed.
52: 6 day of the fourth month the *f*
La 4: 9 off than those who die of *f*;
Eze 5: 12 or perish by *f* inside you;
5: 16 I will bring more and more *f*
5: 16 and destructive arrows of *f*,
5: 17 I will send *f* and wild beasts
6: 11 for they will fall by the sword, *f*
6: 12 survives and is spared will die of *f*.
7: 15 in the city will be devoured by *f*
7: 15 inside are plague and *f*;
12: 16 a few of them from the sword, *f*
14: 13 and send *f* upon it and kill its men
14: 21 sword and *f* and wild beasts
34: 29 they will no longer be victims of *f*
36: 29 and will not bring *f* upon you.
36: 30 among the nations because of *f*.
Am 8: 11 but a *f* of hearing the words
8: 11 not a *f* of food or a thirst for water,
8: 11 "when I will send a *f*
Lk 4: 25 and there was a severe *f*
15: 14 there was a severe *f*
Ac 7: 11 "Then a *f* struck all Egypt
11: 28 that a severe *f* would spread
Ro 8: 35 or persecution or *f* or nakedness
Rev 6: 8 *f* and plague, and by the wild beasts
18: 8 death, mourning and *f*.

FAMINES (FAMINE)

Mt 24: 7 There will be *f* and earthquakes
Mk 13: 8 in various places, and *f*.
Lk 21: 11 *f* and pestilences in various places,

FAMISHED

Ge 25: 29 came in from the open country, *f*.
25: 30 I'm *f*!" (That is why he was
Isa 8: 21 when they are *f*, they will become

FAMOUS (FAME)

Ru 4: 11 in Ephratah and be *f* in Bethlehem.
4: 14 May he become *f* throughout Israel
2Sa 8: 13 David became *f* after he returned
23: 18 and so he became as *f* as the Three.
23: 22 as *f* as the three mighty men.
1Ki 1: 47 God make Solomon's name more *f*
1Ch 5: 24 They were brave warriors, *f* men,
11: 20 and so he became as *f* as the Three.
11: 24 as *f* as the three mighty men.
12: 30 brave warriors, *f* in their own clans
Isa 66: 19 and Lydians (*f* as archers),

FAN (FANS)

2Ti 1: 6 you to *f* into flame the gift of God,

FANGS

Dt 32: 24 against them the *f* of wild beasts,
Job 20: 16 the *f* of an adder will kill him.
29: 17 I broke the *f* of the wicked
Ps 58: 6 O LORD, the *f* of the lions!
Joel 1: 6 the *f* of a lioness.

FANS (FAN)

Isa 54: 16 who *f* the coals into flame

FANTASIES

Ps 73: 20 you will despise them as *f*.

Pr 12: 11 but he who chases *f* lacks judgment
28: 19 one who chases *f* will have his fill

FARE (FARED)

Isa 55: 2 soul will delight in the richest of *f*.
Jnh 1: 3 After paying the *f*, he went aboard

FARED (FARE)

Ge 30: 29 and how your livestock has *f*
Isa 10: 9 'Has not Calno *f* like Carchemish?

FAREWELL

Ac 15: 29 *F*.

FARM (FARMED FARMER FARMERS)

2Sa 9: 10 and your servants are to *f* the land
2Ch 31: 19 who lived on the *f* lands
Eze 48: 19 from the city who *f* it will come

FARMED (FARM)

1Ch 27: 26 of the field workers who *f* the land.
Heb 6: 7 whom it is *f* receives the blessing

FARMER (FARM)

Isa 28: 24 When a *f* plows for planting,
Jer 51: 23 with you I shatter *f* and oxen,
Zec 13: 5 I am a *f*; the land has been my
Mt 13: 3 "A *f* went out to sow his seed.
Mk 4: 3 A *f* went out to sow his seed.
4: 14 any parable? The *f* sows the word.
Lk 8: 5 "A *f* went out to sow his seed.
2Ti 2: 6 hardworking *f* should be the first
Jas 5: 7 See how the *f* waits for the land

FARMERS (FARM)

Jer 14: 4 the *f* are dismayed
31: 5 the *f* will plant them
31: 24 *f* and those who move about
Joel 1: 11 Despair, you *f*,
Am 5: 16 The *f* will be summoned to weep
Mt 21: 33 he rented the vineyard to some *f*
Mk 12: 1 he rented the vineyard to some *f*
Lk 20: 9 rented it to some *f* and went away

FASHION (FASHIONED FASHIONING FASHIONS)

Ex 28: 15 "*F* a breastpiece for making

FASHIONED (FASHION FASHIONING FASHIONS)

Ex 39: 8 They *f* the breastpiece—the work
2Ki 19: 18 and stone, *f* by men's hands.
Isa 37: 19 and stone, *f* by human hands.
45: 18 he who *f* and made the earth,
Hos 13: 2 cleverly *f* images,

FASHIONING (FASHION FASHIONED)

Ex 32: 4 in the shape of a calf, *f* it with a tool

FASHIONS (FASHION FASHIONED)

Job 15: 35 their womb *f* deceit."
Isa 40: 19 and *f* silver chains for it.
44: 15 But he also *f* a god and worships it;

FAST (FASTED FASTING FASTS)

Dt 4: 4 but all of you who held *f*
10: 20 Hold *f* to him and take your oaths
11: 22 in all his ways and to hold *f* to him
13: 4 serve him and hold *f* to him.
30: 20 to his voice, and hold *f* to him.
Jos 22: 5 to hold *f* to him and to serve him
23: 8 to hold *f* to the LORD your God,
Jdg 4: 21 quietly to him while he lay *f* asleep,
2Sa 12: 23 why should I *f*? Can I bring him
1Ki 11: 2 Solomon held *f* to them in love.
21: 12 They proclaimed a *f* and seated
2Ki 18: 6 He held *f* to the LORD
2Ch 20: 3 and he proclaimed a *f* for all Judah.
Ezr 8: 21 the Ahava Canal, I proclaimed a *f*,
Est 4: 16 I and my maids will *f* as you do.
4: 16 are in Susa, and *f* for me.
8: 10 who rode *f* horses especially bred
Job 18: 9 a snare holds him *f*.
36: 8 held *f* by cords of affliction,
41: 17 They are joined *f* to one another;
Ps 69: 10 When I weep and *f*,
119: 31 I hold *f* to your statutes, O LORD;
139: 10 your right hand will hold me *f*.
Pr 5: 22 the cords of his sin hold him *f*.
Isa 56: 2 the man who holds it *f*,

Isa 56: 4 and hold *f* to my covenant—
56: 6 and who hold *f* to my covenant—
58: 4 You cannot *f* as you do today
58: 5 Is that what you call a *f*,
58: 5 Is this the kind of *f* I have chosen,
Jer 14: 12 Although they *f*, I will not listen
50: 33 All their captors hold them *f*,
Joel 1: 14 Declare a holy *f*;
2: 15 declare a holy *f*,
Jnh 3: 5 They declared a *f*, and all of them,
Zec 7: 3 "Should I mourn and *f*
Mt 6: 16 "When you *f*, do not look somber
6: 17 when you *f*, put oil on your head
9: 14 but your disciples do not *f*?"
9: 14 is it that we and the Pharisees *f*,
9: 15 taken from them; then they will *f*.
Mk 2: 19 of the bridegroom *f* while he is
2: 20 and on that day they will *f*.
Lk 5: 33 "John's disciples often *f* and pray,
5: 34 of the bridegroom *f* while he is
5: 35 from them; in those days they will *f*
18: 12 I *f* twice a week and give a tenth
Ac 27: 9 because by now it was after the *F*.
27: 41 bow stuck *f* and would not move,
1Pe 5: 12 Stand *f* in it.

FASTED (FAST)

Jdg 20: 26 They *f* that day until evening
1Sa 7: 6 On that day they *f* and there they
31: 13 at Jabesh, and they *f* seven days.
2Sa 1: 12 and wept and *f* till evening for Saul
12: 16 He *f* and went into his house
12: 21 While the child was alive, you *f*
12: 22 "While the child was still alive, I *f*
1Ki 21: 27 put on sackcloth and *f*.
1Ch 10: 12 in Jabesh, and they *f* seven days.
Ezr 8: 23 we *f* and petitioned our God about
Ne 1: 4 For some days I mourned and *f*
Isa 58: 3 'Why have we *f*,' they say,
Zec 7: 5 was it really for me that you *f*?
7: 5 'When you *f* and mourned
Ac 13: 3 So after they had *f* and prayed,

FASTEN (FASTENED FASTENS)

Ex 25: 12 for it and *f* them to its four feet,
25: 26 and *f* them to the four corners,
26: 6 use them to *f* the curtains together
26: 11 in the loops to *f* the tent together
28: 12 and *f* them on the shoulder pieces
28: 23 and *f* them to two corners
28: 24 *F* the two gold chains to the rings
28: 37 *F* a blue cord to it to attach it
29: 5 *F* the ephod on him
36: 13 and used them to *f* the two sets
36: 18 clasps to *f* the tent together
Job 13: 27 You *f* my feet in shackles;
Pr 6: 21 *f* them around your neck.
Isa 22: 21 and *f* your sash around him
Jer 10: 4 they *f* it with hammer and nails

FASTENED (FASTEN)

Ex 28: 7 to two of its corners, so it can be *f*.
37: 3 for it and *f* them to its four feet,
37: 13 and *f* them to the four corners,
39: 4 to two of its corners, so it could be *f*
39: 7 they *f* them on the shoulder pieces
39: 16 and *f* the rings to two of the corners
39: 17 They *f* the two gold chains
39: 31 they *f* a blue cord to it to attach it
Lev 8: 7 so it was *f* on him.
Nu 19: 15 without a lid *f* on it will be unclean.
Jdg 15: 4 He then *f* a torch to every pair
1Sa 17: 39 David *f* on his sword over the tunic
31: 10 and *f* his body to the wall of Beth
Est 1: 6 *f* with cords of white linen
Eze 24: 17 Keep your turban *f* and your
Lk 4: 20 in the synagogue were *f* on him,
Jn 19: 19 Pilate had a notice prepared and *f*
Ac 16: 24 and *f* their feet in the stocks.
28: 3 out by the heat, *f* itself on his hand.

FASTENS (FASTEN)

Job 16: 9 my opponent *f* on me his piercing
33: 11 He *f* my feet in shackles;

FASTING (FAST)

1Ki 21: 9 a day of *f* and seat Naboth
Ne 9: 1 *f* and wearing sackcloth

Est 4: 3 with *f*, weeping and wailing.
9: 31 in regard to their times of *f*
Ps 35: 13 and humbled myself with *f*.
109: 24 My knees give way from *f*;
Isa 58: 3 "Yet on the day of your *f*, you do
58: 4 Your *f* ends in quarreling and strife
58: 6 the kind of *f* I have chosen:
Jer 36: 6 house of the LORD on a day of *f*
36: 9 a time of *f* before the LORD was
Da 9: 3 in *f*, and in sackcloth and ashes.
Joel 2: 12 with *f* and weeping and mourning."
Mt 4: 2 After *f* forty days and forty nights,
6: 16 faces to show men they are *f*.
6: 18 obvious to men that you are *f*,
Mk 2: 18 disciples and the Pharisees were *f*.
2: 18 the disciples of the Pharisees are *f*,
Lk 2: 37 but worshiped night and day, *f*
Ac 13: 2 were worshiping the Lord and *f*,
14: 23 and *f*, committed them to the Lord

FASTS (FAST)

Zec 8: 19 the LORD Almighty says: "The *f*

FAT (FATTENED FATTENING)

Ge 4: 4 Abel brought *f* portions from some
41: 2 *f*, and they grazed among the reeds
41: 4 gaunt ate up the seven sleek, *f* cows
41: 18 *f* and sleek, and they grazed
41: 20 ate up the seven *f* cows that came
45: 18 you can enjoy the *f* of the land.'
Ex 23: 18 *f* of my festival offerings must not
29: 13 kidneys with the *f* around them,
29: 13 take all the *f* around the inner parts
29: 22 kidneys with the *f* around them,
29: 22 the *f* around the inner parts,
29: 22 "Take from this ram the *f*, the *f* tail,
Lev 1: 8 including the head and the *f*,
1: 12 including the head and the *f*,
3: 3 all the *f* that covers the inner parts
3: 4 kidneys with the *f* around them
3: 9 all the *f* that covers the inner parts
3: 9 its *f*, the entire *f* tail cut off close
3: 10 kidneys with the *f* around them
3: 14 all the *f* that covers the inner parts
3: 15 both kidneys with the *f* on them
3: 16 All the *f* is the LORD's.
3: 17 You must not eat any *f*
4: 8 He shall remove all the *f*
4: 8 the *f* that covers the inner parts
4: 9 both kidneys with the *f* on them
4: 10 as the *f* is removed from the cow
4: 19 He shall remove all the *f* from it
4: 26 He shall burn all the *f* on the altar
4: 26 as he burned the *f* of the fellowship
4: 31 He shall remove all the *f*, just
4: 31 *f* is removed from the fellowship
4: 35 He shall remove all the *f*, just
4: 35 as the *f* is removed from the lamb
6: 12 and burn the *f* of the fellowship
7: 3 All its *f* shall be offered: the *f* tail
7: 3 the *f* that covers the inner parts,
7: 4 kidneys with the *f* around them
7: 23 'Do not eat any of the *f* of cattle,
7: 24 The *f* of an animal found dead
7: 25 Anyone who eats the *f* of an animal
7: 30 is to bring the *f*, together
7: 31 The priest shall burn the *f*
7: 33 the *f* of the fellowship offering shall
8: 16 and both kidneys and their *f*,
8: 16 took all the *f* around the inner parts
8: 20 the head, the pieces and the *f*.
8: 25 He took the *f*, the *f* tail, all the *f*
8: 25 both kidneys and their *f*
8: 26 he put these on the *f* portions
9: 10 On the altar he burned the *f*,
9: 19 But the *f* portions of the cow
9: 19 of the cow and the ram—the *f* tail,
9: 19 the layer of *f*, the kidneys
9: 20 and then Aaron burned the *f*
9: 24 and the *f* portions on the altar.
10: 15 brought with the *f* portions
16: 25 also burn the *f* of the sin offering
17: 6 and burn the *f* as an aroma pleasing
Nu 18: 17 burn their *f* as an offering made
Dt 32: 15 Jeshurun grew *f* and kicked;
32: 38 the gods who ate the *f*
Jdg 3: 17 of Moab, who was a very *f* man.
3: 22 and the *f* closed in over it.
1Sa 2: 15 But even before the *f* was burned,
2: 16 "Let the *f* be burned up first,
15: 9 *f* calves and lambs—everything
15: 22 to heed is better than the *f* of rams.
1Ki 8: 64 the *f* of the fellowship offerings,
8: 64 the *f* of the fellowship offerings.
2Ch 7: 7 grain offerings and the *f* portions.
7: 7 the *f* of the fellowship offerings,
29: 35 together with the *f*
35: 14 and the *f* portions until nightfall.
Job 15: 27 "Though his face is covered with *f*
Ps 66: 15 I will sacrifice *f* animals to you
Isa 1: 11 and the *f* of fattened animals;
10: 27 because you have grown so *f*.
17: 4 the *f* of his body will waste away.
34: 6 it is covered with *f*—
34: 6 *f* from the kidneys of rams.
34: 7 and the dust will be soaked with *f*.
43: 24 on me the *f* of your sacrifices.
Jer 5: 28 and have grown *f* and sleek.
Eze 34: 20 judge between the *f* sheep
39: 19 you will eat *f* till you are glutted
44: 7 *f* and blood, and you broke my
44: 15 before me to offer sacrifices of *f*

FATAL

Jer 42: 20 today that you made a *f* mistake
Na 3: 19 your injury is *f*.
Rev 13: 3 but the *f* wound had been healed.
13: 3 seemed to have had a *f* wound,
13: 12 whose *f* wound had been healed.

FATE

Est 7: 7 the king had already decided his *f*,
Job 12: 5 *f* of those whose feet are slipping.
18: 20 of the west are appalled at his *f*;
20: 29 Such is the *f* God allots the wicked,
21: 17 the *f* God allots in his anger?
27: 13 "Here is the *f* God allots
27: 14 his children, their *f* is the sword;
Ps 49: 13 This is the *f* of those who trust
Ecc 2: 14 that the same *f* overtakes them
2: 15 "The *f* of the fool will overtake me
3: 19 Man's *f* is like that of the animals;
3: 19 the same *f* awaits them both:
Isa 14: 16 they ponder your *f*:

FATHER (FATHER-IN-LAW FATHER'S FATHERED FATHERLESS FATHERS FATHERS' FOREFATHER FOREFATHER'S FOREFATHERS GRANDFATHER GRANDFATHER'S)

Ge 2: 24 this reason a man will leave his *f*
4: 18 Mehujael was the *f* of Methushael,
4: 18 Methushael was the *f* of Lamech.
4: 18 and Irad was the *f* of Mehujael,
4: 20 he was the *f* of those who live
4: 21 he was the *f* of all who play
5: 6 he became the *f* of Enosh.
5: 7 And after he became the *f* of Enosh
5: 9 he became the *f* of Kenan.
5: 10 after he became the *f* of Kenan,
5: 12 he became the *f* of Mahalalel.
5: 13 after he became the *f* of Mahalalel,
5: 15 had lived 65 years, he became the *f*
5: 16 And after he became the *f* of Jared,
5: 18 he became the *f* of Enoch.
5: 19 after he became the *f* of Enoch,
5: 21 he became the *f* of Methuselah.
5: 22 And after he became the *f*
5: 25 he became the *f* of Lamech.
5: 26 after he became the *f* of Lamech,
5: 32 he became the *f* of Shem, Ham
9: 18 (Ham was the *f* of Canaan.)
9: 22 the *f* of Canaan, saw his father's
10: 8 Cush was the *f* of Nimrod,
10: 13 Mizraim was the *f* of the Ludites,
10: 15 Canaan was the *f* of Sidon his
10: 24 Arphaxad was the *f* of Shelah,
10: 24 of Shelah, and Shelah the *f* of Eber.
10: 26 Joktan was the *f* of Almodad,
11: 10 he became the *f* of Arphaxad.
11: 11 after he became the *f* of Arphaxad,
11: 12 he became the *f* of Shelah.
11: 13 after he became the *f* of Shelah,
11: 14 had lived 30 years, he became the *f*
11: 15 And after he became the *f* of Eber,
11: 16 had lived 34 years, he became the *f*
Ge 11: 17 And after he became the *f* of Peleg,
11: 18 had lived 30 years, he became the *f*
11: 19 And after he became the *f* of Reu,
11: 20 had lived 32 years, he became the *f*
11: 21 And after he became the *f* of Serug,
11: 22 he became the *f* of Nahor.
11: 23 after he became the *f* of Nahor,
11: 24 had lived 29 years, he became the *f*
11: 25 And after he became the *f* of Terah
11: 26 he became the *f* of Abram,
11: 27 And Haran became the *f* of Lot.
11: 27 Terah became the *f* of Abram,
11: 28 While his *f* Terah was still alive,
11: 29 the *f* of both Milcah and Iscah.
17: 4 You will be the *f* of many nations.
17: 5 for I have made you a *f*
17: 20 He will be the *f* of twelve rulers,
19: 31 said to the younger, "Our *f* is old,
19: 32 Let's get our *f* to drink wine
19: 32 our family line through our *f*."
19: 33 That night they got their *f*
19: 34 our family line through our *f*."
19: 34 "Last night I lay with my *f*.
19: 35 they got their *f* to drink wine that
19: 36 became pregnant by their *f*.
19: 37 he is the *f* of the Moabites of today.
19: 38 he is the *f* of the Ammonites
20: 12 the daughter of my *f* though not
22: 7 and said to his *f* Abraham,
22: 7 "*F?*" "Yes, my son?" Abraham
22: 21 Kemuel (the *f* of Aram), Kesed,
22: 23 Bethuel became the *f* of Rebekah.
25: 3 Jokshan was the *f* of Sheba
25: 19 Abraham became the *f* of Isaac,
26: 3 swore to your *f* Abraham.
26: 15 dug in the time of his *f* Abraham,
26: 18 dug in the time of his *f* Abraham,
26: 18 same names his *f* had given them.
26: 24 "I am the God of your *f* Abraham.
27: 6 I overheard your *f* say
27: 9 prepare some tasty food for your *f*,
27: 10 Then take it to your *f* to eat,
27: 12 if my *f* touches me? I would appear
27: 14 food, just the way his *f* liked it.
27: 18 He went to his *f* and said, "My *f*."
27: 19 to his *f*, "I am Esau your firstborn.
27: 22 Jacob went close to his *f* Isaac,
27: 26 Then his *f* Isaac said to him,
27: 31 Then he said to him, "My *f*,
27: 31 tasty food and brought it to his *f*.
27: 32 His *f* Isaac asked him, "Who are
27: 34 and bitter cry and said to his *f*,
27: 34 me too, my *f*!" But he said,
27: 38 my son?" Esau said to his *f*,
27: 38 my *f*? Bless me too, my *f*!"
27: 39 His *f* Isaac answered him,
27: 41 days of mourning for my *f* are near;
27: 41 of the blessing his *f* had given him.
28: 2 house of your mother's *f* Bethuel.
28: 7 and that Jacob had obeyed his *f*
28: 8 women were to his *f* Isaac;
28: 13 the God of your *f* Abraham
29: 12 So she ran and told her *f*.
29: 12 that he was a relative of her *f*
31: 1 from what belonged to our *f*."
31: 1 has taken everything our *f* owned
31: 5 the God of my *f* has been with me.
31: 6 for your *f* with all my strength,
31: 7 yet your *f* has cheated me
31: 16 away from our *f* belongs to us
31: 18 to go to his *f* Isaac
31: 29 the God of your *f* said to me,
31: 35 said to her *f*, "Don't be angry,
31: 42 God of my *f*, the God of Abraham
31: 53 God of their *f*, judge between us."
31: 53 the name of the Fear of his *f* Isaac.
32: 9 God of my *f* Isaac, O LORD,
32: 9 "O God of my *f* Abraham,
33: 19 sons of Hamor, the *f* of Shechem,
34: 4 And Shechem said to his *f* Hamor,
34: 6 Then Shechem's *f* Hamor went out
34: 11 Then Shechem said to Dinah's *f*
34: 13 to Shechem and his *f* Hamor.
35: 18 But his *f* named him Benjamin.
35: 27 home to his *f* Isaac in Mamre,
36: 9 of Esau the *f* of the Edomites
36: 24 the donkeys of his *f* Zibeon.
36: 43 This was Esau, the *f*

Ge 37: 1 in the land where his *f* had stayed,
37: 2 and he brought their *f* a bad report
37: 4 saw that their *f* loved him more
37: 10 When he told his *f* as well
37: 10 his *f* rebuked him and said,
37: 11 but his *f* kept the matter in mind.
37: 22 and take him back to his *f*.
37: 32 the ornamented robe back to their *f*
37: 35 So his *f* wept for him.
42: 13 The youngest is now with our *f*,
42: 29 came to their *f* Jacob in the land
42: 32 now with our *f* in Canaan.'
42: 32 were twelve brothers, sons of one *f*.
42: 35 and their *f* saw the money pouches,
42: 36 Their *f* Jacob said to them,
42: 37 Then Reuben said to his *f*,
43: 2 their *f* said to them, "Go back
43: 7 'Is your *f* still living?' he asked us.
43: 8 Then Judah said to Israel his *f*,
43: 11 Then their *f* Israel said to them,
43: 23 of your *f* has given you treasure
43: 27 "How is your aged *f* you told me
43: 28 "Your servant our *f* is still alive
44: 17 go back to your *f* in peace."
44: 19 'Do you have a *f* or a brother?'
44: 20 sons left, and his *f* loves him.'
44: 20 we answered, 'We have an aged *f*,
44: 22 if he leaves him, his *f* will die.'
44: 22 'The boy cannot leave his *f*;
44: 24 back to your servant my *f*,
44: 25 "Then our *f* said, 'Go back
44: 27 "Your servant my *f* said to us,
44: 30 to your servant my *f* and if my *f*,
44: 31 head of our *f* down to the grave
44: 32 my *f*, all my life!' "Now then,
44: 32 the boy's safety to my *f*.
44: 34 back to my *f* if the boy is not
44: 34 that would come upon my *f*."
45: 3 "I am Joseph! Is my *f* still living?"
45: 8 He made me *f* to Pharaoh,
45: 9 hurry back to my *f* and say to him,
45: 13 And bring my *f* down here quickly
45: 13 Tell my *f* about all the honor
45: 18 bring your *f* and your families back
45: 19 and your wives, and get your *f*
45: 23 And this is what he sent to his *f*:
45: 25 came to their *f* Jacob in the land
45: 27 the spirit of their *f* Jacob revived.
46: 1 sacrifices to the God of his *f* Isaac.
46: 3 the God of your *f*," he said.
46: 5 and Israel's sons took their *f* Jacob
46: 29 he threw his arms around his *f*
46: 29 went to Goshen to meet his *f* Israel
47: 1 told Pharaoh, "My *f* and brothers,
47: 5 "Your *f* and your brothers have
47: 6 settle your *f* and your brothers
47: 7 Then Joseph brought his *f* Jacob in
47: 11 So Joseph settled his *f*
47: 12 also provided his *f* and his brothers
48: 1 Joseph was told, "Your *f* is ill."
48: 9 me here," Joseph said to his *f*.
48: 10 his *f* kissed them and embraced
48: 17 Joseph saw his *f* placing his right
48: 18 "No, my *f*, this one is the firstborn;
48: 19 But his *f* refused and said, "I know,
49: 2 listen to your *f* Israel.
49: 28 and this is what their *f* said to them
50: 1 Joseph threw himself upon his *f*
50: 2 in his service to embalm his *f* Israel
50: 5 Now let me go up and bury my *f*;
50: 5 'My *f* made me swear an oath
50: 6 said, "Go up and bury your *f*,
50: 7 So Joseph went up to bury his *f*.
50: 10 period of mourning for his *f*.
50: 14 burying his *f*, Joseph returned
50: 14 gone with him to bury his *f*.
50: 15 brothers saw that their *f* was dead,
50: 16 "Your *f* left these instructions
50: 17 of the servants of the God of your *f*
Ex 2: 18 the girls returned to Reuel their *f*,
3: 6 of your *f*, the God of Abraham,
20: 12 "Honor your *f* and your mother,
21: 15 "Anyone who attacks his *f*
21: 17 "Anyone who curses his *f*
22: 17 If her *f* absolutely refuses
40: 15 them just as you anointed their *f*,
Lev 16: 32 and ordained to succeed his *f*
18: 7 " 'Do not dishonor your *f*
Lev 18: 8 that would dishonor your *f*.
18: 11 born to your *f*; she is your sister.
19: 3 you must respect his mother and *f*,
20: 9 He has cursed his *f* or his mother,
20: 9 " 'If anyone curses his *f* or mother,
20: 11 wife, he has dishonored his *f*.
20: 17 the daughter of either his *f*
20: 19 either your mother or your *f*,
21: 2 his mother or *f*, his son or daughter
21: 9 she disgraces her *f*; she must be
21: 11 himself unclean, even for his *f*
24: 10 and an Egyptian *f* went out
Nu 3: 4 during the lifetime of their *f* Aaron.
6: 7 Even if his own *f* or mother
12: 14 "If her *f* had spit in her face,
26: 29 the Makirite clan (Makir was the *f*
26: 60 Aaron was the *f* of Nadab
27: 3 and said, "Our *f* died in the desert.
27: 11 If his *f* had no brothers, give his
30: 4 her *f* hears about her vow or pledge
30: 5 But if her *f* forbids her
30: 5 because her *f* has forbidden her.
30: 16 between a *f* and his young daughter
36: 6 within the tribal clan of their *f*.
Dt 1: 31 carried you, as a *f* carries his son,
5: 16 "Honor your *f* and your mother,
21: 13 and mourned her *f* and mother
21: 18 son who does not obey his *f*
21: 19 his *f* and mother shall take hold
22: 15 then the girl's *f* and mother shall
22: 16 The girl's *f* will say to the elders,
22: 19 and give them to the girl's *f*,
22: 29 he shall pay the girl's *f* fifty shekels
26: 5 "My *f* was a wandering Aramean,
27: 16 is the man who dishonors his *f*
27: 22 daughter of his *f* or the daughter
32: 6 Is he not your *F*, your Creator,
32: 7 Ask your *f* and he will tell you,
33: 9 He said of his *f* and mother,
Jos 2: 13 that you will spare the lives of my *f*
2: 18 and unless you have brought your *f*
6: 23 her *f* and mother and brothers
15: 18 him to ask her *f* for a field.
17: 4 along with the brothers of their *f*,
24: 2 including Terah the *f* of Abraham
24: 3 But I took your *f* Abraham
24: 32 sons of Hamor, the *f* of Shechem.
Jdg 1: 14 him to ask her *f* for a field.
8: 32 the tomb of his *f* Joash in Ophrah
9: 17 to think that my *f* fought for you,
9: 28 Shechem's *f*! Why should we serve
9: 56 to his *f* by murdering his seventy
11: 1 His *f* was Gilead; his mother was
11: 36 "My *f*," she replied, "you have
11: 39 she returned to her *f* and he did
14: 2 he said to his *f* and mother,
14: 3 But Samson said to his *f*, "Get her
14: 3 His *f* and mother replied, "Isn't
14: 5 down to Timnah together with his *f*
14: 6 But he told neither his *f*
14: 10 his *f* went down to see the woman.
14: 16 explained it to my *f* or mother,"
15: 1 But her *f* would not let him go in.
15: 6 and burned her and her *f* to death.
16: 31 in the tomb of Manoah his *f*.
17: 10 "Live with me and be my *f*
18: 19 Come with us, and be our *f*
19: 3 and when her *f* saw him, he gladly
19: 4 His father-in-law, the girl's *f*,
19: 5 but the girl's *f* said to his son-in-law
19: 6 Afterward the girl's *f* said,
19: 8 the girl's *f* said, "Refresh yourself.
19: 9 the girl's *f*, said, "Now look,
Ru 2: 11 how you left your *f* and mother
4: 17 He was the *f* of Jesse, the *f* of David
4: 18 Perez was the *f* of Hezron,
4: 19 Hezron the *f* of Ram, Ram
4: 19 Ram the *f* of Amminadab,
4: 20 Amminadab the *f* of Nahshon,
4: 20 Nahshon the *f* of Salmon,
4: 21 of Salmon, Salmon the *f* of Boaz,
4: 22 of Jesse, and Jesse the *f* of David.
1Sa 2: 28 I chose your *f* out of all the tribes
9: 3 to Saul's *f* Kish were lost,
9: 5 or my *f* will stop thinking about
10: 2 now your *f* has stopped thinking
10: 12 "And who is their *f*?" So it became
14: 1 But he did not tell his *f*.
1Sa 14: 27 not heard that his *f* had bound
14: 28 "Your *f* bound the army
14: 29 "My *f* has made trouble
14: 51 Saul's *f* Kish and Abner's *f* Ner
19: 2 "My *f* Saul is looking for a chance
19: 3 with my *f* in the field where you are
19: 4 well of David to Saul his *f*
20: 1 How have I wronged your *f*,
20: 2 Look, my *f* doesn't do anything,
20: 3 "Your *f* knows very well that I
20: 6 If your *f* misses me at all, tell him,
20: 8 Why hand me over to your *f*?"
20: 9 inkling that my *f* was determined
20: 10 me if your *f* answers you harshly?"
20: 12 I will surely sound out my *f*
20: 13 But if my *f* is inclined to harm you,
20: 13 as he has been with my *f*.
20: 32 has he done?" Jonathan asked his *f*.
20: 33 Jonathan knew that his *f* intended
22: 3 you let my *f* and mother come
23: 17 Even my *f* Saul knows this."
23: 17 "My *f* Saul will not lay a hand
24: 11 my *f*, look at this piece of your robe
2Sa 3: 8 loyal to the house of your *f* Saul
6: 21 who chose me rather than your *f*
7: 14 I will be his *f*, and he will be my son
9: 7 for the sake of your *f* Jonathan.
10: 2 just as his *f* showed kindness to me
10: 2 to Hanun concerning his *f*.
10: 3 you think David is honoring your *f*
13: 5 "When your *f* comes to see you,
16: 19 I served your *f*, so I will serve you."
17: 8 You know your *f* and his men;
17: 8 your *f* is an experienced fighter;
17: 10 Israel knows that your *f* is a fighter
19: 37 town near the tomb of my *f*
21: 14 in the tomb of Saul's *f* Kish,
1Ki 1: 6 His *f* had never interfered with him
2: 12 sat on the throne of his *f* David,
2: 24 on the throne of my *f* David
2: 26 LORD before my *f* David
2: 32 of my *f* David he attacked two men
2: 44 the wrong you did to my *f* David.
3: 3 to the statutes of his *f* David,
3: 6 to your servant, my *f* David,
3: 7 king in place of my *f* David
3: 14 commands as David your *f* did,
5: 1 king to succeed his *f* David,
5: 3 against my *f* David from all sides,
5: 5 as the LORD told my *f* David,
6: 12 the promise I gave to David your *f*
7: 14 and whose *f* was a man of Tyre
7: 51 the things his *f* David had
8: 15 with his own mouth to my *f* David.
8: 17 "My *f* David had it in his heart
8: 18 But the LORD said to my *f* David,
8: 20 I have succeeded David my *f*
8: 24 to your servant David my *f*;
8: 25 servant David my *f* the promises
8: 26 servant David my *f* come true.
9: 4 as David your *f* did, and do all I
9: 5 as I promised David your *f*
11: 4 as the heart of David his *f* had been
11: 6 as David his *f* had done.
11: 12 for the sake of David your *f*,
11: 17 officials who had served his *f*.
11: 27 in the wall of the city of David his *f*
11: 33 and laws as David, Solomon's *f*,
11: 43 was buried in the city of David his *f*
12: 4 "Your *f* put a heavy yoke on us,
12: 6 who had served his *f* Solomon
12: 9 'Lighten the yoke your *f* put on us
12: 10 'Your *f* put a heavy yoke on us,
12: 11 My *f* laid on you a heavy yoke;
12: 11 My *f* scourged you with whips;
12: 14 My *f* scourged you with whips;
12: 14 "My *f* made your yoke heavy,
13: 11 also told their *f* what he had said
13: 12 Their *f* asked them, "Which way
15: 3 all the sins his *f* had done
15: 11 LORD, as his *f* David had done.
15: 15 that he and his *f* had dedicated.
15: 19 there was between my *f* and your *f*.
15: 24 with them in the city of his *f* David.
15: 26 walking in the ways of his *f*
19: 20 me kiss my *f* and mother good-by,"
20: 34 areas in Damascus, as my *f* did
20: 34 the cities my *f* took from your *f*,"

1Ki 22: 43 walked in the ways of his *f* Asa
22: 46 even after the reign of his *f* Asa.
22: 50 with them in the city of David his *f*.
22: 52 he walked in the ways of his *f*
22: 53 to anger, just as his *f* had done.
2Ki 2: 12 My *f!* The chariots and horsemen
2: 12 saw this and cried out, "My *f!*
3: 2 not as his *f* and mother had done.
3: 2 stone of Baal that his *f* had made.
3: 13 Go to the prophets of your *f*
4: 18 and one day he went out to his *f*,
4: 19 His *f* told a servant, "Carry him
4: 19 My head!" he said to his *f*.
5: 13 went to him and said, "My *f*,
6: 21 I kill them, my *f?* Shall I kill
9: 25 in chariots behind Ahab his *f*
13: 14 "My *f!* My *f!*" he cried.
13: 25 taken in battle from his *f* Jehoahaz.
14: 3 but not as his *f* David had done.
14: 3 the example of his *f* Joash.
14: 5 who had murdered his *f* the king.
14: 21 king in place of his *f* Amaziah.
15: 3 just as his *f* Amaziah had done.
15: 34 just as his *f* Uzziah had done.
15: 38 the City of David, the city of his *f*.
16: 2 Unlike David his *f*, he did not do
18: 3 just as his *f* David had done.
20: 5 the God of your *f* David, says:
21: 3 the high places his *f* Hezekiah had
21: 20 as his *f* Manasseh had done.
21: 21 He walked in all the ways of his *f*;
21: 21 the idols his *f* had worshiped,
22: 2 in all the ways of his *f* David,
23: 30 and made him king in place of his *f*.
23: 34 king in place of his *f* Josiah
24: 9 of the LORD, just as his *f* had done
1Ch 1: 10 Cush was the *f* of Nimrod,
1: 11 Mizraim was the *f* of the Ludites,
1: 13 Canaan was the *f* of Sidon his
1: 18 Arphaxad was the *f* of Shelah,
1: 18 of Shelah, and Shelah the *f* of Eber.
1: 20 Joktan was the *f* of Almodad,
1: 34 Abraham was the *f* of Isaac.
2: 10 Ram was the *f* of Amminadab,
2: 10 and Amminadab the *f* of Nahshon,
2: 11 Nahshon was the *f* of Salmon,
2: 11 of Salmon, Salmon the *f* of Boaz,
2: 12 Boaz the *f* of Obed and Obed
2: 12 of Obed and Obed the *f* of Jesse.
2: 13 Jesse was the *f* of Eliab his firstborn
2: 17 whose *f* was Jether the Ishmaelite.
2: 20 Hur was the *f* of Uri, and Uri
2: 20 of Uri, and Uri the *f* of Bezalel.
2: 21 with the daughter of Makir the *f*
2: 22 Segub was the *f* of Jair, who
2: 23 of Makir the *f* of Gilead.
2: 24 of Hezron bore him Ashhur the *f*
2: 31 Ishi, who was the *f* of Sheshan.
2: 31 Sheshan was the *f* of Ahlai.
2: 36 Attai was the *f* of Nathan,
2: 36 Nathan the *f* of Zabad, Zabad
2: 37 of Zabad, Zabad the *f* of Ephlal,
2: 38 of Jehu, Jehu the *f* of Azariah,
2: 38 the *f* of Obed, Obed the *f* of Jehu,
2: 39 of Azariah, Azariah the *f* of Helez,
2: 39 of Helez, Helez the *f* of Eleasah,
2: 40 of Eleasah, Eleasah the *f* of Sismai,
2: 40 of Sismai, Sismai the *f* of Shallum,
2: 41 Shallum the *f* of Jekamiah,
2: 41 and Jekamiah the *f* of Elishama.
2: 42 Mesha his firstborn, who was the *f*
2: 42 his son Mareshah, who was the *f*
2: 44 Rekem was the *f* of Shammai.
2: 44 Shema was the *f* of Raham,
2: 44 and Raham the *f* of Jorkeam.
2: 45 Maon was the *f* of Beth Zur.
2: 46 Haran was the *f* of Gazez.
2: 49 and to Sheva the *f* of Macbenah
2: 49 to Shaaph the *f* of Madmannah
2: 50 Shobal the *f* of Kiriath Jearim,
2: 51 Salma the *f* of Bethlehem,
2: 51 of Bethlehem, and Hareph the *f*
2: 52 The descendants of Shobal the *f*
2: 55 the *f* of the house of Recab.
4: 2 and Jahath the *f* of Ahumai
4: 2 son of Shobal was the *f* of Jahath,
4: 4 Penuel was the *f* of Gedor,
4: 4 of Ephrathah and *f* of Bethlehem.

1Ch 4: 4 of Gedor, and Ezer the *f* of Hushah
4: 5 Ashhur the *f* of Tekoa had two
4: 8 who was the *f* of Anub
4: 11 Shuhah's brother, was the *f*
4: 11 of Mehir, who was the *f* of Eshton.
4: 12 Eshton was the *f* of Beth Rapha,
4: 12 Tehinnah the *f* of Ir Nahash.
4: 14 Meonothai was the *f* of Ophrah.
4: 14 the *f* of Joab, the *f* of Ge
4: 17 and Ishbah the *f* of Eshtemoa.
4: 18 Heber the *f* of Soco, and Jekuthiel
4: 18 and Jekuthiel the *f* of Zanoah.)
4: 18 birth to Jered the *f* of Gedor,
4: 19 the *f* of Keilah the Garmite,
4: 21 Laadah the *f* of Mareshah
4: 21 son of Judah: Er the *f* of Lecah,
6: 4 Eleazar was the *f* of Phinehas,
6: 4 Phinehas the *f* of Abishua,
6: 5 of Abishua, Abishua the *f* of Bukki,
6: 5 of Bukki, Bukki the *f* of Uzzi,
6: 6 Zerahiah the *f* of Meraioth,
6: 6 of Uzzi, Uzzi the *f* of Zerahiah,
6: 7 the *f* of Amariah, Amariah the *f*
6: 8 of Ahitub, Ahitub the *f* of Zadok,
6: 8 of Zadok, Zadok the *f* of Ahimaaz,
6: 9 the *f* of Azariah, Azariah the *f*
6: 10 Johanan the *f* of Azariah (it was he
6: 11 the *f* of Amariah, Amariah the *f*
6: 12 of Ahitub, Ahitub the *f* of Zadok,
6: 13 the *f* of Shallum, Shallum the *f*
6: 14 and Seraiah the *f* of Jehozadak.
6: 14 the *f* of Azariah, Azariah the *f*
7: 14 birth to Makir the *f* of Gilead.
7: 22 Their *f* Ephraim mourned
7: 31 Malkiel, who was the *f* of Birzaith.
7: 32 Heber was the *f* of Japhlet,
8: 1 Benjamin was the *f*
8: 7 who was the *f* of Uzza and Ahihud.
8: 29 Jeiel the *f* of Gibeon lived
8: 32 who was the *f* of Shimeah.
8: 33 and Saul the *f* of Jonathan,
8: 33 the *f* of Kish, Kish the *f* of Saul,
8: 34 Merib-Baal, who was the *f*
8: 36 Ahaz was the *f* of Jehoaddah,
8: 36 Jehoaddah was the *f* of Alemeth,
8: 36 and Zimri was the *f* of Moza.
8: 37 Moza was the *f* of Binea; Raphah
9: 35 Jeiel the *f* of Gibeon lived
9: 38 Mikloth was the *f* of Shimeam.
9: 39 and Saul the *f* of Jonathan,
9: 39 the *f* of Kish, Kish the *f* of Saul,
9: 40 Merib-Baal, who was the *f*
9: 42 Ahaz was the *f* of Jadah, Jadah was
9: 42 Jadah was the *f* of Alemeth,
9: 42 and Zimri was the *f* of Moza.
9: 43 Moza was the *f* of Binea; Rephaiah
14: 3 and became the *f* of more sons
17: 13 I will be his *f*, and he will be my son
19: 2 his *f* showed kindness to me."
19: 2 to Hanun concerning his *f*.
19: 3 you think David is honoring your *f*
22: 10 will be my son, and I will be his *f*.
24: 2 and Abihu died before their *f* did,
25: 3 the supervision of their *f* Jeduthun,
26: 10 his *f* had appointed him the first),
28: 6 to be my son, and I will be his *f*.
28: 9 acknowledge the God of your *f*,
29: 10 God of our *f* Israel,
29: 23 as king in place of his *f* David.
2Ch 1: 8 great kindness to David my *f*
1: 9 to my *f* David be confirmed,
2: 3 as you did for my *f* David
2: 7 whom my *f* David provided.
2: 14 and whose *f* was from Tyre.
2: 14 with those of my lord, David your *f*
2: 17 the census his *f* David had taken;
3: 1 had appeared to his *f* David.
5: 1 the things his *f* David had
6: 4 with his mouth to my *f* David.
6: 7 "My *f* David had it in his heart
6: 8 But the LORD said to my *f* David,
6: 10 I have succeeded David my *f*
6: 15 to your servant David my *f*;
6: 16 servant David my *f* the promises
7: 17 before me as David your *f* did,
7: 18 with David your *f* when I said,
8: 14 the ordinance of his *f* David,
9: 31 was buried in the city of David his *f*

2Ch 10: 4 "Your *f* put a heavy yoke on us,
10: 6 who had served his *f* Solomon
10: 9 'Lighten the yoke your *f* put on us
10: 10 'Your *f* put a heavy yoke on us,
10: 11 My *f* laid on you a heavy yoke;
10: 11 My *f* scourged you with whips;
10: 14 My *f* scourged you with whips;
10: 14 "My *f* made your yoke heavy;
15: 18 that he and his *f* had dedicated.
16: 3 there was between my *f* and your *f*.
17: 2 Ephraim that his *f* Asa had
17: 3 the ways his *f* David had followed.
17: 4 but sought the God of his *f*
20: 32 He walked in the ways of his *f* Asa
21: 3 Their *f* had given them many gifts
21: 12 in the ways of your *f* Jehoshaphat
21: 12 the God of your *f* David, says:
24: 22 kindness Zechariah's *f* Jehoiada
25: 3 who had murdered his *f* the king.
26: 1 king in place of his *f* Amaziah.
26: 4 just as his *f* Amaziah had done.
27: 2 just as his *f* Uzziah had done,
28: 1 Unlike David his *f*, he did not do
29: 2 just as his *f* David had done.
33: 3 the high places his *f* Hezekiah had
33: 22 as his *f* Manasseh had done.
33: 23 But unlike his *f* Manasseh,
34: 2 walked in the ways of his *f* David,
34: 3 to seek the God of his *f* David.
36: 1 king in Jerusalem in place of his *f*.
Ne 12: 10 Jeshua was the *f* of Joiakim,
12: 10 Joiakim the *f* of Eliashib, Eliashib
12: 10 of Eliashib, Eliashib the *f* of Joiada,
12: 11 and Jonathan the *f* of Jaddua.
12: 11 of Joiada, Joiada the *f* of Jonathan,
Est 2: 7 as his own daughter when her *f*
2: 7 she had neither *f* nor mother.
Job 15: 10 men even older than your *f*.
17: 14 if I say to corruption, 'You are my *f*
29: 16 I was a *f* to the needy;
31: 18 my youth I reared him as would a *f*,
38: 28 Does the rain have a *f?*
42: 15 their *f* granted them an inheritance
Ps 2: 7 today I have become your *F*.
27: 10 Though my *f* and mother forsake
68: 5 A *f* to the fatherless, a defender
89: 26 to me, 'You are my *F*,
103: 13 As a *f* has compassion
Pr 3: 12 as a *f* the son he delights in.
10: 1 A wise son brings joy to his *f*,
15: 20 A wise son brings joy to his *f*,
17: 21 there is no joy for the *f* of a fool.
17: 25 A foolish son brings grief to his *f*
19: 26 He who robs his *f* and drives out
20: 20 If a man curses his *f* or mother,
23: 22 Listen to your *f*, who gave you life,
23: 24 *f* of a righteous man has great joy;
23: 25 May your *f* and mother be glad;
27: 10 your friend and the friend of your *f*,
28: 7 of gluttons disgraces his *f*.
28: 24 He who robs his *f* or mother
29: 3 loves wisdom brings joy to his *f*,
30: 17 "The eye that mocks a *f*,
Isa 7: 17 house of your *f* a time unlike any
8: 4 the boy knows how to say 'My *f*'
9: 6 Everlasting *F*, Prince of Peace.
22: 21 He will be a *f* to those who live
22: 23 seat of honor for the house of his *f*.
38: 5 the God of your *f* David, says:
43: 27 Your first *f* sinned;
45: 10 Woe to him who says to his *f*,
51: 2 look to Abraham, your *f*,
58: 14 on the inheritance of your *f* Jacob."
63: 16 But you are our *F*,
63: 16 you, O LORD, are our *F*,
64: 8 Yet, O LORD, you are our *F*.
Jer 2: 27 They say to wood, 'You are my *f*,'
3: 4 'My *F*, my friend from my youth,
3: 19 I thought you would call me '*F*'
16: 7 not even for a *f* or a mother—
20: 15 man who brought my *f* the news,
22: 11 who succeeded his *f* as king
22: 15 Did not your *f* have food and drink
31: 9 because I am Israel's *f*,
Eze 16: 3 your *f* was an Amorite
16: 45 a Hittite and your *f* an Amorite.
18: 4 living soul belongs to me, the *f*
18: 11 the *f* has done none of them):

Eze 18: 14 who sees all the sins his *f* commits,
18: 18 But his *f* will die for his own sin,
18: 19 the son not share the guilt of his *f*?'
18: 20 son will not share the guilt of the *f*,
18: 20 will the *f* share the guilt of the son.
22: 7 In you they have treated *f*
44: 25 if the dead person was his *f*
Da 5: 2 Nebuchadnezzar his *f* had taken
5: 11 In the time of your *f* he was found
5: 11 your *f*— your *f* the king,
5: 13 of the exiles my *f* the king brought
5: 18 gave your *f* Nebuchadnezzar
11: 6 her *f* and the one who supported
Am 2: 7 *F* and son use the same girl
Mic 7: 6 For a son dishonors his *f*,
Zec 13: 3 And if anyone still prophesies, his *f*
Mal 1: 6 If I am a *f*, where is the honor due
1: 6 son honors his *f*, and a servant his
2: 10 we not all one *F*? Did not one God
Mt 1: 2 Jacob the *f* of Judah and his
1: 2 the *f* of Isaac, Isaac the *f* of Jacob,
1: 3 Judah the *f* of Perez and Zerah,
1: 3 mother was Tamar, Perez the *f*
1: 3 of Hezron, Hezron the *f* of Ram,
1: 4 Amminadab the *f* of Nahshon,
1: 4 Nahshon the *f* of Salmon,
1: 4 Ram the *f* of Amminadab,
1: 5 Salmon the *f* of Boaz, whose
1: 5 mother was Rahab, Boaz the *f*
1: 5 mother was Ruth, Obed the *f*
1: 6 David was the *f* of Solomon,
1: 6 and Jesse the *f* of King David.
1: 7 Rehoboam the *f* of Abijah,
1: 7 Solomon the *f* of Rehoboam,
1: 7 of Abijah, Abijah the *f* of Asa,
1: 8 Jehoshaphat the *f* of Joram,
1: 8 of Asa, Asa the *f* of Jehoshaphat,
1: 8 of Joram, Joram the *f* of Uzziah,
1: 9 of Ahaz, Ahaz the *f* of Hezekiah,
1: 9 of Jotham, Jotham the *f* of Ahaz,
1: 9 of Uzziah, Uzziah the *f* of Jotham,
1: 10 Hezekiah the *f* of Manasseh,
1: 10 of Amon, Amon the *f* of Josiah,
1: 10 of Manasseh, Manasseh the *f*
1: 11 and Josiah the *f* of Jeconiah
1: 12 Jeconiah was the *f* of Shealtiel,
1: 12 Shealtiel the *f* of Zerubbabel,
1: 13 Zerubbabel the *f* of Abiud,
1: 13 of Abiud, Abiud the *f* of Eliakim,
1: 13 of Eliakim, Eliakim the *f* of Azor,
1: 14 of Akim, Akim the *f* of Eliud,
1: 14 of Azor, Azor the *f* of Zadok,
1: 14 of Zadok, Zadok the *f* of Akim,
1: 15 of Matthan, Matthan the *f* of Jacob
1: 15 the *f* of Eleazar, Eleazar the *f*
1: 16 and Jacob the *f* of Joseph,
2: 22 in Judea in place of his *f* Herod,
3: 9 'We have Abraham as our *f*.'
4: 21 were in a boat with their *f* Zebedee,
4: 22 and their *f* and followed him.
5: 16 and praise your *F* in heaven.
5: 45 sons of your *F* in heaven.
5: 48 as your heavenly *F* is perfect.
6: 1 reward from your *F* in heaven.
6: 4 your *F*, who sees what is done
6: 6 close the door and pray to your *F*
6: 6 your *F*, who sees what is done
6: 8 for your *F* knows what you need
6: 9 " 'Our *F* in heaven,
6: 14 your heavenly *F* will also forgive
6: 15 your *F* will not forgive your sins.
6: 18 but only to your *F*, who is unseen;
6: 18 who is unseen; and your *F*,
6: 26 yet your heavenly *F* feeds them.
6: 32 your heavenly *F* knows that you
7: 11 how much more will your *F*
7: 21 the will of my *F* who is in heaven.
8: 21 "Lord, first let me go and bury my *f*
10: 20 of your *F* speaking through you.
10: 21 brother to death, and a *f* his child;
10: 29 apart from the will of your *F*.
10: 32 him before my *F* in heaven.
10: 33 him before my *F* in heaven.
10: 35 " 'a man against his *f*,
10: 37 "Anyone who loves his *f*
11: 25 *F*, Lord of heaven and earth,
11: 26 *F*, for this was your good pleasure.
11: 27 No one knows the Son except the *F*
Mt 11: 27 been committed to me by my *F*.
11: 27 no one knows the *F* except the Son
12: 50 of my *F* in heaven is my brother
13: 43 the sun in the kingdom of their *F*.
15: 4 and 'Anyone who curses his *f*
15: 4 'Honor your *f* and mother'
15: 5 you say that if a man says to his *f*
15: 6 he is not to 'honor his *f*' with it.
15: 13 that my heavenly *F* has not planted
16: 17 by man, but by my *F* in heaven.
18: 10 the face of my *F* in heaven.
18: 14 In the same way your *F*
18: 19 done for you by my *F* in heaven.
18: 35 how my heavenly *F* will treat each
19: 5 this reason a man will leave his *f*
19: 19 honor your *f* and mother,'
19: 29 or brothers or sisters or *f* or mother
20: 23 they have been prepared by my *F*."
21: 30 "Then the *f* went to the other son
21: 31 of the two did what his *f* wanted?"
23: 9 And do not call anyone on earth '*f*,'
23: 9 for you have one *F*, and he is
24: 36 nor the Son, but only the *F*.
25: 34 you who are blessed by my *F*;
26: 39 to the ground and prayed, "My *F*,
26: 42 a second time and prayed, "My *F*,
26: 53 Do you think I cannot call on my *F*
28: 19 baptizing them in the name of the *F*
Mk 1: 20 they left their *f* Zebedee in the boat
5: 40 he took the child's *f* and mother
7: 10 and, 'Anyone who curses his *f*
7: 10 'Honor your *f* and mother,' and,
7: 11 you say that if a man says to his *f*
7: 12 longer let him do anything for his *f*
9: 21 asked the boy's *f*, "How long has
9: 24 Immediately the boy's *f* exclaimed,
10: 7 this reason a man will leave his *f*
10: 19 honor your *f* and mother.' "
10: 29 or sisters or mother or *f* or children
11: 10 coming kingdom of our *f* David!"
11: 25 so that your *F* in heaven may
13: 12 brother to death, and a *f* his child.
13: 32 nor the Son, but only the *F*.
14: 36 *F*," he said, "everything is possible
15: 21 the *f* of Alexander and Rufus,
Lk 1: 32 give him the throne of his *f* David,
1: 59 to name him after his *f* Zechariah,
1: 62 Then they made signs to his *f*,
1: 67 His *f* Zechariah was filled
1: 73 the oath he swore to our *f* Abraham
2: 33 The child's *f* and mother marveled
2: 48 Your *f* and I have been anxiously
3: 8 'We have Abraham as our *f*.'
6: 36 merciful, just as your *F* is merciful.
8: 51 and the child's *f* and mother.
9: 26 and in the glory of the *F*
9: 42 and gave him back to his *f*.
9: 59 "Lord, first let me go and bury my *f*
10: 21 *F*, Lord of heaven and earth,
10: 21 *F*, for this was your good pleasure.
10: 22 and no one knows who the *F* is
10: 22 been committed to me by my *F*.
10: 22 knows who the Son is except the *F*,
11: 2 " '*F*, hallowed be your name,
11: 13 how much more will your *F*
12: 30 your *F* knows that you need them.
12: 32 for your *F* has been pleased
12: 53 *f* against son and son against *f*,
14: 26 and does not hate his *f* and mother,
15: 12 The younger one said to his *f*,
15: 12 younger one said to his father, '*F*,
15: 18 and go back to my *f* and say to him:
15: 18 *F*, I have sinned against heaven
15: 20 So he got up and went to his *f*.
15: 20 his *f* saw him and was filled
15: 21 '*F*, I have sinned against heaven
15: 22 "But the *f* said to his servants,
15: 27 your *f* has killed the fattened calf
15: 28 So his *f* went out and pleaded
15: 29 But he answered his *f*, 'Look!
15: 31 the *f* said, 'you are always with me,
16: 24 So he called to him, '*F* Abraham,
16: 27 "He answered, 'Then I beg you, *f*,
16: 30 " 'No, *f* Abraham,' he said,
18: 20 honor your *f* and mother.' "
22: 29 just as my *F* conferred one on me,
22: 42 knelt down and prayed, "*F*,
23: 34 Jesus said, "*F*, forgive them,
Lk 23: 46 out with a loud voice, "*F*,
24: 49 send you what my *F* has promised;
Jn 1: 14 who came from the *F*, full of grace
3: 35 The *F* loves the Son and has placed
4: 12 Are you greater than our *f* Jacob,
4: 21 you will worship the *F* neither
4: 23 the kind of worshipers the *F* seeks.
4: 23 true worshipers will worship the *F*
4: 53 *f* realized that this was the exact
5: 17 "My *F* is always at his work
5: 18 he was even calling God his own *F*,
5: 19 do only what he sees his *F* doing,
5: 19 whatever the *F* does the Son
5: 20 For the *F* loves the Son
5: 21 For just as the *F* raises the dead
5: 22 Moreover, the *F* judges no one,
5: 23 the Son does not honor the *F*,
5: 23 the Son just as they honor the *F*.
5: 26 For as the *F* has life in himself,
5: 36 testifies that the *F* has sent me.
5: 36 very work that the *F* has given me
5: 37 *F* who sent me has himself testified
5: 45 I will accuse you before the *F*.
6: 27 On him God the *F* has placed his
6: 32 it is my *F* who gives you the true
6: 37 All that the *F* gives me will come
6: 42 whose *f* and mother we know?
6: 44 the *F* who sent me draws him,
6: 45 Everyone who listens to the *F*
6: 46 No one has seen the *F*
6: 46 from God; only he has seen the *F*.
6: 57 Just as the living *F* sent me
6: 57 and I live because of the *F*,
6: 65 unless the *F* has enabled him."
8: 16 I stand with the *F* who sent me.
8: 18 is the one who sent me—the *F*."
8: 19 they asked him, "Where is your *f*?"
8: 19 you would know my *F* also."
8: 19 "You do not know me or my *F*,"
8: 27 he was telling them about his *F*.
8: 28 speak just what the *F* has taught me
8: 38 what you have heard from your *f*."
8: 39 Abraham is our *f*," they answered.
8: 41 The only *F* we have is God himself
8: 41 doing the things your own *f* does."
8: 42 God were your *F*, you would love
8: 44 You belong to your *f*, the devil,
8: 44 for he is a liar and the *f* of lies.
8: 49 I honor my *F* and you dishonor me.
8: 53 greater than our *f* Abraham?
8: 54 My *F*, whom you claim
8: 56 Your *f* Abraham rejoiced
10: 15 just as the *F* knows me
10: 15 knows me and I know the *F*
10: 17 reason my *F* loves me is that I lay
10: 18 command I received from my *F*."
10: 29 My *F*, who has given them to me,
10: 30 I and the *F* are one."
10: 32 many great miracles from the *F*.
10: 36 about the one whom the *F* set apart
10: 37 me unless I do what my *F* does.
10: 38 and understand that the *F* is in me,
10: 38 is in me, and I in the *F*."
11: 41 Then Jesus looked up and said, "*F*,
12: 26 My *F* will honor the one who
12: 27 '*F*, save me from this hour'?
12: 28 *F*, glorify your name!"
12: 49 the *F* who sent me commanded me
12: 50 I say is just what the *F* has told me
13: 1 to leave this world and go to the *F*.
13: 3 Jesus knew that the *F* had put all
14: 6 No one comes to the *F*
14: 7 you would know my *F* as well.
14: 8 show us the *F* and that will be
14: 9 How can you say, 'Show us the *F*'?
14: 9 who has seen me has seen the *F*.
14: 10 Rather, it is the *F*, living in me,
14: 10 am in the *F*, and that the *F* is in me?
14: 11 am in the *F* and the *F* is in me;
14: 12 because I am going to the *F*.
14: 13 the Son may bring glory to the *F*.
14: 16 I will ask the *F*, and he will give
14: 20 you will realize that I am in my *F*,
14: 21 loves me will be loved by my *F*,
14: 23 My *F* will love him, and we will
14: 24 they belong to the *F* who sent me.
14: 26 whom the *F* will send in my name,
14: 28 be glad that I am going to the *F*,

Jn 14: 28 for the F is greater than I.
14: 31 exactly what my F has commanded
14: 31 world must learn that I love the F
15: 1 true vine and my F is the gardener
15: 9 "As the F has loved me,
15: 15 from my F I have made known
15: 16 F will give you whatever you ask
15: 23 He who hates me hates my F
15: 24 they have hated both me and my F.
15: 26 of truth who goes out from the F,
15: 26 whom I will send to you from the F
16: 3 they have not known the F or me.
16: 10 because I am going to the F,
16: 15 All that belongs to the F is mine.
16: 17 and 'Because I am going to the F'?"
16: 23 my F will give you whatever you
16: 25 but will tell you plainly about my F.
16: 26 I am not saying that I will ask the F
16: 27 the F himself loves you
16: 28 from the F and entered the world;
16: 28 the world and going back to the F."
16: 32 for my F is with me.
17: 1 toward heaven and prayed: "F,
17: 5 F, glorify me in your presence
17: 11 Holy F, protect them by the power
17: 21 that all of them may be one, F,
17: 24 "F, I want those you have given me
17: 25 "Righteous F, though the world
18: 11 drink the cup the F has given me?"
20: 17 for I have not yet returned to the F.
20: 17 'I am returning to my F and your F,
20: 21 be with you! As the F has sent me,
Ac 1: 4 but wait for the gift my F promised,
1: 7 or dates the F has set
2: 33 from the F the promised Holy
4: 25 of your servant, our f David:
7: 2 of glory appeared to our f Abraham
7: 4 the death of his f, God sent him
7: 8 Abraham became the f of Isaac
7: 8 Later Isaac became the f of Jacob,
7: 8 and Jacob became the f
7: 14 Joseph sent for his f Jacob
13: 33 today I have become your F.'
16: 1 a believer, but whose f was a Greek
16: 3 all knew that his f was a Greek.
28: 8 His f was sick in bed, suffering
Ro 1: 7 and peace to you from God our F
4: 11 he is the f of all who believe
4: 12 of the faith that our f Abraham had
4: 12 f of the circumcised who not only
4: 16 He is the f of us all.
4: 17 He is our f in the sight of God,
4: 17 "I have made you a f
4: 18 so became the f of many nations,
6: 4 the dead through the glory of the F,
8: 15 And by him we cry, "Abba, F."
9: 10 and the same f, our f Isaac.
15: 6 and F of our Lord Jesus Christ.
1Co 1: 3 and peace to you from God our F
4: 15 for in Christ Jesus I became your f
8: 6 for us there is but one God, the F,
15: 24 over the kingdom to God the F
2Co 1: 2 and peace to you from God our F
1: 3 and F of our Lord Jesus Christ,
1: 3 the F of compassion and the God
6: 18 "I will be a F to you,
11: 31 The God and F of the Lord Jesus,
Gal 1: 1 but by Jesus Christ and God the F,
1: 3 and peace to you from God our F
1: 4 to the will of our God and F,
4: 2 trustees until the time set by his f.
4: 6 the Spirit who calls out, "Abba, F."
Eph 1: 2 and peace to you from God our F
1: 3 and F of our Lord Jesus Christ,
1: 17 glorious F, may give you the Spirit
2: 18 access to the F by one Spirit.
3: 14 For this reason I kneel before the F
4: 6 one baptism; one God and F of all,
5: 20 thanks to God the F for everything,
5: 31 this reason a man will leave his f
6: 2 "Honor your f and mother"—
6: 23 and love with faith from God the F
Php 1: 2 and peace to you from God our F
2: 11 to the glory of God the F.
2: 22 as a son with his f he has served
4: 20 To our God and F be glory for ever
Col 1: 2 and peace to you from God our F.
1: 3 the F of our Lord Jesus Christ,
Col 1: 12 and joyfully giving thanks to the F,
3: 17 thanks to God the F through him.
1Th 1: 1 of the Thessalonians in God the F
1: 3 and F your work produced by faith,
2: 11 as a f deals with his own children,
3: 11 Now may our God and F himself
3: 13 and F when our Lord Jesus comes
2Th 1: 1 of the Thessalonians in God our F
1: 2 and peace to you from God the F
2: 16 Christ himself and God our F,
1Ti 1: 2 and peace from God the F
5: 1 but exhort him as if he were your f.
2Ti 1: 2 and peace from God the F
Tit 1: 4 and peace from God the F
Phm : 3 and peace from God our F
Heb 1: 5 today I have become your F"?
1: 5 "I will be his F,
5: 5 today I have become your F."
7: 3 Without f or mother,
11: 11 was enabled to become a f
12: 7 what son is not disciplined by his f?
12: 9 submit to the F of our spirits
Jas 1: 17 coming down from the F
1: 27 Religion that God our F accepts
3: 9 tongue we praise our Lord and F,
1Pe 1: 2 to the foreknowledge of God the F,
1: 3 and F of our Lord Jesus Christ!
1: 17 on a F who judges each man's work
2Pe 1: 17 and glory from God the F
1Jn 1: 2 was with the F and has appeared
1: 3 And our fellowship is with the F
2: 1 speaks to the F in our defense—
2: 13 because you have known the F.
2: 15 the love of the F is not in him.
2: 16 comes not from the F
2: 22 he denies the F and the Son.
2: 23 acknowledges the Son has the F
2: 23 one who denies the Son has the F;
2: 24 will remain in the Son and in the F.
3: 1 great is the love the F has lavished
4: 14 testify that the F has sent his Son
5: 1 who loves the f loves his child
2Jn : 3 and peace from God the F
: 4 just as the F commanded us.
: 9 in the teaching has both the F
Jude : 1 who are loved by God the F
Rev 1: 6 priests to serve his God and F—
2: 27 have received authority from my F.
3: 5 acknowledge his name before my F
3: 21 sat down with my F on his throne.

FATHER-IN-LAW (FATHER)

Ge 38: 13 "Your f is on his way to Timnah
38: 25 she sent a message to her f.
Ex 3: 1 tending the flock of Jethro his f,
4: 18 Moses went back to Jethro his f
18: 1 the priest of Midian and f of Moses
18: 2 his f Jethro received her
18: 5 Moses' f, together
18: 6 word to him, "I, your f Jethro,
18: 7 So Moses went out to meet his f
18: 8 Moses told his f about everything
18: 12 Moses' f, brought a burnt offering
18: 12 bread with Moses' f in the presence
18: 14 When his f saw all that Moses was
18: 17 Moses' f replied, "What you are
18: 24 Moses listened to his f
18: 27 Then Moses sent his f on his way,
Nu 10: 29 of Reuel the Midianite, Moses' f,
Jdg 1: 16 The descendants of Moses' f,
19: 4 His f, the girl's father, prevailed
19: 7 his f persuaded him,
19: 9 his f, the girl's father, said,
1Sa 4: 19 that her f and her husband were
4: 21 the deaths of her f and her husband
Jn 18: 13 who was the f of Caiaphas,

FATHER'S (FATHER)

Ge 9: 22 saw his f nakedness and told his
9: 23 and covered their f nakedness.
9: 23 would not see their f nakedness.
12: 1 your people and your f household
20: 13 wander from my f household,
24: 7 out of my f household
24: 23 is there room in your f house for us
24: 38 to my f family and to my own clan,
24: 40 my own clan and from my f family.
26: 15 the wells that his f servants had dug
Ge 27: 30 had scarcely left his f presence,
27: 34 When Esau heard his f words,
28: 21 so that I return safely to my f house
29: 9 Rachel came with her f sheep,
31: 5 "I see that your f attitude
31: 9 has taken away your f livestock
31: 14 in the inheritance of our f estate?
31: 19 Rachel stole her f household gods.
31: 30 longed to return to your f house.
34: 19 honored of all his f household,
35: 22 slept with his f concubine Bilhah,
37: 2 and the sons of Zilpah, his f wives,
37: 12 gone to graze their f flocks
38: 11 Tamar went to live in her f house.
38: 11 as a widow in your f house
41: 51 trouble and all my f household."
46: 31 and to his f household,
46: 31 'My brothers and my f household,
47: 12 and all his f household with food,
48: 17 hold of his f hand to move it
49: 4 for you went up onto your f bed,
49: 8 your f sons will bow down to you.
49: 25 of your f God, who helps you,
49: 26 Your f blessings are greater
50: 8 those belonging to his f household.
50: 22 along with all his f family.
Ex 2: 16 the troughs to water their f flock.
6: 20 married his f sister Jochebed,
15: 2 my f God, and I will exalt him.
18: 4 "My f God was my helper;
Lev 18: 8 sexual relations with your f wife;
18: 9 either your f daughter
18: 11 with the daughter of your f wife,
18: 12 sexual relations with your f sister;
18: 12 she is your f close relative.
18: 14 " 'Do not dishonor your f brother
20: 11 " 'If a man sleeps with his f wife,
22: 13 she returns to live in her f house
22: 13 youth, she may eat of her f food.
Nu 18: 1 and your f family are to bear
27: 4 Why should our f name disappear
27: 4 property among our f relatives."
27: 7 and turn their f inheritance
27: 7 inheritance among their f relatives
27: 10 his inheritance to his f brothers.
30: 3 living in her f house makes a vow
36: 8 someone in her f tribal clan,
36: 11 their cousins on their f side.
36: 12 inheritance remained in their f clan
Dt 21: 17 son is the first sign of his f strength.
22: 21 brought to the door of her f house
22: 21 while still in her f house.
22: 30 A man is not to marry his f wife;
22: 30 he must not dishonor his f bed.
27: 20 for he dishonors his f bed."
27: 20 the man who sleeps with his f wife,
Jdg 6: 25 Tear down your f altar to Baal
6: 25 the second bull from your f herd,
9: 5 He went to his f home in Ophrah
9: 18 revolted against my f family,
11: 7 and drive me from my f house?
14: 15 and your f household to death.
14: 19 anger, he went up to his f house.
16: 31 and his f whole family went
19: 2 back to her f house in Bethlehem,
19: 3 She took him into her f house,
1Sa 2: 25 did not listen to their f rebuke,
2: 27 to your f house when they were
2: 28 gave your f house all the offerings
2: 30 and your f house would minister
2: 31 and the strength of your f house,
9: 20 if not to you and all your f family?"
17: 15 to tend his f sheep at Bethlehem.
17: 25 will exempt his f family from taxes
17: 34 has been keeping his f sheep.
18: 2 did not let him return to his f house
18: 18 and what is my family or my f clan
20: 34 grieved at his f shameful treatment
22: 1 and his f household heard about it,
22: 11 of Ahitub and his f whole family,
22: 15 your servant or any of his f family,
22: 16 you and your f whole family."
22: 22 for the death of your f whole family
24: 21 name from my f family."
2Sa 2: 32 him in his f tomb at Bethlehem.
3: 7 sleep with my f concubine?"
3: 29 of Joab and upon all his f house!
14: 9 rest on me and on my f family,

2Sa 15:34 I was your *f* servant in the past,
16:21 with your *f* concubines whom he
16:21 yourself a stench in your *f* nostrils,
16:22 and he lay with his *f* concubines
17:23 and was buried in his *f* tomb
1Ki 2:26 and shared all my *f* hardships."
2:31 and my *f* house of the guilt
12:10 finger is thicker than my *f* waist.
18:18 "But you and your *f* family have.
2Ki 10:3 and set him on his *f* throne.
1Ch 5:1 when he defiled his *f* marriage bed,
26:6 who were leaders in their *f* family
28:4 and from my *f* sons he was pleased
2Ch 10:10 finger is thicker than my *f* waist.
21:4 firmly over his *f* kingdom,
21:13 of your *f* house, men who were
22:4 after his *f* death they became his
Ne 1:6 including myself and my *f* house,
Est 4:14 you and your *f* family will perish.
Ps 45:10 your people and your *f* house.
Pr 1:8 my son, to your *f* instruction
4:1 Listen, my sons, to a *f* instruction;
4:3 When I was a boy in my *f* house,
6:20 My son, keep your *f* commands
13:1 A wise son heeds his *f* instruction,
15:5 A fool spurns his *f* discipline,
19:13 A foolish son is his *f* ruin,
Isa 3:6 brothers at his *f* home, and say,
Eze 18:17 He will not die for his *f* sin;
22:11 his sister, his own *f* daughter.
Mt 16:27 going to come in his *F* glory
26:29 anew with you in my *F* kingdom."
Mk 8:38 him when he comes in his *F* glory
Lk 2:49 had to be in my *F* house?"
15:17 many of my *f* hired men have food
16:27 father, send Lazarus to my *f* house,
Jn 1:18 at the *F* side, has made him known.
2:16 How dare you turn my *F* house
5:43 I have come in my *F* name,
6:40 For my *F* will is that everyone who
8:38 what I have seen in the *F* presence,
8:44 you want to carry out your *f* desire.
10:25 do in my *F* name speak for me,
10:29 can snatch them out of my *F* hand.
14:2 In my *F* house are many rooms,
15:8 to my *F* glory, that you bear much
15:10 as I have obeyed my *F* commands
Ac 7:20 he was cared for in his *f* house.
1Co 5:1 pagans: A man has his *f* wife.
2Jn :3 the *F* Son, will be with us in truth
Rev 14:1 and his *F* name written

FATHERED (FATHER)

Dt 32:18 You deserted the Rock, who *f* you;

FATHERLESS (FATHER)

Ex 22:24 widows and your children *f*.
Dt 10:18 He defends the cause of the *f*
14:29 the *f* and the widows who live
16:11 the *f* and the widows living
16:14 the *f* and the widows who live
24:17 Do not deprive the alien or the *f*
24:19 Leave it for the alien, the *f*
24:20 what remains for the alien, the *f*
24:21 what remains for the alien, the *f*
26:12 the alien, the *f* and the widow,
26:13 the alien, the *f* and the widow,
27:19 justice from the alien, the *f*
Job 6:27 You would even cast lots for the *f*
22:9 and broke the strength of the *f*.
24:9 The *f* child is snatched
29:12 the *f* who had none to assist him.
31:17 not sharing it with the *f*—
31:21 I have raised my hand against the *f*,
Ps 10:14 you are the helper of the *f*.
10:18 defending the *f* and the oppressed,
68:5 A father to the *f*, a defender
82:3 Defend the cause of the weak and *f*
94:6 they murder the *f*.
109:9 May his children be *f*
109:12 or take pity on his *f* children.
146:9 and sustains the *f* and the widow,
Pr 23:10 or encroach on the fields of the *f*,
Isa 1:17 Defend the cause of the *f*,
1:23 do not defend the cause of the *f*;
9:17 nor will he pity the *f* and widows,
10:2 and robbing the *f*.
Jer 5:28 they do not plead the case of the *f*
7:6 the *f* or the widow and do not shed
22:3 or violence to the alien, the *f*
La 5:3 We have become orphans and *f*,
Eze 22:7 mistreated the *f* and the widow.
Hos 14:3 for in you the *f* find compassion."
Zec 7:10 Do not oppress the widow or the *f*,
Mal 3:5 who oppress the widows and the *f*,

FATHERS (FATHER)

Ge 15:15 will go to your *f* in peace
31:3 "Go back to the land of your *f*
46:34 boyhood on, just as our *f* did.'
47:3 to Pharaoh, "just as our *f* were."
47:9 years of the pilgrimage of my *f*."
47:30 but when I rest with my *f*,
48:15 "May the God before whom my *f*
48:16 and the names of my *f* Abraham
48:21 take you back to the land of your *f*.
49:29 Bury me with my *f* in the cave
Ex 3:13 'The God of your *f* has sent me
3:15 the God of your *f*— the God
3:16 the God of your *f*, the God
4:5 the God of their *f*— the God
10:6 something neither your *f*
20:5 for the sin of the *f* to the third
34:7 for the sin of the *f* to the third
Lev 26:40 their sins and the sins of their *f*—
Nu 14:18 for the sin of the *f* to the third
20:15 Egyptians mistreated us and our *f*,
32:8 This is what your *f* did
32:14 standing in the place of your *f*
36:8 will possess the inheritance of his *f*.
Dt 1:8 swore he would give to your *f*—
1:11 May the LORD, the God of your *f*,
1:21 the God of your *f*, told you.
4:1 the God of your *f*, is giving you.
5:3 with our *f* that the LORD made
5:9 for the sin of the *f* to the third
6:3 the God of your *f*, promised you.
6:10 into the land he swore to your *f*,
8:3 neither you nor your *f* had known,
8:16 something your *f* had never known
9:5 what he swore to your *f*,
10:11 swore to their *f* to give them."
12:1 the God of your *f*, has given you
13:6 neither you nor your *f* have known,
24:16 *F* shall not be put to death
24:16 nor children put to death for their *f*
26:7 of our *f*, and the LORD heard our
27:3 the God of your *f*, promised you.
28:36 a nation unknown to you or your *f*.
28:64 neither you nor your *f* have known.
29:13 you and as he swore to your *f*,
29:25 of their *f*, the covenant he made
30:5 and numerous than your *f*.
30:5 to the land that belonged to your *f*,
30:9 just as he delighted in your *f*,
30:20 the land he swore to give to your *f*,
31:16 "You are going to rest with your *f*,
32:17 gods your *f* did not fear.
Jos 4:21 when your descendants ask their *f*,
5:6 he had solemnly promised their *f*
18:3 the God of your *f*, has given you?
22:28 which our *f* built, not
24:6 When I brought your *f* out of Egypt
Jdg 2:10 had been gathered to their *f*,
2:12 of their *f*, who had brought them
2:17 Unlike their *f*, they quickly turned
2:17 way in which their *f* had walked,
2:19 more corrupt than those of their *f*,
6:13 his wonders that our *f* told us about
21:22 When their *f* or brothers complain
1Sa 12:7 by the LORD for you and your *f*.
12:15 against you, as it was against your *f*
2Sa 7:12 are over and you rest with your *f*,
1Ki 1:21 the king is laid to rest with his *f*,
2:10 Then David rested with his *f*
8:21 with our *f* when he brought them
8:34 back to the land you gave to their *f*.
8:40 live in the land you gave our *f*.
8:48 toward the land you gave their *f*,
8:53 brought our *f* out of Egypt."
8:57 be with us as he was with our *f*;
8:58 and regulations he gave our *f*.
9:9 who brought their *f* out of Egypt,
11:21 heard that David rested with his *f*
11:43 Then he rested with his *f*
13:22 buried in the tomb of your *f*.'"
14:20 years and then rested with his *f*.
14:22 more than their *f* had done.
14:31 And Rehoboam rested with his *f*
15:8 And Abijah rested with his *f*
15:12 rid of all the idols his *f* had made.
15:24 Then Asa rested with his *f*
16:6 Baasha rested with his *f*
16:28 Omri rested with his *f*
21:3 give you the inheritance of my *f*."
21:4 give you the inheritance of my *f*."
22:40 of Israel? Ahab rested with his *f*.
22:50 Then Jehoshaphat rested with his *f*
2Ki 8:24 Jehoram rested with his *f*
9:28 buried him with his *f* in his tomb
10:35 rested with his *f* and was buried
12:18 sacred objects dedicated by his *f*—
12:21 was buried with his *f* in the City
13:9 Jehoahaz rested with his *f*
13:13 Jehoash rested with his *f*,
14:6 nor children put to death for their *f*
14:6 "*F* shall not be put to death
14:16 Jehoash rested with his *f*
14:20 was buried in Jerusalem with his *f*,
14:22 after Amaziah rested with his *f*.
14:29 Jeroboam rested with his *f*,
15:7 Azariah rested with his *f*
15:9 of the LORD, as his *f* had done.
15:22 Menahem rested with his *f*.
15:38 Jotham rested with his *f*
16:20 Ahaz rested with his *f*
17:13 Law that I commanded your *f*
17:14 and were as stiff-necked as their *f*,
17:15 covenant he had made with their *f*
17:41 continue to do as their *f* did.
20:17 and all that your *f* have stored up
20:21 Hezekiah rested with his *f*.
21:18 Manasseh rested with his *f*
21:22 the LORD, the God of his *f*,
22:13 our *f* have not obeyed the words
22:20 I will gather you to your *f*,
23:32 of the LORD, just as his *f* had done
23:37 of the LORD, just as his *f* had done
24:6 Jehoiakim rested with his *f*.
1Ch 5:25 unfaithful to the God of their *f*
6:19 Levites listed according to their *f*:
9:19 as their *f* had been responsible
12:17 may the God of our *f* see it
17:11 and you go to be with your *f*,
25:6 supervision of their *f* for the music
29:18 God of our *f* Abraham, Isaac
29:20 the LORD, the God of their *f*;
2Ch 6:25 gave to them and their *f*.
6:31 live in the land you gave our *f*.
6:38 toward the land you gave their *f*,
7:22 of their *f*, who brought them out
9:31 Then he rested with his *f*
11:16 to the LORD, the God of their *f*.
12:16 Rehoboam rested with his *f*
13:12 the God of your *f*,
13:18 on the LORD, the God of their *f*.
14:1 And Abijah rested with his *f*
14:4 the God of their *f*,
15:12 the God of their *f*,
16:13 Asa died and rested with his *f*.
19:4 to the LORD, the God of their *f*.
20:6 of our *f*, are you not the God who is
20:33 hearts on the God of their *f*.
21:1 Then Jehoshaphat rested with his *f*
21:10 the LORD, the God of his *f*.
21:19 in his honor, as they had for his *f*.
24:18 of their *f*, and worshiped Asherah
24:24 of their *f*, judgment was executed
25:4 nor children put to death for their *f*
25:4 "*F* shall not be put to death
25:28 was buried with his *f* in the City
26:2 after Amaziah rested with his *f*.
26:23 Uzziah rested with his *f*
27:9 Jotham rested with his *f*
28:6 the LORD, the God of their *f*.
28:9 the God of your *f*, was angry
28:25 the LORD, the God of his *f*,
28:27 Ahaz rested with his *f*
29:5 of the LORD, the God of your *f*.
29:6 Our *f* were unfaithful; they did evil
29:9 This is why our *f* have fallen
30:7 Do not be like your *f* and brothers,
30:7 the God of their *f*,
30:8 your *f* were; submit to the LORD.

2Ch 30: 19 the LORD, the God of his f—
30: 22 the LORD, the God of their f.
32: 13 my f have done to all the peoples
32: 14 nations that my f destroyed has
32: 15 from my hand or the hand of my f.
32: 33 Hezekiah rested with his f
33: 12 greatly before the God of his f.
33: 20 Manasseh rested with his f
34: 21 our f have not kept the word
34: 28 Now I will gather you to your f,
34: 32 of God, the God of their f.
34: 33 the LORD, the God of their f.
35: 24 He was buried in the tombs of his f,
36: 15 The LORD, the God of their f,
Ezr 5: 12 our f angered the God of heaven,
7: 27 be to the LORD, the God of our f,
8: 28 to the LORD, the God of your f.
10: 11 the God of your f, and do his will.
Ne 2: 3 the city where my f are buried lies
2: 5 city in Judah where my f are buried
9: 2 and the wickedness of their f.
9: 23 into the land that you told their f
9: 32 upon our f and all your people,
9: 34 and our f did not follow your law;
Job 8: 8 and find out what their f learned,
15: 18 nothing received from their f
30: 1 whose f I would have disdained
38: 28 Who f the drops of dew?
Ps 22: 4 In you our f put their trust;
39: 12 a stranger, as all my f were.
44: 1 our f have told us
44: 2 and made our f flourish.
44: 2 and planted our f;
45: 16 sons will take the place of your f;
49: 19 he will join the generation of his f,
78: 3 things our f have told us.
78: 12 in the sight of their f
78: 57 Like their f they were disloyal
79: 8 hold against us the sins of the f;
95: 9 where your f tested and tried me,
106: 6 We have sinned, even as our f did;
106: 7 When our f were in Egypt,
109: 14 of his f be remembered
Pr 30: 11 "There are those who curse their f
Isa 38: 19 f tell their children
39: 6 and all that your f have stored up
49: 23 Kings will be your foster f,
64: 11 temple, where our f praised you,
65: 7 both your sins and the sins of your f
Jer 2: 5 "What fault did your f find in me,
3: 25 both we and our f;
6: 21 F and sons alike will stumble
7: 14 the place I gave to you and your f.
7: 18 gather wood, the f light the fire,
9: 14 the Baals, as their f taught them."
9: 16 they nor their f have known,
13: 14 f and sons alike, declares
14: 20 and the guilt of our f;
16: 3 and the men who are their f:
16: 11 'It is because your f forsook me,'
16: 12 more wickedly than your f.
16: 13 neither you nor your f have known,
16: 19 "Our f possessed nothing
19: 4 nor their f nor the kings
23: 27 as their f forgot my name
23: 39 the city I gave to you and your f.
24: 10 gave to them and their f.' "
25: 5 and your f for ever and ever.
31: 29 'The f have eaten sour grapes,
34: 5 fire in honor of your f,
34: 14 Your f, however, did not listen
35: 15 given to you and your f."
44: 3 nor you nor your f ever knew.
44: 9 wickedness committed by your f
44: 10 set before you and your f.
44: 17 offerings to her just as we and our f,
44: 21 of Jerusalem by you and your f,
47: 3 F will not turn to help their
50: 7 the LORD, the hope of their f.'
La 5: 7 Our f sinned and are no more,
Eze 2: 3 and their f have been in revolt
5: 10 and children will eat their f.
5: 10 in your midst f will eat their
18: 2 " 'The f eat sour grapes,
20: 4 the detestable practices of their f
20: 18 Do not follow the statutes of your f
20: 27 also your f blasphemed me
20: 30 yourselves the way your f did
Eze 20: 36 As I judged your f in the desert
20: 42 with uplifted hand to give to your f.
37: 25 the land where your f lived.
Da 2: 23 and praise you, O God of my f:
9: 6 and our f, and to all the people
9: 8 and our f are covered with shame
9: 16 of our f have made Jerusalem
11: 24 and will achieve what neither his f
11: 37 regard for the gods of his f
11: 38 unknown to his f he will honor
Hos 9: 10 when I saw your f,
Mic 7: 20 as you pledged on oath to our f
Zec 8: 14 pity when your f angered me,"
Mal 2: 10 covenant of our f by breaking faith
4: 6 the hearts of the children to their f;
4: 6 the hearts of the f to their children,
Lk 1: 17 the hearts of the f to their children
1: 55 even as he said to our f."
1: 72 to show mercy to our f
6: 23 is how their f treated the prophets.
6: 26 that is how their f treated the false
11: 11 "Which of you f, if your son asks
Jn 4: 20 Our f worshiped on this mountain,
Ac 3: 13 of our f, has glorified his servant
3: 25 covenant God made with your f.
5: 30 The God of our f raised Jesus
7: 2 "Brothers and f, listen to me!
7: 11 and our f could not find food.
7: 12 he sent our f on their first visit.
7: 15 to Egypt, where he and our f died.
7: 32 of your f, the God of Abraham,
7: 38 with our f and with the angel who
7: 39 "But our f refused to obey him.
7: 45 our f under Joshua brought it
7: 51 just like your f: You always resist
7: 52 a prophet your f did not persecute?
13: 17 of the people of Israel chose our f
13: 32 God promised our f he has fulfilled
13: 36 he was buried with his f
15: 10 nor our f have been able to bear?
22: 1 and f, listen now to my defense."
22: 3 trained in the law of our f
22: 14 'The God of our f has chosen you
24: 14 that I worship the God of our f,
26: 6 God has promised our f that I am
1Co 4: 15 you do not have many f,
Gal 1: 14 zealous for the traditions of my f.
Eph 6: 4 F, do not exasperate your children;
Col 3: 21 F, do not embitter your children,
1Ti 1: 9 for those who kill their f or mothers
Heb 3: 9 where your f tested and tried me
12: 9 all had human f who disciplined us
12: 10 Our f disciplined us for a little
2Pe 3: 4 he promised? Ever since our f died,
1Jn 2: 13 I write to you, f,
2: 14 I write to you, f,

FATHERS' (FATHER)

Lev 26: 39 of their f' sins they will waste away.
Jer 3: 24 the fruits of our f' labor—
32: 18 for the f' sins into the laps
Eze 20: 24 their eyes ⌊lusted⌋ after their f' idols
22: 10 are those who dishonor their f' bed;

FATHOM (FATHOMED)

Job 11: 7 "Can you f the mysteries of God?
Ps 145: 3 his greatness no one can f.
Ecc 3: 11 yet they cannot f what God has
Isa 40: 28 and his understanding no one can f
1Co 13: 2 and can f all mysteries and all

FATHOMED (FATHOM)

Job 5: 9 performs wonders that cannot be f,
9: 10 performs wonders that cannot be f,

FATTENED (FAT)

Dt 32: 14 and with f lambs and goats,
1Sa 28: 24 The woman had a f calf
2Sa 6: 13 he sacrificed a bull and a f calf.
1Ki 1: 9 f calves at the Stone of Zoheleth
1: 19 great numbers of cattle, f calves,
1: 25 great numbers of cattle, f calves,
Pr 15: 17 than a f calf with hatred.
Isa 1: 11 of rams and the fat of f animals;
Jer 46: 21 are like f calves.
Eze 39: 18 all of them f animals from Bashan.
Am 6: 4 and f calves.
Mt 22: 4 and f cattle have been butchered,
Lk 15: 23 Bring the f calf and kill it.
15: 27 'and your father has killed the f calf
15: 30 you kill the f calf for him!'
Jas 5: 5 You have f yourselves in the day

FATTENING (FAT)

1Sa 2: 29 more than me by f yourselves

FAULT (FAULTS FAULTY)

Ex 5: 16 but the f is with your own people."
1Sa 29: 3 I have found no f in him."
29: 6 I have found no f in you,
Job 33: 10 Yet God has found f with me;
Jer 2: 5 What f did your fathers find in me,
17: 4 Through your own f you will lose
Jnh 1: 12 that it is my f that this great storm
Mt 18: 15 and show him his f, just
Php 2: 15 of God without f in a crooked
Heb 8: 8 But God found f with the people
Jas 1: 5 generously to all without finding f,
3: 2 never at f in what he says,
Jude : 24 his glorious presence without f

FAULTFINDERS

Jude : 16 These men are grumblers and f;

FAULTLESS

Pr 8: 9 they are f to those who have
Php 3: 6 as for legalistic righteousness, f.
Jas 1: 27 Father accepts as pure and f is this:

FAULTS (FAULT)

Job 10: 6 that you must search out my f
Ps 19: 12 Forgive my hidden f.

FAULTY (FAULT)

Ps 78: 57 as unreliable as a f bow.
Hos 7: 16 they are like a f bow.

FAVOR (FAVORABLE FAVORED FAVORITE FAVORITISM FAVORS)

Ge 4: 4 The LORD looked with f on Abel
4: 5 his offering he did not look with f.
6: 8 But Noah found f in the eyes
18: 3 "If I have found f in your eyes,
19: 19 Your servant has found f
30: 27 "If I have found f in your eyes,
32: 5 that I may find f in your eyes.' "
33: 8 "To find f in your eyes, my lord,"
33: 10 "If I have found f in your eyes,
33: 15 "Just let me find f in the eyes
34: 11 "Let me find f in your eyes,
39: 4 Joseph found f in his eyes
39: 21 and granted him f in the eyes
47: 25 "May we find f in the eyes
47: 29 "If I have found f in your eyes,
50: 4 "If I have found f in your eyes,
Ex 32: 11 But Moses sought the f
33: 12 and you have found f with me.'
33: 13 If I have found f in your eyes,
33: 13 and continue to find f with you.
34: 9 if I have found f in your eyes,"
Lev 26: 9 " 'I will look on you with f
Nu 11: 15 if I have found f in your eyes—
32: 5 If we have found f in your eyes,"
Dt 33: 16 and the f of him who dwelt
33: 23 abounding with the f of the LORD
Jos 15: 19 She replied, "Do me a special f.
Jdg 1: 15 She replied, "Do me a special f.
6: 17 "If now I have found f in your eyes,
Ru 2: 2 anyone in whose eyes I find f."
2: 10 "Why have I found such f
2: 13 continue to find f in your eyes,
1Sa 1: 18 "May your servant find f
2: 26 in f with the LORD and with men.
13: 12 I have not sought the LORD's f.'
20: 3 knows very well that I have found f
20: 29 If I have found f in your eyes,
27: 5 "If I have found f in your eyes,
29: 4 better could he regain his master's f
2Sa 2: 6 and I too will show you the same f
14: 22 servant knows that he has found f
15: 25 If I find f in the LORD's eyes,
16: 4 "May I find f in your eyes,
2Ki 13: 4 Jehoahaz sought the LORD's f,
2Ch 33: 12 In his distress he sought the f
Ezr 7: 28 who has extended his good f to me
Ne 1: 11 by granting him f in the presence

Ne 2: 5 and if your servant has found *f*
5: 19 Remember me with *f*, O my God,
13: 31 Remember me with *f*, O my God.
Est 2: 9 The girl pleased him and won his *f*.
2: 15 Esther won the *f* of everyone who
2: 17 she won his *f* and approval more
5: 8 If the king regards me with *f*
7: 3 "If I have found *f* with you, O king,
8: 5 "and if he regards me with *f*
Job 11: 19 and many will court your *f*.
33: 26 prays to God and finds *f* with him,
34: 19 does not *f* the rich over the poor,
Ps 5: 12 you surround them with your *f*
30: 5 but his *f* lasts a lifetime;
45: 12 men of wealth will seek your *f*.
69: 13 in the time of your *f*;
77: 7 Will he never show his *f* again?
84: 9 look with *f* on your anointed one.
84: 11 the LORD bestows *f* and honor;
85: 1 You showed *f* to your land,
89: 17 and by your *f* you exalt our horn.
90: 17 May the *f* of the Lord our God rest
102: 13 for it is time to show *f* to her;
106: 4 when you show *f* to your people,
Pr 3: 4 you will win *f* and a good name
8: 35 and receives *f* from the LORD.
12: 2 A good man obtains *f*
13: 15 Good understanding wins *f*,
16: 15 his *f* is like a rain cloud in spring.
18: 22 and receives *f* from the LORD.
19: 6 Many curry *f* with a ruler,
19: 12 but his *f* is like dew on the grass.
28: 23 in the end gain more *f*
Ecc 9: 11 or *f* to the learned;
Isa 27: 11 and their Creator shows them no *f*.
49: 8 the time of my *f* I will answer you,
60: 10 in *f* I will show you compassion.
61: 2 proclaim the year of the LORD's *f*
Jer 16: 13 and night, for I will show you no *f*.'
26: 19 fear the LORD and seek his *f*?
31: 2 will find *f* in the desert;
La 4: 16 the elders no *f*.
Eze 5: 11 I myself will withdraw my *f*;
36: 9 and will look on you with *f*;
Da 1: 9 had caused the official to show *f*
7: 22 and pronounced judgment in *f*
9: 13 yet we have not sought the *f*
9: 17 with *f* on your desolate sanctuary.
11: 30 and show *f* to those who forsake
Hos 12: 4 he wept and begged for his *f*.
Zec 11: 7 called one *F* and the other Union,
11: 10 I took my staff called *F* and broke it
Mt 20: 20 kneeling down, asked a *f* of him.
Lk 1: 25 "In these days he has shown his *f*
1: 30 Mary, you have found *f* with God.
2: 14 to men on whom his *f* rests."
2: 52 and in *f* with God and men.
4: 19 to proclaim the year of the Lord's *f*
Jn 5: 32 is another who testifies in my *f*,
Ac 2: 47 and enjoying the *f* of all the people.
7: 46 who enjoyed God's *f* and asked
24: 27 to grant a *f* to the Jews, he
25: 3 urgently requested Festus, as a *f*
25: 9 wishing to do the Jews a *f*,
2Co 1: 11 behalf for the gracious *f* granted us
6: 2 now is the time of God's *f*,
6: 2 "In the time of my *f* I heard you,
Eph 6: 6 only to win their *f* when their eye is
Col 3: 22 is on you and to win their *f*,
Phm : 14 so that any *f* you do will be
Rev 2: 6 But you have this in your *f*:

FAVORABLE (FAVOR)

Ge 40: 16 Joseph had given a *f* interpretation,
1Sa 25: 8 Therefore be *f* toward my young
1Ki 12: 7 them and give them a *f* answer,
2Ch 10: 7 them and give them a *f* answer,
Jer 42: 6 Whether it is *f* or unfavorable,

FAVORED (FAVOR)

Dt 33: 8 belong to the man you *f*.
33: 24 let him be *f* by his brothers,
Ps 30: 7 O LORD, when you *f* me,
Eze 32: 19 'Are you more *f* than others?
Lk 1: 28 "Greetings, you who are highly *f*!
1: 43 But why am I so *f*, that the mother

FAVORITE (FAVOR)

SS 6: 9 the *f* of the one who bore her.

FAVORITISM (FAVOR)

Ex 23: 3 and do not show *f* to a poor man
Lev 19: 15 to the poor or *f* to the great,
Ac 10: 34 true it is that God does not show *f*
Ro 2: 11 For God does not show *f*.
Eph 6: 9 and there is no *f* with him.
Col 3: 25 for his wrong, and there is no *f*.
1Ti 5: 21 and to do nothing out of *f*.
Jas 2: 1 Lord Jesus Christ, don't show *f*.
2: 9 But if you show *f*, you sin

FAVORS (FAVOR)

2Sa 20: 11 "Whoever *f* Joab, and whoever is
Ecc 9: 7 for it is now that God *f* what you do
Jer 3: 13 you have scattered your *f*
Eze 16: 15 You lavished your *f*
16: 33 from everywhere for your illicit *f*.
16: 34 no one runs after you for your *f*.

FAWN (FAWNS)

Job 39: 1 watch when the doe bears her *f*?
Jer 14: 5 deserts her newborn *f*

FAWNS (FAWN)

Ge 49: 21 that bears beautiful *f*.
SS 4: 5 Your two breasts are like two *f*,
4: 5 like twin *f* of a gazelle
7: 3 Your breasts are like two *f*,

FEAR (AFRAID FEARED FEARFUL FEARFULLY FEARING FEARS FEARSOME FRIGHT FRIGHTEN FRIGHTENED FRIGHTENING GOD-FEARING)

Ge 9: 2 The *f* and dread of you will fall
20: 11 'There is surely no *f* of God
22: 12 Now I know that you *f* God,
31: 42 of Abraham and the *F* of Isaac,
31: 53 name of the *F* of his father Isaac.
32: 7 In great *f* and distress Jacob
42: 18 for I *f* God: If you are honest men,
Ex 9: 30 still do not *f* the LORD God."
18: 21 men who *f* God, trustworthy men
20: 18 in smoke, they trembled with *f*.
20: 20 so that the *f* of God will be
Lev 19: 14 in front of the blind, but *f* your God
25: 17 of each other, but *f* your God.
25: 36 kind from him, but *f* your God,
25: 43 them ruthlessly, but *f* your God.
Dt 2: 25 and *f* of you on all the nations
5: 29 hearts would be inclined to *f* me
6: 2 after them may *f* the LORD your
6: 13 *F* the LORD your God, serve him
6: 24 and to *f* the LORD our God,
7: 19 same to all the peoples you now *f*.
10: 12 but to *f* the LORD your God,
10: 20 *F* the LORD your God
11: 25 and *f* of you on the whole land,
25: 18 behind; they had no *f* of God.
28: 10 of the LORD, and they will *f* you
31: 12 and learn to *f* the LORD your God
31: 13 and learn to *f* the LORD your God
32: 17 gods your fathers did not *f*.
Jos 2: 9 live in this country are melting in *f*
2: 9 that a great *f* of you has fallen on us
2: 24 all the people are melting in *f*
4: 24 you might always *f* the LORD
14: 8 the hearts of the people melt with *f*.
22: 24 it for *f* that some day your
24: 14 "Now *f* the LORD and serve him
Jdg 7: 3 trembles with *f* may turn back
1Sa 12: 14 If you *f* the LORD and serve
12: 24 But be sure to *f* the LORD
13: 7 with him were quaking with *f*.
17: 24 they all ran from him in great *f*.
28: 20 with *f* because of Samuel's words.
2Sa 17: 10 the heart of a lion, will melt with *f*,
23: 3 when he rules in the *f* of God,
1Ki 1: 50 But Adonijah, in *f* of Solomon,
8: 40 so that they will *f* you all the time
8: 43 may know your name and *f* you,
2Ki 25: 26 to Egypt for *f* of the Babylonians.
1Ch 14: 17 LORD made all the nations *f* him.
2Ch 6: 31 so that they will *f* you and walk
6: 33 may know your name and *f* you,
2Ch 12: 5 in Jerusalem for *f* of Shishak,
17: 10 The *f* of the LORD fell
19: 7 let the *f* of the LORD be upon you.
19: 9 and wholeheartedly in the *f*
20: 29 The *f* of God came
26: 5 who instructed him in the *f* of God.
Ezr 3: 3 Despite their *f* of the peoples
10: 3 and of those who *f* the commands
Ne 5: 9 walk in the *f* of our God
Est 5: 9 nor showed *f* in his presence,
8: 17 *f* of the Jews had seized them.
9: 3 *f* of Mordecai had seized them.
Job 1: 9 "Does Job *f* God for nothing?"
4: 14 *f* and trembling seized me
5: 21 need not *f* when destruction comes
5: 22 need not *f* the beasts of the earth.
6: 14 he forsakes the *f* of the Almighty.
9: 35 I would speak up without *f* of him,
11: 15 you will stand firm and without *f*.
19: 29 you should *f* the sword yourselves;
21: 9 homes are safe and free from *f*;
23: 15 when I think of all this, I *f* him.
28: 28 The *f* of the Lord—that is wisdom,
31: 23 for *f* of his splendor I could not do
33: 7 No *f* of me should alarm you,
39: 22 He laughs at *f*, afraid of nothing;
41: 33 a creature without *f*.
Ps 2: 11 Serve the LORD with *f*
3: 6 I will not *f* the tens of thousands
15: 4 but honors those who *f* the LORD,
19: 9 The *f* of the LORD is pure,
22: 23 You who *f* the LORD, praise him!
22: 25 before those who *f* you will I fulfill
23: 4 I will *f* no evil,
25: 14 in those who *f* him;
27: 1 whom shall I *f*?
27: 3 my heart will not *f*;
31: 19 up for those who *f* you,
33: 8 Let all the earth *f* the LORD;
33: 18 are on those who *f* him,
34: 7 around those who *f* him,
34: 9 *F* the LORD, you his saints,
34: 9 for those who *f* him lack nothing.
34: 11 I will teach you the *f* of the LORD.
36: 1 There is no *f* of God
40: 3 Many will see and *f*
46: 2 Therefore we will not *f*,
49: 5 Why should I *f* when evil days
52: 6 The righteous will see and *f*;
55: 5 *F* and trembling have beset me;
55: 19 and have no *f* of God.
60: 4 for those who *f* you, you have
61: 5 of those who *f* your name.
64: 4 at him suddenly, without *f*.
64: 9 All mankind will *f*;
65: 8 living far away *f* your wonders;
66: 16 Come and listen, all you who *f* God
67: 7 all the ends of the earth will *f* him.
85: 9 near those who *f* him,
86: 11 that I may *f* your name.
90: 11 great as the *f* that is due you.
91: 5 You will not *f* the terror of night,
102: 15 The nations will *f* the name
103: 11 love for those who *f* him;
103: 13 compassion on those who *f* him;
103: 17 is with those who *f* him,
111: 5 for those who *f* him;
111: 10 *f* of the LORD is the beginning
112: 7 He will have no *f* of bad news;
112: 8 heart is secure, he will have no *f*;
115: 11 You who *f* him, trust in the LORD
115: 13 will bless those who *f* the LORD—
118: 4 Let those who *f* the LORD say:
119: 63 I am a friend to all who *f* you,
119: 74 May they who *f* you rejoice
119: 79 May those who *f* you turn to me,
119: 120 My flesh trembles in *f* of you;
128: 1 Blessed are all who *f* the LORD,
135: 20 you who *f* him, praise the LORD.
145: 19 of those who *f* him;
147: 11 delights in those who *f* him,
Pr 1: 7 *f* of the LORD is the beginning
1: 29 and did not choose to *f* the LORD,
1: 33 and be at ease, without *f* of harm."
2: 5 then you will understand the *f*
3: 7 *f* the LORD and shun evil.
3: 25 Have no *f* of sudden disaster
8: 13 To *f* the LORD is to hate evil;

Pr 9: 10 *f* of the LORD is the beginning
10: 27 The *f* of the LORD adds length
14: 27 The *f* of the LORD is a fountain
15: 16 with the *f* of the LORD
15: 33 *f* of the LORD teaches a man
16: 6 through the *f* of the LORD a man
19: 23 The *f* of the LORD leads to life:
22: 4 Humility and the *f* of the LORD
23: 17 for the *f* of the LORD.
24: 21 *F* the LORD and the king, my son,
29: 25 *F* of man will prove to be a snare,
31: 21 she has no *f* for her household;
Ecc 8: 13 because the wicked do not *f* God,
12: 13 *F* God and keep his
Isa 7: 25 you will no longer go there for *f*
8: 12 do not *f* what they *f*,
8: 13 he is the one you are to *f*,
11: 2 and of the *f* of the LORD—
11: 3 delight in the *f* of the LORD.
19: 16 They will shudder with *f*
21: 4 *f* makes me tremble;
33: 6 the *f* of the LORD is the key
35: 4 "Be strong, do not *f*;
41: 5 The islands have seen it and *f*;
41: 10 So do not *f*, for I am with you;
41: 13 and says to you, Do not *f*;
41: 23 will be dismayed and filled with *f*.
43: 1 "*F* not, for I have redeemed you;
51: 7 Do not *f* the reproach of men
51: 12 Who are you that you *f* mortal men
54: 4 Do not *f* disgrace; you will not be
54: 14 you will have nothing to *f*.
57: 11 that you do not *f* me?
59: 19 men will *f* the name of the LORD,
Jer 3: 8 her unfaithful sister Judah had no *f*;
5: 22 Should you not *f* me?" declares
5: 24 'Let us *f* the LORD our God,
10: 5 Do not *f* them;
17: 8 It does not *f* when heat comes;
22: 25 you *f*— to Nebuchadnezzar king
26: 19 Did not Hezekiah *f* the LORD
26: 21 heard of it and fled in *f* to Egypt.
30: 5 " 'Cries of *f* are heard—
30: 10 " 'So do not *f*, O Jacob my servant;
32: 39 so that they will always *f* me
32: 40 and I will inspire them to *f* me,
36: 16 they looked at each other in *f*
36: 24 heard all these words showed no *f*,
39: 17 handed over to those you *f*.
42: 11 king of Babylon, whom you now *f*.
42: 16 the sword you *f* will overtake you
46: 27 "Do not *f*, O Jacob my servant;
46: 28 Do not *f*, O Jacob my servant,
La 3: 57 and you said, "Do not *f*."
Eze 11: 8 You *f* the sword, and the sword is
12: 18 in *f* as you drink your water.
27: 35 and their faces are distorted with *f*.
30: 13 I will spread *f* throughout the land.
Da 6: 26 part of my kingdom people must *f*
Hos 10: 5 The people who live in Samaria *f*
Am 3: 8 who will not *f*?
Mic 6: 9 and to *f* your name is wisdom—
7: 17 turn in *f* to the LORD our God
Na 2: 11 and the cubs, with nothing to *f*?
Zep 3: 7 'Surely you will *f* me
3: 15 never again will you *f* any harm.
3: 16 "Do not *f*, O Zion;
Hag 2: 5 Do not *f*.'
Zec 9: 5 Ashkelon will see it and *f*;
Mal 3: 5 but do not *f* me," says the LORD
Mt 14: 26 they said, and cried out in *f*.
Mk 5: 33 with *f*, told him the whole truth.
Lk 1: 12 startled and was gripped with *f*.
1: 50 to those who *f* him,
1: 74 to enable us to serve him without *f*
8: 25 In *f* and amazement they asked one
8: 37 because they were overcome with *f*
12: 5 I will show you whom you should *f*:
12: 5 Yes, I tell you, *f* him.
12: 5 *F* him who, after the killing
18: 4 'Even though I don't *f* God
23: 40 "Don't you *f* God," he said,
Jn 3: 20 for *f* that his deeds will be exposed.
7: 13 anything publicly about him for *f*
12: 42 faith for *f* they would be put out
20: 19 with the doors locked for *f*
Ac 5: 5 great *f* seized all who heard what
5: 11 Great *f* seized the whole church
Ac 7: 32 Moses trembled with *f*
9: 31 living in the *f* of the Lord.
10: 4 Cornelius stared at him in *f*.
10: 35 men from every nation who *f* him
19: 17 they were all seized with *f*,
Ro 3: 18 "There is no *f* of God
8: 15 that makes you a slave again to *f*,
13: 3 want to be free from *f* of the one
1Co 2: 3 I came to you in weakness and *f*,
16: 10 nothing to *f* while he is with you,
2Co 5: 11 we know what it is to *f* the Lord,
7: 15 receiving him with *f* and trembling.
12: 20 I *f* that there may be quarreling,
Gal 2: 2 for *f* that I was running
4: 11 I *f* for you, that somehow I have
Eph 6: 5 masters with respect and *f*,
Php 2: 12 to work out your salvation with *f*
Heb 2: 15 held in slavery by their *f* of death.
11: 7 in holy *f* built an ark
12: 21 said, "I am trembling with *f*."
1Pe 1: 17 as strangers here in reverent *f*.
2: 17 brotherhood of believers, *f* God,
3: 6 is right and do not give way to *f*.
3: 14 "Do not *f* what they *f*; do not be
1Jn 4: 18 But perfect love drives out *f*,
4: 18 There is no *f* in love.
4: 18 *f* has to do with punishment.
Jude : 23 to others show mercy, mixed with *f*
Rev 14: 7 "*F* God and give him glory,
15: 4 Who will not *f* you, O Lord,
19: 5 you who *f* him,

FEARED (FEAR)

Ex 1: 17 *f* God and did not do what the king
1: 21 And because the midwives *f* God,
9: 20 officials of Pharaoh who *f* the word
14: 31 the people *f* the LORD
Dt 9: 19 I *f* the anger and wrath
Jos 9: 24 So we *f* for our lives because of you
1Sa 4: 13 his heart *f* for the ark of God.
14: 26 his mouth, because they *f* the oath.
1Ch 16: 25 he is to be *f* above all gods.
Ne 7: 2 and *f* God more than most men do.
Job 1: 1 he *f* God and shunned evil.
3: 25 What I *f* has come upon me;
31: 34 because I so *f* the crowd
Ps 76: 7 You alone are to be *f*.
76: 8 and the land *f* and was quiet—
76: 11 bring gifts to the One to be *f*.
76: 12 he is *f* by the kings of the earth.
89: 7 of the holy ones God is greatly *f*;
96: 4 he is to be *f* above all gods.
119: 38 so that you may be *f*.
130: 4 therefore you are *f*.
Isa 18: 2 to a people *f* far and wide,
18: 7 from a people *f* far and wide,
57: 11 "Whom have you so dreaded and *f*
Da 5: 19 every language dreaded and *f* him.
Jnh 1: 16 this the men greatly *f* the LORD,
Hab 1: 7 They are a *f* and dreaded people;
Hag 1: 12 And the people *f* the LORD.
Mal 1: 14 is to be *f* among the nations.
3: 16 concerning those who *f* the LORD
3: 16 those who *f* the LORD talked
Mk 6: 20 because Herod *f* John
11: 18 for they *f* him, because the whole
11: 32 (They *f* the people,
Lk 18: 2 was a judge who neither *f* God
Jn 19: 38 but secretly because he *f* the Jews.
Ac 5: 26 they *f* that the people would stone

FEARFUL (FEAR)

Lev 26: 36 I will make their hearts so *f*
Dt 28: 59 the LORD will send *f* plagues
Job 32: 6 that is why I was *f*,
Isa 8: 22 and darkness and *f* gloom,
35: 4 say to those with *f* hearts,
Lk 21: 11 and *f* events and great signs
Heb 10: 27 only a *f* expectation of judgment

FEARFULLY (FEAR)

Ps 139: 14 I am *f* and wonderfully made;

FEARING (FEAR)

Jos 22: 25 ours to stop *f* the LORD.
Ac 27: 17 *F* that they would run aground
27: 29 *F* that we would be dashed
Heb 11: 27 left Egypt, not *f* the king's anger;

FEARS (FEAR)

Job 1: 8 a man who *f* God and shuns evil."
2: 3 a man who *f* God and shuns evil.
Ps 25: 12 then, is the man that *f* the LORD?
34: 4 he delivered me from all my *f*.
112: 1 is the man who *f* the LORD,
128: 4 who *f* the LORD.
Pr 14: 2 whose walk is upright *f* the LORD,
14: 16 A wise man *f* the LORD
14: 26 He who *f* the LORD has a secure
28: 14 the man who always *f* the LORD,
31: 30 a woman who *f* the LORD is
Ecc 7: 18 man who *f* God will avoid all
Isa 50: 10 Who among you *f* the LORD
2Co 7: 5 conflicts on the outside, *f* within.
1Jn 4: 18 The man who *f* is not made perfect

FEARSOME (FEAR)

Job 41: 14 ringed about with his *f* teeth?

FEAST (FEASTED FEASTING FEASTS)

Ge 21: 8 weaned Abraham held a great *f*.
26: 30 Isaac then made a *f* for them,
29: 22 the people of the place and gave a *f*.
40: 20 and he gave a *f* for all his officials.
Ex 12: 17 the *F* of Unleavened Bread,
23: 15 the *F* of Unleavened Bread;
23: 16 "Celebrate the *F* of Harvest
23: 16 "Celebrate the *F* of Ingathering
34: 18 the *F* of Unleavened Bread.
34: 22 and the *F* of Ingathering at the turn
34: 22 "Celebrate the *F* of Weeks
34: 25 from the Passover *F* remain
Lev 23: 6 day of that month the LORD's *F*
23: 34 the seventh month the LORD's *F*
Nu 28: 26 of new grain during the *F* of Weeks
Dt 16: 10 Then celebrate the *F* of Weeks
16: 13 Celebrate the *F* of Tabernacles
16: 14 Be joyful at your *F*— you,
16: 15 For seven days celebrate the *F*
16: 16 at the *F* of Unleavened Bread,
16: 16 the *F* of Weeks and the *F*
31: 10 during the *F* of Tabernacles,
33: 19 they will *f* on the abundance
Jdg 14: 10 And Samson made a *f* there,
14: 12 within the seven days of the *f*,
14: 17 cried the whole seven days of the *f*.
2Sa 3: 20 David prepared a *f* for him
1Ki 1: 41 as they were finishing their *f*.
3: 15 Then he gave a *f* for all his court.
2Ki 6: 23 So he prepared a great *f* for them,
2Ch 8: 13 the *F* of Unleavened Bread,
8: 13 the *F* of Weeks and the *F*
30: 13 the *F* of Unleavened Bread
30: 21 in Jerusalem celebrated the *F*
35: 17 the *F* of Unleavened Bread
Ezr 3: 4 they celebrated the *F*
6: 22 joy the *F* of Unleavened Bread,
Ne 8: 14 live in booths during the *f*
8: 18 They celebrated the *f*
Job 39: 30 His young ones *f* on blood,
Ps 22: 29 All the rich of the earth will *f*
36: 8 They *f* on the abundance
81: 3 on the day of our *F*;
Pr 5: 10 lest strangers *f* on your wealth
15: 15 the cheerful heart has a continual *f*.
Ecc 5: 11 except to *f* his eyes on them?
10: 16 and whose princes *f* in the morning
10: 19 A *f* is made for laughter,
Isa 25: 6 a *f* of rich food for all peoples,
58: 14 and to *f* on the inheritance
Jer 51: 39 I will set out a *f* for them
La 2: 7 as on the day of an appointed *f*.
2: 22 "As you summon to a *f* day,
Eze 45: 21 a *f* lasting seven days,
45: 23 during the seven days of the *F* he is
45: 25 " 'During the seven days of the *F*,
Zec 14: 16 to celebrate the *F* of Tabernacles.
14: 18 to celebrate the *F* of Tabernacles.
14: 19 to celebrate the *F* of Tabernacles.
Mt 8: 11 places at the *f* with Abraham,
26: 5 "But not during the *F*," they said,
26: 17 day of the *F* of Unleavened Bread,
27: 15 at the *F* to release a prisoner
Mk 14: 1 *F* of Unleavened Bread were only
14: 2 "But not during the *F*," they said,
14: 12 day of the *F* of Unleavened Bread,

Mk 15: 6 Now it was the custom at the *F*
Lk 2: 41 for the *F* of the Passover.
2: 42 to the *F*, according to the custom.
2: 43 the *F* was over, while his parents
13: 29 at the *f* in the kingdom of God.
14: 8 invites you to a wedding *f*,
14: 15 at the *f* in the kingdom of God."
15: 23 Let's have a *f* and celebrate.
22: 1 Now the *F* of Unleavened Bread,
Jn 2: 23 was in Jerusalem at the Passover *F*,
4: 45 in Jerusalem at the Passover *F*,
5: 1 up to Jerusalem for a *f* of the Jews.
6: 4 The Jewish Passover *F* was near.
7: 2 But when the Jewish *F*
7: 8 I am not yet going up to this *F*,
7: 8 You go to the *F*.
7: 10 after his brothers had left for the *F*,
7: 11 at the *F* the Jews were watching
7: 14 through the *F* did Jesus go up
7: 37 the last and greatest day of the *F*,
10: 22 Then came the *F* of Dedication
11: 56 Isn't he coming to the *F* at all?"
12: 12 come for the *F* heard that Jesus was
12: 20 up to worship at the *F*.
13: 1 It was just before the Passover *F*.
13: 29 to buy what was needed for the *F*,
Ac 12: 3 during the *F* of Unleavened Bread.
20: 6 after the *F* of Unleavened Bread,
2Pe 2: 13 pleasures while they *f* with you.

FEASTED (FEAST)

Ge 43: 34 So they *f* and drank freely with him

FEASTING (FEAST)

Est 8: 17 gladness among the Jews, with *f*
9: 17 and made it a day of *f* and joy.
9: 18 and made it a day of *f* and joy.
9: 19 of Adar as a day of joy and *f*,
9: 22 to observe the days as days of *f*
Job 1: 5 a period of *f* had run its course,
1: 13 Job's sons and daughters were *f*
1: 18 "Your sons and daughters were *f*
Pr 17: 1 than a house full of *f*, with strife.
Ecc 7: 2 mourning than to go to a house of *f*,
Jer 16: 8 not enter a house where there is *f*
Am 6: 7 your *f* and lounging will end.
Zec 7: 6 were you not just *f* for yourselves?

FEASTS (FEAST)

Lev 23: 2 the appointed *f* of the LORD,
23: 2 'These are my appointed *f*,
23: 4 These are the LORD's appointed *f*,
23: 37 These are the LORD's appointed *f*,
23: 44 to the Israelites the appointed *f*
Nu 10: 10 your appointed *f* and New Moon
29: 39 for the LORD at your appointed *f*:
1Ch 23: 31 Moon festivals and at appointed *f*.
2Ch 2: 4 at the appointed *f* of the LORD our
8: 13 New Moons and the three annual *f*
31: 3 New Moons and appointed *f*
Ezr 3: 5 for all the appointed *f* of the LORD
Ne 10: 33 Moon festivals and appointed *f*;
Job 1: 4 used to take turns holding *f*
24: 20 the worm *f* on them;
Isa 1: 14 festivals and your appointed *f*
La 1: 4 for no one comes to her appointed *f*
2: 6 her appointed *f* and her Sabbaths;
Eze 36: 38 Jerusalem during her appointed *f*.
44: 24 my decrees for all my appointed *f*,
45: 17 at all the appointed *f* of the house
46: 9 the LORD at the appointed *f*,
46: 11 At the festivals and the appointed *f*
Hos 2: 11 Sabbath days—all her appointed *f*.
9: 5 do on the day of your appointed *f*,
12: 9 as in the days of your appointed *f*.
Am 5: 21 "I hate, I despise your religious *f*;
8: 10 I will turn your religious *f*
Zep 3: 18 "The sorrows for the appointed *f*
Jude : 12 men are blemishes at your love *f*,

FEAT

2Ki 8: 13 a mere dog, accomplish such a *f*?"

FEATHERS

Job 39: 13 with the pinions and *f* of the stork.
39: 18 Yet when she spreads her *f* to run,
Ps 68: 13 its *f* with shining gold."
91: 4 He will cover you with his *f*,
Eze 17: 3 long *f* and full plumage
Da 4: 33 heaven until his hair grew like the *f*

FEATURES

1Sa 16: 12 a fine appearance and handsome *f*.
Est 2: 7 as Esther, was lovely in form and *f*,
Job 38: 14 its *f* stand out like those

FED (FEED)

Dt 32: 13 and *f* him with the fruit of the fields
Jdg 19: 21 into his house and *f* his donkeys.
Ps 80: 5 You have *f* them with the bread
81: 16 you would be *f* with the finest
Da 4: 12 from it every creature was *f*.
Hos 13: 6 When I *f* them, they were satisfied;
Na 2: 11 the place where they *f* their young,
Lk 6: 25 Woe to you who are well *f* now,
Php 4: 12 whether well *f* or hungry,
Jas 2: 16 keep warm and well *f*,"

FEE

Nu 22: 7 with them the *f* for divination.
Eze 16: 33 Every prostitute receives a *f*,

FEEBLE (FEEBLEST)

Ne 4: 2 "What are those *f* Jews doing?
Job 4: 3 you have strengthened *f* hands.
26: 2 you have saved the arm that is *f*!
Ps 38: 8 I am *f* and utterly crushed;
Isa 16: 14 her survivors will be very few and *f*
35: 3 Strengthen the *f* hands,
Jer 49: 24 Damascus has become *f*,
Heb 12: 12 strengthen your *f* arms

FEEBLEST (FEEBLE)

Zec 12: 8 so that the *f* among them will be

FEED (FED FEEDING FEEDS OVERFED PASTURE-FED STALL-FED WELL-FED)

Ge 42: 27 sack to get *f* for his donkey,
1Ki 14: 11 of the air will *f* on those who die
16: 4 of the air will *f* on those who die
17: 4 ordered the ravens to *f* you there."
21: 24 of the air will *f* on those who die
Ps 49: 14 and death will *f* on them.
80: 13 and the creatures of the field *f* on it.
Pr 27: 27 milk to *f* you and your family
Isa 5: 17 lambs will *f* among the ruins
9: 20 Each will *f* on the flesh
9: 21 Manasseh will *f* on Ephraim,
11: 7 The cow will *f* with the bear,
18: 6 the birds will *f* on them all summer,
49: 9 "They will *f* beside the roads
61: 6 You will *f* on the wealth of nations,
65: 25 and the lamb will *f* together,
Eze 34: 10 can no longer *f* themselves.
34: 14 there they will *f* in a rich pasture
34: 18 for you to *f* on the good pasture?
34: 19 Must my flock *f* on what you have
Hos 4: 8 They *f* on the sins of my people
9: 2 winepresses will not *f* the people;
11: 4 and bent down to *f* them.
Mic 7: 14 Let them *f* in Bashan and Gilead
Zec 11: 16 or heal the injured, or *f* the healthy,
Mt 15: 33 place to *f* such a crowd?"
25: 37 did we see you hungry and *f* you,
Mk 8: 4 get enough bread to *f* them?"
Lk 15: 15 who sent him to his fields to *f* pigs.
Jn 21: 15 Jesus said, "*F* my lambs."
21: 17 Jesus said, "*F* my sheep.
Ro 12: 20 "If your enemy is hungry, *f* him;
Jude : 12 shepherds who *f* only themselves.

FEEDING (FEED)

Dt 8: 3 and then *f* you with manna,
Mt 8: 30 from them a large herd of pigs was *f*
Mk 5: 11 of pigs was *f* on the nearby hillside.
Lk 8: 32 of pigs was *f* there on the hillside.

FEEDS (FEED)

Job 40: 15 and which *f* on grass like an ox.
Pr 15: 14 but the mouth of a fool *f* on folly.
Isa 44: 20 He *f* on ashes, a deluded heart
Hos 12: 1 Ephraim *f* on the wind;
Mic 3: 5 if one *f* them,
Mt 6: 26 yet your heavenly Father *f* them.
Lk 12: 24 storeroom or barn; yet God *f* them.
Jn 6: 57 so the one who *f* on me will live
6: 58 but he who *f* on this bread will live
Eph 5: 29 ever hated his own body, but he *f*

FEEL (FEELING FEELINGS FEELS FELT)

Ge 41: 55 all Egypt began to *f* the famine,
Jdg 16: 26 me where I can *f* the pillars that
1Sa 16: 16 upon you, and you will *f* better."
16: 23 come to Saul; he would *f* better,
2Ki 9: 15 Jehu said, "If this is the way you *f*,
Ps 58: 9 Before your pots can *f* the heat
115: 7 they have hands, but cannot *f*,
Pr 23: 35 They beat me, but I don't *f* it!
Isa 32: 9 you daughters who *f* secure,
32: 10 you who *f* secure will tremble;
32: 11 you daughters who *f* secure!
Da 8: 25 When they *f* secure, he will destroy
11: 21 kingdom when its people *f* secure,
11: 24 the richest provinces *f* secure,
Am 6: 1 and to you who *f* secure
Zec 1: 15 with the nations that *f* secure.
2Co 11: 29 I do not *f* weak? Who is led into sin,
Php 1: 7 right for me to *f* this way about all
2Th 3: 14 in order that he may *f* ashamed.

FEELING (FEEL)

Job 24: 23 He may let them rest in a *f*
Isa 59: 10 *f* our way like men without eyes.

FEELINGS (FEEL)

Nu 5: 14 and if *f* of jealousy come
5: 30 or when *f* of jealousy come

FEELS (FEEL)

Ex 23: 9 you yourselves know how it *f*
Job 14: 22 He *f* but the pain of his own body
1Co 7: 36 and he *f* he ought to marry,

FEET (FOOT)

Ge 6: 15 450 *f* long, 75 *f* wide and 45 *f* high.
7: 20 to a depth of more than twenty *f*.
8: 9 dove could find no place to set its *f*
18: 4 and then you may all wash your *f*
19: 2 You can wash your *f* and spend
24: 32 and his men to wash their *f*.
43: 24 gave them water to wash their *f*
49: 10 the ruler's staff from between his *f*,
49: 33 he drew his *f* up into the bed,
Ex 4: 25 and touched Moses' *f* with it.
12: 11 your sandals on your *f*
24: 10 Under his *f* was something like
25: 12 and fasten them to its four *f*,
29: 20 and on the big toes of their right *f*.
30: 19 are to wash their hands and *f*
30: 21 and *f* so that they will not die.
37: 3 and fastened them to its four *f*,
40: 31 it to wash their hands and *f*.
Lev 8: 24 and on the big toes of their right *f*.
11: 42 or walks on all fours or on many *f*;
Nu 11: 31 to about three *f* above the ground,
35: 4 will extend out fifteen hundred *f*
35: 5 measure three thousand *f*
Dt 1: 36 descendants the land he set his *f*
3: 11 than thirteen *f* long and six *f* wide.
8: 4 and your *f* did not swell
22: 4 Help him get it to its *f*.
28: 35 from the soles of your *f* to the top
29: 5 nor did the sandals on your *f*.
33: 3 At your *f* they all bow down,
33: 24 and let him bathe his *f* in oil
Jos 3: 15 their *f* touched the water's edge,
4: 18 No sooner had they set their *f*
9: 5 and patched sandals on their *f*
10: 24 and placed their *f* on their necks.
10: 24 and put your *f* on the necks
14: 9 on which your *f* have walked will
Jdg 5: 27 At her *f* he sank,
5: 27 At her *f* he sank, he fell;
19: 21 After they had washed their *f*,
Ru 3: 4 go and uncover his *f* and lie down.
3: 7 uncovered his *f* and lay down.
3: 8 discovered a woman lying at his *f*.
3: 14 So she lay at his *f* until morning,
1Sa 2: 9 He will guard the *f* of his saints,
14: 13 and *f*, with his armor-bearer right
17: 4 He was over nine *f* tall.
25: 24 She fell at his *f* and said: "My lord,
25: 41 wash the *f* of my master's servants
2Sa 3: 34 your *f* were not fettered.

2Sa 4: 4 had a son who was lame in both *f*.
4: 12 They cut off their hands and *f*
9: 3 of Jonathan; he is crippled in both *f*
9: 13 and he was crippled in both *f*.
11: 8 to your house and wash your *f*.''
19: 24 He had not taken care of his *f*
22: 10 dark clouds were under his *f*.
22: 34 He makes my *f* like the *f* of a deer;
22: 39 they fell beneath my *f*.
22: 40 made my adversaries bow at my *f*.
1Ki 2: 5 his waist and the sandals on his *f*.
5: 3 LORD put his enemies under his *f*.
15: 23 however, his *f* became diseased.
2Ki 4: 27 mountain, she took hold of his *f*.
4: 37 fell at his *f* and bowed
9: 35 her skull, her *f* and her hands.
13: 21 came to life and stood up on his *f*.
14: 13 a section about six hundred *f* long.
19: 24 With the soles of my *f*
21: 8 I will not again make the *f*
25: 17 and a half *f* high and was decorated
25: 17 pillar was twenty-seven *f* high.
1Ch 11: 23 who was seven and a half *f* tall.
28: 2 King David rose to his *f* and said:
2Ch 3: 13 on their *f*, facing the main hall.
16: 12 afflicted with a disease in his *f*.
25: 23 a section about six hundred *f* long.
33: 8 I will not again make the *f*
Ezr 6: 3 be ninety *f* high and ninety *f* wide,
Ne 9: 21 nor did their *f* become swollen.
Est 5: 14 a gallows built, seventy-five *f* high,
7: 9 gallows seventy-five *f* high stands
8: 3 falling at his *f* and weeping.
Job 2: 7 from the soles of his *f* to the top
9: 13 cohorts of Rahab cowered at his *f*.
12: 5 fate of those whose *f* are slipping.
13: 27 You fasten my *f* in shackles;
13: 27 marks on the soles of my *f*.
18: 8 His *f* thrust him into a net
23: 11 My *f* have closely followed his
29: 8 and the old men rose to their *f*;
29: 15 and *f* to the lame.
30: 12 they lay snares for my *f*,
33: 11 He fastens my *f* in shackles;
Ps 8: 6 you put everything under his *f*:
9: 15 their *f* are caught in the net they
17: 5 my *f* have not slipped.
18: 9 dark clouds were under his *f*.
18: 33 He makes my *f* like the *f* of a deer;
18: 38 they fell beneath my *f*.
18: 39 made my adversaries bow at my *f*.
22: 16 have pierced my hands and my *f*.
25: 15 for only he will release my *f*
26: 12 My *f* stand on level ground;
31: 8 have set my *f* in a spacious place.
37: 31 his *f* do not slip.
40: 2 he set my *f* on a rock
44: 18 our *f* had not strayed
45: 5 let the nations fall beneath your *f*.
47: 3 peoples under our *f*.
56: 13 and my *f* from stumbling,
57: 6 They spread a net for my *f*—
58: 10 when they bathe their *f*
66: 9 and kept our *f* from slipping.
68: 23 that you may plunge your *f*
73: 2 as for me, my *f* had almost slipped;
105: 18 They bruised his *f* with shackles,
110: 1 a footstool for your *f*.''
115: 7 *f*, but they cannot walk;
116: 8 my *f* from stumbling,
119:101 I have kept my *f* from every evil
119:105 Your word is a lamp to my *f*
122: 2 Our *f* are standing
140: 4 who plan to trip my *f*.
Pr 1: 16 for their *f* rush into sin,
4: 26 Make level paths for your *f*
5: 5 Her *f* go down to death;
6: 13 signals with his *f*
6: 18 *f* that are quick to rush into evil,
6: 28 coals without his *f* being scorched?
7: 11 her *f* never stay at home;
26: 6 Like cutting off one's *f*
29: 5 is spreading a net for his *f*.
SS 5: 3 I have washed my *f*—
7: 1 How beautiful your sandaled *f*,
Isa 6: 2 with two they covered their *f*,
20: 2 and the sandals from your *f*.''
23: 7 whose *f* have taken her
Isa 26: 6 *F* trample it down—
26: 6 the *f* of the oppressed,
37: 25 With the soles of my *f*
41: 3 by a path his *f* have not traveled
49: 23 they will lick the dust at your *f*.
52: 7 are the *f* of those who bring good
58: 13 ''If you keep your *f*
59: 7 Their *f* rush into sin;
60: 13 and I will glorify the place of my *f*.
60: 14 you will bow down at your *f*
Jer 2: 25 Do not run until your *f* are bare
13: 16 before your *f* stumble
14: 10 they do not restrain their *f*.
18: 22 and have hidden snares for my *f*.
38: 22 Your *f* are sunk in the mud;
La 1: 13 He spread a net for my *f*
Eze 1: 7 their *f* were like those of a calf
2: 1 stand up on your *f* and I will speak
2: 2 into me and raised me to my *f*,
3: 24 into me and raised me to my *f*.
6: 11 stamp your *f* and cry out ''Alas!''
24: 17 and your sandals on your *f*;
24: 23 and your sandals on your *f*.
25: 6 your hands and stamped your *f*,
32: 2 churning the water with your *f*
34: 18 also muddy the rest with your *f*?
34: 18 rest of your pasture with your *f*?
34: 19 you have muddied with your *f*?
37: 10 to life and stood up on their *f*—
43: 7 and the place for the soles of my *f*.
Da 2: 33 its *f* partly of iron and partly
2: 34 It struck the statue on its *f* of iron
2: 41 Just as you saw that the *f*
3: 1 ninety *f* high and nine *f* wide,
3: 24 leaped to his *f* in amazement
7: 4 so that it stood on two *f* like a man,
8: 18 touched me and raised me to my *f*.
Na 1: 3 and clouds are the dust of his *f*.
1: 15 the *f* of one who brings good news,
Hab 3: 19 he makes my *f* like the *f* of a deer,
Zec 5: 2 thirty *f* long and fifteen *f* wide.''
14: 4 On that day his *f* will stand
14: 12 they are still standing on their *f*,
Mal 4: 3 under the soles of your *f* on the day
Mt 7: 6 may trample them under their *f*,
10: 14 shake the dust off your *f*
15: 30 them at his *f*; and he healed them.
18: 8 or two *f* and be thrown
22: 44 enemies under your *f*.'' '
28: 9 clasped his *f* and worshiped him.
Mk 5: 4 and broke the irons on his *f*.
5: 22 fell at his *f* and pleaded earnestly
5: 33 fell at his *f* and, trembling with fear
6: 11 the dust off your *f* when you leave,
7: 25 an evil spirit came and fell at his *f*.
9: 27 by the hand and lifted him to his *f*,
9: 45 crippled than to have two *f*
10: 49 On your *f*! He's calling you.''
10: 50 he jumped to his *f* and came
12: 36 enemies under your *f*.'' '
Lk 1: 79 to guide our *f* into the path of peace
7: 38 she began to wet his *f* with her tears
7: 38 stood behind him at his *f* weeping,
7: 44 but she wet my *f* with her tears
7: 44 did not give me any water for my *f*,
7: 45 has not stopped kissing my *f*.
7: 46 she has poured perfume on my *f*.
8: 28 he cried out and fell at his *f*,
8: 35 sitting at Jesus' *f*, dressed
8: 41 came and fell at Jesus' *f*,
8: 47 came trembling and fell at his *f*.
9: 5 shake the dust off your *f*
10: 11 to our *f* we wipe off against you.
10: 39 who sat at the Lord's *f* listening
15: 22 on his finger and sandals on his *f*.
17: 16 He threw himself at Jesus' *f*
20: 43 a footstool for your *f*.'' '
24: 39 Look at my hands and my *f*.
24: 40 he showed them his hands and *f*.
Jn 11: 2 and wiped his *f* with her hair.
11: 32 she fell at his *f* and said, ''Lord,
11: 44 and *f* wrapped with strips of linen,
12: 3 and wiped his *f* with her hair.
12: 3 she poured it on Jesus' *f*
13: 5 and began to wash his disciples' *f*,
13: 6 are you going to wash my *f*?''
13: 8 ''you shall never wash my *f*.''
13: 9 ''not just my *f* but my hands
Jn 13: 10 had a bath needs only to wash his *f*;
13: 12 he had finished washing their *f*,
13: 14 also should wash one another's *f*.
13: 14 and Teacher, have washed your *f*,
Ac 2: 35 a footstool for your *f*.'' '
3: 7 and instantly the man's *f*
3: 8 He jumped to his *f* and began
4: 35 and put it at the apostles' *f*,
4: 37 and put it at the apostles' *f*.
5: 2 and put it at the apostles' *f*.
5: 9 The *f* of the men who buried your
5: 10 that moment she fell down at his *f*
7: 58 at the *f* of a young man named Saul
9: 41 by the hand and helped her to her *f*.
10: 25 and fell at his *f* in reverence.
13: 51 from their *f* in protest against them
14: 8 there sat a man crippled in his *f*,
14: 10 ''Stand up on your *f*!'' At that,
16: 24 and fastened their *f* in the stocks.
21: 11 tied his own hands and *f* with it
26: 16 'Now get up and stand on your *f*.
27: 28 and found it was ninety *f* deep.
27: 28 was a hundred and twenty *f* deep.
Ro 3: 15 ''Their *f* are swift to shed blood;
10: 15 ''How beautiful are the *f*
16: 20 will soon crush Satan under your *f*.
1Co 12: 21 And the head cannot say to the *f*,
15: 25 has put all his enemies under his *f*.
15: 27 ''has put everything under his *f*.''
Eph 1: 22 God placed all things under his *f*
6: 15 your *f* fitted with the readiness
1Ti 5: 10 washing the *f* of the saints,
Heb 1: 13 a footstool for your *f*'?
2: 8 and put everything under his *f*.''
12: 13 ''Make level paths for your *f*,''
Jas 2: 3 or ''Sit on the floor by my *f*,''
Rev 1: 13 in a robe reaching down to his *f*
1: 15 His *f* were like bronze glowing
1: 17 I fell at his *f* as though dead.
2: 18 whose *f* are like burnished bronze.
3: 9 at your *f* and acknowledge that I
11: 11 and they stood on their *f*,
12: 1 with the moon under her *f*
13: 2 but had *f* like those of a bear
19: 10 At this I fell at his *f* to worship him.
22: 8 I fell down to worship at the *f*

FEIGNED

1Sa 21: 13 So he *f* insanity in their presence;

FELIX

Ac 23: 24 be taken safely to Governor *F*.''
23: 26 To His Excellency, Governor *F*:
24: 2 presented his case before *F*:
24: 3 most excellent *F*, we acknowledge
24: 22 Then *F*, who was well acquainted
24: 24 Several days later *F* came
24: 25 the judgment to come, *F* was afraid
24: 27 because *F* wanted to grant a favor
24: 27 *F* was succeeded by Porcius
25: 14 ''There is a man here whom *F* left

FELL (FALL)

Ge 7: 12 And rain *f* on the earth forty days
14: 10 some of the men *f* into them
15: 12 Abram *f* into a deep sleep,
17: 3 Abram *f* facedown, and God said
17: 17 Abraham *f* facedown; he laughed
35: 5 and the terror of God *f*
41: 5 He *f* asleep again and had a second
Ex 9: 24 hail *f* and lightning flashed back
Lev 9: 24 shouted for joy and *f* facedown.
Nu 3: 4 *f* dead before the LORD
14: 5 and Aaron *f* facedown in front
16: 4 Moses heard this, he *f* facedown.
16: 22 But Moses and Aaron *f* facedown
16: 45 And they *f* facedown.
20: 3 died when our brothers *f* dead
20: 6 Tent of Meeting and *f* facedown,
22: 31 So he bowed low and *f* facedown.
Dt 9: 18 Then once again I *f* prostrate
19: 5 and as he swings his ax to *f* a tree,
Jos 5: 14 Joshua *f* facedown to the ground
7: 6 and *f* facedown to the ground
8: 25 men and women *f* that day—
21: 10 because the first lot *f* to them):
22: 17 a plague *f* on the community
Jdg 4: 16 the troops of Sisera *f* by the sword;

Jdg 5: 27 At her feet he sank, he *f*;
5: 27 he *f*; there he lay.
5: 27 where he sank, there he *f*— dead.
8: 11 and *f* upon the unsuspecting army.
9: 40 and many *f* wounded in the flight
13: 20 and his wife *f* with their faces
16: 4 he *f* in love with a woman
19: 26 *f* down at the door and lay there
20: 31 so that about thirty men *f*
20: 44 Eighteen thousand Benjamites *f*,
20: 46 thousand Benjamite swordsmen *f*,
1Sa 4: 18 Eli *f* backward off his chair
11: 7 of the LORD *f* on the people,
14: 13 The Philistines *f* before Jonathan,
17: 49 and he *f* facedown on the ground.
25: 24 She *f* at his feet and said: "My lord,
28: 20 Immediately Saul *f* full length
31: 1 and many *f* slain on Mount Gilboa.
31: 4 so Saul took his own sword and *f*
31: 5 he too *f* on his sword and died
2Sa 1: 2 he *f* to the ground to pay him honor
1: 4 Many of them *f* and died.
2: 16 and they *f* down together.
2: 23 He *f* there and died on the spot.
3: 34 *f* as one falls before wicked men."
4: 4 he *f* and became crippled.
11: 17 some of the men in David's army *f*;
13: 1 Amnon son of David *f* in love
14: 4 she *f* with her face to the ground
14: 22 Joab *f* with his face to the ground
19: 18 he *f* prostrate before the king
21: 9 All seven of them *f* together;
21: 22 and they *f* at the hands of David
22: 39 they *f* beneath my feet.
1Ki 18: 38 Then the fire of the LORD *f*
18: 39 they *f* prostrate and cried,
19: 5 down under the tree and *f* asleep.
2Ki 1: 10 Then fire *f* from heaven
1: 12 Then the fire of God *f* from heaven
1: 13 and *f* on his knees before Elijah.
4: 37 *f* at his feet and bowed
6: 5 the iron axhead *f* into the water.
1Ch 5: 22 and many others *f* slain,
10: 1 and many *f* slain on Mount Gilboa.
10: 4 so Saul took his own sword and *f*
10: 5 he too *f* on his sword and died.
20: 8 and they *f* at the hands of David
21: 14 thousand men of Israel *f* dead.
21: 16 clothed in sackcloth, *f* facedown.
24: 7 The first lot *f* to Jehoiarib,
25: 9 which was for Asaph, *f* to Joseph,
26: 14 for the East Gate *f* to Shelemiah.
26: 14 the lot for the North Gate *f* to him.
26: 15 The lot for the South Gate *f*
26: 15 lot for the storehouse *f* to his sons.
26: 16 on the upper road *f* to Shuppim
29: 20 and *f* prostrate before the LORD
2Ch 14: 13 of Cushites *f* that they could not
17: 10 of the LORD *f* on all the kingdoms
20: 18 and Jerusalem *f* down in worship
Ezr 9: 5 and *f* on my knees with my hands
Ne 13: 19 When evening shadows *f*
Est 3: 7 And the lot *f* on the twelfth month,
Job 1: 16 "The fire of God *f* from the sky
1: 20 Then he *f* to the ground in worship
29: 22 my words *f* gently on their ears.
Ps 18: 38 they *f* beneath my feet.
105: 44 and they *f* heir to what others had
137: 7 on the day Jerusalem *f*.
La 1: 7 When her people *f*
Eze 1: 28 When I saw it, I *f* facedown,
3: 23 the Kebar River, and I *f* facedown.
9: 8 I *f* facedown, crying out, "Ah,
11: 13 Then I *f* facedown and cried out
31: 12 Its boughs *f* on the mountains
39: 23 and they all *f* by the sword.
43: 3 the Kebar River, and I *f* facedown.
44: 4 of the LORD, and I *f* facedown.
Da 2: 46 King Nebuchadnezzar *f* prostrate
3: 7 and men of every language *f* down
3: 23 firmly tied, *f* into the blazing
7: 20 before which three of them *f*—
8: 17 I was terrified and *f* prostrate.
10: 9 to him, I *f* into a deep sleep,
Jnh 1: 5 lay down and *f* into a deep sleep.
1: 7 They cast lots and the lot *f*
Mt 7: 27 and it *f* with a great crash."
13: 4 he was scattering the seed, some *f*
Mt 13: 5 Some *f* on rocky places, where it
13: 7 Other seed *f* among thorns,
13: 8 Still other seed *f* on good soil,
17: 6 they *f* facedown to the ground,
18: 26 "The servant *f* on his knees
18: 29 "His fellow servant *f* to his knees
25: 5 all became drowsy and *f* asleep.
26: 39 he *f* with his face to the ground
Mk 3: 11 they *f* down before him
4: 4 he was scattering the seed, some *f*
4: 5 Some *f* on rocky places, where it
4: 7 Other seed *f* among thorns,
4: 8 Still other seed *f* on good soil.
5: 6 and *f* on his knees in front of him.
5: 22 he *f* at his feet and pleaded
5: 33 came and *f* at his feet and,
7: 25 by an evil spirit came and *f*
9: 20 He *f* to the ground and rolled
10: 17 and *f* on his knees before him.
10: 22 At this the man's face *f*.
14: 35 he *f* to the ground and prayed that
Lk 5: 8 he *f* at Jesus' knees and said,
5: 12 he *f* with his face to the ground
8: 5 he was scattering the seed, some *f*
8: 6 Some *f* on rock, and when it came
8: 7 Other seed *f* among thorns,
8: 8 Still other seed *f* on good soil.
8: 14 seed that *f* among thorns stands
8: 23 As they sailed, he *f* asleep.
8: 28 he cried out and *f* at his feet,
8: 41 ruler of the synagogue, came and *f*
8: 47 came trembling and *f* at his feet.
10: 30 when he *f* into the hands of robbers
10: 36 to the man who *f* into the hands
13: 4 the tower in Siloam *f* on them—
16: 21 and longing to eat what *f*
Jn 11: 32 she *f* at his feet and said, "Lord,
18: 6 they drew back and *f* to the ground
Ac 1: 18 bought a field; there he *f* headlong,
1: 26 Then they drew lots, and the lot *f*
5: 5 When Ananias heard this, he *f*
5: 10 At that moment she *f*
7: 60 Then he *f* on his knees
7: 60 When he had said this, he *f* asleep.
9: 4 He *f* to the ground and heard
9: 18 something like scales *f*
10: 10 the meal was being prepared, he *f*
10: 25 and *f* at his feet in reverence.
12: 7 and the chains *f* off Peter's wrists.
13: 36 he *f* asleep; he was buried
16: 29 and *f* trembling before Paul
19: 35 which *f* from heaven? Therefore,
20: 9 he *f* to the ground from the third
22: 7 I *f* to the ground and heard a voice
22: 17 I *f* into a trance and saw the Lord
26: 14 We all *f* to the ground,
Ro 11: 22 sternness to those who *f*,
Heb 3: 17 whose bodies *f* in the desert?
11: 30 By faith the walls of Jericho *f*,
Rev 1: 17 I *f* at his feet as though dead.
5: 8 and the twenty-four elders *f*
5: 14 the elders *f* down and worshiped.
6: 13 and the stars in the sky *f* to earth,
7: 11 They *f* down on their faces
8: 10 *f* from the sky on a third
11: 16 *f* on their faces and worshiped God
16: 21 of about a hundred pounds each *f*
19: 4 the four living creatures *f* down
19: 10 At this I *f* at his feet to worship him
22: 8 I *f* down to worship at the feet

FELLED (FALL)

Isa 9: 10 the fig trees have been *f*,
10: 33 The lofty trees will be *f*,

FELLING (FALL)

1Ki 5: 6 one so skilled in *f* timber

FELLOWSHIP

Ex 20: 24 burnt offerings and *f* offerings,
24: 5 as *f* offerings to the LORD.
29: 28 to the LORD from their *f* offerings.
32: 6 offerings and presented *f* offerings.
Lev 3: 1 If someone's offering is a *f* offering,
3: 3 From the *f* offering he is
3: 6 as a *f* offering to the LORD,
3: 9 From the *f* offering he is
4: 10 the cow sacrificed as a *f* offering.
Lev 4: 26 he burned the fat of the *f* offering.
4: 31 removed from the *f* offering,
4: 35 from the lamb of the *f* offering,
6: 12 burn the fat of the *f* offerings on it.
7: 11 for the *f* offering a person may
7: 13 Along with his *f* offering
7: 14 the blood of the *f* offerings.
7: 15 The meat of his *f* offering
7: 18 If any meat of the *f* offering is eaten
7: 20 meat of the *f* offering belonging
7: 21 the meat of the *f* offering belonging
7: 29 'Anyone who brings a *f* offering
7: 32 of your *f* offerings to the priest
7: 33 of the *f* offering shall have the right
7: 34 From the *f* offerings
7: 37 offering and the *f* offering,
9: 4 a ram for a *f* offering to sacrifice
9: 18 as the *f* offering for the people.
9: 22 the burnt offering and the *f* offering
10: 14 share of the Israelites' *f* offerings.
17: 5 and sacrifice them as *f* offerings.
19: 5 " 'When you sacrifice a *f* offering
22: 21 or flock a *f* offering to the LORD
23: 19 each a year old, for a *f* offering.
Nu 6: 14 a ram without defect for a *f* offering
6: 17 as a *f* offering to the LORD,
6: 18 under the sacrifice of the *f* offering.
7: 17 to be sacrificed as a *f* offering.
7: 23 to be sacrificed as a *f* offering.
7: 29 to be sacrificed as a *f* offering.
7: 35 to be sacrificed as a *f* offering.
7: 41 to be sacrificed as a *f* offering.
7: 47 to be sacrificed as a *f* offering.
7: 53 to be sacrificed as a *f* offering.
7: 59 to be sacrificed as a *f* offering.
7: 65 to be sacrificed as a *f* offering.
7: 71 to be sacrificed as a *f* offering.
7: 77 to be sacrificed as a *f* offering.
7: 83 to be sacrificed as a *f* offering.
7: 88 the sacrifice of the *f* offering came
10: 10 burnt offerings and *f* offerings,
15: 8 or a *f* offering to the LORD,
29: 39 drink offerings and *f* offerings.' "
Dt 27: 7 Sacrifice *f* offerings there,
Jos 8: 31 offerings and sacrificed *f* offerings.
22: 23 or to sacrifice *f* offerings on it,
22: 27 offerings, sacrifices and *f* offerings.
Jdg 20: 26 and *f* offerings to the LORD.
21: 4 burnt offerings and *f* offerings.
1Sa 10: 8 burnt offerings and *f* offerings,
11: 15 There they sacrificed *f* offerings
13: 9 burnt offering and the *f* offerings."
2Sa 6: 17 and *f* offerings before the LORD.
6: 18 the burnt offerings and *f* offerings,
24: 25 burnt offerings and *f* offerings.
1Ki 3: 15 burnt offerings and *f* offerings.
8: 63 of *f* offerings to the LORD:
8: 64 and the fat of the *f* offerings,
8: 64 and the fat of the *f* offerings.
9: 25 *f* offerings on the altar he had built
2Ki 16: 13 blood of his *f* offerings on the altar.
1Ch 16: 1 and *f* offerings before God.
16: 2 the burnt offerings and *f* offerings,
21: 26 burnt offerings and *f* offerings.
2Ch 7: 7 and the fat of the *f* offerings,
29: 35 with the fat of the *f* offerings
30: 22 and offered *f* offerings and praised
31: 2 burnt offerings and *f* offerings,
33: 16 and sacrificed *f* and thank offerings
Ps 55: 14 with whom I once enjoyed sweet *f*
Pr 7: 14 "I have *f* offerings at home;
Eze 43: 27 and *f* offerings on the altar.
45: 15 and *f* offerings to make atonement
45: 17 and *f* offerings to make atonement
46: 2 burnt offering and his *f* offerings.
46: 12 a burnt offering or *f* offerings—
46: 12 his burnt offering or his *f* offerings
Am 5: 22 you bring choice *f* offerings,
Ac 2: 42 the apostles' teaching and to the *f*,
1Co 1: 9 who has called you into *f*
5: 2 out of your *f* the man who did this?
2Co 6: 14 what *f* can light have with darkness
13: 14 and the *f* of the Holy Spirit be
Gal 2: 9 and Barnabas the right hand of *f*
Php 2: 1 if any *f* with the Spirit,
3: 10 the *f* of sharing in his sufferings,
1Jn 1: 3 And our *f* is with the Father
1: 3 so that you also may have *f* with us.

1Jn 1: 6 claim to have *f* with him yet walk
1: 7 we have *f* with one another,

FELT (FEEL)

Ge 2: 25 both naked, and they *f* no shame.
Ex 2: 6 He was crying, and she *f* sorry
10: 21 Egypt—darkness that can be *f*."
1Sa 13: 12 So I *f* compelled to offer the burnt
2Ki 8: 11 gaze until Hazael *f* ashamed.
Ps 30: 6 When I *f* secure, I said,
Jer 5: 3 You struck them, but they *f* no pain
22: 21 I warned you when you *f* secure,
Na 3: 19 for who has not *f*
Mk 5: 29 she *f* in her body that she was freed
2Co 1: 9 in our hearts we *f* the sentence
Heb 10: 2 and would no longer have *f* guilty
Jude : 3 I *f* I had to write and urge you

FEMALE (FEMALES)

Ge 1: 27 male and *f* he created them.
5: 2 He created them male and *f*;
6: 19 and *f*, to keep them alive with you.
7: 3 *f*, to keep their various kinds alive
7: 9 male and *f*, came to Noah
7: 16 and *f* of every living thing,
12: 16 male and *f* donkeys, menservants
20: 14 and cattle and male and *f* slaves
30: 35 spotted *f* goats (all that had white
32: 14 two hundred *f* goats and twenty
32: 15 and twenty *f* donkeys and ten male
32: 15 thirty *f* camels with their young,
45: 23 ten *f* donkeys loaded with grain
Ex 21: 20 "If a man beats his male or *f* slave
21: 32 If the bull gores a male or *f* slave,
Lev 3: 1 from the herd, whether male or *f*,
3: 6 to offer a male or *f* without defect.
4: 28 for the sin he committed a *f* goat
4: 32 he is to bring a *f* without defect.
5: 6 bring to the LORD a *f* lamb
25: 44 and *f* slaves are to come
27: 4 and if it is a *f*, set her value
27: 5 and of a *f* at ten shekels.
27: 6 that of a *f* at three shekels of silver.
27: 7 and of a *f* at ten shekels.
Nu 5: 3 Send away male and *f* alike;
15: 27 he must bring a year-old *f* goat
Dt 23: 18 bring the earnings of a *f* prostitute
28: 68 your enemies as male and *f* slaves,
Est 7: 4 been sold as male and *f* slaves,
Ecc 2: 7 I bought male and *f* slaves
Jer 34: 9 his Hebrew slaves, both male and *f*;
34: 10 *f* slaves and no longer hold them
34: 16 and *f* slaves you had set free
Mt 19: 4 Creator 'made them male and *f*,'
Mk 10: 6 God 'made them male and *f*.'
Gal 3: 28 *f*, for you are all one in Christ Jesus

FEMALES (FEMALE)

Ge 30: 41 Whenever the stronger *f* were

FENCE

Ps 62: 3 this leaning wall, this tottering *f*?

FERMENTED

Lev 10: 9 or other *f* drink whenever you go
Nu 6: 3 abstain from wine and other *f* drink
6: 3 from wine or from other *f* drink.
28: 7 of a hin of *f* drink with each lamb.
Dt 14: 26 cattle, sheep, wine or other *f* drink,
29: 6 and drank no wine or other *f* drink.
Jdg 13: 4 or other *f* drink and that you do not
13: 7 drink no wine or other *f* drink
13: 14 nor drink any wine or other *f* drink
Lk 1: 15 never to take wine or other *f* drink,

FEROCIOUS

Ge 37: 20 say that a *f* animal devoured him.
37: 33 Some *f* animal has devoured him.
Isa 35: 9 nor will any *f* beast get up on it;
Mt 7: 15 but inwardly they are *f* wolves.

FERTILE (FERTILIZE)

Nu 13: 20 How is the soil? Is it *f* or poor?
2Ch 26: 10 in the hills and in the *f* lands,
Ne 9: 25 captured fortified cities and *f* land;
9: 35 in the spacious and *f* land you gave
Isa 5: 1 a vineyard on a *f* hillside.
10: 18 splendor of his forests and *f* fields
Isa 28: 1 set on the head of a *f* valley—
28: 4 set on the head of a *f* valley,
29: 17 and the *f* field seem like a forest?
29: 17 not Lebanon be turned into a *f* field
32: 15 and the desert becomes a *f* field,
32: 15 and the *f* field seems like a forest.
32: 16 and righteousness live in the *f* field.
Jer 2: 7 I brought you into a *f* land
Eze 17: 5 of your land and put it in *f* soil.
Mic 7: 14 in *f* pasturelands.

FERTILIZE (FERTILE)

Lk 13: 8 and I'll dig around it and *f* it.

FERVENT (FERVOR)

Pr 26: 23 are *f* lips with an evil heart.

FERVOR (FERVENT)

Ac 18: 25 and he spoke with great *f*
Ro 12: 11 but keep your spiritual *f*, serving

FESTAL (FESTIVAL)

Ps 118: 27 in hand, join in the *f* procession

FESTER (FESTERING)

Ps 38: 5 My wounds *f* and are loathsome

FESTERING (FESTER)

Ex 9: 9 and *f* boils will break out on men
9: 10 and *f* boils broke out on men
Lev 21: 20 or who has *f* or running sores
22: 22 or anything with warts or *f*
Dt 28: 27 *f* sores and the itch,
Job 7: 5 my skin is broken and *f*.

FESTIVAL (FESTAL FESTIVALS FESTIVE)

Ex 5: 1 so that they may hold a *f* to me
10: 9 are to celebrate a *f* to the LORD."
12: 14 to come you shall celebrate it as a *f*
13: 6 and on the seventh day hold a *f*
23: 14 are to celebrate a *f* to me.
23: 18 of my *f* offerings must not be kept
32: 5 "Tomorrow there will be a *f*
Lev 23: 39 celebrate the *f* to the LORD
23: 41 *f* to the LORD for seven days each
Nu 15: 3 or freewill offerings or *f* offerings—
28: 17 day of this month there is to be a *f*;
29: 12 Celebrate a *f* to the LORD
Jdg 9: 27 they held a *f* in the temple
21: 19 there is the annual *f* of the LORD
1Sa 20: 5 tomorrow is the New Moon *f*,
20: 18 "Tomorrow is the New Moon *f*.
20: 24 and when the New Moon *f* came,
1Ki 8: 2 at the time of the *f* in the month
8: 65 So Solomon observed the *f*
12: 32 He instituted a *f* on the fifteenth
12: 32 like the *f* held in Judah,
12: 33 he instituted the *f* for the Israelites
2Ch 5: 3 time of the *f* in the seventh month.
7: 8 So Solomon observed the *f*
7: 9 and the *f* for seven days more.
30: 23 to celebrate the *f* seven more days;
Isa 30: 29 on the night you celebrate a holy *f*;
Hos 7: 5 On the day of the *f* of our king
9: 5 on the *f* days of the LORD?
Mal 2: 3 the offal from your *f* sacrifices,
1Co 5: 8 Therefore let us keep the *F*,
Col 2: 16 or with regard to a religious *f*,

FESTIVALS (FESTIVAL)

Nu 10: 10 feasts and New Moon *f*—
1Ch 23: 31 Moon *f* and at appointed feasts.
Ne 10: 33 New Moon *f* and appointed feasts;
Isa 1: 14 Your New Moon *f* and your
29: 1 and let your cycle of *f* go on.
33: 20 Look upon Zion, the city of our *f*;
Eze 45: 17 and drink offerings at the *f*,
46: 11 At the *f* and the appointed feasts,
Hos 2: 11 her yearly *f*, her New Moons,
5: 7 Now their New Moon *f*
Na 1: 15 Celebrate your *f*, O Judah,
Zec 8: 19 and glad occasions and happy *f*

FESTIVE (FESTIVAL)

1Sa 25: 8 since we come at a *f* time.
Ps 42: 4 thanksgiving among the *f* throng.

FESTOONED

1Ki 7: 17 of interwoven chains *f* the capitals

FESTUS

Ac 25: 1 *F* went up from Caesarea
25: 3 They urgently requested *F*,
25: 4 *F* answered, "Paul is being held
25: 9 *F*, wishing to do the Jews a favor,
25: 12 After *F* had conferred
25: 13 Caesarea to pay their respects to *F*.
25: 14 *F* discussed Paul's case
25: 22 Agrippa said to *F*, "I would like
25: 23 command of *F*, Paul was brought
25: 24 *F* said: "King Agrippa,
26: 24 At this point *F* interrupted Paul's
26: 25 most excellent *F*," Paul replied.
26: 32 to *F*, "This man could have been

FETTERED (FETTERS)

2Sa 3: 34 your feet were not *f*.

FETTERS (FETTERED)

Job 36: 13 when he *f* them, they do not cry
Ps 2: 3 "and throw off their *f*."
149: 8 to bind their kings with *f*,

FEVER (FEVERISH)

Lev 26: 16 and *f* that will destroy your sight
Dt 28: 22 with *f* and inflammation,
Job 30: 30 my body burns with *f*.
Mt 8: 14 mother-in-law lying in bed with a *f*.
8: 15 touched her hand and the *f* left her,
Mk 1: 30 mother-in-law was in bed with a *f*,
1: 31 The *f* left her and she began to wait
Lk 4: 38 was suffering from a high *f*,
4: 39 he bent over her and rebuked the *f*,
Jn 4: 52 "The *f* left him yesterday
Ac 28: 8 suffering from *f* and dysentery.

FEVERISH (FEVER)

La 5: 10 *f* from hunger.

FIELD (BATTLEFIELD FIELDS GRAINFIELD GRAINFIELDS)

Ge 2: 5 no plant of the *f* had yet sprung up;
2: 5 no shrub of the *f* had yet appeared
2: 19 of the ground all the beasts of the *f*
2: 20 of the air and all the beasts of the *f*.
3: 18 and you will eat the plants of the *f*.
4: 8 Abel, "Let's go out to the *f*."
4: 8 And while they were in the *f*,
23: 9 to him and is in the end of his *f*.
23: 11 "Listen to me; I give you the *f*,
23: 13 I will pay the price of the *f*.
23: 17 So Ephron's *f* in Machpelah
23: 17 both the *f* and the cave in it,
23: 17 trees within the borders of the *f*—
23: 19 in the cave in the *f* of Machpelah
23: 20 the *f* and the cave in it were deeded
24: 63 to the *f* one evening to meditate,
24: 65 man in the *f* coming to meet us?"
25: 9 in the *f* of Ephron son
25: 10 the *f* Abraham had bought
27: 27 is like the smell of a *f*
29: 2 There he saw a well in the *f*,
37: 7 sheaves of grain out in the *f*
39: 5 both in the house and in the *f*.
49: 29 cave in the *f* of Ephron the Hittite,
49: 30 the Hittite, along with the *f*.
49: 30 the cave in the *f* of Machpelah,
49: 32 The *f* and the cave
50: 13 in the cave in the *f* of Machpelah,
50: 13 the Hittite, along with the *f*.
Ex 9: 3 plague on your livestock in the *f*—
9: 19 and everything you have in the *f*
9: 19 brought in and is still out in the *f*,
9: 21 their slaves and livestock in the *f*.
22: 5 and they graze in another man's *f*,
22: 5 from the best of his own *f*
22: 5 "If a man grazes his livestock in a *f*
22: 6 or standing grain or the whole *f*,
23: 16 gather in your crops from the *f*.
23: 16 of the crops you sow in your *f*.
Lev 19: 9 reap to the very edges of your *f*
19: 19 Do not plant your *f* with two kinds
23: 22 reap to the very edges of your *f*
26: 4 and the trees of the *f* their fruit.
27: 17 If he dedicates his *f*

Lev 27: 18 But if he dedicates his *f*
27: 19 and the *f* will again become his.
27: 19 the man who dedicates the *f* wishes
27: 20 however, he does not redeem the *f*,
27: 21 When the *f* is released
27: 21 like a *f* devoted to the LORD;
27: 22 to the LORD a *f* he has bought,
27: 24 the Year of Jubilee the *f* will revert
Nu 20: 17 We will not go through any *f*
21: 22 We will not turn aside into any *f*
22: 4 as an ox licks up the grass of the *f*.''
22: 23 she turned off the road into a *f*.
23: 14 So he took him to the *f* of Zophim
Dt 20: 19 Are the trees of the *f* people,
21: 1 in a *f* in the land the LORD your
24: 19 When you are harvesting in your *f*
28: 38 You will sow much seed in the *f*
Jos 15: 18 him to ask her father for a *f*.
Jdg 1: 14 him to ask her father for a *f*.
5: 18 on the heights of the *f*.
13: 9 woman while she was out in the *f*;
20: 31 about thirty men fell in the open *f*
Ru 2: 3 working in a *f* belonging to Boaz,
2: 7 into the *f* and has worked steadily
2: 8 Don't go and glean in another *f*
2: 9 Watch the *f* where the men are
2: 17 Ruth gleaned in the *f* until evening.
2: 22 in someone else's *f* you might be
1Sa 6: 14 The cart came to the *f* of Joshua
6: 18 in the *f* of Joshua of Beth Shemesh.
14: 15 those in the camp and *f*,
17: 44 of the air and the beasts of the *f*!''
19: 3 father in the *f* where you are.
20: 5 and hide in the *f* until the evening
20: 11 said, "let's go out into the *f*."
20: 24 So David hid in the *f*,
20: 35 to the *f* for his meeting with David.
30: 11 They found an Egyptian in a *f*
2Sa 14: 6 into a fight with each other in the *f*,
14: 30 Absalom's servants set the *f* on fire
14: 30 "Look, Joab's *f* is next to mine,
14: 31 "Why have your servants set my *f*
18: 6 marched into the *f* to fight Israel,
20: 12 him from the road into a *f*
23: 11 at a place where there was a *f* full
23: 12 stand in the middle of the *f*
2Ki 3: 19 and ruin every good *f* with stones.''
3: 25 a stone on every good *f* until it was
9: 25 throw him on the *f* that belonged
18: 17 his *f* commander with a large army,
18: 17 on the road to the Washerman's *F*
18: 19 The *f* commander said to them,
18: 26 and Joah said to the *f* commander,
18: 37 him what the *f* commander had
19: 4 the words of the *f* commander,
19: 8 When the *f* commander heard that
19: 26 They are like plants in the *f*,
1Ch 11: 13 At a place where there was a *f* full
11: 14 stand in the middle of the *f*.
27: 26 charge of the *f* workers who farmed
2Ch 26: 23 them in a *f* for burial that belonged
Job 5: 23 with the stones of the *f*,
Ps 8: 7 and the beasts of the *f*,
50: 11 and the creatures of the *f* are mine.
72: 6 will be like rain falling on a mown *f*,
72: 16 let it thrive like the grass of the *f*.
80: 13 and the creatures of the *f* feed on it.
103: 15 he flourishes like a flower of the *f*;
104: 11 to all the beasts of the *f*;
Pr 13: 23 poor man's *f* may produce
24: 30 I went past the *f* of the sluggard,
27: 26 and the goats with the price of a *f*.
31: 16 She considers a *f* and buys it;
SS 2: 7 and by the does of the *f*:
3: 5 and by the does of the *f*:
Isa 1: 8 like a hut in a *f* of melons,
5: 8 and join *f* to *f*
7: 3 on the road to the Washerman's *F*.
19: 7 Every sown *f* along the Nile
28: 25 and spelt in its *f*?
29: 17 Lebanon be turned into a fertile *f*
29: 17 and the fertile *f* seem like a forest?
32: 15 and the desert becomes a fertile *f*,
32: 15 and the fertile *f* seems like a forest.
32: 16 righteousness live in the fertile *f*.
36: 2 of Assyria sent his *f* commander
36: 2 on the road to the Washerman's *F*,
36: 4 The *f* commander said to them,
Isa 36: 11 and Joah said to the *f* commander,
36: 22 him what the *f* commander had
37: 4 the words of the *f* commander,
37: 8 When the *f* commander heard that
37: 27 They are like plants in the *f*,
40: 6 glory is like the flowers of the *f*.
55: 12 and all the trees of the *f*
56: 9 Come, all you beasts of the *f*,
Jer 4: 17 surround her like men guarding a *f*,
7: 20 on the trees of the *f* and on the fruit
9: 22 like refuse on the open *f*,
12: 4 and the grass in every *f* be withered
12: 10 and trample down my *f*;
12: 10 they will turn my pleasant *f*
14: 5 Even the doe in the *f*
26: 18 " 'Zion will be plowed like a *f*,
32: 7 'Buy my *f* at Anathoth, because
32: 8 'Buy my *f* at Anathoth
32: 9 so I bought the *f* at Anathoth
32: 25 'Buy the *f* with silver and have
41: 8 oil and honey, hidden in a *f*.''
La 4: 9 away for lack of food from the *f*.
Eze 16: 5 were thrown out into the open *f*,
16: 7 made you grow like a plant of the *f*.
17: 24 of the *f* will know that I the LORD
29: 5 You will fall on the open *f*
31: 4 channels to all the trees of the *f*.
31: 5 higher than all the trees of the *f*;
31: 6 all the beasts of the *f*
31: 13 of the *f* were among its branches.
31: 15 all the trees of the *f* withered away.
32: 4 and hurl you on the open *f*.
34: 27 trees of the *f* will yield their fruit
36: 30 of the trees and the crops of the *f*,
38: 20 of the *f*, every creature that moves
39: 5 You will fall in the open *f*,
Da 2: 38 and the beasts of the *f* and the birds
4: 12 the beasts of the *f* found shelter,
4: 15 in the ground, in the grass of the *f*.
4: 21 giving shelter to the beasts of the *f*,
4: 23 grass of the *f*, while its roots remain
Hos 2: 18 them with the beasts of the *f*
4: 3 the beasts of the *f* and the birds
10: 4 like poisonous weeds in a plowed *f*.
12: 11 stones on a plowed *f*.
Joel 1: 11 the harvest of the *f* is destroyed.
1: 12 all the trees of the *f*— are dried up.
1: 19 burned up all the trees of the *f*.
Am 4: 7 One *f* had rain;
Mic 3: 12 Zion will be plowed like a *f*,
4: 10 the city to camp in the open *f*.
Zec 10: 1 and plants of the *f* to everyone.
Mt 6: 28 See how the lilies of the *f* grow.
6: 30 how God clothes the grass of the *f*,
9: 38 workers into his harvest *f*.''
13: 24 man who sowed good seed in his *f*.
13: 27 didn't you sow good seed in your *f*?
13: 31 a man took and planted in his *f*.
13: 36 the parable of the weeds in the *f*.''
13: 38 *f* is the world, and the good seed
13: 44 is like treasure hidden in a *f*.
13: 44 sold all he had and bought that *f*.
22: 5 one to his *f*, another to his business.
24: 18 Let no one in the *f* go back
24: 40 be in the *f*; one will be taken
27: 7 the money to buy the potter's *f*
27: 8 That is why it has been called the *F*
27: 10 they used them to buy the potter's *f*
Mk 13: 16 Let no one in the *f* go back
Lk 10: 2 send out workers into his harvest *f*.
12: 28 how God clothes the grass of the *f*,
14: 18 I have just bought a *f*, and I must go
15: 25 the older son was in the *f*.
17: 7 when he comes in from the *f*,
17: 31 no one in the *f* should go back
Ac 1: 18 Judas bought a *f*; there he fell
1: 19 so they called that *f*
1: 19 their language Akeldama, that is, *F*
4: 37 sold a *f* he owned and brought
1Co 3: 9 you are God's *f*, God's building.
2Co 10: 13 a *f* that reaches even to you.
10: 13 to the *f* God has assigned to us,
1Pe 1: 24 glory is like the flowers of the *f*;

FIELDS (FIELD)

Ge 30: 14 Reuben went out into the *f*
30: 16 came in from the *f* that evening,
31: 4 out to the *f* where his flocks were.
34: 5 were in the *f* with his livestock;
34: 7 Jacob's sons had come in from the *f*
34: 28 of theirs in the city and out in the *f*.
37: 15 him wandering around in the *f*
41: 48 grown in the *f* surrounding it.
47: 20 Egyptians, one and all, sold their *f*,
47: 24 as seed for the *f* and as food
Ex 1: 14 and with all kinds of work in the *f*;
8: 13 in the courtyards and in the *f*.
9: 22 growing in the *f* of Egypt.''
9: 25 down everything growing in the *f*
9: 25 hail struck everything in the *f*—
10: 5 every tree that is growing in your *f*.
10: 12 devour everything growing in the *f*,
10: 15 everything growing in the *f*
23: 10 "For six years you are to sow your *f*
Lev 14: 7 to release the live bird in the open *f*
14: 53 bird in the open *f* outside the town.
17: 5 they are now making in the open *f*.
25: 3 For six years sow your *f*,
25: 4 Do not sow your *f* or prune your
25: 12 what is taken directly from the *f*.
Nu 16: 14 or given us an inheritance of *f*
Dt 11: 15 grass in the *f* for your cattle,
14: 22 of all that your *f* produce each year.
32: 13 and fed him with the fruit of the *f*.
32: 32 and from the *f* of Gomorrah.
Jos 8: 24 killing all the men of Ai in the *f*
21: 12 *f* and villages around the city they
Jdg 9: 27 After they had gone out into the *f*
9: 32 should come and lie in wait in the *f*.
9: 42 of Shechem went out to the *f*,
9: 43 and set an ambush in the *f*.
9: 44 rushed upon those in the *f*
19: 16 came in from his work in the *f*.
Ru 2: 2 go to the *f* and pick up the leftover
2: 3 in the *f* behind the harvesters.
1Sa 8: 14 He will take the best of your *f*
11: 5 then Saul was returning from the *f*,
22: 7 the son of Jesse give all of you *f*
25: 15 out in the *f* near them nothing was
2Sa 1: 21 nor *f* that yield offerings
11: 11 men are camped in the open *f*.
19: 29 I order you and Ziba to divide the *f*
1Ki 2: 26 "Go back to your *f* in Anathoth.
2Ki 4: 39 out into the *f* to gather herbs
23: 4 them outside Jerusalem in the *f*
23: 12 land to work the vineyards and *f*.
1Ch 6: 56 *f* and villages around the city were
16: 32 let the *f* be jubilant, and everything
2Ch 26: 10 He had people working his *f*
31: 5 honey and all that the *f* produced.
Ne 5: 3 "We are mortgaging our *f*,
5: 4 to pay the king's tax on our *f*
5: 5 our *f* and our vineyards belong
5: 11 back to them immediately their *f*,
11: 25 As for the villages with their *f*,
11: 30 in Lachish and its *f*, and in Azekah
12: 44 From the *f* around the towns they
13: 10 had gone back to their own *f*.
Job 24: 6 They gather fodder in the *f*
Ps 37: 20 will be like the beauty of the *f*,
96: 12 let the *f* be jubilant, and everything
107: 37 They sowed *f* and planted
132: 6 we came upon it in the *f* of Jaar:
144: 13 by tens of thousands in our *f*;
Pr 8: 26 before he made the earth or its *f*
23: 10 encroach on the *f* of the fatherless,
24: 27 and get your *f* ready;
Ecc 5: 9 the king himself profits from the *f*.
Isa 1: 7 your *f* are being stripped
6: 11 and the *f* ruined and ravaged,
10: 18 splendor of his forests and fertile *f*
16: 8 The *f* of Heshbon wither,
32: 12 Beat your breasts for the pleasant *f*,
61: 5 foreigners will work your *f*
Jer 6: 12 with their *f* and their wives,
6: 25 Do not go out to the *f*
8: 10 and their *f* to new owners.
13: 27 acts on the hills and in the *f*.
32: 15 *f* and vineyards will again be
32: 43 Once more *f* will be bought
32: 44 *F* will be bought for silver,
35: 9 or had vineyards, *f* or crops.
39: 10 time he gave them vineyards and *f*.
48: 33 from the orchards and *f* of Moab.
52: 16 land to work the vineyards and *f*.
Eze 39: 10 need to gather wood from the *f*

Hos 5: 7 will devour them and their *f*.
Joel 1: 10 The *f* are ruined,
Ob : 19 They will occupy the *f* of Ephraim
Mic 2: 2 They covet *f* and seize them,
2: 4 He assigns our *f* to traitors.' "
Hab 3: 17 and the *f* produce no food,
Hag 1: 11 I called for a drought on the *f*
Mal 3: 11 in your *f* will not cast their fruit,"
Mt 19: 29 or *f* for my sake will receive
Mk 10: 29 or father or children or *f* for me
10: 30 mothers, children and *f*—
11: 8 branches they had cut in the *f*.
Lk 2: 8 were shepherds living out in the *f*
15: 15 who sent him to his *f* to feed pigs.
Jn 4: 35 open your eyes and look at the *f!*
Jas 5: 4 who mowed your *f* are crying out

FIELDSTONES (STONE)

Dt 27: 6 altar of the LORD your God with *f*

FIERCE (FIERCE-LOOKING FIERCER FIERCEST)

Ge 49: 7 Cursed be their anger, so *f*,
Ex 32: 12 Turn from your *f* anger; relent
Nu 25: 4 that the LORD's *f* anger may turn
Dt 13: 17 LORD will turn from his *f* anger;
29: 23 the LORD overthrew in *f* anger.
29: 24 Why this *f*, burning anger?"
Jos 7: 26 the LORD turned from his *f* anger.
1Sa 20: 34 up from the table in *f* anger;
28: 18 or carry out his *f* wrath
31: 3 The fighting grew *f* around Saul,
2Sa 2: 17 The battle that day was very *f*,
17: 8 *f* as a wild bear robbed of her cubs.
2Ki 23: 26 away from the heat of his *f* anger,
1Ch 10: 3 The fighting grew *f* around Saul,
2Ch 28: 11 for the LORD's *f* anger rests
28: 13 and his *f* anger rests on Israel."
29: 10 so that his *f* anger will turn away
30: 8 so that his *f* anger will turn away
Ezr 10: 14 until the *f* anger of our God
Job 41: 10 No one is *f* enough to rouse him.
Ps 59: 3 *F* men conspire against me
69: 24 let your *f* anger overtake them.
85: 3 and turned from your *f* anger.
Pr 26: 13 a *f* lion roaming the streets!"
Isa 7: 4 because of the *f* anger of Rezin
13: 9 a cruel day, with wrath and *f*
19: 4 and a *f* king will rule over them,"
27: 1 his *f*, great and powerful sword,
27: 8 with his *f* blast he drives her out,
49: 24 or captives rescued from the *f?*
49: 25 and plunder retrieved from the *f;*
Jer 4: 8 for the *f* anger of the LORD
4: 26 before his *f* anger.
12: 13 because of the LORD's *f* anger."
25: 37 of the *f* anger of the LORD.
25: 38 and because of the LORD's *f* anger
30: 24 *f* anger of the LORD will not turn
44: 6 my *f* anger was poured out;
49: 37 even my *f* anger,"
51: 45 Run from the *f* anger of the LORD.
La 1: 12 me in the day of his *f* anger?
2: 3 In *f* anger he has cut off
2: 6 in his *f* anger he has spurned
4: 11 he has poured out his *f* anger.
Hos 11: 9 I will not carry out my *f* anger,
Jnh 3: 9 compassion turn from his *f* anger
Na 1: 6 Who can endure his *f* anger?
Zep 2: 2 before the *f* anger of the LORD
3: 8 all my *f* anger.

FIERCE-LOOKING (FIERCE)

Dt 28: 50 a *f* nation without respect

FIERCER (FIERCE)

Hab 1: 8 *f* than wolves at dusk.

FIERCEST (FIERCE)

2Sa 11: 15 front line where the fighting is *f*.

FIERY (FIRE)

Ps 11: 6 *f* coals and burning sulfur;
21: 9 you will make them like a *f* furnace
Eze 21: 31 breathe out my *f* anger against you;
22: 20 a furnace to melt it with a *f* blast,
22: 21 I will blow on you with my *f* wrath,
22: 31 consume them with my *f* anger,
Eze 28: 14 you walked among the *f* stones.
28: 16 from among the *f* stones.
38: 19 and *f* wrath I declare that
Mt 13: 42 them into the *f* furnace,
13: 50 and throw them into the *f* furnace,
Rev 6: 4 another horse came out, a *f* red one
9: 17 Their breastplates were *f* red,
10: 1 and his legs were like *f* pillars.
19: 20 into the *f* lake of burning sulfur.
21: 8 be in the *f* lake of burning sulfur.

FIG (FIGS SYCAMORE-FIG SYCAMORE-FIGS)

Ge 3: 7 so they sewed *f* leaves together
Dt 8: 8 vines and *f* trees, pomegranates,
Jdg 9: 10 "Next, the trees said to the *f* tree,
9: 11 *f* tree replied, 'Should I give up my
1Ki 4: 25 man under his own vine and *f* tree.
2Ki 18: 31 and *f* tree and drink water
1Ch 12: 40 *f* cakes, raisin cakes, wine, oil,
Ps 105: 33 struck down their vines and *f* trees
Pr 27: 18 He who tends a *f* tree will eat its
SS 2: 13 The *f* tree forms its early fruit;
Isa 9: 10 the *f* trees have been felled,
28: 4 will be like a *f* ripe before harvest—
34: 4 like shriveled figs from the *f* tree.
36: 16 and *f* tree and drink water
Jer 5: 17 devour your vines and *f* trees.
Hos 2: 12 I will ruin her vines and her *f* trees,
9: 10 the early fruit on the *f* tree.
Joel 1: 7 and ruined my *f* trees.
1: 12 and the *f* tree is withered;
2: 22 the *f* tree and the vine yield their
Am 4: 9 Locusts devoured your *f*
Mic 4: 4 and under his own *f* tree,
Na 3: 12 All your fortresses are like *f* trees
Hab 3: 17 Though the *f* tree does not bud
Hag 2: 19 Until now, the vine and the *f* tree,
Zec 3: 10 to sit under his vine and *f* tree,'
Mt 21: 19 Seeing a *f* tree by the road,
21: 20 "How did the *f* tree wither
21: 21 you do what was done to the *f* tree,
24: 32 learn this lesson from the *f* tree:
Mk 11: 13 in the distance a *f* tree in leaf,
11: 20 they saw the *f* tree withered
11: 21 The *f* tree you cursed has withered
13: 28 learn this lesson from the *f* tree:
Lk 13: 6 "A man had a *f* tree, planted
13: 7 to look for fruit on this *f* tree
21: 29 "Look at the *f* tree and all the trees.
Jn 1: 48 under the *f* tree before Philip called
1: 50 told you I saw you under the *f* tree.
Jas 3: 12 brothers, can a *f* tree bear olives,
Rev 6: 13 drop from a *f* tree when shaken

FIGHT (FIGHTER FIGHTERS FIGHTING FIGHTS FOUGHT)

Ex 1: 10 *f* against us and leave the country."
14: 14 The LORD will *f* for you; you need
17: 9 and go out to *f* the Amalekites.
Lev 24: 10 and a *f* broke out in the camp
Nu 22: 11 then I will be able to *f* them
32: 27 cross over to *f* before the LORD,
Dt 1: 30 going before you, will *f* for you,
1: 41 and *f*, as the LORD our God
1: 42 "Tell them, 'Do not go up and *f*,
3: 22 the LORD your God himself will *f*
20: 4 goes with you to *f* for you
29: 7 of Bashan came out to *f* against us,
Jos 10: 25 to all the enemies you are going to *f*
11: 5 of Merom, to *f* against Israel.
24: 9 prepared to *f* against Israel,
Jdg 1: 1 *f* for us against the Canaanites?"
1: 3 to *f* against the Canaanites.
1: 9 to *f* against the Canaanites living
2: 15 Whenever Israel went out to *f*,
8: 1 us when you went to *f* Midian?"
9: 38 you ridiculed? Go out and *f* them!"
10: 9 the Jordan to *f* against Judah,
11: 6 so we can *f* the Ammonites."
11: 8 come with us to *f* the Ammonites,
11: 9 back to *f* the Ammonites
11: 25 quarrel with Israel or *f* with them?
11: 32 went over to *f* the Ammonites,
12: 1 go to *f* the Ammonites
12: 3 crossed over to *f* the Ammonites,
12: 3 have you come up today to *f* me?"
15: 10 "Why have you come to *f* us?"
Jdg 18: 23 that you called out your men to *f?*"
20: 14 at Gibeah to *f* against the Israelites.
20: 18 first to *f* against the Benjamites?"
20: 20 out to *f* the Benjamites
1Sa 4: 1 out to *f* against the Philistines.
4: 9 and *f!*" So the Philistines fought,
8: 20 to go out before us and *f* our battles
13: 5 Philistines assembled to *f* Israel,
17: 9 If he is able to *f* and kill me,
17: 10 me a man and let us *f* each other."
17: 32 your servant will go and *f* him."
17: 33 against this Philistine and *f* him;
18: 17 and *f* the battles of the LORD."
28: 1 gathered their forces to *f*
29: 8 and *f* against the enemies
2Sa 2: 14 and *f* hand to hand in front of us."
2: 28 Israel, nor did they *f* anymore.
10: 12 and let us *f* bravely for our people
10: 13 advanced to *f* the Arameans,
11: 20 get so close to the city to *f?*
14: 6 They got into a *f* with each other
18: 6 marched into the field to *f* Israel,
21: 15 men to *f* against the Philistines,
1Ki 12: 24 up to *f* against your brothers,
20: 23 But if we *f* them on the plains,
20: 25 so we can *f* Israel on the plains.
20: 26 up to Aphek to *f* against Israel.
22: 4 to *f* against Ramoth Gilead?"
22: 31 "Do not *f* with anyone, small
2Ki 3: 7 go with me to *f* against Moab?"
3: 21 heard that the kings had come to *f*
10: 3 Then *f* for your master's house."
16: 5 up to *f* against Jerusalem
19: 9 was marching out to *f* against him.
1Ch 12: 19 went with the Philistines to *f*
19: 13 and let us *f* bravely for our people
19: 14 advanced to *f* the Arameans,
2Ch 11: 4 up to *f* against your brothers.
13: 12 do not *f* against the LORD,
18: 30 "Do not *f* with anyone, small
20: 17 You will not have to *f* this battle.
25: 8 and *f* courageously in battle,
32: 8 to help us and to *f* our battles."
35: 20 up to *f* at Carchemish
35: 22 but went to *f* him on the plain
Ne 4: 8 to come and *f* against Jerusalem
4: 14 awesome, and *f* for your brothers,
4: 20 Our God will *f* for us!"
Ps 35: 1 *f* against those who *f* against me.
Isa 7: 1 up to *f* against Jerusalem,
19: 2 brother will *f* against brother,
29: 7 the hordes of all the nations that *f*
29: 8 that *f* against Mount Zion.
37: 9 was marching out to *f* against him.
Jer 1: 19 They will *f* against you
15: 20 they will *f* against you
21: 4 using to *f* the king of Babylon
21: 5 I myself will *f* against you
32: 5 If you *f* against the Babylonians,
33: 5 in the *f* with the Babylonians:
34: 22 They will *f* against it, take it
41: 12 went to *f* Ishmael son of Nethaniah
Da 10: 20 return to *f* against the prince
11: 7 he will *f* against them and be
11: 11 and *f* against the king of the North,
Zec 10: 5 they will *f* and overthrow
14: 2 nations to Jerusalem to *f* against it;
14: 3 and *f* against those nations,
14: 14 Judah too will *f* at Jerusalem.
Jn 18: 36 my servants would *f*
1Co 9: 26 I do not *f* like a man beating the air.
2Co 10: 4 The weapons we *f*
1Ti 1: 18 them you may *f* the good *f*,
6: 12 Fight the good *f* of the faith.
6: 12 *F* the good fight of the faith.
2Ti 4: 7 fought the good *f*, I have finished
Jas 4: 2 You quarrel and *f*.
Rev 2: 16 will *f* against them with the sword

FIGHTER (FIGHT)

2Sa 17: 8 your father is an experienced *f;*
17: 10 Israel knows that your father is a *f*
23: 20 son of Jehoiada was a valiant *f*
1Ch 11: 22 son of Jehoiada was a valiant *f*

FIGHTERS (FIGHT)

Jos 10: 2 and all its men were good *f*.
Jdg 20: 44 fell, all of them valiant *f*.

Jdg 20: 46 fell, all of them valiant *f*.
2Sa 17: 8 your father and his men; they are *f*,

FIGHTING (FIGHT)

Ex 2: 13 went out and saw two Hebrews *f*.
14: 25 The LORD is *f* for them
21: 22 "If men who are *f* hit a pregnant
Nu 31: 42 apart from that of the *f* men—
Dt 2: 14 generation of *f* men had perished
2: 16 Now when the last of these *f* men
20: 19 a city for a long time, *f* against it
25: 11 If two men are *f* and the wife of one
Jos 1: 14 but all your *f* men, fully armed,
6: 2 along with its king and its *f* men.
8: 3 thirty thousand of his best *f* men
10: 7 including all the best *f* men.
10: 14 Surely the LORD was *f* for Israel!
Jdg 20: 17 swordsmen, all of them *f* men.
20: 34 *f* was so heavy that the Benjamites
21: 10 sent twelve thousand *f* men
1Sa 17: 19 of Elah, *f* against the Philistines."
17: 33 he has been a *f* man from his youth
23: 1 the Philistines are *f* against Keilah
28: 15 "The Philistines are *f* against me,
29: 4 he will turn against us during the *f*.
31: 3 The *f* grew fierce around Saul,
2Sa 10: 7 out with the entire army of *f* men.
10: 14 returned from *f* the Ammonites
11: 15 the front line where the *f* is fiercest.
24: 2 to Beersheba and enroll the *f* men,
24: 4 king to enroll the *f* men of Israel.
24: 9 number of the *f* men to the king:
24: 10 after he had counted the *f* men,
1Ki 9: 22 they were his *f* men, his
11: 15 when David was *f* with Edom,
12: 21 and eighty thousand *f* men—
22: 34 around and get me out of the *f*.
2Ki 19: 8 found the king *f* against Libnah.
24: 14 all the officers and *f* men,
24: 16 force of seven thousand *f* men,
25: 19 the officer in charge of the *f* men
1Ch 5: 20 They were helped in *f* them,
7: 2 *f* men in their genealogy numbered
7: 5 relatives who were *f* men belonging
7: 7 record listed 22,034 *f* men.
7: 9 heads of families and 20,200 *f* men.
7: 11 *f* men ready to go out to war.
10: 3 The *f* grew fierce around Saul,
12: 38 All these were *f* men who
19: 8 out with the entire army of *f* men.
21: 5 the number of the *f* men to David:
21: 17 Was it not I who ordered the *f* men
2Ch 8: 9 they were his *f* men, commanders
11: 1 and eighty thousand *f* men—
13: 3 four hundred thousand able *f* men,
14: 8 All these were brave *f* men.
17: 13 also kept experienced *f* men
17: 14 with 300,000 *f* men; next,
18: 33 around and get me out of the *f*.
25: 6 hired a hundred thousand *f* men
26: 12 leaders over the *f* men was 2,600.
32: 21 who annihilated all the *f* men
Isa 37: 8 found the king *f* against Libnah.
Jer 34: 1 in the empire he ruled were *f*
34: 7 of Babylon was *f* against Jerusalem
51: 30 Babylon's warriors have stopped *f*;
52: 25 the officer in charge of the *f* men,
Joel 3: 9 Let all the *f* men draw near
Ac 5: 39 you will only find yourselves *f*
7: 26 upon two Israelites who were *f*.

FIGHTS (FIGHT)

Jos 23: 10 the LORD your God *f* for you,
Jdg 6: 31 Whoever *f* for him shall be put
1Sa 25: 28 because he *f* the LORD's battles.
Isa 30: 32 he *f* them in battle with the blows
Zec 14: 3 as he *f* in the day of battle.
Jas 4: 1 What causes *f* and quarrels

FIGS (FIG)

Nu 13: 23 with some pomegranates and *f*.
20: 5 or *f*, grapevines or pomegranates.
1Sa 25: 18 two hundred cakes of pressed *f*,
30: 12 part of a cake of pressed *f*
2Sa 16: 1 a hundred cakes of *f* and a skin
2Ki 20: 7 Isaiah said, "Prepare a poultice of *f*
Ne 13: 15 *f* and all other kinds of loads.
Isa 34: 4 like shriveled *f* from the fig tree.
Isa 38: 21 "Prepare a poultice of *f*
Jer 8: 13 There will be no *f* on the tree,
24: 1 of *f* placed in front of the temple
24: 2 One basket had very good *f*,
24: 2 the other basket had very poor *f*,
24: 3 Jeremiah?" "*F*," I answered.
24: 5 of Israel, says: 'Like these good *f*,
24: 8 " 'But like the poor *f*, which are
29: 17 will make them like poor *f* that are
Mic 7: 1 none of the early *f* that I crave.
Na 3: 12 the *f* fall into the mouth of the eater
Mt 7: 16 grapes from thornbushes, or *f*
Mk 11: 13 because it was not the season for *f*.
Lk 6: 44 People do not pick *f*
Jas 3: 12 grapevine bear *f*? Neither can a salt
Rev 6: 13 as late *f* drop from a fig tree

FIGURE (FIGURES)

Eze 1: 26 on the throne was a *f* like that
8: 2 and I saw a *f* like that of a man.
Jn 7: 4 to become a public *f* acts in secret.
10: 6 Jesus used this *f* of speech,

FIGUREHEAD

Ac 28: 11 with the *f* of the twin gods Castor

FIGURES (FIGURE)

2Ch 4: 3 Below the rim, *f* of bulls encircled
Eze 23: 14 *f* of Chaldeans portrayed in red,
Jn 16: 29 and without *f* of speech.

FILIGREE

Ex 28: 11 mount the stones in gold *f* settings
28: 13 Make gold *f* settings and two
28: 20 Mount them in gold *f* settings.
39: 6 the onyx stones in gold *f* settings
39: 13 were mounted in gold *f* settings.
39: 16 They made two gold *f* settings

FILL (FILLED FILLING FILLS FULL FULLNESS FULLY)

Ge 1: 22 and *f* the water in the seas,
1: 28 and increase in number; *f* the earth
9: 1 increase in number and *f* the earth.
42: 25 Joseph gave orders to *f* their bags
44: 1 "*F* the men's sacks with
Ex 2: 16 *f* the troughs to water their father's
10: 6 They will *f* your houses
Lev 25: 19 and you will eat your *f*
Dt 28: 67 of the terror that will *f* your hearts
31: 20 when they eat their *f* and thrive,
1Sa 16: 1 *F* your horn with oil and be
1Ki 18: 33 "*F* four large jars with water
Job 8: 21 He will yet *f* your mouth
15: 2 or *f* his belly with the hot east wind
15: 21 Terrifying sounds *f* his ears;
15: 24 and anguish *f* him with terror;
23: 4 and *f* my mouth with arguments.
31: 31 Who has not had his *f* of Job's meat
41: 7 Can you *f* his hide with harpoons
Ps 16: 11 you will *f* me with joy
74: 20 haunts of violence *f* the dark places
81: 10 wide your mouth and I will *f* it.
129: 7 it the reaper cannot *f* his hands,
129: 7 nor the one who gathers *f* his arms.
Pr 1: 13 and *f* our houses with plunder;
12: 21 the wicked have their *f* of trouble.
26: 25 for seven abominations *f* his heart.
28: 19 who chases fantasies will have his *f*
Ecc 1: 8 or the ear its *f* of hearing.
SS 5: 1 drink your *f*, O lovers.
Isa 13: 21 jackals will *f* her houses;
27: 6 and *f* all the world with fruit.
33: 5 he will *f* Zion with justice
34: 5 My sword has drunk its *f*
44: 16 he roasts his meat and eats his *f*.
56: 12 Let us drink our *f* of beer!
65: 11 *f* bowls of mixed wine for Destiny,
Jer 13: 13 to *f* with drunkenness all who live
23: 16 they *f* you with false hopes.
23: 24 "Do not I *f* heaven and earth?"
46: 12 your cries will *f* the earth.
50: 10 who plunder her will have their *f*,"
51: 14 I will surely *f* you with men,
Eze 3: 3 and *f* your stomach with it."
7: 19 or *f* their stomachs with it,
8: 17 also *f* the land with violence
9: 7 and *f* the courts with the slain.
Eze 10: 2 *F* your hands with burning coals
20: 26 that I might *f* them with horror
24: 4 *F* it with the best of these bones;
30: 11 and *f* the land with the slain.
32: 5 and *f* the valleys with your remains
35: 8 I will *f* your mountains
39: 20 At my table you will eat your *f*
Da 7: 5 'Get up and eat your *f* of flesh!'
Zep 1: 9 who *f* the temple of their gods
Hag 1: 6 You drink, but never have your *f*.
2: 7 and I will *f* this house with glory,'
Zec 9: 13 and *f* it with Ephraim.
Mt 23: 32 *F* up, then, the measure of the sin
Lk 15: 16 He longed to *f* his stomach
Jn 2: 7 said to the servants, "*F* the jars
6: 26 you ate the loaves and had your *f*.
Ac 2: 28 you will *f* me with joy
Ro 15: 13 the God of hope *f* you with all joy
Eph 4: 10 in order to *f* the whole universe.)
Col 1: 9 and asking God to *f* you
1: 24 and I *f* up in my flesh what is still

FILLED (FILL)

Ge 6: 6 and his heart was *f* with pain.
6: 13 for the earth is *f* with violence
21: 19 she went and *f* the skin with water
24: 16 *f* her jar and came up again.
34: 7 They were *f* with grief and fury,
Ex 1: 7 so that the land was *f* with them.
16: 12 and in the morning you will be *f*
31: 3 I have *f* him with the Spirit of God,
35: 31 he has *f* him with the Spirit of God,
35: 35 He has *f* them with skill
40: 34 of the LORD *f* the tabernacle.
40: 35 of the LORD *f* the tabernacle.
Lev 19: 29 turn to prostitution and be *f*
Nu 7: 13 each *f* with fine flour mixed
7: 14 *f* with incense; one young bull,
7: 19 each *f* with fine flour mixed
7: 20 *f* with incense; one young bull,
7: 25 each *f* with fine flour mixed
7: 26 *f* with incense; one young bull,
7: 31 each *f* with fine flour mixed
7: 32 *f* with incense; one young bull,
7: 37 each *f* with fine flour mixed
7: 38 *f* with incense; one young bull,
7: 43 each *f* with fine flour mixed
7: 44 *f* with incense; one young bull,
7: 49 each *f* with fine flour mixed
7: 50 *f* with incense; one young bull,
7: 55 each *f* with fine flour mixed
7: 56 *f* with incense; one young bull,
7: 61 each *f* with fine flour mixed
7: 62 *f* with incense; one young bull,
7: 67 each *f* with fine flour mixed
7: 68 *f* with incense; one young bull,
7: 73 each *f* with fine flour mixed
7: 74 *f* with incense; one young bull,
7: 79 each *f* with fine flour mixed
7: 80 *f* with incense; one young bull,
7: 86 The twelve gold ladles *f*
22: 3 Moab was *f* with dread
22: 18 "Even if Balak gave me his palace *f*
24: 13 'Even if Balak gave me his palace *f*
Dt 6: 11 houses *f* with all kinds
28: 66 *f* with dread both night and day,
32: 15 *f* with food, he became heavy
32: 32 Their grapes are *f* with poison,
34: 9 son of Nun was *f* with the spirit
Jos 9: 13 these wineskins that we *f* were new
Ru 2: 9 from the water jars the men have *f*
1Sa 5: 11 For death had *f* the city with panic;
28: 5 he was afraid; terror *f* his heart.
28: 20 *f* with fear because of Samuel's
1Ki 3: 26 woman whose son was alive was *f*
8: 10 the cloud *f* the temple
8: 11 glory of the LORD *f* his temple.
11: 27 and had *f* in the gap in the wall
18: 35 the altar and even *f* the trench.
2Ki 3: 17 yet this valley will be *f* with water,
3: 20 And the land was *f* with water.
4: 4 and as each is *f*, put it to one side."
4: 39 some of its gourds and *f* the fold
21: 16 innocent blood that he *f* Jerusalem
24: 4 For he had *f* Jerusalem
2Ch 5: 13 of the LORD was *f* with a cloud,
5: 14 of the LORD *f* the temple of God.
7: 1 the glory of the LORD *f* the temple

2Ch 7: 2 because the glory of the LORD *f* it.
Ezr 6: 22 the LORD had *f* them with joy
9: 11 detestable practices they have *f* it
Ne 9: 25 of houses *f* with all kinds
Est 5: 9 he was *f* with rage
Job 3: 15 who *f* their houses with silver.
3: 22 who are *f* with gladness
20: 23 When he has *f* his belly,
22: 18 Yet it was he who *f* their houses
Ps 4: 7 You have *f* my heart
5: 9 their heart is *f* with destruction.
38: 7 My back is *f* with searing pain;
48: 10 your right hand is *f*
65: 4 We are *f* with the good things
65: 9 streams of God are *f* with water
71: 8 My mouth is *f* with your praise,
72: 19 may the whole earth be *f*
80: 9 and it took root and *f* the land.
119: 64 The earth is *f* with your love,
126: 2 Our mouths were *f* with laughter,
126: 3 and we are *f* with joy.
144: 13 Our barns will be *f*
Pr 1: 31 be *f* with the fruit of their schemes.
3: 10 then your barns will be *f*
7: 20 He took his purse *f* with money
8: 30 I was *f* with delight day after day,
12: 14 of his lips a man is *f*
18: 20 of his mouth a man's stomach is *f*;
24: 4 through knowledge its rooms are *f*
Ecc 8: 11 of the people are *f* with schemes
Isa 6: 1 the train of his robe *f* the temple.
6: 4 and the temple was *f* with smoke.
41: 23 so that we will be dismayed and *f*
51: 20 They are *f* with the wrath
Jer 6: 6 it is *f* with oppression.
13: 12 Every wineskin should be *f*
13: 12 that every wineskin should be *f*
15: 17 and you had *f* me with indignation.
16: 18 and have *f* my inheritance
19: 4 and they have *f* this place
25: 15 "Take from my hand this cup *f*
31: 14 my people will be *f* with my bounty
33: 5 'They will be *f* with the dead bodies
41: 9 Ishmael son of Nethaniah *f* it
50: 2 Marduk *f* with terror.
50: 2 and her idols *f* with terror.'
50: 36 They will be *f* with terror.
51: 34 *f* his stomach with our delicacies,
La 3: 15 He has *f* me with bitter herbs
3: 30 and let him be *f* with disgrace.
Eze 10: 3 and a cloud *f* the inner court.
10: 4 The cloud *f* the temple,
11: 6 and *f* its streets with the dead.
23: 33 You will be *f* with drunkenness
27: 25 You are *f* with heavy cargo
28: 16 you were *f* with violence,
32: 6 the ravines will be *f* with your flesh.
36: 38 So will the ruined cities be *f*
43: 5 the glory of the LORD *f* the temple
Da 2: 35 a huge mountain and *f* the whole
11: 12 of the South will be *f* with pride
Joel 2: 24 The threshing floors will be *f*
Am 4: 10 I *f* your nostrils with the stench
Mic 3: 8 But as for me, I am *f* with power,
Na 1: 2 LORD takes vengeance and is *f*
Hab 2: 14 For the earth will be *f*
2: 16 You will be *f* with shame instead
3: 3 and his praise *f* the earth.
Zec 8: 5 The city streets will be *f* with boys
Mt 5: 6 for they will be *f*.
9: 8 they were *f* with awe; and they
17: 23 And the disciples were *f* with grief.
22: 10 the wedding hall was *f* with guests.
27: 48 He *f* it with wine vinegar, put it
28: 8 afraid yet *f* with joy, and ran
Mk 1: 41 *F* with compassion, Jesus reached
15: 36 *f* a sponge with wine vinegar,
Lk 1: 15 and he will be *f* with the Holy Spirit
1: 41 and Elizabeth was *f* with the Holy
1: 53 He has *f* the hungry
1: 65 The neighbors were all *f* with awe,
1: 67 His father Zechariah was *f*
2: 40 and became strong; he was *f*
3: 5 Every valley shall be *f* in,
5: 7 *f* both boats so full that they began
5: 26 They were *f* with awe and said,
7: 16 They were all *f* with awe
15: 20 and was *f* with compassion for him;
Jn 2: 7 so they *f* them to the brim.
6: 13 *f* twelve baskets with the pieces
12: 3 the house was *f* with the fragrance
16: 6 I have said these things, you are *f*
Ac 2: 2 *f* the whole house where they were
2: 4 All of them were *f*
2: 43 Everyone was *f* with awe,
3: 10 and they were *f* with wonder
4: 8 Then Peter, *f* with the Holy Spirit,
4: 31 they were all *f* with the Holy Spirit
5: 3 so *f* your heart that you have lied
5: 17 the party of the Sadducees, were *f*
5: 28 "Yet you have *f* Jerusalem
9: 17 and be *f* with the Holy Spirit."
13: 9 called Paul, *f* with the Holy Spirit,
13: 45 they were *f* with jealousy
13: 52 And the disciples were *f* with joy
16: 34 and the whole family was *f* with joy
Ro 1: 29 They have become *f*
1Co 5: 2 Shouldn't you rather have been *f*
Eph 3: 19 that you may be *f* to the measure
5: 18 Instead, be *f* with the Spirit.
Php 1: 11 *f* with the fruit of righteousness
2Ti 1: 4 so that I may be *f* with joy.
1Pe 1: 8 and are *f* with an inexpressible
Rev 8: 5 *f* it with fire from the altar,
12: 12 He is *f* with fury,
15: 7 seven angels seven golden bowls *f*
15: 8 And the temple was *f* with smoke
16: 19 gave her the cup *f* with the wine
17: 4 *f* with abominable things

FILLING (FILL)

Ge 26: 15 the Philistines stopped up, *f* them
Eze 44: 4 the glory of the LORD *f* the temple
Na 2: 12 *f* his lairs with the kill

FILLS (FILL)

Nu 14: 21 of the LORD *f* the whole earth,
Job 20: 11 The youthful vigor that *f* his bones
36: 32 He *f* his hands with lightning
Ps 107: 9 and *f* the hungry with good things.
Ac 14: 17 and *f* your hearts with joy."
Eph 1: 23 fullness of him who *f* everything

FILTH (FILTHINESS FILTHY)

2Ki 18: 27 will have to eat their own *f*
Pr 30: 12 and yet are not cleansed of their *f*;
Isa 4: 4 The Lord will wash away the *f*
28: 8 and there is not a spot without *f*.
36: 12 will have to eat their own *f*
Na 3: 6 I will pelt you with *f*,
Zep 1: 17 and their entrails like *f*.
Jas 1: 21 rid of all moral *f* and the evil that is
Rev 17: 4 and the *f* of her adulteries.

FILTHINESS (FILTH)

La 1: 9 Her *f* clung to her skirts;

FILTHY (FILTH)

Isa 64: 6 all our righteous acts are like *f* rags;
Zec 3: 3 Joshua was dressed in *f* clothes
3: 4 before him, "Take off his *f* clothes
Col 3: 8 and *f* language from your lips.
2Pe 2: 7 by the *f* lives of lawless men

FINAL (FINALITY)

Ru 4: 7 transfer of property to become *f*,
Ps 73: 17 then I understood their *f* destiny.
Isa 41: 22 and know their *f* outcome.
Mt 12: 45 the *f* condition of that man is worse
Lk 11: 26 the *f* condition of that man is worse
Ac 28: 25 Paul had made this *f* statement:

FINALITY (FINAL)

Ro 9: 28 on earth with speed and *f*."

FINANCIAL

1Ti 6: 5 that godliness is a means to *f* gain.

FIND (FINDING FINDS FOUND)

Ge 8: 9 But the dove could *f* no place
18: 26 "If I *f* fifty righteous people
18: 28 "If I *f* forty-five there," he said,
18: 30 "I will not do it if I *f* thirty there."
19: 11 so that they could not *f* the door.
27: 20 How did you *f* it so quickly, my son
31: 32 if you *f* anyone who has your gods,
31: 35 but could not *f* the household gods.
32: 5 that I may *f* favor in your eyes.' "
33: 8 "To *f* favor in your eyes, my lord,"
33: 15 "Just let me *f* favor in the eyes
34: 11 "Let me *f* favor in your eyes,
38: 20 the woman, but he did not *f* her.
38: 22 to Judah and said, "I didn't *f* her.
38: 23 young goat, but you didn't *f* her."
41: 38 "Can we *f* anyone like this man,
44: 15 that a man like me can *f* things out
47: 25 "May we *f* favor in the eyes
Ex 5: 11 own straw wherever you can *f* it,
16: 25 You will not *f* any of it
33: 13 and continue to *f* favor with you.
Nu 9: 8 "Wait until I *f* out what the LORD
10: 33 those three days to *f* them a place
22: 19 I will *f* out what else the LORD
32: 23 be sure that your sin will *f* you out.
Dt 4: 29 you will *f* him if you look for him
13: 3 your God is testing you to *f* out
14: 21 eat anything you *f* already dead.
22: 3 if you *f* your brother's donkey
22: 14 I did not *f* proof of her virginity,"
22: 17 'I did not *f* your daughter
28: 65 those nations you will *f* no repose,
Jos 2: 16 hills so the pursuers will not *f* you.
20: 3 and *f* protection from the avenger
Jdg 18: 8 "How did you *f* things?" They
18: 10 you will *f* an unsuspecting people
Ru 1: 9 each of you will *f* rest in the home
2: 2 anyone in whose eyes I *f* favor."
2: 13 "May I continue to *f* favor
3: 1 should I not try to *f* a home for you,
3: 18 until you *f* out what happens.
1Sa 1: 18 "May your servant *f* favor
9: 4 Benjamin, but they did not *f* them.
9: 4 Shalisha, but they did not *f* them.
9: 13 you should *f* him about this time."
9: 13 you will *f* him before he goes up
14: 38 and let us *f* out what sin has been
16: 17 "*F* someone who plays well
17: 56 "*F* out whose son this young man is
19: 3 and will tell you what I *f* out."
20: 21 and say, 'Go, *f* the arrows.'
20: 36 "Run and *f* the arrows I shoot."
21: 3 of bread, or whatever you can *f*."
23: 16 and helped him *f* strength in God.
23: 22 *F* out where David usually goes
23: 23 *F* out about all the hiding places he
25: 8 your son David whatever you can *f*
28: 7 "*F* me a woman who is a medium,
2Sa 3: 25 *f* out everything you are doing."
11: 3 someone to *f* out about her.
15: 25 If I *f* favor in the LORD's eyes,
16: 4 "May I *f* favor in your eyes,
20: 6 or he will *f* fortified cities
1Ki 18: 5 Maybe we can *f* some grass
18: 10 them swear they could not *f* you.
18: 12 and tell Ahab and he doesn't *f* you,
22: 25 "You will *f* out on the day you go
2Ki 2: 17 for three days but did not *f* him.
6: 13 *f* out where he is," the king ordered
7: 13 them to *f* out what happened."
7: 14 "Go and *f* out what has happened."
2Ch 18: 24 "You will *f* out on the day you go
20: 16 and you will *f* them at the end
32: 4 kings of Assyria come and *f* plenty
Ezr 2: 62 but they could not *f* them
4: 15 records you will *f* that this city
Ne 5: 8 because they could *f* nothing to say
7: 64 but they could not *f* them
Est 2: 11 the harem to *f* out how Esther was
4: 5 him to *f* out what was troubling
Job 5: 24 property and *f* nothing missing.
8: 8 and *f* out what their fathers learned
9: 14 How can I *f* words to argue
17: 10 I will not *f* a wise man among you.
22: 26 Surely then you will *f* delight
23: 3 If only I knew where to *f* him;
23: 5 I would *f* out what he would
23: 8 if I go to the west, I do not *f* him.
27: 10 Will he *f* delight in the Almighty?
32: 20 I must speak and *f* relief;
Ps 17: 3 you test me, you will *f* nothing;
36: 7 *f* refuge in the shadow
62: 5 *F* rest, O my soul, in God alone;
91: 4 under his wings you will *f* refuge;
119: 35 for there I *f* delight.

Ps 119: 52 and I *f* comfort in them.
132: 5 till I *f* a place for the LORD,
Pr 1: 28 for me but will not *f* me.
2: 5 and *f* the knowledge of God.
4: 22 life to those who *f* them
8: 17 and those who seek me *f* me.
8: 36 whoever fails to *f* me harms himself
14: 7 for you will not *f* knowledge
14: 22 those who plan what is good *f* love
20: 6 but a faithful man who can *f*?
23: 35 up so I can *f* another drink?''
24: 14 if you *f* it, there is a future hope
25: 16 If you *f* honey, eat just enough—
31: 10 A wife of noble character who can *f*
Ecc 2: 1 with pleasure to *f* out what is good
2: 24 drink and *f* satisfaction in his work.
2: 25 who can eat or *f* enjoyment?
3: 13 and *f* satisfaction in all his toil—
5: 18 and to *f* satisfaction in his toilsome
7: 26 I *f* more bitter than death
11: 1 after many days you will *f* it again.
12: 1 "I *f* no pleasure in them"—
12: 10 searched to *f* just the right words,
SS 3: 1 I looked for him but did not *f* him.
3: 2 I looked for him but did not *f* him.
5: 6 I looked for him but did not *f* him.
5: 8 if you *f* my lover,
Isa 14: 30 of the poor will *f* pasture,
14: 32 his afflicted people will *f* refuge.''
23: 12 even there you will *f* no rest.''
34: 14 and *f* for themselves places of rest.
41: 12 you will not *f* them.
49: 9 and *f* pasture on every barren hill.
57: 2 they *f* rest as they lie in death.
58: 14 then you will *f* your joy
59: 11 We look for justice, but *f* none;
Jer 2: 5 What fault did your fathers *f* in me,
2: 24 at mating time they will *f* her.
2: 34 On your clothes men *f*
5: 1 If you can *f* but one person
6: 10 they *f* no pleasure in it.
6: 16 and you will *f* rest for your souls.
14: 3 but *f* no water.
23: 11 in my temple I *f* their wickedness,''
29: 6 *f* wives for your sons and give your
29: 13 and *f* me when you seek me
31: 2 will *f* favor in the desert;
45: 3 out with groaning and *f* no rest.' ''
La 1: 6 that *f* no pasture;
2: 9 and her prophets no longer *f*
5: 5 we are weary and *f* no rest.
Eze 17: 23 they will *f* shelter in the shade
Da 6: 4 They could *f* no corruption in him,
6: 4 tried to *f* grounds for charges
6: 5 "We will never *f* any basis
Hos 2: 6 in so that she cannot *f* her way.
2: 7 for them but not *f* them.
5: 6 they will not *f* him;
12: 8 With all my wealth they will not *f*
14: 3 in you the fatherless *f* compassion
Am 8: 12 but they will not *f* it.
Jnh 1: 7 lots to *f* out who is responsible
Na 3: 7 Where can I *f* anyone
Zep 2: 7 there they will *f* pasture.
Zec 2: 2 to *f* out how wide and how long it is
Mt 2: 8 As soon as you *f* him, report to me,
7: 7 seek and you will *f*; knock
7: 14 leads to life, and only a few *f* it.
10: 39 life for my sake will *f* it.
11: 29 and you will *f* rest for your souls.
12: 43 seeking rest and does not *f* it.
16: 25 loses his life for me will *f* it.
17: 27 and you will *f* a four-drachma coin.
21: 2 and at once you will *f* a donkey tied
22: 9 invite to the banquet anyone you *f*.'
22: 10 gathered all the people they could *f*
26: 60 But they did not *f* any,
Mk 11: 2 you will *f* a colt tied there,
11: 13 he went to *f* out if it had any fruit.
13: 36 do not let him *f* you sleeping.
14: 55 to death, but they did not *f* any.
Lk 1: 62 to *f* out what he would like
2: 12 You will *f* a baby wrapped in strips
2: 45 they did not *f* him, they went
5: 19 When they could not *f* a way
9: 12 countryside and *f* food and lodging
11: 9 seek and you will *f*; knock
11: 24 seeking rest and does not *f* it.
Lk 13: 6 for fruit on it, but did not *f* any.
18: 8 will he *f* faith on the earth?''
19: 15 order to *f* out what they had gained
19: 30 you will *f* a colt tied there,
19: 48 Yet they could not *f* any way
23: 4 "I *f* no basis for a charge
24: 3 they did not *f* the body
24: 23 this morning but didn't *f* his body.
Jn 1: 41 was to *f* his brother Simon
4: 27 and were surprised to *f* him talking
7: 17 he will *f* out whether my teaching
7: 34 you will not *f* me; and where I am,
7: 35 intend to go that we cannot *f* him?
7: 36 but you will not *f* me,'
7: 51 him to *f* out what he is doing?''
7: 52 you will *f* that a prophet does not
10: 9 come in and go out, and *f* pasture.
18: 38 I *f* no basis for a charge against him
19: 4 you to let you know that I *f* no basis
19: 6 I *f* no basis for a charge against him
21: 6 of the boat and you will *f* some.''
Ac 5: 22 the officers did not *f* them there.
5: 39 you will only *f* yourselves fighting
7: 11 and our fathers could not *f* food.
12: 19 made for him and did not *f* him,
16: 13 where we expected to *f* a place
17: 6 But when they did not *f* them,
17: 27 out for him and *f* him,
22: 24 order to *f* out why the people were
22: 30 to *f* out exactly why Paul was being
23: 9 "We *f* nothing wrong with this man
24: 12 My accusers did not *f* me arguing
24: 25 When I *f* it convenient, I will send
Ro 7: 21 I *f* this law at work: When I want
1Co 4: 19 then I will *f* out not only how these
2Co 2: 13 I did not *f* my brother Titus there.
9: 4 with me and *f* you unprepared,
12: 20 that when I come I may not *f* you
12: 20 you may not *f* me as you want me
Eph 5: 10 and *f* out what pleases the Lord.
1Th 3: 5 I sent to *f* out about your faith.
2Ti 1: 18 the Lord grant that he will *f* mercy
Heb 4: 16 and *f* grace to help us in our time
Jas 3: 16 there you *f* disorder and every evil
1Pe 1: 11 trying to *f* out the time
2Jn : 4 to *f* some of your children walking
Rev 9: 6 but will not *f* it; they will long to die

FINDING (FIND)

Ex 15: 22 in the desert without *f* water.
Jos 2: 22 and returned without *f* them.
Jdg 5: 30 'Are they not *f* and dividing
15: 15 *F* a fresh jawbone of a donkey,
Job 36: 26 of his years is past *f* out.
Ps 107: 4 *f* no way to a city where they could
Ecc 7: 28 but not *f*—
Hos 9: 10 it was like *f* grapes in the desert;
Jn 1: 43 *F* Philip, he said to him, "Follow
Ac 5: 10 came in and, *f* her dead,
21: 4 *F* the disciples there, we stayed
Jas 1: 5 generously to all without *f* fault,

FINDS (FIND)

Ge 4: 14 and whoever *f* me will kill me.''
Lev 6: 3 or if he *f* lost property
Nu 35: 27 and the avenger of blood *f* him
Dt 24: 1 he *f* something indecent about her,
Jdg 9: 33 do whatever your hand *f* to do.''
1Sa 10: 7 do whatever your hand *f* to do,
24: 19 When a man *f* his enemy, does he
Job 33: 20 that his very being *f* food repulsive
33: 26 prays to God and *f* favor with him,
Ps 55: 15 for evil *f* lodging among them.
62: 1 My soul *f* rest in God alone;
112: 1 who *f* great delight
119: 162 like one who *f* great spoil.
Pr 3: 13 Blessed is the man who *f* wisdom,
8: 35 For whoever *f* me *f* life
10: 23 A fool *f* pleasure in evil conduct,
11: 27 He who seeks good *f* good will,
14: 6 mocker seeks wisdom and *f* none,
15: 23 A man *f* joy in giving an apt reply
18: 2 A fool *f* no pleasure
18: 22 He who *f* a wife *f* what is good
20: 4 harvest time he looks but *f* nothing.
21: 21 *f* life, prosperity and honor.
28: 13 renounces them *f* mercy.
Ecc 9: 10 Whatever your hand *f* to do,
Isa 38: 16 and my spirit *f* life in them too.
La 1: 3 she *f* no resting place.
Mt 7: 8 he who seeks *f*; and to him who
10: 39 Whoever *f* his life will lose it
12: 44 it *f* the house unoccupied,
18: 13 And if he *f* it, I tell you the truth,
24: 46 servant whose master *f* him doing
Lk 11: 10 he who seeks *f*; and to him who
11: 25 it *f* the house swept clean
12: 37 whose master *f* them watching
12: 38 whose master *f* them ready,
12: 43 servant whom the master *f* doing
15: 4 go after the lost sheep until he *f* it?
15: 5 And when he *f* it, he joyfully puts it
15: 8 and search carefully until she *f* it?
15: 9 when she *f* it, she calls her friends
22: 16 until it *f* fulfillment in the kingdom
1Co 14: 16 how can one who *f* himself

FINE (FINED FINERY FINES FINEST)

Ge 18: 6 "get three seahs of *f* flour
41: 42 He dressed him in robes of *f* linen
Ex 2: 2 When she saw that he was a *f* child,
9: 9 It will become *f* dust
25: 4 purple and scarlet yarn and *f* linen;
28: 5 purple and scarlet yarn, and *f* linen.
28: 39 and make the turban of *f* linen.
28: 39 "Weave the tunic of *f* linen
29: 2 from *f* wheat flour, without yeast,
29: 40 a tenth of an ephah of *f* flour mixed
30: 23 "Take the following *f* spices:
35: 6 purple and scarlet yarn and *f* linen;
35: 23 purple or scarlet yarn or *f* linen,
35: 25 purple or scarlet yarn or *f* linen.
35: 35 purple and scarlet yarn and *f* linen,
38: 23 purple and scarlet yarn and *f* linen
39: 3 purple and scarlet yarn and *f* linen
39: 27 they made tunics of *f* linen—
39: 28 weaver—and the turban of *f* linen,
Lev 2: 1 his offering is to be of *f* flour.
2: 2 shall take a handful of the *f* flour
2: 4 is to consist of *f* flour: cakes made
2: 5 to be made of *f* flour mixed with oil
2: 7 it is to be made of *f* flour and oil.
5: 11 a tenth of an ephah of *f* flour
6: 15 is to take a handful of *f* flour
6: 20 a tenth of an ephah of *f* flour
7: 12 and cakes of *f* flour well-kneaded
14: 10 of an ephah of *f* flour mixed
14: 21 a tenth of an ephah of *f* flour mixed
23: 13 of an ephah of *f* flour mixed
23: 17 of two-tenths of an ephah of *f* flour,
24: 5 Take *f* flour and bake twelve loaves
Nu 6: 15 cakes made of *f* flour mixed
7: 13 each filled with *f* flour mixed
7: 19 each filled with *f* flour mixed
7: 25 each filled with *f* flour mixed
7: 31 each filled with *f* flour mixed
7: 37 each filled with *f* flour mixed
7: 43 each filled with *f* flour mixed
7: 49 each filled with *f* flour mixed
7: 55 each filled with *f* flour mixed
7: 61 each filled with *f* flour mixed
7: 67 each filled with *f* flour mixed
7: 73 each filled with *f* flour mixed
7: 79 each filled with *f* flour mixed
8: 8 offering of *f* flour mixed with oil;
15: 4 a tenth of an ephah of *f* flour mixed
15: 6 of an ephah of *f* flour mixed
15: 9 of an ephah of *f* flour mixed
28: 5 a tenth of an ephah of *f* flour mixed
28: 9 of an ephah of *f* flour mixed
28: 12 of an ephah of *f* flour mixed
28: 12 of an ephah of *f* flour mixed
28: 13 a tenth of an ephah of *f* flour mixed
28: 20 of an ephah of *f* flour mixed
28: 28 of an ephah of *f* flour mixed
29: 3 of an ephah of *f* flour mixed
29: 9 of an ephah of *f* flour mixed
29: 14 of an ephah of *f* flour mixed
Dt 3: 25 that *f* hill country and Lebanon.''
8: 12 when you build *f* houses
9: 21 and ground it to powder as *f* as dust
22: 19 They shall *f* him a hundred shekels
1Sa 16: 12 with a *f* appearance and handsome
2Sa 22: 43 *f* as the dust of the earth;
1Ki 4: 22 were thirty cors of *f* flour
10: 18 with ivory and overlaid with *f* gold.

2Ki 20: 13 the gold, the spices and the *f* oil—
1Ch 15: 27 clothed in a robe of *f* linen,
29: 2 and all kinds of *f* stone and marble
2Ch 2: 14 blue and crimson yarn and *f* linen.
3: 5 it with *f* gold and decorated it
3: 8 with six hundred talents of *f* gold.
3: 14 and crimson yarn and *f* linen,
5: 12 in *f* linen and playing cymbals,
Ezr 8: 27 two *f* articles of polished bronze,
Est 8: 15 and a purple robe of *f* linen.
Job 16: 4 I could make *f* speeches
Ps 18: 42 *f* as dust borne on the wind;
92: 10 *f* oils have been poured upon me.
Pr 8: 19 My fruit is better than *f* gold;
25: 12 of gold or an ornament of *f* gold
31: 22 she is clothed in *f* linen and purple.
Ecc 7: 1 name is better than *f* perfume,
Isa 3: 22 the *f* robes and the capes
3: 24 instead of *f* clothing, sackcloth;
5: 9 the *f* mansions left
19: 9 the weavers of *f* linen will lose hope
23: 18 for abundant food and *f* clothes.
29: 5 enemies will become like *f* dust,
39: 2 the gold, the spices, the *f* oil,
40: 15 as though they were *f* dust.
Jer 22: 7 they will cut up your *f* cedar beams
25: 34 and be shattered like *f* pottery.
La 4: 1 the *f* gold become dull!
Eze 16: 10 I dressed you in *f* linen
16: 13 Your food was *f* flour, honey
16: 13 your clothes were of *f* linen
16: 17 also took the *f* jewelry I gave you,
16: 19 provided for you—the *f* flour,
16: 39 take your *f* jewelry and leave you
23: 26 clothes and take your *f* jewelry.
26: 12 and demolish your *f* houses
27: 7 *F* embroidered linen
27: 16 embroidered work, *f* linen,
Mt 11: 8 A man dressed in *f* clothes? No,
11: 8 those who wear *f* clothes are
13: 45 like a merchant looking for *f* pearls.
Mk 7: 9 "You have a *f* way of setting
Lk 7: 25 A man dressed in *f* clothes? No,
13: 9 If it bears fruit next year, *f!* If not,
16: 19 *f* linen and lived in luxury every
Gal 4: 18 It is *f* to be zealous, provided
Jas 2: 2 wearing a gold ring and *f* clothes,
2: 3 to the man wearing *f* clothes
1Pe 3: 3 of gold jewelry and *f* clothes.
Rev 18: 12 precious stones and pearls; *f* linen,
18: 13 and olive oil, of *f* flour and wheat;
18: 16 dressed in *f* linen, purple
19: 8 *F* linen, bright and clean,
19: 8 (*F* linen stands for the righteous
19: 14 white horses and dressed in *f* linen,

FINE-LOOKING (LOOK)

1Sa 16: 18 He speaks well and is a *f* man.

FINE-SOUNDING (SOUND)

Col 2: 4 may deceive you by *f* arguments.

FINED (FINE)

Ex 21: 22 the offender must be *f* whatever

FINERY (FINE)

2Sa 1: 24 who clothed you in scarlet and *f*,
Isa 3: 18 the Lord will snatch away their *f:*

FINES (FINE)

Am 2: 8 they drink wine taken as *f*.

FINEST (FINE)

Nu 18: 12 all the *f* new wine and grain they
18: 12 "I give you all the *f* olive oil
Dt 32: 14 and the *f* kernels of wheat.
33: 14 and the *f* the moon can yield;
Jdg 20: 34 of Israel's *f* men made a frontal
2Ki 8: 9 of all the *f* wares of Damascus.
19: 23 the *f* of its forests.
Job 28: 15 It cannot be bought with the *f* gold,
Ps 81: 16 with the *f* of wheat;
147: 14 satisfies you with the *f* of wheat.
SS 4: 14 and all the *f* spices.
Isa 17: 10 though you set out the *f* plants
25: 6 the best of meats and the *f* of wines.
37: 24 the *f* of its forests.
Jer 48: 15 her *f* young men will go
Eze 27: 22 merchandise they exchanged the *f*
Da 10: 5 a belt of the *f* gold around his waist.
Joel 3: 5 and carried off my *f* treasures
Am 6: 6 and use the *f* lotions,

FINGER (FINGERS)

Ge 41: 42 from his *f* and put it on Joseph's *f*.
Ex 8: 19 to Pharaoh, "This is the *f* of God."
29: 12 on the horns of the altar with your *f*
31: 18 of stone inscribed by the *f* of God.
Lev 4: 6 He is to dip his *f* into the blood
4: 17 He shall dip his *f* into the blood
4: 25 blood of the sin offering with his *f*
4: 30 to take some of the blood with his *f*
4: 34 blood of the sin offering with his *f*
8: 15 with his *f* he put it on all the horns
9: 9 and he dipped his *f* into the blood
14: 16 and with his *f* sprinkle some of it
16: 14 some of it with his *f* seven times
16: 14 with his *f* sprinkle it on the front
16: 19 blood on it with his *f* seven times
Nu 19: 4 is to take some of its blood on his *f*
Dt 9: 10 two stone tablets inscribed by the *f*
1Ki 12: 10 'My little *f* is thicker
2Ch 10: 10 'My little *f* is thicker
Est 3: 10 king took the signet ring off his *f*
Job 1: 12 on the man himself do not lay a *f*."
Isa 58: 9 with the pointing *f* and malicious
Mt 23: 4 willing to lift a *f* to move them.
Lk 11: 20 But if I drive out demons by the *f*
11: 46 you yourselves will not lift one *f*
15: 22 Put a ring on his *f* and sandals
16: 24 to dip the tip of his *f* in water
Jn 8: 6 to write on the ground with his *f*.
20: 25 and put my *f* where the nails were,
20: 27 "Put your *f* here; see my hands.

FINGERS (FINGER)

2Sa 21: 20 man with six *f* on each hand
1Ch 20: 6 man with six *f* on each hand
Ps 8: 3 the work of your *f*,
144: 1 my *f* for battle.
Pr 6: 13 and motions with his *f*,
7: 3 Bind them on your *f;*
31: 19 and grasps the spindle with her *f*.
SS 5: 5 my *f* with flowing myrrh,
Isa 2: 8 to what their *f* have made.
17: 8 the incense altars their *f* have made
59: 3 your *f* with guilt.
Jer 52: 21 each was four *f* thick, and hollow.
Da 5: 5 Suddenly the *f* of a human hand
Mk 7: 33 Jesus put his *f* into the man's ears.

FINISH (FINISHED FINISHING)

Ge 6: 16 and *f* the ark to within 18 inches
29: 27 *F* out this daughter's bridal week;
Ru 2: 21 until they *f* harvesting all my grain
1Ch 27: 24 to count the men but did not *f*.
Ne 4: 2 they offer sacrifices? Will they *f*
Ps 90: 9 we *f* our years with a moan.
Pr 24: 27 *F* your outdoor work
Jer 51: 63 When you *f* reading this scroll,
Da 9: 24 your holy city to *f* transgression,
Mt 10: 23 you will not *f* going
Lk 14: 29 foundation and is not able to *f* it,
14: 30 to build and was not able to *f*.'
Jn 4: 34 him who sent me and to *f* his work.
5: 36 that the Father has given me to *f*,
Ac 20: 24 if only I may *f* the race
2Co 8: 11 Now *f* the work, so that your eager
9: 5 and *f* the arrangements
Jas 1: 4 Perseverance must *f* its work

FINISHED (FINISH)

Ge 2: 2 seventh day God had *f* the work he
17: 22 When he had *f* speaking
18: 33 When the LORD had *f* speaking
24: 15 Before he had *f* praying, Rebekah
24: 19 until they have *f* drinking."
24: 22 When the camels had *f* drinking,
24: 45 "Before I *f* praying in my heart,
27: 30 After Isaac *f* blessing him
29: 28 He *f* out the week with Leah,
49: 33 Jacob had *f* giving instructions
Ex 31: 18 When the LORD *f* speaking
34: 33 When Moses *f* speaking to them,
40: 33 And so Moses *f* the work.
Lev 16: 20 Aaron has *f* making atonement
Nu 4: 15 his sons have *f* covering the holy
7: 1 When Moses *f* setting up
16: 31 As soon as he *f* saying all this,
Dt 20: 9 When the officers have *f* speaking
26: 12 When you have *f* setting
31: 24 After Moses *f* writing
32: 45 When Moses *f* reciting all these
Jos 4: 1 the whole nation had *f* crossing
8: 24 When Israel had *f* killing all
19: 49 When they had *f* dividing the land
19: 51 And so they *f* dividing the land.
Jdg 15: 17 When he *f* speaking, he threw away
Ru 2: 23 and wheat harvests were *f*.
3: 3 there until he has *f* eating
3: 7 When Boaz had *f* eating
1Sa 1: 9 Once when they had *f* eating
13: 10 Just as he *f* making the offering,
18: 1 After David had *f* talking with Saul
24: 16 When David *f* saying this,
2Sa 6: 18 After he had *f* sacrificing the burnt
11: 19 "When you have *f* giving the king
13: 36 As he *f* speaking, the king's sons
15: 24 all the people had *f* leaving the city.
1Ki 3: 1 David until he *f* building his palace
6: 38 the temple was *f* in all its details
7: 40 So Huram *f* all the work he had
7: 51 for the temple of the LORD was *f*,
8: 54 When Solomon had *f* all these
9: 1 When Solomon had *f* building
13: 23 When the man of God had *f* eating
2Ki 6: 23 after they had *f* eating and drinking
10: 25 as Jehu had *f* making the burnt
16: 11 and *f* it before King Ahaz returned.
1Ch 16: 2 After David had *f* sacrificing
28: 20 of the temple of the LORD is *f*.
2Ch 4: 11 So Huram *f* the work he had
5: 1 for the temple of the LORD was *f*,
7: 1 When Solomon *f* praying,
7: 11 When Solomon had *f* the temple
8: 16 So the temple of the LORD was *f*.
20: 23 After they *f* slaughtering the men
24: 14 When they had *f*, they brought
29: 29 When the offerings were *f*,
29: 34 them until the task was *f*
31: 7 and *f* in the seventh month.
Ezr 5: 11 king of Israel built and *f*.
5: 16 under construction but is not yet *f*
6: 14 They *f* building the temple
10: 17 of the first month they *f* dealing
Isa 10: 12 When the Lord has *f* all his work
Jer 26: 8 as Jeremiah *f* telling all the people
43: 1 When Jeremiah *f* telling the people
Eze 4: 6 "After you have *f* this, lie
4: 8 the other until you have *f* the days
42: 15 When he had *f* measuring what was
43: 23 When you have *f* purifying it,
Mt 7: 28 When Jesus had *f* saying these
11: 1 After Jesus had *f* instructing his
13: 53 When Jesus had *f* these parables,
19: 1 When Jesus had *f* saying these
26: 1 When Jesus had *f* saying all these
Lk 4: 13 the devil had *f* all this tempting,
5: 4 When he had *f* speaking, he said
7: 1 When Jesus had *f* saying all this
11: 1 When he *f*, one of his disciples said
11: 37 When Jesus had *f* speaking,
Jn 12: 36 When he had *f* speaking, Jesus left
13: 12 When he had *f* washing their feet,
18: 1 When he had *f* praying, Jesus left
19: 30 the drink, Jesus said, "It is *f*."
21: 15 When they had *f* eating, Jesus said
Ac 12: 25 and Saul had *f* their mission,
15: 13 When they *f*, James spoke up:
2Ti 4: 7 I have *f* the race, I have kept
Heb 4: 3 And yet his work has been *f*
Rev 11: 7 when they have *f* their testimony,

FINISHING (FINISH)

1Ki 1: 41 as they were *f* their feast.
2Ch 29: 17 *f* on the sixteenth day

FINS

Lev 11: 9 you may eat any that have *f*
11: 10 or streams that do not have *f*
11: 12 in the water that does not have *f*
Dt 14: 9 you may eat any that has *f*
14: 10 But anything that does not have *f*

FIR (FIRS)

Isa 41: 19 the *f* and the cypress together,
60: 13 the *f* and the cypress together,

FIRE (AFIRE CAMPFIRES FIERY FIREBRANDS FIRELIGHT FIREPANS FIREPOT FIRES FIREWOOD)

Ge 15: 17 smoking *f* pot with a blazing torch
22: 6 and he himself carried the *f*
22: 7 "The *f* and wood are here,"
Ex 3: 2 in flames of *f* from within a bush.
3: 2 the bush was on *f* it did not burn up
12: 8 to eat the meat roasted over the *f*,
12: 9 but roast it over the *f*— head,
13: 21 in a pillar of *f* to give them light,
13: 22 the pillar of *f* by night left its place
14: 24 looked down from the pillar of *f*
19: 18 the LORD descended on it in *f*.
22: 6 who started the *f* must make
22: 6 "If a *f* breaks out and spreads
24: 17 LORD looked like a consuming *f*
29: 18 an offering made to the LORD by *f*
29: 25 an offering made to the LORD by *f*
29: 41 an offering made to the LORD by *f*
30: 20 made to the LORD by *f*,
32: 20 had made and burned it in the *f*;
32: 24 into the *f*, and out came this calf!"
35: 3 Do not light a *f* in any
40: 38 and *f* was in the cloud by night,
Lev 1: 7 and arrange wood on the *f*.
1: 7 are to put *f* on the altar
1: 9 made by *f*, an aroma pleasing
1: 13 made by *f*, an aroma pleasing
1: 17 is on the *f* on the altar.
1: 17 made by *f*, an aroma pleasing
2: 2 made by *f*, an aroma pleasing
2: 3 made to the LORD by *f*.
2: 9 as an offering made by *f*,
2: 10 made to the LORD by *f*.
2: 11 made to the LORD by *f*.
2: 14 heads of new grain roasted in the *f*.
2: 16 an offering made to the LORD by *f*
3: 3 made to the LORD by *f*:
3: 5 made by *f*, an aroma pleasing
3: 9 made to the LORD by *f*:
3: 11 an offering made to the LORD by *f*
3: 14 offering to the LORD by *f*:
3: 16 made by *f*, a pleasing aroma.
4: 12 burn it in a wood *f* on the ash heap.
4: 35 made to the LORD by *f*.
5: 12 made to the LORD by *f*.
6: 9 and the *f* must be kept burning
6: 10 offering that the *f* has consumed
6: 12 arrange the burnt offering on the *f*
6: 12 *f* on the altar must be kept burning;
6: 13 The *f* must be kept burning
6: 17 of the offerings made to me by *f*.
6: 18 the LORD by *f* for the generations
7: 5 an offering made to the LORD by *f*
7: 25 an offering by *f* may be made
7: 30 made to the LORD by *f*;
7: 35 the LORD by *f* that were allotted
8: 21 an offering made to the LORD by *f*
8: 28 an offering made to the LORD by *f*
9: 24 *F* came out from the presence
10: 1 and they offered unauthorized *f*
10: 1 put *f* in them and added incense;
10: 2 So *f* came out from the presence
10: 6 the LORD has destroyed by *f*.
10: 12 offerings made to the LORD by *f*
10: 13 made to the LORD by *f*;
10: 15 portions of the offerings made by *f*,
13: 55 it with *f*, whether the mildew has
13: 57 the mildew must be burned with *f*.
16: 13 incense on the *f* before the LORD,
20: 14 and they must be burned in the *f*,
21: 6 made to the LORD by *f*,
21: 9 she must be burned in the *f*.
21: 21 made to the LORD by *f*.
22: 22 an offering made to the LORD by *f*
22: 27 an offering made to the LORD by *f*
23: 8 made to the LORD by *f*.
23: 13 an offering made to the LORD by *f*
23: 18 made by *f*, an aroma pleasing
23: 25 made to the LORD by *f*.' "
23: 27 made to the LORD by *f*.
23: 36 made to the LORD by *f*.
Lev 23: 36 made to the LORD by *f*.
23: 37 made to the LORD by *f*—
24: 7 made to the LORD by *f*.
24: 9 made to the LORD by *f*."
Nu 3: 4 with unauthorized *f* before him
6: 18 and put it in the *f* that is
9: 15 above the tabernacle looked like *f*.
9: 16 and at night it looked like *f*.
11: 1 Then *f* from the LORD burned
11: 2 to the LORD and the *f* died down.
11: 3 *f* from the LORD had burned
14: 14 by day and a pillar of *f* by night.
15: 3 to the LORD offerings made by *f*,
15: 10 It will be an offering made by *f*,
15: 13 he brings an offering made by *f*
15: 14 you presents an offering made by *f*
15: 25 their wrong an offering made by *f*
16: 7 Take censers and tomorrow put *f*
16: 18 So each man took his censer, put *f*
16: 35 And *f* came out from the LORD
16: 46 along with *f* from the altar,
18: 9 offerings that is kept from the *f*.
18: 17 as an offering made by *f*,
21: 28 "*F* went out from Heshbon,
26: 10 when the *f* devoured the 250 men.
26: 61 the LORD with unauthorized *f*.)
28: 2 food for my offerings made by *f*,
28: 3 made by *f* that you are to present
28: 6 an offering made to the LORD by *f*
28: 8 This is an offering made by *f*,
28: 13 an offering made to the LORD by *f*
28: 19 to the LORD an offering made by *f*
28: 24 the offering made by *f* every day
29: 6 made to the LORD by *f*—
29: 13 Present an offering made by *f*
29: 36 Present an offering made by *f*
31: 23 cannot withstand *f* must be
31: 23 *f* must be put through the *f*,
Dt 1: 33 in *f* by night and in a cloud by day,
4: 11 the mountain while it blazed with *f*
4: 12 spoke to you out of the *f*.
4: 15 spoke to you at Horeb out of the *f*.
4: 24 LORD your God is a consuming *f*,
4: 33 the voice of God speaking out of *f*,
4: 36 On earth he showed you his great *f*,
4: 36 heard his words from out of the *f*.
5: 4 to face out of the *f* on the mountain
5: 5 because you were afraid of the *f*
5: 22 on the mountain from out of the *f*,
5: 23 the mountain was ablaze with *f*,
5: 24 we have heard his voice from the *f*.
5: 25 This great *f* will consume us,
5: 26 of the living God speaking out of *f*,
7: 5 and burn their idols in the *f*.
7: 25 their gods you are to burn in the *f*.
9: 3 ahead of you like a devouring *f*.
9: 10 to you on the mountain out of the *f*,
9: 15 while it was ablaze with *f*.
9: 21 had made, and burned it in the *f*.
10: 4 out of the *f*, on the day
12: 3 burn their Asherah poles in the *f*;
12: 31 and daughters in the *f* as sacrifices
18: 1 made to the LORD by *f*,
18: 10 his son or daughter in the *f*,
18: 16 nor see this great *f* anymore,
32: 22 For a *f* has been kindled
Jos 7: 15 things shall be destroyed by *f*,
8: 8 you have taken the city, set it on *f*.
8: 19 captured it and quickly set it on *f*.
13: 14 made by *f* to the LORD,
Jdg 1: 8 the city to the sword and set it on *f*.
6: 21 *F* flared from the rock, consuming
9: 15 then let *f* come out
9: 20 and let *f* come out from you,
9: 20 let *f* come out from Abimelech
9: 49 set it on *f* over the people inside.
9: 52 entrance to the tower to set it on *f*,
20: 48 came across they set on *f*.
1Sa 2: 28 made with *f* by the Israelites.
30: 3 they found it destroyed by *f*
2Sa 14: 30 Go and set it on *f*."
14: 30 servants set the field on *f*.
14: 31 your servants set my field on *f*?"
22: 9 consuming *f* came from his mouth,
1Ki 9: 16 He had set it on *f*.
16: 18 and set the palace on *f* around him.
18: 23 put it on the wood but not set *f* to it
18: 23 put it on the wood but not set *f* to it
1Ki 18: 24 The god who answers by *f*—
18: 25 of your god, but do not light the *f*."
18: 38 Then the *f* of the LORD fell
19: 12 After the earthquake came a *f*,
19: 12 after the *f* came a gentle whisper.
19: 12 but the LORD was not in the *f*.
2Ki 1: 10 Then *f* fell from heaven
1: 10 may *f* come down from heaven
1: 12 Then the *f* of God fell from heaven
1: 12 "may *f* come down from heaven
1: 14 *f* has fallen from heaven
2: 11 horses of *f* appeared and separated
2: 11 suddenly a chariot of *f*
6: 17 and chariots of *f* all around Elisha.
8: 12 "You will set *f* to their fortified
16: 3 and even sacrificed his son in the *f*,
17: 17 their sons and daughters in the *f*.
17: 31 burned their children in the *f*
19: 18 have thrown their gods into the *f*
21: 6 He sacrificed his own son in the *f*,
23: 10 or daughter in the *f* to Molech.
25: 9 He set *f* to the temple of the LORD
1Ch 14: 12 orders to burn them in the *f*.
21: 26 him with *f* from heaven
2Ch 7: 1 *f* came down from heaven
7: 3 all the Israelites saw the *f* coming
16: 14 they made a huge *f* in his honor.
21: 19 His people made no *f* in his honor,
28: 3 and sacrificed his sons in the *f*,
33: 6 sons in the *f* in the Valley of Ben
35: 13 the Passover animals over the *f*
36: 19 They set *f* to God's temple
Ne 1: 3 its gates have been burned with *f*."
2: 3 its gates have been destroyed by *f*
2: 13 which had been destroyed by *f*.
2: 17 its gates have been burned with *f*.
9: 12 with a pillar of *f* to give them light
9: 19 nor the pillar of *f* by night to shine
Job 1: 16 "The *f* of God fell from the sky
15: 34 *f* will consume the tents
18: 5 the flame of his *f* stops burning.
18: 15 *F* resides in his tent;
20: 26 A *f* unfanned will consume him
22: 20 and *f* devours their wealth.'
28: 5 is transformed below as by *f*;
31: 12 It is a *f* that burns to Destruction;
41: 19 sparks of *f* shoot out.
41: 20 from a boiling pot over a *f* of reeds.
Ps 18: 8 consuming *f* came from his mouth,
21: 9 and his *f* will consume them.
39: 3 and as I meditated, the *f* burned;
46: 9 he burns the shields with *f*.
50: 3 a *f* devours before him,
66: 12 we went through *f* and water,
68: 2 as wax melts before the *f*,
78: 14 and with light from the *f* all night.
78: 21 his *f* broke out against Jacob,
78: 63 *F* consumed their young men,
79: 5 long will your jealousy burn like *f*?
80: 16 down, it is burned with *f*;
83: 14 As *f* consumes the forest
89: 46 long will your wrath burn like *f*?
97: 3 *F* goes before him
104: 4 flames of *f* his servants.
105: 39 and a *f* to give light at night.
106: 18 *F* blazed among their followers;
140: 10 may they be thrown into the *f*,
Pr 6: 27 Can a man scoop *f* into his lap
16: 27 and his speech is like a scorching *f*.
26: 20 Without wood a *f* goes out;
26: 21 to embers and as wood to *f*,
30: 16 and *f*, which never says, 'Enough!'
SS 8: 6 It burns like blazing *f*,
Isa 1: 7 your cities burned with *f*;
1: 31 with no one to quench the *f*."
4: 4 a spirit of judgment and a spirit of *f*.
4: 5 and a glow of flaming *f* by night;
5: 24 as tongues of *f* lick up straw
9: 5 will be fuel for the *f*.
9: 18 Surely wickedness burns like a *f*;
9: 19 and the people will be fuel for the *f*;
10: 16 under his pomp a *f* will be kindled
10: 17 The Light of Israel will become a *f*,
26: 11 let the *f* reserved for your enemies
27: 4 I would set them all on *f*.
29: 6 and flames of a devouring *f*.
30: 27 and his tongue is a consuming *f*.
30: 30 with raging anger and consuming *f*,

Isa 30: 33 Its *f* pit has been made deep
30: 33 with an abundance of *f* and wood;
31: 9 whose *f* is in Zion,
33: 11 breath is a *f* that consumes you.
33: 14 dwell with the consuming *f*?
37: 19 have thrown their gods into the *f*
43: 2 When you walk through the *f*,
44: 15 he kindles a *f* and bakes bread.
44: 16 Half of the wood he burns in the *f*;
44: 16 "Ah! I am warm; I see the *f*."
47: 14 here is no *f* to sit by.
47: 14 the *f* will burn them up.
64: 2 As when *f* sets twigs ablaze
64: 11 has been burned with *f*,
65: 5 a *f* that keeps burning all day.
66: 15 See, the LORD is coming with *f*,
66: 15 and his rebuke with flames of *f*.
66: 16 For with *f* and with his sword
66: 24 nor will their *f* be quenched,
Jer 4: 4 wrath will break out and burn like *f*
5: 14 make my words in your mouth a *f*
6: 29 to burn away the lead with *f*,
7: 18 gather wood, the fathers light the *f*,
7: 31 their sons and daughters in the *f*—
11: 16 he will set it on *f*,
15: 14 for my anger will kindle a *f*
17: 27 I will kindle an unquenchable *f*
19: 5 of Baal to burn their sons in the *f*
20: 9 is in my heart like a burning *f*,
21: 10 and he will destroy it with *f*.'
21: 12 wrath will break out and burn like *f*
21: 14 I will kindle a *f* in your forests
22: 7 and throw them into the *f*.
23: 29 my word like *f*," declares
29: 22 king of Babylon burned in the *f*.'
32: 29 this city will come in and set it on *f*;
34: 5 As people made a funeral *f*
34: 5 so they will make a *f* in your honor
36: 22 with a *f* burning in the firepot
36: 23 entire scroll was burned in the *f*.
36: 32 king of Judah had burned in the *f*.
39: 8 The Babylonians set *f*
43: 12 He will set *f* to the temples
48: 45 for a *f* has gone out from Heshbon,
49: 2 villages will be set on *f*.
49: 27 I will set *f* to the walls of Damascus
50: 32 I will kindle a *f* in her towns
51: 30 Her dwellings are set on *f*;
51: 32 the marshes set on *f*,
51: 58 and her high gates set on *f*;
52: 13 He set *f* to the temple of the LORD
La 1: 13 "From on high he sent *f*,
2: 3 burned in Jacob like a flaming *f*
2: 4 he has poured out his wrath like *f*
4: 11 He kindled a *f* in Zion
Eze 1: 4 of the *f* looked like glowing metal,
1: 5 in the *f* was what looked like four
1: 13 *F* moved back and forth
1: 13 was like burning coals of *f*
1: 27 as if full of *f*, and that from there
1: 27 from there down he looked like *f*;
5: 2 of the hair with *f* inside the city.
5: 4 A *f* will spread from there
5: 4 them into the *f* and burn them up.
8: 2 to be his waist down he was like *f*,
10: 6 "Take *f* from among the wheels,
10: 7 hand to the *f* that was among them.
15: 4 after it is thrown on the *f* as fuel
15: 4 as fuel and the *f* burns both ends
15: 5 useful when the *f* has burned it
15: 6 trees of the forest as fuel for the *f*,
15: 7 the *f* will yet consume them.
15: 7 they have come out of the *f*,
19: 12 and *f* consumed them.
19: 14 *F* spread from one
20: 31 the sacrifice of your sons in the *f*—
20: 47 I am about to set *f* to you,
21: 32 You will be fuel for the *f*,
23: 25 who are left will be consumed by *f*.
24: 10 and kindle the *f*.
24: 12 not even by *f*.
28: 18 So I made a *f* come out from you,
30: 8 when I set *f* to Egypt
30: 14 set *f* to Zoan
30: 16 I will set *f* to Egypt;
39: 6 I will send *f* on Magog
46: 23 with places for *f* built all
Da 3: 22 of the *f* killed the men who took up
Da 3: 24 we tied up and threw into the *f*?"
3: 25 four men walking around in the *f*,
3: 26 and Abednego came out of the *f*,
3: 27 and there was no smell of *f* on them
3: 27 saw that the *f* had not harmed
7: 9 His throne was flaming with *f*,
7: 10 A river of *f* was flowing,
7: 11 and thrown into the blazing *f*.
Hos 7: 4 whose *f* the baker need not stir
7: 6 morning it blazes like a flaming *f*.
8: 14 But I will send *f* upon their cities
Joel 1: 19 for *f* has devoured the open
1: 20 *f* has devoured the open pastures.
2: 3 Before them *f* devours,
2: 5 a crackling *f* consuming stubble,
2: 30 blood and *f* and billows of smoke.
Am 1: 4 I will send *f* upon the house
1: 7 I will send *f* upon the walls of Gaza
1: 10 I will send *f* upon the walls of Tyre
1: 12 I will send *f* upon Teman
1: 14 I will set *f* to the walls of Rabbah
2: 2 I will send *f* upon Moab
2: 5 I will send *f* upon Judah
4: 11 a burning stick snatched from the *f*,
5: 6 through the house of Joseph like a *f*
7: 4 calling for judgment by *f*;
Ob : 18 The house of Jacob will be a *f*
: 18 they will set it on *f* and consume it.
Mic 1: 4 like wax before the *f*,
1: 7 temple gifts will be burned with *f*;
Na 1: 6 His wrath is poured out like *f*;
3: 13 *f* has consumed their bars.
3: 15 There the *f* will devour you;
Hab 2: 13 people's labor is only fuel for the *f*,
Zep 1: 18 In the *f* of his jealousy
3: 8 by the *f* of my jealous anger.
Zec 2: 5 I myself will be a wall of *f* around it
3: 2 stick snatched from the *f*?"
9: 4 and she will be consumed by *f*.
11: 1 so that *f* may devour your cedars!
13: 9 This third I will bring into the *f*;
Mal 3: 2 For he will be like a refiner's *f*
4: 1 that is coming will set them on *f*,"
Mt 3: 10 cut down and thrown into the *f*.
3: 11 you with the Holy Spirit and with *f*.
3: 12 the chaff with unquenchable *f*."
5: 22 will be in danger of the *f* of hell.
6: 30 and tomorrow is thrown into the *f*,
7: 19 cut down and thrown into the *f*.
13: 40 are pulled up and burned in the *f*,
17: 15 He often falls into the *f*
18: 8 and be thrown into eternal *f*.
18: 9 and be thrown into the *f* of hell.
25: 41 into the eternal *f* prepared
Mk 9: 22 "It has often thrown him into *f*
9: 43 where the *f* never goes out.
9: 48 and the *f* is not quenched.'
9: 49 Everyone will be salted with *f*.
14: 54 and warmed himself at the *f*.
Lk 3: 9 cut down and thrown into the *f*."
3: 16 you with the Holy Spirit and with *f*.
3: 17 the chaff with unquenchable *f*."
9: 54 us to call *f* down from heaven
12: 28 and tomorrow is thrown into the *f*,
12: 49 I have come to bring *f* on the earth,
16: 24 because I am in agony in this *f*.'
17: 29 *f* and sulfur rained
22: 55 But when they had kindled a *f*
Jn 15: 6 thrown into the *f* and burned.
18: 18 stood around a *f* they had made
21: 9 they saw a *f* of burning coals there
Ac 2: 3 to be tongues of *f* that separated
2: 19 blood and *f* and billows of smoke.
28: 2 They built a *f* and welcomed us all
28: 3 and, as he put it on the *f*, a viper,
28: 5 Paul shook the snake off into the *f*
1Co 3: 13 It will be revealed with *f*,
3: 13 and the *f* will test the quality
1Th 5: 19 Do not put out the Spirit's *f*;
2Th 1: 7 revealed from heaven in blazing *f*
Heb 1: 7 his servants flames of *f*."
10: 27 and of raging *f* that will consume
12: 18 touched and that is burning with *f*;
12: 29 for our God is a consuming *f*.
Jas 3: 5 set on *f* by a small spark.
3: 6 also is a *f*, a world of evil
3: 6 and is itself set on *f* by hell.
3: 6 sets the whole course of his life on *f*
Jas 5: 3 against you and eat your flesh like *f*
1Pe 1: 7 even though refined by *f*—
2Pe 3: 7 and earth are reserved for *f*,
3: 10 the elements will be destroyed by *f*,
3: 12 the destruction of the heavens by *f*,
Jude : 7 suffer the punishment of eternal *f*.
: 23 snatch others from the *f*
Rev 1: 14 and his eyes were like blazing *f*.
2: 18 whose eyes are like blazing *f*
3: 18 to buy from me gold refined in the *f*
8: 5 filled it with *f* from the altar,
8: 7 and there came hail and *f* mixed
9: 17 and out of their mouths came *f*,
9: 18 killed by the three plagues of *f*,
11: 5 *f* comes from their mouths
13: 13 *f* to come down from heaven
14: 18 angel, who had charge of the *f*,
15: 2 a sea of glass mixed with *f*
16: 8 power to scorch people with *f*.
17: 16 eat her flesh and burn her with *f*.
18: 8 She will be consumed by *f*,
19: 12 His eyes are like blazing *f*,
20: 9 But *f* came down from heaven
20: 14 The lake of *f* is the second death.
20: 14 were thrown into the lake of *f*.
20: 15 he was thrown into the lake of *f*.

FIREBRANDS (FIRE)

Job 41: 19 *F* stream from his mouth;
Pr 26: 18 *f* or deadly arrows

FIRELIGHT (FIRE)

Lk 22: 56 girl saw him seated there in the *f*.

FIREPANS (FIRE)

Ex 27: 3 sprinkling bowls, meat forks and *f*.
38: 3 sprinkling bowls, meat forks and *f*.
Nu 4: 14 including the *f*, meat forks,

FIREPOT (FIRE)

Jer 36: 22 burning in the *f* in front of him.
36: 23 and threw them into the *f*,
Zec 12: 6 of Judah like a *f* in a woodpile,

FIRES (FIRE)

Isa 27: 11 women come and make *f*
40: 16 Lebanon is not sufficient for altar *f*,
50: 11 But now, all you who light *f*
50: 11 go, walk in the light of your *f*
Mal 1: 10 that you would not light useless *f*

FIREWOOD (FIRE)

Lev 6: 12 Every morning the priest is to add *f*
Isa 7: 4 of these two smoldering stubs of *f*

FIRM

Ex 14: 13 Stand *f* and you will see
15: 8 surging waters stood *f* like a wall;
Jos 3: 17 the covenant of the LORD stood *f*
2Ch 20: 17 stand *f* and see the deliverance
Ezr 9: 8 giving us a *f* place in his sanctuary,
Job 11: 15 you will stand *f* and without fear.
36: 5 he is mighty, and *f* in his purpose.
41: 23 they are *f* and immovable.
Ps 20: 8 but we rise up and stand *f*.
30: 7 you made my mountain stand *f*;
33: 9 he commanded, and it stood *f*.
33: 11 of the LORD stand *f* forever,
37: 23 whose steps he has made *f*;
40: 2 and gave me a *f* place to stand.
75: 3 it is I who hold its pillars *f*.
78: 13 made the water stand *f* like a wall.
89: 2 that your love stands *f* forever,
89: 4 and make your throne *f*
93: 5 Your statutes stand *f*;
119: 89 it stands *f* in the heavens.
Pr 4: 26 and take only ways that are *f*.
10: 25 but the righteous stand *f* forever.
12: 7 the house of the righteous stands *f*.
Isa 7: 9 If you do not stand *f* in your faith,
22: 17 about to take *f* hold of you
22: 23 drive him like a peg into a *f* place;
22: 25 into the *f* place will give way;
Eze 13: 5 so that it will stand *f* in the battle
Zec 8: 23 nations will take *f* hold of one Jew
Mt 10: 22 he who stands *f* to the end will be
24: 13 he who stands *f* to the end will be
Mk 13: 13 he who stands *f* to the end will be

Lk 21: 19 By standing *f* you will save
1Co 10: 12 So, if you think you are standing *f*,
15: 58 my dear brothers, stand *f*.
16: 13 on your guard; stand *f* in the faith;
2Co 1: 7 for you is *f*, because we know that
1: 21 who makes both us and you stand *f*
1: 24 because it is by faith you stand *f*.
Gal 5: 1 Stand *f*, then, and do not let
Eph 6: 14 Stand *f* then, with the belt
Php 1: 27 I will know that you stand *f*
4: 1 that is how you should stand *f*
Col 1: 23 in your faith, established and *f*,
2: 5 and how *f* your faith in Christ is.
4: 12 that you may stand *f* in all the will
1Th 3: 8 since you are standing *f* in the Lord
2Th 2: 15 stand *f* and hold to the teachings
1Ti 6: 19 a *f* foundation for the coming age,
2Ti 2: 19 God's solid foundation stands *f*,
Heb 6: 19 an anchor for the soul, *f* and secure
Jas 5: 8 You too, be patient and stand *f*,
1Pe 5: 9 Resist him, standing *f* in the faith,
5: 10 make you strong, *f* and steadfast.

FIRS (FIR)

SS 1: 17 our rafters are *f*.

FIRST

Ge 1: 5 and there was morning—the *f* day.
2: 11 The name of the *f* is the Pishon;
8: 5 and on the *f* day of the tenth month
8: 13 By the *f* day of the *f* month
8: 13 of Noah's six hundred and *f* year,
10: 10 The *f* centers of his kingdom were
13: 4 and where he had *f* built an altar.
25: 25 The *f* to come out was red,
25: 31 "*F* sell me your birthright."
25: 33 But Jacob said, "Swear to me *f*."
38: 28 and said, "This one came out *f*."
41: 20 the seven fat cows that came up *f*.
43: 18 back into our sacks the *f* time.
43: 20 down here the *f* time to buy food.
49: 3 my might, the *f* sign of my strength
Ex 4: 8 attention to the *f* miraculous sign,
12: 2 be for you the *f* month, the *f* month
12: 15 On the *f* day remove the yeast
12: 15 with yeast in it from the *f* day
12: 16 On the *f* day hold a sacred
12: 18 In the *f* month you are
13: 2 The *f* offspring of every womb
13: 12 over to the LORD the *f* offspring
13: 15 to the LORD the *f* male offspring
21: 10 he must not deprive the *f* one
25: 35 the *f* pair of branches extending
28: 17 In the *f* row there shall be a ruby,
29: 40 With the *f* lamb offer a tenth
34: 1 two stone tablets like the *f* ones,
34: 1 words that were on the *f* tablets,
34: 4 out two stone tablets like the *f* ones
34: 19 *f* offspring of every womb belongs
37: 21 the *f* pair of branches extending
39: 10 In the *f* row there was a ruby,
40: 2 on the *f* day of the *f* month.
40: 17 up on the *f* day of the *f* month
Lev 4: 21 and burn it as he burned the *f* bull.
5: 8 who shall *f* offer the one
9: 15 sin offering as he did with the *f* one.
23: 5 the fourteenth day of the *f* month.
23: 7 On the *f* day hold a sacred
23: 10 a sheaf of the *f* grain you harvest.
23: 24 'On the *f* day of the seventh month
23: 35 The *f* day is a sacred assembly;
23: 39 for seven days; the *f* day is a day
23: 40 On the *f* day you are
Nu 1: 1 the Desert of Sinai on the *f* day
1: 18 on the *f* day of the second month.
2: 9 They will set out *f*.
3: 12 in place of the *f* male offspring
7: 12 on the *f* day was Nahshon son
8: 16 the *f* male offspring
9: 1 the Desert of Sinai in the *f* month
9: 5 the fourteenth day of the *f* month.
10: 13 this *f* time, at the LORD's
10: 14 of the camp of Judah went *f*,
13: 20 the season for the *f* ripe grapes.)
15: 20 from the *f* of your ground meal
15: 21 from the *f* of your ground meal.
18: 15 The *f* offspring of every womb,
20: 1 In the *f* month the whole Israelite
22: 15 and more distinguished than the *f*.
24: 20 "Amalek was *f* among the nations,
28: 11 " 'On the *f* of every month,
28: 16 day of the *f* month the LORD's
28: 18 On the *f* day hold a sacred
29: 1 " 'On the *f* day of the seventh
33: 3 on the fifteenth day of the *f* month,
33: 38 where he died on the *f* day
Dt 1: 3 on the *f* day of the eleventh month,
10: 1 out two stone tablets like the *f* ones
10: 2 words that were on the *f* tablets,
10: 3 two stone tablets like the *f* ones,
10: 10 as I did the *f* time, and the LORD
13: 9 Your hand must be the *f*
16: 4 of the *f* day remain until morning.
17: 7 of the witnesses must be the *f*
18: 4 and the *f* wool from the shearing
21: 17 That son is the *f* sign
24: 4 then her *f* husband, who divorced
25: 6 The *f* son she bears shall carry
Jos 4: 19 of the *f* month the people went up
21: 4 The *f* lot came out
21: 10 because the *f* lot fell to them):
Jdg 1: 1 "Who will be the *f* to go up
20: 18 LORD replied, "Judah shall go *f*."
20: 18 "Who of us shall go *f* to fight
20: 22 had stationed themselves the *f* day.
20: 39 defeating them as in the *f* battle."
1Sa 2: 16 "Let the fat be burned up *f*,
14: 14 In that *f* attack Jonathan
14: 35 it was the *f* time he had done this.
22: 15 Was that day the *f* time I inquired
2Sa 17: 9 If he should attack your troops *f*,
18: 27 seems to me that the *f* one runs like
19: 20 the *f* of the whole house of Joseph
19: 43 Were we not the *f* to speak
21: 9 put to death during the *f* days
1Ki 3: 22 But the *f* one insisted, "No!
3: 27 the living baby to the *f* woman.
6: 24 of the *f* cherub was five cubits long,
17: 13 *f* make a small cake of bread for me
18: 25 one of the bulls and prepare it *f*,
20: 9 do all you demanded the *f* time,
20: 17 provincial commanders went out *f*.
22: 5 "*F* seek the counsel of the LORD."
2Ki 1: 14 and consumed the *f* two captains
4: 42 baked from the *f* ripe grain,
17: 25 When they *f* lived there, they did
1Ch 6: 54 because the *f* lot was for them):
9: 2 *f* to resettle on their own property
11: 6 Joab son of Zeruiah went up *f*,
12: 15 Jordan in the *f* month when it was
15: 13 bring it up the *f* time that
16: 7 That day David *f* committed
23: 8 Jehiel the *f*, Zetham and Joel—
23: 11 Jahath was the *f* and Ziza
23: 16 of Gershom: Shubael was the *f*.
23: 17 of Eliezer: Rehabiah was the *f*.
23: 18 sons of Izhar: Shelomith was the *f*.
23: 19 Jeriah the *f*, Amariah the second,
23: 20 Micah the *f* and Isshiah the second
24: 7 *f* lot fell to Jehoiarib, the second
24: 21 from his sons: Isshiah was the *f*.
24: 23 Jeriah the *f*, Amariah the second,
25: 9 The *f* lot, which was for Asaph,
26: 10 Shimri the *f* (although he was not
26: 10 his father had appointed him the *f*),
27: 2 In charge of the *f* division,
27: 2 for the *f* month, was Jashobeam
27: 3 the army officers for the *f* month.
2Ch 3: 11 of the *f* cherub was five cubits long
3: 12 touched the wing of the *f* cherub.
18: 4 "*F* seek the counsel of the LORD."
29: 3 In the *f* month of the *f* year
29: 17 on the sixteenth day of the *f* month
29: 17 on the *f* day of the *f* month,
35: 1 the fourteenth day of the *f* month.
36: 22 In the *f* year of Cyrus king of Persia
Ezr 1: 1 In the *f* year of Cyrus king of Persia
3: 6 On the *f* day of the seventh month
5: 13 in the *f* year of Cyrus king
6: 3 In the *f* year of King Cyrus,
6: 19 the fourteenth day of the *f* month,
7: 9 arrived in Jerusalem on the *f* day
7: 9 on the *f* day of the *f* month,
8: 31 day of the *f* month we set out
10: 16 On the *f* day of the tenth month
10: 17 by the *f* day of the *f* month they
Ne 4: 21 from the *f* light of dawn
7: 5 record of those who had been the *f*
8: 2 on the *f* day of the seventh month
8: 18 after day, from the *f* day to the last,
10: 37 to the priests, the *f*
Est 3: 7 in the *f* month, the month of Nisan,
3: 12 of the *f* month the royal secretaries
Job 3: 9 and not see the *f* rays of dawn,
15: 7 "Are you the *f* man ever born?
40: 19 He ranks *f* among the works
42: 12 part of Job's life more than the *f*.
42: 14 The *f* daughter he named Jemimah,
Pr 4: 18 of the righteous is like the *f* gleam
18: 17 *f* to present his case seems right,
Isa 41: 4 I, the LORD—with the *f* of them
41: 27 I was the *f* to tell Zion, 'Look,
43: 27 Your *f* father sinned;
44: 6 I am the *f* and I am the last;
48: 12 I am the *f* and I am the last.
48: 16 "From the *f* announcement I have
52: 4 "At *f* my people went
Jer 4: 31 a groan as of one bearing her *f* child
7: 12 in Shiloh where I *f* made a dwelling
25: 1 which was the *f* year
36: 28 the words that were on the *f* scroll,
50: 17 The *f* to devour him
Eze 26: 1 on the *f* day of the month,
29: 17 in the *f* month on the *f* day,
30: 20 in the *f* month on the seventh day,
31: 1 in the third month on the *f* day,
32: 1 in the twelfth month on the *f* day,
40: 21 as those of the *f* gateway.
44: 30 are to give them the *f* portion
45: 18 In the *f* month on the *f* day you are
45: 21 " 'In the *f* month on the fourteenth
Da 1: 21 until the *f* year of King Cyrus.
6: 19 At the *f* light of dawn, the king got
7: 1 In the *f* year of Belshazzar king
7: 4 "The *f* was like a lion, and it had
7: 8 three of the *f* horns were uprooted
8: 21 horn between his eyes is the *f* king.
9: 1 In the *f* year of Darius son
9: 2 in the *f* year of his reign, I, Daniel,
10: 4 twenty-fourth day of the *f* month,
10: 12 Since the *f* day that you set your
10: 21 but *f* I will tell you what is written
11: 1 in the *f* year of Darius the Mede,
11: 13 than the *f*; and after several years,
Hos 2: 7 I will go back to my husband as at *f*,
Am 6: 7 among the *f* to go into exile;
Na 3: 12 trees with their *f* ripe fruit;
Hag 1: 1 on the *f* day of the sixth month,
Zec 6: 2 The *f* chariot had red horses,
12: 7 will save the dwellings of Judah *f*,
14: 10 Gate to the site of the *F* Gate,
Mt 5: 24 *F* go and be reconciled
6: 33 But seek *f* his kingdom
7: 5 *f* take the plank out
8: 21 *f* let me go and bury my father."
10: 2 the names of the twelve apostles: *f*,
12: 29 unless he *f* ties up the strong man?
12: 45 of that man is worse than the *f*.
13: 30 *F* collect the weeds and tie them
17: 10 law say that Elijah must come *f*?"
17: 25 into the house, Jesus was the *f*
17: 27 Take the *f* fish you catch; open its
19: 30 But many who are *f* will be last,
19: 30 and many who are last will be *f*.
20: 8 ones hired and going on to the *f*.'
20: 10 when those came who were hired *f*,
20: 16 last will be *f*, and the *f* will be last."
20: 27 wants to be *f* must be your slave—
21: 28 He went to the *f* and said, 'Son,
21: 31 what his father wanted?" "The *f*,"
21: 36 than the *f* time, and the tenants
22: 25 The *f* one married and died,
22: 38 This is the *f* and greatest
23: 26 *F* clean the inside of the cup
26: 17 On the *f* day of the Feast
27: 64 deception will be worse than the *f*."
28: 1 at dawn on the *f* day of the week,
Mk 3: 27 unless he *f* ties up the strong man.
4: 28 soil produces grain—*f* the stalk,
7: 27 "*F* let the children eat all they want
9: 11 law say that Elijah must come *f*?"
9: 12 Elijah does come *f*, and restores all
9: 35 to be *f*, he must be the very last,
10: 31 are *f* will be last, and the last *f*."

Mk 10: 44 wants to be *f* must be slave
12: 20 The *f* one married and died
13: 10 And the gospel must *f* be preached
14: 12 On the *f* day of the Feast
16: 2 Very early on the *f* day of the week,
16: 9 he appeared *f* to Mary Magdalene,
16: 9 rose early on the *f* day of the week,
Lk 1: 2 who from the *f* were eyewitnesses
2: 2 (This was the *f* census that took
6: 42 *f* take the plank out of your eye,
9: 59 *f* let me go and bury my father.''
9: 61 *f* let me go back and say good-by
10: 5 ''When you enter a house, *f* say,
11: 26 of that man is worse than the *f*.''
11: 38 noticing that Jesus did not *f* wash
12: 1 began to speak *f* to his disciples,
13: 30 will be *f*, and *f* who will be last.''
14: 18 *f* said, 'I have just bought a field,
14: 28 Will he not *f* sit down and estimate
14: 31 Will he not *f* sit down and consider
16: 5 He asked the *f*, 'How much do you
17: 25 But *f* he must suffer many things
19: 16 ''The *f* one came and said, 'Sir,
20: 29 The *f* one married a woman
21: 9 These things must happen *f*,
24: 1 On the *f* day of the week, very
Jn 1: 41 The *f* thing Andrew did was
2: 10 brings out the choice wine *f*
2: 11 This, the *f* of his miraculous signs,
7: 51 a man without *f* hearing him
8: 7 let him be the *f* to throw a stone
8: 9 older ones *f*, until only Jesus was
12: 16 At *f* his disciples did not
15: 18 keep in mind that it hated me *f*.
16: 4 I did not tell you this at *f*
18: 13 and brought him *f* to Annas,
19: 32 the legs of the *f* man who had been
20: 1 Early on the *f* day of the week,
20: 4 Peter and reached the tomb *f*.
20: 8 who had reached the tomb *f*,
20: 19 evening of that *f* day of the week,
Ac 3: 26 he sent him *f* to you to bless you
7: 12 he sent our fathers on their *f* visit.
11: 26 disciples were *f* called Christians
12: 10 They passed the *f* and second
13: 46 to speak the word of God to you *f*.
15: 14 God at *f* showed his concern
20: 7 On the *f* day of the week we came
20: 18 from the *f* day I came
26: 20 *F* to those in Damascus, then
26: 23 and, as the *f* to rise from the dead,
27: 43 swim to jump overboard *f*
Ro 1: 8 *F*, I thank my God
1: 16 *f* for the Jew, then for the Gentile.
1: 17 is by faith from *f* to last,
2: 9 *f* for the Jew, then for the Gentile;
2: 10 *f* for the Jew, then for the Gentile.
3: 2 Much in every way! *F* of all,
10: 19 did Israel not understand? *F*,
13: 11 now than when we *f* believed.
16: 5 who was the *f* convert to Christ
1Co 11: 18 In the *f* place, I hear that
12: 28 in the church God has appointed *f*
14: 30 down, the *f* speaker should stop.
15: 3 on to you as of *f* importance:
15: 45 ''The *f* man Adam became a living
15: 46 The spiritual did not come *f*,
15: 47 The *f* man was of the dust
16: 2 On the *f* day of every week,
16: 15 of Stephanas were the *f* converts
2Co 1: 15 I planned to visit you *f*
8: 5 they gave themselves *f* to the Lord
8: 10 Last year you were the *f* not only
Gal 4: 13 illness that I *f* preached the gospel
Eph 1: 12 who were the *f* to hope in Christ,
6: 2 which is the *f* commandment
Php 1: 5 the gospel from the *f* day until now,
1Th 4: 16 and the dead in Christ will rise *f*.
1Ti 2: 1 I urge, then, *f* of all, that requests,
2: 13 For Adam was formed *f*, then Eve.
3: 10 They must *f* be tested;
5: 4 these should learn *f* of all
5: 12 they have broken their *f* pledge.
2Ti 1: 5 which *f* lived in your grandmother
2: 6 hardworking farmer should be the *f*
4: 16 At my *f* defense, no one came
Heb 2: 3 which was *f* announced
3: 14 the end the confidence we had at *f*.
Heb 7: 2 *F*, his name means ''king
7: 27 day after day, *f* for his own sins,
8: 7 wrong with that *f* covenant,
8: 13 he has made the *f* one obsolete;
9: 1 the *f* covenant had regulations
9: 2 In its *f* room were the lampstand,
9: 8 the *f* tabernacle was still standing.
9: 15 committed under the *f* covenant.
9: 18 even the *f* covenant was not put
10: 8 *F* he said, ''Sacrifices and offerings,
10: 9 He sets aside the *f*
10: 15 *F* he says: ''This is the covenant I
Jas 3: 17 comes from heaven is *f* of all pure;
2Pe 3: 3 *F* of all, you must understand that
1Jn 4: 19 We love because he *f* loved us.
3Jn : 9 but Diotrephes, who loves to be *f*,
Rev 1: 17 I am the *F* and the Last.
2: 4 You have forsaken your *f* love.
2: 5 and do the things you did at *f*.
2: 8 the words of him who is the *F*
2: 19 now doing more than you did at *f*.
4: 1 the voice I had *f* heard speaking
4: 7 The *f* living creature was like a lion,
6: 1 as the Lamb opened the *f*
8: 7 The *f* angel sounded his trumpet,
9: 12 *f* woe is past; two other woes are
13: 12 its inhabitants worship the *f* beast,
13: 12 of the *f* beast on his behalf,
13: 14 to do on behalf of the *f* beast,
13: 15 breath to the image of the *f* beast,
16: 2 *f* angel went and poured out his
20: 5 This is the *f* resurrection.
20: 6 part in the *f* resurrection.
21: 1 for the *f* heaven and the *f* earth had
21: 19 The *f* foundation was jasper,
22: 13 and the Omega, the *F* and the Last,

FIRSTBORN

Ge 4: 4 from some of the *f* of his flock.
10: 15 was the father of Sidon his *f*,
22: 21 Uz the *f*, Buz his brother, Kemuel
25: 13 Nebaioth the *f* of Ishmael, Kedar,
27: 19 to his father, ''I am Esau your *f*.
27: 32 he answered, ''your *f*, Esau.''
35: 23 Reuben the *f* of Jacob, Simeon,
36: 15 The sons of Eliphaz the *f* of Esau:
38: 6 his *f*, and her name was Tamar.
38: 7 Judah's *f*, was wicked
41: 51 Joseph named his *f* Manasseh
43: 33 from the *f* to the youngest;
46: 8 to Egypt: Reuben the *f* of Jacob.
48: 14 even though Manasseh was the *f*.
48: 18 ''No, my father, this one is the *f*;
49: 3 ''Reuben, you are my *f*,
Ex 4: 22 Israel is my *f* son, and I told you,
4: 23 so I will kill your *f* son.' ''
6: 14 The sons of Reuben the *f* son
11: 5 Every *f* son in Egypt will die,
11: 5 and all the *f* of the cattle as well.
11: 5 from the *f* son of Pharaoh,
11: 5 to the *f* son of the slave girl,
12: 12 Egypt and strike down every *f*—
12: 29 and the *f* of all the livestock as well.
12: 29 from the *f* of Pharaoh, who sat
12: 29 struck down all the *f* in Egypt,
12: 29 to the *f* of the prisoner,
13: 2 ''Consecrate to me every *f* male.
13: 12 All the *f* males of your livestock
13: 13 Redeem every *f* among your sons.
13: 13 with a lamb every *f* donkey,
13: 15 and redeem each of my *f* sons.'
13: 15 the LORD killed every *f* in Egypt,
22: 29 ''You must give me the *f*
34: 19 including all the *f* males
34: 20 Redeem all your *f* sons.
34: 20 Redeem the *f* donkey with a lamb,
Lev 27: 26 may dedicate the *f* of an animal,
27: 26 since the *f* already belongs
Nu 1: 20 of Reuben the *f* son of Israel:
3: 2 the sons of Aaron were Nadab the *f*
3: 13 apart for myself every *f* in Israel,
3: 13 for all the *f* are mine.
3: 13 struck down all the *f* in Egypt,
3: 40 ''Count all the *f* Israelite males who
3: 41 in place of all the *f* of the Israelites,
3: 41 in place of all the *f* of the livestock
3: 42 So Moses counted all the *f*
3: 43 number of *f* males a month old
Nu 3: 45 Levites in place of all the *f* of Israel,
3: 46 redeem the 273 *f* Israelites who
3: 50 From the *f* of the Israelites he
8: 16 as my own in place of the *f*,
8: 17 Every *f* male in Israel,
8: 17 struck down all the *f* in Egypt,
8: 18 in place of all the *f* sons in Israel.
18: 15 But you must redeem every *f* son
18: 15 every *f* male of unclean animals.
18: 17 you must not redeem the *f* of an ox,
26: 5 of Reuben, the *f* son of Israel,
33: 4 who were burying all their *f*,
Dt 12: 6 and the *f* of your herds and flocks.
12: 17 or the *f* of your herds and flocks,
14: 23 and the *f* of your herds
15: 19 Do not put the *f* of your oxen
15: 19 do not shear the *f* of your sheep.
15: 19 the LORD your God every *f* male
21: 15 *f* is the son of the wife he does not
21: 16 he must not give the rights of the *f*
21: 16 loves in preference to his actual *f*,
21: 17 The right of the *f* belongs to him.
21: 17 the *f* by giving him a double share
33: 17 In majesty he is like a *f* bull;
Jos 6: 26 ''At the cost of his *f* son
17: 1 that is, for Makir, Manasseh's *f*.
17: 1 the tribe of Manasseh as Joseph's *f*,
1Sa 8: 2 The name of his *f* was Joel
17: 13 The *f* was Eliab; the second,
2Sa 3: 2 His *f* was Amnon the son
1Ki 16: 34 at the cost of his *f* son Abiram,
2Ki 3: 27 Then he took his *f* son, who was
1Ch 1: 13 was the father of Sidon his *f*,
1: 29 Nebaioth the *f* of Ishmael, Kedar,
2: 3 Judah's *f*, was wicked
2: 13 Jesse was the father of Eliab his *f*;
2: 25 Ram his *f*, Bunah, Oren, Ozem
2: 25 sons of Jerahmeel the *f* of Hezron:
2: 27 The sons of Ram the *f* of Jerahmeel
2: 42 Mesha his *f*, who was the father
2: 50 The sons of Hur the *f* of Ephrathah
3: 1 The *f* was Amnon the son
3: 15 Johanan the *f*, Jehoiakim
4: 4 the *f* of Ephrathah and father
5: 1 as *f* were given to the sons
5: 1 the *f* of Israel (he was the *f*,
5: 2 of the *f* belonged to Joseph)—
5: 3 the sons of Reuben the *f* of Israel:
6: 28 Joel the *f* and Abijah the second
8: 1 was the father of Bela his *f*,
8: 30 and his *f* son was Abdon, followed
8: 39 of his brother Eshek: Ulam his *f*,
9: 5 Of the Shilonites: Asaiah the *f*
9: 31 the *f* son of Shallum the Korahite,
9: 36 and his *f* son was Abdon, followed
26: 2 Zechariah the *f*, Jediael the second,
26: 4 Shemaiah the *f*, Jehozabad
26: 10 the first (although he was not the *f*,
2Ch 21: 3 Jehoram because he was his *f* son.
Ne 10: 36 we will bring the *f* of our sons
Job 18: 13 death's *f* devours his limbs.
Ps 78: 51 He struck down all the *f* of Egypt,
89: 27 I will also appoint him my *f*,
105: 36 down all the *f* in their land,
135: 8 He struck down the *f* of Egypt,
135: 8 the *f* of men and animals.
136: 10 down the *f* of Egypt
Jer 31: 9 and Ephraim is my *f* son.
Eze 20: 26 gifts—the sacrifice of every *f*—
Mic 6: 7 I offer my *f* for my transgression,
Zec 12: 10 as one grieves for a *f* son.
Lk 2: 7 and she gave birth to her *f*, a son.
2: 23 ''Every *f* male is to be consecrated
Ro 8: 29 that he might be the *f*
Col 1: 15 image of the invisible God, the *f*
1: 18 and the *f* from among the dead,
Heb 1: 6 when God brings his *f*
11: 28 of the *f* would not touch the *f*
12: 23 of the *f*, whose names are written
Rev 1: 5 who is the faithful witness, the *f*

FIRSTFRUITS

Ex 23: 16 the Feast of Harvest with the *f*
23: 19 ''Bring the best of the *f* of your soil
34: 22 the Feast of Weeks with the *f*
34: 26 ''Bring the best of the *f* of your soil
Lev 2: 12 to the LORD as an offering of the *f*
2: 14 offering of *f* to the LORD,

Lev 23: 17 a wave offering of f to the LORD.
23: 20 together with the bread of the f.
Nu 18: 12 grain they give the LORD as the f
18: 13 All the land's f that they bring
28: 26 On the day of f, when you present
Dt 18: 4 are to give them the f of your grain,
26: 2 of the f of all that you produce
26: 10 now I bring the f of the soil that
2Ch 31: 5 the Israelites generously gave the f
Ne 10: 35 house of the LORD each year the f
12: 44 storerooms for the contributions, f
13: 31 at designated times, and for the f.
Ps 78: 51 the f of manhood in the tents
105: 36 the f of all their manhood.
Pr 3: 9 with the f of all your crops;
Jer 2: 3 the f of his harvest;
Eze 44: 30 The best of all the f
Ro 8: 23 who have the f of the Spirit,
11: 16 of the dough offered as f is holy,
1Co 15: 20 f of those who have fallen asleep.
15: 23 Christ, the f; then, when he comes,
Jas 1: 18 a kind of f of all he created.
Rev 14: 4 offered as f to God and the Lamb.

FISH (FISHERS FISHING)

Ge 1: 26 let them rule over the f of the sea
1: 28 Rule over the f of the sea
9: 2 and upon all the f of the sea;
Ex 7: 18 The f in the Nile will die,
7: 21 The f in the Nile died,
Nu 11: 5 We remember the f we ate in Egypt
11: 22 if all the f in the sea were caught
Dt 4: 18 or any f in the water below.
1Ki 4: 33 animals and birds, reptiles and f.
2Ch 33: 14 as far as the entrance of the F Gate
Ne 3: 3 The F Gate was rebuilt by the sons
12: 39 the Jeshanah Gate, the F Gate,
13: 16 in Jerusalem were bringing in f
Job 12: 8 or let the f of the sea inform you.
Ps 8: 8 and the f of the sea,
105: 29 causing their f to die.
Ecc 9: 12 As f are caught in a cruel net,
Isa 50: 2 their f rot for lack of water
Eze 29: 4 make the f of your streams stick
29: 4 with all the f sticking to your scales
29: 5 you and all the f of your streams.
38: 20 The f of the sea, the birds of the air,
47: 9 There will be large numbers of f,
47: 10 The f will be of many kinds—
47: 10 like the f of the Great Sea.
Hos 4: 3 and the f of the sea are dying.
Jnh 1: 17 But the LORD provided a great f
1: 17 Jonah was inside the f three days
2: 1 From inside the f Jonah prayed
2: 10 And the LORD commanded the f,
Hab 1: 14 You have made men like f
Zep 1: 3 and the f of the sea.
1: 10 "a cry will go up from the F Gate,
Mt 7: 10 asks for a f, will give him a snake?
12: 40 three nights in the belly of a huge f,
13: 47 the lake and caught all kinds of f.
13: 48 and collected the good f in baskets,
14: 17 loaves of bread and two f,"
14: 19 the two f and looking up to heaven,
15: 34 they replied, "and a few small f."
15: 36 he took the seven loaves and the f,
17: 27 Take the first f you catch; open its
Mk 6: 38 they said, "Five—and two f."
6: 41 divided the two f among them all.
6: 41 the two f and looking up to heaven,
6: 43 of broken pieces of bread and f.
8: 7 They had a few small f as well;
Lk 5: 6 of f that their nets began to break.
5: 9 at the catch of f they had taken,
9: 13 loaves of bread and two f—
9: 16 the two f and looking up to heaven,
11: 11 for a f, will give him a snake instead
24: 42 They gave him a piece of broiled f,
Jn 6: 9 small barley loaves and two small f,
6: 11 He did the same with the f.
21: 3 out to f," Simon Peter told them,
21: 5 haven't you any f?" "No,"
21: 6 because of the large number of f.
21: 8 towing the net full of f,
21: 9 of burning coals there with f on it,
21: 10 of the f you have just caught."
21: 11 It was full of large f, 153, but
21: 13 and did the same with the f.

1Co 15: 39 birds another and f another.

FISHERMEN

Isa 19: 8 The f will groan and lament,
Jer 16: 16 "But now I will send for many f,"
Eze 47: 10 F will stand along the shore;
Mt 4: 18 a net into the lake, for they were f.
13: 48 the f pulled it up on the shore.
Mk 1: 16 a net into the lake, for they were f.
Lk 5: 2 by the f, who were washing their

FISHERS (FISH)

Mt 4: 19 "and I will make you f of men."
Mk 1: 17 "and I will make you f of men."

FISHHOOK (HOOK)

Job 41: 1 pull in the leviathan with a f

FISHHOOKS (HOOK)

Am 4: 2 the last of you with f.

FISHING (FISH)

Job 41: 7 or his head with f spears?

FISHNETS (NET)

Eze 26: 5 she will become a place to spread f,
26: 14 you will become a place to spread f.

FIST (FISTS TIGHTFISTED)

Ex 21: 18 or with his f and he does not die
Nu 35: 21 him with his f so that he dies,
Job 15: 25 because he shakes his f at God
Isa 10: 32 they will shake their f

FISTS (FIST)

Isa 58: 4 in striking each other with wicked f
Zep 2: 15 and shake their f.
Mt 26: 67 and struck him with their f.
Mk 14: 65 struck him with their f, and said,

FIT (FITS FITTED FITTING FITTINGS)

Ge 49: 20 he will provide delicacies f
Dt 12: 8 here today, everyone as he sees f,
Jdg 5: 25 in a bowl f for nobles she brought
17: 6 no king; everyone did as he saw f.
21: 25 no king; everyone did as he saw f.
2Ki 24: 16 f for war, and a thousand craftsmen
Isa 54: 16 and forges a weapon f for its work.
Eze 19: 11 f for a ruler's scepter.
19: 14 f for a ruler's scepter.'
Mt 3: 11 whose sandals I am not f to carry.
Lk 9: 62 and looks back is f for service
14: 35 It is f neither for the soil
Ac 22: 22 earth of him! He's not f to live!"

FITS (FIT)

Gal 5: 20 hatred, discord, jealousy, f of rage,

FITTED (FIT)

Ex 26: 24 f into a single ring; both shall be
36: 29 to the top and f into a single ring;
Eph 6: 15 with your feet f with the readiness

FITTING (FIT)

Ps 33: 1 it is f for the upright to praise him.
147: 1 how pleasant and f to praise him!
Pr 10: 32 of the righteous know what is f,
19: 10 It is not f for a fool to live in luxury
26: 1 honor is not f for a fool.
1Co 14: 40 everything should be done in a f
Col 3: 18 to your husbands, as is f in the Lord
Heb 2: 10 sons to glory, it was f that God,

FITTINGS (FIT)

1Ch 22: 3 doors of the gateways and for the f,

FIX (AFFIXING FIXED)

Dt 11: 18 F these words of mine
Job 14: 3 Do you f your eye on such a one?
Pr 4: 25 f your gaze directly before you.
Isa 46: 8 "Remember this, f it in mind,
Am 9: 4 I will f my eyes upon them
2Co 4: 18 we f our eyes not on what is seen,
Heb 3: 1 heavenly calling, f your thoughts
12: 2 Let us f our eyes on Jesus,

FIXED (FIX)

2Ki 8: 11 stared at him with a f gaze
Job 38: 10 when I f limits for it

Ps 141: 8 my eyes are f on you, O Sovereign
Pr 8: 28 f securely the fountains of the deep
Jer 33: 25 and night and the f laws of heaven
Lk 16: 26 and you a great chasm has been f,

FLAGSTAFF

Isa 30: 17 like a f on a mountaintop,

FLAKES

Ex 16: 14 thin f like frost on the ground

FLAME (AFLAME FLAMED FLAMES FLAMING)

Jdg 13: 20 As the f blazed up from the altar
13: 20 of the LORD ascended in the f.
16: 9 snaps when it comes close to a f.
Job 15: 30 a f will wither his shoots,
18: 5 the f of his fire stops burning.
Ps 83: 14 or a f sets the mountains ablaze,
106: 18 a f consumed the wicked.
SS 8: 6 like a mighty f.
Isa 10: 16 like a blazing f.
10: 17 their Holy One a f;
47: 14 themselves from the power of the f.
54: 16 who fans the coals into f
Eze 20: 47 The blazing f will not be quenched,
Joel 2: 3 behind them a f blazes.
Ob : 18 and the house of Joseph a f;
2Ti 1: 6 you to fan into f the gift of God,

FLAMED (FLAME)

Am 1: 11 and his fury f unchecked,

FLAMES (FLAME)

Ex 3: 2 him in f of fire from within a bush.
Job 41: 21 and f dart from his mouth.
Ps 104: 4 f of fire his servants.
Isa 5: 24 and as dry grass sinks down in the f
29: 6 tempest and f of a devouring fire.
42: 25 in f, yet they did not understand;
43: 2 the f will not set you ablaze.
66: 15 and his rebuke with f of fire.
Jer 51: 58 nations' labor is only fuel for the f."
Da 3: 22 and the furnace so hot that the f
Joel 1: 19 and f have burned up all the trees
Ac 7: 30 to Moses in the f of a burning bush
1Co 3: 15 only as one escaping through the f.
13: 3 and surrender my body to the f,
Heb 1: 7 his servants f of fire."
11: 34 quenched the fury of the f,

FLAMING (FLAME)

Ge 3: 24 and a f sword flashing back
Ps 7: 13 he makes ready his f arrows.
Isa 4: 5 and a glow of f fire by night;
50: 11 provide yourselves with f torches,
La 2: 3 He has burned in Jacob like a f fire
Da 7: 9 His throne was f with fire,
10: 6 lightning, his eyes like f torches,
Hos 7: 6 in the morning it blazes like a f fire.
Na 2: 4 They look like f torches;
Zec 12: 6 like a f torch among sheaves.
Eph 6: 16 you can extinguish all the f arrows

FLANK

Eze 25: 9 I will expose the f of Moab,
34: 21 Because you shove with f

FLAP (FLAPPED)

Job 39: 13 "The wings of the ostrich f joyfully,

FLAPPED (FLAP)

Isa 10: 14 not one f a wing,

FLARE (FLARED)

2Sa 11: 20 the king's anger may f up,
Ps 2: 12 for his wrath can f up in a moment.

FLARED (FLARE)

Jdg 6: 21 Fire f from the rock, consuming
1Sa 20: 30 Saul's anger f up at Jonathan
Ps 124: 3 when their anger f against us,

FLASH (FLASHED FLASHES FLASHING)

Job 15: 12 and why do your eyes f,
37: 15 and makes his lightning f?
Eze 21: 15 Oh! It is made to f like lightning,
21: 28 and to f like lightning!

Hos 11: 6 Swords will *f* in their cities,
Zec 9: 14 his arrow will *f* like lightning.
Lk 9: 29 as bright as a *f* of lightning.
1Co 15: 52 in a *f*, in the twinkling of an eye,

FLASHED (FLASH)

Ex 9: 23 and lightning *f* down to the ground.
9: 24 and lightning *f* back and forth.
Ps 77: 17 your arrows *f* back and forth.
Eze 1: 13 it was bright, and lightning *f* out
Hos 6: 5 my judgments *f* like lightning
Hab 3: 4 rays *f* from his hand,
Ac 9: 3 a light from heaven *f* around him.
22: 6 light from heaven *f* around me.

FLASHES (FLASH)

Job 41: 18 His sneezing throws out *f* of light;
Ps 29: 7 with *f* of lightning.
Eze 1: 14 and forth like *f* of lightning.
Am 5: 9 he *f* destruction on the stronghold
Na 2: 3 The metal on the chariots *f*
Mt 24: 27 from the east and *f* to the west,
Lk 17: 24 which *f* and lights up the sky
Rev 4: 5 From the throne came *f*
8: 5 *f* of lightning and an earthquake.
11: 19 And there came *f* of lightning,
16: 18 Then there came *f* of lightning,

FLASHING (FLASH)

Ge 3: 24 and a flaming sword *f* back
Dt 32: 41 when I sharpen my *f* sword
Job 39: 23 along with the *f* spear and lance.
Ps 76: 3 There he broke the *f* arrows,
Eze 1: 4 an immense cloud with *f* lightning
21: 10 polished, and *f* like lightning!
Na 3: 3 *f* swords
Hab 3: 11 at the lightning of your *f* spear.

FLASK

1Sa 10: 1 Then Samuel took a *f* of oil
2Ki 9: 1 take this *f* of oil with you
9: 3 Then take the *f* and pour the oil

FLAT (FLATS FLATTENS)

Hos 7: 8 Ephraim is a *f* cake not turned over

FLATS (FLAT)

Job 39: 6 the salt *f* as his habitat.

FLATTENS (FLAT)

Isa 32: 19 Though hail *f* the forest

FLATTER (FLATTERING FLATTERS FLATTERY)

Job 32: 21 nor will I *f* any man;
Ps 78: 36 But then they would *f* him
Jude : 16 *f* others for their own advantage.

FLATTERING (FLATTER)

Ps 12: 2 their *f* lips speak with deception.
12: 3 May the LORD cut off all *f* lips
Pr 26: 28 and a *f* mouth works ruin.
28: 23 than he who has a *f* tongue.
Eze 12: 24 or *f* divinations among the people

FLATTERS (FLATTER)

Ps 36: 2 For in his own eyes he *f* himself
Pr 29: 5 Whoever *f* his neighbor

FLATTERY (FLATTER)

Job 32: 22 for if I were skilled in *f*,
Da 11: 32 With *f* he will corrupt those who
Ro 16: 18 and *f* they deceive the minds
1Th 2: 5 You know we never used *f*,

FLAVOR

Job 6: 6 or is there *f* in the white of an egg?

FLAW

Dt 15: 21 or blind, or has any serious *f*,
17: 1 a sheep that has any defect or *f* in it
SS 4: 7 there is no *f* in you.

FLAWLESS

2Sa 22: 31 the word of the LORD is *f*.
Job 11: 4 You say to God, 'My beliefs are *f*
Ps 12: 6 And the words of the LORD are *f*,
18: 30 the word of the LORD is *f*.
Pr 30: 5 "Every word of God is *f*;
SS 5: 2 my dove, my *f* one.

FLAX

Ex 9: 31 barley had headed and the *f* was
9: 31 (The *f* and barley were destroyed,
Jos 2: 6 the stalks of *f* she had laid out
Jdg 15: 14 on his arms became like charred *f*,
Pr 31: 13 She selects wool and *f*
Isa 19: 9 with combed *f* will despair,

FLEA

1Sa 24: 14 you pursuing? A dead dog? A *f*?
26: 20 has come out to look for a *f*—

FLED (FLEE)

Ge 14: 10 into them and the rest *f* to the hills.
14: 10 kings of Sodom and Gomorrah *f*,
16: 6 Sarai mistreated Hagar; so she *f*
31: 21 So he *f* with all he had,
31: 22 Laban was told that Jacob had *f*.
31: 40 at night, and sleep *f* from my eyes.
Ex 2: 15 but Moses *f* from Pharaoh
14: 5 was told that the people had *f*,
Nu 16: 34 all the Israelites around them *f*,
35: 25 to the city of refuge to which he *f*.
35: 26 the city of refuge to which he has *f*
35: 32 for anyone who has *f* to a city
Jos 8: 15 and they *f* toward the desert.
10: 11 As they *f* before Israel on the road
10: 16 Now the five kings had *f*
20: 6 in the town from which he *f*."
Jdg 1: 6 Adoni-Bezek *f*, but they chased
4: 15 Sisera abandoned his chariot and *f*
4: 17 *f* on foot to the tent of Jael,
7: 21 ran, crying out as they *f*.
7: 22 The army *f* to Beth Shittah
8: 12 the two kings of Midian, *f*,
9: 21 Then Jotham *f*, escaping to Beer,
9: 51 all the people of the city—*f*.
11: 3 So Jephthah *f* from his brothers
20: 42 So they *f* before the Israelites
20: 45 and *f* toward the desert to the rock
20: 47 and *f* into the desert to the rock
1Sa 4: 10 and every man *f* to his tent.
4: 16 come from the battle line; I *f*
4: 17 "Israel *f* before the Philistines,
19: 8 them with such force that they *f*
19: 12 down through a window, and he *f*
19: 18 When David had *f* and made his
20: 1 David *f* from Naioth at Ramah
21: 10 That day David *f* from Saul
22: 20 escaped and *f* to join David.
23: 6 down with him when he *f* to David
27: 4 Saul was told that David had *f*
30: 17 rode off on camels and *f*.
31: 1 the Israelites *f* before them,
31: 7 saw that the Israelite army had *f*
31: 7 they abandoned their towns and *f*.
2Sa 1: 4 "The men *f* from the battle.
4: 3 the people of Beeroth *f* to Gittaim
4: 4 His nurse picked him up and *f*,
10: 13 to fight the Arameans, and they *f*
10: 14 they *f* before Abishai and went
10: 18 But they *f* before Israel,
13: 29 mounted their mules and *f*.
13: 34 Meanwhile, Absalom had *f*.
13: 37 Absalom *f* and went to Talmai son
13: 38 After Absalom *f* and went
18: 17 all the Israelites *f* to their homes.
19: 8 the Israelites had *f* to their homes.
19: 9 But now he has *f* the country
23: 11 Israel's troops *f* from them.
1Ki 2: 7 me when I *f* from your brother
2: 28 he *f* to the tent of the LORD
2: 29 Solomon was told that Joab had *f*
11: 17 *f* to Egypt with some Edomite
11: 23 who had *f* from his master,
11: 40 but Jeroboam *f* to Egypt,
12: 2 where he had *f* from King Solomon
20: 20 the Arameans *f*, with the Israelites
20: 30 And Ben-Hadad *f* to the city
2Ki 3: 24 and fought them until they *f*.
7: 7 So they got up and *f* in the dusk
8: 21 his army, however, *f* back home.
9: 23 Joram turned about and *f*,
9: 27 had happened, he *f* up the road
14: 12 and every man *f* to his home.
14: 19 in Jerusalem, and he *f* to Lachish,
2Ki 25: 4 They *f* toward the Arabah,
25: 4 and the whole army *f* at night
25: 26 *f* to Egypt for fear
1Ch 10: 1 the Israelites *f* before them,
10: 7 the valley saw that the army had *f*
10: 7 they abandoned their towns and *f*.
11: 13 the troops *f* from the Philistines.
19: 14 to fight the Arameans, and they *f*
19: 15 they too *f* before his brother
19: 18 But they *f* before Israel,
2Ch 10: 2 where he had *f* from King Solomon
13: 16 The Israelites *f* before Judah,
14: 12 The Cushites *f*, and Asa
25: 22 and every man *f* to his home.
25: 27 in Jerusalem and he *f* to Lachish,
Ps 48: 5 they *f* in terror.
104: 7 But at your rebuke the waters *f*,
114: 3 The sea looked and *f*,
114: 5 Why was it, O sea, that you *f*,
Isa 20: 6 those we *f* to for help
22: 3 All your leaders have *f* together;
22: 3 having *f* while the enemy was still
Jer 9: 10 The birds of the air have *f*
26: 21 heard of it and *f* in fear to Egypt.
39: 4 all the soldiers saw them, they *f*;
41: 15 escaped from Johanan and *f*
52: 7 They *f* toward the Arabah,
52: 7 through, and the whole army *f*.
La 1: 6 in weakness they have *f*
Da 10: 7 overwhelmed them that they *f*
Hos 12: 12 Jacob *f* to the country of Aram;
Am 5: 19 as though a man *f* from a lion
Zec 14: 5 as you *f* from the earthquake
Mt 26: 56 all the disciples deserted him and *f*.
Mk 14: 50 Then everyone deserted him and *f*.
14: 52 When they seized him, he *f* naked,
16: 8 the women went out and *f*
Ac 7: 29 When Moses heard this, he *f*
14: 6 *f* to the Lycaonian cities of Lystra
Heb 6: 18 we who have *f* to take hold
Rev 12: 6 The woman *f* into the desert
16: 20 Every island *f* away
20: 11 Earth and sky *f* from his presence,

FLEE (FLED FLEEING FLEES)

Ge 19: 17 *F* to the mountains or you will be
19: 17 one of them said, "*F* for your lives!
19: 19 But I can't *f* to the mountains;
19: 20 Let me *f* to it—it is very small,
19: 22 *f* there quickly, because I cannot
27: 43 *F* at once to my brother Laban
Ex 21: 13 he is to *f* to a place I will designate.
Lev 26: 17 and you will *f* even when no one is
Nu 10: 35 may your foes *f* before you."
35: 6 who has killed someone may *f*.
35: 11 killed someone accidentally may *f*.
35: 15 another accidentally can *f* there.
Dt 4: 42 He could *f* into one of these cities
4: 42 who had killed a person could *f*
19: 3 who kills a man may *f* there.
19: 5 That man may *f* to one
28: 7 from one direction but *f* from you
28: 25 from one direction but *f* from them
Jos 8: 5 did before, we will *f* from them.
8: 6 So when we *f* from them, you are
20: 3 and unintentionally may *f* there
20: 9 someone accidentally could *f*
2Sa 15: 14 We must *f*, or none
17: 2 then all the people with him will *f*.
18: 3 to *f*, they won't care about us.
19: 3 ashamed when they *f* from battle.
2Ki 19: 21 tosses her head as you *f*.
Job 41: 28 Arrows do not make him *f*;
Ps 11: 1 "*F* like a bird to your mountain.
31: 11 me on the street *f* from me.
55: 7 I would *f* far away
68: 1 may his foes *f* before him.
68: 12 "Kings and armies *f* in haste;
139: 7 Where can I *f* from your presence?
SS 2: 17 and the shadows *f*,
4: 6 and the shadows *f*,
Isa 2: 19 Men will *f* to caves in the rocks
2: 21 They will *f* to caverns in the rocks
13: 14 each will *f* to his native land.
15: 5 her fugitives *f* as far as Zoar,
17: 13 he rebukes them they *f* far away,
21: 15 They *f* from the sword,
30: 16 Therefore you will *f*!

Isa 30: 16 You said, 'No, we will *f* on horses.'
30: 17 A thousand will *f*
30: 17 you will all *f* away,
31: 8 They will *f* before the sword
33: 3 of your voice, the peoples *f*;
35: 10 and sorrow and sighing will *f* away.
37: 22 tosses her head as you *f*.
48: 20 *f* from the Babylonians!
51: 11 and sorrow and sighing will *f* away.
Jer 4: 5 Let us *f* to the fortified cities!'
4: 6 *F* for safety without delay!
6: 1 *F* from Jerusalem!
6: 1 "*F* for safety, people of Benjamin!
8: 14 Let us *f* to the fortified cities
25: 35 shepherds will have nowhere to *f*,
46: 5 They *f* in haste
46: 6 "The swift cannot *f*
46: 21 They too will turn and *f* together,
48: 6 *F*! Run for your lives;
49: 8 Turn and *f*, hide in deep caves,
49: 24 she has turned to *f*
49: 30 "*F* quickly away!
50: 3 both men and animals will *f* away
50: 8 "*F* out of Babylon;
50: 16 let everyone *f* to his own land.
51: 6 "*F* from Babylon!
La 4: 15 When they *f* and wander about,
Da 4: 14 Let the animals *f* from under it
Am 2: 16 will *f* naked on that day,"
Jnh 1: 3 for Tarshish to *f* from the LORD.
4: 2 was so quick to *f* to Tarshish.
Na 3: 7 All who see you will *f* from you
Zec 2: 6 Come! *F* from the land of the north
14: 5 You will *f* as you fled
14: 5 You will *f* by my mountain valley,
Mt 3: 7 Who warned you to *f*
10: 23 in one place, *f* to another.
24: 16 are in Judea *f* to the mountains.
Mk 13: 14 are in Judea *f* to the mountains.
Lk 3: 7 Who warned you to *f*
21: 21 are in Judea *f* to the mountains,
1Co 6: 18 *F* from sexual immorality.
10: 14 my dear friends, *f* from idolatry.
1Ti 6: 11 But you, man of God, *f* from all this
2Ti 2: 22 *F* the evil desires of youth,
Jas 4: 7 Resist the devil, and he will *f*

FLEECE

Jdg 6: 37 I will place a wool *f*
6: 37 If there is dew only on the *f*
6: 38 he squeezed the *f* and wrung out
6: 39 Allow me one more test with the *f*.
6: 39 This time make the *f* dry
6: 40 Only the *f* was dry; all the ground
Job 31: 20 him with the *f* from my sheep,

FLEEING (FLEE)

Ge 35: 1 when you were *f* from your brother
35: 7 when he was *f* from his brother.
Ex 14: 27 The Egyptians were *f* toward it,
Lev 26: 36 as though *f* from the sword,
26: 37 as though *f* from the sword,
Jos 8: 20 for the Israelites who had been *f*
1Sa 22: 17 They knew he was *f*, yet they did
2Sa 10: 14 saw that the Arameans were *f*,
24: 13 months of *f* from your enemies
1Ch 19: 15 saw that the Arameans were *f*,
Jer 46: 22 Egypt will hiss like a *f* serpent
48: 19 Ask the man *f* and the woman
Eze 17: 21 All his *f* troops will fall

FLEES (FLEE)

Dt 19: 4 and *f* there to save his life—
19: 11 and then *f* to one of these cities,
Jos 20: 4 "When he *f* to one of these cities,
Job 20: 24 Though he *f* from an iron weapon,
27: 22 as he *f* headlong from its power.
Pr 28: 1 The wicked man *f* though no one
Isa 10: 29 Gibeah of Saul *f*.
24: 18 Whoever *f* at the sound of terror
Jer 48: 44 "Whoever *f* from the terror

FLEET (FLEETING)

1Ki 9: 27 serve in the *f* with Solomon's men.
10: 22 The king had a *f* of trading ships
22: 48 Now Jehoshaphat built a *f*
2Ch 9: 21 The king had a *f* of trading ships
20: 36 to construct a *f* of trading ships.
Da 11: 40 and cavalry and a great *f* of ships.

FLEET-FOOTED (FOOT)

2Sa 2: 18 Asahel was as *f* as a wild gazelle.
Am 2: 15 the *f* soldier will not get away,

FLEETING (FLEET)

Job 14: 2 like a *f* shadow, he does not endure
Ps 39: 4 let me know how *f* is my life.
89: 47 Remember how *f* is my life.
144: 4 his days are like a *f* shadow.
Pr 21: 6 is a *f* vapor and a deadly snare.
31: 30 Charm is deceptive, and beauty is *f*

FLESH

Ge 2: 21 and closed up the place with *f*.
2: 23 and *f* of my *f*;
2: 24 and they will become one *f*.
17: 13 My covenant in your *f* is
17: 14 has not been circumcised in the *f*,
29: 14 "You are my own *f* and blood."
37: 27 he is our brother, our own *f*
40: 19 And the birds will eat away your *f*
Ex 4: 7 it was restored, like the rest of his *f*.
29: 14 But burn the bull's *f* and its hide
Lev 4: 11 But the hide of the bull and all its *f*,
6: 27 any of the *f* will become holy,
8: 17 But the bull with its hide and its *f*
9: 11 the *f* and the hide he burned up
13: 10 and if there is raw *f* in the swelling,
13: 14 But whenever raw *f* appears on him
13: 15 The raw *f* is unclean; he has
13: 15 When the priest sees the raw *f*,
13: 16 Should the raw *f* change
13: 24 appears in the raw *f* of the burn,
16: 27 *f* and offal are to be burned up.
26: 29 You will eat the *f* of your sons
26: 29 and the *f* of your daughters.
Nu 12: 12 womb with its *f* half eaten away."
19: 5 its hide, *f*, blood and offal.
Dt 28: 53 the *f* of the sons and daughters
28: 55 give to one of them any of the *f*
32: 42 while my sword devours *f*:
Jdg 8: 7 I will tear your *f* with desert thorns
9: 2 Remember, I am your *f* and blood
1Sa 17: 44 I'll give your *f* to the birds of the air
2Sa 1: 22 from the *f* of the mighty,
5: 1 "We are your own *f* and blood.
16: 11 who is of my own *f*, is trying
19: 12 You are my brothers, my own *f*
19: 13 'Are you not my own *f* and blood?
1Ki 8: 19 who is your own *f* and blood—
2Ki 5: 10 and your *f* will be restored
5: 14 and his *f* was restored and became
9: 36 dogs will devour Jezebel's *f*.
20: 18 of your descendants, your own *f*
1Ch 11: 1 "We are your own *f* and blood.
2Ch 6: 9 who is your own *f* and blood—
32: 8 With him is only the arm of *f*,
Ne 5: 5 Although we are of the same *f*
Job 2: 5 out your hand and strike his *f*
6: 12 Is my *f* bronze?
10: 4 Do you have eyes of *f*?
10: 11 clothe me with skin and *f*
15: 27 and his waist bulges with *f*,
19: 22 Will you never get enough of my *f*?
19: 26 yet in my *f* I will see God;
33: 21 His *f* wastes away to nothing,
33: 25 then his *f* is renewed like a child's;
41: 23 The folds of his *f* are tightly joined,
Ps 27: 2 me to devour my *f*,
50: 13 Do I eat the *f* of bulls
73: 26 My *f* and my heart may fail,
78: 39 remembered that they were but *f*,
79: 2 the *f* of your saints to the beasts
84: 2 my heart and my *f* cry out
119: 120 My *f* trembles in fear of you;
Pr 5: 11 when your *f* and body are spent.
Isa 9: 20 feed on the *f* of his own offspring:
31: 3 their horses are *f* and not spirit.
39: 7 your own *f* and blood who will be
49: 26 your oppressors eat their own *f*;
58: 7 not to turn away from your own *f*
65: 4 who eat the *f* of pigs,
66: 17 midst of those who eat the *f* of pigs
Jer 9: 25 are circumcised only in the *f*—
17: 5 who depends on *f* for his strength
19: 9 I will make them eat the *f*
Jer 19: 9 and they will eat one another's *f*
51: 35 to our *f* be upon Babylon,"
La 3: 4 made my skin and my *f* grow old
Eze 11: 19 of stone and give them a heart of *f*.
32: 5 I will spread your *f*
32: 6 the ravines will be filled with your *f*
36: 26 of stone and give you a heart of *f*.
37: 6 and make *f* come upon you
37: 8 tendons and *f* appeared on them
39: 17 you will eat *f* and drink blood.
39: 18 You will eat the *f* of mighty men
40: 43 were for the *f* of the offerings.
44: 7 in heart and *f* into my sanctuary,
44: 9 and *f* is to enter my sanctuary,
Da 7: 5 'Get up and eat your fill of *f*!'
Mic 3: 2 and the *f* from their bones;
3: 3 like *f* for the pot?"
3: 3 who eat my people's *f*,
Zec 11: 9 who are left eat one another's *f*."
14: 12 Their *f* will rot while they are still
Mal 2: 15 In *f* and spirit they are his.
Mt 19: 5 and the two will become one *f*?
Mk 10: 8 and the two will become one *f*.'
Lk 24: 39 a ghost does not have *f* and bones,
Jn 1: 14 The Word became *f* and lived for a
3: 6 *F* gives birth to *f*,
6: 51 This bread is my *f*, which I will give
6: 52 "How can this man give us his *f*
6: 53 you eat the *f* of the Son of Man
6: 54 Whoever eats my *f* and drinks my
6: 55 For my *f* is real food and my blood
6: 56 Whoever eats my *f* and drinks my
6: 63 The Spirit gives life; the *f* counts
1Co 6: 16 "The two will become one *f*."
15: 39 All *f* is not the same: Men have one
15: 39 kind of *f*, animals have another,
15: 50 that *f* and blood cannot inherit
2Co 12: 7 there was given me a thorn in my *f*,
Gal 6: 13 that they may boast about your *f*.
Eph 2: 15 by abolishing in his *f* the law
5: 31 and the two will become one *f*."
6: 12 For our struggle is not against *f*
Php 3: 2 do evil, those mutilators of the *f*.
3: 3 and who put no confidence in the *f*
3: 4 reasons to put confidence in the *f*,
Col 1: 24 I fill up in my *f* what is still lacking
Heb 2: 14 Since the children have *f* and blood
Jas 5: 3 against you and eat your *f* like fire.
1Jn 4: 2 come in the *f* is from God,
2Jn : 7 Jesus Christ as coming in the *f*,
Jude : 23 the clothing stained by corrupted *f*.
Rev 17: 16 they will eat her *f* and burn her
19: 18 and the *f* of all people, free
19: 18 so that you may eat the *f* of kings,
19: 21 birds gorged themselves on their *f*.

FLEW (FLY)

2Sa 22: 11 He mounted the cherubim and *f*;
Ps 18: 10 He mounted the cherubim and *f*;
Isa 6: 6 Then one of the seraphs *f* to me
Ac 16: 26 At once all the prison doors *f* open,

FLIES (FLY)

Ex 8: 21 I will send swarms of *f* on you
8: 21 of the Egyptians will be full of *f*,
8: 22 no swarms of *f* will be there,
8: 24 Dense swarms of *f* poured
8: 24 Egypt the land was ruined by the *f*.
8: 29 tomorrow the *f* will leave Pharaoh
8: 31 The *f* left Pharaoh and his officials
Dt 4: 17 or any bird that *f* in the air,
Job 20: 8 Like a dream he *f* away, no more
Ps 78: 45 of *f* that devoured them
91: 5 nor the arrow that *f* by day,
105: 31 and there came swarms of *f*,
Ecc 10: 1 As dead *f* give perfume a bad smell,
Isa 7: 18 for *f* from the distant streams
51: 6 and its inhabitants die like *f*.

FLIGHT (FLY)

Lev 26: 36 wind-blown leaf will put them to *f*.
Dt 32: 30 or two put ten thousand to *f*,
Jdg 9: 40 and many fell wounded in the *f*—
2Sa 22: 41 my enemies turn their backs in *f*,
2Ki 7: 15 away in their headlong *f*.
1Ch 12: 15 and they put to *f* everyone living
Job 39: 26 "Does the hawk take *f*
Ps 18: 40 my enemies turn their backs in *f*,

Ps 104: 7 of your thunder they took to *f*;
Isa 10: 31 Madmenah is in *f*;
52: 12 or go in *f*;
Jer 4: 29 every town takes to *f*.
Eze 40: 49 It was reached by a *f* of stairs,
Da 9: 21 to me in swift *f* about the time
Mt 24: 20 Pray that your *f* will not take place

FLIMSY

Eze 13: 10 and because, when a *f* wall is built,

FLINGING (FLUNG)

Ac 22: 23 throwing off their cloaks and *f* dust

FLINT (FLINTY)

Ex 4: 25 But Zipporah took a *f* knife,
Jos 5: 2 "Make *f* knives and circumcise
5: 3 So Joshua made *f* knives
Isa 5: 28 their horses' hoofs seem like *f*,
50: 7 Therefore have I set my face like *f*,
Jer 17: 1 inscribed with a *f* point,
Eze 3: 9 the hardest stone, harder than *f*.
Zec 7: 12 They made their hearts as hard as *f*

FLINTY (FLINT)

Dt 32: 13 and with oil from the *f* crag,
Job 28: 9 Man's hand assaults the *f* rock

FLIRTING

Isa 3: 16 *f* with their eyes,

FLOAT (FLOATED)

1Ki 5: 9 and I will *f* them in rafts by sea
2Ki 6: 6 threw it there, and made the iron *f*.
2Ch 2: 16 and will *f* them in rafts by sea
Hos 10: 7 Samaria and its king will *f* away

FLOATED (FLOAT)

Ge 7: 18 the ark *f* on the surface of the water

FLOCK (FLOCKING FLOCKS)

Ge 4: 4 from some of the firstborn of his *f*.
21: 28 apart seven ewe lambs from the *f*,
27: 9 to the *f* and bring me two choice
30: 40 the young of the *f* by themselves,
31: 10 mating with the *f* were streaked,
31: 12 mating with the *f* are streaked,
38: 17 send you a young goat from my *f*,"
Ex 2: 16 the troughs to water their father's *f*.
2: 17 to their rescue and watered their *f*.
2: 19 drew water for us and watered the *f*
3: 1 Now Moses was tending the *f*
3: 1 and he led the *f* to the far side
34: 19 livestock, whether from herd or *f*.
Lev 1: 2 from either the herd or the *f*.
1: 10 is a burnt offering from the *f*,
3: 6 " 'If he offers an animal from the *f*
5: 6 or goat from the *f* as a sin offering;
5: 15 as a penalty a ram from the *f*,
5: 18 as a guilt offering a ram from the *f*,
6: 6 his guilt offering, a ram from the *f*,
22: 21 or *f* a fellowship offering
27: 32 The entire tithe of the herd and *f*—
Nu 15: 3 from the herd or the *f*,
Dt 15: 14 Supply him liberally from your *f*,
16: 2 your God an animal from your *f*
32: 14 curds and milk from herd and *f*
1Sa 17: 20 in the morning David left the *f*
17: 34 and carried off a sheep from the *f*,
2Sa 7: 8 and from following the *f* to be ruler
1Ch 17: 7 and from following the *f*,
Ezr 10: 19 each presented a ram from the *f*
Job 21: 11 send forth their children as a *f*;
Ps 77: 20 You led your people like a *f*
78: 52 he brought his people out like a *f*;
80: 1 you who lead Joseph like a *f*;
95: 7 the *f* under his care.
SS 1: 7 I love, where you graze your *f*
4: 1 Your hair is like a *f* of goats
4: 2 Your teeth are like a *f*
6: 5 Your hair is like a *f* of goats
6: 6 Your teeth are like a *f* of sheep
Isa 40: 11 He tends his *f* like a shepherd:
63: 11 with the shepherd of his *f*?
Jer 10: 21 and all their *f* is scattered.
13: 17 the LORD's *f* will be taken captive.
13: 20 Where is the *f* that was entrusted
23: 2 "Because you have scattered my *f*
Jer 23: 3 will gather the remnant of my *f* out
25: 34 roll in the dust, you leaders of the *f*.
25: 35 the leaders of the *f* no place
25: 36 the wailing of the leaders of the *f*,
31: 10 watch over his *f* like a shepherd.'
49: 20 of the *f* will be dragged away;
50: 8 and be like the goats that lead the *f*.
50: 17 "Israel is a scattered *f*
50: 45 of the *f* will be dragged away;
51: 23 with you I shatter shepherd and *f*,
Eze 24: 5 take the pick of the *f*.
34: 2 not shepherds take care of the *f*?
34: 3 but you do not take care of the *f*.
34: 8 because my *f* lacks a shepherd
34: 8 for themselves rather than for my *f*,
34: 8 shepherds did not search for my *f*
34: 10 hold them accountable for my *f*.
34: 10 them from tending the *f*
34: 10 will rescue my *f* from their mouths,
34: 12 after his scattered *f* when he is
34: 16 I will shepherd the *f* with justice.
34: 17 my *f*, this is what the Sovereign
34: 19 Must my *f* feed on what you have
34: 22 I will save my *f*, and they will no
43: 23 a young bull and a ram from the *f*,
43: 25 a young bull and a ram from the *f*,
45: 15 taken from every *f* of two hundred
Am 7: 15 me from tending the *f*
Jnh 3: 7 not let any man or beast, herd or *f*,
Mic 2: 12 like a *f* in its pasture;
4: 8 As for you, O watchtower of the *f*,
5: 4 He will stand and shepherd his *f*
7: 14 the *f* of your inheritance,
Zec 9: 16 as the *f* of his people.
10: 3 care for his *f*, the house of Judah,
11: 4 Pasture the *f* marked for slaughter.
11: 7 So I pastured the *f* marked
11: 7 other Union, and I pastured the *f*.
11: 7 particularly the oppressed of the *f*.
11: 8 *f* detested me, and I grew weary
11: 11 of the *f* who were watching me
11: 17 who deserts the *f*!
Mal 1: 14 who has an acceptable male in his *f*
Mt 26: 31 the sheep of the *f* will be scattered.'
Lk 12: 32 little *f*, for your Father has been
Jn 10: 12 the wolf attacks the *f* and scatters it
10: 16 shall be one *f* and one shepherd.
Ac 20: 28 all the *f* of which the Holy Spirit
20: 29 among you and will not spare the *f*.
1Co 9: 7 Who tends a *f* and does not drink
1Pe 5: 2 Be shepherds of God's *f* that is
5: 3 but being examples to the *f*.

FLOCKING (FLOCK)

Hos 7: 12 When I hear them *f* together,

FLOCKS (FLOCK)

Ge 4: 2 Now Abel kept *f*, and Cain worked
13: 5 also had *f* and herds and tents.
26: 14 He had so many *f* and herds
29: 2 the *f* were watered from that well.
29: 2 with three *f* of sheep lying near it
29: 3 When all the *f* were gathered there,
29: 7 time for the *f* to be gathered.
29: 8 "until all the *f* are gathered
30: 31 I will go on tending your *f*
30: 32 Let me go through all your *f* today
30: 36 to tend the rest of Laban's *f*.
30: 38 When the *f* were in heat
30: 38 in front of the *f* when they came
30: 40 Thus he made separate *f*
30: 43 and came to own large *f*,
31: 4 out to the fields where his *f* were.
31: 8 then all the *f* bore streaked young.
31: 8 then all the *f* gave birth
31: 38 nor have I eaten rams from your *f*.
31: 41 daughters and six years for your *f*,
31: 43 are my children, and the *f* are my *f*.
32: 7 and the *f* and herds and camels
34: 28 They seized their *f* and herds
37: 2 was tending the *f* with his brothers,
37: 12 gone to graze their father's *f*
37: 13 your brothers are grazing the *f*
37: 14 with your brothers and with the *f*,
37: 16 me where they are grazing their *f*?"
45: 10 grandchildren, your *f* and herds,
46: 32 and they have brought along their *f*
47: 1 with their *f* and herds
Ge 47: 4 your servants' *f* have no pasture.
50: 8 Only their children and their *f*
Ex 10: 9 daughters, and with our *f* and herds
10: 24 only leave your *f* and herds behind
12: 32 Take your *f* and herds,
12: 38 as large droves of livestock, both *f*
34: 3 the *f* and herds may graze in front
Nu 11: 22 Would they have enough if *f*
31: 9 and took all the Midianite herds, *f*
32: 1 who had very large herds and *f*,
32: 24 for your *f*, but do what you have
32: 26 our *f* and herds will remain here
32: 36 cities, and built pens for their *f*.
35: 3 *f* and all their other livestock.
Dt 7: 13 and the lambs of your *f*
8: 13 when your herds and *f* grow large
12: 6 the firstborn of your herds and *f*.
12: 17 or the firstborn of your herds and *f*,
12: 21 and *f* the LORD has given you,
14: 23 and *f* in the presence of the LORD
15: 19 male of your herds and *f*.
28: 4 your herds and the lambs of your *f*.
28: 18 your herds and the lambs of your *f*.
28: 51 lambs of your *f* until you are ruined
Jos 14: 4 with pasturelands for their *f*
Jdg 5: 16 to hear the whistling for the *f*?
1Sa 8: 17 He will take a tenth of your *f*,
30: 20 He took all the *f* and herds,
1Ki 20: 27 opposite them like two small *f*
2Ki 5: 26 olive groves, vineyards, *f*, herds,
1Ch 4: 39 in search of pasture for their *f*.
4: 41 there was pasture for their *f*.
27: 31 the Hagrite was in charge of the *f*.
2Ch 17: 11 and the Arabs brought him *f*:
31: 6 brought a tithe of their herds and *f*
32: 28 kinds of cattle, and pens for the *f*.
32: 29 and acquired great numbers of *f*
Ne 10: 36 of our *f* to the house of our God,
Job 1: 10 so that his *f* and herds are spread
24: 2 they pasture *f* they have stolen.
Ps 8: 7 all *f* and herds,
65: 13 The meadows are covered with *f*
107: 41 and increased their families like *f*.
Pr 27: 23 you know the condition of your *f*,
Ecc 2: 7 and *f* than anyone in Jerusalem
SS 1: 7 beside the *f* of your friends?
Isa 13: 20 no shepherd will rest his *f* there.
17: 2 and left to *f*, which will lie down,
32: 14 delight of donkeys, a pasture for *f*,
60: 7 All Kedar's *f* will be gathered
61: 5 Aliens will shepherd your *f*;
65: 10 Sharon will become a pasture for *f*,
Jer 3: 24 their *f* and herds,
5: 17 they will devour your *f* and herds,
6: 3 Shepherds with their *f* will come
31: 12 the young of the *f* and herds.
31: 24 those who move about with their *f*.
33: 12 for shepherds to rest their *f*.
33: 13 *f* will again pass under the hand
49: 29 Their tents and their *f* will be taken
Eze 36: 38 as the *f* for offerings at Jerusalem
36: 38 will the ruined cities be filled with *f*
Hos 5: 6 When they go with their *f*
Joel 1: 18 even the *f* of sheep are suffering.
Mic 5: 8 like a young lion among *f* of sheep,
Zep 2: 14 *F* and herds will lie down there,
Lk 2: 8 keeping watch over their *f* at night.
Jn 4: 12 did also his sons and his *f* and herds

FLOG (FLOGGED FLOGGING FLOGGINGS)

Pr 17: 26 or to *f* officials for their integrity.
19: 25 *F* a mocker, and the simple will
Mt 10: 17 and *f* you in their synagogues.
23: 34 you will *f* in your synagogues
Mk 10: 34 and spit on him, *f* him and kill him.
Lk 18: 32 spit on him, *f* him and kill him.
Ac 22: 25 As they stretched him out to *f* him,
22: 25 to *f* a Roman citizen who hasn't

FLOGGED (FLOG)

Dt 25: 2 and have him *f* in his presence
25: 3 If he is *f* more than that, your
Mt 20: 19 to the Gentiles to be mocked and *f*
27: 26 But he had Jesus *f*, and handed him
Mk 13: 9 over to the local councils and *f*
15: 15 He had Jesus *f*, and handed him
Jn 19: 1 Pilate took Jesus and had him *f*.

Ac 5: 40 the apostles in and had them *f*.
16: 23 After they had been severely *f*,
22: 24 He directed that he be *f*
2Co 11: 23 frequently, been *f* more severely,

FLOGGING (FLOG)

Ps 89: 32 their iniquity with *f*;
Heb 11: 36 *f*, while still others were chained

FLOGGINGS (FLOG)

2Sa 7: 14 rod of men, with *f* inflicted by men.

FLOOD (FLOODED FLOODGATES FLOODING FLOODS FLOODWATERS)

Ge 7: 7 ark to escape the waters of the *f*.
7: 17 For forty days the *f* kept coming
9: 11 cut off by the waters of a *f*;
9: 11 never again will there be a *f*
9: 15 again will the waters become a *f*
9: 28 After the *f* Noah lived 350 years.
10: 1 themselves had sons after the *f*.
10: 32 out over the earth after the *f*.
11: 10 Two years after the *f*,
Jos 3: 15 Now the Jordan is at *f* stage all
4: 18 and ran at *f* stage as before.
Job 20: 28 A *f* will carry off his house,
22: 11 and why a *f* of water covers you.
22: 16 foundations washed away by a *f*.
27: 20 Terrors overtake him like a *f*;
38: 34 and cover yourself with a *f* of water
Ps 6: 6 all night long I *f* my bed
29: 10 LORD sits enthroned over the *f*;
88: 17 day long they surround me like a *f*;
124: 4 the *f* would have engulfed us,
Isa 8: 7 the mighty *f* waters of the River—
59: 19 For he will come like a pent-up *f*
Da 9: 26 The end will come like a *f*:
11: 10 sweep on like an irresistible *f*
11: 40 and sweep through them like a *f*.
Hos 5: 10 like a *f* of water.
Na 1: 8 but with an overwhelming *f*
Mal 2: 13 You *f* the LORD's altar with tears.
Mt 24: 38 For in the days before the *f*,
24: 39 would happen until the *f* came
Lk 6: 48 When a *f* came, the torrent struck
17: 27 the *f* came and destroyed them all.
1Pe 4: 4 them into the same *f* of dissipation,
2Pe 2: 5 world when he brought the *f*

FLOODED (FLOOD)

Ge 7: 24 The waters *f* the earth

FLOODGATES (FLOOD)

Ge 7: 11 the *f* of the heavens were opened.
8: 2 *f* of the heavens had been closed,
2Ki 7: 2 if the LORD should open the *f*
7: 19 if the LORD should open the *f*
Isa 24: 18 The *f* of the heavens are opened,
Mal 3: 10 see if I will not throw open the *f*

FLOODING (FLOOD)

Isa 28: 2 a driving rain and a *f* downpour,
66: 12 the wealth of nations like a *f* stream

FLOODS (FLOOD)

Ps 69: 2 the *f* engulf me.

FLOODWATERS (FLOOD)

Ge 6: 17 I am going to bring *f* on the earth
7: 6 old when the *f* came on the earth.
7: 10 after the seven days the *f* came
Ps 69: 15 Do not let the *f* engulf me

FLOOR (FLOORS)

Ge 50: 10 When they reached the threshing *f*
50: 11 at the threshing *f* of Atad,
Ex 16: 14 ground appeared on the desert *f*.
Nu 5: 17 from the tabernacle *f* into the water
15: 20 as an offering from the threshing *f*.
18: 27 as grain from the threshing *f*
18: 30 as the product of the threshing *f*
Dt 15: 14 your threshing *f* and your
16: 13 the produce of your threshing *f*
Jdg 3: 25 they saw their lord fallen to the *f*,
6: 37 fleece on the threshing *f*.
Ru 3: 2 barley on the threshing *f*.
3: 3 Then go down to the threshing *f*,
3: 6 she went down to the threshing *f*
Ru 3: 14 came to the threshing *f*."
2Sa 6: 6 came to the threshing *f* of Nacon,
24: 16 then at the threshing *f* of Araunah
24: 18 on the threshing *f* of Araunah
24: 21 "To buy your threshing *f*,"
24: 24 So David bought the threshing *f*
1Ki 6: 6 The lowest *f* was five cubits wide,
6: 6 six cubits and the third *f* seven.
6: 6 the middle *f* six cubits
6: 8 The entrance to the lowest *f* was
6: 15 and covered the *f* of the temple
6: 15 them from the *f* of the temple
6: 16 with cedar boards from *f* to ceiling
7: 7 it with cedar from *f* to ceiling.
22: 10 at the threshing *f* by the entrance
22: 35 ran onto the *f* of the chariot,
2Ki 6: 27 From the threshing *f*? From
1Ch 13: 9 came to the threshing *f* of Kidon,
21: 15 at the threshing *f* of Araunah
21: 18 on the threshing *f* of Araunah
21: 21 he left the threshing *f* and bowed
21: 22 the site of your threshing *f*
21: 28 him on the threshing *f* of Araunah
2Ch 3: 1 was on the threshing *f* of Araunah
18: 9 at the threshing *f* by the entrance
Job 39: 12 and gather it to your threshing *f*?
Isa 21: 10 crushed on the threshing *f*,
Jer 51: 33 of Babylon is like a threshing *f*
Eze 37: 2 bones on the *f* of the valley,
41: 7 to the top *f* through the middle *f*.
41: 7 up from the lowest *f* to the top *f*
41: 16 The *f*, the wall up to the windows,
41: 20 From the *f* to the area
42: 6 rooms on the third *f* had no pillars,
42: 6 smaller in *f* space than those
Da 2: 35 on a threshing *f* in the summer.
6: 24 before they reached the *f* of the den
Hos 9: 1 a prostitute at every threshing *f*.
13: 3 swirling from a threshing *f*,
Mic 4: 12 like sheaves to the threshing *f*.
Mt 3: 12 and he will clear his threshing *f*.
Lk 3: 17 in his hand to clear his threshing *f*
Jas 2: 3 or "Sit on the *f* by my feet,"

FLOORS (FLOOR)

1Sa 23: 1 and are looting the threshing *f*,"
1Ki 6: 30 also covered the *f* of both the inner
Eze 42: 5 and middle *f* of the building.
42: 6 those on the lower and middle *f*.
Hos 9: 2 Threshing *f* and winepresses will
Joel 2: 24 The threshing *f* will be filled

FLORAL (FLOWER)

1Ki 7: 49 the gold *f* work and lamps
2Ch 4: 21 the gold *f* work and lamps

FLOUR

Ge 18: 6 "get three seahs of fine *f*
Ex 29: 2 from fine wheat *f*, without yeast,
29: 40 ephah of fine *f* mixed with a fourth
Lev 2: 1 his offering is to be of fine *f*.
2: 2 shall take a handful of the fine *f*
2: 4 is to consist of fine *f*: cakes made
2: 5 to be made of fine *f* mixed with oil,
2: 7 it is to be made of fine *f* and oil.
5: 11 an ephah of fine *f* for a sin offering.
6: 15 is to take a handful of fine *f*
6: 20 a tenth of an ephah of fine *f*
7: 12 and cakes of fine *f* well-kneaded
14: 10 of an ephah of fine *f* mixed with oil
14: 21 of an ephah of fine *f* mixed with oil
23: 13 of an ephah of fine *f* mixed with oil
23: 17 of two-tenths of an ephah of fine *f*,
24: 5 "Take fine *f* and bake twelve loaves
Nu 5: 15 an ephah of barley *f* on her behalf.
6: 15 cakes made of fine *f* mixed with oil,
7: 13 filled with fine *f* mixed with oil
7: 19 filled with fine *f* mixed with oil
7: 25 filled with fine *f* mixed with oil
7: 31 filled with fine *f* mixed with oil
7: 37 filled with fine *f* mixed with oil
7: 43 filled with fine *f* mixed with oil
7: 49 filled with fine *f* mixed with oil
7: 55 filled with fine *f* mixed with oil
7: 61 filled with fine *f* mixed with oil
7: 67 filled with fine *f* mixed with oil
7: 73 filled with fine *f* mixed with oil
7: 79 filled with fine *f* mixed with oil
Nu 8: 8 offering of fine *f* mixed with oil;
15: 4 ephah of fine *f* mixed with a fourth
15: 6 ephah of fine *f* mixed with a third
15: 9 of an ephah of fine *f* mixed
28: 5 ephah of fine *f* mixed with a fourth
28: 9 of an ephah of fine *f* mixed with oil.
28: 12 of an ephah of fine *f* mixed with oil;
28: 12 of an ephah of fine *f* mixed with oil;
28: 13 of an ephah of fine *f* mixed with oil.
28: 20 of an ephah of fine *f* mixed with oil;
28: 28 of an ephah of fine *f* mixed with oil;
29: 3 of an ephah of fine *f* mixed with oil;
29: 9 of an ephah of fine *f* mixed with oil;
29: 14 of an ephah of fine *f* mixed with oil;
Jdg 6: 19 from an ephah of *f* he made bread
1Sa 1: 24 an ephah of *f* and a skin of wine,
28: 24 She took some *f*, kneaded it
2Sa 17: 28 and barley, *f* and roasted grain,
1Ki 4: 22 provisions were thirty cors of fine *f*
17: 12 only a handful of *f* in a jar
17: 14 'The jar of *f* will not be used up
17: 16 For the jar of *f* was not used up
2Ki 4: 41 Elisha said, "Get some *f*."
7: 1 a seah of *f* will sell for a shekel
7: 16 So a seah of *f* sold for a shekel,
7: 18 a seah of *f* will sell for a shekel
1Ch 9: 29 as well as the *f* and wine,
12: 40 There were plentiful supplies of *f*,
23: 29 the *f* for the grain offerings,
Isa 47: 2 Take millstones and grind *f*;
Eze 16: 13 Your food was fine *f*, honey
16: 19 provided for you—the fine *f*,
46: 14 third of a hin of oil to moisten the *f*.
Hos 8: 7 it will produce no *f*.
Mt 13: 33 amount of *f* until it worked all
Lk 13: 21 amount of *f* until it worked all
Rev 18: 13 of fine *f* and wheat; cattle

FLOURISH (FLOURISHES FLOURISHING)

Ge 26: 22 has given us room and we will *f*
Job 15: 32 and his branches will not *f*.
Ps 44: 2 and made our fathers *f*.
72: 7 In his days the righteous will *f*,
72: 16 Let its fruit *f* like Lebanon;
92: 7 and all evildoers *f*,
92: 12 The righteous will *f* like a palm tree
92: 13 they will *f* in the courts of our God.
Pr 14: 11 but the tent of the upright will *f*.
Isa 55: 10 and making it bud and *f*,
66: 14 and you will *f* like grass;
Eze 17: 24 green tree and make the dry tree *f*.
Hos 14: 7 He will *f* like the grain.

FLOURISHES (FLOURISH)

Ps 103: 15 he *f* like a flower of the field;
Pr 12: 12 but the root of the righteous *f*.

FLOURISHING (FLOURISH)

Dt 6: 10 with large, *f* cities you did not build
Ps 37: 35 *f* like a green tree in its native soil,
52: 8 *f* in the house of God;
Ecc 2: 6 to water groves of *f* trees.

FLOW (FLOWED FLOWING FLOWS)

Ex 14: 26 sea so that the waters may *f* back
Lev 12: 7 clean from her *f* of blood.
15: 19 " 'When a woman has her regular *f*
15: 24 and her monthly *f* touches him,
20: 18 he has exposed the source of her *f*,
Nu 13: 27 and it does *f* with milk and honey!
24: 7 Water will *f* from their buckets;
Jos 4: 7 tell them that the *f*
Job 6: 17 but that cease to *f* in the dry season
Ps 78: 16 and made water *f* down like rivers.
119:136 Streams of tears *f* from my eyes,
147: 18 up his breezes, and the waters *f*.
Ecc 1: 7 All streams *f* into the sea,
Isa 30: 25 streams of water will *f*
41: 18 I will make rivers *f*
48: 21 he made water *f* for them
Jer 18: 14 ever cease to *f*?
48: 33 I have stopped the *f* of wine
La 2: 18 let your tears *f* like a river
3: 48 Streams of tears *f* from my eyes
3: 49 My eyes will *f* unceasingly,
Eze 28: 23 and make blood *f* in her streets.
32: 14 and make her streams *f* like oil,

Joel 3:18 A fountain will *f* out
3:18 and the hills will *f* with milk;
Am 9:13 and *f* from all the hills.
Zec 14: 8 On that day living water will *f* out
Jn 7:38 streams of living water will *f*
19:34 bringing a sudden *f* of blood
2Co 1: 5 as the sufferings of Christ *f*
Jas 3:11 salt water *f* from the same spring?

FLOWED (FLOW)

Ge 2:10 A river watering the garden *f*
Ex 14:28 The water *f* back and covered
Dt 9:21 the dust into a stream that *f*
1Ki 18:28 until their blood *f*.
2Ch 32: 4 the stream that *f* through the land.
Ps 78:20 and streams *f* abundantly.
104: 8 they *f* over the mountains,
105: 41 like a river it *f* in the desert.
Eze 31: 4 their streams *f*
Rev 14:20 and blood *f* out of the press,

FLOWER (FLORAL FLOWERLIKE FLOWERS)

Job 14: 2 up like a *f* and withers away;
Ps 103: 15 he flourishes like a *f* of the field;
Isa 18: 5 and the *f* becomes a ripening grape,
28: 1 to the fading *f*, his glorious beauty,
28: 4 That fading *f*, his glorious beauty,
Jas 1:10 he will pass away like a wild *f*.

FLOWERLIKE (FLOWER)

Ex 25:31 its *f* cups, buds and blossoms shall
37:17 its *f* cups, buds and blossoms were

FLOWERS (FLOWER)

Ex 25:33 Three cups shaped like almond *f*
25:34 be four cups shaped like almond *f*
37:19 Three cups shaped like almond *f*
37:20 four cups shaped like almond *f*
1Ki 6:18 carved with gourds and open *f*.
6:29 cherubim, palm trees and open *f*.
6:32 palm trees and open *f*,
6:35 palm trees and open *f* on them
SS 2:12 *F* appear on the earth;
Isa 5:24 and their *f* blow away like dust;
40: 6 and all their glory is like the *f*
40: 7 The grass withers and the *f* fall,
40: 8 The grass withers and the *f* fall,
1Pe 1:24 and all their glory is like the *f*
1:24 the grass withers and the *f* fall,

FLOWING (FLOW)

Ex 3: 8 a land *f* with milk and honey—
3:17 a land *f* with milk and honey.'
13: 5 a land *f* with milk and honey—
33: 3 Go up to the land *f* with milk
Lev 15: 3 Whether it continues *f*
20:24 a land *f* with milk and honey."
Nu 14: 8 a land *f* with milk and honey,
16:13 out of a land *f* with milk
16:14 us into a land *f* with milk
Dt 6: 3 greatly in a land *f* with milk
8: 7 with springs *f* in the valleys
11: 9 a land *f* with milk and honey.
21: 4 and where there is a *f* stream.
26: 9 a land *f* with milk and honey;
26:15 a land *f* with milk and honey."
27: 3 a land *f* with milk and honey,
31:20 them into the land *f* with milk
Jos 3:13 the water *f* downstream will be cut
3:16 the water from upstream stopped *f*.
3:16 while the water *f* down to the Sea
5: 6 a land *f* with milk and honey.
2Ki 3:20 water *f* from the direction of Edom
4: 6 Then the oil stopped *f*.
Job 20:17 the rivers *f* with honey and cream.
39:19 or clothe his neck with a *f* mane?
Ps 74:15 you dried up the ever *f* rivers.
107: 33 *f* springs into thirsty ground,
107: 35 the parched ground into *f* springs;
SS 4:15 a well of *f* water
5: 5 my fingers with *f* myrrh,
7: 9 *f* gently over lips and teeth.
Isa 8: 6 the gently *f* waters of Shiloah
27:12 from the *f* Euphrates to the Wadi
44: 4 like poplar trees by *f* streams.
Jer 11: 5 to give them a land *f* with milk
32:22 a land *f* with milk and honey.
Eze 20: 6 a land *f* with milk and honey,
20:15 a land *f* with milk and honey,
23:15 and *f* turbans on their heads;
32: 6 drench the land with your *f* blood
47: 2 the water was *f* from the south side.
Da 7:10 A river of fire was *f*,
Mk 12:38 They like to walk around in *f* robes
Lk 20:46 They like to walk around in *f* robes
Rev 22: 1 *f* from the throne of God

FLOWN (FLY)

Jer 4:25 every bird in the sky had *f* away.

FLOWS (FLOW)

Ezr 8:15 at the canal that *f* toward Ahava,
Ps 58: 7 them vanish like water that *f* away;
104: 10 it *f* between the mountains.
Eze 47: 8 "This water *f* toward the eastern
47: 9 because this water *f* there
47: 9 where the river *f* everything will
47: 9 will live wherever the river *f*.
47:12 water from the sanctuary *f* to them.

FLUENT

Isa 32: 4 the stammering tongue will be *f*

FLUNG (FLINGING)

Am 8: 3 many bodies—*f* everywhere!
Rev 12: 4 of the sky and *f* them to the earth.

FLUTE (FLUTES)

Ge 4:21 of all who play the harp and *f*.
Job 21:12 to the sound of the *f*.
30:31 and my *f* to the sound of wailing.
Ps 150: 4 praise him with the strings and *f*,
Jer 48:36 laments like a *f* for the men of
48:36 my heart laments for Moab like a *f*;
Da 3: 5 *f*, zither, lyre, harp, pipes
3: 7 *f*, zither, lyre, harp and all kinds
3:10 who hears the sound of the horn, *f*,
3:15 you hear the sound of the horn, *f*,
Mt 9:23 and saw the *f* players and the noisy
11:17 " 'We played the *f* for you,
Lk 7:32 " 'We played the *f* for you,
1Co 14: 7 that make sounds, such as the *f*
Rev 18:22 musicians, *f* players

FLUTES (FLUTE)

1Sa 10: 5 *f* and harps being played
1Ki 1:40 playing *f* and rejoicing greatly,
Isa 5:12 tambourines and *f* and wine,
30:29 as when people go up with *f*

FLUTTERING

Pr 26: 2 Like a *f* sparrow or a darting
Isa 16: 2 Like *f* birds

FLY (FLEW FLIES FLIGHT FLOWN FLYING)

Ge 1:20 and let birds *f* above the earth
Ex 8:31 and his people; not a *f* remained.
Dt 19: 5 head may *f* off and hit his neighbor
Job 5: 7 as surely as sparks *f* upward.
9:25 they *f* away without a glimpse
Ps 55: 6 I would *f* away and be at rest—
90:10 they quickly pass, and we *f* away.
Pr 23: 5 and *f* off to the sky like an eagle.
Isa 60: 8 "Who are these that *f*
Hos 9:11 Ephraim's glory will *f* away like
Na 3:16 and then *f* away.
3:17 when the sun appears they *f* away,
Hab 1: 8 They *f* like a vulture swooping
Rev 12:14 so that she might *f*

FLYING (FLY)

Ge 8: 7 and it kept *f* back and forth
Lev 11:20 " 'All *f* insects that walk
Dt 14:19 All *f* insects that swarm are
Ps 78:27 *f* birds like sand on the seashore.
148: 10 small creatures and *f* birds,
Isa 6: 2 and with two they were *f*.
Hab 3:11 at the glint of your *f* arrows,
Zec 5: 1 and there before me was a *f* scroll!
5: 2 I answered, "I see a *f* scroll,
Rev 4: 7 the fourth was like a *f* eagle.
8:13 I heard an eagle that was *f*
14: 6 I saw another angel *f* in midair,
19:17 voice to all the birds *f* in midair,

FOAL

Zec 9: 9 on a colt, the *f* of a donkey.
Mt 21: 5 on a colt, the *f* of a donkey.' "

FOAM (FOAMING FOAMS)

Job 24:18 "Yet they are *f* on the surface
Ps 46: 3 though its waters roar and *f*

FOAMING (FOAM)

Ps 75: 8 full of *f* wine mixed with spices;
Mk 9:20 and rolled around, *f* at the mouth.
Jude :13 *f* up their shame; wandering stars,

FOAMS (FOAM)

Mk 9:18 He *f* at the mouth, gnashes his
Lk 9:39 so that he *f* at the mouth.

FODDER

Ge 24:25 "We have plenty of straw and *f*,
24:32 and *f* were brought for the camels,
43:24 and provided *f* for their donkeys.
Jdg 19:19 We have both straw and *f*
Job 6: 5 or an ox bellow when it has *f*?
24: 6 They gather *f* in the fields
Isa 30:24 that work the soil will eat *f*

FOE (FOES)

Ps 7: 4 or without cause have robbed my *f*
8: 2 to silence the *f* and the avenger.
55:12 if a *f* were raising himself
61: 3 a strong tower against the *f*.
74:10 Will the *f* revile your name forever
106: 10 from the hand of the *f*;
107: 2 redeemed from the hand of the *f*,
La 1: 5 captive before the *f*.
2: 4 Like a *f* he has slain
Hab 1:15 The wicked *f* pulls all of them up

FOES (FOE)

Nu 10:35 may your *f* flee before you."
Dt 33: 7 Oh, be his help against his *f*!"
33:11 strike his *f* till they rise no more."
2Sa 22:18 from my *f*, who were too strong
22:41 and I destroyed my *f*.
22:49 You exalted me above my *f*;
2Ki 21:14 and plundered by all their *f*,
Job 22:20 'Surely our *f* are destroyed,
Ps 3: 1 O LORD, how many are my *f*!
6: 7 they fail because of all my *f*.
13: 4 and my *f* will rejoice when I fall.
17: 7 refuge in you from their *f*.
18:17 from my *f*, who were too strong
18:40 and I destroyed my *f*.
18:48 You exalted me above my *f*;
21: 8 your right hand will seize your *f*.
27: 2 my enemies and my *f* attack me,
27:12 me over to the desire of my *f*,
34:21 *f* of the righteous will be
41: 2 him to the desire of his *f*.
42:10 as my *f* taunt me,
44: 5 your name we trample our *f*.
54: 7 in triumph on my *f*.
68: 1 may his *f* flee before him.
68:23 feet in the blood of your *f*,
69:18 redeem me because of my *f*.
74: 4 Your *f* roared in the place where
81:14 and turn my hand against their *f*!
83: 2 how your *f* rear their heads.
89:23 I will crush his *f* before him
89:42 have exalted the right hand of his *f*;
92:11 have heard the rout of my wicked *f*.
97: 3 and consumes his *f* on every side.
105: 24 them too numerous for their *f*,
106: 41 and their *f* ruled over them.
112: 8 in triumph on his *f*.
119:157 Many are the *f* who persecute me,
138: 7 hand against the anger of my *f*,
143: 12 destroy all my *f*,
Isa 1:24 "Ah, I will get relief from my *f*
9:11 LORD has strengthened Rezin's *f*
59:18 and retribution to his *f*;
66:14 but his fury will be shown to his *f*.
Jer 46:10 for vengeance on his *f*.
49:37 I will shatter Elam before their *f*,
La 1: 5 Her *f* have become her masters;
1:17 that his neighbors become his *f*;
2:17 he has exalted the horn of your *f*.
4:12 that enemies and *f* could enter

Mic 5: 9 and all your *f* will be destroyed.
Na 1: 2 LORD takes vengeance on his *f*
1: 8 he will pursue his *f* into darkness.

FOILS

Ps 33: 10 The LORD *f* the plans
Isa 44: 25 who *f* the signs of false prophets

FOLD (ENFOLDS FOLDED FOLDING FOLDS)

Ex 26: 9 *F* the sixth curtain double
2Ki 4: 39 and filled the *f* of his cloak.
Hag 2: 12 and that *f* touches some bread
2: 12 meat in the *f* of his garment,

FOLDED (FOLD)

Ex 28: 16 and a span wide—and *f* double.
39: 9 and a span wide—and *f* double.
Jn 20: 7 The cloth was *f* up by itself,

FOLDING (FOLD)

Pr 6: 10 a little *f* of the hands to rest—
24: 33 a little *f* of the hands to rest—

FOLDS (FOLD)

Ne 5: 13 I also shook out the *f* of my robe
Job 41: 23 The *f* of his flesh are tightly joined;
Ps 74: 11 Take it from the *f* of your garment
Ecc 4: 5 The fool *f* his hands
Eze 5: 3 away in the *f* of your garment.

FOLIAGE

Eze 19: 11 high above the thick *f*,
31: 3 its top above the thick *f*.
31: 10 lifting its top above the thick *f*,
31: 14 lifting their tops above the thick *f*.

FOLLOW (FOLLOWED FOLLOWER FOLLOWERS FOLLOWING FOLLOWS)

Ge 41: 30 seven years of famine will *f* them.
Ex 11: 8 you and all the people who *f* you!'
16: 4 they will *f* my instructions.
23: 2 Do not *f* the crowd in doing wrong.
23: 24 worship them or *f* their practices.
Lev 18: 3 Do not *f* their practices.
18: 4 and be careful to *f* my decrees.
18: 30 and do not *f* any of the detestable
19: 37 and all my laws and *f* them.
20: 5 *f* him in prostituting themselves
20: 8 Keep my decrees and *f* them.
20: 22 all my decrees and laws and *f* them,
22: 31 "Keep my commands and *f* them.
25: 18 " '*F* my decrees and be careful
26: 3 If you *f* my decrees and are careful
Nu 9: 12 they must *f* all the regulations.
Dt 4: 1 *F* them so that you may live
4: 5 so that you may *f* them
4: 13 which he commanded you to *f*
4: 14 are to *f* in the land that you are
5: 1 Learn them and be sure to *f* them.
5: 31 and laws you are to teach them to *f*
6: 14 Do not *f* other gods, the gods
7: 11 take care to *f* the commands,
7: 12 laws and are careful to *f* them,
8: 1 to *f* every command I am giving
8: 19 and *f* other gods and worship
11: 22 commands I am giving you to *f*—
12: 1 and laws you must be careful to *f*
13: 2 "Let us *f* other gods" (gods you
13: 4 is the LORD your God you must *f*,
13: 5 your God commanded you to *f*.
15: 5 to *f* all these commands I am giving
16: 12 and *f* carefully these decrees.
16: 20 *F* justice and justice alone,
17: 19 *f* carefully all the words of this law
19: 9 you carefully *f* all these laws I
20: 18 to *f* all the detestable things they
24: 8 You must *f* carefully what I have
26: 16 you this day to *f* these decrees
27: 10 your God and *f* his commands
28: 1 carefully *f* all his commands I give
28: 13 you this day and carefully *f* them,
28: 15 do not carefully *f* all his commands
28: 58 you do not carefully *f* all the words
29: 9 Carefully *f* the terms
29: 22 Your children who *f* you
29: 29 that we may *f* all the words
30: 8 *f* all his commands I am giving you
Dt 31: 12 *f* carefully all the words of this law.
Jos 3: 3 out from your positions and *f* it.
22: 27 and you and the generations that *f*,
Jdg 3: 28 "*F* me," he ordered,
6: 34 summoning the Abiezrites to *f* him
7: 17 "*F* my lead.
9: 3 they were inclined to *f* Abimelech,
Ru 2: 9 the men are harvesting, and *f*
1Sa 11: 7 oxen of anyone who does not *f* Saul
12: 14 over you *f* the LORD your God—
25: 19 "Go on ahead; I'll *f* you."
25: 27 be given to the men who *f* you.
30: 21 had been too exhausted to *f* him
2Sa 17: 9 among the troops who *f* Absalom.'
20: 2 David to *f* Sheba son of Bicri.
20: 11 is for David, let him *f* Joab!"
1Ki 6: 12 if you *f* my decrees,
11: 6 he did not *f* the LORD completely,
11: 10 forbidden Solomon to *f* other gods,
18: 21 If the LORD is God, *f* him;
18: 21 but if Baal is God, *f* him."
19: 21 Then he set out to *f* Elijah
2Ki 6: 19 *F* me, and I will lead you
18: 6 and did not cease to *f* him;
23: 3 to *f* the LORD and keep his
1Ch 28: 8 Be careful to *f* all the commands
2Ch 34: 31 to *f* the LORD and keep his
34: 33 they did not fail to *f* the LORD,
Ne 9: 34 and our fathers did not *f* your law;
10: 29 an oath to *f* the Law of God given
Est 2: 20 to *f* Mordecai's instructions
Job 21: 33 all men *f* after him,
Ps 23: 6 Surely goodness and love will *f* me
45: 14 her virgin companions *f* her
81: 12 to *f* their own devices.
81: 13 if Israel would *f* my ways,
89: 30 and do not *f* my statutes,
94: 15 and all the upright in heart will *f* it.
111: 10 all who *f* his precepts have good
119: 33 O LORD, to *f* your decrees;
119: 63 to all who *f* your precepts.
119:106 that I will *f* your righteous laws.
119:166 and I *f* your commands.
Ecc 1: 11 remembered by those who *f*.
11: 9 *F* the ways of your heart
SS 1: 8 *f* the tracks of the sheep
Isa 8: 11 warning me not to *f* the way
42: 24 For they would not *f* his ways;
Jer 3: 17 longer will they *f* the stubbornness
7: 6 and if you do not *f* other gods
7: 9 *f* other gods you have not known,
11: 6 terms of this covenant and *f* them.
11: 8 I had commanded them to *f*
13: 10 who *f* the stubbornness
18: 12 each of us will *f* the stubbornness
23: 10 The prophets *f* an evil course
23: 17 And to all who *f* the stubbornness
25: 6 Do not *f* other gods to serve
26: 4 listen to me and *f* my law,
32: 23 they did not obey you or *f* your law
35: 15 do not *f* other gods to serve them.
42: 16 and the famine you dread will *f* you
Eze 9: 5 "*F* him through the city and kill,
11: 20 Then they will *f* my decrees
13: 3 foolish prophets who *f* their own
20: 13 They did not *f* my decrees
20: 16 and did not *f* my decrees
20: 18 "Do not *f* the statutes
20: 19 *f* my decrees and be careful
20: 21 They did not *f* my decrees,
36: 27 and move you to *f* my decrees
37: 24 They will *f* my laws and be careful
43: 11 to its design and *f* all its regulations
48: 1 it will *f* the Hethlon road to Lebo
Hos 11: 10 They will *f* the LORD;
Mt 4: 19 *f* me," Jesus said, "and I will make
8: 19 I will *f* you wherever you go."
8: 22 But Jesus told him, "*F* me,
9: 9 "*F* me," he told him, and Matthew
10: 38 and *f* me is not worthy of me.
16: 24 and take up his cross and *f* me.
19: 21 Then come, *f* me."
19: 27 "We have left everything to *f* you!
Mk 1: 17 *f* me," Jesus said, "and I will make
2: 14 "*F* me," Jesus told him,
5: 37 He did not let anyone *f* him
8: 34 and take up his cross and *f* me.
10: 21 Then come, *f* me."
Mk 10: 28 "We have left everything to *f* you!"
14: 13 *F* him.
Lk 5: 27 "*F* me," Jesus said to him,
9: 23 take up his cross daily and *f* me.
9: 57 "I will *f* you wherever you go."
9: 59 He said to another man, "*F* me."
9: 61 Still another said, "I will *f* you,
14: 27 and *f* me cannot be my disciple.
18: 22 Then come, *f* me."
18: 28 "We have left all we had to *f* you!"
21: 8 Do not *f* them.
22: 10 *F* him to the house that he enters,
Jn 1: 43 Philip, he said to him, "*F* me."
10: 4 his sheep *f* him because they know
10: 5 But they will never *f* a stranger;
10: 27 I know them, and they *f* me.
12: 26 Whoever serves me must *f* me;
13: 36 cannot *f* now, but you will *f* later."
13: 37 "Lord, why can't I *f* you now?
21: 19 Then he said to him, "*F* me!"
21: 22 what is that to you? You must *f* me
Ac 12: 8 cloak around you and *f* me,"
Ro 2: 8 and who reject the truth and *f* evil,
15: 5 yourselves as you *f* Christ Jesus,
1Co 1: 12 Cephas"; still another, "I *f* Christ."
1: 12 One of you says, "I *f* Paul";
1: 12 another, "I *f* Apollos"; another,
1: 12 another, "I *f* Cephas"; still another,
3: 4 For when one says, "I *f* Paul,"
3: 4 and another, "I *f* Apollos,"
11: 1 as I *f* the example of Christ.
11: 1 *F* my example, as I follow
14: 1 *F* the way of love and eagerly
2Co 12: 18 same spirit and *f* the same course?
Gal 2: 14 Gentiles to *f* Jewish customs?
6: 16 and mercy to all who *f* this rule,
2Th 3: 7 how you ought to *f* our example.
3: 9 ourselves a model for you to *f*.
1Ti 4: 1 and *f* deceiving spirits and things
5: 15 fact already turned away to *f* Satan.
1Pe 1: 11 and the glories that would *f*.
2: 21 that you should *f* in his steps.
2Pe 1: 16 We did not *f* cleverly invented
2: 2 Many will *f* their shameful ways
2: 10 of those who *f* the corrupt desire
2: 15 and wandered off to *f* the way
Jude : 16 they *f* their own evil desires;
: 18 scoffers who will *f* their own
: 19 who *f* mere natural instincts
Rev 14: 4 They *f* the Lamb wherever he goes.
14: 13 for their deeds will *f* them."

FOLLOWED (FOLLOW)

Ge 32: 19 and all the others who *f* the herds:
Ex 14: 23 and horsemen *f* them into the sea.
14: 28 of Pharaoh that had *f* the Israelites
15: 20 and all the women *f* her,
Nu 16: 25 and the elders of Israel *f* him.
25: 8 and *f* the Israelite into the tent.
31: 16 the ones who *f* Balaam's advice
32: 11 they have not *f* me wholeheartedly,
32: 12 for they *f* the LORD
Dt 1: 36 he *f* the LORD wholeheartedly."
4: 3 you everyone who *f* the Baal
Jos 6: 8 of the LORD's covenant *f* them.
6: 9 and the rear guard *f* the ark.
6: 13 and the rear guard *f* the ark
14: 8 *f* the LORD my God
14: 9 you have *f* the LORD my God
14: 14 he *f* the LORD, the God of Israel,
Jdg 2: 12 They *f* and worshiped various gods
3: 28 So they *f* him down and, taking
4: 10 Ten thousand men *f* him,
4: 14 went down Mount Tabor, *f*
5: 14 with the people who *f* you.
9: 49 men cut branches and *f* Abimelech.
10: 3 He was *f* by Jair of Gilead,
11: 3 gathered around him and *f* him.
13: 11 Manoah got up and *f* his wife.
1Sa 6: 12 The rulers of the Philistines *f* them
14: 13 and his armor-bearer *f*
17: 13 Jesse's three oldest sons had *f* Saul
17: 14 The three oldest *f* Saul,
26: 3 he saw that Saul had *f* him there,
2Sa 2: 10 house of Judah, however, *f* David.
17: 23 saw that his advice had not been *f*,
20: 14 who gathered together and *f* him.
1Ki 11: 5 He *f* Ashtoreth the goddess

1Ki 12: 14 he *f* the advice of the young men
14: 8 and *f* me with all his heart,
18: 18 commands and have *f* the Baals.
2Ki 4: 30 So he got up and *f* her.
7: 15 They *f* them as far as the Jordan,
14: 3 In everything he *f* the example
17: 8 and *f* the practices of the nations
17: 15 They *f* worthless idols
17: 19 They *f* the practices Israel had
1Ch 8: 30 and his firstborn son was Abdon, *f*
9: 36 and his firstborn son was Abdon, *f*
2Ch 10: 14 he *f* the advice of the young men
11: 16 *f* the Levites to Jerusalem
17: 3 in the ways his father David had *f*.
17: 4 and *f* his commands rather
22: 5 also *f* their counsel when he went
26: 17 priests of the LORD *f* him in.
Ne 12: 32 half the leaders of Judah *f* them,
12: 38 I *f* them on top of the wall,
Est 2: 4 appealed to the king, and he *f* it.
Job 23: 11 My feet have closely *f* his steps;
Pr 7: 22 All at once he *f* her
Ecc 4: 15 walked under the sun *f* the youth,
Jer 2: 2 and *f* me through the desert,
2: 5 They *f* worthless idols
7: 24 they *f* the stubborn inclinations
8: 2 which they have *f* and consulted
9: 13 have not obeyed me or *f* my law.
9: 14 they have *f* the Baals, as their
9: 14 they have *f* the stubbornness
11: 8 they *f* the stubbornness
11: 10 They have *f* other gods
16: 11 'and *f* other gods and served
35: 18 and have *f* all his instructions
44: 10 nor have they *f* my law
44: 23 have not obeyed him or *f* his law
Eze 5: 6 my laws and has not *f* my decrees.
5: 7 and have not *f* my decrees
11: 12 for you have not *f* my decrees
Am 2: 4 the gods their ancestors *f*,
Mic 6: 16 and you have *f* their traditions.
Hab 3: 5 pestilence *f* his steps.
Mal 2: 9 because you have not *f* my ways
Mt 4: 20 once they left their nets and *f* him.
4: 22 and their father and *f* him.
4: 25 the region across the Jordan *f* him.
8: 1 mountainside, large crowds *f* him.
8: 23 into the boat and his disciples *f* him
9: 9 and Matthew got up and *f* him.
9: 27 two blind men *f* him, calling out,
12: 15 Many *f* him, and he healed all their
14: 13 the crowds *f* him on foot
19: 2 Large crowds *f* him, and he healed
19: 28 you who have *f* me will
20: 29 Jericho, a large crowd *f* him.
20: 34 they received their sight and *f* him.
21: 9 of him and those that *f* shouted,
26: 58 But Peter *f* him at a distance,
27: 55 They had *f* Jesus from Galilee
Mk 1: 18 once they left their nets and *f* him.
1: 20 boat with the hired men and *f* him.
2: 14 and Levi got up and *f* him.
2: 15 for there were many who *f* him.
3: 7 and a large crowd from Galilee *f*.
5: 24 A large crowd *f* and pressed
10: 32 while those who *f* were afraid.
10: 52 and *f* Jesus along the road.
11: 9 ahead and those who *f* shouted,
14: 54 Peter *f* him at a distance, right
15: 41 In Galilee these women had *f* him
Lk 5: 11 on shore, left everything and *f* him.
5: 28 got up, left everything and *f* him.
9: 11 crowds learned about it and *f* him.
18: 43 he received his sight and *f* Jesus,
22: 39 of Olives, and his disciples *f* him.
22: 54 Peter *f* at a distance.
23: 27 A large number of people *f* him,
23: 49 the women who had *f* him
23: 55 with Jesus from Galilee *f* Joseph
Jn 1: 37 heard him say this, they *f* Jesus.
1: 40 John had said and who had *f* Jesus.
6: 2 and a great crowd of people *f* him
6: 66 turned back and no longer *f* him.
11: 31 she got up and went out, they *f* her,
21: 8 The other disciples *f* in the boat,
Ac 8: 11 They *f* him because he had amazed
8: 13 And he *f* Philip everywhere,
12: 9 Peter *f* him out of the prison,
Ac 13: 43 devout converts to Judaism *f* Paul
16: 17 This girl *f* Paul and the rest of us,
21: 36 The crowd that *f* kept shouting,
27: 11 *f* the advice of the pilot
Ro 5: 16 The judgment *f* one sin
5: 16 but the gift *f* many trespasses
Eph 2: 2 used to live when you *f* the ways
1Ti 4: 6 the good teaching that you have *f*.
Rev 13: 3 was astonished and *f* the beast.
14: 8 A second angel *f* and said, "Fallen!
14: 9 A third angel *f* them and said

FOLLOWER (FOLLOW)

Ac 24: 14 *f* of the Way, which they call a sect.

FOLLOWERS (FOLLOW)

Nu 16: 5 Then he said to Korah and all his *f*:
16: 6 Korah, and all your *f* are to do this:
16: 11 all your *f* have banded together.
16: 16 and all your *f* are to appear
16: 19 When Korah had gathered all his *f*
16: 40 would become like Korah and his *f*.
26: 9 and were among Korah's *f*
26: 10 whose *f* died when the fire
27: 3 He was not among Korah's *f*,
Jdg 9: 4 adventurers, who became his *f*.
1Sa 30: 22 among David's *f* said,
1Ki 16: 22 But Omri's *f* proved stronger
Ne 11: 8 and his *f*, Gabbai and Sallai—
Ps 49: 13 of their *f*, who approve their
106: 18 Fire blazed among their *f*;
Da 11: 24 loot and wealth among his *f*.
Lk 11: 19 by whom do your *f* drive them out?
22: 49 When Jesus' *f* saw what was going
Ac 5: 36 was killed, all his *f* were dispersed,
5: 37 and all his *f* were scattered.
9: 25 But his *f* took him by night
17: 34 A few men became *f* of Paul
22: 4 I persecuted the *f* of this Way
Rev 17: 14 his called, chosen and faithful *f*."

FOLLOWING (FOLLOW)

Ge 47: 18 they came to him the *f* year
Ex 30: 23 "Take the *f* fine spices: 500 shekels
Lev 20: 6 to prostitute himself by *f* them,
23: 32 month until the *f* evening you are
Nu 32: 15 If you turn away from *f* him,
Dt 7: 4 from *f* me to serve other gods,
11: 28 you today by *f* other gods,
28: 14 *f* other gods and serving them.
Jos 18: 21 had the *f* cities: Jericho, Beth
21: 3 gave the Levites the *f* towns
21: 9 Simeon they allotted the *f* towns
Jdg 2: 19 *f* other gods and serving
1Sa 5: 4 But the *f* morning when they rose,
2Sa 7: 8 and from *f* the flock to be ruler
15: 12 and Absalom's *f* kept on increasing
15: 16 with his entire household *f* him;
15: 17 with all the people *f* him,
1Ki 8: 66 On the *f* day he sent the people
2Ki 13: 2 the eyes of the LORD by *f* the sins
16: 3 *f* the detestable ways
17: 21 Israel away from *f* the LORD
21: 2 *f* the detestable practices
1Ch 6: 71 The Gershonites received the *f*:
6: 77 rest of the Levites) received the *f*:
17: 7 the pasture and from *f* the flock,
2Ch 8: 14 *F* the ordinance of his father David
25: 27 away from *f* the LORD,
28: 3 *f* the detestable ways
29: 15 as the king had ordered, *f* the word
30: 12 his officials had ordered, *f* the word
33: 2 *f* the detestable practices
36: 14 *f* all the detestable practices
Ezr 2: 59 of Solomon 392 The *f* came up
10: 18 the *f* had married foreign women:
Ne 7: 61 of Solomon 392 The *f* came up
Job 34: 27 because they turned from *f* him
Ps 119: 14 I rejoice in *f* your statutes
Isa 66: 17 *f* the one in the midst
Jer 2: 8 *f* worthless idols.
3: 19 and not turn away from *f* me.
16: 12 each of you is *f* the stubbornness
Zep 1: 6 who turn back from *f* the LORD
Mt 8: 10 astonished and said to those *f* him,
10: 5 out with the *f* instructions:
Mk 13: 24 "But in those days, *f* that distress,
14: 51 but a linen garment, was *f* Jesus.
Lk 7: 9 and turning to the crowd *f* him,
Jn 1: 38 Jesus saw them *f* and asked,
18: 15 and another disciple were *f* Jesus.
21: 20 whom Jesus loved was *f* them.
Ac 10: 9 About noon the *f* day as they were
10: 24 The *f* day he arrived in Caesarea.
15: 23 With them they sent the *f* letter:
15: 28 beyond the *f* requirements:
20: 15 and on the *f* day arrived at Miletus.
23: 11 The *f* night the Lord stood
28: 13 on the *f* day we reached Puteoli.
1Co 11: 17 In the *f* directives I have no praise
Eph 2: 3 and *f* its desires and thoughts.
Php 3: 17 Join with others in *f* my example,
1Ti 1: 18 by *f* them you may fight the good
Heb 4: 11 by *f* their example of disobedience.
2Pe 3: 3 scoffing and *f* their own evil desires
Rev 6: 8 and Hades was *f* close behind him.
19: 14 The armies of heaven were *f* him,

FOLLOWS (FOLLOW)

Ge 41: 31 the famine that *f* it will be so severe
Nu 14: 24 spirit and *f* me wholeheartedly,
2Ki 11: 15 put to the sword anyone who *f* her
2Ch 17: 14 enrollment by families was as *f*:
23: 14 put to the sword anyone who *f* her
Ezr 4: 8 to Artaxerxes the king as *f*:
5: 7 The report they sent him read as *f*:
Jer 4: 20 Disaster *f* disaster;
51: 31 One courier *f* another
51: 31 and messenger *f* messenger
Eze 18: 9 He *f* my decrees
18: 17 He keeps my laws and *f* my decrees
33: 15 *f* the decrees that give life,
Hos 4: 2 and bloodshed *f* bloodshed.
Jn 8: 12 Whoever *f* me will never walk
Ac 23: 25 He wrote a letter as *f*: Claudius

FOLLY (FOOL)

1Sa 25: 25 his name is Fool, and *f* goes
Job 42: 8 deal with you according to your *f*.
Ps 38: 5 because of my sinful *f*.
69: 5 You know my *f*, O God;
85: 8 but let them not return to *f*.
Pr 5: 23 led astray by his own great *f*.
9: 13 The woman *F* is loud;
12: 23 but the heart of fools blurts out *f*.
13: 16 but a fool exposes his *f*.
14: 8 but the *f* of fools is deception.
14: 18 The simple inherit *f*,
14: 24 but the *f* of fools yields *f*.
14: 29 a quick-tempered man displays *f*.
15: 2 but the mouth of the fool gushes *f*.
15: 14 but the mouth of a fool feeds on *f*.
15: 21 *F* delights a man who lacks
16: 22 but *f* brings punishment to fools.
17: 12 than a fool in his *f*.
18: 13 that is his *f* and his shame.
19: 3 A man's own *f* ruins his life,
22: 15 *F* is bound up in the heart of a child
24: 9 The schemes of *f* are sin,
26: 4 not answer a fool according to his *f*,
26: 5 Answer a fool according to his *f*,
26: 11 so a fool repeats his *f*.
27: 22 you will not remove his *f* from him.
Ecc 1: 17 and also of madness and *f*,
2: 3 and embracing *f*— my mind still
2: 12 and also madness and *f*.
2: 13 I saw that wisdom is better than *f*,
7: 25 and the madness of *f*.
10: 1 so a little *f* outweighs wisdom
10: 13 At the beginning his words are *f*;
Isa 32: 6 For the fool speaks *f*,
Mk 7: 22 envy, slander, arrogance and *f*.
2Ti 3: 9 their *f* will be clear to everyone.

FOMENTING

Isa 59: 13 *f* oppression and revolt,

FOND

1Sa 19: 1 But Jonathan was very *f* of David

FONDLED

Eze 23: 3 In that land their breasts were *f*
23: 21 caressed and your young breasts *f*.

FOOD (FOODS)

Ge 1: 29 They will be yours for *f*.

Ge 1:30 I give every green plant for *f*."
2: 9 pleasing to the eye and good for *f*.
3: 6 the fruit of the tree was good for *f*
3:19 you will eat your *f*
6:21 and store it away as *f* for you
6:21 are to take every kind of *f* that is
9: 3 and moves will be *f* for you.
14:11 and Gomorrah and all their *f*;
21:14 morning Abraham took some *f*
24:33 Then *f* was set before him,
27: 4 Prepare me the kind of tasty *f* I like
27: 7 and prepare me some tasty *f* to eat,
27: 9 so I can prepare some tasty *f*
27:14 and she prepared some tasty *f*,
27:17 handed to her son Jacob the tasty *f*
27:31 He too prepared some tasty *f*
28:20 I am taking and will give me *f*
39: 6 with anything except the *f* he ate.
41:35 They should collect all the *f*
41:35 to be kept in the cities for *f*.
41:36 This *f* should be held in reserve
41:48 In each city he put the *f* grown
41:48 Joseph collected all the *f* produced
41:54 land of Egypt there was *f*.
41:55 the people cried to Pharaoh for *f*.
42: 7 of Canaan," they replied, "to buy *f*
42:10 "Your servants have come to buy *f*.
42:33 take *f* for your starving households
43: 2 Go back and buy us a little more *f*."
43: 4 we will go down and buy *f* for you.
43:20 down here the first time to buy *f*.
43:22 additional silver with us to buy *f*.
43:31 himself, said, "Serve the *f*."
44: 1 as much *f* as they can carry,
44:25 'Go back and buy a little more *f*.'
47:12 all his father's household with *f*,
47:13 There was no *f*, however,
47:15 to Joseph and said, "Give us *f*.
47:16 "I will sell you *f* in exchange
47:17 and he gave them *f* in exchange
47:17 year with *f* in exchange
47:19 and our land in exchange for *f*,
47:22 had *f* enough from the allotment
47:24 and as *f* for yourselves and your
49:20 "Asher's *f* will be rich;
Ex 12:16 to prepare *f* for everyone to eat—
12:39 time to prepare *f* for themselves.
16: 3 and ate all the *f* we wanted,
21:10 not deprive the first one of her *f*,
23:11 poor among your people may get *f*
23:25 and his blessing will be on your *f*
Lev 3:11 shall burn them on the altar as *f*,
3:16 shall burn them on the altar as *f*,
11:34 Any *f* that could be eaten
21: 6 the *f* of their God, they are
21: 8 they offer up the *f* of your God.
21:17 come near to offer the *f* of his God.
21:21 come near to offer the *f* of his God.
21:22 He may eat the most holy *f*
21:22 as well as the holy *f*; yet
22: 7 sacred offerings, for they are his *f*.
22:11 household, that slave may eat his *f*.
22:13 she may eat of her father's *f*.
22:25 offer them as the *f* of your God.
25: 6 during the sabbath year will be *f*
25:37 at interest or sell him *f* at a profit.
26: 5 and you will eat all the *f* you want
Nu 11: 4 with them began to crave other *f*,
11:34 the people who had craved other *f*
15:19 and you eat the *f* of the land,
21: 5 And we detest this miserable *f*!"
28: 2 me at the appointed time the *f*
28:24 In this way prepare the *f*
Dt 2: 6 them in silver for the *f* you eat
2:28 Sell us *f* to eat and water to drink
10:18 giving him *f* and clothing.
23:19 whether on money or *f*
28:26 Your carcasses will be *f*
32:15 filled with *f*, he became heavy
Jos 5:12 after they ate this *f* from the land;
9: 5 the bread of their *f* supply was dry
Jdg 13:16 I will not eat any of your *f*.
17:10 a year, your clothes and your *f*."
Ru 1: 6 people by providing *f* for them,
1Sa 2: 5 were full hire themselves out for *f*,
2:36 office so I can have *f* to eat." ' "
9: 7 The *f* in our sacks is gone.
14:24 So none of the troops tasted *f*.
1Sa 14:24 "Cursed be any man who eats *f*
14:28 be any man who eats *f* today!'
28:22 and let me give you some *f*
30:11 water to drink and *f* to eat—
30:12 for he had not eaten any *f*
2Sa 3:29 falls by the sword or who lacks *f*."
12: 3 It shared his *f*, drank from his cup
12:17 he would not eat any *f* with them.
12:20 and at his request they served him *f*
13: 5 Let her prepare the *f* in my sight
13: 7 and prepare some *f* for him."
13:10 "Bring the *f* here into my bedroom
1Ki 5: 9 wish by providing *f* for my royal
5:11 of wheat as *f* for his household,
10: 5 the *f* on his table, the seating
11:18 and land and provided him with *f*.
17: 9 in that place to supply you with *f*."
17:15 So there was *f* every day for Elijah
18: 4 had supplied them with *f* and water
18:13 and supplied them with *f* and water
19: 8 by that *f*, he traveled forty days
2Ki 6:22 Set *f* and water before them
25: 3 so severe that there was no *f*
1Ch 12:40 and Naphtali came bringing *f*
2Ch 9: 4 the *f* on his table, the seating
11:11 with supplies of *f*, olive oil
28:15 *f* and drink, and healing balm.
Ezr 2:63 any of the most sacred *f*
3: 7 and gave *f* and drink and oil
10: 6 he ate no *f* and drank no water,
Ne 5:14 nor my brothers ate the *f* allotted
5:15 of silver from them in addition to *f*
5:18 I never demanded the *f* allotted
7:65 not to eat any of the most sacred *f*
8:10 enjoy choice *f* and sweet drinks,
8:12 portions of *f* and to celebrate
13: 2 had not met the Israelites with *f*
13:15 them against selling *f* on that day.
Est 2: 9 beauty treatments and special *f*.
9:22 giving presents of *f* to one another
Job 3:24 comes to me instead of *f*;
6: 6 Is tasteless *f* eaten without salt,
6: 7 such *f* makes me ill.
12:11 as the tongue tastes *f*?
15:23 He wanders about—*f* for vultures;
20:14 yet his *f* will turn sour
22: 7 you withheld *f* from the hungry,
24: 5 go about their labor of foraging *f*;
24: 5 the wasteland provides *f*
28: 5 The earth, from which *f* comes,
30: 4 their *f* was the root
33:20 that his very being finds *f* repulsive
34: 3 as the tongue tastes *f*.
36:16 of your table laden with choice *f*.
36:31 and provides *f* in abundance.
38:41 Who provides *f* for the raven
38:41 and wander about for lack of *f*?
39:29 From there he seeks out his *f*;
Ps 42: 3 My tears have been my *f*
59:15 They wander about for *f*
63:10 and become *f* for jackals.
69:21 They put gall in my *f*
74:14 *f* to the creatures of the desert.
78:18 by demanding the *f* they craved.
78:20 But can he also give us *f*?
78:25 he sent them all the *f* they could eat
78:30 turned from the *f* they craved,
79: 2 as *f* to the birds of the air,
102: 4 I forget to eat my *f*.
102: 9 For I eat ashes as my *f*
104: 14 bringing forth *f* from the earth:
104: 21 and seek their *f* from God.
104: 27 to give them their *f*
105: 16 and destroyed all their supplies of *f*
107: 18 They loathed all *f*
111: 5 He provides *f* for those who fear
127: 2 toiling for *f* to eat—
132: 15 her poor will I satisfy with *f*.
136: 25 and who gives *f* to every creature.
145: 15 you give them their *f*
146: 7 and gives *f* to the hungry.
147: 9 He provides *f* for the cattle
Pr 6: 8 and gathers its *f* at harvest.
9: 5 "Come, eat my *f*
9:17 *f* eaten in secret is delicious!"
12: 9 to be somebody and have no *f*.
12:11 his land will have abundant *f*,
13:23 field may produce abundant *f*,
Pr 20:13 you will have *f* to spare.
20:17 *F* gained by fraud tastes sweet
21:20 of the wise are stores of choice *f*
22: 9 for he shares his *f* with the poor.
23: 3 for that *f* is deceptive.
23: 6 Do not eat the *f* of a stingy man,
25:21 If your enemy is hungry, give him *f*
28:19 his land will have abundant *f*,
30:22 a fool who is full of *f*,
30:25 yet they store up their *f*
31:14 bringing her *f* from afar.
31:15 she provides *f* for her family
Ecc 9: 7 Go, eat your *f* with gladness,
9:11 nor does *f* come to the wise
Isa 3: 1 all supplies of *f* and all supplies
3: 7 I have no *f* or clothing in my house;
4: 1 and say, "We will eat our own *f*
21:14 bring *f* for the fugitives.
23:18 for abundant *f* and fine clothes.
25: 6 a feast of rich *f* for all peoples,
30:23 *f* that comes from the land will be
58: 7 not to share your *f* with the hungry
62: 8 as *f* for your enemies,
65:25 but dust will be the serpent's *f*.
Jer 5:17 will devour your harvests and *f*,
7:33 of this people will become *f*
9:15 I will make this people eat bitter *f*
16: 4 and their dead bodies will become *f*
16: 7 No one will offer *f*
19: 7 as *f* to the birds of the air
22:15 Did not your father have *f*
23:15 "I will make them eat bitter *f*
34:20 Their dead bodies will become *f*
44:17 At that time we had plenty of *f*
52: 6 so severe that there was no *f*
La 1:11 they barter their treasures for *f*
1:19 the city while they searched for *f*
4: 9 away for lack of *f* from the field.
4:10 who became their *f*
Eze 4:10 shekels of *f* to eat each day
4:12 Eat the *f* as you would a barley
4:13 people of Israel will eat defiled *f*
4:16 The people will eat rationed *f*
4:16 cut off the supply of *f* in Jerusalem.
4:17 for *f* and water will be scarce.
5:16 and cut off your supply of *f*.
12:18 of man, tremble as you eat your *f*,
12:19 They will eat their *f* in anxiety
14:13 against it to cut off its *f* supply
16:13 Your *f* was fine flour, honey
16:19 Also the *f* I provided for you—
16:20 sacrificed them as *f* to the idols.
18: 7 but gives his *f* to the hungry
18:16 but gives his *f* to the hungry
23:37 bore to me, as *f* for them.
24:17 eat the customary *f* ⌞of mourners⌟."
24:22 eat the customary *f* ⌞of mourners⌟.
29: 5 I will give you as *f*
34: 5 they were scattered they became *f*
34: 8 and has become *f* for all the wild
34:10 and it will no longer be *f* for them.
39: 4 as *f* to all kinds of carrion birds
44: 7 temple while you offered me *f*,
47:12 Their fruit will serve for *f*
48:18 Its produce will supply *f*
Da 1: 5 assigned them a daily amount of *f*
1: 8 to defile himself with the royal *f*
1:10 who has assigned your *f* and drink.
1:13 the young men who eat the royal *f*,
1:15 the young men who ate the royal *f*.
1:16 the guard took away their choice *f*
4:12 its fruit abundant, and on it was *f*
4:21 abundant fruit, providing *f* for all,
10: 3 I ate no choice *f*; no meat
Hos 2: 5 who give me my *f* and my water,
9: 3 and eat unclean *f* in Assyria.
9: 4 This *f* will be for themselves;
Joel 1:16 Has not the *f* been cut off
Am 8:11 not a famine of *f* or a thirst
Hab 1:16 and enjoys the choicest *f*.
3:17 and the fields produce no *f*,
Hag 2:12 other *f*, does it become consecrated
Zec 9: 7 *f* from between their teeth.
Mal 1: 7 "You place defiled *f* on my altar.
1:12 and of its *f*, 'It is contemptible.'
3:10 that there may be *f* in my house.
Mt 3: 4 His *f* was locusts and wild honey.
6:25 Is not life more important than *f*,

Mt 14:15 and buy themselves some *f*."
24:45 household to give them their *f*
Mk 7: 2 some of his disciples eating *f*
7: 5 their *f* with 'unclean' hands'?"
Lk 3:11 one who has *f* should do the same."
9:12 countryside and find *f* and lodging,
9:13 we go and buy *f* for all this crowd."
12:23 more than *f*, and the body more
12:42 to give them their *f* allowance
15:17 of my father's hired men have *f*
Jn 4: 8 gone into the town to buy *f*.)
4:32 "I have *f* to eat that you know
4:34 have brought him *f*?" "My *f*,"
6:27 Do not work for *f* that spoils,
6:27 but for *f* that endures to eternal life,
6:55 my flesh is real *f* and my blood is
Ac 6: 1 in the daily distribution of *f*.
7:11 and our fathers could not find *f*.
9:19 after taking some *f*, he regained his
12:20 king's country for their *f* supply.
14:17 he provides you with plenty of *f*
15:20 to abstain from *f* polluted by idols,
15:29 to abstain from *f* sacrificed to idols,
21:25 abstain from *f* sacrificed to idols,
27:21 had gone a long time without *f*,
27:33 and have gone without *f*—
27:34 Now I urge you to take some *f*.
27:36 and ate some *f* themselves.
Ro 14:14 fully convinced that no *f* is unclean
14:20 All *f* is clean, but it is wrong
14:20 the work of God for the sake of *f*.
1Co 3: 2 I gave you milk, not solid *f*,
6:13 *F* for the stomach and the stomach
6:13 stomach and the stomach for *f*'—
8: 1 Now about *f* sacrificed to idols:
8: 4 about eating *f* sacrificed to idols:
8: 7 when they eat such *f* they think
8: 8 But *f* does not bring us near to God
9: 4 Don't we have the right to *f*
9:13 work in the temple get their *f*
10: 3 They all ate the same spiritual *f*
2Co 9:10 and bread for *f* will also supply
11:27 and have often gone without *f*;
2Th 3: 8 nor did we eat anyone's *f*
1Ti 6: 8 But if we have *f* and clothing,
Heb 5:12 You need milk, not solid *f*!
5:14 But solid *f* is for the mature,
9:10 They are only a matter of *f*
Jas 2:15 sister is without clothes and daily *f*.
Rev 2:14 to sin by eating *f* sacrificed to idols
2:20 the eating of *f* sacrificed to idols.

FOODS (FOOD)

Ps 63: 5 with the richest of *f*;
Mk 7:19 Jesus declared all *f* "clean.")
1Ti 4: 3 them to abstain from certain *f*,
Heb 13: 9 not by ceremonial *f*, which are

FOOL (FOLLY FOOL'S FOOLISH FOOLISHLY FOOLISHNESS FOOLS)

Nu 22:29 "You have made a *f* of me!
Jdg 16:10 "You have made a *f* of me;
16:13 you have been making a *f* of me
16:15 is the third time you have made a *f*
1Sa 25:25 his name is *F*, and folly goes
26:21 Surely I have acted like a *f*
Job 5: 2 Resentment kills a *f*,
5: 3 I myself have seen a *f* taking root,
Ps 14: 1 The *f* says in his heart,
53: 1 The *f* says in his heart,
Pr 10: 8 but a chattering *f* comes to ruin.
10:10 and a chattering *f* comes to ruin.
10:14 but the mouth of a *f* invites ruin.
10:18 and whoever spreads slander is a *f*.
10:23 A *f* finds pleasure in evil conduct,
11:29 and the *f* will be servant to the wise
12:15 The way of a *f* seems right to him,
12:16 A *f* shows his annoyance at once,
13:16 but a *f* exposes his folly.
14:16 but a *f* is hotheaded and reckless.
15: 2 but the mouth of the *f* gushes folly.
15: 5 A *f* spurns his father's discipline,
15:14 but the mouth of a *f* feeds on folly.
17: 7 Arrogant lips are unsuited to a *f*—
17:10 more than a hundred lashes a *f*.
17:12 than a *f* in his folly.
17:16 use is money in the hand of a *f*,
17:21 To have a *f* for a son brings grief;
Pr 17:21 there is no joy for the father of a *f*.
17:28 Even a *f* is thought wise
18: 2 A *f* finds no pleasure
19: 1 than a *f* whose lips are perverse.
19:10 fitting for a *f* to live in luxury—
20: 3 but every *f* is quick to quarrel.
23: 9 Do not speak to a *f*,
24: 7 Wisdom is too high for a *f*;
26: 1 honor is not fitting for a *f*.
26: 4 Do not answer a *f* according
26: 5 Answer a *f* according to his folly,
26: 6 of a message by the hand of a *f*.
26: 7 is a proverb in the mouth of a *f*.
26: 8 is the giving of honor to a *f*.
26: 9 is a proverb in the mouth of a *f*.
26:10 is he who hires a *f* or any passer-by.
26:11 so a *f* repeats his folly.
26:12 for a *f* than for him.
27: 3 provocation by a *f* is heavier
27:22 Though you grind a *f* in a mortar,
28:26 He who trusts in himself is a *f*,
29: 9 If a wise man goes to court with a *f*,
29: 9 *f* rages and scoffs, and there is no
29:11 A *f* gives full vent to his anger,
29:20 for a *f* than for him.
30:22 a *f* who is full of food,
30:32 "If you have played the *f*
Ecc 2:14 while the *f* walks in the darkness;
2:15 "The fate of the *f* will overtake me
2:16 Like the *f*, the wise man too must
2:16 like the *f*, will not be long
2:19 he will be a wise man or a *f*?
4: 5 The *f* folds his hands
5: 3 so the speech of a *f*
6: 8 man over a *f*?
7: 7 Extortion turns a wise man into a *f*,
7:17 and do not be a *f*—
10: 2 but the heart of the *f* to the left.
10: 3 the *f* lacks sense
10:12 but a *f* is consumed by his own lips.
10:14 and the *f* multiplies words.
Isa 32: 5 No longer will the *f* be called noble
32: 6 For the *f* speaks folly,
Jer 17:11 in the end he will prove to be a *f*.
Hos 9: 7 the prophet is considered a *f*,
Mt 5:22 But anyone who says, 'You *f*!'
Lk 12:20 "But God said to him, 'You *f*!
1Co 3:18 he should become a "*f*"
2Co 11:16 I repeat: Let no one take me for a *f*.
11:16 receive me just as you would a *f*,
11:17 as the Lord would, but as a *f*.
11:21 I am speaking as a *f*—I
12: 6 would not be a *f*, because I would
12:11 I have made a *f* of myself,

FOOL'S (FOOL)

Pr 14: 3 A *f* talk brings a rod to his back,
17:24 a *f* eyes wander to the ends
18: 6 A *f* lips bring him strife,
18: 7 A *f* mouth is his undoing,
Ecc 10:15 A *f* work wearies him;

FOOLISH (FOOL)

Ge 31:28 You have done a *f* thing.
Dt 32: 6 O *f* and unwise people?
2Sa 24:10 I have done a very *f* thing."
1Ch 21: 8 I have done a very *f* thing."
2Ch 16: 9 You have done a *f* thing,
Job 2:10 "You are talking like a *f* woman.
Ps 49:10 the *f* and the senseless alike perish
74:18 how *f* people have reviled your
Pr 8: 5 you who are *f*, gain understanding.
10: 1 but a *f* son grief to his mother.
14: 1 her own hands the *f* one tears hers
14: 7 Stay away from a *f* man,
14:17 quick-tempered man does *f* things,
15:20 but a *f* man despises his mother.
17:25 A *f* son brings grief to his father
19:13 A *f* son is his father's ruin,
21:20 but a *f* man devours all he has.
Ecc 2: 2 "Laughter," I said, "is *f*.
4:13 *f* king who no longer knows how
Jer 5: 4 they are *f*,
5:21 you *f* and senseless people,
10: 8 They are all senseless and *f*;
Eze 13: 3 to the *f* prophets who follow their
Zec 11:15 the equipment of a *f* shepherd.
Mt 7:26 practice is like a *f* man who built
Mt 25: 2 of them were *f* and five were wise.
25: 3 The *f* ones took their lamps
25: 8 The *f* ones said to the wise,
Lk 11:40 You *f* people! Did not the one who
24:25 He said to them, "How *f* you are,
Ro 1:14 both to the wise and the *f*.
1:21 and their *f* hearts were darkened.
2:20 an instructor of the *f*, a teacher
1Co 1:20 Has not God made *f* the wisdom
1:27 God chose the *f* things of the world
15:36 of body will they come?" How *f*!
Gal 3: 1 died for nothing!" You *f* Galatians!
3: 3 Are you so *f*? After beginning
Eph 5: 4 should there be obscenity, *f* talk
5:17 Therefore do not be *f*,
1Ti 6: 9 and a trap and into many *f*
2Ti 2:23 Don't have anything to do with *f*
Tit 3: 3 At one time we too were *f*,
3: 9 But avoid *f* controversies
Jas 2:20 You *f* man, do you want evidence
1Pe 2:15 silence the ignorant talk of *f* men.

FOOLISHLY (FOOL)

Nu 12:11 us the sin we have so *f* committed.
1Sa 13:13 "You acted *f*," Samuel said.

FOOLISHNESS (FOOL)

2Sa 15:31 turn Ahithophel's counsel into *f*."
1Co 1:18 of the cross is *f* to those who are
1:21 through the *f* of what was preached
1:23 block to Jews and *f* to Gentiles,
1:25 For the *f* of God is wiser
2:14 for they are *f* to him, and he cannot
3:19 of this world is *f* in God's sight.
2Co 11: 1 up with a little of my *f*;

FOOLS (FOOL)

2Sa 13:13 one of the wicked *f* in Israel.
Job 12:17 and makes *f* of judges.
Ps 39: 8 do not make me the scorn of *f*.
74:22 remember how *f* mock you all day
92: 6 *f* do not understand,
94: 8 you *f*, when will you become wise?
107:17 became *f* through their rebellious
Pr 1: 7 but *f* despise wisdom and discipline
1:22 and *f* hate knowledge?
1:32 of *f* will destroy them;
3:35 but *f* he holds up to shame.
10:21 but *f* die for lack of judgment.
12:23 but the heart of *f* blurts out folly.
13:19 but *f* detest turning from evil.
13:20 but a companion of *f* suffers harm.
14: 8 but the folly of *f* is deception.
14: 9 *F* mock at making amends for sin,
14:24 but the folly of *f* yields folly.
14:33 among *f* she lets herself be known.
15: 7 not so the hearts of *f*.
16:22 but folly brings punishment to *f*.
19:29 and beatings for the backs of *f*.
26: 3 and a rod for the backs of *f*!
Ecc 5: 1 than to offer the sacrifice of *f*,
5: 4 pleasure in *f*; fulfill your vow.
7: 4 the heart of *f* is in the house
7: 5 than to listen to the song of *f*.
7: 6 so is the laughter of *f*.
7: 9 for anger resides in the lap of *f*.
9:17 than the shouts of a ruler of *f*.
10: 6 *F* are put in many high positions,
Isa 19:11 of Zoan are nothing but *f*;
19:13 officials of Zoan have become *f*,
35: 8 wicked *f* will not go about on it.
44:25 and makes *f* of diviners,
Jer 4:22 "My people are *f*;
50:36 They will become *f*.
Mt 23:17 You blind *f*! Which is greater:
Ro 1:22 they became *f* and exchanged
1Co 4:10 We are *f* for Christ, but you are
2Co 11:19 up with *f* since you are

FOOT (FEET FLEET-FOOTED FOOTHOLD FOOTINGS FOOTPRINTS FOUR-FOOTED UNDERFOOT)

Ge 41:44 your word no one will lift hand or *f*
Ex 12:37 six hundred thousand men on *f*,
19:12 go up the mountain or touch the *f*
19:17 they stood at the *f* of the mountain.
21:24 hand for hand, *f* for *f*, burn for burn
24: 4 an altar at the *f* of the mountain

Ex 32: 19 to pieces at the *f* of the mountain.
Lev 8: 23 and on the big toe of his right *f*.
13: 12 the infected person from head to *f*,
14: 14 and on the big toe of his right *f*.
14: 17 and on the big toe of his right *f*.
14: 25 and on the big toe of his right *f*.
14: 28 and on the big toe of his right *f*.
21: 19 no man with a crippled *f* or hand,
Nu 11: 21 six hundred thousand men on *f*,
20: 19 We only want to pass through on *f*
22: 25 crushing Balaam's *f* against it.
Dt 2: 5 not even enough to put your *f* on.
2: 28 Only let us pass through on *f*—
4: 11 and stood at the *f* of the mountain
11: 10 it by *f* as in a vegetable garden.
11: 24 where you set your *f* will be yours:
19: 21 for tooth, hand for hand, *f* for *f*.
28: 56 the ground with the sole of her *f*—
28: 65 place for the sole of your *f*.
32: 35 In due time their *f* will slip;
Jos 1: 3 every place where you set your *f*,
3: 13 of all the earth—set *f* in the Jordan
18: 16 The boundary went down to the *f*
Jdg 3: 16 a double-edged sword about a *f*
4: 15 his chariot and fled on *f*.
4: 17 fled on *f* to the tent of Jael,
1Sa 4: 10 lost thirty thousand *f* soldiers.
15: 4 two hundred thousand *f* soldiers
2Sa 8: 4 and twenty thousand *f* soldiers.
10: 6 thousand Aramean *f* soldiers
10: 18 forty thousand of their *f* soldiers.
14: 25 sole of his *f* there was no blemish
21: 20 on each hand and six toes on each *f*
1Ki 14: 12 When you set *f* in your city,
20: 29 on the Aramean *f* soldiers
2Ki 13: 7 and ten thousand *f* soldiers,
1Ch 18: 4 and twenty thousand *f* soldiers.
19: 18 forty thousand of their *f* soldiers.
20: 6 on each hand and six toes on each *f*
Job 28: 4 in places forgotten by the *f* of man;
28: 8 Proud beasts do not set *f* on it,
31: 5 or my *f* has hurried after deceit—
39: 15 unmindful that a *f* may crush them,
Ps 36: 11 May the *f* of the proud not come
38: 16 over me when my *f* slips."
66: 6 they passed through the river on *f*
91: 12 so that you will not strike your *f*
94: 18 When I said, "My *f* is slipping,"
121: 3 He will not let your *f* slip—
Pr 1: 15 do not set *f* on their paths;
3: 23 and your *f* will not stumble;
3: 26 will keep your *f* from being snared.
4: 14 Do not set *f* on the path
4: 27 keep your *f* from evil.
25: 17 Seldom set *f* in your neighbor's
25: 19 Like a bad tooth or a lame *f*
Ecc 10: 7 while princes go on *f* like slaves.
Isa 1: 6 From the sole of your *f* to the top
Jer 12: 5 "If you have raced with men on *f*
Eze 29: 11 No *f* of man or animal will pass
32: 13 longer to be stirred by the *f* of man
Hab 3: 13 you stripped him from head to *f*.
Mt 4: 6 so that you will not strike your *f*
14: 13 him on *f* from the towns.
18: 8 or your *f* causes you to sin,
22: 13 and *f*, and throw him outside,
Mk 5: 4 had often been chained hand and *f*,
6: 33 and ran on *f* from all the towns
9: 45 And if your *f* causes you to sin,
Lk 4: 11 so that you will not strike your *f*
8: 29 and *f* and kept under guard,
Jn 20: 12 at the head and the other at the *f*.
Ac 7: 5 no inheritance here, not even a *f*
20: 13 because he was going there on *f*.
1Co 12: 15 If the *f* should say, "Because I am
Heb 10: 29 trampled the Son of God under *f*,
Rev 10: 2 He planted his right *f* on the sea
10: 2 on the sea and his left *f* on the land,

FOOTHILLS (HILL)

Dt 1: 7 in the mountains, in the western *f*,
Jos 9: 1 in the hill country, in the western *f*,
10: 40 western *f* and the mountain slopes,
11: 2 western *f* and in Naphoth Dor
11: 16 region of Goshen, the western *f*,
11: 16 the mountains of Israel with their *f*,
12: 8 the western *f*, the Arabah,
15: 33 In the western *f*: Eshtaol, Zorah,
Jdg 1: 9 the Negev and the western *f*.
1Ki 10: 27 as sycamore-fig trees in the *f*.
1Ch 27: 28 sycamore-fig trees in the western *f*.
2Ch 1: 15 as sycamore-fig trees in the *f*.
9: 27 as sycamore-fig trees in the *f*.
26: 10 he had much livestock in the *f*
28: 18 had raided towns in the *f*
Jer 17: 26 of Benjamin and the western *f*,
32: 44 of the western *f* and of the Negev,
33: 13 of the western *f* and of the Negev,
Ob : 19 and people from the *f* will possess
Zec 7: 7 and the western *f* were settled?' "

FOOTHOLD (FOOT)

Ps 69: 2 where there is no *f*.
73: 2 I had nearly lost my *f*.
Eph 4: 27 and do not give the devil a *f*.

FOOTINGS (FOOT)

Job 38: 6 On what were its *f* set,

FOOTPRINTS (FOOT)

Ps 77: 19 though your *f* were not seen.
Hos 6: 8 stained with *f* of blood.

FOOTSTEPS (STEP)

1Ki 14: 6 the sound of her *f* at the door,
2Ki 6: 32 of his master's *f* behind him?"
Ps 119:133 Direct my *f* according
Isa 26: 6 the *f* of the poor
Ro 4: 12 in the *f* of the faith that our father

FOOTSTOOL (STOOL)

1Ch 28: 2 for the *f* of our God, and I made
2Ch 9: 18 and a *f* of gold was attached to it.
Ps 99: 5 and worship at his *f*;
110: 1 a *f* for your feet."
132: 7 let us worship at his *f*—
Isa 66: 1 and the earth is my *f*.
La 2: 1 he has not remembered his *f*
Mt 5: 35 for it is his *f*; or by Jerusalem,
Lk 20: 43 a *f* for your feet." '
Ac 2: 35 a *f* for your feet." '
7: 49 and the earth is my *f*.
Heb 1: 13 a *f* for your feet"?
10: 13 for his enemies to be made his *f*,

FORAGING

Job 24: 5 poor go about their labor of *f* food;

FORBEARANCE

Ro 3: 25 because in his *f* he had left the sins

FORBID (FORBIDDEN FORBIDS)

Nu 30: 11 nothing to her and does not *f* her,
1Sa 24: 6 LORD *f* that I should do such
26: 11 LORD *f* that I should lay a hand
1Ki 21: 3 LORD *f* that I should give you
1Ch 11: 19 "God *f* that I should do this!"
1Co 14: 39 and do not *f* speaking in tongues.
1Ti 4: 3 They *f* people to marry

FORBIDDEN (FORBID)

Lev 4: 2 and does what is *f* in any
4: 13 and does what is *f* in any
4: 22 and does what is *f* in any
4: 27 and does what is *f* in any
5: 17 and does what is *f* in any
19: 23 of fruit tree, regard its fruit as *f*.
19: 23 three years you are to consider it *f*;
Nu 30: 5 her because her father has *f* her.
Dt 4: 23 the LORD your God has *f*.
23: 2 No one born of a *f* marriage
1Ki 11: 10 Although he had *f* Solomon
2Ki 17: 15 the things the LORD had *f* them
Est 2: 10 Mordecai had *f* her to do so.
La 1: 10 those you had *f*
Zec 9: 7 the *f* food from between their teeth

FORBIDS (FORBID)

Nu 30: 5 if her father *f* her when he hears
30: 8 But if her husband *f* her
Jn 5: 10 the law *f* you to carry your mat."

FORCE (ENFORCE FORCED FORCEFUL FORCES FORCING)

Ge 31: 31 your daughters away from me by *f*.
47: 26 still in *f* today—that a fifth
Ex 9: 14 or this time I will send the full *f*
19: 21 people so they do not *f* their way
19: 24 and the people must not *f* their way
Jos 8: 11 The entire *f* that was
Jdg 7: 13 the tent with such *f* that the tent
8: 10 with a *f* of about fifteen thousand
1Sa 2: 16 if you don't, I'll take it by *f*."
19: 8 them with such *f* that they fled
2Sa 5: 17 up in full *f* to search for him,
13: 12 "Don't *f* me.
1Ki 9: 21 conscripted for his slave labor *f*,
11: 28 of the whole labor *f* of the house
2Ki 6: 14 and chariots and a strong *f* there.
24: 16 deported to Babylon the entire *f*
1Ch 14: 8 up in full *f* to search for him,
2Ch 8: 8 conscripted for his slave labor *f*,
13: 3 Abijah went into battle with a *f*
26: 13 a powerful *f* to support the king
32: 4 A large *f* of men assembled,
Ezr 4: 23 and compelled them by *f* to stop.
Est 8: 11 and annihilate any armed *f*
Job 19: 12 His troops advance in *f*;
20: 22 the full *f* of misery will come
24: 4 *f* all the poor of the land into hiding
28: 25 When he established the *f*
Jer 46: 22 as the enemy advances in *f*;
Am 5: 11 and *f* him to give you grain.
Ob : 7 All your allies will *f* you
Jn 6: 15 to come and make him king by *f*,
Ac 5: 26 did not use *f*, because they feared
23: 10 and take him away from them by *f*
26: 11 and I tried to *f* them to blaspheme.
27: 14 a wind of hurricane *f*, called
Gal 2: 14 that you *f* Gentiles
Heb 9: 17 in *f* only when somebody has died;

FORCED (FORCE)

Ge 49: 15 and submit to *f* labor.
Ex 1: 11 them to oppress them with *f* labor,
Dt 20: 11 in it shall be subject to *f* labor
Jos 16: 10 but are required to do *f* labor.
17: 13 subjected the Canaanites to *f* labor
Jdg 1: 28 pressed the Canaanites into *f* labor
1: 30 but they did subject them to *f* labor
1: 33 became *f* laborers for them.
1: 35 they too were pressed into *f* labor.
2Sa 18: 3 if we are *f* to flee, they won't care
20: 24 Adoniram was in charge of *f* labor;
1Ki 4: 6 son of Abda—in charge of *f* labor.
5: 14 was in charge of the *f* labor.
9: 15 of the *f* labor King Solomon
12: 18 who was in charge of *f* labor,
2Ch 10: 18 who was in charge of *f* labor,
Job 30: 6 They were *f* to live
Ps 69: 4 I am *f* to restore
Isa 31: 8 young men will be put to *f* labor.
Jer 34: 16 You have *f* them to become your
Mt 27: 32 and they *f* him to carry the cross.
Mk 15: 21 and they *f* him to carry the cross.
Phm : 14 do will be spontaneous and not *f*.
Rev 13: 16 He also *f* everyone, small and great

FORCEFUL (FORCE)

Mt 11: 12 forcefully advancing, and *f* men lay
2Co 10: 10 "His letters are weighty and *f*,

FORCES (FORCE)

Ge 14: 3 All these latter kings joined *f*
21: 22 of his *f* said to Abraham,
21: 32 of his *f* returned to the land
26: 26 and Phicol the commander of his *f*.
34: 30 and if they join *f* against me
Jos 10: 5 Lachish and Eglon—joined *f*.
10: 6 from the hill country have joined *f*
11: 5 All these kings joined *f*
Jdg 6: 33 and other eastern peoples joined *f*
12: 1 men of Ephraim called out their *f*,
1Sa 4: 2 The Philistines deployed their *f*
14: 17 "Muster the *f* and see who has left
17: 1 the Philistines gathered their *f*
23: 3 to Keilah against the Philistine *f*!"
23: 8 Saul called up all his *f* for battle,
23: 26 and his *f* were closing in on David
28: 1 days the Philistines gathered their *f*
29: 1 The Philistines gathered all their *f*
30: 23 handed over to us the *f* that came
1Ki 11: 24 rebels when David destroyed the *f*
15: 20 of his *f* against the towns

1Ch 20: 1 off to war, Joab led out the armed *f*.
2Ch 14: 13 before the LORD and his *f*.
16: 4 of his *f* against the towns
32: 9 and all his *f* were laying siege
Job 10: 17 your *f* come against me wave
25: 3 Can his *f* be numbered?
Ps 48: 4 When the kings joined *f*,
55: 11 Destructive *f* are at work
Da 11: 7 He will attack the *f* of the king
11: 15 *f* of the South will be powerless
11: 31 "His armed *f* will rise up
Joel 2: 11 his *f* are beyond number,
Zec 9: 8 against marauding *f*.
Mt 5: 41 If someone *f* you to go one mile,
Eph 6: 12 and against the spiritual *f* of evil

FORCING (FORCE)

Lk 16: 16 and everyone is *f* his way into it.
Ac 7: 19 our forefathers by *f* them

FORD (FORDED FORDS)

Ge 32: 22 and crossed the *f* of the Jabbok.
2Sa 19: 18 They crossed at the *f*

FORDED (FORD)

Jos 2: 23 *f* the river and came to Joshua son

FORDS (FORD)

Jos 2: 7 leads to the *f* of the Jordan,
Jdg 3: 28 and, taking possession of the *f*
12: 5 The Gileadites captured the *f*
12: 6 killed him at the *f* of the Jordan.
2Sa 15: 28 I will wait at the *f* in the desert
17: 16 the night at the *f* in the desert;
Isa 16: 2 Moab at the *f* of the Arnon.

FOREFATHER (FATHER)

Nu 26: 58 (Kohath was the *f* of Amram;
Jos 15: 13 (Arba was the *f* of Anak.)
19: 47 and named it Dan after their *f*.)
21: 11 (Arba was the *f* of Anak.)
Jdg 18: 29 named it Dan after their *f* Dan,
1Ki 15: 3 as the heart of David his *f* had been
1Ch 24: 19 for them by their *f* Aaron,
Jer 35: 6 our *f* Jonadab son of Recab gave us
35: 8 everything our *f* Jonadab son
35: 10 everything our *f* Jonadab
35: 16 the command their *f* gave them,
35: 18 the command of your *f* Jonadab
Ro 4: 1 our *f*, discovered in this matter? If,

FOREFATHER'S (FATHER)

Jer 35: 14 they obey their *f* command.

FOREFATHERS (FATHER)

Ex 10: 6 nor your *f* have ever seen
13: 5 swore to your *f* to give you,
13: 11 on oath to you and your *f*,
Lev 25: 41 and to the property of his *f*.
Nu 11: 12 promised on oath to their *f*?
14: 23 land I promised on oath to their *f*.
20: 15 Our *f* went down into Egypt,
36: 4 from the tribal inheritance of our *f*
36: 7 the tribal land inherited from his *f*.
Dt 1: 35 good land I swore to give your *f*,
4: 31 or forget the covenant with your *f*,
4: 37 Because he loved your *f*
6: 18 LORD promised on oath to your *f*,
6: 23 that he promised on oath to our *f*.
7: 8 to your *f* that he brought you out
7: 12 with you, as he swore to your *f*.
7: 13 swore to your *f* to give you.
8: 1 LORD promised on oath to your *f*.
8: 18 which he swore to your *f*,
10: 15 LORD set his affection on your *f*
10: 22 *f* who went down into Egypt were
11: 9 swore to your *f* to give to them
11: 21 the LORD swore to give your *f*,
13: 17 as he promised on oath to your *f*,
19: 8 as he promised on oath to your *f*,
26: 3 swore to our *f* to give us."
26: 15 as you promised on oath to our *f*,
28: 11 swore to your *f* to give you.
31: 7 swore to their *f* to give them,
31: 20 land I promised on oath to their *f*,
Jos 1: 6 swore to their *f* to give them.
21: 43 land he had sworn to give their *f*,
21: 44 just as he had sworn to their *f*.
Jos 24: 2 of Israel, says: 'Long ago your *f*,
24: 14 away the gods your *f* worshiped
24: 15 whether the gods your *f* served
24: 17 who brought us and our *f* up out
Jdg 2: 1 land that I swore to give to your *f*.
2: 20 that I laid down for their *f*
2: 22 and walk in it as their *f* did."
3: 4 which he had given their *f*
1Sa 12: 6 and brought your *f* up out of Egypt.
12: 8 who brought your *f* out of Egypt
1Ki 14: 15 good land that he gave to their *f*
2Ki 19: 12 destroyed by my *f* deliver them:
21: 8 wander from the land I gave their *f*,
21: 15 anger from the day their *f* came out
1Ch 29: 15 in your sight, as were all our *f*.
2Ch 33: 8 leave the land I assigned to your *f*,
Ezr 9: 7 From the days of our *f* until now,
Ne 9: 9 "You saw the suffering of our *f*
9: 16 our *f*, became arrogant
9: 36 slaves in the land you gave our *f*
13: 18 Didn't your *f* do the same things,
Ps 78: 5 which he commanded our *f*
78: 8 They would not be like their *f*—
Pr 22: 28 set up by your *f*.
Isa 14: 21 sons for the sins of their *f*;
37: 12 destroyed by my *f* deliver them—
Jer 3: 18 land to the land I gave your *f*
7: 7 in the land I gave your *f* for ever
7: 22 when I brought your *f* out of Egypt
7: 25 From the time your *f* left Egypt
7: 26 and did more evil than their *f*.'
11: 4 the terms I commanded your *f*
11: 5 fulfill the oath I swore to your *f*,
11: 7 From the time I brought your *f* up
11: 10 returned to the sins of their *f*,
11: 10 the covenant I made with their *f*.
16: 15 them to the land I gave their *f*.
17: 22 day holy, as I commanded your *f*.
30: 3 to the land I gave their *f* to possess
31: 32 I made with their *f*
32: 22 land you had sworn to give their *f*,
34: 13 with your *f* when I brought them
Eze 36: 28 live in the land I gave your *f*;
47: 14 hand to give it to your *f*,
Da 11: 24 neither his fathers nor his *f* did.
Joel 1: 2 or in the days of your *f*?
Zec 1: 2 LORD was very angry with your *f*.
1: 4 Do not be like your *f*,
1: 5 Where are your *f* now?
1: 6 overtake your *f*? "Then they
Mal 3: 7 of your *f* you have turned away
Mt 23: 30 'If we had lived in the days of our *f*,
23: 32 the measure of the sin of your *f*!
Lk 11: 47 and it was your *f* who killed them.
11: 48 approve of what your *f* did;
Jn 6: 31 Our *f* ate the manna in the desert;
6: 49 Your *f* ate the manna in the desert,
6: 58 Our *f* ate manna and died,
Ac 7: 19 oppressed our *f* by forcing them
7: 44 "Our *f* had the tabernacle
28: 25 the truth to your *f* when he said
1Co 10: 1 that our *f* were all under the cloud
2Ti 1: 3 whom I serve, as my *f* did,
Heb 1: 1 spoke to our *f* through the prophets
8: 9 I made with their *f*
1Pe 1: 18 handed down to you from your *f*,

FOREFINGER

Lev 14: 16 dip his right *f* into the oil
14: 27 and with his right *f* sprinkle some

FOREHEAD (FOREHEADS)

Ex 13: 9 a reminder on your *f* that the law
13: 16 on your *f* that the LORD brought
28: 38 It will be on Aaron's *f* continually
28: 38 It will be on Aaron's *f*,
Lev 13: 41 front of his scalp and has a bald *f*,
13: 42 breaking out on his head or *f*.
13: 42 sore on his bald head or *f*,
13: 43 *f* is reddish-white like an infectious
1Sa 17: 49 The stone sank into his *f*,
17: 49 and struck the Philistine on the *f*.
2Ch 26: 19 leprosy broke out on his *f*.
26: 20 saw that he had leprosy on his *f*,
Isa 48: 4 your *f* was bronze.
Eze 3: 9 I will make your *f* like the hardest
Rev 13: 16 a mark on his right hand or on his *f*,
14: 9 and receives his mark on the *f*
Rev 17: 5 This title was written on her *f*:

FOREHEADS (FOREHEAD)

Nu 24: 17 He will crush the *f* of Moab,
Dt 6: 8 hands and bind them on your *f*.
11: 18 hands and bind them on your *f*.
Jer 48: 45 it burns the *f* of Moab,
Eze 9: 4 a mark on the *f* of those who grieve
Rev 7: 3 on the *f* of the servants of our God
9: 4 not have the seal of God on their *f*.
14: 1 his Father's name written on their *f*
20: 4 not received his mark on their *f*
22: 4 and his name will be on their *f*.

FOREIGN (FOREIGNER FOREIGNERS FOREIGNERS')

Ge 35: 2 "Get rid of the *f* gods you have
35: 4 gave Jacob all the *f* gods they had
Ex 2: 22 I have become an alien in a *f* land."
18: 3 I have become an alien in a *f* land";
Dt 31: 16 to the *f* gods of the land they are
32: 12 no *f* god was with him.
32: 16 made him jealous with their *f* gods
Jos 24: 20 the LORD and serve *f* gods,
24: 23 "throw away the *f* gods that are
Jdg 10: 16 rid of the *f* gods among them
1Sa 7: 3 then rid yourselves of the *f* gods
1Ki 11: 1 loved many *f* women
11: 8 He did the same for all his *f* wives,
2Ki 19: 24 I have dug wells in *f* lands
2Ch 14: 3 He removed the *f* altars
33: 15 He got rid of the *f* gods
Ezr 9: 7 humiliation at the hand of *f* kings,
10: 2 God by marrying *f* women
10: 10 you have married *f* women,
10: 11 around you and from your *f* wives
10: 14 who has married a *f* woman come
10: 17 men who had married *f* women.
10: 18 the following had married *f* women
10: 44 All these had married *f* women,
Ne 13: 3 Israel all who were of *f* descent.
13: 26 he was led into sin by *f* women.
13: 27 to our God by marrying *f* women?"
13: 30 and the Levites of everything *f*,
Ps 44: 20 or spread out our hands to a *f* god,
81: 9 You shall have no *f* god among you
114: 1 of Jacob from a people of *f* tongue,
137: 4 the LORD while in a *f* land?
Isa 28: 11 with *f* lips and strange tongues
37: 25 I have dug wells in *f* lands
43: 12 I, and not some *f* god among you.
Jer 2: 25 I love *f* gods,
3: 13 scattered your favors to *f* gods
5: 19 and served *f* gods in your own land,
8: 19 with their worthless *f* idols?"
19: 4 and made this a place of *f* gods;
25: 20 all the *f* people there; all the kings
25: 24 the kings of the *f* people who live
Eze 31: 12 the most ruthless of *f* nations cut it
Da 11: 39 fortresses with the help of a *f* god
Zep 1: 8 clad in *f* clothes.
Hag 2: 22 the power of the *f* kingdoms.
Mal 2: 11 by marrying the daughter of a *f* god
Ac 17: 18 He seems to be advocating *f* gods."
26: 11 went to *f* cities to persecute them.
Heb 11: 9 land like a stranger in a *f* country;
11: 34 in battle and routed *f* armies.

FOREIGNER (FOREIGN)

Ge 17: 12 or bought with money from a *f*—
17: 27 in his household or bought from a *f*,
Ex 12: 43 for the Passover: "No *f* is to eat
Lev 22: 25 animals from the hand of a *f*
Dt 14: 21 may eat it, or you may sell it to a *f*.
15: 3 You may require payment from a *f*,
17: 15 Do not place a *f* over you,
23: 20 You may charge a *f* interest,
Ru 2: 10 eyes that you notice me—a *f*?"
2Sa 15: 19 You are a *f*, an exile
1Ki 8: 41 "As for the *f* who does not belong
8: 43 and do whatever the *f* asks of you,
2Ch 6: 32 "As for the *f* who does not belong
6: 33 and do whatever the *f* asks of you,
Isa 56: 3 Let no *f* who has joined himself
Eze 44: 9 No *f* uncircumcised in heart
Lk 17: 18 give praise to God except this *f*?"
Ac 7: 29 where he settled as a *f*
1Co 14: 11 I am a *f* to the speaker,

1Co 14: 11 to the speaker, and he is a *f* to me.

FOREIGNERS (FOREIGN)

Ge 31: 15 Does he not regard us as *f*?
Ex 21: 8 He has no right to sell her to *f*,
Dt 29: 22 *f* who come from distant lands will
2Sa 22: 45 and *f* come cringing to me;
Ne 9: 2 separated themselves from all *f*.
Ps 18: 44 *f* cringe before me.
144: 7 from the hands of *f*
144: 11 me from the hands of *f*
Isa 1: 7 your fields are being stripped by *f*
25: 5 You silence the uproar of *f*;
56: 6 And *f* who bind themselves
60: 10 "*F* will rebuild your walls,
61: 5 *f* will work your fields
62: 8 never again will *f* drink the new
Jer 5: 19 so now you will serve *f*
30: 8 no longer will *f* enslave them.
50: 37 and all the *f* in her ranks!
51: 2 I will send *f* to Babylon
51: 51 because *f* have entered
La 5: 2 our homes to *f*.
Eze 7: 21 I will hand it all over as plunder to *f*
11: 9 over to *f* and inflict punishment
28: 7 I am going to bring *f* against you,
28: 10 at the hands of *f*.
30: 12 by the hand of *f*
44: 7 you brought *f* uncircumcised
44: 9 the *f* who live among the Israelites.
Hos 7: 9 *F* sap his strength,
8: 7 *f* would swallow it up.
Joel 3: 17 never again will *f* invade her.
Ob : 11 and *f* entered his gates
Zec 9: 6 *F* will occupy Ashdod,
Mt 27: 7 potter's field as a burial place for *f*.
Ac 17: 21 *f* who lived there spent their time
1Co 14: 21 and through the lips of *f*
Eph 2: 12 *f* to the covenants of the promise,
2: 19 you are no longer *f* and aliens,

FOREIGNERS' (FOREIGN)

Isa 25: 2 the *f* stronghold a city no more;

FOREKNEW (KNOW)

Ro 8: 29 For those God *f* he
11: 2 not reject his people, whom he *f*.

FOREKNOWLEDGE (KNOW)

Ac 2: 23 to you by God's set purpose and *f*;
1Pe 1: 2 to the *f* of God the Father,

FOREMAN (FOREMEN)

Ru 2: 5 Boaz asked the *f* of his harvesters,
2: 6 woman is that?" The *f* replied,
Mt 20: 8 owner of the vineyard said to his *f*,

FOREMEN (FOREMAN)

Ex 5: 6 and *f* in charge of the people:
5: 10 the slave drivers and the *f* went out
5: 14 The Israelite *f* appointed
5: 15 Then the Israelite *f* went
5: 19 The Israelite *f* realized they were
1Ki 5: 16 as thirty-three hundred *f* who
2Ch 2: 2 thirty-six hundred as *f* over them.
2: 18 *f* over them to keep the people

FORESAIL (SAIL)

Ac 27: 40 Then they hoisted the *f* to the wind

FORESAW (FORESEE)

Gal 3: 8 Scripture *f* that God would justify

FORESEE (FORESAW FORESIGHT)

Isa 47: 11 a catastrophe you cannot *f*

FORESIGHT (FORESEE)

Ac 24: 2 your *f* has brought about reforms

FORESKIN (FORESKINS)

Ex 4: 25 cut off her son's *f*

FORESKINS (FORESKIN)

1Sa 18: 25 bride than a hundred Philistine *f*.
18: 27 He brought their *f* and presented
2Sa 3: 14 the price of a hundred Philistine *f*."

FOREST (FORESTED FORESTS)

Dt 19: 5 go into the *f* with his neighbor
Jos 17: 15 go up into the *f* and clear land
1Sa 22: 5 and went to the *f* of Hereth
2Sa 18: 6 place in the *f* of Ephraim.
18: 8 the *f* claimed more lives that day
18: 17 threw him into a big pit in the *f*
1Ki 7: 2 He built the Palace of the *F*
10: 17 in the Palace of the *F* of Lebanon.
10: 21 articles in the Palace of the *F*
1Ch 16: 33 Then the trees of the *f* will sing,
2Ch 9: 16 in the Palace of the *F* of Lebanon.
9: 20 articles in the Palace of the *F*
Ne 2: 8 to Asaph, keeper of the king's *f*,
Ps 50: 10 for every animal of the *f* is mine,
80: 13 Boars from the *f* ravage it
83: 14 As fire consumes the *f*
96: 12 all the trees of the *f* will sing for joy
104: 20 and all the beasts of the *f* prowl.
SS 2: 3 among the trees of the *f*
Isa 7: 2 as the trees of the *f* are shaken
9: 18 it sets the *f* thickets ablaze,
10: 34 down the *f* thickets with an ax;
22: 8 the weapons in the Palace of the *F*;
29: 17 and the fertile field seem like a *f*?
32: 15 and the fertile field seems like a *f*.
32: 19 Though hail flattens the *f*
44: 14 grow among the trees of the *f*,
56: 9 and devour, all you beasts of the *f*!
Jer 5: 6 a lion from the *f* will attack them,
10: 3 they cut a tree out of the *f*,
12: 8 like a lion in the *f*.
46: 23 They will chop down her *f*,"
Eze 15: 2 branch on any of the trees in the *f*?
15: 6 of the vine among the trees of the *f*
20: 46 and prophesy against the *f*
20: 47 to the southern *f*: 'Hear the word
31: 3 branches overshadowing the *f*;
Mic 5: 8 like a lion among the beasts of the *f*
7: 14 which lives by itself in a *f*,
Zec 11: 2 the dense *f* has been cut down!
Jas 3: 5 Consider what a great *f* is set

FORESTED (FOREST)

Jos 17: 18 but the *f* hill country as well.

FORESTS (FOREST)

2Ki 19: 23 the finest of its *f*.
Ps 29: 9 and strips the *f* bare.
Isa 10: 18 splendor of his *f* and fertile fields
10: 19 of his *f* will be so few
37: 24 the finest of its *f*.
44: 23 you *f* and all your trees,
Jer 21: 14 I will kindle a fire in your *f*
Eze 34: 25 and sleep in the *f* in safety.
39: 10 from the fields or cut it from the *f*,

FORETELL (FORETELLS FORETOLD)

Isa 44: 7 yes, let him *f* what will come.
44: 8 not proclaim this and *f* it long ago?

FORETELLS (FORETELL)

Dt 13: 1 If a prophet, or one who *f*

FORETOLD (FORETELL)

2Ki 7: 17 of God had *f* when the king came
23: 16 the man of God who *f* these things.
Ps 105: 19 till what he *f* came to pass,
Isa 41: 26 no one *f* it,
43: 9 Which of them *f* this
45: 21 Who *f* this long ago,
48: 3 I *f* the former things long ago,
48: 14 of [the idols] has *f* these things?
52: 6 that it is I who *f* it.
Ac 3: 18 is how God fulfilled what he had *f*
3: 24 as have spoken, have *f* these days.
Jude : 17 apostles of our Lord Jesus Christ *f*.

FOREVER (EVER)

Ge 3: 22 the tree of life and eat, and live *f*."
6: 3 Spirit will not contend with man *f*,
13: 15 give to you and your offspring *f*.
Ex 3: 15 This is my name *f*, the name
31: 17 between me and the Israelites *f*,
32: 13 and it will be their inheritance *f*.'"
Dt 5: 29 with them and their children *f*!
13: 16 is to remain a ruin *f*, never
28: 46 to you and your descendants *f*.
29: 29 belong to us and to our children *f*,
32: 40 As surely as I live *f*,
Jos 4: 7 memorial to the people of Israel *f*."
14: 9 and that of your children *f*,
1Sa 2: 30 house would minister before me *f*.'
3: 13 him that I would judge his family *f*
20: 23 witness between you and me *f*."
20: 42 and my descendants *f*.'"
27: 12 that he will be my servant *f*."
2Sa 2: 26 "Must the sword devour *f*?
3: 28 and my kingdom are *f* innocent
7: 13 the throne of his kingdom *f*.
7: 16 and your kingdom will endure *f*
7: 16 your throne will be established *f*.'"
7: 24 people Israel as your very own *f*,
7: 25 keep *f* the promise you have made
7: 26 so that your name will be great *f*.
7: 29 of your servant will be blessed *f*."
7: 29 that it may continue *f* in your sight;
22: 51 to David and his descendants *f*."
1Ki 1: 31 "May my lord King David live *f*!"
2: 33 head of Joab and his descendants *f*.
2: 33 may there be the LORD's peace *f*."
2: 45 secure before the LORD *f*."
8: 13 a place for you to dwell *f*."
9: 3 by putting my Name there *f*.
9: 5 your royal throne over Israel *f*,
11: 39 because of this, but not *f*.'"
2Ki 5: 27 and to your descendants *f*."
8: 19 for David and his descendants *f*.
21: 7 of Israel, I will put my Name *f*.
1Ch 15: 2 and to minister before him *f*."
16: 15 He remembers his covenant *f*,
16: 34 his love endures *f*.
16: 41 "for his love endures *f*."
17: 12 and I will establish his throne *f*.
17: 14 his throne will be established *f*.'"
17: 14 over my house and my kingdom *f*;
17: 22 your people Israel your very own *f*,
17: 23 and his house be established *f*.
17: 24 and that your name will be great *f*.
17: 27 blessed it, and it will be blessed *f*."
17: 27 that it may continue *f* in your sight;
22: 10 of his kingdom over Israel *f*.'
23: 13 and his descendants *f*,
23: 13 pronounce blessings in his name *f*.
23: 25 has come to dwell in Jerusalem *f*,
28: 4 family to be king over Israel *f*.
28: 7 I will establish his kingdom *f*
28: 8 inheritance to your descendants *f*.
28: 9 forsake him, he will reject you *f*.
29: 18 in the hearts of your people *f*,
2Ch 5: 13 his love endures *f*."
6: 2 a place for you to dwell *f*."
7: 3 his love endures *f*."
7: 6 saying, "His love endures *f*."
7: 16 so that my Name may be there *f*.
9: 8 and his desire to uphold them *f*,
13: 5 his descendants *f* by a covenant
20: 7 and give it *f* to the descendants
20: 21 for his love endures *f*."
21: 7 for David and his descendants *f*.
30: 8 which he has consecrated *f*.
33: 4 Name will remain in Jerusalem *f*."
33: 7 of Israel, I will put my Name *f*.
Ezr 3: 11 his love to Israel endures *f*."
Ne 2: 3 to the king, "May the king live *f*!
Job 4: 20 unnoticed, they perish *f*.
7: 16 I despise my life; I would not live *f*.
19: 24 or engraved in rock *f*!
20: 7 he will perish *f*, like his own dung;
23: 7 I would be delivered *f*
36: 7 and exalts them *f*.
Ps 9: 7 The LORD reigns *f*;
12: 7 and protect us from such people *f*.
13: 1 O LORD? Will you forget me *f*?
18: 50 to David and his descendants *f*.
19: 9 enduring *f*.
22: 26 may your hearts live *f*!
23: 6 dwell in the house of the LORD *f*.
28: 9 be their shepherd and carry them *f*.
29: 10 the LORD is enthroned as King *f*.
30: 12 my God, I will give you thanks *f*.
33: 11 the plans of the LORD stand firm *f*
37: 18 and their inheritance will endure *f*.
37: 28 They will be protected *f*,
37: 29 and dwell in it *f*.
41: 12 and set me in your presence *f*.

Ps 44: 8 and we will praise your name *f.*
44: 23 Rouse yourself! Do not reject us *f.*
45: 2 since God has blessed you *f.*
48: 8 God makes her secure *f.*
49: 9 that he should live on *f*
49: 11 tombs will remain their houses *f,*
52: 9 I will praise you *f* for what you
55: 19 God, who is enthroned *f,*
61: 4 I long to dwell in your tent *f*
61: 7 in God's presence *f;*
66: 7 He rules *f* by his power,
68: 16 the LORD himself will dwell *f?*
69: 23 and their backs be bent *f.*
72: 17 May his name endure *f;*
72: 19 Praise be to his glorious name *f;*
73: 26 and my portion *f.*
74: 1 Why have you rejected us *f,* O God
74: 10 Will the foe revile your name *f?*
74: 19 of your afflicted people *f.*
75: 9 As for me, I will declare this *f;*
77: 7 "Will the Lord reject us *f?*
77: 8 Has his unfailing love vanished *f?*
78: 69 like the earth that he established *f.*
79: 5 O LORD? Will you be angry *f?*
79: 13 will praise you *f;*
81: 15 and their punishment would last *f.*
85: 5 Will you be angry with us *f?*
86: 12 I will glorify your name *f.*
89: 1 of the LORD's great love *f;*
89: 2 that your love stands firm *f,*
89: 4 'I will establish your line *f*
89: 28 I will maintain my love to him *f,*
89: 29 I will establish his line *f,*
89: 36 that his line will continue *f*
89: 37 will be established *f* like the moon,
89: 46 O LORD? Will you hide yourself *f*
89: 52 Praise be to the LORD *f!* Amen
92: 7 they will be *f* destroyed.
92: 8 But you, O LORD, are exalted *f.*
100: 5 is good and his love endures *f;*
102: 12 But you, O LORD, sit enthroned *f;*
103: 9 nor will he harbor his anger *f;*
104: 31 of the LORD endure *f;*
105: 8 He remembers his covenant *f,*
106: 1 his love endures *f.*
107: 1 his love endures *f.*
109: 19 like a belt tied *f* around him.
110: 4 "You are a priest *f,*
111: 3 and his righteousness endures *f.*
111: 5 he remembers his covenant *f.*
111: 9 he ordained his covenant *f*—
112: 3 and his righteousness endures *f.*
112: 6 man will be remembered *f.*
112: 9 his righteousness endures *f;*
117: 2 of the LORD endures *f.*
118: 1 his love endures *f.*
118: 2 "His love endures *f.*"
118: 3 "His love endures *f.*"
118: 4 "His love endures *f.*"
118: 29 his love endures *f.*
119:111 Your statutes are my heritage *f;*
119:144 Your statutes are *f* right;
119:152 that you established them to last *f.*
125: 1 cannot be shaken but endures *f.*
135: 13 Your name, O LORD, endures *f,*
136: 1 *His love endures f.*
136: 2 *His love endures f.*
136: 3 *His love endures f.*
136: 4 *His love endures f.*
136: 5 *His love endures f.*
136: 6 *His love endures f.*
136: 7 *His love endures f.*
136: 8 *His love endures f.*
136: 9 *His love endures f.*
136: 10 *His love endures f.*
136: 11 *His love endures f.*
136: 12 *His love endures f.*
136: 13 *His love endures f.*
136: 14 *His love endures f.*
136: 15 *His love endures f.*
136: 16 *His love endures f.*
136: 17 *His love endures f.*
136: 18 *His love endures f.*
136: 19 *His love endures f.*
136: 20 *His love endures f.*
136: 21 *His love endures f.*
136: 22 *His love endures f.*
136: 23 *His love endures f.*
Ps 136: 24 *His love endures f.*
136: 25 *His love endures f.*
136: 26 *His love endures f.*
138: 8 your love, O LORD, endures *f*—
146: 6 the LORD, who remains faithful *f.*
146: 10 The LORD reigns *f,*
Pr 6: 21 Bind them upon your heart *f;*
10: 25 but the righteous stand firm *f.*
12: 19 Truthful lips endure *f,*
21: 28 listens to him will be destroyed *f.*
27: 24 for riches do not endure *f,*
Ecc 1: 4 but the earth remains *f.*
3: 14 everything God does will endure *f;*
Isa 9: 7 from that time on and *f.*
25: 8 he will swallow up death *f.*
26: 4 Trust in the LORD *f,*
28: 28 so one does not go on threshing it *f.*
32: 14 will become a wasteland *f,*
32: 17 will be quietness and confidence *f.*
34: 10 its smoke will rise *f.*
34: 17 They will possess it *f*
40: 8 but the word of our God stands *f.*"
47: 7 You said, 'I will continue *f*—
51: 6 But my salvation will last *f,*
51: 8 But my righteousness will last *f,*
57: 15 he who lives *f,* whose name is holy:
57: 16 I will not accuse *f,*
59: 21 from this time on and *f,*"
60: 21 and they will possess the land *f.*
64: 9 do not remember our sins *f.*
65: 18 But be glad and rejoice *f*
Jer 3: 5 Will your wrath continue *f?*'
3: 12 'I will not be angry *f.*
17: 4 and it will burn *f.*"
17: 25 and this city will be inhabited *f.*
20: 17 her womb enlarged *f.*
25: 12 "and will make it desolate *f.*
33: 11 his love endures *f.*"
49: 13 and all its towns will be in ruins *f.*"
49: 33 a desolate place *f.*
51: 26 for you will be desolate *f,*"
51: 39 then sleep *f* and not awake,"
51: 57 they will sleep *f* and not awake,"
51: 62 live in it; it will be desolate *f.*'
La 3: 31 by the Lord *f.*
5: 19 You, O LORD, reign *f;*
Eze 35: 9 I will make you desolate *f;*
37: 25 children's children will live there *f,*
37: 25 my servant will be their prince *f.*
37: 26 put my sanctuary among them *f.*
37: 28 my sanctuary is among them *f.*' "
43: 7 live among the Israelites *f.*
43: 9 and I will live among them *f.*
Da 2: 4 live *f!* Tell your servants the dream
2: 44 to an end, but it will itself endure *f.*
3: 9 live *f!* You have issued a decree,
4: 34 and glorified him who lives *f.*
5: 10 "O king, live *f!*" she said.
6: 6 live *f!* The royal administrators,
6: 21 Daniel answered, "O king, live *f!*
6: 26 and he endures *f;*
7: 18 the kingdom and will possess it *f*—
7: 26 and completely destroyed *f.*
12: 7 swear by him who lives *f,*
Hos 2: 19 I will betroth you to me *f;*
Joel 3: 20 Judah will be inhabited *f*
Ob : 10 you will be destroyed *f.*
Jnh 2: 6 the earth beneath barred me in *f.*
Mic 2: 9 blessing from their children *f.*
4: 7 Zion from that day and *f.*
7: 18 You do not stay angry *f*
Zep 2: 9 a wasteland *f.*
Zec 1: 5 And the prophets, do they live *f?*
Lk 1: 33 reign over the house of Jacob *f;*
1: 55 to Abraham and his descendants *f,*
Jn 6: 51 eats of this bread, he will live *f.*
6: 58 feeds on this bread will live *f.*"
8: 35 the family, but a son belongs to it *f.*
12: 34 Law that the Christ will remain *f,*
14: 16 Counselor to be with you *f*—
Ro 1: 25 than the Creator—who is *f* praised
9: 5 who is God over all, *f* praised!
11: 10 and their backs be bent *f.*"
11: 36 To him be the glory *f!* Amen.
16: 27 to the only wise God be glory *f*
1Co 9: 25 it to get a crown that will last *f.*
2Co 9: 9 his righteousness endures *f.*"
11: 31 to be praised *f,* knows that I am not
1Th 4: 17 And so we will be with the Lord *f.*
1Ti 6: 16 To him be honor and might *f.*
Heb 5: 6 "You are a priest *f,*
6: 20 He has become a high priest *f,*
7: 3 Son of God he remains a priest *f.*
7: 17 "You are a priest *f,*
7: 21 'You are a priest *f.*' "
7: 24 Jesus lives *f,* he has a permanent
7: 28 who has been made perfect *f.*
10: 14 has made perfect *f* those who are
13: 8 same yesterday and today and *f.*
1Pe 1: 25 but the word of the Lord stands *f.*"
2Pe 3: 18 To him be glory both now and *f!*
1Jn 2: 17 who does the will of God lives *f.*
2Jn : 2 lives in us and will be with us *f:*
Jude : 13 darkness has been reserved *f.*

FOREVERMORE (EVER)

Ps 113: 2 both now and *f.*
115: 18 both now and *f.*
121: 8 both now and *f.*
125: 2 both now and *f.*
131: 3 both now and *f.*
133: 3 even life *f.*
Jude : 25 before all ages, now and *f!* Amen.

FORFEIT (FORFEITING FORFEITS)

Ezr 10: 8 three days would *f* all his property,
Jnh 2: 8 *f* the grace that could be theirs.
Mk 8: 36 the whole world, yet *f* his soul?
Lk 9: 25 and yet lose or *f* his very self?

FORFEITING (FORFEIT)

Hab 2: 10 your own house and *f* your life.

FORFEITS (FORFEIT)

Pr 20: 2 he who angers him *f* his life.
Mt 16: 26 yet *f* his soul? Or what can a man

FORGAVE (FORGIVE)

Ps 32: 5 and you *f*
85: 2 You *f* the iniquity of your people
Eph 4: 32 just as in Christ God *f* you.
Col 2: 13 He *f* us all our sins, having
3: 13 Forgive as the Lord *f* you.

FORGED (FORGES)

Ge 4: 22 who *f* all kinds of tools out
Isa 54: 17 no weapon *f* against you will

FORGES (FORGED)

Isa 44: 12 he *f* it with the might of his arm.
54: 16 and *f* a weapon fit for its work.

FORGET (FORGETS FORGETTING FORGOT FORGOTTEN)

Ge 41: 51 God has made me *f* all my trouble
Dt 4: 9 that you do not *f* the things your
4: 23 Be careful not to *f* the covenant
4: 31 or *f* the covenant with your
6: 12 that you do not *f* the LORD,
8: 11 that you do not *f* the LORD your
8: 14 you will *f* the LORD your God,
8: 19 If you ever *f* the LORD your God
9: 7 and never *f* how you provoked
25: 19 Do not *f!* When you have entered
1Sa 1: 11 and not *f* your servant
2Ki 17: 38 Do not *f* the covenant I have made
Job 8: 13 Such is the destiny of all who *f* God
9: 27 If I say, 'I will *f* my complaint,
11: 16 You will surely *f* your trouble,
Ps 9: 17 all the nations that *f* God.
10: 12 Do not *f* the helpless.
13: 1 O LORD? Will you *f* me forever?
44: 24 and *f* our misery and oppression?
45: 10 *F* your people and your father's
50: 22 "Consider this, you who *f* God,
59: 11 or my people will *f.*
74: 19 do not *f* the lives of your afflicted
78: 7 and would not *f* his deeds
102: 4 I *f* to eat my food.
103: 2 and *f* not all his benefits.
119: 61 I will not *f* your law.
119: 83 I do not *f* your decrees.
119: 93 I will never *f* your precepts,
119:109 I will not *f* your law.
119:141 I do not *f* your precepts.
137: 5 If I *f* you, O Jerusalem,

Ps 137: 5 may my right hand *f* ⌊its skill⌋.
Pr 3: 1 My son, do not *f* my teaching,
4: 5 do not *f* my words or swerve
31: 5 and *f* what the law decrees,
31: 7 let them drink and *f* their poverty
Isa 43: 18 "*F* the former things;
44: 21 O Israel, I will not *f* you.
49: 15 I will not *f* you!
49: 15 Though she may *f*,
49: 15 "Can a mother *f* the baby
51: 13 that you *f* the LORD your Maker,
54: 4 You will *f* the shame of your youth
65: 11 and *f* my holy mountain,
Jer 2: 32 Does a maiden *f* her jewelry,
23: 27 will make my people *f* my name,
23: 39 I will surely *f* you and cast you out
La 2: 6 The LORD has made Zion *f*
5: 20 Why do you always *f* us?
Eze 39: 26 They will *f* their shame
Am 8: 7 "I will never *f* anything they have
Mic 6: 10 Am I still to *f*, O wicked house,
Heb 6: 10 he will not *f* your work
13: 2 Do not *f* to entertain strangers,
13: 16 And do not *f* to do good
2Pe 3: 5 they deliberately *f* that long ago
3: 8 But do not *f* this one thing,

FORGETS (FORGET)

Ge 27: 45 and *f* what you did to him,
Job 24: 20 The womb *f* them,
Jn 16: 21 her baby is born she *f* the anguish
Jas 1: 24 immediately *f* what he looks like.

FORGETTING (FORGET)

Php 3: 13 *F* what is behind and straining
Jas 1: 25 to do this, not *f* what he has heard,

FORGIVE (FORGAVE FORGIVEN FORGIVENESS FORGIVES FORGIVING)

Ge 50: 17 I ask you to *f* your brothers the sins
50: 17 please *f* the sins of the servants
Ex 10: 17 Now *f* my sin once more
23: 21 he will not *f* your rebellion,
32: 32 But now, please *f* their sin—
34: 9 *f* our wickedness and our sin,
Nu 14: 19 with your great love, *f* the sin
Dt 29: 20 will never be willing to *f* him;
Jos 24: 19 He will not *f* your rebellion
1Sa 15: 25 *f* my sin and come back with me,
25: 28 Please *f* your servant's offense,
1Ki 8: 30 place, and when you hear, *f*.
8: 34 and *f* the sin of your people Israel
8: 36 and *f* the sin of your servants,
8: 39 *F* and act; deal with each man
8: 50 *f* all the offenses they have
8: 50 *f* your people, who have sinned
2Ki 5: 18 But may the LORD *f* your servant
5: 18 may the LORD *f* your servant
24: 4 and the LORD was not willing to *f*.
2Ch 6: 21 place; and when you hear, *f*.
6: 25 and *f* the sin of your people Israel
6: 27 and *f* the sin of your servants,
6: 30 *F*, and deal with each man
6: 39 *f* your people, who have sinned
7: 14 will *f* their sin and will heal their
Job 7: 21 and *f* my sins?
Ps 19: 12 *F* my hidden faults.
25: 11 *f* my iniquity, though it is great.
Isa 2: 9 do not *f* them.
Jer 5: 1 I will *f* this city.
5: 7 "Why should I *f* you?
18: 23 Do not *f* their crimes
31: 34 "For I will *f* their wickedness
33: 8 and will *f* all their sins of rebellion
36: 3 then I will *f* their wickedness
50: 20 for I will *f* the remnant I spare.
Da 9: 19 O Lord, listen! O Lord, *f*! O Lord,
Hos 1: 6 that I should at all *f* them.
14: 2 "*F* all our sins
Am 7: 2 *f*! How can Jacob survive?
Mt 6: 12 *F* us our debts,
6: 14 For if you *f* men when they sin
6: 14 heavenly Father will also *f* you.
6: 15 But if you do not *f* men their sins,
6: 15 your Father will not *f* your sins.
9: 6 authority on earth to *f* sins..
18: 21 many times shall I *f* my brother
18: 35 you *f* your brother from your heart
Mk 2: 7 Who can *f* sins but God alone?"
2: 10 authority on earth to *f* sins
11: 25 anything against anyone, *f* him,
11: 25 in heaven may *f* you your sins."
Lk 5: 21 Who can *f* sins but God alone?"
5: 24 authority on earth to *f* sins..
6: 37 *F*, and you will be forgiven.
11: 4 *F* us our sins,
11: 4 *f* everyone who sins against us.
17: 3 rebuke him, and if he repents, *f* him
17: 4 and says, 'I repent,' *f* him."
23: 34 Jesus said, "Father, *f* them,
Jn 20: 23 If you *f* anyone his sins, they are
20: 23 if you do not *f* them, they are not
Ac 8: 22 Perhaps he will *f* you
2Co 2: 7 you ought to *f* and comfort him,
2: 10 If you *f* anyone, I also *f* him.
2: 10 if there was anything to *f*—
12: 13 a burden to you? *F* me this wrong!
Col 3: 13 and *f* whatever grievances you may
3: 13 *F* as the Lord forgave you.
Heb 8: 12 For I will *f* their wickedness
1Jn 1: 9 and just and will *f* us our sins

FORGIVEN (FORGIVE)

Lev 4: 20 for them, and they will be *f*.
4: 26 for the man's sin, and he will be *f*.
4: 31 atonement for him, and he will be *f*.
4: 35 he has committed, and he will be *f*.
5: 10 he has committed, and he will be *f*.
5: 13 he has committed, and he will be *f*.
5: 16 as a guilt offering, and he will be *f*.
5: 18 unintentionally, and he will be *f*.
6: 7 and he will be *f* for any
19: 22 committed, and his sin will be *f*.
Nu 14: 20 "I have *f* them, as you asked.
15: 25 community, and they will be *f*,
15: 26 living among them will be *f*,
15: 28 made for him, he will be *f*.
Ps 32: 1 whose transgressions are *f*,
Isa 33: 24 of those who dwell there will be *f*.
La 3: 42 and you have not *f*.
Mt 6: 12 as we also have *f* our debtors.
9: 2 "Take heart, son; your sins are *f*."
9: 5 to say, 'Your sins are *f*,' or to say,
12: 31 against the Spirit will not be *f*.
12: 31 and blasphemy will be *f* men,
12: 32 against the Holy Spirit will not be *f*,
12: 32 against the Son of Man will be *f*,
Mk 2: 5 paralytic, "Son, your sins are *f*."
2: 9 'Your sins are *f*,' or to say, 'Get up,
3: 28 blasphemies of men will be *f* them.
3: 29 the Holy Spirit will never be *f*;
4: 12 otherwise they might turn and be *f*
Lk 5: 20 he said, "Friend, your sins are *f*."
5: 23 to say, 'Your sins are *f*,' or to say,
6: 37 Forgive, and you will be *f*.
7: 47 he who has been *f* little loves little
7: 47 her many sins have been *f*—
7: 48 Jesus said to her, "Your sins are *f*."
12: 10 against the Holy Spirit will not be *f*.
12: 10 against the Son of Man will be *f*,
Jn 20: 23 not forgive them, they are not *f*."
20: 23 they are *f*; if you do not forgive
Ac 2: 38 Christ so that your sins may be *f*.
Ro 4: 7 whose transgressions are *f*,
2Co 2: 10 And what I have *f*— if there was
2: 10 I have *f* in the sight of Christ
Heb 10: 18 And where these have been *f*,
Jas 5: 15 If he has sinned, he will be *f*.
1Jn 2: 12 your sins have been *f* on account

FORGIVENESS (FORGIVE)

Ps 130: 4 But with you there is *f*;
Mt 26: 28 out for many for the *f* of sins.
Mk 1: 4 of repentance for the *f* of sins.
Lk 1: 77 salvation through the *f* of their sins,
3: 3 of repentance for the *f* of sins.
24: 47 and *f* of sins will be preached
Ac 5: 31 that he might give repentance and *f*
10: 43 believes in him receives *f* of sins
13: 38 that through Jesus the *f*
26: 18 so that they may receive *f* of sins
Eph 1: 7 through his blood, the *f* of sins,
Col 1: 14 in whom we have redemption, the *f*
Heb 9: 22 the shedding of blood there is no *f*.

FORGIVES (FORGIVE)

Ps 103: 3 He *f* all my sins
Mic 7: 18 pardons sin and *f* the transgression
Lk 7: 49 "Who is this who even *f* sins?"

FORGIVING (FORGIVE)

Ex 34: 7 and *f* wickedness, rebellion and sin.
Nu 14: 18 abounding in love and *f* sin
Ne 9: 17 But you are a *f* God, gracious
Ps 86: 5 You are kind and *f*, O Lord,
99: 8 you were to Israel a *f* God,
Da 9: 9 The Lord our God is merciful and *f*
Eph 4: 32 to one another, *f* each other,

FORGO

Ne 10: 31 year we will *f* working the land

FORGOT (FORGET)

Ge 40: 23 did not remember Joseph; he *f* him.
Dt 32: 18 you *f* the God who gave you birth.
Jdg 3: 7 they *f* the LORD their God
1Sa 12: 9 "But they *f* the LORD their God;
Ps 78: 11 They *f* what he had done,
106: 13 But they soon *f* what he had done
106: 21 They *f* the God who saved them,
Jer 23: 27 as their fathers *f* my name
50: 6 and *f* their own resting place.
Hos 2: 13 but me she *f*,"
13: 6 then they *f* me.
Mt 16: 5 the disciples *f* to take bread.

FORGOTTEN (FORGET)

Ge 41: 30 all the abundance in Egypt will be *f*
Dt 26: 13 your commands nor have I *f* any
31: 21 it will not be *f* by their descendants
Job 11: 6 God has even *f* some of your sin.
19: 14 my friends have *f* me.
28: 4 in places *f* by the foot of man;
Ps 9: 18 But the needy will not always be *f*,
10: 11 He says to himself, "God has *f*;
31: 12 I am *f* by them as though I were
42: 9 "Why have you *f* me?
44: 17 though we had not *f* you
44: 20 If we had *f* the name of our God
77: 9 Has God *f* to be merciful?
119: 153 for I have not *f* your law.
119: 176 I have not *f* your commandments.
Ecc 2: 16 in days to come both will be *f*.
9: 5 and even the memory of them is *f*.
Isa 17: 10 You have *f* God your Savior;
23: 15 At that time Tyre will be *f*
23: 16 O prostitute *f*;
49: 14 the Lord has *f* me."
65: 16 For the past troubles will be *f*
Jer 2: 32 Yet my people have *f* me,
3: 21 and have *f* the LORD their God.
13: 25 "because you have *f* me
18: 15 Yet my people have *f* me;
20: 11 their dishonor will never be *f*.
23: 40 everlasting shame that will not be *f*
30: 14 All your allies have *f* you;
44: 9 Have you *f* the wickedness
50: 5 that will not be *f*.
La 3: 17 I have *f* what prosperity is.
Eze 22: 12 And you have *f* me, declares
23: 35 Since you have *f* me and thrust me
Hos 8: 14 Israel has *f* his Maker
Mk 8: 14 The disciples had *f* to bring bread,
Lk 12: 6 Yet not one of them is *f* by God.
Heb 12: 5 And you have *f* that word
2Pe 1: 9 and has *f* that he has been cleansed

FORK (FORKS)

1Sa 2: 13 with a three-pronged *f* in his hand.
2: 14 himself whatever the *f* brought up.
Isa 30: 24 spread out with *f* and shovel.
Jer 15: 7 with a winnowing *f*
Eze 21: 21 stop at the *f* in the road,
Mt 3: 12 His winnowing *f* is in his hand,
Lk 3: 17 His winnowing *f* is in his hand

FORKS (FORK)

Ex 27: 3 sprinkling bowls, meat *f*
38: 3 sprinkling bowls, meat *f*
Nu 4: 14 including the firepans, meat *f*,
1Sa 13: 21 a third of a shekel for sharpening *f*
1Ch 28: 17 the weight of pure gold for the *f*,
2Ch 4: 16 meat *f* and all related articles.

FORLORN

Ps 35: 12 and leave my soul *f*.

FORM (FORMATION FORMED FORMING FORMS)

Ge 29: 17 but Rachel was lovely in *f*,
Ex 20: 4 idol in the *f* of anything in heaven
Nu 12: 8 he sees the *f* of the LORD.
Dt 4: 12 the sound of words but saw no *f*;
4: 15 You saw no *f* of any kind the day
4: 23 make for yourselves an idol in the *f*
5: 8 idol in the *f* of anything in heaven
1Ki 6: 16 boards from floor to ceiling to *f*
Est 2: 7 was lovely in *f* and features,
Job 4: 16 A *f* stood before my eyes,
31: 15 Did not the same one *f* us both
41: 12 his strength and his graceful *f*.
Ps 83: 5 they *f* an alliance against you—
Isa 44: 13 He shapes it in the *f* of man,
45: 7 I *f* the light and create darkness,
52: 14 *f* marred beyond human likeness—
Jer 11: 16 with fruit beautiful in *f*.
Eze 1: 5 In appearance their *f* was that
Mk 16: 12 in a different *f* to two of them
Lk 3: 22 on him in bodily *f* like a dove.
Jn 5: 37 heard his voice nor seen his *f*,
Ac 7: 41 the time they made an idol in the *f*
14: 11 come down to us in human *f*!"
Ro 6: 17 you wholeheartedly obeyed the *f*
12: 5 we who are many *f* one body,
1Co 7: 31 in its present *f* is passing away.
12: 12 its parts are many, they *f* one body.
Eph 4: 31 along with every *f* of malice.
Col 2: 9 of the Deity lives in bodily *f*,
2Ti 3: 5 having a *f* of godliness

FORMATION (FORM)

2Sa 10: 8 drew up in battle *f* at the entrance
1Ch 19: 9 drew up in battle *f* at the entrance
Jer 6: 23 they come like men in battle *f*
50: 42 they come like men in battle *f*

FORMED (FORM)

Ge 2: 7 And the LORD God *f* man
2: 8 and there he put the man he had *f*.
2: 19 Now the LORD God had *f* out
Dt 4: 16 whether *f* like a man or a woman,
32: 6 who made you and *f* you?
Jos 18: 20 The Jordan *f* the boundary
2Sa 2: 25 They *f* themselves into a group
10: 17 The Arameans *f* their battle lines
1Ch 19: 17 David *f* his lines to meet
19: 17 and *f* his battle lines opposite them.
Job 1: 17 Chaldeans *f* three raiding parties
Ps 65: 6 who *f* the mountains
94: 9 Does he who *f* the eye not see?
95: 5 and his hands *f* the dry land.
103: 14 for he knows how we are *f*,
104: 26 which you *f* to frolic there.
119: 73 Your hands made me and *f* me;
Ecc 11: 5 or how the body is *f* in a mother's
Isa 29: 16 Shall what is *f* say to him who *f* it,
43: 1 he who *f* you, O Israel:
43: 7 whom I *f* and made."
43: 10 Before me no god was *f*,
43: 21 the people I *f* for myself
44: 2 he who made you, who *f* you
44: 24 your Redeemer, who *f* you
45: 18 but *f* it to be inhabited—
49: 5 he who *f* me in the womb
Jer 1: 5 "Before I *f* you in the womb I knew
18: 4 so the potter *f* it into another pot,
33: 2 the LORD who *f* it and established
Eze 16: 7 Your breasts were *f* and your hair
45: 7 of the area *f* by the sacred district
48: 21 of the area *f* by the sacred portion
Mt 13: 26 the wheat sprouted and *f* heads,
Ac 17: 5 *f* a mob and started a riot in the city
23: 12 morning the Jews *f* a conspiracy
Ro 9: 20 "Shall what is *f* say to him who *f* it,
Gal 4: 19 of childbirth until Christ is *f* in you,
1Ti 2: 13 For Adam was *f* first, then Eve.
Heb 11: 3 understand that the universe was *f*
2Pe 3: 5 and the earth was *f* out of water

FORMING (FORM)

Isa 30: 1 *f* an alliance, but not by my Spirit,
Eze 41: 8 *f* the foundation of the side rooms.
Zec 14: 4 from east to west, *f* a great valley,

FORMLESS

Ge 1: 2 Now the earth was *f* and empty,
Jer 4: 23 and it was *f* and empty;

FORMS (FORM)

Ge 41: 32 in two *f* is that the matter has been
Lev 26: 30 on the lifeless *f* of your idols,
Ps 33: 15 he who *f* the hearts of all,
49: 14 their *f* will decay in the grave,
SS 2: 13 The fig tree *f* its early fruit;
Jer 16: 18 land with the lifeless *f* of their vile
Am 4: 13 He who *f* the mountains,
Zec 12: 1 who *f* the spirit of man within him,
1Pe 4: 10 God's grace in its various *f*.

FORMULA

Ex 30: 32 do not make any oil with the same *f*
30: 37 incense with this *f* for yourselves;

FORSAKE (FORSAKEN FORSAKES FORSAKING FORSOOK)

Dt 31: 6 he will never leave you nor *f* you."
31: 8 he will never leave you nor *f* you.
31: 16 They will *f* me and break
31: 17 angry with them and *f* them;
Jos 1: 5 I will never leave you or *f* you.
24: 16 "Far be it from us to *f* the LORD
24: 20 If you *f* the LORD and serve
1Ki 8: 57 may he never leave or *f* us.
2Ki 21: 14 I will *f* the remnant
1Ch 28: 9 but if you *f* him, he will reject you
28: 20 or *f* you until all the work
2Ch 7: 19 if you turn away and *f* the decrees
15: 2 but if you *f* him, he will *f* you.
Ezr 8: 22 is against all who *f* him."
Ps 27: 9 Do not reject me or *f* me,
27: 10 Though my father and mother *f* me
37: 28 and will not *f* his faithful ones.
38: 21 O LORD, do not *f* me;
71: 9 do not *f* me when my strength is
71: 18 do not *f* me, O God,
89: 30 "If his sons *f* my law
94: 14 he will never *f* his inheritance.
119: 8 do not utterly *f* me.
Pr 1: 8 do not *f* your mother's teaching.
4: 2 so do not *f* my teaching.
4: 6 Do not *f* wisdom, and she will
6: 20 do not *f* your mother's teaching.
27: 10 Do not *f* your friend and the friend
28: 4 Those who *f* the law praise
Isa 1: 28 those who *f* the LORD will perish.
41: 17 I, the God of Israel, will not *f* them.
42: 16 I will not *f* them.
55: 7 Let the wicked *f* his way
65: 11 "But as for you who *f* the LORD
Jer 2: 19 when you *f* the LORD your God
12: 7 "I will *f* my house,
14: 9 do not *f* us!
17: 13 all who *f* you will be put to shame.
23: 33 'What oracle? I will *f* you,
La 5: 20 Why do you *f* us so long?
Eze 20: 8 nor did they *f* the idols of Egypt.
Da 11: 30 to those who *f* the holy covenant.
Heb 13: 5 never will I *f* you."

FORSAKEN (FORSAKE)

Jdg 10: 13 But you have *f* me and served other
1Sa 12: 10 we have *f* the LORD and served
1Ki 9: 9 'Because they have *f* the LORD
11: 33 will do this because they have *f* me
2Ki 22: 17 Because they have *f* me
2Ch 7: 22 'Because they have *f* the LORD,
13: 10 is our God, and we have not *f* him.
13: 11 But you have *f* him.
21: 10 because Jehoram had *f* the LORD,
24: 20 Because you have *f* the LORD,
24: 20 the LORD, he has *f* you.' "
24: 24 Because Judah had *f* the LORD,
28: 6 because Judah had *f* the LORD,
34: 25 Because they have *f* me
Ps 9: 10 have never *f* those who seek you.
22: 1 my God, why have you *f* me?
37: 25 I have never seen the righteous *f*
71: 11 They say, "God has *f* him;
119: 53 who have *f* your law.
119: 87 but I have not *f* your precepts.
Isa 1: 4 They have *f* the LORD;
6: 12 and the land is utterly *f*.
27: 10 an abandoned settlement, *f* like
49: 14 Zion said, "The LORD has *f* me,
58: 2 has not *f* the commands of its God.
60: 15 "Although you have been *f*
Jer 2: 13 They have *f* me,
5: 7 Your children have *f* me
5: 19 'As you have *f* me and served
9: 13 "It is because they have *f* my law,
17: 13 because they have *f* the LORD,
19: 4 For they have *f* me and made this
22: 9 'Because they have *f* the covenant
51: 5 and Judah have not been *f*
Eze 8: 12 the LORD has *f* the land.' "
9: 9 'The LORD has *f* the land;
Mt 27: 46 my God, why have you *f* me?"
Mk 15: 34 my God, why have you *f* me?"
Rev 2: 4 You have *f* your first love.

FORSAKES (FORSAKE)

Job 6: 14 he *f* the fear of the Almighty.

FORSAKING (FORSAKE)

Dt 28: 20 of the evil you have done in *f* him.
Jdg 10: 10 *f* our God and serving the Baals."
1Sa 8: 8 *f* me and serving other gods,
Isa 57: 8 *F* me, you uncovered your bed,
Jer 1: 16 because of their wickedness in *f* me
2: 17 by *f* the LORD your God
Eze 20: 27 fathers blasphemed me by *f* me:

FORSOOK (FORSAKE)

Jdg 2: 12 They *f* the LORD, the God
2: 13 because they *f* him and served Baal
10: 6 because the Israelites *f* the LORD
2Ki 17: 16 They *f* all the commands
21: 22 He *f* the LORD, the God
2Ch 29: 6 of the LORD our God and *f* him.
Jer 16: 11 They *f* me and did not keep my law
16: 11 'It is because your fathers *f* me,'

FORTIETH (FORTY)

Nu 33: 38 day of the fifth month of the *f* year
Dt 1: 3 In the *f* year, on the first day
1Ch 26: 31 In the *f* year of David's reign

FORTIFICATIONS (FORTRESS)

2Sa 20: 15 and it stood against the outer *f*.

FORTIFIED (FORTRESS)

Nu 13: 19 Are they unwalled or *f*? How is
13: 28 and the cities are *f* and very large.
21: 24 because their border was *f*.
32: 17 and children will live in *f* cities,
32: 36 and Beth Haran as *f* cities,
Dt 3: 5 All these cities were *f*
28: 52 land until the high *f* walls
Jos 10: 20 who were left reached their *f* cities.
14: 12 and their cities were large and *f*,
19: 29 and went to the *f* city of Tyre,
19: 35 The *f* cities were Ziddim, Zer,
1Sa 6: 18 *f* towns with their country villages.
2Sa 20: 6 or he will find *f* cities and escape
1Ki 12: 25 Then Jeroboam *f* Shechem
15: 17 and *f* Ramah to prevent anyone
22: 39 inlaid with ivory, and the cities he *f*
2Ki 3: 19 You will overthrow every *f* city
8: 12 "You will set fire to their *f* places,
10: 2 and horses, a *f* city and weapons,
17: 9 to *f* city they built themselves high
18: 8 From watchtower to *f* city,
18: 13 of Assyria attacked all the *f* cities
19: 25 that you have turned *f* cities
2Ch 8: 5 and Lower Beth Horon as *f* cities,
11: 10 These were *f* cities in Judah
11: 23 Benjamin, and to all the *f* cities.
12: 4 he captured the *f* cities of Judah
14: 6 He built up the *f* cities of Judah,
16: 1 and *f* Ramah to prevent anyone
17: 2 troops in all the *f* cities of Judah
17: 19 in the *f* cities throughout Judah.
19: 5 in each of the *f* cities of Judah.
21: 3 as well as *f* cities in Judah,
26: 9 the angle of the wall, and he *f* them.
32: 1 He laid siege to the *f* cities,
33: 14 in all the *f* cities in Judah.
Ne 9: 25 They captured *f* cities

Ps 60: 9 Who will bring me to the f city?
108: 10 Who will bring me to the f city?
Pr 10: 15 The wealth of the rich is their f city
18: 11 The wealth of the rich is their f city
18: 19 is more unyielding than a f city,
Isa 2: 15 and every f wall,
17: 3 The f city will disappear
25: 2 the f town a ruin,
25: 12 bring down your high f walls
27: 10 The f city stands desolate,
36: 1 of Assyria attacked all the f cities
37: 26 that you have turned f cities
Jer 1: 18 Today I have made you a f city,
4: 5 Let us flee to the f cities!'
5: 17 the f cities in which you trust.
8: 14 Let us flee to the f cities
15: 20 a f wall of bronze;
34: 7 These were the only f cities left
48: 18 and ruin your f cities.
Eze 21: 20 against Judah and f Jerusalem.
36: 35 destroyed, are now f and inhabited
Da 11: 15 ramps and will capture a f city.
Hos 8: 14 Judah has f many towns.
Am 5: 9 and brings the f city to ruin),
Hab 1: 10 They laugh at all f cities;
Zep 1: 16 cry against the f cities

FORTIFIES (FORTRESS)

Jer 51: 53 and f her lofty stronghold,

FORTRESS (FORTIFICATIONS FORTIFIED FORTIFIES FORTRESSES FORTS)

2Sa 5: 7 David captured the f of Zion,
5: 9 then took up residence in the f
22: 2 "The LORD is my rock, my f
24: 7 they went toward the f of Tyre
1Ch 11: 5 David captured the f of Zion,
11: 7 then took up residence in the f,
Ps 18: 2 The LORD is my rock, my f
28: 8 a f of salvation for his anointed one
31: 2 a strong f to save me.
31: 3 Since you are my rock and my f,
46: 7 the God of Jacob is our f.
46: 11 the God of Jacob is our f.
48: 3 he has shown himself to be her f.
59: 9 you, O God, are my f,
59: 16 for you are my f,
59: 17 O God, are my f, my loving God.
62: 2 he is my f, I will never be shaken.
62: 6 he is my f, I will not be shaken.
71: 3 for you are my rock and my f.
91: 2 "He is my refuge and my f,
94: 22 But the LORD has become my f,
144: 2 He is my loving God and my f,
Pr 14: 26 who fears the LORD has a secure f,
Isa 17: 10 not remembered the Rock, your f.
23: 4 O Sidon, and you, O f of the sea,
23: 14 your f is destroyed!
29: 7 that attack her and her f
32: 14 The f will be abandoned,
33: 16 refuge will be the mountain f.
Jer 16: 19 O LORD, my strength and my f,
Da 11: 7 king of the North and enter his f;
11: 10 and carry the battle as far as his f.
11: 31 up to desecrate the temple f
Na 2: 1 Guard the f,
Zec 9: 12 Return to your f, O prisoners

FORTRESSES (FORTRESS)

Isa 23: 11 that her f be destroyed.
23: 13 they stripped its f bare
Jer 6: 5 and destroy her f!"
9: 21 and has entered our f;
17: 27 that will consume her f.' "
49: 27 it will consume the f of Ben-Hadad
Da 11: 19 toward the f of his own country
11: 24 He will plot the overthrow of f—
11: 38 of them, he will honor a god of f;
11: 39 He will attack the mightiest f
Hos 8: 14 that will consume their f."
10: 14 so that all your f will be devastated
Am 1: 4 that will consume the f
1: 7 that will consume her f
1: 10 that will consume her f."
1: 12 that will consume the f of Bozrah."
1: 14 that will consume her f
2: 2 that will consume the f of Kerioth.
Am 2: 5 that will consume the f
3: 9 Proclaim to the f of Ashdod
3: 9 and to the f of Egypt:
3: 10 hoard plunder and loot in their f."
3: 11 and plunder your f."
6: 8 and detest his f;
Mic 5: 5 and marches through our f,
Na 3: 12 All your f are like fig trees

FORTS (FORTRESS)

2Ch 17: 12 he built f and store cities in Judah
27: 4 f and towers in the wooded areas.

FORTUNATE (FORTUNE)

Ac 26: 2 I consider myself f to stand

FORTUNATUS

1Co 16: 17 I was glad when Stephanas, F

FORTUNE (FORTUNATE FORTUNE-TELLING FORTUNES)

Ge 30: 11 Then Leah said, "What good f!"
Job 31: 25 the f my hands had gained,
Pr 21: 6 A f made by a lying tongue
Isa 65: 11 who spread a table for F

FORTUNE-TELLING (FORTUNE)

Ac 16: 16 deal of money for her owners by f.

FORTUNES (FORTUNE)

Dt 30: 3 your God will restore your f
Ps 14: 7 When the LORD restores the f
53: 6 When God restores the f
85: 1 you restored the f of Jacob.
126: 4 Restore our f, O LORD,
Jer 30: 18 " 'I will restore the f
32: 44 because I will restore their f,
33: 11 For I will restore the f of the land
33: 26 For I will restore their f
48: 47 "Yet I will restore the f of Moab
49: 6 restore the f of the Ammonites,"
49: 39 "Yet I will restore the f of Elam
Eze 16: 53 I will restore the f of Sodom
16: 53 and your f along with them,
Hos 7: 1 "Whenever I would restore the f
Joel 3: 1 when I restore the f of Judah
Mic 3: 11 and her prophets tell f for money.
Zep 2: 7 he will restore their f.
3: 20 the earth when I restore your f

FORTY (FORTIETH 40)

Ge 7: 4 on the earth for f days and f nights,
7: 12 fell on the earth f days and f nights.
7: 17 For f days the flood kept coming
8: 6 After f days Noah opened
18: 29 "For the sake of f, I will not do it."
18: 29 "What if only f are found there?"
25: 20 and Isaac was f years old
26: 34 When Esau was f years old,
32: 15 camels with their young, f cows
50: 3 embalmed him, taking a full f days,
Ex 16: 35 The Israelites ate manna f years,
24: 18 on the mountain f days and f nights
26: 19 and make f silver bases to go
26: 21 twenty frames and f silver bases—
34: 28 and f nights without eating bread
34: 28 there with the LORD f days
36: 24 and made f silver bases to go
36: 26 twenty frames and f silver bases
Nu 13: 25 At the end of f days they returned
14: 33 will be shepherds here for f years,
14: 34 For f years—one year for each
14: 34 of the f days you explored the land
32: 13 wander in the desert f years,
Dt 2: 7 These f years the LORD your God
8: 2 the way in the desert these f years,
8: 4 swell during these f years.
9: 9 on the mountain f days and f nights
9: 11 the end of the f days and f nights,
9: 18 the LORD for f days and f nights;
9: 25 LORD those f days and f nights
10: 10 stayed on the mountain f days
25: 3 not give him more than f lashes.
29: 5 During the f years that I led you
Jos 4: 13 About f thousand armed
5: 6 about in the desert f years
14: 7 I was f years old when Moses
Jdg 3: 11 So the land had peace for f years,
Jdg 5: 8 seen among f thousand in Israel.
5: 31 Then the land had peace f years.
8: 28 the land enjoyed peace f years.
12: 14 He had f sons and thirty grandsons,
13: 1 hands of the Philistines for f years.
1Sa 4: 18 He had led Israel f years.
17: 16 For f days the Philistine came
2Sa 2: 10 son of Saul was f years old
5: 4 king, and he reigned f years.
10: 18 f thousand of their foot soldiers.
1Ki 2: 11 He had reigned f years over Israel
6: 17 front of this room was f cubits long.
7: 38 each holding f baths and measuring
11: 42 in Jerusalem over all Israel f years.
19: 8 he traveled f days and f nights
2Ki 8: 9 as a gift f camel-loads
12: 1 and he reigned in Jerusalem f years
1Ch 19: 18 f thousand of their foot soldiers.
29: 27 He ruled over Israel f years—
2Ch 9: 30 in Jerusalem over all Israel f years.
24: 1 and he reigned in Jerusalem f years
Ne 5: 15 took f shekels of silver from them
9: 21 For f years you sustained them
Job 42: 16 Job lived a hundred and f years;
Ps 95: 10 For f years I was angry
Eze 29: 11 no one will live there for f years.
29: 12 her cities will lie desolate f years
29: 13 the end of f years I will gather
41: 2 it was f cubits long and twenty
46: 22 f cubits long and thirty cubits wide;
Am 2: 10 and I led you f years in the desert
5: 25 f years in the desert, O house
Jnh 3: 4 "F more days and Nineveh will be
Mt 4: 2 After fasting f days and f nights,
Mk 1: 13 and he was in the desert f days,
Lk 4: 2 where for f days he was tempted
Ac 1: 3 to them over a period of f days
4: 22 healed was over f years old.
7: 23 "When Moses was f years old,
7: 30 "After f years had passed,
7: 36 and for f years in the desert.
7: 42 f years in the desert, O house
13: 18 and endured their conduct f years
13: 21 of Benjamin, who ruled f years.
23: 13 More than f men were involved
23: 21 more than f of them are waiting
2Co 11: 24 the Jews the f lashes minus one.
Heb 3: 9 and for f years saw what I did.
3: 17 with whom was he angry for f years

FORUM

Ac 28: 15 and they traveled as far as the F

FOSTER

Isa 49: 23 Kings will be your f fathers,

FOUGHT (FIGHT)

Ex 17: 10 So Joshua f the Amalekites
Nu 21: 23 When he reached Jahaz, he f
21: 26 who had f against the former king
31: 7 They f against Midian,
31: 28 From the soldiers who f
31: 36 of those who f in the battle was:
Jos 10: 42 the God of Israel, f for Israel.
23: 3 it was the LORD your God who f
24: 8 They f against you, but I gave them
24: 11 citizens of Jericho f against you,
Jdg 1: 5 that they found Adoni-Bezek and f
5: 19 the kings of Canaan f
5: 19 "Kings came, they f;
5: 20 From the heavens the stars f,
5: 20 from their courses they f
9: 17 to think that my father f for you,
9: 39 of Shechem and f Abimelech.
11: 20 at Jahaz and f with Israel.
12: 4 of Gilead and f against Ephraim.
1Sa 4: 10 and fight!" So the Philistines f,
12: 9 king of Moab, who f against them.
14: 47 he f against their enemies
14: 48 He f valiantly and defeated
19: 8 went out and f the Philistines.
23: 5 f the Philistines and carried
30: 17 David f them from dusk
31: 1 Now the Philistines f against Israel
2Sa 8: 3 David f Hadadezer son of Rehob,
10: 17 to meet David and f against him.
11: 17 the men of the city came out and f
12: 26 Meanwhile Joab f against Rabbah

2Sa 12: 27 "I have f against Rabbah
2Ki 3: 23 "Those kings must have f
3: 24 the Israelites rose up and f them
1Ch 10: 1 Now the Philistines f against Israel
18: 3 David f Hadadezer king of Zobah,
19: 17 in battle, and they f against him.
22: 8 much blood and have f many wars.
2Ch 20: 29 they heard how the LORD had f
Isa 63: 10 and he himself f against them.
Zec 14: 12 will strike all the nations that f
1Co 15: 32 If I f wild beasts in Ephesus
2Ti 4: 7 I have f the good fight, I have
Rev 12: 7 and his angels f against the dragon,
12: 7 the dragon and his angels f back.

FOUND (FIND)

Ge 2: 20 for Adam no suitable helper was f.
4: 15 that no one who f him would kill
6: 8 But Noah f favor in the eyes
7: 1 because I have f you righteous
9: 24 f out what his youngest son had
11: 2 they f a plain in Shinar
16: 7 of the LORD f Hagar near a spring
18: 3 "If I have f favor in your eyes,
18: 29 "What if only forty are f there?"
18: 30 What if only thirty can be f there?"
18: 31 what if only twenty can be f there
18: 32 What if only ten can be f there?"
19: 19 Your servant has f favor
24: 30 and f him standing by the camels
26: 32 They said, "We've f water!"
30: 14 and f some mandrake plants,
30: 27 "If I have f favor in your eyes,
31: 33 two maidservants, but he f nothing.
31: 34 in the tent but f nothing.
31: 37 what have you f that belongs
33: 10 "If I have f favor in your eyes,
37: 15 a man f him wandering
37: 17 went after his brothers and f them
37: 32 to their father and said, "We f this.
39: 4 Joseph f favor in his eyes
43: 21 and each of us f his silver—
44: 8 the land of Canaan the silver we f
44: 9 any of your servants is f to have it,
44: 10 Whoever is f to have it will become
44: 12 the cup was f in Benjamin's sack.
44: 16 the one who was f to have the cup."
44: 17 Only the man who was f
47: 14 all the money that was to be f
47: 29 "If I have f favor in your eyes,
50: 4 "If I have f favor in your eyes,
Ex 5: 20 they f Moses and Aaron waiting
9: 7 men to investigate and f that not
12: 19 is to be f in your houses.
16: 27 day to gather it, but they f none.
22: 4 "If the stolen animal is f alive
22: 8 But if the thief is not f, the owner
33: 12 and you have f favor with me.'
33: 13 If I have f favor in your eyes,
34: 9 if I have f favor in your eyes,"
Lev 6: 4 or the lost property he f,
7: 24 The fat of an animal f dead
10: 16 and f that it had been burned up,
17: 15 who eats anything f dead
22: 8 He must not eat anything f dead
Nu 11: 15 if I have f favor in your eyes—
15: 32 a man was f gathering wood
15: 33 Those who f him gathering wood
23: 6 f him standing beside his offering,
23: 17 f him standing beside his offering,
32: 5 If we have f favor in your eyes,"
Dt 13: 17 those condemned things shall be f
15: 9 and you will be f guilty of sin.
16: 4 Let no yeast be f in your possession
17: 2 the LORD gives you is f doing evil
18: 10 Let no one be f among you who
21: 1 If a man is f slain, lying in a field
22: 20 proof of the girl's virginity can be f,
22: 22 If a man is f sleeping
22: 27 for the man f the girl out
32: 10 In a desert land he f him,
Jos 10: 17 the five kings had been f hiding
Jdg 1: 5 was there that they f Adoni-Bezek
3: 24 and f the doors of the upper room
6: 17 "If now I have f favor in your eyes,
20: 48 and everything else they f.
21: 9 they f that none of the people
21: 12 They f among the people living

Ru 2: 3 she f herself working
2: 10 "Why have I f such favor
1Sa 9: 20 about them; they have been f.
10: 2 out to look for have been f.
10: 14 when we saw they were not to be f,
10: 16 us that the donkeys had been f."
10: 21 looked for him, he was not to be f.
12: 5 that you have not f anything
13: 19 Not a blacksmith could be f
14: 20 They f the Philistines
20: 3 knows very well that I have f favor
20: 29 If I have f favor in your eyes,
25: 28 Let no wrongdoing be f in you
27: 5 "If I have f favor in your eyes,
29: 3 until now, I have f no fault in him."
29: 6 until now, I have f no fault in you,
29: 8 have you f against your servant
30: 3 they f it destroyed by fire
30: 6 David f strength in the LORD his
30: 11 They f an Egyptian in a field
31: 8 they f Saul and his three sons fallen
2Sa 2: 30 of David's men were f missing.
7: 27 So your servant has f courage
14: 22 servant knows that he has f favor
17: 12 attack him wherever he may be f,
17: 13 until not even a piece of it can be f
17: 20 The men searched but f no one,
1Ki 1: 3 for a beautiful girl and f Abishag,
1: 52 but if evil is f in him, he will die."
13: 14 He f him sitting under an oak tree
13: 28 and f the body thrown
14: 13 God of Israel, has f anything good.
19: 19 and f Elisha son of Shaphat.
20: 36 a lion f him and killed him.
20: 37 The prophet f another man
21: 20 "I have f you," he answered,
21: 20 "So you have f me, my enemy!"
2Ki 4: 39 to gather herbs and f a wild vine.
7: 15 and they f the whole road strewn
9: 5 he f the army officers sitting
9: 35 they f nothing except her skull,
12: 5 used to repair whatever damage is f
12: 18 and all the gold f in the treasuries
14: 14 and all the articles f in the temple
16: 8 gold f in the temple of the LORD
18: 15 gave him all the silver that was f
19: 8 f the king fighting against Libnah.
20: 13 everything f among his treasures.
22: 8 "I have f the Book of the Law
22: 13 written in this book that has been f.
23: 2 which had been f in the temple
25: 19 of his men who were f in the city.
1Ch 4: 40 They f rich, good pasture,
10: 8 they f Saul and his sons fallen
17: 25 your servant has f courage to pray
20: 2 its weight was f to be a talent
24: 4 f among Eleazar's descendants
26: 31 men among the Hebronites were f
28: 9 If you seek him, he will be f by you;
2Ch 2: 17 and they were f to be 153,600.
15: 2 If you seek him, he will be f by you,
15: 4 sought him, and he was f by them.
15: 15 sought God eagerly, and he was f
20: 25 they f among them a great amount
21: 17 off all the goods f in the king's
22: 8 he f the princes of Judah
25: 5 f that there were three hundred
25: 24 and all the articles f in the temple
29: 16 everything unclean that they f
34: 14 Hilkiah the priest f the Book
34: 15 "I have f the Book of the Law
34: 21 written in this book that has been f.
34: 30 which had been f in the temple
36: 8 and all that was f against him,
Ezr 4: 19 and it was f that this city has a long
6: 2 A scroll was f in the citadel
8: 15 and the priests, I f no Levites there.
Ne 2: 5 and if your servant has f favor
7: 5 I f the genealogical record
7: 5 This is what I f written there:
8: 14 They f written in the Law,
9: 8 You f his heart faithful to you,
13: 1 and there it was f written that no
Est 2: 22 But Mordecai f out about the plot
2: 23 the report was investigated and f
6: 2 It was f recorded there that
7: 3 "If I have f favor with you, O king,
Job 9: 29 Since I am already f guilty,

Job 12: 12 Is not wisdom f among the aged?
20: 8 he flies away, no more to be f,
28: 12 "But where can wisdom be f?
28: 13 it cannot be f in the land
32: 3 they had f no way to refute Job,
32: 13 Do not say, 'We have f wisdom;
33: 10 Yet God has f fault with me;
33: 24 I have f a ransom for him'—
42: 15 in all the land were there f women
Ps 10: 15 that would not be f out.
32: 6 you while you may be f;
37: 10 for them, they will not be f.
37: 36 I looked for him, he could not be f.
69: 20 for comforters, but I f none.
84: 3 Even the sparrow has f a home,
89: 20 I have f David my servant;
109: 7 When he is tried, let him be f guilty
109: 17 he f no pleasure in blessing—
Pr 7: 15 I looked for you and have f you!
10: 9 takes crooked paths will be f out.
10: 13 Wisdom is f on the lips
13: 10 wisdom is f in those who take
14: 9 but good will is f among the upright
19: 7 they are nowhere to be f.
30: 28 yet it is f in kings' palaces.
Ecc 7: 28 I f one upright man
7: 29 This only have I f:
SS 3: 3 The watchmen f me
3: 4 when I f the one my heart loves.
5: 7 The watchmen f me
8: 1 Then, if I f you outside,
Isa 30: 14 its pieces not a fragment will be f
35: 9 they will not be f there.
37: 8 f the king fighting against Libnah.
39: 2 everything f among his treasures.
45: 25 will be f righteous and will exult.
51: 3 Joy and gladness will be f in her,
55: 6 Seek the LORD while he may be f;
57: 10 You f renewal of your strength,
59: 15 Truth is nowhere to be f,
65: 1 I was f by those who did not seek
65: 8 "As when juice is still f in a cluster
Jer 29: 14 I will be f by you," declares
40: 1 He had f Jeremiah bound in chains
40: 2 of the guard f Jeremiah,
50: 7 Whoever f them devoured them;
50: 20 but none will be f,
50: 24 you were f and captured
52: 25 of his men who were f in the city.
Eze 4: 14 I have never eaten anything f dead
16: 37 with whom you f pleasure,
22: 30 have to destroy it, but I f none.
26: 21 but you will never again be f,
28: 15 till wickedness was f in you.
44: 31 f dead or torn by wild animals.
Da 1: 19 and he f none equal to Daniel,
1: 20 he f them ten times better
2: 25 "I have f a man among the exiles
4: 12 the beasts of the field f shelter,
5: 11 the time of your father he was f
5: 12 was f to have a keen mind
5: 27 on the scales and f wanting.
6: 11 as a group and f Daniel praying
6: 22 I was f innocent in his sight.
6: 23 no wound was f on him,
12: 1 everyone whose name is f written
Hos 9: 10 "When I f Israel,
12: 4 He f him at Bethel
Jnh 1: 3 where he f a ship bound
Mic 1: 13 were f in you.
Zep 3: 13 nor will deceit be f in their mouths.
Zec 1: 11 and f the whole world at rest
Mal 2: 6 and nothing false was f on his lips.
Mt 1: 18 she was f to be with child
2: 7 and f out from them the exact time
8: 10 I have not f anyone in Israel
13: 44 When a man f it, he hid it again,
13: 46 When he f one of great value,
18: 28 he f one of his fellow servants who
20: 6 and f still others standing around.
21: 19 but f nothing on it except leaves.
26: 40 to his disciples and f them sleeping.
26: 43 back, he again f them sleeping,
Mk 1: 37 when they f him, they exclaimed:
6: 38 When they f out, they said, "Five
7: 30 and f her child lying on the bed,
11: 4 and f a colt outside in the street,
11: 13 When he reached it, he f nothing

Mk 14: 16 went into the city and *f* things just
14: 37 to his disciples and *f* them sleeping.
14: 40 back, he again *f* them sleeping,
Lk 1: 30 Mary, you have *f* favor with God.
2: 16 So they hurried off and *f* Mary
2: 46 After three days they *f* him
4: 17 he *f* the place where it is written:
7: 9 I have not *f* such great faith
7: 10 to the house and *f* the servant well.
8: 35 they *f* the man from whom
9: 36 they *f* that Jesus was alone.
13: 7 on this fig tree and haven't *f* any.
15: 6 with me; I have *f* my lost sheep.'
15: 9 with me; I have *f* my lost coin.'
15: 24 is alive again; he was lost and is *f*.'
15: 32 is alive again; he was lost and is *f*.' "
17: 18 Was no one *f* to return
19: 32 were sent ahead went and *f* it just
22: 13 They left and *f* things just
22: 45 he *f* them asleep, exhausted
23: 2 "We have *f* this man subverting our
23: 14 have *f* no basis for your charges
23: 22 I have *f* in him no grounds
24: 2 They *f* the stone rolled away
24: 24 and *f* it just as the women had said,
24: 33 There they *f* the Eleven
Jn 1: 41 "We have *f* the Messiah" (that is,
1: 45 Philip *f* Nathanael and told him,
1: 45 "We have *f* the one Moses wrote
2: 14 the temple courts he *f* men selling
5: 14 Later Jesus *f* him at the temple
6: 25 When they *f* him on the other side
9: 35 and when he *f* him, he said,
11: 17 Jesus *f* that Lazarus had already
11: 57 if anyone *f* out where Jesus was,
12: 9 of Jews *f* out that Jesus was there
12: 14 Jesus *f* a young donkey
19: 33 and *f* that he was already dead,
Ac 4: 12 Salvation is *f* in no one else,
5: 23 when we opened them, we *f* no one
5: 23 "We *f* the jail securely locked,
9: 2 that if he *f* any there who belonged
9: 33 There he *f* a man named Aeneas,
10: 17 by Cornelius *f* out where Simon's
10: 27 and *f* a large gathering of people.
11: 26 and when he *f* him, he brought him
13: 22 'I have *f* David son of Jesse a man
13: 28 Though they *f* no proper ground
14: 6 But they *f* out about it
17: 23 even *f* an altar with this inscription:
19: 1 There he *f* some disciples
21: 2 We *f* a ship crossing
22: 25 who hasn't even been *f* guilty?"
23: 29 I *f* that the accusation had to do
24: 5 "We have *f* this man
24: 18 ceremonially clean when they *f* me
24: 20 here should state what crime they *f*
25: 25 I *f* he had done nothing deserving
27: 6 the centurion *f* an Alexandrian
27: 28 and *f* it was ninety feet deep.
27: 28 and *f* that the water was a hundred
28: 1 we *f* out that the island was called
28: 14 There we *f* some brothers who
Ro 7: 10 I *f* that the very commandment
10: 20 "I was *f* by those who did not seek
1Co 15: 15 we are then *f* to be false witnesses
2Co 2: 12 *f* that the Lord had opened a door
5: 3 are clothed, we will not be *f* naked.
Php 2: 8 And being *f* in appearance as a man
3: 9 that I may gain Christ and be *f*
Col 2: 17 the reality, however, is *f* in Christ.
2Ti 1: 17 hard for me until he *f* me.
Heb 3: 3 Jesus has been *f* worthy
4: 1 of you be *f* to have fallen short of it.
8: 8 But God *f* fault with the people
11: 5 he could not be *f*, because God had
Jas 2: 8 If you really keep the royal law *f*
1Pe 2: 22 and no deceit was *f* in his mouth."
2Pe 3: 14 make every effort to be *f* spotless,
Rev 2: 2 but are not, and have *f* them false.
3: 2 I have not *f* your deeds complete
5: 4 no one was *f* who was worthy
14: 5 No lie was *f* in their mouths;
16: 20 and the mountains could not be *f*.
18: 21 never to be *f* again.
18: 22 will ever be *f* in you again.
18: 24 In her was *f* the blood of prophets
20: 15 If anyone's name was not *f* written
Rev 21: 16 with the rod and *f* it to be 12,000

FOUNDATION (FOUNDATIONS FOUNDED)

1Ki 5: 17 to provide a *f* of dressed stone
6: 37 The *f* of the temple
7: 9 to the great courtyard and from *f*
2Ch 3: 3 The *f* Solomon laid
8: 16 from the day the *f* of the temple
23: 5 palace and a third at the *F* Gate,
Ezr 3: 3 they built the altar on its *f*
3: 6 *f* of the LORD's temple had not
3: 10 When the builders laid the *f*
3: 11 the *f* of the house of the LORD was
3: 12 aloud when they saw the *f*
Job 38: 4 when I laid the earth's *f*?
Ps 87: 1 He has set his *f* on the holy
89: 14 justice are the *f* of your throne;
97: 2 justice are the *f* of his throne.
Isa 28: 16 a precious cornerstone for a sure *f*;
33: 6 He will be the sure *f* for your times,
Jer 51: 26 nor any stone for a *f*,
Eze 13: 14 ground so that its *f* will be laid bare.
41: 8 forming the *f* of the side rooms.
Am 9: 6 and sets its *f* on the earth,
Hag 2: 18 thought to the day when the *f*
Zec 4: 9 hands of Zerubbabel have laid the *f*
8: 9 when the *f* was laid for the house
12: 1 who lays the *f* of the earth,
Mt 7: 25 because it had its *f* on the rock.
Lk 6: 48 down deep and laid the *f* on rock.
6: 49 a house on the ground without a *f*.
14: 29 For if he lays the *f* and is not able
Ro 15: 20 building on someone else's *f*.
1Co 3: 10 I laid a *f* as an expert builder,
3: 11 For no one can lay any *f* other
3: 12 builds on this *f* using gold,
Eph 2: 20 built on the *f* of the apostles
1Ti 3: 15 the pillar and *f* of the truth.
6: 19 as a firm *f* for the coming age,
2Ti 2: 19 God's solid *f* stands firm,
Heb 6: 1 not laying again the *f* of repentance
Rev 21: 19 The first *f* was jasper, the second

FOUNDATIONS (FOUNDATION)

Dt 32: 22 and set afire the *f* of the mountains
Jos 6: 26 will he lay its *f*;
1Sa 2: 8 "For the *f* of the earth are
2Sa 22: 8 the *f* of the heavens shook;
22: 16 and the *f* of the earth laid bare
1Ki 7: 10 The *f* were laid with large stones
16: 34 He laid its *f* at the cost
Ezr 4: 12 the walls and repairing the *f*.
5: 16 and laid the *f* of the house of God
6: 3 sacrifices, and let its *f* be laid.
Job 4: 19 whose *f* are in the dust,
22: 16 their *f* washed away by a flood.
Ps 11: 3 When the *f* are being destroyed,
18: 7 and the *f* of the mountains shook;
18: 15 and the *f* of the earth laid bare
82: 5 all the *f* of the earth are shaken.
102: 25 In the beginning you laid the *f*
104: 5 He set the earth on its *f*;
137: 7 "tear it down to its *f*!"
Pr 3: 19 the LORD laid the earth's *f*,
8: 29 and when he marked out the *f*
Isa 24: 18 the *f* of the earth shake.
44: 28 and of the temple, "Let its *f* be laid
48: 13 My own hand laid the *f* of the earth
51: 13 and laid the *f* of the earth,
51: 16 who laid the *f* of the earth,
54: 11 your *f* with sapphires.
58: 12 and will raise up the age-old *f*;
Jer 31: 37 *f* of the earth below be searched out
La 4: 11 that consumed her *f*.
Eze 30: 4 and her *f* torn down.
Mic 1: 6 and lay bare her *f*.
6: 2 listen, you everlasting *f* of the earth
Ac 16: 26 such a violent earthquake that the *f*
Heb 1: 10 O Lord, you laid the *f* of the earth,
11: 10 looking forward to the city with *f*,
Rev 21: 14 The wall of the city had twelve *f*,
21: 19 *f* of the city walls were decorated

FOUNDED (FOUNDATION)

Ex 9: 18 from the day it was *f* till now.
1Ki 2: 24 and has *f* a dynasty for me
Ps 24: 2 for he *f* it upon the seas
Ps 89: 11 you *f* the world and all that is in it.
94: 15 Judgment will again be *f*
107: 36 and they *f* a city where they could
Isa 40: 21 understood since the earth was *f*?
45: 18 he *f* it;
Jer 10: 12 he *f* the world by his wisdom
51: 15 he *f* the world by his wisdom
Heb 8: 6 and it is *f* on better promises.

FOUNTAIN (FOUNTAINS)

Ne 2: 14 I moved on toward the *F* Gate
3: 15 The *F* Gate was repaired
12: 37 At the *F* Gate they continued
Ps 36: 9 For with you is the *f* of life;
Pr 5: 18 May your *f* be blessed,
10: 11 of the righteous is a *f* of life,
13: 14 of the wise is a *f* of life,
14: 27 The fear of the LORD is a *f* of life,
16: 22 Understanding is a *f* of life
18: 4 the *f* of wisdom is a bubbling brook.
SS 4: 12 are a spring enclosed, a sealed *f*.
4: 15 You are a garden *f*,
Jer 9: 1 and my eyes a *f* of tears!
Joel 3: 18 A *f* will flow out of the LORD's
Zec 13: 1 "On that day a *f* will be opened

FOUNTAINS (FOUNTAIN)

Ps 87: 7 "All my *f* are in you."
Pr 8: 28 and fixed securely the *f* of the deep,

FOUR-DRACHMA (DRACHMAS)

Mt 17: 27 its mouth and you will find a *f* coin.

FOUR-FOOTED (FOOT)

Ac 10: 12 It contained all kinds of *f* animals,
11: 6 and saw *f* animals of the earth,

FOWL (FOWLER FOWLER'S)

1Ki 4: 23 gazelles, roebucks and choice *f*.

FOWLER (FOWL)

Pr 6: 5 like a bird from the snare of the *f*.

FOWLER'S (FOWL)

Ps 91: 3 he will save you from the *f* snare
124: 7 out of the *f* snare;

FOX (FOXES)

Ne 4: 3 if even a *f* climbed up on it,
Lk 13: 32 He replied, "Go tell that *f*,

FOXES (FOX)

Jdg 15: 4 and caught three hundred *f*
15: 5 let the *f* loose in the standing grain
SS 2: 15 Catch for us the *f*,
2: 15 the little *f*
Mt 8: 20 "*F* have holes and birds
Lk 9: 58 "*F* have holes and birds

FRACTION

Mk 12: 42 small copper coins, worth only a *f*

FRACTURE (FRACTURES)

Lev 24: 20 *f* for *f*, eye for eye, tooth for tooth.

FRACTURES (FRACTURE)

Ps 60: 2 mend its *f*, for it is quaking.

FRAGILE

Job 8: 14 What he trusts in is *f*;

FRAGMENT

Isa 30: 14 its pieces not a *f* will be found

FRAGRANCE (FRAGRANT)

Ex 30: 38 it to enjoy its *f* must be cut
SS 1: 3 Pleasing is the *f* of your perfumes;
1: 12 my perfume spread its *f*.
2: 13 the blossoming vines spread their *f*.
4: 10 and the *f* of your perfume
4: 11 The *f* of your garments is like that
4: 16 that its *f* may spread abroad.
7: 8 the *f* of your breath like apples,
7: 13 The mandrakes send out their *f*,
Isa 3: 24 Instead of *f* there will be a stench;
Hos 14: 6 his *f* like a cedar of Lebanon.
Jn 12: 3 filled with the *f* of the perfume.
2Co 2: 14 us spreads everywhere the *f*
2: 16 of death; to the other, the *f* of life.

FRAGRANT (FRAGRANCE)
Ex 25: 6 anointing oil and for the *f* incense;
30: 7 "Aaron must burn *f* incense
30: 23 shekels of *f* cane, 500 shekels
30: 23 shekels) of *f* cinnamon,
30: 25 a *f* blend, the work of a perfumer.
30: 34 "Take *f* spices—gum resin,
30: 35 and make a *f* blend of incense,
31: 11 and *f* incense for the Holy Place.
35: 8 anointing oil and for the *f* incense;
35: 15 the anointing oil and the *f* incense;
35: 28 anointing oil and for the *f* incense.
37: 29 *f* incense—the work of a perfumer.
39: 38 the anointing oil, the *f* incense,
40: 27 and burned *f* incense on it,
Lev 4: 7 of the altar of *f* incense that is
16: 12 handfuls of finely ground *f* incense
Nu 4: 16 *f* incense, the regular grain offering
2Ch 2: 4 for burning *f* incense before him,
13: 11 and *f* incense to the LORD.
Ps 45: 8 All your robes are *f* with myrrh
Isa 43: 24 You have not bought any *f* calamus
Eze 6: 13 places where they offered *f* incense
8: 11 and a *f* cloud of incense was rising.
16: 19 as *f* incense before them.
20: 28 presented their *f* incense
20: 41 as *f* incense when I bring you out
Eph 5: 2 as a *f* offering and sacrifice to God.
Php 4: 18 They are a *f* offering, an acceptable

FRAME (FRAMES)
Ex 26: 16 Each *f* is to be ten cubits long
26: 19 two bases for each *f*, one
26: 21 silver bases—two under each *f*.
26: 25 silver bases—two under each *f*.
36: 21 Each *f* was ten cubits long
36: 24 two bases for each *f*, one
36: 26 silver bases—two under each *f*.
36: 30 silver bases—two under each *f*.
Nu 4: 10 sea cows and put it on a carrying *f*.
4: 12 and put them on a carrying *f*.
1Ki 7: 31 that had a circular *f* one cubit deep.
Job 17: 7 my whole *f* is but a shadow.
Ps 139: 15 My *f* was not hidden from you
Isa 58: 11 and will strengthen your *f*.

FRAMES (FRAME)
Ex 26: 15 "Make upright *f* of acacia wood
26: 17 Make all the *f* of the tabernacle
26: 18 Make twenty *f* for the south side
26: 20 make twenty *f* and forty silver
26: 22 Make six *f* for the far end, that is,
26: 23 and make two *f* for the corners
26: 25 will be eight *f* and sixteen silver
26: 26 five for the *f* on one side
26: 27 and five for the *f* on the west,
26: 28 end to end at the middle of the *f*.
26: 29 Overlay the *f* with gold
35: 11 clasps, *f*, crossbars, posts and bases
36: 20 They made upright *f*
36: 22 They made all the *f*
36: 23 They made twenty *f*
36: 25 they made twenty *f* and forty silver
36: 27 They made six *f* for the far end,
36: 28 two *f* were made for the corners
36: 29 these two corners the *f* were double
36: 30 there were eight *f* and sixteen silver
36: 31 five for the *f* on one side
36: 32 and five for the *f* on the west,
36: 33 end to end at the middle of the *f*.
36: 34 They overlaid the *f* with gold
39: 33 *f*, crossbars, posts and bases;
40: 18 the bases in place, erected the *f*,
Nu 3: 36 care of the *f* of the tabernacle,
4: 31 to carry the *f* of the tabernacle,
1Ki 7: 5 All the doorways had rectangular *f*;

FRANKINCENSE (INCENSE)
Ex 30: 34 and pure *f*, all in equal amounts,
Rev 18: 13 myrrh and *f*, of wine and olive oil,

FRANTIC
1Ki 18: 29 they continued their *f* prophesying

FRAUD
Pr 20: 17 Food gained by *f* tastes sweet
Jer 10: 14 His images are a *f*;
51: 17 His images are a *f*;

FRAY
Job 39: 21 and charges into the *f*.

FREE (FREED FREEDMAN FREEDMEN FREEDOM FREEING FREELY)
Ge 2: 16 "You are *f* to eat from any tree
44: 10 the rest of you will be *f* from blame
49: 21 "Naphtali is a doe set *f*
Ex 6: 6 I will *f* you from being slaves
21: 2 shall go *f*, without paying anything.
21: 3 he comes alone, he is to go *f* alone;
21: 4 and only the man shall go *f*.
21: 5 children and do not want to go *f*,'
21: 7 she is not to go *f* as menservants do
21: 11 she is to go *f*, without any payment
21: 26 he must let the servant go *f*
21: 27 he must let the servant go *f*
Nu 5: 28 has not defiled herself and is *f*
32: 22 and be *f* from your obligation
Dt 7: 15 The LORD will keep you *f*
15: 12 seventh year you must let him go *f*.
15: 18 a hardship to set your servant *f*,
24: 5 is to be *f* to stay at home
32: 36 and no one is left, slave or *f*.
Jdg 16: 20 as before and shake myself *f*."
2Sa 22: 49 who sets me *f* from my enemies.
1Ki 14: 10 male in Israel—slave or *f*.
20: 34 basis of a treaty I will set you *f*."
20: 42 'You have set *f* a man I had
21: 21 male in Israel—slave or *f*.
2Ki 9: 8 male in Israel—slave or *f*.
14: 26 whether slave or *f*, was suffering;
1Ch 4: 10 harm so that I will be *f* from pain."
12: 17 when my hands are *f* from violence
Job 10: 1 I will give *f* rein to my complaint
16: 17 yet my hands have been *f*
21: 9 Their homes are safe and *f*
33: 9 I am clean and *f* from guilt.
36: 16 distress to a spacious place *f*
39: 5 "Who let the wild donkey go *f*?
Ps 25: 17 *f* me from my anguish.
31: 4 *F* me from the trap that is set
73: 5 They are *f* from the burdens
81: 6 their hands were set *f*
105: 20 the ruler of peoples set him *f*.
118: 5 and he answered by setting me *f*.
119: 32 for you have set my heart *f*.
129: 4 he has cut me *f* from the cords
142: 7 Set me *f* from my prison,
146: 7 The LORD sets prisoners *f*,
Pr 6: 3 then do this, my son, to *f* yourself,
6: 5 *F* yourself, like a gazelle
11: 21 those who are righteous will go *f*.
19: 5 he who pours out lies will not go *f*.
Isa 32: 20 your oxen and donkeys range *f*.
42: 7 to *f* captives from prison
45: 13 and set my exiles *f*,
49: 9 and to those in darkness, 'Be *f*!'
51: 14 prisoners will soon be set *f*;
52: 2 *F* yourself from the chains
58: 6 to set the oppressed *f*
Jer 2: 31 Why do my people say, 'We are *f*
34: 9 was to *f* his Hebrew slaves,
34: 10 They agreed, and set them *f*.
34: 10 agreed that they would *f* their male
34: 14 of you must *f* any fellow Hebrew
34: 14 six years, you must let him go *f*.'
34: 16 and female slaves you had set *f*
37: 4 Now Jeremiah was *f* to come
La 5: 8 there is none to *f* us
Eze 13: 20 I will set *f* the people that you
Zec 9: 11 I will *f* your prisoners
Lk 13: 12 you are set *f* from your infirmity."
13: 16 be set *f* on the Sabbath day
Jn 8: 32 and the truth will set you *f*."
8: 33 can you say that we shall be set *f*?"
8: 36 if the Son sets you *f*, you will be *f*
19: 10 either to *f* you or to crucify you?"
19: 12 Pilate tried to set Jesus *f*,
Ac 7: 34 and have come down to set them *f*.
26: 32 "This man could have been set *f*,
Ro 6: 18 You have been set *f* from sin
6: 20 you were *f* from the control
6: 22 But now that you have been set *f*
8: 2 of life set me *f* from the law of sin
13: 3 Do you want to be *f* from fear
1Co 7: 22 he who was a *f* man
7: 32 you to be *f* from concern.
7: 39 she is *f* to marry anyone she wishes
9: 1 Am I not *f*? Am I not an apostle?
9: 18 preaching the gospel I may offer it *f*
9: 19 Though I am *f* and belong
9: 21 (though I am not *f* from God's law
12: 13 whether Jews or Greeks, slave or *f*
2Co 11: 7 gospel of God to you *f* of charge?
Gal 3: 28 slave nor *f*, male nor female,
4: 22 and the other by the *f* woman.
4: 23 his son by the *f* woman was born
4: 26 But the Jerusalem that is above is *f*,
4: 30 with the *f* woman's son."
4: 31 slave woman, but of the *f* woman.
5: 1 for freedom that Christ has set us *f*.
5: 13 my brothers, were called to be *f*.
Eph 6: 8 he does, whether he is slave or *f*.
Col 1: 22 without blemish and *f*
3: 11 barbarian, Scythian, slave or *f*,
Heb 2: 15 *f* those who all their lives were held
9: 15 ransom to set them *f* from the sins
13: 5 Keep your lives *f* from the love
1Pe 2: 16 *f* men, but do not use your freedom
Rev 6: 15 and every *f* man hid in caves
13: 16 rich and poor, *f* and slave,
19: 18 *f* and slave, small and great."
20: 3 he must be set *f* for a short time.
22: 17 let him take the *f* gift of the water

FREED (FREE)
Lev 19: 20 because she had not been *f*.
Job 3: 19 and the slave is *f* from his master.
Ps 116: 16 you have *f* me from my chains.
136: 24 and *f* us from our enemies,
Jer 34: 11 and took back the slaves they had *f*
52: 31 and *f* him from prison
Mk 5: 29 felt in her body that she was *f*
5: 34 and be *f* from your suffering."
Ro 6: 7 anyone who has died has been *f*
Rev 1: 5 has *f* us from our sins by his blood,

FREEDMAN (FREE)
1Co 7: 22 called by the Lord is the Lord's *f*;

FREEDMEN (FREE)
Ac 6: 9 members of the Synagogue of the *F*

FREEDOM (FREE)
Lev 19: 20 not been ransomed or given her *f*,
Ps 119: 45 I will walk about in *f*,
Isa 61: 1 to proclaim *f* for the captives
Jer 34: 8 to proclaim *f* for the slaves.
34: 15 Each of you proclaimed *f*
34: 17 So I now proclaim '*f*' for you,
34: 17 declares the LORD—'*f*' to fall
34: 17 you have not proclaimed *f*
Eze 46: 17 may keep it until the year of *f*;
Lk 4: 18 me to proclaim *f* for the prisoners
Ac 24: 23 to give him some *f* and permit his
Ro 8: 21 into the glorious *f* of the children
1Co 7: 21 although if you can gain your *f*,
8: 9 exercise of your *f* does not become
10: 29 For why should my *f* be judged
2Co 3: 17 the Spirit of the Lord is, there is *f*.
Gal 2: 4 ranks to spy on the *f* we have
5: 1 It is for *f* that Christ has set us free.
5: 13 But do not use your *f* to indulge
Eph 3: 12 him we may approach God with *f*
Jas 1: 25 into the perfect law that gives *f*,
2: 12 to be judged by the law that gives *f*,
1Pe 2: 16 but do not use your *f* as a cover-up
2Pe 2: 19 They promise them *f*,

FREEING (FREE)
Jer 40: 4 today I am *f* you from the chains
Ac 2: 24 *f* him from the agony of death,

FREELY (FREE)
Ge 43: 34 they feasted and drank *f* with him.
Dt 15: 8 and *f* lend him whatever he needs.
23: 23 because you made your vow *f*
1Ch 29: 9 had given *f* and wholeheartedly
Ezr 7: 15 and his advisers have *f* given
Ps 12: 8 The wicked *f* strut about
37: 26 are always generous and lend *f*;
112: 5 to him who is generous and lends *f*,
Pr 11: 24 One man gives *f*, yet gains
Isa 55: 7 and to our God, for he will *f* pardon

Hos 14: 4 and love them *f*.
Mt 10: 8 Freely you have received, *f* give.
Mk 1:45 he went out and began to talk *f*,
Jn 1:20 confessed *f*, "I am not the Christ."
Ac 9:28 and moved about *f* in Jerusalem,
26:26 with these things, and I can speak *f*
Ro 3:24 and are justified *f* by his grace
1Co 2:12 what God has *f* given us.
2Co 6:11 have spoken *f* to you, Corinthians,
10: 8 I boast somewhat *f* about
Eph 1: 6 which he has *f* given us

FREEWILL (WILL)

Ex 35:29 brought to the LORD *f* offerings
36: 3 to bring *f* offerings morning
Lev 7:16 the result of a vow or is a *f* offering,
22:18 to fulfill a vow or as a *f* offering,
22:21 a special vow or as a *f* offering,
22:23 present as a *f* offering a cow
23:38 and all the *f* offerings you give
Nu 15: 3 for special vows or *f* offerings
29:39 what you vow and your *f* offerings,
Dt 12: 6 vowed to give and your *f* offerings,
12:17 or your *f* offerings or special gifts.
16:10 by giving a *f* offering in proportion
2Ch 31:14 in charge of the *f* offerings given
Ezr 1: 4 and with *f* offerings for the temple
1: 6 in addition to all the *f* offerings.
2:68 of the families gave *f* offerings
3: 5 as *f* offerings to the LORD.
7:16 well as the *f* offerings of the people
8:28 gold are a *f* offering to the LORD,
Ps 54: 6 I will sacrifice a *f* offering to you;
Eze 46:12 the prince provides a *f* offering
Am 4: 5 and brag about your *f* offerings—

FRENZIED

Job 39:24 In *f* excitement he eats up

FRESH

Ge 26:19 discovered a well of *f* water there.
Lev 14: 5 killed over *f* water in a clay pot.
14: 6 that was killed over the *f* water.
14:50 one of the birds over *f* water
14:51 of the dead bird and the *f* water,
14:52 the *f* water, the live bird, the cedar
15:13 and bathe himself with *f* water,
Nu 19:17 and pour *f* water over them.
Jdg 15:15 Finding a *f* jawbone of a donkey,
16: 7 with seven *f* thongs that have not
16: 8 brought her seven *f* thongs that had
Job 29:20 My glory will remain *f* in me,
Ps 92:14 they will stay *f* and green,
Eze 47: 8 the water there becomes *f*.
47: 9 and makes the salt water *f*;
47:11 and marshes will not become *f*;
Jas 3:11 Can both *f* water and salt water
3:12 can a salt spring produce *f* water.

FRESH-CUT

Ge 30:37 took *f* branches from poplar,

FRET

Ps 37: 1 Do not *f* because of evil men
37: 7 do not *f* when men succeed
37: 8 do not *f*— it leads only to evil.
Pr 24:19 Do not *f* because of evil men

FRICTION

1Ti 6: 5 and constant *f* between men

FRIEND (FRIENDLY FRIENDS FRIENDSHIP)

Ge 38:12 his *f* Hirah the Adullamite went
38:20 by his *f* the Adullamite in order
Ex 32:27 each killing his brother and *f*
33:11 as a man speaks with his *f*.
Dt 13: 6 your closest *f* secretly entices you,
Jdg 7:13 as a man was telling a *f* his dream.
7:14 His *f* responded, "This can be
14:20 to the *f* who had attended him
15: 2 he said, "that I gave her to your *f*.
15: 6 because his wife was given to his *f*
Ru 4: 1 "Come over here, my *f*.
2Sa 13: 3 Amnon had a *f* named Jonadab son
15:37 So David's *f* Hushai arrived
16:16 Then Hushai the Arkite, David's *f*,
16:17 Why didn't you go with your *f*?"
2Sa 16:17 "Is this the love you show your *f*?
1Ki 16:11 a single male, whether relative or *f*.
1Ch 27:33 Hushai the Arkite was the king's *f*.
2Ch 20: 7 descendants of Abraham your *f*?
Job 6:27 and barter away your *f*.
16:20 My intercessor is my *f*
16:21 as a man pleads for his *f*.
Ps 35:14 as though for my *f* or brother.
41: 9 Even my close *f*, whom I trusted,
55:13 my companion, my close *f*,
88:18 the darkness is my closest *f*.
119:63 I am a *f* to all who fear you,
Pr 17:17 A *f* loves at all times,
18:24 there is a *f* who sticks closer
19: 4 but a poor man's *f* deserts him.
19: 6 everyone is the *f* of a man who
22:11 will have the king for his *f*.
27: 6 but faithful are the wounds of a *f*.
27: 9 the pleasantness of one's *f* springs
27:10 Do not forsake your *f* and the *f*
Ecc 4:10 his *f* can help him up.
SS 5:16 This is my lover, this my *f*,
Isa 41: 8 you descendants of Abraham my *f*,
Jer 3: 4 'My Father, my *f* from my youth,
9: 4 and every *f* a slanderer.
9: 5 *F* deceives *f*,
23:35 each of you keeps on saying to his *f*
Mic 7: 5 put no confidence in a *f*.
Mt 11:19 a *f* of tax collectors and "sinners." '
20:13 "But he answered one of them, '*F*,
22:12 '*F*,' he asked, 'how did you get
26:50 "*F*, do what you came for."
Lk 5:20 he said, "*F*, your sins are forgiven."
7:34 a *f* of tax collectors and "sinners." '
11: 5 '*F*, lend me three loaves of bread,
11: 5 "Suppose one of you has a *f*,
11: 6 a *f* of mine on a journey has come
11: 8 him the bread because he is his *f*.
14:10 '*F*, move up to a better place.'
Jn 3:29 *f* who attends the bridegroom waits
11:11 "Our *f* Lazarus has fallen asleep;
19:12 "If you let this man go, you are no *f*
Ro 16: 5 Greet my dear *f* Epenetus,
16: 9 in Christ, and my dear *f* Stachys.
16:12 Greet my dear *f* Persis, another
Col 4:14 Our dear *f* Luke, the doctor,
Phm : 1 To Philemon our dear *f*
Jas 2:23 and he was called God's *f*.
4: 4 Anyone who chooses to be a *f*
3Jn : 1 The elder, To my dear *f* Gaius,
: 2 Dear *f*, I pray that you may enjoy
: 5 Dear *f*, you are faithful
:11 Dear *f*, do not imitate what is evil

FRIENDLY (FRIEND)

Ge 34:21 "These men are *f* toward us,"
Jdg 4:17 because there were *f* relations
1Ki 5: 1 been on *f* terms with David.

FRIENDS (FRIEND)

Ge 19: 7 behind him and said, "No, my *f*.
Jdg 11:37 roam the hills and weep with my *f*,
19:23 "No, my *f*, don't be so vile.
1Sa 30:26 the elders of Judah, who were his *f*,
2Sa 3: 8 and to his family and *f*.
2Ki 10:11 his close *f* and his priests, leaving
Est 5:10 Calling together his *f* and Zeresh,
5:14 His wife Zeresh and all his *f* said
6:13 and all his *f* everything that had
Job 2:11 When Job's three *f*, Eliphaz
6:14 should have the devotion of his *f*,
12: 4 become a laughingstock to my *f*,
17: 5 If a man denounces his *f* for reward
19:14 my *f* have forgotten me.
19:19 All my intimate *f* detest me;
19:21 "Have pity on me, my *f*, have pity,
24:17 they make *f* with the terrors
32: 3 He was also angry with the three *f*,
35: 4 and to your *f* with you.
42: 7 I am angry with you and your two *f*
42:10 After Job had prayed for his *f*,
Ps 31:11 I am a dread to my *f*—
38:11 My *f* and companions avoid me
55:20 My companion attacks his *f*;
88: 8 from me my closest *f*
122: 8 For the sake of my brothers and *f*,
Pr 14:20 but the rich have many *f*.
Pr 16:28 and a gossip separates close *f*.
17: 9 the matter separates close *f*.
19: 4 Wealth brings many *f*,
19: 7 how much more do his *f* avoid him!
22:24 Do not make *f* with a hot-tempered
SS 1: 7 woman beside the flocks of your *f*?
5: 1 Eat, O *f*, and drink;
8:13 the gardens with *f* in attendance,
Jer 6:21 neighbors and *f* will perish."
9: 4 "Beware of your *f*;
20: 4 terror to yourself and to all your *f*;
20: 6 and all your *f* to whom you have
20:10 All my *f*
38:22 those trusted *f* of yours.
38:22 your *f* have deserted you.'
La 1: 2 All her *f* have betrayed her;
Da 2:13 and his *f* to put them to death.
2:17 the matter to his *f* Hananiah,
2:18 and his *f* might not be executed
Ob : 7 your *f* will deceive and overpower
Zec 13: 6 given at the house of my *f*.'
Lk 2:44 for him among their relatives and *f*.
7: 6 when the centurion sent *f* to say
12: 4 my *f*, do not be afraid
14:12 do not invite your *f*, your brothers
15: 6 Then he calls his *f* and neighbors
15: 9 she calls her *f* and neighbors
15:29 goat so I could celebrate with my *f*.
16: 9 wealth to gain *f* for yourselves,
21:16 by parents, brothers, relatives and *f*
23:12 day Herod and Pilate became *f*—
Jn 15:13 that one lay down his life for his *f*.
15:14 You are my *f* if you do what I
15:15 Instead, I have called you *f*,
21: 5 "*F*, haven't you any fish?"
Ac 10:24 together his relatives and close *f*.
15:25 to you with our dear *f* Barnabas
19:31 officials of the province, *f* of Paul,
24:23 and permit his *f* to take care
27: 3 to go to his *f* so they might provide
Ro 12:19 Do not take revenge, my *f*,
1Co 10:14 my dear *f*, flee from idolatry.
2Co 7: 1 we have these promises, dear *f*,
12:19 dear *f*, is for your strengthening.
Php 2:12 my dear *f*, as you have always
4: 1 firm in the Lord, dear *f*!
Heb 6: 9 though we speak like this, dear *f*,
1Pe 2:11 Dear *f*, I urge you, as aliens
4:12 Dear *f*, do not be surprised
2Pe 3: 1 Dear *f*, this is now my second letter
3: 8 do not forget this one thing, dear *f*:
3:14 dear *f*, since you are looking
3:17 dear *f*, since you already know this,
1Jn 2: 7 Dear *f*, I am not writing you a new
3: 2 Dear *f*, now we are children of God
3:21 Dear *f*, if our hearts do not
4: 1 Dear *f*, do not believe every spirit,
4: 7 Dear *f*, let us love one another,
4:11 Dear *f*, since God so loved us,
3Jn :14 Greet the *f* there by name.
:14 The *f* here send their greetings.
Jude : 3 Dear *f*, although I was very eager
:17 dear *f*, remember what the apostles
:20 dear *f*, build yourselves up

FRIENDSHIP (FRIEND)

1Sa 20:42 for we have sworn *f*
Job 29: 4 when God's intimate *f* blessed my
Ps 109: 4 In return for my *f* they accuse me,
109: 5 and hatred for my *f*.
Pr 12:26 A righteous man is cautious in *f*,
Jas 4: 4 don't you know that *f*

FRIGHT (FEAR)

Lk 24: 5 In their *f* the women bowed

FRIGHTEN (FEAR)

Dt 28:26 there will be no one to *f* them away
Ne 6: 9 They were all trying to *f* us,
Job 7:14 even then you *f* me with dreams
9:34 that his terror would *f* me no more.
Jer 7:33 there will be no one to *f* them away
Eze 30: 9 out from me in ships to *f* Cush out
2Co 10: 9 to be trying to *f* you with my letters

FRIGHTENED (FEAR)

Ge 42:35 the money pouches, they were *f*.
43:18 men were *f* when they were taken

Isa 31: 4 he is not *f* by their shouts
Da 5: 6 was so *f* that his knees knocked
Mk 9: 6 what to say, they were so *f*.)
Lk 21: 9 and revolutions, do not be *f*.
24: 37 and *f*, thinking they saw a ghost.
Php 1: 28 gospel without being *f* in any way
1Pe 3: 14 fear what they fear; do not be *f*."

FRIGHTENING (FEAR)

Job 13: 21 and stop *f* me with your terrors.
Da 7: 7 terrifying and *f* and very powerful.

FRINGE

Job 26: 14 but the outer *f* of his works;

FROGS

Ex 8: 2 plague your whole country with *f*.
8: 3 The Nile will teem with *f*.
8: 4 The *f* will go up on you
8: 5 and make *f* come up on the land
8: 6 the *f* came up and covered the land
8: 7 also made *f* come up on the land
8: 8 LORD to take the *f* away from me
8: 9 your houses may be rid of the *f*,
8: 11 *f* will leave you and your houses,
8: 12 LORD about the *f* he had brought
8: 13 The *f* died in the houses,
Ps 78: 45 and *f* that devastated them.
105: 30 Their land teemed with *f*,
Rev 16: 13 three evil spirits that looked like *f*;

FROLIC

Ps 104: 26 which you formed to *f* there.
Jer 50: 11 you *f* like a heifer threshing grain

FRONDS

Lev 23: 40 and palm *f*, leafy branches

FRONTIER (FRONTIERS)

Eze 25: 9 beginning at its *f* towns—
48: 1 At the northern *f*, Dan will have

FRONTIERS (FRONTIER)

Ne 9: 22 to them even the remotest *f*.

FROST

Ex 16: 14 thin flakes like *f* on the ground
Job 38: 29 birth to the *f* from the heavens
Ps 147: 16 and scatters the *f* like ashes.
Jer 36: 30 the heat by day and the *f* by night.
Zec 14: 6 there will be no light, no cold or *f*.

FROWN

Jer 3: 12 'I will *f* on you no longer,

FROZE (FROZEN)

2Sa 23: 10 till his hand grew tired and *f*

FROZEN (FROZE)

Job 37: 10 and the broad waters become *f*.
38: 30 when the surface of the deep is *f*?

FRUIT (FRUITAGE FRUITFUL FRUITION FRUITS)

Ge 1: 11 on the land that bear *f* with seed
1: 12 and trees bearing *f* with seed
1: 29 every tree that has *f* with seed in it.
3: 2 "We may eat *f* from the trees
3: 3 'You must not eat *f*
3: 6 When the woman saw that the *f*
3: 12 she gave me some *f* from the tree,
Ex 10: 15 in the fields and the *f* on the trees.
Lev 19: 23 plant any kind of *f* tree, regard its *f*
19: 24 the fourth year all its *f* will be holy,
19: 25 in the fifth year you may eat its *f*.
23: 40 are to take choice *f* from the trees,
25: 19 Then the land will yield its *f*,
26: 4 and the trees of the field their *f*.
26: 20 the trees of the land yield their *f*.
27: 30 from the soil or *f* from the trees,
Nu 13: 20 some of the *f* of the land."
13: 26 and showed them the *f* of the land.
13: 27 with milk and honey! Here is its *f*.
Dt 1: 25 with them some of the *f* of the land,
7: 13 He will bless the *f* of your womb,
20: 19 because you can eat their *f*.
20: 20 trees that you know are not *f* trees
22: 9 the *f* of the vineyard will be defiled.
Dt 28: 4 The *f* of your womb will be blessed,
28: 11 in the *f* of your womb,
28: 18 The *f* of your womb will be cursed,
28: 30 will not even begin to enjoy its *f*.
28: 53 you will eat the *f* of the womb,
30: 9 and in the *f* of your womb,
32: 13 and fed him with the *f* of the fields.
Jdg 9: 11 'Should I give up my *f*, so good
2Sa 16: 2 and *f* are for the men to eat,
2Ki 19: 29 plant vineyards and eat their *f*.
19: 30 below and bear *f* above.
Ne 9: 25 olive groves and *f* trees
9: 36 forefathers so they could eat its *f*
10: 35 of our crops and of every *f* tree.
10: 37 of the *f* of all our trees
Ps 1: 3 which yields its *f* in season
72: 3 the hills the *f* of righteousness.
72: 16 Let its *f* flourish like Lebanon;
92: 14 They will still bear *f* in old age,
104: 13 by the *f* of his work.
128: 2 You will eat the *f* of your labor;
148: 9 *f* trees and all cedars,
Pr 1: 31 be filled with the *f* of their schemes
1: 31 they will eat the *f* of their ways
8: 19 My *f* is better than fine gold;
11: 30 The *f* of the righteous is a tree
12: 14 From the *f* of his lips a man is filled
13: 2 From the *f* of his lips a man enjoys
18: 20 From the *f* of his mouth a man's
18: 21 and those who love it will eat its *f*.
27: 18 He who tends a fig tree will eat its *f*
Ecc 2: 5 planted all kinds of *f* trees in them.
SS 2: 3 and his *f* is sweet to my taste.
2: 13 The fig tree forms its early *f*;
7: 7 and your breasts like clusters of *f*.
7: 8 I will take hold of its *f*."
8: 11 Each was to bring for its *f*
8: 12 are for those who tend its *f*.
Isa 3: 10 for they will enjoy the *f*
4: 2 the *f* of the land will be the pride
5: 2 but it yielded only bad *f*.
11: 1 from his roots a Branch will bear *f*.
14: 29 its *f* will be a darting, venomous
16: 9 shouts of joy over your ripened *f*
27: 6 and fill all the world with *f*.
32: 10 and the harvest of *f* will not come.
32: 17 The *f* of righteousness will be peace
37: 30 plant vineyards and eat their *f*.
37: 31 below and bear *f* above.
65: 21 will plant vineyards and eat their *f*.
Jer 2: 7 land to eat its *f* and rich produce.
6: 19 the *f* of their schemes,
7: 20 and on the *f* of the ground,
11: 16 with *f* beautiful in form.
11: 19 "Let us destroy the tree and its *f*;
12: 2 they grow and bear *f*.
17: 8 and never fails to bear *f*."
31: 5 and enjoy their *f*.
40: 10 are to harvest the wine, summer *f*
40: 12 abundance of wine and summer *f*.
48: 32 fallen on your ripened *f* and grapes.
Eze 17: 8 bear *f* and become a splendid vine.'
17: 9 stripped of its *f* so that it withers?
17: 23 bear *f* and become a splendid cedar
19: 12 it was stripped of its *f*;
19: 14 and consumed its *f*.
25: 4 they will eat your *f* and drink your
34: 27 trees of the field will yield their *f*
36: 8 and *f* for my people Israel,
36: 30 I will increase the *f* of the trees
47: 12 Their *f* will serve for food
47: 12 *F* trees of all kinds will grow
47: 12 will not wither, nor will their *f* fail.
Da 4: 12 were beautiful, its *f* abundant,
4: 14 strip off its leaves and scatter its *f*.
4: 21 beautiful leaves and abundant *f*,
Hos 9: 10 the early *f* on the fig tree.
9: 16 they yield no *f*.
10: 1 As his *f* increased,
10: 1 he brought forth *f* for himself.
10: 12 reap the *f* of unfailing love,
10: 13 you have eaten the *f* of deception.
14: 2 that we may offer the *f* of our lips.
Joel 2: 22 The trees are bearing their *f*;
Am 2: 9 I destroyed his *f* above
6: 12 and the *f* of righteousness
8: 1 showed me: a basket of ripe *f*.
8: 2 "A basket of ripe *f*," I answered.
Am 9: 14 will make gardens and eat their *f*.
Mic 6: 7 the *f* of my body for the sin
7: 1 am like one who gathers summer *f*
Na 3: 12 trees with their first ripe *f*;
Hag 2: 19 and the olive tree have not borne *f*.
Zec 8: 12 vine will yield its *f*, the ground will
Mal 3: 11 in your fields will not cast their *f*,"
Mt 3: 8 Produce *f* in keeping
3: 10 does not produce good *f* will be cut
7: 16 By their *f* you will recognize them.
7: 17 good *f*, but a bad tree bears bad *f*.
7: 18 A good tree cannot bear bad *f*,
7: 18 and a bad tree cannot bear good *f*.
7: 19 tree that does not bear good *f* is cut
7: 20 by their *f* you will recognize them.
12: 33 a tree good and its *f* will be good,
12: 33 for a tree is recognized by its *f*.
12: 33 make a tree bad and its *f* will be bad
21: 19 "May you never bear *f* again!"
21: 34 to the tenants to collect his *f*.
21: 43 to a people who will produce its *f*.
26: 29 drink of this *f* of the vine from now
Mk 11: 13 he went to find out if it had any *f*.
11: 14 "May no one ever eat *f*
12: 2 some of the *f* of the vineyard.
14: 25 of the *f* of the vine until that day
Lk 3: 8 Produce *f* in keeping
3: 9 does not produce good *f* will be cut
6: 43 nor does a bad tree bear good *f*.
6: 43 "No good tree bears bad *f*,
6: 44 Each tree is recognized by its own *f*
13: 6 and he went to look for *f* on it,
13: 7 coming to look for *f* on this fig tree
13: 9 If it bears *f* next year, fine! If not,
20: 10 some of the *f* of the vineyard.
22: 18 again of the *f* of the vine
Jn 15: 2 branch in me that bears no *f*,
15: 2 that does bear *f* he trims clean
15: 4 Neither can you bear *f*
15: 4 No branch can bear *f* by itself;
15: 5 he will bear much *f*; apart
15: 8 bear much *f*, showing yourselves
15: 16 and bear *f*—*f* that will last.
Ro 7: 4 in order that we might bear *f*
7: 5 so that we bore *f* for death.
15: 28 sure that they have received this *f*,
Gal 5: 22 But the *f* of the Spirit is love, joy,
Eph 5: 9 light (for the *f* of the light consists
Php 1: 11 with the *f* of righteousness that
Col 1: 6 the world this gospel is producing *f*
1: 10 bearing *f* in every good work,
Heb 13: 15 the *f* of lips that confess his name.
Jas 3: 17 and good *f*, impartial and sincere.
Jude : 12 autumn trees, without *f*
Rev 18: 14 'The *f* you longed for is gone
22: 2 of *f*, yielding its *f* every month.

FRUITAGE (FRUIT)

Isa 27: 9 this will be the full *f* of the removal

FRUITFUL (FRUIT FRUITFULNESS)

Ge 1: 22 "Be *f* and increase in number
1: 28 "Be *f* and increase in number;
8: 17 be *f* and increase in number upon it
9: 1 "Be *f* and increase in number
9: 7 be *f* and increase in number;
17: 6 will make you very *f*; I will make
17: 20 I will make him *f* and will greatly
28: 3 Almighty bless you and make you *f*
35: 11 be *f* and increase in number.
41: 52 God has made me *f* in the land
47: 27 and were *f* and increased greatly
48: 4 'I am going to make you *f*
49: 22 a *f* vine near a spring,
49: 22 "Joseph is a *f* vine,
Ex 1: 7 the Israelites were *f* and multiplied
Lev 26: 9 and make you *f* and increase your
Ps 105: 24 The LORD made his people very *f*;
107: 34 and *f* land into a salt waste,
107: 37 that yielded a *f* harvest;
128: 3 Your wife will be like a *f* vine
Isa 17: 6 four or five on the *f* boughs,"
27: 2 "Sing about a *f* vineyard:
32: 12 for the *f* vines
Jer 4: 26 and the *f* land was a desert;
23: 3 where they will be *f* and increase
49: 4 boast of your valleys so *f*?
Eze 19: 10 it was *f* and full of branches

Eze 36: 11 and they will be *f* and become
Jn 15: 2 clean so that it will be even more *f*.
Php 1: 22 this will mean *f* labor for me.

FRUITFULNESS (FRUIT FRUITFUL)

Dt 33: 15 and the *f* of the everlasting hills;
Hos 14: 8 your *f* comes from me."

FRUITION (FRUIT)

2Sa 23: 5 Will he not bring to *f* my salvation

FRUITLESS

Eph 5: 11 to do with the *f* deeds of darkness,

FRUITS (FRUIT)

Ge 4: 3 of time Cain brought some of the *f*
Ps 109: 11 may strangers plunder the *f*
SS 4: 13 pomegranates with choice *f*,
4: 16 and taste its choice *f*.
Jer 3: 24 the *f* of our fathers' labor—

FRUSTRATE (FRUSTRATED FRUSTRATES FRUSTRATING FRUSTRATION)

2Sa 17: 14 to *f* the good advice of Ahithophel
Ezr 4: 5 *f* their plans during the entire reign
Ps 14: 6 You evildoers *f* the plans
1Co 1: 19 of the intelligent I will *f*."

FRUSTRATED (FRUSTRATE)

2Sa 13: 2 Amnon became *f* to the point
Ne 4: 15 of their plot and that God had *f* it,
Eze 24: 12 It has *f* all efforts;

FRUSTRATES (FRUSTRATE)

Ps 146: 9 but he *f* the ways of the wicked.
Pr 22: 12 but he *f* the words of the unfaithful.

FRUSTRATING (FRUSTRATE)

2Sa 15: 34 me by *f* Ahithophel's advice.

FRUSTRATION (FRUSTRATE)

Ecc 5: 17 with great *f*, affliction and anger.
Ro 8: 20 For the creation was subjected to *f*,

FUEL

Isa 9: 5 will be *f* for the fire.
9: 19 and the people will be *f* for the fire;
44: 15 It is man's *f* for burning;
44: 19 "Half of it I used for *f*;
Jer 51: 58 the nations' labor is only *f*
Eze 4: 12 using human excrement for *f*."
15: 4 as *f* and the fire burns both ends
15: 6 trees of the forest as *f* for the fire,
21: 32 You will be *f* for the fire,
39: 9 weapons for *f* and burn them up—
39: 9 years they will use them for *f*.
39: 10 they will use the weapons for *f*.
Hab 2: 13 that the people's labor is only *f*

FUGITIVE (FUGITIVES)

Pr 28: 17 will be a *f* till death;
Eze 24: 26 on that day a *f* will come

FUGITIVES (FUGITIVE)

Nu 21: 29 He has given up his sons as *f*
Jos 8: 22 them neither survivors nor *f*.
Isa 15: 5 her *f* flee as far as Zoar,
15: 9 a lion upon the *f* of Moab
16: 3 Hide the *f*,
16: 4 Let the Moabite *f* stay with you;
21: 14 bring food for the *f*.
43: 14 bring down as *f* all the Babylonians
45: 20 assemble, you *f* from the nations.
Jer 44: 14 none will return except a few *f*."
48: 45 the *f* stand helpless,
49: 5 and no one will gather the *f*.
50: 28 Listen to the *f* and refugees
Ob : 14 the crossroads to cut down their *f*,

FULFILL (FULFILLED FULFILLING FULFILLMENT FULFILLS)

Ge 38: 8 your brother's wife and *f* your duty
Lev 22: 18 to *f* a vow or as a freewill offering,
22: 21 to the LORD to *f* a special vow
Nu 6: 21 He must *f* the vow he has made,
23: 19 Does he promise and not *f*?
Dt 25: 5 *f* the duty of a brother-in-law to her
25: 7 He will not *f* the duty
1Sa 1: 21 to the LORD and to *f* his vow,
2Sa 15: 7 and *f* a vow I made to the LORD.
1Ki 6: 12 I will *f* through you the promise I
12: 15 to *f* the word the LORD had
2Ki 23: 24 This he did to *f* the requirements
2Ch 10: 15 to *f* the word the LORD had
36: 22 in order to *f* the word
Ezr 1: 1 in order to *f* the word
Est 5: 8 grant my petition and *f* my request,
Job 22: 27 and you will *f* your vows.
Ps 22: 25 who fear you will I *f* my vows.
50: 14 *f* your vows to the Most High,
61: 8 and *f* my vows day after day.
66: 13 and *f* my vows to you—
76: 11 to the LORD your God and *f* them
116: 14 I will *f* my vows to the LORD
116: 18 I will *f* my vows to the LORD
119: 38 *F* your promise to your servant,
138: 8 The LORD will *f* ⌊his purpose⌋
Ecc 5: 4 pleasure in fools; *f* your vow.
5: 5 than to make a vow and not *f* it.
Isa 46: 11 far-off land, a man to *f* my purpose.
Jer 11: 5 Then I will *f* the oath I swore
28: 6 May the LORD *f* the words you
29: 10 and *f* my gracious promise
33: 14 'when I will *f* the gracious promise
39: 16 I am about to *f* my words
Eze 12: 25 house, I will *f* whatever I say,
Na 1: 15 and *f* your vows.
Mt 1: 22 place to *f* what the Lord had said
3: 15 us to do this to *f* all righteousness."
4: 14 *f* what was said
5: 17 come to abolish them but to *f* them.
8: 17 This was to *f* what was spoken
12: 17 This was to *f* what was spoken
21: 4 place to *f* what was spoken
Jn 12: 38 This was to *f* the word
13: 18 But this is to *f* the scripture:
15: 25 But this is to *f* what is written
Ac 7: 17 drew near for God to *f* his promise
1Co 7: 3 husband should *f* his marital duty
Gal 6: 2 and in this way you will *f* the law
2Th 1: 11 power he may *f* every good

FULFILLED (FULFILL)

Jos 21: 45 of Israel failed; every one was *f*.
23: 14 Every promise has been *f*;
Jdg 13: 12 him, "When your words are *f*,
1Sa 10: 7 these signs are *f*, do whatever your
10: 9 and all these signs were *f* that day.
1Ki 8: 15 own hand has *f* what he promised
8: 24 and with your hand you have *f* it—
9: 25 and so *f* the temple obligations.
2Ki 15: 12 of the LORD spoken to Jehu was *f*:
2Ch 6: 4 his hands has *f* what he promised
6: 15 and with your hand you have *f* it—
Ps 65: 1 to you our vows will be *f*.
Pr 7: 14 today I *f* my vows.
13: 12 but a longing *f* is a tree of life.
13: 19 A longing *f* is sweet to the soul,
Jer 1: 12 watching to see that my word is *f*."
17: 15 Let it now be *f*!"
25: 12 "But when the seventy years are *f*,
34: 18 and have not *f* the terms
39: 16 At that time they will be *f*
La 2: 17 he has *f* his word,
Eze 12: 23 near when every vision will be *f*.
12: 25 and it shall be *f* without delay.
12: 28 say will be *f*, declares the Sovereign
13: 6 yet they expect their words to be *f*.
Da 4: 33 said about Nebuchadnezzar was *f*.
8: 13 take for the vision to be *f*—
9: 12 You have *f* the words spoken
12: 6 these astonishing things are *f*?"
Mt 2: 15 so was *f* what the Lord had said
2: 17 the prophet Jeremiah was *f*:
2: 23 So was *f* what was said
13: 14 In them is *f* the prophecy of Isaiah:
13: 35 So was *f* what was spoken
26: 54 would the Scriptures be *f* that say it
26: 56 of the prophets might be *f*."
27: 9 by Jeremiah the prophet was *f*:
Mk 13: 4 that they are all about to be *f*?"
14: 49 But the Scriptures must be *f*."
Lk 1: 1 of the things that have been *f*
4: 21 "Today this scripture is *f*
18: 31 about the Son of Man will be *f*.
21: 24 until the times of the Gentiles are *f*.
22: 37 I tell you that this must be *f* in me.
24: 44 Everything must be *f* that is
Jn 17: 12 so that Scripture would be *f*.
18: 9 words he had spoken would be *f*:
18: 32 he was going to die would be *f*.
19: 24 the Scripture might be *f* which said,
19: 28 and so that the Scripture would be *f*
19: 36 so that the Scripture would be *f*:
Ac 1: 16 to be *f* which the Holy Spirit spoke
3: 18 But this is how God *f* what he had
13: 27 condemning him they *f* the words
13: 33 God promised our fathers he has *f*
23: 1 I have *f* my duty to God
26: 7 our twelve tribes are hoping to see *f*
Ro 13: 8 loves his fellow man has *f* the law.
Jas 2: 23 And the scripture was *f* that says,
Rev 17: 17 to rule, until God's words are *f*.

FULFILLING (FULFILL)

Nu 3: 8 *f* the obligations of the Israelites
1Ki 2: 27 *f* the word the LORD had spoken
Ecc 5: 4 a vow to God, do not delay in *f* it.

FULFILLMENT (FULFILL)

Lev 22: 23 it will not be accepted in *f* of a vow.
2Ch 36: 21 seventy years were completed in *f*
Da 11: 14 your own people will rebel in *f*
Lk 9: 31 about to bring to *f* at Jerusalem.
21: 22 the time of punishment in *f*
22: 16 again until it finds *f* in the kingdom
22: 37 written about me is reaching its *f*."
Ro 13: 10 Therefore love is the *f* of the law.
1Co 10: 11 on whom the *f* of the ages has come
Eph 1: 10 times will have reached their *f*—

FULFILLS (FULFILL)

Ps 57: 2 to God, who *f* ⌊his purpose⌋ for me.
145: 19 He *f* the desires of those who fear
Isa 44: 26 *f* the predictions of his messengers,

FULL (FILL)

Ge 6: 11 in God's sight and was *f* of violence
14: 10 Valley of Siddim was *f* of tar pits,
15: 16 has not yet reached its *f* measure."
23: 9 him to sell it to me for the *f* price
25: 8 an old man and *f* of years;
35: 29 to his people, old and *f* of years.
41: 1 When two *f* years had passed,
41: 7 up the seven healthy, *f* heads
41: 22 *f* and good, growing
50: 3 him, taking a *f* forty days,
Ex 5: 18 yet you must produce your *f* quota
8: 21 of the Egyptians will be *f* of flies,
9: 14 or this time I will send the *f* force
16: 20 but it was *f* of maggots
23: 26 I will give you a *f* life span.
Lev 6: 5 He must make restitution in *f*,
16: 12 is to take a censer *f* of burning coals
23: 15 offering, count off seven *f* weeks.
25: 29 of redemption a *f* year after its sale.
25: 30 before a *f* year has passed,
Nu 5: 7 He must make *f* restitution
33: 3 They marched out boldly in *f* view
Dt 21: 13 father and mother for a *f* month,
33: 23 and is *f* of his blessing;
Jos 10: 13 delayed going down about a *f* day
Jdg 8: 2 than the *f* grape harvest of Abiezer
Ru 1: 21 I went away *f*, but the LORD has
1Sa 2: 5 Those who were *f* hire themselves
18: 27 presented the *f* number to the king
28: 20 Immediately Saul fell *f* length
2Sa 5: 17 they went up in *f* force to search
11: 18 Joab sent David a *f* account
23: 11 at a place where there was a field *f*
2Ki 3: 16 Make this valley *f* of ditches.
4: 6 When all the jars were *f*, she said
6: 17 and saw the hills *f* of horses
10: 21 of Baal until it was *f* from one end
1Ch 11: 13 At a place where there was a field *f*
14: 8 they went up in *f* force to search
21: 22 Sell it to me at the *f* price."
21: 24 "No, I insist on paying the *f* price.
23: 1 When David was old and *f* of years,
2Ch 24: 10 them into the chest until it was *f*.
24: 15 Jehoiada was old and *f* of years,
Ne 9: 25 to the *f* and were well-nourished;
Est 1: 4 For a *f* 180 days he displayed
9: 29 wrote with *f* authority

Est 10: 2 together with a *f* account
Job 5: 26 to the grave in *f* vigor,
10: 15 for I am *f* of shame
14: 1 is of few days and *f* of trouble.
15: 32 Before his time he will be paid in *f*.
20: 22 the *f* force of misery will come
21: 23 One man dies in *f* vigor,
21: 27 I know *f* well what you are thinking
26: 9 He covers the face of the *f* moon,
32: 12 I gave you my *f* attention.
32: 18 For I am *f* of words,
42: 17 And so he died, old and *f* of years.
Ps 10: 7 His mouth is *f* of curses and lies
26: 10 whose right hands are *f* of bribes.
31: 23 but the proud he pays back in *f*.
33: 5 the earth is *f* of his unfailing love.
75: 8 *f* of foaming wine mixed
78: 38 and did not stir up his *f* wrath.
81: 3 and when the moon is *f*, on the day
88: 3 For my soul is *f* of trouble
94: 4 all the evildoers are *f* of boasting.
104: 24 the earth is *f* of your creatures.
116: 5 our God is *f* of compassion.
127: 5 whose quiver is *f* of them.
130: 7 and with him is *f* redemption.
139: 14 I know that *f* well.
144: 8 whose mouths are *f* of lies,
144: 11 whose mouths are *f* of lies,
Pr 1: 17 a net in *f* view of all the birds!
4: 18 till the *f* light of day.
5: 21 are in *f* view of the LORD,
7: 20 and will not be home till *f* moon."
8: 21 and making their treasuries *f*.
17: 1 and quiet than a house *f* of feasting,
20: 17 he ends up with a mouth *f* of gravel
27: 7 He who is *f* loathes honey,
29: 11 A fool gives *f* vent to his anger,
30: 22 a fool who is *f* of food,
31: 11 Her husband has *f* confidence
Ecc 1: 7 yet the sea is never *f*.
9: 3 are *f* of evil and there is madness
11: 3 If clouds are *f* of water,
Isa 1: 15 Your hands are *f* of blood;
1: 21 She once was *f* of justice;
2: 6 They are *f* of superstitions
2: 7 Their land is *f* of horses;
2: 7 Their land is *f* of silver and gold;
2: 8 Their land is *f* of idols;
6: 3 the whole earth is *f* of his glory."
11: 9 for the earth will be *f*
15: 9 Dimon's waters are *f* of blood,
22: 2 O town *f* of commotion,
22: 7 Your choicest valleys are *f*
27: 9 and this will be the *f* fruitage
30: 26 like the light of seven *f* days,
30: 27 his lips are *f* of wrath,
47: 9 come upon you in *f* measure,
65: 6 keep silent but will pay back in *f*;
65: 7 *f* payment for their former deeds."
Jer 5: 27 Like cages *f* of birds,
5: 27 their houses are *f* of deceit;
6: 11 I am *f* of the wrath of the LORD,
23: 10 The land is *f* of adulterers;
35: 5 Then I set bowls *f* of wine
51: 5 though their land is *f* of guilt
51: 56 he will repay in *f*.
La 1: 1 once so *f* of people!
4: 11 The LORD has given *f* vent
Eze 1: 18 and all four rims were *f* of eyes all
1: 27 as if *f* of fire, and that from there
7: 23 and the city is *f* of violence.
7: 23 because the land is *f* of bloodshed
9: 9 and the city is *f* of injustice.
9: 9 the land is *f* of bloodshed
10: 4 and the court was *f* of the radiance
10: 12 were completely *f* of eyes,
17: 3 *f* plumage of varied colors came
17: 7 with powerful wings and *f* plumage
19: 10 it was fruitful and *f* of branches
22: 5 O infamous city, *f* of turmoil.
23: 12 in *f* dress, mounted horsemen,
28: 12 *f* of wisdom and perfect in beauty.
37: 1 middle of a valley; it was *f* of bones.
Joel 2: 26 plenty to eat, until you are *f*,
3: 13 for the winepress is *f*
Na 3: 1 *f* of lies,
3: 1 *f* of plunder,
Zec 9: 15 they will be *f* like a bowl
Mt 6: 2 have received their reward in *f*.
6: 5 have received their reward in *f*.
6: 16 have received their reward in *f*.
6: 22 your whole body will be *f* of light.
6: 23 your whole body will be *f*
13: 48 When it was *f*, the fishermen pulled
23: 25 but inside they are *f* of greed
23: 27 the inside are *f* of dead men's bones
23: 28 on the inside you are *f* of hypocrisy
Mk 2: 12 walked out in *f* view of them all.
4: 28 then the *f* kernel in the head.
Lk 4: 1 Jesus, *f* of the Holy Spirit,
5: 7 boats so *f* that they began
6: 34 expecting to be repaid in *f*.
10: 21 *f* of joy through the Holy Spirit,
11: 34 your body also is *f* of darkness.
11: 34 your whole body also is *f* of light.
11: 36 if your whole body is *f* of light,
11: 39 but inside you are *f* of greed
14: 23 so that my house will be *f*.
Jn 1: 14 came from the Father, *f* of grace
3: 29 and is *f* of joy when he hears
10: 10 may have life, and have it to the *f*.
13: 1 he now showed them the *f* extent
17: 13 that they may have the *f* measure
21: 8 towing the net *f* of fish,
21: 11 It was *f* of large fish, 153, but
Ac 5: 2 With his wife's *f* knowledge he
5: 20 "and tell the people the *f* message
5: 21 the *f* assembly of the elders
6: 3 known to be *f* of the Spirit
6: 5 a man *f* of faith and of the Holy
6: 8 a man *f* of God's grace and power,
7: 55 But Stephen, *f* of the Holy Spirit,
8: 23 For I see that you are *f* of bitterness
11: 24 *f* of the Holy Spirit and faith,
13: 10 You are *f* of all kinds of deceit
17: 16 to see that the city was *f* of idols.
Ro 1: 29 They are *f* of envy, murder, strife,
3: 14 "Their mouths are *f* of cursing
11: 25 in part until the *f* number
13: 6 who give their *f* time to governing.
15: 14 that you yourselves are *f*
15: 29 in the *f* measure of the blessing
16: 19 so I am *f* of joy over you;
Gal 4: 5 that we might receive the *f* rights
Eph 6: 11 Put on the *f* armor of God
6: 13 put on the *f* armor of God,
Php 4: 18 I have received *f* payment and
Col 2: 2 so that they may have the *f* riches
4: 6 Let your conversation be always *f*
1Ti 1: 15 saying that deserves *f* acceptance:
2: 11 learn in quietness and *f* submission.
4: 9 saying that deserves *f* acceptance
6: 1 their masters worthy of *f* respect,
Phm : 6 you will have a *f* understanding
Heb 10: 22 heart in *f* assurance of faith,
Jas 3: 8 It is a restless evil, *f*
3: 17 submissive, *f* of mercy
5: 11 The Lord is *f* of compassion
2Pe 2: 14 With eyes *f* of adultery, they never
Rev 5: 8 they were holding golden bowls *f*
13: 13 heaven to earth in *f* view of men.
14: 10 which has been poured *f* strength
21: 9 angels who had the seven bowls *f*

FULL-GROWN (GROW)

Jas 1: 15 when it is *f*, gives birth to death.

FULLNESS (FILL)

Dt 33: 16 gifts of the earth and its *f*
Jn 1: 16 From the *f* of his grace we have all
Ro 11: 12 greater riches will their *f* bring!
Eph 1: 23 the *f* of him who fills everything
3: 19 to the measure of all the *f* of God.
4: 13 to the whole measure of the *f*
Col 1: 19 to have all his *f* dwell in him,
1: 25 to you the word of God in its *f*—
2: 9 in Christ all the *f* of the Deity lives
2: 10 and you have been given *f* in Christ

FULLY (FILL)

Ex 19: 5 Now if you obey me *f* and keep my
Dt 15: 5 if only you *f* obey the LORD your
28: 1 If you *f* obey the LORD your God
Jos 1: 14 but all your fighting men, *f* armed,
1: 17 Just as we *f* obeyed Moses,
1Ki 8: 61 your hearts must be *f* committed
1Ki 11: 4 and his heart was not *f* devoted
15: 3 his heart was not *f* devoted
15: 14 Asa's heart was *f* committed
1Ch 12: 38 They came to Hebron *f* determined
2Ch 15: 17 Asa's heart was *f* committed
16: 9 whose hearts are *f* committed
Ezr 6: 8 of these men are to be *f* paid out
Ps 62: 4 They *f* intend to topple him
106: 2 or *f* declare his praise?
119: 4 that are to be *f* obeyed.
119: 138 they are *f* trustworthy.
Pr 13: 4 of the diligent are *f* satisfied.
14: 14 The faithless will be *f* repaid
28: 5 seek the LORD understand it *f*.
Isa 21: 7 *f* alert."
Jer 23: 20 back until he *f* accomplishes
30: 24 back until he *f* accomplishes
35: 10 and have *f* obeyed everything our
Eze 38: 4 horses, your horsemen *f* armed,
Da 11: 13 with a huge army *f* equipped.
Joel 2: 19 enough to satisfy you *f*;
Lk 6: 40 everyone who is *f* trained will be
9: 32 but when they became *f* awake,
11: 21 "When a strong man, *f* armed,
Ro 4: 21 being *f* persuaded that God had
8: 4 of the law might be *f* met in us,
14: 5 Each one should be *f* convinced
14: 14 I am *f* convinced that no food is
15: 19 I have *f* proclaimed the gospel
1Co 13: 12 shall know *f*, even as I am *f* known.
15: 58 Always give yourselves *f*
2Co 1: 14 to understand *f* that you can boast
Gal 4: 4 But when the time had *f* come,
Col 4: 12 will of God, mature and *f* assured.
2Ti 4: 17 the message might be *f* proclaimed
Tit 2: 10 to show that they can be *f* trusted,
1Pe 1: 13 set your hope *f* on the grace
2Jn : 8 but that you may be rewarded *f*.

FUN

Ac 2: 13 however, made *f* of them and said,

FUNCTION

Ex 27: 19 whatever their *f*, including all
Ro 12: 4 do not all have the same *f*,

FUNERAL

Jer 16: 5 a house where there is a *f* meal;
34: 5 As people made a *f* fire in honor

FURIOUS (FURY)

Dt 29: 28 In *f* anger and in great wrath
2Sa 13: 21 King David heard all this, he was *f*.
2Ch 25: 10 They were *f* with Judah
Est 1: 12 Then the king became *f*
Jer 32: 37 where I banish them in my *f* anger
Da 2: 12 and *f* that he ordered the execution
3: 13 *F* with rage, Nebuchadnezzar
3: 19 Then Nebuchadnezzar was *f*
Mt 2: 16 outwitted by the Magi, he was *f*,
8: 24 a *f* storm came up on the lake,
Mk 4: 37 A *f* squall came up, and the waves
Lk 4: 28 the people in the synagogue were *f*
6: 11 they were *f* and began to discuss
Ac 5: 33 they were *f* and wanted to put them
7: 54 they were *f* and gnashed their teeth
19: 28 they were *f* and began shouting:

FURNACE

Ge 19: 28 from the land, like smoke from a *f*.
Ex 9: 8 "Take handfuls of soot from a *f*
9: 10 So they took soot from a *f*
19: 18 up from it like smoke from a *f*,
Dt 4: 20 out of the iron-smelting *f*,
1Ki 8: 51 out of that iron-smelting *f*.
Ps 12: 6 like silver refined in a *f* of clay,
21: 9 you will make them like a fiery *f*.
Pr 17: 3 for silver and the *f* for gold,
27: 21 for silver and the *f* for gold,
Isa 31: 9 whose *f* is in Jerusalem.
48: 10 in the *f* of affliction.
Jer 11: 4 out of the iron-smelting *f*.'
Eze 22: 18 tin, iron and lead left inside a *f*.
22: 20 and tin into a *f* to melt it
22: 22 melted in a *f*, so you will be melted
Da 3: 6 be thrown into a blazing *f*."
3: 11 will be thrown into a blazing *f*.
3: 15 immediately into a blazing *f*.

Da 3: 17 If we are thrown into the blazing *f*.
3: 19 He ordered the *f* heated seven
3: 20 and throw them into the blazing *f*.
3: 21 and thrown into the blazing *f*.
3: 22 and the *f* so hot that the flames
3: 23 firmly tied, fell into the blazing *f*.
3: 26 the opening of the blazing *f*
Mal 4: 1 day is coming; it will burn like a *f*.
Mt 13: 42 will throw them into the fiery *f*,
13: 50 and throw them into the fiery *f*,
Rev 1: 15 feet were like bronze glowing in a *f*,
9: 2 it like the smoke from a gigantic *f*.

FURNISHED (FURNISHINGS)

Eze 16: 52 for you have *f* some justification
Mk 14: 15 will show you a large upper room, *f*
Lk 22: 12 show you a large upper room, all *f*.
Ac 28: 10 they *f* us with the supplies we

FURNISHINGS (FURNISHED)

Ex 25: 9 all its *f* exactly like the pattern I
31: 7 and all the other *f* of the tent—
39: 33 the tent and all its *f*, its clasps,
39: 40 all the *f* for the tabernacle,
40: 9 consecrate it and all its *f*,
Nu 1: 50 over all its *f* and everything
1: 50 to carry the tabernacle and all its *f*;
3: 8 of all the *f* of the Tent of Meeting,
4: 15 have finished covering the holy *f*
4: 16 including its holy *f* and articles."
7: 1 and consecrated it and all its *f*.
18: 3 go near the *f* of the sanctuary
19: 18 and sprinkle the tent and all the *f*
1Ki 7: 48 also made all the *f* that were
7: 51 the silver and gold and the *f*—
8: 4 of Meeting and all the sacred *f* in it.
1Ch 9: 29 assigned to take care of the *f*
2Ch 4: 19 also made all the *f* that were
5: 1 the silver and gold and all the *f*—
5: 5 of Meeting and all the sacred *f* in it.
28: 24 Ahaz gathered together the *f*
Jer 27: 18 Almighty that the *f* remaining
27: 19 the other *f* that are left in this city,

FURROW (FURROWS)

Job 39: 10 him to the *f* with a harness?

FURROWS (FURROW)

Job 31: 38 and all its *f* are wet with tears,
Ps 65: 10 You drench its *f*
129: 3 and made their *f* long.

FURY (FURIOUS)

Ge 27: 44 until your brother's *f* subsides
34: 7 They were filled with grief and *f*,
49: 7 and their *f*, so cruel!
2Ki 3: 27 The *f* against Israel was great;
Est 7: 10 Then the king's *f* subsided.
Job 40: 11 Unleash the *f* of your wrath,
Pr 6: 34 for jealousy arouses a husband's *f*,
22: 8 the rod of his *f* will be destroyed.
27: 4 Anger is cruel and *f* overwhelming,
Isa 14: 4 How his *f* has ended!
14: 6 and in *f* subdued nations
66: 14 but his *f* will be shown to his foes.
66: 15 he will bring down his anger with *f*,
Jer 21: 5 and a mighty arm in anger and *f*
Eze 13: 13 of rain will fall with destructive *f*.
19: 12 But it was uprooted in *f*
23: 25 and they will deal with you in *f*
Da 11: 30 vent his *f* against the holy covenant
Am 1: 11 and his *f* flamed unchecked,
Heb 11: 34 quenched the *f* of the flames,
Rev 12: 12 He is filled with *f*,
14: 10 will drink of the wine of God's *f*,
16: 19 with the wine of the *f* of his wrath.
19: 15 the winepress of the *f* of the wrath

FUTILE (FUTILITY)

Ps 94: 11 he knows that they are *f*.
Jer 48: 30 I know her insolence but it is *f*,"
Mal 3: 14 You have said, 'It is *f* to serve God.
Ro 1: 21 but their thinking became *f*
1Co 3: 20 that the thoughts of the wise are *f*."
15: 17 your faith is *f*; you are still

FUTILITY (FUTILE)

Job 7: 3 so I have been allotted months of *f*,
Ps 78: 33 So he ended their days in *f*
89: 47 For what *f* you have created all
Eph 4: 17 in the *f* of their thinking.

FUTURE

Ge 30: 33 honesty will testify for me in the *f*,
Dt 6: 20 In the *f*, when your son asks you,
Jos 4: 6 In the *f*, when your children ask
4: 21 "In the *f* when your descendants
22: 27 in the *f* your descendants will not
2Sa 7: 19 spoken about the *f* of the house
1Ch 17: 17 you have spoken about the *f*
Job 8: 7 so prosperous will your *f* be.
Ps 22: 30 *f* generations will be told about
37: 37 there is a *f* for the man of peace.
37: 38 the *f* of the wicked will be cut off.
102: 18 this be written for a *f* generation,
Pr 23: 18 There is surely a *f* hope for you,
24: 14 if you find it, there is a *f* hope
24: 20 for the evil man has no *f* hope,
Ecc 7: 14 anything about his *f*.
8: 7 Since no man knows the *f*,
Isa 9: 1 but in the *f* he will honor Galilee
41: 23 tell us what the *f* holds,
Jer 29: 11 plans to give you hope and a *f*.
31: 17 So there is hope for your *f*,"
La 1: 9 she did not consider her *f*.
Eze 12: 27 he prophesies about the distant *f*.'
38: 8 In *f* years you will invade a land
Da 2: 45 king what will take place in the *f*.
8: 26 for it concerns the distant *f*."
10: 14 happen to your people in the *f*,
Mt 26: 64 In the *f* you will see the Son
Ac 16: 16 spirit by which she predicted the *f*.
Ro 8: 38 neither the present nor the *f*,
1Co 3: 22 life or death or the present or the *f*
Heb 3: 5 to what would be said in the *f*.
11: 20 and Esau in regard to their *f*.

GAAL

Jdg 9: 26 Now *G* son of Ebed moved
9: 28 Then *G* son of Ebed said, "Who is
9: 30 of the city heard what *G* son
9: 31 "*G* son of Ebed and his brothers
9: 33 When *G* and his men come out
9: 35 Now *G* son of Ebed had gone out
9: 36 When *G* saw them, he said to Zebul
9: 37 But *G* spoke up again: "Look,
9: 39 *G* led out the citizens of Shechem
9: 41 Zebul drove *G* and his brothers out

GAASH

Jos 24: 30 of Ephraim, north of Mount *G*.
Jdg 2: 9 of Ephraim, north of Mount *G*.
2Sa 23: 30 Hiddai from the ravines of *G*,
1Ch 11: 32 Hurai from the ravines of *G*,

GABBAI

Ne 11: 8 and his followers, *G* and Sallai—

GABBATHA

Jn 19: 13 Pavement (which in Aramaic is *G*).

GABRIEL

Da 8: 16 "*G*, tell this man the meaning
9: 21 while I was still in prayer, *G*,
Lk 1: 19 The angel answered, "I am *G*.
1: 26 God sent the angel *G* to Nazareth,

GAD (GAD'S GADITES)

Ge 30: 11 fortune!" So she named him *G*.
35: 26 of Leah's maidservant Zilpah: *G*
46: 16 The sons of *G*: Zephon, Haggi,
49: 19 "*G* will be attacked by a band
Ex 1: 4 Dan and Naphtali; *G* and Asher.
Nu 1: 14 from *G*, Eliasaph son of Deuel;
1: 24 From the descendants of *G*:
1: 25 from the tribe of *G* was 45,650.
2: 14 The tribe of *G* will be next.
2: 14 of the people of *G* is Eliasaph son
7: 42 the leader of the people of *G*,
10: 20 over the division of the tribe of *G*.
13: 15 from the tribe of *G*, Geuel son
26: 15 The descendants of *G*
26: 18 These were the clans of *G*;
34: 14 the tribe of *G* and the half-tribe
Dt 27: 13 Reuben, *G*, Asher, Zebulun,
33: 20 About *G* he said:
33: 20 *G* lives there like a lion,
Jos 4: 12 *G* and the half-tribe
13: 24 Moses had given to the tribe of *G*,
18: 7 And *G*, Reuben and the half-tribe
20: 8 Ramoth in Gilead in the tribe of *G*,
21: 7 towns from the tribes of Reuben, *G*
21: 38 four towns; from the tribe of *G*,
22: 13 *G* and the half-tribe of Manasseh.
22: 15 *G* and the half-tribe of Manasseh—
22: 21 *G* and the half-tribe
22: 30 *G* and Manasseh had to say,
22: 31 said to Reuben, *G* and Manasseh,
1Sa 13: 7 crossed the Jordan to the land of *G*
22: 5 But the prophet *G* said to David,
2Sa 24: 5 and then went through *G*
24: 11 LORD had come to *G* the prophet,
24: 13 So *G* went to David and said to him
24: 14 David said to *G*, "I am
24: 18 On that day *G* went to David
24: 19 had commanded through *G*.
2Ki 10: 33 the land of Gilead (the region of *G*,
1Ch 2: 2 Benjamin, Naphtali, *G* and Asher.
6: 63 towns from the tribes of Reuben, *G*
6: 80 tribe of *G* they received Ramoth
12: 37 *G* and the half-tribe of Manasseh,
21: 9 The LORD said to *G*, David's seer,
21: 11 So *G* went to David and said to him
21: 13 David said to *G*, "I am
21: 18 the angel of the LORD ordered *G*
21: 19 to the word that *G* had spoken
29: 29 and the records of *G* the seer,
2Ch 29: 25 and *G* the king's seer and Nathan
Jer 49: 1 has Molech taken possession of *G*?
Eze 48: 27 "*G* will have one portion; it will
48: 28 boundary of *G* will run south
48: 34 will be three gates: the gate of *G*,
Rev 7: 5 from the tribe of *G* 12,000,

GAD'S (GAD)

Dt 33: 20 is he who enlarges *G* domain!

GADARENES

Mt 8: 28 side in the region of the *G*,

GADDI

Nu 13: 11 *G* son of Susi; from the tribe of Dan

GADDIEL

Nu 13: 10 the tribe of Zebulun, *G* son of Sodi;

GADFLY

Jer 46: 20 but a *g* is coming

GADI

2Ki 15: 14 Then Menahem son of *G* went
15: 17 Menahem son of *G* became king

GADITES (GAD)

Nu 32: 1 and *G*, who had very large herds
32: 6 said to the *G* and Reubenites,
32: 25 The *G* and Reubenites said
32: 29 He said to them, "If the *G*
32: 31 The *G* and Reubenites answered,
32: 33 Then Moses gave to the *G*,
32: 34 The *G* built up Dibon, Ataroth,
Dt 3: 12 the *G* the territory north of Aroer
3: 16 the *G* I gave the territory extending
4: 43 for the *G*; and Golan in Bashan,
29: 8 the *G* and the half-tribe
Jos 1: 12 the *G* and the half-tribe
12: 6 the *G* and the half-tribe
13: 8 *G* had received the inheritance that
13: 28 were the inheritance of the *G*,
22: 1 the *G* and the half-tribe
22: 9 the *G* and the half-tribe
22: 10 the *G* and the half-tribe
22: 25 and *G*! You have no share
22: 32 and *G* in Gilead and reported
22: 33 the Reubenites and the *G* lived.
22: 34 and the *G* gave the altar this name:
1Ch 5: 11 The *G* lived next to them in Bashan
5: 16 The *G* lived in Gilead, in Bashan
5: 18 the *G* and the half-tribe
5: 26 the *G* and the half-tribe
12: 8 Some *G* defected to David
12: 14 These *G* were army commanders;
26: 32 the *G* and the half-tribe

GAHAM
Ge 22: 24 Tebah, G, Tahash and Maacah.

GAHAR
Ezr 2: 47 Hanan, Giddel, G, Reaiah, Rezin,

GAHER
Ne 7: 49 Hanan, Giddel, G, Reaiah, Rezin,

GAIETY
Isa 24: 8 The g of the tambourines is stilled,
24: 11 all g is banished from the earth.

GAIN (GAINED GAINING GAINS REGAIN REGAINED)
Ge 15: 8 can I know that I will g possession
37: 26 "What will we g if we kill our
Ex 14: 4 But I will g glory for myself
14: 17 And I will g glory through Pharaoh
14: 18 when I g glory through Pharaoh,
18: 21 men who hate dishonest g—
1Sa 8: 3 They turned aside after dishonest g
2Ki 15: 19 talents of silver to g his support
Job 21: 15 What would we g by praying
22: 3 What would he g if your ways were
35: 3 and what do I g by not sinning?'
Ps 30: 9 "What g is there in my destruction,
60: 12 With God we will g the victory,
90: 12 that we may g a heart of wisdom.
108: 13 With God we will g the victory,
119: 36 and not toward selfish g.
119:104 g understanding from your
Pr 1: 19 end of all who go after ill-gotten g;
4: 1 pay attention and g understanding.
8: 5 You who are simple, g prudence;
8: 5 who are foolish, g understanding.
11: 16 but ruthless men g only wealth.
16: 8 than much g with injustice.
19: 25 man, and he will g knowledge.
21: 11 is punished, the simple g wisdom;
28: 16 he who hates ill-gotten g will enjoy
28: 23 in the end g more favor
Ecc 1: 3 What does man g from all his labor
2: 15 What then do I g by being wise?"
3: 9 What does the worker g
5: 16 and what does he g,
6: 8 What does a poor man g
Isa 29: 24 in spirit will g understanding;
33: 15 who rejects g from extortion
56: 11 each seeks his own g.
63: 12 to g for himself everlasting renown
Jer 6: 13 all are greedy for g;
8: 10 all are greedy for g;
12: 13 wear themselves out but g nothing.
22: 17 are set only on dishonest g,
Eze 22: 12 make unjust g from your neighbors
22: 13 at the unjust g you have made
22: 27 and kill people to make unjust g.
28: 22 and I will g glory within you.
33: 31 their hearts are greedy for unjust g.
Da 2: 8 that you are trying to g time,
10: 12 mind to g understanding
11: 43 He will g control of the treasures
Hab 2: 9 who builds his realm by unjust g
Mal 3: 14 What did we g by carrying out his
Mk 8: 36 it for a man to g the whole world,
Lk 9: 25 it for a man to g the whole world,
16: 9 wealth to g friends for yourselves,
Jn 7: 18 does so to g honor for himself,
Ac 7: 10 and enabled him to g the goodwill
1Co 7: 21 although if you can g your freedom
13: 3 but have not love, I g nothing.
Php 1: 21 to live is Christ and to die is g.
3: 8 that I may g Christ and be found
1Ti 3: 8 and not pursuing dishonest g.
3: 13 have served well g an excellent
6: 5 godliness is a means to financial g.
6: 6 with contentment is great g.
2Ti 3: 6 g control over weak-willed women,
Tit 1: 7 violent, not pursuing dishonest g.
1: 11 and that for the sake of dishonest g.
Heb 11: 35 that they might g a better

GAINED (GAIN)
Ge 31: 1 and has g all this wealth
2Sa 15: 12 And so the conspiracy g strength,
2Ch 32: 8 And the people g confidence
Job 31: 25 the fortune my hands had g,
Ps 129: 2 but they have not g the victory
Pr 20: 17 Food g by fraud tastes sweet
20: 21 An inheritance quickly g
Ecc 2: 11 nothing was g under the sun.
Isa 26: 15 You have g glory for yourself;
Jer 32: 20 have g the renown that is still yours
Eze 28: 4 you have g wealth for yourself
Da 11: 2 When he has g power by his wealth
Mt 25: 16 money to work and g five more.
25: 17 with the two talents g two more.
25: 20 See, I have g five more.'
25: 22 talents; see, I have g two more.'
Lk 19: 15 to find out what they had g with it.
Ro 5: 2 through whom we have g access
1Co 15: 32 what have I g? If the dead are not
2Co 12: 1 Although there is nothing to be g,
Gal 2: 21 for if righteousness could be g
Heb 11: 33 and g what was promised;
Rev 18: 15 g their wealth from her will stand

GAINING (GAIN)
Ge 3: 6 and also desirable for g wisdom,
Ps 44: 12 g nothing from their sale.
Jn 4: 1 Pharisees heard that Jesus was g

GAINS (GAIN)
Pr 3: 13 the man who g understanding,
11: 16 A kindhearted woman g respect,
11: 24 One man gives freely, yet g
15: 32 heeds correction g understanding.
29: 23 but a man of lowly spirit g honor.
Jer 17: 11 is the man who g riches
Mic 4: 13 You will devote their ill-gotten g
Mt 16: 26 for a man if he g the whole world,

GAIUS
Ac 19: 29 people seized G and Aristarchus,
20: 4 G from Derbe, Timothy also,
Ro 16: 23 G, whose hospitality I
1Co 1: 14 any of you except Crispus and G,
3Jn : 1 The elder, To my dear friend G,

GALAL
1Ch 9: 15 G and Mattaniah son of Mica,
9: 16 the son of G, the son of Jeduthun;
Ne 11: 17 the son of G, the son of Jeduthun.

GALATIA (GALATIAN GALATIANS)
Ac 16: 6 the region of Phrygia and G,
18: 23 to place throughout the region of G
Gal 1: 2 with me, To the churches in G:
2Ti 4: 10 Crescens has gone to G,
1Pe 1: 1 scattered throughout Pontus, G,

GALATIAN (GALATIA)
1Co 16: 1 Do what I told the G churches

GALATIANS (GALATIA)
Gal 3: 1 You foolish G! Who has bewitched

GALBANUM
Ex 30: 34 and g— and pure frankincense,

GALE
Job 21: 18 like chaff swept away by a g?
Isa 17: 13 like tumbleweed before a g.
41: 16 and a g will blow them away.

GALEED
Ge 31: 47 and Jacob called it G.
31: 48 That is why it was called G.

GALILEAN (GALILEE)
Mk 14: 70 one of them, for you are a G."
Lk 22: 59 was with him, for he is a G."
23: 6 Pilate asked if the man was a G.
Ac 5: 37 Judas the G appeared in the days

GALILEANS (GALILEE)
Lk 13: 1 Jesus about the G whose blood
13: 2 sinners than all the other G
13: 2 think that these G were worse
Jn 4: 45 in Galilee, the G welcomed him.
Ac 2: 7 all these men who are speaking G?

GALILEE (GALILEAN GALILEANS)
Jos 20: 7 Kedesh in G in the hill country
21: 32 Kedesh in G (a city of refuge
1Ki 9: 11 towns in G to Hiram king of Tyre,
2Ki 15: 29 and G— all the land of Naphtali—
1Ch 6: 76 they received Kedesh in G,
Isa 9: 1 but in the future he will honor G
Mt 2: 22 he withdrew to the district of G,
3: 13 Jesus came from G to the Jordan
4: 12 put in prison, he returned to G.
4: 15 G of the Gentiles—
4: 18 walking beside the Sea of G,
4: 23 Jesus went throughout G, teaching
4: 25 crowds from G, the Decapolis,
11: 1 and preach in the towns of G.
15: 29 and went along the Sea of G.
17: 22 When they came together in G,
19: 1 he left G and went into the region
21: 11 the prophet from Nazareth in G."
26: 32 I will go ahead of you into G."
26: 69 "You also were with Jesus of G,"
27: 55 They had followed Jesus from G
28: 7 and is going ahead of you into G.
28: 10 Go and tell my brothers to go to G;
28: 16 the eleven disciples went to G,
Mk 1: 9 came from Nazareth in G
1: 14 into G, proclaiming the good news
1: 16 walked beside the Sea of G,
1: 28 quickly over the whole region of G.
1: 39 So he traveled throughout G,
3: 7 and a large crowd from G followed.
6: 21 and the leading men of G.
7: 31 to the Sea of G and into the region
9: 30 that place and passed through G.
14: 28 I will go ahead of you into G."
15: 41 In G these women had followed
16: 7 'He is going ahead of you into G.
Lk 1: 26 Gabriel to Nazareth, a town in G,
2: 4 town of Nazareth in G to Judea,
2: 39 they returned to G
3: 1 of G, his brother Philip tetrarch
4: 14 Jesus returned to G in the power
4: 31 down to Capernaum, a town in G,
5: 17 come from every village of G
8: 26 which is across the lake from G.
17: 11 the border between Samaria and G.
23: 5 in G and has come all the way here
23: 49 who had followed him from G,
23: 55 with Jesus from G followed Joseph
24: 6 while he was still with you in G:
Jn 1: 43 day Jesus decided to leave for G.
2: 1 a wedding took place at Cana in G.
2: 11 Jesus performed in Cana of G.
4: 3 and went back once more to G.
4: 43 After the two days he left for G.
4: 45 in G, the Galileans welcomed him.
4: 46 Once more he visited Cana in G,
4: 47 heard that Jesus had arrived in G
4: 54 having come from Judea to G.
6: 1 shore of the Sea of G (that is,
7: 1 After this, Jesus went around in G,
7: 9 Having said this, he stayed in G.
7: 41 How can the Christ come from G?
7: 52 a prophet does not come out of G."
7: 52 "Are you from G, too? Look into it,
12: 21 who was from Bethsaida in G,
21: 2 Nathanael from Cana in G,
Ac 1: 11 of G," they said, "why do you
9: 31 G and Samaria enjoyed a time
10: 37 in G after the baptism that John
13: 31 with him from G to Jerusalem.

GALL (GALLED)
Job 16: 13 and spills my g on the ground.
Ps 69: 21 They put g in my food
Pr 5: 4 but in the end she is bitter as g,
La 3: 15 and sated me with g.
3: 19 the bitterness and the g.
Mt 27: 34 mixed with g; but after tasting it,

GALLED (GALL)
1Sa 18: 8 was very angry; this refrain g him.

GALLERIES (GALLERY)
Eze 41: 15 including its g on each side;
41: 16 and g around the three of them—
42: 5 for the g took more space

GALLERY (GALLERIES)
Eze 42: 3 g faced g at the three levels.

GALLEY
Isa 33:21 No *g* with oars will ride them,

GALLIM
1Sa 25:44 son of Laish, who was from *G.*
Isa 10:30 Cry out, O Daughter of *G!*

GALLIO
Ac 18:12 While *G* was proconsul of Achaia,
18:14 about to speak, *G* said to the Jews,
18:17 *G* showed no concern whatever.

GALLONS
Lk 16:6 " 'Eight hundred *g* of olive oil,'
Jn 2:6 holding from twenty to thirty *g.*

GALLOP (GALLOPING GALLOPS)
Joel 2:4 they *g* along like cavalry.

GALLOPING (GALLOP)
Jdg 5:22 *g, g* go his mighty steeds.
Jer 47:3 the sound of the hoofs of *g* steeds,
Na 3:2 *g* horses

GALLOPS (GALLOP)
Hab 1:8 Their cavalry *g* headlong;

GALLOWS
Est 2:23 two officials were hanged on a *g.*
5:14 Haman, and he had the *g* built.
5:14 "Have a *g* built, seventy-five feet
6:4 on the *g* he had erected for him.
7:9 "A *g* seventy-five feet high stands
7:10 Haman on the *g* he had prepared
8:7 and they have hanged him on the *g*
9:13 Haman's ten sons be hanged on *g.*"
9:25 his sons should be hanged on the *g.*

GAMALIEL
Nu 1:10 from Manasseh, *G* son of Pedahzur
2:20 of Manasseh is *G* son of Pedahzur.
7:54 On the eighth day *G* son
7:59 the offering of *G* son of Pedahzur.
10:23 *G* son of Pedahzur was
Ac 5:34 But a Pharisee named *G,* a teacher
22:3 Under *G* I was thoroughly trained

GAME (GAMES)
Ge 25:28 who had a taste for wild *g,*
27:3 to hunt some wild *g* for me.
27:5 left for the open country to hunt *g*
27:7 'Bring me some *g* and prepare me
27:19 of my *g* so that you may give me
27:25 bring me some of your *g* to eat,
27:31 sit up and eat some of my *g,*
27:33 that hunted *g* and brought it to me?
Ps 76:4 than mountains rich with *g.*
Pr 12:27 The lazy man does not roast his *g,*

GAMES (GAME)
1Co 9:25 in the *g* goes into strict training.

GAMMAD
Eze 27:11 men of *G*

GAMUL
1Ch 24:17 to Jakin, the twenty-second to *G,*

GANGRENE
2Ti 2:17 Their teaching will spread like *g.*

GAP (GAPS)
Jdg 21:15 because the LORD had made a *g*
1Ki 11:27 and had filled in the *g* in the wall
Ne 6:1 rebuilt the wall and not a *g* was left
Eze 22:30 stand before me in the *g* on behalf

GAPE (GAPING)
Ps 35:21 They *g* at me and say, "Aha! Aha!

GAPING (GAPE)
Job 30:14 through a *g* breach;

GAPS (GAP)
Ne 4:7 and that the *g* were being closed,

GARDEN (GARDENER GARDENS)
Ge 2:8 the LORD God had planted a *g*
2:9 In the middle of the *g* were the tree
2:10 A river watering the *g* flowed
2:15 put him in the *G* of Eden to work it
2:16 free to eat from any tree in the *g;*
3:1 eat from any tree in the *g'?"*
3:2 fruit from the trees in the *g,*
3:3 is in the middle of the *g,*
3:8 God among the trees of the *g.*
3:8 he was walking in the *g* in the cool
3:10 He answered, "I heard you in the *g*
3:23 him from the *G* of Eden
3:24 side of the *G* of Eden cherubim
13:10 like the *g* of the LORD, like
Dt 11:10 it by foot as in a vegetable *g.*
1Ki 21:2 vineyard to use for a vegetable *g,*
2Ki 21:18 in his palace *g,* the *g* of Uzza.
21:26 buried in his grave in the *g* of Uzza.
25:4 the two walls near the king's *g,*
Ne 3:15 by the King's *G,* as far
Est 1:5 in the enclosed *g* of the king's
1:6 The *g* had hangings of white
7:7 and went out into the palace *g.*
7:8 from the palace *g* to the banquet
Job 8:16 spreading its shoots over the *g;*
SS 4:12 You are a *g* locked up, my sister,
4:15 You are a *g* fountain,
4:16 Blow on my *g,*
4:16 Let my lover come into his *g*
5:1 I have come into my *g,* my sister,
6:2 My lover has gone down to his *g,*
Isa 1:30 like a *g* without water.
5:7 are the *g* of his delight.
51:3 her wastelands like the *g*
58:11 You will be like a well-watered *g,*
61:11 and a *g* causes seeds to grow,
Jer 31:12 They will be like a well-watered *g,*
39:4 city at night by way of the king's *g,*
52:7 the two walls near the king's *g,*
La 2:6 has laid waste his dwelling like a *g;*
Eze 28:13 the *g* of God;
31:8 The cedars in the *g* of God
31:8 no tree in the *g* of God
31:9 Eden in the *g* of God.
36:35 laid waste has become like the *g*
Joel 2:3 Before them the land is like the *g*
Mt 13:32 it is the largest of *g* plants
Mk 4:32 becomes the largest of all *g* plants,
Lk 11:42 rue and all other kinds of *g* herbs,
13:19 a man took and planted in his *g.*
Jn 19:41 there was a *g,* and in the *g* a new

GARDENER (GARDEN)
Jn 15:1 true vine and my Father is the *g.*
20:15 Thinking he was the *g,* she said,

GARDENS (GARDEN)
Nu 24:6 like *g* beside a river,
Ecc 2:5 I made *g* and parks and planted all
SS 6:2 to browse in the *g*
8:13 You who dwell in the *g*
Isa 1:29 will be disgraced because of the *g*
65:3 offering sacrifices in *g*
66:17 purify themselves to go into the *g,*
Jer 29:5 plant *g* and eat what they produce.
29:28 plant *g* and eat what they produce
Am 4:9 "Many times I struck your *g*
9:14 they will make *g* and eat their fruit.

GAREB
2Sa 23:38 *G* the Ithrite and Uriah the Hittite
1Ch 11:40 Ira the Ithrite, *G* the Ithrite,
Jer 31:39 from there straight to the hill of *G*

GARLAND
Pr 1:9 They will be a *g* to grace your head
4:9 She will set a *g* of grace

GARLIC
Nu 11:5 melons, leeks, onions and *g.*

GARMENT (GARMENTS UNDERGARMENT UNDERGARMENTS)
Ge 9:23 But Shem and Japheth took a *g*
25:25 his whole body was like a hairy *g;*
Ex 22:9 *g,* or any other lost property about
Lev 6:27 any of the blood is spattered on a *g,*
Nu 31:20 Purify every *g* as well as everything
Jdg 8:25 So they spread out a *g,*
Ru 3:9 the corner of your *g* over me,
1Sa 19:13 it with a *g* and putting some goats'
2Sa 13:18 the kind of *g* the virgin daughters
20:12 into a field and threw a *g* over him.
2Ki 1:8 "He was a man with a *g* of hair
Job 13:28 like a *g* eaten by moths.
30:18 he binds me like the neck of my *g.*
31:19 or a needy man without a *g,*
38:9 when I made the clouds its *g*
38:14 features stand out like those of a *g.*
Ps 74:11 Take it from the folds of your *g*
102:26 they will all wear out like a *g.*
104:2 in light as with a *g;*
104:6 with the deep as with a *g;*
109:18 He wore cursing as his *g;*
Pr 20:16 Take the *g* of one who puts up
25:20 Like one who takes away a *g*
27:13 Take the *g* of one who puts up
Isa 9:5 and every *g* rolled in blood
50:9 They will all wear out like a *g;*
51:6 the earth will wear out like a *g*
51:8 the moth will eat them up like a *g;*
61:3 and a *g* of praise
Jer 43:12 As a shepherd wraps his *g*
Eze 5:3 away in the folds of your *g.*
16:8 I spread the corner of my *g*
44:17 they must not wear any woolen *g*
Hag 2:12 meat in the fold of his *g,*
Zec 13:4 put on a prophet's *g* of hair in order
Mal 2:16 with violence as well as with his *g,*"
Mt 9:16 of unshrunk cloth on an old *g,*
9:16 the patch will pull away from the *g,*
Mk 2:21 of unshrunk cloth on an old *g.*
14:51 wearing nothing but a linen *g,*
14:52 he fled naked, leaving his *g* behind.
Lk 5:36 he will have torn the new *g,*
5:36 "No one tears a patch from a new *g*
Jn 19:23 This *g* was seamless, woven
21:7 he wrapped his outer *g* around him
Heb 1:11 they will all wear out like a *g.*
1:12 like a *g* they will be changed.

GARMENTS (GARMENT)
Ge 3:21 The LORD God made *g* of skin
49:11 he will wash his *g* in wine,
Ex 28:2 Make sacred *g* for your brother
28:3 are to make *g* for Aaron,
28:4 These are the *g* they are to make:
28:4 are to make these sacred *g*
29:5 Take the *g* and dress Aaron
29:21 and on his sons and their *g.*
29:21 and sprinkle it on Aaron and his *g*
29:21 and their *g* will be consecrated.
29:29 "Aaron's sacred *g* will belong
31:10 both the sacred *g* for Aaron
31:10 its stand—and also the woven *g,*
31:10 the *g* for his sons when they serve
35:19 both the sacred *g* for Aaron
35:19 the woven *g* worn for ministering
35:19 the *g* for his sons when they serve
35:21 all its service, and for the sacred *g.*
39:1 They also made sacred *g* for Aaron
39:1 scarlet yarn they made woven *g*
39:41 and the *g* for his sons when serving
39:41 both the sacred *g* for Aaron
39:41 the woven *g* worn for ministering
40:13 Then dress Aaron in the sacred *g,*
Lev 8:2 "Bring Aaron and his sons, their *g,*
8:30 and his *g* and his sons and their *g.*
8:30 and on his sons and their *g*
8:30 sprinkled them on Aaron and his *g*
16:4 These are sacred *g;*
16:23 and take off the linen *g* he put
16:24 holy place and put on his regular *g.*
16:32 He is to put on the sacred linen *g*
21:10 ordained to wear the priestly *g,*
Nu 15:38 tassels on the corners of your *g,*
20:26 Remove Aaron's *g* and put them
20:28 Moses removed Aaron's *g*
Jdg 5:30 colorful *g* as plunder for Sisera,
5:30 colorful *g* embroidered,
5:30 highly embroidered *g* for my neck
8:26 and the purple *g* worn by the kings
14:12 I will give you thirty linen *g*
14:13 you must give me thirty linen *g*
2Sa 1:24 who adorned your *g*
10:4 cut off their *g* in the middle
1Ch 19:4 cut off their *g* in the middle
Ezr 2:69 minas of silver and 100 priestly *g.*

Ne 7: 70 50 bowls and 530 *g* for priests.
7: 72 minas of silver and 67 *g* for priests.
Est 8: 15 the king's presence wearing royal *g*
Ps 22: 18 They divide my *g* among them
45: 14 In embroidered *g* she is led
Pr 31: 24 She makes linen *g* and sells them,
SS 4: 11 The fragrance of your *g* is like that
Isa 3: 23 and the linen *g* and tiaras
52: 1 Put on your *g* of splendor,
59: 17 he put on the *g* of vengeance
61: 10 me with *g* of salvation
63: 1 with his *g* stained crimson?
63: 2 Why are your *g* red,
63: 3 their blood spattered my *g*,
La 4: 14 that no one dares to touch their *g*.
Eze 16: 10 and covered you with costly *g*.
16: 16 You took some of your *g*
26: 16 and take off their embroidered *g*.
27: 24 traded with you beautiful *g*,
42: 14 behind the *g* in which they minister
44: 19 the people by means of their *g*.
Joel 2: 13 and not your *g*.
Am 2: 8 on *g* taken in pledge.
Zec 3: 4 and I will put rich *g* on you."
Jn 19: 24 "They divided my *g* among them

GARMITE

1Ch 4: 19 the father of Keilah the *G*,

GARRISON (GARRISONS)

2Sa 23: 14 the Philistine *g* was at Bethlehem.
1Ch 11: 16 the Philistine *g* was at Bethlehem.

GARRISONS (GARRISON)

2Sa 8: 6 He put *g* in the Aramean kingdom
8: 14 He put *g* throughout Edom,
1Ch 18: 6 He put *g* in the Aramean kingdom
18: 13 He put *g* in Edom, and all
2Ch 17: 2 cities of Judah and put *g* in Judah

GASP (GASPING)

Job 11: 20 their hope will become a dying *g*."
Isa 42: 14 I cry out, I *g* and pant.

GASPING (GASP)

Jer 4: 31 the Daughter of Zion *g* for breath,

GATAM

Ge 36: 11 Omar, Zepho, *G* and Kenaz.
36: 16 Kenaz, Korah, *G* and Amalek.
1Ch 1: 36 Omar, Zepho, *G* and Kenaz;

GATE (GATES)

Ge 23: 10 come to the *g* of his city.
23: 18 come to the *g* of the city.
28: 17 of God; this is the *g* of heaven."
34: 20 went to the *g* of their city to speak
34: 24 of the city *g* agreed with Hamor
Dt 17: 5 done this evil deed to your city *g*
21: 19 to the elders at the *g* of his town.
22: 15 a virgin to the town elders at the *g*.
22: 24 both of them to the *g* of that town
25: 7 go to the elders at the town *g*
Jos 2: 5 when it was time to close the city *g*,
2: 7 had gone out, the *g* was shut.
7: 5 the Israelites from the city *g*
8: 29 down at the entrance of the city *g*.
20: 4 stand in the entrance of the city *g*
Jdg 9: 35 at the entrance to the city *g* just
9: 40 all the way to the entrance to the *g*.
9: 44 at the entrance to the city *g*.
16: 2 wait for him all night at the city *g*.
16: 3 took hold of the doors of the city *g*,
18: 16 stood at the entrance to the *g*.
18: 17 stood at the entrance to the *g*.
Ru 4: 1 Boaz went up to the town *g*
4: 11 the elders and all those at the *g* said
1Sa 4: 18 off his chair by the side of the *g*.
21: 13 making marks on the doors of the *g*
2Sa 10: 8 at the entrance to their city *g*,
11: 23 back to the entrance to the city *g*.
15: 2 of the road leading to the city *g*.
18: 4 So the king stood beside the *g*
23: 15 the well near the *g* of Bethlehem!"
23: 16 the well near the *g* of Bethlehem
1Ki 4: 13 cities with bronze *g* bars);
17: 10 When he came to the town *g*,
22: 10 by the entrance of the *g* of Samaria,
2Ki 7: 1 for a shekel at the *g* of Samaria."
7: 3 at the entrance of the city *g*.
7: 17 leaned in charge of the *g*,
7: 18 for a shekel at the *g* of Samaria."
9: 31 As Jehu entered the *g*, she asked,
10: 8 of the city *g* until morning."
11: 6 a third at the Sur *G*, and a third
11: 6 a third at the *g* behind the guard,
11: 19 by way of the *g* of the guards.
14: 13 Ephraim *G* to the Corner *G*—
15: 35 Jotham rebuilt the Upper *G*
23: 8 at the entrance to the *G* of Joshua,
23: 8 which is on the left of the city *g*.
25: 4 fled at night through the *g*
1Ch 9: 18 at the King's *G* on the east,
11: 17 the well near the *g* of Bethlehem!"
11: 18 the well near the *g* of Bethlehem
16: 42 of Jeduthun were stationed at the *g*
26: 13 cast for each *g*, according
26: 14 lot for the East *G* fell to Shelemiah.
26: 14 the lot for the North *G* fell to him.
26: 15 for the South *G* fell to Obed-Edom,
26: 16 Shalleketh *G* on the upper road fell
26: 16 The lots for the West *G*
2Ch 18: 9 by the entrance to the *g* of Samaria,
23: 5 and a third at the Foundation *G*,
23: 15 of the Horse *G* on the palace
23: 20 the palace through the Upper *G*
24: 8 at the *g* of the temple of the LORD
25: 23 Ephraim *G* to the Corner *G*—
26: 9 at the Valley *G* and at the angle
26: 9 in Jerusalem at the Corner *G*,
27: 3 Jotham rebuilt the Upper *G*
31: 14 the Levite, keeper of the East *G*,
32: 6 him in the square at the city *g*
33: 14 as the entrance of the Fish *G*
35: 15 gatekeepers at each *g* did not need
Ne 2: 13 out through the Valley *G*
2: 13 the Jackal Well and the Dung *G*,
2: 14 I moved on toward the Fountain *G*
2: 15 reentered through the Valley *G*.
3: 1 to work and rebuilt the Sheep *G*.
3: 3 The Fish *G* was rebuilt by the sons
3: 6 The Jeshanah *G* was repaired
3: 13 The Valley *G* was repaired
3: 13 of the wall as far as the Dung *G*.
3: 14 The Dung *G* was repaired
3: 15 The Fountain *G* was repaired
3: 26 a point opposite the Water *G*
3: 28 Above the Horse *G*, the priests
3: 29 guard at the East *G*, made repairs.
3: 31 opposite the Inspection *G*,
3: 32 and the Sheep *G* the goldsmiths
8: 1 in the square before the Water *G*.
8: 3 before the Water *G* in the presence
8: 16 and in the square by the Water *G*
8: 16 and the one by the *G* of Ephraim.
12: 31 to the right, toward the Dung *G*.
12: 37 At the Fountain *G* they continued
12: 37 of David to the Water *G* on the east
12: 39 At the *G* of the Guard they
12: 39 over the *G* of Ephraim,
12: 39 the Hundred, as far as the Sheep *G*.
12: 39 the Jeshanah *G*, the Fish *G*,
Est 2: 19 Mordecai was sitting at the king's *g*
2: 21 was sitting at the king's *g*,
3: 2 officials at the king's *g* knelt down
3: 3 at the king's *g* asked Mordecai,
4: 2 he went only as far as the king's *g*,
4: 6 of the city in front of the king's *g*.
5: 9 he saw Mordecai at the king's *g*
5: 13 Mordecai sitting at the king's *g*."
6: 10 the Jew, who sits at the king's *g*.
6: 12 Mordecai returned to the king's *g*.
Job 29: 7 "When I went to the *g* of the city
Ps 69: 12 Those who sit at the *g* mock me,
118: 20 This is the *g* of the LORD
127: 5 with their enemies in the *g*.
Pr 17: 19 builds a high *g* invites destruction.
24: 7 at the *g* he has nothing
31: 23 husband is respected at the city *g*,
31: 31 works bring her praise at the city *g*.
SS 7: 4 Heshbon by the *g* of Bath Rabbim.
Isa 14: 31 Wail, O *g*! Howl, O city!
24: 12 its *g* is battered to pieces.
28: 6 who turn back the battle at the *g*.
Jer 7: 2 at the *g* of the LORD's house
17: 19 Go and stand at the *g* of the people,
Jer 19: 2 the entrance of the Potsherd *G*.
20: 2 stocks at the Upper *G* of Benjamin
26: 10 of the New *G* of the LORD's house
31: 38 Tower of Hananel to the Corner *G*.
31: 40 as far as the corner of the Horse *G*,
36: 10 of the New *G* of the temple,
37: 13 *G*, the captain of the guard,
38: 7 sitting in the Benjamin *G*,
39: 3 and took seats in the Middle *G*:
39: 4 through the *g* between the two
52: 7 the city at night through the *g*
La 5: 14 The elders are gone from the city *g*;
Eze 8: 3 to the north *g* of the inner court,
8: 5 and in the entrance north of the *g*
8: 14 to the north *g* of the house
9: 2 from the direction of the upper *g*,
10: 19 to the east *g* of the LORD's house,
11: 1 brought me to the *g* of the house
11: 1 to the *g* were twenty-five men,
26: 2 Aha! The *g* to the nations is broken
40: 6 Then he went to the *g* facing east.
40: 6 measured the threshold of the *g*;
40: 7 And the threshold of the *g* next
40: 10 Inside the east *g* were three alcoves
40: 20 and width of the *g* facing north,
40: 22 as those of the *g* facing east.
40: 23 He measured from one *g* to
40: 23 There was a *g* to the inner court
40: 23 the inner court facing the north *g*,
40: 24 and I saw a *g* facing south.
40: 27 and he measured from this *g*
40: 27 court also had a *g* facing south,
40: 27 to the outer *g* on the south side;
40: 28 and he measured the south *g*;
40: 28 court through the south *g*,
40: 35 Then he brought me to the north *g*
40: 44 Outside the inner *g*,
40: 44 another at the side of the south *g*
40: 44 one at the side of the north *g*
42: 15 he led me out by the east *g*
43: 1 me to the *g* facing east,
43: 4 temple through the *g* facing east.
44: 1 to the outer *g* of the sanctuary,
44: 2 to me, "This *g* is to remain shut.
44: 4 by way of the north *g* to the front
46: 1 *g* of the inner court facing east is
46: 2 the *g* will not be shut until evening.
46: 9 but each is to go out the opposite *g*.
46: 9 enters by the north *g* to worship is
46: 9 is to go out the north *g*.
46: 9 is to return through the *g*
46: 9 to worship is to go out the south *g*;
46: 9 whoever enters by the south *g* is
46: 12 he has gone out, the *g* will be shut.
46: 12 the *g* facing east is to be opened
46: 19 the entrance at the side of the *g*
47: 2 out through the north *g*
47: 2 outside to the outer *g* facing east,
48: 31 gates on the north side will be the *g*
48: 31 the *g* of Judah and the *g* of Levi.
48: 32 the *g* of Benjamin and the *g* of Dan.
48: 32 the *g* of Benjamin and the *g* of Dan.
48: 32 will be three gates: the *g* of Joseph,
48: 33 the *g* of Issachar and the *g*
48: 33 will be three gates: the *g* of Simeon,
48: 34 of Asher and the *g* of Naphtali.
48: 34 the *g* of Asher and the *g*
48: 34 will be three gates: the *g* of Gad,
Am 1: 5 break down the *g* of Damascus;
Mic 1: 9 It has reached the very *g*
1: 12 even to the *g* of Jerusalem.
2: 13 they will break through the *g*
Zep 1: 10 "a cry will go up from the Fish *G*,
Zec 14: 10 *G* to the site of the First *G*,
14: 10 the Corner *G*, and from the Tower
Mt 7: 13 For wide is the *g* and broad is
7: 13 "Enter through the narrow *g*.
7: 14 small is the *g* and narrow the road
Lk 7: 12 As he approached the town *g*,
16: 20 At his *g* was laid a beggar named
Jn 5: 2 Jerusalem near the Sheep *G* a pool,
10: 1 not enter the sheep pen by the *g*,
10: 2 enters by the *g* is the shepherd
10: 3 The watchman opens the *g* for him,
10: 7 "I tell you the truth, I am the *g*
10: 9 I am the *g*; whoever enters
Ac 3: 2 to the temple *g* called Beautiful,
3: 10 at the temple *g* called Beautiful,

Ac 10: 17 house was and stopped at the *g*.
12: 10 and came to the iron *g* leading
16: 13 went outside the city *g* to the river,
Heb 13: 12 also suffered outside the city *g*
Rev 21: 21 each *g* made of a single pearl.

GATEKEEPER (GATEKEEPERS)

2Sa 18: 26 and he called down to the *g*, "Look
1Ch 9: 21 son of Meshelemiah was the *g*

GATEKEEPERS (GATEKEEPER)

2Ki 7: 10 and called out to the city *g*
7: 11 The *g* shouted the news,
1Ch 9: 17 The *g*: Shallum, Akkub, Talmon,
9: 18 These were the *g* belonging
9: 19 and his fellow *g* from his family
9: 20 of Eleazar was in charge of the *g*,
9: 22 The *g* had been assigned
9: 22 those chosen to be *g*
9: 24 The *g* were on the four sides: east,
9: 26 four principal *g*, who were Levites,
15: 18 Obed-Edom and Jeiel, the *g*.
16: 38 Jeduthun, and also Hosah, were *g*.
23: 5 Four thousand are to be *g*
26: 1 of the *g*: From the Korahites:
26: 12 These divisions of the *g*,
26: 19 of the *g* who were descendants
2Ch 8: 14 also appointed the *g* by divisions
35: 15 The *g* at each gate did not need
Ezr 2: 42 of Asaph 128 The *g* of the temple:
2: 70 *g* and the temple servants settled
7: 7 singers, *g* and temple servants,
7: 24 of the priests, Levites, singers, *g*,
10: 24 From the *g*: Shallum, Telem
Ne 7: 1 *g* and the singers and the Levites
7: 3 While the *g* are still on duty,
7: 45 descendants of Asaph 148 The *g*:
7: 73 The priests, the Levites, the *g*,
10: 28 priests, Levites, *g*, singers,
10: 39 the *g* and the singers stay.
11: 19 The *g*: Akkub, Talmon
12: 25 and Akkub were *g* who guarded
12: 45 as did also the singers and *g*,
12: 47 portions for the singers and *g*.
13: 5 and *g*, as well as the contributions

GATEPOST (GATEPOSTS)

Eze 46: 2 of the gateway and stand by the *g*.

GATEPOSTS (GATEPOST)

Eze 45: 19 and on the *g* of the inner court.

GATES (GATE)

Ge 24: 60 the *g* of their enemies."
Ex 20: 10 nor the alien within your *g*.
Dt 3: 5 fortified with high walls and with *g*
5: 14 nor the alien within your *g*,
6: 9 of your houses and on your *g*.
11: 20 of your houses and on your *g*,
20: 11 If they accept and open their *g*,
33: 25 The bolts of your *g* will be iron
Jos 6: 26 will he set up its *g*."
Jdg 5: 8 war came to the city *g*,
5: 11 went down to the city *g*.
1Sa 17: 52 of Gath and to the *g* of Ekron.
23: 7 himself by entering a town with *g*
2Sa 18: 24 between the inner and outer *g*,
1Ki 16: 34 and he set up its *g* at the cost
2Ki 15: 16 they refused to open their *g*.
23: 8 He broke down the shrines at the *g*
1Ch 9: 23 of guarding the *g* of the house
2Ch 8: 5 walls and with *g* and bars, as
8: 14 by divisions for the various *g*,
14: 7 walls around them, with towers, *g*
23: 19 also stationed doorkeepers at the *g*
31: 2 at the *g* of the LORD's dwelling.
Ne 1: 3 its *g* have been burned with fire."
2: 3 its *g* have been destroyed by fire?"
2: 8 beams for the *g* of the citadel
2: 13 its *g*, which had been destroyed
2: 17 its *g* have been burned with fire.
6: 1 I had not set the doors in the *g*—
7: 3 "The *g* of Jerusalem are not
11: 19 who kept watch at the *g*— 172 men
12: 25 guarded the storerooms at the *g*.
12: 30 they purified the people, the *g*
13: 19 fell on the *g* of Jerusalem
13: 19 some of my own men at the *g*
Ne 13: 22 and guard the *g* in order
Job 17: 16 Will it go down to the *g* of death?
38: 17 Have the *g* of death been shown
38: 17 Have you seen the *g* of the shadow
Ps 9: 13 and lift me up from the *g* of death,
9: 14 in the *g* of the Daughter of Zion
24: 7 Lift up your heads, O you *g*;
24: 9 Lift up your heads, O you *g*;
87: 2 the LORD loves the *g* of Zion
100: 4 Enter his *g* with thanksgiving
107: 16 for he breaks down *g* of bronze
107: 18 and drew near the *g* of death.
118: 19 Open for me the *g* of righteousness
122: 2 in your *g*, O Jerusalem.
147: 13 he strengthens the bars of your *g*
Pr 8: 3 beside the *g* leading into the city,
14: 19 the wicked at the *g* of the righteous
18: 19 disputes are like the barred *g*
Isa 3: 26 The *g* of Zion will lament
13: 2 them to enter the *g* of the nobles.
22: 7 horsemen are posted at the city *g*;
26: 2 Open the *g*
38: 10 must I go through the *g* of death
45: 1 him so that *g* will not be shut:
45: 2 I will break down *g* of bronze
54: 12 your *g* of sparkling jewels,
60: 11 Your *g* will always stand open,
60: 18 and your *g* Praise.
62: 10 Pass through, pass through the *g*!
Jer 1: 15 the entrance of the *g* of Jerusalem;
7: 2 come through these *g* to worship
15: 7 at the city *g* of the land.
17: 19 also at all the other *g* of Jerusalem.
17: 20 who come through these *g*.
17: 21 bring it through the *g* of Jerusalem.
17: 24 load through the *g* of this city
17: 25 come through the *g* of this city
17: 27 come through the *g* of Jerusalem
17: 27 fire in the *g* of Jerusalem that will
22: 2 people who come through these *g*.
22: 4 come through the *g* of this palace,
22: 19 outside the *g* of Jerusalem."
49: 31 a nation that has neither *g* nor bars;
51: 30 the bars of her *g* are broken.
51: 58 and her high *g* set on fire;
La 2: 9 Her *g* have sunk into the ground;
4: 12 the *g* of Jerusalem.
Eze 21: 15 slaughter at all their *g*.
21: 22 to set battering rams against the *g*,
26: 10 and chariots when he enters your *g*
38: 11 living without walls and without *g*
44: 11 charge of the *g* of the temple
44: 17 garment while ministering at the *g*
44: 17 " 'When they enter the *g*
48: 31 the *g* of the city will be named
48: 31 three *g* on the north side will be
48: 32 will be three *g*: the gate of Joseph,
48: 33 will be three *g*: the gate of Simeon,
48: 34 will be three *g*: the gate of Gad,
Hos 11: 6 will destroy the bars of their *g*
Ob : 11 and foreigners entered his *g*
: 13 march through the *g* of my people
Na 2: 6 The river *g* are thrown open
3: 13 The *g* of your land
Mt 16: 18 the *g* of Hades will not overcome it
Ac 9: 24 on the city *g* in order to kill him.
14: 13 wreaths to the city *g* because he
21: 30 and immediately the *g* were shut.
Rev 21: 12 On the *g* were written the names
21: 12 and with twelve angels at the *g*.
21: 12 high wall with twelve *g*,
21: 13 There were three *g* on the east,
21: 15 of gold to measure the city, its *g*
21: 21 The twelve *g* were twelve pearls,
21: 25 On no day will its *g* ever be shut,
22: 14 may go through the *g* into the city.

GATEWAY (GATEWAYS)

Ge 19: 1 Lot was sitting in the *g* of the city.
1Sa 9: 18 Saul approached Samuel in the *g*
2Sa 3: 27 Joab took him aside into the *g*,
18: 24 up to the roof of the *g* by the wall.
18: 33 He went up to the room over the *g*
19: 8 got up and took his seat in the *g*.
19: 8 "The king is sitting in the *g*,"
2Ki 7: 17 the people trampled him in the *g*,
7: 20 the people trampled him in the *g*,
Eze 27: 3 situated at the *g* to the sea,
Eze 40: 3 standing in the *g* with a linen cord
40: 8 he measured the portico of the *g*;
40: 9 portico of the *g* faced the temple.
40: 11 the width of the entrance to the *g*;
40: 13 he measured the *g* from the top
40: 14 all around the inside of the *g*—
40: 15 the entrance of the *g* to the far end
40: 16 walls inside the *g* were surmounted
40: 19 the inside of the lower *g* to the
40: 21 as those of the first *g*.
40: 25 The *g* and its portico had narrow
40: 29 *g* and its portico had openings all
40: 32 he measured the *g*; it had the same
40: 33 *g* and its portico had openings all
40: 39 the portico of the *g* were two tables
40: 40 outside wall of the portico of the *g*,
40: 40 to the north *g* were two tables,
40: 41 tables on one side of the *g*
44: 3 enter by way of the portico of the *g*
44: 3 inside the *g* to eat in the presence
46: 2 outside through the portico of the *g*
46: 2 to worship at the threshold of the *g*
46: 3 LORD at the entrance to that *g*.
46: 8 go in through the portico of the *g*,
Mt 26: 71 Then he went out to the *g*,

GATEWAYS (GATEWAY)

1Ch 22: 3 to make nails for the doors of the *g*
Pr 1: 21 in the *g* of the city she makes her
La 1: 4 All her *g* are desolate,
Eze 40: 18 It abutted the sides of the *g*
40: 30 (The porticoes of the *g*
40: 38 by the portico in each of the inner *g*

GATH

Jos 11: 22 *G* and Ashdod did any survive.
13: 3 Ashdod, Ashkelon, *G* and Ekron—
1Sa 5: 8 of the god of Israel moved to *G*."
6: 17 Gaza, Ashkelon, *G* and Ekron.
7: 14 Ekron to *G* that the Philistines had
17: 4 who was from *G*, came out
17: 23 the Philistine champion from *G*,
17: 52 along the Shaaraim road to *G*
17: 52 the Philistines to the entrance of *G*
21: 10 and went to Achish king of *G*.
21: 12 afraid of Achish king of *G*.
22: 1 David left *G* and escaped
27: 2 to Achish son of Maoch king of *G*.
27: 3 his men settled in *G* with Achish.
27: 4 was told that David had fled to *G*,
27: 11 or woman alive to be brought to *G*,
2Sa 1: 20 "Tell it not in *G*,
15: 18 from *G* marched before the king.
21: 20 battle, which took place at *G*,
21: 22 were descendants of Rapha in *G*,
1Ki 2: 39 king of *G*, and Shimei was told,
2: 39 was told, "Your slaves are in *G*."
2: 40 and went to Achish at *G* in search
2: 40 brought the slaves back from *G*.
2: 41 gone from Jerusalem to *G*
2Ki 12: 17 and attacked *G* and captured it.
1Ch 7: 21 killed by the native-born men of *G*,
8: 13 who drove out the inhabitants of *G*.
18: 1 and he took *G* and its surrounding
20: 6 battle, which took place at *G*,
20: 8 were descendants of Rapha in *G*,
2Ch 11: 8 Soco, Adullam, *G*, Mareshah,
26: 6 and broke down the walls of *G*,
Am 6: 2 and then go down to *G* in Philistia.
Mic 1: 10 Tell it not in *G*;

GATH HEPHER

Jos 19: 13 Then it continued eastward to *G*
2Ki 14: 25 of Amittai, the prophet from *G*.

GATH RIMMON

Jos 19: 45 Baalath, Jehud, Bene Berak, *G*,
21: 24 Gibbethon, Aijalon and *G*,
21: 25 they received Taanach and *G*,
1Ch 6: 69 Beth Horon, Aijalon and *G*,

GATHER (GATHERED GATHERING GATHERS INGATHERING)

Ge 31: 46 to his relatives, "*G* some stones."
49: 1 "*G* around so I can tell you what
Ex 5: 7 let them go and *g* their own straw.
5: 12 all over Egypt to *g* stubble to use
16: 4 and *g* enough for that day.

Ex 16: 5 much as they *g* on the other days.''
16: 16 'Each one is to *g* as much
16: 26 Six days you are to *g* it,
16: 27 out on the seventh day to *g* it,
23: 16 when you *g* in your crops
Lev 8: 3 and *g* the entire assembly
19: 9 or *g* the gleanings of your harvest.
23: 22 or *g* the gleanings of your harvest.
25: 3 your vineyards and *g* their crops.
Nu 10: 7 To *g* the assembly, blow
19: 9 who is clean shall *g* up the ashes
20: 8 your brother Aaron *g* the assembly
21: 16 "*G* the people together
Dt 11: 14 so that you may *g* in your grain,
13: 16 *G* all the plunder of the town
28: 39 not drink the wine or *g* the grapes,
30: 3 *g* you again from all the nations
30: 4 the LORD your God will *g* you
Ru 2: 7 and *g* among the sheaves
2Ki 4: 39 out into the fields to *g* herbs
22: 20 Therefore I will *g* you
1Ch 16: 35 *g* us and deliver us from the nations
2Ch 34: 28 Now I will *g* you to your fathers,
Ne 1: 9 I will *g* them from there
Est 4: 16 *g* together all the Jews who are
Job 24: 6 They *g* fodder in the fields
39: 12 and *g* it to your threshing floor?
Ps 2: 2 and the rulers *g* together
7: 7 Let the assembled peoples *g*
50: 5 "*G* to me my consecrated ones,
104: 28 they *g* it up;
106: 47 and *g* us from the nations,
142: 7 Then the righteous will *g* about me
Ecc 3: 5 scatter stones and a time to *g* them,
SS 6: 2 and to *g* lilies.
Isa 10: 14 as men *g* abandoned eggs,
11: 12 and *g* the exiles of Israel;
34: 15 there also the falcons will *g*,
34: 16 and his Spirit will *g* them together.
43: 5 and *g* you from the west.
43: 9 All the nations *g* together
45: 20 "*G* together and come;
49: 5 and *g* Israel to himself,
49: 18 all your sons *g* and come to you.
56: 8 "I will *g* still others to them
62: 9 those who *g* the grapes will drink it
66: 18 and *g* all nations and tongues,
Jer 3: 17 and all nations will *g* in Jerusalem
4: 5 '*G* together!
7: 18 children *g* wood, the fathers light
8: 14 *G* together!
9: 22 with no one to *g* them.' "
10: 17 *G* up your belongings
12: 9 Go and *g* all the wild beasts;
21: 4 And I will *g* them inside this city.
23: 3 "I myself will *g* the remnant
29: 14 I will *g* you from all the nations
31: 8 *g* them from the ends of the earth.
31: 10 who scattered Israel will *g* them
32: 37 I will surely *g* them
49: 5 and no one will *g* the fugitives.
Eze 11: 17 I will *g* you from the nations
16: 37 I am going to *g* all your lovers,
16: 37 I will *g* them against you from all
20: 34 *g* you from the countries where
20: 41 *g* you from the countries where
22: 19 I will *g* you into Jerusalem.
22: 20 As men *g* silver, copper, iron,
22: 20 so will I *g* you in my anger
22: 21 I will *g* you and I will blow on you
28: 25 When I *g* the people of Israel
29: 13 of forty years I will *g* the Egyptians
34: 13 and *g* them from the countries,
36: 24 I will *g* you from all the countries
37: 21 I will *g* them from all around
39: 10 need to *g* wood from the fields
39: 28 I will *g* them to their own land,
Hos 7: 14 They *g* together for grain
8: 10 I will now *g* them together.
9: 6 Egypt will *g* them,
Joel 2: 16 *G* the people,
2: 16 *g* the children,
3: 2 I will *g* all nations
Mic 2: 12 "I will surely *g* all of you, O Jacob;
4: 6 "I will *g* the lame;
Na 3: 18 mountains with no one to *g* them.
Hab 1: 9 and *g* prisoners like sand.
Zep 2: 1 *G* together, *g* together,
Zep 3: 8 to *g* the kingdoms
3: 19 *g* those who have been scattered.
3: 20 At that time I will *g* you;
Zec 10: 8 and *g* them in.
10: 10 and *g* them from Assyria.
14: 2 I will *g* all the nations to Jerusalem
Mt 12: 30 he who does not *g* with me scatters
13: 30 then *g* the wheat and bring it
23: 37 longed to *g* your children together,
24: 28 a carcass, there the vultures will *g*.
24: 31 and they will *g* his elect
25: 26 *g* where I have not scattered seed?
Mk 13: 27 and *g* his elect from the four winds,
Lk 3: 17 and to *g* the wheat into his barn,
11: 23 and he who does not *g* with me,
13: 34 longed to *g* your children together,
17: 37 body, there the vultures will *g*."
Jn 6: 12 "*G* the pieces that are left over.
Ac 4: 26 and the rulers *g* together
2Ti 4: 3 they will *g* around them a great
Rev 14: 18 and *g* the clusters of grapes
16: 14 to *g* them for the battle
19: 17 *g* together for the great supper
20: 8 and Magog—to *g* them for battle.

GATHERED (GATHER)

Ge 1: 9 under the sky be *g* to one place,
1: 10 and the *g* waters he called "seas."
25: 8 and he was *g* to his people.
25: 17 and he was *g* to his people.
29: 3 When all the flocks were *g* there,
29: 7 it is not time for the flocks to be *g*.
29: 8 "until all the flocks are *g*
35: 29 and died and was *g* to his people,
37: 7 while your sheaves *g* around mine
49: 29 "I am about to be *g* to my people.
49: 33 breathed his last and was *g*
Ex 16: 17 as they were told; some *g* much,
16: 18 Each one *g* as much as he needed.
16: 18 and he who *g* little did not have too
16: 18 he who *g* much did not have too
16: 21 Each morning everyone *g* as much
16: 22 On the sixth day, they *g* twice
32: 1 they *g* around Aaron and said,
Lev 8: 4 and the assembly *g* at the entrance
23: 39 after you have *g* the crops
Nu 11: 32 No one *g* less than ten homers.
11: 32 the people went out and *g* quail.
14: 5 whole Israelite assembly *g* there.
16: 19 When Korah had *g* all his followers
16: 42 when the assembly *g* in opposition
20: 2 and the people *g* in opposition
20: 10 and Aaron *g* the assembly together
20: 24 "Aaron will be *g* to his people.
20: 26 for Aaron will be *g* to his people;
27: 13 you too will be *g* to your people,
31: 2 you will be *g* to your people."
Dt 16: 13 days after you have *g* the produce
32: 50 died on Mount Hor and was *g*
32: 50 have climbed you will die and be *g*
Jos 18: 1 of the Israelites *g* at Shiloh
22: 12 assembly of Israel *g* at Shiloh to go
Jdg 2: 10 that whole generation had been *g*
4: 13 Sisera *g* together his nine hundred
9: 6 Beth Millo *g* beside the great tree
9: 27 and *g* the grapes and trodden them,
11: 3 group of adventurers *g* around him
Ru 2: 17 she threshed the barley she had *g*,
2: 18 saw how much she had *g*.
1Sa 8: 4 So all the elders of Israel *g* together
17: 1 Now the Philistines *g* their forces
17: 47 All those *g* here will know that it is
22: 2 or discontented *g* around him,
28: 1 days the Philistines *g* their forces
28: 4 while Saul *g* all the Israelites
29: 1 The Philistines *g* all their forces
2Sa 10: 17 told of this, he *g* all Israel,
17: 11 sand on the seashore—be *g* to you,
20: 14 who *g* together and followed him.
21: 13 been killed and exposed were *g* up.
23: 6 which are not *g* with the hand.
23: 9 when they taunted the Philistines *g*
1Ki 8: 5 of Israel that had *g* about him were
11: 24 He *g* men around him
2Ki 4: 39 He *g* some of its gourds
1Ch 11: 13 Philistines *g* there for battle.
19: 17 he *g* all Israel and crossed
23: 2 *g* together all the leaders of Israel,
2Ch 5: 6 of Israel that had *g* about him were
13: 7 Some worthless scoundrels *g*
23: 2 Judah and *g* the Levites
28: 24 Ahaz *g* together the furnishings
29: 20 morning King Hezekiah *g* the city
Ezr 7: 28 *g* leading men from Israel to go up
9: 4 of the God of Israel *g* around me
10: 1 and children—*g* around him.
10: 9 and Benjamin had *g* in Jerusalem.
Ne 8: 13 *g* around Ezra the scribe
9: 1 month, the Israelites *g* together,
Job 5: 26 like sheaves *g* in season.
24: 24 are brought low and *g* up like all
30: 4 In the brush they *g* salt herbs,
Ps 35: 15 But when I stumbled, they *g* in glee
35: 15 attackers *g* against me
107: 3 those he *g* from the lands,
Pr 27: 25 and the grass from the hills is *g* in,
30: 4 Who has *g* up the wind
SS 5: 1 I have *g* my myrrh with my spice.
Isa 10: 14 so I *g* all the countries;
27: 12 O Israelites, will be *g* up one by one
56: 8 them besides those already *g*."
60: 7 All Kedar's flocks will be *g* to you,
Jer 6: 11 and on the young men *g* together;
8: 2 They will not be *g* up or buried,
25: 33 They will not be mourned or *g* up
40: 15 and cause all the Jews who are *g*
Eze 29: 5 and not be *g* or picked up.
38: 7 you and all the hordes *g* about you,
38: 8 whose people were *g*
38: 12 and the people *g* from the nations,
38: 13 Have you *g* your hordes to loot,
39: 27 have *g* them from the countries
Hos 10: 10 nations will be *g* against them
Mic 1: 7 Since she *g* her gifts
4: 11 are *g* against you.
Zec 12: 3 of the earth are *g* against her,
Mt 13: 2 Such large crowds *g*
16: 9 and how many basketfuls you *g*?
16: 10 and how many basketfuls you *g*?
22: 10 *g* all the people they could find,
22: 41 the Pharisees were *g* together,
25: 32 All the nations will be *g* before him
27: 17 So when the crowd had *g*,
27: 27 *g* the whole company of soldiers
Mk 1: 33 The whole town *g* at the door,
2: 2 many *g* that there was no room left,
3: 20 a house, and again a crowd *g*,
4: 1 The crowd that *g* around him was
5: 21 a large crowd *g* around him.
6: 30 The apostles *g* around Jesus
7: 1 from Jerusalem *g* around Jesus
8: 1 those days another large crowd *g*.
Lk 12: 1 a crowd of many thousands had *g*,
23: 48 When all the people who had *g*
Jn 6: 13 So they *g* them and filled twelve
8: 2 where all the people *g* around him,
10: 24 The Jews *g* around him, saying,
Ac 5: 16 Crowds *g* also from the towns
6: 2 Twelve *g* all the disciples together
12: 12 where many people had *g*
13: 44 Sabbath almost the whole city *g*
14: 20 But after the disciples had *g*
14: 27 they *g* the church together
15: 30 where they *g* the church together
16: 13 to the women who had *g* there.
28: 3 Paul *g* a pile of brushwood and,
2Co 8: 15 and he that *g* little did not have too
8: 15 "He that *g* much did not have too
2Th 2: 1 Lord Jesus Christ and our being *g*
Rev 14: 19 *g* its grapes and threw them
16: 16 Then they *g* the kings together
19: 19 and their armies *g* together

GATHERING (GATHER)

Nu 11: 8 The people went around *g* it,
15: 32 a man was found *g* wood
15: 33 who found him *g* wood brought
1Ki 17: 10 a widow was there *g* sticks.
17: 12 I am *g* a few sticks to take home
Ecc 2: 26 to the sinner he gives the task of *g*
Jer 6: 9 like one *g* grapes."
Mt 3: 12 *g* the wheat into his barn
25: 24 and *g* where you have not scattered
Lk 8: 4 While a large crowd was *g*
15: 1 and "sinners" were all *g*
Ac 10: 27 and found a large *g* of people.

GATHERS (GATHER)

Nu 19: 10 The man who *g* up the ashes
Ru 2: 15 "Even if she *g* among the sheaves,
Ps 33: 7 He *g* the waters of the sea into jars;
41: 6 while his heart *g* slander;
129: 7 nor the one who *g* fill his arms.
147: 2 he *g* the exiles of Israel.
Pr 6: 8 and *g* its food at harvest.
10: 5 He who *g* crops in summer is a wise
13: 11 he who *g* money little
Isa 17: 5 when a reaper *g* the standing grain
40: 11 He *g* the lambs in his arms
56: 8 he who *g* the exiles of Israel:
Mic 4: 12 he who *g* them like sheaves
7: 1 I am like one who *g* summer fruit
Hab 1: 15 he *g* them up in his dragnet;
2: 5 he *g* to himself all the nations
Mt 23: 37 a hen *g* her chicks under her wings,
Lk 13: 34 a hen *g* her chicks under her wings,

GAUDY

Eze 16: 16 garments to make *g* high places,

GAUNT (GAUNTNESS)

Ge 41: 3 seven other cows, ugly and *g*,
41: 4 and *g* ate up the seven sleek,
Ps 109: 24 my body is thin and *g*.

GAUNTNESS (GAUNT)

Job 16: 8 my *g* rises up and testifies

GAVE (GIVE)

Ge 2: 20 man *g* names to all the livestock,
3: 6 She also *g* some to her husband,
3: 12 she *g* me some fruit from the tree,
4: 1 she conceived and *g* birth to Cain.
4: 2 Later she *g* birth to his brother
4: 17 she became pregnant and *g* birth
4: 20 Adah *g* birth to Jabal; he was
4: 25 and she *g* birth to a son
9: 3 Just as I *g* you the green plants,
12: 20 Pharaoh *g* orders about Abram
14: 20 Abram *g* him a tenth of everything.
16: 3 *g* her to her husband to be his wife.
16: 13 She *g* this name to the LORD who
16: 15 and Abram *g* the name Ishmael
18: 7 tender calf and *g* it to a servant,
20: 14 and female slaves and *g* them
21: 3 Abraham *g* the name Isaac
21: 14 skin of water and *g* them to Hagar.
21: 19 with water and *g* the boy a drink.
21: 27 cattle and *g* them to Abimelech,
24: 18 jar to her hands and *g* him a drink.
24: 53 he also *g* costly gifts to her brother
24: 53 of clothing and *g* them to Rebekah;
25: 6 he *g* gifts to the sons
25: 26 old when Rebekah *g* birth to them.
25: 34 Then Jacob *g* Esau some bread
26: 11 So Abimelech *g* orders
26: 18 and he *g* them the same names his
27: 20 The LORD your God *g* me success
28: 4 the land God *g* to Abraham."
29: 22 people of the place and *g* a feast.
29: 23 took his daughter Leah and *g* her
29: 24 And Laban *g* his servant girl Zilpah
29: 28 and then Laban *g* him his daughter
29: 29 Laban *g* his servant girl Bilhah
29: 32 Leah became pregnant and *g* birth
29: 33 am not loved, he *g* me this one
29: 33 when she *g* birth to a son she said,
29: 34 when she *g* birth to a son she said,
29: 35 when she *g* birth to a son she said,
30: 4 So she *g* him her servant Bilhah
30: 9 her maidservant Zilpah and *g* her
30: 21 Some time later she *g* birth
30: 23 She became pregnant and *g* birth
30: 25 After Rachel *g* birth to Joseph,
31: 8 then all the flocks *g* birth
35: 4 So they *g* Jacob all the foreign gods
35: 12 The land I *g* to Abraham
38: 3 she became pregnant and *g* birth
38: 4 She conceived again and *g* birth
38: 5 She *g* birth to still another son
38: 5 at Kezib that she *g* birth to him.
38: 18 he *g* them to her and slept with her,
39: 3 and that the LORD *g* him success
39: 23 *g* him success in whatever he did.
40: 20 and he *g* a feast for all his officials.
Ge 41: 45 Pharaoh *g* Joseph the name
41: 45 and *g* him Asenath daughter
42: 25 Joseph *g* orders to fill their bags
43: 24 *g* them water to wash their feet
44: 1 Now Joseph *g* these instructions
45: 21 Joseph *g* them carts, as Pharaoh
45: 21 *g* them provisions for their journey
45: 22 To each of them he *g* new clothing,
45: 22 to Benjamin he *g* three hundred
47: 11 *g* them property in the best part
47: 17 and he *g* them food in exchange
47: 22 from the allotment Pharaoh *g* them
49: 29 Then he *g* them these instructions:
Ex 1: 21 he *g* them families of their own.
1: 22 Then Pharaoh *g* this order
2: 2 she became pregnant and *g* birth
2: 21 who *g* his daughter Zipporah
2: 22 Zipporah *g* birth to a son,
4: 11 to him, "Who *g* man his mouth?
5: 6 same day Pharaoh *g* this order
12: 36 they *g* them what they asked for;
16: 32 so they can see the bread I *g* you
31: 18 he *g* him the two tablets
32: 24 Then they *g* me the gold,
34: 32 and he *g* them all the commands
36: 6 Then Moses *g* an order
Lev 7: 38 which the LORD *g* Moses
27: 34 the commands the LORD *g* Moses
Nu 3: 51 Moses *g* the redemption money
7: 6 oxen and *g* them to the Levites.
7: 7 He *g* two carts and four oxen
7: 8 and he *g* four carts and eight oxen
13: 16 (Moses *g* Hoshea son
13: 27 They *g* Moses this account:
15: 22 commands the LORD *g* Moses—
15: 23 from the day the LORD *g* them
17: 6 their leaders *g* him twelve staffs,
21: 3 and *g* the Canaanites over to them.
22: 18 Even if Balak *g* me his palace filled
22: 40 and *g* some to Balaam
24: 13 'Even if Balak *g* me his palace filled
30: 16 the LORD *g* Moses concerning
31: 21 of the law that the LORD *g* Moses:
31: 41 Moses *g* the tribute
31: 47 and *g* them to the Levites,
32: 28 Then Moses *g* orders about them
32: 33 Then Moses *g* to the Gadites,
32: 38 They *g* names to the cities they
32: 40 So Moses *g* Gilead to the Makirites
36: 5 command Moses *g* this order
36: 13 and regulations the LORD *g*
Dt 2: 12 did in the land the LORD *g* them
2: 36 The LORD our God *g* us all
3: 3 *g* into our hands Og king of Bashan
3: 12 I *g* the Reubenites and the Gadites
3: 13 I *g* to the half tribe of Manasseh.
3: 15 And I *g* Gilead to Makir.
3: 16 Gadites I *g* the territory extending
4: 45 and laws Moses *g* them
5: 22 on two stone tablets and *g* them
8: 16 He *g* you manna to eat in the desert
9: 10 The LORD *g* me two stone tablets
9: 11 LORD *g* me the two stone tablets,
10: 4 And the LORD *g* them to me.
22: 16 "I *g* my daughter in marriage
26: 9 us to this place and *g* us this land,
28: 45 commands and decrees he *g* you.
29: 8 We took their land and *g* it
31: 9 down this law and *g* it to the priests
31: 23 The LORD *g* this command
31: 25 he *g* this command
32: 8 the Most High *g* the nations their
32: 18 forgot the God who *g* you birth.
33: 4 the law that Moses *g* us,
Jos 1: 7 the law my servant Moses *g* you;
1: 13 the servant of the LORD *g* you:
1: 14 in the land that Moses *g* you east
1: 15 servant of the LORD *g* you east
6: 20 when the people *g* a loud shout,
8: 33 when he *g* instructions
10: 12 the day the LORD *g* the Amorites
10: 27 At sunset Joshua *g* the order
10: 30 The LORD also *g* that city
11: 8 the LORD *g* them into the hand
11: 23 and he *g* it as an inheritance
12: 6 servant of the LORD *g* their land
12: 7 toward Seir (their lands Joshua *g*
13: 14 tribe of Levi he *g* no inheritance,
Jos 14: 13 *g* him Hebron as his inheritance.
15: 13 Joshua *g* to Caleb son
15: 17 so Caleb *g* his daughter Acsah
15: 19 So Caleb *g* her the upper
17: 4 So Joshua *g* them an inheritance
18: 7 servant of the LORD *g* it to them."
19: 49 the Israelites *g* Joshua son
19: 50 They *g* him the town he asked for
21: 3 the Israelites *g* the Levites
21: 11 They *g* them Kiriath Arba
21: 13 the priest they *g* Hebron (a city
21: 17 of Benjamin they *g* them Gibeon,
21: 43 LORD *g* Israel all the land he had
21: 44 The LORD *g* them rest
22: 3 the LORD your God *g* you.
22: 4 the servant of the LORD *g* you
22: 5 the servant of the LORD *g* you:
22: 7 half of the tribe Joshua *g* land
22: 34 the Gadites *g* the altar this name:
23: 14 LORD your God *g* you has failed.
24: 3 I *g* him Isaac, and to Isaac I *g* Jacob
24: 3 and *g* him many descendants.
24: 8 but I *g* them into your hands.
24: 11 but I *g* them into your hands.
24: 13 I *g* you a land on which you did not
Jdg 1: 4 the LORD *g* the Canaanites
1: 13 so Caleb *g* his daughter Acsah
1: 15 Then Caleb *g* her the upper
3: 6 *g* their own daughters to their sons,
3: 10 LORD *g* Cushan-Rishathaim king
3: 12 this evil the LORD *g* Eglon king
3: 15 and he *g* them a deliverer—Ehud,
4: 19 a skin of milk, *g* him a drink,
5: 25 for water, and she *g* him milk;
6: 1 and for seven years he *g* them
6: 9 before you and *g* you their land.
8: 3 God *g* Oreb and Zeeb,
9: 4 They *g* him seventy silver shekels
11: 21 *g* Sihon and all his men
11: 32 the LORD *g* them into his hands.
12: 3 and the LORD *g* me the victory
12: 9 He *g* his daughters away
13: 24 The woman *g* birth to a boy
14: 9 his parents, he *g* them some,
14: 19 *g* their clothes to those who had
15: 2 he said, "that I *g* her to your friend.
17: 4 and *g* them to a silversmith,
Ru 1: 12 a husband tonight and then *g* birth
2: 15 to glean, Boaz *g* orders to his men,
2: 18 and *g* her what she had left
3: 17 "He *g* me these six measures
4: 7 off his sandal and *g* it to the other.
4: 13 her to conceive, and she *g* birth
1Sa 1: 5 to Hannah he *g* a double portion
1: 20 time Hannah conceived and *g* birth
2: 20 prayed for and *g* to the LORD."
2: 21 she conceived and *g* birth
2: 28 also *g* your father's house all
4: 19 she went into labor and *g* birth,
9: 23 "Bring the piece of meat I *g* you,
13: 13 the LORD your God *g* you;
15: 24 of the people and so I *g* in to them.
18: 4 off the robe he was wearing and *g* it
18: 5 successfully that Saul *g* him a high
18: 13 *g* him command over a thousand
18: 27 Saul *g* him his daughter Michal
20: 40 Jonathan *g* his weapons to the boy
21: 6 priest *g* him the consecrated bread,
22: 10 he also *g* him provisions
24: 22 So David *g* his oath to Saul.
25: 9 they *g* Nabal this message
27: 6 So on that day Achish *g* him Ziklag
30: 11 They *g* him water to drink
2Sa 3: 15 So Ish-Bosheth *g* orders
4: 10 That was the reward I *g* him
4: 12 So David *g* an order to his men,
6: 19 he *g* a loaf of bread, a cake of dates
8: 6 The LORD *g* David victory
8: 14 The LORD *g* David victory
12: 8 I *g* you the house of Israel
12: 8 I *g* your master's house to you,
12: 24 She *g* birth to a son, and they
13: 25 to go, but *g* him his blessing.
14: 16 son from the inheritance God *g* us.'
16: 23 the advice Ahithophel *g* was like
19: 28 but you *g* your servant a place
19: 39 kissed Barzillai and *g* him his
1Ki 1: 7 and they *g* him their support.

1Ki 2: 1 he *g* a charge to Solomon his son.
2: 25 So King Solomon *g* orders
2: 43 and obey the command I *g* you?"
2: 46 the king *g* the order to Benaiah son
3: 15 Then he *g* a feast for all his court.
3: 25 He then *g* an order: "Cut the living
3: 27 Then the king *g* his ruling:
4: 29 God *g* Solomon wisdom
5: 11 Solomon *g* Hiram twenty thousand
5: 12 The LORD *g* Solomon wisdom,
6: 12 fulfill through you the promise I *g*
8: 34 to the land you *g* to their fathers.
8: 36 rain on the land you *g* your people
8: 40 live in the land you *g* our fathers.
8: 48 toward the land you *g* their fathers,
8: 56 failed of all the good promises he *g*
8: 58 and regulations he *g* our fathers.
9: 11 King Solomon *g* twenty towns
9: 16 Canaanite inhabitants and then *g* it
10: 10 queen of Sheba *g* to King Solomon.
10: 10 she *g* the king 120 talents of gold,
10: 13 King Solomon *g* the queen
11: 18 who *g* Hadad a house and land
11: 19 with Hadad that he *g* him a sister
12: 8 rejected the advice the elders *g* him
13: 3 same day the man of God *g* a sign:
13: 21 the LORD your God *g* you.
14: 8 the house of David and *g* it to you,
14: 15 Israel from this good land that he *g*
15: 4 the LORD his God *g* him a lamp
17: 23 He *g* him to his mother and said,
19: 21 to cook the meat and *g* it
2Ki 4: 17 about that same time she *g* birth
5: 23 He *g* them to two of his servants,
11: 10 he *g* the commanders the spears
12: 11 they *g* the money to the men
12: 15 those to whom they *g* the money
15: 19 Menahem *g* him a thousand talents
16: 15 King Ahaz then *g* these orders
17: 20 and *g* them into the hands
17: 27 the king of Assyria *g* this order:
17: 34 that the LORD *g* the descendants
18: 15 Hezekiah *g* him all the silver that
18: 16 and *g* it to the king of Assyria.
21: 8 from the land I *g* their forefathers,
21: 8 that my servant Moses *g* them."
22: 8 He *g* it to Shaphan, who read it.
22: 12 He *g* these orders to Hilkiah
23: 21 The king *g* this order
25: 28 and *g* him a seat of honor higher
25: 30 day the king *g* Jehoiachin a regular
1Ch 2: 35 Sheshan *g* his daughter in marriage
2: 49 also *g* birth to Shaaph the father
4: 9 saying, "I *g* birth to him in pain."
4: 17 of Mered's wives *g* birth to Miriam
4: 18 (His Judean wife *g* birth
6: 64 Israelites *g* the Levites these towns
6: 70 of Manasseh the Israelites *g* Aner
7: 14 She *g* birth to Makir the father
7: 16 Makir's wife Maacah *g* birth
7: 18 His sister Hammoleketh *g* birth
7: 23 she became pregnant and *g* birth
11: 10 *g* his kingship strong support
14: 12 and David *g* orders to burn them
16: 3 he *g* a loaf of bread, a cake of dates
18: 6 The LORD *g* David victory
18: 13 The LORD *g* David victory
22: 2 So David *g* orders to assemble
22: 13 and laws that the LORD *g* Moses
25: 5 God *g* Heman fourteen sons
28: 11 David *g* his son Solomon the plans
28: 12 He *g* him the plans
28: 13 He *g* him instructions
28: 18 also *g* him the plan for the chariot,
28: 19 and he *g* me understanding
29: 6 of the king's work *g* willingly.
29: 7 They *g* toward the work
29: 8 who had precious stones *g* them
2Ch 2: 1 Solomon *g* orders to build a temple
6: 25 back to the land you *g* to them
6: 27 rain on the land you *g* your people
6: 31 live in the land you *g* our fathers.
6: 38 toward the land you *g* their fathers,
7: 3 and *g* thanks to the LORD,
7: 6 which were used when he *g* thanks,
9: 9 queen of Sheba *g* to King Solomon.
9: 9 she *g* the king 120 talents of gold,
9: 12 King Solomon *g* the queen

2Ch 9: 12 he *g* her more than she had brought
10: 8 rejected the advice the elders *g* him
11: 23 He *g* them abundant provisions
14: 6 for the LORD *g* him rest.
15: 15 So the LORD *g* them rest
19: 9 He *g* them these orders: "You must
20: 11 out of the possession you *g* us
23: 9 Then he *g* the commanders of units
24: 12 and Jehoiada *g* it to the men who
26: 5 the LORD, God *g* him success.
28: 9 he *g* them into your hand.
28: 14 So the soldiers *g* up the prisoners
28: 20 but he *g* him trouble instead of help
29: 27 Hezekiah *g* the order
31: 5 the Israelites generously *g*
31: 11 Hezekiah *g* orders
32: 24 and *g* him a miraculous sign.
34: 9 and *g* him the money that had been
34: 11 also *g* money to the carpenters
34: 15 He *g* it to Shaphan.
34: 20 He *g* these orders to Hilkiah,
35: 8 *g* the priests twenty-six hundred
Ezr 2: 68 of the families *g* freewill offerings
2: 69 According to their ability they *g*
3: 7 Then they *g* money to the masons
3: 7 and *g* food and drink and oil
3: 11 And all the people *g* a great shout
5: 11 This is the answer they *g* us:
5: 14 "Then King Cyrus *g* them
8: 36 who then *g* assistance to the people
9: 11 disregarded the commands you *g*
10: 19 (They all *g* their hands in pledge
Ne 1: 7 laws you *g* your servant Moses.
1: 8 the instruction you *g* your servant
2: 1 I took the wine and *g* it to the king.
2: 9 and *g* them the king's letters.
6: 4 and each time I *g* them the same
7: 70 governor *g* to the treasury 1,000
7: 71 of the families *g* to the treasury
9: 13 You *g* them regulations
9: 14 Sabbath and *g* them commands,
9: 15 In their hunger you *g* them bread
9: 20 You *g* your good Spirit
9: 20 you *g* them water for their thirst.
9: 22 You *g* them kingdoms and nations,
9: 27 compassion you *g* them deliverers,
9: 34 or the warnings you *g* them.
9: 35 and fertile land you *g* them,
9: 36 in the land you *g* our forefathers
12: 40 two choirs that *g* thanks then took
13: 9 I *g* orders to purify the rooms,
Est 1: 3 year of his reign he *g* a banquet
1: 5 the king *g* a banquet, lasting seven
1: 9 also *g* a banquet for the women
2: 18 And the king *g* a great banquet,
3: 10 *g* it to Haman son of Hammedatha,
4: 8 *g* him a copy of the text of the edict
5: 12 the king to the banquet she *g*.
8: 1 day King Xerxes *g* Queen Esther
Job 1: 21 LORD *g* and the LORD has taken
8: 4 he *g* them over to the penalty
10: 12 You *g* me life and showed me
22: 7 You *g* no water to the weary
32: 12 I *g* you my full attention.
38: 36 or *g* understanding to the mind?
39: 6 I *g* him the wasteland as his home,
42: 10 prosperous again and *g* him twice
42: 11 and each one *g* him a piece of silver
Ps 21: 4 for life, and you *g* it to him—
21: 5 Through the victories you *g*,
40: 2 and *g* me a firm place to stand.
44: 11 You *g* us up to be devoured like
68: 9 You *g* abundant showers, O God;
69: 21 and *g* me vinegar for my thirst.
74: 14 *g* him as food to the creatures
78: 15 and *g* them water as abundant
78: 23 Yet he *g* a command to the skies
78: 24 he *g* them the grain of heaven.
78: 46 He *g* their crops to the grasshopper
78: 48 He *g* over their cattle to the hail,
78: 50 but *g* them over to the plague.
78: 62 He *g* his people over to the sword;
81: 12 I *g* them over to their stubborn
99: 7 the decrees he *g* them.
105: 44 he *g* them the lands of the nations,
106: 7 they *g* no thought to your miracles;
106: 14 In the desert they *g*
106: 15 So he *g* them what they asked for,

Ps 135: 12 he *g* their land as an inheritance,
136: 21 and *g* their land as an inheritance,
148: 6 he *g* a decree that will never pass
Pr 1: 24 no one *g* heed when I stretched out
8: 29 when he *g* the sea its boundary
23: 22 to your father, who *g* you life,
23: 25 may she who *g* you birth rejoice!
Ecc 12: 7 the spirit returns to God who *g* it.
SS 8: 5 was in labor *g* you birth.
Isa 8: 3 she conceived and *g* birth to a son.
22: 16 and who *g* you permission
26: 18 but we *g* birth to wind.
41: 27 I *g* to Jerusalem a messenger
47: 6 I *g* them into your hand,
51: 2 and to Sarah, who *g* you birth.
63: 5 was appalled that no one *g* support;
Jer 2: 27 and to stone, 'You *g* me birth.'
3: 8 I *g* faithless Israel her certificate
3: 18 land to the land I *g* your forefathers
7: 7 in the land I *g* your forefathers
7: 14 place I *g* to you and your fathers.
7: 23 but I *g* them this command:
12: 14 the inheritance I *g* my people
15: 10 my mother, that you *g* me birth,
16: 15 to the land I *g* their forefathers.
17: 4 the inheritance I *g* you.
22: 26 and the mother who *g* you birth
23: 39 along with the city I *g* to you
24: 10 from the land I *g* to them
25: 5 stay in the land the LORD *g* to you
27: 12 I *g* the same message
30: 3 to the land I *g* their forefathers
32: 12 and I *g* this deed to Baruch son
32: 13 their presence I *g* Baruch these
32: 22 You *g* them this land you had
35: 6 son of Recab *g* us this command:
35: 16 command their forefather *g* them,
36: 32 and *g* it to the scribe Baruch son
37: 21 King Zedekiah then *g* orders
39: 10 at that time he *g* them vineyards
40: 5 the commander *g* him provisions
50: 12 she who *g* you birth will be
51: 59 This is the message Jeremiah *g*
52: 32 and *g* him a seat of honor higher
52: 34 of Babylon *g* Jehoiachin a regular
La 2: 14 The oracles they *g* you
Eze 3: 2 and he *g* me the scroll to eat.
16: 8 I *g* you my solemn oath
16: 17 also took the fine jewelry I *g* you,
16: 19 olive oil and honey I *g* you to eat—
16: 27 I *g* you over to the greed
16: 36 you *g* them your children's blood,
20: 11 I *g* them my decrees and made
20: 12 Also I *g* them my Sabbaths
20: 25 *g* them over to statutes that were
23: 4 They were mine and *g* birth to sons
23: 7 She *g* herself as a prostitute
28: 25 which I *g* to my servant Jacob.
31: 6 *g* birth under its branches;
36: 28 live in the land I *g* your forefathers;
37: 25 in the land I *g* to my servant Jacob,
Da 1: 7 chief official *g* them new names:
1: 16 and *g* them vegetables instead.
1: 17 four young men God *g* knowledge
5: 1 King Belshazzar *g* a great banquet
5: 2 he *g* orders to bring in the gold
5: 6 together and his legs *g* way.
5: 18 the Most High God *g* your father
5: 19 of the high position he *g* him,
6: 16 So the king *g* the order,
6: 23 and *g* orders to lift Daniel out
7: 16 and *g* me the interpretation
7: 23 "He *g* me this explanation:
9: 10 or kept the laws he *g* us
10: 18 touched me and *g* me strength.
Hos 1: 6 Gomer conceived again and *g* birth
2: 8 who *g* her the grain, the new wine
12: 10 *g* them many visions
13: 11 So in my anger I *g* you a king,
Am 4: 6 "I *g* you empty stomachs
Hag 1: 13 *g* this message of the LORD
Zec 3: 6 angel of the LORD *g* this charge
Mal 2: 5 and peace, and I *g* them to him;
4: 4 laws I *g* him at Horeb for all Israel.
Mt 1: 25 And he *g* him the name Jesus.
1: 25 with her until she *g* birth to a son.
2: 16 and he *g* orders to kill all the boys
8: 18 he *g* orders to cross

Mt 10: 1 *g* them authority to drive out evil
14: 19 Then he *g* them to the disciples,
14: 19 he *g* thanks and broke the loaves.
14: 19 the disciples *g* them to the people.
15: 36 and *g* them to the disciples,
20: 14 was hired last the same as I *g* you.
21: 23 "And who *g* you this authority?"
25: 15 To one he *g* five talents of money,
25: 35 and you *g* me something to drink,
25: 35 and you *g* me something to eat,
25: 42 and you *g* me nothing to drink,
25: 42 and you *g* me nothing to eat,
26: 26 Jesus took bread, *g* thanks
26: 26 and *g* it to his disciples, saying,
26: 27 *g* thanks and offered it to them,
27: 12 and the elders, he *g* no answer.
27: 50 in a loud voice, he *g* up his spirit.
28: 12 they *g* the soldiers a large sum
Mk 2: 26 he also *g* some to his companions."
3: 12 But he *g* them strict orders not
3: 16 (to whom he *g* the name Peter);
3: 17 (to them he *g* the name Boanerges,
5: 13 He *g* them permission,
5: 43 He *g* strict orders not
6: 7 *g* them authority over evil spirits.
6: 21 On his birthday Herod *g* a banquet
6: 28 and she *g* it to her mother.
6: 41 he *g* thanks and broke the loaves.
6: 41 he *g* them to his disciples to set
8: 6 and *g* them to his disciples to set
8: 7 he *g* thanks for them also
9: 9 Jesus *g* them orders not
11: 28 And who *g* you authority to do this
12: 44 They all *g* out of their wealth,
14: 22 Jesus took bread, *g* thanks
14: 22 and *g* it to his disciples, saying,
14: 23 *g* thanks and offered it to them,
14: 57 *g* this false testimony against him:
14: 61 remained silent and *g* no answer.
15: 45 was so, he *g* the body to Joseph.
Lk 1: 57 to have her baby, she *g* birth
2: 7 and she *g* birth to her firstborn,
2: 38 she *g* thanks to God and spoke
4: 20 *g* it back to the attendant
5: 26 Everyone was amazed and *g* praise
6: 4 he also *g* some to his companions."
7: 15 and Jesus *g* him back to his mother.
7: 21 *g* sight to many who were blind.
8: 32 and he *g* them permission.
9: 1 he *g* them power and authority
9: 16 he *g* thanks and broke them.
9: 16 he *g* them to the disciples to set
9: 42 and *g* him back to his father.
10: 35 and *g* them to the innkeeper.
11: 27 is the mother who *g* you birth
15: 16 but no one *g* him anything.
15: 29 Yet you never *g* me even a young
19: 13 his servants and *g* them ten minas.
20: 2 "Who *g* you this authority?"
21: 4 All these people *g* their gifts out
22: 17 After taking the cup, he *g* thanks
22: 19 And he took bread, *g* thanks
22: 19 and broke it, and *g* it to them,
23: 9 but Jesus *g* him no answer.
24: 30 *g* thanks, broke it and began
24: 42 They *g* him a piece of broiled fish,
Jn 1: 12 he *g* the right to become children
1: 32 Then John *g* this testimony:
3: 16 so loved the world that he *g* his one
4: 12 who *g* us the well and drank
5: 19 Jesus *g* them this answer: "I tell
5: 35 was a lamp that burned and *g* light,
6: 11 then took the loaves, *g* thanks,
6: 31 'He *g* them bread from heaven
7: 22 because Moses *g* you circumcision
13: 26 of bread, he *g* it to Judas Iscariot,
17: 4 by completing the work you *g* me
17: 6 you to those whom you *g* me out
17: 6 you *g* them to me and they have
17: 8 For I *g* them the words you *g* me
17: 11 of your name—the name you *g* me
17: 12 safe by that name you *g* me.
17: 22 them the glory that you *g* me,
18: 9 one of those you *g* me."
19: 9 but Jesus *g* him no answer.
19: 30 bowed his head and *g* up his spirit.
21: 13 took the bread and *g* it to them,
Ac 1: 3 *g* many convincing proofs that he
Ac 1: 4 eating with them, he *g* them this
2: 45 they *g* to anyone as he had need.
3: 5 So the man *g* them his attention,
5: 28 We *g* you strict orders not to teach
7: 5 He *g* him no inheritance here,
7: 8 Then he *g* Abraham the covenant
7: 10 He *g* Joseph wisdom and enabled
7: 42 and *g* them over to the worship
8: 10 *g* him their attention
10: 2 he *g* generously to those in need
11: 17 *g* them the same gift as he *g* us,
13: 19 and *g* their land to his people
13: 20 God *g* them judges until the time
13: 21 and he *g* them Saul son of Kish,
19: 16 He *g* them such a beating that they
21: 14 he would not be dissuaded, we *g* up
27: 15 so we *g* way to it and were driven
27: 20 we finally *g* up all hope
27: 35 *g* thanks to God in front of them all
Ro 1: 21 as God nor *g* thanks to him,
1: 24 Therefore God *g* them
1: 26 God *g* them over to shameful lusts.
1: 28 he *g* them over to a depraved mind,
4: 20 in his faith and *g* glory to God,
8: 32 not spare his own Son, but *g* him up
11: 8 "God *g* them a spirit of stupor,
15: 15 because of the grace God *g* me
1Co 3: 2 I *g* you milk, not solid food,
2Co 5: 18 *g* us the ministry of reconciliation:
8: 3 For I testify that they *g* as much
8: 5 they *g* themselves first to the Lord
10: 8 about the authority the Lord *g* us
13: 2 I already *g* you a warning
13: 10 the authority the Lord *g* me
Gal 1: 4 who *g* himself for our sins
2: 9 *g* me and Barnabas the right hand
2: 20 who loved me and *g* himself for me
3: 18 God in his grace *g* it to Abraham
Eph 4: 8 and *g* gifts to men."
4: 11 It was he who *g* some to be apostles
5: 2 as Christ loved us and *g* himself up
5: 25 and *g* himself up for her
Php 2: 9 and *g* him the name that is
3: 17 according to the pattern we *g* you.
Col 1: 25 by the commission God *g* me
1Th 1: 9 kind of reception you *g* us.
4: 2 know what instructions we *g* you
2Th 2: 16 and by his grace *g* us eternal
3: 10 were with you, we *g* you this rule.
1Ti 2: 6 who *g* himself as a ransom
2Ti 4: 17 stood at my side and *g* me strength,
Tit 2: 14 who *g* himself for us to redeem us
Heb 7: 2 and Abraham *g* him a tenth
7: 4 the patriarch Abraham *g* him
11: 22 and *g* instructions about his bones.
Jas 2: 25 did when she *g* lodging to the spies
5: 18 he prayed, and the heavens *g* rain,
2Pe 3: 15 with the wisdom that God *g* him.
1Jn 3: 24 We know it by the Spirit he *g* us.
3Jn : 3 It *g* me great joy to have some
Jude : 7 surrounding towns *g* themselves up
Rev 1: 1 which God *g* him to show his
10: 3 and he *g* a loud shout like the roar
11: 13 and *g* glory to the God of heaven.
12: 5 She *g* birth to a son, a male child,
13: 2 The dragon *g* the beast his power
15: 7 one of the four living creatures *g*
16: 19 *g* her the cup filled with the wine
18: 7 the glory and luxury she *g* herself.
20: 13 The sea *g* up the dead that were
20: 13 and Hades *g* up the dead that were

GAZA

Ge 10: 19 Sidon toward Gerar as far as *G*,
Dt 2: 23 lived in villages as far as *G*,
Jos 10: 41 from Kadesh Barnea to *G*
11: 22 in *G*, Gath and Ashdod did any
13: 3 of the five Philistine rulers in *G*,
15: 47 and *G*, its settlements and villages,
Jdg 1: 18 The men of Judah also took *G*,
6: 4 ruined the crops all the way to *G*
16: 1 One day Samson went to *G*,
16: 2 The people of *G* were told,
16: 21 his eyes and took him down to *G*.
1Sa 6: 17 one each for Ashdod, *G*, Ashkelon,
1Ki 4: 24 from Tiphsah to *G*, and had peace
2Ki 18: 8 as far as *G* and its territory.
Jer 25: 20 *G*, Ekron, and the people left
Jer 47: 1 before Pharaoh attacked *G*:
47: 5 *G* will shave her head in mourning;
Am 1: 6 "For three sins of *G*,
1: 7 I will send fire upon the walls of *G*
Zep 2: 4 *G* will be abandoned
Zec 9: 5 *G* will lose her king
9: 5 *G* will writhe in agony,
Ac 8: 26 goes down from Jerusalem to *G*."

GAZE (GAZING)

2Ki 8: 11 him with a fixed *g* until Hazael felt
Job 35: 5 *g* at the clouds so high above you.
36: 25 men *g* on it from afar.
Ps 27: 4 to *g* upon the beauty of the LORD
68: 16 Why *g* in envy, O rugged
Pr 4: 25 fix your *g* directly before you.
23: 31 Do not *g* at wine when it is red,
SS 6: 13 come back, that we may *g* on you!
6: 13 would you *g* on the Shulammite
Hab 2: 15 so that he can *g* on their naked
Rev 11: 9 and nation will *g* on their bodies

GAZELLE (GAZELLES)

Dt 12: 15 as if it were *g* or deer, according
12: 22 Eat them as you would *g* or deer.
14: 5 the deer, the *g*, the roe deer,
15: 22 the clean may eat it, as if it were *g*
2Sa 2: 18 as fleet-footed as a wild *g*.
Pr 6: 5 like a *g* from the hand of the hunter
SS 2: 9 My lover is like a *g* or a young stag.
2: 17 and be like a *g*
4: 5 like twin fawns of a *g*
7: 3 twins of a *g*.
8: 14 and be like a *g*

GAZELLES (GAZELLE)

1Ki 4: 23 *g*, roebucks and choice fowl.
1Ch 12: 8 as swift as *g* in the mountains.
SS 2: 7 by the *g* and by the does of the field
3: 5 by the *g* and by the does of the field

GAZEZ

1Ch 2: 46 Haran was the father of *G*.
2: 46 the mother of Haran, Moza and *G*.

GAZING (GAZE)

SS 2: 9 *g* through the windows,
Da 10: 8 So I was left alone, *g* at this great
2Co 3: 13 to keep the Israelites from *g* at it

GAZZAM

Ezr 2: 48 Rezin, Nekoda, *G*, Uzza, Paseah,
Ne 7: 51 Rezin, Nekoda, *G*, Uzza, Paseah,

GE HARASHIM

1Ch 4: 14 the father of Joab, the father of *G*.

GEBA

Jos 18: 24 Kephar Ammoni, Ophni and *G*—
21: 17 *G*, Anathoth and Almon, together
1Sa 13: 3 the Philistine outpost at *G*,
13: 16 men with them were staying in *G*
14: 5 the other to the south toward *G*.
1Ki 15: 22 With them King Asa built up *G*
2Ki 23: 8 from *G* to Beersheba, where
1Ch 6: 60 *G*, Alemeth and Anathoth,
8: 6 of families of those living in *G*
2Ch 16: 6 With them he built up *G*
Ezr 2: 26 *G* 621 of Micmash 122 of Bethel
Ne 7: 30 *G* 621 of Micmash 122 of Bethel
11: 31 from *G* lived in Micmash,
12: 29 from the area of *G* and Azmaveth,
Isa 10: 29 "We will camp overnight at *G*."
Zec 14: 10 from *G* to Rimmon,

GEBAL (GEBALITES)

1Ki 5: 18 and Hiram and the men of *G* cut
Ps 83: 7 *G*, Ammon and Amalek,
Eze 27: 9 Veteran craftsmen of *G* were

GEBALITES (GEBAL)

Jos 13: 5 the area of the *G*; and all Lebanon

GEBER

1Ki 4: 19 in Benjamin; *G* son of Uri—

GEBIM

Isa 10: 31 the people of *G* take cover.

GECKO

Lev 11: 30 any kind of great lizard, the g,

GEDALIAH (GEDALIAH'S)

2Ki 25: 22 king of Babylon appointed G son
25: 23 king of Babylon had appointed G
25: 23 they came to G at Mizpah—
25: 24 G took an oath to reassure them
25: 25 with ten men and assassinated G
1Ch 25: 3 from his sons: G, Zeri, Jeshaiah,
25: 9 12 the second to G, he
Ezr 10: 18 Maaseiah, Eliezer, Jarib and G.
Jer 38: 1 son of Mattan, G son of Pashhur,
39: 14 him over to G son of Ahikam,
40: 5 "Go back to G son of Ahikam,
40: 6 Jeremiah went to G son of Ahikam
40: 7 of Babylon had appointed G son
40: 8 they came to G at Mizpah—
40: 9 G son of Ahikam, the son
40: 11 had appointed G son of Ahikam,
40: 12 the land of Judah, to G at Mizpah,
40: 13 still in the open country came to G
40: 14 G son of Ahikam did not believe
40: 15 son of Kareah said privately to G
40: 16 But G son of Ahikam said
41: 1 with ten men to G son of Ahikam
41: 2 and struck down G son of Ahikam,
41: 3 were with G at Mizpah,
41: 6 he said, "Come to G son of Ahikam
41: 9 with G was the one King Asa had
41: 10 guard had appointed G son
41: 16 after he had assassinated G son
41: 18 son of Nethaniah had killed G son
43: 6 left with G son of Ahikam,
Zep 1: 1 the son of G, the son of Amariah,

GEDALIAH'S (GEDALIAH)

Jer 41: 4 The day after G assassination,

GEDER (GEDERITE)

Jos 12: 13 one the king of G one the king

GEDERAH (GEDERATHITE)

Jos 15: 36 Adithaim and G (or Gederothaim
1Ch 4: 23 potters who lived at Netaim and G;

GEDERATHITE (GEDERAH)

1Ch 12: 4 Jozabad the G, Eluzai, Jerimoth,

GEDERITE (GEDER)

1Ch 27: 28 Baal-Hanan the G was in charge

GEDEROTH

Jos 15: 41 Cabbon, Lahmas, Kitlish, G,
2Ch 28: 18 Aijalon and G, as well as Soco,

GEDEROTHAIM

Jos 15: 36 Adithaim and Gederah (or G)—

GEDOR

Jos 15: 58 Halhul, Beth Zur, G, Maarath,
1Ch 4: 4 Penuel was the father of G,
4: 18 birth to Jered the father of G,
4: 39 to the outskirts of G to the east
8: 31 Kish, Baal, Ner, Nadab, G, Ahio,
9: 37 Kish, Baal, Ner, Nadab, G, Ahio,
12: 7 the sons of Jeroham from G.

GEHAZI

2Ki 4: 12 said to his servant G, "Call
4: 14 G said, "Well, she has no son
4: 25 man of God said to his servant G,
4: 27 G came over to push her away,
4: 29 Elisha said to G, "Tuck your cloak
4: 31 So G went back to meet Elisha
4: 31 G went on ahead and laid the staff
4: 36 Elisha summoned G and said,
5: 20 had traveled some distance, G,
5: 21 So G hurried after Naaman.
5: 22 is all right," G answered.
5: 23 He urged G to accept them,
5: 23 and they carried them ahead of G.
5: 24 When G came to the hill, he took
5: 25 didn't go anywhere," G answered.
5: 25 "Where have you been, G?"
5: 27 G went from Elisha's presence
8: 4 The king was talking to G,
8: 5 G said, "This is the woman,
2Ki 8: 5 G was telling the king how Elisha

GELILOTH

Jos 18: 17 to En Shemesh, continued to G,
22: 10 came to G near the Jordan
22: 11 of Canaan at G near the Jordan

GEM (GEMS)

Ex 28: 11 stones the way a g cutter engraves

GEMALLI

Nu 13: 12 Ammiel son of G; from the tribe

GEMARIAH

Jer 29: 3 of Shaphan and to G son of Hilkiah
36: 10 From the room of G son
36: 11 When Micaiah son of G, the son
36: 12 son of Acbor, G son of Shaphan,
36: 25 and G urged the king not

GEMS (GEM)

Ex 25: 7 and other g to be mounted
35: 9 and other g to be mounted
35: 27 and other g to be mounted
La 4: 1 The sacred g are scattered

GENEALOGICAL (GENEALOGY)

1Ch 4: 33 And they kept a g record.
5: 1 listed in the g record in accordance
5: 7 listed according to their g records:
5: 17 in the g records during the reigns
7: 7 Their g record listed 22,034
7: 9 Their g record listed the heads
26: 31 to the g records of their families.
2Ch 31: 16 were in the g records—
31: 17 by their families in the g records
31: 18 listed in these g records.
Ne 7: 5 I found the g record

GENEALOGIES (GENEALOGY)

1Ch 9: 1 listed in the g recorded in the book
2Ch 12: 15 of Iddo the seer that deal with g?
31: 19 recorded in the g of the Levites.
1Ti 1: 4 themselves to myths and endless g.
Tit 3: 9 avoid foolish controversies and g

GENEALOGY (GENEALOGICAL GENEALOGIES)

1Ch 7: 2 men in their g numbered 22,600.
7: 4 According to their family g,
7: 5 as listed in their g, were 87,000
7: 40 as listed in their g, was 26,000.
8: 28 chiefs as listed in their g,
9: 9 as listed in their g, numbered 956.
9: 22 registered by g in their villages.
9: 34 chiefs as listed in their g,
Mt 1: 1 of the g of Jesus Christ the son
Heb 7: 3 father or mother, without g,

GENERALS

Rev 6: 15 the princes, the g, the rich,
19: 18 g, and mighty men, of horses

GENERATION (GENERATIONS)

Ge 7: 1 I have found you righteous in this g
15: 16 In the fourth g your descendants
50: 23 the third g of Ephraim's children.
Ex 1: 6 all his brothers and all that g died,
3: 15 am to be remembered from g to g.
17: 16 against the Amalekites from g to g
20: 5 and fourth g of those who hate me,
34: 7 fathers to the third and fourth g."
Nu 14: 18 fathers to the third and fourth g.'
32: 13 until the whole g of those who had
Dt 1: 35 of this evil g shall see the good land
2: 14 that entire g of fighting men had
5: 9 and fourth g of those who hate me,
23: 2 even down to the tenth g.
23: 3 even down to the tenth g.
23: 8 The third g of children born
32: 5 but a warped and crooked g.
32: 20 for they are a perverse g,
Jdg 2: 10 After that whole g had been
2: 10 to their fathers, another g grew up,
2Ki 10: 30 throne of Israel to the fourth g."
15: 12 throne of Israel to the fourth g."
Est 9: 28 and observed in every g
Job 42: 16 and their children to the fourth g.
Ps 24: 6 Such is the g of those who seek him
48: 13 tell of them to the next g.
49: 19 he will join the g of his fathers,
71: 18 I declare your power to the next g,
73: 15 I would have betrayed this g
78: 4 we will tell the next g
78: 6 so the next g would know them,
78: 8 a stubborn and rebellious g,
79: 13 from g to g we will recount
95: 10 forty years I was angry with that g;
102: 18 Let this be written for a future g,
109: 13 names blotted out from the next g.
112: 2 each g of the upright will be blessed
145: 4 One g will commend your works
Isa 34: 10 From g to g it will lie desolate;
34: 17 and dwell there from g to g.
Jer 2: 31 "You of this g, consider the word
7: 29 and abandoned this g that is
50: 39 or lived in from g to g.
La 5: 19 your throne endures from g to g.
Da 4: 3 his dominion endures from g to g.
4: 34 his kingdom endures from g to g.
Joel 1: 3 and their children to the next g.
Mt 11: 16 "To what can I compare this g?
12: 39 adulterous g asks for a miraculous
12: 41 up at the judgment with this g
12: 42 rise at the judgment with this g
12: 45 be with this wicked g."
16: 4 and adulterous g looks
17: 17 "O unbelieving and perverse g,"
23: 36 all this will come upon this g.
24: 34 this g will certainly not pass away
Mk 8: 12 "Why does this g ask
8: 38 in this adulterous and sinful g,
9: 19 "O unbelieving g," Jesus replied,
13: 30 this g will certainly not pass away
Lk 1: 50 who fear him, from g to g.
7: 31 can I compare the people of this g?
9: 41 "O unbelieving and perverse g,"
11: 29 Jesus said, "This is a wicked g.
11: 30 will the Son of Man be to this g.
11: 31 the judgment with the men of this g
11: 32 up at the judgment with this g
11: 50 Therefore this g will be held
11: 51 this g will be held responsible
17: 25 things and be rejected by this g.
21: 32 this g will certainly not pass away
Ac 2: 40 Save yourselves from this corrupt g
13: 36 served God's purpose in his own g,
Php 2: 15 fault in a crooked and depraved g,
Heb 3: 10 That is why I was angry with that g

GENERATIONS (GENERATION)

Ge 9: 12 a covenant for all g to come:
17: 7 after you for the g to come,
17: 9 after you for the g to come.
17: 12 For the g to come every male
Ex 12: 14 for the g to come you shall
12: 17 as a lasting ordinance for the g
12: 42 vigil to honor the LORD for the g
16: 32 and keep it for the g to come,
16: 33 to be kept for the g to come."
27: 21 among the Israelites for the g
29: 42 "For the g to come this burnt
30: 8 before the LORD for the g to come
30: 10 of the atoning sin offering for the g
30: 21 his descendants for the g to come."
30: 31 be my sacred anointing oil for the g
31: 13 and you for the g to come,
31: 16 celebrating it for the g to come
40: 15 continue for all g to come."
Lev 3: 17 This is a lasting ordinance for the g
6: 18 LORD by fire for the g to come.
7: 36 as their regular share for the g
10: 9 This is a lasting ordinance for the g
17: 7 for them and for the g to come.'
21: 17 'For the g to come none
22: 3 "Say to them: 'For the g to come,
23: 14 is to be a lasting ordinance for the g
23: 21 is to be a lasting ordinance for the g
23: 31 is to be a lasting ordinance for the g
23: 41 is to be a lasting ordinance for the g
24: 3 is to be a lasting ordinance for the g
Nu 10: 8 for you and the g to come.
15: 14 For the g to come, whenever
15: 15 this is a lasting ordinance for the g
15: 21 Throughout the g to come you are
15: 23 continuing through the g to come

Nu 15:38 'Throughout the *g* to come you are
18:23 This is a lasting ordinance for the *g*
35:29 for you throughout the *g* to come,
Dt 7: 9 covenant of love to a thousand *g*
29:22 children who follow you in later *g*
32: 7 consider the *g* long past.
Jos 22:27 and you and the *g* that follow,
1Ch 16:15 he commanded, for a thousand *g*,
Job 8: 8 "Ask the former *g*
Ps 22:30 future *g* will be told about the Lord
33:11 of his heart through all *g*.
45:17 your memory through all *g*;
49:11 their dwellings for endless *g*,
61: 6 his years for many *g*.
72: 5 as long as the moon, through all *g*.
85: 5 prolong your anger through all *g*?
89: 1 faithfulness known through all *g*.
89: 4 your throne firm through all *g*.' "
90: 1 throughout all *g*.
100: 5 continues through all *g*.
102: 12 your renown endures through all *g*.
102: 24 your years go on through all *g*.
105: 8 he commanded, for a thousand *g*,
106: 31 for endless *g* to come.
119: 90 continues through all *g*;
135: 13 renown, O LORD, through all *g*.
145: 13 dominion endures through all *g*.
146: 10 your God, O Zion, for all *g*.
Pr 27:24 and a crown is not secure for all *g*.
Ecc 1: 4 *G* come and *g* go,
Isa 13:20 or lived in through all *g*;
41: 4 forth the *g* from the beginning?
51: 8 my salvation through all *g*."
51: 9 as in *g* of old.
60:15 and the joy of all *g*.
61: 4 that have been devastated for *g*.
Joel 3:20 and Jerusalem through all *g*.
Mt 1:17 Thus there were fourteen *g* in all
Lk 1:48 now on all *g* will call me blessed,
Eph 3: 5 not made known to men in other *g*
3:21 in Christ Jesus throughout all *g*,
Col 1:26 been kept hidden for ages and *g*,

GENEROSITY (GENEROUS)

2Co 8: 2 poverty welled up in rich *g*.
9:11 and through us your *g* will result
9:13 and for your *g* in sharing with them

GENEROUS (GENEROSITY)

Ps 37:26 They are always *g* and lend freely;
112: 5 Good will come to him who is *g*
Pr 11:25 A *g* man will prosper;
22: 9 A *g* man will himself be blessed,
Mt 20:15 Or are you envious because I am *g*
2Co 9: 5 Then it will be ready as a *g* gift,
9: 5 for the *g* gift you had promised.
9:11 way so that you can be *g*
1Ti 6:18 and to be *g* and willing to share.

GENITALS

Eze 23:20 whose *g* were like those of donkeys

GENNESARET

Mt 14:34 crossed over, they landed at *G*.
Mk 6:53 landed at *G* and anchored there.
Lk 5: 1 was standing by the Lake of *G*,

GENTILE (GENTILES)

Ezr 6:21 of their *G* neighbors in order
Ne 5: 9 the reproach of our *G* enemies?
Ac 10:28 law for a Jew to associate with a *G*
15:23 To the *G* believers in Antioch,
21:25 As for the *G* believers, we have
Ro 1:16 first for the Jew, then for the *G*.
2: 9 first for the Jew, then for the *G*;
2:10 first for the Jew, then for the *G*.
10:12 difference between Jew and *G*—
Gal 2:14 yet you live like a *G* and not like
2:15 not '*G* sinners' know that a man is

GENTILES (GENTILE)

Ne 5: 8 brothers who were sold to the *G*.
Isa 9: 1 he will honor Galilee of the *G*,
42: 6 and a light for the *G*,
49: 6 also make you a light for the *G*,
49:22 "See, I will beckon to the *G*,
Mt 4:15 Galilee of the *G*—
10: 5 "Do not go among the *G*
Mt 10:18 as witnesses to them and to the *G*.
20:19 him over to the *G* to be mocked
20:25 rulers of the *G* lord it over them,
Mk 10:33 and will hand him over to the *G*,
10:42 as rulers of the *G* lord it over them,
Lk 2:32 a light for revelation to the *G*
18:32 He will be handed over to the *G*.
21:24 on by the *G* until the times
21:24 until the times of the *G* are fulfilled
22:25 "The kings of the *G* lord it
Ac 4:27 Pilate met together with the *G*
9:15 to carry my name before the *G*
10:45 been poured out even on the *G*.
11: 1 throughout Judea heard that the *G*
11:18 granted the *G* repentance unto life
13:16 and you *G* who worship God,
13:26 Abraham, and you God-fearing *G*,
13:46 of eternal life, we now turn to the *G*
13:47 I have made you a light for the *G*,
13:48 When the *G* heard this, they were
14: 1 number of Jews and *G* believed.
14: 2 refused to believe stirred up the *G*
14: 5 was a plot afoot among the *G*
14:27 opened the door of faith to the *G*.
15: 3 told how the *G* had been
15: 5 "The *G* must be circumcised
15: 7 among you that the *G* might hear
15:12 done among the *G* through them.
15:14 by taking from the *G* a people
15:17 and all the *G* who bear my name,
15:19 for the *G* who are turning to God.
18: 6 From now on I will go to the *G*."
21:11 and will hand him over to the *G*.' "
21:19 among the *G* through his ministry.
21:21 live among the *G* to turn away
22:21 I will send you far away to the *G*.' "
26:17 your own people and from the *G*.
26:20 and in all Judea, and to the *G* also,
26:23 to his own people and to the *G*."
28:28 salvation has been sent to the *G*,
Ro 1: 5 people from among all the *G*
1:13 as I have had among the other *G*.
2:14 when *G*, who do not have the law,
2:24 name is blasphemed among the *G*
3: 9 and *G* alike are all under sin.
3:29 Is he not the God of *G* too? Yes,
3:29 of *G* too, since there is only one
9:24 from the Jews but also from the *G*?
9:30 That the *G*, who did not pursue
11:11 to the *G* to make Israel envious.
11:12 their loss means riches for the *G*,
11:13 as I am the apostle to the *G*,
11:13 bring! I am talking to you *G*.
11:25 number of the *G* has come in.
15: 9 I will praise you among the *G*;
15: 9 so that the *G* may glorify God
15:10 "Rejoice, O *G*, with his people."
15:11 "Praise the Lord, all you *G*,
15:12 the *G* will hope in him."
15:16 so that the *G* might become
15:16 to the *G* with the priestly duty
15:18 me in leading the *G* to obey God
15:27 For if the *G* have shared
16: 4 of the *G* are grateful to them.
1Co 1:23 block to Jews and foolishness to *G*,
2Co 11:26 in danger from *G*; in danger
Gal 1:16 I might preach him among the *G*,
2: 2 gospel that I preach among the *G*.
2: 7 of preaching the gospel to the *G*,
2: 8 my ministry as an apostle to the *G*.
2: 9 agreed that we should go to the *G*,
2:12 James, he used to eat with the *G*.
2:12 and separate himself from the *G*
2:14 that you force *G* to follow Jewish
3: 8 that God would justify the *G*
3:14 to the *G* through Christ Jesus,
Eph 2:11 that formerly you who are *G*
3: 1 Jesus for the sake of you *G*—
3: 6 the gospel the *G* are heirs together
3: 8 to the *G* the unsearchable riches
4:17 must no longer live as the *G* do,
Col 1:27 among the *G* the glorious riches
1Th 2:16 us from speaking to the *G*
1Ti 2: 7 a teacher of the true faith to the *G*.
2Ti 4:17 and all the *G* might hear it.
Rev 11: 2 because it has been given to the *G*.

GENTLE (GENTLENESS)

Dt 28:54 Even the most *g* and sensitive man
28:56 The most *g* and sensitive woman
28:56 and *g* that she would not venture
2Sa 18: 5 Be *g* with the young man Absalom
1Ki 19:12 And after the fire came a *g* whisper
Job 41: 3 Will he speak to you with *g* words?
Pr 15: 1 A *g* answer turns away wrath,
25:15 and a *g* tongue can break a bone.
Jer 11:19 I had been like a *g* lamb led
Zec 9: 9 *g* and riding on a donkey,
Mt 11:29 for I am *g* and humble in heart,
21: 5 *g* and riding on a donkey,
Ac 27:13 When a *g* south wind began
1Co 4:21 or in love and with a *g* spirit?
Eph 4: 2 Be completely humble and *g*;
1Th 2: 7 but we were *g* among you,
1Ti 3: 3 not violent but *g*, not quarrelsome,
1Pe 3: 4 the unfading beauty of a *g*

GENTLENESS (GENTLE)

2Co 10: 1 By the meekness and *g* of Christ,
Gal 5:23 faithfulness, *g* and self-control.
Php 4: 5 Let your *g* be evident to all.
Col 3:12 kindness, humility, *g* and patience.
1Ti 6:11 faith, love, endurance and *g*.
1Pe 3:15 But do this with *g* and respect,

GENUBATH

1Ki 11:20 Tahpenes bore him a son named *G*,
11:20 There *G* lived with Pharaoh's own

GENUINE

2Co 6: 8 *g*, yet regarded as impostors;
Php 2:20 who takes a *g* interest
1Pe 1: 7 may be proved *g* and may result

GERA

Ge 46:21 Beker, Ashbel, *G*, Naaman, Ehi,
Jdg 3:15 the son of *G* the Benjamite,
2Sa 16: 5 His name was Shimei son of *G*,
19:16 Shimei son of *G*, the Benjamite
19:18 son of *G* crossed the Jordan,
1Ki 2: 8 you have with you Shimei son of *G*,
1Ch 8: 3 Addar, *G*, Abihud, Abishua,
8: 5 Abishua, Naaman, Ahoah, *G*,
8: 7 and *G*, who deported them

GERAHS

Ex 30:13 shekel, which weighs twenty *g*.
Lev 27:25 to the sanctuary shekel, twenty *g*
Nu 3:47 shekel, which weighs twenty *g*
18:16 shekel, which weighs twenty *g*.
Eze 45:12 The shekel is to consist of twenty *g*

GERAR

Ge 10:19 reached from Sidon toward *G*
20: 1 For a while he stayed in *G*,
20: 2 Abimelech king of *G* sent for Sarah
26: 1 king of the Philistines in *G*.
26: 6 So Isaac stayed in *G*.
26:17 and encamped in the Valley of *G*
26:20 But the herdsmen of *G* quarreled
26:26 had come to him from *G*,
2Ch 14:13 his army pursued them as far as *G*.
14:14 destroyed all the villages around *G*,

GERASENES

Mk 5: 1 the lake to the region of the *G*.
Lk 8:26 They sailed to the region of the *G*,
8:37 of the region of the *G* asked Jesus

GERIZIM

Dt 11:29 on Mount *G* the blessings,
27:12 on Mount *G* to bless the people:
Jos 8:33 stood in front of Mount *G*
Jdg 9: 7 up on the top of Mount *G*

GERSHOM

Ex 2:22 and Moses named him *G*, saying,
18: 3 One son was named *G*,
Jdg 18:30 and Jonathan son of *G*, the son
1Ch 23:15 The sons of Moses: *G* and Eliezer.
23:16 of *G*: Shubael was the first.
26:24 a descendant of *G* son of Moses,
Ezr 8: 2 of the descendants of Phinehas, *G*;

GERSHON (GERSHONITE GERSHONITES)

Ge 46: 11 The sons of Levi: *G*, Kohath
Ex 6: 16 according to their records: *G*,
6: 17 The sons of *G*, by clans, were Libni
Nu 3: 17 the names of the sons of Levi: *G*,
3: 21 To *G* belonged the clans
26: 57 through *G*, the Gershonite clan;
Jos 21: 6 of *G* were allotted thirteen towns
1Ch 6: 1 The sons of Levi: *G*, Kohath
6: 16 The sons of Levi: *G*, Kohath
6: 17 are the names of the sons of *G*:
6: 20 Of *G*: Libni his son, Jehath his son,
6: 43 the son of *G*, the son of Levi;
6: 62 The descendants of *G*, clan by clan,
15: 7 from the descendants of *G*,
23: 6 to the sons of Levi: *G*,

GERSHONITE (GERSHON)

Nu 3: 18 were the names of the *G* clans:
3: 21 Shimeites; these were the *G* clans.
3: 23 The *G* clans were to camp
4: 24 "This is the service of the *G* clans
4: 28 service of the *G* clans at the Tent
4: 41 of those in the *G* clans who served
26: 57 through Gershon, the *G* clan;
Jos 21: 33 towns of the *G* clans were thirteen,
1Ch 26: 21 families belonging to Ladan the *G*,
29: 8 in the custody of Jehiel the *G*.

GERSHONITES (GERSHON)

Nu 3: 24 families of the *G* was Eliasaph son
3: 25 of Meeting the *G* were responsible
4: 22 of the *G* by their families and clans.
4: 26 The *G* are to do all that needs
4: 38 The *G* were counted by their clans
7: 7 two carts and four oxen to the *G*,
10: 17 the *G* and Merarites, who carried it
Jos 21: 27 clans of the *G* were given:
1Ch 6: 71 The *G* received the following:
23: 7 Belonging to the *G*: Ladan
26: 21 who were *G* through Ladan
2Ch 29: 12 from the *G*, Joah son of Zimmah

GERUTH KIMHAM

Jer 41: 17 stopping at *G* near Bethlehem on

GESHAN

1Ch 2: 47 *G*, Pelet, Ephah and Shaaph.

GESHEM

Ne 2: 19 and *G* the Arab heard about it,
6: 1 *G* the Arab and the rest
6: 2 and *G* sent me this message:
6: 6 the nations—and *G* says it is

GESHUR (GESHURITES)

Jos 12: 5 to the border of the people of *G*
13: 11 the territory of the people of *G*
13: 13 did not drive out the people of *G*
2Sa 3: 3 daughter of Talmai king of *G*;
13: 37 son of Ammihud, the king of *G*.
13: 38 After Absalom fled and went to *G*,
14: 23 to *G* and brought Absalom back
14: 32 "Why have I come from *G*?
15: 8 While your servant was living at *G*
1Ch 2: 23 But *G* and Aram captured Havvoth
3: 2 daughter of Talmai king of *G*;

GESHURITES (GESHUR)

Dt 3: 14 of the *G* and the Maacathites;
Jos 13: 2 regions of the Philistines and *G*:
1Sa 27: 8 his men went up and raided the *G*,

GET (GETS GETTING GOT ILL-GOTTEN)

Ge 18: 5 Let me *g* you something to eat,
18: 6 "*g* three seahs of fine flour
19: 9 "*G* out of our way," they replied.
19: 12 belongs to you? *G* them out of here,
19: 14 "Hurry and *g* out of this place,
19: 32 Let's *g* our father to drink wine
19: 34 Let's *g* him to drink wine again
21: 10 "*G* rid of that slave woman
24: 3 that you will not *g* a wife
24: 4 and *g* a wife for my son Isaac."
24: 7 so that you can *g* a wife for my son
24: 37 'You must not *g* a wife for my son
24: 38 and to my own clan, and *g* a wife
Ge 24: 40 so that you can *g* a wife for my son
24: 48 road to *g* the granddaughter
27: 3 Now then, *g* your weapons—
27: 13 Just do what I say; go and *g* them
29: 20 served seven years to *g* Rachel,
34: 4 "*G* me this girl as my wife."
35: 2 "*G* rid of the foreign gods you have
38: 20 in order to *g* his pledge back
40: 14 and *g* me out of this prison.
42: 16 of your number to *g* your brother;
42: 27 sack to *g* feed for his donkey,
45: 19 and *g* your father and come.
46: 28 to Joseph to *g* directions to Goshen
Ex 2: 5 and sent her slave girl to *g* it.
2: 7 and *g* one of the Hebrew women
5: 4 *G* back to your work!"
5: 11 *g* your own straw wherever you
5: 18 Now *g* to work.
7: 24 along the Nile to *g* drinking water,
8: 20 "*G* up early in the morning
9: 13 "*G* up early in the morning,
10: 26 until we *g* there we will not know
10: 28 Pharaoh said to Moses, "*G* out
14: 25 "Let's *g* away from the Israelites!
16: 24 it did not stink or *g* maggots in it.
23: 11 among your people may *g* food
32: 25 and that Aaron had let them *g* out
Nu 11: 13 Where can I *g* meat
16: 10 trying to *g* the priesthood too.
16: 45 "*G* away from this assembly
17: 2 and *g* twelve staffs from them,
20: 25 *G* Aaron and his son Eleazar
22: 23 Balaam beat her to *g* her back
Dt 2: 13 *g* up and cross the Zered Valley."
6: 7 lie down and when you *g* up.
11: 19 lie down and when you *g* up.
17: 16 return to Egypt to *g* more of them,
22: 4 Help him *g* it to its feet.
24: 10 house to *g* what he is offering
24: 19 a sheaf, do not go back to *g* it.
30: 12 Who will ascend into heaven to *g* it
30: 13 "Who will cross the sea to *g* it
Jos 1: 2 *g* ready to cross the Jordan River
1: 11 tell the people, '*G* your supplies
18: 7 do not *g* a portion among you,
22: 26 'Let us *g* ready and build an altar—
Jdg 1: 24 "Show us how to *g* into the city
7: 9 "*G* up, go down against the camp,
7: 15 of Israel and called out, "*G* up!
7: 17 When I *g* to the edge of the camp,
9: 29 Then I would *g* rid of him.
11: 2 going to *g* any inheritance
11: 5 of Gilead went to *g* Jephthah
14: 2 now *g* her for me as my wife."
14: 3 Philistines to *g* a wife?"
14: 3 said to his father, "*G* her for me.
15: 3 "This time I have a right to *g*
15: 7 stop until I *g* my revenge on you."
16: 28 me with one blow *g* revenge
16: 31 whole family went down to *g* him.
18: 10 When you *g* there, you will find
19: 9 tomorrow morning you can *g* up
19: 28 He said to her, "*G* up; let's go."
20: 10 to *g* provisions for the army.
21: 22 we did not *g* wives for them
Ru 2: 9 and *g* a drink from the water jars
1Sa 1: 14 keep on getting drunk? *G* rid
6: 7 "Now then, *g* a new cart ready,
9: 26 "*G* ready, and I will send you
18: 8 more can he *g* but the kingdom?"
19: 17 "He said to me, 'Let me *g* away.
20: 29 let me *g* away to see my brothers.'
23: 26 hurrying to *g* away from Saul.
24: 19 does he let him *g* away unharmed?
26: 11 *g* the spear and water jug that are
26: 22 young men come over and *g* it.
29: 10 Now *g* up early, along with your
2Sa 2: 14 some of the young men *g* up
4: 6 of the house as if to *g* some wheat,
5: 6 to David, "You will not *g* in here;
5: 6 "David cannot *g* in here."
11: 4 David sent messengers to *g* her.
11: 20 'Why did you *g* so close to the city
11: 21 Why did you *g* so close to the wall
12: 17 stood beside him to *g* him up
12: 21 you *g* up and eat!" He answered,
13: 13 Where could I *g* rid of my disgrace
13: 15 Amnon said to her, "*G* up
2Sa 13: 15 "Get up and *g* out!" "No!"
13: 17 "*G* this woman out of here
14: 7 then we will *g* rid of the heir as well
15: 2 He would *g* up early and stand
16: 7 Shimei said, "*G* out, *g* out,
20: 18 to say, '*G* your answer at Abel,'
23: 15 that someone would *g* me a drink
1Ki 12: 18 managed to *g* into his chariot
17: 11 As she was going to *g* it, he called,
18: 23 *G* two bulls for us.
18: 40 Don't let anyone *g* away!"
19: 5 angel touched him and said, "*G* up
19: 7 "*G* up and eat, for the journey is
19: 15 When you *g* there, anoint Hazael
20: 33 "Go and *g* him," the king said.
21: 7 I'll *g* you the vineyard
21: 7 as king over Israel? *G* up and eat!
21: 15 "*G* up and take possession
22: 34 and *g* me out of the fighting.
2Ki 4: 41 Elisha said, "*G* some flour."
5: 20 and *g* something from him."
6: 2 where each of us can *g* a pole;
6: 27 where can I *g* help for you?
7: 12 then we will take them alive and *g*
9: 2 When you *g* there, look
9: 2 *g* him away from his companions
9: 17 "*G* a horseman," Joram ordered.
13: 15 "*G* a bow and some arrows,"
22: 4 have him *g* ready the money that
1Ch 11: 5 to David, "You will not *g* in here."
11: 17 that someone would *g* me a drink
2Ch 10: 18 managed to *g* into his chariot
18: 33 and *g* me out of the fighting.
Ne 2: 6 and when will you *g* back?"
2: 14 room for my mount to *g* through;
5: 2 and stay alive, we must *g* grain."
5: 3 and our homes to *g* grain
6: 7 this report will *g* back to the king;
6: 9 "Their hands will *g* too weak
Est 6: 10 "*G* the robe and the horse
9: 16 and *g* relief from their enemies.
Job 7: 4 I think, 'How long before I *g* up?'
15: 31 for he will *g* nothing in return.
19: 7 been wronged!' I *g* no response;
19: 22 Will you never *g* enough
33: 27 but I did not *g* what I deserved.
36: 3 I *g* my knowledge from afar;
Ps 39: 6 not knowing who will *g* it.
41: 8 he will never *g* up from the place
Pr 1: 5 and let the discerning *g* guidance—
1: 13 we will *g* all sorts of valuable things
1: 19 away the lives of those who *g* it.
4: 5 *G* wisdom, *g* understanding;
4: 7 cost all you have, *g* understanding.
4: 7 is supreme; therefore *g* wisdom.
6: 9 When will you *g* up
16: 16 better to *g* wisdom than gold,
17: 16 since he has no desire to *g* wisdom?
22: 25 and *g* yourself ensnared.
23: 4 Do not wear yourself out to *g* rich;
23: 23 *g* wisdom, discipline
24: 27 and *g* your fields ready;
28: 20 to *g* rich will not go unpunished.
28: 22 A stingy man is eager to *g* rich
Ecc 2: 22 What does a man *g* for all the toil
8: 14 and wicked men who *g* what
8: 14 righteous men who *g* what
SS 3: 2 I will *g* up now and go about
Isa 1: 24 "Ah, I will *g* relief from my foes
21: 5 *G* up, you officers,
30: 11 *g* off this path,
35: 9 will any ferocious beast *g* up on it;
56: 12 each one cries, "let me *g* wine!
Jer 1: 17 "*G* yourself ready! Stand up
8: 4 fall down, do they not *g* up?
13: 6 *g* the belt I told you to hide there."
25: 27 says: Drink, *g* drunk and vomit,
28: 13 in its place you will *g* a yoke of iron
35: 3 So I went to *g* Jaazaniah son
36: 21 The king sent Jehudi to *g* the scroll
37: 12 territory of Benjamin to *g* his share
46: 11 "Go up to Gilead and *g* balm,
46: 14 'Take your positions and *g* ready,
46: 16 They will say, '*G* up, let us go back
51: 8 *G* balm for her pain;
51: 61 said to Seraiah, "When you *g*
La 3: 44 so that no prayer can *g* through.
5: 6 to *g* enough bread.

La 5: 9 We g our bread at the risk
Eze 3: 22 "G up and go out to the plain,
7: 14 trumpet and g everything ready,
7: 26 They will try to g a vision
17: 15 envoys to Egypt to g horses
18: 31 and g a new heart and a new spirit.
20: 7 g rid of the vile images you have set
20: 8 they did not g rid of the vile images
38: 7 " 'G ready; be prepared, you
Da 7: 5 'G up and eat your fill of flesh!'
Hos 12: 12 Israel served to g a wife,
Am 2: 15 fleet-footed soldier will not g away,
4: 8 but did not g enough to drink,
7: 12 Amaziah said to Amos, "G out,
9: 1 Not one will g away,
Jnh 1: 6 G up and call on your god!
Mic 2: 10 G up, go away!
Zep 2: 10 This is what they will g in return
Mt 2: 13 "G up," he said, "take the child
2: 20 G up, take the child and his mother
5: 26 you will not g out until you have
5: 46 what reward will you g? Are not
9: 5 or to say, 'G up and walk'?
9: 6 he said to the paralytic, "G up,
13: 54 "Where did this man g this wisdom
13: 56 did this man g all these things?"
14: 22 Jesus made the disciples g
15: 33 "Where could we g enough bread
17: 7 "G up," he said.
19: 16 thing must I do to g eternal life?"
22: 12 'how did you g in here
24: 18 in the field go back to g his cloak.
24: 32 As soon as its twigs g tender
Mk 2: 4 Since they could not g him to Jesus
2: 9 'G up, take your mat and walk'?
2: 11 g up, take your mat and go home."
5: 41 "Little girl, I say to you, g up!").
6: 2 "Where did this man g these things
6: 31 to a quiet place and g some rest."
6: 45 Jesus made his disciples g
8: 4 place can anyone g enough bread
13: 16 in the field go back to g his cloak.
13: 28 As soon as its twigs g tender
15: 24 lots to see what each would g.
16: 18 on sick people, and they will g well
Lk 5: 23 or to say, 'G up and walk'?
5: 24 g up, take your mat and go home."
6: 8 G up and stand in front of everyone
6: 35 expecting to g anything back.
7: 14 "Young man, I say to you, g up!"
8: 19 they were not able to g near him
8: 54 g up!" Her spirit returned,
9: 52 village to g things ready for him,
11: 7 I can't g up and give you anything.'
11: 8 the man's persistence he will g up
11: 8 though he will not g up
12: 20 who will g what you have prepared
12: 45 and to eat and drink and g drunk.
12: 47 master's will and does not g ready
12: 59 you will not g out until you have
14: 24 men who were invited will g a taste
17: 8 g yourself ready and wait on me
17: 31 should go down to g them.
18: 8 he will see that they g justice,
18: 12 a week and give a tenth of all I g.'
21: 21 let those in the city g out,
22: 2 for some way to g rid of Jesus,
22: 46 "G up and pray so that you will not
Jn 2: 16 sold doves he said, "G these out
4: 11 Where can you g this living water?
4: 15 water so that I won't g thirsty
5: 6 "Do you want to g well?" "Sir,"
5: 7 trying to g in, someone else goes
5: 8 Then Jesus said to him, "G up!
6: 25 when did you g here?" Jesus
7: 15 "How did this man g such learning
11: 12 Lord, if he sleeps, he will g better."
19: 24 "Let's decide by lot who will g it."
20: 15 have put him, and I will g him."
Ac 3: 5 expecting to g something
9: 6 "Now g up and go into the city,
9: 34 G up and take care of your mat."
9: 40 woman, he said, "Tabitha, g up."
10: 13 Then a voice told him, "G up, Peter
10: 20 So g up and go downstairs.
10: 26 But Peter made him g up.
11: 7 I heard a voice telling me, 'G up,
12: 7 g up!" he said, and the chains fell
Ac 16: 37 want to g rid of us quietly?
21: 34 since the commander could not g
22: 10 " 'G up,' the Lord said,
22: 16 now what are you waiting for? G up
23: 23 "G ready a detachment
23: 35 case when your accusers g here."
26: 16 'Now g up and stand on your feet.
27: 43 swim to jump overboard first and g
27: 44 The rest were to g there on planks
1Co 5: 7 G rid of the old yeast that you may
7: 36 They should g married.
9: 13 work in the temple g their food
9: 24 Run in such a way as to g the prize.
9: 25 it to g a crown that will last forever.
9: 25 it to g a crown that will not last;
14: 8 who will g ready for battle?
2Co 10: 14 for we did g as far as you
Gal 1: 18 up to Jerusalem to g acquainted
4: 30 "G rid of the slave woman
Eph 4: 31 G rid of all bitterness, rage
5: 18 Do not g drunk on wine, which
1Th 5: 7 and those who g drunk, g drunk
1Ti 5: 13 they g into the habit of being idle
6: 9 People who want to g rich fall
2Ti 3: 9 But they will not g very far because
4: 11 G Mark and bring him with you,
4: 21 best to g here before winter.
Jas 1: 21 g rid of all moral filth and the evil
4: 2 You want something but don't g it.
4: 3 that you may spend what you g

GETHER

Ge 10: 23 The sons of Aram: Uz, Hul, G
1Ch 1: 17 The sons of Aram: Uz, Hul, G

GETHSEMANE

Mt 26: 36 disciples to a place called G,
Mk 14: 32 They went to a place called G,

GETS (GET)

Ex 21: 19 held responsible if the other g up
21: 21 if the slave g up after a day
2Sa 15: 4 and I would see that he g justice."
Pr 13: 4 The sluggard craves and g nothing,
19: 8 He who g wisdom loves his own
21: 10 his neighbor g no mercy from him.
21: 11 man is instructed, he g knowledge.
29: 26 from the LORD that man g justice.
31: 15 She g up while it is still dark;
Isa 44: 12 He g hungry and loses his strength;
Mt 28: 14 If this report g to the governor,
Mk 4: 27 whether he sleeps or g up,
Lk 13: 25 Once the owner of the house g up
18: 5 I will see that she g justice,
Ac 23: 15 ready to kill him before he g here."
1Co 9: 24 but only one g the prize? Run
11: 21 remains hungry, another g drunk.
2Ti 2: 4 as a soldier g involved

GETTING (GET)

Jdg 3: 13 G the Ammonites and Amalekites
1Sa 1: 14 How long will you keep on g drunk
1Ki 16: 9 g drunk in the home of Arza,
20: 16 were in their tents g drunk.
Jnh 1: 11 The sea was g rougher and rougher
Mt 14: 15 place, and it's already g late.
27: 24 Pilate saw that he was g nowhere,
Mk 5: 18 As Jesus was g into the boat,
5: 26 instead of g better she grew worse.
Lk 23: 41 for we are g what our deeds
Jn 12: 19 "See, this is g us nowhere.
1Co 7: 36 and if she is g along in years
3Jn : 2 even as your soul is g along well.

GEUEL

Nu 13: 15 the tribe of Gad, G son of Maki.

GEZER

Jos 10: 33 Horam king of G had come up
12: 12 one the king of G one the king
16: 3 Lower Beth Horon and on to G,
16: 10 the Canaanites living in G;
21: 21 for one accused of murder) and G,
Jdg 1: 29 out the Canaanites living in G,
2Sa 5: 25 the way from Gibeon to G.
1Ki 9: 15 and Hazor, Megiddo and G.
9: 16 had attacked and captured G.
9: 17 And Solomon rebuilt G.)
1Ch 6: 67 and G, Jokmeam, Beth Horon,
7: 28 G and its villages to the west,
14: 16 all the way from Gibeon to G.
20: 4 out with the Philistines, at G.

GHOST (GHOSTLIKE)

Mt 14: 26 "It's a g," they said, and cried out
Mk 6: 49 the lake, they thought he was a g.
Lk 24: 37 frightened, thinking they saw a g.
24: 39 a g does not have flesh and bones,

GHOSTLIKE (GHOST)

Isa 29: 4 Your voice will come g

GIAH

2Sa 2: 24 near G on the way to the wasteland

GIBBAR

Ezr 2: 20 of Hashum 223 of G 95 the men

GIBBETHON

Jos 19: 44 Ekron, Eltekeh, G, Baalath, Jehud,
21: 23 G, Aijalon and Gath Rimmon,
1Ki 15: 27 and he struck him down at G,
16: 15 The army was encamped near G,
16: 17 with him withdrew from G

GIBEA (GIBEATHITE)

1Ch 2: 49 the father of Macbenah and G.

GIBEAH

Jos 15: 57 Zanoah, Kain, G and Timnah—
18: 28 Jerusalem), G and Kiriath—
24: 33 of Aaron died and was buried at G,
Jdg 19: 12 We will go on to G."
19: 13 let's try to reach G or Ramah
19: 14 as they neared G in Benjamin.
19: 16 who was living in G (the men
20: 4 and my concubine came to G
20: 5 the men of G came after me
20: 9 But now this is what we'll do to G:
20: 10 Then, when the army arrives at G
20: 13 surrender those wicked men of G
20: 14 at G to fight against the Israelites.
20: 15 men from those living in G.
20: 19 got up and pitched camp near G.
20: 20 positions against them at G.
20: 21 The Benjamites came out of G
20: 25 out from G to oppose them,
20: 29 Israel set an ambush around G.
20: 30 and took up positions against G
20: 31 to Bethel and the other to G.
20: 33 out of its place on the west of G.
20: 34 men made a frontal attack on G
20: 36 on the ambush they had set near G,
20: 37 made a sudden dash into G,
20: 43 in the vicinity of G on the east.
1Sa 10: 5 After that you will go to G of God,
10: 10 they arrived at G, a procession
10: 26 Saul also went to his home in G,
11: 4 When the messengers came to G
13: 2 with Jonathan at G of Benjamin.
13: 15 and went up to G of Benjamin,
14: 2 staying on the outskirts of G
14: 16 Saul's lookouts at G
15: 34 up to his home in G of Saul.
22: 6 the tamarisk tree on the hill at G,
23: 19 The Ziphites went up to Saul at G
26: 1 The Ziphites went to Saul at G
2Sa 21: 6 before the LORD at G of Saul—
23: 29 son of Ribai from G of Benjamin,
1Ch 11: 31 son of Ribai from G of Benjamin,
2Ch 13: 2 Maacah, a daughter of Uriel of G.
Isa 10: 29 G of Saul flees.
Hos 5: 8 "Sound the trumpet in G,
9: 9 as in the days of G.
10: 9 the days of G, you have sinned,
10: 9 the evildoers in G?

GIBEATH HAARALOTH

Jos 5: 3 and circumcised the Israelites at G.

GIBEATHITE (GIBEA)

1Ch 12: 3 Joash the sons of Shemaah the G;

GIBEON (GIBEONITE GIBEONITES)

Jos 9: 3 of G heard what Joshua had done
9: 17 G, Kephirah, Beeroth

Jos 10: 1 the people of G had made a treaty
10: 2 because G was an important city,
10: 4 "Come up and help me attack G,"
10: 5 and took up positions against G
10: 10 them in a great victory at G.
10: 12 "O sun, stand still over G,
10: 41 the whole region of Goshen to G.
11: 19 Except for the Hivites living in G,
18: 25 G, Ramah, Beeroth, Mizpah,
21: 17 of Benjamin they gave them G,
2Sa 2: 12 left Mahanaim and went to G.
2: 13 and met them at the pool of G.
2: 16 that place in G was called Helkath
2: 24 on the way to the wasteland of G.
3: 30 Asahel in the battle at G.)
5: 25 the Philistines all the way from G
20: 8 were at the great rock in G,
1Ki 3: 4 went to G to offer sacrifices,
3: 5 At G the LORD appeared
9: 2 as he had appeared to him at G.
1Ch 6: 60 of Benjamin they were given G,
8: 29 Jeiel the father of G lived in G.
9: 35 Jeiel the father of G lived in G.
14: 16 all the way from G to Gezer.
16: 39 in G to present burnt offerings
21: 29 at that time on the high place at G.
2Ch 1: 3 went to the high place at G,
1: 5 had made was in G in front
1: 13 Jerusalem from the high place at G,
Ne 3: 7 Melatiah of G and Jadon
3: 7 repairs were made by men from G
7: 25 of Hariph 112 of G 95 the men
Isa 28: 21 as in the Valley of G—
Jer 28: 1 son of Azzur, who was from G,
41: 12 with him near the great pool in G.
41: 16 officials he had brought from G.

GIBEONITE (GIBEON)
1Ch 12: 4 Anathothite, and Ishmaiah the G,

GIBEONITES (GIBEON)
Jos 9: 16 they made the treaty with the G,
9: 22 Joshua summoned the G and said,
9: 27 day he made the G woodcutters
10: 6 The G then sent word to Joshua
2Sa 21: 1 it is because he put the G to death."
21: 2 Now the G were not a part of Israel
21: 2 The king summoned the G
21: 3 David asked the G, "What shall I
21: 4 inheritance?" The G answered
21: 9 He handed them over to the G,

GIDDALTI
1Ch 25: 4 Eliathah, G and Romamti-Ezer;
25: 29 12 the twenty-second to G,

GIDDEL
Ezr 2: 47 Shalmai, Hanan, G, Gahar, Reaiah,
2: 56 Jaala, Darkon, G, Shephatiah,
Ne 7: 49 Shalmai, Hanan, G, Gaher, Reaiah,
7: 58 Jaala, Darkon, G, Shephatiah,

GIDEON (GIDEON'S)
Jdg 6: 11 where his son G was threshing
6: 12 angel of the LORD appeared to G,
6: 13 G replied, "if the LORD is with us,
6: 15 G asked, "how can I save Israel?
6: 17 G replied, "If now I have found
6: 19 G went in, prepared a young goat,
6: 20 And G did so.
6: 22 When G realized that it was
6: 24 G built an altar to the LORD there
6: 27 So G took ten of his servants
6: 29 they were told, "G son
6: 32 that day they called G "Jerub-Baal
6: 34 Spirit of the LORD came upon G,
6: 36 G said to God, "If you will save
6: 38 G rose early the next day; he
6: 39 G said to God, "Do not be angry
7: 1 G) and all his men camped
7: 2 to G, "You have too many men
7: 4 to G, "There are still too many men
7: 5 G took the men down to the water.
7: 7 to G, "With the three hundred men
7: 8 So G sent the rest of the Israelites
7: 9 that night the LORD said to G,
7: 13 G arrived just as a man was telling
7: 14 than the sword of G son of Joash,
Jdg 7: 15 When G heard the dream
7: 18 'For the LORD and for G.' "
7: 19 G and the hundred men
7: 20 "A sword for the LORD and for G
7: 24 G sent messengers
7: 25 the heads of Oreb and Zeeb to G,
8: 1 Now the Ephraimites asked G,
8: 4 G and his three hundred men,
8: 7 Then G replied, "Just for that,
8: 11 G went up by the route
8: 13 G son of Joash then returned
8: 15 Then G came and said to the men
8: 19 G replied, "Those were my
8: 21 So G stepped forward
8: 22 said to G, "Rule over us—
8: 23 But G told them, "I will not rule
8: 27 and it became a snare to G
8: 27 G made the gold into an ephod,
8: 32 G son of Joash died
8: 33 No sooner had G died
8: 35 G) for all the good things he had
Heb 11: 32 I do not have time to tell about G,

GIDEON'S (GIDEON)
Jdg 8: 28 During G lifetime, the land

GIDEONI
Nu 1: 11 Abidan son of G; from Dan,
2: 22 of Benjamin is Abidan son of G.
7: 60 On the ninth day Abidan son of G,
7: 65 the offering of Abidan son of G.
10: 24 and Abidan son of G was

GIDOM
Jdg 20: 45 G and struck down two thousand

GIFT (GIFTED GIFTS)
Ge 30: 20 has presented me with a precious g.
32: 13 had with him he selected a g
32: 18 They are a g sent to my lord Esau,
33: 10 in your eyes, accept this g from me.
34: 12 and the g I am to bring as great
43: 11 take them down to the man as a g
Lev 22: 18 presents a g for a burnt offering
Nu 18: 6 among the Israelites as a g to you,
18: 7 the service of the priesthood as a g.
31: 52 a g to the LORD weighed 16,750
Dt 16: 17 of you must bring a g in proportion
1Sa 9: 7 We have no g to take to the man
25: 27 let this g, which your servant has
2Sa 11: 8 and a g from the king was sent
1Ki 9: 16 as a wedding g to his daughter,
10: 25 everyone who came brought a g—
13: 7 to eat, and I will give you a g."
15: 19 I am sending you a g of silver
2Ki 5: 15 Please accept now a g
8: 8 "Take a g with you and go
8: 9 as a g forty camel-loads
16: 8 sent it as a g to the king of Assyria.
20: 12 sent Hezekiah letters and a g,
2Ch 9: 24 everyone who came brought a g—
Ps 45: 12 of Tyre will come with a g,
Pr 18: 16 A g opens the way for the giver
21: 14 A g given in secret soothes anger,
Ecc 3: 13 in all his toil—this is the g of God.
5: 19 in his work—this is a g of God.
Isa 39: 1 sent Hezekiah letters and a g,
Eze 45: 13 This is the special g you are to offer
45: 16 in this special g for the use
46: 16 If the prince makes a g
46: 17 he makes a g from his inheritance
48: 8 are to present as a special g.
48: 12 It will be a special g to them
48: 20 As a special g you will set
Mt 5: 23 if you are offering your g
5: 24 leave your g there in front
5: 24 then come and offer your g.
8: 4 and offer the g Moses commanded,
15: 5 from me is a g devoted to God,'
23: 18 but if anyone swears by the g on it,
23: 19 blind men! Which is greater: the g,
23: 19 or the altar that makes the g sacred
Mk 7: 11 me is Corban' (that is, a g devoted
Jn 4: 10 "If you knew the g of God
Ac 1: 4 wait for the g my Father promised,
2: 38 And you will receive the g
8: 20 you thought you could buy the g
10: 45 Peter were astonished that the g
Ac 11: 17 So if God gave them the same g
11: 30 sending their g to the elders
Ro 1: 11 impart to you some spiritual g
4: 4 are not credited to him as a g,
5: 15 But the g is not like the trespass.
5: 15 and the g that came by the grace
5: 16 but the g followed many trespasses
5: 16 the g of God is not like the result
5: 17 and of the g of righteousness reign
6: 23 but the g of God is eternal life
12: 6 If a man's g is prophesying,
1Co 1: 7 you do not lack any spiritual g
7: 7 each man has his own g from God;
7: 7 one has this g, another has that.
13: 2 If I have the g of prophecy
14: 1 especially the g of prophecy.
16: 3 them with your g to Jerusalem.
2Co 8: 12 the g is acceptable according
8: 20 way we administer this liberal g.
9: 5 for the generous g you had
9: 5 it will be ready as a generous g,
9: 15 be to God for his indescribable g!
Eph 2: 8 it is the g of God—not by works,
3: 7 a servant of this gospel by the g
Php 4: 17 Not that I am looking for a g,
1Ti 4: 14 not neglect your g, which was
2Ti 1: 6 you to fan into flame the g of God,
Heb 6: 4 who have tasted the heavenly g,
Jas 1: 17 and perfect g is from above,
1Pe 3: 7 with you of the gracious g of life,
4: 10 should use whatever g he has
Rev 22: 17 let him take the free g of the water

GIFTED (GIFT)
1Co 14: 37 he is a prophet or spiritually g,

GIFTS (GIFT)
Ge 24: 53 he also gave costly g to her brother
25: 6 he gave g to the sons
32: 20 with these g I am sending on ahead
32: 21 So Jacob's g went on ahead of him,
43: 15 So the men took the g
43: 25 They prepared their g
43: 26 to him the g they had brought
Ex 28: 38 in the sacred g the Israelites
28: 38 whatever their g may be.
Lev 23: 38 to your g and whatever you have
Nu 5: 10 Each man's sacred g are his own,
7: 3 as their g before the LORD six
8: 19 I have given the Levites as g
18: 9 From all the g they bring me
18: 11 from the g of all the wave offerings
Dt 12: 6 special g, what you have vowed
12: 11 sacrifices, your tithes and special g,
12: 17 your freewill offerings or special g.
33: 15 with the choicest g
33: 16 with the best g of the earth
1Sa 10: 27 him and brought him no g.
2Ki 12: 18 and the g he himself had dedicated
2Ch 17: 5 all Judah brought g to Jehoshaphat
17: 11 Philistines brought Jehoshaphat g
21: 3 father had given them many g
31: 12 tithes and dedicated g.
31: 14 and also the consecrated g.
32: 23 and valuable g for Hezekiah king
Ezr 1: 6 and livestock, and with valuable g,
Est 2: 18 distributed g with royal liberality.
9: 22 to one another and g to the poor.
Ps 68: 18 you received g from men,
68: 29 kings will bring you g.
72: 10 will present him g.
76: 11 bring g to the One to be feared.
112: 9 He has scattered abroad his g
Pr 19: 6 of a man who gives g.
22: 16 and he who gives g to the rich—
25: 14 of g he does not give.
Isa 1: 23 and chase after g.
18: 7 At that time g will be brought
18: 7 the g will be brought
Eze 16: 33 but you give g to all your lovers,
20: 26 become defiled through their g—
20: 31 you offer your g— the sacrifice
20: 39 profane my holy name with your g
20: 40 your offerings and your choice g,
44: 30 and of all your special g will belong
Da 2: 6 you will receive from me g
2: 48 and lavished many g on him.
5: 17 "You may keep your g for yourself

Da 11:38 with precious stones and costly *g*.
Mic 1: 7 Since she gathered her *g*
1: 7 all her temple *g* will be burned
1:14 Therefore you will give parting *g*
7: 3 the ruler demands *g*,
Mt 2:11 and presented him with *g* of gold
7:11 Father in heaven give good *g*
7:11 to give good *g* to your children,
Lk 11:13 to give good *g* to your children,
21: 1 Jesus saw the rich putting their *g*
21: 4 All these people gave their *g* out
21: 5 and with *g* dedicated to God.
Ac 10: 4 and *g* to the poor have come up
10:31 remembered your *g* to the poor.
24:17 to bring my people *g* for the poor
Ro 11:29 for God's *g* and his call are
12: 6 We have different *g*, according
1Co 12: 1 Now about spiritual *g*, brothers,
12: 4 There are different kinds of *g*,
12: 9 to another *g* of healing
12:28 also those having *g* of healing,
12:28 those with *g* of administration,
12:30 all work miracles? Do all have *g*
12:31 But eagerly desire the greater *g*.
14: 1 and eagerly desire spiritual *g*,
14:12 eager to have spiritual *g*,
14:12 excel in *g* that build up the church.
2Co 9: 9 "He has scattered abroad his *g*
Eph 4: 8 and gave *g* to men."
Php 4:18 from Epaphroditus the *g* you sent.
Heb 2: 4 and *g* of the Holy Spirit distributed
5: 1 to offer *g* and sacrifices for sins.
8: 3 priest is appointed to offer both *g*
8: 4 men who offer the *g* prescribed
9: 9 indicating that the *g* and sacrifices
Rev 11:10 celebrate by sending each other *g*,

GIGANTIC

Rev 9: 2 it like the smoke from a *g* furnace.

GIHON

Ge 2:13 name of the second river is the *G*;
1Ki 1:33 own mule and take him down to *G*.
1:38 mule and escorted him to *G*.
1:45 have anointed him king at *G*.
2Ch 32:30 the upper outlet of the *G* spring
33:14 west of the *G* spring in the valley,

GILALAI

Ne 12:36 Azarel, Milalai, *G*, Maai, Nethanel

GILBOA

1Sa 28: 4 the Israelites and set up camp at *G*.
31: 1 and many fell slain on Mount *G*.
31: 8 his three sons fallen on Mount *G*.
2Sa 1: 6 "I happened to be on Mount *G*,"
1:21 "O mountains of *G*,
21:12 after they struck Saul down on *G*.)
1Ch 10: 1 and many fell slain on Mount *G*.
10: 8 and his sons fallen on Mount *G*.

GILEAD (GILEAD'S GILEADITE GILEADITES)

Ge 31:21 he headed for the hill country of *G*.
31:23 with him in the hill country of *G*.
31:25 of *G* when Laban overtook him,
37:25 of Ishmaelites coming from *G*.
Nu 26:29 clan (Makir was the father of *G*);
26:29 through *G*, the Gileadite clan.
26:30 These were the descendants of *G*.
27: 1 the son of *G*, the son of Makir,
32: 1 and *G* were suitable for livestock.
32:26 will remain here in the cities of *G*.
32:29 give them the land of *G*
32:39 son of Manasseh went to *G*,
32:40 So Moses gave *G* to the Makirites,
36: 1 of the clan of *G* son of Makir,
Dt 2:36 as *G*, not one town was too strong
3:10 and all *G*, and all Bashan as far
3:12 including half the hill country of *G*,
3:13 The rest of *G* and also all of Bashan
3:15 And I gave *G* to Makir.
3:16 from *G* down to the Arnon Gorge
4:43 Ramoth in *G*, for the Gadites;
34: 1 from *G* to Dan, all of Naphtali,
Jos 12: 2 This included half of *G*.
12: 5 and half of *G* to the border
13:11 also included *G*, the territory
13:25 towns of *G* and half the Ammonite
13:31 in Bashan, sixty towns, half of *G*,
17: 1 who had received *G* and Bashan
17: 3 the son of *G*, the son of Makir,
17: 5 of ten tracts of land besides *G*
17: 6 The land of *G* belonged to the rest
20: 8 Ramoth in *G* in the tribe of Gad,
21:38 Ramoth in *G* (a city of refuge
22: 9 at Shiloh in Canaan to return to *G*,
22:13 to the land of *G*— to Reuben,
22:15 When they went to *G*— to Reuben,
22:32 and Gadites in *G* and reported
Jdg 5:17 *G* stayed beyond the Jordan.
7: 3 turn back and leave Mount *G*.' "
10: 3 He was followed by Jair of *G*,
10: 4 They controlled thirty towns in *G*,
10: 8 on the east side of the Jordan in *G*,
10:17 called to arms and camped in *G*,
10:18 The leaders of the people of *G* said
10:18 the head of all those living in *G*."
11: 1 His father was *G*; his mother was
11: 5 the elders of *G* went
11: 8 The elders of *G* said to him,
11: 8 head over all who live in *G*."
11:10 of *G* replied, "The LORD is our
11:11 Jephthah went with the elders of *G*
11:29 He crossed *G* and Manasseh,
11:29 passed through Mizpah of *G*,
12: 4 then called together the men of *G*
12: 5 the men of *G* asked him, "Are you
12: 7 and was buried in a town in *G*.
20: 1 and from the land of *G* came out
1Sa 13: 7 Jordan to the land of Gad and *G*.
2Sa 2: 9 He made him king over *G*,
17:26 Absalom camped in the land of *G*.
24: 6 They went to *G* and the region
1Ki 2: 7 to the sons of Barzillai of *G*
4:13 son of Manasseh in *G* were his,
4:19 in *G* (the country of Sihon king
17: 1 from Tishbe in *G*, said to Ahab,
2Ki 10:33 Gorge through *G* to Bashan.
10:33 the land of *G* (the region of Gad,
15:25 Taking fifty men of *G* with him,
15:29 He took *G* and Galilee—all
1Ch 2:21 the father of *G* (he had married her
2:22 twenty-three towns in *G*.
2:23 of Makir the father of *G*.
5: 9 their livestock had increased in *G*.
5:10 the entire region east of *G*.
5:14 the son of *G*, the son of Michael,
5:16 The Gadites lived in *G*, in Bashan
6:80 of Gad they received Ramoth in *G*,
7:14 birth to Makir the father of *G*.
7:17 the sons of *G* son of Makir,
26:31 were found at Jazer in *G*.
27:21 the half-tribe of Manasseh in *G*:
Ps 60: 7 *G* is mine, and Manasseh is mine;
108: 8 *G* is mine, Manasseh is mine;
SS 4: 1 descending from Mount *G*.
6: 5 descending from *G*.
Jer 8:22 Is there no balm in *G*?
22: 6 "Though you are like *G* to me,
46:11 "Go up to *G* and get balm,
50:19 on the hills of Ephraim and *G*.
Eze 47:18 along the Jordan between *G*
Hos 6: 8 *G* is a city of wicked men,
12:11 Is *G* wicked?
Am 1: 3 Because she threshed *G*
1:13 open the pregnant women of *G*
Ob :19 and Benjamin will possess *G*.
Mic 7:14 Let them feed in Bashan and *G*
Zec 10:10 I will bring them to *G* and Lebanon

GILEAD'S (GILEAD)

Jdg 11: 2 *G* wife also bore him sons,

GILEADITE (GILEAD)

Nu 26:29 through Gilead, the *G* clan.
Jdg 11: 1 Jephthah the *G* was a mighty
11:40 the daughter of Jephthah the *G*.
12: 7 Then Jephthah the *G* died,
2Sa 17:27 the *G* from Rogelim brought
19:31 Barzillai the *G* also came
Ezr 2:61 a daughter of Barzillai the *G*
Ne 7:63 a daughter of Barzillai the *G*

GILEADITES (GILEAD)

Jos 17: 1 Makir was the ancestor of the *G*,
Jdg 12: 4 The *G* struck them down
12: 4 "You *G* are renegades
12: 5 The *G* captured the fords

GILGAL

Dt 11:30 in the Arabah in the vicinity of *G*.
Jos 4:19 camped at *G* on the eastern border
4:20 up at *G* the twelve stones they had
5: 9 So the place has been called *G*
5:10 while camped at *G* on the plains
9: 6 went to Joshua in the camp at *G*
10: 6 word to Joshua in the camp at *G*:
10: 7 So Joshua marched up from *G*
10: 9 After an all-night march from *G*,
10:15 with all Israel to the camp at *G*.
10:43 with all Israel to the camp at *G*.
12:23 of Goyim in *G* one the king of
14: 6 of Judah approached Joshua at *G*,
15: 7 of Achor and turned north to *G*,
Jdg 2: 1 of the LORD went up from *G*
3:19 idols near *G* he himself turned back
1Sa 7:16 circuit from Bethel to *G* to Mizpah,
10: 8 "Go down ahead of me to *G*.
11:14 go to *G* and there reaffirm
11:15 So all the people went to *G*
13: 4 were summoned to join Saul at *G*.
13: 7 remained at *G*, and all the troops
13: 8 but Samuel did not come to *G*,
13:12 come down against me at *G*,
13:15 Then Samuel left *G* and went up
15:12 has turned and gone on down to *G*
15:21 to the LORD your God at *G*."
15:33 to death before the LORD at *G*.
2Sa 19:15 of Judah had come to *G* to go out
19:40 When the king crossed over to *G*,
2Ki 2: 1 Elisha were on their way from *G*.
4:38 to *G* and there was a famine
Hos 4:15 "Do not go to *G*;
9:15 of all their wickedness in *G*,
12:11 Do they sacrifice bulls in *G*?
Am 4: 4 go to *G* and sin yet more.
5: 5 For *G* will surely go into exile,
5: 5 do not go to *G*,
Mic 6: 5 from Shittim to *G*,

GILOH

Jos 15:51 Anim, Goshen, Holon and *G*—
2Sa 15:12 to come from *G*, his home town.

GILONITE

2Sa 15:12 he also sent for Ahithophel the *G*,
23:34 Eliam son of Ahithophel the *G*,

GIMZO

2Ch 28:18 *G*, with their surrounding villages.

GINATH

1Ki 16:21 half supported Tibni son of *G*
16:22 than those of Tibni son of *G*.

GINNETHON (GINNETHON'S)

Ne 10: 6 Obadiah, Daniel, *G*, Baruch,
12: 4 Meremoth, Iddo, *G*, Abijah,

GINNETHON'S (GINNETHON)

Ne 12:16 Zechariah; of *G*, Meshullam;

GIRD

Ps 45: 3 *G* your sword upon your side,

GIRGASHITES

Ge 10:16 Jebusites, Amorites, *G*, Hivites,
15:21 Canaanites, *G* and Jebusites."
Dt 7: 1 the Hittites, *G*, Amorites,
Jos 3:10 Hittites, Hivites, Perizzites, *G*,
24:11 Perizzites, Canaanites, Hittites, *G*,
1Ch 1:14 Jebusites, Amorites, *G*, Hivites,
Ne 9: 8 Perizzites, Jebusites and *G*.

GIRZITES

1Sa 27: 8 the *G* and the Amalekites.

GISHPA

Ne 11:21 Ziha and *G* were in charge of them.

GITTAIM

2Sa 4: 3 the people of Beeroth fled to *G*
Ne 11:33 in Hazor, Ramah and *G*, in Hadid,

GITTITE (GITTITES)

2Sa 6: 10 to the house of Obed-Edom the *G*.
6: 11 the house of Obed-Edom the *G*
15: 19 The king said to Ittai the *G*,
15: 22 So Ittai the *G* marched
18: 2 and a third under Ittai the *G*.
21: 19 Bethlehemite killed Goliath the *G*,
1Ch 13: 13 to the house of Obed-Edom the *G*.
20: 5 the brother of Goliath the *G*,

GITTITES (GITTITE)

2Sa 15: 18 the six hundred *G* who had

GIVE (GAVE GIVEN GIVER GIVES GIVING LIFE-GIVING)

Ge 1: 15 of the sky to *g* light on the earth."
1: 17 of the sky to *g* light on the earth,
1: 29 "I *g* you every seed-bearing plant
1: 30 I *g* every green plant for food."
3: 16 with pain you will *g* birth
9: 3 plants, I now *g* you everything.
12: 7 "To your offspring I will *g* this land
13: 15 All the land that you see I will *g*
14: 21 "*G* me the people and keep
15: 2 what can you *g* me
15: 7 of the Chaldeans to *g* you this land
15: 18 "To your descendants I *g* this land,
17: 8 I will *g* as an everlasting possession
17: 16 and will surely *g* you a son by her.
23: 11 I *g* it to you in the presence
23: 11 and I *g* you the cave that is in it.
23: 11 "Listen to me; I *g* you the field,
24: 7 'To your offspring I will *g* this land
24: 12 my master Abraham, *g* me success
24: 17 "Please *g* me a little water
24: 41 if they refuse to *g* her to you—
24: 45 I said to her, 'Please *g* me a drink.'
25: 24 the time came for her to *g* birth,
26: 3 descendants I will *g* all these lands
26: 4 and will *g* them all these lands,
27: 4 so that I may *g* you my blessing
27: 7 so that I may *g* you my blessing
27: 10 so that he may *g* you his blessing
27: 19 so that you may *g* me your blessing
27: 25 so that I may *g* you my blessing."
27: 28 May God *g* you of heaven's dew
27: 31 so that you may *g* me your blessing
28: 4 May he *g* you and your
28: 13 I will *g* you and your descendants
28: 20 I am taking and will *g* me food
28: 22 that you *g* me I will *g* you a tenth."
29: 19 "It's better to *g* her to you
29: 21 said to Laban, "*G* me my wife.
29: 26 here to *g* the younger daughter
29: 27 then we will *g* you the younger one
30: 1 she said to Jacob, "*G* me children,
30: 14 "Please *g* me some
30: 26 *G* me my wives and children,
30: 31 "Don't *g* me anything," Jacob
30: 31 "What shall I *g* you?" he asked.
34: 8 Please *g* her to him as his wife.
34: 9 *g* us your daughters and take our
34: 11 and I will *g* you whatever you ask.
34: 12 Only *g* me the girl as my wife."
34: 14 we can't *g* our sister
34: 15 We will *g* our consent to you
34: 16 Then we will *g* you our daughters
34: 23 So let us *g* our consent to them,
35: 12 gave to Abraham and Isaac I also *g*
35: 12 will *g* this land to your descendants
35: 16 Rachel began to *g* birth
38: 16 "And what will you *g* me to sleep
38: 17 "Will you *g* me something
38: 18 "What pledge should I *g* you?"
38: 26 since I wouldn't *g* her
38: 27 the time came for her to *g* birth,
41: 16 God will *g* Pharaoh the answer he
42: 22 Now we must *g* an accounting
42: 25 and to *g* them provisions
42: 34 I will *g* your brother back to you,
45: 18 I will *g* you the best of the land
47: 15 to Joseph and said, "*G* us food.
47: 19 *G* us seed so that we may live
47: 24 when the crop comes in, *g* a fifth
48: 4 I will *g* this land as an everlasting
48: 22 I *g* the ridge of land I took
Ex 1: 19 *g* birth before the midwives arrive
Ex 5: 10 'I will not *g* you any more straw.
6: 4 with them to *g* them the land
6: 8 I will *g* it to you as a possession.
6: 8 with uplifted hand to *g* to Abraham
9: 19 *G* an order now to bring your
12: 25 the land that the LORD will *g* you
13: 5 swore to your forefathers to *g* you,
13: 12 are to *g* over to the LORD the first
13: 21 in a pillar of fire to *g* them light,
17: 2 and said, "*G* us water to drink."
18: 19 and I will *g* you some advice,
20: 16 "You shall not *g* false testimony
22: 17 father absolutely refuses to *g* her
22: 29 "You must *g* me the firstborn
22: 30 but *g* them to me on the eighth day.
23: 2 When you *g* testimony in a lawsuit,
23: 26 I will *g* you a full life span.
24: 12 and I will *g* you the tablets of stone,
25: 2 man whose heart prompts him to *g*.
25: 16 the Testimony, which I will *g* you.
25: 21 the Testimony, which I will *g* you.
25: 22 and *g* you all my commands
28: 2 to *g* him dignity and honor.
28: 40 to *g* them dignity and honor.
30: 13 counted is to *g* a half shekel,
30: 14 are to *g* an offering to the LORD.
30: 15 The rich are not to *g* more
30: 15 and the poor are not to *g* less
32: 13 I will *g* your descendants all this
33: 1 'I will *g* it to your descendants.'
33: 14 go with you, and I will *g* you rest."
Lev 5: 16 to that and *g* it all to the priest,
6: 5 and *g* it all to the owner
6: 9 "*G* Aaron and his sons this
7: 32 You are to *g* the right thigh
7: 36 that the Israelites *g* this
15: 14 of Meeting and *g* them to the priest
18: 21 " 'Do not *g* any of your children
20: 24 I will *g* it to you as an inheritance,
23: 10 enter the land I am going to *g* you
23: 38 and all the freewill offerings you *g*
25: 2 enter the land I am going to *g* you,
25: 38 out of Egypt to *g* you the land
Nu 3: 9 *G* the Levites to Aaron
3: 48 *G* the money for the redemption
5: 7 and *g* it all to the person he has
6: 26 and *g* you peace." '
7: 5 *G* them to the Levites
7: 9 But Moses did not *g* any
10: 29 which the LORD said, 'I will *g* it
11: 12 these people? Did I *g* them birth?
11: 13 wailing to me, '*G* us meat to eat!'
11: 18 Now the LORD will *g* you meat,
11: 21 'I will *g* them meat to eat
14: 8 and honey, and will *g* it to us.
15: 21 to come you are to *g* this offering
18: 8 offerings the Israelites *g* me I *g*
18: 11 I *g* this to you and your sons
18: 12 and grain they *g* the LORD
18: 12 "I *g* you all the finest olive oil
18: 19 present to the LORD I *g* to you
18: 21 "I *g* to the Levites all the tithes
18: 24 I *g* to the Levites as their
18: 26 from the Israelites the tithe I *g* you
18: 28 tithes you must *g* the LORD's
19: 3 *G* it to Eleazar the priest; it is
20: 12 into the land I *g* them."
20: 24 not enter the land I *g* the Israelites,
21: 16 together and I will *g* them water."
23: 5 to Balak and *g* him this message."
23: 16 to Balak and *g* him this message."
26: 54 a larger group *g* a larger
27: 4 *G* us property among our father's
27: 7 must certainly *g* them property
27: 9 *g* his inheritance to his brothers.
27: 10 *g* his inheritance to his father's
27: 11 *g* his inheritance to the nearest
27: 20 *G* him some of your authority
28: 2 "*G* this command to the Israelites
31: 29 and *g* it to Eleazar the priest
31: 30 *G* them to the Levites, who are
32: 29 *g* them the land of Gilead
33: 54 a larger group *g* a larger
33: 55 They will *g* you trouble
35: 2 And *g* them pasturelands
35: 2 the Israelites to *g* the Levites towns
35: 4 towns that you *g* the Levites will
35: 6 of the towns you *g* the Levites will
Nu 35: 6 *g* them forty-two other towns.
35: 7 all you must *g* the Levites
35: 8 The towns you *g* the Levites
35: 13 These six towns you *g* will be your
35: 14 *G* three on this side of the Jordan
36: 2 commanded my lord to *g* the land
36: 2 he ordered you to *g* the inheritance
Dt 1: 8 that the LORD swore he would *g*
1: 35 swore to *g* your forefathers,
1: 36 I will *g* him and his descendants
1: 39 I will *g* it to them and they will take
2: 4 *G* the people these orders:
2: 5 for I will not *g* you any of their land
2: 9 for I will not *g* you any part
2: 19 for I will not *g* you possession
2: 30 in order to *g* him into your hands,
4: 2 the LORD your God that I *g* you.
4: 38 you into their land to *g* it to you
5: 20 "You shall not *g* false testimony
5: 31 me so that I may *g* you all
6: 2 and commands that I *g* you,
6: 6 commandments that I *g* you today
6: 10 Isaac and Jacob, to *g* you—
6: 23 and *g* us the land that he promised
7: 3 Do not *g* your daughters
7: 11 decrees and laws I *g* you today.
7: 13 swore to your forefathers to *g* you.
7: 24 He will *g* their kings into your hand
10: 11 swore to their fathers to *g* them."
11: 9 to your forefathers to *g* to them
11: 21 swore to *g* your forefathers,
12: 6 what you have vowed to *g*
12: 10 and he will *g* you rest from all your
12: 17 or whatever you have vowed to *g*,
12: 26 and whatever you have vowed to *g*,
14: 21 You may *g* it to an alien living
15: 9 needy brother and *g* him nothing.
15: 10 *G* generously to him and do
15: 14 *G* to him as the LORD your God
15: 15 That is why I *g* you this command
17: 9 and they will *g* you the verdict.
17: 10 to the decisions they *g* you
17: 11 and the decisions they *g* you.
18: 4 You are to *g* them the firstfruits
20: 3 or *g* way to panic before them.
20: 4 your enemies to *g* you victory."
21: 16 he must not *g* the rights
22: 2 Then *g* it back to him.
22: 19 and *g* them to the girl's father,
25: 3 but he must not *g* him more
26: 3 swore to our forefathers to *g* us."
26: 12 you shall *g* it to the Levite,
27: 1 commands that I *g* you today.
27: 10 and decrees that I *g* you today."
28: 1 all his commands I *g* you today,
28: 11 swore to your forefathers to *g* you.
28: 13 your God that I *g* you this day
28: 14 of the commands I *g* you today,
28: 55 he will not *g* to one of them any
28: 65 the LORD will *g* you an anxious
30: 20 and he will *g* you many years
30: 20 swore to *g* to your fathers,
31: 7 to their forefathers to *g* them,
32: 38 Let them *g* you shelter!
34: 4 'I will *g* it to your descendants.'
Jos 1: 2 River into the land I am about to *g*
1: 3 I will *g* you every place where you
1: 6 to their forefathers to *g* them.
2: 12 *G* me a sure sign that you will spare
5: 6 promised their fathers to *g* us,
6: 5 have all the people *g* a loud shout;
6: 10 the people, "Do not *g* a war cry,
7: 19 God of Israel, and *g* him the praise.
7: 19 "My son, *g* glory to the LORD,
8: 7 The LORD your God will *g* it
9: 24 Moses to *g* you the whole land
14: 12 Now *g* me this hill country that
15: 16 "I will *g* my daughter Acsah
15: 19 *g* me also springs of water."
17: 4 Moses to *g* us an inheritance
20: 4 and *g* him a place to live with them.
21: 2 through Moses that you *g* us towns
21: 43 sworn to *g* their forefathers,
Jdg 1: 12 "I will *g* my daughter Acsah
1: 15 *g* me also springs of water."
2: 1 swore to *g* to your forefathers.
2: 19 refused to *g* up their evil practices
4: 7 and *g* him into your hands.' "

Jdg 4: 19 "Please *g* me some water."
6: 17 *g* me a sign that it is really you
7: 7 *g* the Midianites into your hands.
7: 9 I am going to *g* it into your hands.
8: 5 *G* my troops some bread;
8: 6 Why should we *g* bread
8: 15 Why should we *g* bread
8: 24 that each of you *g* me an earring
8: 25 "We'll be glad to *g* them."
9: 9 answered, 'Should I *g* up my oil,
9: 11 replied, 'Should I *g* up my fruit,
9: 13 answered, 'Should I *g* up my wine,
11: 13 Now *g* it back peaceably."
11: 17 '*G* us permission to go
11: 30 "If you *g* the Ammonites
11: 37 *G* me two months to roam the hills
13: 5 you will conceive and *g* birth
13: 7 'You will conceive and *g* birth
14: 12 I will *g* you thirty linen garments
14: 12 "If you can *g* me the answer
14: 13 you must *g* me thirty linen
14: 14 days they could not *g* the answer.
16: 5 one of us will *g* you eleven hundred
17: 3 I will *g* it back to you."
17: 10 and I'll *g* you ten shekels
20: 7 speak up and *g* your verdict."
20: 10 it can *g* them what they deserve
20: 28 for tomorrow I will *g* them
21: 1 one of us will *g* his daughter
21: 7 by the LORD not to *g* them any
21: 18 We can't *g* them our daughters
21: 22 since you did not *g* your daughters
1Sa 1: 4 he would *g* portions of the meat
1: 11 forget your servant but *g* her a son,
1: 11 then I will *g* him to the LORD
1: 28 So now I *g* him to the LORD.
2: 10 "He will *g* strength to his king
2: 15 "*G* the priest some meat to roast;
2: 20 "May the LORD *g* you children
8: 6 But when they said, "*G* us a king
8: 14 and *g* them to his attendants.
8: 15 and of your vintage and *g* it
8: 22 Listen to them and *g* them a king."
9: 7 "If we go, what can we *g* the man?
9: 8 I will *g* it to the man of God
9: 27 so that I may *g* you a message
11: 3 "*G* us seven days so we can send
14: 37 Will you *g* them into Israel's hand
14: 41 of Israel, "*G* me the right answer."
17: 10 *G* me a man and let us fight each
17: 25 The king will *g* great wealth
17: 25 also *g* him his daughter in marriage
17: 44 "and I'll *g* your flesh to the birds
17: 46 Today I will *g* the carcasses
17: 47 he will *g* all of you into our hands."
18: 17 I will *g* her to you in marriage;
18: 21 "I will *g* her to him," he thought,
21: 3 *G* me five loaves of bread,
21: 9 "There is none like it; *g* it to me."
22: 7 the son of Jesse *g* all of you fields
23: 4 for I am going to *g* the Philistines
23: 14 God did not *g* David into his hands
24: 4 'I will *g* your enemy
25: 8 Please *g* your servants
25: 11 and *g* it to men coming
25: 14 to *g* our master his greetings,
27: 1 Then Saul will *g* up searching
28: 22 and let me *g* you some food
2Sa 2: 23 Asahel refused to *g* up the pursuit,
3: 14 demanding, "*G* me my wife Michal
7: 11 *g* you rest from all your enemies.
12: 11 *g* them to one who is close to you,
13: 5 and *g* me something to eat.
16: 3 house of Israel will *g* me back my
16: 20 to Ahithophel, "*G* us your advice.
17: 6 If not, *g* us your opinion."
18: 3 now for you to *g* us support
18: 11 had to *g* you ten shekels
21: 6 the king said, "I will *g* them to you
22: 36 You *g* me your shield of victory;
1Ki 2: 17 to *g* me Abishag the Shunammite
3: 5 for whatever you want me to *g* you
3: 9 *g* your servant a discerning heart
3: 12 I will *g* you a wise and discerning
3: 13 I will *g* you what you have not
3: 14 father did, I will *g* you a long life."
3: 25 child in two and *g* half to one
3: 26 my lord, *g* her the living baby!

1Ki 3: 27 "*G* the living baby
5: 6 "So *g* orders that cedars
8: 28 Yet *g* attention to your servant's
8: 46 and *g* them over to the enemy,
11: 11 *g* it to one of your subordinates.
11: 13 but will *g* him one tribe for the sake
11: 31 Solomon's hand and *g* you ten
11: 35 son's hands and *g* you ten tribes.
11: 36 I will *g* one tribe to his son
11: 38 for David and will *g* Israel to you.
12: 7 and *g* them a favorable answer,
12: 27 they will again *g* their allegiance
13: 7 to eat, and I will *g* you a gift."
13: 8 were to *g* me half your possessions,
14: 5 and you are to *g* her such
14: 16 And he will *g* Israel up
17: 19 "*G* me your son," Elijah replied.
20: 10 remains in Samaria to *g* each
20: 13 I will *g* it into your hand today,
21: 2 In exchange I will *g* you a better
21: 3 that I should *g* you the inheritance
21: 4 "I will not *g* you the inheritance
21: 6 I will *g* you another vineyard
21: 6 'I will not *g* you my vineyard.'"
22: 6 "for the Lord will *g* it
22: 12 "for the LORD will *g* it
22: 15 "for the LORD will *g* it
22: 27 and *g* him nothing but bread
2Ki 4: 42 "*G* it to the people to eat,"
4: 43 But Elisha answered, "*G* it
5: 22 Please *g* them a talent of silver
6: 28 '*G* up your son so we may eat him
6: 29 '*G* up your son so we may eat him,'
8: 6 "*G* back everything that belonged
10: 15 said Jehu, "*g* me your hand."
14: 9 '*G* your daughter to my son
18: 23 I will *g* you two thousand horses,
19: 16 *G* ear, O LORD, and hear;
1Ch 16: 4 to make petition, to *g* thanks,
16: 8 *G* thanks to the LORD, call
16: 18 "To you I will *g* the land of Canaan
16: 34 *G* thanks to the LORD,
16: 35 that we may *g* thanks
16: 41 designated by name to *g* thanks
21: 23 I will *g* all this."
21: 23 I will *g* the oxen for the burnt
22: 9 and I will *g* him rest from all his
22: 12 May the LORD *g* you discretion
29: 3 God I now *g* my personal treasures
29: 12 power to exalt and *g* strength to all.
29: 13 Now, our God, we *g* you thanks,
29: 14 that we should be able to *g*
29: 19 And *g* my son Solomon
2Ch 1: 7 for whatever you want me to *g* you
1: 10 *G* me wisdom and knowledge,
1: 12 And I will also *g* you wealth,
2: 10 I will *g* your servants,
5: 13 to *g* praise and thanks
6: 19 Yet *g* attention to your servant's
6: 36 and *g* them over to the enemy,
10: 7 and *g* them a favorable answer,
12: 7 but will soon *g* them deliverance.
15: 7 be strong and do not *g* up,
18: 5 "for God will *g* it into the king's
18: 11 "for the LORD will *g* it
18: 26 and *g* him nothing but bread
19: 6 with you whenever you *g* a verdict.
20: 7 and *g* it forever to the descendants
20: 17 deliverance the LORD will *g* you,
20: 21 "*G* thanks to the LORD,
25: 9 "The LORD can *g* you much more
25: 18 '*G* your daughter to my son
30: 12 was on the people to *g* them unity
31: 2 to *g* thanks and to sing praises
31: 4 to *g* the portion due the priests
35: 12 to *g* them to the subdivisions
Ezr 9: 12 do not *g* your daughters
Ne 1: 11 *G* your servant success today
2: 8 so he will *g* me timber
2: 20 God of heaven will *g* us success.
4: 4 *G* them over as plunder in a land
5: 11 *G* back to them immediately their
5: 12 "We will *g* it back," they said.
6: 13 then they would *g* me a bad name
8: 13 scribe to *g* attention to the words
9: 6 You *g* life to everything,
9: 8 to *g* to his descendants the land
9: 12 with a pillar of fire to *g* them light

Ne 9: 15 with uplifted hand to *g* them.
10: 30 We promise not to *g* our daughters
10: 32 out the commands to *g* a third
12: 24 stood opposite them to *g* praise
12: 31 two large choirs to *g* thanks.
13: 25 "You are not to *g* your daughters
Est 1: 19 let the king *g* her royal position
9: 13 "*g* the Jews in Susa permission
Job 2: 4 "A man will *g* all he has
6: 22 '*G* something on my behalf,
7: 17 that you *g* him so much attention,
9: 16 believe he would *g* me a hearing.
10: 1 I will *g* free rein to my complaint
15: 35 They conceive trouble and *g* birth
17: 3 "*G* me, O God, the pledge you
20: 10 own hands must *g* back his wealth.
20: 18 for he must *g* back uneaten;
21: 2 let this be the consolation you *g* me
22: 3 pleasure would it *g* the Almighty
31: 37 I would *g* him an account
35: 7 If you are righteous, what do you *g*
39: 1 when the mountain goats *g* birth?
39: 2 Do you know the time they *g* birth
39: 17 or *g* her a share of good sense.
39: 19 "Do you *g* the horse his strength
Ps 4: 1 *G* me relief from my distress;
5: 1 *G* ear to my words, O LORD,
7: 17 I will *g* thanks to the LORD
13: 3 *G* light to my eyes, or I will sleep
17: 1 *G* ear to my prayer—
17: 6 *g* ear to me and hear my prayer.
18: 35 You *g* me your shield of victory,
20: 4 May he *g* you the desire
21: 1 joy in the victories you *g*!
28: 7 and I will *g* thanks to him in song.
30: 12 I will *g* you thanks forever.
35: 18 I will *g* you thanks
36: 8 you *g* them drink from your river
37: 4 he will *g* you the desires
37: 21 but the righteous *g* generously;
44: 7 you *g* us victory over our enemies,
45: 10 O daughter, consider and *g* ear:
46: 2 not fear, though the earth *g* way
49: 3 from my heart will *g* understanding
49: 7 or *g* to God a ransom for him—
60: 11 *G* us aid against the enemy,
71: 3 *g* the command to save me,
75: 1 We *g* thanks to you, O God,
75: 1 we *g* thanks, for your Name is near
78: 20 But can he also *g* us food?
85: 12 LORD will indeed *g* what is good,
86: 11 *g* me an undivided heart,
86: 17 *G* me a sign of your goodness,
100: 4 *g* thanks to him and praise his
104: 11 They *g* water to all the beasts
104: 27 to *g* them their food
104: 28 When you *g* it to them,
105: 1 *G* thanks to the LORD, call
105: 11 "To you I will *g* the land of Canaan
105: 39 and a fire to *g* light at night.
106: 1 *G* thanks to the LORD,
106: 47 that we may *g* thanks
107: 1 *G* thanks to the LORD,
107: 8 Let them *g* thanks to the LORD
107: 15 Let them *g* thanks to the LORD
107: 21 Let them *g* thanks to the LORD
107: 31 Let them *g* thanks to the LORD
108: 12 *G* us aid against the enemy,
109: 24 My knees *g* way from fasting;
118: 1 *G* thanks to the LORD,
118: 19 *g* thanks to the LORD.
118: 21 I will *g* you thanks,
118: 28 my God, and I will *g* you thanks;
118: 29 *G* thanks to the LORD,
119: 34 *G* me understanding, and I will
119: 62 At midnight I rise to *g* you thanks
119: 73 *g* me understanding
119:125 am your servant; *g* me discernment
119:144 *g* me understanding that I may live
119:169 *g* me understanding according
136: 1 *G* thanks to the LORD,
136: 2 *G* thanks to the God of gods.
136: 3 *G* thanks to the Lord of lords:
136: 26 *G* thanks to the God of heaven.
141: 8 do not *g* me over to death.
145: 15 you *g* them their food
Pr 1: 10 do not *g* in to them.
3: 28 Come back later; I'll *g* it tomorrow

Pr 4: 2 I *g* you sound learning,
5: 9 you *g* your best strength to others
14: 8 to *g* thought to their ways,
21: 26 but the righteous *g* without sparing
22: 21 so that you can *g* sound answers
23: 26 My son, *g* me your heart
25: 14 of gifts he does not *g*.
25: 21 if he is thirsty, *g* him water to drink
25: 21 your enemy is hungry, *g* him food
27: 23 *g* careful attention to your herds;
29: 17 your son, and he will *g* you peace;
30: 8 but *g* me only my daily bread.
30: 8 *g* me neither poverty nor riches,
30: 15 '*G! G!*' they cry.
31: 6 *G* beer to those who are perishing,
31: 31 *G* her the reward she has earned,
Ecc 3: 6 a time to search and a time to *g* up,
10: 1 As dead flies *g* perfume a bad smell
11: 2 *G* portions to seven, yes to eight,
11: 9 let your heart *g* you joy in the days
SS 7: 12 there I will *g* you my love.
8: 2 I would *g* you spiced wine to drink,
8: 7 If one were to *g*
8: 12 But my own vineyard is mine to *g*;
Isa 7: 14 the Lord himself will *g* you a sign:
7: 14 with child and will *g* birth to a son,
7: 22 of the abundance of the milk they *g*
11: 4 with justice he will *g* decisions
12: 4 "*G* thanks to the LORD, call
13: 10 and the moon will not *g* its light.
16: 3 "*G* us counsel,
19: 11 of Pharaoh *g* senseless advice.
22: 25 into the firm place will *g* way;
24: 15 Therefore in the east *g* glory
26: 17 with child and about to *g* birth
26: 19 the earth will *g* birth to her dead.
29: 11 if you *g* the scroll to someone who
29: 12 if you *g* the scroll to someone who
30: 10 "*G* us no more visions
33: 11 you *g* birth to straw;
34: 2 he will *g* them over to slaughter.
35: 3 steady the knees that *g* way;
36: 8 I will *g* you two thousand horses,
37: 17 *G* ear, O LORD, and hear;
41: 28 no one among them to *g* counsel,
41: 28 no one to *g* answer
42: 8 I will not *g* my glory to another
42: 12 Let them *g* glory to the LORD
43: 3 I *g* Egypt for your ransom,
43: 4 I will *g* men in exchange for you,
43: 6 I will say to the north, '*G* them up!'
43: 20 to *g* drink to my people, my chosen
45: 3 I will *g* you the treasures
45: 11 or *g* me orders about the work
49: 20 *g* us more space to live in.'
53: 12 Therefore I will *g* him a portion
55: 3 *G* ear and come to me;
56: 5 I will *g* them an everlasting name
56: 5 to them I will *g* within my temple
56: 7 *g* them joy in my house of prayer.
59: 4 they conceive trouble and *g* birth
62: 6 *g* yourselves no rest,
62: 7 and *g* him no rest till he establishes
62: 8 "Never again will I *g* your grain
65: 15 servants he will *g* another name.
66: 9 not *g* delivery?" says the LORD.
Jer 3: 15 Then I will *g* you shepherds
3: 19 and *g* you a desirable land,
6: 10 whom can I speak and *g* warning?
7: 22 did not just *g* them commands
8: 10 Therefore I will *g* their wives
11: 5 to *g* them a land flowing with milk
12: 7 I will *g* the one I love
13: 16 *G* glory to the LORD your God
14: 13 I will *g* you lasting peace
15: 13 I will *g* as plunder, without charge,
16: 7 nor will anyone *g* them a drink
17: 3 I will *g* away as plunder,
18: 2 and there I will *g* you my message
18: 21 So *g* their children over to famine;
19: 7 and I will *g* their carcasses
20: 13 *G* praise to the LORD!
24: 7 I will *g* them a heart to know me,
27: 4 *G* them a message for their masters
27: 5 and I *g* it to anyone I please.
28: 14 *g* him control over the wild animals
29: 6 and *g* your daughters in marriage,
29: 11 plans to *g* you hope and a future.

Jer 31: 2 I will come to *g* rest to Israel."
31: 13 I will *g* them comfort and joy
32: 22 sworn to *g* their forefathers,
32: 39 I will *g* them singleness of heart
32: 42 so I will *g* them all the prosperity I
33: 11 "*G* thanks to the LORD Almighty,
34: 22 to *g* the order, declares the LORD,
35: 2 and *g* them wine to drink."
38: 15 Even if I did *g* you counsel,
38: 15 to Zedekiah, "If I *g* you an answer,
La 2: 18 *g* yourself no relief,
Eze 2: 8 your mouth and eat what I *g* you."
3: 17 and *g* them warning from me.
11: 17 and I will *g* you back the land
11: 19 I will *g* them an undivided heart
11: 19 and *g* them a heart of flesh.
16: 33 but you *g* gifts to all your lovers,
16: 34 for you *g* payment and none is
16: 61 I will *g* them to you as daughters,
20: 28 into the land I had sworn to *g* them
20: 42 hand to *g* to your fathers.
21: 22 to *g* the command to slaughter,
21: 27 belongs; to him I will *g* it.'
23: 8 She did not *g* up the prostitution
23: 46 a mob against them and *g* them
25: 4 I am going to *g* you to the people
25: 7 *g* you as plunder to the nations.
25: 10 *g* Moab along with the Ammonites
29: 5 I will *g* you as food
29: 19 I am going to *g* Egypt
32: 7 and the moon will not *g* its light.
33: 7 and *g* them warning from me.
33: 15 follows the decrees that *g* life,
33: 27 out in the country I will *g*
35: 6 I will *g* you over to bloodshed
36: 26 I will *g* you a new heart
36: 26 of stone and *g* you a heart of flesh.
39: 4 I will *g* you as food to all kinds
39: 11 that day I will *g* Gog a burial place
43: 19 You are to *g* a young bull
44: 5 *G* attention to the entrance
44: 5 *g* attention to everything I tell you
44: 28 You are to *g* them no possession
44: 30 You are to *g* them the first portion
45: 6 " 'You are to *g* the city
45: 9 *G* up your violence and oppression
46: 7 as much as he wants to *g*,
46: 18 is to *g* his sons their inheritance out
47: 14 swore with uplifted hand to *g* it
47: 23 are to *g* him his inheritance,"
Da 1: 12 *G* us nothing but vegetables to eat
3: 28 willing to *g* up their lives rather
5: 16 able to *g* interpretations
5: 17 *g* your rewards to someone else.
9: 18 *G* ear, O God, and hear; open your
9: 22 I have now come to *g* you insight
11: 17 And he will *g* him a daughter
Hos 2: 5 who *g* me my food and my water,
2: 15 There I will *g* her back her
4: 10 the LORD to *g* themselves
5: 7 they *g* birth to illegitimate children
9: 14 *G* them wombs that miscarry
9: 14 *G* them, O LORD—
9: 14 what will you *g* them?
11: 8 "How can I *g* you up, Ephraim?
13: 10 '*G* me a king and princes'?
Am 2: 10 to *g* you the land of the Amorites.
5: 11 and force him to *g* you grain.
9: 9 "For I will *g* the command,
Jnh 3: 2 proclaim to it the message I *g* you."
3: 8 Let them *g* up their evil ways
4: 6 over Jonah to *g* shade for his head
Mic 1: 14 Therefore you will *g* parting gifts
4: 13 I will *g* you hoofs of bronze
4: 13 for I will *g* you horns of iron;
6: 14 what you save I will *g* to the sword.
6: 16 Therefore I will *g* you over to ruin
Na 2: 10 Hearts melt, knees *g* way,
Hab 2: 1 am to *g* to this complaint.
2: 19 Can it *g* guidance?
Zep 3: 19 I will *g* them praise and honor
3: 20 I will *g* you honor and praise
Hag 1: 5 "*G* careful thought to your ways.
1: 7 "*G* careful thought to your ways.
2: 15 " 'Now *g* careful thought to this
2: 18 *G* careful thought: Is there yet any
2: 18 *g* careful thought to the day
Zec 3: 7 and I will *g* you a place

Zec 8: 12 I will *g* all these things
10: 2 they *g* comfort in vain.
11: 12 "If you think it best, *g* me my pay;
Mal 1: 14 male in his flock and vows to *g* it,
Mt 1: 21 She will *g* birth to a son,
1: 21 you are to *g* him the name Jesus,
1: 23 with child and will *g* birth to a son,
4: 9 "All this I will *g* you," he said,
5: 31 his wife must *g* her a certificate
5: 42 *G* to the one who asks you,
6: 2 "So when you *g* to the needy,
6: 3 But when you *g* to the needy,
6: 11 *G* us today our daily bread.
7: 6 "Do not *g* dogs what is sacred;
7: 9 asks for bread, will *g* him a stone?
7: 10 will *g* him a snake? If you, then,
7: 11 Father in heaven *g* good gifts
7: 11 know how to *g* good gifts
10: 8 Freely you have received, freely *g*.
10: 12 enter the home, *g* it your greeting.
11: 28 and burdened, and I will *g* you rest.
12: 36 have to *g* account on the day
14: 7 oath to *g* her whatever she asked.
14: 8 "*G* me here on a platter the head
14: 16 You *g* them something to eat."
16: 19 I will *g* you the keys
16: 26 Or what can a man *g* in exchange
17: 27 Take it and *g* it to them for my tax
19: 7 command that a man *g* his wife
19: 18 not steal, do not *g* false testimony,
19: 21 sell your possessions and *g*
20: 14 to *g* the man who was hired last
20: 28 to *g* his life as a ransom for many."
21: 41 who will *g* him his share of the crop
22: 21 "*G* to Caesar what is Caesar's,
23: 23 You *g* a tenth of your spices—
24: 29 and the moon will not *g* its light;
24: 45 household to *g* them their food
25: 8 to the wise, '*G* us some of your oil;
25: 28 and *g* it to the one who has the ten
25: 37 and *g* you something to drink?
26: 15 "What are you willing to *g* me
27: 64 So *g* the order for the tomb
Mk 5: 43 told them to *g* her something to eat
6: 22 for anything you want, and I'll *g* it
6: 23 "Whatever you ask I will *g* you,
6: 25 you to *g* me right now the head
6: 37 on bread and *g* it to them to eat?"
6: 37 "You *g* them something to eat."
7: 3 they *g* their hands a ceremonial
8: 37 Or what can a man *g* in exchange
10: 19 not steal, do not *g* false testimony,
10: 21 sell everything you have and *g*
10: 45 to *g* his life as a ransom for many."
12: 9 and *g* the vineyard to others.
12: 17 "*G* to Caesar what is Caesar's
13: 24 and the moon will not *g* its light;
14: 11 and promised to *g* him money.
Lk 1: 13 you are to *g* him the name John.
1: 31 be with child and *g* birth to a son,
1: 31 you are to *g* him the name Jesus.
1: 32 Lord God will *g* him the throne
1: 77 to *g* his people the knowledge
4: 6 and I can *g* it to anyone I want to.
4: 6 "I will *g* you all their authority
6: 30 *G* to everyone who asks you,
6: 38 *G*, and it will be given to you.
7: 44 You did not *g* me any water
7: 45 You did not *g* me a kiss,
8: 55 Jesus told them to *g* her something
9: 13 "You *g* them something to eat."
10: 7 and drinking whatever they *g* you,
11: 3 *G* us each day our daily bread.
11: 7 I can't get up and *g* you anything.'
11: 8 and *g* him as much as he needs.
11: 8 will not get up and *g* him the bread
11: 11 will *g* him a snake instead?
11: 12 will *g* him a scorpion? If you then,
11: 13 Father in heaven *g* the Holy Spirit
11: 13 know how to *g* good gifts
11: 41 also? But *g* what is inside ⌊the dish⌋
11: 42 you *g* God a tenth of your mint,
12: 32 pleased to *g* you the kingdom.
12: 33 Sell your possessions and *g*
12: 42 to *g* them their food allowance
13: 15 and lead it out to *g* it water?
14: 9 say to you, '*G* this man your seat.'
14: 12 "When you *g* a luncheon or dinner,

Lk 14: 13 But when you *g* a banquet,
14: 33 who does not *g* up everything he
15: 12 Father, *g* me my share of the estate
16: 2 *G* an account of your management,
16: 12 who will *g* you property
17: 18 and *g* praise to God except this
18: 1 should always pray and not *g* up.
18: 12 I fast twice a week and *g* a tenth
18: 20 not steal, do not *g* false testimony,
18: 22 Sell everything you have and *g*
19: 8 and now I *g* half of my possessions
19: 24 *g* it to the one who has ten minas.'
20: 10 tenants so they would *g* him some
20: 16 and *g* the vineyard to others."
20: 25 "Then *g* to Caesar what is Caesar's,
21: 15 For I will *g* you words
22: 5 and agreed to *g* him money.
24: 30 broke it and began to *g* it to them.
Jn 1: 22 *G* us an answer to take back
4: 7 to her, "Will you *g* me a drink?"
4: 14 drinks the water I *g* him will never
4: 14 the water I *g* him will become
4: 15 *g* me this water so that I won't get
5: 21 life to whom he is pleased to *g* it.
6: 27 which the Son of Man will *g* you.
6: 30 sign then will you *g* that we may
6: 34 "from now on *g* us this bread."
6: 51 which I will *g* for the life
6: 52 "How can this man *g* us his flesh
9: 24 "*G* glory to God," they said.
10: 28 I *g* them eternal life, and they shall
11: 22 now God will *g* you whatever you
13: 26 to whom I will *g* this piece of bread
13: 29 or to *g* something to the poor.
13: 34 "A new commandment I *g* you:
14: 16 he will *g* you another Counselor
14: 27 I do not *g* to you as the world gives.
14: 27 leave with you; my peace I *g* you.
15: 16 Father will *g* you whatever you ask
16: 23 my Father will *g* you whatever you
17: 2 people that he might *g* eternal life
18: 40 "No, not him! *G* us Barabbas!"
Ac 3: 6 not have, but what I have I *g* you.
5: 31 Savior that he might *g* repentance
6: 4 and will *g* our attention to prayer
8: 19 "*G* me also this ability
12: 23 Herod did not *g* praise to God,
13: 34 " 'I will *g* you the holy
20: 32 and *g* you an inheritance
20: 35 blessed to *g* than to receive.' "
21: 26 to the temple to *g* notice of the date
23: 21 Don't *g* in to them, because more
24: 23 but to *g* him some freedom
Ro 2: 6 God "will *g* to each person
2: 7 immortality, he will *g* eternal life.
8: 11 also *g* life to your mortal bodies
8: 32 with him, graciously *g* us all things
12: 8 let him *g* generously;
12: 20 *g* him something to drink.
13: 6 who *g* their full time to governing.
13: 7 *G* everyone what you owe him:
14: 12 each of us will *g* an account
15: 5 and encouragement *g* you a spirit
16: 2 and to *g* her any help she may need
1Co 7: 10 the married I *g* this command (not
7: 25 but I *g* a judgment as one who
10: 16 thanksgiving for which we *g* thanks
11: 34 I come I will *g* further directions.
13: 3 If I *g* all I possess to the poor
15: 58 Always *g* yourselves fully
16: 3 I will *g* letters of introduction
2Co 1: 11 many will *g* thanks on our behalf
4: 6 shine in our hearts to *g* us the light
8: 10 you were the first not only to *g*
9: 2 you in Achaia were ready to *g*;
9: 7 Each man should *g* what he has
9: 7 he has decided in his heart to *g*,
Gal 2: 5 We did not *g* in to them
3: 5 Does God *g* you his Spirit
6: 9 reap a harvest if we do not *g* up.
Eph 1: 17 may *g* you the Spirit of wisdom
4: 27 and do not *g* the devil a foothold.
Php 2: 30 up for the help you could not *g* me.
Col 4: 15 *G* my greetings to the brothers
1Th 5: 18 *g* thanks in all circumstances,
2Th 1: 7 *g* relief to you who are troubled,
3: 16 Lord of peace himself *g* you peace
1Ti 1: 18 I *g* you this instruction in keeping
1Ti 4: 15 *g* yourself wholly to them,
5: 3 *G* proper recognition
5: 7 *G* the people these instructions,
5: 14 and to *g* the enemy no opportunity
2Ti 1: 7 For God did not *g* us a spirit
2: 7 for the Lord will *g* you insight
4: 1 I *g* you this charge: Preach
Heb 4: 13 of him to whom we must *g* account
6: 14 and *g* you many descendants."
10: 25 Let us not *g* up meeting together,
13: 17 as men who must *g* an account.
Jas 1: 18 He chose to *g* us birth
1Pe 3: 6 do what is right and do not *g* way
3: 15 Always be prepared to *g* an answer
3: 15 who asks you to *g* the reason
4: 5 But they will have to *g* account
1Jn 5: 16 pray and God will *g* him life.
Rev 2: 7 I will *g* the right to eat
2: 10 and I will *g* you the crown of life.
2: 17 I will *g* some of the hidden manna.
2: 17 also *g* him a white stone
2: 26 I will *g* authority over the nations
2: 28 I will also *g* him the morning star.
3: 21 I will *g* the right to sit with me
4: 9 the living creatures *g* glory,
10: 9 asked him to *g* me the little scroll.
11: 3 I will *g* power to my two witnesses,
11: 17 "We *g* thanks to you, Lord God
12: 2 as she was about to *g* birth.
12: 4 woman who was about to *g* birth,
13: 15 power to *g* breath to the image
14: 7 "Fear God and *g* him glory,
17: 13 one purpose and will *g* their power
17: 17 agreeing to *g* the beast their power
18: 6 *G* back to her as she has given;
18: 7 *G* her as much torture and grief
19: 7 and *g* him glory!
21: 6 To him who is thirsty I will *g*
22: 5 for the Lord God will *g* them light.
22: 12 and I will *g* to everyone according
22: 16 angel to *g* you this testimony

GIVEN (GIVE)

Ge 9: 2 they are *g* into your hands.
15: 3 "You have *g* me no children;
24: 19 After she had *g* him a drink,
24: 35 He has *g* him sheep and cattle,
24: 36 he has *g* him everything he owns.
26: 18 same names his father had *g* them.
26: 22 "Now the LORD has *g* us room
27: 41 of the blessing his father had *g* him.
30: 6 to my plea and *g* me a son."
31: 9 father's livestock and has *g* them
33: 5 has graciously *g* your servant."
38: 14 she had not been *g* to him
38: 30 and he was *g* the name Zerah.
40: 16 that Joseph had *g* a favorable
41: 32 The reason the dream was *g*
43: 23 of your father has *g* you treasure
46: 18 whom Laban had *g*
46: 25 whom Laban had *g*
48: 9 are the sons God has *g* me here,"
Ex 4: 21 wonders I have *g* you the power
5: 16 Your servants are *g* no straw,
5: 18 You will not be *g* any straw,
16: 15 It is the bread the LORD has *g* you
16: 29 the LORD has *g* you the Sabbath;
28: 3 men to whom I have *g* wisdom
31: 6 I have *g* skill to all the craftsmen
34: 32 commands the LORD had *g* him
35: 34 And he has *g* both him
36: 1 to whom the LORD has *g* skill
36: 2 to whom the LORD had *g* ability
Lev 6: 17 I have *g* it as their share
7: 34 have *g* them to Aaron the priest
10: 11 the decrees the LORD has *g* them
10: 14 they have been *g* to you
10: 17 it was *g* to you to take away
17: 11 have *g* it to you to make atonement
19: 20 been ransomed or *g* her freedom,
26: 25 and you will be *g* into enemy hands
27: 9 such an animal *g* to the LORD
Nu 1: 17 men whose names had been *g*,
3: 9 are to be *g* wholly to him.
5: 8 and must be *g* to the priest,
8: 16 are to be *g* wholly to me.
8: 19 I have *g* the Levites as gifts
16: 14 or *g* us an inheritance of fields
Nu 18: 29 holiest part of everything *g* to you.'
21: 29 He has *g* up his sons as fugitives
27: 12 see the land I have *g* the Israelites.
32: 5 "let this land be *g* to your servants
32: 7 into the land the LORD has *g* them
32: 9 the land the LORD had *g* them.
33: 53 for I have *g* you the land to possess.
34: 13 The LORD has ordered that it be *g*
35: 8 are to be *g* in proportion
Dt 1: 8 See, I have *g* you this land.
1: 21 your God has *g* you the land.
2: 5 I have *g* Esau the hill country
2: 9 I have *g* Ar to the descendants
2: 19 I have *g* it as a possession
2: 24 I have *g* into your hand Sihon
3: 18 your God has *g* you this land
3: 19 stay in the towns I have *g* you,
3: 20 to the possession I have *g* you."
6: 17 and decrees he has *g* you.
8: 10 for the good land he has *g* you.
9: 23 of the land I have *g* you."
12: 1 the God of your fathers, has *g* you
12: 21 and flocks the LORD has *g* you,
16: 10 the LORD your God has *g* you.
22: 19 this man has *g* an Israelite virgin
26: 10 that you, O LORD, have *g* me."
26: 11 things the LORD your God has *g*
26: 13 and have *g* it to the Levite,
26: 15 and the land you have *g* us
28: 31 Your sheep will be *g*
28: 32 and daughters will be *g*
28: 53 the LORD your God has *g* you.
29: 4 the LORD has not *g* you a mind
29: 26 not know, gods he had not *g* them.
32: 30 unless the LORD had *g* them up?
Jos 2: 9 that the LORD has *g* this land
2: 24 LORD has surely *g* the whole land
6: 16 For the LORD has *g* you the city!
9: 19 "We have *g* them our oath
10: 8 I have *g* them into your hand.
10: 19 the LORD your God has *g* them
13: 8 that Moses had *g* them east
13: 15 This is what Moses had *g*
13: 24 This is what Moses had *g*
13: 29 This is what Moses had *g*
13: 32 This is the inheritance Moses had *g*
13: 33 Moses had *g* no inheritance;
15: 19 Since you have *g* me land
17: 14 "Why have you *g* us only one
18: 3 the God of your fathers, has *g* you?
21: 12 villages around the city they had *g*
21: 21 Ephraim they were *g* Shechem
21: 26 and their pasturelands were *g*
21: 27 clans of the Gershonites were *g*:
21: 34 (the rest of the Levites) were *g*:
22: 4 your God has *g* your brothers rest
22: 7 Moses had *g* land in Bashan,
23: 1 and the LORD had *g* Israel rest
23: 13 the LORD your God has *g* you.
23: 15 from this good land he has *g* you.
23: 16 from the good land he has *g* you."
Jdg 1: 2 I have *g* the land into their hands."
1: 15 Since you have *g* me land
1: 20 had promised, Hebron was *g*
3: 4 which he had *g* their forefathers
3: 28 "for the LORD has *g* Moab,
4: 14 is the day the LORD has *g* Sisera
7: 14 God has *g* the Midianites
7: 15 LORD has *g* the Midianite camp
8: 7 when the LORD has *g* Zebah
11: 24 the LORD our God has *g* us,
11: 36 "you have *g* your word
14: 11 he was *g* thirty companions.
14: 16 You've *g* my people a riddle,
14: 20 And Samson's wife was *g*
15: 6 because his wife was *g* to his friend
15: 18 "You have *g* your servant this
20: 36 Now the men of Israel had *g* way
21: 14 and were *g* the women
Ru 2: 13 "You have *g* me comfort
4: 15 than seven sons, has *g* him birth."
1Sa 1: 28 For his whole life he will be *g*
4: 20 you have *g* birth to a son."
14: 10 our sign that the LORD has *g* them
14: 12 the LORD has *g* them
15: 28 has *g* it to one of your neighbors—
18: 19 Saul's daughter, to be *g* to David,
18: 19 she was *g* in marriage to Adriel

1Sa 25:27 be *g* to the men who follow you.
25:44 But Saul had *g* his daughter Michal
28:17 and *g* it to one of your neighbors—
30:23 that with what the LORD has *g* us.
2Sa 7:1 and the LORD had *g* him rest
7:28 and you have *g* this good promise
9:9 "I have *g* your master's grandson
12:8 I would have *g* you even more.
13:28 Have not I *g* you this order?
17:6 "Ahithophel has *g* this advice.
17:7 advice Ahithophel has *g* is not
21:6 of his male descendants be *g* to us
1Ki 2:21 "Let Abishag the Shunammite be *g*
3:6 and have *g* him a son to sit
3:28 heard the verdict the king had *g*,
5:4 the LORD my God has *g* me peace
5:7 for he has *g* David a wise son
8:56 who has *g* rest to his people Israel
9:6 and decrees I have *g* you and go
9:7 Israel from the land I have *g* them
9:12 the towns that Solomon had *g* him,
9:13 of towns are these you have *g* me,
10:13 besides what he had *g* her out
12:13 Rejecting the advice *g* him
13:5 to the sign *g* by the man of God
13:26 The LORD has *g* him
15:29 to the word of the LORD *g*
18:26 So they took the bull *g* them
20:27 also mustered and *g* provisions,
2Ki 5:1 him the LORD had *g* victory
5:17 be *g* as much earth as a pair
15:20 shekels of silver to be *g* to the king
17:15 and the warnings he had *g* them.
18:6 the LORD had *g* Moses.
18:30 this city will not be *g* into the hand
22:10 "Hilkiah the priest has *g* me a book
1Ch 5:1 as firstborn were *g* to the sons
6:55 They were *g* Hebron in Judah
6:56 around the city were *g* to Caleb son
6:57 of Aaron were *g* Hebron (a city
6:60 of Benjamin they were *g* Gibeon,
6:66 Some of the Kohathite clans were *g*
6:67 Ephraim they were *g* Shechem
16:40 the LORD, which he had *g* Israel.
17:26 You have *g* this good promise
25:5 were *g* him through the promises
28:5 and the LORD has *g* me many—
29:9 for they had *g* freely
29:14 we have *g* you only what comes
29:17 All these things have I *g* willingly
29:17 your people who are here have *g*
2Ch 1:12 and knowledge will be *g* you.
2:12 He has *g* King David a wise son,
2:14 can execute any design *g* to him.
7:19 and commands I have *g* you
7:20 from my land, which I have *g* them
8:2 the villages that Hiram had *g* him,
13:5 has *g* the kingship of Israel
14:7 and he has *g* us rest on every side."
18:14 "for they will be *g* into your hand."
20:27 for the LORD had *g* them cause
20:30 for his God had *g* him rest
21:3 Their father had *g* them many gifts
21:3 he had *g* the kingdom to Jehoram
28:5 also *g* into the hands of the king
31:14 of the freewill offerings *g* to God,
32:29 for God had *g* him very great
33:8 and ordinances *g* through Moses."
34:14 Law of the LORD that had been *g*
34:18 "Hilkiah the priest has *g* me a book
36:23 has *g* me all the kingdoms
Ezr 1:2 has *g* me all the kingdoms
6:9 must be *g* them daily without fail,
7:6 LORD, the God of Israel, had *g*.
7:11 of the letter King Artaxerxes had *g*
7:15 and his advisers have freely *g*
9:9 and he has *g* us a wall of protection
9:13 and have *g* us a remnant like this.
Ne 7:72 The total *g* by the rest
10:29 the Law of God *g* through Moses
12:43 because God had *g* them great joy.
13:10 to the Levites had not been *g*
Est 2:3 let beauty treatments be *g* to them.
2:13 Anything she wanted was *g* her
5:3 to half the kingdom, it will be *g* you
5:6 is your petition? It will be *g* you.
7:2 is your petition? It will be *g* you.
8:7 I have *g* his estate to Esther,
Est 9:12 is your petition? It will be *g* you.
Job 3:20 "Why is light *g* to those in misery,
3:23 Why is life *g* to a man
15:19 (to whom alone the land was *g*
38:12 "Have you ever *g* orders
Ps 60:3 you have *g* us wine that makes us
61:5 you have *g* me the heritage
63:10 They will be *g* over to the sword
72:15 May gold from Sheba be *g* him.
74:9 We are *g* no miraculous signs;
78:29 for he had *g* them what they craved
79:2 They have *g* the dead bodies
94:17 Unless the LORD had *g* me help,
105:42 *g* to his servant Abraham.
115:16 but the earth he has *g* to man.
118:18 but he has not *g* me over to death.
119:49 for you have *g* me hope.
122:4 according to the statute *g* to Israel.
Pr 8:24 there were no oceans, I was *g* birth,
8:25 before the hills, I was *g* birth,
21:14 A gift *g* in secret soothes anger,
23:2 throat if you are *g* to gluttony.
Ecc 5:18 days of life God has *g* him—
8:15 the days of the life God has *g* him
9:9 life that God has *g* you
12:11 like firmly embedded nails—*g*
Isa 1:4 children *g* to corruption.
8:18 the children the LORD has *g* me.
9:6 to us a son is *g*,
14:32 What answer shall be *g*
23:4 been in labor nor *g* birth;
23:11 He has *g* an order concerning
26:18 we have not *g* birth to people
34:16 it is his mouth that has *g* the order,
35:2 The glory of Lebanon will be *g* to it
36:15 this city will not be *g* into the hand
50:4 Sovereign LORD has *g* me
63:14 they were *g* rest by the Spirit
Jer 4:31 my life is *g* over to murderers."
8:13 What I have *g* them
8:14 and *g* us poisoned water to drink,
21:10 It will be *g* into the hands
32:16 "After I had *g* the deed of purchase
35:15 live in the land I have *g* to you
37:21 and *g* bread from the street
38:16 LORD lives, who has *g* us breath,
39:11 king of Babylon had *g* these orders
La 4:11 The LORD has *g* full vent
Eze 11:15 this land was *g* to us as our
11:24 in the vision *g* by the Spirit
15:6 As I have *g* the wood of the vine
16:14 the splendor I had *g* you made your
16:34 for you give payment and none is *g*
17:18 Because he had *g* his hand
20:15 them into the land I had *g* them—
29:20 I have *g* him Egypt as a reward
33:24 surely the land has been *g* to us
35:12 have been *g* over to us to devour."
46:5 The grain offering *g* with the ram is
Da 2:23 You have *g* me wisdom and power,
2:37 God of heaven has *g* you dominion
4:16 let him be *g* the mind of an animal,
5:21 and *g* the mind of an animal;
5:28 Your kingdom is divided and *g*
7:4 and the heart of a man was *g* to it.
7:6 and it was *g* authority to rule.
7:14 He was *g* authority, glory
8:12 the daily sacrifice were *g* over to it.
8:26 that has been *g* you is true,
9:2 word of the LORD *g* to Jeremiah
9:23 answer was *g*, which I have come
10:1 a revelation was *g*
10:19 since you have *g* me strength."
11:4 his empire will be uprooted and *g*
11:21 who has not been *g* the honor
Hos 6:10 There Ephraim is *g* to prostitution
8:13 They offer sacrifices *g* to me
Joel 2:23 for he has *g* you
Am 6:11 For the LORD has *g* the command
9:15 from the land I have *g* them,"
Mic 1:1 The word of the LORD *g* to Micah
Na 1:14 LORD has *g* a command
Zec 6:8 north country have *g* my Spirit rest
6:14 The crown will be *g* to Heldai,
13:6 'The wounds I was *g* at the house
Mt 6:33 and all these things will be *g* to you
7:7 "Ask and it will be *g* to you;
9:8 who had *g* such authority to men.
Mt 10:19 At that time you will be *g* what
12:39 But none will be *g* it except the sign
13:11 of heaven has been *g* to you,
13:12 Whoever has will be *g* more,
14:11 in on a platter and *g* to the girl,
15:36 and when he had *g* thanks,
16:4 but none will be *g* it except the sign
19:11 only those to whom it has been *g*.
21:43 *g* to a people who will produce its
22:30 people will neither marry nor be *g*
25:29 everyone who has will be *g* more,
26:9 and the money *g* to the poor."
27:58 Pilate ordered that it be *g* to him.
28:18 and on earth has been *g* to me.
Mk 4:11 kingdom of God has been *g* to you.
4:25 Whoever has will be *g* more;
6:2 this wisdom that has been *g* him,
6:17 For Herod himself had *g* orders
8:6 the seven loaves and *g* thanks,
8:12 I tell you the truth, no sign will be *g*
12:25 they will neither marry nor be *g*
12:28 that Jesus had *g* them a good
13:11 Just say whatever is *g* you
14:5 and the money *g* to the poor."
Lk 2:21 the name the angel had *g* him
4:6 for it has been *g* to me,
6:38 Give, and it will be *g* to you.
8:10 kingdom of God has been *g* to you,
8:18 Whoever has will be *g* more;
10:19 I have *g* you authority to trample
11:9 Ask and it will be *g* to you;
11:29 but none will be *g* it except the sign
12:31 these things will be *g* to you as well
12:48 everyone who has been *g* much,
17:27 and being *g* in marriage up
19:15 to whom he had *g* the money,
19:26 more will be *g*, but
20:34 people of this age marry and are *g*
20:35 dead will neither marry nor be *g*
22:19 saying, "This is my body *g* for you;
Jn 1:17 For the law was *g* through Moses;
3:27 man can receive only what is *g* him
4:5 the plot of ground Jacob had *g*
4:10 he would have *g* you living water."
5:27 he has *g* him authority to judge
5:36 very work that the Father has *g* me
6:23 bread after the Lord had *g* thanks.
6:32 not Moses who has *g* you the bread
6:39 none of all that he has *g* me,
7:19 Has not Moses *g* you the law?
7:39 that time the Spirit had not been *g*,
10:29 My Father, who has *g* them to me,
11:57 and Pharisees had *g* orders that
12:2 Here a dinner was *g* in Jesus' honor
12:5 and the money *g* to the poor?
12:18 that he had *g* this miraculous sign,
15:7 you wish, and it will be *g* you.
17:2 life to all those you have *g* him.
17:7 everything you have *g* me comes
17:9 but for those you have *g* me,
17:14 I have *g* them your word
17:22 I have *g* them the glory that you
17:24 I want those you have *g* me to be
17:24 the glory you have *g* me
18:11 the cup the Father has *g* me?"
19:11 if it were not *g* to you from above.
19:35 man who saw it has *g* testimony,
Ac 3:16 him that has *g* this complete
4:12 name under heaven *g* to men
5:32 whom God has *g* to those who
8:18 Simon saw that the Spirit was *g*
17:31 He has *g* proof of this to all men
20:24 the task the Lord Jesus has *g* me—
27:24 God has graciously *g* you the lives
Ro 5:5 the Holy Spirit, whom he has *g* us.
5:13 for before the law was *g*, sin was
11:35 "Who has ever *g* to God,
12:3 For by the grace *g* me I say
12:3 the measure of faith God has *g* you.
12:6 according to the grace *g* us.
1Co 1:4 of his grace *g* you in Christ Jesus.
2:12 what God has freely *g* us.
3:10 By the grace God has *g* me,
4:2 those who have been *g* a trust must
11:15 For long hair is *g* to her
11:24 and when he had *g* thanks,
12:7 of the Spirit is *g* for the common
12:8 To one there is *g* through the Spirit

1Co 12:13 we were all *g* the one Spirit to drink
12:24 and has *g* greater honor
2Co 4:11 we who are alive are always being *g*
5:5 and has *g* us the Spirit as a deposit,
7:7 also by the comfort you had *g* him.
8:1 that God has *g* the Macedonian
9:5 gift, not as one grudgingly *g*.
9:14 surpassing grace God has *g* you.
12:7 there was *g* me a thorn in my flesh,
Gal 2:7 as Peter had been *g* the task
2:7 they saw that I had been *g* the task
2:9 when they recognized the grace *g*
3:14 us in order that the blessing *g*
3:21 a law had been *g* that could impart
3:22 being *g* through faith
3:22 might be *g* to those who believe.
4:15 have torn out your eyes and *g* them
Eph 1:6 which he has freely *g* us
1:21 and every title that can be *g*,
3:2 of God's grace that was *g* to me
3:7 the gift of God's grace *g* me
3:8 this grace was *g* me: to preach
4:7 to each one of us grace has been *g*
4:19 they have *g* themselves
6:19 words may be *g* me
Php 1:19 and the help *g* by the Spirit
Col 2:10 you have been *g* fullness in Christ,
1Th 1:6 with the joy *g* by the Holy Spirit.
1Ti 1:12 who has *g* me strength, that he
2:6 the testimony *g* in its proper time.
3:3 able to teach, not *g* to much wine,
4:14 was *g* you through a prophetic
2Ti 1:9 This grace was *g* us in Christ Jesus
Tit 1:7 not quick-tempered, not *g*
Phm :7 Your love has *g* me great joy
Heb 2:13 and the children God has *g* me."
4:8 For if Joshua had *g* them rest,
7:11 of it the law was *g* to the people),
Jas 1:5 finding fault, and it will be *g*
1Pe 1:3 great mercy he has *g* us new birth
1:13 fully on the grace to be *g* you
2Pe 1:3 divine power has *g* us everything
1:4 Through these he has *g* us his very
3:2 and the command *g* by our Lord
1Jn 4:13 because he has *g* us of his Spirit.
4:21 And he has *g* us this command:
5:9 which he has *g* about his Son.
5:10 testimony God has *g* about his Son.
5:11 the testimony: God has *g* us eternal
5:20 and has *g* us understanding,
2Jn :4 It has *g* me great joy to find some
Rev 2:21 I have *g* her time to repent
6:2 held a bow, and he was *g* a crown,
6:4 Its rider was *g* power to take peace
6:4 To him was *g* a large sword
6:8 They were *g* power over a fourth
6:11 each of them was *g* a white robe,
7:2 four angels who had been *g* power
8:2 and to them were *g* seven trumpets
8:3 He was *g* much incense to offer,
9:1 The star was *g* the key to the shaft
9:3 were *g* power like that of scorpions
9:5 They were not *g* power to kill them
11:1 I was *g* a reed like a measuring rod
11:2 it has been *g* to the Gentiles.
12:13 the woman who had *g* birth
12:14 The woman was *g* the two wings
13:4 he had *g* authority to the beast,
13:5 The beast was *g* a mouth
13:7 He was *g* power to make war
13:7 he was *g* authority over every tribe,
13:14 of the signs he was *g* power to do
13:15 He was *g* power to give breath
15:2 They held harps *g* them by God
16:6 you have *g* them blood to drink
16:8 and the sun was *g* power
18:6 Give back to her as she has *g*;
19:8 was *g* her to wear."
20:4 those who had been *g* authority

GIVER (GIVE)

Pr 18:16 A gift opens the way for the *g*
2Co 9:7 for God loves a cheerful *g*.

GIVES (GIVE)

Ex 4:11 Who *g* him sight or makes him
13:11 of the Canaanites and *g* it to you,
16:8 LORD when he *g* you meat to eat
16:29 on the sixth day he *g* you bread
21:4 If his master *g* him a wife
21:22 and she *g* birth prematurely
22:7 "If a man *g* his neighbor silver
22:10 "If a man *g* a donkey, an ox,
Lev 12:2 and *g* birth to a son will be
12:5 If she *g* birth to a daughter,
12:7 for the woman who *g* birth to a boy
20:2 in Israel who *g* any of his children
20:4 eyes when that man *g* one
Nu 5:10 what he *g* to the priest will belong
10:32 good things the LORD *g* us."
22:8 back the answer the LORD *g* me."
Dt 3:20 until the LORD *g* rest
4:40 land the LORD your God *g* you
7:16 the peoples the LORD your God *g*
8:18 for it is he who *g* you the ability
12:15 the LORD your God *g* you.
16:5 town the LORD your God *g* you
17:2 towns the LORD *g* you is found
19:8 *g* you the whole land he promised
20:14 the LORD your God *g* you
22:14 slanders her and *g* her a bad name,
24:1 *g* it to her and sends her
24:3 *g* it to her and sends her
25:19 the LORD your God *g* you rest
Jos 1:15 until the LORD *g* them rest,
2:14 when the LORD *g* us the land."
Jdg 11:9 and the LORD *g* them to me—
11:24 what your god Chemosh *g* you?
21:18 'Cursed be anyone who *g* a wife
Ru 4:12 the offspring the LORD *g* you
2Sa 22:51 He *g* his king great victories;
24:23 Araunah *g* all this to the king."
1Ki 17:14 dry until the day the LORD *g* rain
Ezr 9:8 and so our God *g* light to our eyes
Est 5:13 But all this *g* me no satisfaction
Job 8:15 He leans on his web, but it *g* way;
32:8 that *g* him understanding.
33:4 of the Almighty *g* me life.
35:10 who *g* songs in the night,
36:6 but *g* the afflicted their rights.
38:29 Who *g* birth to the frost
Ps 7:14 conceives trouble *g* birth
18:50 He *g* his king great victories;
29:11 The LORD *g* strength
68:35 the God of Israel *g* power
82:1 he *g* judgment among the "gods":
119:130 The entrance of your words *g* light;
119:130 it *g* understanding to the simple.
136:25 and who *g* food to every creature.
144:10 to the One who *g* victory to kings,
146:7 and *g* food to the hungry.
146:8 the LORD *g* sight to the blind,
Pr 2:6 For the LORD *g* wisdom,
3:34 but *g* grace to the humble.
5:6 She *g* no thought to the way of life;
11:24 One man *g* freely, yet gains
12:17 truthful witness *g* honest
14:15 a prudent man *g* thought
14:30 A heart at peace *g* life to the body,
15:30 good news *g* health to the bones.
16:20 *g* heed to instruction prospers,
17:8 a charm to the one who *g* it;
19:6 of a man who *g* gifts.
19:11 A man's wisdom *g* him patience;
21:29 an upright man *g* thought
22:16 and he who *g* gifts to the rich—
25:18 is the man who *g* false testimony
25:26 is a righteous man who *g* way
28:27 He who *g* to the poor will lack
29:4 justice a king *g* a country stability,
29:11 A fool *g* full vent to his anger,
29:13 The LORD *g* sight to the eyes
Ecc 2:26 God *g* wisdom, knowledge
2:26 but to the sinner he *g* the task
5:19 when God *g* any man wealth
6:2 God *g* a man wealth, possessions
Isa 14:3 On the day the LORD *g* you relief
21:9 And he *g* back the answer:
30:20 Although the Lord *g* you the bread
40:29 He *g* strength to the weary
42:5 who *g* breath to its people,
66:7 she *g* birth;
66:8 than she *g* birth to her children.
Jer 5:24 who *g* autumn and spring rains
La 4:4 but no one *g* it to them.
Eze 18:7 but *g* his food to the hungry
Eze 18:16 but *g* his food to the hungry
33:15 if he *g* back what he took in pledge
Da 2:21 He *g* wisdom to the wise
4:17 and *g* them to anyone he wishes
4:25 and *g* them to anyone he wishes.
4:32 and *g* them to anyone he wishes."
Mic 5:3 when she who is in labor *g* birth
Hab 2:15 "Woe to him who *g* drink
Zec 10:1 He *g* showers of rain to men,
Mt 5:15 it *g* light to everyone in the house.
10:42 And if anyone *g* a cup of cold water
26:73 for your accent *g* you away."
Mk 1:27 He even *g* orders to evil spirits
9:41 anyone who *g* you a cup of water
Lk 4:36 power he *g* orders to evil spirits
Jn 1:9 The true light that *g* light
3:6 Flesh *g* birth to flesh, but the Spirit
3:6 but the Spirit *g* birth to spirit.
3:34 to him God *g* the Spirit
5:21 even so the Son *g* life to whom he is
5:21 raises the dead and *g* them life,
6:32 is my Father who *g* you the true
6:33 comes down from heaven and *g* life
6:37 All that the Father *g* me will come
6:63 The Spirit *g* life; the flesh counts
14:27 I do not give to you as the world *g*.
Ac 17:25 because he himself *g* all men life
Ro 4:17 the God who *g* life to the dead
14:6 so to the Lord and *g* thanks to God
14:6 to the Lord, for he *g* thanks to God
15:5 May the God who *g* endurance
1Co 12:11 and he *g* them to each one,
15:38 But God *g* it a body as he has
15:38 kind of seed he *g* its own body.
15:57 He *g* us the victory
2Co 3:6 the letter kills, but the Spirit *g* life.
Php 4:13 through him who *g* me strength.
1Th 4:8 who *g* you his Holy Spirit.
1Ti 6:13 of God, who *g* life to everything,
Jas 1:5 who *g* generously to all
1:15 desire has conceived, it *g* birth
1:15 when it is full-grown, *g* birth
1:25 into the perfect law that *g* freedom,
2:12 judged by the law that *g* freedom,
4:6 but *g* grace to the humble."
4:6 he *g* us more grace? That is why
1Pe 5:5 but *g* grace to the humble."
Rev 21:23 for the glory of God *g* it light,

GIVING (GIVE)

Ge 13:17 of the land, for I am *g* it to you."
20:16 "I am *g* your brother a thousand
30:18 me for *g* my maidservant
38:28 As she was *g* birth, one
41:12 *g* each man the interpretation
49:28 *g* each the blessing appropriate
49:33 Jacob had finished *g* instructions
Ex 20:12 land the LORD your God is *g* you.
Lev 14:34 which I am *g* you as your
20:3 for by *g* his children to Molech,
27:2 the LORD by *g* equivalent values,
Nu 13:2 which I am *g* to the Israelites.
15:2 After you enter the land I am *g* you
18:7 I am *g* you the service
Dt 1:20 which the LORD our God is *g* us.
1:25 that the LORD our God is *g* us."
2:29 land the LORD our God is *g* us."
3:20 the LORD your God is *g* them,
4:1 the God of your fathers, is *g* you.
4:21 land the LORD your God is *g* you
4:40 which I am *g* you today,
5:16 land the LORD your God is *g* you.
5:31 in the land I am *g* them to possess."
8:1 every command I am *g* you today,
8:11 his decrees that I am *g* you this day
9:6 LORD your God is *g* you this good
10:13 and decrees that I am *g* you today
10:18 and loves the alien, *g* him food
11:8 all the commands I am *g* you today
11:13 the commands I am *g* you today—
11:17 the good land the LORD is *g* you.
11:22 all these commands I am *g* you
11:27 your God that I am *g* you today;
11:31 land the LORD your God is *g* you.
12:9 the LORD your God is *g* you.
12:10 land the LORD your God is *g* you
12:28 all these regulations I am *g* you,
13:12 the LORD your God is *g* you

Dt 13: 18 commands that I am *g* you today
15: 4 land the LORD your God is *g* you
15: 5 these commands I am *g* you today.
15: 7 that the LORD your God is *g* you,
16: 10 God by *g* a freewill offering
16: 18 the LORD your God is *g* you,
16: 20 land the LORD your God is *g* you.
17: 14 land the LORD your God is *g* you
18: 9 land the LORD your God is *g* you,
19: 1 the nations whose land he is *g* you,
19: 2 land the LORD your God is *g* you
19: 3 land the LORD your God is *g* you
19: 10 the LORD your God is *g* you
19: 14 land the LORD your God is *g* you
19: 18 *g* false testimony against his
20: 16 the LORD your God is *g* you
21: 1 land the LORD your God is *g* you
21: 17 firstborn by *g* him a double share
21: 23 land the LORD your God is *g* you
24: 4 land the LORD your God is *g* you
25: 15 land the LORD your God is *g* you.
25: 19 in the land he is *g* you to possess
26: 1 land the LORD your God is *g* you
26: 2 land the LORD your God is *g* you
27: 2 land the LORD your God is *g* you,
27: 3 land the LORD your God is *g* you,
28: 8 you in the land he is *g* you.
28: 15 and decrees I am *g* you today,
28: 52 land the LORD your God is *g* you.
30: 8 all his commands I am *g* you today.
32: 49 the land I am *g* the Israelites
32: 52 you will not enter the land I am *g*
Jos 1: 11 land the LORD your God is *g* you
1: 13 'The LORD your God is *g* you rest
1: 15 the LORD your God is *g* them.
3: 3 throughout the camp, *g* orders
Jdg 2: 23 at once by *g* them into the hands
1Sa 22: 13 *g* him bread and a sword
2Sa 11: 19 you have finished *g* the king this
18: 5 heard the king *g* orders concerning
24: 12 says: I am *g* you three options.
1Ch 21: 10 says: I am *g* you three options.
Ezr 9: 8 *g* us a firm place in his sanctuary,
Ne 4: 10 The strength of the laborers is *g* out
8: 8 *g* the meaning so that the people
Est 2: 22 it to the king, *g* credit to Mordecai.
3: 1 and *g* him a seat of honor higher
9: 19 a day for *g* presents to each other.
9: 22 *g* presents of food to one another
Ps 19: 8 *g* joy to the heart.
19: 8 *g* light to the eyes.
106: 5 join your inheritance in *g* praise.
111: 6 *g* them the lands of other nations.
Pr 1: 4 for *g* prudence to the simple,
15: 23 A man finds joy in *g* an apt reply—
26: 8 is the *g* of honor to a fool.
Eze 3: 3 eat this scroll I am *g* you
11: 2 and *g* wicked advice in this city.
16: 54 done in *g* them comfort.
Da 4: 21 *g* shelter to the beasts of the field,
6: 10 *g* thanks to his God, just
9: 13 and *g* attention to your truth.
Mt 6: 4 so that your *g* may be in secret.
24: 38 marrying and *g* in marriage,
Jn 16: 21 A woman *g* birth to a child has pain
Ac 1: 2 after *g* instructions
8: 1 And Saul was there, *g* approval
14: 17 by *g* you rain from heaven
15: 8 them by *g* the Holy Spirit to them,
22: 20 I stood there *g* my approval
1Co 14: 17 You may be *g* thanks well enough,
2Co 5: 12 but are *g* you an opportunity
8: 7 also excel in this grace of *g*.
Eph 1: 16 I have not stopped *g* thanks for you
5: 20 always *g* thanks to God the Father
Php 4: 15 shared with me in the matter of *g*
Col 1: 12 and joyfully *g* thanks to the Father,
3: 17 *g* thanks to God the Father

GIZONITE

1Ch 11: 34 the sons of Hashem the *G*,

GLAD (GLADDENS GLADNESS)

Ex 4: 14 his heart will be *g* when he sees you
Jos 22: 33 They were *g* to hear the report
Jdg 8: 25 "We'll be *g* to give them."
18: 20 household?" Then the priest was *g*.
1Sa 19: 5 and you saw it and were *g*.
2Sa 1: 20 daughters of the Philistines be *g*,
1Ki 8: 66 and *g* in heart for all the good
1Ch 16: 31 heavens rejoice, let the earth be *g*;
2Ch 7: 10 and *g* in heart for the good things
Ps 5: 11 let all who take refuge in you be *g*;
9: 2 I will be *g* and rejoice in you;
14: 7 let Jacob rejoice and Israel be *g*!
16: 9 Therefore my heart is *g*
21: 6 made him *g* with the joy
31: 7 I will be *g* and rejoice in your love,
32: 11 Rejoice in the LORD and be *g*,
40: 16 rejoice and be *g* in you;
45: 8 music of the strings makes you *g*.
46: 4 whose streams make *g* the city
48: 11 the villages of Judah are *g*
53: 6 let Jacob rejoice and Israel be *g*!
58: 10 The righteous will be *g*
67: 4 May the nations be *g* and sing
68: 3 But may the righteous be *g*
69: 32 The poor will see and be *g*—
70: 4 rejoice and be *g* in you;
90: 14 for joy and be *g* all our days.
90: 15 Make us *g* for as many days
92: 4 For you make me *g* by your deeds,
96: 11 heavens rejoice, let the earth be *g*;
97: 1 LORD reigns, let the earth be *g*;
97: 8 and the villages of Judah are *g*
105: 38 Egypt was *g* when they left,
107: 30 They were *g* when it grew calm,
118: 24 let us rejoice and be *g* in it.
149: 2 of Zion be *g* in their King.
Pr 23: 15 then my heart will be *g*;
23: 25 May your father and mother be *g*;
29: 6 a righteous one can sing and be *g*.
Ecc 8: 15 sun than to eat and drink and be *g*.
Isa 25: 9 let us rejoice and be *g*
35: 1 and the parched land will be *g*;
65: 18 But be *g* and rejoice forever
66: 10 with Jerusalem and be *g* for her,
Jer 20: 15 who made him very *g*, saying,
31: 13 Then maidens will dance and be *g*,
41: 13 were with him, they were *g*.
50: 11 "Because you rejoice and are *g*,
La 4: 21 be *g*, O Daughter of Edom,
Joel 2: 21 be *g* and rejoice.
2: 23 Be *g*, O people of Zion,
Hab 1: 15 and so he rejoices and is *g*.
Zep 3: 14 Be *g* and rejoice with all your heart
Zec 2: 10 and be *g*, O Daughter of Zion.
8: 19 will become joyful and *g* occasions
10: 7 their hearts will be *g* as with wine.
Mt 5: 12 be *g*, because great is your reward
Lk 15: 32 But we had to celebrate and be *g*,
Jn 4: 36 and the reaper may be *g* together.
8: 56 my day; he saw it and was *g*."
11: 15 for your sake I am *g* I was not there
14: 28 you would be *g* that I am going
Ac 2: 26 Therefore my heart is *g*
2: 46 together with *g* and sincere hearts,
11: 23 he was *g* and encouraged them all
13: 48 they were *g* and honored the word
15: 3 news made all the brothers very *g*.
15: 31 were *g* for its encouraging message.
1Co 16: 17 was *g* when Stephanas, Fortunatus
2Co 2: 2 who is left to make me *g*
7: 16 I am *g* I can have complete
13: 9 We are *g* whenever we are weak
Gal 4: 27 "Be *g*, O barren woman,
Php 2: 17 I am *g* and rejoice with all of you.
2: 18 So you too should be *g* and rejoice
2: 28 you see him again you may be *g*
Rev 19: 7 Let us rejoice and be *g*

GLADDENS (GLAD)

Ps 104: 15 wine that *g* the heart of man,

GLADNESS (GLAD)

2Ch 29: 30 So they sang praises with *g*
Est 8: 16 a time of happiness and joy, *g*
8: 17 there was joy and *g*
Job 3: 22 who are filled with *g*
Ps 35: 27 shout for joy and *g*;
45: 15 They are led in with joy and *g*;
51: 8 Let me hear joy and *g*;
65: 12 the hills are clothed with *g*.
100: 2 Serve the LORD with *g*;
Ecc 5: 20 God keeps him occupied with *g*
9: 7 Go, eat your food with *g*,
Isa 16: 10 *g* are taken away from the orchards
35: 10 *G* and joy will overtake them,
51: 3 Joy and *g* will be found in her,
51: 11 *G* and joy will overtake them,
61: 3 the oil of *g*
Jer 7: 34 and *g* and to the voices of bride
16: 9 and *g* and to the voices of bride
25: 10 from them the sounds of joy and *g*,
31: 13 I will turn their mourning into *g*;
33: 11 once more the sounds of joy and *g*,
48: 33 Joy and *g* are gone
Joel 1: 16 joy and *g*

GLANCE (GLANCES GLANCING)

Pr 23: 5 but a *g* at riches, and they are gone,
SS 4: 9 heart with one *g* of your eyes,

GLANCES (GLANCE)

Pr 30: 13 whose *g* are so disdainful;

GLANCING (GLANCE)

Ex 2: 12 *G* this way and that and seeing no

GLASS

Rev 4: 6 was what looked like a sea of *g*,
15: 2 a sea of *g* mixed with fire
21: 18 the city of pure gold, as pure as *g*.
21: 21 of pure gold, like transparent *g*.

GLAZE

Pr 26: 23 of *g* over earthenware

GLEAM (GLEAMED GLEAMING)

Pr 4: 18 of the righteous is like the first *g*
Da 10: 6 legs like the *g* of burnished bronze,

GLEAMED (GLEAM)

Eze 1: 7 and *g* like burnished bronze.
Lk 24: 4 men in clothes that *g* like lightning

GLEAMING (GLEAM)

Job 20: 25 the *g* point out of his liver.

GLEAN (GLEANED GLEANING GLEANINGS GLEANS)

Ru 2: 3 and began to *g* in the fields
2: 7 'Please let me *g* and gather
2: 8 Don't go and *g* in another field
2: 15 up to *g*, Boaz gave orders
2: 19 "Where did you *g* today? Where
2: 23 girls of Boaz to *g* until the barley
Job 24: 6 *g* in the vineyards of the wicked.
Jer 6: 9 "Let them *g* the remnant of Israel

GLEANED (GLEAN)

Ru 2: 17 So Ruth *g* in the field until evening.

GLEANING (GLEAN)

Mic 7: 1 fruit at the *g* of the vineyard;

GLEANINGS (GLEAN)

Lev 19: 9 or gather the *g* of your harvest.
23: 22 or gather the *g* of your harvest.
Jdg 8: 2 Aren't the *g* of Ephraim's grapes
Isa 17: 6 Yet some *g* will remain,
24: 13 or as when *g* are left after the grape

GLEANS (GLEAN)

Isa 17: 5 as when a man *g* heads of grain

GLEE

Ps 35: 15 I stumbled, they gathered in *g*;
Eze 36: 5 for with *g* and with malice

GLIDE (GLIDED GLIDING)

Dt 32: 24 venom of vipers that *g* in the dust.

GLIDED (GLIDE)

Job 4: 15 A spirit *g* past my face,

GLIDING (GLIDE)

Job 26: 13 his hand pierced the *g* serpent.
Isa 27: 1 Leviathan the *g* serpent,

GLIMPSE

Job 9: 25 they fly away without a *g* of joy.
23: 9 to the south, I catch no *g* of him.

GLINT

Hab 3: 11 at the *g* of your flying arrows,

GLISTENING

Job 41: 32 Behind him he leaves a *g* wake,

GLITTERING

Na 3: 3 and *g* spears!
Rev 17: 4 was *g* with gold, precious stones
18: 16 and *g* with gold, precious stones

GLOAT (GLOATED GLOATING GLOATS)

Ps 22: 17 people stare and *g* over me.
30: 1 did not let my enemies *g* over me.
35: 19 Let not those *g* over me
35: 24 do not let them *g* over me.
35: 26 May all who *g* over my distress
38: 16 For I said, "Do not let them *g*
59: 10 and will let me *g* over those who
Pr 24: 17 Do not *g* when your enemy falls;
La 2: 17 he has let the enemy *g* over you,
Mic 4: 11 let our eyes *g* over Zion!"
7: 8 Do not *g* over me, my enemy!
Rev 11: 10 of the earth will *g* over them

GLOATED (GLOAT)

Job 31: 29 *g* over the trouble that came to him

GLOATING (GLOAT)

Hab 3: 14 *g* as though about to devour

GLOATS (GLOAT)

Pr 17: 5 whoever *g* over disaster will not go

GLOOM (GLOOMY)

Job 10: 21 to the land of *g* and deep shadow,
Ps 107: 10 sat in darkness and the deepest *g*,
107: 14 of darkness and the deepest *g*
Isa 8: 22 and darkness and fearful *g*,
9: 1 there will be no more *g*
24: 11 all joy turns to *g*,
29: 18 and out of *g* and darkness
Jer 13: 16 and change it to deep *g*.
Eze 31: 15 of it I clothed Lebanon with *g*,
Joel 2: 2 a day of darkness and *g*,
Zep 1: 15 a day of darkness and *g*,
Heb 12: 18 *g* and storm; to a trumpet blast
Jas 4: 9 to mourning and your joy to *g*.

GLOOMY (GLOOM)

2Pe 2: 4 putting them into *g* dungeons

GLORIES (GLORY)

1Pe 1: 11 and the *g* that would follow.

GLORIFIED (GLORY)

Isa 66: 5 'Let the LORD be *g*,
Eze 39: 13 day I am *g* will be a memorable day
Da 4: 34 and *g* him who lives forever.
Jn 7: 39 since Jesus had not yet been *g*.
11: 4 glory so that God's Son may be *g*
12: 16 after Jesus was *g* did they realize
12: 23 come for the Son of Man to be *g*.
12: 28 "I have *g* it, and will glorify it again
13: 31 Son of Man *g* and God is *g* in him.
13: 32 If God is *g* in him, God will glorify
Ac 3: 13 our fathers, has *g* his servant Jesus.
Ro 1: 21 they neither *g* him as God
8: 30 those he justified, he also *g*.
2Th 1: 10 comes to be *g* in his holy people
1: 12 of our Lord Jesus may be *g* in you,
1Pe 1: 21 him from the dead and *g* him,

GLORIFIES (GLORY)

Jn 8: 54 as your God, is the one who *g* me.

GLORIFY (GLORY)

Ps 34: 3 *G* the LORD with me;
63: 3 my lips will *g* you.
69: 30 and *g* him with thanksgiving.
86: 12 I will *g* your name forever.
Isa 60: 13 and I will *g* the place of my feet.
Da 4: 37 and exalt and *g* the King of heaven,
Jn 8: 54 Jesus replied, "If I *g* myself,
12: 28 glorified it, and will *g* it again."
12: 28 *g* your name!" Then a voice came
13: 32 God will *g* the Son in himself,
13: 32 in himself, and will *g* him at once.
17: 1 *G* your Son, that your Son may
17: 1 your Son, that your Son may *g* you.
17: 5 *g* me in your presence
21: 19 death by which Peter would *g* God.
Ro 15: 6 and mouth you may *g* the God
15: 9 so that the Gentiles may *g* God
1Pe 2: 12 and *g* God on the day he visits us.
Rev 16: 9 they refused to repent and *g* him.

GLORIFYING (GLORY)

Lk 2: 20 *g* and praising God

GLORIOUS (GLORY)

Dt 28: 58 not revere this *g* and awesome
33: 29 and your *g* sword.
1Ch 29: 13 and praise your *g* name.
Ne 9: 5 "Blessed be your *g* name,
Ps 3: 3 my *G* One, who lifts up my head.
16: 3 they are the *g* ones
45: 13 All *g* is the princess
72: 19 Praise be to his *g* name forever;
87: 3 *G* things are said of you,
111: 3 *G* and majestic are his deeds,
145: 5 of the *g* splendor of your majesty,
145: 12 the *g* splendor of your kingdom.
Isa 3: 8 defying his *g* presence.
4: 2 the LORD will be beautiful and *g*,
11: 10 and his place of rest will be *g*.
12: 5 for he has done *g* things;
28: 1 to the fading flower, his *g* beauty,
28: 4 That fading flower, his *g* beauty,
28: 5 will be a *g* crown,
42: 21 to make his law great and *g*.
60: 7 and I will adorn my *g* temple.
63: 12 who sent his *g* arm of power
63: 14 to make for yourself a *g* name.
63: 15 from your lofty throne, holy and *g*.
64: 11 *g* temple, where our fathers praised
Jer 13: 18 for your *g* crowns
14: 21 do not dishonor your *g* throne.
17: 12 A *g* throne, exalted
48: 17 how broken the *g* staff!'
Mt 19: 28 the Son of Man sits on his *g* throne,
Lk 9: 31 appeared in *g* splendor, talking
Ac 2: 20 of the great and *g* day of the Lord.
Ro 8: 21 and brought into the *g* freedom
2Co 3: 8 of the Spirit be even more *g*?
3: 9 how much more *g* is the ministry
3: 9 ministry that condemns men is *g*,
3: 10 For what was *g* has no glory now
Eph 1: 6 to the praise of his *g* grace,
1: 17 *g* Father, may give you the Spirit
1: 18 the riches of his *g* inheritance
3: 16 of his *g* riches he may strengthen
Php 3: 21 so that they will be like his *g* body.
4: 19 to his *g* riches in Christ Jesus.
Col 1: 11 all power according to his *g* might
1: 27 among the Gentiles the *g* riches
1Ti 1: 11 to the *g* gospel of the blessed God,
Tit 2: 13 the *g* appearing of our great God
Jas 2: 1 believers in our *g* Lord Jesus Christ
1Pe 1: 8 with an inexpressible and *g* joy,
Jude : 24 before his *g* presence without fault

GLORIOUSLY (GLORY)

Isa 24: 23 and before its elders, *g*.

GLORY (GLORIES GLORIFIED GLORIFIES GLORIFY GLORIFYING GLORIOUS GLORIOUSLY)

Ex 14: 4 But I will gain *g* for myself
14: 17 And I will gain *g* through Pharaoh
14: 18 when I gain *g* through Pharaoh,
15: 11 awesome in *g*,
16: 7 in the morning you will see the *g*
16: 10 and there was the *g* of the LORD
24: 16 and the *g* of the LORD settled
24: 17 To the Israelites the *g*
29: 43 place will be consecrated by my *g*.
33: 18 Moses said, "Now show me your *g*
33: 22 When my *g* passes
40: 34 and the *g* of the LORD filled
40: 35 and the *g* of the LORD filled
Lev 9: 6 so that the *g* of the LORD may
9: 23 and the *g* of the LORD appeared
Nu 14: 10 Then the *g* of the LORD appeared
14: 21 the *g* of the LORD fills the whole
14: 22 not one of the men who saw my *g*
Nu 16: 19 the *g* of the LORD appeared
16: 42 and the *g* of the LORD appeared.
20: 6 and the *g* of the LORD appeared
Dt 5: 24 LORD our God has shown us his *g*
Jos 7: 19 "My son, give *g* to the LORD,
1Sa 4: 21 "The *g* has departed from Israel"—
4: 22 "The *g* has departed from Israel,
15: 29 He who is the *G* of Israel does not
2Sa 1: 19 "Your *g*, O Israel, lies slain
1Ki 8: 11 for the *g* of the LORD filled his
2Ki 14: 10 *G* in your victory, but stay at home
1Ch 16: 10 *G* in his holy name;
16: 24 Declare his *g* among the nations,
16: 28 ascribe to the LORD *g*
16: 29 to the LORD the *g* due his name.
16: 35 that we may *g* in your praise."
29: 11 and the *g* and the majesty
2Ch 5: 14 for the *g* of the LORD filled
7: 1 *g* of the LORD filled the temple.
7: 2 the *g* of the LORD filled it.
7: 3 and the *g* of the LORD
Est 1: 4 the splendor and *g* of his majesty.
Job 29: 20 My *g* will remain fresh in me,
40: 10 adorn yourself with *g* and splendor
Ps 4: 2 will you turn my *g* into shame?
8: 1 You have set your *g*
8: 5 and crowned him with *g* and honor
19: 1 The heavens declare the *g* of God;
21: 5 victories you gave, his *g* is great;
24: 7 that the King of *g* may come in.
24: 8 Who is this King of *g*?
24: 9 that the King of *g* may come in.
24: 10 Who is he, this King of *g*?
24: 10 he is the King of *g*.
26: 8 the place where your *g* dwells.
29: 1 ascribe to the LORD *g*
29: 2 to the LORD the *g* due his name;
29: 3 the God of *g* thunders,
29: 9 And in his temple all cry, "*G*!"
57: 5 let your *g* be over all the earth.
57: 11 let your *g* be over all the earth
63: 2 and beheld your power and your *g*.
66: 2 Sing to the *g* of his name;
66: 2 offer him *g* and praise!
72: 19 the whole earth be filled with his *g*.
73: 24 afterward you will take me into *g*.
79: 9 for the *g* of your name;
85: 9 that his *g* may dwell in our land.
86: 9 they will bring *g* to your name.
89: 17 For you are their *g* and strength,
96: 3 Declare his *g* among the nations,
96: 6 strength and *g* are in his sanctuary.
96: 7 ascribe to the LORD *g*
96: 8 to the LORD the *g* due his name;
97: 6 and all the peoples see his *g*.
102: 15 of the earth will revere your *g*.
102: 16 and appear in his *g*.
104: 31 May the *g* of the LORD endure
105: 3 *G* in his holy name;
106: 20 They exchanged their *G*
106: 47 and *g* in your praise.
108: 5 and let your *g* be over all the earth.
113: 4 his *g* above the heavens.
115: 1 but to your name be the *g*,
138: 5 for the *g* of the LORD is great.
145: 11 tell of the *g* of your kingdom
149: 9 This is the *g* of all his saints.
Pr 14: 28 A large population is a king's *g*,
19: 11 it is to his *g* to overlook an offense.
20: 29 *g* of young men is their strength,
25: 2 It is the *g* of God to conceal
25: 2 to search out a matter is the *g*
Isa 4: 2 *g* of the survivors in Israel.
4: 5 over all the *g* will be a canopy.
6: 3 the whole earth is full of his *g*."
13: 19 the *g* of the Babylonians' pride,
17: 3 like the *g* of the Israelites,"
17: 4 In that day the *g* of Jacob will fade;
22: 24 All the *g* of his family will hang
23: 9 to bring low the pride of all *g*
24: 15 in the east give *g* to the LORD;
24: 16 "*G* to the Righteous One."
26: 15 You have gained *g* for yourself;
35: 2 The *g* of Lebanon will be given to it
35: 2 they will see the *g* of the LORD,
40: 5 the *g* of the LORD will be revealed
40: 6 and all their *g* is like the flowers
41: 16 and *g* in the Holy One of Israel.

Isa 42: 8 I will not give my *g* to another
42: 12 Let them give *g* to the LORD
43: 7 whom I created for my *g*,
44: 13 of man in all his *g*,
44: 23 he displays his *g* in Israel.
48: 11 I will not yield my *g* to another.
58: 8 *g* of the LORD will be your rear
59: 19 of the sun, they will revere his *g*.
60: 1 the *g* of the LORD rises upon you.
60: 2 and his *g* appears over you.
60: 13 The *g* of Lebanon will come to you,
60: 19 and your God will be your *g*.
62: 2 and all kings your *g*;
66: 18 and they will come and see my *g*.
66: 19 They will proclaim my *g*
66: 19 heard of my fame or seen my *g*.
Jer 2: 11 my people have exchanged their *G*
4: 2 and in him they will *g*."
13: 16 Give *g* to the LORD your God
48: 18 "Come down from your *g*
Eze 1: 28 the likeness of the *g* of the LORD.
3: 12 May the *g* of the LORD be praised
3: 23 like the *g* I had seen
3: 23 *g* of the LORD was standing there,
8: 4 before me was the *g* of the God
9: 3 the *g* of the God of Israel went up
10: 4 Then the *g* of the LORD rose
10: 4 the radiance of the *g* of the LORD.
10: 18 Then the *g* of the LORD departed
10: 19 and the *g* of the God of Israel was
11: 22 and the *g* of the God of Israel was
11: 23 The *g* of the LORD went up
24: 25 and *g*, the delight of their eyes,
25: 9 Kiriathaim—the *g* of that land.
28: 22 and I will gain *g* within you.
39: 21 "I will display my *g*
43: 2 and I saw the *g* of the God
43: 2 and the land was radiant with his *g*.
43: 4 *g* of the LORD entered the temple
43: 5 *g* of the LORD filled the temple.
44: 4 and saw the *g* of the LORD filling
Da 2: 37 and power and might and *g*;
4: 30 and for the *g* of my majesty?"
4: 36 to me for the *g* of my kingdom.
5: 18 and greatness and *g* and splendor.
5: 20 royal throne and stripped of his *g*.
7: 14 He was given authority, *g*
Hos 4: 7 they exchanged their *G*
9: 11 Ephraim's *g* will fly away like
Mic 1: 15 He who is the *g* of Israel
Hab 2: 14 knowledge of the *g* of the LORD,
2: 16 and disgrace will cover your *g*.
2: 16 filled with shame instead of *g*.
3: 3 His *g* covered the heavens
Hag 2: 3 who saw this house in its former *g*?
2: 7 and I will fill this house with *g*,'
2: 9 than the *g* of the former house,'
2: 9 'The *g* of this present house will be
Zec 2: 5 'and I will be its *g* within.'
Mt 16: 27 in his Father's *g* with his angels,
24: 30 of the sky, with power and great *g*.
25: 31 sit on his throne in heavenly *g*.
25: 31 the Son of Man comes in his *g*,
Mk 8: 38 in his Father's *g* with the holy
10: 37 the other at your left in your *g*."
13: 26 in clouds with great power and *g*.
Lk 2: 9 and the *g* of the Lord shone
2: 14 saying, "*G* to God in the highest,
2: 32 and for *g* to your people Israel."
9: 26 and in the *g* of the Father
9: 26 of him when he comes in his *g*
9: 32 they saw his *g* and the two men
19: 38 in heaven and *g* in the highest!"
21: 27 in a cloud with power and great *g*.
24: 26 these things and then enter his *g*?"
Jn 1: 14 We have seen his *g*, the *g* of the one
2: 11 He thus revealed his *g*,
8: 50 I am not seeking *g* for myself;
8: 54 myself, my *g* means nothing.
9: 24 "Give *g* to God," they said.
11: 4 for God's *g* so that God's Son may
11: 40 you would see the *g* of God?"
12: 41 he saw Jesus' *g* and spoke about
14: 13 so that the Son may bring *g*
15: 8 is to my Father's *g*, that you bear
16: 14 He will bring *g* to me by taking
17: 4 I have brought you *g* on earth
17: 5 presence with the *g* I had with you
Jn 17: 10 *g* has come to me through them.
17: 22 given them the *g* that you gave
17: 24 to see my *g*, the *g* you have given
Ac 7: 2 The God of *g* appeared
7: 55 up to heaven and saw the *g* of God,
Ro 1: 23 exchanged the *g* of the immortal
2: 7 by persistence in doing good seek *g*
2: 10 then for the Gentile; but *g*,
3: 7 truthfulness and so increases his *g*,
3: 23 and fall short of the *g* of God,
4: 20 in his faith and gave *g* to God,
5: 2 rejoice in the hope of the *g* of God.
6: 4 dead through the *g* of the Father,
8: 17 that we may also share in his *g*.
8: 18 with the *g* that will be revealed
9: 4 theirs the divine *g*, the covenants,
9: 23 riches of his *g* known to the objects
9: 23 whom he prepared in advance for *g*
11: 36 To him be the *g* forever! Amen.
15: 17 Therefore I *g* in Christ Jesus
16: 27 to the only wise God be *g* forever
1Co 2: 7 for our *g* before time began.
2: 8 not have crucified the Lord of *g*.
10: 31 whatever you do, do it all for the *g*
11: 7 but the woman is the *g* of man.
11: 7 since he is the image and *g* of God;
11: 15 it is her *g*? For long hair is given
15: 31 as I *g* over you in Christ Jesus our
15: 43 it is raised in *g*; it is sown
2Co 1: 20 spoken by us to the *g* of God.
3: 7 in letters on stone, came with *g*,
3: 7 the face of Moses because of its *g*,
3: 10 comparison with the surpassing *g*.
3: 10 what was glorious has no *g* now
3: 11 how much greater is the *g*
3: 11 what was fading away came with *g*,
3: 18 faces all reflect the Lord's *g*,
3: 18 likeness with ever-increasing *g*,
4: 4 of the gospel of the *g* of Christ,
4: 6 of the knowledge of the *g* of God
4: 15 to overflow to the *g* of God.
4: 17 us an eternal *g* that far outweighs
6: 8 through *g* and dishonor, bad report
Gal 1: 5 to whom be *g* for ever and ever.
Eph 1: 12 might be for the praise of his *g*.
1: 14 to the praise of his *g*.
3: 13 for you, which are your *g*.
3: 21 to him be *g* in the church
Php 1: 11 to the *g* and praise of God.
2: 11 to the *g* of God the Father.
3: 3 of God, who *g* in Christ Jesus,
3: 19 and their *g* is in their shame.
4: 20 and Father be *g* for ever and ever.
Col 1: 27 Christ in you, the hope of *g*.
3: 4 also will appear with him in *g*.
1Th 2: 12 you into his kingdom and *g*.
2: 19 in which we will *g* in the presence
2: 20 Indeed, you are our *g* and joy.
2Th 2: 14 in the *g* of our Lord Jesus Christ.
1Ti 1: 17 be honor and *g* for ever and ever.
3: 16 was taken up in *g*.
2Ti 2: 10 is in Christ Jesus, with eternal *g*.
4: 18 To him be *g* for ever and ever.
Heb 1: 3 The Son is the radiance of God's *g*
2: 7 you crowned him with *g* and honor
2: 9 now crowned with *g* and honor
2: 10 In bringing many sons to *g*,
5: 5 take upon himself the *g*
9: 5 the ark were the cherubim of the *G*,
13: 21 to whom be *g* for ever and ever.
1Pe 1: 7 *g* and honor when Jesus Christ is
1: 24 and all their *g* is like the flowers
4: 11 To him be the *g* and the power
4: 13 overjoyed when his *g* is revealed.
4: 14 for the Spirit of *g* and of God rests
5: 1 will share in the *g* to be revealed:
5: 4 of *g* that will never fade away
5: 10 you to his eternal *g* in Christ,
2Pe 1: 3 of him who called us by his own *g*
1: 17 and *g* from God the Father
1: 17 came to him from the Majestic *G*,
3: 18 To him be *g* both now and forever!
Jude : 25 to the only God our Savior be *g*,
Rev 1: 6 to him be *g* and power for ever
4: 9 the living creatures give *g*,
4: 11 to receive *g* and honor and power,
5: 12 and honor and *g* and praise!"
5: 13 and honor and *g* and power,
Rev 7: 12 Praise and *g*
11: 13 and gave *g* to the God of heaven.
14: 7 "Fear God and give him *g*,
15: 4 and bring *g* to your name?
15: 8 with smoke from the *g* of God
18: 7 as the *g* and luxury she gave herself
19: 1 *g* and power belong to our God,
19: 7 and give him *g*!
21: 11 It shone with the *g* of God,
21: 23 for the *g* of God gives it light,
21: 26 *g* and honor of the nations will be

GLOW (GLOWING GLOWS)
Isa 4: 5 and a *g* of flaming fire by night;

GLOWING (GLOW)
Ps 102: 3 my bones burn like *g* embers.
Eze 1: 4 of the fire looked like *g* metal,
1: 27 his waist up he looked like *g* metal,
8: 2 was as bright as *g* metal.
Rev 1: 15 His feet were like bronze *g*

GLOWS (GLOW)
Eze 24: 11 till it becomes hot and its copper *g*

GLUTTED (GLUTTON)
Eze 39: 19 you will eat fat till you are *g*

GLUTTON (GLUTTED GLUTTONS GLUTTONY)
Mt 11: 19 'Here is a *g* and a drunkard,
Lk 7: 34 'Here is a *g* and a drunkard,

GLUTTONS (GLUTTON)
Pr 23: 21 for drunkards and *g* become poor,
28: 7 of *g* disgraces his father.
Tit 1: 12 always liars, evil brutes, lazy *g*."

GLUTTONY (GLUTTON)
Pr 23: 2 throat if you are given to *g*.

GNASH (GNASHED GNASHES GNASHING)
Ps 37: 12 and *g* their teeth at them;
112: 10 he will *g* his teeth and waste away;
La 2: 16 they scoff and *g* their teeth

GNASHED (GNASH)
Ps 35: 16 they *g* their teeth at me.
Ac 7: 54 they were furious and *g* their teeth

GNASHES (GNASH)
Job 16: 9 and *g* his teeth at me;
Mk 9: 18 *g* his teeth and becomes rigid.

GNASHING (GNASH)
Mt 8: 12 where there will be weeping and *g*
13: 42 where there will be weeping and *g*
13: 50 where there will be weeping and *g*
22: 13 where there will be weeping and *g*
24: 51 where there will be weeping and *g*
25: 30 where there will be weeping and *g*
Lk 13: 28 There will be weeping there, and *g*

GNAT (GNATS)
Mt 23: 24 You strain out a *g* but swallow

GNATS (GNAT)
Ex 8: 16 of Egypt the dust will become *g*."
8: 17 the land of Egypt became *g*.
8: 17 *g* came upon men and animals.
8: 18 And the *g* were on men
8: 18 to produce *g* by their secret arts,
Ps 105: 31 and *g* throughout their country.

GNAWED (GNAWING)
Rev 16: 10 Men *g* their tongues in agony

GNAWING (GNAWED)
Job 30: 17 my *g* pains never rest.

GOADS
1Sa 13: 21 and axes and for repointing *g*.
Ecc 12: 11 The words of the wise are like *g*,
Ac 26: 14 hard for you to kick against the *g*.'

GOAH
Jer 31: 39 hill of Gareb and then turn to *G*.

GOAL

Lk 13: 32 on the third day I will reach my *g*.'
2Co 5: 9 So we make it our *g* to please him,
Gal 3: 3 to attain your *g* by human effort?
Php 3: 14 on toward the *g* to win the prize
1Ti 1: 5 The *g* of this command is love,
1Pe 1: 9 for you are receiving the *g*

GOAT (GOAT'S GOATS GOATS' HE-GOAT SCAPEGOAT)

Ge 15: 9 "Bring me a heifer, a *g* and a ram,
30: 32 and every spotted or speckled *g*.
30: 33 Any *g* in my possession that is not
37: 31 slaughtered a *g* and dipped
38: 17 "I'll send you a young *g*
38: 20 Meanwhile Judah sent the young *g*
38: 23 I did send her this young *g*,
Ex 23: 19 "Do not cook a young *g*
25: 4 scarlet yarn and fine linen; *g* hair;
26: 7 Make curtains of *g* hair for the tent
34: 26 "Do not cook a young *g*
35: 6 scarlet yarn and fine linen; *g* hair;
35: 23 scarlet yarn or fine linen, or *g* hair,
35: 26 and had the skill spun the *g* hair.
36: 14 They made curtains of *g* hair
Lev 3: 12 " 'If his offering is a *g*, he is
4: 23 his offering a male *g* without defect
4: 28 for the sin he committed a female *g*
5: 6 or *g* from the flock as a sin offering;
9: 3 'Take a male *g* for a sin offering,
9: 15 He took the *g* for the people's sin
10: 16 When Moses inquired about the *g*
10: 18 you should have eaten the *g*
16: 9 shall bring the *g* whose lot falls
16: 10 But the *g* chosen by lot
16: 15 "He shall then slaughter the *g*
16: 20 he shall bring forward the live *g*.
16: 21 He shall send the *g* away
16: 21 hands on the head of the live *g*
16: 22 *g* will carry on itself all their sins
16: 26 "The man who releases the *g*
16: 27 and the *g* for the sin offerings,
17: 3 a lamb or a *g* in the camp
17: 7 any of their sacrifices to the *g* idols
22: 27 When a cow, a sheep or a *g* is born,
23: 19 Then sacrifice one male *g*
Nu 7: 16 one male *g* for a sin offering;
7: 22 one male *g* for a sin offering;
7: 28 one male *g* for a sin offering;
7: 34 one male *g* for a sin offering;
7: 40 one male *g* for a sin offering;
7: 46 one male *g* for a sin offering;
7: 52 one male *g* for a sin offering;
7: 58 one male *g* for a sin offering;
7: 64 one male *g* for a sin offering;
7: 70 one male *g* for a sin offering;
7: 76 one male *g* for a sin offering;
7: 82 one male *g* for a sin offering;
15: 11 or young *g*, is to be prepared
15: 24 and a male *g* for a sin offering.
15: 27 he must bring a year-old female *g*
18: 17 a sheep or a *g*; they are holy.
28: 15 one male *g* is to be presented
28: 22 Include one male *g* as a sin offering
28: 30 Include one male *g*
29: 5 Include one male *g* as a sin offering
29: 11 Include one male *g* as a sin offering
29: 16 Include one male *g* as a sin offering
29: 19 Include one male *g* as a sin offering
29: 22 Include one male *g* as a sin offering
29: 25 Include one male *g* as a sin offering
29: 28 Include one male *g* as a sin offering
29: 31 Include one male *g* as a sin offering
29: 34 Include one male *g* as a sin offering
29: 38 Include one male *g* as a sin offering
31: 20 everything made of leather, *g* hair
Dt 14: 4 the *g*, the deer, the gazelle,
14: 5 the roe deer, the wild *g*, the ibex,
14: 21 Do not cook a young *g*
Jdg 6: 19 went in, prepared a young *g*,
13: 15 until we prepare a young *g* for you
13: 19 Then Manoah took a young *g*,
14: 6 as he might have torn a young *g*.
15: 1 Samson took a young *g*
1Sa 16: 20 a skin of wine and a young *g*
2Ch 11: 15 for the *g* and calf idols he had made
Isa 11: 6 the leopard will lie down with the *g*
Eze 43: 22 are to offer a male *g* without defect
43: 25 are to provide a male *g* daily
45: 23 and a male *g* for a sin offering.
Da 8: 5 suddenly a *g* with a prominent
8: 7 the *g* knocked him to the ground
8: 8 The *g* became very great,
8: 21 The shaggy *g* is the king of Greece,
Lk 15: 29 even a young *g* so I could celebrate
Rev 6: 12 black like sackcloth made of *g* hair,

GOAT'S (GOAT)

Lev 4: 24 He is to lay his hand on the *g* head
16: 18 and some of the *g* blood and put it
16: 21 and put them on the *g* head.

GOATS (GOAT)

Ge 27: 9 and bring me two choice young *g*,
30: 35 all the male *g* that were streaked
30: 35 spotted female *g* (all that had white
31: 10 and saw that the male *g* mating
31: 12 and see that all the male *g* mating
31: 38 and *g* have not miscarried,
32: 5 sheep and *g*, menservants
32: 14 female *g* and twenty male *g*,
47: 17 their sheep and *g*, their cattle
Ex 9: 3 and on your cattle and sheep and *g*.
12: 5 them from the sheep or the *g*.
20: 24 your sheep and *g* and your cattle.
Lev 1: 10 from either the sheep or the *g*,
7: 23 any of the fat of cattle, sheep or *g*.
16: 5 to take two male *g* for a sin offering
16: 7 Then he is to take the two *g*
16: 8 He is to cast lots for the two *g*—
22: 19 *g* in order that it may be accepted
Nu 7: 17 five male *g* and five male lambs
7: 23 five male *g* and five male lambs
7: 29 five male *g* and five male lambs
7: 35 five male *g* and five male lambs
7: 41 five male *g* and five male lambs
7: 47 five male *g* and five male lambs
7: 53 five male *g* and five male lambs
7: 59 five male *g* and five male lambs
7: 65 five male *g* and five male lambs
7: 71 five male *g* and five male lambs
7: 77 five male *g* and five male lambs
7: 83 five male *g* and five male lambs
7: 87 Twelve male *g* were used
7: 88 sixty male *g* and sixty male lambs
31: 28 cattle, donkeys, sheep or *g*.
31: 30 donkeys, sheep, *g* or other animals.
Dt 32: 14 and with fattened lambs and *g*,
1Sa 10: 3 One will be carrying three young *g*,
24: 2 men near the Crags of the Wild *G*.
25: 2 had a thousand *g* and three
1Ki 4: 23 and a hundred sheep and *g*,
8: 63 and twenty thousand sheep and *g*.
20: 27 them like two small flocks of *g*,
2Ch 7: 5 and twenty thousand sheep and *g*.
14: 15 carried off droves of sheep and *g*
15: 11 and *g* from the plunder they had
17: 11 seven thousand seven hundred *g*.
29: 21 seven male lambs and seven male *g*
29: 23 *g* for the sin offering were brought
29: 24 The priests then slaughtered the *g*
29: 33 and three thousand sheep and *g*.
30: 24 and seven thousand sheep and *g*
30: 24 and ten thousand sheep and *g*.
35: 7 and *g* for the Passover offerings,
Ezr 6: 17 twelve male *g*, one for each
8: 35 and as a sin offering, twelve male *g*.
Job 39: 1 when the mountain *g* give birth?
Ps 50: 9 or of *g* from your pens,
50: 13 or drink the blood of *g*?
66: 15 I will offer bulls and *g*.
104: 18 mountains belong to the wild *g*;
Pr 27: 26 and the *g* with the price of a field.
SS 1: 8 and graze your young *g*
4: 1 Your hair is like a flock of *g*
6: 5 Your hair is like a flock of *g*
Isa 1: 11 the blood of bulls and lambs and *g*.
7: 21 keep alive a young cow and two *g*.
13: 21 and there the wild *g* will leap about
34: 6 the blood of lambs and *g*,
34: 14 and wild *g* will bleat to each other;
Jer 50: 8 and be like the *g* that lead the flock.
51: 40 like rams and *g*.
Eze 27: 21 with you in lambs, rams and *g*.
34: 17 another, and between rams and *g*.
39: 18 *g* and bulls—all of them fattened
Mt 25: 32 separates the sheep from the *g*.
25: 33 on his right and the *g* on his left.
Heb 9: 12 enter by means of the blood of *g*
9: 13 The blood of *g* and bulls
10: 4 of bulls and *g* to take away sins.

GOATS' (GOAT)

1Sa 19: 13 putting some *g'* hair at the head.
19: 16 and at the head was some *g'* hair.
Pr 27: 27 You will have plenty of *g'* milk

GOATSKINS

Ge 27: 16 part of his neck with the *g*.
Heb 11: 37 about in sheepskins and *g*,

GOB

2Sa 21: 18 battle with the Philistines, at *G*.
21: 19 battle with the Philistines at *G*,

GOBLET (GOBLETS)

SS 7: 2 Your navel is a rounded *g*
Isa 51: 17 the *g* that makes men stagger.
51: 22 from that cup, the *g* of my wrath,

GOBLETS (GOBLET)

1Ki 10: 21 All King Solomon's *g* were gold,
2Ch 9: 20 All King Solomon's *g* were gold,
Est 1: 7 Wine was served in *g* of gold,
Da 5: 2 silver *g* that Nebuchadnezzar his
5: 3 in the gold *g* that had been taken
5: 23 You had the *g* from his temple

GOD (GOD'S GODDESS GODLINESS GODLY GODS')

Ge 1: 1 In the beginning *G* created
1: 2 and the Spirit of *G* was hovering
1: 3 And *G* said, "Let there be light,"
1: 4 *G* saw that the light was good,
1: 5 *G* called the light "day"
1: 6 *G* said, "Let there be an expanse
1: 7 So *G* made the expanse
1: 8 *G* called the expanse "sky."
1: 9 And *G* said, "Let the water
1: 10 And *G* saw that it was good.
1: 10 *G* called the dry ground "land,"
1: 11 Then *G* said, "Let the land produce
1: 12 And *G* saw that it was good.
1: 14 And *G* said, "Let there be lights
1: 16 *G* made two great lights—
1: 17 *G* set them in the expanse
1: 18 And *G* saw that it was good.
1: 20 And *G* said, "Let the water teem
1: 21 And *G* saw that it was good.
1: 21 So *G* created the great creatures
1: 22 *G* blessed them and said, "Be
1: 24 And *G* said, "Let the land produce
1: 25 And *G* saw that it was good.
1: 25 *G* made the wild animals according
1: 26 Then *G* said, "Let us make man
1: 27 So *G* created man in his own image
1: 27 in the image of *G* he created him;
1: 28 *G* blessed them and said to them,
1: 29 Then *G* said, "I give you every
1: 31 *G* saw all that he had made,
2: 2 By the seventh day *G* had finished
2: 3 And *G* blessed the seventh day
2: 4 When the LORD *G* made the earth
2: 5 the LORD *G* had not sent rain
2: 7 And the LORD *G* formed man
2: 8 the LORD *G* had planted a garden
2: 9 And the LORD *G* made all kinds
2: 15 The LORD *G* took the man
2: 16 the LORD *G* commanded the man
2: 18 The LORD *G* said, "It is not good
2: 19 Now the LORD *G* had formed out
2: 21 So the LORD *G* caused the man
2: 22 Then the LORD *G* made a woman
3: 1 animals the LORD *G* had made.
3: 1 to the woman, "Did *G* really say,
3: 3 trees in the garden, but *G* did say,
3: 5 you will be like *G*, knowing good
3: 5 "For *G* knows that when you eat
3: 8 from the LORD *G* among the trees
3: 8 heard the sound of the LORD *G*
3: 9 But the LORD *G* called to the man
3: 13 the LORD *G* said to the woman,
3: 14 So the LORD *G* said to the serpent

Ge 3: 21 The LORD G made garments
3: 22 LORD G said, "The man has now
3: 23 So the LORD G banished him
4: 25 "G has granted me another child
5: 1 When G created man, he made him
5: 1 he made him in the likeness of G.
5: 22 Enoch walked with G 300 years
5: 24 because G took him away.
5: 24 with G; then he was no more,
6: 2 sons of G saw that the daughters
6: 4 when the sons of G went
6: 9 of his time, and he walked with G.
6: 12 G saw how corrupt the earth had
6: 13 So G said to Noah, "I am going
6: 22 just as G commanded him.
7: 9 as G had commanded Noah.
7: 16 as G had commanded Noah.
8: 1 But G remembered Noah
8: 15 Then G said to Noah, "Come out
9: 1 Then G blessed Noah and his sons,
9: 6 for in the image of G
9: 6 has G made man.
9: 8 G said to Noah and to his sons
9: 12 And G said, "This is the sign
9: 16 everlasting covenant between G
9: 17 So G said to Noah, "This is the sign
9: 26 "Blessed be the LORD, the G
9: 27 May G extend the territory
14: 18 He was priest of G Most High,
14: 19 Blessed be Abram by G Most High,
14: 20 And blessed be G Most High,
14: 22 G Most High, Creator of heaven
16: 13 "You are the G who sees me,"
17: 1 "I am G Almighty; walk before me
17: 3 Abram fell facedown, and G said
17: 7 to be your G and the G
17: 8 after you; and I will be their G."
17: 9 G said to Abraham, "As for you,
17: 15 G also said to Abraham, "As
17: 18 to G, "If only Ishmael might live
17: 19 under your blessing!" Then G said,
17: 22 speaking with Abraham, G went up
17: 23 circumcised them, as G told him.
19: 29 So when G destroyed the cities
20: 3 But G came to Abimelech
20: 6 Then G said to him in the dream,
20: 11 'There is surely no fear of G
20: 13 And when G had me wander
20: 17 to G, and G healed Abimelech,
21: 2 the very time G had promised him.
21: 4 him, as G commanded him.
21: 6 "G has brought me laughter,
21: 12 But G said to him, "Do not be
21: 17 and the angel of G called to Hagar
21: 17 G has heard the boy crying
21: 17 G heard the boy crying,
21: 19 Then G opened her eyes
21: 20 G was with the boy as he grew up.
21: 22 G is with you in everything you do.
21: 23 here before G that you will not deal
21: 33 name of the LORD, the Eternal G.
22: 1 Some time later G tested Abraham.
22: 2 Then G said, "Take your son,
22: 3 for the place G had told him about.
22: 8 "G himself will provide the lamb
22: 9 reached the place G had told him
22: 12 Now I know that you fear G,
24: 3 the G of heaven and the G of earth,
24: 7 "The LORD, the G of heaven,
24: 12 G of my master Abraham,
24: 27 the G of my master Abraham,
24: 42 G of my master Abraham,
24: 48 the G of my master Abraham,
25: 11 Abraham's death, G blessed his
26: 24 I am the G of your father Abraham.
27: 20 LORD your G gave me success,"
27: 28 May G give you of heaven's dew
28: 3 May G Almighty bless you
28: 4 the land G gave to Abraham."
28: 12 and the angels of G were ascending
28: 13 of your father Abraham and the G
28: 13 the G of your father Abraham
28: 17 other than the house of G;
28: 20 If G will be with me and will watch
28: 21 then the LORD will be my G.
30: 2 in the place of G, who has kept you
30: 6 Rachel said, "G has vindicated me;
30: 17 G listened to Leah, and she became
Ge 30: 18 "G has rewarded me
30: 20 "G has presented me
30: 22 Then G remembered Rachel;
30: 23 "G has taken away my disgrace."
31: 5 but the G of my father has been
31: 7 G has not allowed him to harm me.
31: 9 So G has taken away your father's
31: 11 The angel of G said to me
31: 13 I am the G of Bethel, where you
31: 16 So do whatever G has told you."
31: 16 all the wealth that G took away
31: 24 G came to Laban the Aramean
31: 29 last night the G of your father said
31: 42 But G has seen my hardship
31: 42 If the G of my father, the G
31: 50 remember that G is a witness
31: 53 May the G of Abraham
31: 53 of Abraham and the G of Nahor,
31: 53 the G of their father, judge
32: 1 and the angels of G met him.
32: 2 "This is the camp of G!"
32: 9 G of my father Abraham, G
32: 28 because you have struggled with G
32: 30 "It is because I saw G face to face,
33: 5 are the children G has graciously
33: 10 face is like seeing the face of G,
33: 11 for G has been gracious to me
35: 1 and build an altar there to G,
35: 1 like a prostitute?" Then G said
35: 3 where I will build an altar to G,
35: 5 and the terror of G fell
35: 7 it was there that G revealed himself
35: 9 Aram, G appeared to him again
35: 10 G said to him, "Your name is Jacob
35: 11 G said to him, "I am G Almighty;
35: 13 Then G went up from him
35: 14 at the place where G had talked
35: 15 the place where G had talked
39: 9 a wicked thing and sin against G?"
40: 8 Do not interpretations belong to G
41: 16 G will give Pharaoh the answer he
41: 25 G has revealed to Pharaoh what he
41: 28 G has shown Pharaoh what he is
41: 32 decided by G, and G will do it soon.
41: 38 one in whom is the spirit of G?"
41: 39 "Since G has made all this known
41: 51 G has made me forget all my
41: 52 G has made me fruitful in the land
42: 18 for I fear G: If you are honest men,
42: 28 "What is this that G has done to us
43: 14 may G Almighty grant you mercy
43: 23 Your G and the G of your father
43: 29 And he said, "G be gracious to you,
44: 16 G has uncovered your servants'
45: 5 to save lives that G sent me ahead
45: 7 G sent me ahead of you to preserve
45: 8 not you who sent me here, but G.
45: 9 G has made me lord of all Egypt.
46: 1 to the G of his father Isaac.
46: 2 And G spoke to Israel in a vision
46: 3 "I am G, the G of your father,"
48: 3 G Almighty appeared to me at Luz
48: 9 "They are the sons G has given me
48: 11 and now G has allowed me
48: 15 the G who has been my Shepherd
48: 15 "May the G before whom my
48: 20 'May G make you like Ephraim
48: 21 but G will be with you
49: 25 because of your father's G,
50: 17 servants of the G of your father."
50: 19 I in the place of G? You intended
50: 20 but G intended it for good
50: 24 But G will surely come to your aid
50: 25 "G will surely come to your aid,
Ex 1: 17 feared G and did not do what
1: 20 So G was kind to the midwives
1: 21 because the midwives feared G,
2: 23 of their slavery went up to G.
2: 24 G heard their groaning
2: 25 So G looked on the Israelites
3: 1 came to Horeb, the mountain of G.
3: 4 G called to him
3: 5 "Do not come any closer," G said.
3: 6 because he was afraid to look at G.
3: 6 of your father, the G of Abraham,
3: 6 the G of Isaac and the G of Jacob."
3: 6 "I am the G of your father,
3: 11 But Moses said to G, "Who am I,
Ex 3: 12 And G said, "I will be with you.
3: 12 you will worship G
3: 13 Moses said to G, "Suppose I go
3: 13 'The G of your fathers has sent me
3: 14 what shall I tell them?" G said
3: 15 G also said to Moses, "Say
3: 15 the G of Isaac and the G of Jacob—
3: 15 the G of your fathers—the G
3: 16 the G of Abraham, Isaac and Jacob
3: 16 'The LORD, the G of your fathers,
3: 18 sacrifices to the LORD our G.'
3: 18 'The LORD, the G of the Hebrews,
4: 5 the G of Isaac and the G of Jacob—
4: 5 the G of their fathers—the G
4: 16 and as if you were G to him.
4: 20 he took the staff of G in his hand.
4: 27 he met Moses at the mountain of G
5: 1 "This is what the LORD, the G
5: 3 sacrifices to the LORD our G,
5: 3 "The G of the Hebrews has met
5: 8 'Let us go and sacrifice to our G.'
6: 2 G also said to Moses, "I am
6: 3 and to Jacob as G Almighty,
6: 7 know that I am the LORD your G,
6: 7 own people, and I will be your G.
7: 1 I have made you like G to Pharaoh,
7: 16 'The LORD, the G of the Hebrews,
8: 10 is no one like the LORD our G.
8: 19 to Pharaoh, "This is the finger of G
8: 25 sacrifice to your G here in the land
8: 26 the LORD our G would be
8: 27 sacrifices to the LORD our G,
8: 28 to the LORD your G in the desert,
9: 1 the G of the Hebrews, says:
9: 13 the G of the Hebrews, says:
9: 30 still do not fear the LORD G."
10: 3 the G of the Hebrews, says:
10: 7 may worship the LORD their G.
10: 8 worship the LORD your G,"
10: 16 sinned against the LORD your G
10: 17 and pray to the LORD your G
10: 25 to present to the LORD our G.
10: 26 in worshiping the LORD our G,
13: 17 For G said, "If they face war,
13: 17 G did not lead them on the road
13: 18 So G led the people
13: 19 "G will surely come to your aid,
14: 19 angel of G, who had been traveling
15: 2 He is my G, and I will praise him,
15: 2 my father's G, and I will exalt him.
15: 26 to the voice of the LORD your G
16: 12 that I am the LORD your G.' "
17: 9 with the staff of G in my hands."
18: 1 heard of everything G had done
18: 4 "My father's G was my helper;
18: 5 camped near the mountain of G.
18: 12 father-in-law in the presence of G.
18: 12 offering and other sacrifices to G,
18: 19 people's representative before G
18: 19 you some advice, and may G be
18: 21 men who fear G, trustworthy men
18: 23 If you do this and G so commands,
19: 3 Then Moses went up to G,
19: 17 out of the camp to meet with G,
19: 19 and the voice of G answered him.
20: 1 And G spoke all these words:
20: 2 the LORD your G, who brought
20: 5 the LORD your G, am a jealous G,
20: 7 the name of the LORD your G,
20: 10 a Sabbath to the LORD your G.
20: 12 the LORD your G is giving you.
20: 19 But do not have G speak to us
20: 20 G has come to test you,
20: 20 the fear of G will be with you
20: 21 the thick darkness where G was.
21: 13 it intentionally, but G lets it
22: 20 "Whoever sacrifices to any g other
22: 28 "Do not blaspheme G
23: 19 to the house of the LORD your G.
23: 25 Worship the LORD your G,
24: 10 of Israel went up and saw the G
24: 11 But G did not raise his hand
24: 11 they saw G, and they ate and drank
24: 13 up on the mountain of G.
29: 45 among the Israelites and be their G
29: 46 I am the LORD their G.
29: 46 know that I am the LORD their G,
31: 3 him with the Spirit of G,

Ex 31:18 inscribed by the finger of *G*.
32:11 the favor of the LORD his *G*.
32:16 The tablets were the work of *G*;
32:16 the writing was the writing of *G*,
32:27 "This is what the LORD, the *G*
34: 6 the compassionate and gracious *G*,
34:14 Do not worship any other *g*,
34:14 name is Jealous, is a jealous *G*.
34:23 before the Sovereign LORD, the *G*
34:24 to appear before the LORD your *G*
34:26 to the house of the LORD your *G*.
35:31 him with the Spirit of *G*,
Lev 2:13 salt of the covenant of your *G* out
4:22 the commands of the LORD his *G*,
11:44 the LORD your *G*; consecrate
11:45 out of Egypt to be your *G*;
18: 2 to them: 'I am the LORD your *G*.
18: 4 I am the LORD your *G*.
18:21 not profane the name of your *G*.
18:30 I am the LORD your *G*.' "
19: 2 the LORD your *G*, am holy.
19: 3 I am the LORD your *G*.
19: 4 I am the LORD your *G*.
19:10 I am the LORD your *G*.
19:12 and so profane the name of your *G*.
19:14 front of the blind, but fear your *G*.
19:25 I am the LORD your *G*.
19:31 I am the LORD your *G*.
19:32 for the elderly and revere your *G*.
19:34 I am the LORD your *G*.
19:36 the LORD your *G*, who brought
20: 7 because I am the LORD your *G*.
20:24 am the LORD your *G*, who has set
21: 6 They must be holy to their *G*
21: 6 not profane the name of their *G*.
21: 6 the food of their *G*, they are
21: 7 because priests are holy to their *G*.
21: 8 they offer up the food of your *G*.
21:12 by the anointing oil of his *G*.
21:12 nor leave the sanctuary of his *G*
21:17 near to offer the food of his *G*.
21:21 near to offer the food of his *G*.
21:22 eat the most holy food of his *G*,
22:25 offer them as the food of your *G*.
22:33 out of Egypt to be your *G*.
23:14 you bring this offering to your *G*.
23:22 I am the LORD your *G*.' "
23:28 for you before the LORD your *G*.
23:40 rejoice before the LORD your *G*
23:43 I am the LORD your *G*.' "
24:15 'If anyone curses his *G*, he will be
24:22 I am the LORD your *G*.' "
25:17 I am the LORD your *G*.
25:17 of each other, but fear your *G*.
25:36 but fear your *G*, so that your
25:38 land of Canaan and to be your *G*.
25:38 the LORD your *G*, who brought
25:43 them ruthlessly, but fear your *G*.
25:55 I am the LORD your *G*.
26: 1 I am the LORD your *G*.
26:12 walk among you and be your *G*,
26:13 the LORD your *G*, who brought
26:44 I am the LORD their *G*.
26:45 sight of the nations to be their *G*.
Nu 6: 7 of his separation to *G* is on his head
10: 9 remembered by the LORD your *G*
10:10 I am the LORD your *G*."
10:10 a memorial for you before your *G*.
12:13 out to the LORD, "O *G*,
15:40 and will be consecrated to your *G*.
15:41 I am the LORD your *G*.' "
15:41 out of Egypt to be your *G*.
15:41 the LORD your *G*, who brought
16: 9 for you that the *G* of Israel has
16:22 O *G*, *G* of the spirits of all mankind,
21: 5 they spoke against *G*
22: 9 *G* came to Balaam and asked,
22:10 Balaam said to *G*, "Balak son
22:12 But *G* said to Balaam, "Do not go
22:18 the command of the LORD my *G*.
22:20 That night *G* came to Balaam
22:22 *G* was very angry when he went,
22:38 I must speak only what *G* puts
23: 4 *G* met with him, and Balaam said,
23: 8 those whom *G* has not cursed?
23:19 *G* is not a man, that he should lie,
23:21 The LORD their *G* is with them;
23:22 *G* brought them out of Egypt;
Nu 23:23 and of Israel, 'See what *G* has done
23:27 Perhaps it will please *G*
24: 2 the Spirit of *G* came upon him
24: 4 of one who hears the words of *G*,
24: 8 "*G* brought them out of Egypt;
24:16 of one who hears the words of *G*,
24:23 who can live when *G* does this?
25:13 zealous for the honor of his *G*
27:16 the *G* of the spirits of all mankind,
Dt 1: 6 The LORD our *G* said to us
1:10 LORD your *G* has increased your
1:11 May the LORD, the *G*
1:17 for judgment belongs to *G*.
1:19 as the LORD our *G* commanded us
1:20 which the LORD our *G* is giving us
1:21 the *G* of your fathers, told you.
1:21 the LORD your *G* has given you
1:25 that the LORD our *G* is giving us."
1:26 command of the LORD your *G*.
1:30 The LORD your *G*, who is going
1:31 the LORD your *G* carried you,
1:32 trust in the LORD your *G*,
1:41 as the LORD our *G* commanded us
2: 7 The LORD your *G* has blessed you
2: 7 years the LORD your *G* has been
2:29 land the LORD our *G* is giving us."
2:30 the LORD your *G* had made his
2:33 the LORD our *G* delivered him
2:36 The LORD our *G* gave us all
2:37 the command of the LORD our *G*.
3: 3 So the LORD our *G* also gave
3:18 LORD your *G* has given you this
3:20 the LORD your *G* is giving them,
3:21 all that the LORD your *G* has done
3:22 LORD your *G* himself will fight
3:24 For what *g* is there in heaven
4: 1 the *G* of your fathers, is giving you.
4: 2 of the LORD your *G* that I give
4: 3 The LORD your *G* destroyed
4: 4 to the LORD your *G* are still alive
4: 5 the LORD my *G* commanded me,
4: 7 them the way the LORD our *G* is
4:10 before the LORD your *G* at Horeb,
4:19 the LORD your *G* has apportioned
4:21 the LORD your *G* is giving you
4:23 of the LORD your *G* that he made
4:23 the LORD your *G* has forbidden.
4:24 is a consuming fire, a jealous *G*.
4:24 the LORD your *G* is a consuming
4:25 in the eyes of the LORD your *G*
4:29 there you seek the LORD your *G*,
4:30 return to the LORD your *G*
4:31 the LORD your *G* is a merciful *G*;
4:32 from the day *G* created man
4:33 the voice of *G* speaking out of fire,
4:34 Has any *g* ever tried to take
4:34 the things the LORD your *G* did
4:35 might know that the LORD is *G*;
4:39 heart this day that the LORD is *G*
4:40 land the LORD your *G* gives you
5: 2 The LORD our *G* made a covenant
5: 6 the LORD your *G*, who brought
5: 9 the LORD your *G*, am a jealous *G*,
5:11 the name of the LORD your *G*,
5:12 the LORD your *G* has commanded
5:14 a Sabbath to the LORD your *G*.
5:15 the LORD your *G* brought you out
5:15 the LORD your *G* has commanded
5:16 the LORD your *G* has commanded
5:16 the LORD your *G* is giving you
5:24 even if *G* speaks with him.
5:24 LORD our *G* has shown us his
5:25 of the LORD our *G* any longer.
5:26 of the living *G* speaking out of fire,
5:27 the LORD our *G* tells you.
5:27 to all that the LORD our *G* says.
5:32 the LORD your *G* has commanded
5:33 the LORD your *G* has commanded
6: 1 the LORD your *G* directed me
6: 2 them may fear the LORD your *G*
6: 3 the LORD, the *G* of your fathers,
6: 4 LORD our *G*, the LORD is one.
6: 5 Love the LORD your *G*
6:10 the LORD your *G* brings you
6:13 the LORD your *G*, serve him only
6:15 for the LORD your *G*, who is
6:15 is a jealous *G* and his anger will
6:16 Do not test the LORD your *G*
Dt 6:17 commands of the LORD your *G*
6:20 the LORD our *G* has commanded
6:24 and to fear the LORD our *G*,
6:25 law before the LORD our *G*,
7: 1 the LORD your *G* brings you
7: 2 the LORD your *G* has delivered
7: 6 holy to the LORD your *G*.
7: 6 LORD your *G* has chosen you out
7: 9 your *G* is *G*; he is the faithful *G*,
7:12 the LORD your *G* will keep his
7:16 peoples the LORD your *G* gives
7:18 well what the LORD your *G* did
7:19 LORD your *G* will do the same
7:19 the LORD your *G* brought you
7:20 LORD your *G* will send the hornet
7:21 for the LORD your *G*, who is
7:21 is a great and awesome *G*.
7:22 LORD your *G* will drive out those
7:23 LORD your *G* will deliver them
7:25 detestable to the LORD your *G*.
8: 2 how the LORD your *G* led you all
8: 5 the LORD your *G* disciplines you.
8: 6 commands of the LORD your *G*,
8: 7 the LORD your *G* is bringing you
8:10 praise the LORD your *G*
8:11 do not forget the LORD your *G*,
8:14 you will forget the LORD your *G*,
8:18 But remember the LORD your *G*,
8:19 you ever forget the LORD your *G*
8:20 for not obeying the LORD your *G*.
9: 3 that the LORD your *G* is the one
9: 4 the LORD your *G* has driven them
9: 5 LORD your *G* will drive them out
9: 6 the LORD your *G* is giving you
9: 7 you provoked the LORD your *G*
9:10 inscribed by the finger of *G*.
9:16 sinned against the LORD your *G*;
9:23 command of the LORD your *G*.
10: 9 as the LORD your *G* told them.)
10:12 but to fear the LORD your *G*,
10:12 to serve the LORD your *G*
10:12 what does the LORD your *G* ask
10:14 the LORD your *G* belong
10:17 For the LORD your *G* is *G* of gods
10:17 the great *G*, mighty and awesome,
10:20 Fear the LORD your *G*
10:21 He is your praise; he is your *G*,
10:22 the LORD your *G* has made you
11: 1 Love the LORD your *G*
11: 2 discipline of the LORD your *G*:
11:12 It is a land the LORD your *G* cares
11:12 the LORD your *G* are continually
11:13 to love the LORD your *G*
11:22 to love the LORD your *G*,
11:25 The LORD your *G*, as he promised
11:27 of the LORD your *G* that I am
11:28 commands of the LORD your *G*
11:29 the LORD your *G* has brought you
11:31 the LORD your *G* is giving you.
12: 1 the *G* of your fathers, has given you
12: 4 not worship the LORD your *G*
12: 5 the LORD your *G* will choose
12: 7 the LORD your *G* has blessed you.
12: 7 the presence of the LORD your *G*,
12: 9 the LORD your *G* is giving you.
12:10 the LORD your *G* is giving you
12:11 the LORD your *G* will choose
12:12 rejoice before the LORD your *G*,
12:15 the LORD your *G* gives you.
12:18 the LORD your *G* will choose
12:18 the presence of the LORD your *G*
12:18 to rejoice before the LORD your *G*
12:20 the LORD your *G* has enlarged
12:21 where the LORD your *G* chooses
12:27 on the altar of the LORD your *G*,
12:27 the altar of the LORD your *G*,
12:28 in the eyes of the LORD your *G*.
12:29 The LORD your *G* will cut
12:31 not worship the LORD your *G*
13: 3 The LORD your *G* is testing you
13: 4 the LORD your *G* you must
13: 5 against the LORD your *G*,
13: 5 LORD your *G* commanded you
13:10 away from the LORD your *G*,
13:12 the LORD your *G* is giving you
13:16 offering to the LORD your *G*.
13:18 you obey the LORD your *G*,
14: 1 the children of the LORD your *G*.

Dt 14: 2 holy to the LORD your *G*.
14: 21 holy to the LORD your *G*.
14: 23 the presence of the LORD your *G*
14: 23 to revere the LORD your *G* always
14: 24 blessed by the LORD your *G*
14: 25 the LORD your *G* will choose.
14: 26 the presence of the LORD your *G*
14: 29 the LORD your *G* may bless you
15: 4 the LORD your *G* is giving you
15: 5 you fully obey the LORD your *G*
15: 6 the LORD your *G* will bless you
15: 7 the LORD your *G* is giving you,
15: 10 the LORD your *G* will bless you
15: 14 the LORD your *G* has blessed you.
15: 15 the LORD your *G* redeemed you.
15: 18 the LORD your *G* will bless you
15: 19 the LORD your *G* every firstborn
15: 20 the presence of the LORD your *G*
15: 21 it to the LORD your *G*.
16: 1 the Passover of the LORD your *G*,
16: 2 to the LORD your *G* an animal
16: 5 town the LORD your *G* gives you
16: 7 the LORD your *G* will choose.
16: 8 an assembly to the LORD your *G*
16: 10 Weeks to the LORD your *G*
16: 10 the LORD your *G* has given you.
16: 11 rejoice before the LORD your *G*
16: 15 the Feast to the LORD your *G*
16: 15 the LORD your *G* will bless you
16: 16 appear before the LORD your *G*
16: 17 the LORD your *G* has blessed you.
16: 18 the LORD your *G* is giving you,
16: 20 the LORD your *G* is giving you.
16: 21 build to the LORD your *G*,
16: 22 for these the LORD your *G* hates.
17: 1 to the LORD your *G* an ox
17: 2 of the LORD your *G* in violation
17: 8 the LORD your *G* will choose.
17: 12 to the LORD your *G* must be put
17: 14 the LORD your *G* is giving you
17: 15 king the LORD your *G* chooses.
17: 19 learn to revere the LORD his *G*
18: 5 the LORD your *G* has chosen
18: 7 of the LORD his *G* like all his
18: 9 the LORD your *G* is giving you,
18: 12 the LORD your *G* will drive out
18: 13 before the LORD your *G*.
18: 14 LORD your *G* has not permitted
18: 15 The LORD your *G* will raise up
18: 16 of the LORD your *G* at Horeb
18: 16 the voice of the LORD our *G*
19: 1 the LORD your *G* has destroyed
19: 2 the LORD your *G* is giving you
19: 3 the LORD your *G* is giving you
19: 8 the LORD your *G* enlarges your
19: 9 to love the LORD your *G*
19: 10 the LORD your *G* is giving you
19: 14 the LORD your *G* is giving you
20: 1 because the LORD your *G*,
20: 4 For the LORD your *G* is the one
20: 13 When the LORD your *G* delivers it
20: 14 the LORD your *G* gives you
20: 16 the LORD your *G* is giving you
20: 17 the LORD your *G* has commanded
20: 18 sin against the LORD your *G*.
21: 1 the LORD your *G* is giving you
21: 5 the LORD your *G* has chosen
21: 10 the LORD your *G* delivers them
21: 23 the LORD your *G* is giving you
22: 5 the LORD your *G* detests anyone
23: 5 the LORD your *G* loves you.
23: 5 the LORD your *G* would not listen
23: 14 the LORD your *G* moves about
23: 18 LORD your *G* detests them both.
23: 18 the house of the LORD your *G*
23: 20 the LORD your *G* may bless you
23: 21 a vow to the LORD your *G*,
23: 21 the LORD your *G* will certainly
23: 23 freely to the LORD your *G*
24: 4 the LORD your *G* is giving you
24: 9 what the LORD your *G* did
24: 13 in the sight of the LORD your *G*.
24: 18 the LORD your *G* redeemed you
24: 19 the LORD your *G* may bless you
25: 15 the LORD your *G* is giving you.
25: 16 the LORD your *G* detests anyone
25: 18 behind; they had no fear of *G*.
25: 19 the LORD your *G* gives you rest

Dt 26: 1 the LORD your *G* is giving you
26: 2 the LORD your *G* is giving you
26: 2 the LORD your *G* will choose
26: 3 to the LORD your *G* that I have
26: 4 of the altar of the LORD your *G*.
26: 5 declare before the LORD your *G*:
26: 7 to the LORD, the *G* of our fathers,
26: 10 basket before the LORD your *G*
26: 11 things the LORD your *G* has given
26: 13 Then say to the LORD your *G*:
26: 14 I have obeyed the LORD my *G*;
26: 16 LORD your *G* commands you this
26: 17 this day that the LORD is your *G*
26: 19 holy to the LORD your *G*,
27: 2 the LORD your *G* is giving you,
27: 3 the LORD your *G* is giving you,
27: 3 the LORD, the *G* of your fathers,
27: 5 an altar to the LORD your *G*,
27: 6 on it to the LORD your *G*.
27: 6 the altar of the LORD your *G*
27: 7 the presence of the LORD your *G*.
27: 9 the people of the LORD your *G*.
27: 10 Obey the LORD your *G*
28: 1 If you fully obey the LORD your *G*
28: 1 the LORD your *G* will set you high
28: 2 you if you obey the LORD your *G*:
28: 8 The LORD your *G* will bless you
28: 9 commands of the LORD your *G*
28: 13 of the LORD your *G* that I give
28: 15 you do not obey the LORD your *G*
28: 45 did not obey the LORD your *G*
28: 47 serve the LORD your *G* joyfully
28: 52 the LORD your *G* is giving you.
28: 53 the LORD your *G* has given you.
28: 58 LORD your *G*— the LORD will
28: 62 did not obey the LORD your *G*.
29: 6 know that I am the LORD your *G*.
29: 10 presence of the LORD your *G*—
29: 12 a covenant with the LORD your *G*,
29: 13 that he may be your *G*
29: 15 in the presence of the LORD our *G*
29: 18 away from the LORD our *G* to go
29: 25 of the LORD, the *G* of their fathers
29: 29 belong to the LORD our *G*,
30: 1 the LORD your *G* disperses you
30: 2 return to the LORD your *G*
30: 3 the LORD your *G* will restore your
30: 4 the LORD your *G* will gather you
30: 6 The LORD your *G* will circumcise
30: 7 LORD your *G* will put all these
30: 9 LORD your *G* will make you most
30: 10 and turn to the LORD your *G*
30: 10 if you obey the LORD your *G*
30: 16 the LORD your *G* will bless you
30: 16 today to love the LORD your *G*,
30: 20 you may love the LORD your *G*,
31: 3 LORD your *G* himself will cross
31: 6 for the LORD your *G* goes
31: 11 to appear before the LORD your *G*
31: 12 and learn to fear the LORD your *G*
31: 13 and learn to fear the LORD your *G*
31: 17 come upon us because our *G* is not
31: 26 the covenant of the LORD your *G*.
32: 3 Oh, praise the greatness of our *G*!
32: 4 A faithful *G* who does no wrong,
32: 12 no foreign *g* was with him.
32: 15 He abandoned the *G* who made
32: 17 to demons, which are not *G*—
32: 18 you forgot the *G* who gave you
32: 21 made me jealous by what is no *g*
32: 39 There is no *g* besides me.
33: 1 of *G* pronounced on the Israelites
33: 26 "There is no one like the *G*
33: 27 The eternal *G* is your refuge,
Jos 1: 9 for the LORD your *G* will be
1: 11 the LORD your *G* is giving you
1: 13 LORD your *G* is giving you rest
1: 15 the LORD your *G* is giving them.
1: 17 Only may the LORD your *G* be
2: 11 for the LORD your *G* is *G*
3: 3 the covenant of the LORD your *G*,
3: 9 to the words of the LORD your *G*.
3: 10 you will know that the living *G* is
4: 5 the ark of the LORD your *G*
4: 23 For the LORD your *G* dried up
4: 23 The LORD your *G* did
4: 24 always fear the LORD your *G*."
7: 13 for this is what the LORD, the *G*

Jos 7: 19 glory to the LORD, the *G* of Israel,
7: 20 against the LORD, the *G* of Israel.
8: 7 The LORD your *G* will give it
8: 30 altar to the LORD, the *G* of Israel,
9: 9 of the fame of the LORD your *G*.
9: 18 by the LORD, the *G* of Israel.
9: 19 *G* of Israel, and we cannot touch
9: 23 carriers for the house of my *G*."
9: 24 LORD your *G* had commanded
10: 19 the LORD your *G* has given them
10: 40 the *G* of Israel, had commanded.
10: 42 because the LORD, the *G* of Israel,
13: 14 *G* of Israel, are their inheritance,
13: 33 the LORD, the *G* of Israel,
14: 6 said to Moses the man of *G*
14: 8 the LORD my *G* wholeheartedly.
14: 9 the LORD my *G* wholeheartedly.'
14: 14 the *G* of Israel, wholeheartedly.
18: 3 the *G* of your fathers, has given you
18: 6 in the presence of the LORD our *G*
22: 3 the LORD your *G* gave you.
22: 4 the LORD your *G* has given your
22: 5 to love the LORD your *G*,
22: 16 faith with the *G* of Israel like this?
22: 19 than the altar of the LORD our *G*.
22: 22 The Mighty One, *G*, the LORD!
22: 22 "The Mighty One, *G*, the LORD!
22: 24 do with the LORD, the *G* of Israel?
22: 29 of the LORD our *G* that stands
22: 33 to hear the report and praised *G*.
22: 34 BETWEEN US THAT THE LORD IS *G*.
23: 3 the LORD your *G* has done
23: 3 was the LORD your *G* who fought
23: 5 as the LORD your *G* promised you
23: 5 LORD your *G* himself will drive
23: 8 to hold fast to the LORD your *G*,
23: 10 the LORD your *G* fights for you,
23: 11 careful to love the LORD your *G*.
23: 13 the LORD your *G* has given you.
23: 13 the LORD your *G* will no longer
23: 14 the LORD your *G* gave you has
23: 15 of the LORD your *G* has come true
23: 16 the covenant of the LORD your *G*,
24: 1 presented themselves before *G*.
24: 2 "This is what the LORD, the *G*
24: 17 the LORD our *G* himself who
24: 18 the LORD, because he is our *G*."
24: 19 He is a holy *G*; he is a jealous *G*.
24: 23 to the LORD, the *G* of Israel."
24: 24 "We will serve the LORD our *G*
24: 26 things in the Book of the Law of *G*.
24: 27 you if you are untrue to your *G*."
Jdg 1: 7 *G* has paid me back for what I did
2: 12 They forsook the LORD, the *G*
3: 7 they forgot the LORD their *G*
3: 20 "I have a message from *G* for you."
4: 6 "The LORD, the *G* of Israel,
4: 23 On that day *G* subdued Jabin,
5: 3 to the LORD, the *G* of Israel.
5: 5 before the LORD, the *G* of Israel.
6: 8 "This is what the LORD, the *G*
6: 10 the LORD your *G*; do not worship
6: 20 The angel of *G* said to him,
6: 26 to the LORD your *G* on the top
6: 31 Baal really is a *g*, he can defend
6: 36 said to *G*, "If you will save Israel
6: 39 said to *G*, "Do not be angry
6: 40 That night *G* did so.
7: 14 *G* has given the Midianites
7: 15 its interpretation, he worshiped *G*.
8: 3 *G* gave Oreb and Zeeb,
8: 33 They set up Baal-Berith as their *g*
8: 34 not remember the LORD their *G*,
9: 7 so that *G* may listen to you.
9: 23 *G* sent an evil spirit
9: 24 *G* did this in order that the crime
9: 27 a festival in the temple of their *g*.
9: 56 Thus *G* repaid the wickedness that
9: 57 *G* also made the men
10: 10 forsaking our *G* and serving
11: 21 "Then the LORD, the *G* of Israel,
11: 23 since the LORD, the *G* of Israel,
11: 24 take what your *g* Chemosh gives
11: 24 the LORD our *G* has given us,
13: 5 is to be a Nazirite, set apart to *G*
13: 6 He looked like an angel of *G*,
13: 6 told him, "A man of *G* came to me.
13: 7 of *G* from birth until the day

Jdg 13: 8 let the man of *G* you sent
13: 9 and the angel of *G* came again
13: 9 *G* heard Manoah, and the angel
13: 22 "We have seen *G!*" But his wife
15: 19 *G* opened up the hollow place
16: 17 have been a Nazirite set apart to *G*
16: 23 a great sacrifice to Dagon their *g*
16: 23 "Our *g* has delivered Samson,
16: 24 they praised their *g*, saying,
16: 24 "Our *g* has delivered our enemy
16: 28 O *G*, please strengthen me just
18: 5 "Please inquire of *G* to learn
18: 10 and a spacious land that *G* has put
18: 31 the house of *G* was in Shiloh.
20: 2 in the assembly of the people of *G*,
20: 18 up to Bethel and inquired of *G*.
20: 27 ark of the covenant of *G* was there,
21: 2 sat before *G* until evening,
21: 3 "O LORD, the *G* of Israel,"
Ru 1: 16 be my people and your *G* my *G*.
2: 12 by the LORD, the *G* of Israel,
1Sa 1: 17 may the *G* of Israel grant you what
2: 2 there is no Rock like our *G*.
2: 3 for the LORD is a *G* who knows,
2: 25 another man, *G* may mediate
2: 27 Now a man of *G* came to Eli
2: 30 "Therefore the LORD, the *G*
3: 3 The lamp of *G* had not yet gone out
3: 3 the LORD, where the ark of *G* was.
3: 17 May *G* deal with you, be it ever
4: 4 with the ark of the covenant of *G*.
4: 7 "A *g* has come into the camp,"
4: 11 The ark of *G* was captured,
4: 13 his heart feared for the ark of *G*.
4: 17 and the ark of *G* has been captured
4: 18 When he mentioned the ark of *G*,
4: 19 the ark of *G* had been captured
4: 21 of the capture of the ark of *G*
4: 22 for the ark of *G* has been captured
5: 1 had captured the ark of *G*,
5: 7 of the *g* of Israel must not stay here
5: 7 upon us and upon Dagon our *g*."
5: 8 So they moved the ark of the *G*
5: 8 do with the ark of the *g* of Israel?"
5: 8 the ark of the *g* of Israel moved
5: 10 As the ark of *G* was entering Ekron
5: 10 So they sent the ark of *G* to Ekron.
5: 10 ark of the *g* of Israel around to us
5: 11 Send the ark of the *g* of Israel away
6: 3 "If you return the ark of the *g*
6: 5 and pay honor to Israel's *g*.
6: 19 *G* struck down some of the men
6: 20 this holy *G?* To whom will the ark
7: 8 out to the LORD our *G* for us,
9: 6 in this town there is a man of *G*;
9: 7 gift to take to the man of *G*.
9: 8 I will give it to the man of *G*
9: 9 if a man went to inquire of *G*,
9: 10 the town where the man of *G* was.
9: 27 I may give you a message from *G*."
10: 3 Three men going up to *G*
10: 5 that you will go to Gibeah of *G*,
10: 7 finds to do, for *G* is with you.
10: 9 to leave Samuel, *G* changed Saul's
10: 10 the Spirit of *G* came upon him
10: 18 "This is what the LORD, the *G*
10: 19 But you have now rejected your *G*,
10: 26 men whose hearts *G* had touched.
11: 6 the Spirit of *G* came upon him
12: 9 But they forgot the LORD their *G*;
12: 12 the LORD your *G* was your king.
12: 14 over you follow the LORD your *G*
12: 19 "Pray to the LORD your *G*
13: 13 the LORD your *G* gave you;
14: 15 It was a panic sent by *G*.
14: 18 to Ahijah, "Bring the ark of *G*."
14: 36 "Let us inquire of *G* here."
14: 37 But *G* did not answer him that day.
14: 37 So Saul asked *G*, "Shall I go
14: 41 to the LORD, the *G* of Israel,
14: 44 Saul said, "May *G* deal with me,
15: 15 to sacrifice to the LORD your *G*,
15: 21 the best of what was devoted to *G*,
15: 21 to the LORD your *G* at Gilgal."
15: 30 I may worship the LORD your *G*."
16: 15 spirit from *G* is tormenting you.
16: 16 spirit from *G* comes upon you,
16: 23 the spirit from *G* came upon Saul,

1Sa 17: 26 defy the armies of the living *G?*"
17: 36 defied the armies of the living *G*.
17: 45 the *G* of the armies of Israel,
17: 46 world will know that there is a *G*
18: 10 from *G* came forcefully upon Saul.
19: 20 the Spirit of *G* came
19: 23 But the Spirit of *G* came
20: 12 "By the LORD, the *G* of Israel,
22: 3 until I learn what *G* will do for me
22: 13 a sword and inquiring of *G* for him,
22: 15 day the first time I inquired of *G*
23: 7 "*G* has handed him over to me,
23: 10 David said, "O LORD, *G* of Israel,
23: 11 *G* of Israel, tell your servant."
23: 14 *G* did not give David into his hands
23: 16 and helped him find strength in *G*.
25: 22 May *G* deal with David, be it ever
25: 29 of the living by the LORD your *G*.
25: 32 be to the LORD, the *G* of Israel,
25: 34 surely as the LORD, the *G* of Israel
26: 8 Today *G* has delivered your enemy
28: 15 and *G* has turned away from me.
29: 9 in my eyes as an angel of *G*;
30: 6 strength in the LORD his *G*.
30: 15 before *G* that you will not kill me
2Sa 2: 27 answered, "As surely as *G* lives,
3: 9 May *G* deal with Abner, be it ever
3: 35 saying, "May *G* deal with me,
5: 10 the LORD *G* Almighty was
6: 2 to bring up from there the ark of *G*,
6: 3 They set the ark of *G* on a new cart
6: 4 cart with the ark of *G* on it,
6: 6 and took hold of the ark of *G*,
6: 7 he died there beside the ark of *G*.
6: 7 therefore *G* struck him down
6: 12 he has, because of the ark of *G*."
6: 12 the ark of *G* from the house
7: 2 while the ark of *G* remains in a tent
7: 22 and there is no *G* but you,
7: 23 on earth that *G* went out to redeem
7: 24 O LORD, have become their *G*.
7: 25 LORD *G*, keep forever
7: 26 'The LORD Almighty is *G*
7: 27 "O LORD Almighty, *G* of Israel,
7: 28 you are *G!* Your words are
10: 12 our people and the cities of our *G*.
12: 7 This is what the LORD, the *G*
12: 16 David pleaded with *G* for the child.
14: 11 the king invoke the LORD his *G*
14: 13 this against the people of *G?*
14: 14 But *G* does not take away life;
14: 16 from the inheritance *G* gave us.'
14: 17 May the LORD your *G* be
14: 17 an angel of *G* in discerning good
14: 20 that of an angel of *G*—
15: 24 They set down the ark of *G*,
15: 24 the ark of the covenant of *G*.
15: 25 Take the ark of *G* back into the city
15: 29 the ark of *G* back to Jerusalem
15: 32 where people used to worship *G*,
16: 23 that of one who inquires of *G*.
18: 28 "Praise be to the LORD your *G!*
19: 13 May *G* deal with me, be it ever
19: 27 lord the king is like an angel of *G*;
21: 14 *G* answered prayer in behalf
22: 3 my *G* is my rock, in whom I take
22: 7 I called out to my *G*.
22: 22 by turning from my *G*.
22: 30 with my *G* I can scale a wall.
22: 31 "As for *G*, his way is perfect,
22: 32 And who is the Rock except our *G*
22: 32 For who is *G* besides the LORD?
22: 33 It is *G* who arms me with strength
22: 47 Exalted be *G*, the Rock, my Savior!
22: 48 He is the *G* who avenges me,
23: 1 the man anointed by the *G* of Jacob
23: 3 The *G* of Israel spoke,
23: 3 when he rules in the fear of *G*,
23: 5 "Is not my house right with *G?*
24: 3 the LORD your *G* multiply
24: 23 May the LORD your *G* accept you
24: 24 the LORD my *G* burnt offerings
1Ki 1: 17 servant by the LORD your *G*:
1: 30 *G* of Israel: Solomon your son shall
1: 36 the *G* of my lord the king,
1: 47 'May your *G* make Solomon's
1: 48 be to the LORD, the *G* of Israel,
2: 3 what the LORD your *G* requires:

1Ki 2: 23 swore by the LORD: "May *G* deal
3: 5 and *G* said, "Ask for whatever you
3: 7 O LORD my *G*, you have made
3: 11 So *G* said to him, "Since you have
3: 28 from *G* to administer justice.
4: 29 *G* gave Solomon wisdom
5: 3 the Name of the LORD his *G*
5: 4 now the LORD my *G* has given me
5: 5 for the Name of the LORD my *G*,
8: 15 be to the LORD, the *G* of Israel,
8: 17 of the LORD, the *G* of Israel.
8: 20 of the LORD, the *G* of Israel.
8: 23 and said: "O LORD, *G* of Israel,
8: 23 there is no *G* like you in heaven
8: 25 "Now LORD, *G* of Israel,
8: 26 O *G* of Israel, let your word that
8: 27 "But will *G* really dwell on earth?
8: 28 his plea for mercy, O LORD my *G*.
8: 57 May the LORD our *G* be with us
8: 59 be near to the LORD our *G* day
8: 60 may know that the LORD is *G*
8: 61 committed to the LORD our *G*,
8: 65 it before the LORD our *G*
9: 9 have forsaken the LORD their *G*,
10: 9 Praise be to the LORD your *G*,
10: 24 to hear the wisdom *G* had put
11: 4 devoted to the LORD his *G*,
11: 5 and Molech the detestable *g*
11: 7 and for Molech the detestable *g*
11: 7 place for Chemosh the detestable *g*
11: 9 the *G* of Israel, who had appeared
11: 23 And *G* raised up against Solomon
11: 31 for this is what the LORD, the *G*
11: 33 Chemosh the *g* of the Moabites,
11: 33 Molech the *g* of the Ammonites,
12: 22 But this word of *G* came
12: 22 came to Shemaiah the man of *G*:
13: 1 of *G* came from Judah to Bethel,
13: 3 same day the man of *G* gave a sign:
13: 4 man of *G* cried out against the altar
13: 5 given by the man of *G* by the word
13: 6 So the man of *G* interceded
13: 6 Then the king said to the man of *G*,
13: 6 "Intercede with the LORD your *G*
13: 7 The king said to the man of *G*,
13: 8 the man of *G* answered the king,
13: 11 man of *G* had done there that day.
13: 12 man of *G* from Judah had taken
13: 14 and rode after the man of *G*.
13: 14 man of *G* who came from Judah?"
13: 16 man of *G* said, "I cannot turn back
13: 19 So the man of *G* returned with him
13: 21 out to the man of *G* who had come
13: 21 the LORD your *G* gave you.
13: 23 the man of *G* had finished eating
13: 26 the man of *G* who defied the word
13: 29 up the body of the man of *G*,
13: 31 grave where the man of *G* is buried;
14: 7 that this is what the LORD, the *G*
14: 13 the *G* of Israel, has found anything
15: 3 devoted to the LORD his *G*,
15: 4 sake the LORD his *G* gave him
15: 30 he provoked the LORD, the *G*
16: 13 the *G* of Israel to anger
16: 26 they provoked the LORD, the *G*
16: 33 the *G* of Israel, to anger
17: 1 As the LORD, the *G* of Israel, lives
17: 12 as the LORD your *G* lives,"
17: 14 For this is what the LORD, the *G*
17: 18 have against me, man of *G?*
17: 20 to the LORD, "O LORD my *G*,
17: 21 "O LORD my *G*, let this boy's life
17: 24 I know that you are a man of *G*
18: 10 as the LORD your *G* lives,
18: 21 If the LORD is *G*, follow him;
18: 21 but if Baal is *G*, follow him."
18: 24 The *g* who answers by fire—
18: 24 answers by fire—he is *G*."
18: 24 you call on the name of your *g*,
18: 25 Call on the name of your *g*,
18: 27 Surely he is a *g!* Perhaps he is deep
18: 36 it be known today that you are *G*
18: 36 "O LORD, *G* of Abraham,
18: 37 are *G*, and that you are turning
18: 39 The LORD—he is *G!* The LORD
18: 39 he is *G!*" Then Elijah commanded
19: 8 reached Horeb, the mountain of *G*.
19: 10 for the LORD *G* Almighty.

1Ki 19: 14 for the LORD G Almighty.
20: 28 The man of G came up
20: 28 a g of the hills and not a g
21: 10 testify that he has cursed both G
21: 13 "Naboth has cursed both G
22: 53 and provoked the LORD, the G
2Ki 1: 2 consult Baal-Zebub, the g of Ekron
1: 3 there is no G in Israel that you are
1: 3 g of Ekron?' Therefore this is what
1: 6 there is no G in Israel that you are
1: 6 g of Ekron? Therefore you will not
1: 9 "Man of G, the king says, 'Come
1: 10 the captain, "If I am a man of G,
1: 11 Man of G, this is what the king says
1: 12 If I am a man of G," Elijah replied,
1: 12 Then the fire of G fell from heaven
1: 13 of G," he begged, "please have
1: 16 the g of Ekron? Because you have
1: 16 there is no G in Israel for you
2: 14 the G of Elijah?" he asked.
4: 7 She went and told the man of G,
4: 9 comes our way is a holy man of G.
4: 16 man of G!" But the woman became
4: 21 laid him on the bed of the man of G
4: 22 so I can go to the man of G quickly
4: 25 of G said to his servant Gehazi,
4: 25 to the man of G at Mount Carmel.
4: 27 man of G said, "Leave her alone!
4: 27 the man of G at the mountain,
4: 40 they cried out, "O man of G,
4: 42 the man of G twenty loaves
5: 7 he tore his robes and said, "Am I G
5: 8 the man of G heard that the king
5: 11 on the name of the LORD his G,
5: 14 as the man of G had told him,
5: 15 went back to the man of G.
5: 15 "Now I know that there is no G
5: 17 and sacrifices to any other g
5: 20 the servant of Elisha the man of G,
6: 6 of G asked, "Where did it fall?"
6: 9 The man of G sent word to the king
6: 10 place indicated by the man of G.
6: 15 the servant of the man of G got up
6: 31 He said, "May G deal with me,
7: 2 was leaning said to the man of G,
7: 17 as the man of G had foretold
7: 18 the man of G had said to the king:
7: 19 The man of G had replied,
7: 19 officer had said to the man of G,
8: 2 to do as the man of G said.
8: 4 the servant of the man of G,
8: 7 of G has come all the way up here,"
8: 8 and go to meet the man of G.
8: 11 Then the man of G began to weep.
9: 6 "This is what the LORD, the G
10: 31 the G of Israel, with all his heart.
13: 19 The man of G was angry with him
14: 25 word of the LORD, the G of Israel,
16: 2 in the eyes of the LORD his G.
17: 7 sinned against the LORD their G,
17: 9 the LORD their G that were not
17: 14 trust in the LORD their G.
17: 16 commands of the LORD their G
17: 19 commands of the LORD their G.
17: 26 of Samaria do not know what the g
17: 27 and teach the people what the g
17: 39 Rather, worship the LORD your G
18: 5 in the LORD, the G of Israel.
18: 12 had not obeyed the LORD their G,
18: 22 depending on the LORD our G"—
18: 33 Has the g of any nation ever
19: 4 has sent to ridicule the living G,
19: 4 that the LORD your G will hear all
19: 4 the LORD your G has heard.
19: 10 Do not let the g you depend
19: 15 G of Israel, enthroned
19: 15 you alone are G over all
19: 16 sent to insult the living G.
19: 19 Now, O LORD our G, deliver us
19: 19 that you alone, O LORD, are G."
19: 20 "This is what the LORD, the G
19: 37 in the temple of his g Nisroch,
20: 5 the G of your father David, says:
21: 12 this is what the LORD, the G
21: 22 He forsook the LORD, the G
22: 15 "This is what the LORD, the G
22: 18 'This is what the LORD, the G
23: 13 and for Molech the detestable g
2Ki 23: 13 for Chemosh the vile g of Moab,
23: 16 of G who foretold these things.
23: 17 tomb of the man of G who came
23: 21 the Passover to the LORD your G,
1Ch 4: 10 And G granted his request.
4: 10 Jabez cried out to the G of Israel,
5: 20 and G handed the Hagrites
5: 25 unfaithful to the G of their fathers
5: 25 whom G had destroyed
5: 26 the G of Israel stirred up the spirit
6: 48 of the tabernacle, the house of G.
6: 49 the servant of G had commanded.
9: 11 official in charge of the house of G;
9: 13 for ministering in the house of G.
9: 26 and treasuries in the house of G.
9: 27 stationed around the house of G,
11: 2 And the LORD your G said to you,
11: 19 "G forbid that I should do this!"
12: 17 may the G of our fathers see it
12: 18 for your G will help you."
13: 2 if it is the will of the LORD our G,
13: 3 the ark of our G back to us,
13: 5 the ark of G from Kiriath Jearim.
13: 6 from there the ark of G the LORD,
13: 7 ark of G from Abinadab's house
13: 8 with all their might before G,
13: 10 So he died there before G.
13: 12 David was afraid of G that day
13: 12 "How can I ever bring the ark of G
13: 14 The ark of G remained
14: 10 so David inquired of G: "Shall I go
14: 11 G has broken out against my
14: 14 of G again, and G answered him,
14: 15 that will mean G has gone out
14: 16 David did as G commanded him,
15: 1 he prepared a place for the ark of G
15: 2 the Levites may carry the ark of G,
15: 12 the G of Israel, to the place I have
15: 13 that the LORD our G broke out
15: 14 ark of the LORD, the G of Israel.
15: 15 the ark of G with the poles
15: 24 trumpets before the ark of G.
15: 26 Because G had helped the Levites
16: 1 They brought the ark of G
16: 1 and fellowship offerings before G.
16: 4 to praise the LORD, the G of Israel
16: 6 before the ark of the covenant of G.
16: 14 He is the LORD our G;
16: 35 Cry out, "Save us, O G our Savior;
16: 36 to the LORD, the G of Israel,
17: 2 in mind, do it, for G is with you."
17: 3 the word of G came to Nathan,
17: 16 O LORD G, and what is my family
17: 17 enough in your sight, O G,
17: 17 exalted of men, O LORD G.
17: 20 and there is no G but you,
17: 21 nation on earth whose G went out
17: 22 O LORD, have become their G.
17: 24 the G over Israel, is Israel's G!'
17: 25 my G, have revealed
17: 26 you are G! You have given this
19: 13 our people and the cities of our G.
21: 7 was also evil in the sight of G;
21: 8 said to G, "I have sinned greatly
21: 15 And G sent an angel to destroy
21: 17 have they done? O LORD my G,
21: 17 to G, "Was it not I who ordered
21: 30 go before it to inquire of G,
22: 1 house of the LORD G is to be here,
22: 2 stone for building the house of G.
22: 6 for the LORD, the G of Israel.
22: 7 for the Name of the LORD my G.
22: 11 the house of the LORD your G,
22: 12 the law of the LORD your G.
22: 18 Is not the LORD your G with you?
22: 19 soul to seeking the LORD your G.
22: 19 the sacred articles belonging to G
22: 19 the sanctuary of the LORD G,
23: 14 the man of G were counted
23: 25 "Since the LORD, the G of Israel,
23: 28 of other duties at the house of G.
24: 5 of G among the descendants
24: 19 as the LORD, the G of Israel,
25: 5 G gave Heman fourteen sons
25: 5 him through the promises of G
25: 6 for the ministry at the house of G.
26: 5 (For G had blessed Obed-Edom.)
26: 20 of the treasuries of the house of G
1Ch 26: 32 for every matter pertaining to G
28: 2 for the footstool of our G,
28: 3 But G said to me, 'You are not
28: 4 "Yet the LORD, the G of Israel,
28: 8 and in the hearing of our G:
28: 8 commands of the LORD your G,
28: 9 acknowledge the G of your father,
28: 12 for the treasuries of the temple of G
28: 20 for the LORD G, my G, is with you
28: 21 for all the work on the temple of G,
29: 1 not for man but for the LORD G.
29: 1 the one whom G has chosen,
29: 2 provided for the temple of my G—
29: 3 and silver for the temple of my G,
29: 3 of my G I now give my personal
29: 7 temple of G five thousand talents
29: 10 G of our father Israel,
29: 13 Now, our G, we give you thanks,
29: 16 O LORD our G, as for all this
29: 17 my G, that you test the heart
29: 18 G of our fathers Abraham,
29: 20 they all praised the LORD, the G
29: 20 "Praise the LORD your G."
2Ch 1: 1 for the LORD his G was with him
1: 4 David had brought up the ark of G
1: 7 That night G appeared to Solomon
1: 8 Solomon answered G, "You have
1: 9 Now, LORD G, let your promise
1: 11 of yours?" G said to Solomon,
2: 4 feasts of the LORD our G.
2: 4 for the Name of the LORD my G
2: 5 our G is greater than all other gods.
2: 12 be to the LORD, the G of Israel,
3: 3 temple of G was sixty cubits long
4: 11 Solomon in the temple of G:
5: 14 of the LORD filled the temple of G
6: 4 be to the LORD, the G of Israel,
6: 7 of the LORD, the G of Israel.
6: 10 of the LORD, the G of Israel.
6: 14 He said: "O LORD, G of Israel,
6: 14 there is no G like you in heaven
6: 16 "Now LORD, G of Israel,
6: 17 And now, O LORD, G of Israel,
6: 18 "But will G really dwell on earth
6: 19 his plea for mercy, O LORD my G.
6: 40 my G, may your eyes be open
6: 41 O LORD G, and come
6: 41 O LORD G, be clothed
6: 42 O LORD G, do not reject your
7: 5 people dedicated the temple of G.
7: 22 have forsaken the LORD, the G
8: 14 David the man of G had ordered.
9: 8 Praise be to the LORD your G,
9: 8 king to rule for the LORD your G.
9: 8 of the love of your G for Israel
9: 23 to hear the wisdom G had put
10: 15 for this turn of events was from G,
11: 2 came to Shemaiah the man of G:
11: 16 G of Israel, followed the Levites
11: 16 to the LORD, the G of their fathers
13: 5 you know that the LORD, the G
13: 10 LORD is our G, and we have not
13: 11 requirements of the LORD our G.
13: 12 fight against the LORD, the G
13: 12 G is with us; he is our leader.
13: 15 G routed Jeroboam and all Israel
13: 16 G delivered them into their hands.
13: 18 relied on the LORD, the G
14: 2 in the eyes of the LORD his G.
14: 4 Judah to seek the LORD, the G
14: 7 we have sought the LORD our G;
14: 11 Asa called to the LORD his G
14: 11 O LORD our G, for we rely on you
14: 11 you are our G; do not let man
15: 1 The Spirit of G came
15: 3 was without the true G,
15: 4 the G of Israel, and sought him,
15: 6 because G was troubling them
15: 9 they saw that the LORD his G was
15: 12 the G of their fathers,
15: 13 would not seek the LORD, the G
15: 15 They sought G eagerly,
15: 18 into the temple of G the silver
16: 7 and not on the LORD your G,
17: 4 but sought the G of his father
18: 5 "for G will give it into the king's
18: 13 I can tell him only what my G says
18: 31 G drew them away from him,

2Ch 19: 3 have set your heart on seeking *G.*''
19: 4 to the LORD, the *G* of their fathers
19: 7 with the LORD our *G* there is no
20: 6 are you not the *G* who is in heaven?
20: 6 "O LORD, *G* of our fathers,
20: 7 O our *G*, did you not drive out
20: 12 O our *G*, will you not judge them?
20: 19 *G* of Israel, with very loud voice.
20: 20 Have faith in the LORD your *G*
20: 29 The fear of *G* came
20: 30 for his *G* had given him rest
20: 33 hearts on the *G* of their fathers.
21: 10 had forsaken the LORD, the *G*
21: 12 the *G* of your father David, says:
22: 7 *G* brought about Ahaziah's
22: 12 at the temple of *G* for six years
23: 3 with the king at the temple of *G*.
23: 9 and that were in the temple of *G*.
24: 5 to repair the temple of your *G*.
24: 7 broken into the temple of *G*
24: 9 servant of *G* had required of Israel
24: 13 rebuilt the temple of *G* according
24: 16 good he had done in Israel for *G*
24: 18 of the LORD, the *G* of their fathers
24: 20 Then the Spirit of *G* came
24: 20 "This is what *G* says: 'Why do you
24: 24 had forsaken the LORD, the *G*
24: 27 of the temple of *G* are written
25: 7 But a man of *G* came to him
25: 8 for *G* has the power to help
25: 8 *G* will overthrow you
25: 9 Amaziah asked the man of *G*,
25: 9 of *G* replied, "The LORD can give
25: 16 "I know that *G* has determined
25: 20 for *G* so worked that he might hand
25: 24 in the temple of *G* that had been
26: 5 He sought *G* during the days
26: 5 sought the LORD, *G* gave him
26: 5 who instructed him in the fear of *G*
26: 7 *G* helped him
26: 16 unfaithful to the LORD his *G*,
26: 18 honored by the LORD *G*."
27: 6 before the LORD his *G*.
28: 5 the LORD his *G* handed him
28: 6 had forsaken the LORD, the *G*
28: 9 "Because the LORD, the *G*
28: 10 of sins against the LORD your *G*?
28: 24 furnishings from the temple of *G*
28: 25 the *G* of his fathers, to anger.
29: 5 of the LORD, the *G* of your fathers
29: 6 evil in the eyes of the LORD our *G*
29: 7 at the sanctuary to the *G* of Israel.
29: 10 with the LORD, the *G* of Israel,
29: 36 at what *G* had brought about
30: 1 to the LORD, the *G* of Israel.
30: 5 to the LORD, the *G* of Israel.
30: 6 to the LORD, the *G* of Abraham,
30: 7 to the LORD, the *G* of their fathers
30: 8 Serve the LORD your *G*,
30: 9 for the LORD your *G* is gracious
30: 12 the hand of *G* was on the people
30: 16 in the Law of Moses the man of *G*.
30: 19 the LORD, the *G* of his fathers—
30: 19 who sets his heart on seeking *G*—
30: 22 and praised the LORD, the *G*
30: 27 and *G* heard them, for their prayer
31: 6 dedicated to the LORD their *G*,
31: 13 in charge of the temple of *G*.
31: 14 of the freewill offerings given to *G*,
31: 20 faithful before the LORD his *G*.
31: 21 he sought his *G* and worked
32: 8 but with us is the LORD our *G*
32: 11 'The LORD our *G* will save us
32: 14 How then can your *g* deliver you
32: 15 for no *g* of any nation or kingdom
32: 15 much less will your *g* deliver you
32: 16 further against the LORD *G*
32: 17 so the *g* of Hezekiah will not rescue
32: 17 the *G* of Israel, and saying this
32: 19 They spoke about the *G*
32: 21 went into the temple of his *g*,
32: 29 for *G* had given him very great
32: 31 *G* left him to test him
33: 7 of which *G* had said to David
33: 12 greatly before the *G* of his fathers.
33: 12 the favor of the LORD his *G*
33: 13 knew that the LORD is *G*.
33: 16 to serve the LORD, the *G* of Israel.

2Ch 33: 17 but only to the LORD their *G*.
33: 18 including his prayer to his *G*
33: 18 the *G* of Israel, are written
33: 19 how *G* was moved by his entreaty,
34: 3 to seek the *G* of his father David.
34: 8 the temple of the LORD his *G*.
34: 9 brought into the temple of *G*,
34: 23 "This is what the LORD, the *G*
34: 26 'This is what the LORD, the *G*
34: 27 and you humbled yourself before *G*
34: 32 of *G*, the *G* of their fathers.
34: 33 fail to follow the LORD, the *G*
34: 33 in Israel serve the LORD their *G*.
35: 3 Now serve the LORD your *G*
35: 21 *G* has told me to hurry;
35: 21 so stop opposing *G*, who is with me
36: 5 evil in the eyes of the LORD his *G*.
36: 12 evil in the eyes of the LORD his *G*
36: 13 turn to the LORD, the *G* of Israel.
36: 15 The LORD, the *G* of their fathers,
36: 17 *G* handed all of them
36: 18 the articles from the temple of *G*,
36: 23 may the LORD his *G* be with him,
36: 23 " 'The LORD, the *G* of heaven,
Ezr 1: 2 " 'The LORD, the *G* of heaven,
1: 3 people among you—may his *G* be
1: 3 the *G* of Israel, the *G* who is
1: 4 for the temple of *G* in Jerusalem.' "
1: 5 whose heart *G* had moved—
1: 7 had placed in the temple of his *g*.
2: 68 of the house of *G* on its site.
3: 2 in the Law of Moses the man of *G*.
3: 2 to build the altar of the *G* of Israel
3: 8 at the house of *G* in Jerusalem,
3: 9 working on the house of *G*.
4: 1 the *G* of Israel, they came
4: 2 we seek your *G* and have been
4: 3 the *G* of Israel, as King Cyrus,
4: 3 us in building a temple to our *G*.
4: 24 the house of *G* in Jerusalem came
5: 1 in the name of the *G* of Israel,
5: 2 the house of *G* in Jerusalem.
5: 2 the prophets of *G* were with them,
5: 5 the eye of their *G* was watching
5: 8 to the temple of the great *G*.
5: 11 the servants of the *G* of heaven
5: 12 because our fathers angered the *G*
5: 13 a decree to rebuild this house of *G*.
5: 14 silver articles of the house of *G*,
5: 15 rebuild the house of *G* on its site.'
5: 16 of the house of *G* in Jerusalem.
5: 17 house of *G* in Jerusalem.
6: 3 the temple of *G* in Jerusalem:
6: 5 silver articles of the house of *G*,
6: 5 to be deposited in the house of *G*.
6: 7 elders rebuild this house of *G*
6: 7 with the work on this temple of *G*.
6: 8 the construction of this house of *G*:
6: 9 offerings to the *G* of heaven,
6: 10 pleasing to the *G* of heaven
6: 12 May *G*, who has caused his Name
6: 14 to the command of the *G* of Israel
6: 16 of the house of *G* with joy.
6: 17 of *G* they offered a hundred bulls,
6: 18 for the service of *G* at Jerusalem,
6: 21 to seek the LORD, the *G* of Israel.
6: 22 on the house of *G*, the *G* of Israel.
7: 6 of the LORD his *G* was on him.
7: 6 which the LORD, the *G* of Israel,
7: 9 hand of his *G* was on him.
7: 12 of the Law of the *G* of heaven:
7: 14 with regard to the Law of your *G*,
7: 15 advisers have freely given to the *G*
7: 16 the temple of their *G* in Jerusalem.
7: 17 the temple of your *G* in Jerusalem.
7: 18 accordance with the will of your *G*.
7: 19 Deliver to the *G* of Jerusalem all
7: 19 for worship in the temple of your *G*
7: 20 of your *G* that you may have
7: 21 of the Law of the *G* of heaven,
7: 23 Whatever the *G* of heaven has
7: 23 for the temple of the *G* of heaven.
7: 24 or other workers at this house of *G*.
7: 25 all who know the laws of your *G*.
7: 25 with the wisdom of your *G*,
7: 26 does not obey the law of your *G*
7: 27 to the LORD, the *G* of our fathers,
7: 28 of the LORD my *G* was on me,

Ezr 8: 17 to us for the house of our *G*.
8: 18 hand of our *G* was on us,
8: 21 humble ourselves before our *G*
8: 22 "The good hand of our *G* is
8: 23 and petitioned our *G* about this,
8: 25 donated for the house of our *G*.
8: 28 to the LORD, the *G* of your fathers
8: 30 to the house of our *G* in Jerusalem.
8: 31 The hand of our *G* was on us,
8: 33 in the house of our *G*,
8: 35 sacrificed burnt offerings to the *G*
8: 36 to the people and to the house of *G*.
9: 4 words of the *G* of Israel gathered
9: 5 out to the LORD my *G*
9: 6 to lift up my face to you, my *G*,
9: 6 "O my *G*, I am too ashamed
9: 8 and so our *G* gives light to our eyes
9: 8 the LORD our *G* has been gracious
9: 9 life to rebuild the house of our *G*
9: 9 our *G* has not deserted us
9: 10 O our *G*, what can we say after this
9: 13 our *G*, you have punished us less
9: 15 *G* of Israel, you are righteous!
10: 1 down before the house of *G*,
10: 2 to our *G* by marrying foreign
10: 3 before our *G* to send away all these
10: 3 who fear the commands of our *G*.
10: 6 from before the house of *G*
10: 9 in the square before the house of *G*,
10: 11 to the LORD, the *G* of your fathers
10: 14 until the fierce anger of our *G*
Ne 1: 4 and prayed before the *G* of heaven.
1: 5 I said: "O LORD, *G* of heaven,
1: 5 the great and awesome *G*,
2: 4 Then I prayed to the *G* of heaven,
2: 8 hand of my *G* was upon me,
2: 12 not told anyone what my *G* had put
2: 18 about the gracious hand of my *G*
2: 20 *G* of heaven will give us success.
4: 4 O our *G*, for we are despised.
4: 9 But we prayed to our *G*
4: 15 and that *G* had frustrated it,
4: 20 Our *G* will fight for us!"
5: 9 fear of our *G* to avoid the reproach
5: 13 "In this way may *G* shake out
5: 15 for *G* I did not act like that.
5: 19 Remember me with favor, O my *G*,
6: 10 "Let us meet in the house of *G*,
6: 12 I realized that *G* had not sent him,
6: 14 Tobiah and Sanballat, O my *G*,
6: 16 done with the help of our *G*.
7: 2 feared *G* more than most men do.
7: 5 So my *G* put it into my heart
8: 6 praised the LORD, the great *G*;
8: 8 from the Book of the Law of *G*,
8: 9 sacred to the LORD your *G*.
8: 16 in the courts of the house of *G*
8: 18 from the Book of the Law of *G*.
9: 3 in worshiping the LORD their *G*.
9: 3 of the LORD their *G* for a fourth
9: 4 voices to the LORD their *G*.
9: 5 and praise the LORD your *G*,
9: 7 are the LORD *G*, who chose
9: 17 But you are a forgiving *G*,
9: 18 'This is your *g*, who brought you up
9: 31 you are a gracious and merciful *G*.
9: 32 Now therefore, O our *G*, the great,
9: 32 the great, mighty and awesome *G*,
10: 28 for the sake of the Law of *G*,
10: 29 and decrees of the LORD our *G*.
10: 29 oath to follow the Law of *G* given
10: 29 through Moses the servant of *G*
10: 32 the service of the house of our *G*:
10: 33 the duties of the house of our *G*.
10: 34 is to bring to the house of our *G*
10: 34 on the altar of the LORD our *G*,
10: 36 of our flocks to the house of our *G*,
10: 37 storerooms of the house of our *G*,
10: 38 up to the house of our *G*,
10: 39 not neglect the house of our *G*."
11: 11 supervisor in the house of *G*,
11: 16 the outside work of the house of *G*;
11: 22 for the service of the house of *G*.
12: 24 prescribed by David the man of *G*.
12: 36 by David the man of *G*.
12: 40 took their places in the house of *G*;
12: 43 *G* had given them great joy.
12: 45 performed the service of their *G*

Ne 12:46 of praise and thanksgiving to *G*.
13: 1 admitted into the assembly of *G*,
13: 2 (Our *G*, however, turned the curse
13: 4 storerooms of the house of our *G*.
13: 7 in the courts of the house of *G*.
13: 9 the equipment of the house of *G*,
13:11 Why is the house of *G* neglected?''
13:14 Remember me for this, O my *G*,
13:14 done for the house of my *G*
13:18 so that our *G* brought all this
13:22 me for this also, O my *G*,
13:26 He was loved by his *G*,
13:26 *G* made him king over all Israel,
13:27 to our *G* by marrying foreign
13:29 Remember them, O my *G*,
13:31 Remember me with favor, O my *G*.
Job 1: 1 he feared *G* and shunned evil.
1: 5 and cursed *G* in their hearts.''
1: 8 a man who fears *G* and shuns evil.''
1: 9 ''Does Job fear *G* for nothing?''
1:16 ''The fire of *G* fell from the sky
1:22 by charging *G* with wrongdoing.
2: 3 a man who fears *G* and shuns evil.
2: 9 Curse *G* and die!'' He replied,
2:10 Shall we accept good from *G*,
3: 4 may *G* above not care about it;
3:23 whom *G* has hedged in?
4: 9 of *G* they are destroyed;
4:17 a mortal be more righteous than *G?*
4:18 If *G* places no trust in his servants,
5: 8 But if it were I, I would appeal to *G;*
5:17 is the man whom *G* corrects;
6: 8 that *G* would grant what I hope for,
6: 9 that *G* would be willing to crush me
7: 7 O *G*, that my life is but a breath;
8: 3 Does *G* pervert justice?
8: 5 But if you will look to *G*
8:13 of all who forget *G;*
8:20 ''Surely *G* does not reject
9: 2 a mortal be righteous before *G?*
9:13 *G* does not restrain his anger;
10: 2 to *G:* Do not condemn me,
11: 4 say to *G*, 'My beliefs are flawless
11: 5 how I wish that *G* would speak,
11: 6 *G* has even forgotten some
11: 7 Can you fathom the mysteries of *G*
12: 4 I called upon *G* and he answered—
12: 6 those who carry their *g*
12: 6 those who provoke *G* are secure—
12:13 ''To *G* belong wisdom and power;
13: 3 and to argue my case with *G*.
13: 8 Will you argue the case for *G?*
13:20 grant me these two things, O *G*,
15: 4 and hinder devotion to *G*.
15:13 that you vent your rage against *G*
15:15 If *G* places no trust in his holy ones
15:25 because he shakes his fist at *G*
16: 7 Surely, O *G*, you have worn me out
16: 9 *G* assails me and tears me
16:11 *G* has turned me over to evil men
16:20 as my eyes pour out tears to *G;*
16:21 on behalf of a man he pleads with *G*
17: 3 O *G*, the pledge you demand.
17: 6 ''*G* has made me a byword
18:21 of one who knows not *G*.''
19: 6 then know that *G* has wronged me
19:21 for the hand of *G* has struck me.
19:22 Why do you pursue me as *G* does?
19:26 yet in my flesh I will see *G;*
20:15 *G* will make his stomach vomit
20:23 *G* will vent his burning anger
20:29 Such is the fate *G* allots the wicked,
20:29 heritage appointed for them by *G*.''
21: 9 the rod of *G* is not upon them.
21:14 Yet they say to *G*, 'Leave us alone!
21:17 the fate *G* allots in his anger?
21:19 '*G* stores up a man's punishment
21:22 Can anyone teach knowledge to *G*,
22: 2 ''Can a man be of benefit to *G?*
22:12 ''Is not *G* in the heights of heaven?
22:13 Yet you say, 'What does *G* know?
22:17 They said to *G*, 'Leave us alone!
22:21 ''Submit to *G* and be at peace
22:26 and will lift up your face to *G*.
23:16 *G* has made my heart faint;
24:12 *G* charges no one with wrongdoing
24:22 *G* drags away the mighty
25: 2 ''Dominion and awe belong to *G;*

Job 25: 4 can a man be righteous before *G?*
26: 6 Death is naked before *G;*
27: 2 *G* lives, who has denied me justice,
27: 3 the breath of *G* in my nostrils,
27: 8 when *G* takes away his life?
27: 9 Does *G* listen to his cry
27:10 Will he call upon *G* at all times?
27:11 teach you about the power of *G;*
27:13 ''Here is the fate *G* allots
28:23 *G* understands the way to it
29: 2 the days when *G* watched over me,
30:11 Now that *G* has unstrung my bow
30:18 his great power ⌊*G*⌋ becomes like
30:20 O *G*, but you do not answer;
31: 2 For what is man's lot from *G* above
31: 6 let *G* weigh me in honest scales
31:14 do when *G* confronts me?
31:23 For I dreaded destruction from *G*,
31:28 I would have been unfaithful to *G*
32: 2 for justifying himself rather than *G*.
32:13 let *G* refute him, not man.'
33: 4 The Spirit of *G* has made me;
33: 6 I am just like you before *G;*
33:10 Yet *G* has found fault with me;
33:12 for *G* is greater than man.
33:14 For *G* does speak—now one way,
33:26 He prays to *G* and finds favor
33:26 he is restored by *G*
33:29 ''*G* does all these things to a man—
34: 5 but *G* denies me justice.
34: 9 when he tries to please *G*.'
34:10 Far be it from *G* to do evil,
34:12 is unthinkable that *G* would do
34:23 *G* has no need to examine men
34:31 ''Suppose a man says to *G*,
34:33 Should *G* then reward you
34:37 and multiplies his words against *G*
35: 2 You say, 'I will be cleared by *G*.'
35:10 no one says, 'Where is *G* my Maker
35:13 *G* does not listen to their empty
36: 5 ''*G* is mighty, but does not despise
36:22 ''*G* is exalted in his power.
36:26 is *G*— beyond our understanding!
37:10 The breath of *G* produces ice,
37:15 you know how *G* controls
37:22 *G* comes in awesome majesty.
38:41 raven when its young cry out to *G*
39:17 for *G* did not endow her
40: 2 Let him who accuses *G* answer him
40:19 among the works of *G*,
Ps 3: 2 ''*G* will not deliver him.''
3: 7 Deliver me, O my *G!*
4: 1 O my righteous *G*.
5: 2 my King and my *G*,
5: 4 You are not a *G* who takes pleasure
5:10 Declare them guilty, O *G!*
7: 1 O LORD my *G*, I take refuge
7: 3 O LORD my *G*, if I have done this
7: 6 Awake, my *G;* decree justice.
7: 9 O righteous *G*,
7:10 My shield is *G* Most High,
7:11 *G* is a righteous judge,
7:11 *G* who expresses his wrath every
9:17 all the nations that forget *G*.
10: 4 his thoughts there is no room for *G*.
10:11 to himself, ''*G* has forgotten;
10:12 LORD! Lift up your hand, O *G*.
10:13 Why does the wicked man revile *G*
10:14 O *G*, do see trouble and grief;
13: 3 and answer, O LORD my *G*.
14: 1 ''There is no *G*.''
14: 2 any who seek *G*.
14: 5 for *G* is present in the company
16: 1 Keep me safe, O *G*,
17: 6 O *G*, for you will answer me;
18: 2 my *G* is my rock, in whom I take
18: 6 I cried to my *G* for help.
18:21 by turning from my *G*.
18:28 my *G* turns my darkness into light.
18:29 with my *G* I can scale a wall.
18:30 As for *G*, his way is perfect;
18:31 And who is the Rock except our *G*
18:31 For who is *G* besides the LORD?
18:32 It is *G* who arms me with strength
18:46 Exalted be *G* my Savior!
18:47 He is the *G* who avenges me,
19: 1 The heavens declare the glory of *G;*
20: 1 of the *G* of Jacob protect you.

Ps 20: 5 in the name of our *G*.
20: 7 in the name of the LORD our *G*.
22: 1 *G*, my *G*, why have you forsaken
22: 2 O my *G*, I cry out by day,
22:10 womb you have been my *G*.
24: 5 and vindication from *G* his Savior.
24: 6 who seek your face, O *G* of Jacob.
25: 2 in you I trust, O my *G*.
25: 5 for you are *G* my Savior,
25:22 Redeem Israel, O *G*,
27: 9 O *G* my Savior.
29: 3 the *G* of glory thunders,
30: 2 O LORD my *G*, I called to you
30:12 O LORD my *G*, I will give you
31: 5 redeem me, O LORD, the *G*
31:14 I say, ''You are my *G*.''
33:12 the nation whose *G* is the LORD,
35:23 Contend for me, my *G* and Lord.
35:24 righteousness, O LORD my *G;*
36: 1 There is no fear of *G*
37:31 The law of his *G* is in his heart;
38:15 you will answer, O Lord my *G*.
38:21 be not far from me, O my *G*.
40: 3 a hymn of praise to our *G*.
40: 5 Many, O LORD my *G*,
40: 8 I desire to do your will, O my *G;*
40:17 O my *G*, do not delay.
41:13 to the LORD, the *G* of Israel,
42: 1 so my soul pants for you, O *G*.
42: 2 When can I go and meet with *G?*
42: 2 thirsts for *G*, for the living *G*.
42: 3 ''Where is your *G?*''
42: 4 the procession to the house of *G*,
42: 5 Put your hope in *G*,
42: 6 and my *G*.
42: 8 a prayer to the *G* of my life.
42: 9 I say to *G* my Rock,
42:10 ''Where is your *G?*''
42:11 Put your hope in *G*,
42:11 my Savior and my *G*.
43: 1 Vindicate me, O *G*,
43: 2 You are *G* my stronghold.
43: 4 O *G*, my *G*.
43: 4 Then will I go to the altar of *G*,
43: 4 to *G*, my joy and my delight.
43: 5 Put your hope in *G*,
43: 5 my Savior and my *G*.
44: 1 We have heard with our ears, O *G;*
44: 4 You are my King and my *G*,
44: 8 In *G* we make our boast all day
44:20 had forgotten the name of our *G*
44:20 spread out our hands to a foreign *g*,
44:21 would not *G* have discovered it,
45: 2 since *G* has blessed you forever.
45: 6 O *G*, will last for ever and ever;
45: 7 therefore *G*, your *G*, has set you
46: 1 *G* is our refuge and strength,
46: 4 streams make glad the city of *G*,
46: 5 *G* is within her, she will not fall;
46: 5 *G* will help her at break of day.
46: 7 the *G* of Jacob is our fortress.
46:10 ''Be still, and know that I am *G;*
46:11 the *G* of Jacob is our fortress.
47: 1 shout to *G* with cries of joy.
47: 5 *G* has ascended amid shouts of joy,
47: 6 Sing praises to *G*, sing praises;
47: 7 For *G* is the King of all the earth;
47: 8 *G* is seated on his holy throne.
47: 8 *G* reigns over the nations;
47: 9 as the people of the *G* of Abraham,
47: 9 the kings of the earth belong to *G;*
48: 1 of our *G*, his holy mountain.
48: 3 *G* is in her citadels;
48: 8 *G* makes her secure forever.
48: 8 in the city of our *G:*
48: 9 Within your temple, O *G*,
48:10 Like your name, O *G*,
48:14 For this *G* is our *G* for ever
49: 7 or give to *G* a ransom for him—
49:15 *G* will redeem my soul
50: 1 The Mighty One, *G*, the LORD,
50: 2 *G* shines forth.
50: 3 Our *G* comes and will not be silent;
50: 6 for *G* himself is judge.
50: 7 I am *G*, your *G*.
50:14 Sacrifice thank offerings to *G*,
50:16 But to the wicked, *G* says:
50:22 ''Consider this, you who forget *G*,

Ps 50: 23 may show him the salvation of G.''
51: 1 Have mercy on me, O G,
51: 10 Create in me a pure heart, O G,
51: 14 Save me from bloodguilt, O G,
51: 14 the G who saves me,
51: 17 O G, you will not despise.
51: 17 sacrifices of G are a broken spirit;
52: 1 are a disgrace in the eyes of G?
52: 5 Surely G will bring you
52: 7 who did not make G his stronghold
52: 8 flourishing in the house of G;
53: 1 "There is no G."
53: 2 any who seek G.
53: 2 G looks down from heaven
53: 4 and who do not call on G?
53: 5 G scattered the bones
53: 5 to shame, for G despised them.
53: 6 When G restores the fortunes
54: 1 Save me, O G, by your name;
54: 2 Hear my prayer, O G;
54: 3 men without regard for G.
54: 4 Surely G is my help;
55: 1 Listen to my prayer, O G,
55: 14 with the throng at the house of G.
55: 16 But I call to G,
55: 19 and have no fear of G.
55: 19 G, who is enthroned forever,
55: 23 O G, will bring down the wicked
56: 1 O G, for men hotly pursue me;
56: 4 In G, whose word I praise,
56: 4 in G I trust; I will not be afraid.
56: 7 O G, bring down the nations.
56: 9 By this I will know that G is for me.
56: 10 In G, whose word I praise,
56: 11 in G I trust; I will not be afraid.
56: 12 I am under vows to you, O G;
56: 13 that I may walk before G
57: 1 on me, O G, have mercy on me,
57: 2 I cry out to G Most High,
57: 2 to G, who fulfills his purpose
57: 3 G sends his love and his
57: 5 Be exalted, O G, above the heavens
57: 7 My heart is steadfast, O G,
57: 11 Be exalted, O G, above the heavens
58: 6 the teeth in their mouths, O G;
58: 11 surely there is a G who judges
59: 1 Deliver me from my enemies, O G;
59: 5 O LORD G Almighty, the G
59: 9 you, O G, are my fortress,
59: 10 G will go before me
59: 10 my loving G.
59: 13 that G rules over Jacob.
59: 17 are my fortress, my loving G.
59: 17 you, O G, are my fortress,
60: 1 You have rejected us, O G,
60: 6 G has spoken from his sanctuary:
60: 10 O G, you who have rejected us
60: 12 With G we will gain the victory,
61: 1 Hear my cry, O G;
61: 5 For you have heard my vows, O G;
62: 1 My soul finds rest in G alone;
62: 5 Find rest, O my soul, in G alone;
62: 7 my honor depend on G;
62: 8 for G is our refuge.
62: 11 One thing G has spoken,
62: 11 that you, O G, are strong,
63: 1 O G, you are my G,
63: 11 But the king will rejoice in G;
64: 1 O G, as I voice my complaint;
64: 7 But G will shoot them with arrows;
64: 9 they will proclaim the works of G
65: 1 Praise awaits you, O G, in Zion;
65: 5 O G our Savior,
65: 9 The streams of G are filled
66: 1 Shout with joy to G, all the earth!
66: 3 Say to G, "How awesome are your
66: 5 Come and see what G has done,
66: 8 Praise our G, O peoples,
66: 10 For you, O G, tested us;
66: 16 listen, all you who fear G;
66: 19 but G has surely listened
66: 20 Praise be to G,
67: 1 May G be gracious to us
67: 3 May the peoples praise you, O G;
67: 5 May the peoples praise you, O G;
67: 6 and G, our G, will bless us.
67: 7 G will bless us,
68: 1 May G arise, may his enemies be

Ps 68: 2 may the wicked perish before G.
68: 3 and rejoice before G;
68: 4 Sing to G, sing praise to his name,
68: 5 is G in his holy dwelling.
68: 6 G sets the lonely in families,
68: 7 out before your people, O G,
68: 8 before G, the One of Sinai,
68: 8 before G, the G of Israel.
68: 9 You gave abundant showers, O G;
68: 10 and from your bounty, O G,
68: 16 at the mountain where G chooses
68: 17 The chariots of G are tens
68: 18 O LORD G, might dwell there.
68: 19 to the Lord, to G our Savior,
68: 20 Our G is a G who saves;
68: 21 Surely G will crush the heads
68: 24 has come into view, O G,
68: 24 the procession of my G
68: 26 Praise G in the great congregation;
68: 28 Summon your power, O G;
68: 28 show us your strength, O G,
68: 31 Cush will submit herself to G.
68: 32 Sing to G, O kingdoms of the earth,
68: 34 Proclaim the power of G,
68: 35 Praise be to G!
68: 35 You are awesome, O G,
68: 35 the G of Israel gives power
69: 1 Save me, O G,
69: 3 looking for my G.
69: 5 You know my folly, O G;
69: 6 O G of Israel.
69: 13 in your great love, O G,
69: 29 your salvation, O G, protect me.
69: 32 you who seek G, may your hearts
69: 35 for G will save Zion
70: 1 Hasten, O G, to save me;
70: 4 "Let G be exalted!"
70: 5 come quickly to me, O G.
71: 4 O my G, from the hand
71: 11 They say, "G has forsaken him;
71: 12 Be not far from me, O G;
71: 12 come quickly, O my G, to help me.
71: 17 my youth, O G, you have taught
71: 18 do not forsake me, O G,
71: 19 Who, O G, is like you?
71: 19 reaches to the skies, O G,
71: 22 harp for your faithfulness, O my G;
72: 1 with your justice, O G,
72: 18 to the LORD G, the G of Israel,
73: 1 Surely G is good to Israel,
73: 11 They say, "How can G know?
73: 17 me till I entered the sanctuary of G;
73: 26 but G is the strength of my heart
73: 28 as for me, it is good to be near G.
74: 1 have you rejected us forever, O G?
74: 8 place where G was worshiped
74: 10 will the enemy mock you, O G?
74: 12 O G, are my king from of old;
74: 22 O G, and defend your cause;
75: 1 We give thanks to you, O G,
75: 7 But it is G who judges:
75: 9 I will sing praise to the G of Jacob.
76: 1 In Judah G is known;
76: 6 At your rebuke, O G of Jacob,
76: 9 when you, O G, rose up to judge,
76: 11 Make vows to the LORD your G
77: 1 I cried out to G for help;
77: 1 I cried out to G to hear me.
77: 3 I remembered you, O G,
77: 9 Has G forgotten to be merciful?
77: 13 What god is so great as our G?
77: 13 What g is so great as our God?
77: 13 Your ways, O G, are holy.
77: 14 You are the G who performs
77: 16 The waters saw you, O G,
78: 7 they would put their trust in G
78: 8 whose hearts were not loyal to G,
78: 18 They willfully put G to the test
78: 19 Can G spread a table in the desert?
78: 19 They spoke against G, saying,
78: 22 for they did not believe in G
78: 34 Whenever G slew them, they
78: 35 They remembered that G was their
78: 35 that G Most High was their
78: 41 and again they put G to the test;
78: 56 But they put G to the test
78: 59 When G heard them, he was very
79: 1 O G, the nations have invaded

Ps 79: 9 Help us, O G our Savior,
79: 10 "Where is their G?"
80: 3 Restore us, O G;
80: 4 O LORD G Almighty,
80: 7 Restore us, O G Almighty;
80: 14 Return to us, O G Almighty!
80: 19 Restore us, O LORD G Almighty;
81: 1 Sing for joy to G our strength;
81: 1 shout aloud to the G of Jacob!
81: 4 an ordinance of the G of Jacob.
81: 9 You shall have no foreign g
81: 9 bow down to an alien g.
81: 10 I am the LORD your G,
82: 1 G presides in the great assembly;
82: 8 Rise up, O G, judge the earth,
83: 1 O G, do not keep silent;
83: 1 be not quiet, O G, be not still.
83: 12 of the pasturelands of G."
83: 13 them like tumbleweed, O my G,
84: 2 out for the living G.
84: 3 Almighty, my King and my G.
84: 7 till each appears before G in Zion.
84: 8 listen to me, O G of Jacob.
84: 8 my prayer, O LORD G Almighty;
84: 9 Look upon our shield, O G;
84: 10 a doorkeeper in the house of my G
84: 11 For the LORD G is a sun
85: 4 Restore us again, O G our Savior,
85: 8 to what G the LORD will say;
86: 2 You are my G; save your servant
86: 10 you alone are G.
86: 12 O Lord my G, with all my heart;
86: 14 arrogant are attacking me, O G;
86: 15 a compassionate and gracious G,
87: 3 O city of G: Selah
88: 1 O LORD, the G who saves me,
89: 7 of the holy ones G is greatly feared;
89: 8 O LORD G Almighty, who is like
89: 26 my G, the Rock my Savior.'
90: 2 to everlasting you are G.
90: 17 of the Lord our G rest upon us;
91: 2 my G, in whom I trust."
92: 13 flourish in the courts of our G.
94: 1 O G who avenges, shine forth.
94: 1 O LORD, the G who avenges,
94: 7 the G of Jacob pays no heed."
94: 22 my G the rock in whom I take
94: 23 the LORD our G will destroy them
95: 3 For the LORD is the great G,
95: 7 for he is our G
98: 3 the salvation of our G.
99: 5 Exalt the LORD our G
99: 8 O LORD our G,
99: 8 you were to Israel a forgiving G,
99: 9 Exalt the LORD our G
99: 9 for the LORD our G is holy.
100: 3 Know that the LORD is G.
102: 24 O my G, in the midst of my days;
104: 1 O LORD my G, you are very great,
104: 21 and seek their food from G.
104: 33 I will sing praise to my G as long
105: 7 He is the LORD our G;
106: 14 in the wasteland they put G
106: 21 They forgot the G who saved them,
106: 33 rebelled against the Spirit of G,
106: 47 Save us, O LORD our G,
106: 48 to the LORD, the G of Israel,
107: 11 rebelled against the words of G
108: 1 My heart is steadfast, O G;
108: 5 Be exalted, O G, above the heavens
108: 7 G has spoken from his sanctuary:
108: 11 O G, you who have rejected us
108: 13 With G we will gain the victory,
109: 1 O G, whom I praise,
109: 26 Help me, O LORD my G;
113: 5 Who is like the LORD our G,
114: 7 at the presence of the G of Jacob,
115: 2 "Where is their G?"
115: 3 Our G is in heaven;
116: 5 our G is full of compassion.
118: 27 The LORD is G,
118: 28 You are my G, and I will give you
118: 28 you are my G, and I will exalt you.
119:115 may keep the commands of my G!
122: 9 of the house of the LORD our G,
123: 2 look to the LORD our G,
135: 2 in the courts of the house of our G.
136: 2 Give thanks to the G of gods.

Ps 136: 26 Give thanks to the *G* of heaven.
139: 17 to me are your thoughts, O *G!*
139: 19 you would slay the wicked, O *G!*
139: 23 Search me, O *G*, and know my
140: 6 I say to you, "You are my *G*."
143: 10 for you are my *G;*
144: 2 He is my loving *G* and my fortress,
144: 9 I will sing a new song to you, O *G;*
144: 15 the people whose *G* is the LORD.
145: 1 I will exalt you, my *G* the King;
146: 2 I will sing praise to my *G* as long
146: 5 Blessed is he whose help is the *G*
146: 5 whose hope is in the LORD his *G*,
146: 10 your *G*, O Zion, for all generations.
147: 1 is to sing praises to our *G*,
147: 7 make music to our *G* on the harp.
147: 12 praise your *G*, O Zion,
149: 6 May the praise of *G* be
150: 1 Praise *G* in his sanctuary;
Pr 2: 5 and find the knowledge of *G*.
2: 17 the covenant she made before *G*.
3: 4 in the sight of *G* and man.
14: 31 to the needy honors *G*.
25: 2 of *G* to conceal a matter;
30: 5 "Every word of *G* is flawless;
30: 9 and so dishonor the name of my *G*.
Ecc 1: 13 What a heavy burden *G* has laid
2: 24 the hand of *G*, for without him,
2: 26 *G* gives wisdom, knowledge
2: 26 it over to the one who pleases *G*.
3: 10 I have seen the burden *G* has laid
3: 11 cannot fathom what *G* has done
3: 13 in all his toil—this is the gift of *G*.
3: 14 *G* does it, so men will revere him.
3: 14 know that everything *G* does will
3: 15 and *G* will call the past to account.
3: 17 "*G* will bring to judgment
3: 18 *G* tests them so that they may see
5: 1 when you go to the house of *G*.
5: 2 *G* is in heaven
5: 2 heart to utter anything before *G*.
5: 4 When you make a vow to *G*,
5: 6 Why should *G* be angry
5: 7 Therefore stand in awe of *G*.
5: 18 days of life *G* has given him—
5: 19 in his work—this is a gift of *G*.
5: 19 when *G* gives any man wealth
5: 20 because *G* keeps him occupied
6: 2 but *G* does not enable him
6: 2 on men: *G* gives a man wealth,
7: 13 Consider what *G* has done:
7: 14 *G* has made the one
7: 18 man who fears *G* will avoid all
7: 26 man who pleases *G* will escape her,
7: 29 *G* made mankind upright,
8: 2 because you took an oath before *G*.
8: 12 who are reverent before *G*.
8: 13 because the wicked do not fear *G*,
8: 15 the days of the life *G* has given him
8: 17 then I saw all that *G* has done.
9: 7 it is now that *G* favors what you do.
9: 9 meaningless life that *G* has given
11: 5 cannot understand the work of *G*,
11: 9 *G* will bring you to judgment.
12: 7 the spirit returns to *G* who gave it.
12: 13 Fear *G* and keep his
12: 14 For *G* will bring every deed
Isa 1: 10 listen to the law of our *G*,
2: 3 to the house of the *G* of Jacob.
5: 16 the holy *G* will show himself holy
5: 19 to those who say, "Let *G* hurry,
7: 11 "Ask the LORD your *G* for a sign,
7: 13 Will you try the patience of my *G*
8: 10 for *G* is with us.
8: 19 not a people inquire of their *G?*
8: 21 will curse their king and their *G*.
9: 6 Wonderful Counselor, Mighty *G*,
10: 21 will return to the Mighty *G*.
12: 2 Surely *G* is my salvation;
13: 19 will be overthrown by *G*
14: 13 throne above the stars of *G;*
17: 6 declares the LORD, the *G* of Israel
17: 10 You have forgotten *G* your Savior;
21: 10 from the *G* of Israel.
21: 17 The LORD, the *G* of Israel,
24: 15 name of the LORD, the *G* of Israel,
25: 1 O LORD, you are my *G;*
25: 9 "Surely this is our *G;*

Isa 25: 11 *G* will bring down their pride
26: 1 *G* makes salvation
26: 13 our *G*, other lords
28: 11 *G* will speak to this people,
28: 26 His *G* instructs him
29: 23 will stand in awe of the *G* of Israel.
30: 18 For the LORD is a *G* of justice.
31: 3 the Egyptians are men and not *G;*
34: 11 *G* will stretch out over Edom
35: 2 the splendor of our *G*.
35: 4 your *G* will come,
36: 7 depending on the LORD our *G*"—
36: 18 Has the *g* of any nation ever
37: 4 has sent to ridicule the living *G*,
37: 4 that the LORD your *G* will hear
37: 4 the LORD your *G* has heard.
37: 10 Do not let the *g* you depend
37: 16 you alone are *G* over all
37: 16 "O LORD Almighty, *G* of Israel,
37: 17 sent to insult the living *G*.
37: 20 Now, O LORD our *G*, deliver us
37: 20 that you alone, O LORD, are *G*."
37: 21 "This is what the LORD, the *G*
37: 38 in the temple of his *g* Nisroch,
38: 5 the *G* of your father David, says:
40: 1 says your *G*.
40: 3 a highway for our *G*.
40: 8 the word of our *G* stands forever."
40: 9 "Here is your *G!*"
40: 18 then, will you compare *G?*
40: 27 my cause is disregarded by my *G*"?
40: 28 The LORD is the everlasting *G*,
41: 10 not be dismayed, for I am your *G*.
41: 13 For I am the LORD, your *G*,
41: 17 *G* of Israel, will not forsake them.
42: 5 This is what *G* the LORD says—
43: 3 For I am the LORD, your *G*,
43: 10 Before me no *g* was formed,
43: 12 and not some foreign *g* among you.
43: 12 declares the LORD, "that I am *G*.
44: 6 apart from me there is no *G*.
44: 8 Is there any *G* besides me?
44: 10 Who shapes a *g* and casts an idol,
44: 15 he also fashions a *g* and worships it;
44: 17 From the rest he makes a *g*, his idol
44: 17 "Save me; you are my *g*."
45: 3 the *G* of Israel, who calls you
45: 5 apart from me there is no *G*.
45: 14 'Surely *G* is with you, and there is
45: 14 there is no other *g*.' "
45: 15 O *G* and Savior of Israel.
45: 15 you are a *G* who hides himself,
45: 18 he is *G;*
45: 21 And there is no *G* apart from me,
45: 21 a righteous *G* and a Savior;
45: 22 for I am *G*, and there is no other.
46: 6 a goldsmith to make it into a *g*,
46: 9 I am *G*, and there is no other;
46: 9 I am *G*, and there is none like me.
48: 1 and invoke the *G* of Israel—
48: 2 and rely on the *G* of Israel—
48: 5 and metal *g* ordained them.'
48: 17 "I am the LORD your *G*,
49: 4 and my reward is with my *G*."
49: 5 and my *G* has been my strength—
50: 10 and rely on his *G*.
51: 15 For I am the LORD your *G*,
51: 20 and the rebuke of your *G*.
51: 22 your *G*, who defends his people:
52: 7 "Your *G* reigns!"
52: 10 the salvation of our *G*.
52: 12 *G* of Israel will be your rear guard.
53: 4 we considered him stricken by *G*,
54: 5 he is called the *G* of all the earth.
54: 6 only to be rejected," says your *G*.
55: 5 because of the LORD your *G*,
55: 7 to our *G*, for he will freely pardon.
57: 21 says my *G*, "for the wicked."
58: 2 and seem eager for *G* to come
58: 2 forsaken the commands of its *G*.
59: 2 you from your *G;*
59: 13 turning our backs on our *G*,
60: 9 to the honor of the LORD your *G*,
60: 19 and your *G* will be your glory.
61: 2 and the day of vengeance of our *G*,
61: 6 will be named ministers of our *G*.
61: 10 my soul rejoices in my *G*.
62: 3 in the hand of your *G*.

Isa 62: 5 so will your *G* rejoice over you.
64: 4 no eye has seen any *G* besides you,
65: 16 will do so by the *G* of truth;
65: 16 will swear by the *G* of truth.
66: 9 bring to delivery?" says your *G*.
Jer 2: 17 by forsaking the LORD your *G*
2: 19 you forsake the LORD your *G*
3: 13 rebelled against the LORD your *G*,
3: 21 have forgotten the LORD their *G*.
3: 22 for you are the LORD our *G*.
3: 23 surely in the LORD our *G*
3: 25 not obeyed the LORD our *G*."
3: 25 sinned against the LORD our *G*,
5: 4 the requirements of their *G*.
5: 5 the requirements of their *G*."
5: 14 what the LORD *G* Almighty says:
5: 19 has the LORD our *G* done all this
5: 24 'Let us fear the LORD our *G*,
7: 3 is what the LORD Almighty, the *G*
7: 21 the *G* of Israel, says: Go ahead,
7: 23 I will be your *G* and you will be my
7: 28 has not obeyed the LORD its *G*
8: 14 the LORD our *G* has doomed us
9: 15 the *G* of Israel, says: "See,
10: 10 But the LORD is the true *G;*
10: 10 he is the living *G*, the eternal King.
10: 12 But *G* made the earth by his power;
11: 3 that this is what the LORD, the *G*
11: 4 be my people, and I will be your *G*.
11: 13 incense to that shameful *g* Baal are
13: 12 'This is what the LORD, the *G*
13: 16 Give glory to the LORD your *G*
14: 22 No, it is you, O LORD our *G*.
15: 16 O LORD *G* Almighty.
16: 9 is what the LORD Almighty, the *G*
16: 10 against the LORD our *G?*'
19: 3 the *G* of Israel, says: Listen!
19: 15 the *G* of Israel, says: 'Listen!
21: 4 'This is what the LORD, the *G*
22: 9 the covenant of the LORD their *G*
23: 2 this is what the LORD, the *G*
23: 23 "Am I only a *G* nearby,"
23: 23 "and not a *G* far away?
23: 36 distort the words of the living *G*,
23: 36 the LORD Almighty, our *G*.
24: 5 "This is what the LORD, the *G*
24: 7 be my people, and I will be their *G*,
25: 15 the *G* of Israel, said to me:
25: 27 the *G* of Israel, says: Drink,
26: 13 and obey the LORD your *G*.
26: 16 in the name of the LORD our *G*."
27: 4 is what the LORD Almighty, the *G*
27: 21 is what the LORD Almighty, the *G*
28: 2 is what the LORD Almighty, the *G*
28: 14 is what the LORD Almighty, the *G*
29: 4 is what the LORD Almighty, the *G*
29: 8 is what the LORD Almighty, the *G*
29: 21 is what the LORD Almighty, the *G*
29: 25 is what the LORD Almighty, the *G*
30: 2 "This is what the LORD, the *G*
30: 9 they will serve the LORD their *G*
30: 22 and I will be your *G*.' "
31: 1 "I will be the *G* of all the clans
31: 6 to the LORD our *G*.' "
31: 18 because you are the LORD my *G*.
31: 23 is what the LORD Almighty, the *G*
31: 33 I will be their *G*,
32: 14 the *G* of Israel, says: Take these
32: 15 the *G* of Israel, says: Houses,
32: 18 and powerful *G*, whose name is
32: 27 "I am the LORD, the *G*
32: 36 but this is what the LORD, the *G*
32: 38 be my people, and I will be their *G*.
33: 4 For this is what the LORD, the *G*
34: 2 "This is what the LORD, the *G*
34: 13 "This is what the LORD, the *G*
35: 4 son of Igdaliah the man of *G*.
35: 13 is what the LORD Almighty, the *G*
35: 17 the *G* of Israel, says: 'Listen!
35: 17 this is what the LORD *G* Almighty
35: 18 is what the LORD Almighty, the *G*
35: 19 is what the LORD Almighty, the *G*
37: 3 pray to the LORD our *G* for us."
37: 7 "This is what the LORD, the *G*
38: 17 the LORD *G* Almighty, the *G*
39: 16 is what the LORD Almighty, the *G*
40: 2 "The LORD your *G* decreed this
42: 2 and pray to the LORD your *G*

Jer 42: 3 that the LORD your G will tell us
42: 4 pray to the LORD your G
42: 5 the LORD your G sends you
42: 6 for we will obey the LORD our G."
42: 6 we will obey the LORD our G
42: 9 "This is what the LORD, the G
42: 13 and so disobey the LORD your G,
42: 15 is what the LORD Almighty, the G
42: 18 is what the LORD Almighty, the G
42: 20 me to the LORD your G
42: 20 'Pray to the LORD our G for us;
42: 21 have not obeyed the LORD your G
43: 1 the words of the LORD their G—
43: 2 The LORD our G has not sent you
43: 10 is what the LORD Almighty, the G
44: 2 is what the LORD Almighty, the G
44: 7 the LORD G Almighty, the G
44: 11 is what the LORD Almighty, the G
44: 25 is what the LORD Almighty, the G
45: 2 the G of Israel, says to you,
46: 25 The LORD Almighty, the G
46: 25 punishment on Amon g of Thebes,
48: 1 is what the LORD Almighty, the G
50: 4 in tears to seek the LORD their G.
50: 18 is what the LORD Almighty, the G
50: 28 the LORD our G has taken
50: 40 As G overthrew Sodom
51: 5 by their G, the LORD Almighty,
51: 10 what the LORD our G has done.'
51: 33 is what the LORD Almighty, the G
51: 56 For the LORD is a G of retribution
La 3: 41 hands to G in heaven, and say:
Eze 1: 1 opened and I saw visions of G.
8: 3 and in visions of G he took me
8: 4 before me was the glory of the G
9: 3 the glory of the G of Israel went up
10: 5 like the voice of G Almighty
10: 19 and the glory of the G of Israel was
10: 20 seen beneath the G of Israel
11: 20 be my people, and I will be their G.
11: 22 and the glory of the G of Israel was
11: 24 the vision given by the Spirit of G.
14: 11 will be their G, declares
20: 5 "I am the LORD your G."
20: 7 I am the LORD your G."
20: 19 the LORD your G; follow my
20: 20 that I am the LORD your G."
28: 2 But you are a man and not a g,
28: 2 I sit on the throne of a g
28: 2 you say, "I am a g;
28: 2 you think you are as wise as a g.
28: 6 as wise as a g,
28: 9 Will you then say, "I am a g,"
28: 9 You will be but a man, not a g,
28: 13 the garden of G;
28: 14 You were on the holy mount of G;
28: 16 in disgrace from the mount of G,
28: 26 that I am the LORD their G.' "
31: 8 The cedars in the garden of G
31: 8 no tree in the garden of G
31: 9 Eden in the garden of G.
34: 24 I the LORD will be their G,
34: 30 the LORD their G, am with them
34: 31 and I am your G, declares
36: 28 be my people, and I will be your G.
37: 23 be my people, and I will be their G.
37: 27 I will be their G, and they will be
39: 22 know that I am the LORD their G.
39: 28 know that I am the LORD their G,
40: 2 In visions of G he took me
43: 2 the glory of the G of Israel coming
44: 2 the G of Israel, has entered
Da 1: 2 of the articles from the temple of G
1: 2 put in the treasure house of his g.
1: 2 to the temple of his g in Babylonia
1: 9 Now G had caused the official
1: 17 four young men G gave knowledge
2: 18 plead for mercy from the G
2: 19 Daniel praised the G of heaven
2: 20 Praise be to the name of G for ever
2: 23 and praise you, O G of my fathers:
2: 28 there is a G in heaven who reveals
2: 37 The G of heaven has given you
2: 44 G of heaven will set up a kingdom
2: 45 great G has shown the king what
2: 47 "Surely your G is the G of gods
3: 15 what g will be able to rescue you
3: 17 the G we serve is able to save us
Da 3: 26 servants of the Most High G,
3: 28 any god except their own G.
3: 28 or worship any g except their own
3: 28 "Praise be to the G of Shadrach,
3: 29 against the G of Shadrach,
3: 29 for no other g can save in this way
4: 2 the Most High G has performed
4: 8 after the name of my g,
5: 3 from the temple of G in Jerusalem,
5: 18 the Most High G gave your father
5: 21 that the Most High G is sovereign
5: 23 you did not honor the G who holds
5: 26 G has numbered the days
6: 5 to do with the law of his G."
6: 7 that anyone who prays to any g
6: 10 giving thanks to his G, just
6: 11 found Daniel praying and asking G
6: 12 days anyone who prays to any g
6: 16 "May your G, whom you serve
6: 20 servant of the living G, has your G,
6: 22 live forever! My G sent his angel,
6: 23 because he had trusted in his G.
6: 26 and reverence the G of Daniel.
6: 26 "For he is the living G
9: 3 So I turned to the Lord G
9: 4 I prayed to the LORD my G
9: 4 O Lord, the great and awesome G,
9: 9 The Lord our G is merciful
9: 10 have not obeyed the LORD our G
9: 11 servant of G, have been poured out
9: 13 of the LORD our G by turning
9: 14 for the LORD our G is righteous
9: 15 O Lord our G, who brought your
9: 17 "Now, our G, hear the prayers
9: 18 O G, and hear; open your eyes
9: 19 your sake, O my G, do not delay,
9: 20 to the LORD my G for his holy hill
10: 12 to humble yourself before your G,
11: 32 who know their G will firmly resist
11: 36 and magnify himself above every g
11: 36 things against the G of gods.
11: 37 nor will he regard any g,
11: 38 a g unknown to his fathers he will
11: 38 he will honor a g of fortresses;
11: 39 with the help of a foreign g
Hos 1: 7 but by the LORD their G."
1: 9 my people, and I am not your G.
1: 10 will be called 'sons of the living G.'
2: 23 and they will say, 'You are my G'
3: 5 and seek the LORD their G
4: 1 no acknowledgment of G
4: 6 you have ignored the law of your G
4: 12 they are unfaithful to their G.
5: 4 to return to their G.
6: 6 acknowledgment of G rather
7: 10 return to the LORD his G
8: 2 'O our G, we acknowledge you!'
8: 6 it is not G.
9: 1 you have been unfaithful to your G;
9: 8 The prophet, along with my G,
9: 8 and hostility in the house of his G.
9: 9 G will remember their wickedness
9: 17 My G will reject them
11: 9 For I am G, and not man—
11: 12 And Judah is unruly against G,
12: 3 as a man he struggled with G.
12: 5 the LORD G Almighty,
12: 6 But you must return to your G;
12: 6 and wait for your G always.
12: 9 "I am the LORD your G,
13: 4 You shall acknowledge no G
13: 4 "But I am the LORD your G,
13: 16 they have rebelled against their G.
14: 1 O Israel, to the LORD your G.
Joel 1: 13 withheld from the house of your G.
1: 13 you who minister before my G;
1: 14 to the house of the LORD your G,
1: 16 gladness from the house of our G?
2: 13 Return to the LORD your G,
2: 14 offerings for the LORD your G.
2: 17 'Where is their G?' "
2: 23 rejoice in the LORD your G,
2: 26 the name of the LORD your G,
2: 27 that I am the LORD your G,
3: 17 know that I, the LORD your G,
Am 2: 8 In the house of their g
3: 13 the Lord, the LORD G Almighty.
4: 12 prepare to meet your G, O Israel."
Am 4: 13 the LORD G Almighty is his name
5: 14 the LORD G Almighty will be
5: 15 the LORD G Almighty will
5: 16 the LORD G Almighty, says:
5: 26 the star of your g
5: 27 whose name is G Almighty.
6: 8 the LORD G Almighty declares:
6: 14 the LORD G Almighty declares,
8: 14 'As surely as your g lives, O Dan,'
8: 14 as the g of Beersheba lives'—
9: 15 says the LORD your G.
Jnh 1: 5 and each cried out to his own g.
1: 6 Get up and call on your g!
1: 9 the G of heaven, who made the sea
2: 1 prayed to the LORD his G.
2: 6 O LORD my G.
3: 5 The Ninevites believed G.
3: 8 Let everyone call urgently on G.
3: 9 G may yet relent
3: 10 When G saw what they did
4: 2 a G who relents from sending
4: 2 a gracious and compassionate G,
4: 6 Then the LORD G provided a vine
4: 7 the next day G provided a worm,
4: 8 G provided a scorching east wind,
4: 9 But G said to Jonah, "Do you have
Mic 3: 7 because there is no answer from G
4: 2 to the house of the G of Jacob.
4: 5 our G for ever and ever.
5: 4 of the name of the LORD his G.
6: 6 and bow down before the exalted G
6: 8 and to walk humbly with your G.
7: 4 the day G visits you.
7: 7 I wait for G my Savior;
7: 7 my G will hear me.
7: 10 "Where is the LORD your G?"
7: 17 turn in fear to the LORD our G
7: 18 Who is a G like you,
Na 1: 2 LORD is a jealous and avenging G;
Hab 1: 11 whose own strength is their g."
1: 12 My G, my Holy One, we will not
3: 3 G came from Teman,
3: 18 I will be joyful in G my Savior.
Zep 2: 7 The LORD their G will care
2: 9 the LORD Almighty, the G
3: 2 she does not draw near to her G.
3: 17 The LORD your G is with you,
Hag 1: 12 the LORD their G had sent him.
1: 12 the voice of the LORD their G
1: 14 of the LORD Almighty, their G,
Zec 4: 7 capstone to shouts of 'G bless it!
4: 7 G bless it!' " Then the word
6: 15 obey the LORD your G."
8: 8 and righteous to them as their G."
8: 23 we have heard that G is with you
9: 7 who are left will belong to our G
9: 16 The LORD their G will save them
10: 6 for I am the LORD their G
11: 4 This is what the LORD my G says.
12: 5 the LORD Almighty is their G.'
12: 8 the house of David will be like G,
13: 9 they will say, 'The LORD is our G
14: 5 Then the LORD my G will come,
Mal 1: 9 Now implore G to be gracious to us
2: 10 Father? Did not one G create us?
2: 11 the daughter of a foreign g.
2: 16 says the LORD G of Israel,
2: 17 or "Where is the G of justice?"
3: 8 Will a man rob G? Yet you rob me.
3: 14 have said, 'It is futile to serve G.
3: 15 even those who challenge G escape
3: 18 between those who serve G
Mt 1: 23 which means, "G with us."
3: 9 out of these stones G can raise up
3: 16 Spirit of G descending like a dove
4: 3 the Son of G, tell these stones
4: 4 comes from the mouth of G.' "
4: 6 "If you are the Son of G," he said,
4: 7 'Do not put the Lord your G
4: 10 'Worship the Lord your G,
5: 8 for they will see G.
5: 9 for they will be called sons of G.
6: 24 You cannot serve both G
6: 30 If that is how G clothes the grass
8: 29 want with us, Son of G?"
9: 8 they praised G, who had given such
12: 4 He entered the house of G,
12: 28 out demons by the Spirit of G,

Mt 12:28 then the kingdom of G has come
14:33 saying, "Truly you are the Son of G
15: 3 of G for the sake of your tradition?
15: 4 sake of your tradition? For G said,
15: 5 from me is a gift devoted to G,'
15: 6 Thus you nullify the word of G
15:31 And they praised the G of Israel.
16:16 the Christ, the Son of the living G."
16:23 have in mind the things of G,
19: 6 Therefore what G has joined
19:24 man to enter the kingdom of G."
19:26 but with G all things are possible."
21:31 the kingdom of G ahead of you.
21:43 of G will be taken away from you
22:16 of G in accordance with the truth.
22:21 and to G what is God's."
22:29 the Scriptures or the power of G.
22:31 have you not read what G said
22:32 He is not the G of the dead
22:32 of Isaac, and the G of Jacob'?
22:32 the G of Abraham, the G of Isaac,
22:37 " 'Love the Lord your G
26:61 able to destroy the temple of G
26:63 if you are the Christ, the Son of G."
26:63 you under oath by the living G:
27:40 of G!" In the same way the chief
27:43 He trusts in G.
27:43 Let G rescue him now
27:43 for he said, 'I am the Son of G.' "
27:46 which means, "My G, my G,
27:54 "Surely he was the Son of G!"
Mk 1: 1 about Jesus Christ, the Son of G.
1:14 proclaiming the good news of G.
1:15 "The kingdom of G is near.
1:24 the Holy One of G!" "Be quiet!"
2: 7 Who can forgive sins but G alone?"
2:12 everyone and they praised G,
2:26 he entered the house of G
3:11 cried out, "You are the Son of G."
4:11 of the kingdom of G has been given
4:26 is what the kingdom of G is like.
4:30 we say the kingdom of G is like,
5: 7 Jesus, Son of the Most High G?
5: 7 to G that you won't torture me!"
7: 8 go of the commands of G
7: 9 aside the commands of G in order
7:11 to G), then you no longer let him
7:13 Thus you nullify the word of G
8:33 have in mind the things of G,
9: 1 kingdom of G come with power."
9:47 you to enter the kingdom of G
10: 6 of creation G 'made them male
10: 9 Therefore what G has joined
10:14 the kingdom of G belongs to such
10:15 of G like a little child will never
10:18 "No one is good—except G alone.
10:23 rich to enter the kingdom of G!"
10:24 is to enter the kingdom of G!
10:25 man to enter the kingdom of G."
10:27 all things are possible with G."
10:27 not with G; all things are possible
11:22 "Have faith in G," Jesus answered.
12:14 the way of G in accordance
12:17 and to G what is God's."
12:24 the Scriptures or the power of G?
12:26 of Isaac, and the G of Jacob'?
12:26 of the bush, how G said to him,
12:26 the G of Abraham, the G of Isaac,
12:27 He is not the G of the dead,
12:29 the Lord our G, the Lord is one.
12:30 Love the Lord your G
12:32 right in saying that G is one
12:34 far from the kingdom of G."
13:19 when G created the world,
14:25 anew in the kingdom of G."
15:34 which means, "My G, my G,
15:39 Surely this man was the Son of G!"
15:43 waiting for the kingdom of G,
16:19 and he sat at the right hand of G.
Lk 1: 6 them were upright in the sight of G,
1: 8 he was serving as priest before G,
1:16 back to the Lord their G.
1:19 I stand in the presence of G,
1:26 G sent the angel Gabriel
1:30 Mary, you have found favor with G
1:32 Lord G will give him the throne
1:35 be born will be called the Son of G.
1:37 For nothing is impossible with G."

Lk 1:47 my spirit rejoices in G my Savior,
1:64 and he began to speak, praising G.
1:68 to the Lord, the G of Israel,
1:78 of the tender mercy of our G,
2:13 praising G and saying, "Glory
2:14 "Glory to G in the highest,
2:20 praising G for all the things they
2:28 in his arms and praised G,
2:38 to G and spoke about the child
2:40 and the grace of G was upon him.
2:52 and in favor with G and men.
3: 2 the word of G came to John son
3: 8 out of these stones G can raise up
3:38 the son of G.
4: 3 the Son of G, tell this stone
4: 8 'Worship the Lord your G
4: 9 "If you are the Son of G," he said,
4:12 'Do not put the Lord your G
4:34 the Holy One of G!" "Be quiet!"
4:41 shouting, "You are the Son of G!"
4:43 news of the kingdom of G
5: 1 and listening to the word of G,
5:21 Who can forgive sins but G alone?"
5:25 and went home praising G.
5:26 was amazed and gave praise to G.
6: 4 He entered the house of G,
6:12 and spent the night praying to G.
6:20 for yours is the kingdom of G.
7:16 filled with awe and praised G.
7:16 "G has come to help his people."
7:28 least in the kingdom of G is greater
8: 1 news of the kingdom of G.
8:10 of the kingdom of G has been given
8:11 The seed is the word of G.
8:28 Son of the Most High G? I beg you,
8:39 tell how much G has done for you."
9: 2 out to preach the kingdom of G
9:11 to them about the kingdom of G,
9:20 Peter answered, "The Christ of G."
9:27 before they see the kingdom of G."
9:43 amazed at the greatness of G.
9:60 and proclaim the kingdom of G."
9:62 for service in the kingdom of G."
10: 9 'The kingdom of G is near you.'
10:11 The kingdom of G is near.'
10:27 " 'Love the Lord your G
11:20 demons by the finger of G,
11:20 then the kingdom of G has come
11:28 are those who hear the word of G
11:42 neglect justice and the love of G.
11:42 you give G a tenth of your mint,
11:49 Because of this, G
12: 6 one of them is forgotten by G.
12: 8 him before the angels of G.
12: 9 disowned before the angels of G.
12:20 "But G said to him, 'You fool!
12:21 but is not rich toward G."
12:24 or barn; yet G feeds them.
12:28 If that is how G clothes the grass
13:13 she straightened up and praised G.
13:18 "What is the kingdom of G like?
13:20 shall I compare the kingdom of G
13:28 the prophets in the kingdom of G,
13:29 at the feast in the kingdom of G.
14:15 at the feast in the kingdom of G."
15:10 of G over one sinner who repents."
16:13 You cannot serve both G
16:15 of men, but G knows your hearts.
16:16 kingdom of G is being preached,
17:15 praising G in a loud voice.
17:18 praise to G except this foreigner?"
17:20 of G does not come visibly,
17:20 the kingdom of G would come,
17:21 the kingdom of G is within you."
18: 2 was a judge who neither feared G
18: 4 I don't fear G or care about men,
18: 7 And will not G bring about justice
18:11 and prayed about himself; 'G,
18:13 but beat his breast and said, 'G,
18:14 went home justified before G.
18:16 the kingdom of G belongs to such
18:17 of G like a little child will never
18:19 "No one is good—except G alone.
18:24 the rich to enter the kingdom of G!
18:25 man to enter the kingdom of G."
18:27 with men is possible with G."
18:29 sake of the kingdom of G will fail
18:43 and followed Jesus, praising G.

Lk 18:43 people saw it, they also praised G.
19:11 of G was going to appear at once.
19:37 to praise G in loud voices
20:21 teach the way of G in accordance
20:25 and to G what is God's."
20:37 for he calls the Lord 'the G
20:37 the G of Isaac, and the G of Jacob.'
20:38 He is not the G of the dead,
21: 5 and with gifts dedicated to G.
21:31 you know that the kingdom of G is
22:16 fulfillment in the kingdom of G."
22:18 until the kingdom of G comes."
22:69 at the right hand of the mighty G."
22:70 "Are you then the Son of G?"
23:35 himself if he is the Christ of G,
23:40 "Don't you fear G," he said,
23:47 what had happened, praised G
23:51 waiting for the kingdom of G.
24:19 deed before G and all the people.
24:53 at the temple, praising G.
Jn 1: 1 was with G, and the Word was G.
1: 2 He was with G in the beginning.
1: 6 came a man who was sent from G;
1:12 right to become children of G—
1:13 or a husband's will, but born of G.
1:18 ever seen G, but G the only ⌞Son⌟,
1:29 Lamb of G, who takes away the sin
1:34 I testify that this is the Son of G."
1:36 he said, "Look, the Lamb of G!"
1:49 "Rabbi, you are the Son of G;
1:51 and the angels of G ascending
3: 2 a teacher who has come from G.
3: 2 doing if G were not with him."
3: 3 he cannot see the kingdom of G."
3: 5 he cannot enter the kingdom of G.
3:16 "For G so loved the world that he
3:17 For G did not send his Son
3:21 done has been done through G."
3:33 it has certified that G is truthful.
3:34 has sent speaks the words of G;
3:34 the one whom G has sent speaks
3:34 to him G gives the Spirit
4:10 "If you knew the gift of G
4:24 G is spirit, and his worshipers must
5:18 even calling G his own Father,
5:18 making himself equal with G.
5:25 will hear the voice of the Son of G
5:42 the love of G in your hearts.
5:44 praise that comes from the only G?
6:27 On him G the Father has placed his
6:28 do to do the works G requires?"
6:29 answered, "The work of G is this:
6:33 For the bread of G is he who comes
6:45 'They will all be taught by G.'
6:46 except the one who is from G;
6:69 that you are the Holy One of G."
7:17 my teaching comes from G or
8:40 you the truth that I heard from G.
8:41 only Father we have is G himself."
8:42 for I came from G and now am here
8:42 to them, "If G were your Father,
8:47 belongs to G hears what G says.
8:47 is that you do not belong to G."
8:54 whom you claim as your G,
9: 3 the work of G might be displayed
9:16 "This man is not from G,
9:24 "Give glory to G," they said.
9:29 We know that G spoke to Moses,
9:31 We know that G does not listen
9:33 If this man were not from G,
10:33 a mere man, claim to be G."
10:35 to whom the word of G came—
11:22 now G will give you whatever you
11:27 the Son of G, who was to come
11:40 you would see the glory of G?"
11:52 also for the scattered children of G,
12:43 from men more than praise from G.
13: 3 from G and was returning to G;
13:31 of Man glorified and G is glorified
13:32 If G is glorified in him, G will
14: 1 Trust in G; trust also in me.
16: 2 think he is offering a service to G.
16:27 have believed that I came from G.
16:30 us believe that you came from G."
17: 3 the only true G, and Jesus Christ,
19: 7 he claimed to be the Son of G."
20:17 your Father, to my G and your G
20:28 "My Lord and my G!"

Jn 20: 31 the Son of *G*, and that
21: 19 by which Peter would glorify *G*.
Ac 1: 3 and spoke about the kingdom of *G*.
2: 11 wonders of *G* in our own tongues!''
2: 17 '' 'In the last days, *G* says,
2: 22 accredited by *G* to you by miracles,
2: 22 which *G* did among you
2: 24 But *G* raised him from the dead,
2: 30 and knew that *G* had promised him
2: 32 *G* has raised this Jesus to life,
2: 33 Exalted to the right hand of *G*,
2: 36 *G* has made this Jesus, whom you
2: 39 all whom the Lord our *G* will call.''
2: 47 praising *G* and enjoying the favor
3: 8 and jumping, and praising *G*.
3: 9 saw him walking and praising *G*,
3: 13 The *G* of Abraham, Isaac
3: 13 and Jacob, the *G* of our fathers,
3: 15 but *G* raised him from the dead.
3: 18 this is how *G* fulfilled what he had
3: 19 Repent, then, and turn to *G*,
3: 21 comes for *G* to restore everything,
3: 22 'The Lord your *G* will raise up
3: 25 and of the covenant *G* made
3: 26 When *G* raised up his servant,
4: 10 but whom *G* raised from the dead,
4: 19 sight to obey you rather than *G*.
4: 21 all the people were praising *G*
4: 24 voices together in prayer to *G*.
4: 31 and spoke the word of *G* boldly.
5: 4 You have not lied to men but to *G*
5: 29 ''We must obey *G* rather than men!
5: 30 The *G* of our fathers raised Jesus
5: 31 *G* exalted him to his own right
5: 32 whom *G* has given
5: 39 find yourselves fighting against *G*.''
5: 39 if it is from *G*, you will not be able
6: 2 of the word of *G* in order to wait
6: 7 So the word of *G* spread.
6: 11 against Moses and against *G*.''
7: 2 The *G* of glory appeared
7: 3 country and your people,' *G* said,
7: 4 *G* sent him to this land where you
7: 5 But *G* promised him that he
7: 6 *G* spoke to him in this way:
7: 7 nation they serve as slaves,' *G* said,
7: 9 *G* was with him and rescued him
7: 17 near for *G* to fulfill his promise
7: 25 would realize that *G* was using him
7: 32 'I am the *G* of your fathers,
7: 32 the *G* of Abraham, Isaac and Jacob
7: 35 and deliverer by *G* himself,
7: 37 '*G* will send you a prophet like me
7: 42 But *G* turned away and gave them
7: 43 and the star of your *g* Rephan.
7: 44 been made as *G* directed Moses,
7: 45 land from the nations *G* drove out
7: 46 place for the *G* of Jacob.
7: 55 standing at the right hand of *G*.
7: 55 to heaven and saw the glory of *G*,
7: 56 standing at the right hand of *G*.''
8: 12 news of the kingdom of *G*
8: 14 had accepted the word of *G*,
8: 20 thought you could buy the gift of *G*
8: 21 your heart is not right before *G*.
9: 20 that Jesus is the Son of *G*.
10: 2 and prayed to *G* regularly.
10: 3 He distinctly saw an angel of *G*,
10: 4 as a remembrance before *G*.
10: 15 anything impure that *G* has made
10: 28 *G* has shown me that I should not
10: 31 *G* has heard your prayer
10: 33 here in the presence of *G* to listen
10: 34 true it is that *G* does not show
10: 36 This is the message *G* sent
10: 38 how *G* anointed Jesus of Nazareth
10: 38 power of the devil, because *G* was
10: 40 but *G* raised him from the dead
10: 41 by witnesses whom *G* had already
10: 42 he is the one whom *G* appointed
10: 46 speaking in tongues and praising *G*.
11: 1 also had received the word of *G*.
11: 9 anything impure that *G* has made
11: 17 I to think that I could oppose *G*!''
11: 17 So if *G* gave them the same gift
11: 18 further objections and praised *G*,
11: 18 *G* has even granted the Gentiles
11: 23 saw the evidence of the grace of *G*,

Ac 12: 5 church was earnestly praying to *G*
12: 22 the voice of a *g*, not of a man.''
12: 23 Herod did not give praise to *G*,
12: 24 But the word of *G* continued
13: 5 of *G* in the Jewish synagogues.
13: 7 he wanted to hear the word of *G*.
13: 16 and you Gentiles who worship *G*,
13: 17 The *G* of the people
13: 20 *G* gave them judges until the time
13: 23 man's descendants *G* has brought
13: 30 But *G* raised him from the dead,
13: 32 What *G* promised our fathers he
13: 34 The fact that *G* raised him
13: 37 But the one whom *G* raised
13: 43 them to continue in the grace of *G*.
13: 46 to speak the word of *G* to you first.
14: 15 worthless things to the living *G*,
14: 22 to enter the kingdom of *G*,''
14: 26 of *G* for the work they had now
14: 27 and reported all that *G* had done
15: 4 reported everything *G* had done
15: 7 some time ago *G* made a choice
15: 8 *G*, who knows the heart, showed
15: 10 to test *G* by putting on the necks
15: 12 and wonders *G* had done
15: 14 to us how *G* at first showed his
15: 19 the Gentiles who are turning to *G*.
16: 10 concluding that *G* had called us
16: 14 who was a worshiper of *G*.
16: 17 servants of the Most High *G*,
16: 25 praying and singing hymns to *G*,
16: 34 they had come to believe in *G*.
17: 13 Paul was preaching the word of *G*
17: 23 TO AN UNKNOWN *G*.
17: 24 ''The *G* who made the world
17: 27 *G* did this so that men would seek
17: 30 In the past *G* overlooked such
18: 7 Titius Justus, a worshiper of *G*.
18: 11 teaching them the word of *G*.
18: 13 to worship *G* in ways contrary
18: 26 the way of *G* more adequately.
19: 8 about the kingdom of *G*.
19: 11 *G* did extraordinary miracles
20: 21 turn to *G* in repentance
20: 27 to you the whole will of *G*.
20: 28 Be shepherds of the church of *G*,
20: 32 ''Now I commit you to *G*
21: 19 reported in detail what *G* had done
21: 20 they heard this, they praised *G*.
22: 3 and was just as zealous for *G*
22: 14 *G* of our fathers has chosen you
23: 1 duty to *G* in all good conscience
23: 3 Paul said to him, ''*G* will strike you,
24: 14 I admit that I worship the *G*
24: 15 and I have the same hope in *G*
24: 16 keep my conscience clear before *G*
26: 6 in what *G* has promised our fathers
26: 7 as they earnestly serve *G* day
26: 8 it incredible that *G* raises the dead?
26: 18 and from the power of Satan to *G*,
26: 20 to *G* and prove their repentance
26: 29 I pray *G* that not only you
27: 23 an angel of the *G* whose I am
27: 24 and *G* has graciously given you
27: 25 faith in *G* that it will happen just
27: 35 and gave thanks to *G* in front
28: 6 their minds and said he was a *g*.
28: 15 sight of these men Paul thanked *G*
28: 23 declared to them the kingdom of *G*
28: 31 he preached the kingdom of *G*
Ro 1: 1 and set apart for the gospel of *G*—
1: 4 the Son of *G* by his resurrection
1: 7 To all in Rome who are loved by *G*
1: 7 peace to you from *G* our Father
1: 8 I thank my *G* through Jesus Christ
1: 9 *G*, whom I serve with my whole
1: 16 the power of *G* for the salvation
1: 17 a righteousness from *G* is revealed,
1: 18 The wrath of *G* is being revealed
1: 19 *G* has made it plain to them.
1: 19 may be known about *G* is plain
1: 21 For although they knew *G*,
1: 21 they neither glorified him as *G*
1: 23 of the immortal *G* for images made
1: 24 Therefore *G* gave them
1: 25 They exchanged the truth of *G*
1: 26 *G* gave them over to shameful lusts
1: 28 to retain the knowledge of *G*,

Ro 2: 6 *G* ''will give to each person
2: 11 For *G* does not show favoritism.
2: 16 when *G* will judge men's secrets
2: 17 brag about your relationship to *G*;
2: 23 do you dishonor *G*
2: 29 not from men, but from *G*.
3: 2 entrusted with the very words of *G*.
3: 4 Let *G* be true, and every man a liar.
3: 5 That *G* is unjust in bringing his
3: 6 how could *G* judge the world?
3: 11 no one who seeks *G*.
3: 18 fear of *G* before their eyes.''
3: 19 world held accountable to *G*.
3: 21 But now a righteousness from *G*,
3: 22 This righteousness from *G* comes
3: 23 and fall short of the glory of *G*,
3: 25 *G* presented him as a sacrifice
3: 29 Is *G* the *G* of Jews only? Is he not
3: 29 Is he not the *G* of Gentiles too? Yes
3: 30 since there is only one *G*,
4: 2 to boast about—but not before *G*.
4: 3 say? ''Abraham believed *G*,
4: 5 trusts *G* who justifies the wicked,
4: 6 to whom *G* credits righteousness
4: 17 He is our father in the sight of *G*,
4: 17 the *G* who gives life to the dead
4: 20 in his faith and gave glory to *G*,
4: 20 regarding the promise of *G*,
4: 21 fully persuaded that *G* had power
4: 24 to whom *G* will credit
5: 1 we have peace with *G*
5: 2 in the hope of the glory of *G*.
5: 5 because *G* has poured out his love
5: 8 *G* demonstrates his own love for us
5: 11 in *G* through our Lord Jesus Christ,
5: 16 the gift of *G* is not like the result
6: 10 but the life he lives, he lives to *G*.
6: 11 but alive to *G* in Christ Jesus.
6: 13 but rather offer yourselves to *G*,
6: 17 But thanks be to *G* that,
6: 22 and have become slaves to *G*,
6: 23 but the gift of *G* is eternal life
7: 4 order that we might bear fruit to *G*.
7: 25 be to *G*— through Jesus Christ our
8: 3 *G* did by sending his own Son
8: 7 the sinful mind is hostile to *G*.
8: 8 the sinful nature cannot please *G*.
8: 9 if the Spirit of *G* lives in you.
8: 14 led by the Spirit of *G* are sons of *G*.
8: 17 heirs of *G* and co-heirs with Christ,
8: 19 for the sons of *G* to be revealed.
8: 21 freedom of the children of *G*.
8: 28 in all things *G* works for the good
8: 29 For those *G* foreknew he
8: 31 in response to this? If *G* is for us,
8: 33 against those whom *G* has chosen?
8: 33 has chosen? It is *G* who justifies.
8: 34 is at the right hand of *G* and is
8: 39 us from the love of *G* that is
9: 5 who is *G* over all, forever praised!
9: 14 What then shall we say? Is *G* unjust
9: 18 Therefore *G* has mercy
9: 19 ''Then why does *G* still blame us?
9: 20 O man, to talk back to *G*?
9: 22 What if *G*, choosing
9: 26 be called 'sons of the living *G*.' ''
10: 1 to *G* for the Israelites is that they
10: 2 them that they are zealous for *G*,
10: 3 righteousness that comes from *G*
10: 9 in your heart that *G* raised him
11: 1 I ask then, Did *G* reject his people?
11: 2 *G* did not reject his people,
11: 2 how he appealed to *G* against Israel
11: 8 ''*G* gave them a spirit of stupor,
11: 21 For if *G* did not spare the natural
11: 22 the kindness and sternness of *G*:
11: 23 for *G* is able to graft them in again.
11: 30 to *G* have now received mercy
11: 32 For *G* has bound all men
11: 33 of the wisdom and knowledge of *G*
11: 35 that *G* should repay him?''
11: 35 ''Who has ever given to *G*,
12: 1 to *G*— which is your spiritual
12: 3 measure of faith *G* has given you.
13: 1 exist have been established by *G*.
13: 1 that which *G* has established.
13: 2 against what *G* has instituted,
14: 3 for *G* has accepted him.

Ro 14: 6 for he gives thanks to G;
14: 6 to the Lord and gives thanks to G.
14: 11 every tongue will confess to G.' "
14: 12 give an account of himself to G.
14: 17 the kingdom of G is not a matter
14: 18 Christ in this way is pleasing to G
14: 20 the work of G for the sake of food.
14: 22 keep between yourself and G.
15: 5 May the G who gives endurance
15: 6 and mouth you may glorify the G
15: 7 in order to bring praise to G.
15: 9 so that the Gentiles may glorify G
15: 13 May the G of hope fill you
15: 15 because of the grace G gave me
15: 16 an offering acceptable to G,
15: 16 of proclaiming the gospel of G,
15: 17 in Christ Jesus in my service to G.
15: 18 to obey G by what I have said
15: 30 struggle by praying to G for me.
15: 33 The G of peace be with you all.
16: 20 G of peace will soon crush Satan
16: 26 by the command of the eternal G,
16: 27 to the only wise G be glory forever
1Co 1: 1 of Christ Jesus by the will of G,
1: 2 To the church of G in Corinth,
1: 3 peace to you from G our Father
1: 4 I always thank G for you
1: 9 G, who has called you
1: 18 are being saved it is the power of G.
1: 20 Has not G made foolish
1: 21 G was pleased
1: 21 since in the wisdom of G the world
1: 24 but to those whom G has called,
1: 24 power of G and the wisdom of G.
1: 25 For the foolishness of G is wiser
1: 25 and the weakness of G is stronger
1: 27 But G chose the foolish things
1: 27 G chose the weak things
1: 30 become for us wisdom from G—
2: 1 to you the testimony about G.
2: 7 and that G destined for our glory
2: 9 what G has prepared
2: 10 even the deep things of G.
2: 10 G has revealed it to us by his Spirit.
2: 11 of G except the Spirit of G.
2: 12 but the Spirit who is from G,
2: 12 may understand what G has freely
2: 14 come from the Spirit of G,
3: 6 watered it, but G made it grow.
3: 7 but only G, who makes things grow
3: 10 By the grace G has given me,
3: 17 God's temple, G will destroy
3: 23 you are of Christ, and Christ is of G
4: 1 with the secret things of G.
4: 5 each will receive his praise from G.
4: 9 to me that G has put us apostles
4: 20 the kingdom of G is not a matter
5: 13 G will judge those outside.
6: 9 will not inherit the kingdom of G?
6: 10 will inherit the kingdom of G.
6: 11 and by the Spirit of our G.
6: 13 but G will destroy them both.
6: 14 By his power G raised the Lord
6: 19 whom you have received from G?
6: 20 Therefore honor G with your body.
7: 7 each man has his own gift from G;
7: 15 G has called us to live in peace.
7: 17 and to which G has called him.
7: 20 was in when G called him.
7: 24 each man, as responsible to G,
7: 24 in the situation G called him to.
7: 40 that I too have the Spirit of G.
8: 3 man who loves G is known by G.
8: 4 and that there is no G but one.
8: 6 yet for us there is but one G,
8: 8 food does not bring us near to G;
9: 9 Is it about oxen that G is concerned
10: 5 G was not pleased with most
10: 13 G is faithful; he will not let you be
10: 20 offered to demons, not to G,
10: 30 of something I thank G for?
10: 31 do it all for the glory of G.
10: 32 Greeks or the church of G—
11: 3 and the head of Christ is G.
11: 7 since he is the image and glory of G
11: 12 But everything comes from G.
11: 13 to G with her head uncovered?
11: 16 nor do the churches of G.
1Co 11: 22 Or do you despise the church of G
12: 3 speaking by the Spirit of G says,
12: 6 but the same G works all of them
12: 18 But in fact G has arranged the parts
12: 24 But G has combined the members
12: 28 in the church G has appointed first
14: 2 does not speak to men but to G.
14: 16 If you are praising G
14: 18 I thank G that I speak
14: 25 So he will fall down and worship G,
14: 25 exclaiming, "G is really among you
14: 28 and speak to himself and G.
14: 33 For G is not a G of disorder
14: 36 the word of G originate with you?
15: 9 I persecuted the church of G.
15: 10 but the grace of G that was with me
15: 10 by the grace of G I am what I am,
15: 15 have testified about G that he
15: 15 to be false witnesses about G,
15: 24 over the kingdom to G the Father
15: 27 this does not include G himself,
15: 28 so that G may be all in all.
15: 34 are some who are ignorant of G—
15: 38 But G gives it a body as he has
15: 50 cannot inherit the kingdom of G,
15: 57 be to G! He gives us the victory
2Co 1: 1 To the church of G in Corinth,
1: 1 of Christ Jesus by the will of G,
1: 2 peace to you from G our Father
1: 3 Father of compassion and the G
1: 3 Praise be to the G and Father
1: 4 ourselves have received from G.
1: 9 rely on ourselves but on G,
1: 12 and sincerity that are from G.
1: 18 no"? But as surely as G is faithful,
1: 19 For the Son of G, Jesus Christ,
1: 20 how many promises G has made,
1: 20 spoken by us to the glory of G.
1: 21 Now it is G who makes both us
1: 23 I call G as my witness that it was
2: 14 be to G, who always leads us
2: 15 For we are to G the aroma of Christ
2: 17 sincerity, like men sent from G.
2: 17 speak before G with sincerity,
2: 17 we do not peddle the word of G
3: 3 but with the Spirit of the living G,
3: 4 this is ours through Christ before G
3: 5 but our competence comes from G.
4: 2 man's conscience in the sight of G.
4: 2 nor do we distort the word of G.
4: 4 of Christ, who is the image of G.
4: 4 g of this age has blinded the minds
4: 6 For G, who said, "Let light shine
4: 6 of the glory of G in the face
4: 7 this all-surpassing power is from G
4: 15 to overflow to the glory of G.
5: 1 we have a building from G,
5: 5 Now it is G who has made us
5: 11 What we are is plain to G,
5: 13 it is for the sake of G; if we are
5: 18 new has come! All this is from G,
5: 19 that G was reconciling the world
5: 20 Christ's behalf: Be reconciled to G.
5: 20 though G were making his appeal
5: 21 become the righteousness of G.
5: 21 G made him who had no sin
6: 4 of G we commend ourselves
6: 7 and in the power of G;
6: 16 As G has said: "I will live
6: 16 I will be their G, and they will be
6: 16 there between the temple of G
6: 16 we are the temple of the living G.
7: 1 out of reverence for G.
7: 6 But G, who comforts the downcast,
7: 9 became sorrowful as G intended
7: 12 rather that before G you could see
8: 1 about the grace that G has given
8: 16 I thank G, who put into the heart
9: 7 for G loves a cheerful giver.
9: 8 G is able to make all grace abound
9: 11 result in thanksgiving to G.
9: 12 in many expressions of thanks to G
9: 13 men will praise G for the obedience
9: 14 the surpassing grace G has given
9: 15 be to G for his indescribable gift!
10: 5 up against the knowledge of G,
10: 13 to the field G has assigned to us,
11: 7 you by preaching the gospel of G
2Co 11: 11 I do not love you? G knows I do!
11: 31 The G and Father of the Lord Jesus
12: 2 body I do not know—G knows.
12: 3 but G knows—was caught up
12: 19 been speaking in the sight of G
12: 21 I come again my G will humble me
13: 7 to G that you will not do anything
13: 11 And the G of love and peace will be
13: 14 the love of G, and the fellowship
Gal 1: 1 by Jesus Christ and G the Father,
1: 3 peace to you from G our Father
1: 4 according to the will of our G
1: 10 of G? Or am I trying to please men
1: 13 I persecuted the church of G
1: 15 But when G, who set me apart
1: 20 before G that what I am writing
1: 24 And they praised G because of me.
2: 6 G does not judge by external
2: 8 For G, who was at work
2: 19 to the law so that I might live for G.
2: 20 I live by faith in the Son of G,
2: 21 I do not set aside the grace of G,
3: 5 Does G give you his Spirit
3: 6 Abraham: "He believed G,
3: 8 foresaw that G would justify
3: 11 justified before G by the law,
3: 17 previously established by G
3: 18 G in his grace gave it to Abraham
3: 20 just one party; but G is one.
3: 21 opposed to the promises of G?
3: 26 You are all sons of G through faith
4: 4 had fully come, G sent his Son,
4: 6 G sent the Spirit of his Son
4: 7 G has made you also an heir.
4: 8 when you did not know G,
4: 9 But now that you know G—
4: 9 or rather are known by G—
4: 14 as if I were an angel of G,
5: 21 will not inherit the kingdom of G.
6: 7 not be deceived: G cannot be
6: 16 this rule, even to the Israel of G.
Eph 1: 1 of Christ Jesus by the will of G,
1: 2 peace to you from G our Father
1: 3 Praise be to the G and Father
1: 17 I keep asking that the G
1: 22 G placed all things under his feet
2: 4 because of his great love for us, G,
2: 6 And G raised us up with Christ
2: 8 it is the gift of G— not by works,
2: 10 which G prepared in advance for us
2: 12 and without G in the world.
2: 16 of them to G through the cross,
2: 22 in which G lives by his Spirit.
3: 9 for ages past was kept hidden in G,
3: 10 of G should be made known
3: 12 faith in him we may approach G
3: 19 the measure of all the fullness of G.
4: 6 one baptism; one G and Father
4: 13 in the knowledge of the Son of G
4: 18 and separated from the life of G
4: 24 to be like G in true righteousness
4: 30 do not grieve the Holy Spirit of G,
4: 32 just as in Christ G forgave you.
5: 1 Be imitators of G, therefore,
5: 2 fragrant offering and sacrifice to G.
5: 5 in the kingdom of Christ and of G.
5: 20 giving thanks to G the Father
6: 6 doing the will of G from your heart.
6: 11 Put on the full armor of G
6: 13 put on the full armor of G,
6: 17 of the Spirit, which is the word of G
6: 23 love with faith from G the Father
Php 1: 2 peace to you from G our Father
1: 3 I thank my G every time I
1: 8 G can testify how I long for all
1: 11 to the glory and praise of G.
1: 14 the word of G more courageously
1: 28 you will be saved—and that by G.
2: 6 Who, being in very nature G,
2: 6 with G something to be grasped,
2: 9 Therefore G exalted him
2: 11 to the glory of G the Father.
2: 13 for it is G who works in you to will
2: 15 children of G without fault
2: 27 But G had mercy on him,
3: 3 we who worship by the Spirit of G,
3: 9 righteousness that comes from G
3: 14 the prize for which G has called me

Php 3: 15 that too G will make clear to you.
3: 19 is destruction, their g is their
4: 6 present your requests to G.
4: 7 peace of G, which transcends all
4: 9 the G of peace will be with you.
4: 18 acceptable sacrifice, pleasing to G.
4: 19 And my G will meet all your needs
4: 20 To our G and Father be glory
Col 1: 1 of Christ Jesus by the will of G,
1: 2 peace to you from G our Father.
1: 3 We always thank G, the Father
1: 9 and asking G to fill you
1: 10 growing in the knowledge of G,
1: 15 He is the image of the invisible G,
1: 19 For G was pleased
1: 21 Once you were alienated from G
1: 25 by the commission G gave me
1: 25 to you the word of G in its fullness
1: 27 To them G has chosen
2: 2 they may know the mystery of G,
2: 12 faith in the power of G,
2: 13 G made you alive with Christ.
2: 19 grows as G causes it to grow.
3: 1 seated at the right hand of G.
3: 3 life is now hidden with Christ in G.
3: 6 of these, the wrath of G is coming.
3: 16 with gratitude in your hearts to G.
3: 17 giving thanks to G the Father
4: 3 that G may open a door
4: 11 workers for the kingdom of G,
4: 12 firm in all the will of G,
1Th 1: 1 the Thessalonians in G the Father
1: 2 We always thank G for all of you,
1: 3 continually remember before our G
1: 4 by G, we know that he has chosen
1: 8 faith in G has become known
1: 9 They tell how you turned to G
1: 9 idols to serve the living and true G,
2: 2 but with the help of our G we dared
2: 4 men approved by G to be entrusted
2: 4 trying to please men but G,
2: 5 cover up greed—G is our witness.
2: 8 with you not only the gospel of G
2: 9 while we preached the gospel of G
2: 10 You are witnesses, and so is G,
2: 12 urging you to live lives worthy of G
2: 13 also thank G continually because,
2: 13 but as it actually is, the word of G,
2: 13 when you received the word of G,
2: 15 They displease G and are hostile
2: 16 The wrath of G has come
3: 9 How can we thank G enough
3: 9 have in the presence of our G
3: 11 may our G and Father himself
3: 13 and holy in the presence of our G
4: 1 how to live in order to please G,
4: 5 the heathen, who do not know G;
4: 7 For G did not call us to be impure,
4: 8 does not reject man but G,
4: 9 taught by G to love each other.
4: 14 and so we believe that G will bring
4: 16 and with the trumpet call of G,
5: 9 For G did not appoint us
5: 23 May G himself, the G of peace,
2Th 1: 1 the Thessalonians in G our Father
1: 2 peace to you from G the Father
1: 3 always to thank G for you,
1: 5 worthy of the kingdom of G,
1: 6 G is just: He will pay back trouble
1: 8 punish those who do not know G
1: 11 that our G may count you worthy
1: 12 according to the grace of our G
2: 4 over everything that is called G
2: 4 proclaiming himself to be G.
2: 11 For this reason G sends them
2: 13 from the beginning G chose you
2: 13 we ought always to thank G for you
2: 16 Christ himself and G our Father,
1Ti 1: 1 by the command of G our Savior
1: 2 and peace from G the Father
1: 11 glorious gospel of the blessed G,
1: 17 immortal, invisible, the only G,
2: 3 is good, and pleases G our Savior,
2: 5 one mediator between G and men,
2: 5 there is one G and one mediator
2: 10 women who profess to worship G.
3: 15 which is the church of the living G,
4: 3 which G created to be received

1Ti 4: 4 For everything G created is good,
4: 5 it is consecrated by the word of G
4: 10 have put our hope in the living G,
5: 4 for this is pleasing to G.
5: 5 and left all alone puts her hope in G
5: 5 day to pray and to ask G for help.
5: 21 in the sight of G and Christ Jesus
6: 11 man of G, flee from all this,
6: 13 In the sight of G, who gives life
6: 15 G, the blessed and only Ruler,
6: 15 which G will bring about
6: 17 but to put their hope in G,
2Ti 1: 1 of Christ Jesus by the will of G,
1: 2 and peace from G the Father
1: 3 I thank G, whom I serve,
1: 6 you to fan into flame the gift of G,
1: 7 For G did not give us a spirit
1: 8 the power of G, who has saved us
2: 14 Warn them before G
2: 15 best to present yourself to G
2: 25 in the hope that G will grant them
3: 4 of pleasure rather than lovers of G
3: 17 of G may be thoroughly equipped
4: 1 In the presence of G
Tit 1: 1 a servant of G and an apostle
1: 2 which G, who does not lie,
1: 3 by the command of G our Savior,
1: 4 Grace and peace from G the Father
1: 16 They claim to know G,
2: 5 no one will malign the word of G.
2: 10 the teaching about G our Savior
2: 11 grace of G that brings salvation has
2: 13 glorious appearing of our great G
3: 4 and love of G our Savior appeared,
3: 8 trusted in G may be careful
Phm : 3 and peace from G our Father
: 4 I always thank my G as I remember
Heb 1: 1 In the past G spoke
1: 5 which of the angels did G ever say,
1: 6 when G brings his firstborn
1: 8 O G, will last for ever and ever,
1: 9 therefore G, your G, has set you
1: 13 which of the angels did G ever say,
2: 4 G also testified to it by signs,
2: 8 G left nothing that is not subject
2: 9 the grace of G he might taste death
2: 10 it was fitting that G, for whom
2: 13 and the children G has given me."
2: 17 faithful high priest in service to G,
3: 4 but G is the builder of everything.
3: 12 that turns away from the living G.
3: 18 to whom did G swear that they
4: 3 enter that rest, just as G has said,
4: 4 "And on the seventh day G rested
4: 7 Therefore G again set a certain day
4: 8 G would not have spoken later
4: 9 a Sabbath-rest for the people of G;
4: 10 from his own work, just as G did
4: 12 For the word of G is living
4: 14 the Son of G, let us hold firmly
5: 1 them in matters related to G,
5: 4 he must be called by G, just
5: 5 But G said to him,
5: 10 and was designated by G
6: 1 in G, instruction about baptisms,
6: 3 And G permitting, we will do so.
6: 5 the goodness of the word of G
6: 6 the Son of G all over again
6: 7 farmed receives the blessing of G.
6: 10 G is not unjust; he will not forget
6: 13 When G made his promise
6: 17 Because G wanted
6: 18 G did this so that, by two
6: 18 in which it is impossible for G to lie
7: 1 and priest of G Most High.
7: 3 of G he remains a priest forever.
7: 19 by which we draw near to G.
7: 21 with an oath when G said to him:
7: 25 come to G through him,
8: 8 But G found fault with the people
8: 10 I will be their G,
9: 14 offered himself unblemished to G,
9: 14 so that we may serve the living G!
9: 20 which G has commanded you
10: 7 I have come to do your will, O G
10: 12 he sat down at the right hand of G.
10: 21 priest over the house of G,
10: 22 draw near to G with a sincere heart

Heb 10: 27 will consume the enemies of G.
10: 29 who has trampled the Son of G
10: 31 to fall into the hands of the living G
10: 36 when you have done the will of G,
11: 4 faith Abel offered G a better
11: 4 when G spoke well of his offerings.
11: 5 because G had taken him away.
11: 5 commended as one who pleased G.
11: 6 faith it is impossible to please G,
11: 10 whose architect and builder is G.
11: 16 Therefore G is not ashamed
11: 16 ashamed to be called their G,
11: 17 when G tested him,
11: 18 even though G had said to him,
11: 19 reasoned that G could raise
11: 25 along with the people of G rather
11: 40 G had planned something better
12: 2 at the right hand of the throne of G.
12: 7 as discipline; G is treating you
12: 10 but G disciplines us for our good,
12: 15 it that no one misses the grace of G
12: 22 Jerusalem, the city of the living G.
12: 23 You have come to G, the judge
12: 28 and so worship G acceptably
12: 29 for our G is a consuming fire.
13: 4 for G will judge the adulterer
13: 5 what you have, because G has said,
13: 7 who spoke the word of G to you.
13: 15 offer to G a sacrifice of praise—
13: 16 for with such sacrifices G is pleased
13: 20 May the G of peace, who
Jas 1: 1 of G and of the Lord Jesus Christ,
1: 5 he should ask G, who gives
1: 12 crown of life that G has promised
1: 13 For G cannot be tempted by evil,
1: 13 one should say, "G is tempting
1: 20 the righteous life that G desires.
1: 27 Religion that G our Father accepts
2: 5 Has not G chosen those who are
2: 19 You believe that there is one G.
2: 23 "Abraham believed G,
4: 2 because you do not ask G.
4: 4 the world becomes an enemy of G.
4: 4 with the world is hatred toward G?
4: 6 "G opposes the proud
4: 7 Submit yourselves, then, to G.
4: 8 Come near to G and he will come
1Pe 1: 2 the foreknowledge of G the Father,
1: 3 Praise be to the G and Father
1: 21 Through him you believe in G,
1: 21 and so your faith and hope are in G
1: 23 the living and enduring word of G.
2: 4 chosen by G and precious to him—
2: 5 to G through Jesus Christ.
2: 9 nation, a people belonging to G,
2: 10 but now you are the people of G;
2: 12 glorify G on the day he visits us.
2: 16 for evil; live as servants of G.
2: 17 brotherhood of believers, fear G,
2: 19 because he is conscious of G.
2: 20 this is commendable before G.
3: 5 hope in G used to make themselves
3: 18 the unrighteous, to bring you to G.
3: 20 ago when G waited patiently
3: 21 of a good conscience toward G.
4: 2 but rather for the will of G.
4: 6 but live according to G in regard
4: 11 it with the strength G provides,
4: 11 one speaking the very words of G.
4: 11 that in all things G may be praised
4: 14 of glory and of G rests on you.
4: 16 praise G that you bear that name.
4: 17 to begin with the family of G;
4: 17 who do not obey the gospel of G?
5: 2 you are willing, as G wants you
5: 5 because, "G opposes the proud
5: 10 the G of all grace, who called you
5: 12 that this is the true grace of G.
2Pe 1: 1 through the righteousness of our G
1: 2 through the knowledge of G
1: 17 and glory from G the Father
1: 21 but men spoke from G
2: 4 For if G did not spare angels
3: 12 as you look forward to the day of G
3: 15 with the wisdom that G gave him.
1Jn 1: 5 G is light; in him there is no
2: 14 and the word of G lives in you,
2: 17 the will of G lives forever.

1Jn 3: 1 we should be called children of *G!*
3: 2 now we are children of *G*,
3: 8 the Son of *G* appeared was
3: 9 because he has been born of *G*.
3: 9 born of *G* will continue to sin,
3: 10 do what is right is not a child of *G;*
3: 10 we know who the children of *G* are
3: 17 how can the love of *G* be in him?
3: 20 For *G* is greater than our hearts,
3: 21 we have confidence before *G*
4: 1 to see whether they are from *G*,
4: 2 come in the flesh is from *G*,
4: 2 you can recognize the Spirit of *G:*
4: 3 acknowledge Jesus is not from *G*.
4: 4 from *G* and have overcome them,
4: 6 are from *G*, and whoever knows *G*
4: 6 not from *G* does not listen
4: 7 born of *G* and knows *G*.
4: 7 for love comes from *G*.
4: 8 not know *G*, because *G* is love.
4: 9 This is how *G* showed his love
4: 10 This is love: not that we loved *G*,
4: 11 Dear friends, since *G* so loved us,
4: 12 No one has ever seen *G;*
4: 12 *G* lives in us and his love is made
4: 15 *G* lives in him and he in *G*.
4: 15 that Jesus is the Son of *G*,
4: 16 and rely on the love *G* has for us.
4: 16 *G* is love.
4: 16 in love lives in *G*, and *G* in him.
4: 20 cannot love *G*, whom he has not
4: 20 "I love *G*," yet hates his brother,
4: 21 Whoever loves *G* must
5: 1 that Jesus is the Christ is born of *G*,
5: 2 by loving *G* and carrying out his
5: 2 that we love the children of *G:*
5: 3 love for *G:* to obey his commands.
5: 4 born of *G* overcomes the world.
5: 5 believes that Jesus is the Son of *G*.
5: 9 because it is the testimony of *G*,
5: 10 believed the testimony *G* has given
5: 10 does not believe *G* has made him
5: 10 in the Son of *G* has this testimony
5: 11 *G* has given us eternal life,
5: 12 the Son of *G* does not have life.
5: 13 believe in the name of the Son of *G*
5: 14 have in approaching *G:*
5: 16 he should pray and *G* will give him
5: 18 born of *G* does not continue to sin;
5: 18 born of *G* keeps him safe,
5: 19 We know that we are children of *G*,
5: 20 He is the true *G* and eternal life.
5: 20 also that the Son of *G* has come
2Jn : 3 and peace from *G* the Father
: 9 teaching of Christ does not have *G;*
3Jn : 6 way in a manner worthy of *G*.
: 11 does what is evil has not seen *G*.
: 11 who does what is good is from *G*.
Jude : 1 who are loved by *G* the Father
: 4 the grace of our *G* into a license
: 25 to the only *G* our Savior be glory,
Rev 1: 1 which *G* gave him
1: 2 the word of *G* and the testimony
1: 6 priests to serve his *G* and Father—
1: 8 says the Lord *G*, "who is,
1: 9 of the word of *G* and the testimony
2: 7 which is in the paradise of *G*.
2: 18 are the words of the Son of *G*,
3: 1 who holds the seven spirits of *G*
3: 2 complete in the sight of my *G*.
3: 12 a pillar in the temple of my *G*.
3: 12 and the name of the city of my *G*,
3: 12 down out of heaven from my *G;*
3: 12 write on him the name of my *G*
4: 5 These are the seven spirits of *G*.
4: 8 holy is the Lord *G* Almighty,
4: 11 "You are worthy, our Lord and *G*,
5: 6 are the seven spirits of *G* sent out
5: 9 blood you purchased men for *G*
5: 10 priests to serve our *G*,
6: 9 of *G* and the testimony they had
7: 2 having the seal of the living *G*.
7: 3 of the servants of our *G*."
7: 10 "Salvation belongs to our *G*,
7: 11 before the throne and worshiped *G*
7: 12 be to our *G* for ever and ever.
7: 15 "they are before the throne of *G*
7: 17 *G* will wipe away every tear
Rev 8: 2 seven angels who stand before *G*,
8: 4 up before *G* from the angel's hand.
9: 4 the seal of *G* on their foreheads.
9: 13 of the golden altar that is before *G*.
10: 7 mystery of *G* will be accomplished,
11: 1 and measure the temple of *G*
11: 11 breath of life from *G* entered them,
11: 13 and gave glory to the *G* of heaven.
11: 16 fell on their faces and worshiped *G*,
11: 16 seated on their thrones before *G*,
11: 17 thanks to you, Lord *G* Almighty,
12: 5 her child was snatched up to *G*
12: 6 to a place prepared for her by *G*,
12: 10 accuses them before our *G* day
12: 10 and the kingdom of our *G*,
13: 6 opened his mouth to blaspheme *G*,
14: 4 as firstfruits to *G* and the Lamb.
14: 7 "Fear *G* and give him glory,
15: 2 They held harps given them by *G*
15: 3 Lord *G* Almighty.
15: 3 the song of Moses the servant of *G*
15: 7 filled with the wrath of *G*,
15: 8 with smoke from the glory of *G*
16: 7 "Yes, Lord *G* Almighty,
16: 9 and they cursed the name of *G*,
16: 11 and cursed the *G* of heaven
16: 14 on the great day of *G* Almighty.
16: 19 *G* remembered Babylon the Great
16: 21 And they cursed *G* on account
17: 17 For *G* has put it into their hearts
18: 5 and *G* has remembered her crimes.
18: 8 is the Lord *G* who judges her.
18: 20 *G* has judged her for the way she
19: 1 glory and power belong to our *G*,
19: 4 fell down and worshiped *G*,
19: 5 "Praise our *G*,
19: 6 For our Lord *G* Almighty reigns.
19: 9 "These are the true words of *G*."
19: 10 Worship *G!* For the testimony
19: 13 and his name is the Word of *G*.
19: 15 fury of the wrath of *G* Almighty.
19: 17 together for the great supper of *G*,
20: 4 and because of the word of *G*.
20: 6 but they will be priests of *G*
21: 2 coming down out of heaven from *G*
21: 3 Now the dwelling of *G* is with men,
21: 3 and *G* himself will be with them
21: 3 be with them and be their *G*.
21: 7 I will be his *G* and he will be my
21: 10 coming down out of heaven from *G*
21: 11 It shone with the glory of *G*,
21: 22 because the Lord *G* Almighty
21: 23 for the glory of *G* gives it light,
22: 1 flowing from the throne of *G*
22: 3 throne of *G* and of the Lamb will be
22: 5 for the Lord *G* will give them light.
22: 6 the *G* of the spirits of the prophets,
22: 9 Worship *G!*" Then he told me,
22: 18 *G* will add to him the plagues
22: 19 *G* will take away from him his

GOD-BREATHED (BREATH)

2Ti 3: 16 All Scripture is *G* and is useful

GOD-FEARING (FEAR)

Ecc 8: 12 that it will go better with *G* men,
Ac 2: 5 staying in Jerusalem *G* Jews
10: 2 all his family were devout and *G;*
10: 22 He is a righteous and *G* man,
13: 26 of Abraham, and you *G* Gentiles,
13: 50 But the Jews incited the *G* women
17: 4 as did a large number of *G* Greeks
17: 17 with the Jews and the *G* Greeks,

GOD-HATERS (HATE)

Ro 1: 30 They are gossips, slanderers, *G*,

GOD'S (GOD)

Ge 6: 11 the earth was corrupt in *G* sight
28: 22 as a pillar will be *G* house,
Ex 18: 15 come to me to seek *G* will.
18: 16 inform them of *G* decrees and laws
Dt 21: 23 hung on a tree is under *G* curse.
1Sa 5: 11 *G* hand was very heavy upon it.
14: 45 for he did this today with *G* help."
2Sa 9: 3 to whom I can show *G* kindness?"
1Ch 5: 22 fell slain, because the battle was *G*.
2Ch 1: 3 for *G* Tent of Meeting was there,
2Ch 4: 19 furnishings that were in *G* temple:
5: 1 them in the treasuries of *G* temple.
20: 15 For the battle is not yours, but *G*.
24: 18 *G* anger came upon Judah
31: 21 in the service of *G* temple
32: 12 himself remove this *g* high places
33: 7 had made and put it in *G* temple,
35: 8 the administrators of *G* temple,
35: 22 what Neco had said at *G* command
36: 13 made him take an oath in *G* name.
36: 16 But they mocked *G* messengers,
36: 19 They set fire to *G* temple
Ne 13: 25 made them take an oath in *G* name
Job 6: 4 *G* terrors are marshaled against me
9: 34 someone to remove *G* rod from me
13: 7 you speak wickedly on *G* behalf?
15: 8 Do you listen in on *G* council?
15: 11 Are *G* consolations not enough
15: 30 of *G* mouth will carry him away.
20: 28 on the day of *G* wrath.
29: 4 when *G* intimate friendship blessed
33: 26 he sees *G* face and shouts for joy;
36: 2 to be said in *G* behalf.
37: 5 *G* voice thunders in marvelous
37: 14 stop and consider *G* wonders.
38: 33 Can you set up ⌊*G*⌋ dominion
40: 9 Do you have an arm like *G*,
Ps 52: 8 I trust in *G* unfailing love
61: 7 in *G* presence forever;
63: 11 swear by *G* name will praise him,
69: 30 I will praise *G* name in song
78: 10 they did not keep *G* covenant
78: 31 *G* anger rose against them;
114: 2 Judah became *G* sanctuary,
Ecc 9: 1 and what they do are in *G* hands,
Mt 5: 34 for it is *G* throne; or by the earth,
22: 21 and to God what is *G*."
23: 22 by heaven swears by *G* throne
Mk 3: 35 Whoever does *G* will is my brother
12: 17 and to God what is *G*."
Lk 3: 6 all mankind will see *G* salvation.' "
7: 29 acknowledged that *G* way was
7: 30 in the law rejected *G* purpose
8: 21 are those who hear *G* word
16: 15 among men is detestable in *G* sight.
19: 44 the time of *G* coming to you."
20: 25 and to God what is *G*."
20: 36 They are *G* children,
Jn 3: 18 believed in the name of *G* one
3: 36 for *G* wrath remains on him."
7: 17 If any one chooses to do *G* will,
10: 36 'I am *G* Son'? Do not believe me
11: 4 is for *G* glory so that *G* Son may be
Ac 2: 23 over to you by *G* set purpose
4: 19 whether it is right in *G* sight
6: 8 a man full of *G* grace and power,
7: 46 who enjoyed *G* favor and asked
13: 36 when David had served *G* purpose
17: 29 Therefore since we are *G* offspring,
18: 21 "I will come back if it is *G* will."
20: 24 testifying to the gospel of *G* grace.
23: 4 "You dare to insult *G* high priest?"
26: 22 I have had *G* help to this very day,
28: 28 to know that *G* salvation has been
Ro 1: 10 by *G* will the way may be opened
1: 20 of the world *G* invisible qualities—
1: 32 they know *G* righteous decree
2: 2 Now we know that *G* judgment
2: 3 think you will escape *G* judgment?
2: 4 not realizing that *G* kindness leads
2: 5 yourself for the day of *G* wrath,
2: 13 law who are righteous in *G* sight,
2: 24 "*G* name is blasphemed
3: 3 lack of faith nullify *G* faithfulness?
3: 5 brings out *G* righteousness more
3: 7 falsehood enhances *G* truthfulness
5: 9 saved from *G* wrath through him!
5: 10 For if, when we were *G* enemies,
5: 15 how much more did *G* grace
5: 17 who receive *G* abundant provision
7: 22 in my inner being I delight in *G* law
7: 25 in my mind am a slave to *G* law,
8: 7 It does not submit to *G* law,
8: 16 our spirit that we are *G* children.
8: 27 saints in accordance with *G* will.
9: 6 as though *G* word had failed.
9: 8 children who are *G* children,
9: 11 in order that *G* purpose

Ro 9: 16 or effort, but on *G* mercy.
10: 3 submit to *G* righteousness.
11: 4 And what was *G* answer to him?
11: 29 for *G* gifts and his call are
11: 31 as a result of *G* mercy to you
12: 1 brothers, in view of *G* mercy,
12: 2 and approve what *G* will is—
12: 13 Share with *G* people who are
12: 19 but leave room for *G* wrath,
13: 4 For he is *G* servant to do you good.
13: 4 He is *G* servant, an agent of wrath
13: 6 for the authorities are *G* servants,
14: 10 stand before *G* judgment seat.
15: 8 of the Jews on behalf of *G* truth,
15: 32 so that by *G* will I may come to you
1Co 2: 5 on men's wisdom, but on *G* power.
2: 7 No, we speak of *G* secret wisdom,
3: 9 For we are *G* fellow workers;
3: 9 you are *G* field, *G* building.
3: 16 and that *G* Spirit lives in you?
3: 16 that you yourselves are *G* temple
3: 17 If anyone destroys *G* temple,
3: 17 for *G* temple is sacred,
3: 19 this world is foolishness in *G* sight.
7: 19 Keeping *G* commands is what
9: 21 (though I am not free from *G* law
11: 19 which of you have *G* approval.
16: 1 about the collection for *G* people:
2Co 1: 12 wisdom but according to *G* grace.
4: 1 through *G* mercy we have this
6: 1 As *G* fellow workers we urge you
6: 1 not to receive *G* grace in vain.
6: 2 now is the time of *G* favor,
8: 5 then to us in keeping with *G* will.
9: 12 supplying the needs of *G* people
13: 4 weakness, yet he lives by *G* power.
13: 4 yet by *G* power we will live
Eph 1: 7 riches of *G* grace that he lavished
1: 14 of those who are *G* possession—
2: 10 For we are *G* workmanship,
2: 19 and members of *G* household,
2: 19 but fellow citizens with *G* people
3: 2 of *G* grace that was given to me
3: 5 by the Spirit to *G* holy apostles
3: 7 by the gift of *G* grace given me
3: 8 less than the least of all *G* people,
4: 12 to prepare *G* people for works
5: 3 improper for *G* holy people.
5: 6 of such things *G* wrath comes
Php 1: 7 all of you share in *G* grace with me.
Col 1: 6 understood *G* grace in all its truth.
3: 12 Therefore, as *G* chosen people,
1Th 2: 14 became imitators of *G* churches
3: 2 and *G* fellow worker in spreading
4: 3 It is *G* will that you should be holy;
5: 18 for this is *G* will for you
2Th 1: 4 among *G* churches we boast about
1: 5 is evidence that *G* judgment is
2: 4 even sets himself up in *G* temple,
3: 5 Lord direct your hearts into *G* love
1Ti 1: 4 rather than *G* work—
3: 5 how can he take care of *G* church?)
3: 15 themselves in *G* household,
6: 1 so that *G* name and our teaching
2Ti 2: 9 But *G* word is not chained.
2: 19 *G* solid foundation stands firm,
Tit 1: 1 Christ for the faith of *G* elect
1: 7 overseer is entrusted with *G* work,
Heb 1: 3 The Son is the radiance of *G* glory
1: 6 "Let all *G* angels worship him."
3: 2 Moses was faithful in all *G* house.
3: 5 as a servant in all *G* house,
3: 6 is faithful as a son over *G* house.
4: 10 for anyone who enters *G* rest
4: 13 all creation is hidden from *G* sight.
5: 12 truths of *G* word all over again.
9: 24 now to appear for us in *G* presence.
11: 3 was formed at *G* command,
13: 24 all your leaders and all *G* people.
Jas 2: 23 and he was called *G* friend.
3: 9 who have been made in *G* likeness.
1Pe 1: 1 To *G* elect, strangers in the world,
1: 5 by *G* power until the coming
2: 15 For it is *G* will that
3: 4 which is of great worth in *G* sight.
3: 17 if it is *G* will, to suffer
3: 22 into heaven and is at *G* right hand
4: 10 faithfully administering *G* grace
1Pe 4: 19 according to *G* will should commit
5: 2 Be shepherds of *G* flock that is
5: 6 therefore, under *G* mighty hand,
2Pe 3: 5 ago by *G* word the heavens existed
1Jn 2: 5 *G* love is truly made complete
3: 9 because *G* seed remains in him;
5: 9 but *G* testimony is greater
Jude : 21 Keep yourselves in *G* love
Rev 3: 14 true witness, the ruler of *G* creation
11: 19 *G* temple in heaven was opened,
12: 17 those who obey *G* commandments
14: 10 too, will drink of the wine of *G* fury
14: 12 saints who obey *G* commandments
14: 19 into the great winepress of *G* wrath
15: 1 with them *G* wrath is completed.
16: 1 bowls of *G* wrath on the earth."
17: 17 until *G* words are fulfilled.
20: 9 surrounded the camp of *G* people,
22: 21 of the Lord Jesus be with *G* people.

GODDESS (GOD)

1Ki 11: 5 He followed Ashtoreth the *g*
11: 33 and worshiped Ashtoreth the *g*
2Ki 23: 13 built for Ashtoreth the vile *g*
Ac 19: 27 and the *g* herself, who is worshiped
19: 27 of the great *g* Artemis will be
19: 37 temples nor blasphemed our *g*.

GODLESS (GODLESSNESS)

Job 8: 13 so perishes the hope of the *g*.
13: 16 for no *g* man would dare come
15: 34 of the *g* will be barren,
20: 5 the joy of the *g* lasts but a moment.
27: 8 For what hope has the *g*
34: 30 to keep a *g* man from ruling,
36: 13 "The *g* in heart harbor resentment;
Pr 11: 9 his mouth the *g* destroys his
Isa 10: 6 I send him against a *g* nation,
33: 14 trembling grips the *g*:
Jer 23: 11 "Both prophet and priest are *g*;
1Ti 4: 7 Have nothing to do with *g* myths
6: 20 Turn away from *g* chatter
2Ti 2: 16 Avoid *g* chatter, because those
Heb 12: 16 sexually immoral, or is *g* like Esau,
Jude : 4 They are *g* men, who change

GODLESSNESS (GODLESS)

Ro 1: 18 from heaven against all the *g*
11: 26 he will turn *g* away from Jacob.

GODLINESS (GOD)

Ac 3: 12 or *g* we had made this man walk?
1Ti 2: 2 and quiet lives in all *g* and holiness.
3: 16 question, the mystery of *g* is great:
4: 8 but *g* has value for all things,
6: 5 and who think that *g* is a means
6: 6 *g* with contentment is great gain.
6: 11 and pursue righteousness, *g*, faith,
2Ti 3: 5 a form of *g* but denying its power.
Tit 1: 1 of the truth that leads to *g*—
2Pe 1: 3 and *g* through our knowledge
1: 6 and to perseverance, *g*;
1: 7 and to *g*, brotherly kindness;

GODLY (GOD)

Ps 4: 3 that the LORD has set apart the *g*
12: 1 LORD, for the *g* are no more;
32: 6 let everyone who is *g* pray
Mic 7: 2 The *g* have been swept
Mal 2: 15 Because he was seeking *g* offspring
Jn 9: 31 to the *g* man who does his will.
Ac 8: 2 *G* men buried Stephen
2Co 7: 10 *G* sorrow brings repentance that
7: 11 See what this *g* sorrow has
11: 2 jealous for you with a *g* jealousy.
1Ti 4: 7 rather, train yourself to be *g*.
6: 3 Jesus Christ and to *g* teaching,
2Ti 3: 12 everyone who wants to live a *g* life
Tit 2: 12 and *g* lives in this present age,
2Pe 2: 9 how to rescue *g* men from trials
3: 11 You ought to live holy and *g* lives

GODS (GOD)

Ge 31: 19 stole her father's household *g*.
31: 30 But why did you steal my *g*?"
31: 32 if you find anyone who has your *g*,
31: 32 know that Rachel had stolen the *g*.
31: 34 Rachel had taken the household *g*
Ge 31: 35 but could not find the household *g*.
35: 2 of the foreign *g* you have with you,
35: 4 Jacob all the foreign *g* they had
Ex 12: 12 judgment on all the *g* of Egypt.
15: 11 "Who among the *g* is like you,
18: 11 LORD is greater than all other *g*,
20: 3 "You shall have no other *g*
20: 23 Do not make any *g* to be
20: 23 *g* of silver or *g* of gold.
23: 13 Do not invoke the names of other *g*
23: 24 Do not bow down before their *g*
23: 32 covenant with them or with their *g*.
23: 33 *g* will certainly be a snare
32: 1 make us *g* who will go before us.
32: 4 "These are your *g*, O Israel,
32: 8 'These are your *g*, O Israel,
32: 23 'Make us *g* who will go before us.
32: 31 They have made themselves *g*
34: 15 prostitute themselves to their *g*
34: 16 prostitute themselves to their *g*,
Lev 19: 4 make *g* of cast metal for yourselves
Nu 25: 2 and bowed down before these *g*.
25: 2 them to the sacrifices to their *g*.
33: 4 had brought judgment on their *g*.
Dt 4: 7 to have their *g* near them the way
4: 28 you will worship man-made *g*
5: 7 "You shall have no other *g*
6: 14 Do not follow other *g*, the *g*
7: 4 from following me to serve other *g*,
7: 16 with pity and do not serve their *g*,
7: 25 The images of their *g* you are
8: 19 and follow other *g* and worship
10: 17 the LORD your God is God of *g*
11: 16 and worship other *g* and bow
11: 28 today by following other *g*,
12: 2 are dispossessing worship their *g*.
12: 3 cut down the idols of their *g*
12: 30 How do these nations serve their *g*
12: 30 by inquiring about their *g*,
12: 31 because in worshiping their *g*,
12: 31 in the fire as sacrifices to their *g*.
13: 2 "Let us follow other *g*" (*g* you have
13: 6 worship other *g*" (*g* that neither
13: 7 *g* of the peoples around you,
13: 13 worship other *g*" (*g* you have not
17: 3 command has worshiped other *g*,
18: 20 speaks in the name of other *g*,
20: 18 do in worshiping their *g*,
28: 14 following other *g* and serving them
28: 36 There you will worship other *g*, *g*
28: 64 There you will worship other *g*— *g*
29: 18 and worship the *g* of those nations;
29: 26 and worshiped other *g* and bowed
29: 26 *g* they did not know, *g* he had not
30: 17 away to bow down to other *g*
31: 16 to the foreign *g* of the land they are
31: 18 wickedness in turning to other *g*.
31: 20 they will turn to other *g*
32: 16 with their foreign *g*
32: 17 *g* that recently appeared,
32: 17 *g* they had not known,
32: 17 *g* your fathers did not fear.
32: 37 will say: "Now where are their *g*,
32: 38 the *g* who ate the fat
Jos 23: 7 do not invoke the names of their *g*
23: 16 and go and serve other *g*
24: 2 the River and worshiped other *g*.
24: 14 Throw away the *g* your forefathers
24: 15 or the *g* of the Amorites,
24: 15 the *g* your forefathers served
24: 16 the LORD to serve other *g*!
24: 20 the LORD and serve foreign *g*,
24: 23 "throw away the foreign *g* that are
Jdg 2: 3 and their *g* will be a snare to you."
2: 12 worshiped various *g* of the peoples
2: 17 prostituted themselves to other *g*
2: 19 following other *g* and serving
3: 6 to their sons, and served their *g*.
5: 8 When they chose new *g*,
6: 10 do not worship the *g*
9: 9 by which both *g* and men are
9: 13 which cheers both *g* and men,
10: 6 and the *g* of Aram, the *g* of Sidon,
10: 6 and the *g* of the Philistines.
10: 6 the *g* of Moab,
10: 6 the *g* of the Ammonites
10: 13 forsaken me and served other *g*,
10: 14 cry out to the *g* you have chosen.

Jdg 10: 16 rid of the foreign *g* among them
18: 14 other household *g*, a carved image
18: 17 the other household *g*
18: 18 the other household *g*
18: 20 the other household *g*
18: 24 He replied, "You took the *g* I made
Ru 1: 15 back to her people and her *g*.
1Sa 4: 8 They are the *g* who struck
4: 8 from the hand of these mighty *g?*
6: 5 hand from you and your *g*
7: 3 then rid yourselves of the foreign *g*
8: 8 forsaking me and serving other *g*,
17: 43 the Philistine cursed David by his *g*
26: 19 and have said, 'Go, serve other *g*.'
2Sa 7: 23 their *g* from before your people,
1Ki 9: 6 and go off to serve other *g*
9: 9 and have embraced other *g*,
11: 2 turn your hearts after their *g*."
11: 4 turned his heart after other *g*,
11: 8 and offered sacrifices to their *g*.
11: 10 Solomon to follow other *g*,
12: 28 Here are your *g*, O Israel, who
14: 9 You have made for yourself other *g*
19: 2 "May the *g* deal with me, be it ever
20: 10 "May the *g* deal with me, be it ever
20: 23 "Their *g* are *g* of the hills.
2Ki 17: 7 They worshiped other *g*
17: 29 each national group made its own *g*
17: 31 Anammelech, the *g* of Sepharvaim.
17: 33 served their own *g* in accordance
17: 35 "Do not worship any other *g*
17: 37 Do not worship other *g*.
17: 38 and do not worship other *g*.
18: 34 Where are the *g* of Hamath
18: 34 Where are the *g* of Sepharvaim,
18: 35 of all the *g* of these countries has
19: 12 Did the *g* of the nations that were
19: 12 the *g* of Gozan, Haran, Rezeph
19: 18 They have thrown their *g*
19: 18 for they were not *g* but only wood
22: 17 and burned incense to other *g*
23: 24 and spiritists, the household *g*,
1Ch 5: 25 themselves to the *g* of the peoples
10: 10 armor in the temple of their *g*
14: 12 had abandoned their *g* there,
16: 25 he is to be feared above all *g*.
16: 26 For all the *g* of the nations are idols
2Ch 2: 5 our God is greater than all other *g*.
7: 19 and go off to serve other *g*
7: 22 and have embraced other *g*,
13: 8 that Jeroboam made to be your *g*.
13: 9 become a priest of what are not *g*.
25: 14 He set them up as his own *g*,
25: 14 he brought back the *g* of the people
25: 15 Why do you consult this people's *g*
25: 20 because they sought the *g* of Edom
28: 23 sacrifices to the *g* of Damascus,
28: 23 "Since the *g* of the kings
28: 25 places to burn sacrifices to other *g*
32: 13 Were the *g* of those nations ever
32: 14 of all the *g* of these nations that my
32: 17 as the *g* of the peoples
32: 19 as they did about the *g*
33: 15 He got rid of the foreign *g*
34: 25 and burned incense to other *g*
Ps 4: 2 love delusions and seek false *g?*
16: 4 who run after other *g*.
40: 4 to those who turn aside to false *g*.
82: 1 he gives judgment among the "*g*":
82: 6 "I said, 'You are "*g*";
86: 8 Among the *g* there is none like you
95: 3 the great King above all *g*.
96: 4 he is to be feared above all *g*.
96: 5 For all the *g* of the nations are idols
97: 7 worship him, all you *g!*
97: 9 you are exalted far above all *g*.
106: 28 ate sacrifices offered to lifeless *g;*
135: 5 that our Lord is greater than all *g*.
136: 2 Give thanks to the God of *g*.
138: 1 before the "*g*" I will sing your
Isa 21: 9 All the images of its *g*
36: 19 Where are the *g* of Hamath
36: 19 Where are the *g* of Sepharvaim?
36: 20 of all the *g* of these countries has
37: 12 Did the *g* of the nations that were
37: 12 the *g* of Gozan, Haran, Rezeph
37: 19 They have thrown their *g*
37: 19 for they were not *g* but only wood
Isa 41: 23 so we may know that you are *g*.
42: 17 who say to images, 'You are our *g*,'
45: 20 who pray to *g* that cannot save.
Jer 1: 16 in burning incense to other *g*
2: 11 Has a nation ever changed its *g?*
2: 11 (Yet they are not *g* at all.)
2: 25 I love foreign *g*,
2: 28 For you have as many *g*
2: 28 Where then are the *g* you made
3: 13 scattered your favors to foreign *g*
3: 24 youth shameful *g* have consumed
5: 7 and sworn by *g* that are not *g*.
5: 19 served foreign *g* in your own land,
7: 6 and if you do not follow other *g*
7: 9 follow other *g* you have not known
7: 18 to other *g* to provoke me to anger.
10: 11 'These *g*, who did not make
11: 10 They have followed other *g*
11: 12 to the *g* to whom they burn incense
11: 13 as many *g* as you have towns,
13: 10 and go after other *g* to serve
13: 25 and trusted in false *g*.
16: 11 'and followed other *g* and served
16: 13 there you will serve other *g* day
16: 19 possessed nothing but false *g*,
16: 20 Do men make their own *g?*
16: 20 Yes, but they are not *g!*"
19: 4 and made this a place of foreign *g;*
19: 4 sacrifices in it to *g* that neither they
19: 13 out drink offerings to other *g*.' "
22: 9 have worshiped and served other *g*
25: 6 Do not follow other *g* to serve
32: 29 out drink offerings to other *g*.
35: 15 do not follow other *g* to serve them
43: 12 temples and take their *g* captive.
43: 12 to the temples of the *g* of Egypt;
43: 13 down the temples of the *g* of Egypt
44: 3 by worshiping other *g* that neither
44: 5 or stop burning incense to other *g*.
44: 8 burning incense to other *g* in Egypt
44: 15 were burning incense to other *g*,
46: 25 on Egypt and her *g* and her kings,
48: 35 and burn incense to their *g*,"
Da 2: 11 it to the king except the *g*,
2: 47 "Surely your God is the God of *g*
3: 12 They neither serve your *g*
3: 14 that you do not serve my *g*
3: 18 that we will not serve your *g*
3: 25 the fourth looks like a son of the *g*
4: 8 and the spirit of the holy *g* is in him
4: 9 the spirit of the holy *g* is in you,
4: 18 the spirit of the holy *g* is in you."
5: 4 they praised the *g* of gold
5: 11 and wisdom like that of the *g*.
5: 11 the spirit of the holy *g* in him.
5: 14 have heard that the spirit of the *g* is
5: 23 You praised the *g* of silver and gold
11: 8 seize their *g*, their metal images
11: 36 things against the God of *g*.
11: 37 regard for the *g* of his fathers
Hos 3: 1 though they turn to other *g*
14: 3 We will never again say 'Our *g*'
Am 2: 4 the *g* their ancestors followed,
2: 4 they have been led astray by false *g*
Mic 4: 5 walk in the name of their *g;*
Na 1: 14 that are in the temple of your *g*.
Zep 1: 9 who fill the temple of their *g*
2: 11 when he destroys all the *g*
Jn 10: 34 have said you are *g*'? If he called
10: 35 If he called them '*g*,'
Ac 7: 40 'Make us *g* who will go before us.
14: 11 "The *g* have come down to us
17: 18 seems to be advocating foreign *g*."
19: 26 He says that man-made *g* are no *g*
28: 11 the figurehead of the twin *g* Castor
1Co 8: 5 For even if there are so-called *g*,
8: 5 (as indeed there are many "*g*"
Gal 4: 8 to those who by nature are not *g*.

GOG

1Ch 5: 4 Shemaiah his son, *G* his son,
Eze 38: 2 set your face against *G*, of the land
38: 3 O *G*, chief prince of Meshech
38: 14 son of man, prophesy and say to *G*:
38: 16 O *G*, I will bring you
38: 18 When *G* attacks the land of Israel,
38: 21 against *G* on all my mountains,
39: 1 O *G*, chief prince of Meshech
Eze 39: 1 prophesy against *G* and say:
39: 11 *G* and all his hordes will be buried
39: 11 that day I will give *G* a burial place
Rev 20: 8 *G* and Magog—to gather them

GOIIM (GOYIM)

Ge 14: 1 and Tidal king of *G* went to war
14: 9 Tidal king of *G*, Amraphel king

GOLAN

Dt 4: 43 for the Gadites; and *G* in Bashan,
Jos 20: 8 and *G* in Bashan in the tribe
21: 27 *G* in Bashan (a city of refuge
1Ch 6: 71 of Manasseh they received *G*

GOLD (GOLDEN)

Ge 2: 11 land of Havilah, where there is *g*.
2: 12 (The *g* of that land is good;
13: 2 in livestock and in silver and *g*.
24: 22 and two *g* bracelets weighing ten
24: 22 took out a *g* nose ring weighing
24: 35 silver and *g*, menservants
24: 53 Then the servant brought out *g*
41: 42 and put a *g* chain around his neck.
44: 8 or *g* from your master's house?
Ex 3: 22 house for articles of silver and *g*
11: 2 for articles of silver and *g*."
12: 35 for articles of silver and *g*
20: 23 gods of silver or gods of *g*.
25: 3 are to receive from them: *g*,
25: 11 Overlay it with pure *g*, both inside
25: 11 and make a *g* molding around it.
25: 12 Cast four *g* rings for it
25: 13 wood and overlay them with *g*.
25: 17 an atonement cover of pure *g*—
25: 18 out of hammered *g* at the ends
25: 24 Overlay it with pure *g*
25: 24 and make a *g* molding around it.
25: 25 and put a *g* molding on the rim.
25: 26 Make four *g* rings for the table
25: 28 them with *g* and carry the table
25: 29 make its plates and ladles of pure *g*,
25: 31 "Make a lampstand of pure *g*
25: 36 hammered out of pure *g*.
25: 38 and trays are to be of pure *g*.
25: 39 A talent of pure *g* is to be used
26: 6 Then make fifty *g* clasps
26: 29 Also overlay the crossbars with *g*.
26: 29 Overlay the frames with *g*
26: 29 make *g* rings to hold the crossbars.
26: 32 Hang it with *g* hooks on four posts
26: 32 of acacia wood overlaid with *g*
26: 37 Make *g* hooks for this curtain
26: 37 of acacia wood overlaid with *g*.
28: 5 Have them use *g*, and blue,
28: 6 "Make the ephod of *g*, and of blue,
28: 8 with the ephod and made with *g*,
28: 11 the stones in *g* filigree settings
28: 13 Make *g* filigree settings
28: 14 and two braided chains of pure *g*,
28: 15 Make it like the ephod: of *g*,
28: 20 Mount them in *g* filigree settings.
28: 22 make braided chains of pure *g*,
28: 23 Make two *g* rings for it
28: 24 Fasten the two *g* chains to the rings
28: 26 Make two *g* rings and attach them
28: 27 Make two more *g* rings
28: 33 with *g* bells between them.
28: 34 *g* bells and the pomegranates are
28: 36 "Make a plate of pure *g*
30: 3 and make a *g* molding around it.
30: 3 and the horns with pure *g*,
30: 4 Make two *g* rings for the altar
30: 5 wood and overlay them with *g*.
31: 4 make artistic designs for work in *g*,
31: 8 the pure *g* lampstand and all its
32: 2 off the *g* earrings that your wives,
32: 24 Then they gave me the *g*,
32: 24 'Whoever has any *g* jewelry,
32: 31 have made themselves gods of *g*.
35: 5 to the LORD an offering of *g*,
35: 22 They all presented their *g*
35: 22 and brought *g* jewelry of all kinds:
35: 32 make artistic designs for work in *g*,
36: 13 Then they made fifty *g* clasps
36: 34 They overlaid the frames with *g*
36: 34 also overlaid the crossbars with *g*.
36: 34 made *g* rings to hold the crossbars.

Ex 36: 36 They made *g* hooks for them
36: 36 for it and overlaid them with *g*.
36: 38 with *g* and made their five bases
37: 2 He overlaid it with pure *g*.
37: 2 and made a *g* molding around it.
37: 3 He cast four *g* rings for it
37: 4 wood and overlaid them with *g*.
37: 6 the atonement cover of pure *g*—
37: 7 out of hammered *g* at the ends
37: 11 Then they overlaid it with pure *g*
37: 11 and made a *g* molding around it.
37: 12 and put a *g* molding on the rim.
37: 13 They cast four *g* rings for the table
37: 15 wood and were overlaid with *g*.
37: 16 they made from pure *g* the articles
37: 17 They made the lampstand of pure *g*
37: 22 hammered out of pure *g*.
37: 23 wick trimmers and trays, of pure *g*.
37: 24 from one talent of pure *g*.
37: 26 and made a *g* molding around it.
37: 26 and the horns with pure *g*,
37: 27 They made two *g* rings
37: 28 wood and overlaid them with *g*.
38: 24 The total amount of the *g*
39: 2 They made the ephod of *g*,
39: 3 hammered out thin sheets of *g*
39: 5 with the ephod and made with *g*,
39: 6 stones in *g* filigree settings
39: 8 They made it like the ephod: of *g*,
39: 13 mounted in *g* filigree settings.
39: 15 made braided chains of pure *g*,
39: 16 They made two *g* filigree settings
39: 16 filigree settings and two *g* rings,
39: 17 They fastened the two *g* chains
39: 19 They made two *g* rings
39: 20 Then they made two more *g* rings
39: 25 And they made bells of pure *g*
39: 30 out of pure *g* and engraved on it,
39: 37 the pure *g* lampstand with its row
39: 38 the *g* altar, the anointing oil,
40: 5 Place the *g* altar of incense in front
40: 26 Moses placed the *g* altar
Lev 8: 9 on Aaron's head and set the *g* plate
24: 4 The lamps on the pure *g* lampstand
24: 6 table of pure *g* before the LORD.
Nu 4: 11 "Over the *g* altar they are
7: 14 one *g* ladle weighing ten shekels,
7: 20 one *g* ladle weighing ten shekels,
7: 26 one *g* ladle weighing ten shekels,
7: 32 one *g* ladle weighing ten shekels,
7: 38 one *g* ladle weighing ten shekels,
7: 44 one *g* ladle weighing ten shekels,
7: 50 one *g* ladle weighing ten shekels,
7: 56 one *g* ladle weighing ten shekels,
7: 62 one *g* ladle weighing ten shekels,
7: 68 one *g* ladle weighing ten shekels,
7: 74 one *g* ladle weighing ten shekels,
7: 80 one *g* ladle weighing ten shekels,
7: 84 bowls and twelve *g* ladles.
7: 86 The twelve *g* ladles filled
7: 86 the *g* ladles weighed a hundred
8: 4 It was made of hammered *g*—
22: 18 his palace filled with silver and *g*,
24: 13 his palace filled with silver and *g*,
31: 22 *G*, silver, bronze, iron, tin,
31: 50 to the LORD the *g* articles each
31: 51 accepted from them the *g*—
31: 52 All the *g* from the commanders
31: 54 Eleazar the priest accepted the *g*
Dt 7: 25 Do not covet the silver and *g*
8: 13 and your silver and *g* increase
17: 17 large amounts of silver and *g*.
29: 17 of wood and stone, of silver and *g*.
Jos 6: 19 and *g* and the articles of bronze
6: 24 but they put the silver and *g*
7: 21 a wedge of *g* weighing fifty shekels,
7: 24 the silver, the robe, the *g* wedge,
22: 8 with silver, *g*, bronze and iron,
Jdg 8: 24 the Ishmaelites to wear *g* earrings.)
8: 26 The weight of the *g* rings he asked
8: 27 Gideon made the *g* into an ephod,
1Sa 6: 4 "Five *g* tumors and five *g* rats,
6: 8 beside it put the *g* objects you are
6: 11 it the chest containing the *g* rats
6: 15 the chest containing the *g* objects,
6: 17 These are the *g* tumors
6: 18 number of the *g* rats was according
2Sa 1: 24 garments with ornaments of *g*.

2Sa 8: 7 David took the *g* shields that
8: 10 with him articles of silver and *g*
8: 11 and *g* from all the nations he had
12: 30 its weight was a talent of *g*,
21: 4 or *g* from Saul or his family,
1Ki 6: 20 He overlaid the inside with pure *g*,
6: 21 and he extended *g* chains
6: 21 inside of the temple with pure *g*,
6: 21 which was overlaid with *g*.
6: 22 overlaid the whole interior with *g*.
6: 22 with *g* the altar that belonged
6: 28 He overlaid the cherubim with *g*.
6: 30 outer rooms of the temple with *g*.
6: 32 and palm trees with beaten *g*.
6: 35 them with *g* hammered evenly
7: 49 the lampstands of pure *g* (five
7: 49 the *g* floral work and lamps
7: 50 and the *g* sockets for the doors
7: 50 the pure *g* dishes, wick trimmers,
7: 51 the silver and *g* and the furnishings
9: 11 and pine and *g* he wanted.
9: 14 sent to the king 120 talents of *g*.
9: 28 and brought back 420 talents of *g*,
10: 2 of *g*, and precious stones—
10: 10 she gave the king 120 talents of *g*,
10: 11 (Hiram's ships brought *g*
10: 14 of the *g* that Solomon received
10: 16 large shields of hammered *g*;
10: 16 six hundred bekas of *g* went
10: 17 small shields of hammered *g*,
10: 17 with three minas of *g* in each shield
10: 18 with ivory and overlaid with fine *g*.
10: 21 All King Solomon's goblets were *g*,
10: 21 the Forest of Lebanon were pure *g*.
10: 22 three years it returned carrying *g*,
10: 25 articles of silver and *g*, robes,
14: 26 including all the *g* shields Solomon
15: 15 and *g* and the articles that he
15: 18 and *g* that was left in the treasuries
15: 19 sending you a gift of silver and *g*.
20: 3 'Your silver and *g* are mine,
20: 5 'I sent to demand your silver and *g*,
20: 7 and my *g*, I did not refuse him."
22: 48 of trading ships to go to Ophir for *g*
2Ki 5: 5 six thousand shekels of *g*
7: 8 carried away silver, *g* and clothes,
12: 13 trumpets or any other articles of *g*
12: 18 and all the *g* found in the treasuries
14: 14 He took all the *g* and silver
16: 8 *g* found in the temple of the LORD
18: 14 of silver and thirty talents of *g*.
18: 16 king of Judah stripped off the *g*
20: 13 the *g*, the spices and the fine oil—
23: 33 talents of silver and a talent of *g*.
23: 35 and *g* from the people of the land
23: 35 the silver and *g* he demanded.
24: 13 away all the *g* articles that
25: 15 all that were made of *g* or silver.
1Ch 18: 7 David took the *g* shields carried
18: 10 brought all kinds of articles of *g*
18: 11 and *g* he had taken from all these
20: 2 was found to be a talent of *g*,
21: 25 Araunah six hundred shekels of *g*
22: 14 a hundred thousand talents of *g*,
22: 16 skilled in every kind of work in *g*
28: 14 of *g* for all the *g* articles to be used
28: 15 weight of *g* for the *g* lampstands
28: 16 the weight of *g* for each table
28: 17 the weight of pure *g* for the forks,
28: 17 the weight of *g* for each *g* dish;
28: 18 of *g* that spread their wings
28: 18 weight of the refined *g* for the altar
29: 2 *g* for the *g* work, silver
29: 3 give my personal treasures of *g*
29: 4 three thousand talents of *g* (*g*
29: 5 for the *g* work and the silver work,
29: 7 and ten thousand darics of *g*,
2Ch 1: 15 and *g* as common in Jerusalem
2: 7 a man skilled to work in *g*
2: 14 He is trained to work in *g*
3: 4 He overlaid the inside with pure *g*.
3: 5 it with fine *g* and decorated it
3: 6 the *g* he used was *g* of Parvaim.
3: 7 and doors of the temple with *g*,
3: 8 with six hundred talents of fine *g*.
3: 9 The *g* nails weighed fifty shekels.
3: 9 overlaid the upper parts with *g*.
3: 10 and overlaid them with *g*.

2Ch 4: 7 made ten *g* lampstands according
4: 8 made a hundred *g* sprinkling bowls
4: 20 of pure *g* with their lamps,
4: 21 lamps and tongs (they were solid *g*
4: 21 the *g* floral work and lamps
4: 22 and the *g* doors of the temple:
4: 22 the pure *g* wick trimmers,
5: 1 and *g* and all the furnishings—
8: 18 four hundred and fifty talents of *g*,
9: 1 of *g*, and precious stones—
9: 9 she gave the king 120 talents of *g*,
9: 10 of Solomon brought *g* from Ophir;
9: 13 of the *g* that Solomon received
9: 14 the governors of the land brought *g*
9: 15 bekas of hammered *g* went
9: 15 large shields of hammered *g*;
9: 16 bekas of *g* in each shield.
9: 16 small shields of hammered *g*,
9: 17 with ivory and overlaid with pure *g*
9: 18 a footstool of *g* was attached to it.
9: 20 All King Solomon's goblets were *g*,
9: 20 the Forest of Lebanon were pure *g*.
9: 21 carrying *g*, silver and ivory,
9: 24 articles of silver and *g*, and robes,
12: 9 including the *g* shields Solomon
13: 11 on the *g* lampstand every evening.
15: 18 and *g* and the articles that he
16: 2 and *g* out of the treasuries
16: 3 See, I am sending you silver and *g*.
21: 3 and *g* and articles of value,
24: 14 and other objects of *g* and silver.
25: 24 He took all the *g* and silver
32: 27 and *g* and for his precious stones,
36: 3 talents of silver and a talent of *g*.
Ezr 1: 4 to provide him with silver and *g*,
1: 6 them with articles of silver and *g*,
1: 9 *g* dishes 30 silver dishes 1,000
1: 10 silver pans 29 *g* bowls 30 matching
1: 11 there were 5,400 articles of *g*
2: 69 drachmas of *g*, 5,000 minas
5: 14 from the temple of Babylon the *g*
6: 5 Also, the *g* and silver articles
7: 15 you the silver and *g* that the king
7: 16 and *g* you may obtain
7: 18 with the rest of the silver and *g*,
8: 25 and *g* and the articles that the king,
8: 26 talents of *g*, 20 bowls
8: 27 bowls of *g* valued at 1,000
8: 27 of polished bronze, as precious as *g*
8: 28 and *g* are a freewill offering
8: 30 Levites received the silver and *g*
8: 33 we weighed out the silver and *g*
Ne 7: 70 drachmas of *g*, 50 bowls
7: 71 drachmas of *g* and 2,200 minas
7: 72 drachmas of *g*, 2,000 minas
Est 1: 6 There were couches of *g*
1: 7 Wine was served in goblets of *g*,
4: 11 king to extend the *g* scepter to him
5: 2 out to her the *g* scepter that was
8: 4 the king extended the *g* scepter
8: 15 crown of *g* and a purple robe
Job 3: 15 with rulers who had *g*,
22: 24 your *g* of Ophir to the rocks
22: 25 then the Almighty will be your *g*,
23: 10 tested me, I will come forth as *g*.
28: 1 and a place where *g* is refined.
28: 6 and its dust contains nuggets of *g*.
28: 15 cannot be bought with the finest *g*,
28: 16 with the *g* of Ophir,
28: 17 Neither *g* nor crystal can compare
28: 17 nor can it be had for jewels of *g*.
28: 19 it cannot be bought with pure *g*.
31: 24 said to pure *g*, 'You are my security
31: 24 "If I have put my trust in *g*
42: 11 a piece of silver and a *g* ring.
Ps 19: 10 They are more precious than *g*,
19: 10 than much pure *g*;
21: 3 of pure *g* on his head.
45: 9 right hand is the royal bride in *g*
45: 13 her gown is interwoven with *g*.
68: 13 its feathers with shining *g*."
72: 15 May *g* from Sheba be given him.
105: 37 out Israel, laden with silver and *g*,
115: 4 But their idols are silver and *g*,
119: 72 of pieces of silver and *g*.
119:127 more than *g*, more than pure *g*,
135: 15 of the nations are silver and *g*,
Pr 3: 14 and yields better returns than *g*.

Pr 8: 10 knowledge rather than choice *g*,
8: 19 My fruit is better than fine *g*;
11: 22 Like a *g* ring in a pig's snout
16: 16 better to get wisdom than *g*,
17: 3 for silver and the furnace for *g*,
20: 15 *G* there is, and rubies in abundance
22: 1 esteemed is better than silver or *g*.
25: 11 is like apples of *g* in settings
25: 12 of *g* or an ornament of fine *g*
27: 21 for silver and the furnace for *g*,
Ecc 2: 8 I amassed silver and *g* for myself,
SS 1: 11 We will make you earrings of *g*,
3: 10 its base of *g*.
5: 11 His head is purest *g*;
5: 14 His arms are rods of *g*
5: 15 set on bases of pure *g*.
Isa 2: 7 Their land is full of silver and *g*;
2: 20 their idols of silver and idols of *g*,
13: 12 more rare than the *g* of Ophir.
13: 12 will make man scarcer than pure *g*,
13: 17 and have no delight in *g*.
30: 22 and your images covered with *g*;
31: 7 and *g* your sinful hands have made.
39: 2 the silver, the *g*, the spices,
40: 19 and a goldsmith overlays it with *g*
46: 6 Some pour out *g* from their bags
60: 6 bearing *g* and incense
60: 9 with their silver and *g*,
60: 17 Instead of bronze I will bring you *g*
Jer 4: 30 and put on jewels of *g*?
10: 4 They adorn it with silver and *g*;
10: 9 and *g* from Uphaz.
51: 7 Babylon was a *g* cup
52: 19 all that were made of *g* or silver.
La 4: 1 How the *g* has lost its luster,
4: 1 the fine *g* become dull!
4: 2 once worth their weight in *g*,
Eze 7: 19 and their *g* will be an unclean thing
7: 19 and *g* will not be able to save them
16: 13 you were adorned with *g* and silver
16: 17 the jewelry made of my *g* and silver
27: 22 and precious stones, and *g*.
28: 4 and amassed *g* and silver
28: 13 and mountings were made of *g*;
38: 13 and *g*, to take away livestock
Da 2: 32 of the statue was made of pure *g*,
2: 35 and the *g* were broken to pieces
2: 38 You are that head of *g*.
2: 45 the silver and the *g* to pieces.
3: 1 made an image of *g*,
3: 5 of *g* that King Nebuchadnezzar has
3: 7 of *g* that King Nebuchadnezzar
3: 10 and worship the image of *g*,
3: 12 the image of *g* you have set up."
3: 14 or worship the image of *g* I have set
3: 18 the image of *g* you have set up."
5: 2 he gave orders to bring in the *g*
5: 3 in the *g* goblets that had been taken
5: 4 they praised the gods of *g*
5: 7 and have a *g* chain placed
5: 16 and have a *g* chain placed
5: 23 praised the gods of silver and *g*,
5: 29 a *g* chain was placed
10: 5 belt of the finest *g* around his waist.
11: 8 valuable articles of silver and *g*
11: 38 to his fathers he will honor with *g*
11: 43 control of the treasures of *g*
Hos 2: 8 lavished on her the silver and *g*—
8: 4 With their silver and *g*
Joel 3: 5 For you took my silver and my *g*
Na 2: 9 Plunder the *g*!
Hab 2: 19 It is covered with *g* and silver;
Zep 1: 18 Neither their silver nor their *g*
Hag 2: 8 The silver is mine and the *g* is mine
Zec 4: 2 "I see a solid *g* lampstand
4: 12 beside the two *g* pipes that pour
6: 10 and *g* from the exiles Heldai,
6: 11 Take the silver and *g* and make
9: 3 and *g* like the dirt of the streets.
13: 9 and test them like *g*.
14: 14 great quantities of *g* and silver
Mal 3: 3 and refine them like *g* and silver.
Mt 2: 11 and presented him with gifts of *g*
10: 9 Do not take along any *g* or silver
23: 16 swears by the *g* of the temple,
23: 17 blind fools! Which is greater: the *g*,
23: 17 the temple that makes the *g* sacred
Ac 3: 6 "Silver or *g* I do not have,
17: 29 think that the divine being is like *g*
20: 33 not coveted anyone's silver or *g*
1Co 3: 12 builds on this foundation using *g*,
1Ti 2: 9 not with braided hair or *g* or pearls
2Ti 2: 20 there are articles not only of *g*
Heb 9: 4 This ark contained the *g* jar
Jas 2: 2 into your meeting wearing a *g* ring
5: 3 Your *g* and silver are corroded.
1Pe 1: 7 worth than *g*, which perishes
1: 18 or *g* that you were redeemed
3: 3 and the wearing of *g* jewelry
Rev 3: 18 to buy from me *g* refined in the fire,
4: 4 and had crowns of *g* on their heads.
9: 7 wore something like crowns of *g*,
9: 20 and idols of *g*, silver, bronze,
14: 14 with a crown of *g* on his head
17: 4 glittering with *g*, precious stones
18: 12 cargoes of *g*, silver, precious stones
18: 16 glittering with *g*, precious stones
21: 15 rod of *g* to measure the city,
21: 18 the city of pure *g*, as pure as glass.
21: 21 The street of the city was of pure *g*,

GOLD-COVERED (COVER)

Heb 9: 4 and the *g* ark of the covenant.

GOLDEN (GOLD)

1Ki 7: 48 the *g* altar; the *g* table
12: 28 the king made two *g* calves.
2Ki 10: 29 worship of the *g* calves at Bethel
2Ch 4: 19 the *g* altar; the tables
13: 8 and have with you the *g* calves that
Job 37: 22 of the north he comes in *g* splendor
Ecc 12: 6 or the *g* bowl is broken;
Zec 4: 12 two gold pipes that pour out *g* oil?"
Heb 9: 4 which had the *g* altar of incense
Rev 1: 12 I turned I saw seven *g* lampstands,
1: 13 and with a *g* sash around his chest.
1: 20 of the seven *g* lampstands is this:
2: 1 among the seven *g* lampstands:
5: 8 and they were holding *g* bowls full
8: 3 Another angel, who had a *g* censer,
8: 3 on the *g* altar before the throne.
9: 13 from the horns of the *g* altar that is
15: 6 wore *g* sashes around their chests.
15: 7 seven angels seven *g* bowls filled
17: 4 She held a *g* cup in her hand,

GOLDSMITH (GOLDSMITHS)

Isa 40: 19 and a *g* overlays it with gold
41: 7 The craftsman encourages the *g*,
46: 6 they hire a *g* to make it into a god,
Jer 10: 9 the craftsman and *g* have made
10: 14 every *g* is shamed by his idols.
51: 17 every *g* is shamed by his idols.

GOLDSMITHS (GOLDSMITH)

Ne 3: 8 of the *g*, repaired the next section;
3: 31 Next to him, Malkijah, one of the *g*
3: 32 Sheep Gate the *g* and merchants

GOLGOTHA

Mt 27: 33 to a place called *G* (which means
Mk 15: 22 to the place called *G* (which means
Jn 19: 17 (which in Aramaic is called *G*).

GOLIATH

1Sa 17: 4 A champion named *G*, who was
17: 8 *G* stood and shouted to the ranks
17: 23 *G*, the Philistine champion
21: 9 "The sword of *G* the Philistine,
22: 10 and the sword of *G* the Philistine."
2Sa 21: 19 Bethlehemite killed *G* the Gittite,
1Ch 20: 5 Lahmi the brother of *G* the Gittite,

GOMER

Ge 10: 2 The sons of Japheth: *G*, Magog,
10: 3 The sons of *G*: Ashkenaz, Riphath
1Ch 1: 5 The sons of Japheth: *G*, Magog,
1: 6 The sons of *G*: Ashkenaz, Riphath
Eze 38: 6 helmets, also *G* with all its troops,
Hos 1: 3 he married *G* daughter of Diblaim,
1: 6 *G* conceived again and gave birth
1: 8 weaned Lo-Ruhamah, *G* had

GOMORRAH

Ge 10: 19 and then toward Sodom, *G*,
13: 10 LORD destroyed Sodom and *G*.)
14: 2 Birsha king of *G*, Shinab king
14: 8 the king of *G*, the king of Admah,
14: 10 the kings of Sodom and *G* fled,
14: 11 all the goods of Sodom and *G*
18: 20 against Sodom and *G* is so great
19: 24 sulfur on Sodom and *G*—
19: 28 down toward Sodom and *G*,
Dt 29: 23 the destruction of Sodom and *G*,
32: 32 and from the fields of *G*.
Isa 1: 9 we would have been like *G*.
1: 10 you people of *G*!
13: 19 like Sodom and *G*.
Jer 23: 14 the people of Jerusalem are like *G*
49: 18 As Sodom and *G* were overthrown,
50: 40 As God overthrew Sodom and *G*
Am 4: 11 as I overthrew Sodom and *G*.
Zep 2: 9 the Ammonites like *G*—
Mt 10: 15 and *G* on the day of judgment
Ro 9: 29 and we would have been like *G*."
2Pe 2: 6 and *G* by burning them to ashes,
Jude : 7 *G* and the surrounding towns gave

GONG

1Co 13: 1 I am only a resounding *g*

GOOD (GOODNESS)

Ge 1: 4 God saw that the light was *g*,
1: 10 And God saw that it was *g*.
1: 12 And God saw that it was *g*.
1: 18 And God saw that it was *g*.
1: 21 And God saw that it was *g*.
1: 25 And God saw that it was *g*.
1: 31 he had made, and it was very *g*.
2: 9 and the tree of the knowledge of *g*
2: 9 pleasing to the eye and *g* for food.
2: 12 (The gold of that land is *g*;
2: 17 from the tree of the knowledge of *g*
2: 18 "It is not *g* for the man to be alone.
3: 5 you will be like God, knowing *g*
3: 6 the fruit of the tree was *g* for food
3: 22 become like one of us, knowing *g*
15: 15 and be buried at a *g* old age.
20: 3 as *g* as dead because of the woman
24: 10 kinds of *g* things from his master.
25: 8 his last and died at a *g* old age,
25: 32 "What *g* is the birthright to me?"
30: 11 Then Leah said, "What *g* fortune!"
31: 24 to say anything to Jacob, either *g*
31: 29 to say anything to Jacob, either *g*
34: 18 Their proposal seemed *g* to Hamor
41: 5 Seven heads of grain, healthy and *g*
41: 22 full and *g*, growing on a single stalk
41: 24 swallowed up the seven *g* heads.
41: 26 The seven *g* cows are seven years,
41: 26 seven *g* heads of grain are seven
41: 35 of these *g* years that are coming
41: 37 The plan seemed *g* to Pharaoh
44: 4 'Why have you repaid *g* with evil?
49: 15 When he sees how *g* is his resting
50: 20 but God intended it for *g*
Ex 3: 8 out of that land into a *g*
18: 9 about all the *g* things the LORD
18: 17 "What you are doing is not *g*.
Lev 5: 4 *g* or evil—in any matter one might
27: 10 or a bad one for a *g* one;
27: 10 or substitute a *g* one for a bad one,
27: 12 who will judge its quality as *g*
27: 14 the priest will judge its quality as *g*
27: 33 He must not pick out the *g*
Nu 10: 29 the LORD has promised *g* things
10: 32 share with you whatever *g* things
13: 19 kind of land do they live in? Is it *g*
14: 7 and explored is exceedingly *g*.
24: 13 anything of my own accord, *g*
Dt 1: 14 "What you propose to do is *g*."
1: 23 The idea seemed *g* to me;
1: 25 "It is a *g* land that the LORD our
1: 35 shall see the *g* land I swore
1: 39 children who do not yet know *g*
3: 25 see the *g* land beyond the Jordan—
4: 21 enter the *g* land the LORD your
4: 22 and take possession of that *g* land.
5: 28 Everything they said was *g*.
6: 11 of *g* things you did not provide,
6: 18 and *g* in the LORD's sight,
6: 18 over the *g* land that the LORD
8: 7 God is bringing you into a *g* land—
8: 10 for the *g* land he has given you.

Dt 9: 6 your God is giving you this *g* land
10: 13 giving you today for your own *g?*
11: 17 from the *g* land the LORD is
12: 28 because you will be doing what is *g*
18: 17 said to me: "What they say is *g*.
23: 6 Do not seek peace or *g* relations
26: 11 in all the *g* things the LORD your
Jos 9: 25 Do to us whatever seems *g*
10: 2 and all its men were *g* fighters.
21: 45 one of all the LORD's *g* promises
23: 13 until you perish from this *g* land,
23: 14 of all the *g* promises the LORD
23: 15 every *g* promise of the LORD your
23: 15 from this *g* land he has given you.
23: 16 from the *g* land he has given you."
24: 20 after he has been *g* to you."
Jdg 8: 32 son of Joash died at a *g* old age
8: 35 for all the *g* things he had done
9: 11 'Should I give up my fruit, so *g*
9: 16 and in *g* faith when you made
9: 19 and in *g* faith toward Jerub-Baal
17: 13 I know that the LORD will be *g*
18: 9 have seen that the land is very *g*.
Ru 2: 22 "It will be *g* for you, my daughter,
3: 7 and drinking and was in *g* spirits,
3: 13 morning if he wants to redeem, *g;*
1Sa 1: 23 may the LORD make *g* his word."
2: 24 it is not a *g* report that I hear
2: 32 Although *g* will be done to Israel,
3: 18 let him do what is *g* in his eyes."
9: 10 "*G*," Saul said to his servant.
11: 10 do to us whatever seems *g* to you."
12: 14 *g!* But if you do not obey
12: 21 They can do you no *g*,
12: 23 I will teach you the way that is *g*
15: 9 and lambs—everything that was *g*.
19: 10 night David made *g* his escape.
24: 18 me of the *g* you did to me;
25: 6 And *g* health to all that is yours!
25: 6 *G* health to you and your
25: 15 Yet these men were very *g* to us.
25: 21 He has paid me back evil for *g*.
25: 30 my master every *g* thing he
25: 33 blessed for your *g* judgment
26: 16 What you have done is not *g*.
2Sa 3: 13 "*G*," said David.
4: 10 thought he was bringing *g* news,
7: 28 and you have given this *g* promise
10: 12 The LORD will do what is *g*
13: 22 a word to Amnon, either *g*
14: 17 an angel of God in discerning *g*
15: 26 to me whatever seems *g* to him."
16: 12 me with *g* for the cursing I am
17: 4 This plan seemed *g* to Absalom
17: 7 has given is not *g* this time.
17: 14 to frustrate the *g* advice
18: 25 If he is alone, he must have *g* news
18: 26 "He must be bringing *g* news, too."
18: 27 "He comes with *g* news."
18: 27 "He's a *g* man," the king said.
18: 31 My lord the king, hear the *g* news!
19: 35 the difference between what is *g*
1Ki 1: 42 like you must be bringing *g* news."
2: 38 the king, "What you say is *g*.
2: 42 said to me, 'What you say is *g*.
7: 10 laid with large stones of *g* quality,
8: 56 failed of all the *g* promises he gave
8: 66 for all the *g* the LORD had done
14: 13 of Israel, has found anything *g*.
14: 15 Israel from this *g* land that he gave
18: 24 people said, "What you say is *g*."
20: 33 The men took this as a *g* sign
22: 8 prophesies anything *g* about me,
22: 18 prophesies anything *g* about me,
2Ki 3: 19 You will cut down every *g* tree,
3: 19 and ruin every *g* field with stones."
3: 25 a stone on every *g* field until it was
3: 25 and cut down every *g* tree.
7: 9 This is a day of *g* news
20: 3 have done what is *g* in your eyes."
20: 19 of the LORD you have spoken is *g*
1Ch 4: 40 They found rich, *g* pasture,
13: 2 "If it seems *g* to you
16: 34 to the LORD, for he is *g;*
17: 26 You have given this *g* promise
19: 13 The LORD will do what is *g*
28: 8 that you may possess this *g* land
29: 28 at a *g* old age, having enjoyed long
2Ch 5: 13 "He is *g;*
7: 3 "He is *g;*
7: 10 for the *g* things the LORD had
12: 12 Indeed, there was some *g* in Judah.
14: 2 Asa did what was *g* and right
18: 7 prophesies anything *g* about me,
18: 17 prophesies anything *g* about me,
19: 3 There is, however, some *g* in you,
24: 16 of the *g* he had done in Israel
30: 18 saying, "May the LORD, who is *g*,
30: 22 who showed *g* understanding
31: 20 doing what was *g* and right
Ezr 3: 11 "He is *g;*
7: 9 for the *g* hand of his God was
7: 28 who has extended his *g* favor to me
8: 18 Because the *g* hand of our God was
8: 22 "The *g* hand of our God is
9: 12 and eat the *g* things of the land
Ne 2: 18 So they began this *g* work.
5: 5 though our sons are as *g* as theirs,
6: 19 kept reporting to me his *g* deeds
9: 13 decrees and commands that are *g*.
9: 20 You gave your *g* Spirit
9: 25 filled with all kinds of *g* things,
9: 36 and the other *g* things it produces.
Est 9: 30 words of *g* will and assurance—
10: 3 he worked for the *g* of his people
Job 2: 10 Shall we accept *g* from God,
21: 25 never having enjoyed anything *g*.
22: 18 filled their houses with *g* things,
30: 26 Yet when I hoped for *g*, evil came;
34: 4 let us learn together what is *g*.
39: 17 or give her a share of *g* sense.
Ps 4: 6 "Who can show us any *g?*"
13: 6 for he has been *g* to me.
14: 1 there is no one who does *g*.
14: 3 there is no one who does *g*,
16: 2 apart from you I have no *g* thing."
25: 7 for you are *g*, O LORD.
25: 8 *G* and upright is the LORD;
34: 8 Taste and see that the LORD is *g;*
34: 10 seek the LORD lack no *g* thing.
34: 12 and desires to see many *g* days,
34: 14 Turn from evil and do *g;*
35: 12 They repay me evil for *g*
36: 3 to be wise and to do *g*.
37: 3 Trust in the LORD and do *g;*
37: 27 Turn from evil and do *g;*
38: 20 Those who repay my *g* with evil
38: 20 slander me when I seek what is *g*.
39: 2 not even saying anything *g*,
51: 18 In your *g* pleasure make Zion
52: 3 You love evil rather than *g*,
52: 9 for your name is *g*.
53: 1 there is no one who does *g*.
53: 3 there is no one who does *g*,
54: 6 for it is *g*.
65: 4 with the *g* things of your house,
73: 1 Surely God is *g* to Israel,
73: 28 But as for me, it is *g* to be near God
84: 11 no *g* thing does he withhold
85: 12 LORD will indeed give what is *g*,
92: 1 It is *g* to praise the LORD
100: 5 For the LORD is *g* and his love
103: 5 satisfies my desires with *g* things,
104: 28 they are satisfied with *g* things.
106: 1 thanks to the LORD, for he is *g;*
107: 1 to the LORD, for he is *g;*
107: 9 and fills the hungry with *g* things.
109: 5 They repay me evil for *g*,
111: 10 his precepts have *g* understanding.
112: 5 *G* will come to him who is
116: 7 for the LORD has been *g* to you.
118: 1 to the LORD, for he is *g;*
118: 29 to the LORD, for he is *g;*
119: 17 Do *g* to your servant, and I will live
119: 39 for your laws are *g*.
119: 65 Do *g* to your servant
119: 66 me knowledge and *g* judgment,
119: 68 You are *g*, and what you do is *g;*
119: 71 It was *g* for me to be afflicted
125: 4 Do *g*, O LORD, to those who are
125: 4 O LORD, to those who are *g*,
133: 1 How *g* and pleasant it is
135: 3 for the LORD is *g;*
136: 1 thanks to the LORD, for he is *g*.
143: 10 may your *g* Spirit
145: 9 The LORD is *g* to all;
Ps 147: 1 How *g* it is to sing praises
Pr 2: 9 and fair—every *g* path.
2: 20 in the ways of *g* men
3: 4 you will win favor and a *g* name
3: 27 Do not withhold *g*
11: 23 of the righteous ends only in *g*,
11: 27 He who seeks *g* finds *g* will,
12: 2 A *g* man obtains favor
12: 14 his lips a man is filled with *g* things
13: 2 of his lips a man enjoys *g* things,
13: 15 *G* understanding wins favor,
13: 22 A *g* man leaves an inheritance
14: 9 *g* will is found among the upright.
14: 14 and the *g* man rewarded for his.
14: 19 down in the presence of the *g*,
14: 22 those who plan what is *g* find love
15: 3 on the wicked and the *g*.
15: 23 and how *g* is a timely word!
15: 30 *g* news gives health to the bones.
16: 29 leads him down a path that is not *g*.
17: 13 If a man pays back evil for *g*,
17: 22 A cheerful heart is *g* medicine,
17: 26 It is not *g* to punish an innocent
18: 5 It is not *g* to be partial
18: 22 He who finds a wife finds what is *g*
19: 2 It is not *g* to have zeal
20: 14 It's no *g*, it's no *g!*" says the buyer;
22: 1 A *g* name is more desirable
24: 13 Eat honey, my son, for it is *g;*
24: 23 partiality in judging is not *g:*
25: 25 is *g* news from a distant land.
25: 27 It is not *g* to eat too much honey,
28: 10 will receive a *g* inheritance.
28: 21 To show partiality is not *g*—
31: 12 She brings him *g*, not harm,
Ecc 2: 1 with pleasure to find out what is *g*
3: 12 than to be happy and do *g*
4: 9 they have a *g* return for their work:
5: 18 Then I realized that it is *g*
6: 12 For who knows what is *g* for a man
7: 1 A *g* name is better
7: 3 because a sad face is *g* for the heart.
7: 11 like an inheritance, is a *g* thing
7: 14 When times are *g*, be happy;
7: 18 It is *g* to grasp the one
9: 2 As it is with the *g* man,
9: 2 and the wicked, the *g* and the bad,
9: 18 but one sinner destroys much *g*.
12: 14 whether it is *g* or evil.
Isa 5: 2 he looked for a crop of *g* grapes,
5: 4 When I looked for *g* grapes,
5: 20 Woe to those who call evil *g*
5: 20 and *g* evil,
38: 3 have done what is *g* in your eyes."
39: 8 of the LORD you have spoken is *g*
40: 9 You who bring *g* tidings
40: 9 You who bring *g* tidings to Zion,
41: 7 He says of the welding, "It is *g*."
41: 23 Do something, whether *g* or bad,
41: 27 Jerusalem a messenger of *g* tidings.
52: 7 the feet of those who bring *g* news,
52: 7 who bring *g* tidings,
55: 2 listen to me, and eat what is *g*,
61: 1 me to preach *g* news to the poor.
63: 7 yes, the many *g* things he has done
65: 2 who walk in ways not *g*,
65: 8 there is yet some *g* in it,'
Jer 4: 22 they know not how to do *g*."
5: 25 your sins have deprived you of *g*.
6: 16 ask where the *g* way is,
8: 15 but no *g* has come,
10: 5 nor can they do any *g*."
13: 23 Neither can you do *g*
14: 19 but no *g* has come,
15: 11 I will deliver you for a *g* purpose;
16: 19 worthless idols that did them no *g*.
18: 10 will reconsider the *g* I had
18: 20 Should *g* be repaid with evil?
21: 10 to do this city harm and not *g*,
24: 2 One basket had very *g* figs,
24: 3 "The *g* ones are very *g*,
24: 5 I regard as *g* the exiles from Judah,
24: 5 of Israel, says: 'Like these *g* figs,
24: 6 watch over them for their *g*,
26: 14 do with me whatever you think is *g*
29: 32 nor will he see the *g* things I will do
32: 39 the *g* of their children after them.
32: 39 will always fear me for their own *g*

Jer 32: 40 I will never stop doing g to them,
32: 41 I will rejoice in doing them g
33: 9 hear of all the g things I do for it;
33: 11 for the LORD is g;
38: 4 This man is not seeking the g
44: 27 over them for harm, not for g;
La 3: 25 LORD is g to those whose hope is
3: 26 it is g to wait quietly
3: 27 It is g for a man to bear the yoke
3: 38 both calamities and g things come?
Eze 17: 8 planted in g soil by abundant water
20: 25 over to statutes that were not g
30: 22 the g arm as well as the broken one,
34: 14 I will tend them in a g pasture,
34: 14 lie down in g grazing land,
34: 18 for you to feed on the g pasture?
Da 3: 15 worship the image I made, very g.
Hos 8: 3 But Israel has rejected what is g;
Am 5: 14 Seek g, not evil,
5: 15 Hate evil, love g;
9: 4 them for evil and not for g."
Jnh 2: 9 What I have vowed I will make g.
Mic 2: 7 "Do not my words do g
3: 2 you who hate g and love evil;
6: 8 has showed you, O man, what is g.
Na 1: 7 The LORD is g,
1: 15 the feet of one who brings g news,
Zep 1: 12 either g or bad.'
Zec 8: 15 to do g again to Jerusalem
Mal 2: 17 "All who do evil are g in the eyes
Mt 3: 10 does not produce g fruit will be
4: 23 preaching the g news
5: 13 It is no longer g for anything,
5: 16 that they may see your g deeds
5: 45 sun to rise on the evil and the g,
6: 22 If your eyes are g, your whole body
7: 11 Father in heaven give g gifts
7: 11 know how to give g gifts
7: 17 Likewise every g tree bears g fruit,
7: 18 A g tree cannot bear bad fruit,
7: 18 and a bad tree cannot bear g fruit.
7: 19 tree that does not bear g fruit is cut
9: 35 preaching the g news
11: 5 the g news is preached to the poor.
11: 26 Father, for this was your g pleasure
12: 12 lawful to do g on the Sabbath."
12: 33 Make a tree g and its fruit will be g,
12: 33 "Make a tree g and its fruit will be
12: 34 you who are evil say anything g?
12: 35 The g man brings g things out
12: 35 out of the g stored up in him,
13: 8 Still other seed fell on g soil,
13: 23 on g soil is the man who hears
13: 24 is like a man who sowed g seed
13: 27 didn't you sow g seed in your field?
13: 37 "The one who sowed the g seed is
13: 38 and the g seed stands for the sons
13: 48 and collected the g fish in baskets,
16: 26 What g will it be for a man
17: 4 "Lord, it is g for us to be here.
19: 16 what g thing must I do
19: 17 Why do you ask me about what is g
19: 17 "There is only One who is g.
22: 10 both g and bad, and the wedding
24: 46 It will be g for that servant whose
25: 21 'Well done, g and faithful servant!
25: 23 'Well done, g and faithful servant!
Mk 1: 14 proclaiming the g news of God.
1: 15 Repent and believe the g news!"
3: 4 lawful on the Sabbath: to do g
4: 8 Still other seed fell on g soil.
4: 20 sown on g soil, hear the word,
8: 36 What g is it for a man
9: 5 "Rabbi, it is g for us to be here.
9: 50 "Salt is g, but if it loses its saltiness,
10: 17 "G teacher," he asked, "what must
10: 18 do you call me g?" Jesus answered.
10: 18 "No one is g— except God alone.
12: 28 Jesus had given them a g answer,
16: 15 preach the g news to all creation.
Lk 1: 3 it seemed g also to me
1: 19 and to tell you this g news.
1: 53 has filled the hungry with g things
2: 10 I bring you g news
3: 9 does not produce g fruit will be
3: 18 and preached the g news to them.
4: 18 me to preach g news to the poor.
4: 43 "I must preach the g news

Lk 6: 9 lawful on the Sabbath: to do g
6: 27 do g to those who hate you,
6: 33 And if you do g to those who are g
6: 35 love your enemies, do g to them,
6: 38 A g measure, pressed down,
6: 43 nor does a bad tree bear g fruit.
6: 43 "No g tree bears bad fruit,
6: 45 The g man brings g things out
6: 45 out of the g stored up in his heart,
7: 22 the g news is preached to the poor.
8: 1 proclaiming the g news
8: 8 Still other seed fell on g soil.
8: 15 for those with a noble and g heart,
8: 15 the seed on g soil stands for those
9: 25 What g is it for a man
9: 33 "Master, it is g for us to be here.
10: 21 Father, for this was your g pleasure
11: 13 know how to give g gifts
11: 34 your eyes are g, your whole body
12: 16 rich man produced a g crop.
12: 19 You have plenty of g things laid up
12: 37 It will be g for those servants
12: 38 It will be g for those servants
12: 43 It will be g for that servant whom
14: 34 "Salt is g, but if it loses its saltiness,
16: 16 the g news of the kingdom
16: 25 lifetime you received your g things,
18: 18 ruler asked him, "G teacher,
18: 19 do you call me g?" Jesus answered.
18: 19 "No one is g— except God alone.
19: 17 " 'Well done, my g servant!'
23: 50 a member of the Council, a g
Jn 1: 46 Can anything g come from there?"
5: 29 those who have done g will rise
7: 12 Some said, "He is a g man."
10: 11 The g shepherd lays down his life
10: 11 "I am the g shepherd.
10: 14 "I am the g shepherd; I know my
16: 7 It is for your g that I am going away
18: 14 advised the Jews that it would be g
Ac 5: 42 proclaiming the g news that Jesus
8: 12 as he preached the g news
8: 35 told him the g news about Jesus.
9: 36 who was always doing g
10: 33 and it was g of you to come.
10: 36 telling the g news of peace
10: 38 and how he went around doing g
11: 20 also, telling them the g news about
11: 24 He was a g man, full
13: 32 tell you the g news: What God
14: 7 continued to preach the g news.
14: 15 We are bringing you g news,
14: 21 They preached the g news
15: 28 It seemed g to the Holy Spirit
17: 18 was preaching the g news about
19: 25 you know we receive a g income
19: 27 that our trade will lose its g name,
23: 1 duty to God in all g conscience
Ro 2: 7 persistence in doing g seek glory,
2: 10 peace for everyone who does g:
3: 8 "Let us do evil that g may result"?
3: 12 there is no one who does g,
4: 19 the fact that his body was as g
5: 7 though for a g man someone might
7: 12 is holy, righteous and g.
7: 13 death in me through what was g,
7: 13 that which is g, then, become death
7: 16 want to do, I agree that the law is g.
7: 18 I have the desire to do what is g,
7: 18 I know that nothing g lives in me,
7: 19 For what I do is not the g I want
7: 21 want to do g, evil is right there
8: 28 for the g of those who love him,
9: 11 or had done anything g or bad—
10: 15 feet of those who bring g news!"
10: 16 the Israelites accepted the g news.
12: 2 his g, pleasing and perfect will.
12: 9 Hate what is evil; cling to what is g.
12: 21 by evil, but overcome evil with g.
13: 4 For he is God's servant to do you g
14: 16 Do not allow what you consider g
15: 2 please his neighbor for his g,
16: 19 you to be wise about what is g,
1Co 5: 6 Your boasting is not g.
7: 1 It is g for a man not to marry.
7: 8 It is g for them to stay unmarried,
7: 26 I think that it is g for you to remain
7: 35 I am saying this for your own g,

1Co 10: 24 should seek his own g, but the g
10: 33 For I am not seeking my own g
10: 33 am not seeking my own g but the g
11: 17 meetings do more harm than g.
12: 7 given for the common g.
14: 6 speak in tongues, what g will I be
15: 33 Bad company corrupts g character
2Co 5: 10 done while in the body, whether g
6: 8 bad report and g report; genuine,
9: 8 you will abound in every g work.
Gal 4: 17 to win you over, but for no g.
4: 18 provided the purpose is g,
5: 7 You were running a g race.
6: 6 in the word must share all g things
6: 9 us not become weary in doing g,
6: 10 as we have opportunity, let us do g
6: 12 to make a g impression outwardly
Eph 1: 9 his will according to his g pleasure,
2: 10 in Christ Jesus to do g works,
6: 8 everyone for whatever g he does,
Php 1: 6 that he who began a g work
1: 15 and rivalry, but others out of g will.
2: 13 to act according to his g purpose.
4: 14 Yet it was g of you to share
Col 1: 10 bearing fruit in every g work,
1Th 3: 6 and has brought g news about your
5: 21 Hold on to the g.
2Th 1: 11 he may fulfill every g purpose
2: 16 eternal encouragement and g hope,
2: 17 and strengthen you in every g deed
1Ti 1: 5 a g conscience and a sincere faith.
1: 8 We know that the law is g
1: 9 that law is made not for g men
1: 18 them you may fight the g fight,
1: 19 on to faith and a g conscience.
2: 3 This is g, and pleases God our
2: 10 but with g deeds, appropriate
3: 7 have a g reputation with outsiders,
4: 4 For everything God created is g,
4: 6 and of the g teaching that you have
4: 6 you will be a g minister
5: 10 and is well known for her g deeds,
5: 10 herself to all kinds of g deeds.
5: 25 the same way, g deeds are obvious,
6: 12 Fight the g fight of the faith.
6: 12 when you made your g confession
6: 13 Pilate made the g confession,
6: 18 them to do g, to be rich in g deeds,
2Ti 1: 14 Guard the g deposit that was
2: 3 hardship with us like a g soldier
2: 21 and prepared to do any g work.
3: 3 not lovers of the g, treacherous,
3: 17 equipped for every g work.
4: 7 I have fought the g fight, I have
Tit 1: 8 loves what is g, who is
1: 16 and unfit for doing anything g.
2: 3 but to teach what is g.
2: 7 an example by doing what is g.
2: 14 his very own, eager to do what is g.
3: 1 to be ready to do whatever is g,
3: 8 themselves to doing what is g.
3: 14 themselves to doing what is g,
Phm : 6 of every g thing we have in Christ.
: 15 you might have him back for g—
Heb 5: 14 to distinguish g from evil.
9: 11 of the g things that are already here
10: 1 of the g things that are coming—
10: 24 on toward love and g deeds.
11: 12 so from this one man, and he as g
12: 10 but God disciplines us for our g,
13: 9 It is g for our hearts
13: 16 do not forget to do g and to share
13: 21 equip you with everything g
Jas 1: 17 Every g and perfect gift is
2: 3 "Here's a g seat for you,"
2: 14 over judgment! What g is it,
2: 16 what g is it? In the same way,
2: 19 G! Even the demons believe that—
3: 13 Let him show it by his g life,
3: 17 full of mercy and g fruit, impartial
4: 17 who knows the g he ought to do
1Pe 2: 3 you have tasted that the Lord is g.
2: 12 Live such g lives among the pagans
2: 12 they may see your g deeds
2: 15 that by doing g you should silence
2: 18 not only to those who are g
2: 20 But if you suffer for doing g
3: 10 and see g days

1Pe 3:11 He must turn from evil and do *g*;
3:13 to harm you if you are eager to do *g*
3:16 against your *g* behavior
3:17 to suffer for doing *g*
3:21 of a *g* conscience toward God
4:19 Creator and continue to do *g*.
3Jn :2 I pray that you may enjoy *g* health
:11 Anyone who does what is *g* is
:11 imitate what is evil but what is *g*.

GOOD-BY

Ge 31:28 grandchildren and my daughters *g*.
Ru 1:14 Orpah kissed her mother-in-law *g*,
1Ki 19:20 me kiss my father and mother *g*,"
Lk 9:61 but first let me go back and say *g*
Ac 20:1 said *g* and set out for Macedonia.
21:6 After saying *g* to each other,
2Co 2:13 So I said *g* to them and went
13:11 Finally, brothers, *g*.

GOODNESS (GOOD)

Ex 33:19 I will cause all my *g* to pass in front
2Ch 6:41 may your saints rejoice in your *g*.
Ne 9:25 they reveled in your great *g*.
9:35 enjoying your great *g* to them
Ps 23:6 Surely *g* and love will follow me
27:13 I will see the *g* of the LORD
31:19 How great is your *g*,
69:16 O LORD, out of the *g* of your love;
86:17 Give me a sign of your *g*,
109:21 of the *g* of your love, deliver me.
116:12 the LORD for all his *g* to me?
142:7 because of your *g* to me.
145:7 will celebrate your abundant *g*
Ro 15:14 that you yourselves are full of *g*,
Gal 5:22 patience, kindness, *g*, faithfulness,
Eph 5:9 fruit of the light consists in all *g*,
Heb 6:5 who have tasted the *g* of the word
2Pe 1:3 us by his own glory and *g*.
1:5 effort to add to your faith *g*;
1:5 to *g*, knowledge; and to knowledge

GOODS

Ge 14:11 The four kings seized all the *g*
14:16 He recovered all the *g*
14:21 and keep the *g* for yourself."
31:18 with all the *g* he had accumulated
31:37 have searched through all my *g*,
36:6 all the *g* he had acquired in Canaan
40:17 kinds of baked *g* for Pharaoh,
Ex 22:7 a man gives his neighbor silver or *g*
Nu 31:9 the Midianite herds, flocks and *g*
2Ch 21:17 and carried off all the *g* found
Ezr 1:4 with *g* and livestock,
1:6 with *g* and livestock,
Ne 13:8 threw all Tobiah's household *g* out
13:20 of all kinds of *g* spent the night
Est 3:13 of Adar, and to plunder their *g*.
Ps 62:10 or take pride in stolen *g*;
Ecc 5:11 As *g* increase,
Jer 49:29 off with all their *g* and camels.
Eze 27:12 because of your great wealth of *g*;
27:18 products and great wealth of *g*,
38:12 *g*, living at the center of the land."
38:13 to take away livestock and *g*
Hab 2:6 to him who piles up stolen *g*
Lk 12:18 I will store all my grain and my *g*.
17:31 with his *g* inside, should go
Ac 2:45 Selling their possessions and *g*,

GOODWILL

Ac 7:10 him to gain the *g* of Pharaoh king

GORE (GORES GORING)

Dt 33:17 with them he will *g* the nations,
1Ki 22:11 these you will *g* the Arameans
2Ch 18:10 these you will *g* the Arameans

GORES (GORE)

Ex 21:28 "If a bull *g* a man or a woman
21:31 also applies if the bull *g* a son
21:32 If the bull *g* a male or female slave,

GORGE (GORGED)

Ex 15:9 I will *g* myself on them.
Dt 2:24 Set out now and cross the Arnon *G*
2:36 and from the town in the *g*,
2:36 *G*, and from the town in the gorge,
Dt 3:8 from the Arnon *G* as far
3:12 *G*, including half the hill country
3:16 down to the Arnon *G* (the middle
3:16 middle of the *g* being the border)
4:48 of the Arnon *G* to Mount Siyon
Jos 12:1 from the Arnon *G*
12:2 from the middle of the *g*—
12:2 *G*—from the middle of the gorge
13:9 Aroer on the rim of the Arnon *G*,
13:9 the town in the middle of the *g*,
13:16 Aroer on the rim of the Arnon *G*,
13:16 the town in the middle of the *g*,
15:7 Pass of Adummim south of the *g*.
2Sa 24:5 south of the town in the *g*,
2Ki 10:33 by the Arnon *G* through Gilead
2Ch 20:16 at the end of the *g* in the Desert
Pr 23:20 or *g* themselves on meat,
Eze 32:4 of the earth *g* themselves on you.

GORGED (GORGE)

Rev 19:21 and all the birds *g* themselves

GORING (GORE)

Ex 21:29 the bull has had the habit of *g*
21:36 that the bull had the habit of *g*,

GOSHEN

Ge 45:10 You shall live in the region of *G*
46:28 arrived in the region of *G*,
46:28 to Joseph to get directions to *G*,
46:29 went to *G* to meet his father Israel.
46:34 allowed to settle in the region of *G*,
47:1 land of Canaan and are now in *G*."
47:4 please let your servants settle in *G*
47:6 Let them live in *G*.
47:27 settled in Egypt in the region of *G*.
50:8 flocks and herds were left in *G*.
Ex 8:22 differently with the land of *G*,
9:26 it did not hail was the land of *G*,
Jos 10:41 and from the whole region of *G*
11:16 region of *G*, the western foothills,
15:51 Eshtemoh, Anim, *G*, Holon

GOSPEL

Mt 24:14 And this *g* of the kingdom will be
26:13 wherever this *g* is preached
Mk 1:1 of the *g* about Jesus Christ,
8:35 life for me and for the *g* will save it.
10:29 the *g* will fail to receive a hundred
13:10 And the *g* must first be preached
14:9 wherever the *g* is preached
Lk 9:6 preaching the *g* and healing people
20:1 temple courts and preaching the *g*,
Ac 8:25 preaching the *g* in many Samaritan
8:40 preaching the *g* in all the towns
15:7 from my lips the message of the *g*
16:10 us to preach the *g* to them.
20:24 of testifying to the *g* of God's grace
Ro 1:1 and set apart for the *g* of God—
1:2 the *g* he promised beforehand
1:9 heart in preaching the *g* of his Son,
1:15 am so eager to preach the *g*
1:16 I am not ashamed of the *g*,
1:17 For in the *g* a righteousness
2:16 Jesus Christ, as my *g* declares.
11:28 As far as the *g* is concerned,
15:16 duty of proclaiming the *g* of God,
15:19 I have fully proclaimed the *g*
15:20 to preach the *g* where Christ was
16:25 able to establish you by my *g*
1Co 1:17 to preach the *g*—not with words
4:15 I became your father through the *g*.
9:12 rather than hinder the *g* of Christ.
9:14 receive their living from the *g*.
9:14 who preach the *g* should receive
9:16 Woe to me if I do not preach the *g*!
9:16 when I preach the *g*, I cannot boast
9:18 in preaching the *g* I may offer it
9:23 I do all this for the sake of the *g*,
15:1 you of the *g* I preached to you,
15:2 By this *g* you are saved,
2Co 2:12 to Troas to preach the *g* of Christ
4:3 And even if our *g* is veiled,
4:4 light of the *g* of the glory of Christ,
8:18 churches for his service to the *g*.
9:13 your confession of the *g*
10:14 as far as you with the *g* of Christ.
10:16 so that we can preach the *g*
2Co 11:4 or a different *g* from the one you
11:7 you by preaching the *g* of God
Gal 1:7 a different *g*—which is really no *g*
1:7 are trying to pervert the *g* of Christ
1:8 heaven should preach a *g* other
1:9 to you a *g* other than what you
1:11 that the *g* I preached is not
2:2 set before them the *g* that I preach
2:5 of the *g* might remain with you.
2:7 of preaching the *g* to the Gentiles,
2:7 task of preaching the *g* to the Jews.
2:14 in line with the truth of the *g*,
3:8 and announced the *g* in advance
4:13 an illness that I first preached the *g*
Eph 1:13 of truth, the *g* of your salvation.
3:6 through the *g* the Gentiles are heirs
3:7 a servant of this *g* by the gift
6:15 comes from the *g* of peace.
6:19 make known the mystery of the *g*,
Php 1:5 in the *g* from the first day
1:7 or defending and confirming the *g*,
1:12 has really served to advance the *g*.
1:16 here for the defense of the *g*.
1:27 in a manner worthy of the *g*
1:27 of the *g* without being frightened
2:22 with me in the work of the *g*.
4:3 at my side in the cause of the *g*,
4:15 of your acquaintance with the *g*,
Col 1:5 the *g* that has come to you.
1:6 the world this *g* is producing fruit
1:23 This is the *g* that you heard
1:23 from the hope held out in the *g*.
1Th 1:5 our *g* came to you not simply
2:2 dared to tell you his *g* in spite
2:4 by God to be entrusted with the *g*.
2:8 with you not only the *g* of God
2:9 while we preached the *g* of God
3:2 worker in spreading the *g* of Christ,
2Th 1:8 do not obey the *g* of our Lord Jesus
2:14 He called you to this through our *g*,
1Ti 1:11 to the glorious *g* of the blessed God
2Ti 1:8 join with me in suffering for the *g*,
1:10 immortality to light through the *g*.
1:11 of this *g* I was appointed a herald
2:8 This is my *g*, for which I am
Phm :13 me while I am in chains for the *g*.
Heb 4:2 also have had the *g* preached to us,
4:6 who formerly had the *g* preached
1Pe 1:12 by those who have preached the *g*
4:6 is the reason the *g* was preached
4:17 be for those who do not obey the *g*
Rev 14:6 he had the eternal *g* to proclaim

GOSSIP (GOSSIPING GOSSIPS)

Pr 11:13 A *g* betrays a confidence,
16:28 and a *g* separates close friends.
18:8 of a *g* are like choice morsels;
20:19 A *g* betrays a confidence;
26:20 without *g* a quarrel dies down.
26:22 of a *g* are like choice morsels;
2Co 12:20 slander, *g*, arrogance and disorder.

GOSSIPING (GOSSIP)

3Jn :10 he is doing, *g* maliciously about us.

GOSSIPS (GOSSIP)

Ro 1:29 They are *g*, slanderers, God-haters,
1Ti 5:13 but also *g* and busybodies,

GOT (GET)

Ge 18:16 When the men *g* up to leave,
19:1 he *g* up to meet them and bowed
19:27 the next morning Abraham *g* up
19:33 That night they *g* their father
19:33 lay down or when she *g* up.
19:35 So they *g* their father
19:35 lay down or when she *g* up.
21:21 his mother *g* a wife for him
22:3 the next morning Abraham *g* up
24:54 When they *g* up the next morning,
24:61 Rebekah and her maids *g* ready
24:64 She *g* down from her camel
25:34 and drank, and then *g* up and left.
27:14 So he went and *g* them
32:22 That night Jacob *g* up and took his
37:31 Then they *g* Joseph's robe,
38:6 Judah *g* a wife for Er, his firstborn,
Ex 2:3 she *g* a papyrus basket for him

Ex 2: 8 girl went and *g* the baby's mother.
2: 17 but Moses *g* up and came
12: 30 and all the Egyptians *g* up
24: 4 He *g* up early the next morning
32: 6 drink and *g* up to indulge in revelry
Nu 16: 25 Moses *g* up and went to Dathan
22: 13 The next morning Balaam *g* up
22: 21 Balaam *g* up in the morning,
24: 25 Balaam *g* up and returned home
Jos 6: 12 Joshua *g* up early the next morning
6: 15 they *g* up at daybreak and marched
15: 18 When she *g* off the donkey,
Jdg 1: 14 When she *g* off her donkey,
3: 26 While they waited, Ehud *g* away.
6: 28 when the men of the town *g* up,
7: 6 All the rest *g* down on their knees
10: 16 Then they *g* rid of the foreign gods
13: 11 Manoah *g* up and followed his wife
16: 3 he *g* up and took hold of the doors
19: 5 On the fourth day they *g* up early
19: 7 And when the man *g* up to go,
19: 9 *g* up to leave, his father-in-law,
19: 27 When her master *g* up
20: 11 So all the men of Israel *g* together
20: 19 next morning the Israelites *g* up
Ru 2: 15 As she *g* up to glean, Boaz gave
3: 14 but *g* up before anyone could be
1Sa 3: 6 And Samuel *g* up and went to Eli
3: 8 and Samuel *g* up and went to Eli
9: 26 When Saul *g* ready, he
15: 12 Early in the morning Samuel *g* up
20: 34 Jonathan *g* up from the table
20: 41 David *g* up from the south side
25: 23 she quickly *g* off her donkey
25: 42 Abigail quickly *g* on a donkey and,
28: 23 He *g* up from the ground
28: 25 That same night they *g* up and left.
29: 11 his men *g* up early in the morning
30: 17 and none of them *g* away,
2Sa 11: 2 One evening David *g* up
12: 20 Then David *g* up from the ground.
13: 29 Then all the king's sons *g* up,
14: 6 They *g* into a fight with each other
18: 9 Absalom's head *g* caught
19: 8 So the king *g* up and took his seat
24: 11 Before David *g* up the next
1Ki 1: 5 So he *g* chariots and horses ready,
3: 20 she *g* up in the middle of the night
3: 21 The next morning, I *g* up
14: 17 Then Jeroboam's wife *g* up and left
15: 12 *g* rid of all the idols his fathers had
19: 8 So he *g* up and ate and drank.
21: 16 *g* up and went down to take
2Ki 1: 15 So Elijah *g* up and went
3: 2 He *g* rid of the sacred stone
3: 22 they *g* up early in the morning,
4: 30 So he *g* up and followed her.
4: 34 Then he *g* on the bed and lay
4: 35 in the room and then *g* on the bed
5: 21 he *g* down from the chariot
5: 26 the man *g* down from his chariot
6: 15 the servant of the man of God *g* up
7: 5 At dusk they *g* up and went
7: 7 So they *g* up and fled in the dusk
7: 12 The king *g* up in the night
9: 6 Jehu *g* up and went into the house.
9: 16 Then he *g* into his chariot
19: 35 When the people *g* up the next
23: 24 Josiah *g* rid of the mediums
2Ch 33: 15 He *g* rid of the foreign gods
Est 6: 11 So Haman *g* the robe and the horse
7: 7 king *g* up in a rage, left his wine
9: 1 and the Jews *g* the upper hand
9: 22 as the time when the Jews *g* relief
Job 1: 20 Job *g* up and tore his robe
Isa 37: 36 When the people *g* up the next
Jer 41: 2 ten men who were with him *g* up
Eze 3: 23 So I *g* up and went out to the plain.
29: 18 and his army *g* no reward
Da 6: 10 Three times a day he *g*
6: 19 the king *g* up and hurried
8: 27 I *g* up and went about the king's
Zec 11: 8 In one month I *g* rid
Mt 2: 14 So he *g* up, took the child
2: 21 So he *g* up, took the child
8: 15 she *g* up and began to wait on him.
8: 23 Then he *g* into the boat
8: 26 he *g* up and rebuked the winds
Mt 9: 7 And the man *g* up and went home.
9: 9 Matthew *g* up and followed him.
9: 19 Jesus *g* up and went with him,
9: 25 the girl by the hand, and she *g* up.
13: 2 around him that he *g* into a boat
14: 29 Then Peter *g* down out of the boat
15: 39 he *g* into the boat and went
22: 34 the Pharisees *g* together.
27: 48 one of them ran and *g* a sponge.
Mk 1: 35 while it was still dark, Jesus *g* up,
2: 12 He *g* up, took his mat and walked
2: 14 and Levi *g* up and followed him.
4: 1 was so large that he *g* into a boat
4: 39 care if we drown?'' He *g* up,
5: 2 When Jesus *g* out of the boat,
6: 33 and *g* there ahead of them.
6: 54 As soon as they *g* out of the boat,
8: 10 he *g* into the boat with his disciples
8: 13 *g* back into the boat and crossed
Lk 1: 39 At that time Mary *g* ready
4: 29 They *g* up, drove him out
4: 39 She *g* up at once and began to wait
5: 3 He *g* into one of the boats,
5: 28 Jesus said to him, and Levi *g* up,
6: 8 So he *g* up and stood there.
8: 22 So they *g* into a boat and set out.
8: 24 He *g* up and rebuked the wind
8: 37 So he *g* into the boat and left.
14: 20 Still another said, 'I just *g* married,
15: 13 younger son *g* together all he had,
15: 20 So he *g* up and went to his father.
24: 12 however, *g* up and ran to the tomb.
24: 33 They *g* up and returned at once
Jn 4: 52 to the time when his son *g* better,
6: 17 where they *g* into a boat
6: 24 they *g* into the boats and went
11: 29 she *g* up quickly and went to him.
11: 31 noticed how quickly she *g* up
13: 4 so he *g* up from the meal, took
21: 3 they went out and *g* into the boat,
Ac 1: 18 (With the reward he *g*
5: 8 and Ananias *g* for the land?''
9: 8 Saul *g* up from the ground,
9: 18 He *g* up and was baptized,
9: 34 Immediately Aeneas *g* up.
9: 40 then he *g* down on his knees
14: 20 he *g* up and went back into the city.
15: 7 Peter *g* up and addressed them:
16: 10 we *g* ready at once to leave
21: 15 we *g* ready and went up
25: 18 When his accusers *g* up to speak,
28: 16 When we *g* to Rome, Paul was
1Co 10: 7 *g* up to indulge in pagan revelry.''

GOUGE (GOUGED)

Nu 16: 14 Will you *g* out the eyes
1Sa 11: 2 the condition that I *g* out the right
Mt 5: 29 *g* it out and throw it away.
18: 9 *g* it out and throw it away.

GOUGED (GOUGE)

Jdg 16: 21 *g* out his eyes and took him

GOURDS

1Ki 6: 18 carved with *g* and open flowers.
7: 24 Below the rim, *g* encircled it—
7: 24 The *g* were cast in two rows
2Ki 4: 39 He gathered some of its *g*

GOVERN (GOVERNED GOVERNING GOVERNMENT GOVERNOR GOVERNOR'S GOVERNORS GOVERNS)

Ge 1: 16 and the lesser light to *g* the night.
1: 16 the greater light to *g* the day
1: 18 to *g* the day and the night,
1Sa 9: 17 to you about; he will *g* my people.''
1Ki 3: 9 a discerning heart to *g* your people
3: 9 able to *g* this great people
2Ch 1: 10 able to *g* this great people
1: 11 and knowledge to *g* my people
Job 34: 17 Can he who hates justice *g*?
Ps 9: 8 he will *g* the peoples with justice.
136: 8 the sun to *g* the day,
136: 9 the moon and stars to *g* the night;
Pr 8: 16 by me princes *g*,
Isa 3: 4 mere children will *g* them.
Ob : 21 to *g* the mountains of Esau.
Zec 3: 7 then you will *g* my house
Ro 12: 8 it is leadership, let him *g* diligently;

GOVERNED (GOVERN)

Jdg 9: 22 After Abimelech had *g* Israel three
2Ki 15: 5 and *g* the people of the land.
2Ch 26: 21 and *g* the people of the land.

GOVERNING (GOVERN)

Ro 13: 1 himself to the *g* authorities,
13: 6 who give their full time to *g*.

GOVERNMENT (GOVERN)

1Ki 9: 22 his *g* officials, his officers,
Isa 9: 6 and the *g* will be on his shoulders.
9: 7 Of the increase of his *g* and peace
Da 6: 4 Daniel in his conduct of *g* affairs,

GOVERNOR (GOVERN)

Ge 42: 6 Now Joseph was the *g* of the land,
Jdg 9: 30 When Zebul the *g*
1Ki 4: 19 He was the only *g* over the district.
2Ki 10: 5 the palace administrator, the city *g*
23: 8 the city *g*, which is on the left
25: 23 had appointed Gedaliah as *g*,
Ezr 2: 63 The *g* ordered them not to eat any
5: 3 At that time Tattenai, *g*
5: 6 *g* of Trans-Euphrates,
5: 14 whom he had appointed *g*,
6: 6 Tattenai, *g* of Trans-Euphrates,
6: 7 Let the *g* of the Jews
6: 13 Tattenai, *g* of Trans-Euphrates,
Ne 3: 7 of the *g* of Trans-Euphrates.
5: 14 ate the food allotted to the *g*.
5: 14 to be their *g* in the land of Judah,
5: 18 the food allotted to the *g*,
7: 65 The *g*, therefore, ordered them not
7: 70 The *g* gave to the treasury 1,000
8: 9 Nehemiah the *g*, Ezra the priest
10: 1 Nehemiah the *g*, the son
12: 26 and in the days of Nehemiah the *g*
Isa 60: 17 I will make peace your *g*
Jer 40: 7 as *g* over the land and had put him
40: 11 the son of Shaphan, as *g* over them,
41: 2 king of Babylon had appointed as *g*
41: 18 king of Babylon had appointed as *g*
Hag 1: 1 *g* of Judah, and to Joshua son
1: 14 *g* of Judah, and the spirit
2: 2 son of Shealtiel, *g* of Judah,
2: 21 ''Tell Zerubbabel *g*
Mal 1: 8 Try offering them to your *g*!
Mt 27: 2 handed him over to Pilate, the *g*.
27: 11 before the *g*, and the *g* asked him,
27: 14 to the great amazement of the *g*.
27: 21 me to release to you?'' asked the *g*.
28: 14 If this report gets to the *g*,
Lk 2: 2 while Quirinius was *g* of Syria.)
3: 1 when Pontius Pilate was *g* of Judea
20: 20 to the power and authority of the *g*.
Jn 18: 28 to the palace of the Roman *g*.
Ac 23: 24 he may be taken safely to *G* Felix.''
23: 26 To His Excellency, *G* Felix:
23: 33 they delivered the letter to the *g*
23: 34 *g* read the letter and asked what
24: 1 charges against Paul before the *g*.
24: 10 When the *g* motioned for him
26: 30 and with him the *g* and Bernice
2Co 11: 32 In Damascus the *g*

GOVERNOR'S (GOVERN)

Mt 27: 15 it was the *g* custom at the Feast
27: 27 Then the *g* soldiers took Jesus

GOVERNORS (GOVERN)

1Ki 4: 7 had twelve district *g* over all Israel,
10: 15 all the Arabian kings and the *g*
2Ch 9: 14 and the *g* of the land brought gold
Ezr 8: 36 and to the *g* of Trans-Euphrates,
Ne 2: 7 letters to the *g* of Trans-Euphrates,
2: 9 I went to the *g* of Trans-Euphrates
5: 15 the earlier *g*— those preceding me
Est 3: 12 the *g* of the various provinces
8: 9 *g* and nobles of the 127 provinces
9: 3 the *g* and the king's administrators
Jer 51: 23 with you I shatter *g* and officials.
51: 28 their *g* and all their officials,
51: 57 her *g*, officers and warriors as well;
Eze 23: 6 warriors clothed in blue, *g*
23: 12 lusted after the Assyrians—*g*

Eze 23: 23 all of them *g* and commanders,
Da 3: 2 prefects, *g*, advisers, treasurers,
3: 3 prefects, *g*, advisers, treasurers,
3: 27 *g* and royal advisers crowded
6: 7 and *g* have all agreed that the king
Mt 10: 18 you will be brought before *g*
Mk 13: 9 of me you will stand before *g*
Lk 21: 12 brought before kings and *g*,
1Pe 2: 14 as the supreme authority, or to *g*,

GOVERNS (GOVERN)

Job 36: 31 This is the way he *g* the nations

GOWN

Ps 45: 13 her *g* is interwoven with gold.

GOYIM (GOIIM)

Jos 12: 23 the king of *G* in Gilgal one the king

GOZAN

2Ki 17: 6 in *G* on the Habor River
18: 11 in *G* on the Habor River
19: 12 the gods of *G*, Haran, Rezeph
1Ch 5: 26 Habor, Hara and the river of *G*,
Isa 37: 12 the gods of *G*, Haran, Rezeph

GRABBED

Jdg 15: 15 he *g* it and struck down a thousand
2Sa 2: 16 Then each man *g* his opponent
13: 11 he *g* her and said, "Come to bed
Mt 18: 28 He *g* him and began to choke him.

GRACE (GRACIOUS)

Ps 45: 2 lips have been anointed with *g*,
Pr 1: 9 will be a garland to *g* your head
3: 22 an ornament to *g* your neck.
3: 34 but gives *g* to the humble.
4: 9 She will set a garland of *g*
Isa 26: 10 Though *g* is shown to the wicked,
Jnh 2: 8 forfeit the *g* that could be theirs.
Zec 12: 10 of Jerusalem a spirit of *g*
Lk 2: 40 and the *g* of God was upon him.
Jn 1: 14 who came from the Father, full of *g*
1: 16 of his *g* we have all received one
1: 17 *g* and truth came through Jesus
Ac 4: 33 and much *g* was upon them all.
6: 8 a man full of God's *g* and power,
11: 23 saw the evidence of the *g* of God,
13: 43 them to continue in the *g* of God.
14: 3 message of his *g* by enabling them
14: 26 they had been committed to the *g*
15: 11 We believe it is through the *g*
15: 40 by the brothers to the *g* of the Lord
18: 27 to those who by *g* had believed.
20: 24 testifying to the gospel of God's *g*.
20: 32 to God and to the word of his *g*,
Ro 1: 5 we received *g* and apostleship
1: 7 *G* and peace to you
3: 24 and are justified freely by his *g*
4: 16 be by *g* and may be guaranteed
5: 2 access by faith into this *g*
5: 15 came by the *g* of the one man,
5: 15 how much more did God's *g*
5: 17 God's abundant provision of *g*
5: 20 where sin increased, *g* increased all
5: 21 also *g* might reign
6: 1 on sinning so that *g* may increase?
6: 14 you are not under law, but under *g*.
6: 15 we are not under law but under *g*?
11: 5 there is a remnant chosen by *g*.
11: 6 if by *g*, then it is no longer by works
11: 6 if it were, *g* would no longer be *g*.
12: 3 For by the *g* given me I say
12: 6 according to the *g* given us.
15: 15 because of the *g* God gave me
16: 20 The *g* of our Lord Jesus be
1Co 1: 3 *G* and peace to you
1: 4 of his *g* given you in Christ Jesus.
3: 10 By the *g* God has given me,
15: 10 But by the *g* of God I am what I am
15: 10 but the *g* of God that was with me.
15: 10 his *g* to me was not without effect.
16: 23 The *g* of the Lord Jesus be with you
2Co 1: 2 *G* and peace to you
1: 12 wisdom but according to God's *g*.
4: 15 so that the *g* that is reaching more
6: 1 not to receive God's *g* in vain.
8: 1 to know about the *g* that God has
2Co 8: 6 also to completion this act of *g*
8: 7 also excel in this *g* of giving.
8: 9 For you know the *g*
9: 8 able to make all *g* abound to you,
9: 14 of the surpassing *g* God has given
12: 9 "My *g* is sufficient for you,
13: 14 May the *g* of the Lord Jesus Christ,
Gal 1: 3 *G* and peace to you
1: 6 the one who called you by the *g*
1: 15 from birth and called me by his *g*,
2: 9 when they recognized the *g* given
2: 21 I do not set aside the *g* of God,
3: 18 God in his *g* gave it to Abraham
5: 4 you have fallen away from *g*.
6: 18 The *g* of our Lord Jesus Christ be
Eph 1: 2 *G* and peace to you
1: 6 to the praise of his glorious *g*,
1: 7 riches of God's *g* that he lavished
2: 5 it is by *g* you have been saved.
2: 7 the incomparable riches of his *g*,
2: 8 For it is by *g* you have been saved,
3: 2 of God's *g* that was given to me
3: 7 by the gift of God's *g* given me
3: 8 God's people, this *g* was given me:
4: 7 to each one of us *g* has been given
6: 24 *G* to all who love our Lord Jesus
Php 1: 2 *G* and peace to you
1: 7 all of you share in God's *g* with me.
4: 23 The *g* of the Lord Jesus Christ be
Col 1: 2 *G* and peace to you
1: 6 understood God's *g* in all its truth.
4: 6 conversation be always full of *g*,
4: 18 *G* be with you.
1Th 1: 1 and the Lord Jesus Christ: *G*
5: 28 The *g* of our Lord Jesus Christ be
2Th 1: 2 *G* and peace to you
1: 12 according to the *g* of our God
2: 16 and by his *g* gave us eternal
3: 18 The *g* of our Lord Jesus Christ be
1Ti 1: 2 my true son in the faith: *G*,
1: 14 The *g* of our Lord was poured out
6: 21 *G* be with you.
2Ti 1: 2 To Timothy, my dear son: *G*,
1: 9 This *g* was given us in Christ Jesus
1: 9 because of his own purpose and *g*.
2: 1 be strong in the *g* that is
4: 22 *G* be with you.
Tit 1: 4 *G* and peace from God the Father
2: 11 For the *g* of God that brings
3: 7 having been justified by his *g*,
3: 15 *G* be with you all.
Phm : 3 *G* to you and peace
: 25 The *g* of the Lord Jesus Christ be
Heb 2: 9 that by the *g* of God he might taste
4: 16 find *g* to help us in our time of need
4: 16 the throne of *g* with confidence,
10: 29 and who has insulted the Spirit of *g*
12: 15 See to it that no one misses the *g*
13: 9 hearts to be strengthened by *g*,
13: 25 *G* be with you all.
Jas 4: 6 but gives *g* to the humble."
4: 6 but he gives us more *g*? That is why
1Pe 1: 2 *G* and peace be yours in abundance
1: 10 who spoke of the *g* that was
1: 13 fully on the *g* to be given you
4: 10 faithfully administering God's *g*
5: 5 but gives *g* to the humble."
5: 10 the God of all *g*, who called you
5: 12 and testifying that this is the true *g*
2Pe 1: 2 *G* and peace be yours in abundance
3: 18 But grow in the *g* and knowledge
2Jn : 3 and will be with us forever: *G*,
Jude : 4 who change the *g* of our God
Rev 1: 4 *G* and peace to you
22: 21 The *g* of the Lord Jesus be

GRACEFUL

Job 41: 12 his strength and his *g* form.
Pr 5: 19 A loving doe, a *g* deer—
SS 7: 1 Your *g* legs are like jewels,

GRACIOUS (GRACE)

Ge 21: 1 Now the LORD was *g* to Sarah
33: 11 for God has been *g* to me
43: 29 "God be *g* to you, my son."
Ex 34: 6 the compassionate and *g* God,
Nu 6: 25 and be *g* to you;
1Sa 2: 21 And the LORD was *g* to Hannah;
2Sa 1: 23 in life they were loved and *g*,
12: 22 The LORD may be *g* to me
2Ki 13: 23 But the LORD was *g* to them
2Ch 30: 9 for the LORD your God is *g*
Ezr 9: 8 the LORD our God has been *g*
Ne 2: 8 the *g* hand of my God was upon me
2: 18 also told them about the *g* hand
9: 17 But you are a forgiving God, *g*
9: 31 for you are a *g* and merciful God.
Job 33: 24 to be *g* to him and say,
Ps 25: 16 Turn to me and be *g* to me,
67: 1 May God be *g* to us and bless us
86: 15 are a compassionate and *g* God,
103: 8 The LORD is compassionate and *g*
111: 4 the LORD is *g* and compassionate.
112: 4 for the *g* and compassionate
116: 5 The LORD is *g* and righteous;
119: 29 be *g* to me through your law.
119: 58 be *g* to me according
145: 8 The LORD is *g* and compassionate
Pr 22: 11 a pure heart and whose speech is *g*
Ecc 10: 12 from a wise man's mouth are *g*,
Isa 30: 18 Yet the LORD longs to be *g* to you
30: 19 How *g* he will be when you cry
33: 2 O LORD, be *g* to us;
Jer 29: 10 and fulfill my *g* promise
33: 14 I will fulfill the *g* promise I made
Joel 2: 13 for he is *g* and compassionate,
Jnh 4: 2 I knew that you are a *g*
Mal 1: 9 "Now implore God to be *g* to us.
Lk 4: 22 amazed at the *g* words that came
2Co 1: 11 behalf for the *g* favor granted us
1Pe 3: 7 as heirs with you of the *g* gift of life,

GRAFT (GRAFTED)

Ro 11: 23 for God is able to *g* them in again.

GRAFTED (GRAFT)

Ro 11: 17 have been *g* in among the others
11: 19 broken off so that I could be *g* in."
11: 23 they will be *g* in, for God is able
11: 24 and contrary to nature were *g*
11: 24 be *g* into their own olive tree!

GRAIN (GRAINS GRANARIES)

Ge 27: 28 an abundance of *g* and new wine.
27: 37 and I have sustained him with *g*
37: 7 sheaves of *g* out in the field
41: 5 Seven heads of *g*, healthy and good
41: 6 seven other heads of *g* sprouted—
41: 7 heads of *g* swallowed up the seven
41: 22 dreams I also saw seven heads of *g*,
41: 24 of *g* swallowed up the seven good
41: 26 heads of *g* are seven years;
41: 27 of *g* scorched by the east wind:
41: 35 store up the *g* under the authority
41: 49 stored up huge quantities of *g*,
41: 56 and sold *g* to the Egyptians,
41: 57 to Egypt to buy *g* from Joseph,
42: 1 Jacob learned that there was *g*
42: 2 "I have heard that there is *g*
42: 3 went down to buy *g* from Egypt.
42: 5 among those who went to buy *g*,
42: 6 the one who sold *g* to all its people.
42: 19 and take *g* back for your starving
42: 25 orders to fill their bags with *g*,
42: 26 they loaded their *g*
43: 2 eaten all the *g* they had brought
44: 2 along with the silver for his *g*."
45: 23 ten female donkeys loaded with *g*
47: 14 for the *g* they were buying,
Ex 22: 6 or standing *g* or the whole field,
22: 6 so that it burns shocks of *g*
29: 41 at twilight with the same *g* offering
30: 9 or any burnt offering or *g* offering,
40: 29 on it burnt offerings and *g* offerings
Lev 2: 1 When someone brings a *g* offering
2: 3 The rest of the *g* offering belongs
2: 4 " 'If you bring a *g* offering baked
2: 5 If your *g* offering is prepared
2: 6 and pour oil on it; it is a *g* offering.
2: 7 If your *g* offering is cooked in a pan
2: 8 Bring the *g* offering made
2: 9 portion from the *g* offering
2: 10 The rest of the *g* offering belongs
2: 11 " 'Every *g* offering you bring
2: 13 Season all your *g* offerings with salt
2: 13 of your God out of your *g* offerings

Lev 2: 14 heads of new *g* roasted in the fire.
2: 14 " 'If you bring a *g* offering
2: 15 and incense on it; it is a *g* offering.
2: 16 memorial portion of the crushed *g*
5: 13 as in the case of the *g* offering.' "
6: 14 the regulations for the *g* offering:
6: 15 all the incense on the *g* offering,
6: 20 of fine flour as a regular *g* offering,
6: 21 and present the *g* offering broken
6: 23 Every *g* offering of a priest shall be
7: 9 Every *g* offering baked in an oven
7: 10 every *g* offering, whether mixed
7: 37 the *g* offering, the sin offering,
9: 4 together with a *g* offering mixed
9: 17 He also brought the *g* offering,
10: 12 "Take the *g* offering left
14: 10 mixed with oil for a *g* offering,
14: 20 together with the *g* offering,
14: 21 mixed with oil for a *g* offering,
14: 31 together with the *g* offering.
23: 10 a sheaf of the first *g* you harvest.
23: 13 together with its *g* offering
23: 14 eat any bread, or roasted or new *g*,
23: 16 an offering of new *g* to the LORD.
23: 18 together with their *g* offerings
23: 37 the burnt offerings and *g* offerings,
27: 30 whether *g* from the soil
Nu 4: 16 the regular *g* offering
5: 15 it is a *g* offering for jealousy,
5: 18 the *g* offering for jealousy,
5: 25 take from her hands the *g* offering
5: 26 to take a handful of the *g* offering
6: 15 together with their *g* offerings
6: 17 together with its *g* offering
7: 13 mixed with oil as a *g* offering;
7: 19 mixed with oil as a *g* offering;
7: 25 mixed with oil as a *g* offering;
7: 31 mixed with oil as a *g* offering;
7: 37 mixed with oil as a *g* offering;
7: 43 mixed with oil as a *g* offering;
7: 49 mixed with oil as a *g* offering;
7: 55 mixed with oil as a *g* offering;
7: 61 mixed with oil as a *g* offering;
7: 67 mixed with oil as a *g* offering;
7: 73 mixed with oil as a *g* offering;
7: 79 mixed with oil as a *g* offering;
7: 87 together with their *g* offering.
8: 8 bull with its *g* offering of fine flour
15: 4 to the LORD a *g* offering of a tenth
15: 6 " 'With a ram prepare a *g* offering
15: 9 bring with the bull a *g* offering
15: 24 along with its prescribed *g* offering
18: 9 whether *g* or sin or guilt offerings,
18: 12 and *g* they give the LORD
18: 27 as *g* from the threshing floor
20: 5 It has no *g* or figs, grapevines
28: 5 together with a *g* offering of a tenth
28: 8 with the same kind of *g* offering
28: 9 and a *g* offering of two-tenths
28: 12 a *g* offering of two-tenths
28: 12 is to be a *g* offering of three-tenths
28: 13 a *g* offering of a tenth of an ephah
28: 20 With each bull prepare a *g* offering
28: 26 of new *g* during the Feast of Weeks
28: 28 is to be a *g* offering of three-tenths
28: 31 burnt offering and its *g* offering.
29: 3 With the bull prepare a *g* offering
29: 6 offerings with their *g* offerings
29: 9 With the bull prepare a *g* offering
29: 11 offering with its *g* offering,
29: 14 thirteen bulls prepare a *g* offering
29: 16 burnt offering with its *g* offering
29: 18 prepare their *g* offerings
29: 19 offering with its *g* offering,
29: 21 prepare their *g* offerings
29: 22 burnt offering with its *g* offering
29: 24 prepare their *g* offerings
29: 25 burnt offering with its *g* offering
29: 27 prepare their *g* offerings
29: 28 burnt offering with its *g* offering
29: 30 prepare their *g* offerings
29: 31 burnt offering with its *g* offering
29: 33 prepare their *g* offerings
29: 34 burnt offering with its *g* offering
29: 37 prepare their *g* offerings
29: 38 burnt offering with its *g* offering
29: 39 your burnt offerings, *g* offerings,
Dt 7: 13 your *g*, new wine and oil—
11: 14 so that you may gather in your *g*,
12: 17 your own towns the tithe of your *g*
14: 23 Eat the tithe of your *g*, new wine
16: 9 to put the sickle to the standing *g*.
18: 4 give them the firstfruits of your *g*,
23: 25 not put a sickle to his standing *g*.
25: 4 an ox while it is treading out the *g*.
28: 51 They will leave you no *g*, new wine
33: 28 secure in a land of *g* and new wine,
Jos 5: 11 unleavened bread and roasted *g*.
22: 23 burnt offerings and *g* offerings,
22: 29 *g* offerings and sacrifices, other
Jdg 13: 19 together with the *g* offering,
13: 23 and *g* offering from our hands,
15: 5 in the standing *g* of the Philistines.
15: 5 up the shocks and standing *g*,
Ru 2: 2 and pick up the leftover *g*
2: 14 he offered her some roasted *g*.
2: 21 until they finish harvesting all my *g*
3: 7 lie down at the far end of the *g* pile.
1Sa 8: 15 He will take a tenth of your *g*
17: 17 "Take this ephah of roasted *g*
25: 18 sheep, five seahs of roasted *g*,
2Sa 1: 21 fields that yield offerings ⌞of *g*⌟.
17: 19 of the well and scattered *g* over it.
17: 28 flour and roasted *g*, beans
1Ki 8: 64 the *g* offerings and the fat
8: 64 *g* offerings and the fat
2Ki 4: 42 along with some heads of new *g*.
4: 42 baked from the first ripe *g*,
16: 13 up his burnt offering and *g* offering,
16: 15 and the evening *g* offering,
16: 15 and their *g* offering and their drink
16: 15 burnt offering and his *g* offering,
18: 32 a land of *g* and new wine, a land
1Ch 21: 23 and the wheat for the *g* offering.
23: 29 the flour for the *g* offerings,
2Ch 7: 7 the *g* offerings and the fat portions.
31: 5 gave the firstfruits of their *g*,
32: 28 buildings to store the harvest of *g*,
Ezr 7: 17 together with their *g* offerings
Ne 5: 2 and stay alive, we must get *g*."
5: 3 homes to get *g* during the famine."
5: 10 lending the people money and *g*.
5: 11 the hundredth part of the money, *g*
10: 31 or *g* to sell on the Sabbath,
10: 33 for the regular *g* offerings
10: 37 of our ⌞*g*⌟ offerings,
10: 39 are to bring their contributions of *g*
13: 5 and also the tithes of *g*, new wine
13: 5 used to store the *g* offerings
13: 9 with the *g* offerings
13: 12 All Judah brought the tithes of *g*,
13: 15 and bringing in *g* and loading it
Job 24: 24 they are cut off like heads of *g*.
31: 10 my wife grind another man's *g*,
39: 12 you trust him to bring in your *g*
Ps 4: 7 when their *g* and new wine abound.
65: 9 water to provide the people with *g*,
65: 13 and the valleys are mantled with *g*;
72: 16 Let *g* abound throughout the land;
78: 24 he gave them the *g* of heaven.
Pr 11: 26 People curse the man who hoards *g*
27: 22 grinding him like *g* with a pestle,
Isa 5: 10 a homer of seed only an ephah of *g*
17: 5 a reaper gathers the standing *g*
17: 5 and harvests the *g* with his arm—
17: 5 as when a man gleans heads of *g*
19: 21 with sacrifices and *g* offerings;
23: 3 came the *g* of the Shihor;
28: 28 *G* must be ground to make bread;
36: 17 a land of *g* and new wine, a land
43: 23 not burdened you with *g* offerings
57: 6 and offered *g* offerings.
62: 8 "Never again will I give your *g*
66: 3 whoever makes a *g* offering
66: 20 the Israelites bring their *g* offerings
Jer 9: 22 like cut *g* behind the reaper,
14: 12 burnt offerings and *g* offerings,
17: 26 and sacrifices, *g* offerings,
23: 28 For what has straw to do with *g*?"
31: 12 the *g*, the new wine and the oil,
33: 18 to burn *g* offerings
41: 5 bringing *g* offerings and incense
50: 11 you frolic like a heifer threshing *g*
50: 26 pile her up like heaps of *g*.
Eze 36: 29 call for the *g* and make it plentiful
42: 13 the *g* offerings, the sin offerings
Eze 44: 29 They will eat the *g* offerings,
45: 15 used for the *g* offerings,
45: 17 the sin offerings, *g* offerings,
45: 17 *g* offerings and drink offerings
45: 24 a *g* offering an ephah for each bull
45: 25 burnt offerings, *g* offerings and oil.
46: 5 The *g* offering given
46: 5 and the *g* offering with the lambs is
46: 7 a *g* offering one ephah with the bull
46: 11 the *g* offering is to be an ephah
46: 14 The presenting of this *g* offering
46: 14 morning by morning a *g* offering,
46: 15 So the lamb and the *g* offering
46: 20 sin offering and bake the *g* offering,
Hos 2: 8 who gave her the *g*, the new wine
2: 9 "Therefore I will take away my *g*
2: 22 and the earth will respond to the *g*,
7: 14 They gather together for *g*
8: 7 Were it to yield *g*,
14: 7 He will flourish like the *g*.
Joel 1: 9 *G* offerings and drink offerings
1: 10 the *g* is destroyed,
1: 13 for the *g* offerings and drink
1: 17 for the *g* has dried up.
2: 14 *g* offerings and drink offerings
2: 19 "I am sending you *g*, new wine
2: 24 floors will be filled with *g*;
Am 2: 13 a cart crushes when loaded with *g*.
5: 11 and force him to give you *g*.
5: 22 me burnt offerings and *g* offerings,
8: 5 that we may sell *g*,
9: 9 as *g* is shaken in a sieve,
Hag 1: 11 on the *g*, the new wine, the oil
Zec 9: 17 *G* will make the young men thrive,
Mt 12: 1 and began to pick some heads of *g*
Mk 2: 23 they began to pick some heads of *g*.
4: 7 so that they did not bear *g*.
4: 28 All by itself the soil produces *g*—
4: 29 the *g* is ripe, he puts the sickle to it,
Lk 6: 1 began to pick some heads of *g*,
12: 18 and there I will store all my *g*
17: 35 women will be grinding *g* together;
Ac 7: 12 When Jacob heard that there was *g*
27: 38 ship by throwing the *g* into the sea.
1Co 9: 9 ox while it is treading out the *g*."
1Ti 5: 18 ox while it is treading out the *g*,"

GRAINFIELD (FIELD)

Dt 23: 25 If you enter your neighbor's *g*,

GRAINFIELDS (FIELD)

Mt 12: 1 went through the *g* on the Sabbath.
Mk 2: 23 Jesus was going through the *g*,
Lk 6: 1 Jesus was going through the *g*,

GRAINS (GRAIN)

Job 29: 18 numerous as the *g* of sand.
Ps 139: 18 they would outnumber the *g*
Isa 48: 19 your children like its numberless *g*;

GRANARIES (GRAIN)

Ex 22: 29 not hold back offerings from your *g*
Jer 50: 26 Break open her *g*;
Joel 1: 17 the *g* have been broken down,

GRANDCHILDREN (CHILD)

Ge 31: 28 let me kiss my *g* and my daughters
31: 55 next morning Laban kissed his *g*
45: 10 your children and *g*, your flocks
Ex 10: 2 and *g* how I dealt harshly
Dt 4: 25 After you have had children and *g*
2Ki 17: 41 day their children and *g* continue
1Ti 5: 4 But if a widow has children or *g*,

GRANDDAUGHTER (DAUGHTER)

Ge 24: 48 to get the *g* of my master's brother
36: 2 and *g* of Zibeon the Hivite—
36: 14 daughter of Anah and *g* of Zibeon,
2Ki 8: 26 mother's name was Athaliah, a *g*
2Ch 22: 2 mother's name was Athaliah, a *g*

GRANDDAUGHTERS (DAUGHTER)

Ge 46: 7 grandsons and his daughters and *g*

GRANDFATHER (FATHER)

2Sa 9: 7 land that belonged to your *g* Saul,

GRANDFATHER'S (FATHER)

2Sa 16: 3 will give me back my *g* kingdom.' "
19: 28 All my *g* descendants deserved

GRANDMOTHER (MOTHER)

1Ki 15: 13 even deposed his *g* Maacah
2Ch 15: 16 also deposed his *g* Maacah
2Ti 1: 5 which first lived in your *g* Lois

GRANDMOTHER'S (MOTHER)

1Ki 15: 10 His *g* name was Maacah daughter

GRANDPARENTS (PARENTS)

1Ti 5: 4 so repaying their parents and *g*,

GRANDSON (SON)

Ge 11: 31 took his son Abram, his *g* Lot son
29: 5 Nahor's *g?*" "Yes, we know him,"
Jdg 8: 22 you, your son and your *g*—
2Sa 9: 9 your master's *g* everything that
9: 10 Mephibosheth, *g* of your master,
9: 10 that your master's *g* may be
16: 3 "Where is your master's *g?*"
19: 24 Saul's *g*, also went
Jer 27: 7 and his *g* until the time

GRANDSONS (SON)

Ge 36: 12 These were *g* of Esau's wife Adah.
36: 13 These were *g* of Esau's wife
36: 16 in Edom; they were *g* of Adah.
36: 17 they were *g* of Esau's wife
46: 7 and *g* and his daughters
Jdg 12: 14 He had forty sons and thirty *g*,
1Ch 8: 40 They had many sons and *g*—

GRANT (GRANTED GRANTING GRANTS)

Ge 19: 21 "Very well, I will *g* this request too;
24: 42 please *g* success to the journey
43: 14 may God Almighty *g* you mercy
Ex 21: 9 he must *g* her the rights
Lev 26: 6 " 'I will *g* peace in the land,
Dt 28: 7 LORD will *g* that the enemies who
28: 11 The LORD will *g* you abundant
Jdg 11: 37 But *g* me this one request,"
Ru 1: 9 May the LORD *g* that each
1Sa 1: 17 God of Israel *g* you what you have
2Sa 23: 5 and *g* me my every desire?
1Ki 5: 9 And you are to *g* my wish
1Ch 22: 9 and I will *g* Israel peace
Est 5: 8 it pleases the king to *g* my petition
7: 3 pleases your majesty, *g* me my
Job 6: 8 that God would *g* what I hope for,
13: 20 Only *g* me these two things, O God
Ps 20: 2 and *g* you support from Zion.
20: 5 May the LORD *g* all your requests
51: 12 *g* me a willing spirit, to sustain me.
85: 7 and *g* us your salvation.
86: 16 *g* your strength to your servant
94: 13 you *g* him relief from days
118: 25 O LORD, *g* us success.
140: 8 do not *g* the wicked their desires,
Isa 46: 13 I will *g* salvation to Zion,
Hag 2: 9 'And in this place I will *g* peace,'
Mt 20: 21 "*G* that one of these two sons
20: 23 at my right or left is not for me to *g*.
Mk 10: 40 at my right or left is not for me to *g*.
Lk 18: 3 *G* me justice against my adversary.'
23: 24 Pilate decided to *g* their demand.
Ac 24: 27 because Felix wanted to *g* a favor
2Ti 1: 18 May the Lord *g* that he will find
2: 25 that God will *g* them repentance

GRANTED (GRANT)

Ge 4: 25 "God has *g* me another child
24: 56 now that the LORD has *g* success
39: 21 and *g* him favor in the eyes
Jos 1: 13 you rest and has *g* you this land.'
14: 3 Moses had *g* the two-and-a-half
14: 3 but had not *g* the Levites
1Sa 1: 27 the LORD has *g* me what I asked
25: 35 your words and *g* your request."
2Sa 14: 22 the king has *g* his servant's request
1Ch 4: 10 And God *g* his request.
22: 18 has he not *g* you rest on every side?
23: 25 has *g* rest to his people
Ezr 7: 6 The king had *g* him everything he
9: 9 He has *g* us new life
Ne 2: 8 upon me, the king *g* my requests.
Est 5: 6 to half the kingdom, it will be *g*."
7: 2 to half the kingdom, it will be *g*."
8: 11 The king's edict *g* the Jews
9: 12 is your request? It will also be *g*."
Job 42: 15 their father *g* them an inheritance
Ps 21: 2 You have *g* him the desire
21: 6 Surely you have *g* him eternal
Pr 10: 24 what the righteous desire will be *g*.
Mt 14: 9 he ordered that her request be *g*
15: 28 great faith! Your request is *g*."
Jn 5: 26 so he has *g* the Son to have life
17: 2 For you *g* him authority
Ac 11: 18 *g* the Gentiles repentance unto life
Ro 11: 20 *G*. But they were broken off
2Co 1: 11 behalf for the gracious favor *g* us
Php 1: 29 For it has been *g* to you on behalf

GRANTING (GRANT)

Ne 1: 11 by *g* him favor in the presence

GRANTS (GRANT)

Ps 127: 2 for he *g* sleep to those he loves.
147: 14 He *g* peace to your borders

GRAPE (GRAPES)

Lev 26: 5 and the *g* harvest will continue
26: 5 will continue until *g* harvest
Nu 6: 3 He must not drink *g* juice
Dt 32: 14 You drank the red blood of the *g*.
Jdg 8: 2 than the full *g* harvest of Abiezer?
Isa 18: 5 the flower becomes a ripening *g*,
24: 13 left after the *g* harvest.
32: 10 the *g* harvest will fail,
Jer 49: 9 If *g* pickers came to you,
Ob : 5 If *g* pickers came to you,

GRAPES (GRAPE)

Ge 40: 10 and its clusters ripened into *g*.
40: 11 was in my hand, and I took the *g*,
49: 11 his robes in the blood of *g*.
Lev 19: 10 or pick up the *g* that have fallen.
25: 5 or harvest the *g* of your untended
Nu 6: 3 must not drink grape juice or eat *g*
13: 20 It was the season for the first ripe *g*
13: 23 branch bearing a single cluster of *g*.
13: 24 of the cluster of *g* the Israelites cut
Dt 23: 24 you may eat all the *g* you want,
24: 21 When you harvest the *g*
28: 39 not drink the wine or gather the *g*,
32: 32 Their *g* are filled with poison,
Jdg 8: 2 the gleanings of Ephraim's *g* better
9: 27 gathered the *g* and trodden them,
Ne 13: 15 *g*, figs and all other kinds of loads.
Job 15: 33 like a vine stripped of its unripe *g*,
Ps 80: 12 so that all who pass by pick its *g?*
Isa 5: 2 he looked for a crop of good *g*,
5: 4 When I looked for good *g*,
62: 9 those who gather the *g* will drink it
65: 8 juice is still found in a cluster of *g*
Jer 6: 9 like one gathering *g*."
8: 13 There will be no *g* on the vine.
25: 30 shout like those who tread the *g*,
31: 29 'The fathers have eaten sour *g*,
31: 30 whoever eats sour *g*— his own
48: 32 fallen on your ripened fruit and *g*.
49: 9 would they not leave a few *g?*
Eze 18: 2 " 'The fathers eat sour *g*,
Hos 9: 10 it was like finding *g* in the desert;
Joel 3: 13 Come, trample the *g*,
Am 9: 13 the planter by the one treading *g*.
Ob : 5 would they not leave a few *g?*
Mic 6: 15 you will crush *g* but not drink
7: 1 there is no cluster of *g* to eat,
Hab 3: 17 and there are no *g* on the vines,
Mt 7: 16 Do people pick *g* from thornbushes
Lk 6: 44 from thornbushes, or *g* from briers.
1Co 9: 7 vineyard and does not eat of its *g?*
Rev 14: 18 and gather the clusters of *g*
14: 18 earth's vine, because its *g* are ripe."
14: 19 gathered its *g* and threw them

GRAPEVINE (GRAPEVINES)

Nu 6: 4 anything that comes from the *g*,
Jdg 13: 14 anything that comes from the *g*,
Jas 3: 12 fig tree bear olives, or a *g* bear figs?

GRAPEVINES (GRAPEVINE)

Nu 20: 5 or figs, *g* or pomegranates.

GRASP (GRASPED GRASPING GRASPS)

2Ki 14: 5 the kingdom was firmly in his *g*,
Ps 71: 4 from the *g* of evil and cruel men.
Ecc 7: 18 It is good to *g* the one
Jer 15: 21 redeem you from the *g* of the cruel
34: 3 You will not escape from his *g*
Lk 9: 45 from them, so that they did not *g* it,
Jn 10: 39 to seize him, but he escaped their *g*
1Co 14: 11 If then I do not *g* the meaning
Eph 3: 18 to *g* how wide and long and high

GRASPED (GRASP)

Ge 19: 16 the men *g* his hand and the hands
Eze 21: 11 to be *g* with the hand;
21: 15 it is *g* for slaughter.
29: 7 When they *g* you with their hands,
Hos 12: 3 In the womb he *g* his brother's heel
Php 2: 6 with God something to be *g*,

GRASPING (GRASP)

Ge 25: 26 with his hand *g* Esau's heel;
Jdg 7: 20 *G* the torches in their left hands
Pr 27: 16 or *g* oil with the hand.

GRASPS (GRASP)

Dt 32: 41 and my hand *g* it in judgment,
Pr 31: 19 and *g* the spindle with her fingers.

GRASS

Nu 22: 4 as an ox licks up the *g* of the field."
Dt 11: 15 I will provide *g* in the fields
32: 2 like showers on new *g*,
2Sa 23: 4 that brings the *g* from the earth.'
1Ki 18: 5 Maybe we can find some *g*
2Ki 19: 26 like *g* sprouting on the housetops,
Job 5: 25 your descendants like the *g*
6: 5 a wild donkey bray when it has *g*,
8: 12 they wither more quickly than *g*.
38: 27 and make it sprout with *g?*
40: 15 and which feeds on *g* like an ox.
Ps 37: 2 for like the *g* they will soon wither,
72: 16 let it thrive like the *g* of the field.
90: 5 they are like the new *g*
92: 7 though the wicked spring up like *g*
102: 4 is blighted and withered like *g*;
102: 11 I wither away like *g*.
103: 15 As for man, his days are like *g*,
104: 14 He makes *g* grow for the cattle,
106: 20 for an image of a bull, which eats *g*.
129: 6 May they be like *g*
147: 8 and makes *g* grow on the hills.
Pr 19: 12 but his favor is like dew on the *g*.
27: 25 the *g* from the hills is gathered in,
Isa 5: 24 as dry *g* sinks down in the flames,
15: 6 and the *g* is withered;
35: 7 *g* and reeds and papyrus will grow.
37: 27 like *g* sprouting on the housetops,
40: 6 "All men are like *g*,
40: 7 Surely the people are *g*.
40: 7 The *g* withers and the flowers fall,
40: 8 The *g* withers and the flowers fall,
44: 4 They will spring up like *g*
51: 12 the sons of men, who are but *g*,
66: 14 and you will flourish like *g*;
Jer 12: 4 and the *g* in every field be withered
14: 5 because there is no *g*.
Da 4: 15 in the ground, in the *g* of the field.
4: 23 and bronze, in the *g* of the field,
4: 25 you will eat *g* like cattle
4: 32 animals; you will eat *g* like cattle.
4: 33 from people and ate *g* like cattle.
5: 21 wild donkeys and ate *g* like cattle;
Mic 5: 7 like showers on the *g*,
Mt 6: 30 If that is how God clothes the *g*
14: 19 the people to sit down on the *g*.
Mk 6: 39 sit down in groups on the green *g*.
Lk 12: 28 If that is how God clothes the *g*
Jn 6: 10 There was plenty of *g* in that place,
1Pe 1: 24 the *g* withers and the flowers fall,
1: 24 "All men are like *g*,
Rev 8: 7 and all the green *g* was burned up.
9: 4 not to harm the *g* of the earth

GRASSHOPPER (GRASSHOPPERS)

Lev 11: 22 of locust, katydid, cricket or *g*.
Ps 78: 46 He gave their crops to the *g*,
Ecc 12: 5 and the *g* drags himself along

GRASSHOPPERS (GRASSHOPPER)

Nu 13: 33 We seemed like *g* in our own eyes,
1Ki 8: 37 or blight or mildew, locusts or *g*,
2Ch 6: 28 or blight or mildew, locusts or *g*,
Ps 105: 34 *g* without number;
Isa 40: 22 and its people are like *g*.
Na 3: 15 Multiply like *g*,
3: 15 and, like *g*, consume you.

GRASSLANDS (LAND)

Ps 65: 12 The *g* of the desert overflow;

GRATEFUL (GRATIFY GRATIFYING GRATITUDE)

Ro 16: 4 of the Gentiles are *g* to them.

GRATIFY (GRATEFUL)

Ro 13: 14 think about how to *g* the desires
Gal 5: 16 and you will not *g* the desires

GRATIFYING (GRATEFUL)

Eph 2: 3 *g* the cravings of our sinful nature

GRATING

Ex 27: 4 Make a *g* for it, a bronze network,
35: 16 of burnt offering with its bronze *g*,
38: 4 They made a *g* for the altar,
38: 5 for the four corners of the bronze *g*.
38: 30 the bronze altar with its bronze *g*
39: 39 the bronze altar with its bronze *g*,

GRATITUDE (GRATEFUL)

Jdg 8: 35 also failed to show *g* to the family
Ac 24: 3 acknowledge this with profound *g*.
Col 3: 16 and spiritual songs with *g*

GRAVE (GRAVES)

Ge 37: 35 go down to the *g* to my son."
42: 38 head down to the *g* in sorrow."
44: 29 head down to the *g* in misery.'
44: 31 father down to the *g* in sorrow.
Nu 16: 30 and they go down alive into the *g*,
16: 33 They went down alive into the *g*,
19: 16 who touches a human bone or a *g*,
19: 18 a *g* or someone who has been killed
Dt 34: 6 day no one knows where his *g* is.
1Sa 2: 6 he brings down to the *g*
2Sa 22: 6 of the *g* coiled around me;
1Ki 2: 6 go down to the *g* in peace.
2: 9 head down to the *g* in blood."
13: 31 bury me in the *g* where the man
2Ki 21: 26 buried in his *g* in the garden
Job 3: 22 and rejoice when they reach the *g?*
5: 26 You will come to the *g* in full vigor,
7: 9 down to the *g* does not return.
10: 19 straight from the womb to the *g!*
11: 8 deeper than the depths of the *g*—
14: 13 "If only you would hide me in the *g*
17: 1 the *g* awaits me.
17: 13 If the only home I hope for is the *g*,
21: 13 and go down to the *g* in peace.
21: 32 He is carried to the *g*,
24: 19 so the *g* snatches away those who
40: 13 shroud their faces in the *g*.
Ps 5: 9 Their throat is an open *g;*
6: 5 Who praises you from the *g?*
9: 17 The wicked return to the *g*,
16: 10 you will not abandon me to the *g*,
18: 5 of the *g* coiled around me;
30: 3 you brought me up from the *g;*
31: 17 and lie silent in the *g*.
49: 14 sheep they are destined for the *g*,
49: 14 their forms will decay in the *g*,
49: 15 will redeem my soul from the *g;*
55: 15 let them go down alive to the *g*,
86: 13 from the depths of the *g*.
88: 3 and my life draws near the *g*.
88: 5 like the slain who lie in the *g*,
88: 11 Is your love declared in the *g*,
89: 48 himself from the power of the *g?*
107: 20 he rescued them from the *g*.
116: 3 the anguish of the *g* came upon me;
141: 7 at the mouth of the *g*."
Pr 1: 12 let's swallow them alive, like the *g*,
5: 5 her steps lead straight to the *g*.
7: 27 Her house is a highway to the *g*,
9: 18 are in the depths of the *g*.
15: 24 him from going down to the *g*.
Pr 30: 16 the *g*, the barren womb,
Ecc 9: 10 for in the *g*, where you are going,
SS 8: 6 its jealousy unyielding as the *g*.
Isa 5: 14 Therefore the *g* enlarges its
14: 9 The *g* below is all astir
14: 11 has been brought down to the *g*,
14: 15 But you are brought down to the *g*,
22: 16 hewing your *g* on the height
22: 16 to cut out a *g* for yourself here,
28: 15 with the *g* we have made
28: 18 with the *g* will not stand.
38: 18 For the *g* cannot praise you,
53: 9 He was assigned a *g*
57: 9 you descended to the *g* itself!
Jer 5: 16 Their quivers are like an open *g;*
20: 17 with my mother as my *g*,
Eze 31: 15 to the *g* I covered the deep springs
31: 16 it down to the *g* with those who go
31: 17 had also gone down to the *g* with it,
32: 21 within the *g* the mighty leaders will
32: 23 and her army lies around her *g*.
32: 24 with all her hordes around her *g*.
32: 25 with all her hordes around her *g*.
32: 27 down to the *g* with their weapons
Hos 13: 14 Where, O *g*, is your destruction?
13: 14 from the power of the *g;*
Am 9: 2 down to the depths of the *g*,
Jnh 2: 2 the depths of the *g* I called for help,
Na 1: 14 I will prepare your *g*,
Hab 2: 5 Because he is as greedy as the *g*
Jn 11: 44 "Take off the *g* clothes
Ac 2: 27 you will not abandon me to the *g*,
2: 31 that he was not abandoned to the *g*,

GRAVEDIGGERS (DIG)

Eze 39: 15 beside it until the *g* have buried it

GRAVEL

Pr 20: 17 he ends up with a mouth full of *g*.
La 3: 16 He has broken my teeth with *g;*

GRAVES (GRAVE)

Ex 14: 11 there were no *g* in Egypt that you
2Ki 23: 6 over the *g* of the common people.
2Ch 34: 4 and scattered over the *g*
Isa 65: 4 who sit among the *g*
Jer 8: 1 will be removed from their *g*.
Eze 32: 22 surrounded by the *g* of all her slain,
32: 23 Their *g* are in the depths of the pit
32: 26 with all their hordes around their *g*.
37: 12 I am going to open your *g*
37: 13 when I open your *g* and bring you
Mt 23: 29 and decorate the *g* of the righteous.
Lk 11: 44 because you are like unmarked *g*,
Jn 5: 28 are in their *g* will hear his voice
Ro 3: 13 "Their throats are open *g;*

GRAY

Ge 42: 38 you will bring my *g* head
44: 29 you will bring my *g* head
44: 31 Your servants will bring the *g* head
1Sa 12: 2 As for me, I am old and *g*,
1Ki 2: 6 but do not let his *g* head go
2: 9 Bring his *g* head down to the grave
Ps 71: 18 Even when I am old and *g*,
Pr 16: 31 *G* hair is a crown of splendor;
20: 29 *g* hair the splendor of the old.
Isa 46: 4 Even to your old age and *g* hairs
Hos 7: 9 His hair is sprinkled with *g*,

GRAY-HAIRED (HAIR)

Dt 32: 25 infants and *g* men.
Job 15: 10 The *g* and the aged are on our side,

GRAZE (GRAZED GRAZES GRAZING)

Ge 37: 12 gone to *g* their father's flocks
Ex 22: 5 and they *g* in another man's field,
34: 3 and herds may *g* in front
SS 1: 7 I love, where you *g* your flock
1: 8 and *g* your young goats
Isa 5: 17 sheep will *g* as in their own pasture;
27: 10 there the calves *g*,
30: 23 In that day your cattle will *g*
Jer 50: 19 and he will *g* on Carmel

GRAZED (GRAZE)

Ge 41: 2 and they *g* among the reeds.
41: 18 and they *g* among the reeds.

GRAZES (GRAZE)

Ex 22: 5 "If a man *g* his livestock in a field

GRAZING (GRAZE)

Ge 36: 24 desert while he was *g* the donkeys
37: 13 your brothers are *g* the flocks
37: 16 me where they are *g* their flocks?"
1Ch 27: 29 in charge of the herds *g* in Sharon.
Job 1: 14 and the donkeys were *g* nearby,
Eze 34: 14 lie down in good *g* land,
34: 14 of Israel will be their *g* land.

GREAT (GREATER GREATEST GREATNESS)

Ge 1: 16 God made two *g* lights—
1: 21 So God created the *g* creatures
6: 5 saw how *g* man's wickedness
7: 11 springs of the *g* deep burst forth,
10: 12 and Calah; that is the *g* city.
12: 2 I will make your name *g*,
12: 2 "I will make you into a *g* nation
12: 6 as the site of the *g* tree of Moreh
13: 6 were so *g* that they were not able
13: 18 to live near the *g* trees of Mamre
14: 13 Abram was living near the *g* trees
15: 1 your very *g* reward."
15: 14 out with *g* possessions.
15: 18 the river of Egypt to the *g* river,
17: 20 and I will make him into a *g* nation.
18: 1 near the *g* trees of Mamre
18: 18 Abraham will surely become a *g*
18: 20 Sodom and Gomorrah is so *g*
19: 13 is so *g* that he has sent us
19: 19 you have shown *g* kindness to me
20: 9 that you have brought such *g* guilt
21: 8 weaned Abraham held a *g* feast.
21: 18 for I will make him into a *g* nation
30: 8 "I have had a *g* struggle
32: 7 In *g* fear and distress Jacob divided
34: 12 and the gift I am to bring as *g*
35: 16 to give birth and had *g* difficulty.
35: 17 And as she was having *g* difficulty
36: 7 Their possessions were too *g*
41: 29 years of *g* abundance are coming
45: 7 lives by a *g* deliverance.
46: 3 you into a *g* nation there.
48: 19 a people, and he too will become *g*.
Ex 10: 14 area of the country in *g* numbers.
14: 31 the Israelites saw the *g* power
32: 10 I will make you into a *g* nation."
32: 11 out of Egypt with *g* power
32: 21 that you led them into such a *g* sin?"
32: 30 "You have committed a *g* sin.
32: 31 what a *g* sin these people have
Lev 11: 17 the cormorant, the *g* owl, the white
11: 29 any kind of *g* lizard, the gecko,
19: 15 to the poor or favoritism to the *g*,
Nu 13: 32 people we saw there are of *g* size.
14: 19 In accordance with your *g* love,
22: 18 I could not do anything *g*
34: 6 boundary will be the coast of the *G*
34: 7 a line from the *G* Sea to Mount Hor
Dt 1: 7 as far as the *g* river, the Euphrates.
1: 17 hear both small and *g* alike.
3: 5 also a *g* many unwalled villages.
4: 6 "Surely this *g* nation is a wise
4: 7 What other nation is so *g*
4: 8 And what other nation is so *g*
4: 32 so *g* as this ever happened,
4: 34 or by *g* and awesome deeds,
4: 36 On earth he showed you his *g* fire,
4: 37 by his Presence and his *g* strength,
5: 25 This *g* fire will consume us,
6: 22 and wonders—*g* and terrible—
7: 19 saw with your own eyes the *g* trials,
7: 21 who is among you, is a *g*
7: 23 throwing them into *g* confusion
9: 26 you redeemed by your *g* power
9: 29 you brought out by your *g* power
10: 17 the *g* God, mighty and awesome,
10: 21 who performed for you those *g*
11: 7 saw all these *g* things the LORD
11: 30 near the *g* trees of Moreh,
14: 16 little owl, the *g* owl, the white owl,
17: 16 must not acquire *g* numbers
18: 16 nor see this *g* fire anymore,
19: 6 him if the distance is too *g*,

Dt 26: 5 lived there and became a *g* nation,
26: 8 *g* terror and with miraculous signs
29: 3 miraculous signs and *g* wonders.
29: 3 own eyes you saw those *g* trials,
29: 28 in *g* wrath the LORD uprooted
Jos 1: 4 and from Lebanon to the *g* river,
1: 4 and to the *G* Sea on the west.
2: 9 that a *g* fear of you has fallen on us,
3: 16 up in a heap a *g* distance away,
7: 9 do for your own *g* name?"
9: 1 along the entire coast of the *G* Sea
10: 10 them in a *g* victory at Gibeon.
15: 12 boundary is the coastline of the *G*
15: 47 of Egypt and the coastline of the *G*
17: 1 the Makirites were *g* soldiers.
22: 8 and a *g* quantity of clothing—
22: 8 to your homes with your *g* wealth
23: 4 between the Jordan and the *G* Sea
23: 9 LORD has driven out before you *g*
24: 17 and performed those *g* signs
Jdg 2: 7 had seen all the *g* things the LORD
2: 15 They were in *g* distress.
4: 11 tent by the *g* tree in Zaanannim
9: 6 beside the *g* tree at the pillar
10: 9 and Israel was in *g* distress.
12: 2 in a *g* struggle with the Ammonites
15: 18 given your servant this *g* victory.
16: 5 you the secret of his *g* strength
16: 6 the secret of your *g* strength
16: 15 the secret of your *g* strength."
16: 23 assembled to offer a *g* sacrifice
20: 38 that they should send up a *g* cloud
1Sa 1: 16 praying here out of my *g* anguish
2: 17 sin of the young men was very *g*
4: 5 Israel raised such a *g* shout that
4: 10 slaughter was very *g*; Israel lost
5: 9 throwing it into a *g* panic.
6: 9 LORD has brought this *g* disaster
10: 3 until you reach the *g* tree of Tabor.
11: 15 the Israelites held a *g* celebration.
12: 16 see this *g* thing the LORD is about
12: 22 of his *g* name the LORD will not
12: 24 consider what *g* things he has done
14: 45 brought about this *g* deliverance
17: 24 they all ran from him in *g* fear.
17: 25 The king will give *g* wealth
18: 14 everything he did he had *g* success,
19: 5 The LORD won a *g* victory
19: 22 and went to the *g* cistern at Secu.
20: 2 my father doesn't do anything, *g*
26: 25 you will do *g* things and surely
28: 15 "I am in *g* distress," Saul said
30: 16 of the *g* amount of plunder they
2Sa 3: 22 with them a *g* deal of plunder.
3: 38 a *g* man has fallen in Israel this day
7: 9 Now I will make your name *g*,
7: 21 you have done this *g* thing
7: 22 "How *g* you are, O Sovereign
7: 23 and to perform *g* and awesome
7: 26 so that your name will be *g* forever.
8: 8 King David took a *g* quantity
12: 30 He took a *g* quantity of plunder
18: 7 and the casualties that day were *g*
18: 29 "I saw *g* confusion just
20: 8 were at the *g* rock in Gibeon,
22: 36 you stoop down to make me *g*.
22: 51 He gives his king *g* victories;
23: 10 brought about a *g* victory that day.
23: 12 LORD brought about a *g* victory.
23: 20 who performed *g* exploits.
24: 14 for his mercy is *g*; but do not let me
1Ki 1: 19 He has sacrificed *g* numbers
1: 25 and sacrificed *g* numbers of cattle,
3: 6 have continued this *g* kindness
3: 6 "You have shown *g* kindness
3: 8 a *g* people, too numerous to count
3: 9 to govern this *g* people of yours?"
4: 29 wisdom and very *g* insight,
5: 7 son to rule over this *g* nation."
7: 9 from the outside to the *g* courtyard
7: 12 The *g* courtyard was surrounded
8: 42 for men will hear of your *g* name
10: 2 at Jerusalem with a very *g* caravan
10: 11 from there they brought *g* cargoes
10: 18 the king made a *g* throne inlaid
19: 11 Then a *g* and powerful wind tore
22: 31 small or *g*, except the king of Israel
2Ki 3: 27 The fury against Israel was *g*;
2Ki 5: 1 He was a *g* man in the sight
5: 13 you to do some *g* thing,
6: 23 So he prepared a *g* feast for them,
6: 25 There was a *g* famine in the city;
7: 6 of chariots and horses and a *g* army
8: 4 me about all the *g* things Elisha has
10: 19 going to hold a *g* sacrifice for Baal.
17: 21 and caused them to commit a *g* sin.
18: 19 " 'This is what the *g* king, the king
18: 28 "Hear the word of the *g* king,
22: 13 *G* is the LORD's anger that burns
1Ch 10: 12 bones under the *g* tree in Jabesh,
11: 14 LORD brought about a *g* victory.
11: 22 who performed *g* exploits.
12: 22 until he had a *g* and mighty army.
16: 25 For *g* is the LORD and most
17: 19 made known all these *g* promises.
17: 19 you have done this *g* thing
17: 21 and to perform *g* and awesome
17: 24 that your name will be *g* forever.
18: 8 David took a *g* quantity of bronze,
20: 2 He took a *g* quantity of plunder
21: 13 for his mercy is very *g*;
22: 5 be of *g* magnificence
22: 14 and iron too *g* to be weighed,
22: 14 "I have taken *g* pains to provide
29: 1 The task is *g*, because this palatial
29: 22 drank with *g* joy in the presence
2Ch 1: 1 and made him exceedingly *g*.
1: 8 "You have shown *g* kindness
1: 10 to govern this *g* people of yours?"
2: 5 I am going to build will be *g*,
2: 13 you Huram-Abi, a man of *g* skill,
6: 32 of your *g* name and your mighty
9: 1 Arriving with a very *g* caravan—
9: 17 the king made a *g* throne inlaid
14: 13 Such a *g* number of Cushites fell
15: 5 of the lands were in *g* turmoil.
15: 13 whether small or *g*, man or woman.
16: 8 army with *g* numbers of chariots
17: 5 so that he had *g* wealth and honor.
18: 1 Now Jehoshaphat had *g* wealth
18: 30 small or *g*, except the king of Israel
20: 25 found among them a *g* amount
21: 19 of the disease, and he died in *g* pain
24: 11 collected a *g* amount of money.
25: 10 and left for home in a *g* rage.
25: 13 carried off *g* quantities of plunder.
28: 8 They also took a *g* deal of plunder,
28: 13 For our guilt is already *g*,
30: 21 for seven days with *g* rejoicing,
30: 24 A *g* number of priests consecrated
30: 26 There was *g* joy in Jerusalem,
31: 5 They brought a *g* amount,
31: 10 and this *g* amount is left over."
32: 27 Hezekiah had very *g* riches
32: 29 God had given him very *g* riches.
32: 29 and acquired *g* numbers of flocks
34: 21 *G* is the LORD's anger that is
Ezr 3: 11 And all the people gave a *g* shout
4: 10 and the other people whom the *g*
5: 8 to the temple of the *g* God.
5: 11 one that a *g* king of Israel built
8: 22 but his *g* anger is against all who
9: 7 until now, our guilt has been *g*.
9: 13 of our evil deeds and our *g* guilt,
Ne 1: 3 in the province are in *g* trouble
1: 5 of heaven, the *g* and awesome God
1: 10 redeemed by your *g* strength
3: 27 from the *g* projecting tower
4: 14 Remember the Lord, who is *g*
5: 1 and their wives raised a *g* outcry
6: 3 "I am carrying on a *g* project
8: 6 Ezra praised the LORD, the *g* God
8: 12 and to celebrate with *g* joy,
8: 17 And their joy was very *g*.
9: 19 of your *g* compassion you did not
9: 25 they reveled in your *g* goodness.
9: 27 and in your *g* compassion you gave
9: 31 in your *g* mercy you did not put
9: 32 the *g*, mighty and awesome God,
9: 35 enjoying your *g* goodness to them
9: 37 We are in *g* distress.
12: 43 because God had given them *g* joy
12: 43 that day they offered *g* sacrifices,
13: 22 to me according to your *g* love.
Est 2: 18 And the king gave a *g* banquet,
4: 3 there was *g* mourning
Est 4: 4 Mordecai, she was in *g* distress.
Job 2: 13 they saw how *g* his suffering was.
3: 19 The small and the *g* are there,
4: 10 of the *g* lions are broken.
12: 23 He makes nations *g*, and destroys
21: 28 'Where now is the *g* man's house,
22: 5 Is not your wickedness *g*?
23: 6 Would he oppose me with *g* power
26: 3 what *g* insight you have displayed!
30: 18 In his *g* power ⌊God⌋ becomes like
31: 25 if I have rejoiced over my *g* wealth,
36: 26 *g* is God—beyond our
37: 5 *g* things beyond our
37: 23 in his justice and *g* righteousness,
39: 11 rely on him for his *g* strength?
Ps 5: 7 But I, by your *g* mercy,
17: 7 Show the wonder of your *g* love,
17: 12 like a *g* lion crouching in cover.
18: 14 *g* bolts of lightning and routed
18: 35 you stoop down to make me *g*.
18: 50 He gives his king *g* victories;
19: 11 in keeping them there is *g* reward.
19: 13 innocent of *g* transgression.
21: 1 How *g* is his joy in the victories
21: 5 victories you gave, his glory is *g*;
22: 25 in the *g* assembly;
25: 6 O LORD, your *g* mercy and love,
25: 11 forgive my iniquity, though it is *g*.
26: 12 in the *g* assembly I will praise
31: 19 How *g* is your goodness,
33: 16 warrior escapes by his *g* strength.
33: 17 despite all its *g* strength it cannot
35: 18 in the *g* assembly;
36: 6 your justice like the *g* deep.
37: 11 and enjoy *g* peace.
40: 9 righteousness in the *g* assembly;
40: 10 truth from the *g* assembly.
47: 2 the *g* King over all the earth!
48: 1 *G* is the LORD, and most worthy
48: 2 the city of the *G* King.
49: 6 and boast of their *g* riches?
51: 1 according to your *g* compassion
52: 7 but trusted in his *g* wealth
57: 10 For *g* is your love, reaching
66: 3 So *g* is your power
68: 11 and *g* was the company
68: 26 Praise God in the *g* congregation;
68: 27 there the *g* throng
69: 13 in your *g* love, O God,
69: 16 in your *g* mercy turn to me.
71: 19 you who have done *g* things.
76: 1 his name is *g* in Israel.
77: 13 What god is so *g* as our God?
82: 1 God presides in the *g* assembly;
86: 10 For you are *g* and do marvelous
86: 13 For *g* is your love toward me;
89: 1 of the LORD's *g* love forever;
89: 49 where is your former *g* love,
90: 11 *g* as the fear that is due you.
91: 13 you will trample the *g* lion
92: 5 How *g* are your works, O LORD,
93: 4 than the thunder of the *g* waters,
94: 19 When anxiety was *g* within me,
95: 3 For the LORD is the *g* God,
95: 3 the *g* King above all gods.
96: 4 For *g* is the LORD and most
99: 2 *G* is the LORD in Zion;
99: 3 Let them praise your *g*
102: 10 because of your *g* wrath,
103: 11 so *g* is his love for those who fear
104: 1 O LORD my God, you are very *g*;
106: 21 who had done *g* things in Egypt,
106: 45 and out of his *g* love he relented.
107: 43 consider the *g* love of the LORD.
108: 4 For *g* is your love, higher
109: 30 in the *g* throng I will praise him.
111: 2 *G* are the works of the LORD;
112: 1 who finds *g* delight
115: 13 small and *g* alike.
116: 6 when I was in *g* need, he saved me.
117: 2 For *g* is his love toward us,
119: 14 as one rejoices in *g* riches.
119:156 Your compassion is *g*, O LORD;
119:162 like one who finds *g* spoil.
119:165 *G* peace have they who love your
126: 2 "The LORD has done *g* things
126: 3 The LORD has done *g* things
131: 1 not concern myself with *g* matters

Ps 135: 5 I know that the LORD is *g*,
136: 4 to him who alone does *g* wonders,
136: 7 who made the *g* lights—
136: 17 who struck down *g* kings,
138: 5 for the glory of the LORD is *g*.
145: 3 *G* is the LORD and most worthy
145: 6 and I will proclaim your *g* deeds.
147: 5 *G* is our Lord and mighty in power;
148: 7 you *g* sea creatures and all ocean
Pr 5: 23 led astray by his own *g* folly.
6: 35 refuse the bribe, however *g* it is.
13: 7 to be poor, yet has *g* wealth.
14: 29 A patient man has *g* understanding
15: 6 of the righteous contains *g* treasure
15: 16 than *g* wealth with turmoil.
18: 16 into the presence of the *g*.
21: 14 in the cloak pacifies *g* wrath.
22: 1 is more desirable than *g* riches;
23: 24 of a righteous man has *g* joy;
24: 5 A wise man has *g* power,
25: 6 do not claim a place among *g* men;
28: 12 triumph, there is *g* elation;
Ecc 2: 4 I undertook *g* projects: I built
2: 21 is meaningless and a *g* misfortune.
5: 17 with *g* frustration, affliction
10: 4 calmness can lay *g* errors to rest.
Isa 5: 9 "Surely the *g* houses will become
9: 2 have seen a *g* light;
10: 33 off the boughs with *g* power.
12: 6 for *g* is the Holy One of Israel
13: 4 like that of a *g* multitude!
17: 12 roar like the roaring of *g* waters!
23: 3 On the *g* waters
27: 1 his fierce, *g* and powerful sword,
27: 13 in that day a *g* trumpet will sound.
29: 6 and earthquake and *g* noise,
29: 15 Woe to those who go to *g* depths
30: 25 In the day of *g* slaughter,
31: 1 in the *g* strength of their horsemen,
31: 4 a *g* lion over his prey—
32: 2 and the shadow of a *g* rock
34: 6 and a *g* slaughter in Edom.
34: 7 the bull calves and the *g* bulls.
34: 11 *g* owl and the raven will nest there.
36: 4 'This is what the *g* king, the king
36: 13 "Hear the words of the *g* king,
40: 26 Because of his *g* power
42: 21 to make his law *g* and glorious.
51: 10 the waters of the *g* deep,
53: 12 give him a portion among the *g*,
54: 13 and *g* will be your children's peace.
Jer 2: 12 and shudder with *g* horror,"
2: 31 or a land of *g* darkness?
5: 6 for their rebellion is *g*
6: 22 a *g* nation is being stirred up
9: 19 How *g* is our shame!
10: 6 you are *g*,
10: 22 a *g* commotion from the land
13: 9 and the *g* pride of Jerusalem.
14: 7 For our backsliding is *g*;
16: 10 LORD decreed such a *g* disaster
21: 5 arm in anger and fury and *g* wrath.
22: 8 done such a thing to this *g* city?'
22: 14 'I will build myself a *g* palace
25: 14 by many nations and *g* kings;
27: 5 With my *g* power and outstretched
27: 7 and *g* kings will subjugate him.
28: 8 many countries and *g* kingdoms.
30: 14 because your guilt is so *g*
30: 15 Because of your *g* guilt
31: 8 a *g* throng will return.
31: 15 mourning and *g* weeping,
31: 20 I have *g* compassion for him,"
32: 17 and the earth by your *g* power
32: 18 O *g* and powerful God, whose
32: 19 *g* are your purposes and mighty are
32: 21 outstretched arm and with *g* terror.
32: 37 in my furious anger and *g* wrath;
32: 42 I have brought all this *g* calamity
33: 3 and I will answer you and tell you *g*
36: 7 people by the LORD are *g*."
41: 12 with him near the *g* pool in Gibeon
44: 2 You saw the *g* disaster I brought
44: 7 Why bring such *g* disaster
44: 26 by my *g* name,' says the LORD,
45: 5 Should you then seek *g* things
48: 3 cries of *g* havoc and destruction.
50: 9 an alliance of *g* nations
Jer 50: 22 the noise of *g* destruction!
50: 41 a *g* nation and many kings
51: 54 the sound of *g* destruction
51: 55 ⌞of enemies⌟ will rage like *g* waters;
La 1: 1 who once was *g* among the nations
3: 22 of the LORD's *g* love we are not
3: 23 *g* is your faithfulness.
3: 32 so *g* is his unfailing love.
Eze 9: 9 and Judah is exceedingly *g*;
14: 4 in keeping with his *g* idolatry.
17: 3 A *g* eagle with powerful wings,
17: 7 " 'But there was another *g* eagle
17: 17 *g* horde will be of no help to him
21: 14 a sword for *g* slaughter,
25: 17 I will carry out *g* vengeance
26: 7 with horsemen and a *g* army.
27: 12 because of your *g* wealth of goods;
27: 18 your many products and *g* wealth
27: 33 with your *g* wealth and your wares
28: 5 By your *g* skill in trading
29: 3 you *g* monster lying
31: 6 all the *g* nations
32: 3 " 'With a *g* throng of people
36: 23 show the holiness of my *g* name,
37: 2 I saw a *g* many bones on the floor
38: 4 and a *g* horde with large
38: 15 of them riding on horses, a *g* horde,
38: 19 time there shall be a *g* earthquake
39: 17 the *g* sacrifice on the mountains
47: 7 I saw a *g* number of trees
47: 10 many kinds—like the fish of the *G*
47: 15 run from the *G* Sea by the Hethlon
47: 19 along the Wadi ⌞of Egypt⌟ to the *G*
47: 20 the *G* Sea will be the boundary
48: 28 along the Wadi ⌞of Egypt⌟ to the *G*
Da 2: 6 me gifts and rewards and *g* honor.
2: 10 No king, however *g* and mighty,
2: 45 *g* God has shown the king what
4: 3 How *g* are his signs,
4: 22 You have become *g* and strong;
4: 30 "Is not this the *g* Babylon I have
5: 1 King Belshazzar gave a *g* banquet
7: 2 of heaven churning up the *g* sea.
7: 3 Four *g* beasts, each different
7: 17 four *g* beasts are four kingdoms
8: 4 He did as he pleased and became *g*.
8: 6 and charged at him in *g* rage.
8: 8 The goat became very *g*,
8: 11 as *g* as the Prince of the host;
9: 4 "O Lord, the *g* and awesome God,
9: 12 by bringing upon us *g* disaster.
9: 18 but because of your *g* mercy.
10: 1 was true and it concerned a *g* war.
10: 4 standing on the bank of the *g* river,
10: 8 at this *g* vision; I had no strength
11: 3 who will rule with *g* power and do
11: 5 his own kingdom with *g* power.
11: 10 for war and assemble a *g* army,
11: 28 to his own country with *g* wealth,
11: 40 and cavalry and a *g* fleet of ships.
11: 44 he will set out in a *g* rage to destroy
12: 1 *g* prince who protects your people,
Hos 1: 11 for *g* will be the day of Jezreel.
5: 13 and sent to the *g* king for help.
5: 14 like a *g* lion to Judah.
9: 7 and your hostility so *g*,
10: 6 as tribute for the *g* king.
10: 15 because your wickedness is *g*.
Joel 1: 4 the *g* locusts have eaten;
1: 4 what the *g* locusts have left
2: 11 The day of the LORD is *g*;
2: 20 Surely he has done *g* things.
2: 21 the LORD has done *g* things.
2: 25 my *g* army that I sent among you.
2: 25 the *g* locust and the young locust,
2: 31 blood before the coming of the *g*
3: 13 so *g* is their wickedness!"
Am 2: 2 Moab will go down in *g* tumult
3: 9 see the *g* unrest within her
5: 12 and how *g* your sins.
6: 2 go from there to *g* Hamath,
6: 11 and he will smash the *g* house
7: 4 it dried up the *g* deep and devoured
Jnh 1: 2 "Go to the *g* city of Nineveh
1: 4 the LORD sent a *g* wind on the sea
1: 12 my fault that this *g* storm has come
1: 17 But the LORD provided a *g* fish
3: 2 "Go to the *g* city of Nineveh
Jnh 4: 11 be concerned about that *g* city?"
Na 1: 3 to anger and *g* in power;
3: 10 all her *g* men were put in chains.
Hab 3: 15 churning the *g* waters.
Zep 1: 14 "The *g* day of the LORD is near—
3: 17 He will take *g* delight in you,
Zec 2: 4 because of the *g* number of men
12: 11 the weeping in Jerusalem will be *g*,
14: 4 forming a *g* valley, with half
14: 13 by the LORD with *g* panic.
14: 14 *g* quantities of gold and silver
Mal 1: 5 '*G* is the LORD—
1: 11 My name will be *g*
1: 11 because my name will be *g*
1: 14 For I am a *g* king," says the LORD
4: 5 the prophet Elijah before that *g*
Mt 2: 18 weeping and *g* mourning,
4: 16 have seen a *g* light;
5: 12 because *g* is your reward in heaven,
5: 19 these commands will be called *g*
5: 35 for it is the city of the *G* King.
6: 23 is darkness, how *g* is that darkness!
7: 27 house, and it fell with a *g* crash."
8: 10 anyone in Israel with such *g* faith.
13: 46 When he found one of *g* value,
15: 28 "Woman, you have *g* faith!
15: 30 *G* crowds came to him, bringing
19: 22 away sad, because he had *g* wealth.
20: 26 whoever wants to become *g*
24: 21 For then there will be *g* distress,
24: 24 and perform *g* signs and miracles
24: 30 of the sky, with power and *g* glory.
27: 14 to the *g* amazement
27: 19 for I have suffered a *g* deal today
Mk 5: 26 She had suffered a *g* deal
10: 22 away sad, because he had *g* wealth.
10: 43 whoever wants to become *g*
13: 2 "Do you see all these *g* buildings?"
13: 26 coming in clouds with *g* power
Lk 1: 15 for he will be *g* in the sight
1: 32 He will be *g* and will be called
1: 49 the Mighty One has done *g* things
1: 58 the Lord had shown her *g* mercy,
2: 10 news of *g* joy that will be
2: 13 Suddenly a *g* company
5: 29 Levi held a *g* banquet for Jesus
6: 17 and a *g* number of people from all
6: 23 because *g* is your reward in heaven.
6: 35 Then your reward will be *g*,
7: 9 I have not found such *g* faith
7: 16 "A *g* prophet has appeared
8: 23 and they were in *g* danger.
14: 16 man was preparing a *g* banquet
16: 26 and you a *g* chasm has been fixed,
18: 23 because he was a man of *g* wealth.
21: 11 There will be *g* earthquakes,
21: 11 and fearful events and *g* signs
21: 23 There will be *g* distress in the land
21: 27 in a cloud with power and *g* glory.
24: 52 returned to Jerusalem with *g* joy.
Jn 5: 3 Here a *g* number of disabled people
6: 2 a *g* crowd of people followed him
6: 5 saw a *g* crowd coming toward him,
10: 32 I have shown you many *g* miracles
12: 12 The next day the *g* crowd that had
Ac 2: 20 blood before the coming of the *g*
4: 29 to speak your word with *g* boldness
4: 33 With *g* power the apostles
5: 5 *g* fear seized all who heard what
5: 11 *G* fear seized the whole church
6: 8 did *g* wonders and miraculous
7: 11 bringing *g* suffering, and our
8: 1 that day a *g* persecution broke out
8: 8 So there was *g* joy in that city.
8: 9 He boasted that he was someone *g*,
8: 10 divine power known as the *G* Power
8: 13 astonished by the *g* signs
11: 21 and a *g* number of people believed
11: 24 a *g* number of people were brought
11: 26 and taught *g* numbers of people.
12: 18 there was a *g* commotion
14: 1 so effectively that a *g* number
16: 16 She earned a *g* deal of money
17: 11 the message with *g* eagerness
18: 25 and he spoke with *g* fervor
18: 27 he was a *g* help to those who
19: 23 there arose a *g* disturbance about
19: 27 of the *g* goddess Artemis will be

Ac 19: 28 "*G* is Artemis of the Ephesians!"
19: 34 "*G* is Artemis of the Ephesians!"
19: 35 of the temple of the *g* Artemis
20: 19 I served the Lord with *g* humility
21: 35 of the mob was so *g* he had
23: 9 There was a *g* uproar, and some
25: 23 and Bernice came with *g* pomp
26: 22 and testify to small and *g* alike.
26: 24 "Your *g* learning is driving you
27: 10 and bring *g* loss to ship and cargo,
Ro 9: 2 I have *g* sorrow and unceasing
9: 22 bore with *g* patience the objects
16: 2 for she has been a *g* help
1Co 16: 9 a *g* door for effective work has
2Co 1: 8 We were under *g* pressure,
2: 4 For I wrote you out of *g* distress
6: 4 in *g* endurance; in troubles,
7: 4 I have *g* confidence in you;
7: 4 in you; I take *g* pride in you.
8: 22 because of his *g* confidence in you.
12: 7 of these surpassingly *g* revelations,
12: 12 among you with *g* perseverance.
Eph 1: 19 and his incomparably *g* power
2: 4 But because of his *g* love for us,
Php 2: 29 him in the Lord with *g* joy,
Col 1: 11 so that you may have *g* endurance
2: 18 into *g* detail about what he has seen
1Ti 3: 13 and *g* assurance in their faith
3: 16 the mystery of godliness is *g*:
6: 6 with contentment is *g* gain.
2Ti 4: 2 with *g* patience and careful
4: 3 gather around them a *g* number
4: 14 the metalworker did me a *g* deal
Tit 2: 13 glorious appearing of our *g* God
Phm : 7 Your love has given me *g* joy
Heb 2: 3 if we ignore such a *g* salvation?
4: 14 since we have a *g* high priest who
7: 4 Just think how *g* he was: Even
10: 21 and since we have a *g* priest
10: 32 ground in a *g* contest in the face
12: 1 by such a *g* cloud of witnesses,
13: 20 that *g* Shepherd of the sheep,
Jas 3: 5 Consider what a *g* forest is set
3: 5 of the body, but it makes *g* boasts.
1Pe 1: 3 In his *g* mercy he has given us new
3: 4 which is of *g* worth in God's sight.
2Pe 1: 4 these he has given us his very *g*
1Jn 3: 1 How *g* is the love the Father has
2Jn : 4 It has given me *g* joy to find some
3Jn : 3 It gave me *g* joy to have some
Jude : 6 chains for judgment on the *g* Day.
: 24 without fault and with *g* joy—
Rev 6: 12 There was a *g* earthquake.
6: 17 For the *g* day of their wrath has
7: 9 me was a *g* multitude that no
7: 14 out of the *g* tribulation;
8: 10 and a *g* star, blazing like a torch,
9: 14 bound at the *g* river Euphrates."
11: 8 lie in the street of the *g* city,
11: 17 you have taken your *g* power
11: 18 both small and *g*—
11: 19 an earthquake and a *g* hailstorm.
12: 1 A *g* and wondrous sign appeared
12: 9 The *g* dragon was hurled down—
12: 14 given the two wings of a *g* eagle,
13: 2 and his throne and *g* authority.
13: 13 he performed *g* and miraculous
13: 16 small and *g*, rich and poor,
14: 8 "Fallen! Fallen is Babylon the *G*,
14: 19 threw them into the *g* winepress
15: 1 I saw in heaven another *g*
15: 3 "*G* and marvelous are your deeds,
16: 12 bowl on the *g* river Euphrates,
16: 14 on the *g* day of God Almighty.
16: 19 God remembered Babylon the *G*
16: 19 The *g* city split into three parts,
17: 1 the punishment of the *g* prostitute,
17: 5 MYSTERY BABYLON THE *G*
17: 18 you saw is the *g* city that rules
18: 1 He had *g* authority, and the earth
18: 2 "Fallen! Fallen is Babylon the *G*!
18: 10 " 'Woe! Woe, O *g* city,
18: 16 " 'Woe! Woe, O *g* city,
18: 17 In one hour such *g* wealth has been
18: 18 there ever a city like this *g* city?'
18: 19 " 'Woe! Woe, O *g* city,
18: 21 *g* city of Babylon will be thrown
18: 23 merchants were the world's *g* men.
Rev 19: 1 of a *g* multitude in heaven shouting
19: 2 He has condemned the *g* prostitute
19: 5 both small and *g*!"
19: 6 what sounded like a *g* multitude,
19: 17 together for the *g* supper of God,
19: 18 free and slave, small and *g*."
20: 1 and holding in his hand a *g* chain.
20: 11 Then I saw a *g* white throne
20: 12 And I saw the dead, *g* and small,
21: 10 away in the Spirit to a mountain *g*
21: 12 It had a *g*, high wall
22: 2 middle of the *g* street of the city.

GREATER (GREAT)

Ge 1: 16 the *g* light to govern the day
39: 9 No one is *g* in this house than I am.
41: 40 to the throne will I be *g* than you."
48: 19 his younger brother will be *g*
49: 26 Your father's blessings are *g*
Ex 18: 11 Now I know that the LORD is *g*
Nu 14: 12 but I will make you into a nation *g*
24: 7 "Their king will be *g* than Agag;
Dt 4: 38 to drive out before you nations *g*
9: 1 dispossess nations *g* and stronger
20: 1 chariots and an army *g* than yours,
Jos 11: 8 them all the way to *G* Sidon,
19: 28 and Kanah, as far as *G* Sidon.
Ru 3: 10 "This kindness is *g*
1Sa 14: 30 of the Philistines have been even *g*
2Sa 13: 16 me away would be a *g* wrong
19: 43 we have a *g* claim on David
23: 19 held in *g* honor than the Three?
23: 23 He was held in *g* honor than any
1Ki 1: 37 *g* than the throne of my lord King
1: 47 and his throne *g* than yours!'
4: 30 Solomon's wisdom was *g*
4: 30 and *g* than all the wisdom of Egypt.
10: 23 King Solomon was *g* in riches
1Ch 11: 25 He was held in *g* honor than any
2Ch 2: 5 our God is *g* than all other gods.
9: 22 King Solomon was *g* in riches
32: 7 for there is a *g* power with us
Job 33: 12 for God is *g* than man.
Ps 4: 7 You have filled my heart with *g* joy
135: 5 that our Lord is *g* than all gods.
Ecc 2: 9 I became *g* by far than anyone
La 4: 6 is *g* than that of Sodom,
Da 2: 30 I have *g* wisdom than other living
4: 36 and became even *g* than before.
Hag 2: 9 glory of this present house will be *g*
Zec 12: 7 inhabitants may not be *g*
Mt 11: 11 the kingdom of heaven is *g* than he.
11: 11 there has not risen anyone *g*
12: 6 I tell you that one *g*
12: 41 and now one *g* than Jonah is here.
12: 42 now one *g* than Solomon is here.
23: 17 You blind fools! Which is *g*:
23: 19 You blind men! Which is *g*: the gift
Mk 12: 31 There is no commandment *g*
Lk 7: 28 born of women there is no one *g*
7: 28 in the kingdom of God is *g* than he
11: 31 now one *g* than Solomon is here.
11: 32 and now one *g* than Jonah is here.
22: 27 For who is *g*, the one who is
Jn 1: 50 You shall see *g* things than that."
3: 30 He must become *g*; I must become
4: 12 Are you *g* than our father Jacob,
5: 20 he will show him even *g* things
8: 53 Are you *g* than our father
10: 29 them to me, is *g* than all;
13: 16 is a messenger *g* than the one who
13: 16 no servant is *g* than his master,
14: 12 He will do even *g* things than these
14: 28 for the Father is *g* than I.
15: 13 *G* love has no one than this,
15: 20 'No servant is *g* than his master.'
19: 11 me over to you is guilty of a *g* sin."
Ro 11: 12 how much *g* riches will their
1Co 12: 24 has given *g* honor to the parts that
12: 31 But eagerly desire the *g* gifts.
14: 5 He who prophesies is *g*
2Co 3: 11 how much *g* is the glory
7: 7 so that my joy was *g* than ever.
7: 15 his affection for you is all the *g*
Heb 3: 3 the builder of a house has *g* honor
3: 3 worthy of *g* honor than Moses,
6: 13 since there was no one *g* for him
6: 16 by someone *g* than themselves,
Heb 7: 7 lesser person is blessed by the *g*.
9: 11 he went through the *g*
11: 26 as of *g* value than the treasures
1Pe 1: 7 of *g* worth than gold,
1Jn 3: 20 For God is *g* than our hearts,
4: 4 is in you is *g* than the one who is
5: 9 but God's testimony is *g*
3Jn : 4 I have no *g* joy than to hear that my

GREATEST (GREAT)

Jos 14: 15 who was the *g* man
2Sa 7: 9 names of the *g* men of the earth.
2Ki 23: 2 the people from the least to the *g*.
25: 26 the people from the least to the *g*,
1Ch 12: 14 a match for a hundred, and the *g*
17: 8 names of the *g* men of the earth.
2Ch 34: 30 the people from the least to the *g*.
Est 1: 5 the people from the least to the *g*,
1: 20 from the least to the *g*."
Job 1: 3 He was the *g* man among all
Jer 6: 13 "From the least to the *g*,
8: 10 From the least to the *g*,
31: 7 shout for the *g* of the nations.
31: 34 from the least of them to the *g*,"
42: 1 least to the *g* approached Jeremiah
42: 8 the people from the least to the *g*.
44: 12 the least to the *g*, they will die
Jnh 3: 5 all of them, from the *g* to the least,
Mt 18: 1 "Who is the *g* in the kingdom
18: 4 himself like this child is the *g*
22: 36 which is the *g* commandment
22: 38 is the first and *g* commandment.
23: 11 *g* among you will be your servant.
Mk 9: 34 had argued about who was the *g*.
Lk 9: 46 as to which of them would be the *g*.
9: 48 least among you all—he is the *g*."
22: 24 of them was considered to be *g*.
22: 26 the *g* among you should be like
Jn 7: 37 On the last and *g* day of the Feast,
1Co 13: 13 But the *g* of these is love.
Heb 8: 11 from the least of them to the *g*.
1Pe 1: 10 intently and with the *g* care,

GREATNESS (GREAT)

Ex 15: 7 In the *g* of your majesty
Dt 3: 24 to show to your servant your *g*
32: 3 Oh, praise the *g* of our God!
1Ch 29: 11 O LORD, is the *g* and the power
2Ch 9: 6 half the *g* of your wisdom was told
Est 10: 2 account of the *g* of Mordecai
Ps 145: 3 his *g* no one can fathom.
150: 2 praise him for his surpassing *g*.
Isa 63: 1 forward in the *g* of his strength?
Eze 38: 23 I will show my *g* and my holiness,
Da 4: 22 your *g* has grown until it reaches
5: 18 and *g* and glory and splendor.
7: 27 and *g* of the kingdoms
Mic 5: 4 will live securely, for then his *g*
Lk 9: 43 And they were all amazed at the *g*
Php 3: 8 compared to the surpassing *g*

GREAVES

1Sa 17: 6 on his legs he wore bronze *g*,

GRECIAN (GREECE)

Ac 6: 1 *G* Jews among them complained
9: 29 and debated with the *G* Jews,

GREECE (GRECIAN GREEK GREEKS)

Isa 66: 19 as archers), to Tubal and *G*,
Eze 27: 13 " '*G*, Tubal and Meshech traded
Da 8: 21 The shaggy goat is the king of *G*,
10: 20 the prince of *G* will come;
11: 2 against the kingdom of *G*.
Zec 9: 13 against your sons, O *G*,
Ac 20: 2 in *G*, where he stayed three months

GREED (GREEDY)

Isa 57: 17 I was enraged by his sinful *g*;
Eze 16: 27 you over to the *g* of your enemies,
Mt 23: 25 but inside they are full of *g*
Mk 7: 22 murder, adultery, *g*, malice, deceit,
Lk 11: 39 but inside you are full of *g*
12: 15 on your guard against all kinds of *g*
Ro 1: 29 kind of wickedness, evil, *g*
Eph 5: 3 or of any kind of impurity, or of *g*,
Col 3: 5 evil desires and *g*, which is idolatry
1Th 2: 5 did we put on a mask to cover up *g*

2Pe 2: 3 In their *g* these teachers will
2: 14 experts in *g*— an accursed brood!

GREEDY (GREED)

Ps 10: 3 he blesses the *g* and reviles
Pr 15: 27 A *g* man brings trouble
28: 25 A *g* man stirs up dissension,
29: 4 one who is *g* for bribes tears it
Jer 6: 13 all are *g* for gain;
8: 10 all are *g* for gain;
Eze 33: 31 their hearts are *g* for unjust gain.
Hab 2: 5 Because he is as *g* as the grave
1Co 5: 10 or the *g* and swindlers, or idolaters.
5: 11 but is sexually immoral or *g*,
6: 10 nor thieves nor the *g* nor drunkards
Eph 5: 5 No immoral, impure or *g* person—
1Pe 5: 2 not *g* for money, but eager to serve;

GREEK (GREECE)

Mk 7: 26 The woman was a *G*, born
Jn 19: 20 written in Aramaic, Latin and *G*.
Ac 16: 1 but whose father was a *G*.
16: 3 all knew that his father was a *G*.
17: 12 *G* women and many *G* men.
21: 37 "Do you speak *G?*" he replied.
Gal 2: 3 even though he was a *G*.
3: 28 There is neither Jew nor *G*,
Col 3: 11 Here there is no *G* or Jew,
Rev 9: 11 in Hebrew is Abaddon, and in *G*,

GREEKS (GREECE)

Eze 27: 19 and *G* from Uzal bought your
Joel 3: 6 of Judah and Jerusalem to the *G*,
Jn 7: 35 people live scattered among the *G*,
7: 35 teach the *G?* What did he mean
12: 20 Now there were some *G*
Ac 11: 20 and began to speak to *G* also,
17: 4 a large number of God-fearing *G*
17: 17 the Jews and the God-fearing *G*,
18: 4 trying to persuade Jews and *G*.
19: 10 and *G* who lived in the province
19: 17 to the Jews and *G* living in Ephesus
20: 21 and *G* that they must turn to God
21: 28 he has brought *G* into the temple
Ro 1: 14 I am obligated both to *G*
1Co 1: 22 miraculous signs and *G* look
1: 24 God has called, both Jews and *G*,
10: 32 *G* or the church of God—
12: 13 whether Jews or *G*, slave or free—

GREEN (GREENISH)

Ge 1: 30 I give every *g* plant for food."
9: 3 Just as I gave you the *g* plants,
Ex 10: 15 Nothing *g* remained on tree
2Ki 19: 26 like tender *g* shoots,
Job 39: 8 and searches for any *g* thing.
Ps 23: 2 makes me lie down in *g* pastures,
37: 2 like *g* plants they will soon die
37: 35 flourishing like a *g* tree
58: 9 whether they be *g* or dry—
92: 14 they will stay fresh and *g*,
105: 35 they ate up every *g* thing
Pr 11: 28 righteous will thrive like a *g* leaf.
Isa 15: 6 and nothing *g* is left.
37: 27 like tender *g* shoots,
Jer 17: 8 its leaves are always *g*.
Eze 17: 24 I dry up the *g* tree and make
20: 47 will consume all your trees, both *g*
Hos 14: 8 I am like a *g* pine tree;
Joel 2: 22 the open pastures are becoming *g*.
Mk 6: 39 sit down in groups on the *g* grass.
Lk 23: 31 things when the tree is *g*,
Rev 8: 7 and all the *g* grass was burned up.

GREENISH (GREEN)

Lev 13: 49 any leather article, is *g* or reddish,
14: 37 if it has *g* or reddish depressions

GREET (GREETED GREETING GREETINGS GREETS)

1Sa 10: 4 They will *g* you and offer you two
13: 10 and Saul went out to *g* him.
25: 5 at Carmel and *g* him in my name.
2Sa 8: 10 Joram to King David to *g* him
2Ki 4: 29 If you meet anyone, do not *g* him,
10: 13 come down to *g* the families
1Ch 18: 10 Hadoram to King David to *g* him
Isa 14: 9 spirits of the departed to *g* you—
Mt 5: 47 And if you *g* only your brothers,
Mk 9: 15 with wonder and ran to *g* him.
Lk 10: 4 and do not *g* anyone on the road.
Ro 16: 3 *G* Priscilla and Aquila, my fellow
16: 5 *G* also the church that meets
16: 5 *G* my dear friend Epenetus,
16: 6 *G* Mary, who worked very hard
16: 7 *G* Andronicus and Junias,
16: 8 *G* Ampliatus, whom I love
16: 9 *G* Urbanus, our fellow worker
16: 10 *G* Apelles, tested and approved
16: 10 *G* those who belong
16: 11 *G* Herodion, my relative.
16: 11 *G* those in the household
16: 12 *G* Tryphena and Tryphosa,
16: 12 *G* my dear friend Persis, another
16: 13 *G* Rufus, chosen in the Lord,
16: 14 *G* Asyncritus, Phlegon, Hermes,
16: 15 *G* Philologus, Julia, Nereus
16: 16 *G* one another with a holy kiss.
16: 22 down this letter, *g* you in the Lord.
1Co 16: 19 Priscilla *g* you warmly in the Lord,
16: 20 *G* one another with a holy kiss.
2Co 13: 12 *G* one another with a holy kiss.
Php 4: 21 *G* all the saints in Christ Jesus.
1Th 5: 26 *G* all the brothers with a holy kiss.
2Ti 4: 19 *G* Priscilla and Aquila
Tit 3: 15 *G* those who love us in the faith.
Heb 13: 24 *G* all your leaders and all God's
1Pe 5: 14 *G* one another with a kiss of love.
3Jn : 14 *G* the friends there by name.

GREETED (GREET)

Ex 18: 7 They *g* each other and then went
Jdg 18: 15 Levite at Micah's place and *g* him.
Ru 2: 4 Bethlehem and *g* the harvesters,
1Sa 17: 22 the battle lines and *g* his brothers.
30: 21 his men approached, he *g* them.
2Ki 10: 15 Jehu *g* him and said, "Are you
Mt 23: 7 love to be *g* in the marketplaces
Mk 12: 38 and be *g* in the marketplaces,
Lk 1: 40 Zechariah's home and *g* Elizabeth.
20: 46 love to be *g* in the marketplaces
Ac 18: 22 he went up and *g* the church
21: 7 where we *g* the brothers
21: 19 Paul *g* them and reported

GREETING (GREET)

Mt 10: 12 you enter the home, give it your *g*.
Lk 1: 29 kind of *g* this might be.
1: 41 When Elizabeth heard Mary's *g*,
1: 44 sound of your *g* reached my ears,
1Co 16: 21 I, Paul, write this *g* in my own hand
Col 4: 18 I, Paul, write this *g* in my own hand
2Th 3: 17 I, Paul, write this *g* in my own hand

GREETINGS (GREET)

1Sa 25: 14 the desert to give our master his *g*,
Ezr 4: 17 elsewhere in Trans-Euphrates: *G*.
5: 7 To King Darius: Cordial *g*.
7: 12 of the Law of the God of heaven: *G*
Mt 26: 49 "*G*, Rabbi!" and kissed him.
28: 9 "*G*," he said.
Lk 1: 28 "*G*, you who are highly favored!
11: 43 and *g* in the marketplaces.
Ac 15: 23 in Antioch, Syria and Cilicia: *G*.
23: 26 Excellency, Governor Felix: *G*.
Ro 16: 16 All the churches of Christ send *g*.
16: 21 my fellow worker, sends his *g*
16: 23 brother Quartus send you their *g*.
16: 23 church here enjoy, sends you his *g*.
1Co 16: 19 in the province of Asia send you *g*.
16: 20 All the brothers here send you *g*.
2Co 13: 13 All the saints send their *g*.
Php 4: 21 brothers who are with me send *g*.
4: 22 saints send you *g*, especially those
Col 4: 10 Aristarchus sends you his *g*,
4: 11 who is called Justus, also sends *g*.
4: 12 a servant of Christ Jesus, sends *g*.
4: 14 the doctor, and Demas send *g*.
4: 15 Give my *g* to the brothers
Tit 3: 15 Everyone with me sends you *g*.
Phm : 23 for Christ Jesus, sends you *g*.
Heb 13: 24 Those from Italy send you their *g*.
Jas 1: 1 scattered among the nations: *G*.
1Pe 5: 13 sends you her *g*, and so does my
2Jn : 13 of your chosen sister send their *g*.
3Jn : 14 The friends here send their *g*.

GREETS (GREET)

2Ki 4: 29 and if anyone *g* you, do not answer.
2Ti 4: 21 Eubulus *g* you, and so do Pudens,

GREW (GROW)

Ge 10: 8 who *g* to be a mighty warrior
21: 8 The child *g* and was weaned,
21: 20 God was with the boy as he *g* up.
25: 27 The boys *g* up, and Esau became
30: 43 the man *g* exceedingly prosperous
Ex 2: 10 When the child *g* older, she took
16: 21 when the sun *g* hot, it melted away.
17: 12 When Moses' hands *g* tired,
19: 19 the sound of the trumpet *g* louder
Nu 21: 4 the people *g* impatient on the way;
Dt 32: 15 Jeshurun *g* fat and kicked;
Jos 17: 13 when the Israelites *g* stronger,
Jdg 2: 10 fathers, another generation *g* up,
4: 24 the hand of the Israelites *g* stronger
13: 24 He *g* and the LORD blessed him,
Ru 1: 13 would you wait until they *g* up?
1Sa 2: 21 the boy Samuel *g* up
3: 19 was with Samuel as he *g* up,
8: 1 When Samuel *g* old, he appointed
31: 3 The fighting *g* fierce around Saul,
2Sa 3: 1 David *g* stronger and stronger,
3: 1 while the house of Saul *g* weaker
12: 3 it *g* up with him and his children.
23: 10 the Philistines till his hand *g* tired
1Ki 11: 4 As Solomon *g* old, his wives turned
17: 17 He *g* worse and worse,
18: 45 the sky *g* black with clouds,
2Ki 4: 18 child *g*, and one day he went out
4: 34 upon him, the boy's body *g* warm.
1Ch 1: 10 who *g* to be a mighty warrior
10: 3 The fighting *g* fierce around Saul,
2Ch 13: 21 But Abijah *g* in strength.
27: 6 Jotham *g* powerful because he
Ps 39: 3 My heart *g* hot within me,
52: 7 and *g* strong by destroying others
77: 3 I mused, and my spirit *g* faint.
106: 16 In the camp they *g* envious
107: 30 They were glad when it *g* calm,
Isa 38: 14 My eyes *g* weak as I looked
53: 2 He *g* up before him like a tender
Eze 16: 7 You *g* up and developed
16: 7 were formed and your hair *g*,
17: 10 wither away in the plot where it *g*
31: 5 and its branches *g* long,
Da 4: 11 The tree *g* large and strong
4: 20 The tree you saw, which *g* large
4: 33 until his hair *g* like the feathers
5: 9 terrified and his face *g* more pale.
8: 3 longer than the other but *g* up later.
8: 8 its place four prominent horns *g* up
8: 9 but *g* in power to the south
8: 10 It *g* until it reached the host
Jnh 1: 13 for the sea *g* even wilder
1: 15 and the raging sea *g* calm.
4: 8 on Jonah's head so that he *g* faint.
Zec 11: 8 and I *g* weary of them and said,
Mt 13: 7 which *g* up and choked the plants.
Mk 4: 7 which *g* up and choked the plants,
4: 8 It came up, *g* and produced a crop,
5: 26 of getting better she *g* worse.
Lk 1: 80 And the child *g* and became strong
2: 40 And the child *g* and became strong
2: 52 And Jesus *g* in wisdom and stature,
8: 7 which *g* up with it and choked
13: 19 It *g*, became a tree, and the birds
Jn 6: 18 blowing and the waters *g* rough.
Ac 4: 4 and the number of men *g*
9: 22 Yet Saul *g* more and more
9: 31 by the Holy Spirit, it *g* in numbers,
16: 5 in the faith and *g* daily in numbers.
19: 20 of the Lord spread widely and *g*
Rev 18: 3 the merchants of the earth *g* rich

GRIDDLE

Lev 2: 5 grain offering is prepared on a *g*,
6: 21 with oil on a *g*; bring it well-mixed
7: 9 or on a *g* belongs to the priest who

GRIEF (GRIEFS GRIEVANCE GRIEVANCES GRIEVE GRIEVED GRIEVES GRIEVING GRIEVOUS)

Ge 26: 35 They were a source of *g* to Isaac

Ge 34: 7 They were filled with *g* and fury,
38: 12 Judah had recovered from his *g*,
1Sa 1: 16 out of my great anguish and *g*."
Est 6: 12 with his head covered in *g*,
Job 17: 7 My eyes have grown dim with *g*;
Ps 10: 14 O God, do see trouble and *g*;
31: 9 my soul and my body with *g*.
35: 14 I bowed my head in *g*
88: 9 my eyes are dim with *g*.
Pr 10: 1 but a foolish son *g* to his mother.
10: 10 He who winks maliciously causes *g*
14: 13 and joy may end in *g*.
17: 21 To have a fool for a son brings *g*;
17: 25 A foolish son brings *g* to his father
29: 21 he will bring *g* in the end.
Ecc 1: 18 the more knowledge, the more *g*.
2: 23 All his days his work is pain and *g*;
La 1: 5 The LORD has brought her *g*
3: 32 Though he brings *g*, he will show
3: 33 or *g* to the children of men.
3: 51 What I see brings *g* to my soul
Eze 13: 22 when I had brought them no *g*,
21: 6 with broken heart and bitter *g*.
Mic 4: 6 and those I have brought to *g*.
Mt 17: 23 And the disciples were filled with *g*
Jn 16: 6 these things, you are filled with *g*.
16: 20 but your *g* will turn to joy.
16: 22 So with you: Now is your time of *g*,
1Co 5: 2 you rather have been filled with *g*
2Co 2: 5 If anyone has caused *g*, he has not
1Pe 1: 6 had to suffer *g* in all kinds of trials.
Rev 18: 7 Give her as much torture and *g*

GRIEFS (GRIEF)

1Ti 6: 10 pierced themselves with many *g*.

GRIEVANCE (GRIEF)

Job 31: 13 when they had a *g* against me,
Ac 19: 38 and his fellow craftsmen have a *g*

GRIEVANCES (GRIEF)

Col 3: 13 forgive whatever *g* you may have

GRIEVE (GRIEF)

1Sa 2: 33 eyes with tears and to *g* your heart,
2Sa 1: 26 I *g* for you, Jonathan my brother;
Ne 8: 10 Do not *g*, for the joy
8: 11 Do not *g*."
Isa 16: 7 Lament and *g*
61: 3 provide for those who *g* in Zion—
La 1: 4 her maidens *g*,
Eze 7: 12 the buyer rejoice nor the seller *g*,
9: 4 on the foreheads of those who *g*
Joel 1: 11 *g* for the wheat and the barley,
Am 6: 6 but you do not *g* over the ruin
Zec 12: 10 *g* bitterly for him as one grieves
Jn 16: 20 You will *g*, but your grief will turn
2Co 2: 2 For if I *g* you, who is left
2: 4 not to *g* you but to let you know
Eph 4: 30 do not *g* the Holy Spirit of God,
1Th 4: 13 or to *g* like the rest of men,
Jas 4: 9 *G*, mourn and wail.

GRIEVED (GRIEF)

Ge 6: 6 LORD was *g* that he had made
6: 7 for I am *g* that I have made them."
Dt 34: 8 The Israelites *g* for Moses
Jdg 21: 6 the Israelites *g* for their brothers,
21: 15 The people *g* for Benjamin,
1Sa 15: 11 "I am *g* that I have made Saul king,
15: 35 the LORD was *g* that he had made
20: 3 must not know this or he will be *g*.'
20: 34 he was *g* at his father's shameful
2Sa 24: 16 was *g* because of the calamity
1Ch 21: 15 and was *g* because of the calamity
Job 30: 25 Has not my soul *g* for the poor?
Ps 73: 21 When my heart was *g*
78: 40 and *g* him in the wasteland!
Isa 63: 10 and *g* his Holy Spirit.
Jer 42: 10 for I am *g* over the disaster I have
Eze 6: 9 how I have been *g*
Ac 20: 38 What *g* them most was his
2Co 2: 2 me glad but you whom I have *g*?
2: 5 so much *g* me as he has *g* all of you,
12: 21 and I will be *g* over many who have

GRIEVES (GRIEF)

Zec 12: 10 as one *g* for a firstborn son.

GRIEVING (GRIEF)

2Sa 14: 2 woman who has spent many days *g*
19: 2 "The king is *g* for his son."
Joel 1: 8 *g* for the husband of her youth.

GRIEVOUS (GRIEF)

Ge 18: 20 their sin so *g* that I will go down
Ecc 2: 17 under the sun was *g* to me.
5: 13 I have seen a *g* evil under the sun:
5: 16 This too is a *g* evil:
6: 2 This is meaningless, a *g* evil.
Jer 14: 17 has suffered a *g* wound,
15: 18 and my wound *g* and incurable?

GRIND (GRINDERS GRINDING)

Ex 30: 36 *G* some of it to powder
Job 31: 10 may my wife *g* another man's
Pr 27: 22 Though you *g* a fool in a mortar,
Isa 28: 28 his horses do not *g* it.
47: 2 Take millstones and *g* flour;

GRINDERS (GRIND)

Ecc 12: 3 when the *g* cease because they are

GRINDING (GRIND)

Jdg 16: 21 they set him to *g* in the prison.
Pr 27: 22 *g* him like grain with a pestle,
Ecc 12: 4 and the sound of *g* fades;
Isa 3: 15 and *g* the faces of the poor?"
Mt 24: 41 Two women will be *g*
Lk 17: 35 women will be *g* grain together;

GRIP (GRIPPED GRIPS)

Ex 15: 14 anguish will *g* the people
Job 30: 16 days of suffering *g* me.
Isa 13: 8 pain and anguish will *g* them;
Jer 13: 21 Will not pain *g* you

GRIPPED (GRIP)

Jer 6: 24 Anguish has *g* us,
49: 24 and panic has *g* her;
50: 43 Anguish has *g* him,
Lk 1: 12 he was startled and was *g* with fear.

GRIPS (GRIP)

Ps 119: 53 *g* me because of the wicked,
Isa 33: 14 trembling *g* the godless:
Jer 8: 21 I mourn, and horror *g* me.

GROAN (GROANED GROANING GROANS)

Ps 38: 8 I *g* in anguish of heart.
Pr 5: 11 At the end of your life you will *g*,
29: 2 when the wicked rule, the people *g*.
Isa 19: 8 The fishermen will *g* and lament,
24: 7 all the merrymakers *g*.
Jer 4: 31 a *g* as of one bearing her first child
22: 23 how you will *g* when pangs come
51: 52 the wounded will *g*.
La 1: 4 her priests *g*,
1: 11 All her people *g*
Eze 21: 6 *G* before them with broken heart
21: 6 "Therefore *g*, son of man!
24: 17 *G* quietly; do not mourn
24: 23 your sins and *g* among yourselves.
26: 15 when the wounded *g*
30: 24 he will *g* before him like a mortally
Ro 8: 23 *g* inwardly as we wait eagerly
2Co 5: 2 Meanwhile we *g*, longing
5: 4 For while we are in this tent, we *g*

GROANED (GROAN)

Ex 2: 23 The Israelites *g* in their slavery
Jdg 2: 18 they *g* under those who oppressed
Ps 77: 3 I remembered you, O God, and I *g*;

GROANING (GROAN)

Ex 2: 24 God heard their *g* and he
6: 5 I have heard the *g* of the Israelites,
Job 23: 2 his hand is heavy in spite of my *g*.
Ps 6: 6 I am worn out from *g*;
12: 5 and the *g* of the needy,
22: 1 so far from the words of my *g*?
31: 10 and my years by *g*;
32: 3 away through my *g* all day long.
102: 5 Because of my loud *g*
Isa 21: 2 bring to an end all the *g* she caused.
Jer 45: 3 out with *g* and find no rest.' "

La 1: 21 "People have heard my *g*,
Eze 21: 7 'Why are you *g*?' you shall say,
Ac 7: 34 I have heard their *g* and have come
Ro 8: 22 that the whole creation has been *g*

GROANS (GROAN)

Job 3: 24 my *g* pour out like water.
24: 12 The *g* of the dying rise
Ps 79: 11 May the *g* of the prisoners come
102: 20 to hear the *g* of the prisoners
La 1: 8 she herself *g*
1: 22 My *g* are many
Ro 8: 26 with *g* that words cannot express.

GROPE (GROPED)

Dt 28: 29 At midday you will *g* about like
Job 5: 14 at noon they *g* as in the night.
12: 25 They *g* in darkness with no light;
Isa 59: 10 Like the blind we *g* along the wall,
La 4: 14 Now they *g* through the streets

GROPED (GROPE)

Ac 13: 11 came over him, and he *g* about,

GROUND (AGROUND GROUNDS)

Ge 1: 9 to one place, and let dry *g* appear."
1: 10 God called the dry *g* "land,"
1: 24 creatures that move along the *g*,
1: 25 along the *g* according to their kinds
1: 26 creatures that move along the *g*."
1: 28 creature that moves on the *g*."
1: 30 all the creatures that move on the *g*
2: 5 there was no man to work the *g*,
2: 6 watered the whole surface of the *g*.
2: 7 man from the dust of the *g*
2: 9 kinds of trees grow out of the *g*—
2: 19 of the *g* all the beasts of the field
3: 17 "Cursed is the *g* because of you;
3: 19 food until you return to the *g*,
3: 23 the Garden of Eden to work the *g*
4: 10 blood cries out to me from the *g*.
4: 11 a curse and driven from the *g*,
4: 12 When you work the *g*, it will no
5: 29 by the *g* the LORD has cursed."
6: 7 creatures that move along the *g*,
6: 20 moves along the *g* will come to you
7: 8 all creatures that move along the *g*,
7: 14 along the *g* according to its kind
7: 23 the creatures that move along the *g*
8: 8 receded from the surface of the *g*.
8: 13 that the surface of the *g* was dry.
8: 17 creatures that move along the *g*—
8: 19 the creatures that move along the *g*
8: 21 "Never again will I curse the *g*
9: 2 creature that moves along the *g*,
18: 2 meet them and bowed low to the *g*.
19: 1 bowed down with his face to the *g*.
24: 52 down to the *g* before the LORD.
33: 3 bowed down to the *g* seven times
33: 19 plot of *g* where he pitched his tent.
37: 10 bow down to the *g* before you?"
38: 9 *g* to keep from producing offspring
42: 6 to him with their faces to the *g*.
43: 26 bowed down before him to the *g*.
44: 11 quickly lowered his sack to the *g*
44: 14 themselves to the *g* before him.
47: 23 seed for you so you can plant the *g*.
48: 12 bowed down with his face to the *g*.
Ex 3: 5 where you are standing is holy *g*."
4: 3 Moses threw it on the *g*
4: 3 LORD said, "Throw it on the *g*."
4: 9 river will become blood on the *g*."
4: 9 the Nile and pour it on the dry *g*.
8: 16 and strike the dust of the *g*,'
8: 17 and struck the dust of the *g*,
8: 21 and even the *g* where they are.
9: 23 and lightning flashed down to the *g*
10: 5 of the *g* so that it cannot be seen.
10: 15 They covered all the *g*
14: 16 go through the sea on dry *g*.
14: 22 went through the sea on dry *g*,
14: 29 went through the sea on dry *g*,
15: 19 walked through the sea on dry *g*.
16: 14 frost on the *g* appeared
16: 25 any of it on the *g* today.
32: 20 then he *g* it to powder, scattered it
34: 8 Moses bowed to the *g* at once
Lev 5: 2 creatures that move along the *g*—

Lev 11: 21 legs for hopping on the *g*.
11: 29 animals that move about on the *g*,
11: 31 Of all those that move along the *g*,
11: 41 about on the *g* is detestable;
11: 42 creature that moves about on the *g*,
11: 44 creature that moves about on the *g*.
11: 46 creature that moves about on the *g*.
16: 12 of finely *g* fragrant incense
20: 25 anything that moves along the *g*—
26: 4 and the *g* will yield its crops
26: 19 and the *g* beneath you like bronze.
Nu 11: 8 and then *g* it in a handmill
11: 31 to about three feet above the *g*,
15: 20 a cake from the first of your *g* meal
15: 21 from the first of your *g* meal.
16: 31 the *g* under them split apart
Dt 4: 18 creature that moves along the *g*
9: 21 I crushed it and *g* it to powder
11: 17 and the *g* will yield no produce,
12: 16 pour it out on the *g* like water.
12: 24 pour it out on the *g* like water.
15: 23 pour it out on the *g* like water.
22: 6 either in a tree or on the *g*,
28: 11 livestock and the crops of your *g*—
28: 23 your head will be bronze, the *g*
28: 56 venture to touch the *g* with the sole
Jos 3: 17 completed the crossing on dry *g*.
3: 17 firm on dry *g* in the middle
4: 18 feet on the dry *g* than the waters
4: 22 Israel crossed the Jordan on dry *g*.'
5: 14 facedown to the *g* in reverence,
7: 6 facedown to the *g* before the ark
7: 21 hidden in the *g* inside my tent,
Jdg 4: 21 peg through his temple into the *g*,
6: 37 on the fleece and all the *g* is dry,
6: 39 and the *g* covered with dew."
6: 40 all the *g* was covered with dew.
13: 20 his wife fell with their faces to the *g*
Ru 2: 10 bowed down with her face to the *g*.
1Sa 3: 19 he let none of his words fall to the *g*
4: 5 such a great shout that the *g* shook.
5: 3 on his face on the *g* before the ark
5: 4 on his face on the *g* before the ark
8: 12 to plow his *g* and reap his harvest,
14: 15 raiding parties—and the *g* shook.
14: 25 and there was honey on the *g*.
14: 32 they butchered them on the *g*
14: 45 a hair of his head will fall to the *g*,
17: 49 and he fell facedown on the *g*.
20: 41 with his face to the *g*.
24: 8 himself with his face to the *g*.
25: 23 before David with her face to the *g*.
25: 41 bowed down with her face to the *g*
26: 7 stuck in the *g* near his head.
26: 8 him to the *g* with one thrust
26: 20 fall to the *g* far from the presence
28: 13 I see a spirit coming up out of the *g*
28: 14 himself with his face to the *g*.
28: 20 Saul fell full length on the *g*,
28: 23 He got up from the *g* and sat
2Sa 1: 2 he fell to the *g* to pay him honor.
8: 2 He made them lie down on the *g*
12: 16 and spent the nights lying on the *g*.
12: 17 beside him to get him up from the *g*
12: 20 Then David got up from the *g*.
13: 31 his clothes and lay down on the *g*;
14: 4 face to the *g* to pay him honor,
14: 11 of your son's head will fall to the *g*
14: 14 Like water spilled on the *g*,
14: 22 face to the *g* to pay him honor,
14: 33 face to the *g* before the king.
17: 12 fall on him as dew settles on the *g*.
18: 11 him to the *g* right there?
18: 28 the king with his face to the *g*
20: 10 his intestines spilled out on the *g*.
23: 10 but he stood his *g* and struck
24: 20 the king with his face to the *g*.
1Ki 1: 23 and bowed with his face to the *g*.
1: 31 low with her face to the *g*
1: 40 so that the *g* shook with the sound.
1: 52 a hair of his head will fall to the *g*;
18: 7 bowed down to the *g*, and said,
18: 42 bent down to the *g* and put his face
2Ki 2: 8 two of them crossed over on dry *g*.
2: 15 and bowed to the *g* before him.
4: 37 fell at his feet and bowed to the *g*.
8: 12 dash their little children to the *g*,
9: 10 her on the plot of *g* at Jezreel,
2Ki 9: 21 at the plot of *g* that had belonged
9: 26 pay for it on this plot of *g*,
9: 36 plot of *g* at Jezreel dogs will devour
9: 37 on the *g* in the plot at Jezreel,
13: 18 Elisha told him, "Strike the *g*."
13: 19 "You should have struck the *g* five
23: 6 He *g* it to powder and scattered
23: 15 He burned the high place and *g* it
1Ch 21: 21 before David with his face to the *g*.
2Ch 2: 10 twenty thousand cors of *g* wheat,
7: 3 pavement with their faces to the *g*,
20: 18 bowed with his face to the *g*,
20: 24 only dead bodies lying on the *g*;
Ne 8: 6 the LORD with their faces to the *g*.
9: 11 passed through it on dry *g*,
10: 37 the first of our *g* meal,
Job 1: 20 he fell to the *g* in worship and said:
2: 13 Then they sat on the *g* with him
3: 16 in the *g* like a stillborn child,
5: 6 nor does trouble sprout from the *g*.
14: 8 Its roots may grow old in the *g*
16: 13 and spills my gall on the *g*.
18: 10 A noose is hidden for him on the *g*;
30: 6 the rocks and in holes in the *g*.
39: 14 She lays her eggs on the *g*
39: 24 excitement he eats up the *g*;
Ps 7: 5 let him trample my life to the *g*
17: 11 to throw me to the *g*.
26: 12 My feet stand on level *g*;
44: 25 our bodies cling to the *g*.
73: 18 you place them on slippery *g*;
74: 7 burned your sanctuary to the *g*;
80: 9 You cleared the *g* for it,
83: 10 and became like refuse on the *g*.
89: 44 and cast his throne to the *g*.
107: 33 flowing springs into thirsty *g*,
107: 35 the parched *g* into flowing springs;
143: 3 he crushes me to the *g*;
143: 10 lead me on level *g*.
146: 4 spirit departs, they return to the *g*;
147: 6 but casts the wicked to the *g*.
Pr 24: 31 the *g* was covered with weeds,
Ecc 12: 7 returns to the *g* it came from,
Isa 2: 10 hide in the *g*
2: 19 and to holes in the *g*
3: 26 destitute, she will sit on the *g*.
21: 9 lie shattered on the *g*!' "
25: 12 he will bring them down to the *g*,
26: 5 he levels it to the *g*
28: 2 he will throw it forcefully to the *g*.
28: 28 Grain must be *g* to make bread;
29: 4 you will speak from the *g*;
30: 23 rain for the seed you sow in the *g*,
35: 7 the thirsty *g* bubbling springs.
40: 4 the rough *g* shall become level,
40: 24 no sooner do they take root in the *g*
41: 18 and the parched *g* into springs.
44: 3 and streams on the dry *g*;
45: 9 among the potsherds on the *g*.
47: 1 sit on the *g* without a throne,
49: 23 before you with their faces to the *g*;
51: 23 And you made your back like the *g*
53: 2 and like a root out of dry *g*.
63: 6 and poured their blood on the *g*."
Jer 4: 3 "Break up your unplowed *g*
7: 20 of the field and on the fruit of the *g*,
8: 2 but will be like refuse lying on the *g*
14: 4 The *g* is cracked
16: 4 will be like refuse lying on the *g*.
25: 33 but will be like refuse lying on the *g*
46: 21 they will not stand their *g*,
48: 18 and sit on the parched *g*,
La 2: 2 princes down to the *g* in dishonor.
2: 9 Her gates have sunk into the *g*;
2: 10 have bowed their heads to the *g*.
2: 10 sit on the *g* in silence;
2: 11 my heart is poured out on the *g*
Eze 1: 15 on the *g* beside each creature
1: 19 the living creatures rose from the *g*,
1: 21 when the creatures rose from the *g*,
10: 16 their wings to rise from the *g*,
10: 19 their wings and rose from the *g*,
13: 14 and will level it to the *g*
19: 12 and thrown to the *g*.
24: 7 she did not pour it on the *g*,
26: 11 your strong pillars will fall to the *g*.
26: 16 on the *g*, trembling every moment,
28: 18 and I reduced you to ashes on the *g*
Eze 34: 27 and the *g* will yield its crops;
38: 20 and every wall will fall to the *g*.
38: 20 creature that moves along the *g*,
39: 14 bury those that remain on the *g*.
43: 14 From the gutter on the *g* up
44: 30 of your *g* meal so that a blessing
Da 4: 15 remain in the *g*, in the grass
4: 23 while its roots remain in the *g*.
7: 4 lifted from the *g* so that it stood
8: 5 earth without touching the *g*.
8: 7 the goat knocked him to the *g*
8: 12 and truth was thrown to the *g*.
8: 18 with my face to the *g*.
10: 9 into a deep sleep, my face to the *g*.
10: 15 I bowed with my face toward the *g*
Hos 2: 18 the creatures that move along the *g*
10: 11 and Jacob must break up the *g*.
10: 12 and break up your unplowed *g*;
10: 14 dashed to the *g* with their children.
13: 16 little ones will be dashed to the *g*,
Joel 1: 10 the *g* is dried up;
Am 2: 7 as upon the dust of the *g*
2: 15 The archer will not stand his *g*,
3: 5 Does a bird fall into a trap on the *g*
3: 14 and fall to the *g*.
5: 7 and cast righteousness to the *g*
9: 9 but not a kernel will fall to the *g*.
Ob : 3 'Who can bring me down to the *g*?'
Mic 7: 17 like creatures that crawl on the *g*.
Hag 1: 11 and whatever the *g* produces,
Zec 4: 7 you will become level *g*.
8: 12 the *g* will produce its crops,
Mt 10: 29 fall to the *g* apart from the will
15: 35 the crowd to sit down on the *g*.
17: 6 they fell facedown to the *g*,
25: 18 in the *g* and hid his master's money
25: 25 and hid your talent in the *g*.
26: 39 he fell with his face to the *g*
Mk 4: 26 A man scatters seed on the *g*.
4: 31 smallest seed you plant in the *g*.
8: 6 the crowd to sit down on the *g*.
9: 18 it seizes him, it throws him to the *g*.
9: 20 He fell to the *g* and rolled around,
14: 35 he fell to the *g* and prayed that
Lk 5: 12 he fell with his face to the *g*
6: 49 on the *g* without a foundation.
9: 42 him to the *g* in a convulsion.
12: 16 *g* of a certain rich man produced
19: 44 They will dash you to the *g*,
22: 44 drops of blood falling to the *g*.
24: 5 down with their faces to the *g*,
Jn 4: 5 near the plot of *g* Jacob had given
8: 6 to write on the *g* with his finger.
8: 8 stooped down and wrote on the *g*.
9: 6 he spit on the *g*, made some mud
12: 24 a kernel of wheat falls to the *g*
18: 6 they drew back and fell to the *g*.
Ac 7: 5 here, not even a foot of *g*.
7: 33 where you are standing is holy *g*.
9: 4 fell to the *g* and heard a voice say
9: 8 Saul got up from the *g*,
13: 28 Though they found no proper *g*
20: 9 he fell to the *g* from the third story
22: 7 I fell to the *g* and heard a voice say
26: 14 to the *g*, and I heard a voice saying
2Co 11: 12 doing in order to cut the *g*
Eph 6: 13 you may be able to stand your *g*,
Heb 10: 32 when you stood your *g*
11: 38 and in caves and holes in the *g*.

GROUNDS (GROUND)

2Ki 11: 16 the horses enter the palace *g*,
2Ch 23: 15 of the Horse Gate on the palace *g*,
Da 6: 4 to find *g* for charges against Daniel
Lk 23: 22 in him no *g* for the death penalty.
Jn 8: 59 slipping away from the temple *g*.

GROUP (GROUPS REGROUPED)

Ge 32: 8 the *g* that is left may escape."
32: 8 "If Esau comes and attacks one *g*,
48: 19 his descendants will become a *g*
Nu 16: 3 They came as a *g* to oppose Moses
26: 54 To a larger *g* give a larger
26: 54 and to a smaller *g* a smaller one;
26: 55 What each *g* inherits will be
33: 54 To a larger *g* give a larger
33: 54 and to a smaller *g* a smaller one.
Jdg 11: 3 where a *g* of adventurers gathered

1Sa 19:20 But when they saw a *g*
2Sa 2:13 One *g* sat down on one side
2:13 and one *g* on the other side.
2:25 They formed themselves into a *g*
2Ki 17:29 each national *g* made its own gods
2Ch 35:5 place with a *g* of Levites
Da 6:6 the satraps went as a *g* to the king
6:11 as a *g* and found Daniel praying
6:15 the men went as a *g* to the king
Jn 8:3 They made her stand before the *g*
Ac 1:15 the believers (a *g* numbering about
6:5 This proposal pleased the whole *g*.
17:18 A *g* of Epicurean and Stoic
Gal 2:12 belonged to the circumcision *g*.
Tit 1:10 those of the circumcision *g*.

GROUPS (GROUP)

Ge 32:7 were with him into two *g*,
32:10 but now I have become two *g*.
Nu 26:56 among the larger and smaller *g*.''
1Ch 23:6 into *g* corresponding to the sons
Ezr 6:18 the Levites in their *g* for the service
Mk 6:39 sit down in *g* on the green grass.
6:40 So they sat down in *g* of hundreds
Lk 9:14 sit down in *g* of about fifty each.''

GROVE (GROVES)

Ex 23:11 your vineyard and your olive *g*.
SS 6:11 I went down to the *g* of nut trees
Jn 18:1 the other side there was an olive *g*,
18:3 to the *g*, guiding a detachment
18:26 you with him in the olive *g*?''

GROVES (GROVE)

Dt 6:11 and olive *g* you did not plant—
Jos 24:13 and olive *g* that you did not plant.'
Jdg 15:5 with the vineyards and olive *g*.
1Sa 8:14 and olive *g* and give them
2Ki 5:26 olive *g*, vineyards, flocks, herds,
Ne 5:11 vineyards, olive *g* and houses,
9:25 olive *g* and fruit trees in abundance
Ecc 2:6 to water *g* of flourishing trees.

GROW (FULL-GROWN GREW GROWERS GROWING GROWN GROWS GROWTH OVERGROWN)

Ge 2:9 kinds of trees *g* out of the ground—
26:13 and his wealth continued to *g*
27:40 But when you *g* restless,
Nu 6:5 the hair of his head *g* long.
24:18 but Israel will *g* strong.
Dt 8:13 and flocks *g* large and your silver
Jdg 16:22 hair on his head began to *g* again
1Sa 2:26 the boy Samuel continued to *g*
Ezr 4:22 Why let this threat *g*,
Job 8:11 Can papyrus *g* tall where there is
8:19 and from the soil other plants *g*.
14:8 Its roots may *g* old in the ground
17:9 with clean hands will *g* stronger.
31:16 let the eyes of the widow *g* weary,
39:4 Their young thrive and *g* strong
Ps 6:7 My eyes *g* weak with sorrow;
31:9 my eyes *g* weak with sorrow,
31:10 and my bones *g* weak.
34:10 The lions may *g* weak and hungry,
92:12 they will *g* like a cedar of Lebanon;
104:14 He makes grass *g* for the cattle,
129:6 which withers before it can *g*;
132:17 "Here I will make a horn *g*
147:8 and makes grass *g* on the hills.
Pr 13:11 by little makes it *g*.
20:13 not love sleep or you will *g* poor;
Ecc 12:2 and the moon and the stars *g* dark,
12:3 through the windows *g* dim;
12:4 but all their songs *g* faint;
Isa 5:6 and briers and thorns will *g* there.
17:11 set them out, you make them *g*,
29:22 no longer will their faces *g* pale.
35:7 grass and reeds and papyrus will *g*.
40:28 He will not *g* tired or weary,
40:30 Even youths *g* tired and weary,
40:31 they will run and not *g* weary,
44:14 He let it *g* among the trees
44:14 a pine, and the rain made it *g*.
45:8 let righteousness *g* with it;
55:13 instead of briers the myrtle will *g*.
55:13 the thornbush will *g* the pine tree,
57:16 of man would *g* faint before me—
Isa 61:11 and a garden causes seeds to *g*,
Jer 4:28 and the heavens above *g* dark,
6:4 and the shadows of evening *g* long.
12:2 they *g* and bear fruit.
15:9 The mother of seven will *g* faint
La 3:4 made my skin and my flesh *g* old
5:17 of these things our eyes *g* dim
Eze 16:7 I made you *g* like a plant
17:24 and make the low tree *g* tall.
29:21 "On that day I will make a horn *g*
31:4 deep springs made it *g* tall;
44:20 their heads or let their hair *g* long,
47:12 of all kinds will *g* on both banks
Hos 10:8 Thorns and thistles will *g* up
14:6 his young shoots will *g*.
Jnh 4:6 and made it *g* up over Jonah
4:10 you did not tend it or make it *g*.
Zec 8:12 seed will *g* well, the vine will yield
Mt 6:28 See how the lilies of the field *g*.
13:30 Let both *g* together
24:12 the love of most will *g* cold,
Lk 12:27 "Consider how the lilies *g*.
1Co 3:6 watered it, but God made it *g*.
3:7 but only God, who makes things *g*.
2Co 10:15 as your faith continues to *g*,
Eph 4:15 we will in all things *g* up
Col 2:19 grows as God causes it to *g*.
Heb 12:3 so that you will not *g* weary
1Pe 2:2 that by it you may *g* up
2Pe 3:18 But *g* in the grace and knowledge

GROWERS (GROW)

Joel 1:11 wail, you vine *g*;

GROWING (GROW)

Ge 41:5 and good, were *g* on a single stalk.
41:22 full and good, *g* on a single stalk.
Ex 9:22 and on everything *g* in the fields
9:25 down everything *g* in the fields
10:5 including every tree that is *g*
10:12 devour everything *g* in the fields,
10:15 everything *g* in the fields
Dt 29:23 nothing sprouting, no vegetation *g*
Job 8:12 While still *g* and uncut,
21:7 *g* old and increasing in power?
Col 1:6 this gospel is producing fruit and *g*,
1:10 *g* in the knowledge of God,
2Th 1:3 your faith is *g* more and more,

GROWL (GROWLED GROWLS)

Job 4:10 The lions may roar and *g*,
Isa 5:29 they *g* as they seize their prey
59:11 We all *g* like bears;
Jer 51:38 they *g* like lion cubs.
Am 3:4 Does he *g* in his den

GROWLED (GROWL)

Jer 2:15 they have *g* at him.

GROWLS (GROWL)

Isa 31:4 "As a lion *g*,

GROWN (GROW)

Ge 38:14 though Shelah had now *g* up,
41:48 In each city he put the food *g*
Ex 2:11 One day, after Moses had *g* up,
Lev 13:37 it is unchanged and black hair has *g*
Jdg 11:2 when they were *g* up, they drove
2Sa 10:5 at Jericho till your beards have *g*,
1Ki 12:8 the young men who had *g* up
12:10 The young men who had *g* up
1Ch 19:5 at Jericho till your beards have *g*,
2Ch 10:8 the young men who had *g* up
10:10 The young men who had *g* up
Job 17:7 My eyes have *g* dim with grief;
Ecc 1:16 I have *g* and increased
SS 8:8 and her breasts are not yet *g*.
Isa 10:27 because you have *g* so fat.
Jer 5:28 and have *g* fat and sleek.
Eze 7:11 Violence has *g* into a rod
28:5 your heart has *g* proud.
Da 4:22 your greatness has *g*
Heb 11:24 By faith Moses, when he had *g* up,
Rev 2:3 for my name, and have not *g* weary

GROWS (GROW)

Ge 38:11 house until my son Shelah *g* up.''
Lev 25:5 Do not reap what *g* of itself
Lev 25:11 and do not reap what *g* of itself
1Ki 4:33 to the hyssop that *g* out of walls.
2Ki 19:26 scorched before it *g* up.
19:29 This year you will eat what *g*
Job 30:30 My skin *g* black and peels;
Ps 49:16 overawed when a man *g* rich,
61:2 I call as my heart *g* faint;
142:3 When my spirit *g* faint within me,
143:4 So my spirit *g* faint within me;
Pr 13:20 He who walks with the wise *g* wise,
Isa 5:27 Not one of them *g* tired
37:27 scorched before it *g* up.
37:30 "This year you will eat what *g*
44:12 he drinks no water and *g* faint.
Na 2:10 bodies tremble, every face *g* pale.
Mt 13:32 yet when it *g*, it is the largest
Mk 4:27 the seed sprouts and *g*,
4:32 it *g* and becomes the largest
Eph 4:16 *g* and builds itself up in love,
Col 2:19 *g* as God causes it to grow.
Heb 12:15 and that no bitter root *g* up

GROWTH (GROW)

Pr 27:25 hay is removed and new *g* appears
SS 6:11 to look at the new *g* in the valley,
Eze 17:9 it withers? All its new *g* will wither.

GRUDGE (GRUDGING)

Ge 27:41 Esau held a *g* against Jacob
50:15 What if Joseph holds a *g* against us
Lev 19:18 bear a *g* against one of your people,
Mk 6:19 Herodias nursed a *g* against John

GRUDGING (GRUDGE)

Dt 15:10 and do so without a *g* heart;

GRUMBLE (GRUMBLED GRUMBLERS GRUMBLING)

Ex 16:7 that you should *g* against us?''
Nu 14:27 long will this wicked community *g*
14:36 and made the whole community *g*
16:11 Who is Aaron that you should *g*
Mt 20:11 began to *g* against the landowner.
Jn 6:41 this the Jews began to *g* about him
1Co 10:10 And do not *g*, as some of them did
Jas 5:9 Don't *g* against each other,

GRUMBLED (GRUMBLE)

Ex 15:24 So the people *g* against Moses,
16:2 the desert the whole community *g*
17:3 and they *g* against Moses.
Nu 14:2 All the Israelites *g* against Moses
14:29 and who has *g* against me
16:41 the whole Israelite community *g*
Dt 1:27 You *g* in your tents and said,
Jos 9:18 The whole assembly *g*
Ps 106:25 They *g* in their tents

GRUMBLERS (GRUMBLE)

Jude :16 These men are *g* and faultfinders;

GRUMBLING (GRUMBLE)

Ex 16:7 he has heard your *g* against him.
16:8 Who are we? You are not *g*
16:8 he has heard your *g* against him.
16:9 for he has heard your *g*.' ''
16:12 I have heard the *g* of the Israelites.
Nu 14:27 the complaints of these *g* Israelites.
17:5 of this constant *g* against you
17:10 an end to their *g* against me,
Jn 6:43 "Stop *g* among yourselves,''
6:61 that his disciples were *g* about this,
1Pe 4:9 to one another without *g*.

GUARANTEE (GUARANTEED GUARANTEEING)

Ge 43:9 I myself will *g* his safety; you can
Heb 7:22 Jesus has become the *g*

GUARANTEED (GUARANTEE)

Ge 44:32 Your servant *g* the boy's safety
Ro 4:16 and may be *g* to all Abraham's

GUARANTEEING (GUARANTEE)

2Co 1:22 as a deposit, *g* what is to come.
5:5 as a deposit, *g* what is to come.
Eph 1:14 who is a deposit *g* our inheritance

GUARD (BODYGUARD GUARDED GUARDIAN GUARDIANS GUARDING GUARDROOM GUARDS SAFEGUARD)

Ge 3: 24 forth to *g* the way to the tree of life.
37: 36 officials, the captain of the *g*.
39: 1 the captain of the *g*, bought him
40: 3 in the house of the captain of the *g*,
40: 4 The captain of the *g* assigned them
41: 10 in the house of the captain of the *g*.
41: 12 a servant of the captain of the *g*.
Ex 23: 20 of you to *g* you along the way
Nu 10: 25 as the rear *g* for all the units,
Jos 6: 7 with the armed *g* going ahead
6: 9 The armed *g* marched ahead
6: 9 and the rear *g* followed the ark.
6: 13 and the rear *g* followed the ark
10: 18 and post some men there to *g* it.
Jdg 7: 19 just after they had changed the *g*.
1Sa 2: 9 He will *g* the feet of his saints,
7: 1 Eleazar his son to *g* the ark
19: 2 Be on your *g* tomorrow morning;
26: 15 Why didn't you *g* your lord
26: 16 because you did not *g* your master,
2Sa 16: 6 the special *g* were on David's right
20: 3 and put them in a house under *g*.
20: 10 not on his *g* against the dagger
1Ki 1: 8 and David's special *g* did not join
1: 10 or Benaiah or the special *g*
14: 27 these to the commanders of the *g*
20: 39 with a captive and said, '*G* this man
2Ki 6: 10 was on his *g* in such places.
11: 6 and a third at the gate behind the *g*,
11: 7 all to *g* the temple for the king.
25: 8 commander of the imperial *g*,
25: 10 the commander of the imperial *g*,
25: 11 the commander of the *g* carried
25: 15 of the imperial *g* took away
25: 18 The commander of the *g* took
1Ch 9: 27 because they had to *g* it;
26: 16 *G* was alongside of *g*:
2Ch 12: 10 these to the commanders of the *g*
23: 6 to *g* what the LORD has assigned
Ezr 8: 29 *G* them carefully until you weigh
Ne 3: 25 palace near the court of the *g*.
3: 29 son of Shecaniah, the *g*
4: 9 and posted a *g* day and night
12: 39 At the Gate of the *G* they stopped.
13: 22 and *g* the gates in order
Job 7: 12 that you put me under *g*?
Ps 25: 20 *G* my life and rescue me;
86: 2 *G* my life, for I am devoted to you.
91: 11 you to *g* you in all your ways;
127: 1 the watchmen stand *g* in vain.
141: 3 Set a *g* over my mouth, O LORD;
Pr 2: 11 and understanding will *g* you.
4: 13 *g* it well, for it is your life.
4: 23 Above all else, *g* your heart,
7: 2 *g* my teachings as the apple
Ecc 5: 1 *G* your steps when you go
Isa 27: 3 I *g* it day and night
52: 12 the God of Israel will be your rear *g*
58: 8 of the LORD will be your rear *g*.
Jer 32: 2 of the *g* in the royal palace
32: 8 to me in the courtyard of the *g*
32: 12 sitting in the courtyard of the *g*.
33: 1 confined in the courtyard of the *g*,
37: 13 Gate, the captain of the *g*,
37: 21 placed in the courtyard of the *g*
37: 21 remained in the courtyard of the *g*.
38: 6 which was in the courtyard of the *g*
38: 13 remained in the courtyard of the *g*.
38: 28 remained in the courtyard of the *g*
39: 9 of the imperial *g* carried into exile
39: 10 the commander of the *g* left
39: 11 commander of the imperial *g*:
39: 13 the commander of the *g*,
39: 14 out of the courtyard of the *g*.
39: 15 confined in the courtyard of the *g*,
40: 1 of the imperial *g* had released him
40: 2 of the *g* found Jeremiah,
41: 10 of the imperial *g* had appointed
43: 6 of the imperial *g* had left
51: 12 Reinforce the *g*,
52: 12 commander of the imperial *g*,
52: 14 commander of the imperial *g* broke
52: 15 of the *g* carried into exile some
52: 19 of the imperial *g* took away
Jer 52: 24 The commander of the *g* took
52: 30 the commander of the imperial *g*.
Da 1: 11 to the *g* whom the chief official had
1: 16 the *g* took away their choice food
2: 14 the commander of the king's *g*,
Na 2: 1 *G* the fortress,
Mal 2: 15 So *g* yourself in your spirit,
2: 16 So *g* yourself in your spirit,
Mt 10: 17 But be on your *g* against men;
16: 6 "Be on your *g* against the yeast
16: 11 But be on your *g* against the yeast
16: 12 to *g* against the yeast used in bread,
27: 65 "Take a *g*," Pilate answered.
27: 66 seal on the stone and posting the *g*.
Mk 13: 9 "You must be on your *g*.
13: 23 So be on your *g*; I have told you
13: 33 Be on *g*! Be alert! You do not know
14: 44 and lead him away under *g*."
Lk 4: 10 you to *g* you carefully;
8: 29 and foot and kept under *g*,
12: 1 "Be on your *g* against the yeast
12: 15 Be on your *g* against all kinds
22: 4 and the officers of the temple *g*
22: 52 the officers of the temple *g*,
Ac 4: 1 and the captain of the temple *g*
5: 24 the captain of the temple *g*
12: 6 and sentries stood *g* at the entrance
16: 23 commanded to *g* them carefully.
20: 31 So be on your *g*! Remember that
23: 35 kept under *g* in Herod's palace.
24: 23 the centurion to keep Paul under *g*
28: 16 by himself, with a soldier to *g* him.
1Co 16: 13 Be on your *g*; stand firm in the faith
Php 1: 13 throughout the whole palace *g*
4: 7 will *g* your hearts and your minds
1Ti 6: 20 *g* what has been entrusted
2Ti 1: 12 to *g* what I have entrusted to him
1: 14 *G* the good deposit that was
1: 14 *g* it with the help of the Holy Spirit
4: 15 be on your *g* against him,
2Pe 3: 17 be on your *g* so that you may not be

GUARDED (GUARD)

Dt 32: 10 he *g* him as the apple of his eye,
33: 9 and *g* your covenant.
2Ki 12: 9 The priests who *g* the entrance put
Ne 12: 25 gatekeepers who *g* the storerooms
Est 2: 21 king's officers who *g* the doorway,
6: 2 who *g* the doorway and who had
Ac 12: 4 him over to be *g* by four squads
2Co 11: 32 city of the Damascenes *g* in order

GUARDIAN (GUARD)

Eze 28: 14 You were anointed as a *g* cherub,
28: 16 and I expelled you, O *g* cherub,
Ac 19: 35 of Ephesus is the *g* of the temple

GUARDIANS (GUARD)

2Ki 10: 1 and to the *g* of Ahab's children.
10: 5 and the *g* sent this message to Jehu:
1Co 4: 15 you have ten thousand *g* in Christ,
Gal 4: 2 He is subject to *g* and trustees

GUARDING (GUARD)

2Ki 11: 5 a third of you *g* the royal palace,
11: 6 who take turns *g* the temple—
1Ch 9: 19 for *g* the entrance to the dwelling
9: 19 for *g* the thresholds of the tent just
9: 23 were in charge of *g* the gates
Jer 4: 17 surround her like men *g* a field,
Mt 27: 54 with him who were *g* Jesus saw
Lk 22: 63 The men who were *g* Jesus began
Ac 22: 20 *g* the clothes of those who were

GUARDROOM (GUARD)

1Ki 14: 28 they returned them to the *g*.
2Ch 12: 11 they returned them to the *g*.

GUARDS (GUARD)

1Sa 22: 17 the king ordered the *g* at his side:
1Ki 14: 28 the LORD's temple, the *g* bore
2Ki 10: 25 he ordered the *g* and officers:
10: 25 *g* and officers threw the bodies out
11: 4 the *g* and had them brought to him
11: 11 The *g*, each with his weapon
11: 13 heard the noise made by the *g*
11: 18 Then Jehoiada the priest posted *g*
11: 19 entering by way of the gate of the *g*
2Ki 11: 19 the *g* and all the people of the land,
2Ch 12: 11 the *g* went with him, bearing
Ne 4: 22 so they can serve us as *g* by night
4: 23 the *g* with me took off our clothes;
7: 3 appoint residents of Jerusalem as *g*,
Ps 97: 10 for he *g* the lives of his faithful ones
Pr 2: 8 for he *g* the course of the just
13: 3 He who *g* his lips *g* his soul,
13: 6 Righteousness *g* the man
16: 17 he who *g* his way *g* his soul.
19: 16 who obeys instructions *g* his soul,
21: 23 He who *g* his mouth and his tongue
22: 5 he who *g* his soul stays far
24: 12 Does not he who *g* your life know
Eze 9: 1 "Bring the *g* of the city here,
40: 7 alcoves for the *g* were one rod long
Na 3: 17 Your *g* are like locusts,
Mt 26: 58 and sat down with the *g*
28: 4 The *g* were so afraid
28: 11 some of the *g* went into the city
Mk 14: 54 There he sat with the *g*
14: 65 And the *g* took him and beat him.
Lk 11: 21 fully armed, *g* his own house,
Jn 7: 32 and the Pharisees sent temple *g*
7: 45 Finally the temple *g* went back
7: 46 this man does," the *g* declared.
Ac 5: 23 with the *g* standing at the doors;
12: 10 They passed the first and second *g*
12: 19 he cross-examined the *g*

GUDGODAH

Dt 10: 7 From there they traveled to *G*

GUEST (GUESTS)

Lev 22: 10 nor may the *g* of a priest
Jdg 19: 23 this man is my *g*, don't do this
Est 1: 8 command each *g* was allowed
Mk 14: 14 Teacher asks: Where is my *g* room,
Lk 19: 7 He has gone to be the *g* of a 'sinner
22: 11 Teacher asks: Where is the *g* room,
Ac 10: 32 He is a *g* in the home
Phm : 22 one thing more: Prepare a *g* room

GUESTS (GUEST)

1Sa 9: 24 the time I said, 'I have invited *g*.' "
2Sa 15: 11 as *g* and went quite innocently,
1Ki 1: 41 and all the *g* who were
1: 49 all Adonijah's *g* rose in alarm
Job 19: 15 My *g* and my maidservants count
Pr 9: 18 that her *g* are in the depths
Mt 9: 15 "How can the *g* of the bridegroom
14: 9 of his oaths and his dinner *g*,
22: 10 the wedding hall was filled with *g*.
22: 11 when the king came in to see the *g*,
Mk 2: 19 "How can the *g* of the bridegroom
6: 22 she pleased Herod and his dinner *g*
6: 26 of his oaths and his dinner *g*,
Lk 5: 34 "Can you make the *g*
7: 49 The other *g* began to say
14: 7 noticed how the *g* picked
14: 10 in the presence of all your fellow *g*.
14: 16 great banquet and invited many *g*.
Jn 2: 10 wine after the *g* have had too much
Ac 10: 23 the men into the house to be his *g*.

GUIDANCE (GUIDE)

2Ki 16: 15 use the bronze altar for seeking *g*."
1Ch 10: 13 even consulted a medium for *g*,
Pr 1: 5 and let the discerning get *g*—
11: 14 For lack of *g* a nation falls,
20: 18 if you wage war, obtain *g*.
24: 6 for waging war you need *g*,
Hab 2: 19 Can it give *g*?

GUIDE (GUIDANCE GUIDED GUIDEPOSTS GUIDES GUIDING)

Ex 13: 21 of cloud to *g* them on their way
15: 13 In your strength you will *g* them
Ne 9: 19 cease to *g* them on their path,
Ps 25: 5 *g* me in your truth and teach me,
31: 3 of your name lead and *g* me.
43: 3 let them *g* me;
48: 14 he will be our *g* even to the end.
67: 4 and *g* the nations of the earth.
73: 24 You *g* me with your counsel,
139: 10 even there your hand will *g* me,
Pr 4: 11 I *g* you in the way of wisdom
6: 22 When you walk, they will *g* you;

Isa 9: 16 Those who *g* this people mislead
42: 16 unfamiliar paths I will *g* them;
49: 10 compassion on them will *g* them
51: 18 there was none to *g* her;
57: 18 I will *g* him and restore comfort
58: 11 The LORD will *g* you always;
Lk 1: 79 to *g* our feet into the path of peace
Jn 16: 13 comes, he will *g* you into all truth.
Ac 1: 16 as *g* for those who arrested Jesus—
Ro 2: 19 you are convinced that you are a *g*

GUIDED (GUIDE)

Job 31: 18 and from my birth I *g* the widow—
Ps 78: 14 He *g* them with the cloud by day
78: 53 He *g* them safely, so they were
107: 30 he *g* them to their desired haven.
Isa 9: 16 and those who are *g* are led astray.
63: 14 This is how you *g* your people

GUIDEPOSTS (GUIDE)

Jer 31: 21 put up *g*.

GUIDES (GUIDE)

Ps 23: 3 He *g* me in paths of righteousness
25: 9 He *g* the humble in what is right
Pr 11: 3 The integrity of the upright *g* them,
16: 23 A wise man's heart *g* his mouth,
Isa 3: 12 my people, your *g* lead you astray;
Mt 15: 14 Leave them; they are blind *g*.
23: 16 "Woe to you, blind *g*! You say,
23: 24 You blind *g*! You strain out a gnat

GUIDING (GUIDE)

2Sa 6: 3 were *g* the new cart with the ark
1Ch 13: 7 with Uzzah and Ahio *g* it.
Ecc 2: 3 my mind still *g* me with wisdom.
Jn 18: 3 *g* a detachment of soldiers

GUILT (BLOODGUILT GUILTLESS GUILTY)

Ge 20: 9 that you have brought such great *g*
26: 10 you would have brought *g* upon us
44: 16 has uncovered your servants' *g*.
Ex 28: 38 and he will bear the *g* involved
28: 43 so that they will not incur *g* and die
Lev 4: 3 the anointed priest sins, bringing *g*
5: 15 It is a *g* offering.
5: 16 for him with the ram as a *g* offering
5: 18 as a *g* offering a ram from the flock,
5: 19 It is a *g* offering; he has been guilty
6: 5 the day he presents his *g* offering.
6: 6 that is, to the LORD, his *g* offering
6: 17 the sin offering and the *g* offering,
7: 1 the regulations for the *g* offering,
7: 2 The *g* offering is to be slaughtered
7: 5 It is a *g* offering.
7: 7 the sin offering and the *g* offering:
7: 37 the *g* offering,
10: 17 you to take away the *g*
14: 12 and offer it as a *g* offering,
14: 13 the *g* offering belongs to the priest;
14: 14 some of the blood of the *g* offering
14: 17 on top of the blood of the *g* offering
14: 21 as a *g* offering to be waved
14: 24 to take the lamb for the *g* offering,
14: 25 the lamb for the *g* offering
14: 28 the blood of the *g* offering—
19: 17 so you will not share in his *g*.
19: 21 the Tent of Meeting for a *g* offering
19: 22 ram of the *g* offering the priest is
22: 16 upon them *g* requiring payment.
Nu 5: 15 offering to draw attention to *g*.
5: 28 she will be cleared of *g*
6: 12 year-old male lamb as a *g* offering.
15: 31 cut off; his *g* remains on him.' "
18: 9 whether grain or sin or *g* offerings,
30: 15 then he is responsible for her *g*."
Dt 19: 13 Israel the *g* of shedding innocent
21: 9 purge from yourselves the *g*
22: 8 so that you may not bring the *g*
1Sa 3: 14 'The *g* of Eli's house will never be
6: 3 but by all means send a *g* offering
6: 4 "What *g* offering should we send
6: 8 back to him as a *g* offering.
6: 17 as a *g* offering to the LORD—
2Sa 14: 9 and his throne be without *g*."
24: 10 take away the *g* of your servant.
1Ki 2: 31 and my father's house of the *g*
1Ki 2: 33 May the *g* of their blood rest
2Ki 12: 16 The money from the *g* offerings
1Ch 21: 3 Why should he bring *g* on Israel?"
21: 8 take away the *g* of your servant.
2Ch 24: 18 of their *g*, God's anger came
28: 13 For our *g* is already great,
28: 13 intend to add to our sin and *g*?
33: 23 the LORD; Amon increased his *g*.
Ezr 9: 6 our *g* has reached to the heavens.
9: 7 until now, our *g* has been great.
9: 13 of our evil deeds and our great *g*,
9: 15 Here we are before you in our *g*,
10: 10 women, adding to Israel's *g*.
10: 19 and for their *g* they each presented
10: 19 ram from the flock as a *g* offering.)
Ne 4: 5 Do not cover up their *g*
Job 20: 27 The heavens will expose his *g*;
31: 33 by hiding my *g* in my heart
33: 9 I am clean and free from *g*.
Ps 7: 3 and there is *g* on my hands—
32: 5 the *g* of my sin.
38: 4 My *g* has overwhelmed me
69: 5 my *g* is not hidden from you
Pr 28: 17 tormented by the *g* of murder
Isa 1: 4 a people loaded with *g*,
6: 7 your *g* is taken away and your sin
24: 6 its people must bear their *g*.
24: 20 upon it is the *g* of its rebellion
27: 9 then, will Jacob's *g* be atoned for,
53: 10 LORD makes his life a *g* offering,
59: 3 your fingers with *g*.
Jer 2: 22 the stain of your *g* is still before me
3: 13 Only acknowledge your *g*—
14: 20 and the *g* of our fathers;
25: 12 for their *g*," declares the LORD,
26: 15 you will bring the *g*
30: 14 because your *g* is so great
30: 15 Because of your great *g*
50: 20 "search will be made for Israel's *g*,
51: 5 though their land is full of *g*
Eze 14: 10 will bear their *g*— the prophet will
18: 19 'Why does the son not share the *g*
18: 20 The son will not share the *g*
18: 20 nor will the father share the *g*
21: 23 but he will remind them of their *g*
21: 24 to mind your *g* by your open
40: 39 and *g* offerings were slaughtered.
42: 13 the sin offerings and the *g* offerings
44: 29 the sin offerings and the *g* offerings
46: 20 the priests will cook the *g* offering
Hos 5: 15 until they admit their *g*.
10: 2 and now they must bear their *g*.
12: 14 upon him the *g* of his bloodshed
13: 12 The *g* of Ephraim is stored up,
13: 16 of Samaria must bear their *g*,
Jn 9: 41 claim you can see, your *g* remains.
16: 8 the world of *g* in regard to sin

GUILTLESS (GUILT)

Ex 20: 7 not hold anyone *g* who misuses his
Dt 5: 11 not hold anyone *g* who misuses his
1Sa 26: 9 on the LORD's anointed and be *g*?
Job 34: 6 although I am *g*,

GUILTY (GUILT)

Ge 38: 24 "Your daughter-in-law Tamar is *g*
Ex 22: 2 the defender is not *g* of bloodshed;
22: 3 after sunrise, he is *g* of bloodshed.
22: 9 the judges declare *g* must pay back
23: 7 to death, for I will not acquit the *g*
34: 7 does not leave the *g* unpunished;
Lev 4: 13 unaware of the matter, they are *g*.
4: 22 of the LORD his God, he is *g*.
4: 27 of the LORD's commands, he is *g*.
5: 2 he has become unclean and is *g*.
5: 3 when he learns of it he will be *g*.
5: 4 when he learns of it he will be *g*.
5: 5 " 'When anyone is *g* in any
5: 17 he is *g* and will be held responsible.
5: 19 he has been *g* of wrongdoing
6: 4 when he thus sins and becomes *g*,
6: 7 things he did that made him *g*."
17: 4 that man shall be considered *g*
22: 9 so that they do not become *g*
Nu 5: 6 that person is *g* and must confess
14: 18 does not leave the *g* unpunished;
18: 32 of it you will not be *g* in this matter;
35: 27 accused without being *g* of murder.
Dt 15: 9 and you will be found *g* of sin.
19: 10 and so that you will not be *g*
21: 8 and do not hold your people *g*
21: 22 If a man *g* of a capital offense is put
23: 21 it of you and you will be *g* of sin.
23: 22 making a vow, you will not be *g*.
24: 15 against you, and you will be *g* of sin
25: 1 innocent and condemning the *g*.
25: 2 If the *g* man deserves to be beaten,
1Sa 20: 8 If I am *g*, then kill me yourself!
24: 11 and recognize that I am not *g*
26: 18 and what wrong am I *g* of?
2Sa 14: 32 if I am *g* of anything, let him put
19: 19 "May my lord not hold me *g*.
1Ki 8: 32 Declare the innocent not *g*,
8: 32 condemning the *g* and bringing
2Ch 6: 23 Declare the innocent not *g*
6: 23 repaying the *g* by bringing
20: 35 of Israel, who was *g* of wickedness.
28: 10 *g* of sins against the LORD your
28: 13 "or we will be *g* before the LORD.
Job 9: 20 it would pronounce me *g*.
9: 29 Since I am already found *g*,
10: 7 though you know that I am not *g*
10: 15 If I am *g*— woe to me!
34: 31 'I am *g* but will offend no more.
Ps 5: 10 Declare them *g*, O God!
109: 7 he is tried, let him be found *g*,
Pr 17: 15 Acquitting the *g* and condemning
21: 8 The way of the *g* is devious,
24: 24 to the *g*, "You are innocent"—
24: 25 with those who convict the *g*,
Isa 5: 23 who acquit the *g* for a bribe,
29: 21 with a word make a man out to be *g*
Jer 2: 3 all who devoured her were held *g*,
50: 7 their enemies said, 'We are not *g*,
Eze 14: 10 the prophet will be as *g*
18: 24 of the unfaithfulness he is *g* of
22: 4 you have become *g*
25: 12 and became very *g* by doing so,
Hos 1: 2 the land is *g* of the vilest adultery
4: 15 let not Judah become *g*.
13: 1 But he became *g* of Baal worship
Na 1: 3 will not leave the *g* unpunished.
Hab 1: 11 *g* men, whose own strength is their
Mk 3: 29 Spirit will never be forgiven; he is *g*
Lk 13: 4 do you think they were more *g*
Jn 8: 46 Can any of you prove me *g* of sin?
9: 41 you were blind, you would not be *g*
15: 22 they would not be *g* of sin.
15: 24 they would not be *g* of sin.
19: 11 over to you is *g* of a greater sin."
Ac 5: 28 to make us *g* of this man's blood."
22: 25 who hasn't even been found *g*?"
25: 11 I am *g* of doing anything deserving
28: 18 I was not *g* of any crime deserving
1Co 11: 27 in an unworthy manner will be *g*
Heb 10: 2 and would no longer have felt *g*
10: 22 to cleanse us from a *g* conscience
Jas 2: 10 at just one point is *g* of breaking all

GULF

Isa 11: 15 the *g* of the Egyptian sea;

GULL

Lev 11: 16 the screech owl, the *g*, any kind
Dt 14: 15 the screech owl, the *g*, any kind

GULPS

Pr 19: 28 of the wicked *g* down evil.

GUM

Ex 30: 34 "Take fragrant spices—*g* resin,

GUNI (GUNITE)

Ge 46: 24 Jahziel, *G*, Jezer and Shillem.
Nu 26: 48 through *G*, the Gunite clan;
1Ch 5: 15 the son of *G*, was head
7: 13 Jahziel, *G*, Jezer and Shillem—

GUNITE (GUNI)

Nu 26: 48 through Guni, the *G* clan;

GUR

2Ki 9: 27 on the way up to *G* near Ibleam,

GUR BAAL

2Ch 26: 7 against the Arabs who lived in *G*

GUSH (GUSHED GUSHES)
Isa 35: 6 Water will *g* forth in the wilderness

GUSHED (GUSH)
Nu 20: 11 Water *g* out, and the community
Ps 78: 20 he struck the rock, water *g* out,
105: 41 opened the rock, and water *g* out;
Isa 48: 21 and water *g* out.

GUSHES (GUSH)
Pr 15: 2 but the mouth of the fool *g* folly.
15: 28 but the mouth of the wicked *g* evil.

GUTTER
Eze 43: 13 Its *g* is a cubit deep and a cubit
43: 14 From the *g* on the ground up
43: 17 and a *g* of a cubit all around.

HAAHASHTARI
1Ch 4: 6 Ahuzzam, Hepher, Temeni and *H*.

HABAKKUK
Hab 1: 1 oracle that *H* the prophet received.
3: 1 A prayer of *H* the prophet.

HABAZZINIAH
Jer 35: 3 the son of *H*, and his brothers

HABIT
Ex 21: 29 the bull has had the *h* of goring
21: 36 was known that the bull had the *h*
Nu 22: 30 Have I been in the *h* of doing this
1Ti 5: 13 they get into the *h* of being idle
Heb 10: 25 as some are in the *h* of doing,

HABITAT (INHABIT)
Job 39: 6 the salt flats as his *h*.

HABOR
2Ki 17: 6 in Gozan on the *H* River
18: 11 in Gozan on the *H* River
1Ch 5: 26 He took them to Halah, *H*,

HACALIAH
Ne 1: 1 The words of Nehemiah son of *H*:
10: 1 the governor, the son of *H*.

HACK
Eze 16: 40 *h* you to pieces with their swords.

HACMONI (HACMONITE)
1Ch 27: 32 Jehiel son of *H* took care

HACMONITE (HACMONI)
1Ch 11: 11 a *H*, was chief of the officers;

HADAD
Ge 25: 15 Dumah, Massa, *H*, Tema, Jetur,
36: 35 When Husham died, *H* son
36: 36 When *H* died, Samlah
36: 39 of Acbor died, *H* succeeded him
1Ki 11: 14 *H* the Edomite, from the royal line
11: 17 *H*, still only a boy, fled to Egypt
11: 18 who gave *H* a house and land
11: 19 with *H* that he gave him a sister
11: 21 *H* heard that David rested
11: 21 *H* said to Pharaoh, "Let me go,
11: 22 *H* replied, "but do let me go!"
11: 25 adding to the trouble caused by *H*.
1Ch 1: 30 Dumah, Massa, *H*, Tema, Jetur,
1: 46 When Husham died, *H* son
1: 47 When *H* died, Samlah
1: 50 Baal-Hanan died, *H* succeeded
1: 51 *H* also died.

HADAD RIMMON
Zec 12: 11 like the weeping of *H*

HADADEZER (HADADEZER'S)
2Sa 8: 3 David fought *H* son of Rehob,
8: 5 came to help *H* king of Zobah,
8: 7 belonged to the officers of *H*
8: 8 towns that belonged to *H*,
8: 9 had defeated the entire army of *H*,
8: 10 him on his victory in battle over *H*,
8: 12 taken from *H* son of Rehob,
10: 16 *H* had Arameans brought
10: 19 vassals of *H* saw that they had been
1Ki 11: 23 from his master, *H* king of Zobah.
1Ch 18: 3 David fought *H* king of Zobah,
18: 5 came to help *H* king of Zobah,
18: 7 carried by the officers of *H*
18: 8 towns that belonged to *H*,
18: 9 army of *H* king of Zobah,
18: 10 him on his victory in battle over *H*,
19: 19 vassals of *H* saw that they had been

HADADEZER'S (HADADEZER)
2Sa 10: 16 of *H* army leading them.
1Ch 19: 16 of *H* army leading them.

HADASHAH
Jos 15: 37 Zenan, *H*, Migdal Gad, Dilean,

HADASSAH
Est 2: 7 Mordecai had a cousin named *H*,

HADES
Mt 16: 18 the gates of *H* will not overcome it.
Rev 1: 18 And I hold the keys of death and *H*
6: 8 *H* was following close behind him.
20: 13 and *H* gave up the dead that were
20: 14 *H* were thrown into the lake of fire.

HADID
Ezr 2: 33 *H* and Ono 725 of Jericho 345
Ne 7: 37 *H* and Ono 721 of Senaah 3,930
11: 34 in *H*, Zeboim and Neballat,

HADLAI
2Ch 28: 12 of Shallum, and Amasa son of *H*—

HADORAM
Ge 10: 27 Hazarmaveth, Jerah, *H*, Uzal,
1Ch 1: 21 Hazarmaveth, Jerah, *H*, Uzal,
18: 10 *H* brought all kinds of articles
18: 10 he sent his son *H* to King David

HADRACH
Zec 9: 1 is against the land of *H*

HAELEPH
Jos 18: 28 Rekem, Irpeel, Taralah, Zelah, *H*,

HAGAB
Ezr 2: 46 Hagabah, Akkub, *H*, Shalmai,

HAGABA
Ne 7: 48 Padon, Lebana, *H*, Shalmai, Hanan

HAGABAH
Ezr 2: 45 Padon, Lebanah, *H*, Akkub, Hagab

HAGAR
Ge 16: 1 Egyptian maidservant named *H*;
16: 3 took her Egyptian maidservant *H*
16: 4 He slept with *H*, and she conceived
16: 6 Sarai mistreated *H*; so she fled
16: 7 The angel of the LORD found *H*
16: 8 And he said, "*H*, servant of Sarai,
16: 15 So *H* bore Abram a son,
16: 16 old when *H* bore him Ishmael.
21: 9 the son whom *H* the Egyptian had
21: 14 a skin of water and gave them to *H*.
21: 17 of God called to *H* from heaven
21: 17 "What is the matter, *H*? Do not be
25: 12 Sarah's maidservant, *H*
Ps 83: 6 of Moab and the descendants of *H*,
Gal 4: 24 are to be slaves: This is *H*.
4: 25 *H* stands for Mount Sinai in Arabia

HAGGAI
Ezr 5: 1 Now *H* the prophet and Zechariah
6: 14 the preaching of *H* the prophet
Hag 1: 1 came through the prophet *H*
1: 3 came through the prophet *H*:
1: 12 and the message of the prophet *H*,
1: 13 Then *H*, the LORD's messenger,
2: 1 came through the prophet *H*:
2: 10 the LORD came to the prophet *H*:
2: 13 Then *H* said, "If a person defiled
2: 14 *H* said, " 'So it is with this people
2: 20 came to *H* a second time

HAGGARD
2Sa 13: 4 look so *h* morning after morning?
Job 30: 3 *H* from want and hunger,

HAGGEDOLIM
Ne 11: 14 chief officer was Zabdiel son of *H*.

HAGGI (HAGGITE)
Ge 46: 16 Zephon, *H*, Shuni, Ezbon, Eri,
Nu 26: 15 through *H*, the Haggite clan;

HAGGIAH
1Ch 6: 30 *H* his son and Asaiah his son.

HAGGITE (HAGGI)
Nu 26: 15 through Haggi, the *H* clan;

HAGGITH
2Sa 3: 4 Adonijah the son of *H*; the fifth,
1Ki 1: 5 Adonijah, whose mother was *H*,
1: 11 heard that Adonijah, the son of *H*,
2: 13 the son of *H*, went to Bathsheba,
1Ch 3: 2 Adonijah the son of *H*; the fifth,

HAGRI (HAGRITE HAGRITES)
2Sa 23: 36 the son of *H*, Zelek the Ammonite,
1Ch 11: 38 son of *H*, Zelek the Ammonite,

HAGRITE (HAGRI)
1Ch 27: 31 Jaziz the *H* was in charge

HAGRITES (HAGRI)
1Ch 5: 10 of the *H* throughout the entire
5: 10 they waged war against the *H*,
5: 19 They waged war against the *H*,
5: 20 and God handed the *H*
5: 21 They seized the livestock of the *H*

HAIL (HAILSTONES HAILSTORM)
Ex 9: 19 the *h* will fall on every man
9: 22 toward the sky so that *h* will fall all
9: 23 So the LORD rained *h* on the land
9: 23 the LORD sent thunder and *h*,
9: 24 *h* fell and lightning flashed back
9: 25 Throughout Egypt *h* struck
9: 26 only place it did not *h* was the land
9: 28 have had enough thunder and *h*.
9: 29 and there will be no more *h*,
9: 33 the thunder and *h* stopped,
9: 34 and *h* and thunder had stopped,
10: 5 what little you have left after the *h*,
10: 12 the fields, everything left by the *h*."
10: 15 all that was left after the *h*—
Job 38: 22 or seen the storehouses of the *h*,
Ps 78: 47 He destroyed their vines with *h*
78: 48 He gave over their cattle to the *h*,
105: 32 He turned their rain into *h*,
147: 17 He hurls down his *h* like pebbles.
148: 8 lightning and *h*, snow and clouds,
Isa 28: 17 *h* will sweep away your refuge,
30: 30 cloudburst, thunderstorm and *h*.
32: 19 Though *h* flattens the forest
Hag 2: 17 and *h*, yet you did not turn to me,'
Mt 27: 29 "*H*, King of the Jews!" they said.
Mk 15: 18 they began to call out to him, "*H*,
Jn 19: 3 saying, "*H*, O king of the Jews!"
Rev 8: 7 and there came *h* and fire mixed
16: 21 God on account of the plague of *h*,

HAILSTONES (HAIL)
Jos 10: 11 died from the *h* than were killed
10: 11 the LORD hurled large *h*
Ps 18: 12 with *h* and bolts of lightning.
Eze 13: 11 and I will send *h* hurtling down,
13: 13 and in my anger *h* and torrents
38: 22 *h* and burning sulfur on him
Rev 16: 21 From the sky huge *h*

HAILSTORM (HAIL)
Ex 9: 18 will send the worst *h* that has ever
Isa 28: 2 Like a *h* and a destructive wind,
Rev 11: 19 an earthquake and a great *h*.

HAIR (GRAY-HAIRED HAIRS HAIRY)
Ex 25: 4 scarlet yarn and fine linen; goat *h*;
26: 7 Make curtains of goat *h* for the tent
35: 6 scarlet yarn and fine linen; goat *h*;
35: 23 scarlet yarn or fine linen, or goat *h*,
35: 26 and had the skill spun the goat *h*.
36: 14 curtains of goat *h* for the tent
Lev 10: 6 Do not let your *h* become unkempt
13: 3 if the *h* in the sore has turned white

Lev 13: 4 and the *h* in it has not turned white,
13: 10 the skin that has turned the *h* white
13: 20 and the *h* in it has turned white,
13: 21 there is no white *h* in it
13: 25 and if the *h* in it has turned white,
13: 26 and there is no white *h* in the spot
13: 30 and the *h* in it is yellow and thin,
13: 31 and there is no black *h* in it,
13: 32 and there is no yellow *h* in it
13: 36 need to look for yellow *h;*
13: 37 and black *h* has grown in it,
13: 40 "When a man has lost his *h*
13: 41 If he has lost his *h* from the front
13: 45 let his *h* be unkempt, cover
14: 8 shave off all his *h* and bathe
14: 9 day he must shave off all his *h;*
14: 9 his eyebrows and the rest of his *h.*
19: 27 " 'Do not cut the *h* at the sides
21: 10 must not let his *h* become unkempt
Nu 5: 18 he shall loosen her *h* and place
6: 5 he must let the *h* of his head grow
6: 9 thus defiling the *h* he has dedicated
6: 18 He is to take the *h* and put it
6: 18 shave off the *h* that he dedicated.
6: 19 shaved off the *h* of his dedication,
31: 20 everything made of leather, goat *h*
Jdg 16: 19 shave off the seven braids of his *h,*
16: 22 But the *h* on his head began
20: 16 of whom could sling a stone at a *h*
1Sa 14: 45 not a *h* of his head will fall
17: 35 I seized it by its *h,* struck it
19: 13 putting some goats' *h* at the head.
19: 16 and at the head was some goats' *h.*
2Sa 14: 11 "not one *h* of your son's head will
14: 26 Whenever he cut the *h* of his head
14: 26 used to cut his *h* from time to time
1Ki 1: 52 not a *h* of his head will fall
2Ki 1: 8 "He was a man with a garment of *h*
9: 30 arranged her *h* and looked out
Ezr 9: 3 pulled *h* from my head and beard
Ne 13: 25 of the men and pulled out their *h.*
Job 4: 15 and the *h* on my body stood on end
41: 32 would think the deep had white *h.*
Pr 16: 31 Gray *h* is a crown of splendor;
20: 29 gray *h* the splendor of the old.
SS 4: 1 Your *h* is like a flock of goats
5: 2 my *h* with the dampness
5: 11 his *h* is wavy
6: 5 Your *h* is like a flock of goats
7: 5 Your *h* is like royal tapestry;
Isa 3: 24 instead of well-dressed *h,* baldness;
7: 20 to shave your head and the *h*
22: 12 to tear out your *h* and put
Jer 7: 29 Cut off your *h* and throw it away;
Eze 5: 1 a set of scales and divide up the *h.*
5: 2 burn a third of the *h* with fire
5: 3 But take a few strands of *h*
8: 3 and took me by the *h* of my head.
16: 7 were formed and your *h* grew,
44: 20 are to keep the *h* of their heads
44: 20 their heads or let their *h* grow long,
Da 3: 27 nor was a *h* of their heads singed;
4: 33 until his *h* grew like the feathers
7: 9 *h* of his head was white like wool.
Hos 7: 9 His *h* is sprinkled with gray,
Zec 13: 4 garment of *h* in order to deceive.
Mt 3: 4 clothes were made of camel's *h,*
5: 36 you cannot make even one *h* white
Mk 1: 6 wore clothing made of camel's *h,*
Lk 7: 38 Then she wiped them with her *h,*
7: 44 and wiped them with her *h.*
21: 18 But not a *h* of your head will perish
Jn 11: 2 and wiped his feet with her *h.*
12: 3 and wiped his feet with her *h.*
Ac 18: 18 he had his *h* cut off at Cenchrea
27: 34 one of you will lose a single *h*
1Co 11: 6 for a woman to have her *h* cut
11: 6 she should have her *h* cut off;
11: 14 that if a man has long *h,*
11: 15 For long *h* is given to her
11: 15 but that if a woman has long *h,*
1Ti 2: 9 not with braided *h* or gold or pearls
1Pe 3: 3 as braided *h* and the wearing
Rev 1: 14 and *h* were white like wool,
6: 12 like sackcloth made of goat *h,*
9: 8 Their *h* was like women's *h,*

HAIRS (HAIR)

Ps 40: 12 more than the *h* of my head,
69: 4 outnumber the *h* of my head;
Isa 46: 4 Even to your old age and gray *h*
Mt 10: 30 even the very *h* of your head are all
Lk 12: 7 the very *h* of your head are all

HAIRY (HAIR)

Ge 25: 25 whole body was like a *h* garment;
27: 11 "But my brother Esau is a *h* man,
27: 23 for his hands were *h* like those
Ps 68: 21 the *h* crowns of those who go

HAKILAH

1Sa 23: 19 on the hill of *H,* south of Jeshimon?
26: 1 Is not David hiding on the hill of *H*
26: 3 on the hill of *H* facing Jeshimon,

HAKKATAN

Ezr 8: 12 Johanan son of *H,*

HAKKOZ

1Ch 24: 10 the seventh to *H,* the eighth
Ezr 2: 61 *H* and Barzillai (a man who had
Ne 3: 4 son of *H,* repaired the next section.
3: 21 son of *H,* repaired another section,
7: 63 *H* and Barzillai (a man who had

HAKUPHA

Ezr 2: 51 Nephussim, Bakbuk, *H,* Harhur,
Ne 7: 53 Nephussim, Bakbuk, *H,* Harhur,

HALAH

2Ki 17: 6 He settled them in *H,* in Gozan
18: 11 to Assyria and settled them in *H,*
1Ch 5: 26 He took them to *H,* Habor,

HALAK

Jos 11: 17 from Mount *H,* which rises
12: 7 the Valley of Lebanon to Mount *H,*

HALF (HALFWAY HALVES)

Ge 15: 10 however, he did not cut in *h.*
Ex 24: 6 Moses took *h* of the blood
24: 6 and the other *h* he sprinkled
25: 10 a *h* wide, and a cubit and a *h* high.
25: 10 two and a *h* cubits long, a cubit
25: 17 long and a cubit and a *h* wide.
25: 17 two and a *h* cubits long and a cubit
25: 23 cubit wide and a cubit and a *h* high.
26: 12 the *h* curtain that is left over is
26: 16 long and a cubit and a *h* wide.
30: 13 This *h* shekel is an offering
30: 13 counted is to give a *h* shekel,
30: 15 not to give more than a *h* shekel
30: 23 shekels of liquid myrrh, *h*
36: 21 long and a cubit and a *h* wide,
37: 1 a *h* wide, and a cubit and a *h* high.
37: 1 two and a *h* cubits long, a cubit
37: 6 long and a cubit and a *h* wide.
37: 6 two and a *h* cubits long and a cubit
37: 10 wide, and a cubit and a *h* high.
38: 26 beka per person, that is, *h* a shekel,
Lev 6: 20 *h* of it in the morning and *h*
Nu 12: 12 womb with its flesh *h* eaten away."
15: 9 mixed with *h* a hin of oil.
15: 10 Also bring *h* a hin of wine
28: 14 is to be a drink offering of *h* a hin
31: 29 Take this tribute from their *h* share
31: 30 From the Israelites' *h,* select one
31: 36 The *h* share of those who fought
31: 42 The *h* belonging to the Israelites,
31: 43 the community's *h*— was 337,500
31: 47 the Israelites' *h,* Moses selected
34: 13 given to the nine and a *h* tribes,
34: 15 and a *h* tribes have received their
Dt 3: 12 including *h* the hill country
3: 13 I gave to the *h* tribe of Manasseh.
Jos 8: 33 *H* of the people stood in front
8: 33 *h* of them in front of Mount Ebal,
12: 2 This included *h* of Gilead.
12: 5 and *h* of Gilead to the border
13: 7 and *h* of the tribe of Manasseh."
13: 8 The other *h* of Manasseh,
13: 25 and *h* the Ammonite country as far
13: 29 to *h* the family of the descendants
13: 31 for *h* of the sons of Makir,
13: 31 in Bashan, sixty towns, *h* of Gilead,
Jos 21: 5 the tribes of Ephraim, Dan and *h*
21: 25 From *h* the tribe of Manasseh they
22: 7 to the other *h* of the tribe Joshua
Jdg 3: 16 sword about a foot and a *h* long,
1Sa 14: 14 men in an area of about *h* an acre.
2Sa 10: 4 shaved off *h* of each man's beard,
18: 3 Even if *h* of us die, they won't care;
19: 40 and *h* the troops of Israel had taken
1Ki 3: 25 give *h* to one and *h* to the other."
7: 31 it measured a cubit and a *h.*
7: 32 of each wheel was a cubit and a *h.*
7: 35 was a circular band *h* a cubit deep.
10: 7 Indeed, not even *h* was told me;
13: 8 to give me *h* your possessions,
16: 9 had command of *h* his chariots,
16: 21 and the other *h* supported Omri.
16: 21 *h* supported Tibni son of Ginath
2Ki 25: 17 a *h* feet high and was decorated
1Ch 2: 52 Haroeh, *h* the Manahathites,
2: 54 *h* the Manahathites,
6: 61 towns from the clans of *h* the tribe
6: 70 And from *h* the tribe of Manasseh
11: 23 who was seven and a *h* feet tall.
12: 31 men of *h* the tribe of Manasseh,
27: 20 over *h* the tribe of Manasseh:
2Ch 9: 6 *h* the greatness of your wisdom was
Ne 3: 17 ruler of *h* the district of Keilah,
4: 6 till all of it reached *h* its height,
4: 16 while the other *h* were equipped
4: 16 *h* of my men did the work,
4: 21 with *h* the men holding spears,
12: 32 and *h* the leaders of Judah followed
12: 38 together with *h* the people—
12: 40 together with *h* the officials,
13: 24 *H* of their children spoke
Est 5: 3 Even up to *h* the kingdom,
5: 6 Even up to *h* the kingdom,
7: 2 Even up to *h* the kingdom,
Ps 55: 23 will not live out *h* their days.
Isa 44: 16 *H* of the wood he burns in the fire;
44: 19 "*H* of it I used for fuel;
Jer 17: 11 When his life is *h* gone, they will
Eze 16: 51 did not commit *h* the sins you
40: 42 and a *h* wide and a cubit high
40: 42 each a cubit and a *h* long, a cubit
43: 17 with a rim of *h* a cubit and a gutter
Da 7: 25 him for a time, times and *h* a time.
12: 7 be for a time, times and *h* a time.
Zec 14: 2 *H* of the city will go into exile,
14: 4 moving north and *h* moving south.
14: 4 with *h* of the mountain moving
14: 8 *h* to the eastern sea and *h*
Mk 6: 23 up to *h* my kingdom."
Lk 4: 25 shut for three and a *h* years
10: 30 went away, leaving him *h* dead.
19: 8 and now I give *h* of my possessions
Jn 6: 19 rowed three or three and a *h* miles,
Ac 18: 11 So Paul stayed for a year and a *h,*
Jas 5: 17 on the land for three and a *h* years.
Rev 8: 1 in heaven for about *h* an hour.
11: 9 a *h* days men from every people,
11: 11 and a *h* days a breath of life
12: 14 *h* a time, out of the serpent's reach.

HALF-DISTRICT (DISTRICT)

Ne 3: 9 ruler of a *h* of Jerusalem, repaired
3: 12 ruler of a *h* of Jerusalem,
3: 16 ruler of a *h* of Beth Zur,
3: 18 ruler of the other *h* of Keilah.

HALF-TRIBE (TRIBE)

Nu 32: 33 and the *h* of Manasseh son
34: 14 *h* of Manasseh have received their
Dt 29: 8 the Gadites and the *h* of Manasseh.
Jos 1: 12 the Gadites and the *h* of Manasseh,
4: 12 the *h* of Manasseh crossed over,
12: 6 and the *h* of Manasseh
13: 29 given to the *h* of Manasseh,
18: 7 the *h* of Manasseh have already
21: 6 and the *h* of Manasseh in Bashan.
21: 27 from the *h* of Manasseh,
22: 1 the Gadites and the *h* of Manasseh
22: 7 (To the *h* of Manasseh
22: 9 *h* of Manasseh left the Israelites
22: 10 *h* of Manasseh built an imposing
22: 13 Gad and the *h* of Manasseh.
22: 15 Gad and the *h* of Manasseh—
22: 21 and the *h* of Manasseh replied

1Ch 5: 18 and the *h* of Manasseh had 44,760
5: 23 The people of the *h*
5: 26 and the *h* of Manasseh into exile.
6: 71 From the clan of the *h*
12: 37 Gad and the *h* of Manasseh,
26: 32 and the *h* of Manasseh
27: 21 over the *h* of Manasseh in Gilead:

HALFWAY (HALF)

Ex 27: 5 the altar so that it is *h* up the altar.
38: 4 to be under its ledge, *h* up the altar.
Jn 7: 14 until *h* through the Feast did Jesus

HALHUL

Jos 15: 58 *H,* Beth Zur, Gedor, Maarath,

HALI

Jos 19: 25 Helkath, *H,* Beten, Acshaph,

HALL

1Sa 9: 22 Saul and his servant into the *h*
1Ki 6: 3 portico at the front of the main *h*
6: 5 Against the walls of the main *h*
6: 17 The main *h* in front
6: 33 for the entrance to the main *h.*
7: 7 He built the throne hall, the *H*
7: 7 He built the throne *h,* the Hall
7: 8 also made a palace like this *h*
7: 50 doors of the main *h* of the temple.
2Ch 3: 5 He paneled the main *h* with pine
3: 13 on their feet, facing the main *h.*
4: 22 and the doors of the main *h.*
Est 5: 1 in front of the king's *h.*
5: 1 sitting on his royal throne in the *h,*
7: 8 the palace garden to the banquet *h,*
SS 2: 4 He has taken me to the banquet *h,*
Da 5: 10 his nobles, came into the banquet *h*
Mt 22: 10 and the wedding *h* was filled
Ac 19: 9 daily in the lecture *h* of Tyrannus.

HALLELUJAH

Rev 19: 1 great multitude in heaven shouting: *"H!*
19: 3 And again they shouted: *"H!*
19: 4 And they cried: "Amen, *H!"*
19: 6 loud peals of thunder, shouting: *"H!*

HALLOHESH

Ne 3: 12 Shallum son of *H,* ruler
10: 24 Hananiah, Hasshub, *H,* Pilha,

HALLOWED (HOLY)

Mt 6: 9 *h* be your name,
Lk 11: 2 *h* be your name,

HALT (HALTED)

2Sa 2: 28 and all the men came to a *h;*
20: 12 all the troops came to a *h* there.
Job 38: 11 here is where your proud waves *h'?*
Isa 10: 32 This day they will *h* at Nob;

HALTED (HALT)

2Sa 15: 17 and they *h* at a place some distance
18: 16 pursuing Israel, for Joab *h* them.

HALTER

Pr 26: 3 for the horse, a *h* for the donkey,

HALVES (HALF)

Ge 15: 10 arranged the *h* opposite each other;
SS 4: 3 are like the *h* of a pomegranate.
6: 7 are like the *h* of a pomegranate.

HAM (HAMITES)

Ge 5: 32 he became the father of Shem, *H*
6: 10 Noah had three sons: Shem, *H*
7: 13 and his sons, Shem, *H* and Japheth,
9: 18 out of the ark were Shem, *H*
9: 18 *(H* was the father of Canaan.)
9: 22 *H,* the father of Canaan, saw his
10: 1 *H* and Japheth, Noah's sons,
10: 6 The sons of *H:* Cush, Mizraim,
10: 20 the descendants of *H* by their clans
14: 5 the Zuzites in *H,*
1Ch 1: 4 The sons of Noah: Shem, *H*
1: 8 The sons of *H:* Cush, Mizraim,
Ps 78: 51 of manhood in the tents of *H.*
105: 23 an alien in the land of *H.*
105: 27 his wonders in the land of *H.*
106: 22 miracles in the land of *H*

HAMAN (HAMAN'S)

Est 3: 1 King Xerxes honored *H* son
3: 2 knelt down and paid honor to *H,*
3: 4 Therefore they told *H* about it
3: 5 When *H* saw that Mordecai would
3: 6 Instead *H* looked for a way
3: 7 in the presence of *H* to select a day
3: 8 Then *H* said to King Xerxes,
3: 10 gave it to *H* son of Hammedatha,
3: 11 the money," the king said to *H,*
3: 15 The king and *H* sat down to drink,
4: 7 of money *H* had promised to pay
5: 4 "let the king, together with *H,*
5: 5 *H* went to the banquet Esther had
5: 5 "Bring *H* at once," the king said,
5: 8 and *H* come tomorrow
5: 9 *H* went out that day happy
5: 10 *H* restrained himself and went
5: 11 *H* boasted to them about his vast
5: 12 "And that's not all," *H* added.
5: 14 This suggestion delighted *H,*
6: 4 *H* had just entered the outer court
6: 5 *"H* is standing in the court."
6: 6 Now *H* thought to himself,
6: 6 When *H* entered, the king asked
6: 10 at once," the king commanded *H.*
6: 11 So *H* got the robe and the horse.
6: 12 But *H* rushed home, with his head
6: 14 and hurried *H* away to the banquet
7: 1 *H* went to dine with Queen Esther,
7: 6 and enemy is this vile *H."*
7: 6 *H* was terrified before the king
7: 7 But *H,* realizing that the king had
7: 8 *H* was falling on the couch where
7: 10 they hanged *H* on the gallows he
8: 1 gave Queen Esther the estate of *H,*
8: 2 which he had reclaimed from *H,*
8: 3 to the evil plan of *H* the Agagite,
8: 5 the dispatches that *H* son
8: 7 "Because *H* attacked the Jews,
9: 10 sons of *H* son of Hammedatha,
9: 12 and the ten sons of *H* in the citadel
9: 14 and they hanged the ten sons of *H.*
9: 24 For *H* son of Hammedatha,
9: 25 that the evil scheme *H* had devised

HAMAN'S (HAMAN)

Est 3: 12 of each people all *H* orders
7: 8 king's mouth, they covered *H* face.
7: 9 feet high stands by *H* house.
8: 2 appointed him over *H* estate.
9: 13 also, and let *H* ten sons be hanged

HAMATH (HAMATHITES)

2Sa 8: 9 king of *H* heard that David had
2Ki 14: 28 for Israel both Damascus and *H,*
17: 24 *H* and Sepharvaim and settled
17: 30 and the men from *H* made Ashima;
18: 34 Where are the gods of *H*
19: 13 the king of *H,* the king of Arpad,
23: 33 at Riblah in the land of *H* so
25: 21 of *H,* the king had them executed.
1Ch 18: 3 king of Zobah, as far as *H,*
18: 9 king of *H* heard that David had
2Ch 8: 4 all the store cities he had built in *H.*
Isa 10: 9 Is not *H* like Arpad,
11: 11 from *H* and from the islands
36: 19 Where are the gods of *H*
37: 13 the king of *H,* the king of Arpad,
Jer 39: 5 Babylon at Riblah in the land of *H,*
49: 23 *"H* and Arpad are dismayed,
52: 9 Babylon at Riblah in the land of *H,*
52: 27 of *H,* the king had them executed.
Eze 47: 16 border between Damascus and *H),*
47: 17 with the border of *H* to the north.
48: 1 of Damascus next to *H* will be part
Am 6: 2 go from there to great *H,*
Zec 9: 2 upon *H* too, which borders on it,

HAMATH ZOBAH

2Ch 8: 3 Solomon then went to *H* and

HAMATHITES (HAMATH)

Ge 10: 18 Arvadites, Zemarites and *H.*
1Ch 1: 16 Arvadites, Zemarites and *H.*

HAMITES (HAM)

1Ch 4: 40 Some *H* had lived there formerly.
4: 41 They attacked the *H*

HAMMATH

Jos 19: 35 Zer, *H,* Rakkath, Kinnereth,
1Ch 2: 55 are the Kenites who came from *H,*

HAMMEDATHA

Est 3: 1 Xerxes honored Haman son of *H,*
3: 10 and gave it to Haman son of *H,*
8: 5 dispatches that Haman son of *H,*
9: 10 the ten sons of Haman son of *H,*
9: 24 For Haman son of *H,* the Agagite,

HAMMER (HAMMERED HAMMERS)

Ex 25: 31 of pure gold and *h* it out,
Nu 16: 38 *H* the censers into sheets
Jdg 4: 21 picked up a tent peg and a *h*
5: 26 her right hand for the workman's *h*
1Ki 6: 7 at the quarry were used, and no *h,*
Isa 41: 7 and he who smooths with the *h*
Jer 10: 4 they fasten it with *h* and nails
23: 29 like a *h* that breaks a rock in pieces
50: 23 is the *h* of the whole earth!

HAMMERED (HAMMER)

Ex 25: 18 out of *h* gold at the ends
25: 36 piece with the lampstand, *h* out
37: 7 out of *h* gold at the ends
37: 17 of pure gold and *h* it out,
37: 22 piece with the lampstand, *h* out
39: 3 They *h* out thin sheets of gold
Nu 8: 4 It was made of *h* gold—
10: 2 "Make two trumpets of *h* silver,
16: 39 and he had them *h* out
1Ki 6: 35 overlaid them with gold *h* evenly
7: 29 and bulls were wreaths of *h* work.
10: 16 hundred large shields of *h* gold;
10: 17 hundred small shields of *h* gold,
2Ch 9: 15 hundred large shields of *h* gold;
9: 15 six hundred bekas of *h* gold went
9: 16 hundred small shields of *h* gold,
Jer 10: 9 *H* silver is brought from Tarshish

HAMMERS (HAMMER)

Isa 44: 12 he shapes an idol with *h,*

HAMMOLEKETH

1Ch 7: 18 His sister *H* gave birth to Ishhod,

HAMMON

Jos 19: 28 It went to Abdon, Rehob, *H*
1Ch 6: 76 *H* and Kiriathaim, together

HAMMOTH DOR

Jos 21: 32 *H* and Kartan, together with

HAMMUEL

1Ch 4: 26 descendants of Mishma: *H* his son,

HAMON GOG

Eze 39: 11 So it will be called the Valley of *H.*
39: 15 it in the Valley of *H.*

HAMONAH

Eze 39: 16 Also a town called *H* will be there.)

HAMOR

Ge 33: 19 he bought from the sons of *H,*
34: 2 Shechem son of *H* the Hivite,
34: 4 And Shechem said to his father *H,*
34: 6 Then Shechem's father *H* went out
34: 8 *H* said to them, "My son Shechem
34: 13 to Shechem and his father *H.*
34: 18 Their proposal seemed good to *H*
34: 20 So *H* and his son Shechem went
34: 24 out of the city gate agreed with *H*
34: 26 They put *H* and his son Shechem
Jos 24: 32 pieces of silver from the sons of *H,*
Jdg 9: 28 the men of *H,* Shechem's father!
Ac 7: 16 from the sons of *H* at Shechem

HAMPERED

Pr 4: 12 you walk, your steps will not be *h;*

HAMSTRING (HAMSTRUNG)

Jos 11: 6 You are to *h* their horses

HAMSTRUNG (HAMSTRING)

Ge 49: 6 and *h* oxen as they pleased.
Jos 11: 9 He *h* their horses and burned their
2Sa 8: 4 He *h* all but a hundred
1Ch 18: 4 He *h* all but a hundred

HAMUL (HAMULITE)

Ge 46: 12 The sons of Perez: Hezron and *H*.
Nu 26: 21 through *H*, the Hamulite clan.
1Ch 2: 5 The sons of Perez: Hezron and *H*.

HAMULITE (HAMUL)

Nu 26: 21 through Hamul, the *H* clan.

HAMUTAL

2Ki 23: 31 His mother's name was *H* daughter
24: 18 His mother's name was *H* daughter
Jer 52: 1 His mother's name was *H* daughter

HANAMEL

Jer 32: 7 *H* son of Shallum your uncle is
32: 8 my cousin *H* came to me
32: 9 at Anathoth from my cousin *H*
32: 12 in the presence of my cousin *H*

HANAN

1Ch 8: 23 Abdon, Zicri, *H*, Hananiah, Elam,
8: 38 Ishmael, Sheariah, Obadiah and *H*.
9: 44 Ishmael, Sheariah, Obadiah and *H*.
11: 43 thirty with him, *H* son of Maacah,
Ezr 2: 46 Hagab, Shalmai, *H*, Giddel, Gahar,
Ne 7: 49 Hagaba, Shalmai, *H*, Giddel,
8: 7 Azariah, Jozabad, *H* and Pelaiah—
10: 10 Kelita, Pelaiah, *H*, Mica, Rehob,
10: 22 Jaddua, Pelatiah, *H*, Anaiah,
10: 26 Maaseiah, Ahiah, *H*, Anan,
13: 13 and made *H* son of Zaccur,
Jer 35: 4 the room of the sons of *H* son

HANANEL

Ne 3: 1 and as far as the Tower of *H*.
12: 39 the Tower of *H* and the Tower
Jer 31: 38 me from the Tower of *H*
Zec 14: 10 and from the Tower of *H*

HANANI

1Ki 16: 1 to Jehu son of *H* against Baasha:
16: 7 through the prophet Jehu son of *H*
1Ch 25: 4 and Jerimoth; Hananiah, *H*,
25: 25 12 the eighteenth to *H*, his sons
2Ch 16: 7 At that time *H* the seer came
19: 2 Jehu the seer, the son of *H*,
20: 34 in the annals of Jehu son of *H*,
Ezr 10: 20 From the descendants of Immer: *H*
Ne 1: 2 while I was in the citadel of Susa, *H*
7: 2 charge of Jerusalem my brother *H*,
12: 36 Maai, Nethanel, Judah and *H*—

HANANIAH

1Ch 3: 19 of Zerubbabel: Meshullam and *H*.
3: 21 The descendants of *H*: Pelatiah
8: 24 Hanan, *H*, Elam, Anthothijah,
25: 4 Shubael and Jerimoth; *H*, Hanani,
25: 23 12 the sixteenth to *H*, his sons
2Ch 26: 11 officer under the direction of *H*,
Ezr 10: 28 Jehohanan, *H*, Zabbai and Athlai.
Ne 3: 8 and *H*, one of the perfume-makers,
3: 30 Next to him, *H* son of Shelemiah,
7: 2 along with *H* the commander
10: 23 Anaiah, Hoshea, *H*, Hasshub,
12: 12 of Jeremiah's, *H*; of Ezra's,
12: 41 and *H* with their trumpets—
Jer 28: 1 the prophet *H* son of Azzur,
28: 5 to the prophet *H* before the priests
28: 10 Then the prophet *H* took the yoke
28: 12 after the prophet *H* had broken
28: 13 and tell *H*, 'This is what the Lord
28: 15 Jeremiah said to *H* the prophet,
28: 15 *H!* The Lord has not sent you,
28: 17 that same year, *H* the prophet died.
36: 12 son of *H*, and all the other officials.
37: 13 the son of *H*, arrested him and said,
Da 1: 6 Daniel, *H*, Mishael and Azariah.
1: 7 to *H*, Shadrach; to Mishael,
1: 11 *H*, Mishael and Azariah, "Please
Da 1: 19 he found none equal to Daniel, *H*,
2: 17 the matter to his friends *H*,

HAND (HANDBREADTH HANDED HANDFUL HANDFULS HANDING HANDS LEFT-HANDED OPENHANDED RIGHT-HANDED)

Ge 3: 22 not be allowed to reach out his *h*
4: 11 your brother's blood from your *h*.
8: 9 He reached out his *h* and took
14: 20 your enemies into your *h*."
14: 22 "I have raised my *h* to the Lord,
16: 12 and everyone's *h* against him,
16: 12 his *h* will be against everyone
19: 16 the men grasped his *h*
21: 18 the boy up and take him by the *h*,
21: 30 these seven lambs from my *h*
22: 10 Then he reached out his *h*
22: 12 Do not lay a *h* on the boy," he said.
24: 2 "Put your *h* under my thigh.
24: 9 So the servant put his *h*
25: 26 with his *h* grasping Esau's heel;
32: 11 from the *h* of my brother Esau,
37: 22 here in the desert, but don't lay a *h*
38: 18 the staff in your *h*," she answered.
38: 28 one of them put out his *h*;
38: 29 But when he drew back his *h*,
39: 12 But he left his cloak in her *h*
39: 13 that he had left his cloak in her *h*
40: 11 Pharaoh's cup was in my *h*,
40: 11 cup and put the cup in his *h*."
40: 13 you will put Pharaoh's cup in his *h*,
40: 21 again put the cup into Pharaoh's *h*,
41: 44 without your word no one will lift *h*
46: 4 Joseph's own *h* will close your eyes
47: 29 put your *h* under my thigh
48: 13 on his left toward Israel's right *h*,
48: 13 on his right toward Israel's left *h*
48: 14 But Israel reached out his right *h*
48: 14 put his left *h* on Manasseh's head,
48: 17 hold of his father's *h* to move it
48: 17 saw his father placing his right *h*
48: 18 put your right *h* on his head."
49: 8 your *h* will be on the neck
49: 24 because of the *h* of the Mighty One
Ex 3: 8 them from the *h* of the Egyptians
3: 19 unless a mighty *h* compels him.
3: 20 So I will stretch out my *h*
4: 2 What is that in your *h*?" "A staff,"
4: 4 it turned back into a staff in his *h*.
4: 4 "Reach out your *h* and take it
4: 6 So Moses put his *h* into his cloak,
4: 6 "Put your *h* inside your cloak."
4: 7 Moses put his *h* back into his cloak,
4: 17 But take this staff in your *h*
4: 20 he took the staff of God in his *h*.
5: 21 have put a sword in their *h* to kill us
6: 1 of my mighty *h* he will drive them
6: 1 of my mighty *h* he will let them go;
6: 8 with uplifted *h* to give to Abraham,
7: 4 Then I will lay my *h* on Egypt
7: 5 the Lord when I stretch out my *h*
7: 15 in your *h* the staff that was changed
7: 17 is in my *h* I will strike the water
7: 19 stretch out your *h* over the waters
8: 5 "Stretch out your *h* with your staff
8: 6 So Aaron stretched out his *h*
8: 17 when Aaron stretched out his *h*
9: 3 *h* of the Lord will bring a terrible
9: 15 I could have stretched out my *h*
9: 22 "Stretch out your *h* toward the sky
10: 12 "Stretch out your *h* over Egypt
10: 21 "Stretch out your *h* toward the sky
10: 22 So Moses stretched out his *h*
11: 5 is at her *h* mill, and all the firstborn
12: 11 your feet and your staff in your *h*.
13: 3 out of it with a mighty *h*.
13: 9 be for you like a sign on your *h*
13: 9 out of Egypt with his mighty *h*.
13: 14 'With a mighty *h* the Lord
13: 16 And it will be like a sign on your *h*
13: 16 out of Egypt with his mighty *h*."
14: 16 and stretch out your *h* over the sea
14: 21 Then Moses stretched out his *h*
14: 26 "Stretch out your *h* over the sea
14: 27 Moses stretched out his *h*
15: 6 Your right *h*, O Lord,
15: 6 "Your right *h*, O Lord,
Ex 15: 9 and my *h* will destroy them.'
15: 12 You stretched out your right *h*
15: 20 took a tambourine in her *h*,
16: 3 died by the Lord's *h* in Egypt!
17: 5 and take in your *h* the staff
18: 9 them from the *h* of the Egyptians.
18: 10 people from the *h* of the Egyptians.
18: 10 you from the *h* of the Egyptians
19: 13 not a *h* is to be laid on him.
21: 24 tooth for tooth, *h* for *h*, foot
23: 31 I will *h* over to you the people who
24: 11 But God did not raise his *h*
32: 11 with great power and a mighty *h*?
33: 22 and cover you with my *h*
33: 23 Then I will remove my *h*
Lev 1: 4 He is to lay his *h* on the head
3: 2 He is to lay his *h* on the head
3: 8 He is to lay his *h* on the head
3: 13 He is to lay his *h* on its head
4: 4 He is to lay his *h* on its head
4: 24 He is to lay his *h* on the goat's head
4: 29 He is to lay his *h* on the head
4: 33 He is to lay his *h* on its head
8: 23 on the thumb of his right *h*
14: 14 on the thumb of his right *h*
14: 15 pour it in the palm of his own left *h*,
14: 17 on the thumb of his right *h*
14: 25 on the thumb of his right *h*
14: 26 oil into the palm of his own left *h*,
14: 28 on the thumb of his right *h*
21: 19 no man with a crippled foot or *h*,
22: 25 animals from the *h* of a foreigner
Nu 14: 30 with uplifted *h* to make your home,
22: 23 road with a drawn sword in his *h*,
22: 29 in my *h*, I would kill you right now
25: 7 in his *h* and followed the Israelite
27: 18 whom is the spirit, and lay your *h*
35: 17 a stone in his *h* that could kill,
35: 18 object in his *h* that could kill,
Dt 2: 15 The Lord's *h* was against them
2: 24 into your *h* Sihon the Amorite,
3: 24 your greatness and your strong *h*.
4: 34 by a mighty *h* and an outstretched
5: 15 out of there with a mighty *h*
6: 21 out of Egypt with a mighty *h*.
7: 8 he brought you out with a mighty *h*
7: 19 the mighty *h* and outstretched arm,
7: 24 He will give their kings into your *h*,
9: 26 out of Egypt with a mighty *h*.
11: 2 his mighty *h*, his outstretched arm;
12: 7 in everything you have put your *h*
12: 18 in everything you put your *h* to.
13: 9 Your *h* must be the first
15: 10 in everything you put your *h* to.
15: 18 as much as that of a hired *h*.
19: 12 *h* him over to the avenger of blood
19: 21 tooth for tooth, *h* for *h*, foot for foot.
20: 13 your God delivers it into your *h*,
23: 15 do not *h* him over to his master.
23: 20 you in everything you put your *h*
25: 12 parts, you shall cut off her *h*.
26: 8 out of Egypt with a mighty *h*
28: 8 on everything you put your *h* to.
28: 20 in everything you put your *h* to,
28: 32 day after day, powerless to lift a *h*.
32: 27 and say, 'Our *h* has triumphed;
32: 39 and no one can deliver from my *h*.
32: 40 I lift my *h* to heaven and declare:
32: 41 and my *h* grasps it in judgment,
33: 3 all the holy ones are in your *h*.
Jos 2: 19 be on our head if a *h* is laid on him.
4: 24 of the earth might know that the *h*
5: 13 of him with a drawn sword in his *h*.
8: 7 your God will give it into your *h*.
8: 18 Ai the javelin that is in your *h*,
8: 18 into your *h* I will deliver the city."
8: 26 not draw back the *h* that held out
10: 8 I have given them into your *h*.
10: 19 God has given them into your *h*."
10: 30 and its king into Israel's *h*.
11: 6 by this time tomorrow I will *h* all
11: 8 them into the *h* of Israel.
22: 31 the Israelites from the Lord's *h*."
24: 10 and I delivered you out of his *h*.
Jdg 2: 15 the *h* of the Lord was
3: 21 Ehud reached with his left *h*,
4: 9 for the Lord will *h* Sisera
4: 24 the *h* of the Israelites grew stronger

Jdg 5: 26 Her *h* reached for the tent peg,
5: 26 her right *h* for the workman's
6: 9 from the *h* of all your oppressors.
6: 13 and put us into the *h* of Midian.''
6: 14 and save Israel out of Midian's *h*.
6: 21 the tip of the staff that was in his *h*,
6: 36 ''If you will save Israel by my *h*
6: 37 that you will save Israel by my *h*,
8: 7 Zebah and Zalmunna into my *h*,
8: 22 out of the *h* of Midian.''
9: 17 to rescue you from the *h* of Midian
9: 33 do whatever your *h* finds to do.''
15: 12 and *h* you over to the Philistines.''
15: 13 ''We will only tie you up and *h* you
16: 26 said to the servant who held his *h*,
16: 29 and his left *h* on the other,
16: 29 his right *h* on the one and his left
Ru 1: 13 the LORD's *h* has gone out
1Sa 2: 13 with a three-pronged fork in his *h*.
2: 16 would then answer, ''No, *h* it
4: 3 save us from the *h* of our enemies.''
4: 8 us from the *h* of these mighty gods?
5: 6 The LORD's *h* was heavy
5: 7 because his *h* is heavy upon us
5: 9 the LORD's *h* was against that city
5: 11 God's *h* was very heavy upon it.
6: 3 will know why his *h* has not been
6: 5 Perhaps he will lift his *h* from you
6: 9 that it was not his *h* that struck us
7: 3 out of the *h* of the Philistines.''
7: 8 us from the *h* of the Philistines.''
7: 13 the *h* of the LORD was
9: 16 from the *h* of the Philistines.
10: 7 do whatever your *h* finds to do,
12: 3 From whose *h* have I accepted
12: 4 anything from anyone's *h*.''
12: 5 have not found anything in my *h*.''
12: 9 so he sold them into the *h* of Sisera,
12: 15 against his commands, his *h* will be
13: 22 had a sword or spear in his *h*;
14: 12 them into the *h* of Israel.''
14: 19 to the priest, ''Withdraw your *h*.''
14: 26 yet no one put his *h* to his mouth,
14: 27 He raised his *h* to his mouth,
14: 27 the end of the staff that was in his *h*
14: 37 Will you give them into Israel's *h*
17: 37 me from the *h* of this Philistine.''
17: 40 Then he took his staff in his *h*,
17: 40 in his *h*, approached the Philistine.
17: 46 This day the LORD will *h* you
17: 50 without a sword in his *h* he struck
18: 10 Saul had a spear in his *h*
18: 17 ''I will not raise a *h* against him.
18: 21 so that the *h* of the Philistines may
19: 9 in his house with his spear in his *h*.
20: 8 Why *h* me over to your father?''
21: 3 have on *h*? Give me five loaves
21: 4 have any ordinary bread on *h*;
22: 6 spear in *h*, was seated
22: 17 to raise a *h* to strike the priests
23: 4 to give the Philistines into your *h*.''
23: 17 ''My father Saul will not lay a *h*
24: 6 the LORD's anointed, or lift my *h*
24: 10 'I will not lift my *h*
24: 11 at this piece of your robe in my *h*!
24: 12 but my *h* will not touch you.
24: 13 so my *h* will not touch you.
24: 15 me by delivering me from your *h*.''
25: 35 from her *h* what she had brought
26: 9 Who can lay a *h* on the LORD's
26: 11 LORD forbid that I should lay a *h*
26: 23 but I would not lay a *h*
27: 1 and I will slip out of his *h*.''
27: 1 days I will be destroyed by the *h*
28: 19 The LORD will *h* over both Israel
28: 19 also *h* over the army of Israel
30: 15 or *h* me over to my master,
2Sa 1: 14 afraid to lift your *h* to destroy
2: 14 and fight *h* to *h* in front of us.''
3: 18 Israel from the *h* of the Philistines
3: 18 from the *h* of all their enemies.' ''
4: 11 now demand his blood from your *h*
5: 19 Will you *h* them over to me?''
5: 19 for I will surely *h* the Philistines
12: 7 I delivered you from the *h* of Saul.
13: 5 and then eat it from her *h*.' ''
13: 6 in my sight, so I may eat from her *h*
13: 10 so I may eat from your *h*.''
2Sa 13: 19 She put her *h* on her head
14: 7 '*H* over the one who struck his
14: 16 to deliver his servant from the *h*
14: 19 ''Isn't the *h* of Joab with you
15: 5 Absalom would reach out his *h*,
18: 12 I would not lift my *h*
18: 14 So he took three javelins in his *h*
18: 19 him from the *h* of his enemies.''
19: 9 us from the *h* of our enemies;
19: 9 us from the *h* of the Philistines.
20: 9 beard with his right *h* to kiss him.
20: 10 against the dagger in Joab's *h*,
20: 21 *H* over this one man, and I'll
20: 21 has lifted up his *h* against the king,
21: 20 man with six fingers on each *h*
22: 1 and from the *h* of Saul.
22: 1 him from the *h* of all his enemies
23: 6 which are not gathered with the *h*.
23: 10 the Philistines till his *h* grew tired
23: 21 the Egyptian had a spear in his *h*,
23: 21 the spear from the Egyptian's *h*
24: 16 When the angel stretched out his *h*
24: 16 ''Enough! Withdraw your *h*.''
24: 17 Let your *h* fall upon me
1Ki 2: 19 and she sat down at his right *h*.
8: 15 with his own *h* has fulfilled what he
8: 24 with your *h* you have fulfilled it—
8: 42 and your mighty *h* and your
11: 12 I will tear it out of the *h* of your son
11: 31 the kingdom out of Solomon's *h*
11: 34 kingdom out of Solomon's *h*;
13: 4 But the *h* he stretched out
13: 4 he stretched out his *h*
13: 6 and the king's *h* was restored
13: 6 for me that my *h* may be restored.''
18: 44 as a man's *h* is rising from the sea.''
20: 13 I will give it into your *h* today,
22: 6 it into the king's *h*.''
22: 12 it into the king's *h*.''
22: 15 it into the king's *h*.''
2Ki 3: 10 only to *h* us over to Moab?''
3: 13 together to *h* us over to Moab.''
3: 15 the *h* of the LORD came
3: 18 he will also *h* Moab over to you.
4: 29 take my staff in your *h* and run.
5: 11 wave his *h* over the spot
6: 7 Then the man reached out his *h*
10: 15 said Jehu, ''give me your *h*.''
11: 8 each man with his weapon in his *h*.
11: 11 each with his weapon in his *h*,
12: 7 *h* it over for repairing the temple.''
14: 27 them by the *h* of Jeroboam son
16: 7 and save me out of the *h* of the king
17: 39 from the *h* of all your enemies.''
18: 21 which pierces a man's *h*
18: 29 He cannot deliver you from my *h*.
18: 30 into the *h* of the king of Assyria.'
18: 33 from the *h* of the king of Assyria?
18: 34 they rescued Samaria from my *h*?
18: 35 deliver Jerusalem from my *h*?''
19: 19 our God, deliver us from his *h*,
20: 6 and this city from the *h* of the king
21: 14 and *h* them over to their enemies.
1Ch 4: 10 enlarge my territory! Let your *h* be
6: 15 exile by the *h* of Nebuchadnezzar.
6: 39 served at his right *h*: Asaph son
6: 44 at his left *h*: Ethan son of Kishi,
11: 23 a spear like a weaver's rod in his *h*,
11: 23 the spear from the Egyptian's *h*
13: 9 Uzzah reached out his *h*
13: 10 because he had put his *h* on the ark.
14: 10 Will you *h* them over to me?''
14: 10 ''Go, I will *h* them over to you.''
14: 11 out against my enemies by my *h*.''
20: 6 man with six fingers on each *h*
21: 15 ''Enough! Withdraw your *h*.''
21: 16 in his *h* extended over Jerusalem.
21: 17 let your *h* fall upon me
28: 19 the *h* of the LORD was upon me,
29: 14 you only what comes from your *h*.
29: 16 it comes from your *h*, and all
2Ch 6: 15 with your *h* you have fulfilled it—
6: 32 and your mighty *h* and your
16: 7 of Aram has escaped from your *h*.
16: 8 he delivered them into your *h*.
18: 5 for God will give it into the king's *h*
18: 11 it into the king's *h*.''
18: 14 for they will be given into your *h*.''
2Ch 20: 6 Power and might are in your *h*,
23: 7 each man with his weapons in his *h*
23: 10 each with his weapon in his *h*,
25: 15 their own people from your *h*?''
25: 20 so worked that he might *h* them
26: 19 in his *h* ready to burn incense,
28: 9 Judah, he gave them into your *h*.
30: 6 escaped from the *h* of the kings
30: 12 Also in Judah the *h* of God was
32: 11 from the *h* of the king of Assyria,'
32: 13 to deliver their land from my *h*?
32: 14 your god deliver you from my *h*?
32: 15 from my *h* or the *h* of my fathers.
32: 15 your god deliver you from my *h*!''
32: 17 not rescue his people from my *h*.''
32: 17 not rescue their people from my *h*,
32: 22 and from the *h* of all others.
32: 22 from the *h* of Sennacherib king
Ezr 6: 12 or people who lifts a *h*
7: 6 for the *h* of the LORD his God was
7: 9 for the good *h* of his God was
7: 14 of your God, which is in your *h*.
7: 28 Because the *h* of the LORD my
8: 18 Because the good *h* of our God was
8: 22 ''The good *h* of our God is
8: 31 The *h* of our God was on us,
9: 7 and humiliation at the *h*
Ne 1: 10 great strength and your mighty *h*.
2: 8 the gracious *h* of my God was
2: 18 also told them about the gracious *h*
4: 17 materials did their work with one *h*
6: 5 and in his *h* was an unsealed letter
9: 15 sworn with uplifted *h* to give them.
9: 27 them from the *h* of their enemies.
9: 28 them to the *h* of their enemies
Est 5: 2 the gold scepter that was in his *h*.
9: 1 and the Jews got the upper *h*
Job 1: 11 But stretch out your *h*
2: 5 But stretch out your *h*
6: 9 to let loose his *h* and cut me off!
6: 23 deliver me from the *h* of the enemy
9: 33 to lay his *h* upon us both,
10: 7 no one can rescue me from your *h*?
11: 14 put away the sin that is in your *h*
12: 9 that the *h* of the LORD has done
12: 10 In his *h* is the life of every creature
13: 21 Withdraw your *h* far from me,
15: 23 of darkness is at *h*.
19: 21 for the *h* of God has struck me.
21: 5 clap your *h* over your mouth.
23: 2 his *h* is heavy in spite
26: 13 his *h* pierced the gliding serpent.
28: 9 Man's *h* assaults the flinty rock
29: 20 the bow ever new in my *h*.'
30: 21 of your *h* you attack me.
30: 24 ''Surely no one lays a *h*
31: 21 if I have raised my *h*
31: 27 my *h* offered them a kiss of homage
33: 7 should my *h* be heavy upon you.
34: 20 removed without human *h*.
35: 7 what does he receive from your *h*?
40: 4 I put my *h* over my mouth.
40: 14 that your own right *h* can save you.
41: 8 If you lay a *h* on him,
Ps 10: 12 LORD! Lift up your *h*, O God.
10: 14 you consider it to take it in *h*.
16: 8 Because he is at my right *h*,
16: 11 eternal pleasures at your right *h*.
17: 7 you who save by your right *h*
17: 14 by your *h* save me from such men,
18: 35 and your right *h* sustains me;
20: 6 with the saving power of his right *h*
21: 8 Your *h* will lay hold
21: 8 your right *h* will seize your foes.
32: 4 your *h* was heavy upon me;
36: 11 the *h* of the wicked drive me away.
37: 24 the LORD upholds him with his *h*.
38: 2 your *h* has come down upon me.
39: 10 by the blow of your *h*.
44: 2 With your *h* you drove out
44: 3 it was your right *h*, your arm,
45: 4 let your right *h* display awesome
45: 9 at your right *h* is the royal bride
48: 10 your right *h* is filled
60: 5 help us with your right *h*,
63: 8 your right *h* upholds me.
71: 4 from the *h* of the wicked,
73: 23 you hold me by my right *h*.

Ps 74:11 you hold back your *h*, your right *h*?
74:19 Do not *h* over the life of your dove
75: 8 In the *h* of the LORD is a cup
77:10 of the right *h* of the Most High."
77:20 by the *h* of Moses and Aaron
78:54 hill country his right *h* had taken.
80:15 the root your right *h* has planted,
80:17 Let your *h* rest on the man
80:17 on the man at your right *h*,
81:14 and turn my *h* against their foes!
82: 4 from the *h* of the wicked.
89:13 *h* is strong, your right *h*
89:21 My *h* will sustain him;
89:25 I will set his *h* over the sea,
89:25 his right *h* over the rivers.
89:42 You have exalted the right *h*
91: 7 ten thousand at your right *h*,
95: 4 In his *h* are the depths of the earth,
97:10 them from the *h* of the wicked.
98: 1 his right *h* and his holy arm
104: 28 when you open your *h*,
106: 10 from the *h* of the enemy he
106: 10 from the *h* of the foe;
106: 26 So he swore to them with uplifted *h*
107: 2 redeemed from the *h* of the foe,
108: 6 help us with your right *h*,
109: 6 let an accuser stand at his right *h*.
109: 27 Let them know that it is your *h*,
109: 31 at the right *h* of the needy one,
110: 1 "Sit at my right *h*
110: 5 The Lord is at your right *h*;
118: 15 LORD's right *h* has done mighty
118: 16 The LORD's right *h* is lifted high;
118: 16 LORD's right *h* has done mighty
118: 27 With boughs in *h*, join
119:173 May your *h* be ready to help me,
121: 5 is your shade at your right *h*;
123: 2 look to the *h* of her mistress,
123: 2 look to the *h* of their master,
136: 12 with a mighty *h* and outstretched
137: 5 may my right *h* forget its skill.
138: 7 with your right *h* you save me.
138: 7 you stretch out your *h*
139: 5 you have laid your *h* upon me.
139: 10 even there your *h* will guide me,
139: 10 your right *h* will hold me fast.
144: 7 Reach down your *h* from on high;
145: 16 You open your *h*
Pr 1:24 heed when I stretched out my *h*,
3:16 Long life is in her right *h*;
3:16 in her left *h* are riches and honor.
6: 5 from the *h* of the hunter,
17:16 Of what use is money in the *h*
19:24 The sluggard buries his *h*
21: 1 is in the *h* of the LORD;
26: 6 of a message by the *h* of a fool.
26: 9 Like a thornbush in a drunkard's *h*
26:15 The sluggard buries his *h*
27:16 or grasping oil with the *h*.
30:28 a lizard can be caught with the *h*,
30:32 clap your *h* over your mouth!
31:19 In her *h* she holds the distaff
Ecc 2:24 I see, is from the *h* of God,
2:26 and storing up wealth to *h* it
5:15 that he can carry in his *h*.
9:10 Whatever your *h* finds to do,
SS 5: 4 My lover thrust his *h*
Isa 1:25 I will turn my *h* against you;
5:25 his *h* is raised and he strikes them
5:25 his *h* is still upraised.
6: 6 flew to me with a live coal in his *h*,
8:11 to me with his strong *h* upon me,
9:12 his *h* is still upraised.
9:17 his *h* is still upraised.
9:21 his *h* is still upraised.
10: 4 his *h* is still upraised.
10: 5 in whose *h* is the club of my wrath!
10:10 As my *h* seized the kingdoms
10:13 strength of my *h* I have done this,
10:14 so my *h* reached for the wealth
11: 8 the young child put his *h*
11:11 will reach out his *h* a second time
11:15 scorching wind he will sweep his *h*
13:22 Her time is at *h*,
14:26 this is the *h* stretched out
14:27 His *h* is stretched out,
19: 4 I will *h* the Egyptians over
19:16 at the uplifted *h* that the LORD
Isa 22:21 and *h* your authority over to him.
23:11 The LORD has stretched out his *h*
25:10 The *h* of the LORD will rest
26:11 O LORD, your *h* is lifted high,
28: 4 someone sees it and takes it in his *h*
31: 3 the LORD stretches out his *h*,
33:15 keeps his *h* from accepting bribes,
34:17 his *h* distributes them by measure.
36: 6 which pierces a man's *h*
36:15 into the *h* of the king of Assyria.'
36:18 from the *h* of the king of Assyria?
36:19 they rescued Samaria from my *h*?
36:20 deliver Jerusalem from my *h*?"
37:20 our God, deliver us from his *h*,
38: 6 and this city from the *h* of the king
40: 2 received from the LORD's *h*
40:12 of his *h* marked off the heavens?
40:12 the waters in the hollow of his *h*,
41:10 you with my righteous right *h*.
41:13 who takes hold of your right *h*
41:20 that the *h* of the LORD has done
42: 6 I will take hold of your *h*.
43:13 No one can deliver out of my *h*.
44: 5 still another will write on his *h*,
44:20 "Is not this thing in my right *h* a lie
45: 1 whose right *h* I take hold of
47: 6 I gave them into your *h*,
48:13 My own *h* laid the foundations
48:13 my right *h* spread out the heavens;
49: 2 in the shadow of his *h* he hid me;
49: 4 what is due me is in the LORD's *h*,
50:11 what you shall receive from my *h*:
51:16 you with the shadow of my *h*—
51:17 drunk from the *h* of the LORD
51:18 there was none to take her by the *h*.
51:22 "See, I have taken out of your *h*
53:10 of the LORD will prosper in his *h*.
56: 1 for my salvation is close at *h*
56: 2 and keeps his *h* from doing any evil
62: 3 in the *h* of your God.
62: 3 of splendor in the LORD's *h*,
62: 8 LORD has sworn by his right *h*
63:12 power to be at Moses' right *h*,
64: 8 we are all the work of your *h*.
66: 2 Has not my *h* made all these things
66:14 the *h* of the LORD will be made
Jer 1: 9 Then the LORD reached out his *h*
6: 9 pass your *h* over the branches
6:12 when I stretch out my *h*
15:17 I sat alone because your *h* was
18: 6 you in my *h*, O house of Israel.
18: 6 "Like clay in the *h* of the potter,
18:21 *h* them over to the power
20: 4 I will *h* all Judah over to the king
20: 5 I will *h* over to their enemies all
21: 5 against you with an outstretched *h*
21: 7 I will *h* over Zedekiah king
21:12 rescue from the *h* of his oppressor
22: 3 Rescue from the *h*
22:24 were a signet ring on my right *h*,
22:25 I will *h* you over to those who seek
25:15 "Take from my *h* this cup filled
25:17 I took the cup from the LORD's *h*
25:28 refuse to take the cup from your *h*
27: 6 Now I will *h* all your countries
27: 8 until I destroy it by his *h*.
29:21 *h* them over to Nebuchadnezzar
31:11 from the *h* of those stronger
31:32 when I took them by the *h*
32: 3 I am about to *h* this city
32:21 by a mighty *h* and an outstretched
32:28 I am about to *h* this city
33:13 flocks will again pass under the *h*
34: 2 I am about to *h* this city
34:20 I will *h* over to their enemies who
34:21 "I will *h* Zedekiah king of Judah
36:14 to them with the scroll in his *h*
38:16 nor *h* you over to those who are
38:19 for the Babylonians may *h* me
38:20 "They will not *h* you over,"
43: 3 us to *h* us over to the Babylonians,
44:30 going to *h* Pharaoh Hophra king
46:26 I will *h* them over to those who
48:16 "The fall of Moab is at *h*;
48:37 every *h* is slashed
51: 7 was a gold cup in the LORD's *h*;
51:25 I will stretch out my *h* against you,
La 2: 3 He has withdrawn his right *h*
La 2: 4 his right *h* is ready.
2: 8 and did not withhold his *h*
3: 3 he has turned his *h* against me
4: 6 without a *h* turned to help her.
Eze 1: 3 There the *h* of the LORD was
2: 9 and I saw a *h* stretched out to me.
3:14 with the strong *h* of the LORD
3:22 The *h* of the LORD was
6:14 I will stretch out my *h* against them
7:17 Every *h* will go limp, and every
7:21 I will *h* it all over as plunder
8: 1 *h* of the Sovereign LORD came
8: 3 stretched out what looked like a *h*
8:11 Each had a censer in his *h*,
9: 1 each with a weapon in his *h*."
9: 2 each with a deadly weapon in his *h*.
10: 7 of the cherubim reached out his *h*
11: 9 and *h* you over to foreigners
13: 9 My *h* will be against the prophets
14: 9 I will stretch out my *h* against him
14:13 I stretch out my *h* against it to cut
16:27 So I stretched out my *h* against you
16:39 I will *h* you over to your lovers,
17:18 Because he had given his *h*
18: 8 He withholds his *h*
18:17 He withholds his *h* from sin
20: 5 With uplifted *h* I said to them,
20: 5 with uplifted *h* to the descendants
20:15 with uplifted *h* I swore to them
20:22 I withheld my *h*, and for the sake
20:23 with uplifted *h* I swore to them
20:33 I will rule over you with a mighty *h*
20:34 with a mighty *h*
20:42 sworn with uplifted *h* to give
21: 7 heart will melt and every *h* go limp;
21:11 made ready for the *h* of the slayer.
21:11 to be grasped with the *h*;
21:22 Into his right *h* will come the lot
21:31 I will *h* you over to brutal men,
23:28 I am about to *h* you
23:31 so I will put her cup into your *h*.
25: 7 I will stretch out my *h* against you
25:13 I will stretch out my *h*
25:14 vengeance on Edom by the *h*
25:16 about to stretch out my *h*
30:10 by the *h* of Nebuchadnezzar king
30:12 by the *h* of foreigners
30:22 and make the sword fall from his *h*.
30:24 and put my sword in his *h*,
30:25 into the *h* of the king of Babylon
33:22 the *h* of the LORD was upon me,
35: 3 I will stretch out my *h* against you
36: 7 with uplifted *h* that the nations
37: 1 The *h* of the LORD was upon me,
37:17 they will become one in your *h*.
37:19 and they will become one in my *h*.'
37:19 which is in Ephraim's *h*—
38:12 and turn my *h* against the resettled
39: 3 drop from your right *h*.
39: 3 strike your bow from your left *h*
39:21 and the *h* I lay upon them.
40: 1 on that very day the *h*
40: 3 and a measuring rod in his *h*.
40: 5 in the man's *h* was six long cubits,
44:12 with uplifted *h* that they must bear
47: 3 with a measuring line in his *h*,
47:14 swore with uplifted *h* to give it
Da 1: 2 king of Judah into his *h*,
3:15 able to rescue you from my *h*?"
3:17 and he will rescue us from your *h*,
4:35 No one can hold back his *h*
5: 5 The king watched the *h* as it wrote.
5: 5 the fingers of a human *h* appeared
5:23 God who holds in his *h* your life
5:24 Therefore he sent the *h* that wrote
9:15 out of Egypt with a mighty *h*
10:10 *h* touched me and set me trembling
11:41 will be delivered from his *h*.
12: 7 lifted his right *h* and his left *h*
Hos 9: 7 the days of reckoning are at *h*.
11: 8 How can I *h* you over, Israel?
Joel 2: 1 It is close at *h*—
Am 1: 8 I will turn my *h* against Ekron
5:19 and rested his *h* on the wall
7: 7 to plumb, with a plumb line in his *h*
9: 2 from there my *h* will take them.
Ob :14 nor *h* over their survivors
Jnh 4:11 people who cannot tell their right *h*

Mic 4: 10 out of the *h* of your enemies.
5: 9 Your *h* will be lifted up in triumph
Hab 2: 16 from the LORD's right *h* is coming
3: 4 rays flashed from his *h*,
Zep 1: 4 "I will stretch out my *h*
2: 13 He will stretch out his *h*
Zec 2: 1 man with a measuring line in his *h!*
2: 9 I will surely raise my *h*
4: 10 line in the *h* of Zerubbabel.
8: 4 each with cane in *h*
11: 6 "I will *h* everyone
13: 7 I will turn my *h* against the little
14: 13 Each man will seize the *h*
Mt 3: 12 His winnowing fork is in his *h*,
5: 25 and the judge may *h* you
5: 25 or he may *h* you over to the judge,
5: 30 if your right *h* causes you to sin,
6: 3 know what your right *h* is doing,
6: 3 not let your left *h* know what your
8: 3 Jesus reached out his *h*
8: 15 He touched her *h* and the fever left
9: 18 But come and put your *h* on her,
9: 25 went in and took the girl by the *h*,
10: 17 they will *h* you over to the local
12: 10 a man with a shriveled *h* was there.
12: 13 to the man, "Stretch out your *h*."
14: 31 Jesus reached out his *h*
18: 8 If your *h* or your foot causes you
22: 13 'Tie him *h* and foot, and throw him
22: 44 "Sit at my right *h*
24: 41 will be grinding with a *h* mill;
26: 15 to give me if I *h* him over to you?"
26: 16 for an opportunity to *h* him over.
26: 23 "The one who has dipped his *h*
26: 64 at the right *h* of the Mighty One
27: 29 They put a staff in his right *h*
Mk 1: 31 took her *h* and helped her up.
1: 41 Jesus reached out his *h*
3: 1 a man with a shriveled *h* was there.
3: 3 to the man with the shriveled *h*,
3: 5 and his *h* was completely restored.
3: 5 to the man, "Stretch out your *h*."
5: 4 For he had often been chained *h*
5: 41 her by the *h* and said to her,
7: 32 him to place his *h* on the man.
8: 23 He took the blind man by the *h*
9: 27 But Jesus took him by the *h*
9: 43 If your *h* causes you to sin, cut it off
10: 33 and will *h* him over to the Gentiles,
12: 36 "Sit at my right *h*
14: 11 for an opportunity to *h* him over.
14: 62 at the right *h* of the Mighty One
16: 19 and he sat at the right *h* of God.
Lk 1: 66 For the Lord's *h* was with him.
1: 71 and from the *h* of all who hate us—
1: 74 us from the *h* of our enemies,
3: 17 in his *h* to clear his threshing floor
5: 13 Jesus reached out his *h*
6: 6 there whose right *h* was shriveled.
6: 8 to the man with the shriveled *h*,
6: 10 and his *h* was completely restored.
6: 10 to the man, "Stretch out your *h*."
8: 29 though he was chained *h* and foot
8: 54 But he took her by the *h* and said,
9: 62 "No one who puts his *h* to the plow
20: 20 said so that they might *h* him
20: 42 "Sit at my right *h*
22: 6 for an opportunity to *h* Jesus
22: 21 But the *h* of him who is going
22: 53 and you did not lay a *h* on me.
22: 69 at the right *h* of the mighty God."
Jn 7: 30 but no one laid a *h* on him,
7: 44 but no one laid a *h* on him.
10: 12 hired *h* is not the shepherd who
10: 13 he is a hired *h* and cares nothing
10: 28 one can snatch them out of my *h*.
10: 29 snatch them out of my Father's *h*.
20: 25 and put my *h* into his side,
20: 27 Reach out your *h* and put it
Ac 2: 25 Because he is at my right *h*,
2: 33 Exalted to the right *h* of God,
2: 34 "Sit at my right *h*
3: 7 Taking him by the right *h*,
4: 30 Stretch out your *h* to heal
5: 31 God exalted him to his own right *h*
7: 50 Has not my *h* made all these things
7: 55 Jesus standing at the right *h* of God
7: 56 standing at the right *h* of God."
Ac 9: 8 him by the *h* into Damascus.
9: 41 her by the *h* and helped her
11: 21 The Lord's *h* was with them,
12: 17 Peter motioned with his *h* for them
13: 11 someone to lead him by the *h*.
13: 11 the *h* of the Lord is against you.
13: 16 Paul motioned with his *h* and said:
21: 11 will *h* him over to the Gentiles.' "
22: 11 me by the *h* into Damascus,
23: 19 took the young man by the *h*,
25: 11 the right to *h* me over to them.
25: 16 custom to *h* over any man
26: 1 So Paul motioned with his *h*
28: 3 by the heat, fastened itself on his *h*.
28: 4 saw the snake hanging from his *h*,
Ro 8: 34 is at the right *h* of God and is
1Co 5: 5 Lord Jesus is present, *h* this man
12: 15 I am not a *h*, I do not belong
12: 21 The eye cannot say to the *h*,
16: 21 write this greeting in my own *h*.
2Co 6: 7 of righteousness in the right *h*
Gal 2: 9 Barnabas the right *h* of fellowship
6: 11 as I write to you with my own *h!*
Eph 1: 20 him at his right *h* in the heavenly
Col 3: 1 seated at the right *h* of God.
4: 18 write this greeting in my own *h*.
2Th 3: 17 write this greeting in my own *h*,
Phm : 19 am writing this with my own *h*.
Heb 1: 3 down at the right *h* of the Majesty
1: 13 "Sit at my right *h*
8: 1 down at the right *h* of the throne
8: 9 when I took them by the *h*
10: 12 he sat down at the right *h* of God.
12: 2 down at the right *h* of the throne
1Pe 3: 22 into heaven and is at God's right *h*
5: 6 therefore, under God's mighty *h*,
Rev 1: 16 In his right *h* he held seven stars,
1: 17 Then he placed his right *h* on me
1: 20 stars that you saw in my right *h*
2: 1 holds the seven stars in his right *h*
5: 1 I saw in the right *h* of him who sat
5: 7 from the right *h* of him who sat
6: 5 was holding a pair of scales in his *h*.
8: 4 up before God from the angel's *h*.
10: 2 little scroll, which lay open in his *h*.
10: 5 and on the land raised his right *h*
10: 8 open in the *h* of the angel who is
10: 10 scroll from the angel's *h*
13: 16 to receive a mark on his right *h*
14: 9 mark on the forehead or on the *h*,
14: 14 and a sharp sickle in his *h*.
17: 4 She held a golden cup in her *h*,
20: 1 and holding in his *h* a great chain.

HANDBREADTH (HAND)

Ex 25: 25 Also make around it a rim a *h* wide
37: 12 also made around it a rim a *h* wide
1Ki 7: 26 It was a *h* in thickness,
2Ch 4: 5 It was a *h* in thickness,
Ps 39: 5 You have made my days a mere *h*;
Eze 40: 5 each of which was a cubit and a *h*.
40: 43 hooks, each a *h* long,
43: 13 that cubit being a cubit and a *h*:

HANDED (HAND)

Ge 27: 17 she *h* to her son Jacob the tasty
Ex 32: 4 He took what they *h* him
Lev 9: 12 His sons *h* him the blood,
9: 13 They *h* him the burnt offering
9: 18 His sons *h* him the blood,
Nu 21: 34 for I have *h* him over to you,
Dt 3: 2 for I have *h* him over to you
Jos 10: 32 The LORD *h* Lachish
21: 44 the LORD *h* all their enemies
Jdg 2: 14 against Israel the LORD *h* them
1Sa 23: 7 "God has *h* him over to me,
30: 23 *h* over to us the forces that came
2Sa 3: 8 I haven't *h* you over to David.
16: 8 The LORD has *h* the kingdom
21: 9 He *h* them over to the Gibeonites,
2Ki 19: 10 'Jerusalem will not be *h*
1Ch 5: 20 and God *h* the Hagrites
22: 18 For he has *h* the inhabitants
2Ch 28: 5 the LORD his God *h* him
30: 16 The priests sprinkled the blood *h*
35: 11 the priests sprinkled the blood *h*
36: 17 *h* all of them
Ezr 5: 12 he *h* them over to Nebuchadnezzar
Ne 9: 24 you *h* the Canaanites over to them,
9: 27 you *h* them over to their enemies,
9: 30 you *h* them over to the neighboring
Ps 31: 8 You have not *h* me
106: 41 He *h* them over to the nations,
Isa 37: 10 'Jerusalem will not be *h*
42: 24 Who *h* Jacob over to become loot,
Jer 26: 24 so he was not *h* over to the people
32: 4 will certainly be *h* over to the king
32: 24 will be *h* over to the Babylonians
32: 25 will be *h* over to the Babylonians,
32: 36 plague it will be *h* over to the king
32: 43 been *h* over to the Babylonians.'
34: 3 but will surely be captured and *h*
37: 17 "you will be *h* over to the king
38: 3 'This city will certainly be *h*
38: 18 will be *h* over to the Babylonians
39: 17 you will not be *h* over to those you
44: 30 as I *h* Zedekiah king of Judah
46: 24 *h* over to the people of the north."
La 1: 14 He has *h* me over
2: 7 He has *h* over to the enemy
Eze 23: 9 Therefore I *h* her over to her lovers
31: 11 I *h* it over to the ruler of the nations
39: 23 and *h* them over to their enemies,
Da 7: 25 The saints will be *h* over to him
7: 27 under the whole heaven will be *h*
11: 6 In those days she will be *h* over,
Mt 24: 9 you will be *h* over to be persecuted
26: 2 Man will be *h* over to be crucified."
27: 2 led him away and *h* him
27: 18 out of envy that they had *h* Jesus
27: 26 and *h* him over to be crucified.
Mk 7: 13 by your tradition that you have *h*
13: 9 You will be *h* over to the local
15: 1 led him away and *h* him
15: 10 that the chief priests had *h* Jesus
15: 15 and *h* him over to be crucified.
Lk 1: 2 as they were *h* down to us
4: 17 of the prophet Isaiah was *h* to him.
18: 32 He will be *h* over to the Gentiles.
24: 20 rulers *h* him over to be sentenced
Jn 18: 30 "we would not have *h* him
18: 35 and your chief priests who *h* you
19: 11 Therefore the one who *h* me
19: 16 Finally Pilate *h* him over to them
Ac 2: 23 This man was *h* over to you
3: 13 You *h* him over to be killed,
6: 14 and change the customs Moses *h*
23: 33 letter to the governor and *h* Paul
27: 1 and some other prisoners were *h*
28: 17 and *h* over to the Romans.
1Ti 1: 20 whom I have *h* over to Satan
1Pe 1: 18 way of life *h* down to you

HANDFUL (HAND)

Lev 2: 2 The priest shall take a *h*
5: 12 who shall take a *h* of it
6: 15 The priest is to take a *h* of fine flour
9: 17 took a *h* of it and burned it
Nu 5: 26 to take a *h* of the grain offering
1Ki 17: 12 only a *h* of flour in a jar
20: 10 to give each of my men a *h*."
Ecc 4: 6 Better one *h* with tranquillity

HANDFULS (HAND)

Ex 9: 8 "Take *h* of soot from a furnace
Lev 16: 12 and two *h* of finely ground fragrant
Ecc 4: 6 tranquillity than two *h* with toil
Eze 13: 19 people for a few *h* of barley

HANDING (HAND)

1Sa 23: 20 we will be responsible for *h* him
1Ki 18: 9 "that you are *h* your servant
Ac 12: 4 *h* him over to be guarded

HANDIWORK

Isa 19: 25 Assyria my *h*, and Israel my

HANDKERCHIEFS

Ac 19: 12 *H* and aprons that had touched

HANDLE (HANDLED HANDLES HANDLING)

Ex 18: 18 for you; you cannot *h* it alone.
Jdg 3: 22 Even the *h* sank in after the blade,
2Sa 24: 9 men who could *h* a sword,
1Ch 5: 18 men who could *h* shield

1Ch 8: 40 warriors who could h the bow.
12: 8 and able to h the shield and spear.
21: 5 men who could h a sword,
2Ch 25: 5 able to h the spear and shield.
Eze 27: 29 All who h the oars
Col 2: 21 "Do not h! Do not taste! Do not

HANDLED (HANDLE)

Jer 8: 8 has h it falsely?

HANDLES (HANDLE)

1Ki 7: 34 Each stand had four h, one
SS 5: 5 on the h of the lock.
2Ti 2: 15 who correctly h the word of truth.

HANDLING (HANDLE)

Lk 16: 11 trustworthy in h worldly wealth,

HANDMILL (MILL)

Nu 11: 8 and then ground it in a h

HANDS (HAND)

Ge 5: 29 and painful toil of our h caused
9: 2 they are given into your h.
16: 6 "Your servant is in your h,"
19: 16 the men grasped his hand and the h
20: 5 with a clear conscience and clean h
24: 18 quickly lowered the jar to her h
27: 16 She also covered his h
27: 22 but the h are the h of Esau."
27: 23 for his h were hairy like those
31: 42 my hardship and the toil of my h,
37: 21 he tried to rescue him from their h.
37: 27 to the Ishmaelites and not lay our h
Ex 9: 29 I will spread out my h in prayer
9: 33 He spread out his h
14: 30 Israel from the h of the Egyptians,
15: 17 O Lord, your h established.
17: 9 hill with the staff of God in my h."
17: 11 As long as Moses held up his h,
17: 11 but whenever he lowered his h,
17: 12 Aaron and Hur held his h up—
17: 12 When Moses' h grew tired,
17: 12 so that his h remained steady
17: 16 "For h were lifted up to the throne
22: 8 he has laid his h on the other man's
22: 11 that the neighbor did not lay h
29: 10 his sons shall lay their h on its head
29: 15 his sons shall lay their h on its head
29: 19 his sons shall lay their h on its head
29: 20 on the thumbs of their right h,
29: 24 Put all these in the h of Aaron
29: 25 Then take them from their h
30: 19 and his sons are to wash their h
30: 21 they shall wash their h
32: 15 tablets of the Testimony in his h.
32: 19 he threw the tablets out of his h,
34: 4 the two stone tablets in his h.
34: 29 tablets of the Testimony in his h,
35: 25 skilled woman spun with her h
40: 31 and his sons used it to wash their h
Lev 4: 15 are to lay their h on the bull's head
7: 30 With his own h he is
8: 14 and his sons laid their h on its head.
8: 18 and his sons laid their h on its head.
8: 22 and his sons laid their h on its head.
8: 24 on the thumbs of their right h
8: 27 He put all these in the h of Aaron
8: 28 Moses took them from their h
9: 22 lifted his h toward the people
15: 11 touches without rinsing his h
16: 21 He is to lay both h on the head
24: 14 are to lay their h on his head,
26: 25 and you will be given into enemy h.
Nu 5: 18 place in her h the reminder offering
5: 25 take from her h the grain offering
6: 19 is to place in his h a boiled shoulder
8: 10 are to lay their h on them.
8: 12 "After the Levites lay their h
21: 2 will deliver these people into our h,
24: 10 He struck his h together
27: 23 Then he laid his h on him
Dt 1: 27 us into the h of the Amorites
2: 7 you in all the work of your h.
2: 30 in order to give him into your h,
3: 3 gave into our h Og king of Bashan
6: 8 Tie them as symbols on your h
8: 17 of my h have produced this wealth
Dt 9: 15 of the covenant were in my h.
9: 17 and threw them out of my h,
10: 3 with the two tablets in my h.
11: 18 tie them as symbols on your h
13: 9 and then the h of all the people.
13: 17 things shall be found in your h,
14: 29 you in all the work of your h.
16: 15 and in all the work of your h,
17: 7 and then the h of all the people.
17: 7 h of the witnesses must be the first
21: 6 nearest the body shall wash their h
21: 7 "Our h did not shed this blood,
21: 10 God delivers them into your h
23: 25 you may pick kernels with your h,
24: 19 you in all the work of your h.
26: 4 shall take the basket from your h
27: 15 the work of the craftsman's h—
28: 12 and to bless all the work of your h.
30: 9 in all the work of your h
31: 29 to anger by what your h have made
33: 7 With his own h he defends his
33: 11 be pleased with the work of his h.
34: 9 Moses had laid his h on him.
Jos 2: 24 given the whole land into our h;
6: 2 have delivered Jericho into your h,
7: 7 us into the h of the Amorites
8: 1 into your h the king of Ai,
9: 25 We are now in your h.
24: 8 but I gave them into your h.
24: 11 but I gave them into your h.
Jdg 1: 2 I have given the land into their h."
1: 4 and Perizzites into their h
2: 16 out of the h of these raiders.
2: 18 out of the h of their enemies
2: 23 by giving them into the h of Joshua
3: 8 the h of Cushan-Rishathaim king
3: 10 king of Aram into the h of Othniel,
3: 28 your enemy, into your h."
4: 2 them into the h of Jabin,
4: 7 and give him into your h.' "
4: 14 has given Sisera into your h.
6: 1 them into the h of the Midianites.
7: 2 me to deliver Midian into their h.
7: 6 lapped with their h to their mouths.
7: 7 give the Midianites into your h.
7: 9 I am going to give it into your h.
7: 14 and the whole camp into his h."
7: 15 the Midianite camp into your h."
7: 16 empty jars in the h of all of them,
7: 19 broke the jars that were in their h.
7: 20 Grasping the torches in their left h
7: 20 in their right h the trumpets they
8: 3 the Midianite leaders, into your h.
8: 6 "Do you already have the h
8: 15 'Do you already have the h
8: 34 from the h of all their enemies
10: 7 them into the h of the Philistines
10: 12 did I not save you from their h?
11: 21 and all his men into Israel's h,
11: 30 you give the Ammonites into my h,
11: 32 the LORD gave them into his h.
12: 2 you didn't save me out of their h.
12: 3 I took my life in my h and crossed
13: 1 them into the h of the Philistines
13: 5 from the h of the Philistines."
13: 23 and grain offering from our h,
14: 6 tore the lion apart with his bare h
14: 9 which he scooped out with his h
15: 14 the bindings dropped from his h.
15: 18 fall into the h of the uncircumcised
16: 18 returned with the silver in their h.
16: 23 Samson, our enemy, into our h."
16: 24 enemy into our h,
18: 10 land that God has put into your h,
19: 27 with her h on the threshold.
20: 28 I will give them into your h."
1Sa 5: 4 His head and h had been broken off
12: 9 and into the h of the Philistines
12: 10 us from the h of our enemies,
12: 11 you from the h of your enemies
14: 10 LORD has given them into our h."
14: 13 Jonathan climbed up, using his h
14: 48 delivering Israel from the h
17: 47 he will give all of you into our h."
18: 25 fall by the h of the Philistines.
19: 5 life in his h when he killed
21: 13 in their h he acted like a madman,
23: 14 God did not give David into his h.
1Sa 24: 4 into your h for you to deal with
24: 10 you into my h in the cave.
24: 18 LORD delivered me into your h,
24: 20 Israel will be established in your h.
25: 26 avenging yourself with your own h,
25: 33 avenging myself with my own h.
26: 8 delivered your enemy into your h.
26: 23 delivered you into my h today,
28: 17 has torn the kingdom out of your h
28: 21 in my h and did what you told me
2Sa 3: 34 Your h were not bound,
4: 12 They cut off their h and feet
16: 21 the h of everyone with you will be
18: 12 were weighed out into my h,
18: 28 up the men who lifted their h
21: 22 and they fell at the h of David
22: 21 of my h he has rewarded me.
22: 35 He trains my h for battle;
24: 14 Let us fall into the h of the LORD,
24: 14 do not let me fall into the h of men
1Ki 2: 46 firmly established in Solomon's h.
8: 22 spread out his h toward heaven
8: 38 and spreading out his h
8: 54 kneeling with his h spread out
11: 35 take the kingdom from his son's h
20: 28 deliver this vast army into your h,
2Ki 3: 11 to pour water on the h of Elijah."
4: 34 to mouth, eyes to eyes, h to h.
9: 35 except her skull, her feet and her h.
10: 24 men I am placing in your h escape,
11: 12 and the people clapped their h
13: 16 Elisha put his h on the king's h.
13: 16 "Take the bow in your h."
17: 20 gave them into the h of plunderers,
19: 18 and stone, fashioned by men's h.
22: 17 by all the idols their h have made,
1Ch 5: 10 who were defeated at their h;
12: 17 when my h are free from violence,
20: 8 and they fell at the h of David
21: 13 Let me fall into the h of the LORD,
21: 13 do not let me fall into the h of men
29: 12 In your h are strength and power
2Ch 6: 4 who with his h has fulfilled what he
6: 12 of Israel and spread out his h
6: 13 spread out his h toward heaven.
6: 29 and spreading out his h
13: 8 is in the h of David's descendants.
13: 16 God delivered them into their h.
23: 18 of the LORD in the h of the priests,
24: 24 into their h a much larger army.
28: 5 given into the h of the king of Israel
29: 23 and they laid their h on them.
32: 19 of the world—the work of men's h.
34: 25 anger by all that their h have made,
Ezr 8: 33 articles into the h of Meremoth son
9: 5 on my knees with my h spread out
10: 4 Rise up; this matter is in your h.
10: 19 (They all gave their h in pledge
Ne 6: 9 I prayed, "Now strengthen my h."
6: 9 "Their h will get too weak
8: 6 and all the people lifted their h
13: 21 If you do this again, I will lay h
Est 9: 10 But they did not lay their h
9: 15 but they did not lay their h
9: 16 did not lay their h on the plunder.
Job 1: 10 You have blessed the work of his h,
1: 12 then, everything he has is in your h
2: 6 is in your h; but you must spare his
4: 3 you have strengthened feeble h.
5: 12 so that their h achieve no success.
5: 18 he injures, but his h also heal.
8: 20 or strengthen the h of evildoers.
9: 24 into the h of the wicked,
9: 30 and my h with washing soda,
10: 3 to spurn the work of your h,
10: 8 "Your h shaped me and made me.
11: 13 and stretch out your h to him,
12: 6 those who carry their god in their h
13: 14 and take my life in my h?
14: 15 for the creature your h have made.
16: 17 yet my h have been free of violence
17: 9 with clean h will grow stronger.
20: 10 his own h must give back his
21: 16 prosperity is not in their own h,
22: 30 through the cleanness of your h."
27: 23 It claps its h in derision
29: 9 covered their mouths with their h;
30: 2 what use was the strength of their h

Job 31: 7 or if my *h* have been defiled,
31: 25 the fortune my *h* had gained,
34: 19 for they are all the work of his *h?*
34: 37 scornfully he claps his *h* among us
36: 32 He fills his *h* with lightning
Ps 7: 3 and there is guilt on my *h*—
8: 6 ruler over the works of your *h;*
9: 16 by the work of their *h.*
18: 20 of my *h* he has rewarded me.
18: 24 to the cleanness of my *h* in his sight
18: 34 He trains my *h* for battle;
19: 1 the skies proclaim the work of his *h*
22: 16 they have pierced my *h*
24: 4 He who has clean *h* and a pure
26: 6 I wash my *h* in innocence,
26: 10 in whose *h* are wicked schemes,
26: 10 whose right *h* are full of bribes.
28: 2 as I lift up my *h*
28: 4 them for what their *h* have done
28: 5 and what his *h* have done,
31: 5 Into your *h* I commit my spirit;
31: 15 My times are in your *h;*
44: 20 or spread out our *h* to a foreign god
47: 1 Clap your *h*, all you nations;
58: 2 and your *h* mete out violence
63: 4 and in your name I will lift up my *h*
73: 13 in vain have I washed my *h*
76: 5 can lift his *h.*
77: 2 at night I stretched out untiring *h*
78: 61 into the *h* of the enemy.
78: 72 with skillful *h* he led them.
81: 6 their *h* were set free
88: 9 I spread out my *h* to you.
90: 17 establish the work of our *h* for us—
90: 17 yes, establish the work of our *h.*
91: 12 they will lift you up in their *h,*
92: 4 I sing for joy at the works of your *h.*
95: 5 and his *h* formed the dry land.
98: 8 Let the rivers clap their *h,*
102: 25 the heavens are the work of your *h.*
111: 7 The works of his *h* are faithful
115: 4 made by the *h* of men.
115: 7 they have *h*, but cannot feel,
119: 48 out my *h* for your commandments,
119: 73 Your *h* made me and formed me;
119:109 I constantly take my life in my *h,*
125: 3 their *h* to do evil.
127: 4 Like arrows in the *h* of a warrior
129: 7 with it the reaper cannot fill his *h,*
134: 2 Lift up your *h* in the sanctuary
135: 15 made by the *h* of men.
138: 8 not abandon the works of your *h.*
140: 4 O LORD, from the *h* of the wicked
141: 2 of my *h* be like the evening
143: 5 consider what your *h* have done.
143: 6 I spread out my *h* to you;
144: 1 who trains my *h* for war,
144: 7 from the *h* of foreigners
144: 8 whose right *h* are deceitful.
144: 11 me from the *h* of foreigners
144: 11 whose right *h* are deceitful.
149: 6 a double-edged sword in their *h,*
Pr 6: 1 if you have struck *h* in pledge
6: 3 fallen into your neighbor's *h:*
6: 10 a little folding of the *h* to rest—
6: 17 *h* that shed innocent blood,
10: 4 Lazy *h* make a man poor,
10: 4 but diligent *h* bring wealth.
11: 15 whoever refuses to strike *h*
12: 14 the work of his *h* rewards him.
12: 24 Diligent *h* will rule,
14: 1 but with her own *h* the foolish one
17: 18 in judgment strikes *h* in pledge
21: 25 because his *h* refuse to work.
22: 26 Do not be a man who strikes *h*
24: 33 a little folding of the *h* to rest—
30: 4 the wind in the hollow of his *h?*
31: 13 and works with eager *h.*
31: 20 and extends her *h* to the needy.
Ecc 2: 11 I surveyed all that my *h* had done
4: 5 The fool folds his *h*
5: 6 and destroy the work of your *h?*
7: 26 and whose *h* are chains.
9: 1 and what they do are in God's *h,*
10: 18 if his *h* are idle, the house leaks.
11: 6 at evening let not your *h* be idle,
SS 5: 5 and my *h* dripped with myrrh,
7: 1 the work of a craftsman's *h.*

Isa 1: 15 When you spread out your *h*
1: 15 Your *h* are full of blood;
2: 6 and clasp *h* with pagans.
2: 8 bow down to the work of their *h,*
3: 11 back for what their *h* have done.
5: 12 no respect for the work of his *h.*
11: 14 They will lay *h* on Edom and Moab
13: 7 Because of this, all *h* will go limp,
17: 8 the work of their *h,*
25: 11 They will spread out their *h* in it,
25: 11 a swimmer spreads out his *h*
25: 11 despite the cleverness of their *h.*
29: 23 the work of my *h,*
31: 7 and gold your sinful *h* have made.
35: 3 Strengthen the feeble *h,*
37: 19 and stone, fashioned by human *h.*
41: 2 He *h* nations over to him
45: 9 'He has no *h*'?
45: 11 me orders about the work of my *h?*
45: 12 My own *h* stretched out
49: 16 you on the palms of my *h;*
51: 23 it into the *h* of your tormentors,
55: 12 will clap their *h.*
59: 3 For your *h* are stained with blood,
59: 6 and acts of violence are in their *h.*
60: 21 the work of my *h,*
65: 2 All day long I have held out my *h*
65: 22 the works of their *h.*
Jer 1: 16 what their *h* have made.
2: 37 place with your *h* on your head,
4: 31 stretching out her *h* and saying,
6: 24 and our *h* hang limp.
11: 21 or you will die by our *h*'—
12: 7 love into the *h* of her enemies.
15: 6 I will lay *h* on you and destroy you;
15: 21 from the *h* of the wicked
18: 4 from the clay was marred in his *h;*
19: 7 at the *h* of those who seek their
20: 13 the needy from the *h* of the wicked.
21: 4 weapons of war that are in your *h,*
21: 10 into the *h* of the king of Babylon,
23: 14 They strengthen the *h* of evildoers,
25: 6 anger with what your *h* have made.
25: 7 me with what your *h* have made,
25: 14 deeds and the work of their *h.*"
26: 14 in your *h;* do with me whatever you
30: 6 man with his *h* on his stomach like
32: 4 out of the *h* of the Babylonians
32: 30 me with what their *h* have made,
38: 5 is in your *h,*" King Zedekiah
38: 18 will not escape from their *h.*' "
38: 23 will not escape from their *h*
42: 11 and deliver you from his *h.*
44: 8 anger with what your *h* have made,
47: 3 their *h* will hang limp.
50: 43 and his *h* hang limp.
La 1: 7 When her people fell into enemy *h,*
1: 10 The enemy laid *h*
1: 14 by his *h* they were woven together.
1: 17 Zion stretches out her *h,*
2: 15 clap their *h* at you;
2: 19 Lift up your *h* to him
3: 41 Let us lift up our hearts and our *h*
3: 64 for what their *h* have done.
4: 2 the work of a potter's *h!*
4: 10 their own *h* compassionate women
5: 8 there is none to free us from their *h*
5: 12 have been hung up by their *h;*
Eze 1: 8 on their four sides they had the *h*
6: 11 Strike your *h* together
7: 27 and the *h* of the people
10: 2 Fill your *h* with burning coals
10: 7 put it into the *h* of the man in linen,
10: 8 be seen what looked like the *h*
10: 12 including their backs, their *h*
10: 21 wings was what looked like the *h*
12: 7 dug through the wall with my *h.*
13: 21 and save my people from your *h,*
13: 23 I will save my people from your *h.*
21: 14 and strike your *h* together.
21: 17 I too will strike my *h* together,
22: 13 " 'I will surely strike my *h* together
22: 14 or your *h* be strong in the day I deal
23: 37 adultery and blood is on their *h.*
23: 45 adulterous and blood is on their *h.*
25: 6 Because you have clapped your *h*
28: 9 in the *h* of those who slay you.
28: 10 at the *h* of foreigners.

Eze 29: 7 they grasped you with their *h,*
34: 27 and rescue them from the *h*
48: 14 and must not pass into other *h,*
Da 2: 34 was cut out, but not by human *h.*
2: 38 in your *h* he has placed mankind
2: 45 by human *h*— a rock that broke
10: 10 and set me trembling on my *h*
Hos 2: 10 no one will take her out of my *h.*
7: 5 and he joins *h* with the mockers.
14: 3 to what our own *h* have made,
Mic 5: 13 down to the work of your *h.*
7: 3 Both *h* are skilled in doing evil;
7: 16 They will lay their *h*
Na 3: 19 claps his *h* at your fall,
Zep 3: 16 do not let your *h* hang limp.
Hag 1: 11 and on the labor of your *h.*"
2: 17 the work of your *h* with blight,
Zec 4: 9 his *h* will also complete it.
4: 9 "The *h* of Zerubbabel have laid
8: 9 let your *h* be strong
8: 13 be afraid, but let your *h* be strong."
11: 6 I will not rescue them from their *h*
Mal 1: 9 With such offerings from your *h,*
1: 10 will accept no offering from your *h.*
1: 13 should I accept them from your *h*
2: 13 them with pleasure from your *h.*
Mt 4: 6 and they will lift you up in their *h,*
15: 2 They don't wash their *h*
15: 20 with unwashed *h* does not make
16: 21 things at the *h* of the elders,
17: 12 of Man is going to suffer at their *h*
17: 22 to be betrayed into the *h* of men.
18: 8 or crippled than to have two *h*
19: 13 for him to place his *h* on them
19: 15 When he had placed his *h* on them,
26: 45 betrayed into the *h* of sinners.
27: 24 washed his *h* in front of the crowd.
Mk 5: 23 put your *h* on her so that she will be
6: 5 lay his *h* on a few sick people
7: 2 that is, ceremonially unwashed—*h*
7: 3 they give their *h* a ceremonial
7: 5 food with 'unclean' *h?*"
8: 23 spit on the man's eyes and put his *h*
8: 25 Once more Jesus put his *h*
9: 31 to be betrayed into the *h* of men.
9: 43 than with two *h* to go into hell,
10: 16 put his *h* on them and blessed them
14: 41 betrayed into the *h* of sinners.
16: 18 they will place their *h*
16: 18 will pick up snakes with their *h;*
Lk 4: 11 they will lift you up in their *h,*
4: 40 and laying his *h* on each one,
6: 1 them in their *h* and eat the kernels.
9: 44 to be betrayed into the *h* of men."
10: 30 when he fell into the *h* of robbers.
10: 36 fell into the *h* of robbers?"
13: 13 Then he put his *h* on her,
21: 12 they will lay *h* on you
23: 46 into your *h* I commit my spirit."
24: 7 delivered into the *h* of sinful men,
24: 39 Look at my *h* and my feet.
24: 40 he showed them his *h* and feet.
24: 50 he lifted up his *h* and blessed them.
Jn 3: 35 and has placed everything in his *h.*
11: 44 his *h* and feet wrapped with strips
13: 9 but my *h* and my head as well!"
20: 20 he showed them his *h* and side.
20: 25 Unless I see the nail marks in his *h*
20: 27 "Put your finger here; see my *h.*
21: 18 are old you will stretch out your *h,*
Ac 6: 6 who prayed and laid their *h*
7: 41 in honor of what their *h* had made.
8: 17 and John placed their *h* on them,
8: 18 at the laying on of the apostles' *h,*
8: 19 whom I lay my *h* may receive
9: 12 and place his *h* on him
9: 17 Placing his *h* on Saul, he said,
13: 3 they placed their *h* on them
17: 24 does not live in temples built by *h.*
17: 25 And he is not served by human *h,*
19: 6 When Paul placed his *h* on them,
20: 34 You yourselves know that these *h*
21: 11 tied his own *h* and feet with it
27: 19 tackle overboard with their own *h.*
28: 8 placed his *h* on him and healed him
Ro 10: 21 "All day long I have held out my *h*
1Co 4: 12 We work hard with our own *h.*
15: 24 when he *h* over the kingdom

2Co 5: 1 in heaven, not built by human *h*.
11: 33 the wall and slipped through his *h*.
Eph 2: 11 in the body by the *h* of men)—
4: 28 something useful with his own *h*,
Col 2: 11 with a circumcision done by the *h*
1Th 4: 11 and to work with your *h*,
1Ti 2: 8 to lift up holy *h* in prayer,
4: 14 body of elders laid their *h* on you.
5: 22 hasty in the laying on of *h*,
2Ti 1: 6 you through the laying on of my *h*.
Heb 1: 10 the heavens are the work of your *h*.
6: 2 the laying on of *h*, the resurrection
10: 31 to fall into the *h* of the living God.
Jas 4: 8 Wash your *h*, you sinners,
1Jn 1: 1 at and our *h* have touched—
Rev 7: 9 holding palm branches in their *h*.
9: 20 repent of the work of their *h*;
20: 4 mark on their foreheads or their *h*.

HANDSOME

Ge 39: 6 Now Joseph was well-built and *h*,
1Sa 16: 12 a fine appearance and *h* features.
17: 42 ruddy and *h*, and he despised him.
2Sa 14: 25 praised for his *h* appearance
1Ki 1: 6 also very *h* and was born next
SS 1: 16 How *h* you are, my lover!
Eze 23: 6 all of them *h* young men,
23: 12 horsemen, all *h* young men.
23: 23 with them, *h* young men,
Da 1: 4 without any physical defect, *h*,
Zec 11: 13 the *h* price at which they priced me

HANES

Isa 30: 4 and their envoys have arrived in *H*,

HANG (HANGED HANGING HANGINGS HANGS HUNG OVERHANG OVERHANGING OVERHANGS)

Ge 40: 19 off your head and *h* you on a tree.
Ex 26: 12 left over is to *h* down at the rear
26: 13 what is left will *h* over the sides
26: 32 *H* it with gold hooks on four posts
26: 33 *H* the curtain from the clasps
Est 7: 9 The king said, "*H* him on it!"
Job 37: 16 you know how the clouds *h* poised,
Pr 26: 7 Like a lame man's legs that *h* limp
SS 4: 4 on it *h* a thousand shields,
Isa 22: 24 glory of his family will *h* on him:
Jer 6: 24 and our hands *h* limp.
47: 3 their hands will *h* limp.
50: 43 and his hands *h* limp.
Eze 15: 3 pegs from it to *h* things on?
Zep 3: 16 do not let your hands *h* limp.
Mt 22: 40 and the Prophets *h* on these two

HANGED (HANG)

Ge 40: 22 hand, but he *h* the chief baker,
41: 13 and the other man was *h*."
2Sa 17: 23 house in order and then *h* himself.
Est 2: 23 the two officials were *h*
5: 14 morning to have Mordecai *h* on it.
7: 10 So they *h* Haman on the gallows he
8: 7 and they have *h* him on the gallows
9: 13 also, and let Haman's ten sons be *h*
9: 14 and they *h* the ten sons of Haman.
9: 25 his sons should be *h* on the gallows.
Mt 27: 5 Then he went away and *h* himself.

HANGING (HANG)

Jos 10: 26 and they were left *h* on the trees
1Sa 25: 17 disaster is *h* over our master
2Sa 18: 9 He was left *h* in midair,
18: 10 I just saw Absalom *h* in an oak tree
Est 6: 4 speak to the king about *h* Mordecai
Isa 22: 25 the load *h* on it will be cut down."
Ac 5: 30 killed by *h* him on a tree.
10: 39 They killed him by *h* him on a tree,
28: 4 the islanders saw the snake *h*
2Pe 2: 3 condemnation has long been *h*

HANGINGS (HANG)

Est 1: 6 The garden had *h* of white

HANGS (HANG)

Isa 33: 23 Your rigging *h* loose:

HANNAH

1Sa 1: 2 had children, but *H* had none.
1: 2 one was called *H* and the other
1: 5 But to *H* he gave a double portion
1: 7 Whenever *H* went up to the house
1: 8 "*H*, why are you weeping?
1: 9 and drinking in Shiloh, *H* stood up.
1: 10 In bitterness of soul *H* wept much
1: 13 *H* was praying in her heart,
1: 15 "Not so, my lord," *H* replied,
1: 19 Elkanah lay with *H* his wife,
1: 20 in the course of time *H* conceived
1: 22 and to fulfill his vow, *H* did not go.
2: 1 Then *H* prayed and said:
2: 21 And the LORD was gracious to *H*;

HANNATHON

Jos 19: 14 went around on the north to *H*

HANNIEL

Nu 34: 23 the tribe of Dan; *H* son of Ephod,
1Ch 7: 39 The sons of Ulla: Arah, *H*

HANOCH (HANOCHITE)

Ge 25: 4 Epher, *H*, Abida and Eldaah.
46: 9 The sons of Reuben: *H*, Pallu,
Ex 6: 14 the firstborn son of Israel were *H*
Nu 26: 5 through *H*, the Hanochite clan;
1Ch 1: 33 Epher, *H*, Abida and Eldaah.
5: 3 *H*, Pallu, Hezron and Carmi.

HANOCHITE (HANOCH)

Nu 26: 5 through Hanoch, the *H* clan;

HANUN

2Sa 10: 1 and his son *H* succeeded him
10: 2 kindness to *H* son of Nahash,
10: 2 to *H* concerning his father.
10: 3 nobles said to *H* their lord,
10: 4 So *H* seized David's men,
1Ch 19: 2 When David's men came to *H*
19: 2 kindness to *H* son of Nahash,
19: 2 to *H* concerning his father.
19: 3 the Ammonite nobles said to *H*,
19: 4 So *H* seized David's men,
19: 6 *H* and the Ammonites sent
Ne 3: 13 The Valley Gate was repaired by *H*
3: 30 Hananiah son of Shelemiah, and *H*

HAPHARAIM

Jos 19: 19 Kesulloth, Shunem, *H*, Shion,

HAPPIER (HAPPY)

Ecc 4: 2 are *h* than the living,
Mt 18: 13 he is *h* about that one sheep
1Co 7: 40 she is *h* if she stays as she is—

HAPPINESS (HAPPY)

Dt 24: 5 bring *h* to the wife he has married.
Est 8: 16 For the Jews it was a time of *h*
Job 7: 7 my eyes will never see *h* again.
Ecc 2: 26 gives wisdom, knowledge and *h*,
Mt 25: 21 Come and share your master's *h*!'
25: 23 Come and share your master's *h*!'

HAPPIZZEZ

1Ch 24: 15 the eighteenth to *H*, the nineteenth

HAPPY (HAPPIER HAPPINESS)

Ge 30: 13 The women will call me *h*."
30: 13 Then Leah said, "How *h* I am!
1Ki 4: 20 they drank and they were *h*.
10: 8 How *h* your men must be!
10: 8 men must be! How *h* your officials,
2Ch 9: 7 How *h* your men must be!
9: 7 men must be! How *h* your officials,
Est 5: 9 Haman went out that day *h*
5: 14 the king to the dinner and be *h*."
Ps 10: 6 I'll always be *h* and never have
68: 3 may they be *h* and joyful.
113: 9 as a *h* mother of children.
137: 8 *h* is he who repays you
Pr 15: 13 A *h* heart makes the face cheerful,
Ecc 3: 12 better for men than to be *h*
5: 19 to accept his lot and be *h*
7: 14 When times are good, be *h*;
11: 9 Be *h*, young man, while you are
Jnh 4: 6 Jonah was very *h* about the vine.
Zec 8: 19 and glad occasions and *h* festivals
1Co 7: 30 those who are *h*, as if they were not
2Co 7: 9 yet now I am *h*, not because you
7: 13 delighted to see how *h* Titus was,
Jas 5: 13 Is anyone *h*? Let him sing songs

HARA

1Ch 5: 26 Habor, *H* and the river of Gozan,

HARADAH

Nu 33: 24 Mount Shepher and camped at *H*.
33: 25 They left *H* and camped

HARAN

Ge 11: 26 the father of Abram, Nahor and *H*.
11: 27 And *H* became the father of Lot.
11: 27 the father of Abram, Nahor and *H*.
11: 28 *H* died in Ur of the Chaldeans,
11: 29 she was the daughter of *H*,
11: 31 But when they came to *H*,
11: 31 his grandson Lot son of *H*,
11: 32 lived 205 years, and he died in *H*.
12: 4 old when he set out from *H*.
12: 5 the people they had acquired in *H*,
27: 43 at once to my brother Laban in *H*.
28: 10 left Beersheba and set out for *H*.
29: 4 "We're from *H*," they replied.
2Ki 19: 12 *H*, Rezeph and the people
1Ch 2: 46 Ephah was the mother of *H*,
2: 46 *H* was the father of Gazez.
23: 9 Shelomoth, Haziel and *H*—
Isa 37: 12 *H*, Rezeph and the people
Eze 27: 23 " '*H*, Canneh and Eden
Ac 7: 2 before he lived in *H*.
7: 4 of the Chaldeans and settled in *H*.

HARARITE

2Sa 23: 11 was Shammah son of Agee the *H*.
23: 33 Ahiam son of Sharar the *H*,
23: 33 Jonathan son of Shammah the *H*,
1Ch 11: 34 Jonathan son of Shagee the *H*,
11: 35 Ahiam son of Sacar the *H*,

HARASS (HARASSED)

Dt 2: 9 "Do not *h* the Moabites
2: 19 do not *h* them or provoke them

HARASSED (HARASS)

Mt 9: 36 because they were *h* and helpless,
2Co 7: 5 but we were *h* at every turn—

HARBONA

Est 1: 10 Mehuman, Biztha, *H*, Bigtha,
7: 9 *H*, one of the eunuchs attending

HARBOR (HARBORED HARBORS)

Dt 15: 9 not to *h* this wicked thought:
Job 36: 13 The godless in heart *h* resentment;
Ps 28: 3 but *h* malice in their hearts.
103: 9 nor will he *h* his anger forever;
Isa 23: 1 and left without house or *h*.
Jer 4: 14 long will you *h* wicked thoughts?
Ac 27: 12 Since the *h* was unsuitable
27: 12 This was a *h* in Crete, facing both
Jas 3: 14 But if you *h* bitter envy

HARBORED (HARBOR)

Eze 35: 5 Because you *h* an ancient hostility

HARBORS (HARBOR)

Pr 26: 24 but in his heart he *h* deceit.

HARD (HARDEN HARDENED HARDENING HARDENS HARDER HARDEST HARDSHIP HARDSHIPS)

Ge 18: 14 Is anything too *h* for the LORD?
33: 13 If they are driven *h* just one day,
Ex 1: 14 bitter with *h* labor in brick
1: 14 in all their *h* labor the Egyptians
2: 11 and watched them at their *h* labor.
7: 13 Yet Pharaoh's heart became *h*
7: 22 and Pharaoh's heart became *h*;
8: 19 But Pharaoh's heart was *h*
9: 35 So Pharaoh's heart was *h*
Dt 1: 17 Bring me any case too *h* for you,
8: 15 He brought you water out of *h* rock
26: 6 us suffer, putting us to *h* labor.
1Sa 13: 6 and that their army was *h* pressed,
31: 2 The Philistines pressed *h* after Saul
1Ki 10: 1 came to test him with *h* questions.

1Ki 10: 3 nothing was too *h* for the king
1Ch 10: 2 The Philistines pressed *h* after Saul
2Ch 9: 1 to test him with *h* questions.
9: 2 nothing was too *h* for him
32: 5 Then he worked *h* repairing all
Job 7: 1 "Does not man have *h* service
14: 14 All the days of my *h* service
37: 18 *h* as a mirror of cast bronze?
38: 30 when the waters become *h* as stone
38: 38 heavens when the dust becomes *h*
41: 24 His chest is *h* as rock,
41: 24 *h* as a lower millstone.
Ps 114: 8 the *h* rock into springs of water.
Pr 13: 15 but the way of the unfaithful is *h*.
14: 23 All *h* work brings a profit,
Ecc 8: 1 and changes its *h* appearance.
Isa 40: 2 that her *h* service has been
Jer 32: 17 Nothing is too *h* for you.
32: 27 anything too *h* for me? Therefore,
Eze 29: 18 army in a *h* campaign against Tyre;
Zec 7: 12 They made their hearts as *h* as flint
Mt 19: 8 wives because your hearts were *h*.
19: 23 it is *h* for a rich man
25: 24 'I knew that you are a *h* man,
Mk 10: 5 your hearts were *h* that Moses
10: 23 "How *h* it is for the rich
10: 24 how *h* it is to enter the kingdom
Lk 5: 5 we've worked *h* all night
12: 58 try *h* to be reconciled to him
18: 24 "How *h* it is for the rich
19: 21 of you, because you are a *h* man.
19: 22 did you, that I am a *h* man,
Jn 4: 38 Others have done the *h* work,
6: 60 disciples said, "This is a *h* teaching.
Ac 20: 35 of *h* work we must help the weak,
26: 14 It is *h* for you to kick
Ro 16: 6 who worked very *h* for you.
16: 12 those women who work *h*
16: 12 woman who has worked very *h*
1Co 4: 12 We work *h* with our own hands.
2Co 4: 8 We are *h* pressed on every side,
6: 5 imprisonments and riots; in *h* work
8: 13 relieved while you are *h* pressed,
Col 4: 13 for him that he is working *h* for you
1Th 5: 12 to respect those who work *h*
2Ti 1: 17 he searched *h* for me
Heb 5: 11 it is *h* to explain because you are
1Pe 4: 18 And, "If it is *h* for the righteous
2Pe 3: 16 contain some things that are *h*
Rev 2: 2 your *h* work and your

HARDEN (HARD)

Ex 4: 21 I will *h* his heart so that he will not
7: 3 But I will *h* Pharaoh's heart,
14: 4 And I will *h* Pharaoh's heart,
14: 17 I will *h* the hearts of the Egyptians
1Sa 6: 6 Why do you *h* your hearts
Ps 95: 8 do not *h* your hearts as you did
Isa 63: 17 *h* our hearts so we do not revere
Ro 9: 18 he hardens whom he wants to *h*.
Heb 3: 8 do not *h* your hearts
3: 15 do not *h* your hearts
4: 7 do not *h* your hearts."

HARDENED (HARD)

Ex 8: 15 he *h* his heart and would not listen
8: 32 this time also Pharaoh *h* his heart
9: 12 But the LORD *h* Pharaoh's heart
9: 34 He and his officials *h* their hearts.
10: 1 for I have *h* his heart and the hearts
10: 20 But the LORD *h* Pharaoh's heart,
10: 27 But the LORD *h* Pharaoh's heart,
11: 10 but the LORD *h* Pharaoh's heart,
14: 8 The LORD *h* the heart
Jos 11: 20 LORD himself who *h* their hearts
2Ch 36: 13 stiff-necked and *h* his heart
Jer 6: 28 They are all *h* rebels,
Eze 3: 7 for the whole house of Israel is *h*
3: 8 as unyielding and *h* as they are.
Da 5: 20 his heart became arrogant and *h*
Mk 6: 52 the loaves; their hearts were *h*.
8: 17 Are your hearts *h*? Do you have
Ro 11: 7 The others were *h*, as it is written:
Heb 3: 13 may be *h* by sin's deceitfulness.

HARDENING (HARD)

Ro 11: 25 Israel has experienced a *h* in part
Eph 4: 18 in them due to the *h* of their hearts.

HARDENS (HARD)

Pr 28: 14 he who *h* his heart falls into trouble
Ro 9: 18 and he *h* whom he wants to harden.

HARDER (HARD)

Ex 5: 9 Make the work *h* for the men
Jer 5: 3 They made their faces *h* than stone
Eze 3: 9 forehead like the hardest stone, *h*
Jn 5: 18 this reason the Jews tried all the *h*
1Co 15: 10 No, I worked *h* than all of them—
2Co 11: 23 I have worked much *h*, been

HARDEST (HARD)

Eze 3: 9 your forehead like the *h* stone,

HARDHEARTED (HEART)

Dt 15: 7 do not be *h* or tightfisted

HARDSHIP (HARD)

Ge 31: 42 But God has seen my *h*
Dt 15: 18 Do not consider it a *h*
Ne 9: 32 do not let all this *h* seem trifling
9: 32 the *h* that has come upon us,
Job 5: 6 For *h* does not spring from the soil,
Isa 30: 6 Through a land of *h* and distress,
La 3: 5 with bitterness and *h*.
Ro 8: 35 Shall trouble or *h* or persecution
1Th 2: 9 remember, brothers, our toil and *h*;
2Ti 2: 3 Endure *h* with us like a good
4: 5 endure *h*, do the work
Heb 12: 7 Endure *h* as discipline; God is

HARDSHIPS (HARD)

Ex 18: 8 and about all the *h* they had met
Nu 11: 1 people complained about their *h*
20: 14 about all the *h* that have come
1Ki 2: 26 and shared all my father's *h*."
Ps 132: 1 and all the *h* he endured.
Ac 14: 22 go through many *h* to enter
20: 23 me that prison and *h* are facing me.
2Co 1: 8 about the *h* we suffered
6: 4 in troubles, *h* and distresses;
12: 10 in insults, in *h*, in persecutions,
Rev 2: 3 and have endured *h* for my name,

HARDWORKING (WORK)

2Ti 2: 6 The *h* farmer should be the first

HAREM

Est 2: 3 into the *h* at the citadel of Susa.
2: 8 to Hegai, who had charge of the *h*.
2: 9 maids into the best place in the *h*.
2: 11 forth near the courtyard of the *h*
2: 13 take with her from the *h*
2: 14 to another part of the *h* to the care
2: 15 was in charge of the *h*,
Ecc 2: 8 women singers, and a *h* as well—

HAREPH

1Ch 2: 51 of Bethlehem, and *H* the father

HARHAIAH

Ne 3: 8 Uzziel son of *H*, one

HARHAS

2Ki 22: 14 the son of *H*, keeper

HARHUR

Ezr 2: 51 Bakbuk, Hakupha, *H*, Bazluth,
Ne 7: 53 Bakbuk, Hakupha, *H*, Bazluth,

HARIM (HARIM'S)

1Ch 24: 8 the third to *H*, the fourth to Seorim
Ezr 2: 32 of *H* 320 of Lod, Hadid
2: 39 of Pashhur 1,247 of *H* 1,017
10: 21 From the descendants of *H*:
10: 31 From the descendants of *H*:
Ne 3: 11 son of *H* and Hasshub son
7: 35 of *H* 320 of Jericho 345 of Lod,
7: 42 of Pashhur 1,247 of *H* 1,017
10: 5 Shebaniah, Malluch, *H*, Meremoth
10: 27 Anan, Malluch, *H* and Baanah.

HARIM'S (HARIM)

Ne 12: 15 Joseph; of *H*, Adna; of Meremoth's

HARIPH

Ne 7: 24 of Bezai 324 of *H* 112
10: 19 Hashum, Bezai, *H*, Anathoth,

HARLOT (HARLOTS)

Isa 1: 21 the faithful city has become a *h*!
Na 3: 4 all because of the wanton lust of a *h*

HARLOTS (HARLOT)

Hos 4: 14 the men themselves consort with *h*

HARM (HARMED HARMFUL HARMING HARMS)

Ge 26: 29 with you that you will do us no *h*,
31: 7 God has not allowed him to *h* me.
31: 29 I have the power to *h* you;
31: 52 and pillar to my side to *h* me.
31: 52 heap to your side to *h* you
42: 4 he was afraid that *h* might come
42: 38 If *h* comes to him on the journey
44: 29 from me too and *h* comes to him,
48: 16 who has delivered me from all *h*
50: 20 of God? You intended to *h* me,
Nu 5: 19 water that brings a curse not *h* you.
35: 23 and he did not intend to *h* him,
Jdg 15: 3 Philistines; I will really *h* them."
1Sa 20: 7 sure that he is determined to *h* me.
20: 9 father was determined to *h* you,
20: 13 But if my father is inclined to *h* you
25: 26 to *h* my master be like Nabal.
26: 21 I will not try to *h* you again.
2Sa 18: 32 to *h* you be like that young man."
20: 6 son of Bicri will do us more *h*
2Ki 8: 12 "Because I know the *h* you will do
1Ch 4: 10 me from *h* so that I will be free
16: 22 do my prophets no *h*."
Ne 6: 2 But they were scheming to *h* me;
Job 5: 19 in seven no *h* will befall you.
Ps 38: 12 those who would *h* me talk
56: 5 they are always plotting to *h* me.
71: 13 may those who want to *h* me
71: 24 for those who wanted to *h* me
91: 10 then no *h* will befall you,
105: 15 do my prophets no *h*."
121: 6 the sun will not *h* you by day,
121: 7 LORD will keep you from all *h*—
Pr 1: 33 and be at ease, without fear of *h*."
3: 29 not plot *h* against your neighbor,
3: 30 when he has done you no *h*.
11: 17 but a cruel man brings himself *h*.
12: 21 No *h* befalls the righteous,
13: 20 but a companion of fools suffers *h*.
31: 12 She brings him good, not *h*,
Ecc 5: 13 hoarded to the *h* of its owner,
8: 5 his command will come to no *h*,
Isa 11: 9 They will neither *h* nor destroy
27: 3 and night so that no one may *h* it.
65: 25 They will neither *h* nor destroy
Jer 5: 12 No *h* will come to us;
7: 6 follow other gods to your own *h*,
10: 5 they can do no *h*
21: 10 I have determined to do this city *h*
23: 17 they say, 'No *h* will come to you.'
25: 6 Then I will not *h* you."
25: 7 you have brought *h* to yourselves."
29: 11 to prosper you and not to *h* you,
39: 12 don't *h* him but do
44: 17 were well off and suffered no *h*.
44: 27 For I am watching over them for *h*,
44: 29 of *h* against you will surely stand.'
Zep 3: 15 never again will you fear any *h*.
Lk 10: 19 of the enemy; nothing will *h* you.
Ac 9: 13 all the *h* he has done to your saints
16: 28 Paul shouted, "Don't *h* yourself!
18: 10 no one is going to attack and *h* you,
Ro 13: 10 Love does no *h* to its neighbor.
1Co 11: 17 for your meetings do more *h*
2Ti 4: 14 did me a great deal of *h*.
1Pe 3: 13 Who is going to *h* you
2Pe 2: 13 with *h* for the *h* they have done.
Rev 7: 2 had been given power to *h* the land
7: 3 "Do not *h* the land or the sea
9: 4 They were told not to *h* the grass
11: 5 tries to *h* them, fire comes
11: 5 wants to *h* them must die.

HARMED (HARM)

Ru 2: 22 else's field you might be *h*."
Da 3: 27 that the fire had not *h* their bodies,
2Co 7: 9 and so were not *h* in any way by us.

HARMFUL (HARM)
2Ki 4:41 And there was nothing *h* in the pot.
Ps 52: 4 You love every *h* word,
1Ti 6: 9 *h* desires that plunge men into ruin

HARMING (HARM)
1Sa 24: 9 men say, 'David is bent on *h* you'?
25:34 lives, who has kept me from *h* you,
Jer 7:19 Are they not rather *h* themselves,

HARMLESS
Lev 13:39 it is a *h* rash that has broken out
Pr 1:11 let's waylay some *h* soul;

HARMON
Am 4: 3 and you will be cast out toward *H,*"

HARMONY
Zec 6:13 there will be *h* between the two.'
Ro 12:16 Live in *h* with one another.
2Co 6:15 What *h* is there between Christ
1Pe 3: 8 live in *h* with one another;

HARMS (HARM)
Pr 8:36 whoever fails to find me *h* himself;

HARNEPHER
1Ch 7:36 Suah, *H,* Shual, Beri, Imrah, Bezer,

HARNESS (HARNESSED)
Job 39:10 him to the furrow with a *h?*
Ps 50:19 and *h* your tongue to deceit.
Jer 46: 4 *H* the horses,
Mic 1:13 *h* the team to the chariot.

HARNESSED (HARNESS)
SS 1: 9 *h* to one of the chariots of Pharaoh.

HAROD (HARODITE)
Jdg 7: 1 camped at the spring of *H.*

HARODITE (HAROD)
2Sa 23:25 Elika the *H,* Helez the Paltite,
23:25 Shammah the *H,* Elika

HAROEH
1Ch 2:52 *H,* half the Manahathites,

HARORITE
1Ch 11:27 Shammoth the *H,* Helez

HAROSHETH HAGGOYIM
Jdg 4: 2 army was Sisera, who lived in *H.*
4:13 from *H* to the Kishon River.
4:16 the chariots and army as far as *H,*

HARP (HARPIST HARPISTS HARPS)
Ge 4:21 the father of all who play the *h*
1Sa 16:16 for someone who can play the *h.*
16:18 who knows how to play the *h.*
16:23 David would take his *h* and play.
18:10 while David was playing the *h,*
19: 9 While David was playing the *h,*
1Ch 25: 3 using the *h* in thanking
Job 21:12 to the music of tambourine and *h;*
30:31 My *h* is tuned to mourning,
Ps 33: 2 Praise the LORD with the *h;*
43: 4 I will praise you with the *h,*
49: 4 with the *h* I will expound my riddle
57: 8 Awake, *h* and lyre!
71:22 I will praise you with the *h*
81: 2 play the melodious *h* and lyre.
92: 3 and the melody of the *h.*
98: 5 music to the LORD with the *h,*
98: 5 with the *h* and the sound of singing
108: 2 Awake, *h* and lyre!
147: 7 make music to our God on the *h.*
149: 3 to him with tambourine and *h.*
150: 3 praise him with the *h* and lyre,
Isa 16:11 My heart laments for Moab like a *h*
23:16 Take up a *h,* walk through the city,
23:16 play the *h* well, sing many a song,
24: 8 the joyful *h* is silent.
Da 3: 5 lyre, *h,* pipes and all kinds of music
3: 7 lyre, *h* and all kinds of music,
3:10 of the horn, flute, zither, lyre, *h,*
3:15 lyre, *h,* pipes and all kinds of music
1Co 14: 7 make sounds, such as the flute or *h,*
Rev 5: 8 Each one had a *h* and they were

HARPIST (HARP)
2Ki 3:15 But now bring me a *h.*"
3:15 While the *h* was playing, the hand

HARPISTS (HARP)
Rev 14: 2 that of *h* playing their harps.
18:22 The music of *h* and musicians,

HARPOONS
Job 41: 7 Can you fill his hide with *h*

HARPS (HARP)
Ge 31:27 to the music of tambourines and *h?*
1Sa 10: 5 and *h* being played before them,
2Sa 6: 5 with songs and with *h,* lyres,
1Ki 10:12 and to make *h* and lyres
1Ch 13: 8 with songs and with *h,* lyres,
15:16 by musical instruments: lyres, *h*
15:21 and Azaziah were to play the *h,*
15:28 and the playing of lyres and *h.*
16: 5 They were to play the lyres and *h,*
25: 1 accompanied by *h,* lyres
25: 6 with cymbals, lyres and *h,*
2Ch 5:12 and playing cymbals, *h* and lyres.
9:11 and to make *h* and lyres
20:28 to the temple of the LORD with *h*
29:25 *h* and lyres in the way prescribed
Ne 12:27 and with the music of cymbals, *h*
Ps 137: 2 we hung our *h,*
Isa 5:12 They have *h* and lyres
14:11 along with the noise of your *h;*
30:32 to the music of tambourines and *h,*
Eze 26:13 of your *h* will be heard no more.
Am 5:23 to the music of your *h.*
6: 5 on your *h* like David
Rev 14: 2 that of harpists playing their *h.*
15: 2 They held *h* given them by God

HARROWING
Isa 28:24 keep on breaking up and *h* the soil?

HARSH
Dt 28:59 *h* and prolonged disasters,
1Ki 12: 4 but now lighten the *h* labor
2Ch 10: 4 but now lighten the *h* labor
Pr 15: 1 but a *h* word stirs up anger.
Isa 66: 4 will choose *h* treatment for them
La 1: 3 After affliction and *h* labor,
Da 2:15 did the king issue such a *h* decree?"
Mal 3:13 "You have said *h* things against me
2Co 13:10 to be *h* in my use of authority—
Col 2:23 and their *h* treatment of the body,
3:19 and do not be *h* with them.
1Pe 2:18 but also to those who are *h.*
Jude :15 of all the *h* words ungodly sinners

HARSHA
Ezr 2:52 Bazluth, Mehida, *H,* Barkos, Sisera
Ne 7:54 Bazluth, Mehida, *H,* Barkos, Sisera

HARUM
1Ch 4: 8 of the clans of Aharhel son of *H.*

HARUMAPH
Ne 3:10 Jedaiah son of *H* made repairs

HARUPHITE
1Ch 12: 5 Shemariah and Shephatiah the *H;*

HARUZ
2Ki 21:19 was Meshullemeth daughter of *H;*

HARVEST (HARVESTED HARVESTERS HARVESTING HARVESTS)
Ge 8:22 seedtime and *h,*
30:14 During wheat *h,* Reuben went out
41:34 land to take a fifth of the *h* of Egypt
Ex 23:10 to sow your fields and *h* the crops,
23:16 the Feast of *H* with the firstfruits
34:21 the plowing season and *h* you must
34:22 with the firstfruits of the wheat *h,*
Lev 19: 9 When you reap the *h* of your land,
19: 9 or gather the gleanings of your *h.*
19:25 In this way your *h* will be increased
23:10 a sheaf of the first grain you *h.*
23:10 to give you and you reap its *h,*
Lev 23:22 When you reap the *h* of your land,
23:22 or gather the gleanings of your *h.*
25: 5 or *h* the grapes of your untended
25:11 of itself or *h* the untended vines.
25:20 if we do not plant or *h* our crops?"
25:22 until the *h* of the ninth year comes
26: 5 and the grape *h* will continue
26: 5 will continue until grape *h*
26:10 You will still be eating last year's *h*
Nu 18:12 as the firstfruits of their *h.*
Dt 16:15 God will bless you in all your *h*
24:21 When you *h* the grapes
28:38 in the field but you will *h* little,
Jos 3:15 is at flood stage all during *h.*
Jdg 8: 2 than the full grape *h* of Abiezer?
15: 1 Later on, at the time of wheat *h,*
Ru 1:22 as the barley *h* was beginning.
1Sa 8:12 to plow his ground and reap his *h,*
12:17 Is it not wheat *h* now? I will call
2Sa 21: 9 death during the first days of the *h,*
21: 9 just as the barley *h* was beginning.
21:10 of the *h* till the rain poured
23:13 During *h* time, three
2Ch 32:28 buildings to store the *h* of grain,
Ne 9:37 its abundant *h* goes
Job 5: 5 The hungry consume his *h,*
31:12 it would have uprooted my *h.*
Ps 67: 6 Then the land will yield its *h,*
85:12 and our land will yield its *h.*
107:37 that yielded a fruitful *h,*
Pr 6: 8 and gathers its food at *h.*
10: 5 during *h* is a disgraceful son.
14: 4 of an ox comes an abundant *h.*
18:20 with the *h* from his lips he is
20: 4 at *h* time he looks but finds nothing
25:13 Like the coolness of snow at *h* time
26: 1 Like snow in summer or rain in *h,*
Isa 9: 3 as people rejoice at the *h,*
17:11 yet the *h* will be as nothing
18: 4 like a cloud of dew in the heat of *h*
18: 5 before the *h,* when the blossom is
23: 3 the *h* of the Nile was the revenue
24:13 gleanings are left after the grape *h.*
28: 4 will be like a fig ripe before *h*—
32:10 and the *h* of fruit will not come.
32:10 the grape *h* will fail,
62: 9 but those who *h* it will eat it
Jer 2: 3 the firstfruits of his *h;*
5:24 us of the regular weeks of *h.'*
8:13 " 'I will take away their *h,*
8:20 "The *h* is past,
12:13 So bear the shame of your *h*
40:10 you are to *h* the wine, summer fruit
50:16 and the reaper with his sickle at *h.*
51:33 the time to *h* her will soon come."
Hos 6:11 a *h* is appointed.
Joel 1:11 the *h* of the field is destroyed.
3:13 for the *h* is ripe.
Am 4: 7 when the *h* was still three months
Mic 6:15 You will plant but not *h;*
Mt 9:37 *h* is plentiful but the workers are
9:38 Ask the Lord of the *h,* therefore,
9:38 to send out workers into his *h* field
13:30 Let both grow together until the *h.*
13:39 The *h* is the end of the age,
21:34 When the *h* time approached,
21:41 share of the crop at *h* time."
25:26 you knew that I *h* where I have not
Mk 4:29 to it, because the *h* has come."
12: 2 At *h* time he sent a servant
Lk 10: 2 Ask the Lord of the *h,* therefore,
10: 2 He told them, "The *h* is plentiful,
10: 2 to send out workers into his *h* field.
20:10 At *h* time he sent a servant
Jn 4:35 at the fields! They are ripe for *h.*
4:35 'Four months more and then the *h*
Ro 1:13 in order that I might have a *h*
1Co 9:10 so in the hope of sharing in the *h.*
9:11 if we reap a material *h* from you?
2Co 9:10 the *h* of your righteousness.
Gal 6: 9 at the proper time we will reap a *h*
Heb 12:11 it produces a *h* of righteousness
Jas 3:18 in peace raise a *h* of righteousness.
Rev 14:15 for the *h* of the earth is ripe."

HARVESTED (HARVEST)
Isa 33: 4 O nations, is *h* as by young locusts;
Jer 40:12 And they *h* an abundance of wine

Am 7: 1 after the king's share had been *h*
Hag 1: 6 planted much, but have *h* little.
Rev 14: 16 over the earth, and the earth was *h*.

HARVESTERS (HARVEST)

Ru 2: 3 to glean in the fields behind the *h*.
2: 4 from Bethlehem and greeted the *h*,
2: 5 Boaz asked the foreman of his *h*,
2: 7 among the sheaves behind the *h*.'
2: 14 When she sat down with the *h*,
Mt 13: 30 At that time I will tell the *h*:
13: 39 end of the age, and the *h* are angels.
Jas 5: 4 cries of the *h* have reached the ears

HARVESTING (HARVEST)

Lev 25: 15 number of years left for *h* crops.
Dt 24: 19 When you are *h* in your field
Ru 2: 9 the field where the men are *h*,
2: 21 until they finish *h* all my grain.' "
1Sa 6: 13 Beth Shemesh were *h* their wheat
Mt 25: 24 *h* where you have not sown

HARVESTS (HARVEST)

Dt 32: 22 It will devour the earth and its *h*
Ru 2: 23 and wheat *h* were finished.
Isa 16: 9 and over your *h* have been stilled.
17: 5 and *h* the grain with his arm—
Jer 5: 17 They will devour your *h* and food,
Jn 4: 36 now he *h* the crop for eternal life,

HASADIAH

1Ch 3: 20 Berekiah, *H* and Jushab-Hesed.

HASHABIAH

1Ch 6: 45 the son of *H*, the son of Amaziah,
9: 14 son of *H*, a Merarite; Bakbakkar,
25: 3 Shimei, *H* and Mattithiah,
25: 19 the twelfth to *H*, his sons
26: 30 From the Hebronites: *H*
27: 17 over Levi: *H* son of Kemuel;
2Ch 35: 9 his brothers, and *H*, Jeiel
Ezr 8: 19 and brothers, 18 men; and *H*,
8: 24 *H* and ten of their brothers,
Ne 3: 17 *H*, ruler of half the district
10: 11 Rehob, *H*, Zaccur, Sherebiah,
11: 15 the son of *H*, the son of Bunni;
11: 22 the son of *H*, the son of Mattaniah,
12: 21 Eber; of Hilkiah's, *H*; of Jedaiah's,
12: 24 the leaders of the Levites were *H*,

HASHABNAH

Ne 10: 25 Shobek, Rehum, *H*, Maaseiah,

HASHABNEIAH

Ne 3: 10 son of *H* made repairs next
9: 5 Kadmiel, Bani, *H*, Sherebiah,

HASHBADDANAH

Ne 8: 4 Mishael, Malkijah, Hashum, *H*,

HASHEM

1Ch 11: 34 the sons of *H* the Gizonite,

HASHMONAH

Nu 33: 29 left Mithcah and camped at *H*.
33: 30 They left *H* and camped

HASHUBAH

1Ch 3: 20 There were also five others: *H*,

HASHUM

Ezr 2: 19 of Jorah 112 of *H* 223
10: 33 From the descendants of *H*:
Ne 7: 22 (through Hezekiah) 98 of *H* 328
8: 4 Malkijah, *H*, Hashbaddanah,
10: 18 Azzur, Hodiah, *H*, Bezai, Hariph,

HASRAH

2Ch 34: 22 the son of *H*, keeper

HASSENAAH

Ne 3: 3 Gate was rebuilt by the sons of *H*.

HASSENUAH

1Ch 9: 7 the son of *H*; Ibneiah son
Ne 11: 9 and Judah son of *H* was

HASSHUB

1Ch 9: 14 Shemaiah son of *H*, the son
Ne 3: 11 *H* son of Pahath-Moab repaired
3: 23 and *H* made repairs in front
10: 23 Hoshea, Hananiah, *H*, Hallohesh,
11: 15 Shemaiah son of *H*, the son

HASSOPHERETH

Ezr 2: 55 *H*, Peruda, Jaala, Darkon,

HASTE (HASTEN HASTY)

Ex 12: 11 it in *h*; it is the LORD's Passover.
Dt 16: 3 because you left Egypt in *h*—
Ps 68: 12 "Kings and armies flee in *h*;
Pr 21: 5 as surely as *h* leads to poverty.
29: 20 Do you see a man who speaks in *h*?
Isa 52: 12 But you will not leave in *h*
Jer 46: 5 They flee in *h*

HASTEN (HASTE)

Ps 70: 1 *H*, O God, to save me;
119: 60 I will *h* and not delay
Isa 5: 19 let him *h* his work
49: 17 Your sons *h* back,
55: 5 nations that do not know you will *h*

HASTY (HASTE)

Pr 19: 2 nor to be *h* and miss the way.
Ecc 5: 2 do not be *h* in your heart
1Ti 5: 22 Do not be *h* in the laying

HASUPHA

Ezr 2: 43 *H*, Tabbaoth, Keros, Siaha,
Ne 7: 46 the descendants of Ziha, *H*,

HATCH (HATCHED HATCHES)

Isa 34: 15 she will *h* them, and care
59: 5 They *h* the eggs of vipers

HATCHED (HATCH)

Isa 59: 5 when one is broken, an adder is *h*.

HATCHES (HATCH)

Jer 17: 11 Like a partridge that *h* eggs it did

HATCHETS

Ps 74: 6 with their axes and *h*.

HATE (GOD-HATERS HATED HATES HATING HATRED)

Ex 18: 21 men who *h* dishonest gain—
20: 5 generation of those who *h* me,
Lev 19: 17 " 'Do not *h* your brother
26: 17 those who *h* you will rule over you,
Dt 5: 9 generation of those who *h* me,
7: 10 But those who *h* him he will repay
7: 10 to their face those who *h* him.
7: 15 will inflict them on all who *h* you.
30: 7 curses on your enemies who *h*
32: 41 and repay those who *h* me.
Jdg 11: 7 "Didn't you *h* me and drive me
14: 16 "You *h* me! You don't really love
2Sa 19: 6 You love those who *h* you
19: 6 and *h* those who love you.
1Ki 22: 8 but I *h* him because he never
2Ch 18: 7 but I *h* him because he never
19: 2 and love those who *h* the LORD?
Ps 5: 5 you *h* all who do wrong.
25: 19 and how fiercely they *h* me!
31: 6 I *h* those who cling
35: 19 let not those who *h* me
36: 2 too much to detect or *h* his sin.
38: 19 those who *h* me without reason are
45: 7 righteousness and *h* wickedness;
50: 17 You *h* my instruction
69: 4 Those who *h* me without reason
69: 14 deliver me from those who *h* me,
81: 15 Those who *h* the LORD would
97: 10 those who love the LORD *h* evil,
101: 3 The deeds of faithless men I *h*;
105: 25 hearts he turned to *h* his people,
119:104 therefore I *h* every wrong path.
119:113 I *h* double-minded men,
119:128 I *h* every wrong path.
119:163 I *h* and abhor falsehood
120: 6 lived among those who *h* peace.
129: 5 May all who *h* Zion
139: 21 Do I not *h* those who *h* you,
Pr 1: 22 and fools *h* knowledge?
8: 13 I *h* pride and arrogance,
8: 13 To fear the LORD is to *h* evil;
8: 36 all who *h* me love death."
9: 8 rebuke a mocker or he will *h* you;
13: 5 The righteous *h* what is false,
25: 17 too much of you, and he will *h* you.
29: 10 Bloodthirsty men *h* a man
Ecc 3: 8 a time to love and a time to *h*,
9: 1 whether love or *h* awaits him.
9: 6 Their love, their *h*
Isa 61: 8 I *h* robbery and iniquity.
66: 5 "Your brothers who *h* you,
Jer 12: 8 therefore I *h* her.
44: 4 do this detestable thing that I *h*!'
Eze 23: 28 to hand you over to those you *h*,
35: 6 Since you did not *h* bloodshed,
Am 5: 10 you *h* the one who reproves
5: 15 *H* evil, love good;
5: 21 "I *h*, I despise your religious feasts;
Mic 3: 2 you who *h* good and love evil;
Zec 8: 17 I *h* all this," declares the LORD.
Mal 2: 16 "I *h* divorce," says the LORD God
2: 16 "and I *h* a man's covering himself
Mt 5: 43 your neighbor and *h* your enemy.'
6: 24 Either he will *h* the one
10: 22 All men will *h* you because of me,
24: 10 and will betray and *h* each other,
Mk 13: 13 All men will *h* you because of me,
Lk 1: 71 and from the hand of all who *h* us
6: 22 Blessed are you when men *h* you,
6: 27 do good to those who *h* you,
14: 26 does not *h* his father and mother,
16: 13 Either he will *h* the one
21: 17 All men will *h* you because of me.
Jn 7: 7 The world cannot *h* you,
Ro 7: 15 to do I do not do, but what I *h* I do.
12: 9 *H* what is evil; cling to what is good
Rev 2: 6 You *h* the practices
2: 6 of the Nicolaitans, which I also *h*.
17: 16 horns you saw will *h* the prostitute.

HATED (HATE)

Ge 37: 4 they *h* him and could not speak
37: 5 it to his brothers, they *h* him all
37: 8 And they *h* him all the more
Dt 9: 28 he *h* them, he brought them out
Jdg 15: 2 I was so sure you thoroughly *h* her
2Sa 13: 15 Amnon *h* her with intense hatred.
13: 15 he *h* her more than he had loved
13: 22 he *h* Amnon because he had
Est 9: 1 hand over those who *h* them.
9: 5 pleased to those who *h* them.
Pr 1: 29 Since they *h* knowledge
5: 12 You will say, "How I *h* discipline!
14: 17 and a crafty man is *h*.
Ecc 2: 17 I *h* life, because the work that is
2: 18 I *h* all the things I had toiled
Isa 60: 15 you have been forsaken and *h*,
Eze 16: 37 you loved as well as those you *h*.
Hos 9: 15 I *h* them there.
Mal 1: 3 loved Jacob, but Esau I have *h*,
Mt 24: 9 and you will be *h* by all nations
Lk 19: 14 "But his subjects *h* him
Jn 15: 18 keep in mind that it *h* me first.
15: 24 and yet they have *h* both me
15: 25 'They *h* me without reason.'
17: 14 word and the world has *h* them,
Ro 9: 13 "Jacob I loved, but Esau I *h*."
Eph 5: 29 no one ever *h* his own body,
Tit 3: 3 being *h* and hating one another.
Heb 1: 9 righteousness and *h* wickedness;

HATES (HATE)

Ex 23: 5 of someone who *h* you fallen
Dt 1: 27 and said, "The LORD *h* us;
12: 31 of detestable things the LORD *h*.
16: 22 for these the LORD your God *h*.
19: 11 But if a man *h* his neighbor
Job 34: 17 Can he who *h* justice govern?
Ps 11: 5 his soul *h*.
Pr 6: 16 There are six things the LORD *h*,
12: 1 but he who *h* correction is stupid.
13: 24 He who spares the rod *h* his son,
15: 10 he who *h* correction will die.
15: 27 but he who *h* bribes will live.
26: 28 A lying tongue *h* those it hurts,
28: 16 he who *h* ill-gotten gain will enjoy
Isa 1: 14 my soul *h*.
Jn 3: 20 Everyone who does evil *h* the light,

Jn 7: 7 it *h* me because I testify that what
12: 25 while the man who *h* his life
15: 18 "If the world *h* you, keep
15: 19 That is why the world *h* you.
15: 23 He who *h* me *h* my Father as well,
1Jn 2: 9 *h* his brother is still in the darkness.
2: 11 But whoever *h* his brother is
3: 13 my brothers, if the world *h* you.
3: 15 Anyone who *h* his brother is
4: 20 "I love God," yet *h* his brother,

HATHACH

Est 4: 5 Then Esther summoned *H*,
4: 6 So *H* went out to Mordecai
4: 9 *H* went back and reported

HATHATH

1Ch 4: 13 The sons of Othniel: *H*

HATING (HATE)

Tit 3: 3 being hated and *h* one another.
Jude : 23 *h* even the clothing stained

HATIPHA

Ezr 2: 54 *H* The descendants of the servants
Ne 7: 56 *H* The descendants of the servants

HATITA

Ezr 2: 42 *H* and Shobai 139 The temple
Ne 7: 45 *H* and Shobai 138 The temple

HATRED (HATE)

2Sa 13: 15 Amnon hated her with intense *h*.
Ps 109: 3 With words of *h* they surround me;
109: 5 and *h* for my friendship.
139: 22 I have nothing but *h* for them;
Pr 10: 12 *H* stirs up dissension,
10: 18 who conceals his *h* has lying lips,
15: 17 than a fattened calf with *h*.
Eze 23: 29 They will deal with you in *h*
35: 11 and jealousy you showed in your *h*
Gal 5: 20 idolatry and witchcraft; *h*, discord,
Jas 4: 4 with the world is *h* toward God?

HATTIL

Ezr 2: 57 Darkon, Giddel, Shephatiah, *H*,
Ne 7: 59 Darkon, Giddel, Shephatiah, *H*,

HATTUSH

1Ch 3: 22 Shemaiah and his sons: *H*, Igal,
Ezr 8: 2 *H* of the descendants of Shecaniah;
Ne 3: 10 and *H* son of Hashabneiah made
10: 4 Amariah, Malkijah, *H*, Shebaniah,
12: 2 Amariah, Malluch, *H*, Shecaniah,

HAUGHTINESS (HAUGHTY)

Jer 48: 29 and the *h* of her heart

HAUGHTY (HAUGHTINESS)

2Sa 22: 28 on the *h* to bring them low.
Job 41: 34 He looks down on all that are *h*;
Ps 10: 5 he is *h* and your laws are far
18: 27 bring low those whose eyes are *h*.
101: 5 whoever has *h* eyes and a proud
131: 1 my eyes are not *h*;
Pr 6: 17 *h* eyes,
16: 18 a *h* spirit before a fall.
21: 4 *H* eyes and a proud heart,
30: 13 those whose eyes are ever so *h*,
Isa 3: 16 "The women of Zion are *h*,
10: 12 pride of his heart and the *h* look
13: 11 an end to the arrogance of the *h*
Eze 16: 50 They were *h* and did detestable
Zep 3: 11 Never again will you be *h*

HAUL

1Ki 5: 9 My men will *h* them
Eze 32: 3 and they will *h* you up in my net.
Jn 21: 6 they were unable to *h* the net in

HAUNT (HAUNTS)

Ps 44: 19 made us a *h* for jackals
Isa 34: 13 She will become a *h* for jackals,
Jer 9: 11 a *h* of jackals;
10: 22 a *h* of jackals.
49: 33 "Hazor will become a *h* of jackals,
51: 37 a *h* of jackals,
Rev 18: 2 and a *h* for every evil spirit,
Rev 18: 2 *h* for every unclean and detestable

HAUNTS (HAUNT)

Ps 74: 20 *h* of violence fill the dark places
SS 4: 8 and the mountain *h* of the leopards
Isa 35: 7 In the *h* where jackals once lay,

HAURAN

Eze 47: 16 which is on the border of *H*.
47: 18 the boundary will run between *H*

HAVEN

Ge 49: 13 and become a *h* for ships;
Ps 107: 30 he guided them to their desired *h*.
Isa 23: 10 will no longer be a *h* for you.

HAVILAH

Ge 2: 11 winds through the entire land of *H*,
10: 7 *H*, Sabtah, Raamah and Sabtecah.
10: 29 Sheba, Ophir, *H* and Jobab.
25: 18 settled in the area from *H* to Shur,
1Sa 15: 7 the Amalekites all the way from *H*
1Ch 1: 9 *H*, Sabta, Raamah and Sabteca.
1: 23 Sheba, Ophir, *H* and Jobab.

HAVOC

Isa 54: 16 created the destroyer to work *h*;
Jer 48: 3 cries of great *h* and destruction.
Ac 9: 21 "Isn't he the man who raised *h*

HAVVOTH JAIR

Nu 32: 41 settlements and called them *H*.
Dt 3: 14 that to this day Bashan is called *H*.
Jdg 10: 4 which to this day are called *H*.
1Ch 2: 23 But Geshur and Aram captured *H*,

HAWK

Lev 11: 16 the gull, any kind of *h*, the little owl
Dt 14: 15 the gull, any kind of *h*, the little owl
Job 39: 26 "Does the *h* take flight

HAY

Pr 27: 25 When the *h* is removed
1Co 3: 12 costly stones, wood, *h* or straw,

HAZAEL

1Ki 19: 15 anoint *H* king over Aram.
19: 17 any who escape the sword of *H*,
2Ki 8: 8 he said to *H*, "Take a gift with you
8: 9 recover from this illness?' " *H* went
8: 11 gaze until *H* felt ashamed.
8: 12 Why is my lord weeping?" asked *H*
8: 13 *H* said, "How could your servant,
8: 14 Then *H* left Elisha and returned
8: 14 say to you?" *H* replied,
8: 15 Then *H* succeeded him as king.
8: 28 to war against *H* king of Aram
8: 29 in his battle with *H* king of Aram.
9: 14 against *H* king of Aram,
9: 15 in the battle with *H* king of Aram.)
10: 32 *H* overpowered the Israelites
12: 17 About this time *H* king
12: 18 he sent them to *H* king of Aram,
13: 3 under the power of *H* king of Aram
13: 22 *H* king of Aram oppressed Israel
13: 24 *H* king of Aram died,
13: 25 son of *H* the towns he had taken
2Ch 22: 5 to war against *H* king of Aram
22: 6 in his battle with *H* king of Aram.
Am 1: 4 I will send fire upon the house of *H*

HAZAIAH

Ne 11: 5 the son of *H*, the son of Adaiah,

HAZAR ADDAR

Nu 34: 4 it will go to *H* and over to Azmon,

HAZAR ENAN

Nu 34: 9 continue to Ziphron and end at *H*.
34: 10 run a line from *H* to Shepham.
Eze 47: 17 extend from the sea to *H*,
48: 1 *H* and the northern border

HAZAR GADDAH

Jos 15: 27 Shema, Moladah, *H*, Heshmon,

HAZAR SHUAL

Jos 15: 28 Beth Pelet, *H*, Beersheba,
19: 3 Moladah, *H*, Balah, Ezem,
1Ch 4: 28 Moladah, *H*, Bilhah, Ezem, Tolad,
Ne 11: 27 in *H*, in Beersheba and

HAZAR SUSAH

Jos 19: 5 Ziklag, Beth Marcaboth, *H*,

HAZAR SUSIM

1Ch 4: 31 Ziklag, Beth Marcaboth, *H*,

HAZARMAVETH

Ge 10: 26 Sheleph, *H*, Jerah, Hadoram, Uzal,
1Ch 1: 20 Sheleph, *H*, Jerah, Hadoram, Uzal,

HAZAZON TAMAR

2Ch 20: 2 in *H*" (that is, En Gedi).

HAZER HATTICON

Eze 47: 16 as *H*, which is on the border of

HAZEROTH

Nu 11: 35 the people traveled to *H*
12: 16 the people left *H* and encamped
33: 17 and camped at *H*.
33: 18 They left *H* and camped
Dt 1: 1 Tophel, Laban, *H* and Dizahab.

HAZEZON TAMAR

Ge 14: 7 the Amorites who were living in *H*.

HAZIEL

1Ch 23: 9 Shelomoth, *H* and Haran—

HAZO

Ge 22: 22 *H*, Pildash, Jidlaph and Bethuel."

HAZOR

Jos 11: 1 When Jabin king of *H* heard of this,
11: 10 and captured *H* and put its king
11: 10 (*H* had been the head
11: 11 and he burned up *H* itself.
11: 13 except *H*, which Joshua burned.
12: 19 one the king of *H* one the king
15: 23 Adadah, Kedesh, *H*, Ithnan, Ziph,
15: 25 Kerioth Hezron (that is, *H*),
19: 36 Adamah, Ramah, *H*, Kedesh,
Jdg 4: 2 a king of Canaan, who reigned in *H*
4: 17 relations between Jabin king of *H*
1Sa 12: 9 the commander of the army of *H*,
1Ki 9: 15 and *H*, Megiddo and Gezer.
2Ki 15: 29 Janoah, Kedesh and *H*.
Ne 11: 33 in *H*, Ramah and Gittaim,
Jer 49: 28 Kedar and the kingdoms of *H*,
49: 30 in deep caves, you who live in *H*,"
49: 33 "*H* will become a haunt of jackals,

HAZOR HADATTAH

Jos 15: 25 Ithnan, Ziph, Telem, Bealoth, *H*,

HAZZELELPONI

1Ch 4: 3 Their sister was named *H*.

HAZZOBEBAH

1Ch 4: 8 who was the father of Anub and *H*

HE-GOAT (GOAT)

Pr 30: 31 a strutting rooster, a *h*,

HEAD (HEADED HEADING HEADS HOTHEADED)

Ge 3: 15 he will crush your *h*,
28: 11 he put it under his *h* and lay
28: 18 the stone he had placed under his *h*
40: 13 days Pharaoh will lift up your *h*
40: 16 On my *h* were three baskets
40: 17 out of the basket on my *h*."
40: 19 days Pharaoh will lift off your *h*
42: 38 you will bring my gray *h*
44: 29 you will bring my gray *h*
44: 31 Your servants will bring the gray *h*
48: 14 and put it on Ephraim's *h*,
48: 14 put his left hand on Manasseh's *h*,
48: 17 from Ephraim's *h* to Manasseh's *h*.
48: 17 on Ephraim's *h* he was displeased;
48: 18 put your right hand on his *h*."
49: 26 Let all these rest on the *h* of Joseph
Ex 12: 9 but roast it over the fire—*h*,
22: 1 he must pay back five *h* of cattle
28: 32 an opening for the *h* in its center.
29: 6 Put the turban on his *h*

Ex 29: 7 anoint him by pouring it on his *h*.
29: 10 sons shall lay their hands on its *h*.
29: 15 sons shall lay their hands on its *h*.
29: 17 putting them with the *h*
29: 19 sons shall lay their hands on its *h*.
Lev 1: 4 hand on the *h* of the burnt offering,
1: 8 including the *h* and the fat,
1: 12 including the *h* and the fat,
1: 15 wring off the *h* and burn it
3: 2 hand on the *h* of his offering
3: 8 hand on the *h* of his offering
3: 13 He is to lay his hand on its *h*
4: 4 He is to lay his hand on its *h*
4: 11 as the *h* and legs, the inner parts
4: 15 on the bull's *h* before the LORD,
4: 24 He is to lay his hand on the goat's *h*
4: 29 hand on the *h* of the sin offering
4: 33 He is to lay his hand on its *h*
5: 8 He is to wring its *h* from its neck,
8: 9 he placed the turban on Aaron's *h*
8: 12 of the anointing oil on Aaron's *h*
8: 14 his sons laid their hands on its *h*.
8: 18 his sons laid their hands on its *h*.
8: 20 ram into pieces and burned the *h*,
8: 22 his sons laid their hands on its *h*.
9: 13 including the *h*, and he burned
13: 12 skin of the infected person from *h*
13: 29 or woman has a sore on the *h*
13: 30 an infectious disease of the *h*
13: 42 a reddish-white sore on his bald *h*
13: 42 disease breaking out on his *h*
13: 43 and, if the swollen sore on his *h*
13: 44 because of the sore on his *h*.
14: 9 he must shave his *h*, his beard,
14: 18 on the *h* of the one to be cleansed
14: 29 on the *h* of the one to be cleansed,
16: 21 and put them on the goat's *h*.
16: 21 hands on the *h* of the live goat
19: 27 the hair at the sides of your *h*
20: 9 and his blood will be on his own *h*.
21: 10 the anointing oil poured on his *h*
24: 14 are to lay their hands on his *h*,
Nu 1: 4 man from each tribe, each the *h*
6: 5 no razor may be used on his *h*.
6: 5 the hair of his *h* grow long.
6: 7 of his separation to God is on his *h*.
6: 9 he must shave his *h* on the day
6: 11 is to consecrate his *h*.
17: 3 for the *h* of each ancestral tribe.
Dt 19: 5 *h* may fly off and hit his neighbor
21: 12 home and have her shave her *h*,
28: 13 The LORD will make you the *h*,
28: 23 The sky over your *h* will be bronze,
28: 35 of your feet to the top of your *h*.
28: 44 He will be the *h*, but you will be
33: 16 Let all these rest on the *h* of Joseph
33: 20 tearing at arm or *h*.
Jos 2: 19 be on our *h* if a hand is laid
2: 19 his blood will be on his own *h*;
11: 10 (Hazor had been the *h*
22: 14 each the *h* of a family division
Jdg 5: 26 She struck Sisera, she crushed his *h*
8: 28 and did not raise its *h* again.
9: 53 an upper millstone on his *h*
10: 18 the Ammonites will be the *h*
11: 8 you will be our *h* over all who live
11: 9 will I really be your *h*?" The elders
11: 11 and the people made him *h*
12: 1 down your house over your *h*."
13: 5 No razor may be used on his *h*,
16: 13 braids of my *h* into the fabric
16: 13 took the seven braids of his *h*,
16: 17 If my *h* were shaved, my strength
16: 17 razor has ever been used on my *h*,"
16: 22 But the hair on his *h* began
1Sa 1: 11 no razor will ever be used on his *h*
4: 12 his clothes torn and dust on his *h*.
5: 4 His *h* and hands had been broken
9: 2 a *h* taller than any of the others.
9: 22 and seated them at the *h*
10: 1 it on Saul's *h* and kissed him,
10: 23 among the people he was a *h* taller
14: 45 not a hair of his *h* will fall
15: 17 did you not become the *h*
17: 5 He had a bronze helmet on his *h*
17: 38 and a bronze helmet on his *h*.
17: 46 you down and cut off your *h*.
17: 51 he cut off his *h* with the sword.
1Sa 17: 54 David took the Philistine's *h*
17: 57 still holding the Philistine's *h*.
19: 13 putting some goats' hair at the *h*.
19: 16 and at the *h* was some goats' hair.
21: 7 the Edomite, Saul's *h* shepherd.
25: 39 wrongdoing down on his own *h*."
26: 7 stuck in the ground near his *h*.
26: 11 and water jug that are near his *h*,
26: 12 and water jug near Saul's *h*,
26: 16 water jug that were near his *h*?"
31: 9 They cut off his *h* and stripped
2Sa 1: 2 and with dust on his *h*.
1: 10 I took the crown that was on his *h*
1: 16 "Your blood be on your own *h*.
2: 16 man grabbed his opponent by the *h*
3: 8 "Am I a dog's *h*— on Judah's side?
3: 29 fall upon the *h* of Joab
4: 7 and killed him, they cut off his *h*.
4: 8 They brought the *h* of Ish-Bosheth
4: 8 "Here is the *h* of Ish-Bosheth son
4: 12 But they took the *h* of Ish-Bosheth
12: 30 and it was placed on David's *h*.
12: 30 crown from the *h* of their king—
13: 19 She put her hand on her *h*
13: 19 Tamar put ashes on her *h*
14: 11 hair of your son's *h* will fall
14: 25 From the top of his *h* to the sole
14: 26 Whenever he cut the hair of his *h*—
15: 30 his *h* was covered and he was
15: 32 his robe torn and dust on his *h*.
16: 9 Let me go over and cut off his *h*."
18: 9 Absalom's *h* got caught in the tree.
20: 21 "His *h* will be thrown to you
20: 22 and they cut off the *h* of Sheba son
22: 44 you have preserved me as the *h*
1Ki 1: 52 not a hair of his *h* will fall
2: 6 but do not let his gray *h* go
2: 9 Bring his gray *h* down to the grave
2: 33 of their blood rest on the *h* of Joab
2: 37 your blood will be on your own *h*."
4: 23 ten *h* of stall-fed cattle, twenty
8: 32 on his own *h* what he has done.
19: 6 and there by his *h* was a cake
2Ki 4: 19 My *h*! My *h*!" he said to his father.
6: 25 so long that a donkey's *h* sold
6: 31 if the *h* of Elisha son
6: 32 sending someone to cut off my *h*?
9: 3 pour the oil on his *h* and declare,
9: 6 prophet poured the oil on Jehu's *h*
19: 21 tosses her *h* as you flee.
1Ch 5: 15 son of Guni, was *h* of their family.
10: 9 and took his *h* and his armor,
10: 10 and hung up his *h* in the temple
15: 22 Kenaniah the *h* Levite was
20: 2 and it was placed on David's *h*.
20: 2 crown from the *h* of their king—
29: 11 you are exalted as *h* over all.
2Ch 6: 23 on his own *h* what he has done.
7: 5 of twenty-two thousand *h* of cattle
15: 11 to the LORD seven hundred *h*
20: 21 they went out at the *h* of the army,
35: 9 and five hundred *h* of cattle
Ezr 9: 3 pulled hair from my *h* and beard
Ne 6: 8 are just making it up out of your *h*."
Est 2: 17 So he set a royal crown on her *h*
6: 8 with a royal crest placed on its *h*.
6: 12 with his *h* covered in grief,
9: 25 should come back onto his own *h*,
Job 1: 20 and tore his robe and shaved his *h*.
2: 7 soles of his feet to the top of his *h*.
10: 15 if I am innocent, I cannot lift my *h*,
10: 16 If I hold my *h* high, you stalk me
16: 4 and shake my *h* at you.
19: 9 and removed the crown from my *h*.
20: 6 and his *h* touches the clouds,
29: 3 when his lamp shone upon my *h*
41: 7 or his *h* with fishing spears?
Ps 3: 3 Glorious One, who lifts up my *h*.
7: 16 down on his own *h*.
18: 43 you have made me the *h* of nations;
21: 3 of pure gold on his *h*.
23: 5 You anoint my *h* with oil;
27: 6 Then my *h* will be exalted
35: 14 I bowed my *h* in grief
40: 12 more than the hairs of my *h*,
69: 4 outnumber the hairs of my *h*;
110: 7 therefore he will lift up his *h*.
132: 18 on his *h* will be resplendent."
Ps 133: 2 is like precious oil poured on the *h*,
140: 7 who shields my *h* in the day
141: 5 My *h* will not refuse it.
141: 5 him rebuke me—it is oil on my *h*.
Pr 1: 9 will be a garland to grace your *h*
1: 21 at the *h* of the noisy streets she
4: 9 of grace on your *h*
10: 6 Blessings crown the *h*
25: 22 will heap burning coals on his *h*,
Ecc 2: 14 The wise man has eyes in his *h*,
9: 8 and always anoint your *h* with oil.
SS 2: 6 His left arm is under my *h*,
5: 2 My *h* is drenched with dew,
5: 11 His *h* is purest gold;
7: 5 Your *h* crowns you like Mount
8: 3 His left arm is under my *h*
Isa 1: 5 Your whole *h* is injured,
1: 6 of your foot to the top of your *h*
7: 8 for the *h* of Aram is Damascus,
7: 8 the *h* of Damascus is only Rezin.
7: 9 The *h* of Ephraim is Samaria,
7: 9 *h* of Samaria is only Remaliah's
7: 20 to shave your *h* and the hair
9: 14 cut off from Israel both *h*
9: 15 and prominent men are the *h*,
15: 2 Every *h* is shaved
19: 15 *h* or tail, palm branch or reed.
28: 1 set on the *h* of a fertile valley—
28: 4 set on the *h* of a fertile valley,
37: 22 tosses her *h* as you flee.
51: 20 they lie at the *h* of every street,
58: 5 only for bowing one's *h* like a reed
59: 17 and the helmet of salvation on his *h*
61: 10 as a bridegroom adorns his *h* like
Jer 2: 16 have shaved the crown of your *h*.
2: 37 place with your hands on your *h*,
9: 1 that my *h* were a spring of water
16: 6 one will cut himself or shave his *h*
47: 5 Gaza will shave her *h* in mourning;
48: 27 that you shake your *h* in scorn
48: 37 Every *h* is shaved
La 2: 19 hunger at the *h* of every street.
3: 54 the waters closed over my *h*,
4: 1 scattered at the *h* of every street.
5: 16 The crown has fallen from our *h*.
Eze 5: 1 as a barber's razor to shave your *h*
8: 3 and took me by the hair of my *h*.
10: 11 in whatever direction the *h* faced,
16: 12 and a beautiful crown on your *h*.
16: 25 At the *h* of every street you built
16: 31 mounds at the *h* of every street
16: 43 on your *h* what you have done,
17: 19 on his *h* my oath that he despised
18: 13 and his blood will be on his own *h*.
29: 18 every *h* was rubbed bare
33: 4 his blood will be on his own *h*.
33: 5 his blood will be on his own *h*.
Da 1: 10 The king would then have my *h*
2: 32 The *h* of the statue was made
2: 38 You are that *h* of gold.
7: 9 hair of his *h* was white like wool.
7: 20 know about the ten horns on its *h*
Hos 8: 7 The stalk has no *h*;
Joel 2: 11 thunders at the *h* of his army;
Ob : 15 deeds will return upon your own *h*.
Jnh 2: 5 seaweed was wrapped around my *h*
4: 6 for his *h* to ease his discomfort,
4: 8 and the sun blazed on Jonah's *h*
Mic 2: 13 the LORD at their *h*."
Na 3: 10 pieces at the *h* of every street.
Hab 3: 13 you stripped him from *h* to foot.
3: 14 his own spear you pierced his *h*
Zec 1: 21 so that no one could raise his *h*,
3: 5 So they put a clean turban on his *h*
3: 5 "Put a clean turban on his *h*."
6: 11 and set it on the *h* of the high priest
Mt 5: 36 And do not swear by your *h*,
6: 17 oil on your *h* and wash your face,
8: 20 of Man has no place to lay his *h*."
10: 25 If the *h* of the house has been
10: 30 hairs of your *h* are all numbered.
14: 8 here on a platter the *h* of John
14: 11 His *h* was brought in on a platter
26: 7 which she poured on his *h*
27: 29 crown of thorns and set it on his *h*.
27: 30 struck him on the *h* again and again
27: 37 Above his *h* they placed
Mk 4: 28 then the full kernel in the *h*.

Mk 4:28 then the *h,* then the full kernel
6:24 "The *h* of John the Baptist,"
6:25 you to give me right now the *h*
6:27 with orders to bring John's *h.*
6:28 and brought back his *h* on a platter.
12: 4 they struck this man on the *h*
14: 3 and poured the perfume on his *h.*
15:19 him on the *h* with a staff
Lk 7:46 You did not put oil on my *h,*
9:58 of Man has no place to lay his *h.*"
12: 7 hairs of your *h* are all numbered.
21:18 But not a hair of your *h* will perish.
Jn 13: 9 but my hands and my *h* as well!"
19: 2 crown of thorns and put it on his *h.*
19:30 he bowed his *h* and gave up his
20: 7 that had been around Jesus' *h.*
20:12 one at the *h* and the other
Ac 27:15 and could not *h* into the wind;
27:34 will lose a single hair from his *h.*"
Ro 12:20 will heap burning coals on his *h.*"
1Co 11: 3 and the *h* of Christ is God.
11: 3 and the *h* of the woman is man,
11: 3 you to realize that the *h*
11: 4 with his *h* covered dishonors his *h.*
11: 5 as though her *h* were shaved.
11: 5 her *h* uncovered dishonors her *h*—
11: 6 If a woman does not cover her *h,*
11: 6 shaved off, she should cover her *h.*
11: 7 A man ought not to cover his *h,*
11:10 to have a sign of authority on her *h.*
11:13 pray to God with her *h* uncovered?
12:21 And the *h* cannot say to the feet,
Eph 1:10 and on earth together under one *h,*
1:22 him to be *h* over everything
4:15 up into him who is the *H,*
5:23 For the husband is the *h* of the wife
5:23 as Christ is the *h* of the church,
Col 1:18 And he is the *h* of the body,
2:10 who is the *h* over every power
2:19 He has lost connection with the *H,*
2Ti 4: 5 keep your *h* in all situations,
Rev 1:14 His *h* and hair were white like wool
10: 1 with a rainbow above his *h;*
12: 1 a crown of twelve stars on her *h.*
13: 1 and on each *h* a blasphemous name
14:14 with a crown of gold on his *h*
19:12 and on his *h* are many crowns.

HEADBAND (HEADBANDS)

1Ki 20:38 with his *h* down over his eyes.
20:41 the prophet quickly removed the *h*

HEADBANDS (HEADBAND)

Ex 28:40 sashes and *h* for Aaron's sons,
29: 9 them in tunics and put *h* on them.
39:28 the linen *h* and the undergarments
Lev 8:13 around them and put *h* on them,
Isa 3:18 and *h* and crescent necklaces,

HEADDRESSES

Isa 3:20 the *h* and ankle chains and sashes,

HEADED (HEAD)

Ge 31:21 he *h* for the hill country of Gilead.
Ex 9:31 since the barley had *h*
Jos 15: 9 From the hilltop the boundary *h*
18:12 and *h* west into the hill country,
Jer 39: 4 and *h* toward the Arabah.
Jnh 1: 3 from the LORD and *h* for Tarshish

HEADING (HEAD)

Lk 9:53 because he was *h* for Jerusalem.
Jn 6:21 the shore where they were *h.*

HEADLONG

2Ki 7:15 had thrown away in their *h* flight.
Job 27:22 as he flees *h* from its power.
Hab 1: 8 Their cavalry gallops *h;*
Ac 1:18 Judas bought a field; there he fell *h,*

HEADS (HEAD)

Ge 40:20 He lifted up the *h* of the chief
41: 5 Seven *h* of grain, healthy and good,
41: 6 seven other *h* of grain sprouted—
41: 7 The thin *h* of grain swallowed up
41: 7 up the seven healthy, full *h.*
41:22 "In my dreams I also saw seven *h*
41:23 After them, seven other *h* sprouted
Ge 41:24 The thin *h* of grain swallowed up
41:24 swallowed up the seven good *h.*
41:26 the seven good *h* of grain are seven
41:27 and so are the seven worthless *h*
Ex 6:14 These were the *h* of their families:
6:25 These were the *h* of the Levite
Lev 2:14 offer crushed *h* of new grain
20:11 their blood will be on their own *h.*
20:12 their blood will be on their own *h.*
20:13 their blood will be on their own *h.*
20:16 their blood will be on their own *h.*
20:27 their blood will be on their own *h*
21: 5 " 'Priests must not shave their *h*
26:13 you to walk with *h* held high.
Nu 1:16 They were the *h* of the clans
7: 2 *h* of families who were the tribal
8:12 hands on the *h* of the bulls,
10: 4 the *h* of the clans of Israel—
30: 1 Moses said to the *h* of the tribes
31:26 the family *h* of the community are
32:28 and to the family *h* of the Israelite
36: 1 The family *h* of the clan
36: 1 the *h* of the Israelite families.
Dt 14: 1 the front of your *h* for the dead,
32:42 the *h* of the enemy leaders."
33:21 When the *h* of the people
Jos 7: 6 and sprinkled dust on their *h.*
14: 1 and the *h* of the tribal clans
19:51 and the *h* of the tribal clans
21: 1 family *h* of the Levites approached
21: 1 the *h* of the other tribal families
22:21 replied to the *h* of the clans
22:30 the *h* of the clans of the Israelites—
Jdg 7:25 and brought the *h* of Oreb
1Sa 29: 4 favor than by taking the *h*
2Sa 15:30 with him covered their *h* too
1Ki 8: 1 all the *h* of the tribes and the chiefs
20:31 our waists and ropes around our *h.*
20:32 waists and ropes around their *h,*
2Ki 4:42 along with some *h* of new grain.
10: 6 take the *h* of your master's sons
10: 7 They put their *h* in baskets
10: 8 "They have brought the *h*
1Ch 5:24 These were the *h* of their families:
5:24 famous men, and *h* of their families
7: 2 and Samuel—*h* of their families.
7: 7 Jerimoth and Iri, *h* of families—
7: 9 genealogical record listed the *h*
7:11 sons of Jediael were *h* of families.
7:40 of Asher—*h* of families,
8: 6 who were *h* of families
8:10 These were his sons, *h* of families.
8:13 who were *h* of families
8:28 All these were *h* of families,
9: 9 All these men were *h*
9:13 The priests, who were *h* of families,
9:33 Those who were musicians, *h*
9:34 All these were *h* of Levite families,
12:19 "It will cost us our *h* if he deserts
15:12 "You are the *h* of the Levitical
23: 9 These were the *h* of the families
23:24 the *h* of families as they were
24: 4 and eight *h* of families
24: 4 sixteen *h* of families
24: 6 and the *h* of families of the priests
24:31 and the *h* of families of the priests
26:21 who were *h* of families belonging
26:26 by the *h* of families who were
26:32 who were able men and *h*
27: 1 list of the Israelites—*h* of families,
2Ch 1: 2 leaders in Israel, the *h* of families—
5: 2 all the *h* of the tribes and the chiefs
19: 8 and *h* of Israelite families
23: 2 and the *h* of Israelite families
29:30 and bowed their *h* and worshiped.
Ezr 1: 5 Then the family *h* of Judah
2:68 some of the *h* of the families gave
3:12 priests and Levites and family *h,*
4: 2 to the *h* of the families and said,
4: 3 and the rest of the *h* of the families
8: 1 These are the family *h*
8:29 and the family *h* of Israel."
9: 6 our sins are higher than our *h*
10:16 selected men who were family *h,*
Ne 4: 4 their insults back on their own *h.*
7:70 of the *h* of the families contributed
7:71 Some of the *h* of the families gave
8:13 day of the month, the *h*
Ne 9: 1 and having dust on their *h.*
11:13 who were *h* of families—242 men;
11:16 two of the *h* of the Levites,
12:12 these were the *h* of the priestly
12:22 The family *h* of the Levites
12:23 family *h* among the descendants
Job 2:12 and sprinkled dust on their *h.*
24:24 they are cut off like *h* of grain.
Ps 22: 7 they hurl insults, shaking their *h:*
24: 7 Lift up your *h,* O you gates;
24: 9 Lift up your *h,* O you gates;
44:14 the peoples shake their *h* at us.
64: 8 all who see them will shake their *h*
66:12 You let men ride over our *h;*
68:21 Surely God will crush the *h*
74:13 you broke the *h* of the monster
74:14 It was you who crushed the *h*
83: 2 how your foes rear their *h.*
109:25 they see me, they shake their *h.*
140: 9 Let the *h* of those who surround
Isa 3:17 on the *h* of the women of Zion;
17: 5 as when a man gleans *h* of grain
29:10 he has covered your *h* (the seers).
35:10 everlasting joy will crown their *h.*
51:11 everlasting joy will crown their *h.*
Jer 13:18 will fall from your *h.*"
14: 3 they cover their *h.*
14: 4 and cover their *h.*
18:16 and will shake their *h.*
23:19 down on the *h* of the wicked.
30:23 down on the *h* of the wicked.
La 2:10 have bowed their *h* to the ground.
2:10 they have sprinkled dust on their *h*
2:15 they scoff and shake their *h*
Eze 1:22 Spread out above the *h*
1:25 above the expanse over their *h*
1:26 over their *h* was what looked like
7:18 and their *h* will be shaved.
9:10 on their own *h* what they have
10: 1 was over the *h* of the cherubim.
11:21 on their own *h* what they have
13:18 lengths for their *h* in order
22:31 on their own *h* all they have done,
23:15 and flowing turbans on their *h;*
23:42 and beautiful crowns on their *h.*
24:23 will keep your turbans on your *h*
27:30 they will sprinkle dust on their *h*
27:31 They will shave their *h*
32:27 swords were placed under their *h?*
44:18 are to wear linen turbans on their *h*
44:20 to keep the hair of their *h* trimmed.
44:20 " 'They must not shave their *h*
Da 3:27 nor was a hair of their *h* singed;
7: 6 This beast had four *h,* and it was
Joel 3: 4 on your own *h* what you have done
3: 7 on your own *h* what you have done
Am 2: 7 They trample on the *h* of the poor
8:10 and shave your *h.*
9: 1 "Cut off the *h* of all the people—
Mic 1:16 Shave your *h* in mourning
Mt 12: 1 and began to pick some *h* of grain
13:26 the wheat sprouted and formed *h,*
27:39 shaking their *h* and saying,
Mk 2:23 they began to pick some *h* of grain.
15:29 shaking their *h* and saying, "So!
Lk 6: 1 began to pick some *h* of grain,
21:28 stand up and lift up your *h,*
Ac 18: 6 "Your blood be on your own *h!*
21:24 that they can have their *h* shaved.
Rev 4: 4 and had crowns of gold on their *h.*
9: 7 On their *h* they wore something
9:17 The *h* of the horses resembled
9:17 of the horses resembled the *h*
9:19 having *h* with which they inflict
12: 3 and seven crowns on his *h.*
12: 3 enormous red dragon with seven *h*
13: 1 He had ten horns and seven *h,*
13: 3 One of the *h* of the beast seemed
17: 3 and had seven *h* and ten horns.
17: 7 which has the seven *h*
17: 9 The seven *h* are seven hills
18:19 They will throw dust on their *h,*

HEADSTREAMS (STREAM)

Ge 2:10 from there it divided; it had four *h.*

HEADWAY

Ac 27: 7 We made slow *h* for many days

HEAL (HEALED HEALING HEALS)

Nu 12: 13 please *h* her!'' The LORD replied
Dt 32: 39 I have wounded and I will *h,*
2Ki 20: 5 and seen your tears; I will *h* you.
20: 8 the sign that the LORD will *h* me
2Ch 7: 14 their sin and will *h* their land.
Job 5: 18 he injures, but his hands also *h.*
Ps 6: 2 *h* me, for my bones are in agony.
41: 4 *h* me, for I have sinned against you
Ecc 3: 3 a time to kill and a time to *h,*
Isa 19: 22 he will strike them and *h* them.
19: 22 respond to their pleas and *h* them.
57: 18 seen his ways, but I will *h* him;
57: 19 ''And I will *h* them.''
Jer 17: 14 *H* me, O LORD, and I will be
30: 17 and *h* your wounds,'
33: 6 I will *h* my people and will let them
La 2: 13 Who can *h* you?
Hos 5: 13 not able to *h* your sores.
6: 1 but he will *h* us;
7: 1 whenever I would *h* Israel,
14: 4 ''I will *h* their waywardness
Na 3: 19 Nothing can *h* your wound;
Zec 11: 16 or seek the young, or *h* the injured,
Mt 8: 7 said to him, ''I will go and *h* him.''
10: 1 to *h* every disease and sickness.
10: 8 *H* the sick, raise the dead,
12: 10 ''Is it lawful to *h* on the Sabbath?''
13: 15 and turn, and I would *h* them.'
17: 16 but they could not *h* him.''
Mk 3: 2 if he would *h* him on the Sabbath.
6: 5 on a few sick people and *h* them.
Lk 4: 23 to me: 'Physician, *h* yourself!
5: 17 present for him to *h* the sick.
6: 7 to see if he would *h* on the Sabbath.
7: 3 him to come and *h* his servant.
8: 43 years, but no one could *h* her.
9: 2 kingdom of God and to *h* the sick.
10: 9 *H* the sick who are there
13: 32 and *h* people today and tomorrow,
14: 3 ''Is it lawful to *h* on the Sabbath
Jn 4: 47 begged him to come and *h* his son,
12: 40 nor turn—and I would *h* them.''
Ac 4: 30 Stretch out your hand to *h*
28: 27 and turn and I would *h* them.'

HEALED (HEAL)

Ge 20: 17 to God, and God *h* Abimelech,
Ex 21: 19 and see that he is completely *h.*
Lev 13: 37 hair has grown in it, the itch is *h.*
14: 3 If the person has been *h*
Jos 5: 8 were in camp until they were *h.*
1Sa 6: 3 you will be *h,* and you will know
2Ki 2: 21 LORD says: 'I have *h* this water.
2Ch 30: 20 heard Hezekiah and *h* the people.
Ps 30: 2 and you *h* me.
107: 20 He sent forth his word and *h* them;
Isa 6: 10 and turn and be *h.*''
53: 5 and by his wounds we are *h.*
Jer 14: 19 us so that we cannot be *h?*
17: 14 Heal me, O LORD, and I will be *h;*
51: 8 perhaps she can be *h.*
51: 9 but she cannot be *h;*
51: 9 '' 'We would have *h* Babylon,
Eze 34: 4 the weak or *h* the sick
Hos 11: 3 it was I who *h* them.
Mt 4: 24 and the paralytics, and he *h* them.
8: 8 the word, and my servant will be *h.*
8: 13 his servant was *h* at that very hour.
8: 16 with a word and *h* all the sick.
9: 21 If I only touch his cloak, I will be *h*
9: 22 he said, ''your faith has *h* you.''
9: 22 woman was *h* from that moment.
12: 15 him, and he *h* all their sick,
12: 22 Jesus *h* him, so that he could both
14: 14 on them and *h* their sick.
14: 36 and all who touched him were *h.*
15: 28 And her daughter was *h*
15: 30 laid them at his feet; and he *h* them
17: 18 and he was *h* from that moment.
19: 2 followed him, and he *h* them there.
21: 14 to him at the temple, and he *h* them
Mk 1: 34 and Jesus *h* many who had various
3: 10 For he had *h* many, so that those
5: 23 hands on her so that she will be *h*
5: 28 If I just touch his clothes, I will be *h*
5: 34 ''Daughter, your faith has *h* you.
Mk 6: 13 people with oil and *h* them.
6: 56 and all who touched him were *h.*
10: 52 said Jesus, ''your faith has *h* you.''
Lk 4: 40 hands on each one, he *h* them.
5: 15 and to be *h* of their sicknesses.
6: 18 and to be *h* of their diseases.
7: 7 the word, and my servant will be *h.*
8: 47 and how she had been instantly *h.*
8: 48 ''Daughter, your faith has *h* you.
8: 50 just believe, and she will be *h.*''
9: 11 and *h* those who needed healing.
9: 42 *h* the boy and gave him back
13: 14 Jesus had *h* on the Sabbath,
13: 14 So come and be *h* on those days,
14: 4 he *h* him and sent him away.
17: 15 when he saw he was *h,* came back,
18: 42 your sight; your faith has *h* you.''
22: 51 touched the man's ear and *h* him.
Jn 5: 10 said to the man who had been *h,*
5: 13 man who was *h* had no idea who it
Ac 4: 9 and are asked how he was *h,*
4: 10 stands before you completely *h.*
4: 14 who had been *h* standing there
4: 22 man who was miraculously *h* was
5: 16 evil spirits, and all of them were *h.*
8: 7 paralytics and cripples were *h.*
14: 9 saw that he had faith to be *h*
28: 8 placed his hands on him and *h* him.
Heb 12: 13 may not be disabled, but rather *h.*
Jas 5: 16 for each other so that you may be *h*
1Pe 2: 24 by his wounds you have been *h.*
Rev 13: 3 but the fatal wound had been *h.*
13: 12 whose fatal wound had been *h.*

HEALING (HEAL)

2Ch 28: 15 food and drink, and *h* balm.
Pr 12: 18 but the tongue of the wise brings *h.*
13: 17 but a trustworthy envoy brings *h.*
15: 4 The tongue that brings *h* is a tree
16: 24 sweet to the soul and *h* to the bones
Isa 58: 8 and your *h* will quickly appear;
Jer 8: 15 for a time of *h*
8: 22 Why then is there no *h*
14: 19 for a time of *h*
30: 12 your injury beyond *h.*
30: 13 no *h* for you.
33: 6 I will bring health and *h* to it;
46: 11 there is no *h* for you.
Eze 30: 21 It has not been bound up for *h*
47: 12 for food and their leaves for *h.*''
Mal 4: 2 rise with *h* in its wings.
Mt 4: 23 and *h* every disease and sickness
9: 35 and *h* every disease and sickness.
Lk 6: 19 coming from him and *h* them all.
9: 6 gospel and *h* people everywhere.
9: 11 and healed those who needed *h.*
Jn 7: 23 angry with me for *h* the whole man
Ac 3: 16 him that has given this complete *h*
10: 38 *h* all who were under the power
1Co 12: 9 to another gifts of *h*
12: 28 also those having gifts of *h,*
12: 30 Do all have gifts of *h?* Do all speak
Rev 22: 2 are for the *h* of the nations.

HEALS (HEAL)

Ex 15: 26 for I am the LORD who *h* you.''
Lev 13: 18 a boil on his skin and it *h,*
Ps 103: 3 and *h* all my diseases;
147: 3 He *h* the brokenhearted
Isa 30: 26 and *h* the wounds he inflicted.
Ac 9: 34 said to him, ''Jesus Christ *h* you.

HEALTH (HEALTHIER HEALTHY)

1Sa 25: 6 And good *h* to all that is yours!
25: 6 Good *h* to you and your household
Ps 38: 3 of your wrath there is no *h*
38: 7 there is no *h* in my body.
Pr 3: 8 This will bring *h* to your body
4: 22 and *h* to a man's whole body.
15: 30 and good news gives *h* to the bones
Isa 38: 16 You restored me to *h*
Jer 30: 17 But I will restore you to *h*
33: 6 I will bring *h* and healing to it;
3Jn : 2 I pray that you may enjoy good *h*

HEALTHIER (HEALTH)

Da 1: 15 end of the ten days they looked *h*

HEALTHY (HEALTH)

Ge 41: 5 Seven heads of grain, *h* and good,
41: 7 of grain swallowed up the seven *h,*
Ps 73: 4 their bodies are *h* and strong.
Zec 11: 16 or heal the injured, or feed the *h,*
Mt 9: 12 ''It is not the *h* who need a doctor,
Mk 2: 17 ''It is not the *h* who need a doctor,
Lk 5: 31 ''It is not the *h* who need a doctor,

HEAP (HEAPED HEAPING HEAPS)

Ge 31: 46 and they ate there by the *h.*
31: 46 took stones and piled them in a *h,*
31: 48 ''This *h* is a witness between you
31: 51 also said to Jacob, ''Here is this *h,*
31: 52 This *h* is a witness, and this pillar is
31: 52 and that you will not go past this *h*
31: 52 that I will not go past this *h*
Lev 4: 12 burn it in a wood fire on the ash *h.*
Dt 32: 23 ''I will *h* calamities upon them
Jos 3: 13 cut off and stand up in a *h.*''
3: 16 up in a *h* a great distance away,
8: 28 and made it a permanent *h* of ruins,
1Sa 2: 8 and lifts the needy from the ash *h;*
2Sa 18: 17 piled up a large *h* of rocks over him
Ps 113: 7 and lifts the needy from the ash *h;*
Pr 25: 22 you will *h* burning coals
Isa 3: 6 take charge of this *h* of ruins!''
17: 1 but will become a *h* of ruins.
25: 2 You have made the city a *h*
Jer 9: 11 ''I will make Jerusalem a *h* of ruins,
26: 18 Jerusalem will become a *h*
51: 37 Babylon will be a *h* of ruins,
Eze 24: 10 So *h* on the wood
Mic 1: 6 ''Therefore I will make Samaria a *h*
3: 12 Jerusalem will become a *h*
Hag 2: 16 came to a *h* of twenty measures,
Ro 12: 20 you will *h* burning coals
1Th 2: 16 this way they always *h* up their sins
1Pe 4: 4 of dissipation, and they *h* abuse

HEAPED (HEAP)

Jos 7: 26 Over Achan they *h* up a large pile
2Ki 19: 23 you have *h* insults on the Lord.
Isa 37: 24 you have *h* insults on the Lord.
Zec 9: 3 she has *h* up silver like dust,
Mt 27: 44 with him also *h* insults on him.
Mk 15: 32 with him also *h* insults on him.

HEAPING (HEAP)

Ps 110: 6 judge the nations, *h* up the dead
Isa 30: 1 *h* sin upon sin;

HEAPS (HEAP)

Ex 8: 14 They were piled into *h,*
2Ch 31: 6 God, and they piled them in *h.*
31: 8 his officials came and saw the *h,*
31: 9 the priests and Levites about the *h;*
Ne 4: 2 to life from those *h* of rubble—
Job 27: 16 Though he *h* up silver like dust
Ps 39: 6 he *h* up wealth, not knowing who
Jer 50: 26 pile her up like *h* of grain.
La 4: 5 now lie on ash *h.*
Zep 1: 3 The wicked will have only *h*

HEAR (HEARD HEARERS HEARING HEARS OVERHEARD)

Ge 4: 23 wives of Lamech, *h* my words.
41: 15 that when you *h* a dream you can
Ex 15: 14 The nations will *h* and tremble;
18: 9 to *h* about all the good things
19: 9 that the people will *h* me speaking
22: 23 I will certainly *h* their cry.
22: 27 I will *h,* for I am compassionate.
32: 18 it is the sound of singing that I *h.*''
Nu 14: 13 Then the Egyptians will *h* about it!
23: 18 *h* me, son of Zippor.
Dt 1: 16 *H* the disputes between your
1: 17 hard for you, and I will *h* it.
1: 17 *h* both small and great alike.
2: 25 They will *h* reports of you
4: 1 *H* now, O Israel, the decrees
4: 6 who will *h* about all these decrees
4: 10 people before me to *h* my words
4: 28 which cannot see or *h* or eat
4: 36 heaven he made you *h* his voice
5: 1 summoned all Israel and said: *H,*
5: 25 and we will die if we *h* the voice
6: 3 *H,* O Israel, and be careful to obey

Dt 6: 4 H, O Israel: The LORD our God,
9: 1 H, O Israel.
13: 11 Then all Israel will h and be afraid,
13: 12 If you h it said about one
17: 13 All the people will h and be afraid,
18: 16 "Let us not h the voice
19: 20 The rest of the people will h of this
20: 3 He shall say: "H, O Israel,
21: 21 All Israel will h of it and be afraid.
29: 4 or eyes that see or ears that h.
31: 13 must h it and learn
32: 1 h, O earth, the words of my mouth.
33: 7 "H, O LORD, the cry of Judah;
Jos 6: 5 When you h them sound a long
7: 9 of the country will h about this
22: 33 They were glad to h the report
Jdg 5: 3 "H this, you kings! Listen,
5: 16 to h the whistling for the flocks?
14: 13 "Let's h it."
1Sa 2: 23 I h from all the people about these
2: 24 not a good report that I h spreading
13: 3 "Let the Hebrews h!"
15: 14 lowing of cattle that I h?"
16: 2 Saul will h about it and kill me."
25: 7 I h that it is sheep-shearing time.
25: 24 h what your servant has to say.
2Sa 5: 24 as you h the sound of marching
15: 3 of the king to h you."
15: 10 as you h the sound of the trumpets,
15: 35 Tell them anything you h
15: 36 them to me with anything you h."
16: 21 all Israel will h that you have made
17: 5 so we can h what he has to say."
18: 31 My lord the king, h the good news!
19: 35 Can I still h the voices of men
22: 45 as soon as they h me, they obey me
1Ki 1: 45 That's the noise you h.
8: 28 H the cry and the prayer that your
8: 29 so that you will h the prayer your
8: 30 dwelling place, and when you h,
8: 30 H from heaven, your dwelling
8: 30 H the supplication of your servant
8: 32 then h from heaven and act.
8: 34 then h from heaven and forgive
8: 36 then h from heaven and forgive
8: 39 then h from heaven, your dwelling
8: 42 for men will h of your great name
8: 43 then h from heaven, your dwelling
8: 45 then h from heaven their prayer
8: 49 h their prayer and their plea,
10: 8 before you and h your wisdom!
10: 24 to h the wisdom God had put
22: 19 Therefore h the word of the LORD
2Ki 7: 1 "H the word of the LORD.
7: 6 to h the sound of chariots
18: 28 "H the word of the great king,
19: 4 your God will h all the words
19: 16 O LORD, and h; open your eyes,
20: 16 "H the word of the LORD:
1Ch 14: 15 as you h the sound of marching
2Ch 6: 19 H the cry and the prayer that your
6: 20 May you h the prayer your servant
6: 21 dwelling place; and when you h,
6: 21 H from heaven, your dwelling
6: 21 H the supplications of your servant
6: 23 then h from heaven and act.
6: 25 then h from heaven and forgive
6: 27 then h from heaven and forgive
6: 30 then h from heaven, your dwelling
6: 33 then h from heaven, your dwelling
6: 35 then h from heaven their prayer
6: 39 h their prayer and their pleas,
7: 14 then will I h from heaven
9: 7 before you and h your wisdom!
9: 23 to h the wisdom God had put
18: 18 Therefore h the word of the LORD
20: 9 and you will h us and save us.'
Ne 1: 6 open to h the prayer your servant is
4: 4 down their wall of stones!" H us,
4: 20 Wherever you h the sound
13: 27 Must we h now that you too are
Job 3: 18 they no longer h the slave driver's
5: 27 So h it and apply it to yourself."
13: 6 H now my argument;
20: 3 I h a rebuke that dishonors me,
22: 27 to him, and he will h you,
26: 14 how faint the whisper we h of him!
31: 35 ("Oh, that I had someone to h me!
Job 34: 2 Then Elihu said: "H my words,
34: 16 "If you have understanding, h this;
34: 34 wise men who h me say to me,
39: 7 he does not h a driver's shout
Ps 4: 1 Be merciful to me and h my prayer.
4: 3 the LORD will h when I call to him
5: 3 O LORD, you h my voice;
10: 17 You h, O LORD, the desire
17: 1 H, O LORD, my righteous plea;
17: 6 give ear to me and h my prayer.
18: 44 they h me, they obey me;
27: 7 H my voice when I call, O LORD;
28: 2 H my cry for mercy
30: 10 H, O LORD, and be merciful
31: 13 For I h the slander of many;
34: 2 let the afflicted h and rejoice.
38: 13 I am like a deaf man, who cannot h,
38: 14 become like a man who does not h,
39: 12 "H my prayer, O LORD,
49: 1 H this, all you peoples;
50: 7 "H, O my people, and I will speak,
51: 8 Let me h joy and gladness;
54: 2 H my prayer, O God;
55: 2 h me and answer me.
55: 19 will h them and afflict them—
59: 7 and they say, "Who can h us?"
61: 1 H my cry, O God;
64: 1 H me, O God, as I voice my
65: 2 O you who h prayer,
77: 1 I cried out to God to h me.
78: 1 O my people, h my teaching;
80: 1 H us, O Shepherd of Israel,
81: 8 "H, O my people, and I will warn
84: 8 H my prayer, O LORD God
86: 1 H, O LORD, and answer me,
86: 6 H my prayer, O LORD;
94: 9 he who implanted the ear not h?
95: 7 Today, if you h his voice,
102: 1 H my prayer, O LORD;
102: 20 to h the groans of the prisoners
115: 6 they have ears, but cannot h,
119:149 H my voice in accordance
130: 2 O LORD; O Lord, h my voice.
135: 17 they have ears, but cannot h,
138: 4 when they h the words
140: 6 H, O LORD, my cry for mercy.
141: 1 H my voice when I call to you.
143: 1 O LORD, h my prayer,
Pr 20: 12 Ears that h and eyes that see—
Ecc 7: 21 or you may h your servant cursing
SS 2: 14 let me h your voice;
8: 13 let me h your voice!
Isa 1: 2 H, O heavens! Listen, O earth!
1: 10 H the word of the LORD,
6: 10 h with their ears,
7: 13 Then Isaiah said, "H now,
18: 3 you will h it.
21: 3 I am staggered by what I h.
24: 16 of the earth we h singing:
28: 14 Therefore h the word of the LORD
28: 23 Listen and h my voice;
28: 23 pay attention and h what I say.
29: 18 that day the deaf will h the words
30: 21 your ears will h a voice behind you,
30: 30 men to h his majestic voice
32: 3 the ears of those who h will listen.
32: 9 h what I have to say!
33: 13 who are far away, h what I have
34: 1 Let the earth h, and all that is in it,
36: 13 "H the words of the great king,
37: 4 LORD your God will h the words
37: 17 O LORD, and h; open your eyes,
39: 5 "H the word of the LORD
42: 18 "H, you deaf;
42: 20 ears are open, but you h nothing."
43: 9 so that others may h and say,
49: 1 h this you distant nations.
51: 4 h me, my nation:
51: 7 H me, you who know what is right,
51: 21 Therefore h this, you afflicted one,
55: 3 h me, that your soul may live.
59: 1 nor his ear too dull to h.
59: 2 so that he will not h.
65: 24 while they are still speaking I will h
66: 5 H the word of the LORD,
66: 6 H that uproar from the city,
66: 6 h that noise from the temple!
Jer 2: 4 H the word of the LORD,
Jer 4: 21 and h the sound of the trumpet?
4: 31 I h a cry as of a woman in labor,
5: 21 H this, you foolish and senseless
5: 21 who have ears but do not h:
6: 10 closed so they cannot h.
6: 18 Therefore h, O nations;
6: 19 H, O earth:
7: 2 " 'H the word of the LORD,
9: 20 O women, h the word
10: 1 H what the LORD says to you,
13: 15 H and pay attention,
17: 20 'H the word of the LORD,
18: 19 h what my accusers are saying!
19: 3 and say, 'H the word of the LORD,
20: 10 I h many whispering,
20: 16 May he h wailing in the morning,
21: 11 'H the word of the LORD;
22: 2 'H the word of the LORD,
22: 29 h the word of the LORD!
23: 18 the LORD to see or to h his word?
25: 36 H the cry of the shepherds,
29: 20 Therefore, h the word
31: 10 "H the word of the LORD,
33: 9 before all nations on earth that h
34: 4 " 'Yet h the promise of the LORD,
36: 3 of Judah h about every disaster I
38: 25 If the officials h that I talked
42: 2 "Please h our petition
42: 14 will not see war or h the trumpet
42: 15 then h the word of the LORD,
44: 24 "H the word of the LORD,
44: 26 But h the word of the LORD,
46: 12 The nations will h of your shame;
49: 20 h what the LORD has planned
50: 45 h what the LORD has planned
Eze 3: 17 so h the word I speak and give
6: 3 h the word of the Sovereign LORD
12: 2 not see and ears to h but do not h,
13: 2 'H the word of the LORD!
16: 35 you prostitute, h the word
18: 25 H, O house of Israel: Is my way
20: 47 'H the word of the LORD.
25: 3 'H the word of the Sovereign
33: 7 so h the word I speak and give
33: 30 and h the message that has come
33: 32 for they h your words but do not
34: 7 you shepherds, h the word
34: 9 therefore, O shepherds, h the word
36: 1 'O mountains of Israel, h the word
36: 4 h the word of the Sovereign LORD
36: 15 longer will I make you h the taunts
37: 4 'Dry bones, h the word
40: 4 look with your eyes and h
Da 3: 5 as you h the sound of the horn,
3: 15 when you h the sound of the horn,
5: 23 which cannot see or h
9: 17 h the prayers and petitions
9: 18 and h; open your eyes
9: 19 O Lord, forgive! O Lord, h and act!
Hos 4: 1 H the word of the LORD,
5: 1 "H this, you priests!
7: 12 When I h them flocking together,
Joel 1: 2 H this, you elders;
Am 3: 1 H this word the LORD has spoken
3: 13 H this and testify against the house
4: 1 H this word, you cows of Bashan
5: 1 H this word, O house of Israel,
7: 16 then, h the word of the LORD.
8: 4 flung everywhere! Silence!" H this
Mic 1: 2 H, O peoples, all of you,
3: 9 H this, you leaders of the house
6: 1 let the hills h what you have to say.
6: 2 H, O mountains, the LORD's
7: 7 my God will h me.
Zec 8: 9 "You who now h these words
Mt 11: 4 report to John what you h and see:
11: 5 the deaf h, the dead are raised,
11: 15 He who has ears, let him h.
12: 19 no one will h his voice in the streets
13: 9 He who has ears, let him h."
13: 13 they do not h or understand.
13: 15 they hardly h with their ears,
13: 15 h with their ears,
13: 16 and your ears because they h.
13: 17 and to h what you h but did not h it
13: 43 He who has ears, let him h.
21: 16 "Do you h what these children are
24: 6 You will h of wars and rumors

Mt 27:13 "Don't you *h* how many things
Mk 4: 9 "He who has ears to *h*, let him *h*."
4:15 As soon as they *h* it, Satan comes
4:16 *h* the word and at once receive it
4:18 sown among thorns, *h* the word;
4:20 sown on good soil, *h* the word,
4:23 If anyone has ears to *h*, let him *h*."
4:24 "Consider carefully what you *h*,"
7:37 makes the deaf *h* and the dumb
8:18 fail to *h?* And don't you remember
12:29 answered Jesus, "is this: '*H*,
13: 7 When you *h* of wars and rumors
14:11 They were delighted to *h* this
15:44 to *h* that he was already dead.
Lk 5:15 crowds of people came to *h* him
6:18 who had come to *h* him
6:27 I tell you who *h* me: Love your
7:22 the deaf *h*, the dead are raised,
8: 8 "He who has ears to *h*, let him *h*."
8:12 along the path are the ones who *h*,
8:13 the word with joy when they *h* it,
8:14 thorns stands for those who *h*,
8:15 who *h* the word, retain it,
8:21 are those who *h* God's word
9: 9 then, is this I *h* such things about?"
10:24 and to *h* what you *h* but did not *h* it
11:28 rather are those who *h* the word
14:35 "He who has ears to *h*, let him *h*."
15: 1 were all gathering around to *h* him.
16: 2 'What is this I *h* about you?
21: 9 When you *h* of wars
21:38 early in the morning to *h* him
Jn 3: 8 You *h* its sound, but you cannot
5:25 of God and those who *h* will live.
5:25 when the dead will *h* the voice
5:28 are in their graves will *h* his voice
5:30 as I *h*, and my judgment is just,
8:43 you are unable to *h* what I say.
8:47 reason you do not *h* is that you do
9:27 Why do you want to *h* it again?
11:42 I knew that you always *h* me,
14:24 These words you *h* are not my own
Ac 2:11 we *h* them declaring the wonders
2:33 out what you now see and *h*.
10:22 so that he could *h* what you have
13: 7 he wanted to *h* the word of God.
13:44 gathered to *h* the word of the Lord.
15: 7 you that the Gentiles might *h*
17:32 "We want to *h* you again
19:26 and *h* how this fellow Paul has
21:22 They will certainly *h* that you have
22:14 and to *h* words from his mouth.
23:35 "I will *h* your case
24: 4 you be kind enough to *h* us briefly.
25:22 I would like to *h* this man myself."
25:22 "Tomorrow you will *h* him."
28:22 we want to *h* what your views are,
28:27 they hardly *h* with their ears,
28:27 *h* with their ears,
Ro 2:13 is not those who *h* the law who are
10:14 they *h* without someone preaching
10:18 Did they not *h?* Of course they did
11: 8 and ears so that they could not *h*,
1Co 11:18 I *h* that when you come together
Php 1:27 or only *h* about you in my absence,
1:30 and now *h* that I still have.
2Th 3:11 We *h* that some among you are idle
2Ti 4: 3 what their itching ears want to *h*.
4:17 and all the Gentiles might *h* it.
Phm : 5 because I *h* about your faith
Heb 3: 7 "Today, if you *h* his voice,
3:15 "Today, if you *h* his voice,
4: 7 "Today, if you *h* his voice,
3Jn : 4 to *h* that my children are walking
Rev 1: 3 and blessed are those who *h* it
2: 7 let him *h* what the Spirit says
2:11 let him *h* what the Spirit says
2:17 let him *h* what the Spirit says
2:29 let him *h* what the Spirit says
3: 6 let him *h* what the Spirit says
3:13 let him *h* what the Spirit says
3:22 let him *h* what the Spirit says
9:20 idols that cannot see or *h* or walk.
13: 9 He who has an ear, let him *h*.

HEARD (HEAR)

Ge 3: 8 and his wife *h* the sound
3:10 He answered, "I *h* you
14:14 When Abram *h* that his relative
16:11 for the LORD has *h* of your misery
17:20 And as for Ishmael, I have *h* you:
21:17 God has *h* the boy crying
21:17 God *h* the boy crying,
21:26 and I *h* about it only today."
24:30 had *h* Rebekah tell what the man
24:52 Abraham's servant *h* what they
27:34 When Esau *h* his father's words,
29:13 as Laban *h* the news about Jacob,
29:33 "Because the LORD *h* that I am
31: 1 Jacob *h* that Laban's sons were
34: 5 When Jacob *h* that his daughter
34: 7 soon as they *h* what had happened.
35:22 concubine Bilhah, and Israel *h*
37:17 "I *h* them say, 'Let's go to Dothan
37:21 When Reuben *h* this, he tried
39:15 When he *h* me scream for help,
39:19 When his master *h* the story his
41:15 But I have *h* it said of you that
42: 2 I have *h* that there is grain in Egypt
43:25 because they had *h* that they were
45: 2 and Pharaoh's household *h* about it
45: 2 so loudly that the Egyptians *h* him,
Ex 2:15 When Pharaoh *h* of this, he tried
2:24 God *h* their groaning and he
3: 7 I have *h* them crying out
4:31 when they *h* that the LORD was
6: 5 I have *h* the groaning
16: 7 because he has *h* your grumbling
16: 8 because he has *h* your grumbling
16: 9 for he has *h* your grumbling.' "
16:12 "I have *h* the grumbling
18: 1 *h* of everything God had done
20:18 and lightning and *h* the trumpet
23:13 do not let them be *h* on your lips.
28:35 The sound of the bells will be *h*
32:17 When Joshua *h* the noise
33: 4 the people *h* these distressing
Lev 10:20 When Moses *h* this, he was
24:14 All those who *h* him are
Nu 7:89 he *h* the voice speaking to him
11: 1 and when he *h* them his anger was
11:10 Moses *h* the people
11:18 The LORD *h* you when you wailed
12: 2 through us?" And the LORD *h* this
14:14 They have already *h* that you,
14:15 the nations who have *h* this report
14:27 I have *h* the complaints
14:28 to you the very things I *h* you say:
16: 4 When Moses *h* this, he fell
20:16 he *h* our cry and sent an angel
21: 1 *h* that Israel was coming
22:36 When Balak *h* that Balaam was
33:40 *h* that the Israelites were coming.
Dt 1:34 When the LORD *h* what you said,
4:12 You *h* the sound of words
4:32 has anything like it ever been *h* of?
4:33 Has any other people *h* the voice
4:36 you *h* his words from out of the fire
5:23 When you *h* the voice out
5:24 we have *h* his voice from the fire.
5:26 mortal man has ever *h* the voice
5:28 The LORD *h* you when you spoke
5:28 "I have *h* what this people said
9: 2 about them and have *h* it said:
26: 7 and the LORD *h* our voice
Jos 2:10 We have *h* how the LORD dried
2:11 When we *h* of it, our hearts sank
5: 1 kings along the seacoast *h* how
9: 1 of the Jordan *h* about these things
9: 3 of Gibeon *h* what Joshua had done
9: 9 For we have *h* reports of him:
9:16 the Israelites *h* that they were
10: 1 of Jerusalem *h* that Joshua had
11: 1 When Jabin king of Hazor *h* of this,
14:12 You yourself *h* then that
22:11 when the Israelites *h* that they had
22:30 of the Israelites—*h* what Reuben,
24:27 It has *h* all the words the LORD
Jdg 7:15 When Gideon *h* the dream
9:30 of the city *h* what Gaal son
9:47 When Abimelech *h* that they had
13: 9 God *h* Manoah, and the angel
17: 2 about which I *h* you utter a curse—
20: 3 Benjamites *h* that the Israelites had
Ru 1: 6 When she *h* in Moab that
1Sa 1:13 moving but her voice was not *h*.
2:22 *h* about everything his sons were
4:14 Eli *h* the outcry and asked,
4:19 When she *h* the news that the ark
7: 7 And when the Israelites *h* of it,
7: 7 When the Philistines *h* that Israel
8:21 When Samuel *h* all that the people
11: 6 When Saul *h* their words, the Spirit
13: 3 and the Philistines *h* about it.
13: 4 hear!" So all Israel *h* the news:
14:22 of Ephraim *h* that the Philistines
14:27 Jonathan had not *h* that his father
17:23 his usual defiance, and David *h* it.
17:28 *h* him speaking with the men,
22: 1 his father's household *h* about it,
22: 6 Now Saul *h* that David
23:10 your servant has *h* definitely that
23:11 as your servant has *h?* O LORD,
23:25 When Saul *h* this, he went
25: 4 he *h* that Nabal was shearing sheep
25:35 I have *h* your words and granted
25:39 When David *h* that Nabal was
31:11 the people of Jabesh Gilead *h*
2Sa 3:28 Later, when David *h* about this,
4: 1 son of Saul *h* that Abner had died
5:17 When the Philistines *h* that David
5:17 but David *h* about it and went
7:22 as we have *h* with our own ears.
8: 9 king of Hamath *h* that David had
11:26 When Uriah's wife *h* that her
13:21 When King David *h* all this,
18: 5 And all the troops *h* the king giving
19: 2 on that day the troops *h* it said,
22: 7 From his temple he *h* my voice;
1Ki 1:11 "Have you not *h* that Adonijah,
1:41 the guests who were with him *h* it
3:28 When all Israel *h* the verdict
4:34 the kings of the world, who had *h*
5: 1 of Tyre *h* that Solomon had been
5: 7 When Hiram *h* Solomon's message
6: 7 or any other iron tool was *h*
9: 3 "I have *h* the prayer and plea you
10: 1 queen of Sheba *h* about the fame
10: 6 report I *h* in my own country about
10: 7 have far exceeded the report I *h*.
11:21 Hadad *h* that David rested
12: 2 son of Nebat *h* this (he was still
12:20 all the Israelites *h* that Jeroboam
13: 4 When King Jeroboam *h* what
13:26 back from his journey *h* of it,
14: 6 So when Ahijah *h* the sound
15:21 When Baasha *h* this, he stopped
16:16 in the camp *h* that Zimri had
17:22 The LORD *h* Elijah's cry,
18:13 Haven't you *h*, my lord, what I did
19:13 When Elijah *h* it, he pulled his
20:12 Ben-Hadad *h* this message
20:31 we have *h* that the kings
21:15 as Jezebel *h* that Naboth had been
21:16 When Ahab *h* that Naboth was
21:27 When Ahab *h* these words,
2Ki 3:21 the Moabites had *h* that the kings
5: 8 the man of God *h* that the king
6:30 When the king *h* the woman's
9:30 When Jezebel *h* about it, she
11:13 When Athaliah *h* the noise made
19: 1 When King Hezekiah *h* this,
19: 4 words the LORD your God has *h*.
19: 6 afraid of what you have *h*—
19: 8 the field commander *h* that
19:11 Surely you have *h* what the kings
19:20 I have *h* your prayer concerning
19:25 " 'Have you not *h?*
20: 5 I have *h* your prayer and seen your
20:12 he had *h* of Hezekiah's illness.
22:11 When the king *h* the words
22:18 says concerning the words you *h:*
22:19 I have *h* you, declares the LORD.
22:19 when you *h* what I have spoken
25:23 and their men *h* that the king
1Ch 10:11 of Jabesh Gilead *h* of everything
14: 8 When the Philistines *h* that David
14: 8 but David *h* about it and went out
17:20 as we have *h* with our own ears.
18: 9 king of Hamath *h* that David had
2Ch 7:12 "I have *h* your prayer and have
9: 1 of Sheba *h* of Solomon's fame,
9: 5 report I *h* in my own country about
9: 6 have far exceeded the report I *h*.

2Ch 10: 2 son of Nebat *h* this (he was
15: 8 When Asa *h* these words
16: 5 When Baasha *h* this, he stopped
20: 29 when they *h* how the LORD had
23: 12 When Athaliah *h* the noise
30: 20 And the LORD *h* Hezekiah
30: 27 and God *h* them, for their prayer
34: 19 When the king *h* the words
34: 26 says concerning the words you *h*:
34: 27 God when you *h* what he spoke
34: 27 I have *h* you, declares the LORD.
Ezr 3: 13 And the sound was *h* far away.
4: 1 Benjamin *h* that the exiles were
9: 3 When I *h* this, I tore my tunic
Ne 1: 4 When I *h* these things, I sat down
2: 10 the Ammonite official *h* about this,
2: 19 and Geshem the Arab *h* about it,
4: 1 When Sanballat *h* that we were
4: 7 men of Ashdod *h* that the repairs
4: 15 When our enemies *h* that we were
5: 6 When I *h* their outcry
6: 16 When all our enemies *h* about this
9: 9 you *h* their cry at the Red Sea.
9: 27 From heaven you *h* them,
9: 28 to you again, you *h* from heaven,
12: 43 in Jerusalem could be *h* far away.
13: 3 When the people *h* this law,
Est 1: 18 the nobility who have *h* about
Job 2: 11 *h* about all the troubles that had
3: 7 may no shout of joy be *h* in it.
4: 16 and I *h* a hushed voice:
13: 1 my ears have *h* and understood it.
16: 2 "I have *h* many things like these;
29: 11 Whoever *h* me spoke well of me,
33: 8 I *h* the very words—
34: 28 so that he *h* the cry of the needy.
42: 5 My ears had *h* of you
Ps 6: 8 for the LORD has *h* my weeping.
6: 9 The LORD has *h* my cry for mercy
18: 6 From his temple he *h* my voice;
19: 3 where their voice is not *h*.
28: 6 for he has *h* my cry for mercy.
31: 22 Yet you *h* my cry for mercy
34: 6 man called, and the LORD *h* him;
40: 1 he turned to me and *h* my cry.
44: 1 We have *h* with our ears, O God;
48: 8 As we have *h*,
61: 5 For you have *h* my vows, O God;
62: 11 two things have I *h*:
66: 8 let the sound of his praise be *h*;
66: 19 and *h* my voice in prayer.
77: 18 Your thunder was *h*
78: 3 things we have *h* and known,
78: 21 When the LORD *h* them,
78: 59 When God *h* them, he was very
81: 5 where we *h* a language we did not
92: 11 my ears have *h* the rout
106: 44 distress when he *h* their cry;
116: 1 for he *h* my voice;
116: 1 he *h* my cry for mercy.
132: 6 We *h* it in Ephrathah,
Ecc 12: 13 Now all has been *h*;
SS 2: 12 is *h* in our land.
Isa 5: 7 for righteousness, but *h* cries
6: 8 I *h* the voice of the Lord saying,
15: 4 their voices are *h* all the way
16: 6 We have *h* of Moab's pride—
21: 10 I tell you what I have *h*
37: 1 When King Hezekiah *h* this,
37: 4 words the LORD your God has *h*,
37: 6 afraid of what you have *h*—
37: 8 the field commander *h* that
37: 9 When he *h* it, he sent messengers
37: 11 Surely you have *h* what the kings
37: 26 "Have you not *h*?
38: 5 I have *h* your prayer and seen your
39: 1 because he had *h* of his illness
40: 21 Have you not *h*?
40: 28 Have you not *h*?
41: 26 no one *h* any words from you.
48: 6 You have *h* these things; look
48: 7 you have not *h* of them
48: 8 You have neither *h* nor understood
52: 15 and what they have not *h*,
58: 4 expect your voice to be *h* on high.
60: 18 No longer will violence be *h*
64: 4 Since ancient times no one has *h*,
65: 19 will be *h* in it no more.
Isa 66: 8 Who has ever *h* of such a thing?
66: 19 the distant islands that have not *h*
Jer 3: 21 A cry is *h* on the barren heights,
4: 19 For I have *h* the sound
4: 19 I have *h* the battle cry.
6: 24 We have *h* reports about them,
8: 16 is *h* from Dan;
9: 10 and the lowing of cattle is not *h*.
9: 19 sound of wailing is *h* from Zion:
18: 13 Who has ever *h* anything like this?
18: 22 Let a cry be *h* from their houses
20: 1 *h* Jeremiah prophesying these
22: 20 let your voice be *h* in Bashan,
23: 18 Who has listened and *h* his word?
23: 25 "I have *h* what the prophets say
26: 7 all the people *h* Jeremiah speak
26: 10 of Judah *h* about these things,
26: 11 You have *h* it with your own ears!"
26: 12 this city all the things you have *h*.
26: 21 But Uriah *h* of it and fled in fear
26: 21 officers and officials *h* his words,
30: 5 " 'Cries of fear are *h*—
31: 7 Make your praises *h*, and say,
31: 15 "A voice is *h* in Ramah,
31: 18 I have surely *h* Ephraim's moaning
33: 10 there will be *h* once more
36: 11 *h* all the words of the LORD
36: 13 everything he had *h* Baruch read
36: 16 When they *h* all these words,
36: 24 his attendants who *h* all these
37: 5 besieging Jerusalem *h* the report
38: 1 of Malkijah *h* what Jeremiah was
38: 7 *h* that they had put Jeremiah
38: 27 for no one had *h* his conversation
40: 7 in the open country *h* that the king
40: 11 the other countries *h* that the king
41: 11 with him *h* about all the crimes
42: 4 "I have *h* you," replied Jeremiah
48: 5 cries over the destruction are *h*.
48: 29 "We have *h* of Moab's pride—
49: 14 I have *h* a message from the LORD
49: 23 for they have *h* bad news.
50: 43 of Babylon has *h* reports about
51: 46 when rumors are *h* in the land;
La 1: 21 All my enemies have *h*
1: 21 "People have *h* my groaning,
3: 56 You *h* my plea: "Do not close your
3: 61 O LORD, you have *h* their insults,
Eze 1: 24 I *h* the sound of their wings,
1: 28 and I *h* the voice of one speaking.
2: 2 and I *h* him speaking to me.
3: 12 I *h* behind me a loud rushing sound
9: 1 I *h* him call out in a loud voice,
10: 5 wings of the cherubim could be *h*
10: 13 I *h* the wheels being called
19: 4 The nations *h* about him,
19: 9 so his roar was *h* no longer
26: 13 of your harps will be *h* no more.
33: 5 Since he *h* the sound
35: 12 the LORD have *h* all
35: 13 me without restraint, and I *h* it.
43: 6 I *h* someone speaking to me
Da 3: 7 as they *h* the sound of the horn,
5: 14 I have *h* that the spirit
5: 16 Now I have *h* that you are able
6: 14 When the king *h* this, he was
8: 13 Then I *h* a holy one speaking,
8: 16 I *h* a man's voice from the Ulai
10: 9 Then I *h* him speaking, and
10: 12 your words were *h*, and I have
12: 7 and I *h* him swear by him who lives
12: 8 I *h*, but I did not understand.
Ob : 1 We have *h* a message
Na 2: 13 will no longer be *h*."
Hab 3: 2 LORD, I have *h* of your fame;
3: 16 I *h* and my heart pounded,
Zep 2: 8 "I have *h* the insults of Moab
Zec 8: 23 we have *h* that God is with you.' "
Mal 3: 16 and the LORD listened and *h*.
Mt 2: 3 When King Herod *h* this he was
2: 9 After they had *h* the king,
2: 18 was fulfilled: "A voice is *h*
2: 22 But when he *h* that Archelaus was
4: 12 When Jesus *h* that John had been
5: 21 "You have *h* that it was said
5: 27 "You have *h* that it was said,
5: 33 you have *h* that it was said
5: 38 "You have *h* that it was said,
Mt 5: 43 "You have *h* that it was said,
6: 7 for they think they will be *h*
8: 10 When Jesus *h* this, he was
11: 2 When John *h* in prison what Christ
12: 24 But when the Pharisees *h* this,
14: 1 Herod the tetrarch *h* the reports
14: 13 When Jesus *h* what had happened,
15: 12 offended when they *h* this?"
17: 6 When the disciples *h* this,
19: 22 When the young man *h* this,
19: 25 When the disciples *h* this,
20: 24 When the ten *h* about this,
20: 30 when they *h* that Jesus was going
21: 45 and the Pharisees *h* Jesus' parables,
22: 22 When they *h* this, they were
22: 33 When the crowds *h* this, they were
26: 65 now you have *h* the blasphemy.
27: 47 some of those standing there *h* this,
Mk 2: 1 people *h* that he had come home.
3: 8 When they *h* all he was doing,
3: 21 When his family *h* about this,
5: 27 When she *h* about Jesus, she came
6: 2 and many who *h* him were amazed.
6: 14 King Herod *h* about this,
6: 16 But when Herod *h* this, he said,
6: 20 When Herod *h* John, he was
6: 55 on mats to wherever they *h* he was.
7: 25 In fact, as soon as she *h* about him,
10: 41 When the ten *h* about this,
10: 47 When he *h* that it was Jesus
11: 14 And his disciples *h* him say it.
11: 18 and the teachers of the law *h* this
12: 28 the law came and *h* them debating.
14: 58 against him: "We *h* him say,
14: 64 "You have *h* the blasphemy.
15: 35 some of those standing near *h* this,
15: 39 *h* his cry and saw how he died,
16: 11 When they *h* that Jesus was alive
Lk 1: 13 Zechariah; your prayer has been *h*.
1: 41 When Elizabeth *h* Mary's greeting,
1: 58 and relatives *h* that the Lord had
1: 66 Everyone who *h* this wondered
2: 18 and all who *h* it were amazed
2: 20 God for all the things they had *h*
2: 47 Everyone who *h* him was amazed
4: 23 town what we have *h* that you did
4: 28 were furious when they *h* this.
7: 3 The centurion *h* of Jesus
7: 9 When Jesus *h* this, he was amazed
7: 22 to John what you have seen and *h*:
7: 29 when they *h* Jesus' words,
9: 7 Herod the tetrarch *h* about all that
12: 3 in the dark will be *h* in the daylight,
14: 15 of those at the table with him *h* this
15: 25 came near the house, he *h* music
16: 14 *h* all this and were sneering at Jesus
18: 22 When Jesus *h* this, he said to him,
18: 23 When he *h* this, he became very
18: 26 Those who *h* this asked, "Who
18: 36 When he *h* the crowd going by,
20: 16 When the people *h* this, they said,
22: 71 We have *h* it from his own lips."
23: 8 From what he had *h* about him,
Jn 1: 37 the two disciples *h* him say this,
1: 40 of the two who *h* what John had
3: 32 testifies to what he has seen and *h*,
4: 1 Pharisees *h* that Jesus was gaining
4: 42 now we have *h* for ourselves,
4: 47 When this man *h* that Jesus had
5: 37 You have never *h* his voice
7: 32 Pharisees *h* the crowd whispering
8: 9 those who *h* began to go away one
8: 26 and what I have *h* from him I tell
8: 38 and you do what you have *h*
8: 40 who has told you the truth that I *h*
9: 32 Nobody has ever *h*
9: 35 Jesus *h* that they had thrown him
9: 40 were with him *h* him say this
11: 4 When he *h* this, Jesus said,
11: 6 when he *h* that Lazarus was sick,
11: 20 When Martha *h* that Jesus was
11: 29 When Mary *h* this, she got up
11: 41 I thank you that you have *h* me.
12: 12 come for the Feast *h* that Jesus was
12: 18 they had *h* that he had given this
12: 29 and *h* it said it had thundered;
12: 34 "We have *h* from the Law that
14: 28 "You *h* me say, 'I am going away

Jn 18:21 question me? Ask those who *h* me.
19: 8 When Pilate *h* this, he was
19:13 When Pilate *h* this, he brought
21: 7 As soon as Simon Peter *h* him say,
Ac 1: 4 which you have *h* me speak about.
1:19 Everyone in Jerusalem *h* about this
2: 6 When they *h* this sound, a crowd
2: 6 because each one *h* them speaking
2:37 When the people *h* this, they were
4: 4 many who *h* the message believed,
4:20 about what we have seen and *h*.''
4:24 When they *h* this, they raised their
5: 5 When Ananias *h* this, he fell down
5: 5 seized all who *h* what had
5:11 and all who *h* about these events.
5:33 When they *h* this, they were
6:11 ''We have *h* Stephen speak words
6:14 For we have *h* him say that this
7:12 When Jacob *h* that there was grain
7:29 When Moses *h* this, he fled
7:31 more closely, he *h* the Lord's
7:34 I have *h* their groaning
7:54 When they *h* this, they were
8: 6 When the crowds *h* Philip
8:14 in Jerusalem *h* that Samaria had
8:30 and *h* the man reading Isaiah
9: 4 fell to the ground and *h* a voice say
9: 7 they *h* the sound but did not see
9:13 ''I have *h* many reports about this
9:21 All those who *h* him were
9:38 when the disciples *h* that Peter was
10:31 God has *h* your prayer
10:44 came on all who *h* the message.
10:46 For they *h* them speaking
11: 1 brothers throughout Judea *h* that
11: 7 Then I *h* a voice telling me, 'Get up
11:18 When they *h* this, they had no
13:48 When the Gentiles *h* this,
14:14 the apostles Barnabas and Paul *h*
15:24 We have *h* that some went out
16:38 and when they *h* that Paul
17: 8 When they *h* this, the crowd
17:32 When they *h* about
18: 8 Corinthians who *h* him believed
18:26 When Priscilla and Aquila *h* him,
19: 2 even *h* that there is a Holy Spirit.''
19:10 in the province of Asia *h* the word
19:28 When they *h* this, they were
21:12 When we *h* this, we and the people
21:20 When they *h* this, they praised
22: 2 When they *h* him speak to them
22: 7 fell to the ground and *h* a voice say
22:15 men of what you have seen and *h*.
22:26 When the centurion *h* this,
23:16 son of Paul's sister *h* of this plot,
26:14 I *h* a voice saying to me in Aramaic
28:15 brothers there had *h* that we were
Ro 10:14 in the one of whom they have not *h*
10:17 the message is *h* through the word
15:21 who have not *h* will understand.''
16:19 Everyone has *h* about your
1Co 2: 9 no ear has *h*,
2Co 6: 2 ''In the time of my favor I *h* you,
12: 4 He *h* inexpressible things,
Gal 1:13 For you have *h* of my previous way
1:23 They only *h* the report: ''The man
3: 2 or by believing what you *h*?
3: 5 or because you believe what you *h*?
Eph 1:13 in Christ when you *h* the word
1:15 ever since I *h* about your faith
3: 2 Surely you have *h* about
4:21 Surely you *h* of him and were
Php 2:26 distressed because you *h* he was ill.
4: 9 or received or *h* from me,
Col 1: 4 because we have *h* of your faith
1: 5 and that you have already *h* about
1: 6 among you since the day you *h* it
1: 9 since the day we *h* about you,
1:23 This is the gospel that you *h*
1Th 2:13 word of God, which you *h* from us,
2Ti 1:13 What you *h* from me, keep
2: 2 And the things you have *h* me say
Heb 2: 1 therefore, to what we have *h*,
2: 3 to us by those who *h* him.
3:16 Who were they who *h* and rebelled
4: 2 the message they *h* was of no value
4: 2 those who *h* did not combine it
5: 7 he was *h* because of his reverent
Heb 12:19 so that those who *h* it begged that
Jas 1:25 not forgetting what he has *h*,
5:11 You have *h* of Job's perseverance
2Pe 1:18 We ourselves *h* this voice that
2: 8 by the lawless deeds he saw and *h*
1Jn 1: 1 which we have *h*, which we have
1: 3 to you what we have seen and *h*,
1: 5 This is the message we have *h*
2: 7 is the message you have *h*.
2:18 as you have *h* that the antichrist is
2:24 See that what you have *h*
3:11 This is the message you *h*
4: 3 which you have *h* is coming and
2Jn : 6 As you have *h* from the beginning,
Rev 1:10 and I *h* behind me a loud voice like
3: 3 what you have received and *h*;
4: 1 the voice I had first *h* speaking
5:11 and *h* the voice of many angels,
5:13 Then I *h* every creature in heaven
6: 1 I *h* one of the four living creatures
6: 3 I *h* the second living creature say,
6: 5 I *h* the third living creature say,
6: 6 Then I *h* what sounded like a voice
6: 7 I *h* the voice of the fourth living
7: 4 I *h* the number of those who were
8:13 I *h* an eagle that was flying
9:13 I *h* a voice coming from the horns
9:16 I *h* their number.
10: 4 but I *h* a voice from heaven say,
10: 8 Then the voice that I had *h*
11:12 Then they *h* a loud voice
12:10 Then I *h* a loud voice in heaven say
14: 2 And I *h* a sound from heaven like
14: 2 The sound I *h* was like that
14:13 Then I *h* a voice from heaven say,
16: 1 I *h* a loud voice from the temple
16: 5 Then I *h* the angel in charge
16: 7 And I *h* the altar respond:
18: 4 I *h* another voice from heaven say:
18:22 will never be *h* in you again.
18:22 will never be *h* in you again.
18:23 will never be *h* in you again.
19: 1 After this I *h* what sounded like
19: 6 Then I *h* what sounded like a great
21: 3 I *h* a loud voice from the throne
22: 8 And when I had *h* and seen them,
22: 8 am the one who *h* and saw these

HEARERS (HEAR)

1Ti 4:16 will save both yourself and your *h*.

HEARING (HEAR)

Ge 23:10 and he replied to Abraham in the *h*
23:13 and he said to Ephron in their *h*,
23:16 named in the *h* of the Hittites:
Nu 11: 1 hardships in the *h* of the LORD,
Dt 5: 1 and laws I declare in your *h* today.
31:11 law before them in their *h*.
31:28 I can speak these words in their *h*
31:30 end in the *h* of the whole assembly
32:44 of this song in the *h* of the people.
Jdg 9:46 On *h* this, the citizens in the tower
1Sa 4: 6 *H* the uproar, the Philistines asked,
17:11 On *h* the Philistine's words,
2Sa 10: 7 On *h* this, David sent Joab out
18:12 In our *h* the king commanded you
1Ki 1:41 On *h* the sound of the trumpet,
2Ki 18:26 us in Hebrew in the *h* of the people
23: 2 He read in their *h* all the words
1Ch 19: 8 On *h* this, David sent Joab out
28: 8 and in the *h* of our God: Be careful
2Ch 34:30 He read in their *h* all the words
Ne 13: 1 aloud in the *h* of the people
Job 9:16 not believe he would give me a *h*.
33: 8 ''But you have said in my *h*—
Ecc 1: 8 or the ear its fill of *h*.
Isa 5: 9 Almighty has declared in my *h*:
6: 9 Be ever *h*, but never understanding
22:14 has revealed this in my *h*:
36:11 us in Hebrew in the *h* of the people
49:20 will yet say in your *h*,
Jer 2: 2 and proclaim in the *h* of Jerusalem:
26:15 to speak all these words in your *h*.''
28: 7 and in the *h* of all the people:
28: 7 to what I have to say in your *h*
Da 5:10 *h* the voices of the king
Am 8:11 but a famine of *h* the words
Mt 9:12 and 'sinners'?'' On *h* this,
Mt 13:13 though *h*, they do not hear
13:14 will be ever *h* but never
14:13 *H* of this, the crowds followed him
22:34 *H* that Jesus had silenced
Mk 2:17 On *h* this, Jesus said to them,
4:12 ever *h* but never understanding;
6:29 On *h* of this, John's disciples came
Lk 4:21 this scripture is fulfilled in your *h*.''
7: 1 this in the *h* of the people,
8:10 though *h*, they may not understand
8:50 *H* this, Jesus said to Jairus,
23: 6 On *h* this, Pilate asked
Jn 6:60 On *h* it, many of his disciples said,
7:40 On *h* his words, some
7:51 a man without first *h* him
Ac 5:24 On *h* this report, the captain
19: 5 On *h* this, they were baptized
28:26 will be ever *h* but never
Ro 10:17 faith comes from *h* the message,
1Co 12:17 where would the sense of *h* be?

HEARS (HEAR)

Ge 21: 6 and everyone who *h* about this will
Ex 17:14 and make sure that Joshua *h* it,
Lev 5: 1 when he *h* a public charge to testify
Nu 24: 4 of one who *h* the words of God,
24:16 of one who *h* the words of God,
30: 4 and her father *h* about her vow
30: 5 her when he *h* about it,
30: 7 and her husband *h* about it
30: 8 her when he *h* about it,
30:11 and her husband *h* about it
30:12 them when he *h* about them,
30:14 to her when he *h* about them.
30:15 time after he *h* about them,
Dt 29:19 When such a person *h* the words
1Sa 3:11 ears of everyone who *h* of it tingle.
2Sa 17: 9 whoever *h* about it will say,
2Ki 19: 7 that when he *h* a certain report,
21:12 of everyone who *h* of it will tingle.
Ps 34:17 cry out, and the LORD *h* them;
55:17 and he *h* my voice.
69:33 The LORD *h* the needy
97: 8 Zion *h* and rejoices
145: 19 he *h* their cry and saves them.
Pr 13: 8 but a poor man *h* no threat.
15:29 but he *h* the prayer of the righteous
25:10 or he who *h* it may shame you
Isa 11: 3 decide by what he *h* with his ears;
30:19 As soon as he *h*, he will answer you
37: 7 so that when he *h* a certain report,
Jer 19: 3 ears of everyone who *h* of it tingle.
Eze 33: 4 then if anyone *h* the trumpet
Da 3:10 that everyone who *h* the sound
Na 3:19 Everyone who *h* the news about
Mt 7:24 everyone who *h* these words
7:26 But everyone who *h* these words
13:19 When anyone *h* the message about
13:20 places is the man who *h* the word
13:22 thorns is the man who *h* the word,
13:23 soil is the man who *h* the word
Lk 6:47 and *h* my words and puts them
6:49 But the one who *h* my words
Jn 3:29 when he *h* the bridegroom's voice.
5:24 whoever *h* my word and believes
8:47 belongs to God *h* what God says.
12:47 As for the person who *h* my words
16:13 he will speak only what he *h*,
Ac 2: 8 each of us *h* them in his own native
1Jn 5:14 according to his will, he *h* us.
5:15 And if we know that he *h* us—
Rev 3:20 If anyone *h* my voice and opens
22:17 And let him who *h* say, ''Come!''
22:18 I warn everyone who *h* the words

HEART (BROKENHEARTED DISHEARTENED DOWNHEARTED FAINT-HEARTED HARDHEARTED HEART'S HEARTACHE HEARTS HEARTS' KINDHEARTED SIMPLEHEARTED STOUTHEARTED STUBBORN-HEARTED WHOLEHEARTED WHOLEHEARTEDLY)

Ge 6: 5 of his *h* was only evil all the time.
6: 6 and his *h* was filled with pain.
8:21 every inclination of his *h* is evil
8:21 pleasing aroma and said in his *h*:
24:45 ''Before I finished praying in my *h*,

Ge 34: 3 *h* was drawn to Dinah daughter
34: 8 "My son Shechem has his *h* set
Ex 4: 14 his *h* will be glad when he sees you.
4: 21 But I will harden his *h*
7: 3 But I will harden Pharaoh's *h*,
7: 13 Yet Pharaoh's *h* became hard
7: 14 "Pharaoh's *h* is unyielding;
7: 22 and Pharaoh's *h* became hard;
7: 23 and did not take even this to *h*.
8: 15 he hardened his *h* and would not
8: 19 But Pharaoh's *h* was hard
8: 32 also Pharaoh hardened his *h*
9: 7 Yet his *h* was unyielding
9: 12 the LORD hardened Pharaoh's *h*
9: 35 So Pharaoh's *h* was hard
10: 1 for I have hardened his *h*
10: 20 the LORD hardened Pharaoh's *h*,
10: 27 the LORD hardened Pharaoh's *h*,
11: 10 the LORD hardened Pharaoh's *h*,
14: 4 And I will harden Pharaoh's *h*,
14: 8 The LORD hardened the *h*
15: 8 congealed in the *h* of the sea.
25: 2 each man whose *h* prompts him
28: 29 Israel over his *h* on the breastpiece
28: 30 over Aaron's *h* whenever he enters
28: 30 over his *h* before the LORD.
35: 21 and whose *h* moved him came
Lev 19: 17 Do not hate your brother in your *h*.
Dt 1: 28 Our brothers have made us lose *h*.
2: 30 his *h* obstinate in order to give him
4: 9 or let them slip from your *h* as long
4: 29 if you look for him with all your *h*
4: 39 to *h* this day that the LORD is God
6: 5 LORD your God with all your *h*
8: 2 order to know what was in your *h*,
8: 5 Know then in your *h* that
8: 14 then your *h* will become proud
10: 12 LORD your God with all your *h*
11: 3 the things he did in the *h* of Egypt,
11: 13 and to serve him with all your *h*
13: 3 you love him with all your *h*
15: 10 and do so without a grudging *h*;
17: 17 or his *h* will be led astray
26: 16 observe them with all your *h*
28: 65 with longing, and a despairing *h*.
29: 18 you today whose *h* turns away
30: 1 to *h* wherever the LORD your
30: 2 and obey him with all your *h*
30: 6 you may love him with all your *h*
30: 10 LORD your God with all your *h*
30: 14 and in your *h* so you may obey it.
30: 17 But if your *h* turns away
32: 46 to *h* all the words I have solemnly
Jos 22: 5 and to serve him with all your *h*
23: 14 You know with all your *h*
Jdg 5: 9 My *h* is with Israel's princes,
5: 15 there was much searching of *h*.
5: 16 there was much searching of *h*.
1Sa 1: 13 Hannah was praying in her *h*,
2: 1 "My *h* rejoices in the LORD;
2: 33 with tears and to grieve your *h*,
2: 35 will do according to what is in my *h*
4: 13 his *h* feared for the ark of God.
9: 19 will tell you all that is in your *h*.
10: 9 God changed Saul's *h*,
12: 20 serve the LORD with all your *h*.
12: 24 serve him faithfully with all your *h*;
13: 14 sought out a man after his own *h*
14: 7 I am with you *h* and soul."
16: 7 but the LORD looks at the *h*."
17: 28 and how wicked your *h* is;
17: 32 "Let no one lose *h* on account
21: 12 David took these words to *h*
25: 37 his *h* failed him and he became like
28: 5 he was afraid; terror filled his *h*.
2Sa 3: 21 rule over all that your *h* desires."
6: 16 she despised him in her *h*.
13: 20 Don't take this thing to *h*."
14: 1 knew that the king's *h* longed
17: 10 whose *h* is like the *h* of a lion,
18: 14 plunged them into Absalom's *h*
22: 46 They all lose *h*;
1Ki 2: 4 faithfully before me with all their *h*
2: 44 in your *h* all the wrong you did
3: 6 and righteous and upright in *h*.
3: 9 So give your servant a discerning *h*
3: 12 give you a wise and discerning *h*,
8: 17 it in his *h* to build a temple
1Ki 8: 18 was in your *h* to build a temple
8: 18 you did well to have this in your *h*.
8: 38 of the afflictions of his own *h*,
8: 39 since you know his *h*
8: 47 and if they have a change of *h*
8: 48 back to you with all their *h*
8: 66 in *h* for all the good the LORD had
9: 3 and my *h* will always be there.
9: 4 walk before me in integrity of *h*
10: 24 the wisdom God had put in his *h*.
11: 4 and his *h* was not fully devoted
11: 4 his wives turned his *h*
11: 4 the *h* of David his father had been.
11: 9 because his *h* had turned away
11: 37 rule over all that your *h* desires;
14: 8 and followed me with all his *h*,
15: 3 his *h* was not fully devoted
15: 3 *h* of David his forefather had been.
15: 14 Asa's *h* was fully committed
2Ki 9: 24 The arrow pierced his *h*
10: 31 the God of Israel, with all his *h*.
22: 19 Because your *h* was responsive
23: 3 with all his *h* and all his soul,
23: 25 with all his *h* and with all his soul
1Ch 15: 29 she despised him in her *h*.
22: 7 I had it in my *h* to build a house
22: 19 Now devote your *h* and soul
28: 2 I had it in my *h* to build a house
28: 9 for the LORD searches every *h*
29: 17 that you test the *h* and are pleased
2Ch 6: 7 it in his *h* to build a temple
6: 8 was in your *h* to build a temple
6: 8 you did well to have this in your *h*
6: 30 since you know his *h*
6: 37 and if they have a change of *h*
6: 38 back to you with all their *h*
7: 10 in *h* for the good things the LORD
7: 16 and my *h* will always be there.
9: 23 the wisdom God had put in his *h*.
12: 14 because he had not set his *h*
15: 12 of their fathers, with all their *h*
15: 17 Asa's *h* was fully committed
17: 6 His *h* was devoted to the ways
19: 3 have set your *h* on seeking God."
22: 9 sought the LORD with all his *h*."
30: 19 pardon everyone who sets his *h*
32: 25 But Hezekiah's *h* was proud
32: 26 repented of the pride of his *h*,
32: 31 know everything that was in his *h*.
34: 27 Because your *h* was responsive
34: 31 with all his *h* and all his soul,
36: 13 stiff-necked and hardened his *h*
36: 22 the LORD moved the *h*
Ezr 1: 1 the LORD moved the *h*
1: 5 everyone whose *h* God had moved
7: 27 it into the king's *h* to bring honor
Ne 2: 2 can be nothing but sadness of *h*."
2: 12 put in my *h* to do for Jerusalem.
4: 6 the people worked with all their *h*.
7: 5 it into my *h* to assemble the nobles,
9: 8 You found his *h* faithful to you,
Job 10: 13 is what you concealed in your *h*,
11: 13 "Yet if you devote your *h* to him
15: 12 Why has your *h* carried you away,
17: 11 and so are the desires of my *h*.
19: 27 How my *h* yearns within me!
22: 22 and lay up his words in your *h*.
23: 16 God has made my *h* faint;
29: 13 I made the widow's *h* sing.
31: 7 if my *h* has been led by my eyes,
31: 9 "If my *h* has been enticed
31: 20 and his *h* did not bless me
31: 27 so that my *h* was secretly enticed
31: 33 by hiding my guilt in my *h*
33: 3 My words come from an upright *h*;
36: 13 The godless in *h* harbor resentment
37: 1 "At this my *h* pounds
37: 24 for all the wise in *h*?"
38: 36 Who endowed the *h* with wisdom
Ps 4: 7 You have filled my *h*
5: 9 their *h* is filled with destruction.
7: 10 who saves the upright in *h*.
9: 1 you, O LORD, with all my *h*;
10: 3 He boasts of the cravings of his *h*;
11: 2 the shadows at the upright in *h*.
13: 2 and every day have sorrow in my *h*
13: 5 my *h* rejoices in your salvation.
14: 1 The fool says in his *h*,
Ps 15: 2 who speaks the truth from his *h*
16: 7 even at night my *h* instructs me.
16: 9 Therefore my *h* is glad
17: 3 Though you probe my *h*
18: 45 They all lose *h*;
19: 8 giving joy to the *h*.
19: 14 and the meditation of my *h*
20: 4 he give you the desire of your *h*
21: 2 granted him the desire of his *h*
22: 14 My *h* has turned to wax;
24: 4 who has clean hands and a pure *h*,
25: 17 of my *h* have multiplied;
26: 2 examine my *h* and my mind;
27: 3 my *h* will not fear;
27: 8 My *h* says of you, "Seek his face!"
27: 14 be strong and take *h*
28: 7 My *h* leaps for joy
28: 7 my *h* trusts in him, and I am helped
30: 12 that my *h* may sing to you
31: 24 Be strong and take *h*,
32: 11 sing, all you who are upright in *h*!
33: 11 of his *h* through all generations.
36: 1 An oracle is within my *h*
36: 10 to the upright in *h*.
37: 4 will give you the desires of your *h*.
37: 31 The law of his God is in his *h*;
38: 8 I groan in anguish of *h*.
38: 10 My *h* pounds, my strength fails me;
39: 3 My *h* grew hot within me,
40: 8 your law is within my *h*."
40: 10 hide your righteousness in my *h*;
40: 12 and my *h* fails within me.
41: 6 while his *h* gathers slander;
44: 21 since he knows the secrets of the *h*
45: 1 My *h* is stirred by a noble theme
46: 2 fall into the *h* of the sea,
49: 3 from my *h* will give understanding.
51: 10 Create in me a pure *h*, O God,
51: 17 a broken and contrite *h*,
53: 1 The fool says in his *h*,
55: 4 My *h* is in anguish within me;
55: 21 yet war is in his *h*;
57: 7 My *h* is steadfast, O God,
57: 7 my *h* is steadfast;
58: 2 No, in your *h* you devise injustice,
61: 2 I call as my *h* grows faint;
62: 10 do not set your *h* on them.
64: 6 and *h* of man are cunning.
64: 10 let all the upright in *h* praise him!
66: 18 If I had cherished sin in my *h*,
69: 20 Scorn has broken my *h*
73: 1 to those who are pure in *h*.
73: 13 in vain have I kept my *h* pure;
73: 21 When my *h* was grieved
73: 26 My flesh and my *h* may fail,
73: 26 but God is the strength of my *h*
77: 6 My *h* mused and my spirit inquired
78: 72 with integrity of *h*;
84: 2 my *h* and my flesh cry out
86: 11 give me an undivided *h*,
86: 12 O Lord my God, with all my *h*;
89: 50 how I bear in my *h* the taunts
90: 12 that we may gain a *h* of wisdom.
94: 15 all the upright in *h* will follow it.
97: 11 and joy on the upright in *h*.
101: 2 house with blameless *h*.
101: 4 Men of perverse *h* shall be far
101: 5 has haughty eyes and a proud *h*,
102: 4 My *h* is blighted and withered like
104: 15 and bread that sustains his *h*.
104: 15 wine that gladdens the *h* of man,
108: 1 My *h* is steadfast, O God;
109: 22 and my *h* is wounded within me.
111: 1 I will extol the LORD with all my *h*
112: 7 his *h* is steadfast, trusting
112: 8 His *h* is secure, he will have no fear
119: 2 and seek him with all their *h*.
119: 7 I will praise you with an upright *h*
119: 10 I seek you with all my *h*;
119: 11 I have hidden your word in my *h*
119: 30 I have set my *h* on your laws.
119: 32 for you have set my *h* free.
119: 34 and obey it with all my *h*.
119: 36 Turn my *h* toward your statutes
119: 58 sought your face with all my *h*;
119: 69 I keep your precepts with all my *h*.
119: 80 May my *h* be blameless
119:111 they are the joy of my *h*.

Ps 119:112 My *h* is set on keeping your
119:145 I call with all my *h;* answer me,
119:161 but my *h* trembles at your word.
125: 4 to those who are upright in *h*.
131: 1 My *h* is not proud, O LORD,
138: 1 you, O LORD, with all my *h;*
139: 23 Search me, O God, and know my *h*
141: 4 Let not my *h* be drawn
143: 4 my *h* within me is dismayed.
148: 14 of Israel, the people close to his *h*.
Pr 1: 23 I would have poured out my *h*
2: 2 applying your *h* to understanding,
2: 10 For wisdom will enter your *h*,
3: 1 but keep my commands in your *h*,
3: 3 write them on the tablet of your *h*.
3: 5 Trust in the LORD with all your *h*
4: 4 hold of my words with all your *h;*
4: 21 keep them within your *h;*
4: 23 Above all else, guard your *h*,
5: 12 How my *h* spurned correction!
6: 14 who plots evil with deceit in his *h*
6: 18 a *h* that devises wicked schemes,
6: 21 Bind them upon your *h* forever;
6: 25 lust in your *h* after her beauty
7: 3 write them on the tablet of your *h*.
7: 25 Do not let your *h* turn to her ways
10: 8 The wise in *h* accept commands,
10: 20 the *h* of the wicked is of little value.
11: 20 LORD detests men of perverse *h*
12: 23 but the *h* of fools blurts out folly.
12: 25 An anxious *h* weighs a man down,
13: 12 Hope deferred makes the *h* sick,
14: 10 Each *h* knows its own bitterness,
14: 13 Even in laughter the *h* may ache,
14: 30 A *h* at peace gives life to the body,
14: 33 in the *h* of the discerning
15: 13 A happy *h* makes the face cheerful,
15: 14 The discerning *h* seeks knowledge,
15: 15 the cheerful *h* has a continual feast.
15: 28 *h* of the righteous weighs its
15: 30 A cheerful look brings joy to the *h*,
16: 1 To man belong the plans of the *h*,
16: 5 LORD detests all the proud of *h*.
16: 9 In his *h* a man plans his course,
16: 21 The wise in *h* are called discerning,
16: 23 A wise man's *h* guides his mouth,
17: 3 but the LORD tests the *h*.
17: 20 of perverse *h* does not prosper;
17: 22 A cheerful *h* is good medicine,
18: 12 his downfall a man's *h* is proud,
18: 15 The *h* of the discerning acquires
19: 3 yet his *h* rages against the LORD.
19: 21 Many are the plans in a man's *h*,
20: 5 of a man's *h* are deep waters,
20: 9 can say, "I have kept my *h* pure;
21: 1 The king's *h* is in the hand
21: 2 but the LORD weighs the *h*.
21: 4 Haughty eyes and a proud *h*,
22: 11 He who loves a pure *h*
22: 15 Folly is bound up in the *h* of a child
22: 17 apply your *h* to what I teach,
22: 18 when you keep them in your *h*
23: 7 but his *h* is not with you.
23: 12 Apply your *h* to instruction
23: 15 My son, if your *h* is wise,
23: 15 then my *h* will be glad;
23: 17 Do not let your *h* envy sinners,
23: 19 and keep your *h* on the right path.
23: 26 My son, give me your *h*
24: 12 he who weighs the *h* perceive it?
24: 17 stumbles, do not let your *h* rejoice,
24: 32 I applied my *h* to what I observed
25: 20 is one who sings songs to a heavy *h*.
26: 23 are fervent lips with an evil *h*.
26: 24 but in his *h* he harbors deceit.
26: 25 for seven abominations fill his *h*.
27: 9 incense bring joy to the *h*,
27: 11 my son, and bring joy to my *h;*
27: 19 so a man's *h* reflects the man.
28: 14 he who hardens his *h* falls
Ecc 2: 1 I thought in my *h*, "Come now,
2: 8 the delights of the *h* of man.
2: 10 I refused my *h* no pleasure.
2: 10 My *h* took delight in all my work,
2: 15 I said in my *h*,
2: 15 Then I thought in my *h*,
2: 20 So my *h* began to despair
3: 17 I thought in my *h*,
Ecc 5: 2 do not be hasty in your *h*
5: 20 occupied with gladness of *h*.
6: 2 that he lacks nothing his *h* desires,
7: 2 the living should take this to *h*.
7: 3 because a sad face is good for the *h*.
7: 4 The *h* of the wise is in the house
7: 4 the *h* of fools is in the house
7: 7 and a bribe corrupts the *h*.
7: 22 for you know in your *h*
7: 26 whose *h* is a trap
8: 5 wise *h* will know the proper time
9: 7 and drink your wine with a joyful *h*
10: 2 The *h* of the wise inclines
10: 2 but the *h* of the fool to the left.
11: 9 Follow the ways of your *h*
11: 9 let your *h* give you joy in the days
11: 10 banish anxiety from your *h*
SS 3: 1 I looked for the one my *h* loves;
3: 2 I will search for the one my *h* loves.
3: 3 "Have you seen the one my *h* loves
3: 4 when I found the one my *h* loves.
3: 11 the day his *h* rejoiced.
4: 9 You have stolen my *h*, my sister,
4: 9 you have stolen my *h*
5: 2 I slept but my *h* was awake
5: 4 my *h* began to pound for him.
5: 6 My *h* had gone out to him
8: 6 Place me like a seal over your *h*,
Isa 1: 5 your whole *h* afflicted.
6: 10 Make the *h* of this people calloused
7: 4 Do not lose *h* because of these two
9: 9 and arrogance of *h*,
10: 12 Assyria for the willful pride of his *h*
13: 7 every man's *h* will melt.
14: 13 You said in your *h*,
15: 5 My *h* cries out over Moab;
16: 11 My *h* laments for Moab like a harp,
19: 3 The Egyptians will lose *h*,
19: 10 the wage earners will be sick at *h*.
19: 19 to the LORD in the *h* of Egypt,
21: 4 My *h* falters,
40: 11 and carries them close to his *h;*
42: 25 but they did not take it to *h*.
44: 20 a deluded *h* misleads him;
46: 8 take it to *h*, you rebels.
49: 21 Then you will say in your *h*,
57: 1 and no one ponders it in his *h;*
57: 15 and to revive the *h* of the contrite.
60: 5 your *h* will throb and swell with joy
63: 4 of vengeance was in my *h*,
65: 14 out from anguish of *h*
66: 14 you see this, your *h* will rejoice
Jer 3: 10 return to me with all her *h*,
3: 15 give you shepherds after my own *h*,
4: 9 the king and the officials will lose *h*
4: 14 wash the evil from your *h*
4: 18 How it pierces to the *h!*"
4: 19 My *h* pounds within me,
4: 19 Oh, the agony of my *h!*
8: 18 my *h* is faint within me.
9: 8 but in his *h* he sets a trap for him.
9: 26 of Israel is uncircumcised in *h*."
11: 20 and test the *h* and mind,
15: 1 my *h* would not go out
16: 12 of his evil *h* instead of obeying me.
17: 5 and whose *h* turns away
17: 9 The *h* is deceitful above all things
17: 10 "I the LORD search the *h*
18: 12 the stubbornness of his evil *h*.' "
20: 9 is in my *h* like a burning fire,
20: 12 and probe the *h* and mind,
22: 17 "But your eyes and your *h*
23: 9 My *h* is broken within me;
23: 20 the purposes of his *h*.
24: 7 I will give them a *h* to know me,
24: 7 return to me with all their *h*.
29. 13 when you seek me with all your *h*.
30: 24 the purposes of his *h*.
31: 20 Therefore my *h* yearns for him;
32: 39 I will give them singleness of *h*
32: 41 them in this land with all my *h*
48: 29 and the haughtiness of her *h*.
48: 36 my *h* laments for Moab like a flute;
48: 41 will be like the *h* of a woman
49: 16 pride of your *h* have deceived you,
49: 22 will be like the *h* of a woman
51: 46 Do not lose *h* or be afraid
La 1: 20 and in my *h* I am disturbed,
La 1: 22 and my *h* is faint."
2: 11 my *h* is poured out on the ground
2: 19 pour out your *h* like water
3: 13 He pierced my *h*
Eze 3: 10 and take to *h* all the words I speak
11: 19 I will give them an undivided *h*
11: 19 and give them a *h* of flesh.
11: 19 remove from them their *h* of stone
14: 4 any Israelite sets up idols in his *h*
14: 7 idols in his *h* and puts a wicked
18: 31 and get a new *h* and a new spirit.
21: 6 Groan before them with broken *h*
21: 7 Every *h* will melt and every hand
25: 6 of your *h* against the land of Israel,
27: 25 cargo in the *h* of the sea.
27: 26 pieces in the *h* of the sea.
27: 27 will sink into the *h* of the sea
28: 2 a god in the *h* of the seas."
28: 2 " 'In the pride of your *h*
28: 5 your *h* has grown proud.
28: 8 death in the *h* of the seas.
28: 17 Your *h* became proud
36: 26 I will give you a new *h*
36: 26 of stone and give you a *h* of flesh.
36: 26 remove from you your *h* of stone
44: 7 foreigners uncircumcised in *h*
44: 9 No foreigner uncircumcised in *h*
Da 5: 20 But when his *h* became arrogant
7: 4 and the *h* of a man was given to it.
11: 28 but his *h* will be set against the holy
11: 30 will oppose him, and he will lose *h*.
Hos 5: 4 A spirit of prostitution is in their *h;*
10: 2 Their *h* is deceitful,
11: 8 My *h* is changed within me;
Joel 2: 12 "return to me with all your *h*,
2: 13 Rend your *h*
Am 7: 10 against you in the very *h* of Israel.
Ob : 3 pride of your *h* has deceived you,
Jnh 2: 3 into the very *h* of the seas,
Hab 3: 16 I heard and my *h* pounded,
Zep 3: 14 Be glad and rejoice with all your *h*,
Mal 2: 2 and if you do not set your *h*
2: 2 because you have not set your *h*
Mt 5: 8 Blessed are the pure in *h*,
5: 28 adultery with her in his *h*.
6: 21 treasure is, there your *h* will be
9: 2 Take *h*, son; your sins are forgiven
9: 22 "Take *h*, daughter," he said,
11: 29 for I am gentle and humble in *h*,
12: 34 of the *h* the mouth speaks.
12: 40 three nights in the *h* of the earth.
13: 15 For this people's *h* has become
13: 19 away what was sown in his *h*.
15: 18 out of the mouth come from the *h*,
15: 19 For out of the *h* come evil thoughts
18: 35 forgive your brother from your *h*."
22: 37 the Lord your God with all your *h*
Mk 7: 19 For it doesn't go into his *h*
11: 23 and does not doubt in his *h*
12: 30 the Lord your God with all your *h*
12: 33 To love him with all your *h*,
Lk 2: 19 and pondered them in her *h*.
2: 51 treasured all these things in her *h*.
6: 45 out of the evil stored up in his *h*.
6: 45 out of the good stored up in his *h*,
6: 45 overflow of his *h* his mouth speaks.
7: 13 his *h* went out to her and he said,
8: 15 for those with a noble and good *h*,
10: 27 the Lord your God with all your *h*
12: 29 do not set your *h* on what you will
12: 34 treasure is, there your *h* will be
24: 25 of *h* to believe all that the prophets
Jn 12: 27 "Now my *h* is troubled,
16: 33 take *h!* I have overcome the world
Ac 1: 24 "Lord, you know everyone's *h*.
2: 26 Therefore my *h* is glad
2: 37 they were cut to the *h*
4: 32 All the believers were one in *h*
5: 3 so filled your *h* that you have lied
8: 21 your *h* is not right before God.
8: 22 for having such a thought in your *h*
13: 22 son of Jesse a man after my own *h;*
15: 8 who knows the *h*, showed that he
16: 14 The Lord opened her *h* to respond
21: 13 you weeping and breaking my *h?*
28: 27 For this people's *h* has become
Ro 1: 9 with my whole *h* in preaching
2: 5 and your unrepentant *h*,

Ro 2:29 is circumcision of the *h*,
9: 2 and unceasing anguish in my *h*.
10: 6 say in your *h*, 'Who will ascend
10: 8 it is in your mouth and in your *h*,''
10: 9 in your *h* that God raised him
10:10 is with your *h* that you believe
15: 6 with one *h* and mouth you may
1Co 14:25 the secrets of his *h* will be laid bare.
2Co 2: 4 anguish of *h* and with many tears,
4: 1 this ministry, we do not lose *h*.
4:16 Therefore we do not lose *h*.
5:12 rather than in what is in the *h*.
8:16 who put into the *h*
9: 7 give what he has decided in his *h*
Eph 1:18 eyes of your *h* may be enlightened
5:19 make music in your *h* to the Lord,
6: 5 and with sincerity of *h*, just
6: 6 doing the will of God from your *h*.
Php 1: 7 since I have you in my *h*; for
Col 2: 2 is that they may be encouraged in *h*
3:22 but with sincerity of *h*
3:23 work at it with all your *h*,
1Ti 1: 5 which comes from a pure *h*
3: 1 If anyone sets his *h*
2Ti 2:22 call on the Lord out of a pure *h*.
Phm :12 who is my very *h*— back to you.
:20 in the Lord; refresh my *h* in Christ.
Heb 3:12 unbelieving *h* that turns away
4:12 the thoughts and attitudes of the *h*.
10:22 with a sincere *h* in full assurance
12: 3 you will not grow weary and lose *h*.
12: 5 do not lose *h* when he rebukes you,
1Pe 1:22 one another deeply, from the *h*.
1Jn 5:10 of God has this testimony in his *h*.
Rev 1: 3 and take to *h* what is written in it,
18: 7 In her *h* she boasts,

HEART'S (HEART)

2Ch 1:11 "Since this is your *h* desire
Jer 15:16 they were my joy and my *h* delight,
Eze 24:25 delight of their eyes, their *h* desire,
Ro 10: 1 my *h* desire and prayer to God

HEARTACHE (HEART)

Pr 15:13 but *h* crushes the spirit.

HEARTH

Lev 6: 9 on the altar *h* throughout the night,
Isa 29: 2 she will be to me like an altar *h*.
30:14 found for taking coals from a *h*
Eze 43:15 The altar *h* is four cubits high,
43:15 horns project upward from the *h*.
43:16 altar *h* is square, twelve cubits long

HEARTLESS

La 4: 3 but my people have become *h*
Ro 1:31 they are senseless, faithless, *h*,

HEARTS (HEART)

Ge 42:28 Their *h* sank and they turned
Ex 9:34 and his officials hardened their *h*.
10: 1 and the *h* of his officials
14:17 I will harden the *h* of the Egyptians
Lev 26:36 I will make their *h* so fearful
26:41 their uncircumcised *h* are humbled
Nu 15:39 going after the lusts of your own *h*
Dt 5:29 that their *h* would be inclined
6: 6 are to be upon your *h*.
10:16 Circumcise your *h*, therefore,
11:18 Fix these words of mine in your *h*
28:67 of the terror that will fill your *h*
30: 6 and the *h* of your descendants,
30: 6 your God will circumcise your *h*
Jos 2:11 our *h* sank and everyone's courage
5: 1 their *h* sank and they no longer had
7: 5 At this the *h* of the people melted
11:20 himself who hardened their *h*
14: 8 up with me made the *h*
24:23 and yield your *h* to the LORD,
1Sa 6: 6 Why do you harden your *h*
7: 3 to the LORD with all your *h*,
10:26 valiant men whose *h* God had
2Sa 15: 6 and so he stole the *h* of the men
15:13 "The *h* of the men of Israel are
19:14 He won over the *h* of all the men
1Ki 8:39 for you alone know the *h* of all men
8:58 May he turn our *h* to him,
8:61 your *h* must be fully committed
1Ki 11: 2 they will surely turn your *h*
18:37 are turning their *h* back again."
1Ch 16:10 let the *h* of those who seek
29:18 and keep their *h* loyal to you.
29:18 in the *h* of your people forever,
2Ch 6:30 (for you alone know the *h* of men),
11:16 tribe of Israel who set their *h*
16: 9 strengthen those whose *h* are fully
20:33 the people still had not set their *h*
29:31 all whose *h* were willing brought
Job 1: 5 and cursed God in their *h*."
Ps 4: 4 search your *h* and be silent.
7: 9 who searches minds and *h*,
17:10 They close up their callous *h*,
22:26 may your *h* live forever!
28: 3 but harbor malice in their *h*.
33:15 he who forms the *h* of all,
33:21 In him our *h* rejoice,
37:15 their swords will pierce their own *h*
44:18 Our *h* had not turned back;
45: 5 Let your sharp arrows pierce the *h*
62: 4 but in their *h* they curse.
62: 8 pour out your *h* to him,
69:32 you who seek God, may your *h* live
73: 7 their callous *h* comes iniquity;
74: 8 in their *h*, "We will crush them
78: 8 whose *h* were not loyal to God,
78:37 their *h* were not loyal to him,
81:12 over to their stubborn *h*
84: 5 who have set their *h* on pilgrimage.
95: 8 do not harden your *h* as you did
95:10 are a people whose *h* go astray,
105: 3 let the *h* of those who seek
105:25 whose *h* he turned
119:70 Their *h* are callous and unfeeling,
140: 2 who devise evil plans in their *h*
Pr 12:20 There is deceit in the *h*
15: 7 not so the *h* of fools.
15:11 how much more the *h* of men!
24: 2 for their *h* plot violence,
25: 3 so the *h* of kings are unsearchable.
Ecc 3:11 also set eternity in the *h* of men;
8:11 the *h* of the people are filled
9: 3 The *h* of men, moreover, are full
9: 3 madness in their *h* while they live,
Isa 6:10 understand with their *h*,
7: 2 so the *h* of Ahaz and his people
15: 4 and their *h* are faint.
19: 1 and the *h* of the Egyptians melt
26: 8 are the desire of our *h*.
29:13 but their *h* are far from me.
30:29 your *h* will rejoice
35: 4 say to those with fearful *h*,
51: 7 people who have my law in your *h*:
57:11 nor pondered this in your *h*?
59:13 uttering lies our *h* have conceived.
63:17 harden our *h* so we do not revere
65:14 out of the joy of their *h*,
Jer 3:17 the stubbornness of their evil *h*.
4: 4 circumcise your *h*,
5:23 have stubborn and rebellious *h*;
7:24 inclinations of their evil *h*.
9:14 the stubbornness of their *h*;
11: 8 the stubbornness of their evil *h*.
12: 2 but far from their *h*.
13:10 follow the stubbornness of their *h*
17: 1 on the tablets of their *h*
23:17 follow the stubbornness of their *h*
23:26 in the *h* of these lying prophets,
31:33 and write it on their *h*.
48:41 that day the *h* of Moab's warriors
49:22 that day the *h* of Edom's warriors
La 2:18 The *h* of the people
3:41 Let us lift up our *h* and our hands
3:65 Put a veil over their *h*,
5:15 Joy is gone from our *h*;
5:17 Because of this our *h* are faint,
Eze 6: 9 grieved by their adulterous *h*,
11:21 as for those whose *h* are devoted
14: 3 men have set up idols in their *h*
14: 5 this to recapture the *h* of the people
20:16 For their *h* were devoted
21:15 So that *h* may melt
25:15 took revenge with malice in their *h*
32: 9 " 'I will trouble the *h*
33:31 their *h* are greedy for unjust gain.
36: 5 in their *h* they made my land their
Da 11:27 with their *h* bent on evil,
Hos 7: 6 Their *h* are like an oven;
7:14 to me from their *h*
Na 2:10 *H* melt, knees give way,
Zec 7:10 In your *h* do not think evil
7:12 They made their *h* as hard as flint
10: 7 and their *h* will be glad
10: 7 their *h* will rejoice in the LORD.
12: 5 leaders of Judah will say in their *h*,
Mal 4: 6 He will turn the *h* of the fathers
4: 6 and the *h* of the children
Mt 9: 4 entertain evil thoughts in your *h*?
13:15 understand with their *h*
15: 8 but their *h* are far from me.
19: 8 wives because your *h* were hard.
Mk 2: 8 what they were thinking in their *h*,
3: 5 distressed at their stubborn *h*,
6:52 the loaves; their *h* were hardened.
7: 6 but their *h* are far from me.
7:21 out of men's *h*, come evil thoughts,
8:17 understand? Are your *h* hardened?
10: 5 your *h* were hard that Moses wrote
Lk 1:17 to turn the *h* of the fathers
2:35 of many *h* will be revealed.
3:15 and were all wondering in their *h*
5:22 thinking these things in your *h*?
8:12 takes away the word from their *h*,
16:15 of men, but God knows your *h*.
21:34 or your *h* will be weighed
24:32 "Were not our *h* burning within us
Jn 5:42 not have the love of God in your *h*.
12:40 and deadened their *h*,
12:40 nor understand with their *h*,
14: 1 "Do not let your *h* be troubled.
14:27 Do not let your *h* be troubled
Ac 2:46 together with glad and sincere *h*,
7:39 in their *h* turned back to Egypt.
7:51 with uncircumcised *h* and ears!
11:23 true to the Lord with all their *h*.
14:17 of food and fills your *h* with joy."
15: 9 for he purified their *h* by faith.
28:27 understand with their *h*
Ro 1:21 and their foolish *h* were darkened.
1:24 desires of their *h* to sexual impurity
2:15 of the law are written on their *h*,
5: 5 love into our *h* by the Holy Spirit,
8:27 who searches our *h* knows
1Co 4: 5 will expose the motives of men's *h*.
10: 6 us from setting our *h* on evil things
2Co 1: 9 in our *h* we felt the sentence
1:22 put his Spirit in our *h* as a deposit,
3: 2 written on our *h*, known
3: 3 but on tablets of human *h*.
3:15 Moses is read, a veil covers their *h*.
4: 6 shine in our *h* to give us the light
6:11 and opened wide our *h* to you.
6:13 to my children—open wide your *h*
7: 2 Make room for us in your *h*.
7: 3 a place in our *h* that we would live
9:14 for you their *h* will go out to you,
Gal 4: 6 the Spirit of his Son into our *h*,
Eph 3:17 dwell in your *h* through faith.
4:18 due to the hardening of their *h*.
Php 4: 7 will guard your *h* and your minds
Col 3: 1 set your *h* on things above,
3:15 the peace of Christ rule in your *h*,
3:16 with gratitude in your *h* to God.
4: 8 and that he may encourage your *h*.
1Th 2: 4 men but God, who tests our *h*.
3:13 May he strengthen your *h*
2Th 2:17 encourage your *h* and strengthen
3: 5 May the Lord direct your *h*
Phm : 7 have refreshed the *h* of the saints.
Heb 3: 8 do not harden your *h*
3:10 'Their *h* are always going astray,
3:15 do not harden your *h*
4: 7 do not harden your *h*."
8:10 and write them on their *h*.
10:16 I will put my laws in their *h*,
10:22 having our *h* sprinkled
13: 9 good for our *h* to be strengthened
Jas 3:14 and selfish ambition in your *h*,
4: 8 purify your *h*, you double-minded.
1Pe 3:15 But in your *h* set apart Christ
2Pe 1:19 the morning star rises in your *h*.
1Jn 3:19 and how we set our *h* at rest
3:20 For God is greater than our *h*,
3:20 whenever our *h* condemn us.
3:21 if our *h* do not condemn us,

Rev 2: 23 know that I am he who searches *h*
17: 17 it into their *h* to accomplish his

HEARTS' (HEART)

Pr 13: 25 to their *h'* content,

HEAT (HEATED)

Ge 8: 22 cold and *h*,
18: 1 to his tent in the *h* of the day.
30: 38 When the flocks were in *h*
30: 41 the stronger females were in *h*,
31: 40 The *h* consumed me in the daytime
Dt 28: 22 with scorching *h* and drought,
1Sa 11: 11 them until the *h* of the day.
2Sa 4: 5 there in the *h* of the day
2Ki 23: 26 away from the *h* of his fierce anger,
Job 6: 17 in the *h* vanish from their channels.
24: 19 As *h* and drought snatch away
Ps 19: 6 nothing is hidden from its *h*.
32: 4 as in the *h* of summer.
58: 9 Before your pots can feel the *h*
Isa 4: 6 and shade from the *h* of the day,
18: 4 a cloud of dew in the *h* of harvest.''
18: 4 like shimmering *h* in the sunshine,
21: 15 and from the *h* of battle.
25: 4 and a shade from the *h*.
25: 5 and like the *h* of the desert.
25: 5 as *h* is reduced by the shadow
49: 10 will the desert *h* or the sun beat
Jer 2: 24 in her *h* who can restrain her?
17: 8 It does not fear when *h* comes;
36: 30 and exposed to the *h* by day
Hos 13: 5 in the land of burning *h*.
Mt 20: 12 of the work and the *h* of the day.'
Ac 28: 3 driven out by the *h*, fastened itself
Jas 1: 11 For the sun rises with scorching *h*
2Pe 3: 12 and the elements will melt in the *h*.
Rev 7: 16 nor any scorching *h*.
16: 9 They were seared by the intense *h*

HEATED (HEAT)

Da 3: 19 ordered the furnace *h* seven times

HEATHEN

1Th 4: 5 not in passionate lust like the *h*,

HEAVEN (HEAVEN'S HEAVENLY HEAVENS HEAVENWARD)

Ge 14: 19 Creator of *h* and earth.
14: 22 God Most High, Creator of *h*
21: 17 of God called to Hagar from *h*
22: 11 LORD called out to him from *h*,
22: 15 to Abraham from *h* a second time
24: 3 the God of *h* and the God of earth,
24: 7 ''The LORD, the God of *h*,
27: 39 away from the dew of *h* above.
28: 12 with its top reaching to *h*,
28: 17 house of God; this is the gate of *h*.''
Ex 16: 4 rain down bread from *h* for you.
17: 14 of the Amalekites from under *h*.''
20: 4 in the form of anything in *h* above
20: 22 that I have spoken to you from *h*:
Dt 2: 25 of you on all the nations under *h*.
3: 24 For what god is there in *h*
4: 19 to all the nations under *h*.
4: 26 I call *h* and earth as witnesses
4: 36 From *h* he made you hear his voice
4: 39 this day that the LORD is God in *h*
5: 8 in the form of anything in *h* above
7: 24 wipe out their names from under *h*.
9: 14 blot out their name from under *h*.
11: 11 and valleys that drinks rain from *h*.
25: 19 memory of Amalek from under *h*.
26: 15 from *h*, your holy dwelling place,
29: 20 blot out his name from under *h*.
30: 12 It is not up in *h*, so that you have
30: 12 ''Who will ascend into *h* to get it
30: 19 This day I call *h* and earth
31: 28 and call *h* and earth to testify
32: 40 I lift my hand to *h* and declare:
33: 13 land with the precious dew from *h*
Jos 2: 11 the LORD your God is God in *h*
Jdg 13: 20 up from the altar toward *h*,
1Sa 2: 10 thunder against them from *h*;
5: 12 the outcry of the city went up to *h*.
2Sa 22: 14 The LORD thundered from *h*;
1Ki 8: 22 spread out his hands toward *h*
8: 23 there is no God like you in *h* above
1Ki 8: 27 the highest *h*, cannot contain you.
8: 30 Hear from *h*, your dwelling place,
8: 32 in this temple, then hear from *h*
8: 34 hear from *h* and forgive the sin
8: 36 hear from *h* and forgive the sin
8: 39 hear from *h*, your dwelling place.
8: 43 hear from *h*, your dwelling place,
8: 45 then hear from *h* their prayer
8: 49 then from *h*, your dwelling place,
8: 54 with his hands spread out toward *h*
22: 19 the host of *h* standing around him
2Ki 1: 10 from *h* and consumed the captain
1: 10 may fire come down from *h*
1: 12 Then the fire of God fell from *h*
1: 12 ''may fire come down from *h*
1: 14 from *h* and consumed the first two
2: 1 up to *h* in a whirlwind,
2: 11 Elijah went up to *h* in a whirlwind.
14: 27 the name of Israel from under *h*,
19: 15 You have made *h* and earth.
1Ch 21: 16 of the LORD standing between *h*
21: 26 him with fire from *h* on the altar
29: 11 everything in *h* and earth is yours.
2Ch 2: 12 the God of Israel, who made *h*
6: 13 and spread out his hands toward *h*.
6: 14 there is no God like you in *h*
6: 21 Hear from *h*, your dwelling place;
6: 23 in this temple, then hear from *h*
6: 25 hear from *h* and forgive the sin
6: 27 hear from *h* and forgive the sin
6: 30 hear from *h*, your dwelling place.
6: 33 hear from *h*, your dwelling place,
6: 35 then hear from *h* their prayer
6: 39 then from *h*, your dwelling place,
7: 1 fire came down from *h*
7: 14 then will I hear from *h*
18: 18 the host of *h* standing on his right
20: 6 are you not the God who is in *h*?
28: 9 them in a rage that reaches to *h*.
30: 27 for their prayer reached *h*,
32: 20 out in prayer to *h* about this.
36: 23 '' 'The LORD, the God of *h*,
Ezr 1: 2 '' 'The LORD, the God of *h*,
5: 11 We are the servants of the God of *h*
5: 12 our fathers angered the God of *h*,
6: 9 for burnt offerings to the God of *h*,
6: 10 sacrifices pleasing to the God of *h*
7: 12 teacher of the Law of the God of *h*:
7: 21 teacher of the Law of the God of *h*,
7: 23 for the temple of the God of *h*.
7: 23 the God of *h* has prescribed,
Ne 1: 4 and prayed before the God of *h*.
1: 5 of *h*, the great and awesome God,
2: 4 Then I prayed to the God of *h*,
2: 20 ''The God of *h* will give us success.
9: 6 the multitudes of *h* worship you.
9: 13 you spoke to them from *h*.
9: 15 you gave them bread from *h*
9: 27 From *h* you heard them,
9: 28 you heard from *h*,
Job 16: 19 Even now my witness is in *h*;
22: 12 ''Is not God in the heights of *h*?
25: 2 order in the heights of *h*.
37: 3 beneath the whole *h*
41: 11 Everything under *h* belongs to me.
Ps 2: 4 The One enthroned in *h* laughs;
14: 2 The LORD looks down from *h*
18: 13 The LORD thundered from *h*;
20: 6 he answers him from his holy *h*
33: 13 From *h* the LORD looks down
53: 2 God looks down from *h*
57: 3 He sends from *h* and saves me,
69: 34 Let *h* and earth praise him,
73: 9 Their mouths lay claim to *h*,
73: 25 Whom have I in *h* but you?
75: 5 Do not lift your horns against *h*;
76: 8 From *h* you pronounced judgment,
78: 24 he gave them the grain of *h*.
80: 14 Look down from *h* and see!
85: 11 righteousness looks down from *h*.
89: 2 your faithfulness in *h* itself.
102: 19 from *h* he viewed the earth,
103: 19 has established his throne in *h*,
105: 40 satisfied them with the bread of *h*.
115: 3 Our God is in *h*;
115: 15 the Maker of *h* and earth.
121: 2 the Maker of *h* and earth.
123: 1 to you whose throne is in *h*.
Ps 124: 8 the Maker of *h* and earth.
134: 3 May the LORD, the Maker of *h*
136: 26 Give thanks to the God of *h*.
146: 6 the Maker of *h* and earth,
Pr 30: 4 up to *h* and come down?
Ecc 1: 13 by wisdom all that is done under *h*.
2: 3 to do under *h* during the few days
3: 1 a season for every activity under *h*:
5: 2 God is in *h*
Isa 13: 10 of *h* and their constellations
14: 12 How you have fallen from *h*,
14: 13 ''I will ascend to *h*;
37: 16 You have made *h* and earth.
55: 10 come down from *h*,
63: 15 Look down from *h* and see
66: 1 ''*H* is my throne
Jer 7: 18 cakes of bread for the Queen of *H*.
23: 24 ''Do not I fill *h* and earth?''
33: 25 and the fixed laws of *h* and earth,
44: 17 incense to the Queen of *H*
44: 18 incense to the Queen of *H*
44: 19 incense to the Queen of *H*
44: 25 offerings to the Queen of *H*.'
51: 48 *h* and earth and all that is in them
La 2: 1 Israel from *h* to earth;
3: 41 hands to God in *h*, and say:
3: 50 down from *h* and sees.
Eze 8: 3 up between earth and *h*
Da 2: 18 God of *h* concerning this mystery,
2: 19 Then Daniel praised the God of *h*
2: 28 a God in *h* who reveals mysteries.
2: 37 God of *h* has given you dominion
2: 44 of *h* will set up a kingdom that will
4: 13 a holy one, coming down from *h*.
4: 15 drenched with the dew of *h*,
4: 23 coming down from *h* and saying,
4: 23 drenched with the dew of *h*;
4: 25 and be drenched with the dew of *h*.
4: 26 you acknowledge that *H* rules.
4: 31 lips when a voice came from *h*,
4: 33 the dew of *h* until his hair grew like
4: 34 raised my eyes toward *h*,
4: 35 pleases with the powers of *h*
4: 37 and exalt and glorify the King of *h*,
5: 21 drenched with the dew of *h*,
5: 23 up against the Lord of *h*.
7: 2 of *h* churning up the great sea.
7: 13 coming with the clouds of *h*.
7: 27 under the whole *h* will be handed
8: 8 up toward the four winds of *h*.
9: 12 Under the whole *h* nothing has
11: 4 out toward the four winds of *h*.
12: 7 and his left hand toward *h*,
Jnh 1: 9 the God of *h*, who made the sea
Zec 2: 6 you to the four winds of *h*,''
5: 9 they lifted up the basket between *h*
6: 5 ''These are the four spirits of *h*,
Mal 3: 10 not throw open the floodgates of *h*
Mt 3: 2 for the kingdom of *h* is near.''
3: 16 At that moment *h* was opened,
3: 17 voice from *h* said, ''This is my Son,
4: 17 for the kingdom of *h* is near.''
5: 3 for theirs is the kingdom of *h*.
5: 10 for theirs is the kingdom of *h*.
5: 12 because great is your reward in *h*,
5: 16 and praise your Father in *h*.
5: 18 until *h* and earth disappear,
5: 19 great in the kingdom of *h*.
5: 19 least in the kingdom of *h*,
5: 20 not enter the kingdom of *h*.
5: 34 either by *h*, for it is God's throne;
5: 45 sons of your Father in *h*.
6: 1 reward from your Father in *h*.
6: 9 '' 'Our Father in *h*,
6: 10 done on earth as it is in *h*.
6: 20 up for yourselves treasures in *h*,
7: 11 Father in *h* give good gifts
7: 21 Lord,' will enter the kingdom of *h*,
7: 21 the will of my Father who is in *h*.
8: 11 and Jacob in the kingdom of *h*.
10: 7 'The kingdom of *h* is near.'
10: 32 him before my Father in *h*.
10: 33 him before my Father in *h*.
11: 11 least in the kingdom of *h* is greater
11: 12 of *h* has been forcefully advancing,
11: 25 Father, Lord of *h* and earth,
12: 50 will of my Father in *h* is my brother
13: 11 of the kingdom of *h* has been given

Mt 13: 24 of *h* is like a man who sowed good
13: 31 of *h* is like a mustard seed,
13: 33 of *h* is like yeast that a woman took
13: 44 of *h* is like treasure hidden
13: 45 of *h* is like a merchant looking
13: 47 of *h* is like a net that was let
13: 52 the kingdom of *h* is like the owner
14: 19 the two fish and looking up to *h*,
16: 1 him to show them a sign from *h*.
16: 17 you by man, but by my Father in *h*.
16: 19 bind on earth will be bound in *h*,
16: 19 loose on earth will be loosed in *h*.''
16: 19 the keys of the kingdom of *h;*
18: 1 the greatest in the kingdom of *h?*''
18: 3 will never enter the kingdom of *h*.
18: 4 the greatest in the kingdom of *h*.
18: 10 angels in *h* always see the face
18: 10 the face of my Father in *h*.
18: 14 Father in *h* is not willing that any
18: 18 bind on earth will be bound in *h*,
18: 18 loose on earth will be loosed in *h*.
18: 19 done for you by my Father in *h*.
18: 23 of *h* is like a king who wanted
19: 12 because of the kingdom of *h*.
19: 14 the kingdom of *h* belongs to such
19: 21 and you will have treasure in *h*.
19: 23 man to enter the kingdom of *h*.
20: 1 of *h* is like a landowner who went
21: 25 Was it from *h*, or from men?''
21: 25 ''If we say, 'From *h*,' he will ask,
22: 2 of *h* is like a king who prepared
22: 30 they will be like the angels in *h*.
23: 9 you have one Father, and he is in *h*.
23: 13 the kingdom of *h* in men's faces.
23: 22 And he who swears by *h* swears
24: 35 *H* and earth will pass away,
24: 36 even the angels in *h*, nor the Son,
25: 1 of *h* will be like ten virgins who
26: 64 and coming on the clouds of *h*.''
28: 2 of the Lord came down from *h*
28: 18 ''All authority in *h*
Mk 1: 10 he saw *h* being torn open
1: 11 And a voice came from *h:*
6: 41 the two fish and looking up to *h*,
7: 34 He looked up to *h*
8: 11 they asked him for a sign from *h*.
10: 21 and you will have treasure in *h*.
11: 25 in *h* may forgive you your sins.''
11: 30 was it from *h*, or from men?
11: 31 ''If we say, 'From *h*,' he will ask,
12: 25 they will be like the angels in *h*.
13: 31 *H* and earth will pass away,
13: 32 even the angels in *h*, nor the Son,
14: 62 and coming on the clouds of *h*.''
16: 19 he was taken up into *h*
Lk 1: 78 rising sun will come to us from *h*
2: 15 had left them and gone into *h*,
3: 21 *h* was opened and the Holy Spirit
3: 22 And a voice came from *h:*
6: 23 because great is your reward in *h*.
9: 16 the two fish and looking up to *h*,
9: 51 for him to be taken up to *h*,
9: 54 fire down from *h* to destroy them?''
10: 18 saw Satan fall like lightning from *h*.
10: 20 that your names are written in *h*.''
10: 21 Father, Lord of *h* and earth,
11: 13 Father in *h* give the Holy Spirit
11: 16 him by asking for a sign from *h*.
12: 33 in *h* that will not be exhausted,
15: 7 in *h* over one sinner who repents
15: 18 I have sinned against *h*
15: 21 I have sinned against *h*
16: 17 It is easier for *h* and earth
17: 29 and sulfur rained down from *h*
18: 13 He would not even look up to *h*,
18: 22 and you will have treasure in *h*.
19: 38 Peace in *h* and glory in the highest
20: 4 was it from *h*, or from men?''
20: 5 ''If we say, 'From *h*,' he will ask,
21: 11 events and great signs from *h*.
21: 33 *H* and earth will pass away,
22: 43 An angel from *h* appeared to him
24: 51 left them and was taken up into *h*.
Jn 1: 32 I saw the Spirit come down from *h*
1: 51 you the truth, you shall see *h* open,
3: 13 No one has ever gone into *h*
3: 13 except the one who came from *h*—
3: 27 only what is given him from *h*.
Jn 3: 31 comes from *h* is above all.
6: 31 'He gave them bread from *h* to eat
6: 32 gives you the true bread from *h*.
6: 32 has given you the bread from *h*.
6: 33 God is he who comes down from *h*
6: 38 down from *h* not to do my will
6: 41 the bread that came down from *h*.''
6: 42 down from *h'?*'' ''Stop grumbling
6: 50 the bread that comes down from *h*,
6: 51 bread that came down from *h*.
6: 58 the bread that came down from *h*.
12: 28 Then a voice came from *h*,
17: 1 he looked toward *h* and prayed:
Ac 1: 2 until the day he was taken up to *h*,
1: 11 has been taken from you into *h*,
1: 11 way you have seen him go into *h*.''
2: 2 of a violent wind came from *h*
2: 5 Jews from every nation under *h*.
2: 19 I will show wonders in the *h* above
2: 34 For David did not ascend to *h*,
3: 21 He must remain in *h*
4: 12 name under *h* given to men
4: 24 ''you made the *h* and the earth
7: 49 the prophet says: '' '*H* is my
7: 55 looked up to *h* and saw the glory
7: 56 ''I see *h* open and the Son
9: 3 a light from *h* flashed around him.
10: 11 He saw *h* opened and something
10: 16 the sheet was taken back to *h*.
11: 5 let down from *h* by its four corners,
11: 9 spoke from *h* a second time,
11: 10 then it was all pulled up to *h* again.
14: 15 who made *h* and earth and sea
14: 17 kindness by giving you rain from *h*
17: 24 and everything in it is the Lord of *h*
19: 35 which fell from *h?* Therefore,
22: 6 light from *h* flashed around me.
26: 13 light from *h*, brighter than the sun,
26: 19 disobedient to the vision from *h*.
Ro 1: 18 from *h* against all the godlessness
10: 6 'Who will ascend into *h?*' '' (that is,
1Co 8: 5 whether in *h* or on earth
15: 47 the earth, the second man from *h*.
15: 48 and as is the man from *h*, so
15: 48 so also are those who are of *h*.
15: 49 the likeness of the man from *h*.
2Co 5: 1 an eternal house in *h*, not built
12: 2 ago was caught up to the third *h*.
Gal 1: 8 from *h* should preach a gospel
Eph 1: 10 to bring all things in *h*
3: 15 from whom his whole family in *h*
6: 9 both their Master and yours is in *h*,
Php 2: 10 in *h* and on earth and under the earth,
3: 20 But our citizenship is in *h*.
Col 1: 5 hope that is stored up for you in *h*
1: 16 things in *h* and on earth, visible
1: 20 things on earth or things in *h*,
1: 23 to every creature under *h*.
4: 1 that you also have a Master in *h*.
1Th 1: 10 and to wait for his Son from *h*,
4: 16 himself will come down from *h*,
2Th 1: 7 revealed from *h* in blazing fire
Heb 1: 3 hand of the Majesty in *h*.
8: 1 of the throne of the Majesty in *h*,
8: 5 and shadow of what is in *h*.
9: 24 he entered *h* itself, now to appear
9: 25 Nor did he enter *h*
12: 23 whose names are written in *h*.
12: 25 from him who warns us from *h?*
Jas 3: 15 does not come down from *h*
3: 17 wisdom that comes from *h* is first
5: 12 not by *h* or by earth
1Pe 1: 4 spoil or fade—kept in *h* for you,
1: 12 you by the Holy Spirit sent from *h*.
3: 22 who has gone into *h* and is
2Pe 1: 18 from *h* when we were with him
3: 13 we are looking forward to a new *h*
Rev 3: 12 down out of *h* from my God;
4: 1 me was a door standing open in *h*.
4: 2 in *h* with someone sitting on it.
5: 3 But no one in *h* or on earth
5: 13 Then I heard every creature in *h*
8: 1 there was silence in *h*
10: 1 mighty angel coming down from *h*.
10: 4 but I heard a voice from *h* say,
10: 5 the land raised his right hand to *h*.
10: 8 from *h* spoke to me once more:
11: 12 And they went up to *h* in a cloud,
Rev 11: 12 voice from *h* saying to them,
11: 13 and gave glory to the God of *h*.
11: 15 and there were loud voices in *h*,
11: 19 God's temple in *h* was opened,
12: 1 and wondrous sign appeared in *h:*
12: 3 Then another sign appeared in *h:*
12: 7 And there was war in *h*.
12: 8 and they lost their place in *h*.
12: 10 Then I heard a loud voice in *h* say:
13: 6 place and those who live in *h*.
13: 13 fire to come down from *h* to earth
14: 2 I heard a sound from *h* like the roar
14: 13 Then I heard a voice from *h* say,
14: 17 out of the temple in *h*,
15: 1 I saw in *h* another great
15: 5 this I looked and in *h* the temple,
16: 11 and cursed the God of *h*
18: 1 angel coming down from *h*.
18: 4 I heard another voice from *h* say:
18: 5 for her sins are piled up to *h*,
18: 20 Rejoice over her, O *h!*
19: 1 of a great multitude in *h* shouting:
19: 11 I saw *h* standing open and there
19: 14 The armies of *h* were following him
20: 1 an angel coming down out of *h*,
20: 9 But fire came down from *h*
21: 1 Then I saw a new *h* and a new earth
21: 1 for the first *h* and the first earth
21: 2 coming down out of *h* from God,
21: 10 coming down out of *h* from God.

HEAVEN'S (HEAVEN)

Ge 27: 28 May God give you of *h* dew

HEAVENLY (HEAVEN)

Dt 4: 19 and the stars—all the *h* array—
Ps 8: 5 him a little lower than the *h* beings
11: 4 the LORD is on his *h* throne.
89: 6 the LORD among the *h* beings?
103: 21 Praise the LORD, all his *h* hosts,
148: 2 praise him, all his *h* hosts.
Mt 5: 48 as your *h* Father is perfect.
6: 14 your *h* Father will also forgive you.
6: 26 and yet your *h* Father feeds them.
6: 32 your *h* Father knows that you need
15: 13 plant that my *h* Father has not
18: 35 ''This is how my *h* Father will treat
24: 29 and the *h* bodies will be shaken.'
25: 31 he will sit on his throne in *h* glory.
Mk 13: 25 and the *h* bodies will be shaken.'
Lk 2: 13 of the *h* host appeared
21: 26 for the *h* bodies will be shaken.
Jn 3: 12 believe if I speak of *h* things?
Ac 7: 42 over to the worship of the *h* bodies.
1Co 15: 40 There are also *h* bodies
15: 40 of the *h* bodies is one kind,
2Co 5: 2 to be clothed with our *h* dwelling,
5: 4 to be clothed with our *h* dwelling,
Eph 1: 3 in the *h* realms with every spiritual
1: 20 at his right hand in the *h* realms,
2: 6 us with him in the *h* realms
3: 10 and authorities in the *h* realms,
6: 12 forces of evil in the *h* realms.
2Ti 4: 18 bring me safely to his *h* kingdom.
Heb 3: 1 who share in the *h* calling,
6: 4 who have tasted the *h* gift,
9: 23 but the *h* things themselves
9: 23 copies of the *h* things to be purified
11: 16 for a better country—a *h* one.
12: 22 to the *h* Jerusalem, the city
Jas 1: 17 from the Father of the *h* lights,

HEAVENS (HEAVEN)

Ge 1: 1 In the beginning God created the *h*
2: 1 Thus the *h* and the earth were
2: 4 God made the earth and the *h*,
2: 4 This is the account of the *h*
6: 17 earth to destroy all life under the *h*,
7: 11 floodgates of the *h* were opened.
7: 19 under the entire *h* were covered.
8: 2 of the *h* had been closed,
11: 4 with a tower that reaches to the *h*,
15: 5 up at the *h* and count the stars—
19: 24 from the LORD out of the *h*.
49: 25 you with blessings of the *h* above,
Ex 20: 11 in six days the LORD made the *h*
31: 17 in six days the LORD made the *h*
Dt 4: 11 blazed with fire to the very *h*,

Dt 4: 32 from one end of the *h* to the other.
10: 14 even the highest *h*, the earth
10: 14 the LORD your God belong the *h*,
11: 17 he will shut the *h* so that it will not
11: 21 as the days that the *h* are
28: 12 The LORD will open the *h*,
30: 4 the most distant land under the *h*,
32: 1 Listen, O *h*, and I will speak;
33: 26 who rides on the *h* to help you
33: 28 where the *h* drop dew.
Jdg 5: 4 the earth shook, the *h* poured,
5: 20 From the *h* the stars fought,
2Sa 21: 10 down from the *h* on the bodies,
22: 8 the foundations of the *h* shook;
22: 10 He parted the *h* and came down;
1Ki 8: 27 The *h*, even the highest heaven,
8: 35 "When the *h* are shut up
2Ki 7: 2 open the floodgates of the *h*,
7: 19 open the floodgates of the *h*,
1Ch 16: 26 but the LORD made the *h*.
16: 31 Let the *h* rejoice, let the earth be
2Ch 2: 6 since the *h*, even the highest
2: 6 the highest *h*, cannot contain him?
6: 18 The *h*, even the highest *h*,
6: 26 "When the *h* are shut up
7: 13 "When I shut up the *h*
Ezr 9: 6 and our guilt has reached to the *h*.
Ne 9: 6 You made the *h*, even the highest
9: 6 highest *h*, and all their starry host,
Job 9: 8 He alone stretches out the *h*
11: 8 They are higher than the *h*—
14: 12 till the *h* are no more, men will not
15: 15 even the *h* are not pure in his eyes,
20: 6 Though his pride reaches to the *h*
20: 27 The *h* will expose his guilt;
22: 14 as he goes about in the vaulted *h*.'
26: 11 The pillars of the *h* quake,
28: 24 and sees everything under the *h*.
35: 5 Look up at the *h* and see;
38: 29 birth to the frost from the *h*
38: 33 Do you know the laws of the *h?*
38: 37 tip over the water jars of the *h*
Ps 8: 1 set your glory above the *h*.
8: 3 When I consider your *h*,
18: 9 He parted the *h* and came down;
19: 1 The *h* declare the glory of God;
19: 4 In the *h* he has pitched a tent
19: 6 It rises at one end of the *h*
33: 6 of the LORD were the *h* made,
36: 5 O LORD, reaches to the *h*,
50: 4 He summons the *h* above,
50: 6 the *h* proclaim his righteousness,
57: 5 Be exalted, O God, above the *h;*
57: 10 is your love, reaching to the *h;*
57: 11 Be exalted, O God, above the *h;*
68: 8 the *h* poured down rain,
78: 23 and opened the doors of the *h;*
78: 26 let loose the east wind from the *h*
89: 5 The *h* praise your wonders,
89: 11 The *h* are yours, and yours
89: 29 his throne as long as the *h* endure.
96: 5 but the LORD made the *h*.
96: 11 Let the *h* rejoice, let the earth be
97: 6 The *h* proclaim his righteousness,
102: 25 the *h* are the work of your hands.
103: 11 as high as the *h* are above the earth,
104: 2 he stretches out the *h* like a tent
107: 26 They mounted up to the *h*
108: 4 is your love, higher than the *h;*
108: 5 Be exalted, O God, above the *h*,
113: 4 his glory above the *h*.
113: 6 look on the *h* and the earth?
115: 16 The highest *h* belong to the LORD
119: 89 it stands firm in the *h*.
135: 6 in the *h* and on the earth,
136: 5 by his understanding made the *h*,
139: 8 If I go up to the *h*, you are there;
144: 5 Part your *h*, O LORD,
148: 1 Praise the LORD from the *h*,
148: 4 Praise him, you highest *h*
148: 13 is above the earth and the *h*.
150: 1 praise him in his mighty *h*.
Pr 3: 19 by understanding he set the *h*
8: 27 there when he set the *h* in place,
25: 3 As the *h* are high and the earth is
Isa 1: 2 Hear, O *h!* Listen, O earth!
13: 5 from the ends of the *h*—
13: 13 I will make the *h* tremble;
Isa 24: 18 The floodgates of the *h* are opened,
24: 21 the powers in the *h* above
34: 4 the stars of the *h* will be dissolved
34: 5 My sword has drunk its fill in the *h;*
38: 14 grew weak as I looked to the *h*.
40: 12 of his hand marked off the *h?*
40: 22 stretches out the *h* like a canopy,
40: 26 Lift your eyes and look to the *h:*
42: 5 who created the *h* and stretched
44: 23 O *h*, for the LORD has done this;
44: 24 who alone stretched out the *h*,
45: 8 "You *h* above, rain
45: 12 My own hands stretched out the *h;*
45: 18 he who created the *h*,
48: 13 and my right hand spread out the *h*
49: 13 Shout for joy, O *h;*
51: 6 Lift up your eyes to the *h*,
51: 6 the *h* will vanish like smoke,
51: 13 who stretched out the *h*
51: 16 I who set the *h* in place,
55: 9 "As the *h* are higher than the earth,
64: 1 that you would rend the *h*
65: 17 new *h* and a new earth.
66: 22 "As the new *h* and the new earth
Jer 2: 12 Be appalled at this, O *h*,
4: 23 and at the *h*,
4: 28 and the *h* above grow dark,
8: 2 the moon and all the stars of the *h*,
10: 11 and from under the *h*.' "
10: 11 who did not make the *h*
10: 12 and stretched out the *h*
10: 13 thunders, the waters in the *h* roar;
31: 37 if the *h* above can be measured
32: 17 you have made the *h* and the earth
49: 36 from the four quarters of the *h;*
51: 15 and stretched out the *h*
51: 16 thunders, the waters in the *h* roar;
La 3: 66 from under the *h* of the LORD.
Eze 1: 1 *h* were opened and I saw visions
32: 7 I snuff you out, I will cover the *h*
32: 8 All the shining lights in the *h*
Da 6: 27 wonders in the *h* and on the earth.
8: 10 until it reached the host of the *h*,
12: 3 shine like the brightness of the *h*,
Joel 2: 30 I will show wonders in the *h*
Am 9: 2 Though they climb up to the *h*,
9: 6 who builds his lofty palace in the *h*
Hab 3: 3 His glory covered the *h*
3: 11 Sun and moon stood still in the *h*
Hag 1: 10 of you the *h* have withheld their
2: 6 while I will once more shake the *h*
2: 21 of Judah that I will shake the *h*
Zec 8: 12 and the *h* will drop their dew.
12: 1 LORD, who stretches out the *h*,
Mt 24: 31 from one end of the *h* to the other.
Mk 13: 27 of the earth to the ends of the *h*.
Eph 4: 10 who ascended higher than all the *h*,
Heb 1: 10 the *h* are the work of your hands.
4: 14 priest who has gone through the *h*,
7: 26 from sinners, exalted above the *h*.
12: 26 not only the earth but also the *h*."
Jas 5: 18 he prayed, and the *h* gave rain,
2Pe 3: 5 ago by God's word the *h* existed
3: 7 By the same word the present *h*
3: 10 The *h* will disappear with a roar;
3: 12 bring about the destruction of the *h*
Rev 10: 6 who created the *h* and all that is
12: 12 Therefore rejoice, you *h*
14: 7 Worship him who made the *h*,

HEAVENWARD (HEAVEN)

Php 3: 14 for which God has called me *h*

HEAVIER (HEAVY)

1Ki 12: 11 a heavy yoke; I will make it even *h*.
12: 14 yoke heavy; I will make it even *h*.
2Ch 10: 11 a heavy yoke; I will make it even *h*.
10: 14 yoke heavy; I will make it even *h*.
Pr 27: 3 provocation by a fool is *h* than both
Isa 28: 22 or your chains will become *h;*

HEAVY (HEAVIER)

Ex 18: 18 The work is too *h* for you;
Nu 11: 14 the burden is too *h* for me.
Dt 1: 9 "You are too *h* a burden for me
25: 13 weights in your bag—one *h*,
32: 15 filled with food, he became *h*
Jdg 20: 34 so *h* that the Benjamites did not
1Sa 4: 17 and the army has suffered *h* losses.
4: 18 for he was an old man and *h*.
5: 6 The LORD's hand was *h*
5: 7 because his hand is *h* upon us
5: 11 God's hand was very *h* upon it.
6: 19 of the *h* blow the LORD had dealt
23: 5 He inflicted *h* losses
2Sa 14: 26 when it became too *h* for him—
1Ki 12: 4 and the *h* yoke he put on us,
12: 4 "Your father put a *h* yoke on us,
12: 10 'Your father put a *h* yoke on us,
12: 11 My father laid on you a *h* yoke;
12: 14 "My father made your yoke *h;*
18: 41 for there is the sound of a *h* rain."
18: 45 a *h* rain came on and Ahab rode
20: 21 inflicted *h* losses on the Arameans.
2Ch 10: 4 and the *h* yoke he put on us,
10: 4 "Your father put a *h* yoke on us,
10: 10 'Your father put a *h* yoke on us,
10: 11 My father laid on you a *h* yoke;
10: 14 "My father made your yoke *h;*
13: 17 his men inflicted *h* losses on them,
21: 14 that is yours, with a *h* blow.
28: 5 who inflicted *h* casualties on him.
Ne 5: 15 placed a *h* burden on the people
5: 18 because the demands were *h*
Job 23: 2 his hand is *h* in spite
33: 7 nor should my hand be *h* upon you.
39: 11 Will you leave your *h* work to him?
Ps 32: 4 your hand was *h* upon me;
38: 4 like a burden too *h* to bear.
144: 14 our oxen will draw *h* loads.
Pr 25: 20 is one who sings songs to a *h* heart.
27: 3 Stone is *h* and sand a burden,
Ecc 1: 13 What a *h* burden God has laid
Isa 24: 20 so *h* upon it is the guilt
47: 6 you laid a very *h* yoke.
Eze 24: 12 its *h* deposit has not been removed,
27: 25 You are filled with *h* cargo
Mt 23: 4 They tie up *h* loads and put them
26: 43 because their eyes were *h*.
Mk 14: 40 because their eyes were *h*.

HEBER (HEBER'S HEBERITE)

Ge 46: 17 The sons of Beriah: *H* and Malkiel.
Nu 26: 45 through *H*, the Heberite clan;
Jdg 4: 11 *H* the Kenite had left the other
4: 17 and the clan of *H* the Kenite.
4: 17 of Jael, the wife of *H* the Kenite,
5: 24 the wife of *H* the Kenite,
1Ch 4: 18 *H* the father of Soco, and Jekuthiel
7: 31 The sons of Beriah: *H* and Malkiel,
7: 32 *H* was the father of Japhlet,
8: 17 Meshullam, Hizki, *H*, Ishmerai,

HEBER'S (HEBER)

Jdg 4: 21 *H* wife, picked up a tent peg

HEBERITE (HEBER)

Nu 26: 45 through Heber, the *H* clan;

HEBREW (HEBREWS)

Ge 14: 13 and reported this to Abram the *H*.
39: 14 "this *H* has been brought to us
39: 17 "That *H* slave you brought us came
41: 12 Now a young *H* was there with us,
Ex 1: 15 of Egypt said to the *H* midwives,
1: 16 "When you help the *H* women
1: 19 "*H* women are not like Egyptian
2: 6 "This is one of the *H* babies,"
2: 7 and get one of the *H* women
2: 11 He saw an Egyptian beating a *H*,
2: 13 Why are you hitting your fellow *H*
21: 2 "If you buy a *H* servant, he is
Dt 15: 12 If a fellow *H*, a man or a woman,
1Sa 4: 6 all this shouting in the *H* camp?"
2Ki 18: 26 speak to us in *H* in the hearing
18: 28 stood and called out in *H:*
2Ch 32: 18 they called out in *H* to the people
Isa 36: 11 speak to us in *H* in the hearing
36: 13 stood and called out in *H*,
Jer 34: 9 Everyone was to free his *H* slaves,
34: 14 free any fellow *H* who has sold
Jnh 1: 9 I am a *H* and I worship the LORD,
Php 3: 5 tribe of Benjamin, a *H* of Hebrews;
Rev 9: 11 whose name in *H* is Abaddon,
16: 16 that in *H* is called Armageddon.

HEBREWS (HEBREW)
Ge 40: 15 carried off from the land of the *H*,
43: 32 Egyptians could not eat with *H*,
Ex 2: 13 went out and saw two *H* fighting.
3: 18 the God of the *H*, has met with us.
5: 3 The God of the *H* has met with us.
7: 16 'The LORD, the God of the *H*,
9: 1 of the *H*, says: "Let my people go,
9: 13 of the *H*, says: Let my people go,
10: 3 what the LORD, the God of the *H*,
1Sa 4: 9 or you will be subject to the *H*,
13: 3 "Let the *H* hear!" So all Israel
13: 7 Some *H* even crossed the Jordan
13: 19 Otherwise the *H* will make swords
14: 11 "The *H* are crawling out
14: 21 Those *H* who had previously been
29: 3 about these *H*?" Achish replied,
2Co 11: 22 Are they *H*? So am I.
Php 3: 5 a Hebrew of *H*; in regard to the law

HEBRON (HEBRONITE HEBRONITES)
Ge 13: 18 near the great trees of Mamre at *H*,
23: 2 died at Kiriath Arba (that is, *H*)
23: 19 near Mamre (which is at *H*)
35: 27 *H*), where Abraham and Isaac had
37: 14 him off from the Valley of *H*.
Ex 6: 18 of Kohath were Amram, Izhar, *H*
Nu 3: 19 Amram, Izhar, *H* and Uzziel.
13: 22 through the Negev and came to *H*,
13: 22 (*H* had been built seven years
Jos 10: 3 appealed to Hoham king of *H*,
10: 5 the kings of Jerusalem, *H*, Jarmuth
10: 23 the kings of Jerusalem, *H*, Jarmuth
10: 36 with him went up from Eglon to *H*
10: 39 to Libnah and its king and to *H*.
11: 21 from *H*, Debir and Anab,
12: 10 one the king of *H* one the king
14: 13 and gave him *H* as his inheritance.
14: 14 So *H* has belonged to Caleb son
14: 15 (*H* used to be called Kiriath Arba
15: 13 Kiriath Arba, that is, *H*.
15: 14 From *H* Caleb drove out
15: 54 Kiriath Arba (that is, *H*)
20: 7 *H*) in the hill country of Judah.
21: 11 Kiriath Arba (that is, *H*),
21: 13 the priest they gave *H* (a city
Jdg 1: 10 *H* (formerly called Kiriath Arba)
1: 20 Moses had promised, *H* was given
16: 3 to the top of the hill that faces *H*.
1Sa 30: 31 Bor Ashan, Athach and *H*;
2Sa 2: 1 "To *H*," the LORD answered.
2: 3 and they settled in *H* and its towns.
2: 4 Then the men of Judah came to *H*
2: 11 king in *H* over the house
2: 32 and arrived at *H* by daybreak.
3: 2 Sons were born to David in *H*:
3: 5 These were born to David in *H*.
3: 19 to *H* to tell David everything that
3: 20 David at *H*, David prepared a feast
3: 22 was no longer with David in *H*,
3: 27 Now when Abner returned to *H*,
3: 32 They buried Abner in *H*,
4: 1 heard that Abner had died in *H*,
4: 8 head of Ish-Bosheth to David at *H*
4: 12 and buried it in Abner's tomb at *H*.
4: 12 hung the bodies by the pool in *H*.
5: 1 tribes of Israel came to David at *H*
5: 3 come to King David at *H*,
5: 3 with them at *H* before the LORD,
5: 5 In *H* he reigned over Judah seven
5: 13 After he left *H*, David took more
15: 7 go to *H* and fulfill a vow I made
15: 8 I will worship the LORD in *H*.' "
15: 9 So he went to *H*.
15: 10 then say, 'Absalom is king in *H*.' "
1Ki 2: 11 seven years in *H* and thirty-three
1Ch 2: 42 who was the father of *H*.
2: 43 The sons of *H*: Korah, Tappuah,
3: 1 the sons of David born to him in *H*:
3: 4 These six were born to David in *H*,
6: 2 Amram, Izhar, *H* and Uzziel.
6: 18 Amram, Izhar, *H* and Uzziel.
6: 55 They were given *H* in Judah
6: 57 of Aaron were given *H* (a city
11: 1 Israel came together to David at *H*
11: 3 come to King David at *H*,
11: 3 with them at *H* before the LORD,
12: 23 David at *H* to turn Saul's kingdom
12: 38 They came to *H* fully determined
15: 9 from the descendants of *H*,
23: 12 Amram, Izhar, *H* and Uzziel—
23: 19 The sons of *H*: Jeriah the first,
24: 23 The sons of *H*: Jeriah the first,
29: 27 seven in *H* and thirty-three
2Ch 11: 10 Azekah, Zorah, Aijalon and *H*.

HEBRONITE (HEBRON)
Nu 26: 58 the Libnite clan, the *H* clan,

HEBRONITES (HEBRON)
Nu 3: 27 Izharites, *H* and Uzzielites;
1Ch 26: 23 Izharites, the *H* and the Uzzielites:
26: 30 From the *H*: Hashabiah
26: 31 As for the *H*, Jeriah was their chief
26: 31 men among the *H* were found

HEDGE (HEDGED)
Job 1: 10 "Have you not put a *h* around him
Isa 5: 5 I will take away its *h*,
Mic 7: 4 most upright worse than a thorn *h*.

HEDGED (HEDGE)
Job 3: 23 whom God has *h* in?

HEED (HEEDED HEEDS)
1Sa 15: 22 to *h* is better than the fat of rams.
Ps 58: 5 that will not *h* the tune
94: 7 the God of Jacob pays no *h*."
94: 8 Take *h*, you senseless ones
107: 43 is wise, let him *h* these things
Pr 1: 24 no one gave *h* when I stretched out
16: 20 gives *h* to instruction prospers,
Ecc 7: 5 It is better to *h* a wise man's rebuke
Mic 6: 9 "*H* the rod and the One who

HEEDED (HEED)
Ecc 9: 16 and his words are no longer *h*.
9: 17 of the wise are more to be *h*

HEEDS (HEED)
Pr 10: 17 He who *h* discipline shows the way
13: 1 wise son *h* his father's instruction,
13: 18 whoever *h* correction is honored.
15: 5 whoever *h* correction shows
15: 32 whoever *h* correction gains

HEEL (HEELS)
Ge 3: 15 and you will strike his *h*."
25: 26 with his hand grasping Esau's *h*;
Job 18: 9 A trap seizes him by the *h*;
Ps 41: 9 has lifted up his *h* against me.
Hos 12: 3 womb he grasped his brother's *h*;
Jn 13: 18 shares my bread has lifted up his *h*

HEELS (HEEL)
Ge 49: 17 that bites the horse's *h*
49: 19 but he will attack them at their *h*.
La 5: 5 Those who pursue us are at our *h*;

HEGAI
Est 2: 3 placed under the care of *H*,
2: 8 and put under the care of *H*.
2: 8 king's palace and entrusted to *H*,
2: 15 for nothing other than what *H*,

HEIFER (HEIFER'S)
Ge 15: 9 "Bring me a *h*, a goat and a ram,
Nu 19: 2 to bring you a red *h* without defect
19: 5 While he watches, the *h* is
19: 6 throw them onto the burning *h*.
19: 9 shall gather up the ashes of the *h*
19: 10 gathers up the ashes of the *h* must
Dt 21: 3 body shall take a *h* that has never
21: 6 over the *h* whose neck was broken
Jdg 14: 18 "If you had not plowed with my *h*,
1Sa 16: 2 "Take a *h* with you and say,
Jer 46: 20 "Egypt is a beautiful *h*,
50: 11 you frolic like a *h* threshing grain
Hos 4: 16 like a stubborn *h*.
10: 11 Ephraim is a trained *h*
Heb 9: 13 and the ashes of a *h* sprinkled

HEIFER'S (HEIFER)
Dt 21: 4 are to break the *h* neck.

HEIGHT (HEIGHTS)
Nu 23: 3 Then he went off to a barren *h*.
1Sa 16: 7 consider his appearance or his *h*,
1Ki 6: 10 The *h* of each was five cubits,
6: 26 *h* of each cherub was ten cubits.
Ne 4: 6 wall till all of it reached half its *h*,
Isa 22: 16 hewing your grave on the *h*
Eze 19: 11 conspicuous for its *h*
31: 10 and because it was proud of its *h*,
31: 14 are ever to reach such a *h*;
43: 13 And this is the *h* of the altar:
Da 4: 10 Its *h* was enormous.
8: 8 at the *h* of his power his large horn
Ro 8: 39 any powers, neither *h* nor depth,
Rev 2: 5 Remember the *h* from which you

HEIGHTS (HEIGHT)
Nu 21: 28 the citizens of Arnon's *h*.
23: 9 from the *h* I view them.
Dt 32: 13 on the *h* of the land
Jdg 5: 18 so did Naphtali on the *h* of the field
2Sa 1: 19 O Israel, lies slain on your *h*.
1: 25 Jonathan lies slain on your *h*.
22: 34 he enables me to stand on the *h*.
2Ki 19: 23 I have ascended the *h*
19: 23 the utmost *h* of Lebanon.
Job 22: 12 "Is not God in the *h* of heaven?
25: 2 order in the *h* of heaven.
Ps 18: 33 he enables me to stand on the *h*
42: 6 the *h* of Hermon—
48: 2 Like the utmost *h* of Zaphon is
148: 1 praise him in the *h* above.
Pr 8: 2 On the *h* along the way,
Ecc 12: 5 when men are afraid of *h*
Isa 7: 11 deepest depths or in the highest *h*."
14: 13 on the utmost *h* of the sacred
31: 4 battle on Mount Zion and on its *h*.
33: 16 is the man who will dwell on the *h*,
37: 24 I have ascended the *h*
37: 24 I have reached its remotest *h*,
37: 24 the utmost *h* of Lebanon.
41: 18 I will make rivers flow on barren *h*,
58: 14 you to ride on the *h* of the land
Jer 3: 2 "Look up to the barren *h* and see.
3: 21 A cry is heard on the barren *h*,
4: 11 from the barren *h* in the desert
7: 29 take up a lament on the barren *h*,
12: 12 Over all the barren *h* in the desert
14: 6 donkeys stand on the barren *h*
31: 12 and shout for joy on the *h* of Zion;
49: 16 who occupy the *h* of the hill.
Eze 17: 23 On the mountain *h*
34: 14 mountain *h* of Israel will be their
36: 2 The ancient *h* have become our
Ob : 3 and make your home on the *h*,
Hab 3: 19 he enables me to go on the *h*.

HEIR (INHERIT)
Ge 15: 3 in my household will be my *h*."
15: 4 from your own body will be your *h*
15: 4 "This man will not be your *h*,
2Sa 14: 7 then we will get rid of the *h* as well
Ps 105: 44 and they fell *h* to what others had
Mt 21: 38 said to each other, 'This is the *h*.
Mk 12: 7 said to one another, 'This is the *h*.
Lk 20: 14 'This is the *h*,' they said.
Ro 4: 13 the promise that he would be *h*
Gal 4: 1 as long as the *h* is a child,
4: 7 God has made you also an *h*.
Heb 1: 2 whom he appointed *h* of all things,
11: 7 became *h* of the righteousness that

HEIRS (INHERIT)
Jdg 21: 17 Benjamite survivors must have *h*,"
Jer 49: 1 Has she no *h*?
Ac 3: 25 And you are *h* of the prophets
Ro 4: 14 For if those who live by law are *h*,
8: 17 then we are *h*—*h* of God
Gal 3: 29 and *h* according to the promise.
Eph 3: 6 gospel the Gentiles are *h* together
Tit 3: 7 we might become *h* having
Heb 6: 17 to the *h* of what was promised,
11: 9 who were *h* with him
1Pe 3: 7 as *h* with you of the gracious gift

HELAH
1Ch 4: 5 father of Tekoa had two wives, *H*
4: 7 The sons of *H*: Zereth, Zohar,

HELAM

2Sa 10: 16 went to *H*, with Shobach
10: 17 crossed the Jordan and went to *H*.

HELBAH

Jdg 1: 31 or Ahlab or Aczib or *H* or Aphek

HELBON

Eze 27: 18 business with you in wine from *H*

HELD (HOLD)

Ge 21: 8 was weaned Abraham *h* a great
27: 41 Esau *h* a grudge against Jacob
39: 22 charge of all those *h* in the prison,
40: 5 who were being *h* in prison—
41: 36 This food should be *h* in reserve
Ex 17: 11 As long as Moses *h* up his hands,
17: 12 Aaron and Hur *h* his hands up—
21: 19 the blow will not be *h* responsible
21: 28 of the bull will not be *h* responsible.
Lev 5: 1 about, he will be *h* responsible.
5: 17 is guilty and will be *h* responsible.
7: 18 any of it will be *h* responsible.
17: 16 he will be *h* responsible.' "
19: 8 eats it will be *h* responsible
20: 17 his sister and will be *h* responsible.
20: 19 both of you would be *h* responsible.
20: 20 They will be *h* responsible;
24: 15 his God, he will be *h* responsible;
26: 13 you to walk with heads *h* high.
Nu 28: 16 the LORD's Passover is to be *h*.
Dt 4: 4 but all of you who *h* fast
Jos 8: 18 Joshua *h* out his javelin toward Ai.
8: 26 back the hand that *h* out his javelin
21: 41 in the territory *h* by the Israelites
Jdg 4: 5 She *h* court under the Palm
7: 21 While each man *h* his position
9: 27 they *h* a festival in the temple
16: 26 said to the servant who *h* his hand,
1Sa 11: 15 and all the Israelites *h* a great
2Sa 6: 22 spoke of, I will be *h* in honor."
23: 19 Was he not *h* in greater honor
23: 23 He was *h* in greater honor than any
1Ki 3: 28 the king had given, they *h* the king
7: 26 It *h* two thousand baths.
8: 47 the land where they are *h* captive,
11: 2 Solomon *h* fast to them in love.
12: 32 like the festival *h* in Judah,
2Ki 18: 6 He *h* fast to the LORD
1Ch 11: 25 He was *h* in greater honor than any
2Ch 4: 5 It *h* three thousand baths.
6: 37 the land where they are *h* captive,
7: 9 the eighth day they *h* an assembly,
Ne 4: 17 and *h* a weapon in the other,
Est 5: 2 *h* out to her the gold scepter that
8: 15 city of Susa *h* a joyous celebration.
10: 3 and *h* in high esteem by his many
Job 36: 8 *h* fast by cords of affliction,
Ps 17: 5 My steps have *h* to your paths;
106: 46 by all who *h* them captive.
SS 3: 4 I *h* him and would not let him go
7: 5 the king is *h* captive by its tresses.
Isa 33: 23 The mast is not *h* secure,
40: 12 Who has *h* the dust of the earth
42: 14 have been quiet and *h* myself back.
65: 2 All day long I have *h* out my hands
Jer 2: 3 all who devoured her were *h* guilty,
Eze 31: 15 I *h* back its streams, and its
Mt 21: 46 the people *h* that he was a prophet.
Mk 11: 32 for everyone *h* that John really was
Lk 5: 29 Levi *h* a great banquet for Jesus
11: 50 generation will be *h* responsible
11: 51 generation will be *h* responsible
Ac 3: 11 While the beggar *h* on to Peter
7: 41 and *h* a celebration in honor
19: 17 the name of the Lord Jesus was *h*
25: 4 "Paul is being *h* at Caesarea,
25: 21 I ordered him *h* until I could send
25: 21 to be *h* over for the Emperor's
27: 32 cut the ropes that *h* the lifeboat
27: 40 untied the ropes that *h* the rudders.
Ro 3: 19 and the whole world *h* accountable
10: 21 day long I have *h* out my hands
Gal 3: 23 we were *h* prisoners by the law,
Eph 4: 16 and *h* together by every supporting
Col 1: 23 from the hope *h* out in the gospel.
2: 19 and *h* together by its ligaments
2Ti 4: 16 May it not be *h* against them.
Heb 2: 15 free those who all their lives were *h*
2Pe 2: 4 dungeons to be *h* for judgment;
Rev 1: 16 In his right hand he *h* seven stars,
6: 2 Its rider *h* a bow, and he was given
15: 2 They *h* harps given them by God
17: 4 She *h* a golden cup in her hand,

HELDAI

1Ch 27: 15 month, was *H* the Netophathite,
Zec 6: 10 and gold from the exiles *H*,
6: 14 The crown will be given to *H*,

HELECH

Eze 27: 11 Men of Arvad and *H*

HELED

2Sa 23: 29 *H* son of Baanah the Netophathite,
1Ch 11: 30 *H* son of Baanah the Netophathite,

HELEK (HELEKITE)

Nu 26: 30 through *H*, the Helekite clan;
Jos 17: 2 the clans of Abiezer, *H*, Asriel,

HELEKITE (HELEK)

Nu 26: 30 through Helek, the *H* clan;

HELEM

1Ch 7: 35 The sons of his brother *H*: Zophah,

HELEPH

Jos 19: 33 Their boundary went from *H*

HELEZ

2Sa 23: 26 Elika the Harodite, *H* the Paltite,
1Ch 2: 39 of *H*, *H* the father of Eleasah,
11: 27 the Harorite, *H* the Pelonite,
27: 10 was *H* the Pelonite, an Ephraimite.

HELI

Lk 3: 23 the son of *H*,

HELIOPOLIS

Eze 30: 17 The young men of *H* and Bubastis

HELKAI

Ne 12: 15 Adna; of Meremoth's, *H*; of Iddo's,

HELKATH

Jos 19: 25 Their territory included: *H*, Hali,
21: 31 Mishal, Abdon, *H* and Rehob,

HELKATH HAZZURIM

2Sa 2: 16 that place in Gibeon was called *H*.

HELL

Mt 5: 22 will be in danger of the fire of *h*.
5: 29 body to be thrown into *h*.
5: 30 for your whole body to go into *h*.
10: 28 destroy both soul and body in *h*.
18: 9 and be thrown into the fire of *h*.
23: 15 as much a son of *h* as you are.
23: 33 you escape being condemned to *h*?
Mk 9: 43 than with two hands to go into *h*,
9: 45 have two feet and be thrown into *h*.
9: 47 two eyes and be thrown into *h*,
Lk 12: 5 has power to throw you into *h*.
16: 23 In *h*, where he was in torment,
Jas 3: 6 and is itself set on fire by *h*.
2Pe 2: 4 but sent them to *h*, putting them

HELMET (HELMETS)

1Sa 17: 5 He had a bronze *h* on his head
17: 38 and a bronze *h* on his head.
Ps 60: 7 Ephraim is my *h*,
108: 8 Ephraim is my *h*,
Isa 59: 17 and the *h* of salvation on his head;
Eph 6: 17 Take the *h* of salvation
1Th 5: 8 and the hope of salvation as a *h*.

HELMETS (HELMET)

2Ch 26: 14 Uzziah provided shields, spears, *h*,
Jer 46: 4 positions with *h* on!
Eze 23: 24 and small shields and with *h*.
27: 10 They hung their shields and *h*
38: 5 *h*, also Gomer with all its troops,

HELON

Nu 1: 9 from Zebulun, Eliab son of *H*;
2: 7 of Zebulun is Eliab son of *H*.
7: 24 On the third day, Eliab son of *H*,
7: 29 was the offering of Eliab son of *H*.
10: 16 and Eliab son of *H* was

HELP (HELPED HELPER HELPERS HELPFUL HELPING HELPLESS HELPS)

Ge 4: 1 "With the *h* of the LORD I have
39: 15 When he heard me scream for *h*,
39: 18 But as soon as I screamed for *h*,
Ex 1: 16 "When you *h* the Hebrew women
2: 23 for *h* because of their slavery went
4: 12 I will *h* you speak and will teach
4: 15 I will *h* both of you speak
23: 1 Do not *h* a wicked man
23: 5 leave it there; be sure you *h* him
31: 6 of the tribe of Dan, to *h* him.
Lev 25: 35 *h* him as you would an alien
Nu 1: 4 the head of his family, is to *h* you.
11: 17 They will *h* you carry the burden
34: 18 from each tribe to *h* assign the land
Dt 22: 4 *H* him get it to its feet.
22: 24 in a town and did not scream for *h*,
32: 38 Let them rise up to *h* you!
33: 7 Oh, be his *h* against his foes!"
33: 26 who rides on the heavens to *h* you
Jos 1: 14 You are to *h* your brothers
10: 4 Come up and *h* me attack Gibeon,"
10: 6 up to us quickly and save us! *H* us,
10: 33 of Gezer had come up to *h* Lachish
24: 7 But they cried to the LORD for *h*,
Jdg 4: 3 they cried to the LORD for *h*,
5: 23 they did not come to *h* the LORD,
5: 23 to *h* the LORD against the mighty
6: 6 out to the LORD for *h*.
10: 12 you and you cried to me for *h*,
12: 3 When I saw that you wouldn't *h*,
1Sa 12: 8 they cried to the LORD for *h*,
14: 45 for he did this today with God's *h*."
2Sa 3: 12 and I will *h* you bring all Israel
8: 5 came to *h* Hadadezer king
10: 19 to *h* the Ammonites anymore.
14: 4 and she said, "*H* me, O king!"
15: 34 then you can *h* me
22: 30 With your *h* I can advance
22: 42 for *h*, but there was no one
2Ki 4: 2 "How can I *h* you? Tell me,
6: 26 a woman cried to him, "*H* me,
6: 27 where can I get *h* for you?
6: 27 "If the LORD does not *h* you,
14: 26 there was no one to *h* them.
23: 29 to *h* the king of Assyria.
1Ch 12: 17 come to me in peace, to *h* me,
12: 18 and success to those who *h* you,
12: 18 for your God will *h* you."
12: 19 his men did not *h* the Philistines
12: 22 after day men came to *h* David,
12: 33 to *h* David with undivided loyalty
18: 5 came to *h* Hadadezer king
19: 19 to *h* the Ammonites anymore.
22: 17 of Israel to *h* his son Solomon.
23: 28 was to *h* Aaron's descendants
24: 3 With the *h* of Zadok a descendant
28: 21 skilled in any craft will *h* you
2Ch 14: 11 *H* us, O LORD our God,
14: 11 you to *h* the powerless
16: 12 even in his illness he did not seek *h*
19: 2 "Should you *h* the wicked
20: 4 together to seek *h* from the LORD;
25: 8 for God has the power to *h*
28: 16 sent to the king of Assyria for *h*.
28: 20 he gave him trouble instead of *h*.
28: 21 of Assyria, but that did not *h* him.
28: 23 to them so they will *h* me."
32: 8 us is the LORD our God to *h* us
Ezr 4: 2 "Let us *h* you build because,
Ne 3: 12 section with the *h* of his daughters.
6: 16 done with the *h* of our God.
Est 7: 9 who spoke up to *h* the king."
Job 6: 13 Do I have any power to *h* myself,
6: 21 you too have proved to be of no *h*;
19: 7 I call for *h*, there is no justice.
24: 12 of the wounded cry out for *h*.
29: 12 I rescued the poor who cried for *h*,
30: 24 when he cries for *h* in his distress.
30: 28 in the assembly and cry for *h*.
36: 13 fetters them, they do not cry for *h*.
Ps 5: 2 Listen to my cry for *h*,

Ps 12: 1 *H*, LORD, for the godly are no
18: 6 I cried to my God for *h*.
18: 29 With your *h* I can advance
18: 41 for *h*, but there was no one
20: 2 May he send you *h*
22: 11 and there is no one to *h*.
22: 19 Strength, come quickly to *h* me.
22: 24 but has listened to his cry for *h*.
28: 2 as I call to you for *h*,
30: 2 my God, I called to you for *h*
30: 10 O LORD, be my *h*."
31: 22 mercy when I called to you for *h*.
33: 20 he is our *h* and our shield.
38: 22 Come quickly to *h* me,
39: 12 listen to my cry for *h*;
40: 13 O LORD, come quickly to *h* me.
40: 17 You are my *h* and my deliverer;
44: 26 Rise up and *h* us;
46: 1 an ever present *h* in trouble.
46: 5 God will *h* her at break of day.
54: 4 Surely God is my *h*;
56: 9 back when I call for *h*.
59: 4 Arise to *h* me; look on my plight!
60: 5 *h* us with your right hand,
60: 11 for the *h* of man is worthless.
63: 7 Because you are my *h*,
69: 3 I am worn out calling for *h*;
70: 1 O LORD, come quickly to *h* me.
70: 5 You are my *h* and my deliverer;
71: 12 come quickly, O my God, to *h* me.
72: 12 the afflicted who have no one to *h*.
77: 1 I cried out to God for *h*;
79: 9 *H* us, O God our Savior,
88: 13 But I cry to you for *h*, O LORD;
94: 17 Unless the LORD had given me *h*,
102: 1 let my cry for *h* come to you.
107: 12 and there was no one to *h*.
108: 6 *h* us with your right hand,
108: 12 for the *h* of man is worthless.
109: 26 *H* me, O LORD my God;
115: 9 he is their *h* and shield.
115: 10 he is their *h* and shield.
115: 11 he is their *h* and shield.
119: 86 *h* me, for men persecute me
119:147 I rise before dawn and cry for *h*;
119:173 May your hand be ready to *h* me,
121: 1 where does my *h* come from?
121: 2 My *h* comes from the LORD,
124: 8 Our *h* is in the name of the LORD,
146: 5 Blessed is he whose *h* is the God
Ecc 4: 10 and has no one to *h* him up!
4: 10 his friend can *h* him up.
Isa 10: 3 To whom will you run for *h*?
20: 6 fled to for *h* and deliverance
30: 2 look for *h* to Pharaoh's protection,
30: 5 who bring neither *h* nor advantage,
30: 7 to Egypt, whose *h* is utterly useless
30: 19 be when you cry for *h*!
31: 1 go down to Egypt for *h*,
31: 1 or seek *h* from the LORD.
31: 2 against those who *h* evildoers.
41: 10 I will strengthen you and *h* you;
41: 13 I will *h* you.
41: 14 for I myself will *h* you," declares
44: 2 and who will *h* you:
49: 8 in the day of salvation I will *h* you;
57: 13 When you cry out for *h*,
58: 9 you will cry for *h*, and he will say:
63: 5 I looked, but there was no one to *h*,
64: 5 You come to the *h*
Jer 11: 12 but they will not *h* them at all
47: 3 turn to *h* their children;
47: 4 who could *h* Tyre and Sidon.
50: 32 and no one will *h* her up;
La 1: 7 there was no one to *h* her.
3: 8 Even when I call out or cry for *h*,
3: 11 and left me without *h*.
4: 6 without a hand turned to *h* her.
4: 17 looking in vain for *h*;
Eze 16: 49 they did not *h* the poor and needy.
17: 17 be of no *h* to him in war,
29: 16 of their sin in turning to her for *h*.
Da 6: 11 praying and asking God for *h*.
10: 13 of the chief princes, came to *h* me,
11: 17 his plans will not succeed or *h* him.
11: 34 they will receive a little *h*,
11: 39 with the *h* of a foreign god
11: 45 to his end, and no one will *h* him.
Hos 5: 13 and sent to the great king for *h*.
Jnh 2: 2 depths of the grave I called for *h*,
Hab 1: 2 O LORD, must I call for *h*,
Zec 6: 15 *h* to build the temple of the LORD,
Mt 8: 5 came to him, asking for *h*.
15: 5 'Whatever *h* you might otherwise
15: 25 "Lord, *h* me!" she said.
25: 44 and did not *h* you?' "He will reply,
Mk 7: 11 'Whatever *h* you might otherwise
9: 22 anything, take pity on us and *h* us."
9: 24 *h* me overcome my unbelief!"
14: 7 you can *h* them any time you want.
Lk 4: 38 and they asked Jesus to *h* her.
5: 7 boat to come and *h* them,
7: 16 "God has come to *h* his people."
10: 40 Tell her to *h* me!" "Martha,
11: 46 will not lift one finger to *h* them.
Jn 5: 7 I have no one to *h* me into the pool
12: 6 he used to *h* himself
Ac 2: 23 and you, with the *h* of wicked men,
4: 20 For we cannot *h* speaking about
11: 29 decided to provide *h*
16: 9 Come over to Macedonia and *h* us
18: 27 he was a great *h* to those who
20: 35 of hard work we must *h* the weak,
21: 28 shouting, "Men of Israel, *h* us!
26: 22 I have had God's *h* to this very day,
Ro 16: 2 and to give her any *h* she may need
16: 2 for she has been a great *h*
1Co 12: 28 those able to *h* others, those
16: 6 so that you can *h* me
2Co 1: 11 as you *h* us by your prayers.
8: 19 and to show our eagerness to *h*.
9: 2 For I know your eagerness to *h*,
Php 1: 19 and the *h* given by the Spirit
2: 30 up for the *h* you could not give me.
4: 3 *h* these women who have
1Th 2: 2 but with the *h* of our God we dared
5: 14 encourage the timid, *h* the weak,
2Th 3: 9 we do not have the right to such *h*,
1Ti 5: 5 day to pray and to ask God for *h*.
5: 16 she should *h* them and not let
5: 16 the church can *h* those widows
2Ti 1: 14 guard it with the *h*
Tit 3: 13 can to *h* Zenas the lawyer
Heb 2: 18 to *h* those who are being tempted.
4: 16 and find grace to *h* us in our time
6: 10 his people and continue to *h* them.
1Pe 5: 12 With the *h* of Silas, whom I regard
3Jn : 7 receiving no *h* from the pagans.

HELPED (HELP)

Jdg 9: 24 who had *h* him murder his brothers
1Sa 7: 12 "Thus far has the LORD *h* us."
23: 16 and *h* him find strength in God.
2Ki 10: 15 and Jehu *h* him up into the chariot.
1Ch 5: 20 They were *h* in fighting them,
12: 1 among the warriors who *h* him
12: 21 *h* David against raiding bands,
15: 26 Because God had *h* the Levites
2Ch 18: 31 cried out, and the LORD *h* him.
20: 23 they *h* to destroy one another.
26: 7 God *h* him against the Philistines
26: 15 for he was greatly *h*
28: 23 of the kings of Aram have *h* them,
29: 34 their kinsmen the Levites *h* them
32: 3 outside the city, and they *h* him.
Est 9: 3 king's administrators *h* the Jews,
Job 26: 2 "How you have *h* the powerless!
26: 4 Who has *h* you utter these words?
Ps 28: 7 my heart trusts in him, and I am *h*.
86: 17 have *h* me and comforted me.
118: 13 but the LORD *h* me.
Isa 31: 3 he who is *h* will fall;
Jer 2: 37 you will not be *h* by them.
Mk 1: 31 took her hand and *h* her up.
Lk 1: 54 He has *h* his servant Israel,
Ac 3: 7 him by the right hand, he *h* him up,
9: 41 by the hand and *h* her to her feet.
2Co 6: 2 and in the day of salvation I *h* you
2Ti 1: 18 well in how many ways he *h* me
Heb 6: 10 you have *h* his people and continue
Rev 12: 16 But the earth *h* the woman

HELPER (HELP)

Ge 2: 18 I will make a *h* suitable for him."
2: 20 for Adam no suitable *h* was found.
Ex 18: 4 "My father's God was my *h*;
Dt 33: 29 He is your shield and *h*
Ne 4: 22 his *h* stay inside Jerusalem at night,
Ps 10: 14 you are the *h* of the fatherless.
27: 9 you have been my *h*.
118: 7 The LORD is with me; he is my *h*.
Hos 13: 9 you are against me, against your *h*.
Ac 13: 5 John was with them as their *h*.
Heb 13: 6 Lord is my *h*; I will not be afraid.

HELPERS (HELP)

Eze 30: 8 and all her *h* are crushed.
Ac 19: 22 He sent two of his *h*, Timothy

HELPFUL (HELP)

Ac 20: 20 to preach anything that would be *h*
Eph 4: 29 only what is *h* for building others
2Ti 4: 11 he is *h* to me in my ministry.

HELPING (HELP)

Jos 14: 12 LORD *h* me, I will drive them out
Jdg 21: 22 'Do us a kindness by *h* them,
Ezr 5: 2 of God were with them, *h* them.
Job 30: 13 without anyone's *h* them.
Lk 8: 3 These women were *h*
Ac 9: 36 always doing good and *h* the poor.
1Ti 5: 10 *h* those in trouble and devoting
Phm : 13 place in *h* me while I am in chains

HELPLESS (HELP)

Ps 10: 9 he catches the *h* and drags them
10: 9 he lies in wait to catch the *h*;
10: 12 Do not forget the *h*.
69: 20 and has left me *h*;
Pr 28: 15 wicked man ruling over a *h* people.
Jer 48: 45 the fugitives stand *h*,
Da 10: 8 turned deathly pale and I was *h*.
10: 16 of the vision, my lord, and I am *h*.
Mt 9: 36 because they were harassed and *h*,

HELPS (HELP)

Ge 49: 25 of your father's God, who *h* you,
Ps 37: 40 LORD *h* them and delivers them,
Isa 31: 3 he who *h* will stumble,
41: 6 each *h* the other
50: 7 the Sovereign LORD *h* me,
50: 9 is the Sovereign LORD who *h* me.
Ro 8: 26 the Spirit *h* us in our weakness.
Heb 2: 16 For surely it is not angels he *h*,

HEM (HEMMED)

Ex 28: 33 yarn around the *h* of the robe,
28: 34 alternate around the *h* of the robe.
39: 24 linen around the *h* of the robe.
39: 25 the *h* between the pomegranates.
39: 26 alternated around the *h* of the robe
Ps 139: 5 You *h* me in—behind and before;
Hab 1: 4 The wicked *h* in the righteous,
Lk 19: 43 and *h* you in on every side.

HEMAN (HEMAN'S)

1Ki 4: 31 wiser than *H*, Calcol and Darda,
1Ch 2: 6 Zimri, Ethan, *H*, Calcol and Darda
6: 33 the Kohathites: *H*, the musician,
15: 17 the Levites appointed *H* son of Joel
15: 19 The musicians *H*, Asaph
16: 41 With them were *H* and Jeduthun
16: 42 *H* and Jeduthun were responsible
25: 1 *H* and Jeduthun for the ministry
25: 4 As for *H*, from his sons: Bukkiah,
25: 5 God gave *H* fourteen sons
25: 5 sons of *H* the king's seer.
25: 6 and *H* were under the supervision
2Ch 5: 12 *H*, Jeduthun and their sons
29: 14 from the descendants of *H*,
35: 15 *H* and Jeduthun the king's seer.

HEMAN'S (HEMAN)

1Ch 6: 39 of Israel; and *H* associate Asaph,

HEMDAN

Ge 36: 26 The sons of Dishon: *H*, Eshban,
1Ch 1: 41 The sons of Dishon: *H*, Eshban,

HEMMED (HEM)

Ex 14: 3 in confusion, *h* in by the desert.'

HEN

Zec 6: 14 Jedaiah and *H* son of Zephaniah

Mt 23: 37 as a *h* gathers her chicks
Lk 13: 34 as a *h* gathers her chicks

HENA

2Ki 18: 34 are the gods of Sepharvaim, *H*
19: 13 of the city of Sepharvaim, or of *H*
Isa 37: 13 of the city of Sepharvaim, or of *H*

HENADAD

Ezr 3: 9 and the sons of *H* and their sons
Ne 3: 18 under Binnui son of *H*,
3: 24 son of *H* repaired another section,
10: 9 Binnui of the sons of *H*, Kadmiel,

HENNA

SS 1: 14 to me a cluster of *h* blossoms
4: 13 with *h* and nard,

HEPHER (HEPHERITE)

Nu 26: 32 through *H*, the Hepherite clan.
26: 33 (Zelophehad son of *H* had no sons;
27: 1 daughters of Zelophehad son of *H*,
Jos 12: 17 one the king of *H* one the king
17: 2 Asriel, Shechem, *H* and Shemida.
17: 3 Now Zelophehad son of *H*,
1Ki 4: 10 and all the land of *H* were his);
1Ch 4: 6 *H*, Temeni and Haahashtari.
11: 36 son of Ur, *H* the Mekerathite,

HEPHERITE (HEPHER)

Nu 26: 32 through Hepher, the *H* clan.

HEPHZIBAH

2Ki 21: 1 His mother's name was *H*.
Isa 62: 4 But you will be called *H*,

HERALD

Da 3: 4 Then the *h* loudly proclaimed,
Hab 2: 2 tablets so that a *h* may run with it.
1Ti 2: 7 for this purpose I was appointed a *h*
2Ti 1: 11 of this gospel I was appointed a *h*

HERBS

Ex 12: 8 with bitter *h*, and bread made
Nu 9: 11 with unleavened bread and bitter *h*
2Ki 4: 39 out into the fields to gather *h*
Job 30: 4 In the brush they gathered salt *h*,
La 3: 15 He has filled me with bitter *h*
Lk 11: 42 rue and all other kinds of garden *h*,

HERD (HERDED HERDING HERDS HERDSMEN)

Ge 18: 7 ran to the *h* and selected a choice,
32: 16 each *h* by itself, and said
Ex 34: 19 of your livestock, whether from *h*
Lev 1: 2 an animal from either the *h*
1: 3 is a burnt offering from the *h*,
3: 1 and he offers an animal from the *h*,
22: 21 When anyone brings from the *h*
27: 32 The entire tithe of the *h* and flock
Nu 15: 3 from the *h* or the flock,
Dt 16: 2 or *h* at the place the LORD will
32: 14 with curds and milk from *h*
Jdg 6: 25 bull from your father's *h*,
Ps 68: 30 the *h* of bulls among the calves
Jnh 3: 7 Do not let any man or beast, *h*
Mt 8: 30 distance from them a large *h*
8: 31 send us into the *h* of pigs."
8: 32 and the whole *h* rushed
Mk 5: 11 A large *h* of pigs was feeding on
5: 13 The *h*, about two thousand
Lk 8: 32 A large *h* of pigs was feeding there
8: 33 the *h* rushed down the steep bank

HERDED (HERD)

Isa 24: 22 They will be *h* together

HERDING (HERD)

1Sa 25: 16 us all the time we were *h* our sheep

HERDS (HERD)

Ge 13: 5 also had flocks and *h* and tents.
26: 14 He had so many flocks and *h*
32: 7 and the flocks and *h* and camels
32: 16 keep some space between the *h*."
32: 19 all the others who followed the *h*:
34: 28 They seized their flocks and *h*
45: 10 your flocks and *h*, and all you have.
46: 32 and *h* and everything they own.'
47: 1 with their flocks and *h*
50: 8 and *h* were left in Goshen.
Ex 10: 9 and with our flocks and *h*,
10: 24 only leave your flocks and *h*
12: 32 Take your flocks and *h*,
12: 38 of livestock, both flocks and *h*.
34: 3 and *h* may graze in front
Nu 11: 22 and *h* were slaughtered for them?
31: 9 and took all the Midianite *h*,
32: 1 who had very large *h* and flocks,
32: 26 and *h* will remain here in the cities
Dt 7: 13 the calves of your *h* and the lambs
8: 13 when your *h* and flocks grow large
12: 6 the firstborn of your *h* and flocks.
12: 17 or the firstborn of your *h* and flocks
12: 21 may slaughter animals from the *h*
14: 23 and the firstborn of your *h*
15: 19 God every firstborn male of your *h*
28: 4 the calves of your *h* and the lambs
28: 18 and the calves of your *h*
28: 51 nor any calves of your *h*
Jos 14: 4 pasturelands for their flocks and *h*.
22: 8 with large *h* of livestock,
1Sa 30: 20 He took all the flocks and *h*,
2Ki 5: 26 olive groves, vineyards, flocks, *h*,
1Ch 27: 29 charge of the *h* grazing in Sharon.
27: 29 in charge of the *h* in the valleys.
2Ch 31: 6 brought a tithe of their *h* and flocks
32: 29 great numbers of flocks and *h*,
Ne 10: 36 of our *h* and of our flocks
Job 1: 10 *h* are spread throughout the land.
Ps 8: 7 all flocks and *h*,
107: 38 and he did not let their *h* diminish.
Pr 27: 23 give careful attention to your *h*;
Ecc 2: 7 also owned more *h* and flocks
Isa 60: 6 *H* of camels will cover your land,
65: 10 of Achor a resting place for *h*,
Jer 3: 24 their flocks and *h*,
5: 17 they will devour your flocks and *h*,
31: 12 the young of the flocks and *h*.
49: 32 and their large *h* will be booty.
Hos 5: 6 go with their flocks and *h*
Joel 1: 18 The *h* mill about
Zep 2: 14 Flocks and *h* will lie down there,
Jn 4: 12 also his sons and his flocks and *h*?"

HERDSMEN (HERD)

Ge 13: 7 arose between Abram's *h* and the *h*
13: 8 or between your *h* and mine,
26: 20 But the *h* of Gerar quarreled
26: 20 of Gerar quarreled with Isaac's *h*
2Ch 14: 15 also attacked the camps of the *h*

HERES

Jdg 1: 35 also to hold out in Mount *H*,
8: 13 from the battle by the Pass of *H*.

HERESH

1Ch 9: 15 a Merarite; Bakbakkar, *H*,

HERESIES

2Pe 2: 1 secretly introduce destructive *h*,

HERETH

1Sa 22: 5 and went to the forest of *H*.

HERITAGE (INHERIT)

Job 20: 29 the *h* appointed for them by God."
27: 13 the *h* a ruthless man receives
31: 2 his *h* from the Almighty on high?
Ps 61: 5 you have given me the *h*
119:111 Your statutes are my *h* forever;
127: 3 Sons are a *h* from the LORD,
Isa 54: 17 This is the *h* of the servants

HERMAS

Ro 16: 14 *H* and the brothers with them.

HERMES

Ac 14: 12 and Paul they called *H*
Ro 16: 14 Greet Asyncritus, Phlegon, *H*,

HERMOGENES

2Ti 1: 15 including Phygelus and *H*.

HERMON

Dt 3: 8 Arnon Gorge as far as Mount *H*.
3: 9 *H* is called Sirion by the Sidonians;
4: 48 *H*), and included all the Arabah
Jos 11: 3 the Hivites below *H* in the region
11: 17 of Lebanon below Mount *H*.
12: 1 from the Arnon Gorge to Mount *H*
12: 5 He ruled over Mount *H*, Salecah,
13: 5 below Mount *H* to Lebo Hamath.
13: 11 all of Mount *H* and all Bashan
1Ch 5: 23 that is, to Senir (Mount *H*).
Ps 42: 6 the heights of *H*—
89: 12 *H* sing for joy at your name.
133: 3 It is as if the dew of *H*
SS 4: 8 the top of Senir, the summit of *H*,

HERO (HEROES)

1Sa 17: 51 saw that their *h* was dead,
Isa 3: 2 the *h* and warrior,

HEROD (HEROD'S HERODIANS)

Mt 2: 1 during the time of King *H*,
2: 3 When King *H* heard this he was
2: 7 Then *H* called the Magi secretly
2: 12 in a dream not to go back to *H*,
2: 13 for *H* is going to search
2: 15 stayed until the death of *H*.
2: 16 When *H* realized that he had been
2: 19 After *H* died, an angel
2: 22 in Judea in place of his father *H*,
14: 1 At that time *H* the tetrarch heard
14: 3 Now *H* had arrested John
14: 5 *H* wanted to kill John,
14: 6 and pleased *H* so much that he
Mk 6: 14 King *H* heard about this,
6: 16 But when *H* heard this, he said,
6: 17 For *H* himself had given orders
6: 18 For John had been saying to *H*,
6: 20 When *H* heard John, he was
6: 20 because *H* feared John
6: 21 On his birthday *H* gave a banquet
6: 22 she pleased *H* and his dinner guests
8: 15 of the Pharisees and that of *H*."
Lk 1: 5 In the time of *H* king
3: 1 of Judea, *H* tetrarch of Galilee,
3: 19 when John rebuked *H* the tetrarch
3: 20 things he had done, *H* added this
9: 7 *H* the tetrarch heard about all that
9: 9 But *H* said, "I beheaded John.
13: 31 *H* wants to kill you."
23: 7 he sent him to *H*, who was
23: 8 When *H* saw Jesus, he was greatly
23: 11 Then *H* and his soldiers ridiculed
23: 12 That day *H* and Pilate became
23: 15 Neither has *H*, for he sent him
Ac 4: 27 Indeed *H* and Pontius Pilate met
12: 1 time that King *H* arrested some
12: 4 *H* intended to bring him out
12: 6 The night before *H* was
12: 19 After *H* had a thorough search
12: 19 *H* went from Judea to Caesarea
12: 21 the appointed day *H*, wearing his
12: 23 *H* did not give praise to God,
13: 1 up with *H* the tetrarch)

HEROD'S (HEROD)

Mt 14: 6 On *H* birthday the daughter
Lk 8: 3 the manager of *H* household;
23: 7 was under *H* jurisdiction,
Ac 12: 11 and rescued me from *H* clutches
23: 35 kept under guard in *H* palace.

HERODIANS (HEROD)

Mt 22: 16 disciples to him along with the *H*.
Mk 3: 6 plot with the *H* how they might kill
12: 13 and *H* to Jesus to catch him

HERODIAS

Mt 14: 3 and put him in prison because of *H*,
14: 6 the daughter of *H* danced for them
Mk 6: 17 of *H*, his brother Philip's wife,
6: 19 So *H* nursed a grudge against John
6: 22 When the daughter of *H* came in
Lk 3: 19 Herod the tetrarch because of *H*,

HERODION

Ro 16: 11 Greet *H*, my relative.

HEROES (HERO)

Ge 6: 4 They were the *h* of old, men

Ne 3: 16 pool and the House of the *H*.
Isa 5: 22 to those who are *h* at drinking wine

HERON

Lev 11: 19 any kind of *h*, the hoopoe
Dt 14: 18 any kind of *h*, the hoopoe

HESHBON

Nu 21: 25 including *H* and all its surrounding
21: 26 *H* was the city of Sihon king
21: 27 "Come to *H* and let it be rebuilt;
21: 28 "Fire went out from *H*,
21: 30 *H* is destroyed all the way to Dibon
21: 34 of the Amorites, who reigned in *H*
32: 3 Jazer, Nimrah, *H*, Elealeh, Sebam,
32: 37 And the Reubenites rebuilt *H*,
Dt 1: 4 who reigned in *H*,
2: 24 king of *H*, and his country.
2: 26 to Sihon king of *H* offering peace
2: 30 But Sihon king of *H* refused
3: 2 of the Amorites, who reigned in *H*
3: 6 we had done with Sihon king of *H*,
4: 46 who reigned in *H* and was defeated
29: 7 Sihon king of *H* and Og king
Jos 9: 10 Sihon king of *H*, and Og king
12: 2 of the Amorites, who reigned in *H*.
12: 5 to the border of Sihon king of *H*.
13: 10 who ruled in *H*, out to the border
13: 17 whole plateau past Medeba to *H*
13: 21 of the Amorites, who ruled at *H*.
13: 26 and from *H* to Ramath Mizpah
13: 27 of Sihon king of *H* (the east side
21: 39 *H* and Jazer, together
Jdg 11: 19 who ruled in *H*, and said to him,
11: 26 hundred years Israel occupied *H*,
1Ch 6: 81 *H* and Jazer, together
Ne 9: 22 over the country of Sihon king of *H*
SS 7: 4 Your eyes are the pools of *H*
Isa 15: 4 *H* and Elealeh cry out,
16: 8 The fields of *H* wither,
16: 9 O *H*, O Elealeh,
Jer 48: 2 in *H* men will plot her downfall:
48: 34 rises from *H* to Elealeh and Jahaz,
48: 45 for a fire has gone out from *H*,
48: 45 "In the shadow of *H*
49: 3 "Wail, O *H*, for Ai is destroyed!

HESHMON

Jos 15: 27 Hazar Gaddah, *H*, Beth Pelet,

HESITATE (HESITATED HESITATION)

Jdg 18: 9 Don't *h* to go there and take it over
Job 30: 10 they do not *h* to spit in my face.
Da 9: 14 The LORD did not *h*
Ac 10: 20 Do not *h* to go with them,

HESITATED (HESITATE)

Ge 19: 16 When he *h*, the men grasped his
Ac 20: 20 You know that I have not *h*
20: 27 For I have not *h* to proclaim

HESITATION (HESITATE)

Ac 11: 12 to have no *h* about going with them

HETHLON

Eze 47: 15 Great Sea by the *H* road
48: 1 the *H* road to Lebo Hamath;

HEWING (HEWN)

Isa 22: 16 *h* your grave on the height

HEWN (HEWING)

Pr 9: 1 she has *h* out its seven pillars.
Isa 51: 1 the quarry from which you were *h*;

HEZEKIAH (HEZEKIAH'S)

2Ki 16: 20 And *H* his son succeeded him
18: 1 *H* son of Ahaz king of Judah began
18: 5 *H* trusted in the LORD, the God
18: 14 *H* king of Judah sent this message
18: 14 of Assyria exacted from *H* king
18: 15 *H* gave him all the silver that was
18: 16 At this time *H* king
18: 17 Lachish to King *H* at Jerusalem.
18: 19 "Tell *H*: " 'This is what the great
18: 22 high places and altars *H* removed,
18: 29 Do not let *H* deceive you.
18: 30 Do not let *H* persuade you to trust
2Ki 18: 31 "Do not listen to *H*.
18: 32 "Do not listen to *H*,
18: 37 of Asaph the recorder went to *H*,
19: 1 When King *H* heard this, he tore
19: 3 told him, "This is what *H* says:
19: 9 messengers to *H* with this word:
19: 10 "Say to *H* king of Judah:
19: 14 *H* received the letter
19: 15 And *H* prayed to the LORD:
19: 20 son of Amoz sent a message to *H*:
19: 29 "This will be the sign for you, O *H*:
20: 1 In those days *H* became ill
20: 2 *H* turned his face to the wall
20: 3 And *H* wept bitterly.
20: 5 and tell *H*, the leader of my people,
20: 8 *H* had asked Isaiah, "What will be
20: 10 to go forward ten steps," said *H*.
20: 12 king of Babylon sent *H* letters
20: 13 *H* received the messengers
20: 13 his kingdom that *H* did not show
20: 14 Isaiah the prophet went to King *H*
20: 14 "From a distant land," *H* replied.
20: 15 everything in my palace," *H* said.
20: 16 Isaiah said to *H*, "Hear the word
20: 19 have spoken is good," *H* replied.
20: 21 of Judah? *H* rested with his fathers.
21: 3 places his father *H* had destroyed;
1Ch 3: 13 *H* his son, Manasseh his son,
4: 41 in the days of *H* king of Judah.
2Ch 28: 27 And *H* his son succeeded him
29: 1 *H* was twenty-five years old
29: 18 Then they went in to King *H*
29: 20 the next morning King *H* gathered
29: 27 *H* gave the order to sacrifice
29: 30 King *H* and his officials ordered
29: 31 *H* said, "You have now dedicated
29: 36 *H* and all the people rejoiced
30: 1 *H* sent word to all Israel and Judah
30: 18 But *H* prayed for them, saying,
30: 20 And the LORD heard *H*
30: 22 *H* spoke encouragingly
30: 24 *H* king of Judah provided
31: 2 *H* assigned the priests
31: 8 When *H* and his officials came
31: 9 *H* asked the priests and Levites
31: 11 *H* gave orders to prepare
31: 13 by appointment of King *H*
31: 20 This is what *H* did
32: 1 After all that *H* had
32: 2 When *H* saw that Sennacherib had
32: 8 from what *H* the king of Judah said
32: 9 message for *H* king of Judah
32: 11 under siege? When *H* says,
32: 12 Did not *H* himself remove this
32: 15 Now do not let *H* deceive you
32: 16 and against his servant *H*.
32: 17 god of *H* will not rescue his people
32: 20 King *H* and the prophet Isaiah son
32: 22 So the LORD saved *H*
32: 23 valuable gifts for *H* king of Judah.
32: 24 In those days *H* became ill
32: 26 *H* repented of the pride of his heart
32: 26 upon them during the days of *H*.
32: 27 *H* had very great riches and honor,
32: 30 It was *H* who blocked the upper
32: 33 *H* rested with his fathers
33: 3 his father *H* had demolished;
Ezr 2: 16 of Ater (through *H*) 98
Ne 7: 21 of Ater (through *H*) 98
10: 17 Adin, Ater, *H*, Azzur, Hodiah,
Pr 25: 1 by the men of *H* king of Judah:
Isa 1: 1 Ahaz and *H*, kings of Judah.
36: 2 Lachish to King *H* at Jerusalem.
36: 4 Tell *H*, 'This is what the great king,
36: 7 high places and altars *H* removed,
36: 14 Do not let *H* deceive you.
36: 15 Do not let *H* persuade you to trust
36: 16 "Do not listen to *H*.
36: 18 "Do not let *H* mislead you
36: 22 of Asaph the recorder went to *H*,
37: 1 When King *H* heard this, he tore
37: 3 told him, "This is what *H* says:
37: 9 messengers to *H* with this word:
37: 10 "Say to *H* king of Judah:
37: 14 *H* received the letter
37: 15 And *H* prayed to the LORD:
37: 21 son of Amoz sent a message to *H*:
37: 30 "This will be the sign for you, O *H*:
Isa 38: 1 In those days *H* became ill
38: 2 *H* turned his face to the wall
38: 3 And *H* wept bitterly.
38: 5 tell *H*, 'This is what the LORD,
38: 9 A writing of *H* king of Judah
38: 22 *H* had asked, "What will be
39: 1 king of Babylon sent *H* letters
39: 2 *H* received the envoys gladly
39: 2 his kingdom that *H* did not show
39: 3 Isaiah the prophet went to King *H*
39: 3 "From a distant land," *H* replied.
39: 4 everything in my palace," *H* said.
39: 5 Isaiah said to *H*, "Hear the word
39: 8 have spoken is good," *H* replied.
Jer 15: 4 son of *H* king of Judah did
26: 18 in the days of *H* king of Judah.
26: 19 Did *H* king of Judah or anyone else
26: 19 Did not *H* fear the LORD
Hos 1: 1 Ahaz and *H*, kings of Judah,
Mic 1: 1 Ahaz and *H*, kings of Judah—
Zep 1: 1 the son of Amariah, the son of *H*,
Mt 1: 9 Ahaz the father of *H*, *H* the father

HEZEKIAH'S (HEZEKIAH)

2Ki 18: 9 In King *H* fourth year, which was
18: 10 was captured in *H* sixth year,
18: 13 fourteenth year of King *H* reign,
19: 5 When King *H* officials came
20: 12 because he had heard of *H* illness.
20: 20 As for the other events of *H* reign,
2Ch 32: 25 But *H* heart was proud
32: 32 The other events of *H* reign
Isa 36: 1 fourteenth year of King *H* reign,
37: 5 When King *H* officials came

HEZION

1Ki 15: 18 the son of *H*, the king of Aram,

HEZIR

1Ch 24: 15 seventeenth to *H*, the eighteenth
Ne 10: 20 Meshullam, *H*, Meshezabel,

HEZRO

2Sa 23: 35 *H* the Carmelite, Paarai the Arbite,
1Ch 11: 37 the Pelonite, *H* the Carmelite,

HEZRON (HEZRONITE)

Ge 46: 9 Hanoch, Pallu, *H* and Carmi.
46: 12 The sons of Perez: *H* and Hamul.
Ex 6: 14 of Israel were Hanoch and Pallu, *H*
Nu 26: 6 through *H*, the Hezronite clan;
26: 21 through *H*, the Hezronite clan;
Jos 15: 3 Then it ran past *H* up to Addar
Ru 4: 18 father of *H*, *H* the father of Ram,
1Ch 2: 5 The sons of Perez: *H* and Hamul.
2: 9 born to *H* were: Jerahmeel,
2: 18 Caleb son of *H* had children
2: 21 *H* lay with the daughter
2: 24 *H* died in Caleb Ephrathah,
2: 24 of *H* bore him Ashhur the father
2: 25 of Jerahmeel the firstborn of *H*:
4: 1 Perez, *H*, Carmi, Hur and Shobal.
5: 3 Hanoch, Pallu, *H* and Carmi.
Mt 1: 3 father of *H*, *H* the father of Ram,
Lk 3: 33 the son of *H*, the son of Perez,

HEZRONITE (HEZRON)

Nu 26: 6 through Hezron, the *H* clan;
26: 21 through Hezron, the *H* clan;

HID (HIDE)

Ge 3: 8 and they *h* from the LORD God
3: 10 afraid because I was naked; so I *h*."
Ex 2: 2 she *h* him for three months.
2: 12 he killed the Egyptian and *h* him
3: 6 Moses *h* his face, because he was
Jos 6: 17 because she *h* the spies we sent.
6: 25 she *h* the men Joshua had sent
1Sa 13: 6 they *h* in caves and thickets,
20: 19 go to the place where you *h*
20: 24 So David *h* in the field,
1Ki 18: 13 I *h* a hundred of the LORD's
20: 30 to the city and *h* in an inner room.
2Ki 7: 8 clothes, and went off and *h* them.
7: 8 things from it and *h* them
1Ch 21: 20 were with him *h* themselves.
2Ch 22: 11 she *h* the child from Athaliah
Ps 30: 7 but when you *h* your face,

Ps 35: 7 Since they *h* their net for me
35: 8 may the net they *h* entangle them,
Isa 49: 2 in the shadow of his hand he *h* me;
54: 8 I *h* my face from you for a moment,
57: 17 I punished him, and *h* my face
Jer 13: 5 So I went and *h* it at Perath,
Eze 39: 23 So I *h* my face from them
39: 24 and I *h* my face from them.
Da 10: 7 that they fled and *h* themselves.
Mt 13: 44 When a man found it, he *h* it again,
25: 18 and *h* his master's money.
25: 25 and *h* your talent in the ground.
Jn 8: 59 but Jesus *h* himself, slipping away
12: 36 Jesus left and *h* himself from them.
Ac 1: 9 and a cloud *h* him from their sight.
Heb 11: 23 By faith Moses' parents *h* him
Rev 6: 15 and every free man *h* in caves

HIDDAI

2Sa 23: 30 *H* from the ravines of Gaash,

HIDDEN (HIDE)

Ge 4: 14 and I will be *h* from your presence;
Nu 5: 13 and this is *h* from her husband
Dt 33: 19 on the treasures *h* in the sand."
Jos 2: 4 had taken the two men and *h* them.
2: 6 and *h* them under the stalks
7: 21 They are *h* in the ground
7: 22 and there it was, *h* in his tent,
10: 16 and *h* in the cave at Makkedah.
Jdg 16: 9 With men *h* in the room, she called
16: 12 Then, with men *h* in the room,
1Sa 10: 22 has *h* himself among the baggage."
14: 22 When all the Israelites who had *h*
2Sa 17: 9 he is *h* in a cave or some other
18: 13 and nothing is *h* from the king—
1Ki 18: 4 a hundred prophets and *h* them
2Ki 4: 27 but the LORD has *h* it from me
6: 29 may eat him,' but she had *h* him."
11: 3 He remained *h* with his nurse
2Ch 22: 12 He remained *h* with them
Job 3: 16 why was I not *h* in the ground like
3: 21 for it more than for *h* treasure,
3: 23 whose way is *h*,
18: 10 A noose is *h* for him on the ground;
28: 7 No bird of prey knows that *h* path,
28: 11 and brings *h* things to light.
28: 21 It is *h* from the eyes
33: 21 his bones, once *h*, now stick out.
40: 21 *h* among the reeds in the marsh.
Ps 9: 15 in the net they have *h*.
19: 6 nothing is *h* from its heat.
19: 12 Forgive my *h* faults.
22: 24 he has not *h* his face from him
38: 9 my sighing is not *h* from you.
69: 5 my guilt is not *h* from you.
78: 2 I will utter things *h* from of old—
119: 11 I have *h* your word in my heart
139: 15 My frame was not *h* from you
140: 5 Proud men have *h* a snare for me;
142: 3 men have *h* a snare for me.
Pr 2: 4 and search for it as for *h* treasure,
27: 5 rebuke than *h* love.
Ecc 12: 14 including every *h* thing,
Isa 30: 20 your teachers will be *h* no more;
40: 27 "My way is *h* from the LORD;
42: 22 or *h* away in prisons.
48: 6 of *h* things unknown to you.
59: 2 your sins have *h* his face from you,
64: 7 for you have *h* your face from us
65: 16 and *h* from my eyes.
Jer 13: 7 it from the place where I had *h* it,
16: 17 are on all their ways; they are not *h*
18: 22 and have *h* snares for my feet.
36: 26 But the LORD had *h* them.
41: 8 oil and honey, *h* in a field."
Eze 28: 3 Is no secret *h* from you?
Da 2: 22 He reveals deep and *h* things;
Hos 5: 3 Israel is not *h* from me.
Ob : 6 his *h* treasures pillaged!
Hab 3: 4 where his power was *h*.
Mt 5: 14 A city on a hill cannot be *h*.
10: 26 or *h* that will not be made known.
11: 25 because you have *h* these things
13: 35 I will utter things *h*
13: 44 of heaven is like treasure *h*
Mk 4: 22 For whatever is *h* is meant
Lk 8: 17 For there is nothing *h* that will not
9: 45 It was *h* from them,
10: 21 because you have *h* these things
11: 33 puts it in a place where it will be *h*,
12: 2 or *h* that will not be made known.
18: 34 Its meaning was *h* from them,
19: 42 but now it is *h* from your eyes.
Ro 16: 25 of the mystery *h* for long ages past,
1Co 2: 7 a wisdom that has been *h*
4: 5 bring to light what is *h* in darkness
Eph 3: 9 for ages past was kept *h* in God,
Col 1: 26 the mystery that has been kept *h*
2: 3 in whom are *h* all the treasures
3: 3 and your life is now *h* with Christ
1Ti 5: 25 even those that are not cannot be *h*
Heb 4: 13 in all creation is *h* from God's sight
Rev 2: 17 I will give some of the *h* manna.

HIDE (HID HIDDEN HIDES HIDING)

Ge 18: 17 "Shall I *h* from Abraham what I am
47: 18 "We cannot *h* from our lord
Ex 2: 3 when she could *h* him no longer,
29: 14 But burn the bull's flesh and its *h*
Lev 4: 11 But the *h* of the bull and all its flesh
7: 8 offering for anyone may keep its *h*
8: 17 But the bull with its *h* and its flesh
9: 11 and the *h* he burned up
11: 32 it is made of wood, cloth, *h*
Nu 19: 5 its *h*, flesh, blood and offal.
Dt 7: 20 even the survivors who *h*
31: 17 I will *h* my face from them,
31: 18 And I will certainly *h* my face
32: 20 "I will *h* my face from them,"
Jos 2: 16 *H* yourselves there three days
7: 19 me what you have done; do not *h* it
Jdg 21: 20 "Go and *h* in the vineyards
1Sa 3: 17 if you *h* from me anything he told
3: 17 "Do not *h* it from me.
20: 2 Why would he *h* this from me?
20: 5 and *h* in the field until the evening
1Ki 17: 3 turn eastward and *h* in the Kerith
22: 25 go to *h* in an inner room."
2Ki 7: 12 the camp to *h* in the countryside,
11: 2 a bedroom to *h* him from Athaliah;
2Ch 18: 24 go to *h* in an inner room."
Job 3: 10 me to *h* trouble from my eyes.
13: 20 and then I will not *h* from you:
13: 24 Why do you *h* your face
14: 13 "If only you would *h* me
34: 22 where evildoers can *h*.
41: 7 Can you fill his *h* with harpoons
Ps 10: 1 Why do you *h* yourself in times
13: 1 How long will you *h* your face
17: 8 *h* me in the shadow of your wings
27: 5 he will *h* me in the shelter
27: 9 Do not *h* your face from me,
31: 20 of your presence you *h* them
40: 10 I do not *h* your righteousness
44: 24 Why do you *h* your face
51: 9 *H* your face from my sins
55: 12 I could *h* from him.
64: 2 *H* me from the conspiracy
69: 17 Do not *h* your face
78: 4 We will not *h* them
88: 14 and *h* your face from me?
89: 46 Will you *h* yourself forever?
102: 2 Do not *h* your face from me
104: 29 When you *h* your face,
119: 19 do not *h* your commands from me.
139: 11 "Surely the darkness will *h* me
143: 7 Do not *h* your face from me
143: 9 for I *h* myself in you.
Isa 1: 15 I will *h* my eyes from you;
2: 10 *h* in the ground
3: 9 they do not *h* it.
16: 3 *H* the fugitives,
26: 20 *h* yourselves for a little while
29: 15 to *h* their plans from the LORD,
50: 6 I did not *h* my face
53: 3 one from whom men *h* their faces
Jer 13: 4 *h* it there in a crevice in the rocks."
13: 6 get the belt I told you to *h* there."
23: 24 Can anyone *h* in secret places
33: 5 I will *h* my face from this city
36: 19 "You and Jeremiah, go and *h*.
38: 14 "Do not *h* anything from me."
38: 25 do not *h* it from us or we will kill
49: 8 Turn and flee, *h* in deep caves,
Eze 39: 29 I will no longer *h* my face
Am 9: 3 Though they *h* from me
9: 3 Though they *h* themselves
Mic 3: 4 At that time he will *h* his face
Rev 6: 16 *h* us from the face of him who sits

HIDES (HIDE)

Ex 25: 5 ram skins dyed red and *h*
26: 14 and over that a covering of *h*
35: 7 ram skins dyed red and *h*
35: 23 or *h* of sea cows brought them.
36: 19 and over that a covering of *h*
39: 34 the covering of *h* of sea cows
Lev 16: 27 taken outside the camp; their *h*,
Nu 4: 6 are to cover this with *h* of sea cows,
4: 8 cover that with *h* of sea cows
4: 10 in a covering of *h* of sea cows
4: 11 and cover that with *h* of sea cows
4: 12 cover that with *h* of sea cows
4: 14 are to spread a covering of *h*
4: 25 the outer covering of *h* of sea cows,
Job 20: 12 and he *h* it under his tongue,
34: 29 If he *h* his face, who can see him?
Isa 45: 15 Truly you are a God who *h* himself,
Lk 8: 16 "No one lights a lamp and *h* it

HIDING (HIDE)

Jos 10: 17 the five kings had been found *h*
10: 27 the cave where they had been *h*.
Jdg 9: 5 son of Jerub-Baal, escaped by *h*.
9: 35 out from their *h* place.
1Sa 3: 18 told him everything, *h* nothing
14: 11 out of the holes they were *h* in."
19: 2 guard tomorrow morning; go into *h*
23: 19 "Is not David *h* among us
23: 23 out about all the *h* places he uses
26: 1 "Is not David *h* on the hill
2Ch 22: 9 him while he was *h* in Samaria.
Job 15: 18 *h* nothing received
24: 4 force all the poor of the land into *h*.
31: 33 by *h* my guilt in my heart
Ps 32: 7 You are my *h* place;
64: 5 they talk about *h* their snares;
Pr 28: 12 to power, men go into *h*.
28: 28 to power, people go into *h*;
SS 2: 14 in the *h* places on the mountainside
Isa 4: 6 a refuge and *h* place from the storm
8: 17 who is *h* his face from the house
28: 15 and falsehood our *h* place."
28: 17 water will overflow your *h* place.
Jer 49: 10 I will uncover his *h* places,
La 3: 10 like a lion in *h*,
Am 6: 10 and asks anyone still *h* there,
Na 3: 11 you will go into *h*
Hab 3: 14 the wretched who were in *h*.

HIEL

1Ki 16: 34 *H* of Bethel rebuilt Jericho.

HIERAPOLIS

Col 4: 13 and for those at Laodicea and *H*.

HIGGAION

Ps 9: 16 *H*.

HIGH

Ge 14: 18 He was priest of God Most *H*,
14: 19 Blessed be Abram by God Most *H*,
14: 20 And blessed be God Most *H*,
14: 22 God Most *H*, Creator of heaven
Nu 24: 16 has knowledge from the Most *H*,
Dt 32: 8 When the Most *H* gave the nations
2Sa 22: 14 the voice of the Most *H* resounded.
23: 1 of the man exalted by the Most *H*,
Ps 7: 8 to my integrity, O Most *H*.
7: 10 My shield is God Most *H*,
7: 17 to the name of the LORD Most *H*.
9: 2 to your name, O Most *H*.
18: 13 the voice of the Most *H* resounded.
21: 7 the unfailing love of the Most *H*
46: 4 place where the Most *H* dwells.
47: 2 awesome is the LORD Most *H*,
50: 14 fulfill your vows to the Most *H*,
57: 2 I cry out to God Most *H*,
73: 11 Does the Most *H* have knowledge
77: 10 of the right hand of the Most *H*."
78: 17 in the desert against the Most *H*.
78: 35 that God Most *H* was their
78: 56 and rebelled against the Most *H*;

Ps 82: 6 you are all sons of the Most *H*.'
83: 18 that you alone are the Most *H*
87: 5 Most *H* himself will establish her.''
91: 1 in the shelter of the Most *H*
91: 9 make the Most *H* your dwelling—
92: 1 music to your name, O Most *H*,
97: 9 are the Most *H* over all the earth;
107: 11 despised the counsel of the Most *H*
Isa 14: 14 I will make myself like the Most *H*
La 3: 35 rights before the Most *H*,
3: 38 not from the mouth of the Most *H*
Da 3: 26 servants of the Most *H* God,
4: 2 that the Most *H* God has
4: 17 know that the Most *H* is sovereign
4: 24 is the decree the Most *H* has issued
4: 25 that the Most *H* is sovereign
4: 32 that the Most *H* is sovereign
4: 34 Then I praised the Most *H*;
5: 18 the Most *H* God gave your father
5: 21 that the Most *H* God is sovereign
7: 18 saints of the Most *H* will receive
7: 22 in favor of the saints of the Most *H*,
7: 25 He will speak against the Most *H*
7: 27 the people of the Most *H*.
Hos 7: 16 They do not turn to the Most *H*;
11: 7 Even if they call to the Most *H*,
Mk 5: 7 Jesus, Son of the Most *H* God?
Lk 1: 32 be called the Son of the Most *H*.
1: 35 of the Most *H* will overshadow you
1: 76 be called a prophet of the Most *H*;
6: 35 and you will be sons of the Most *H*,
8: 28 Son of the Most *H* God? I beg you,
Ac 7: 48 the Most *H* does not live
16: 17 servants of the Most *H* God,
Heb 7: 1 and priest of God Most *H*.

HIGH-GRADE

1Ki 7: 9 of blocks of *h* stone cut to size
7: 11 Above were *h* stones, cut to size,

HIGHBORN (BEAR)

Ps 62: 9 the *h* are but a lie;

HIGHWAY (HIGHWAYS)

Nu 20: 17 We will travel along the king's *h*
21: 22 along the king's *h* until we have
Pr 7: 27 Her house is a *h* to the grave,
15: 19 but the path of the upright is a *h*.
16: 17 The *h* of the upright avoids evil;
Isa 11: 16 There will be a *h* for the remnant
19: 23 In that day there will be a *h*
35: 8 And a *h* will be there;
40: 3 a *h* for our God.
62: 10 Build up, build up the *h*!
Jer 31: 21 Take note of the *h*,

HIGHWAYS (HIGHWAY)

Isa 33: 8 The *h* are deserted,
49: 11 and my *h* will be raised up.

HILEN

1Ch 6: 58 Jattir, Eshtemoa, *H*, Debir, Ashan,

HILKIAH (HILKIAH'S)

2Ki 18: 18 son of *H* the palace administrator,
18: 26 Eliakim son of *H*, and Shebna
18: 37 son of *H* the palace administrator,
22: 4 "Go up to *H* the high priest
22: 8 *H* the high priest said
22: 10 *H* the priest has given me a book.''
22: 12 gave these orders to *H* the priest,
22: 14 *H* the priest, Ahikam, Acbor,
23: 4 The king ordered *H* the high priest,
23: 24 in the book that *H* the priest had
1Ch 6: 13 of *H*, *H* the father of Azariah,
6: 45 the son of *H*, the son of Amzi,
9: 11 Azariah son of *H*, the son
26: 11 him the first), *H* the second,
2Ch 34: 9 They went to *H* the high priest
34: 14 *H* the priest found the Book
34: 15 *H* said to Shaphan the secretary,
34: 18 *H* the priest has given me a book.''
34: 20 He gave these orders to *H*,
34: 22 *H* and those the king had sent
35: 8 *H*, Zechariah and Jehiel,
Ezr 7: 1 the son of *H*, the son of Shallum,
Ne 8: 4 Anaiah, Uriah, *H* and Maaseiah;
11: 11 Seraiah son of *H*, the son
12: 7 Sallu, Amok, *H* and Jedaiah.
Isa 22: 20 my servant, Eliakim son of *H*.
36: 3 son of *H* the palace administrator,
36: 22 son of *H* the palace administrator,
Jer 1: 1 The words of Jeremiah son of *H*
29: 3 and to Gemariah son of *H*,

HILKIAH'S (HILKIAH)

Ne 12: 21 Eber; of *H*, Hashabiah; of Jedaiah's

HILL (FOOTHILLS HILLS HILLSIDE HILLTOP HILLTOPS)

Ge 10: 30 in the eastern *h* country.
14: 6 the Horites in the *h* country of Seir,
31: 21 headed for the *h* country of Gilead.
31: 23 with him in the *h* country of Gilead
31: 25 tent in the *h* country of Gilead
31: 54 a sacrifice there in the *h* country
36: 8 settled in the *h* country of Seir.
36: 9 Edomites in the *h* country of Seir.
Ex 17: 9 stand on top of the *h* with the staff
17: 10 and Hur went to the top of the *h*.
Nu 13: 17 and on into the *h* country.
13: 29 and Amorites live in the *h* country;
14: 40 up toward the high *h* country.
14: 44 up toward the high *h* country,
14: 45 lived in that *h* country came down
Dt 1: 7 and advance into the *h* country
1: 19 and went toward the *h* country
1: 20 "You have reached the *h* country
1: 24 and went up into the *h* country,
1: 41 easy to go up into the *h* country.
1: 43 up into the *h* country.
2: 1 way around the *h* country of Seir.
2: 3 around this *h* country long enough;
2: 5 I have given Esau the *h* country
3: 12 including half the *h* country
3: 25 that fine *h* country and Lebanon.''
Jos 9: 1 those in the *h* country,
10: 6 from the *h* country have joined
10: 40 including the *h* country, the Negev
11: 3 and Jebusites in the *h* country;
11: 16 the *h* country, all the Negev,
11: 21 and from all the *h* country of Israel.
11: 21 from all the *h* country of Judah,
11: 21 the Anakites from the *h* country:
12: 8 the *h* country, the western foothills
13: 19 Zereth Shahar on the *h*
14: 12 Now give me this *h* country that
15: 8 climbed to the top of the *h* west
15: 48 In the *h* country: Shamir, Jattir,
16: 1 desert into the *h* country of Bethel.
17: 15 if the *h* country of Ephraim is too
17: 16 The *h* country is not enough for us,
17: 18 but the forested *h* country as well.
18: 12 headed west into the *h* country,
18: 13 the *h* south of Lower Beth Horon.
18: 14 From the *h* facing Beth Horon
18: 16 the foot of the *h* facing the Valley
19: 50 in the *h* country of Ephraim.
20: 7 Hebron) in the *h* country of Judah.
20: 7 Shechem in the *h* country
20: 7 in the *h* country of Naphtali,
21: 11 in the *h* country of Judah.
21: 21 In the *h* country of Ephraim they
24: 4 I assigned the *h* country of Seir
24: 30 in the *h* country of Ephraim,
24: 33 in the *h* country of Ephraim.
Jdg 1: 9 Canaanites living in the *h* country,
1: 19 took possession of the *h* country,
1: 34 the Danites to the *h* country,
2: 9 in the *h* country of Ephraim,
3: 27 in the *h* country of Ephraim,
4: 5 Bethel in the *h* country of Ephraim
7: 1 in the valley near the *h* of Moreh.
7: 24 throughout the *h* country
10: 1 in the *h* country of Ephraim.
12: 15 in the *h* country of the Amalekites.
16: 3 the top of the *h* that faces Hebron.
17: 1 from the *h* country of Ephraim said
17: 8 house in the *h* country of Ephraim.
18: 2 The men entered the *h* country
18: 13 on to the *h* country of Ephraim
19: 1 in a remote area in the *h* country
19: 16 from the *h* country of Ephraim,
19: 18 to a remote area in the *h* country
1Sa 1: 1 from the *h* country of Ephraim,
7: 1 it to Abinadab's house on the *h*
9: 4 through the *h* country of Ephraim
9: 11 As they were going up the *h*
13: 2 and in the *h* country of Bethel,
14: 22 in the *h* country of Ephraim heard
17: 3 The Philistines occupied one *h*
22: 6 tree on the *h* at Gibeah,
23: 19 on the *h* of Hakilah, south
26: 1 hiding on the *h* of Hakilah,
26: 3 the road on the *h* of Hakilah facing
26: 13 on top of the *h* some distance away
2Sa 2: 24 they came to the *h* of Ammah,
2: 25 and took their stand on top of a *h*.
6: 3 of Abinadab, which was on the *h*.
13: 34 coming down the side of the *h*.
13: 34 of Horonaim, on the side of the *h*.''
20: 21 from the *h* country of Ephraim,
21: 9 them on a *h* before the LORD.
1Ki 4: 8 in the *h* country of Ephraim;
11: 7 On a *h* east of Jerusalem, Solomon
12: 25 in the *h* country of Ephraim
14: 23 and Asherah poles on every high *h*
16: 24 He bought the *h* of Samaria
16: 24 name of the former owner of the *h*.
16: 24 of silver and built a city on the *h*,
2Ki 1: 9 who was sitting on the top of a *h*,
5: 22 me from the *h* country of Ephraim.
5: 24 When Gehazi came to the *h*,
17: 10 and Asherah poles on every high *h*
23: 13 on the south of the *H* of Corruption
1Ch 4: 42 invaded the *h* country of Seir.
6: 67 In the *h* country of Ephraim they
2Ch 13: 4 in the *h* country of Ephraim,
19: 4 to the *h* country of Ephraim
27: 3 work on the wall at the *h* of Ophel.
32: 33 buried on the *h* where the tombs
33: 14 and encircling the *h* of Ophel;
33: 15 altars he had built on the temple *h*
Ne 3: 26 on the *h* of Ophel made repairs up
8: 15 "Go out into the *h* country
11: 21 lived on the *h* of Ophel,
Ps 2: 6 King on Zion, my holy *h*.''
3: 4 and he answers me from his holy *h*.
15: 1 Who may live on your holy *h*?
24: 3 ascend the *h* of the LORD?
78: 54 to the *h* country his right hand had
SS 4: 6 and to the *h* of incense.
Isa 10: 32 at the *h* of Jerusalem.
30: 17 like a banner on a *h*.''
30: 25 high mountain and every lofty *h*.
40: 4 every mountain and *h* made low;
49: 9 and find pasture on every barren *h*.
57: 7 bed on a high and lofty *h*;
Jer 2: 20 Indeed, on every high *h*
3: 6 She has gone up on every high *h*
16: 16 and *h* and from the crevices
17: 26 from the *h* country and the Negev,
26: 18 the temple *h* a mound overgrown
31: 39 stretch from there straight to the *h*
32: 44 and in the towns of the *h* country,
33: 13 In the towns of the *h* country,
49: 16 who occupy the heights of the *h*.
50: 6 wandered over mountain and *h*
Eze 6: 13 on every high *h* and on all
20: 28 they saw any high *h* or any leafy
34: 6 the mountains and on every high *h*.
34: 26 and the places surrounding my *h*.
Da 9: 16 Jerusalem, your city, your holy *h*.
9: 20 LORD my God for his holy *h*—
Joel 2: 1 sound the alarm on my holy *h*.
3: 17 dwell in Zion, my holy *h*.
Ob : 16 Just as you drank on my holy *h*,
Mic 3: 12 the temple *h* a mound overgrown
Zep 3: 11 haughty on my holy *h*.
Mt 5: 14 A city on a *h* cannot be hidden.
Lk 1: 39 to a town in the *h* country of Judah,
1: 65 and throughout the *h* country
3: 5 every mountain and *h* made low.
4: 29 him to the brow of the *h*
19: 29 Bethany at the *h* called the Mount
21: 37 on the *h* called the Mount of Olives
Ac 1: 12 from the *h* called the Mount

HILLEL

Jdg 12: 13 Abdon son of *H*, from Pirathon,
12: 15 Then Abdon son of *H* died,

HILLS (HILL)

Ge 12: 8 went on toward the *h* east of Bethel

Ge 14: 10 into them and the rest fled to the *h*.
49: 26 than the bounty of the age-old *h*.
Dt 1: 44 in those *h* came out against you;
2: 37 nor that around the towns in the *h*.
8: 7 flowing in the valleys and *h;*
8: 9 you can dig copper out of the *h*.
12: 2 on the high mountains and on the *h*
33: 15 the fruitfulness of the everlasting *h;*
Jos 2: 16 to the *h* so the pursuers will not
2: 22 into the *h* and stayed there three
2: 23 They went down out of the *h*,
Jdg 3: 27 went down with him from the *h*,
11: 37 Give me two months to roam the *h*
11: 38 the girls went into the *h* and wept
1Sa 23: 14 and in the *h* of the Desert of Ziph.
1Ki 5: 15 thousand stonecutters in the *h*,
20: 23 "Their gods are gods of the *h*.
20: 28 think the LORD is a god of the *h*
22: 17 scattered on the *h* like sheep
2Ki 6: 17 and saw the *h* full of horses
2Ch 2: 2 in the *h* and thirty-six hundred
2: 18 to be stonecutters in the *h*,
15: 8 captured in the *h* of Ephraim.
18: 16 scattered on the *h* like sheep
21: 11 built high places on the *h* of Judah
26: 10 and vineyards in the *h*
27: 4 He built towns in the Judean *h*
Job 15: 7 you brought forth before the *h?*
39: 8 He ranges the *h* for his pasture
40: 20 The *h* bring him their produce,
Ps 50: 10 and the cattle on a thousand *h*.
65: 12 the *h* are clothed with gladness.
72: 3 the *h* the fruit of righteousness.
72: 16 on the tops of the *h* may it sway.
114: 4 the *h* like lambs.
114: 6 you *h*, like lambs?
121: 1 I lift up my eyes to the *h*—
147: 8 and makes grass grow on the *h*.
148: 9 you mountains and all *h*,
Pr 8: 25 before the *h*, I was given birth,
27: 25 the grass from the *h* is gathered in,
SS 2: 8 bounding over the *h*.
2: 17 stag on the rugged *h*.
Isa 2: 2 it will be raised above the *h*,
2: 14 and all the high *h*,
7: 25 As for all the *h* once cultivated
17: 13 before the wind like chaff on the *h*,
40: 12 and the *h* in a balance?
41: 15 and reduce the *h* to chaff.
42: 15 will lay waste the mountains and *h*
54: 10 and the *h* be removed,
55: 12 the mountains and *h*
65: 7 and defied me on the *h*,
Jer 3: 23 ˻idolatrous˼ commotion on the *h*
4: 15 disaster from the *h* of Ephraim.
4: 24 all the *h* were swaying.
13: 16 stumble on the darkening *h*.
13: 27 acts on the *h* and in the fields.
17: 2 and on the high *h*.
31: 5 vineyards on the *h* of Samaria;
31: 6 out on the *h* of Ephraim,
50: 19 on the *h* of Ephraim and Gilead.
Eze 6: 3 says to the mountains and *h*,
35: 8 by the sword will fall on your *h*
36: 4 says to the mountains and *h*,
36: 6 and say to the mountains and *h*,
Hos 4: 13 and burn offerings on the *h*,
10: 8 and to the *h*, "Fall on us!"
Joel 3: 18 and the *h* will flow with milk;
Am 9: 13 and flow from all the *h*.
Mic 4: 1 it will be raised above the *h*,
6: 1 let the *h* hear what you have to say.
Na 1: 5 and the *h* melt away.
Hab 3: 6 and the age-old *h* collapsed.
Zep 1: 10 and a loud crash from the *h*.
Mt 14: 23 up into the *h* by himself to pray.
15: 29 he went up into the *h* and sat down.
18: 12 not leave the ninety-nine on the *h*
Mk 3: 13 Jesus went up into the *h*
5: 5 and in the *h* he would cry out
6: 46 he went into the *h* to pray.
Lk 6: 12 out into the *h* to pray,
23: 30 and to the *h*, "Cover us!" '
Jn 6: 15 again into the *h* by himself.
Rev 17: 9 The seven heads are seven *h*

HILLSIDE (HILL)

2Sa 16: 13 going along the *h* opposite him,
2Ki 23: 16 the tombs that were there on the *h*,
Isa 5: 1 a vineyard on a fertile *h*.
Mk 5: 11 of pigs was feeding on the nearby *h*
Lk 8: 32 of pigs was feeding there on the *h*.
Jn 6: 3 Then Jesus went up on the *h*

HILLTOP (HILL)

Jos 15: 9 From the *h* the boundary headed
Isa 13: 2 Raise a banner on a bare *h*,

HILLTOPS (HILL)

Jdg 9: 25 men on the *h* to ambush
2Ki 16: 4 on the *h* and under every spreading
2Ch 28: 4 on the *h* and under every spreading

HIN

Ex 29: 40 and a fourth of a *h* of wine
29: 40 mixed with a fourth of a *h* of oil
30: 24 to the sanctuary shekel—and a *h*
Lev 19: 36 an honest ephah and an honest *h*.
23: 13 offering of a fourth of a *h* of wine.
Nu 15: 4 mixed with a fourth of a *h* of oil.
15: 5 prepare a fourth of a *h* of wine
15: 6 mixed with a third of a *h* of oil,
15: 7 and a third of a *h* of wine
15: 9 mixed with half a *h* of oil.
15: 10 Also bring half a *h* of wine
28: 5 mixed with a fourth of a *h* of oil
28: 7 a fourth of a *h* of fermented drink
28: 14 a third of a *h;* and with each lamb,
28: 14 and with each lamb, a fourth of a *h*.
28: 14 offering of half a *h* of wine;
Eze 4: 11 measure out a sixth of a *h* of water
45: 24 along with a *h* of oil for each ephah.
46: 5 along with a *h* of oil for each ephah.
46: 7 along with a *h* of oil
46: 11 along with a *h* of oil for each ephah.
46: 14 an ephah with a third of a *h* of oil

HINDER (HINDERED HINDERS HINDRANCE)

1Sa 14: 6 Nothing can *h* the LORD
Job 15: 4 and *h* devotion to God.
Mt 19: 14 come to me, and do not *h* them,
Mk 10: 14 come to me, and do not *h* them,
Lk 18: 16 come to me, and do not *h* them,
1Co 9: 12 anything rather than *h* the gospel
1Pe 3: 7 so that nothing will *h* your prayers.

HINDERED (HINDER)

Lk 11: 52 and you have *h* those who were
Ro 15: 22 This is why I have often been *h*

HINDERS (HINDER)

Heb 12: 1 let us throw off everything that *h*

HINDQUARTERS

1Ki 7: 25 and their *h* were toward the center.
2Ch 4: 4 and their *h* were toward the center.

HINDRANCE (HINDER)

Ac 28: 31 and without *h* he preached

HINGED (HINGES)

Eze 41: 24 two *h* leaves for each door.

HINGES (HINGED)

Pr 26: 14 As a door turns on its *h*,

HINNOM (BEN HINNOM)

Jos 15: 8 of the *H* Valley at the northern end
18: 16 It continued down the *H* Valley
Ne 11: 30 from Beersheba to the Valley of *H*.

HINT

Eph 5: 3 even a *h* of sexual immorality,

HIP

Ge 32: 25 *h* so that his *h* was wrenched
32: 31 and he was limping because of his *h*
32: 32 attached to the socket of the *h*,
32: 32 socket of Jacob's *h* was touched

HIRAH

Ge 38: 1 with a man of Adullam named *H*.
38: 12 his friend *H* the Adullamite went

HIRAM (HIRAM'S)

2Sa 5: 11 *H* king of Tyre sent messengers
1Ki 5: 1 When *H* king of Tyre heard that
5: 2 sent back this message to *H:*
5: 7 When *H* heard Solomon's message
5: 8 So *H* sent word to Solomon:
5: 10 In this way *H* kept Solomon
5: 11 Solomon gave *H* twenty thousand
5: 11 to do this for *H* year after year.
5: 12 were peaceful relations between *H*
5: 18 The craftsmen of Solomon and *H*
9: 11 because *H* had supplied him
9: 11 towns in Galilee to *H* king of Tyre,
9: 12 But when *H* went from Tyre
9: 14 *H* had sent to the king 120 talents
9: 27 *H* sent his men—sailors who knew
10: 22 at sea along with the ships of *H*.
1Ch 14: 1 *H* king of Tyre sent messengers
2Ch 2: 3 message to *H* king of Tyre:
2: 11 *H* king of Tyre replied by letter
2: 12 *H* added: "Praise be to the LORD,
8: 2 the villages that *H* had given him,
8: 18 And *H* sent him ships commanded
9: 10 (The men of *H* and the men

HIRAM'S (HIRAM)

1Ki 10: 11 *(H* ships brought gold from Ophir;
2Ch 9: 21 of trading ships manned by *H* men.

HIRE (HIRED HIRES)

Ex 22: 15 paid for the *h* covers the loss.
Jdg 9: 4 them to *h* reckless adventurers,
1Sa 2: 5 who were full *h* themselves out
1Ch 19: 6 talents of silver to *h* chariots
Isa 23: 17 She will return to her *h*
46: 6 they *h* a goldsmith to make it
Mt 20: 1 in the morning to *h* men to work

HIRED (HIRE)

Ge 30: 16 "I have *h* you with my son's
Ex 12: 45 and a *h* worker may not eat of it.
22: 15 the animal was *h*, the money paid
Lev 19: 13 the wages of a *h* man overnight.
22: 10 of a priest or his *h* worker eat it.
25: 6 *h* worker and temporary resident
25: 40 He is to be treated as a *h* worker
25: 50 paid to a *h* man for that number
25: 53 as a man *h* from year to year;
Dt 15: 18 as much as that of a *h* hand.
23: 4 and they *h* Balaam son of Beor
24: 14 advantage of a *h* man who is poor
Jdg 18: 4 "He has *h* me and I am his priest."
2Sa 10: 6 they *h* twenty thousand Aramean
2Ki 7: 6 the king of Israel has *h* the Hittite
1Ch 19: 7 They *h* thirty-two thousand
2Ch 24: 12 They *h* masons and carpenters
25: 6 *h* a hundred thousand fighting men
Ezr 4: 5 They *h* counselors to work
Ne 6: 12 Tobiah and Sanballat had *h* him.
6: 13 He had been *h* to intimidate me
13: 2 but had *h* Balaam to call a curse
Job 7: 1 not his days like those of a *h* man?
7: 2 or a *h* man waiting eagerly
14: 6 in his time like a *h* man.
Isa 7: 20 that day the Lord will use a razor *h*
Mt 20: 7 " 'Because no one has *h* us,'
20: 8 beginning with the last ones *h*
20: 9 "The workers who were *h* about
20: 10 when those came who were *h* first,
20: 12 men who were *h* last worked only
20: 14 the man who was *h* last the same
Mk 1: 20 Zebedee in the boat with the *h* men
Lk 15: 15 and *h* himself out to a citizen
15: 17 of my father's *h* men have food
15: 19 make me like one of your *h* men.'
Jn 10: 12 *h* hand is not the shepherd who
10: 13 he is a *h* hand and cares nothing

HIRES (HIRE)

Pr 26: 10 is he who *h* a fool or any passer-by.

HISS (HISSES)
Jer 46: 22 Egypt will *h* like a fleeing serpent
Eze 27: 36 among the nations *h* at you;

HISSES (HISS)
Job 27: 23 and *h* him out of his place.

HISTORIC (HISTORY)
Ne 2: 20 or any claim or *h* right to it.''

HISTORY (HISTORIC)
Ezr 4: 19 found that this city has a long *h*

HIT (HITS HITTING)
Ex 21: 22 who are fighting *h* a pregnant
Dt 19: 5 and *h* his neighbor and kill him.
1Ki 22: 34 and *h* the king of Israel
2Ch 18: 33 and *h* the king of Israel
Pr 23: 35 "They *h* me," you will say,
Mt 26: 68 Who *h* you?'' Now Peter was
Lk 22: 64 demanded, ''Prophesy! Who *h* you

HITCH (HITCHED)
1Sa 6: 7 *H* the cows to the cart,
1Ki 18: 44 '*H* up your chariot and go
2Ki 9: 21 "*H* up my chariot,'' Joram ordered.

HITCHED (HITCH)
1Sa 6: 10 took two such cows and *h* them
2Ki 9: 21 And when it was *h* up, Joram king

HITS (HIT)
Ex 21: 18 and one *h* the other with a stone
21: 26 "If a man *h* a manservant
Nu 35: 18 and he *h* someone so that he dies,
35: 21 if in hostility he *h* him with his fist

HITTING (HIT)
Ex 2: 13 Why are you *h* your fellow Hebrew

HITTITE (HITTITES)
Ge 23: 10 Ephron the *H* was sitting
25: 9 field of Ephron son of Zohar the *H*,
26: 34 Basemath daughter of Elon the *H*.
26: 34 Judith daughter of Beeri the *H*,
27: 46 because of these *H* women.
27: 46 from *H* women like these,
36: 2 Adah daughter of Elon the *H*,
49: 29 cave in the field of Ephron the *H*,
49: 30 a burial place from Ephron the *H*,
50: 13 a burial place from Ephron the *H*,
Jos 1: 4 the Euphrates—all the *H* country
1Sa 26: 6 then asked Ahimelech the *H*
2Sa 11: 3 and the wife of Uriah the *H*?''
11: 6 to Joab. "Send me Uriah the *H*.''
11: 17 moreover, Uriah the *H* was dead.
11: 21 your servant Uriah the *H* is dead
11: 24 your servant Uriah the *H* is dead.''
12: 9 down Uriah the *H* with the sword
12: 10 of Uriah the *H* to be your own.'
23: 39 Gareb the Ithrite and Uriah the *H*.
1Ki 15: 5 except in the case of Uriah the *H*.
2Ki 7: 6 the king of Israel has hired the *H*
1Ch 11: 41 Uriah the *H*, Zabad son of Ahlai,
Eze 16: 3 an Amorite and your mother a *H*.
16: 45 mother was a *H* and your father

HITTITES (HITTITE)
Ge 10: 15 and of the *H*, Jebusites, Amorites,
15: 20 Kadmonites, *H*, Perizzites,
23: 3 his dead wife and spoke to the *H*.
23: 5 The *H* replied to Abraham, "Sir,
23: 7 before the people of the land, the *H*
23: 10 hearing of all the *H* who had come
23: 16 named in the hearing of the *H*:
23: 18 of all the *H* who had come
23: 20 deeded to Abraham by the *H*
25: 10 Abraham had bought from the *H*.
49: 32 cave in it were bought from the *H*.''
Ex 3: 8 the home of the Canaanites, *H*,
3: 17 *H*, Amorites, Perizzites, Hivites
13: 5 *H*, Amorites, Hivites and Jebusites
23: 23 *H*, Perizzites, Canaanites,
23: 28 Canaanites and *H* out of your way.
33: 2 *H*, Perizzites, Hivites and Jebusites
34: 11 Canaanites, *H*, Perizzites,
Nu 13: 29 live in the Negev; the *H*,
Dt 7: 1 the *H*, Girgashites, Amorites,
20: 17 the *H*, Amorites, Canaanites,
Jos 3: 10 *H*, Hivites, Perizzites, Girgashites,
9: 1 far as Lebanon (the kings of the *H*,
11: 3 *H*, Perizzites and Jebusites
12: 8 the lands of the *H*, Amorites,
24: 11 Canaanites, *H*, Girgashites,
Jdg 1: 26 He then went to the land of the *H*,
3: 5 *H*, Amorites, Perizzites, Hivites
1Ki 9: 20 left from the Amorites, *H*,
10: 29 them to all the kings of the *H*
11: 1 Edomites, Sidonians and *H*.
1Ch 1: 13 and of the *H*, Jebusites, Amorites,
2Ch 1: 17 them to all the kings of the *H*
8: 7 All the people left from the *H*,
Ezr 9: 1 *H*, Perizzites, Jebusites,
Ne 9: 8 *H*, Amorites, Perizzites, Jebusites

HIVITE (HIVITES)
Ge 34: 2 Shechem son of Hamor the *H*,
36: 2 granddaughter of Zibeon the *H*—

HIVITES (HIVITE)
Ge 10: 17 Amorites, Girgashites, *H*, Arkites,
Ex 3: 8 Perizzites, *H* and Jebusites.
3: 17 Perizzites, *H* and Jebusites—
13: 5 Hittites, Amorites, *H* and Jebusites
23: 23 Canaanites, *H* and Jebusites,
23: 28 ahead of you to drive the *H*,
33: 2 Perizzites, *H* and Jebusites.
34: 11 Perizzites, *H* and Jebusites.
Dt 7: 1 Perizzites, *H* and Jebusites,
20: 17 Perizzites, *H* and Jebusites—
Jos 3: 10 Hittites, *H*, Perizzites, Girgashites,
9: 1 Perizzites, *H* and Jebusites)—
9: 7 The men of Israel said to the *H*,
11: 3 and to the *H* below Hermon
11: 19 Except for the *H* living in Gibeon,
12: 8 Perizzites, *H* and Jebusites):
24: 11 Girgashites, *H* and Jebusites,
Jdg 3: 3 *H* living in the Lebanon mountains
3: 5 Perizzites, *H* and Jebusites.
2Sa 24: 7 the towns of the *H* and Canaanites.
1Ki 9: 20 *H* and Jebusites (these peoples
1Ch 1: 15 Amorites, Girgashites, *H*, Arkites,
2Ch 8: 7 *H* and Jebusites (these peoples

HIZKI
1Ch 8: 17 Zebadiah, Meshullam, *H*, Heber,

HIZKIAH
1Ch 3: 23 Elioenai, *H* and Azrikam—

HOARD (HOARDED HOARDS)
Am 3: 10 "who *h* plunder and loot

HOARDED (HOARD)
Ecc 5: 13 wealth *h* to the harm of its owner,
Isa 23: 18 they will not be stored up or *h*.
Jas 5: 3 You have *h* wealth in the last days.

HOARDS (HOARD)
Pr 11: 26 People curse the man who *h* grain,

HOBAB
Nu 10: 29 Now Moses said to *H* son
Jdg 4: 11 of *H*, Moses' brother-in-law,

HOBAH
Ge 14: 15 pursuing them as far as *H*,

HOBAIAH
Ezr 2: 61 the priests: The descendants of *H*,
Ne 7: 63 the priests: the descendants of *H*,

HOD
1Ch 7: 37 Imrah, Bezer, *H*, Shamma,

HODAVIAH
1Ch 3: 24 *H*, Eliashib, Pelaiah, Akkub,
5: 24 Azriel, Jeremiah, *H* and Jahdiel.
9: 7 the son of *H*, the son of Hassenuah;
Ezr 2: 40 the line of *H*) 74 The singers:
3: 9 and his sons (descendants of *H*)
Ne 7: 43 the line of *H*) 74 The singers:

HODESH
1Ch 8: 9 By his wife *H* he had Jobab, Zibia,

HODIAH (HODIAH'S)
Ne 8: 7 Akkub, Shabbethai, *H*, Maaseiah,
9: 5 Bani, Hashabneiah, Sherebiah, *H*,
10: 10 Shebaniah, *H*, Kelita, Pelaiah
10: 13 Zaccur, Sherebiah, Shebaniah, *H*,
10: 18 Hezekiah, Azzur, *H*, Hashum,

HODIAH'S (HODIAH)
1Ch 4: 19 The sons of *H* wife, the sister

HOE
Isa 7: 25 the hills once cultivated by the *h*,

HOGLAH
Nu 26: 33 Noah, *H*, Milcah and Tirzah.)
27: 1 Noah, *H*, Milcah and Tirzah.
36: 11 Tirzah, *H*, Milcah and Noah—
Jos 17: 3 Noah, *H*, Milcah and Tirzah.

HOHAM
Jos 10: 3 appealed to *H* king of Hebron,

HOISTED
Ac 27: 17 When the men had *h* it aboard,
27: 40 they *h* the foresail to the wind

HOLD (HELD HOLDING HOLDS)
Ge 43: 9 you can *h* me personally
48: 17 so he took *h* of his father's hand
Ex 4: 4 So Moses reached out and took *h*
5: 1 so that they may *h* a festival to me
9: 2 and continue to *h* them back,
12: 16 the first day *h* a sacred assembly,
13: 6 and on the seventh day *h* a festival
20: 7 LORD will not *h* anyone guiltless
22: 29 "Do not *h* back offerings
25: 27 close to the rim to *h* the poles used
26: 29 make gold rings to *h* the crossbars.
30: 4 to *h* the poles used to carry it.
36: 34 made gold rings to *h* the crossbars.
37: 14 close to the rim to *h* the poles used
37: 27 to *h* the poles used to carry it.
38: 5 cast bronze rings to *h* the poles
Lev 19: 13 " 'Do not *h* back the wages
23: 7 the first day *h* a sacred assembly
23: 8 the seventh day *h* a sacred
23: 27 *H* a sacred assembly and deny
23: 36 the eighth day *h* a sacred assembly
25: 24 Throughout the country that you *h*
25: 33 a house sold in any town they *h*—
Nu 12: 11 do not *h* against us the sin we have
28: 18 the first day *h* a sacred assembly
28: 25 the seventh day *h* a sacred
28: 26 *h* a sacred assembly and do no
29: 1 the seventh month *h* a sacred
29: 7 this seventh month *h* a sacred
29: 12 *h* a sacred assembly and do no
29: 35 " 'On the eighth day *h* an assembly
Dt 5: 11 LORD will not *h* anyone guiltless
10: 20 *H* fast to him and take your oaths
11: 22 in all his ways and to *h* fast to him
13: 4 serve him and *h* fast to him.
16: 8 on the seventh day *h* an assembly
21: 8 and do not *h* your people guilty
21: 19 and mother shall take *h* of him
30: 20 listen to his voice, and *h* fast to him
Jos 8: 18 "*H* out toward Ai the javelin that is
22: 5 to *h* fast to him and to serve him
23: 8 to *h* fast to the LORD your God,
Jdg 1: 35 also to *h* out in Mount Heres,
16: 3 took *h* of the doors of the city gate,
Ru 3: 15 you are wearing and *h* it out.''
1Sa 15: 27 Saul caught *h* of the edge
17: 51 He took *h* of the Philistine's sword
2Sa 1: 11 with him took *h* of their clothes
6: 6 and took *h* of the ark of God,
15: 5 take *h* of him and kiss him.
19: 19 "May my lord not *h* me guilty.
22: 17 from on high and took *h* of me;
1Ki 1: 50 and took *h* of the horns of the altar.
2: 28 and took *h* of the horns of the altar.
8: 64 small to *h* the burnt offerings,
11: 30 Ahijah took *h* of the new cloak he
18: 32 enough to *h* two seahs of seed.
2Ki 2: 12 Then he took *h* of his own clothes
4: 16 "you will *h* a son in your arms.''
4: 27 God at the mountain, she took *h*
6: 32 shut the door and *h* it shut

2Ki 10: 19 I am going to *h* a great sacrifice
15: 19 and strengthen his own *h*
2Ch 7: 7 made could not *h* the burnt
Job 8: 15 he clings to it, but it does not *h*.
9: 28 I know you will not *h* me innocent.
10: 16 If I *h* my head high, you stalk me
17: 9 the righteous will *h* to their ways,
36: 17 justice have taken *h* of you.
39: 10 Can you *h* him to the furrow
Ps 18: 16 from on high and took *h* of me;
21: 8 Your hand will lay *h*
73: 23 you *h* me by my right hand.
74: 11 Why do you *h* back your hand,
75: 3 it is I who *h* its pillars firm.
79: 8 Do not *h* against us the sins
119: 31 I *h* fast to your statutes, O LORD;
139: 10 your right hand will *h* me fast.
Pr 3: 18 those who lay *h* of her will be
4: 4 "Lay *h* of my words
4: 13 *H* on to instruction, do not let it go;
5: 22 the cords of his sin *h* him fast.
7: 13 She took *h* of him and kissed him
20: 16 *h* it in pledge if he does it
24: 11 *h* back those staggering
27: 13 *h* it in pledge if he does it
SS 7: 8 I will take *h* of its fruit."
Isa 4: 1 will take *h* of one man
22: 17 about to take firm *h* of you
41: 13 who takes *h* of your right hand
42: 6 I will take *h* of your hand.
43: 6 to the south, 'Do not *h* them back.'
45: 1 whose right hand I take *h* of
48: 9 of my praise I *h* it back from you,
54: 2 do not *h* back;
56: 4 and *h* fast to my covenant—
56: 6 and who *h* fast to my covenant—
58: 1 "Shout it aloud, do not *h* back.
64: 7 or strives to lay *h* of you;
64: 12 O LORD, will you *h* yourself back?
65: 4 and whose pots *h* broth
Jer 2: 13 broken cisterns that cannot *h* water
6: 11 and I cannot *h* it in.
34: 9 no one was to *h* a fellow Jew
34: 10 and no longer *h* them in bondage.
50: 33 All their captors *h* them fast,
Eze 3: 18 and I will *h* you accountable
3: 20 and I will *h* you accountable
17: 3 Taking *h* of the top of a cedar,
24: 14 I will not *h* back; I will not have
30: 9 Anguish will take *h* of them
30: 21 strong enough to *h* a sword.
33: 6 I will *h* the watchman accountable
33: 8 and I will *h* you accountable
34: 10 and will *h* them accountable
37: 20 *H* before their eyes the sticks you
Da 4: 35 No one can *h* back his hand
Jnh 1: 14 Do not *h* us accountable
Zec 8: 23 nations will take firm *h* of one Jew
Mt 11: 12 and forceful men lay *h* of it.
12: 11 will you not take *h* of it
21: 26 for they all *h* that John was
Mk 11: 25 if you *h* anything against anyone,
Lk 14: 4 taking *h* of the man, he healed him
Jn 8: 31 Jesus said, "If you *h* to my teaching
14: 30 He has no *h* on me, but the world
20: 17 Jesus said, "Do not *h* on to me,
Ac 2: 24 for death to keep its *h* on him.
7: 60 Lord, do not *h* this sin against them
27: 7 did not allow us to *h* our course,
27: 17 under the ship itself to *h* it together
Ro 13: 3 For rulers *h* no terror
1Co 15: 2 if you *h* firmly to the word I
Php 2: 16 as you *h* out the word of life—
3: 12 but I press on to take *h* of that
3: 12 for which Christ Jesus took *h* of me
3: 13 yet to have taken *h* of it.
Col 1: 17 and in him all things *h* together
1Th 5: 13 *H* them in the highest regard
5: 21 *H* on to the good.
2Th 2: 15 and *h* to the teachings we passed
1Ti 3: 9 They must keep *h*
6: 12 Take *h* of the eternal life
6: 19 so that they may take *h*
Tit 1: 9 must *h* firmly to the trustworthy
Heb 3: 6 if we *h* on to our courage
3: 14 to share in Christ if we *h* firmly
4: 14 let us *h* firmly to the faith we
6: 18 fled to take *h* of the hope offered
Heb 10: 23 Let us *h* unswervingly
2Pe 2: 9 to *h* the unrighteous for the day
Rev 1: 18 And I *h* the keys of death
2: 4 Yet I *h* this against you: You have
2: 14 You have people there who *h*
2: 15 have those who *h* to the teaching
2: 24 to you who do not *h*
2: 25 Only *h* on to what you have
3: 11 *H* on to what you have,
12: 17 and *h* to the testimony of Jesus.
19: 10 and with your brothers who *h*

HOLDING (HOLD)

Ge 50: 11 "The Egyptians are *h* a solemn
Jdg 7: 20 *h* in their right hands the trumpets
1Sa 17: 57 with David still *h* the Philistine's
25: 36 in the house *h* a banquet like that
1Ki 7: 38 each *h* forty baths and measuring
Ne 4: 21 work with half the men *h* spears,
Job 1: 4 used to take turns *h* feasts
2: 9 Are you still *h* on to your integrity?
Jer 20: 9 I am weary of *h* it in;
34: 7 of Judah that were still *h* out—
Mk 7: 3 *h* to the tradition of the elders.
7: 8 are *h* on to the traditions of men."
Jn 2: 6 each *h* from twenty
8: 44 murderer from the beginning, not *h*
1Co 11: 2 and for *h* to the teachings,
2Th 2: 6 now you know what is *h* him back,
1Ti 1: 19 *h* on to faith and a good conscience
4: 8 *h* promise for both the present life
Rev 5: 8 and they were *h* golden bowls full
6: 5 Its rider was *h* a pair of scales
7: 1 *h* back the four winds of the earth
7: 9 and were *h* palm branches
10: 2 He was *h* a little scroll, which lay
20: 1 and *h* in his hand a great chain.

HOLDS (HOLD)

Ge 50: 15 "What if Joseph *h* a grudge
Nu 5: 18 while he himself *h* the bitter water
Job 12: 15 If he *h* back the waters, there is
18: 9 a snare *h* him fast.
37: 4 he *h* nothing back.
Pr 2: 7 He *h* victory in store
3: 35 but fools he *h* up to shame.
10: 19 but he who *h* his tongue is wise.
11: 12 of understanding *h* his tongue.
17: 28 and discerning if he *h* his tongue.
31: 19 In her hand she *h* the distaff
Isa 41: 23 tell us what the future *h*,
56: 2 the man who *h* it fast,
Eze 23: 32 for it *h* so much.
Da 5: 23 you did not honor the God who *h*
Am 1: 5 who *h* the scepter in Beth Eden.
1: 8 the one who *h* the scepter
2Th 2: 7 but the one who now *h* it back will
Heb 2: 14 destroy him who *h* the power
Rev 2: 1 words of him who *h* the seven stars
3: 1 of him who *h* the seven spirits
3: 7 and true, who *h* the key of David.

HOLE (HOLES)

Dt 23: 13 dig a *h* and cover up your
2Ki 12: 9 priest took a chest and bored a *h*
Ps 7: 15 He who digs a *h* and scoops it out
Isa 11: 8 near the *h* of the cobra,
Eze 8: 7 I looked, and I saw a *h* in the wall.
12: 12 a *h* will be dug in the wall for him
Mt 25: 18 dug a *h* in the ground and hid his

HOLES (HOLE)

1Sa 14: 11 out of the *h* they were hiding in."
Job 30: 6 in *h* in the ground.
Isa 2: 19 and to *h* in the ground
7: 19 thornbushes and at all the water *h*.
Hag 1: 6 to put them in a purse with *h* in it."
Mt 8: 20 "Foxes have *h* and birds
Lk 9: 58 "Foxes have *h* and birds
Heb 11: 38 and in caves and *h* in the ground.

HOLIDAY

Est 2: 18 He proclaimed a *h*

HOLIEST (HOLY)

Nu 18: 29 *h* part of everything given to you.'

HOLINESS (HOLY)

Ex 15: 11 majestic in *h*,
Dt 32: 51 because you did not uphold my *h*
1Ch 16: 29 the LORD in the splendor of his *h*.
2Ch 20: 21 him for the splendor of his *h*
Ps 29: 2 in the splendor of his *h*.
89: 35 Once for all, I have sworn by my *h*
93: 5 *h* adorns your house
96: 9 in the splendor of his *h*;
Isa 29: 23 they will acknowledge the *h*
35: 8 it will be called the Way of *H*.
Eze 36: 23 I will show the *h* of my great name,
38: 23 I will show my greatness and my *h*,
Am 4: 2 LORD has sworn by his *h*:
Lk 1: 75 fear in *h* and righteousness
Ro 1: 4 the Spirit of *h* was declared
6: 19 to righteousness leading to *h*.
6: 22 the benefit you reap leads to *h*,
1Co 1: 30 our righteousness, *h*
2Co 1: 12 in the *h* and sincerity that are
7: 1 perfecting *h* out of reverence
Eph 4: 24 God in true righteousness and *h*.
1Ti 2: 2 quiet lives in all godliness and *h*.
2: 15 love and *h* with propriety.
Heb 12: 10 that we may share in his *h*.
12: 14 without *h* no one will see the Lord.

HOLLOW

Ex 27: 8 Make the altar *h*, out of boards.
38: 7 They made it *h*, out of boards.
Jdg 15: 19 God opened up the *h* place in Lehi,
Pr 30: 4 the wind in the *h* of his hands?
Isa 40: 12 the waters in the *h* of his hand,
Jer 52: 21 each was four fingers thick, and *h*.
2Co 9: 3 in this matter should not prove *h*,
Col 2: 8 no one takes you captive through *h*

HOLON

Jos 15: 51 Anim, Goshen, *H* and Giloh—
21: 15 Jattir, Eshtemoa, *H*, Debir, Ain,
Jer 48: 21 to *H*, Jahzah and Mephaath,

HOLY (HALLOWED HOLIEST HOLINESS)

Ge 2: 3 the seventh day and made it *h*,
Ex 3: 5 you are standing is *h* ground."
15: 13 them to your *h* dwelling.
16: 23 a *h* Sabbath to the LORD.
19: 6 kingdom of priests and a *h* nation.'
19: 23 mountain and set it apart as *h*.' "
20: 8 the Sabbath day by keeping it *h*.
20: 11 the Sabbath day and made it *h*.
22: 31 "You are to be my *h* people.
26: 33 Place from the Most *H* Place.
26: 33 curtain will separate the *H* Place
26: 34 Testimony in the Most *H* Place.
28: 29 Aaron enters the *H* Place,
28: 35 heard when he enters the *H* Place
28: 36 SEAL: *H* TO THE LORD.
28: 43 the altar to minister in the *H* Place,
29: 30 to minister in the *H* Place is
29: 37 Then the altar will be most *h*,
29: 37 and whatever touches it will be *h*.
30: 10 It is most *h* to the LORD."
30: 29 them so they will be most *h*,
30: 29 whatever touches them will be *h*.
30: 36 It shall be most *h* to you.
30: 37 consider it *h* to the LORD.
31: 11 fragrant incense for the *H* Place.
31: 13 I am the LORD, who makes you *h*.
31: 14 the Sabbath, because it is *h*
31: 15 a Sabbath of rest, *h* to the LORD.
35: 2 the seventh day shall be your *h* day
39: 30 SEAL: *H* TO THE LORD.
40: 9 all its furnishings, and it will be *h*.
40: 10 the altar, and it will be most *h*.
Lev 2: 3 it is a most *h* part of the offerings
2: 10 it is a most *h* part of the offerings
5: 15 to any of the LORD's *h* things,
5: 16 to do in regard to the *h* things,
6: 16 eaten without yeast in a *h* place;
6: 17 and the guilt offering, it is most *h*.
6: 18 Whatever touches it will become *h*
6: 25 offering is slaughtered; it is most *h*.
6: 26 it is to be eaten in a *h* place,
6: 27 any of the flesh will become *h*,
6: 27 you must wash it in a *h* place.

Lev 6:29 family may eat it; it is most *h*.
6:30 in the *H* Place must not be eaten;
7:1 the guilt offering, which is most *h*:
7:6 eaten in a *h* place; it is most *h*.
10:3 I will show myself *h*;
10:10 must distinguish between the *h*
10:12 beside the altar, for it is most *h*.
10:13 in a *h* place, because it is your share
10:17 in the sanctuary area? It is most *h*;
10:18 was not taken into the *H* Place,
11:44 and be *h*, because I am *h*.
11:45 therefore be *h*, because I am *h*.
14:13 belongs to the priest; it is most *h*.
14:13 lamb in the *h* place where the sin
16:2 chooses into the Most *H* Place
16:16 atonement for the Most *H* Place
16:17 atonement in the Most *H* Place
16:20 atonement for the Most *H* Place,
16:23 he entered the Most *H* Place,
16:24 himself with water in a *h* place
16:27 brought into the Most *H* Place
16:33 atonement for the Most *H* Place,
19:2 'Be *h* because I, the LORD your
19:2 the LORD your God, am *h*.
19:8 he has desecrated what is *h*
19:24 the fourth year all its fruit will be *h*,
20:3 and profaned my *h* name.
20:7 " 'Consecrate yourselves and be *h*,
20:8 I am the LORD, who makes you *h*.
20:26 You are to be *h* to me because I,
20:26 to me because I, the LORD, am *h*,
21:6 They must be *h* to their God
21:6 food of their God, they are to be *h*.
21:7 because priests are *h* to their God.
21:8 Consider them *h*, because I
21:8 as *h*, because they offer up the food
21:8 LORD, who makes you *h*, am *h*.
21:15 I am the LORD, who makes him *h*
21:22 He may eat the most *h* food
21:22 as well as the *h* food; yet
21:23 the LORD, who makes them *h*.' "
22:2 so they will not profane my *h* name
22:9 am the LORD, who makes them *h*.
22:16 the LORD, who makes them *h*.' "
22:32 Do not profane my *h* name.
22:32 I must be acknowledged as *h*
22:32 who makes you *h* and who brought
24:9 it is a most *h* part of their regular
24:9 who are to eat it in a *h* place,
25:12 For it is a jubilee and is to be *h*
27:9 given to the LORD becomes *h*.
27:10 both it and the substitute become *h*
27:14 as something *h* to the LORD,
27:21 it will become *h*, like a field
27:23 as something *h* to the LORD.
27:28 so devoted is most *h* to the LORD.
27:30 to the LORD; it is *h* to the LORD.
27:32 the shepherd's rod—will be *h*
27:33 and its substitute become *h*
Nu 4:4 the care of the most *h* things.
4:15 finished covering the *h* furnishings
4:15 furnishings and all the *h* articles,
4:15 they must not touch the *h* things
4:16 including its *h* furnishings
4:19 come near the most *h* things,
4:20 go in to look at the *h* things,
5:17 Then he shall take some *h* water
6:5 He must be *h* until the period
6:20 they are *h* and belong to the priest,
7:9 on their shoulders the *h* things,
10:21 set out, carrying the *h* things.
16:3 The whole community is *h*,
16:5 belongs to him and who is *h*,
16:7 chooses will be the one who is *h*.
16:37 for the censers are *h*— the censers
16:38 the LORD and have become *h*.
18:8 all the *h* offerings the Israelites
18:9 of the most *h* offerings that is kept
18:9 they bring me as most *h* offerings,
18:10 Eat it as something most *h*;
18:10 You must regard it as *h*.
18:17 a sheep or a goat; they are *h*.
18:19 from the *h* offerings the Israelites
18:32 you will not defile the *h* offerings
20:12 as *h* in the sight of the Israelites,
20:13 and where he showed himself *h*
27:14 to honor me as *h* before their eyes
35:25 who was anointed with the *h* oil.
Dt 5:12 the Sabbath day by keeping it *h*,
7:6 For you are a people *h*
14:2 for you are a people *h*
14:21 But you are a people *h*
23:14 Your camp must be *h*,
26:15 from heaven, your *h* dwelling place
26:19 and that you will be a people *h*
28:9 will establish you as his *h* people,
33:2 He came with myriads of *h* ones
33:3 all the *h* ones are in your hand.
Jos 5:15 place where you are standing is *h*."
24:19 He is a *h* God; he is a jealous God.
24:26 oak near the *h* place of the LORD.
1Sa 2:2 "There is no one *h* like the LORD;
6:20 of the LORD, this *h* God?
21:5 The men's things are *h*
21:5 even on missions that are not *h*.
1Ki 6:16 inner sanctuary, the Most *H* Place.
7:50 room, the Most *H* Place,
8:6 the Most *H* Place, and put it
8:8 but not from outside the *H* Place;
8:8 seen from the *H* Place in front
8:10 priests withdrew from the *H* Place,
2Ki 4:9 often comes our way is a *h* man
19:22 Against the *H* One of Israel!
1Ch 6:49 done in the Most *H* Place,
16:10 Glory in his *h* name;
16:35 may give thanks to your *h* name,
23:13 to consecrate the most *h* things,
23:32 *H* Place and, under their brothers
29:3 I have provided for this *h* temple:
29:16 a temple for your *H* Name,
2Ch 3:8 He built the Most *H* Place,
3:10 In the Most *H* Place he made a pair
4:22 doors to the Most *H* Place
5:7 the Most *H* Place, and put it
5:9 but not from outside the *H* Place;
5:11 then withdrew from the *H* Place.
8:11 of the LORD has entered are *h*."
30:27 heaven, his *h* dwelling place.
31:6 a tithe of the *h* things dedicated
35:5 "Stand in the *h* place with a group
35:13 and boiled the *h* offerings in pots,
Ezr 9:2 and have mingled the *h* race
Ne 9:14 known to them your *h* Sabbath
10:31 on the Sabbath or on any *h* day.
10:33 appointed feasts; for the *h* offerings
11:1 the *h* city, while the remaining nine
11:18 Levites in the *h* city totaled 284.
13:22 in order to keep the Sabbath day *h*.
Job 5:1 which of the *h* ones will you turn?
6:10 not denied the words of the *H* One.
15:15 If God places no trust in his *h* ones,
Ps 2:6 King on Zion, my *h* hill."
3:4 and he answers me from his *h* hill
5:7 down toward your *h* temple.
11:4 The LORD is in his *h* temple;
15:1 Who may live on your *h* hill?
16:10 will you let your *H* One see decay.
20:6 he answers him from his *h* heaven
22:3 you are enthroned as the *H* One;
24:3 Who may stand in his *h* place?
28:2 hands toward your Most *H* Place.
30:4 praise his *h* name.
33:21 for we trust in his *h* name.
43:3 me to your *h* mountain,
46:4 *h* place where the Most High
47:8 God is seated on his *h* throne.
48:1 of our God, his *h* mountain.
51:11 or take your *H* Spirit from me.
65:4 of your *h* temple.
68:5 is God in his *h* dwelling.
71:22 O *H* One of Israel.
77:13 Your ways, O God, are *h*.
78:41 they vexed the *H* One of Israel.
78:54 to the border of his *h* land,
79:1 they have defiled your *h* temple,
87:1 on the *h* mountain;
89:5 in the assembly of the *h* ones.
89:7 of the *h* ones God is greatly feared;
89:18 our king to the *H* One of Israel.
97:12 and praise his *h* name.
98:1 his right hand and his *h* arm
99:3 he is *h*.
99:5 he is *h*.
99:9 and worship at his *h* mountain,
99:9 for the LORD our God is *h*.
103:1 inmost being, praise his *h* name.
Ps 105:3 Glory in his *h* name;
105:42 For he remembered his *h* promise
106:47 we may give thanks to your *h* name
110:3 Arrayed in *h* majesty,
111:9 *h* and awesome is his name.
138:2 bow down toward your *h* temple
145:21 every creature praise his *h* name
Pr 9:10 of the *H* One is understanding.
30:3 nor have I knowledge of the *H* One
Ecc 8:10 to come and go from the *h* place
Isa 1:4 they have spurned the *H* One
4:3 in Jerusalem, will be called *h*,
5:16 the *h* God will show himself *h*
5:19 plan of the *H* One of Israel come,
5:24 the word of the *H* One of Israel.
6:3 *H*, *h*, *h* is the LORD Almighty;
6:13 so the *h* seed will be the stump
8:13 is the one you are to regard as *h*,
10:17 their *H* One a flame;
10:20 the *H* One of Israel.
11:9 nor destroy on all my *h* mountain,
12:6 for great is the *H* One of Israel
13:3 I have commanded my *h* ones;
17:7 to the *H* One of Israel.
27:13 on the *h* mountain in Jerusalem.
29:19 in the *H* One of Israel.
29:23 the holiness of the *H* One of Jacob,
29:23 they will keep my name *h*;
30:11 us with the *H* One of Israel!"
30:12 this is what the *H* One
30:15 the Sovereign LORD, the *H* One
30:29 the night you celebrate a *h* festival;
31:1 do not look to the *H* One of Israel,
37:23 Against the *H* One of Israel!
40:25 who is my equal?" says the *H* One.
41:14 your Redeemer, the *H* One
41:16 and glory in the *H* One of Israel.
41:20 that the *H* One of Israel has
43:3 the *H* One of Israel, your Savior;
43:14 your Redeemer, the *H* One
43:15 I am the LORD, your *H* One,
45:11 the *H* One of Israel, and its Maker:
47:4 is the *H* One of Israel.
48:2 yourselves citizens of the *h* city
48:17 your Redeemer, the *H* One
49:7 *H* One of Israel, who has chosen
49:7 the Redeemer and *H* One of Israel
52:1 O Jerusalem, the *h* city
52:10 The LORD will lay bare his *h* arm
54:5 *H* One of Israel is your Redeemer;
55:5 the *H* One of Israel,
56:7 these I will bring to my *h* mountain
57:13 and possess my *h* mountain."
57:15 who lives forever, whose name is *h*:
57:15 "I live in a high and *h* place,
58:13 and the LORD's *h* day honorable,
58:13 as you please on my *h* day,
60:9 the *H* One of Israel,
60:14 Zion of the *H* One of Israel.
62:12 They will be called The *H* People,
63:10 and grieved his *H* Spirit.
63:11 his *H* Spirit among them,
63:15 from your lofty throne, *h*
63:18 people possessed your *h* place,
64:11 Our *h* and glorious temple,
65:11 and forget my *h* mountain,
65:25 nor destroy in all my *h* mountain,"
66:20 to my *h* mountain in Jerusalem
Jer 2:3 Israel was *h* to the LORD,
17:22 but keep the Sabbath day *h*,
17:24 but keep the Sabbath day *h*
17:27 me to keep the Sabbath day *h*
23:9 and his *h* words.
25:30 voice from his *h* dwelling
31:40 corner of the Horse Gate, will be *h*
50:29 the *H* One of Israel.
51:5 guilt before the *H* One of Israel.
51:51 the *h* places of the LORD's house
Eze 20:12 that I the LORD made them *h*.
20:20 Keep my Sabbaths *h*, that they
20:39 and no longer profane my *h* name
20:40 For on my *h* mountain, the high
20:40 along with all your *h* sacrifices.
20:41 I will show myself *h* among you
22:8 You have despised my *h* things
22:26 do not distinguish between the *h*
22:26 to my law and profane my *h* things;
28:14 You were on the *h* mount of God;

Eze 28:22 and show myself *h* within her.
28:25 I will show myself *h* among them
36:20 nations they profaned my *h* name,
36:21 I had concern for my *h* name,
36:22 but for the sake of my *h* name,
36:23 when I show myself *h* through you
37:28 that I the LORD make Israel *h,*
38:16 when I show myself *h* through you
39:7 longer let my *h* name be profaned,
39:7 that I the LORD am the *H* One
39:7 " 'I will make known my *h* name
39:25 and I will be zealous for my *h* name
39:27 I will show myself *h* through them
41:4 "This is the Most *H* Place."
41:21 of the Most *H* Place was similar.
41:23 the Most *H* Place had double doors
42:13 guilt offerings—for the place is *h.*
42:13 they will put the most *h* offerings—
42:13 will eat the most *h* offerings.
42:14 the priests enter the *h* precincts,
42:14 they minister, for these are *h.*
42:20 to separate the *h* from the common
43:7 never again defile my *h* name—
43:8 they defiled my *h* name
43:12 top of the mountain will be most *h.*
44:8 duty in regard to my *h* things,
44:13 my *h* things or my most *h* offerings;
44:23 the difference between the *h*
44:24 and they are to keep my Sabbaths *h*
45:1 wide; the entire area will be *h.*
45:3 the sanctuary, the Most *H* Place.
45:4 well as a *h* place for the sanctuary.
48:12 a most *h* portion, bordering
48:14 because it is *h* to the LORD.
Da 4:8 and the spirit of the *h* gods is in him
4:9 the spirit of the *h* gods is in you,
4:13 a *h* one, coming down from heaven
4:17 the *h* ones declare the verdict,
4:18 the spirit of the *h* gods is in you."
4:23 O king, saw a messenger, a *h* one,
5:11 the spirit of the *h* gods in him.
8:13 Then I heard a *h* one speaking,
8:13 and another *h* one said to him,
8:24 the mighty men and the *h* people.
9:16 Jerusalem, your city, your *h* hill.
9:20 to the LORD my God for his *h* hill
9:24 prophecy and to anoint the most *h.*
9:24 your *h* city to finish transgression,
11:28 set against the *h* covenant.
11:30 fury against the *h* covenant.
11:30 those who forsake the *h* covenant.
11:45 seas at the beautiful *h* mountain.
12:7 of the *h* people has been finally
Hos 11:9 the *H* One among you.
11:12 even against the faithful *H* One.
Joel 1:14 Declare a *h* fast;
2:1 sound the alarm on my *h* hill.
2:15 declare a *h* fast,
3:17 Jerusalem will be *h;*
3:17 dwell in Zion, my *h* hill.
Am 2:7 and so profane my *h* name.
Ob :16 Just as you drank on my *h* hill,
:17 it will be *h,*
Jnh 2:4 again toward your *h* temple.'
2:7 to your *h* temple.
Mic 1:2 the Lord from his *h* temple.
Hab 1:12 my *H* One, we will not die.
2:20 But the LORD is in his *h* temple;
3:3 the *H* One from Mount Paran.
Zep 3:11 haughty on my *h* hill.
Zec 2:12 as his portion in the *h* land
2:13 himself from his *h* dwelling."
8:3 will be called The *H* Mountain."
14:5 and all the *h* ones with him.
14:20 On that day *H* TO THE LORD
14:21 and Judah will be *h* to the LORD
Mt 1:18 be with child through the *H* Spirit.
1:20 in her is from the *H* Spirit.
3:11 will baptize you with the *H* Spirit
4:5 the devil took him to the *h* city
12:32 against the *H* Spirit will not be
24:15 in the *h* place 'the abomination
27:52 of many *h* people who had died
27:53 they went into the *h* city
28:19 and of the Son and of the *H* Spirit,
Mk 1:8 you with the *H* Spirit."
1:24 the *H* One of God!" "Be quiet!"
3:29 against the *H* Spirit will never be
Mk 6:20 him to be a righteous and *h* man.
8:38 glory with the *h* angels."
12:36 speaking by the *H* Spirit, declared:
13:11 not you speaking, but the *H* Spirit.
Lk 1:15 he will be filled with the *H* Spirit
1:35 the *h* one to be born will be called
1:35 "The *H* Spirit will come upon you,
1:41 was filled with the *H* Spirit.
1:49 *h* is his name.
1:67 was filled with the *H* Spirit
1:70 (as he said through his *h* prophets
1:72 and to remember his *h* covenant,
2:25 and the *H* Spirit was upon him.
2:26 by the *H* Spirit that he would not
3:16 will baptize you with the *H* Spirit
3:22 and the *H* Spirit descended on him
4:1 full of the *H* Spirit, returned
4:34 the *H* One of God!" "Be quiet!"
9:26 of the Father and of the *h* angels.
10:21 full of joy through the *H* Spirit, said
11:13 Father in heaven give the *H* Spirit
12:10 against the *H* Spirit will not be
12:12 for the *H* Spirit will teach you
Jn 1:33 baptize with the *H* Spirit.'
6:69 and know that you are the *H* One
14:26 But the Counselor, the *H* Spirit,
17:11 *H* Father, protect them
20:22 and said, "Receive the *H* Spirit.
Ac 1:2 instructions through the *H* Spirit
1:5 baptized with the *H* Spirit."
1:8 when the *H* Spirit comes on you;
1:16 fulfilled which the *H* Spirit spoke
2:4 them were filled with the *H* Spirit
2:27 will you let your *H* One see decay.
2:33 the Father the promised *H* Spirit
2:38 will receive the gift of the *H* Spirit.
3:14 disowned the *H* and Righteous
3:21 ago through his *h* prophets.
4:8 filled with the *H* Spirit, said
4:25 You spoke by the *H* Spirit
4:27 against your *h* servant Jesus,
4:30 the name of your *h* servant Jesus."
4:31 were all filled with the *H* Spirit
5:3 that you have lied to the *H* Spirit
5:32 these things, and so is the *H* Spirit,
6:5 full of faith and of the *H* Spirit;
6:13 speaking against the *h* place
7:33 you are standing is *h* ground.
7:51 You always resist the *H* Spirit!
7:55 But Stephen, full of the *H* Spirit,
8:15 they might receive the *H* Spirit,
8:16 the *H* Spirit had not yet come
8:17 and they received the *H* Spirit.
8:19 hands may receive the *H* Spirit."
9:17 and be filled with the *H* Spirit."
9:31 and encouraged by the *H* Spirit,
10:22 A *h* angel told him
10:38 Jesus of Nazareth with the *H* Spirit
10:44 the *H* Spirit came on all who heard
10:45 of the *H* Spirit had been poured out
10:47 have received the *H* Spirit just
11:15 the *H* Spirit came on them
11:16 baptized with the *H* Spirit.'
11:24 full of the *H* Spirit and faith,
13:2 and fasting, the *H* Spirit said,
13:4 sent on their way by the *H* Spirit,
13:9 with the *H* Spirit, looked straight
13:34 " 'I will give you the *h*
13:35 will not let your *H* One see decay.'
13:52 with joy and with the *H* Spirit.
15:8 by giving the *H* Spirit to them,
15:28 It seemed good to the *H* Spirit
16:6 having been kept by the *H* Spirit
19:2 even heard that there is a *H* Spirit."
19:2 "Did you receive the *H* Spirit
19:6 the *H* Spirit came on them,
20:23 in every city the *H* Spirit warns me
20:28 of which the *H* Spirit has made you
21:11 and said, "The *H* Spirit says,
21:28 area and defiled this *h* place."
28:25 "The *H* Spirit spoke the truth
Ro 1:2 prophets in the *H* Scriptures
5:5 love into our hearts by the *H* Spirit,
7:12 and the commandment is *h,*
7:12 law is *h,* and the commandment is
9:1 confirms it in the *H* Spirit—
11:16 if the root is *h,* so are the branches.
11:16 the dough offered as firstfruits is *h,*
Ro 11:16 then the whole batch is *h;*
12:1 as living sacrifices, *h* and pleasing
14:17 peace and joy in the *H* Spirit,
15:13 hope by the power of the *H* Spirit.
15:16 sanctified by the *H* Spirit.
16:16 Greet one another with a *h* kiss.
1Co 1:2 in Christ Jesus and called to be *h,*
6:19 body is a temple of the *H* Spirit,
7:14 be unclean, but as it is, they are *h.*
12:3 is Lord," except by the *H* Spirit.
16:20 Greet one another with a *h* kiss.
2Co 6:6 in the *H* Spirit and in sincere love;
13:12 Greet one another with a *h* kiss.
13:14 the fellowship of the *H* Spirit be
Eph 1:4 the creation of the world to be *h*
1:13 with a seal, the promised *H* Spirit,
2:21 and rises to become a *h* temple
3:5 by the Spirit to God's *h* apostles
4:30 do not grieve the *H* Spirit of God,
5:3 improper for God's *h* people.
5:26 up for her to make her *h,*
5:27 or any other blemish, but *h*
Col 1:2 To the *h* and faithful brothers
1:22 death to present you *h* in his sight,
3:12 as God's chosen people, *h*
1Th 1:5 *H* Spirit and with deep conviction.
1:6 with the joy given by the *H* Spirit.
2:10 and so is God, of how *h,*
3:13 and *h* in the presence of our God
3:13 comes with all his *h* ones.
4:3 It is God's will that you should be *h*
4:4 his own body in a way that is *h*
4:7 us to be impure, but to live a *h* life.
4:8 who gives you his *H* Spirit.
5:26 Greet all the brothers with a *h* kiss.
2Th 1:10 to be glorified in his *h* people
1Ti 2:8 to lift up *h* hands in prayer,
2Ti 1:9 saved us and called us to a *h* life—
1:14 the help of the *H* Spirit who lives
2:21 for noble purposes, made *h,*
3:15 you have known the *h* Scriptures,
Tit 1:8 upright, *h* and disciplined.
3:5 and renewal by the *H* Spirit,
Heb 2:4 and gifts of the *H* Spirit distributed
2:11 Both the one who makes men *h*
2:11 and those who are made *h* are
3:1 *h* brothers, who share
3:7 So, as the *H* Spirit says:
6:4 who have shared in the *H* Spirit,
7:26 one who is *h,* blameless, pure,
9:2 this was called the *H* Place.
9:3 a room called the Most *H* Place,
9:8 The *H* Spirit was showing
9:8 into the Most *H* Place had not yet
9:12 he entered the Most *H* Place once
9:25 enters the Most *H* Place every year
10:10 we have been made *h*
10:14 those who are being made *h.*
10:15 The *H* Spirit also testifies
10:19 to enter the Most *H* Place
11:7 in *h* fear built an ark
12:14 in peace with all men and to be *h;*
13:11 of animals into the Most *H* Place
13:12 gate to make the people *h*
1Pe 1:12 gospel to you by the *H* Spirit sent
1:15 But just as he who called you is *h,*
1:15 so be *h* in all you do;
1:16 is written: "Be *h,* because I am *h.*"
2:5 house to be a *h* priesthood,
2:9 a royal priesthood, a *h* nation,
3:5 For this is the way the *h* women
2Pe 1:21 carried along by the *H* Spirit.
3:2 in the past by the *h* prophets
3:11 You ought to live *h* and godly lives
1Jn 2:20 have an anointing from the *H* One,
Jude :14 upon thousands of his *h* ones
:20 holy faith and pray in the *H* Spirit.
:20 up in your most *h* faith
Rev 3:7 are the words of him who is *h*
4:8 "*H, h, h* is the Lord God
6:10 Sovereign Lord, *h* and true,
11:2 on the *h* city for 42 months.
14:10 in the presence of the *h* angels
15:4 For you alone are *h.*
16:5 and who were, the *H* One,
20:6 and *h* are those who have part
21:2 I saw the *H* City, the new
21:10 and showed me the *H* City,

Rev 22: 11 let him who is *h* continue to be *h*.''
22: 19 in the tree of life and in the *h* city,

HOMAGE

2Ch 24: 17 officials of Judah came and paid *h*
Job 31: 27 my hand offered them a kiss of *h*,

HOMAM

Ge 36: 22 The sons of Lotan: Hori and *H*.
1Ch 1: 39 The sons of Lotan: Hori and *H*.

HOME (HOMELAND HOMES)

Ge 18: 33 he left, and Abraham returned *h*.
29: 13 him and brought him to his *h*,
31: 55 Then he left and returned *h*.
34: 5 it until they came *h*.
35: 27 Jacob came *h* to his father Isaac
39: 16 beside her until his master came *h*.
43: 26 Joseph came *h*, they presented
Ex 3: 8 the *h* of the Canaanites, Hittites,
18: 23 all these people will go *h* satisfied.''
Lev 18: 9 whether she was born in the same *h*
Nu 14: 30 with uplifted hand to make your *h*,
15: 2 as a *h* and you present
24: 11 Now leave at once and go *h!*
24: 25 Balaam got up and returned *h*
Dt 6: 7 Talk about them when you sit at *h*
11: 19 about them when you sit at *h*
20: 5 Let him go *h*, or he may die
20: 6 Let him go *h*, or he may die
20: 7 Let him go *h*, or he may die
20: 8 Let him go *h* so that his brothers
21: 12 into your *h* and have her shave her
22: 2 take it *h* with you and keep it
24: 5 is to be free to stay at *h*
Jos 9: 12 warm when we packed it at *h*
20: 6 back to his own *h* in the town
22: 7 When Joshua sent them *h*,
Jdg 8: 29 son of Joash went back *h* to live.
9: 5 He went to his father's *h* in Ophrah
9: 55 Abimelech was dead, they went *h*.
11: 34 returned to his *h* in Mizpah,
18: 26 turned around and went back *h*.
19: 9 can get up and be on your way *h*.''
19: 15 them into his *h* for the night.
19: 28 her on his donkey and set out for *h*.
19: 29 When he reached *h*, he took a knife
20: 8 saying, ''None of us will go *h*.
21: 24 went *h* to their tribes and clans,
Ru 1: 6 prepared to return *h* from there.
1: 8 each of you, to your mother's *h*.
1: 9 rest in the *h* of another husband.''
1: 11 ''Return *h*, my daughters.
1: 12 become your husbands? Return *h*,
3: 1 should I not try to find a *h* for you,
4: 11 coming into your *h* like Rachel
1Sa 1: 19 then went back to their *h* at Ramah
1: 23 So the woman stayed at *h*
2: 11 Then Elkanah went *h* to Ramah,
2: 20 Then they would go *h*.
7: 17 where his *h* was, and there he
10: 25 the people, each to his own *h*.
10: 26 Saul also went to his *h* in Gibeah,
15: 34 up to his *h* in Gibeah of Saul.
18: 6 When the men were returning *h*
20: 6 to hurry to Bethlehem, his *h* town,
23: 18 Then Jonathan went *h*,
24: 22 Then Saul returned *h*, but David
25: 1 they buried him at his *h* in Ramah.
25: 35 had brought him and said, ''Go *h*
26: 25 on his way, and Saul returned *h*.
2Sa 3: 16 ''Go back *h!*'' So he went back.
6: 20 When David returned *h*
7: 10 them so that they can have a *h*
11: 4 Then she went back *h*.
11: 10 Uriah did not go *h*,'' he asked him,
11: 10 Why didn't you go *h?*'' Uriah said
11: 13 master's servants; he did not go *h*.
12: 15 After Nathan had gone *h*,
14: 8 The king said to the woman, ''Go *h*
15: 12 to come from Giloh, his *h* town.
17: 23 set out for his house in his *h* town.
19: 30 lord the king has arrived *h* safely.''
19: 39 and Barzillai returned to his *h*.
20: 22 the city, each returning to his *h*.
1Ki 1: 53 and Solomon said, ''Go to your *h*.''
5: 14 in Lebanon and two months at *h*.
8: 66 blessed the king and then went *h*,
1Ki 12: 16 So the Israelites went *h*.
12: 24 Go *h*, every one of you,
12: 24 of the LORD and went *h* again,
13: 7 ''Come *h* with me and have
13: 15 ''Come *h* with me and eat.''
14: 12 ''As for you, go back *h*.
16: 9 getting drunk in the *h* of Arza,
17: 12 am gathering a few sticks to take *h*
17: 13 Go *h* and do as you have said.
21: 4 So Ahab went *h*, sullen and angry
22: 17 Let each one go *h* in peace.' ''
2Ki 4: 13 I have a *h* among my own people.''
8: 21 his army, however, fled back *h*.
14: 10 Glory in your victory, but stay at *h*
14: 12 and every man fled to his *h*.
1Ch 16: 43 and David returned *h* to bless his
16: 43 for his own *h*, and David returned
17: 9 them so that they can have a *h*
2Ch 10: 16 So all the Israelites went *h*.
11: 4 Go *h*, every one of you,
18: 16 Let each one go *h* in peace.' ''
25: 10 and left for *h* in a great rage.
25: 10 from Ephraim and sent them *h*.
25: 19 But stay at *h!* Why ask for trouble
25: 22 and every man fled to his *h*.
Ne 6: 10 who was shut in at his *h*.
Est 5: 10 restrained himself and went *h*.
6: 12 But Haman rushed *h*, with his head
Job 17: 13 If the only *h* I hope for is the grave,
39: 6 I gave him the wasteland as his *h*,
Ps 84: 3 Even the sparrow has found a *h*,
104: 17 the stork has its *h* in the pine trees.
113: 9 settles the barren woman in her *h*
Pr 3: 33 but he blesses the *h* of the righteous
7: 11 her feet never stay at *h*;
7: 14 ''I have fellowship offerings at *h*;
7: 19 My husband is not at *h*;
7: 20 and will not be *h* till full moon.''
15: 31 will be at *h* among the wise.
27: 8 is a man who strays from his *h*.
30: 26 yet they make their *h* in the crags;
Ecc 12: 5 Then man goes to his eternal *h*
Isa 3: 6 brothers at his father's *h*, and say,
14: 17 and would not let his captives go *h*
34: 13 a *h* for owls.
Jer 39: 14 to take him back to his *h*.
Eze 36: 8 for they will soon come *h*.
Da 4: 4 Nebuchadnezzar, was at *h*
6: 10 he went *h* to his upstairs room
Ob : 3 and make your *h* on the heights,
Jnh 4: 2 said when I was still at *h?*
Mic 2: 2 They defraud a man of his *h*,
Zep 3: 20 at that time I will bring you *h*.
Hag 1: 9 What you brought *h*, I blew away.
Mt 1: 20 do not be afraid to take Mary *h*
1: 24 and took Mary *h* as his wife.
8: 6 ''my servant lies at *h* paralyzed
9: 6 ''Get up, take your mat and go *h*.''
9: 7 And the man got up and went *h*.
10: 12 As you enter the *h*, give it your
10: 13 If the *h* is deserving, let your peace
10: 14 off your feet when you leave that *h*
13: 54 to his *h* town, he began teaching
13: 57 ''Only in his *h* town
26: 6 in Bethany in the *h* of a man known
Mk 1: 29 and John to the *h* of Simon
2: 1 people heard that he had come *h*.
2: 11 get up, take your mat and go *h*.''
5: 19 ''Go *h* to your family and tell them
5: 38 to the *h* of the synagogue ruler,
6: 1 left there and went to his *h* town,
6: 4 said to them, ''Only in his *h* town,
7: 30 She went *h* and found her child
8: 3 If I send them *h* hungry, they will
8: 26 Jesus sent him *h*, saying, ''Don't go
10: 29 ''no one who has left *h* or brothers
14: 3 the table in the *h* of a man known
Lk 1: 23 was completed, he returned *h*.
1: 40 where she entered Zechariah's *h*
1: 56 three months and then returned *h*.
2: 43 while his parents were returning *h*,
4: 23 in your *h* town what we have heard
4: 24 prophet is accepted in his *h* town.
4: 38 and went to the *h* of Simon.
5: 24 get up, take your mat and go *h*.''
5: 25 lying on and went *h* praising God.
8: 39 ''Return *h* and tell how much God
10: 38 named Martha opened her *h*
Lk 15: 6 it on his shoulders and goes *h*.
15: 30 property with prostitutes comes *h*,
18: 14 went *h* justified before God.
18: 29 ''no one who has left *h* or wife
19: 15 king, however, and returned *h*.
23: 56 they went *h* and prepared spices
Jn 7: 53 Then each went to his own *h*.
9: 7 and washed, and came *h* seeing.
11: 20 to meet him, but Mary stayed at *h*.
14: 23 to him and make our *h* with him.
16: 32 will be scattered, each to his own *h*.
19: 27 this disciple took her into his *h*.
Ac 8: 28 and on his way *h* was sitting
10: 32 guest in the *h* of Simon the tanner,
16: 15 baptized, she invited us to her *h*.
18: 26 they invited him to their *h*
20: 12 people took the young man *h* alive
21: 6 the ship, and they returned *h*.
21: 16 and brought us to the *h* of Mnason,
28: 7 He welcomed us to his *h*
1Co 11: 34 is hungry, he should eat at *h*,
14: 35 ask their own husbands at *h*;
2Co 5: 6 we are at *h* in the body we are away
5: 8 and at *h* with the Lord.
5: 9 whether we are at *h* in the body
Tit 2: 5 to be busy at *h*, to be kind,
Phm : 2 to the church that meets in your *h*:
Heb 11: 9 By faith he made his *h*
2Pe 3: 13 a new earth, the *h* of righteousness.
Jude : 6 but abandoned their own *h*
Rev 18: 2 She has become a *h* for demons

HOMELAND (HOME)

Ge 30: 25 way so I can go back to my own *h*.
Ru 2: 11 your father and mother and your *h*
2Sa 15: 19 a foreigner, an exile from your *h*.
2Ki 17: 23 from their *h* into exile in Assyria,
Ps 79: 7 and destroyed his *h*.
Jer 10: 25 and destroyed his *h*.
Joel 3: 6 might send them far from their *h*.

HOMELESS

1Co 4: 11 we are brutally treated, we are *h*.

HOMER (HOMERS)

Lev 27: 16 of silver to a *h* of barley seed.
Isa 5: 10 a *h* of seed only an ephah of grain.''
Eze 45: 11 and the ephah a tenth of a *h*;
45: 11 the bath containing a tenth of a *h*
45: 11 the *h* is to be the standard measure
45: 13 of an ephah from each *h* of barley
45: 13 of an ephah from each *h* of wheat
45: 14 consists of ten baths or one *h*,
45: 14 for ten baths are equivalent to a *h*).
Hos 3: 2 about a *h* and a lethek of barley.

HOMERS (HOMER)

Nu 11: 32 No one gathered less than ten *h*.

HOMES (HOME)

Ex 12: 27 and spared our *h* when he struck
Nu 32: 18 We will not return to our *h*
Dt 32: 25 in their *h* terror will reign.
Jos 22: 4 to your *h* in the land that Moses
22: 6 away, and they went to their *h*.
22: 8 ''Return to your *h*
1Sa 13: 2 of the men he sent back to their *h*.
2Sa 6: 19 And all the people went to their *h*.
18: 17 all the Israelites fled to their *h*.
19: 8 the Israelites had fled to their *h*.
2Ki 13: 5 the Israelites lived in their own *h*
2Ch 7: 10 he sent the people to their *h*,
Ne 4: 14 daughters, your wives and your *h*.''
5: 3 our *h* to get grain during the famine
Job 1: 4 take turns holding feasts in their *h*,
2: 11 they set out from their *h*
21: 9 Their *h* are safe and free from fear;
36: 20 to drag people away from their *h*.
Ps 78: 55 the tribes of Israel in their *h*.
109: 10 from their ruined *h*.
Isa 32: 18 in secure *h*,
La 5: 2 our *h* to foreigners.
Hos 11: 11 I will settle them in their *h*,''
Mic 2: 9 from their pleasant *h*.
Mk 10: 30 as much in this present age (*h*,
Jn 20: 10 the disciples went back to their *h*,
Ac 2: 46 They broke bread in their *h*
1Co 11: 22 Don't you have *h* to eat

1Ti 5: 14 to manage their *h* and to give
2Ti 3: 6 kind who worm their way into *h*

HOMOSEXUAL

1Co 6: 9 male prostitutes nor *h* offenders

HONEST (HONESTY)

Ge 42: 11 Your servants are *h* men, not spies
42: 19 for I fear God: If you are *h* men,
42: 31 'We are *h* men; we are not spies.
42: 33 I will know whether you are *h* men:
42: 34 that you are not spies but *h* men.
Ex 23: 7 do not put an innocent or *h* person
Lev 19: 36 Use *h* scales and *h* weights,
19: 36 weights, an *h* ephah and an *h* hin.
Dt 25: 15 and *h* weights and measures,
1Ch 29: 17 I given willingly and with *h* intent.
Job 6: 25 How painful are *h* words!
31: 6 let God weigh me in *h* scales
Pr 12: 17 truthful witness gives *h* testimony,
16: 11 *H* scales and balances are
16: 13 Kings take pleasure in *h* lips;
24: 26 An *h* answer
Lk 20: 20 sent spies, who pretended to be *h*.

HONESTY (HONEST)

Ge 30: 33 And my *h* will testify for me
2Ki 12: 15 they acted with complete *h*.
Isa 59: 14 *h* cannot enter.

HONEY (HONEYCOMB)

Ge 43: 11 a little *h*, some spices and myrrh,
Ex 3: 8 a land flowing with milk and *h*—
3: 17 a land flowing with milk and *h*.'
13: 5 a land flowing with milk and *h*—
16: 31 and tasted like wafers made with *h*.
33: 3 to the land flowing with milk and *h*
Lev 2: 11 *h* in an offering made to the LORD
20: 24 a land flowing with milk and *h*.''
Nu 13: 27 and it does flow with milk and *h!*
14: 8 a land flowing with milk and *h*,
16: 13 and *h* to kill us in the desert?
16: 14 and *h* or given us an inheritance
Dt 6: 3 in a land flowing with milk and *h*,
8: 8 pomegranates, olive oil and *h;*
11: 9 a land flowing with milk and *h*.
26: 9 a land flowing with milk and *h;*
26: 15 a land flowing with milk and *h*.''
27: 3 a land flowing with milk and *h*,
31: 20 the land flowing with milk and *h*,
32: 13 him with *h* from the rock,
Jos 5: 6 a land flowing with milk and *h*.
Jdg 14: 8 a swarm of bees and some *h*,
14: 9 tell them that he had taken the *h*
14: 18 ''What is sweeter than *h?*
1Sa 14: 25 and there was *h* on the ground.
14: 26 they saw the *h* oozing out,
14: 29 when I tasted a little of this *h*.
14: 43 ''I merely tasted a little *h*
2Sa 17: 29 beans and lentils, *h* and curds,
1Ki 14: 3 and a jar of *h*, and go to him.
2Ki 18: 32 a land of olive trees and *h*.
2Ch 31: 5 *h* and all that the fields produced.
Job 20: 17 the rivers flowing with *h* and cream
Ps 19: 10 than *h* from the comb.
19: 10 they are sweeter than *h*,
81: 16 with *h* from the rock I would
119:103 sweeter than *h* to my mouth!
Pr 5: 3 For the lips of an adulteress drip *h*,
24: 13 Eat *h*, my son, for it is good;
24: 13 *h* from the comb is sweet
25: 16 If you find *h*, eat just enough—
25: 27 It is not good to eat too much *h*,
27: 7 He who is full loathes *h*,
SS 4: 11 milk and *h* are under your tongue.
5: 1 eaten my honeycomb and my *h;*
Isa 7: 15 and *h* when he knows enough
7: 22 in the land will eat curds and *h*.
Jer 11: 5 flowing with milk and *h*'—
32: 22 a land flowing with milk and *h*.
41: 8 oil and *h*, hidden in a field.''
Eze 3: 3 it tasted as sweet as *h* in my mouth.
16: 13 Your food was fine flour, *h*
16: 19 olive oil and *h* I gave you to eat—
20: 6 a land flowing with milk and *h*,
20: 15 a land flowing with milk and *h*,
27: 17 *h*, oil and balm for your wares.
Mt 3: 4 His food was locusts and wild *h*.
Mk 1: 6 and he ate locusts and wild *h*.
Rev 10: 9 mouth it will be as sweet as *h*.''
10: 10 It tasted as sweet as *h* in my mouth,

HONEYCOMB (HONEY)

1Sa 14: 27 in his hand and dipped it into the *h*.
Pr 16: 24 Pleasant words are a *h*,
SS 4: 11 Your lips drop sweetness as the *h*,
5: 1 I have eaten my *h* and my honey;

HONOR (HONORABLE HONORABLY HONORED HONORING HONORS)

Ge 30: 20 my husband will treat me with *h*,
43: 28 And they bowed low to pay him *h*.
45: 13 father about all the *h* accorded me
49: 3 excelling in *h*, excelling in power.
Ex 8: 9 to you the *h* of setting the time
12: 42 are to keep vigil to *h* the LORD
20: 12 ''*H* your father and your mother,
28: 2 to give him dignity and *h*.
28: 40 to give them dignity and *h*.
Nu 20: 12 trust in me enough to *h* me
25: 11 as I am for my *h* among them,
25: 13 he was zealous for the *h* of his God
27: 14 disobeyed my command to *h* me
Dt 5: 16 ''*H* your father and your mother,
26: 19 *h* high above all the nations he has
Jdg 4: 9 going about this, the *h* will not be
13: 17 so that we may *h* you
1Sa 2: 8 and has them inherit a throne of *h*.
2: 29 Why do you *h* your sons more
2: 30 Those who *h* me I will *h*,
6: 5 destroying the country, and pay *h*
15: 12 has set up a monument in his own *h*
15: 30 But please *h* me before the elders
2Sa 1: 2 he fell to the ground to pay him *h*.
6: 22 spoke of, I will be held in *h*.''
9: 6 he bowed down to pay him *h*.
14: 4 face to the ground to pay him *h*,
14: 22 face to the ground to pay him *h*,
23: 19 held in greater *h* than the Three?
23: 23 He was held in greater *h* than any
1Ki 3: 13 *h*— so that in your lifetime you will
2Ki 10: 20 ''Call an assembly in *h* of Baal.''
25: 28 a seat of *h* higher than those
1Ch 11: 25 He was held in greater *h* than any
29: 12 Wealth and *h* come from you;
29: 28 enjoyed long life, wealth and *h*.
2Ch 1: 11 or *h*, nor for the death
1: 12 also give you wealth, riches and *h*,
16: 14 and they made a huge fire in his *h*.
17: 5 so that he had great wealth and *h*.
18: 1 had great wealth and *h*,
21: 19 His people made no fire in his *h*,
32: 27 had very great riches and *h*,
Ezr 7: 27 heart to bring *h* to the house
Est 3: 1 a seat of *h* higher than that
3: 2 kneel down or pay him *h*.
3: 2 knelt down and paid *h* to Haman,
3: 5 kneel down or pay him *h*,
6: 3 ''What *h* and recognition has
6: 6 for the man the king delights to *h*
6: 6 there that the king would rather *h*
6: 7 For the man the king delights to *h*,
6: 9 for the man the king delights to *h*
6: 9 robe the man the king delights to *h*,
6: 11 for the man the king delights to *h!*''
8: 16 happiness and joy, gladness and *h*.
Job 19: 9 He has stripped me of my *h*
40: 10 clothe yourself in *h* and majesty.
Ps 8: 5 and crowned him with glory and *h*.
22: 23 you descendants of Jacob, *h* him!
45: 11 *h* him, for he is your lord.
50: 15 deliver you, and you will *h* me.''
62: 7 my *h* depend on God;
71: 21 You will increase my *h*
84: 11 the LORD bestows favor and *h;*
91: 15 I will deliver him and *h* him.
112: 9 his horn will be lifted high in *h*.
149: 5 Let the saints rejoice in this *h*
Pr 3: 9 *H* the LORD with your wealth,
3: 16 in her left hand are riches and *h*.
3: 35 The wise inherit *h*,
4: 8 embrace her, and she will *h* you.
8: 18 With me are riches and *h*,
15: 33 and humility comes before *h*.
18: 12 but humility comes before *h*.
20: 3 It is to a man's *h* to avoid strife,
Pr 21: 21 finds life, prosperity and *h*.
22: 4 bring wealth and *h* and life.
25: 27 is it honorable to seek one's own *h*.
26: 1 *h* is not fitting for a fool.
26: 8 is the giving of *h* to a fool.
29: 23 but a man of lowly spirit gains *h*.
Ecc 6: 2 a man wealth, possessions and *h*,
10: 1 folly outweighs wisdom and *h*.
Isa 9: 1 but in the future he will *h* Galilee
22: 23 he will be a seat of *h* for the house
25: 3 strong peoples will *h* you;
26: 13 but your name alone do we *h*.
29: 13 and *h* me with their lips,
43: 20 The wild animals *h* me,
45: 4 and bestow on you a title of *h*,
58: 13 if you *h* it by not going your own
60: 9 to the *h* of the LORD your God,
Jer 3: 17 gather in Jerusalem to *h* the name
13: 11 for my renown and praise and *h*.
30: 19 I will bring them *h*,
33: 9 and *h* before all nations
34: 5 fire in *h* of your fathers,
34: 5 so they will make a fire in your *h*
52: 32 a seat of *h* higher than those
La 4: 16 The priests are shown no *h*,
Da 2: 6 me gifts and rewards and great *h*.
2: 46 and paid him *h* and ordered that
4: 36 my *h* and splendor were returned
5: 23 you did not *h* the God who holds
11: 21 who has not been given the *h*
11: 38 he will *h* a god of fortresses;
11: 38 to his fathers he will *h* with gold
11: 39 and will greatly *h* those who
Hab 1: 7 and promote their own *h*.
Zep 3: 19 I will give them praise and *h*
3: 20 I will give you *h* and praise
Zec 12: 7 so that the *h* of the house of David
Mal 1: 6 where is the *h* due me? If I am
2: 2 not set your heart to *h* my name,''
2: 2 you have not set your heart to *h* me
Mt 13: 57 own house is a prophet without *h*.''
15: 4 '*H* your father and mother'
15: 6 he is not to '*h* his father' with it.
15: 8 These people *h* me with their lips,
19: 19 *h* your father and mother,'
23: 6 they love the place of *h* at banquets
Mk 6: 4 own house is a prophet without *h*.''
7: 6 These people *h* me with their lips,
7: 10 '*H* your father and mother,'
10: 19 *h* your father and mother.' ''
12: 39 and the places of *h* at banquets.
Lk 14: 7 the guests picked the places of *h*
14: 8 do not take the place of *h*,
18: 20 *h* your father and mother.' ''
20: 46 and the places of *h* at banquets.
Jn 4: 44 pointed out that a prophet has no *h*
5: 23 He who does not *h* the Son does
5: 23 that all may *h* the Son just
5: 23 the Son does not *h* the Father,
5: 23 the Son just as they *h* the Father.
7: 18 but he who works for the *h*
7: 18 does so to gain *h* for himself,
8: 49 I *h* my Father and you dishonor me
12: 2 Here a dinner was given in Jesus' *h*.
12: 26 My Father will *h* the one who
Ac 7: 41 and held a celebration in *h*
19: 17 the Lord Jesus was held in high *h*.
Ro 2: 7 *h* and immortality, he will give
2: 10 *h* and peace for everyone who does
12: 10 *H* one another above yourselves.
13: 7 if respect, then respect; if *h*, then *h*.
1Co 6: 20 Therefore *h* God with your body.
12: 23 honorable we treat with special *h*.
12: 24 and has given greater *h*
2Co 8: 19 in order to *h* the Lord himself
8: 23 of the churches and an *h* to Christ.
Eph 6: 2 ''*H* your father and mother''—
Php 2: 29 with great joy, and *h* men like him,
1Ti 1: 17 be *h* and glory for ever and ever.
5: 17 well are worthy of double *h*,
6: 16 To him be *h* and might forever.
Heb 2: 7 you crowned him with glory and *h*
2: 9 and *h* because he suffered death,
3: 3 the builder of a house has greater *h*
3: 3 worthy of greater *h* than Moses,
5: 4 No one takes this *h* upon himself;
1Pe 1: 7 *h* when Jesus Christ is revealed.
2: 17 of believers, fear God, *h* the king.

2Pe 1:17 For he received *h* and glory
Rev 4: 9 *h* and thanks to him who sits
4:11 to receive glory and *h* and power,
5:12 and *h* and glory and praise!"
5:13 be praise and *h* and glory
7:12 and wisdom and thanks and *h*
13:14 them to set up an image in *h*
21:26 and *h* of the nations will be brought

HONORABLE (HONOR)

1Ch 4: 9 Jabez was more *h* than his brothers
Ezr 4:10 and *h* Ashurbanipal deported
Pr 25:27 nor is it *h* to seek one's own honor.
Isa 3: 5 the base against the *h*.
58:13 and the LORD's holy day *h*,
1Co 12:23 that we think are less *h* we treat
1Th 4: 4 body in a way that is holy and *h*,

HONORABLY (HONOR)

Jdg 9:16 "Now if you have acted *h*
9:19 if then you have acted *h*
Heb 13:18 and desire to live *h* in every way.

HONORED (HONOR)

Ge 34:19 who was the most *h*
Ex 20:24 Wherever I cause my name to be *h*,
Lev 10: 3 I will be *h*.' "
Jdg 9: 9 by which both gods and men are *h*,
1Ch 11:21 He was doubly *h* above the Three
2Ch 26:18 and you will not be *h* by the LORD
32:33 and the people of Jerusalem *h* him
Est 3: 1 King Xerxes *h* Haman son
5:11 and all the ways the king had *h* him
Job 14:21 If his sons are *h*, he does not know
22: 8 an *h* man, living on it.
Ps 12: 8 when what is vile is *h* among men.
45: 9 of kings are among your *h* women;
Pr 13:18 but whoever heeds correction is *h*.
27:18 after his master will be *h*.
Isa 43: 4 Since you are precious and *h*
43:23 nor *h* me with your sacrifices.
49: 5 for I am *h* in the eyes of the LORD
La 1: 8 All who *h* her despise her,
Da 4:34 I *h* and glorified him who lives
Hag 1: 8 I may take pleasure in it and be *h*,"
Zec 2: 8 "After he has *h* me and has sent me
Mal 3:16 feared the LORD and *h* his name.
Mt 6: 2 and on the streets, to be *h* by men.
Lk 14:10 Then you will be *h* in the presence
Ac 5:34 who was *h* by all the people,
13:48 and *h* the word of the Lord;
28:10 They *h* us in many ways
1Co 4:10 You are *h*, we are dishonored!
12:26 if one part is *h*, every part rejoices
2Th 3: 1 Lord may spread rapidly and be *h*,
Heb 13: 4 Marriage should be *h* by all,

HONORING (HONOR)

2Sa 10: 3 you think David is *h* your father
1Ch 17:18 say to you for *h* your servant?
19: 3 you think David is *h* your father

HONORS (HONOR)

Ps 15: 4 but *h* those who fear the LORD,
50:23 sacrifices thank offerings *h* me,
Pr 14:31 to the needy *h* God.
Mal 1: 6 son *h* his father, and a servant his

HOOF (HOOFS)

Ex 10:26 not a *h* is to be left behind.
Lev 11: 3 has a split *h* completely divided
11: 4 chew the cud or only have a split *h*,
11: 4 not have a split *h*; it is ceremonially
11: 5 does not have a split *h*; it is unclean
11: 6 does not have a split *h*; it is unclean
11: 7 it has a split *h* completely divided,
11:26 has a split *h* not completely divided
Dt 14: 6 animal that has a split *h* divided
14: 7 have a split *h* completely divided
14: 7 they do not have a split *h*;
14: 8 it has a split *h*, it does not chew

HOOFS (HOOF)

Jdg 5:22 Then thundered the horses' *h*—
Ps 69:31 than a bull with its horns and *h*.
Isa 5:28 their horses' *h* seem like flint,
Jer 47: 3 sound of the *h* of galloping steeds,
Eze 26:11 *h* of his horses will trample all your
Eze 32:13 or muddied by the *h* of cattle.
Mic 4:13 I will give you *h* of bronze
Zec 11:16 choice sheep, tearing off their *h*.

HOOK (FISHHOOK FISHHOOKS HOOKS)

2Ki 19:28 I will put my *h* in your nose
2Ch 33:11 took Manasseh prisoner, put a *h*
Job 41: 2 or pierce his jaw with a *h*?
Isa 37:29 I will put my *h* in your nose

HOOKS (HOOK)

Ex 26:32 Hang it with gold *h* on four posts
26:37 Make gold *h* for this curtain
27:10 and with silver *h* and bands
27:11 and with silver *h* and bands
27:17 are to have silver bands and *h*,
36:36 They made gold *h* for them
36:38 and they made five posts with *h*
38:10 and with silver *h* and bands
38:11 with silver *h* and bands
38:12 with silver *h* and bands
38:17 The *h* and bands on the posts were
38:19 Their *h* and bands were silver,
38:28 shekels to make the *h* for the posts,
Isa 2: 4 and their spears into pruning *h*.
19: 8 all who cast *h* into the Nile;
Eze 19: 4 They led him with *h*
19: 9 With *h* they pulled him into a cage
29: 4 But I will put *h* in your jaws
38: 4 put *h* in your jaws and bring you
40:43 And double-pronged *h*, each
Joel 3:10 and your pruning *h* into spears.
Am 4: 2 you will be taken away with *h*,
Mic 4: 3 and their spears into pruning *h*.
Hab 1:15 all of them up with *h*,

HOOPOE

Lev 11:19 any kind of heron, the *h*
Dt 14:18 any kind of heron, the *h*

HOPE (HOPED HOPES HOPING)

Ru 1:12 if I thought there was still *h* for me
1Ch 29:15 earth are like a shadow, without *h*.
Ezr 10: 2 of this, there is still *h* for Israel.
Job 4: 6 and your blameless ways your *h*?
5:16 So the poor have *h*,
6: 8 that God would grant what I *h* for,
6:11 do I have, that I should still *h*?
6:19 of Sheba look in *h*.
7: 6 and they come to an end without *h*.
8:13 so perishes the *h* of the godless.
11:18 will be secure, because there is *h*;
11:20 their *h* will become a dying gasp."
13:15 Though he slay me, yet will I *h*
14: 7 "At least there is *h* for a tree:
14:19 so you destroy man's *h*.
17:13 If the only home I *h* for is the grave
17:15 Who can see any *h* for me?
17:15 where then is my *h*?
19:10 he uproots my *h* like a tree.
27: 8 For what *h* has the godless
41: 9 Any *h* of subduing him is false;
Ps 9:18 the *h* of the afflicted ever perish.
25: 3 No one whose *h* is in you
25: 5 and my *h* is in you all day long.
25:21 because my *h* is in you.
31:24 all you who *h* in the LORD.
33:17 A horse is a vain *h* for deliverance;
33:18 on those whose *h* is
33:20 We wait in *h* for the LORD;
33:22 even as we put our *h* in you.
37: 9 those who *h* in the LORD will
39: 7 My *h* is in you.
42: 5 Put your *h* in God,
42:11 Put your *h* in God,
43: 5 Put your *h* in God,
52: 9 in your name I will *h*,
62: 5 my *h* comes from him.
65: 5 the *h* of all the ends of the earth
69: 6 May those who *h* in you
71: 5 have been my *h*, O Sovereign
71:14 But as for me, I will always have *h*;
119: 43 for I have put my *h* in your laws.
119: 49 for you have given me *h*.
119: 74 for I have put my *h* in your word.
119: 81 but I have put my *h* in your word.
119:114 I have put my *h* in your word.
119:147 I have put my *h* in your word.
Ps 130: 5 and in his word I put my *h*.
130: 7 O Israel, put your *h* in the LORD,
131: 3 O Israel, put your *h* in the LORD
146: 5 whose *h* is in the LORD his God,
147:11 who put their *h* in his unfailing love
Pr 11: 7 a wicked man dies, his *h* perishes;
11:23 the *h* of the wicked only in wrath.
13:12 *H* deferred makes the heart sick,
19:18 for in that there is *h*;
23:18 There is surely a future *h* for you,
23:18 and your *h* will not be cut off.
24:14 and your *h* will not be cut off.
24:14 there is a future *h* for you,
24:20 for the evil man has no future *h*,
26:12 There is more *h* for a fool
29:20 There is more *h* for a fool
Ecc 9: 4 is among the living has *h*—
Isa 19: 9 the weavers of fine linen will lose *h*
38:18 cannot *h* for your faithfulness.
40:31 but those who *h* in the LORD
42: 4 his law the islands will put their *h*."
49:23 those who *h* in me will not be
51: 5 and wait in *h* for my arm.
Jer 13:16 You *h* for light,
14: 8 O *H* of Israel,
14:22 Therefore our *h* is in you,
17:13 O LORD, the *h* of Israel,
29:11 plans to give you *h* and a future.
31:17 So there is *h* for your future,"
50: 7 the LORD, the *h* of their fathers.'
La 3:21 and therefore I have *h*:
3:25 good to those whose *h* is in him,
3:29 there may yet be *h*.
Eze 19: 5 " 'When she saw her *h* unfulfilled,
37:11 are dried up and our *h* is gone;
Hos 2:15 of Achor a door of *h*.
Mic 7: 7 I watch in *h* for the LORD,
Zec 9: 5 and Ekron too, for her *h* will wither
9:12 to your fortress, O prisoners of *h*;
Mt 12:21 name the nations will put their *h*."
Ac 2:26 my body also will live in *h*,
16:19 of the slave girl realized that their *h*
23: 6 because of my *h* in the resurrection
24:15 and I have the same *h* in God
26: 6 of my *h* in what God has promised
26: 7 of this *h* that the Jews are accusing
27:20 we finally gave up all *h*
28:20 of the *h* of Israel that I am bound
Ro 4:18 Abraham in *h* believed
4:18 Against all *h*, Abraham
5: 2 And we rejoice in the *h* of the glory
5: 4 character; and character, *h*
5: 5 And *h* does not disappoint us,
8:20 in *h* that the creation itself will be
8:24 But *h* that is seen is no *h* at all.
8:24 For in this *h* we were saved.
8:25 if we *h* for what we do not yet have,
11:14 in the *h* that I may somehow
12:12 Be joyful in *h*, patient in affliction,
15: 4 of the Scriptures we might have *h*.
15:12 the Gentiles will *h* in him."
15:13 May the God of *h* fill you
15:13 overflow with *h* by the power
15:24 I *h* to visit you while passing
1Co 9:10 ought to do so in the *h* of sharing
9:13 this in the *h* that you will do such
13:13 now these three remain: faith, *h*
15:19 for this life we have *h* in Christ,
16: 7 I *h* to spend some time with you,
2Co 1: 7 And our *h* for you is firm,
1:10 we have set our *h* that he will
1:13 I *h* that, as you have understood us
3:12 we have such a *h*, we are very bold.
5:11 *h* it is also plain to your conscience.
10:15 Our *h* is that, as your faith
11: 1 I *h* you will put up with a little
Gal 5: 5 the righteousness for which we *h*.
Eph 1:12 who were the first to *h* in Christ,
1:18 in order that you may know the *h*
2:12 without *h* and without God
4: 4 to one *h* when you were called—
Php 1:20 *h* that I will in no way be ashamed,
2:19 I *h* in the Lord Jesus
2:23 I *h*, therefore, to send him as soon
Col 1: 5 spring from the *h* that is stored up
1:23 not moved from the *h* held out
1:27 Christ in you, the *h* of glory.
1Th 1: 3 and your endurance inspired by *h*

1Th 2: 19 For what is our *h*, our joy,
4: 13 the rest of men, who have no *h*.
5: 8 and the *h* of salvation as a helmet.
2Th 2: 16 encouragement and good *h*,
1Ti 1: 1 and of Christ Jesus our *h*,
3: 14 Although I *h* to come to you soon,
4: 10 that we have put our *h*
5: 5 and left all alone puts her *h* in God
6: 17 but to put their *h* in God,
6: 17 nor to put their *h* in wealth,
2Ti 2: 25 in the *h* that God will grant them
Tit 1: 2 resting on the *h* of eternal life,
2: 13 while we wait for the blessed *h*—
3: 7 might become heirs having the *h*
Phm : 22 I *h* to be restored to you in answer
Heb 3: 6 and the *h* of which we boast.
6: 11 in order to make your *h* sure.
6: 18 fled to take hold of the *h* offered
6: 19 We have this *h* as an anchor
7: 19 and a better *h* is introduced,
10: 23 unswervingly to the *h* we profess,
11: 1 faith is being sure of what we *h* for
1Pe 1: 3 a living *h* through the resurrection
1: 13 set your *h* fully on the grace
1: 21 and so your faith and *h* are in God.
3: 5 women of the past who put their *h*
3: 15 the reason for the *h* that you have.
1Jn 3: 3 Everyone who has this *h*
2Jn : 12 I *h* to visit you and talk
3Jn : 14 I *h* to see you soon, and we will talk

HOPED (HOPE)

Est 9: 1 the Jews had *h* to overpower them,
Job 30: 26 Yet when I *h* for good, evil came;
Jer 8: 15 We *h* for peace
14: 19 We *h* for peace
La 3: 18 all that I had *h* from the LORD."
Lk 20: 20 They *h* to catch Jesus
23: 8 he *h* to see him perform some
24: 21 we had *h* that he was the one who

HOPELESS

Isa 57: 10 but you would not say, 'It is *h*.'

HOPES (HOPE)

2Ki 4: 28 'Don't raise my *h*'?" Elisha said
Ps 119:116 do not let my *h* be dashed.
Pr 10: 28 the *h* of the wicked come
Jer 23: 16 they fill you with false *h*.
Jn 5: 45 on whom your *h* are set.
Ro 8: 24 Who *h* for what he already has?
1Co 13: 7 always *h*, always perseveres.

HOPHNI

1Sa 1: 3 where *H* and Phinehas, the two
2: 34 what happens to your two sons, *H*
4: 4 Eli's two sons, *H* and Phinehas,
4: 11 and Eli's two sons, *H* and Phinehas
4: 17 your two sons, *H* and Phinehas,

HOPHRA

Jer 44: 30 to hand Pharaoh *H* king of Egypt

HOPING (HOPE)

Da 2: 9 *h* the situation will change.
Ac 24: 26 time he was *h* that Paul would
26: 7 the promise our twelve tribes are *h*
27: 12 *h* to reach Phoenix and winter

HOPPING

Lev 11: 21 legs for *h* on the ground.

HOR

Nu 20: 22 Kadesh and came to Mount *H*.
20: 23 At Mount *H*, near the border
20: 25 and take them up Mount *H*.
20: 27 They went up Mount *H* in the sight
21: 4 from Mount *H* along the route
33: 37 Kadesh and camped at Mount *H*,
33: 38 the priest went up Mount *H*,
33: 39 old when he died on Mount *H*.
33: 41 They left Mount *H* and camped
34: 7 from the Great Sea to Mount *H*
34: 8 from Mount *H* to Lebo Hamath.
Dt 32: 50 brother Aaron died on Mount *H*

HOR HAGGIDGAD

Nu 33: 32 left Bene Jaakan and camped at *H*.
Nu 33: 33 They left *H* and camped at

HORAM

Jos 10: 33 *H* king of Gezer had come up

HORDE (HORDES)

Nu 22: 4 "This *h* is going to lick up
Eze 17: 17 great *h* will be of no help to him
38: 4 and a great *h* with large
38: 15 of them riding on horses, a great *h*,

HORDES (HORDE)

Isa 29: 5 the ruthless *h* like blown chaff.
29: 7 the *h* of all the nations that fight
29: 8 be with the *h* of all the nations
Eze 30: 10 " 'I will put an end to the *h*
30: 15 and cut off the *h* of Thebes.
31: 2 king of Egypt and to his *h*:
31: 18 " 'This is Pharaoh and all his *h*,
32: 12 I will cause your *h* to fall
32: 12 and all her *h* will be overthrown.
32: 16 and all her *h* they will chant it,
32: 18 wail for the *h* of Egypt
32: 20 let her be dragged off with all her *h*.
32: 24 with all her *h* around her grave.
32: 25 with all her *h* around her grave.
32: 26 with all their *h* around their graves.
32: 31 for all his *h* that were killed
32: 32 and all his *h* will be laid
38: 7 and all the *h* gathered about you,
38: 13 Have you gathered your *h* to loot,
39: 11 and all his *h* will be buried there.
Hab 1: 9 Their *h* advance like a desert wind

HOREB

Ex 3: 1 side of the desert and came to *H*.
17: 6 there before you by the rock at *H*.
33: 6 off their ornaments at Mount *H*.
Dt 1: 2 to go from *H* to Kadesh Barnea
1: 6 The LORD our God said to us at *H*
1: 19 we set out from *H* and went
4: 10 before the LORD your God at *H*,
4: 15 spoke to you at *H* out of the fire.
5: 2 God made a covenant with us at *H*.
9: 8 At *H* you aroused the LORD's
18: 16 asked of the LORD your God at *H*
29: 1 he had made with them at *H*.
1Ki 8: 9 that Moses had placed in it at *H*,
19: 8 forty nights until he reached *H*,
2Ch 5: 10 that Moses had placed in it at *H*,
Ps 106: 19 At *H* they made a calf
Mal 4: 4 laws I gave him at *H* for all Israel.

HOREM

Jos 19: 38 Iron, Migdal El, *H*,

HORESH

1Sa 23: 15 was at *H* in the Desert
23: 16 son Jonathan went to David at *H*
23: 18 but David remained at *H*.
23: 19 among us in the strongholds at *H*,

HORI (HORITE HORITES)

Ge 36: 22 The sons of Lotan: *H* and Homam.
Nu 13: 5 Shaphat son of *H*; from the tribe
1Ch 1: 39 The sons of Lotan: *H* and Homam.

HORITE (HORI)

Ge 36: 20 These were the sons of Seir the *H*,
36: 21 of Seir in Edom were *H* chiefs.
36: 29 These were the *H* chiefs: Lotan,
36: 30 These were the *H* chiefs, according

HORITES (HORI)

Ge 14: 6 the *H* in the hill country of Seir,
Dt 2: 12 They destroyed the *H*
2: 12 *H* used to live in Seir,
2: 22 when he destroyed the *H*

HORIZON

Ne 1: 9 exiled people are at the farthest *h*,
Job 26: 10 He marks out the *h* on the face
Pr 8: 27 when he marked out the *h*

HORMAH

Nu 14: 45 beat them down all the way to *H*.
21: 3 so the place was named *H*.
Dt 1: 44 down from Seir all the way to *H*.
Jos 12: 14 one the king of *H* one the king
15: 30 Kesil, *H*, Ziklag, Madmannah,
19: 4 Eltolad, Bethul, *H*, Ziklag,
Jdg 1: 17 Therefore it was called *H*.
1Sa 30: 30 to those in *H*, Bor Ashan, Athach
1Ch 4: 30 Tolad, Bethuel, *H*, Ziklag,

HORN (HORNED HORNS TWO-HORNED)

Ex 19: 13 when the ram's *h* sounds a long
27: 2 Make a *h* at each of the four
38: 2 They made a *h* at each
1Sa 2: 1 in the LORD my *h* is lifted high.
2: 10 and exalt the *h* of his anointed."
16: 1 Fill your *h* with oil and be
16: 13 So Samuel took the *h* of oil
2Sa 22: 3 my shield and the *h* of my salvation
1Ki 1: 39 Zadok the priest took the *h* of oil
Ps 18: 2 He is my shield and the *h*
81: 3 Sound the ram's *h*
89: 17 and by your favor you exalt our *h*.
89: 24 my name his *h* will be exalted.
92: 10 You have exalted my *h* like that
98: 6 and the blast of the ram's *h*—
112: 9 his *h* will be lifted high in honor.
132: 17 "Here I will make a *h* grow
148: 14 He has raised up for his people a *h*,
Jer 48: 25 Moab's *h* is cut off;
La 2: 3 every *h* of Israel.
2: 17 he has exalted the *h* of your foes.
Eze 29: 21 "On that day I will make a *h* grow
Da 3: 5 as you hear the sound of the *h*,
3: 7 as they heard the sound of the *h*,
3: 10 who hears the sound of the *h*,
3: 15 when you hear the sound of the *h*,
7: 8 This *h* had eyes like the eyes
7: 8 there before me was another *h*,
7: 11 boastful words the *h* was speaking.
7: 20 and about the other *h* that came up,
7: 20 the *h* that looked more imposing
7: 21 this *h* was waging war
8: 5 a goat with a prominent *h*
8: 8 of his power his large *h* was broken
8: 9 Out of one of them came another *h*
8: 21 large *h* between his eyes is the first
Hos 5: 8 the *h* in Ramah.
Lk 1: 69 He has raised up a *h* of salvation

HORNED (HORN)

Lev 11: 16 the *h* owl, the screech owl,
Dt 14: 15 the *h* owl, the screech owl,

HORNET

Ex 23: 28 I will send the *h* ahead of you
Dt 7: 20 LORD your God will send the *h*
Jos 24: 12 I sent the *h* ahead of you, which

HORNS (HORN)

Ge 22: 13 he saw a ram caught by its *h*.
Ex 27: 2 so that the *h* and the altar are
29: 12 and put it on the *h* of the altar
30: 2 two cubits high—its *h* of one piece
30: 3 and all the sides and the *h*
30: 10 shall make atonement on its *h*.
37: 25 two cubits high—its *h* of one piece
37: 26 and all the sides and the *h*
38: 2 so that the *h* and the altar were
Lev 4: 7 of the blood on the *h* of the altar
4: 18 some of the blood on the *h*
4: 25 and put it on the *h* of the altar
4: 30 and put it on the *h* of the altar
4: 34 and put it on the *h* of the altar
8: 15 it on all the *h* of the altar
9: 9 and put it on the *h* of the altar;
16: 18 and put it on all the *h* of the altar.
Dt 33: 17 his *h* are the *h* of a wild ox,
Jos 6: 4 of rams' *h* in front of the ark.
1Ki 1: 50 and took hold of the *h* of the altar.
1: 51 and is clinging to the *h* of the altar.
2: 28 and took hold of the *h* of the altar.
22: 11 son of Kenaanah had made iron *h*
1Ch 15: 28 with the sounding of rams' *h*
2Ch 15: 14 and with trumpets and *h*.
18: 10 son of Kenaanah had made iron *h*,
Ps 22: 21 save me from the *h*
69: 31 more than a bull with its *h*
75: 4 the wicked, 'Do not lift up your *h*.
75: 5 Do not lift your *h* against heaven;
75: 10 I will cut off the *h* of all the wicked,

Ps 75:10 *h* of the righteous will be lifted up.
118:27 up to the *h* of the altar.
Jer 17:1 and on the *h* of their altars.
Eze 34:21 with your *h* until you have driven
43:15 and four *h* project upward
43:20 and put it on the four *h* of the altar
Da 7:7 the former beasts, and it had ten *h*.
7:8 three of the first *h* were uprooted
7:8 "While I was thinking about the *h*,
7:20 to know about the ten *h* on its head
7:24 ten *h* are ten kings who will come
8:3 One of the *h* was longer
8:3 before me was a ram with two *h*,
8:3 the canal, and the *h* were long.
8:7 the ram and shattering his two *h*.
8:8 its place four prominent *h* grew up
8:22 four *h* that replaced the one that
Am 3:14 the *h* of the altar will be cut off
Mic 4:13 for I will give you *h* of iron;
Zec 1:18 and there before me were four *h*!
1:19 "These are the *h* that scattered
1:21 and throw down these *h*
1:21 of the nations who lifted up their *h*
1:21 "These are the *h* that scattered
Rev 5:6 He had seven *h* and seven eyes,
9:13 from the *h* of the golden altar that
12:3 and ten *h* and seven crowns
13:1 He had ten *h* and seven heads,
13:1 with ten crowns on his *h*,
13:11 He had two *h* like a lamb,
17:3 and had seven heads and ten *h*.
17:7 has the seven heads and ten *h*.
17:12 ten *h* you saw are ten kings who
17:16 and the ten *h* you saw will hate

HORONAIM

2Sa 13:34 "I see men in the direction of *H*,
Isa 15:5 on the road to *H*
Jer 48:3 Listen to the cries from *H*,
48:5 on the road down to *H*
48:34 from Zoar as far as *H*

HORONITE

Ne 2:10 When Sanballat the *H*
2:19 But when Sanballat the *H*,
13:28 son-in-law to Sanballat the *H*.

HORRIBLE (HORROR)

Dt 7:15 on you the *h* diseases you knew
Jer 5:30 "A *h* and shocking thing
18:13 A most *h* thing has been done
23:14 I have seen something *h*:
Eze 26:21 I will bring you to a *h* end
27:36 you have come to a *h* end
28:19 you have come to a *h* end
Hos 6:10 I have seen a *h* thing

HORRIFIED (HORROR)

Jer 4:9 the priests will be *h*,
50:13 All who pass Babylon will be *h*

HORROR (HORRIBLE HORRIFIED)

Dt 28:25 a thing of *h* to all the kingdoms
28:37 You will become a thing of *h*
2Ch 29:8 them an object of dread and *h*
30:7 so that he made them an object of *h*
Job 18:20 men of the east are seized with *h*.
Ps 55:5 *h* has overwhelmed me.
Isa 21:4 has become a *h* to me.
Jer 2:12 and shudder with great *h*,"
8:21 I mourn, and *h* grips me.
25:9 make them an object of *h* and scorn
25:18 and an object of *h* and scorn
29:18 and an object of cursing and *h*,
42:18 will be an object of cursing and *h*,
44:12 become an object of cursing and *h*,
48:39 an object of *h* to all those
49:13 become a ruin and an object of *h*,
49:17 "Edom will become an object of *h*;
51:37 an object of *h* and scorn,
51:41 What a *h* Babylon will be
Eze 5:15 and an object of *h* to the nations
20:26 that I might fill them with *h*
27:35 their kings shudder with *h*
32:10 and their kings will shudder with *h*

HORSE (HORSE'S HORSEBACK HORSES HORSES' WAR-HORSES)

Ex 15:1 The *h* and its rider
15:21 The *h* and its rider
1Ki 10:29 and a *h* for a hundred and fifty.
20:25 *h* for *h* and chariot for chariot—
2Ki 14:20 He was brought back by *h*
2Ch 1:17 and a *h* for a hundred and fifty.
23:15 of the *H* Gate on the palace
25:28 He was brought back by *h*
Ne 3:28 Above the *H* Gate, the priests
Est 6:8 and a *h* the king has ridden,
6:9 and *h* be entrusted to one
6:9 on the *h* through the city streets,
6:10 "Get the robe and the *h* and do just
6:11 So Haman got the robe and the *h*.
Job 39:18 she laughs at *h* and rider.
39:19 "Do you give the *h* his strength
Ps 32:9 Do not be like the *h* or the mule,
33:17 A *h* is a vain hope for deliverance;
76:6 both *h* and chariot lie still.
147:10 not in the strength of the *h*,
Pr 21:31 The *h* is made ready for the day
26:3 A whip for the *h*, a halter
Isa 63:13 Like a *h* in open country,
Jer 8:6 like a *h* charging into battle.
31:40 as far as the corner of the *H* Gate,
51:21 with you I shatter *h* and rider,
Zec 1:8 before me was a man riding a red *h*
10:3 make them like a proud *h* in battle.
12:4 On that day I will strike every *h*
Rev 6:2 and there before me was a white *h*!
6:4 Come!" Then another *h* came out,
6:5 and there before me was a black *h*!
6:8 and there before me was a pale *h*!
19:11 and there before me was a white *h*,
19:19 war against the rider on the *h*
19:21 of the mouth of the rider on the *h*,

HORSE'S (HORSE)

Ge 49:17 that bites the *h* heels

HORSEBACK (HORSE)

1Ki 20:20 of Aram escaped on *h* with some
Est 6:11 him on *h* through the city streets,
Ecc 10:7 I have seen slaves on *h*,

HORSEMAN (HORSEMEN)

2Ki 9:17 "Get a *h*," Joram ordered.
9:18 The *h* rode off to meet Jehu
9:19 So the king sent out a second *h*
Am 2:15 and the *h* will not save his life

HORSEMEN (HORSEMAN)

Ge 50:9 and *h* also went up with him.
Ex 14:9 and chariots, *h* and troops—
14:17 through his chariots and his *h*.
14:18 Pharaoh, his chariots and his *h*."
14:23 and *h* followed them into the sea.
14:26 and their chariots and *h*."
14:28 and covered the chariots and *h*—
15:19 chariots and *h* went into the sea,
Jos 24:6 them with chariots and *h*
1Ki 20:20 on horseback with some of his *h*.
2Ki 2:12 The chariots and *h* of Israel!"
13:7 army of Jehoahaz except fifty *h*,
13:14 "The chariots and *h* of Israel!"
18:24 on Egypt for chariots and *h*?
2Ch 12:3 and sixty thousand *h*
16:8 numbers of chariots and *h*?
Ezr 8:22 and *h* to protect us from enemies
Isa 22:7 and *h* are posted at the city gates;
31:1 and in the great strength of their *h*,
36:9 on Egypt for chariots and *h*?
Jer 4:29 At the sound of *h* and archers
Eze 23:6 young men, and mounted *h*.
23:12 mounted *h*, all handsome young
26:7 chariots, with *h* and a great army.
38:4 your horses, your *h* fully armed,
Hos 1:7 *h*, but by the LORD their God."
Hab 1:8 their *h* come from afar.
Zec 10:5 they will fight and overthrow the *h*.
Ac 23:23 seventy *h* and two hundred

HORSES (HORSE)

Ge 47:17 food in exchange for their *h*,
Ex 9:3 on your *h* and donkeys and camels
14:9 all Pharaoh's *h* and chariots,
14:23 and all Pharaoh's *h* and chariots
15:19 When Pharaoh's *h*, chariots
Dt 11:4 did to the Egyptian army, to its *h*
17:16 not acquire great numbers of *h*
20:1 and see *h* and chariots and an army
Jos 11:4 a large number of *h* and chariots—
11:6 You are to hamstring their *h*
11:9 He hamstrung their *h* and burned
1Sa 8:11 serve with his chariots and *h*,
2Sa 8:4 but a hundred of the chariot *h*.
15:1 himself with a chariot and *h*
1Ki 1:5 So he got chariots and *h* ready,
4:26 chariot *h*, and twelve thousand *h*.
4:28 for the chariot *h* and the other *h*.
9:19 for his chariots and for his *h*—
10:25 and spices, and *h* and mules.
10:26 accumulated chariots and *h*;
10:26 chariots and twelve thousand *h*,
10:28 Solomon's *h* were imported
18:5 can find some grass to keep the *h*
20:1 by thirty-two kings with their *h*
20:21 overpowered the *h* and chariots
22:4 as your people, my *h* as your *h*."
2Ki 2:11 of fire and *h* of fire appeared
3:7 as your people, my *h* as your *h*."
5:9 So Naaman went with his *h*
6:14 Then he sent *h* and chariots
6:15 an army with *h* and chariots had
6:17 saw the hills full of *h* and chariots
7:6 to hear the sound of chariots and *h*
7:7 abandoned their tents and their *h*
7:10 only tethered *h* and donkeys,
7:13 five of the *h* that are left in the city.
7:14 selected two chariots with their *h*,
9:33 *h* as they trampled her underfoot.
10:2 and you have chariots and *h*,
11:16 place where the *h* enter the palace
18:23 I will give you two thousand *h*,
23:11 of the LORD the *h* that the kings
1Ch 18:4 but a hundred of the chariot *h*.
2Ch 1:14 accumulated chariots and *h*;
1:14 chariots and twelve thousand *h*,
1:16 Solomon's *h* were imported
8:6 for his chariots and for his *h*
9:24 and spices, and *h* and mules.
9:25 chariots, and twelve thousand *h*,
9:25 had four thousand stalls for *h*
9:28 Solomon's *h* were imported
Ezr 2:66 They had 736 *h*, 245 mules,
Ne 7:68 There were 736 *h*, 245 mules,
Est 8:10 who rode fast *h* especially bred
8:14 riding the royal *h*, raced out,
Ps 20:7 in chariots and some in *h*,
Isa 2:7 Their land is full of *h*;
21:7 chariots with teams of *h*,
21:9 with a team of *h*.
22:6 with her charioteers and *h*;
28:28 his *h* do not grind it.
30:16 You said, 'No, we will flee on *h*.'
30:16 'We will ride off on swift *h*.'
31:1 who rely on *h*,
31:3 their *h* are flesh and not spirit.
36:8 I will give you two thousand *h*,
43:17 who drew out the chariots and *h*,
66:20 on *h*, in chariots and wagons,
Jer 4:13 his *h* are swifter than eagles.
6:23 as they ride on their *h*;
8:16 The snorting of the enemy's *h*
12:5 how can you compete with *h*?
17:25 riding in chariots and on *h*,
22:4 riding in chariots and on *h*,
46:4 Harness the *h*,
46:9 Charge, O *h*!
50:37 A sword against her *h* and chariots
50:42 as they ride on their *h*;
51:27 send up *h* like a swarm of locusts.
Eze 17:15 his envoys to Egypt to get *h*
23:20 whose emission was like that of *h*.
23:23 men of high rank, all mounted on *h*
26:7 king of kings, with *h* and chariots,
26:10 His *h* will be so many that they will
26:10 tremble at the noise of the war *h*,
26:11 of his *h* will trample all your streets
27:14 Beth Togarmah exchanged work *h*,
27:14 *h* and mules for your merchandise.
38:4 your *h*, your horsemen fully armed
38:15 of them riding on *h*, a great horde,
39:20 my table you will eat your fill of *h*

Hos 1: 7 or battle, or by *h* and horsemen,
Joel 2: 4 They have the appearance of *h;*
Am 4: 10 along with your captured *h*.
6: 12 Do *h* run on the rocky crags?
Mic 5: 10 "I will destroy your *h*
Na 3: 2 galloping *h*
Hab 1: 8 Their *h* are swifter than leopards,
3: 8 the sea when you rode with your *h*
3: 15 You trampled the sea with your *h*,
Hag 2: 22 *h* and their riders will fall,
Zec 1: 8 him were red, brown and white *h*.
6: 2 The first chariot had red *h*,
6: 6 The one with the black *h* is going
6: 6 and the one with the dappled *h*
6: 6 with the white *h* toward the west,
6: 7 When the powerful *h* went out,
12: 4 I will blind all the *h* of the nations.
14: 15 A similar plague will strike the *h*
14: 20 inscribed on the bells of the *h*,
Jas 3: 3 bits into the mouths of *h*
Rev 9: 7 The locusts looked like *h* prepared
9: 9 was like the thundering of many *h*
9: 17 The *h* and riders I saw
9: 17 heads of the *h* resembled the heads
9: 19 The power of the *h* was
18: 13 cattle and sheep; *h* and carriages;
19: 14 riding on white *h* and dressed
19: 18 mighty men, of *h* and their riders,

HORSES' (HORSE)

Jdg 5: 22 Then thundered the *h'* hoofs—
Isa 5: 28 their *h'* hoofs seem like flint,
Rev 14: 20 as the *h'* bridles for a distance

HOSAH

Jos 19: 29 turned toward *H* and came out
1Ch 16: 38 and also *H*, were gatekeepers.
26: 10 *H* the Merarite had sons: Shimri
26: 11 and relatives of *H* were 13 in all.
26: 16 fell to Shuppim and *H*.

HOSANNA

Mt 21: 9 "*H* to the Son of David!" Blessed is
21: 9 name of the Lord!" "*H* in the highest!"
21: 15 "*H* to the Son of David," they
Mk 11: 9 those who followed shouted, "*H!*"
11: 10 kingdom of our father David!" "*H*
Jn 12: 13 went out to meet him, shouting, "*H!*"

HOSEA

Hos 1: 1 of the LORD that came to *H* son
1: 2 began to speak through *H*,
1: 4 Then the LORD said to *H*,
1: 6 Then the LORD said to *H*,
Ro 9: 25 from the Gentiles? As he says in *H:*

HOSHAIAH

Ne 12: 32 *H* and half the leaders
Jer 42: 1 of Kareah and Jezaniah son of *H*,
43: 2 Azariah son of *H* and Johanan son

HOSHAMA

1Ch 3: 18 Jekamiah, *H* and Nedabiah.

HOSHEA (JOSHUA)

Nu 13: 8 tribe of Ephraim, *H* son of Nun;
13: 16 (Moses gave *H* son
2Ki 15: 30 Then *H* son of Elah conspired
17: 1 *H* son of Elah became king
17: 3 of Assyria came up to attack *H*,
17: 4 Assyria discovered that *H* was
17: 6 In the ninth year of *H*, the king
18: 1 year of *H* son of Elah king
18: 9 year of *H* son of Elah king
18: 10 year of *H* king of Israel.
1Ch 27: 20 over the Ephraimites: *H* son
Ne 10: 23 Hanan, Anaiah, *H*, Hananiah,

HOSPITABLE (HOSPITALITY)

1Ti 3: 2 self-controlled, respectable, *h*,
Tit 1: 8 Rather he must be *h*, one who loves

HOSPITABLY (HOSPITALITY)

Ac 28: 7 and for three days entertained us *h*.

HOSPITALITY (HOSPITABLE HOSPITABLY)

Ro 12: 13 Practice *h*.
16: 23 whose *h* I and the whole church
1Ti 5: 10 as bringing up children, showing *h*,
1Pe 4: 9 Offer *h* to one another
3Jn : 8 therefore to show *h* to such men

HOST (HOSTS)

1Ki 22: 19 with all the *h* of heaven standing
2Ch 18: 18 with all the *h* of heaven standing
Ne 9: 6 heavens, and all their starry *h*,
Ps 33: 6 their starry *h* by the breath
Isa 34: 4 all the starry *h* will fall
40: 26 He who brings out the starry *h* one
Da 8: 10 grew until it reached the *h*
8: 10 of the starry *h* down to the earth
8: 11 as great as the Prince of the *h;*
8: 12 the *h* of the saints and the daily
8: 13 and of the *h* that will be trampled
Zep 1: 5 housetops to worship the starry *h*,
Lk 2: 13 of the heavenly *h* appeared
14: 9 the *h* who invited both
14: 10 so that when your *h* comes,
14: 12 said to his *h*, "When you give

HOSTAGES

2Ki 14: 14 took *h* and returned to Samaria.
2Ch 25: 24 with the palace treasures and the *h*,

HOSTILE (HOSTILITY)

Ge 26: 27 since you were *h* to me
Lev 26: 21 " 'If you remain *h* toward me
26: 23 but continue to be *h* toward me,
26: 24 I myself will be *h* toward you
26: 27 but continue to be *h* toward me,
26: 28 in my anger I will be *h* toward you,
26: 41 which made me *h* toward them
Nu 24: 8 They devour *h* nations
Jdg 6: 31 replied to the *h* crowd around him,
1Ki 11: 25 in Aram and was *h* toward Israel.
Isa 11: 13 nor Judah *h* toward Ephraim.
Ro 8: 7 the sinful mind is *h* to God.
1Th 2: 15 and are *h* to all men in their effort

HOSTILITY (HOSTILE)

Ge 16: 12 and he will live in *h*
25: 18 lived in *h* toward all their brothers.
49: 23 they shot at him with *h*.
Lev 26: 40 against me and their *h* toward me,
Nu 35: 21 or if in *h* he hits him with his fist
35: 22 if without *h* someone suddenly
2Ch 21: 16 aroused against Jehoram the *h*
Job 17: 2 my eyes must dwell on their *h*.
Ps 78: 49 his wrath, indignation and *h*—
Eze 25: 15 and with ancient *h* sought
35: 5 Because you harbored an ancient *h*
Hos 9: 7 and your *h* so great,
9: 8 and *h* in the house of his God.
Eph 2: 14 wall of *h*, by abolishing
2: 16 by which he put to death their *h*.

HOSTS (HOST)

2Ki 17: 16 bowed down to all the starry *h*,
21: 3 He bowed down to all the starry *h*
21: 5 he built altars to all the starry *h*.
23: 4 and Asherah and all the starry *h*.
23: 5 and to all the starry *h*.
2Ch 33: 3 He bowed down to all the starry *h*
33: 5 he built altars to all the starry *h*.
Ps 103: 21 the LORD, all his heavenly *h*,
148: 2 praise him, all his heavenly *h*.
Isa 45: 12 I marshaled their starry *h*.
Jer 19: 13 on the roofs to all the starry *h*

HOT (HOTTER)

Ge 36: 24 Anah who discovered the *h* springs
Ex 11: 8 Then Moses, *h* with anger,
16: 21 the sun grew *h*, it melted away.
1Sa 11: 9 'By the time the sun is *h* tomorrow,
14: 22 they joined the battle in *h* pursuit.
21: 6 and replaced by *h* bread
1Ki 19: 6 a cake of bread baked over *h* coals,
Ne 7: 3 not to be opened until the sun is *h*.
Job 15: 2 or fill his belly with the *h* east wind
Ps 39: 3 My heart grew *h* within me,
78: 49 against them his *h* anger,
Pr 6: 28 Can a man walk on *h* coals
La 5: 10 Our skin is *h* as an oven,
Eze 24: 11 till it becomes *h* and its copper
38: 18 my *h* anger will be aroused,
Da 3: 22 the furnace so *h* that the flames
Hos 7: 7 All of them are *h* as an oven;
Lk 12: 55 you say, 'It's going to be *h*,' and it is
1Ti 4: 2 have been seared as with a *h* iron.
Rev 3: 15 that you are neither cold nor *h*.
3: 16 you are lukewarm—neither *h*

HOT-TEMPERED (TEMPER)

Jdg 18: 25 or some *h* men will attack you,
Pr 15: 18 A *h* man stirs up dissension,
19: 19 A *h* man must pay the penalty;
22: 24 Do not make friends with a *h* man,
29: 22 and a *h* one commits many sins.

HOTHAM

1Ch 7: 32 and *H* and of their sister Shua.
11: 44 Jeiel the sons of *H* the Aroerite,

HOTHEADED (HEAD)

Pr 14: 16 but a fool is *h* and reckless.

HOTHIR

1Ch 25: 4 Mallothi, *H* and Mahazioth.
25: 28 12 the twenty-first to *H*, his sons

HOTTER (HOT)

Da 3: 19 the furnace heated seven times *h*

HOUND (HOUNDED)

Job 19: 28 "If you say, 'How we will *h* him,

HOUNDED (HOUND)

Ps 109: 16 but *h* to death the poor
Eze 36: 3 and *h* you from every side

HOUR (HOURS)

Ecc 9: 12 knows when his *h* will come:
Mt 6: 27 you by worrying can add a single *h*
8: 13 servant was healed at that very *h*.
15: 28 was healed from that very *h*.
20: 3 "About the third *h* he went out
20: 5 He went out again about the sixth *h*
20: 5 the ninth *h* and did the same thing.
20: 6 About the eleventh *h* he went out
20: 9 hired about the eleventh *h* came
20: 12 were hired last worked only one *h*,'
24: 36 No one knows about that day or *h*,
24: 44 the Son of Man will come at an *h*
24: 50 and at an *h* he is not aware of.
25: 13 you do not know the day or the *h*.
26: 40 watch with me for one *h?*"
26: 45 and resting? Look, the *h* is near,
27: 45 From the sixth *h* until the ninth
27: 45 until the ninth *h* darkness came
27: 46 About the ninth *h* Jesus cried out
Mk 13: 32 No one knows about that day or *h*,
14: 35 that if possible the *h* might pass
14: 37 you not keep watch for one *h?*
14: 41 Enough! The *h* has come.
15: 25 was the third *h* when they crucified
15: 33 At the sixth *h* darkness came
15: 33 the whole land until the ninth *h*.
15: 34 And at the ninth *h* Jesus cried out
Lk 12: 25 you by worrying can add a single *h*
12: 39 at what *h* the thief was coming,
12: 40 the Son of Man will come at an *h*
12: 46 and at an *h* he is not aware of.
22: 14 When the *h* came, Jesus
22: 53 is your *h*— when darkness reigns."
22: 59 About an *h* later another asserted,
23: 44 It was now about the sixth *h*,
23: 44 the whole land until the ninth *h*,
Jn 1: 39 It was about the tenth *h*.
4: 6 It was about the sixth *h*.
4: 52 him yesterday at the seventh *h*."
12: 23 The *h* has come for the Son of Man
12: 27 'Father, save me from this *h*'? No,
12: 27 for this very reason I came to this *h*
19: 14 Passover Week, about the sixth *h*.
Ac 10: 30 was in my house praying at this *h*,
16: 33 At that *h* of the night the jailer took
Ro 13: 11 The *h* has come for you to wake up
1Co 4: 11 To this very *h* we go hungry
15: 30 do we endanger ourselves every *h?*
1Jn 2: 18 Dear children, this is the last *h;*

1Ki 2:31 and my father's *h* of the guilt
2:33 and his descendants, his *h*
2:36 "Build yourself a *h* in Jerusalem
3:17 this woman and I live in the same *h*
3:18 there was no one in the *h*
8:43 may know that this *h* I have built
11:18 who gave Hadad a *h* and land
11:28 force of the *h* of Joseph.
12:16 Look after your own *h*, O David!"
12:19 in rebellion against the *h* of David
12:20 of Judah remained loyal to the *h*
12:21 he mustered the whole *h* of Judah
12:21 to make war against the *h* of Israel
12:23 to the whole *h* of Judah
12:26 will now likely revert to the *h*
13: 2 named Josiah will be born to the *h*
13:18 back with you to your *h*
13:19 and ate and drank in his *h*.
13:34 sin of the *h* of Jeroboam that led
14: 4 and went to Ahijah's *h* in Shiloh.
14: 8 away from the *h* of David
14:10 I will burn up the *h* of Jeroboam
14:10 disaster on the *h* of Jeroboam.
14:13 one in the *h* of Jeroboam
14:17 stepped over the threshold of the *h*,
15:27 Ahijah of the *h* of Issachar plotted
16: 3 and I will make your *h* like that
16: 3 to consume Baasha and his *h*,
16: 7 becoming like the *h* of Jeroboam—
16: 7 son of Hanani to Baasha and his *h*,
17:17 who owned the *h* became ill.
17:23 down from the room into the *h*.
20:31 kings of the *h* of Israel are merciful.
21:22 I will make your *h* like that
21:29 I will bring it on his *h* in the days
2Ki 4: 2 what do you have in your *h*?"
4:32 When Elisha reached the *h*,
5: 9 stopped at the door of Elisha's *h*.
5:24 and put them away in the *h*.
6:32 Now Elisha was sitting in his *h*,
7:17 when the king came down to his *h*.
8: 3 went to the king to beg for her *h*
8: 5 came to beg the king for her *h*
8:18 as the *h* of Ahab had done,
8:27 as the *h* of Ahab had done,
8:27 in the ways of the *h* of Ahab
9: 6 Jehu got up and went into the *h*.
9: 7 are to destroy the *h* of Ahab your
9: 8 The whole *h* of Ahab will perish.
9: 9 I will make the *h* of Ahab like
9: 9 like the *h* of Baasha son of Ahijah.
9: 9 of Ahab like the *h* of Jeroboam son
10: 1 in Samaria seventy sons of the *h*
10: 3 Then fight for your master's *h*."
10:10 against the *h* of Ahab will fail.
10:11 in Jezreel who remained of the *h*
10:30 and have done to the *h*
13: 6 from the sins of the *h* of Jeroboam,
15: 5 and he lived in a separate *h*.
17:21 away from the *h* of David,
19:30 Once more a remnant of the *h*
20: 1 Put your *h* in order, because you
21:13 used against the *h* of Ahab.
1Ch 2:55 the father of the *h* of Recab.
6:31 of the music in the *h* of the LORD
6:48 of the tabernacle, the *h* of God.
9:11 official in charge of the *h* of God;
9:13 for ministering in the *h* of God.
9:23 the gates of the *h* of the LORD—
9:23 the LORD—the *h* called the Tent.
9:26 and treasuries in the *h* of God.
9:27 stationed around the *h* of God,
10: 6 and all his *h* died together.
12:29 loyal to Saul's *h* until then;
13: 7 the ark of God from Abinadab's *h*
13:13 to the *h* of Obed-Edom the Gittite.
13:14 in his *h* for three months,
15:25 LORD from the *h* of Obed-Edom,
17: 4 the one to build me a *h* to dwell in.
17: 5 I have not dwelt in a *h*
17: 6 "Why have you not built me a *h*
17:10 you that the LORD will build a *h*
17:12 He is the one who will build a *h*
17:14 I will set him over my *h*
17:17 the future of the *h* of your servant.
17:23 and his *h* be established forever.
17:24 the *h* of your servant David will be
17:25 your servant that you will build a *h*
1Ch 17:27 to bless the *h* of your servant,
22: 1 "The *h* of the LORD God is
22: 2 stone for building the *h* of God.
22: 5 *h* to be built for the LORD should
22: 6 him to build a *h* for the LORD,
22: 7 heart to build a *h* for the Name
22: 8 not to build a *h* for my Name,
22:10 He is the one who will build a *h*
22:11 build the *h* of the LORD your God
23:28 of other duties at the *h* of God.
25: 6 for the ministry at the *h* of God.
26:20 of the treasuries of the *h* of God
28: 2 I had it in my heart to build a *h*
28: 3 not to build a *h* for my Name,
28: 4 from the *h* of Judah he chose my
28: 6 son is the one who will build my *h*
2Ch 6:33 may know that this *h* I have built
10:16 Look after your own *h*, O David!"
10:19 in rebellion against the *h* of David
11: 1 he mustered the *h* of Judah
21: 6 as the *h* of Ahab had done,
21: 7 willing to destroy the *h* of David.
21:13 members of your father's *h*,
21:13 prostitute themselves, just as the *h*
22: 3 in the ways of the *h* of Ahab,
22: 4 as the *h* of Ahab had done,
22: 7 anointed to destroy the *h* of Ahab.
22: 8 was executing judgment on the *h*
22: 9 one in the *h* of Ahaziah powerful
22:10 the whole royal family of the *h*
26:21 He lived in a separate *h*—
35:21 but the *h* with which I am at war.
Ezr 1: 5 and build the *h* of the LORD
2:68 arrived at the *h* of the LORD
2:68 toward the rebuilding of the *h*
3: 8 at the *h* of God in Jerusalem,
3: 8 the building of the *h* of the LORD.
3: 9 supervising those working on the *h*
3:11 because the foundation of the *h*
4:24 Thus the work on the *h* of God
5: 2 work to rebuild the *h* of God
5:13 a decree to rebuild this *h* of God.
5:14 and silver articles of the *h* of God,
5:15 And rebuild the *h* of God on its site
5:16 of the *h* of God in Jerusalem.
5:17 a decree to rebuild this *h* of God
6: 5 and silver articles of the *h* of God,
6: 5 are to be deposited in the *h* of God.
6: 7 and the Jewish elders rebuild this *h*
6: 8 in the construction of this *h* of God
6:11 And for this crime his *h* is
6:11 a beam is to be pulled from his *h*
6:16 of the *h* of God with joy.
6:17 For the dedication of this *h*
6:22 them in the work on the *h* of God,
7:24 or other workers at this *h* of God.
7:27 honor to the *h* of the LORD
8:17 to us for the *h* of our God.
8:25 donated for the *h* of our God.
8:29 chambers of the *h* of the LORD
8:30 out to be taken to the *h* of our God
8:33 in the *h* of our God,
8:36 to the people and to the *h* of God.
9: 9 life to rebuild the *h* of our God
10: 1 himself down before the *h* of God,
10: 6 withdrew from before the *h* of God
10: 9 in the square before the *h* of God,
Ne 1: 6 including myself and my father's *h*,
3:10 made repairs opposite his *h*,
3:16 as the artificial pool and the *H*
3:20 the angle to the entrance of the *h*
3:21 entrance of Eliashib's *h* to the end
3:23 made repairs beside his *h*.
3:23 made repairs in front of their *h*;
3:24 from Azariah's *h* to the angle
3:28 each in front of his own *h*.
3:29 Immer made repairs opposite his *h*.
3:31 far as the *h* of the temple servants
5:13 way may God shake out of his *h*
6:10 went to the *h* of Shemaiah son
6:10 "Let us meet in the *h* of God,
8:16 in the courts of the *h* of God
10:32 for the service of the *h* of our God:
10:33 the duties of the *h* of our God.
10:34 is to bring to the *h* of our God
10:35 responsibility for bringing to the *h*
10:36 of our flocks to the *h* of our God,
10:37 the storerooms of the *h* of our God,
Ne 10:38 of the tithes up to the *h* of our God,
10:39 "We will not neglect the *h*
11:11 supervisor in the *h* of God,
11:16 of the outside work of the *h* of God
11:22 for the service of the *h* of God.
12:37 and passed above the *h* of David
12:40 then took their places in the *h*
13: 4 the storerooms of the *h* of our God.
13: 7 room in the courts of the *h* of God.
13: 9 into them the equipment of the *h*
13:11 "Why is the *h* of God neglected?"
13:14 done for the *h* of my God
Est 4:13 you are in the king's *h* you alone
7: 8 while she is with me in the *h*?"
7: 9 feet high stands by Haman's *h*.
Job 1:13 wine at the oldest brother's *h*,
1:18 wine at the oldest brother's *h*,
1:19 struck the four corners of the *h*.
5: 3 but suddenly his *h* was cursed.
7:10 He will never come to his *h* again;
20:28 A flood will carry off his *h*,
21:28 'Where now is the great man's *h*,
27:18 *h* he builds is like a moth's cocoon,
29: 4 intimate friendship blessed my *h*,
29:18 "I thought, 'I will die in my own *h*,
42:11 came and ate with him in his *h*.
Ps 5: 7 will come into your *h*;
23: 6 I will dwell in the *h* of the LORD
26: 8 I love the *h* where you live,
27: 4 dwell in the *h* of the LORD
36: 8 on the abundance of your *h*;
42: 4 leading the procession to the *h*
45:10 your people and your father's *h*.
49:16 the splendor of his *h* increases;
52: 8 flourishing in the *h* of God;
55:14 with the throng at the *h* of God.
65: 4 with the good things of your *h*,
69: 9 for zeal for your *h* consumes me,
84: 4 are those who dwell in your *h*;
84:10 a doorkeeper in the *h* of my God
92:13 planted in the *h* of the LORD,
93: 5 holiness adorns your *h*
98: 3 his faithfulness to the *h* of Israel;
101: 2 I will walk in my *h*
101: 7 will dwell in my *h*;
112: 3 Wealth and riches are in his *h*,
114: 1 the *h* of Jacob from a people
115: 9 O *h* of Israel, trust in the LORD—
115:10 O *h* of Aaron, trust in the LORD—
115:12 He will bless the *h* of Israel,
115:12 he will bless the *h* of Aaron,
116:19 in the courts of the *h* of the LORD
118: 3 Let the *h* of Aaron say:
118:26 From the *h* of the LORD we bless
122: 1 "Let us go to the *h* of the LORD."
122: 5 the thrones of the *h* of David.
122: 9 For the sake of the *h*
127: 1 Unless the LORD builds the *h*,
128: 3 vine within your *h*;
132: 3 "I will not enter my *h*
134: 1 by night in the *h* of the LORD.
135: 2 in the courts of the *h* of our God.
135: 2 minister in the *h* of the LORD,
135:19 O *h* of Aaron, praise the LORD;
135:19 O *h* of Israel, praise the LORD;
135:20 O *h* of Levi, praise the LORD;
Pr 2:18 For her *h* leads down to death
3:33 on the *h* of the wicked,
4: 3 When I was a boy in my father's *h*,
5: 8 do not go near the door of her *h*,
5:10 your toil enrich another man's *h*.
6:31 it costs him all the wealth of his *h*.
7: 6 At the window of my *h*
7: 8 along in the direction of her *h*
7:27 Her *h* is a highway to the grave,
9: 1 Wisdom has built her *h*;
9:14 She sits at the door of her *h*,
12: 7 the *h* of the righteous stands firm.
14: 1 The wise woman builds her *h*,
14:11 *h* of the wicked will be destroyed,
15: 6 *h* of the righteous contains great
15:25 down the proud man's *h*
17: 1 than a *h* full of feasting, with strife.
17:13 evil will never leave his *h*.
21: 9 than share a *h* with a quarrelsome
21:12 of the *h* of the wicked
21:20 In the *h* of the wise are stores
24: 3 By wisdom a *h* is built,

Pr 24: 15 outlaw against a righteous man's *h*,
24: 27 after that, build your *h*.
25: 17 in your neighbor's *h*—
25: 24 than share a *h* with a quarrelsome
27: 10 go to your brother's *h*
Ecc 2: 7 slaves who were born in my *h*.
5: 1 steps when you go to the *h* of God.
7: 2 It is better to go to a *h* of mourning
7: 2 than to go to a *h* of feasting,
7: 4 of fools is in the *h* of pleasure.
7: 4 of the wise is in the *h* of mourning,
10: 18 if his hands are idle, the *h* leaks.
12: 3 when the keepers of the *h* tremble,
SS 1: 17 of our *h* are cedars;
3: 4 had brought him to my mother's *h*,
8: 2 and bring you to my mother's *h*—
8: 7 all the wealth of his *h* for love,
Isa 2: 3 to the *h* of the God of Jacob.
2: 5 Come, O *h* of Jacob,
2: 6 the *h* of Jacob.
3: 7 I have no food or clothing in my *h*;
5: 7 is the *h* of Israel,
5: 8 Woe to you who add *h* to *h*
7: 2 Now the *h* of David was told,
7: 13 "Hear now, you *h* of David!
7: 17 and on the *h* of your father a time
8: 17 from the *h* of Jacob.
10: 20 the survivors of the *h* of Jacob,
14: 1 and unite with the *h* of Jacob.
14: 2 *h* of Israel will possess the nations
16: 5 one from the *h* of David—
22: 18 you disgrace to your master's *h*!
22: 21 in Jerusalem and to the *h* of Judah.
22: 22 on his shoulder the key to the *h*
22: 23 seat of honor for the *h* of his father.
23: 1 and left without *h* or harbor.
24: 10 the entrance to every *h* is barred.
29: 22 redeemed Abraham, says to the *h*
31: 2 up against the *h* of the wicked,
37: 31 Once more a remnant of the *h*
38: 1 is what the LORD says: Put your *h*
38: 12 Like a shepherd's tent my *h*
46: 3 all you who remain of the *h*
46: 3 "Listen to me, O *h* of Jacob,
48: 1 "Listen to this, O *h* of Jacob,
56: 7 a *h* of prayer for all nations."
56: 7 and give them joy in my *h* of prayer
56: 7 for my *h* will be called
58: 1 and to the *h* of Jacob their sins.
63: 7 done for the *h* of Israel,
66: 1 Where is the *h* you will build
Jer 2: 4 all you clans of the *h* of Israel.
2: 4 of the LORD, O *h* of Jacob,
2: 26 so the *h* of Israel is disgraced—
3: 18 In those days the *h*
3: 18 of Judah will join the *h* of Israel,
3: 20 unfaithful to me, O *h* of Israel,"
5: 11 The *h* of Israel and the *h* of Judah
5: 15 O *h* of Israel," declares the LORD,
5: 20 "Announce this to the *h* of Jacob
7: 2 "Stand at the gate of the LORD's *h*
7: 10 and stand before me in this *h*,
7: 11 Has this *h*, which bears my Name,
7: 14 do to the *h* that bears my Name,
7: 30 idols in the *h* that bears my Name
9: 26 whole *h* of Israel is uncircumcised
10: 1 says to you, O *h* of Israel.
11: 10 Both the *h* of Israel and the *h*
11: 17 and the *h* of Judah have done evil
11: 17 because the *h* of Israel
12: 7 "I will forsake my *h*,
12: 14 and I will uproot the *h* of Judah
13: 11 and the whole *h* of Judah to me,'
13: 11 so I bound the whole *h* of Israel
16: 5 "Do not enter a *h* where there is
16: 8 do not enter a *h* where there is
17: 26 offerings to the *h* of the LORD.
18: 2 "Go down to the potter's *h*,
18: 3 So I went down to the potter's *h*,
18: 6 came to me: "O *h* of Israel,
18: 6 so are you in my hand, O *h* of Israel
20: 6 live in your *h* will go into exile
21: 11 say to the royal *h* of Judah,
21: 12 word of the LORD; O *h* of David,
26: 2 in the courtyard of the LORD's *h*
26: 2 to worship in the *h* of the LORD.
26: 6 then I will make this *h* like Shiloh
26: 7 words in the *h* of the LORD.

Jer 26: 9 Jeremiah in the *h* of the LORD.
26: 9 name that this *h* will be like
26: 10 of the New Gate of the LORD's *h*.
26: 10 palace to the *h* of the LORD
26: 12 me to prophesy against this *h*
27: 16 from the LORD's *h* will be brought
27: 18 remaining in the *h* of the LORD
27: 21 left in the *h* of the LORD
28: 1 said to me in the *h* of the LORD
28: 3 the LORD's *h* that
28: 5 standing in the *h* of the LORD.
28: 6 the articles of the LORD's *h*
29: 26 be in charge of the *h* of the LORD;
31: 27 the *h* of Judah with the offspring
31: 27 "when I will plant the *h* of Israel
31: 31 and with the *h* of Judah.
31: 31 covenant with the *h* of Israel
31: 33 with the *h* of Israel
32: 34 idols in the *h* that bears my Name
33: 11 offerings to the *h* of the LORD,
33: 14 gracious promise I made to the *h*
33: 14 of Israel and to the *h* of Judah.
33: 17 sit on the throne of the *h* of Israel,
34: 15 me in the *h* that bears my Name.
35: 2 rooms of the *h* of the LORD
35: 4 them into the *h* of the LORD,
36: 6 So you go to the *h* of the LORD
37: 15 and imprisoned in the *h*
37: 20 to the *h* of Jonathan the secretary,
38: 26 back to Jonathan's *h* to die there.' "
41: 5 with them to the *h* of the LORD.
48: 13 as the *h* of Israel was ashamed
51: 51 the holy places of the LORD's *h*."
La 2: 7 a shout in the *h* of the LORD
Eze 2: 5 for they are a rebellious *h*—
2: 6 though they are a rebellious *h*.
2: 8 Do not rebel like that rebellious *h*;
3: 1 then go and speak to the *h* of Israel
3: 4 go now to the *h* of Israel
3: 5 but to the *h* of Israel—not
3: 7 But the *h* of Israel is not willing
3: 7 for the whole *h* of Israel is
3: 9 though they are a rebellious *h*."
3: 17 made you a watchman for the *h*
3: 24 "Go, shut yourself inside your *h*.
3: 26 though they are a rebellious *h*.
3: 27 for they are a rebellious *h*.
4: 3 This will be a sign to the *h* of Israel.
4: 4 sin of the *h* of Israel upon yourself.
4: 5 days you will bear the sin of the *h*
4: 6 and bear the sin of the *h* of Judah.
5: 4 from there to the whole *h* of Israel.
6: 11 and detestable practices of the *h*
8: 1 while I was sitting in my *h*
8: 6 the utterly detestable things the *h*
8: 10 and all the idols of the *h* of Israel.
8: 11 them stood seventy elders of the *h*
8: 12 elders of the *h* of Israel are doing
8: 14 gate of the *h* of the LORD,
8: 16 court of the *h* of the LORD,
8: 17 Is it a trivial matter for the *h*
9: 9 "The sin of the *h* of Israel
10: 19 to the east gate of the LORD's *h*,
11: 1 me to the gate of the *h*
11: 5 That is what you are saying, O *h*
11: 15 and the whole *h* of Israel—
12: 3 though they are a rebellious *h*.
12: 6 a sign to the *h* of Israel."
12: 9 did not that rebellious *h*
12: 10 the whole *h* of Israel who are there
12: 25 For in your days, you rebellious *h*,
12: 27 Son of man, the *h* of Israel is saying
13: 5 wall to repair it for the *h* of Israel
13: 9 in the records of the *h* of Israel,
14: 6 "Therefore say to the *h* of Israel,
17: 2 and tell the *h* of Israel a parable.
17: 12 to this rebellious *h*, 'Do you not
18: 6 or look to the idols of the *h* of Israel
18: 15 or look to the idols of the *h* of Israel
18: 25 O *h* of Israel: Is my way unjust?
18: 29 Are my ways unjust, O *h* of Israel?
18: 29 Yet the *h* of Israel says, 'The way
18: 30 O *h* of Israel, I will judge you,
18: 31 Why will you die, O *h* of Israel?
20: 5 hand to the descendants of the *h*
20: 30 "Therefore say to the *h* of Israel:
20: 31 O *h* of Israel? As surely as I live,
20: 39 " 'As for you, O *h* of Israel,

Eze 20: 40 there in the land the entire *h*
20: 44 O *h* of Israel, declares
22: 18 the *h* of Israel has become dross
23: 39 That is what they did in my *h*.
24: 3 Tell this rebellious *h* a parable
24: 21 Say to the *h* of Israel, 'This is what
25: 8 the *h* of Judah has become like all
25: 12 Edom took revenge on the *h*
29: 6 a staff of reed for the *h* of Israel.
29: 21 I will make a horn grow for the *h*
33: 7 made you a watchman for the *h*
33: 10 "Son of man, say to the *h* of Israel,
33: 11 O *h* of Israel?' "Therefore,
33: 20 Yet, O *h* of Israel, you say,
34: 30 the *h* of Israel, are my people,
35: 15 of the *h* of Israel became desolate,
36: 10 even the whole *h* of Israel.
36: 21 which the *h* of Israel profaned
36: 22 It is not for your sake, O *h* of Israel,
36: 22 "Therefore say to the *h* of Israel,
36: 32 for your conduct, O *h* of Israel!
36: 37 yield to the plea of the *h* of Israel
37: 11 these bones are the whole *h*
37: 16 and all the *h* of Israel associated
39: 12 " 'For seven months the *h*
39: 22 From that day forward the *h*
39: 29 I will pour out my Spirit on the *h*
40: 4 Tell the *h* of Israel everything you
43: 7 *h* of Israel will never again defile
44: 6 Say to the rebellious *h* of Israel,
44: 6 of your detestable practices, O *h*
44: 12 made the *h* of Israel fall into sin,
45: 6 belong to the whole *h* of Israel.
45: 8 but will allow the *h* of Israel
45: 17 at all the appointed feasts of the *h*
45: 17 to make atonement for the *h*
Da 1: 2 and put in the treasure *h* of his god.
2: 17 Then Daniel returned to his *h*
Hos 1: 4 I will soon punish the *h* of Jehu
1: 6 I will no longer show love to the *h*
1: 7 Yet I will show love to the *h*
5: 1 Listen, O royal *h*!
6: 10 in the *h* of Israel.
8: 1 is over the *h* of the LORD
9: 8 and hostility in the *h* of his God.
9: 15 I will drive them out of my *h*.
11: 12 the *h* of Israel with deceit.
Joel 1: 9 are cut off from the *h* of the LORD
1: 13 withheld from the *h* of your God.
1: 14 to the *h* of the LORD your God,
1: 16 gladness from the *h* of our God?
3: 18 will flow out of the LORD's *h*
Am 1: 4 fire upon the *h* of Hazael
2: 8 In the *h* of their god
3: 13 and testify against the *h* of Jacob,"
3: 15 *h* along with the summer *h*;
5: 1 Hear this word, O *h* of Israel,
5: 4 is what the LORD says to the *h*
5: 6 or he will sweep through the *h*
5: 19 as though he entered his *h*
5: 25 years in the desert, O *h* of Israel?
6: 9 If ten men are left in one *h*,
6: 10 comes to carry them out of the *h*
6: 11 and he will smash the great *h*
6: 11 and the small *h* into bits.
6: 14 a nation against you, O *h* of Israel,
7: 9 rise against the *h* of Jeroboam."
7: 16 preaching against the *h* of Isaac.'
9: 8 the *h* of Jacob,"
9: 9 and I will shake the *h* of Israel
Ob : 17 and the *h* of Jacob
: 18 The *h* of Jacob will be a fire
: 18 and the *h* of Joseph a flame;
: 18 survivors from the *h* of Esau."
: 18 the *h* of Esau will be stubble,
Mic 1: 5 because of the sins of the *h* of Israel
2: 7 Should it be said, O *h* of Jacob:
3: 1 you rulers of the *h* of Israel.
3: 9 you leaders of the *h* of Jacob,
3: 9 you rulers of the *h* of Israel,
4: 2 to the *h* of the God of Jacob.
6: 10 Am I still to forget, O wicked *h*,
6: 16 and all the practices of Ahab's *h*,
Hab 2: 10 shaming your own *h* and forfeiting
Zep 2: 7 to the remnant of the *h* of Judah;
Hag 1: 2 for the LORD's *h* to be built.' "
1: 4 while this *h* remains a ruin?"
1: 8 bring down timber and build the *h*,

Hag 1: 9 each of you is busy with his own *h*.
1: 9 of my *h*, which remains a ruin,
1: 14 on the *h* of the LORD Almighty,
2: 3 'Who of you is left who saw this *h*
2: 7 and I will fill this *h* with glory,'
2: 9 of this present *h* will be greater
2: 9 than the glory of the former *h*,'
Zec 1: 16 and there my *h* will be rebuilt.
3: 7 then you will govern my *h*
5: 4 and it will enter the *h* of the thief
5: 4 and the *h* of him who swears falsely
5: 4 remain in his *h* and destroy it,
5: 11 of Babylonia to build a *h* for it.
6: 10 to the *h* of Josiah son of Zephaniah.
7: 3 of the *h* of the LORD Almighty
8: 9 for the *h* of the LORD Almighty,
9: 8 But I will defend my *h*
10: 3 care for his flock, the *h* of Judah,
10: 6 I will strengthen the *h* of Judah
10: 6 and save the *h* of Joseph.
11: 13 them into the *h* of the LORD
12: 4 eye over the *h* of Judah,
12: 7 so that the honor of the *h* of David
12: 8 and the *h* of David will be like God
12: 10 I will pour out on the *h* of David
12: 12 the clan of the *h* of David
12: 12 the clan of the *h* of Nathan
12: 13 the clan of the *h* of Levi
13: 1 a fountain will be opened to the *h*
13: 6 given at the *h* of my friends.'
14: 20 pots in the LORD's *h* will be like
14: 21 in the *h* of the LORD Almighty.
Mal 3: 10 that there may be food in my *h*.
Mt 2: 11 coming to the *h*, they saw the child
5: 15 it gives light to everyone in the *h*.
7: 24 is like a wise man who built his *h*
7: 25 winds blew and beat against that *h*;
7: 26 is like a foolish man who built his *h*
7: 27 winds blew and beat against that *h*,
8: 14 When Jesus came into Peter's *h*,
9: 10 was having dinner at Matthew's *h*,
9: 23 When Jesus entered the ruler's *h*
10: 11 and stay at his *h* until you leave.
10: 25 of the *h* has been called Beelzebub,
12: 4 He entered the *h* of God, and he
12: 29 can anyone enter a strong man's *h*
12: 29 strong man? Then he can rob his *h*.
12: 44 'I will return to the *h* I left.'
12: 44 it arrives, it finds the *h* unoccupied,
13: 1 same day Jesus went out of the *h*
13: 36 left the crowd and went into the *h*.
13: 52 the owner of a *h* who brings out
13: 57 and in his own *h* is a prophet
17: 25 When Peter came into the *h*,
21: 13 My *h* will be called a *h* of prayer,'
23: 38 Look, your *h* is left to you desolate.
24: 17 down to take anything out of the *h*.
24: 17 one on the roof of his *h* go
24: 43 If the owner of the *h* had known
24: 43 would not have let his *h* be broken
26: 18 with my disciples at your *h*.' "
Mk 1: 35 left the *h* and went
2: 15 was having dinner at Levi's *h*,
2: 26 he entered the *h* of God
3: 20 Then Jesus entered a *h*,
3: 25 If a *h* is divided against itself,
3: 25 against itself, that *h* cannot stand.
3: 27 Then he can rob his *h*.
3: 27 no one can enter a strong man's *h*
5: 35 came from the *h* of Jairus,
6: 4 and in his own *h* is a prophet
6: 10 Whenever you enter a *h*, stay there
7: 17 left the crowd and entered the *h*,
7: 24 He entered a *h* and did not want
9: 33 was in the *h*, he asked them,
10: 10 When they were in the *h* again,
11: 17 a *h* of prayer for all nations'?
11: 17 " 'My *h* will be called
13: 15 one on the roof of his *h* go down
13: 15 or enter the *h* to take anything out.
13: 34 He leaves his *h* in charge
13: 35 owner of the *h* will come back—
14: 14 Say to the owner of the *h* he enters,
Lk 1: 33 reign over the *h* of Jacob forever;
1: 69 us in the *h* of his servant David
2: 4 he belonged to the *h* and line
2: 49 had to be in my Father's *h*?"
5: 18 to take him into the *h* to lay him
Lk 5: 29 a great banquet for Jesus at his *h*,
6: 4 He entered the *h* of God,
6: 48 He is like a man building a *h*,
6: 48 the torrent struck that *h*
6: 49 moment the torrent struck that *h*,
6: 49 practice is like a man who built a *h*
7: 6 from the *h* when the centurion sent
7: 10 had been sent returned to the *h*
7: 36 so he went to the Pharisee's *h*
7: 37 eating at the Pharisee's *h*,
7: 44 this woman? I came into your *h*.
8: 27 not worn clothes or lived in a *h*,
8: 41 pleading with him to come to his *h*
8: 49 someone came from the *h* of Jairus,
8: 51 When he arrived at the *h* of Jairus,
9: 4 Whatever *h* you enter, stay there
10: 5 enter a *h*, first say, 'Peace to this *h*.'
10: 7 Do not move around from *h* to *h*.
10: 7 Stay in that *h*, eating and drinking
11: 17 a *h* divided against itself will fall.
11: 21 guards his own *h*, his possessions
11: 24 'I will return to the *h* I left.'
11: 25 it finds the *h* swept clean
12: 39 If the owner of the *h* had known
12: 39 would not have let his *h* be broken
13: 25 Once the owner of the *h* gets up
13: 35 Look, your *h* is left to you desolate.
14: 1 in the *h* of a prominent Pharisee,
14: 21 the owner of the *h* became angry
14: 23 come in, so that my *h* will be full.
15: 8 sweep the *h* and search carefully
15: 25 When he came near the *h*,
16: 27 send Lazarus to my father's *h*,
17: 31 is on the roof of his *h*,
19: 5 I must stay at your *h* today."
19: 9 Today salvation has come to this *h*,
19: 46 " 'My *h* will be a *h* of prayer';
22: 10 Follow him to the *h* that he enters,
22: 11 and say to the owner of the *h*,
22: 54 and took him into the *h*
Jn 2: 16 How dare you turn my Father's *h*
2: 17 "Zeal for your *h* will consume me."
11: 31 been with Mary in the *h*,
12: 3 the *h* was filled with the fragrance
14: 2 In my Father's *h* are many rooms;
20: 26 his disciples were in the *h* again,
Ac 2: 2 filled the whole *h* where they were
5: 42 the temple courts and from *h* to *h*,
7: 20 cared for in his father's *h*.
7: 42 years in the desert, O *h* of Israel?
7: 47 But it was Solomon who built the *h*
7: 49 What kind of *h* will you build
8: 3 Going from *h* to *h*, he dragged
9: 11 "Go to the *h* of Judas
9: 17 Then Ananias went to the *h*
10: 6 with Simon the tanner, whose *h* is
10: 17 found out where Simon's *h* was
10: 22 him to have you come to his *h*
10: 23 the men into the *h* to be his guests.
10: 25 Peter entered the *h*, Cornelius met
10: 30 was in my *h* praying at this hour,
11: 3 into the *h* of uncircumcised men
11: 11 at the *h* where I was staying.
11: 12 and we entered the man's *h*.
11: 13 had seen an angel appear in his *h*
12: 12 went to the *h* of Mary the mother
16: 15 she said, "come and stay at my *h*."
16: 32 and to all the others in his *h*.
16: 34 The jailer brought them into his *h*
16: 40 went to Lydia's *h*, where they met
17: 5 They rushed to Jason's *h* in search
17: 7 has welcomed them into his *h*.
18: 7 went next door to the *h* of Titius
19: 16 that they ran out of the *h* naked
20: 20 you publicly and from *h* to *h*.
21: 8 at the *h* of Philip the evangelist,
28: 30 there in his own rented *h*
Ro 16: 5 the church that meets at their *h*.
1Co 16: 19 the church that meets at their *h*.
2Co 5: 1 an eternal *h* in heaven, not built
Col 4: 15 to Nympha and the church in her *h*
1Ti 5: 13 and going about from *h* to *h*.
2Ti 2: 20 In a large *h* there are articles not
Heb 3: 2 Moses was faithful in all God's *h*.
3: 3 has greater honor than the *h* itself.
3: 3 the builder of a *h* has greater honor
3: 4 For every *h* is built by someone,
3: 5 as a servant in all God's *h*,
Heb 3: 6 And we are his *h*, if we hold
3: 6 is faithful as a son over God's *h*.
8: 8 and with the *h* of Judah.
8: 8 covenant with the *h* of Israel
8: 10 with the *h* of Israel
10: 21 priest over the *h* of God,
1Pe 2: 5 built into a spiritual *h* to be a holy
2Jn : 10 do not take him into your *h*

HOUSEHOLD (HOUSE)

Ge 12: 1 your people and your father's *h*
12: 17 his *h* because of Abram's wife Sarai
14: 14 the 318 trained men born in his *h*
15: 3 so a servant in my *h* will be my heir
17: 12 including those born in your *h*
17: 13 Whether born in your *h*
17: 23 all those born in his *h* or bought
17: 23 in his *h*, and circumcised them,
17: 27 And every male in Abraham's *h*,
17: 27 including those born in his *h*
18: 19 and his *h* after him to keep the way
20: 13 wander from my father's *h*,
20: 18 up every womb in Abimelech's *h*
24: 2 He said to the chief servant in his *h*
24: 7 brought me out of my father's *h*
24: 28 and told her mother's *h* about these
30: 30 I do something for my own *h*?"
31: 19 Rachel stole her father's *h* gods.
31: 34 Now Rachel had taken the *h* gods
31: 35 but could not find the *h* gods.
31: 37 you found that belongs to your *h*?
31: 41 for the twenty years I was in your *h*
34: 19 honored of all his father's *h*,
34: 30 I and my *h* will be destroyed."
35: 2 So Jacob said to his *h*
36: 6 and all the members of his *h*,
39: 4 Potiphar put him in charge of his *h*,
39: 5 the LORD blessed the *h*
39: 5 time he put him in charge of his *h*
39: 11 none of the *h* servants was inside.
39: 14 house, she called her *h* servants.
41: 51 my trouble and all my father's *h*."
45: 2 and Pharaoh's *h* heard about it.
45: 8 lord of his entire *h* and ruler
45: 11 Otherwise you and your *h*
46: 31 'My brothers and my father's *h*,
46: 31 to his brothers and to his father's *h*,
47: 12 and all his father's *h* with food,
50: 8 all the members of Joseph's *h*
50: 8 those belonging to his father's *h*.
Ex 12: 3 lamb for his family, one for each *h*.
12: 4 If any *h* is too small
12: 48 the males in his *h* circumcised;
23: 12 and the slave born in your *h*,
Lev 16: 6 atonement for himself and his *h*.
16: 11 atonement for himself and his *h*,
16: 17 his *h* and the whole community
22: 11 or if a slave is born in his *h*,
Nu 18: 11 in your *h* who is ceremonially
18: 13 in your *h* who is ceremonially
Dt 6: 22 and Pharaoh and his whole *h*.
14: 26 and your *h* shall eat there
26: 11 given to you and your *h*.
Jos 24: 15 my *h*, we will serve the LORD."
Jdg 14: 15 and your father's *h* to death.
18: 14 other *h* gods, a carved image
18: 17 the other *h* gods and the cast idol
18: 18 the other *h* gods and the cast idol,
18: 19 priest rather than just one man's *h*
18: 20 other *h* gods and the carved image
1Sa 22: 1 and his father's *h* heard about it,
22: 14 and highly respected in your *h*?
25: 6 Good health to you and your *h*!
25: 17 over our master and his whole *h*.
2Sa 6: 11 blessed him and his entire *h*.
6: 12 "The LORD has blessed the *h*
6: 20 returned home to bless his *h*,
9: 2 a servant of Saul's *h* named Ziba.
9: 12 members of Ziba's *h* were servants
12: 11 'Out of your own *h* I am going
12: 17 elders of his *h* stood beside him
15: 16 with his entire *h* following him;
16: 2 are for the king's *h* to ride on,
16: 8 for all the blood you shed in the *h*
19: 17 with Ziba, the steward of Saul's *h*,
19: 18 at the ford to take the king's *h* over
19: 41 and his *h* across the Jordan,
1Ki 4: 7 for the king and the royal *h*.

1Ki 5: 9 by providing food for my royal *h*.''
5: 11 cors of wheat as food for his *h*,
10: 21 and all the *h* articles in the Palace
2Ki 23: 24 mediums and spiritists, the *h* gods,
1Ch 13: 14 and the LORD blessed his *h*
2Ch 9: 20 and all the *h* articles in the Palace
Ne 13: 8 and threw all Tobiah's *h* goods out
Est 1: 22 should be ruler over his own *h*.
Job 1: 10 and his *h* and everything he has?
16: 7 you have devastated my entire *h*.
31: 31 if the men of my *h* have never said,
Ps 105: 21 He made him master of his *h*,
Pr 31: 21 it snows, she has no fear for her *h*;
31: 27 over the affairs of her *h*
Jer 23: 34 I will punish that man and his *h*.
Eze 44: 30 that a blessing may rest on your *h*.
Mic 7: 6 are the members of his own *h*.
Mt 10: 25 much more the members of his *h*!
10: 36 will be the members of his own *h*.'
12: 25 or *h* divided against itself will not
24: 45 charge of the servants in his *h*
Lk 8: 3 the manager of Herod's *h*; Susanna
Jn 4: 53 So he and all his *h* believed.
Ac 11: 14 and all your *h* will be saved.'
16: 15 members of her *h* were baptized,
16: 31 you will be saved—you and your *h*
18: 8 his entire *h* believed in the Lord;
Ro 16: 10 belong to the *h* of Aristobulus.
16: 11 Greet those in the *h*
1Co 1: 11 from Chloe's *h* have informed me
1: 16 I also baptized the *h* of Stephanas;
16: 15 You know that the *h*
Eph 2: 19 people and members of God's *h*,
Php 4: 22 those who belong to Caesar's *h*.
1Ti 3: 12 manage his children and his *h* well.
3: 15 to conduct themselves in God's *h*,
2Ti 1: 16 mercy to the *h* of Onesiphorus,
4: 19 Aquila and the *h* of Onesiphorus.

HOUSEHOLDS (HOUSE)

Ge 42: 19 take grain back for your starving *h*.
42: 33 and take food for your starving *h*
47: 24 and your *h* and your children.''
Nu 16: 32 with their *h* and all Korah's men
18: 31 and your *h* may eat the rest
Dt 11: 6 swallowed them up with their *h*,
Tit 1: 11 because they are ruining whole *h*

HOUSES (HOUSE)

Ge 34: 29 as plunder everything in the *h*.
Ex 8: 3 into the *h* of your officials
8: 9 and your *h* may be rid of the frogs,
8: 11 The frogs will leave you and your *h*
8: 13 died in the *h*, in the courtyards
8: 21 The *h* of the Egyptians will be full
8: 21 on your people and into your *h*.
8: 24 and into the *h* of his officials,
10: 6 They will fill your *h* and those
12: 7 of the *h* where they eat the lambs
12: 13 for you on the *h* where you are;
12: 15 day remove the yeast from your *h*,
12: 19 is to be found in your *h*.
12: 23 the destroyer to enter your *h*
12: 27 passed over the *h* of the Israelites
Lev 25: 31 But *h* in villages without walls
25: 32 to redeem their *h* in the Levitical
25: 33 because the *h* in the towns
Dt 6: 9 them on the doorframes of your *h*
6: 11 *h* filled with all kinds
8: 12 when you build fine *h* and settle
11: 20 them on the doorframes of your *h*
19: 1 and settled in their towns and *h*,
Jdg 18: 14 one of these *h* has an ephod,
1Ki 20: 6 and the *h* of your officials.
2Ki 25: 9 and all the *h* of Jerusalem.
Ne 5: 11 vineyards, olive groves and *h*,
7: 3 and some near their own *h*.''
7: 4 and the *h* had not yet been rebuilt.
9: 25 they took possession of *h* filled
Job 3: 15 who filled their *h* with silver.
4: 19 much more those who live in *h*
15: 28 and *h* where no one lives,
15: 28 *h* crumbling to rubble.
20: 19 he has seized *h* he did not build.
22: 18 Yet it was he who filled their *h*
24: 16 In the dark, men break into *h*,
Ps 49: 11 tombs will remain their *h* forever,
Pr 1: 13 and fill our *h* with plunder;
Pr 19: 14 *H* and wealth are inherited
Ecc 2: 4 I built *h* for myself and planted
Isa 3: 14 plunder from the poor is in your *h*.
5: 9 "Surely the great *h* will become
6: 11 until the *h* are left deserted
8: 14 but for both *h* of Israel he will be
13: 16 their *h* will be looted and their
13: 21 jackals will fill her *h*;
22: 10 tore down *h* to strengthen the wall.
32: 13 yes, mourn for all *h* of merriment
65: 21 They will build *h* and dwell in them
65: 22 No longer will they build *h*
Jer 5: 7 and thronged to the *h* of prostitutes
5: 27 their *h* are full of deceit;
6: 12 Their *h* will be turned
9: 19 because our *h* are in ruins.' ''
17: 22 Do not bring a load out of your *h*
18: 22 Let a cry be heard from their *h*
19: 13 The *h* in Jerusalem and those
19: 13 all the *h* where they burned
29: 5 "Build *h* and settle
29: 28 Therefore build *h* and settle down;
32: 15 the God of Israel, says: *H*,
32: 29 along with the *h* where the people
33: 4 says about the *h* in this city
35: 7 Also you must never build *h*,
35: 9 built *h* to live in or had vineyards,
39: 8 fire to the royal palace and the *h*
52: 13 and all the *h* of Jerusalem.
Eze 7: 24 to take possession of their *h*;
11: 3 'Will it not soon be time to build *h*?
16: 41 They will burn down your *h*
23: 47 daughters and burn down their *h*.
26: 12 demolish your fine *h* and throw
28: 26 will build *h* and plant vineyards;
33: 30 and at the doors of the *h*,
45: 4 It will be a place for their *h* as well
48: 15 the common use of the city, for *h*
Da 2: 5 your *h* turned into piles of rubble.
3: 29 and their *h* be turned into piles
Hos 7: 1 thieves break into *h*,
Joel 2: 9 They climb into the *h*;
Am 3: 15 the *h* adorned with ivory will be
Mic 2: 2 and *h*, and take them.
Zep 1: 13 They will build *h*
1: 13 their *h* demolished.
2: 7 down in the *h* of Ashkelon.
Hag 1: 4 to be living in your paneled *h*,
Zec 14: 2 the *h* ransacked, and the women
Mt 19: 29 everyone who has left *h* or brothers
Mk 12: 40 They devour widows' *h*
Lk 16: 4 will welcome me into their *h*.'
20: 47 They devour widows' *h*
Ac 4: 34 who owned lands or *h* sold them,
7: 48 live in *h* made by men

HOUSETOP (HOUSE)

Ps 102: 7 like a bird alone on a *h*.

HOUSETOPS (HOUSE)

2Ki 19: 26 like grass sprouting on the *h*,
Ps 129: 6 May they be like grass on the *h*,
Isa 22: 1 that you have all gone up on the *h*,
37: 27 like grass sprouting on the *h*,
Jer 48: 38 On all the *h* in Moab
Zep 1: 5 those who bow down on the *h*
Mt 10: 27 in your ear, proclaim from the *h*.
Lk 12: 3 will be proclaimed from the *h*.

HOVERING (HOVERS)

Ge 1: 2 of God was *h* over the waters.
Isa 31: 5 Like birds *h* overhead,

HOVERS (HOVERING)

Dt 32: 11 and *h* over its young,

HOWL (HOWLING)

Ps 59: 15 and *h* if not satisfied.
Isa 13: 22 Hyenas will *h* in her strongholds,
14: 31 Wail, O gate! *H*, O city!
Mic 1: 8 I will *h* like a jackal

HOWLING (HOWL)

Dt 32: 10 in a barren and *h* waste.

HUBBAH

1Ch 7: 34 Ahi, Rohgah, *H* and Aram.

HUBS

1Ki 7: 33 spokes and *h* were all of cast metal.

HUDDLED

Job 30: 7 and *h* in the underbrush.

HUG

Job 24: 8 and *h* the rocks for lack of shelter.

HUGE

Ge 41: 49 Joseph stored up *h* quantities
Jos 11: 4 a *h* army, as numerous
2Sa 21: 20 there was a *h* man with six fingers
23: 21 And he struck down a *h* Egyptian.
1Ch 20: 6 there was a *h* man with six fingers
2Ch 16: 14 and they made a *h* fire in his honor.
Ecc 9: 14 and built *h* siegeworks against it.
Da 2: 35 the statue became a *h* mountain
11: 13 with a *h* army fully equipped.
Mt 12: 40 three nights in the belly of a *h* fish,
Rev 8: 8 and something like a *h* mountain,
16: 21 From the sky *h* hailstones

HUKKOK

Jos 19: 34 and came out at *H*.

HUKOK

1Ch 6: 75 *H* and Rehob, together

HUL

Ge 10: 23 Uz, *H*, Gether and Meshech.
1Ch 1: 17 Uz, *H*, Gether and Meshech.

HULDAH

2Ki 22: 14 went to speak to the prophetess *H*,
2Ch 34: 22 went to speak to the prophetess *H*,

HUMAN (HUMANITY)

Lev 5: 3 " 'Or if he touches *h* uncleanness—
7: 21 whether *h* uncleanness
24: 17 If anyone takes the life of a *h* being,
Nu 19: 16 or anyone who touches a *h* bone
19: 18 anyone who has touched a *h* bone
1Ki 13: 2 and *h* bones will be burned on you
2Ki 23: 14 and covered the sites with *h* bones.
23: 20 and burned *h* bones on them.
Job 34: 20 are removed without *h* hand.
Ps 73: 5 they are not plagued by *h* ills.
Isa 37: 19 and stone, fashioned by *h* hands.
52: 14 his form marred beyond *h* likeness
Eze 4: 12 using *h* excrement for fuel.''
4: 15 manure instead of *h* excrement.''
39: 15 and one of them sees a *h* bone,
Da 2: 34 was cut out, but not by *h* hands.
2: 45 not by *h* hands—a rock that broke
5: 5 the fingers of a *h* hand appeared
8: 25 be destroyed, but not by *h* power.
Hos 11: 4 I led them with cords of *h* kindness
13: 2 "They offer *h* sacrifice
Jn 1: 13 of *h* decision or a husband's will,
5: 34 Not that I accept *h* testimony;
8: 15 You judge by *h* standards;
Ac 5: 38 purpose or activity is of *h* origin,
14: 11 come down to us in *h* form!''
14: 15 We too are only men, *h* like you.
17: 25 And he is not served by *h* hands,
Ro 1: 3 as to his *h* nature was a descendant
2: 9 for every *h* being who does evil:
3: 5 (I am using a *h* argument.)
6: 19 in *h* terms because you are weak
9: 5 from them is traced the *h* ancestry
1Co 1: 17 not with words of *h* wisdom,
1: 26 of you were wise by *h* standards;
2: 13 not in words taught us by *h* wisdom
4: 3 judged by you or by any *h* court;
9: 8 merely from a *h* point of view?
15: 32 in Ephesus for merely *h* reasons,
2Co 3: 3 of stone but on tablets of *h* hearts.
5: 1 in heaven, not built by *h* hands.
Gal 3: 3 to attain your goal by *h* effort?
3: 15 to a *h* covenant that has been duly
Php 2: 7 being made in *h* likeness.
Col 2: 8 which depends on *h* tradition
2: 22 they are based on *h* commands
Heb 12: 9 have all had *h* fathers who
1Pe 4: 2 of his earthly life for evil *h* desires,
2Pe 2: 18 lustful desires of sinful *h* nature,
Rev 9: 7 and their faces resembled *h* faces.

HUMANITY (HUMAN)

Heb 2:14 he too shared in their *h* so that

HUMBLE (HUMBLED HUMBLES HUMILITY)

Ex 10: 3 refuse to *h* yourself before me?
Nu 12: 3 more *h* than anyone else
12: 3 (Now Moses was a very *h* man,
Dt 8: 2 to *h* you and to test you in order
8:16 to *h* and to test you so that
2Sa 22:28 You save the *h*,
1Ki 11:39 I will *h* David's descendants
2Ch 7:14 will *h* themselves and pray
33:23 he did not *h* himself
36:12 did not *h* himself before Jeremiah
Ezr 8:21 so that we might *h* ourselves
Job 8: 7 Your beginnings will seem *h*,
40:12 look at every proud man and *h* him
Ps 18:27 You save the *h*
25: 9 He guides the *h* in what is right
147: 6 The LORD sustains the *h*
149: 4 he crowns the *h* with salvation.
Pr 3:34 but gives grace to the *h*.
6: 3 Go and *h* yourself;
Isa 13:11 and will *h* the pride of the ruthless.
23: 9 and to *h* all who are renowned
29:19 Once more the *h* will rejoice
58: 5 only a day for a man to *h* himself?
66: 2 he who is *h* and contrite in spirit,
Da 4:37 walk in pride he is able to *h*.
5:19 those he wanted to *h*, he humbled.
10:12 and to *h* yourself before your God,
Zep 2: 3 Seek the LORD, all you *h*
3:12 the meek and *h*,
Mt 11:29 for I am gentle and *h* in heart,
Lk 1:48 of the *h* state of his servant.
1:52 but has lifted up the *h*.
2Co 12:21 I come again my God will *h* me
Eph 4: 2 Be completely *h* and gentle;
Jas 1: 9 brother in *h* circumstances ought
4: 6 but gives grace to the *h*."
4:10 *H* yourselves before the Lord,
1Pe 3: 8 brothers, be compassionate and *h*.
5: 5 but gives grace to the *h*."
5: 6 *H* yourselves,

HUMBLED (HUMBLE)

Lev 26:41 their uncircumcised hearts are *h*
Dt 8: 3 He *h* you, causing you to hunger
1Ki 21:29 Because he has *h* himself, I will not
21:29 noticed how Ahab has *h* himself
2Ki 22:19 you *h* yourself before the LORD
2Ch 12: 6 and the king *h* themselves and said,
12: 7 LORD saw that they *h* themselves,
12: 7 "Since they have *h* themselves,
12:12 Because Rehoboam *h* himself,
28:19 The LORD had *h* Judah
30:11 and Zebulun *h* themselves
33:12 *h* himself greatly before the God
33:19 and idols before he *h* himself—
34:27 and you *h* yourself before God
34:27 because you *h* yourself before me
Ps 35:13 and *h* myself with fasting.
44: 9 But now you have rejected and *h* us
68:30 *H*, may it bring bars of silver.
107:39 decreased, and they were *h*
Isa 2: 9 and mankind *h*—
2:11 eyes of the arrogant man will be *h*
2:12 (and they will be *h*),
2:17 and the pride of men *h*;
5:15 and mankind *h*,
5:15 the eyes of the arrogant *h*.
9: 1 In the past he *h* the land of Zebulun
58: 3 Why have we *h* ourselves,
Jer 44:10 day they have not *h* themselves
Da 5:19 those he wanted to humble, he *h*.
5:22 O Belshazzar, have not *h* yourself,
Mt 23:12 whoever exalts himself will be *h*,
Lk 14:11 who exalts himself will be *h*,
18:14 who exalts himself will be *h*,
Php 2: 8 he *h* himself

HUMBLES (HUMBLE)

1Sa 2: 7 he *h* and he exalts.
Isa 26: 5 He *h* those who dwell on high,
Mt 18: 4 whoever *h* himself like this child is
Mt 23:12 whoever *h* himself will be exalted.
Lk 14:11 he who *h* himself will be exalted."
18:14 he who *h* himself will be exalted."

HUMILIATE (HUMILATED HUMILIATION)

Pr 25: 7 than for him to *h* you
1Co 11:22 and *h* those who have nothing?

HUMILIATED (HUMILIATE)

2Sa 6:22 and I will be *h* in my own eyes.
10: 5 for they were greatly *h*.
19: 5 "Today you have *h* all your men,
1Ch 19: 5 for they were greatly *h*.
Isa 54: 4 not fear disgrace; you will not be *h*.
Jer 15: 9 she will be disgraced and *h*.
31:19 I was ashamed and *h*
Mal 2: 9 and *h* before all the people,
Lk 13:17 said this, all his opponents were *h*,
14: 9 *h*, you will have to take the least

HUMILIATION (HUMILIATE)

Ezr 9: 7 and *h* at the hand of foreign kings,
Job 19: 5 and use my *h* against me,
Eze 16:63 your mouth because of your *h*,
Ac 8:33 In his *h* he was deprived of justice.

HUMILITY (HUMBLE)

Ps 45: 4 of truth, *h* and righteousness;
Pr 11: 2 but with *h* comes wisdom.
15:33 and *h* comes before honor.
18:12 but *h* comes before honor.
22: 4 *H* and the fear of the LORD
Zep 2: 3 Seek righteousness, seek *h*;
Ac 20:19 I served the Lord with great *h*
Php 2: 3 but in *h* consider others better
Col 2:18 let anyone who delights in false *h*
2:23 their false *h* and their harsh
3:12 *h*, gentleness and patience.
Tit 3: 2 and to show true *h* toward all men.
Jas 3:13 in the *h* that comes from wisdom.
1Pe 5: 5 Clothe yourselves with *h*

HUMPS

Isa 30: 6 their treasures on the *h* of camels,

HUMTAH

Jos 15:54 *H*, Kiriath Arba (that is, Hebron)

HUNCHBACKED

Lev 21:20 or who is *h* or dwarfed,

HUNG (HANG)

Ex 40:21 and *h* the shielding curtain
Dt 21:22 and his body is *h* on a tree,
21:23 anyone who is *h* on a tree is
Jos 8:29 He *h* the king of Ai on a tree
10:26 and killed the kings and *h* them
2Sa 4:12 *h* the bodies by the pool in Hebron.
21:12 the Philistines had *h* them
1Ch 10:10 and *h* up his head in the temple
Ps 137: 2 we *h* our harps,
La 5:12 Princes have been *h* up
Eze 27:10 They *h* their shields and helmets
27:11 They *h* their shields
Mt 18: 6 him to have a large millstone *h*
Lk 19:48 all the people *h* on his words.
23:39 the criminals who *h* there hurled
Gal 3:13 "Cursed is everyone who is *h*

HUNGER (HUNGRY)

Dt 8: 3 you to *h* and then feeding you
28:48 in *h* and thirst, in nakedness
1Sa 2: 5 those who were hungry *h* no more.
2Ch 32:11 to let you die of *h* and thirst.
Ne 9:15 In their *h* you gave them bread
Job 30: 3 Haggard from want and *h*,
38:39 and satisfy the *h* of the lions
Ps 17:14 You still the *h* of those you cherish;
Pr 6:30 to satisfy his *h* when he is starving.
16:26 his *h* drives him on.
Isa 5:13 their men of rank will die of *h*
29: 8 but he awakens, and his *h* remains;
49:10 They will neither *h* nor thirst,
La 2:19 who faint from *h*
4: 9 racked with *h*, they waste away
5:10 feverish from *h*.
Eze 7:19 They will not satisfy their *h*
Mt 5: 6 Blessed are those who *h*
Lk 6:21 Blessed are you who *h* now,
2Co 6: 5 sleepless nights and *h*; in purity,
11:27 I have known *h* and thirst
Rev 7:16 Never again will they *h*;

HUNGRY (HUNGER)

1Sa 2: 5 those who were *h* hunger no more.
2Sa 17:29 "The people have become *h*
Job 5: 5 The *h* consume his harvest,
18:12 Calamity is *h* for him;
22: 7 and you withheld food from the *h*,
24:10 carry the sheaves, but still go *h*.
Ps 17:12 They are like a lion *h* for prey,
34:10 The lions may grow weak and *h*,
50:12 If I were *h* I would not tell you,
107: 5 They were *h* and thirsty,
107: 9 and fills the *h* with good things.
107:36 there he brought the *h* to live,
146: 7 and gives food to the *h*.
Pr 10: 3 does not let the righteous go *h*
13:25 the stomach of the wicked goes *h*.
19:15 and the shiftless man goes *h*.
25:21 If your enemy is *h*, give him food
27: 7 to the *h* even what is bitter tastes
Isa 8:21 *h*, they will roam through the land;
9:20 but still be *h*;
29: 8 as when a *h* man dreams that he is
32: 6 the *h* he leaves empty
44:12 He gets *h* and loses his strength;
58: 7 not to share your food with the *h*
58:10 spend yourselves in behalf of the *h*
65:13 but you will go *h*;
Jer 42:14 hear the trumpet or be *h* for bread,'
Eze 18: 7 but gives his food to the *h*
18:16 but gives his food to the *h*
Mt 4: 2 and forty nights, he was *h*.
12: 1 His disciples were *h* and began
12: 3 and his companions were *h*?
15:32 I do not want to send them away *h*,
21:18 back to the city, he was *h*.
25:35 For I was *h* and you gave me
25:37 when did we see you *h*
25:42 For I was *h* and you gave me
25:44 when did we see you *h* or thirsty
Mk 2:25 his companions were *h* and in need
8: 3 send them home *h*, they will
11:12 were leaving Bethany, Jesus was *h*.
Lk 1:53 He has filled the *h* with good things
4: 2 and at the end of them he was *h*.
6: 3 and his companions were *h*?
6:25 for you will go *h*.
Jn 6:35 comes to me will never go *h*,
Ac 10:10 He became *h* and wanted
Ro 12:20 "If your enemy is *h*, feed him;
1Co 4:11 To this very hour we go *h*
11:21 One remains *h*, another gets drunk.
11:34 If anyone is *h*, he should eat
Php 4:12 whether well fed or *h*,

HUNT (HUNTED HUNTER HUNTERS HUNTING HUNTS)

Ge 27: 3 country to *h* some wild game
27: 5 left for the open country to *h* game
31:36 sin have I committed that you *h* me
Job 38:39 "Do you *h* the prey for the lioness
Ps 140:11 may disaster *h* down men
Jer 16:16 *h* them down on every mountain
Am 9: 3 there I will *h* them down

HUNTED (HUNT)

Ge 27:33 that *h* game and brought it to me?
Isa 13:14 Like *h* antelope,
La 3:52 *h* me like a bird.

HUNTER (HUNT)

Ge 10: 9 He was a mighty *h*
10: 9 a mighty *h* before the LORD."
25:27 and Esau became a skillful *h*,
Pr 6: 5 from the hand of the *h*,

HUNTERS (HUNT)

Jer 16:16 After that I will send for many *h*,

HUNTING (HUNT)

Ge 27:30 his brother Esau came in from *h*.
1Sa 24:11 you are *h* me down to take my life.

HUNTS (HUNT)

Lev 17:13 among you who *h* any animal
1Sa 26:20 one *h* a partridge in the mountains
Ps 10:2 In his arrogance the wicked man *h*
Mic 7:2 each *h* his brother with a net.

HUPHAM (HUPHAMITE)

Nu 26:39 through *H*, the Huphamite clan.

HUPHAMITE (HUPHAM)

Nu 26:39 through Hupham, the *H* clan.

HUPPAH

1Ch 24:13 the thirteenth to *H*, the fourteenth

HUPPIM

Ge 46:21 Ehi, Rosh, Muppim, *H* and Ard.

HUPPITES

1Ch 7:12 and *H* were the descendants of Ir,
7:15 a wife from among the *H*

HUR

Ex 17:10 and *H* went to the top of the hill.
17:12 Aaron and *H* held his hands up—
24:14 Aaron and *H* are with you,
31:2 the son of *H*, of the tribe of Judah,
35:30 the son of *H*, of the tribe of Judah,
38:22 the son of *H*, of the tribe of Judah,
Nu 31:8 Rekem, Zur, *H* and Reba—
Jos 13:21 Evi, Rekem, Zur, *H* and Reba—
1Ch 2:19 married Ephrath, who bore him *H*.
2:20 *H* was the father of Uri,
2:50 The sons of *H* the firstborn
4:1 Hezron, Carmi, *H* and Shobal.
4:4 These were the descendants of *H*,
2Ch 1:5 son of Uri, the son of *H*,
Ne 3:9 Rephaiah son of *H*, ruler

HURAI

1Ch 11:32 *H* from the ravines of Gaash,

HURAM

1Ki 7:13 sent to Tyre and brought *H*,
7:14 *H* was highly skilled
7:40 So *H* finished all the work he had
7:45 All these objects that *H* made
1Ch 8:5 Ahoah, Gera, Shephuphan and *H*.
2Ch 4:11 So *H* finished the work he had

HURAM-ABI

2Ch 2:13 "I am sending you *H*, a man
4:16 All the objects that *H* made

HURI

1Ch 5:14 the sons of Abihail son of *H*,

HURL (HURLED HURLS)

1Sa 25:29 of your enemies he will *h* away
2Ch 26:15 to shoot arrows and *h* large stones.
Ps 22:7 they *h* insults, shaking their heads:
Isa 22:17 *h* you away, O you mighty man.
Jer 10:18 "At this time I will *h* out
22:26 I will *h* you and the mother who
Eze 32:4 and *h* you on the open field.
Mic 7:19 *h* all our iniquities into the depths

HURLED (HURL)

Ex 15:1 he has *h* into the sea
15:4 he has *h* into the sea.
15:21 he has *h* into the sea."
Jos 10:11 the LORD *h* large hailstones
1Sa 18:11 a spear in his hand and he *h* it,
20:33 Saul *h* his spear at him to kill him.
25:14 his greetings, but he *h* insults
Ne 9:11 but you *h* their pursuers
Ps 79:12 the reproach they have *h* at you,
Jer 22:28 will he and his children be *h* out,
La 2:1 He has *h* down the splendor
Jnh 2:3 You *h* me into the deep,
Mt 27:39 passed by *h* insults at him,
Mk 15:29 passed by *h* insults at him,
Lk 23:39 criminals who hung there *h* insults
Jn 9:28 Then they *h* insults at him and said
1Pe 2:23 When they *h* their insults at him,
Rev 8:5 from the altar, and *h* it on the earth
8:7 and it was *h* down upon the earth.
12:9 He was *h* to the earth,
Rev 12:9 The great dragon was *h* down—
12:10 has been *h* down.
12:13 the dragon saw that he had been *h*

HURLS (HURL)

Job 27:22 It *h* itself against him
Ps 147:17 He *h* down his hail like pebbles.

HURRICANE

Ac 27:14 of *h* force, called the "Northeaster

HURRIED (HURRY)

Ge 18:2 he *h* from the entrance of his tent
18:6 Abraham *h* into the tent to Sarah.
18:7 it to a servant, who *h* to prepare it.
24:17 The servant *h* to meet her and said,
24:29 he *h* out to the man at the spring.
29:13 his sister's son, he *h* to meet him.
43:15 They *h* down to Egypt
43:30 Joseph *h* out and looked for a place
Ex 9:20 of the LORD *h* to bring their slaves
Jos 4:10 The people *h* over, and as soon
8:14 the city *h* out early in the morning
Jdg 13:10 The woman *h* to tell her husband,
1Sa 4:14 of this uproar?" The man *h*
2Sa 4:4 but as she *h* to leave, he fell
19:16 *h* down with the men of Judah
2Ki 5:21 So Gehazi *h* after Naaman.
9:13 They *h* and took their cloaks
2Ch 26:20 on his forehead, so they *h* him out.
Est 6:14 and *h* Haman away to the banquet
Job 31:5 or my foot has *h* after deceit—
Da 6:19 the king got up and *h*
Mt 28:8 the women *h* away from the tomb,
Mk 6:25 At once the girl *h* in to the king
Lk 1:39 and *h* to a town in the hill country
2:16 So they *h* off and found Mary

HURRIES (HURRY)

Ecc 1:5 and *h* back to where it rises.

HURRY (HURRIED HURRIES HURRYING)

Ge 19:14 "*H* and get out of this place,
19:15 the angels urged Lot, saying, "*H!*
45:9 Now *h* back to my father
Ex 12:33 Egyptians urged the people to *h*
Nu 16:46 and *h* to the assembly to make
1Sa 9:12 *H* now; he has just come
17:17 bread for your brothers and *h*
20:6 permission to *h* to Bethlehem,
20:38 Then he shouted, "*H!* Go quickly!
2Ch 35:21 me to *h*; so stop opposing God,
Ps 55:8 I would *h* to my place of shelter,
Ecc 8:3 in a *h* to leave the king's presence.
SS 1:4 Take me away with you—let us *h!*
Isa 5:19 to those who say, "Let God *h*,
Ac 20:16 for he was in a *h* to reach Jerusalem

HURRYING (HURRY)

1Sa 23:26 on the other side, *h* to get away

HURT (HURTS)

Ps 69:26 talk about the pain of those you *h*.
Pr 23:35 you will say, "but I'm not *h!*
Ecc 8:9 it over others to his own *h*.
Da 6:22 They have not *h* me, because I was
Mk 16:18 deadly poison, it will not *h* them
Jn 21:17 Peter was *h* because Jesus asked
Ac 7:26 why do you want to *h* each other?'
2Co 7:8 I see that my letter *h* you,
Rev 2:11 He who overcomes will not be *h*

HURTLING

Eze 13:11 and I will send hailstones *h* down,

HURTS (HURT)

Ps 15:4 even when it *h*,
Pr 26:28 A lying tongue hates those it *h*,

HUSBAND (HUSBAND'S HUSBANDS)

Ge 3:6 She also gave some to her *h*,
3:16 Your desire will be for your *h*,
16:3 and gave her to her *h* to be his wife.
29:32 Surely my *h* will love me now."
29:34 at last my *h* will become attached
30:15 enough that you took away my *h?*
30:18 for giving my maidservant to my *h*
Ge 30:20 This time my *h* will treat me
Ex 21:22 whatever the woman's *h* demands
Lev 21:3 on him since she has no *h*—
Nu 5:13 and this is hidden from her *h*
5:14 of jealousy come over her *h*
5:19 impure while married to your *h*,
5:20 astray while married to your *h*
5:20 with a man other than your *h*"—
5:27 and been unfaithful to her *h*,
5:29 herself while married to her *h*,
5:31 The *h* will be innocent
30:7 and her *h* hears about it but says
30:8 But if her *h* forbids her
30:10 living with her *h* makes a vow
30:11 and her *h* hears about it but says
30:12 But if her *h* nullifies them
30:12 Her *h* has nullified them,
30:13 Her *h* may confirm or nullify any
30:14 if her *h* says nothing to her about it
Dt 21:13 be her *h* and she shall be your wife.
24:3 and her second *h* dislikes her
24:4 then her first *h*, who divorced her,
25:11 to rescue her *h* from his assailant,
28:56 will begrudge the *h* she loves
Jdg 13:6 Then the woman went to her *h*
13:9 but her *h* Manoah was not with her
13:10 The woman hurried to tell her *h*,
14:15 "Coax your *h* into explaining
19:3 her *h* went to her to persuade her
20:4 the *h* of the murdered woman,
Ru 1:3 Now Elimelech, Naomi's *h*, died,
1:5 left without her two sons and her *h*.
1:9 rest in the home of another *h*."
1:12 I am too old to have another *h*.
1:12 even if I had a *h* tonight
2:11 since the death of your *h*—
1Sa 1:8 Elkanah her *h* would say to her,
1:22 to her *h*, "After the boy is weaned,
1:23 to you," Elkanah her *h* told her.
2:19 up with her *h* to offer the annual
4:19 father-in-law and her *h* were dead,
4:21 of her father-in-law and her *h*.
25:3 and beautiful woman, but her *h*,
25:19 But she did not tell her *h* Nabal.
2Sa 3:15 from her *h* Paltiel son of Laish.
3:16 Her *h*, however, went with her,
11:26 wife heard that her *h* was dead,
14:5 I am indeed a widow; my *h* is dead.
14:7 leaving my *h* neither name
2Ki 4:1 "Your servant my *h* is dead,
4:9 said to her *h*, "I know that this man
4:14 she has no son and her *h* is old."
4:22 She called her *h* and said, "Please
4:26 Are you all right? Is your *h* all right
Pr 7:19 My *h* is not at home;
31:11 Her *h* has full confidence in her
31:23 Her *h* is respected at the city gate,
31:28 her *h* also, and he praises her:
Isa 54:1 woman than of her who has a *h*,"
54:5 For your Maker is your *h*—
Jer 3:14 the LORD, "for I am your *h*.
3:20 like a woman unfaithful to her *h*,
6:11 both *h* and wife will be caught in it,
31:32 though I was a *h* to them,"
Eze 16:32 You prefer strangers to your own *h*
16:45 who despised her *h* and her
Hos 2:2 and I am not her *h*.
2:7 'I will go back to my *h* as at first,
2:16 "you will call me 'my *h*';
Joel 1:8 grieving for the *h* of her youth.
Mt 1:16 the father of Joseph, the *h* of Mary,
1:19 Because Joseph her *h* was
19:10 "If this is the situation between a *h*
Mk 10:12 she divorces her *h* and marries
Lk 2:36 lived with her *h* seven years
Jn 4:16 "Go, call your *h* and come back."
4:17 right when you say you have no *h*.
4:17 "I have no *h*," she replied.
4:18 man you now have is not your *h*.
Ac 5:9 of the men who buried your *h* are
5:10 and buried her beside her *h*.
Ro 7:2 a married woman is bound to her *h*
7:2 but if her *h* dies, she is released
7:3 But if her *h* dies, she is released
7:3 man while her *h* is still alive,
1Co 7:2 and each woman her own *h*.
7:3 The *h* should fulfill his marital duty
7:3 and likewise the wife to her *h*.

IDENTICAL

1Ki 6:25 for the two cherubim were *i* in size
7:37 and were *i* in size and shape.

IDLE (IDLENESS IDLERS)

Dt 32:47 They are not just *i* words for you—
Job 11:3 Will your *i* talk reduce men
Ecc 10:18 if his hands are *i*, the house leaks.
11:6 at evening let not your hands be *i*,
Isa 58:13 as you please or speaking *i* words,
Col 2:18 mind puffs him up with *i* notions.
1Th 5:14 those who are *i*, encourage
2Th 3:6 away from every brother who is *i*
3:7 We were not *i* when we were
3:11 We hear that some among you are *i*
1Ti 5:13 they get into the habit of being *i*

IDLENESS (IDLE)

Pr 31:27 and does not eat the bread of *i*.

IDLERS (IDLE)

1Ti 5:13 And not only do they become *i*,

IDOL (CALF-IDOL CALF-IDOLS IDOL'S IDOLATER IDOLATERS IDOLATRIES IDOLATROUS IDOLATRY IDOLS)

Ex 20:4 make for yourself an *i* in the form
32:4 made it into an *i* cast in the shape
32:8 have made themselves an *i* cast
Dt 4:16 and make for yourselves an *i*,
4:23 for yourselves an *i* in the form
4:25 corrupt and make any kind of *i*,
5:8 make for yourself an *i* in the form
9:12 have made a cast *i* for themselves."
9:16 for yourselves an *i* cast in the shape
27:15 who carves an image or casts an *i*—
Jdg 17:3 to make a carved image and a cast *i*
17:4 them into the image and the *i*.
18:14 a carved image and a cast *i*?
18:17 and the cast *i* while the priest
18:18 household gods and the cast *i*,
1Sa 19:13 Then Michal took an *i*
19:16 the men entered, there was the *i*
Ps 24:4 who does not lift up his soul to an *i*
106:19 and worshiped an *i* cast from metal
Isa 40:19 As for an *i*, a craftsman casts it,
40:20 to set up an *i* that will not topple.
41:7 He nails down the *i*
44:10 Who shapes a god and casts an *i*,
44:12 he shapes an *i* with hammers,
44:15 he makes an *i* and bows down to it.
44:17 From the rest he makes a god, his *i*,
66:3 like one who worships an *i*.
Eze 8:3 where the *i* that provokes
8:5 of the altar I saw this *i* of jealousy.
8:12 each at the shrine of his own *i*?
Hos 3:4 sacred stones, without ephod or *i*.
4:12 They consult a wooden *i*
9:10 to that shameful *i* and
Hab 2:18 "Of what value is an *i*,
Ac 7:41 That was the time they made an *i*
1Co 8:4 We know that an *i* is nothing at all
8:7 as having been sacrificed to an *i*,
10:19 offered to an *i* is anything,
10:19 or that an *i* is anything? No,

IDOL'S (IDOL)

1Co 8:10 knowledge eating in an *i* temple,

IDOLATER (IDOL)

1Co 5:11 an *i* or a slanderer, a drunkard
Eph 5:5 greedy person—such a man is an *i*

IDOLATERS (IDOL)

1Co 5:10 or the greedy and swindlers, or *i*.
6:9 Neither the sexually immoral nor *i*
10:7 Do not be *i*, as some of them were;
Rev 21:8 those who practice magic arts, the *i*
22:15 the *i* and everyone who loves

IDOLATRIES (IDOL)

Jer 14:14 *i* and the delusions

IDOLATROUS (IDOL)

Jer 3:23 Surely the ⌞*i*⌟ commotion
Hos 10:5 and so will its *i* priests,
Zep 1:4 of the pagan and the *i* priests—

IDOLATRY (IDOL)

1Sa 15:23 and arrogance like the evil of *i*.
2Ki 9:22 as all the *i* and witchcraft
Eze 14:4 myself in keeping with his great *i*
23:49 the consequences of your sins of *i*.
1Co 10:14 my dear friends, flee from *i*.
Gal 5:20 and debauchery; *i* and witchcraft;
Col 3:5 evil desires and greed, which is *i*.
1Pe 4:3 orgies, carousing and detestable *i*.

IDOLS (IDOL)

Ex 34:17 "Do not make cast *i*.
Lev 17:7 to the goat *i* to whom they
19:4 " 'Do not turn to *i* or make gods
26:1 " 'Do not make *i* or set up an image
26:30 on the lifeless forms of your *i*,
Nu 33:52 carved images and their cast *i*,
Dt 7:5 and burn their *i* in the fire.
12:3 cut down the *i* of their gods
29:17 them their detestable images and *i*
32:16 angered him with their detestable *i*.
32:21 angered me with their worthless *i*.
Jdg 3:19 At the *i* near Gilgal he himself
3:26 He passed by the *i* and escaped
17:5 and he made an ephod and some *i*
18:30 up for themselves the *i*,
18:31 to use the *i* Micah had made,
1Sa 12:21 Do not turn away after useless *i*.
31:9 the news in the temple of their *i*
2Sa 5:21 Philistines abandoned their *i* there,
1Ki 14:9 for yourself other gods, *i* made
15:12 rid of all the *i* his fathers had made.
16:13 Israel to anger by their worthless *i*.
16:26 to anger by their worthless *i*.
21:26 in the vilest manner by going after *i*
2Ki 11:18 They smashed the altars and *i*
17:12 They worshiped *i*,
17:15 They followed worthless *i*
17:16 and made for themselves two *i* cast
17:41 LORD, they were serving their *i*.
21:11 has led Judah into sin with his *i*.
21:21 he worshiped the *i* his father had
22:17 by all the *i* their hands have made,
23:24 *i* and all the other detestable things
1Ch 10:9 to proclaim the news among their *i*
16:26 For all the gods of the nations are *i*,
2Ch 11:15 for the goat and calf *i* he had made.
15:8 He removed the detestable *i*
23:17 They smashed the altars and *i*
24:18 and worshiped Asherah poles and *i*
28:2 and also made cast *i* for worshiping
33:19 and *i* before he humbled himself—
33:22 to all the *i* Manasseh had made.
34:3 Asherah poles, carved *i*
34:4 smashed the Asherah poles, the *i*
34:7 and crushed the *i* to powder
34:33 Josiah removed all the detestable *i*
Ps 31:6 hate those who cling to worthless *i*;
78:58 aroused his jealousy with their *i*.
96:5 For all the gods of the nations are *i*,
97:7 those who boast in *i*—
106:36 They worshiped their *i*,
106:38 sacrificed to the *i* of Canaan,
115:4 But their *i* are silver and gold,
135:15 The *i* of the nations are silver
Isa 2:8 Their land is full of *i*;
2:18 and the *i* will totally disappear.
2:20 their *i* of silver and *i* of gold,
10:10 hand seized the kingdoms of the *i*,
10:11 as I dealt with Samaria and her *i*
19:1 The *i* of Egypt tremble before him,
19:3 will consult the *i* and the spirits
30:22 Then you will defile your *i* overlaid
31:7 one of you will reject the *i* of silver
41:22 "Bring in ⌞your *i*⌟ to tell us
42:8 or my praise to *i*.
42:17 But those who trust in *i*,
44:9 All who make *i* are nothing,
45:16 All the makers of *i* will be put
45:20 are those who carry about *i*
46:1 their *i* are borne by beasts
48:5 'My *i* did them;
48:14 of ⌞the *i*⌟ has foretold these things?
57:6 ⌞The *i*⌟ among the smooth stones
57:13 let your collection ⌞of *i*⌟ save you!
Jer 2:5 They followed worthless *i*
2:8 following worthless *i*.
2:11 Glory for worthless *i*.
4:1 "If you put your detestable *i* out
7:30 They have set up their detestable *i*
8:19 with their worthless foreign *i*?"
10:5 their *i* cannot speak;
10:8 by worthless wooden *i*.
10:14 every goldsmith is shamed by his *i*.
14:22 Do any of the worthless *i*
16:18 with their detestable *i*."
16:19 worthless *i* that did them no good.
18:15 they burn incense to worthless *i*,
32:34 They set up their abominable *i*
50:2 and her *i* filled with terror.'
50:38 For it is a land of *i*,
50:38 *i* that will go mad with terror.
51:17 every goldsmith is shamed by his *i*.
51:47 when I will punish the *i* of Babylon;
51:52 "when I will punish her *i*,
Eze 5:9 Because of all your detestable *i*,
6:4 slay your people in front of your *i*.
6:5 of the Israelites in front of their *i*,
6:6 your *i* smashed and ruined,
6:9 which have lusted after their *i*.
6:13 among their *i* around their altars,
6:13 fragrant incense to all their *i*.
7:20 used it to make their detestable *i*
8:10 and all the *i* of the house of Israel.
11:18 all its vile images and detestable *i*.
11:21 to their vile images and detestable *i*
14:3 these men have set up *i*
14:4 When any Israelite sets up *i*
14:5 who have all deserted me for their *i*
14:6 from your *i* and renounce all your
14:7 from me and sets up *i* in his heart
16:17 and you made for yourself male *i*
16:20 sacrificed them as food to the *i*.
16:21 and sacrificed them to the *i*.
16:36 and because of all your detestable *i*,
18:6 look to the *i* of the house of Israel.
18:12 He looks to the *i*.
18:15 look to the *i* of the house of Israel.
20:7 yourselves with the *i* of Egypt
20:8 nor did they forsake the *i* of Egypt.
20:16 their hearts were devoted to their *i*.
20:18 or defile yourselves with their *i*.
20:24 after their fathers' *i*.
20:31 with all your *i* to this day.
20:39 and serve your *i*, every one of you!
20:39 name with your gifts and *i*.
21:21 will consult his *i*, he will examine
22:3 and defiles herself by making *i*,
22:4 defiled by the *i* you have made.
23:7 with all the *i* of everyone she lusted
23:30 and defiled yourself with their *i*.
23:37 committed adultery with their *i*;
23:39 sacrificed their children to their *i*,
30:13 " 'I will destroy the *i*
33:25 and look to your *i* and shed blood,
36:18 they had defiled it with their *i*.
36:25 your impurities and from all your *i*.
37:23 defile themselves with their *i*
43:7 and the lifeless *i* of their kings
43:9 and the lifeless *i* of their kings,
44:10 me after their *i* must bear
44:12 them in the presence of their *i*
Hos 4:17 Ephraim is joined to *i*;
5:11 intent on pursuing *i*.
8:4 they make *i* for themselves
10:6 will be ashamed of its wooden *i*.
13:2 they make *i* for themselves
14:8 what more have I to do with *i*?
Am 5:26 the pedestal of your *i*,
Jnh 2:8 "Those who cling to worthless *i*
Mic 1:7 All her *i* will be broken to pieces;
Na 1:14 the carved images and cast *i*
Hab 2:18 he makes *i* that cannot speak.
Zec 10:2 The *i* speak deceit,
13:2 the names of the *i* from the land,
Ac 7:43 the *i* you made to worship.
15:20 to abstain from food polluted by *i*,
15:29 to abstain from food sacrificed to *i*,
17:16 to see that the city was full of *i*.
21:25 abstain from food sacrificed to *i*,
Ro 2:22 You who abhor *i*, do you rob
1Co 8:1 Now about food sacrificed to *i*:
8:4 about eating food sacrificed to *i*:
8:7 still so accustomed to *i* that
8:10 to eat what has been sacrificed to *i*

1Co 12: 2 and led astray to dumb *i*.
2Co 6: 16 between the temple of God and *i*?
1Th 1: 9 to God from *i* to serve the living
1Jn 5: 21 children, keep yourselves from *i*.
Rev 2: 14 to sin by eating food sacrificed to *i*
2: 20 the eating of food sacrificed to *i*.
9: 20 and *i* of gold, silver, bronze,
9: 20 *i* that cannot see or hear or walk.

IDUMEA

Mk 3: 8 to him from Judea, Jerusalem, *I*,

IEZER (IEZERITE)

Nu 26: 30 through *I*, the Iezerite clan;

IEZERITE (IEZER)

Nu 26: 30 the *I* clan; through Helek,

IGAL

Nu 13: 7 tribe of Issachar, *I* son of Joseph;
2Sa 23: 36 *I* son of Nathan from Zobah,
1Ch 3: 22 *I*, Bariah, Neariah and Shaphat—

IGDALIAH

Jer 35: 4 of Hanan son of *I* the man of God.

IGNOBLE

2Ti 2: 20 for noble purposes and some for *i*.

IGNORANCE (IGNORE)

Eze 45: 20 sins unintentionally or through *i*;
Ac 3: 17 I know that you acted in *i*,
17: 30 In the past God overlooked such *i*,
Eph 4: 18 because of the *i* that is in them due
1Ti 1: 13 because I acted in *i* and unbelief.
Heb 9: 7 sins the people had committed in *i*.
1Pe 1: 14 had when you lived in *i*.

IGNORANT (IGNORE)

Ps 73: 22 I was senseless and *i*;
Pr 30: 2 "I am the most *i* of men;
Isa 44: 9 they are *i*, to their own shame.
45: 20 *I* are those who carry about idols
Ro 11: 25 you to be *i* of this mystery,
1Co 10: 1 For I do not want you to be *i*
12: 1 brothers, I do not want you to be *i*.
15: 34 for there are some who are *i* of God
1Th 4: 13 to be *i* about those who fall asleep,
Heb 5: 2 to deal gently with those who are *i*
1Pe 2: 15 good you should silence the *i* talk
2Pe 3: 16 which *i* and unstable people distort

IGNORE (IGNORANCE IGNORANT IGNORED IGNORES IGNORING)

Dt 22: 1 do not *i* it but be sure
22: 3 Do not *i* it.
22: 4 his ox fallen on the road, do not *i* it.
Ps 9: 12 he does not *i* the cry of the afflicted
55: 1 do not *i* my plea;
74: 23 Do not *i* the clamor
119: 139 for my enemies *i* your words.
Pr 8: 33 do not *i* it.
Hos 4: 6 I also will *i* your children.
Heb 2: 3 if we *i* such a great salvation?

IGNORED (IGNORE)

Ex 9: 21 But those who *i* the word
Pr 1: 25 since you *i* all my advice
2: 17 and *i* the covenant she made
Hos 4: 6 you have *i* the law of your God,
1Co 14: 38 he ignores this, he himself will be *i*.

IGNORES (IGNORE)

Pr 10: 17 whoever *i* correction leads others
13: 18 He who *i* discipline comes
15: 32 He who *i* discipline despises
1Co 14: 38 If he *i* this, he himself will be

IGNORING (IGNORE)

Mk 5: 36 the teacher any more?" *I* what they

IIM

Jos 15: 29 Baalah, *I*, Ezem, Eltolad,

IJON

1Ki 15: 20 He conquered *I*, Dan,
2Ki 15: 29 king of Assyria came and took *I*,
2Ch 16: 4 They conquered *I*, Dan,

IKKESH

2Sa 23: 26 Ira son of *I* from Tekoa, Abiezer
1Ch 11: 28 Ira son of *I* from Tekoa, Abiezer
27: 9 was Ira the son of *I* the Tekoite.

ILAI

1Ch 11: 29 the Hushathite, *I* the Ahohite,

ILL (ILLNESS ILLNESSES ILLS)

Ge 48: 1 Joseph was told, "Your father is *i*."
Dt 15: 9 so that you do not show *i* will
1Sa 19: 14 David, Michal said, "He is *i*."
30: 13 when I became *i* three days ago.
2Sa 12: 15 borne to David, and he became *i*.
13: 5 "Go to bed and pretend to be *i*,"
13: 6 lay down and pretended to be *i*.
1Ki 14: 1 son of Jeroboam became *i*,
14: 5 for he is *i*, and you are
17: 17 who owned the house became *i*.
2Ki 8: 7 and Ben-Hadad king of Aram was *i*
20: 1 In those days Hezekiah became *i*
2Ch 21: 15 You yourself will be very *i*
32: 24 In those days Hezekiah became *i*
Ne 2: 2 look so sad when you are not *i*?
Job 6: 7 such food makes me *i*.
Ps 35: 13 Yet when they were *i*, I put
Isa 33: 24 in Zion will say, "I am *i*";
38: 1 In those days Hezekiah became *i*
Da 8: 27 was exhausted and lay *i*
Mt 4: 24 brought to him all who were *i*
Ac 28: 5 the fire and suffered no *i* effects.
Php 2: 26 because you heard he was *i*.
2: 27 Indeed he was *i*, and almost died.

ILL-GOTTEN (GET)

Pr 1: 19 the end of all who go after *i* gain;
10: 2 *I* treasures are of no value,
28: 16 he who hates *i* gain will enjoy
Mic 4: 13 You will devote their *i* gains
6: 10 your *i* treasures

ILL-TEMPERED (TEMPER)

Pr 21: 19 than with a quarrelsome and *i* wife.

ILLEGAL

Ex 22: 9 In all cases of *i* possession of an ox,

ILLEGITIMATE

Hos 5: 7 they give birth to *i* children.
Jn 8: 41 "We are not *i* children," they
Heb 12: 8 then you are *i* children

ILLICIT

Eze 16: 33 from everywhere for your *i* favors.

ILLNESS (ILL)

2Sa 13: 2 to the point of *i* on account
2Ki 8: 8 'Will I recover from this *i*?' "
8: 9 'Will I recover from this *i*?' "
13: 14 from the *i* from which he died.
20: 12 he had heard of Hezekiah's *i*.
2Ch 16: 12 even in his *i* he did not seek help
Ps 41: 3 and restore him from his bed of *i*.
Isa 38: 9 king of Judah after his *i*
39: 1 he had heard of his *i* and recovery.
Gal 4: 13 because of an *i* that I first preached
4: 14 Even though my *i* was a trial to you

ILLNESSES (ILL)

Dt 28: 59 and severe and lingering *i*.
Ac 19: 12 and their *i* were cured
1Ti 5: 23 your stomach and your frequent *i*.

ILLS (ILL)

Ps 73: 5 they are not plagued by human *i*.

ILLUMINATED

Rev 18: 1 and the earth was *i* by his splendor.

ILLUSIONS

Isa 30: 10 prophesy *i*.

ILLUSTRATION

Heb 9: 9 This is an *i* for the present time,

ILLYRICUM

Ro 15: 19 Jerusalem all the way around to *I*.

IMAGE (IMAGES)

Ge 1: 26 "Let us make man in our *i*,
1: 27 So God created man in his own *i*,
1: 27 in the *i* of God he created him;
5: 3 in his own *i*; and he named him
9: 6 for in the *i* of God
Lev 26: 1 or set up an *i* or a sacred stone
Dt 4: 16 *i* of any shape, whether formed like
27: 15 "Cursed is the man who carves an *i*
Jdg 17: 3 for my son to make a carved *i*
17: 4 who made them into the *i*
18: 14 other household gods, a carved *i*
18: 17 went inside and took the carved *i*,
18: 18 house and took the carved *i*,
18: 20 and the carved *i* and went
2Ch 33: 7 He took the carved *i* he had made
33: 15 and removed the *i* from the temple
Ne 9: 18 cast for themselves an *i* of a calf
Ps 106: 20 for an *i* of a bull, which eats grass.
Isa 40: 18 What *i* will you compare him to?
48: 5 my wooden *i* and metal god
Jer 44: 19 we were making cakes like her *i*
Da 3: 1 King Nebuchadnezzar made an *i*
3: 2 dedication of the *i* he had set up.
3: 3 of the *i* that King Nebuchadnezzar
3: 5 and worship the *i* of gold that King
3: 7 worshiped the *i* of gold that King
3: 10 fall down and worship the *i* of gold,
3: 12 worship the *i* of gold you have set
3: 14 worship the *i* of gold I have set up?
3: 15 fall down and worship the *i* I made,
3: 18 worship the *i* of gold you have set
Hab 2: 18 Or an *i* that teaches lies?
Ac 17: 29 an *i* made by man's design and skill
19: 35 of the great Artemis and of her *i*,
1Co 11: 7 since he is the *i* and glory of God;
2Co 4: 4 glory of Christ, who is the *i* of God.
Col 1: 15 He is the *i* of the invisible God,
3: 10 in knowledge in the *i* of its Creator.
Rev 13: 14 them to set up an *i* in honor
13: 15 breath to the *i* of the first beast,
13: 15 to worship the *i* to be killed.
14: 9 anyone worships the beast and his *i*
14: 11 who worship the beast and his *i*,
15: 2 and his *i* and over the number
16: 2 of the beast and worshiped his *i*.
19: 20 of the beast and worshiped his *i*.
20: 4 had not worshiped the beast or his *i*

IMAGES (IMAGE)

Nu 33: 52 Destroy all their carved *i*
Dt 7: 25 The *i* of their gods you are to burn
29: 17 saw among them their detestable *i*
2Ch 34: 3 poles, carved idols and cast *i*.
34: 4 Asherah poles, the idols and the *i*.
Ps 97: 7 All who worship *i* are put to shame,
Isa 10: 10 kingdoms whose *i* excelled those
10: 11 deal with Jerusalem and her *i*
21: 9 All the *i* of its gods
30: 22 and your *i* covered with gold;
41: 29 their *i* are but wind and confusion.
42: 17 who say to *i*, 'You are our gods,'
46: 1 The *i* that are carried about are
Jer 8: 19 me to anger with their *i*,
10: 14 His *i* are a fraud;
16: 18 with the lifeless forms of their vile *i*
50: 2 Her *i* will be put to shame
51: 17 His *i* are a fraud;
Eze 5: 11 sanctuary with all your vile *i*
7: 20 their detestable idols and vile *i*.
11: 18 all its vile *i* and detestable idols.
11: 21 hearts are devoted to their vile *i*
20: 7 of the vile *i* you have set your eyes
20: 8 of the vile *i* they had set their eyes
20: 30 did and lust after their vile *i*?
30: 13 and put an end to the *i* in Memphis
37: 23 vile *i* or with any of their offenses,
Da 4: 5 the *i* and visions that passed
11: 8 their metal *i* and their valuable
Hos 11: 2 and they burned incense to *i*.
13: 2 cleverly fashioned *i*,
Mic 1: 7 I will destroy all her *i*.
5: 13 I will destroy your carved *i*
Na 1: 14 I will destroy the carved *i*
Ro 1: 23 of the immortal God for *i* made

IMAGINATION (IMAGINE)
Eze 13: 2 who prophesy out of their own *i:*
13: 17 who prophesy out of their own *i.*

IMAGINATIONS (IMAGINE)
Isa 65: 2 pursuing their own *i*—
66: 18 because of their actions and their *i,*

IMAGINE (IMAGINATION IMAGINATIONS)
Ps 41: 7 they *i* the worst for me, saying,
Pr 18: 11 they *i* it an unscalable wall.
23: 33 and your mind *i* confusing things.
Eph 3: 20 more than all we ask or *i,*

IMITATE (IMITATED IMITATORS)
Dt 18: 9 learn to *i* the detestable ways
Eze 23: 48 may take warning and not *i* you.
1Co 4: 16 Therefore I urge you to *i* me.
Heb 6: 12 but to *i* those who through faith
13: 7 of their way of life and *i* their faith.
3Jn : 11 do not *i* what is evil but what is

IMITATED (IMITATE)
2Ki 17: 15 They *i* the nations around them

IMITATORS (IMITATE)
Eph 5: 1 Be *i* of God, therefore,
1Th 1: 6 You became *i* of us and of the Lord
2: 14 became *i* of God's churches

IMLAH
1Ki 22: 8 He is Micaiah son of *I.*"
22: 9 "Bring Micaiah son of *I* at once."
2Ch 18: 7 He is Micaiah son of *I.*"
18: 8 "Bring Micaiah son of *I* at once."

IMMANUEL
Isa 7: 14 birth to a son, and will call him *I.*
8: 8 O *I!*"
Mt 1: 23 and they will call him *I*"—

IMMEDIATE
1Ti 5: 8 and especially for his *i* family,

IMMENSE
Eze 1: 4 an *i* cloud with flashing lightning

IMMER
1Ch 9: 12 son of Meshillemith, the son of *I.*
24: 14 the sixteenth to *I,* the seventeenth
Ezr 2: 37 the family of Jeshua) 973 of *I* 1,052
2: 59 Kerub, Addon and *I,*
10: 20 From the descendants of *I:*
Ne 3: 29 Zadok son of *I* made repairs
7: 40 the family of Jeshua) 973 of *I* 1,052
7: 61 but they could not show that
11: 13 the son of *I,* and his associates,
Jer 20: 1 When the priest Pashhur son of *I,*

IMMORAL (IMMORALITY)
Pr 6: 24 keeping you from the *i* woman,
1Co 5: 9 to associate with sexually *i* people
5: 10 the people of this world who are *i,*
5: 11 but is sexually *i* or greedy,
6: 9 Neither the sexually *i* nor idolaters
Eph 5: 5 No *i,* impure or greedy person—
Heb 12: 16 See that no one is sexually *i,*
13: 4 the adulterer and all the sexually *i.*
Rev 21: 8 the murderers, the sexually *i,*
22: 15 the sexually *i,* the murderers,

IMMORALITY (IMMORAL)
Nu 25: 1 in sexual *i* with Moabite women,
Jer 3: 9 Because Israel's *i* mattered so little
Mt 15: 19 murder, adultery, sexual *i,* theft,
Mk 7: 21 sexual *i,* theft, murder, adultery,
Ac 15: 20 from sexual *i,* from the meat
15: 29 animals and from sexual *i.*
21: 25 animals and from sexual *i.*"
Ro 13: 13 not in sexual *i* and debauchery,
1Co 5: 1 reported that there is sexual *i*
6: 13 The body is not meant for sexual *i,*
6: 18 Flee from sexual *i.*
7: 2 But since there is so much *i,*
10: 8 We should not commit sexual *i,*
Gal 5: 19 sexual *i,* impurity and debauchery;
Eph 5: 3 must not be even a hint of sexual *i,*
Col 3: 5 sexual *i,* impurity, lust, evil desires
1Th 4: 3 that you should avoid sexual *i;*
Jude : 4 grace of our God into a license for *i*
: 7 gave themselves up to sexual *i*
Rev 2: 14 and by committing sexual *i.*
2: 20 misleads my servants into sexual *i*
2: 21 given her time to repent of her *i,*
9: 21 their sexual *i* or their thefts.

IMMORTAL (IMMORTALITY)
Ro 1: 23 glory of the *i* God for images made
1Ti 1: 17 Now to the King eternal, *i,*
6: 16 who alone is *i* and who lives

IMMORTALITY (IMMORTAL)
Pr 12: 28 along that path is *i.*
Ro 2: 7 honor and *i,* he will give eternal life
1Co 15: 53 and the mortal with *i.*
15: 54 with *i,* then the saying that is
2Ti 1: 10 and *i* to light through the gospel.

IMMOVABLE
Job 41: 23 they are firm and *i.*
Zec 12: 3 I will make Jerusalem an *i* rock

IMNA
1Ch 7: 35 Zophah, *I,* Shelesh and Amal.

IMNAH (IMNITE)
Ge 46: 17 The sons of Asher: *I,* Ishvah,
Nu 26: 44 through *I,* the Imnite clan;
1Ch 7: 30 The sons of Asher: *I,* Ishvah,
2Ch 31: 14 Kore son of *I* the Levite, keeper

IMNITE (IMNAH)
Nu 26: 44 through Imnah, the *I* clan;

IMPALED
Ezr 6: 11 and he is to be lifted up and *i* on it.

IMPART (IMPARTED IMPARTS)
Ro 1: 11 you so that I may *i* to you some
Gal 3: 21 law had been given that could *i* life,

IMPARTED (IMPART)
Ecc 12: 9 also he *i* knowledge to the people.

IMPARTIAL
Jas 3: 17 and good fruit, *i* and sincere.

IMPARTS (IMPART)
Pr 29: 15 The rod of correction *i* wisdom,

IMPATIENT
Nu 21: 4 But the people grew *i* on the way;
Job 4: 2 a word with you, will you be *i?*
21: 4 Why should I not be *i?*

IMPERFECT
1Co 13: 10 perfection comes, the *i* disappears.

IMPERIAL (EMPIRE)
2Ki 25: 8 commander of the *i* guard,
25: 10 the commander of the *i* guard,
25: 15 of the *i* guard took away
Jer 39: 9 commander of the *i* guard carried
39: 11 commander of the *i* guard:
40: 1 of the *i* guard had released him
41: 10 of the *i* guard had appointed
43: 6 commander of the *i* guard had left
52: 12 commander of the *i* guard,
52: 14 commander of the *i* guard broke
52: 19 of the *i* guard took away the basins,
52: 30 the commander of the *i* guard.
Ac 27: 1 who belonged to the *I* Regiment.

IMPERISHABLE
1Co 15: 42 it is raised *i;* it is sown in dishonor,
15: 50 nor does the perishable inherit the *i*
15: 52 the dead will be raised *i,*
15: 53 must clothe itself with the *i,*
15: 54 has been clothed with the *i,*
1Pe 1: 23 not of perishable seed, but of *i,*

IMPETUOUS
Job 6: 3 no wonder my words have been *i.*
Hab 1: 6 that ruthless and *i* people,

IMPLANTED
Ps 94: 9 Does he who *i* the ear not hear?

IMPLORE
Mal 1: 9 "Now *i* God to be gracious to us.
2Co 5: 20 We *i* you on Christ's behalf:

IMPORTANCE (IMPORTANT)
1Co 15: 3 passed on to you as of first *i:*

IMPORTANT (IMPORTANCE)
Jos 10: 2 because Gibeon was an *i* city,
1Ki 3: 4 for that was the most *i* high place,
2Ki 25: 9 Every *i* building he burned down.
Jer 52: 13 Every *i* building he burned down.
Mt 6: 25 Is not life more *i* than food,
6: 25 and the body more *i* than clothes?
23: 6 the most *i* seats in the synagogues;
23: 23 have neglected the more *i* matters
Mk 12: 28 is the most *i?*" "The most
12: 29 "The most *i* one," answered Jesus,
12: 33 as yourself is more *i* than all burnt
12: 39 and have the most *i* seats
Lk 11: 43 because you love the most *i* seats
14: 9 have to take the least *i* place.
20: 46 and have the most *i* seats
Ac 8: 27 an *i* official in charge
Gal 2: 6 As for those who seemed to be *i*—
Php 1: 18 The *i* thing is that in every way,

IMPORTED
1Ki 10: 12 much almugwood has never been *i*
10: 28 Solomon's horses were *i*
10: 29 They *i* a chariot from Egypt
2Ch 1: 16 Solomon's horses were *i*
1: 17 They *i* a chariot from Egypt
9: 28 Solomon's horses were *i*
Isa 17: 10 and plant *i* vines,

IMPOSE (IMPOSED IMPOSING SELF-IMPOSED)
Ezr 7: 24 you have no authority to *i* taxes,
Rev 2: 24 (I will not *i* any other burden

IMPOSED (IMPOSE)
2Ki 23: 33 and he *i* on Judah a levy
2Ch 24: 6 and Jerusalem the tax *i*
36: 3 and *i* on Judah a levy of a hundred
Est 10: 1 King Xerxes *i* tribute
Jer 19: 9 the stress of the siege *i* on them

IMPOSING (IMPOSE)
Jos 22: 10 of Manasseh built an *i* altar there
1Ki 9: 8 And though this temple is now *i,*
2Ch 7: 21 And though this temple is now so *i,*
Da 7: 20 the horn that looked more *i*

IMPOSSIBLE
Ge 11: 6 plan to do will be *i* for them.
Jdg 6: 5 It was *i* to count the men
2Sa 13: 2 it seemed *i* for him to do anything
Mt 17: 20 Nothing will be *i* for you."
19: 26 "With man this is *i,*
Mk 10: 27 "With man this is *i,* but not
Lk 1: 37 For nothing is *i* with God."
18: 27 "What is *i* with men is possible
Ac 2: 24 it was *i* for death to keep its hold
Heb 6: 4 It is *i* for those who have once been
6: 18 things in which it is *i* for God to lie,
10: 4 because it is *i* for the blood of bulls
11: 6 without faith it is *i* to please God,

IMPOSTORS
2Co 6: 8 genuine, yet regarded as *i;* known,
2Ti 3: 13 and *i* will go from bad to worse,

IMPOVERISHED (POVERTY)
Jdg 6: 6 so *i* the Israelites that they cried

IMPRESS (IMPRESSED IMPRESSES IMPRESSION IMPRESSIVE)
Dt 6: 7 *I* them on your children.

IMPRESSED (IMPRESS)
Ecc 9: 13 of wisdom that greatly *i* me:

IMPRESSES (IMPRESS)
Pr 17: 10 A rebuke *i* a man of discernment

IMPRESSION (IMPRESS)

Gal 6: 12 make a good *i* outwardly are trying

IMPRESSIVE (IMPRESS)

1Sa 9: 2 an *i* young man without equal

IMPRISON (PRISON)

Ac 22: 19 from one synagogue to another to *i*

IMPRISONED (PRISON)

Ge 41: 10 and he *i* me and the chief baker
1Sa 23: 7 for David has *i* himself
Jer 32: 3 king of Judah had *i* him there,
37: 15 and *i* in the house of Jonathan

IMPRISONMENT (PRISON)

Ezr 7: 26 confiscation of property, or *i*.
Ac 23: 29 him that deserved death or *i*.
26: 31 anything that deserves death or *i*."

IMPRISONMENTS (PRISON)

2Co 6: 5 distresses; in beatings, *i* and riots;

IMPRISONS (PRISON)

Job 12: 14 the man he *i* cannot be released.

IMPROPER

Eph 5: 3 these are *i* for God's holy people.

IMPROVISE

Am 6: 5 and *i* on musical instruments.

IMPURE (IMPURITIES IMPURITY)

Lev 7: 18 for it is *i;* the person who eats any
19: 7 it is *i* and will not be accepted.
Nu 5: 14 he suspects his wife and she is *i*—
5: 14 her even though she is not *i*—
5: 19 and become *i* while married
Dt 23: 9 keep away from everything *i*.
Job 14: 4 can bring what is pure from the *i?*
Ac 10: 14 "I have never eaten anything *i*
10: 15 not call anything *i* that God has
10: 28 me that I should not call any man *i*
11: 8 Nothing *i* or unclean has ever
11: 9 not call anything *i* that God has
Eph 5: 5 No immoral, *i* or greedy person—
1Th 2: 3 spring from error or *i* motives,
4: 7 For God did not call us to be *i*,
Rev 21: 27 Nothing *i* will ever enter it,

IMPURITIES (IMPURE)

Isa 1: 25 and remove your *i*.
Eze 24: 11 glows so its *i* may be melted
36: 25 I will cleanse you from all your *i*

IMPURITY (IMPURE)

Lev 15: 19 the *i* of her monthly period will last
20: 21 of *i;* he has dishonored his brother.
Nu 5: 13 and her *i* is undetected
5: 28 defiled herself and is free from *i*,
Ezr 9: 11 it with their *i* from one end
Eze 24: 13 would not be cleansed from your *i*,
24: 13 " 'Now your *i* is lewdness.
Zec 13: 1 to cleanse them from sin and *i*.
13: 2 and the spirit of *i* from the land.
Ro 1: 24 hearts to sexual *i* for the degrading
6: 19 parts of your body in slavery to *i*
2Co 12: 21 and have not repented of the *i*,
Gal 5: 19 sexual immorality, *i*
Eph 4: 19 as to indulge in every kind of *i*,
5: 3 or of any kind of *i*, or of greed,
Col 3: 5 *i*, lust, evil desires and greed,

IMRAH

1Ch 7: 36 Shual, Beri, *I*, Bezer, Hod,

IMRI

1Ch 9: 4 the son of *I*, the son of Bani,
Ne 3: 2 Zaccur son of *I* built next to them.

INCAPABLE

Hos 8: 5 How long will they be *i* of purity?

INCENSE (FRANKINCENSE INCENSED)

Ex 25: 6 anointing oil and for the fragrant *i;*
30: 1 altar of acacia wood for burning *i*.
30: 7 "Aaron must burn fragrant *i*
30: 8 He must burn *i* again
Ex 30: 8 at twilight so *i* will burn regularly
30: 9 offer on this altar any other *i*
30: 27 and its accessories, the altar of *i*,
30: 35 and make a fragrant blend of *i*,
30: 37 Do not make any *i*
31: 8 the altar of *i*, the altar
31: 11 and fragrant *i* for the Holy Place.
35: 8 anointing oil and for the fragrant *i;*
35: 15 the altar of *i* with its poles,
35: 15 the anointing oil and the fragrant *i;*
35: 28 anointing oil and for the fragrant *i*.
37: 25 the altar of *i* out of acacia wood.
37: 29 fragrant *i*— the work of a perfumer
39: 38 the anointing oil, the fragrant *i*,
40: 5 Place the gold altar of *i* in front
40: 27 and burned fragrant *i* on it,
Lev 2: 1 put *i* on it and take it
2: 2 together with all the *i*,
2: 15 and *i* on it; it is a grain offering.
2: 16 together with all the *i*,
4: 7 of the altar of fragrant *i* that is
5: 11 He must not put oil or *i* on it,
6: 15 together with all the *i*
10: 1 put fire in them and added *i;*
16: 12 handfuls of finely ground fragrant *i*
16: 13 He is to put the *i* on the fire
16: 13 of the *i* will conceal the atonement
24: 7 Along each row put some pure *i*
26: 30 cut down your *i* altars
Nu 4: 16 fragrant *i*, the regular grain offering
5: 15 oil on it or put *i* on it,
7: 14 filled with *i;* one young bull,
7: 20 filled with *i;* one young bull,
7: 26 filled with *i;* one young bull,
7: 32 filled with *i;* one young bull,
7: 38 filled with *i;* one young bull,
7: 44 filled with *i;* one young bull,
7: 50 filled with *i;* one young bull,
7: 56 filled with *i;* one young bull,
7: 62 filled with *i;* one young bull,
7: 68 filled with *i;* one young bull,
7: 74 filled with *i;* one young bull,
7: 80 filled with *i;* one young bull,
7: 86 with *i* weighed ten shekels each,
16: 7 and *i* in them before the LORD.
16: 17 is to take his censer and put *i* in it—
16: 18 man took his censer, put fire and *i*
16: 35 men who were offering the *i*.
16: 40 come to burn *i* before the LORD,
16: 46 "Take your censer and put *i* in it,
16: 47 but Aaron offered the *i*
Dt 33: 10 He offers *i* before you
1Sa 2: 28 to go up to my altar, to burn *i*,
1Ki 3: 3 and burned *i* on the high places.
9: 25 burning *i* before the LORD
11: 8 who burned *i* and offered sacrifices
22: 43 to offer sacrifices and burn *i* there.
2Ki 12: 3 to offer sacrifices and burn *i* there.
14: 4 to offer sacrifices and burn *i* there.
15: 4 to offer sacrifices and burn *i* there.
15: 35 to offer sacrifices and burn *i* there.
16: 4 and burned *i* at the high places,
17: 11 At every high place they burned *i*,
18: 4 the Israelites had been burning *i*
22: 17 and burned *i* to other gods
23: 5 Judah to burn *i* on the high places
23: 5 those who burned *i* to Baal,
23: 8 where the priests had burned *i*.
1Ch 6: 49 and on the altar of *i* in connection
9: 29 and wine, and the oil, *i* and spices.
28: 18 of the refined gold for the altar of *i*.
2Ch 2: 4 for burning fragrant *i* before him,
13: 11 and fragrant *i* to the LORD.
14: 5 and *i* altars in every town in Judah,
26: 16 LORD to burn *i* on the altar of *i*.
26: 18 Uzziah, to burn *i* to the LORD.
26: 18 have been consecrated to burn *i*.
26: 19 a censer in his hand ready to burn *i*,
26: 19 in their presence before the *i* altar
28: 4 and burned *i* at the high places,
29: 7 They did not burn *i* or present any
29: 11 minister before him and to burn *i*."
30: 14 and cleared away the *i* altars
34: 4 cut to pieces the *i* altars that were
34: 7 and cut to pieces all the *i* altars
34: 25 and burned *i* to other gods
Ne 13: 5 to store the grain offerings and *i*
13: 9 with the grain offerings and the *i*.
Ps 141: 2 my prayer be set before you like *i;*
Pr 27: 9 *i* bring joy to the heart,
SS 3: 6 perfumed with myrrh and *i*
4: 6 and to the hill of *i*.
4: 14 with every kind of *i* tree,
Isa 1: 13 Your *i* is detestable to me.
17: 8 the *i* altars their fingers have made.
27: 9 no Asherah poles or *i* altars
43: 23 wearied you with demands for *i*.
60: 6 bearing gold and *i*
65: 3 and burning *i* on altars of brick;
66: 3 and whoever burns memorial *i*,
Jer 1: 16 in burning *i* to other gods
6: 20 What do I care about *i* from Sheba
7: 9 burn *i* to Baal and follow other
11: 12 to the gods to whom they burn *i*,
11: 13 to burn *i* to that shameful god Baal
11: 17 me to anger by burning *i* to Baal.
17: 26 *i* and thank offerings to the house
18: 15 they burn *i* to worthless idols,
19: 13 all the houses where they burned *i*
32: 29 to anger by burning *i* on the roofs
41: 5 and *i* with them to the house
44: 3 me to anger by burning *i*
44: 5 or stop burning *i* to other gods.
44: 8 burning *i* to other gods in Egypt,
44: 15 that their wives were burning *i*
44: 17 We will burn *i* to the Queen
44: 18 ever since we stopped burning *i*
44: 19 "When we burned *i* to the Queen
44: 21 and think about the *i* burned
44: 23 Because you have burned *i*
44: 25 out the vows we made to burn *i*
48: 35 and burn *i* to their gods,"
Eze 6: 4 and your *i* altars will be smashed;
6: 6 your *i* altars broken down,
6: 13 where they offered fragrant *i*
8: 11 and a fragrant cloud of *i* was rising.
16: 18 and you offered my oil and *i*
16: 19 as fragrant *i* before them.
20: 28 presented their fragrant *i*
20: 41 as fragrant *i* when I bring you out
23: 41 it on which you had placed the *i*
Da 2: 46 that an offering and *i* be presented
Hos 2: 13 she burned *i* to the Baals;
11: 2 and they burned *i* to images.
Hab 1: 16 and burns *i* to his dragnet,
Mal 1: 11 In every place *i* and pure offerings
Mt 2: 11 him with gifts of gold and of *i*
Lk 1: 9 the temple of the Lord and burn *i*.
1: 10 the time for the burning of *i* came,
1: 11 at the right side of the altar of *i*.
Heb 9: 4 which had the golden altar of *i*
Rev 5: 8 were holding golden bowls full of *i*,
8: 3 He was given much *i* to offer,
8: 4 The smoke of the *i*, together
18: 13 of *i*, myrrh and frankincense,

INCENSED (INCENSE)

Ne 4: 1 he became angry and was greatly *i*.

INCHES

Ge 6: 16 the ark to within 18 *i* of the top.

INCIDENT

1Ki 21: 1 there was an *i* involving a vineyard

INCITED (INCITING)

1Sa 22: 8 me that my son has *i* my servant
26: 19 If the LORD has *i* you against me,
2Sa 24: 1 and he *i* David against them,
1Ch 21: 1 *i* David to take a census of Israel.
Job 2: 3 you *i* me against him to ruin him
Ac 13: 50 the Jews *i* the God-fearing women

INCITING (INCITED)

Jer 43: 3 son of Neriah is *i* you against us
Lk 23: 14 as one who was *i* the people

INCLINATION (INCLINATIONS INCLINED INCLINES)

Ge 6: 5 and that every *i* of the thoughts
8: 21 though every *i* of his heart is evil

INCLINATIONS (INCLINATION)

Jer 7: 24 they followed the stubborn *i*

INCLINED (INCLINATION)
Dt 5: 29 that their hearts would be *i*
Jdg 9: 3 they were *i* to follow Abimelech,
1Sa 20: 13 But if my father is *i* to harm you,

INCLINES (INCLINATION)
Ecc 10: 2 The heart of the wise *i* to the right,

INCLUDE (INCLUDED)
Nu 28: 22 *I* one male goat as a sin offering
28: 30 *I* one male goat to make atonement
29: 5 *I* one male goat as a sin offering
29: 11 *I* one male goat as a sin offering,
29: 16 *I* one male goat as a sin offering,
29: 19 *I* one male goat as a sin offering,
29: 22 *I* one male goat as a sin offering,
29: 25 *I* one male goat as a sin offering,
29: 28 *I* one male goat as a sin offering,
29: 31 *I* one male goat as a sin offering,
29: 34 *I* one male goat as a sin offering,
29: 38 *I* one male goat as a sin offering,

INCLUDED (INCLUDE)
Jos 19: 15 *I* were Kattath, Nahalal, Shimron,

INCOME
2Ki 8: 6 including all the *i* from her land
Pr 10: 16 *i* of the wicked brings them
15: 6 *i* of the wicked brings them
Ecc 5: 10 wealth is never satisfied with his *i*.
Ac 19: 25 you know we receive a good *i*
1Co 16: 2 sum of money in keeping with his *i*,

INCOMPARABLE
Eph 2: 7 ages he might show the *i* riches

INCOMPREHENSIBLE
Isa 33: 19 with their strange, *i* tongue.

INCREASE (EVER-INCREASING INCREASED INCREASES INCREASING)
Ge 1: 22 and let the birds *i* on the earth."
1: 22 "Be fruitful and *i* in number
1: 28 "Be fruitful and *i* in number;
3: 16 "I will greatly *i* your pains
6: 1 When men began to *i* in number
8: 17 be fruitful and *i* in number upon it
9: 1 "Be fruitful and *i* in number
9: 7 be fruitful and *i* in number;
9: 7 multiply on the earth and *i* upon it
16: 10 so *i* your descendants that they will
17: 2 and will greatly *i* your numbers."
17: 20 and will greatly *i* his numbers.
24: 60 "Our sister, may you *i*
26: 24 *I* the number of your descendants
28: 3 *i* your numbers until you become
35: 11 be fruitful and *i* in number.
48: 4 fruitful and will *i* your numbers.
48: 16 and may they *i* greatly
Lev 25: 16 are many, you are to *i* the price,
26: 9 you fruitful and *i* your numbers,
Dt 1: 11 *i* you a thousand times
6: 3 and that you may *i* greatly
7: 13 and bless you and *i* your numbers.
8: 1 so that you may live and *i*
8: 13 gold *i* and all you have is multiplied
13: 17 on you, and *i* your numbers,
28: 63 LORD to make you prosper and *i*
30: 16 and laws; then you will live and *i*,
Job 10: 17 and *i* your anger toward me;
Ps 16: 4 The sorrows of those will *i*
61: 6 *I* the days of the king's life,
62: 10 though your riches *i*,
71: 21 You will *i* my honor
73: 12 always carefree, they *i* in wealth.
115: 14 May the LORD make you *i*,
144: 13 Our sheep will *i* by thousands,
Pr 22: 16 oppresses the poor to *i* his wealth
Ecc 5: 9 The *i* from the land is taken by all;
5: 11 As goods *i*,
Isa 9: 7 Of the *i* of his government
Jer 23: 3 where they will be fruitful and *i*
29: 6 *I* in number there; do not decrease.
Eze 36: 11 I will *i* the number of men
36: 30 I will *i* the fruit of the trees
37: 26 establish them and *i* their numbers,
Da 12: 4 and there to *i* knowledge."
Hos 4: 10 engage in prostitution but not *i*,
Mt 24: 12 Because of the *i* of wickedness,
Lk 17: 5 said to the Lord, "*I* our faith!"
Ac 12: 24 But the word of God continued to *i*
Ro 5: 20 added so that the trespass might *i*.
6: 1 go on sinning so that grace may *i*?
2Co 9: 10 also supply and *i* your store of seed
1Th 3: 12 May the Lord make your love *i*

INCREASED (INCREASE)
Ge 7: 17 the waters *i* they lifted the ark high
7: 18 The waters rose and *i* greatly
30: 30 had before I came has *i* greatly,
47: 27 and were fruitful and *i* greatly
Ex 1: 20 and the people *i* and became
23: 30 *i* enough to take possession
Lev 19: 25 In this way your harvest will be *i*.
Dt 1: 10 your God has *i* your numbers
Jdg 1: 35 the power of the house of Joseph *i*,
1Sa 14: 19 in the Philistine camp *i* more
1Ch 4: 38 Their families *i* greatly,
5: 9 their livestock had *i* in Gilead.
2Ch 33: 23 before the LORD; Amon *i* his guilt
Ps 25: 19 See how my enemies have *i*
39: 2 my anguish *i*.
107: 38 and their numbers greatly *i*,
107: 41 and *i* their families like flocks.
Ecc 1: 16 *i* in wisdom more than anyone who
Isa 9: 3 and *i* their joy;
57: 9 and *i* your perfumes.
Jer 3: 16 when your numbers have *i* greatly
Eze 16: 29 Then you *i* your promiscuity
28: 5 you have *i* your wealth,
31: 5 its boughs *i*
Hos 4: 7 The more the priests *i*,
10: 1 As his fruit *i*,
Na 3: 16 You have *i* the number
Lk 11: 29 As the crowds *i*, Jesus said,
Ac 6: 7 of disciples in Jerusalem *i* rapidly,
7: 17 of our people in Egypt greatly *i*.
Ro 5: 20 But where sin *i*, grace *i* all the more

INCREASES (INCREASE)
Ps 49: 16 when the splendor of his house *i*;
Pr 24: 5 and a man of knowledge *i* strength;
28: 8 He who *i* his wealth
Isa 40: 29 and *i* the power of the weak.
Ro 3: 7 truthfulness and so *i* his glory,

INCREASING (INCREASE)
2Sa 15: 12 and Absalom's following kept on *i*.
Job 21: 7 growing old and *i* in power?
Eze 16: 25 body with *i* promiscuity
16: 26 to anger with your *i* promiscuity.
Ac 6: 1 when the number of disciples was *i*,
2Th 1: 3 one of you has for each other is *i*.
2Pe 1: 8 these qualities in *i* measure,

INCREDIBLE
Ac 26: 8 of you consider it *i* that God raises

INCUR (INCURS)
Ex 28: 43 so that they will not *i* guilt and die.

INCURABLE
2Ch 21: 18 with an *i* disease of the bowels.
Job 34: 6 his arrow inflicts an *i* wound.'
Isa 17: 11 in the day of disease and *i* pain.
Jer 10: 19 My wound is *i*!
15: 18 and my wound grievous and *i*?
30: 12 " 'Your wound is *i*,
Mic 1: 9 For her wound is *i*;

INCURS (INCUR)
Pr 9: 7 rebukes a wicked man *i* abuse.
14: 35 but a shameful servant *i* his wrath.

INDECENT
Dt 23: 14 see among you anything *i*
24: 1 he finds something *i* about her,
Ro 1: 27 Men committed *i* acts

INDECISIVE
2Ch 13: 7 and *i* and not strong enough

INDEPENDENT
1Co 11: 11 however, woman is not *i* of man,
11: 11 of man, nor is man *i* of woman.

INDESCRIBABLE
2Co 9: 15 Thanks be to God for his *i* gift!

INDESTRUCTIBLE
Heb 7: 16 on the basis of the power of an *i* life

INDIA
Est 1: 1 provinces stretching from *I*
8: 9 the 127 provinces stretching from *I*

INDICATE (INDICATED INDICATING)
1Sa 16: 3 You are to anoint for me the one I *i*
Jn 21: 19 Jesus said this to *i* the kind of death
Heb 12: 27 words "once more" *i* the removing

INDICATED (INDICATE)
Nu 1: 18 The people *i* their ancestry
2Ki 6: 10 on the place *i* by the man of God.

INDICATING (INDICATE)
Jn 18: 32 words Jesus had spoken *i* the kind
Heb 9: 9 *i* that the gifts and sacrifices being

INDICTMENT
Job 31: 35 let my accuser put his *i* in writing.

INDIGNANT (INDIGNATION)
Mt 20: 24 they were *i* with the two brothers.
21: 15 to the Son of David," they were *i*.
26: 8 the disciples saw this, they were *i*.
Mk 10: 14 When Jesus saw this, he was *i*.
10: 41 they became *i* with James and John
Lk 13: 14 *I* because Jesus had healed

INDIGNATION (INDIGNANT)
Ps 78: 49 his wrath, *i* and hostility—
90: 7 and terrified by your *i*.
119: 53 *I* grips me because of the wicked,
Jer 15: 17 and you had filled me with *i*.
Na 1: 6 Who can withstand his *i*?
2Co 7: 11 what *i*, what alarm, what longing,

INDISPENSABLE
1Co 12: 22 seem to be weaker are *i*,

INDULGE (INDULGED INDULGENCE INDULGING SELF-INDULGENCE)
Ex 32: 6 and drink and got up to *i* in revelry.
Nu 25: 1 began to *i* in sexual immorality
Lk 7: 25 and *i* in luxury are in palaces.
1Co 10: 7 and got up to *i* in pagan revelry."
Gal 5: 13 freedom to *i* the sinful nature;
Eph 4: 19 as to *i* in every kind of impurity,
2Ti 2: 16 those who *i* in it will become more

INDULGED (INDULGE)
2Co 12: 21 debauchery in which they have *i*.

INDULGENCE (INDULGE)
Col 2: 23 value in restraining sensual *i*.

INDULGING (INDULGE)
1Ti 3: 8 sincere, not *i* in much wine,

INEFFECTIVE
2Pe 1: 8 they will keep you from being *i*

INEXPERIENCED
1Ch 22: 5 "My son Solomon is young and *i*,
29: 1 God has chosen, is young and *i*.

INEXPRESSIBLE
2Co 12: 4 He heard *i* things, things that man
1Pe 1: 8 are filled with an *i* and glorious joy,

INFAMOUS (INFAMY)
Eze 22: 5 far away will mock you, O *i* city,

INFAMY (INFAMOUS)
Isa 44: 11 brought down to terror and *i*.

INFANCY (INFANT)
2Ti 3: 15 from *i* you have known the holy

INFANT (INFANCY INFANT'S INFANTS)
Nu 11: 12 as a nurse carries an *i*,
12: 12 let her be like a stillborn *i* coming
Job 3: 16 like an *i* who never saw the light
24: 9 the *i* of the poor is seized for a debt.

Isa 11: 8 The *i* will play near the hole
65: 20 an *i* that lives but a few days,
Heb 5: 13 lives on milk, being still an *i*,

INFANT'S (INFANT)
La 4: 4 Because of thirst the *i* tongue

INFANTS (INFANT)
Dt 32: 25 *i* and gray-haired men.
1Sa 15: 3 children and *i*, cattle and sheep,
22: 19 its children and *i*, and its cattle,
Ps 8: 2 From the lips of children and *i*
137: 9 he who seizes your *i*
Isa 13: 16 Their *i* will be dashed to pieces
13: 18 they will have no mercy on *i*
Jer 44: 7 and *i*, and so leave yourselves
La 2: 11 because children and *i* faint
Na 3: 10 Her *i* were dashed to pieces
Mt 21: 16 " 'From the lips of children and *i*
Ro 2: 20 of the foolish, a teacher of *i*,
1Co 3: 1 but as worldly—mere *i* in Christ.
14: 20 In regard to evil be *i*,
Eph 4: 14 Then we will no longer be *i*,

INFECTED
Lev 13: 4 is to put the *i* person in isolation
13: 12 of the *i* person from head to foot,
13: 17 shall pronounce the *i* person clean;
13: 31 is to put the *i* person in isolation

INFECTION
Lev 13: 46 as he has the *i* he remains unclean.

INFECTIOUS
Lev 13: 2 that may become an *i* skin disease,
13: 3 skin deep, it is an *i* skin disease.
13: 8 him unclean; it is an *i* disease.
13: 9 When anyone has an *i* skin disease,
13: 15 flesh is unclean; he has an *i* disease.
13: 20 It is an *i* skin disease that has
13: 22 shall pronounce him unclean; it is *i*.
13: 25 him unclean; it is an *i* skin disease.
13: 25 it is an *i* disease that has broken out
13: 27 him unclean; it is an *i* skin disease.
13: 30 an *i* disease of the head or chin.
13: 42 it is an *i* disease breaking out
13: 43 reddish-white like an *i* skin disease,
13: 45 with such an *i* disease must wear
14: 3 healed of his *i* skin disease,
14: 7 one to be cleansed of the *i* disease
14: 32 anyone who has an *i* skin disease
14: 54 regulations for any *i* skin disease,
14: 57 the regulations for *i* skin diseases
22: 4 of Aaron has an *i* skin disease
Nu 5: 2 anyone who has an *i* skin disease

INFERIOR
Job 12: 3 I am not *i* to you.
13: 2 I am not *i* to you.
Da 2: 39 another kingdom will rise, *i*
2Co 11: 5 least *i* to those "super-apostles."
12: 11 in the least *i* to the "super-apostles
12: 13 How were you *i* to the other

INFILTRATED
Gal 2: 4 some false brothers had *i* our ranks

INFIRMITIES
Isa 53: 4 Surely he took up our *i*
Mt 8: 17 "He took up our *i*

INFIRMITY
Lk 13: 12 you are set free from your *i*."

INFLAMED (INFLAME)
Isa 5: 11 night till they are *i* with wine.
Hos 7: 5 the princes become *i* with wine,
Ro 1: 27 were *i* with lust for one another.

INFLAMMATION (INFLAME)
Dt 28: 22 fever and *i*, with scorching heat

INFLICT (INFLICTED INFLICTS)
Dt 7: 15 He will not *i* on you the horrible
7: 15 he will *i* them on all who hate you.
28: 53 the suffering that your enemy will *i*
28: 55 of the suffering your enemy will *i*
28: 57 the distress that your enemy will *i*
Jdg 20: 31 They began to *i* casualties
20: 39 begun to *i* casualties on the men
Ps 149: 7 to *i* vengeance on the nations
Jer 18: 8 and not *i* on it the disaster I had
36: 3 hear about every disaster I plan to *i*
Eze 5: 8 and I will *i* punishment on you
5: 10 I will *i* punishment on you
5: 15 you when I *i* punishment on you
11: 9 to foreigners and *i* punishment
16: 41 *i* punishment on you in the sight
25: 11 and I will *i* punishment on Moab.
28: 22 when I *i* punishment on her
28: 26 live in safety when I *i* punishment
30: 14 and *i* punishment on Thebes.
30: 19 So I will *i* punishment on Egypt,
39: 21 nations will see the punishment I *i*
Rev 9: 19 heads with which they *i* injury.

INFLICTED (INFLICT)
Ge 12: 17 But the LORD *i* serious diseases
1Sa 14: 47 he turned, he *i* punishment
23: 5 He *i* heavy losses on the Philistines
2Sa 7: 14 of men, with floggings *i* by men.
1Ki 20: 21 *i* heavy losses on the Arameans.
20: 29 The Israelites *i* a hundred thousand
2Ki 8: 29 the wounds the Arameans had *i*
9: 15 the wounds the Arameans had *i*
2Ch 13: 17 his men *i* heavy losses on them,
22: 6 from the wounds they had *i* on him
28: 5 who *i* heavy casualties on him.
Isa 30: 26 and heals the wounds he *i*.
Jer 42: 10 over the disaster I have *i* on you.
La 1: 12 that was *i* on me,
Eze 23: 10 and punishment was *i* on her.
2Co 2: 6 The punishment *i* on him

INFLICTS (INFLICT)
Job 34: 6 his arrow *i* an incurable wound.'
Zec 14: 18 bring on them the plague he *i*

INFLUENCE (INFLUENCED INFLUENTIAL)
Job 31: 21 knowing that I had *i* in court,

INFLUENCED (INFLUENCE)
1Co 12: 2 somehow or other you were *i*

INFLUENTIAL (INFLUENCE)
1Co 1: 26 not many were *i*; not many were

INFORM (INFORMATION INFORMED)
Ex 18: 16 and *i* them of God's decrees
1Sa 27: 11 "They might *i* on us and say,
2Sa 15: 28 until word comes from you to *i* me
17: 17 A servant girl was to go and *i* them,
17: 21 the well and went to *i* King David.
Ezr 4: 14 sending this message to *i* the king,
4: 16 We *i* the king that
Job 12: 8 or let the fish of the sea *i* you.

INFORMATION (INFORM)
1Sa 23: 23 come back to me with definite *i*.
Ezr 5: 10 names of their leaders for your *i*.
Ac 23: 15 wanting more accurate *i* about his
23: 20 more accurate *i* about him.

INFORMED (INFORM)
2Ki 22: 10 Shaphan the secretary *i* the king,
2Ch 34: 18 Shaphan the secretary *i* the king,
Da 1: 4 well *i*, quick to understand,
Ac 21: 21 They have been *i* that you teach all
23: 30 When I was *i* of a plot
1Co 1: 11 Chloe's household have *i* me that

INGATHERING (GATHER)
Ex 23: 16 "Celebrate the Feast of *I* at the end
34: 22 the Feast of *I* at the turn of the year

INHABIT (HABITAT INHABITANT INHABITANTS INHABITED)
Job 15: 28 he will *i* ruined towns
Ac 17: 26 that they should *i* the whole earth;

INHABITANT (INHABIT)
Isa 6: 11 and without *i*,
Jer 4: 7 ruins without *i*.
46: 19 and lie in ruins without *i*.

INHABITANTS (INHABIT)
Lev 18: 25 and the land vomited out its *i*.
25: 10 throughout the land to all its *i*.
Nu 14: 14 they will tell the *i* of this land about
32: 17 for protection from the *i* of the land
33: 52 drive out all the *i* of the land
33: 55 " 'But if you do not drive out the *i*
Jos 9: 24 to wipe out all its *i* from before you.
13: 6 for all the *i* of the mountain regions
Jdg 1: 32 among the Canaanite *i* of the land.
1: 33 among the Canaanite *i* of the land,
1Ki 9: 16 He killed its Canaanite *i*
2Ki 16: 9 He deported its *i* to Kir
1Ch 8: 13 and who drove out the *i* of Gath.
10: 11 the *i* of Jabesh Gilead heard
22: 18 For he has handed the *i* of the land
2Ch 15: 5 for all the *i* of the lands were
20: 7 did you not drive out the *i*
34: 9 Benjamin and the *i* of Jerusalem.
Isa 9: 9 Ephraim and the *i* of Samaria—
24: 1 and scatter its *i*—
24: 6 Therefore earth's *i* are burned up,
51: 6 and its *i* die like flies.
Jer 25: 9 its *i* and against all the surrounding
44: 22 and a desolate waste without *i*,
48: 18 O *i* of the Daughter of Dibon,
49: 3 Cry out, O *i* of Rabbah!
51: 35 say the *i* of Zion.
Mic 7: 13 become desolate because of its *i*,
Zec 8: 20 the *i* of many cities will yet come,
8: 21 the *i* of one city will go to another
12: 7 of Jerusalem's *i* may not be greater
12: 10 the *i* of Jerusalem a spirit of grace
13: 1 of David and the *i* of Jerusalem,
Rev 6: 10 until you judge the *i* of the earth
8: 13 Woe! Woe to the *i* of the earth,
11: 10 The *i* of the earth will gloat
13: 8 All *i* of the earth will worship
13: 12 and its *i* worship the first beast,
13: 14 he deceived the *i* of the earth.
17: 2 the *i* of the earth were intoxicated
17: 8 *i* of the earth whose names have

INHABITED (INHABIT)
Isa 13: 20 She will never be *i*
44: 26 who says of Jerusalem, 'It shall be *i*
45: 18 but formed it to be *i*—
Jer 17: 25 and this city will be *i* forever.
22: 6 like towns not *i*.
33: 10 *i* by neither men nor animals,
46: 26 Egypt will be *i* as in times past,"
50: 13 the LORD's anger she will not be *i*
50: 39 It will never again be *i*
Eze 12: 20 The *i* towns will be laid waste
26: 19 desolate city, like cities no longer *i*,
35: 9 forever; your towns will not be *i*.
36: 10 The towns will be *i* and the ruins
36: 35 destroyed, are now fortified and *i*."
Joel 3: 20 Judah will be *i* forever
Zec 14: 11 It will be *i*; never again will it be

INHERIT (CO-HEIRS HEIR HEIRS HERITAGE INHERITANCE INHERITANCES INHERITED INHERITS)
Ge 15: 2 one who will *i* my estate is Eliezer
48: 6 in the territory they *i* they will be
Nu 14: 24 and his descendants will *i* it.
32: 32 but the property we *i* will be
Dt 1: 38 because he will lead Israel to *i* it.
3: 28 to *i* the land that you will see."
33: 23 he will *i* southward to the lake."
Jos 1: 6 people to *i* the land I swore
1Sa 2: 8 and has them *i* a throne of honor.
2Ki 2: 9 "Let me *i* a double portion
1Ch 16: 18 as the portion you will *i*."
Job 13: 26 and make me *i* the sins of my youth
Ps 25: 13 and his descendants will *i* the land.
37: 9 in the LORD will *i* the land.
37: 11 But the meek will *i* the land
37: 22 the LORD blesses will *i* the land,
37: 29 the righteous will *i* the land
69: 36 the children of his servants will *i* it,
105: 11 as the portion you will *i*."
Pr 3: 35 The wise *i* honor,
11: 29 on his family will *i* only wind,
14: 18 The simple *i* folly,
Isa 14: 21 they are not to rise to *i* the land

Isa 57: 13 will *i* the land
61: 7 and so they will *i* a double portion
65: 9 my chosen people will *i* them,
Zep 2: 9 of my nation will *i* their land."
Zec 2: 12 The LORD will *i* Judah
Mt 5: 5 for they will *i* the earth.
19: 29 as much and will *i* eternal life.
Mk 10: 17 "what must I do to *i* eternal life?"
Lk 10: 25 "what must I do to *i* eternal life?"
18: 18 what must I do to *i* eternal life?"
1Co 6: 9 the wicked will not *i* the kingdom
6: 10 nor swindlers will *i* the kingdom
15: 50 blood cannot *i* the kingdom of God
15: 50 the perishable *i* the imperishable.
Gal 5: 21 live like this will not *i* the kingdom
Heb 1: 14 to serve those who will *i* salvation?
6: 12 patience *i* what has been promised.
12: 17 when he wanted to *i* this blessing,
Jas 2: 5 to *i* the kingdom he promised those
1Pe 3: 9 called so that you may *i* a blessing.
Rev 21: 7 He who overcomes will *i* all this,

INHERITANCE (INHERIT)

Ge 21: 10 share in the *i* with my son Isaac."
31: 14 share in the *i* of our father's estate?
Ex 15: 17 them on the mountain of your *i*—
32: 13 and it will be their *i* forever.' "
34: 9 and our sin, and take us as your *i*."
Lev 20: 24 I will give it to you as an *i*,
Nu 16: 14 given us an *i* of fields and vineyards
18: 20 and your *i* among the Israelites.
18: 20 "You will have no *i* in their land,
18: 21 their *i* in return for the work they
18: 23 They will receive no *i*
18: 24 their *i* the tithes that the Israelites
18: 24 'They will have no *i*
18: 26 the tithe I give you as your *i*,
26: 53 an *i* based on the number of names.
26: 54 To a larger group give a larger *i*,
26: 54 is to receive its *i* according
26: 56 Each *i* is to be distributed by lot
26: 62 they received no *i* among them.
27: 7 an *i* among their father's relatives
27: 7 turn their father's *i* over to them.
27: 8 turn his *i* over to his daughter.
27: 9 If he has no daughter, give his *i*
27: 10 give his *i* to his father's brothers.
27: 11 give his *i* to the nearest relative
32: 18 every Israelite has received his *i*.
32: 19 We will not receive any *i*
32: 19 because our *i* has come to us
33: 54 To a larger group give a larger *i*,
34: 2 as an *i* will have these boundaries:
34: 13 "Assign this land by lot as an *i*.
34: 14 of Manasseh have received their *i*.
34: 15 a half tribes have received their *i*
34: 17 to assign the land for you as an *i*:
34: 29 to assign the *i* to the Israelites
35: 2 from the *i* the Israelites will possess
35: 8 in proportion to the *i* of each tribe:
36: 2 as an *i* to the Israelites by lot,
36: 2 you to give the *i* of our brother
36: 3 And so part of the *i* allotted
36: 3 taken from our ancestral *i*
36: 3 then their *i* will be taken
36: 4 from the tribal *i* of our forefathers
36: 4 their *i* will be added to that
36: 7 No *i* in Israel is to pass from tribe
36: 8 every Israelite will possess the *i*
36: 9 No *i* may pass from tribe to tribe,
36: 12 their *i* remained in their father's
Dt 4: 20 to be the people of his *i*,
4: 21 your God is giving you as your *i*.
4: 38 land to give it to you for your *i*,
9: 26 your own *i* that you redeemed
9: 29 your *i* that you brought out
10: 9 or *i* among their brothers;
10: 9 the LORD is their *i*, as the LORD
12: 9 the *i* the LORD your God is giving
12: 10 your God is giving you as an *i*,
12: 12 who have no allotment or *i*
14: 27 for they have no allotment or *i*
14: 29 or *i* of their own) and the aliens,
15: 4 you to possess as your *i*,
18: 1 are to have no allotment or *i*
18: 1 LORD by fire, for that is their *i*.
18: 2 They shall have no *i*
18: 2 LORD is their *i*, as he promised
Dt 19: 3 your God is giving you as an *i*,
19: 10 your God is giving you as your *i*,
19: 14 predecessors in the *i* you receive
20: 16 your God is giving you as an *i*,
21: 23 your God is giving you as an *i*.
24: 4 your God is giving you as an *i*.
25: 19 he is giving you to possess as an *i*,
26: 1 an *i* and have taken possession of it
29: 8 gave it as an *i* to the Reubenites,
31: 7 it among them as their *i*.
32: 8 Most High gave the nations their *i*,
32: 9 Jacob his allotted *i*.
Jos 11: 23 as an *i* to Israel according
12: 7 an *i* to the tribes of Israel according
13: 6 allocate this land to Israel for an *i*,
13: 7 as an *i* among the nine tribes
13: 8 had received the *i* that Moses had
13: 14 But to the tribe of Levi he gave no *i*
13: 14 are their *i*, as he promised them.
13: 23 and their villages were the *i*
13: 28 and their villages were the *i*
13: 32 This is the *i* Moses had given
13: 33 Moses had given no *i*; the LORD,
13: 33 is their *i*, as he promised them.
14: 1 as an *i* in the land of Canaan,
14: 3 had not granted the Levites an *i*
14: 3 two-and-a-half tribes their *i* east
14: 9 feet have walked will be your *i*
14: 13 and gave him Hebron as his *i*.
15: 20 This is the *i* of the tribe of Judah,
16: 4 of Joseph, received their *i*.
16: 5 The boundary of their *i* went
16: 8 This was the *i* of the tribe
16: 9 within the *i* of the Manassites.
17: 4 So Joshua gave them an *i*
17: 4 to give us an *i* among our brothers
17: 6 the tribe of Manasseh received an *i*
17: 14 allotment and one portion for an *i*?
18: 2 who had not yet received their *i*.
18: 4 according to the *i* of each.
18: 7 have already received their *i*
18: 7 service of the LORD is their *i*.
18: 20 boundaries that marked out the *i*
18: 28 This was the *i* of Benjamin
19: 1 Their *i* lay within the territory
19: 8 This was the *i* of the tribe
19: 9 So the Simeonites received their *i*
19: 9 The *i* of the Simeonites was taken
19: 10 The boundary of their *i* went as far
19: 16 their villages were the *i* of Zebulun,
19: 23 their villages were the *i* of the tribe
19: 31 their villages were the *i* of the tribe
19: 39 their villages were the *i* of the tribe
19: 41 The territory of their *i* included:
19: 48 their villages were the *i* of the tribe
19: 49 son of Nun an *i* among them,
21: 3 and pasturelands out of their own *i*:
23: 4 as an *i* for your tribes all the land
24: 28 the people away, each to his own *i*.
24: 30 they buried him in the land of his *i*,
24: 32 the *i* of Joseph's descendants.
Jdg 2: 6 of the land, each to his own *i*.
2: 9 they buried him in the land of his *i*,
11: 2 going to get any *i* in our family,"
18: 1 into an *i* among the tribes of Israel.
20: 6 piece to each region of Israel's *i*,
21: 23 Then they returned to their *i*
21: 24 and clans, each to his own *i*.
1Sa 10: 1 anointed you leader over his *i*?
26: 19 me from my share in the LORD's *i*
2Sa 14: 16 my son from the *i* God gave us.'
20: 19 to swallow up the LORD's *i*?"
21: 3 so that you will bless the LORD's *i*
1Ki 8: 36 land you gave your people for an *i*.
8: 51 for they are your people and your *i*,
8: 53 of the world to be your own *i*,
21: 3 forbid that I should give you the *i*
21: 4 "I will not give you the *i*
2Ki 21: 14 I will forsake the remnant of my *i*
1Ch 28: 8 as an *i* to your descendants forever.
2Ch 6: 27 land you gave your people for an *i*.
20: 11 the possession you gave us as an *i*.
Ezr 9: 12 to your children as an everlasting *i*
Job 42: 15 and their father granted them an *i*
Ps 2: 8 and I will make the nations your *i*,
16: 6 surely I have a delightful *i*.
28: 9 Save your people and bless your *i*;
33: 12 the people he chose for his *i*.
Ps 37: 18 and their *i* will endure forever.
47: 4 He chose our *i* for us,
68: 9 you refreshed your weary *i*.
74: 2 the tribe you redeemed as your *i*—
78: 55 allotted their lands to them as an *i*;
78: 62 he was very angry with his *i*.
78: 71 of Israel his *i*.
79: 1 the nations have invaded your *i*;
82: 8 for all the nations are your *i*.
94: 5 they oppress your *i*.
94: 14 he will never forsake his *i*.
106: 5 and join your *i* in giving praise.
106: 40 and abhorred his *i*.
135: 12 an *i* to his people Israel.
135: 12 and he gave their land as an *i*,
136: 21 and gave their land as an *i*,
136: 22 an *i* to his servant Israel;
Pr 13: 22 A good man leaves an *i*
17: 2 will share the *i* as one
20: 21 An *i* quickly gained
28: 10 the blameless will receive a good *i*.
Ecc 7: 11 Wisdom, like an *i*, is a good thing
Isa 19: 25 my handiwork, and Israel my *i*."
47: 6 and desecrated my *i*;
58: 14 feast on the *i* of your father Jacob."
61: 7 they will rejoice in their *i*;
63: 17 the tribes that are your *i*.
Jer 2: 7 and made my *i* detestable.
3: 18 land I gave your forefathers as an *i*.
3: 19 the most beautiful *i* of any nation.'
10: 16 including Israel, the tribe of his *i*—
12: 7 abandon my *i*;
12: 8 My *i* has become to me
12: 9 Has not my *i* become to me
12: 14 neighbors who seize the *i* I gave my
12: 15 each of them back to his own *i*
16: 18 filled my *i* with their detestable
17: 4 the *i* I gave you.
50: 11 you who pillage my *i*,
51: 19 including the tribe of his *i*—
La 5: 2 Our *i* has been turned
Eze 35: 15 rejoiced when the *i* of the house
36: 12 possess you, and you will be their *i*;
44: 28 am to be the only *i* the priests have.
45: 1 " 'When you allot the land as an *i*,
46: 16 a gift from his *i* to one of his sons,
46: 16 it is to be their property by *i*.
46: 17 His *i* belongs to his sons only;
46: 17 from his *i* to one of his servants,
46: 18 any of the *i* of the people,
46: 18 is to give his sons their *i* out
47: 13 for an *i* among the twelve tribes
47: 14 this land will become your *i*.
47: 22 are to allot it as an *i* for yourselves
47: 22 to be allotted an *i* among the tribes
47: 23 there you are to give him his *i*,"
48: 29 as an *i* to the tribes of Israel,
Da 12: 13 rise to receive your allotted *i*."
Joel 2: 17 Do not make your *i* an object
3: 2 concerning my *i*, my people Israel,
Ob : 17 will possess its *i*.
Mic 2: 2 a fellowman of his *i*.
7: 14 the flock of your *i*,
7: 18 of the remnant of his *i*?
Zec 8: 12 an *i* to the remnant of this people.
Mal 1: 3 and left his *i* to the desert jackals."
Mt 21: 38 Come, let's kill him and take his *i*.'
25: 34 blessed by my Father; take your *i*,
Mk 12: 7 let's kill him, and the *i* will be ours.'
Lk 12: 13 brother to divide the *i* with me."
20: 14 Let's kill him, and the *i* will be ours
Ac 7: 5 He gave him no *i* here, not
13: 19 land to his people as their *i*.
20: 32 give you an *i* among all those who
Gal 3: 18 For if the *i* depends on the law,
4: 30 in the *i* with the free woman's son."
Eph 1: 14 who is a deposit guaranteeing our *i*
1: 18 riches of his glorious *i* in the saints,
5: 5 has any *i* in the kingdom of Christ
Col 1: 12 you to share in the *i* of the saints
3: 24 you know that you will receive an *i*
Heb 9: 15 receive the promised eternal *i*—
11: 8 he would later receive as his *i*,
12: 16 for a single meal sold his *i* rights
1Pe 1: 4 and into an *i* that can never perish,

INHERITANCES (INHERIT)

Jos 14: 2 Their *i* were assigned by lot

Isa 49: 8 and to reassign its desolate *i*,

INHERITED (INHERIT)

Lev 25:46 them to your children as *i* property
Nu 36: 7 Israelite shall keep the tribal land *i*
Pr 19:14 wealth are *i* from parents,
Heb 1: 4 as the name he has *i* is superior

INHERITS (INHERIT)

Nu 26:55 What each group *i* will be
36: 8 Every daughter who *i* land
36: 9 is to keep the land it *i*."

INIQUITIES (INIQUITY)

Ps 78:38 he atoned for their *i*
90: 8 You have set our *i* before you,
103: 10 or repay us according to our *i*.
107: 17 suffered affliction because of their *i*
Isa 53: 5 he was crushed for our *i*;
53:11 and he will bear their *i*.
59: 2 But your *i* have separated
59:12 and we acknowledge our *i*:
La 4:13 and the *i* of her priests,
Da 9:16 and the *i* of our fathers have made
Mic 7:19 and hurl all our *i* into the depths

INIQUITY (INIQUITIES)

Ps 25:11 forgive my *i*, though it is great.
32: 5 and did not cover up my *i*.
38:18 I confess my *i*;
51: 2 Wash away all my *i*
51: 9 and blot out all my *i*.
73: 7 From their callous hearts comes *i*;
85: 2 You forgave the *i* of your people
89:32 their *i* with flogging;
109: 14 May the *i* of his fathers be
Isa 53: 6 the *i* of us all.
61: 8 I hate robbery and *i*.
Hos 12: 8 any *i* or sin."
Mic 2: 1 Woe to those who plan *i*,
Zec 5: 6 "This is the *i* of the people

INITIATIVE

2Co 8:17 much enthusiasm and on his own *i*.

INJURE (INJURED INJURES INJURING INJURY)

Zec 12: 3 try to move it will *i* themselves.

INJURED (INJURE)

Ex 21:19 he must pay the *i* man for the loss
22:10 or is *i* or is taken away
22:14 it is *i* or dies while the owner is not
Lev 22:22 offer to the LORD the blind, the *i*
24:20 As he has *i* the other, so he is to be *i*
2Ki 1: 2 room in Samaria and *i* himself.
Ecc 10: 9 Whoever quarries stones may be *i*
Isa 1: 5 Your whole head is *i*,
28:13 be *i* and snared and captured.
Eze 34: 4 healed the sick or bound up the *i*.
34:16 will bind up the *i* and strengthen
Hos 6: 1 he has *i* us
Zec 11:16 or heal the *i*, or feed the healthy,
Mal 1:13 "When you bring *i*, crippled
2Co 7:12 who did the wrong or of the *i* party,

INJURES (INJURE)

Ex 21:35 "If a man's bull *i* the bull of another
Lev 24:19 If anyone *i* his neighbor, whatever
Job 5:18 he *i*, but his hands also heal.

INJURING (INJURE)

Ge 4:23 a young man for *i* me.
Lk 4:35 and came out without *i* him.

INJURY (INJURE)

Ex 21:22 but there is no serious *i*,
21:23 But if there is serious *i*, you are
2Ki 1: 2 to see if I will recover from this *i*."
Jer 10:19 Woe to me because of my *i*!
30:12 your *i* beyond healing.
Na 3:19 your *i* is fatal.
Rev 9:19 heads with which they inflict *i*.

INJUSTICE

2Ch 19: 7 the LORD our God there is no *i*
Job 5:16 and *i* shuts its mouth.
Ps 58: 2 No, in your heart you devise *i*,
Ps 64: 6 They plot *i* and say,
Pr 13:23 but *i* sweeps it away.
16: 8 than much gain with *i*.
Isa 58: 6 to loose the chains of *i*
Jer 22:13 his upper rooms by *i*,
Eze 9: 9 of bloodshed and the city is full of *i*
Hab 1: 3 Why do you make me look at *i*?

INK

Jer 36:18 and I wrote them in *i* on the scroll
2Co 3: 3 not with *i* but with the Spirit
2Jn :12 but I do not want to use paper and *i*
3Jn :13 want to do so with pen and *i*.

INKLING

1Sa 20: 9 I had the least *i* that my father was

INLAID

1Ki 10:18 the king made a great throne *i*
22:39 the palace he built and *i* with ivory,
2Ch 9:17 the king made a great throne *i*
SS 3:10 its interior lovingly *i*
Eze 27: 6 they made your deck, *i* with ivory.
Am 6: 4 You lie on beds *i* with ivory

INN (INNKEEPER)

Lk 2: 7 there was no room for them in the *i*
10:34 took him to an *i* and took care

INNKEEPER (INN)

Lk 10:35 silver coins and gave them to the *i*.

INNOCENCE (INNOCENT)

Ge 44:16 we prove our *i*? God has
1Ki 8:32 not guilty, and so establish his *i*.
2Ch 6:23 not guilty and so establish his *i*.
Ps 26: 6 I wash my hands in *i*,
73:13 in vain have I washed my hands in *i*
Isa 43:26 state the case for your *i*.

INNOCENT (INNOCENCE)

Ge 20: 4 Lord, will you destroy an *i* nation?
Ex 23: 7 do not put an *i* or honest person
Nu 5:31 The husband will be *i*
Dt 19:10 this so that *i* blood will not be shed
19:13 the guilt of shedding *i* blood,
21: 8 guilty of the blood of an *i* man."
21: 9 the guilt of shedding *i* blood,
25: 1 acquitting the *i* and condemning
27:25 a bribe to kill an *i* person."
Jdg 21:22 you are *i*, since you did not give
1Sa 19: 5 wrong to an *i* man like David
2Sa 3:28 and my kingdom are forever *i*
4:11 wicked men have killed an *i* man
1Ki 2: 9 But now, do not consider him *i*.
2:31 guilt of the *i* blood that Joab shed.
8:32 Declare the *i* not guilty,
2Ki 10: 9 all the people and said, "You are *i*.
21:16 shed so much *i* blood that he filled
24: 4 had filled Jerusalem with *i* blood,
24: 4 including the shedding of *i* blood.
2Ch 6:23 Declare the *i* not guilty
Job 4: 7 Who, being *i*, has ever perished?
9:15 Though I were *i*, I could not
9:20 Even if I were *i*, my mouth would
9:23 he mocks the despair of the *i*.
9:28 for I know you will not hold me *i*.
10:15 Even if I am *i*, I cannot lift my head
17: 8 *i* are aroused against the ungodly.
22:19 the *i* mock them, saying,
22:30 will deliver even one who is not *i*,
27:17 and the *i* will divide his silver.
34: 5 "Job says, 'I am *i*,
Ps 10: 8 from ambush he murders the *i*,
15: 5 does not accept a bribe against the *i*
19:13 *i* of great transgression.
64: 4 from ambush at the *i* man;
94:21 and condemn the *i* to death.
106: 38 They shed *i* blood,
Pr 6:17 hands that shed *i* blood,
16: 2 All a man's ways seem *i* to him,
17:15 the guilty and condemning the *i*—
17:26 It is not good to punish an *i* man,
18: 5 or to deprive the *i* of justice.
21: 8 but the conduct of the *i* is upright.
24:24 says to the guilty, "You are *i*"—
Isa 5:23 but deny justice to the *i*.
29:21 with false testimony deprive the *i*
Isa 59: 7 they are swift to shed *i* blood.
Jer 2:34 the lifeblood of the *i* poor,
2:35 you say, 'I am *i*;
7: 6 do not shed *i* blood in this place,
19: 4 place with the blood of the *i*.
22: 3 do not shed *i* blood in this place.
22:17 on shedding *i* blood
26:15 the guilt of *i* blood on yourselves
Da 6:22 because I was found *i* in his sight.
Joel 3:19 in whose land they shed *i* blood.
Jnh 1:14 accountable for killing an *i* man,
Mt 10:16 shrewd as snakes and as *i* as doves.
12: 5 desecrate the day and yet are *i*?
12: 7 would not have condemned the *i*.
27: 4 "for I have betrayed *i* blood."
27:19 anything to do with that *i* man,
27:24 I am *i* of this man's blood," he said.
Ac 20:26 declare to you today that I am *i*
Ro 16:19 what is good, and *i* about what is
1Co 4: 4 but that does not make me *i*.
2Co 7:11 yourselves to be *i* in this matter.
Jas 5: 6 condemned and murdered *i* men,

INNUMERABLE

2Ch 12: 3 and the *i* troops of Libyans,

INQUIRE (INQUIRED INQUIRES INQUIRING INQUIRY)

Ge 25:22 So she went to *i* of the LORD.
Dt 13:14 then you must *i*, probe
17: 9 *I* of them and they will give you
Jos 9:14 but did not *i* of the LORD.
Jdg 18: 5 "Please *i* of God to learn
1Sa 9: 9 went to *i* of God, he would say,
14:36 But the priest said, "Let us *i*
28: 7 so I may go and *i* of her."
1Ki 22: 7 of the LORD here whom we can *i*
22: 8 man through whom we can *i*
2Ki 3:11 that we may *i* of the LORD
22:13 "Go and *i* of the LORD for me
22:18 who sent you to *i* of the LORD,
1Ch 10:14 and did not *i* of the LORD.
13: 3 for we did not *i* of it
15:13 We did not *i* of him about how
21:30 go before it to *i* of God,
2Ch 18: 6 of the LORD here whom we can *i*
18: 7 man through whom we can *i*
20: 3 Jehoshaphat resolved to *i*
34:21 "Go and *i* of the LORD for me
34:26 who sent you to *i* of the LORD,
Ezr 7:14 his seven advisers to *i* about Judah
Isa 8:19 should not a people *i* of their God?
Jer 10:21 and do not *i* of the LORD;
18:13 "*I* among the nations:
21: 2 "*I* now of the LORD for us
37: 7 you to *i* of me, 'Pharaoh's army,
Eze 14: 3 Should I let them *i* of me at all?
14: 7 then goes to a prophet to *i* of me,
20: 1 of Israel came to *i* of the LORD,
20: 3 Have you come to *i* of me?
20: 3 I will not let you *i* of me, declares
20:31 Am I to let you *i* of me, O house
20:31 LORD, I will not let you *i*
Zep 1: 6 and neither seek the LORD nor *i*
1Co 14:35 If they want to *i* about something,

INQUIRED (INQUIRE)

Lev 10:16 When Moses *i* about the goat
Jdg 13:17 Then Manoah *i* of the angel
20:18 up to Bethel and *i* of God.
20:23 LORD until evening, and they *i*
20:27 And the Israelites *i* of the LORD.
1Sa 10:22 So they *i* further of the LORD,
22:10 Ahimelech *i* of the LORD for him;
22:15 Was that day the first time I *i*
23: 2 he *i* of the LORD, saying,
23: 4 Once again David *i* of the LORD,
28: 6 He *i* of the LORD, but the LORD
30: 8 and David *i* of the LORD,
2Sa 2: 1 of time, David *i* of the LORD.
5:19 so David *i* of the LORD, "Shall I
5:23 so David *i* of the LORD,
1Ch 14:10 so David *i* of God: "Shall I go
14:14 so David *i* of God again,
2Ch 1: 5 and the assembly *i* of him there.
Ps 77: 6 My heart mused and my spirit *i*:
Mt 19:18 "Which ones?" the man *i*.
Jn 4:52 When he *i* as to the time

INQUIRES (INQUIRE)

2Sa 16: 23 that of one who *i* of God.

INQUIRING (INQUIRE)

Ex 33: 7 Anyone *i* of the LORD would go
Nu 27: 21 decisions for him by *i* of the Urim
Dt 12: 30 to be ensnared by *i* about their gods
1Sa 22: 13 and a sword and *i* of God for him,

INQUIRY (INQUIRE)

Job 34: 24 Without *i* he shatters the mighty

INSANE (INSANITY)

1Sa 21: 14 He is *i!* Why bring him to me?
Ac 26: 24 Your great learning is driving you *i*
26: 25 I am not *i*, most excellent Festus,"

INSANITY (INSANE)

1Sa 21: 13 So he feigned *i* in their presence;

INSATIABLE

Eze 16: 28 because you were *i;* and

INSCRIBE (INSCRIBED INSCRIPTION)

Isa 30: 8 *i* it on a scroll,

INSCRIBED (INSCRIBE)

Ex 31: 18 the tablets of stone *i* by the finger
32: 15 They were *i* on both sides,
Dt 9: 10 LORD gave me two stone tablets *i*
Job 19: 24 that they were *i* with an iron tool
Jer 17: 1 *i* with a flint point,
Zec 14: 20 HOLY TO THE LORD will be *i*

INSCRIPTION (INSCRIBE)

Ex 39: 30 like an *i* on a seal:
Da 5: 24 he sent the hand that wrote the *i*.
5: 25 "This is the *i* that was written:
Zec 3: 9 and I will engrave an *i* on it,'
Mt 22: 20 And whose *i?*" "Caesar's,"
Mk 12: 16 And whose *i?*" "Caesar's,"
Lk 20: 24 Whose portrait and *i* are on it?"
Ac 17: 23 I even found an altar with this *i:*
2Ti 2: 19 with this *i:* "The Lord knows those

INSECTS

Lev 11: 20 " 'All flying *i* that walk
Dt 14: 19 All flying *i* that swarm are unclean

INSERT (INSERTED)

Ex 25: 14 *I* the poles into the rings

INSERTED (INSERT)

Ex 27: 7 The poles are to be *i* into the rings
37: 5 And he *i* the poles into the rings
38: 7 They *i* the poles into the rings
40: 18 *i* the crossbars and set up the posts.
1Ki 6: 6 temple so that nothing would be *i*
Eze 41: 6 so that the supports were not *i*

INSIGHT (INSIGHTS)

1Ki 4: 29 Solomon wisdom and very great *i*,
1Ch 27: 32 was a counselor, a man of *i*
Job 26: 3 what great *i* you have displayed!
34: 35 his words lack *i*.'
Ps 119: 99 I have more *i* than all my teachers,
Pr 1: 2 for understanding words of *i;*
2: 3 and if you call out for *i*
5: 1 listen well to my words of *i*,
21: 30 There is no wisdom, no *i*, no plan
Da 5: 11 your father he was found to have *i*
5: 14 is in you and that you have *i*,
9: 22 I have now come to give you *i*
Eph 3: 4 able to understand my *i*
Php 1: 9 more in knowledge and depth of *i*,
2Ti 2: 7 for the Lord will give you *i*
Rev 13: 18 If anyone has *i*, let him calculate

INSIGHTS (INSIGHT)

Job 15: 9 What *i* do you have that we do not

INSIST (INSISTED INSISTING)

2Sa 24: 24 "No, I *i* on paying you for it.
1Ch 21: 24 "No, I *i* on paying the full price.
Eph 4: 17 So I tell you this, and *i* on it

INSISTED (INSIST)

Ge 19: 3 he *i* so strongly that they did go
Ge 33: 11 because Jacob *i*, Esau accepted it.
1Ki 3: 22 first one *i*, "No! The dead one is
Mk 14: 31 But Peter *i* emphatically, "Even
Lk 23: 5 they *i*, "He stirs up the people all
Jn 9: 9 But he himself *i*, "I am the man."
19: 7 The Jews *i*, "We have a law,

INSISTING (INSIST)

Ac 12: 15 When she kept *i* that it was so,

INSOLENCE (INSOLENT)

2Ki 19: 28 and your *i* has reached my ears,
Isa 16: 6 her pride and her *i*—
37: 29 because your *i* has reached my ears
Jer 48: 30 I know her *i* but it is futile,"
Da 11: 18 and will turn his *i* back upon him.
11: 18 commander will put an end to his *i*

INSOLENT (INSOLENCE)

Nu 16: 1 became *i* and rose up
Hos 7: 16 because of their *i* words.
Ro 1: 30 God-haters, *i*, arrogant

INSPECT (INSPECTED INSPECTION)

Lev 14: 36 is to go in and *i* the house.
14: 39 priest shall return to *i* the house.

INSPECTED (INSPECT)

Ex 39: 43 Moses *i* the work and saw that they

INSPECTION (INSPECT)

Ne 3: 31 opposite the *I* Gate, and as far

INSPIRE (INSPIRED INSPIRES)

Jer 32: 40 and I will *i* them to fear me,
49: 16 The terror you *i*

INSPIRED (INSPIRE)

Hos 9: 7 the *i* man a maniac.
1Th 1: 3 and your endurance *i* by hope

INSPIRES (INSPIRE)

Job 20: 3 my understanding *i* me to reply.

INSTALLED

Jdg 17: 5 and some idols and *i* one of his sons
17: 12 Then Micah *i* the Levite,
1Ki 12: 32 *i* priests at the high places he had
Ezr 6: 18 they *i* the priests in their divisions
Ps 2: 6 "I have *i* my King

INSTANCE

Dt 19: 5 For *i*, a man may go into the forest

INSTANT

Job 7: 19 or let me alone even for an *i?*
34: 20 They die in an *i*, in the middle
Pr 6: 15 disaster will overtake him in an *i;*
Isa 29: 5 Suddenly, in an *i*,
30: 13 that collapses suddenly, in an *i*.
Jer 4: 20 In an *i* my tents are destroyed,
49: 19 Edom from its land in an *i*.
50: 44 Babylon from its land in an *i*.
Lk 4: 5 him in an *i* all the kingdoms

INSTINCT (INSTINCTS)

2Pe 2: 12 are like brute beasts, creatures of *i*,
Jude : 10 things they do understand by *i*,

INSTINCTS (INSTINCT)

Jude : 19 who follow mere natural *i*

INSTITUTED

Nu 28: 6 This is the regular burnt offering *i*
1Ki 12: 32 He *i* a festival on the fifteenth day
12: 33 So he *i* the festival for the Israelites
Ro 13: 2 rebelling against what God has *i*,
1Pe 2: 13 to every authority *i* among men:

INSTRUCT (INSTRUCTED INSTRUCTING INSTRUCTION INSTRUCTIONS INSTRUCTOR INSTRUCTORS INSTRUCTS)

Dt 24: 8 the priests, who are Levites, *i* you.
Ne 9: 20 gave your good Spirit to *i* them.
Job 8: 10 Will they not *i* you and tell you?
Ps 25: 12 He will *i* him in the way chosen
32: 8 I will *i* you and teach you
Pr 9: 9 *I* a wise man and he will be wiser
Da 11: 33 "Those who are wise will *i* many,
Ro 15: 14 and competent to *i* one another.
1Co 2: 16 that he may *i* him?"
14: 19 to *i* others than ten thousand words
2Ti 2: 25 who oppose him he must gently *i*,

INSTRUCTED (INSTRUCT)

Ge 32: 4 He *i* them: "This is what you are
32: 17 He *i* the one in the lead: "When my
32: 19 He also *i* the second, the third
Ex 12: 35 The Israelites did as Moses *i*
Nu 5: 4 as the LORD had *i* Moses.
27: 23 as the LORD *i* through Moses.
Jos 8: 27 as the LORD had *i* Joshua.
13: 6 for an inheritance, as I have *i* you,
18: 8 to map out the land, Joshua *i* them,
20: 2 as I *i* you through Moses,
Jdg 21: 20 So they *i* the Benjamites, saying,
2Sa 11: 19 He *i* the messenger: "When you
14: 19 it was your servant Joab who *i* me
2Ki 12: 2 the years Jehoiada the priest *i* him.
2Ch 26: 5 who *i* him in the fear of God.
35: 3 who *i* all Israel and who had been
Ne 8: 7 *i* the people in the Law
Est 1: 8 for the king *i* all the wine stewards
4: 10 Then she *i* him to say to Mordecai,
Job 4: 3 Think how you have *i* many,
Pr 21: 11 a wise man is *i*, he gets knowledge.
Isa 40: 13 or *i* him as his counselor?
50: 4 LORD has given me an *i* tongue,
Jer 9: 12 Who has been *i* by the LORD
Da 9: 22 He *i* me and said to me, "Daniel,
Mt 13: 52 who has been *i* about the kingdom
17: 9 down the mountain, Jesus *i* them,
21: 6 and did as Jesus had *i* them.
28: 15 the money and did as they were *i*.
Ac 18: 25 He had been *i* in the way
Ro 2: 18 what is superior because you are *i*
1Co 14: 31 in turn so that everyone may be *i*
1Th 4: 1 we *i* you how to live in order

INSTRUCTING (INSTRUCT)

Ne 8: 9 Levites who were *i* the people said
Mt 11: 1 Jesus had finished *i* his twelve

INSTRUCTION (INSTRUCT)

Ex 24: 12 I have written for their *i*."
Dt 33: 3 and from you receive *i*,
Ne 1: 8 "Remember the *i* you gave your
Job 22: 22 Accept *i* from his mouth
Ps 50: 17 You hate my *i*
Pr 1: 8 Listen, my son, to your father's *i*
4: 1 Listen, my sons, to a father's *i;*
4: 13 Hold on to *i*, do not let it go;
8: 10 Choose my *i* instead of silver,
8: 33 Listen to my *i* and be wise;
13: 1 A wise son heeds his father's *i*,
13: 13 He who scorns *i* will pay for it,
16: 20 Whoever gives heed to *i* prospers,
16: 21 and pleasant words promote *i*.
16: 23 and his lips promote *i*.
19: 20 Listen to advice and accept *i*,
19: 27 Stop listening to *i*, my son,
23: 12 Apply your heart to *i*
31: 26 and faithful *i* is on her tongue.
Isa 29: 24 those who complain will accept *i*."
30: 9 to listen to the LORD's *i*.
Mal 2: 6 True *i* was in his mouth
2: 7 from his mouth men should seek *i*
1Co 14: 6 or prophecy or word of *i?*
14: 26 or a word of *i*, a revelation,
Gal 6: 6 Anyone who receives *i*
Eph 6: 4 up in the training and *i* of the Lord.
1Th 4: 8 he who rejects this *i* does not reject
2Th 3: 14 If anyone does not obey our *i*
1Ti 1: 18 I give you this *i* in keeping
6: 3 to the sound *i* of our Lord Jesus
2Ti 4: 2 with great patience and careful *i*.
Heb 6: 2 of faith in God, *i* about baptisms,

INSTRUCTIONS (INSTRUCT)

Ge 44: 1 Joseph gave these *i* to the steward
49: 29 Then he gave them these *i:*
49: 33 When Jacob had finished giving *i*
50: 16 "Your father left these *i*
Ex 12: 24 Obey these *i* as a lasting ordinance
16: 4 see whether they will follow my *i*.
16: 28 to keep my commands and my *i?*

Jos 8: 33 when he gave *i* to bless the people
Jdg 21: 10 men with *i* to go to Jabesh Gilead
1Sa 15: 11 and has not carried out my *i*.''
15: 13 I have carried out the LORD's *i*.''
15: 24 the LORD's command and your *i*.
21: 2 about your mission and your *i*.'
1Ch 23: 27 According to the last *i* of David,
28: 13 He gave him *i* for the divisions
Est 2: 20 continued to follow Mordecai's *i*
4: 17 and carried out all of Esther's *i*.
Pr 19: 16 He who obeys *i* guards his soul,
Jer 32: 13 presence I gave Baruch these *i*:
35: 18 followed all his *i* and have done
Mt 10: 5 out with the following *i*:
Mk 6: 8 These were his *i*: ''Take nothing
Ac 1: 2 after giving *i* through the Holy
17: 15 and then left with *i* for Silas
19: 33 some of the crowd shouted *i* to him
Col 4: 10 (You have received *i* about him;
1Th 4: 2 You know what *i* we gave you
1Ti 3: 14 I am writing you these *i* so that,
5: 7 Give the people these *i*, too,
5: 21 to keep these *i* without partiality,
Heb 11: 22 and gave *i* about his bones.

INSTRUCTOR (INSTRUCT)
Ro 2: 20 an *i* of the foolish, a teacher
Gal 6: 6 share all good things with his *i*.

INSTRUCTORS (INSTRUCT)
Pr 5: 13 or listen to my *i*.

INSTRUCTS (INSTRUCT)
Ps 16: 7 even at night my heart *i* me.
25: 8 therefore he *i* sinners in his ways.
Isa 28: 26 His God *i* him

INSTRUMENT (INSTRUMENTS)
Eze 33: 32 beautiful voice and plays an *i* well,
Ac 9: 15 This man is my chosen *i*
2Ti 2: 21 he will be an *i* for noble purposes,

INSTRUMENTS (INSTRUMENT)
1Ch 15: 16 accompanied by musical *i*: lyres,
16: 42 of the other *i* for sacred song.
23: 5 with the musical *i* I have provided
2Ch 5: 13 by trumpets, cymbals and other *i*,
7: 6 with the LORD's musical *i*,
23: 13 singers with musical *i* were leading
29: 26 Levites stood ready with David's *i*,
29: 27 and the *i* of David king of Israel.
30: 21 by the LORD's *i* of praise.
34: 12 skilled in playing musical *i*—
Ne 12: 36 with musical *i* prescribed
Isa 38: 20 and we will sing with stringed *i*
Am 6: 5 and improvise on musical *i*.
Hab 3: 19 On my stringed *i*.
Ro 6: 13 as *i* of wickedness, but rather offer
6: 13 body to him as *i* of righteousness.

INSULT (INSULTED INSULTING INSULTS)
2Ki 19: 16 sent to *i* the living God.
Ps 69: 9 of those who *i* you fall on me.
Pr 9: 7 corrects a mocker invites *i*;
12: 16 but a prudent man overlooks an *i*.
Isa 37: 17 sent to *i* the living God.
Jer 20: 8 *i* and reproach all day long.
Mt 5: 11 Blessed are you when people *i* you,
Lk 6: 22 when they exclude you and *i* you
11: 45 when you say these things, you *i* us
18: 32 They will mock him, *i* him,
Ac 23: 4 ''You dare to *i* God's high priest?''
Ro 15: 3 of those who *i* you have fallen
Heb 10: 33 you were publicly exposed to *i*
1Pe 3: 9 evil with evil or *i* with *i*,

INSULTED (INSULT)
2Ki 19: 22 is it you have *i* and blasphemed?
Isa 37: 23 is it you have *i* and blasphemed?
Jer 51: 51 for we have been *i*
Zep 2: 8 who *i* my people
1Th 2: 2 had previously suffered and been *i*
Heb 10: 29 and who has *i* the Spirit of grace?
Jas 2: 6 love him? But you have *i* the poor.
1Pe 4: 14 If you are *i* because of the name

INSULTING (INSULT)
2Ch 32: 17 also wrote letters *i* the LORD,
Ps 55: 12 If an enemy were *i* me,
Zep 2: 10 for *i* and mocking the people
Lk 22: 65 And they said many other *i* things

INSULTS (INSULT)
1Sa 25: 14 his greetings, but he hurled *i*
2Ki 19: 23 you have heaped *i* on the Lord.
Ne 4: 4 Turn their *i* back on their own
4: 5 for they have thrown *i* in the face
Ps 22: 7 they hurl *i*, shaking their heads:
69: 9 the *i* of those who insult you fall
Pr 22: 10 quarrels and *i* are ended.
Isa 37: 24 you have heaped *i* on the Lord.
51: 7 or be terrified by their *i*.
La 3: 61 O LORD, you have heard their *i*,
Eze 21: 28 about the Ammonites and their *i*:
Zep 2: 8 ''I have heard the *i* of Moab
Mt 27: 39 passed by hurled *i* at him,
27: 44 with him also heaped *i* on him.
Mk 15: 29 passed by hurled *i* at him,
15: 32 with him also heaped *i* on him.
Lk 23: 39 criminals who hung there hurled *i*
Jn 9: 28 Then they hurled *i* at him and said,
Ro 15: 3 ''The *i* of those who insult you have
2Co 12: 10 in *i*, in hardships, in persecutions,
1Pe 2: 23 When they hurled their *i* at him,

INSURRECTION (INSURRECTIONISTS)
Lk 23: 19 into prison for an *i* in the city,
23: 25 had been thrown into prison for *i*

INSURRECTIONISTS (INSURRECTION)
Mk 15: 7 with the *i* who had committed

INTACT
Pr 15: 25 he keeps the widow's boundaries *i*.
Zec 12: 6 Jerusalem will remain *i* in her place

INTEGRITY
Dt 9: 5 or your *i* that you are going
1Ki 9: 4 if you walk before me in *i* of heart
1Ch 29: 17 the heart and are pleased with *i*.
Ne 7: 2 because he was a man of *i*
Job 2: 3 And he still maintains his *i*,
2: 9 ''Are you still holding on to your *i*?
6: 29 reconsider, for my *i* is at stake.
27: 5 till I die, I will not deny my *i*.
Ps 7: 8 according to my *i*, O Most High.
25: 21 May *i* and uprightness protect me,
41: 12 In my *i* you uphold me
78: 72 David shepherded them with *i*
Pr 10: 9 The man of *i* walks securely,
11: 3 The *i* of the upright guides them,
13: 6 Righteousness guards the man of *i*,
17: 26 or to flog officials for their *i*.
29: 10 Bloodthirsty men hate a man of *i*
Isa 45: 23 my mouth has uttered in all *i*
59: 4 no one pleads his case with *i*.
Mt 22: 16 ''we know you are a man of *i*
Mk 12: 14 we know you are a man of *i*.
Tit 2: 7 your teaching show *i*, seriousness

INTELLIGENCE (INTELLIGENT)
2Ch 2: 12 endowed with *i* and discernment,
Isa 29: 14 the *i* of the intelligent will vanish.''
Da 5: 11 *i* and wisdom like that of the gods.
5: 14 *i* and outstanding wisdom.
1Co 1: 19 *i* of the intelligent I will frustrate.''

INTELLIGENT (INTELLIGENCE)
1Sa 25: 3 She was an *i* and beautiful woman,
Isa 29: 14 the intelligence of the *i* will vanish
Ac 13: 7 an *i* man, sent for Barnabas
1Co 1: 19 of the *i* I will frustrate.''

INTELLIGIBLE
1Co 14: 9 Unless you speak *i* words
14: 19 I would rather speak five *i* words

INTEND (INTENDED INTENDING INTENDS INTENT INTENTION INTENTIONAL INTENTIONALLY)
Ge 37: 8 ''Do you *i* to reign over us?
Nu 35: 23 and he did not *i* to harm him,
1Sa 25: 26 all who *i* to harm my master be like
1Ki 5: 5 I *i*, therefore, to build a temple
2Ch 28: 10 And now you *i* to make the men
28: 13 Do you *i* to add to our sin and guilt
29: 10 Now I *i* to make a covenant
Ps 62: 4 They fully *i* to topple him
Jn 7: 35 ''Where does this man *i*
14: 22 why do you *i* to show yourself to us
Ac 5: 35 consider carefully what you *i* to do

INTENDED (INTEND)
Ge 50: 20 place of God? You *i* to harm me,
50: 20 *i* it for good to accomplish what
Dt 19: 19 as he *i* to do to his brother.
1Sa 14: 4 of the pass that Jonathan *i* to cross
20: 33 Jonathan knew that his father *i*
2Ch 32: 2 that he *i* to make war on Jerusalem,
Jer 18: 10 I will reconsider the good I had *i*
Hos 2: 9 *i* to cover her nakedness.
Jn 6: 15 knowing that they *i* to come
Ac 12: 4 Herod *i* to bring him out
20: 7 because he *i* to leave the next day,
Ro 7: 10 the very commandment that was *i*
2Co 7: 9 For you became sorrowful as God *i*

INTENDING (INTEND)
Jdg 20: 5 surrounded the house, *i* to kill me.
Ac 12: 1 to the church, *i* to persecute them.

INTENDS (INTEND)
Dt 28: 57 For she *i* to eat them secretly
Isa 10: 7 But this is not what he *i*,

INTENSE
2Sa 13: 15 Amnon hated her with *i* hatred.
1Th 2: 17 out of our *i* longing we made every
Rev 16: 9 They were seared by the *i* heat

INTENT (INTEND)
Ex 32: 12 with evil *i* that he brought them out
1Ch 29: 17 I given willingly and with honest *i*.
Ps 139: 20 They speak of you with evil *i*;
Pr 7: 10 like a prostitute and with crafty *i*.
21: 27 more so when brought with evil *i*!
Hos 5: 11 *i* on pursuing idols.
Mt 22: 18 knowing their evil *i*, said, ''You
Eph 3: 10 His *i* was that now,

INTENTION (INTEND)
2Sa 13: 32 been Absalom's expressed *i* ever
Job 34: 14 If it were his *i*

INTENTIONAL (INTEND)
Nu 15: 25 for it was not *i* and they have

INTENTIONALLY (INTEND)
Ex 21: 13 he does not do it *i*, but God lets it
Nu 35: 20 or throws something at him *i*

INTERCEDE (INTERCEDED INTERCEDES INTERCEDING INTERCESSION INTERCESSOR)
Ge 23: 8 and *i* with Ephron son of Zohar
1Sa 2: 25 who will *i* for him?'' His sons,
7: 5 I will *i* with the LORD for you.''
1Ki 13: 6 ''*I* with the LORD your God
Isa 59: 16 appalled that there was no one to *i*;
Heb 7: 25 he always lives to *i* for them.

INTERCEDED (INTERCEDE)
1Ki 13: 6 the man of God *i* with the LORD,

INTERCEDES (INTERCEDE)
Ro 8: 26 but the Spirit himself *i* for us
8: 27 because the Spirit *i* for the saints

INTERCEDING (INTERCEDE)
Ro 8: 34 hand of God and is also *i* for us.

INTERCESSION (INTERCEDE)
Isa 53: 12 and made *i* for the transgressors.
1Ti 2: 1 *i* and thanksgiving be made

INTERCESSOR (INTERCEDE)
Job 16: 20 My *i* is my friend

INTERCOURSE
Lev 18: 20 not have *i* with your neighbor's

INTEREST (INTERESTS)
Ex 22: 25 a moneylender; charge him no *i*.

Lev 25: 36 Do not take *i* of any kind from him,
25: 37 You must not lend him money at *i*
Dt 23: 19 Do not charge your brother *i*,
23: 19 or anything else that may earn *i*.
23: 20 You may charge a foreigner *i*
Est 3: 8 in the king's best *i* to tolerate them.
Pr 28: 8 increases his wealth by exorbitant *i*
Eze 18: 8 or take excessive *i*.
18: 13 at usury and takes excessive *i*.
18: 17 and takes no usury or excessive *i*.
22: 12 you take usury and excessive *i*
Mt 25: 27 would have received it back with *i*.
Lk 19: 23 I could have collected it with *i*?'
Php 2: 20 who takes a genuine *i*
1Ti 6: 4 He has an unhealthy *i*

INTERESTS (INTEREST)

Ezr 4: 22 to the detriment of the royal *i*?
1Co 7: 34 his wife—and his *i* are divided.
Php 2: 4 only to your own *i*, but also to the *i*
2: 21 everyone looks out for his own *i*,

INTERFERE (INTERFERED)

Ezr 6: 7 Do not *i* with the work

INTERFERED (INTERFERE)

1Ki 1: 6 (His father had never *i* with him

INTERIOR

1Ki 6: 15 He lined its *i* walls
6: 22 he overlaid the whole *i* with gold.
SS 3: 10 its *i* lovingly inlaid
Ac 19: 1 Paul took the road through the *i*

INTERMARRY (MARRY)

Ge 34: 9 *I* with us; give us your daughters
Dt 7: 3 Do not *i* with them.
Jos 23: 12 if you *i* with them and associate
1Ki 11: 2 "You must not *i* with them,
Ezr 9: 14 and *i* with the peoples who commit

INTERMITTENT

Job 6: 15 as undependable as *i* streams,

INTERPRET (INTERPRETATION INTERPRETATIONS INTERPRETED INTERPRETER INTERPRETERS INTERPRETS)

Ge 40: 8 "but there is no one to *i* them."
41: 8 but no one could *i* them for him.
41: 15 when you hear a dream you can *i* it
41: 15 "I had a dream, and no one can *i* it
Da 2: 4 the dream, and we will *i* it."
2: 5 tell me what my dream was and *i* it,
2: 6 So tell me the dream and *i* it for me
2: 7 the dream, and we will *i* it."
2: 9 I will know that you can *i* it for me
2: 16 so that he might *i* the dream
2: 24 and I will *i* his dream for him."
2: 26 saw in my dream and *i* it?"
2: 36 and now we will *i* it to the king.
4: 6 before me to *i* the dream for me.
4: 7 but they could not *i* it for me.
4: 9 Here is my dream; *i* it for me.
4: 18 men in my kingdom can *i* it for me.
5: 12 and also the ability to *i* dreams,
Mt 16: 3 You know how to *i* the appearance
16: 3 you cannot *i* the signs of the times.
Lk 12: 56 You know how to *i* the appearance
12: 56 how to *i* this present time?
1Co 12: 30 Do all *i*? But eagerly desire
14: 13 pray that he may *i* what he says.
14: 27 one at a time, and someone must *i*.

INTERPRETATION (INTERPRET)

Ge 40: 16 that Joseph had given a favorable *i*,
40: 22 as Joseph had said to them in his *i*.
41: 12 giving each man the *i* of his dream.
Jdg 7: 15 Gideon heard the dream and its *i*,
Da 2: 30 may know the *i* and that you may
2: 45 is true and the *i* is trustworthy."
4: 24 "This is the *i*, O king, and this is
7: 16 and gave me the *i* of these things:
1Co 12: 10 and to still another the *i* of tongues.
14: 26 a revelation, a tongue or an *i*.
2Pe 1: 20 about by the prophet's own *i*.

INTERPRETATIONS (INTERPRET)

Ge 40: 8 to them, "Do not *i* belong to God?
Da 5: 16 heard that you are able to give *i*

INTERPRETED (INTERPRET)

Ge 41: 12 told him our dreams, and he *i* them
41: 13 turned out exactly as he *i* them

INTERPRETER (INTERPRET)

Ge 42: 23 since he was using an *i*.
1Co 14: 28 If there is no *i*, the speaker should

INTERPRETERS (INTERPRET)

Jer 27: 9 your diviners, your *i* of dreams,

INTERPRETS (INTERPRET)

Dt 18: 10 *i* omens, engages in witchcraft,
1Co 14: 5 he *i*, so that the church may be

INTERRUPTED

Ac 26: 24 this point Festus *i* Paul's defense.

INTERSECTING

Eze 1: 16 to be made like a wheel *i* a wheel.
10: 10 each was like a wheel *i* a wheel.

INTERVALS

Eze 41: 17 at regular *i* all around the inner

INTERVENED

Ps 106: 30 But Phinehas stood up and *i*,

INTERWOVEN (WEAVE)

1Ki 7: 17 of *i* chains festooned the capitals
2Ch 3: 16 He made *i* chains and put them
Ps 45: 13 her gown is *i* with gold.

INTESTINES

2Sa 20: 10 and his *i* spilled out on the ground.
Ac 1: 18 burst open and all his *i* spilled out.

INTIMATE

1Ki 1: 4 the king had no *i* relations with her.
Job 19: 19 All my *i* friends detest me;
29: 4 when God's *i* friendship blessed
Hos 3: 3 you must not be a prostitute or be *i*

INTIMIDATE

Ne 6: 13 He had been hired to *i* me
6: 14 who have been trying to *i* me.
6: 19 And Tobiah sent letters to *i* me.

INTOXICATED

Rev 17: 2 of the earth were *i* with the wine

INTRIGUE (INTRIGUES)

Da 8: 23 a stern-faced king, a master of *i*,
11: 21 and he will seize it through *i*.
Hos 7: 6 they approach him with *i*.

INTRIGUES (INTRIGUE)

Ps 5: 10 Let their *i* be their downfall.
31: 20 them from the *i* of men;

INTRODUCE (INTRODUCED INTRODUCTION)

2Pe 2: 1 will secretly *i* destructive heresies,

INTRODUCED (INTRODUCE)

2Ki 17: 8 which the kings of Israel had *i*.
17: 19 followed the practices Israel had *i*.
Gal 3: 17 The law, *i* 430 years later,
Heb 7: 19 better hope is *i*, by which we draw

INTRODUCTION (INTRODUCE)

1Co 16: 3 I will give letters of *i*

INVADE (INVADED INVADER INVADERS INVADES INVADING)

Dt 12: 29 you the nations you are about to *i*
1Sa 7: 13 did not *i* Israelite territory again.
2Ch 20: 10 to *i* when they came from Egypt;
Isa 7: 6 your ruin, saying, "Let us *i* Judah;
Eze 38: 8 future years you will *i* a land that
38: 11 "I will *i* a land of unwalled villages;
Da 11: 9 king of the North will *i* the realm
11: 21 He will *i* the kingdom
11: 24 he will *i* them and will achieve
11: 29 time he will *i* the South again,
11: 40 He will *i* many countries
11: 41 He will also *i* the Beautiful Land.
Joel 3: 17 never again will foreigners *i* her.
Na 1: 15 No more will the wicked *i* you;

INVADED (INVADE)

Ex 10: 14 they *i* all Egypt and settled
Jdg 6: 3 other eastern peoples *i* the country.
6: 5 they *i* the land to ravage it.
2Ki 3: 24 And the Israelites *i* the land
15: 19 Then Pul king of Assyria *i* the land,
17: 5 king of Assyria *i* the entire land,
24: 1 king of Babylon *i* the land,
1Ch 4: 42 the sons of Ishi, *i* the hill country
2Ch 21: 17 *i* it and carried off all the goods
24: 23 *i* Judah and Jerusalem
32: 1 king of Assyria came and *i* Judah.
Ps 79: 1 the nations have *i* your inheritance
Jer 35: 11 king of Babylon *i* this land,
48: 15 will be destroyed and her towns *i*;
Joel 1: 6 A nation has *i* my land,

INVADER (INVADE)

Isa 21: 1 an *i* comes from the desert,
Da 11: 16 The *i* will do as he pleases;

INVADERS (INVADE)

Jer 18: 22 houses when you suddenly bring *i*

INVADES (INVADE)

Mic 5: 5 When the Assyrian *i* our land
5: 6 the Assyrian when he *i* our land

INVADING (INVADE)

2Ch 20: 22 and Mount Seir who were *i* Judah,
Hab 3: 16 to come on the nation *i* us.

INVALID

Jn 5: 5 One who was there had been an *i*
5: 7 to get well?" "Sir," the *i* replied,

INVENT (INVENTED)

Ro 1: 30 boastful; they *i* ways of doing evil;

INVENTED (INVENT)

2Pe 1: 16 We did not follow cleverly *i* stories

INVENTORY

Ezr 1: 9 This was the *i*: gold dishes 30 silver

INVESTIGATE (INVESTIGATED INVESTIGATION)

Ex 9: 7 Pharaoh sent men to *i*
Dt 13: 14 inquire, probe and *i* it thoroughly.
17: 4 then you must *i* it thoroughly.
Ezr 10: 16 sat down to *i* the cases,
Ecc 7: 25 to *i* and to search out wisdom
Ac 25: 20 I was at a loss how to *i* such matters

INVESTIGATED (INVESTIGATE)

Jdg 6: 29 When they carefully *i*, they were
Est 2: 23 And when the report was *i*
Lk 1: 3 I myself have carefully *i* everything

INVESTIGATION (INVESTIGATE)

Dt 19: 18 The judges must make a thorough *i*
Ac 25: 26 of this *i* I may have something

INVISIBLE

Ro 1: 20 of the world God's *i* qualities—
Col 1: 15 He is the image of the *i* God,
1: 16 and on earth, visible and *i*,
1Ti 1: 17 immortal, *i*, the only God,
Heb 11: 27 because he saw him who is *i*.

INVITATION (INVITE)

2Sa 11: 13 At David's *i*, he ate and drank

INVITE (INVITATION INVITED INVITES INVITING)

Ex 2: 20 *I* him to have something to eat."
34: 15 they will *i* you and you will eat
Jdg 14: 15 Did you *i* us here to rob us?"
1Sa 16: 3 *I* Jesse to the sacrifice,
1Ki 1: 10 he did not *i* Nathan the prophet
1: 26 your servant Solomon he did not *i*.
Job 1: 4 and they would *i* their three sisters
Jer 35: 2 and *i* them to come to one
Zec 3: 10 each of you will *i* his neighbor to sit

Mt 22: 9 *i* to the banquet anyone you find.'
25: 38 did we see you a stranger and *i* you
25: 43 was a stranger and you did not *i* me
Lk 14: 12 do not *i* your friends, your brothers
14: 12 they may *i* you back
14: 13 you give a banquet, *i* the poor,

INVITED (INVITE)

Ge 31: 54 and *i* his relatives to a meal.
Nu 25: 2 who *i* them to the sacrifices
1Sa 9: 13 afterward, those who are *i* will eat.
9: 22 at the head of those who were *i*—
9: 24 from the time I said, 'I have *i* guests
16: 5 his sons and *i* them to the sacrifice.
2Sa 13: 23 he *i* all the king's sons
15: 11 They had been *i* as guests
1Ki 1: 9 He *i* all his brothers, the king's sons
1: 19 and has *i* all the king's sons,
1: 19 he has not *i* Solomon your servant.
1: 25 He has *i* all the king's sons,
Est 5: 12 I'm the only person Queen Esther *i*
5: 12 she has *i* me along with the king
Zep 1: 7 he has consecrated those he has *i*.
Mt 22: 3 servants to those who had been *i*
22: 4 those who have been *i* that I have
22: 8 those I *i* did not deserve to come.
22: 14 For many are *i*, but few are chosen
25: 35 I was a stranger and you *i* me in,
Lk 7: 36 Now one of the Pharisees *i* Jesus
7: 39 Pharisee who had *i* him saw this,
11: 37 a Pharisee *i* him to eat with him;
14: 8 than you may have been *i*.
14: 9 the host who *i* both
14: 10 But when you are *i*, take the lowest
14: 16 a great banquet and *i* many guests.
14: 17 to tell those who had been *i*,
14: 24 those men who were *i* will get
Jn 2: 2 also been *i* to the wedding.
Ac 8: 31 So he *i* Philip to come up
10: 23 Peter *i* the men into the house
13: 42 the people *i* them to speak further
16: 15 household were baptized, she *i* us
18: 26 they *i* him to their home
28: 14 we found some brothers who *i* us
Rev 19: 9 'Blessed are those who are *i*

INVITES (INVITE)

Pr 9: 7 Whoever corrects a mocker *i* insult
10: 14 but the mouth of a fool *i* ruin.
17: 19 builds a high gate *i* destruction.
18: 6 and his mouth *i* a beating.
Lk 14: 8 "When someone *i* you
1Co 10: 27 If some unbeliever *i* you to a meal

INVITING (INVITE)

2Ch 30: 1 *i* them to come to the temple

INVOKE (INVOKED INVOKES INVOKING)

Ex 23: 13 Do not *i* the names of other gods;
Jos 23: 7 do not *i* the names of their gods
2Sa 14: 11 let the king *i* the LORD his God
Isa 48: 1 and *i* the God of Israel—
Jer 44: 26 in Egypt will ever again *i* my name
Ac 19: 13 to *i* the name of the Lord Jesus

INVOKED (INVOKE)

Hos 2: 17 no longer will their names be *i*.

INVOKES (INVOKE)

Dt 29: 19 he *i* a blessing on himself and
Isa 65: 16 Whoever *i* a blessing in the land

INVOKING (INVOKE)

Job 31: 30 sin by *i* a curse against his life—

INVOLVE (INVOLVED INVOLVES INVOLVING)

Jn 2: 4 why do you *i* me?" Jesus replied,

INVOLVED (INVOLVE)

Ex 24: 14 and anyone *i* in a dispute can go
28: 38 and he will bear the guilt *i*
Nu 15: 26 because all the people were *i*
Dt 19: 17 the two men *i* in the dispute must
Ac 23: 13 than forty men were *i* in this plot.
24: 18 nor was I *i* in any disturbance.
2Ti 2: 4 a soldier gets *i* in civilian affairs—

INVOLVES (INVOLVE)

Ac 18: 15 But since it *i* questions about words

INVOLVING (INVOLVE)

2Sa 3: 8 me of an offense *i* this woman!
1Ki 21: 1 was an incident *i* a vineyard

IPHDEIAH

1Ch 8: 25 *I* and Penuel were the sons

IPHTAH

Jos 15: 43 Ether, Ashan, *I*, Ashnah, Nezib,

IPHTAH EL

Jos 19: 14 and ended at the Valley of *I*
19: 27 Zebulun and the Valley of *I*

IR

1Ch 7: 12 Huppites were the descendants of *I*

IR NAHASH

1Ch 4: 12 and Tehinnah the father of *I*.

IR SHEMESH

Jos 19: 41 Zorah, Eshtaol, *I*, Shaalabbin,

IRA

2Sa 20: 26 and *I* the Jairite was David's priest.
23: 26 *I* son of Ikkesh from Tekoa,
23: 38 of Joab son of Zeruiah, *I* the Ithrite
1Ch 11: 28 *I* son of Ikkesh from Tekoa,
11: 40 *I* the Ithrite, Gareb the Ithrite,
27: 9 was *I* the son of Ikkesh the Tekoite.

IRAD

Ge 4: 18 To Enoch was born *I*, and *I* was

IRAM

Ge 36: 43 Teman, Mibzar, Magdiel and *I*.
1Ch 1: 54 Teman, Mibzar, Magdiel and *I*.

IRI

1Ch 7: 7 Jerimoth and *I*, heads of families—

IRIJAH

Jer 37: 13 whose name was *I* son
37: 14 But *I* would not listen to him;

IRON (IRON-SMELTING IRONS NECK-IRONS)

Ge 4: 22 kinds of tools out of bronze and *i*.
Lev 26: 19 and make the sky above you like *i*
Nu 31: 22 Gold, silver, bronze, *i*, tin,
35: 16 with an *i* object so that he dies,
Dt 3: 11 His bed was made of *i*
8: 9 a land where the rocks are *i*
27: 5 Do not use any *i* tool upon them.
28: 23 the ground beneath you *i*.
28: 48 He will put an *i* yoke on your neck
33: 25 The bolts of your gates will be *i*
Jos 6: 19 and *i* are sacred to the LORD
6: 24 and *i* into the treasury
8: 31 on which no *i* tool had been used.
17: 16 live in the plain have *i* chariots,
17: 18 the Canaanites have *i* chariots and
19: 38 Edrei, En Hazor, *I*, Migdal El,
22: 8 with silver, gold, bronze and *i*,
Jdg 1: 19 because they had *i* chariots.
4: 3 he had nine hundred *i* chariots
4: 13 his nine hundred *i* chariots
1Sa 17: 7 and its *i* point weighed six hundred
2Sa 12: 31 to labor with saws and with *i* picks
23: 7 uses a tool of *i* or the shaft
1Ki 6: 7 or any other *i* tool was heard
22: 11 son of Kenaanah had made *i* horns
2Ki 6: 5 the *i* axhead fell into the water.
6: 6 threw it there, and made the *i* float.
1Ch 20: 3 to labor with saws and with *i* picks
22: 3 He provided a large amount of *i*
22: 14 and *i* too great to be weighed,
22: 16 and *i*— craftsmen beyond number.
29: 2 *i* for the *i* and wood for the wood,
29: 7 a hundred thousand talents of *i*.
2Ch 2: 7 bronze and *i*, and in purple,
2: 14 bronze and *i*, stone and wood,
18: 10 son of Kenaanah had made *i* horns,
24: 12 and also workers in *i* and bronze
Job 19: 24 inscribed with an *i* tool on lead,
20: 24 Though he flees from an *i* weapon,
28: 2 *I* is taken from the earth,
40: 18 his limbs like rods of *i*.
41: 27 *I* he treats like straw
Ps 2: 9 will rule them with an *i* scepter;
107: 10 prisoners suffering in *i* chains;
107: 16 and cuts through bars of *i*.
149: 8 their nobles with shackles of *i*,
Pr 27: 17 As *i* sharpens *i*,
Isa 45: 2 and cut through bars of *i*.
48: 4 the sinews of your neck were *i*,
60: 17 and silver in place of *i*.
60: 17 and *i* in place of stones.
Jer 1: 18 an *i* pillar and a bronze wall
6: 28 They are bronze and *i*;
15: 12 "Can a man break *i*—
15: 12 *i* from the north—or bronze?
17: 1 sin is engraved with an *i* tool,
28: 13 in its place you will get a yoke of *i*.
28: 14 I will put an *i* yoke on the necks
Eze 4: 3 Then take an *i* pan, place it
4: 3 place it as an *i* wall between you
22: 18 tin, *i* and lead left inside a furnace.
22: 20 As men gather silver, copper, *i*,
27: 12 *i*, tin and lead for your
27: 19 they exchanged wrought *i*,
Da 2: 33 and thighs of bronze, its legs of *i*,
2: 33 its feet partly of *i* and partly
2: 34 It struck the statue on its feet of *i*
2: 35 Then the *i*, the clay, the bronze,
2: 40 and as *i* breaks things to pieces,
2: 40 strong as *i*— for *i* breaks
2: 41 even as you saw *i* mixed with clay.
2: 41 partly of baked clay and partly of *i*,
2: 41 some of the strength of *i* in it,
2: 42 As the toes were partly *i*
2: 43 any more than *i* mixes with clay.
2: 43 as you saw the *i* mixed
2: 45 a rock that broke the *i*, the bronze,
4: 15 bound with *i* and bronze, remain
4: 23 but leave the stump, bound with *i*
5: 4 of bronze, *i*, wood and stone.
5: 23 of bronze, *i*, wood and stone,
7: 7 It had large *i* teeth; it crushed
7: 19 with its *i* teeth and bronze claws—
Am 1: 3 Gilead with sledges having *i* teeth,
Mic 4: 13 for I will give you horns of *i*;
Ac 12: 10 and came to the *i* gate leading
1Ti 4: 2 have been seared as with a hot *i*.
Rev 2: 27 He will rule them with an *i* scepter;
9: 9 breastplates like breastplates of *i*,
12: 5 all the nations with an *i* scepter.
18: 12 costly wood, bronze, *i* and marble;
19: 15 He will rule them with an *i* scepter

IRON-SMELTING (IRON)

Dt 4: 20 brought you out of the *i* furnace,
1Ki 8: 51 out of Egypt, out of that *i* furnace.
Jer 11: 4 out of Egypt, out of the *i* furnace.'

IRONS (IRON)

Ps 105: 18 his neck was put in *i*,
Mk 5: 4 and broke the *i* on his feet.

IRPEEL

Jos 18: 27 Mozah, Rekem, *I*, Taralah, Zelah,

IRRELIGIOUS

1Ti 1: 9 and sinful, the unholy and *i*;

IRRESISTIBLE

Da 11: 10 which will sweep on like an *i* flood

IRREVERENT

2Sa 6: 7 against Uzzah because of his *i* act;

IRREVOCABLE

Ro 11: 29 for God's gifts and his call are *i*.

IRRIGATED (IRRIGATE)

Dt 11: 10 you planted your seed and *i* it

IRRITATE

1Sa 1: 6 provoking her in order to *i* her.

IRU

1Ch 4: 15 sons of Caleb son of Jephunneh: *I*,

ISAAC (ISAAC'S)

Ge 17: 19 you a son, and you will call him *I*.

Ge 17:21 my covenant I will establish with *I*,
21: 3 Abraham gave the name *I*
21: 4 When his son *I* was eight days old,
21: 5 old when his son *I* was born to him.
21: 8 on the day *I* was weaned Abraham
21: 10 in the inheritance with my son *I*.''
21: 12 is through *I* that your offspring will
22: 2 your only son *I*, whom you love,
22: 3 two of his servants and his son *I*.
22: 6 offering and placed it on his son *I*,
22: 7 The fire and wood are here,'' *I* said,
22: 7 *I* spoke up and said
22: 9 He bound his son *I* and laid him
24: 4 and get a wife for my son *I*.''
24: 14 chosen for your servant *I*.
24: 62 *I* had come from Beer Lahai Roi,
24: 64 Rebekah also looked up and saw *I*.
24: 66 the servant told *I* all he had done.
24: 67 *I* brought her into the tent
24: 67 *I* was comforted after his mother's
25: 5 left everything he owned to *I*.
25: 6 away from his son *I* to the land
25: 9 His sons *I* and Ishmael buried him
25: 11 blessed his son *I*, who then lived
25: 19 Abraham became the father of *I*,
25: 19 the account of Abraham's son *I*.
25: 20 and *I* was forty years old
25: 21 *I* prayed to the LORD on behalf
25: 26 *I* was sixty years old
25: 28 *I*, who had a taste for wild game,
26: 1 and *I* went to Abimelech king
26: 2 The LORD appeared to *I* and said,
26: 6 So *I* stayed in Gerar.
26: 8 When *I* had been there a long time,
26: 8 saw *I* caressing his wife Rebekah.
26: 9 Abimelech summoned *I* and said,
26: 9 'She is my sister'?'' *I* answered him,
26: 12 *I* planted crops in that land
26: 16 Then Abimelech said to *I*,
26: 17 So *I* moved away from there
26: 18 *I* reopened the wells that had been
26: 25 *I* built an altar there and called
26: 27 *I* asked them, ''Why have you
26: 30 *I* then made a feast for them,
26: 31 Then *I* sent them on their way,
26: 35 They were a source of grief to *I*
27: 1 When *I* was old and his eyes were
27: 2 *I* said, ''I am now an old man
27: 5 as *I* spoke to his son Esau.
27: 20 *I* asked his son, ''How did you find
27: 21 Then *I* said to Jacob, ''Come
27: 22 Jacob went close to his father *I*,
27: 26 Then his father *I* said to him,
27: 27 When *I* caught the smell
27: 30 After *I* finished blessing him
27: 32 His father *I* asked him, ''Who are
27: 33 *I* trembled violently and said,
27: 37 blessing for me?'' *I* answered Esau,
27: 39 His father *I* answered him,
27: 46 Rebekah said to *I*, ''I'm disgusted
28: 1 *I* called for Jacob and blessed him
28: 5 Then *I* sent Jacob on his way,
28: 6 Esau learned that *I* had blessed
28: 8 women were to his father *I*;
28: 13 father Abraham and the God of *I*.
31: 18 to go to his father *I* in the land
31: 42 God of Abraham and the Fear of *I*,
31: 53 the name of the Fear of his father *I*.
32: 9 God of my father *I*, O LORD,
35: 12 The land I gave to Abraham and *I*
35: 27 home to his father *I* in Mamre,
35: 27 where Abraham and *I* had stayed.
35: 28 *I* lived a hundred and eighty years.
46: 1 sacrifices to the God of his father *I*.
48: 15 Abraham and *I* walked,
48: 16 of my fathers Abraham and *I*,
49: 31 there *I* and his wife Rebekah were
50: 24 promised on oath to Abraham, *I*
Ex 2: 24 covenant with Abraham, with *I*
3: 6 the God of *I* and the God of Jacob
3: 15 the God of *I* and the God of Jacob
3: 16 the God of Abraham, *I* and Jacob,
4: 5 the God of *I* and the God of Jacob
6: 3 to *I* and to Jacob as God Almighty,
6: 8 hand to give to Abraham, to *I*
32: 13 your servants Abraham, *I*
33: 1 *I* and Jacob, saying, 'I will give it
Lev 26: 42 covenant with *I* and my covenant
Nu 32: 11 *I* and Jacob—not one
Dt 1: 8 to Abraham, *I* and Jacob—
6: 10 *I* and Jacob, to give you—
9: 5 to your fathers, to Abraham, *I*
9: 27 your servants Abraham, *I*
29: 13 swore to your fathers, Abraham, *I*
30: 20 to give to your fathers, Abraham, *I*
34: 4 promised on oath to Abraham, *I*
Jos 24: 3 I gave him *I*, and to *I* I gave Jacob
1Ki 18: 36 God of Abraham, *I* and Israel,
2Ki 13: 23 of his covenant with Abraham, *I*
1Ch 1: 28 The sons of Abraham: *I*
1: 34 Abraham was the father of *I*.
1: 34 The sons of *I*: Esau and Israel.
16: 16 the oath he swore to *I*.
29: 18 God of our fathers Abraham, *I*
2Ch 30: 6 the God of Abraham, *I* and Israel,
Ps 105: 9 the oath he swore to *I*.
Jer 33: 26 the descendants of Abraham, *I*
Am 7: 9 places of *I* will be destroyed
7: 16 preaching against the house of *I*.'
Mt 1: 2 the father of *I*, *I* the father of Jacob,
8: 11 *I* and Jacob in the kingdom
22: 32 the God of *I*, and the God of Jacob
Mk 12: 26 the God of *I*, and the God of Jacob
Lk 3: 34 the son of *I*, the son of Abraham,
13: 28 *I* and Jacob and all the prophets
20: 37 the God of *I*, and the God of Jacob
Ac 3: 13 The God of Abraham, *I* and Jacob,
7: 8 Abraham became the father of *I*
7: 8 Later *I* became the father of Jacob,
7: 32 the God of Abraham, *I* and Jacob.'
Ro 9: 7 is through *I* that your offspring will
9: 10 and the same father, our father *I*.
Gal 4: 28 Now you, brothers, like *I*,
Heb 11: 9 he lived in tents, as did *I* and Jacob,
11: 17 when God tested him, offered *I*
11: 18 is through *I* that your offspring will
11: 19 he did receive *I* back from death.
11: 20 By faith *I* blessed Jacob
Jas 2: 21 did when he offered his son *I*

ISAAC'S (ISAAC)

Ge 26: 19 *I* servants dug in the valley
26: 20 Gerar quarreled with *I* herdsmen
26: 32 That day *I* servants came

ISAIAH

2Ki 19: 2 to the prophet *I* son of Amoz.
19: 5 Hezekiah's officials came to *I*,
19: 6 *I* said to them, ''Tell your master,
19: 20 Then *I* son of Amoz sent a message
20: 1 The prophet *I* son of Amoz went
20: 4 Before *I* had left the middle court,
20: 7 *I* said, ''Prepare a poultice of figs.''
20: 8 Hezekiah had asked *I*, ''What will
20: 9 *I* answered, ''This is the LORD's
20: 11 Then the prophet *I* called
20: 14 Then *I* the prophet went
20: 16 *I* said to Hezekiah, ''Hear the word
2Ch 26: 22 by the prophet *I* son of Amoz.
32: 20 prophet *I* son of Amoz cried out
32: 32 vision of the prophet *I* son of Amoz
Isa 1: 1 Jerusalem that *I* son of Amoz saw
2: 1 This is what *I* son of Amoz saw
7: 3 Then the LORD said to *I*, ''Go out,
7: 13 Then *I* said, ''Hear now, you house
13: 1 concerning Babylon that *I* son
20: 2 spoke through *I* son of Amoz.
20: 3 as my servant *I* has gone stripped
37: 2 to the prophet *I* son of Amoz.
37: 5 Hezekiah's officials came to *I*,
37: 6 *I* said to them, ''Tell your master,
37: 21 Then *I* son of Amoz sent a message
38: 1 The prophet *I* son of Amoz went
38: 4 the word of the LORD came to *I*:
38: 21 *I* said, ''Prepare a poultice of figs
39: 3 Then *I* the prophet went
39: 5 *I* said to Hezekiah, ''Hear the word
Mt 3: 3 spoken of through the prophet *I*:
4: 14 said through the prophet *I*:
8: 17 spoken through the prophet *I*:
12: 17 spoken through the prophet *I*:
13: 14 them is fulfilled the prophecy of *I*:
15: 7 *I* was right when he prophesied
Mk 1: 2 It is written in *I* the prophet:
7: 6 ''*I* was right when he prophesied
Lk 3: 4 book of the words of *I* the prophet:
Lk 4: 17 of the prophet *I* was handed to him
Jn 1: 23 in the words of *I* the prophet,
12: 38 to fulfill the word of *I* the prophet:
12: 39 because, as *I* says elsewhere:
12: 41 *I* said this because he saw Jesus'
Ac 8: 28 reading the book of *I* the prophet.
8: 30 the man reading *I* the prophet.
28: 25 when he said through *I* the prophet
Ro 9: 27 *I* cries out concerning Israel:
9: 29 It is just as *I* said previously:
10: 16 For *I* says, ''Lord, who has
10: 20 And *I* boldly says,
15: 12 And again, *I* says,

ISCAH

Ge 11: 29 the father of both Milcah and *I*.

ISCARIOT

Mt 10: 4 Simon the Zealot and Judas *I*,
26: 14 the one called Judas *I*— went
Mk 3: 19 Simon the Zealot and Judas *I*,
14: 10 Then Judas *I*, one of the Twelve,
Lk 6: 16 and Judas *I*, who became a traitor.
22: 3 called *I*, one of the Twelve.
Jn 6: 71 *I*, who, though one of the Twelve,
12: 4 But one of his disciples, Judas *I*,
13: 2 had already prompted Judas *I*,
13: 26 he gave it to Judas *I*, son of Simon.
14: 22 Then Judas (not Judas *I*) said, ''But

ISH-BOSHETH

2Sa 2: 8 had taken *I* son of Saul
2: 10 *I* son of Saul was forty years old
2: 12 with the men of *I* son of Saul,
2: 15 for Benjamin and *I* son of Saul,
3: 7 And *I* said to Abner, ''Why did you
3: 8 of what *I* said and he answered,
3: 11 *I* did not dare to say another word
3: 14 David sent messengers to *I* son
3: 15 So *I* gave orders and had her taken
4: 1 When *I* son of Saul heard that
4: 5 set out for the house of *I*,
4: 8 the head of *I* to David at Hebron
4: 8 ''Here is the head of *I* son of Saul,
4: 12 But they took the head of *I*

ISHBAH

1Ch 4: 17 and *I* the father of Eshtemoa.

ISHBAK

Ge 25: 2 Medan, Midian, *I* and Shuah.
1Ch 1: 32 Medan, Midian, *I* and Shuah.

ISHBI-BENOB

2Sa 21: 16 *I*, one of the descendants of Rapha,

ISHHOD

1Ch 7: 18 Hammoleketh gave birth to *I*,

ISHI

1Ch 2: 31 *I*, who was the father of Sheshan.
4: 20 The descendants of *I*: Zoheth
4: 42 Rephaiah and Uzziel, the sons of *I*,
5: 24 Epher, *I*, Eliel, Azriel, Jeremiah,

ISHIJAH

Ezr 10: 31 Eliezer, *I*, Malkijah, Shemaiah,

ISHMA

1Ch 4: 3 the sons of Etam: Jezreel, *I*

ISHMAEL (ISHMAELITE ISHMAELITES)

Ge 16: 11 You shall name him *I*,
16: 15 and Abram gave the name *I*
16: 16 old when Hagar bore him *I*.
17: 18 ''If only *I* might live
17: 20 And as for *I*, I have heard you:
17: 23 very day Abraham took his son *I*
17: 25 and his son *I* was thirteen;
17: 26 his son *I* were both circumcised
25: 9 and *I* buried him in the cave
25: 12 the account of Abraham's son *I*,
25: 13 Nebaioth the firstborn of *I*, Kedar,
25: 13 are the names of the sons of *I*,
25: 16 These were the sons of *I*,
25: 17 *I* lived a hundred and thirty-seven
28: 9 and daughter of *I* son of Abraham,
28: 9 went to *I* and married Mahalath,

Ge 36: 3 also Basemath daughter of *I*
2Ki 25: 23 at Mizpah—*I* son of Nethaniah,
25: 25 however, *I* son of Nethaniah,
1Ch 1: 28 The sons of Abraham: Isaac and *I*.
1: 29 Nebaioth the firstborn of *I*, Kedar,
1: 31 These were the sons of *I*.
8: 38 Azrikam, Bokeru, *I*, Sheariah,
9: 44 Azrikam, Bokeru, *I*, Sheariah,
2Ch 19: 11 and Zebadiah son of *I*, the leader
23: 1 of Jeroham, *I* son of Jehohanan,
Ezr 10: 22 Elioenai, Maaseiah, *I*, Nethanel,
Jer 40: 8 at Mizpah—*I* son of Nethaniah,
40: 14 of the Ammonites has sent *I* son
40: 15 and kill *I* son of Nethaniah,
40: 16 you are saying about *I* is not true."
41: 1 In the seventh month *I* son
41: 2 *I* son of Nethaniah and the ten men
41: 3 *I* also killed all the Jews who were
41: 6 *I* son of Nethaniah went out
41: 7 *I* son of Nethaniah and the men
41: 8 ten of them said to *I*, "Don't kill us
41: 9 *I* son of Nethaniah filled it
41: 10 *I* made captives of all the rest
41: 10 *I* son of Nethaniah took them
41: 11 heard about all the crimes *I* son
41: 12 went to fight *I* son of Nethaniah.
41: 13 When all the people *I* had
41: 14 All the people *I* had taken captive
41: 15 But *I* son of Nethaniah
41: 16 recovered from *I* son of Nethaniah
41: 18 *I* son of Nethaniah had killed

ISHMAELITE (ISHMAEL)

1Ch 2: 17 whose father was Jether the *I*.
27: 30 Obil the *I* was in charge

ISHMAELITES (ISHMAEL)

Ge 37: 25 a caravan of *I* coming from Gilead.
37: 27 him to the *I* and not lay our hands
37: 28 for twenty shekels of silver to the *I*,
39: 1 from the *I* who had taken him there
Jdg 8: 24 of the *I* to wear gold earrings.)
Ps 83: 6 the tents of Edom and the *I*,

ISHMAIAH

1Ch 12: 4 Anathothite, and *I* the Gibeonite,
27: 19 over Zebulun: *I* son of Obadiah;

ISHMERAI

1Ch 8: 18 Meshullam, Hizki, Heber, *I*,

ISHPAH

1Ch 8: 16 *I* and Joha were the sons of Beriah.

ISHPAN

1Ch 8: 22 *I*, Eber, Eliel, Abdon, Zicri, Hanan,

ISHVAH

Ge 46: 17 Imnah, *I*, Ishvi and Beriah.
1Ch 7: 30 Imnah, *I*, Ishvi and Beriah.

ISHVI (ISHVITE)

Ge 46: 17 Imnah, Ishvah, *I* and Beriah.
Nu 26: 44 through *I*, the Ishvite clan;
1Sa 14: 49 Saul's sons were Jonathan, *I*
1Ch 7: 30 Imnah, Ishvah, *I* and Beriah.

ISHVITE (ISHVI)

Nu 26: 44 the *I* clan; through Beriah,

ISLAND (ISLANDERS ISLANDS)

Isa 23: 2 Be silent, you people of the *i*
23: 6 wail, you people of the *i*.
Ac 13: 6 traveled through the whole *i*
27: 14 swept down from the *i*.
27: 16 to the lee of a small *i* called Cauda,
27: 26 we must run aground on some *i*."
28: 1 out that the *i* was called Malta.
28: 7 to Publius, the chief official of the *i*.
28: 9 the rest of the sick on the *i* came
28: 11 in a ship that had wintered in the *i*.
Rev 1: 9 was on the *i* of Patmos
6: 14 and *i* was removed from its place.
16: 20 Every *i* fled away

ISLANDERS (ISLAND)

Ac 28: 2 The *i* showed us unusual kindness.
28: 4 When the *i* saw the snake hanging

ISLANDS (ISLAND)

Isa 11: 11 and from the *i* of the sea.
24: 15 in the *i* of the sea.
40: 15 he weighs the *i* as though they were
41: 1 "Be silent before me, you *i!*
41: 5 The *i* have seen it and fear;
42: 4 In his law the *i* will put their hope."
42: 10 you *i*, and all who live in them.
42: 12 and proclaim his praise in the *i*.
42: 15 I will turn rivers into *i*
49: 1 Listen to me, you *i;*
51: 5 The *i* will look to me
59: 18 he will repay the *i* their due.
60: 9 Surely the *i* look to me;
66: 19 to the distant *i* that have not heard
Eze 26: 18 the *i* in the sea

ISMAKIAH

2Ch 31: 13 Asahel, Jerimoth, Jozabad, Eliel, *I*,

ISOLATE (ISOLATION)

Lev 13: 50 *i* the affected article for seven days.
13: 54 he is to *i* it for another seven days.

ISOLATION (ISOLATE)

Lev 13: 4 person in *i* for seven days.
13: 5 to keep him in *i* another seven days
13: 11 He is not to put him in *i*,
13: 21 is to put him in *i* for seven days.
13: 26 is to put him in *i* for seven days.
13: 31 person in *i* for seven days.
13: 33 to keep him in *i* another seven days

ISRAEL (ISRAEL'S ISRAELITE ISRAELITES ISRAELITES')

Ge 32: 28 name will no longer be Jacob, but *I*,
34: 7 in *I* by lying with Jacob's daughter
35: 10 So he named him *I*.
35: 10 called Jacob; your name will be *I*."
35: 21 *I* moved on again and pitched his
35: 22 While *I* was living in that region,
35: 22 concubine Bilhah, and *I* heard
37: 3 Now *I* loved Joseph more than any
37: 13 and *I* said to Joseph, "As you know
43: 6 *I* asked, "Why did you bring this
43: 8 Then Judah said to *I* his father,
43: 11 Then their father *I* said to them,
45: 21 So the sons of *I* did this.
45: 28 And *I* said, "I'm convinced!
46: 1 So *I* set out with all that was his,
46: 2 God spoke to *I* in a vision at night
46: 29 went to Goshen to meet his father *I*
46: 30 *I* said to Joseph, "Now I am ready
47: 29 When the time drew near for *I*
47: 31 *I* worshiped as he leaned on the top
48: 2 *I* rallied his strength and sat up
48: 8 When *I* saw the sons of Joseph,
48: 9 Then *I* said, "Bring them to me
48: 11 *I* said to Joseph, "I never expected
48: 14 But *I* reached out his right hand
48: 20 your name will *I* pronounce this
48: 21 *I* said to Joseph, "I am about to die,
49: 2 listen to your father *I*.
49: 7 and disperse them in *I*.
49: 16 as one of the tribes of *I*.
49: 24 of the Shepherd, the Rock of *I*,
49: 28 All these are the twelve tribes of *I*,
50: 2 in his service to embalm his father *I*
50: 25 made the sons of *I* swear an oath
Ex 1: 1 of the sons of *I* who entered Egypt
3: 16 assemble the elders of *I*
3: 18 "The elders of *I* will listen to you.
4: 22 the LORD says: *I* is my firstborn
5: 1 God of *I*, says: 'Let my people go,
5: 2 that I should obey him and let *I* go?
5: 2 the LORD and I will not let *I* go."
6: 14 the firstborn son of *I* were Hanoch
9: 4 between the livestock of *I*
11: 7 a distinction between Egypt and *I*.
12: 3 Tell the whole community of *I* that
12: 6 of *I* must slaughter them
12: 15 the seventh must be cut off from *I*.
12: 19 cut off from the community of *I*,
12: 21 summoned all the elders of *I*
12: 47 community of *I* must celebrate it.
13: 19 the sons of *I* swear an oath.
14: 20 between the armies of Egypt and *I*.
14: 30 That day the LORD saved *I*
14: 30 and *I* saw the Egyptians lying dead
15: 22 Then Moses led *I* from the Red Sea
16: 31 people of *I* called the bread manna.
17: 5 with you some of the elders of *I*
17: 6 this in the sight of the elders of *I*.
18: 1 for Moses and for his people *I*,
18: 1 how the LORD had brought *I* out
18: 9 done for *I* in rescuing them
18: 11 who had treated *I* arrogantly."
18: 12 with all the elders of *I* to eat bread
18: 25 He chose capable men from all *I*
19: 2 and *I* camped there in the desert
19: 3 what you are to tell the people of *I*:
24: 1 and seventy of the elders of *I*.
24: 4 representing the twelve tribes of *I*.
24: 9 and the seventy elders of *I* went up
24: 10 went up and saw the God of *I*.
28: 9 names of the sons of *I* in the order
28: 11 Engrave the names of the sons of *I*
28: 12 memorial stones for the sons of *I*.
28: 21 each of the names of the sons of *I*,
28: 29 of the sons of *I* over his heart
32: 4 "These are your gods, O *I*,
32: 8 'These are your gods, O *I*,
32: 13 servants Abraham, Isaac and *I*,
32: 27 is what the LORD, the God of *I*,
34: 23 Sovereign LORD, the God of *I*.
34: 27 a covenant with you and with *I*."
39: 6 seal with the names of the sons of *I*.
39: 7 memorial stones for the sons of *I*,
39: 14 each of the names of the sons of *I*,
40: 38 house of *I* during all their travels.
Lev 9: 1 and his sons and the elders of *I*.
10: 6 your relatives, all the house of *I*,
16: 17 and the whole community of *I*.
19: 2 "Speak to the entire assembly of *I*
20: 2 any alien living in *I* who gives any
22: 18 an Israelite or an alien living in *I*—
Nu 1: 3 the men in *I* twenty years old
1: 16 were the heads of the clans of *I*.
1: 20 of Reuben the firstborn son of *I*:
1: 44 Aaron and the twelve leaders of *I*,
3: 13 for myself every firstborn in *I*,
3: 45 in place of all the firstborn of *I*,
4: 46 leaders of *I* counted all the Levites
7: 2 Then the leaders of *I*, the heads
8: 17 Every firstborn male in *I*,
8: 18 in place of all the firstborn sons in *I*
10: 4 the heads of the clans of *I*—
10: 29 has promised good things to *I*."
10: 36 to the countless thousands of *I*."
11: 30 the elders of *I* returned to the camp
16: 9 the God of *I* has separated you
16: 25 and the elders of *I* followed him.
18: 14 "Everything in *I* that is devoted
18: 21 give to the Levites all the tithes in *I*
19: 13 That person must be cut off from *I*.
20: 14 "This is what your brother *I* says:
20: 21 *I* turned away from them.
20: 29 the entire house of *I* mourned
21: 1 heard that *I* was coming
21: 2 *I* made this vow to the LORD:
21: 17 Then *I* sang this song:
21: 21 *I* sent messengers to say
21: 23 But Sihon would not let *I* pass
21: 23 he reached Jahaz, he fought with *I*.
21: 23 out into the desert against *I*.
21: 24 *I*, however, put him to the sword
21: 25 *I* captured all the cities
21: 31 So *I* settled in the land
22: 2 of Zippor saw all that *I* had done
23: 7 come, denounce *I*.'
23: 10 or number the fourth part of *I*?
23: 21 no misery observed in *I*.
23: 23 and of *I*, 'See what God has done!'
23: 23 no divination against *I*.
24: 1 that it pleased the LORD to bless *I*,
24: 2 and saw *I* encamped tribe by tribe,
24: 5 your dwelling places, O *I!*
24: 17 a scepter will rise out of *I*.
24: 18 but *I* will grow strong.
25: 1 While *I* was staying in Shittim,
25: 3 So *I* joined in worshiping the Baal
25: 4 anger may turn away from *I*."
25: 6 and the whole assembly of *I*
26: 2 able to serve in the army of *I*."
26: 5 the firstborn son of *I*, were:

Nu 26:51 of the men of *I* was 601,730.
30: 1 said to the heads of the tribes of *I:*
31: 4 men from each of the tribes of *I*.''
31: 5 were supplied from the clans of *I*.
32: 4 subdued before the people of *I*—
32: 13 LORD's anger burned against *I*
32: 14 the LORD even more angry with *I*.
32: 22 obligation to the LORD and to *I*.
36: 7 No inheritance in *I* is to pass
Dt 1: 1 spoke to all *I* in the desert east
1: 38 because he will lead *I* to inherit it.
2: 12 as *I* did in the land the LORD gave
4: 1 O *I*, the decrees and laws I am
5: 1 all *I* and said: Hear, O *I*,
6: 3 O *I*, and be careful to obey
6: 4 Hear, O *I:* The LORD our God,
9: 1 Hear, O *I*.
10: 12 O *I*, what does the LORD your
11: 6 right in the middle of all *I*
13: 11 Then all *I* will hear and be afraid,
17: 4 detestable thing has been done in *I*,
17: 12 You must purge the evil from *I*.
17: 20 time over his kingdom in *I*.
18: 1 no allotment or inheritance with *I*.
18: 6 anywhere in *I* where he is living,
19: 13 You must purge from *I* the guilt
20: 3 O *I*, today you are going into battle
21: 8 this atonement for your people *I*,
21: 21 All *I* will hear of it and be afraid.
22: 21 thing in *I* by being promiscuous
22: 22 You must purge the evil from *I*.
25: 6 name will not be blotted out from *I*.
25: 7 to carry on his brother's name in *I*.
25: 10 That man's line shall be known in *I*
26: 15 and bless your people *I*
27: 1 elders of *I* commanded the people:
27: 9 said to all *I*, "Be silent, O *I*,
27: 14 to all the people of *I* in a loud voice:
29: 10 and all the other men of *I*,
29: 21 from all the tribes of *I* for disaster,
31: 1 and spoke these words to all *I:*
31: 7 said to him in the presence of all *I*,
31: 9 and to all the elders of *I*.
31: 11 when all *I* comes to appear
31: 30 hearing of the whole assembly of *I:*
32: 8 to the number of the sons of *I*.
32: 45 reciting all these words to all *I*,
32: 52 giving to the people of *I*.''
33: 5 along with the tribes of *I*
33: 10 and your law to *I*.
33: 21 and his judgments concerning *I*.''
33: 28 So *I* will live in safety alone;
33: 29 Blessed are you, O *I!*
34: 10 prophet has risen in *I* like Moses,
34: 12 did in the sight of all *I*.
Jos 3: 7 to exalt you in the eyes of all *I*,
3: 12 men from the tribes of *I*,
3: 17 all *I* passed by until the whole
4: 7 to the people of *I* forever.''
4: 14 Joshua in the sight of all *I;*
4: 22 *I* crossed the Jordan on dry ground
6: 18 the camp of *I* liable to destruction
6: 23 in a place outside the camp of *I*.
7: 1 the LORD's anger burned against *I*
7: 6 The elders of *I* did the same,
7: 8 now that *I* has been routed
7: 11 *I* has sinned; they have violated my
7: 13 is devoted is among you, O *I*.
7: 13 of *I*, says: That which is devoted is
7: 15 has done a disgraceful thing in *I!*' ''
7: 16 Joshua had *I* come forward
7: 19 God of *I*, and give him the praise.
7: 20 against the LORD, the God of *I*.
7: 24 Then Joshua, together with all *I*,
7: 25 Then all *I* stoned him,
8: 10 and the leaders of *I* marched
8: 14 in the morning to meet *I* in battle
8: 15 all *I* let themselves be driven back
8: 17 city open and went in pursuit of *I*.
8: 17 or Bethel who did not go after *I*.
8: 21 all *I* saw that the ambush had taken
8: 22 *I* cut them down, leaving them
8: 24 When *I* had finished killing all
8: 27 But *I* did carry off for themselves
8: 30 the God of *I*, as Moses the servant
8: 33 All *I*, aliens and citizens alike,
8: 33 instructions to bless the people of *I*.
8: 35 read to the whole assembly of *I*,

Jos 9: 2 to make war against Joshua and *I*.
9: 6 and said to him and the men of *I*,
9: 7 The men of *I* said to the Hivites,
9: 14 men of *I* sampled their provisions
9: 18 them by the LORD, the God of *I*.
9: 19 of *I*, and we cannot touch them
10: 1 had made a treaty of peace with *I*
10: 10 *I* pursued them along the road
10: 10 them into confusion before *I*,
10: 11 As they fled before *I* on the road
10: 12 gave the Amorites over to *I*,
10: 12 to the LORD in the presence of *I:*
10: 14 Surely the LORD was fighting for *I*
10: 15 returned with all *I* to the camp
10: 24 he summoned all the men of *I*
10: 29 and all *I* with him moved
10: 31 and all *I* with him moved
10: 32 LORD handed Lachish over to *I*,
10: 34 and all *I* with him moved
10: 36 all *I* with him went up from Eglon
10: 38 and all *I* with him turned around
10: 40 the God of *I*, had commanded.
10: 42 LORD, the God of *I*, fought for *I*.
10: 43 returned with all *I* to the camp
11: 5 of Merom, to fight against *I*.
11: 6 I will hand all of them over to *I*,
11: 8 them into the hand of *I*.
11: 13 Yet *I* did not burn any
11: 16 and the mountains of *I*
11: 20 hearts to wage war against *I*,
11: 21 and from all the hill country of *I*.
11: 23 as an inheritance to *I* according
12: 7 to the tribes of *I* according
13: 6 land to *I* for an inheritance,
13: 14 the God of *I*, are their inheritance,
13: 33 the God of *I*, is their inheritance,
14: 1 clans of *I* allotted to them.
14: 10 while *I* moved about in the desert.
14: 14 the God of *I*, wholeheartedly.
19: 51 clans of *I* assigned by lot
21: 1 families of *I* at Shiloh in Canaan
21: 43 LORD gave *I* all the land he had
21: 45 promises to the house of *I* failed;
22: 12 assembly of *I* gathered at Shiloh
22: 14 one for each of the tribes of *I*,
22: 16 faith with the God of *I* like this?
22: 18 with the whole community of *I*.
22: 20 upon the whole community of *I?*
22: 21 to the heads of the clans of *I:*
22: 22 He knows! And let *I* know!
22: 24 to do with the LORD, the God of *I*
23: 1 and the LORD had given *I* rest
23: 2 summoned all *I*— their elders,
24: 1 Joshua assembled all the tribes of *I*
24: 1 leaders, judges and officials of *I*,
24: 2 the God of *I*, says: 'Long ago your
24: 9 prepared to fight against *I*,
24: 23 hearts to the LORD, the God of *I*.''
24: 31 *I* served the LORD
24: 31 the LORD had done for *I*.
Jdg 1: 28 When *I* became strong, they
2: 7 things the LORD had done for *I*.
2: 10 nor what he had done for *I*.
2: 14 against *I* the LORD handed them
2: 15 Whenever *I* went out to fight,
2: 20 the LORD was very angry with *I*
2: 22 I will use them to test *I* and see
3: 8 of the LORD burned against *I*
3: 12 king of Moab power over *I*.
3: 13 Eglon came and attacked *I*,
3: 30 day Moab was made subject to *I*,
3: 31 He too saved *I*.
4: 4 was leading *I* at that time.
4: 6 the God of *I*, commands you: 'Go,
5: 2 When the princes in *I* take the lead,
5: 3 music to the LORD, the God of *I*.
5: 5 before the LORD, the God of *I*.
5: 7 Village life in *I* ceased,
5: 7 arose a mother in *I*.
5: 8 seen among forty thousand in *I*.
5: 11 acts of his warriors in *I*.
6: 4 did not spare a living thing for *I*,
6: 8 is what the LORD, the God of *I*,
6: 14 and save *I* out of Midian's hand.
6: 15 Gideon asked, "how can I save *I?*
6: 36 "If you will save *I* by my hand
6: 37 I will know that you will save *I*
7: 2 In order that *I* may not boast

Jdg 7: 15 He returned to the camp of *I*
8: 27 All *I* prostituted themselves
9: 22 had governed *I* three years,
10: 1 the son of Dodo, rose to save *I*.
10: 2 He led *I* twenty-three years;
10: 3 who led *I* twenty-two years.
10: 9 and *I* was in great distress.
11: 4 the Ammonites made war on *I*,
11: 13 "When *I* came up out of Egypt,
11: 15 *I* did not take the land of Moab
11: 16 *I* went through the desert
11: 17 So *I* stayed at Kadesh.
11: 17 Then *I* sent messengers to the king
11: 19 *I* sent messengers to Sihon king
11: 20 at Jahaz and fought with *I*.
11: 20 did not trust *I* to pass
11: 21 *I* took over all the land
11: 21 "Then the LORD, the God of *I*,
11: 23 Now since the LORD, the God of *I*
11: 23 out before his people *I*,
11: 25 Did he ever quarrel with *I*
11: 26 hundred years *I* occupied
11: 33 Thus *I* subdued Ammon.
11: 40 women of *I* go out for four days.
12: 7 Jephthah led *I* six years.
12: 8 Ibzan of Bethlehem led *I*.
12: 9 Ibzan led *I* seven years.
12: 11 Elon the Zebulunite led *I* ten years.
12: 13 son of Hillel, from Pirathon, led *I*.
12: 14 He led *I* eight years.
13: 5 the deliverance of *I* from the hands
14: 4 at that time they were ruling over *I*
15: 20 Samson led *I* for twenty years
16: 31 He had led *I* twenty years.
17: 6 In those days *I* had no king;
18: 1 In those days *I* had no king.
18: 1 inheritance among the tribes of *I*.
18: 19 and clan in *I* as priest rather
18: 29 born to *I*— though the city used
19: 1 In those days *I* had no king.
19: 29 sent them into all the areas of *I*.
20: 2 of the tribes of *I* took their places
20: 6 this lewd and disgraceful act in *I*.
20: 10 for all this vileness done in *I*.''
20: 10 hundred from all the tribes of *I*,
20: 11 So all the men of *I* got together
20: 12 The tribes of *I* sent men
20: 13 and purge the evil from *I*.''
20: 17 *I*, apart from Benjamin, mustered
20: 20 The men of *I* went out
20: 22 men of *I* encouraged one another
20: 29 *I* set an ambush around Gibeah.
20: 33 All the men of *I* moved
20: 35 defeated Benjamin before *I*,
20: 36 Now the men of *I* had given way
20: 38 The men of *I* had arranged
20: 39 and then the men of *I* would turn
20: 39 on the men of *I* (about thirty),
20: 41 Then the men of *I* turned on them,
20: 42 And the men of *I* who came out
20: 48 The men of *I* went back
21: 1 The men of *I* had taken an oath
21: 3 O LORD, the God of *I*,'' they cried
21: 3 one tribe be missing from *I* today?''
21: 3 "why has this happened to *I?*
21: 5 tribes of *I* has failed to assemble
21: 6 "Today one tribe is cut off from *I*,''
21: 8 of the tribes of *I* failed to assemble
21: 15 had made a gap in the tribes of *I*.
21: 17 a tribe of *I* will not be wiped out.
21: 25 In those days *I* had no king;
Ru 2: 12 of *I*, under whose wings you have
4: 7 (Now in earlier times in *I*,
4: 7 of legalizing transactions in *I*.)
4: 11 together built up the house of *I*.
4: 14 he become famous throughout *I!*
1Sa 1: 17 of *I* grant you what you have asked
2: 22 his sons were doing to all *I*
2: 28 of all the tribes of *I* to be my priest,
2: 29 offering made by my people *I?*'
2: 30 Therefore the LORD, the God of *I*,
2: 32 Although good will be done to *I*,
3: 11 in *I* that will make the ears
3: 20 *I* from Dan to Beersheba
4: 1 And Samuel's word came to all *I*.
4: 2 deployed their forces to meet *I*,
4: 2 *I* was defeated by the Philistines,
4: 3 to camp, the elders of *I* asked,

1Sa 4: 5 all *I* raised such a great shout that
4: 10 *I* lost thirty thousand foot soldiers.
4: 17 "*I* fled before the Philistines,
4: 18 He had led *I* forty years.
4: 21 "The glory has departed from *I*"—
4: 22 "The glory has departed from *I*,
5: 7 of the god of *I* must not stay here
5: 8 ark of the god of *I* moved to Gath."
5: 8 do with the ark of the god of *I*?"
5: 8 they moved the ark of the God of *I*.
5: 10 the ark of the god of *I* around to us
5: 11 "Send the ark of the god of *I* away;
6: 3 If you return the ark of the god of *I*,
7: 2 all the people of *I* mourned
7: 3 Samuel said to the whole house of *I*
7: 5 "Assemble all *I* at Mizpah
7: 6 Samuel was leader of *I* at Mizpah.
7: 7 heard that *I* had assembled
7: 10 drew near to engage *I* in battle.
7: 11 The men of *I* rushed out of Mizpah
7: 14 And there was peace between *I*
7: 14 and *I* delivered the neighboring
7: 14 from *I* were restored to her,
7: 15 judge over *I* all the days of his life.
7: 16 judging *I* in all those places.
7: 17 and there he also judged *I*.
8: 1 appointed his sons as judges for *I*.
8: 4 all the elders of *I* gathered together
8: 22 Then Samuel said to the men of *I*,
9: 9 (Formerly in *I*, if a man went
9: 16 him leader over my people *I*;
9: 20 to whom is all the desire of *I* turned
9: 21 from the smallest tribe of *I*,
10: 17 Samuel summoned the people of *I*
10: 18 is what the LORD, the God of *I*,
10: 18 says: 'I brought *I* up out of Egypt,
10: 20 Samuel brought all the tribes of *I*
11: 2 and so bring disgrace on all *I*."
11: 3 can send messengers throughout *I*;
11: 7 pieces by messengers throughout *I*,
11: 8 men of *I* numbered three hundred
11: 13 this day the LORD has rescued *I*."
12: 1 said to all *I*, "I have listened
13: 1 and he reigned over *I*
13: 2 chose three thousand men from *I*;
13: 4 and now *I* has become a stench
13: 4 hear!" So all *I* heard the news:
13: 5 The Philistines assembled to fight *I*
13: 6 of *I* saw that their situation was
13: 13 kingdom over *I* for all time.
13: 19 found in the whole land of *I*,
13: 20 all *I* went down to the Philistines
14: 12 them into the hand of *I*."
14: 23 So the LORD rescued *I* that day,
14: 24 men of *I* were in distress that day,
14: 39 as the LORD who rescues *I* lives,
14: 41 of *I*, "Give me the right answer."
14: 45 about this great deliverance in *I*?
14: 47 After Saul had assumed rule over *I*,
14: 48 delivering *I* from the hands
15: 1 to anoint you king over his people *I*
15: 2 did to *I* when they waylaid them
15: 17 become the head of the tribes of *I*?
15: 17 LORD anointed you king over *I*.
15: 26 has rejected you as king over *I*!"
15: 28 the kingdom of *I* from you today
15: 29 who is the Glory of *I* does not lie
15: 30 elders of my people and before *I*;
15: 35 that he had made Saul king over *I*.
16: 1 I have rejected him as king over *I*?
17: 8 and shouted to the ranks of *I*,
17: 10 "This day I defy the ranks of *I*!
17: 19 and all the men of *I* in the Valley
17: 21 *I* and the Philistines were drawing
17: 25 his father's family from taxes in *I*."
17: 25 out? He comes out to defy *I*.
17: 26 and removes this disgrace from *I*?
17: 45 the God of the armies of *I*,
17: 46 will know that there is a God in *I*.
17: 52 men of *I* and Judah surged forward
18: 6 the towns of *I* to meet King Saul
18: 16 But all *I* and Judah loved David,
18: 18 my family or my father's clan in *I*,
19: 5 LORD won a great victory for all *I*,
20: 12 "By the LORD, the God of *I*,
23: 10 David said, "O LORD, God of *I*,
23: 11 God of *I*, tell your servant."
23: 17 You will be king over *I*,

1Sa 24: 2 thousand chosen men from all *I*
24: 14 whom has the king of *I* come out?
24: 20 the kingdom of *I* will be established
25: 1 and all *I* assembled and mourned
25: 30 has appointed him leader over *I*,
25: 32 be to the LORD, the God of *I*,
25: 34 surely as the LORD, the God of *I*,
26: 2 three thousand chosen men of *I*,
26: 15 aren't you? And who is like you in *I*
26: 20 The king of *I* has come out to look
27: 1 searching for me anywhere in *I*,
28: 1 their forces to fight against *I*.
28: 3 and all *I* had mourned for him
28: 19 The LORD will hand over both *I*
28: 19 over the army of *I* to the Philistines
29: 1 *I* camped by the spring in Jezreel.
29: 3 who was an officer of Saul king of *I*
30: 25 and ordinance for *I* from that day
31: 1 the Philistines fought against *I*;
2Sa 1: 12 of the LORD and the house of *I*,
1: 19 O *I*, lies slain on your heights.
1: 24 "O daughters of *I*,
2: 9 over Ephraim, Benjamin and all *I*.
2: 10 old when he became king over *I*,
2: 17 and the men of *I* were defeated
2: 28 they no longer pursued *I*,
3: 10 and establish David's throne over *I*
3: 12 and I will help you bring all *I*
3: 17 conferred with the elders of *I*
3: 18 David I will rescue my people *I*
3: 19 to tell David everything that *I*
3: 21 assemble all *I* for my lord the king,
3: 37 all *I* knew that the king had no part
3: 38 a great man has fallen in *I* this day?
4: 1 and all *I* became alarmed.
5: 1 All the tribes of *I* came to David
5: 2 you were the one who led *I*
5: 2 'You will shepherd my people *I*,
5: 3 When all the elders of *I* had come
5: 3 they anointed David king over *I*.
5: 5 in Jerusalem he reigned over all *I*
5: 12 for the sake of his people *I*.
5: 12 had established him as king over *I*
5: 17 had been anointed king over *I*,
6: 1 together out of *I* chosen men,
6: 5 house of *I* were celebrating
6: 15 house of *I* brought up the ark
6: 20 king of *I* has distinguished himself
6: 21 ruler over the LORD's people *I*—
7: 7 to shepherd my people *I*,
7: 8 flock to be ruler over my people *I*.
7: 10 will provide a place for my people *I*
7: 11 leaders over my people *I*.
7: 23 And who is like your people *I*—
7: 24 You have established your people *I*
7: 26 LORD Almighty is God over *I*!'
7: 27 "O LORD Almighty, God of *I*,
8: 15 over all *I*, doing what was just
10: 9 some of the best troops in *I*
10: 15 saw that they had been routed by *I*,
10: 17 he gathered all *I*, crossed
10: 18 But they fled before *I*,
10: 19 that they had been defeated by *I*,
11: 11 *I* and Judah are staying in tents,
12: 7 God of *I*, says: 'I anointed you king
12: 7 says: 'I anointed you king over *I*,
12: 8 I gave you the house of *I* and Judah
12: 12 in broad daylight before all *I*.' "
13: 12 a thing should not be done in *I*!
13: 13 one of the wicked fools in *I*.
14: 25 In all *I* there was not a man
15: 2 is from one of the tribes of *I*."
15: 6 he stole the hearts of the men of *I*.
15: 10 throughout the tribes of *I* to say,
15: 13 of the men of *I* are with Absalom."
16: 3 the house of *I* will give me back my
16: 15 all the men of *I* came to Jerusalem,
16: 18 by all the men of *I*—his I will be,
16: 21 all *I* will hear that you have made
16: 22 concubines in the sight of all *I*.
17: 4 and to all the elders of *I*.
17: 10 for all *I* knows that your father is
17: 11 Let all *I*, from Dan to Beersheba—
17: 13 then all *I* will bring ropes
17: 14 Absalom and all the men of *I* said,
17: 15 the elders of *I* to do such and such,
17: 24 the Jordan with all the men of *I*.
18: 6 marched into the field to fight *I*,

2Sa 18: 7 There the army of *I* was defeated
18: 16 and the troops stopped pursuing *I*,
19: 9 Throughout the tribes of *I*,
19: 11 throughout *I* has reached the king
19: 22 know that today I am king over *I*?"
19: 22 put to death in *I* today?
19: 40 the troops of *I* had taken the king
19: 41 Soon all the men of *I* were coming
19: 42 of Judah answered the men of *I*,
19: 43 more harshly than the men of *I*.
19: 43 the men of *I* answered the men
20: 1 Every man to his tent, O *I*!"
20: 2 So all the men of *I* deserted David
20: 14 tribes of *I* to Abel Beth Maacah
20: 19 are the peaceful and faithful in *I*.
20: 19 destroy a city that is a mother in *I*.
21: 2 but Saul in his zeal for *I*
21: 2 the Gibeonites were not a part of *I*
21: 4 right to put anyone in *I* to death."
21: 5 and have no place anywhere in *I*,
21: 15 between the Philistines and *I*.
21: 17 lamp of *I* will not be extinguished."
21: 21 When he taunted *I*, Jonathan son
23: 3 The God of *I* spoke,
23: 3 the Rock of *I* said to me:
23: 9 Then the men of *I* retreated,
24: 1 of the LORD burned against *I*,
24: 1 saying, "Go and count *I* and Judah
24: 2 "Go throughout the tribes of *I*
24: 4 king to enroll the fighting men of *I*.
24: 9 In *I* there were eight hundred
24: 15 a plague on *I* from that morning
24: 25 and the plague on *I* was stopped.
1Ki 1: 3 Then they searched throughout *I*
1: 20 the eyes of all *I* are on you,
1: 30 of *I*: Solomon your son shall be
1: 34 the prophet anoint him king over *I*.
1: 35 I have appointed him ruler over *I*
1: 48 be to the LORD, the God of *I*,
2: 4 to have a man on the throne of *I*.'
2: 11 He had reigned forty years over *I*
2: 15 All *I* looked to me as their king.
3: 28 When all *I* heard the verdict
4: 1 So King Solomon ruled over all *I*.
4: 7 twelve district governors over all *I*,
4: 20 The people of Judah and *I* were
4: 25 Solomon's lifetime Judah and *I*,
5: 13 conscripted laborers from all *I*—
6: 1 year of Solomon's reign over *I*,
6: 13 and will not abandon my people *I*."
8: 1 at Jerusalem the elders of *I*,
8: 2 All the men of *I* came together
8: 3 When all the elders of *I* had arrived
8: 5 of *I* that had gathered about him
8: 14 assembly of *I* was standing there,
8: 15 be to the LORD, the God of *I*,
8: 16 David to rule my people *I*.'
8: 16 the day I brought my people *I* out
8: 16 tribe of *I* to have a temple built
8: 17 Name of the LORD, the God of *I*.
8: 20 Name of the LORD, the God of *I*.
8: 20 and now I sit on the throne of *I*,
8: 22 in front of the whole assembly of *I*,
8: 23 and said: "O LORD, God of *I*,
8: 25 of *I*, keep for your servant David
8: 25 to sit before me on the throne of *I*,
8: 26 God of *I*, let your word that you
8: 30 of your people *I* when they pray
8: 33 "When your people *I* have been
8: 34 and forgive the sin of your people *I*
8: 36 sin of your servants, your people *I*.
8: 38 made by any of your people *I*—
8: 41 does not belong to your people *I*
8: 43 as do your own people *I*,
8: 52 and to the plea of your people *I*,
8: 55 assembly of *I* in a loud voice,
8: 56 rest to his people *I* just
8: 59 the cause of his people *I* according
8: 62 and all *I* with him offered sacrifices
8: 65 all *I* with him—a vast assembly,
8: 66 his servant David and his people *I*.
9: 5 to have a man on the throne of *I*.'
9: 5 your royal throne over *I* forever,
9: 7 *I* will then become a byword
9: 7 then I will cut off *I*
10: 9 and placed you on the throne of *I*.
10: 9 of the LORD's eternal love for *I*,
11: 9 the God of *I*, who had appeared

1Ki 11:25 in Aram and was hostile toward *I*.
11:31 is what the LORD, the God of *I*,
11:32 out of all the tribes of *I*,
11:37 desires; you will be king over *I*.
11:38 for David and will give *I* to you.
11:42 in Jerusalem over all *I* forty years.
12: 3 assembly of *I* went to Rehoboam
12:16 To your tents, O *I*!
12:16 When all *I* saw that the king
12:18 but all *I* stoned him to death.
12:19 So *I* has been in rebellion
12:20 and made him king over all *I*.
12:21 to make war against the house of *I*
12:28 O *I*, who brought you up out
14: 7 is what the LORD, the God of *I*,
14: 7 you a leader over my people *I*.
14:10 from Jeroboam every last male in *I*
14:13 All *I* will mourn for him
14:13 God of *I*, has found anything good.
14:14 a king over *I* who will cut
14:15 And the LORD will strike *I*,
14:15 He will uproot *I* from this good
14:16 and has caused *I* to commit."
14:16 he will give *I* up because of the sins
14:18 and all *I* mourned for him,
14:19 book of the annals of the kings of *I*.
14:21 out of all the tribes of *I* in which
15: 9 year of Jeroboam king of *I*,
15:16 king of *I* throughout their reigns.
15:17 Baasha king of *I* went up
15:19 treaty with Baasha king of *I*
15:20 of his forces against the towns of *I*.
15:25 and he reigned over *I* two years.
15:25 king of *I* in the second year
15:26 which he had caused *I* to commit.
15:27 and all *I* were besieging it.
15:30 and had caused *I* to commit,
15:30 provoked the LORD, the God of *I*,
15:31 of the annals of the kings of *I*?
15:32 king of *I* throughout their reigns.
15:33 son of Ahijah became king of all *I*
15:34 which he had caused *I* to commit.
16: 2 and caused my people *I* to sin
16: 2 made you leader of my people *I*,
16: 5 of the annals of the kings of *I*?
16: 8 son of Baasha became king of *I*,
16:13 and had caused *I* to commit,
16:13 the God of *I* to anger
16:14 of the annals of the kings of *I*?
16:16 king over *I* that very day there
16:19 and had caused *I* to commit.
16:20 of the annals of the kings of *I*?
16:21 Then the people of *I* were split
16:23 Omri became king of *I*,
16:26 the God of *I*, to anger
16:26 which he had caused *I* to commit,
16:27 of the annals of the kings of *I*?
16:29 Ahab son of Omri became king of *I*
16:29 in Samaria over *I* twenty-two years
16:33 anger than did all the kings of *I*
16:33 the God of *I*, to anger
17: 1 the God of *I*, lives, whom I serve,
17:14 is what the LORD, the God of *I*,
18:17 "Is that you, you troubler of *I*?"
18:18 "I have not made trouble for *I*,"
18:19 people from all over *I* to meet me
18:20 So Ahab sent word throughout all *I*
18:31 saying, "Your name shall be *I*."
18:36 God of Abraham, Isaac and *I*,
18:36 known today that you are God in *I*
19:16 son of Nimshi king over *I*,
19:18 Yet I reserve seven thousand in *I*—
20: 2 into the city to Ahab king of *I*,
20: 4 The king of *I* answered, "Just
20: 7 king of *I* summoned all the elders
20:11 The king of *I* answered, "Tell him:
20:13 a prophet came to Ahab king of *I*
20:21 The king of *I* advanced
20:22 the prophet came to the king of *I*
20:25 so we can fight *I* on the plains.
20:26 went up to Aphek to fight against *I*.
20:28 God came up and told the king of *I*,
20:31 go to the king of *I* with sackcloth
20:31 kings of the house of *I* are merciful.
20:32 they went to the king of *I* and said,
20:40 your sentence," the king of *I* said.
20:41 and the king of *I* recognized him
20:43 the king of *I* went to his palace
1Ki 21: 7 "Is this how you act as king over *I*?
21:18 "Go down to meet Ahab king of *I*,
21:21 off from Ahab every last male in *I*
21:22 to anger and have caused *I* to sin.'
21:26 the LORD drove out before *I*.)
22: 1 war between Aram and *I*.
22: 2 went down to see the king of *I*.
22: 3 The king of *I* had said
22: 4 replied to the king of *I*,
22: 5 also said to the king of *I*,
22: 6 of *I* brought together the prophets
22: 8 king of *I* answered Jehoshaphat,
22: 9 So the king of *I* called one
22:10 the king of *I* and Jehoshaphat king
22:17 "I saw all *I* scattered
22:18 The king of *I* said to Jehoshaphat,
22:26 The king of *I* then ordered,
22:29 the king of *I* and Jehoshaphat king
22:30 So the king of *I* disguised himself
22:30 The king of *I* said to Jehoshaphat,
22:31 small or great, except the king of *I*
22:32 "Surely this is the king of *I*."
22:33 saw that he was not the king of *I*
22:34 the king of *I* between the sections
22:39 of the annals of the kings of *I*?
22:41 in the fourth year of Ahab king of *I*.
22:44 also at peace with the king of *I*.
22:51 and he reigned over *I* two years.
22:51 son of Ahab became king of *I*
22:52 son of Nebat, who caused *I* to sin
22:53 the God of *I*, to anger, just
2Ki 1: 1 death, Moab rebelled against *I*.
1: 3 God in *I* that you are going
1: 6 God in *I* that you are sending men
1:16 there is no God in *I* for you
1:18 of the annals of the kings of *I*?
2:12 The chariots and horsemen of *I*!"
3: 1 son of Ahab became king of *I*
3: 3 which he had caused *I* to commit;
3: 4 had to supply the king of *I*
3: 5 rebelled against the king of *I*.
3: 6 from Samaria and mobilized all *I*.
3: 9 the king of *I* set out with the king
3:10 "What!" exclaimed the king of *I*.
3:11 An officer of the king of *I* answered
3:12 So the king of *I* and Jehoshaphat
3:13 Elisha said to the king of *I*,
3:13 "No," the king of *I* answered,
3:24 Moabites came to the camp of *I*,
3:27 The fury against *I* was great;
5: 2 taken captive a young girl from *I*,
5: 4 him what the girl from *I* had said.
5: 5 I will send a letter to the king of *I*."
5: 6 took to the king of *I* read:
5: 7 as the king of *I* read the letter,
5: 8 know that there is a prophet in *I*."
5: 8 the king of *I* had torn his robes,
5:12 better than any of the waters of *I*?
5:15 God in all the world except in *I*.
6: 8 the king of Aram was at war with *I*.
6: 9 of God sent word to the king of *I*:
6:10 So the king of *I* checked
6:11 of us is on the side of the king of *I*
6:12 but Elisha, the prophet who is in *I*,
6:12 king of *I* the very words you speak
6:21 When the king of *I* saw them,
6:26 As the king of *I* was passing
7: 6 the king of *I* has hired the Hittite
8:16 of Joram son of Ahab king of *I*,
8:18 in the ways of the kings of *I*,
8:25 of Joram son of Ahab king of *I*,
8:26 a granddaughter of Omri king of *I*.
9: 3 says: I anoint you king over *I*.'
9: 6 is what the LORD, the God of *I*,
9: 6 king over the LORD's people *I*.
9: 8 off from Ahab every last male in *I*
9:12 I anoint you king over *I*.' "
9:14 (Now Joram and all *I*
9:21 Joram king of *I* and Ahaziah king
10:21 Then he sent word throughout *I*,
10:28 Jehu destroyed Baal worship in *I*.
10:29 which he had caused *I* to commit—
10:30 of *I* to the fourth generation."
10:31 the God of *I*, with all his heart.
10:31 which he had caused *I* to commit.
10:32 began to reduce the size of *I*.
10:34 of the annals of the kings of *I*?
10:36 over *I* in Samaria was twenty-eight
2Ki 13: 1 son of Jehu became king of *I*
13: 2 which he had caused *I* to commit,
13: 3 the LORD's anger burned against *I*
13: 4 the king of Aram was oppressing *I*.
13: 5 LORD provided a deliverer for *I*,
13: 6 which he had caused *I* to commit;
13: 8 of the annals of the kings of *I*?
13:10 son of Jehoahaz became king of *I*
13:11 which he had caused *I* to commit;
13:12 of the annals of the kings of *I*?
13:13 in Samaria with the kings of *I*.
13:14 Jehoash king of *I* went
13:14 "The chariots and horsemen of *I*!"
13:16 hands," he said to the king of *I*.
13:22 king of Aram oppressed *I*
14: 1 son of Jehoahaz king of *I*,
14: 8 king of *I*, with the challenge:
14: 9 But Jehoash king of *I* replied
14:11 so Jehoash king of *I* attacked.
14:12 Judah was routed by *I*,
14:13 king of *I* captured Amaziah king
14:15 of the annals of the kings of *I*?
14:16 in Samaria with the kings of *I*.
14:17 son of Jehoahaz king of *I*.
14:23 of Jehoash king of *I* became king
14:24 which he had caused *I* to commit.
14:25 of *I* from Lebo Hamath to the Sea
14:25 the God of *I*, spoken
14:26 seen how bitterly everyone in *I*,
14:27 the name of *I* from under heaven,
14:28 of the annals of the kings of *I*?
14:28 recovered for *I* both Damascus
14:29 with his fathers, the kings of *I*
15: 1 year of Jeroboam king of *I*,
15: 8 son of Jeroboam became king of *I*
15: 9 which he had caused *I* to commit.
15:11 book of the annals of the kings of *I*.
15:12 of *I* to the fourth generation."
15:15 book of the annals of the kings of *I*.
15:17 son of Gadi became king of *I*,
15:18 which he had caused *I* to commit.
15:20 exacted this money from *I*.
15:21 of the annals of the kings of *I*?
15:23 son of Menahem became king of *I*
15:24 which he had caused *I* to commit.
15:26 book of the annals of the kings of *I*.
15:27 son of Remaliah became king of *I*
15:28 which he had caused *I* to commit.
15:29 In the time of Pekah king of *I*,
15:31 of the annals of the kings of *I*?
15:32 of Pekah son of Remaliah king of *I*,
16: 3 walked in the ways of the kings of *I*
16: 5 of Remaliah king of *I* marched up
16: 7 king of Aram and of the king of *I*,
17: 1 son of Elah became king of *I*
17: 2 the kings of *I* who preceded him.
17: 8 the kings of *I* had introduced.
17:13 The LORD warned *I* and Judah
17:18 the LORD was very angry with *I*
17:19 the practices *I* had introduced.
17:20 LORD rejected all the people of *I*;
17:21 Jeroboam enticed *I* away
17:21 When he tore *I* away
17:23 So the people of *I* were taken
17:34 of Jacob, whom he named *I*.
18: 1 of Hoshea son of Elah king of *I*,
18: 5 trusted in the LORD, the God of *I*.
18: 9 of Hoshea son of Elah king of *I*,
18:10 year of Hoshea king of *I*.
18:11 of Assyria deported *I* to Assyria
19:15 God of *I*, enthroned
19:20 is what the LORD, the God of *I*,
19:22 Against the Holy One of *I*!
21: 3 as Ahab king of *I* had done.
21: 7 out of all the tribes of *I*,
21:12 is what the LORD, the God of *I*,
22:15 is what the LORD, the God of *I*,
22:18 of *I*, says concerning the words you
23:13 ones Solomon king of *I* had built
23:15 who had caused *I* to sin—
23:19 the kings of *I* had built in the towns
23:22 the days of the judges who led *I*,
23:22 the days of the kings of *I*
23:27 from my presence as I removed *I*,
24:13 king of *I* had made for the temple
1Ch 1:34 The sons of Isaac: Esau and *I*.
2: 1 These were the sons of *I*: Reuben,
2: 7 who brought disaster on *I*

1Ch 4: 10 Jabez cried out to the God of *I*,
5: 1 firstborn of *I* (he was the firstborn,
5: 1 given to the sons of Joseph son of *I;*
5: 3 sons of Reuben the firstborn of *I:*
5: 17 of Judah and Jeroboam king of *I*.
5: 26 So the God of *I* stirred up the spirit
6: 38 of *I;* and Heman's associate Asaph,
6: 49 atonement for *I*, in accordance
7: 29 of Joseph son of *I* lived
9: 1 All *I* was listed in the genealogies
9: 1 in the book of the kings of *I*.
10: 1 the Philistines fought against *I;*
11: 1 All *I* came together to David
11: 2 you were the one who led *I*
11: 2 'You will shepherd my people *I*,
11: 3 When all the elders of *I* had come
11: 3 they anointed David king over *I*,
11: 10 men—they, together with all *I*,
12: 32 and knew what *I* should do—
12: 38 to make David king over all *I*.
12: 40 and sheep, for there was joy in *I*.
13: 2 said to the whole assembly of *I*,
13: 2 throughout the territories of *I*,
14: 2 exalted for the sake of his people *I*.
14: 2 had established him as king over *I*
14: 8 had been anointed king over all *I*,
15: 3 David assembled all *I* in Jerusalem
15: 12 of *I*, to the place I have prepared
15: 14 the ark of the LORD, the God of *I*.
15: 25 So David and the elders of *I*
15: 28 So all *I* brought up the ark
16: 4 the God of *I:* Asaph was the chief,
16: 13 O descendants of *I* his servant,
16: 17 to *I* as an everlasting covenant:
16: 36 to the LORD, the God of *I*,
16: 40 of the LORD, which he had given *I*
17: 5 from the day I brought *I* up out
17: 7 to be ruler over my people *I*.
17: 9 will provide a place for my people *I*
17: 10 leaders over my people *I*.
17: 21 And who is like your people *I*—
17: 22 made your people *I* your very own
17: 24 the God over *I*, is Israel's God!'
18: 14 over all *I*, doing what was just
19: 10 some of the best troops in *I*
19: 16 saw that they had been routed by *I*,
19: 17 he gathered all *I* and crossed
19: 18 But they fled before *I*,
19: 19 that they had been defeated by *I*,
20: 7 When he taunted *I*, Jonathan son
21: 1 Satan rose up against *I*
21: 1 incited David to take a census of *I*.
21: 3 Why should he bring guilt on *I?*"
21: 4 so Joab left and went throughout *I*
21: 5 In all *I* there were one million one
21: 7 the sight of God; so he punished *I*.
21: 12 LORD ravaging every part of *I*.'
21: 14 So the LORD sent a plague on *I*,
21: 14 thousand men of *I* fell dead.
22: 1 also the altar of burnt offering for *I*
22: 2 to assemble the aliens living in *I*,
22: 6 house for the LORD, the God of *I*.
22: 9 and I will grant *I* peace
22: 10 of his kingdom over *I* forever.'
22: 12 you in command over *I*,
22: 13 that the LORD gave Moses for *I*.
22: 17 of *I* to help his son Solomon.
23: 1 made his son Solomon king over *I*.
23: 2 together all the leaders of *I*,
23: 25 "Since the LORD, the God of *I*,
24: 19 the God of *I*, had commanded him.
26: 29 as officials and judges over *I*.
26: 30 were responsible in *I* west
27: 16 The officers over the tribes of *I:*
27: 22 the officers over the tribes of *I*.
27: 23 the LORD had promised to make *I*
27: 24 Wrath came on *I* on account
28: 1 of *I* to assemble at Jerusalem:
28: 4 family to be king over *I* forever.
28: 4 pleased to make me king over all *I*.
28: 4 "Yet the LORD, the God of *I*,
28: 5 the kingdom of the LORD over *I*.
28: 8 you in the sight of all *I*
29: 6 the officers of the tribes of *I*,
29: 10 God of our father *I*,
29: 18 of our fathers Abraham, Isaac and *I*
29: 21 sacrifices in abundance for all *I*.
29: 23 He prospered and all *I* obeyed him.
1Ch 29: 25 Solomon in the sight of all *I*
29: 25 as no king over *I* ever had before.
29: 26 son of Jesse was king over all *I*.
29: 27 He ruled over *I* forty years—
29: 30 that surrounded him and *I*
2Ch 1: 2 Then Solomon spoke to all *I*—
1: 2 and to all the leaders in *I*,
1: 13 And he reigned over *I*.
2: 4 This is a lasting ordinance for *I*.
2: 12 the God of *I*, who made heaven
2: 17 of all the aliens who were in *I*,
5: 2 to Jerusalem the elders of *I*,
5: 3 And all the men of *I* came together
5: 4 When all the elders of *I* had arrived
5: 6 of *I* that had gathered about him
6: 3 assembly of *I* was standing there,
6: 4 be to the LORD, the God of *I*,
6: 5 to be the leader over my people *I*.
6: 5 tribe of *I* to have a temple built
6: 6 David to rule my people *I*.'
6: 7 Name of the LORD, the God of *I*.
6: 10 Name of the LORD, the God of *I*.
6: 10 and now I sit on the throne of *I*,
6: 11 made with the people of *I*."
6: 12 in front of the whole assembly of *I*
6: 13 before the whole assembly of *I*
6: 14 He said: "O LORD, God of *I*,
6: 16 of *I*, keep for your servant David
6: 16 to sit before me on the throne of *I*,
6: 17 And now, O LORD, God of *I*,
6: 21 of your people *I* when they pray
6: 24 "When your people *I* have been
6: 25 and forgive the sin of your people *I*
6: 27 sin of your servants, your people *I*.
6: 29 made by any of your people *I*—
6: 32 does not belong to your people *I*
6: 33 as do your own people *I*,
7: 8 all *I* with him—a vast assembly,
7: 10 and Solomon and for his people *I*.
7: 18 fail to have a man to rule over *I*.'
7: 20 then I will uproot *I* from my land,
8: 11 in the palace of David king of *I*,
9: 8 of the love of your God for *I*
9: 30 in Jerusalem over all *I* forty years.
10: 3 and he and all *I* went to Rehoboam
10: 16 To your tents, O *I!*
10: 16 When all *I* saw that the king
10: 19 So *I* has been in rebellion
11: 1 to make war against *I*
11: 16 the God of *I*, followed the Levites
11: 16 tribe of *I* who set their hearts
12: 1 all *I* with him abandoned the law
12: 6 leaders of *I* and the king humbled
12: 13 out of all the tribes of *I* in which
13: 4 "Jeroboam and all *I*, listen to me!
13: 5 has given the kingship of *I*
13: 5 that the LORD, the God of *I*,
13: 12 Men of *I*, do not fight
13: 15 and all *I* before Abijah and Judah.
13: 18 The men of *I* were subdued
15: 3 For a long time *I* was
15: 4 the God of *I*, and sought him,
15: 9 come over to him from *I*
15: 13 the God of *I*, were to be put
15: 17 not remove the high places from *I*,
16: 1 king of *I* went up against Judah
16: 3 treaty with Baasha king of *I*
16: 4 of his forces against the towns of *I*.
16: 11 book of the kings of Judah and *I*.
17: 1 and strengthened himself against *I*.
17: 4 rather than the practices of *I*.
18: 3 king of *I* asked Jehoshaphat king
18: 4 also said to the king of *I*,
18: 5 of *I* brought together the prophets
18: 7 king of *I* answered Jehoshaphat,
18: 8 So the king of *I* called one
18: 9 the king of *I* and Jehoshaphat king
18: 16 "I saw all *I* scattered
18: 17 The king of *I* said to Jehoshaphat,
18: 19 'Who will lure Ahab king of *I*
18: 25 The king of *I* then ordered,
18: 28 the king of *I* and Jehoshaphat king
18: 29 So the king of *I* disguised himself
18: 29 The king of *I* said to Jehoshaphat,
18: 30 small or great, except the king of *I*
18: 31 they thought, "This is the king of *I*
18: 32 saw that he was not the king of *I*,
18: 33 the king of *I* between the sections
2Ch 18: 34 the king of *I* propped himself up
20: 7 of this land before your people *I*
20: 10 territory you would not allow *I*
20: 19 the God of *I*, with very loud voice.
20: 29 fought against the enemies of *I*.
20: 34 in the book of the kings of *I*.
20: 35 an alliance with Ahaziah king of *I*,
21: 2 sons of Jehoshaphat king of *I*.
21: 4 along with some of the princes of *I*.
21: 6 in the ways of the kings of *I*,
21: 13 in the ways of the kings of *I*,
22: 5 son of Ahab king of *I* to war
24: 5 the money due annually from all *I*,
24: 6 by the assembly of *I* for the Tent
24: 9 servant of God had required of *I*
24: 16 of the good he had done in *I*
25: 6 men from *I* for a hundred talents
25: 7 for the LORD is not with *I*—
25: 7 these troops from *I* must not march
25: 17 the son of Jehu, king of *I:* "Come,
25: 18 But Jehoash king of *I* replied
25: 21 So Jehoash king of *I* attacked.
25: 22 Judah was routed by *I*,
25: 23 king of *I* captured Amaziah king
25: 25 son of Jehoahaz king of *I*.
25: 26 book of the kings of Judah and *I?*
27: 7 written in the book of the kings of *I*
28: 2 walked in the ways of the kings of *I*
28: 5 given into the hands of the king of *I*
28: 13 and his fierce anger rests on *I*."
28: 19 Judah because of Ahaz king of *I*,
28: 23 downfall and the downfall of all *I*.
28: 26 book of the kings of Judah and *I*.
28: 27 in the tombs of the kings of *I*.
29: 7 at the sanctuary to the God of *I*.
29: 10 of *I*, so that his fierce anger will
29: 24 and the sin offering for all *I*.
29: 24 for a sin offering to atone for all *I*,
29: 27 the instruments of David king of *I*.
30: 1 Hezekiah sent word to all *I*
30: 1 to the LORD, the God of *I*.
30: 5 send a proclamation throughout *I*,
30: 5 to the LORD, the God of *I*.
30: 6 couriers went throughout *I*
30: 6 the God of Abraham, Isaac and *I*,
30: 6 "People of *I*, return to the LORD,
30: 25 and all who had assembled from *I*,
30: 25 the aliens who had come from *I*
30: 26 of *I* there had been nothing like
31: 6 The men of *I* and Judah who lived
31: 8 LORD and blessed his people *I*.
32: 17 the God of *I*, and saying this
32: 32 book of the kings of Judah and *I*.
33: 7 out of all the tribes of *I*,
33: 16 to serve the LORD, the God of *I*.
33: 18 in the annals of the kings of *I*.
33: 18 the God of *I*, are written
34: 7 all the incense altars throughout *I*.
34: 9 and the entire remnant of *I*
34: 21 for me and for the remnant in *I*
34: 23 is what the LORD, the God of *I*,
34: 26 of *I*, says concerning the words you
34: 33 in *I* serve the LORD their God.
35: 3 LORD your God and his people *I*.
35: 3 son of David king of *I* built.
35: 3 who instructed all *I* and who had
35: 4 written by David king of *I*
35: 18 *I* who were there with the people
35: 18 kings of *I* had ever celebrated such
35: 18 this in *I* since the days
35: 25 These became a tradition in *I*
35: 27 written in the book of the kings of *I*
36: 8 written in the book of the kings of *I*
36: 13 turn to the LORD, the God of *I*.
Ezr 1: 3 the God of *I*, the God who is
2: 2 list of the men of the people of *I:*
2: 59 families were descended from *I:*
3: 2 God of *I* to sacrifice burnt offerings
3: 10 as prescribed by David king of *I*.
3: 11 his love to *I* endures forever."
4: 1 the God of *I*, they came
4: 3 heads of the families of *I* answered,
4: 3 the God of *I*, as King Cyrus,
5: 1 in the name of the God of *I*,
5: 11 one that a great king of *I* built
6: 14 to the command of the God of *I*
6: 16 Then the people of *I*— the priests,
6: 17 offering for all *I*, twelve male goats,

Ezr 6: 17 one for each of the tribes of *I*.
6: 21 to seek the LORD, the God of *I*.
6: 22 on the house of God, the God of *I*.
7: 6 which the LORD, the God of *I*,
7: 10 to teaching its decrees and laws in *I*
7: 11 and decrees of the LORD for *I*:
7: 15 have freely given to the God of *I*,
7: 28 and gathered leading men from *I*
8: 18 the son of *I*, and Sherebiah's sons
8: 25 and all *I* present there had donated
8: 29 and the family heads of *I*."
8: 35 bulls for all *I*, ninety-six rams,
8: 35 burnt offerings to the God of *I*:
9: 1 people of *I*, including the priests
9: 4 of the God of *I* gathered around me
9: 15 God of *I*, you are righteous!
10: 2 spite of this, there is still hope for *I*.
10: 5 and all *I* under oath to do what had
Ne 1: 6 for your servants, the people of *I*.
7: 7 list of the men of *I*: the descendants
7: 61 families were descended from *I*:
8: 1 the LORD had commanded for *I*.
10: 33 offerings to make atonement for *I*;
10: 39 people of *I*, including the Levites,
12: 47 all *I* contributed the daily portions
13: 3 they excluded from *I* all who were
13: 18 wrath against *I* by desecrating
13: 26 and God made him king over all *I*,
13: 26 that Solomon king of *I* sinned?
Ps 14: 7 let Jacob rejoice and *I* be glad!
14: 7 that salvation for *I* would come out
22: 3 you are the praise of *I*.
22: 23 him, all you descendants of *I*!
25: 22 Redeem *I*, O God,
41: 13 to the LORD, the God of *I*,
50: 7 O *I*, and I will testify against you:
53: 6 let Jacob rejoice and *I* be glad!
53: 6 that salvation for *I* would come out
59: 5 God Almighty, the God of *I*,
68: 8 before God, the God of *I*.
68: 26 in the assembly of *I*.
68: 34 whose majesty is over *I*,
68: 35 the God of *I* gives power
69: 6 O God of *I*.
71: 22 O Holy One of *I*.
72: 18 to the LORD God, the God of *I*,
73: 1 Surely God is good to *I*,
76: 1 his name is great in *I*.
78: 5 and established the law in *I*,
78: 21 and his wrath rose against *I*,
78: 31 cutting down the young men of *I*.
78: 41 they vexed the Holy One of *I*.
78: 55 the tribes of *I* in their homes.
78: 59 he rejected *I* completely.
78: 71 of *I* his inheritance.
80: 1 Hear us, O Shepherd of *I*,
81: 4 this is a decree for *I*,
81: 8 if you would but listen to me, O *I*!
81: 11 *I* would not submit to me.
81: 13 if *I* would follow my ways,
83: 4 of *I* be remembered no more."
89: 18 our king to the Holy One of *I*.
98: 3 his faithfulness to the house of *I*;
99: 8 you were to *I* a forgiving God,
103: 7 his deeds to the people of *I*:
105: 10 to *I* as an everlasting covenant:
105: 23 Then *I* entered Egypt;
105: 37 He brought out *I*, laden with silver
105: 38 dread of *I* had fallen on them.
106: 48 to the LORD, the God of *I*,
114: 1 When *I* came out of Egypt,
114: 2 *I* his dominion.
115: 9 O house of *I*, trust in the LORD—
115: 12 He will bless the house of *I*,
118: 2 Let *I* say:
121: 4 indeed, he who watches over *I*
122: 4 according to the statute given to *I*.
124: 1 let *I* say—
125: 5 Peace be upon *I*.
128: 6 Peace be upon *I*.
129: 1 let *I* say—
130: 7 O *I*, put your hope in the LORD,
130: 8 He himself will redeem *I*
131: 3 O *I*, put your hope in the LORD
135: 4 *I* to be his treasured possession.
135: 12 an inheritance to his people *I*.
135: 19 O house of *I*, praise the LORD;
136: 11 brought *I* out from among them

Ps 136: 14 brought *I* through the midst of it,
136: 22 an inheritance to his servant *I*;
147: 2 he gathers the exiles of *I*.
147: 19 his laws and decrees to *I*.
148: 14 of *I*, the people close to his heart.
149: 2 Let *I* rejoice in their Maker;
Pr 1: 1 king of *I*: for attaining wisdom
Ecc 1: 12 was king over *I* in Jerusalem.
SS 3: 7 the noblest of *I*,
Isa 1: 3 but *I* does not know,
1: 4 have spurned the Holy One of *I*
1: 24 the Mighty One of *I*, declares:
4: 2 glory of the survivors in *I*.
5: 7 is the house of *I*,
5: 19 the plan of the Holy One of *I* come,
5: 24 the word of the Holy One of *I*.
7: 1 of Remaliah king of *I* marched up
8: 14 but for both houses of *I* he will be
8: 18 in *I* from the LORD Almighty,
9: 8 it will fall on *I*.
9: 12 have devoured *I* with open mouth.
9: 14 cut off from *I* both head
10: 17 The Light of *I* will become a fire,
10: 20 In that day the remnant of *I*,
10: 20 the Holy One of *I*.
10: 22 O *I*, be like the sand by the sea,
11: 12 and gather the exiles of *I*;
11: 16 as there was for *I*
12: 6 for great is the Holy One of *I*
14: 1 once again he will choose *I*
14: 2 house of *I* will possess the nations
17: 6 declares the LORD, the God of *I*.
17: 7 turn their eyes to the Holy One of *I*
19: 24 In that day *I* will be the third,
19: 25 handiwork, and *I* my inheritance."
21: 10 from the God of *I*.
21: 17 The LORD, the God of *I*,
24: 15 name of the LORD, the God of *I*,
27: 6 *I* will bud and blossom
29: 19 in the Holy One of *I*.
29: 23 will stand in awe of the God of *I*.
30: 11 us with the Holy One of *I*!"
30: 12 this is what the Holy One of *I* says.
30: 15 LORD, the Holy One of *I*,
30: 29 to the Rock of *I*.
31: 1 do not look to the Holy One of *I*,
37: 16 God of *I*, enthroned
37: 21 is what the LORD, the God of *I*,
37: 23 Against the Holy One of *I*!
40: 27 and complain, O *I*,
41: 8 "But you, O *I*, my servant,
41: 14 O little *I*,
41: 14 your Redeemer, the Holy One of *I*.
41: 16 and glory in the Holy One of *I*.
41: 17 the God of *I*, will not forsake them.
41: 20 One of *I* has created it.
42: 24 and *I* to the plunderers?
43: 1 he who formed you, O *I*:
43: 3 the Holy One of *I*, your Savior;
43: 14 your Redeemer, the Holy One of *I*:
43: 22 not wearied yourselves for me, O *I*.
43: 28 and *I* to scorn.
44: 1 *I*, whom I have chosen.
44: 5 and will take the name *I*.
44: 21 O *I*, I will not forget you.
44: 21 for you are my servant, O *I*.
44: 23 he displays his glory in *I*.
45: 3 the God of *I*, who calls you
45: 4 of *I* my chosen,
45: 11 the Holy One of *I*, and its Maker:
45: 15 O God and Savior of *I*.
45: 17 But *I* will be saved by the LORD
45: 25 the LORD all the descendants of *I*
46: 3 you who remain of the house of *I*,
46: 13 my splendor to *I*.
47: 4 is the Holy One of *I*.
48: 1 and invoke the God of *I*—
48: 1 you who are called by the name of *I*
48: 2 and rely on the God of *I*—
48: 12 *I*, whom I have called:
48: 17 your Redeemer, the Holy One of *I*:
49: 3 *I*, in whom I will display my
49: 5 and gather *I* to himself,
49: 6 bring back those of *I* I have kept.
49: 7 One of *I*, who has chosen you."
49: 7 the Redeemer and Holy One of *I*—
52: 12 the God of *I* will be your rear guard
54: 5 One of *I* is your Redeemer;

Isa 55: 5 the Holy One of *I*,
56: 8 he who gathers the exiles of *I*:
57: 19 on the lips of the mourners in *I*.
60: 9 the Holy One of *I*,
60: 14 Zion of the Holy One of *I*.
63: 7 done for the house of *I*,
63: 16 or *I* acknowledge us;
Jer 2: 3 *I* was holy to the LORD,
2: 4 all you clans of the house of *I*.
2: 14 Is *I* a servant, a slave by birth?
2: 26 so the house of *I* is disgraced—
2: 31 "Have I been a desert to *I*
3: 6 you seen what faithless *I* has done?
3: 8 I gave faithless *I* her certificate
3: 11 "Faithless *I* is more righteous
3: 12 faithless *I*,' declares the LORD,
3: 18 of Judah will join the house of *I*,
3: 20 unfaithful to me, O house of *I*,"
3: 21 and pleading of the people of *I*,
3: 23 is the salvation of *I*.
4: 1 "If you will return, O *I*,
5: 11 The house of *I* and the house
5: 15 O house of *I*," declares the LORD,
6: 9 "Let them glean the remnant of *I*
7: 3 God of *I*, says: Reform your ways
7: 12 of the wickedness of my people *I*.
7: 21 the God of *I*, says: Go ahead,
9: 15 the LORD Almighty, the God of *I*,
9: 26 house of *I* is uncircumcised
10: 1 says to you, O house of *I*.
10: 16 including *I*, the tribe
11: 3 is what the LORD, the God of *I*,
11: 10 Both the house of *I* and the house
11: 17 because the house of *I*
12: 14 the inheritance I gave my people *I*,
13: 11 so I bound the whole house of *I*
13: 12 is what the LORD, the God of *I*,
14: 8 O Hope of *I*,
16: 9 the LORD Almighty, the God of *I*,
17: 13 O LORD, the hope of *I*,
18: 6 O house of *I*, can I not do with you
18: 6 so are you in my hand, O house of *I*
18: 13 done by Virgin *I*.
19: 3 the God of *I*, says: Listen!
19: 15 the God of *I*, says: 'Listen!
21: 4 is what the LORD, the God of *I*,
23: 2 of *I*, says to the shepherds who
23: 6 and *I* will live in safety.
23: 8 brought the descendants of *I* up out
23: 13 and led my people *I* astray.
24: 5 of *I*, says: 'Like these good figs,
25: 15 is what the LORD, the God of *I*,
25: 27 God of *I*, says: Drink, get drunk
27: 4 the God of *I*, says: "Tell this
27: 21 the LORD Almighty, the God of *I*,
28: 2 the LORD Almighty, the God of *I*,
28: 14 the LORD Almighty, the God of *I*,
29: 4 the LORD Almighty, the God of *I*,
29: 8 the LORD Almighty, the God of *I*,
29: 21 the LORD Almighty, the God of *I*,
29: 23 have done outrageous things in *I*;
29: 25 the LORD Almighty, the God of *I*,
30: 2 is what the LORD, the God of *I*,
30: 3 'when I will bring my people *I*
30: 4 the LORD spoke concerning *I*
30: 10 do not be dismayed, O *I*,'
31: 1 I will be the God of all the clans of *I*
31: 2 I will come to give rest to *I*."
31: 4 and you will be rebuilt, O Virgin *I*.
31: 7 the remnant of *I*.'
31: 10 'He who scattered *I* will gather
31: 21 Return, O Virgin *I*,
31: 23 of *I*, says: "When I bring them back
31: 27 "when I will plant the house of *I*
31: 31 covenant with the house of *I*
31: 33 with the house of *I*
31: 36 the descendants of *I* ever cease
31: 37 will I reject all the descendants of *I*
32: 14 of *I*, says: Take these documents,
32: 15 the God of *I*, says: Houses,
32: 20 both in *I* and among all mankind,
32: 21 You brought your people *I* out
32: 30 of *I* and Judah have done nothing
32: 30 the people of *I* have done nothing
32: 32 of *I* and Judah have provoked me
32: 36 is what the LORD, the God of *I*,
33: 4 is what the LORD, the God of *I*,
33: 7 I will bring Judah and *I* back

Jer 33: 14 promise I made to the house of *I*
33: 17 sit on the throne of the house of *I*,
34: 2 is what the LORD, the God of *I*,
34: 13 is what the LORD, the God of *I*,
35: 13 the LORD Almighty, the God of *I*,
35: 17 the God of *I*, says: 'Listen!
35: 18 the LORD Almighty, the God of *I*,
35: 19 the LORD Almighty, the God of *I*,
36: 2 spoken to you concerning *I*,
37: 7 the God of *I*, says: Tell the king
38: 17 God Almighty, the God of *I*,
39: 16 the LORD Almighty, the God of *I*,
41: 9 defense against Baasha king of *I*.
42: 9 is what the LORD, the God of *I*,
42: 15 the LORD Almighty, the God of *I*,
42: 18 the LORD Almighty, the God of *I*,
43: 10 the LORD Almighty, the God of *I*,
44: 2 the LORD Almighty, the God of *I*,
44: 7 God Almighty, the God of *I*,
44: 11 the LORD Almighty, the God of *I*,
44: 25 the LORD Almighty, the God of *I*,
45: 2 the God of *I*, says to you, Baruch:
46: 25 The LORD Almighty, the God of *I*
46: 27 do not be dismayed, O *I*.
48: 1 the LORD Almighty, the God of *I*,
48: 13 as the house of *I* was ashamed
48: 27 Was not *I* the object
49: 1 "Has *I* no sons?
49: 2 Then *I* will drive out
50: 4 "the people of *I* and the people
50: 17 "*I* is a scattered flock
50: 18 the LORD Almighty, the God of *I*,
50: 19 But I will bring *I* back to his own
50: 29 the Holy One of *I*.
50: 33 "The people of *I* are oppressed,
51: 5 For *I* and Judah have not been
51: 5 guilt before the Holy One of *I*.
51: 33 the LORD Almighty, the God of *I*,
La 2: 1 hurled down the splendor of *I*
2: 3 every horn of *I*.
2: 5 he has swallowed up *I*.
Eze 3: 1 then go and speak to the house of *I*
3: 4 go now to the house of *I*
3: 5 but to the house of *I*— not
3: 7 the house of *I* is not willing to listen
3: 7 the whole house of *I* is hardened
3: 17 you a watchman for the house of *I*;
4: 3 This will be a sign to the house of *I*.
4: 4 sin of the house of *I* upon yourself.
4: 5 will bear the sin of the house of *I*.
4: 13 the people of *I* will eat defiled food
5: 4 from there to the whole house of *I*.
6: 2 face against the mountains of *I*;
6: 3 'O mountains of *I*, hear the word
6: 11 practices of the house of *I*,
7: 2 LORD says to the land of *I*:
8: 4 me was the glory of the God of *I*,
8: 6 things the house of *I* is doing here,
8: 10 and all the idols of the house of *I*.
8: 11 seventy elders of the house of *I*,
8: 12 elders of the house of *I* are doing
9: 3 the glory of the God of *I* went up
9: 8 remnant of *I* in this outpouring
9: 9 "The sin of the house of *I*
10: 19 of the God of *I* was above them.
10: 20 seen beneath the God of *I*
11: 5 what you are saying, O house of *I*,
11: 10 on you at the borders of *I*.
11: 11 on you at the borders of *I*.
11: 13 destroy the remnant of *I*?"
11: 15 and the whole house of *I*—
11: 17 give you back the land of *I* again.'
11: 22 of the God of *I* was above them.
12: 6 a sign to the house of *I*."
12: 9 that rebellious house of *I* ask you,
12: 10 the whole house of *I* who are there
12: 19 in Jerusalem and in the land of *I*:
12: 22 proverb you have in the land of *I*:
12: 23 and they will no longer quote it in *I*
12: 24 divinations among the people of *I*.
12: 27 Son of man, the house of *I* is saying
13: 2 of *I* who are now prophesying.
13: 4 O *I*, are like jackals among ruins.
13: 5 house of *I* so that it will stand firm
13: 9 in the records of the house of *I*,
13: 9 nor will they enter the land of *I*.
13: 16 those prophets of *I* who prophesied
14: 1 Some of the elders of *I* came to me

Eze 14: 5 the hearts of the people of *I*,
14: 6 "Therefore say to the house of *I*,
14: 7 living in *I* separates himself
14: 9 him from among my people *I*.
14: 11 the people of *I* will no longer stray
17: 2 and tell the house of *I* a parable.
17: 23 mountain heights of *I* I will plant
18: 2 this proverb about the land of *I*:
18: 3 no longer quote this proverb in *I*.
18: 6 or look to the idols of the house of *I*
18: 15 or look to the idols of the house of *I*
18: 25 O house of *I*: Is my way unjust?
18: 29 Are my ways unjust, O house of *I*?
18: 29 Yet the house of *I* says, 'The way
18: 30 O house of *I*, I will judge you,
18: 31 Why will you die, O house of *I*?
19: 1 lament concerning the princes of *I*
19: 9 longer on the mountains of *I*.
20: 1 of the elders of *I* came to inquire
20: 3 speak to the elders of *I*
20: 5 LORD says: On the day I chose *I*,
20: 13 the people of *I* rebelled against me
20: 27 speak to the people of *I*
20: 30 "Therefore say to the house of *I*:
20: 31 O house of *I*? As surely as I live,
20: 38 yet they will not enter the land of *I*.
20: 39 " 'As for you, O house of *I*,
20: 40 of *I*, declares the Sovereign LORD
20: 40 the entire house of *I* will serve me,
20: 42 when I bring you into the land of *I*,
20: 44 of *I*, declares the Sovereign LORD
21: 2 Prophesy against the land of *I*
21: 12 it is against all the princes of *I*.
21: 25 O profane and wicked prince of *I*,
22: 6 each of the princes of *I* who are
22: 18 the house of *I* has become dross
24: 21 of *I*, 'This is what the Sovereign
25: 3 the land of *I* when it was laid waste
25: 6 of your heart against the land of *I*,
25: 14 Edom by the hand of my people *I*,
27: 17 " 'Judah and *I* traded with you;
28: 24 of *I* have malicious neighbors who
28: 25 When I gather the people of *I*
29: 6 a staff of reed for the house of *I*.
29: 16 of confidence for the people of *I*
29: 21 a horn grow for the house of *I*,
33: 7 you a watchman for the house of *I*;
33: 10 of *I*, 'This is what you are saying:
33: 11 O house of *I*?' "Therefore,
33: 20 Yet, O house of *I*, you say,
33: 24 ruins in the land of *I* are saying,
33: 28 of *I* will become desolate
34: 2 prophesy against the shepherds of *I*
34: 2 shepherds of *I* who only take care
34: 13 them on the mountains of *I*,
34: 14 of *I* will be their grazing land.
34: 14 pasture on the mountains of *I*.
34: 30 the house of *I*, are my people,
35: 12 said against the mountains of *I*.
35: 15 of the house of *I* became desolate,
36: 1 'O mountains of *I*, hear the word
36: 1 prophesy to the mountains of *I*
36: 4 therefore, O mountains of *I*,
36: 6 prophesy concerning the land of *I*
36: 8 branches and fruit for my people *I*,
36: 8 " 'But you, O mountains of *I*,
36: 10 even the whole house of *I*.
36: 12 my people *I*, to walk upon you.
36: 17 when the people of *I* were living
36: 21 which the house of *I* profaned
36: 22 O house of *I*, that I am going
36: 22 "Therefore say to the house of *I*,
36: 32 of *I*! " 'This is what the Sovereign
36: 37 yield to the plea of the house of *I*
37: 11 bones are the whole house of *I*.
37: 12 will bring you back to the land of *I*.
37: 16 the house of *I* associated with him.'
37: 22 in the land, on the mountains of *I*.
37: 28 that I the LORD make *I* holy,
38: 8 nations to the mountains of *I*,
38: 14 when my people *I* are living
38: 16 against my people *I* like a cloud
38: 17 by my servants the prophets of *I*?
38: 18 When Gog attacks the land of *I*,
38: 19 a great earthquake in the land of *I*.
39: 2 you against the mountains of *I*.
39: 4 On the mountains of *I* you will fall,
39: 7 I the LORD am the Holy One in *I*.

Eze 39: 7 name among my people *I*.
39: 9 live in the towns of *I* will go out
39: 11 I will give Gog a burial place in *I*,
39: 12 the house of *I* will be burying them
39: 17 sacrifice on the mountains of *I*.
39: 22 of *I* will know that I am the LORD
39: 23 of *I* went into exile for their sin,
39: 25 compassion on all the people of *I*,
39: 29 out my Spirit on the house of *I*,
40: 2 of God he took me to the land of *I*
40: 4 the house of *I* everything you see."
43: 2 the glory of the God of *I* coming
43: 7 of *I* will never again defile my holy
43: 10 the temple to the people of *I*,
44: 2 the God of *I*, has entered through it
44: 6 Say to the rebellious house of *I*,
44: 6 detestable practices, O house of *I*!
44: 10 far from me when *I* went astray
44: 12 made the house of *I* fall into sin,
44: 28 are to give them no possession in *I*;
44: 29 and everything in *I* devoted
45: 6 belong to the whole house of *I*.
45: 8 This land will be his possession in *I*
45: 8 but will allow the house of *I*
45: 9 gone far enough, O princes of *I*!
45: 15 from the well-watered pastures of *I*
45: 16 gift for the use of the prince in *I*.
45: 17 appointed feasts of the house of *I*.
45: 17 make atonement for the house of *I*.
47: 13 among the twelve tribes of *I*,
47: 18 between Gilead and the land of *I*,
47: 21 according to the tribes of *I*.
47: 22 inheritance among the tribes of *I*.
48: 19 come from all the tribes of *I*.
48: 29 as an inheritance to the tribes of *I*,
48: 31 named after the tribes of *I*.
Da 9: 7 and people of Jerusalem and all *I*,
9: 11 All *I* has transgressed your law
9: 20 my sin and the sin of my people *I*
Hos 1: 1 son of Jehoash king of *I*:
1: 4 an end to the kingdom of *I*.
1: 6 longer show love to the house of *I*,
1: 11 and the people of *I* will be reunited,
4: 15 Though you commit adultery, O *I*,
5: 3 *I* is corrupt.
5: 3 *I* is not hidden from me.
5: 9 Among the tribes of *I*
6: 10 and *I* is defiled.
6: 10 in the house of *I*.
7: 1 whenever I would heal *I*,
8: 2 *I* cries out to me,
8: 3 But *I* has rejected what is good;
8: 6 They are from *I*!
8: 8 *I* is swallowed up;
8: 14 *I* has forgotten his Maker
9: 1 Do not rejoice, O *I*;
9: 7 Let *I* know this.
9: 10 "When I found *I*,
10: 1 *I* was a spreading vine;
10: 6 *I* will be ashamed of its wooden
10: 8 it is the sin of *I*.
10: 9 of Gibeah, you have sinned, O *I*,
10: 15 of *I* will be completely destroyed.
11: 1 "When *I* was a child, I loved him,
11: 2 But the more I called *I*,
11: 8 How can I hand you over, *I*?
11: 12 the house of *I* with deceit.
12: 12 *I* served to get a wife,
12: 13 to bring *I* up from Egypt,
13: 1 he was exalted in *I*.
13: 9 "I will destroy you, O *I*,
14: 1 O *I*, to the LORD your God.
14: 5 I will be like the dew to *I*;
Joel 2: 27 Then you will know that I am in *I*,
3: 2 my inheritance, my people *I*,
3: 16 a stronghold for the people of *I*.
Am 1: 1 he saw concerning *I* two years
1: 1 son of Jehoash was king of *I*.
2: 6 "For three sins of *I*,
2: 11 Is this not true, people of *I*?"
3: 1 of *I*— against the whole family I
3: 14 "On the day I punish *I* for her sins,
4: 12 prepare to meet your God, O *I*."
4: 12 this is what I will do to you, *I*,
5: 1 Hear this word, O house of *I*,
5: 2 concerning you: "Fallen is Virgin *I*,
5: 3 out a thousand strong for *I*
5: 4 the LORD says to the house of *I*:

Am 5:25 years in the desert, O house of *I*?
6: 1 to whom the people of *I* come!
6:14 a nation against you, O house of *I*,
7: 8 line among my people *I*;
7: 9 the sanctuaries of *I* will be ruined;
7:10 a message to Jeroboam king of *I*:
7:10 against you in the very heart of *I*.
7:11 and *I* will surely go into exile,
7:15 'Go, prophesy to my people *I*.'
7:16 " 'Do not prophesy against *I*,
7:17 And *I* will certainly go into exile,
8: 2 "The time is ripe for my people *I*;
9: 7 "Did I not bring *I* up from Egypt,
9: 9 and I will shake the house of *I*
9:14 I will bring back my exiled people *I*
9:15 I will plant *I* in their own land,
Mic 1: 5 because of the sins of the house of *I*
1:13 for the transgressions of *I*
1:14 deceptive to the kings of *I*.
1:15 He who is the glory of *I*
2:12 bring together the remnant of *I*.
3: 1 you rulers of the house of *I*.
3: 8 to *I* his sin.
3: 9 you rulers of the house of *I*,
5: 2 one who will be ruler over *I*,
5: 3 Therefore *I* will be abandoned
6: 2 he is lodging a charge against *I*.
Na 2: 2 like the splendor of *I*,
Zep 2: 9 the LORD Almighty, the God of *I*,
3:13 The remnant of *I* will do no wrong;
3:14 shout aloud, O *I*!
3:15 The LORD, the King of *I*,
Zec 1:19 the horns that scattered Judah, *I*
8:13 O Judah and *I*, so will I save you,
9: 1 eyes of men and all the tribes of *I*
11:14 brotherhood between Judah and *I*.
12: 1 word of the LORD concerning *I*.
Mal 1: 1 of the LORD to *I* through Malachi.
1: 5 even beyond the borders of *I*!'
2:11 thing has been committed in *I*
2:16 divorce," says the LORD God of *I*,
4: 4 laws I gave him at Horeb for all *I*.
Mt 2: 6 be the shepherd of my people *I*.' "
2:20 his mother and go to the land of *I*,
2:21 mother and went to the land of *I*.
8:10 anyone in *I* with such great faith.
9:33 like this has ever been seen in *I*."
10: 6 Go rather to the lost sheep of *I*.
10:23 the cities of *I* before the Son
15:24 only to the lost sheep of *I*."
15:31 And they praised the God of *I*.
19:28 judging the twelve tribes of *I*.
27: 9 set on him by the people of *I*,
27:42 He's the king of *I*! Let him come
Mk 12:29 'Hear, O *I*, the Lord our God,
15:32 Let this Christ, this King of *I*,
Lk 1:16 of the people of *I* will he bring back
1:54 He has helped his servant *I*,
1:68 Praise be to the Lord, the God of *I*,
1:80 until he appeared publicly to *I*.
2:25 waiting for the consolation of *I*,
2:32 and for glory to your people *I*."
2:34 the falling and rising of many in *I*,
4:25 widows in *I* in Elijah's time,
4:27 there were many in *I* with leprosy
7: 9 found such great faith even in *I*."
22:30 judging the twelve tribes of *I*.
24:21 the one who was going to redeem *I*.
Jn 1:31 was that he might be revealed to *I*."
1:49 Son of God; you are the King of *I*."
12:13 "Blessed is the King of *I*!"
Ac 1: 6 going to restore the kingdom to *I*?"
2:22 "Men of *I*, listen to this: Jesus
2:36 Therefore let all *I* be assured of this
3:12 of *I*, why does this surprise you?
4:10 you and everyone else in *I*:
4:27 and the people of *I* in this city
5:21 the full assembly of the elders of *I*
5:31 and forgiveness of sins to *I*.
5:35 he addressed them: "Men of *I*,
7:42 years in the desert, O house of *I*?
9:15 and before the people of *I*.
10:36 God sent to the people of *I*,
13:16 of *I* and you Gentiles who worship
13:17 of the people of *I* chose our fathers
13:23 God has brought to *I* the Savior
13:24 and baptism to all the people of *I*
21:28 shouting, "Men of *I*, help us!
Ac 28:20 of the hope of *I* that I am bound
Ro 9: 4 of my own race, the people of *I*.
9: 6 all who are descended from *I* are *I*.
9:27 Isaiah cries out concerning *I*:
9:31 but *I*, who pursued a law
10:19 did *I* not understand? First,
10:21 But concerning *I* he says,
11: 2 how he appealed to God against *I*:
11: 7 What *I* sought so earnestly it did
11:11 to the Gentiles to make *I* envious.
11:25 *I* has experienced a hardening
11:26 And so all *I* will be saved,
1Co 10:18 people of *I*: Do not those who eat
Gal 6:16 who follow this rule, even to the *I*
Eph 2:12 excluded from citizenship in *I*
3: 6 Gentiles are heirs together with *I*,
Php 3: 5 of the people of *I*, of the tribe
Heb 8: 8 covenant with the house of *I*
8:10 with the house of *I*
11:28 would not touch the firstborn of *I*.
Rev 7: 4 from all the tribes of *I*.
21:12 the names of the twelve tribes of *I*.

ISRAEL'S (ISRAEL)

Ge 42: 5 *I* sons were among those who went
46: 5 and *I* sons took their father Jacob
48:10 Now *I* eyes were failing
48:12 Joseph removed them from *I* knees
48:13 on his left toward *I* right hand,
48:13 on his right toward *I* left hand
Ex 14:19 traveling in front of *I* army,
18: 8 and the Egyptians for *I* sake
Nu 1:45 in *I* army were counted according
11:16 seventy of *I* elders who are known
21: 3 The LORD listened to *I* plea
25: 5 So Moses said to *I* judges,
Jos 10:30 that city and its king into *I* hand.
Jdg 3:10 so that he became *I* judge
5: 9 My heart is with *I* princes,
10:16 he could bear *I* misery no longer.
11:21 and all his men into *I* hands,
20: 6 to each region of *I* inheritance,
20:34 of *I* finest men made a frontal
1Sa 6: 5 country, and pay honor to *I* god.
7: 9 out to the LORD on *I* behalf,
14:37 Will you give them into *I* hand?"
2Sa 20:23 Joab was over *I* entire army;
23: 1 *I* singer of songs:
23:11 of lentils, *I* troops fled from them.
1Ki 2: 5 to the two commanders of *I* armies,
2:32 son of Ner, commander of *I* army,
11:25 Rezon was *I* adversary as long
2Ki 6:23 Aram stopped raiding *I* territory.
1Ch 17:24 the God over Israel, is *I* God!'
2Ch 13:17 casualties among *I* able men.
Ezr 10:10 foreign women, adding to *I* guilt.
Isa 43:15 *I* Creator, your King."
44: 6 *I* King and Redeemer, the LORD
56:10 *I* watchmen are blind,
Jer 3: 9 Because *I* immorality mattered
31: 9 because I am *I* father,
50:20 "search will be made for *I* guilt,
51:49 Babylon must fall because of *I* slain
Hos 1: 5 In that day I will break *I* bow
5: 5 *I* arrogance testifies against them;
7:10 *I* arrogance testifies against him,
Mic 5: 1 They will strike *I* ruler
Jn 3:10 "You are *I* teacher," said Jesus,

ISRAELITE (ISRAEL)

Ge 36:31 in Edom before any *I* king reigned:
Ex 5:14 The *I* foremen appointed
5:15 Then the *I* foremen went
5:19 The *I* foremen realized they were
12:40 length of time the *I* people lived
16: 1 The whole *I* community set out
16: 9 "Say to the entire *I* community,
16:10 to the whole *I* community,
17: 1 The whole *I* community set out
24: 5 Then he sent young *I* men,
35: 1 assembled the whole *I* community
35: 4 said to the whole *I* community,
35:20 the whole *I* community withdrew
35:29 All the *I* men and women who
Lev 4:13 " 'If the whole *I* community sins
16: 5 From the *I* community he is
17: 3 Any *I* who sacrifices a cow,
17: 8 'Any *I* or any alien living
Lev 17:10 " 'Any *I* or any alien living
17:13 " 'Any *I* or any alien living
20: 2 'Any *I* or any alien living
22:18 an *I* or an alien living in Israel—
24:10 Now the son of an *I* mother
24:10 in the camp between him and an *I*.
24:11 son of the *I* woman blasphemed
Nu 1: 2 a census of the whole *I* community
1:53 fall on the *I* community.
3:12 offspring of every *I* woman.
3:40 all the firstborn *I* males who are
7:84 of the *I* leaders for the dedication
8: 9 assemble the whole *I* community.
8:16 offspring from every *I* woman.
8:20 and the whole *I* community did
10:28 order of march for the *I* divisions
13:26 the whole *I* community at Kadesh
14: 5 of the whole *I* assembly gathered
14: 7 and said to the entire *I* assembly,
15:25 for the whole *I* community,
15:26 The whole *I* community
15:29 he is a native-born *I* or an alien.
16: 2 With them were 250 *I* men,
16: 9 from the rest of the *I* community
16:41 the whole *I* community grumbled
19: 9 kept by the *I* community for use
20: 1 the whole *I* community arrived
20:22 The whole *I* community set out
25: 6 an *I* man brought to his family
25: 8 and followed the *I* into the tent.
25: 8 through the *I* and into the woman's
25:14 The name of the *I* who was killed
26: 2 a census of the whole *I* community
27:20 so the whole *I* community will
31:12 and the *I* assembly at their camp
32:18 until every *I* has received his
32:28 to the family heads of the *I* tribes.
36: 1 the heads of the *I* families.
36: 3 men from other *I* tribes;
36: 7 for every *I* shall keep the tribal land
36: 8 in any *I* tribe must marry someone
36: 8 so that every *I* will possess
36: 9 for each *I* tribe is to keep the land it
Dt 15: 2 loan he has made to his fellow *I*
15: 2 require payment from his fellow *I*
17:15 one who is not a brother *I*.
22:19 man has given an *I* virgin a bad
23:17 No *I* man or woman is
23:20 interest, but not a brother *I*,
24:14 whether he is a brother *I*
Jos 11:22 No Anakites were left in *I* territory
18: 2 were still seven *I* tribes who had
22:11 near the Jordan on the *I* side,
22:14 division among the *I* clans.
Jdg 7:14 of Gideon son of Joash, the *I*.
11:39 this comes the *I* custom that each
20:33 and the *I* ambush charged out
1Sa 7:13 did not invade *I* territory again.
31: 7 Jordan saw that the *I* army had fled
2Sa 1: 3 "I have escaped from the *I* camp."
11: 1 king's men and the whole *I* army.
17:25 an *I* who had married Abigail,
1Ki 8: 1 and the chiefs of the *I* families,
2Ki 13:25 and so he recovered the *I* towns.
1Ch 1:43 in Edom before any *I* king reigned:
16: 3 and a cake of raisins to each *I* man
2Ch 5: 2 and the chiefs of the *I* families,
19: 8 and heads of *I* families
23: 2 and the heads of *I* families
25: 9 paid for these *I* troops?"
Ne 9: 2 Those of *I* descent had separated
Eze 14: 4 When any *I* sets up idols
14: 7 " 'When any *I* or any alien living
37:19 of the *I* tribes associated with him,
44:22 marry only virgins of *I* descent
Ob :20 This company of *I* exiles who are
Jn 1:47 "Here is a true *I*, in whom there is
Ro 11: 1 I am an *I* myself, a descendant

ISRAELITES (ISRAEL)

Ge 32:32 to this day the *I* do not eat
46: 8 These are the names of the *I* (Jacob
47:27 the *I* settled in Egypt in the region
Ex 1: 7 the *I* were fruitful and multiplied
1: 9 *I* have become much too numerous
1:12 the Egyptians came to dread the *I*
2:23 The *I* groaned in their slavery
2:25 So God looked on the *I*

Ex 3: 9 the cry of the *I* has reached me,
3: 10 to bring my people the *I* out
3: 11 and bring the *I* out of Egypt?"
3: 13 "Suppose I go to the *I*
3: 14 This is what you are to say to the *I:*
3: 15 "Say to the *I*, 'The LORD,
4: 29 together all the elders of the *I*,
6: 5 I have heard the groaning of the *I*,
6: 6 say to the *I:* 'I am the LORD
6: 9 Moses reported this to the *I*,
6: 11 king of Egypt to let the *I* go out
6: 12 "If the *I* will not listen to me,
6: 13 and Aaron about the *I* and Pharaoh
6: 13 them to bring the *I* out of Egypt.
6: 26 "Bring the *I* out of Egypt
6: 27 of Egypt about bringing the *I* out
7: 2 to let the *I* go out of his country.
7: 4 out my divisions, my people the *I*.
7: 5 against Egypt and bring the *I* out
9: 4 belonging to the *I* will die.' "
9: 6 one animal belonging to the *I* died.
9: 7 one of the animals of the *I* had died
9: 26 land of Goshen, where the *I* were.
9: 35 and he would not let the *I* go,
10: 20 and he would not let the *I* go.
10: 23 Yet all the *I* had light
11: 7 But among the *I* not a dog will bark
11: 10 and he would not let the *I* go out
12: 27 over the houses of the *I* in Egypt
12: 28 The *I* did just what the LORD
12: 31 Leave my people, you and the *I!*
12: 35 The *I* did as Moses instructed
12: 37 The *I* journeyed from Rameses
12: 42 on this night all the *I* are
12: 50 All the *I* did just what the LORD
12: 51 day the LORD brought the *I* out
13: 2 womb among the *I* belongs to me,
13: 18 The *I* went up out of Egypt armed
14: 2 "Tell the *I* to turn back
14: 3 'The *I* are wandering
14: 4 So the *I* did this.
14: 5 We have let the *I* go and have lost
14: 8 he pursued the *I*, who were
14: 9 pursued the *I* and overtook them
14: 10 approached, the *I* looked up,
14: 15 out to me? Tell the *I* to move on.
14: 16 so that the *I* can go through the sea
14: 22 and the *I* went through the sea
14: 25 "Let's get away from the *I!*
14: 28 of Pharaoh that had followed the *I*
14: 29 But the *I* went through the sea
14: 31 when the *I* saw the great power
15: 1 the *I* sang this song to the LORD:
15: 19 but the *I* walked through the sea
16: 3 *I* said to them, "If only we had died
16: 6 Moses and Aaron said to all the *I*,
16: 12 I have heard the grumbling of the *I*.
16: 15 When the *I* saw it, they said
16: 17 The *I* did as they were told;
16: 35 The *I* ate manna forty years,
17: 7 Meribah because the *I* quarreled
17: 8 and attacked the *I* at Rephidim.
17: 11 *I* were winning, but whenever he
19: 1 month after the *I* left Egypt—
19: 6 are to speak to the *I*."
20: 22 said to Moses, "Tell the *I* this:
24: 11 hand against these leaders of the *I;*
24: 17 To the *I* the glory of the LORD
25: 2 "Tell the *I* to bring me an offering.
25: 22 give you all my commands for the *I*
27: 20 "Command the *I* to bring you clear
27: 21 among the *I* for the generations
28: 1 brought to you from among the *I*,
28: 30 decisions for the *I* over his heart
28: 38 in the sacred gifts the *I* consecrate,
29: 28 It is the contribution the *I* are
29: 28 share from the *I* for Aaron
29: 43 there also I will meet with the *I*,
29: 45 Then I will dwell among the *I*
30: 12 a census of the *I* to count them,
30: 16 for the *I* before the LORD,
30: 16 the atonement money from the *I*
30: 31 Say to the *I*, 'This is
31: 13 to the *I*, 'You must observe my
31: 16 The *I* are to observe the Sabbath,
31: 17 sign between me and the *I* forever,
32: 20 the water and made the *I* drink it.
33: 5 "Tell the *I*, 'You are a stiff-necked

Ex 33: 6 the *I* stripped off their ornaments
34: 30 Aaron and all the *I* saw Moses,
34: 32 Afterward all the *I* came near him,
34: 34 and told the *I* what he had been
35: 30 Then Moses said to the *I*, "See,
36: 3 all the offerings the *I* had brought
39: 32 The *I* did everything just
39: 42 The *I* had done all the work just
40: 36 of the *I*, whenever the cloud lifted
Lev 1: 2 "Speak to the *I* and say to them:
4: 2 said to Moses, "Say to the *I:*
7: 23 said to Moses, "Say to the *I:*
7: 29 said to Moses, "Say to the *I:*
7: 34 as their regular share from the *I*.' "
7: 34 the fellowship offerings of the *I*,
7: 36 commanded that the *I* give this
7: 38 on the day he commanded the *I*
9: 3 say to the *I:* 'Take a male goat
10: 11 you must teach the *I* all the decrees
11: 2 to the *I:* 'Of all the animals that live
12: 2 said to Moses, "Say to the *I:*
15: 2 "Speak to the *I* and say to them:
15: 31 " 'You must keep the *I* separate
16: 16 uncleanness and rebellion of the *I*,
16: 19 it from the uncleanness of the *I*.
16: 21 wickedness and rebellion of the *I*—
16: 34 a year for all the sins of the *I*."
17: 2 and to all the *I* and say to them:
17: 5 This is so the *I* will bring
17: 12 Therefore I say to the *I*, "None
17: 14 That is why I have said to the *I*,
18: 2 "Speak to the *I* and say to them:
20: 2 said to Moses, "Say to the *I:*
21: 24 and his sons and to all the *I*.
22: 2 sacred offerings the *I* consecrate
22: 3 offerings that the *I* consecrate
22: 15 the sacred offerings the *I* present
22: 18 and to all the *I* and say to them:
22: 32 be acknowledged as holy by the *I*.
23: 2 "Speak to the *I* and say to them:
23: 10 "Speak to the *I* and say to them:
23: 24 said to Moses, "Say to the *I:*
23: 34 said to Moses, "Say to the *I:*
23: 42 All native-born *I* are to live
23: 43 will know that I had the *I* live
23: 44 to the *I* the appointed feasts
24: 2 "Command the *I* to bring you clear
24: 8 of the *I*, as a lasting covenant.
24: 10 father went out among the *I*,
24: 15 to the *I:* 'If anyone curses his God,
24: 23 Then Moses spoke to the *I*,
24: 23 *I* did as the LORD commanded
25: 2 "Speak to the *I* and say to them:
25: 33 are their property among the *I*.
25: 42 Because the *I* are my servants,
25: 46 rule over your fellow *I* ruthlessly.
25: 55 for the *I* belong to me as servants.
26: 46 Sinai between himself and the *I*
27: 2 "Speak to the *I* and say to them:
27: 34 Moses on Mount Sinai for the *I*.
Nu 1: 1 year after the *I* came out of Egypt.
1: 45 All the *I* twenty years old
1: 49 them in the census of the other *I*.
1: 52 The *I* are to set up their tents
1: 54 The *I* did all this just as the LORD
2: 2 The *I* are to camp around the Tent
2: 32 These are the *I*, counted according
2: 33 counted along with the other *I*,
2: 34 So the *I* did everything the LORD
3: 8 of the *I* by doing the work
3: 9 they are the *I* who are
3: 12 Levites from among the *I* in place
3: 38 of the sanctuary on behalf of the *I*.
3: 41 firstborn of the livestock of the *I*.
3: 41 in place of all the firstborn of the *I*,
3: 42 counted all the firstborn of the *I*,
3: 46 the 273 firstborn *I* who exceed
3: 48 of the additional *I* to Aaron
3: 50 firstborn of the *I* he collected silver
5: 2 "Command the *I* to send away
5: 4 The *I* did this; they sent them
5: 6 said to Moses, "Say to the *I:*
5: 9 the sacred contributions the *I* bring
5: 12 "Speak to the *I* and say to them:
6: 2 "Speak to the *I* and say to them:
6: 23 'This is how you are to bless the *I*.
6: 27 "So they will put my name on the *I*,
8: 6 the Levites from among the other *I*

Nu 8: 10 the *I* are to lay their hands on them
8: 11 as a wave offering from the *I*,
8: 14 the Levites apart from the other *I*,
8: 16 They are the *I* who are
8: 19 Of all the *I*, I have given
8: 19 Tent of Meeting on behalf of the *I*
8: 19 so that no plague will strike the *I*
9: 2 "Have the *I* celebrate the Passover
9: 4 So Moses told the *I* to celebrate
9: 5 The *I* did everything just
9: 7 with the other *I* at the appointed
9: 10 said to Moses, "Tell the *I:*
9: 17 the cloud settled, the *I* encamped.
9: 17 the *I* set out; wherever the cloud
9: 18 LORD's command the *I* set out,
9: 19 the *I* obeyed the LORD's order
9: 22 the *I* would remain in camp
10: 12 Then the *I* set out from the Desert
11: 4 and again the *I* started wailing
13: 2 which I am giving to the *I*.
13: 3 All of them were leaders of the *I*.
13: 24 cluster of grapes the *I* cut off there.
13: 32 among the *I* a bad report about
14: 2 All the *I* grumbled against Moses
14: 10 at the Tent of Meeting to all the *I*.
14: 27 complaints of these grumbling *I*.
14: 39 Moses reported this to all the *I*,
15: 2 "Speak to the *I* and say to them:
15: 18 "Speak to the *I* and say to them:
15: 32 While the *I* were in the desert,
15: 38 "Speak to the *I* and say to them:
16: 34 all the *I* around them fled, shouting
16: 38 Let them be a sign to the *I*."
16: 40 was to remind the *I* that no one
17: 2 Speak to the *I* and get twelve staffs
17: 5 grumbling against you by the *I*."
17: 6 So Moses spoke to the *I*,
17: 9 the LORD's presence to all the *I*.
17: 12 The *I* said to Moses, "We will die!
18: 5 wrath will not fall on the *I* again.
18: 6 fellow Levites from among the *I*
18: 8 the holy offerings the *I* give me I
18: 11 of all the wave offerings of the *I*.
18: 19 the holy offerings the *I* present
18: 20 and your inheritance among the *I*.
18: 22 From now on the *I* must not go
18: 23 no inheritance among the *I*.
18: 24 have no inheritance among the *I*.' "
18: 24 the tithes that the *I* present
18: 26 from the *I* the tithe I give you
18: 28 the tithes you receive from the *I*.
18: 32 defile the holy offerings of the *I*,
19: 2 Tell the *I* to bring you a red heifer
19: 10 be a lasting ordinance both for the *I*
20: 12 as holy in the sight of the *I*,
20: 13 where the *I* quarreled
20: 19 The *I* replied: "We will go
20: 24 will not enter the land I give the *I*,
21: 1 he attacked the *I* and captured
21: 6 they bit the people and many *I* died
21: 10 The *I* moved on and camped
21: 32 the *I* captured its surrounding
22: 1 the *I* traveled to the plains of Moab
22: 3 filled with dread because of the *I*.
25: 8 plague against the *I* was stopped;
25: 11 turned my anger away from the *I;*
25: 13 and made atonement for the *I*."
26: 4 These were the *I* who came out
26: 62 counted along with the other *I*
26: 63 the priest when they counted the *I*
26: 64 the priest when they counted the *I*
26: 65 had told those *I* they would surely
27: 8 "Say to the *I*, 'If a man dies
27: 11 to be a legal requirement for the *I*,
27: 12 and see the land I have given the *I*.
27: 21 community of the *I* will go out,
28: 2 "Give this command to the *I*
29: 40 Moses told the *I* all that the LORD
31: 2 on the Midianites for the *I*.
31: 9 *I* captured the Midianite women
31: 16 the means of turning the *I* away
31: 42 The half belonging to the *I*,
31: 54 for the *I* before the LORD.
32: 7 Why do you discourage the *I*
32: 9 they discouraged the *I*
32: 17 of the *I* until we have brought them
33: 1 of the *I* when they came out
33: 3 The *I* set out from Rameses

Nu 33: 5 The *I* left Rameses and camped
33: 38 year after the *I* came out of Egypt.
33: 40 heard that the *I* were coming.
33: 51 "Speak to the *I* and say to them:
34: 2 "Command the *I* and say to them:
34: 13 commanded the *I*: "Assign this
34: 29 to the *I* in the land of Canaan.
35: 2 the inheritance the *I* will possess.
35: 2 "Command the *I* to give
35: 8 from the land the *I* possess are
35: 10 "Speak to the *I* and say to them:
35: 15 towns will be a place of refuge for *I*,
35: 34 for I, the LORD, dwell among the *I*
36: 2 as an inheritance to the *I* by lot,
36: 4 the Year of Jubilee for the *I* comes,
36: 5 Moses gave this order to the *I*:
36: 13 Moses to the *I* on the plains
Dt 1: 3 to the *I* all that the LORD had
1: 16 the case is between brother *I*
3: 18 cross over ahead of your brother *I*.
4: 44 is the law Moses set before the *I*.
4: 46 was defeated by Moses and the *I*
10: 6 (The *I* traveled from the wells
24: 7 kidnapping one of his brother *I*
29: 1 Moses to make with the *I* in Moab,
29: 2 Moses summoned all the *I*
31: 19 it to the *I* and have them sing it,
31: 22 song that day and taught it to the *I*.
31: 23 for you will bring the *I*
32: 49 the land I am giving the *I*
32: 51 the presence of the *I* at the waters
32: 51 uphold my holiness among the *I*.
33: 1 on the *I* before his death.
34: 8 The *I* grieved for Moses
34: 9 So the *I* listened to him
Jos 1: 2 about to give to them—to the *I*.
2: 2 of the *I* have come here tonight
3: 1 and all the *I* set out from Shittim
3: 9 Joshua said to the *I*, "Come here
4: 4 men he had appointed from the *I*,
4: 5 to the number of the tribes of the *I*,
4: 8 *I* did as Joshua commanded them.
4: 8 to the number of the tribes of the *I*,
4: 12 of the *I*, as Moses had directed
4: 21 He said to the *I*, "In the future
5: 1 before the *I* until we had crossed
5: 1 had the courage to face the *I*.
5: 2 and circumcise the *I* again."
5: 3 and circumcised the *I* at Gibeath
5: 6 The *I* had moved about
5: 10 the *I* celebrated the Passover.
5: 12 was no longer any manna for the *I*,
6: 1 tightly shut up because of the *I*.
6: 25 she lives among the *I* to this day.
7: 1 the *I* acted unfaithfully in regard
7: 5 They chased the *I*
7: 12 That is why the *I* cannot stand
7: 23 them to Joshua and all the *I*
8: 20 for the *I* who had been fleeing
8: 22 in the middle, with *I* on both sides.
8: 24 all the *I* returned to Ai
8: 31 the LORD had commanded the *I*.
8: 32 There in the presence of the *I*,
9: 16 *I* heard that they were neighbors,
9: 17 *I* set out and on the third day came
9: 18 But the *I* did not attack them,
9: 26 So Joshua saved them from the *I*,
10: 4 peace with Joshua and the *I*."
10: 11 killed by the swords of the *I*.
10: 20 the *I* destroyed them completely—
10: 21 no one uttered a word against the *I*.
11: 14 The *I* carried off for themselves all
11: 19 a treaty of peace with the *I*,
12: 1 the land whom the *I* had defeated
12: 6 and the *I* conquered them.
12: 7 the *I* conquered on the west side
13: 6 drive them out before the *I*.
13: 13 the *I* did not drive out the people
13: 13 to live among the *I* to this day.
13: 22 *I* had put to the sword Balaam son
14: 1 these are the areas the *I* received
14: 5 So the *I* divided the land, just
17: 13 However, when the *I* grew stronger
18: 1 of the *I* gathered at Shiloh
18: 3 to the *I*: "How long will you wait
18: 10 to the *I* according to their tribal
19: 49 the *I* gave Joshua son
20: 2 "Tell the *I* to designate the cities
Jos 20: 9 Any of the *I* or any alien living
21: 3 the *I* gave the Levites the following
21: 8 the *I* allotted to the Levites these
21: 41 held by the *I* were forty-eight in all,
22: 9 of Manasseh left the *I* at Shiloh
22: 11 when the *I* heard that they had
22: 13 the *I* sent Phinehas son of Eleazar,
22: 30 the heads of the clans of the *I*—
22: 31 Now you have rescued the *I*
22: 32 in Gilead and reported to the *I*.
24: 32 which the *I* had brought up
Jdg 1: 1 of Joshua, the *I* asked the LORD,
2: 4 had spoken these things to all the *I*,
2: 6 After Joshua had dismissed the *I*,
2: 11 Then the *I* did evil in the eyes
3: 1 left to test all those *I* who had not
3: 2 of the *I* who had not had previous
3: 4 They were left to test the *I* to see
3: 5 The *I* lived among the Canaanites,
3: 7 The *I* did evil in the eyes
3: 8 to whom the *I* were subject
3: 12 Once again the *I* did evil
3: 14 The *I* were subject to Eglon king
3: 15 Again the *I* cried out to the LORD,
3: 15 The *I* sent him with tribute
3: 27 and the *I* went down with him
4: 1 the *I* once again did evil in the eyes
4: 3 and had cruelly oppressed the *I*
4: 5 *I* came to her to have their disputes
4: 23 the Canaanite king, before the *I*.
4: 24 the hand of the *I* grew stronger
6: 1 Again the *I* did evil in the eyes
6: 2 the *I* prepared shelters
6: 3 Whenever the *I* planted their crops
6: 6 so impoverished the *I* that they
6: 7 When the *I* cried to the LORD
7: 8 the rest of the *I* to their tents
7: 23 *I* from Naphtali, Asher
8: 22 The *I* said to Gideon, "Rule
8: 28 Midian was subdued before the *I*
8: 33 died than the *I* again prostituted
9: 55 When the *I* saw that Abimelech
10: 6 Again the *I* did evil in the eyes
10: 6 because the *I* forsook the LORD
10: 8 years they oppressed all the *I*
10: 10 Then the *I* cried out to the LORD,
10: 15 But the *I* said to the LORD,
10: 17 the *I* assembled and camped
11: 27 the dispute this day between the *I*
13: 1 Again the *I* did evil in the eyes
19: 12 alien city, whose people are not *I*.
19: 30 not since the day the *I* came up out
20: 1 all the *I* from Dan to Beersheba
20: 3 heard that the *I* had gone up
20: 3 *I* said, "Tell us how this awful thing
20: 7 all you *I*, speak up and give your
20: 13 would not listen to their fellow *I*.
20: 14 at Gibeah to fight against the *I*.
20: 18 The *I* went up to Bethel
20: 19 The next morning the *I* got up
20: 21 cut down twenty-two thousand *I*
20: 23 The *I* went up and wept
20: 24 Then the *I* drew near to Benjamin
20: 25 down another eighteen thousand *I*,
20: 26 Then the *I*, all the people, went up
20: 27 And the *I* inquired of the LORD.
20: 31 began to inflict casualties on the *I*
20: 32 as before," the *I* were saying,
20: 35 and on that day the *I* struck
20: 42 fled before the *I* in the direction
20: 45 the *I* cut down five thousand men
21: 5 Then the *I* asked, "Who
21: 6 the *I* grieved for their brothers,
21: 18 since we *I* have taken this oath:
21: 24 At that time the *I* left that place
1Sa 2: 14 they treated all the *I* who came
2: 28 offerings made with fire by the *I*.
4: 1 Now the *I* went out to fight
4: 1 The *I* camped at Ebenezer,
4: 10 and the *I* were defeated
6: 6 did they not send the *I* out
7: 4 So the *I* put away their Baals
7: 7 And when the *I* heard of it,
7: 10 that they were routed before the *I*.
9: 2 man without equal among the *I*—
11: 15 all the *I* held a great celebration.
14: 18 (At that time it was with the *I*.)
14: 21 over to the *I* who were with Saul
1Sa 14: 22 When all the *I* who had hidden
14: 31 after the *I* had struck
14: 40 to all the *I*, "You stand over there;
15: 6 to all the *I* when they came up out
17: 2 Saul and the *I* assembled
17: 3 one hill and the *I* another,
17: 11 Saul and all the *I* were dismayed
17: 24 When the *I* saw the man, they all
17: 25 Now the *I* had been saying,
17: 53 When the *I* returned
27: 12 the *I*, that he will be my servant
28: 4 while Saul gathered all the *I*
31: 1 fought against Israel; the *I* fled
31: 7 When the *I* along the valley
2Sa 6: 19 person in the whole crowd of *I*,
7: 6 from the day I brought the *I* up out
7: 7 I have moved with all the *I*,
10: 19 they made peace with the *I*
15: 6 way toward all the *I* who came
17: 26 The *I* and Absalom camped
18: 17 all the *I* fled to their homes.
19: 8 the *I* had fled to their homes.
21: 2 the *I* had sworn to spare them,
1Ki 6: 1 year after the *I* had come out
6: 13 And I will live among the *I*
8: 9 with the *I* after they came out
8: 63 and all the *I* dedicated the temple
9: 20 Jebusites (these peoples were not *I*
9: 21 whom the *I* could not exterminate
9: 22 did not make slaves of any of the *I*;
11: 2 which the LORD had told the *I*,
11: 16 all the *I* stayed there for six months
12: 1 for all the *I* had gone there
12: 16 So the *I* went home.
12: 17 But as for the *I* who were living
12: 20 When all the *I* heard that Jeroboam
12: 24 to fight against your brothers, the *I*.
12: 33 he instituted the festival for the *I*
14: 24 LORD had driven out before the *I*.
16: 16 When the *I* in the camp heard that
16: 17 and all the *I* with him withdrew
19: 10 The *I* have rejected your covenant,
19: 14 The *I* have rejected your covenant,
20: 15 Then he assembled the rest of the *I*,
20: 20 with the *I* in pursuit.
20: 27 When the *I* were also mustered
20: 27 *I* camped opposite them like two
20: 29 The *I* inflicted a hundred thousand
2Ki 3: 24 And the *I* invaded the land
3: 24 the *I* rose up and fought them
7: 13 be like all these *I* who are doomed.
7: 13 that of all the *I* left here—
8: 12 the harm you will do to the *I*,"
10: 32 Hazael overpowered the *I*
13: 5 So the *I* lived in their own homes
13: 21 while some *I* were burying a man,
16: 3 LORD had driven out before the *I*.
17: 6 and deported the *I* to Assyria.
17: 7 the *I* had sinned against the LORD
17: 9 The *I* secretly did things
17: 22 The *I* persisted in all the sins
17: 24 towns of Samaria to replace the *I*.
17: 35 LORD made a covenant with the *I*,
18: 4 to that time the *I* had been burning
21: 2 LORD had driven out before the *I*.
21: 8 feet of the *I* wander from the land I
21: 9 LORD had destroyed before the *I*.
1Ch 6: 64 the *I* gave the Levites these towns
6: 70 tribe of Manasseh the *I* gave Aner
9: 2 in their own towns were some *I*,
10: 1 fought against Israel; the *I* fled
10: 7 When all the *I* in the valley saw
11: 4 and all the *I* marched to Jerusalem,
12: 38 All the rest of the *I* were
13: 5 So David assembled all the *I*,
13: 6 all the *I* with him went to Baalah
13: 8 and all the *I* were celebrating
17: 6 I have moved with all the *I*,
21: 2 count the *I* from Beersheba to Dan.
27: 1 the list of the *I*—heads of families,
2Ch 5: 10 with the *I* after they came out
7: 3 When all the *I* saw the fire coming
7: 6 and all the *I* were standing.
8: 2 Hiram had given him, and settled *I*
8: 7 Jebusites (these peoples were not *I*
8: 8 whom the *I* had not destroyed—
8: 9 slaves of the *I* for his work;
10: 1 for all the *I* had gone there

2Ch 10: 16 So all the I went home.
10: 17 But as for the I who were living
10: 18 but the I stoned him to death.
11: 3 to all the I in Judah and Benjamin,
13: 16 The I fled before Judah,
28: 3 LORD had driven out before the I.
28: 8 The I took captive
30: 21 The I who were present
31: 1 the I returned to their own towns
31: 1 the I who were there went out
31: 5 the I generously gave the firstfruits
33: 2 LORD had driven out before the I.
33: 8 of the I leave the land I assigned
33: 9 LORD had destroyed before the I.
34: 33 all the territory belonging to the I,
35: 17 The I who were present celebrated
Ezr 2: 70 and the rest of the I settled
3: 1 and the I had settled in their towns,
6: 21 So the I who had returned
7: 7 Some of the I, including priests,
7: 13 any of the I in my kingdom,
10: 1 a large crowd of I— men, women
10: 25 And among the other I: From
Ne 1: 6 the sins we I, including myself
2: 10 to promote the welfare of the I.
7: 73 and the I had settled in their towns,
7: 73 of the people and the rest of the I,
8: 14 that the I were to live in booths
8: 17 the I had not celebrated it like this.
9: 1 month, the I gathered together,
11: 3 settled in Jerusalem (now some I,
11: 20 The rest of the I, with the priests
13: 2 they had not met the I with food
Isa 17: 3 like the glory of the I,"
17: 9 which they left because of the I,
27: 12 O I, will be gathered up one by one.
31: 6 so greatly revolted against, O I.
66: 20 as the I bring their grain offerings,
Jer 16: 14 who brought the I up out of Egypt,'
16: 15 who brought the I up out
23: 7 who brought the I up out of Egypt,'
Eze 2: 3 of man, I am sending you to the I,
6: 5 of the I in front of their idols,
20: 9 to the I by bringing them out
35: 5 delivered the I over to the sword
37: 16 and the I associated with him.'
37: 21 I will take the I out
43: 7 live among the I forever.
44: 9 the foreigners who live among the I
44: 15 when the I went astray from me,
47: 22 to consider them as native-born I;
48: 11 did when the I went astray.
Da 1: 3 some of the I from the royal family
Hos 1: 10 "Yet the I will be like the sand
3: 1 Love her as the LORD loves the I,
3: 4 For the I will live many days
3: 5 Afterward the I will return
4: 1 Hear the word of the LORD, you I,
4: 16 The I are stubborn,
5: 1 Pay attention, you I!
5: 5 the I, even Ephraim, stumble
Am 3: 12 so will the I be saved,
4: 5 boast about them, you I,
9: 7 "Are not you I
Mic 5: 3 return to join the I.
Ac 7: 23 he decided to visit his fellow I.
7: 26 upon two I who were fighting.
7: 37 This is that Moses who told the I,
Ro 9: 27 the number of the I be like the sand
10: 1 for the I is that they may be saved.
10: 16 But not all the I accepted the good
2Co 3: 7 so that the I could not look steadily
3: 13 face to keep the I from gazing at it
11: 22 Are they I? So am I.
Heb 11: 22 the exodus of the I from Egypt
Rev 2: 14 Balak to entice the I to sin

ISRAELITES' (ISRAEL)

Lev 10: 14 share of the I' fellowship offerings.
Nu 31: 30 From the I' half, select one out
31: 47 From the I' half, Moses selected

ISSACHAR

Ge 30: 18 So she named him I.
35: 23 Levi, Judah, I and Zebulun.
46: 13 The sons of I: Tola, Puah, Jashub
49: 14 "I is a rawboned donkey
Ex 1: 3 Levi and Judah; I, Zebulun
Nu 1: 8 from I, Nethanel son of Zuar;
1: 28 From the descendants of I:
1: 29 from the tribe of I was 54,400.
2: 5 The tribe of I will camp next
2: 5 of the people of I is Nethanel son
7: 18 the leader of I, brought his offering.
10: 15 over the division of the tribe of I,
13: 7 from the tribe of I, Igal son
26: 23 The descendants of I
26: 25 of I; those numbered were 64,300.
34: 26 the leader from the tribe of I;
Dt 27: 12 Judah, I, Joseph and Benjamin.
33: 18 and you, I, in your tents.
Jos 17: 10 on the north and I on the east
17: 11 Within I and Asher, Manasseh
19: 17 The fourth lot came out for I,
19: 23 the inheritance of the tribe of I,
21: 6 from the clans of the tribes of I,
21: 28 from the tribe of I, Kishion,
Jdg 5: 15 The princes of I were
5: 15 yes, I was with Barak,
10: 1 the time of Abimelech a man of I,
1Ki 4: 17 Jehoshaphat son of Paruah—in I;
15: 27 the house of I plotted against him,
1Ch 2: 1 Levi, Judah, I, Zebulun, Dan,
6: 62 towns from the tribes of I,
6: 72 the tribe of I they received Kedesh,
7: 1 The sons of I: Tola, Puah, Jashub
7: 5 belonging to all the clans of I,
12: 32 of I, who understood the times
12: 40 neighbors from as far away as I,
26: 5 I the seventh and Peullethai
27: 18 over I: Omri son of Michael;
2Ch 30: 18 I and Zebulun had not purified
Eze 48: 25 "I will have one portion; it will
48: 26 the territory of I from east to west.
48: 33 the gate of I and the gate
Rev 7: 7 from the tribe of I 12,000,

ISSHIAH

1Ch 7: 3 Michael, Obadiah, Joel and I.
12: 6 the Haruphite; Elkanah, I,
23: 20 Micah the first and I the second.
24: 21 from his sons: I was the first.
24: 25 I; from the sons of I:

ISSUE (ISSUED ISSUES ISSUING)

Ex 22: 11 the i between them will be settled
2Sa 14: 8 and I will i an order in your behalf
Ezr 4: 21 Now i an order to these men
5: 17 if King Cyrus did in fact i a decree
Est 1: 19 let him i a royal decree
Isa 10: 1 to those who i oppressive decrees,
Da 2: 15 "Why did the king i such a harsh
6: 7 that the king should i an edict
6: 8 i the decree and put it in writing
6: 26 "I i a decree that in every part

ISSUED (ISSUE)

1Ki 15: 22 King Asa i an order to all Judah—
2Ch 24: 9 A proclamation was then i
Ezr 4: 19 I i an order and a search was made,
5: 13 King Cyrus i a decree
6: 1 King Darius then i an order,
6: 3 the king i a decree concerning
10: 7 A proclamation was then i
Est 3: 9 let a decree be i to destroy them,
3: 14 of the text of the edict was to be i
3: 15 the edict was i in the citadel of Susa
8: 13 of the text of the edict was to be i
8: 14 also i in the citadel of Susa.
9: 14 An edict was i in Susa,
9: 25 he i written orders that the evil
Da 2: 13 decree was i to put the wise men
3: 10 live forever! You have i a decree,
4: 24 is the decree the Most High has i
Jnh 3: 7 he i a proclamation in Nineveh:
Lk 2: 1 days Caesar Augustus i a decree

ISSUES (ISSUE)

Da 6: 15 edict that the king i can be changed

ISSUING (ISSUE)

Da 9: 25 From the i of the decree to restore

ITALIAN (ITALY)

Ac 10: 1 what was known as the I Regiment.

ITALY (ITALIAN)

Ac 18: 2 come from I with his wife Priscilla,
27: 1 decided that we would sail for I,
27: 6 an Alexandrian ship sailing for I
Heb 13: 24 from I send you their greetings.

ITCH (ITCHING)

Lev 13: 30 it is an i, an infectious disease
13: 32 and if the i has not spread
13: 34 day the priest is to examine the i
13: 35 But if the i does spread in the skin
13: 36 and if the i has spread in the skin,
13: 37 grown in it, the i is healed.
14: 54 for an i, for mildew in clothing
Dt 28: 27 i, from which you cannot be cured.

ITCHING (ITCH)

2Ti 4: 3 to say what their i ears want to hear

ITHAI

2Sa 23: 29 I son of Ribai from Gibeah
1Ch 11: 31 I son of Ribai from Gibeah

ITHAMAR (ITHAMAR'S)

Ex 6: 23 Nadab and Abihu, Eleazar and I.
28: 1 and I, so they may serve me
38: 21 Levites under the direction of I son
Lev 10: 6 and his sons Eleazar and I,
10: 12 his remaining sons, Eleazar and I,
10: 16 he was angry with Eleazar and I,
Nu 3: 2 firstborn and Abihu, Eleazar and I.
3: 4 so only Eleazar and I served
4: 28 be under the direction of I son
4: 33 under the direction of I son
7: 8 all under the direction of I son
26: 60 of Nadab and Abihu, Eleazar and I
1Ch 6: 3 Nadab, Abihu, Eleazar and I.
24: 1 were Nadab, Abihu, Eleazar and I.
24: 2 so Eleazar and I served
24: 3 and Ahimelech a descendant of I,
24: 5 descendants of both Eleazar and I.
24: 6 from Eleazar and then one from I.
Ezr 8: 2 of the descendants of I, Daniel;

ITHAMAR'S (ITHAMAR)

1Ch 24: 4 descendants than among I,
24: 4 of families from I descendants.

ITHIEL

Ne 11: 7 the son of I, the son of Jeshaiah,
Pr 30: 1 This man declared to I,
30: 1 to I and to Ucal:

ITHLAH

Jos 19: 42 Shaalabbin, Aijalon, I, Elon,

ITHMAH

1Ch 11: 46 the sons of Elnaam, I the Moabite,

ITHNAN

Jos 15: 23 Kedesh, Hazor, I, Ziph, Telem,

ITHRAN

Ge 36: 26 Hemdan, Eshban, I and Keran.
1Ch 1: 41 Hemdan, Eshban, I and Keran.
7: 37 Shamma, Shilshah, I and Beera.

ITHREAM

2Sa 3: 5 I the son of David's wife Eglah.
1Ch 3: 3 and the sixth, I, by his wife Eglah.

ITHRITE (ITHRITES)

2Sa 23: 38 Ira the I, Gareb the I and Uriah
1Ch 11: 40 Ira the I, Gareb the I, Uriah

ITHRITES (ITHRITE)

1Ch 2: 53 the I, Puthites, Shumathites

ITTAI

2Sa 15: 19 The king said to I the Gittite,
15: 21 I replied to the king, "As surely
15: 22 David said to I, "Go ahead,
15: 22 So I the Gittite marched
18: 2 and a third under I the Gittite.
18: 5 commanded Joab, Abishai and I,
18: 12 you and Abishai and I,

ITUREA
Lk 3: 1 his brother Philip tetrarch of *I*

IVORY
1Ki 10: 18 made a great throne inlaid with *i*
10: 22 silver and *i*, and apes and baboons.
22: 39 the palace he built and inlaid with *i*
2Ch 9: 17 made a great throne inlaid with *i*
9: 21 carrying gold, silver and *i*,
Ps 45: 8 from palaces adorned with *i*
SS 5: 14 His body is like polished *i*
7: 4 Your neck is like an *i* tower.
Eze 27: 6 they made your deck, inlaid with *i*.
27: 15 they paid you with *i* tusks
Am 3: 15 adorned with *i* will be destroyed
6: 4 You lie on beds inlaid with *i*
Rev 18: 12 and articles of every kind made of *i*

IVVAH
2Ki 18: 34 and *I?* Have they rescued Samaria
19: 13 or *I?*" Hezekiah received the letter
Isa 37: 13 or *I?*" Hezekiah received the letter

IYE ABARIM
Nu 21: 11 out from Oboth and camped in *I*,
33: 44 They left Oboth and camped at *I*,

IYIM
Nu 33: 45 left *I* and camped at Dibon Gad.

IZHAR (IZHARITES)
Ex 6: 18 The sons of Kohath were Amram, *I*
6: 21 The sons of *I* were Korah,
Nu 3: 19 Amram, *I*, Hebron and Uzziel.
16: 1 Korah son of *I*, the son of Kohath,
1Ch 6: 2 Amram, *I*, Hebron and Uzziel.
6: 18 Amram, *I*, Hebron and Uzziel.
6: 38 the son of *I*, the son of Kohath,
23: 12 Amram, *I*, Hebron and Uzziel—
23: 18 sons of *I*: Shelomith was the first.

IZHARITES (IZHAR)
Nu 3: 27 *I*, Hebronites and Uzzielites,
1Ch 24: 22 From the *I*: Shelomoth;
26: 23 From the Amramites, the *I*,
26: 29 From the *I*: Kenaniah

IZLIAH
1Ch 8: 18 *I* and Jobab were the sons of Elpaal

IZRAHIAH
1Ch 7: 3 The son of Uzzi: *I*.
7: 3 The sons of *I*: Michael, Obadiah,

IZRAHITE
1Ch 27: 8 the commander Shamhuth the *I*.

IZRI
1Ch 25: 11 12 the fourth to *I*, his sons

IZZIAH
Ezr 10: 25 Ramiah, *I*, Malkijah, Mijamin,

JAAKANITES
Dt 10: 6 from the wells of the *J* to Moserah.

JAAKOBAH
1Ch 4: 36 also Elioenai, *J*, Jeshohaiah,

JAALA
Ezr 2: 56 Hassophereth, Peruda, *J*, Darkon,
Ne 7: 58 Sophereth, Perida, *J*, Darkon,

JAAR
Ps 132: 6 we came upon it in the fields of *J*:

JAARE-OREGIM
2Sa 21: 19 son of *J* the Bethlehemite killed

JAARESHIAH
1Ch 8: 27 Shehariah, Athaliah, *J*,

JAASIEL
1Ch 11: 47 Eliel, Obed and *J* the Mezobaite.
27: 21 over Benjamin: *J* son of Abner;

JAASU
Ezr 10: 37 Mattaniah, Mattenai and *J*.

JAAZANIAH
2Ki 25: 23 *J* the son of the Maacathite,
Jer 35: 3 So I went to get *J* son of Jeremiah,
40: 8 and *J* the son of the Maacathite,
Eze 8: 11 and *J* son of Shaphan was standing
11: 1 I saw among them *J* son of Azzur

JAAZIAH
1Ch 24: 26 The son of *J*: Beno.
24: 27 The sons of Merari: from *J*: Beno,

JAAZIEL
1Ch 15: 18 Zechariah, *J*, Shemiramoth, Jehiel,

JABAL
Ge 4: 20 birth to *J*; he was the father

JABBOK
Ge 32: 22 and crossed the ford of the *J*.
Nu 21: 24 land from the Arnon to the *J*,
Dt 2: 37 the land along the course of the *J*
3: 16 and out to the *J* River,
Jos 12: 2 of the gorge—to the *J* River
Jdg 11: 13 land from the Arnon to the *J*,
11: 22 all of it from the Arnon to the *J*

JABESH
1Sa 11: 1 And all the men of *J* said to him,
11: 3 The elders of *J* said to him,
11: 5 to him what the men of *J* had said.
11: 9 and reported this to the men of *J*,
31: 12 wall of Beth Shan and went to *J*,
31: 13 them under a tamarisk tree at *J*,
2Ki 15: 10 Shallum son of *J* conspired
15: 13 Shallum son of *J* became king
15: 14 He attacked Shallum son of *J*
1Ch 10: 12 and his sons and brought them to *J*.
10: 12 bones under the great tree in *J*,

JABESH GILEAD
Jdg 21: 8 that no one from *J* had come to
21: 9 none of the people of *J* were there.
21: 10 men with instructions to go to *J*
21: 12 in *J* four hundred young women
21: 14 women of *J* who had been spared.
1Sa 11: 1 Ammonite went up and besieged *J*.
11: 9 "Say to the men of *J*,
31: 11 When the people of *J* heard of
2Sa 2: 4 the men of *J* who had buried Saul,
2: 5 to the men of *J* to say to them,
21: 12 Jonathan from the citizens of *J*.
1Ch 10: 11 the inhabitants of *J* heard

JABEZ
1Ch 2: 55 the clans of scribes who lived at *J*:
4: 9 His mother had named him *J*,
4: 9 *J* was more honorable
4: 10 *J* cried out to the God of Israel,

JABIN (JABIN'S)
Jos 11: 1 When *J* king of Hazor heard of this
Jdg 4: 2 them into the hands of *J*,
4: 17 relations between *J* king of Hazor
4: 23 On that day God subdued *J*,
4: 24 stronger and stronger against *J*,
Ps 83: 9 to Sisera and *J* at the river Kishon,

JABIN'S (JABIN)
Jdg 4: 7 the commander of *J* army,

JABNEEL
Jos 15: 11 to Mount Baalah and reached *J*.
19: 33 passing Adami Nekeb and *J*

JABNEH
2Ch 26: 6 broke down the walls of Gath, *J*

JACAN
1Ch 5: 13 Meshullam, Sheba, Jorai, *J*,

JACINTH
Ex 28: 19 in the third row a *j*, an agate
39: 12 in the third row a *j*, an agate
Rev 21: 20 the eleventh *j*, and the twelfth

JACKAL (JACKALS)
Ne 2: 13 Gate toward the *J* Well
Mic 1: 8 I will howl like a *j*

JACKALS (JACKAL)
Job 30: 29 I have become a brother of *j*,
Ps 44: 19 us and made us a haunt for *j*
63: 10 and become food for *j*.
Isa 13: 21 *j* will fill her houses;
13: 22 *j* in her luxurious palaces.
34: 13 She will become a haunt for *j*,
35: 7 In the haunts where *j* once lay,
43: 20 the *j* and the owls,
Jer 9: 11 a haunt of *j*;
10: 22 a haunt of *j*.
14: 6 and pant like *j*;
49: 33 "Hazor will become a haunt of *j*,
51: 37 a haunt of *j*,
La 4: 3 Even *j* offer their breasts
5: 18 with *j* prowling over it.
Eze 13: 4 O Israel, are like *j* among ruins.
Mal 1: 3 left his inheritance to the desert *j*."

JACOB (JACOB'S)
Ge 25: 26 so he was named *J*.
25: 27 while *J* was a quiet man,
25: 28 loved Esau, but Rebekah loved *J*.
25: 29 when *J* was cooking some stew,
25: 30 said to *J*, "Quick, let me have some
25: 31 *J* replied, "First sell me your
25: 33 But *J* said, "Swear to me first."
25: 33 to him, selling his birthright to *J*.
25: 34 Then *J* gave Esau some bread
27: 6 Rebekah said to her son *J*, "Look,
27: 11 *J* said to Rebekah his mother,
27: 15 and put them on her younger son *J*
27: 17 handed to her son *J* the tasty food
27: 19 "Who is it?" *J* said to his father,
27: 21 Then Isaac said to *J*, "Come
27: 22 *J* went close to his father Isaac,
27: 22 "The voice is the voice of *J*,
27: 25 *J* brought it to him and he ate;
27: 30 and *J* had scarcely left his father's
27: 36 "Isn't he rightly named *J*?
27: 41 Esau held a grudge against *J*
27: 41 then I will kill my brother *J*."
27: 42 she sent for her younger son *J*
27: 46 *J* takes a wife
28: 1 Isaac called for *J* and blessed him
28: 5 Then Isaac sent *J* on his way,
28: 5 who was the mother of *J* and Esau.
28: 6 learned that Isaac had blessed *J*
28: 7 and that *J* had obeyed his father
28: 10 *J* left Beersheba and set out
28: 16 When *J* awoke from his sleep,
28: 18 the next morning *J* took the stone
28: 20 Then *J* made a vow, saying,
29: 1 Then *J* continued on his journey
29: 4 *J* asked the shepherds, "My
29: 6 Then *J* asked them, "Is he well?"
29: 10 When *J* saw Rachel daughter
29: 11 Then *J* kissed Rachel and began
29: 13 as Laban heard the news about *J*,
29: 13 there *J* told him all these things.
29: 14 After *J* had stayed with him
29: 18 *J* was in love with Rachel and said,
29: 20 *J* served seven years to get Rachel,
29: 21 *J* said to Laban, "Give me my wife.
29: 23 gave her to *J*, and *J* lay with her.
29: 25 there was Leah! So *J* said to Laban,
29: 28 And *J* did so.
29: 30 *J* lay with Rachel also,
30: 1 So she said to *J*, "Give me children
30: 1 she was not bearing *J* any children,
30: 2 *J* became angry with her and said,
30: 4 *J* slept with her, and she became
30: 7 again and bore *J* a second son.
30: 9 and gave her to *J* as a wife.
30: 10 Leah's servant Zilpah bore *J* a son.
30: 12 servant Zilpah bore *J* a second son.
30: 16 when *J* came in from the fields that
30: 17 pregnant and bore *J* a fifth son.
30: 19 again and bore *J* a sixth son.
30: 25 birth to Joseph, *J* said to Laban,
30: 29 *J* said to him, "You know how I
30: 31 Don't give me anything," *J* replied.
30: 36 journey between himself and *J*,
30: 36 while *J* continued to tend the rest
30: 37 *J*, however, took fresh-cut
30: 40 *J* set apart the young of the flock
30: 41 *J* would place the branches

Ge 30:42 to Laban and the strong ones to J.
31: 1 J heard that Laban's sons were
31: 1 "J has taken everything our father
31: 2 J noticed that Laban's attitude
31: 3 Then the LORD said to J,
31: 4 So J sent word to Rachel
31:11 of God said to me in the dream, 'J.'
31:17 Then J put his children
31:20 J deceived Laban the Aramean
31:22 day Laban was told that J had fled.
31:23 he pursued J for seven days
31:24 Be careful not to say anything to J,
31:25 J had pitched his tent
31:26 said to J, "What have you done?
31:29 'Be careful not to say anything to J,
31:31 J answered Laban, "I was afraid,
31:32 J did not know that Rachel had
31:36 J was angry and took Laban to task
31:43 Laban answered J, "The women
31:45 So J took a stone and set it up
31:47 and J called it Galeed.
31:51 also said to J, "Here is this heap,
31:53 So J took an oath in the name
32: 1 J also went on his way,
32: 2 When J saw them, he said,
32: 3 J sent messengers ahead of him
32: 4 master Esau: 'Your servant J says,
32: 6 When the messengers returned to J
32: 7 distress J divided the people who
32: 9 Then J prayed, "O God
32:18 'They belong to your servant J.
32:20 Your servant J is coming behind us
32:22 That night J got up and took his
32:24 So J was left alone, and a man
32:26 But J replied, "I will not let you go
32:27 "What is your name?" "J,"
32:28 "Your name will no longer be J,
32:29 J said, "Please tell me your name."
32:30 So J called the place Peniel, saying,
33: 1 J looked up and there was Esau,
33: 4 ran to meet J and embraced him;
33: 5 J answered, "They are the children
33:10 "No, please!" said J.
33:11 J insisted, Esau accepted it.
33:13 J said to him, "My lord knows that
33:15 "But why do that?" J asked.
33:17 J, however, went to Succoth,
33:18 After J came from Paddan Aram,
34: 1 the daughter Leah had borne to J,
34: 3 drawn to Dinah daughter of J,
34: 5 When J heard that his daughter
34: 6 Hamor went out to talk with J.
34:27 The sons of J came
34:30 Then J said to Simeon and Levi,
35: 1 God said to J, "Go up to Bethel
35: 2 So J said to his household
35: 4 So they gave J all the foreign gods
35: 4 and J buried them under the oak
35: 6 J and all the people with him came
35: 9 J returned from Paddan Aram,
35:10 God said to him, "Your name is J,
35:10 but you will no longer be called J;
35:14 J set up a stone pillar
35:15 J named the place where God had
35:20 Over her tomb J set up a pillar,
35:22 J had twelve sons: The sons
35:23 Reuben the firstborn of J, Simeon,
35:26 the sons of J, who were born
35:27 J came home to his father Isaac
35:29 his sons Esau and J buried him.
36: 6 distance from his brother J.
37: 1 J lived in the land where his father
37: 2 This is the account of J.
37:34 J tore his clothes, put on sackcloth
42: 1 When J learned that there was
42: 4 But J did not send Benjamin,
42:29 came to their father J in the land
42:36 Their father J said to them,
42:38 But J said, "My son will not go
45:25 came to their father J in the land
45:26 J was stunned; he did not believe
45:27 the spirit of their father J revived.
46: 2 "J! J!" "Here I am," he replied.
46: 5 Then J left Beersheba,
46: 5 and Israel's sons took their father J
46: 6 and J and all his offspring went
46: 8 Reuben the firstborn of J.
46: 8 the names of the Israelites (J
Ge 46:15 These were the sons Leah bore to J
46:18 These were the children born to J
46:22 of Rachel who were born to J—
46:25 These were the sons born to J
46:26 All those who went to Egypt with J
46:28 Now J sent Judah ahead of him
47: 7 After J blessed Pharaoh, Pharaoh
47: 7 Then Joseph brought his father J in
47: 9 "How old are you?" And J said
47:10 Then J blessed Pharaoh
47:28 J lived in Egypt seventeen years,
48: 2 When J was told, "Your son
48: 3 J said to Joseph, "God Almighty
49: 1 Then J called for his sons and said.
49: 2 "Assemble and listen, sons of J;
49: 7 I will scatter them in J
49:24 of the hand of the Mighty One of J,
49:33 When J had finished giving
50:24 on oath to Abraham, Isaac and J."
Ex 1: 1 of Israel who entered Egypt with J,
1: 5 of J numbered seventy
2:24 with Isaac and with J.
3: 6 the God of Isaac and the God of J
3:15 the God of Isaac and the God of J
3:16 Isaac and J, appeared to me
4: 5 the God of Isaac and the God of J
6: 3 to Isaac and to J as God Almighty,
6: 8 give to Abraham, to Isaac and to J.
19: 3 are to say to the house of J
33: 1 and J, saying, 'I will give it
Lev 26:42 will remember my covenant with J
Nu 23: 7 'Come,' he said, 'curse J for me;
23:10 Who can count the dust of J
23:21 "No misfortune is seen in J,
23:23 It will now be said of J
23:23 There is no sorcery against J,
24: 5 "How beautiful are your tents, O J,
24:17 A star will come out of J;
24:19 A ruler will come out of J
32:11 and J— not one except Caleb son
Dt 1: 8 to Abraham, Isaac and J—
6:10 Isaac and J, to give you—
9: 5 to Abraham, Isaac and J.
9:27 servants Abraham, Isaac and J.
29:13 fathers, Abraham, Isaac and J.
30:20 fathers, Abraham, Isaac and J.
32: 9 J his allotted inheritance.
33: 4 the possession of the assembly of J.
33:10 He teaches your precepts to J
34: 4 and J when I said, 'I will give it
Jos 24: 4 and to Isaac I gave J and Esau.
24: 4 J and his sons went down to Egypt.
24:32 the tract of land that J bought
1Sa 12: 8 "After J entered Egypt, they cried
2Sa 23: 1 the man anointed by the God of J,
1Ki 18:31 of the tribes descended from J,
2Ki 13:23 with Abraham, Isaac and J.
17:34 LORD gave the descendants of J,
1Ch 16:13 O sons of J, his chosen ones.
16:17 He confirmed it to J as a decree,
Ps 14: 7 let J rejoice and Israel be glad!
20: 1 of the God of J protect you.
22:23 you descendants of J, honor him!
24: 6 who seek your face, O God of J.
44: 4 who decrees victories for J.
46: 7 the God of J is our fortress.
46:11 the God of J is our fortress.
47: 4 the pride of J, whom he loved.
53: 6 let J rejoice and Israel be glad!
59:13 that God rules over J.
75: 9 I will sing praise to the God of J.
76: 6 At your rebuke, O God of J,
77:15 the descendants of J and Joseph.
78: 5 He decreed statutes for J
78:21 his fire broke out against J,
78:71 to be the shepherd of his people J,
79: 7 for they have devoured J
81: 1 shout aloud to the God of J!
81: 4 an ordinance of the God of J.
84: 8 listen to me, O God of J.
85: 1 you restored the fortunes of J.
87: 2 more than all the dwellings of J.
94: 7 the God of J pays no heed."
99: 4 in J you have done
105: 6 O sons of J, his chosen ones.
105: 10 He confirmed it to J as a decree,
105: 23 J lived as an alien in the land
114: 1 the house of J from a people
Ps 114: 7 at the presence of the God of J,
132: 2 made a vow to the Mighty One of J
132: 5 a dwelling for the Mighty One of J
135: 4 For the LORD has chosen J
146: 5 is he whose help is the God of J,
147: 19 He has revealed his word to J,
Isa 2: 3 to the house of the God of J.
2: 5 Come, O house of J,
2: 6 the house of J.
8:17 from the house of J.
9: 8 Lord has sent a message against J;
10:20 the survivors of the house of J,
10:21 remnant will return, a remnant of J
14: 1 and unite with the house of J.
14: 1 LORD will have compassion on J;
17: 4 In that day the glory of J will fade;
27: 6 In days to come J will take root,
29:22 Abraham, says to the house of J:
29:22 "No longer will J be ashamed;
29:23 the holiness of the Holy One of J,
40:27 Why do you say, O J,
41: 8 J, whom I have chosen,
41:14 Do not be afraid, O worm J,
42:24 Who handed J over to become loot
43: 1 he who created you, O J,
43:22 you have not called upon me, O J,
43:28 and I will consign J to destruction
44: 1 "But now listen, O J, my servant,
44: 2 Do not be afraid, O J, my servant,
44: 5 will call himself by the name of J;
44:21 "Remember these things, O J,
44:23 for the LORD has redeemed J,
45: 4 For the sake of J my servant,
46: 3 "Listen to me, O house of J,
48: 1 "Listen to this, O house of J,
48:12 "Listen to me, O J,
48:20 has redeemed his servant J."
49: 5 servant to bring J back to him
49: 6 servant to restore the tribes of J
49:26 Redeemer, the Mighty One of J."
58: 1 and to the house of J their sins.
58:14 on the inheritance of your father J
59:20 to those in J who repent
60:16 Redeemer, the Mighty One of J.
65: 9 bring forth descendants from J,
Jer 2: 4 of the LORD, O house of J,
5:20 "Announce this to the house of J
10:16 the Portion of J is not like these,
10:25 For they have devoured J;
30: 7 It will be a time of trouble for J,
30:10 J will again have peace
30:10 " 'So do not fear, O J my servant;
31: 7 "Sing with joy for J;
31:11 For the LORD will ransom J
33:26 I will reject the descendants of J
33:26 of Abraham, Isaac and J.
46:27 J will again have peace
46:27 "Do not fear, O J my servant;
46:28 Do not fear, O J my servant,
51:19 the Portion of J is not like these,
La 1:17 The LORD has decreed for J
2: 2 all the dwellings of J;
2: 3 burned in J like a flaming fire
Eze 20: 5 the descendants of the house of J
28:25 which I gave to my servant J.
37:25 in the land I gave to my servant J,
39:25 I will now bring J back
Hos 10:11 and J must break up the ground.
12: 2 he will punish J according
12:12 J fled to the country of Aram;
Am 3:13 and testify against the house of J,"
6: 8 "I abhor the pride of J
7: 2 forgive! How can J survive?
7: 5 How can J survive? He is so small
8: 7 LORD has sworn by the Pride of J:
9: 8 the house of J,"
Ob :10 the violence against your brother J,
:17 and the house of J
:18 The house of J will be a fire
Mic 2: 7 Should it be said, O house of J:
2:12 "I will surely gather all of you, O J;
3: 1 "Listen, you leaders of J,
3: 8 to declare to J his transgression,
3: 9 you leaders of the house of J,
4: 2 to the house of the God of J.
5: 7 The remnant of J will be
5: 8 The remnant of J will be
7:20 You will be true to J,

Na 2: 2 will restore the splendor of *J*
Mal 1: 2 "Yet I have loved *J*, but Esau I
2: 12 him off from the tents of *J*—
3: 6 of *J*, are not destroyed.
Mt 1: 2 Isaac the father of *J*, *J* the father
1: 15 Matthan the father of *J*,
1: 16 and *J* the father of Joseph,
8: 11 and *J* in the kingdom of heaven.
22: 32 the God of Isaac, and the God of *J*
Mk 12: 26 the God of Isaac, and the God of *J*
Lk 1: 33 reign over the house of *J* forever;
3: 34 the son of *J*,
13: 28 and *J* and all the prophets
20: 37 the God of Isaac, and the God of *J*
Jn 4: 5 near the plot of ground *J* had given
4: 12 Are you greater than our father *J*,
Ac 3: 13 Isaac and *J*, the God of our fathers,
7: 8 Later Isaac became the father of *J*,
7: 8 and *J* became the father
7: 12 When *J* heard that there was grain
7: 14 Joseph sent for his father *J*
7: 15 Then *J* went down to Egypt,
7: 32 the God of Abraham, Isaac and *J*.'
7: 46 a dwelling place for the God of *J*.
Ro 9: 13 Just as it is written: "*J* I loved,
11: 26 will turn godlessness away from *J*.
Heb 11: 9 he lived in tents, as did Isaac and *J*,
11: 20 By faith Isaac blessed *J*
11: 21 By faith *J*, when he was dying,

JACOB'S (JACOB)

Ge 31: 33 So Laban went into *J* tent
32: 21 So *J* gifts went on ahead of him,
32: 25 he touched the socket of *J* hip
32: 32 the socket of *J* hip was touched
34: 7 in Israel by lying with *J* daughter—
34: 7 *J* sons had come in from the fields
34: 13 *J* sons replied deceitfully
34: 19 he was delighted with *J* daughter.
34: 25 two of *J* sons, Simeon and Levi,
46: 19 The sons of *J* wife Rachel:
46: 27 members of *J* family, which went
50: 12 *J* sons did as he had commanded
Dt 33: 28 *J* spring is secure
Isa 27: 9 then, will *J* guilt be atoned for,
41: 21 your arguments," says *J* King.
45: 19 I have not said to *J* descendants,
Jer 30: 18 will restore the fortunes of *J* tents
Mic 1: 5 What is *J* transgression?
1: 5 of *J* transgression,
Mal 1: 2 "Was not Esau *J* brother?"
Jn 4: 6 *J* well was there, and Jesus,

JADA

1Ch 2: 28 The sons of Onam: Shammai and *J*
2: 32 The sons of *J*, Shammai's brother:

JADAH

1Ch 9: 42 the father of *J*, *J* was the father

JADDAI

Ezr 10: 43 Mattithiah, Zabad, Zebina, *J*,

JADDUA

Ne 10: 21 Meshezabel, Zadok, *J*, Pelatiah,
12: 11 and Jonathan the father of *J*.
12: 22 Johanan and *J*, as well

JADON

Ne 3: 7 of Gibeon and *J* of Meronoth

JAEL

Jdg 4: 17 fled on foot to the tent of *J*,
4: 18 *J* went out to meet Sisera
4: 21 *J*, Heber's wife, picked up a tent
4: 22 and *J* went out to meet him.
5: 6 of *J*, the roads were abandoned;
5: 24 "Most blessed of women be *J*,

JAGGED

Job 41: 30 His undersides are *j* potsherds,

JAGUR

Jos 15: 21 Kabzeel, Eder, *J*, Kinah, Dimonah,

JAHATH

1Ch 4: 2 and *J* the father of Ahumai
4: 2 son of Shobal was the father of *J*,
6: 43 the son of *J*, the son of Gershon,
23: 10 *J*, Ziza, Jeush and Beriah.
23: 11 *J* was the first and Ziza the second,
24: 22 from the sons of Shelomoth: *J*.
2Ch 34: 12 Over them to direct them were *J*

JAHAZ

Nu 21: 23 When he reached *J*, he fought
Dt 2: 32 out to meet us in battle at *J*,
Jos 13: 18 *J*, Kedemoth, Mephaath,
21: 36 Bezer, *J*, Kedemoth and Mephaath
Jdg 11: 20 and encamped at *J* and fought
Isa 15: 4 voices are heard all the way to *J*.
Jer 48: 34 from Heshbon to Elealeh and *J*,

JAHAZIEL

1Ch 12: 4 *J*, Johanan, Jozabad
16: 6 and *J* the priests were to blow
23: 19 *J* the third and Jekameam
24: 23 *J* the third and Jekameam
2Ch 20: 14 came upon *J* son of Zechariah,
Ezr 8: 5 Shecaniah son of *J*,

JAHDAI

1Ch 2: 47 The sons of *J*: Regem, Jotham,

JAHDIEL

1Ch 5: 24 Azriel, Jeremiah, Hodaviah and *J*.

JAHDO

1Ch 5: 14 the son of *J*, the son of Buz.

JAHLEEL (JAHLEELITE)

Ge 46: 14 sons of Zebulun: Sered, Elon and *J*.
Nu 26: 26 through *J*, the Jahleelite clan.

JAHLEELITE (JAHLEEL)

Nu 26: 26 through Jahleel, the *J* clan.

JAHMAI

1Ch 7: 2 Jeriel, *J*, Ibsam and Samuel—

JAHZAH

1Ch 6: 78 *J*, Kedemoth and Mephaath,
Jer 48: 21 to Holon, *J* and Mephaath,

JAHZEEL (JAHZEELITE)

Nu 26: 48 through *J*, the Jahzeelite clan;

JAHZEELITE (JAHZEEL)

Nu 26: 48 through Jahzeel, the *J* clan;

JAHZEIAH

Ezr 10: 15 son of Asahel and *J* son of Tikvah,

JAHZERAH

1Ch 9: 12 the son of *J*, the son of Meshullam,

JAHZIEL

Ge 46: 24 The sons of Naphtali: *J*, Guni,
1Ch 7: 13 The sons of Naphtali: *J*, Guni,

JAIL (JAILER JAILERS)

Ac 4: 3 them in *j* until the next day.
5: 18 and put them in the public *j*.
5: 19 the Lord opened the doors of the *j*
5: 21 and sent to the *j* for the apostles.
5: 22 at the *j*, the officers did not find
5: 23 "We found the *j* securely locked,
5: 25 The men you put in *j* are standing

JAILER (JAIL)

Ac 16: 23 and the *j* was commanded
16: 27 The *j* woke up, and when he saw
16: 29 We are all here!" The *j* called
16: 33 hour of the night the *j* took them
16: 34 The *j* brought them into his house
16: 35 officers to the *j* with the order:
16: 36 *j* told Paul, "The magistrates have

JAILERS (JAIL)

Mt 18: 34 to the *j* until he should pay back all

JAIR (JAIRITE)

Nu 32: 41 *J*, a descendant of Manasseh,
Dt 3: 14 *J*, a descendant of Manasseh,
Jos 13: 30 all the settlements of *J* in Bashan,
Jdg 10: 3 He was followed by *J* of Gilead,
10: 5 When *J* died, he was buried
1Ki 4: 13 settlements of *J* son of Manasseh
1Ch 2: 22 of *J*, who controlled twenty-three
20: 5 son of *J* killed Lahmi the brother
Est 2: 5 named Mordecai son of *J*,

JAIRITE (JAIR)

2Sa 20: 26 and Ira the *J* was David's priest.

JAIRUS

Mk 5: 22 of the synagogue rulers, named *J*,
5: 35 came from the house of *J*,
Lk 8: 41 Just then a man named *J*, a ruler
8: 49 someone came from the house of *J*,
8: 50 Jesus said to *J*, "Don't be afraid;
8: 51 When he arrived at the house of *J*,

JAKEH

Pr 30: 1 The sayings of Agur son of *J*—

JAKIM

1Ch 8: 19 *J*, Zicri, Zabdi, Elienai, Zillethai,
24: 12 the twelfth to *J*, the thirteenth

JAKIN (JAKINITE)

Ge 46: 10 of Simeon: Jemuel, Jamin, Ohad, *J*,
Ex 6: 15 were Jemuel, Jamin, Ohad, *J*,
Nu 26: 12 through *J*, the Jakinite clan;
1Ki 7: 21 The pillar to the south he named *J*
1Ch 9: 10 *J*; Azariah son of Hilkiah,
24: 17 to *J*, the twenty-second
2Ch 3: 17 The one to the south he named *J*
Ne 11: 10 the son of Joiarib; *J*; Seraiah son

JAKINITE (JAKIN)

Nu 26: 12 the *J* clan; through Zerah,

JALAM

Ge 36: 5 and Oholibamah bore Jeush, *J*
36: 14 whom she bore to Esau: Jeush, *J*
36: 18 Chiefs Jeush, *J* and Korah.
1Ch 1: 35 Eliphaz, Reuel, Jeush, *J* and Korah

JALON

1Ch 4: 17 Jether, Mered, Epher and *J*.

JAMBRES

2Ti 3: 8 as Jannes and *J* opposed Moses,

JAMBS

1Ki 6: 31 of olive wood with five-sided *j*.
6: 33 the same way he made four-sided *j*
Eze 40: 9 and its *j* were two cubits thick.
40: 24 He measured its *j* and its portico,
40: 31 palm trees decorated its *j*,
40: 34 palm trees decorated the *j* on
40: 37 palm trees decorated the *j* on
40: 48 and measured the *j* of the portico;
40: 49 pillars on each side of the *j*.
41: 1 sanctuary and measured the *j*;
41: 1 the width of the *j* was six cubits
41: 3 and measured the *j* of the entrance;

JAMES

Mt 4: 21 *J* son of Zebedee and his brother
10: 2 *J* son of Zebedee, and his brother
10: 3 *J* son of Alphaeus, and Thaddaeus;
13: 55 and aren't his brothers *J*, Joseph,
17: 1 *J* and John the brother of *J*,
27: 56 Mary the mother of *J* and Joseph,
Mk 1: 19 he saw *J* son of Zebedee
1: 29 they went with *J* and John
3: 17 he gave the name Peter); *J* son
3: 18 Thomas, *J* son of Alphaeus,
5: 37 *J* and John the brother of *J*.
6: 3 Mary's son and the brother of *J*,
9: 2 *J* and John with him and led them
10: 35 *J* and John, the sons of Zebedee,
10: 41 they became indignant with *J*
13: 3 *J*, John and Andrew asked him
14: 33 *J* and John along with him,
15: 40 Mary the mother of *J* the younger
16: 1 Magdalene, Mary the mother of *J*,
Lk 5: 10 and so were *J* and John, the sons
6: 14 his brother Andrew, *J*, John, Philip
6: 15 Thomas, *J* son of Alphaeus,
6: 16 Judas son of *J*, and Judas Iscariot,
8: 51 John and *J*, and the child's father
9: 28 and *J* with him and went up

Lk 9: 54 When the disciples *J* and John saw
24: 10 Joanna, Mary the mother of *J*,
Ac 1: 13 Those present were Peter, John, *J*
1: 13 *J* son of Alphaeus and Simon
1: 13 the Zealot, and Judas son of *J*.
12: 2 He had *J*, the brother of John,
12: 17 Tell *J* and the brothers about this,''
15: 13 When they finished, *J* spoke up:
21: 18 and the rest of us went to see *J*,
1Co 15: 7 Then he appeared to *J*, then
Gal 1: 19 only *J*, the Lord's brother.
2: 9 *J*, Peter and John, those reputed
2: 12 Before certain men came from *J*,
Jas 1: 1 *J*, a servant of God
Jude : 1 of Jesus Christ and a brother of *J*,

JAMIN (JAMINITE)

Ge 46: 10 The sons of Simeon: Jemuel, *J*,
Ex 6: 15 The sons of Simeon were Jemuel, *J*
Nu 26: 12 through *J*, the Jaminite clan;
1Ch 2: 27 the firstborn of Jerahmeel: Maaz, *J*
4: 24 Nemuel, *J*, Jarib, Zerah and Shaul;
Ne 8: 7 Bani, Sherebiah, *J*, Akkub,

JAMINITE (JAMIN)

Nu 26: 12 through Jamin, the *J* clan;

JAMLECH

1Ch 4: 34 *J*, Joshah son of Amaziah,

JANAI

1Ch 5: 12 Shapham the second, then *J*

JANIM

Jos 15: 53 Arab, Dumah, Eshan, *J*,

JANNAI

Lk 3: 24 the son of *J*, the son of Joseph,

JANNES

2Ti 3: 8 as *J* and Jambres opposed Moses,

JANOAH

Jos 16: 6 passing by it to *J* on the east.
16: 7 it went down from *J* to Ataroth
2Ki 15: 29 *J*, Kedesh and Hazor.

JAPHETH

Ge 5: 32 the father of Shem, Ham and *J*.
6: 10 had three sons: Shem, Ham and *J*.
7: 13 and his sons, Shem, Ham and *J*,
9: 18 of the ark were Shem, Ham and *J*.
9: 23 But Shem and *J* took a garment
9: 27 May God extend the territory of *J*;
9: 27 may *J* live in the tents of Shem,
10: 1 the account of Shem, Ham and *J*,
10: 2 The sons of *J*: Gomer, Magog,
10: 21 whose older brother was *J*;
1Ch 1: 4 sons of Noah: Shem, Ham and *J*.
1: 5 The sons of *J*: Gomer, Magog,

JAPHIA

Jos 10: 3 *J* king of Lachish and Debir king
19: 12 went on to Daberath and up to *J*.
2Sa 5: 15 Elishua, Nepheg, *J*, Elishama,
1Ch 3: 7 Nogah, Nepheg, *J*, Elishama,
14: 6 Nogah, Nepheg, *J*, Elishama,

JAPHLET (JAPHLET'S JAPHLETITES)

1Ch 7: 32 Heber was the father of *J*,
7: 33 The sons of *J*: Pasach, Bimhal

JAPHLET'S (JAPHLET)

1Ch 7: 33 These were *J* sons.

JAPHLETITES (JAPHLET)

Jos 16: 3 westward to the territory of the *J*

JAR (JARS)

Ge 24: 14 let down your *j* that I may have
24: 15 out with her *j* on her shoulder.
24: 16 filled her *j* and came up again.
24: 17 give me a little water from your *j*.''
24: 18 quickly lowered the *j* to her hands
24: 20 So she quickly emptied her *j*
24: 43 drink a little water from your *j*,''
24: 45 with her *j* on her shoulder.
24: 46 "She quickly lowered her *j*
Ex 16: 33 Take a *j* and put an omer of manna
Nu 5: 17 take some holy water in a clay *j*
19: 17 burned purification offering into a *j*
1Ki 14: 3 some cakes and a *j* of honey,
17: 10 water in a *j* so I may have a drink?''
17: 12 only a handful of flour in a *j*
17: 14 'The *j* of flour will not be used up
17: 16 For the *j* of flour was not used up
19: 6 over hot coals, and a *j* of water.
2Ki 4: 6 But he replied, "There is not a *j* left
Jer 19: 1 "Go and buy a clay *j* from a potter.
19: 10 break the *j* while those who go
19: 11 as this potter's *j* is smashed
32: 14 and put them in a clay *j*
48: 11 not poured from one *j* to another—
48: 38 like a *j* that no one wants,''
51: 34 he has made us an empty *j*.
Eze 4: 9 put them in a storage *j*
Mt 26: 7 him with an alabaster *j*
Mk 14: 3 She broke the *j* and poured
14: 3 came with an alabaster *j*
14: 13 and a man carrying a *j*
Lk 7: 37 she brought an alabaster *j*
8: 16 hides it in a *j* or puts it under a bed.
22: 10 a man carrying a *j*
Jn 4: 28 her?'' Then, leaving her water *j*,
19: 29 A *j* of wine vinegar was there,
Heb 9: 4 This ark contained the gold *j*

JARED

Ge 5: 15 he became the father of *J*.
5: 16 And after he became the father of *J*
5: 18 When *J* had lived 162 years,
5: 19 *J* lived 800 years and had other
5: 20 Altogether, *J* lived 962 years,
1Ch 1: 2 Kenan, Mahalalel, *J*, Enoch,
Lk 3: 37 the son of *J*, the son of Mahalaleel,

JARHA

1Ch 2: 34 had an Egyptian servant named *J*.
2: 35 in marriage to his servant *J*,

JARIB

1Ch 4: 24 Nemuel, Jamin, *J*, Zerah and Shaul
Ezr 8: 16 Shemaiah, Elnathan, *J*, Elnathan,
10: 18 Maaseiah, Eliezer, *J* and Gedaliah.

JARMUTH

Jos 10: 3 Piram king of *J*, Japhia king
10: 5 Hebron, *J*, Lachish and Eglon—
10: 23 Hebron, *J*, Lachish and Eglon.
12: 11 one the king of *J* one the king
15: 35 Enam, *J*, Adullam, Socoh,
21: 29 Kishion, Daberath, *J*
Ne 11: 29 in *J*, Zanoah, Adullam

JAROAH

1Ch 5: 14 the son of *J*, the son of Gilead,

JARS (JAR)

Ex 7: 19 in the wooden buckets and stone *j*
Nu 4: 7 and the *j* for drink offerings;
4: 9 all its *j* for the oil used to supply it.
Jdg 7: 16 empty *j* in the hands of all of them,
7: 19 broke the *j* that were in their hands
7: 20 the trumpets and smashed the *j*.
Ru 2: 9 from the water *j* the men have
1Ki 18: 33 "Fill four large *j* with water
2Ki 4: 3 ask all your neighbors for empty *j*.
4: 4 Pour oil into all the *j*, and
4: 5 They brought the *j* to her
4: 6 When all the *j* were full, she said
Job 38: 37 tip over the water *j* of the heavens
Ps 33: 7 gathers the waters of the sea into *j*;
Isa 22: 24 from the bowls to all the *j*.
Jer 14: 3 They return with their *j* unfilled;
40: 10 and put them in your storage *j*,
48: 12 I will send men who pour from *j*,
48: 12 they will empty her *j*
Mt 25: 4 took oil in *j* along with their lamps.
Jn 2: 6 Nearby stood six stone water *j*,
2: 7 said to the servants, "Fill the *j*
2Co 4: 7 we have this treasure in *j* of clay

JASHAR

Jos 10: 13 as it is written in the Book of *J*.
2Sa 1: 18 bow (it is written in the Book of *J*):

JASHEN

2Sa 23: 32 the Shaalbonite, the sons of *J*,

JASHOBEAM

1Ch 11: 11 *J*, a Hacmonite, was chief
12: 6 Azarel, Joezer and *J* the Korahites;
27: 2 for the first month, was *J* son

JASHUB (JASHUBITE)

Ge 46: 13 Tola, Puah, *J* and Shimron.
Nu 26: 24 through *J*, the Jashubite clan;
1Ch 7: 1 Tola, Puah, *J* and Shimron—
Ezr 10: 29 Meshullam, Malluch, Adaiah, *J*,

JASHUBI LEHEM

1Ch 4: 22 Saraph, who ruled in Moab and *J*.

JASHUBITE (JASHUB)

Nu 26: 24 through Jashub, the *J* clan;

JASON (JASON'S)

Ac 17: 6 they dragged *J* and some other
17: 7 and *J* has welcomed them
17: 9 they made *J* and the others post
Ro 16: 21 as do Lucius, *J* and Sosipater,

JASON'S (JASON)

Ac 17: 5 They rushed to *J* house in search

JASPER

Ex 28: 20 row a chrysolite, an onyx and a *j*.
39: 13 row a chrysolite, an onyx and a *j*.
Job 28: 18 *j* are not worthy of mention;
Eze 28: 13 chrysolite, onyx and *j*,
Rev 4: 3 sat there had the appearance of *j*
21: 11 of a very precious jewel, like a *j*,
21: 18 The wall was made of *j*,
21: 19 The first foundation was *j*,

JATHNIEL

1Ch 26: 2 Zebadiah the third, *J* the fourth,

JATTIR

Jos 15: 48 Shamir, *J*, Socoh, Dannah,
21: 14 Libnah, *J*, Eshtemoa, Holon, Debir
1Sa 30: 27 Bethel, Ramoth Negev and *J*;
1Ch 6: 57 and Libnah, *J*, Eshtemoa, Hilen,

JAVAN

Ge 10: 2 Gomer, Magog, Madai, *J*, Tubal,
10: 4 The sons of *J*: Elishah, Tarshish,
1Ch 1: 5 Gomer, Magog, Madai, *J*, Tubal,
1: 7 The sons of *J*: Elishah, Tarshish,

JAVELIN (JAVELINS)

Jos 8: 18 So Joshua held out his *j* toward Ai.
8: 18 "Hold out toward Ai the *j* that is
8: 26 back the hand that held out his *j*
1Sa 17: 6 a bronze *j* was slung on his back.
17: 45 me with sword and spear and *j*,
Job 41: 26 does the spear or the dart or the *j*.
Ps 35: 3 Brandish spear and *j*

JAVELINS (JAVELIN)

2Sa 18: 14 So he took three *j* in his hand

JAW (JAWBONE JAWS)

Job 41: 2 or pierce his *j* with a hook?
Ps 3: 7 struck all my enemies on the *j*;

JAWBONE (JAW)

Jdg 15: 15 Finding a fresh *j* of a donkey,
15: 16 With a donkey's *j*
15: 16 "With a donkey's *j*
15: 17 he threw away the *j*; and the place

JAWS (JAW)

Job 36: 16 you from the *j* of distress
Pr 30: 14 and whose *j* are set with knives
Isa 30: 28 he places in the *j* of the peoples
Eze 29: 4 But I will put hooks in your *j*
38: 4 hooks in your *j* and bring you out

JAZER

Nu 21: 32 After Moses had sent spies to *J*,
32: 1 saw that the lands of *J*
32: 3 "Ataroth, Dibon, *J*, Nimrah,
32: 35 Atroth Shophan, *J*, Jogbehah,

Jos 13: 25 clan by clan: The territory of *J*,
21: 39 Mahanaim, Heshbon and *J*,
2Sa 24: 5 then went through Gad and on to *J*
1Ch 6: 81 Mahanaim, Heshbon and *J*,
26: 31 the Hebronites were found at *J*
Isa 16: 8 which once reached *J*
16: 9 So I weep, as *J* weeps,
Jer 48: 32 I weep for you, as *J* weeps,
48: 32 they reached as far as the sea of *J*.

JAZIZ

1Ch 27: 31 *J* the Hagrite was in charge

JEALOUS (JEALOUSY)

Ge 30: 1 she became *j* of her sister.
37: 11 His brothers were *j* of him,
Ex 20: 5 the LORD your God, am a *j* God,
34: 14 whose name is *J* is a *j* God.
Nu 5: 14 or if he is *j* and suspects her even
11: 29 But Moses replied, "Are you *j*
Dt 4: 24 God is a consuming fire, a *j* God.
5: 9 the LORD your God, am a *j* God,
6: 15 is a *j* God and his anger will burn
32: 16 They made him *j* with their foreign
32: 21 They made me *j* by what is no god
Jos 24: 19 He is a holy God; he is a *j* God.
1Sa 18: 9 time on Saul kept a *j* eye on David.
1Ki 14: 22 they stirred up his *j* anger more
Isa 11: 13 Ephraim will not be *j* of Judah,
Eze 16: 38 of my wrath and *j* anger.
16: 42 my *j* anger will turn away from you
23: 25 I will direct my *j* anger against you,
36: 6 in my *j* wrath because you have
Joel 2: 18 the LORD will be *j* for his land
Na 1: 2 LORD is a *j* and avenging God;
Zep 3: 8 consumed by the fire of my *j* anger.
Zec 1: 14 I am very *j* for Jerusalem and Zion,
8: 2 "I am very *j* for Zion; I am burning
Ac 7: 9 "Because the patriarchs were *j*
17: 5 Jews were *j*; so they rounded up
2Co 11: 2 I am *j* for you with a godly jealousy

JEALOUSY (JEALOUS)

Nu 5: 14 and if feelings of *j* come
5: 15 because it is a grain offering for *j*,
5: 18 the grain offering for *j*,
5: 25 her hands the grain offering for *j*,
5: 29 law of *j* when a woman goes astray
5: 30 when feelings of *j* come over a man
Ps 78: 58 they aroused his *j* with their idols.
79: 5 How long will your *j* burn like fire?
Pr 6: 34 for *j* arouses a husband's fury,
27: 4 but who can stand before *j*?
Ecc 9: 6 their *j* have long since vanished;
SS 8: 6 its *j* unyielding as the grave.
Isa 11: 13 Ephraim's *j* will vanish,
Eze 8: 3 the idol that provokes to *j* stood.
8: 5 gate of the altar I saw this idol of *j*.
35: 11 and *j* you showed in your hatred
Zep 1: 18 In the fire of his *j*
Zec 8: 2 I am burning with *j* for her."
Ac 5: 17 of the Sadducees, were filled with *j*.
13: 45 they were filled with *j*
Ro 13: 13 debauchery, not in dissension and *j*
1Co 3: 3 For since there is *j* and quarreling
10: 22 trying to arouse the Lord's *j*?
2Co 11: 2 I am jealous for you with a godly *j*.
12: 20 *j*, outbursts of anger, factions,
Gal 5: 20 hatred, discord, *j*, fits of rage,

JEARIM

Jos 15: 10 slope of Mount *J* (that is,

JEATHERAI

1Ch 6: 21 Zerah his son and *J* his son.

JEBEREKIAH

Isa 8: 2 son of *J* as reliable witnesses

JEBUS (JEBUSITE JEBUSITES)

Jdg 19: 10 and went toward *J* (that is,
19: 11 When they were near *J*
1Ch 11: 4 marched to Jerusalem, that is, *J*.

JEBUSITE (JEBUS)

Jos 15: 8 slope of the *J* city (that is,
18: 16 the southern slope of the *J* city
Jos 18: 28 Zelah, Haeleph, the *J* city (that is,
2Sa 24: 16 threshing floor of Araunah the *J*.
24: 18 floor of Araunah the *J*."
1Ch 21: 15 threshing floor of Araunah the *J*.
21: 18 threshing floor of Araunah the *J*.
21: 28 threshing floor of Araunah the *J*,
2Ch 3: 1 threshing floor of Araunah the *J*,

JEBUSITES (JEBUS)

Ge 10: 16 *J*, Amorites, Girgashites, Hivites,
15: 21 Canaanites, Girgashites and *J*."
Ex 3: 8 Amorites, Perizzites, Hivites and *J*
3: 17 Amorites, Perizzites, Hivites and *J*
13: 5 Hittites, Amorites, Hivites and *J*—
23: 23 Canaanites, Hivites and *J*,
33: 2 Hittites, Perizzites, Hivites and *J*.
34: 11 Hittites, Perizzites, Hivites and *J*.
Nu 13: 29 *J* and Amorites live
Dt 7: 1 Perizzites, Hivites and *J*,
20: 17 Perizzites, Hivites and *J*—
Jos 3: 10 Girgashites, Amorites and *J*.
9: 1 Perizzites, Hivites and *J*)—
11: 3 Perizzites and *J* in the hill country;
12: 8 Perizzites, Hivites and *J*):
15: 63 Judah could not dislodge the *J*,
15: 63 to this day the *J* live there
24: 11 Hittites, Girgashites, Hivites and *J*
Jdg 1: 21 however, failed to dislodge the *J*,
1: 21 to this day the *J* live there
3: 5 Amorites, Perizzites, Hivites and *J*
19: 11 let's stop at this city of the *J*
2Sa 5: 6 *J* said to David, "You will not get
5: 6 to Jerusalem to attack the *J*,
5: 8 who conquers the *J* will have
1Ki 9: 20 *J* (these peoples were not Israelites
1Ch 1: 14 *J*, Amorites, Girgashites, Hivites,
11: 4 The *J* who lived there said
11: 6 the attack on the *J* will become
2Ch 8: 7 *J* (these peoples were not Israelites
Ezr 9: 1 Hittites, Perizzites, *J*, Ammonites,
Ne 9: 8 Perizzites, *J* and Girgashites.
Zec 9: 7 and Ekron will be like the *J*.

JECOLIAH

2Ki 15: 2 His mother's name was *J*;
2Ch 26: 3 His mother's name was *J*;

JECONIAH

Mt 1: 11 and Josiah the father of *J*
1: 12 *J* was the father of Shealtiel,

JEDAIAH (JEDAIAH'S)

1Ch 4: 37 the son of *J*, the son of Shimri,
9: 10 Of the priests: *J*; Jehoiarib; Jakin;
24: 7 the second to *J*, the third to Harim,
Ezr 2: 36 the descendants of *J*
Ne 3: 10 *J* son of Harumaph made repairs
7: 39 the descendants of *J*
11: 10 From the priests: *J*; the son
12: 6 Shemaiah, Joiarib, *J*, Sallu, Amok,
12: 7 Sallu, Amok, Hilkiah and *J*.
Zec 6: 10 *J*, who have arrived from Babylon.
6: 14 *J* and Hen son of Zephaniah

JEDAIAH'S (JEDAIAH)

Ne 12: 19 Mattenai; of *J*, Uzzi; of Sallu's,
12: 21 Hashabiah; of *J*, Nethanel.

JEDIAEL

1Ch 7: 6 of Benjamin: Bela, Beker and *J*.
7: 10 The son of *J*: Bilhan.
7: 11 All these sons of *J* were heads
11: 45 *J* son of Shimri, his brother Joha
12: 20 Adnah, Jozabad, *J*, Michael,
26: 2 the firstborn, *J* the second,

JEDIDAH

2Ki 22: 1 His mother's name was *J* daughter

JEDIDIAH

2Sa 12: 25 Nathan the prophet to name him *J*.

JEDUTHUN

1Ch 9: 16 the son of *J*; and Berekiah son
16: 38 Obed-Edom son of *J*, and
16: 41 With them were Heman and *J*
16: 42 The sons of *J* were stationed
16: 42 *J* were responsible for the sounding
1Ch 25: 1 *J* for the ministry of prophesying,
25: 3 As for *J*, from his sons: Gedaliah,
25: 3 the supervision of their father *J*,
25: 6 *J* and Heman were
2Ch 5: 12 *J* and their sons and relatives—
29: 14 from the descendants of *J*,
35: 15 Heman and *J* the king's seer.
Ne 11: 17 the son of Galal, the son of *J*.

JEER (JEERED JEERS)

Job 16: 10 Men open their mouths to *j* at me;

JEERED (JEER)

2Ki 2: 23 out of the town and *j* at him.

JEERS (JEER)

Heb 11: 36 Some faced *j* and flogging,

JEGAR SAHADUTHA

Ge 31: 47 Laban called it *J*, and Jacob called

JEHALLELEL

1Ch 4: 16 The sons of *J*: Ziph, Ziphah,
2Ch 29: 12 son of Abdi and Azariah son of *J*;

JEHATH

1Ch 6: 20 Gershon: Libni his son, *J* his son,

JEHDEIAH

1Ch 24: 20 from the sons of Shubael: *J*.
27: 30 *J* the Meronothite was in charge

JEHEZKEL

1Ch 24: 16 the twentieth to *J*, the twenty-first

JEHIAH

1Ch 15: 24 Obed-Edom and *J* were

JEHIEL

1Ch 15: 18 Jaaziel, Shemiramoth, *J*, Unni,
15: 20 Aziel, Shemiramoth, *J*, Unni, Eliab
16: 5 Shemiramoth, *J*, Mattithiah, Eliab,
23: 8 The sons of Ladan: *J* the first,
27: 32 *J* son of Hacmoni took care
29: 8 in the custody of *J* the Gershonite.
2Ch 21: 2 were Azariah, *J*, Zechariah,
29: 14 from the descendants of Heman, *J*
31: 13 *J*, Azaziah, Nahath, Asahel,
35: 8 and *J*, the administrators
Ezr 8: 9 son of *J*, and with him 218 men;
10: 2 Then Shecaniah son of *J*, one
10: 21 Elijah, Shemaiah, *J* and Uzziah.
10: 26 Mattaniah, Zechariah, *J*, Abdi,

JEHIELI

1Ch 26: 21 were *J*, the sons of *J*, Zetham

JEHIZKIAH

2Ch 28: 12 of Meshillemoth, *J* son of Shallum,

JEHOADDAH

1Ch 8: 36 the father of *J*, *J* was the father

JEHOADDIN

2Ki 14: 2 His mother's name was *J*;
2Ch 25: 1 His mother's name was *J*;

JEHOAHAZ

2Ki 10: 35 And *J* his son succeeded him
13: 1 *J* son of Jehu became king of Israel
13: 4 Then *J* sought the LORD's favor,
13: 7 had been left of the army of *J*
13: 8 the other events of the reign of *J*,
13: 9 *J* rested with his fathers
13: 10 Jehoash son of *J* became king
13: 22 Israel throughout the reign of *J*.
13: 25 Then Jehoash son of *J* recaptured
13: 25 taken in battle from his father *J*.
14: 1 of Jehoash son of *J* king of Israel,
14: 8 messengers to Jehoash son of *J*,
14: 17 of Jehoash son of *J* king of Israel.
23: 30 of the land took *J* son of Josiah
23: 31 *J* was twenty-three years old
23: 34 But he took *J* and carried him
2Ch 25: 17 challenge to Jehoash son of *J*,
25: 25 of Jehoash son of *J* king of Israel.
36: 1 of the land took *J* son of Josiah
36: 2 *J* was twenty-three years old
36: 4 But Neco took Eliakim's brother *J*

2Ch 36: 4 made Eliakim, a brother of *J*,

JEHOASH

2Ki 13: 9 And *J* his son succeeded him
13: 10 *J* son of Jehoahaz became king
13: 12 the other events of the reign of *J*,
13: 13 *J* rested with his fathers,
13: 13 *J* was buried in Samaria
13: 14 *J* king of Israel went
13: 25 Then *J* son of Jehoahaz recaptured
13: 25 Three times *J* defeated him,
14: 1 year of *J* son of Jehoahaz king
14: 8 messengers to *J* son of Jehoahaz,
14: 9 But *J* king of Israel replied
14: 11 so *J* king of Israel attacked.
14: 13 Then *J* went to Jerusalem
14: 13 *J* king of Israel captured Amaziah
14: 15 the other events of the reign of *J*,
14: 16 *J* rested with his fathers
14: 17 years after the death of *J* son
14: 23 Jeroboam son of *J* king
14: 27 by the hand of Jeroboam son of *J*.
2Ch 25: 17 challenge to *J* son of Jehoahaz,
25: 18 But *J* king of Israel replied
25: 20 he might hand them over to *J*,
25: 21 So *J* king of Israel attacked.
25: 23 Then *J* brought him to Jerusalem
25: 23 *J* king of Israel captured Amaziah
25: 25 years after the death of *J* son
Hos 1: 1 of Jeroboam son of *J* king of Israel:
Am 1: 1 and Jeroboam son of *J* was king

JEHOHANAN

1Ch 26: 3 *J* the sixth and Eliehoenai
2Ch 17: 15 men; next, *J* the commander,
23: 1 Ishmael son of *J*, Azariah son
28: 12 Azariah son of *J*, Berekiah son
Ezr 10: 6 to the room of *J* son of Eliashib.
10: 28 *J*, Hananiah, Zabbai and Athlai.
Ne 6: 18 his son *J* had married the daughter
12: 13 of Amariah's, *J*; of Malluch's,
12: 42 Eleazar, Uzzi, *J*, Malkijah,

JEHOIACHIN (JEHOIACHIN'S)

2Ki 24: 6 And *J* his son succeeded him
24: 8 *J* was eighteen years old
24: 12 *J* king of Judah, his mother,
24: 12 of Babylon, he took *J* prisoner.
24: 15 Nebuchadnezzar took *J* captive
25: 27 he released *J* from prison
25: 27 year of the exile of *J* king of Judah,
25: 29 So *J* put aside his prison clothes
25: 30 the king gave *J* a regular allowance
1Ch 3: 16 successors of Jehoiakim: *J* his son,
3: 17 The descendants of *J* the captive:
2Ch 36: 8 And *J* his son succeeded him
36: 9 *J* was eighteen years old
Est 2: 6 captive with *J* king of Judah.
Jer 22: 24 *J* son of Jehoiakim king of Judah,
22: 28 Is this man *J* a despised, broken
24: 1 After *J* son of Jehoiakim king
27: 20 away when he carried *J* son
28: 4 back to this place *J* son
29: 2 (This was after King *J*
37: 1 in place of *J* son of Jehoiakim.
52: 31 he released *J* king of Judah
52: 31 year of the exile of *J* king of Judah,
52: 33 So *J* put aside his prison clothes
52: 34 king of Babylon gave *J* a regular
Eze 1: 2 year of the exile of King *J*—

JEHOIACHIN'S (JEHOIACHIN)

2Ki 24: 17 He made Mattaniah, *J* uncle,
2Ch 36: 10 and he made *J* uncle, Zedekiah,

JEHOIADA

2Sa 8: 18 Benaiah son of *J* was
20: 23 Benaiah son of *J* was
23: 20 son of *J* was a valiant fighter
23: 22 the exploits of Benaiah son of *J*;
1Ki 1: 8 son of *J*, Nathan the prophet,
1: 26 the priest, and Benaiah son of *J*,
1: 32 the prophet and Benaiah son of *J*."
1: 36 Benaiah son of *J* answered the king
1: 38 the prophet, Benaiah son of *J*,
1: 44 Benaiah son of *J*, the Kerethites
2: 25 orders to Benaiah son of *J*,
2: 29 Solomon ordered Benaiah son of *J*,
1Ki 2: 34 So Benaiah son of *J* went up
2: 35 son of *J* over the army
2: 46 the order to Benaiah son of *J*,
4: 4 Benaiah son of *J*— commander
2Ki 11: 4 In the seventh year *J* sent
11: 9 did just as *J* the priest ordered.
11: 9 off duty—and came to *J* the priest.
11: 12 *J* brought out the king's son
11: 15 *J* the priest ordered
11: 17 *J* then made a covenant
11: 18 Then *J* the priest posted guards
12: 2 all the years *J* the priest instructed
12: 7 King Joash summoned *J* the priest
12: 9 *J* the priest took a chest
1Ch 11: 22 son of *J* was a valiant fighter
11: 24 the exploits of Benaiah son of *J*;
12: 27 men of Levi—4,600, including *J*,
18: 17 Benaiah son of *J* was
27: 5 was Benaiah son of *J* the priest.
27: 34 succeeded by *J* son of Benaiah
2Ch 22: 11 Jehoram and wife of the priest *J*,
23: 1 the seventh year *J* showed his
23: 3 *J* said to them, "The king's son
23: 8 did just as *J* the priest ordered.
23: 8 for *J* the priest had not released
23: 11 *J* and his sons brought out
23: 14 *J* the priest sent out
23: 16 *J* then made a covenant that he
23: 18 Then *J* placed the oversight
24: 2 LORD all the years of *J* the priest.
24: 3 *J* chose two wives for him,
24: 6 the king summoned *J* the chief
24: 12 *J* gave it to the men who carried
24: 14 as *J* lived, burnt offerings were
24: 14 rest of the money to the king and *J*,
24: 15 Now *J* was old and full of years,
24: 17 After the death of *J*, the officials
24: 20 upon Zechariah son of *J* the priest.
24: 22 Zechariah's father *J* had shown
24: 25 murdering the son of *J* the priest,
Jer 29: 26 priest in place of *J* to be in charge

JEHOIAKIM (JEHOIAKIM'S)

2Ki 23: 34 and changed Eliakim's name to *J*.
23: 35 *J* paid Pharaoh Neco the silver
23: 36 *J* was twenty-five years old
24: 1 *J* became his vassal for three years.
24: 6 of Judah? *J* rested with his fathers.
24: 19 of the LORD, just as *J* had done.
1Ch 3: 15 Johanan the firstborn, *J* the second
3: 16 successors of *J*: Jehoiachin his son,
2Ch 36: 4 and changed Eliakim's name to *J*.
36: 5 *J* was twenty-five years old
Jer 1: 3 and through the reign of *J* son
22: 18 is what the LORD says about *J* son
22: 24 Jehoiachin son of *J* king of Judah,
24: 1 After Jehoiachin son of *J* king
25: 1 year of *J* son of Josiah king
26: 1 in the reign of *J* son of Josiah king
26: 21 When King *J* and all his officers
26: 22 King *J*, however, sent Elnathan
26: 23 of Egypt and took him to King *J*,
27: 20 son of *J* king of Judah into exile
28: 4 this place Jehoiachin son of *J* king
35: 1 LORD during the reign of *J* son
36: 1 year of *J* son of Josiah king
36: 9 year of *J* son of Josiah king
36: 28 which *J* king of Judah burned up.
36: 29 tell *J* king of Judah, 'This is what
36: 30 what the LORD says about *J* king
36: 32 the words of the scroll that *J* king
37: 1 in place of Jehoiachin son of *J*.
45: 1 year of *J* son of Josiah king
46: 2 year of *J* son of Josiah king
52: 2 of the LORD, just as *J* had done.
Da 1: 1 year of the reign of *J* king of Judah,
1: 2 the Lord delivered *J* king of Judah

JEHOIAKIM'S (JEHOIAKIM)

2Ki 24: 1 During *J* reign, Nebuchadnezzar
24: 5 As for the other events of *J* reign,
2Ch 36: 8 The other events of *J* reign,

JEHOIARIB

1Ch 9: 10 Of the priests: Jedaiah; *J*; Jakin;
24: 7 fell to *J*, the second to Jedaiah,

JEHONADAB

2Ki 10: 15 am with you?" "I am," *J* answered.
10: 15 he came upon *J* son of Recab,
10: 23 and *J* son of Recab went

JEHONATHAN

2Ch 17: 8 Asahel, Shemiramoth, *J*, Adonijah
Ne 12: 18 of Shemaiah's, *J*; of Joiarib's,

JEHORAM (JEHORAM'S)

1Ki 22: 50 And *J* his son succeeded him.
2Ki 1: 17 year of *J* son of Jehoshaphat king
8: 16 *J* son of Jehoshaphat began his
8: 20 In the time of *J*, Edom rebelled
8: 21 *J* went to Zair with all his chariots.
8: 24 *J* rested with his fathers
8: 25 Ahaziah son of *J* king
8: 29 Then Ahaziah son of *J* king
11: 2 the daughter of King *J*
12: 18 Jehoshaphat, *J* and Ahaziah,
1Ch 3: 11 Jehoshaphat his son, *J* his son,
2Ch 17: 8 and the priests Elishama and *J*.
21: 1 And *J* his son succeeded him
21: 3 but he had given the kingdom to *J*
21: 4 When *J* established himself firmly
21: 5 *J* was thirty-two years old
21: 8 In the time of *J*, Edom rebelled
21: 9 So *J* went there with his officers
21: 10 because *J* had forsaken the LORD,
21: 12 *J* received a letter
21: 16 aroused against *J* the hostility
21: 18 the LORD afflicted *J*
21: 20 *J* was thirty-two years old
22: 1 So Ahaziah son of *J* king
22: 6 Then Ahaziah son of *J* king
22: 11 Jehosheba, the daughter of King *J*,
22: 11 the daughter of King *J*

JEHORAM'S (JEHORAM)

2Ki 8: 23 As for the other events of *J* reign,
2Ch 21: 2 *J* brothers, the sons of Jehoshaphat
22: 1 made Ahaziah, *J* youngest son,

JEHOSHAPHAT (JEHOSHAPHAT'S)

2Sa 8: 16 *J* son of Ahilud was recorder;
20: 24 *J* son of Ahilud was recorder;
1Ki 4: 3 secretaries; *J* son of Ahilud—
4: 17 and in Aloth; *J* son of Paruah—
15: 24 And *J* his son succeeded him
22: 2 But in the third year *J* king
22: 4 he asked *J*, "Will you go with me
22: 4 *J* replied to the king of Israel,
22: 5 But *J* also said to the king of Israel,
22: 7 But *J* asked, "Is there not a prophet
22: 8 The king of Israel answered *J*,
22: 8 should not say that," *J* replied.
22: 10 and *J* king of Judah were sitting
22: 18 The king of Israel said to *J*,
22: 29 *J* king of Judah went up to Ramoth
22: 30 The king of Israel said to *J*,
22: 32 the chariot commanders saw *J*,
22: 32 to attack him, but when *J* cried out,
22: 41 *J* son of Asa became king of Judah
22: 42 *J* was thirty-five years old
22: 44 *J* was also at peace with the king
22: 48 *J* built a fleet of trading ships to go
22: 49 Ahaziah son of Ahab said to *J*,
22: 49 sail with your men," but *J* refused.
22: 50 Then *J* rested with his fathers
22: 51 year of *J* king of Judah,
2Ki 1: 17 of Jehoram son of *J* king of Judah.
3: 1 year of *J* king of Judah,
3: 7 message to *J* king of Judah:
3: 11 But *J* asked, "Is there no prophet
3: 12 So the king of Israel and *J*
3: 12 *J* said, "The word of the LORD is
3: 14 for the presence of *J* king of Judah,
8: 16 Jehoram son of *J* began his reign
8: 16 when *J* was king of Judah,
9: 2 for Jehu son of *J*, the son of Nimshi
9: 14 So Jehu son of *J*, the son of Nimshi
12: 18 *J*, Jehoram and Ahaziah, the kings
1Ch 3: 10 *J* his son, Jehoram his son,
18: 15 *J* son of Ahilud was recorder;
2Ch 17: 1 *J* his son succeeded him as king
17: 3 The LORD was with *J*
17: 5 and all Judah brought gifts to *J*,
17: 10 that they did not make war with *J*.

2Ch 17: 11 Some Philistines brought *J* gifts
17: 12 *J* became more and more powerful;
18: 1 Now *J* had great wealth and honor,
18: 3 *J* replied, "I am as you are,
18: 3 of Israel asked *J* king of Judah,
18: 4 But *J* also said to the king of Israel,
18: 6 But *J* asked, "Is there not a prophet
18: 7 The king of Israel answered *J*,
18: 7 should not say that," *J* replied.
18: 9 and *J* king of Judah were sitting
18: 17 The king of Israel said to *J*,
18: 28 *J* king of Judah went up to Ramoth
18: 29 The king of Israel said to *J*,
18: 31 the chariot commanders saw *J*,
18: 31 to attack him, but *J* cried out,
19: 1 When *J* king of Judah returned
19: 4 *J* lived in Jerusalem, and he went
19: 8 *J* appointed some of the Levites,
20: 1 Meunites came to make war on *J*.
20: 2 Some men came and told *J*,
20: 3 *J* resolved to inquire of the LORD,
20: 5 *J* stood up in the assembly of Judah
20: 15 King *J* and all who live in Judah
20: 18 *J* bowed with his face to the ground
20: 20 As they set out, *J* stood and said,
20: 21 *J* appointed men to sing
20: 25 So *J* and his men went to carry
20: 27 Then, led by *J*, all the men of Judah
20: 30 And the kingdom of *J* was at peace
20: 31 So *J* reigned over Judah.
20: 35 *J* king of Judah made an alliance
20: 37 of Mareshah prophesied against *J*,
21: 1 Then *J* rested with his fathers
21: 2 sons of *J* king of Israel.
21: 2 the sons of *J*, were Azariah, Jehiel,
21: 12 walked in the ways of your father *J*
22: 9 for they said, "He was a son of *J*,
Joel 3: 2 bring them down to the Valley of *J*.
3: 12 advance into the Valley of *J*,
Mt 1: 8 father of *J*, *J* the father of Joram,

JEHOSHAPHAT'S (JEHOSHAPHAT)

1Ki 22: 45 As for the other events of *J* reign,
2Ch 20: 34 The other events of *J* reign,

JEHOSHEBA

2Ki 11: 2 *J*, the daughter of King Jehoram
2Ch 22: 11 Because *J*, the daughter
22: 11 *J*, the daughter of King Jehoram,

JEHOZABAD

2Ki 12: 21 of Shimeath and *J* son of Shomer.
1Ch 26: 4 the firstborn, *J* the second,
2Ch 17: 18 *J*, with 180,000 men armed
24: 26 and *J*, son of Shimrith a Moabite

JEHOZADAK

1Ch 6: 14 and Seraiah the father of *J*.
6: 15 *J* was deported when the LORD
Hag 1: 1 to Joshua son of *J*, the high priest:
1: 12 Joshua son of *J*, the high priest,
1: 14 and the spirit of Joshua son of *J*,
2: 2 to Joshua son of *J*, the high priest,
2: 4 O Joshua son of *J*, the high priest.
Zec 6: 11 of the high priest, Joshua son of *J*.

JEHU (JEHU'S)

1Ki 16: 1 came to *J* son of Hanani
16: 7 came through the prophet *J* son
16: 12 Baasha through the prophet *J*—
19: 16 Also, anoint *J* son of Nimshi king
19: 17 any who escape the sword of *J*.
19: 17 *J* will put to death any who escape
2Ki 9: 2 look for *J* son of Jehoshaphat,
9: 5 "For which of us?" asked *J*.
9: 6 *J* got up and went into the house.
9: 11 When *J* went out to his fellow
9: 11 sort of things he says," *J* replied.
9: 12 *J* said, "Here is what he told me:
9: 14 *J* is king!" So *J* son of Jehoshaphat,
9: 15 *J* said, "If this is the way you feel,
9: 18 The horseman rode off to meet *J*
9: 18 have to do with peace?" *J* replied.
9: 19 Do you come in peace?' " *J* replied
9: 20 that of *J* son of Nimshi—
9: 21 each in his own chariot, to meet *J*.
9: 22 How can there be peace," *J* replied
9: 22 When Joram saw *J* he asked,
2Ki 9: 22 "Have you come in peace, *J*?"
9: 24 *J* drew his bow and shot Joram
9: 25 *J* said to Bidkar, his chariot officer,
9: 27 *J* chased him, shouting, "Kill him
9: 30 Then *J* went to Jezreel.
9: 31 As *J* entered the gate, she asked,
9: 33 "Throw her down!" *J* said.
9: 34 *J* went in and ate and drank.
9: 36 They went back and told *J*,
10: 1 So *J* wrote letters and sent them
10: 5 guardians sent this message to *J*:
10: 6 Then *J* wrote them a second letter,
10: 7 and sent them to *J* in Jezreel.
10: 8 *J* ordered, "Put them in two piles
10: 8 the messenger arrived, he told *J*,
10: 9 The next morning *J* went out.
10: 11 So *J* killed everyone in Jezreel who
10: 12 *J* then set out and went
10: 15 If so," said *J*, "give me your hand."
10: 15 *J* greeted him and said, "Are you
10: 15 *J* helped him up into the chariot.
10: 16 *J* said, "Come with me
10: 17 When *J* came to Samaria, he killed
10: 18 *J* brought all the people together
10: 18 served Baal a little; *J* will serve him
10: 19 *J* was acting deceptively in order
10: 20 *J* said, "Call an assembly in honor
10: 22 And *J* said to the keeper
10: 23 Then *J* and Jehonadab son
10: 23 *J* said to the ministers of Baal,
10: 24 Now *J* had posted eighty men
10: 25 as *J* had finished making the burnt
10: 28 *J* destroyed Baal worship in Israel.
10: 30 to *J*, "Because you have done well
10: 31 Yet *J* was not careful
10: 35 *J* rested with his fathers
10: 36 The time that *J* reigned over Israel
12: 1 year of *J*, Joash became king,
13: 1 Jehoahaz son of *J* became king
14: 8 the son of *J*, king of Israel,
15: 12 LORD spoken to *J* was fulfilled:
1Ch 2: 38 father of *J*, *J* the father of Azariah,
4: 35 son of Amaziah, Joel, *J* son
12: 3 Beracah, *J* the Anathothite,
2Ch 19: 2 *J* the seer, the son of Hanani,
20: 34 in the annals of *J* son of Hanani,
22: 7 Joram to meet *J* son of Nimshi,
22: 8 While *J* was executing judgment
22: 9 He was brought to *J* and put
25: 17 the son of *J*, king of Israel: "Come,
Hos 1: 4 of *J* for the massacre at Jezreel,

JEHU'S (JEHU)

2Ki 9: 6 prophet poured the oil on *J* head
9: 17 Jezreel saw *J* troops approaching,
10: 34 As for the other events of *J* reign,

JEHUCAL

Jer 37: 3 sent *J* son of Shelemiah
38: 1 son of Pashhur, *J* son of Shelemiah,

JEHUD

Jos 19: 45 Eltekeh, Gibbethon, Baalath, *J*,

JEHUDI

Jer 36: 14 all the officials sent *J* son
36: 21 The king sent *J* to get the scroll,
36: 21 and *J* brought it from the room
36: 23 Whenever *J* had read three

JEIEL

1Ch 5: 7 genealogical records: *J* the chief,
8: 29 *J* the father of Gibeon lived
9: 35 *J* the father of Gibeon lived
11: 44 *J* the sons of Hotham the Aroerite,
15: 18 Obed-Edom and *J*, the gatekeepers
15: 21 *J* and Azaziah were
16: 5 Eliab, Benaiah, Obed-Edom and *J*.
16: 5 then *J*, Shemiramoth, Jehiel,
2Ch 20: 14 the son of *J*, the son of Mattaniah,
26: 11 as mustered by *J* the secretary
29: 13 *J*; from the descendants of Asaph,
35: 9 and Hashabiah, *J* and Jozabad,
Ezr 10: 43 *J*, Mattithiah, Zabad, Zebina,

JEKABZEEL

Ne 11: 25 in *J* and its villages, in Jeshua,

JEKAMEAM

1Ch 23: 19 Jahaziel the third and *J* the fourth.
24: 23 Jahaziel the third and *J* the fourth.

JEKAMIAH

1Ch 2: 41 Shallum the father of *J*,
2: 41 and *J* the father of Elishama.
3: 18 Malkiram, Pedaiah, Shenazzar, *J*,

JEKUTHIEL

1Ch 4: 18 and *J* the father of Zanoah.)

JEMIMAH

Job 42: 14 The first daughter he named *J*,

JEMUEL

Ge 46: 10 The sons of Simeon: *J*, Jamin,
Ex 6: 15 The sons of Simeon were *J*, Jamin,

JEOPARDY

2Sa 18: 13 And if I had put my life in *j*—
Job 13: 14 Why do I put myself in *j*

JEPHTHAH (JEPHTHAH'S)

Jdg 11: 1 *J* the Gileadite was a mighty
11: 2 were grown up, they drove *J* away.
11: 3 So *J* fled from his brothers
11: 5 went to get *J* from the land
11: 7 *J* said to them, "Didn't you hate
11: 9 *J* answered, "Suppose you take me
11: 11 So *J* went with the elders of Gilead
11: 12 Then *J* sent messengers
11: 14 *J* sent back messengers
11: 15 saying: "This is what *J* says:
11: 28 to the message *J* sent him.
11: 29 Spirit of the LORD came upon *J*.
11: 30 And *J* made a vow to the LORD:
11: 32 Then *J* went over to fight
11: 34 When *J* returned to his home
11: 40 the daughter of *J* the Gileadite
12: 1 over to Zaphon and said to *J*,
12: 2 *J* answered, "I and my people were
12: 4 *J* then called together the men
12: 7 Then *J* the Gileadite died,
12: 7 *J* led Israel six years.
1Sa 12: 11 LORD sent Jerub-Baal, Barak, *J*
Heb 11: 32 *J*, David, Samuel and the prophets,

JEPHTHAH'S (JEPHTHAH)

Jdg 11: 13 answered *J* messengers,

JEPHUNNEH

Nu 13: 6 Caleb son of *J*; from the tribe
14: 6 son of Nun and Caleb son of *J*,
14: 30 Caleb son of *J* and Joshua son
14: 38 and Caleb son of *J* survived.
26: 65 Caleb son of *J* and Joshua son
32: 12 except Caleb son of *J* the Kenizzite
34: 19 Caleb son of *J*, from the tribe
Dt 1: 36 forefathers, except Caleb son of *J*.
Jos 14: 6 Caleb son of *J* the Kenizzite said
14: 13 Then Joshua blessed Caleb son of *J*
14: 14 to Caleb son of *J* the Kenizzite ever
15: 13 to Caleb son of *J* a portion in Judah
21: 12 they had given to Caleb son of *J*
1Ch 4: 15 The sons of Caleb son of *J*: Iru,
6: 56 city were given to Caleb son of *J*
7: 38 The sons of Jether: *J*, Pispah

JERAH

Ge 10: 26 Hazarmaveth, *J*, Hadoram,
1Ch 1: 20 Hazarmaveth, *J*, Hadoram,

JERAHMEEL (JERAHMEELITES)

1Sa 27: 10 or "Against the Negev of *J*"
1Ch 2: 9 The sons born to Hezron were: *J*,
2: 25 The sons of *J* the firstborn
2: 26 *J* had another wife, whose name
2: 27 The sons of Ram the firstborn of *J*:
2: 33 These were the descendants of *J*.
2: 42 The sons of Caleb the brother of *J*:
24: 29 From Kish: the son of Kish: *J*.
Jer 36: 26 Instead, the king commanded *J*,

JERAHMEELITES (JERAHMEEL)

1Sa 30: 29 to those in the towns of the *J*

JERED
1Ch 4: 18 birth to *J* the father of Gedor,

JEREMAI
Ezr 10: 33 Mattattah, Zabad, Eliphelet, *J*,

JEREMIAH (JEREMIAH'S)
2Ki 23: 31 name was Hamutal daughter of *J*;
24: 18 name was Hamutal daughter of *J*;
1Ch 5: 24 Azriel, *J*, Hodaviah and Jahdiel.
12: 4 *J*, Jahaziel, Johanan, Jozabad
12: 10 Mishmannah the fourth, *J* the fifth,
12: 13 *J* the tenth and Macbannai
2Ch 35: 25 *J* composed laments for Josiah,
36: 12 himself before *J* the prophet,
36: 21 word of the LORD spoken by *J*.
36: 22 word of the LORD spoken by *J*,
Ezr 1: 1 word of the LORD spoken by *J*,
Ne 10: 2 Seraiah, Azariah, *J*, Pashhur,
12: 1 Seraiah, *J*, Ezra, Amariah,
12: 34 Judah, Benjamin, Shemaiah, *J*,
Jer 1: 1 The words of *J* son of Hilkiah,
1: 11 *J*?" "I see the branch
7: 1 came to *J* from the LORD:
11: 1 came to *J* from the LORD:
14: 1 to *J* concerning the drought:
18: 1 came to *J* from the LORD:
18: 18 "Come, let's make plans against *J*;
19: 14 *J* then returned from Topheth,
20: 1 heard *J* prophesying these things,
20: 2 he had *J* the prophet beaten
20: 3 him from the stocks, *J* said to him,
21: 1 came to *J* from the LORD
21: 3 *J* answered them, "Tell Zedekiah,
24: 3 "What do you see, *J*?" "Figs,"
25: 1 came to *J* concerning all the people
25: 2 *J* the prophet said to all the people
25: 13 by *J* against all the nations.
26: 7 the people heard *J* speak these
26: 8 as *J* finished telling all the people
26: 9 crowded around *J* in the house
26: 12 Then *J* said to all the officials
26: 20 this city and this land as *J* did.
26: 24 son of Shaphan supported *J*,
27: 1 came to *J* from the LORD:
28: 5 Then the prophet *J* replied
28: 10 yoke off the neck of the prophet *J*
28: 11 the prophet *J* went on his way.
28: 12 the word of the LORD came to *J*:
28: 12 yoke off the neck of the prophet *J*,
28: 15 Then the prophet *J* said
29: 1 of the letter that the prophet *J* sent
29: 27 why have you not reprimanded *J*
29: 29 read the letter to *J* the prophet.
29: 30 the word of the LORD came to *J*:
30: 1 came to *J* from the LORD:
32: 1 came to *J* from the LORD
32: 2 and *J* the prophet was confined
32: 6 *J* said, "The word
32: 26 the word of the LORD came to *J*:
33: 1 While *J* was still confined
33: 19 The word of the LORD came to *J*:
33: 23 The word of the LORD came to *J*:
34: 1 came to *J* from the LORD:
34: 6 Then *J* the prophet told all this
34: 8 came to *J* from the LORD
34: 12 the word of the LORD came to *J*:
35: 1 came to *J* from the LORD
35: 3 So I went to get Jaazaniah son of *J*,
35: 12 the word of the LORD came to *J*,
35: 18 Then *J* said to the family
36: 1 came to *J* from the LORD:
36: 4 So *J* called Baruch son of Neriah,
36: 4 and while *J* dictated all the words
36: 5 *J* told Baruch, "I am restricted;
36: 8 did everything *J* the prophet
36: 10 the words of *J* from the scroll.
36: 17 Did *J* dictate it?" "Yes," Baruch
36: 19 said to Baruch, "You and *J*,
36: 26 the scribe and *J* the prophet.
36: 27 the word of the LORD came to *J*:
36: 32 So *J* took another scroll
36: 32 son of Neriah, and as *J* dictated,
37: 2 spoken through *J* the prophet.
37: 3 son of Maaseiah to *J* the prophet
37: 4 Now *J* was free to come
37: 6 the LORD came to *J* the prophet:
Jer 37: 12 *J* started to leave the city to go
37: 14 he arrested *J* and brought him
37: 14 "That's not true!" *J* said.
37: 15 They were angry with *J*
37: 16 *J* was put into a vaulted cell
37: 17 from the LORD?" "Yes," *J* replied
37: 18 Then *J* said to King Zedekiah,
37: 21 So *J* remained in the courtyard
37: 21 Zedekiah then gave orders for *J*
38: 1 Malkijah heard what *J* was telling
38: 6 So they took *J* and put him
38: 6 They lowered *J* by ropes
38: 6 and *J* sank down into the mud.
38: 7 heard that they had put *J*
38: 9 all they have done to *J* the prophet.
38: 10 lift *J* the prophet out of the cistern
38: 11 down with ropes to *J* in the cistern.
38: 12 Ebed-Melech the Cushite said to *J*,
38: 12 *J* did so, and they pulled him up
38: 13 And *J* remained in the courtyard
38: 14 Zedekiah sent for *J* the prophet
38: 14 you something," the king said to *J*.
38: 15 *J* said to Zedekiah, "If I give you
38: 16 swore this oath secretly to *J*:
38: 17 *J* said to Zedekiah, "This is what
38: 19 Zedekiah said to *J*, "I am afraid
38: 20 will not hand you over," *J* replied.
38: 24 said to *J*, "Do not let anyone know
38: 27 All the officials did come to *J*
38: 28 And *J* remained in the courtyard
39: 11 had given these orders about *J*
39: 14 had *J* taken out of the courtyard
39: 15 While *J* had been confined
40: 1 He had found *J* bound in chains
40: 1 came to *J* from the LORD
40: 2 commander of the guard found *J*,
40: 5 However, before *J* turned to go,
40: 6 *J* went to Gedaliah son of Ahikam
42: 2 greatest approached *J* the prophet
42: 4 heard you," replied *J* the prophet.
42: 5 to *J*, "May the LORD be a true
42: 7 the word of the LORD came to *J*.
43: 1 When *J* finished telling the people
43: 2 and all the arrogant men said to *J*,
43: 6 and *J* the prophet and Baruch son
43: 8 the word of the LORD came to *J*:
44: 1 to *J* concerning all the Jews living
44: 15 and Upper Egypt, said to *J*,
44: 20 Then *J* said to all the people,
44: 24 Then *J* said to all the people,
45: 1 This is what *J* the prophet told
45: 1 a scroll the words *J* was then
46: 1 came to *J* the prophet concerning
46: 13 to *J* the prophet about the coming
47: 1 came to *J* the prophet concerning
49: 34 to *J* the prophet concerning Elam,
50: 1 through *J* the prophet concerning
51: 59 This is the message *J* gave
51: 60 *J* had written on a scroll about all
51: 64 The words of *J* end here.
52: 1 name was Hamutal daughter of *J*;
Da 9: 2 the LORD given to *J* the prophet,
Mt 2: 17 through the prophet *J* was fulfilled:
16: 14 still others, *J* or one of the prophets
27: 9 by *J* the prophet was fulfilled:

JEREMIAH'S (JEREMIAH)
Ne 12: 12 Meraiah; of *J*, Hananiah; of Ezra's,
Jer 36: 27 Baruch had written at *J* dictation,

JEREMOTH
1Ch 7: 8 Eliezer, Elioenai, Omri, *J*, Abijah,
8: 14 Ahio, Shashak, *J*, Zebadiah, Arad,
23: 23 Mahli, Eder and *J*— three in all.
Ezr 10: 26 Jehiel, Abdi, *J* and Elijah.
10: 27 Elioenai, Eliashib, Mattaniah, *J*,
10: 29 Adaiah, Jashub, Sheal and *J*.

JERIAH
1Ch 23: 19 The sons of Hebron: *J* the first,
24: 23 The sons of Hebron: *J* the first,
26: 31 *J* was their chief according
26: 32 *J* had twenty-seven hundred

JERIBAI
1Ch 11: 46 *J* and Joshaviah the sons

JERICHO
Nu 22: 1 along the Jordan across from *J*.
26: 3 Moab by the Jordan across from *J*,
26: 63 Moab by the Jordan across from *J*.
31: 12 by the Jordan across from *J*.
33: 48 Moab by the Jordan across from *J*.
33: 50 across from *J* the LORD said
34: 15 on the east side of the Jordan of *J*,
35: 1 Moab by the Jordan across from *J*,
36: 13 Moab by the Jordan across from *J*.
Dt 32: 49 across from *J*, and view Canaan,
34: 1 to the top of Pisgah, across from *J*.
34: 3 region from the Valley of *J*,
Jos 2: 1 the land," he said, "especially *J*."
2: 2 The king of *J* was told, "Look!
2: 3 So the king of *J* sent this message
3: 16 the people crossed over opposite *J*.
4: 13 LORD to the plains of *J* for war.
4: 19 at Gilgal on the eastern border of *J*.
5: 10 camped at Gilgal on the plains of *J*,
5: 13 Now when Joshua was near *J*,
6: 1 Now *J* was tightly shut up
6: 2 I have delivered *J* into your hands,
6: 25 men Joshua had sent as spies to *J*—
6: 26 undertakes to rebuild this city, *J*:
7: 2 Now Joshua sent men from *J* to Ai,
8: 2 its king as you did to *J* and its king,
9: 3 heard what Joshua had done to *J*
10: 1 as he had done to *J* and its king,
10: 28 as he had done to the king of *J*.
10: 30 as he had done to the king of *J*.
12: 9 the king of *J* one the king of Ai
13: 32 of Moab across the Jordan east of *J*
16: 1 east of the waters of *J*,
16: 1 for Joseph began at the Jordan of *J*,
16: 7 touched *J* and came out
18: 12 passed the northern slope of *J*
18: 21 had the following cities: *J*,
20: 8 Jordan of *J* they designated Bezer
24: 11 The citizens of *J* fought
24: 11 crossed the Jordan and came to *J*.
2Sa 10: 5 at *J* till your beards have grown,
1Ki 16: 34 Hiel of Bethel rebuilt *J*.
2Ki 2: 4 Elisha; the LORD has sent me to *J*
2: 4 So they went to *J*.
2: 5 of the prophets at *J* went up
2: 15 company of the prophets from *J*,
2: 18 who was staying in *J*, he said
25: 5 and overtook him in the plains of *J*.
1Ch 6: 78 east of *J* they received Bezer
19: 5 at *J* till your beards have grown,
2Ch 28: 15 to their fellow countrymen at *J*,
Ezr 2: 34 Ono 725 of *J* 345 of Senaah 3,630
Ne 3: 2 of *J* built the adjoining section,
7: 36 of Harim 320 of *J* 345 of Lod,
Jer 39: 5 Zedekiah in the plains of *J*.
52: 8 and overtook him in the plains of *J*.
Mt 20: 29 and his disciples were leaving *J*,
Mk 10: 46 Then they came to *J*.
Lk 10: 30 going down from Jerusalem to *J*,
18: 35 As Jesus approached *J*, a blind
19: 1 Jesus entered *J* and was passing
Heb 11: 30 By faith the walls of *J* fell,

JERIEL
1Ch 7: 2 Uzzi, Rephaiah, *J*, Jahmai,

JERIMOTH
1Ch 7: 7 Ezbon, Uzzi, Uzziel, *J* and Iri,
12: 5 Jozabad the Gederathite, Eluzai, *J*,
24: 30 sons of Mushi: Mahli, Eder and *J*.
25: 4 Shubael and *J*; Hananiah, Hanani,
25: 22 12 the fifteenth to *J*, his sons
27: 19 over Naphtali: *J* son of Azriel;
2Ch 11: 18 was the daughter of David's son *J*
31: 13 Nahath, Asahel, *J*, Jozabad, Eliel,

JERIOTH
1Ch 2: 18 by his wife Azubah (and by *J*).

JEROBOAM (JEROBOAM'S)
1Ki 11: 26 Also, *J* son of Nebat rebelled
11: 28 Now *J* was a man of standing,
11: 29 About that time *J* was going out
11: 31 Then he said to *J*, "Take ten pieces
11: 40 tried to kill *J*, but *J* fled to Egypt,
12: 2 When *J* son of Nebat heard this (he
12: 3 So they sent for *J*, and he

1Ki 12: 12 Three days later J and all
12: 15 to J son of Nebat through Ahijah
12: 20 heard that J had returned,
12: 25 Then J fortified Shechem
12: 26 J thought to himself,
12: 31 J built shrines on high places
13: 1 as J was standing by the altar
13: 4 When King J heard what the man
13: 33 J did not change his evil ways,
13: 34 the sin of the house of J that led
14: 1 time Abijah son of J became ill,
14: 2 and J said to his wife, "Go,
14: 2 be recognized as the wife of J.
14: 6 he said, "Come in, wife of J.
14: 7 tell J that this is what the LORD,
14: 10 I will burn up the house of J
14: 10 I will cut off from J every last male
14: 10 to bring disaster on the house of J.
14: 11 belonging to J who die in the city,
14: 13 belonging to J who will be buried,
14: 13 the house of J in whom the LORD,
14: 14 cut off the family of J.
14: 16 of the sins J has committed
14: 30 warfare between Rehoboam and J.
15: 1 year of the reign of J son of Nebat,
15: 6 J throughout ⌞Abijah's⌟ lifetime.
15: 7 war between Abijah and J.
15: 9 year of J king of Israel,
15: 25 Nadab son of J became king
15: 29 did not leave J anyone that
15: 30 of the sins J had committed
15: 34 walking in the ways of J
16: 2 but you walked in the ways of J
16: 3 make your house like that of J son
16: 7 and becoming like the house of J—
16: 19 and walking in the ways of J
16: 26 in all the ways of J son of Nebat
16: 31 trivial to commit the sins of J son
21: 22 make your house like that of J son
22: 52 and in the ways of J son of Nebat,
2Ki 3: 3 clung to the sins of J son of Nebat,
9: 9 of Ahab like the house of J son
10: 29 from the sins of J son of Nebat,
10: 31 away from the sins of J,
13: 2 by following the sins of J son
13: 6 from the sins of the house of J,
13: 11 any of the sins of J son of Nebat,
13: 13 and J succeeded him on the throne
14: 16 And J his son succeeded him
14: 23 J son of Jehoash king
14: 24 any of the sins of J son of Nebat,
14: 27 by the hand of J son of Jehoash.
14: 29 J rested with his fathers, the kings
15: 1 year of J king of Israel,
15: 8 Zechariah son of J became king
15: 9 from the sins of J son of Nebat,
15: 18 from the sins of J son of Nebat,
15: 24 from the sins of J son of Nebat,
15: 28 from the sins of J son of Nebat,
17: 21 J enticed Israel away
17: 21 they made J son of Nebat their
17: 22 persisted in all the sins of J
23: 15 made by J son of Nebat,
1Ch 5: 17 king of Judah and J king of Israel.
2Ch 9: 29 of Iddo the seer concerning J son
10: 2 When J son of Nebat heard this (he
10: 3 So they sent for J, and he
10: 12 Three days later J and all
10: 15 to J son of Nebat through Ahijah
11: 4 back from marching against J.
11: 14 to Judah and Jerusalem because J
12: 15 warfare between Rehoboam and J.
13: 1 eighteenth year of the reign of J,
13: 2 war between Abijah and J.
13: 3 J drew up a battle line against him
13: 4 and said, "J and all Israel,
13: 6 Yet J son of Nebat, an officia!
13: 8 you the golden calves that J made
13: 13 Now J had sent troops
13: 15 God routed J and all Israel
13: 19 Abijah pursued J and took
13: 20 J did not regain power
Hos 1: 1 and during the reign of J son
Am 1: 1 J son of Jehoash was king of Israel.
7: 9 rise against the house of J."
7: 10 a message to J king of Israel:
7: 11 " 'J will die by the sword,

JEROBOAM'S (JEROBOAM)

1Ki 14: 4 So J wife did what he said
14: 5 "J wife is coming to ask you about
14: 17 Then J wife got up and left
14: 19 The other events of J reign,
15: 29 to reign, he killed J whole family.
2Ki 14: 28 As for the other events of J reign,

JEROHAM

1Sa 1: 1 whose name was Elkanah son of J,
1Ch 6: 27 his son, Eliab his son, J his son,
6: 34 the son of J, the son of Eliel,
8: 27 Elijah and Zicri were the sons of J.
9: 8 Ibneiah son of J; Elah son of Uzzi,
9: 12 Adaiah son of J, the son of Pashhur
12: 7 Zebadiah the sons of J from Gedor.
27: 22 over Dan: Azarel son of J.
2Ch 23: 1 Azariah son of J, Ishmael son
Ne 11: 12 Adaiah son of J, the son of Pelaliah

JERUB-BAAL (JERUB-BAAL'S)

Jdg 6: 32 So that day they called Gideon "J
7: 1 Early in the morning, J (that is,
8: 29 J son of Joash went back home
8: 35 gratitude to the family of J (that is,
9: 1 Abimelech son of J went
9: 5 his seventy brothers, the sons of J.
9: 5 son of J, escaped by hiding.
9: 16 and if you have been fair to J
9: 19 and in good faith toward J
9: 57 of Jotham son of J came on them.
1Sa 12: 11 Then the LORD sent J, Barak,

JERUB-BAAL'S (JERUB-BAAL)

Jdg 9: 2 seventy of J sons rule over you,
9: 24 the crime against J seventy sons,
9: 28 Isn't he J son, and isn't Zebul his

JERUB-BESHETH

2Sa 11: 21 Who killed Abimelech son of J?

JERUEL

2Ch 20: 16 end of the gorge in the Desert of J.

JERUSALEM (JERUSALEM'S)

Jos 10: 1 of J heard that Joshua had taken Ai
10: 3 So Adoni-Zedek king of J appealed
10: 5 the kings of J, Hebron, Jarmuth,
10: 23 the kings of J, Hebron, Jarmuth,
12: 10 one the king of J one the king
15: 8 of the Jebusite city (that is, J).
15: 63 the Jebusites, who were living in J;
18: 28 the Jebusite city (that is, J),
Jdg 1: 7 They brought him to J,
1: 8 The men of Judah attacked J also
1: 21 the Jebusites, who were living in J;
19: 10 J), with his two saddled donkeys
1Sa 17: 54 head and brought it to J,
2Sa 5: 5 and in J he reigned over all Israel
5: 6 and his men marched to J
5: 13 more concubines and wives in J,
8: 7 Hadadezer and brought them to J.
9: 13 And Mephibosheth lived in J,
10: 14 the Ammonites and came to J.
11: 1 But David remained in J.
11: 12 So Uriah remained in J that day
12: 31 and his entire army returned to J.
14: 23 and brought Absalom back to J.
14: 28 Absalom lived two years in J
15: 8 'If the LORD takes me back to J,
15: 11 from J had accompanied Absalom.
15: 14 officials who were with him in J,
15: 29 took the ark of God back to J
15: 37 David's friend Hushai arrived at J
16: 3 staying in J, because he thinks,
16: 15 and all the men of Israel came to J,
17: 20 found no one, so they returned to J
19: 19 on the day my lord the king left J.
19: 25 When he came from J
19: 33 over with me and stay with me in J,
19: 34 up to J with the king?
20: 2 the way from the Jordan to J.
20: 3 David returned to his palace in J,
20: 7 They marched out from J
20: 22 Joab went back to the king in J.
24: 8 they came back to J at the end
24: 16 stretched out his hand to destroy J,
1Ki 2: 11 in Hebron and thirty-three in J.
1Ki 2: 36 "Build yourself a house in J
2: 38 Shimei stayed in J for a long time.
2: 41 told that Shimei had gone from J
3: 1 the LORD, and the wall around J.
3: 15 He returned to J, stood
8: 1 into his presence at J the elders
9: 15 the wall of J, and Hazor, Megiddo
9: 19 whatever he desired to build in J,
10: 2 at J with a very great caravan—
10: 26 cities and also with him in J.
10: 27 as common in J as stones,
11: 7 of J, Solomon built a high place
11: 13 my servant and for the sake of J,
11: 29 time Jeroboam was going out of J,
11: 32 my servant David and the city of J,
11: 36 always have a lamp before me in J,
11: 42 Solomon reigned in J
12: 18 get into his chariot and escape to J.
12: 21 When Rehoboam arrived in J,
12: 27 at the temple of the LORD in J,
12: 28 It is too much for you to go up to J.
14: 21 and he reigned seventeen years in J
14: 25 Shishak king of Egypt attacked J.
15: 2 and he reigned in J three years.
15: 4 a lamp in J by raising up a son
15: 4 and by making J strong.
15: 10 and he reigned in J forty-one years.
22: 42 he reigned in J twenty-five years.
2Ki 8: 17 and he reigned in J eight years.
8: 26 and he reigned in J one year.
9: 28 servants took him by chariot to J
12: 1 and he reigned in J forty years.
12: 17 Then he turned to attack J.
12: 18 who then withdrew from J.
14: 2 he reigned in J twenty-nine years.
14: 2 was Jehoaddin; she was from J.
14: 13 Then Jehoash went to J
14: 13 and broke down the wall of J
14: 19 They conspired against him in J,
14: 20 was buried in J with his fathers,
15: 2 and he reigned in J fifty-two years.
15: 2 name was Jecoliah; she was from J.
15: 33 and he reigned in J sixteen years.
16: 2 and he reigned in J sixteen years.
16: 5 Israel marched up to fight against J
18: 2 he reigned in J twenty-nine years.
18: 17 Lachish to King Hezekiah at J.
18: 17 They came up to J and stopped
18: 22 and J, "You must worship
18: 22 worship before this altar in J"?
18: 35 How then can the LORD deliver J
19: 10 'J will not be handed
19: 21 The Daughter of J
19: 31 For out of J will come a remnant,
21: 1 and he reigned in J fifty-five years.
21: 4 "In J I will put my Name."
21: 7 and in J, which I have chosen out
21: 12 going to bring such disaster on J
21: 13 I will wipe out J as one wipes a dish
21: 13 out over J the measuring line used
21: 16 innocent blood that he filled J
21: 19 and he reigned in J two years.
22: 1 he reigned in J thirty-one years.
22: 14 lived in J, in the Second District.
23: 1 all the elders of Judah and J.
23: 2 the people of J, the priests
23: 4 them outside J in the fields
23: 5 of Judah and on those around J—
23: 6 to the Kidron Valley outside J
23: 9 serve at the altar of the LORD in J,
23: 13 east of J on the south of the Hill
23: 20 Then he went back to J.
23: 23 celebrated to the LORD in J.
23: 24 things seen in Judah and J.
23: 27 and I will reject J, the city I chose,
23: 30 in a chariot from Megiddo to J
23: 31 and he reigned in J three months.
23: 33 so that he might not reign in J,
23: 36 and he reigned in J eleven years.
24: 4 For he had filled J
24: 8 and he reigned in J three months.
24: 8 of Elnathan; she was from J.
24: 10 king of Babylon advanced on J
24: 14 He carried into exile all J:
24: 15 took from J to Babylon the king's
24: 18 and he reigned in J eleven years.
24: 20 anger that all this happened to J
25: 1 king of Babylon marched against J

2Ki 25: 8 of the king of Babylon, came to *J*.
25: 9 royal palace and all the houses of *J*.
25: 10 broke down the walls around *J*.
1Ch 3: 4 reigned in *J* thirty-three years,
6: 10 in the temple Solomon built in *J*),
6: 15 and *J* into exile by the hand
6: 32 the temple of the LORD in *J*.
8: 28 genealogy, and they lived in *J*.
8: 32 lived near their relatives in *J*.
9: 3 and Manasseh who lived in *J* were:
9: 34 genealogy, and they lived in *J*.
9: 38 lived near their relatives in *J*.
11: 4 and all the Israelites marched to *J*,
14: 3 In *J* David took more wives
15: 3 David assembled all Israel in *J*
18: 7 Hadadezer and brought them to *J*.
19: 15 So Joab went back to *J*.
20: 1 it, but David remained in *J*.
20: 3 and his entire army returned to *J*.
21: 4 Israel and then came back to *J*.
21: 15 And God sent an angel to destroy *J*
21: 16 sword in his hand extended over *J*.
23: 25 and has come to dwell in *J* forever,
28: 1 officials of Israel to assemble at *J*:
29: 27 in Hebron and thirty-three in *J*.
2Ch 1: 4 he had pitched a tent for it in *J*.
1: 13 Then Solomon went to *J*
1: 14 cities and also with him in *J*.
1: 15 and gold as common in *J* as stones,
2: 7 and *J* with my skilled craftsmen,
2: 16 You can then take them up to *J*."
3: 1 the LORD in *J* on Mount Moriah,
5: 2 Solomon summoned to *J* the elders
6: 6 now I have chosen *J* for my Name
8: 6 whatever he desired to build in *J*,
9: 1 she came to *J* to test him
9: 25 cities and also with him in *J*.
9: 27 as common in *J* as stones,
9: 30 Solomon reigned in *J*
10: 18 get into his chariot and escape to *J*.
11: 1 When Rehoboam arrived in *J*,
11: 5 lived in *J* and built up towns
11: 14 to Judah and *J* because Jeroboam
11: 16 the Levites to *J* to offer sacrifices
12: 2 of Egypt attacked *J* in the fifth year
12: 4 cities of Judah and came as far as *J*.
12: 5 assembled in *J* for fear of Shishak,
12: 7 out on *J* through Shishak.
12: 9 king of Egypt attacked *J*,
12: 13 and he reigned seventeen years in *J*
12: 13 established himself firmly in *J*
13: 2 and he reigned in *J* three years.
14: 15 Then they returned to *J*.
15: 10 They assembled at *J*
17: 13 kept experienced fighting men in *J*.
19: 1 returned safely to his palace in *J*,
19: 4 Jehoshaphat lived in *J*,
19: 8 And they lived in *J*.
19: 8 In *J* also, Jehoshaphat appointed
20: 5 and *J* at the temple of the LORD
20: 15 and all who live in Judah and *J*!
20: 17 will give you, O Judah and *J*.
20: 18 and *J* fell down in worship
20: 20 Listen to me, Judah and people of *J*
20: 27 and *J* returned joyfully to *J*,
20: 28 They entered *J* and went
20: 31 he reigned in *J* twenty-five years.
21: 5 and he reigned in *J* eight years.
21: 11 of *J* to prostitute themselves
21: 13 of *J* to prostitute themselves,
21: 20 and he reigned in *J* eight years.
22: 1 The people of *J* made Ahaziah,
22: 2 and he reigned in *J* one year.
23: 2 to *J*, the whole assembly made
24: 1 and he reigned in *J* forty years.
24: 6 and *J* the tax imposed by Moses
24: 9 and *J* that they should bring
24: 18 came upon Judah and *J*.
24: 23 it invaded Judah and *J*
25: 1 he reigned in *J* twenty-nine years.
25: 1 was Jehoaddin; she was from *J*.
25: 23 Then Jehoash brought him to *J*
25: 23 and broke down the wall of *J*
25: 27 they conspired against him in *J*
26: 3 and he reigned in *J* fifty-two years.
26: 3 name was Jecoliah; she was from *J*.
26: 9 Uzziah built towers in *J*
26: 15 In *J* he made machines designed
2Ch 27: 1 and he reigned in *J* sixteen years.
27: 8 and he reigned in *J* sixteen years.
28: 1 and he reigned in *J* sixteen years.
28: 10 women of Judah and *J* your slaves.
28: 24 altars at every street corner in *J*.
28: 27 and was buried in the city of *J*,
29: 1 he reigned in *J* twenty-nine years.
29: 8 LORD has fallen on Judah and *J*;
30: 1 to the temple of the LORD in *J*
30: 2 the whole assembly in *J* decided
30: 3 the people had not assembled in *J*.
30: 5 calling the people to come to *J*
30: 11 humbled themselves and went to *J*.
30: 13 crowd of people assembled in *J*
30: 14 They removed the altars in *J*
30: 21 present in *J* celebrated the Feast
30: 26 had been nothing like this in *J*.
30: 26 joy in *J*, for since the days
31: 4 He ordered the people living in *J*
32: 2 that he intended to make war on *J*,
32: 9 officers to *J* with this message
32: 10 that you remain in *J* under siege?
32: 12 and *J*, 'You must worship
32: 18 to the people of *J* who were
32: 19 They spoke about the God of *J*
32: 22 and the people of *J* from the hand
32: 23 offerings to *J* for the LORD
32: 25 was on him and on Judah and *J*.
32: 26 of his heart, as did the people of *J*;
32: 33 and the people of *J* honored him
33: 1 and he reigned in *J* fifty-five years.
33: 4 "My Name will remain in *J* forever
33: 7 and in *J*, which I have chosen out
33: 9 and the people of *J* astray,
33: 13 so he brought him back to *J*
33: 15 built on the temple hill and in *J*;
33: 21 and he reigned in *J* two years.
34: 1 he reigned in *J* thirty-one years.
34: 3 to purge Judah and *J* of high places
34: 5 and so he purged Judah and *J*.
34: 7 Then he went back to *J*.
34: 9 Benjamin and the inhabitants of *J*.
34: 22 lived in *J*, in the Second District.
34: 29 all the elders of Judah and *J*.
34: 30 the people of *J*, the priests
34: 32 Then he had everyone in *J*
34: 32 the people of *J* did this
35: 1 the Passover to the LORD in *J*,
35: 18 there with the people of *J*.
35: 24 all Judah and *J* mourned for him.
35: 24 he had and brought him to *J*,
36: 1 and made him king in *J* in place
36: 2 and he reigned in *J* three months.
36: 3 king of Egypt dethroned him in *J*
36: 4 king over Judah and *J*
36: 5 and he reigned in *J* eleven years.
36: 9 and he reigned in *J* three months
36: 10 Zedekiah, king over Judah and *J*.
36: 11 and he reigned in *J* eleven years.
36: 14 which he had consecrated in *J*.
36: 19 and broke down the wall of *J*;
36: 23 a temple for him at *J* in Judah.
Ezr 1: 2 a temple for him at *J* in Judah.
1: 3 God of Israel, the God who is in *J*.
1: 3 and let him go up to *J* in Judah
1: 4 for the temple of God in *J*.' "
1: 5 build the house of the LORD in *J*.
1: 7 had carried away from *J*
1: 11 up from Babylon to *J*.
2: 1 to Babylon (they returned to *J*
2: 68 at the house of the LORD in *J*,
3: 1 people assembled as one man in *J*.
3: 8 arrival at the house of God in *J*,
3: 8 the captivity to *J*) began the work,
4: 6 against the people of Judah and *J*.
4: 8 against *J* to Artaxerxes the king
4: 12 up to us from you have gone to *J*
4: 20 *J* has had powerful kings ruling
4: 23 went immediately to the Jews in *J*
4: 24 of God in *J* came to a standstill
5: 1 *J* in the name of the God of Israel,
5: 2 to rebuild the house of God in *J*.
5: 14 taken from the temple in *J*
5: 15 deposit them in the temple in *J*.
5: 16 of the house of God in *J*.
5: 17 to rebuild this house of God in *J*.
6: 3 concerning the temple of God in *J*:
6: 5 to their places in the temple in *J*;
Ezr 6: 5 took from the temple in *J*
6: 9 as requested by the priests in *J*—
6: 12 or to destroy this temple in *J*.
6: 18 groups for the service of God at *J*,
7: 7 came up to *J* in the seventh year
7: 8 Ezra arrived in *J* in the fifth month
7: 9 and he arrived in *J* on the first day
7: 13 who wish to go to *J* with you,
7: 14 and *J* with regard to the Law
7: 15 whose dwelling is in *J*, together
7: 16 for the temple of their God in *J*.
7: 17 of the temple of your God in *J*.
7: 19 God of *J* all the articles entrusted
7: 27 house of the LORD in *J* in this way
8: 29 in *J* before the leading priests
8: 30 taken to the house of our God in *J*.
8: 31 from the Ahava Canal to go to *J*.
8: 32 in *J*, where we rested three days.
9: 9 a wall of protection in Judah and *J*.
10: 7 and *J* for all the exiles to assemble
10: 7 for all the exiles to assemble in *J*.
10: 9 and Benjamin had gathered in *J*.
Ne 1: 2 the exile, and also about *J*.
1: 3 The wall of *J* is broken down,
2: 11 to *J*, and after staying there three
2: 12 put in my heart to do for *J*.
2: 13 walls of *J*, which had been broken
2: 17 Come, let us rebuild the wall of *J*,
2: 17 You see the trouble we are in: *J* lies
2: 20 you have no share in *J* or any claim
3: 8 They restored *J* as far as the Broad
3: 9 ruler of a half-district of *J*,
3: 12 ruler of a half-district of *J*,
4: 8 fight against *J* and stir up trouble
4: 22 his helper stay inside *J* at night,
6: 7 this proclamation about you in *J*:
7: 2 in charge of *J* my brother Hanani,
7: 3 The gates of *J* are not to be opened
7: 3 appoint residents of *J* as guards,
7: 6 taken captive (they returned to *J*
8: 15 it throughout their towns and in *J*:
11: 1 leaders of the people settled in *J*,
11: 1 out of every ten to live in *J*,
11: 2 men who volunteered to live in *J*.
11: 3 settled in *J* (now some Israelites,
11: 4 Judah and Benjamin lived in *J*):
11: 6 lived in *J* totaled 468 brave men.
11: 22 of the Levites in *J* was Uzzi son
12: 27 At the dedication of the wall of *J*,
12: 27 brought to *J* to celebrate joyfully
12: 28 from the region around *J*—
12: 29 villages for themselves around *J*.
12: 43 in *J* could be heard far away.
13: 6 all this was going on, I was not in *J*,
13: 7 his permission and came back to *J*.
13: 15 this into *J* on the Sabbath.
13: 16 lived in *J* were bringing in fish
13: 16 selling them in *J* on the Sabbath
13: 19 on the gates of *J* before the Sabbath
13: 20 of goods spent the night outside *J*.
Est 2: 6 from *J* by Nebuchadnezzar king
Ps 51: 18 build up the walls of *J*.
68: 29 Because of your temple at *J*
79: 1 they have reduced *J* to rubble.
79: 3 all around *J*,
102: 21 and his praise in *J*
116: 19 in your midst, O *J*.
122: 2 in your gates, O *J*.
122: 3 *J* is built like a city
122: 6 Pray for the peace of *J*:
125: 2 As the mountains surround *J*,
128: 5 may you see the prosperity of *J*,
135: 21 to him who dwells in *J*.
137: 5 If I forget you, O *J*,
137: 6 if I do not consider *J*
137: 7 on the day *J* fell.
147: 2 The LORD builds up *J*;
147: 12 Extol the LORD, O *J*;
Ecc 1: 1 in *J*: "Meaningless! Meaningless!"
1: 12 Teacher, was king over Israel in *J*.
1: 16 than anyone who has ruled over *J*
2: 7 flocks than anyone in *J* before me.
2: 9 by far than anyone in *J* before me.
SS 1: 5 O daughters of *J*,
2: 7 Daughters of *J*, I charge you
3: 5 Daughters of *J*, I charge you
3: 10 inlaid by the daughters of *J*.
5: 8 O daughters of *J*, I charge you—

Mal 2: 11 been committed in Israel and in *J:*
3: 4 *J* will be acceptable to the LORD,
Mt 2: 1 Magi from the east came to *J*
2: 3 this he was disturbed, and all *J*
3: 5 People went out to him from *J*
4: 25 from Galilee, the Decapolis, *J,*
5: 35 for it is his footstool; or by *J,*
15: 1 of the law came to Jesus from *J*
16: 21 to his disciples that he must go to *J*
20: 17 Now as Jesus was going up to *J,*
20: 18 said to them, "We are going up to *J*
21: 1 As they approached *J*
21: 10 When Jesus entered *J,* the whole
23: 37 "O *J, J,* you who kill the prophets
Mk 1: 5 all the people of *J* went out to him.
3: 8 came to him from Judea, *J,*
3: 22 came down from *J* said,
7: 1 from *J* gathered around Jesus
10: 32 They were on their way up to *J,*
10: 33 "We are going up to *J,*" he said,
11: 1 As they approached *J*
11: 11 Jesus entered *J* and went
11: 15 On reaching *J,* Jesus entered
11: 27 They arrived again in *J,*
15: 41 up with him to *J* were
Lk 2: 22 Mary took him to *J* to present him
2: 25 there was a man in *J* called Simeon
2: 38 forward to the redemption of *J.*
2: 41 Every year his parents went to *J*
2: 43 the boy Jesus stayed behind in *J,*
2: 45 they went back to *J* to look for him.
4: 9 The devil led him to *J*
5: 17 of Galilee and from Judea and *J,*
6: 17 from *J,* and from the seacoast
9: 31 about to bring to fulfillment at *J.*
9: 51 Jesus resolutely set out for *J,*
9: 53 because he was heading for *J.*
10: 30 going down from *J* to Jericho,
13: 4 than all the others living in *J?*
13: 22 teaching as he made his way to *J.*
13: 34 die outside *J!* "O *J, J,*
17: 11 on his way to *J,* Jesus traveled
18: 31 told them, "We are going up to *J,*
19: 11 because he was near *J*
19: 28 he went on ahead, going up to *J.*
19: 41 As he approached *J* and saw
21: 20 "When you see *J* surrounded
21: 24 *J* will be trampled
23: 7 who was also in *J* at that time.
23: 28 Daughters of *J,* do not weep for me
24: 13 about seven miles from *J.*
24: 18 in *J* who doesn't know the things
24: 33 got up and returned at once to *J.*
24: 47 name to all nations, beginning at *J.*
24: 52 and returned to *J* with great joy.
Jn 1: 19 when the Jews of *J* sent priests
2: 13 Passover, Jesus went up to *J.*
2: 23 was in *J* at the Passover Feast,
4: 20 where we must worship is in *J.*"
4: 21 neither on this mountain nor in *J.*
4: 45 done in *J* at the Passover Feast,
5: 1 Jesus went up to *J* for a feast
5: 2 is in *J* near the Sheep Gate a pool,
7: 25 of the people of *J* began to ask,
10: 22 came the Feast of Dedication at *J.*
11: 18 less than two miles from *J,*
11: 55 up from the country to *J*
12: 12 that Jesus was on his way to *J.*
Ac 1: 4 this command: "Do not leave *J,*
1: 8 and you will be my witnesses in *J,*
1: 12 Then they returned to *J*
1: 19 Everyone in *J* heard about this,
2: 5 staying in *J* God-fearing Jews
2: 14 and all of you who are in *J,*
4: 5 and teachers of the law met in *J.*
4: 16 living in *J* knows they have done
5: 16 also from the towns around *J,*
5: 28 "Yet you have filled *J*
6: 7 of disciples in *J* increased rapidly,
8: 1 out against the church at *J,*
8: 14 in *J* heard that Samaria had
8: 25 Peter and John returned to *J,*
8: 26 that goes down from *J* to Gaza."
8: 27 This man had gone to *J* to worship,
9: 2 might take them as prisoners to *J.*
9: 13 done to your saints in *J.*
9: 21 havoc in *J* among those who call
9: 26 When he came to *J,* he tried
Ac 9: 28 and moved about freely in *J,*
10: 39 in the country of the Jews and in *J.*
11: 2 So when Peter went up to *J,*
11: 22 the ears of the church at *J,*
11: 27 came down from *J* to Antioch.
12: 25 they returned from *J,* taking
13: 13 where John left them to return to *J.*
13: 27 people of *J* and their rulers did not
13: 31 with him from Galilee to *J.*
15: 2 to go up to *J* to see the apostles
15: 4 came to *J,* they were welcomed
16: 4 elders in *J* for the people to obey.
19: 21 decided to go to *J,* passing
20: 16 for he was in a hurry to reach *J,*
20: 22 by the Spirit, I am going to *J,*
21: 4 they urged Paul not to go on to *J.*
21: 11 the Jews of *J* will bind the owner
21: 12 pleaded with Paul not to go up to *J.*
21: 13 but also to die in *J* for the name
21: 15 we got ready and went up to *J.*
21: 17 at *J,* the brothers received us
21: 31 city of *J* was in an uproar.
22: 5 as prisoners to *J* to be punished.
22: 17 "When I returned to *J*
22: 18 'Leave *J* immediately,
23: 11 As you have testified about me in *J*
24: 11 than twelve days ago I went up to *J*
24: 17 I came to *J* to bring my people gifts
25: 1 Festus went up from Caesarea to *J,*
25: 3 to have Paul transferred to *J,*
25: 7 down from *J* stood around him,
25: 9 "Are you willing to go up to *J*
25: 15 When I went to *J,* the chief priests
25: 20 if he would be willing to go to *J*
25: 24 has petitioned me about him in *J*
26: 4 in my own country, and also in *J.*
26: 10 And that is just what I did in *J.*
26: 20 then to those in *J* and in all Judea,
28: 17 I was arrested in *J* and handed
Ro 15: 19 So from *J* all the way
15: 25 I am on my way to *J* in the service
15: 26 for the poor among the saints in *J.*
15: 31 service in *J* may be acceptable
1Co 16: 3 and send them with your gift to *J.*
Gal 1: 17 to *J* to see those who were apostles
1: 18 I went up to *J* to get acquainted
2: 1 years later I went up again to *J,*
4: 25 corresponds to the present city of *J*
4: 26 But the *J* that is above is free,
Heb 12: 22 to the heavenly *J,* the city
Rev 3: 12 the new *J,* which is coming
21: 2 I saw the Holy City, the new *J,*
21: 10 and showed me the Holy City, *J,*

JERUSALEM'S (JERUSALEM)

Ne 4: 7 repairs to *J* walls had gone ahead
Isa 62: 1 for *J* sake I will not remain quiet,
Zec 12: 7 of *J* inhabitants may not be greater

JERUSHA

2Ki 15: 33 His mother's name was *J* daughter
2Ch 27: 1 His mother's name was *J* daughter

JESARELAH

1Ch 25: 14 the seventh to *J,* his sons

JESHAIAH

1Ch 3: 21 and *J,* and the sons of Rephaiah,
25: 3 Gedaliah, Zeri, *J,* Shimei,
25: 15 the eighth to *J,* his sons
26: 25 Rehabiah his son, *J* his son,
Ezr 8: 7 of Elam, *J* son of Athaliah,
8: 19 with *J* from the descendants
Ne 11: 7 the son of *J,* and his followers,

JESHANAH

2Ch 13: 19 *J* and Ephron, with their
Ne 3: 6 The *J* Gate was repaired
12: 39 the *J* Gate, the Fish Gate,

JESHEBEAB

1Ch 24: 13 the fourteenth to *J,* the fifteenth

JESHER

1Ch 2: 18 These were her sons: *J,* Shobab

JESHIMON

1Sa 23: 19 on the hill of Hakilah, south of *J?*
1Sa 23: 24 of Maon, in the Arabah south of *J.*
26: 1 which faces *J?*" So Saul went
26: 3 road on the hill of Hakilah facing *J,*

JESHISHAI

1Ch 5: 14 the son of *J,* the son of Jahdo,

JESHOHAIAH

1Ch 4: 36 Jaakobah, *J,* Asaiah, Adiel,

JESHUA

1Ch 24: 11 the ninth to *J,* the tenth
2Ch 31: 15 Eden, Miniamin, *J,* Shemaiah,
Ezr 2: 2 *J,* Nehemiah, Seraiah, Reelaiah,
2: 6 (through the line of *J*
2: 36 (through the family of *J*) 973
2: 40 the descendants of *J* and Kadmiel
3: 2 Then *J* son of Jozadak
3: 8 *J* son of Jozadak and the rest
3: 9 *J* and his sons and brothers
4: 3 *J* and the rest of the heads
5: 2 and *J* son of Jozadak set to work
8: 33 were the Levites Jozabad son of *J*
10: 18 descendants of *J* son of Jozadak,
Ne 3: 19 Ezer son of *J,* ruler of Mizpah,
7: 7 *J,* Nehemiah, Azariah, Raamiah,
7: 11 (through the line of *J*
7: 39 (through the family of *J*) 973
7: 43 descendants of *J* (through Kadmiel
8: 7 The Levites—*J,* Bani, Sherebiah,
9: 4 *J,* Bani, Kadmiel, Shebaniah,
9: 5 And the Levites—*J,* Kadmiel,
10: 9 The Levites: *J* son of Azaniah,
11: 26 in Jekabzeel and its villages, in *J,*
12: 1 son of Shealtiel and with *J:*
12: 7 their associates in the days of *J.*
12: 8 The Levites were *J,* Binnui,
12: 10 *J* was the father of Joiakim,
12: 24 Sherebiah, *J* son of Kadmiel,
12: 26 in the days of Joiakim son of *J,*

JESHURUN

Dt 32: 15 *J* grew fat and kicked;
33: 5 He was king over *J*
33: 26 "There is no one like the God of *J,*
Isa 44: 2 *J,* whom I have chosen.

JESIMIEL

1Ch 4: 36 Asaiah, Adiel, *J,* Benaiah,

JESSE (JESSE'S)

Ru 4: 17 the father of *J,* the father of David.
4: 22 the father of *J,* and *J* the father
1Sa 16: 1 I am sending you to *J* of Bethlehem
16: 3 Invite *J* to the sacrifice,
16: 5 Then he consecrated *J* and his sons
16: 8 Then *J* called Abinadab
16: 9 *J* then had Shammah pass by,
16: 10 *J* had seven of his sons pass
16: 11 he asked *J,* "Are these all the sons
16: 11 is still the youngest," *J* answered,
16: 18 of *J* of Bethlehem who knows how
16: 19 Saul sent messengers to *J* and said,
16: 20 *J* took a donkey loaded with bread,
16: 22 Then Saul sent word to *J,* saying,
17: 12 *J* had eight sons, and in Saul's time
17: 12 the son of an Ephrathite named *J,*
17: 17 Now *J* said to his son David,
17: 20 and set out, as *J* had directed.
17: 58 of your servant *J* of Bethlehem."
20: 27 the son of *J* come to the meal,
20: 30 the son of *J* to your own shame
20: 31 as the son of *J* lives on this earth,
22: 7 Will the son of *J* give all
22: 8 makes a covenant with the son of *J.*
22: 9 son of *J* come to Ahimelech son
22: 13 against me, you and the son of *J,*
25: 10 is this David? Who is this son of *J?*
2Sa 23: 1 "The oracle of David son of *J,*
1Ch 2: 12 of Obed and Obed the father of *J.*
2: 13 *J* was the father of Eliab his
10: 14 kingdom over to David son of *J.*
12: 18 We are with you, O son of *J!*
29: 26 David son of *J* was king
Ps 72: 20 the prayers of David son of *J.*
Isa 11: 1 up from the stump of *J;*
11: 10 In that day the Root of *J* will stand
Mt 1: 5 the father of *J,* and *J* the father

Lk 3: 32 the son of *J*,
Ac 13: 22 'I have found David son of *J* a man
Ro 15: 12 "The root of *J* will spring up,

JESSE'S (JESSE)

1Sa 17: 13 *J* three oldest sons had followed
2Sa 20: 1 no part in *J* son!
1Ki 12: 16 what part in *J* son?
2Ch 10: 16 what part in *J* son?
11: 18 the daughter of *J* son Eliab.

JESUS (JESUS')

Mt 1: 1 of the genealogy of *J* Christ the son
1: 16 of whom was born *J*, who is called
1: 18 the birth of *J* Christ came about.
1: 21 and you are to give him the name *J*,
1: 25 And he gave him the name *J*.
2: 1 After *J* was born in Bethlehem
3: 13 *J* came from Galilee to the Jordan
3: 15 and do you come to me?" *J* replied,
3: 16 As soon as *J* was baptized,
4: 1 Then *J* was led by the Spirit
4: 4 *J* answered, "It is written:
4: 7 *J* answered him, "It is also written:
4: 10 *J* said to him, "Away from me,
4: 12 When *J* heard that John had been
4: 17 time on *J* began to preach,
4: 18 As *J* was walking beside the Sea
4: 19 "Come, follow me," *J* said,
4: 21 *J* called them, and immediately
4: 23 *J* went throughout Galilee,
7: 28 When *J* had finished saying these
8: 3 *J* reached out his hand
8: 4 *J* said to him, "See that you don't
8: 5 When *J* had entered Capernaum,
8: 7 *J* said to him, "I will go
8: 10 When *J* heard this, he was
8: 13 Then *J* said to the centurion, "Go!
8: 14 When *J* came into Peter's house,
8: 18 When *J* saw the crowd around him,
8: 20 *J* replied, "Foxes have holes
8: 22 But *J* told him, "Follow me,
8: 24 But *J* was sleeping.
8: 31 demons begged *J*, "If you drive us
8: 34 the whole town went out to meet *J*.
9: 1 *J* stepped into a boat, crossed over
9: 2 When *J* saw their faith, he said
9: 4 Knowing their thoughts, *J* said,
9: 9 As *J* went on from there, he saw
9: 10 While *J* was having dinner
9: 12 *J* said, "It is not the healthy who
9: 15 disciples do not fast?" *J* answered,
9: 19 *J* got up and went with him,
9: 22 *J* turned and saw her.
9: 23 When *J* entered the ruler's house
9: 27 As *J* went on from there, two blind
9: 30 *J* warned them sternly, "See that
9: 32 could not talk was brought to *J*.
9: 35 *J* went through all the towns
10: 5 These twelve *J* sent out
11: 1 After *J* had finished instructing his
11: 4 expect someone else?" *J* replied,
11: 7 *J* began to speak to the crowd
11: 20 *J* began to denounce the cities
11: 25 At that time *J* said, "I praise you,
12: 1 At that time *J* went
12: 10 Looking for a reason to accuse *J*,
12: 14 and plotted how they might kill *J*.
12: 15 *J* withdrew from that place.
12: 22 *J* healed him, so that he could both
12: 25 *J* knew their thoughts
12: 46 While *J* was still talking
13: 1 That same day *J* went out
13: 24 *J* told them another parable:
13: 34 *J* spoke all these things
13: 51 all these things?" *J* asked.
13: 53 When *J* had finished these parables
13: 57 But *J* said to them, "Only
14: 1 tetrarch heard the reports about *J*,
14: 12 Then they went and told *J*.
14: 13 When *J* heard what had happened,
14: 14 When *J* landed and saw a large
14: 16 *J* replied, "They do not need
14: 22 Immediately *J* made the disciples
14: 25 of the night *J* went out to them,
14: 27 But *J* immediately said to them:
14: 29 and walked on the water to *J*.
14: 31 Immediately *J* reached out his

Mt 14: 35 the men of that place recognized *J*,
15: 1 came to *J* from Jerusalem
15: 3 hands before they eat!" *J* replied,
15: 10 *J* called the crowd to him and said,
15: 16 Are you still so dull?" *J* asked them
15: 21 *J* withdrew to the region of Tyre
15: 23 *J* did not answer a word.
15: 28 Then *J* answered, "Woman,
15: 29 *J* left there and went along the Sea
15: 32 *J* called his disciples to him
15: 34 loaves do you have?" *J* asked.
15: 39 After *J* had sent the crowd away,
16: 1 Pharisees and Sadducees came to *J*
16: 4 *J* then left them and went away.
16: 6 "Be careful," *J* said to them.
16: 8 Aware of their discussion, *J* asked,
16: 13 When *J* came to the region
16: 17 *J* replied, "Blessed are you,
16: 21 time on *J* began to explain
16: 23 *J* turned and said to Peter,
16: 24 Then *J* said to his disciples,
17: 1 After six days *J* took
17: 3 Moses and Elijah, talking with *J*.
17: 4 Peter said to *J*, "Lord, it is good
17: 7 But *J* came and touched them.
17: 8 up, they saw no one except *J*.
17: 9 the mountain, *J* instructed them,
17: 11 *J* replied, "To be sure, Elijah
17: 14 a man approached *J* and knelt
17: 17 perverse generation," *J* replied,
17: 18 *J* rebuked the demon,
17: 19 the disciples came to *J* in private
17: 24 After *J* and his disciples arrived
17: 25 came into the house, *J* was the first
17: 26 the sons are exempt," *J* said to him
18: 1 At that time the disciples came to *J*
18: 21 Then Peter came to *J* and asked,
18: 22 Up to seven times?" *J* answered,
19: 1 When *J* had finished saying these
19: 8 *J* replied, "Moses permitted you
19: 11 *J* replied, "Not everyone can
19: 13 little children were brought to *J*
19: 14 *J* said, "Let the little children come
19: 16 Now a man came up to *J* and asked
19: 17 me about what is good?" *J* replied.
19: 18 *J* replied, " 'Do not murder,
19: 21 "What do I still lack?" *J* answered,
19: 23 Then *J* said to his disciples,
19: 26 *J* looked at them and said,
19: 28 be for us?" *J* said to them,
20: 17 as *J* was going up to Jerusalem,
20: 20 of Zebedee's sons came to *J*
20: 22 know what you are asking," *J* said
20: 23 *J* said to them, "You will indeed
20: 25 *J* called them together and said,
20: 29 As *J* and his disciples were leaving
20: 30 when they heard that *J* was going
20: 32 *J* stopped and called them.
20: 34 *J* had compassion on them
21: 1 *J* sent two disciples, saying to them
21: 6 and did as *J* had instructed them.
21: 7 cloaks on them, and *J* sat on them.
21: 10 When *J* entered Jerusalem,
21: 11 The crowds answered, "This is *J*,
21: 12 *J* entered the temple area
21: 16 replied *J*, "have you never read,
21: 21 *J* replied, "I tell you the truth,
21: 23 *J* entered the temple courts, and,
21: 24 gave you this authority?" *J* replied,
21: 27 they answered *J*, "We don't know
21: 31 *J* said to them, "I tell you the truth,
21: 42 *J* said to them, "Have you never
22: 1 *J* spoke to them again in parables,
22: 18 But *J*, knowing their evil intent,
22: 29 married to her?" *J* replied,
22: 34 Hearing that *J* had silenced
22: 37 in the Law?" *J* replied:
22: 41 gathered together, *J* asked them,
23: 1 Then *J* said to the crowds
24: 1 *J* left the temple and was walking
24: 3 As *J* was sitting on the Mount
24: 4 *J* answered: "Watch out that no
26: 1 When *J* had finished saying all
26: 4 and they plotted to arrest *J*
26: 6 While *J* was in Bethany
26: 10 Aware of this, *J* said to them,
26: 17 the disciples came to *J* and asked,
26: 19 the disciples did as *J* had directed

Mt 26: 20 *J* was reclining at the table
26: 23 "Surely not I, Lord?" *J* replied,
26: 25 Rabbi?" *J* answered, "Yes,
26: 26 they were eating, *J* took bread,
26: 31 *J* told them, "This very night you
26: 34 *J* answered, "this very night,
26: 36 Then *J* went with his disciples
26: 49 Going at once to *J*, Judas said,
26: 50 *J* replied, "Friend, do what you
26: 50 seized *J* and arrested him.
26: 52 back in its place," *J* said to him,
26: 55 At that time *J* said to the crowd,
26: 57 Those who had arrested *J* took him
26: 59 looking for false evidence against *J*
26: 62 high priest stood up and said to *J*,
26: 63 you?" But *J* remained silent.
26: 64 "Yes, it is as you say," *J* replied.
26: 69 "You also were with *J* of Galilee,"
26: 71 This fellow was with *J* of Nazareth
26: 75 the word *J* had spoken:
27: 1 to the decision to put *J* to death.
27: 3 saw that *J* was condemned,
27: 11 Meanwhile *J* stood
27: 11 "Yes, it is as you say," *J* replied.
27: 14 But *J* made no reply, not
27: 17 Barabbas, or *J* who is called Christ
27: 18 out of envy that they had handed *J*
27: 20 and to have *J* executed.
27: 22 then, with *J* who is called Christ?"
27: 26 he had *J* flogged, and handed him
27: 27 Then the governor's soldiers took *J*
27: 37 THIS IS *J*, THE KING
27: 46 About the ninth hour *J* cried out
27: 48 and offered it to *J* to drink.
27: 50 And when *J* had cried out again
27: 54 who were guarding *J* saw
27: 55 They had followed *J* from Galilee
27: 57 had himself become a disciple of *J*.
28: 5 I know that you are looking for *J*,
28: 9 Suddenly *J* met them.
28: 10 *J* said to them, "Do not be afraid.
28: 16 the mountain where *J* had told
28: 18 Then *J* came to them and said,
Mk 1: 1 of the gospel about *J* Christ,
1: 9 At that time *J* came from Nazareth
1: 10 As *J* was coming up out
1: 14 put in prison, *J* went into Galilee,
1: 16 As *J* walked beside the Sea
1: 17 "Come, follow me," *J* said,
1: 21 *J* went into the synagogue
1: 24 want with us, *J* of Nazareth?
1: 25 "Be quiet!" said *J* sternly.
1: 30 and they told *J* about her.
1: 32 the people brought to *J* all the sick
1: 34 *J* healed many who had various
1: 35 while it was still dark, *J* got up,
1: 38 looking for you!" *J* replied,
1: 41 *J* reached out his hand
1: 43 *J* sent him away at once
1: 45 *J* could no longer enter a town
2: 1 when *J* again entered Capernaum,
2: 4 Since they could not get him to *J*
2: 4 an opening in the roof above *J*
2: 5 When *J* saw their faith, he said
2: 8 Immediately *J* knew
2: 13 Once again *J* went out
2: 14 *J* told him, and Levi got up
2: 15 While *J* was having dinner
2: 17 On hearing this, *J* said to them,
2: 18 Some people came and asked *J*
2: 19 but yours are not?" *J* answered,
2: 23 One Sabbath *J* was going
3: 2 looking for a reason to accuse *J*,
3: 3 *J* said to the man with the shriveled
3: 4 *J* asked them, "Which is lawful
3: 6 Herodians how they might kill *J*.
3: 7 *J* withdrew with his disciples
3: 13 *J* went up into the hills
3: 20 Then *J* entered a house,
3: 23 So *J* called them and spoke to them
4: 1 On another occasion *J* began
4: 9 *J* said, "He who has ears to hear,
4: 13 Then *J* said to them, "Don't you
4: 33 many similar parables *J* spoke
4: 38 *J* was in the stern, sleeping
5: 2 When *J* got out of the boat,
5: 6 When he saw *J* from a distance,
5: 7 "What do you want with me, *J*,

Mk 5: 8 torture me!" For *J* was saying
5: 9 you evil spirit!" Then *J* asked him,
5: 10 And he begged *J* again
5: 12 The demons begged *J*, "Send us
5: 15 to *J*, they saw the man who had
5: 17 to plead with *J* to leave their region
5: 18 As *J* was getting into the boat,
5: 19 *J* did not let him, but said,
5: 20 Decapolis how much *J* had done
5: 21 When *J* had again crossed
5: 22 Seeing *J*, he fell at his feet
5: 24 So *J* went with him.
5: 27 she heard about *J*, she came up
5: 30 At once *J* realized that power had
5: 32 *J* kept looking around to see who
5: 35 While *J* was still speaking,
5: 36 *J* told the synagogue ruler,
5: 38 *J* saw a commotion,
6: 1 *J* left there and went
6: 4 *J* said to them, "Only
6: 6 Then *J* went around teaching
6: 30 The apostles gathered around *J*
6: 34 When *J* landed and saw a large
6: 39 Then *J* directed them to have all
6: 45 Immediately *J* made his disciples
6: 54 of the boat, people recognized *J*.
7: 1 from Jerusalem gathered around *J*
7: 5 and teachers of the law asked *J*,
7: 14 Again *J* called the crowd to him
7: 19 *J* declared all foods "clean.")
7: 24 *J* left that place and went
7: 26 She begged *J* to drive the demon
7: 31 Then *J* left the vicinity of Tyre
7: 33 *J* put his fingers into the man's ears
7: 36 *J* commanded them not
8: 1 *J* called his disciples to him
8: 5 loaves do you have?" *J* asked.
8: 11 came and began to question *J*.
8: 15 "Be careful," *J* warned them.
8: 17 of their discussion, *J* asked them:
8: 22 and begged *J* to touch him.
8: 23 *J* asked, "Do you see anything?"
8: 25 Once more *J* put his hands
8: 26 *J* sent him home, saying, "Don't go
8: 27 *J* and his disciples went
8: 30 *J* warned them not
8: 33 But when *J* turned and looked
9: 2 After six days *J* took Peter,
9: 4 Moses, who were talking with *J*.
9: 5 Peter said to *J*, "Rabbi, it is good
9: 8 anyone with them except *J*.
9: 9 *J* gave them orders not
9: 12 *J* replied, "To be sure, Elijah does
9: 15 As soon as all the people saw *J*,
9: 19 unbelieving generation," *J* replied,
9: 20 the spirit saw *J*, it immediately
9: 21 *J* asked the boy's father, "How
9: 23 " 'If you can'?" said *J*.
9: 25 When *J* saw that a crowd was
9: 27 But *J* took him by the hand
9: 28 After *J* had gone indoors, his
9: 30 *J* did not want anyone
9: 35 *J* called the Twelve and said,
9: 39 "Do not stop him," *J* said.
10: 1 *J* then left that place and went
10: 5 wrote you this law," *J* replied.
10: 10 the disciples asked *J* about this.
10: 13 to *J* to have him touch them,
10: 14 When *J* saw this, he was indignant.
10: 17 As *J* started on his way, a man ran
10: 18 do you call me good?" *J* answered.
10: 21 *J* looked at him and loved him.
10: 23 *J* looked around and said
10: 24 But *J* said again, "Children,
10: 27 *J* looked at them and said,
10: 29 "I tell you the truth," *J* replied,
10: 32 with *J* leading the way,
10: 38 know what you are asking," *J* said.
10: 39 *J* said to them, "You will drink
10: 42 *J* called them together and said,
10: 46 As *J* and his disciples, together
10: 47 When he heard that it was *J*
10: 47 he began to shout, "*J*, Son of David
10: 49 have mercy on me!" *J* stopped
10: 50 he jumped to his feet and came to *J*
10: 51 me to do for you?" *J* asked him.
10: 52 and followed *J* along the road.
10: 52 said *J*, "your faith has healed you."

Mk 11: 1 *J* sent two of his disciples,
11: 6 They answered as *J* had told them
11: 7 When they brought the colt to *J*
11: 11 *J* entered Jerusalem and went
11: 12 leaving Bethany, *J* was hungry.
11: 15 *J* entered the temple area
11: 21 Peter remembered and said to *J*,
11: 22 "Have faith in God," *J* answered.
11: 27 and while *J* was walking
11: 29 *J* replied, "I will ask you one
11: 33 *J* said, "Neither will I tell you
11: 33 they answered *J*, "We don't know
12: 13 and Herodians to *J* to catch him
12: 15 But *J* knew their hypocrisy.
12: 17 Then *J* said to them, "Give
12: 24 married to her?" *J* replied,
12: 28 Noticing that *J* had given them
12: 29 answered *J*, "is this: 'Hear,
12: 34 When *J* saw that he had answered
12: 35 While *J* was teaching
12: 38 *J* said, "Watch out for the teachers
12: 41 *J* sat down opposite the place
12: 43 Calling his disciples to him, *J* said,
13: 2 these great buildings?" replied *J*.
13: 3 As *J* was sitting on the Mount
13: 5 *J* said to them: "Watch out that no
14: 1 looking for some sly way to arrest *J*
14: 6 "Leave her alone," said *J*.
14: 10 priests to betray *J* to them.
14: 16 things just as *J* had told them.
14: 17 *J* arrived with the Twelve.
14: 22 they were eating, *J* took bread,
14: 27 You will all fall away," *J* told them,
14: 30 *J* answered, "today—yes, tonight
14: 32 and *J* said to his disciples,
14: 45 Going at once to *J*, Judas said,
14: 46 The men seized *J* and arrested him.
14: 48 "Am I leading a rebellion," said *J*,
14: 51 a linen garment, was following *J*.
14: 53 They took *J* to the high priest,
14: 55 looking for evidence against *J*
14: 60 up before them and asked *J*,
14: 61 But *J* remained silent and gave no
14: 62 of the Blessed One?" "I am," said *J*
14: 67 also were with that Nazarene, *J*,"
14: 72 the word *J* had spoken
15: 1 They bound *J*, led him away
15: 2 "Yes, it is as you say," *J* replied.
15: 5 But *J* still made no reply,
15: 10 that the chief priests had handed *J*
15: 15 He had *J* flogged, and handed him
15: 16 The soldiers led *J* away
15: 22 They brought *J* to the place called
15: 34 And at the ninth hour *J* cried out
15: 36 and offered it to *J* to drink.
15: 37 With a loud cry, *J* breathed his last.
15: 39 who stood there in front of *J*,
15: 44 he asked him if *J* had already died.
16: 6 You are looking for *J* the Nazarene
16: 9 When *J* rose early on the first day
16: 11 When they heard that *J* was alive
16: 12 Afterward *J* appeared
16: 14 Later *J* appeared to the Eleven
16: 19 After the Lord *J* had spoken
Lk 1: 31 and you are to give him the name *J*.
2: 21 to circumcise him, he was named *J*,
2: 27 in the child *J* to do
2: 43 boy *J* stayed behind in Jerusalem,
2: 52 And *J* grew in wisdom and stature,
3: 21 being baptized, *J* was baptized
3: 23 *J* himself was about thirty years old
4: 1 *J*, full of the Holy Spirit, returned
4: 4 *J* answered, "It is written:
4: 8 *J* answered, "It is written:
4: 12 *J* answered, "It says: 'Do not put
4: 14 *J* returned to Galilee in the power
4: 23 *J* said to them, "Surely you will
4: 34 want with us, *J* of Nazareth?
4: 35 "Be quiet!" *J* said sternly.
4: 38 and they asked *J* to help her.
4: 38 *J* left the synagogue and went
4: 40 to *J* all who had various kinds
4: 42 At daybreak *J* went out
5: 1 as *J* was standing by the Lake
5: 10 *J* said to Simon, "Don't be afraid;
5: 12 When he saw *J*, he fell with his face
5: 12 While *J* was in one of the towns,
5: 13 *J* reached out his hand

Lk 5: 14 *J* ordered him, "Don't tell anyone,
5: 16 *J* often withdrew to lonely places
5: 18 into the house to lay him before *J*.
5: 19 of the crowd, right in front of *J*.
5: 20 When *J* saw their faith, he said,
5: 22 *J* knew what they were thinking
5: 27 *J* went out and saw a tax collector
5: 27 "Follow me," *J* said to him,
5: 29 Levi held a great banquet for *J*
5: 31 and 'sinners'?" *J* answered them,
5: 34 *J* answered, "Can you make
6: 1 One Sabbath *J* was going
6: 3 on the Sabbath?" *J* answered them,
6: 5 Then *J* said to them, "The Son
6: 7 looking for a reason to accuse *J*,
6: 8 *J* knew what they were thinking
6: 9 Then *J* said to them, "I ask you,
6: 11 another what they might do to *J*.
6: 12 One of those days *J* went out
7: 1 When *J* had finished saying all this
7: 3 The centurion heard of *J*
7: 4 came to *J*, they pleaded earnestly
7: 6 So *J* went with them.
7: 9 When *J* heard this, he was amazed
7: 11 *J* went to a town called Nain,
7: 15 and *J* gave him back to his mother.
7: 17 This news about *J* spread
7: 20 When the men came to *J*, they said
7: 21 that very time *J* cured many who
7: 24 *J* began to speak to the crowd
7: 36 Now one of the Pharisees invited *J*
7: 37 that town learned that *J* was eating
7: 40 *J* answered him, "Simon, I have
7: 43 You have judged correctly," *J* said.
7: 48 Then *J* said to her, "Your sins are
7: 50 forgives sins?" *J* said to the woman
8: 1 *J* traveled about from one town
8: 4 people were coming to *J* from town
8: 22 One day *J* said to his disciples,
8: 27 When *J* stepped ashore, he was
8: 28 When he saw *J*, he cried out
8: 28 "What do you want with me, *J*,
8: 29 For *J* had commanded the evil
8: 30 *J* asked him, "What is your name?"
8: 32 The demons begged *J*
8: 35 came to *J*, they found the man
8: 37 region of the Gerasenes asked *J*
8: 38 but *J* sent him away, saying,
8: 39 over town how much *J* had done
8: 40 Now when *J* returned, a crowd
8: 42 As *J* was on his way, the crowds
8: 45 "Who touched me?" *J* asked.
8: 46 But *J* said, "Someone touched me;
8: 49 While *J* was still speaking,
8: 50 Hearing this, *J* said to Jairus,
8: 52 "Stop wailing," *J* said.
8: 55 *J* told them to give her something
9: 1 When *J* had called the Twelve
9: 10 reported to *J* what they had done.
9: 18 Once when *J* was praying
9: 21 *J* strictly warned them not
9: 28 About eight days after *J* said this,
9: 31 in glorious splendor, talking with *J*.
9: 33 As the men were leaving *J*,
9: 36 they found that *J* was alone.
9: 41 perverse generation," *J* replied,
9: 42 But *J* rebuked the evil spirit,
9: 43 was marveling at all that *J* did,
9: 47 *J*, knowing their thoughts,
9: 50 "Do not stop him," *J* said,
9: 51 *J* resolutely set out for Jerusalem,
9: 55 But *J* turned and rebuked them,
9: 58 *J* replied, "Foxes have holes
9: 60 *J* said to him, "Let the dead bury
9: 62 *J* replied, "No one who puts his
10: 21 At that time *J*, full of joy
10: 25 expert in the law stood up to test *J*.
10: 28 answered correctly," *J* replied.
10: 29 so he asked *J*, "And who is my
10: 30 is my neighbor?" In reply *J* said:
10: 37 *J* told him, "Go and do likewise."
10: 38 As *J* and his disciples were
11: 1 One day *J* was praying
11: 14 *J* was driving out a demon that was
11: 17 *J* knew their thoughts
11: 27 As *J* was saying these things,
11: 29 As the crowds increased, *J* said,
11: 37 When *J* had finished speaking,

Lk 11: 38 noticing that *J* did not first wash
11: 46 *J* replied, "And you experts
11: 53 When *J* left there, the Pharisees
12: 1 *J* began to speak first
12: 14 *J* replied, "Man, who appointed
12: 22 Then *J* said to his disciples:
13: 1 time who told *J* about
13: 2 *J* answered, "Do you think that
13: 10 On a Sabbath *J* was teaching in one
13: 12 When *J* saw her, he called her
13: 14 *J* had healed on the Sabbath,
13: 18 *J* asked, "What is the kingdom
13: 22 Then *J* went through the towns
13: 31 that time some Pharisees came to *J*
14: 1 when *J* went to eat in the house
14: 3 *J* asked the Pharisees and experts
14: 12 *J* said to his host, "When you give
14: 15 with him heard this, he said to *J*,
14: 16 *J* replied: "A certain man was
14: 25 Large crowds were traveling with *J*
15: 3 Then *J* told them this parable:
15: 11 *J* continued: "There was a man
16: 1 *J* told his disciples: "There was
16: 14 all this and were sneering at *J*.
17: 1 *J* said to his disciples: "Things that
17: 11 *J* traveled along the border
17: 13 "*J*, Master, have pity on us!"
17: 17 *J* asked, "Were not all ten cleansed
17: 20 *J* replied, "The kingdom
18: 1 Then *J* told his disciples a parable
18: 9 *J* told this parable: "Two men went
18: 15 also bringing babies to *J*
18: 16 But *J* called the children to him
18: 19 do you call me good?" *J* answered.
18: 22 When *J* heard this, he said to him,
18: 24 *J* looked at him and said, "How
18: 27 Who then can be saved?" *J* replied,
18: 29 I tell you the truth," *J* said to them,
18: 31 *J* took the Twelve aside
18: 35 As *J* approached Jericho, a blind
18: 37 "*J* of Nazareth is passing by."
18: 38 He called out, "*J*, Son of David,
18: 40 When he came near, *J* asked him,
18: 40 *J* stopped and ordered the man
18: 42 *J* said to him, "Receive your sight;
18: 43 received his sight and followed *J*,
19: 1 *J* entered Jericho and was passing
19: 3 He wanted to see who *J* was,
19: 4 since *J* was coming that way.
19: 5 When *J* reached the spot, he
19: 9 *J* said to him, "Today salvation has
19: 28 After *J* had said this, he went
19: 35 cloaks on the colt and put *J* on it.
19: 35 it to *J*, threw their cloaks
19: 39 in the crowd said to *J*,
20: 8 *J* said, "Neither will I tell you
20: 17 *J* looked directly at them
20: 20 They hoped to catch *J*
20: 27 came to *J* with a question.
20: 34 married to her?" *J* replied,
20: 41 *J* said to them, "How is it that they
20: 45 all the people were listening, *J* said
21: 1 *J* saw the rich putting their gifts
21: 5 *J* said, "As for what you see here,
21: 37 Each day *J* was teaching
22: 2 for some way to get rid of *J*,
22: 4 with them how he might betray *J*.
22: 6 opportunity to hand *J* over to them
22: 8 *J* sent Peter and John, saying,
22: 13 things just as *J* had told them.
22: 14 *J* and his apostles reclined
22: 25 *J* said to them, "The kings
22: 34 *J* answered, "I tell you, Peter,
22: 35 *J* asked them, "When I sent you
22: 39 *J* went out as usual to the Mount
22: 48 *J* to kiss him, but *J* asked him,
22: 51 But *J* answered, "No more of this
22: 52 Then *J* said to the chief priests,
22: 63 were guarding *J* began mocking
22: 66 and *J* was led before them.
22: 67 *J* answered, "If I tell you, you will
23: 3 Pilate asked *J*, "Are you the king
23: 3 "Yes, it is as you say," *J* replied.
23: 7 When he learned that *J* was
23: 8 When Herod saw *J*, he was greatly
23: 9 but *J* gave him no answer.
23: 20 to release *J*, Pilate appealed
23: 25 and surrendered *J* to their will.

Lk 23: 26 and made him carry it behind *J*.
23: 28 *J* turned and said to them,
23: 34 *J* said, "Father, forgive them,
23: 42 "*J*, remember me when you come
23: 43 *J* answered him, "I tell you
23: 46 *J* called out with a loud voice,
23: 55 come with *J* from Galilee followed
24: 3 did not find the body of the Lord *J*.
24: 15 *J* himself came up and walked
24: 19 About *J* of Nazareth," they replied
24: 28 *J* acted as if he were going farther.
24: 35 and how *J* was recognized by them
24: 36 *J* himself stood among them
Jn 1: 17 and truth came through *J* Christ.
1: 29 The next day John saw *J* coming
1: 36 When he saw *J* passing by, he said,
1: 37 him say this, they followed *J*.
1: 38 *J* saw them following and asked,
1: 40 had said and who had followed *J*.
1: 42 Then he brought Simon to *J*,
1: 43 The next day *J* decided to leave
1: 45 *J* of Nazareth, the son of Joseph."
1: 47 When *J* saw Nathanael
1: 48 *J* answered, "I saw you
1: 50 *J* said, "You believe because I told
2: 4 why do you involve me?" *J* replied,
2: 7 *J* said to the servants, "Fill the jars
2: 11 *J* performed in Cana of Galilee.
2: 13 for the Jewish Passover, *J* went up
2: 19 *J* answered them, "Destroy this
2: 22 and the words that *J* had spoken.
2: 24 But *J* would not entrust himself
3: 2 He came to *J* at night and said,
3: 3 In reply *J* declared, "I tell you
3: 5 *J* answered, "I tell you the truth,
3: 10 "You are Israel's teacher," said *J*,
3: 22 *J* and his disciples went out
4: 1 Pharisees heard that *J* was gaining
4: 2 in fact it was not *J* who baptized,
4: 6 Jacob's well was there, and *J*,
4: 7 came to draw water, *J* said to her,
4: 10 *J* answered her, "If you knew
4: 13 his flocks and herds?" *J* answered,
4: 17 *J* said to her, "You are right
4: 21 *J* declared, "Believe me, woman,
4: 26 Then *J* declared, "I who speak
4: 34 him food?" "My food," said *J*,
4: 44 *J* himself had pointed out that
4: 47 this man heard that *J* had arrived
4: 48 *J* told him, "you will never believe
4: 50 The man took *J* at his word
4: 50 *J* replied, "You may go.
4: 53 time at which *J* had said to him,
4: 54 miraculous sign that *J* performed,
5: 1 *J* went up to Jerusalem for a feast
5: 6 When *J* saw him lying there
5: 8 Then *J* said to him, "Get up!
5: 13 for *J* had slipped away
5: 14 Later *J* found him at the temple
5: 15 Jews that it was *J* who had made
5: 16 because *J* was doing these things
5: 17 *J* said to them, "My Father is
5: 19 *J* gave them this answer: "I tell you
6: 1 *J* crossed to the far shore of the Sea
6: 3 Then *J* went up on the hillside
6: 5 When *J* looked up and saw a great
6: 10 *J* said, "Have the people sit down."
6: 11 *J* then took the loaves, gave thanks
6: 14 saw the miraculous sign that *J* did,
6: 15 *J*, knowing that they intended
6: 17 and *J* had not yet joined them.
6: 19 they saw *J* approaching the boat,
6: 22 and that *J* had not entered it
6: 24 the crowd realized that neither *J*
6: 24 went to Capernaum in search of *J*.
6: 26 did you get here?" *J* answered,
6: 29 *J* answered, "The work
6: 32 *J* said to them, "I tell you the truth,
6: 35 *J* declared, "I am the bread of life.
6: 42 "Is this not *J*, the son of Joseph,
6: 43 among yourselves," *J* answered.
6: 53 *J* said to them, "I tell you the truth,
6: 61 *J* said to them, "Does this offend
6: 64 *J* had known from the beginning
6: 67 do you?" *J* asked the Twelve.
6: 70 *J* replied, "Have I not chosen you,
7: 1 After this, *J* went around in Galilee
7: 6 Therefore *J* told them, "The right

Jn 7: 14 through the Feast did *J* go up
7: 16 *J* answered, "My teaching is not
7: 21 trying to kill you?" *J* said to them,
7: 28 Then *J*, still teaching in the temple
7: 33 *J* said, "I am with you
7: 37 *J* stood and said in a loud voice,
7: 39 since *J* had not yet been glorified.
7: 43 people were divided because of *J*.
7: 50 who had gone to *J* earlier
8: 1 But *J* went to the Mount of Olives.
8: 4 before the group and said to *J*,
8: 6 *J* bent down and started to write
8: 9 until only *J* was left,
8: 10 *J* straightened up and asked her,
8: 11 do I condemn you," *J* declared.
8: 12 When *J* spoke again to the people,
8: 14 *J* answered, "Even if I testify
8: 19 or my Father," *J* replied.
8: 21 Once more *J* said to them,
8: 25 been claiming all along," *J* replied.
8: 28 *J* said, "When you have lifted up
8: 31 Jews who had believed him, *J* said,
8: 34 *J* replied, "I tell you the truth,
8: 39 were Abraham's children," said *J*,
8: 42 *J* said to them, "If God were your
8: 49 possessed by a demon," said *J*,
8: 54 *J* replied, "If I glorify myself,
8: 58 "I tell you the truth," *J* answered,
8: 59 to stone him, but *J* hid himself,
9: 3 nor his parents sinned," said *J*,
9: 11 man they call *J* made some mud
9: 14 day on which *J* had made the mud
9: 22 who acknowledged that *J* was
9: 35 *J* heard that they had thrown him
9: 37 *J* said, "You have now seen him;
9: 39 *J* said, "For judgment I have come
9: 41 "What? Are we blind too?" *J* said,
10: 6 *J* used this figure of speech,
10: 7 Therefore *J* said again, "I tell you
10: 23 *J* was in the temple area walking
10: 25 *J* answered, "I did tell you,
10: 32 to stone him, but *J* said to them,
10: 34 *J* answered them, "Is it not written
10: 40 *J* went back across the Jordan
10: 42 in that place many believed in *J*.
11: 3 So the sisters sent word to *J*, "Lord
11: 4 When he heard this, *J* said,
11: 5 *J* loved Martha and her sister
11: 9 are going back there?" *J* answered,
11: 13 *J* had been speaking of his death,
11: 17 *J* found that Lazarus had already
11: 20 Martha heard that *J* was coming,
11: 21 "Lord," Martha said to *J*,
11: 23 *J* said to her, "Your brother will
11: 25 *J* said to her, "I am
11: 30 *J* had not yet entered the village,
11: 32 reached the place where *J* was
11: 33 When *J* saw her weeping,
11: 35 *J* wept.
11: 38 *J*, once more deeply moved,
11: 40 *J* said, "Did I not tell you that
11: 41 Then *J* looked up and said, "Father
11: 43 When he had said this, *J* called
11: 44 *J* said to them, "Take
11: 45 had seen what *J* did, put their faith
11: 46 and told them what *J* had done.
11: 51 he prophesied that *J* would die
11: 54 Therefore *J* no longer moved about
11: 56 They kept looking for *J*, and
11: 57 if anyone found out where *J* was,
12: 1 days before the Passover, *J* arrived
12: 1 whom *J* had raised from the dead.
12: 7 "Leave her alone," *J* replied.
12: 9 of Jews found out that *J* was there
12: 11 of the Jews were going over to *J*
12: 12 come for the Feast heard that *J* was
12: 14 *J* found a young donkey
12: 16 Only after *J* was glorified did they
12: 21 they said, "we would like to see *J*."
12: 22 Andrew and Philip in turn told *J*.
12: 23 *J* replied, "The hour has come
12: 30 *J* said, "This voice was
12: 35 'Son of Man'?" Then *J* told them,
12: 36 *J* left and hid himself from them.
12: 37 Even after *J* had done all these
12: 44 *J* cried out, "When a man believes
13: 1 *J* knew that the time had come
13: 2 son of Simon, to betray *J*.

Jn 13: 3 *J* knew that the Father had put all
13: 7 going to wash my feet?'' *J* replied,
13: 8 *J* answered, ''Unless I wash you,
13: 10 and my head as well!'' *J* answered,
13: 21 *J* was troubled in spirit
13: 23 the disciple whom *J* loved,
13: 25 back against *J*, he asked him,
13: 26 ''Lord, who is it?'' *J* answered,
13: 27 to do, do quickly,'' *J* told him,
13: 28 meal understood why *J* said this
13: 29 some thought *J* was telling him
13: 31 When he was gone, *J* said,
13: 36 where are you going?'' *J* replied,
13: 38 *J* answered, ''Will you really lay
14: 6 we know the way?'' *J* answered,
14: 9 *J* answered: ''Don't you know me,
14: 23 *J* replied, ''If anyone loves me,
16: 19 *J* saw that they wanted
16: 31 ''You believe at last!'' *J* answered.
17: 1 After *J* said this, he looked
17: 3 the only true God, and *J* Christ,
18: 1 *J* left with his disciples
18: 2 because *J* had often met there
18: 4 *J*, knowing all that was going
18: 5 ''I am he,'' *J* said.
18: 5 ''*J* of Nazareth,'' they replied.
18: 6 When *J* said, ''I am he,'' they drew
18: 7 And they said, ''*J* of Nazareth.''
18: 8 told you that I am he,'' *J* answered.
18: 11 *J* commanded Peter, ''Put your
18: 12 and the Jewish officials arrested *J*.
18: 15 another disciple were following *J*.
18: 15 went with *J* into the high priest's
18: 19 high priest questioned *J* about his
18: 20 openly to the world,'' *J* replied.
18: 22 When *J* said this, one
18: 23 I said something wrong,'' *J* replied,
18: 28 Then the Jews led *J* from Caiaphas
18: 32 that the words *J* had spoken
18: 33 summoned *J* and asked him,
18: 34 ''Is that your own idea,'' *J* asked,
18: 36 What is it you have done?'' *J* said,
18: 37 *J* answered, ''You are right
19: 1 Pilate took *J* and had him flogged.
19: 5 When *J* came out wearing
19: 9 he asked *J*, but *J* gave him no
19: 11 or to crucify you?'' *J* answered,
19: 12 Pilate tried to set *J* free,
19: 13 he brought *J* out and sat
19: 16 So the soldiers took charge of *J*.
19: 18 on each side and *J* in the middle.
19: 19 It read, *J* OF NAZARETH,
19: 20 the place where *J* was crucified
19: 23 When the soldiers crucified *J*,
19: 25 the cross of *J* stood his mother,
19: 26 When *J* saw his mother there,
19: 28 Scripture would be fulfilled, *J* said,
19: 30 he had received the drink, *J* said,
19: 32 who had been crucified with *J*,
19: 33 But when they came to *J*
19: 38 Now Joseph was a disciple of *J*,
19: 38 asked Pilate for the body of *J*.
19: 39 the man who earlier had visited *J*
19: 41 At the place where *J* was crucified,
19: 42 was nearby, they laid *J* there.
20: 2 one *J* loved, and said, ''They have
20: 9 from Scripture that *J* had to rise
20: 14 around and saw *J* standing there,
20: 14 but she did not realize that it was *J*.
20: 16 *J* said to her, ''Mary.''
20: 17 *J* said, ''Do not hold on to me,
20: 19 *J* came and stood among them
20: 21 Again *J* said, ''Peace be with you!
20: 24 with the disciples when *J* came.
20: 26 *J* came and stood among them
20: 29 and my God!'' Then *J* told him,
20: 30 *J* did many other miraculous signs
20: 31 may believe that *J* is the Christ,
21: 1 Afterward *J* appeared again
21: 4 Early in the morning, *J* stood
21: 4 did not realize that it was *J*.
21: 7 the disciple whom *J* loved said
21: 10 *J* said to them, ''Bring some
21: 12 *J* said to them, ''Come
21: 13 *J* came, took the bread
21: 14 was now the third time *J* appeared
21: 15 *J* said, ''Feed my lambs.''
21: 15 they had finished eating, *J* said

Jn 21: 16 Again *J* said, ''Simon son of John,
21: 16 *J* said, ''Take care of my sheep.''
21: 17 because *J* asked him the third time,
21: 17 *J* said, ''Feed my sheep.
21: 19 *J* said this to indicate the kind
21: 20 back against *J* at the supper
21: 20 the disciple whom *J* loved was
21: 22 what about him?'' *J* answered,
21: 23 *J* did not say that he would not die;
21: 25 *J* did many other things as well.
Ac 1: 1 I wrote about all that *J* began to do
1: 11 This same *J*, who has been taken
1: 14 and Mary the mother of *J*,
1: 16 as guide for those who arrested *J*—
1: 21 us the whole time the Lord *J* went
1: 22 to the time when *J* was taken up
2: 22 *J* of Nazareth was a man
2: 32 God has raised this *J* to life,
2: 36 has made this *J*, whom you
2: 38 in the name of *J* Christ
3: 6 the name of *J* Christ of Nazareth,
3: 13 has glorified his servant *J*.
3: 16 name of *J*, this man whom you see
3: 20 been appointed for you—even *J*.
4: 2 proclaiming in *J* the resurrection
4: 10 the name of *J* Christ of Nazareth,
4: 13 that these men had been with *J*.
4: 18 or teach at all in the name of *J*.
4: 27 against your holy servant *J*,
4: 30 the name of your holy servant *J*.''
4: 33 to the resurrection of the Lord *J*,
5: 30 The God of our fathers raised *J*
5: 40 not to speak in the name of *J*,
5: 42 the good news that *J* is the Christ.
6: 14 we have heard him say that this *J*
7: 55 *J* standing at the right hand of God
7: 59 ''Lord *J*, receive my spirit.''
8: 12 of God and the name of *J* Christ,
8: 16 into the name of the Lord *J*.
8: 35 told him the good news about *J*.
9: 5 ''I am *J*, whom you are persecuting
9: 17 ''Brother Saul, the Lord—*J*,
9: 20 in the synagogues that *J* is the Son
9: 22 by proving that *J* is the Christ.
9: 27 fearlessly in the name of *J*.
9: 34 said to him, ''*J* Christ heals you.
10: 36 news of peace through *J* Christ,
10: 38 how God anointed *J* of Nazareth
10: 48 baptized in the name of *J* Christ.
11: 17 who believed in the Lord *J* Christ,
11: 20 the good news about the Lord *J*.
13: 23 brought to Israel the Savior *J*,
13: 24 of *J*, John preached repentance
13: 27 their rulers did not recognize *J*,
13: 33 their children, by raising up *J*.
13: 38 that through *J* the forgiveness
15: 11 of our Lord *J* that we are saved,
15: 26 for the name of our Lord *J* Christ.
16: 7 Spirit of *J* would not allow them
16: 18 name of *J* Christ I command you
16: 31 ''Believe in the Lord *J*,
17: 3 ''This *J* I am proclaiming
17: 7 is another king, one called *J*.''
17: 18 preaching the good news about *J*
18: 5 to the Jews that *J* was the Christ.
18: 25 and taught about *J* accurately,
18: 28 the Scriptures that *J* was
19: 4 coming after him, that is, in *J*.''
19: 5 into the name of the Lord *J*.
19: 13 name of *J*, whom Paul preaches,
19: 13 of the Lord *J* over those who were
19: 15 ''*J* I know and Paul I know about,
19: 17 the name of the Lord *J* was held
20: 21 and have faith in our Lord *J*.
20: 24 the task the Lord *J* has given me—
20: 35 the words the Lord *J* himself said:
21: 13 for the name of the Lord *J*.''
22: 8 '' 'I am *J* of Nazareth, whom you
24: 24 as he spoke about faith in Christ *J*.
25: 19 a dead man named *J* who Paul
26: 9 possible to oppose the name of *J*
26: 15 I am *J*, whom you are persecuting,'
28: 23 and tried to convince them about *J*
28: 31 and taught about the Lord *J* Christ.
Ro 1: 1 Paul, a servant of Christ *J*,
1: 4 from the dead: *J* Christ our Lord.
1: 6 called to belong to *J* Christ.
1: 7 and from the Lord *J* Christ.

Ro 1: 8 God through *J* Christ for all
2: 16 men's secrets through *J* Christ,
3: 22 comes through faith in *J* Christ
3: 24 redemption that came by Christ *J*.
3: 26 justifies the man who has faith in *J*.
4: 24 in him who raised *J* our Lord
5: 1 God through our Lord *J* Christ,
5: 11 in God through our Lord *J* Christ,
5: 15 *J* Christ, overflow to the many!
5: 17 life through the one man, *J* Christ.
5: 21 life through *J* Christ our Lord.
6: 3 into Christ *J* were baptized
6: 11 but alive to God in Christ *J*.
6: 23 life in Christ *J* our Lord.
7: 25 through *J* Christ our Lord!
8: 1 for those who are in Christ *J*,
8: 2 because through Christ *J* the law
8: 11 the Spirit of him who raised *J*
8: 34 Christ *J*, who died—more
8: 39 of God that is in Christ *J* our Lord.
10: 9 with your mouth, ''*J* is Lord,''
13: 14 yourselves with the Lord *J* Christ,
14: 14 As one who is in the Lord *J*,
15: 5 yourselves as you follow Christ *J*,
15: 6 and Father of our Lord *J* Christ.
15: 16 minister of Christ *J* to the Gentiles
15: 17 glory in Christ *J* in my service
15: 30 by our Lord *J* Christ
16: 3 my fellow workers in Christ *J*.
16: 20 grace of our Lord *J* be with you.
16: 25 and the proclamation of *J* Christ,
16: 27 be glory forever through *J* Christ!
1Co 1: 1 of Christ *J* by the will of God,
1: 2 on the name of our Lord *J* Christ—
1: 2 to those sanctified in Christ *J*
1: 3 our Father and the Lord *J* Christ.
1: 4 of his grace given you in Christ *J*.
1: 7 for our Lord *J* Christ to be revealed
1: 8 on the day of our Lord *J* Christ.
1: 9 with his Son *J* Christ our Lord,
1: 10 in the name of our Lord *J* Christ,
1: 30 of him that you are in Christ *J*,
2: 2 except *J* Christ and him crucified.
3: 11 one already laid, which is *J* Christ.
4: 15 for in Christ *J* I became your father
4: 17 you of my way of life in Christ *J*,
5: 4 in the name of our Lord *J*
5: 4 the power of our Lord *J* is present,
6: 11 in the name of the Lord *J* Christ
8: 6 and there is but one Lord, *J* Christ,
9: 1 Have I not seen *J* our Lord?
11: 23 The Lord *J*, on the night he was
12: 3 and no one can say, ''*J* is Lord,''
12: 3 ''*J* be cursed,'' and no one can say,
15: 31 over you in Christ *J* our Lord.
15: 57 victory through our Lord *J* Christ.
16: 23 grace of the Lord *J* be with you.
16: 24 My love to all of you in Christ *J*.
2Co 1: 1 an apostle of Christ *J* by the will
1: 2 our Father and the Lord *J* Christ.
1: 3 and Father of our Lord *J* Christ,
1: 14 of you in the day of the Lord *J*.
1: 19 For the Son of God, *J* Christ,
4: 5 not preach ourselves, but *J* Christ
4: 10 around in our body the death of *J*,
4: 10 so that the life of *J* may
4: 14 also raise us with *J* and present us
4: 14 that the one who raised the Lord *J*
8: 9 the grace of our Lord *J* Christ,
11: 4 and preaches a *J* other
11: 4 other than the *J* we preached,
11: 31 The God and Father of the Lord *J*,
13: 5 Do you not realize that Christ *J* is
13: 14 May the grace of the Lord *J* Christ,
Gal 1: 1 but by *J* Christ and God the Father
1: 3 our Father and the Lord *J* Christ,
1: 12 it by revelation from *J* Christ.
2: 4 on the freedom we have in Christ *J*
2: 16 but by faith in *J* Christ.
2: 16 in Christ *J* that we may be justified
3: 1 your very eyes *J* Christ was clearly
3: 14 to the Gentiles through Christ *J*,
3: 22 given through faith in *J* Christ,
3: 26 of God through faith in Christ *J*,
3: 28 for you are all one in Christ *J*.
4: 14 as if I were Christ *J* himself.
5: 6 in Christ *J* neither circumcision
5: 24 to Christ *J* have crucified the sinful

Gal 6: 14 in the cross of our Lord *J* Christ,
6: 17 bear on my body the marks of *J*.
6: 18 The grace of our Lord *J* Christ be
Eph 1: 1 an apostle of Christ *J* by the will
1: 1 in Ephesus, the faithful in Christ *J*:
1: 2 our Father and the Lord *J* Christ.
1: 3 and Father of our Lord *J* Christ,
1: 5 as his sons through *J* Christ,
1: 15 about your faith in the Lord *J*
1: 17 the God of our Lord *J* Christ,
2: 6 in the heavenly realms in Christ *J*,
2: 7 in his kindness to us in Christ *J*.
2: 10 created in Christ *J*
2: 13 in Christ *J* you who once were far
2: 20 with Christ *J* himself as the chief
3: 1 the prisoner of Christ *J* for the sake
3: 6 together in the promise in Christ *J*.
3: 11 accomplished in Christ *J* our Lord.
3: 21 *J* throughout all generations,
4: 21 with the truth that is in *J*.
5: 20 in the name of our Lord *J* Christ.
6: 23 the Father and the Lord *J* Christ.
6: 24 to all who love our Lord *J* Christ
Php 1: 1 and Timothy, servants of Christ *J*,
1: 1 the saints in Christ *J* at Philippi,
1: 2 our Father and the Lord *J* Christ.
1: 6 until the day of Christ *J*.
1: 8 you with the affection of Christ *J*.
1: 11 comes through *J* Christ—
1: 19 given by the Spirit of *J* Christ,
1: 26 joy in Christ *J* will overflow
2: 5 be the same as that of Christ *J*:
2: 10 name of *J* every knee should bow,
2: 11 tongue confess that *J* Christ is
2: 19 in the Lord *J* to send Timothy
2: 21 interests, not those of *J* Christ.
3: 3 glory in Christ *J*, and who put no
3: 8 of knowing Christ *J* my Lord,
3: 12 for which Christ *J* took hold of me.
3: 14 called me heavenward in Christ *J*.
3: 20 from there, the Lord *J* Christ,
4: 7 and your minds in Christ *J*.
4: 19 to his glorious riches in Christ *J*.
4: 21 Greet all the saints in Christ *J*.
4: 23 The grace of the Lord *J* Christ be
Col 1: 1 an apostle of Christ *J* by the will
1: 3 the Father of our Lord *J* Christ,
1: 4 heard of your faith in Christ *J*
2: 6 as you received Christ *J* as Lord,
3: 17 do it all in the name of the Lord *J*,
4: 11 *J*, who is called Justus,
4: 12 of you and a servant of Christ *J*,
1Th 1: 1 the Father and the Lord *J* Christ:
1: 3 by hope in our Lord *J* Christ.
1: 10 whom he raised from the dead—*J*,
2: 14 in Judea, which are in Christ *J*:
2: 15 killed the Lord *J* and the prophets
2: 19 of our Lord *J* when he comes?
3: 11 and our Lord *J* clear the way for us
3: 13 and Father when our Lord *J* comes
4: 1 you in the Lord *J* to do this more
4: 2 you by the authority of the Lord *J*.
4: 14 We believe that *J* died
4: 14 with *J* those who have fallen asleep
5: 9 through our Lord *J* Christ.
5: 18 will for you in Christ *J*.
5: 23 at the coming of our Lord *J* Christ.
5: 28 of our Lord *J* Christ be with you.
2Th 1: 1 our Father and the Lord *J* Christ:
1: 2 the Father and the Lord *J* Christ.
1: 7 when the Lord *J* is revealed
1: 8 not obey the gospel of our Lord *J*.
1: 12 of our God and the Lord *J* Christ.
1: 12 of our Lord *J* may be glorified
2: 1 the coming of our Lord *J* Christ
2: 8 whom the Lord *J* will overthrow
2: 14 in the glory of our Lord *J* Christ.
2: 16 May our Lord *J* Christ himself
3: 6 In the name of the Lord *J* Christ,
3: 12 urge in the Lord *J* Christ to settle
3: 18 The grace of our Lord *J* Christ be
1Ti 1: 1 and of Christ *J* our hope,
1: 1 of Christ *J* by the command
1: 2 the Father and Christ *J* our Lord.
1: 12 I thank Christ *J* our Lord,
1: 14 and love that are in Christ *J*.
1: 15 Christ *J* came into the world
1: 16 Christ *J* might display his
1Ti 2: 5 the man Christ *J*, who gave himself
3: 13 assurance in their faith in Christ *J*.
4: 6 will be a good minister of Christ *J*,
5: 21 and Christ *J* and the elect angels
6: 3 instruction of our Lord *J* Christ
6: 13 life to everything, and of Christ *J*,
6: 14 the appearing of our Lord *J* Christ,
2Ti 1: 1 an apostle of Christ *J* by the will
1: 1 promise of life that is in Christ *J*,
1: 2 the Father and Christ *J* our Lord.
1: 9 us in Christ *J* before the beginning
1: 10 appearing of our Savior, Christ *J*,
1: 13 with faith and love in Christ *J*.
2: 1 in the grace that is in Christ *J*.
2: 3 us like a good soldier of Christ *J*.
2: 8 Remember *J* Christ, raised
2: 10 the salvation that is in Christ *J*,
3: 12 life in Christ *J* will be persecuted,
3: 15 salvation through faith in Christ *J*.
4: 1 presence of God and of Christ *J*,
Tit 1: 1 an apostle of *J* Christ for the faith
1: 4 the Father and Christ *J* our Savior.
2: 13 our great God and Savior, *J* Christ,
3: 6 through *J* Christ our Savior,
Phm : 1 of Christ *J*, and Timothy our
: 3 our Father and the Lord *J* Christ.
: 5 hear about your faith in the Lord *J*
: 9 now also a prisoner of Christ *J*—
: 23 my fellow prisoner for Christ *J*,
: 25 The grace of the Lord *J* Christ be
Heb 2: 9 But we see *J*, who was made a little
2: 11 So *J* is not ashamed to call them
3: 1 fix your thoughts on *J*, the apostle
3: 3 *J* has been found worthy
4: 14 through the heavens, *J* the Son
6: 20 where *J*, who went before us,
7: 22 *J* has become the guarantee
7: 24 but because *J* lives forever,
8: 6 But the ministry *J* has received is
10: 10 of the body of *J* Christ once for all.
10: 19 Most Holy Place by the blood of *J*,
12: 2 Let us fix our eyes on *J*, the author
12: 24 to *J* the mediator of a new
13: 8 *J* Christ is the same yesterday
13: 12 so *J* also suffered outside the city
13: 15 Through *J*, therefore, let us
13: 20 back from the dead our Lord *J*,
13: 21 through *J* Christ, to whom be glory
Jas 1: 1 of God and of the Lord *J* Christ,
2: 1 in our glorious Lord *J* Christ,
1Pe 1: 1 Peter, an apostle of *J* Christ,
1: 2 for obedience to *J* Christ
1: 3 and Father of our Lord *J* Christ!
1: 3 the resurrection of *J* Christ
1: 7 honor when *J* Christ is revealed.
1: 13 you when *J* Christ is revealed.
2: 5 to God through *J* Christ.
3: 21 you by the resurrection of *J* Christ,
4: 11 may be praised through *J* Christ.
2Pe 1: 1 a servant and apostle of *J* Christ,
1: 1 and Savior *J* Christ have received
1: 2 of God and of *J* our Lord.
1: 8 knowledge of our Lord *J* Christ.
1: 11 of our Lord and Savior *J* Christ.
1: 14 as our Lord *J* Christ has made clear
1: 16 and coming of our Lord *J* Christ,
2: 20 and Savior *J* Christ and are again
3: 18 of our Lord and Savior *J* Christ.
1Jn 1: 3 and with his Son, *J* Christ.
1: 7 and the blood of *J*, his Son,
2: 1 *J* Christ, the Righteous One.
2: 6 to live in him must walk as *J* did.
2: 22 who denies that *J* is the Christ.
3: 16 *J* Christ laid down his life for us.
3: 23 in the name of his Son, *J* Christ,
4: 2 acknowledges that *J* Christ has
4: 3 that does not acknowledge *J* is not
4: 15 anyone acknowledges that *J* is
5: 1 who believes that *J* is the Christ
5: 5 he who believes that *J* is the Son
5: 6 by water and blood—*J* Christ.
5: 20 even in his Son *J* Christ.
2Jn : 3 God the Father and from *J* Christ,
: 7 who do not acknowledge *J* Christ
Jude : 1 a servant of *J* Christ and a brother
: 1 the Father and kept by *J* Christ:
: 4 deny *J* Christ our only Sovereign
: 17 of our Lord *J* Christ foretold.
Jude : 21 of our Lord *J* Christ to bring you
: 25 through *J* Christ our Lord,
Rev 1: 1 The revelation of *J* Christ,
1: 2 and the testimony of *J* Christ.
1: 5 from *J* Christ, who is the faithful
1: 9 of God and the testimony of *J*.
1: 9 patient endurance that are ours in *J*
12: 17 and hold to the testimony of *J*.
14: 12 and remain faithful to *J*.
17: 6 of those who bore testimony to *J*.
19: 10 For the testimony of *J* is the spirit
19: 10 hold to the testimony of *J*.
20: 4 of their testimony for *J* and
22: 16 *J*, have sent my angel
22: 20 Come, Lord *J*.
22: 21 of the Lord *J* be with God's people.

JESUS’ (JESUS)

Mt 21: 45 the Pharisees heard *J’* parables,
26: 51 one of *J’* companions reached
27: 53 and after *J’* resurrection they went
27: 58 to Pilate, he asked for *J’* body,
Mk 3: 31 *J’* mother and brothers arrived.
6: 14 for *J’* name had become well
14: 12 Passover lamb, *J’* disciples asked
15: 43 to Pilate and asked for *J’* body.
16: 1 they might go to anoint *J’* body.
Lk 5: 8 he fell at *J’* knees and said,
7: 29 when they heard *J’* words,
8: 19 Now *J’* mother and brothers came
8: 35 sitting at *J’* feet, dressed
8: 41 synagogue, came and fell at *J’* feet,
17: 16 He threw himself at *J’* feet
22: 49 When *J’* followers saw what was
23: 52 to Pilate, he asked for *J’* body.
Jn 2: 1 *J’* mother was there, and *J*
2: 3 the wine was gone, *J’* mother said
7: 3 was near, *J’* brothers said
12: 2 Here a dinner was given in *J’* honor
12: 3 she poured it on *J’* feet
12: 41 he saw *J’* glory and spoke about
16: 29 Then *J’* disciples said,
19: 29 hyssop plant, and lifted it to *J’* lips.
19: 34 one of the soldiers pierced *J’* side
19: 40 Taking *J’* body, the two
20: 7 cloth that had been around *J’* head.
20: 12 seated where *J’* body had been,
Ac 3: 16 It is *J’* name and the faith that
2Co 4: 5 as your servants for *J’* sake.
4: 11 given over to death for *J’* sake,
Heb 5: 7 During the days of *J’* life on earth,

JETHER

Jdg 8: 20 But *J* did not draw his sword,
8: 20 Turning to *J*, his oldest son, he said
2Sa 17: 25 the son of a man named *J*,
1Ki 2: 5 son of Ner and Amasa son of *J*.
2: 32 and Amasa son of *J*, commander
1Ch 2: 17 whose father was *J* the Ishmaelite.
2: 32 Shammai's brother: *J*
2: 32 *J* died without children.
4: 17 The sons of Ezrah: *J*, Mered,
7: 38 The sons of *J*: Jephunneh,

JETHETH

Ge 36: 40 Timna, Alvah, *J*, Oholibamah,
1Ch 1: 51 Timna, Alvah, *J*, Oholibamah,

JETHRO

Ex 3: 1 the flock of *J* his father-in-law,
4: 18 back to *J* his father-in-law
4: 18 *J* said, "Go, and I wish you well."
18: 1 Now *J*, the priest of Midian
18: 2 his father-in-law *J* received her
18: 5 *J*, Moses' father-in-law, together
18: 6 *J* had sent word to him, "I,
18: 6 to him, "I, your father-in-law *J*,
18: 9 *J* was delighted to hear about all
18: 12 Then *J*, Moses' father-in-law,

JETUR

Ge 25: 15 Tema, *J*, Naphish and Kedemah.
1Ch 1: 31 Tema, *J*, Naphish and Kedemah.
5: 19 war against the Hagrites, *J*,

JEUEL

1Ch 9: 6 Of the Zerahites: *J*.
Ezr 8: 13 whose names were Eliphelet, *J*

JEUSH

Ge 36: 5 and Oholibamah bore *J*, Jalam
36: 14 whom she bore to Esau: *J*,
36: 18 Chiefs *J*, Jalam and Korah.
1Ch 1: 35 Eliphaz, Reuel, *J*, Jalam and Korah
7: 10 *J*, Benjamin, Ehud, Kenaanah,
8: 39 *J* the second son and Eliphelet
23: 10 Jahath, Ziza, *J* and Beriah.
23: 11 *J* and Beriah did not have many
2Ch 11: 19 *J*, Shemariah and Zaham.

JEUZ

1Ch 8: 10 Zibia, Mesha, Malcam, *J*,

JEW (JEWESS JEWISH JEWS JEWS' JUDAISM)

Est 2: 5 of Susa a *J* of the tribe of Benjamin,
3: 4 for he had told them he was a *J*.
5: 13 as I see that *J* Mordecai sitting
6: 10 suggested for Mordecai the *J*,
8: 7 and to Mordecai the *J*,
9: 29 along with Mordecai the *J*,
9: 31 Mordecai the *J* and Queen Esther
10: 3 Mordecai the *J* was second in rank
Jer 34: 9 was to hold a fellow *J* in bondage.
Zec 8: 23 of one *J* by the edge of his robe
Jn 3: 25 and a certain *J* over the matter
4: 9 "You are a *J* and I am a Samaritan
18: 35 you think I am a *J*?" Pilate replied.
Ac 10: 28 against our law for a *J* to associate
18: 2 There he met a *J* named Aquila,
18: 24 Meanwhile a *J* named Apollos,
19: 34 But when they realized he was a *J*,
21: 39 "I am a *J*, from Tarsus in Cilicia,
22: 3 "I am a *J*, born in Tarsus of Cilicia,
Ro 1: 16 first for the *J*, then for the Gentile.
2: 9 first for the *J*, then for the Gentile;
2: 10 first for the *J*, then for the Gentile.
2: 17 Now you, if you call yourself a *J*;
2: 28 A man is not a *J* if he is only one
2: 29 a man is a *J* if he is one inwardly;
3: 1 in being a *J*, or what value is there
10: 12 there is no difference between *J*
1Co 9: 20 To the Jews I became like a *J*,
Gal 2: 14 live like a Gentile and not like a *J*.
2: 14 "You are a *J*, yet you live like
3: 28 There is neither *J* nor Greek,
Col 3: 11 Here there is no Greek or *J*,

JEWEL (JEWELRY JEWELS)

Pr 20: 15 that speak knowledge are a rare *j*.
SS 4: 9 with one *j* of your necklace.
Isa 13: 19 Babylon, the *j* of kingdoms,
Rev 21: 11 that of a very precious *j*,

JEWELRY (JEWEL)

Ge 24: 53 and silver *j* and articles of clothing
Ex 32: 24 Whoever has any gold *j*, take it off.'
35: 22 and brought gold *j* of all kinds:
Jer 2: 32 Does a maiden forget her *j*,
Eze 7: 20 proud of their beautiful *j*
16: 11 you with *j*: I put bracelets
16: 17 You also took the fine *j* I gave you,
16: 17 the *j* made of my gold and silver,
16: 39 and take your fine *j* and leave you
23: 26 of your clothes and take your fine *j*.
23: 40 painted your eyes and put on your *j*
Hos 2: 13 she decked herself with rings and *j*,
1Pe 3: 3 wearing of gold *j* and fine clothes.

JEWELS (JEWEL)

Job 28: 17 nor can it be had for *j* of gold.
SS 1: 10 your neck with strings of *j*.
5: 12 mounted like *j*.
7: 1 Your graceful legs are like *j*,
Isa 54: 12 your gates of sparkling *j*,
61: 10 as a bride adorns herself with her *j*.
Jer 4: 30 and put on *j* of gold?
Eze 16: 7 and became the most beautiful of *j*.
Zec 9: 16 like *j* in a crown.

JEWESS (JEW)

Ac 16: 1 whose mother was a *J*
24: 24 with his wife Drusilla, who was a *J*.

JEWISH (JEW)

Ezr 6: 7 and the *J* elders rebuild this house
Ne 1: 2 them about the *J* remnant that
5: 1 outcry against their *J* brothers.
5: 8 bought back our *J* brothers who
Est 6: 13 is of *J* origin, you cannot stand
Jn 2: 13 time for the *J* Passover,
3: 1 a member of the *J* ruling council.
6: 4 The *J* Passover Feast was near.
7: 2 the *J* Feast of Tabernacles was
11: 51 Jesus would die for the *J* nation,
11: 55 time for the *J* Passover,
18: 12 and the *J* officials arrested Jesus.
19: 40 accordance with *J* burial customs.
19: 42 Because it was the *J* day
Ac 10: 22 who is respected by all the *J* people
12: 11 from everything the *J* people were
13: 5 word of God in the *J* synagogues.
13: 6 There they met a *J* sorcerer
14: 1 as usual into the *J* synagogue.
17: 1 where there was a *J* synagogue.
17: 10 they went to the *J* synagogue.
19: 14 sons of Sceva, a *J* chief priest,
25: 2 and *J* leaders appeared before him
25: 24 whole *J* community has petitioned
26: 3 acquainted with all the *J* customs
Gal 2: 14 Gentiles to follow *J* customs?
Tit 1: 14 will pay no attention to *J* myths

JEWS (JEW)

Ezr 4: 12 know that the *J* who came up
4: 23 immediately to the *J* in Jerusalem
5: 1 prophesied to the *J* in Judah
5: 5 watching over the elders of the *J*,
6: 7 Let the governor of the *J*
6: 8 elders of the *J* in the construction
6: 14 elders of the *J* continued to build
7: 18 and your brother *J* may then do
Ne 2: 16 as yet I had said nothing to the *J*
4: 1 He ridiculed the *J*,
4: 2 "What are those feeble *J* doing?
4: 12 the *J* who lived near them came
5: 17 fifty *J* and officials ate at my table,
6: 6 and the *J* are plotting to revolt,
Est 3: 6 *J*, throughout the whole kingdom
3: 10 the Agagite, the enemy of the *J*.
3: 13 kill and annihilate all the *J*—
4: 3 was great mourning among the *J*,
4: 7 for the destruction of the *J*.
4: 13 alone of all the *J* will escape.
4: 14 and deliverance for the *J* will arise
4: 16 gather together all the *J* who are
8: 1 of Haman, the enemy of the *J*.
8: 3 which he had devised against the *J*.
8: 5 and wrote to destroy the *J*
8: 7 "Because Haman attacked the *J*,
8: 8 in the king's name in behalf of the *J*
8: 9 and also to the *J* in their own script
8: 9 out all Mordecai's orders to the *J*,
8: 11 The king's edict granted the *J*
8: 12 appointed for the *J* to do this
8: 13 so that the *J* would be ready
8: 16 For the *J* it was a time of happiness
8: 17 and gladness among the *J*,
8: 17 fear of the *J* had seized them.
8: 17 of other nationalities became *J*
9: 1 and the *J* got the upper hand
9: 1 the enemies of the *J* had hoped
9: 2 The *J* assembled in their cities
9: 3 king's administrators helped the *J*,
9: 5 *J* struck down all their enemies
9: 6 the *J* killed and destroyed five
9: 10 Hammedatha, the enemy of the *J*.
9: 12 The *J* have killed five hundred men
9: 13 "give the *J* in Susa permission
9: 15 The *J* in Susa came together
9: 16 the remainder of the *J* who were
9: 18 *J* in Susa, however, had assembled
9: 19 That is why rural *J*— those living
9: 20 all the *J* throughout the provinces
9: 22 as the time when the *J* got relief
9: 23 So the *J* agreed to continue
9: 24 against the *J* to destroy them
9: 24 the Agagite, the enemy of all the *J*,
9: 25 against the *J* should come back
9: 27 the *J* took it upon themselves
9: 28 cease to be celebrated by the *J*,
9: 30 to all the *J* in the 127 provinces
10: 3 esteem by his many fellow *J*,
10: 3 preeminent among the *J*,
10: 3 spoke up for the welfare of all the *J*.
Jer 32: 12 of all the *J* sitting in the courtyard
38: 19 I am afraid of the *J* who have gone
40: 11 When all the *J* in Moab, Ammon,
40: 15 cause all the *J* who are gathered
41: 3 also killed all the *J* who were
43: 9 "While the *J* are watching,
44: 1 concerning all the *J* living
44: 26 of the LORD, all *J* living in Egypt:
44: 27 the *J* in Egypt will perish by sword
52: 28 *J*; in Nebuchadnezzar's eighteenth
52: 30 745 *J* taken into exile
Da 3: 8 forward and denounced the *J*.
3: 12 there are some *J* whom you have
Mt 2: 2 who has been born king of the *J*?
27: 11 "Are you the king of the *J*?" "Yes,
27: 29 "Hail, King of the *J*!" they said.
27: 37 JESUS, THE KING OF THE *J*.
28: 15 among the *J* to this very day.
Mk 7: 3 Pharisees and all the *J* do not eat
15: 2 "Are you the king of the *J*?"
15: 9 to release to you the king of the *J*?"
15: 12 the one you call the king of the *J*?"
15: 18 out to him, "Hail, King of the *J*!"
15: 26 THE KING OF THE *J*.
Lk 7: 3 sent some elders of the *J* to him,
23: 3 "Are you the king of the *J*?" "Yes,
23: 37 "If you are the king of the *J*,
23: 38 THE KING OF THE *J*.
Jn 1: 19 when the *J* of Jerusalem sent
2: 6 by the *J* for ceremonial washing,
2: 18 Then the *J* demanded of him,
2: 20 *J* replied, "It has taken forty-six
4: 9 (For *J* do not associate
4: 20 you *J* claim that the place where
4: 22 for salvation is from the *J*.
5: 1 up to Jerusalem for a feast of the *J*.
5: 10 so the *J* said to the man who had
5: 15 told the *J* that it was Jesus who had
5: 16 the Sabbath, the *J* persecuted him.
5: 18 For this reason the *J* tried all
6: 41 At this the *J* began
6: 52 Then the *J* began to argue sharply
7: 1 because the *J* there were waiting
7: 11 at the Feast the *J* were watching
7: 13 publicly about him for fear of the *J*.
7: 15 The *J* were amazed and asked,
7: 35 The *J* said to one another,
8: 22 This made the *J* ask, "Will he kill
8: 31 To the *J* who had believed him,
8: 48 *J* answered him, "Aren't we right
8: 52 At this the *J* exclaimed,
8: 57 not yet fifty years old," the *J* said
9: 18 *J* still did not believe that he had
9: 22 because they were afraid of the *J*,
9: 22 for already the *J* had decided that
10: 19 these words the *J* were again
10: 24 The *J* gathered around him, saying,
10: 31 Again the *J* picked up stones
10: 33 replied the *J*, "but for blasphemy,
11: 8 while ago the *J* tried to stone you,
11: 19 and many *J* had come to Martha
11: 31 When the *J* who had been
11: 33 the *J* who had come along with her
11: 36 the *J* said, "See how he loved him
11: 45 many of the *J* who had come
11: 54 moved about publicly among the *J*.
12: 9 of *J* found out that Jesus was there
12: 11 of him many of the *J* were going
13: 33 just as I told the *J*, so I tell you now
18: 14 who had advised the *J* that it would
18: 20 where all the *J* come together.
18: 28 Then the *J* led Jesus from Caiaphas
18: 28 uncleanness the *J* did not
18: 31 to execute anyone," the *J* objected.
18: 33 "Are you the king of the *J*?"
18: 36 fight to prevent my arrest by the *J*.
18: 38 With this he went out again to the *J*
18: 39 me to release 'the king of the *J*'?"
19: 3 saying, "Hail, O king of the *J*!"
19: 4 Pilate came out and said to the *J*,
19: 7 The *J* insisted, "We have a law,
19: 12 Jesus free, but the *J* kept shouting,
19: 14 is your king," Pilate said to the *J*.
19: 19 THE KING OF THE *J*.
19: 20 Many of the *J* read this sign,
19: 21 claimed to be king of the *J*."
19: 21 priests of the *J* protested to Pilate,
19: 21 "Do not write 'The King of the *J*,'

Jn 19: 31 Because the *J* did not want
19: 38 but secretly because he feared the *J*
20: 19 the doors locked for fear of the *J*,
Ac 2: 5 staying in Jerusalem God-fearing *J*
2: 11 visitors from Rome (both *J*
2: 14 "Fellow *J* and all of you who are
6: 1 Grecian *J* among them complained
6: 9 *J* of Cyrene and Alexandria as well
9: 22 baffled the *J* living in Damascus
9: 23 the *J* conspired to kill him,
9: 29 and debated with the Grecian *J*,
10: 39 did in the country of the *J*
11: 19 telling the message only to *J*.
12: 3 he saw that this pleased the *J*,
13: 43 many of the *J* and devout converts
13: 45 When the *J* saw the crowds,
13: 50 *J* incited the God-fearing women
14: 1 effectively that a great number of *J*
14: 2 *J* who refused to believe stirred up
14: 4 some sided with the *J*, others
14: 5 afoot among the Gentiles and *J*,
14: 19 Then some *J* came from Antioch
16: 3 of the *J* who lived in that area,
16: 20 and said, "These men are *J*,
17: 4 Some of the *J* were persuaded
17: 5 But the *J* were jealous;
17: 12 Many of the *J* believed, as did
17: 13 the *J* in Thessalonica learned
17: 17 in the synagogue with the *J*
18: 2 Claudius had ordered all the *J*
18: 4 trying to persuade *J* and Greeks.
18: 5 to the *J* that Jesus was the Christ.
18: 6 But when the *J* opposed Paul
18: 12 the *J* made a united attack on Paul
18: 14 about to speak, Gallio said to the *J*,
18: 14 "If you *J* were making a complaint
18: 19 and reasoned with the *J*.
18: 28 For he vigorously refuted the *J*
19: 10 so that all the *J* and Greeks who
19: 13 *J* who went around driving out
19: 17 When this became known to the *J*
19: 33 The *J* pushed Alexander
20: 3 Because the *J* made a plot
20: 19 tested by the plots of the *J*.
20: 21 I have declared to both *J*
21: 11 'In this way the *J* of Jerusalem will
21: 20 thousands of *J* have believed,
21: 21 that you teach all the *J* who live
21: 27 some *J* from the province
22: 12 respected by all the *J* living there.
22: 30 Paul was being accused by the *J*,
23: 12 The next morning the *J* formed
23: 20 "The *J* have agreed to ask you
23: 27 This man was seized by the *J*
24: 5 among the *J* all over the world
24: 9 The *J* joined in the accusation,
24: 19 there are some *J* from the province
24: 27 to grant a favor to the *J*, he
25: 7 the *J* who had come
25: 8 wrong against the law of the *J*
25: 9 Festus, wishing to do the *J* a favor,
25: 10 I have not done any wrong to the *J*,
25: 11 against me by these *J* are not true,
25: 15 and elders of the *J* brought charges
26: 2 against all the accusations of the *J*,
26: 4 *J* all know the way I have lived
26: 7 hope that the *J* are accusing me.
26: 21 That is why the *J* seized me
28: 17 called together the leaders of the *J*.
28: 19 But when the *J* objected, I was
Ro 3: 9 already made the charge that *J*
3: 29 Is God the God of *J* only?
9: 24 not only from the *J* but
15: 8 of the *J* on behalf of God's truth,
15: 27 they owe it to the *J* to share
1Co 1: 22 *J* demand miraculous signs
1: 23 a stumbling block to *J*
1: 24 those whom God has called, both *J*
9: 20 I became like a Jew, to win the *J*.
9: 20 To the *J* I became like a Jew,
10: 32 *J*, Greeks or the church of God—
12: 13 whether *J* or Greeks, slave or free
2Co 11: 24 from the *J* the forty lashes minus
Gal 1: 14 in Judaism beyond many *J*
2: 7 of preaching the gospel to the *J*.
2: 8 of Peter as an apostle to the *J*,
2: 9 to the Gentiles, and they to the *J*.
2: 13 The other *J* joined him
Gal 2: 15 "We who are *J* by birth
Col 4: 11 These are the only *J*
1Th 2: 14 those churches suffered from the *J*,
Rev 2: 9 slander of those who say they are *J*
3: 9 claim to be *J* though they are not,

JEWS' (JEW)

Ro 15: 27 shared in the *J'* spiritual blessings,

JEZANIAH

Jer 42: 1 of Kareah and *J* son of Hoshaiah,

JEZEBEL (JEZEBEL'S)

1Ki 16: 31 married *J* daughter of Ethbaal king
18: 4 While *J* was killing
18: 13 did while *J* was killing the prophets
19: 1 Ahab told *J* everything Elijah had
19: 2 *J* sent a messenger to Elijah to say,
21: 5 His wife *J* came in and asked him,
21: 7 *J* his wife said, "Is this how you act
21: 11 as *J* directed in the letters she had
21: 14 to *J*: "Naboth has been stoned
21: 15 as *J* heard that Naboth had been
21: 23 also concerning *J* the LORD says:
21: 23 'Dogs will devour *J* by the wall
21: 25 the LORD, urged on by *J* his wife.
2Ki 9: 7 all the LORD's servants shed by *J*.
9: 10 As for *J*, dogs will devour her
9: 22 of your mother *J* abound?"
9: 30 When *J* heard about it, she painted
9: 37 able to say, 'This is *J*.' "
Rev 2: 20 You tolerate that woman *J*,

JEZEBEL'S (JEZEBEL)

1Ki 18: 19 of Asherah, who eat at *J* table."
2Ki 9: 36 at Jezreel dogs will devour *J* flesh.
9: 37 *J* body will be like refuse

JEZER (JEZERITE)

Ge 46: 24 Jahziel, Guni, *J* and Shillem.
Nu 26: 49 through *J*, the Jezerite clan;
1Ch 7: 13 Jahziel, Guni, *J* and Shillem—

JEZERITE (JEZER)

Nu 26: 49 the *J* clan; through Shillem,

JEZIEL

1Ch 12: 3 *J* and Pelet the sons of Azmaveth;

JEZRAHIAH

Ne 12: 42 sang under the direction of *J*.

JEZREEL (JEZREELITE)

Jos 15: 56 Ziph, Juttah, *J*, Jokdeam, Zanoah,
17: 16 and those in the Valley of *J*."
19: 18 Their territory included: *J*,
Jdg 6: 33 and camped in the Valley of *J*.
1Sa 25: 43 also married Ahinoam of *J*,
27: 3 Ahinoam of *J* and Abigail
29: 1 Israel camped by the spring in *J*.
29: 11 and the Philistines went up to *J*.
30: 5 Ahinoam of *J* and Abigail,
2Sa 2: 2 Ahinoam of *J* and Abigail,
2: 9 and *J*, and also over Ephraim,
3: 2 Amnon the son of Ahinoam of *J*;
4: 4 and Jonathan came from *J*.
1Ki 4: 12 next to Zarethan below *J*,
18: 45 came on and Ahab rode off to *J*.
18: 46 ahead of Ahab all the way to *J*.
21: 1 The vineyard was in *J*, close
21: 23 devour Jezebel by the wall of *J*.'
2Ki 8: 29 so King Joram returned to *J*
8: 29 went down to *J* to see Joram son
9: 10 her on the plot of ground at *J*,
9: 15 but King Joram had returned to *J*
9: 15 city to go and tell the news in *J*."
9: 16 he got into his chariot and rode to *J*
9: 17 in *J* saw Jehu's troops approaching,
9: 30 Then Jehu went to *J*.
9: 36 at *J* dogs will devour Jezebel's flesh
9: 37 on the ground in the plot at *J*,
10: 1 to the officials of *J*, to the elders
10: 6 to me in *J* by this time tomorrow."
10: 7 and sent them to Jehu in *J*.
10: 11 everyone in *J* who remained
1Ch 3: 1 Amnon the son of Ahinoam of *J*;
4: 3 These were the sons of Etam: *J*,
2Ch 22: 6 so he returned to *J* to recover
2Ch 22: 6 went down to *J* to see Joram son
Hos 1: 4 house of Jehu for the massacre at *J*,
1: 4 said to Hosea, "Call him *J*,
1: 5 bow in the Valley of *J*."
1: 11 for great will be the day of *J*.
2: 22 and they will respond to *J*.

JEZREELITE (JEZREEL)

1Ki 21: 1 belonging to Naboth the *J*.
21: 4 because Naboth the *J* had said,
21: 6 "Because I said to Naboth the *J*,
21: 7 you the vineyard of Naboth the *J*."
21: 15 of Naboth the *J* that he refused
2Ki 9: 21 that had belonged to Naboth the *J*.
9: 25 that belonged to Naboth the *J*.

JIDLAPH

Ge 22: 22 Hazo, Pildash, *J* and Bethuel."

JINGLING

Isa 3: 16 with ornaments *j* on their ankles.

JOAB (JOAB'S)

2Sa 2: 13 *J* son of Zeruiah and David's men
2: 14 Abner said to *J*, "Let's have some
2: 14 "All right, let them do it," *J* said.
2: 18 sons of Zeruiah were there: *J*,
2: 22 How could I look your brother *J*
2: 24 But *J* and Abishai pursued Abner,
2: 26 out to *J*, "Must the sword devour
2: 27 *J* answered, "As surely
2: 28 So *J* blew the trumpet,
2: 30 *J* returned from pursuing Abner
2: 32 *J* and his men marched all night
3: 22 and *J* returned from a raid
3: 23 When *J* and all the soldiers
3: 24 So *J* went to the king and said,
3: 26 *J* then left David and sent
3: 27 *J* stabbed him in the stomach,
3: 27 *J* took him aside into the gateway,
3: 29 fall upon the head of *J*
3: 30 (*J* and his brother Abishai
3: 31 David said to *J* and all the people
8: 16 *J* son of Zeruiah was over the army
10: 7 David sent *J* out with the entire
10: 9 *J* saw that there were battle lines
10: 11 *J* said, "If the Arameans are too
10: 13 Then *J* and the troops with him
10: 14 So *J* returned from fighting
11: 1 David sent *J* out with the king's
11: 6 And *J* sent him to David.
11: 6 So David sent this word to *J*:
11: 7 David asked him how *J* was,
11: 11 my master *J* and my lord's men are
11: 14 morning David wrote a letter to *J*
11: 16 So while *J* had the city under siege,
11: 17 city came out and fought against *J*,
11: 18 *J* sent David a full account
11: 22 told David everything *J* had sent
11: 25 Say this to encourage *J*."
11: 25 this to *J*: 'Don't let this upset you;
12: 26 Meanwhile *J* fought
12: 27 *J* then sent messengers to David,
14: 1 *J* son of Zeruiah knew that
14: 2 So *J* sent someone to Tekoa
14: 3 And *J* put the words in her mouth.
14: 19 was your servant *J* who instructed
14: 19 "Isn't the hand of *J* with you
14: 20 Your servant *J* did this
14: 21 The king said to *J*, "Very well,
14: 22 *J* fell with his face to the ground
14: 22 *J* said, "Today your servant knows
14: 23 Then *J* went to Geshur
14: 29 Then Absalom sent for *J* in order
14: 29 but *J* refused to come to him.
14: 31 Then *J* did go to Absalom's house
14: 32 Absalom said to *J*, "Look,
14: 33 *J* went to the king and told him this
17: 25 Amasa over the army in place of *J*.
17: 25 sister of Zeruiah the mother of *J*.
18: 2 a third under the command of *J*,
18: 5 The king commanded *J*, Abishai
18: 10 one of the men saw this, he told *J*,
18: 11 *J* said to the man who had told him
18: 14 *J* said, "I'm not going
18: 16 Then *J* sounded the trumpet,
18: 16 for *J* halted them.
18: 20 to take the news today," *J* told him

2Sa 18:21 The Cushite bowed down before J
18:21 Then J said to a Cushite, "Go,
18:22 J replied, "My son, why do you
18:22 son of Zadok again said to J,
18:23 J said, "Run!" Then Ahimaaz ran
18:29 as J was about to send the king's
19: 1 my son, my son!" J was told,
19: 5 J went into the house to the king
19:13 of my army in place of J.' "
20: 8 J was wearing his military tunic,
20: 9 Then J took Amasa by the beard
20: 9 J said to Amasa, "How are you,
20:10 and J plunged it into his belly,
20:10 J and his brother Abishai pursued
20:11 is for David, let him follow J!"
20:11 "Whoever favors J, and whoever is
20:13 went on with J to pursue Sheba son
20:15 All the troops with J came
20:16 Tell J to come here so I can speak
20:17 "Are you J?" "I am," he answered.
20:20 "Far be it from me!" J replied,
20:21 said to J, "His head will be thrown
20:22 And J went back to the king
20:22 son of Bicri and threw it to J.
20:23 J was over Israel's entire army;
23:18 Abishai the brother of J son
23:24 the brother of J, Elhanan son
23:37 the armor-bearer of J son
24: 2 to J and the army commanders
24: 3 But J replied to the king, "May
24: 4 overruled J and the army
24: 9 J reported the number
1Ki 1: 7 Adonijah conferred with J son
1:19 and J the commander of the army,
1:41 the sound of the trumpet, J asked,
2: 5 you yourself know what J son
2:22 for Abiathar the priest and J son
2:28 When the news reached J,
2:29 Solomon was told that J had fled
2:30 the tent of the LORD and said to J,
2:30 "This is how J answered me."
2:31 of the innocent blood that J shed.
2:33 of their blood rest on the head of J
2:34 and struck down J and killed him,
11:15 J the commander of the army,
11:16 J and all the Israelites stayed there
11:21 and that J the commander
1Ch 2:16 three sons were Abishai, J
4:14 Seraiah was the father of J,
11: 6 J son of Zeruiah went up first,
11: 8 while J restored the rest of the city.
11:20 Abishai the brother of J was chief
11:26 the brother of J, Elhanan son
11:39 the armor-bearer of J son
18:15 J son of Zeruiah was over the army
19: 8 David sent J out with the entire
19:10 J saw that there were battle lines
19:12 J said, "If the Arameans are too
19:14 Then J and the troops with him
19:15 So J went back to Jerusalem.
20: 1 J attacked Rabbah and left it
20: 1 J led out the armed forces.
21: 2 said to J and the commanders
21: 3 But J replied, "May the LORD
21: 4 king's word, however, overruled J;
21: 4 so J left and went
21: 5 J reported the number
21: 6 But J did not include Levi
26:28 son of Ner and J son of Zeruiah,
27: 7 was Asahel the brother of J;
27:24 J son of Zeruiah began
27:34 J was the commander
Ezr 2: 6 the line of Jeshua and J) 2,812
8: 9 the descendants of J, Obadiah son
Ne 7:11 the line of Jeshua and J) 2,818

JOAB'S (JOAB)

1Sa 26: 6 Abishai son of Zeruiah, J brother,
2Sa 3:29 May J house never be
14:30 "Look, J field is next to mine,
18: 2 a third under J brother Abishai son
18:15 ten of J armor-bearers surrounded
20: 7 So J men and the Kerethites
20:10 guard against the dagger in J hand,
20:11 One of J men stood beside Amasa
1Ki 2:35 over the army in J position

JOAH

2Ki 18:18 J son of Asaph the recorder went
18:26 and J said to the field commander,
18:37 J son of Asaph the recorder went
1Ch 6:21 Zimmah his son, J his son,
26: 4 Jehozabad the second, J the third,
2Ch 29:12 J son of Zimmah and Eden son
29:12 son of Zimmah and Eden son of J;
34: 8 with J son of Joahaz, the recorder,
Isa 36: 3 J son of Asaph the recorder went
36:11 and J said to the field commander,
36:22 J son of Asaph the recorder went

JOAHAZ

2Ch 34: 8 with Joah son of J, the recorder,

JOANAN

Lk 3:27 the son of J, the son of Rhesa,

JOANNA

Lk 8: 3 J the wife of Cuza, the manager
24:10 It was Mary Magdalene, J,

JOASH

Jdg 6:11 belonged to J the Abiezrite,
6:29 were told, "Gideon son of J did it."
6:30 men of the town demanded of J,
6:31 But J replied to the hostile crowd
7:14 than the sword of Gideon son of J,
8:13 Gideon son of J then returned
8:29 son of J went back home
8:32 Gideon son of J died
8:32 the tomb of his father J in Ophrah
1Ki 22:26 and to J the king's son and say,
2Ki 11: 2 took J son of Ahaziah
11:21 J was seven years old
12: 1 year of Jehu, J became king,
12: 2 J did what was right in the eyes
12: 4 J said to the priests, "Collect all
12: 6 of King J the priests still had not
12: 7 Therefore King J summoned
12:18 J king of Judah took all the sacred
12:19 the other events of the reign of J,
13: 1 year of J son of Ahaziah king
13:10 year of J king of Judah,
14: 1 Amaziah son of J king
14: 3 the example of his father J.
14:13 the son of J, the son of Ahaziah,
14:17 Amaziah son of J king
14:23 of Amaziah son of J king of Judah,
1Ch 3:11 Ahaziah his son, J his son,
4:22 the men of Cozeba, and J
7: 8 Zemirah, J, Eliezer, Elioenai,
12: 3 and J the sons of Shemaah
27:28 J was in charge of the supplies
2Ch 18:25 of the city and to J the king's son,
22:11 took J son of Ahaziah
24: 1 J was seven years old
24: 2 J did what was right in the eyes
24: 4 Some time later J decided
24:22 King J did not remember
24:23 army of Aram marched against J;
24:24 judgment was executed on J.
24:25 they left J severely wounded.
25:23 the son of J, the son of Ahaziah,
25:25 Amaziah son of J king

JOB (JOB'S)

2Ch 34:13 all the workers from j to j.
Job 1: 1 lived a man whose name was J.
1: 5 J would send and have them
1: 8 Have you considered my servant J
1: 9 "Does J fear God for nothing?"
1:14 a messenger came to J and said,
1:20 J got up and tore his robe
1:22 J did not sin by charging God
2: 3 Have you considered my servant J
2: 7 and afflicted J with painful sores
2: 8 J took a piece of broken pottery
2:10 J did not sin in what he said.
3: 1 J opened his mouth and cursed
6: 1 J replied: "If only my anguish
9: 1 J replied: "Indeed, I know that this
12: 1 Then J replied: "Doubtless you are
16: 1 J replied: "I have heard many
19: 1 Then J replied: "How long will you
21: 1 J replied: "Listen carefully
23: 1 J replied: "Even today my
Job 26: 1 J replied: "How you have helped
27: 1 And J continued his discourse:
29: 1 J continued his discourse:
31:40 The words of J are ended.
32: 1 three men stopped answering J,
32: 2 became very angry with J
32: 3 they had found no way to refute J,
32: 4 waited before speaking to J
32:12 not one of you has proved J wrong;
32:14 J has not marshaled his words
33: 1 "But now, J, listen to my words;
33:31 "Pay attention, J, and listen to me;
34: 5 "J says, 'I am innocent,
34: 7 What man is like J,
34:35 'J speaks without knowledge;
34:36 that J might be tested to the utmost
35:16 J opens his mouth with empty talk;
37:14 "Listen to this, J;
38: 1 the LORD answered J out
40: 1 to J: "Will the one who contends
40: 3 Then J answered the LORD:
40: 6 Then the LORD spoke to J out
42: 1 Then J replied to the LORD:
42: 7 LORD had said these things to J,
42: 7 what is right, as my servant J has.
42: 8 My servant J will pray for you,
42: 8 seven rams and go to my servant J
42: 8 what is right, as my servant J has."
42:10 After J had prayed for his friends,
42:16 J lived a hundred and forty years;
Eze 14:14 Noah, Daniel and J— were in it,
14:20 if Noah, Daniel and J were in it,
Lk 16: 3 My master is taking away my j.
16: 4 when I lose my j here, people will

JOB'S (JOB)

Job 1: 5 This was J regular custom.
1:13 when J sons and daughters were
2:11 When J three friends, Eliphaz
31:31 'Who has not had his fill of J meat
42: 9 and the LORD accepted J prayer.
42:12 part of J life more than the first.
42:15 as beautiful as J daughters,
Jas 5:11 You have heard of J perseverance

JOBAB

Ge 10:29 Sheba, Ophir, Havilah and J.
36:33 J son of Zerah from Bozrah
36:34 When J died, Husham
Jos 11: 1 he sent word to J king of Madon,
1Ch 1:23 Sheba, Ophir, Havilah and J.
1:44 J son of Zerah from Bozrah
1:45 When J died, Husham
8: 9 By his wife Hodesh he had J, Zibia,
8:18 Izliah and J were the sons of Elpaal

JOCHEBED

Ex 6:20 Amram married his father's sister J
Nu 26:59 the name of Amram's wife was J,

JODA

Lk 3:26 the son of Josech, the son of J,

JOED

Ne 11: 7 the son of J, the son of Pedaiah,

JOEL

1Sa 8: 2 The name of his firstborn was J
1Ch 4:35 Joshah son of Amaziah, J,
5: 4 of J: Shemaiah his son,
5: 8 the son of Shema, the son of J.
5:12 as far as Salecah: J was the chief,
6:28 J the firstborn and Abijah
6:33 the son of J, the son of Samuel,
6:36 the son of J, the son of Azariah,
7: 3 Michael, Obadiah, J and Isshiah.
11:38 Naarai son of Ezbai, J the brother
15: 7 J the leader and 130 relatives;
15:11 and Uriel, Asaiah, J, Shemaiah,
15:17 Levites appointed Heman son of J;
23: 8 Zetham and J— three in all.
26:22 Zetham and his brother J.
27:20 of Manasseh: J son of Pedaiah;
2Ch 29:12 of Amasai and J son of Azariah;
Ezr 10:43 Zebina, Jaddai, J and Benaiah.
Ne 11: 9 J son of Zicri was their chief officer
Joel 1: 1 came to J son of Pethuel.
Ac 2:16 what was spoken by the prophet J:

JOELAH

1Ch 12: 7 and *J* and Zebadiah the sons

JOEZER

1Ch 12: 6 *J* and Jashobeam the Korahites;

JOGBEHAH

Nu 32:35 Atroth Shophan, Jazer, *J*,
Jdg 8:11 *J* and fell upon the unsuspecting

JOGLI

Nu 34:22 Bukki son of *J*, the leader

JOHA

1Ch 8:16 and *J* were the sons of Beriah.
11:45 his brother *J* the Tizite, Eliel

JOHANAN

2Ki 25:23 son of Nethaniah, *J* son of Kareah,
1Ch 3:15 The sons of Josiah: *J* the firstborn,
3:24 Eliashib, Pelaiah, Akkub, *J*,
6: 9 of Azariah, Azariah the father of *J*,
6:10 *J* the father of Azariah (it was he
12: 4 *J*, Jozabad the Gederathite,
12:12 Eliel the seventh, *J* the eighth,
Ezr 8:12 of Azgad, *J* son of Hakkatan,
Ne 12:22 *J* and Jaddua, as well as those
12:23 up to the time of *J* son
Jer 40: 8 *J* and Jonathan the sons of Kareah,
40:13 *J* son of Kareah and all the army
40:15 *J* son of Kareah said privately
40:16 of Ahikam said to *J* son of Kareah,
41:11 When *J* son of Kareah
41:13 had with him saw *J* son of Kareah
41:14 and went over to *J* son of Kareah.
41:15 eight of his men escaped from *J*
41:16 *J* son of Kareah and all the army
42: 1 including *J* son of Kareah
42: 8 he called together *J* son of Kareah
43: 2 of Hoshaiah and *J* son of Kareah
43: 4 So *J* son of Kareah and all the army
43: 5 *J* son of Kareah and all the army

JOHN (JOHN'S)

Mt 3: 1 In those days *J* the Baptist came,
3:13 to the Jordan to be baptized by *J*.
3:14 But *J* tried to deter him, saying,
3:15 Then *J* consented.
4:12 Jesus heard that *J* had been put
4:21 son of Zebedee and his brother *J*.
10: 2 and his brother *J*; Philip
11: 2 When *J* heard in prison what
11: 4 and report to *J* what you hear
11: 7 to speak to the crowd about *J*:
11:11 greater than *J* the Baptist;
11:12 From the days of *J* the Baptist
11:13 and the Law prophesied until *J*.
11:18 For *J* came neither eating
14: 2 attendants, "This is *J* the Baptist;
14: 3 Herod had arrested *J* and bound
14: 4 for *J* had been saying to him:
14: 5 Herod wanted to kill *J*,
14: 8 a platter the head of *J* the Baptist."
14:10 and had *J* beheaded in the prison.
16:14 replied, "Some say *J* the Baptist;
17: 1 James and *J* the brother of James,
17:13 talking to them about *J* the Baptist.
21:26 they all hold that *J* was a prophet."
21:32 For *J* came to you
Mk 1: 4 And so *J* came, baptizing
1: 6 *J* wore clothing made
1: 9 was baptized by *J* in the Jordan.
1:14 After *J* was put in prison, Jesus
1:19 and his brother *J* in a boat,
1:29 and *J* to the home of Simon
3:17 and his brother *J* (to them he gave
5:37 James and *J* the brother of James.
6:14 "*J* the Baptist has been raised
6:16 he said, "*J*, the man I beheaded,
6:17 orders to have *J* arrested,
6:18 For *J* had been saying to Herod,
6:19 Herodias nursed a grudge against *J*
6:20 When Herod heard *J*, he was
6:20 because Herod feared *J*
6:24 "The head of *J* the Baptist,"
6:25 head of *J* the Baptist on a platter."
6:27 The man went, beheaded *J*
8:28 replied, "Some say *J* the Baptist;
Mk 9: 2 *J* with him and led them up a high
9:38 said *J*, "we saw a man driving out
10:35 James and *J*, the sons of Zebedee,
10:41 indignant with James and *J*.
11:32 for everyone held that *J* really was
13: 3 *J* and Andrew asked him privately,
14:33 James and *J* along with him,
Lk 1:13 and you are to give him the name *J*.
1:60 "No! He is to be called *J*."
1:63 he wrote, "His name is *J*."
3: 2 of God came to *J* son of Zechariah
3: 7 *J* said to the crowds coming out
3:11 *J* answered, "The man
3:15 if *J* might possibly be the Christ.
3:16 *J* answered them all, "I baptize you
3:18 many other words *J* exhorted
3:19 when *J* rebuked Herod the tetrarch
3:20 this to them all: He locked *J* up
5:10 and *J*, the sons of Zebedee,
6:14 James, *J*, Philip, Bartholomew,
7:20 "*J* the Baptist sent us to you to ask,
7:22 and report to *J* what you have seen
7:24 to speak to the crowd about *J*:
7:28 there is no one greater than *J*;
7:29 they had been baptized by *J*.
7:30 they had not been baptized by *J*.)
7:33 For *J* the Baptist came neither
8:51 *J* and James, and the child's father
9: 7 were saying that *J* had been raised
9: 9 But Herod said, "I beheaded *J*.
9:19 replied, "Some say *J* the Baptist;
9:28 *J* and James with him and went up
9:49 said *J*, "we saw a man driving out
9:54 the disciples James and *J* saw this,
11: 1 just as *J* taught his disciples."
16:16 Prophets were proclaimed until *J*.
20: 6 are persuaded that *J* was
22: 8 Jesus sent Peter and *J*, saying,
Jn 1: 6 sent from God; his name was *J*.
1:15 *J* testifies concerning him.
1:23 *J* replied in the words
1:26 "I baptize with water," *J* replied,
1:28 the Jordan, where *J* was baptizing.
1:29 The next day *J* saw Jesus coming
1:32 Then *J* gave this testimony:
1:35 The next day *J* was there again
1:40 the two who heard what *J* had said
1:42 and said, "You are Simon son of *J*.
3:23 Now *J* also was baptizing at Aenon
3:24 This was before *J* was put in prison
3:26 They came to *J* and said to him,
3:27 To this *J* replied, "A man can
4: 1 baptizing more disciples than *J*,
5:33 sent to *J* and he has testified
5:35 *J* was a lamp that burned
5:36 testimony weightier than that of *J*.
10:40 the place where *J* had been
10:41 all that *J* said about this man was
10:41 "Though *J* never performed
21:15 Simon Peter, "Simon son of *J*,
21:16 son of *J*, do you truly love me?"
21:17 "Simon son of *J*, do you love me?"
Ac 1: 5 For *J* baptized with water,
1:13 Those present were Peter, *J*,
3: 1 and *J* were going up to the temple
3: 3 When he saw Peter and *J* about
3: 4 looked straight at him, as did *J*.
3:11 the beggar held on to Peter and *J*,
4: 1 and *J* while they were speaking
4: 3 They seized Peter and *J*, and
4: 6 and so were Caiaphas, *J*,
4: 7 and *J* brought before them
4:13 and *J* and realized that they were
4:19 *J* replied, "Judge for yourselves
4:23 *J* went back to their own people
8:14 they sent Peter and *J* to them.
8:17 and *J* placed their hands on them,
8:25 Peter and *J* returned to Jerusalem,
10:37 after the baptism that *J* preached—
11:16 what the Lord had said, '*J* baptized
12: 2 He had James, the brother of *J*,
12:12 the house of Mary the mother of *J*,
12:25 with them *J*, also called Mark.
13: 5 *J* was with them as their helper.
13:13 where *J* left them to return
13:24 *J* preached repentance
13:25 As *J* was completing his work,
15:37 Barnabas wanted to take *J*,
Ac 18:25 he knew only the baptism of *J*.
Gal 2: 9 and *J*, those reputed to be pillars,
Rev 1: 1 sending his angel to his servant *J*,
1: 4 *J*, To the seven churches
1: 9 *J*, your brother and companion
22: 8 *J*, am the one who heard

JOHN'S (JOHN)

Mt 3: 4 *J* clothes were made of camel's hair
9:14 Then *J* disciples came
11: 7 As *J* disciples were leaving,
14:12 *J* disciples came and took his body
21:25 *J* baptism—where did it come
Mk 2:18 *J* disciples and the Pharisees were
2:18 "How is it that *J* disciples
6:27 with orders to bring *J* head.
6:29 *J* disciples came and took his body
11:30 *J* baptism—was it from heaven,
Lk 5:33 "*J* disciples often fast and pray,
7:18 *J* disciples told him about all these
7:24 After *J* messengers left, Jesus
20: 4 *J* baptism—was it from heaven,
Jn 1:19 this was *J* testimony when the Jews
3:25 between some of *J* disciples
Ac 1:22 beginning from *J* baptism
19: 3 "*J* baptism," they replied.
19: 4 "*J* baptism was a baptism

JOIADA

Ne 3: 6 repaired by *J* son of Paseah
12:11 of *J*, *J* the father of Jonathan,
12:22 *J*, Johanan and Jaddua, as well
13:28 One of the sons of *J* son

JOIAKIM

Ne 12:10 father of *J*, *J* the father of Eliashib,
12:12 the days of *J*, these were the heads
12:26 in the days of *J* son of Jeshua,

JOIARIB (JOIARIB'S)

Ezr 8:16 who were leaders, and *J*
Ne 11: 5 the son of *J*, the son of Zechariah,
11:10 Jedaiah; the son of *J*; Jakin;
12: 6 Bilgah, Shemaiah, *J*, Jedaiah, Sallu

JOIARIB'S (JOIARIB)

Ne 12:19 Jehonathan; of *J*, Mattenai;

JOIN (JOINED JOINING JOINS JUNCTION REJOINED)

Ge 34:30 and if they *j* forces against me
49: 6 let me not *j* their assembly,
Ex 1:10 if war breaks out, will *j* our enemies
26: 3 *J* five of the curtains together,
26: 9 *J* five of the curtains together
Nu 18: 2 from your ancestral tribe to *j* you
18: 4 are to *j* you and be responsible
34: 5 *j* the Wadi of Egypt and end
Jdg 3:13 and Amalekites to *j* him,
21:21 out to *j* in the dancing,
1Sa 13: 4 summoned to *j* Saul at Gilgal.
22:20 escaped and fled to *j* David.
2Sa 13:24 and his officials please *j* me?"
1Ki 1: 8 special guard did not *j* Adonijah.
1Ch 13: 2 and pasturelands, to come and *j* us.
2Ch 18: 3 as your people; we will *j* you
Ne 4:20 sound of the trumpet, *j* us there.
10:29 all these now *j* their brothers
Est 9:27 and all who *j* them should
Job 37:18 can you *j* him in spreading out
Ps 49:19 he will *j* the generation
50:18 When you see a thief, you *j*
106: 5 *j* your inheritance in giving praise.
118:27 With boughs in hand, *j*
Pr 23:20 Do not *j* those who drink too much
24:21 and do not *j* with the rebellious,
Ecc 9: 3 and afterward they *j* the dead.
Isa 5: 8 and *j* field to field
14: 1 Aliens will *j* them
14:20 you will not *j* them in burial,
Jer 3:18 of Judah will *j* the house of Israel,
Eze 37:17 *J* them together into one stick
37:19 with him, and *j* it to Judah's stick,
Da 11:34 who are not sincere will *j* them.
Mic 5: 3 return to *j* the Israelites.
Ac 5:13 No one else dared *j* them,
9:26 he tried to *j* the disciples,
17:15 and Timothy to *j* him as soon

Ac 21: 24 *j* in their purification rites
Ro 15: 30 to *j* me in my struggle by praying
Php 3: 17 *J* with others in following my
2Ti 1: 8 *j* with me in suffering for the gospel

JOINED (JOIN)

Ge 14: 3 All these latter kings *j* forces
Ex 36: 10 They *j* five of the curtains together
36: 16 They *j* five of the curtains
Nu 25: 3 So Israel *j* in worshiping the Baal
25: 5 those of your men who have *j*
Jos 10: 5 Lachish and Eglon—*j* forces.
10: 6 from the hill country have *j* forces
11: 5 All these kings *j* forces
15: 4 along to Azmon and *j* the Wadi
Jdg 6: 33 and other eastern peoples *j* forces
1Sa 10: 10 and he *j* in their prophesying.
14: 22 they *j* the battle in hot pursuit.
28: 23 his men *j* the woman in urging him,
1Ki 20: 29 on the seventh day the battle was *j*.
2Ch 5: 13 The trumpeters and singers *j*
Ezr 3: 9 *j* together in supervising those
Job 41: 17 They are *j* fast to one another;
41: 23 The folds of his flesh are tightly *j*;
Ps 48: 4 When the kings *j* forces,
83: 8 Even Assyria has *j* them
Isa 56: 3 Let no foreigner who has *j* himself
Hos 4: 17 Ephraim is *j* to idols;
Zec 2: 11 "Many nations will be *j*
Mt 19: 6 Therefore what God has *j* together,
Mk 10: 9 Therefore what God has *j* together,
Jn 6: 17 and Jesus had not yet *j* them.
Ac 1: 14 They all *j* together constantly
12: 20 they now *j* together and sought
16: 22 The crowd *j* in the attack
17: 4 the Jews were persuaded and *j* Paul
20: 6 five days later *j* the others at Troas,
24: 9 The Jews *j* in the accusation,
Gal 2: 13 The other Jews *j* him
Eph 2: 21 him the whole building is *j* together
4: 16 *j* and held together

JOINING (JOIN)

Eze 31: 17 *j* those killed by the sword.

JOINS (JOIN)

Hos 7: 5 and he *j* hands with the mockers.
1Co 16: 16 and to everyone who *j* in the work,

JOINT (JOINTED JOINTS)

Job 31: 22 let it be broken off at the *j*.
Ps 22: 14 and all my bones are out of *j*.

JOINTED (JOINT)

Lev 11: 21 those that have *j* legs for hopping

JOINTS (JOINT)

Heb 4: 12 even to dividing soul and spirit, *j*

JOISTS

2Ch 34: 11 and timber for *j* and beams

JOKDEAM

Jos 15: 56 Juttah, Jezreel, *J*, Zanoah, Kain,

JOKIM

1Ch 4: 22 *J*, the men of Cozeba, and Joash

JOKING

Ge 19: 14 his sons-in-law thought he was *j*.
Pr 26: 19 and says, "I was only *j!*"
Eph 5: 4 or coarse *j*, which are out of place,

JOKMEAM

1Ki 4: 12 to Abel Meholah across to *J*;
1Ch 6: 68 and Gezer, *J*, Beth Horon,

JOKNEAM

Jos 12: 22 king of *J* in Carmel one the king
19: 11 and extended to the ravine near *J*.
21: 34 *J*, Kartah, Dimnah and Nahalal,
1Ch 6: 77 tribe of Zebulun they received *J*,

JOKSHAN

Ge 25: 2 She bore him Zimran, *J*, Medan,
25: 3 *J* was the father of Sheba
1Ch 1: 32 The sons of *J*: Sheba and Dedan.
1: 32 Zimran, *J*, Medan, Midian,

JOKTAN

Ge 10: 25 divided; his brother was named *J*.
10: 26 *J* was the father of Almodad,
10: 29 All these were sons of *J*.
1Ch 1: 19 divided; his brother was named *J*.
1: 20 *J* was the father of Almodad,
1: 23 All these were sons of *J*.

JOKTHEEL

Jos 15: 38 Mizpah, *J*, Lachish, Bozkath,
2Ki 14: 7 calling it *J*, the name it has

JOLTING

Na 3: 2 and *j* chariots!

JONADAB

2Sa 13: 3 Amnon had a friend named *J* son
13: 3 *J* was a very shrewd man.
13: 5 and pretend to be ill," *J* said.
13: 32 *J* son of Shimeah, David's brother,
13: 35 *J* said to the king, "See, the king's
Jer 35: 6 because our forefather *J* son
35: 8 everything our forefather *J* son
35: 10 our forefather *J* commanded us.
35: 14 *J* son of Recab ordered his sons not
35: 16 The descendants of *J* son
35: 18 the command of your forefather *J*
35: 19 '*J* son of Recab will never fail

JONAH (JONAH'S)

2Ki 14: 25 spoken through his servant *J* son
Jnh 1: 1 came to *J* son of Amittai:
1: 3 But *J* ran away from the LORD
1: 5 But *J* had gone below deck,
1: 7 They cast lots and the lot fell on *J*.
1: 15 Then they took *J* and threw him
1: 17 and *J* was inside the fish three days
1: 17 provided a great fish to swallow *J*,
2: 1 From inside the fish *J* prayed
2: 10 and it vomited *J* onto dry land.
3: 1 came to *J* a second time:
3: 3 *J* obeyed the word of the LORD
3: 4 *J* started into the city, going a day's
4: 1 But *J* was greatly displeased
4: 5 *J* went out and sat
4: 6 *J* was very happy about the vine.
4: 6 up over *J* to give shade
4: 9 God said to *J*, "Do you have a right
Mt 12: 39 except the sign of the prophet *J*.
12: 40 For as *J* was three days
12: 41 and now one greater than *J* is here.
12: 41 repented at the preaching of *J*,
16: 4 be given it except the sign of *J*."
16: 17 "Blessed are you, Simon son of *J*,
Lk 11: 29 will be given it except the sign of *J*.
11: 30 For as *J* was a sign to the Ninevites
11: 32 and now one greater than *J* is here.
11: 32 repented at the preaching of *J*,

JONAH'S (JONAH)

Jnh 4: 8 and the sun blazed on *J* head

JONAM

Lk 3: 30 the son of *J*, the son of Eliakim,

JONATHAN (JONATHAN'S)

Jdg 18: 30 and *J* son of Gershom, the son
1Sa 13: 2 a thousand were with *J* at Gibeah
13: 3 *J* attacked the Philistine outpost
13: 16 and his son *J* and the men
13: 22 *J* had a sword or spear in his hand;
13: 22 only Saul and his son *J* had them.
14: 1 One day *J* son of Saul said
14: 3 No one was aware that *J* had left.
14: 4 of the pass that *J* intended to cross
14: 6 *J* said to his young armor-bearer,
14: 8 *J* said, "Come, then; we will cross
14: 12 So *J* said to his armor-bearer,
14: 12 men of the outpost shouted to *J*
14: 13 The Philistines fell before *J*,
14: 13 *J* climbed up, using his hands
14: 14 that first attack *J* and his
14: 17 it was *J* and his armor-bearer who
14: 21 who were with Saul and *J*.
14: 27 *J* had not heard that his father had
14: 29 *J* said, "My father has made
14: 39 even if it lies with my son *J*,
14: 40 I and *J* my son will stand over here
1Sa 14: 41 And *J* and Saul were taken by lot,
14: 42 And *J* was taken.
14: 42 the lot between me and *J* my son."
14: 43 *J* told him, "I merely tasted a little
14: 43 to *J*, "Tell me what you have done
14: 44 so severely, if you do not die, *J*."
14: 45 So the men rescued *J*,
14: 45 the men said to Saul, "Should *J* die
14: 49 Saul's sons were *J*, Ishvi
18: 1 *J* became one in spirit with David,
18: 3 *J* made a covenant with David
18: 4 *J* took off the robe he was wearing
19: 1 But *J* was very fond of David
19: 1 Saul told his son *J* and all
19: 4 *J* spoke well of David
19: 6 listened to *J* and took this oath:
19: 7 So *J* called David and told him
20: 1 Naioth at Ramah and went to *J*
20: 2 take my life?" "Never!" *J* replied.
20: 3 '*J* must not know this or he will be
20: 4 *J* said to David, "Whatever you
20: 9 to your father?" "Never!" *J* said.
20: 11 *J* said, "let's go out into the field."
20: 12 *J* said to David: "By the LORD,
20: 16 *J* made a covenant with the house
20: 17 *J* had David reaffirm his oath out
20: 18 *J* said to David: "Tomorrow is
20: 25 *J* sat opposite him, and Abner sat
20: 27 Then Saul said to his son *J*,
20: 28 yesterday or today?" *J* answered,
20: 30 Saul's anger flared up at *J*
20: 32 has he done?" *J* asked his father.
20: 33 *J* knew that his father intended
20: 34 *J* got up from the table
20: 35 In the morning *J* went out
20: 37 *J* called out after him, "Isn't
20: 39 boy knew nothing of all this; only *J*
20: 40 Then *J* gave his weapons to the boy
20: 41 bowed down before *J* three times,
20: 42 and *J* went back to the town.
20: 42 *J* said to David, "Go in peace,
23: 16 And Saul's son *J* went to David
23: 18 *J* went home, but David remained
31: 2 and they killed his sons *J*,
2Sa 1: 4 And Saul and his son *J* are dead."
1: 5 that Saul and his son *J* are dead?"
1: 12 till evening for Saul and his son *J*,
1: 17 concerning Saul and his son *J*,
1: 22 the bow of *J* did not turn back,
1: 23 "Saul and *J*—
1: 25 *J* lies slain on your heights.
1: 26 I grieve for you, *J* my brother;
4: 4 the news about Saul and *J* came
4: 4 (*J* son of Saul had a son who was
9: 3 a son of *J*; he is crippled
9: 6 When Mephibosheth son of *J*,
9: 7 for the sake of your father *J*.
15: 27 with your son Ahimaaz and *J* son
15: 36 of Zadok and *J* son of Abiathar,
17: 17 *J* and Ahimaaz were staying
17: 20 "Where are Ahimaaz and *J*?"
21: 7 between David and *J* son of Saul.
21: 7 spared Mephibosheth son of *J*,
21: 12 bones of Saul and his son *J*
21: 13 of Saul and his son *J* from there,
21: 14 and his son *J* in the tomb
21: 21 When he taunted Israel, *J* son
23: 32 *J* son of Shammah the Hararite,
1Ki 1: 42 *J* son of Abiathar the priest arrived
1: 43 "Not at all!" *J* answered.
1Ch 2: 32 Shammai's brother: Jether and *J*.
2: 33 The sons of *J*: Peleth and Zaza.
8: 33 Saul the father of *J*, Malki-Shua,
8: 34 The son of *J*: Merib-Baal, who was
9: 39 Saul the father of *J*, Malki-Shua,
9: 40 The son of *J*: Merib-Baal, who was
10: 2 and they killed his sons *J*,
11: 34 *J* son of Shagee the Hararite,
20: 7 When he taunted Israel, *J* son
27: 25 *J* son of Uzziah was in charge
27: 32 *J*, David's uncle, was a counselor,
Ezr 8: 6 son of *J*, and with him 50 men;
10: 15 Only *J* son of Asahel and Jahzeiah
Ne 12: 11 the father of *J*, and *J* the father
12: 14 of Malluch's, *J*; of Shecaniah's,
12: 35 and also Zechariah son of *J*,
Jer 37: 15 in the house of *J* the secretary,
37: 20 to the house of *J* the secretary,

Jer 40: 8 Johanan and *J* the sons of Kareah,

JONATHAN'S (JONATHAN)

1Sa 20:37 the place where *J* arrow had fallen,
2Sa 9: 1 I can show kindness for *J* sake?''
Jer 38:26 back to *J* house to die there.' ''

JOPPA

Jos 19:46 and Rakkon, with the area facing *J*.
2Ch 2:16 them in rafts by sea down to *J*.
Ezr 3: 7 logs by sea from Lebanon to *J*,
Jnh 1: 3 to *J*, where he found a ship bound
Ac 9:36 In *J* there was a disciple named
9:38 Lydda was near *J*;
9:42 This became known all over *J*,
9:43 Peter stayed in *J* for some time
10: 5 to *J* to bring back a man named
10: 8 had happened and sent them to *J*.
10:23 of the brothers from *J* went along.
10:32 to *J* for Simon who is called Peter.
11: 5 ''I was in the city of *J* praying,
11:13 to *J* for Simon who is called Peter.

JORAH

Ezr 2:18 of Bezai 323 of *J* 112

JORAI

1Ch 5:13 Meshullam, Sheba, *J*, Jacan,

JORAM

2Sa 8:10 he sent his son *J* to King David
8:10 *J* brought with him articles of silver
2Ki 1:17 *J* succeeded him as king
3: 1 *J* son of Ahab became king
3: 6 So at that time King *J* set out
8:16 year of *J* son of Ahab king
8:25 year of *J* son of Ahab king
8:28 Ahaziah went with *J* son of Ahab
8:28 The Arameans wounded *J*;
8:29 so King *J* returned to Jezreel
8:29 to Jezreel to see *J* son of Ahab,
9:14 *J* and all Israel had been defending
9:14 son of Nimshi, conspired against *J*.
9:15 but King *J* had returned to Jezreel
9:16 because *J* was resting there
9:17 ''Get a horseman,'' *J* ordered.
9:21 *J* king of Israel and Ahaziah king
9:21 ''Hitch up my chariot,'' *J* ordered.
9:22 When *J* saw Jehu he asked,
9:23 *J* turned about and fled, calling out
9:24 and shot *J* between the shoulders.
9:29 (In the eleventh year of *J* son
1Ch 26:25 Jeshaiah his son, *J* his son,
2Ch 22: 5 The Arameans wounded *J*;
22: 5 counsel when he went with *J* son
22: 6 to Jezreel to see *J* son of Ahab
22: 7 Through Ahaziah's visit to *J*,
22: 7 he went out with *J*
Mt 1: 8 father of *J*, *J* the father of Uzziah,

JORDAN (JORDAN'S)

Ge 13:10 plain of the *J* was well watered,
13:11 for himself the whole plain of the *J*
32:10 staff when I crossed this *J*,
50:10 near the *J*, they lamented loudly
50:11 place near the *J* is called Abel
Nu 13:29 live near the sea and along the *J*.''
22: 1 and camped along the *J*
26: 3 Moab by the *J* across from Jericho,
26:63 Moab by the *J* across from Jericho.
31:12 by the *J* across from Jericho.
32: 5 Do not make us cross the *J*.''
32:19 to us on the east side of the *J*.''
32:19 with them on the other side of the *J*
32:21 armed over the *J* before the LORD
32:29 cross over the *J* with you
32:32 be on this side of the *J*.''
33:48 Moab by the *J* across from Jericho.
33:49 along the *J* from Beth Jeshimoth
33:50 Moab by the *J* across from Jericho
33:51 When you cross the *J* into Canaan,
34:12 boundary will go down along the *J*
34:15 on the east side of the *J* of Jericho,
35: 1 Moab by the *J* across from Jericho,
35:10 When you cross the *J* into Canaan,
35:14 Give three on this side of the *J*
36:13 Moab by the *J* across from Jericho.
Dt 1: 1 Israel in the desert east of the *J*—
1: 5 East of the *J* in the territory
2:29 until we cross the *J*
3: 8 Amorites the territory east of the *J*,
3:17 Its western border was the *J*
3:20 God is giving them, across the *J*.
3:25 see the good land beyond the *J*—
3:27 you are not going to cross this *J*.
4:14 the land that you are crossing the *J*
4:21 swore that I would not cross the *J*
4:22 in this land; I will not cross the *J*;
4:26 the land that you are crossing the *J*
4:41 set aside three cities east of the *J*,
4:46 near Beth Peor east of the *J*,
4:47 the two Amorite kings east of the *J*
4:49 all the Arabah east of the *J*,
6: 1 the land that you are crossing the *J*
9: 1 about to cross the *J* to go in
11: 8 the land that you are crossing the *J*
11:11 But the land you are crossing the *J*
11:30 these mountains are across the *J*,
11:31 about to cross the *J* to enter
12:10 But you will cross the *J*
27: 2 When you have crossed the *J*
27: 4 And when you have crossed the *J*,
27:12 When you have crossed the *J*,
30:18 in the land you are crossing the *J*
31: 2 'You shall not cross the *J*.'
31:13 in the land you are crossing the *J*
32:47 in the land you are crossing the *J*
Jos 1: 2 get ready to cross the *J* River
1:11 from now you will cross the *J* here
1:14 that Moses gave you east of the *J*,
1:15 east of the *J* toward the sunrise.''
2: 7 leads to the fords of the *J*,
2:10 kings of the Amorites east of the *J*,
3: 1 out from Shittim and went to the *J*,
3:11 go into the *J* ahead of you.
3:13 of all the earth—set foot in the *J*,
3:14 people broke camp to cross the *J*,
3:15 Now the *J* is at flood stage all
3:15 who carried the ark reached the *J*
3:17 ground in the middle of the *J*,
4: 1 nation had finished crossing the *J*,
4: 3 stones from the middle of the *J*
4: 5 God into the middle of the *J*.
4: 7 When it crossed the *J*, the waters
4: 7 of the *J* was cut off before the ark
4: 7 the waters of the *J* were cut off.
4: 8 stones from the middle of the *J*,
4: 9 been in the middle of the *J*
4:10 standing in the middle of the *J*
4:16 to come up out of the *J*.''
4:17 the priests, ''Come up out of the *J*.''
4:18 of the *J* returned to their place
4:19 the people went up from the *J*
4:20 stones they had taken out of the *J*.
4:22 Israel crossed the *J* on dry ground.'
4:23 did to the *J* just what he had done
4:23 the LORD your God dried up the *J*
5: 1 all the Amorite kings west of the *J*
5: 1 how the LORD had dried up the *J*
7: 7 people across the *J* to deliver us
7: 7 to stay on the other side of the *J*!
9: 1 of the *J* heard about these things—
9:10 of the Amorites east of the *J*—
12: 1 they took over east of the *J*,
12: 7 on the west side of the *J*,
13: 8 had given them east of the *J*,
13:23 Reubenites was the bank of the *J*.
13:27 of Heshbon (the east side of the *J*,
13:32 Moab across the *J* east of Jericho.
14: 3 tribes their inheritance east of the *J*
15: 5 as far as the mouth of the *J*.
15: 5 bay of the sea at the mouth of the *J*,
16: 1 for Joseph began at the *J* of Jericho
16: 7 Jericho and came out at the *J*.
17: 5 Gilead and Bashan east of the *J*,
18: 7 on the east side of the *J*.
18:12 side their boundary began at the *J*,
18:19 at the mouth of the *J* in the south.
18:20 The *J* formed the boundary
19:22 and ended at the *J*.
19:33 to Lakkum and ending at the *J*.
19:34 on the west and the *J* on the east.
20: 8 of the *J* of Jericho they designated
22: 4 you on the other side of the *J*.
22: 7 side of the *J* with their brothers.)
22:10 an imposing altar there by the *J*.
Jos 22:10 to Geliloth near the *J* in the land
22:11 Canaan at Geliloth near the *J*
22:25 LORD has made the *J* a boundary
23: 4 between the *J* and the Great Sea
24: 8 Amorites who lived east of the *J*.
24:11 '' 'Then you crossed the *J*
Jdg 3:28 the fords of the *J* that led to Moab,
5:17 Gilead stayed beyond the *J*.
6:33 and crossed over the *J* and camped
7:24 the waters of the *J* ahead of them
7:24 they took the waters of the *J* as far
7:25 Zeeb to Gideon, who was by the *J*.
8: 4 came to the *J* and crossed it.
10: 8 on the east side of the *J* in Gilead,
10: 9 crossed the *J* to fight against Judah
11:13 to the Jabbok, all the way to the *J*.
11:22 and from the desert to the *J*.
12: 5 fords of the *J* leading to Ephraim,
12: 6 and killed him at the fords of the *J*.
1Sa 13: 7 crossed the *J* to the land of Gad
31: 7 across the *J* saw that the Israelite
2Sa 2:29 They crossed the *J*, continued
10:17 crossed the *J* and went to Helam.
17:22 was left who had not crossed the *J*.
17:22 with him set out and crossed the *J*.
17:24 and Absalom crossed the *J*
19:15 and bring him across the *J*.
19:15 returned and went as far as the *J*.
19:17 to the *J*, where the king was.
19:18 son of Gera crossed the *J*,
19:31 to cross the *J* with the king
19:36 cross over the *J* with the king
19:39 So all the people crossed the *J*,
19:41 and his household across the *J*,
20: 2 the way from the *J* to Jerusalem.
24: 5 After crossing the *J*, they camped
1Ki 2: 8 came down to meet me at the *J*,
7:46 the plain of the *J* between Succoth
17: 3 in the Kerith Ravine, east of the *J*.
17: 5 east of the *J*, and stayed there.
2Ki 2: 6 the LORD has sent me to the *J*.''
2: 7 and Elisha had stopped at the *J*.
2:13 and stood on the bank of the *J*.
5:10 wash yourself seven times in the *J*,
5:14 dipped himself in the *J* seven times
6: 2 Let us go to the *J*, where each
6: 4 They went to the *J* and began
7:15 They followed them as far as the *J*,
10:33 east of the *J* in all the land
1Ch 6:78 tribe of Reuben across the *J* east
12:15 It was they who crossed the *J*
12:37 from east of the *J*, men of Reuben,
19:17 all Israel and crossed the *J*;
26:30 west of the *J* for all the work
2Ch 4:17 the plain of the *J* between Succoth
Job 40:23 the *J* should surge
Ps 42: 6 you from the land of the *J*,
114: 3 the *J* turned back;
114: 5 O *J*, that you turned back,
Isa 9: 1 along the *J*— The people walking
Jer 12: 5 manage in the thickets by the *J*?
Eze 47:18 along the *J* between Gilead
Zec 11: 3 the lush thicket of the *J* is ruined!
Mt 3: 5 and the whole region of the *J*.
3: 6 baptized by him in the *J* River.
3:13 from Galilee to the *J* to be baptized
4:15 the way to the sea, along the *J*,
4:25 region across the *J* followed him.
19: 1 of Judea to the other side of the *J*.
Mk 1: 5 baptized by him in the *J* River.
1: 9 and was baptized by John in the *J*.
3: 8 and the regions across the *J*
10: 1 region of Judea and across the *J*.
Lk 3: 3 into all the country around the *J*,
4: 1 returned from the *J* and was led
Jn 1:28 Bethany on the other side of the *J*,
3:26 with you on the other side of the *J*
10:40 Then Jesus went back across the *J*

JORDAN'S (JORDAN)

Jos 3: 8 you reach the edge of the *J* waters,
Jer 49:19 a lion coming up from *J* thickets
50:44 a lion coming up from *J* thickets

JORIM

Lk 3:29 the son of *J*, the son of Matthat,

JORKEAM

1Ch 2: 44 and Raham the father of *J*.

JOSECH

Lk 3: 26 the son of *J*, the son of Joda,

JOSEPH (JOSEPH'S)

Ge 30: 24 She named him *J*, and said,
30: 25 After Rachel gave birth to *J*,
33: 2 and Rachel and *J* in the rear.
33: 7 Last of all came *J* and Rachel,
35: 24 sons of Rachel: *J* and Benjamin.
37: 2 *J*, a young man of seventeen,
37: 3 Now Israel loved *J* more than any
37: 5 *J* had a dream, and when he told it
37: 13 and Israel said to *J*, "As you know,
37: 14 When *J* arrived at Shechem,
37: 17 So *J* went after his brothers
37: 23 So when *J* came to his brothers,
37: 28 his brothers pulled *J* up out
37: 29 and saw that *J* was not there,
37: 33 *J* has surely been torn to pieces."
37: 36 the Midianites sold *J* in Egypt
39: 1 *J* had been taken down to Egypt.
39: 2 The LORD was with *J*
39: 4 *J* found favor in his eyes
39: 5 of the Egyptian because of *J*.
39: 6 care everything he had; with *J*
39: 6 *J* was well-built and handsome,
39: 7 his master's wife took notice of *J*
39: 10 though she spoke to *J* day after day
39: 20 But while *J* was there in the prison,
39: 22 So the warden put *J* in charge
39: 23 because the LORD was with *J*
40: 3 same prison where *J* was confined.
40: 4 of the guard assigned them to *J*,
40: 6 When *J* came to them the next
40: 8 Then *J* said to them, "Do not
40: 9 chief cupbearer told *J* his dream.
40: 12 "This is what it means," *J* said
40: 16 chief baker saw that *J* had given
40: 16 he said to *J*, "I too had a dream:
40: 18 "This is what it means," *J* said.
40: 22 as *J* had said to them
40: 23 did not remember *J*; he forgot him.
41: 14 So Pharaoh sent for *J*,
41: 15 Pharaoh said to *J*, "I had a dream,
41: 16 "I cannot do it," *J* replied
41: 17 to *J*, "In my dream I was standing
41: 25 *J* said to Pharaoh, "The dreams
41: 39 to *J*, "Since God has made all this
41: 41 said to *J*, "I hereby put you
41: 44 Pharaoh said to *J*, "I am Pharaoh,
41: 45 And *J* went throughout the land
41: 45 Pharaoh gave *J* the name
41: 46 And *J* went out from Pharaoh's
41: 46 *J* was thirty years old
41: 48 *J* collected all the food produced
41: 49 *J* stored up huge quantities of grain
41: 50 born to *J* by Asenath daughter
41: 51 *J* named his firstborn Manasseh
41: 54 of famine began, just as *J* had said.
41: 55 "Go to *J* and do what he tells you."
41: 56 *J* opened the storehouses
41: 57 came to Egypt to buy grain from *J*,
42: 6 *J* was the governor of the land,
42: 7 As soon as *J* saw his brothers,
42: 8 Although *J* recognized his brothers
42: 14 *J* said to them, "It is just
42: 18 On the third day, *J* said to them,
42: 23 not realize that *J* could understand
42: 25 *J* gave orders to fill their bags
42: 36 *J* is no more and Simeon is no more
43: 15 and presented themselves to *J*.
43: 16 When *J* saw Benjamin with them,
43: 17 The man did as *J* told him
43: 26 When *J* came home, they
43: 30 *J* hurried out and looked
44: 1 Now *J* gave these instructions
44: 2 And he did as *J* said.
44: 4 far from the city when *J* said
44: 14 *J* was still in the house when Judah
44: 15 *J* said to them, "What is this you
44: 17 But *J* said, "Far be it from me
45: 1 So there was no one with *J*
45: 1 *J* could no longer control himself
45: 3 *J* said to his brothers, "I am *J*!
Ge 45: 4 Then *J* said to his brothers,
45: 4 he said, "I am your brother *J*,
45: 9 'This is what your son *J* says:
45: 17 said to *J*, "Tell your brothers,
45: 21 *J* gave them carts, as Pharaoh had
45: 26 They told him, "*J* is still alive!
45: 27 they told him everything *J* had said
45: 27 when he saw the carts *J* had sent
45: 28 convinced! My son *J* is still alive.
46: 19 The sons of Jacob's wife Rachel: *J*
46: 20 born to *J* by Asenath daughter
46: 27 two sons who had been born to *J*
46: 28 ahead of him to *J* to get directions
46: 29 As soon as *J* appeared before him,
46: 29 *J* had his chariot made ready
46: 30 Israel said to *J*, "Now I am ready
46: 31 Then *J* said to his brothers
47: 1 *J* went and told Pharaoh, "My
47: 5 Pharaoh said to *J*, "Your father
47: 7 Then *J* brought his father Jacob in
47: 11 *J* settled his father and his brothers
47: 12 *J* also provided his father
47: 14 *J* collected all the money that was
47: 15 all Egypt came to *J* and said,
47: 16 Then bring your livestock," said *J*.
47: 17 So they brought their livestock to *J*
47: 20 So *J* bought all the land in Egypt
47: 21 *J* reduced the people to servitude,
47: 23 *J* said to the people, "Now that I
47: 26 *J* established it as a law concerning
47: 29 called for his son *J* and said to him,
47: 31 Then *J* swore to him, and Israel
48: 1 Some time later *J* was told,
48: 2 "Your son *J* has come to you,"
48: 3 said to *J*, "God Almighty appeared
48: 8 When Israel saw the sons of *J*,
48: 9 God has given me here," *J* said
48: 10 So *J* brought his sons close to him,
48: 11 Israel said to *J*, "I never expected
48: 12 Then *J* removed them from Israel's
48: 13 And *J* took both of them, Ephraim
48: 15 Then he blessed *J* and said,
48: 17 When *J* saw his father placing his
48: 18 *J* said to him, "No, my father,
48: 21 Israel said to *J*, "I am about to die,
49: 22 "*J* is a fruitful vine,
49: 26 Let all these rest on the head of *J*,
50: 1 *J* threw himself upon his father
50: 2 Then *J* directed the physicians
50: 4 of mourning had passed, *J* said
50: 7 So *J* went up to bury his father.
50: 10 and there *J* observed a seven-day
50: 14 After burying his father, *J* returned
50: 15 What if *J* holds a grudge against us
50: 16 So they sent word to *J*, saying,
50: 17 their message came to him, *J* wept.
50: 17 'This is what you are to say to *J*:
50: 19 *J* said to them, "Don't be afraid.
50: 22 *J* stayed in Egypt,
50: 24 Then *J* said to his brothers,
50: 25 *J* made the sons of Israel swear
50: 26 So *J* died at the age of a hundred
Ex 1: 5 in all; *J* was already in Egypt.
1: 6 Now *J* and all his brothers
1: 8 who did not know about *J*,
13: 19 Moses took the bones of *J*
13: 19 because *J* had made the sons
Nu 1: 10 from the sons of *J*: from Ephraim,
1: 32 sons of *J*: From the descendants
13: 7 Igal son of *J*; from the tribe
13: 11 the tribe of Manasseh (a tribe of *J*),
26: 28 The descendants of *J* by their clans
26: 37 the descendants of *J* by their clans.
27: 1 to the clans of Manasseh son of *J*.
32: 33 of Manasseh son of *J* the kingdom
34: 23 from the tribe of Manasseh son of *J*
34: 24 from the tribe of Ephraim son of *J*;
36: 1 the clans of the descendants of *J*,
36: 5 descendants of *J* is saying is right.
36: 12 descendants of Manasseh son of *J*,
Dt 27: 12 Judah, Issachar, *J* and Benjamin.
33: 13 About *J* he said:
33: 16 Let all these rest on the head of *J*,
Jos 14: 4 sons of *J* had become two tribes—
16: 1 The allotment for *J* began
16: 4 of *J*, received their inheritance.
17: 2 of Manasseh son of *J* by their clans
17: 14 The people of *J* said to Joshua,
Jos 17: 16 of *J* replied, "The hill country is
17: 17 But Joshua said to the house of *J*—
18: 5 and the house of *J* in its territory
18: 11 between the tribes of Judah and *J*:
Jdg 1: 22 the house of *J* attacked Bethel,
1: 35 power of the house of *J* increased,
2Sa 19: 20 house of *J* to come down
1Ki 11: 28 whole labor force of the house of *J*.
1Ch 2: 2 Zebulun, Dan, *J*, Benjamin,
5: 1 given to the sons of *J* son of Israel;
5: 2 of the firstborn belonged to *J*)—
7: 29 The descendants of *J* son
25: 2 Zaccur, *J*, Nethaniah and Asarelah
25: 9 fell to *J*, his sons and relatives,
Ezr 10: 42 Shallum, Amariah and *J*.
Ne 12: 14 of Shecaniah's, *J*; of Harim's,
Ps 77: 15 the descendants of Jacob and *J*.
78: 67 Then he rejected the tents of *J*,
80: 1 you who lead *J* like a flock;
81: 5 He established it as a statute for *J*
105: 17 *J*, sold as a slave.
Eze 37: 16 belonging to *J* and all the house
37: 19 I am going to take the stick of *J*—
47: 13 of Israel, with two portions for *J*.
48: 32 will be three gates: the gate of *J*,
Am 5: 6 through the house of *J* like a fire;
5: 15 mercy on the remnant of *J*.
6: 6 you do not grieve over the ruin of *J*
Ob : 18 and the house of *J* a flame;
Zec 10: 6 and save the house of *J*.
Mt 1: 16 Jacob the father of *J*, the husband
1: 18 pledged to be married to *J*,
1: 19 Because *J* her husband was
1: 20 him in a dream and said, "*J* son
1: 24 When *J* woke up, he did what
2: 13 an angel of the Lord appeared to *J*
2: 19 appeared in a dream to *J* in Egypt
13: 55 and aren't his brothers James, *J*,
27: 56 Mary the mother of James and *J*,
27: 57 man from Arimathea, named *J*,
27: 59 *J* took the body, wrapped it
Mk 15: 43 So as evening approached, *J*
15: 45 was so, he gave the body to *J*.
15: 46 So *J* bought some linen cloth,
Lk 1: 27 to be married to a man named *J*,
2: 4 So *J* also went up from the town
2: 16 hurried off and found Mary and *J*,
2: 22 *J* and Mary took him to Jerusalem
2: 39 When *J* and Mary had done
3: 23 so it was thought, of *J*,
3: 24 the son of Jannai, the son of *J*,
3: 30 the son of Judah, the son of *J*,
23: 50 Now there was a man named *J*,
23: 55 with Jesus from Galilee followed *J*
Jn 1: 45 Jesus of Nazareth, the son of *J*."
4: 5 Jacob had given to his son *J*.
6: 42 the son of *J*, whose father
19: 38 Now *J* was a disciple of Jesus,
19: 38 *J* of Arimathea asked Pilate
Ac 1: 23 *J* called Barsabbas (also known
4: 36 *J*, a Levite from Cyprus, whom
7: 9 the patriarchs were jealous of *J*,
7: 10 He gave *J* wisdom and enabled him
7: 13 *J* told his brothers who he was,
7: 14 *J* sent for his father Jacob
7: 18 who knew nothing about *J*,
Heb 11: 22 By faith *J*, when his end was near,
Rev 7: 8 from the tribe of *J* 12,000,

JOSEPH'S (JOSEPH)

Ge 37: 31 I turn now?" Then they got *J* robe,
39: 6 he left in *J* care everything he had;
39: 20 *J* master took him and put him
39: 23 attention to anything under *J* care,
41: 42 his finger and put it on *J* finger.
42: 3 Then ten of *J* brothers went
42: 4 *J* brother, with the others,
42: 6 So when *J* brothers arrived,
43: 17 and took the men to *J* house.
43: 19 So they went up to *J* steward
43: 24 steward took the men into *J* house,
43: 25 gifts for *J* arrival at noon,
43: 34 served to them from *J* table,
45: 16 palace that *J* brothers had
46: 4 *J* own hand will close your eyes."
50: 8 all the members of *J* household
50: 15 When *J* brothers saw that their
50: 23 placed at birth on *J* knees.

Jos 17: 1 tribe of Manasseh as *J* firstborn,
24: 32 *J* bones, which the Israelites had
24: 32 the inheritance of *J* descendants.
Lk 4: 22 "Isn't this *J* son?" they asked.
Ac 7: 13 Pharaoh learned about *J* family.
Heb 11: 21 was dying, blessed each of *J* sons,

JOSES

Mk 6: 3 and the brother of James, *J*,
15: 40 of James the younger and of *J*,
15: 47 mother of *J* saw where he was laid.

JOSHAH

1Ch 4: 34 Jamlech, *J* son of Amaziah,

JOSHAPHAT

1Ch 11: 43 son of Maacah, *J* the Mithnite,
15: 24 Shebaniah, *J*, Nethanel, Amasai,

JOSHAVIAH

1Ch 11: 46 Jeribai and *J* the sons of Elnaam,

JOSHBEKASHAH

1Ch 25: 4 Giddalti and Romamti-Ezer; *J*,
25: 24 the seventeenth to *J*, his sons

JOSHEB-BASSHEBETH

2Sa 23: 8 *J*, a Tahkemonite, was chief

JOSHIBIAH

1Ch 4: 35 Jehu son of *J*, the son of Seraiah,

JOSHUA (HOSHEA)

Ex 17: 9 Moses said to *J*, "Choose some
17: 10 So *J* fought the Amalekites
17: 13 So *J* overcame the Amalekite army
17: 14 and make sure that *J* hears it,
24: 13 Then Moses set out with *J* his aide,
32: 17 When *J* heard the noise
33: 11 but his young aide *J* son
Nu 11: 28 *J* son of Nun, who had been
13: 16 son of Nun the name *J*.)
14: 6 *J* son of Nun and Caleb son
14: 30 of Jephunneh and *J* son of Nun.
14: 38 only *J* son of Nun and Caleb son
26: 65 of Jephunneh and *J* son of Nun.
27: 18 said to Moses, "Take *J* son of Nun,
27: 22 He took *J* and had him stand
32: 12 Jephunneh the Kenizzite and *J* son
32: 28 to Eleazar the priest and *J* son
34: 17 Eleazar the priest and *J* son of Nun
Dt 1: 38 But your assistant, *J* son of Nun,
3: 21 At that time I commanded *J*:
3: 28 But commission *J*, and encourage
31: 3 *J* also will cross over ahead of you,
31: 7 Then Moses summoned *J*
31: 14 Call *J* and present yourselves
31: 14 *J* came and presented themselves
31: 23 LORD gave this command to *J* son
32: 44 Moses came with *J* son of Nun
34: 9 Now *J* son of Nun was filled
Jos 1: 1 the LORD said to *J* son of Nun,
1: 10 *J* ordered the officers of the people
1: 12 the half-tribe of Manasseh, *J* said,
1: 16 they answered *J*, "Whatever you
2: 1 *J* son of Nun secretly sent two
2: 23 forded the river and came to *J* son
2: 24 to *J*, "The LORD has surely given
3: 1 Early in the morning *J*
3: 5 *J* told the people, "Consecrate
3: 6 *J* said to the priests, "Take up
3: 7 said to *J*, "Today I will begin
3: 9 *J* said to the Israelites, "Come here
4: 1 said to *J*, "Choose twelve men
4: 4 *J* called together the twelve men
4: 8 as the LORD had told *J*;
4: 8 did as *J* commanded them.
4: 9 *J* set up the twelve stones that had
4: 10 had commanded *J* was done
4: 10 just as Moses had directed *J*.
4: 14 That day the LORD exalted *J*
4: 15 Then the LORD said to *J*,
4: 17 So *J* commanded the priests,
4: 20 *J* set up at Gilgal the twelve stones
5: 2 At that time the LORD said to *J*,
5: 3 So *J* made flint knives
5: 7 these were the ones *J* circumcised.
5: 9 Then the LORD said to *J*,
Jos 5: 13 Now when *J* was near Jericho,
5: 13 *J* went up to him and asked,
5: 14 Then *J* fell facedown to the ground
5: 15 And *J* did so.
6: 2 Then the LORD said to *J*, "See,
6: 6 So *J* son of Nun called the priests
6: 8 When *J* had spoken to the people,
6: 10 But *J* had commanded the people,
6: 12 *J* got up early the next morning
6: 16 *J* commanded the people, "Shout!
6: 22 *J* said to the two men who had
6: 25 But *J* spared Rahab the prostitute,
6: 25 because she hid the men *J* had sent
6: 26 At that time *J* pronounced this
6: 27 So the LORD was with *J*,
7: 2 Now *J* sent men from Jericho to Ai
7: 3 When they returned to *J*, they said,
7: 6 Then *J* tore his clothes
7: 7 And *J* said, "Ah, Sovereign LORD
7: 10 The LORD said to *J*, "Stand up!
7: 16 the next morning *J* had Israel come
7: 18 *J* had his family come forward man
7: 19 Then *J* said to Achan, "My son,
7: 22 So *J* sent messengers, and they ran
7: 23 them to *J* and all the Israelites
7: 24 Then *J*, together with all Israel,
7: 25 *J* said, "Why have you brought this
8: 1 Then the LORD said to *J*,
8: 3 *J* and the whole army moved out
8: 9 *J* sent them off, and they went
8: 9 *J* spent that night with the people.
8: 10 the next morning *J* mustered his
8: 12 *J* had taken about five thousand
8: 13 That night *J* went into the valley.
8: 15 *J* and all Israel let themselves be
8: 16 and they pursued *J* and were lured
8: 18 So *J* held out his javelin toward Ai.
8: 18 Then the LORD said to *J*,
8: 21 For when *J* and all Israel saw that
8: 23 of Ai alive and brought him to *J*.
8: 26 For *J* did not draw back the hand
8: 27 as the LORD had instructed *J*.
8: 28 So *J* burned Ai and made it
8: 29 *J* ordered them to take his body
8: 30 *J* built on Mount Ebal an altar
8: 32 *J* copied on stones the law
8: 34 *J* read all the words of the law—
8: 35 had commanded that *J* did not
9: 2 together to make war against *J*
9: 3 of Gibeon heard what *J* had done
9: 6 Then they went to *J* in the camp
9: 8 But *J* asked, "Who are you
9: 8 are your servants," they said to *J*.
9: 15 *J* made a treaty of peace with them
9: 22 Then *J* summoned the Gibeonites
9: 24 They answered *J*, "Your servants
9: 26 So *J* saved them from the Israelites
10: 1 Jerusalem heard that *J* had taken
10: 4 "because it has made peace with *J*
10: 6 word to *J* in the camp at Gilgal:
10: 7 So *J* marched up from Gilgal
10: 8 said to *J*, "Do not be afraid
10: 9 march from Gilgal, *J* took them
10: 12 *J* said to the LORD in the presence
10: 15 Then *J* returned with all Israel
10: 17 When *J* was told that the five kings
10: 20 *J* and the Israelites destroyed them
10: 21 to *J* in the camp at Makkedah,
10: 22 *J* said, "Open the mouth
10: 24 they had brought these kings to *J*,
10: 25 *J* said to them, "Do not be afraid;
10: 26 Then *J* struck and killed the kings
10: 27 At sunset *J* gave the order
10: 28 That day *J* took Makkedah.
10: 29 *J* and all Israel with him moved
10: 30 everyone in it *J* put to the sword.
10: 31 *J* and all Israel with him moved
10: 32 and *J* took it on the second day.
10: 33 but *J* defeated him and his army—
10: 34 *J* and all Israel with him moved
10: 36 *J* and all Israel with him went up
10: 38 *J* and all Israel with him turned
10: 40 So *J* subdued the whole region,
10: 41 *J* subdued them from Kadesh
10: 42 and their lands *J* conquered
10: 43 Then *J* returned with all Israel
11: 6 said to *J*, "Do not be afraid
11: 7 So *J* and his whole army came
Jos 11: 9 *J* did to them as the LORD had
11: 10 At that time *J* turned back
11: 12 *J* took all these royal cities
11: 13 except Hazor, which *J* burned
11: 15 Moses commanded *J*, and *J* did it;
11: 16 So *J* took this entire land: the hill
11: 18 *J* waged war against all these kings
11: 21 At that time *J* went and destroyed
11: 21 *J* totally destroyed them
11: 23 So *J* took the entire land, just
12: 7 are the kings of the land that *J*
12: 7 toward Seir (their lands *J* gave
13: 1 When *J* was old and well advanced
14: 1 *J* son of Nun and the heads
14: 6 of Judah approached *J* at Gilgal,
14: 13 *J* blessed Caleb son of Jephunneh
15: 13 *J* gave to Caleb son
17: 4 So *J* gave them an inheritance
17: 4 to Eleazar the priest, *J* son of Nun,
17: 14 The people of Joseph said to *J*,
17: 15 are so numerous," *J* answered,
17: 17 But *J* said to the house of Joseph—
18: 3 *J* said to the Israelites: "How long
18: 8 out the land, *J* instructed them,
18: 9 returned to *J* in the camp at Shiloh.
18: 10 *J* then cast lots for them in Shiloh
19: 49 the Israelites gave *J* son
19: 51 *J* son of Nun and the heads
20: 1 Then the LORD said to *J*:
21: 1 Eleazar the priest, *J* son
22: 1 Then *J* summoned the Reubenites,
22: 6 *J* blessed them and sent them away
22: 7 When *J* sent them home, he
22: 7 half of the tribe *J* gave land
23: 1 *J*, by then old and well advanced
24: 1 *J* assembled all the tribes of Israel
24: 2 *J* said to all the people, "This is
24: 19 *J* said to the people, "You are not
24: 21 But the people said to *J*, "No!
24: 22 Then *J* said, "You are witnesses
24: 23 said *J*, "throw away the foreign
24: 24 to *J*, "We will serve the LORD our
24: 25 On that day *J* made a covenant
24: 26 *J* recorded these things in the Book
24: 28 Then *J* sent the people away,
24: 29 After these things, *J* son of Nun,
24: 31 LORD throughout the lifetime of *J*
Jdg 1: 1 of *J*, the Israelites asked the LORD
2: 6 After *J* had dismissed the Israelites
2: 7 LORD throughout the lifetime of *J*
2: 8 *J* son of Nun, the servant
2: 21 of the nations *J* left when he died.
2: 23 by giving them into the hands of *J*.
1Sa 6: 14 The cart came to the field of *J*
6: 18 in the field of *J* of Beth Shemesh.
1Ki 16: 34 of the LORD spoken by *J* son
2Ki 23: 8 at the entrance to the Gate of *J*,
1Ch 7: 27 Nun his son and *J* his son.
Ne 8: 17 From the days of *J* son of Nun
Hag 1: 1 and to *J* son of Jehozadak,
1: 12 of Shealtiel, *J* son of Jehozadak,
1: 14 and the spirit of *J* son of Jehozadak
2: 2 of Judah, to *J* son of Jehozadak,
2: 4 'Be strong, O *J* son of Jehozadak,
Zec 3: 1 he showed me *J* the high priest
3: 3 Now *J* was dressed in filthy clothes
3: 4 to *J*, "See, I have taken away your
3: 6 of the LORD gave this charge to *J*:
3: 8 O high priest *J* and your associates
3: 9 the stone I have set in front of *J*!
6: 11 the head of the high priest, *J* son
Lk 3: 29 the son of *J*, the son of Eliezer,
Ac 7: 45 our fathers under *J* brought it
Heb 4: 8 For if *J* had given them rest,

JOSIAH (JOSIAH'S)

1Ki 13: 2 'A son named *J* will be born
2Ki 21: 24 and they made *J* his son king
21: 26 And *J* his son succeeded him
22: 1 *J* was eight years old
22: 3 King *J* sent the secretary, Shaphan
23: 8 *J* brought all the priests
23: 11 *J* then burned the chariots
23: 14 *J* smashed the sacred stones
23: 16 Then *J* looked around,
23: 19 *J* removed and defiled all
23: 20 *J* slaughtered all the priests
23: 23 in the eighteenth year of King *J*,

2Ki 23: 24 *J* got rid of the mediums
23: 25 after *J* was there a king like him
23: 29 King *J* marched out to meet him
23: 29 kings of Judah? While *J* was king,
23: 30 of the land took Jehoahaz son of *J*
23: 34 king in place of his father *J*
23: 34 made Eliakim son of *J* king
1Ch 3: 14 his son, Amon his son, *J* his son.
3: 15 sons of *J*: Johanan the firstborn,
2Ch 33: 25 and they made *J* his son king
34: 1 *J* was eight years old
34: 33 *J* removed all the detestable idols
35: 1 *J* celebrated the Passover
35: 7 *J* provided for all the lay people
35: 16 the LORD, as King *J* had ordered.
35: 18 celebrated such a Passover as did *J*,
35: 20 and *J* marched out to meet him
35: 20 when *J* had set the temple in order,
35: 22 *J*, however, would not turn away
35: 23 Archers shot King *J*, and he told
35: 25 Jeremiah composed laments for *J*,
35: 25 women singers commemorate *J*
36: 1 of the land took Jehoahaz son of *J*
Jer 1: 2 of the reign of *J* son of Amon king
1: 3 of Jehoiakim son of *J* king of Judah
1: 3 of Zedekiah son of *J* king of Judah,
3: 6 During the reign of King *J*,
22: 11 says about Shallum son of *J*,
22: 18 son of *J* king of Judah:
25: 1 of Jehoiakim son of *J* king of Judah
25: 3 year of *J* son of Amon king
26: 1 of Jehoiakim son of *J* king of Judah
27: 1 of Zedekiah son of *J* king of Judah,
35: 1 of Jehoiakim son of *J* king of Judah
36: 1 of Jehoiakim son of *J* king of Judah
36: 2 to you in the reign of *J* till now.
36: 9 of Jehoiakim son of *J* king of Judah
37: 1 Zedekiah son of *J* was made king
45: 1 of Jehoiakim son of *J* king of Judah
46: 2 of Jehoiakim son of *J* king of Judah
Zep 1: 1 during the reign of *J* son
Zec 6: 10 to the house of *J* son of Zephaniah.
Mt 1: 10 of Amon, Amon the father of *J*,
1: 11 and *J* the father of Jeconiah

JOSIAH'S (JOSIAH)

2Ki 23: 28 As for the other events of *J* reign,
23: 30 *J* servants brought his body
2Ch 34: 8 In the eighteenth year of *J* reign,
35: 19 in the eighteenth year of *J* reign.
35: 26 The other events of *J* reign

JOSIPHIAH

Ezr 8: 10 Shelomith son of *J*,

JOSTLE (JOSTLED)

Joel 2: 8 They do not *j* each other;

JOSTLED (JOSTLE)

Ge 25: 22 The babies *j* each other within her,

JOTBAH

2Ki 21: 19 daughter of Haruz; she was from *J*.

JOTBATHAH

Nu 33: 33 Hor Haggidgad and camped at *J*.
33: 34 They left *J* and camped at Abronah
Dt 10: 7 traveled to Gudgodah and on to *J*,

JOTHAM (JOTHAM'S)

Jdg 9: 5 *J*, the youngest son of Jerub-Baal,
9: 7 When *J* was told about this,
9: 21 Then *J* fled, escaping to Beer,
9: 57 The curse of *J* son
2Ki 15: 5 *J* the king's son had charge
15: 7 And *J* his son succeeded him
15: 30 year of *J* son of Uzziah.
15: 32 *J* son of Uzziah king
15: 35 *J* rebuilt the Upper Gate
15: 38 *J* rested with his fathers
16: 1 Ahaz son of *J* king of Judah began
1Ch 2: 47 The sons of Jahdai: Regem, *J*,
3: 12 Azariah his son, *J* his son,
5: 17 during the reigns of *J* king of Judah
2Ch 26: 21 *J* his son had charge of the palace
26: 23 And *J* his son succeeded him
27: 1 *J* was twenty-five years old
27: 3 *J* rebuilt the Upper Gate
27: 5 *J* made war on the king
27: 6 *J* grew powerful because he walked
27: 9 *J* rested with his fathers
Isa 1: 1 *J*, Ahaz and Hezekiah, kings
7: 1 When Ahaz son of *J*, the son
Hos 1: 1 *J*, Ahaz and Hezekiah, kings
Mic 1: 1 of Moresheth during the reigns of *J*
Mt 1: 9 father of *J*, *J* the father of Ahaz,

JOTHAM'S (JOTHAM)

2Ki 15: 36 As for the other events of *J* reign,
2Ch 27: 7 The other events in *J* reign,

JOURNEY (JOURNEYED JOURNEYS)

Ge 24: 21 LORD had made his *j* successful.
24: 27 me on the *j* to the house
24: 40 and make your *j* a success,
24: 42 please grant success to the *j*
24: 56 LORD has granted success to my *j*.
28: 20 watch over me on this *j* I am taking
29: 1 Then Jacob continued on his *j*
30: 36 Then he put a three-day *j*
42: 25 to give them provisions for their *j*.
42: 38 to him on the *j* you are taking,
45: 21 gave them provisions for their *j*.
45: 23 bread and other provisions for his *j*.
Ex 3: 18 Let us take a three-day *j*
5: 3 Now let us take a three-day *j*
8: 27 We must take a three-day *j*
Nu 9: 10 of a dead body or are away on a *j*,
9: 13 and not on a *j* fails to celebrate
33: 1 the stages in the *j* of the Israelites
33: 2 This is their *j* by stages:
33: 2 recorded the stages in their *j*.
Dt 1: 33 who went ahead of you on your *j*,
2: 7 over your *j* through this vast desert
25: 18 they met you on your *j*
28: 68 on a *j* I said you should never make
Jos 5: 5 during the *j* from Egypt had not.
9: 11 'Take provisions for your *j*;
9: 13 out by the very long *j*."
24: 17 He protected us on our entire *j*
Jdg 18: 5 whether our *j* will be successful."
18: 6 Your *j* has the LORD's approval."
1Ki 13: 26 back from his *j* heard of it,
19: 4 while he himself went a day's *j*
19: 7 for the *j* is too much for you."
Ezr 7: 9 He had begun his *j* from Babylon
8: 21 and ask him for a safe *j* for us
Ne 2: 6 "How long will your *j* take,
Job 16: 22 before I go on the *j* of no return.
Pr 7: 19 he has gone on a long *j*.
Isa 35: 8 The unclean will not *j* on it;
Am 5: 5 do not *j* to Beersheba.
Jnh 3: 4 going a day's *j*, and he proclaimed:
Mic 6: 5 Remember your *j* from Shittim
Mt 10: 10 take no bag for the *j*, or extra tunic,
21: 33 farmers and went away on a *j*.
25: 14 it will be like a man going on a *j*,
25: 15 Then he went on his *j*.
Mk 6: 8 Take nothing for the *j* except a staff
12: 1 farmers and went away on a *j*.
Lk 9: 3 "Take nothing for the *j*— no staff,
11: 6 of mine on a *j* has come to me,
Jn 4: 6 as he was from the *j*, sat
Ac 9: 3 As he neared Damascus on his *j*,
9: 27 Saul on his *j* had seen the Lord
16: 3 wanted to take him along on the *j*,
Ro 15: 24 to have you assist me on my *j* there
1Co 16: 6 so that you can help me on my *j*,

JOURNEYED (JOURNEY)

Ex 12: 37 The Israelites *j* from Rameses
1Sa 31: 12 all their valiant men *j*
Job 38: 16 "Have you *j* to the springs

JOURNEYS (JOURNEY)

Ac 26: 12 "On one of these *j* I was going

JOWLS

Dt 18: 3 shoulder, the *j* and the inner parts.

JOY (ENJOY ENJOYED ENJOYING ENJOYMENT ENJOYS JOYFUL JOYOUS OVERJOYED REJOICE REJOICED REJOICES REJOICING)

Ge 31: 27 so I could send you away with *j*
Lev 9: 24 shouted for *j* and fell facedown.
Dt 16: 15 and your *j* will be complete.
Jdg 9: 19 may Abimelech be your *j*,
1Ch 12: 40 and sheep, for there was *j* in Israel.
16: 27 strength and *j* in his dwelling place.
16: 33 sing for *j* before the LORD,
29: 17 with *j* how willingly your people
29: 22 drank with great *j* in the presence
2Ch 30: 26 There was great *j* in Jerusalem,
Ezr 3: 12 while many others shouted for *j*.
3: 13 of the shouts of *j* from the sound
6: 16 of the house of God with *j*.
6: 22 with *j* by changing the attitude
6: 22 *j* the Feast of Unleavened Bread,
Ne 8: 10 for the *j* of the LORD is your
8: 12 and to celebrate with great *j*,
8: 17 And their *j* was very great.
12: 43 God had given them great *j*.
Est 8: 16 a time of happiness and *j*,
8: 17 there was *j* and gladness
9: 17 and made it a day of feasting and *j*.
9: 18 and made it a day of feasting and *j*.
9: 19 as a day of *j* and feasting,
9: 22 and *j* and giving presents of food
9: 22 their sorrow was turned into *j*
Job 3: 7 may no shout of *j* be heard in it.
6: 10 my *j* in unrelenting pain—
8: 21 and your lips with shouts of *j*.
9: 25 they fly away without a glimpse of *j*
10: 20 from me so I can have a moment's *j*
20: 5 the *j* of the godless lasts
33: 26 he sees God's face and shouts for *j*;
38: 7 and all the angels shouted for *j*?
Ps 4: 7 have filled my heart with greater *j*
5: 11 let them ever sing for *j*.
16: 11 me with *j* in your presence,
19: 8 giving *j* to the heart.
20: 5 We will shout for *j*
21: 1 How great is his *j* in the victories
21: 6 with the *j* of your presence.
27: 6 will I sacrifice with shouts of *j*;
28: 7 My heart leaps for *j*
30: 11 sackcloth and clothed me with *j*,
33: 3 play skillfully, and shout for *j*.
35: 27 shout for *j* and gladness;
42: 4 with shouts of *j* and thanksgiving
43: 4 to God, my *j* and my delight.
45: 7 by anointing you with the oil of *j*.
45: 15 They are led in with *j* and gladness;
47: 1 shout to God with cries of *j*.
47: 5 God has ascended amid shouts of *j*,
48: 2 the *j* of the whole earth.
51: 8 Let me hear *j* and gladness;
51: 12 to me the *j* of your salvation
65: 8 you call forth songs of *j*.
65: 13 they shout for *j* and sing.
66: 1 Shout with *j* to God, all the earth!
67: 4 the nations be glad and sing for *j*,
71: 23 My lips will shout for *j*
81: 1 Sing for *j* to God our strength;
86: 4 Bring *j* to your servant,
89: 12 Hermon sing for *j* at your name.
90: 14 for *j* and be glad all our days.
92: 4 I sing for *j* at the works
94: 19 your consolation brought *j*
95: 1 let us sing for *j* to the LORD;
96: 12 the trees of the forest will sing for *j*;
97: 11 and *j* on the upright in heart.
98: 4 for *j* to the LORD, all the earth,
98: 6 shout for *j* before the LORD,
98: 8 the mountains sing together for *j*;
100: 1 for *j* to the LORD, all the earth.
105: 43 his chosen ones with shouts of *j*;
106: 5 share in the *j* of your nation
107: 22 and tell of his works with songs of *j*
118: 15 Shouts of *j* and victory
119:111 they are the *j* of my heart.
126: 2 our tongues with songs of *j*.
126: 3 and we are filled with *j*.
126: 5 will reap with songs of *j*.
126: 6 will return with songs of *j*,
132: 9 may your saints sing for *j*."
132: 16 and her saints will ever sing for *j*.
137: 3 tormentors demanded songs of *j*;
137: 6 my highest *j*.
149: 5 and sing for *j* on their beds.
Pr 10: 1 A wise son brings *j* to his father,
10: 28 The prospect of the righteous is *j*,
11: 10 wicked perish, there are shouts of *j*.

Pr 12: 20 but *j* for those who promote peace.
14: 10 and no one else can share its *j*.
14: 13 and *j* may end in grief.
15: 20 A wise son brings *j* to his father,
15: 23 A man finds *j* in giving an apt reply
15: 30 A cheerful look brings *j*
17: 21 there is no *j* for the father of a fool.
21: 15 it brings *j* to the righteous
23: 24 of a righteous man has great *j*;
27: 9 incense bring *j* to the heart,
27: 11 my son, and bring *j* to my heart;
29: 3 A man who loves wisdom brings *j*
Ecc 8: 15 Then *j* will accompany him
11: 9 let your heart give you *j* in the days
Isa 9: 3 and increased their *j*;
12: 3 With *j* you will draw water
12: 6 Shout aloud and sing for *j*,
16: 9 shouts of *j* over your ripened fruit
16: 10 *J* and gladness are taken away
22: 13 But see, there is *j* and revelry,
24: 11 all *j* turns to gloom,
24: 14 raise their voices, they shout for *j*;
26: 19 wake up and shout for *j*.
35: 2 will rejoice greatly and shout for *j*.
35: 6 the tongue of the dumb shout for *j*.
35: 10 Gladness and *j* will overtake them,
35: 10 everlasting *j* will crown their heads
42: 11 Let the people of Sela sing for *j*;
44: 23 Sing for *j*, O heavens,
48: 20 Announce this with shouts of *j*
49: 13 Shout for *j*, O heavens;
51: 3 *J* and gladness will be found in her,
51: 11 Gladness and *j* will overtake them,
51: 11 everlasting *j* will crown their heads
52: 8 together they shout for *j*.
52: 9 Burst into songs of *j* together,
54: 1 burst into song, shout for *j*,
55: 12 You will go out in *j*
56: 7 give them *j* in my house of prayer.
58: 14 then you will find your *j*
60: 5 heart will throb and swell with *j*;
60: 15 and the *j* of all generations.
61: 7 and everlasting *j* will be theirs.
65: 14 out of the *j* of their hearts,
65: 18 and its people a *j*.
66: 5 that we may see your *j*!'
Jer 7: 34 will bring an end to the sounds of *j*
15: 16 they were my *j* and my heart's
16: 9 will bring an end to the sounds of *j*
25: 10 banish from them the sounds of *j*
31: 7 "Sing with *j* for Jacob;
31: 12 shout for *j* on the heights of Zion;
31: 13 give them comfort and *j* instead
33: 9 this city will bring me renown, *j*,
33: 11 be heard once more the sounds of *j*
48: 33 *J* and gladness are gone
48: 33 no one treads them with shouts of *j*
48: 33 they are not shouts of *j*.
51: 48 will shout for *j* over Babylon,
La 2: 15 the *j* of the whole earth?"
5: 15 *J* is gone from our hearts;
Eze 7: 7 not *j*, upon the mountains.
24: 25 their *j* and glory, the delight
Joel 1: 12 Surely the *j* of mankind
1: 16 *j* and gladness
Mt 13: 20 and at once receives it with *j*.
13: 44 in his *j* went and sold all he had
28: 8 afraid yet filled with *j*,
Mk 4: 16 and at once receive it with *j*.
Lk 1: 14 He will be a *j* and delight to you,
1: 44 the baby in my womb leaped for *j*.
1: 58 great mercy, and they shared her *j*.
2: 10 news of great *j* that will be
6: 23 "Rejoice in that day and leap for *j*,
8: 13 the word with *j* when they hear it,
10: 17 The seventy-two returned with *j*
10: 21 full of *j* through the Holy Spirit,
24: 41 still did not believe it because of *j*
24: 52 returned to Jerusalem with great *j*.
Jn 3: 29 That *j* is mine, and it is now
3: 29 full of *j* when he hears
15: 11 and that your *j* may be complete.
15: 11 this so that my *j* may be in you
16: 20 but your grief will turn to *j*.
16: 21 because of her *j* that a child is born
16: 22 and no one will take away your *j*.
16: 24 and your *j* will be complete.
17: 13 measure of my *j* within them.
Ac 2: 28 with *j* in your presence.'
8: 8 So there was great *j* in that city.
13: 52 And the disciples were filled with *j*
14: 17 and fills your hearts with *j*."
16: 34 the whole family was filled with *j*,
Ro 14: 17 peace and *j* in the Holy Spirit,
15: 13 the God of hope fill you with all *j*
15: 32 will I may come to you with *j*
16: 19 so I am full of *j* over you;
2Co 1: 24 but we work with you for your *j*,
2: 3 that you would all share my *j*.
7: 4 our troubles my *j* knows no
7: 7 so that my *j* was greater than ever.
8: 2 their overflowing *j* and their
Gal 4: 15 What has happened to all your *j*?
5: 22 *j*, peace, patience, kindness,
Php 1: 4 I always pray with *j*
1: 25 for your progress and *j* in the faith,
1: 26 being with you again your *j*
2: 2 then make my *j* complete
2: 29 him in the Lord with great *j*,
4: 1 and long for, my *j* and crown,
1Th 1: 6 with the *j* given by the Holy Spirit.
2: 19 For what is our hope, our *j*,
2: 20 Indeed, you are our glory and *j*.
3: 9 you in return for all the *j* we have
2Ti 1: 4 so that I may be filled with *j*.
Phm : 7 Your love has given me great *j*
Heb 1: 9 by anointing you with the oil of *j*."
12: 2 for the *j* set before him endured
13: 17 them so that their work will be a *j*,
Jas 1: 2 Consider it pure *j*, my brothers,
4: 9 to mourning and your *j* to gloom.
1Pe 1: 8 with an inexpressible and glorious *j*
1Jn 1: 4 this to make our *j* complete.
2Jn : 4 It has given me great *j* to find some
: 12 so that our *j* may be complete.
3Jn : 3 It gave me great *j* to have some
: 4 I have no greater *j*
Jude : 24 without fault and with great *j*—

JOYFUL (JOY)

Dt 16: 14 Be *j* at your Feast—you, your sons
1Sa 18: 6 with *j* songs and with tambourines
1Ki 8: 66 *j* and glad in heart
1Ch 15: 16 as singers to sing *j* songs,
2Ch 7: 10 *j* and glad in heart
Ps 68: 3 may they be happy and *j*.
100: 2 come before him with *j* songs.
Ecc 9: 7 and drink your wine with a *j* heart,
Isa 24: 8 the *j* harp is silent.
Jer 31: 4 and go out to dance with the *j*.
Hab 3: 18 I will be *j* in God my Savior.
Zec 8: 19 and tenth months will become *j*
10: 7 Their children will see it and be *j*;
Ro 12: 12 Be *j* in hope, patient in affliction,
1Th 5: 16 Be *j* always; pray continually;
Heb 12: 22 thousands of angels in *j* assembly,

JOYOUS (JOY)

Est 8: 15 the city of Susa held a *j* celebration.

JOZABAD

2Ki 12: 21 who murdered him were *J* son
1Ch 12: 4 Johanan, *J* the Gederathite,
12: 20 Adnah, *J*, Jediael, Michael,
12: 20 Michael, *J*, Elihu and Zillethai,
2Ch 31: 13 Asahel, Jerimoth, *J*, Eliel,
35: 9 and Hashabiah, Jeiel and *J*,
Ezr 8: 33 so were the Levites *J* son of Jeshua
10: 22 Ishmael, Nethanel, *J* and Elasah.
10: 23 Among the Levites: *J*, Shimei,
Ne 8: 7 Maaseiah, Kelita, Azariah, *J*,
11: 16 the son of Bunni; Shabbethai and *J*,

JOZADAK

Ezr 3: 2 son of *J* and his fellow priests
3: 8 Jeshua son of *J* and the rest
5: 2 and Jeshua son of *J* set to work
10: 18 the descendants of Jeshua son of *J*,
Ne 12: 26 son of Jeshua, the son of *J*,

JUBAL

Ge 4: 21 His brother's name was *J*;

JUBILANT

1Ch 16: 32 let the fields be *j*, and everything
Ps 94: 3 how long will the wicked be *j*?
96: 12 let the fields be *j*, and everything
98: 4 burst into *j* song with music;
Hos 9: 1 do not be *j* like the other nations.

JUBILEE

Lev 25: 10 It shall be a *j* for you; each one
25: 11 The fiftieth year shall be a *j* for you;
25: 12 For it is a *j* and is to be holy for you
25: 13 " 'In this Year of *J* everyone is
25: 15 of the number of years since the *J*.
25: 28 It will be returned in the *J*,
25: 28 of the buyer until the Year of *J*.
25: 30 It is not to be returned in the *J*.
25: 31 and they are to be returned in the *J*
25: 33 and is to be returned in the *J*,
25: 40 to work for you until the Year of *J*.
25: 50 he sold himself up to the Year of *J*.
25: 52 remain until the Year of *J*,
25: 54 are to be released in the Year of *J*,
27: 17 field during the Year of *J*,
27: 18 if he dedicates his field after the *J*,
27: 18 remain until the next Year of *J*,
27: 21 When the field is released in the *J*,
27: 23 its value up to the Year of *J*,
27: 24 In the Year of *J* the field will revert
Nu 36: 4 When the Year of *J*

JUDAH (JUDAH'S JUDEA JUDEAN)

Ge 29: 35 So she named him *J*.
35: 23 Levi, *J*, Issachar and Zebulun.
37: 26 *J* said to his brothers, "What will
38: 1 *J* left his brothers and went
38: 2 There *J* met the daughter
38: 6 *J* got a wife for Er, his firstborn,
38: 8 Then *J* said to Onan, "Lie
38: 11 *J* then said to his daughter-in-law
38: 12 When *J* had recovered
38: 15 When *J* saw her, he thought she
38: 20 Meanwhile *J* sent the young goat
38: 22 So he went back to *J* and said,
38: 23 *J* said, "Let her keep what she has,
38: 24 *J* said, "Bring her out and have her
38: 24 three months later *J* was told,
38: 26 *J* recognized them and said,
43: 3 *J* said to him, "The man warned us
43: 8 Then *J* said to Israel his father,
44: 14 still in the house when *J*
44: 16 say to my lord?" *J* replied.
44: 18 Then *J* went up to him and said:
46: 12 The sons of *J*: Er, Onan, Shelah,
46: 28 Now Jacob sent *J* ahead of him
49: 8 "*J*, your brothers will praise you;
49: 9 You are a lion's cub, O *J*;
49: 10 The scepter will not depart from *J*,
Ex 1: 2 Simeon, Levi and *J*; Issachar,
31: 2 the son of Hur, of the tribe of *J*,
35: 30 the son of Hur, of the tribe of *J*,
38: 22 of *J*, made everything the LORD
Nu 1: 7 from *J*, Nahshon son
1: 26 From the descendants of *J*:
1: 27 from the tribe of *J* was 74,600.
2: 3 of the camp of *J* are to encamp
2: 3 of the people of *J* is Nahshon son
2: 9 the men assigned to the camp of *J*,
7: 12 son of Amminadab of the tribe of *J*.
10: 14 of the camp of *J* went first,
13: 6 from the tribe of *J*, Caleb son
26: 19 Er and Onan were sons of *J*,
26: 20 The descendants of *J*
26: 22 These were the clans of *J*;
34: 19 from the tribe of *J*; Shemuel son
Dt 27: 12 Simeon, Levi, *J*, Issachar,
33: 7 And this he said about *J*:
33: 7 "Hear, O LORD, the cry of *J*;
34: 2 land of *J* as far as the western sea,
Jos 7: 1 of the tribe of *J*, took some of them
7: 16 forward by tribes, and *J* was taken.
7: 17 The clans of *J* came forward,
7: 18 of the tribe of *J*, was taken.
11: 21 from all the hill country of *J*,
14: 6 the men of *J* approached Joshua
15: 1 The allotment for the tribe of *J*,
15: 12 the people of *J* by their clans.
15: 13 son of Jephunneh a portion in *J*—
15: 20 is the inheritance of the tribe of *J*,
15: 21 towns of the tribe of *J* in the Negev
15: 63 *J* could not dislodge the Jebusites,
15: 63 there with the people of *J*.

Jos 18: 5 *J* is to remain in its territory
18: 11 lay between the tribes of *J*
18: 14 a town of the people of *J*.
19: 1 lay within the territory of *J*.
19: 9 taken from the share of *J*,
19: 9 within the territory of *J*.
20: 7 Hebron) in the hill country of *J*.
21: 4 towns from the tribes of *J*,
21: 9 of *J* and Simeon they allotted
21: 11 in the hill country of *J*.
Jdg 1: 2 The LORD answered, "*J* is to go;
1: 3 of *J* said to the Simeonites their
1: 4 When *J* attacked, the LORD gave
1: 8 The men of *J* attacked Jerusalem
1: 9 the men of *J* went down to fight
1: 16 Palms with the men of *J* to live
1: 16 of the Desert of *J* in the Negev
1: 17 Then the men of *J* went
1: 18 The men of *J* also took Gaza,
1: 19 The LORD was with the men of *J*.
10: 9 the Jordan to fight against *J*,
15: 9 went up and camped in *J*,
15: 10 of *J* asked, "Why have you come
15: 11 three thousand men from *J* went
17: 7 Levite from Bethlehem in *J*,
17: 7 living within the clan of *J*,
17: 9 I'm a Levite from Bethlehem in *J*,"
18: 12 near Kiriath Jearim in *J*.
19: 1 a concubine from Bethlehem in *J*.
19: 2 her father's house in Bethlehem, *J*.
19: 18 I have been to Bethlehem in *J*
19: 18 way from Bethlehem in *J*
20: 18 The LORD replied, "*J* shall go first
Ru 1: 1 and a man from Bethlehem in *J*,
1: 2 Ephrathites from Bethlehem, *J*.
1: 7 take them back to the land of *J*.
4: 12 of Perez, whom Tamar bore to *J*."
1Sa 11: 8 and the men of *J* thirty thousand.
15: 4 and ten thousand men from *J*.
17: 1 and assembled at Socoh in *J*.
17: 12 who was from Bethlehem in *J*.
17: 52 and *J* surged forward with a shout
18: 16 But all Israel and *J* loved David,
22: 5 Go into the land of *J*."
23: 3 to him, "Here in *J* we are afraid.
23: 23 down among all the clans of *J*."
27: 6 to the kings of *J* ever since.
27: 10 "Against the Negev of *J*"
30: 14 and the territory belonging to *J*
30: 16 land of the Philistines and from *J*.
30: 26 of the plunder to the elders of *J*,
2Sa 1: 18 the men of *J* be taught this lament
2: 1 up to one of the towns of *J*?"
2: 4 Then the men of *J* came to Hebron
2: 4 king over the house of *J*.
2: 7 house of *J* has anointed me king
2: 10 of *J*, however, followed David.
2: 11 over the house of *J* was seven years
3: 10 and *J* from Dan to Beersheba."
5: 5 all Israel and *J* thirty-three years.
5: 5 reigned over *J* seven years
6: 2 out from Baalah of *J* to bring up
11: 11 Israel and *J* are staying in tents,
12: 8 I gave you the house of Israel and *J*
19: 11 the priests: "Ask the elders of *J*,
19: 14 over the hearts of all the men of *J*
19: 15 the men of *J* had come to Gilgal
19: 16 the men of *J* to meet King David.
19: 40 the troops of *J* and half the troops
19: 41 Why did our brothers, the men of *J*
19: 42 All the men of *J* answered the men
19: 43 But the men of *J* responded
19: 43 of Israel answered the men of *J*,
20: 2 But the men of *J* stayed
20: 4 "Summon the men of *J* to come
20: 5 when Amasa went to summon *J*,
21: 2 and *J* had tried to annihilate them.)
24: 1 saying, "Go and count Israel and *J*
24: 7 on to Beersheba in the Negev of *J*.
24: 9 and in *J* five hundred thousand.
1Ki 1: 9 men of *J* who were royal officials,
1: 35 ruler over Israel and *J*."
4: 20 The people of *J* and Israel were
4: 25 During Solomon's lifetime *J*
12: 17 who were living in the towns of *J*,
12: 20 Only the tribe of *J* remained loyal
12: 21 he mustered the whole house of *J*
12: 23 son of Solomon king of *J*,
1Ki 12: 23 to the whole house of *J*
12: 27 to their lord, Rehoboam king of *J*.
12: 32 like the festival held in *J*,
13: 1 man of God came from *J* to Bethel,
13: 12 the man of God from *J* had taken.
13: 14 man of God who came from *J*?"
13: 21 man of God who had come from *J*,
14: 21 son of Solomon was king in *J*.
14: 22 *J* did evil in the eyes of the LORD.
14: 29 of the annals of the kings of *J*?
15: 1 Abijah became king of *J*,
15: 7 of the annals of the kings of *J*?
15: 9 Asa became king of *J*,
15: 17 king of Israel went up against *J*
15: 17 the territory of Asa king of *J*.
15: 22 King Asa issued an order to all *J*—
15: 23 of the annals of the kings of *J*?
15: 25 in the second year of Asa king of *J*,
15: 28 in the third year of Asa king of *J*
15: 33 In the third year of Asa king of *J*,
16: 8 twenty-sixth year of Asa king of *J*,
16: 10 year of Asa king of *J*.
16: 15 year of Asa king of *J*,
16: 23 thirty-first year of Asa king of *J*,
16: 29 thirty-eighth year of Asa king of *J*,
19: 3 When he came to Beersheba in *J*,
22: 2 king of *J* went down to see the king
22: 10 Jehoshaphat king of *J* were sitting
22: 29 and Jehoshaphat king of *J* went up
22: 41 king of *J* in the fourth year
22: 45 of the annals of the kings of *J*?
22: 51 year of Jehoshaphat king of *J*,
2Ki 1: 17 son of Jehoshaphat king of *J*.
3: 1 year of Jehoshaphat king of *J*,
3: 7 message to Jehoshaphat king of *J*:
3: 9 of Israel set out with the king of *J*
3: 14 presence of Jehoshaphat king of *J*,
8: 16 began his reign as king of *J*.
8: 16 when Jehoshaphat was king of *J*,
8: 19 was not willing to destroy *J*.
8: 20 Edom rebelled against *J*
8: 22 been in rebellion against *J*.
8: 23 of the annals of the kings of *J*?
8: 25 of Jehoram king of *J* began to reign
8: 29 son of Jehoram king of *J* went
9: 16 and Ahaziah king of *J* had gone
9: 21 and Ahaziah king of *J* rode out,
9: 27 king of *J* saw what had happened,
9: 29 Ahaziah had become king of *J*.)
10: 13 relatives of Ahaziah king of *J*
12: 18 and Ahaziah, the kings of *J*—
12: 18 king of *J* took all the sacred objects
12: 19 of the annals of the kings of *J*?
13: 1 of Joash son of Ahaziah king of *J*,
13: 10 year of Joash king of *J*,
13: 12 war against Amaziah king of *J*,
14: 1 of Joash king of *J* began to reign.
14: 9 replied to Amaziah king of *J*:
14: 10 your own downfall and that of *J*
14: 11 Amaziah king of *J* faced each other
14: 11 at Beth Shemesh in *J*.
14: 12 *J* was routed by Israel,
14: 13 Israel captured Amaziah king of *J*,
14: 15 war against Amaziah king of *J*,
14: 17 son of Joash king of *J* lived
14: 18 of the annals of the kings of *J*?
14: 21 all the people of *J* took Azariah,
14: 22 it to *J* after Amaziah rested
14: 23 of Amaziah son of Joash king of *J*,
15: 1 king of *J* began to reign.
15: 6 of the annals of the kings of *J*?
15: 8 year of Azariah king of *J*,
15: 13 year of Uzziah king of *J*,
15: 17 year of Azariah king of *J*,
15: 23 year of Azariah king of *J*,
15: 27 year of Azariah king of *J*,
15: 32 of Uzziah king of *J* began to reign.
15: 36 of the annals of the kings of *J*?
15: 37 Pekah son of Remaliah against *J*.)
16: 1 of Jotham king of *J* began to reign.
16: 6 Aram by driving out the men of *J*.
16: 19 of the annals of the kings of *J*?
17: 1 the twelfth year of Ahaz king of *J*,
17: 13 and *J* through all his prophets
17: 18 Only the tribe of *J* was left,
17: 19 even *J* did not keep the commands
18: 1 of Ahaz king of *J* began to reign.
18: 5 him among all the kings of *J*,
2Ki 18: 13 attacked all the fortified cities of *J*
18: 14 king of *J* sent this message
18: 14 king of *J* three hundred talents
18: 16 king of *J* stripped off the gold
18: 22 saying to *J* and Jerusalem,
19: 10 "Say to Hezekiah king of *J*:
19: 30 more a remnant of the house of *J*
20: 20 of the annals of the kings of *J*?
21: 11 and has led *J* into sin with his idols.
21: 11 king of *J* has committed these
21: 12 *J* that the ears of everyone who
21: 16 besides the sin that he had caused *J*
21: 17 of the annals of the kings of *J*?
21: 25 of the annals of the kings of *J*?
22: 13 and for all *J* about what is written
22: 16 in the book the king of *J* has read.
22: 18 Tell the king of *J*, who sent you
23: 1 called together all the elders of *J*
23: 2 of the LORD with the men of *J*
23: 5 by the kings of *J* to burn incense
23: 5 on the high places of the towns of *J*
23: 8 the priests from the towns of *J*
23: 11 kings of *J* had dedicated to the sun.
23: 12 kings of *J* had erected on the roof
23: 17 the man of God who came from *J*
23: 22 kings of Israel and the kings of *J*,
23: 24 other detestable things seen in *J*
23: 26 which burned against *J*
23: 27 remove *J* also from my presence
23: 28 of the annals of the kings of *J*?
23: 33 and he imposed on *J* a levy
24: 2 He sent them to destroy *J*,
24: 3 things happened to *J* according
24: 5 of the annals of the kings of *J*?
24: 12 Jehoiachin king of *J*, his mother,
24: 20 happened to Jerusalem and *J*,
25: 21 So *J* went into captivity, away
25: 22 the people he had left behind in *J*.
25: 25 Gedaliah and also the men of *J*
25: 27 of the exile of Jehoiachin king of *J*,
1Ch 2: 1 Simeon, Levi, *J*, Issachar, Zebulun,
2: 3 The sons of *J*: Er, Onan and Shelah
2: 4 *J* had five sons in all.
2: 10 the leader of the people of *J*.
4: 1 The descendants of *J*: Perez,
4: 21 The sons of Shelah son of *J*:
4: 27 as numerous as the people of *J*.
4: 41 in the days of Hezekiah king of *J*.
5: 2 *J* was the strongest of his brothers
5: 17 the reigns of Jotham king of *J*
6: 15 deported when the LORD sent *J*
6: 55 Hebron in *J* with its surrounding
6: 65 From the tribes of *J*, Simeon
9: 1 The people of *J* were taken captive
9: 3 Those from *J*, from Benjamin,
9: 4 a descendant of Perez son of *J*.
9: 6 The people from *J* numbered 690.
12: 16 Benjamites and some men from *J*
12: 24 men of *J*, carrying shield and spear
13: 6 to Baalah of *J* (Kiriath Jearim)
21: 5 and seventy thousand in *J*.
27: 18 over Aaron: Zadok; over *J*: Elihu,
28: 4 He chose *J* as leader,
28: 4 the house of *J* he chose my family,
2Ch 2: 7 to work in *J* and Jerusalem
9: 11 like them had ever been seen in *J*.)
10: 17 who were living in the towns of *J*,
11: 1 he mustered the house of *J*
11: 3 and to all the Israelites in *J*
11: 3 son of Solomon king of *J*
11: 5 and built up towns for defense in *J*:
11: 10 These were fortified cities in *J*
11: 12 So *J* and Benjamin were his.
11: 14 and came to *J* and Jerusalem
11: 17 strengthened the kingdom of *J*
11: 23 sons throughout the districts of *J*
12: 4 he captured the fortified cities of *J*
12: 5 the leaders of *J* who had assembled
12: 12 Indeed, there was some good in *J*.
13: 1 Abijah became king of *J*,
13: 13 was in front of *J* the ambush was
13: 14 *J* turned and saw that they were
13: 15 and all Israel before Abijah and *J*.
13: 15 the men of *J* raised the battle cry.
13: 16 The Israelites fled before *J*,
13: 18 and the men of *J* were victorious
14: 4 He commanded *J*
14: 5 incense altars in every town in *J*,

2Ch 14: 6 He built up the fortified cities of *J*,
14: 7 he said to *J*, "and put walls
14: 8 hundred thousand men from *J*,
14: 12 the Cushites before Asa and *J*.
14: 13 The men of *J* carried
15: 2 Asa and all *J* and Benjamin.
15: 8 idols from the whole land of *J*
15: 9 he assembled all *J* and Benjamin
15: 15 All *J* rejoiced about the oath
16: 1 king of Israel went up against *J*
16: 1 the territory of Asa king of *J*.
16: 6 King Asa brought all the men of *J*,
16: 7 the seer came to Asa king of *J*
16: 11 written in the book of the kings of *J*
17: 2 put garrisons in *J* and in the towns
17: 2 troops in all the fortified cities of *J*
17: 5 all *J* brought gifts to Jehoshaphat,
17: 6 and the Asherah poles from *J*.
17: 7 Micaiah to teach in the towns of *J*.
17: 9 They taught throughout *J*,
17: 9 went around to all the towns of *J*
17: 10 of the lands surrounding *J*,
17: 12 he built forts and store cities in *J*
17: 13 had large supplies in the towns of *J*.
17: 14 From *J*, commanders of units
17: 19 in the fortified cities throughout *J*.
18: 3 Israel asked Jehoshaphat king of *J*,
18: 9 Jehoshaphat king of *J* were sitting
18: 28 and Jehoshaphat king of *J* went up
19: 1 king of *J* returned safely
19: 5 in each of the fortified cities of *J*.
19: 11 the leader of the tribe of *J*,
20: 3 and he proclaimed a fast for all *J*.
20: 4 The people of *J* came together
20: 4 from every town in *J* to seek him.
20: 5 up in the assembly of *J*
20: 13 All the men of *J*, with their wives
20: 15 all who live in *J* and Jerusalem!
20: 17 the LORD will give you, O *J*
20: 18 and all the people of *J*
20: 20 *J* and people of Jerusalem!
20: 22 Mount Seir who were invading *J*,
20: 24 When the men of *J* came
20: 27 men of *J* and Jerusalem returned
20: 31 So Jehoshaphat reigned over *J*.
20: 31 old when he became king of *J*,
20: 35 king of *J* made an alliance
21: 3 as well as fortified cities in *J*,
21: 8 Edom rebelled against *J*
21: 10 been in rebellion against *J*.
21: 11 built high places on the hills of *J*
21: 11 themselves and had led *J* astray.
21: 12 Jehoshaphat or of Asa king of *J*.
21: 13 and you have led *J* and the people
21: 17 They attacked *J*, invaded it
22: 1 of Jehoram king of *J* began to reign
22: 6 son of Jehoram king of *J* went
22: 8 he found the princes of *J*
22: 10 royal family of the house of *J*.
23: 2 They went throughout *J*
23: 8 and all the men of *J* did just
24: 5 of *J* and collect the money due
24: 6 the Levites to bring in from *J*
24: 9 proclamation was then issued in *J*
24: 17 the officials of *J* came
24: 18 God's anger came upon *J*
24: 23 it invaded *J* and Jerusalem
24: 24 Because *J* had forsaken the LORD
25: 5 called the people of *J* together
25: 5 commanders of hundreds for all *J*
25: 10 They were furious with *J*
25: 12 of *J* also captured ten thousand
25: 17 king of *J* consulted his advisers,
25: 18 replied to Amaziah king of *J*:
25: 19 your own downfall and that of *J*
25: 21 Amaziah king of *J* faced each other
25: 21 at Beth Shemesh in *J*.
25: 22 *J* was routed by Israel,
25: 23 Israel captured Amaziah king of *J*,
25: 25 son of Joash king of *J* lived
25: 26 written in the book of the kings of *J*
25: 28 with his fathers in the City of *J*.
26: 1 all the people of *J* took Uzziah,
26: 2 it to *J* after Amaziah rested
27: 7 book of the kings of Israel and *J*.
28: 6 because *J* had forsaken the LORD,
28: 6 twenty thousand soldiers in *J*—
28: 9 was angry with *J*, he gave them

2Ch 28: 10 of *J* and Jerusalem your slaves.
28: 17 and attacked *J* and carried away
28: 18 the foothills and in the Negev of *J*.
28: 19 The LORD had humbled *J*
28: 19 he had promoted wickedness in *J*
28: 25 town in *J* he built high places
28: 26 written in the book of the kings of *J*
29: 8 anger of the LORD has fallen on *J*
29: 21 for the sanctuary and for *J*.
30: 1 *J* and also wrote letters to Ephraim
30: 6 and *J* with letters from the king
30: 12 Also in *J* the hand of God was
30: 24 king of *J* provided a thousand bulls
30: 25 Israel and those who lived in *J*.
30: 25 The entire assembly of *J* rejoiced,
31: 1 and the altars throughout *J*
31: 1 there went out to the towns of *J*,
31: 6 and *J* who lived in the towns of *J*
31: 20 is what Hezekiah did throughout *J*,
32: 1 of Assyria came and invaded *J*.
32: 8 what Hezekiah the king of *J* said.
32: 9 message for Hezekiah king of *J*
32: 9 the people of *J* who were there:
32: 12 saying to *J* and Jerusalem,
32: 23 gifts for Hezekiah king of *J*.
32: 25 wrath was on him and on *J*
32: 32 Amoz in the book of the kings of *J*
32: 33 All *J* and the people
33: 9 But Manasseh led *J* and the people
33: 14 in all the fortified cities in *J*.
33: 16 and told *J* to serve the LORD,
34: 3 his twelfth year he began to purge *J*
34: 5 and so he purged *J* and Jerusalem
34: 9 and from all the people of *J*
34: 11 of *J* had allowed to fall into ruin.
34: 21 and *J* about what is written
34: 24 in the presence of the king of *J*.
34: 26 Tell the king of *J*, who sent you
34: 29 called together all the elders of *J*
34: 30 of the LORD with the men of *J*,
35: 18 and all *J* and Israel who were there
35: 21 of *J*? It is not you I am attacking
35: 24 and all *J* and Jerusalem mourned
35: 27 book of the kings of Israel and *J*.
36: 3 and imposed on *J* a levy
36: 4 king over *J* and Jerusalem
36: 8 book of the kings of Israel and *J*.
36: 10 king over *J* and Jerusalem.
36: 23 a temple for him at Jerusalem in *J*.
Ezr 1: 2 a temple for him at Jerusalem in *J*.
1: 3 and let him go up to Jerusalem in *J*
1: 5 the family heads of *J* and Benjamin
1: 8 out to Sheshbazzar the prince of *J*.
2: 1 returned to Jerusalem and *J*,
4: 1 When the enemies of *J*
4: 4 out to discourage the people of *J*
4: 6 accusation against the people of *J*
5: 1 prophesied to the Jews in *J*
5: 8 went to the district of *J*,
7: 14 seven advisers to inquire about *J*
9: 9 given us a wall of protection in *J*
10: 7 was then issued throughout *J*
10: 9 of *J* and Benjamin had gathered
10: 23 (that is Kelita), Pethahiah, *J*
Ne 1: 2 came from *J* with some other men,
2: 5 in *J* where my fathers are buried
2: 7 safe conduct until I arrive in *J*?
4: 10 Meanwhile, the people in *J* said,
4: 16 of *J* who were building the wall.
5: 14 to be their governor in the land of *J*
6: 7 in *J*!' Now this report will get back
6: 17 of *J* were sending many letters
6: 18 For many in *J* were under oath
7: 6 returned to Jerusalem and *J*,
11: 3 servants lived in the towns of *J*,
11: 4 From the descendants of *J*:
11: 4 while other people from both *J*
11: 9 and *J* son of Hassenuah was
11: 20 were in all the towns of *J*, each
11: 24 the descendants of Zerah son of *J*,
11: 25 people of *J* lived in Kiriath Arba
11: 36 Levites of *J* settled in Benjamin.
12: 8 Binnui, Kadmiel, Sherebiah, *J*,
12: 31 I had the leaders of *J* go up on top
12: 32 half the leaders of *J* followed them,
12: 34 Ezra, Meshullam, *J*, Benjamin,
12: 36 Maai, Nethanel, *J* and Hanani—
12: 44 *J* was pleased with the ministering

Ne 13: 12 All *J* brought the tithes of grain,
13: 15 men in *J* treading winepresses
13: 16 on the Sabbath to the people of *J*.
13: 17 I rebuked the nobles of *J*
13: 23 men of *J* who had married women
13: 24 how to speak the language of *J*.
Est 2: 6 captive with Jehoiachin king of *J*.
Ps 48: 11 the villages of *J* are glad
60: 7 *J* my scepter.
69: 35 and rebuild the cities of *J*.
76: 1 In *J* God is known;
78: 68 but he chose the tribe of *J*,
97: 8 and the villages of *J* are glad
108: 8 *J* my scepter.
114: 2 *J* became God's sanctuary,
Pr 25: 1 by the men of Hezekiah king of *J*:
Isa 1: 1 Ahaz and Hezekiah, kings of *J*.
1: 1 The vision concerning *J*
2: 1 son of Amoz saw concerning *J*
3: 1 about to take from Jerusalem and *J*
3: 8 *J* is falling;
5: 3 in Jerusalem and men of *J*,
5: 7 and the men of *J*
7: 1 the son of Uzziah, was king of *J*,
7: 6 "Let us invade *J*; let us tear it apart
7: 17 since Ephraim broke away from *J*
8: 8 sweep on into *J*, swirling over it,
9: 21 together they will turn against *J*.
11: 12 assemble the scattered people of *J*
11: 13 Ephraim will not be jealous of *J*,
11: 13 nor *J* hostile toward Ephraim.
19: 17 And the land of *J* will bring terror
19: 17 to whom *J* is mentioned will be
22: 8 the defenses of *J* are stripped away.
22: 21 in Jerusalem and to the house of *J*.
26: 1 song will be sung in the land of *J*:
36: 1 attacked all the fortified cities of *J*
36: 7 saying to *J* and Jerusalem,
37: 10 "Say to Hezekiah king of *J*:
37: 31 more a remnant of the house of *J*
38: 9 king of *J* after his illness
40: 9 say to the towns of *J*,
44: 26 the towns of *J*, 'They shall be built,'
48: 1 and come from the line of *J*,
65: 9 from *J* those who will possess my
Jer 1: 2 of Josiah son of Amon king of *J*,
1: 3 of Jehoiakim son of Josiah king of *J*
1: 3 of Zedekiah son of Josiah king of *J*,
1: 15 and against all the towns of *J*.
1: 18 against the kings of *J*, its officials,
2: 28 as you have towns, O *J*.
3: 7 and her unfaithful sister *J* saw it.
3: 8 her unfaithful sister *J* had no fear;
3: 10 her unfaithful sister *J* did not
3: 11 is more righteous than unfaithful *J*.
3: 18 the house of *J* will join the house
4: 3 the LORD says to the men of *J*
4: 4 you men of *J* and people
4: 5 "Announce in *J* and proclaim
4: 16 cry against the cities of *J*.
5: 11 house of Israel and the house of *J*
5: 20 and proclaim it in *J*:
7: 2 all you people of *J* who come
7: 17 they are doing in the towns of *J*
7: 30 " 'The people of *J* have done evil
7: 34 and bridegroom in the towns of *J*
8: 1 of the kings and officials of *J*,
9: 11 and I will lay waste the towns of *J*
9: 26 Egypt, *J*, Edom, Ammon,
10: 22 It will make the towns of *J* desolate
11: 2 and tell them to the people of *J*
11: 6 all these words in the towns of *J*
11: 9 a conspiracy among the people of *J*
11: 10 of *J* have broken the covenant I
11: 12 The towns of *J* and the people
11: 13 many gods as you have towns, O *J*;
11: 17 and the house of *J* have done evil
12: 14 the house of *J* from among them.
13: 9 same way I will ruin the pride of *J*
13: 11 and the whole house of *J* to me,'
13: 19 All *J* will be carried into exile,
14: 2 the drought: "*J* mourns,
14: 19 Have you rejected *J* completely?
15: 4 king of *J* did in Jerusalem.
17: 19 through which the kings of *J* go in
17: 20 O kings of *J* and all people of *J*
17: 25 accompanied by the men of *J*
17: 26 come from the towns of *J*

Jer 18: 11 to the people of *J* and those living
19: 3 O kings of *J* and people
19: 4 nor the kings of *J* ever knew,
19: 7 this place I will ruin the plans of *J*
19: 13 of *J* will be defiled like this place,
20: 4 I will hand all *J* over to the king
20: 5 all the treasures of the kings of *J*.
21: 7 I will hand over Zedekiah king of *J*,
21: 11 say to the royal house of *J*,
22: 1 down to the palace of the king of *J*
22: 2 O king of *J*, you who sit
22: 6 about the palace of the king of *J*:
22: 11 as king of *J* but has gone
22: 18 son of Josiah king of *J*:
22: 24 son of Jehoiakim king of *J*,
22: 30 or rule anymore in *J*.''
23: 6 In his days *J* will be saved
24: 1 and the artisans of *J* were carried
24: 1 son of Jehoiakim king of *J*
24: 5 I regard as good the exiles from *J*,
24: 8 deal with Zedekiah king of *J*,
25: 1 of Jehoiakim son of Josiah king of *J*
25: 1 the people of *J* in the fourth year
25: 2 said to all the people of *J*
25: 3 son of Amon king of *J*
25: 18 Jerusalem and the towns of *J*,
26: 1 of Jehoiakim son of Josiah king of *J*
26: 2 people of the towns of *J* who come
26: 10 of *J* heard about these things,
26: 18 He told all the people of *J*,
26: 18 in the days of Hezekiah king of *J*.
26: 19 anyone else in *J* put him to death?
26: 19 ''Did Hezekiah king of *J*
27: 1 of Zedekiah son of Josiah king of *J*,
27: 3 to Jerusalem to Zedekiah king of *J*.
27: 12 message to Zedekiah king of *J*.
27: 18 and in the palace of the king of *J*
27: 20 along with all the nobles of *J*
27: 20 of Jehoiakim king of *J* into exile
27: 21 and in the palace of the king of *J*
28: 1 in the reign of Zedekiah king of *J*,
28: 4 from *J* who went to Babylon,'
28: 4 son of Jehoiakim king of *J*
29: 2 and the leaders of *J* and Jerusalem,
29: 3 whom Zedekiah king of *J* sent
29: 22 all the exiles from *J* who are
30: 3 bring my people Israel and *J* back
30: 4 spoke concerning Israel and *J*:
31: 23 the people in the land of *J*
31: 24 People will live together in *J*
31: 27 the house of *J* with the offspring
31: 31 and with the house of *J*.
32: 1 year of Zedekiah king of *J*,
32: 2 of the guard in the royal palace of *J*
32: 3 of *J* had imprisoned him there,
32: 4 king of *J* will not escape out
32: 30 of Israel and *J* have done nothing
32: 32 and *J* have provoked me
32: 32 the men of *J* and the people
32: 35 detestable thing and so make *J* sin.
32: 44 in the towns of *J* and in the towns
33: 4 palaces of *J* that have been torn
33: 7 I will bring *J* and Israel back
33: 10 in the towns of *J* and the streets
33: 13 Jerusalem and in the towns of *J*,
33: 14 of Israel and to the house of *J*.
33: 16 In those days *J* will be saved
34: 2 Go to Zedekiah king of *J*
34: 4 the LORD, O Zedekiah king of *J*.
34: 6 this to Zedekiah king of *J*,
34: 7 of *J* that were still holding out—
34: 7 the only fortified cities left in *J*.
34: 19 The leaders of *J* and Jerusalem,
34: 21 ''I will hand Zedekiah king of *J*
34: 22 of *J* so no one can live there.''
35: 1 of Jehoiakim son of Josiah king of *J*
35: 13 tell the men of *J* and the people
35: 17 I am going to bring on *J*
36: 1 of Jehoiakim son of Josiah king of *J*
36: 2 *J* and all the other nations
36: 3 of *J* hear about every disaster I
36: 6 to all the people of *J* who come
36: 9 come from the towns of *J*.
36: 9 of Jehoiakim son of Josiah king of *J*
36: 28 Jehoiakim king of *J* burned up.
36: 29 Also tell Jehoiakim king of *J*,
36: 30 says about Jehoiakim king of *J*:
36: 31 of *J* every disaster I pronounced
Jer 36: 32 king of *J* had burned in the fire.
37: 1 king of *J* by Nebuchadnezzar king
37: 7 Tell the king of *J*, who sent you
38: 22 of the king of *J* will be brought out
39: 1 year of Zedekiah king of *J*,
39: 4 When Zedekiah king of *J*
39: 6 and also killed all the nobles of *J*.
39: 10 left behind in the land of *J* some
40: 1 *J* who were being carried into exile
40: 5 appointed over the towns of *J*,
40: 11 of Babylon had left a remnant in *J*
40: 12 they all came back to the land of *J*,
40: 15 and the remnant of *J* to perish?''
42: 15 of the LORD, O remnant of *J*.
42: 19 of *J*, the LORD has told you,
43: 4 command to stay in the land of *J*.
43: 5 back to live in the land of *J*
43: 5 of *J* who had come back to live
44: 2 and on all the towns of *J*.
44: 6 it raged against the towns of *J*
44: 7 by cutting off from *J* the men
44: 9 and by the kings and queens of *J*
44: 9 and your wives in the land of *J*
44: 11 disaster on you and to destroy all *J*.
44: 12 of *J* who were determined to go
44: 14 of the remnant of *J* who have gone
44: 14 or survive to return to the land of *J*,
44: 17 our officials did in the towns of *J*
44: 21 incense burned in the towns of *J*
44: 24 all you people of *J* in Egypt.
44: 26 that no one from *J* living anywhere
44: 28 and return to the land of *J*
44: 28 the whole remnant of *J* who came
44: 30 of *J* over to Nebuchadnezzar king
45: 1 of Jehoiakim son of Josiah king of *J*
46: 2 of Jehoiakim son of Josiah king of *J*
49: 34 in the reign of Zedekiah king of *J*:
50: 4 and the people of *J* together
50: 20 and for the sins of *J*,
50: 33 and the people of *J* as well.
51: 5 and *J* have not been forsaken
51: 59 Babylon with Zedekiah king of *J*
52: 3 happened to Jerusalem and *J*,
52: 10 he also killed all the officials of *J*.
52: 27 So *J* went into captivity, away
52: 31 he released Jehoiachin king of *J*
52: 31 of the exile of Jehoiachin king of *J*,
La 1: 3 *J* has gone into exile.
1: 15 the Virgin Daughter of *J*.
2: 2 strongholds of the Daughter of *J*.
2: 5 lamentation for the Daughter of *J*.
5: 11 and virgins in the towns of *J*.
Eze 4: 6 and bear the sin of the house of *J*.
8: 1 and the elders of *J* were sitting
8: 17 it a trivial matter for the house of *J*
9: 9 and *J* is exceedingly great;
21: 20 against *J* and fortified Jerusalem.
25: 3 the people of *J* when they went
25: 8 of *J* has become like all the other
25: 12 took revenge on the house of *J*
25: 15 hostility sought to destroy *J*,
27: 17 '' '*J* and Israel traded with you;
37: 16 to *J* and the Israelites associated
48: 7 ''*J* will have one portion; it will
48: 8 ''Bordering the territory of *J*
48: 22 lie between the border of *J*
48: 31 the gate of *J* and the gate of Levi.
Da 1: 1 of the reign of Jehoiakim king of *J*,
1: 2 king of *J* into his hand,
1: 6 Among these were some from *J*:
2: 25 from *J* who can tell the king what
5: 13 my father the king brought from *J*?
6: 13 who is one of the exiles from *J*,
9: 7 the men of *J* and people
Hos 1: 1 Ahaz and Hezekiah, kings of *J*,
1: 7 I will show love to the house of *J*;
1: 11 The people of *J* and the people
4: 15 let not *J* become guilty.
5: 5 *J* also stumbles with them.
5: 12 like rot to the people of *J*.
5: 13 and *J* his sores,
5: 14 like a great lion to *J*.
6: 4 What can I do with you, *J*?
6: 11 ''Also for you, *J*,
8: 14 *J* has fortified many towns.
10: 11 *J* must plow,
11: 12 And *J* is unruly against God,
12: 2 a charge to bring against *J*;
Joel 3: 1 when I restore the fortunes of *J*
3: 6 You sold the people of *J*
3: 8 and daughters to the people of *J*,
3: 18 all the ravines of *J* will run
3: 19 of violence done to the people of *J*,
3: 20 *J* will be inhabited forever
Am 1: 1 when Uzziah was king of *J*
2: 4 ''For three sins of *J*,
2: 5 I will send fire upon *J*
7: 12 you seer! Go back to the land of *J*.
Ob : 12 nor rejoice over the people of *J*
Mic 1: 1 Ahaz and Hezekiah, kings of *J*—
1: 9 it has come to *J*.
5: 2 you are small among the clans of *J*,
Na 1: 12 I have afflicted you, O *J*,
1: 15 Celebrate your festivals, O *J*,
Zep 1: 1 of Josiah son of Amon king of *J*:
1: 4 will stretch out my hand against *J*
2: 7 to the remnant of the house of *J*;
Hag 1: 1 governor of *J*, and to Joshua son
1: 14 governor of *J*, and the spirit
2: 2 governor of *J*, to Joshua son
2: 21 of *J* that I will shake the heavens
Zec 1: 12 and from the towns of *J*,
1: 19 are the horns that scattered *J*,
1: 21 are the horns that scattered *J*
1: 21 horns against the land of *J*
2: 12 The LORD will inherit *J*
8: 13 O *J* and Israel, so will I save you,
8: 15 again to Jerusalem and *J*.
8: 19 occasions and happy festivals for *J*.
9: 7 and become leaders in *J*,
9: 13 I will bend *J* as I bend my bow
10: 3 care for his flock, the house of *J*,
10: 4 From *J* will come the cornerstone,
10: 6 I will strengthen the house of *J*
11: 14 the brotherhood between *J*
12: 2 *J* will be besieged as well
12: 4 eye over the house of *J*,
12: 5 Then the leaders of *J* will say
12: 6 of *J* like a firepot in a woodpile,
12: 7 may not be greater than that of *J*.
12: 7 will save the dwellings of *J* first,
14: 5 in the days of Uzziah king of *J*.
14: 14 *J* too will fight at Jerusalem.
14: 21 and *J* will be holy to the LORD
Mal 2: 11 *J* has desecrated the sanctuary
2: 11 with one another? *J* has broken
3: 4 offerings of *J* and Jerusalem will be
Mt 1: 2 the father of *J* and his brothers,
1: 3 *J* the father of Perez and Zerah,
2: 6 Bethlehem, in the land of *J*,
2: 6 least among the rulers of *J*;
Lk 1: 39 to a town in the hill country of *J*,
3: 30 the son of *J*, the son of Joseph,
3: 33 the son of *J*,
Heb 7: 14 that our Lord descended from *J*,
8: 8 and with the house of *J*.
Rev 5: 5 of the tribe of *J*, the Root of David,
7: 5 From the tribe of *J* 12,000

JUDAH'S (JUDAH)

Ge 38: 7 *J* firstborn, was wicked
38: 12 a long time *J* wife, the daughter
Jos 19: 9 because *J* portion was more
2Sa 3: 8 ''Am I a dog's head—on *J* side?
1Ki 2: 32 of Jether, commander of *J* army—
1Ch 2: 3 *J* firstborn, was wicked
2: 4 Tamar, *J* daughter-in-law,
Ps 68: 27 there the great throng of *J* princes,
Isa 11: 13 and *J* enemies will be cut off;
Jer 17: 1 ''*J* sin is engraved with an iron tool,
Eze 37: 19 it to *J* stick, making them a single
Hos 5: 10 *J* leaders are like those
Mic 1: 5 What is *J* high place?

JUDAISM (JEW)

Ac 2: 11 (both Jews and converts to *J*);
6: 5 from Antioch, a convert to *J*.
13: 43 devout converts to *J* followed Paul
Gal 1: 13 of my previous way of life in *J*,
1: 14 advancing in *J* beyond many Jews

JUDAS

Mt 10: 4 Simon the Zealot and *J* Iscariot,
13: 55 *J*? Aren't all his sisters with us?
26: 14 the one called *J* Iscariot—
26: 16 From then on *J* watched

Mt 26: 25 *J*, the one who would betray him,
26: 47 While he was still speaking, *J*,
26: 49 *J* said, "Greetings, Rabbi!"
27: 3 When *J*, who had betrayed him,
27: 5 *J* threw the money into the temple
Mk 3: 19 Simon the Zealot and *J* Iscariot,
6: 3 *J* and Simon? Aren't his sisters
14: 10 Then *J* Iscariot, one of the Twelve,
14: 43 Just as he was speaking, *J*,
14: 45 Going at once to Jesus, *J* said,
Lk 6: 16 *J* son of James, and *J* Iscariot,
22: 3 Satan entered *J*, called Iscariot,
22: 4 And *J* went to the chief priests
22: 47 and the man who was called *J*,
22: 48 to kiss him, but Jesus asked him, "*J*
Jn 6: 71 (He meant *J*, the son of Simon
12: 4 But one of his disciples, *J* Iscariot,
13: 2 had already prompted *J* Iscariot,
13: 26 he gave it to *J* Iscariot, son
13: 27 As soon as *J* took the bread,
13: 29 Since *J* had charge of the money,
13: 30 As soon as *J* had taken the bread,
14: 22 Then *J* (not *J* Iscariot) said, "But,
18: 2 Now *J*, who betrayed him,
18: 3 So *J* came to the grove, guiding
18: 5 *J* the traitor was standing there
Ac 1: 13 and Simon the Zealot, and *J* son
1: 16 the mouth of David concerning *J*,
1: 18 *J* bought a field; there he fell
1: 25 which *J* left to go where he belongs
5: 37 *J* the Galilean appeared in the days
9: 11 to the house of *J* on Straight Street
15: 22 They chose *J* (called Barsabbas)
15: 27 Therefore we are sending *J*
15: 32 *J* and Silas, who themselves were

JUDE

Jude : 1 *J*, a servant of Jesus Christ

JUDEA (JUDAH)

Mt 2: 1 born in Bethlehem in *J*,
2: 5 "In Bethlehem in *J*," they replied,
2: 22 in *J* in place of his father Herod,
3: 1 preaching in the Desert of *J*
3: 5 and all *J* and the whole region
4: 25 *J* and the region across the Jordan
19: 1 and went into the region of *J*
24: 16 are in *J* flee to the mountains.
Mk 3: 8 many people came to him from *J*,
10: 1 and went into the region of *J*
13: 14 are in *J* flee to the mountains.
Lk 1: 5 king of *J* there was a priest named
1: 65 of *J* people were talking about all
2: 4 town of Nazareth in Galilee to *J*,
3: 1 Pontius Pilate was governor of *J*,
4: 44 preaching in the synagogues of *J*.
5: 17 and from *J* and Jerusalem,
6: 17 number of people from all over *J*,
7: 17 about Jesus spread throughout *J*
21: 21 are in *J* flee to the mountains,
23: 5 all over *J* by his teaching.
Jn 4: 3 he left *J* and went back once more
4: 47 Jesus had arrived in Galilee from *J*,
4: 54 having come from *J* to Galilee.
7: 1 purposely staying away from *J*
7: 3 You ought to leave here and go to *J*
11: 7 his disciples, "Let us go back to *J*."
Ac 1: 8 and in all *J* and Samaria,
2: 9 residents of Mesopotamia, *J*
8: 1 were scattered throughout *J*
9: 31 Then the church throughout *J*,
10: 37 what has happened throughout *J*,
11: 1 brothers throughout *J* heard that
11: 29 help for the brothers living in *J*.
12: 19 Herod went from *J* to Caesarea
15: 1 came down from *J* to Antioch
21: 10 named Agabus came down from *J*.
26: 20 to those in Jerusalem and in all *J*,
28: 21 letters from *J* concerning you,
Ro 15: 31 rescued from the unbelievers in *J*
2Co 1: 16 have you send me on my way to *J*.
Gal 1: 22 to the churches of *J* that are
1Th 2: 14 imitators of God's churches in *J*,

JUDEAN (JUDAH)

1Ch 4: 18 (His *J* wife gave birth
2Ch 25: 13 part in the war raided *J* towns
27: 4 He built towns in the *J* hills

Mk 1: 5 The whole *J* countryside
Lk 23: 51 from the *J* town of Arimathea
Jn 3: 22 out into the *J* countryside,

JUDGE (JUDGE'S JUDGED JUDGES JUDGING JUDGMENT JUDGMENTS)

Ge 16: 5 May the LORD *j* between you
18: 25 Will not the *J* of all the earth do
19: 9 and now he wants to play the *j*!
31: 37 let them *j* between the two of us.
31: 53 God of their father, *j* between us."
Ex 2: 14 Who made you ruler and *j* over us?
5: 21 look upon you and *j* you!
18: 13 seat to serve as *j* for the people,
18: 14 as *j*, while all these people stand
Lev 19: 15 but *j* your neighbor fairly.
27: 12 who will *j* its quality as good or bad
27: 14 the priest will *j* its quality as good
Nu 35: 24 the assembly must *j* between him
Dt 1: 16 between your brothers and *j* fairly,
16: 18 and they shall *j* the people fairly.
17: 8 that are too difficult for you to *j*—
17: 9 to the *j* who is in office at that time.
17: 12 man who shows contempt for the *j*
25: 2 the *j* shall make him lie down
32: 36 The LORD will *j* his people
Jdg 2: 18 Whenever the LORD raised up a *j*
2: 18 their enemies as long as the *j* lived;
2: 18 was with the *j* and saved them out
2: 19 But when the *j* died, the people
3: 10 so that he became Israel's *j*
11: 27 the *J*, decide the dispute this day
1Sa 2: 10 the LORD will *j* the ends
3: 13 that I would *j* his family forever
7: 15 *j* over Israel all the days of his life.
24: 12 May the LORD *j* between you
24: 15 May the LORD be our *j*
2Sa 15: 4 "If only I were appointed *j*
1Ki 7: 7 Hall of Justice, where he was to *j*,
8: 32 *J* between your servants,
1Ch 12: 17 of our fathers see it and *j* you."
16: 33 for he comes to *j* the earth.
2Ch 6: 23 *J* between your servants, repaying
19: 7 *J* carefully, for with the LORD our
20: 12 O our God, will you not *j* them?
Job 9: 15 plead with my *J* for mercy
22: 13 Does he *j* through such darkness?
23: 7 be delivered forever from my *j*.
Ps 7: 8 *J* me, O LORD, according
7: 8 let the LORD *j* the peoples.
7: 11 God is a righteous *j*,
9: 8 He will *j* the world in righteousness
50: 4 the earth, that he may *j* his people:
50: 6 for God himself is *j*.
51: 4 and justified when you *j*.
58: 1 Do you *j* uprightly among men?
72: 2 He will *j* your people
75: 2 it is I who *j* uprightly.
76: 9 when you, O God, rose up to *j*,
82: 8 Rise up, O God, *j* the earth,
94: 2 Rise up, O *J* of the earth;
96: 10 he will *j* the peoples with equity.
96: 13 He will *j* the world in righteousness
96: 13 he comes to *j* the earth.
98: 9 He will *j* the world in righteousness
98: 9 for he comes to *j* the earth.
110: 6 He will *j* the nations, heaping up
Pr 20: 8 When a king sits on his throne to *j*,
31: 9 Speak up and *j* fairly;
Isa 2: 4 He will *j* between the nations
3: 2 the *j* and prophet,
3: 13 he rises to *j* the people.
5: 3 *j* between me and my vineyard.
11: 3 He will not *j* by what he sees
11: 4 righteousness he will *j* the needy,
33: 22 For the LORD is our *j*,
Jer 11: 20 Almighty, you who *j* righteously
Eze 7: 3 I will *j* you according
7: 8 I will *j* you according
7: 27 by their own standards I will *j* them
18: 30 O house of Israel, I will *j* you,
20: 4 "Will you *j* them? Will you *j* them,
20: 36 so I will *j* you, declares
21: 30 I will *j* you.
22: 2 Will you *j* this city of bloodshed?
22: 2 "Son of man, will you *j* her?
23: 36 will you *j* Oholah and Oholibah?
33: 20 But I will *j* each of you according

Eze 34: 17 I will *j* between one sheep
34: 20 I myself will *j* between the fat
34: 22 I will *j* between one sheep
35: 11 known among them when I *j* you.
Joel 3: 12 sit to *j* all the nations on every side.
Mic 3: 11 Her leaders *j* for a bribe,
4: 3 He will *j* between many peoples
7: 3 the *j* accepts bribes,
Mt 5: 25 and the *j* may hand you
5: 25 or he may hand you over to the *j*,
7: 1 Do not *j*, or you too will be judged.
7: 2 For in the same way you *j* others,
Lk 6: 37 "Do not *j*, and you will not be
12: 14 who appointed me a *j* or an arbiter
12: 57 don't you *j* for yourselves what
12: 58 or he may drag you off to the *j*,
12: 58 the *j* turn you over to the officer,
18: 2 there was a *j* who neither feared
18: 6 "Listen to what the unjust *j* says.
19: 22 'I will *j* you by your own words,
Jn 5: 27 And he has given him authority to *j*
5: 30 By myself I can do nothing; I *j* only
8: 15 You *j* by human standards;
8: 16 But if I do *j*, my decisions are right,
8: 50 is one who seeks it, and he is the *j*.
12: 47 For I did not come to *j* the world,
12: 47 does not keep them, I do not *j* him.
12: 48 There is a *j* for the one who rejects
18: 31 and *j* him by your own law."
Ac 4: 19 "*J* for yourselves whether it is right
7: 27 'Who made you ruler and *j* over us?
7: 35 'Who made you ruler and *j*?'
10: 42 as *j* of the living and the dead.
17: 31 a day when he will *j* the world
18: 15 I will not be a *j* of such things."
23: 3 You sit there to *j* me according
24: 10 number of years you have been a *j*
Ro 2: 1 at whatever point you *j* the other,
2: 16 day when God will *j* men's secrets
3: 6 how could God *j* the world?
14: 4 you to *j* someone else's servant?
14: 10 then, why do you *j* your brother?
1Co 4: 3 indeed, I do not even *j* myself.
4: 5 Therefore *j* nothing
5: 12 Are you not to *j* those inside?
5: 12 mine to *j* those outside the church?
5: 13 inside? God will *j* those outside.
6: 2 And if you are to *j* the world,
6: 2 not competent to *j* trivial cases?
6: 2 that the saints will *j* the world?
6: 3 you not know that we will *j* angels?
6: 5 to *j* a dispute between believers?
10: 15 *j* for yourselves what I say.
11: 13 *J* for yourselves: Is it proper
Gal 2: 6 not *j* by external appearance—
Col 2: 16 Therefore do not let anyone *j* you
2Ti 4: 1 who will *j* the living and the dead,
4: 8 which the Lord, the righteous *J*,
Heb 10: 30 "The Lord will *j* his people."
12: 23 come to God, the *j* of all men,
13: 4 for God will *j* the adulterer
Jas 4: 11 When you *j* the law, you are not
4: 12 There is only one Lawgiver and *J*,
4: 12 who are you to *j* your neighbor?
5: 9 The *J* is standing at the door!
1Pe 4: 5 to him who is ready to *j* the living
Jude : 15 of his holy ones to *j* everyone,
Rev 6: 10 until you *j* the inhabitants
20: 4 who had been given authority to *j*.

JUDGE'S (JUDGE)

Mt 27: 19 Pilate was sitting on the *j* seat,
Jn 19: 13 and sat down on the *j* seat

JUDGED (JUDGE)

1Sa 7: 17 was, and there he also *j* Israel.
Job 31: 11 a sin to be *j*.
31: 28 then these also would be sins to be *j*
Ps 9: 19 let the nations be *j* in your presence
Eze 20: 36 As I *j* your fathers in the desert
24: 14 You will be *j* according
36: 19 I *j* them according to their conduct
Mt 7: 1 "Do not judge, or you too will be *j*.
7: 2 you will be *j*, and with the measure
Lk 6: 37 Do not judge, and you will not be *j*.
7: 43 "You have *j* correctly," Jesus said.
Ro 2: 12 under the law will be *j* by the law.
1Co 4: 3 I care very little if I am *j* by you

1Co 10: 29 For why should my freedom be j
11: 31 But if we j ourselves, we would not
11: 32 When we are j by the Lord,
14: 24 all that he is a sinner and will be j
Jas 2: 12 as those who are going to be j
3: 1 who teach will be j more strictly.
5: 9 other, brothers, or you will be j.
1Pe 4: 6 so that they might be j according
Rev 16: 5 because you have so j;
18: 20 God has j her for the way she
20: 12 The dead were j according
20: 13 and each person was j according

JUDGES (JUDGE)

Ex 18: 22 as j for the people at all times,
18: 26 as j for the people at all times.
21: 6 master must take him before the j.
22: 8 appear before the j to determine
22: 9 are to bring their cases before the j.
22: 9 one whom the j declare guilty must
Nu 25: 5 So Moses said to Israel's j,
Dt 1: 16 And I charged your j at that time:
16: 18 Appoint j and officials for each
19: 17 the j who are in office at the time.
19: 18 The j must make a thorough
21: 2 your elders and j shall go out
25: 1 and the j will decide the case,
Jos 8: 33 with their elders, officials and j,
23: 2 their elders, leaders, j and officials
24: 1 leaders, j and officials of Israel,
Jdg 2: 16 Then the LORD raised up j,
2: 17 Yet they would not listen to their j
Ru 1: 1 In the days when the j ruled,
1Sa 8: 1 he appointed his sons as j for Israel.
2Ki 23: 22 the days of the j who led Israel,
1Ch 23: 4 are to be officials and j.
26: 29 as officials and j over Israel.
2Ch 1: 2 to the j and to all the leaders
19: 5 He appointed j in the land,
Ezr 4: 9 the j and officials over the men
7: 25 and j to administer justice
10: 14 with the elders and j of each town,
Job 9: 24 he blindfolds its j.
12: 17 and makes fools of j.
21: 22 since he j even the highest?
Ps 58: 11 there is a God who j the earth."
75: 7 But it is God who j:
Pr 29: 14 If a king j the poor with fairness,
Isa 1: 26 I will restore your j as in days of old
Eze 18: 8 and j fairly between man and man.
44: 24 the priests are to serve as j
Da 3: 2 governors, advisers, treasurers, j,
3: 3 governors, advisers, treasurers, j,
Mt 12: 27 So then, they will be your j.
Lk 11: 19 So then, they will be your j.
Jn 5: 22 Moreover, the Father j no one,
Ac 13: 20 God gave them j until the time
1Co 4: 4 It is the Lord who j me.
6: 4 as j even men of little account
Heb 4: 12 it j the thoughts and attitudes
Jas 2: 4 and become j with evil thoughts?
4: 11 or j him speaks against the law
4: 11 speaks against the law and j it.
1Pe 1: 17 on a Father who j each man's work
2: 23 himself to him who j justly.
Rev 18: 8 mighty is the Lord God who j her.
19: 11 With justice he j and makes war.

JUDGING (JUDGE)

Dt 1: 17 Do not show partiality in j;
1Sa 7: 16 Bethel to Gilgal to Mizpah, j Israel
2Ch 19: 6 because you are not j for man
Ps 9: 4 on your throne, j righteously.
Pr 24: 23 To show partiality in j is not good:
Isa 16: 5 one who in j seeks justice
Mt 19: 28 j the twelve tribes of Israel.
Lk 22: 30 j the twelve tribes of Israel.
Jn 7: 24 Stop j by mere appearances,
Ro 3: 4 and prevail in your j."
Rev 11: 18 The time has come for j the dead,

JUDGMENT (JUDGE)

Ex 6: 6 and with mighty acts of j.
7: 4 of j I will bring out my divisions,
12: 12 and I will bring j on all the gods
Lev 13: 37 in his j it is unchanged
Nu 33: 4 for the LORD had brought j
Dt 1: 17 of any man, for j belongs to God.
32: 41 and my hand grasps it in j,
1Sa 25: 33 May you be blessed for your good j
2Ch 20: 9 whether the sword of j, or plague
22: 8 While Jehu was executing j
24: 24 of their fathers, j was executed
Job 14: 3 Will you bring him before you for j
19: 29 then you will know that there is j."
24: 1 the Almighty not set times for j?
34: 23 they should come before him for j.
36: 17 with the j due the wicked;
36: 17 j and justice have taken hold of you
Ps 1: 5 the wicked will not stand in the j,
9: 7 he has established his throne for j.
76: 8 From heaven you pronounced j,
82: 1 he gives j among the "gods":
94: 15 J will again be founded
119: 66 Teach me knowledge and good j,
122: 5 There the thrones for j stand,
143: 2 Do not bring your servant into j,
Pr 3: 21 preserve sound j and discernment,
6: 32 man who commits adultery lacks j;
7: 7 a youth who lacked j.
8: 14 Counsel and sound j are mine;
9: 4 she says to those who lack j.
9: 16 she says to those who lack j.
10: 13 for the back of him who lacks j.
10: 21 but fools die for lack of j.
11: 12 man who lacks j derides his
12: 11 but he who chases fantasies lacks j.
15: 21 Folly delights a man who lacks j,
17: 18 A man lacking in j strikes hands
18: 1 he defies all sound j.
24: 30 vineyard of the man who lacks j;
28: 16 A tyrannical ruler lacks j,
Ecc 3: 16 place of j— wickedness was there,
3: 17 "God will bring to j
11: 9 God will bring you to j.
12: 14 God will bring every deed into j,
Isa 3: 14 The LORD enters into j
4: 4 from Jerusalem by a spirit of j
28: 6 justice to him who sits in j,
34: 5 see, it descends in j on Edom,
41: 1 us meet together at the place of j.
53: 8 By oppression and j, he was taken
66: 16 the LORD will execute j
Jer 2: 35 But I will pass j on you
10: 15 when their j comes, they will
25: 31 he will bring j on all mankind
48: 21 J has come to the plateau—
48: 47 Here ends the j on Moab.
51: 9 for her j reaches to the skies,
51: 18 when their j comes, they will
Eze 11: 10 and I will execute j on you
11: 11 I will execute j on you
17: 20 and execute j upon him there
20: 35 to face, I will execute j upon you.
38: 22 I will execute j upon him
Da 7: 22 pronounced j in favor of the saints
Hos 5: 1 This j is against you:
5: 11 trampled in j,
Joel 3: 2 enter into j against them
Am 7: 4 Sovereign LORD was calling for j
Hab 1: 12 have appointed them to execute j;
Zec 8: 16 and sound j in your courts;
Mal 3: 5 "So I will come near to you for j.
Mt 5: 21 who murders will be subject to j.'
5: 22 with his brother will be subject to j.
10: 15 on the day of j than for that town.
11: 22 Sidon on the day of j than for you.
11: 24 on the day of j than for you."
12: 36 have to give account on the day of j
12: 41 up at the j with this generation
12: 42 rise at the j with this generation
Lk 10: 14 and Sidon at the j than for you.
11: 31 rise at the j with the men
11: 32 up at the j with this generation
Jn 5: 22 but has entrusted all j to the Son,
5: 30 as I hear, and my j is just,
7: 24 appearances, and make a right j."
8: 15 judge by human standards; I pass j
8: 26 "I have much to say in j of you.
9: 39 "For j I have come into this world,
12: 31 Now is the time for j on this world;
16: 8 to sin and righteousness and j:
16: 11 in regard to j, because the prince
Ac 15: 19 "It is my j, therefore, that we
24: 25 self-control and the j to come,
Ro 2: 1 you who pass j do the same things.
Ro 2: 1 you who pass j on someone else,
2: 2 Now we know that God's j
2: 3 pass j on them and yet do the same
2: 3 you think you will escape God's j?
2: 5 when his righteous j will be
5: 16 The j followed one sin
12: 3 rather think of yourself with sober j
13: 2 do so will bring j on themselves.
14: 1 passing j on disputable matters.
14: 10 stand before God's j seat.
14: 13 Therefore let us stop passing j
1Co 2: 15 is not subject to any man's j:
5: 3 And I have already passed j
6: 1 it before the ungodly for j instead
7: 25 but I give a j as one who
7: 40 In my j, she is happier if she stays
9: 3 defense to those who sit in j on me.
11: 29 body of the Lord eats and drinks j
11: 31 we would not come under j.
11: 34 meet together it may not result in j.
2Co 5: 10 appear before the j seat of Christ,
2Th 1: 5 is evidence that God's j is right,
1Ti 3: 6 fall under the same j as the devil.
5: 12 Thus they bring j on themselves,
5: 24 the place of j ahead of them;
Heb 6: 2 of the dead, and eternal j.
9: 27 to die once, and after that to face j,
10: 27 but only a fearful expectation of j
Jas 2: 13 triumphs over j! What good is it,
2: 13 j without mercy will be shown
4: 11 are not keeping it, but sitting in j
1Pe 4: 17 For it is time for j to begin
2Pe 2: 4 gloomy dungeons to be held for j;
2: 9 the unrighteous for the day of j,
3: 7 being kept for the day of j
1Jn 4: 17 have confidence on the day of j,
Jude : 6 bound with everlasting chains for j
Rev 14: 7 because the hour of his j has come.

JUDGMENTS (JUDGE)

Dt 33: 21 and his j concerning Israel."
1Ch 16: 12 miracles, and the j he pronounced,
16: 14 his j are in all the earth.
Ps 48: 11 because of your j.
97: 8 because of your j, O LORD.
105: 5 miracles, and the j he pronounced,
105: 7 his j are in all the earth.
Isa 26: 9 When your j come upon the earth,
Jer 1: 16 I will pronounce my j on my people
4: 12 I pronounce my j against them."
Eze 14: 21 Jerusalem my four dreadful j—
Da 9: 11 and sworn j written in the Law
Hos 6: 5 my j flashed like lightning
Ro 11: 33 How unsearchable his j,
1Co 2: 15 spiritual man makes j about all
Rev 16: 5 "You are just in these j,
16: 7 true and just are your j."
19: 2 for true and just are his j.

JUDITH

Ge 26: 34 he married J daughter

JUG (JUGS)

1Sa 26: 11 and water j that are near his head,
26: 12 and water j near Saul's head,
26: 16 water j that were near his head?"
1Ki 17: 12 of flour in a jar and a little oil in a j.
17: 14 and the j of oil will not run dry
17: 16 and the j of oil did not run dry,

JUGS (JUG)

Jer 48: 12 and smash her j.

JUICE

Nu 6: 3 He must not drink grape j
18: 27 grain from the threshing floor or j
Isa 65: 8 "As when j is still found in a cluster

JULIA

Ro 16: 15 Greet Philologus, J, Nereus

JULIUS

Ac 27: 1 over to a centurion named J,
27: 3 and J, in kindness to Paul,

JUMP (JUMPED JUMPING)

Ac 27: 43 swim to j overboard first

JUMPED (JUMP)

Mk 10: 50 he *j* to his feet and came to Jesus.
Jn 21: 7 it off) and *j* into the water.
Ac 3: 8 He *j* to his feet and began to walk.
14: 10 the man *j* up and began to walk.
19: 16 the man who had the evil spirit *j*

JUMPING (JUMP)

Ac 3: 8 walking and *j*, and praising God.

JUNCTION (JOIN)

Eze 21: 21 at the *j* of the two roads,

JUNIAS

Ro 16: 7 and *J*, my relatives who have been

JURISDICTION

Lk 23: 7 that Jesus was under Herod's *j*,

JUSHAB-HESED

1Ch 3: 20 Ohel, Berekiah, Hasadiah and *J*.

JUST (JUSTICE JUSTIFICATION JUSTIFIED JUSTIFIES JUSTIFY JUSTIFYING JUSTLY)

Ge 18: 19 LORD by doing what is right and *j*,
Dt 32: 4 and all his ways are *j*.
32: 4 upright and *j* is he.
2Sa 8: 15 doing what was *j* and right
1Ch 18: 14 doing what was *j* and right
2Ch 12: 6 and said, "The LORD is *j*."
Ne 9: 13 and laws that are *j* and right,
9: 33 you have been *j*; you have acted
Job 34: 17 Will you condemn the *j*
35: 2 Elihu said: "Do you think this is *j*?
Ps 37: 28 For the LORD loves the *j*
37: 30 and his tongue speaks what is *j*.
99: 4 what is *j* and right.
111: 7 of his hands are faithful and *j*;
119:121 I have done what is righteous and *j*;
Pr 1: 3 doing what is right and *j* and fair;
2: 8 for he guards the course of the *j*
2: 9 will understand what is right and *j*
8: 8 All the words of my mouth are *j*;
8: 15 and rulers make laws that are *j*;
12: 5 The plans of the righteous are *j*,
21: 3 To do what is right and *j*
Isa 32: 7 even when the plea of the needy is *j*
58: 2 They ask me for *j* decisions
Jer 4: 2 if in a truthful, *j* and righteous way
22: 3 what the LORD says: Do what is *j*
22: 15 He did what was right and *j*,
23: 5 do what is *j* and right in the land.
33: 15 he will do what is *j* and right
Eze 18: 5 who does what is *j* and right.
18: 19 Since the son has done what is *j*
18: 21 and does what is *j* and right,
18: 25 'The way of the Lord is not *j*.'
18: 27 and does what is *j* and right,
18: 29 'The way of the Lord is not *j*.'
33: 14 and does what is *j* and right—
33: 16 He has done what is *j* and right;
33: 17 But it is their way that is not *j*.
33: 17 'The way of the Lord is not *j*.'
33: 19 and does what is *j* and right,
33: 20 'The way of the Lord is not *j*.'
45: 9 and oppression and do what is *j*
Da 4: 37 does is right and all his ways are *j*.
Jn 5: 30 as I hear, and my judgment is *j*,
Ro 3: 26 as to be *j* and the one who justifies
2Th 1: 6 God is *j*: He will pay back trouble
Heb 2: 2 received its *j* punishment,
1Jn 1: 9 and *j* and will forgive us our sins
Rev 15: 3 *J* and true are your ways,
16: 5 "You are *j* in these judgments,
16: 7 true and *j* are your judgments."
19: 2 for true and *j* are his judgments.

JUSTICE (JUST)

Ge 49: 16 "Dan will provide *j* for his people
Ex 23: 2 do not pervert *j* by siding
23: 6 "Do not deny *j* to your poor people
Lev 19: 15 " 'Do not pervert *j*; do not show
Dt 16: 19 Do not pervert *j* or show partiality.
16: 20 Follow *j* and *j* alone,
24: 17 the alien or the fatherless of *j*,
27: 19 Cursed is the man who withholds *j*
1Sa 8: 3 accepted bribes and perverted *j*.
2Sa 15: 4 and I would see that he gets *j*."
15: 6 came to the king asking for *j*,
1Ki 3: 11 for discernment in administering *j*,
3: 28 wisdom from God to administer *j*.
7: 7 the Hall of *J*, where he was to judge
10: 9 to maintain *j* and righteousness."
2Ch 9: 8 to maintain *j* and righteousness."
Ezr 7: 25 and judges to administer *j*
Est 1: 13 experts in matters of law and *j*,
Job 8: 3 Does God pervert *j*?
9: 19 matter of *j*, who will summon him?
19: 7 though I call for help, there is no *j*.
27: 2 as God lives, who has denied me *j*,
29: 14 *j* was my robe and my turban.
31: 13 "If I have denied *j*
34: 5 but God denies me *j*.
34: 12 that the Almighty would pervert *j*.
34: 17 Can he who hates *j* govern?
36: 3 I will ascribe *j* to my Maker.
36: 17 *j* have taken hold of you.
37: 23 in his *j* and great righteousness,
40: 8 "Would you discredit my *j*?
Ps 7: 6 Awake, my God; decree *j*.
9: 8 he will govern the peoples with *j*.
9: 16 The LORD is known by his *j*;
11: 7 he loves *j*;
33: 5 LORD loves righteousness and *j*;
36: 6 your *j* like the great deep.
37: 6 *j* of your cause like the noonday
45: 6 a scepter of *j* will be the scepter
72: 1 Endow the king with your *j*, O God
72: 2 your afflicted ones with *j*.
89: 14 *j* are the foundation of your throne;
97: 2 *j* are the foundation of his throne.
99: 4 The King is mighty, he loves *j*—
101: 1 I will sing of your love and *j*;
103: 6 and *j* for all the oppressed.
106: 3 Blessed are they who maintain *j*,
112: 5 who conducts his affairs with *j*.
140: 12 I know that the LORD secures *j*
Pr 8: 20 along the paths of *j*,
16: 10 and his mouth should not betray *j*.
17: 23 to pervert the course of *j*.
18: 5 or to deprive the innocent of *j*.
19: 28 A corrupt witness mocks at *j*,
21: 15 When *j* is done, it brings joy
28: 5 Evil men do not understand *j*,
29: 4 By *j* a king gives a country stability
29: 7 The righteous care about *j*
29: 26 from the LORD that man gets *j*.
Ecc 3: 16 place of *j*— wickedness was there.
5: 8 poor oppressed in a district, and *j*
Isa 1: 17 Seek *j*,
1: 21 She once was full of *j*;
1: 27 Zion will be redeemed with *j*,
5: 7 he looked for *j*, but saw bloodshed;
5: 16 Almighty will be exalted by his *j*,
5: 23 but deny *j* to the innocent.
9: 7 it with *j* and righteousness
10: 2 and rob my oppressed people of *j*,
11: 4 with *j* he will give decisions
16: 5 one who in judging seeks *j*
28: 6 He will be a spirit of *j*
28: 17 I will make *j* the measuring line
29: 21 deprive the innocent of *j*.
30: 18 For the LORD is a God of *j*.
32: 1 and rulers will rule with *j*.
32: 16 *J* will dwell in the desert
33: 5 with *j* and righteousness.
42: 1 and he will bring *j* to the nations.
42: 3 In faithfulness he will bring forth *j*;
42: 4 till he establishes *j* on earth.
51: 4 my *j* will become a light
51: 5 my arm will bring *j* to the nations.
56: 1 "Maintain *j*
59: 4 No one calls for *j*;
59: 8 there is no *j* in their paths.
59: 9 So *j* is far from us,
59: 11 We look for *j*, but find none;
59: 14 So *j* is driven back,
59: 15 that there was no *j*.
61: 8 "For I, the LORD, love *j*;
Jer 9: 24 *j* and righteousness on earth,
10: 24 Correct me, LORD, but only with *j*
12: 1 speak with you about your *j*:
21: 12 " 'Administer *j* every morning;
30: 11 I will discipline you but only with *j*;
46: 28 I will discipline you but only with *j*;
La 3: 36 to deprive a man of *j*—
Eze 22: 29 mistreat the alien, denying them *j*.
34: 16 I will shepherd the flock with *j*.
Hos 2: 19 you in righteousness and *j*,
12: 6 maintain love and *j*,
Am 2: 7 and deny *j* to the oppressed.
5: 7 You who turn *j* into bitterness
5: 12 and you deprive the poor of *j*
5: 15 maintain *j* in the courts.
5: 24 But let *j* roll on like a river,
6: 12 But you have turned *j* into poison
Mic 3: 1 Should you not know *j*,
3: 8 and with *j* and might,
3: 9 who despise *j*
7: 9 I will see his *j*.
Hab 1: 4 and *j* never prevails.
1: 4 so that *j* is perverted.
Zep 3: 5 by morning he dispenses his *j*,
Zec 7: 9 'Administer true *j*; show mercy
Mal 2: 17 or "Where is the God of *j*?"
3: 5 and deprive aliens of *j*,
Mt 12: 18 he will proclaim *j* to the nations.
12: 20 till he leads *j* to victory.
23: 23 important matters of the law—*j*,
Lk 11: 42 you neglect *j* and the love of God.
18: 3 'Grant me *j* against my adversary.'
18: 5 I will see that she gets *j*,
18: 7 And will not God bring about *j*
18: 8 he will see that they get *j*,
Ac 8: 33 humiliation he was deprived of *j*.
17: 31 with *j* by the man he has appointed.
28: 4 *J* has not allowed him to live."
Ro 3: 25 He did this to demonstrate his *j*,
3: 26 it to demonstrate his *j*
2Co 7: 11 what readiness to see *j* done.
Heb 11: 33 administered *j*, and gained what
Rev 19: 11 With *j* he judges and makes war.

JUSTIFICATION (JUST)

Eze 16: 52 for you have furnished some *j*
Ro 4: 25 and was raised to life for our *j*.
5: 16 many trespasses and brought *j*.
5: 18 of righteousness was *j* that brings

JUSTIFIED (JUST)

Ps 51: 4 and *j* when you judge.
Lk 18: 14 rather than the other, went home *j*
Ac 13: 39 from everything you could not be *j*
13: 39 him everyone who believes is *j*
Ro 3: 24 and are *j* freely by his grace
3: 28 For we maintain that a man is *j*
4: 2 If, in fact, Abraham was *j* by works,
5: 1 since we have been *j* through faith,
5: 9 Since we have now been *j*
8: 30 those he called, he also *j*; those he *j*,
10: 10 heart that you believe and are *j*,
1Co 6: 11 you were *j* in the name
Gal 2: 16 in Christ Jesus that we may be *j*
2: 16 observing the law no one will be *j*.
2: 16 sinners' know that a man is not *j*
2: 17 "If, while we seek to be *j* in Christ,
3: 11 Clearly no one is *j* before God
3: 24 to Christ that we might be *j* by faith
5: 4 to be *j* by law have been alienated
Tit 3: 7 so that, having been *j* by his grace,
Jas 2: 24 You see that a person is *j*

JUSTIFIES (JUST)

Ro 3: 26 one who *j* the man who has faith
4: 5 but trusts God who *j* the wicked,
8: 33 God has chosen? It is God who *j*.

JUSTIFY (JUST)

Est 7: 4 such distress would *j* disturbing
Job 40: 8 you condemn me to *j* yourself?
Isa 53: 11 my righteous servant will *j* many,
Lk 10: 29 But he wanted to *j* himself,
16: 15 "You are the ones who *j* yourselves
Ro 3: 30 who will *j* the circumcised by faith
Gal 3: 8 that God would *j* the Gentiles

JUSTIFYING (JUST)

Job 32: 2 angry with Job for *j* himself rather

JUSTLY (JUST)

Ps 58: 1 Do you rulers indeed speak *j*?
67: 4 for you rule the peoples *j*
Jer 7: 5 and deal with each other *j*,

Mic 6: 8 To act *j* and to love mercy
Lk 23: 41 We are punished *j*,
1Pe 2: 23 himself to him who judges *j*.

JUSTUS

Ac 1: 23 (also known as *J*) and Matthias.
Col 4: 11 who is called *J*, also sends

JUTTAH

Jos 15: 55 Carmel, Ziph, *J*, Jezreel, Jokdeam,
21: 16 Debir, Ain, *J* and Beth Shemesh,
1Ch 6: 59 Hilen, Debir, Ashan, *J*

KABZEEL

Jos 15: 21 *K*, Eder, Jagur, Kinah, Dimonah,
2Sa 23: 20 was a valiant fighter from *K*,
1Ch 11: 22 was a valiant fighter from *K*,

KADESH

Ge 14: 7 (that is, *K*), and they conquered
16: 14 it is still there, between *K*
20: 1 and lived between *K* and Shur.
Nu 13: 26 community at *K* in the Desert
20: 1 of Zin, and they stayed at *K*.
20: 14 messengers from *K* to the king
20: 16 "Now we are here at *K*, a town
20: 22 Israelite community set out from *K*
27: 14 were the waters of Meribah in *K*,
33: 36 left Ezion Geber and camped at *K*,
33: 37 They left *K* and camped
Dt 1: 46 And so you stayed in *K* many days
Jdg 11: 16 desert to the Red Sea and on to *K*.
11: 17 So Israel stayed at *K*.
Ps 29: 8 the LORD shakes the Desert of *K*.

KADESH BARNEA

Nu 32: 8 I sent them from *K* to look over
34: 4 on to Zin and go south of *K*.
Dt 1: 2 days to go from Horeb to *K*
1: 19 have seen, and so we reached *K*.
2: 14 passed from the time we left *K*
9: 23 the LORD sent you out from *K*,
Jos 10: 41 Joshua subdued them from *K*
14: 6 the man of God at *K* about you
14: 7 me from *K* to explore the land.
15: 3 and went over to the south of *K*.

KADMIEL

Ezr 2: 40 and *K* (through the line
3: 9 and his sons and brothers and *K*
Ne 7: 43 descendants of Jeshua (through *K*
9: 4 Jeshua, Bani, *K*, Shebaniah, Bunni,
9: 5 Jeshua, *K*, Bani, Hashabneiah,
10: 9 *K*, and their associates: Shebaniah,
12: 8 Binnui, *K*, Sherebiah, Judah,
12: 24 son of *K*, and their associates,

KADMONITES

Ge 15: 19 Kenizzites, *K*, Hittites, Perizzites,

KAIN

Jos 15: 57 Jezreel, Jokdeam, Zanoah, *K*,

KALLAI

Ne 12: 20 Uzzi; of Sallu's, *K*; of Amok's, Eber

KAMON

Jdg 10: 5 When Jair died, he was buried in *K*.

KANAH

Jos 16: 8 border went west to the *K* Ravine
17: 9 continued south to the *K* Ravine.
19: 28 Hammon and *K*, as far

KAREAH

2Ki 25: 23 Johanan son of *K*, Seraiah son
Jer 40: 8 and Jonathan the sons of *K*,
40: 13 of *K* and all the army officers still
40: 15 Johanan son of *K* said privately
40: 16 said to Johanan son of *K*,
41: 11 When Johanan son of *K*
41: 13 had with him saw Johanan son of *K*
41: 14 and went over to Johanan son of *K*.
41: 16 Then Johanan son of *K*
42: 1 including Johanan son of *K*
42: 8 called together Johanan son of *K*
43: 2 of Hoshaiah and Johanan son of *K*
43: 4 son of *K* and all the army officers
43: 5 of *K* and all the army officers led

KARKA

Jos 15: 3 to Addar and curved around to *K*.

KARKOR

Jdg 8: 10 Zalmunna were in *K* with a force

KARNAIM

Am 6: 13 "Did we not take *K*

KARTAH

Jos 21: 34 Jokneam, *K*, Dimnah and Nahalal,
1Ch 6: 77 *K*, Rimmono and Tabor, together

KARTAN

Jos 21: 32 *K*, together with their pasturelands

KATTATH

Jos 19: 15 Included were *K*, Nahalal,

KATYDID

Lev 11: 22 you may eat any kind of locust, *k*,

KEBAR

Eze 1: 1 among the exiles by the *K* River,
1: 3 by the *K* River in the land
3: 15 Tel Aviv near the *K* River.
3: 23 the glory I had seen by the *K* River,
10: 15 I had seen by the *K* River.
10: 20 the God of Israel by the *K* River,
10: 22 as those I had seen by the *K* River.
43: 3 visions I had seen by the *K* River,

KEDAR (KEDAR'S)

Ge 25: 13 *K*, Adbeel, Mibsam, Mishma,
1Ch 1: 29 *K*, Adbeel, Mibsam, Mishma,
Ps 120: 5 that I live among the tents of *K*!
SS 1: 5 dark like the tents of *K*,
Isa 21: 16 all the pomp of *K* will come
21: 17 the warriors of *K*, will be few."
42: 11 settlements where *K* lives rejoice.
Jer 2: 10 send to *K* and observe closely;
49: 28 Concerning *K* and the kingdoms
49: 28 "Arise, and attack *K*
Eze 27: 21 princes of *K* were your customers;

KEDAR'S (KEDAR)

Isa 60: 7 All *K* flocks will be gathered to you

KEDEMAH

Ge 25: 15 Tema, Jetur, Naphish and *K*.
1Ch 1: 31 Tema, Jetur, Naphish and *K*.

KEDEMOTH

Dt 2: 26 the desert of *K* I sent messengers
Jos 13: 18 Jahaz, *K*, Mephaath, Kiriathaim,
21: 37 Bezer, Jahaz, *K* and Mephaath,
1Ch 6: 79 Jahzah, *K* and Mephaath,

KEDESH

Jos 12: 22 king of *K* one the king of Jokneam
15: 23 Dimonah, Adadah, *K*, Hazor,
19: 37 Ramah, Hazor, *K*, Edrei,
20: 7 So they set apart *K* in Galilee
21: 32 *K* in Galilee (a city of refuge
Jdg 4: 6 of Abinoam from *K* in Naphtali
4: 9 So Deborah went with Barak to *K*,
4: 11 tree in Zaanannim near *K*.
2Ki 15: 29 Janoah, *K* and Hazor.
1Ch 6: 72 tribe of Issachar they received *K*,
6: 76 tribe of Naphtali they received *K*

KEDORLAOMER

Ge 14: 1 *K* king of Elam and Tidal king
14: 4 years they had been subject to *K*,
14: 5 *K* and the kings allied
14: 9 of Siddim against *K* king of Elam,
14: 17 Abram returned from defeating *K*

KEEN

Da 5: 12 was found to have a *k* mind

KEEP (KEEPER KEEPERS KEEPING KEEPS KEPT SAFEKEEPING)

Ge 6: 19 female, to *k* them alive with you.
7: 3 to *k* their various kinds alive
14: 21 and *k* the goods for yourself."
17: 9 for you, you must *k* my covenant,
17: 10 the covenant you are to *k*:
18: 19 household after him to *k* the way
31: 49 "May the LORD *k* watch
32: 16 *k* some space between the herds."
33: 9 *K* what you have for yourself."
38: 9 to *k* from producing offspring
38: 23 Judah said, "Let her *k* what she has
42: 1 "Why do you just *k* looking
47: 24 The other four-fifths you may *k*
Ex 5: 9 for the men so that they *k* working
5: 17 lazy! That is why you *k* saying,
12: 42 are to *k* vigil to honor the LORD
13: 10 You must *k* this ordinance
15: 26 his commands and *k* all his
16: 19 "No one is to *k* any of it
16: 23 Save whatever is left and *k* it
16: 28 refuse to *k* my commands
16: 32 *k* it for the generations to come,
19: 5 obey me fully and *k* my covenant,
20: 6 and *k* my commandments.
20: 20 with you to *k* you from sinning."
21: 36 the owner did not *k* it penned up,
27: 21 his sons are to *k* the lamps burning
Lev 7: 8 offering for anyone may *k* its hide
13: 5 to *k* him in isolation another seven
13: 33 and the priest is to *k* him
15: 31 You must *k* the Israelites separate
18: 5 *K* my decrees and laws,
18: 26 But you must *k* my decrees
18: 30 *K* my requirements and do not
19: 19 " '*K* my decrees.
19: 37 " '*K* all my decrees and all my laws
20: 8 *K* my decrees and follow them.
20: 22 " '*K* all my decrees and laws
22: 9 are to *k* my requirements
22: 31 *K* my commands and follow them.
26: 9 and I will *k* my covenant with you.
Nu 6: 24 and *k* you;
11: 13 They *k* wailing to me, 'Give us
15: 22 if you unintentionally fail to *k* any
22: 16 Do not let anything *k* you
36: 7 every Israelite shall *k* the tribal
36: 9 is to *k* the land it inherits."
Dt 4: 2 but *k* the commands of the LORD
4: 40 *K* his decrees and commands,
5: 10 and *k* my commandments.
5: 29 and *k* all my commands always,
6: 17 Be sure to *k* the commands
7: 9 who love him and *k* his commands.
7: 12 your God will *k* his covenant
7: 15 The LORD will *k* you free
8: 2 or not you would *k* his commands.
11: 1 your God and *k* his requirements,
13: 4 *K* his commands and obey him;
22: 2 *k* it until he comes looking for it.
23: 9 *k* away from everything impure.
26: 17 that you will *k* his decrees,
26: 18 that you are to *k* all his commands.
27: 1 "*K* all these commands that I give
28: 9 if you *k* the commands
28: 41 daughters but you will not *k* them,
30: 10 your God and *k* his commands
30: 16 and to *k* his commands, decrees
Jos 3: 4 *k* a distance of about a thousand
6: 18 *k* away from the devoted things,
7: 11 which I commanded them to *k*.
22: 5 careful to *k* the commandment
Jdg 2: 22 they will *k* the way of the LORD
6: 11 wheat in a winepress to *k* it
1Sa 1: 14 "How long will you *k*
2: 3 "Do not *k* talking so proudly
6: 9 it on its way, but *k* watching it.
2Sa 7: 25 *k* forever the promise you have
13: 13 will not *k* me from being married
14: 18 "Do not *k* from me the answer
1Ki 1: 1 he could not *k* warm
1: 2 our lord the king may *k* warm."
2: 3 and *k* his decrees and commands,
2: 4 that the LORD may *k* his promise
2: 43 Why then did you not *k* your oath
6: 12 my regulations and *k* all my
8: 23 you who *k* your covenant of love
8: 25 *k* for your servant David my father
8: 58 and to *k* the commands,
11: 10 Solomon did not *k* the LORD's
15: 5 and had not failed to *k* any
18: 5 can find some grass to *k* the horses
2Ki 10: 31 careful to *k* the law of the LORD,

2Ki 17: 19 Judah did not *k* the commands
17: 37 always be careful to *k* the decrees
21: 8 and will *k* the whole Law that my
23: 3 the LORD and *k* his commands,
1Ch 4: 10 *k* me from harm so that I will be
10: 13 he did not *k* the word of the LORD
22: 12 so that you may *k* the law
29: 18 and *k* their hearts loyal to you.
29: 18 *k* this desire in the hearts
29: 19 devotion to *k* your commands,
2Ch 2: 18 over them to *k* the people working.
6: 14 you who *k* your covenant of love
6: 16 *k* for your servant David my father
23: 4 are to *k* watch at the doors,
34: 31 the LORD and *k* his commands,
Ne 5: 13 man who does not *k* this promise.
13: 22 in order to *k* the Sabbath day holy.
Est 3: 8 kingdom who *k* themselves
3: 11 "*K* the money," the king said
Job 4: 2 But who can *k* from speaking?
7: 11 "Therefore I will not *k* silent;
13: 13 "*K* silent and let me speak;
13: 27 you *k* close watch on all my paths
14: 16 but not *k* track of my sin.
16: 3 What ails you that you *k*
22: 15 Will you *k* to the old path
30: 10 detest me and *k* their distance;
33: 17 and *k* him from pride,
34: 30 to *k* a godless man from ruling,
36: 6 He does not *k* the wicked alive
41: 3 Will he *k* begging you for mercy?
Ps 12: 7 O LORD, you will *k* us safe
16: 1 *K* me safe, O God,
17: 8 *K* me as the apple of your eye;
18: 28 You, O LORD, *k* my lamp burning
19: 13 *K* your servant also from willful
22: 29 who cannot *k* themselves alive.
25: 10 for those who *k* the demands
27: 5 he will *k* me safe in his dwelling;
31: 20 in your dwelling you *k* them safe
33: 19 and *k* them alive in famine.
34: 13 *k* your tongue from evil
37: 34 and *k* his way.
39: 1 and *k* my tongue from sin;
78: 7 but would *k* his commands.
78: 10 they did not *k* God's covenant
78: 56 they did not *k* his statutes.
83: 1 O God, do not *k* silent;
89: 31 and fail to *k* my commands,
103: 18 with those who *k* his covenant
105: 45 that they might *k* his precepts
106: 23 *k* his wrath from destroying them.
119: 2 Blessed are they who *k* his statutes
119: 9 can a young man *k* his way pure?
119: 22 for I *k* your statutes.
119: 29 *K* me from deceitful ways;
119: 33 then I will *k* them to the end.
119: 34 and I will *k* your law
119: 55 and I will *k* your law.
119: 69 I *k* your precepts with all my heart.
119:115 that I may *k* the commands
119:146 and I will *k* your statutes.
121: 7 The LORD will *k* you
132: 12 if your sons *k* my covenant
140: 4 *K* me, O LORD, from the hands
141: 3 *k* watch over the door of my lips.
141: 9 *K* me from the snares they have
Pr 2: 20 and *k* to the paths of the righteous.
3: 1 but *k* my commands in your heart,
3: 26 will *k* your foot from being snared.
4: 4 *k* my commands and you will live.
4: 21 *k* them within your heart;
4: 24 *k* corrupt talk far from your lips.
4: 27 *k* your foot from evil.
5: 8 *K* to a path far from her,
6: 20 My son, *k* your father's commands
7: 1 My son, *k* my words
7: 2 *K* my commands and you will live;
7: 5 they will *k* you from the adulteress,
8: 32 blessed are those who *k* my ways.
15: 24 the wise to *k* him from going
20: 28 Love and faithfulness *k* a king safe;
22: 3 but the simple *k* going
22: 12 of the LORD *k* watch
22: 18 when you *k* them in your heart
23: 19 and *k* your heart on the right path.
23: 26 and let your eyes *k* to my ways,
27: 12 but the simple *k* going
Pr 28: 4 but those who *k* the law resist them
30: 8 *K* falsehood and lies far from me;
Ecc 3: 6 a time to *k* and a time
4: 11 But how can one *k* warm alone?
4: 11 down together, they will *k* warm.
12: 13 and *k* his commandments,
Isa 7: 4 *k* calm and don't be afraid.
7: 21 a man will *k* alive a young cow
19: 21 vows to the LORD and *k* them.
26: 3 You will *k* in perfect peace
28: 24 Does he *k* on breaking up
29: 23 they will *k* my name holy;
42: 6 I will *k* you and will make you
47: 12 "*K* on, then, with your magic spells
49: 8 I will *k* you and will make you
56: 4 To the eunuchs who *k* my Sabbaths
56: 6 all who *k* the Sabbath
58: 13 "If you *k* your feet
62: 1 For Zion's sake I will not *k* silent,
64: 12 Will you *k* silent and punish us
65: 5 '*K* away; don't come near me,
65: 6 I will not *k* silent but will pay back
Jer 4: 19 I cannot *k* silent.
11: 8 to follow but that they did not *k*.' "
13: 14 or compassion to *k* me
14: 13 the prophets *k* telling them,
15: 6 "You *k* on backsliding.
16: 11 forsook me and did not *k* my law.
17: 15 They *k* saying to me,
17: 18 but *k* me from shame,
17: 18 but *k* me from terror.
17: 22 but *k* the Sabbath day holy,
17: 24 but *k* the Sabbath day holy
17: 27 me to *k* the Sabbath day holy
23: 17 They *k* saying to those who despise
23: 37 This is what you *k* saying
42: 4 and will *k* nothing back from you."
44: 25 what you promised! *K* your vows!
50: 2 *k* nothing back, but say,
La 1: 11 food to *k* themselves alive.
1: 19 food to *k* themselves alive.
Eze 11: 20 and be careful to *k* my laws.
18: 19 has been careful to *k* all my decrees
20: 9 of my name I did what would *k* it
20: 14 of my name I did what would *k* it
20: 18 or *k* their laws or defile yourselves
20: 19 and be careful to *k* my laws.
20: 20 *K* my Sabbaths holy, that they may
20: 21 they were not careful to *k* my laws
20: 22 of my name I did what would *k* it
24: 17 *K* your turban fastened
24: 23 You will *k* your turbans
36: 27 and be careful to *k* my laws.
37: 24 and be careful to *k* my decrees.
44: 20 but they are to *k* the hair
44: 24 They are to *k* my laws
44: 24 and they are to *k* my Sabbaths holy
46: 17 the servant may *k* it until the year
Da 5: 17 "You may *k* your gifts for yourself
Hab 1: 17 Is he to *k* on emptying his net,
Zec 3: 7 in my ways and *k* my requirements
11: 12 give me my pay; but if not, *k* it."
12: 4 "I will *k* a watchful eye
Mt 5: 33 but *k* the oaths you have made
6: 7 do not *k* on babbling like pagans,
10: 10 for the worker is worth his *k*.
24: 42 "Therefore *k* watch, because you
25: 13 "Therefore *k* watch, because you
26: 38 Stay here and *k* watch with me."
26: 40 "Could you men not *k* watch
28: 14 we will satisfy him and *k* you out
Mk 3: 9 to *k* the people from crowding him.
7: 24 he could not *k* his presence secret.
13: 34 tells the one at the door to *k* watch.
13: 35 "Therefore *k* watch because you
14: 34 "Stay here and *k* watch."
14: 37 Could you not *k* watch
Lk 4: 42 they tried to *k* him
12: 35 and *k* your lamps burning,
13: 33 I must *k* going today
17: 33 tries to *k* his life will lose it,
18: 7 Will he *k* putting them off?
19: 40 he replied, "if they *k* quiet,
Jn 4: 15 and have to *k* coming here
8: 55 but I do know him and *k* his word.
9: 16 for he does not *k* the Sabbath."
10: 24 How long will you *k* us in suspense
12: 25 in this world will *k* it for eternal life
Jn 12: 47 my words but does not *k* them,
15: 18 *k* in mind that it hated me first.
18: 18 a fire they had made to *k* warm.
Ac 2: 24 for death to *k* its hold on him.
10: 47 "Can anyone *k* these people
18: 9 "Do not be afraid; *k* on speaking,
20: 28 *K* watch over yourselves
24: 16 always to *k* my conscience clear
24: 23 centurion to *k* Paul under guard
27: 22 you to *k* up your courage,
27: 25 So *k* up your courage, men,
Ro 2: 26 are not circumcised *k* the law's
7: 19 want to do—this I *k* on doing.
12: 11 but *k* your spiritual fervor,
14: 22 you believe about these things *k*
16: 17 *K* away from them.
1Co 1: 8 He will *k* you strong to the end,
5: 8 Therefore let us *k* the Festival,
7: 30 as if it were not theirs to *k*;
10: 6 to *k* us from setting our hearts
14: 28 the speaker should *k* quiet
2Co 3: 13 veil over his face to *k* the Israelites
11: 12 I will *k* on doing what I am doing
12: 7 To *k* me from becoming conceited
Gal 5: 15 If you *k* on biting and devouring
5: 25 let us *k* in step with the Spirit.
Eph 1: 17 I *k* asking that the God
4: 3 Make every effort to *k* the unity
6: 18 and always *k* on praying
1Th 2: 16 in their effort to *k* us from speaking
2Th 3: 6 to *k* away from every brother who
1Ti 3: 9 They must *k* hold of the deep
5: 21 to *k* these instructions
5: 22 *K* yourself pure.
6: 14 you to *k* this commandment
2Ti 1: 13 *k* as the pattern of sound teaching,
2: 14 *K* reminding them of these things.
4: 5 *k* your head in all situations,
Phm : 13 I would have liked to *k* him
Heb 9: 20 God has commanded you to *k*."
10: 26 If we deliberately *k* on sinning
13: 1 *K* on loving each other as brothers.
13: 5 *K* your lives free from the love
13: 17 They *k* watch over you
Jas 1: 26 and yet does not *k* a tight rein
1: 27 to *k* oneself from being polluted
2: 8 If you really *k* the royal law found
2: 16 I wish you well; *k* warm
3: 2 able to *k* his whole body in check.
1Pe 3: 10 must *k* his tongue from evil
2Pe 1: 8 will *k* you from being ineffective
1Jn 5: 21 Dear children, *k* yourselves
Jude : 6 who did not *k* their positions
: 21 *K* yourselves in God's love
: 24 able to *k* you from falling
Rev 3: 10 also *k* you from the hour
20: 3 to *k* him from deceiving
22: 9 of all who *k* the words of this book.

KEEPER (KEEP)

Ge 4: 9 I my brother's *k*?" The LORD
1Sa 17: 22 things with the *k* of supplies,
2Ki 10: 22 Jehu said to the *k* of the wardrobe,
22: 14 son of Harhas, *k* of the wardrobe.
2Ch 31: 14 son of Imnah the Levite, *k*
34: 22 son of Hasrah, *k* of the wardrobe.
Ne 2: 8 to Asaph, *k* of the king's forest,
Jn 12: 6 as *k* of the money bag, he used

KEEPERS (KEEP)

Ecc 12: 3 when the *k* of the house tremble,

KEEPING (KEEP)

Ge 41: 49 so much that he stopped *k* records
Ex 20: 8 the Sabbath day by *k* it holy.
Dt 5: 12 the Sabbath day by *k* it holy,
6: 2 long as you live by *k* all his decrees
7: 9 *k* his covenant of love
13: 18 *k* all his commands that I am
Jdg 8: 4 exhausted yet *k* up the pursuit,
1Sa 6: 12 *k* on the road and lowing
17: 34 servant has been *k* his father's
25: 33 for *k* me from bloodshed this day
1Ki 11: 38 right in my eyes by *k* my statutes
17: 16 in *k* with the word
2Ki 7: 9 and we are *k* it to ourselves.
Est 1: 7 in *k* with the king's liberality.
Ps 19: 11 in *k* them there is great reward.

Ps 119:112 My heart is set on *k* your decrees
Pr 6: 24 *k* you from the immoral woman,
15: 3 *k* watch on the wicked
Isa 65: 4 spend their nights *k* secret vigil;
Eze 14: 4 myself in *k* with his great idolatry.
17: 14 surviving only by *k* his treaty.
22: 26 eyes to the *k* of my Sabbaths,
Da 9: 16 in *k* with all your righteous acts,
Zec 9: 8 for now I am *k* watch.
Mt 3: 8 Produce fruit in *k* with repentance.
Lk 2: 8 *k* watch over their flocks at night.
2: 24 a sacrifice in *k* with what is said
3: 8 Produce fruit in *k* with repentance.
20: 20 *K* a close watch on him, they sent
Ac 14: 18 they had difficulty *k* the crowd
1Co 7: 19 *K* God's commands is what counts.
16: 2 of money in *k* with his income,
2Co 8: 5 and then to us in *k* with God's will.
1Ti 1: 18 I give you this instruction in *k*
Jas 4: 11 you are not *k* it, but sitting
1Pe 3: 16 and respect, *k* a clear conscience,
2Pe 3: 9 Lord is not slow in *k* his promise,
3: 13 But in *k* with his promise we are

KEEPS (KEEP)

Jdg 5: 29 indeed, she *k* saying to herself,
1Sa 17: 25 see how this man *k* coming out?
Ne 1: 5 who *k* his covenant of love
9: 32 who *k* his covenant of love,
Job 20: 13 and *k* it in his mouth,
24: 15 and he *k* his face concealed.
33: 11 he *k* close watch on all my paths.'
34: 8 He *k* company with evildoers;
Ps 15: 4 who *k* his oath
Pr 11: 13 but a trustworthy man *k* a secret.
12: 23 A prudent man *k* his knowledge
15: 21 of understanding *k* a straight
15: 25 he *k* the widow's boundaries intact.
17: 24 A discerning man *k* wisdom
17: 28 a fool is thought wise if he *k* silent,
18: 18 and *k* strong opponents apart.
21: 23 *k* himself from calamity.
28: 7 He who *k* the law is a discerning
29: 11 a wise man *k* himself under control
29: 18 but blessed is he who *k* the law.
Ecc 5: 20 God *k* him occupied with gladness
Isa 26: 2 the nation that *k* faith.
33: 15 *k* his hand from accepting bribes,
56: 2 and *k* his hand from doing any evil
56: 2 who *k* the Sabbath
65: 5 a fire that *k* burning all day.
Jer 23: 35 of you *k* on saying to his friend
48: 10 A curse on him who *k* his sword
Eze 18: 9 and faithfully *k* my laws.
18: 17 He *k* my laws and follows my
18: 21 *k* all my decrees and does what is
Da 9: 4 who *k* his covenant of love
Am 5: 13 Therefore the prudent man *k* quiet
Mt 15: 23 for she *k* crying out after us."
Lk 18: 5 this widow *k* bothering me,
Jn 7: 19 Yet not one of you *k* the law.
8: 51 if a man *k* my word, he will never
8: 52 that if a man *k* your word,
1Co 13: 5 is not easily angered, it *k* no record
Jas 2: 10 For whoever *k* the whole law
1Jn 3: 6 lives in him *k* on sinning.
5: 18 born of God *k* him safe,
Rev 16: 15 and *k* his clothes with him,
22: 7 Blessed is he who *k* the words

KEHELATHAH

Nu 33: 22 They left Rissah and camped at *K*.
33: 23 They left *K* and camped

KEILAH

Jos 15: 44 Iphtah, Ashnah, Nezib, *K*,
1Sa 23: 1 Philistines are fighting against *K*
23: 2 attack the Philistines and save *K*."
23: 3 to *K* against the Philistine forces!"
23: 4 answered him, "Go down to *K*,
23: 5 So David and his men went to *K*,
23: 5 and saved the people of *K*.
23: 6 him when he fled to David at *K*.)
23: 7 was told that David had gone to *K*,
23: 8 to go down to *K* to besiege David
23: 10 that Saul plans to come to *K*
23: 11 Will the citizens of *K* surrender me
23: 12 Will the citizens of *K* surrender me
1Sa 23: 13 left *K* and kept moving from place
23: 13 that David had escaped from *K*,
1Ch 4: 19 the father of *K* the Garmite,
Ne 3: 17 ruler of half the district of *K*,
3: 18 ruler of the other half-district of *K*.

KELAIAH

Ezr 10: 23 Jozabad, Shimei, *K* (that is Kelita),

KELAL

Ezr 10: 30 Adna, *K*, Benaiah, Maaseiah,

KELITA

Ezr 10: 23 Kelaiah (that is *K*), Pethahiah,
Ne 8: 7 Hodiah, Maaseiah, *K*, Azariah,
10: 10 Shebaniah, Hodiah, *K*, Pelaiah,

KELUB

1Ch 4: 11 *K*, Shuhah's brother, was the father
27: 26 Ezri son of *K* was in charge

KELUHI

Ezr 10: 35 Benaiah, Bedeiah, *K*, Vaniah,

KEMUEL

Ge 22: 21 Buz his brother, *K* (the father
Nu 34: 24 son of Joseph; *K* son of Shiphtan,
1Ch 27: 17 Hashabiah son of *K*; over Aaron:

KENAANAH

1Ki 22: 11 son of *K* had made iron horns
22: 24 Then Zedekiah son of *K* went up
1Ch 7: 10 Jeush, Benjamin, Ehud, *K*, Zethan,
2Ch 18: 10 son of *K* had made iron horns,
18: 23 Then Zedekiah son of *K* went up

KENAN

Ge 5: 9 he became the father of *K*.
5: 10 after he became the father of *K*,
5: 12 When *K* had lived 70 years,
5: 13 *K* lived 840 years and had other
5: 14 Altogether, *K* lived 910 years,
1Ch 1: 2 Seth, Enosh, *K*, Mahalalel, Jared,

KENANI

Ne 9: 4 Bunni, Sherebiah, Bani and *K*—

KENANIAH

1Ch 15: 22 *K* the head Levite was in charge
15: 27 and as were the singers, and *K*,
26: 29 *K* and his sons were assigned

KENATH

Nu 32: 42 And Nobah captured *K*
1Ch 2: 23 *K* with its surrounding settlements

KENAZ

Ge 36: 11 Omar, Zepho, Gatam and *K*.
36: 15 Chiefs Teman, Omar, Zepho, *K*,
36: 42 Elah, Pinon, *K*, Teman, Mibzar,
Jos 15: 17 Othniel son of *K*, Caleb's brother,
Jdg 1: 13 son of *K*, Caleb's younger brother,
3: 9 son of *K*, Caleb's younger brother,
3: 11 until Othniel son of *K* died.
1Ch 1: 36 Zepho, Gatam and *K*; by Timna:
1: 53 Elah, Pinon, *K*, Teman, Mibzar,
4: 13 The sons of *K*: Othniel and Seraiah
4: 15 The son of Elah: *K*.

KENITE (KENITES)

Jdg 1: 16 of Moses' father-in-law, the *K*,
4: 11 Heber the *K* had left the other
4: 17 and the clan of Heber the *K*.
4: 17 of Jael, the wife of Heber the *K*,
5: 24 the wife of Heber the *K*,

KENITES (KENITE)

Ge 15: 19 the land of the *K*, Kenizzites,
Nu 24: 21 he saw the *K* and uttered his oracle
24: 22 yet you *K* will be destroyed
Jdg 4: 11 the Kenite had left the other *K*,
1Sa 15: 6 So the *K* moved away
15: 6 Then he said to the *K*, "Go away,
27: 10 or "Against the Negev of the *K*."
30: 29 of the Jerahmeelites and the *K*;
1Ch 2: 55 These are the *K* who came

KENIZZITE (KENIZZITES)

Nu 32: 12 Caleb son of Jephunneh the *K*
Jos 14: 6 of Jephunneh the *K* said to him,
14: 14 son of Jephunneh the *K* ever since,

KENIZZITES (KENIZZITE)

Ge 15: 19 *K*, Kadmonites, Hittites, Perizzites

KEPHAR AMMONI

Jos 18: 24 Avvim, Parah, Ophrah, *K*, Ophni

KEPHIRAH

Jos 9: 17 Gibeon, *K*, Beeroth
18: 26 Beeroth, Mizpah, *K*, Mozah,
Ezr 2: 25 *K* and Beeroth 743 of Ramah
Ne 7: 29 *K* and Beeroth 743 of Ramah and

KEPT (KEEP)

Ge 4: 2 Abel *k* flocks, and Cain worked
6: 20 come to you to be *k* alive.
7: 17 For forty days the flood *k* coming
8: 7 and it *k* flying back and forth
16: 2 "The LORD has *k* me
19: 9 They *k* bringing pressure on Lot
20: 6 and so I have *k* you from sinning
26: 5 obeyed me and *k* my requirements,
30: 2 has *k* you from having children?"
34: 5 so he *k* quiet about it
37: 11 but his father *k* the matter in mind.
39: 16 She *k* his cloak beside her
41: 35 to be *k* in the cities for food.
42: 16 the rest of you will be *k* in prison,
Ex 5: 13 The slave drivers *k* pressing them,
12: 42 Because the LORD *k* vigil that
16: 20 they *k* part of it until morning,
16: 33 LORD to be *k* for the generations
16: 34 of the Testimony, that it might be *k*
21: 29 but has not *k* it penned up
23: 18 my festival offerings must not be *k*
27: 20 so that the lamps may be *k* burning
Lev 6: 9 and the fire must be *k* burning
6: 12 fire on the altar must be *k* burning;
6: 13 The fire must be *k* burning
24: 2 may be *k* burning continually.
Nu 9: 7 but why should we be *k*
15: 34 and they *k* him in custody,
17: 10 to be *k* as a sign to the rebellious.
18: 9 of the most holy offerings that is *k*
19: 9 They shall be *k* by the Israelite
24: 11 but the LORD has *k* you
Dt 6: 24 always prosper and be *k* alive,
7: 8 and *k* the oath he swore
32: 34 "Have I not *k* this in reserve
33: 21 the leader's portion was *k* for him.
Jos 6: 13 while the trumpets *k* sounding.
9: 21 the leaders' promise to them was *k*.
14: 10 has *k* me alive for forty-five years
Jdg 7: 8 their tents but *k* the three hundred,
20: 45 *k* pressing after the Benjamites
1Sa 1: 6 her rival *k* provoking her in order
1: 12 As she *k* on praying to the LORD,
9: 24 "Here is what has been *k* for you.
10: 27 But Saul *k* silent.
13: 13 "You have not *k* the command
13: 14 you have not *k* the LORD's
17: 41 *k* coming closer to David.
18: 2 From that day Saul *k* David
18: 9 time on Saul *k* a jealous eye
21: 4 the men have *k* themselves
21: 5 "Indeed women have been *k*
23: 13 and *k* moving from place to place.
25: 26 "Now since the LORD has *k* you,
25: 34 who has *k* me from harming you,
25: 39 He has *k* me from doing wrong
2Sa 15: 12 and Absalom's following *k*
18: 9 while the mule he was riding *k*
18: 13 you would have *k* your distance
20: 3 They were *k* in confinement
22: 22 For I have *k* the ways of the LORD
22: 24 and have *k* myself from sin.
1Ki 5: 10 way Hiram *k* Solomon supplied
8: 20 LORD has *k* the promise he made:
8: 24 You have *k* your promise
10: 26 which he *k* in the chariot cities and
11: 11 and you have not *k* my covenant
11: 33 nor *k* my statutes and laws
13: 21 and have not *k* the command
14: 8 who *k* my commands and followed
2Ki 4: 5 the jars to her and she *k* pouring.
13: 3 and for a long time he *k* them

2Ki 18: 6 he *k* the commands the LORD had
25: 2 The city was *k* under siege
1Ch 4: 33 And they *k* a genealogical record.
2Ch 1: 14 which he *k* in the chariot cities and
6: 10 LORD has *k* the promise he made.
6: 15 You have *k* your promise
9: 25 which he *k* in the chariot cities and
17: 13 also *k* experienced fighting men
34: 21 our fathers have not *k* the word
Ezr 9: 1 have not *k* themselves separate
Ne 5: 8 They *k* quiet, because they could
6: 17 and replies from Tobiah *k* coming
6: 19 they *k* reporting to me his good
9: 8 You have *k* your promise
10: 39 the articles for the sanctuary are *k*
11: 19 who *k* watch at the gates—
Est 2: 20 But Esther had *k* secret her family
7: 4 I would have *k* quiet, because no
Job 21: 32 and watch is *k* over his tomb.
23: 11 I have *k* to his way without turning
31: 17 if I have *k* my bread to myself,
31: 34 that I *k* silent and would not go
Ps 17: 4 I have *k* myself
18: 21 For I have *k* the ways of the LORD
18: 23 and have *k* myself from sin.
32: 3 When I *k* silent,
50: 21 things you have done and I *k* silent;
66: 9 and *k* our feet from slipping.
73: 13 in vain have I *k* my heart pure;
77: 4 You *k* my eyes from closing;
78: 32 of all this, they *k* on sinning;
99: 7 they *k* his statutes and the decrees
119: 101 I have *k* my feet from every evil
130: 3 If you, O LORD, *k* a record of sins,
Pr 20: 9 can say, "I have *k* my heart pure;
28: 18 whose walk is blameless is *k* safe,
28: 26 he who walks in wisdom is *k* safe.
29: 25 in the LORD is *k* safe.
Isa 38: 17 In your love you *k* me
42: 14 "For a long time I have *k* silent,
49: 6 bring back those of Israel I have *k*.
57: 17 yet he *k* on in his willful ways.
Jer 5: 25 wrongdoings have *k* these away;
35: 14 and this command has been *k*
52: 5 The city was *k* under siege
Eze 5: 7 followed my decrees or *k* my laws.
11: 12 followed my decrees or *k* my laws
Da 7: 11 I *k* looking until the beast was slain
7: 28 but I *k* the matter to myself."
9: 10 or *k* the laws he gave us
Hos 13: 12 his sins are *k* on record.
Am 2: 4 and have not *k* his decrees,
Mal 3: 7 my decrees and have not *k* them.
Mt 19: 20 these I have *k*," the young man
24: 43 he would have *k* watch
27: 36 they *k* watch over him there.
Mk 5: 32 Jesus *k* looking around to see who
7: 36 the more they *k* talking about it.
9: 10 They *k* the matter to themselves,
9: 34 they *k* quiet because on the way
10: 20 "all these I have *k* since I was a boy
Lk 1: 22 for he *k* making signs to them
4: 44 And he *k* on preaching
8: 29 and foot and *k* under guard,
9: 36 The disciples *k* this to themselves,
13: 16 whom Satan has *k* bound
18: 3 in that town who *k* coming to him
18: 21 All these I have *k* since I was a boy
19: 20 I have *k* it laid away in a piece
23: 21 But they *k* shouting, "Crucify him!
24: 16 they were *k* from recognizing him.
Jn 8: 7 When they *k* on questioning him,
11: 37 of the blind man have *k* this man
11: 56 They *k* looking for Jesus, and
16: 18 to the Father'?" They *k* asking,
17: 12 *k* them safe by that name you gave
19: 12 the Jews *k* shouting, "If you let this
Ac 5: 2 full knowledge he *k* back part
5: 3 and have *k* for yourself some
9: 24 and night they *k* close watch
12: 5 So Peter was *k* in prison,
12: 15 When she *k* insisting that it was so,
12: 16 But Peter *k* on knocking,
16: 6 having been *k* by the Holy Spirit
16: 18 She *k* this up for many days.
20: 7 *k* on talking until midnight.
21: 36 crowd that followed *k* shouting,
23: 35 Then he ordered that Paul be *k*
Ac 27: 43 *k* them from carrying out their plan
2Co 11: 9 I have *k* myself from being
Gal 5: 7 and *k* you from obeying the truth?
Eph 3: 9 for ages past was *k* hidden in God,
Col 1: 26 the mystery that has been *k* hidden
1Th 3: 4 we *k* telling you that we would be
5: 23 body be *k* blameless at the coming
1Ti 2: 15 But women will be *k* safe
2Ti 4: 7 finished the race, I have *k* the faith.
Heb 11: 28 By faith he *k* the Passover
13: 4 and the marriage bed *k* pure,
1Pe 1: 4 spoil or fade—*k* in heaven for you,
2Pe 3: 7 being *k* for the day of judgment
Jude : 1 loved by God the Father and *k*
: 6 these he has *k* in darkness,
Rev 3: 8 yet you have *k* my word
3: 10 Since you have *k* my command
9: 15 four angels who had been *k* ready
14: 4 for they *k* themselves pure.

KERAN

Ge 36: 26 Hemdan, Eshban, Ithran and *K*.
1Ch 1: 41 Hemdan, Eshban, Ithran and *K*.

KEREN-HAPPUCH

Job 42: 14 the second Keziah and the third *K*.

KERETHITE (KERETHITES)

Zep 2: 5 O *K* people;

KERETHITES (KERETHITE)

1Sa 30: 14 We raided the Negev of the *K*
2Sa 8: 18 son of Jehoiada was over the *K*
15: 18 along with all the *K* and Pelethites;
20: 7 men and the *K* and Pelethites
20: 23 son of Jehoiada was over the *K*
1Ki 1: 38 the *K* and the Pelethites went
1: 44 Benaiah son of Jehoiada, the *K*
1Ch 18: 17 son of Jehoiada was over the *K*
Eze 25: 16 and I will cut off the *K*
Zep 2: 6 by the sea, where the *K* dwell,

KERIOTH

Jer 48: 24 Beth Meon, to *K* and Bozrah—
Am 2: 2 will consume the fortresses of *K*.

KERIOTH HEZRON

Jos 15: 25 *K* (that is, Hazor),

KERITH

1Ki 17: 3 turn eastward and hide in the *K*
17: 5 He went to the *K* Ravine, east

KERNEL (KERNELS)

Am 9: 9 but not a *k* will fall to the ground.
Mk 4: 28 then the full *k* in the head.
Jn 12: 24 a *k* of wheat falls to the ground

KERNELS (KERNEL)

Dt 23: 25 you may pick *k* with your hands,
32: 14 and the finest *k* of wheat.
Lk 6: 1 them in their hands and eat the *k*.

KEROS

Ezr 2: 44 Hasupha, Tabbaoth, *K*, Siaha,
Ne 7: 47 Hasupha, Tabbaoth, *K*, Sia, Padon,

KERUB

Ezr 2: 59 Tel Harsha, *K*, Addon
Ne 7: 61 Tel Harsha, *K*, Addon and Immer,

KESALON

Jos 15: 10 Jearim (that is, *K*),

KESED

Ge 22: 22 Kemuel (the father of Aram), *K*,

KESIL

Jos 15: 30 Ezem, Eltolad, *K*, Hormah, Ziklag,

KESULLOTH

Jos 19: 18 Jezreel, *K*, Shunem, Hapharaim,

KETTLE (KETTLES)

1Sa 2: 14 would plunge it into the pan or *k*

KETTLES (KETTLE)

Mk 7: 4 the washing of cups, pitchers and *k*

KETURAH

Ge 25: 1 another wife, whose name was *K*.
25: 4 All these were descendants of *K*.
1Ch 1: 32 born to *K*, Abraham's concubine:
1: 33 All these were descendants of *K*.

KEY (KEYS)

Jdg 3: 25 they took a *k* and unlocked them.
1Ch 9: 27 and they had charge of the *k*
Isa 22: 22 on his shoulder the *k* to the house
33: 6 the fear of the LORD is the *k*
Lk 11: 52 because you have taken away the *k*
Rev 3: 7 who holds the *k* of David.
9: 1 The star was given the *k*
20: 1 having the *k* to the Abyss

KEYS (KEY)

Mt 16: 19 I will give you the *k* of the kingdom
Rev 1: 18 And I hold the *k* of death

KEZIAH

Job 42: 14 the second *K* and the third

KEZIB

Ge 38: 5 It was at *K* that she gave birth

KIBROTH HATTAAVAH

Nu 11: 34 Therefore the place was named *K*.
11: 35 From *K* the people traveled to
33: 16 Desert of Sinai and camped at *K*.
33: 17 They left *K* and camped at
Dt 9: 22 at Taberah, at Massah and at *K*.

KIBZAIM

Jos 21: 22 *K* and Beth Horon, together

KICK (KICKED KICKING)

Ac 26: 14 for you to *k* against the goads.'

KICKED (KICK)

Dt 32: 15 Jeshurun grew fat and *k*;

KICKING (KICK)

Eze 16: 6 and saw you *k* about in your blood,
16: 22 and bare, *k* about in your blood.

KIDNAPPER (KIDNAPPING KIDNAPS)

Dt 24: 7 a slave or sells him, the *k* must die.

KIDNAPPING (KIDNAPPER)

Dt 24: 7 If a man is caught *k* one

KIDNAPS (KIDNAPPER)

Ex 21: 16 "Anyone who *k* another and

KIDNEYS

Ex 29: 13 both *k* with the fat around them,
29: 22 both *k* with the fat around them,
Lev 3: 4 both *k* with the fat around them
3: 4 which he will remove with the *k*.
3: 10 both *k* with the fat around them
3: 10 which he will remove with the *k*.
3: 15 both *k* with the fat on them
3: 15 which he will remove with the *k*.
4: 9 both *k* with the fat on them
4: 9 which he will remove with the *k*—
7: 4 both *k* with the fat around them
7: 4 which is to be removed with the *k*.
8: 16 covering of the liver, and both *k*
8: 25 both *k* and their fat and the right
9: 10 the *k* and the covering of the liver
9: 19 the *k* and the covering of the liver
Job 16: 13 Without pity, he pierces my *k*
Isa 34: 6 fat from the *k* of rams.

KIDON

1Ch 13: 9 came to the threshing floor of *K*,

KIDRON

2Sa 15: 23 The king also crossed the *K* Valley,
1Ki 2: 37 you leave and cross the *K* Valley,
15: 13 and burned it in the *K* Valley.
2Ki 23: 4 in the fields of the *K* Valley
23: 6 to the *K* Valley outside Jerusalem
23: 12 threw the rubble into the *K* Valley.
2Ch 15: 16 and burned it in the *K* Valley.
29: 16 and carried it out to the *K* Valley.
30: 14 and threw them into the *K* Valley.

Jer 31:40 out to the *K* Valley on the east
Jn 18: 1 disciples and crossed the *K* Valley.

KILEAB

2Sa 3: 3 *K* the son of Abigail the widow

KILION

Ru 1: 2 of his two sons were Mahlon and *K*
1: 5 both Mahlon and *K* also died,
4: 9 all the property of Elimelech, *K*

KILL (KILLED KILLING KILLS)

Ge 4: 14 and whoever finds me will *k* me."
4: 15 one who found him would *k* him.
12: 12 they will *k* me but will let you live.
18: 25 to *k* the righteous with the wicked,
20: 11 they will *k* me because of my wife.'
26: 7 "The men of this place might *k* me
27: 41 then I will *k* my brother Jacob."
37: 18 them, they plotted to *k* him.
37: 20 let's *k* him and throw him into one
37: 26 gain if we *k* our brother
Ex 1: 16 if it is a boy, *k* him; but if it is a girl,
2: 15 heard of this, he tried to *k* Moses,
4: 19 wanted to *k* you are dead."
4: 23 so I will *k* your firstborn son.' "
4: 24 met Moses and was about to *k* him.
5: 21 a sword in their hand to *k* us."
22: 24 and I will *k* you with the sword;
32: 12 to *k* them in the mountains
Lev 14: 50 He shall *k* one of the birds
20: 15 and you must *k* the animal.
20: 16 *k* both the woman and the animal.
Nu 16: 13 and honey to *k* us in the desert?
22: 29 I would *k* you right now."
25: 4 *k* them and expose them
25: 17 Midianites as enemies and *k* them,
31: 17 And *k* every woman who has slept
31: 17 Now *k* all the boys.
35: 17 a stone in his hand that could *k*,
35: 18 object in his hand that could *k*,
35: 23 a stone on him that could *k* him,
35: 27 of blood may *k* the accused
Dt 19: 5 and hit his neighbor and *k* him.
19: 6 and *k* him even though he is not
27: 25 a bribe to *k* an innocent person."
Jos 9: 26 Israelites, and they did not *k* them.
Jdg 8: 18 kind of men did you *k* at Tabor?"
8: 19 their lives, I would not *k* you."
8: 20 his oldest son, he said, "*K* them!"
9: 54 "Draw your sword and *k* me,
13: 23 "If the LORD had meant to *k* us,
15: 12 that you won't *k* me yourselves."
15: 13 We will not *k* you."
16: 2 saying, "At dawn we'll *k* him."
20: 5 the house, intending to *k* me.
21: 11 "*K* every male and every woman
1Sa 5: 10 god of Israel around to us to *k* us
5: 11 or it will *k* us and our people."
16: 2 Saul will hear about it and *k* me."
17: 9 If he is able to fight and *k* me,
17: 9 but if I overcome him and *k* him,
19: 1 and all the attendants to *k* David.
19: 2 looking for a chance to *k* you.
19: 11 and to *k* him in the morning.
19: 15 to me in his bed so that I may *k* him
19: 17 Why should I *k* you?' " When
20: 8 If I am guilty, then *k* me yourself!
20: 33 hurled his spear at him to *k* him.
20: 33 that his father intended to *k* David.
22: 17 and *k* the priests of the LORD,
24: 10 Some urged me to *k* you,
24: 11 of your robe but did not *k* you.
24: 18 your hands, but you did not *k* me.
30: 15 before God that you will not *k* me
2Sa 1: 9 'Stand over me and *k* me!
13: 28 'Strike Amnon down,' then *k* him.
21: 16 ⌞sword⌟, said he would *k* David.
1Ki 3: 26 Don't *k* him!" But the other said,
3: 27 Do not *k* him; she is his mother."
11: 40 Solomon tried to *k* Jeroboam,
12: 27 They will *k* me and return
17: 18 me of my sin and *k* my son?"
18: 5 have to *k* any of our animals."
18: 12 he doesn't find you, he will *k* me.
18: 14 He will *k* me!" Elijah said,
19: 10 now they are trying to *k* me too."
19: 14 now they are trying to *k* me too."
1Ki 20: 36 as you leave me a lion will *k* you."
2Ki 5: 7 Can I *k* and bring back to life?
6: 21 my father? Shall I *k* them?"
6: 21 "Shall I *k* them, my father?
6: 22 "Do not *k* them," he answered.
6: 22 "Would you *k* men you have
7: 4 we live; if they *k* us, then we die."
8: 12 *k* their young men with the sword,
9: 27 him, shouting, "*K* him too!"
10: 25 and *k* them; let no one escape."
2Ch 22: 11 Athaliah so she could not *k* him.
30: 17 had to *k* the Passover lambs
Ne 4: 11 and will *k* them and put an end
6: 10 because men are coming to *k* you
6: 10 by night they are coming to *k* you
Est 3: 13 *k* and annihilate all the Jews—
8: 11 *k* and annihilate any armed force
Job 20: 16 the fangs of an adder will *k* him.
Ps 59: 11 do not *k* them, O Lord our shield,
71: 10 to *k* me conspire together.
Pr 1: 32 of the simple will *k* them,
29: 10 and seek to *k* the upright.
Ecc 3: 3 a time to *k* and a time to heal,
Jer 15: 3 "the sword to *k* and the dogs
18: 23 all their plots to *k* me.
20: 17 For he did not *k* me in the womb,
38: 15 will you not *k* me? Even
38: 16 I will neither *k* you nor hand you
38: 25 it from us or we will *k* you,'
40: 15 and *k* Ishmael son of Nethaniah,
41: 8 and did not *k* them with the others.
41: 8 "Don't *k* us! We have wheat
43: 3 so they may *k* us or carry us
50: 21 *k* and completely destroy them,"
50: 27 *K* all her young bulls;
Eze 9: 5 Follow him through the city and *k*,
14: 13 send famine upon it and *k* its men
14: 17 and I *k* its men and their animals,
14: 21 to *k* its men and their animals!
22: 27 and *k* people to make unjust gain.
23: 47 they will *k* their sons
25: 13 and *k* its men and their animals.
26: 11 he will *k* your people
28: 9 in the presence of those who *k* you
29: 8 and *k* your men and their animals.
Am 2: 3 and *k* all her officials with him,"
9: 1 those who are left I will *k*
Na 2: 12 filling his lairs with the *k*
Mt 2: 13 to search for the child to *k* him."
2: 16 and he gave orders to *k* all the boys
10: 28 *k* the body but cannot *k* the soul.
12: 14 plotted how they might *k* Jesus.
14: 5 Herod wanted to *k* John,
17: 23 They will *k* him, and on the third
21: 38 let's *k* him and take his inheritance
23: 34 Some of them you will *k*
23: 37 you who *k* the prophets
26: 4 Jesus in some sly way and *k* him.
Mk 3: 4 or to *k*?" But they remained silent.
3: 6 Herodians how they might *k* Jesus.
6: 19 against John and wanted to *k* him.
9: 22 him into fire or water to *k* him.
9: 31 will *k* him, and after three days
10: 34 spit on him, flog him and *k* him.
11: 18 began looking for a way to *k* him,
12: 7 let's *k* him, and the inheritance will
12: 9 He will come and *k* those tenants
14: 1 way to arrest Jesus and *k* him.
Lk 11: 49 some of whom they will *k*
12: 4 afraid of those who *k* the body
13: 31 Herod wants to *k* you."
13: 34 you who *k* the prophets
15: 23 Bring the fattened calf and *k* it.
15: 30 you *k* the fattened calf for him!'
18: 32 spit on him, flog him and *k* him.
19: 27 and *k* them in front of me.' "
19: 47 the people were trying to *k* him.
20: 14 'Let's *k* him, and the inheritance
20: 16 He will come and *k* those tenants
Jn 5: 18 Jews tried all the harder to *k* him;
7: 19 Why are you trying to *k* me?"
7: 20 "Who is trying to *k* you?"
7: 25 this the man they are trying to *k*?
8: 22 "Will he *k* himself? Is that why he
8: 37 Yet you are ready to *k* me,
8: 40 you are determined to *k* me,
10: 10 The thief comes only to steal and *k*
12: 10 priests made plans to *k* Lazarus
Ac 7: 28 to *k* me as you killed the Egyptian
9: 23 the Jews conspired to *k* him,
9: 24 on the city gates in order to *k* him.
9: 29 Jews, but they tried to *k* him.
10: 13 *K* and eat."
11: 7 *K* and eat.'
16: 27 and was about to *k* himself
21: 31 While they were trying to *k* him,
23: 15 We are ready to *k* him
23: 27 and they were about to *k* him,
25: 3 an ambush to *k* him along the way.
26: 21 temple courts and tried to *k* me.
27: 42 soldiers planned to *k* the prisoners
Ro 11: 3 and they are trying to *k* me"?
1Ti 1: 9 for those who *k* their fathers
Jas 4: 2 You *k* and covet, but you cannot
Rev 6: 8 a fourth of the earth to *k* by sword,
9: 5 were not given power to *k* them,
9: 15 and year were released to *k* a third
11: 7 and overpower and *k* them.

KILLED (KILL)

Ge 4: 8 his brother Abel and *k* him.
4: 23 I have *k* a man for wounding me,
4: 25 in place of Abel, since Cain *k* him."
49: 6 for they have *k* men in their anger
Ex 2: 12 he *k* the Egyptian and hid him
2: 14 of killing me as you *k* the Egyptian
13: 15 the LORD *k* every firstborn
Lev 14: 5 of the birds be *k* over fresh water
14: 6 the blood of the bird that was *k*
Nu 16: 41 "You have *k* the LORD's people,"
19: 16 touches someone who has been *k*
19: 18 a grave or someone who has been *k*
22: 33 I would certainly have *k* you
25: 14 name of the Israelite who was *k*
25: 18 the woman who was *k*
31: 7 Moses, and *k* every man.
31: 8 also *k* Balaam son of Beor
31: 19 anyone who was *k* must stay
31: 19 "All of you who have *k* anyone
35: 6 a person who has *k* someone may
35: 11 who has *k* someone accidentally
35: 15 who has *k* another accidentally
Dt 4: 42 anyone who had *k* a person could
4: 42 had unintentionally *k* his neighbor
21: 1 and it is not known who *k* him,
Jos 7: 5 who *k* about thirty-six of them.
8: 24 and *k* those who were in it.
10: 11 than were *k* by the swords
10: 26 Then Joshua struck and *k* the kings
20: 5 he *k* his neighbor unintentionally
20: 9 and not be *k* by the avenger
20: 9 them who *k* someone accidentally
Jdg 7: 25 They *k* Oreb at the rock of Oreb,
8: 17 and *k* the men of the town.
8: 21 stepped forward and *k* them,
9: 45 he had captured it and *k* its people.
9: 54 they can't say, 'A woman *k* him.' "
12: 6 thousand Ephraimites were *k*
12: 6 *k* him at the fords of the Jordan.
15: 16 I have *k* a thousand men."
16: 30 Thus he *k* many more
1Sa 4: 2 who *k* about four thousand of them
14: 13 his armor-bearer followed and *k*
14: 14 his armor-bearer *k* some twenty
17: 35 it by its hair, struck it and *k* it.
17: 36 Your servant has *k* both the lion
17: 50 down the Philistine and *k* him.
17: 51 After he *k* him, he cut off his head
18: 6 after David had *k* the Philistine,
18: 27 and *k* two hundred Philistines.
19: 5 hands when he *k* the Philistine.
19: 11 life tonight, tomorrow you'll be *k*."
20: 14 so that I may not be *k*,
21: 9 whom you *k* in the Valley of Elah,
22: 18 That day he *k* eighty-five men who
22: 21 David that Saul had *k* the priests
30: 2 They *k* none of them, but carried
31: 2 and they *k* his sons Jonathan,
2Sa 1: 10 "So I stood over him and *k* him,
1: 16 'I *k* the LORD's anointed.' "
2: 31 David's men had *k* three hundred
3: 30 he had *k* their brother Asahel
4: 7 After they stabbed and *k* him,
4: 11 wicked men have *k* an innocent
4: 12 order to his men, and they *k* them.
10: 18 and David *k* seven hundred

2Sa 11: 21 Who *k* Abimelech son
12: 9 You *k* him with the sword
13: 32 think that they *k* all the princes;
14: 6 One struck the other and *k* him.
14: 7 the life of his brother whom he *k*,
18: 15 Absalom, struck him and *k* him.
21: 6 descendants be given to us to be *k*
21: 9 who *k* and exposed them on a hill
21: 13 the bones of those who had been *k*
21: 17 the Philistine down and *k* him.
21: 18 Sibbecai the Hushathite *k* Saph,
21: 19 the Bethlehemite *k* Goliath
21: 21 of Shimeah, David's brother, *k* him
23: 8 whom he *k* in one encounter.
23: 18 whom he *k*, and so he became
23: 20 a pit on a snowy day and *k* a lion.
23: 21 and *k* him with his own spear.
1Ki 2: 5 He *k* them, shedding their blood
2: 32 and *k* them with the sword.
2: 34 and struck down Joab and *k* him,
2: 46 and struck Shimei down and *k* him.
9: 16 He *k* its Canaanite inhabitants
13: 24 him on the road and *k* him,
13: 26 which has mauled him and *k* him,
15: 28 Baasha *k* Nadab in the third year
15: 29 he *k* Jeroboam's whole family.
16: 10 *k* him in the twenty-seventh year
16: 11 he *k* off Baasha's whole family.
19: 1 and how he had *k* all the prophets
20: 36 a lion found him and *k* him.
2Ki 10: 9 against my master and *k* him,
10: 9 but who *k* all these? Know then,
10: 11 So Jehu *k* everyone in Jezreel who
10: 17 he *k* all who were left there
11: 2 from Athaliah; so he was not *k*.
11: 18 *k* Mattan the priest of Baal in front
14: 19 him to Lachish and *k* him there.
15: 25 Pekah *k* Pekahiah and succeeded
17: 25 and they *k* some of the people.
21: 24 of the land *k* all who had plotted
23: 29 but Neco faced him and *k* him
25: 7 They *k* the sons of Zedekiah
1Ch 4: 43 They *k* the remaining Amalekites
7: 21 Elead were *k* by the native-born
10: 2 and they *k* his sons Jonathan,
11: 11 whom he *k* in one encounter.
11: 20 whom he *k*, and so he became
11: 22 a pit on a snowy day and *k* a lion.
11: 23 and *k* him with his own spear.
19: 18 also *k* Shophach the commander
19: 18 and David *k* seven thousand
20: 4 Sibbecai the Hushathite *k* Sippai,
20: 5 son of Jair *k* Lahmi the brother
20: 7 of Shimea, David's brother, *k* him
2Ch 22: 1 into the camp, had *k* all the older
22: 8 attending Ahaziah, and he *k* them.
23: 17 *k* Mattan the priest of Baal in front
24: 22 had shown him but *k* his son,
24: 23 and *k* all the leaders of the people.
24: 25 and they *k* him in his bed.
25: 11 where he *k* ten thousand men
25: 13 They *k* three thousand people
25: 27 him to Lachish and *k* him there.
28: 6 son of Remaliah *k* a hundred
28: 7 *k* Maaseiah the king's son,
33: 25 of the land *k* all who had plotted
36: 17 who *k* their young men
Ne 9: 26 They *k* your prophets, who had
Est 9: 6 Jews *k* and destroyed five hundred
9: 7 They also *k* Parshandatha,
9: 12 The Jews have *k* five hundred men
9: 16 They *k* seventy-five thousand
Ps 135: 10 and *k* mighty kings—
136: 18 and *k* mighty kings—
Isa 14: 20 and *k* your people.
22: 2 Your slain were not *k* by the sword
27: 7 Has she been *k*
27: 7 as those were *k* who *k* her?
Jer 39: 6 and also *k* all the nobles of Judah.
41: 3 also *k* all the Jews who were
41: 9 the bodies of the men he had *k*
41: 18 of Nethaniah had *k* Gedaliah son
52: 10 he also *k* all the officials of Judah.
La 2: 20 Should priest and prophet be *k*
4: 9 Those *k* by the sword are better off
Eze 11: 6 You have *k* many people
13: 19 you have *k* those who should not
23: 10 daughters and *k* her with the sword
Eze 31: 17 joining those *k* by the sword.
31: 18 with those *k* by the sword.
32: 20 fall among those *k* by the sword.
32: 21 with those *k* by the sword.'
32: 25 All of them are uncircumcised, *k*
32: 26 *k* by the sword because they spread
32: 28 with those *k* by the sword.
32: 29 laid with those *k* by the sword.
32: 30 with those *k* by the sword
32: 31 for all his hordes that were *k*
32: 32 with those *k* by the sword,
35: 8 those *k* by the sword will fall
Da 3: 22 of the fire *k* the men who took up
Hos 6: 5 I *k* you with the words
Am 4: 10 I *k* your young men with the sword
Na 2: 12 The lion *k* enough for his cubs
Mt 16: 21 that he must be *k* and on the third
21: 35 *k* another, and stoned a third.
21: 39 out of the vineyard and *k* him.
22: 6 mistreated them and *k* them.
Mk 8: 31 he must be *k* and after three days
12: 5 of them they beat, others they *k*.
12: 5 still another, and that one they *k*.
12: 8 So they took him and *k* him,
Lk 9: 22 he must be *k* and on the third day
11: 47 it was your forefathers who *k* them
11: 48 they *k* the prophets, and you build
11: 51 who was *k* between the altar
15: 27 your father has *k* the fattened calf
20: 15 out of the vineyard and *k* him.
Ac 3: 13 You handed him over to be *k*,
3: 15 You *k* the author of life,
5: 30 whom you had *k* by hanging him
5: 36 He was *k*, all his followers were
5: 37 He too was *k*, and all his followers
7: 28 as you *k* the Egyptian yesterday?'
7: 52 *k* those who predicted the coming
10: 39 They *k* him by hanging him
23: 12 or drink until they had *k* Paul.
23: 14 anything until we have *k* Paul.
23: 21 or drink until they have *k* him.
Ro 11: 3 they have *k* your prophets
1Co 10: 9 as some of them did—and were *k*
10: 10 and were *k* by the destroying angel
2Co 6: 9 beaten, and yet not *k*; sorrowful,
1Th 2: 15 who *k* the Lord Jesus
Heb 11: 31 was not *k* with those who were
Rev 6: 11 and brothers who were to be *k*
9: 18 of mankind was *k* by the three
9: 20 rest of mankind that were not *k*
11: 13 Seven thousand people were *k*
13: 10 If anyone is to be *k* with the sword,
13: 10 with the sword he will be *k*.
13: 15 to worship the image to be *k*.
18: 24 of all who have been *k* on the earth
19: 21 The rest of them were *k*

KILLING (KILL)

Ge 27: 42 himself with the thought of *k* you.
34: 25 unsuspecting city, *k* every male.
Ex 2: 14 Are you thinking of *k* me
32: 27 each *k* his brother and friend
Jos 8: 24 Israel had finished *k* all the men
1Sa 17: 57 returned from *k* the Philistine,
19: 5 David by *k* him for no reason?"
1Ki 18: 4 While Jezebel was *k*
18: 13 while Jezebel was *k* the prophets
2Ki 17: 26 among them, which are *k* them off,
Est 3: 6 the idea of *k* only Mordecai.
9: 5 all their enemies with the sword, *k*
Isa 22: 13 of cattle and *k* of sheep,
Jer 41: 2 *k* the one whom the king
Eze 9: 7 and began *k* throughout the city.
9: 8 While they were *k* and I was left
14: 19 *k* its men and their animals,
Jnh 1: 14 accountable for *k* an innocent man,
Lk 12: 5 after the *k* of the body,
Ac 7: 24 avenged him by *k* the Egyptian.
22: 20 clothes of those who were *k* him.'

KILLS (KILL)

Ge 4: 15 "Not so; if anyone *k* Cain,
Ex 21: 12 *k* him shall surely be put to death.
21: 14 and *k* another man deliberately,
21: 29 kept it penned up and it *k* a man
Lev 24: 21 Whoever *k* an animal must make
24: 21 but whoever *k* a man must be put
Nu 35: 30 Anyone who *k* a person is to be put
Dt 19: 3 so that anyone who *k* a man may
19: 4 concerning the man who *k* another
19: 4 one who *k* his neighbor
19: 11 and *k* him, and then flees to one
27: 24 the man who *k* his neighbor
Jos 20: 3 that anyone who *k* a person
1Sa 17: 25 wealth to the man who *k* him.
17: 26 for the man who *k* this Philistine
17: 27 done for the man who *k* him."
Job 5: 2 Resentment *k* a fool,
24: 14 and *k* the poor and needy;
Isa 66: 3 is like one who *k* a man,
Jn 16: 2 when anyone who *k* you will think
2Co 3: 6 for the letter *k*, but the Spirit gives

KILMAD

Eze 27: 23 Asshur and *K* traded with you.

KIMHAM

2Sa 19: 37 But here is your servant *K*.
19: 38 "*K* shall cross over with me,
19: 40 over to Gilgal, *K* crossed with him.

KIN (KINSMAN KINSMEN)

Ru 3: 12 it is true that I am near of *k*,

KINAH

Jos 15: 22 Eder, Jagur, *K*, Dimonah, Adadah,

KIND (KINDEST KINDNESS KINDNESSES KINDS)

Ge 1: 21 winged bird according to its *k*.
1: 24 animals, each according to its *k*."
6: 20 Two of every *k* of bird,
6: 20 of every *k* of animal
6: 20 of every *k* of creature that moves
6: 21 are to take every *k* of food that is
7: 2 seven of every *k* of clean animal,
7: 2 two of every *k* of unclean animal,
7: 3 and also seven of every *k* of bird,
7: 14 along the ground according to its *k*
7: 14 and every bird according to its *k*,
7: 14 wild animal according to its *k*,
8: 17 Bring out every *k* of living creature
8: 19 out of the ark, one *k* after another.
9: 15 and all living creatures of every *k*
9: 16 creatures of every *k* on the earth."
27: 4 Prepare me the *k* of tasty food I
37: 4 could not speak a *k* word to him.
Ex 1: 20 So God was *k* to the midwives
Lev 7: 14 He is to bring one of each *k*
11: 14 the red kite, any *k* of black kite,
11: 15 any *k* of raven, the horned owl,
11: 16 any *k* of hawk, the little owl,
11: 19 the osprey, the stork, any *k*
11: 22 Of these you may eat any *k*
11: 29 the rat, any *k* of great lizard,
13: 31 when the priest examines this *k*
19: 23 and plant any *k* of fruit tree,
25: 36 interest of any *k* from him,
Nu 5: 2 disease or a discharge of any *k*,
13: 19 What *k* of land do they live in?
13: 19 What *k* of towns do they live in?
28: 8 with the same *k* of grain offering
Dt 4: 15 of any *k* the day the LORD spoke
4: 25 become corrupt and make any *k*
14: 14 any *k* of falcon, any *k* of raven,
14: 15 any *k* of hawk, the little owl,
14: 18 the cormorant, the stork, any *k*
24: 10 a loan of any *k* to your neighbor,
28: 61 bring on you every *k* of sickness
Jdg 6: 26 Then build a proper *k* of altar
8: 18 "What *k* of men did you kill
2Sa 13: 18 for this was the *k* of garment
1Ki 9: 13 "What *k* of towns are these you
2Ki 1: 7 "What *k* of man was it who came
1Ch 22: 15 as men skilled in every *k* of work
2Ch 10: 7 "If you will be *k* to these people
15: 6 them with every *k* of distress.
Job 6: 28 "But now be so *k* as to look at me.
Ps 86: 5 You are *k* and forgiving, O Lord,
144: 13 with every *k* of provision.
Pr 11: 17 A *k* man benefits himself,
12: 25 but a *k* word cheers him up.
14: 21 blessed is he who is *k* to the needy.
14: 31 whoever is *k* to the needy honors
19: 17 He who is *k* to the poor lends
23: 7 for he is the *k* of man

Pr 28: 8 for another, who will be *k*
SS 4: 14 with every *k* of incense tree,
Isa 44: 11 He and his *k* will be put to shame;
58: 5 Is this the *k* of fast I have chosen,
58: 6 "Is not this the *k* of fasting I have
Jer 8: 9 what *k* of wisdom do they have?
Eze 17: 23 Birds of every *k* will nest in it;
39: 17 Call out to every *k* of bird
39: 20 mighty men and soldiers of every *k*
Da 1: 4 aptitude for every *k* of learning,
4: 27 by being *k* to the oppressed.
Zep 2: 14 creatures of every *k*.
Zec 1: 13 So the LORD spoke *k*
Mt 8: 27 and asked, "What *k* of man is this?
Mk 9: 29 This *k* can come out only by prayer
Lk 1: 29 wondered what *k* of greeting this
6: 35 because he is *k* to the ungrateful
7: 39 and what *k* of woman she is—
16: 8 dealing with their own *k* than are
Jn 2: 6 the *k* used by the Jews
4: 23 for they are the *k* of worshipers
12: 33 to show the *k* of death he was going
16: 25 when I will no longer use this *k*
18: 32 Jesus had spoken indicating the *k*
21: 19 this to indicate the *k* of death
Ac 7: 49 What *k* of house will you build
20: 35 I showed you that by this *k*
24: 4 request that you be *k* enough
Ro 1: 29 filled with every *k* of wickedness,
7: 8 in me every *k* of covetous desire.
1Co 5: 1 and of a *k* that does not occur
13: 4 Love is patient, love is *k*.
15: 35 With what *k* of body will they
15: 38 to each *k* of seed he gives its own
15: 39 Men have one *k* of flesh, animals
15: 40 of the heavenly bodies is one *k*,
15: 41 The sun has one *k* of splendor,
Gal 5: 8 That *k* of persuasion does not
Eph 4: 19 to indulge in every *k* of impurity,
4: 32 Be *k* and compassionate
5: 3 or of any *k* of impurity, or of greed,
1Th 1: 9 for they themselves report what *k*
5: 15 but always try to be *k* to each other
5: 22 Avoid every *k* of evil.
2Ti 2: 24 instead, he must be *k* to everyone,
3: 6 They are the *k* who worm their
Tit 2: 5 to be busy at home, to be *k*,
Jas 1: 18 that we might be a *k* of firstfruits
1Pe 2: 1 envy, and slander of every *k*.
4: 15 or thief or any other *k* of criminal,
5: 9 world are undergoing the same *k*
2Pe 3: 11 what *k* of people ought you to be?
Rev 11: 6 the earth with every *k* of plague
18: 12 articles of every *k* made of ivory,
21: 19 with every *k* of precious stone.

KINDEST (KIND)

Pr 12: 10 the *k* acts of the wicked are cruel.

KINDHEARTED (HEART)

Pr 11: 16 A *k* woman gains respect,

KINDLE (KINDLED KINDLES KINDLING)

Jer 15: 14 for my anger will *k* a fire
17: 27 then I will *k* an unquenchable fire
21: 14 I will *k* a fire in your forests
50: 32 I will *k* a fire in her towns
Eze 24: 10 and *k* the fire.

KINDLED (KINDLE)

Dt 32: 22 For a fire has been *k* by my wrath,
Isa 10: 16 under his pomp a fire will be *k*
Jer 17: 4 for you have *k* my anger,
La 4: 11 He *k* a fire in Zion
Eze 20: 48 will see that I the LORD have *k* it;
Lk 12: 49 and how I wish it were already *k!*
22: 55 But when they had *k* a fire

KINDLES (KINDLE)

Isa 44: 15 he *k* a fire and bakes bread.

KINDLING (KINDLE)

Pr 26: 21 so is a quarrelsome man for *k* strife.

KINDNESS (KIND)

Ge 19: 19 and you have shown great *k* to me
21: 23 as an alien the same *k* I have shown
24: 12 and show *k* to my master Abraham
24: 14 I will know that you have shown *k*
24: 27 who has not abandoned his *k*
24: 49 Now if you will show *k*
32: 10 I am unworthy of all the *k*
39: 21 he showed him *k* and granted him
40: 14 remember me and show me *k;*
47: 29 promise that you will show me *k*
Jos 2: 12 because I have shown *k* to you.
2: 12 by the LORD that you will show *k*
Jdg 21: 22 'Do us a *k* by helping them,
Ru 1: 8 May the LORD show *k* to you,
2: 20 has not stopped showing his *k*
3: 10 "This *k* is greater than that which
1Sa 15: 6 for you showed *k* to all
20: 8 As for you, show *k* to your servant,
20: 14 But show me unfailing *k* like that
20: 15 cut off your *k* from my family—
2Sa 2: 5 you for showing this *k*
2: 6 May the LORD now show you *k*
9: 1 Saul to whom I can show *k*
9: 3 to whom I can show God's *k?"*
9: 7 "for I will surely show you *k*
10: 2 just as his father showed *k* to me."
10: 2 "I will show *k* to Hanun son
15: 20 May *k* and faithfulness be with you
22: 51 he shows unfailing *k*
1Ki 2: 7 "But show *k* to the sons of Barzillai
3: 6 You have continued this great *k*
3: 6 "You have shown great *k*
1Ch 19: 2 because his father showed *k* to me
19: 2 "I will show *k* to Hanun son
2Ch 1: 8 "You have shown great *k*
24: 22 remember the *k* Zechariah's father
32: 25 respond to the *k* shown him;
Ezr 9: 9 He has shown us *k* in the sight
Job 10: 12 You gave me life and showed me *k*,
24: 21 and to the widow show no *k*.
Ps 18: 50 he shows unfailing *k*
109: 12 May no one extend *k* to him
109: 16 For he never thought of doing a *k*,
141: 5 righteous man strike me—it is a *k;*
Isa 54: 8 but with everlasting *k*
Jer 9: 24 I am the LORD, who exercises *k*,
Hos 11: 4 I led them with cords of human *k*,
Ac 4: 9 for an act of *k* shown to a cripple
14: 17 He has shown *k* by giving you rain
27: 3 at Sidon; and Julius, in *k* to Paul,
28: 2 The islanders showed us unusual *k*.
Ro 2: 4 contempt for the riches of his *k*,
2: 4 realizing that God's *k* leads you
11: 22 Consider therefore the *k*
11: 22 provided that you continue in his *k*
11: 22 to those who fell, but *k* to you,
2Co 6: 6 understanding, patience and *k;*
Gal 5: 22 peace, patience, *k*, goodness,
Eph 2: 7 expressed in his *k* to us
Col 3: 12 yourselves with compassion, *k*,
Tit 3: 4 But when the *k* and love
2Pe 1: 7 brotherly *k;* and to brotherly *k*,

KINDNESSES (KIND)

2Ch 6: 42 Remember the *k* promised
Ps 106: 7 did not remember your many *k*,
Isa 63: 7 I will tell of the *k* of the LORD,
63: 7 to his compassion and many *k*.

KINDS (KIND)

Ge 1: 11 according to their various *k*."
1: 12 bearing seed according to their *k*
1: 12 with seed in it according to their *k*.
1: 21 to their *k*, and every winged bird
1: 24 creatures according to their *k:*
1: 25 the ground according to their *k*.
1: 25 the livestock according to their *k*,
1: 25 wild animals according to their *k*,
2: 9 And the LORD God made all *k*
4: 22 who forged all *k* of tools out
7: 3 to keep their various *k* alive
7: 14 all livestock according to their *k*,
24: 10 taking with him all *k* of good things
40: 17 In the top basket were all *k*
Ex 1: 14 and with all *k* of work in the fields;
31: 3 and knowledge in all *k* of crafts—
31: 5 to engage in all *k* of craftsmanship.
35: 22 and brought gold jewelry of all *k:*
35: 31 and knowledge in all *k* of crafts—
35: 33 in all *k* of artistic craftsmanship.
35: 35 them with skill to do all *k* of work
Lev 19: 19 Do not mate different *k* of animals.
19: 19 field with two *k* of seed.
19: 19 woven of two *k* of material.
Dt 6: 11 houses filled with all *k*
12: 31 they do all *k* of detestable things
22: 9 Do not plant two *k* of seed
1Sa 4: 8 with all *k* of plagues in the desert.
1Ki 7: 14 experienced in all *k* of bronze work
1Ch 18: 10 Hadoram brought all *k* of articles
28: 14 to be used in various *k* of service:
28: 14 to be used in various *k* of service,
29: 2 and all *k* of fine stone and marble
2Ch 2: 14 experienced in all *k* of engraving
32: 27 shields and all *k* of valuables.
32: 28 stalls for various *k* of cattle,
Ne 5: 18 an abundant supply of wine of all *k*.
9: 25 filled with all *k* of good things,
13: 15 grapes, figs and all other *k* of loads.
13: 16 in fish and all *k* of merchandise
13: 20 of all *k* of goods spent the night
Ecc 2: 5 planted all *k* of fruit trees in them.
Jer 15: 3 "I will send four *k* of destroyers
Eze 8: 10 all over the walls all *k*
27: 22 they exchanged the finest of all *k*
39: 4 as food to all *k* of carrion birds
47: 10 The fish will be of many *k*—
47: 12 Fruit trees of all *k* will grow
Da 1: 17 understanding of all *k* of literature
1: 17 visions and dreams of all *k*.
3: 5 lyre, harp, pipes and all *k* of music,
3: 7 zither, lyre, harp and all *k* of music,
3: 10 and all *k* of music must fall down
3: 15 lyre, harp, pipes and all *k* of music,
Mt 5: 11 falsely say all *k* of evil against you
13: 47 down into the lake and caught all *k*
Lk 4: 40 to Jesus all who had various *k*
11: 42 rue and all other *k* of garden herbs,
12: 15 on your guard against all *k* of greed
Ac 10: 12 all *k* of four-footed animals,
13: 10 You are full of all *k* of deceit
1Co 12: 4 There are different *k* of gifts,
12: 5 There are different *k* of service,
12: 6 There are different *k* of working,
12: 10 to speak in different *k* of tongues,
12: 28 speaking in different *k* of tongues.
Eph 6: 18 occasions with all *k* of prayers
2Th 2: 9 in all *k* of counterfeit miracles,
1Ti 5: 10 herself to all *k* of good deeds.
6: 10 of money is a root of all *k* of evil.
2Ti 3: 6 are swayed by all *k* of evil desires,
3: 11 what *k* of things happened to me
Tit 3: 3 and enslaved by all *k* of passions
Heb 13: 9 away by all *k* of strange teachings.
Jas 1: 2 whenever you face trials of many *k*
3: 7 All *k* of animals, birds, reptiles
1Pe 1: 6 had to suffer grief in all *k* of trials.

KING (KING'S KINGDOM KINGDOMS KINGS KINGS' KINGSHIP)

Ge 14: 1 Kedorlaomer *k* of Elam
14: 1 and Tidal *k* of Goiim went to war
14: 1 *k* of Shinar, Arioch *k* of Ellasar,
14: 2 Birsha *k* of Gomorrah, Shinab *k*
14: 2 and the *k* of Bela (that is, Zoar).
14: 2 of Admah, Shemeber *k* of Zeboiim,
14: 2 to war against Bera *k* of Sodom,
14: 8 of Gomorrah, the *k* of Admah,
14: 8 the *k* of Sodom, the *k* of Gomorrah
14: 8 the *k* of Zeboiim and the *k*
14: 9 Tidal *k* of Goiim, Amraphel *k*
14: 9 against Kedorlaomer *k* of Elam,
14: 9 of Shinar and Arioch *k* of Ellasar—
14: 17 the *k* of Sodom came out
14: 18 Melchizedek *k* of Salem brought
14: 21 The *k* of Sodom said to Abram,
14: 22 But Abram said to the *k* of Sodom,
20: 2 Then Abimelech *k* of Gerar sent
26: 1 to Abimelech *k* of the Philistines
26: 8 Abimelech *k* of the Philistines
36: 31 before any Israelite *k* reigned:
36: 32 son of Beor became *k* of Edom.
36: 33 from Bozrah succeeded him as *k*.
36: 34 the Temanites succeeded him as *k*.
36: 35 of Moab, succeeded him as *k*.
36: 36 from Masrekah succeeded him as *k*
36: 37 on the river succeeded him as *k*.
36: 38 son of Acbor succeeded him as *k*.
36: 39 Hadad succeeded him as *k*.

Ge 40: 1 Egypt offended their master, the *k*
40: 1 of the *k* of Egypt offended their
40: 5 and the baker of the *k* of Egypt,
41: 46 the service of Pharaoh *k* of Egypt.
49: 20 he will provide delicacies fit for a *k*
Ex 1: 8 a new *k*, who did not know about
1: 15 The *k* of Egypt said
1: 17 and did not do what the *k*
1: 18 Then the *k* of Egypt summoned
2: 23 During that long period, the *k*
3: 18 are to go to the *k* of Egypt
3: 19 I know that the *k* of Egypt will not
5: 4 But the *k* of Egypt said, "Moses
6: 11 tell Pharaoh *k* of Egypt
6: 13 about the Israelites and Pharaoh *k*
6: 27 spoke to Pharaoh *k* of Egypt about
6: 29 Pharaoh *k* of Egypt everything
14: 5 When the *k* of Egypt was told that
14: 8 the heart of Pharaoh *k* of Egypt,
Nu 20: 14 from Kadesh to the *k* of Edom,
21: 1 When the Canaanite *k* of Arad,
21: 21 to say to Sihon *k* of the Amorites:
21: 26 against the former *k* of Moab
21: 26 the city of Sihon *k* of the Amorites,
21: 29 to Sihon *k* of the Amorites.
21: 33 Og *k* of Bashan and his whole army
21: 34 did to Sihon *k* of the Amorites,
22: 4 who was *k* of Moab at that time,
22: 10 "Balak son of Zippor, *k* of Moab,
23: 7 the *k* of Moab from the eastern
23: 21 the shout of the *K* is among them.
24: 7 "Their *k* will be greater than Agag;
32: 33 of Sihon *k* of the Amorites
32: 33 the kingdom of Og *k* of Bashan—
33: 40 Canaanite *k* of Arad, who lived
Dt 1: 4 and at Edrei had defeated Og *k*
1: 4 was after he had defeated Sihon *k*
2: 24 *k* of Heshbon, and his country.
2: 26 to Sihon *k* of Heshbon offering
2: 30 But Sihon *k* of Heshbon refused
3: 1 and Og *k* of Bashan with his whole
3: 2 did to Sihon *k* of the Amorites,
3: 3 into our hands Og *k* of Bashan
3: 6 done with Sihon *k* of Heshbon,
3: 11 (Only Og *k* of Bashan was left
4: 46 land of Sihon *k* of the Amorites,
4: 47 and the land of Og *k* of Bashan,
7: 8 the power of Pharaoh *k* of Egypt.
11: 3 both to Pharaoh *k* of Egypt
17: 14 "Let us set a *k* over us like all
17: 15 over you the *k* the LORD your
17: 16 The *k*, moreover, must not acquire
28: 36 and the *k* you set over you
29: 7 Sihon *k* of Heshbon and Og *k*
33: 5 He was *k* over Jeshurun
Jos 2: 2 The *k* of Jericho was told, "Look!
2: 3 the *k* of Jericho sent this message
6: 2 with its *k* and its fighting men.
8: 1 into your hands the *k* of Ai,
8: 2 and its *k* as you did to Jericho
8: 2 as you did to Jericho and its *k*,
8: 14 When the *k* of Ai saw this,
8: 23 But they took the *k* of Ai alive
8: 29 He hung the *k* of Ai on a tree
9: 10 Sihon *k* of Heshbon, and Og *k*
10: 1 Adoni-Zedek *k* of Jerusalem heard
10: 1 and its *k* as he had done to Jericho
10: 1 as he had done to Jericho and its *k*,
10: 3 Piram *k* of Jarmuth, Japhia *k*
10: 3 appealed to Hoham *k* of Hebron,
10: 3 of Lachish and Debir *k* of Eglon.
10: 3 *k* of Jerusalem appealed
10: 28 And he did to the *k* of Makkedah
10: 28 He put the city and its *k*
10: 28 as he had done to the *k* of Jericho.
10: 30 And he did to its *k* as he had done
10: 30 and its *k* into Israel's hand.
10: 30 as he had done to the *k* of Jericho.
10: 33 Horam *k* of Gezer had come up
10: 37 together with its *k*, its villages
10: 39 They did to Debir and its *k*
10: 39 They took the city, its *k*
10: 39 they had done to Libnah and its *k*
11: 1 When Jabin *k* of Hazor heard
11: 1 he sent word to Jobab *k* of Madon,
11: 10 and captured Hazor and put its *k*
12: 2 Sihon *k* of the Amorites, who
12: 4 the territory of Og *k* of Bashan,
Jos 12: 5 the border of Sihon *k* of Heshbon.
12: 9 the *k* of Jericho one the *k* of Ai
12: 10 the *k* of Jerusalem one the *k*
12: 11 the *k* of Jarmuth one the *k*
12: 12 the *k* of Eglon one the *k*
12: 13 the *k* of Debir one the *k*
12: 14 the *k* of Hormah one the *k*
12: 15 the *k* of Libnah one the *k*
12: 16 the *k* of Makkedah one the *k*
12: 17 the *k* of Tappuah one the *k*
12: 18 the *k* of Aphek one the *k*
12: 19 the *k* of Madon one the *k*
12: 20 the *k* of Shimron Meron one the *k*
12: 21 the *k* of Taanach one the *k*
12: 22 of Kedesh one the *k* of Jokneam
12: 23 in Carmel one the *k* of Dor
12: 23 one the *k* of Goyim in Gilgal
12: 24 Goyim in Gilgal one the *k*
13: 10 towns of Sihon *k* of the Amorites,
13: 21 realm of Sihon *k* of the Amorites,
13: 27 the rest of the realm of Sihon *k*
13: 30 the entire realm of Og *k* of Bashan
24: 9 son of Zippor, the *k* of Moab,
Jdg 3: 8 Cushan-Rishathaim *k* of Aram
3: 10 LORD gave Cushan-Rishathaim *k*
3: 12 this evil the LORD gave Eglon *k*
3: 14 subject to Eglon *k* of Moab
3: 15 with tribute to Eglon *k* of Moab.
3: 17 the tribute to Eglon *k* of Moab,
3: 19 The *k* said, "Quiet!" And all his
3: 19 a secret message for you, O *k*."
3: 20 As the *k* rose from his seat,
4: 2 a *k* of Canaan, who reigned
4: 17 relations between Jabin *k* of Hazor
4: 23 Canaanite *k*, before the Israelites.
4: 24 Canaanite *k*, until they destroyed
9: 6 in Shechem to crown Abimelech *k*.
9: 8 out to anoint a *k* for themselves.
9: 8 said to the olive tree, 'Be our *k*.'
9: 10 to the fig tree, 'Come and be our *k*.'
9: 12 to the vine, 'Come and be our *k*.'
9: 14 thornbush, 'Come and be our *k*.'
9: 15 want to anoint me *k* over you,
9: 16 faith when you made Abimelech *k*,
9: 18 *k* over the citizens of Shechem
11: 12 messengers to the Ammonite *k*
11: 13 The *k* of the Ammonites answered
11: 14 messengers to the Ammonite *k*,
11: 17 Israel sent messengers to the *k*
11: 17 They sent also to the *k* of Moab,
11: 17 but the *k* of Edom would not listen.
11: 19 to Sihon *k* of the Amorites,
11: 25 son of Zippor, *k* of Moab?
11: 28 The *k* of Ammon, however,
17: 6 In those days Israel had no *k*;
18: 1 In those days Israel had no *k*.
19: 1 In those days Israel had no *k*.
21: 25 In those days Israel had no *k*;
1Sa 2: 10 "He will give strength to his *k*
8: 5 now appoint a *k* to lead us,
8: 6 "Give us a *k* to lead us," this
8: 7 you they have rejected as their *k*,
8: 9 know what the *k* who will reign
8: 10 who were asking him for a *k*.
8: 11 "This is what the *k* who will reign
8: 18 relief from the *k* you have chosen,
8: 19 "We want a *k* over us.
8: 20 with a *k* to lead us and to go out
8: 22 Listen to them and give them a *k*."
10: 19 you have said, 'No, set a *k* over us.'
10: 24 people shouted, "Long live the *k*!"
11: 15 as *k* in the presence of the LORD.
12: 1 to me and have set a *k* over you.
12: 2 Now you have a *k* as your leader.
12: 9 hands of the Philistines and the *k*
12: 12 'No, we want a *k* to rule over us'—
12: 12 the LORD your God was your *k*.
12: 12 "But when you saw that Nahash *k*
12: 13 Now here is the *k* you have chosen
12: 13 see, the LORD has set a *k* over you
12: 14 the *k* who reigns over you follow
12: 17 LORD when you asked for a *k*."
12: 19 sins the evil of asking for a *k*."
12: 25 and your *k* will be swept away."
13: 1 old when he became *k*,
15: 1 to anoint you *k* over his people
15: 8 He took Agag *k* of the Amalekites
15: 11 grieved that I have made Saul *k*,
1Sa 15: 17 The LORD anointed you *k*
15: 20 and brought back Agag their *k*.
15: 23 he has rejected you as *k*."
15: 26 the LORD has rejected you as *k*
15: 32 Bring me Agag *k* of the Amalekites
15: 35 grieved that he had made Saul *k*
16: 1 one of his sons to be *k*."
16: 1 since I have rejected him as *k*
17: 25 The *k* will give great wealth
17: 55 "As surely as you live, O *k*,
17: 56 *k* said, "Find out whose son this
18: 6 Israel to meet *K* Saul with singing
18: 22 'Look, the *k* is pleased with you,
18: 25 'The *k* wants no other price
18: 27 presented the full number to the *k*
19: 4 "Let not the *k* do wrong
20: 5 I am supposed to dine with the *k*;
20: 24 New Moon festival came, the *k* sat
21: 2 "The *k* charged me
21: 10 and went to Achish *k* of Gath.
21: 11 "Isn't this David, the *k* of the land?
21: 12 afraid of Achish *k* of Gath.
22: 3 and said to the *k* of Moab,
22: 4 So he left them with the *k* of Moab,
22: 11 and they all came to the *k*.
22: 11 *k* sent for the priest Ahimelech son
22: 14 Ahimelech answered the *k*,
22: 15 Let not the *k* accuse your servant
22: 16 But the *k* said, "You will surely die
22: 17 the *k* ordered the guards at his side
22: 18 The *k* then ordered Doeg,
23: 17 You will be *k* over Israel,
23: 20 for handing him over to the *k*."
23: 20 south of Jeshimon? Now, O *k*,
24: 8 My lord the *k*!" When Saul looked
24: 14 "Against whom has the *k*
24: 20 I know that you will surely be *k*
25: 36 holding a banquet like that of a *k*.
26: 14 "Who are you who calls to the *k*?"
26: 15 came to destroy your lord the *k*.
26: 15 didn't you guard your lord the *k*?
26: 17 replied, "Yes it is, my lord the *k*."
26: 19 Now let my lord the *k* listen
26: 20 The *k* of Israel has come out
27: 2 to Achish son of Maoch *k* of Gath.
28: 13 You are Saul!" The *k* said to her,
29: 3 an officer of Saul *k* of Israel?
29: 8 the enemies of my lord the *k*?"
2Sa 2: 4 and there they anointed David *k*
2: 7 house of Judah has anointed me *k*
2: 9 He made him *k* over Gilead,
2: 10 old when he became *k* over Israel,
2: 11 of time David was *k* in Hebron
3: 3 daughter of Talmai *k* of Geshur;
3: 17 wanted to make David your *k*.
3: 21 all Israel for my lord the *k*,
3: 23 and that the *k* had sent him away
3: 23 son of Ner had come to the *k*
3: 24 So Joab went to the *k* and said,
3: 31 *K* David himself walked
3: 32 the *k* wept aloud at Abner's tomb.
3: 33 The *k* sang this lament for Abner:
3: 36 everything the *k* did pleased them.
3: 37 Israel knew that the *k* had no part
3: 38 Then the *k* said to his men,
3: 39 though I am the anointed *k*,
4: 8 David at Hebron and said to the *k*,
4: 8 LORD has avenged my lord the *k*
5: 2 while Saul was *k* over us,
5: 3 come to *K* David at Hebron,
5: 3 the *k* made a compact with them
5: 3 they anointed David *k* over Israel.
5: 4 old when he became *k*,
5: 6 The *k* and his men marched
5: 11 Hiram *k* of Tyre sent messengers
5: 12 LORD had established him as *k*
5: 17 that David had been anointed *k*
6: 12 *K* David was told, "The LORD has
6: 16 when she saw *K* David leaping
6: 20 "How the *k* of Israel has
7: 1 After the *k* was settled in his palace
7: 3 to the *k*, "Whatever you have
7: 18 Then *K* David went in
8: 3 son of Rehob, *k* of Zobah,
8: 5 to help Hadadezer *k* of Zobah,
8: 8 *K* David took a great quantity
8: 9 When Tou *k* of Hamath heard that
8: 10 Joram to *K* David to greet him

2Sa 8: 11 *K* David dedicated these articles
8: 12 son of Rehob, *k* of Zobah.
9: 2 the *k* said to him, "Are you Ziba?"
9: 3 Ziba answered the *k*, "There is still
9: 3 *k* asked, "Is there no one still left
9: 4 "Where is he?" the *k* asked.
9: 5 So *K* David had him brought
9: 9 Then the *k* summoned Ziba,
9: 11 my lord the *k* commands his
9: 11 said to the *k*, "Your servant will do
10: 1 his son Hanun succeeded him as *k*.
10: 1 the *k* of the Ammonites died,
10: 5 The *k* said, "Stay at Jericho
10: 6 *k* of Maacah with a thousand men,
11: 8 a gift from the *k* was sent after him.
11: 19 finished giving the *k* this account
12: 7 says: 'I anointed you *k* over Israel,
12: 30 crown from the head of their *k*—
13: 6 When the *k* came to see him,
13: 13 speak to the *k*; he will not keep me
13: 18 the virgin daughters of the *k* wore.
13: 21 When *K* David heard all this,
13: 24 Absalom went to the *k* and said,
13: 24 Will the *k* and his officials please
13: 25 "No, my son," the *k* replied.
13: 26 *k* asked him, "Why should he go
13: 31 The *k* stood up, tore his clothes
13: 33 My lord the *k* should not be
13: 34 The watchman went and told the *k*
13: 35 Jonadab said to the *k*, "See,
13: 36 *k*, too, and all his servants wept
13: 37 But *K* David mourned
13: 37 son of Ammihud, the *k* of Geshur.
13: 39 And the spirit of the *k* longed to go
14: 3 go to the *k* and speak these words
14: 4 woman from Tekoa went to the *k*,
14: 4 "Help me, O *k*!" The *k* asked her,
14: 8 *k* said to the woman, "Go home,
14: 9 and let the *k* and his throne be
14: 9 said to him, "My lord the *k*,
14: 10 *k* replied, "If anyone says anything
14: 11 let the *k* invoke the LORD his God
14: 12 a word to my lord the *k*."
14: 13 When the *k* says this, does he not
14: 13 for the *k* has not brought back his
14: 15 come to say this to my lord the *k*
14: 15 thought, 'I will speak to the *k*;
14: 16 Perhaps the *k* will agree
14: 17 for my lord the *k* is like an angel
14: 17 of my lord the *k* bring me rest,
14: 18 Then the *k* said to the woman,
14: 18 "Let my lord the *k* speak,"
14: 19 As surely as you live, my lord the *k*
14: 19 The *k* asked, "Isn't the hand
14: 19 from anything my lord the *k* says.
14: 21 The *k* said to Joab, "Very well,
14: 22 him honor, and he blessed the *k*.
14: 22 my lord the *k*, because the *k* has
14: 24 But the *k* said, "He must go
14: 24 and did not see the face of the *k*.
14: 29 Joab in order to send him to the *k*,
14: 32 so I can send you to the *k* to ask,
14: 33 And the *k* kissed Absalom.
14: 33 Then the *k* summoned Absalom,
14: 33 face to the ground before the *k*.
14: 33 went to the *k* and told him this.
15: 2 placed before the *k* for a decision,
15: 3 of the *k* to hear you."
15: 6 came to the *k* asking for justice,
15: 7 of four years, Absalom said to the *k*
15: 9 The *k* said to him, "Go in peace."
15: 10 then say, 'Absalom is *k* in Hebron
15: 15 whatever our lord the *k* chooses."
15: 16 *k* set out, with his entire household
15: 17 So the *k* set out, with all the people
15: 18 from Gath marched before the *k*.
15: 19 Go back and stay with *K* Absalom.
15: 19 The *k* said to Ittai the Gittite,
15: 21 Ittai replied to the *k*, "As surely
15: 21 and as my lord the *k* lives,
15: 21 wherever my lord the *k* may be,
15: 23 *k* also crossed the Kidron Valley,
15: 25 Then the *k* said to Zadok,
15: 27 The *k* also said to Zadok the priest,
15: 34 'I will be your servant, O *k*;
16: 2 The *k* asked Ziba, "Why have you
16: 3 The *k* then asked, "Where is your
16: 4 favor in your eyes, my lord the *k*."

2Sa 16: 4 *k* said to Ziba, "All that belonged
16: 5 As *K* David approached Bahurim,
16: 9 son of Zeruiah said to the *k*,
16: 9 this dead dog curse my lord the *k*?
16: 10 But the *k* said, "What do you
16: 14 The *k* and all the people
16: 16 "Long live the *k*! Long live the *k*!"
17: 2 I would strike down only the *k*
17: 16 or the *k* and all the people
17: 17 they were to go and tell *K* David,
17: 21 and went to inform *K* David.
18: 2 *k* told the troops, "I myself will
18: 4 So the *k* stood beside the gate
18: 4 *k* answered, "I will do whatever
18: 5 The *k* commanded Joab, Abishai
18: 5 troops heard the *k* giving orders
18: 12 our hearing the *k* commanded you
18: 13 and nothing is hidden from the *k*—
18: 19 news to the *k* that the LORD has
18: 21 Go, tell the *k* what you have seen."
18: 25 The watchman called out to the *k*
18: 25 The *k* said, "If he is alone,
18: 26 man running alone!" The *k* said,
18: 27 "He's a good man," the *k* said.
18: 28 Then Ahimaaz called out to the *k*,
18: 28 down before the *k* with his face
18: 28 hands against my lord the *k*."
18: 29 The *k* asked, "Is the young man
18: 30 The *k* said, "Stand aside
18: 31 My lord the *k*, hear the good news!
18: 32 *k* asked the Cushite, "Is the young
18: 32 "May the enemies of my lord the *k*
18: 33 The *k* was shaken.
19: 1 "The *k* is weeping and mourning
19: 2 "The *k* is grieving for his son."
19: 4 The *k* covered his face
19: 5 Joab went into the house to the *k*
19: 8 So the *k* got up and took his seat
19: 8 "The *k* is sitting in the gateway,"
19: 9 "The *k* delivered us from the hand
19: 10 about bringing the *k* back?"
19: 11 Israel has reached the *k*
19: 11 *K* David sent this message
19: 11 to bring the *k* back to his palace,
19: 12 the last to bring back the *k*?'
19: 14 They sent word to the *k*, "Return,
19: 15 Then the *k* returned and went
19: 15 and meet the *k* and bring him
19: 16 the men of Judah to meet *K* David.
19: 17 to the Jordan, where the *k* was.
19: 18 he fell prostrate before the *k*
19: 19 May the *k* put it out of his mind.
19: 19 day my lord the *k* left Jerusalem.
19: 20 down and meet my lord the *k*."
19: 22 Do I not know that today I am *k*
19: 23 And the *k* promised him on oath.
19: 23 *k* said to Shimei, "You shall not
19: 24 also went down to meet the *k*.
19: 24 clothes from the day the *k* left
19: 25 from Jerusalem to meet the *k*,
19: 25 *k* asked him, "Why didn't you go
19: 26 He said, "My lord the *k*,
19: 26 ride on it, so I can go with the *k*.'
19: 27 My lord the *k* is like an angel
19: 27 your servant to my lord the *k*.
19: 28 but death from my lord the *k*,
19: 28 to make any more appeals to the *k*
19: 29 The *k* said to him, "Why say more?
19: 30 Mephibosheth said to the *k*,
19: 30 my lord the *k* has arrived home
19: 31 to cross the Jordan with the *k*
19: 32 provided for the *k* during his stay
19: 33 The *k* said to Barzillai, "Cross
19: 34 But Barzillai answered the *k*,
19: 34 up to Jerusalem with the *k*?
19: 35 an added burden to my lord the *k*?
19: 36 but why should the *K* reward me
19: 36 with the *k* for a short distance,
19: 37 cross over with my lord the *k*.
19: 38 The *k* said, "Kimham shall cross
19: 39 and then the *k* crossed over.
19: 39 *k* kissed Barzillai and gave him his
19: 40 When the *k* crossed over to Gilgal,
19: 40 of Israel had taken the *k* over.
19: 41 men of Israel were coming to the *k*
19: 41 steal the *k* away and bring him
19: 42 the *k* is closely related to us.
19: 43 to speak of bringing back our *k*?"

2Sa 19: 43 "We have ten shares in the *k*;
20: 2 stayed by their *k* all the way
20: 4 Then the *k* said to Amasa,
20: 5 than the time the *k* had set for him.
20: 21 has lifted up his hand against the *k*,
20: 22 back to the *k* in Jerusalem.
21: 2 The *k* summoned the Gibeonites
21: 5 They answered the *k*, "As
21: 6 the *k* said, "I will give them to you
21: 7 The *k* spared Mephibosheth son
21: 8 But the *k* took Armoni
21: 14 did everything the *k* commanded.
22: 51 He gives his *k* great victories;
24: 2 So the *k* said to Joab and the army
24: 3 But why does my lord the *k* want
24: 3 may the eyes of my lord the *k* see it
24: 3 to the *k*, "May the LORD your
24: 4 of the *k* to enroll the fighting men
24: 9 of the fighting men to the *k*:
24: 20 Araunah looked and saw the *k*
24: 20 down before the *k* with his face
24: 21 "Why has my lord the *k* come
24: 22 my lord the *k* take whatever
24: 23 Araunah gives all this to the *k*."
24: 23 O *k*, Araunah gives all this
24: 24 But the *k* replied to Araunah, "No,
1Ki 1: 1 When *K* David was old
1: 2 for a young virgin to attend the *k*
1: 2 our lord the *k* may keep warm."
1: 3 and brought her to the *k*.
1: 4 but the *k* had no intimate relations
1: 4 care of the *k* and waited on him,
1: 5 forward and said, "I will be *k*."
1: 11 has become *k* without our lord
1: 13 Go in to *K* David and say to him,
1: 13 Surely Solomon your son shall be *k*
1: 13 Why then has Adonijah become *k*
1: 13 'My lord the *k*, did you not swear
1: 14 you are still there talking to the *k*,
1: 15 went to see the aged *k* in his room,
1: 16 bowed low and knelt before the *k*.
1: 16 "What is it you want?" the *k* asked.
1: 17 'Solomon your son shall be *k*
1: 18 But now Adonijah has become *k*,
1: 18 my lord the *k*, do not know about it
1: 20 My lord the *k*, the eyes
1: 20 throne of my lord the *k* after him.
1: 21 as my lord the *k* is laid to rest
1: 22 she was still speaking with the *k*,
1: 23 And they told the *k*, "Nathan
1: 23 So he went before the *k*
1: 24 declared that Adonijah shall be *k*
1: 24 "Have you, my lord the *k*,
1: 25 'Long live *K* Adonijah!'
1: 27 something my lord the *k* has done
1: 27 throne of my lord the *k* after him?"
1: 28 *K* David said, "Call in Bathsheba."
1: 29 *k* then took an oath: "As surely
1: 30 Solomon your son shall be *k*
1: 31 and, kneeling before the *k*, said,
1: 31 "May my lord *K* David live forever
1: 32 David live forever!" *K* David said,
1: 32 When they came before the *k*,
1: 34 Nathan the prophet anoint him *k*
1: 34 and shout, 'Long live *K* Solomon!'
1: 36 God of my lord the *k*, so declare it.
1: 36 son of Jehoiada answered the *k*,
1: 37 the throne of my lord *K* David!"
1: 37 was with my lord the *k*,
1: 38 put Solomon on *K* David's mule
1: 39 "Long live *K* Solomon!"
1: 43 King David has made Solomon *k*.
1: 43 "Our lord *K* David has made
1: 44 The *k* has sent with him Zadok
1: 45 the prophet have anointed him *k*
1: 47 the *k* bowed in worship on his bed
1: 47 to congratulate our lord *K* David,
1: 51 'Let *K* Solomon swear
1: 51 "Adonijah is afraid of *K* Solomon
1: 53 Then *K* Solomon sent men,
1: 53 and bowed down to *K* Solomon,
2: 15 All Israel looked to me as their *k*.
2: 17 "Please ask *K* Solomon—
2: 18 "I will speak to the *k* for you."
2: 19 the *k* stood up to meet her,
2: 19 went to *K* Solomon to speak
2: 20 *k* replied, "Make it, my mother;
2: 22 *K* Solomon answered his mother,

1Ki 2: 23 *K* Solomon swore by the LORD:
2: 25 So *K* Solomon gave orders
2: 26 To Abiathar the priest the *k* said,
2: 29 *K* Solomon was told that Joab had
2: 30 Benaiah reported to the *k*,
2: 30 "The *k* says, 'Come out!' "
2: 31 Then the *k* commanded Benaiah,
2: 35 The *k* put Benaiah son of Jehoiada
2: 36 Then the *k* sent for Shimei
2: 38 Shimei answered the *k*, "What you
2: 38 as my lord the *k* has said."
2: 39 *k* of Gath, and Shimei was told,
2: 42 the *k* summoned Shimei
2: 44 The *k* also said to Shimei,
2: 45 But *K* Solomon will be blessed,
2: 46 the *k* gave the order to Benaiah son
3: 1 alliance with Pharaoh *k* of Egypt
3: 4 The *k* went to Gibeon
3: 7 you have made your servant *k*
3: 16 Now two prostitutes came to the *k*
3: 22 And so they argued before the *k*.
3: 23 The *k* said, "This one says,
3: 24 So they brought a sword for the *k*.
3: 24 Then the *k* said, "Bring me a sword
3: 26 for her son and said to the *k*,
3: 27 Then the *k* gave his ruling:
3: 28 the *k* had given, they held the *k*
4: 1 So *K* Solomon ruled over all Israel.
4: 5 and personal adviser to the *k*;
4: 7 who supplied provisions for the *k*
4: 19 country of Sihon *k* of the Amorites
4: 19 the country of Og *k* of Bashan).
4: 27 supplied provisions for *K* Solomon
5: 1 When Hiram *k* of Tyre heard that
5: 1 that Solomon had been anointed *k*
5: 13 *K* Solomon conscripted laborers
6: 2 The temple that *K* Solomon built
7: 13 *K* Solomon sent to Tyre
7: 14 He came to *K* Solomon
7: 40 for *K* Solomon in the temple
7: 45 made for *K* Solomon for the temple
7: 46 The *k* had them cast in clay molds
7: 51 all the work *K* Solomon had done
8: 1 Then *K* Solomon summoned
8: 2 together to *K* Solomon at the time
8: 5 and *K* Solomon and, with him,
8: 14 *k* turned around and blessed them.
8: 62 Then the *k* and all Israel
8: 63 *k* and all the Israelites dedicated
8: 64 same day the *k* consecrated
8: 66 They blessed the *k* and then went
9: 11 in Galilee to Hiram *k* of Tyre,
9: 11 *K* Solomon gave twenty towns
9: 14 sent to the *k* 120 talents of gold.
9: 15 the forced labor *K* Solomon
9: 16 (Pharaoh *k* of Egypt had attacked
9: 26 *K* Solomon also built ships
9: 28 they delivered to *K* Solomon.
10: 3 hard for the *k* to explain to her.
10: 6 said to the *k*, "The report I heard
10: 9 he has made you *k*,
10: 10 queen of Sheba gave to *K* Solomon.
10: 10 she gave the *k* 120 talents of gold,
10: 12 The *k* used the almugwood
10: 13 *K* Solomon gave the queen
10: 16 *K* Solomon made two hundred
10: 17 The *k* put them in the Palace
10: 18 the *k* made a great throne inlaid
10: 21 All *K* Solomon's goblets were gold,
10: 22 The *k* had a fleet of trading ships
10: 23 *K* Solomon was greater in riches
10: 27 The *k* made silver as common
11: 1 *K* Solomon, however, loved many
11: 18 to Egypt, to Pharaoh *k* of Egypt,
11: 23 fled from his master, Hadadezer *k*
11: 26 son of Nebat rebelled against the *k*.
11: 27 of how he rebelled against the *k*:
11: 37 your heart desires; you will be *k*
11: 40 to Shishak the *k*, and stayed there
11: 43 his son succeeded him as *k*.
12: 1 had gone there to make him *k*.
12: 2 where he had fled from *K* Solomon
12: 6 *K* Rehoboam consulted the elders
12: 12 the *k* had said, "Come back to me
12: 13 The *k* answered the people harshly
12: 15 So the *k* did not listen to the people
12: 16 all Israel saw that the *k* refused
12: 16 to them, they answered the *k*:

1Ki 12: 18 *K* Rehoboam sent out Adoniram,
12: 18 *K* Rehoboam, however, managed
12: 20 and made him *k* over all Israel.
12: 23 son of Solomon *k* of Judah,
12: 27 and return to *K* Rehoboam.
12: 27 to their lord, Rehoboam *k* of Judah
12: 28 the *k* made two golden calves.
13: 4 When *K* Jeroboam heard what
13: 6 Then the *k* said to the man of God,
13: 7 The *k* said to the man of God,
13: 8 the man of God answered the *k*,
13: 11 father what he had said to the *k*.
14: 2 the one who told me I would be *k*
14: 14 for himself a *k* over Israel who will
14: 20 Nadab his son succeeded him as *k*.
14: 21 old when he became *k*,
14: 21 son of Solomon was *k* in Judah.
14: 25 In the fifth year of *K* Rehoboam,
14: 25 Shishak *k* of Egypt attacked
14: 27 *K* Rehoboam made bronze shields
14: 28 Whenever the *k* went
14: 31 Abijah his son succeeded him as *k*.
15: 1 Abijah became *k* of Judah,
15: 8 Asa his son succeeded him as *k*.
15: 9 Asa became *k* of Judah,
15: 9 year of Jeroboam *k* of Israel,
15: 16 *k* of Israel throughout their reigns.
15: 17 Baasha *k* of Israel went up
15: 17 the territory of Asa *k* of Judah.
15: 18 the son of Hezion, the *k* of Aram,
15: 19 treaty with Baasha *k* of Israel
15: 20 Ben-Hadad agreed with *K* Asa
15: 22 With them *K* Asa built up Geba
15: 22 *K* Asa issued an order to all Judah
15: 24 his son succeeded him as *k*.
15: 25 son of Jeroboam became *k* of Israel
15: 25 year of Asa *k* of Judah,
15: 28 in the third year of Asa *k* of Judah
15: 28 of Judah and succeeded him as *k*.
15: 32 *k* of Israel throughout their reigns.
15: 33 In the third year of Asa *k* of Judah,
15: 33 son of Ahijah became *k* of all Israel
16: 6 Elah his son succeeded him as *k*.
16: 8 son of Baasha became *k* of Israel,
16: 8 year of Asa *k* of Judah,
16: 10 Then he succeeded him as *k*
16: 10 year of Asa *k* of Judah.
16: 15 year of Asa *k* of Judah,
16: 16 Zimri had plotted against the *k*
16: 16 *k* over Israel that very day there
16: 21 Tibni son of Ginath for *k*,
16: 22 So Tibni died and Omri became *k*.
16: 23 Omri became *k* of Israel,
16: 23 year of Asa *k* of Judah,
16: 28 Ahab his son succeeded him as *k*.
16: 29 son of Omri became *k* of Israel,
16: 29 year of Asa *k* of Judah,
16: 31 of Ethbaal *k* of the Sidonians,
19: 15 anoint Hazael *k* over Aram.
19: 16 son of Nimshi *k* over Israel,
20: 1 Ben-Hadad *k* of Aram mustered
20: 2 into the city to Ahab *k* of Israel,
20: 4 The *k* of Israel answered, "Just
20: 4 "Just as you say, my lord the *k*.
20: 7 *k* of Israel summoned all the elders
20: 9 messengers, "Tell my lord the *k*,
20: 11 The *k* of Israel answered, "Tell him
20: 13 came to Ahab *k* of Israel
20: 20 But Ben-Hadad *k* of Aram escaped
20: 21 The *k* of Israel advanced
20: 22 next spring the *k* of Aram will
20: 22 the prophet came to the *k* of Israel
20: 23 the officials of the *k*
20: 28 man of God came up and told the *k*
20: 31 go to the *k* of Israel with sackcloth
20: 32 The *k* answered, "Is he still alive?
20: 32 they went to the *k* of Israel
20: 33 "Go and get him," the *k* said.
20: 38 stood by the road waiting for the *k*.
20: 39 As the *k* passed by, the prophet
20: 40 "That is your sentence," the *k*
20: 41 and the *k* of Israel recognized him
20: 42 to the *k*, "This is what the LORD
20: 43 the *k* of Israel went to his palace
21: 1 to the palace of Ahab *k* of Samaria.
21: 7 Is this how you act as *k* over Israel?
21: 10 he has cursed both God and the *k*.
21: 13 has cursed both God and the *k*."

1Ki 21: 18 Go down to meet Ahab *k* of Israel,
22: 2 But in the third year Jehoshaphat *k*
22: 2 went down to see the *k* of Israel.
22: 3 The *k* of Israel had said
22: 3 to retake it from the *k* of Aram?"
22: 4 Jehoshaphat replied to the *k*
22: 5 But Jehoshaphat also said to the *k*
22: 6 So the *k* of Israel brought together
22: 8 *k* of Israel answered Jehoshaphat,
22: 8 "The *k* should not say that,"
22: 9 So the *k* of Israel called one
22: 10 the *k* of Israel and Jehoshaphat *k*
22: 13 are predicting success for the *k*.
22: 15 the *k* asked him, "Micaiah,
22: 16 *k* said to him, "How many times
22: 18 The *k* of Israel said to Jehoshaphat,
22: 26 The *k* of Israel then ordered,
22: 27 'This is what the *k* says: Put this
22: 29 the *k* of Israel and Jehoshaphat *k*
22: 30 So the *k* of Israel disguised himself
22: 30 The *k* of Israel said to Jehoshaphat,
22: 31 or great, except the *k* of Israel."
22: 31 the *k* of Aram had ordered his
22: 32 "Surely this is the *k* of Israel."
22: 33 saw that he was not the *k*
22: 34 The *k* told his chariot driver,
22: 34 the *k* of Israel between the sections
22: 35 and the *k* was propped up
22: 37 So the *k* died and was brought
22: 40 his son succeeded him as *k*.
22: 41 son of Asa became *k* of Judah
22: 41 year of Ahab *k* of Israel.
22: 42 old when he became *k*
22: 44 also at peace with the *k* of Israel.
22: 47 There was then no *k* in Edom;
22: 51 son of Ahab became *k* of Israel
22: 51 year of Jehoshaphat *k* of Judah,
2Ki 1: 3 the messengers of the *k* of Samaria
1: 5 the messengers returned to the *k*,
1: 6 'Go back to the *k* who sent you
1: 7 die!' " The *k* asked them,
1: 8 The *k* said, "That was Elijah
1: 9 the *k* says, 'Come down!' "
1: 11 At this the *k* sent to Elijah another
1: 11 this is what the *k* says, 'Come
1: 13 So the *k* sent a third captain
1: 15 and went down with him to the *k*.
1: 16 He told the *k*, "This is what
1: 17 as *k* in the second year
1: 17 son of Jehoshaphat *k* of Judah.
3: 1 son of Ahab became *k* of Israel
3: 1 year of Jehoshaphat *k* of Judah,
3: 4 Mesha *k* of Moab raised sheep,
3: 4 and he had to supply the *k* of Israel
3: 5 rebelled against the *k* of Israel.
3: 5 the *k* of Moab rebelled
3: 6 So at that time *K* Joram set out
3: 7 to Jehoshaphat *k* of Judah:
3: 7 "The *k* of Moab has rebelled
3: 9 So the *k* of Israel set out with the *k*
3: 9 the *k* of Judah and the *k* of Edom.
3: 10 "What!" exclaimed the *k* of Israel.
3: 11 officer of the *k* of Israel answered,
3: 12 So the *k* of Israel and Jehoshaphat
3: 12 the *k* of Edom went down to him.
3: 13 Elisha said to the *k* of Israel,
3: 13 "No," the *k* of Israel answered,
3: 14 of Jehoshaphat *k* of Judah,
3: 26 When the *k* of Moab saw that
3: 26 to break through to the *k* of Edom,
3: 27 who was to succeed him as *k*,
4: 13 speak on your behalf to the *k*
5: 1 of the army of the *k* of Aram.
5: 5 I will send a letter to the *k* of Israel
5: 5 go," the *k* of Aram replied.
5: 6 took to the *k* of Israel read:
5: 7 as the *k* of Israel read the letter,
5: 8 the man of God heard that the *k*
6: 8 Now the *k* of Aram was at war
6: 9 of God sent word to the *k* of Israel:
6: 10 So the *k* of Israel checked
6: 10 and again Elisha warned the *k*,
6: 11 This enraged the *k* of Aram.
6: 11 of us is on the side of the *k* of Israel
6: 12 my lord the *k*," said one
6: 12 tells the *k* of Israel the very words
6: 13 out where he is," the *k* ordered,
6: 21 When the *k* of Israel saw them,

2Ki 6: 24 Ben-Hadad *k* of Aram mobilized
6: 26 As the *k* of Israel was passing
6: 26 my lord the *k!*" The *k* replied,
6: 30 When the *k* heard the woman's
6: 32 The *k* sent a messenger ahead,
6: 33 And ⌞the *k*⌟ said, "This disaster is
7: 2 whose arm the *k* was leaning said
7: 6 the *k* of Israel has hired the Hittite
7: 12 The *k* got up in the night
7: 14 the *k* sent them after the Aramean
7: 15 returned and reported to the *k*.
7: 17 Now the *k* had put the officer
7: 17 the *k* came down to his house.
7: 18 the man of God had said to the *k:*
8: 3 went to the *k* to beg for her house
8: 4 The *k* was talking to Gehazi,
8: 5 came to beg the *k* for her house
8: 5 was telling the *k* how Elisha had
8: 5 "This is the woman, my lord the *k*,
8: 6 The *k* asked the woman about it,
8: 7 When the *k* was told, "The man
8: 7 and Ben-Hadad *k* of Aram was ill.
8: 9 "Your son Ben-Hadad *k*
8: 13 shown me that you will become *k*
8: 15 Then Hazael succeeded him as *k*.
8: 16 of Jehoshaphat began his reign as *k*
8: 16 of Joram son of Ahab *k* of Israel,
8: 16 when Jehoshaphat was *k* of Judah,
8: 17 old when he became *k*,
8: 20 against Judah and set up its own *k*.
8: 24 his son succeeded him as *k*.
8: 25 of Joram son of Ahab *k* of Israel,
8: 25 son of Jehoram *k* of Judah began
8: 26 granddaughter of Omri *k* of Israel.
8: 26 old when he became *k*,
8: 28 to war against Hazael *k* of Aram
8: 29 in his battle with Hazael *k* of Aram
8: 29 so *K* Joram returned to Jezreel
8: 29 son of Jehoram *K* of Judah went
9: 3 I anoint you *k* over Israel.'
9: 6 'I anoint you *k* over the LORD's
9: 12 I anoint you *k* over Israel.' "
9: 13 "Jehu is *k!*" So Jehu son
9: 14 against Hazael *k* of Aram,
9: 15 in the battle with Hazael *k* of Aram
9: 15 *K* Joram had returned to Jezreel
9: 16 and Ahaziah *k* of Judah had gone
9: 18 "This is what the *k* says: 'Do you
9: 19 the *k* sent out a second horseman.
9: 19 "This is what the *k* says: 'Do you
9: 21 Joram *k* of Israel and Ahaziah *k*
9: 27 When Ahaziah *k* of Judah saw
9: 29 Ahaziah had become *k* of Judah.)
10: 5 We will not appoint anyone as *k;*
10: 13 down to greet the families of the *k*
10: 13 relatives of Ahaziah *k* of Judah
10: 35 his son succeeded him as *k*.
11: 2 the daughter of *K* Jehoram
11: 7 all to guard the temple for the *k*.
11: 8 Station yourselves around the *k*,
11: 8 close to the *k* wherever he goes."
11: 10 that had belonged to *K* David
11: 11 stationed themselves around the *k*
11: 12 and shouted, "Long live the *k!*"
11: 12 covenant and proclaimed him *k*.
11: 14 She looked and there was the *k*,
11: 14 the trumpeters were beside the *k*,
11: 17 made a covenant between the *k*
11: 17 *k* and people that they would be
11: 19 The *k* then took his place
11: 19 and together they brought the *k*
12: 1 Joash became *k*, and he reigned
12: 6 of *K* Joash the priests still had not
12: 7 Therefore *K* Joash summoned
12: 17 About this time Hazael *k*
12: 18 Joash *k* of Judah took all the sacred
12: 18 he sent them to Hazael *k* of Aram,
12: 21 his son succeeded him as *k*.
13: 1 of Joash son of Ahaziah *k* of Judah,
13: 1 son of Jehu became *k* of Israel
13: 3 the power of Hazael *k* of Aram
13: 4 for he saw how severely the *k*
13: 7 for the *k* of Aram had destroyed
13: 9 Jehoash his son succeeded him as *k*
13: 10 son of Jehoahaz became *k* of Israel
13: 10 year of Joash *k* of Judah,
13: 12 war against Amaziah *k* of Judah,
13: 14 Jehoash *k* of Israel went

2Ki 13: 16 in your hands," he said to the *k*
13: 18 the arrows," and the *k* took them.
13: 22 Hazael *k* of Aram oppressed Israel
13: 24 Hazael *k* of Aram died,
13: 24 his son succeeded him as *k*.
14: 1 son of Jehoahaz *k* of Israel,
14: 1 son of Joash *k* of Judah began
14: 2 old when he became *k*,
14: 5 who had murdered his father the *k*.
14: 8 the son of Jehu, *k* of Israel,
14: 9 But Jehoash *k* of Israel replied
14: 9 replied to Amaziah *k* of Judah:
14: 11 Amaziah *k* of Judah faced each
14: 11 so Jehoash *k* of Israel attacked.
14: 13 *k* of Israel captured Amaziah *k*
14: 15 war against Amaziah *k* of Judah,
14: 16 his son succeeded him as *k*.
14: 17 son of Jehoahaz *k* of Israel.
14: 17 son of Joash *k* of Judah lived
14: 21 and made him *k* in place
14: 23 of Amaziah son of Joash *k* of Judah
14: 23 *k* of Israel became *k* in Samaria,
14: 29 his son succeeded him as *k*.
15: 1 son of Amaziah *k* of Judah began
15: 1 year of Jeroboam *k* of Israel,
15: 2 old when he became *k*,
15: 5 The LORD afflicted the *k*
15: 7 Jotham his son succeeded him as *k*.
15: 8 son of Jeroboam became *k* of Israel
15: 8 year of Azariah *k* of Judah,
15: 10 him and succeeded him as *k*.
15: 13 son of Jabesh became *k*
15: 13 year of Uzziah *k* of Judah,
15: 14 him and succeeded him as *k*.
15: 17 son of Gadi became *k* of Israel,
15: 17 year of Azariah *k* of Judah,
15: 19 Pul *k* of Assyria invaded the land,
15: 20 So the *k* of Assyria withdrew
15: 20 to be given to the *k* of Assyria.
15: 22 his son succeeded him as *k*.
15: 23 of Menahem became *k* of Israel
15: 23 year of Azariah *k* of Judah,
15: 25 Pekahiah and succeeded him as *k*.
15: 27 son of Remaliah became *k* of Israel
15: 27 year of Azariah *k* of Judah,
15: 29 In the time of Pekah *k* of Israel,
15: 29 Tiglath-Pileser *k* of Assyria came
15: 30 as *k* in the twentieth year
15: 32 son of Remaliah *k* of Israel,
15: 32 son of Uzziah *k* of Judah began
15: 33 old when he became *k*,
15: 37 began to send Rezin *k* of Aram
15: 38 Ahaz his son succeeded him as *k*.
16: 1 son of Jotham *k* of Judah began
16: 2 old when he became *k*,
16: 5 Then Rezin *k* of Aram
16: 5 and Pekah son of Remaliah *k*
16: 6 Rezin *k* of Aram recovered Elath
16: 7 say to Tiglath-Pileser *k* of Assyria,
16: 7 *k* of Aram and of the *k* of Israel,
16: 8 sent it as a gift to the *k* of Assyria.
16: 9 The *k* of Assyria complied
16: 10 Then *K* Ahaz went to Damascus
16: 10 to meet Tiglath-Pileser *k*
16: 11 all the plans that *K* Ahaz had sent
16: 11 finished it before *K* Ahaz returned.
16: 12 When the *k* came back
16: 15 *K* Ahaz then gave these orders
16: 16 did just as *K* Ahaz had ordered.
16: 17 *K* Ahaz took away the side panels
16: 18 in deference to the *k* of Assyria.
16: 20 his son succeeded him as *k*.
17: 1 son of Elah became *k* of Israel
17: 1 year of Ahaz *k* of Judah,
17: 3 Shalmaneser *k* of Assyria came up
17: 4 for he had sent envoys to So *k*
17: 4 the *k* of Assyria discovered that
17: 4 tribute to the *k* of Assyria,
17: 5 The *k* of Assyria invaded the entire
17: 6 the *k* of Assyria captured Samaria
17: 7 the power of Pharaoh *k* of Egypt.
17: 21 Jeroboam son of Nebat their *k*.
17: 24 The *k* of Assyria brought people
17: 26 It was reported to the *k* of Assyria:
17: 27 the *k* of Assyria gave this order:
18: 1 of Hoshea son of Elah *k* of Israel,
18: 1 son of Ahaz *k* of Judah began
18: 2 old when he became *k*,

2Ki 18: 7 rebelled against the *k* of Assyria
18: 9 In *K* Hezekiah's fourth year,
18: 9 Shalmaneser *k* of Assyria marched
18: 9 of Hoshea son of Elah *k* of Israel,
18: 10 year of Hoshea *k* of Israel.
18: 11 The *k* of Assyria deported Israel
18: 13 Sennacherib *k* of Assyria attacked
18: 13 year of *K* Hezekiah's reign,
18: 14 Assyria exacted from Hezekiah *k*
18: 14 So Hezekiah *k* of Judah sent this
18: 14 The *k* of Assyria exacted
18: 14 to the *k* of Assyria at Lachish:
18: 16 At this time Hezekiah *k*
18: 16 and gave it to the *k* of Assyria.
18: 17 The *k* of Assyria sent his supreme
18: 17 from Lachish to *K* Hezekiah
18: 18 called for the *k;* and Eliakim son
18: 19 " 'This is what the great *k*, the *k*
18: 21 Such is Pharaoh *k* of Egypt
18: 23 with my master, the *k* of Assyria:
18: 28 of the great *k*, the *k* of Assyria!
18: 29 This is what the *k* says: Do not let
18: 30 into the hand of the *k* of Assyria.'
18: 31 This is what the *k* of Assyria says:
18: 33 from the hand of the *k* of Assyria?
18: 36 because the *k* had commanded,
19: 1 When *K* Hezekiah heard this,
19: 4 whom his master, the *k* of Assyria,
19: 5 When *K* Hezekiah's officials came
19: 6 underlings of the *k* of Assyria have
19: 8 field commander heard that the *k*
19: 8 found the *k* fighting against Libnah
19: 9 report that Tirhakah, the Cushite *k*
19: 10 handed over to the *k* of Assyria.'
19: 10 "Say to Hezekiah *k* of Judah:
19: 13 the *k* of Hamath, the *k* of Arpad,
19: 13 the *k* of the city of Sepharvaim,
19: 20 prayer concerning Sennacherib *k*
19: 32 the LORD says concerning the *k*
19: 36 So Sennacherib *k* of Assyria broke
19: 37 his son succeeded him as *k*.
20: 6 from the hand of the *k* of Assyria.
20: 12 son of Baladan *k* of Babylon sent
20: 14 the prophet went to *K* Hezekiah
20: 18 in the palace of the *k* of Babylon."
20: 21 his son succeeded him as *k*.
21: 1 old when he became *k*,
21: 3 as Ahab *k* of Israel had done.
21: 11 "Manasseh *k* of Judah has
21: 18 Amon his son succeeded him as *k*.
21: 19 old when he became *k*,
21: 23 assassinated the *k* in his palace.
21: 24 and they made Josiah his son *k*
21: 24 who had plotted against *K* Amon,
21: 26 Josiah his son succeeded him as *k*.
22: 1 old when he became *k*,
22: 3 *K* Josiah sent the secretary,
22: 9 the secretary went to the *k*
22: 10 from it in the presence of the *k*.
22: 10 the secretary informed the *k*,
22: 11 When the *k* heard the words
22: 16 in the book the *k* of Judah has read.
22: 18 Tell the *k* of Judah, who sent you
22: 20 they took her answer back to the *k*.
23: 1 the *k* called together all the elders
23: 3 The *k* stood by the pillar
23: 4 *k* ordered Hilkiah the high priest,
23: 13 the ones Solomon *k*
23: 13 *k* also desecrated the high places
23: 17 *k* asked, "What is that tombstone I
23: 21 The *k* gave this order
23: 23 in the eighteenth year of *K* Josiah,
23: 25 Josiah was there a *k* like him who
23: 29 Josiah was *k*, Pharaoh Neco *k*
23: 29 *K* Josiah marched out to meet him
23: 29 to help the *k* of Assyria.
23: 30 made him *k* in place of his father.
23: 31 old when he became *k*,
23: 34 son of Josiah *k* in place
23: 36 old when he became *k*,
24: 1 Nebuchadnezzar *k*
24: 6 his son succeeded him as *k*.
24: 7 The *k* of Egypt did not march out
24: 7 the *k* of Babylon had taken all his
24: 8 old when he became *k*,
24: 10 the officers of Nebuchadnezzar *k*
24: 12 Jehoiachin *k* of Judah, his mother,
24: 12 of the reign of the *k* of Babylon,

2Ki 24: 13 all the gold articles that Solomon *k*
24: 16 The *k* of Babylon also deported
24: 17 *k* in his place and changed his
24: 18 old when he became *k*,
24: 20 rebelled against the *k* of Babylon
25: 1 Nebuchadnezzar *k*
25: 2 the eleventh year of *K* Zedekiah.
25: 5 the Babylonian army pursued the *k*
25: 6 to the *k* of Babylon at Riblah,
25: 8 an official of the *k* of Babylon,
25: 8 of Nebuchadnezzar *k* of Babylon,
25: 11 gone over to the *k* of Babylon.
25: 20 brought them to the *k* of Babylon
25: 21 land of Hamath, the *k* had them
25: 22 Nebuchadnezzar *k*
25: 23 and their men heard that the *k*
25: 24 and serve the *k* of Babylon,
25: 27 the exile of Jehoiachin *k* of Judah,
25: 27 the year Evil-Merodach became *k*
25: 30 Day by day the *k* gave Jehoiachin
1Ch 1: 43 before any Israelite *k* reigned:
1: 44 from Bozrah succeeded him as *k*.
1: 45 the Temanites succeeded him as *k*.
1: 46 of Moab, succeeded him as *k*.
1: 47 from Masrekah succeeded him as *k*
1: 48 on the river succeeded him as *k*
1: 49 son of Acbor succeeded him as *k*.
1: 50 Hadad succeeded him as *k*.
3: 2 daughter of Talmai *k* of Geshur;
4: 23 stayed there and worked for the *k*.
4: 41 in the days of Hezekiah *k* of Judah.
5: 6 whom Tiglath-Pileser *k*
5: 17 of Judah and Jeroboam *k* of Israel.
5: 17 the reigns of Jotham *k* of Judah
5: 26 Tiglath-Pileser *k* of Assyria),
5: 26 spirit of Pul *k* of Assyria (that is,
11: 2 In the past, even while Saul was *k*,
11: 3 come to *K* David at Hebron,
11: 3 they anointed David *k* over Israel,
12: 31 name to come and make David *k*—
12: 38 also of one mind to make David *k*.
12: 38 to make David *k* over all Israel.
14: 1 Hiram *k* of Tyre sent messengers
14: 2 LORD had established him as *k*
14: 8 that David had been anointed *k*
15: 29 when she saw *K* David dancing
17: 16 Then *K* David went in
18: 3 David fought Hadadezer *k*
18: 5 to help Hadadezer *k* of Zobah,
18: 9 When Tou *k* of Hamath heard that
18: 9 army of Hadadezer *k* of Zobah,
18: 10 Hadoram to *K* David to greet him
18: 11 *K* David dedicated these articles
19: 1 Nahash *k* of the Ammonites died,
19: 1 and his son succeeded him as *k*.
19: 5 The *k* said, "Stay at Jericho
19: 7 as the *k* of Maacah with his troops,
20: 2 crown from the head of their *k*—
21: 3 My lord the *k*, are they not all my
21: 23 my lord the *k* do whatever pleases
21: 24 But *K* David replied to Araunah,
23: 1 he made his son Solomon *k*
24: 6 names in the presence of the *k*
24: 31 in the presence of *K* David
25: 6 under the supervision of the *k*.
26: 26 the things dedicated by *K* David,
26: 32 and for the affairs of the *k*.
26: 32 and *K* David put them in charge
27: 1 who served the *k* in all that
27: 24 the book of the annals of *K* David.
27: 31 in charge of *K* David's property.
28: 1 and livestock belonging to the *k*
28: 1 the divisions in the service of the *k*,
28: 2 *K* David rose to his feet and said:
28: 4 family to be *k* over Israel forever.
28: 4 to make me *k* over all Israel.
29: 1 Then *K* David said to the whole
29: 9 David the *k* also rejoiced greatly.
29: 20 before the LORD and the *k*.
29: 22 son of David as *k* a second time,
29: 23 as *k* in place of his father David.
29: 24 as well as all of *K* David's sons,
29: 24 their submission to *K* Solomon.
29: 25 as no *k* over Israel ever had before.
29: 26 son of Jesse was *k* over all Israel.
29: 28 son Solomon succeeded him as *k*.
29: 29 for the events of *K* David's reign,
2Ch 1: 8 and have made me *k* in his place.
2Ch 1: 9 for you have made me *k*
1: 11 over whom I have made you *k*,
1: 12 no *k* who was before you ever had
1: 15 The *k* made silver and gold
2: 3 message to Hiram *k* of Tyre:
2: 11 Hiram *k* of Tyre replied by letter
2: 11 he has made you their *k*."
2: 12 He has given *K* David a wise son,
4: 11 for *K* Solomon in the temple
4: 16 made for *K* Solomon for the temple
4: 17 The *k* had them cast in clay molds
5: 3 together to the *k* at the time
5: 6 and *K* Solomon and the entire
6: 3 *k* turned around and blessed them.
7: 4 the *k* and all the people offered
7: 5 And *K* Solomon offered a sacrifice
7: 5 the *k* and all the people dedicated
7: 6 which *K* David had made
8: 10 also *K* Solomon's chief officials—
8: 11 in the palace of David *k* of Israel,
8: 18 they delivered to *K* Solomon.
9: 5 said to the *k*, "The report I heard
9: 8 he has made you *k* over them,
9: 8 *k* to rule for the LORD your God.
9: 9 queen of Sheba gave to *K* Solomon.
9: 9 she gave the *k* 120 talents of gold,
9: 11 The *k* used the algumwood
9: 12 *K* Solomon gave the queen
9: 15 *K* Solomon made two hundred
9: 16 The *k* put them in the Palace
9: 17 the *k* made a great throne inlaid
9: 20 All *K* Solomon's goblets were gold,
9: 21 The *k* had a fleet of trading ships
9: 22 *K* Solomon was greater in riches
9: 27 The *k* made silver as common
9: 31 his son succeeded him as *k*.
10: 1 had gone there to make him *k*.
10: 2 where he had fled from *K* Solomon
10: 6 *K* Rehoboam consulted the elders
10: 12 the *k* had said, "Come back to me
10: 13 The *k* answered them harshly.
10: 15 So the *k* did not listen to the people
10: 16 all Israel saw that the *k* refused
10: 16 to them, they answered the *k*:
10: 18 *K* Rehoboam sent out Adoniram,
10: 18 *K* Rehoboam, however, managed
11: 3 son of Solomon *k* of Judah
11: 22 in order to make him *k*.
12: 1 position as *k* was established
12: 2 Shishak *k* of Egypt attacked
12: 2 in the fifth year of *K* Rehoboam.
12: 6 the *k* humbled themselves and said
12: 9 When Shishak *k* of Egypt attacked
12: 10 *K* Rehoboam made bronze shields
12: 11 Whenever the *k* went
12: 13 in Jerusalem and continued as *k*.
12: 13 *K* Rehoboam established himself
12: 13 old when he became *k*,
12: 16 Abijah his son succeeded him as *k*.
13: 1 Abijah became *k* of Judah,
14: 1 Asa his son succeeded him as *k*,
15: 16 *K* Asa also deposed his
16: 1 the territory of Asa *k* of Judah.
16: 1 year of Asa's reign Baasha *k*
16: 2 sent it to Ben-Hadad *k* of Aram,
16: 3 treaty with Baasha *k* of Israel
16: 4 Ben-Hadad agreed with *K* Asa
16: 6 *K* Asa brought all the men of Judah
16: 7 Hanani the seer came to Asa *k*
16: 7 army of the *k* of Aram has escaped
16: 7 "Because you relied on the *k*
17: 1 as *k* and strengthened himself
17: 19 were the men who served the *k*,
18: 3 *k* of Israel asked Jehoshaphat *k*
18: 4 But Jehoshaphat also said to the *k*
18: 5 So the *k* of Israel brought together
18: 7 *k* of Israel answered Jehoshaphat,
18: 7 "The *k* should not say that,"
18: 8 So the *k* of Israel called one
18: 9 the *k* of Israel and Jehoshaphat *k*
18: 12 are predicting success for the *k*.
18: 14 the *k* asked him, "Micaiah,
18: 15 *k* said to him, "How many times
18: 17 The *k* of Israel said to Jehoshaphat,
18: 19 'Who will lure Ahab *k* of Israel
18: 25 The *k* of Israel then ordered,
18: 26 and say, 'This is what the *k* says:
18: 28 the *k* of Israel and Jehoshaphat *k*
2Ch 18: 29 So the *k* of Israel disguised himself
18: 29 The *k* of Israel said to Jehoshaphat,
18: 30 or great, except the *k* of Israel."
18: 30 *k* of Aram had ordered his chariot
18: 31 they thought, "This is the *k*
18: 32 saw that he was not the *k*
18: 33 The *k* told the chariot driver,
18: 33 the *k* of Israel between the sections
18: 34 the *k* of Israel propped himself up
19: 1 When Jehoshaphat *k*
19: 2 out to meet him and said to the *k*,
19: 11 in any matter concerning the *k*,
20: 15 *K* Jehoshaphat and all who live
20: 31 old when he became *k* of Judah,
20: 35 Jehoshaphat *k* of Judah made
20: 35 alliance with Ahaziah *k* of Israel,
21: 1 his son succeeded him as *k*.
21: 2 sons of Jehoshaphat *k* of Israel.
21: 5 old when he became *k*,
21: 8 against Judah and set up its own *k*.
21: 12 or of Asa *k* of Judah.
21: 20 old when he became *k*,
22: 1 Jehoram's youngest son, *k*
22: 1 son of Jehoram *k* of Judah began
22: 2 old when he became *k*,
22: 5 son of Ahab *k* of Israel to war
22: 5 to war against Hazael *k* of Aram
22: 6 in his battle with Hazael *k* of Aram
22: 6 son of Jehoram *k* of Judah went
22: 11 the daughter of *K* Jehoram
22: 11 the daughter of *K* Jehoram,
23: 3 with the *k* at the temple of God.
23: 7 close to the *k* wherever he goes."
23: 7 to station themselves around the *k*,
23: 9 that had belonged to *K* David
23: 10 around the *k*— near the altar
23: 11 and shouted, "Long live the *k*!"
23: 11 covenant and proclaimed him *k*.
23: 12 people running and cheering the *k*,
23: 13 She looked, and there was the *k*,
23: 13 the trumpeters were beside the *k*,
23: 16 the *k* would be the LORD's people
23: 20 seated the *k* on the royal throne,
23: 20 the *k* down from the temple
24: 1 old when he became *k*,
24: 6 Therefore the *k* summoned
24: 12 The *k* and Jehoiada gave it
24: 14 the rest of the money to the *k*
24: 17 came and paid homage to the *k*,
24: 21 by order of the *k* they stoned him
24: 22 *K* Joash did not remember
24: 23 the plunder to their *k* in Damascus.
24: 27 his son succeeded him as *k*.
25: 1 old when he became *k*,
25: 3 who had murdered his father the *k*.
25: 7 "O *k*, these troops
25: 16 appointed you an adviser to the *k*?
25: 16 he was still speaking, the *k* said
25: 17 Amaziah *k* of Judah consulted
25: 17 the son of Jehu, *k* of Israel: "Come,
25: 18 But Jehoash *k* of Israel replied
25: 18 replied to Amaziah *k* of Judah:
25: 21 Amaziah *k* of Judah faced each
25: 21 So Jehoash *k* of Israel attacked.
25: 23 *k* of Israel captured Amaziah *k*
25: 25 son of Jehoahaz *k* of Israel.
25: 25 son of Joash *k* of Judah lived
26: 1 and made him *k* in place
26: 3 old when he became *k*,
26: 13 support the *k* against his enemies.
26: 21 *K* Uzziah had leprosy
26: 23 Jotham his son succeeded him as *k*.
27: 1 old when he became *k*,
27: 5 war on the *k* of the Ammonites
27: 8 old when he became *k*,
27: 9 Ahaz his son succeeded him as *k*.
28: 1 old when he became *k*,
28: 5 him over to the *k* of Aram.
28: 5 into the hands of the *k* of Israel,
28: 7 and Elkanah, second to the *k*.
28: 16 At that time *K* Ahaz sent
28: 16 sent to the *k* of Assyria for help.
28: 19 because of Ahaz *k* of Israel,
28: 20 Tiglath-Pileser *k* of Assyria came
28: 21 presented them to the *k* of Assyria,
28: 22 time of trouble *K* Ahaz became
28: 27 his son succeeded him as *k*.
29: 1 old when he became *k*,

2Ch 29: 15 *k* had ordered, following the word
29: 18 Then they went in to *K* Hezekiah
29: 19 in his unfaithfulness while he was *k*
29: 19 the articles that *K* Ahaz removed
29: 20 the next morning *K* Hezekiah
29: 21 The *k* commanded the priests,
29: 23 offering were brought before the *k*
29: 24 *k* had ordered the burnt offering
29: 27 instruments of David *k* of Israel.
29: 29 the *k* and everyone present
29: 30 *K* Hezekiah and his officials
30: 2 The *k* and his officials
30: 4 plan seemed right both to the *k*
30: 6 and Judah with letters from the *k*
30: 12 of mind to carry out what the *k*
30: 24 Hezekiah *k* of Judah provided
30: 26 days of Solomon son of David *k*
31: 3 The *k* contributed
31: 13 by appointment of *K* Hezekiah
32: 1 Sennacherib *k* of Assyria came
32: 7 because of the *k* of Assyria
32: 8 from what Hezekiah the *k*
32: 9 message for Hezekiah *k* of Judah
32: 9 when Sennacherib *k* of Assyria
32: 10 "This is what Sennacherib *k*
32: 11 from the hand of the *k* of Assyria,'
32: 17 The *k* also wrote letters insulting
32: 20 *K* Hezekiah and the prophet Isaiah
32: 21 in the camp of the Assyrian *k*.
32: 22 hand of Sennacherib *k* of Assyria
32: 23 gifts for Hezekiah *k* of Judah.
32: 33 his son succeeded him as *k*.
33: 1 old when he became *k*,
33: 11 commanders of the *k* of Assyria,
33: 20 Amon his son succeeded him as *k*.
33: 21 old when he became *k*,
33: 25 and they made Josiah his son *k*
33: 25 who had plotted against *K* Amon,
34: 1 old when he became *k*,
34: 16 Shaphan took the book to the *k*
34: 18 from it in the presence of the *k*.
34: 18 the secretary informed the *k*,
34: 19 When the *k* heard the words
34: 22 those the *k* had sent with him went
34: 24 in the presence of the *k* of Judah.
34: 26 Tell the *k* of Judah, who sent you
34: 28 they took her answer back to the *k*.
34: 29 the *k* called together all the elders
34: 31 The *k* stood by his pillar
35: 3 son of David *k* of Israel built.
35: 4 written by David *k* of Israel
35: 10 divisions as the *k* had ordered.
35: 16 as *K* Josiah had ordered.
35: 20 Neco *k* of Egypt went up to fight
35: 21 between you and me, O *k* of Judah
35: 23 Archers shot *K* Josiah,
36: 1 made him *k* in Jerusalem in place
36: 2 old when he became *k*,
36: 3 The *k* of Egypt dethroned him
36: 4 The *k* of Egypt made Eliakim,
36: 4 *k* over Judah and Jerusalem
36: 5 old when he became *k*,
36: 6 Nebuchadnezzar *k*
36: 8 his son succeeded him as *k*.
36: 9 old when he became *k*,
36: 10 *K* Nebuchadnezzar sent for him
36: 10 *k* over Judah and Jerusalem.
36: 11 old when he became *k*,
36: 13 against *K* Nebuchadnezzar,
36: 17 up against them the *k*
36: 18 treasures of the *k* and his officials.
36: 22 the heart of Cyrus *k* of Persia
36: 22 year of Cyrus *k* of Persia,
36: 23 This is what Cyrus *k* of Persia says:
Ezr 1: 1 the heart of Cyrus *k* of Persia
1: 1 year of Cyrus *k* of Persia,
1: 2 This is what Cyrus *k* of Persia says:
1: 7 *K* Cyrus brought out the articles
1: 8 Cyrus *k* of Persia had them
2: 1 whom Nebuchadnezzar *k*
3: 7 as authorized by Cyrus *k* of Persia.
3: 10 as prescribed by David *k* of Israel.
4: 2 time of Esarhaddon *k* of Assyria,
4: 3 as King Cyrus, the *k* of Persia,
4: 3 the God of Israel, as *K* Cyrus,
4: 5 reign of Cyrus *k* of Persia
4: 5 to the reign of Darius *k* of Persia.
4: 7 the days of Artaxerxes *k* of Persia,

Ezr 4: 8 Jerusalem to Artaxerxes the *k*
4: 11 To *K* Artaxerxes, From your
4: 12 *k* should know that the Jews who
4: 13 the *k* should know that
4: 14 for us to see the *k* dishonored,
4: 14 this message to inform the *k*,
4: 16 We inform the *k* that
4: 17 The *k* sent this reply: To Rehum
4: 23 the letter of *K* Artaxerxes was read
4: 24 of the reign of Darius *k* of Persia.
5: 6 Trans-Euphrates, sent to *K* Darius.
5: 7 To *K* Darius: Cordial greetings.
5: 8 The *k* should know that we went
5: 11 one that a great *k* of Israel built
5: 12 Nebuchadnezzar the Chaldean, *k*
5: 13 *K* Cyrus issued a decree
5: 13 year of Cyrus *k* of Babylon,
5: 14 "Then *K* Cyrus gave them
5: 17 Then let the *k* send us his decision
5: 17 if it pleases the *k*, let a search be
5: 17 of Babylon to see if *K* Cyrus did
6: 1 *K* Darius then issued an order,
6: 3 In the first year of *K* Cyrus,
6: 3 the *k* issued a decree concerning
6: 10 and pray for the well-being of the *k*
6: 12 overthrow any *k* or people who
6: 13 of the decree *K* Darius had sent,
6: 15 year of the reign of *K* Darius.
6: 22 the attitude of the *k* of Assyria,
7: 1 the reign of Artaxerxes *k* of Persia,
7: 6 *k* had granted him everything he
7: 7 the seventh year of *K* Artaxerxes.
7: 8 month of the seventh year of the *k*.
7: 11 copy of the letter *K* Artaxerxes had
7: 12 *k* of kings, To Ezra the priest,
7: 14 sent by the *k* and his seven advisers
7: 15 and gold that the *k* and his advisers
7: 21 *K* Artaxerxes, order all
7: 23 wrath against the realm of the *k*
7: 26 of the *k* must surely be punished
7: 28 favor to me before the *k*
8: 1 during the reign of *K* Artaxerxes:
8: 22 ashamed to ask the *k* for soldiers
8: 22 because we had told the *k*,
8: 25 and gold and the articles that the *k*,
Ne 1: 11 I was cupbearer to the *k*.
2: 1 I took the wine and gave it to the *k*.
2: 1 twentieth year of *K* Artaxerxes,
2: 2 presence before; so the *k* asked me,
2: 3 to the *k*, "May the *k* live forever!
2: 4 The *k* said to me, "What is it you
2: 5 of heaven, and I answered the *k*,
2: 5 "If it pleases the *k*
2: 6 It pleased the *k* to send me;
2: 6 Then the *k*, with the queen sitting
2: 7 also said to him, "If it pleases the *k*,
2: 8 the *k* granted my requests.
2: 9 The *k* had also sent army officers
2: 18 and what the *k* had said to me.
2: 19 "Are you rebelling against the *k*?"
5: 14 twentieth year of *K* Artaxerxes,
6: 6 you are about to become their *k*
6: 7 'There is a *k* in Judah!'
6: 7 this report will get back to the *k*;
7: 6 exiles whom Nebuchadnezzar *k*
9: 22 and the country of Og *k* of Bashan.
9: 22 the country of Sihon *k* of Heshbon
13: 6 of Artaxerxes *k* of Babylon I had
13: 6 of Babylon I had returned to the *k*.
13: 26 and God made him *k* over all Israel
13: 26 like these that Solomon *k*
13: 26 nations there was no *k* like him.
Est 1: 2 At that time *K* Xerxes reigned
1: 5 were over, the *k* gave a banquet,
1: 8 for the *k* instructed all the wine
1: 9 in the royal palace of *K* Xerxes.
1: 10 when *K* Xerxes was in high spirits
1: 12 Then the *k* became furious
1: 13 for the *k* to consult experts
1: 14 and were closest to the *k*—
1: 14 who had special access to the *k*
1: 15 of *K* Xerxes that the eunuchs have
1: 16 not only against the *k* but
1: 16 of all the provinces of *K* Xerxes.
1: 16 replied in the presence of the *k*
1: 17 '*K* Xerxes commanded Queen
1: 19 let the *k* give her royal position
1: 19 to enter the presence of *K* Xerxes.

Est 1: 19 "Therefore, if it pleases the *k*,
1: 21 The *k* and his nobles were pleased
1: 21 so the *k* did as Memucan proposed.
2: 1 anger of *K* Xerxes had subsided,
2: 2 beautiful young virgins for the *k*.
2: 3 Let the *k* appoint commissioners
2: 4 This advice appealed to the *k*,
2: 4 who pleases the *k* be queen instead
2: 6 by Nebuchadnezzar *k* of Babylon,
2: 6 captive with Jehoiachin *k* of Judah.
2: 12 came to go in to *K* Xerxes,
2: 13 this is how she would go to the *k*:
2: 14 She would not return to the *k*
2: 15 of his uncle Abihail) to go to the *k*,
2: 16 She was taken to *K* Xerxes
2: 17 the *k* was attracted to Esther more
2: 18 And the *k* gave a great banquet,
2: 21 conspired to assassinate *K* Xerxes.
2: 22 who in turn reported it to the *k*,
2: 23 the annals in the presence of the *k*.
3: 1 *K* Xerxes honored Haman son
3: 2 for the *k* had commanded this
3: 7 In the twelfth year of *K* Xerxes,
3: 8 Then Haman said to *K* Xerxes,
3: 9 If it pleases the *k*, let a decree be
3: 10 So the *k* took the signet ring
3: 11 "Keep the money," the *k* said
3: 12 in the name of *K* Xerxes himself
3: 15 The *k* and Haman sat
4: 3 the edict and order of the *k* came,
4: 11 for the *k* to extend the gold scepter
4: 11 or woman who approaches the *k*
4: 11 since I was called to go to the *k*."
4: 11 without being summoned the *k* has
4: 16 I will go to the *k*, even
5: 1 *k* was sitting on his royal throne
5: 3 Then the *k* asked, "What is it,
5: 4 "If it pleases the *k*," replied Esther,
5: 4 "let the *k*, together with Haman,
5: 5 So the *k* and Haman went
5: 5 "Bring Haman at once," the *k* said,
5: 6 drinking wine, the *k* again asked
5: 8 If the *k* regards me with favor
5: 8 and if it pleases the *k* to grant my
5: 8 let the *k* and Haman come
5: 11 all the ways the *k* had honored him
5: 12 invited to accompany the *k*
5: 12 me along with the *k* tomorrow.
5: 14 Then go with the *k* to the dinner
5: 14 and ask the *k* in the morning
6: 1 That night the *k* could not sleep;
6: 2 conspired to assassinate *K* Xerxes.
6: 3 received for this?" the *k* asked.
6: 4 The *k* said, "Who is in the court?"
6: 4 to the *k* about hanging Mordecai
6: 5 "Bring him in," the *k* ordered.
6: 6 Haman entered, the *k* asked him,
6: 6 for the man the *k* delights to honor
6: 6 there that the *k* would rather honor
6: 7 he answered the *k*, "For the man
6: 7 "For the man the *k* delights
6: 8 and a horse the *k* has ridden,
6: 8 bring a royal robe the *k* has worn
6: 9 for the man the *k* delights to honor
6: 9 them robe the man the *k* delights
6: 10 the *k* commanded Haman.
6: 11 for the man the *k* delights to honor
7: 1 So the *k* and Haman went to dine
7: 2 the *k* again asked, "Queen Esther,
7: 3 O *k*, and if it pleases your majesty,
7: 4 would justify disturbing the *k*."
7: 5 *K* Xerxes asked Queen Esther,
7: 6 Haman was terrified before the *k*
7: 7 The *k* got up in a rage, left his wine
7: 7 realizing that the *k* had already
7: 8 The *k* exclaimed, "Will he
7: 8 *k* returned from the palace garden
7: 9 The *k* said, "Hang him on it!"
7: 9 one of the eunuchs attending the *k*,
7: 9 who spoke up to help the *k*."
8: 1 That same day *K* Xerxes gave
8: 1 came into the presence of the *k*,
8: 2 The *k* took off his signet ring,
8: 3 Esther again pleaded with the *k*,
8: 4 the *k* extended the gold scepter
8: 5 "If it pleases the *k*," she said,
8: 7 *K* Xerxes replied to Queen Esther
8: 10 horses especially bred for the *k*.

Est 8: 10 wrote in the name of *K* Xerxes,
8: 12 of *K* Xerxes was the thirteenth day
8: 17 wherever the edict of the *k* went,
9: 1 the edict commanded by the *k* was
9: 2 in all the provinces of *K* Xerxes
9: 11 reported to the *k* that same day.
9: 12 The *k* said to Queen Esther,
9: 13 it pleases the *k*,'' Esther answered,
9: 14 the *k* commanded that this be done
9: 20 the provinces of *K* Xerxes,
10: 1 *K* Xerxes imposed tribute
10: 2 to which the *k* had raised him,
10: 3 second in rank to *K* Xerxes,
Job 15: 24 overwhelm him, like a *k* poised
18: 14 and marched off to the *k* of terrors.
29: 25 I dwelt as a *k* among his troops;
41: 34 he is *k* over all that are proud.''
Ps 2: 6 ''I have installed my *K*
5: 2 my *K* and my God,
10: 16 The LORD is *K* for ever and ever;
18: 50 He gives his *k* great victories;
20: 9 O LORD, save the *k*!
21: 1 the *k* rejoices in your strength.
21: 7 For the *k* trusts in the LORD;
24: 7 that the *K* of glory may come in.
24: 8 Who is this *K* of glory?
24: 9 that the *K* of glory may come in.
24: 10 Who is he, this *K* of glory?
24: 10 he is the *K* of glory.
29: 10 LORD is enthroned as *K* forever.
33: 16 No *k* is saved by the size
44: 4 You are my *K* and my God,
45: 1 as I recite my verses for the *k*;
45: 11 The *k* is enthralled by your beauty;
45: 14 garments she is led to the *k*;
45: 15 they enter the palace of the *k*.
47: 2 the great *K* over all the earth!
47: 6 sing praises to our *K*, sing praises.
47: 7 For God is the *K* of all the earth;
48: 2 the city of the Great *K*.
63: 11 But the *k* will rejoice in God;
68: 24 my God and *K* into the sanctuary.
72: 1 Endow the *k* with your justice,
74: 12 O God, are my *k* from of old;
84: 3 O LORD Almighty, my *K*
89: 18 our *k* to the Holy One of Israel.
95: 3 the great *K* above all gods.
98: 6 for joy before the LORD, the *K*.
99: 4 The *K* is mighty, he loves justice—
105: 20 The *k* sent and released him,
135: 11 Og *k* of Bashan
135: 11 Sihon *k* of the Amorites,
136: 19 Sihon *k* of the Amorites
136: 20 and Og *k* of Bashan—
145: 1 I will exalt you, my God the *K*;
149: 2 of Zion be glad in their *K*.
Pr 1: 1 son of David, *k* of Israel:
14: 35 A *k* delights in a wise servant,
16: 10 The lips of a *k* speak as an oracle,
20: 8 When a *k* sits on his throne
20: 26 A wise *k* winnows out the wicked;
20: 28 Love and faithfulness keep a *k* safe;
22: 11 will have the *k* for his friend.
24: 21 Fear the LORD and the *k*, my son,
25: 1 by the men of Hezekiah *k* of Judah:
29: 4 By justice a *k* gives a country
29: 14 If a *k* judges the poor with fairness,
30: 22 a servant who becomes *k*,
30: 27 locusts have no *k*,
30: 31 and a *k* with his army around him.
31: 1 The sayings of *K* Lemuel—
Ecc 1: 1 son of David, *k* in Jerusalem:
1: 12 was *k* over Israel in Jerusalem.
4: 13 foolish *k* who no longer knows how
5: 9 the *k* himself profits from the fields
9: 14 And a powerful *k* came against it,
10: 16 O land whose *k* was a servant
10: 17 O land whose *k* is of noble birth
10: 20 Do not revile the *k*
SS 1: 4 The *k* has brought me
1: 12 While the *k* was
3: 9 *K* Solomon made for himself
3: 11 at *K* Solomon wearing the crown,
7: 5 the *k* is held captive by its tresses.
Isa 6: 1 In the year that *K* Uzziah died,
6: 5 and my eyes have seen the *K*,
7: 1 and Pekah son of Remaliah *k*
7: 1 *K* Rezin of Aram and Pekah son
Isa 7: 1 the son of Uzziah, was *k* of Judah,
7: 6 make the son of Tabeel *k* over it.''
7: 17 he will bring the *k* of Assyria.''
7: 20 the *k* of Assyria—
8: 4 carried off by the *k* of Assyria.''
8: 7 the *k* of Assyria with all his pomp.
8: 21 will curse their *k* and their God.
10: 12 ''I will punish the *k* of Assyria
14: 4 taunt against the *k* of Babylon:
14: 28 came in the year *K* Ahaz died:
19: 4 and a fierce *k* will rule over them,''
20: 1 sent by Sargon *k* of Assyria,
20: 4 so the *k* of Assyria will lead away
20: 6 deliverance from the *k* of Assyria!
30: 33 it has been made ready for the *k*.
32: 1 See, a *k* will reign in righteousness
33: 17 Your eyes will see the *k*
33: 22 the LORD is our *k*;
36: 1 Sennacherib *k* of Assyria attacked
36: 1 year of *K* Hezekiah's reign,
36: 2 Then the *k* of Assyria sent his field
36: 2 army from Lachish to *K* Hezekiah
36: 4 the great *k*, the *k* of Assyria,
36: 6 Such is Pharaoh *k* of Egypt
36: 8 with my master, the *k* of Assyria:
36: 13 of the great *k*, the *k* of Assyria!
36: 14 This is what the *k* says: Do not let
36: 15 into the hand of the *k* of Assyria.'
36: 16 This is what the *k* of Assyria says:
36: 18 from the hand of the *k* of Assyria?
36: 21 because the *k* had commanded,
37: 1 When *K* Hezekiah heard this,
37: 4 whom his master, the *k* of Assyria,
37: 5 When *K* Hezekiah's officials came
37: 6 underlings of the *k* of Assyria have
37: 8 field commander heard that the *k*
37: 8 found the *k* fighting against Libnah
37: 9 report that Tirhakah, the Cushite *k*
37: 10 handed over to the *k* of Assyria.'
37: 10 ''Say to Hezekiah *k* of Judah:
37: 13 the *k* of Hamath, the *k* of Arpad,
37: 13 the *k* of the city of Sepharvaim,
37: 21 to me concerning Sennacherib *k*
37: 33 the LORD says concerning the *k*
37: 37 So Sennacherib *k* of Assyria broke
37: 38 his son succeeded him as *k*.
38: 6 from the hand of the *k* of Assyria.
38: 9 A writing of Hezekiah *k* of Judah
39: 1 son of Baladan *k* of Babylon sent
39: 3 the prophet went to *K* Hezekiah
39: 7 in the palace of the *k* of Babylon.''
41: 21 your arguments,'' says Jacob's *K*.
43: 15 Israel's Creator, your *K*.''
44: 6 Israel's *K* and Redeemer,
Jer 1: 2 of Josiah son of Amon *k* of Judah,
1: 3 son of Josiah *k* of Judah,
1: 3 son of Josiah *k* of Judah,
3: 6 During the reign of *K* Josiah,
4: 9 *k* and the officials will lose heart,
8: 19 Is her *K* no longer there?''
10: 7 O *K* of the nations?
10: 10 he is the living God, the eternal *K*.
13: 18 to the *k* and to the queen mother,
15: 4 son of Hezekiah *k* of Judah did
20: 4 Judah over to the *k* of Babylon,
21: 1 the LORD when *K* Zedekiah sent
21: 2 because Nebuchadnezzar *k*
21: 4 using to fight the *k* of Babylon
21: 7 hand over Zedekiah *k* of Judah,
21: 7 to Nebuchadnezzar *k* of Babylon
21: 10 into the hands of the *k* of Babylon,
22: 1 to the palace of the *k* of Judah
22: 2 word of the LORD, O *k* of Judah,
22: 6 says about the palace of the *k*
22: 10 Do not weep for the dead *k*,
22: 11 who succeeded his father as *k*
22: 15 ''Does it make you a *k*
22: 18 son of Josiah *k* of Judah:
22: 24 son of Jehoiakim *k* of Judah,
22: 25 to Nebuchadnezzar *k* of Babylon
23: 5 a *K* who will reign wisely
24: 1 by Nebuchadnezzar *k* of Babylon,
24: 1 son of Jehoiakim *k* of Judah
24: 8 deal with Zedekiah *k* of Judah,
25: 1 of Nebuchadnezzar *k* of Babylon.
25: 1 son of Josiah *k* of Judah,
25: 3 of Josiah son of Amon *k* of Judah
25: 9 and my servant Nebuchadnezzar *k*
Jer 25: 11 and these nations will serve the *k*
25: 12 I will punish the *k* of Babylon
25: 19 Pharaoh *k* of Egypt, his attendants,
25: 26 the *k* of Sheshach will drink it too.
26: 1 son of Josiah *k* of Judah,
26: 18 in the days of Hezekiah *k* of Judah.
26: 19 ''Did Hezekiah *k* of Judah
26: 21 When *K* Jehoiakim and all his
26: 21 the *k* sought to put him to death.
26: 22 *K* Jehoiakim, however, sent
26: 23 and took him to *K* Jehoiakim,
27: 1 son of Josiah *k* of Judah,
27: 3 Jerusalem to Zedekiah *k* of Judah.
27: 6 to my servant Nebuchadnezzar *k*
27: 8 will not serve Nebuchadnezzar *k*
27: 9 You will not serve the *k* of Babylon
27: 11 under the yoke of the *k* of Babylon
27: 12 message to Zedekiah *k* of Judah.
27: 12 under the yoke of the *k* of Babylon;
27: 13 any nation that will not serve the *k*
27: 14 'You will never serve the *k*
27: 17 Serve the *k* of Babylon,
27: 18 and in the palace of the *k* of Judah
27: 20 of Jehoiakim *k* of Judah into exile
27: 20 which Nebuchadnezzar *k*
27: 21 and in the palace of the *k* of Judah
28: 1 in the reign of Zedekiah *k* of Judah,
28: 2 the yoke of the *k* of Babylon.
28: 3 house that Nebuchadnezzar *k*
28: 4 son of Jehoiakim *k* of Judah
28: 4 the yoke of the *k* of Babylon.' ''
28: 11 of Nebuchadnezzar *k* of Babylon
28: 14 them serve Nebuchadnezzar *k*
29: 2 (This was after *K* Jehoiachin
29: 3 to *K* Nebuchadnezzar in Babylon.
29: 3 whom Zedekiah *k* of Judah sent
29: 16 LORD says about the *k* who sits
29: 21 to Nebuchadnezzar *k* of Babylon,
29: 22 whom the *k* of Babylon burned
30: 9 and David their *k*,
32: 1 year of Zedekiah *k* of Judah,
32: 2 The army of the *k*
32: 3 Now Zedekiah *k* of Judah had
32: 3 city over to the *k* of Babylon,
32: 4 Zedekiah *k* of Judah will not
32: 4 handed over to the *k* of Babylon,
32: 28 to Nebuchadnezzar *k* of Babylon,
32: 36 handed over to the *k* of Babylon';
34: 1 While Nebuchadnezzar *k*
34: 2 Go to Zedekiah *k* of Judah
34: 2 city over to the *k* of Babylon,
34: 3 You will see the *k* of Babylon
34: 4 of the LORD, O Zedekiah *k*
34: 6 this to Zedekiah *k* of Judah,
34: 7 of the *k* of Babylon was fighting
34: 8 LORD after *K* Zedekiah had made
34: 21 to the army of the *k* of Babylon,
34: 21 ''I will hand Zedekiah *k* of Judah
35: 1 son of Josiah *k* of Judah:
35: 11 But when Nebuchadnezzar *k*
36: 1 son of Josiah *k* of Judah,
36: 9 son of Josiah *k* of Judah,
36: 16 report all these words to the *k*.''
36: 20 they went to the *k* in the courtyard
36: 21 The *k* sent Jehudi to get the scroll,
36: 21 it to the *k* and all the officials
36: 22 and the *k* was sitting in the winter
36: 23 *k* cut them off with a scribe's knife
36: 24 *k* and all his attendants who heard
36: 25 and Gemariah urged the *k* not
36: 26 Jerahmeel, a son of the *k*,
36: 26 the *k* commanded Jerahmeel,
36: 27 After the *k* burned the scroll
36: 28 which Jehoiakim *k*
36: 29 Also tell Jehoiakim *k* of Judah,
36: 29 on it that the *k* of Babylon would
36: 30 the LORD says about Jehoiakim *k*
36: 32 of the scroll that Jehoiakim *k*
37: 1 by Nebuchadnezzar *k* of Babylon;
37: 1 son of Josiah was made *k* of Judah
37: 3 *K* Zedekiah, however, sent Jehucal
37: 7 of Israel, says: Tell the *k* of Judah,
37: 17 Then *K* Zedekiah sent for him
37: 17 handed over to the *k* of Babylon.''
37: 18 Then Jeremiah said to *K* Zedekiah,
37: 19 *k* of Babylon will not attack you
37: 20 my lord the *k*, please listen.
37: 21 *K* Zedekiah then gave orders

Jer 38: 3 to the army of the *k* of Babylon,
38: 4 Then the officials said to the *k*,
38: 5 your hands,'' *K* Zedekiah
38: 5 ''The *k* can do nothing
38: 7 While the *k* was sitting
38: 9 and said to him, ''My lord the *k*,
38: 10 the *k* commanded Ebed-Melech
38: 14 *K* Zedekiah sent for Jeremiah
38: 14 to ask you something,'' the *k* said
38: 16 But *K* Zedekiah swore this oath
38: 17 to the officers of the *k* of Babylon,
38: 18 to the officers of the *k* of Babylon,
38: 19 *K* Zedekiah said to Jeremiah,
38: 22 left in the palace of the *k*
38: 22 to the officials of the *k* of Babylon.
38: 23 captured by the *k* of Babylon;
38: 25 and what the *k* said to you;
38: 25 'Tell us what you said to the *k*
38: 26 'I was pleading with the *k* not
38: 27 heard his conversation with the *k*.
38: 27 them everything the *k* had ordered
39: 1 Nebuchadnezzar *k*
39: 1 year of Zedekiah *k* of Judah,
39: 3 officials of the *k* of Babylon came
39: 3 officials of the *k* of Babylon.
39: 4 When Zedekiah *k* of Judah
39: 5 to Nebuchadnezzar *k* of Babylon
39: 6 There at Riblah the *k*
39: 11 Now Nebuchadnezzar *k*
39: 13 officers of the *k* of Babylon sent
40: 5 whom the *k* of Babylon has
40: 7 the open country heard that the *k*
40: 9 and serve the *k* of Babylon,
40: 11 other countries heard that the *k*
40: 14 ''Don't you know that Baalis *k*
41: 2 killing the one whom the *k*
41: 9 defense against Baasha *k* of Israel.
41: 9 was the one *K* Asa had made
41: 18 whom the *k* of Babylon had
42: 11 afraid of the *k* of Babylon,
43: 10 for my servant Nebuchadnezzar *k*
44: 30 as I handed Zedekiah *k* of Judah
44: 30 going to hand Pharaoh Hophra *k*
44: 30 to Nebuchadnezzar *k* of Babylon,
45: 1 son of Josiah *k* of Judah,
46: 2 Pharaoh Neco *k* of Egypt,
46: 2 by Nebuchadnezzar *k* of Babylon
46: 2 son of Josiah *k* of Judah:
46: 13 of Nebuchadnezzar *k* of Babylon
46: 17 'Pharaoh *k* of Egypt is only a loud
46: 18 As surely as I live,'' declares the *K*,
46: 26 to Nebuchadnezzar *k* of Babylon
48: 15 declares the *K*, whose name is
49: 28 which Nebuchadnezzar *k*
49: 30 ''Nebuchadnezzar *k*
49: 34 in the reign of Zedekiah *k* of Judah:
49: 38 and destroy her *k* and officials,''
50: 17 was Nebuchadnezzar *k* of Babylon
50: 17 was the *k* of Assyria;
50: 18 as I punished the *k* of Assyria.
50: 18 ''I will punish the *k* of Babylon
50: 43 *k* of Babylon has heard reports
51: 31 to announce to the *k* of Babylon
51: 34 ''Nebuchadnezzar *k*
51: 57 declares the *K*, whose name is
51: 59 Babylon with Zedekiah *k* of Judah
52: 1 old when he became *k*,
52: 3 rebelled against the *k* of Babylon.
52: 4 Nebuchadnezzar *k*
52: 5 the eleventh year of *K* Zedekiah.
52: 8 army pursued *K* Zedekiah
52: 9 taken to the *k* of Babylon at Riblah
52: 10 There at Riblah the *k*
52: 12 of Nebuchadnezzar *k* of Babylon,
52: 12 who served the *k* of Babylon,
52: 15 gone over to the *k* of Babylon.
52: 20 which *K* Solomon had made
52: 26 brought them to the *k* of Babylon
52: 27 land of Hamath, the *k* had them
52: 31 he released Jehoiachin *k* of Judah
52: 31 the exile of Jehoiachin *k* of Judah,
52: 31 the year Evil-Merodach became *k*
52: 34 Day by day the *k* of Babylon gave
La 2: 6 both *k* and priest.
2: 9 Her *k* and her princes are exiled
Eze 1: 2 year of the exile of *K* Jehoiachin—
7: 27 *k* will mourn, the prince will be
17: 12 carried off her *k* and her nobles,
Eze 17: 12 'The *k* of Babylon went
17: 15 But the *k* rebelled against him
17: 16 in the land of the *k* who put him
19: 9 brought him to the *k* of Babylon.
21: 19 sword of the *k* of Babylon to take,
21: 21 For the *k* of Babylon will stop
24: 2 the *k* of Babylon has laid siege
26: 7 against Tyre Nebuchadnezzar *k*
26: 7 *k* of kings, with horses and chariots
28: 12 take up a lament concerning the *k*
29: 2 face against Pharaoh *k* of Egypt
29: 3 against you, Pharaoh *k* of Egypt,
29: 18 Nebuchadnezzar *k*
29: 19 to Nebuchadnezzar *k* of Babylon,
30: 10 of Nebuchadnezzar *k* of Babylon.
30: 21 the arm of Pharaoh *k* of Egypt.
30: 22 I am against Pharaoh *k* of Egypt.
30: 24 the arms of the *k* of Babylon
30: 25 into the hand of the *k* of Babylon
30: 25 the arms of the *k* of Babylon,
31: 2 say to Pharaoh *k* of Egypt
32: 2 up a lament concerning Pharaoh *k*
32: 11 '' 'The sword of the *k* of Babylon
37: 22 There will be one *k* over all of them
37: 24 '' 'My servant David will be *k*
Da 1: 1 Nebuchadnezzar *k* of Babylon
1: 1 the reign of Jehoiakim *k* of Judah,
1: 2 the Lord delivered Jehoiakim *k*
1: 3 Then the *k* ordered Ashpenaz,
1: 5 *k* assigned them a daily amount
1: 10 The *k* would then have my head
1: 10 ''I am afraid of my lord the *k*,
1: 18 set by the *k* to bring them in,
1: 19 The *k* talked with them,
1: 20 which the *k* questioned them,
1: 21 until the first year of *K* Cyrus.
2: 2 So the *k* summoned the magicians,
2: 2 came in and stood before the *k*,
2: 4 the astrologers answered the *k*
2: 4 ''O *k*, live forever! Tell your
2: 5 The *k* replied to the astrologers,
2: 7 ''Let the *k* tell his servants
2: 8 *k* answered, ''I am certain that you
2: 10 No *k*, however great and mighty,
2: 10 The astrologers answered the *k*,
2: 10 earth who can do what the *k* asks!
2: 11 No one can reveal it to the *k*
2: 11 What the *k* asks is too difficult.
2: 12 This made the *k* so angry
2: 15 ''Why did the *k* issue such a harsh
2: 16 Daniel went in to the *k*
2: 23 known to us the dream of the *k*.''
2: 24 me to the *k*, and I will interpret his
2: 24 whom the *k* had appointed
2: 25 Arioch took Daniel to the *k*
2: 25 who can tell the *k* what his dream
2: 26 The *k* asked Daniel (also called
2: 27 to the *k* the mystery he has asked
2: 28 has shown *K* Nebuchadnezzar
2: 29 ''As you were lying there, O *k*,
2: 30 O *k*, may know the interpretation
2: 31 O *k*, and there before you stood
2: 36 now we will interpret it to the *k*.
2: 37 You, O *k*, are the *k* of kings.
2: 45 has shown the *k* what will take
2: 46 *K* Nebuchadnezzar fell prostrate
2: 47 *k* said to Daniel, ''Surely your God
2: 48 Then the *k* placed Daniel
2: 49 request the *k* appointed Shadrach,
3: 1 *K* Nebuchadnezzar made an image
3: 3 image that *K* Nebuchadnezzar had
3: 5 of gold that *K* Nebuchadnezzar has
3: 7 gold that *K* Nebuchadnezzar had
3: 9 They said to *K* Nebuchadnezzar,
3: 9 to King Nebuchadnezzar, ''O *k*,
3: 10 You have issued a decree, O *k*,
3: 12 who pay no attention to you, O *k*.
3: 13 men were brought before the *k*,
3: 16 and Abednego replied to the *k*,
3: 17 us from your hand, O *k*.
3: 18 we want you to know, O *k*,
3: 24 Then *K* Nebuchadnezzar leaped
3: 24 They replied, ''Certainly, O *k*.''
3: 30 Then the *k* promoted Shadrach,
4: 1 *K* Nebuchadnezzar, To the peoples
4: 18 dream that I, *K* Nebuchadnezzar,
4: 19 So the *k* said, ''Belteshazzar,
4: 22 O *k*, are that tree! You have
Da 4: 23 ''You, O *k*, saw a messenger,
4: 24 issued against my lord the *k*:
4: 24 ''This is the interpretation, O *k*,
4: 27 O *k*, be pleased to accept my
4: 28 happened to *K* Nebuchadnezzar.
4: 29 as the *k* was walking on the roof
4: 31 for you, *K* Nebuchadnezzar:
4: 37 exalt and glorify the *K* of heaven,
5: 1 *K* Belshazzar gave a great banquet
5: 2 so that the *k* and his nobles,
5: 3 and the *k* and his nobles, his wives
5: 5 The *k* watched the hand as it wrote
5: 7 The *k* called out for the enchanters
5: 8 or tell the *k* what it meant.
5: 9 So *K* Belshazzar became
5: 10 hearing the voices of the *k*
5: 10 ''O *k*, live forever!'' she said.
5: 11 *K* Nebuchadnezzar your father—
5: 11 your father—your father the *k*,
5: 12 whom the *k* called Belteshazzar,
5: 13 So Daniel was brought before the *k*
5: 13 the exiles my father the *k* brought
5: 13 the *k* said to him, ''Are you Daniel,
5: 17 I will read the writing for the *k*
5: 17 Then Daniel answered the *k*,
5: 18 ''O *k*, the Most High God gave
5: 19 Those the *k* wanted to put to death
5: 30 That very night Belshazzar, *k*
6: 2 so that the *k* might not suffer loss.
6: 3 qualities that the *k* planned
6: 6 as a group to the *k* and said:
6: 6 ''O *K* Darius, live forever!
6: 7 O *k*, shall be thrown
6: 7 all agreed that the *k* should issue
6: 8 O *k*, issue the decree and put it
6: 9 *K* Darius put the decree in writing.
6: 12 O *k*, would be thrown
6: 12 So they went to the *k* and spoke
6: 12 *k* answered, ''The decree stands—
6: 13 Then they said to the *k*, ''Daniel,
6: 13 pays no attention to you, O *k*,
6: 14 When the *k* heard this, he was
6: 15 and said to him, ''Remember, O *k*,
6: 15 as a group to the *k* and said to him,
6: 15 or edict that the *k* issues can be
6: 16 So the *k* gave the order,
6: 16 *k* said to Daniel, ''May your God,
6: 17 *k* sealed it with his own signet ring
6: 18 Then the *k* returned to his palace
6: 19 the *k* got up and hurried
6: 21 answered, ''O *k*, live forever!
6: 22 done any wrong before you, O *k*.''
6: 23 *k* was overjoyed and gave orders
6: 25 *K* Darius wrote to all the peoples,
7: 1 year of Belshazzar *k* of Babylon,
7: 24 After them another *k* will arise,
8: 1 year of *K* Belshazzar's reign,
8: 21 The shaggy goat is the *k* of Greece,
8: 21 horn between his eyes is the first *k*.
8: 23 a stern-faced *k*, a master of intrigue
10: 1 year of Cyrus *k* of Persia,
10: 13 there with the *k* of Persia.
11: 3 Then a mighty *k* will appear,
11: 5 *k* of the South will become strong,
11: 6 The daughter of the *k*
11: 6 go to the *k* of the North
11: 7 the forces of the *k* of the North
11: 8 For some years he will leave the *k*
11: 9 Then the *k* of the North will invade
11: 9 the realm of the *k* of the South
11: 11 fight against the *k* of the North,
11: 11 the *k* of the South will march out
11: 12 the *k* of the South will be filled
11: 13 For the *k* of the North will muster
11: 14 rise against the *k* of the South.
11: 15 Then the *k* of the North will come
11: 17 an alliance with the *k* of the South.
11: 25 The *k* of the South will wage war
11: 25 courage against the *k* of the South.
11: 28 The *k* of the North will return
11: 36 ''The *k* will do as he pleases.
11: 40 of the end the *k* of the South will
11: 40 the *k* of the North will storm out
Hos 1: 1 son of Jehoash *k* of Israel:
3: 4 will live many days without *k*
3: 5 their God and David their *k*.
5: 13 and sent to the great *k* for help.
7: 3 ''They delight the *k*

Hos 7: 5 On the day of the festival of our *k*
8: 10 the oppression of the mighty *k*.
10: 3 But even if we had a *k*,
10: 3 Then they will say, "We have no *k*
10: 6 as tribute for the great *k*
10: 7 Samaria and its *k* will float away
10: 15 the *k* of Israel will be completely
13: 10 Where is your *k*, that he may save
13: 10 'Give me a *k* and princes'?
13: 11 So in my anger I gave you a *k*,
Am 1: 1 son of Jehoash was *k* of Israel.
1: 1 when Uzziah was *k* of Judah
1: 5 I will destroy the *k* who is
1: 8 I will destroy the *k* of Ashdod
1: 15 Her *k* will go into exile,
2: 1 the bones of Edom's *k*,
5: 26 have lifted up the shrine of your *k*,
7: 10 a message to Jeroboam *k* of Israel:
Jnh 3: 6 When the news reached the *k*
3: 7 "By the decree of the *k*
Mic 2: 13 *k* will pass through before them,
4: 9 have you no *k*?
6: 5 *k* of Moab counseled
Na 3: 18 O *k* of Assyria, your shepherds
Zep 1: 1 of Josiah son of Amon *k* of Judah:
3: 15 The LORD, the *K* of Israel,
Hag 1: 1 In the second year of *K* Darius,
1: 15 in the second year of *K* Darius.
Zec 7: 1 In the fourth year of *K* Darius,
9: 5 Gaza will lose her *k*
9: 9 See, your *k* comes to you,
11: 6 over to his neighbor and his *k*.
14: 5 in the days of Uzziah *k* of Judah.
14: 9 The LORD will be *k*
14: 16 year after year to worship the *K*,
14: 17 up to Jerusalem to worship the *K*,
Mal 1: 14 I am a great *k*," says the LORD
Mt 1: 6 and Jesse the father of *K* David.
2: 1 during the time of *K* Herod,
2: 2 is the one who has been born *k*
2: 3 When *K* Herod heard this he was
2: 9 After they had heard the *k*,
5: 35 for it is the city of the Great *K*.
14: 9 The *k* was distressed, but
18: 23 of heaven is like a *k* who wanted
21: 5 'See, your *k* comes to you,
22: 2 heaven is like a *k* who prepared
22: 7 The *k* was enraged.
22: 11 "But when the *k* came in to see
22: 13 "Then the *k* told the attendants,
25: 34 the *K* will say to those on his right,
25: 40 *K* will reply, 'I tell you the truth,
27: 11 "Are you the *k* of the Jews?" "Yes,
27: 29 "Hail, *K* of the Jews!" they said.
27: 37 JESUS, THE *K* OF THE JEWS.
27: 42 he can't save himself! He's the *k*
Mk 6: 14 *K* Herod heard about this,
6: 22 The *k* said to the girl, "Ask me
6: 25 hurried in to the *k* with the request:
6: 26 The *k* was greatly distressed,
15: 2 "Are you the *k* of the Jews?"
15: 9 to release to you the *k* of the Jews
15: 12 with the one you call the *k*
15: 18 out to him, "Hail, *K* of the Jews!"
15: 26 THE *K* OF THE JEWS.
15: 32 Let this Christ, this *K* of Israel,
Lk 1: 5 In the time of Herod *k*
14: 31 suppose a *k* is about to go to war
14: 31 to go to war against another *k*.
19: 12 to have himself appointed *k*
19: 14 We don't want this man to be our *k*
19: 15 "He was made *k*, however,
19: 27 me to be *k* over them—
19: 38 "Blessed is the *k* who comes
23: 2 and claims to be Christ, a *k*."
23: 3 "Are you the *k* of the Jews?" "Yes,
23: 37 "If you are the *k* of the Jews,
23: 38 THE *K* OF THE JEWS.
Jn 1: 49 of God; you are the *K* of Israel."
6: 15 to come and make him *k* by force,
12: 13 "Blessed is the *K* of Israel!"
12: 15 see, your *k* is coming,
18: 33 "Are you the *k* of the Jews?"
18: 37 "You are a *k*, then!" said Pilate.
18: 37 "You are right in saying I am a *k*.
18: 39 me to release 'the *k* of the Jews'?"
19: 3 saying, "Hail, O *k* of the Jews!"
19: 12 claims to be a *k* opposes Caesar."
Jn 19: 14 "Here is your *k*," Pilate said
19: 15 I crucify your *k*?" Pilate asked.
19: 15 "We have no *k* but Caesar,"
19: 19 JESUS OF NAZARETH, THE *K*
19: 21 claimed to be *k* of the Jews."
19: 21 "Do not write 'The *K* of the Jews,'
Ac 7: 10 goodwill of Pharaoh *k* of Egypt;
7: 18 Then another *k*, who knew nothing
12: 1 this time that *K* Herod arrested
12: 20 a trusted personal servant of the *k*,
13: 21 Then the people asked for a *k*,
13: 22 Saul, he made David their *k*.
17: 7 saying that there is another *k*,
25: 13 A few days later *K* Agrippa
25: 14 discussed Paul's case with the *k*.
25: 24 *K* Agrippa, and all who are present
25: 26 especially before you, *K* Agrippa,
26: 2 and began his defense: "*K* Agrippa,
26: 7 O *k*, it is because of this hope that
26: 13 About noon, O *k*, as I was
26: 19 *K* Agrippa, I was not disobedient
26: 26 The *k* is familiar with these things,
26: 27 *K* Agrippa, do you believe
26: 30 *k* rose, and with him the governor
2Co 11: 32 under *K* Aretas had the city
1Ti 1: 17 Now to the *K* eternal, immortal,
6: 15 the *K* of kings and Lord of lords,
Heb 7: 1 This Melchizedek was *k* of Salem
7: 2 his name means "*k*
7: 2 "*k* of Salem" means "*k* of peace."
1Pe 2: 13 to the *k*, as the supreme authority,
2: 17 of believers, fear God, honor the *k*.
Rev 9: 11 *k* over them the angel of the Abyss,
15: 3 *K* of the ages.
17: 11 and now is not, is an eighth *k*.
17: 14 he is Lord of lords and *K* of kings—
19: 16 *K* OF KINGS AND LORD

KING'S (KING)

Ge 14: 17 of Shaveh (that is, the *K* Valley).
39: 20 place where the *k* prisoners were
Nu 20: 17 We will travel along the *k* highway
21: 22 We will travel along the *k* highway
Jdg 3: 21 and plunged it into the *k* belly.
1Sa 18: 18 I should become the *k* son-in-law?"
18: 23 matter to become the *k* son-in-law?
18: 26 to become the *k* son-in-law.
18: 27 he might become the *k* son-in-law.
20: 29 he has not come to the *k* table."
21: 8 because the *k* business was urgent
22: 14 as loyal as David, the *k* son-in-law,
22: 17 But the *k* officials were not willing
26: 16 Where are the *k* spear
26: 22 "Here is the *k* spear," David
2Sa 9: 11 David's table like one of the *k* sons.
9: 13 because he always ate at the *k* table
11: 1 sent Joab out with the *k* men
11: 20 the *k* anger may flare up,
11: 24 and some of the *k* men died.
13: 4 Amnon, "Why do you, the *k* son,
13: 23 invited all the *k* sons to
13: 27 Amnon and the rest of the *k* sons.
13: 29 Then all the *k* sons got up,
13: 30 struck down all the *k* sons;
13: 33 report that all the *k* sons are dead.
13: 35 the king, "See, the *k* sons are here;
13: 36 finished speaking, the *k* sons came
14: 1 knew that the *k* heart longed
14: 28 without seeing the *k* face.
14: 32 Now then, I want to see the *k* face,
15: 15 The *k* officials answered him,
15: 35 anything you hear in the *k* palace.
16: 2 are for the *k* household to ride on,
16: 6 and all the *k* officials with stones,
18: 12 not lift my hand against the *k* son.
18: 18 and erected it in the *K* Valley
18: 20 because the *k* son is dead."
18: 29 about to send the *k* servant
19: 18 ford to take the *k* household over
19: 42 any of the *k* provisions?
24: 4 *k* word, however, overruled Joab
1Ki 1: 9 invited all his brothers, the *k* sons,
1: 19 and has invited all the *k* sons,
1: 25 He has invited all the *k* sons,
1: 28 So she came into the *k* presence
1: 44 they have put him on the *k* mule,
2: 19 a throne brought for the *k* mother,
4: 27 and all who came to the *k* table.
1Ki 5: 17 At the *k* command they removed
13: 6 and the *k* hand was restored
22: 6 Lord will give it into the *k* hand."
22: 12 will give it into the *k* hand."
22: 15 will give it into the *k* hand."
22: 26 and to Joash the *k* son and say,
2Ki 8: 15 and spread it over the *k* face,
9: 34 for she was a *k* daughter."
11: 4 Then he showed them the *k* son.
11: 12 Jehoiada brought out the *k* son
13: 16 Elisha put his hands on the *k* hands
15: 5 Jotham the *k* son had charge
16: 15 the *k* burnt offering and his grain
22: 12 and Asaiah the *k* attendant:
24: 15 to Babylon the *k* mother,
25: 4 walls near the *k* garden,
25: 29 his life ate regularly at the *k* table.
1Ch 9: 18 stationed at the *K* Gate on the east,
18: 17 were chief officials at the *k* side.
21: 4 *k* word, however, overruled Joab;
21: 6 the *k* command was repulsive
25: 2 under the *k* supervision.
25: 5 sons of Heman the *k* seer.
26: 30 of the LORD and for the *k* service.
27: 32 of Hacmoni took care of the *k* sons
27: 33 Ahithophel was the *k* counselor.
27: 33 Hushai the Arkite was the *k* friend.
29: 6 of the *k* work gave willingly.
2Ch 8: 15 deviate from the *k* commands
18: 5 for God will give it into the *k* hand
18: 11 will give it into the *k* hand."
18: 25 of the city and to Joash the *k* son,
21: 17 all the goods found in the *k* palace,
23: 3 to them, "The *k* son shall reign,
23: 11 and his sons brought out the *k* son
24: 8 At the *k* command, a chest was
24: 11 in by the Levites to the *k* officials
28: 7 killed Maaseiah the *k* son,
29: 25 and Gad the *k* seer and Nathan
30: 6 At the *k* command, couriers went
34: 20 and Asaiah the *k* attendant:
35: 7 all from the *k* own possessions.
35: 15 Heman and Jeduthun the *k* seer.
Ezr 7: 27 it into the *k* heart to bring honor
7: 28 and all the *k* powerful officials.
8: 36 also delivered the *k* orders
Ne 2: 8 to Asaph, keeper of the *k* forest,
2: 9 and gave them the *k* letters.
2: 14 the Fountain Gate and the *K* Pool,
3: 15 Pool of Siloam, by the *K* Garden,
5: 4 to pay the *k* tax on our fields
11: 23 were under the *k* orders,
11: 24 was the *k* agent in all affairs
Est 1: 5 enclosed garden of the *k* palace,
1: 7 in keeping with the *k* liberality.
1: 8 By the *k* command each guest was
1: 12 delivered the *k* command,
1: 18 to all the *k* nobles in the same way.
1: 20 when the *k* edict is proclaimed
2: 2 the *k* personal attendants proposed
2: 3 the *k* eunuch, who is in charge
2: 8 When the *k* order and edict had
2: 8 also was taken to the *k* palace
2: 9 maids selected from the *k* palace
2: 13 her from the harem to the *k* palace.
2: 14 the *k* eunuch who was in charge
2: 15 the *k* eunuch who was in charge
2: 19 Mordecai was sitting at the *k* gate.
2: 21 Mordecai was sitting at the *k* gate,
2: 21 two of the *k* officers who guarded
3: 2 officials at the *k* gate knelt down
3: 3 at the *k* gate asked Mordecai,
3: 3 do you disobey the *k* command?"
3: 8 and they do not obey the *k* laws;
3: 8 it is not in the *k* best interest
3: 12 all Haman's orders to the *k* satraps,
3: 13 couriers to all the *k* provinces
3: 15 Spurred on by the *k* command,
4: 2 he went only as far as the *k* gate,
4: 5 one of the *k* eunuchs assigned
4: 6 of the city in front of the *k* gate.
4: 8 her to go into the *k* presence to beg
4: 11 "All the *k* officials and the people
4: 13 you are in the *k* house you alone
5: 1 of the palace, in front of the *k* hall.
5: 8 Then I will answer the *k* question."
5: 9 he saw Mordecai at the *k* gate
5: 13 Mordecai sitting at the *k* gate."

Est 6: 2 two of the *k* officers, who guarded
6: 9 to one of the *k* most noble princes.
6: 10 the Jew, who sits at the *k* gate.
6: 12 Mordecai returned to the *k* gate.
6: 14 the *k* eunuchs arrived
7: 8 as the word left the *k* mouth,
7: 10 Then the *k* fury subsided.
8: 5 the Jews in all the *k* provinces.
8: 8 and seal it with the *k* signet ring—
8: 8 decree in the *k* name in behalf
8: 8 no document written in the *k* name
8: 10 dispatches with the *k* signet ring,
8: 11 The *k* edict granted the Jews
8: 14 spurred on by the *k* command.
8: 15 left the *k* presence wearing
9: 3 *k* administrators helped the Jews,
9: 12 done in the rest of the *k* provinces?
9: 16 were in the *k* provinces
9: 25 came to the *k* attention,
Ps 45: 5 pierce the hearts of the *k* enemies;
61: 6 Increase the days of the *k* life,
Pr 14: 28 A large population is a *k* glory,
16: 14 A *k* wrath is a messenger of death,
16: 15 When a *k* face brightens, it means
19: 12 A *k* rage is like the roar of a lion,
20: 2 A *k* wrath is like the roar of a lion;
21: 1 The *k* heart is in the hand
25: 5 the wicked from the *k* presence,
25: 6 exalt yourself in the *k* presence,
Ecc 2: 12 What more can the *k* successor do
4: 15 the youth, the *k* successor.
8: 2 Obey the *k* command, I say,
8: 3 in a hurry to leave the *k* presence.
8: 4 Since a *k* word is supreme,
Isa 23: 15 seventy years, the span of a *k* life.
Jer 38: 6 the *k* son, which was
39: 4 at night by way of the *k* garden,
41: 1 and had been one of the *k* officers,
41: 10 the *k* daughters along with all
43: 6 *k* daughters whom Nebuzaradan
52: 7 walls near the *k* garden,
52: 33 his life ate regularly at the *k* table.
Da 1: 4 qualified to serve in the *k* palace.
1: 5 and wine from the *k* table.
1: 5 were to enter the *k* service.
1: 19 so they entered the *k* service.
2: 14 the commander of the *k* guard,
2: 15 He asked the *k* officer, "Why did
3: 22 The *k* command was so urgent
3: 28 and defied the *k* command
5: 8 Then all the *k* wise men came in,
6: 24 At the *k* command, the men who
8: 27 and went about the *k* business.
11: 26 eat from the *k* provisions will try
Am 7: 1 locusts after the *k* share had been
7: 13 because this is the *k* sanctuary
Zep 1: 8 and the *k* sons
Ac 12: 20 they depended on the *k* country
Heb 11: 23 they were not afraid of the *k* edict.
11: 27 left Egypt, not fearing the *k* anger;

KINGDOM (KING)

Ge 10: 10 centers of his *k* were Babylon,
20: 9 guilt upon me and my *k?*
Ex 19: 6 you will be for me a *k* of priests
Nu 24: 7 their *k* will be exalted.
32: 33 and the *k* of Og king of Bashan—
32: 33 son of Joseph the *k* of Sihon king
Dt 3: 4 region of Argob, Og's *k* in Bashan.
3: 10 towns of Og's *k* in Bashan.
3: 13 and also all of Bashan, the *k* of Og,
17: 18 When he takes the throne of his *k*,
17: 20 time over his *k* in Israel.
Jos 13: 12 that is, the whole *k* of Og in Bashan
1Sa 13: 13 he would have established your *k*
13: 14 But now your *k* will not endure;
15: 28 The LORD has torn the *k* of Israel
18: 8 What more can he get but the *k?*"
20: 31 nor your *k* will be established.
24: 20 and that the *k* of Israel will be
28: 17 The LORD has torn the *k* out
2Sa 3: 10 and transfer the *k* from the house
3: 28 and my *k* are forever innocent
5: 12 and had exalted his *k* for the sake
7: 12 body, and I will establish his *k*.
7: 13 the throne of his *k* forever.
7: 16 and your *k* will endure forever
8: 6 in the Aramean *k* of Damascus,
2Sa 16: 3 me back my grandfather's *k*.' "
16: 8 The LORD has handed the *k*
1Ki 2: 15 and the *k* has gone to my brother;
2: 15 know," he said, "the *k* was mine.
2: 22 as well request the *k* for him—
2: 46 The *k* was now firmly established
10: 20 ever been made for any other *k*.
11: 11 will most certainly tear the *k* away
11: 13 Yet I will not tear the whole *k*
11: 31 to tear the *k* out of Solomon's hand
11: 34 I will not take the whole *k* out
11: 35 I will take the *k* from his son's
12: 21 to regain the *k* for Rehoboam son
12: 26 "The *k* will now likely revert
14: 8 I tore the *k* away from the house
18: 10 or *k* claimed you were not there,
18: 10 or *k* where my master has not sent
2Ki 14: 5 After the *k* was firmly in his grasp,
15: 19 strengthen his own hold on the *k*.
20: 13 or in all his *k* that Hezekiah did not
1Ch 10: 14 and turned the *k* over to David son
12: 23 to turn Saul's *k* over to him,
14: 2 that his *k* had been highly exalted
16: 20 from one *k* to another.
17: 11 own sons, and I will establish his *k*.
17: 14 over my house and my *k* forever;
18: 6 in the Aramean *k* of Damascus,
22: 10 throne of his *k* over Israel forever.'
28: 5 the throne of the *k* of the LORD
28: 7 I will establish his *k* forever
29: 11 Yours, O LORD, is the *k;*
2Ch 1: 1 himself firmly over his *k*,
9: 19 ever been made for any other *k*.
11: 1 and to regain the *k* for Rehoboam.
11: 17 They strengthened the *k* of Judah
13: 8 plan to resist the *k* of the LORD,
14: 5 and the *k* was at peace under him.
17: 5 The LORD established the *k*
20: 30 the *k* of Jehoshaphat was at peace,
21: 3 but he had given the *k* to Jehoram
21: 4 firmly over his father's *k*,
22: 9 powerful enough to retain the *k*.
25: 3 After the *k* was firmly
29: 21 as a sin offering for the *k*,
32: 15 or *k* has been able to deliver his
33: 13 back to Jerusalem and to his *k*.
36: 20 his sons until the *k* of Persia came
Ezr 7: 13 any of the Israelites in my *k*,
Ne 9: 35 Even while they were in their *k*,
Est 1: 4 displayed the vast wealth of his *k*
1: 14 the king and were highest in the *k*.
1: 22 dispatches to all parts of the *k*,
3: 6 throughout the whole *k* of Xerxes.
3: 8 of your *k* who keep themselves
5: 3 to half the *k*, it will be given you."
5: 6 up to half the *k*, it will be granted."
7: 2 up to half the *k*, it will be granted."
9: 30 provinces of the *k* of Xerxes—
Ps 45: 6 justice will be the scepter of your *k*.
103: 19 and his *k* rules over all.
105: 13 from one *k* to another.
145: 11 They will tell of the glory of your *k*
145: 12 and the glorious splendor of your *k*
145: 13 Your *k* is an everlasting *k*,
Ecc 4: 14 born in poverty within his *k*.
Isa 9: 7 and over his *k*,
19: 2 *k* against *k*.
34: 12 have nothing there to be called a *k*,
39: 2 or in all his *k* that Hezekiah did not
60: 12 *k* that will not serve you will perish
Jer 18: 7 I announce that a nation or *k* is
18: 9 or *k* is to be built up and planted,
27: 8 *k* will not serve Nebuchadnezzar
La 2: 2 has brought her *k* and its princes
Eze 17: 14 so that the *k* would be brought low,
29: 14 There they will be a lowly *k*.
Da 1: 20 and enchanters in his whole *k*.
2: 39 Next, a third *k*, one of bronze,
2: 39 "After you, another *k* will rise,
2: 40 there will be a fourth *k*, strong
2: 41 so this will be a divided *k;*
2: 42 so this *k* will be partly strong
2: 44 will set up a *k* that will never be
4: 3 His *k* is an eternal *k;*
4: 18 in my *k* can interpret it for me.
4: 26 means that your *k* will be restored
4: 34 his *k* endures from generation
4: 36 to me for the glory of my *k*.
Da 5: 7 the third highest ruler in the *k*."
5: 11 a man in your *k* who has the spirit
5: 16 the third highest ruler in the *k*."
5: 28 Your *k* is divided and given
5: 29 the third highest ruler in the *k*.
5: 31 Darius the Mede took over the *k*,
6: 1 satraps to rule throughout the *k*,
6: 3 to set him over the whole *k*.
6: 26 his *k* will not be destroyed,
6: 26 part of my *k* people must fear
7: 14 and his *k* is one that will never be
7: 18 of the Most High will receive the *k*
7: 22 came when they possessed the *k*.
7: 23 beast is a fourth *k* that will appear
7: 24 kings who will come from this *k*.
7: 27 His *k* will be an everlasting *k*,
9: 1 ruler over the Babylonian *k*—
10: 13 prince of the Persian *k* resisted me
11: 2 everyone against the *k* of Greece.
11: 5 and will rule his own *k*
11: 17 come with the might of his entire *k*
11: 17 in order to overthrow the *k*,
11: 21 He will invade the *k*
Hos 1: 4 I will put an end to the *k* of Israel.
Am 7: 13 sanctuary and the temple of the *k*."
9: 8 are on the sinful *k*.
Ob :21 And the *k* will be the LORD's.
Mt 3: 2 Repent, for the *k* of heaven is near
4: 17 Repent, for the *k* of heaven is near
4: 23 preaching the good news of the *k*,
5: 3 for theirs is the *k* of heaven.
5: 10 for theirs is the *k* of heaven.
5: 19 great in the *k* of heaven.
5: 19 least in the *k* of heaven,
5: 20 you will certainly not enter the *k*
6: 10 your *k* come,
6: 33 But seek first his *k* and his
7: 21 Lord,' will enter the *k* of heaven,
8: 11 Isaac and Jacob in the *k* of heaven.
8: 12 the subjects of the *k* will be thrown
9: 35 preaching the good news of the *k*
10: 7 preach this message: 'The *k*
11: 11 least in the *k* of heaven is greater
11: 12 the *k* of heaven has been forcefully
12: 25 "Every *k* divided against itself will
12: 26 How then can his *k* stand?
12: 28 then the *k* of God has come
13: 11 knowledge of the secrets of the *k*
13: 19 hears the message about the *k*
13: 24 "The *k* of heaven is like a man who
13: 31 *k* of heaven is like a mustard seed,
13: 33 "The *k* of heaven is like yeast that
13: 38 stands for the sons of the *k*.
13: 41 of his *k* everything that causes sin
13: 43 the sun in the *k* of their Father.
13: 44 *k* of heaven is like treasure hidden
13: 45 the *k* of heaven is like a merchant
13: 47 *k* of heaven is like a net that was let
13: 52 has been instructed about the *k*
16: 19 the keys of the *k* of heaven;
16: 28 the Son of Man coming in his *k*."
18: 1 the greatest in the *k* of heaven?"
18: 3 you will never enter the *k*
18: 4 the greatest in the *k* of heaven.
18: 23 the *k* of heaven is like a king who
19: 12 because of the *k* of heaven.
19: 14 for the *k* of heaven belongs to such
19: 23 man to enter the *k* of heaven.
19: 24 for a rich man to enter the *k* of God
20: 1 "For the *k* of heaven is like
20: 21 the other at your left in your *k*."
21: 31 the prostitutes are entering the *k*
21: 43 "Therefore I tell you that the *k*
22: 2 "The *k* of heaven is like a king who
23: 13 You shut the *k* of heaven
24: 7 rise against nation, and *k* against *k*.
24: 14 gospel of the *k* will be preached
25: 1 "At that time the *k*
25: 34 the *k* prepared for you
26: 29 anew with you in my Father's *k*."
Mk 1: 15 "The *k* of God is near.
3: 24 If a *k* is divided against itself,
3: 24 against itself, that *k* cannot stand.
4: 11 "The secret of the *k*
4: 26 "This is what the *k* of God is like.
4: 30 "What shall we say the *k*
6: 23 I will give you, up to half my *k*."
9: 1 before they see the *k* of God come

Mk 9:47 better for you to enter the *k* of God
10:14 for the *k* of God belongs to such
10:15 anyone who will not receive the *k*
10:23 for the rich to enter the *k* of God!"
10:24 how hard it is to enter the *k* of God
10:25 for a rich man to enter the *k* of God
11:10 "Blessed is the coming *k*
12:34 "You are not far from the *k* of God
13:8 rise against nation, and *k* against *k*.
14:25 day when I drink it anew in the *k*
15:43 who was himself waiting for the *k*
Lk 1:33 Jacob forever; his *k* will never
4:43 of the *k* of God to the other towns
6:20 for yours is the *k* of God.
7:28 in the *k* of God is greater than he."
8:1 proclaiming the good news of the *k*
8:10 knowledge of the secrets of the *k*
9:2 out to preach the *k* of God
9:11 spoke to them about the *k* of God,
9:27 before they see the *k* of God."
9:60 you go and proclaim the *k* of God
9:62 fit for service in the *k* of God."
10:9 'The *k* of God is near you.'
10:11 sure of this: The *k* of God is near.'
11:2 your *k* come.
11:17 "Any *k* divided against itself will
11:18 himself, how can his *k* stand?
11:20 then the *k* of God has come to you.
12:31 seek his *k*, and these things will be
12:32 has been pleased to give you the *k*.
13:18 "What is the *k* of God like?
13:20 What shall I compare the *k* of God
13:28 all the prophets in the *k* of God,
13:29 places at the feast in the *k* of God.
14:15 eat at the feast in the *k* of God."
16:16 the good news of the *k*
17:20 when the *k* of God would come,
17:20 *k* of God does not come visibly,
17:21 because the *k* of God is within you
18:16 for the *k* of God belongs to such
18:17 anyone who will not receive the *k*
18:24 for the rich to enter the *k* of God!
18:25 for a rich man to enter the *k* of God
18:29 for the sake of the *k* of God will fail
19:11 and the people thought that the *k*
21:10 rise against nation, and *k* against *k*.
21:31 you know that the *k* of God is near.
22:16 until it finds fulfillment in the *k*
22:18 the vine until the *k* of God comes."
22:29 And I confer on you a *k*, just
22:30 and drink at my table in my *k*
23:42 me when you come into your *k*."
23:51 he was waiting for the *k* of God.
Jn 3:3 he cannot see the *k* of God."
3:5 he cannot enter the *k* of God.
18:36 now my *k* is from another place."
18:36 "My *k* is not of this world.
Ac 1:3 and spoke about the *k* of God.
1:6 going to restore the *k* to Israel?"
8:12 he preached the good news of the *k*
14:22 hardships to enter the *k* of God,"
19:8 arguing persuasively about the *k*
20:25 about preaching the *k* will ever see
28:23 and declared to them the *k* of God
28:31 hindrance he preached the *k*
Ro 14:17 For the *k* of God is not a matter
1Co 4:20 For the *k* of God is not a matter
6:9 the wicked will not inherit the *k*
6:10 swindlers will inherit the *k* of God.
15:24 hands over the *k* to God the Father
15:50 blood cannot inherit the *k* of God,
Gal 5:21 live like this will not inherit the *k*
Eph 2:2 and of the ruler of the *k* of the air,
5:5 has any inheritance in the *k*
Col 1:12 of the saints in the *k* of light.
1:13 and brought us into the *k*
4:11 among my fellow workers for the *k*
1Th 2:12 who calls you into his *k* and glory.
2Th 1:5 will be counted worthy of the *k*
2Ti 4:1 in view of his appearing and his *k*,
4:18 bring me safely to his heavenly *k*.
Heb 1:8 will be the scepter of your *k*.
12:28 we are receiving a *k* that cannot be
Jas 2:5 to inherit the *k* he promised those
2Pe 1:11 into the eternal *k* of our Lord
Rev 1:6 has made us to be a *k* and priests
1:9 companion in the suffering and *k*
5:10 You have made them to be a *k*
Rev 11:15 of the world has become the *k*
11:15 "The *k* of the world has become
12:10 the power and the *k* of our God,
16:10 his *k* was plunged into darkness.
17:12 who have not yet received a *k*,

KINGDOMS (KING)

Dt 3:21 to all the *k* over there where you
28:25 thing of horror to all the *k* on earth.
Jos 11:10 had been the head of all these *k*.)
1Sa 10:18 and all the *k* that oppressed you.'
1Ki 4:21 ruled over all the *k* from the River
4:24 over all the *k* west of the River,
2Ki 19:15 God over all the *k* of the earth.
19:19 so that all *k* on earth may know
1Ch 29:30 and the *k* of all the other lands.
2Ch 17:10 fell on all the *k* of the lands
20:6 rule over all the *k* of the nations.
20:29 upon all the *k* of the countries
36:23 has given me all the *k* of the earth
Ezr 1:2 has given me all the *k* of the earth
Ne 9:22 "You gave them *k* and nations,
Ps 46:6 Nations are in uproar, *k* fall;
68:32 Sing to God, O *k* of the earth,
79:6 on the *k*
102:22 when the peoples and the *k*
Isa 10:10 As my hand seized the *k*
10:10 *k* whose images excelled those
13:4 Listen, an uproar among the *k*,
13:19 Babylon, the jewel of *k*,
14:16 and made *k* tremble,
23:11 and made its *k* tremble.
23:17 trade with all the *k* on the face
37:16 God over all the *k* of the earth.
37:20 so that all *k* on earth may know
47:5 queen of *k*.
Jer 1:10 and *k* to uproot and tear down,
1:15 the peoples of the northern *k*,"
10:7 and in all their *k*,
15:4 abhorrent to all the *k* of the earth
24:9 an offense to all the *k* of the earth,
25:26 all the *k* on the face of the earth.
28:8 against many countries and great *k*
29:18 abhorrent to all the *k* of the earth
33:24 has rejected the two *k* he chose'?
34:1 and all his army and all the *k*
34:17 abhorrent to all the *k* of the earth.
49:28 Concerning Kedar and the *k*
51:20 with you I destroy *k*,
51:27 summon against her these *k*:
Eze 29:15 It will be the lowliest of *k*
37:22 or be divided into two *k*.
Da 2:44 It will crush all those *k*
4:17 Most High is sovereign over the *k*
4:25 Most High is sovereign over the *k*
4:32 Most High is sovereign over the *k*
5:21 High God is sovereign over the *k*
7:17 great beasts are four *k* that will rise
7:23 different from all the other *k*
7:27 of the *k* under the whole heaven
8:22 off represent four *k* that will
Am 6:2 Are you better than those *k*?
Na 3:5 and the *k* your shame.
Zep 3:8 to gather the *k*
Hag 2:22 shatter the power of the foreign *k*.
Mt 4:8 showed him all the *k* of the world
Lk 4:5 in an instant all the *k* of the world.
Heb 11:33 who through faith conquered *k*,

KINGS (KING)

Ge 14:3 All these latter *k* joined forces
14:5 and the *k* allied with him went out
14:9 of Ellasar—four *k* against five.
14:10 and when the *k* of Sodom
14:11 The four *k* seized all the goods
14:17 Kedorlaomer and the *k* allied
17:6 and *k* will come from you.
17:16 *k* of peoples will come from her."
35:11 and *k* will come from your body.
36:31 These were the *k* who reigned
Nu 31:8 and Reba—the five *k* of Midian.
Dt 3:8 from these two *k* of the Amorites
3:21 your God has done to these two *k*.
4:47 the two Amorite *k* east
7:24 He will give their *k* into your hand,
31:4 the *k* of the Amorites, whom he
Jos 2:10 the two *k* of the Amorites east
5:1 Now when all the Amorite *k* west
Jos 5:1 and all the Canaanite *k*
9:1 Now when all the *k* west
9:1 as Lebanon (the *k* of the Hittites,
9:10 to the two *k* of the Amorites east
10:5 Then the five *k* of the Amorites—
10:5 the *k* of Jerusalem, Hebron,
10:6 all the Amorite *k* from the hill
10:16 Now the five *k* had fled
10:17 told that the five *k* had been found
10:22 and bring those five *k* out to me."
10:23 So they brought the five *k* out
10:23 the *k* of Jerusalem, Hebron,
10:24 When they had brought these *k*
10:24 feet on the necks of these *k*."
10:26 Joshua struck and killed the *k*
10:40 slopes, together with all their *k*.
10:42 All these *k* and their lands Joshua
11:1 to the *k* of Shimron and Acshaph,
11:2 and to the northern *k* who were
11:5 All these *k* joined forces
11:12 their *k* and put them to the sword.
11:17 He captured all their *k*
11:18 against all these *k* for a long time.
12:1 These are the *k* of the land whom
12:7 These are the *k* of the land that
12:24 of Tirzah one thirty-one *k* in all.
24:12 you—also the two Amorite *k*.
Jdg 1:7 "Seventy *k* with their thumbs
5:3 Hear this, you *k*! Listen, you rulers
5:19 the *k* of Canaan fought
5:19 "*K* came, they fought;
8:5 and Zalmunna, the *k* of Midian."
8:12 Zalmunna, the two *k* of Midian
8:26 worn by the *k* of Midian
1Sa 14:47 the Ammonites, Edom, the *k*
27:6 to the *k* of Judah ever since.
2Sa 10:19 When all the *k* who were vassals
11:1 at the time when *k* go off to war,
1Ki 3:13 you will have no equal among *k*.
4:34 sent by all the *k* of the world,
10:15 traders and from all the Arabian *k*
10:23 than all the other *k* of the earth.
10:29 them to all the *k* of the Hittites
14:19 of the annals of the *k* of Israel.
14:29 of the annals of the *k* of Judah?
15:7 of the annals of the *k* of Judah?
15:23 of the annals of the *k* of Judah?
15:31 of the annals of the *k* of Israel?
16:5 of the annals of the *k* of Israel?
16:14 of the annals of the *k* of Israel?
16:20 of the annals of the *k* of Israel?
16:27 of the annals of the *k* of Israel?
16:33 anger than did all the *k* of Israel
20:1 Accompanied by thirty-two *k*
20:12 the *k* were drinking in their tents,
20:16 and the 32 *k* allied with him were
20:24 all the *k* from their commands
20:31 we have heard that the *k*
22:39 of the annals of the *k* of Israel?
22:45 of the annals of the *k* of Judah?
2Ki 1:18 of the annals of the *k* of Israel?
3:10 called us three *k* together only
3:13 who called us three *k* together
3:21 had heard that the *k* had come
3:23 "Those *k* must have fought
7:6 and Egyptian *k* to attack us!"
8:18 in the ways of the *k* of Israel,
8:23 of the annals of the *k* of Judah?
10:4 "If two *k* could not resist him,
10:34 of the annals of the *k* of Israel?
12:18 and Ahaziah, the *k* of Judah—
12:19 of the annals of the *k* of Judah?
13:8 of the annals of the *k* of Israel?
13:12 of the annals of the *k* of Israel?
13:13 in Samaria with the *k* of Israel.
14:15 of the annals of the *k* of Israel?
14:16 in Samaria with the *k* of Israel.
14:18 of the annals of the *k* of Judah?
14:28 of the annals of the *k* of Israel?
14:29 with his fathers, the *k* of Israel.
15:6 of the annals of the *k* of Judah?
15:11 of the annals of the *k* of Israel.
15:15 of the annals of the *k* of Israel.
15:21 of the annals of the *k* of Israel?
15:26 of the annals of the *k* of Israel.
15:31 of the annals of the *k* of Israel?
15:36 of the annals of the *k* of Judah?
16:3 in the ways of the *k* of Israel

2Ki 16: 19 of the annals of the *k* of Judah?
17: 2 but not like the *k* of Israel who
17: 8 as the practices which the *k*
18: 5 him among all the *k* of Judah,
19: 11 Surely you have heard what the *k*
19: 17 that the Assyrian *k* have laid waste
20: 20 of the annals of the *k* of Judah?
21: 17 of the annals of the *k* of Judah?
21: 25 of the annals of the *k* of Judah?
23: 5 by the *k* of Judah to burn incense
23: 11 of the LORD the horses that the *k*
23: 12 pulled down the altars the *k*
23: 19 shrines at the high places that the *k*
23: 22 of the *k* of Israel and the *k* of Judah
23: 28 of the annals of the *k* of Judah?
24: 5 of the annals of the *k* of Judah?
25: 28 of the other *k* who were with him
1Ch 1: 43 These were the *k* who reigned
9: 1 in the book of the *k* of Israel.
16: 21 for their sake he rebuked *k*:
19: 9 while the *k* who had come were
20: 1 at the time when *k* go off to war,
2Ch 1: 17 them to all the *k* of the Hittites
9: 14 Also all the *k* of Arabia
9: 22 than all the other *k* of the earth.
9: 23 All the *k* of the earth sought
9: 26 ruled over all the *k* from the River
12: 8 and serving the *k* of other lands.''
16: 11 in the book of the *k* of Judah
20: 34 in the book of the *k* of Israel.
21: 6 in the ways of the *k* of Israel,
21: 13 in the ways of the *k* of Israel,
21: 20 but not in the tombs of the *k*.
24: 16 buried with the *k* in the City
24: 25 but not in the tombs of the *k*.
24: 27 annotations on the book of the *k*.
25: 26 in the book of the *k* of Judah
26: 23 for burial that belonged to the *k*,
27: 7 in the book of the *k* of Israel
28: 2 in the ways of the *k* of Israel
28: 23 ''Since the gods of the *k*
28: 26 in the book of the *k* of Judah
28: 27 in the tombs of the *k* of Israel.
30: 6 from the hand of the *k* of Assyria.
32: 4 Why should the *k* of Assyria come
32: 32 Amoz in the book of the *k* of Judah
33: 18 in the annals of the *k* of Israel.
34: 11 beams for the buildings that the *k*
35: 18 and none of the *k* of Israel had ever
35: 27 in the book of the *k* of Israel
36: 8 in the book of the *k* of Israel
Ezr 4: 15 troublesome to *k* and provinces,
4: 19 history of revolt against *k*
4: 20 has had powerful *k* ruling
6: 14 Darius and Artaxerxes, *k* of Persia.
7: 12 king of *k*, To Ezra the priest,
9: 7 and our *k* and our priests have been
9: 7 at the hand of foreign *k*,
9: 9 in the sight of the *k* of Persia:
Ne 9: 24 along with their *k* and the peoples
9: 32 of the *k* of Assyria until today.
9: 32 upon our *k* and leaders,
9: 34 Our *k*, our leaders, our priests
9: 37 to the *k* you have placed over us.
Est 10: 2 of the annals of the *k* of Media
Job 3: 14 with *k* and counselors of the earth,
12: 18 off the shackles put on by *k*
34: 18 Is he not the One who says to *k*,
36: 7 he enthrones them with *k*
Ps 2: 2 The *k* of the earth take their stand
2: 10 Therefore, you *k*, be wise;
45: 9 Daughters of *k* are
47: 9 for the *k* of the earth belong to God
48: 4 When the *k* joined forces,
68: 12 ''*K* and armies flee in haste;
68: 14 the Almighty scattered the *k*
68: 29 *k* will bring you gifts.
72: 10 the *k* of Sheba and Seba
72: 10 *k* of Tarshish and of distant shores
72: 11 All *k* will bow down to him
76: 12 he is feared by the *k* of the earth.
89: 27 of the *k* of the earth.
102: 15 all the *k* of the earth will revere
105: 14 for their sake he rebuked *k*:
110: 5 he will crush *k* on the day
119: 46 speak of your statutes before *k*
135: 10 and killed mighty *k*—
135: 11 and all the *k* of Canaan—
Ps 136: 17 who struck down great *k*,
136: 18 and killed mighty *k*—
138: 4 May all the *k* of the earth praise
144: 10 to the One who gives victory to *k*,
148: 11 *k* of the earth and all nations,
149: 8 to bind their *k* with fetters,
Pr 8: 15 By me *k* reign
16: 12 *K* detest wrongdoing,
16: 13 *K* take pleasure in honest lips;
22: 29 He will serve before *k*;
25: 2 out a matter is the glory of *k*.
25: 3 so the hearts of *k* are unsearchable.
31: 3 your vigor on those who ruin *k*.
31: 4 not for *k* to drink wine,
31: 4 ''It is not for *k*, O Lemuel—
Ecc 2: 8 and the treasure of *k* and provinces
Isa 1: 1 Ahaz and Hezekiah, *k* of Judah.
7: 16 of the two *k* you dread will be laid
10: 8 'Are not my commanders all *k*?'
10: 13 like a mighty one I subdued their *k*.
14: 9 all those who were *k*
14: 18 All the *k* of the nations lie in state,
19: 11 a disciple of the ancient *k*''?
24: 21 and the *k* on the earth below.
37: 11 Surely you have heard what the *k*
37: 18 that the Assyrian *k* have laid waste
41: 2 and subdues *k* before him.
45: 1 and to strip *k* of their armor,
49: 7 ''*K* will see you and rise up,
49: 23 *K* will be your foster fathers,
52: 15 and *k* will shut their mouths
60: 3 *k* to the brightness of your dawn.
60: 10 and their *k* will serve you.
60: 11 their *k* led in triumphal procession.
62: 2 and all *k* your glory;
Jer 1: 15 ''Their *k* will come and set up their
1: 18 against the *k* of Judah, its officials,
2: 26 they, their *k* and their officials,
8: 1 the bones of the *k* and officials
13: 13 including the *k* who sit
17: 19 through which the *k* of Judah go in
17: 20 O *k* of Judah and all people
17: 25 then *k* who sit on David's throne
19: 3 O *k* of Judah and people
19: 4 nor the *k* of Judah ever knew,
19: 13 of the *k* of Judah will be defiled like
20: 5 all the treasures of the *k* of Judah.
22: 4 then *k* who sit on David's throne
25: 14 by many nations and great *k*;
25: 18 and the towns of Judah, its *k*
25: 20 all the *k* of the Philistines (those
25: 20 the foreign people there; all the *k*
25: 22 all the *k* of Tyre and Sidon;
25: 22 the *k* of the coastlands
25: 24 all the *k* of Arabia and all the *k*
25: 25 all the *k* of Zimri, Elam and Media;
25: 26 Media; and all the *k* of the north,
27: 3 Then send word to the *k* of Edom,
27: 7 and great *k* will subjugate him.
32: 32 they, their *k* and officials,
34: 5 the former *k* who preceded you,
44: 9 and by the *k* and queens of Judah
44: 17 our *k* and our officials did
44: 21 your *k* and your officials
46: 25 on Egypt and her gods and her *k*,
50: 41 a great nation and many *k*
51: 11 The LORD has stirred up the *k*
51: 28 the *k* of the Medes,
52: 32 of the other *k* who were with him
La 4: 12 The *k* of the earth did not believe,
Eze 26: 7 king of *k*, with horses and chariots,
27: 33 you enriched the *k* of the earth.
27: 35 their *k* shudder with horror
28: 17 I made a spectacle of you before *k*.
32: 10 their *k* will shudder with horror
32: 29 ''Edom is there, her *k* and all her
43: 7 idols of their *k* at their high places.
43: 7 neither they nor their *k*—
43: 9 and the lifeless idols of their *k*,
Da 2: 21 he sets up *k* and deposes them.
2: 37 You, O king, are the king of *k*.
2: 44 ''In the time of those *k*, the God
2: 47 and the Lord of *k* and a revealer
7: 24 earlier ones; he will subdue three *k*.
7: 24 ten horns are ten *k* who will come
8: 20 ram that you saw represents the *k*
9: 6 who spoke in your name to our *k*,
9: 8 we and our *k*, our princes
Da 11: 2 Three more *k* will appear in Persia,
11: 27 The two *k*, with their hearts bent
Hos 1: 1 Ahaz and Hezekiah, *k* of Judah,
7: 7 All their *k* fall,
8: 4 They set up *k* without my consent;
Mic 1: 1 Ahaz and Hezekiah, *k* of Judah—
1: 14 deceptive to the *k* of Israel.
Hab 1: 10 They deride *k*
Mt 10: 18 and *k* as witnesses to them
17: 25 ''From whom do the *k*
Mk 13: 9 and *k* as witnesses to them.
Lk 10: 24 and *k* wanted to see what you see
21: 12 and you will be brought before *k*
22: 25 ''The *k* of the Gentiles lord it
Ac 4: 26 The *k* of the earth take their stand
9: 15 and their *k* and before the people
1Co 4: 8 You have become *k*—
4: 8 so that we might be *k* with you!
4: 8 wish that you really had become *k*
1Ti 2: 2 for *k* and all those in authority,
6: 15 the King of *k* and Lord of lords,
Heb 7: 1 returning from the defeat of the *k*
Rev 1: 5 and the ruler of the *k* of the earth.
6: 15 Then the *k* of the earth, the princes
10: 11 nations, languages and *k*.''
16: 12 the way for the *k* from the East.
16: 14 out to the *k* of the whole world,
16: 16 Then they gathered the *k* together
17: 2 With her the *k* of the earth
17: 9 They are also seven *k*.
17: 12 as *k* along with the beast.
17: 12 you saw are ten *k* who have not yet
17: 14 he is Lord of lords and King of *k*—
17: 18 rules over the *k* of the earth.''
18: 3 *k* of the earth committed adultery
18: 9 ''When the *k* of the earth who
19: 16 KING OF K AND LORD
19: 18 so that you may eat the flesh of *k*,
19: 19 Then I saw the beast and the *k*
21: 24 the *k* of the earth will bring their

KINGS' (KING)

Pr 30: 28 yet it is found in *k'* palaces.
Mt 11: 8 wear fine clothes are in *k'* palaces.

KINGSHIP (KING)

1Sa 10: 16 what Samuel had said about the *k*.
10: 25 the people the regulations of the *k*.
11: 14 to Gilgal and there reaffirm the *k*.''
1Ch 11: 10 gave his *k* strong support
2Ch 13: 5 has given the *k* of Israel to David
Ecc 4: 14 come from prison to the *k*,
Mic 4: 8 *k* will come to the Daughter

KINNERETH

Nu 34: 11 the slopes east of the Sea of *K*.
Dt 3: 17 from *K* to the Sea of the Arabah
Jos 11: 2 south of *K*, in the western foothills
12: 3 from the Sea of *K* to the Sea
13: 27 up to the end of the Sea of *K*).
19: 35 Hammath, Rakkath, *K*, Adamah,
1Ki 15: 20 and all *K* in addition to Naphtali.

KINSMAN (KIN)

Ru 3: 2 servant girls you have been, a *k*
Pr 7: 4 and call understanding your *k*;

KINSMAN-REDEEMER (REDEEM)

Ru 3: 9 over me, since you are a *k*.''
3: 12 of kin, there is a *k* nearer than I.
4: 1 When the *k* he had mentioned
4: 3 Then he said to the *k*, ''Naomi,
4: 6 *k* said, ''Then I cannot redeem it
4: 8 the *k* said to Boaz, ''Buy it yourself
4: 14 day has not left you without a *k*.

KINSMAN-REDEEMERS (REDEEM)

Ru 2: 20 close relative; he is one of our *k*.''

KINSMEN (KIN)

1Ch 12: 2 they were *k* of Saul from the tribe
12: 29 men of Benjamin, Saul's *k*— 3,000,
2Ch 28: 8 from their *k* two hundred thousand
29: 34 so their *k* the Levites helped them
Ezr 8: 17 what to say to Iddo and his *k*,
Job 19: 14 My *k* have gone away;

KIOS

Ac 20:15 sail from there and arrived off *K*.

KIR

2Ki 16: 9 He deported its inhabitants to *K*
Isa 15: 1 *K* in Moab is ruined,
22: 6 *K* uncovers the shield.
Am 1: 5 of Aram will go into exile to *K*,"
9: 7 and the Arameans from *K*?

KIR HARESETH

2Ki 3:25 Only *K* was left with its stones in
Isa 16: 7 and grieve for the raisin cakes of *K*.
16:11 my inmost being for *K*.
Jer 48:31 I moan for the men of *K*.
48:36 like a flute for the men of *K*.

KIRIATH

Jos 18:28 Jerusalem), Gibeah and *K*—

KIRIATH ARBA

Ge 23: 2 She died at *K* (that is, Hebron) in
35:27 Mamre, near *K* (that is, Hebron),
Jos 14:15 (Hebron used to be called *K*
15:13 Jephunneh a portion in Judah—*K*,
15:54 Humtah, *K* (that is, Hebron)
20: 7 and *K* (that is, Hebron)
21:11 gave them *K* (that is, Hebron),
Jdg 1:10 in Hebron (formerly called *K*)
Ne 11:25 of the people of Judah lived in *K*

KIRIATH BAAL

Jos 15:60 *K* (that is, Kiriath Jearim)
18:14 *K* (that is, Kiriath Jearim),

KIRIATH HUZOTH

Nu 22:39 Then Balaam went with Balak to *K*

KIRIATH JEARIM

Jos 9:17 Gibeon, Kephirah, Beeroth and *K*.
15: 9 down toward Baalah (that is, *K*).
15:60 Kiriath Baal (that is, *K*)
18:14 Kiriath Baal (that is, *K*),
18:15 at the outskirts of *K* on the west,
Jdg 18:12 their way they set up camp near *K*
18:12 west of *K* is called Mahaneh Dan
1Sa 6:21 messengers to the people of *K*,
7: 1 So the men of *K* came and
7: 2 that the ark remained at *K*,
1Ch 2:50 Shobal the father of *K*,
2:52 Shobal the father of *K*
2:53 and the clans of *K*: the Ithrites,
13: 5 to bring the ark of God from *K*.
13: 6 went to Baalah of Judah (*K*)
2Ch 1: 4 the ark of God from *K*
Ezr 2:25 of Azmaveth 42 of *K*,
Ne 7:29 of Beth Azmaveth 42 of *K*,
Jer 26:20 son of Shemaiah from *K*

KIRIATH SANNAH

Jos 15:49 Socoh, Dannah, *K* (that is, Debir),

KIRIATH SEPHER

Jos 15:15 Debir (formerly called *K*).
15:16 man who attacks and captures *K*."
Jdg 1:11 living in Debir (formerly called *K*).
1:12 man who attacks and captures *K*."

KIRIATHAIM

Nu 32:37 rebuilt Heshbon, Elealeh and *K*,
Jos 13:19 Kedemoth, Mephaath, *K*, Sibmah,
1Ch 6:76 *K*, together with their pasturelands
Jer 48: 1 *K* will be disgraced and captured;
48:23 Nebo and Beth Diblathaim, to *K*,
Eze 25: 9 and *K*—the glory of that land.

KISH

1Sa 9: 1 whose name was *K* son of Abiel,
9: 3 and *K* said to his son Saul,
9: 3 to Saul's father *K* were lost,
10:11 that has happened to the son of *K*?
10:21 Finally Saul son of *K* was chosen.
14:51 Saul's father *K* and Abner's father
2Sa 21:14 in the tomb of Saul's father *K*,
1Ch 8:30 followed by Zur, *K*, Baal, Ner,
8:33 father of *K*, *K* the father of Saul,
9:36 followed by Zur, *K*, Baal, Ner,
9:39 father of *K*, *K* the father of Saul,
1Ch 12: 1 of Saul son of *K* (they were
23:21 The sons of Mahli: Eleazar and *K*.
23:22 the sons of *K*, married them.
24:29 From *K*: the son of *K*: Jerahmeel.
26:28 the seer and by Saul son of *K*,
2Ch 29:12 *K* son of Abdi and Azariah son
Est 2: 5 the son of Shimei, the son of *K*,
Ac 13:21 and he gave them Saul son of *K*,

KISHI

1Ch 6:44 Ethan son of *K*, the son of Abdi,

KISHION

Jos 19:20 Anaharath, Rabbith, *K*, Ebez,
21:28 *K*, Daberath, Jarmuth

KISHON

Jdg 4: 7 and his troops to the *K* River
4:13 to the *K* River.
5:21 The river *K* swept them away,
5:21 the age-old river, the river *K*.
1Ki 18:40 brought down to the *K* Valley
Ps 83: 9 to Sisera and Jabin at the river *K*,

KISLEV

Ne 1: 1 In the month of *K*
Zec 7: 1 of the ninth month, the month of *K*

KISLON

Nu 34:21 Elidad son of *K*, from the tribe

KISLOTH TABOR

Jos 19:12 the sunrise to the territory of *K*

KISS (KISSED KISSES KISSING)

Ge 27:26 "Come here, my son, and *k* me."
31:28 even let me *k* my grandchildren
2Sa 15: 5 take hold of him and *k* him.
20: 9 beard with his right hand to *k* him.
1Ki 19:20 "Let me *k* my father and mother
Job 31:27 and my hand offered them a *k*
Ps 2:12 *K* the Son, lest he be angry
85:10 and peace *k* each other.
Pr 24:26 is like a *k* on the lips.
SS 1: 2 Let him *k* me
8: 1 I would *k* you,
Hos 13: 2 and *k* the calf-idols."
Mt 26:48 The one I *k* is the man; arrest him."
Mk 14:44 "The one I *k* is the man; arrest him
Lk 7:45 You did not give me a *k*,
22:47 He approached Jesus to *k* him,
22:48 the Son of Man with a *k*?"
Ro 16:16 Greet one another with a holy *k*.
1Co 16:20 Greet one another with a holy *k*.
2Co 13:12 Greet one another with a holy *k*.
1Th 5:26 Greet all the brothers with a holy *k*
1Pe 5:14 Greet one another with a *k* of love.

KISSED (KISS)

Ge 27:27 So he went to him and *k* him.
29:11 Then Jacob *k* Rachel and began
29:13 He embraced him and *k* him
31:55 morning Laban *k* his
33: 4 arms around his neck and *k* him.
45:15 And he *k* all his brothers
48:10 his father *k* them and embraced
50: 1 and wept over him and *k* him.
Ex 4:27 at the mountain of God and *k* him.
18: 7 and bowed down and *k* him.
Ru 1: 9 she *k* them and they wept aloud
1:14 Then Orpah *k* her mother-in-law
1Sa 10: 1 poured it on Saul's head and *k* him,
20:41 Then they *k* each other
2Sa 14:33 And the king *k* Absalom.
19:39 king *k* Barzillai and gave him his
1Ki 19:18 all whose mouths have not *k* him."
Pr 7:13 She took hold of him and *k* him
Mt 26:49 "Greetings, Rabbi!" and *k* him.
Mk 14:45 Judas said, "Rabbi!" and *k* him.
Lk 7:38 *k* them and poured perfume
15:20 arms around him and *k* him.
Ac 20:37 as they embraced him and *k* him.

KISSES (KISS)

Pr 27: 6 The *k* of an enemy may be profuse,
SS 1: 2 with the *k* of his mouth—

KISSING (KISS)

Lk 7:45 has not stopped *k* my feet.

KIT

Eze 9: 2 in linen who had a writing *k*
9: 3 in linen who had the writing *k*
9:11 the man in linen with the writing *k*

KITCHENS

Eze 46:24 "These are the *k* where those who

KITE

Lev 11:14 any kind of black *k*, any kind
11:14 the black vulture, the red *k*,
Dt 14:13 the black vulture, the red *k*,
14:13 the black *k*, any kind of falcon,

KITLISH

Jos 15:40 Cabbon, Lahmas, *K*, Gederoth,

KITRON

Jdg 1:30 out the Canaanites living in *K*

KITTIM

Ge 10: 4 Tarshish, the *K* and the Rodanim.
Nu 24:24 come from the shores of *K*;
1Ch 1: 7 Tarshish, the *K* and the Rodanim.
Jer 2:10 Cross over to the coasts of *K*

KNEAD (KNEADED KNEADING WELL-KNEADED)

Ge 18: 6 and *k* it and bake some bread."
Jer 7:18 and the women *k* the dough

KNEADED (KNEAD)

1Sa 28:24 *k* it and baked bread without yeast.
2Sa 13: 8 She took some dough, *k* it,

KNEADING (KNEAD)

Ex 8: 3 and into your ovens and *k* troughs.
12:34 shoulders in *k* troughs wrapped
Dt 28: 5 and your *k* trough will be blessed.
28:17 and your *k* trough will be cursed.
Hos 7: 4 from the *k* of the dough till it rises.

KNEE (KNEE DEEP KNEES)

Isa 45:23 Before me every *k* will bow;
Eze 7:17 and every *k* will become as weak
21: 7 every *k* become as weak as water.'
Ro 11: 4 who have not bowed the *k*
14:11 'Every *k* will bow before me;
Php 2:10 name of Jesus every *k* should bow,

KNEE-DEEP (KNEE)

Eze 47: 4 led me through water that was *k*.

KNEEL (KNEELING KNELT)

Ge 24:11 He had the camels *k*
Jdg 7: 5 from those who *k* down to drink."
Est 3: 2 But Mordecai would not *k* down
3: 5 saw that Mordecai would not *k*
Ps 22:29 down to the dust will *k* before him
95: 6 let us *k* before the LORD our
Eph 3:14 For this reason I *k*

KNEELING (KNEEL)

1Ki 1:31 face to the ground and, *k*
8:54 where he had been *k*
Mt 20:20 and, *k* down, asked a favor of him.

KNEES (KNEE)

Ge 48:12 removed them from Israel's *k*
50:23 placed at birth on Joseph's *k*.
Dt 28:35 The LORD will afflict your *k*
Jdg 7: 6 got down on their *k* to drink.
1Ki 18:42 and put his face between his *k*.
19:18 all whose *k* have not bowed
2Ki 1:13 and fell on his *k* before Elijah.
Ezr 9: 5 on my *k* with my hands spread out
Job 3:12 Why were there *k* to receive me
4: 4 you have strengthened faltering *k*.
Ps 20: 8 They are brought to their *k* and fall
109:24 My *k* give way from fasting;
Isa 35: 3 steady the *k* that give way;
66:12 and dandled on her *k*.
Da 5: 6 that his *k* knocked together
6:10 times a day he got down on his *k*
10:10 trembling on my hands and *k*.

Na 2:10 Hearts melt, *k* give way,
Mt 18:26 The servant fell on his *k* before him
18:29 "His fellow servant fell to his *k*
Mk 1:40 to him and begged him on his *k*,
5:6 and fell on his *k* in front of him.
10:17 and fell on his *k* before him.
15:19 on their *k*, they worshiped him.
Lk 5:8 he fell at Jesus' *k* and said,
Ac 7:60 Then he fell on his *k* and cried out,
9:40 then he got down on his *k*
Heb 12:12 your feeble arms and weak *k*.

KNELT (KNEEL)

1Ki 1:16 Bathsheba bowed low and *k*
2Ch 6:13 and then *k* down before the whole
7:3 they *k* on the pavement
29:29 everyone present with him *k* down
Est 3:2 officials at the king's gate *k* down
Mt 8:2 and *k* before him and said,
9:18 a ruler came and *k* before him
15:25 The woman came and *k* before him
17:14 a man approached Jesus and *k*
27:29 *k* in front of him and mocked him.
Lk 22:41 *k* down and prayed, "Father,
Ac 20:36 he *k* down with all of them
21:5 there on the beach we *k* to pray.

KNEW (KNOW)

Ge 8:11 Noah *k* that the water had receded
16:4 When she *k* she was pregnant,
38:9 Onan *k* that the offspring would
Dt 7:15 on you the horrible diseases you *k*
34:10 whom the LORD *k* face to face,
Jdg 2:10 who *k* neither the LORD
1Sa 3:13 because of the sin he *k* about;
20:33 Jonathan *k* that his father intended
20:39 only Jonathan and David *k*.)
20:39 (The boy *k* nothing of all this;
22:17 They *k* he was fleeing, yet they did
22:22 I *k* he would be sure to tell Saul.
26:12 No one saw or *k* about it,
28:14 Then Saul *k* it was Samuel,
2Sa 1:10 I *k* that after he had fallen he could
3:37 and all Israel *k* that the king had no
5:12 And David *k* that the LORD had
11:16 a place where he *k* the strongest
14:1 of Zeruiah *k* that the king's heart
17:19 No one *k* anything about it.
1Ki 9:27 his men—sailors who *k* the sea—
2Ki 4:39 though no one *k* what they were.
1Ch 12:32 and *k* what Israel should do—
14:2 And David *k* that the LORD had
2Ch 8:18 own officers, men who *k* the sea.
33:13 Manasseh *k* that the LORD is God
Ne 9:10 for you *k* how arrogantly
Job 23:3 If only I *k* where to find him;
Ps 31:7 and *k* the anguish of my soul.
Pr 24:12 "But we *k* nothing about this,"
Ecc 6:5 it never saw the sun or *k* anything,
Isa 48:4 For I *k* how stubborn you were;
48:7 'Yes, I *k* of them.'
Jer 1:5 you in the womb I *k* you,
11:18 revealed their plot to me, I *k* it,
19:4 nor the kings of Judah ever *k*,
32:8 "I *k* that this was the word
41:4 before anyone *k* about it,
44:3 nor you nor your fathers ever *k*.
44:15 all the men who *k* that their wives
50:24 you were caught before you *k* it;
Eze 28:19 All the nations who *k* you
Da 5:22 yourself, though you *k* all this.
Jnh 1:10 (They *k* he was running away
4:2 I *k* that you are a gracious
Zec 11:11 who were watching me *k* it was
Mt 7:23 tell them plainly, 'I never *k* you.
12:25 Jesus *k* their thoughts
21:45 they *k* he was talking about them.
24:39 they *k* nothing about what would
25:24 'I *k* that you are a hard man,
25:26 you *k* that I harvest where I have
27:18 For he *k* it was out
Mk 1:34 speak because they *k* who he was.
2:8 Immediately Jesus *k*
12:12 they *k* he had spoken the parable
12:15 But Jesus *k* their hypocrisy.
Lk 4:41 because they *k* he was the Christ.
5:22 Jesus *k* what they were thinking
6:8 Jesus *k* what they were thinking
Lk 11:17 Jesus *k* their thoughts
19:22 you wicked servant! You *k*,
20:19 they *k* he had spoken this parable
23:49 But all those who *k* him, including
Jn 2:9 who had drawn the water *k*.
2:24 himself to them, for he *k* all men.
2:25 for he *k* what was in a man.
4:10 "If you *k* the gift of God
8:19 "If you *k* me, you would know my
11:42 I *k* that you always hear me,
13:1 Jesus *k* that the time had come
13:3 Jesus *k* that the Father had put all
13:11 For he *k* who was going
14:7 If you really *k* me, you would know
17:8 They *k* with certainty that I came
18:2 who betrayed him, *k* the place,
21:12 "Who are you?" They *k* it was
Ac 2:30 and *k* that God had promised him
7:18 who *k* nothing about Joseph,
16:3 for they all *k* that his father was
18:25 he *k* only the baptism of John.
Ro 1:21 For although they *k* God,
Heb 10:34 you *k* that you yourselves had

KNIFE (KNIVES)

Ge 22:6 himself carried the fire and the *k*.
22:10 and took the *k* to slay his son.
Ex 4:25 But Zipporah took a flint *k*,
Jdg 19:29 he took a *k* and cut up his
Pr 23:2 and put a *k* to your throat
Jer 36:23 them off with a scribe's *k*

KNIT (CLOSE-KNIT KNITTED)

Job 10:11 and *k* me together with bones
Ps 139:13 you *k* me together

KNITTED (KNIT)

Lev 13:48 any woven or *k* material of linen
13:49 or leather, or woven or *k* material,
13:51 or the woven or *k* material,
13:52 or the woven or *k* material of wool
13:53 or the woven or *k* material,
13:56 or the woven or *k* material.
13:57 or in the woven or *k* material,
13:58 or the woven or *k* material,
13:59 or *k* material, or any leather article,

KNIVES (KNIFE)

Jos 5:2 "Make flint *k* and circumcise
5:3 So Joshua made flint *k*
Pr 30:14 and whose jaws are set with *k*
Isa 18:5 cut off the shoots with pruning *k*,

KNOCK (KNOCKED KNOCKING KNOCKS)

Mt 7:7 *k* and the door will be opened
Lk 11:9 *k* and the door will be opened
Rev 3:20 I am! I stand at the door and *k*.

KNOCKED (KNOCK)

Da 5:6 that his knees *k* together
8:7 the goat *k* him to the ground
Ac 12:13 Peter *k* at the outer entrance,

KNOCKING (KNOCK)

SS 5:2 Listen! My lover is *k*:
Lk 13:25 you will stand outside *k*
Ac 12:16 kept on *k*, and when they opened

KNOCKS (KNOCK)

Ex 21:27 And if he *k* out the tooth
Mt 7:8 and to him who *k*, the door will be
Lk 11:10 and to him who *k*, the door will be
12:36 and *k* they can immediately open

KNOTTED

Eze 27:24 with cords twisted and tightly *k*.

KNOW (FOREKNEW FOREKNOWLEDGE KNEW KNOWING KNOWLEDGE KNOWN KNOWS WELL-KNOWN)

Ge 4:9 is your brother Abel?" "I don't *k*,"
12:11 I *k* what a beautiful woman you are
15:8 how can I *k* that I will gain
15:13 "*K* for certain that your
18:21 If not, I will *k*."
20:6 I *k* you did this with a clear
21:26 "I don't *k* who has done this.
Ge 22:12 Now I *k* that you fear God,
24:14 By this I will *k* that you have
24:49 so I may *k* which way to turn."
27:2 and don't *k* the day of my death.
27:21 to *k* whether you really are my son
29:5 Do you *k* Laban, Nahor's grandson
29:5 "Yes, we *k* him," they answered.
30:26 You *k* how much work I've done
30:29 "You *k* how I have worked for you
31:6 You *k* that I've worked
31:32 Jacob did not *k* that Rachel had
37:13 Israel said to Joseph, "As you *k*,
42:33 is how I will *k* whether you are
42:34 me so I will *k* that you are not spies
43:7 How were we to *k* he would say,
43:22 We don't *k* who put our silver
44:15 Don't you *k* that a man like me can
44:27 'You *k* that my wife bore me two
47:6 And if you *k* of any among them
48:19 and said, "I *k*, my son, I *k*.
Ex 1:8 who did not *k* about Joseph,
3:19 I *k* that the king of Egypt will not
4:14 Aaron the Levite? I *k* he can speak
5:2 I do not *k* the LORD and I will not
6:7 you will *k* that I am the LORD
7:5 And the Egyptians will *k* that I am
7:17 By this you will *k* that I am
8:10 so that you may *k* there is no one
8:22 so that you will *k* that I, the LORD
9:14 so you may *k* that there is no one
9:29 so you may *k* that the earth is
9:30 I *k* that you and your officials still
10:2 and that you may *k* that I am
10:26 get there we will not *k* what we are
11:7 you will *k* that the LORD makes
14:4 and the Egyptians will *k* that I am
14:18 The Egyptians will *k* that I am
16:6 the evening you will *k* that it was
16:8 "You will *k* that it was the LORD
16:12 you will *k* that I am the LORD
16:15 For they did not *k* what it was.
18:11 Now I *k* that the LORD is greater
23:9 you yourselves *k* how it feels
29:46 They will *k* that I am the LORD
31:13 so you may *k* that I am the LORD,
32:1 we don't *k* what has happened
32:22 "You *k* how prone these people are
32:23 we don't *k* what has happened
33:12 have not let me *k* whom you will
33:12 'I *k* you by name and you have
33:13 teach me your ways so I may *k* you
33:16 How will anyone *k* that you are
33:17 with you and I *k* you by name."
36:1 to *k* how to carry out all the work
Lev 5:17 even though he does not *k* it,
23:43 your descendants will *k* that I had
Nu 10:31 You *k* where we should camp
14:34 and *k* what it is like to have me
16:28 is how you will *k* that the LORD
16:30 then you will *k* that these men
20:14 You *k* about all the hardships that
22:6 For I *k* that those you bless are
Dt 1:39 children who do not yet *k* good
3:19 your livestock (I *k* you have much
4:35 so that you might *k* that the LORD
7:9 *K* therefore that the LORD your
8:2 you in order to *k* what was
8:5 *K* then in your heart that
9:2 You *k* about them and have heard
11:30 As you *k*, these mountains are
18:21 "How can we *k* when a message
20:20 down trees that you *k* are not fruit
22:2 or if you do not *k* who he is,
28:33 that you do not *k* will eat what
29:6 this so that you might *k* that I am
29:16 You yourselves *k* how we lived
29:26 gods they did not *k*, gods he had
31:13 children, who do not *k* this law,
31:21 I *k* what they are disposed to do,
31:27 For I *k* how rebellious
31:29 For I *k* that after my death you are
Jos 2:4 I did not *k* where they had come
2:5 I don't *k* which way they went.
2:9 "I *k* that the LORD has given this
3:4 Then you will *k* which way to go,
3:7 so they may *k* that I am with you
3:10 is how you will *k* that the living
4:24 of the earth might *k* that the hand

Jos 8:14 he did not *k* that an ambush had
14:6 "You *k* what the LORD said
22:22 He knows! And let Israel *k!*
22:31 "Today we *k* that the LORD is
23:14 You *k* with all your heart
Jdg 6:37 then I will *k* that you will save
14:4 (His parents did not *k* that this was
16:20 he did not *k* that the LORD had
17:13 I *k* that the LORD will be good
18:14 a cast idol? Now you *k* what to do
18:14 "Do you *k* that one
Ru 2:11 with a people you did not *k* before.
3:3 but don't let him *k* you are there
3:11 my fellow townsmen *k* that you are
4:4 if you will not, tell me, so I will *k.*
1Sa 3:7 Samuel did not yet *k* the LORD:
6:3 you will *k* why his hand has not
6:9 then we will *k* that it was not his
8:9 let them *k* what the king who will
17:28 I *k* how conceited you are
17:46 the whole world will *k* that there is
17:47 those gathered here will *k* that it is
17:55 as you live, O king, I don't *k.*"
20:3 'Jonathan must not *k* this
20:12 I not send you word and let you *k?*
20:13 do not let you *k* and send you away
20:30 Don't I *k* that you have sided
21:2 is to *k* anything about your mission
24:20 I *k* that you will surely be king
28:9 "Surely you *k* what Saul has done.
29:9 "I *k* that you have been
2Sa 1:5 "How do you *k* that Saul
3:25 he is gone! You *k* Abner son of Ner
3:26 But David did not *k* it.
7:20 For you *k* your servant, O
11:20 Didn't you *k* they would shoot
15:20 when I do not *k* where I am going?
17:8 You *k* your father and his men;
18:29 but I don't *k* what it was."
19:20 For I your servant *k* that I have
19:22 Do I not *k* that today I am king
22:44 People I did not *k* are subject to me
24:2 so that I may *k* how many there are
1Ki 1:18 my lord the king, do not *k* about it.
1:27 letting his servants *k* who should
2:5 you yourself *k* what Joab son
2:9 you will *k* what to do to him.
2:15 "As you *k,*" he said, "the kingdom
2:44 "You *k* in your heart all the wrong
3:7 and do not *k* how to carry out my
5:3 "You *k* that because of the wars
5:6 You *k* that we have no one
8:39 heart (for you alone *k* the hearts
8:39 since you *k* his heart
8:43 may *k* that this house I have built
8:43 of the earth may *k* your name
8:60 of the earth may *k* that the LORD
17:24 Now I *k* that you are a man of God
18:12 I don't *k* where the Spirit
18:37 so these people will *k* that you,
20:13 and then you will *k* that I am
20:28 and you will *k* that I am the LORD
22:3 "Don't you *k* that Ramoth Gilead
2Ki 2:3 "Do you *k* that the LORD is going
2:3 "Yes, I *k,*" Elisha replied,
2:5 I *k,*" he replied, "but do not speak
2:5 "Do you *k* that the LORD is going
4:1 you *k* that he revered the LORD.
4:9 "I *k* that this man who often comes
5:8 and he will *k* that there is a prophet
5:15 "Now I *k* that there is no God
7:12 They *k* we are starving;
8:12 "Because I *k* the harm you will do
9:11 "You *k* the man and the sort
10:10 but who killed all these? *K* then,
17:26 of Samaria do not *k* what the god
17:26 people do not *k* what he requires."
19:19 on earth may *k* that you alone,
19:27 " 'But I *k* where you stay
1Ch 17:18 For you *k* your servant, O LORD.
21:2 so that I may *k* how many there are
29:17 I *k,* my God, that you test the heart
2Ch 2:8 for I *k* that your men are skilled
6:30 since you *k* his heart
6:30 (for you alone *k* the hearts of men),
6:33 may *k* that this house I have built
6:33 of the earth may *k* your name
13:5 Don't you *k* that the LORD,
2Ch 20:12 We do not *k* what to do,
25:16 "I *k* that God has determined
32:13 "Do you not *k* what I and my
32:31 and to *k* everything that was
Ezr 4:12 king should *k* that the Jews who
4:13 the king should *k* that
5:8 The king should *k* that we went
7:24 to *k* that you have no authority
7:25 all who *k* the laws of your God.
7:25 to teach any who do not *k* them.
Ne 2:16 officials did not *k* where I had gone
4:11 "Before they *k* it or see us,
13:24 and did not *k* how to speak
Est 4:11 people of the royal provinces *k* that
Job 5:24 You will *k* that your tent is secure;
5:25 You will *k* that your children will
7:10 his place will *k* him no more.
8:9 born only yesterday and *k* nothing,
9:2 "Indeed, I *k* that this is true.
9:28 for I *k* you will not hold me
10:7 though you *k* that I am not guilty
10:13 and I *k* that this was in your mind:
11:6 *K* this: God has even forgotten
11:8 of the grave—what can you *k?*
12:3 Who does not *k* all these things?
12:9 Which of all these does not *k*
13:2 What you *k,* I also *k;*
13:18 I *k* I will be vindicated.
14:21 sons are honored, he does not *k* it;
15:9 What do you *k* that we do not *k?*
19:6 then *k* that God has wronged me
19:25 I *k* that my Redeemer lives,
19:29 and then you will *k* that there is
20:4 "Surely you *k* how it has been
21:14 We have no desire to *k* your ways.
21:19 so that he will *k* it!
21:27 I *k* full well what you are thinking,
22:13 Yet you say, 'What does God *k?*
24:1 Why must those who *k* him look
24:13 who do not *k* its ways
30:23 I *k* you will bring me
31:6 and he will *k* that I am blameless—
32:6 not daring to tell you what I *k.*
32:10 I too will tell you what I *k.*
32:17 I too will tell what I *k.*
33:3 my lips sincerely speak what I *k.*
34:33 so tell me what you *k.*
37:7 men he has made may *k* his work,
37:15 Do you *k* how God controls
37:16 Do you *k* how the clouds hang
38:5 off its dimensions? Surely you *k!*
38:18 Tell me, if you *k* all this.
38:20 Do you *k* the paths
38:21 Surely you *k,* for you were already
38:33 Do you *k* the laws of the heavens?
39:1 "Do you *k* when the mountain
39:2 Do you *k* the time they give birth?
42:2 "I *k* that you can do all things;
42:3 things too wonderful for me to *k.*
Ps 4:3 *K* that the LORD has set apart
9:10 Those who *k* your name will trust
9:20 let the nations *k* they are but men.
18:43 people I did not *k* are subject to me
20:6 Now I *k* that the LORD saves his
35:11 on things I *k* nothing about.
36:10 to those who *k* you,
39:4 let me *k* how fleeting is my life.
40:9 as you *k,* O LORD.
41:11 I *k* that you are pleased with me,
46:10 "Be still, and *k* that I am God;
50:11 I *k* every bird in the mountains,
51:3 For I *k* my transgressions,
56:9 By this I will *k* that God is for me.
69:5 You *k* my folly, O God;
69:19 You *k* how I am scorned, disgraced
71:15 though I *k* not its measure.
73:7 of their minds *k* no limits.
73:11 They say, "How can God *k?*
78:6 the next generation would *k* them,
82:5 "They *k* nothing, they understand
83:18 Let them *k* that you, whose name
92:6 The senseless man does not *k,*
100:3 *K* that the LORD is God.
109:27 Let them *k* that it is your hand,
119:75 I *k,* O LORD, that your laws are
135:5 I *k* that the LORD is great,
139:1 and you *k* me.
139:2 You *k* when I sit and when I rise;
Ps 139:4 you *k* it completely, O LORD.
139:14 I *k* that full well.
139:23 Search me, O God, and *k* my heart;
139:23 test me and *k* my anxious thoughts.
140:12 I *k* that the LORD secures justice
142:3 it is you who *k* my way.
145:12 so that all men may *k*
147:20 they do not *k* his laws.
Pr 4:19 they do not *k* what makes them
9:18 little do they *k* that the dead are
10:32 of the righteous *k* what is fitting,
24:12 not he who guards your life *k* it?
24:14 *K* also that wisdom is sweet
27:1 for you do not *k* what a day may
27:23 Be sure you *k* the condition
30:4 Tell me if you *k!*
Ecc 3:12 I *k* that there is nothing better
3:14 I *k* that everything God does will
5:1 who do not *k* that they do wrong.
7:22 for you *k* in your heart
8:5 wise heart will *k* the proper time
8:12 I *k* that it will go better
8:16 I applied my mind to *k* wisdom
9:5 For the living *k* that they will die,
9:5 but the dead *k* nothing;
10:15 he does not *k* the way to town.
11:2 for you do not *k* what disaster may
11:5 As you do not *k* the path
11:6 for you do not *k* which will succeed
11:9 but *k* that for all these things
SS 1:8 If you do not *k,* most beautiful
Isa 1:3 but Israel does not *k,*
5:19 so we may *k* it."
9:9 All the people will *k* it—
29:12 he will answer, "I don't *k* how
29:15 "Who sees us? Who will *k?*"
32:4 The mind of the rash will *k*
37:20 on earth may *k* that you alone,
37:28 "But I *k* where you stay
40:21 Do you not *k?*
40:28 Do you not *k?*
41:20 so that people may see and *k,*
41:22 and *k* their final outcome.
41:23 so we may *k* that you are gods.
41:26 from the beginning, so we could *k,*
43:10 so that you may *k* and believe me
44:8 there is no other Rock; I *k* not one
44:18 They *k* nothing, they understand
45:3 so that you may *k* that I am
45:6 men may *k* there is none
47:11 you will not *k* how
48:8 Well do I *k* how treacherous you
49:23 you will *k* that I am the LORD;
49:26 Then all mankind will *k*
50:4 to *k* the word that sustains
50:7 and I *k* I will not be put to shame.
51:7 "Hear me, you who *k* what is right,
52:6 my people will *k* my name;
52:6 therefore in that day they will *k*
55:5 that do not *k* you will hasten
55:5 will summon nations you *k* not,
58:2 they seem eager to *k* my ways,
59:8 The way of peace they do not *k;*
59:8 walks in them will *k* peace.
60:16 Then you will *k* that I, the LORD,
63:16 though Abraham does not *k* us
Jer 1:6 I said, "I do not *k* how to speak;
2:8 deal with the law did not *k* me;
4:22 they do not *k* me.
4:22 they *k* not how to do good."
5:4 for they do not *k* the way
5:5 surely they *k* the way of the LORD
5:15 whose language you do not *k,*
6:15 they do not even *k* how to blush.
8:7 But my people do not *k*
8:12 they do not even *k* how to blush.
10:23 I *k,* O LORD, that a man's life is
12:3 Yet you *k* me, O LORD;
13:12 'Don't we *k* that every wineskin
14:18 have gone to a land they *k* not.' "
15:14 enemies in a land you do not *k,*
16:21 Then they will *k*
17:4 enemies in a land you do not *k,*
17:16 you *k* I have not desired the day
18:23 But you *k,* O LORD,
22:16 Is that not what it means to *k* me?"
22:28 cast into a land they do not *k?*
24:7 I will give them a heart to *k* me,

Jer 29: 11 For I *k* the plans I have for you,"
29: 23 I *k* it and am a witness to it,"
31: 34 because they will all *k* me,
31: 34 his brother, saying, '*K* the LORD,'
33: 3 unsearchable things you do not *k*.'
36: 19 Don't let anyone *k* where you are."
38: 24 not let anyone *k* about this
40: 14 "Don't you *k* that Baalis king
40: 15 of Nethaniah, and no one will *k* it.
44: 19 not our husbands *k* that we were
44: 28 in Egypt will *k* whose word will
44: 29 'so that you will *k* that my threats
48: 17 all who *k* her fame;
48: 30 I *k* her insolence but it is futile,"
Eze 2: 5 they will *k* that a prophet has been
5: 13 they will *k* that I the LORD have
6: 7 and you will *k* that I am the LORD
6: 10 they will *k* that I am the LORD;
6: 13 they will *k* that I am the LORD,
6: 14 they will *k* that I am the LORD.' "
7: 4 you will *k* that I am the LORD.
7: 9 you will *k* that it is I the LORD
7: 27 they will *k* that I am the LORD."
11: 5 *k* what is going through your mind.
11: 10 you will *k* that I am the LORD.
11: 12 you will *k* that I am the LORD,
12: 15 "They will *k* that I am the LORD,
12: 16 they will *k* that I am the LORD."
12: 20 you will *k* that I am the LORD.' "
13: 9 you will *k* that I am the Sovereign
13: 14 and you will *k* that I am the LORD
13: 21 then you will *k* that I am
13: 23 And then you will *k* that I am
14: 8 you will *k* that I am the LORD.
14: 23 for you will *k* that I have done
15: 7 you will *k* that I am the LORD.
16: 62 and you will *k* that I am the LORD
17: 12 'Do you not *k* what these things
17: 21 you will *k* that I the LORD have
17: 24 of the field will *k* that I the LORD
20: 12 so they would *k* that I the LORD
20: 20 you will *k* that I am the LORD
20: 26 horror so they would *k* that I am
20: 38 you will *k* that I am the LORD.
20: 42 you will *k* that I am the LORD,
20: 44 You will *k* that I am the LORD,
21: 5 all people will *k* that I the LORD
22: 16 you will *k* that I am the LORD.' "
22: 22 you will *k* that I the LORD have
23: 49 you will *k* that I am the Sovereign
24: 24 you will *k* that I am the Sovereign
24: 27 they will *k* that I am the LORD."
25: 5 you will *k* that I am the LORD.
25: 7 and you will *k* that I am the LORD
25: 11 they will *k* that I am the LORD.' "
25: 14 they will *k* my vengeance,
25: 17 they will *k* that I am the LORD,
26: 6 they will *k* that I am the LORD.
28: 22 They will *k* that I am the LORD,
28: 23 they will *k* that I am the LORD.
28: 24 they will *k* that I am the Sovereign
28: 26 they will *k* that I am the LORD
29: 6 live in Egypt will *k* that I am
29: 9 they will *k* that I am the LORD.
29: 16 they will *k* that I am the Sovereign
29: 21 they will *k* that I am the LORD."
30: 8 they will *k* that I am the LORD,
30: 19 they will *k* that I am the LORD.' "
30: 25 they will *k* that I am the LORD,
30: 26 they will *k* that I am the LORD."
32: 15 then they will *k* that I am
33: 29 they will *k* that I am the LORD,
33: 33 then they will *k* that a prophet has
34: 27 They will *k* that I am the LORD,
34: 30 they will *k* that I, the LORD their
35: 4 you will *k* that I am the LORD.
35: 9 you will *k* that I am the LORD.
35: 12 you will *k* that I the LORD have
35: 15 they will *k* that I am the LORD.' "
36: 11 you will *k* that I am the LORD.
36: 23 nations will *k* that I am the LORD,
36: 32 you to *k* that I am not doing this
36: 36 you that remain will *k* that I
36: 38 they will *k* that I am the LORD."
37: 3 O Sovereign LORD, you alone *k*."
37: 6 you will *k* that I am the LORD.' "
37: 13 will *k* that I am the LORD,
37: 14 you will *k* that I the LORD have
Eze 37: 28 the nations will *k* that I the LORD
38: 16 so that the nations may *k* me
38: 23 they will *k* that I am the LORD.'
39: 6 they will *k* that I am the LORD.
39: 7 nations will *k* that I the LORD am
39: 22 of Israel will *k* that I am the LORD
39: 23 the nations will *k* that the people
39: 28 they will *k* that I am the LORD
Da 2: 3 and I want to *k* what it means."
2: 9 and I will *k* that you can interpret it
2: 30 may *k* the interpretation
3: 18 we want you to *k*, O king,
4: 9 I *k* that the spirit of the holy gods is
4: 17 that the living may *k* that the Most
7: 19 I wanted to *k* the true meaning
7: 20 wanted to *k* about the ten horns
9: 25 "*K* and understand this: From
10: 20 Do you *k* why I have come to you?
11: 32 people who *k* their God will firmly
Hos 5: 3 I *k* all about Ephraim;
9: 7 Let Israel *k* this.
Joel 2: 27 Then you will *k* that I am in Israel,
3: 17 you will *k* that I, the LORD your
Am 3: 10 "They do not *k* how to do right,"
5: 12 For I *k* how many are your
Jnh 1: 12 I *k* that it is my fault that this great
Mic 3: 1 Should you not *k* justice,
4: 12 But they do not *k*
6: 5 that you may *k* the righteous acts
Zep 3: 5 yet the unrighteous *k* no shame.
Zec 2: 9 Then you will *k* that the LORD
2: 11 and you will *k* that the LORD
4: 5 Do you not *k* what these are?" "No
4: 9 Then you will *k* that the LORD
4: 13 Do you not *k* what these are?" "No
6: 15 and you will *k* that the LORD
Mal 2: 4 you will *k* that I have sent you this
Mt 6: 3 let your left hand *k* what your right
7: 11 *k* how to give good gifts
9: 6 But so that you may *k* that the Son
15: 12 "Do you *k* that the Pharisees were
16: 3 You *k* how to interpret
20: 22 You don't *k* what you are asking,"
20: 25 "You *k* that the rulers
21: 27 they answered Jesus, "We don't *k*
22: 16 "we *k* you are a man of integrity
22: 29 you do not *k* the Scriptures
24: 32 you *k* that summer is near.
24: 33 see all these things, you *k* that it is
24: 42 you do not *k* on what day your
25: 12 'I tell you the truth, I don't *k* you.'
25: 13 because you do not *k* the day
26: 2 "As you *k*, the Passover is two
26: 70 I don't *k* what you're talking about
26: 72 with an oath: "I don't *k* the man!"
26: 74 "I don't *k* the man!" Immediately
27: 65 as secure as you *k* how."
28: 5 for I *k* that you are looking
Mk 1: 24 to destroy us? I *k* who you are—
2: 10 But that you may *k* that the Son
4: 27 though he does not *k* how.
5: 43 not to let anyone *k* about this,
7: 24 and did not want anyone to *k* it;
9: 6 (He did not *k* what to say,
9: 30 anyone to *k* where they were,
10: 19 You *k* the commandments:
10: 38 You don't *k* what you are asking,"
10: 42 You *k* that those who are regarded
11: 33 they answered Jesus, "We don't *k*
12: 14 we *k* you are a man of integrity.
12: 24 you do not *k* the Scriptures
13: 28 you *k* that summer is near.
13: 29 things happening, you *k* that it is
13: 33 You do not *k* when that time will
13: 35 you do not *k* when the owner
14: 40 They did not *k* what to say to him.
14: 68 "I don't *k* or understand what
14: 71 "I don't *k* this man you're talking
Lk 1: 4 so that you may *k* the certainty
2: 49 "Didn't you *k* I had to be
4: 34 to destroy us? I *k* who you are—
5: 24 But that you may *k* that the Son
7: 39 he would *k* who is touching him
8: 46 I *k* that power has gone out
9: 33 (He did not *k* what he was saying.)
11: 13 *k* how to give good gifts
12: 48 But the one who does not *k*
12: 56 How is it that you don't *k* how
Lk 12: 56 You *k* how to interpret
13: 25 'I don't *k* you or where you come
13: 27 'I don't *k* you or where you come
16: 4 ashamed to beg—I *k* what I'll do
18: 20 You *k* the commandments:
18: 34 they did not *k* what he was talking
20: 7 "We don't *k* where it was from."
20: 21 we *k* that you speak and teach
21: 20 you will *k* that its desolation is near
21: 30 and *k* that summer is near.
21: 31 you *k* that the kingdom of God is
22: 34 deny three times that you *k* me."
22: 57 "Woman, I don't *k* him," he said.
22: 60 I don't *k* what you're talking about
23: 34 for they do not *k* what they are
24: 18 Jerusalem who doesn't *k* the things
Jn 1: 26 among you stands one you do not *k*
1: 31 I myself did not *k* him,
1: 48 "How do you *k* me?" Nathanael
3: 2 we *k* you are a teacher who has
3: 11 we speak of what we *k*,
4: 22 we worship what we do *k*,
4: 22 worship what you do not *k*;
4: 25 "I *k* that Messiah" (called Christ)
4: 32 to eat that you *k* nothing about."
4: 42 and we *k* that this man really is
5: 32 I *k* that his testimony about me is
5: 42 I *k* that you do not have the love
5: 42 praise from men, but I *k* you.
6: 42 whose father and mother we *k*?
6: 69 and *k* that you are the Holy One
7: 27 But we *k* where this man is from;
7: 27 no one will *k* where he is from."
7: 28 You do not *k* him, but I *k* him
7: 28 and you *k* where I am from.
7: 28 cried out, "Yes, you *k* me,
8: 14 for I *k* where I came from
8: 19 you would *k* my Father also."
8: 19 "You do not *k* me or my Father,"
8: 28 then you will *k* who I am
8: 32 Then you will *k* the truth,
8: 37 I *k* you are Abraham's descendants
8: 52 we *k* that you are demon-possessed
8: 55 Though you do not *k* him, I *k* him.
8: 55 but I do *k* him and keep his word.
9: 12 "I don't *k*," he said.
9: 20 "We *k* he is our son," the parents
9: 20 "and we *k* he was born blind.
9: 21 or who opened his eyes, we don't *k*
9: 24 "We *k* this man is a sinner."
9: 25 One thing I do *k*.
9: 25 he is a sinner or not, I don't *k*.
9: 29 We *k* that God spoke to Moses,
9: 29 even *k* where he comes from."
9: 30 You don't *k* where he comes from,
9: 31 We *k* that God does not listen
10: 4 him because they *k* his voice.
10: 14 I *k* my sheep and my sheep *k* me—
10: 15 knows me and I *k* the Father—
10: 27 I *k* them, and they follow me.
11: 22 But I *k* that even now God will give
11: 24 "I *k* he will rise again
11: 49 spoke up, "You *k* nothing at all!
12: 35 the dark does not *k* where he is
12: 50 I *k* that his command leads
13: 17 Now that you *k* these things,
13: 18 all of you; I *k* those I have chosen.
13: 22 at a loss to *k* which
13: 35 All men will *k* that you are my
14: 4 You *k* the way to the place where I
14: 5 so how can we *k* the way?"
14: 5 we don't *k* where you are going,
14: 7 you do *k* him and have seen him."
14: 7 you would *k* my Father as well.
14: 9 Jesus answered: "Don't you *k* me,
14: 17 you *k* him, for he lives with you
15: 15 a servant does not *k* his master's
15: 21 for they do not *k* the One who sent
16: 30 we can see that you *k* all things
17: 3 that they may *k* you, the only true
17: 7 they *k* that everything you have
17: 23 to let the world *k* that you sent me
17: 25 and they *k* that you have sent me.
17: 25 the world does not *k* you, I *k* you,
18: 21 Surely they *k* what I said."
19: 4 you to let you *k* that I find no basis
20: 2 we don't *k* where they have put
20: 13 I don't *k* where they have put him

Jn 21: 15 he said, "you *k* that I love you."
21: 16 "Yes, Lord, you *k* that I love you."
21: 17 *k* all things; you *k* that I love you."
21: 24 We *k* that his testimony is true.
Ac 1: 7 "It is not for you to *k* the times
1: 24 "Lord, you *k* everyone's heart.
2: 22 through him, as you yourselves *k*.
3: 16 you see and *k* was made strong.
3: 17 I *k* that you acted in ignorance,
4: 10 then *k* this, you and everyone else
7: 40 we don't *k* what has happened
10: 37 You *k* what has happened
12: 11 I *k* without a doubt that the Lord
13: 38 I want you to *k* that
15: 7 you *k* that some time ago God
17: 19 "May we *k* what this new teaching
17: 20 and we want to *k* what they mean."
19: 15 "Jesus I *k* and Paul I *k* about,
19: 25 you *k* we receive a good income
19: 32 even *k* why they were there.
19: 35 doesn't all the world *k* that the city
20: 18 "You *k* how I lived the whole time
20: 20 You *k* that I have not hesitated
20: 23 I only *k* that in every city the Holy
20: 25 "Now I *k* that none of you
20: 29 I *k* that after I leave, savage wolves
20: 34 You yourselves *k* that these hands
21: 24 everybody will *k* there is no truth
22: 14 fathers has chosen you to *k* his will
22: 19 'these men *k* that I went
23: 28 to *k* why they were accusing him,
24: 10 "I *k* that for a number
25: 10 as you yourself *k* very well.
26: 4 Jews all *k* the way I have lived ever
26: 27 believe the prophets? I *k* you do."
28: 22 for we *k* that people everywhere
28: 28 to *k* that God's salvation has been
Ro 1: 32 Although they *k* God's righteous
2: 2 Now we *k* that God's judgment
2: 18 if you *k* his will and approve
3: 17 and the way of peace they do not *k*
3: 19 we *k* that whatever the law says,
5: 3 we *k* that suffering produces
6: 3 Or don't you *k* that all
6: 6 For we *k* that our old self was
6: 9 For we *k* that since Christ was
6: 16 Don't you *k* that when you offer
7: 1 Do you not *k*, brothers—
7: 1 speaking to men who *k* the law—
7: 14 We *k* that the law is spiritual;
7: 18 I *k* that nothing good lives in me,
8: 22 We *k* that the whole creation has
8: 26 We do not *k* what we ought to pray
8: 28 we *k* that in all things God works
10: 3 they did not *k* the righteousness
11: 2 Don't you *k* what the Scripture
15: 29 I *k* that when I come to you,
1Co 1: 21 through its wisdom did not *k* him,
2: 2 For I resolved to *k* nothing
3: 16 Don't you *k* that you yourselves
5: 6 Don't you *k* that a little yeast
6: 2 Do you not *k* that the saints will
6: 3 Do you not *k* that we will judge
6: 9 Do you not *k* that the wicked will
6: 15 Do you not *k* that your bodies are
6: 16 Do you not *k* that he who unites
6: 19 Do you not *k* that your body is
7: 16 How do you *k*, wife, whether you
7: 16 Or, how do you *k*, husband,
8: 1 We *k* that we all possess
8: 2 does not yet *k* as he ought to *k*.
8: 4 We *k* that an idol is nothing at all
9: 13 Don't you *k* that those who work
9: 24 Do you not *k* that
12: 2 You *k* that when you were pagans,
13: 9 For we *k* in part and we prophesy
13: 12 Now I *k* in part; then I shall *k* fully,
14: 7 how will anyone *k* what tune is
14: 9 how will anyone *k* what you are
14: 16 since he does not *k* what you are
15: 58 because you *k* that your labor
16: 15 You *k* that the household
2Co 1: 7 because we *k* that just
2: 4 to let you *k* the depth of my love
4: 14 we *k* that the one who raised
5: 1 we *k* that if the earthly tent we live
5: 6 we are always confident and *k* that
5: 11 we *k* what it is to fear the Lord,
2Co 8: 1 to *k* about the grace that God has
8: 9 For you *k* the grace
9: 2 For I *k* your eagerness to help,
12: 2 I *k* a man in Christ who fourteen
12: 2 or out of the body I do not *k*—
12: 3 And I *k* that this man—
12: 3 or apart from the body I do not *k*,
Gal 1: 11 you to *k*, brothers, that the gospel I
2: 16 not 'Gentile sinners' *k* that a man
4: 8 Formerly, when you did not *k* God
4: 9 But now that you *k* God—
4: 13 you *k*, it was because of an illness
Eph 1: 17 so that you may *k* him better.
1: 18 in order that you may *k* the hope
3: 19 and to *k* this love that surpasses
4: 20 did not come to *k* Christ that way.
6: 8 you *k* that the Lord will reward
6: 9 since you *k* that he who is both
6: 21 so that you also may *k* how I am
6: 22 that you may *k* how we are,
Php 1: 12 Now I want you to *k*, brothers,
1: 19 for I *k* that through your prayers
1: 22 I do not *k*! I am torn
1: 25 of this, I *k* that I will remain,
1: 27 I will *k* that you stand firm
2: 22 But you *k* that Timothy has proved
3: 10 I want to *k* Christ and the power
4: 12 I *k* what it is to be in need,
4: 12 and I *k* what it is to have plenty.
4: 15 Moreover, as you Philippians *k*,
Col 2: 1 you to *k* how much I am struggling
2: 2 order that they may *k* the mystery
3: 24 since you *k* that you will receive
4: 1 because you *k* that you
4: 6 so that you may *k* how
4: 8 that you may *k* about our
1Th 1: 4 we *k* that he has chosen you,
1: 5 You *k* how we lived among you
2: 1 You *k*, brothers, that our visit
2: 2 been insulted in Philippi, as you *k*,
2: 5 You *k* we never used flattery,
2: 11 For you *k* that we dealt with each
3: 3 You *k* quite well that we were
3: 4 turned out that way, as you well *k*
4: 2 You *k* what instructions we gave
4: 5 the heathen, who do not *k* God;
5: 2 for you *k* very well that the day
2Th 1: 8 punish those who do not *k* God
2: 6 now you *k* what is holding him
3: 7 For you yourselves *k* how you
1Ti 1: 7 they do not *k* what they are talking
1: 8 We *k* that the law is good
1: 9 also *k* that law is made not
3: 5 (If anyone does not *k* how
3: 15 you will *k* how people ought
4: 3 who believe and who *k* the truth.
2Ti 1: 12 because I *k* whom I have believed,
1: 15 You *k* that everyone
1: 18 You *k* very well in how many ways
2: 23 you *k* they produce quarrels.
3: 10 however, *k* all about my teaching,
3: 14 you *k* those from whom you
Tit 1: 16 They claim to *k* God,
Heb 8: 11 because they will all *k* me,
8: 11 his brother, saying, '*K* the Lord,'
10: 30 For we *k* him who said, "It is mine
11: 8 he did not *k* where he was going.
12: 17 as you *k*, when he wanted
13: 23 to *k* that our brother Timothy has
Jas 1: 3 because you *k* that the testing
3: 1 you *k* that we who teach will be
4: 4 don't you *k* that friendship
4: 14 *k* what will happen tomorrow.
5: 11 As you *k*, we consider blessed
1Pe 1: 18 For you *k* that it was not
5: 9 because you *k* that your brothers
2Pe 1: 12 even though you *k* them
1: 14 I *k* that I will soon put it aside,
3: 17 since you already *k* this,
1Jn 2: 3 We *k* that we have come
2: 3 to *k* him if we obey his commands.
2: 4 The man who says, "I *k* him,"
2: 5 This is how we *k* we are in him:
2: 11 he does not *k* where he is going,
2: 18 This is how we *k* it is the last hour.
2: 20 and all of you *k* the truth.
2: 21 because you do not *k* the truth,
2: 21 but because you do *k* it and
1Jn 2: 29 If you *k* that he is righteous,
2: 29 you *k* that everyone who does
3: 1 not *k* us is that it did not *k* him.
3: 2 But we *k* that when he appears,
3: 5 But you *k* that he appeared
3: 10 This is how we *k* who the children
3: 14 We *k* that we have passed
3: 15 you *k* that no murderer has eternal
3: 16 This is how we *k* what love is:
3: 19 then is how we *k* that we belong
3: 24 We *k* it by the Spirit he gave us.
3: 24 this is how we *k* that he lives in us:
4: 8 does not love does not *k* God,
4: 13 We *k* that we live in him
4: 16 so we *k* and rely on the love God
5: 2 This is how we *k* that we love
5: 13 so that you may *k* that you have
5: 15 And if we *k* that he hears us—
5: 15 we *k* that we have what we asked
5: 18 We *k* that anyone born
5: 19 We *k* that we are children of God,
5: 20 We *k* also that the Son
5: 20 so that we may *k* him who is true.
2Jn : 1 but also all who *k* the truth—
3Jn : 12 you *k* that our testimony is true.
Jude : 5 Though you already *k* all this,
Rev 2: 2 I *k* that you cannot tolerate wicked
2: 2 I *k* your deeds, your hard work
2: 9 I *k* the slander of those who say
2: 9 I *k* your afflictions and your
2: 13 I *k* where you live—where Satan
2: 19 I *k* your deeds, your love and faith,
2: 23 all the churches will *k* that I am he
3: 1 I *k* your deeds; you have
3: 3 you will not *k* at what time I will
3: 8 I *k* that you have little strength,
3: 8 I *k* your deeds.
3: 15 I *k* your deeds, that you are neither
7: 14 from?" I answered, "Sir, you *k*."

KNOWING (KNOW)

Ge 3: 5 and you will be like God, *k* good
3: 22 now become like one of us, *k* good
2Sa 15: 11 *k* nothing about the matter.
1Ki 1: 11 king without our lord David's *k* it?
Job 9: 5 moves mountains without their *k* it
31: 21 *k* that I had influence in court,
Ps 39: 6 heaps up wealth, not *k* who will get
Pr 7: 23 little *k* it will cost him his life.
Ecc 6: 8 gain by *k* how to conduct himself
Mt 9: 4 is blaspheming!" *K* their thoughts,
22: 18 But Jesus, *k* their evil intent, said,
Mk 5: 33 *k* what had happened to her,
6: 20 *k* him to be a righteous
15: 10 *k* it was out of envy that the chief
Lk 8: 53 at him, *k* that she was dead.
9: 47 *k* their thoughts, took a little child
11: 44 which men walk over without *k* it."
Jn 6: 15 *k* that they intended to come
18: 4 *k* all that was going to happen
19: 28 *k* that all was now completed,
Ac 5: 7 not *k* what had happened.
20: 22 not *k* what will happen to me there.
23: 6 *k* that some of them were
Php 1: 16 *k* that I am put here for the defense
3: 8 of *k* Christ Jesus my Lord,
Phm : 21 *k* that you will do even more
Heb 13: 2 entertained angels without *k* it.
2Pe 2: 20 of the world by *k* our Lord

KNOWLEDGE (KNOW)

Ge 2: 9 the tree of the *k* of good and evil.
2: 17 eat from the tree of the *k* of good
Ex 31: 3 ability and *k* in all kinds of crafts—
35: 31 ability and *k* in all kinds of crafts—
Nu 24: 16 who has *k* from the Most High,
1Ki 2: 32 without the *k* of my father David
2Ch 1: 10 and *k*, that I may lead this people,
1: 11 and *k* to govern my people
1: 12 wisdom and *k* will be given you.
Job 21: 22 "Can anyone teach *k* to God,
34: 35 'Job speaks without *k*;
35: 16 without *k* he multiplies words."
36: 3 I get my *k* from afar;
36: 4 one perfect in *k* is with you.
36: 12 and die without *k*.
37: 16 of him who is perfect in *k*?
38: 2 counsel with words without *k*?

Job 42: 3 obscures my counsel without *k*?'
Ps 19: 2 night after night they display *k*.
73: 11 Does the Most High have *k*?''
94: 10 Does he who teaches man lack *k*?
119: 66 Teach me *k* and good judgment,
139: 6 Such *k* is too wonderful for me,
Pr 1: 4 *k* and discretion to the young—
1: 7 of the LORD is the beginning of *k*,
1: 22 and fools hate *k*?
1: 29 Since they hated *k*
2: 5 and find the *k* of God.
2: 6 from his mouth come *k*
2: 10 and *k* will be pleasant to your soul.
3: 20 by his *k* the deeps were divided,
5: 2 and your lips may preserve *k*.
8: 9 to those who have *k*.
8: 10 *k* rather than choice gold,
8: 12 I possess *k* and discretion.
9: 10 *k* of the Holy One is understanding
9: 13 she is undisciplined and without *k*.
10: 14 Wise men store up *k*,
11: 9 but through *k* the righteous escape.
12: 1 Whoever loves discipline loves *k*,
12: 23 A prudent man keeps his *k*
13: 16 Every prudent man acts out of *k*,
14: 6 *k* comes easily to the discerning.
14: 7 for you will not find *k* on his lips.
14: 18 but the prudent are crowned with *k*
15: 2 of the wise commends *k*,
15: 7 The lips of the wise spread *k*;
15: 14 The discerning heart seeks *k*,
17: 27 A man of *k* uses words
18: 15 heart of the discerning acquires *k*;
19: 2 to have zeal without *k*,
19: 25 discerning man, and he will gain *k*.
19: 27 you will stray from the words of *k*.
20: 15 lips that speak *k* are a rare jewel.
21: 11 a wise man is instructed, he gets *k*.
22: 12 of the LORD keep watch over *k*,
22: 20 sayings of counsel and *k*,
23: 12 and your ears to words of *k*.
24: 4 through *k* its rooms are filled
24: 5 and a man of *k* increases strength;
28: 2 understanding and *k* maintains
30: 3 nor have I *k* of the Holy One.
Ecc 1: 16 much of wisdom and *k*.''
1: 18 the more *k*, the more grief.
2: 21 may do his work with wisdom, *k*
2: 26 gives wisdom, *k* and happiness,
7: 12 but the advantage of *k* is this:
9: 10 nor planning nor *k* nor wisdom.
12: 9 also he imparted *k* to the people.
Isa 11: 2 the Spirit of *k* and of the fear
11: 9 full of the *k* of the LORD
33: 6 of salvation and wisdom and *k*;
40: 14 Who was it that taught him *k*
44: 19 no one has the *k* or understanding
47: 10 Your wisdom and *k* mislead you
53: 11 by his *k* my righteous servant will
56: 10 they all lack *k*;
Jer 3: 15 who will lead you with *k*
10: 14 is senseless and without *k*;
51: 17 man is senseless and without *k*;
Da 1: 17 these four young men God gave *k*
2: 21 and *k* to the discerning.
5: 12 found to have a keen mind and *k*
12: 4 go here and there to increase *k*.''
Hos 4: 6 are destroyed from lack of *k*.
4: 6 "Because you have rejected *k*,
Hab 2: 14 filled with the *k* of the glory
Mal 2: 7 lips of a priest ought to preserve *k*,
Mt 13: 11 The *k* of the secrets of the kingdom
Lk 1: 77 to give his people the *k* of salvation
8: 10 The *k* of the secrets of the kingdom
11: 52 you have taken away the key to *k*.
Ac 5: 2 With his wife's full *k* he kept back
18: 24 with a thorough *k* of the Scriptures
Ro 1: 28 worthwhile to retain the *k* of God,
2: 20 in the law the embodiment of *k*
10: 2 but their zeal is not based on *k*.
11: 33 riches of the wisdom and *k* of God!
15: 14 complete in *k* and competent
1Co 1: 5 your speaking and in all your *k*—
8: 1 We know that we all possess *k*.
8: 1 *K* puffs up, but love builds up.
8: 10 sees you who have this *k* eating
8: 11 Christ died, is destroyed by your *k*.
12: 8 to another the message of *k*
1Co 13: 2 can fathom all mysteries and all *k*,
13: 8 where there is *k*, it will pass away.
14: 6 I bring you some revelation or *k*
2Co 2: 14 everywhere the fragrance of the *k*
4: 6 light of the *k* of the glory of God
8: 7 in *k*, in complete earnestness
10: 5 up against the *k* of God,
11: 6 a trained speaker, but I do have *k*.
Eph 3: 19 to know this love that surpasses *k*
4: 13 and in the *k* of the Son of God
Php 1: 9 and more in *k* and depth of insight,
Col 1: 9 God to fill you with the *k* of his will
1: 10 every good work, growing in the *k*
2: 3 all the treasures of wisdom and *k*.
3: 10 which is being renewed in *k*
1Ti 2: 4 and to come to a *k* of the truth.
6: 20 ideas of what is falsely called *k*,
2Ti 2: 25 them to a *k* of the truth,
Tit 1: 1 and the *k* of the truth that leads
1: 2 *k* resting on the hope of eternal life,
Heb 10: 26 after we have received the *k*
2Pe 1: 2 in abundance through the *k* of God
1: 3 and godliness through our *k*
1: 5 and to goodness, *k*; and to *k*,
1: 8 and unproductive in your *k*
3: 18 grow in the grace and *k* of our Lord

KNOWN (KNOW)

Ge 41: 39 "Since God has made all this *k*
45: 1 Joseph when he made himself *k*
Ex 2: 14 "What I did must have become *k*."
6: 3 the LORD I did not make myself *k*
21: 36 if it was *k* that the bull had
Nu 11: 16 of Israel's elders who are *k* to you
Dt 3: 13 of Argob in Bashan used to be *k*
8: 3 neither you nor your fathers had *k*,
8: 16 your fathers had never *k*,
9: 24 ever since I have *k* you.
11: 28 other gods, which you have not *k*.
13: 2 other gods'' (gods you have not *k*)
13: 6 you nor your fathers have *k*,
13: 13 other gods'' (gods you have not *k*),
21: 1 and it is not *k* who killed him,
25: 10 That man's line shall be *k* in Israel
28: 64 you nor your fathers have *k*.
32: 17 gods they had not *k*,
Ru 3: 14 "Don't let it be *k* that a woman
1Sa 10: 11 who had formerly *k* him saw him
18: 23 I'm only a poor man and little *k*.''
18: 30 and his name became well *k*.
2Sa 7: 21 and made it *k* to your servant.
1Ki 18: 36 let it be *k* today that you are God
1Ch 16: 8 make *k* among the nations what he
17: 19 made *k* all these great promises.
Ne 8: 12 the words that had been made *k*
9: 14 You made *k* to them your holy
Est 1: 17 the queen's conduct will become *k*
2: 7 This girl, who was also *k* as Esther,
3: 14 and made *k* to the people
8: 13 and made *k* to the people
Job 36: 33 even the cattle make *k* its approach
42: 11 and everyone who had *k* him
Ps 9: 16 The LORD is *k* by his justice;
16: 11 You have made *k* to me the path
25: 14 he makes his covenant *k* to them.
37: 18 of the blameless are *k*
59: 13 it will be *k* to the ends of the earth
67: 2 may your ways be *k* on earth,
76: 1 In Judah God is *k*;
78: 3 things we have heard and *k*,
79: 10 make *k* among the nations
88: 12 Are your wonders *k* in the place
89: 1 I will make your faithfulness *k*
95: 10 and they have not *k* my ways.''
98: 2 LORD has made his salvation *k*
103: 7 He made *k* his ways to Moses,
105: 1 make *k* among the nations what he
106: 8 to make his mighty power *k*.
119: 168 for all my ways are *k* to you.
Pr 1: 23 and made my thoughts *k* to you.
14: 33 among fools she lets herself be *k*.
20: 11 Even a child is *k* by his actions,
24: 8 will be *k* as a schemer.
Ecc 6: 10 and what man is has been *k*;
Isa 12: 4 make *k* among the nations what he
12: 5 let this be *k* to all the world.
19: 12 Let them show you and make *k*
19: 21 So the LORD will make himself *k*
Isa 42: 16 the blind by ways they have not *k*,
46: 10 *k* the end from the beginning,
48: 3 them and I made them *k*;
61: 9 Their descendants will be *k*
64: 2 down to make your name *k*
66: 14 hand of the LORD will be made *k*
Jer 7: 9 follow other gods you have not *k*,
9: 16 they nor their fathers have *k*,
16: 13 you nor your fathers have *k*,
Eze 20: 11 and made *k* to them my laws,
32: 9 among lands you have not *k*.
35: 11 I will make myself *k* among them
38: 23 I will make myself *k* in the sight
39: 7 " 'I will make *k* my holy name
43: 11 make *k* to them the design
Da 2: 23 you have made *k* to me what we
2: 23 you have made *k* to us the dream
Hab 3: 2 in our time make them *k*;
Zec 14: 7 nighttime—a day *k* to the LORD.
Mt 10: 26 or hidden that will not be made *k*.
12: 7 If you had *k* what these words
24: 43 of the house had *k* at what time
26: 6 in Bethany in the home of a man *k*
Mk 6: 14 for Jesus' name had become well *k*.
14: 3 at the table in the home of a man *k*
Lk 8: 17 concealed that will not be *k*
12: 2 or hidden that will not be made *k*.
12: 39 If the owner of the house had *k*
19: 42 had only *k* on this day what would
Jn 1: 18 the Father's side, has made him *k*.
1: 33 I would not have *k* him,
6: 64 For Jesus had *k* from the beginning
15: 15 from my Father I have made *k*
16: 3 they have not *k* the Father or me.
16: 14 from what is mine and making it *k*
16: 15 from what is mine and make it *k*
17: 26 I have made you *k* to them,
17: 26 and will continue to make you *k*
18: 15 Because this disciple was *k*
18: 16 who was *k* to the high priest,
19: 13 on the judge's seat at a place *k*
Ac 1: 23 Joseph called Barsabbas (also *k*
2: 28 You have made *k* to me the paths
6: 3 among you who are *k* to be full
8: 10 "This man is the divine power *k*
9: 42 This became *k* all over Joppa,
10: 1 a centurion in what was *k*
10: 18 asking if Simon who was *k*
15: 18 that have been *k* for ages.
19: 17 When this became *k* to the Jews
26: 5 They have *k* me for a long time
Ro 1: 19 since what may be *k* about God is
3: 21 apart from law, has been made *k*,
7: 7 For I would not have *k* what it was
7: 7 I would not have *k* what sin was
9: 22 his wrath and make his power *k*,
9: 23 riches of his glory *k* to the objects
11: 34 "Who has *k* the mind of the Lord?
15: 20 the gospel where Christ was not *k*,
16: 26 and made *k* through the prophetic
1Co 2: 16 "For who has *k* the mind
8: 3 But the man who loves God is *k*
13: 12 know fully, even as I am fully *k*.
2Co 3: 2 written on our hearts, *k*
6: 9 yet regarded as impostors; *k*,
11: 27 I have *k* hunger and thirst
Gal 4: 9 or rather are *k* by God—
Eph 1: 9 And he made *k* to us the mystery
3: 3 the mystery made *k* to me
3: 5 which was not made *k* to men
3: 10 wisdom of God should be made *k*
6: 19 will fearlessly make *k* the mystery
Col 1: 27 to make *k* among the Gentiles
1Th 1: 8 in God has become *k* everywhere.
1Ti 5: 10 and is well *k* for her good deeds,
2Ti 3: 15 infancy you have *k* the holy
Heb 3: 10 and they have not *k* my ways.'
11: 24 refused to be *k* as the son
2Pe 2: 21 than to have *k* it and then
2: 21 to have *k* the way of righteousness,
1Jn 2: 13 because you have *k* the Father.
2: 13 you have *k* him who is
2: 14 you have *k* him who is
3: 2 we will be has not yet been made *k*.
3: 6 to sin has either seen him or *k* him.
Rev 1: 1 He made it *k* by sending his angel
2: 17 *k* only to him who receives it.

KNOWS (KNOW)

Ge 3: 5 "For God *k* that when you eat
16: 5 and now that she *k* she is pregnant,
33: 13 "My lord *k* that the children are
Dt 34: 6 this day no one *k* where his grave
Jos 22: 22 He *k!* And let Israel know!
1Sa 2: 3 for the LORD is a God who *k*,
16: 18 of Jesse of Bethlehem who *k* how
20: 3 "Your father *k* very well that I
22: 15 for your servant *k* nothing
23: 17 Even my father Saul *k* this."
25: 11 to men coming from who *k* where
2Sa 12: 22 'Who *k?* The LORD may be
14: 20 he *k* everything that happens
14: 22 "Today your servant *k* that he has
17: 10 for all Israel *k* that your father is
Est 4: 14 And who *k* but that you have come
Job 15: 23 he *k* the day of darkness is at hand.
18: 21 of one who *k* not God."
23: 10 But he *k* the way that I take;
28: 7 No bird of prey *k* that hidden path,
28: 23 and he alone *k* where it dwells,
Ps 37: 13 for he *k* their day is coming.
44: 21 since he *k* the secrets of the heart?
74: 9 none of us *k* how long this will be.
90: 11 Who *k* the power of your anger?
94: 11 The LORD *k* the thoughts of man;
94: 11 he *k* that they are futile.
103: 14 for he *k* how we are formed,
104: 19 and the sun *k* when to go down.
138: 6 but the proud he *k* from afar.
Pr 5: 6 paths are crooked, but she *k* it not.
14: 10 Each heart *k* its own bitterness,
24: 22 who *k* what calamities they can
Ecc 2: 19 who *k* whether he will be a wise
3: 21 Who *k* if the spirit
4: 13 foolish king who no longer *k* how
6: 12 For who *k* what is good for a man
8: 1 Who *k* the explanation of things?
8: 7 Since no man *k* the future,
8: 17 Even if a wise man claims he *k*,
9: 1 but no man *k* whether love
9: 12 no man *k* when his hour will come:
10: 14 No one *k* what is coming—
Isa 1: 3 The ox *k* his master,
7: 15 and honey when he *k* enough
7: 16 But before the boy *k* enough
8: 4 Before the boy *k* how
29: 16 "He *k* nothing"?
Jer 8: 7 *k* her appointed seasons,
9: 24 that he understands and *k* me,
Da 2: 22 he *k* what lies in darkness,
Joel 2: 14 Who *k?* He may turn and have pity
Jnh 3: 9 Who *k?* God may yet relent
Na 3: 17 and no one *k* where.
Mt 6: 8 for your Father *k* what you need
6: 32 your heavenly Father *k* that you
9: 30 "See that no one *k* about this."
11: 27 No one *k* the Son
11: 27 and no one *k* the Father
24: 36 "No one *k* about that day or hour,
Mk 13: 32 "No one *k* about that day or hour,
Lk 10: 22 No one *k* who the Son is
10: 22 and no one *k* who the Father is
12: 30 your Father *k* that you need them.
12: 47 "That servant who *k* his master's
16: 15 of men, but God *k* your hearts.
Jn 7: 49 this mob that *k* nothing of the law
10: 15 just as the Father *k* me
14: 17 it neither sees him nor *k* him.
19: 35 He *k* that he tells the truth,
Ac 4: 16 in Jerusalem *k* they have done
15: 8 who *k* the heart, showed that he
Ro 8: 27 who searches our hearts *k* the mind
1Co 2: 11 same way no one *k* the thoughts
2: 11 who among men *k* the thoughts
3: 20 "The Lord *k* that the thoughts
8: 2 who thinks he *k* something does
8: 7 But not everyone *k* this.
2Co 7: 4 our troubles my joy *k* no bounds.
11: 11 I do not love you? God *k* I do!
11: 31 is to be praised forever, *k* that I am
12: 2 of the body I do not know—God *k*
12: 3 God *k*— was caught up to Paradise
2Ti 2: 19 The Lord *k* those who are his," and
Jas 4: 17 who *k* the good he ought to do
2Pe 2: 9 then the Lord *k* how
1Jn 3: 20 our hearts, and he *k* everything.
4: 6 and whoever *k* God listens to us;
4: 7 born of God and *k* God.
Rev 12: 12 because he *k* that his time is short."
19: 12 on him that no one but he himself *k*

KOA

Eze 23: 23 the men of Pekod and Shoa and *K*,

KOHATH (KOHATH'S KOHATHITE KOHATHITES)

Ge 46: 11 The sons of Levi: Gershon, *K*
Ex 6: 16 to their records: Gershon, *K*
6: 18 The sons of *K* were Amram, Izhar,
6: 18 *K* lived 133 years.
Nu 3: 17 of the sons of Levi: Gershon, *K*
3: 27 To *K* belonged the clans
16: 1 the son of *K*, the son of Levi,
26: 57 through *K*, the Kohathite clan;
26: 58 (*K* was the forefather of Amram;
1Ch 6: 1 The sons of Levi: Gershon, *K*
6: 2 The sons of *K:* Amram, Izhar,
6: 16 The sons of Levi: Gershon, *K*
6: 18 The sons of *K:* Amram, Izhar,
6: 22 of *K:* Amminadab his son,
6: 38 the son of *K*, the son of Levi,
15: 5 From the descendants of *K*,
23: 6 to the sons of Levi: Gershon, *K*
23: 12 The sons of *K:* Amram, Izhar,
2Ch 34: 12 Meshullam, descended from *K*.

KOHATH'S (KOHATH)

Jos 21: 5 of *K* descendants were allotted ten
1Ch 6: 61 of *K* descendants were allotted ten

KOHATHITE (KOHATH)

Nu 3: 19 The *K* clans: Amram, Izhar,
3: 27 Uzzielites; these were the *K* clans.
3: 29 The *K* clans were to camp
3: 30 of the *K* clans was Elizaphan son
4: 2 of the *K* branch of the Levites
4: 18 "See that the *K* tribal clans are not
4: 37 those in the *K* clans who served
26: 57 through Kohath, the *K* clan;
Jos 21: 10 from the *K* clans of the Levites,
21: 20 The rest of the *K* clans
21: 26 given to the rest of the *K* clans.
1Ch 6: 54 of Aaron who were from the *K* clan
6: 60 distributed among the *K* clans,
6: 66 Some of the *K* clans were given
6: 70 to the rest of the *K* clans.
9: 32 Some of their *K* brothers were

KOHATHITES (KOHATH)

Nu 3: 28 The *K* were responsible
4: 4 of the *K* in the Tent of Meeting:
4: 15 *K* are to carry those things that are
4: 15 *K* are to come to do the carrying.
4: 20 But the *K* must not go in to look
4: 34 of the community counted the *K*
7: 9 Moses did not give any to the *K*,
10: 21 *K* set out, carrying the holy things.
Jos 21: 4 The first lot came out for the *K*,
1Ch 6: 33 From the *K:* Heman, the musician,
2Ch 20: 19 Then some Levites from the *K*
29: 12 set to work: from the *K*,

KOLAIAH

Ne 11: 7 the son of *K*, the son of Maaseiah,
Jer 29: 21 says about Ahab son of *K*

KORAH (KORAH'S KORAHITE KORAHITES)

Ge 36: 5 bore Jeush, Jalam and *K*.
36: 14 bore to Esau: Jeush, Jalam and *K*.
36: 16 Kenaz, *K*, Gatam and Amalek.
36: 18 Chiefs Jeush, Jalam and *K*.
Ex 6: 21 The sons of Izhar were *K*,
6: 24 The sons of *K* were Assir, Elkanah
Nu 16: 1 *K* son of Izhar, the son of Kohath,
16: 5 he said to *K* and all his followers:
16: 6 *K*, and all your followers are
16: 8 Moses also said to *K*, "Now listen,
16: 16 Moses said to *K*, "You
16: 19 When *K* had gathered all his
16: 24 'Move away from the tents of *K*,
16: 27 away from the tents of *K*,
16: 40 or he would become like *K*
Nu 16: 49 to those who had died because of *K*
26: 10 and swallowed them along with *K*,
26: 11 line of *K*, however, did not die out.
1Ch 1: 35 Eliphaz, Reuel, Jeush, Jalam and *K*
2: 43 The sons of Hebron: *K*, Tappuah,
6: 22 Amminadab his son, *K* his son,
6: 37 the son of *K*, the son of Izhar,
9: 19 the son of Ebiasaph, the son of *K*,
26: 19 who were descendants of *K*

KORAH'S (KORAH)

Nu 16: 32 their households and all *K* men
26: 9 and were among *K* followers
27: 3 He was not among *K* followers,
Jude : 11 been destroyed in *K* rebellion.

KORAHITE (KORAH)

Ex 6: 24 These were the *K* clans.
Nu 26: 58 the Mushite clan, the *K* clan.
1Ch 9: 31 the firstborn son of Shallum the *K*,

KORAHITES (KORAH)

1Ch 9: 19 his family (the *K*) were responsible
12: 6 Joezer and Jashobeam the *K;*
26: 1 From the *K:* Meshelemiah son
2Ch 20: 19 the Kohathites and *K* stood up

KORAZIN

Mt 11: 21 "Woe to you, *K!* Woe to you,
Lk 10: 13 "Woe to you, *K!* Woe to you,

KORE

1Ch 9: 19 Shallum son of *K*, the son
26: 1 Korahites: Meshelemiah son of *K*,
2Ch 31: 14 *K* son of Imnah the Levite,

KOUM

Mk 5: 41 *"Talitha k!"* (which means,

KOZ

1Ch 4: 8 Zereth, Zohar, Ethnan, and *K*,

KUE

1Ki 10: 28 from Egypt and from *K*
10: 28 purchased them from *K*.
2Ch 1: 16 from Egypt and from *K*—
1: 16 purchased them from *K*.

KUSHAIAH

1Ch 15: 17 of *K;* and with them their brothers

LAADAH

1Ch 4: 21 *L* the father of Mareshah

LABAN (LABAN'S)

Ge 24: 29 Rebekah had a brother named *L*,
24: 33 "Then tell us," *L* said.
24: 50 *L* and Bethuel answered, "This is
25: 20 and sister of *L* the Aramean.
27: 43 at once to my brother *L* in Haran.
28: 2 from among the daughters of *L*,
28: 5 *L* son of Bethuel the Aramean,
29: 5 Do you know *L*, Nahor's grandson
29: 10 Jacob saw Rachel daughter of *L*,
29: 13 as *L* heard the news about Jacob,
29: 14 *L* said to him, "You are my own
29: 15 for a whole month, *L* said to him,
29: 16 Now *L* had two daughters;
29: 19 *L* said, "It's better to give her
29: 21 Jacob said to *L*, "Give me my wife.
29: 22 *L* brought together all the people
29: 24 And *L* gave his servant girl Zilpah
29: 25 there was Leah! So Jacob said to *L*,
29: 26 have you deceived me?" *L* replied,
29: 28 and then *L* gave him his daughter
29: 29 *L* gave his servant girl Bilhah
29: 30 worked for *L* another seven years.
30: 25 birth to Joseph, Jacob said to *L*,
30: 27 But *L* said to him, "If I have found
30: 34 "Agreed," said *L*.
30: 40 animals that belonged to *L*.
30: 42 So the weak animals went to *L*
31: 12 have seen all that *L* has been doing
31: 19 When *L* had gone
31: 20 Jacob deceived *L* the Aramean
31: 22 On the third day *L* was told that
31: 24 Then God came to *L* the Aramean
31: 25 *L* and his relatives camped there

Ge 31: 25 of Gilead when *L* overtook him,
31: 26 *L* said to Jacob, "What have you
31: 31 Jacob answered *L*, "I was afraid,
31: 33 So *L* went into Jacob's tent
31: 34 *L* searched through everything
31: 36 Jacob was angry and took *L* to task
31: 36 "What is my crime?" he asked *L*.
31: 43 *L* answered Jacob, "The women
31: 47 *L* called it Jegar Sahadutha,
31: 48 *L* said, "This heap is a witness
31: 51 *L* also said to Jacob, "Here is this
31: 55 the next morning *L* kissed his
32: 4 I have been staying with *L*
46: 18 whom *L* had given
46: 25 whom *L* had given
Dt 1: 1 *L*, Hazeroth and Dizahab.

LABAN'S (LABAN)

Ge 29: 10 his mother's brother, and *L* sheep,
30: 36 to tend the rest of *L* flocks.
30: 40 did not put them with *L* animals.
31: 1 Jacob heard that *L* sons were
31: 2 And Jacob noticed that *L* attitude

LABOR (LABORED LABORER LABORER'S LABORERS LABORING LABORS)

Ge 5: 29 "He will comfort us in the *l*
49: 15 and submit to forced *l*.
Ex 1: 11 to oppress them with forced *l*,
1: 14 all their hard *l* the Egyptians used
1: 14 bitter with hard *l* in brick
2: 11 and watched them at their hard *l*.
5: 4 the people away from their *l*?
20: 9 Six days you shall *l* and do all your
34: 21 "Six days you shall *l*,
Dt 5: 13 Six days you shall *l* and do all your
20: 11 in it shall be subject to forced *l*
26: 6 made us suffer, putting us to hard *l*.
28: 33 eat what your land and *l* produce,
Jos 16: 10 but are required to do forced *l*.
17: 13 the Canaanites to forced *l*
Jdg 1: 28 the Canaanites into forced *l*
1: 30 they did subject them to forced *l*.
1: 35 they too were pressed into forced *l*.
1Sa 4: 19 but was overcome by her *l* pains.
4: 19 she went into *l* and gave birth,
2Sa 12: 31 consigning them to *l* with saws
20: 24 Adoniram was in charge of forced *l*
1Ki 4: 6 of Abda—in charge of forced *l*.
5: 14 was in charge of the forced *l*.
9: 15 of the forced *l* King Solomon
9: 21 conscripted for his slave *l* force,
11: 28 of the whole *l* force of the house
12: 4 but now lighten the harsh *l*
12: 18 who was in charge of forced *l*,
1Ch 20: 3 consigning them to *l* with saws
2Ch 8: 8 conscripted for his slave *l* force,
10: 4 but now lighten the harsh *l*
10: 18 who was in charge of forced *l*,
Job 24: 5 the poor go about their *l*
37: 7 he stops every man from his *l*.
39: 3 their *l* pains are ended.
39: 16 she cares not that her *l* was in vain,
Ps 48: 6 pain like that of a woman in *l*.
104: 23 to his *l* until evening.
107: 12 So he subjected them to bitter *l*;
109: 11 strangers plunder the fruits of his *l*.
127: 1 its builders *l* in vain.
128: 2 You will eat the fruit of your *l*;
Pr 12: 24 but laziness ends in slave *l*.
Ecc 1: 3 What does man gain from all his *l*
2: 10 and this was the reward for all my *l*
2: 20 despair over all my toilsome *l*
4: 4 I saw that all *l* and all achievement
5: 15 He takes nothing from his *l*
5: 18 in his toilsome *l* under the sun
8: 16 and to observe man's *l* on earth—
9: 9 in your toilsome *l* under the sun.
SS 8: 5 was in *l* gave you birth.
Isa 13: 8 they will writhe like a woman in *l*.
21: 3 like those of a woman in *l*;
23: 4 "I have neither been in *l*
31: 8 young men will be put to forced *l*.
54: 1 you who were never in *l*;
55: 2 and your *l* on what does not satisfy
66: 7 "Before she goes into *l*,
66: 8 Yet no sooner is Zion in *l*
Jer 3: 24 the fruits of our fathers' *l*—
4: 31 I hear a cry as of a woman in *l*,
6: 24 pain like that of a woman in *l*.
13: 21 like that of a woman in *l*?
22: 13 not paying them for their *l*.
22: 23 pain like that of a woman in *l*!
30: 6 on his stomach like a woman in *l*,
31: 8 expectant mothers and women in *l*;
48: 41 be like the heart of a woman in *l*.
49: 22 be like the heart of a woman in *l*.
49: 24 pain like that of a woman in *l*.
50: 43 pain like that of a woman in *l*.
51: 58 the nations' *l* is only fuel
La 1: 3 After affliction and harsh *l*,
Mic 4: 9 you like that of a woman in *l*?
4: 10 like a woman in *l*,
5: 3 when she who is in *l* gives birth
Hab 2: 13 that the people's *l* is only fuel
Hag 1: 11 and on the *l* of your hands."
Mt 6: 28 They do not *l* or spin.
Lk 12: 27 They do not *l* or spin.
Jn 4: 38 have reaped the benefits of their *l*."
1Co 3: 8 rewarded according to his own *l*.
15: 58 because you know that your *l*
Gal 4: 27 you who have no *l* pains;
Php 1: 22 this will mean fruitful *l* for me.
2: 16 day of Christ that I did not run or *l*
Col 1: 29 To this end I *l*, struggling
1Th 1: 3 by faith, your *l* prompted by love,
5: 3 as *l* pains on a pregnant woman,
1Ti 4: 10 (and for this we *l* and strive),
Rev 14: 13 "they will rest from their *l*,

LABORED (LABOR)

Isa 47: 12 you have *l* at since childhood.
47: 15 these you have *l* with
49: 4 But I said, "I have *l* to no purpose;
2Co 11: 27 I have *l* and toiled and have often

LABORER (LABOR)

Ecc 5: 12 The sleep of a *l* is sweet,

LABORER'S (LABOR)

Pr 16: 26 The *l* appetite works for him;

LABORERS (LABOR)

Jdg 1: 33 became forced *l* for them.
1Ki 5: 13 King Solomon conscripted *l*
2Ch 34: 13 charge of the *l* and supervised all
Ne 4: 10 "The strength of the *l* is giving out,
Mal 3: 5 against those who defraud *l*

LABORING (LABOR)

2Th 3: 8 *l* and toiling so that we would not

LABORS (LABOR)

Ecc 2: 22 with which he *l* under the sun?
1Co 16: 16 joins in the work, and *l* at it.

LACHISH

Jos 10: 3 Japhia king of *L* and Debir king
10: 5 Hebron, Jarmuth, *L* and Eglon—
10: 23 Hebron, Jarmuth, *L* and Eglon.
10: 31 moved on from Libnah to *L*;
10: 32 The LORD handed *L* over to Israel
10: 33 of Gezer had come up to help *L*,
10: 34 moved on from *L* to Eglon;
10: 35 just as they had done to *L*.
12: 11 one the king of *L* one the king
15: 39 Joktheel, *L*, Bozkath, Eglon,
2Ki 14: 19 but they sent men after him to *L*
14: 19 him in Jerusalem, and he fled to *L*,
18: 14 message to the king of Assyria at *L*:
18: 17 from *L* to King Hezekiah
19: 8 the king of Assyria had left *L*,
2Ch 11: 9 Ziph, Adoraim, *L*, Azekah, Zorah,
25: 27 but they sent men after him to *L*
25: 27 him in Jerusalem and he fled to *L*,
32: 9 all his forces were laying siege to *L*,
Ne 11: 30 their villages, in *L* and its fields,
Isa 36: 2 army from *L* to King Hezekiah
37: 8 the king of Assyria had left *L*,
Jer 34: 7 that were still holding out—*L*
Mic 1: 13 You who live in *L*,

LACK (LACKED LACKING LACKS)

Dt 8: 9 be scarce and you will *l* nothing;
Job 4: 11 The lion perishes for *l* of prey,
24: 8 and hug the rocks for *l* of shelter.
31: 19 I have seen anyone perishing for *l*
34: 35 his words *l* insight.'
38: 41 and wander about for *l* of food?
Ps 23: 1 is my shepherd, I shall *l* nothing.
34: 9 for those who fear him *l* nothing.
34: 10 seek the LORD *l* no good thing.
94: 10 he who teaches man *l* knowledge?
Pr 5: 23 He will die for *l* of discipline,
9: 4 she says to those who *l* judgment.
9: 16 she says to those who *l* judgment.
10: 21 but fools die for *l* of judgment.
11: 14 For *l* of guidance a nation falls,
15: 22 Plans fail for *l* of counsel,
22: 27 if you *l* the means to pay,
28: 27 to the poor will *l* nothing,
Isa 5: 13 exile for *l* of understanding;
34: 16 not one will *l* her mate.
50: 2 Do I *l* the strength to rescue you?
50: 2 their fish rot for *l* of water
51: 14 nor will they *l* bread.
56: 10 they all *l* knowledge;
56: 11 shepherds who *l* understanding;
Jer 14: 6 fails for *l* of pasture."
La 4: 9 away for *l* of food from the field.
Hos 4: 6 from *l* of knowledge.
Am 4: 6 and *l* of bread in every town,
Zec 10: 2 oppressed for *l* of a shepherd.
Mt 13: 58 miracles there because of their *l*
19: 20 What do I still *l*?" Jesus answered,
Mk 6: 6 he was amazed at their *l* of faith.
10: 21 "One thing you *l*," he said.
16: 14 he rebuked them for their *l* of faith
Lk 18: 22 said to him, "You still *l* one thing.
22: 35 did you *l* anything?" "Nothing,"
Ro 3: 3 Will their *l* of faith nullify God's
1Co 1: 7 you do not *l* any spiritual gift
7: 5 because of your *l* of self-control.
Col 2: 23 *l* any value in restraining sensual

LACKED (LACK)

Dt 2: 7 and you have not *l* anything.
Jdg 18: 7 And since their land *l* nothing,
1Ki 11: 22 "What have you *l* here that you
Ne 9: 21 them in the desert; they *l* nothing,
Pr 7: 7 a youth who *l* judgment.
1Co 12: 24 honor to the parts that *l* it,

LACKING (LACK)

1Ki 4: 27 They saw to it that nothing was *l*.
Job 24: 7 *L* clothes, they spend the night
24: 10 *L* clothes, they go about naked;
Pr 17: 18 A man *l* in judgment strikes hands
Ecc 1: 15 what is *l* cannot be counted.
Ro 12: 11 Never be *l* in zeal, but keep your
1Co 16: 17 they have supplied what was *l*
Col 1: 24 in my flesh what is still *l* in regard
1Th 3: 10 and supply what is *l* in your faith.
Jas 1: 4 and complete, not *l* anything.

LACKS (LACK)

Jdg 18: 10 a land that *l* nothing whatever."
2Sa 3: 29 falls by the sword or who *l* food."
Pr 6: 32 who commits adultery *l* judgment;
10: 13 for the back of him who *l* judgment
11: 12 man who *l* judgment derides his
12: 11 he who chases fantasies *l* judgment
15: 21 delights a man who *l* judgment,
24: 30 of the man who *l* judgment;
25: 28 is a man who *l* self-control.
28: 16 A tyrannical ruler *l* judgment,
31: 11 and *l* nothing of value.
Ecc 6: 2 so that he *l* nothing his heart
10: 3 the fool *l* sense
SS 7: 2 that never *l* blended wine.
Eze 34: 8 because my flock *l* a shepherd
Jas 1: 5 any of you *l* wisdom, he should ask

LADAN

1Ch 7: 26 *L* his son, Ammihud his son,
23: 7 Belonging to the Gershonites: *L*
23: 8 The sons of *L*: Jehiel the first,
23: 9 the heads of the families of *L*.
26: 21 belonging to *L* the Gershonite,
26: 21 of *L*, who were Gershonites
26: 21 who were Gershonites through *L*

LADEN (LOAD)
Job 36: 16 of your table *l* with choice food.
36: 17 now you are *l* with the judgment
Ps 105: 37 He brought out Israel, *l* with silver

LADLE (LADLES)
Nu 7: 14 one gold *l* weighing ten shekels,
7: 20 one gold *l* weighing ten shekels,
7: 26 one gold *l* weighing ten shekels,
7: 32 one gold *l* weighing ten shekels,
7: 38 one gold *l* weighing ten shekels,
7: 44 one gold *l* weighing ten shekels,
7: 50 one gold *l* weighing ten shekels,
7: 56 one gold *l* weighing ten shekels,
7: 62 one gold *l* weighing ten shekels,
7: 68 one gold *l* weighing ten shekels,
7: 74 one gold *l* weighing ten shekels,
7: 80 one gold *l* weighing ten shekels,

LADLES (LADLE)
Ex 25: 29 make its plates and *l* of pure gold,
37: 16 its plates and *l* and bowls
Nu 4: 7 *l* and bowls, and the jars
7: 84 sprinkling bowls and twelve gold *l*.
7: 86 The twelve gold *l* filled
7: 86 the gold *l* weighed a hundred
1Ki 7: 50 sprinkling bowls, *l* and censers;
2Ki 25: 14 *l* and all the bronze articles used
2Ch 4: 22 sprinkling bowls, *l* and censers;
24: 14 and also *l* and other objects of gold
Jer 52: 18 *l* and all the bronze articles used
52: 19 *l* and bowls used for drink offerings

LAEL
Nu 3: 24 Gershonites was Eliasaph son of *L*.

LAGGING
Dt 25: 18 and cut off all who were *l* behind;

LAHAD
1Ch 4: 2 Jahath the father of Ahumai and *L*.

LAHMAS
Jos 15: 40 Eglon, Cabbon, *L*, Kitlish,

LAHMI
1Ch 20: 5 son of Jair killed *L* the brother

LAID (LAY)
Ge 9: 23 and *l* it across their shoulders;
22: 9 He bound his son Isaac and *l* him
Ex 19: 13 not a hand is to be *l* on him.
22: 8 he has *l* his hands on the other
Lev 8: 14 his sons *l* their hands on its head.
8: 18 his sons *l* their hands on its head.
8: 22 his sons *l* their hands on its head.
9: 20 these they *l* on the breasts,
26: 33 Your land will be *l* waste,
Nu 27: 23 Then he *l* his hands on him
Dt 24: 5 or have any other duty *l* on him.
34: 9 Moses had *l* his hands on him.
Jos 2: 6 of flax she had *l* out on the roof.)
2: 19 be on our head if a hand is *l* on him.
Jdg 2: 20 has violated the covenant that I *l*
16: 24 the one who *l* waste our land
Ru 4: 16 *l* him in her lap and cared for him.
1Sa 19: 13 Then Michal took an idol and *l* it
2Sa 22: 16 the foundations of the earth *l* bare
1Ki 1: 21 as my lord the king is *l* to rest
6: 37 the temple of the LORD was *l*
7: 10 The foundations were *l*
12: 11 My father *l* on you a heavy yoke;
13: 29 the man of God, *l* it on the donkey,
13: 30 Then he *l* the body in his own tomb
16: 17 from Gibbethon and *l* siege
16: 34 He *l* its foundations at the cost
17: 19 where he was staying, and *l* him
18: 33 into pieces and *l* it on the wood.
2Ki 4: 21 *l* him on the bed of the man of God,
4: 31 and *l* the staff on the boy's face,
6: 24 marched up and *l* siege to Samaria.
17: 5 and *l* siege to it for three years.
18: 9 against Samaria and *l* siege to it.
19: 17 Assyrian kings have *l* waste these
22: 19 become accursed and *l* waste,
24: 10 on Jerusalem and *l* siege to it,
1Ch 6: 32 to the regulations *l* down for them.
20: 1 He *l* waste the land
2Ch 3: 3 The foundation Solomon *l*
8: 16 the temple of the LORD was *l*
10: 11 My father *l* on you a heavy yoke;
16: 14 They *l* him on a bier covered
29: 23 and they *l* their hands on them.
32: 1 He *l* siege to the fortified cities,
Ezr 3: 6 LORD's temple had not yet been *l*.
3: 10 When the builders *l* the foundation
3: 11 of the house of the LORD was *l*.
3: 12 foundation of this temple being *l*,
5: 16 and *l* the foundations of the house
6: 3 and let its foundations be *l*.
Ne 3: 3 They *l* its beams and put its doors
3: 6 They *l* its beams and put its doors
Job 14: 10 But man dies and is *l* low;
16: 18 may my cry never be *l* to rest!
38: 4 when I *l* the earth's foundation?
38: 6 or who *l* its cornerstone—
Ps 18: 15 the foundations of the earth *l* bare
66: 11 and *l* burdens on our backs.
102: 25 beginning you *l* the foundations
119: 4 You have *l* down precepts
119: 25 I am *l* low in the dust;
119:138 The statutes you have *l*
139: 5 you have *l* your hand upon me.
141: 9 from the snares they have *l* for me,
Pr 3: 19 wisdom the LORD *l* the earth's
Ecc 1: 13 What a heavy burden God has *l*
3: 10 I have seen the burden God has *l*
Isa 1: 7 *l* waste as when overthrown
6: 13 it will again be *l* waste.
7: 16 two kings you dread will be *l* waste.
14: 8 "Now that you have been *l* low,
14: 12 you who once *l* low the nations!
24: 3 earth will be completely *l* waste
28: 1 the pride of those *l* low by wine!
37: 18 the Assyrian kings have *l* waste all
44: 28 "Let its foundations be *l*." '
47: 6 you *l* a very heavy yoke.
48: 13 My own hand *l* the foundations
49: 17 those who *l* you waste depart
49: 19 and your land *l* waste,
51: 13 and *l* the foundations of the earth,
51: 16 who *l* the foundations of the earth,
53: 6 and the LORD has *l* on him
Jer 2: 15 They have *l* waste his land;
9: 12 *l* waste like a desert that no one can
12: 11 the whole land will be *l* waste
18: 16 Their land will be *l* waste,
25: 37 peaceful meadows will be *l* waste
39: 1 with his whole army and *l* siege
46: 15 Why will your warriors be *l* low?
46: 19 for Memphis will be *l* waste
48: 9 for she will be *l* waste;
La 1: 10 The enemy *l* hands
2: 6 He has *l* waste his dwelling like
3: 28 for the LORD has *l* it on him.
Eze 6: 6 so that your altars will be *l* waste
6: 6 the towns will be *l* waste
12: 20 The inhabited towns will be *l* waste
13: 14 so that its foundation will be *l* bare.
21: 29 it will be *l* on the necks
24: 2 the king of Babylon has *l* siege
25: 3 land of Israel when it was *l* waste
32: 19 be *l* among the uncircumcised.'
32: 25 they are *l* among the slain.
32: 29 they are *l* with those killed
32: 32 and all his hordes will be *l*
35: 12 "They have been *l* waste
36: 35 land that was *l* waste has become
Hos 5: 9 Ephraim will be *l* waste
Joel 1: 7 It has *l* waste my vines
Mic 5: 1 for a siege is *l* against us.
Na 2: 2 destroyers have *l* them waste
Hag 2: 15 before one stone was *l* on another
2: 18 of the LORD's temple was *l*.
Zec 4: 9 Zerubbabel have *l* the foundation
8: 9 there when the foundation was *l*
Mt 15: 30 many others, and *l* them at his feet;
22: 15 *l* plans to trap him in his words.
Mk 6: 29 took his body and *l* it in a tomb.
15: 47 of Joses saw where he was *l*.
16: 6 See the place where they *l* him.
Lk 6: 48 and *l* the foundation on rock.
12: 19 of good things *l* up for many years.
16: 20 At his gate was *l* a beggar named
19: 20 I have kept it *l* away in a piece
23: 53 one in which no one had yet been *l*.
23: 55 and how his body was *l* in it.
Jn 7: 30 but no one *l* a hand on him,
7: 44 but no one *l* a hand on him.
11: 34 "Where have you *l* him?" he asked.
11: 38 with a stone *l* across the entrance.
19: 41 in which no one had ever been *l*.
19: 42 was nearby, they *l* Jesus there.
Ac 5: 15 into the streets and *l* them on beds
6: 6 and *l* their hands on them.
7: 58 the witnesses *l* their clothes
13: 29 from the tree and *l* him in a tomb.
1Co 3: 10 I *l* a foundation as an expert builder
3: 11 other than the one already *l*,
14: 25 secrets of his heart will be *l* bare.
1Ti 4: 14 body of elders *l* their hands on you.
Heb 1: 10 you *l* the foundations of the earth,
4: 13 and *l* bare before the eyes of him
2Pe 3: 10 and everything in it will be *l* bare.
1Jn 3: 16 Jesus Christ *l* down his life for us.
Rev 21: 16 The city was *l* out like a square,

LAIN (LAY)
Ge 24: 16 a virgin; no man had ever *l* with her
1Sa 26: 5 of the army, had *l* down.

LAIR (LAIRS)
Jer 4: 7 A lion has come out of his *l*;
25: 38 Like a lion he will leave his *l*,
Zep 2: 15 a *l* for wild beasts!

LAIRS (LAIR)
Na 2: 12 filling his *l* with the kill

LAISH
Jdg 18: 7 So the five men left and came to *L*,
18: 14 the land of *L* said to their brothers,
18: 27 went on to *L*, against a peaceful
18: 29 though the city used to be called *L*.
1Sa 25: 44 to Paltiel son of *L*, who was
2Sa 3: 15 from her husband Paltiel son of *L*.

LAISHAH
Isa 10: 30 Listen, O *L*!

LAKE
Dt 33: 23 he will inherit southward to the *l*."
Mt 4: 13 which was by the *l* in the area
4: 18 They were casting a net into the *l*,
8: 18 to cross to the other side of the *l*.
8: 24 a furious storm came up on the *l*,
8: 32 down the steep bank into the *l*
13: 1 out of the house and sat by the *l*.
13: 47 a net that was let down into the *l*
14: 25 out to them, walking on the *l*.
14: 26 disciples saw him walking on the *l*,
16: 5 When they went across the *l*,
17: 27 go to the *l* and throw out your line.
Mk 1: 16 Andrew casting a net into the *l*,
2: 13 again Jesus went out beside the *l*.
3: 7 withdrew with his disciples to the *l*,
4: 1 Jesus began to teach by the *l*.
4: 1 into a boat and sat in it out on the *l*,
5: 1 went across the *l* to the region
5: 13 down the steep bank into the *l*
5: 21 While he was by the *l*, one
5: 21 by boat to the other side of the *l*,
6: 47 the boat was in the middle of the *l*,
6: 48 out to them, walking on the *l*.
6: 49 they saw him walking on the *l*,
Lk 5: 1 standing by the *L* of Gennesaret,
8: 22 go over to the other side of the *l*."
8: 23 A squall came down on the *l*,
8: 26 which is across the *l* from Galilee.
8: 33 down the steep bank into the *l*
Jn 6: 16 his disciples went down to the *l*,
6: 17 set off across the *l* for Capernaum.
6: 22 of the *l* realized that only one boat
6: 25 him on the other side of the *l*,
Rev 19: 20 into the fiery *l* of burning sulfur.
20: 10 thrown into the *l* of burning sulfur,
20: 14 The *l* of fire is the second death.
20: 14 and Hades were thrown into the *l*
20: 15 he was thrown into the *l* of fire.
21: 8 be in the fiery *l* of burning sulfur.

LAKKUM
Jos 19: 33 and Jabneel to *L* and ending

LAMA

Mt 27:46 "Eloi, Eloi, l sabachthani?"—
Mk 15:34 "Eloi, Eloi, l sabachthani?"—

LAMB (LAMB'S LAMBS)

Ge 22: 7 where is the l for the burnt offering
22: 8 "God himself will provide the l
30:32 every dark-colored l and every
30:33 any l that is not dark-colored will
Ex 12: 3 is to take a l for his family,
12: 4 amount of l needed in accordance
12: 4 is too small for a whole l,
12:21 and slaughter the Passover l.
13:13 with a l every firstborn donkey,
29:40 With the first l offer a tenth
29:41 Sacrifice the other l at twilight
34:20 the firstborn donkey with a l,
Lev 3: 7 If he offers a l, he is to present it
4:32 " 'If he brings a l as his sin offering,
4:35 from the l of the fellowship offering
5: 6 bring to the LORD a female l
5: 7 " 'If he cannot afford a l, he is
9: 3 a calf and a l—both a year old
12: 6 the Tent of Meeting a year-old l
12: 8 " 'If she cannot afford a l, she is
14:10 lambs and one ewe l a year old,
14:13 He is to slaughter the l
14:21 he must take one male l
14:24 is to take the l for the guilt offering,
14:25 He shall slaughter the l
17: 3 a l or a goat in the camp
23:12 offering to the LORD a l a year old
Nu 6:12 and must bring a year-old male l
6:14 a year-old ewe l without defect
6:14 a year-old male l without defect
7:15 one ram and one male l a year old,
7:21 one ram and one male l a year old,
7:27 one ram and one male l a year old,
7:33 one ram and one male l a year old,
7:39 one ram and one male l a year old,
7:45 one ram and one male l a year old,
7:51 one ram and one male l a year old,
7:57 one ram and one male l a year old,
7:63 one ram and one male l a year old,
7:69 one ram and one male l a year old,
7:75 one ram and one male l a year old,
7:81 one ram and one male l a year old,
9:11 are to eat the l, together
15: 5 With each l for the burnt offering
15:11 or ram, each l or young goat,
28: 4 Prepare one l in the morning
28: 7 hin of fermented drink with each l.
28: 8 Prepare the second l at twilight,
28:13 and with each l, a grain offering
28:14 and with each l, a fourth of a hin.
1Sa 7: 9 Then Samuel took a suckling l
2Sa 12: 3 one little ewe l he had bought.
12: 4 he took the ewe l that belonged
12: 6 pay for that l four times over,
2Ch 30:15 They slaughtered the Passover l
35: 1 and the Passover l was slaughtered
Ezr 6:20 Levites slaughtered the Passover l
Isa 11: 6 The wolf will live with the l,
53: 7 he was led like a l to the slaughter,
65:25 and the l will feed together,
66: 3 and whoever offers a l,
Jer 11:19 I had been like a gentle l led
Eze 46:13 are to provide a year-old l
46:15 So the l and the grain offering
Mk 14:12 to sacrifice the Passover l,
Lk 22: 7 Bread on which the Passover l had
Jn 1:29 L of God, who takes away the sin
1:36 he said, "Look, the L of God!"
Ac 8:32 as a l before the shearer is silent,
1Co 5: 7 our Passover l, has been sacrificed.
1Pe 1:19 a l without blemish or defect.
Rev 5: 6 Then I saw a L, looking
5: 8 fell down before the L.
5:12 "Worthy is the L, who was slain,
5:13 sits on the throne and to the L
6: 1 as the L opened the first
6: 3 When the L opened the second
6: 5 When the L opened the third seal,
6: 7 When the L opened the fourth seal,
6:16 and from the wrath of the L!
7: 9 the throne and in front of the L.
7:10 and to the L."
Rev 7:14 white in the blood of the L.
7:17 For the L at the center
12:11 him by the blood of the L
13: 8 belonging to the L that was slain
13:11 He had two horns like a l,
14: 1 and there before me was the L,
14: 4 They follow the L wherever he
14: 4 as firstfruits to God and the L.
14:10 of the holy angels and of the L.
15: 3 of God and the song of the L:
17:14 They will make war against the L,
17:14 but the L will overcome them
19: 7 For the wedding of the L has come,
19: 9 to the wedding supper of the L!' "
21: 9 you the bride, the wife of the L."
21:14 of the twelve apostles of the L.
21:22 Almighty and the L are its temple.
21:23 gives it light, and the L is its lamp.
22: 1 and of the L down the middle
22: 3 and of the L will be in the city,

LAMB'S (LAMB)

Rev 21:27 written in the L book of life.

LAMBS (LAMB)

Ge 21:28 Abraham set apart seven ewe l
21:29 of these seven ewe l you have set
21:30 Accept these seven l from my hand
30:35 on them) and all the dark-colored l
Ex 12: 7 of the houses where they eat the l.
29:38 each day: two l a year old.
Lev 14:10 day he must bring two male l
14:12 is to take one of the male l
23:18 with this bread seven male l,
23:19 goat for a sin offering and two l,
23:20 to wave the two l before the LORD
Nu 7:17 goats and five male l a year old,
7:23 goats and five male l a year old,
7:29 goats and five male l a year old,
7:35 goats and five male l a year old,
7:41 goats and five male l a year old,
7:47 goats and five male l a year old,
7:53 goats and five male l a year old,
7:59 goats and five male l a year old,
7:65 goats and five male l a year old,
7:71 goats and five male l a year old,
7:77 goats and five male l a year old,
7:83 goats and five male l a year old,
7:87 and twelve male l a year old,
7:88 and sixty male l a year old.
28: 3 two l a year old without defect,
28: 9 make an offering of two l a year old
28:11 and seven male l a year old,
28:19 and seven male l a year old,
28:21 and with each of the seven l,
28:27 and seven male l a year old
28:29 and with each of the seven l,
29: 2 and seven male l a year old,
29: 4 and with each of the seven l,
29: 8 and seven male l a year old,
29:10 and with each of the seven l,
29:13 and fourteen male l a year old,
29:15 and with each of the fourteen l,
29:17 and fourteen male l a year old,
29:18 With the bulls, rams and l,
29:20 and fourteen male l a year old,
29:21 With the bulls, rams and l,
29:23 and fourteen male l a year old,
29:24 With the bulls, rams and l,
29:26 and fourteen male l a year old,
29:27 With the bulls, rams and l,
29:29 and fourteen male l a year old,
29:30 With the bulls, rams and l,
29:32 and fourteen male l a year old,
29:33 With the bulls, rams and l,
29:36 and seven male l a year old,
29:37 With the bull, the ram and the l,
Dt 7:13 and the l of your flocks
28: 4 the calves of your herds and the l
28:18 the calves of your herds and the l
28:51 l of your flocks until you are ruined
32:14 and with fattened l and goats,
1Sa 15: 9 and l—everything that was good.
2Ki 3: 4 of Israel with a hundred thousand l
1Ch 29:21 rams and a thousand male l,
2Ch 29:21 seven male l and seven male goats
29:22 then they slaughtered the l
29:32 and two hundred male l—
2Ch 30:17 and could not consecrate ⌊their l⌋
30:17 had to kill the Passover l
35: 6 and prepare ⌊the l⌋ for your fellow
35: 6 the Passover l, consecrate
35:11 The Passover l were slaughtered,
Ezr 6: 9 male l for burnt offerings
6:17 hundred rams, four hundred male l
7:17 male l, together with their grain
8:35 rams, seventy-seven male l,
Ps 114: 4 the hills like l.
114: 6 you hills, like l?
Pr 27:26 the l will provide you with clothing
Isa 1:11 in the blood of bulls and l and goats
5:17 l will feed among the ruins
16: 1 Send l as tribute
34: 6 the blood of l and goats,
40:11 He gathers the l in his arms
Jer 51:40 like l to the slaughter,
Eze 27:21 they did business with you in l,
39:18 as if they were rams and l,
46: 4 the Sabbath day is to be six male l
46: 5 the grain offering with the l is to be
46: 6 six l and a ram, all without defect.
46: 7 and with the l as much
46:11 and with the l as much
Hos 4:16 like l in a meadow?
Am 6: 4 You dine on choice l
Lk 10: 3 I am sending you out like l
Jn 21:15 Jesus said, "Feed my l."

LAME

Lev 21:18 or l, disfigured or deformed;
Dt 15:21 If an animal has a defect, is l
2Sa 4: 4 son of Saul had a son who was l
5: 6 the blind and the l can ward you off
5: 8 and l' will not enter the palace."
5: 8 use the water shaft to reach those 'l
19:26 since I your servant am l, I said,
Job 29:15 and feet to the l.
Pr 25:19 Like a bad tooth or a l foot
26: 7 Like a l man's legs that hang limp
Isa 33:23 even the l will carry off plunder.
35: 6 Then will the l leap like a deer,
Jer 31: 8 them will be the blind and the l,
Mic 4: 6 "I will gather the l;
4: 7 I will make the l a remnant,
Zep 3:19 I will rescue the l
Mt 11: 5 The blind receive sight, the l walk,
15:30 bringing the l, the blind,
15:31 the l walking and the blind seeing.
21:14 the l came to him at the temple,
Lk 7:22 The blind receive sight, the l walk,
14:13 the crippled, the l, the blind,
14:21 the crippled, the blind and the l.'
Jn 5: 3 the blind, the l, the paralyzed.
Ac 14: 8 who was l from birth and had never
Heb 12:13 so that the l may not be disabled,

LAMECH

Ge 4:18 and Methushael was the father of L
4:19 L married two women, one named
4:23 L said to his wives,
4:23 wives of L, hear my words.
4:24 then L seventy-seven times."
5:25 he became the father of L.
5:26 after he became the father of L,
5:28 When L had lived 182 years,
5:30 L lived 595 years and had other
5:31 Altogether, L lived 777 years,
1Ch 1: 3 Enoch, Methuselah, L, Noah.
Lk 3:36 the son of Noah, the son of L,

LAMENT (LAMENTATION LAMENTED LAMENTS)

2Sa 1:17 took up this l concerning Saul
1:18 the men of Judah be taught this l
3:33 The king sang this l for Abner:
Ps 56: 8 Record my l;
Isa 3:26 The gates of Zion will l and mourn;
15: 5 they l their destruction.
16: 7 L and grieve
19: 8 The fishermen will groan and l,
29: 2 she will mourn and l,
Jer 4: 8 l and wail,
7:29 take up a l on the barren heights,
9:10 take up a l concerning the desert
9:20 teach one another a l.
34: 5 a fire in your honor and l,

La 2: 8 He made ramparts and walls *l;*
Eze 2: 10 sides of it were written words of *l*
9: 4 *l* over all the detestable things that
19: 1 Take up a *l* concerning the princes
19: 14 This is a *l* and is to be used as a *l.*''
24: 16 Yet do not *l* or weep or shed any
26: 17 will take up a *l* concerning you
27: 2 take up a *l* concerning Tyre.
27: 32 will take up a *l* concerning you:
28: 12 take up a *l* concerning the king
32: 2 take up a *l* concerning Pharaoh
32: 16 This is the *l* they will chant for her.
Am 5: 1 this *l* I take up concerning you:

LAMENTATION (LAMENT)

Est 9: 31 to their times of fasting and *l.*
Isa 15: 8 their *l* as far as Beer Elim.
La 2: 5 He has multiplied mourning and *l*

LAMENTED (LAMENT)

Ge 50: 10 near the Jordan, they *l* loudly

LAMENTS (LAMENT)

2Ch 35: 25 Jeremiah composed *l* for Josiah,
35: 25 commemorate Josiah in the *l.*
35: 25 in Israel and are written in the *L.*
Isa 16: 11 My heart *l* for Moab like a harp,
Jer 48: 36 So my heart *l* for Moab like a flute;
48: 36 it *l* like a flute for the men

LAMP (LAMPS LAMPSTAND LAMPSTANDS)

1Sa 3: 3 The *l* of God had not yet gone out,
2Sa 21: 17 so that the *l* of Israel will not be
22: 29 You are my *l,* O LORD;
1Ki 11: 36 my servant may always have a *l*
15: 4 the LORD his God gave him a *l*
2Ki 4: 10 and a table, a chair and a *l* for him.
8: 19 promised to maintain a *l* for David
2Ch 21: 7 promised to maintain a *l* for David
Job 18: 5 "The *l* of the wicked is snuffed out;
18: 6 the *l* beside him goes out.
21: 17 "Yet how often is the *l*
29: 3 when his *l* shone upon my head
Ps 18: 28 You, O LORD, keep my *l* burning;
119: 105 Your word is a *l* to my feet
132: 17 and set up a *l* for my anointed one.
Pr 6: 23 For these commands are a *l,*
13: 9 the *l* of the wicked is snuffed out.
20: 20 his *l* will be snuffed out
20: 27 *l* of the LORD searches the spirit
21: 4 the *l* of the wicked, are sin!
24: 20 *l* of the wicked will be snuffed out.
31: 18 and her *l* does not go out at night.
Jer 25: 10 of millstones and the light of the *l.*
Mt 5: 15 Neither do people light a *l*
6: 22 "The eye is the *l* of the body.
Mk 4: 21 "Do you bring in a *l* to put it
Lk 8: 16 "No one lights a *l* and hides it
11: 33 "No one lights a *l* and puts it
11: 34 Your eye is the *l* of your body.
11: 36 when the light of a *l* shines on you
15: 8 she not light a *l,* sweep the house
Jn 5: 35 John was a *l* that burned
Rev 18: 23 The light of a *l*
21: 23 gives it light, and the Lamb is its *l.*
22: 5 They will not need the light of a *l*

LAMPS (LAMP)

Ex 25: 37 "Then make its seven *l*
27: 20 so that the *l* may be kept burning.
27: 21 are to keep the *l* burning
30: 7 morning when he tends the *l.*
30: 8 when he lights the *l* at twilight
35: 14 is for light with its accessories, *l*
37: 23 They made its seven *l,* as well
39: 37 gold lampstand with its row of *l*
40: 4 in the lampstand and set up its *l.*
40: 25 and set up the *l* before the LORD,
Lev 24: 2 so that the *l* may be kept burning
24: 3 is to tend the *l* before the LORD
24: 4 The *l* on the pure gold lampstand
Nu 4: 9 with its *l,* its wick trimmers
8: 2 'When you set up the seven *l,*
8: 3 he set up the *l* so that they faced
1Ki 7: 49 the gold floral work and *l* and tongs
1Ch 28: 15 for each silver lampstand and its *l,*
28: 15 for the gold lampstands and their *l,*
1Ch 28: 15 weight for each lampstand and its *l;*
2Ch 4: 20 of pure gold with their *l,*
4: 21 the gold floral work and *l*
13: 11 light the *l* on the gold lampstand
29: 7 of the portico and put out the *l.*
Zep 1: 12 time I will search Jerusalem with *l*
Mt 25: 1 be like ten virgins who took their *l*
25: 3 The foolish ones took their *l*
25: 4 took oil in jars along with their *l.*
25: 7 woke up and trimmed their *l.*
25: 8 of your oil; our *l* are going out.'
Lk 12: 35 for service and keep your *l* burning,
Ac 20: 8 There were many *l*
Rev 4: 5 the throne, seven *l* were blazing.

LAMPSTAND (LAMP)

Ex 25: 31 "Make a *l* of pure gold
25: 32 to extend from the sides of the *l*—
25: 33 six branches extending from the *l.*
25: 34 on the *l* there are to be four cups
25: 35 of branches extending from the *l,*
25: 36 be of one piece with the *l,*
25: 39 of pure gold is to be used for the *l*
26: 35 and put the *l* opposite it
30: 27 its articles, the *l* and its accessories,
31: 8 pure gold *l* and all its accessories,
35: 14 the *l* that is for light
37: 17 They made the *l* of pure gold
37: 18 extended from the sides of the *l*—
37: 19 six branches extending from the *l.*
37: 20 on the *l* were four cups shaped like
37: 21 of branches extending from the *l,*
37: 22 all of one piece with the *l,*
37: 24 They made the *l* and all its
39: 37 the pure gold *l* with its row
40: 4 bring in the *l* and set up its lamps.
40: 24 He placed the *l* in the Tent
Lev 24: 4 The lamps on the pure gold *l*
Nu 3: 31 the *l,* the altars, the articles
4: 9 and cover the *l* that is for light,
8: 2 to light the area in front of the *l.*' ''
8: 3 so that they faced forward on the *l,*
8: 4 This is how the *l* was made:
8: 4 *l* was made exactly like the pattern
1Ch 28: 15 according to the use of each *l;*
28: 15 the weight of silver for each silver *l*
28: 15 with the weight for each *l*
2Ch 13: 11 lamps on the gold *l* every evening.
Da 5: 5 near the *l* in the royal palace.
Zec 4: 2 "I see a solid gold *l* with a bowl
4: 11 on the right and the left of the *l?*''
Heb 9: 2 In its first room were the *l,*
Rev 2: 5 and remove your *l* from its place.

LAMPSTANDS (LAMP)

1Ki 7: 49 the *l* of pure gold (five on the right
1Ch 28: 15 the weight of gold for the gold *l*
2Ch 4: 7 He made ten gold *l* according
4: 20 the *l* of pure gold with their lamps,
Jer 52: 19 censers, sprinkling bowls, pots, *l,*
Rev 1: 12 when I turned I saw seven golden *l,*
1: 13 and among the *l* was someone "like
1: 20 and of the seven golden *l* is this:
1: 20 the seven *l* are the seven churches.
2: 1 walks among the seven golden *l:*
11: 4 the two *l* that stand before the Lord

LANCE

Job 39: 23 along with the flashing spear and *l.*
41: 29 he laughs at the rattling of the *l.*

LAND (BORDERLAND GRASSLANDS LAND'S LANDED LANDOWNER LANDS SHORELANDS WASTELAND WASTELANDS)

Ge 1: 10 God called the dry ground "*l,*''
1: 11 and trees on the *l* that bear fruit
1: 11 "Let the *l* produce vegetation:
1: 12 The *l* produced vegetation:
1: 24 "Let the *l* produce living creatures
2: 11 through the entire *l* of Havilah,
2: 12 (The gold of that *l* is good;
2: 13 winds through the entire *l* of Cush.
4: 14 you are driving me from the *l,*
4: 16 LORD's presence and lived in the *l*
7: 22 on dry *l* that had the breath
10: 11 From that *l* he went to Assyria,
11: 28 in the *l* of his birth.
Ge 12: 1 and go to the *l* I will show you.
12: 5 and they set out for the *l* of Canaan
12: 6 Abram traveled through the *l* as far
12: 6 The Canaanites were then in the *l,*
12: 7 To your offspring I will give this *l.*''
12: 10 Now there was a famine in the *l,*
13: 6 But the *l* could not support them
13: 7 also living in the *l* at that time.
13: 9 Is not the whole *l* before you?
13: 10 like the *l* of Egypt, toward Zoar.
13: 12 Abram lived in the *l* of Canaan,
13: 15 All the *l* that you see I will give
13: 17 the length and breadth of the *l,*
15: 7 to give you this *l* to take possession
15: 18 "To your descendants I give this *l,*
15: 19 the Euphrates—the *l*
17: 8 whole *l* of Canaan, where you are
19: 23 the sun had risen over the *l.*
19: 25 and also the vegetation in the *l.*
19: 28 saw dense smoke rising from the *l,*
19: 28 toward all the *l* of the plain,
20: 15 And Abimelech said, "My *l* is
21: 32 returned to the *l* of the Philistines.
21: 34 stayed in the *l* of the Philistines
23: 2 Hebron) in the *l* of Canaan,
23: 7 down before the people of the *l,*
23: 12 down before the people of the *l*
23: 15 the *l* is worth four hundred shekels
23: 19 is at Hebron) in the *l* of Canaan.
24: 5 to come back with me to this *l?*
24: 7 my native *l* and who spoke to me
24: 7 'To your offspring I will give this *l*
24: 37 in whose *l* I live, but go
25: 6 Isaac to the *l* of the east.
26: 1 Now there was a famine in the *l*—
26: 2 live in the *l* where I tell you to live.
26: 3 Stay in this *l* for a while,
26: 12 Isaac planted crops in that *l*
26: 22 and we will flourish in the *l.*''
27: 46 from among the women of this *l,*
28: 4 of the *l* where you now live
28: 4 the *l* God gave to Abraham.''
28: 13 and your descendants the *l*
28: 15 and I will bring you back to this *l.*
29: 1 came to the *l* of the eastern peoples
31: 3 "Go back to the *l* of your fathers
31: 13 Now leave this *l* at once
31: 13 and go back to your native *l.*' ''
31: 18 Isaac in the *l* of Canaan.
32: 3 to his brother Esau in the *l* of Seir,
34: 1 went out to visit the women of the *l*
34: 10 among us; the *l* is open to you.
34: 21 Let them live in our *l* and trade in it
34: 21 the *l* has plenty of room for them.
34: 30 the people living in this *l.*
35: 6 Bethel) in the *l* of Canaan.
35: 12 The *l* I gave to Abraham
35: 12 will give this *l* to your descendants
36: 6 and moved to a *l* some distance
36: 7 *l* where they were staying could
36: 30 to their divisions, in the *l* of Seir.
36: 34 Husham from the *l*
36: 43 settlements in the *l* they occupied.
37: 1 in the *l* where his father had stayed
37: 1 where his father had stayed, the *l*
40: 15 off from the *l* of the Hebrews,
41: 19 cows in all the *l* of Egypt.
41: 29 coming throughout the *l* of Egypt,
41: 30 and the famine will ravage the *l.*
41: 31 In the *l* will not be remembered,
41: 33 put him in charge of the *l* of Egypt.
41: 34 over the *l* to take a fifth
41: 41 in charge of the whole *l* of Egypt.''
41: 43 in charge of the whole *l* of Egypt.
41: 45 went throughout the *l* of Egypt.
41: 47 abundance the *l* produced
41: 52 fruitful in the *l* of my suffering.''
41: 54 in the whole *l* of Egypt there was
42: 5 for the famine was in the *l*
42: 6 Joseph was the governor of the *l,*
42: 7 "From the *l* of Canaan,'' they
42: 9 to see where our *l* is unprotected.''
42: 12 to see where our *l* is unprotected.''
42: 13 who lives in the *l* of Canaan.
42: 29 Jacob in the *l* of Canaan,
42: 30 as though we were spying on the *l.*
42: 30 lord over the *l* spoke harshly to us
42: 33 lord over the *l* said to us,

Ge 42: 34 and you can trade in the *l*.' "
43: 1 the famine was still severe in the *l*.
43: 11 products of the *l* in your bags
44: 8 brought back to you from the *l*
45: 6 now there has been famine in the *l*,
45: 17 and return to the *l* of Canaan,
45: 18 I will give you the best of the *l*
45: 18 and you can enjoy the fat of the *l*.'
45: 25 Jacob in the *l* of Canaan.
46: 12 Onan had died in the *l* of Canaan).
46: 31 who were living in the *l* of Canaan,
47: 1 have come from the *l* of Canaan
47: 6 and the *l* of Egypt is before you;
47: 6 brothers in the best part of the *l*.
47: 11 property in the best part of the *l*,
47: 18 lord except our bodies and our *l*.
47: 19 and our *l* in exchange for food,
47: 19 before your eyes—we and our *l*
47: 19 that the *l* may not become desolate
47: 19 we with our *l* will be in bondage
47: 20 So Joseph bought all the *l* in Egypt
47: 20 The *l* became Pharaoh's,
47: 22 That is why they did not sell their *l*.
47: 22 he did not buy the *l* of the priests,
47: 23 and your *l* today for Pharaoh,
47: 26 It was only the *l* of the priests that
47: 26 as a law concerning *l* in Egypt—
48: 3 to me at Luz in the *l* of Canaan,
48: 4 I will give this *l* as an everlasting
48: 7 in the *l* of Canaan while we were
48: 21 back to the *l* of your fathers.
48: 22 I give the ridge of *l* I took
49: 15 and how pleasant is his *l*,
50: 5 dug for myself in the *l* of Canaan."
50: 13 They carried him to the *l*
50: 24 out of this *l* to the *l* he promised
Ex 1: 7 so that the *l* was filled with them.
2: 22 become an alien in a foreign *l*."
3: 8 a *l* flowing with milk and honey—
3: 8 of that *l* into a good and spacious *l*,
3: 17 Egypt into the *l* of the Canaanites,
3: 17 a *l* flowing with milk and honey.'
5: 5 people of the *l* are now numerous,
6: 4 them to give them the *l* of Canaan,
6: 8 to the *l* I swore with uplifted hand
8: 5 up on the *l* of Egypt.' "
8: 6 the frogs came up and covered the *l*
8: 7 also made frogs come up on the *l*
8: 14 piled into heaps, and the *l* reeked
8: 16 throughout the *l* of Egypt the dust
8: 17 throughout the *l* of Egypt became
8: 22 differently with the *l* of Goshen,
8: 22 that I, the LORD, am in this *l*.
8: 24 throughout Egypt the *l* was ruined
8: 25 sacrifice to your God here in the *l*."
9: 5 the LORD will do this in the *l*."
9: 9 and animals throughout the *l*."
9: 9 dust over the whole *l* of Egypt,
9: 23 So the LORD rained hail on the *l*
9: 24 storm in all the *l* of Egypt
9: 26 only place it did not hail was the *l*
9: 33 no longer poured down on the *l*.
10: 6 settled in this *l* till now.' "
10: 12 that locusts will swarm over the *l*
10: 13 blow across the *l* all that day
10: 15 or plant in all the *l* of Egypt.
12: 23 goes through the *l* to strike
12: 25 you enter the *l* that the LORD
12: 48 may take part like one born in the *l*.
13: 3 out of Egypt, out of the *l* of slavery,
13: 5 a *l* flowing with milk and honey—
13: 5 the *l* he swore to your forefathers
13: 5 you into the *l* of the Canaanites,
13: 11 you into the *l* of the Canaanites
13: 14 out of Egypt, out of the *l* of slavery.
14: 3 around the *l* in confusion,
14: 21 east wind and turned it into dry *l*.
16: 35 came to a *l* that was settled;
18: 3 become an alien in a foreign *l*";
20: 2 out of Egypt, out of the *l* of slavery.
20: 12 in the *l* the LORD your God is
23: 11 seventh year let the *l* lie unplowed
23: 23 bring you into the *l* of the Amorites
23: 26 will miscarry or be barren in your *l*.
23: 29 the *l* would become desolate
23: 30 enough to take possession of the *l*.
23: 31 to you the people who live in the *l*
23: 33 Do not let them live in your *l*,
Ex 32: 13 descendants all this *l* I promised
33: 1 go up to the *l* I promised on oath
33: 3 Go up to the *l* flowing with milk
34: 12 live in the *l* where you are going,
34: 15 treaty with those who live in the *l*;
34: 24 and no one will covet your *l*
Lev 11: 2 'Of all the animals that live on *l*,
14: 34 mildew in a house in that *l*,
14: 34 "When you enter the *l* of Canaan,
18: 3 as they do in the *l* of Canaan,
18: 25 Even the *l* was defiled;
18: 25 the *l* vomited out its inhabitants.
18: 27 lived in the *l* before you,
18: 27 you, and the *l* became defiled.
18: 28 if you defile the *l*, it will vomit you
19: 9 you reap the harvest of your *l*,
19: 23 " 'When you enter the *l*
19: 29 or the *l* will turn to prostitution
19: 33 lives with you in your *l*,
20: 22 so that the *l* where I am bringing
20: 24 a *l* flowing with milk and honey."
20: 24 to you, "You will possess their *l*;
22: 24 You must not do this in your own *l*,
23: 10 'When you enter the *l* I am going
23: 22 you reap the harvest of your *l*,
23: 39 have gathered the crops of the *l*,
25: 2 the *l* itself must observe a sabbath
25: 2 'When you enter the *l* I am going
25: 4 But in the seventh year the *l* is
25: 5 The *l* is to have a year of rest.
25: 6 Whatever the *l* yields
25: 7 Whatever the *l* produces may be
25: 7 and the wild animals in your *l*.
25: 9 the trumpet throughout your *l*.
25: 10 proclaim liberty throughout the *l*
25: 14 " 'If you sell *l* to one
25: 18 and you will live safely in the *l*.
25: 19 Then the *l* will yield its fruit,
25: 21 year that the *l* will yield enough
25: 23 because the *l* is mine and you are
25: 23 *l* must not be sold permanently,
25: 24 provide for the redemption of the *l*.
25: 38 Egypt to give you the *l* of Canaan
26: 1 in your *l* to bow down before it.
26: 5 and live in safety in your *l*.
26: 6 remove savage beasts from the *l*,
26: 6 " 'I will grant peace in the *l*,
26: 20 the trees of the *l* yield their fruit.
26: 32 I will lay waste the *l*,
26: 33 Your *l* will be laid waste,
26: 34 the *l* will enjoy its sabbath years all
26: 34 then the *l* will rest and enjoy its
26: 35 *l* will have the rest it did not have
26: 38 *l* of your enemies will devour you.
26: 41 them into the *l* of their enemies—
26: 42 and I will remember the *l*.
26: 43 For the *l* will be deserted by them
26: 44 are in the *l* of their enemies,
27: 16 to the LORD part of his family *l*,
27: 22 which is not part of his family *l*,
27: 24 he bought it, the one whose *l* it was.
27: 28 whether man or animal or family *l*
27: 30 " 'A tithe of everything from the *l*,
Nu 10: 9 go into battle in your own *l*
10: 30 I am going back to my own *l*
11: 12 to the *l* you promised on oath
13: 2 men to explore the *l* of Canaan,
13: 16 men Moses sent to explore the *l*.
13: 18 See what the *l* is like and
13: 19 What kind of *l* do they live in?
13: 20 some of the fruit of the *l*."
13: 21 and explored the *l* from the Desert
13: 25 returned from exploring the *l*.
13: 26 and showed them the fruit of the *l*.
13: 27 "We went into the *l*
13: 30 and take possession of the *l*,
13: 32 report about the *l* they had
13: 32 *l* we explored devours those living
14: 3 us to this *l* only to let us fall
14: 6 those who had explored the *l*,
14: 7 "The *l* we passed through
14: 8 us into that *l*, a *l* flowing with milk
14: 9 afraid of the people of the *l*,
14: 14 tell the inhabitants of this *l* about it.
14: 16 people into the *l* he promised them
14: 23 them will ever see the *l* I promised
14: 24 him into the *l* he went to,
14: 30 one of you will enter the *l* I swore
Nu 14: 31 in to enjoy the *l* you have rejected.
14: 34 of the forty days you explored the *l*
14: 36 Moses had sent to explore the *l*,
14: 37 bad report about the *l* were struck
14: 38 the men who went to explore the *l*,
15: 2 'After you enter the *l* I am giving
15: 18 'When you enter the *l*
15: 19 and you eat the food of the *l*,
16: 13 out of a *l* flowing with milk
16: 14 us into a *l* flowing with milk
18: 20 will have no inheritance in their *l*,
20: 12 community into the *l* I give them."
20: 24 will not enter the *l* I give
21: 24 and took over his *l* from the Arnon
21: 26 had taken from him all his *l* as far
21: 31 settled in the *l* of the Amorites.
21: 34 with his whole army and his *l*.
21: 35 And they took possession of his *l*.
22: 5 near the River, in his native *l*.
22: 5 they cover the face of the *l*
22: 11 of Egypt covers the face of the *l*.
26: 53 "The *l* is to be allotted to them
26: 55 Be sure that the *l* is distributed
27: 12 see the *l* I have given the Israelites.
32: 4 the *l* the LORD subdued
32: 5 "let this *l* be given to your servants
32: 7 over into the *l* the LORD has given
32: 8 Kadesh Barnea to look over the *l*.
32: 9 Valley of Eshcol and viewed the *l*,
32: 9 from entering the *l* the LORD had
32: 11 of Egypt will see the *l* I promised
32: 17 from the inhabitants of the *l*.
32: 22 And this *l* will be your possession
32: 22 then when the *l* is subdued
32: 29 give them the *l* of Gilead
32: 29 then when the *l* is subdued
32: 33 the whole *l* with its cities
33: 52 the inhabitants of the *l* before you.
33: 53 Take possession of the *l*
33: 53 for I have given you the *l* to possess
33: 54 Distribute the *l* by lot, according
33: 55 drive out the inhabitants of the *l*,
33: 55 trouble in the *l* where you will live.
34: 2 the *l* that will be allotted to you
34: 12 " 'This will be your *l*,
34: 13 "Assign this *l* by lot
34: 17 are to assign the *l* for you
34: 18 from each tribe to help assign the *l*.
34: 29 to the Israelites in the *l* of Canaan.
35: 8 from the *l* the Israelites possess are
35: 32 live on his own *l* before the death
35: 33 Bloodshed pollutes the *l*,
35: 33 Do not pollute the *l* where you are.
35: 33 cannot be made for the *l*
35: 34 Do not defile the *l* where you live
36: 2 commanded my lord to give the *l*
36: 7 shall keep the tribal *l* inherited
36: 8 Every daughter who inherits *l*
36: 9 is to keep the *l* it inherits."
Dt 1: 7 to the *l* of the Canaanites
1: 8 See, I have given you this *l*.
1: 8 of the *l* that the LORD swore he
1: 21 your God has given you the *l*.
1: 22 ahead to spy out the *l* for us
1: 25 with them some of the fruit of the *l*,
1: 25 "It is a good *l* that the LORD our
1: 35 shall see the good *l* I swore
1: 36 his descendants the *l* he set his feet
1: 39 from bad—they will enter the *l*.
2: 5 for I will not give you any of their *l*,
2: 9 will not give you any part of their *l*.
2: 12 did in the *l* the LORD gave them
2: 19 possession of any *l* belonging
2: 20 (That too was considered a *l*
2: 29 into the *l* the LORD our God is
2: 31 begin to conquer and possess his *l*
2: 37 neither the *l* along the course
2: 37 on any of the *l* of the Ammonites,
3: 2 you with his whole army and his *l*.
3: 12 Of the *l* that we took
3: 13 to be known as a *l* of the Rephaites
3: 18 your God has given you this *l*
3: 20 over the *l* that the LORD your
3: 25 see the good *l* beyond the Jordan—
3: 27 Look at the *l* with your own eyes,
3: 28 to inherit the *l* that you will see."
4: 1 possession of the *l* that the LORD,
4: 5 them in the *l* you are entering

Dt 4:10 as long as they live in the *l*
4:14 follow in the *l* that you are crossing
4:21 enter the good *l* the LORD your
4:22 and take possession of that good *l*.
4:22 in this *l*; I will not cross the Jordan;
4:25 have lived in the *l* a long time—
4:26 from the *l* that you are crossing
4:38 to bring you into their *l* to give it
4:40 in the *l* the LORD your God gives
4:46 the *l* of Sihon king of
4:47 They took possession of his *l*
4:47 and the *l* of Og king of Bashan,
4:48 This *l* extended from Aroer
5: 6 out of Egypt, out of the *l* of slavery.
5:16 you in the *l* the LORD your God is
5:21 on your neighbor's house or *l*,
5:31 to follow in the *l* I am giving them
5:33 days in the *l* that you will possess.
6: 1 in the *l* that you are crossing
6: 3 greatly in a *l* flowing with milk
6:10 into the *l* he swore to your fathers,
6:10 to give you—a *l* with large,
6:12 out of Egypt, out of the *l* of slavery.
6:15 you from the face of the *l*.
6:18 over the good *l* that the LORD
6:23 and give us the *l* that he promised
7: 1 you into the *l* you are entering
7: 8 redeemed you from the *l* of slavery
7:13 of your flocks in the *l* that he swore
7:13 the crops of your *l*— your grain,
8: 1 and possess the *l* that the LORD
8: 7 God is bringing you into a good *l*—
8: 7 a *l* with streams and pools of water,
8: 8 a *l* with wheat and barley,
8: 9 a *l* where bread will not be scarce
8: 9 a *l* where the rocks are iron
8:10 for the good *l* he has given you.
8:14 out of Egypt, out of the *l* of slavery.
8:15 that thirsty and waterless *l*,
9: 4 here to take possession of this *l*
9: 5 in to take possession of their *l*;
9: 6 your God is giving you this good *l*
9:23 of the *l* I have given you."
9:28 into the *l* he had promised them,
10: 7 on to Jotbathah, a *l* with streams
10:11 and possess the *l* that I swore
11: 8 over the *l* that you are crossing
11: 9 a *l* flowing with milk and honey.
11: 9 long in the *l* that the LORD swore
11:10 The *l* you are entering to take
11:10 take over is not like the *l* of Egypt,
11:11 possession of is a *l* of mountains
11:11 the *l* you are crossing the Jordan
11:12 It is a *l* the LORD your God cares
11:14 rain on your *l* in its season,
11:17 from the good *l* the LORD is
11:21 in the *l* that the LORD swore
11:25 and fear of you on the whole *l*,
11:29 you into the *l* you are entering
11:31 of the *l* the LORD your God is
12: 1 as long as you live in the *l*.
12: 1 to follow in the *l* that the LORD,
12:10 in the *l* the LORD your God is
12:19 as long as you live in your *l*.
12:29 them out and settled in their *l*,
13: 5 redeemed you from the *l* of slavery
13: 7 from one end of the *l* to the other),
13:10 out of Egypt, out of the *l* of slavery.
15: 4 for in the *l* the LORD your God is
15: 7 of the *l* that the LORD your God is
15:11 the poor and needy in your *l*.
15:11 will always be poor people in the *l*.
16: 4 in all your *l* for seven days.
16:20 possess the *l* the LORD your God
17:14 you enter the *l* the LORD your
18: 9 you enter the *l* the LORD your
19: 1 the nations whose *l* he is giving
19: 2 in the *l* the LORD your God is
19: 3 three parts the *l* the LORD your
19: 8 you the whole *l* he promised them,
19:10 blood will not be shed in your *l*,
19:14 in the *l* the LORD your God is
21: 1 in the *l* the LORD your God is
21:23 not desecrate the *l* the LORD your
23:20 hand to in the *l* you are entering
24: 4 upon the *l* the LORD your God is
25:15 in the *l* the LORD your God is
25:19 around you in the *l* he is giving you

Dt 26: 1 have entered the *l* the LORD your
26: 2 soil of the *l* the LORD your God is
26: 3 come to the *l* the LORD swore
26: 9 a *l* flowing with milk and honey;
26: 9 us to this place and gave us this *l*,
26:15 a *l* flowing with milk and honey."
26:15 and the *l* you have given us
27: 2 into the *l* the LORD your God is
27: 3 a *l* flowing with milk and honey,
27: 3 to enter the *l* the LORD your God
28: 4 and the crops of your *l*
28: 8 you in the *l* he is giving you.
28:11 the *l* he swore to your forefathers
28:12 to send rain on your *l* in season
28:18 and the crops of your *l*,
28:21 you from the *l* you are entering
28:33 do not know will eat what your *l*
28:42 your trees and the crops of your *l*.
28:51 and the crops of your *l*
28:52 the cities throughout your *l*
28:52 throughout the *l* the LORD your
28:63 from the *l* you are entering
29: 2 to all his officials and to all his *l*.
29: 8 We took their *l* and gave it
29:19 will bring disaster on the watered *l*
29:22 calamities that have fallen on the *l*
29:23 The whole *l* will be a burning waste
29:24 has the LORD done this to this *l*?
29:27 anger burned against this *l*,
29:28 and thrust them into another *l*,
29:28 LORD uprooted them from their *l*
30: 4 banished to the most distant *l*
30: 5 you to the *l* that belonged
30: 9 livestock and the crops of your *l*.
30:16 in the *l* you are entering to possess.
30:18 in the *l* you are crossing the Jordan
30:20 years in the *l* he swore to give
31: 3 you will take possession of their *l*.
31: 4 he destroyed along with their *l*.
31: 7 into the *l* that the LORD swore
31:13 in the *l* you are crossing the Jordan
31:16 gods of the *l* they are entering.
31:20 the *l* I promised on oath
31:20 them into the *l* flowing with milk
31:21 into the *l* I promised them on oath
31:23 into the *l* I promised them on oath,
32:10 In a desert *l* he found him,
32:13 on the heights of the *l*
32:43 and make atonement for his *l*
32:47 in the *l* you are crossing the Jordan
32:49 the *l* I am giving the Israelites
32:52 you will not enter the *l* I am giving
32:52 you will see the *l* only
33:13 "May the LORD bless his *l*
33:21 He chose the best *l* for himself;
33:28 secure in a *l* of grain and new wine,
34: 1 LORD showed him the whole *l*—
34: 2 all the *l* of Judah as far
34: 4 "This is the *l* I promised on oath
34:11 to all his officials and to his whole *l*
Jos 1: 2 River into the *l* I am about to give
1: 6 people to inherit the *l* I swore
1:11 of the *l* the LORD your God is
1:13 and has granted you this *l*.'
1:14 in the *l* that Moses gave you east
1:15 go back and occupy your own *l*,
1:15 of the *l* that the LORD your God is
2: 1 "Go, look over the *l*," he said,
2: 2 come here tonight to spy out the *l*."
2: 3 come to spy out the whole *l*."
2: 9 that the LORD has given this *l*
2:14 when the LORD gives us the *l*."
2:18 when we enter the *l*, you have tied
2:24 LORD has surely given the whole *l*
5: 6 a *l* flowing with milk and honey.
5: 6 would not see the *l* that he had
5:11 some of the produce of the *l*:
5:12 after they ate this food from the *l*;
6:22 two men who had spied out the *l*,
6:27 his fame spread throughout the *l*.
8: 1 his people, his city and his *l*.
9:24 Moses to give you the whole *l*
11:16 So Joshua took this entire *l*:
11:23 So Joshua took the entire *l*,
11:23 Then the *l* had rest from war.
12: 1 of the *l* whom the Israelites had
12: 6 servant of the LORD gave their *l*
12: 7 the kings of the *l* that Joshua

Jos 13: 1 areas of *l* to be taken over.
13: 2 "This is the *l* that remains:
13: 4 all the *l* of the Canaanites,
13: 6 Be sure to allocate this *l* to Israel
13:12 them and taken over their *l*.
14: 1 an inheritance in the *l* of Canaan,
14: 4 Levites received no share of the *l*
14: 5 So the Israelites divided the *l*,
14: 7 Kadesh Barnea to explore the *l*.
14: 9 *l* on which your feet have walked
14:15 Then the *l* had rest from war.
15:19 Since you have given me *l*
17: 5 of ten tracts of *l* besides Gilead
17: 6 The *l* of Gilead belonged to the rest
17: 8 (Manasseh had the *l* of Tappuah,
17:10 On the south the *l* belonged
17:15 and clear *l* for yourselves there
17:15 there in the *l* of the Perizzites
18: 3 possession of the *l* that the LORD,
18: 4 out to make a survey of the *l*
18: 5 are to divide the *l* into seven parts.
18: 6 of the seven parts of the *l*,
18: 8 and make a survey of the *l*
18: 8 on their way to map out the *l*,
18: 9 the men left and went through the *l*
18:10 and there he distributed the *l*
19:49 they had finished dividing the *l*
19:51 And so they finished dividing the *l*.
21:43 gave Israel all the *l* he had sworn
22: 4 in the *l* that Moses the servant
22: 7 Moses had given *l* in Bashan,
22: 7 half of the tribe Joshua gave *l*
22: 9 their own *l*, which they had
22:10 near the Jordan in the *l* of Canaan,
22:13 the priest, to the *l* of Gilead—
22:19 If the *l* you possess is defiled,
22:19 come over to the LORD's *l*,
22:19 tabernacle stands, and share the *l*
23: 4 inheritance for your tribes all the *l*
23: 5 you will take possession of their *l*,
23:13 until you perish from this good *l*,
23:15 from this good *l* he has given you.
23:16 from the good *l* he has given you."
24: 3 from the *l* beyond the River
24: 8 and you took possession of their *l*.
24: 8 " 'I brought you to the *l*
24:13 I gave you a *l* on which you did not
24:15 in whose *l* you are living.
24:17 from that *l* of slavery,
24:18 the Amorites, who lived in the *l*.
24:30 him in the *l* of his inheritance,
24:32 in the tract of *l* that Jacob bought
Jdg 1: 2 I have given the *l* into their hands."
1:15 Since you have given me *l*
1:26 went to the *l* of the Hittites,
1:27 were determined to live in that *l*.
1:32 the Canaanite inhabitants of the *l*.
1:33 the Canaanite inhabitants of the *l*,
2: 1 and led you into the *l* that I swore
2: 2 a covenant with the people of this *l*,
2: 6 went to take possession of the *l*,
2: 9 him in the *l* of his inheritance,
3:11 So the *l* had peace for forty years,
3:30 and the *l* had peace for eighty years
5: 4 marched from the *l* of Edom,
5:31 Then the *l* had peace forty years.
6: 4 They camped on the *l*
6: 5 they invaded the *l* to ravage it.
6: 8 out of Egypt, out of the *l* of slavery.
6: 9 before you and gave you their *l*.
6:10 of the Amorites, in whose *l* you live
8:28 the *l* enjoyed peace forty years.
9:37 down from the center of the *l*,
10: 8 in Gilead, the *l* of the Amorites.
11: 3 and settled in the *l* of Tob,
11: 5 to get Jephthah from the *l* of Tob.
11:13 they took away my *l*
11:15 Israel did not take the *l* of Moab
11:15 or the *l* of the Ammonites.
11:21 Israel took over all the *l*
12:12 in Aijalon in the *l* of Zebulun.
16:24 the one who laid waste our *l*
18: 2 They told them, "Go, explore the *l*
18: 2 and Eshtaol to spy out the *l*
18: 7 And since their *l* lacked nothing,
18: 9 have seen that the *l* is very good.
18:10 a *l* that lacks nothing whatever."
18:10 and a spacious *l* that God has put

Jdg 18: 14 five men who had spied out the *l*
18: 17 men who had spied out the *l* went
18: 30 the time of the captivity of the *l*.
20: 1 and from the *l* of Gilead came out
21: 21 and go to the *l* of Benjamin.
Ru 1: 1 there was a famine in the *l*,
1: 7 that would take them back to the *l*
4: 3 selling the piece of *l* that belonged
4: 5 "On the day you buy the *l*
1Sa 6: 5 from you and your gods and your *l*.
9: 16 a man from the *l* of Benjamin.
13: 3 the trumpet blown throughout the *l*
13: 7 crossed the Jordan to the *l* of Gad
13: 19 found in the whole *l* of Israel,
14: 46 and they withdrew to their own *l*.
21: 11 "Isn't this David, the king of the *l?*
22: 5 Go into the *l* of Judah."
23: 27 The Philistines are raiding the *l*."
27: 1 to escape to the *l* of the Philistines.
27: 8 lived in the *l* extending to Shur
28: 3 mediums and spiritists from the *l*.
28: 9 mediums and spiritists from the *l*.
29: 11 to go back to the *l* of the Philistines
30: 16 taken from the *l* of the Philistines
31: 9 throughout the *l* of the Philistines
2Sa 3: 12 "Whose *l* is it? Make an agreement
9: 7 to you all the *l* that belonged
9: 10 are to farm the *l* for him
10: 2 came to the *l* of the Ammonites,
14: 20 everything that happens in the *l*."
15: 4 I were appointed judge in the *l!*
17: 26 Absalom camped in the *l* of Gilead.
21: 14 answered prayer in behalf of the *l*.
24: 8 gone through the entire *l*,
24: 13 Or three days of plague in your *l?*
24: 13 years of famine in your *l?*
24: 25 answered prayer in behalf of the *l*,
1Ki 2: 34 buried on his own *l* in the desert.
4: 10 and all the *l* of Hepher were his);
4: 21 the River to the *l* of the Philistines,
8: 34 bring them back to the *l* you gave
8: 36 rain on the *l* you gave your people
8: 37 or plague comes to the *l*,
8: 40 live in the *l* you gave our fathers.
8: 41 but has come from a distant *l*
8: 46 takes them captive to his own *l*,
8: 47 in the *l* where they are held captive
8: 47 you in the *l* of their conquerors
8: 48 in the *l* of their enemies who took
8: 48 toward the *l* you gave their fathers,
9: 7 Israel from the *l* I have given them
9: 8 LORD done such a thing to this *l*
9: 13 And he called them the *L* of Cabul,
9: 18 Tadmor in the desert, within his *l*,
9: 21 descendants remaining in the *l*,
10: 15 and the governors of the *l*.
11: 18 and *l* and provided him with food.
14: 15 Israel from this good *l* that he gave
14: 24 male shrine prostitutes in the *l;*
15: 12 male shrine prostitutes from the *l*
17: 7 there had been no rain in the *l*.
17: 14 the LORD gives rain on the *l*.' "
18: 1 and I will send rain on the *l*."
18: 5 "Go through the *l* to all the springs
18: 6 So they divided the *l* they were
20: 7 summoned all the elders of the *l*
22: 36 to his town; everyone to his *l!*"
22: 46 He rid the *l* of the rest
2Ki 2: 19 and the *l* is unproductive."
2: 21 or make the *l* unproductive.' "
3: 20 And the *l* was filled with water.
3: 24 And the Israelites invaded the *l*
3: 27 and returned to their own *l*.
8: 1 in the *l* that will last seven years."
8: 2 in the *l* of the Philistines seven
8: 3 back from the *l* of the Philistines
8: 3 the king to beg for her house and *l*.
8: 5 to beg the king for her house and *l*.
8: 6 including all the income from her *l*
10: 33 in all the *l* of Gilead (the region
11: 3 years while Athaliah ruled the *l*.
11: 14 the people of the *l* were rejoicing
11: 18 people of the *l* went to the temple
11: 19 guards and all the people of the *l*,
11: 20 and all the people of the *l* rejoiced.
15: 5 and governed the people of the *l*.
15: 19 Pul king of Assyria invaded the *l*,
15: 20 and stayed in the *l* no longer.
2Ki 15: 29 Galilee—all the *l* of Naphtali—
16: 15 offering of all the people of the *l*,
17: 5 of Assyria invaded the entire *l*,
17: 27 what the god of the *l* requires."
18: 32 a *l* of grain and new wine, a *l*
18: 32 a *l* of olive trees and honey.
18: 32 and take you to a *l* like your own,
18: 33 of any nation ever delivered his *l*
18: 35 able to save his *l* from me?
19: 37 and they escaped to the *l* of Ararat.
20: 14 a distant *l*," Hezekiah replied.
21: 8 from the *l* I gave their forefathers,
21: 24 of the *l* killed all who had plotted
23: 30 people of the *l* took Jehoahaz son
23: 33 at Riblah in the *l* of Hamath so
23: 35 he taxed the *l* and exacted
23: 35 *l* according to their assessments.
24: 1 king of Babylon invaded the *l*,
24: 14 poorest people of the *l* were left.
24: 15 and the leading men of the *l*.
25: 12 of the *l* to work the vineyards
25: 19 of conscripting the people of the *l*
25: 21 There at Riblah, in the *l* of Hamath
25: 21 into captivity, away from her *l*.
25: 24 down in the *l* and serve the king
1Ch 1: 45 Husham from the *l*
4: 40 pasture, and the *l* was spacious,
5: 9 To the east they occupied the *l* up
5: 22 they occupied the *l* until the exile.
5: 23 they settled in the *l* from Bashan
5: 25 to the gods of the peoples of the *l*,
10: 9 throughout the *l* of the Philistines
11: 10 to extend it over the whole *l*,
14: 17 spread throughout every *l*,
16: 18 "To you I will give the *l* of Canaan
19: 2 Hanun in the *l* of the Ammonites
20: 1 He laid waste the *l*
21: 12 of plague in the *l*, with the angel
22: 18 and the *l* is subject to the LORD
22: 18 the inhabitants of the *l* over to me,
27: 26 the field workers who farmed the *l*.
28: 8 that you may possess this good *l*
2Ch 6: 25 back to the *l* you gave to them
6: 27 rain on the *l* you gave your people
6: 28 or plague comes to the *l*,
6: 31 live in the *l* you gave our fathers.
6: 32 but has come from a distant *l*
6: 36 takes them captive to a *l* far away
6: 37 in the *l* where they are held captive
6: 37 with you in the *l* of their captivity
6: 38 in the *l* of their captivity where
6: 38 toward the *l* you gave their fathers,
7: 13 or command locusts to devour the *l*
7: 14 their sin and will heal their *l*.
7: 20 then I will uproot Israel from my *l*,
7: 21 LORD done such a thing to this *l*
8: 8 descendants remaining in the *l*,
9: 14 the governors of the *l* brought gold
9: 26 the River to the *l* of the Philistines,
14: 6 of Judah, since the *l* was at peace.
14: 7 The *l* is still ours, because we have
15: 8 idols from the whole *l* of Judah
19: 3 for you have rid the *l*
19: 5 He appointed judges in the *l*,
20: 7 of this *l* before your people Israel
22: 12 years while Athaliah ruled the *l*.
23: 13 the people of the *l* were rejoicing
23: 20 people and all the people of the *l*
23: 21 and all the people of the *l* rejoiced.
26: 21 and governed the people of the *l*.
30: 9 and will come back to this *l*,
32: 4 stream that flowed through the *l*.
32: 13 to deliver their *l* from my hand?
32: 21 withdrew to his own *l* in disgrace.
32: 31 sign that had occurred in the *l*,
33: 8 the Israelites leave the *l* I assigned
33: 25 of the *l* killed all who had plotted
34: 8 to purify the *l* and the temple,
36: 1 people of the *l* took Jehoahaz son
36: 21 The *l* enjoyed its Sabbath rests;
Ezr 9: 11 entering to possess is a *l* polluted
9: 11 'The *l* you are entering
9: 12 and eat the good things of the *l*
Ne 4: 4 as plunder in a *l* of captivity.
5: 14 to be their governor in the *l*
5: 16 the work; we did not acquire any *l*.
9: 8 give to his descendants the *l*
9: 10 officials and all the people of his *l*,
Ne 9: 15 possession of the *l* you had sworn
9: 23 into the *l* that you told their fathers
9: 24 and took possession of the *l*.
9: 24 in the *l;* you handed the Canaanites
9: 24 their kings and the peoples of the *l*,
9: 25 fortified cities and fertile *l;*
9: 35 and fertile *l* you gave them,
9: 36 in the *l* you gave our forefathers
10: 31 year we will forgo working the *l*
Job 1: 1 In the *l* of Uz there lived a man
1: 10 herds are spread throughout the *l*.
9: 24 When a *l* falls into the hands
10: 21 to the *l* of gloom and deep shadow,
10: 22 to the *l* of deepest night,
12: 15 them loose, they devastate the *l*.
15: 19 (to whom alone the *l* was given
15: 29 his possessions spread over the *l*.
18: 17 he has no name in the *l*.
22: 8 you were a powerful man, owning *l*
24: 4 of the *l* into hiding.
24: 18 their portion of the *l* is cursed,
28: 13 found in the *l* of the living.
30: 3 they roamed the parched *l*
30: 8 they were driven out of the *l*.
31: 38 "if my *l* cries out against me
37: 17 clothes when the *l* lies hushed
38: 26 to water a *l* where no man lives,
42: 15 in all the *l* were there found women
Ps 10: 16 the nations will perish from his *l*.
16: 3 As for the saints who are in the *l*,
25: 13 his descendants will inherit the *l*.
27: 13 the LORD in the *l* of the living.
35: 20 those who live quietly in the *l*.
37: 3 in the *l* and enjoy safe pasture.
37: 9 in the LORD will inherit the *l*.
37: 11 But the meek will inherit the *l*
37: 22 the LORD blesses will inherit the *l*,
37: 29 the righteous will inherit the *l*
37: 34 He will exalt you to possess the *l;*
41: 2 he will bless him in the *l*
42: 6 you from the *l* of the Jordan,
44: 3 by their sword that they won the *l*,
45: 16 them princes throughout the *l*.
52: 5 you from the *l* of the living.
60: 2 You have shaken the *l*
63: 1 in a dry and weary *l*
65: 9 You care for the *l* and water it;
66: 6 He turned the sea into dry *l*,
67: 6 Then the *l* will yield its harvest,
68: 6 live in a sun-scorched *l*.
68: 14 scattered the kings in the *l*,
72: 16 Let grain abound throughout the *l;*
74: 8 where God was worshiped in the *l*.
74: 20 violence fill the dark places of the *l*.
76: 8 and the *l* feared and was quiet—
76: 9 to save all the afflicted of the *l*.
78: 12 in the *l* of Egypt, in the region
78: 54 to the border of his holy *l*,
80: 9 and it took root and filled the *l*.
85: 1 You showed favor to your *l*,
85: 9 that his glory may dwell in our *l*.
85: 12 and our *l* will yield its harvest.
88: 12 deeds in the *l* of oblivion?
95: 5 and his hands formed the dry *l*.
101: 6 be on the faithful in the *l*,
101: 8 all the wicked in the *l;*
105: 11 "To you I will give the *l* of Canaan
105: 16 He called down famine on the *l*
105: 23 an alien in the *l* of Ham.
105: 27 his wonders in the *l* of Ham.
105: 28 darkness and made the *l* dark—
105: 30 Their *l* teemed with frogs,
105: 32 with lightning throughout their *l;*
105: 35 ate up every green thing in their *l*,
105: 36 down all the firstborn in their *l*,
106: 22 miracles in the *l* of Ham
106: 24 Then they despised the pleasant *l;*
106: 38 the *l* was desecrated by their blood.
107: 34 and fruitful *l* into a salt waste,
112: 2 His children will be mighty in the *l;*
116: 9 the LORD in the *l* of the living.
125: 3 over the *l* allotted to the righteous,
135: 12 he gave their *l* as an inheritance,
136: 21 and gave their *l* as an inheritance,
137: 4 the LORD while in a foreign *l?*
140: 11 not be established in the *l;*
142: 5 my portion in the *l* of the living."
143: 6 for you like a parched *l*.

Pr 2: 21 For the upright will live in the *l*,
2: 22 the wicked will be cut off from the *l*
10: 30 the wicked will not remain in the *l*.
12: 11 who works his *l* will have abundant
25: 25 is good news from a distant *l*.
28: 19 who works his *l* will have abundant
30: 16 *l*, which is never satisfied
31: 23 among the elders of the *l*.
Ecc 5: 9 The increase from the *l* is taken
10: 16 O *l* whose king was a servant
10: 17 O *l* whose king is of noble birth
11: 2 what disaster may come upon the *l*.
SS 2: 12 is heard in our *l*.
Isa 1: 19 you will eat the best from the *l*;
2: 7 Their *l* is full of horses;
2: 7 Their *l* is full of silver and gold;
2: 8 Their *l* is full of idols;
4: 2 the fruit of the *l* will be the pride
5: 8 and you live alone in the *l*.
5: 30 And if one looks at the *l*,
6: 12 and the *l* is utterly forsaken.
6: 13 seed will be the stump in the *l*."
6: 13 though a tenth remains in the *l*,
7: 16 *l* of the two kings you dread will be
7: 18 and for bees from the *l* of Assyria.
7: 22 remain in the *l* will eat curds
7: 24 for the *l* will be covered with briers
8: 8 will cover the breadth of your *l*,
8: 21 they will roam through the *l*;
9: 1 In the past he humbled the *l*
9: 1 of Zebulun and the *l* of Naphtali,
9: 2 living in the *l* of the shadow
9: 19 the *l* will be scorched
10: 23 decreed upon the whole *l*.
13: 9 to make the *l* desolate
13: 14 each will flee to his native *l*.
14: 1 and will settle them in their own *l*.
14: 2 and maidservants in the LORD's *l*.
14: 20 for you have destroyed your *l*
14: 21 they are not to rise to inherit the *l*
14: 25 I will crush the Assyrian in my *l*;
15: 9 and upon those who remain in the *l*
16: 1 as tribute to the ruler of the *l*,
16: 4 the aggressor will vanish from the *l*
18: 1 Woe to the *l* of whirring wings
18: 2 whose *l* is divided by rivers.
18: 7 whose *l* is divided by rivers—
19: 17 And the *l* of Judah will bring terror
19: 20 to the LORD Almighty in the *l*
21: 1 from a *l* of terror.
23: 1 From the *l* of Cyprus
23: 10 Go through your *l*;
23: 13 Look at the *l* of the Babylonians,
26: 1 day this song will be sung in the *l*
26: 10 even in a *l* of uprightness they go
26: 15 extended all the borders of the *l*.
28: 22 decreed against the whole *l*.
30: 6 Through a *l* of hardship
30: 23 comes from the *l* will be rich
32: 2 of a great rock in a thirsty *l*.
32: 13 a *l* overgrown with thorns
32: 13 and for the *l* of my people,
33: 9 The *l* mourns and wastes away,
33: 17 and view a *l* that stretches afar.
34: 7 Their *l* will be drenched with blood
34: 9 her *l* will become blazing pitch!
35: 1 and the parched *l* will be glad;
36: 10 destroy this *l* without the LORD?
36: 17 a *l* of grain and new wine, a *l*
36: 17 and take you to a *l* like your own—
36: 18 of any nation ever delivered his *l*
36: 20 able to save his *l* from me?
37: 38 and they escaped to the *l* of Ararat.
38: 11 the LORD, in the *l* of the living;
39: 3 a distant *l*," Hezekiah replied.
44: 3 I will pour water on the thirsty *l*,
45: 19 from somewhere in a *l* of darkness;
46: 11 from a far-off *l*, a man
49: 8 to restore the *l*
49: 19 and your *l* laid waste,
53: 8 cut off from the *l* of the living;
57: 13 will inherit the *l*
58: 11 needs in a sun-scorched *l*
58: 14 you to ride on the heights of the *l*
60: 6 Herds of camels will cover your *l*,
60: 18 will violence be heard in your *l*,
60: 21 and they will possess the *l* forever.
61: 7 inherit a double portion in their *l*,
Isa 62: 4 and your *l* Beulah;
62: 4 and your *l* will be married.
62: 4 or name your *l* Desolate.
65: 16 Whoever invokes a blessing in the *l*
65: 16 he who takes an oath in the *l*
Jer 1: 14 out on all who live in the *l*.
1: 18 its priests and the people of the *l*.
1: 18 wall to stand against the whole *l*—
2: 2 through a *l* not sown.
2: 6 a *l* of drought and darkness,
2: 6 a *l* where no one travels
2: 6 through a *l* of deserts and rifts,
2: 7 But you came and defiled my *l*
2: 7 I brought you into a fertile *l*
2: 15 They have laid waste his *l*;
2: 31 or a *l* of great darkness?
3: 1 Would not the *l* be completely
3: 2 You have defiled the *l*
3: 9 she defiled the *l* and committed
3: 16 have increased greatly in the *l*,"
3: 18 *l* to the *l* I gave your forefathers
3: 19 and give you a desirable *l*,
4: 5 the trumpet throughout the *l*!"
4: 7 place to lay waste your *l*.
4: 16 army is coming from a distant *l*,
4: 20 the whole *l* lies in ruins.
4: 26 and the fruitful *l* was a desert;
4: 27 "The whole *l* will be ruined,
5: 19 foreigners in a *l* not your own.'
5: 19 served foreign gods in your own *l*,
5: 30 has happened in the *l*:
6: 8 and make your *l* desolate
6: 12 against those who live in the *l*,"
6: 20 or sweet calamus from a distant *l*?
6: 22 coming from the *l* of the north;
7: 7 in the *l* I gave your forefathers
7: 34 for the *l* will become desolate.
8: 16 the whole *l* trembles.
8: 16 the *l* and everything in it,
8: 19 people from a *l* far away:
9: 3 that they triumph in the *l*.
9: 12 Why has the *l* been ruined
9: 19 We must leave our *l*
10: 17 up your belongings to leave the *l*,
10: 18 those who live in this *l*;
10: 22 commotion from the *l* of the north!
11: 5 honey'—the *l* you possess today."
11: 5 to give them a *l* flowing with milk
11: 19 him off from the *l* of the living,
12: 4 How long will the *l* lie parched
12: 11 the whole *l* will be laid waste
12: 12 from one end of the *l* to the other;
13: 13 drunkenness all who live in this *l*,
14: 2 they wail for the *l*,
14: 4 because there is no rain in the *l*;
14: 8 why are you like a stranger in the *l*,
14: 15 or famine will touch this *l*.'
14: 18 have gone to a *l* they know not.' "
15: 7 at the city gates of the *l*.
15: 10 man with whom the whole *l* strives
15: 14 enemies in a *l* you do not know,
16: 3 and daughters born in this *l*
16: 6 Both high and low will die in this *l*.
16: 13 out of this *l* into a *l* neither you
16: 15 out of the *l* of the north
16: 15 to the *l* I gave their forefathers.
16: 18 because they have defiled my *l*
17: 3 My mountain in the *l*
17: 4 enemies in a *l* you do not know,
17: 6 in a salt *l* where no one lives.
18: 16 Their *l* will be laid waste,
22: 10 nor see his native *l* again.
22: 12 he will not see this *l* again."
22: 27 back to the *l* you long to return to."
22: 28 cast into a *l* they do not know?
22: 29 O *l*, *l*, *l*,
23: 5 do what is just and right in the *l*.
23: 8 Then they will live in their own *l*."
23: 8 of Israel up out of the *l* of the north
23: 10 The *l* is full of adulterers;
23: 10 of the curse the *l* lies parched
23: 15 spread throughout the *l*."
24: 5 place to the *l* of the Babylonians.
24: 6 and I will bring them back to this *l*.
24: 8 they remain in this *l* or live
24: 10 destroyed from the *l* I gave to them
25: 5 stay in the *l* the LORD gave
25: 9 "and I will bring them against this *l*
Jer 25: 12 the *l* of the Babylonians,
25: 13 upon that *l* all the things I have
25: 30 and roar mightily against his *l*.
25: 38 and their *l* will become desolate
26: 17 the elders of the *l* stepped forward
26: 20 things against this city and this *l*
27: 7 until the time for his *l* comes;
27: 11 remain in its own *l* to till it
30: 3 to the *l* I gave their forefathers
30: 10 from the *l* of their exile.
31: 8 from the *l* of the north
31: 16 from the *l* of the enemy.
31: 17 children will return to their own *l*.
31: 23 the people in the *l* of Judah
32: 15 will again be bought in this *l*.'
32: 22 a *l* flowing with milk and honey.
32: 22 gave them this *l* you had sworn
32: 41 them in this *l* with all my heart
32: 43 bought in this *l* of which you say,
33: 11 I will restore the fortunes of the *l*
33: 15 do what is just and right in the *l*.
34: 13 out of Egypt, out of the *l* of slavery.
34: 19 all the people of the *l* who walked
35: 7 in the *l* where you are nomads.'
35: 11 king of Babylon invaded this *l*,
35: 15 you will live in the *l* I have given
36: 29 destroy this *l* and cut off both men
37: 2 people of the *l* paid any attention
37: 7 will go back to its own *l*, to Egypt.
37: 19 will not attack you or this *l*'?
39: 5 at Riblah in the *l* of Hamath,
39: 10 left behind in the *l* of Judah some
40: 6 who were left behind in the *l*.
40: 7 over the *l* and had put him
40: 7 who were the poorest in the *l*
40: 9 down in the *l* and serve the king
40: 12 they all came back to the *l* of Judah
41: 2 appointed as governor over the *l*.
41: 18 appointed as governor over the *l*.
42: 10 stay in this *l*, I will build you up
42: 12 on you and restore you to your *l*.'
42: 13 'We will not stay in this *l*,'
43: 4 command to stay in the *l* of Judah.
43: 5 back to live in the *l* of Judah
44: 9 and your wives in the *l* of Judah
44: 14 survive to return to the *l* of Judah,
44: 21 officials and the people of the *l*?
44: 22 your *l* became an object of cursing
44: 28 and return to the *l* of Judah
45: 4 I have planted, throughout the *l*.
46: 10 in the *l* of the north by the River
46: 27 from the *l* of their exile.
47: 2 They will overflow the *l*
47: 2 all who dwell in the *l* will wail
49: 19 Edom from its *l* in an instant.
50: 1 and the *l* of the Babylonians:
50: 3 and lay waste her *l*.
50: 8 leave the *l* of the Babylonians,
50: 9 from the *l* of the north.
50: 12 a wilderness, a dry *l*, a desert.
50: 16 let everyone flee to his own *l*.
50: 18 the king of Babylon and his *l*
50: 21 "Attack the *l* of Merathaim
50: 22 The noise of battle is in the *l*,
50: 25 do in the *l* of the Babylonians.
50: 34 so that he may bring rest to their *l*,
50: 38 For it is a *l* of idols,
50: 44 Babylon from its *l* in an instant.
50: 45 against the *l* of the Babylonians:
51: 2 and to devastate her *l*;
51: 5 though their *l* is full of guilt
51: 9 leave her and each go to his own *l*,
51: 27 "Lift up a banner in the *l*!
51: 29 The *l* trembles and writhes,
51: 29 to lay waste the *l* of Babylon
51: 43 a dry and desert *l*,
51: 43 a *l* where no one lives,
51: 46 rumors of violence in the *l*
51: 46 when rumors are heard in the *l*;
51: 47 her whole *l* will be disgraced
51: 50 Remember the LORD in a distant *l*
51: 52 and throughout her *l*
51: 54 from the *l* of the Babylonians.
52: 9 at Riblah in the *l* of Hamath,
52: 16 of the *l* to work the vineyards
52: 25 of conscripting the people of the *l*
52: 27 There at Riblah, in the *l* of Hamath
52: 27 into captivity, away from her *l*.

La 3:34 all prisoners in the *l*,
4:21 you who live in the *l* of Uz.
Eze 1:3 River in the *l* of the Babylonians.
6:14 and make the *l* a desolate waste
7:2 the Sovereign LORD says to the *l*
7:2 upon the four corners of the *l*.
7:7 upon you—you who dwell in the *l*.
7:13 will not recover the *l* he has sold
7:23 because the *l* is full of bloodshed
7:27 of the people of the *l* will tremble.
8:12 the LORD has forsaken the *l*.' "
8:17 also fill the *l* with violence
9:9 'The LORD has forsaken the *l*;
9:9 the *l* is full of bloodshed
11:15 this *l* was given to us as our
11:17 and I will give you back the *l*
12:6 face so that you cannot see the *l*,
12:12 face so that he cannot see the *l*.
12:13 him to Babylonia, the *l*
12:19 for their *l* will be stripped
12:19 in Jerusalem and in the *l* of Israel:
12:19 of the *l*: 'This is what the Sovereign
12:20 waste and the *l* will be desolate.
12:22 is this proverb you have in the *l*
13:9 nor will they enter the *l* of Israel.
14:16 but the *l* would be desolate.
14:17 the sword pass throughout the *l*,'
14:19 "Or if I send a plague into that *l*
15:8 I will make the *l* desolate
16:3 were in the *l* of the Canaanites;
16:29 to include Babylonia, a *l*
17:4 carried it away to a *l* of merchants,
17:5 He took some of the seed of your *l*
17:13 away the leading men of the *l*,
17:16 in the *l* of the king who put him
18:2 by quoting this proverb about the *l*
19:4 hooks to the *l* of Egypt.
19:7 The *l* and all who were in it
19:13 in a dry and thirsty *l*.
20:6 a *l* flowing with milk and honey,
20:6 of Egypt into a *l* I had searched out
20:15 a *l* flowing with milk and honey,
20:15 them into the *l* I had given them—
20:28 them into the *l* I had sworn
20:36 in the desert of the *l* of Egypt,
20:38 out of the *l* where they are living,
20:38 yet they will not enter the *l*
20:40 there in the *l* the entire house
20:42 when I bring you into the *l* of Israel
20:42 *l* I had sworn with uplifted hand
21:2 Prophesy against the *l* of Israel
21:30 in the *l* of your ancestry,
21:32 your blood will be shed in your *l*,
22:24 to me: "Son of man, say to the *l*,
22:24 'You are a *l* that has had no rain
22:29 people of the *l* practice extortion
22:30 behalf of the *l* so I would not have
23:3 In that *l* their breasts were fondled
23:48 an end to lewdness in the *l*,
25:3 and over the *l* of Israel
25:6 of your heart against the *l* of Israel,
25:9 Kiriathaim—the glory of that *l*.
26:20 take your place in the *l* of the living
28:25 Then they will live in their own *l*,
29:10 I will make the *l* of Egypt a ruin
29:12 I will make the *l* of Egypt desolate
29:14 to Pathros, the *l* of their ancestry.
29:19 plunder the *l* as pay for his army.
30:5 people of the covenant *l* will fall
30:11 and fill the *l* with the slain.
30:11 will be brought in to destroy the *l*.
30:12 and sell the *l* to evil men;
30:12 will lay waste the *l* and everything
30:13 I will spread fear throughout the *l*.
31:12 broken in all the ravines of the *l*.
32:4 I will throw you on the *l*
32:6 will drench the *l* with your flowing
32:8 I will bring darkness over your *l*,
32:15 and strip the *l* of everything in it,
32:23 terror in the *l* of the living are slain,
32:24 terror in the *l* of the living went
32:25 spread in the *l* of the living,
32:26 terror in the *l* of the living.
32:27 stalked through the *l* of the living.
32:32 terror in the *l* of the living,
33:2 and the people of the *l* choose one
33:2 'When I bring the sword against a *l*
33:3 sees the sword coming against the *l*

Eze 33:24 one man, yet he possessed the *l*.
33:24 ruins in the *l* of Israel are saying,
33:24 surely the *l* has been given to us
33:25 should you then possess the *l*?
33:26 Should you then possess the *l*?'
33:28 I will make the *l* a desolate waste,
33:29 I have made the *l* a desolate waste
34:13 I will bring them into their own *l*.
34:13 and in all the settlements in the *l*.
34:14 lie down in good grazing *l*,
34:14 of Israel will be their grazing *l*.
34:25 and rid the *l* of wild beasts
34:27 the people will be secure in their *l*.
34:29 for them a *l* renowned for its crops,
34:29 longer be victims of famine in the *l*
36:5 they made my *l* their own
36:6 prophesy concerning the *l*
36:17 of Israel were living in their own *l*,
36:18 they had shed blood in the *l* and
36:20 and yet they had to leave his *l*.'
36:24 and bring you back into your own *l*.
36:28 live in the *l* I gave your forefathers;
36:34 desolate *l* will be cultivated instead
36:35 "This *l* that was laid waste has
37:12 I will bring you back to the *l*
37:14 and I will settle you in your own *l*.
37:21 bring them back into their own *l*.
37:22 I will make them one nation in the *l*
37:25 They will live in the *l* I gave
37:25 the *l* where your fathers lived.
38:2 against Gog, of the *l* of Magog,
38:8 will invade a *l* that has recovered
38:9 will be like a cloud covering the *l*.
38:11 will invade a *l* of unwalled villages;
38:12 living at the center of the *l*."
38:16 I will bring you against my *l*,
38:16 Israel like a cloud that covers the *l*.
38:18 When Gog attacks the *l* of Israel,
38:19 shall be a great earthquake in the *l*
39:12 them in order to cleanse the *l*.
39:13 the people of the *l* will bury them,
39:14 Some will go throughout the *l* and,
39:14 employed to cleanse the *l*.
39:15 As they go through the *l*
39:16 And so they will cleanse the *l*.'
39:26 lived in safety in their *l* with no one
39:28 I will gather them to their own *l*,
40:2 of God he took me to the *l* of Israel
43:2 and the *l* was radiant with his glory
45:1 to the LORD a portion of the *l*
45:1 " 'When you allot the *l*
45:2 with 50 cubits around it for open *l*.
45:4 portion of the *l* for the priests,
45:7 will have the *l* bordering each side
45:8 Israel to possess the *l* according
45:8 This *l* will be his possession
45:16 the people of the *l* will participate
45:22 and for all the people of the *l*.
46:3 the people of the *l* are to worship
46:9 of the *l* come before the LORD
47:13 to divide the *l* for an inheritance
47:14 this *l* will become your inheritance.
47:15 "This is to be the boundary of the *l*:
47:18 between Gilead and the *l* of Israel,
47:21 this *l* among yourselves according
48:12 from the sacred portion of the *l*,
48:14 This is the best of the *l*
48:29 "This is the *l* you are to allot
Da 4:10 a tree in the middle of the *l*.
6:25 of every language throughout the *l*:
8:9 and toward the Beautiful *L*.
9:6 and to all the people of the *l*.
11:16 establish himself in the Beautiful *L*
11:39 and will distribute the *l* at a price.
11:41 He will also invade the Beautiful *L*.
Hos 1:2 the *l* is guilty of the vilest adultery
1:11 and will come up out of the *l*,
2:3 turn her into a parched *l*,
2:18 I will abolish from the *l*,
2:23 I will plant her for myself in the *l*;
4:1 bring against you who live in the *l*:
4:1 no acknowledgment of God in the *l*
4:3 Because of this the *l* mourns,
7:16 ridiculed in the *l* of Egypt.
9:3 will not remain in the LORD's *l*;
10:1 as his *l* prospered,
13:5 in the *l* of burning heat.
Joel 1:2 listen, all who live in the *l*.

Joel 1:6 A nation has invaded my *l*,
1:14 and all who live in the *l*
2:1 Let all who live in the *l* tremble,
2:3 Before them the *l* is like the garden
2:18 the LORD will be jealous for his *l*
2:20 it into a parched and barren *l*,
2:21 Be not afraid, O *l*;
3:2 and divided up my *l*.
3:19 in whose *l* they shed innocent
Am 2:10 to give you the *l* of the Amorites.
3:11 "An enemy will overrun the *l*;
5:2 deserted in her own *l*,
5:8 out over the face of the *l*—
6:2 Was their *l* larger than yours?
7:2 When they had stripped the *l* clean
7:4 the great deep and devoured the *l*.
7:10 The *l* cannot bear all his words.
7:11 away from their native *l*.' "
7:12 you seer! Go back to the *l* of Judah.
7:17 Your *l* will be measured
7:17 away from their native *l*.' "
8:4 and do away with the poor of the *l*,
8:8 The whole *l* will rise like the Nile;
8:8 "Will not the *l* tremble for this,
8:11 I will send a famine through the *l*—
9:5 the whole *l* rises like the Nile,
9:6 out over the face of the *l*—
9:15 I will plant Israel in their own *l*,
9:15 from the *l* I have given them,"
Ob :19 the *l* of the Philistines.
:20 will possess ⌊the *l*⌋ as far
Jnh 1:9 who made the sea and the *l*."
1:13 men did their best to row back to *l*.
2:10 and it vomited Jonah onto dry *l*.
Mic 2:5 to divide the *l* by lot.
5:5 When the Assyrian invades our *l*
5:6 They will rule the *l* of Assyria
5:6 the Assyrian when he invades our *l*
5:6 the *l* of Nimrod with drawn sword.
5:11 I will destroy the cities of your *l*
6:4 redeemed you from the *l* of slavery
7:2 godly have been swept from the *l*;
Na 3:13 The gates of your *l*
3:16 but like locusts they strip the *l*
Hab 3:13 the leader of the *l* of wickedness,
Zep 2:3 the LORD, all you humble of the *l*,
2:5 O Canaan, *l* of the Philistines.
2:6 *l* by the sea, where the Kerethites
2:8 and made threats against their *l*.
2:9 of my nation will inherit their *l*."
2:11 every one in its own *l*.
2:11 he destroys all the gods of the *l*.
3:19 in every *l* where they were put
Hag 2:4 of the *l*,' declares the LORD,
2:6 and the earth, the sea and the dry *l*.
Zec 1:21 horns against the *l* of Judah
2:6 Come! Flee from the *l* of the north
2:12 as his portion in the holy *l*
3:9 the sin of this *l* in a single day.
5:3 that is going out over the whole *l*;
5:6 of the people throughout the *l*."
6:8 rest in the *l* of the north."
7:5 "Ask all the people of the *l*
7:14 The *l* was left so desolate
7:14 made the pleasant *l* desolate.' "
9:1 is against the *l* of Hadrach
9:16 They will sparkle in his *l*
11:6 They will oppress the *l*,
11:6 pity on the people of the *l*,"
11:16 over the *l* who will not care
12:12 The *l* will mourn, each clan
13:2 the names of the idols from the *l*,
13:2 the spirit of impurity from the *l*.
13:5 the *l* has been my livelihood
13:8 In the whole *l*," declares
14:10 The whole *l*, from Geba
Mal 1:4 They will be called The Wicked *L*,
3:12 for yours will be a delightful *l*,"
4:6 and strike the *l* with a curse."
Mt 2:6 Bethlehem, in the *l* of Judah,
2:20 his mother and go to the *l* of Israel,
2:21 and went to the *l* of Israel.
4:15 *L* of Zebulun and *l* of Naphtali,
4:16 living in the *l* of the shadow
14:24 a considerable distance from *l*,
23:15 You travel over *l* and sea
27:45 hour darkness came over all the *l*.
Mk 6:47 of the lake, and he was alone on *l*.

Mk 15: 33 over the whole *l* until the ninth
Lk 4: 25 a severe famine throughout the *l*.
21: 23 There will be great distress in the *l*
23: 44 over the whole *l* until the ninth
Ac 5: 3 of the money you received for the *l*
5: 8 and Ananias got for the *l*?"
7: 3 'and go to the *l* I will show you.'
7: 4 to this *l* where you are now living.
7: 4 "So he left the *l* of the Chaldeans
7: 5 after him would possess the *l*,
7: 45 It remained in the *l* until the time
7: 45 it with them when they took the *l*
13: 19 and gave their *l* to his people
27: 27 sensed they were approaching *l*.
27: 39 they did not recognize the *l*,
27: 43 to jump overboard first and get to *l*.
27: 44 In this way everyone reached *l*
Heb 6: 7 *L* that drinks in the rain often
6: 8 But *l* that produces thorns
11: 9 in the promised *l* like a stranger
11: 29 through the Red Sea as on dry *l*;
Jas 5: 7 for the *l* to yield its valuable crop
5: 17 and it did not rain on the *l* for three
Rev 7: 1 wind from blowing on the *l*
7: 2 had been given power to harm the *l*
7: 3 "Do not harm the *l* or the sea
10: 2 on the sea and his left foot on the *l*,
10: 5 and on the *l* raised his right hand
10: 8 standing on the sea and on the *l*."
16: 2 and poured out his bowl on the *l*,

LAND'S (LAND)

Nu 18: 13 All the *l* firstfruits that they bring

LANDED (LAND)

Mt 14: 14 When Jesus *l* and saw a large
14: 34 crossed over, they *l* at Gennesaret.
Mk 6: 34 When Jesus *l* and saw a large
6: 53 they *l* at Gennesaret and anchored
Jn 6: 23 Then some boats from Tiberias *l*
21: 9 When they *l*, they saw a fire
Ac 18: 22 When he *l* at Caesarea, he went up
21: 3 We *l* at Tyre, where our ship was
21: 7 from Tyre and *l* at Ptolemais,
27: 3 The next day we *l* at Sidon;
27: 5 Pamphylia, we *l* at Myra in Lycia.

LANDOWNER (LAND)

Mt 20: 1 of heaven is like a *l* who went out
20: 11 they began to grumble against the *l*
21: 33 There was a *l* who planted

LANDS (LAND)

Ge 26: 3 descendants I will give all these *l*
26: 4 and will give them all these *l*,
41: 54 There was famine in all the other *l*,
Lev 26: 36 fearful in the *l* of their enemies that
26: 39 away in the *l* of their enemies
Nu 32: 1 saw that the *l* of Jazer and Gilead
Dt 29: 22 come from distant *l* will see
Jos 10: 42 and their *l* Joshua conquered
12: 7 toward Seir (their *l* Joshua gave
12: 8 the *l* of the Hittites, Amorites,
Jdg 11: 18 skirted the *l* of Edom and Moab,
2Ki 19: 17 laid waste these nations and their *l*.
19: 24 I have dug wells in foreign *l*
1Ch 7: 28 Their *l* and settlements included
29: 30 and the kingdoms of all the other *l*.
2Ch 12: 8 and serving the kings of other *l*."
13: 9 as the peoples of other *l* do?
15: 5 of the *l* were in great turmoil.
17: 10 of the *l* surrounding Judah,
26: 10 in the hills and in the fertile *l*,
31: 19 on the farm *l* around their towns
32: 13 to all the peoples of the other *l*?
32: 17 of the other *l* did not rescue their
Ps 49: 11 they had named *l* after themselves.
76: 11 let all the neighboring *l*
78: 55 and allotted their *l* to them
105: 44 he gave them the *l* of the nations,
106: 27 and scatter them throughout the *l*.
107: 3 those he gathered from the *l*,
111: 6 giving them the *l* of other nations.
Isa 8: 9 Listen, all you distant *l*.
13: 5 They come from faraway *l*,
14: 7 All the *l* are at rest and at peace;
23: 7 her to settle in far-off *l*?
37: 18 waste all these peoples and their *l*.
Isa 37: 25 I have dug wells in foreign *l*
Jer 12: 14 I will uproot them from their *l*
27: 10 to remove you far from your *l*;
32: 37 from all the *l* where I banish them
46: 16 to our own people and our native *l*,
Eze 6: 8 you are scattered among the *l*
20: 6 honey, the most beautiful of all *l*.
20: 15 and honey, most beautiful of all *l*—
29: 12 desolate among devastated *l*,
30: 7 desolate among desolate *l*,
32: 9 among *l* you have not known.
Hab 2: 8 you have destroyed *l* and cities
2: 17 you have destroyed *l* and cities
Zec 10: 9 in distant *l* they will remember me.
Ac 4: 34 time to time those who owned *l*

LANES

Lk 14: 23 country *l* and make them come in,

LANGUAGE (LANGUAGES)

Ge 10: 5 their nations, each with its own *l*.)
11: 1 Now the whole world had one *l*
11: 6 speaking the same *l* they have
11: 7 and confuse their *l* so they will not
11: 9 there the LORD confused the *l*
Dt 28: 49 a nation whose *l* you will not
Ezr 4: 7 script and in the Aramaic *l*.
Ne 13: 24 Half of their children spoke the *l*
13: 24 how to speak the *l* of Judah.
13: 24 or the *l* of one of the other peoples,
Est 1: 22 and to each people in its own *l*,
3: 12 in the *l* of each people all Haman's
8: 9 and the *l* of each people and
8: 9 to the Jews in their own script and *l*
Ps 19: 3 There is no speech or *l*
81: 5 where we heard a *l* we did not
Isa 19: 18 in Egypt will speak the *l* of Canaan
Jer 5: 15 a people whose *l* you do not know,
Eze 3: 5 of obscure speech and difficult *l*,
3: 6 of obscure speech and difficult *l*,
Da 1: 4 He was to teach them the *l*
3: 4 nations and men of every *l*:
3: 7 and men of every *l* fell down
3: 29 *l* who say anything against the God
4: 1 nations and men of every *l*,
5: 19 and men of every *l* dreaded
6: 25 men of every *l* throughout the land:
7: 14 and men of every *l* worshiped him.
Jn 8: 43 Why is my *l* not clear to you?
8: 44 When he lies, he speaks his native *l*
16: 25 I will no longer use this kind of *l*
Ac 1: 19 field in their *l* Akeldama,
2: 6 heard them speaking in his own *l*.
2: 8 of us hears them in his own native *l*
14: 11 they shouted in the Lycaonian *l*,
Col 3: 8 slander, and filthy *l* from your lips.
Rev 5: 9 from every tribe and *l* and people
7: 9 every nation, tribe, people and *l*,
11: 9 *l* and nation will gaze
13: 7 authority over every tribe, people, *l*
14: 6 to every nation, tribe, *l* and people.

LANGUAGES (LANGUAGE)

Ge 10: 20 of Ham by their clans and *l*,
10: 31 sons of Shem by their clans and *l*,
Zec 8: 23 "In those days ten men from all *l*
1Co 14: 10 Undoubtedly there are all sorts of *l*
Rev 10: 11 about many peoples, nations, *l*
17: 15 peoples, multitudes, nations and *l*.

LANGUISH (LANGUISHES)

Isa 24: 4 the exalted of the earth *l*.
Jer 14: 2 her cities *l*;

LANGUISHES (LANGUISH)

Isa 24: 4 the world *l* and withers,

LANTERNS

Jn 18: 3 They were carrying torches, *l*

LAODICEA (LAODICEANS)

Col 2: 1 for you and for those at *L*,
4: 13 and for those at *L* and Hierapolis.
4: 15 greetings to the brothers at *L*,
4: 16 you in turn read the letter from *L*.
Rev 1: 11 Sardis, Philadelphia and *L*."
3: 14 the angel of the church in *L* write:

LAODICEANS (LAODICEA)

Col 4: 16 also read in the church of the *L*

LAP (LAPPED LAPS)

Jdg 7: 5 "Separate those who *l* the water
16: 19 Having put him to sleep on her *l*,
Ru 4: 16 laid him in her *l* and cared for him.
2Ki 4: 20 the boy sat on her *l* until noon,
Pr 6: 27 Can a man scoop fire into his *l*
16: 33 The lot is cast into the *l*,
Ecc 7: 9 for anger resides in the *l* of fools.
Lk 6: 38 will be poured into your *l*.

LAPPED (LAP)

Jdg 7: 6 Three hundred men *l*
7: 7 hundred men that *l* I will save

LAPPIDOTH

Jdg 4: 4 a prophetess, the wife of *L*,

LAPS (LAP)

Ps 79: 12 Pay back into the *l*
Isa 65: 6 I will pay it back into their *l*—
65: 7 I will measure into their *l*
Jer 32: 18 sins into the *l* of their children

LARGE (ENLARGE ENLARGED ENLARGES)

Mt 4: 25 *L* crowds from Galilee,
19: 2 *L* crowds followed him,
Lk 14: 25 *L* crowds were traveling with Jesus

LASEA

Ac 27: 8 near the town of *L*.

LASH (LASHED LASHES)

Job 5: 21 from the *l* of the tongue,
Isa 10: 26 The LORD Almighty will *l* them

LASHA

Ge 10: 19 Admah and Zeboiim, as far as *L*.

LASHARON

Jos 12: 18 one the king of *L* one the king

LASHED (LASH)

Isa 54: 11 *l* by storms and not comforted,

LASHES (LASH)

Dt 25: 2 the number of *l* his crime deserves,
25: 3 not give him more than forty *l*.
Pr 17: 10 more than a hundred *l* a fool.
2Co 11: 24 from the Jews the forty *l* minus one

LAST (LASTED LASTING LASTS LATTER)

Ge 19: 34 "*L* night I lay with my father.
25: 8 Then Abraham breathed his *l*
25: 17 He breathed his *l* and died,
29: 34 "Now at *l* my husband will become
31: 29 *l* night the God of your father said
31: 42 and *l* night he rebuked you."
33: 7 *L* of all came Joseph and Rachel,
35: 18 As she breathed her *l*—
35: 29 Then he breathed his *l* and died
49: 33 breathed his *l* and was gathered
Lev 8: 33 your ordination will *l* seven days.
15: 19 monthly period will *l* seven days,
26: 10 will still be eating *l* year's harvest
Nu 2: 31 They will set out *l*,
14: 33 until the *l* of your bodies lies
24: 20 but he will come to ruin at *l*."
Dt 2: 16 when the *l* of these fighting men
Jos 12: 4 one of the *l* of the Rephaites,
13: 12 as one of the *l* of the Rephaites.
1Sa 11: 11 during the *l* watch
15: 16 the LORD said to me *l* night."
2Sa 19: 11 'Why should you be the *l*
19: 12 So why should you be the *l*
23: 1 These are the *l* words of David:
1Ki 14: 10 off from Jeroboam every *l* male
21: 21 from Ahab every *l* male in Israel—
2Ki 8: 1 in the land that will *l* seven years."
9: 8 from Ahab every *l* male in Israel—
1Ch 23: 27 According to the *l* instructions
Ezr 8: 13 the *l* ones, whose names were
Ne 8: 18 after day, from the first day to the *l*
Job 14: 10 he breathes his *l* and is no more.

Ps 45: 6 O God, will *l* for ever and ever;
76: 5 they sleep their *l* sleep;
81: 15 their punishment would *l* forever.
119:152 you established them to *l* forever.
Isa 2: 2 and Jerusalem: In the *l* days
41: 4 and with the *l*— I am he."
44: 6 I am the first and I am the *l;*
48: 12 I am the first and I am the *l.*
51: 6 But my salvation will *l* forever,
51: 8 But my righteousness will *l* forever
Jer 15: 9 and breathe her *l.*
32: 14 jar so they will *l* a long time.
50: 17 the *l* to crush his bones
Da 9: 2 of Jerusalem would *l* seventy years.
11: 6 and he and his power will not *l.*
Hos 3: 5 and to his blessings in the *l* days.
Am 1: 8 till the *l* of the Philistines is dead,"
4: 2 the *l* of you with fishhooks.
Mic 4: 1 In the *l* days
Mt 5: 26 out until you have paid the *l* penny.
19: 30 But many who are first will be *l,*
19: 30 and many who are *l* will be first.
20: 8 beginning with the *l* ones hired
20: 12 who were hired *l* worked only one
20: 14 the man who was hired *l* the same
20: 16 will be first, and the first will be *l.*"
20: 16 *l* will be first, and the first will be
21: 37 *L* of all, he sent his son to them.
27: 64 This *l* deception will be worse
Mk 4: 17 have no root, they *l* only a short
9: 35 must be the very *l,* and the servant
10: 31 are first will be *l,* and the *l* first."
12: 6 He sent him *l* of all, saying,
12: 22 *L* of all, the woman died too.
15: 37 a loud cry, Jesus breathed his *l.*
Lk 12: 59 until you have paid the *l* penny."
13: 30 are those who are *l* who will be
13: 30 will be first, and first who will be *l.*"
23: 46 he had said this, he breathed his *l.*
Jn 6: 39 but raise them up at the *l* day.
6: 40 and I will raise him up at the *l* day."
6: 44 and I will raise him up at the *l* day.
6: 54 and I will raise him up at the *l* day.
7: 37 On the *l* and greatest day
11: 24 in the resurrection at the *l* day."
12: 48 will condemn him at the *l* day.
15: 16 and bear fruit—fruit that will *l.*
16: 31 You believe at *l!*" Jesus answered.
Ac 2: 17 " 'In the *l* days, God says,
27: 23 *L* night an angel of the God whose
27: 33 "For the *l* fourteen days," he said,
Ro 1: 10 and I pray that now at *l*
1: 17 is by faith from first to *l,*
1Co 9: 25 it to get a crown that will not *l;*
9: 25 it to get a crown that will *l* forever.
15: 8 and *l* of all he appeared to me also,
15: 26 *l* enemy to be destroyed is death.
15: 45 the *l* Adam, a life-giving spirit.
15: 52 of an eye, at the *l* trumpet.
2Co 8: 10 *L* year you were the first not only
9: 2 telling them that since *l* year you
Php 4: 10 that at *l* you have renewed your
1Th 2: 16 of God has come upon them at *l.*
2Ti 3: 1 will be terrible times in the *l* days.
Heb 1: 2 in these *l* days he has spoken to us
1: 8 O God, will *l* for ever and ever,
Jas 5: 3 have hoarded wealth in the *l* days.
1Pe 1: 5 ready to be revealed in the *l* time.
1: 20 but was revealed in these *l* times
2Pe 3: 3 in the *l* days scoffers will come,
1Jn 2: 18 Dear children, this is the *l* hour;
2: 18 This is how we know it is the *l* hour
Jude : 18 "In the *l* times there will be
Rev 1: 17 I am the First and the *L.*
2: 8 of him who is the First and the *L,*
15: 1 angels with the seven *l* plagues—*l,*
21: 9 full of the seven *l* plagues came
22: 13 the First and the *L,* the Beginning

LASTED (LAST)

2Sa 3: 1 the house of David *l* a long time.
2Ki 6: 25 siege *l* so long that a donkey's head

LASTING (LAST)

Ex 12: 14 to the LORD—a *l* ordinance.
12: 17 as a *l* ordinance for the generations
12: 24 these instructions as a *l* ordinance
27: 21 is to be a *l* ordinance
28: 43 is to be a *l* ordinance for Aaron
29: 9 is theirs by a *l* ordinance.
30: 21 is to be a *l* ordinance for Aaron
31: 16 to come as a *l* covenant.
Lev 3: 17 " 'This is a *l* ordinance
10: 9 This is a *l* ordinance
16: 29 "This is to be a *l* ordinance for you:
16: 31 deny yourselves; it is a *l* ordinance.
16: 34 "This is to be a *l* ordinance for you:
17: 7 This is to be a *l* ordinance for them
23: 14 is to be a *l* ordinance
23: 21 is to be a *l* ordinance
23: 31 is to be a *l* ordinance
23: 41 is to be a *l* ordinance
24: 3 is to be a *l* ordinance
24: 8 of the Israelites, as a *l* covenant.
Nu 10: 8 This is to be a *l* ordinance for you
15: 15 this is a *l* ordinance
18: 23 This is a *l* ordinance
19: 10 This will be a *l* ordinance both
19: 21 This is a *l* ordinance for them.
25: 13 have a covenant of a *l* priesthood,
Dt 11: 4 and how the LORD brought *l* ruin
1Sa 25: 28 will certainly make a *l* dynasty
2Ch 2: 4 This is a *l* ordinance for Israel.
Est 1: 5 king gave a banquet, *l* seven days,
Jer 14: 13 I will give you *l* peace in this place
18: 16 an object of *l* scorn;
Eze 45: 21 a feast *l* seven days,
46: 14 to the LORD is a *l* ordinance.
Heb 10: 34 had better and *l* possessions.

LASTS (LAST)

Lev 23: 34 of Tabernacles begins, and it *l*
Job 20: 5 the joy of the godless *l*
Ps 30: 5 For his anger *l* only a moment,
30: 5 but his favor *l* a lifetime;
Pr 12: 19 but a lying tongue *l* only a moment.
Mt 13: 21 has no root, he *l* only a short time.
2Co 3: 11 greater is the glory of that which *l!*

LATCH-OPENING

SS 5: 4 lover thrust his hand through the *l;*

LATIN

Jn 19: 20 the sign was written in Aramaic, *L*

LATRINE

2Ki 10: 27 and people have used it for a *l*

LATTER (LAST)

Ge 14: 3 All these *l* kings joined forces
Job 42: 12 The LORD blessed the *l* part
Da 8: 23 "In the *l* part of their reign,
Mt 23: 23 You should have practiced the *l,*
Lk 11: 42 You should have practiced the *l*
Php 1: 16 *l* do so in love, knowing that I am
2Ti 2: 21 If a man cleanses himself from the *l*

LATTICE

Jdg 5: 28 behind the *l* she cried out,
2Ki 1: 2 through the *l* of his upper room
Pr 7: 6 I looked out through the *l.*
SS 2: 9 peering through the *l.*

LAUGH (LAUGHED LAUGHINGSTOCK LAUGHS LAUGHTER)

Ge 18: 13 "Why did Sarah *l* and say,
18: 15 But he said, "Yes, you did *l.*"
18: 15 so she lied and said, "I did not *l.*"
21: 6 who hears about this will *l*
Job 5: 22 You will *l* at destruction
Ps 52: 6 they will *l* at him, saying,
59: 8 But you, O LORD, *l* at them;
Pr 1: 26 I in turn will *l* at your disaster;
31: 25 she can *l* at the days to come.
Ecc 3: 4 a time to weep and a time to *l,*
Hab 1: 10 They *l* at all fortified cities;
Lk 6: 21 for you will *l.*
6: 25 Woe to you who *l* now,

LAUGHED (LAUGH)

Ge 17: 17 Abraham fell facedown; he *l*
18: 12 So Sarah *l* to herself as she thought,
La 1: 7 and *l* at her destruction.
Mt 9: 24 But they *l* at him.
Mk 5: 40 But they *l* at him.
Lk 8: 53 They *l* at him, knowing that she

LAUGHINGSTOCK (LAUGH)

Ge 38: 23 what she has, or we will become a *l.*
Ex 32: 25 and so become a *l* to their enemies.
Job 12: 4 a mere *l,* though righteous
12: 4 "I have become a *l* to my friends,
La 3: 14 I became the *l* of all my people;
Eze 22: 4 and a *l* to all the countries.

LAUGHS (LAUGH)

Job 39: 7 He *l* at the commotion in the town;
39: 18 she *l* at horse and rider.
39: 22 He *l* at fear, afraid of nothing;
41: 29 he *l* at the rattling of the lance.
Ps 2: 4 The One enthroned in heaven *l;*
37: 13 but the Lord *l* at the wicked,

LAUGHTER (LAUGH)

Ge 21: 6 Sarah said, "God has brought me *l,*
Job 8: 21 He will yet fill your mouth with *l*
Ps 126: 2 Our mouths were filled with *l,*
Pr 14: 13 Even in *l* the heart may ache,
Ecc 2: 2 "*L,*" I said, "is foolish.
7: 3 Sorrow is better than *l,*
7: 6 so is the *l* of fools.
10: 19 A feast is made for *l,*
Jer 51: 39 so that they shout with *l*—
Jas 4: 9 Change your *l* to mourning

LAUNCH

Jdg 10: 18 "Whoever will *l* the attack

LAUNDERER'S

Mal 3: 2 be like a refiner's fire or a *l* soap.

LAVISHED

Isa 43: 24 or *l* on me the fat of your sacrifices.
Eze 16: 15 You *l* your favors on anyone who
Da 2: 48 in a high position and *l* many gifts
Hos 2: 8 who *l* on her the silver and gold—
Eph 1: 8 of God's grace that he *l* on us
1Jn 3: 1 great is the love the Father has *l*

LAW (LAW'S LAWFUL LAWGIVER LAWS LAWYER)

Ge 47: 26 as a *l* concerning land in Egypt—
Ex 12: 49 The same *l* applies
13: 9 on your forehead that the *l*
15: 25 the LORD made a decree and a *l*
21: 31 This *l* also applies if the bull gores
24: 12 with the *l* and commands I have
Lev 7: 7 " 'The same *l* applies
24: 22 are to have the same *l* for the alien
Nu 5: 29 is the *l* of jealousy
5: 30 and is to apply this entire *l* to her.
6: 13 " 'Now this is the *l* for the Nazirite
6: 21 according to the *l* of the Nazirite
6: 21 " 'This is the *l* of the Nazirite who
15: 29 the same *l* applies to everyone who
19: 2 of the *l* that the LORD has
19: 14 "This is the *l* that applies
31: 21 of the *l* that the LORD gave Moses
Dt 1: 5 Moses began to expound this *l,*
4: 44 This is the *l* Moses set
6: 25 to obey all this *l* before the LORD
17: 11 according to the *l* they teach you
17: 18 himself on a scroll a copy of this *l,*
17: 19 carefully all the words of this *l*
17: 20 and turn from the *l* to the right
27: 3 of this *l* when you have crossed
27: 8 of this *l* on these stones you have
27: 26 of this *l* by carrying them out."
28: 58 follow all the words of this *l,*
28: 61 of the *L* until you are destroyed.
29: 21 written in this Book of the *L.*
29: 29 may follow all the words of this *l.*
30: 10 written in this Book of the *L*
31: 9 So Moses wrote down this *l*
31: 11 you shall read this *l* before them
31: 12 carefully all the words of this *l.*
31: 13 children, who do not know this *l,*
31: 24 of this *l* from beginning to end,
31: 26 "Take this Book of the *L*
32: 46 carefully all the words of this *l.*
33: 4 the *l* that Moses gave us,
33: 10 and your *l* to Israel.
Jos 1: 7 to obey all the *l* my servant Moses
1: 8 of the *L* depart from your mouth;
8: 31 in the Book of the *L* of Moses—

Jos 8: 32 copied on stones the *l* of Moses,
8: 34 Joshua read all the words of the *l*—
8: 34 as it is written in the Book of the *L*.
22: 5 and the *l* that Moses the servant
23: 6 in the Book of the *L* of Moses,
24: 26 things in the Book of the *L* of God.
1Ki 2: 3 as written in the *L* of Moses,
2Ki 10: 31 careful to keep the *l* of the LORD,
14: 6 written in the Book of the *L*
17: 13 accordance with the entire *L* that I
21: 8 keep the whole *L* that my servant
22: 8 of the *L* in the temple of the LORD
22: 11 the words of the Book of the *L*,
23: 24 the requirements of the *l* written
23: 25 with all the *L* of Moses.
1Ch 16: 40 written in the *L* of the LORD,
22: 12 so that you may keep the *l*
2Ch 6: 16 walk before me according to my *l*,
12: 1 Israel with him abandoned the *l*
15: 3 a priest to teach and without the *l*.
17: 9 the Book of the *L* of the LORD;
19: 8 to administer the *l* of the LORD
19: 10 or other concerns of the *l*,
23: 18 as written in the *L* of Moses,
25: 4 with what is written in the *L*,
30: 16 as prescribed in the *L*
31: 3 as written in the *L* of the LORD.
31: 4 themselves to the *L* of the LORD.
31: 21 to the *l* and the commands,
34: 14 of the *L* of the LORD that had
34: 15 of the *L* in the temple of the LORD
34: 19 the king heard the words of the *L*,
35: 26 written in the *L* of the LORD—
Ezr 3: 2 written in the *L* of Moses the man
7: 6 versed in the *L* of Moses,
7: 10 observance of the *L* of the LORD,
7: 12 a teacher of the *L* of the God
7: 14 with regard to the *L* of your God,
7: 21 a teacher of the *L* of the God
7: 26 Whoever does not obey the *l*
7: 26 and the *l* of the king must surely be
10: 3 Let it be done according to the *L*.
Ne 8: 1 the Book of the *L* of Moses,
8: 2 Ezra the priest brought the *L*
8: 3 attentively to the Book of the *L*.
8: 7 instructed the people in the *L*
8: 8 from the Book of the *L* of God,
8: 9 they listened to the words of the *L*.
8: 13 attention to the words of the *L*.
8: 14 They found written in the *L*,
8: 18 from the Book of the *L* of God.
9: 3 and read from the Book of the *L*
9: 26 they put your *l* behind their backs.
9: 29 them to return to your *l*,
9: 34 our fathers did not follow your *l*;
10: 28 for the sake of the *L* of God,
10: 29 oath to follow the *L* of God given
10: 34 our God, as it is written in the *L*.
10: 36 "As it is also written in the *L*,
12: 44 required by the *L* for the priests
13: 3 When the people heard this *l*,
Est 1: 13 to consult experts in matters of *l*
1: 15 According to *l*, what must be done
3: 14 to be issued as *l* in every province
4: 11 summoned the king has but one *l*:
4: 16 even though it is against the *l*.
8: 13 to be issued as *l* in every province
Ps 1: 2 and on his *l* he meditates day
1: 2 his delight is in the *l* of the LORD,
19: 7 The *l* of the LORD is perfect,
37: 31 The *l* of his God is in his heart;
40: 8 your *l* is within my heart."
78: 5 and established the *l* in Israel,
78: 10 and refused to live by his *l*.
89: 30 "If his sons forsake my *l*
94: 12 the man you teach from your *l*;
119: 1 to the *l* of the LORD.
119: 18 wonderful things in your *l*.
119: 29 be gracious to me through your *l*.
119: 34 and I will keep your *l*
119: 44 I will always obey your *l*,
119: 51 but I do not turn from your *l*.
119: 53 who have forsaken your *l*.
119: 55 and I will keep your *l*.
119: 61 I will not forget your *l*.
119: 70 but I delight in your *l*.
119: 72 *l* from your mouth is more precious
119: 77 for your *l* is my delight.
Ps 119: 85 contrary to your *l*.
119: 92 If your *l* had not been my delight,
119: 97 Oh, how I love your *l*!
119:109 I will not forget your *l*.
119:113 but I love your *l*.
119:126 your *l* is being broken.
119:136 for your *l* is not obeyed.
119:142 and your *l* is true.
119:150 but they are far from your *l*.
119:153 for I have not forgotten your *l*.
119:163 but I love your *l*.
119:165 peace have they who love your *l*,
119:174 and your *l* is my delight.
Pr 28: 4 those who keep the *l* resist them.
28: 4 who forsake the *l* praise
28: 7 He who keeps the *l* is a discerning
28: 9 If anyone turns a deaf ear to the *l*,
29: 18 but blessed is he who keeps the *l*.
31: 5 and forget what the *l* decrees,
Isa 1: 10 listen to the *l* of our God,
2: 3 The *l* will go out from Zion,
5: 24 for they have rejected the *l*
8: 16 seal up the *l* among my disciples.
8: 20 To the *l* and to the testimony!
42: 4 In his *l* the islands will put their
42: 21 to make his *l* great and glorious.
42: 24 they did not obey his *l*.
51: 4 The *l* will go out from me;
51: 7 you people who have my *l*
Jer 2: 8 deal with the *l* did not know me;
6: 19 and have rejected my *l*.
8: 8 for we have the *l* of the LORD,"
9: 13 because they have forsaken my *l*,
9: 13 not obeyed me or followed my *l*.
16: 11 forsook me and did not keep my *l*.
18: 18 for the teaching of the *l*
26: 4 listen to me and follow my *l*,
31: 33 "I will put my *l* in their minds
32: 23 did not obey you or follow your *l*;
44: 10 nor have they followed my *l*
44: 23 or followed his *l* or his decrees
La 2: 9 the *l* is no more,
Eze 7: 26 the teaching of the *l*
22: 26 Her priests do violence to my *l*
43: 12 Such is the *l* of the temple.
43: 12 "This is the *l* of the temple:
Da 6: 5 to do with the *l* of his God."
6: 15 according to the *l* of the Medes
9: 11 All Israel has transgressed your *l*
9: 11 written in the *L* of Moses,
9: 13 as it is written in the *L* of Moses,
Hos 4: 6 you have ignored the *l* of your God
8: 1 and rebelled against my *l*.
8: 12 for them the many things of my *l*,
Am 2: 4 Because they have rejected the *l*
Mic 4: 2 The *l* will go out from Zion,
Hab 1: 4 Therefore the *l* is paralyzed,
1: 7 they are a *l* to themselves
Zep 3: 4 and do violence to the *l*.
Hag 2: 11 'Ask the priests what the *l* says:
Zec 7: 12 as flint and would not listen to the *l*
Mal 2: 9 partiality in matters of the *l*."
4: 4 "Remember the *l* of my servant
Mt 2: 4 chief priests and teachers of the *l*,
5: 17 that I have come to abolish the *L*
5: 18 from the *L* until everything is
5: 20 Pharisees and the teachers of the *l*,
7: 12 sums up the *L* and the Prophets.
7: 29 and not as their teachers of the *l*.
8: 19 Then a teacher of the *l* came to him
9: 3 teachers of the *l* said to themselves,
11: 13 and the *L* prophesied until John.
12: 5 Or haven't you read in the *L* that
12: 38 and teachers of the *l* said to him,
13: 52 of the *l* who has been instructed
15: 1 and teachers of the *l* came to Jesus
16: 21 chief priests and teachers of the *l*,
17: 10 of the *l* say that Elijah must come
20: 18 priests and the teachers of the *l*.
21: 15 of the *l* saw the wonderful things
22: 35 an expert in the *l*, tested him
22: 36 greatest commandment in the *L*?"
22: 40 All the *L* and the Prophets hang
23: 2 of the *l* and the Pharisees sit
23: 13 teachers of the *l* and Pharisees,
23: 15 teachers of the *l* and Pharisees,
23: 23 more important matters of the *l*—
23: 23 teachers of the *l* and Pharisees,
Mt 23: 25 teachers of the *l* and Pharisees,
23: 27 teachers of the *l* and Pharisees,
23: 29 teachers of the *l* and Pharisees,
26: 57 where the teachers of the *l*
27: 6 "It is against the *l* to put this
27: 41 of the *l* and the elders mocked him.
Mk 1: 22 not as the teachers of the *l*.
2: 6 teachers of the *l* were sitting there,
2: 16 of the *l* who were Pharisees saw
3: 22 And the teachers of the *l* who came
7: 1 the teachers of the *l* who had come
7: 5 and teachers of the *l* asked Jesus,
8: 31 chief priests and teachers of the *l*,
9: 11 of the *l* say that Elijah must come
9: 14 teachers of the *l* arguing with them.
10: 5 hard that Moses wrote you this *l*,"
10: 33 chief priests and teachers of the *l*.
11: 18 and the teachers of the *l* heard this
11: 27 of the *l* and the elders came
12: 28 One of the teachers of the *l* came
12: 35 of the *l* say that the Christ is
12: 38 Watch out for the teachers of the *l*.
14: 1 the teachers of the *l* were looking
14: 43 the teachers of the *l*, and the elders.
14: 53 teachers of the *l* came together.
15: 1 of the *l* and the whole Sanhedrin,
15: 31 the teachers of the *l* mocked him
Lk 2: 22 to the *L* of Moses had been
2: 23 (as it is written in the *L* of the Lord,
2: 24 said in the *L* of the Lord:
2: 27 what the custom of the *L* required,
2: 39 required by the *L* of the Lord,
5: 17 Pharisees and teachers of the *l*,
5: 21 the teachers of the *l* began thinking
5: 30 the teachers of the *l* who belonged
6: 7 the teachers of the *l* were looking
7: 30 in the *l* rejected God's purpose
9: 22 chief priests and teachers of the *l*,
10: 25 in the *l* stood up to test Jesus.
10: 26 "What is written in the *L*?"
10: 37 The expert in the *l* replied,
11: 45 the experts in the *l* answered him,
11: 46 "And you experts in the *l*,
11: 52 "Woe to you experts in the *l*,
11: 53 and the teachers of the *l* began
14: 3 the Pharisees and experts in the *l*,
15: 2 and the teachers of the *l* muttered,
16: 16 "The *L* and the Prophets were
16: 17 stroke of a pen to drop out of the *L*.
19: 47 the teachers of the *l* and the leaders
20: 1 priests and the teachers of the *l*,
20: 19 of the *l* and the chief priests looked
20: 39 of the teachers of the *l* responded,
20: 46 "Beware of the teachers of the *l*.
22: 2 the teachers of the *l* were looking
22: 66 chief priests and teachers of the *l*,
23: 10 of the *l* were standing there,
24: 44 me in the *L* of Moses,
Jn 1: 17 For the *l* was given through Moses;
1: 45 one Moses wrote about in the *L*,
5: 10 the *l* forbids you to carry your mat
7: 19 Has not Moses given you the *l*?
7: 19 Yet not one of you keeps the *l*.
7: 23 on the Sabbath so that the *l*
7: 49 mob that knows nothing of the *l*—
7: 51 "Does our *l* condemn a man
8: 3 of the *l* and the Pharisees brought
8: 5 In the *L* Moses commanded us
8: 17 In your own *L* it is written that
10: 34 "Is it not written in your *L*,
12: 34 from the *L* that the Christ will
15: 25 to fulfill what is written in their *L*:
18: 31 and judge him by your own *l*."
19: 7 The Jews insisted, "We have a *l*,
19: 7 and according to that *l* he must die,
Ac 4: 5 teachers of the *l* met in Jerusalem.
5: 34 a teacher of the *l*, who was honored
6: 12 the elders and the teachers of the *l*.
6: 13 the holy place and against the *l*.
7: 53 have received the *l* that was put
10: 28 against our *l* for a Jew to associate
13: 15 After the reading from the *L*
13: 39 justified from by the *l* of Moses.
15: 5 required to obey the *l* of Moses."
18: 13 God in ways contrary to the *l*."
18: 15 and names and your own *l*—
21: 20 and all of them are zealous for the *l*
21: 24 living in obedience to the *l*.

Ac 21: 28 against our people and our *l*
22: 3 trained in the *l* of our fathers
22: 12 He was a devout observer of the *l*
23: 3 to judge me according to the *l*,
23: 3 yet you yourself violate the *l*
23: 9 of the *l* who were Pharisees stood
23: 29 to do with questions about their *l*,
24: 14 everything that agrees with the *L*
25: 8 wrong against the *l* of the Jews
28: 23 Jesus from the *L* of Moses
Ro 2: 12 All who sin apart from the *l* will
2: 12 also perish apart from the *l*,
2: 12 under the *l* will be judged by the *l*.
2: 13 those who obey the *l* who will be
2: 13 who hear the *l* who are righteous
2: 14 Gentiles, who do not have the *l*,
2: 14 by nature things required by the *l*,
2: 14 even though they do not have the *l*,
2: 14 they are a *l* for themselves,
2: 15 of the *l* are written on their hearts,
2: 17 rely on the *l* and brag about your
2: 18 because you are instructed by the *l*;
2: 20 you have in the *l* the embodiment
2: 23 God by breaking the *l*?
2: 23 You who brag about the *l*,
2: 25 if you break the *l*, you have become
2: 25 value if you observe the *l*,
2: 27 yet obeys the *l* will condemn you
3: 19 it says to those who are under the *l*,
3: 19 we know that whatever the *l* says,
3: 20 in his sight by observing the *l*;
3: 20 through the *l* we become conscious
3: 21 apart from *l*, has been made known
3: 21 to which the *L* and the Prophets
3: 27 On that of observing the *l*? No,
3: 28 by faith apart from observing the *l*.
3: 31 Not at all! Rather, we uphold the *l*.
3: 31 then, nullify the *l* by this faith?
4: 13 It was not through *l* that Abraham
4: 14 For if those who live by *l* are heirs,
4: 15 And where there is no *l* there is no
4: 15 worthless, because *l* brings wrath.
4: 16 not only to those who are of the *l*
5: 13 for before the *l* was given,
5: 13 into account when there is no *l*.
5: 20 *l* was added so that the trespass
6: 14 because you are not under *l*,
6: 15 we are not under *l* but under grace?
7: 1 speaking to men who know the *l*—
7: 1 that the *l* has authority
7: 2 by *l* a married woman is bound
7: 2 released from the *l* of marriage.
7: 3 she is released from that *l*
7: 4 also died to the *l* through the body
7: 5 aroused by the *l* were at work
7: 6 released from the *l* so that we serve
7: 7 then? Is the *l* sin? Certainly not!
7: 7 was to covet if the *l* had not said,
7: 7 what sin was except through the *l*.
7: 8 For apart from *l*, sin is dead.
7: 9 Once I was alive apart from *l*;
7: 12 *l* is holy, and the commandment is
7: 14 We know that the *l* is spiritual;
7: 16 to do, I agree that the *l* is good.
7: 21 I find this *l* at work: When I want
7: 22 my inner being I delight in God's *l*;
7: 23 a prisoner of the *l* of sin at work
7: 23 but I see another *l* at work
7: 23 war against the *l* of my mind
7: 25 in my mind am a slave to God's *l*,
7: 25 in the sinful nature a slave to the *l*
8: 2 because through Christ Jesus the *l*
8: 2 of life set me free from the *l* of sin
8: 3 For what the *l* was powerless to do
8: 4 of the *l* might be fully met in us,
8: 7 It does not submit to God's *l*,
9: 4 covenants, the receiving of the *l*,
9: 31 who pursued a *l* of righteousness,
10: 4 Christ is the end of the *l*
10: 5 the righteousness that is by the *l*:
13: 8 his fellow man has fulfilled the *l*.
13: 10 love is the fulfillment of the *l*.
1Co 6: 6 goes to *l* against another—
9: 8 Doesn't the *L* say the same thing?
9: 9 For it is written in the *L* of Moses:
9: 20 I myself am not under the *l*),
9: 20 so as to win those under the *l*.
9: 20 the *l* I became like one under the *l*
1Co 9: 21 God's *l* but am under Christ's *l*),
9: 21 I became like one not having the *l*
9: 21 so as to win those not having the *l*.
9: 21 those not having the *l* I became like
14: 21 In the *L* it is written:
14: 34 be in submission, as the *L* says.
15: 56 and the power of sin is the *l*.
Gal 2: 16 and not by observing the *l*,
2: 16 by observing the *l* no one will be
2: 16 justified by observing the *l*,
2: 19 For through the *l* I died to the *l*
2: 21 could be gained through the *l*,
3: 2 the Spirit by observing the *l*,
3: 5 you because you observe the *l*,
3: 10 on observing the *l* are under a curse
3: 10 written in the Book of the *L*."
3: 11 justified before God by the *l*,
3: 12 The *l* is not based on faith;
3: 13 curse of the *l* by becoming a curse
3: 17 The *l*, introduced 430 years later,
3: 18 if the inheritance depends on the *l*,
3: 19 The *l* was put into effect
3: 19 then, was the purpose of the *l*?
3: 21 For if a *l* had been given that could
3: 21 Is the *l*, therefore, opposed
3: 21 certainly have come by the *l*.
3: 23 we were held prisoners by the *l*,
3: 24 So the *l* was put in charge to lead us
3: 25 under the supervision of the *l*.
4: 5 under *l*, to redeem those under *l*,
4: 21 aware of what the *l* says?
4: 21 you who want to be under the *l*,
5: 3 obligated to obey the whole *l*.
5: 4 justified by *l* have been alienated
5: 14 The entire *l* is summed up
5: 18 by the Spirit, you are not under *l*.
5: 23 Against such things there is no *l*.
6: 2 and in this way you will fulfill the *l*
6: 13 who are circumcised obey the *l*,
Eph 2: 15 flesh the *l* with its commandments
Php 3: 5 in regard to the *l*, a Pharisee;
3: 9 of my own that comes from the *l*,
1Ti 1: 7 They want to be teachers of the *l*,
1: 8 We know that the *l* is good
1: 9 also know that *l* is made not
Tit 3: 9 arguments and quarrels about the *l*,
Heb 7: 5 Now the *l* requires the descendants
7: 11 of it the *l* was given to the people),
7: 12 there must also be a change of the *l*.
7: 19 (for the *l* made nothing perfect),
7: 28 For the *l* appoints as high priests
7: 28 after the *l*, appointed the Son,
8: 4 offer the gifts prescribed by the *l*.
9: 19 of the *l* to all the people,
9: 22 *l* requires that nearly everything be
10: 1 The *l* is only a shadow
10: 8 the *l* required them to be made).
10: 28 Anyone who rejected the *l*
Jas 1: 25 intently into the perfect *l* that gives
2: 8 If you really keep the royal *l* found
2: 9 convicted by the *l* as lawbreakers.
2: 10 For whoever keeps the whole *l*
2: 12 judged by the *l* that gives freedom,
4: 11 When you judge the *l*, you are not
4: 11 or judges him speaks against the *l*
1Jn 3: 4 Everyone who sins breaks the *l*;

LAW'S (LAW)

Ro 2: 26 keep the *l* requirements,

LAWBREAKER (BREAK)

Ro 2: 27 code and circumcision, are a *l*.
Gal 2: 18 I destroyed, I prove that I am a *l*.
Jas 2: 11 murder, you have become a *l*.

LAWBREAKERS (BREAK)

1Ti 1: 9 not for good men but for *l*
Jas 2: 9 and are convicted by the law as *l*.

LAWFUL (LAW)

Mt 12: 4 which was not *l* for them to do,
12: 10 "Is it *l* to heal on the Sabbath?"
12: 12 Therefore it is *l* to do good
14: 4 "It is not *l* for you to have her."
19: 3 "Is it *l* for a man to divorce his wife
Mk 2: 26 which is *l* only for priests to eat.
3: 4 "Which is *l* on the Sabbath:
6: 18 "It is not *l* for you
Mk 10: 2 "Is it *l* for a man to divorce his wife
Lk 6: 4 he ate what is *l* only for priests
6: 9 I ask you, which is *l* on the Sabbath
14: 3 "Is it *l* to heal on the Sabbath or not

LAWGIVER (LAW)

Isa 33: 22 the LORD is our *l*,
Jas 4: 12 There is only one *L* and Judge,

LAWLESS (LAWLESSNESS)

2Sa 3: 33 Should Abner have died as the *l* die
2Th 2: 8 And then the *l* one will be revealed
2: 9 The coming of the *l* one will be
Heb 10: 17 "Their sins and *l* acts
2Pe 2: 7 by the filthy lives of *l* men
2: 8 soul by the *l* deeds he saw
3: 17 away by the error of *l* men

LAWLESSNESS (LAWLESS)

2Th 2: 3 and the man of *l* is revealed,
2: 7 power of *l* is already at work;
1Jn 3: 4 sins breaks the law; in fact, sin is *l*.

LAWS (LAW)

Ge 26: 5 commands, my decrees and my *l*."
Ex 18: 16 inform them of God's decrees and *l*
18: 20 Teach them the decrees and *l*,
21: 1 "These are the *l* you are to set
24: 3 people all the LORD's words and *l*,
Lev 18: 4 You must obey my *l* and be careful
18: 5 *l*, for the man who obeys them will
18: 26 must keep my decrees and my *l*.
19: 37 and all my *l* and follow them.
20: 22 " 'Keep all my decrees and *l*
25: 18 and be careful to obey my *l*,
26: 15 reject my decrees and abhor my *l*
26: 43 they rejected my *l* and abhorred
26: 46 the *l* and the regulations that
Nu 15: 16 same *l* and regulations will apply
Dt 4: 1 and *l* I am about to teach you.
4: 5 I have taught you decrees and *l*
4: 8 as this body of *l* I am setting
4: 8 have such righteous decrees and *l*
4: 14 and *l* you are to follow
4: 45 and *l* Moses gave them
5: 1 *l* I declare in your hearing today.
5: 31 *l* you are to teach them to follow
6: 1 *l* the LORD your God directed me
6: 20 and *l* the LORD our God has
7: 11 decrees and *l* I give you today.
7: 12 If you pay attention to these *l*
8: 11 his *l* and his decrees that I am
11: 1 his *l* and his commands always.
11: 32 and *l* I am setting before you today.
12: 1 and *l* you must be careful to follow
19: 9 follow all these *l* I command you
26: 16 day to follow these decrees and *l*;
26: 17 and *l*, and that you will obey him.
30: 16 decrees and *l*; then you will live
Jos 24: 25 up for them decrees and *l*.
2Sa 22: 23 All his *l* are before me;
1Ki 2: 3 commands, his *l* and requirements,
9: 4 and observe my decrees and *l*,
11: 33 nor kept my statutes and *l* as David
2Ki 17: 34 *l* and commands that the LORD
17: 37 the *l* and commands he wrote
1Ch 22: 13 and *l* that the LORD gave Moses
28: 7 carrying out my commands and *l*,
2Ch 7: 17 and observe my decrees and *l*,
14: 4 and to obey his *l* and commands.
33: 8 them concerning all the *l*,
Ezr 7: 10 and to teaching its decrees and *l*
7: 25 all who know the *l* of your God.
Ne 1: 7 and *l* you gave your servant Moses.
9: 13 them regulations and *l* that are just
9: 14 and *l* through your servant Moses.
Est 1: 13 the wise men who understood the *l*
1: 19 let it be written in the *l* of Persia
3: 8 and they do not obey the king's *l*;
Job 38: 33 Do you know the *l* of the heavens?
Ps 10: 5 and your *l* are far from him;
18: 22 All his *l* are before me;
50: 16 right have you to recite my *l*
105: 45 and observe his *l*.
119: 7 as I learn your righteous *l*.
119: 13 all the *l* that come
119: 20 for your *l* at all times.
119: 30 I have set my heart on your *l*.

Ps 119: 39 for your *l* are good.
119: 43 for I have put my hope in your *l*.
119: 52 I remember your ancient *l*,
119: 62 for your righteous *l*.
119: 75 O LORD, that your *l* are righteous,
119: 91 Your *l* endure to this day,
119:102 I have not departed from your *l*,
119:106 that I will follow your righteous *l*.
119:108 and teach me your *l*.
119:120 I stand in awe of your *l*.
119:137 and your *l* are right.
119:149 O LORD, according to your *l*.
119:156 renew my life according to your *l*.
119:160 all your righteous *l* are eternal.
119:164 for your righteous *l*.
119:175 and may your *l* sustain me.
147: 19 his *l* and decrees to Israel.
147: 20 they do not know his *l*.
Pr 8: 15 and rulers make *l* that are just;
Isa 10: 1 Woe to those who make unjust *l*,
24: 5 they have disobeyed the *l*,
26: 8 walking in the way of your *l*,
Jer 33: 25 and night and the fixed *l* of heaven
Eze 5: 6 She has rejected my *l* and has not
5: 6 she has rebelled against my *l*
5: 7 followed my decrees or kept my *l*.
11: 12 followed my decrees or kept my *l*
11: 20 and be careful to keep my *l*.
18: 9 and faithfully keeps my *l*.
18: 17 He keeps my *l* and follows my
20: 11 and made known to them my *l*,
20: 13 my decrees but rejected my *l*—
20: 16 because they rejected my *l*
20: 18 or keep their *l* or defile yourselves
20: 19 and be careful to keep my *l*.
20: 21 they were not careful to keep my *l*
20: 24 because they had not obeyed my *l*
20: 25 and *l* they could not live by;
36: 27 and be careful to keep my *l*.
37: 24 will follow my *l* and be careful
43: 11 and all its regulations and *l*.
44: 24 They are to keep my *l*
Da 6: 8 accordance with the *l* of the Medes
6: 12 accordance with the *l* of the Medes
7: 25 to change the set times and the *l*.
9: 5 away from your commands and *l*.
9: 10 or kept the *l* he gave us
Mal 4: 4 *l* I gave him at Horeb for all Israel.
Heb 8: 10 I will put my *l* in their minds
10: 16 I will put my *l* in their hearts,

LAWSUIT (LAWSUITS)

Ex 23: 2 When you give testimony in a *l*,
23: 3 favoritism to a poor man in his *l*.

LAWSUITS (LAWSUIT)

Ex 23: 6 to your poor people in their *l*.
Dt 17: 8 whether bloodshed, *l* or assaults—
Hos 10: 4 therefore *l* spring up
1Co 6: 7 The very fact that you have *l*

LAWYER (LAW)

Ac 24: 1 the elders and a *l* named Tertullus,
Tit 3: 13 can to help Zenas the *l*

LAX

Jer 48: 10 "A curse on him who is *l* in doing

LAY (LAID LAIN LAYER LAYING LAYS)

Ge 4: 1 Adam *l* with his wife Eve,
4: 17 Cain *l* with his wife, and she
4: 25 Adam *l* with his wife again,
9: 21 and *l* uncovered inside his tent.
19: 33 aware of it when she *l* down
19: 33 the older daughter went in and *l*
19: 34 "Last night I *l* with my father.
19: 35 aware of it when she *l* down
19: 35 the younger daughter went and *l*
22: 12 "Do not *l* a hand on the boy,"
28: 11 under his head and *l* down to sleep.
29: 23 her to Jacob, and Jacob *l* with her.
29: 30 Jacob *l* with Rachel also,
37: 22 but don't *l* a hand on him."
37: 27 and not *l* our hands on him;
38: 2 He married her and *l* with her;
38: 9 so whenever he *l* with his brother's
Ex 7: 4 Then I will *l* my hand on Egypt
22: 11 that the neighbor did not *l* hands
29: 10 and his sons shall *l* their hands
29: 15 and his sons shall *l* their hands
29: 19 and his sons shall *l* their hands
Lev 1: 4 He is to *l* his hand on the head
3: 2 He is to *l* his hand on the head
3: 8 He is to *l* his hand on the head
3: 13 He is to *l* his hand on its head
4: 4 He is to *l* his hand on its head
4: 15 the community are to *l* their hands
4: 24 He is to *l* his hand
4: 29 He is to *l* his hand on the head
4: 33 He is to *l* his hand on its head
16: 21 He is to *l* both hands on the head
24: 14 are to *l* their hands on his head,
26: 31 and *l* waste your sanctuaries,
26: 32 I will *l* waste the land,
Nu 8: 10 the Israelites are to *l* their hands
8: 12 "After the Levites *l* their hands
22: 27 she *l* down under Balaam,
27: 18 whom is the spirit, and *l* your hand
Dt 9: 25 I *l* prostrate before the LORD
20: 12 you in battle, *l* siege to that city.
20: 19 When you *l* siege to a city
28: 52 They will *l* siege to all the cities
Jos 2: 8 the spies *l* down for the night,
6: 26 will he *l* its foundations;
8: 9 *l* in wait between Bethel and Ai,
18: 11 Their allotted territory *l*
19: 1 Their inheritance *l*
Jdg 4: 21 to him while he *l* fast asleep,
4: 22 and there *l* Sisera with the tent peg
5: 27 he fell; there he *l*.
7: 8 the camp of Midian *l* below him
16: 2 and *l* in wait for him all night
16: 3 But Samson *l* there only
19: 26 down at the door and *l* there
19: 27 there *l* his concubine, fallen
Ru 3: 7 uncovered his feet and *l* down.
3: 14 So she *l* at his feet until morning,
1Sa 1: 19 Elkanah *l* with Hannah his wife,
3: 5 So he went and *l* down.
3: 9 So Samuel went and *l*
3: 15 Samuel *l* down until morning
9: 23 the one I told you to *l* aside."
19: 24 He *l* that way all that day and night
23: 17 "My father Saul will not *l* a hand
26: 9 Who can *l* a hand on the LORD's
26: 11 LORD forbid that I should *l* a hand
26: 23 but I would not *l* a hand
2Sa 12: 24 and he went to her and *l* with her.
13: 6 So Amnon *l* down and pretended
13: 31 and *l* down on the ground;
16: 22 he *l* with his father's concubines
20: 12 Amasa *l* wallowing in his blood
1Ki 3: 19 woman's son died because she *l*
13: 31 *l* my bones beside his bones.
19: 5 Then he *l* down under the tree
19: 6 and drank and then *l* down again.
21: 4 He *l* on his bed sulking
21: 27 He *l* in sackcloth and went
2Ki 4: 11 up to his room and *l* down there.
4: 29 *L* my staff on the boy's face."
4: 34 got on the bed and *l* upon the boy,
1Ch 2: 21 Hezron *l* with the daughter
7: 23 Then he *l* with his wife again,
2Ch 24: 22 as he *l* dying, "May the LORD see
35: 5 fellow countrymen, the *l* people.
35: 7 for all the *l* people who were there
Ne 13: 21 If you do this again, I will *l* hands
Est 4: 3 Many *l* on sackcloth and ashes.
9: 10 But they did not *l* their hands
9: 15 but they did not *l* their hands
9: 16 did not *l* their hands on the plunder
Job 1: 12 on the man himself do not *l* a finger
5: 8 I would *l* my cause before him.
9: 33 to *l* his hand upon us both,
22: 22 and *l* up his words in your heart.
30: 12 they *l* snares for my feet,
41: 8 If you *l* a hand on him,
Ps 5: 3 by morning I *l* my requests
21: 8 Your hand will *l* hold
22: 15 you *l* me in the dust of death.
73: 9 Their mouths *l* claim to heaven,
Pr 3: 18 those who *l* hold of her will be
4: 4 "*L* hold of my words
Ecc 10: 4 calmness can *l* great errors to rest.
Isa 11: 14 They will *l* hands on Edom
21: 2 Elam, attack! Media, *l* siege!
24: 1 going to *l* waste the earth
25: 12 and *l* them low;
28: 16 "See, I *l* a stone in Zion,
34: 15 The owl will nest there and *l* eggs,
35: 7 In the haunts where jackals once *l*,
42: 15 I will *l* waste the mountains
43: 17 and they *l* there, never to rise again
44: 7 Let him declare and *l* out
52: 10 The LORD will *l* bare his holy arm
64: 7 or strives to *l* hold of you;
Jer 2: 20 you *l* down as a prostitute.
4: 7 place to *l* waste your land.
4: 26 all its towns *l* in ruins
9: 11 I will *l* waste the towns of Judah
15: 6 So I will *l* hands on you
17: 11 that hatches eggs it did not *l*
34: 22 I will *l* waste the towns of Judah
50: 3 and *l* waste her land.
51: 29 to *l* waste the land of Babylon
La 4: 19 and *l* in wait for us in the desert.
Eze 4: 2 Then *l* siege to it: Erect siege works
6: 5 I will *l* the dead bodies
16: 6 as you *l* there in your blood I said
19: 2 She *l* down among the young lions
25: 13 I will *l* it waste, and from Teman
26: 16 and *l* aside their robes and take
30: 12 I will *l* waste the land
30: 14 I will *l* Pathros waste,
31: 12 its branches *l* broken
39: 21 and the hand I *l* upon them.
Da 2: 28 as you *l* on your bed are these:
8: 27 was exhausted and *l* ill
Jnh 1: 5 where he *l* down and fell
Mic 1: 6 and *l* bare her foundations.
7: 16 They will *l* their hands
Mt 8: 20 of Man has no place to *l* his head."
11: 12 and forceful men *l* hold of it.
28: 6 Come and see the place where he *l*.
Mk 6: 5 *l* his hands on a few sick people
Lk 5: 18 into the house to *l* him before Jesus
9: 58 of Man has no place to *l* his head."
21: 12 they will *l* hands on you
22: 53 and you did not *l* a hand on me.
Jn 4: 46 royal official whose son *l* sick
10: 15 and I *l* down my life for the sheep.
10: 17 my Father loves me is that I *l*
10: 18 I have authority to *l* it down
10: 18 but I *l* it down of my own accord.
11: 2 whose brother Lazarus now *l* sick,
13: 37 I will *l* down my life for you."
13: 38 "Will you really *l* down your life
15: 13 that one *l* down his life
Ac 8: 19 on whom I *l* my hands may receive
Ro 9: 33 I *l* in Zion a stone that causes men
1Co 3: 11 no one can *l* any foundation other
7: 17 This is the rule I *l* down in all
1Ti 6: 19 In this way they will *l* up treasure
1Pe 2: 6 "See, I *l* a stone in Zion,
1Jn 3: 16 And we ought to *l* down our lives
Rev 4: 10 They *l* their crowns
10: 2 holding a little scroll, which *l* open

LAYER (LAY)

Ex 16: 13 in the morning there was a *l* of dew
Lev 9: 19 the *l* of fat, the kidneys

LAYING (LAY)

2Ch 32: 9 and all his forces were *l* siege
Job 34: 30 from *l* snares for the people.
Lk 4: 40 and *l* his hands on each one,
Ac 8: 18 at the *l* on of the apostles' hands,
1Ti 5: 22 Do not be hasty in the *l* on of hands
2Ti 1: 6 is in you through the *l*
Heb 6: 1 not *l* again the foundation
6: 2 instruction about baptisms, the *l*

LAYS (LAY)

Job 27: 17 what he *l* up the righteous will wear
28: 9 *l* bare the roots of the mountains.
30: 24 "Surely no one *l* a hand
39: 14 She *l* her eggs on the ground
Ps 104: 3 *l* the beams of his upper chambers
Isa 26: 5 he *l* the lofty city low;
30: 32 Every stroke the LORD *l* on them
Zec 12: 1 who *l* the foundation of the earth,
Lk 14: 29 For if he *l* the foundation
Jn 10: 11 The good shepherd *l* down his life

LAZARUS

Lk 16: 20 his gate was laid a beggar named *L*,
16: 23 with *L* by his side.
16: 24 send *L* to dip the tip of his finger
16: 25 while *L* received bad things,
16: 27 father, send *L* to my father's house,
Jn 11: 1 Now a man named *L* was sick.
11: 2 whose brother *L* now lay sick,
11: 5 loved Martha and her sister and *L*.
11: 6 Yet when he heard that *L* was sick,
11: 11 "Our friend *L* has fallen asleep;
11: 14 he told them plainly, "*L* is dead,
11: 17 Jesus found that *L* had already
11: 43 Jesus called in a loud voice, "*L*,
12: 1 arrived at Bethany, where *L* lived,
12: 2 while *L* was among those reclining
12: 9 because of him but also to see *L*,
12: 10 chief priests made plans to kill *L*
12: 17 the word that he had called *L*

LAZINESS (LAZY)

Pr 12: 24 but *l* ends in slave labor.
19: 15 *L* brings on deep sleep,

LAZY (LAZINESS)

Ex 5: 8 They are *l;* that is why they are
5: 17 "*L*, that's what you are—*l!*
Pr 10: 4 *L* hands make a man poor,
12: 27 The *l* man does not roast his game,
26: 15 he is too *l* to bring it back
Ecc 10: 18 If a man is *l*, the rafters sag;
Mt 25: 26 replied, 'You wicked, *l* servant!
Tit 1: 12 liars, evil brutes, *l* gluttons."
Heb 6: 12 We do not want you to become *l*,

LEAD (LEADER LEADER'S LEADERS LEADERS' LEADERSHIP LEADING LEADS LED RINGLEADER)

Ge 32: 17 He instructed the one in the *l:*
Ex 13: 17 God did not *l* them on the road
15: 10 They sank like *l*
15: 13 "In your unfailing love you will *l*
32: 34 *l* the people to the place I spoke of,
33: 12 been telling me, '*L* these people,'
34: 16 they will *l* your sons to do the same
Nu 14: 8 with us, he will *l* us into that land,
21: 15 that *l* to the site of Ar
27: 17 one who will *l* them out
31: 22 *l* and anything else that can
Dt 1: 38 because he will *l* Israel to inherit it.
3: 28 for he will *l* this people across
10: 11 "and *l* the people on their way,
21: 4 *l* her down to a valley that has not
31: 2 and I am no longer able to *l* you.
Jos 1: 6 because you will *l* these people
Jdg 4: 6 and *l* the way to Mount Tabor.
5: 2 the princes in Israel take the *l*,
7: 17 "Follow my *l*.
1Sa 8: 5 now appoint a king to *l* us,
8: 6 to *l* us," this displeased Samuel;
8: 20 with a king to *l* us and to go out
30: 15 "Can you *l* me down to this raiding
2Ki 4: 24 and said to her servant, "*L* on;
6: 19 and I will *l* you to the man you are
2Ch 1: 10 knowledge, that I may *l* this people
8: 14 and the Levites to *l* the praise
Est 6: 9 and *l* him on the horse
Job 19: 24 inscribed with an iron tool on *l*,
38: 32 or *l* out the Bear with its cubs?
Ps 5: 8 *L* me, O LORD, in your
26: 11 But I *l* a blameless life;
27: 11 *l* me in a straight path
31: 3 for the sake of your name *l*
60: 9 Who will *l* me to Edom?
61: 2 *l* me to the rock that is higher
80: 1 you who *l* Joseph like a flock;
101: 2 I will be careful to *l* a blameless life
108: 10 Who will *l* me to Edom?
139: 24 and *l* me in the way everlasting.
143: 10 *l* me on level ground.
Pr 4: 11 and *l* you along straight paths.
5: 5 her steps *l* straight to the grave.
21: 5 The plans of the diligent *l* to profit
Ecc 5: 6 Do not let your mouth *l* you
SS 8: 2 I would *l* you
Isa 3: 12 people, your guides *l* you astray;
Isa 11: 6 and a little child will *l* them.
20: 4 king of Assyria will *l* away stripped
42: 16 I will *l* the blind by ways they have
43: 8 *L* out those who have eyes
49: 10 and *l* them beside springs of water.
60: 9 in the *l* are the ships of Tarshish,
Jer 3: 15 who will *l* you with knowledge
6: 29 to burn away the *l* with fire,
23: 32 and *l* my people astray
31: 9 I will *l* them beside streams
31: 32 the hand to *l* them out of Egypt,
50: 8 and be like the goats that *l* the flock
Eze 13: 10 " 'Because they *l* my people astray,
22: 18 tin, iron and *l* left inside a furnace.
22: 20 *l* and tin into a furnace to melt it
27: 12 tin and *l* for your merchandise.
Da 12: 3 those who *l* many to righteousness,
Hos 2: 14 I will *l* her into the desert
5: 8 *l* on, O Benjamin.
Mic 3: 5 who *l* my people astray,
6: 4 I sent Moses to *l* you,
Zec 5: 7 Then the cover of *l* was raised,
5: 8 and pushed the *l* cover
Mt 6: 13 And *l* us not into temptation,
Mk 14: 44 and *l* him away under guard."
Lk 6: 39 "Can a blind man *l* a blind man?
11: 4 And *l* us not into temptation.' "
13: 15 and *l* it out to give it water?
Jn 21: 18 *l* you where you do not want to go
Ac 13: 11 seeking someone to *l* him
Gal 3: 24 So the law was put in charge to *l* us
1Th 4: 11 it your ambition to *l* a quiet life,
Heb 6: 1 from acts that *l* to death,
8: 9 the hand to *l* them out of Egypt,
9: 14 from acts that *l* to death,
1Jn 2: 26 who are trying to *l* you astray.
3: 7 do not let anyone *l* you astray.
5: 16 commit a sin that does not *l*
5: 16 refer to those whose sin does not *l*
5: 17 there is sin that does not *l* to death.
Rev 7: 17 he will *l* them to springs

LEADER (LEAD)

Lev 4: 22 " 'When a *l* sins unintentionally
Nu 2: 3 The *l* of the people
2: 5 The *l* of the people
2: 7 The *l* of the people
2: 10 The *l* of the people
2: 12 The *l* of the people
2: 14 The *l* of the people
2: 18 The *l* of the people
2: 20 The *l* of the people
2: 22 The *l* of the people
2: 25 The *l* of the people
2: 27 The *l* of the people
2: 29 The *l* of the people
3: 24 The *l* of the families
3: 30 The *l* of the families
3: 32 chief *l* of the Levites was Eleazar
3: 35 The *l* of the families
7: 3 an ox from each *l* and a cart
7: 11 "Each day one *l* is
7: 18 *l* of Issachar, brought his offering.
7: 24 the *l* of the people of Zebulun,
7: 30 the *l* of the people of Reuben,
7: 36 the *l* of the people of Simeon,
7: 42 the *l* of the people of Gad,
7: 48 the *l* of the people of Ephraim,
7: 54 the *l* of the people of Manasseh,
7: 60 the *l* of the people of Benjamin,
7: 66 the *l* of the people of Dan,
7: 72 the *l* of the people of Asher,
7: 78 the *l* of the people of Naphtali,
14: 4 "We should choose a *l*
17: 2 one from the *l* of each
17: 6 one for the *l* of each
25: 14 the *l* of a Simeonite family.
25: 18 the daughter of a Midianite *l*,
34: 18 And appoint one *l* from each tribe
34: 22 the *l* from the tribe of Dan;
34: 23 the *l* from the tribe
34: 24 the *l* from the tribe of Ephraim son
34: 25 the *l* from the tribe of Zebulun;
34: 26 the *l* from the tribe of Issachar;
34: 27 the *l* from the tribe of Asher;
34: 28 the *l* from the tribe of Naphtali."
1Sa 7: 6 Samuel was *l* of Israel at Mizpah.
9: 16 Anoint him *l* over my people Israel
1Sa 10: 1 Has not the LORD anointed you *l*
12: 2 I have been your *l* from my youth
12: 2 Now you have a king as your *l*.
13: 14 and appointed him *l* of his people,
19: 20 Samuel standing there as their *l*,
22: 2 around him, and he became their *l*.
25: 30 has appointed him *l* over Israel,
1Ki 11: 24 became the *l* of a band of rebels
14: 7 made you a *l* over my people Israel.
16: 2 made you *l* of my people Israel,
2Ki 20: 5 tell Hezekiah, the *l* of my people,
1Ch 2: 10 the *l* of the people of Judah.
5: 6 Beerah was a *l* of the Reubenites.
12: 4 who was a *l* of the Thirty; Jeremiah
12: 27 including Jehoiada, *l* of the family
15: 5 Uriel the *l* and 120 relatives;
15: 6 Asaiah the *l* and 220 relatives;
15: 7 Joel the *l* and 130 relatives;
15: 8 Shemaiah the *l* and 200 relatives;
15: 9 Eliel the *l* and 80 relatives;
15: 10 Amminadab the *l* and 112 relatives
27: 4 Mikloth was the *l* of his division.
28: 4 as *l*, and from the house
2Ch 6: 5 to be the *l* over my people Israel.
13: 12 God is with us; he is our *l*.
19: 11 son of Ishmael, the *l* of the tribe
Ezr 8: 17 them to Iddo, the *l* in Casiphia.
Ne 9: 17 and in their rebellion appointed a *l*
Isa 3: 6 "You have a cloak, you be our *l;*
3: 7 do not make me the *l* of the people
55: 4 a *l* and commander of the peoples.
Jer 30: 21 Their *l* will be one of their own;
Hos 1: 11 and they will appoint one *l*
Hab 3: 13 You crushed the *l* of the land

LEADER'S (LEAD)

Dt 33: 21 the *l* portion was kept for him.

LEADERS (LEAD)

Ex 15: 15 the *l* of Moab will be seized
16: 22 and the *l* of the community came
18: 25 and made them *l* of the people,
24: 11 against these *l* of the Israelites;
34: 31 all the *l* of the community came
35: 27 The *l* brought onyx stones
Nu 1: 16 the *l* of their ancestral tribes.
1: 44 Aaron and the twelve *l* of Israel,
4: 34 the *l* of the community counted
4: 46 *l* of Israel counted all the Levites
7: 2 Then the *l* of Israel, the heads
7: 2 of families who were the tribal *l*
7: 10 the *l* brought their offerings
7: 84 of the Israelite *l* for the dedication
10: 4 If only one is sounded, the *l*—
11: 16 as *l* and officials among the people.
13: 2 ancestral tribe send one of its *l*."
13: 3 All of them were *l* of the Israelites.
16: 2 well-known community *l* who had
17: 6 and their *l* gave him twelve staffs,
25: 4 "Take all the *l* of these people,
27: 2 the *l* and the whole assembly,
31: 13 all the *l* of the community went
32: 2 and to the *l* of the community,
36: 1 and spoke before Moses and the *l*,
Dt 29: 10 your *l* and chief men, your elders
32: 42 the heads of the enemy *l*."
33: 5 when the *l* of the people assembled
Jos 8: 10 the *l* of Israel marched before them
9: 15 and the *l* of the assembly ratified it
9: 18 the *l* of the assembly had sworn
9: 19 against the *l*, but all the *l* answered,
17: 4 Joshua son of Nun, and the *l*
22: 30 and the *l* of the community—
22: 32 and the *l* returned to Canaan
23: 2 their elders, *l*, judges and officials
24: 1 He summoned the elders, *l*,
Jdg 7: 25 captured two of the Midianite *l*,
8: 3 the Midianite *l*, into your hands.
10: 18 The *l* of the people of Gilead said
20: 2 The *l* of all the people of the tribes
1Sa 14: 38 all you who are *l* of the army,
2Sa 4: 2 Saul's son had two men who were *l*
7: 11 ever since the time I appointed *l*
1Ch 4: 38 above by name were *l* of their clans
7: 40 brave warriors and outstanding *l*.
12: 18 made them *l* of his raiding bands.
12: 20 *l* of units of a thousand
15: 16 David told the *l* of the Levites

1Ch 17: 6 any of their *l* whom I commanded
17: 10 ever since the time I appointed *l*
22: 17 David ordered all the *l* of Israel
23: 2 gathered together all the *l* of Israel,
24: 4 A larger number of *l* were found
26: 6 who were *l* in their father's family
29: 6 Then the *l* of families, the officers
29: 9 at the willing response of their *l*,
2Ch 1: 2 and to all the *l* in Israel,
12: 5 and to the *l* of Judah who had
12: 6 *l* of Israel and the king humbled
24: 23 and killed all the *l* of the people.
26: 12 The total number of family *l*
28: 12 Then some of the *l* in Ephraim—
32: 21 all the fighting men and the *l*
35: 9 and Jozabad, the *l* of the Levites,
36: 14 all the *l* of the priests
Ezr 5: 10 of their *l* for your information.
8: 16 who were *l*, and Joiarib
9: 1 the *l* came to me and said,
9: 2 the *l* and officials have led the way
Ne 9: 32 upon our kings and *l*,
9: 34 our *l*, our priests and our fathers
9: 38 putting it in writing, and our *l*,
10: 14 The *l* of the people: Parosh,
11: 1 Now the *l* of the people settled
11: 3 are the provincial *l* who settled
12: 7 These were the *l* of the priests
12: 24 the *l* of the Levites were Hashabiah
12: 31 I had the *l* of Judah go up on top
12: 32 half the *l* of Judah followed them,
Est 1: 3 The military *l* of Persia and Media,
Job 12: 24 He deprives the *l* of the earth
Isa 3: 14 judgment against the elders and *l*
14: 9 all those who were *l* in the world;
19: 13 the *l* of Memphis are deceived;
22: 3 All your *l* have fled together;
Jer 2: 8 the *l* rebelled against me.
5: 5 So I will go to the *l*
25: 34 roll in the dust, you *l* of the flock.
25: 35 the *l* of the flock no place to escape
25: 36 the wailing of the *l* of the flock,
29: 2 and the *l* of Judah and Jerusalem,
34: 19 The *l* of Judah and Jerusalem,
Eze 11: 1 son of Benaiah, *l* of the people.
32: 21 the grave the mighty *l* will say
Da 11: 41 the *l* of Ammon will be delivered
Hos 5: 10 Judah's *l* are like those
7: 16 Their *l* will fall by the sword
9: 15 all their *l* are rebellious.
Mic 3: 1 "Listen, you *l* of Jacob,
3: 9 you *l* of the house of Jacob,
3: 11 Her *l* judge for a bribe,
5: 5 even eight *l* of men.
Zec 9: 7 and become *l* in Judah,
10: 3 and I will punish the *l*;
12: 5 Then the *l* of Judah will say
12: 6 "On that day I will make the *l*
Lk 19: 47 the *l* among the people were trying
Jn 12: 42 even among the *l* believed in him.
Ac 3: 17 acted in ignorance, as did your *l*.
14: 5 together with their *l*,
15: 22 two men who were *l*
25: 2 and Jewish *l* appeared before him
25: 5 Let some of your *l* come with me
28: 17 days later he called together the *l*
Gal 2: 2 to those who seemed to be *l*,
Heb 13: 7 Remember your *l*, who spoke
13: 17 Obey your *l* and submit
13: 24 Greet all your *l* and all God's

LEADERS' (LEAD)

Jos 9: 21 So the *l'* promise to them was kept.

LEADERSHIP (LEAD)

Nu 33: 1 by divisions under the *l* of Moses
Ps 109: 8 may another take his place of *l*.
Ac 1: 20 " 'May another take his place of *l*.'
Ro 12: 8 if it is *l*, let him govern diligently;

LEADING (LEAD)

Dt 1: 15 So I took the *l* men of your tribes,
5: 23 all the *l* men of your tribes
Jdg 3: 27 him from the hills, with him *l* them.
4: 4 the wife of Lappidoth, was *l* Israel
12: 5 fords of the Jordan *l* to Ephraim,
20: 31 the one *l* to Bethel and the other
2Sa 10: 16 of Hadadezer's army *l* them.
2Sa 15: 2 side of the road *l* to the city gate.
17: 11 with you yourself *l* them into battle
2Ki 10: 6 were with the *l* men of the city,
19: 2 the secretary and the *l* priests,
24: 15 his officials and the *l* men
1Ch 19: 16 of Hadadezer's army *l* them.
2Ch 23: 13 instruments were *l* the praises.
Ezr 7: 28 gathered *l* men from Israel to go up
8: 24 I set apart twelve of the *l* priests,
8: 29 in Jerusalem before the *l* priests
10: 5 and put the *l* priests and Levites
Ps 42: 4 *l* the procession to the house
68: 27 tribe of Benjamin, *l* them,
Pr 7: 27 *l* down to the chambers of death.
8: 3 beside the gates *l* into the city,
Isa 37: 2 the *l* priests, all wearing sackcloth,
Eze 17: 13 carried away the *l* men of the land,
40: 20 width of the gate facing north, *l*
Mt 26: 55 to the crowd, "Am I *l* a rebellion,
Mk 6: 21 commanders and the *l* men
10: 32 with Jesus *l* the way,
14: 48 "Am I *l* a rebellion," said Jesus,
Lk 22: 47 one of the Twelve, was *l* them.
22: 52 come for him, "Am I *l* a rebellion,
Ac 12: 10 came to the iron gate *l* to the city.
13: 50 of high standing and the *l* men
16: 12 and the *l* city of that district
25: 23 high ranking officers and the *l* men
Ro 6: 19 to righteousness *l* to holiness.
15: 18 through me in *l* the Gentiles
2Ti 2: 25 will grant them repentance *l* them

LEADS (LEAD)

Dt 27: 18 is the man who *l* the blind astray
Jos 2: 7 spies on the road that *l* to the fords
1Ch 11: 6 "Whoever *l* the attack
Job 12: 17 He *l* counselors away stripped
12: 19 He *l* priests away stripped
Ps 23: 2 he *l* me beside quiet waters,
37: 8 do not fret—it *l* only to evil.
68: 6 he *l* forth the prisoners
Pr 2: 18 For her house *l* down to death
10: 17 ignores correction *l* others astray.
12: 26 the way of the wicked *l* them astray
14: 12 but in the end it *l* to death.
14: 23 but mere talk *l* only to poverty.
15: 24 The path of life *l* upward
16: 25 but in the end it *l* to death.
16: 29 *l* him down a path that is not good.
19: 23 The fear of the LORD *l* to life:
20: 7 righteous man *l* a blameless life;
21: 5 as surely as haste *l* to poverty.
28: 10 He who *l* the upright
Isa 30: 28 a bit that *l* them astray.
40: 11 he gently *l* those that have young.
Hos 4: 12 spirit of prostitution *l* them astray;
Mt 7: 13 and broad is the road that *l*
7: 14 and narrow the road that *l* to life,
12: 20 till he *l* justice to victory.
15: 14 If a blind man *l* a blind man,
Jn 10: 3 sheep by name and *l* them out.
12: 50 I know that his command *l*
Ro 2: 4 realizing that God's kindness *l* you
6: 16 or to obedience, which *l*
6: 16 which *l* to death, or to obedience,
6: 22 the benefit you reap *l* to holiness,
14: 19 effort to do what *l* to peace
2Co 2: 14 always *l* us in triumphal procession
7: 10 sorrow brings repentance that *l*
Eph 5: 18 on wine, which *l* to debauchery.
Tit 1: 1 of the truth that *l* to godliness—
1Jn 5: 16 There is a sin that *l* to death.
Rev 12: 9 who *l* the whole world astray.

LEAF (LEAFY LEAVES)

Ge 8: 11 beak was a freshly plucked olive *l*!
Lev 26: 36 of a wind-blown *l* will put them
Job 13: 25 Will you torment a wind-blown *l*?
Ps 1: 3 and whose *l* does not wither.
Pr 11: 28 righteous will thrive like a green *l*.
Isa 64: 6 we all shrivel up like a *l*,
Mk 11: 13 Seeing in the distance a fig tree in *l*,

LEAFY (LEAF)

Lev 23: 40 and palm fronds, *l* branches
Eze 6: 13 spreading tree and every *l* oak—
17: 6 branches and put out *l* boughs.
20: 28 they saw any high hill or any *l* tree,

LEAH (LEAH'S)

Ge 29: 16 the name of the older was *L*,
29: 17 *L* had weak eyes, but Rachel was
29: 23 he took his daughter *L*
29: 25 When morning came, there was *L*!
29: 28 He finished out the week with *L*,
29: 30 and he loved Rachel more than *L*.
29: 31 LORD saw that *L* was not loved,
29: 32 *L* became pregnant and gave birth
30: 9 When *L* saw that she had stopped
30: 11 Then *L* said, "What good fortune!"
30: 13 Then *L* said, "How happy I am!
30: 14 said to *L*, "Please give me some
30: 14 which he brought to his mother *L*.
30: 16 the fields that evening, *L* went out
30: 17 to *L*, and she became pregnant
30: 18 *L* said, "God has rewarded me
30: 19 *L* conceived again and bore Jacob
30: 20 *L* said, "God has presented me
31: 4 *L* to come out to the fields where
31: 14 Then Rachel and *L* replied,
33: 1 so he divided the children among *L*
33: 2 and their children in front, *L*
33: 7 *L* and her children came
34: 1 the daughter *L* had borne to Jacob,
35: 23 The sons of *L*: Reuben the firstborn
46: 15 These were the sons *L* bore
46: 18 given to his daughter *L*—
49: 31 were buried, and there I buried *L*.
Ru 4: 11 into your home like Rachel and *L*,

LEAH'S (LEAH)

Ge 30: 10 *L* servant Zilpah bore Jacob a son.
30: 12 *L* servant Zilpah bore Jacob
31: 33 After he came out of *L* tent,
31: 33 into Jacob's tent and into *L* tent
35: 26 The sons of *L* maidservant Zilpah:

LEAKS

Ecc 10: 18 if his hands are idle, the house *l*.

LEAN (LEANED LEANING LEANS)

Ge 41: 19 scrawny and very ugly and *l*.
41: 20 *l*, ugly cows ate up the seven fat
41: 27 seven *l*, ugly cows that came up
Jdg 16: 26 so that I may *l* against them."
Pr 3: 5 *l* not on your own understanding;
Eze 34: 20 the fat sheep and the *l* sheep.
Mic 3: 11 Yet they *l* upon the LORD and say

LEANED (LEAN)

Ge 47: 31 as he *l* on the top of his staff.
2Ki 7: 17 officer on whose arm he *l* in charge
Eze 29: 7 when they *l* on you, you broke
Jn 21: 20 (This was the one who had *l* back
Heb 11: 21 as he *l* on the top of his staff.

LEANING (LEAN)

2Sa 1: 6 "and there was Saul, *l* on his spear,
2Ki 5: 18 he is *l* on my arm and I bow there
7: 2 on whose arm the king was *l* said
Ps 62: 3 this *l* wall, this tottering fence?
SS 8: 5 *l* on her lover?
Jn 13: 25 *L* back against Jesus, he asked him,

LEANS (LEAN)

2Sa 3: 29 or leprosy or who *l* on a crutch
2Ki 18: 21 and wounds him if he *l* on it!
Job 8: 15 He *l* on his web, but it gives way;
Isa 36: 6 and wounds him if he *l* on it!

LEAP (LEAPED LEAPING LEAPS)

Job 39: 20 Do you make him *l* like a locust,
Isa 13: 21 there the wild goats will *l* about.
35: 6 Then will the lame *l* like a deer,
Joel 2: 5 they *l* over the mountaintops,
Mal 4: 2 *l* like calves released from the stall.
Lk 6: 23 "Rejoice in that day and *l* for joy,

LEAPED (LEAP)

Da 3: 24 King Nebuchadnezzar *l* to his feet
Lk 1: 41 heard Mary's greeting, the baby *l*
1: 44 the baby in my womb *l* for joy.

LEAPING (LEAP)

2Sa 6: 16 And when she saw King David *l*
SS 2: 8 *l* across the mountains,

LEAPS (LEAP)

Job 37: 1 and *l* from its place.
Ps 28: 7 My heart *l* for joy

LEARN (LEARNED LEARNING LEARNS)

Ge 24: 21 the man watched her closely to *l*
Dt 4: 10 so that they may *l* to revere me
5: 1 *L* them and be sure to follow them.
14: 23 so that you may *l* to revere
17: 19 life so that he may *l* to revere
18: 9 do not *l* to imitate the detestable
31: 12 and *l* to fear the LORD your God
31: 13 and *l* to fear the LORD your God
Jdg 18: 5 "Please inquire of God to *l*
1Sa 22: 3 with you until I *l* what God will do
1Ki 1: 20 to *l* from you who will sit
2Ch 12: 8 so that they may *l* the difference
Job 34: 4 let us *l* together what is good.
Ps 14: 4 Will evildoers never *l*—
53: 4 Will the evildoers never *l*—
119: 7 as I *l* your righteous laws.
119: 71 so that I might *l* your decrees.
119: 73 to *l* your commands.
141: 6 wicked will *l* that my words were
Pr 19: 25 and the simple will *l* prudence;
22: 25 or you may *l* his ways
Isa 1: 17 *l* to do right!
26: 9 of the world *l* righteousness.
26: 10 they do not *l* righteousness;
Jer 2: 33 of women can *l* from your ways.
10: 2 "Do not *l* the ways of the nations
12: 16 if they *l* well the ways of my people
35: 13 'Will you not *l* a lesson
Mt 9: 13 But go and *l* what this means:
11: 29 yoke upon you and *l* from me,
24: 32 Now *l* this lesson from the fig tree:
Mk 13: 28 Now *l* this lesson from the fig tree:
Jn 10: 38 that you may *l* and understand that
14: 31 world must *l* that I love the Father
Ac 24: 8 able to *l* the truth about all these
1Co 4: 6 so that you may *l* from us
Gal 3: 2 I would like to *l* just one thing
1Th 4: 4 that each of you should *l*
1Ti 2: 11 A woman should *l* in quietness
5: 4 these should *l* first of all
Tit 3: 14 Our people must *l*
Heb 5: 11 to explain because you are slow to *l*
Rev 14: 3 No one could *l* the song

LEARNED (LEARN)

Ge 28: 6 Esau *l* that Isaac had blessed Jacob
30: 27 I have *l* by divination that
42: 1 When Jacob *l* that there was grain
Lev 5: 1 something he has seen or *l* about,
Nu 20: 29 the whole community *l* that Aaron
1Sa 4: 6 When they *l* that the ark
23: 9 When David *l* that Saul was
23: 15 he *l* that Saul had come out
26: 4 *l* that Saul had definitely arrived.
Ezr 7: 11 a man *l* in matters concerning
Ne 13: 7 Here I *l* about the evil thing
13: 10 also *l* that the portions assigned
Est 3: 6 Yet having *l* who Mordecai's
4: 1 When Mordecai *l* of all that had
Job 8: 8 and find out what their fathers *l*,
Ps 89: 15 Blessed are those who have *l*
119:152 Long ago I *l* from your statutes
Pr 24: 32 and *l* a lesson from what I saw:
30: 3 I have not *l* wisdom,
Ecc 1: 17 madness and folly, but I *l* that this,
9: 11 or favor to the *l*;
Eze 19: 3 He *l* to tear the prey
19: 6 He *l* to tear the prey
Da 6: 10 when Daniel *l* that the decree had
Mt 2: 16 accordance with the time he had *l*
11: 25 things from the wise and *l*,
Mk 15: 45 When he *l* from the centurion that
Lk 7: 37 in that town *l* that Jesus was eating
9: 11 but the crowds *l* about it
10: 21 things from the wise and *l*,
23: 7 When he *l* that Jesus was
Jn 4: 3 When the Lord *l* of this, he left
5: 6 *l* that he had been in this condition
15: 15 for everything that I *l*
Ac 7: 13 Pharaoh *l* about Joseph's family.
9: 24 to kill him, but Saul *l* of their plan.
9: 30 When the brothers *l* of this,
17: 13 in Thessalonica *l* that Paul was
18: 24 He was a *l* man, with a thorough
23: 27 for I had *l* that he is a Roman
Ro 16: 17 to the teaching you have *l*.
Php 4: 9 Whatever you have *l* or received
4: 11 for I have *l* to be content whatever
4: 12 I have *l* the secret of being content
Col 1: 7 You *l* it from Epaphras, our dear
2Ti 3: 14 continue in what you have *l*
3: 14 those from whom you *l* it,
Heb 5: 8 he *l* obedience from what he
Rev 2: 24 have not *l* Satan's so-called deep

LEARNING (LEARN)

Ezr 8: 16 who were men of *l*, and I sent them
Job 34: 2 listen to me, you men of *l*.
Pr 1: 5 let the wise listen and add to their *l*,
4: 2 I give you sound *l*,
9: 9 man and he will add to his *l*.
Isa 44: 25 who overthrows the *l* of the wise
Da 1: 4 aptitude for every kind of *l*,
1: 17 of all kinds of literature and *l*.
Jn 7: 15 "How did this man get such *l*
Ac 23: 34 *L* that he was from Cilicia, he said,
26: 24 Your great *l* is driving you insane."
2Ti 3: 7 always *l* but never able

LEARNS (LEARN)

Lev 5: 3 when he *l* of it he will be guilty.
5: 4 in any case when he *l*
Jn 6: 45 and *l* from him comes to me.

LEASH

Job 41: 5 or put him on a *l* for your girls?

LEATHER

Lev 13: 48 any *l* or anything made of *l*—
13: 49 or any *l* article, is greenish
13: 49 or *l*, or woven or knitted material,
13: 51 or knitted material, or the *l*,
13: 52 or any *l* article that has
13: 53 or knitted material, or the *l* article,
13: 56 *l*, or the woven or knitted material.
13: 57 or in the *l* article, it is spreading,
13: 58 any *l* article that has been washed
13: 59 or knitted material, or any *l* article,
15: 17 or *l* that has semen on it must be
Nu 31: 20 as well as everything made of *l*,
2Ki 1: 8 and a *l* belt around his waist."
Eze 16: 10 dress and put *l* sandals
Mt 3: 4 and he had a *l* belt around his waist
Mk 1: 6 with a *l* belt around his waist,

LEAVENED

Am 4: 5 Burn *l* bread as a thank offering

LEAVES (LEAF)

Ge 3: 7 so they sewed fig *l* together
1Ki 6: 34 each having two *l* that turned
Isa 1: 30 will be like an oak with fading *l*,
33: 9 Bashan and Carmel drop their *l*.
34: 4 like withered *l* from the vine,
Jer 8: 13 and their *l* will wither.
17: 8 its *l* are always green.
Eze 41: 24 door had two *l*—two hinged *l*
47: 12 Their *l* will not wither,
47: 12 for food and their *l* for healing."
Da 4: 12 Its *l* were beautiful, its fruit
4: 14 strip off its *l* and scatter its fruit.
4: 21 with beautiful *l* and abundant fruit,
Mt 21: 19 but found nothing on it except *l*.
24: 32 twigs get tender and its *l* come out,
Mk 11: 13 reached it, he found nothing but *l*,
13: 28 twigs get tender and its *l* come out,
Lk 21: 30 When they sprout *l*, you can see
Rev 22: 2 the *l* of the tree are for the healing

LEB KAMAI

Jer 51: 1 Babylon and the people of *L*.

LEBANA

Ne 7: 48 Sia, Padon, *L*, Hagaba, Shalmai,

LEBANAH

Ezr 2: 45 Siaha, Padon, *L*, Hagabah, Akkub,

LEBANON

Dt 1: 7 land of the Canaanites and to *L*,
3: 25 that fine hill country and *L*."
11: 24 from the desert to *L*,
Jos 1: 4 and from *L* to the great river,
9: 1 as far as *L* (the kings of the Hittites,
11: 17 Valley of *L* below Mount Hermon.
12: 7 in the Valley of *L* to Mount Halak,
13: 5 the area of the Gebalites; and all *L*
13: 6 regions from *L* to Misrephoth
Jdg 3: 3 living in the *L* mountains
9: 15 and consume the cedars of *L*!'
1Ki 4: 33 from the cedar of *L*
5: 6 cedars of *L* be cut for me.
5: 9 them down from *L* to the sea,
5: 14 He sent them off to *L* in shifts
5: 14 so that they spent one month in *L*
7: 2 Forest of *L* a hundred cubits long,
9: 19 in *L* and throughout all
10: 17 in the Palace of the Forest of *L*.
10: 21 of the Forest of *L* were pure gold.
2Ki 14: 9 Then a wild beast in *L* came along
14: 9 sent a message to a cedar in *L*,
14: 9 "A thistle in *L* sent a message
19: 23 the utmost heights of *L*.
2Ch 2: 8 pine and algum logs from *L*,
2: 16 the logs from *L* that you need
8: 6 in *L* and throughout all
9: 16 in the Palace of the Forest of *L*.
9: 20 of the Forest of *L* were pure gold.
25: 18 Then a wild beast in *L* came along
25: 18 sent a message to a cedar in *L*,
25: 18 "A thistle in *L* sent a message
Ezr 3: 7 logs by sea from *L* to Joppa,
Ps 29: 5 in pieces the cedars of *L*.
29: 6 He makes *L* skip like a calf,
72: 16 Let its fruit flourish like *L*;
92: 12 they will grow like a cedar of *L*;
104: 16 the cedars of *L* that he planted.
SS 3: 9 he made it of wood from *L*.
4: 8 Come with me from *L*, my bride,
4: 8 come with me from *L*.
4: 11 of your garments is like that of *L*.
4: 15 streaming down from *L*.
5: 15 His appearance is like *L*,
7: 4 Your nose is like the tower of *L*
Isa 2: 13 for all the cedars of *L*, tall and lofty
10: 34 *L* will fall before the Mighty One.
14: 8 the pine trees and the cedars of *L*
29: 17 will not *L* be turned
33: 9 *L* is ashamed and withers;
35: 2 The glory of *L* will be given to it,
37: 24 the utmost heights of *L*.
40: 16 *L* is not sufficient for altar fires,
60: 13 "The glory of *L* will come to you,
Jer 18: 14 Does the snow of *L*
22: 6 like the summit of *L*,
22: 20 "Go up to *L* and cry out,
22: 23 You who live in '*L*,'
Eze 17: 3 of varied colors came to *L*.
27: 5 they took a cedar from *L*
31: 3 Assyria, once a cedar in *L*,
31: 15 of it I clothed *L* with gloom,
31: 16 the choicest and best of *L*,
Hos 14: 5 Like a cedar of *L*
14: 6 his fragrance like a cedar of *L*.
14: 7 fame will be like the wine from *L*.
Na 1: 4 and the blossoms of *L* fade.
Hab 2: 17 to *L* will overwhelm you,
Zec 10: 10 I will bring them to Gilead and *L*,
11: 1 Open your doors, O *L*,

LEBAOTH

Jos 15: 32 Madmannah, Sansannah, *L*,

LEBO HAMATH

Nu 13: 21 as far as Rehob, toward *L*.
34: 8 and from Mount Hor to *L*.
Jos 13: 5 below Mount Hermon to *L*.
Jdg 3: 3 from Mount Baal Hermon to *L*.
1Ki 8: 65 from *L* to the Wadi of Egypt.
2Ki 14: 25 of Israel from *L* to the Sea of
1Ch 13: 5 Shihor River in Egypt to *L*,
2Ch 7: 8 people from *L* to the Wadi of
Eze 47: 15 Sea by the Hethlon road past *L* to
47: 20 the boundary to a point opposite *L*.
48: 1 it will follow the Hethlon road to *L*
Am 6: 14 *L* to the valley of the Arabah."

LEBONAH

Jdg 21: 19 to Shechem, and to the south of *L*

LECAH

1Ch 4: 21 son of Judah: Er the father of *L*,

LECTURE

Jn 9: 34 how dare you *l* us!" And they
Ac 19: 9 daily in the *l* hall of Tyrannus.

LED (LEAD)

Ge 19: 16 and *l* them safely out of the city,
24: 27 the LORD has *l* me on the journey
24: 48 who had *l* me on the right road
Ex 3: 1 and he *l* the flock to the far side
13: 18 *l* the people around by the desert
15: 22 Moses *l* Israel from the Red Sea
19: 17 Moses *l* the people out of the camp
32: 21 that you *l* them into such great sin
Dt 8: 2 the LORD your God *l* you all
8: 15 He *l* you through the vast
13: 13 and have *l* the people of their town
17: 17 or his heart will be *l* astray.
29: 5 During the forty years that I *l* you
32: 12 The LORD alone *l* him;
Jos 24: 3 and *l* him throughout Canaan
Jdg 2: 1 and *l* you into the land that I swore
3: 28 fords of the Jordan that *l* to Moab,
9: 39 Gaal *l* out the citizens of Shechem
10: 2 He *l* Israel twenty-three years;
10: 3 who *l* Israel twenty-two years.
12: 7 Jephthah *l* Israel six years.
12: 8 Ibzan of Bethlehem *l* Israel.
12: 9 Ibzan *l* Israel seven years.
12: 11 Elon the Zebulunite *l* Israel ten
12: 13 of Hillel, from Pirathon, *l* Israel.
12: 14 He *l* Israel eight years.
15: 13 and *l* him up from the rock.
15: 20 Samson *l* Israel for twenty years
16: 31 He had *l* Israel twenty years.
1Sa 4: 18 He had *l* Israel forty years.
18: 13 and David *l* the troops
18: 16 he *l* them in their campaigns.
30: 16 He *l* David down, and there they
2Sa 5: 2 you were the one who *l* Israel
1Ki 6: 8 a stairway *l* up to the middle level
11: 3 and his wives *l* him astray.
13: 34 of Jeroboam that *l* to its downfall
2Ki 6: 19 And he *l* them to Samaria.
15: 15 reign, and the conspiracy he *l*,
21: 9 Manasseh *l* them astray,
21: 11 has *l* Judah into sin with his idols.
23: 22 the days of the judges who *l* Israel,
1Ch 4: 42 of these Simeonites, *l* by Pelatiah,
11: 2 you were the one who *l* Israel
20: 1 Joab *l* out the armed forces.
2Ch 20: 27 *l* by Jehoshaphat, all the men
21: 11 themselves and had *l* Judah astray.
21: 13 you have *l* Judah and the people
25: 11 and *l* his army to the Valley of Salt,
26: 16 his pride *l* to his downfall.
33: 9 But Manasseh *l* Judah
Ezr 9: 2 and officials have *l* the way
Ne 9: 12 By day you *l* them with a pillar
11: 17 the director who *l* in thanksgiving
12: 36 Ezra the scribe *l* the procession.
13: 26 he was *l* into sin by foreign women.
Est 6: 11 and *l* him on horseback
Job 31: 7 if my heart has been *l* by my eyes,
Ps 26: 1 for I have *l* a blameless life;
45: 14 In embroidered garments she is *l*
45: 15 They are *l* in with joy and gladness;
68: 18 you *l* captives in your train;
77: 19 Your path *l* through the sea,
77: 20 You *l* your people like a flock
78: 13 He divided the sea and *l* them
78: 26 *l* forth the south wind by his power.
78: 52 he *l* them like sheep
78: 72 with skillful hands he *l* them.
106: 9 he *l* them through the depths
107: 7 He *l* them by a straight way
136: 16 to him who *l* his people
Pr 5: 23 *l* astray by his own great folly.
7: 21 persuasive words she *l* him astray;
20: 1 whoever is *l* astray
24: 11 Rescue those being *l* away to death
Isa 9: 16 those who are guided are *l* astray.
Isa 19: 13 have *l* Egypt astray.
48: 21 when he *l* them through the deserts
53: 7 he was *l* like a lamb to the slaughter
55: 12 and be *l* forth in peace;
60: 11 kings *l* in triumphal procession.
63: 13 who *l* them through the depths?
Jer 2: 6 *l* us through the barren wilderness,
2: 17 God when he *l* you in the way?
11: 19 I had been like a gentle lamb *l*
22: 12 where they have *l* him captive;
23: 13 and *l* my people Israel astray.
29: 31 and has *l* you to believe a lie,
41: 16 with him *l* away all the survivors
43: 5 and all the army officers *l* away all
43: 6 They also *l* away all the men,
50: 6 their shepherds have *l* them astray
Eze 19: 4 They *l* him with hooks
20: 10 Therefore I *l* them out of Egypt
29: 18 reward from the campaign he *l*
37: 2 He *l* me back and forth
40: 22 Seven steps *l* up to it,
40: 24 Then he *l* me to the south side
40: 26 Seven steps *l* up to it,
40: 31 its jambs, and eight steps *l* up
40: 34 side, and eight steps *l* up to it.
40: 37 side, and eight steps *l* up to it.
42: 1 Then the man *l* me northward
42: 15 he *l* me out by the east gate
46: 21 and *l* me around to its four corners,
47: 2 and *l* me
47: 3 then *l* me through water that was
47: 4 and *l* me through water that was
47: 4 and *l* me through water that was up
47: 6 Then he *l* me back to the bank
Da 7: 13 and was *l* into his presence.
Hos 11: 4 I *l* them with cords
Am 2: 4 because they have been *l* astray
2: 10 and I *l* you forty years in the desert
Mt 4: 1 Then Jesus was *l* by the Spirit
17: 1 and *l* them up a high mountain
27: 2 *l* him away and handed him
27: 31 they *l* him away to crucify him.
Mk 8: 23 and *l* him outside the village.
9: 2 and *l* them up a high mountain,
15: 1 *l* him away and handed him
15: 16 The soldiers *l* Jesus away
15: 20 Then they *l* him out to crucify him.
Lk 4: 1 was *l* by the Spirit in the desert,
4: 5 The devil *l* him up to a high place
4: 9 The devil *l* him to Jerusalem
18: 39 Those who *l* the way rebuked him
22: 54 they *l* him away and took him
22: 66 and Jesus was *l* before them.
23: 1 the whole assembly rose and *l* him
23: 26 As they *l* him away, they seized
23: 32 also *l* out with him to be executed.
24: 50 When he had *l* them out
Jn 18: 28 the Jews *l* Jesus from Caiaphas
Ac 5: 37 and *l* a band of people in revolt.
7: 36 He *l* them out of Egypt
7: 40 for this fellow Moses who *l* us out
8: 32 "He was *l* like a sheep
9: 8 So they *l* him by the hand
13: 17 With mighty power he *l* them out
19: 26 and *l* astray large numbers
21: 38 and *l* four thousand terrorists out
22: 11 My companions *l* me by the hand
Ro 8: 14 those who are *l* by the Spirit
1Co 12: 2 and *l* astray to dumb idols.
2Co 7: 9 your sorrow *l* you to repentance
11: 3 minds may somehow be *l* astray
11: 29 I do not feel weak? Who is *l* into sin
Gal 2: 13 even Barnabas was *l* astray.
5: 18 But if you are *l* by the Spirit,
Eph 4: 8 he *l* captives in his train
Heb 3: 16 Were they not all those Moses *l* out
Rev 18: 23 spell all the nations were *l* astray.

LEDGE (LEDGES)

Ex 27: 5 Put it under the *l* of the altar
38: 4 be under its *l*, halfway up the altar.
Eze 43: 14 and from the smaller *l* up
43: 14 to the larger *l* it is four cubits high
43: 14 to the lower *l* it is two cubits high
43: 17 The upper *l* also is square,
43: 20 on the four corners of the upper *l*
45: 19 corners of the upper *l* of the altar
46: 23 for fire built all around under the *l*.
Eze 46: 23 of the four courts was a *l* of stone,

LEDGES (LEDGE)

1Ki 6: 6 He made offset *l* around the
Eze 41: 6 There were *l* all around the wall

LEE

Ac 27: 4 and passed to the *l* of Cyprus
27: 7 we sailed to the *l* of Crete,
27: 16 As we passed to the *l*

LEECH

Pr 30: 15 "The *l* has two daughters.

LEEKS

Nu 11: 5 melons, *l*, onions and garlic.

LEFT

Ge 13: 9 If you go to the *l*, I'll go to the right;
13: 9 if you go to the right, I'll go to the *l*
48: 13 and Manasseh on his *l*
48: 13 on his right toward Israel's *l* hand
48: 14 put his *l* hand on Manasseh's head,
Ex 14: 22 water on their right and on their *l*.
14: 29 water on their right and on their *l*.
Lev 14: 15 it in the palm of his own *l* hand,
14: 26 oil into the palm of his own *l* hand,
Nu 20: 17 or to the *l* until we have passed
Dt 2: 27 turn aside to the right or to the *l*.
5: 32 turn aside to the right or to the *l*.
17: 11 to the right or to the *l*.
17: 20 from the law to the right or to the *l*.
28: 14 or to the *l*, following other gods
Jos 1: 7 turn from it to the right or to the *l*,
19: 27 and Neiel, passing Cabul on the *l*.
23: 6 aside to the right or to the *l*.
Jdg 3: 21 Ehud reached with his *l* hand,
7: 20 the torches in their *l* hands
16: 29 and his *l* hand on the other,
1Sa 6: 12 turn to the right or to the *l*.
2Sa 2: 19 nor to the *l* as he pursued him.
14: 19 or to the *l* from anything my lord
16: 6 were on David's right and *l*.
1Ki 7: 49 (five on the right and five on the *l*,
22: 19 around him on his right and on his *l*
2Ki 2: 8 divided to the right and to the *l*,
2: 14 it divided to the right and to the *l*,
22: 2 aside to the right or to the *l*.
1Ch 6: 44 the Merarites, at his *l* hand:
2Ch 18: 18 standing on his right and on his *l*.
34: 2 aside to the right or to the *l*.
Ne 8: 4 and on his *l* were Pedaiah, Mishael,
Pr 3: 16 in her *l* hand are riches and honor.
4: 27 Do not swerve to the right or the *l*;
Ecc 10: 2 but the heart of the fool to the *l*.
SS 2: 6 His *l* arm is under my head,
8: 3 His *l* arm is under my head
Isa 9: 20 on the *l* they will eat,
30: 21 turn to the right or to the *l*,
54: 3 out to the right and to the *l*;
Eze 1: 10 and on the *l* the face of an ox;
4: 4 "Then lie on your *l* side
21: 16 then to the *l*,
39: 3 strike your bow from your *l* hand
Da 12: 7 and his *l* hand toward heaven,
Jnh 4: 11 tell their right hand from their *l*,
Zec 4: 3 of the bowl and the other on its *l*."
4: 11 and the *l* of the lampstand?"
Mt 6: 3 do not let your *l* hand know what
20: 23 or *l* is not for me to grant.
25: 33 on his right and the goats on his *l*.
25: 41 "Then he will say to those on his *l*,
27: 38 one on his right and one on his *l*.
Mk 10: 37 the other at your *l* in your glory."
10: 40 or *l* is not for me to grant.
15: 27 one on his right and one on his *l*.
Lk 23: 33 one on his right, the other on his *l*.
2Co 6: 7 in the right hand and in the *l*;
Rev 10: 2 on the sea and his *l* foot on the land

LEFT-HANDED (HAND)

Jdg 3: 15 a *l* man, the son of Gera
20: 16 hundred chosen men who were *l*,
1Ch 12: 2 or to sling stones right-handed or *l*;

LEFTOVER

Ru 2: 2 pick up the *l* grain behind anyone

LEG (LEGS)
1Sa 9: 24 So the cook took up the *l*
Eze 24: 4 all the choice pieces—the *l*
Am 3: 12 only two *l* bones or a piece

LEGAL (LEGALISTIC LEGALIZING)
Nu 27: 11 is to be a *l* requirement
35: 29 are to be *l* requirements for you
Ac 19: 39 it must be settled in a *l* assembly.
22: 25 "Is it *l* for you to flog a Roman

LEGALISTIC (LEGAL)
Php 3: 6 as for *l* righteousness, faultless.

LEGALIZING (LEGAL)
Ru 4: 7 method of *l* transactions in Israel.)

LEGION (LEGIONS)
Mk 5: 9 "My name is *L*," he replied,
5: 15 possessed by the *l* of demons,
Lk 8: 30 "What is your name?" "*L*,"

LEGIONS (LEGION)
Mt 26: 53 more than twelve *l* of angels?

LEGS (LEG)
Ex 12: 9 but roast it over the fire—head, *l*
25: 26 four corners, where the four *l* are.
29: 17 and wash the inner parts and the *l*,
37: 13 four corners, where the four *l* were.
Lev 1: 9 is to wash the inner parts and the *l*
1: 13 is to wash the inner parts and the *l*
4: 11 as the head and *l*, the inner parts
8: 21 He washed the inner parts and the *l*
9: 14 He washed the inner parts and the *l*
11: 21 those that have jointed *l*
11: 23 creatures that have four *l* you are
Dt 28: 35 *l* with painful boils that cannot be
1Sa 17: 6 on his *l* he wore bronze greaves,
Ps 147: 10 nor his delight in the *l* of a man;
Pr 26: 7 Like a lame man's *l* that hang limp
SS 5: 15 His *l* are pillars of marble
7: 1 Your graceful *l* are like jewels,
Isa 7: 20 your head and the hair of your *l*,
47: 2 Lift up your skirts, bare your *l*,
Eze 1: 7 Their *l* were straight; their feet
Da 2: 33 and thighs of bronze, its *l* of iron,
5: 6 together and his *l* gave way.
10: 6 and *l* like the gleam of burnished
Hab 3: 16 and my *l* trembled.
Jn 19: 31 Pilate to have the *l* broken
19: 32 broke the *l* of the first man who
19: 33 dead, they did not break his *l*.
Rev 10: 1 and his *l* were like fiery pillars.

LEHABITES
Ge 10: 13 Anamites, *L*, Naphtuhites,
1Ch 1: 11 Anamites, *L*, Naphtuhites,

LEHI
Jdg 15: 9 in Judah, spreading out near *L*.
15: 14 he approached *L*, the Philistines
15: 19 and it is still there in *L*.
15: 19 opened up the hollow place in *L*,

LEMUEL
Pr 31: 1 of King *L*—an oracle his mother
31: 4 "It is not for kings, O *L*—

LEND (LENDER LENDING LENDS LENT MONEYLENDER)
Ex 22: 25 If you *l* money to one of my people
Lev 25: 37 You must not *l* him money
Dt 15: 6 and you will *l* to many nations
15: 8 freely *l* him whatever he needs.
28: 12 You will *l* to many nations
28: 44 He will *l* to you, but you will not
28: 44 to you, but you will not *l* to him.
Ps 37: 26 are always generous and *l* freely;
83: 8 to *l* strength to the descendants
Eze 18: 8 He does not *l* at usury
Lk 6: 34 Even 'sinners' *l* to 'sinners,'
6: 34 if you *l* to those from whom you
6: 35 and *l* to them without expecting
11: 5 'Friend, *l* me three loaves of bread,

LENDER (LEND)
Pr 22: 7 and the borrower is servant to the *l*.
Isa 24: 2 for borrower as for *l*,

LENDING (LEND)
Ne 5: 10 men are also *l* the people money

LENDS (LEND)
Ps 15: 5 who *l* his money without usury
112: 5 to him who is generous and *l* freely,
Pr 19: 17 to the poor *l* to the LORD,
Eze 18: 13 He *l* at usury and takes excessive

LENGTH (LONG)
Ge 13: 17 walk through the *l* and breadth
Ex 12: 40 *l* of time the Israelite people lived
26: 12 As for the additional *l*
Lev 19: 35 standards when measuring *l*,
1Sa 28: 20 Immediately Saul fell full *l*
2Sa 2: 11 The *l* of time David was king
8: 2 and the third *l* was allowed to live.
8: 2 measured them off with a *l* of cord.
2Ch 3: 8 its *l* corresponding to the width
Ps 21: 4 *l* of days, for ever and ever.
90: 10 The *l* of our days is seventy years—
Pr 10: 27 The fear of the LORD adds *l* to life
Eze 40: 5 The *l* of the measuring rod
40: 11 and its *l* was thirteen cubits.
40: 20 Then he measured the *l*
41: 4 And he measured the *l* of the inner
41: 8 It was the *l* of the rod, six long
41: 12 and its *l* was ninety cubits.
41: 15 he measured the *l* of the building
42: 10 side along the *l* of the wall
42: 11 they had the same *l* and width,
48: 8 its *l* from east to west will equal
48: 13 Its total *l* will be 25,000 cubits
48: 18 sacred portion and running the *l*
48: 21 Both these areas running the *l*
Ac 12: 10 When they had walked the *l*
Rev 21: 16 stadia in *l*, and as wide and high

LENGTHEN (LONG)
Ecc 8: 13 their days will not *l* like a shadow.
Isa 54: 2 *l* your cords,

LENGTHS (LONG)
2Sa 8: 2 Every two *l* of them were put
Eze 13: 18 veils of various *l* for their heads

LENGTHWISE (LONG)
Eze 45: 7 running *l* from the western

LENGTHY (LONG)
Mk 12: 40 and for a show make *l* prayers.
Lk 20: 47 and for a show make *l* prayers.

LENT (LEND)
Jer 15: 10 I have neither *l* nor borrowed,

LENTIL (LENTILS)
Ge 25: 34 Esau some bread and some *l* stew.

LENTILS (LENTIL)
2Sa 17: 28 beans and *l*, honey and curds,
23: 11 where there was a field full of *l*,
Eze 4: 9 beans and *l*, millet and spelt;

LEOPARD (LEOPARDS)
Isa 11: 6 the *l* will lie down with the goat,
Jer 5: 6 a *l* will lie in wait near their towns
13: 23 or the *l* its spots?
Da 7: 6 beast, one that looked like a *l*.
Hos 13: 7 like a *l* I will lurk by the path.
Rev 13: 2 The beast I saw resembled a *l*,

LEOPARDS (LEOPARD)
SS 4: 8 and the mountain haunts of the *l*.
Hab 1: 8 Their horses are swifter than *l*,

LEPER (LEPROSY)
Mt 26: 6 of a man known as Simon the *L*,
Mk 14: 3 of a man known as Simon the *L*,

LEPROSY (LEPER LEPROUS)
Nu 12: 10 toward her and saw that she had *l*;
2Sa 3: 29 or *l* or who leans on a crutch
2Ki 5: 1 was a valiant soldier, but he had *l*.
5: 3 He would cure him of his *l*."
5: 6 so that you may cure him of his *l*."
5: 7 someone to me to be cured of his *l*?
2Ki 5: 11 over the spot and cure me of my *l*.
5: 27 Naaman's *l* will cling to you
7: 3 men with *l* at the entrance
7: 8 men who had *l* reached the edge
15: 5 king with *l* until the day he died,
2Ch 26: 19 *l* broke out on his forehead.
26: 20 they saw that he had *l*
26: 21 King Uzziah had *l*
26: 23 for people said, "He had *l*."
Mt 8: 2 A man with *l* came and knelt
8: 3 Immediately he was cured of his *l*.
10: 8 those who have *l*, drive out
11: 5 those who have *l* are cured,
Mk 1: 40 A man with *l* came to him
1: 42 Immediately the *l* left him
Lk 4: 27 many in Israel with *l* in the time
5: 12 along who was covered with *l*.
5: 13 And immediately the *l* left him.
7: 22 those who have *l* are cured,
17: 12 ten men who had *l* met him.

LEPROUS (LEPROSY)
Ex 4: 6 and when he took it out, it was *l*,
Nu 12: 10 there stood Miriam—*l*, like snow.
Dt 24: 8 cases of *l* diseases be very careful
2Ki 5: 27 from Elisha's presence and he was *l*
2Ch 26: 21 He lived in a separate house—

LESHEM
Jos 19: 47 settled in *L* and named it Dan
19: 47 so they went up and attacked *L*,

LESSON
Jdg 8: 16 of Succoth a *l* by punishing them
1Sa 14: 12 up to us and we'll teach you a *l*."
Pr 24: 32 and learned a *l* from what I saw:
Jer 35: 13 you not learn a *l* and obey my
Mt 24: 32 "Now learn this *l* from the fig tree:
Mk 13: 28 "Now learn this *l* from the fig tree:

LETHEK
Hos 3: 2 about a homer and a *l* of barley.

LETTER (LETTERS)
2Sa 11: 14 In the morning David wrote a *l*
2Ki 5: 5 I will send a *l* to the king of Israel."
5: 6 The *l* that he took to the king
5: 6 "With this *l* I am sending my
5: 7 as the king of Israel read the *l*,
10: 2 "As soon as this *l* reaches you,
10: 6 Then Jehu wrote them a second *l*,
10: 7 When the *l* arrived, these men took
19: 14 Hezekiah received the *l*
2Ch 2: 11 of Tyre replied by *l* to Solomon:
21: 12 Jehoram received a *l*
Ezr 4: 7 The *l* was written in Aramaic script
4: 7 the rest of his associates wrote a *l*
4: 8 Shimshai the secretary wrote a *l*
4: 11 This is a copy of the *l* they sent him
4: 18 The *l* you sent us has been read
4: 23 of the *l* of King Artaxerxes was
5: 6 This is a copy of the *l* that Tattenai,
7: 11 of the *l* King Artaxerxes had given
Ne 2: 8 And may I have a *l* to Asaph,
6: 5 and in his hand was an unsealed *l*
Est 9: 26 of everything written in this *l*
9: 29 this second *l* concerning Purim.
Isa 37: 14 Hezekiah received the *l*
Jer 29: 1 of the *l* that the prophet Jeremiah
29: 3 He entrusted the *l* to Elasah son
29: 29 read the *l* to Jeremiah the prophet.
Mt 5: 18 not the smallest *l*, not the least
Ac 15: 23 them they sent the following *l*:
15: 30 together and delivered the *l*.
23: 25 He wrote a *l* as follows: Claudius
23: 33 they delivered the *l* to the governor
23: 34 The governor read the *l*
Ro 16: 22 Tertius, who wrote down this *l*,
1Co 5: 9 you in my *l* not to associate
2Co 3: 2 You yourselves are our *l*, written
3: 3 You show that you are a *l*
3: 6 for the *l* kills, but the Spirit gives
3: 6 not of the *l* but of the Spirit;
7: 8 I see that my *l* hurt you,
7: 8 if I caused you sorrow by my *l*,
Col 4: 16 After this *l* has been read to you,
4: 16 in turn read the *l* from Laodicea.
1Th 5: 27 the Lord to have this *l* read to all

2Th 2: 2 l supposed to have come from us,
2: 15 whether by word of mouth or by l.
3: 14 not obey our instruction in this l,
Heb 13: 22 for I have written you only a short l
2Pe 3: 1 this is now my second l to you.

LETTERS (LETTER)

1Ki 21: 8 So she wrote l in Ahab's name,
21: 9 In those l she wrote: "Proclaim
21: 11 directed in the l she had written
2Ki 10: 1 So Jehu wrote l and sent them
20: 12 king of Babylon sent Hezekiah l
2Ch 30: 1 Judah and also wrote l to Ephraim
30: 6 and Judah with l from the king
32: 17 also wrote l insulting the LORD,
Ne 2: 7 may I have l to the governors
2: 9 and gave them the king's l.
6: 17 of Judah were sending many l
6: 19 And Tobiah sent l to intimidate me
Est 9: 20 and he sent l to all the Jews
9: 30 And Mordecai sent l to all the Jews
Isa 39: 1 king of Babylon sent Hezekiah l
Jer 29: 25 You sent l in your own name
Ac 9: 2 asked him for l to the synagogues
22: 5 even obtained l from them
28: 21 "We have not received any l
1Co 16: 3 I will give l of introduction
2Co 3: 1 l of recommendation to you
3: 7 which was engraved in l on stone,
10: 9 trying to frighten you with my l.
10: 10 "His l are weighty and forceful,
10: 11 are in our l when we are absent,
Gal 6: 11 See what large l I use as I write
2Th 3: 17 the distinguishing mark in all my l.
2Pe 3: 16 He writes the same way in all his l,
3: 16 His l contain some things that are

LETUSHITES

Ge 25: 3 the L and the Leummites.

LEUMMITES

Ge 25: 3 the Letushites and the L.

LEVEL (LEVELED LEVELS)

1Ki 6: 8 a stairway led up to the middle l
Ps 26: 12 My feet stand on l ground;
65: 10 and l its ridges;
143: 10 lead me on l ground.
Pr 4: 26 Make l paths for your feet
Isa 26: 7 The path of the righteous is l;
40: 4 the rough ground shall become l,
45: 2 and will l the mountains;
Jer 31: 9 on a l path where they will not
Eze 13: 14 and will l it to the ground
41: 6 one above another, thirty on each l
41: 7 wider at each successive l.
Zec 4: 7 you will become l ground.
Lk 6: 17 with them and stood on a l place.
Heb 12: 13 "Make l paths for your feet,"

LEVELED (LEVEL)

Isa 28: 25 When he has l the surface,
32: 19 and the city is l completely,
Jer 51: 58 "Babylon's thick wall will be l

LEVELS (LEVEL)

Isa 26: 5 he l it to the ground
Eze 41: 6 The side rooms were on three l,
42: 3 gallery faced gallery at the three l.

LEVI (LEVI'S LEVITE LEVITES LEVITICAL)

Ge 29: 34 So he was named L.
34: 25 Simeon and L, Dinah's brothers,
34: 30 Then Jacob said to Simeon and L,
35: 23 L, Judah, Issachar and Zebulun.
46: 11 The sons of L: Gershon, Kohath
49: 5 "Simeon and L are brothers—
Ex 1: 2 Reuben, Simeon, L and Judah;
2: 1 of L married a Levite woman,
6: 16 L lived 137 years.
6: 16 names of the sons of L according
6: 19 of L according to their records.
Nu 1: 47 The families of the tribe of L,
1: 49 "You must not count the tribe of L
3: 6 the tribe of L and present them
3: 17 were the names of the sons of L:
16: 1 son of L, and certain Reubenites—
Nu 17: 3 the staff of L write Aaron's name,
17: 8 which represented the house of L,
26: 59 a descendant of L, who was born
Dt 10: 8 the tribe of L to carry the ark
18: 1 indeed the whole tribe of L—
21: 5 the sons of L, shall step forward,
27: 12 Simeon, L, Judah, Issachar,
31: 9 the sons of L, who carried the ark
33: 8 About L he said:
Jos 13: 14 tribe of L he gave no inheritance,
13: 33 the tribe of L, Moses had given no
1Ch 2: 1 Reuben, Simeon, L, Judah,
6: 1 The sons of L: Gershon, Kohath
6: 16 The sons of L: Gershon, Kohath
6: 38 the son of L, the son of Israel;
6: 43 son of L; and from their associates,
6: 47 the son of Merari, the son of L.
12: 26 of L— 4,600, including Jehoiada,
21: 6 But Joab did not include L
23: 6 corresponding to the sons of L:
23: 14 counted as part of the tribe of L.
23: 24 of L by their families—
24: 20 for the rest of the descendants of L:
27: 17 over L: Hashabiah son of Kemuel;
Ezr 8: 18 the descendants of Mahli son of L,
Ne 12: 23 among the descendants of L up
Ps 135: 20 O house of L, praise the LORD;
Eze 48: 31 the gate of Judah and the gate of L.
Zec 12: 13 the clan of the house of L
Mal 2: 4 covenant with L may continue,"
2: 8 violated the covenant with L,"
Mk 2: 14 and L got up and followed him.
2: 14 he saw L son of Alphaeus sitting
Lk 3: 24 the son of L, the son of Melki,
3: 29 the son of L,
5: 27 collector by the name of L sitting
5: 28 Jesus said to him, and L got up,
5: 29 L held a great banquet for Jesus
Heb 7: 5 of L who become priests
7: 6 did not trace his descent from L,
7: 9 One might even say that L,
7: 10 L was still in the body
Rev 7: 7 from the tribe of L 12,000,

LEVI'S (LEVI)

Mk 2: 15 was having dinner at L house,

LEVIATHAN

Job 3: 8 those who are ready to rouse L.
41: 1 pull in the l with a fishhook
Ps 74: 14 you who crushed the heads of L
104: 26 the l, which you formed
Isa 27: 1 L the coiling serpent;
27: 1 L the gliding serpent,

LEVITE (LEVI)

Ex 2: 1 house of Levi married a L woman,
4: 14 about your brother, Aaron the L?
6: 25 were the heads of the L families,
Nu 3: 20 These were the L clans, according
26: 58 also were L clans: the Libnite clan,
Dt 18: 6 If a L moves from one
26: 12 you shall give it to the L, the alien,
26: 13 portion and have given it to the L,
Jos 21: 27 L clans of the Gershonites were
Jdg 17: 7 A young L from Bethlehem
17: 9 I'm a L from Bethlehem in Judah,"
17: 11 So the L agreed to live with him,
17: 12 Then Micah installed the L,
17: 13 since this L has become my priest."
18: 3 the voice of the young L;
18: 15 of the young L at Micah's place
19: 1 a L who lived in a remote area
20: 4 So the L, the husband
1Ch 9: 31 L named Mattithiah, the firstborn
9: 33 musicians, heads of L families,
9: 34 All these were heads of L families,
15: 22 Kenaniah the head L was in charge
24: 6 Shemaiah son of Nethanel, a L,
2Ch 20: 14 a L and descendant of Asaph,
31: 12 a L, was in charge of these things,
31: 14 Kore son of Imnah the L, keeper
Ezr 10: 15 Meshullam and Shabbethai the L,
Ne 13: 13 and a L named Pedaiah in charge
Lk 10: 32 a L, when he came to the place
Ac 4: 36 L from Cyprus, whom the apostles

LEVITES (LEVI)

Ex 32: 26 And all the L rallied to him.
32: 28 The L did as Moses commanded,
38: 21 by the L under the direction
Lev 25: 32 " 'The L always have the right
25: 33 the property of the L is redeemable
25: 33 towns of the L are their property
Nu 1: 50 appoint the L to be in charge
1: 51 is to be set up, the L shall do it.
1: 51 to move, the L are to take it down,
1: 53 The L are to be responsible
1: 53 The L, however, are
2: 17 and the camp of the L will set out
2: 33 The L, however, were not counted
3: 9 Give the L to Aaron and his sons;
3: 12 L are mine, for all the firstborn are
3: 12 "I have taken the L
3: 15 "Count the L by their families
3: 32 leader of the L was Eleazar son
3: 39 The total number of L counted
3: 41 Take the L for me in place
3: 41 and the livestock of the L in place
3: 45 The L are to be mine.
3: 45 and the livestock of the L in place
3: 45 "Take the L in place
3: 46 who exceed the number of the L,
3: 49 the number redeemed by the L.
4: 2 branch of the L by their clans
4: 18 clans are not cut off from the L.
4: 46 leaders of Israel counted all the L
7: 5 them to the L as each man's work
7: 6 and oxen and gave them to the L.
8: 6 "Take the L from among the other
8: 9 Bring the L to the front of the Tent
8: 10 to bring the L before the LORD,
8: 11 to present the L before the LORD
8: 12 to make atonement for the L.
8: 12 "After the L lay their hands
8: 13 Have the L stand in front of Aaron
8: 14 Israelites, and the L will be mine.
8: 14 to set the L apart from the other
8: 15 "After you have purified the L
8: 18 And I have taken the L in place
8: 19 I have given the L as gifts to Aaron
8: 20 community did with the L just
8: 21 The L purified themselves
8: 22 They did with the L just
8: 22 the L came to do their work
8: 24 to Moses, "This applies to the L:
8: 26 the responsibilities of the L."
16: 7 You L have gone too far!"
16: 8 said to Korah, "Now listen, you L!
16: 10 and all your fellow L near himself,
18: 2 Bring your fellow L
18: 6 myself have selected your fellow L
18: 21 I give to the L all the tithes in Israel
18: 23 It is the L who are to do the work
18: 24 give to the L as their inheritance
18: 26 "Speak to the L and say to them:
18: 30 "Say to the L: 'When you present
26: 57 These were the L who were
26: 59 who was born to the L in Egypt.
26: 62 All the male L a month old
31: 30 them to the L, who are responsible
31: 47 him, and gave them to the L,
35: 2 Israelites to give the L towns to live
35: 4 that you give the L will extend out
35: 6 towns you give the L will be cities
35: 7 must give the L forty-eight towns,
35: 8 The towns you give the L
Dt 10: 9 That is why the L have no share
12: 12 and the L from your towns,
12: 18 and the L from your towns—
12: 19 Be careful not to neglect the L
14: 27 And do not neglect the L living
14: 29 so that the L (who have no
16: 11 maidservants, the L in your towns,
16: 14 and maidservants, and the L,
17: 9 Go to the priests, who are L,
17: 18 from that of the priests, who are L.
18: 1 who are L— indeed the whole tribe
18: 7 like all his fellow L who serve there
24: 8 as the priests, who are L,
26: 11 and the L and the aliens
27: 9 who are L, said to all Israel,
27: 14 The L shall recite to all the people
31: 25 to the L who carried the ark

Jos 3: 3 and the priests, who are *L*,
8: 33 it—the priests, who were *L*.
14: 3 not granted the *L* an inheritance
14: 4 The *L* received no share of the land
18: 7 *L*, however, do not get a portion
21: 1 heads of the *L* approached Eleazar
21: 3 Israelites gave the *L* the following
21: 4 The *L* who were descendants
21: 8 allotted to the *L* these towns
21: 10 from the Kohathite clans of the *L*,
21: 20 clans of the *L* were allotted towns
21: 34 (the rest of the *L*) were given:
21: 40 who were the rest of the *L*,
21: 41 The towns of the *L*
1Sa 6: 15 The *L* took down the ark
2Sa 15: 24 and all the *L* who were
1Ki 8: 4 The priests and *L* carried them up,
12: 31 even though they were not *L*.
1Ch 6: 19 the clans of the *L* listed according
6: 48 Their fellow *L* were assigned
6: 64 Israelites gave the *L* these towns
6: 77 of the *L*) received the following:
9: 2 priests, *L* and temple servants.
9: 14 Of the *L*: Shemaiah son of Hasshub
9: 18 belonging to the camp of the *L*.
9: 26 principal gatekeepers, who were *L*,
13: 2 *L* who are with them in their towns
15: 2 but the *L* may carry the ark of God,
15: 4 descendants of Aaron and the *L*:
15: 11 Eliel and Amminadab the *L*.
15: 12 *L* are to consecrate yourselves
15: 13 It was because you, the *L*,
15: 14 *L* consecrated themselves in order
15: 15 And the *L* carried the ark of God
15: 16 of the *L* to appoint their brothers
15: 17 the *L* appointed Heman son of Joel
15: 26 had helped the *L* who were
15: 27 as were all the *L* who were carrying
16: 4 some of the *L* to minister
23: 2 as well as the priests and *L*.
23: 3 The *L* thirty years old
23: 6 David divided the *L*
23: 26 the *L* no longer need
23: 27 the *L* were counted
23: 28 The duty of the *L* was
23: 32 And so the *L* carried out their
24: 6 of the priests and of the *L*—
24: 30 These were the *L*, according
24: 31 families of the priests and of the *L*.
26: 17 There were six *L* a day on the east,
26: 20 Their fellow *L* were in charge
28: 13 the divisions of the priests and *L*,
28: 21 and *L* are ready for all the work
2Ch 5: 4 Israel had arrived, the *L* took up
5: 5 who were *L*, carried them up;
5: 12 All the *L* who were musicians—
7: 6 Opposite the *L*, the priests blew
7: 6 did the *L* with the LORD's musical
8: 14 and the *L* to lead the praise
8: 15 or to the *L* in any matter,
11: 13 and *L* from all their districts sided
11: 14 The *L* even abandoned their
11: 16 followed the *L* to Jerusalem
13: 9 the sons of Aaron, and the *L*,
13: 10 of Aaron, and the *L* assist them.
17: 8 With them were certain *L*—
19: 8 appointed some of the *L*,
19: 11 and the *L* will serve as officials
20: 19 Then some *L* from the Kohathites
23: 2 Judah and gathered the *L*
23: 4 and *L* who are going on duty
23: 6 except the priests and *L* on duty;
23: 7 The *L* are to station themselves
23: 8 The *L* and all the men
23: 18 who were *L*, to whom David had
24: 5 But the *L* did not act at once.
24: 5 called together the priests and *L*
24: 6 "Why haven't you required the *L*
24: 11 in by the *L* to the king's officials
29: 4 He brought in the priests and the *L*,
29: 5 *L*! Consecrate yourselves now
29: 12 Then these *L* set to work:
29: 16 The *L* took it and carried it out
29: 25 He stationed the *L* in the temple
29: 26 So the *L* stood ready with David's
29: 30 and his officials ordered the *L*
29: 34 for the *L* had been more
29: 34 so their kinsmen the *L* helped them
2Ch 30: 15 priests and the *L* were ashamed
30: 16 the blood handed to them by the *L*.
30: 17 the *L* had to kill the Passover lambs
30: 21 while the *L* and priests sang
30: 22 spoke encouragingly to all the *L*,
30: 25 along with the priests and *L*
30: 27 and the *L* stood to bless the people,
31: 2 assigned the priests and *L*
31: 2 to their duties as priests or *L*—
31: 4 *L* so they could devote themselves
31: 9 the priests and *L* about the heaps;
31: 17 likewise to the *L* twenty years old
31: 19 in the genealogies of the *L*.
34: 9 which the *L* who were
34: 12 The *L*—all who were skilled
34: 12 *L* descended from Merari,
34: 13 Some of the *L* were secretaries,
34: 30 of Jerusalem, the priests and the *L*
35: 3 to the *L*, who instructed all Israel
35: 5 a group of *L* for each subdivision
35: 8 to the people and the priests and *L*.
35: 9 and Jozabad, the leaders of the *L*,
35: 9 head of cattle for the *L*.
35: 10 places with the *L* in their divisions
35: 11 while the *L* skinned the animals.
35: 14 So the *L* made preparations
35: 15 because their fellow *L* made
35: 18 the *L* and all Judah and Israel who
Ezr 1: 5 *L*—everyone whose heart God
2: 40 of Harim 1,017 The *L*:
2: 70 The priests, the *L*, the singers,
3: 8 appointing *L* twenty years of age
3: 8 brothers (the priests and the *L*
3: 9 all *L*—joined together
3: 10 and the *L* (the sons of Asaph)
3: 12 But many of the older priests and *L*
6: 16 the *L* and the rest of the exiles—
6: 18 the *L* in their groups for the service
6: 20 and *L* had purified themselves
6: 20 *L* slaughtered the Passover lamb
7: 7 including priests, *L*, singers,
7: 13 and *L*, who wish to go to Jerusalem
7: 24 or duty on any of the priests, *L*,
8: 15 and the priests, I found no *L* there.
8: 20 had established to assist the *L*.
8: 29 the *L* and the family heads of Israel
8: 30 priests and *L* received the silver
8: 33 and so were the *L* Jozabad son
9: 1 including the priests and the *L*,
10: 5 and put the leading priests and *L*
10: 23 Among the *L*: Jozabad, Shimei,
Ne 3: 17 by the *L* under Rehum son of Bani.
7: 1 and the *L* were appointed.
7: 43 of Harim 1,017 The *L*:
7: 73 The priests, the *L*, the gatekeepers,
8: 7 The *L*—Jeshua, Bani, Sherebiah,
8: 9 *L* who were instructing the people
8: 11 The *L* calmed all the people, saying
8: 13 along with the priests and the *L*,
9: 4 Standing on the stairs were the *L*—
9: 5 And the *L*—Jeshua, Kadmiel,
9: 38 our *L* and our priests are affixing
10: 9 The *L*: Jeshua son of Azaniah,
10: 28 priests, *L*, gatekeepers, singers,
10: 34 the priests, the *L* and the people—
10: 37 a tithe of our crops to the *L*,
10: 37 for it is the *L* who collect the tithes
10: 38 and the *L* are to bring a tenth
10: 38 is to accompany the *L*
10: 39 people of Israel, including the *L*,
11: 3 (now some Israelites, priests, *L*,
11: 15 From the *L*: Shemaiah son
11: 16 Jozabad, two of the heads of the *L*,
11: 18 The *L* in the holy city totaled 284.
11: 20 *L*, were in all the towns of Judah,
11: 22 The chief officer of the *L*
11: 36 divisions of the *L* of Judah settled
12: 1 *L* who returned with Zerubbabel
12: 8 The *L* were Jeshua, Binnui,
12: 22 heads of the *L* in the days
12: 24 leaders of the *L* were Hashabiah,
12: 27 the *L* were sought out
12: 30 and *L* had purified themselves
12: 44 by the Law for the priests and the *L*
12: 44 with the ministering priests and *L*.
12: 47 and the *L* set aside the portion
12: 47 set aside the portion for the other *L*
13: 5 and oil prescribed for the *L*,
Ne 13: 10 and that all the *L* and singers
13: 10 to the *L* had not been given
13: 22 Then I commanded the *L*
13: 29 of the priesthood and of the *L*.
13: 30 and the *L* of everything foreign,
Isa 66: 21 of them also to be priests and *L*,"
Jer 33: 18 nor will the priests, who are *L*,
33: 21 with the *L* who are priests
33: 22 and the *L* who minister before me
Eze 40: 46 who are the only *L* who may draw
43: 19 who are *L*, of the family of Zadok,
44: 10 " 'The *L* who went far from me
44: 15 who are *L* and descendants
45: 5 cubits wide will belong to the *L*,
48: 11 the *L* did when the Israelites went
48: 12 bordering the territory of the *L*.
48: 13 the *L* will have an allotment 25,000
48: 22 So the property of the *L*
Mal 3: 3 he will purify the *L* and refine them
Jn 1: 19 and *L* to ask him who he was.

LEVITICAL (LEVI)

Lev 25: 32 their houses in the *L* towns,
1Ch 15: 12 You are the heads of the *L* families;
Heb 7: 11 attained through the *L* priesthood

LEVY

2Ki 23: 33 on Judah a *l* of a hundred talents
2Ch 36: 3 and imposed on Judah a *l*

LEWD (LEWDNESS)

Jdg 20: 6 because they committed this *l*
Eze 16: 27 shocked by your *l* conduct.
22: 9 shrines and commit *l* acts.
23: 44 so they slept with those *l* women,

LEWDNESS (LEWD)

Eze 16: 43 Did you not add *l* to all your other
16: 58 bear the consequences of your *l*
23: 21 you longed for the *l* of your youth,
23: 27 So I will put a stop to the *l*
23: 29 Your *l* and promiscuity have
23: 35 bear the consequences of your *l*
23: 48 So I will put an end to *l* in the land,
23: 49 will suffer the penalty for your *l*
24: 13 " 'Now your impurity is *l*.
Hos 2: 10 So now I will expose her *l*
Mk 7: 22 malice, deceit, *l*, envy, slander,

LIABLE

Jos 6: 18 the camp of Israel *l* to destruction
7: 12 because they have been made *l*

LIAR (LIE)

Dt 19: 18 and if the witness proves to be a *l*,
Job 34: 6 I am considered a *l*;
Pr 17: 4 *l* pays attention to a malicious
19: 22 better to be poor than a *l*.
30: 6 will rebuke you and prove you a *l*.
Mic 2: 11 If a *l* and deceiver comes and says,
Jn 8: 44 for he is a *l* and the father of lies.
8: 55 I did not, I would be a *l* like you,
Ro 3: 4 Let God be true, and every man a *l*.
1Jn 1: 10 we make him out to be a *l*
2: 4 not do what he commands is a *l*,
2: 22 Who is the *l*? It is the man who
4: 20 yet hates his brother, he is a *l*.
5: 10 God has made him out to be a *l*,

LIARS (LIE)

Ps 63: 11 the mouths of *l* will be silenced.
116: 11 "All men are *l*."
Isa 57: 4 the offspring of *l*?
Mic 6: 12 her people are *l*
1Ti 1: 10 for slave traders and *l* and perjurers
4: 2 come through hypocritical *l*,
Tit 1: 12 "Cretans are always *l*, evil brutes,
Rev 3: 9 though they are not, but are *l*—
21: 8 magic arts, the idolaters and all *l*—

LIBATIONS

Ps 16: 4 I will not pour out their *l* of blood

LIBERAL (LIBERALITY)

2Co 8: 20 of the way we administer this *l* gift.

LIBERALITY (LIBERAL)

Est 1: 7 in keeping with the king's *l*.

Est 2:18 and distributed gifts with royal *l*.

LIBERATED (LIBERTY)

Ro 8:21 that the creation itself will be *l*

LIBERTY (LIBERATED)

Lev 25:10 and proclaim *l* throughout the land

LIBNAH (LIBNITE LIBNITES)

Nu 33:20 Rimmon Perez and camped at *L*.
33:21 They left *L* and camped at Rissah.
Jos 10:29 moved on from Makkedah to *L*
10:31 moved on from *L* to Lachish;
10:32 the sword, just as he had done to *L*.
10:39 as they had done to *L* and its king
12:15 Arad one the king of *L* one the king
15:42 *L*, Ether, Ashan, Iphtah, Ashnah,
21:13 *L*, Jattir, Eshtemoa, Holon, Debir,
2Ki 8:22 *L* revolted at the same time.
19:8 found the king fighting against *L*.
23:31 of Jeremiah; she was from *L*.
24:18 of Jeremiah; she was from *L*.
1Ch 6:57 and *L*, Jattir, Eshtemoa, Hilen,
2Ch 21:10 *L* revolted at the same time,
Isa 37:8 found the king fighting against *L*.
Jer 52:1 of Jeremiah; she was from *L*.

LIBNI

Ex 6:17 by clans, were *L* and Shimei.
Nu 3:18 names of the Gershonite clans: *L*
1Ch 6:17 names of the sons of Gershon: *L*
6:20 Of Gershon: *L* his son, Jehath his
6:29 of Merari: Mahli, *L* his son,

LIBNITE (LIBNAH)

Nu 26:58 the *L* clan, the Hebronite clan,

LIBNITES (LIBNAH)

Nu 3:21 belonged the clans of the *L*

LIBYA (LIBYANS)

Eze 30:5 *L* and the people of the covenant
Na 3:9 Put and *L* were among her allies.
Ac 2:10 and the parts of *L* near Cyrene;

LIBYANS (LIBYA)

2Ch 12:3 and the innumerable troops of *L*,
16:8 and *L* a mighty army with great
Isa 66:19 to the *L* and Lydians (famous
Da 11:43 with the *L* and Nubians

LICENSE

Jude :4 of our God into a *l* for immorality

LICK (LICKED LICKS)

Nu 22:4 going to *l* up everything around us,
1Ki 21:19 dogs will *l* up your blood—yes,
Ps 72:9 and his enemies will *l* the dust.
Isa 5:24 as tongues of fire *l* up straw
49:23 they will *l* the dust at your feet.
Mic 7:17 They will *l* dust like a snake,

LICKED (LICK)

1Ki 18:38 also *l* up the water in the trench.
21:19 the place where dogs *l* up Naboth's
22:38 and the dogs *l* up his blood,
Lk 16:21 Even the dogs came and *l* his sores.

LICKS (LICK)

Nu 22:4 as an ox *l* up the grass of the field."

LID

Nu 19:15 container without a *l* fastened
2Ki 12:9 a chest and bored a hole in its *l*.

LIE (LIAR LIARS LIED LIES LYING)

Ge 19:31 man around here to *l* with us,
19:32 to drink wine and then *l* with him
19:34 *l* with him so we can preserve our
29:21 time is completed, and I want to *l*
38:8 "*L* with your brother's wife
Ex 23:11 year let the land *l* unplowed
Lev 18:22 " 'Do not *l* with a man
19:11 " 'Do not *l*.
26:6 and you will *l* down and no one will
26:33 and your cities will *l* in ruins.
Nu 21:15 and *l* along the border of Moab."
23:19 God is not a man, that he should *l*,
24:9 Like a lion they crouch and *l* down,
Dt 6:7 when you *l* down and when you get
11:19 when you *l* down and when you get
25:2 the judge shall make him *l* down
33:13 with the deep waters that *l* below,
Jdg 9:32 and your men should come and *l*
Ru 3:4 go and uncover his feet and *l* down.
3:7 went over to *l* down at the far end
3:13 *L* here until morning."
1Sa 3:5 I did not call; go back and *l* down."
3:6 I did not call; go back and *l* down."
3:9 Eli told Samuel, "Go and *l* down,
15:29 the Glory of Israel does not *l*
22:8 servant to *l* in wait for me,
2Sa 8:2 made them *l* down on the ground
11:11 and drink and *l* with my wife?
12:11 and he will *l* with your wives
16:21 "*L* with your father's concubines
20:3 for them, but did not *l* with them.
23:7 they are burned up where they *l*."
1Ki 1:2 She can *l* beside him
Job 6:28 Would I *l* to your face?
7:4 When I *l* down I think, 'How long
7:21 For I will soon *l* down in the dust;
11:19 You will *l* down, with no one
20:11 will *l* with him in the dust.
21:26 Side by side they *l* in the dust,
29:19 the dew will *l* all night
38:40 or *l* in wait in a thicket?
Ps 3:5 I *l* down and sleep;
4:8 I will *l* down and sleep in peace,
23:2 me *l* down in green pastures,
31:17 and *l* silent in the grave.
36:12 See how the evildoers *l* fallen—
37:32 The wicked *l* in wait
38:9 All my longings *l* open before you,
57:4 I *l* among ravenous beasts—
59:3 See how they *l* in wait for me!
62:9 the highborn are but a *l*;
76:5 Valiant men *l* plundered,
76:6 both horse and chariot *l* still.
88:5 like the slain who *l* in the grave,
89:35 and I will not *l* to David—
102:7 I *l* awake; I have become
104:22 return and *l* down in their dens.
Pr 1:11 let's *l* in wait for someone's blood,
1:18 These men *l* in wait
3:24 when you *l* down, you will not be
3:24 when you *l* down, your sleep will
6:9 How long will you *l* there,
12:6 of the wicked *l* in wait for blood,
15:11 and Destruction *l* open
22:5 In the paths of the wicked *l* thorns
24:15 Do not *l* in wait like an outlaw
Ecc 4:11 Also, if two *l* down together,
11:3 place where it falls, there will it *l*.
Isa 6:11 "Until the cities *l* ruined
11:6 leopard will *l* down with the goat,
11:7 their young will *l* down together,
13:21 But desert creatures will *l* there,
14:18 the kings of the nations *l* in state,
14:30 and the needy will *l* down in safety.
17:2 left to flocks, which will *l* down,
21:9 *l* shattered on the ground!' "
27:10 there they *l* down;
28:15 for we have made a *l* our refuge
28:17 will sweep away your refuge, the *l*,
34:10 to generation it will *l* desolate;
44:20 thing in my right hand a *l*?"
50:11 You will *l* down in torment.
51:20 they *l* at the head of every street,
56:10 they *l* around and dream,
57:2 they find rest as they *l* in death.
Jer 3:25 Let us *l* down in our shame,
4:7 Your towns will *l* in ruins
5:6 a leopard will *l* in wait
5:26 who *l* in wait like men who snare
9:5 They have taught their tongues to *l*
9:22 " 'The dead bodies of men will *l*
12:4 How long will the land *l* parched
23:14 They commit adultery and live a *l*.
29:31 and has led you to believe a *l*,
44:2 Today they *l* deserted and in ruins
46:19 and *l* in ruins without inhabitant.
51:47 her slain will all *l* fallen within her.
La 2:21 "Young and old *l* together
4:5 now *l* on ash heaps.
Eze 4:4 number of days you *l* on your side.
4:4 "Then *l* on your left side
4:6 "After you have finished this, *l*
4:9 it during the 390 days you *l*
6:13 when their people *l* slain
13:6 are false and their divinations a *l*.
18:6 *l* with a woman during her period.
29:12 her cities will *l* desolate forty years
30:7 and their cities will *l*
31:18 will *l* among the uncircumcised,
32:21 and they *l* with the uncircumcised,
32:27 Do they not *l* with the other
32:28 will *l* among the uncircumcised,
32:29 They *l* with the uncircumcised,
32:30 They *l* uncircumcised
34:14 they will *l* down in good grazing
34:15 will tend my sheep and have them *l*
48:22 belonging to the prince will *l*
48:22 of the city will *l* in the center
Da 11:27 sit at the same table and *l*
Hos 2:18 so that all may *l* down in safety.
6:9 As marauders *l* in ambush
Am 2:8 They *l* down beside every altar
6:4 You *l* on beds inlaid with ivory
Mic 7:2 All men *l* in wait to shed blood;
Na 3:18 your nobles *l* down to rest.
Zep 2:7 In the evening they will *l* down
2:14 Flocks and herds will *l* down there,
3:13 They will eat and *l* down
Zec 10:2 diviners see visions that *l*;
Jn 5:3 of disabled people used to *l*—
Ro 1:25 exchanged the truth of God for a *l*,
Gal 1:20 that what I am writing you is no *l*.
Col 3:9 Do not *l* to each other,
2Th 2:11 so that they will believe the *l*
Tit 1:2 which God, who does not *l*,
Heb 6:18 which it is impossible for God to *l*,
1Jn 1:6 we *l* and do not live by the truth.
2:21 because no *l* comes from the truth.
Rev 11:8 Their bodies will *l* in the street
14:5 No *l* was found in their mouths;

LIED (LIE)

Ge 18:15 Sarah was afraid, so she *l* and said,
Jos 7:11 they have stolen, they have *l*,
Jdg 16:10 a fool of me; you *l* to me.
Jer 5:12 They have *l* about the LORD;
Ac 5:3 so filled your heart that you have *l*
5:4 You have not *l* to men but to God."

LIES (LIE)

Ge 21:17 heard the boy crying as he *l* there.
49:9 Like a lion he crouches and *l* down,
49:25 blessings of the deep that *l* below,
Ex 5:9 and pay no attention to *l*."
Lev 6:3 finds lost property and *l* about it,
15:4 man with a discharge *l* on will be
15:18 When a man *l* with a woman
15:20 she *l* on during her period
15:24 any bed he *l* on will be unclean.
15:24 " 'If a man *l* with her and her
15:26 bed she *l* on while her discharge
15:33 for a man who *l* with a woman who
18:22 with a man as one *l* with a woman;
20:13 with a man as one *l* with a woman,
20:13 " 'If a man *l* with a man
20:18 " 'If a man *l* with a woman
26:34 years all the time that it *l* desolate
26:35 All the time that it *l* desolate,
26:43 while it *l* desolate without them.
Nu 14:33 last of your bodies *l* in the desert.
Dt 19:11 if a man hates his neighbor and *l*
Ru 3:4 When he *l* down, note the place
1Sa 14:39 even if it *l* with my son Jonathan,
22:13 against me and *l* in wait for me,
2Sa 1:19 O Israel, *l* slain on your heights.
1:25 Jonathan *l* slain on your heights.
Ne 2:3 city where my fathers are buried *l*
2:17 are in: Jerusalem *l* in ruins,
Job 13:4 You, however, smear me with *l*;
14:12 so man *l* down and does not rise;
18:10 a trap *l* in his path.
19:28 the root of the trouble *l* in him,'
20:26 total darkness *l* in wait
26:6 Destruction *l* uncovered.
27:19 He *l* down wealthy, but will do
37:17 clothes when the land *l* hushed
40:21 Under the lotus plants he *l*,
Ps 5:6 You destroy those who tell *l*;
10:7 His mouth is full of curses and *l*

Ps 10: 8 He *l* in wait near the villages;
10: 9 He *l* in wait like a lion in cover;
10: 9 he *l* in wait to catch the helpless;
12: 2 Everyone *l* to his neighbor;
34: 13 and your lips from speaking *l*.
41: 8 up from the place where he *l*.''
55: 11 threats and *l* never leave its streets.
58: 3 they are wayward and speak *l*.
59: 12 For the curses and *l* they utter,
62: 4 they take delight in *l*.
88: 7 Your wrath *l* heavily upon me;
119: 69 arrogant have smeared me with *l*,
144: 8 whose mouths are full of *l*,
144: 11 whose mouths are full of *l*,
Pr 6: 19 a false witness who pours out *l*
12: 17 but a false witness tells *l*.
14: 5 but a false witness pours out *l*.
19: 5 he who pours out *l* will not go free.
19: 9 and he who pours out *l* will perish.
23: 28 Like a bandit she *l* in wait,
29: 12 If a ruler listens to *l*,
30: 8 Keep falsehood and *l* far from me;
Isa 9: 15 prophets who teach *l* are the tail.
24: 10 The ruined city *l* desolate;
32: 7 schemes to destroy the poor with *l*,
59: 3 Your lips have spoken *l*,
59: 4 on empty arguments and speak *l*;
59: 13 uttering *l* our hearts have
64: 11 and all that we treasured *l* in ruins.
Jer 4: 20 the whole land *l* in ruins.
5: 31 The prophets prophesy *l*,
9: 3 like a bow, to shoot *l*;
14: 14 "The prophets are prophesying *l*
20: 6 to whom you have prophesied *l*.' "
23: 10 of the curse the land *l* parched
23: 25 the prophets say who prophesy *l*
23: 32 astray with their reckless *l*,
27: 10 They prophesy *l* to you that will
27: 14 for they are prophesying *l* to you.
27: 15 They are prophesying *l* in my name
27: 16 They are prophesying *l* to you.
28: 15 persuaded this nation to trust in *l*.
29: 9 They are prophesying *l* to you
29: 21 who are prophesying *l* to you
29: 23 and in my name have spoken *l*,
40: 4 the whole country *l* before you;
La 1: 1 How deserted *l* the city,
5: 18 for Mount Zion, which *l* desolate,
Eze 13: 19 lying to my people, who listen to *l*,
13: 22 the righteous with your *l*,
26: 2 now that she *l* in ruins I will
32: 23 and her army *l* around her grave.
47: 16 and Sibraim (which *l* on the border
Da 2: 22 he knows what *l* in darkness,
Hos 7: 3 the princes with their *l*.
7: 13 but they speak *l* against me.
11: 12 Ephraim has surrounded me with *l*,
12: 1 and multiplies *l* and violence.
Mic 7: 5 with her who *l* in your embrace
Na 3: 1 full of *l*,
Hab 2: 18 Or an image that teaches *l*?
Zep 3: 13 they will speak no *l*,
Zec 13: 3 you have told *l* in the LORD's
Mt 8: 6 "my servant *l* at home paralyzed
Jn 8: 44 When he *l*, he speaks his native
8: 44 for he is a liar and the father of *l*.
Rev 10: 8 take the scroll that *l* open

LIFE (LIVE)

Ge 1: 30 everything that has the breath of *l*
2: 7 into his nostrils the breath of *l*,
2: 9 of the garden were the tree of *l*
3: 14 all the days of your *l*.
3: 17 all the days of your *l*.
3: 22 take also from the tree of *l* and eat,
3: 24 to guard the way to the tree of *l*.
6: 17 creature that has the breath of *l*
6: 17 to destroy all *l* under the heavens,
7: 11 the six hundredth year of Noah's *l*,
7: 15 breath of *l* in them came to Noah
7: 22 the breath of *l* in its nostrils died.
9: 5 for the *l* of his fellow man.
9: 11 Never again will all *l* be cut
9: 15 become a flood to destroy all *l*.
9: 17 between me and all *l* on the earth."
12: 13 my *l* will be spared because of you
19: 19 kindness to me in sparing my *l*.
19: 20 isn't it? Then my *l* will be spared."
26: 9 Because I thought I might lose my *l*
27: 46 my *l* will not be worth living."
32: 30 and yet my *l* was spared."
37: 21 "Let's not take his *l*," he said.
42: 21 when he pleaded with us for his *l*,
43: 9 the blame before you all my *l*.
44: 30 is closely bound up with the boy's *l*,
44: 30 whose *l* is closely bound up
44: 32 my father, all my *l*!" "Now then,
47: 28 the years of his *l* were a hundred
48: 15 all my *l* to this day,
Ex 21: 6 Then he will be his servant for *l*.
21: 23 you are to take *l* for *l*, eye for eye,
21: 30 he may redeem his *l*
23: 26 I will give you a full *l* span.
30: 12 for his *l* at the time he is counted.
Lev 17: 11 For the *l* of a creature is
17: 11 that makes atonement for one's *l*.
17: 14 the *l* of every creature is its blood.
17: 14 the *l* of every creature is its blood;
19: 16 that endangers your neighbor's *l*.
24: 17 " 'If anyone takes the *l*
24: 18 Anyone who takes the *l*
24: 18 must make restitution—*l* for *l*.
25: 46 and can make them slaves for *l*,
26: 16 your sight and drain away your *l*.
Nu 35: 31 a ransom for the *l* of a murderer,
Dt 4: 42 one of these cities and save his *l*.
6: 2 and so that you may enjoy long *l*.
12: 23 and you must not eat the *l*
12: 23 because the blood is the *l*,
15: 17 he will become your servant for *l*.
16: 3 days of your *l* you may remember
17: 19 days of his *l* so that he may learn
19: 4 and flees there to save his *l*—
19: 5 to one of these cities and save his *l*.
19: 21 Show no pity: *l* for *l*, eye for eye,
22: 7 and you may have a long *l*.
28: 66 and day, never sure of your *l*.
30: 15 I set before you today *l*
30: 19 Now choose *l*, so that you
30: 19 you that I have set before you *l*
30: 20 For the LORD is your *l*,
32: 39 I put to death and I bring to *l*,
32: 47 words for you—they are your *l*.
Jos 1: 5 against you all the days of your *l*.
4: 14 revered him all the days of his *l*,
Jdg 5: 7 Village *l* in Israel ceased,
9: 17 risked his *l* to rescue you
12: 3 I took my *l* in my hands
13: 12 what is to be the rule for the boy's *l*
Ru 1: 20 has made my *l* very bitter.
4: 15 will renew your *l* and sustain you
1Sa 1: 11 the LORD for all the days of his *l*,
1: 28 For his whole *l* he will be given
2: 33 will die in the prime of *l*.
7: 15 over Israel all the days of his *l*.
19: 5 He took his *l* in his hands
19: 11 "If you don't run for your *l* tonight,
20: 1 that he is trying to take my *l*?"
22: 23 is seeking your *l* is seeking mine
23: 15 Saul had come out to take his *l*.
24: 11 me down to take my *l*.
25: 6 Say to him: 'Long *l* to you!
25: 29 is pursuing you to take your *l*,
25: 29 the *l* of my master will be bound
26: 21 considered my *l* precious today,
26: 24 As surely as I valued your *l* today,
26: 24 so may the LORD value my *l*
28: 2 I will make you my bodyguard for *l*
28: 9 for my *l* to bring about my death?"
28: 21 I took my *l* in my hands
2Sa 1: 23 in *l* they were loved and gracious,
4: 8 enemy, who tried to take your *l*.
14: 7 for the *l* of his brother whom he
14: 14 But God does not take away *l*;
15: 21 whether it means *l* or death,
16: 11 own flesh, is trying to take my *l*.
18: 13 And if I had put my *l* in jeopardy—
19: 5 who have just saved your *l*
1Ki 1: 12 and the *l* of your son Solomon.
1: 12 you how you can save your own *l*
2: 23 pay with his *l* for this request!
3: 11 not for long *l* or wealth for yourself
3: 14 father did, I will give you a long *l*."
4: 21 were Solomon's subjects all his *l*.
4: 33 He described plant *l*,
11: 34 the days of his *l* for the sake
1Ki 15: 5 commands all the days of his *l*—
15: 14 committed to the LORD all his *l*.
17: 21 let this boy's *l* return to him!"
17: 22 and the boy's *l* returned to him,
19: 2 I do not make your *l* like that
19: 3 Elijah was afraid and ran for his *l*.
19: 4 "Take my *l*; I am no better
20: 31 Perhaps he will spare your *l*."
20: 39 it will be your *l* for his *l*,
20: 42 Therefore it is your *l* for his *l*,
2Ki 1: 13 "please have respect for my *l*
1: 14 But now have respect for my *l*!"
5: 7 Can I kill and bring back to *l*?
8: 1 whose son he had restored to *l*,
8: 5 Elisha had restored the dead to *l*,
8: 5 back to *l* came to beg the king
8: 5 son whom Elisha restored to *l*."
10: 24 escape, it will be your *l* for his *l*."
13: 21 the man came to *l* and stood up
18: 32 Choose *l* and not death! "Do not
20: 6 I will add fifteen years to your *l*.
25: 29 and for the rest of his *l* ate regularly
1Ch 29: 28 having enjoyed long *l*, wealth
2Ch 1: 11 you have not asked for a long *l*
15: 17 committed ⌞to the LORD⌟ all his *l*.
Ezr 9: 9 He has granted us new *l*
Ne 4: 2 to *l* from those heaps of rubble—
6: 11 go into the temple to save his *l*?
9: 6 You give *l* to everything,
Est 4: 11 scepter to him and spare his *l*.
7: 3 grant me my *l*— this is my petition.
7: 7 to beg Queen Esther for his *l*.
Job 2: 4 will give all he has for his own *l*.
2: 6 hands; but you must spare his *l*."
3: 20 and *l* to the bitter of soul,
3: 23 Why is *l* given to a man
7: 7 O God, that my *l* is but a breath;
7: 16 I despise my *l*; I would not live
8: 19 Surely its *l* withers away,
9: 21 I despise my own *l*.
10: 1 "I loathe my very *l*;
10: 12 You gave me *l* and showed me
11: 17 *L* will be brighter than noonday,
12: 10 In his hand is the *l*
12: 12 not long *l* bring understanding?
13: 14 and take my *l* in my hands?
24: 22 they have no assurance of *l*.
27: 3 as long as I have *l* within me,
27: 8 when God takes away his *l*?
30: 16 "And now my *l* ebbs away;
31: 30 by invoking a curse against his *l*—
33: 4 of the Almighty gives me *l*.
33: 18 his *l* from perishing by the sword.
33: 22 and his *l* to the messengers of death
33: 30 that the light of *l* may shine on him.
41: 4 you to take him as your slave for *l*?
42: 12 part of Job's *l* more than the first.
Ps 7: 5 let him trample my *l* to the ground
16: 11 known to me the path of *l*;
17: 14 this world whose reward is in this *l*.
21: 4 He asked you for *l*, and you gave it
22: 20 Deliver my *l* from the sword,
22: 20 my precious *l* from the power
23: 6 all the days of my *l*,
25: 20 Guard my *l* and rescue me;
26: 1 for I have led a blameless *l*;
26: 9 or my *l* with bloodthirsty men,
26: 11 But I lead a blameless *l*;
27: 1 LORD is the stronghold of my *l*—
27: 4 all the days of my *l*,
31: 10 My *l* is consumed by anguish
31: 13 and plot to take my *l*.
34: 12 Whoever of you loves *l*
35: 4 May those who seek my *l*
35: 17 Rescue my *l* from their ravages,
35: 17 my precious *l* from these lions.
36: 9 For with you is the fountain of *l*;
38: 12 Those who seek my *l* set their traps
39: 4 let me know how fleeting is my *l*.
39: 5 Each man's *l* is but a breath.
40: 14 May all who seek to take my *l*
41: 2 will protect him and preserve his *l*;
42: 8 a prayer to the God of my *l*.
49: 7 No man can redeem the *l*
49: 8 the ransom for a *l* is costly,
49: 19 who will never see the light ⌞of *l*⌟.
54: 3 ruthless men seek my *l*—
56: 6 eager to take my *l*.

Ps 56: 13 God in the light of *l*.
61: 6 Increase the days of the king's *l*,
63: 3 Because your love is better than *l*,
63: 9 who seek my *l* will be destroyed;
64: 1 protect my *l* from the threat
69: 28 they be blotted out of the book of *l*
70: 2 May those who seek my *l*
71: 20 you will restore my *l* again;
74: 19 over the *l* of your dove
86: 2 Guard my *l*, for I am devoted
86: 14 a band of ruthless men seeks my *l*
88: 3 and my *l* draws near the grave.
89: 47 Remember how fleeting is my *l*.
91: 16 With long *l* will I satisfy him
101: 2 careful to lead a blameless *l*—
102: 23 of my *l* he broke my strength;
103: 4 he redeems my *l* from the pit
104: 33 I will sing to the LORD all my *l*;
109: 31 to save his *l* from those who
119: 25 renew my *l* according to your word
119: 37 renew my *l* according to your word
119: 40 Renew my *l* in your righteousness.
119: 50 Your promise renews my *l*.
119: 88 Preserve my *l* according
119: 93 for by them you have renewed my *l*
119:107 renew my *l*, O LORD, according
119:109 Though I constantly take my *l*
119:149 renew my *l*, O LORD, according
119:154 renew my *l* according
119:156 renew my *l* according to your laws.
119:159 preserve my *l*, O LORD, according
121: 7 he will watch over your *l*;
128: 5 all the days of your *l*;
133: 3 even *l* forevermore.
138: 7 you preserve my *l*;
142: 4 no one cares for my *l*.
143: 11 sake, O LORD, preserve my *l*;
146: 2 I will praise the LORD all my *l*;
Pr 1: 3 a disciplined and prudent *l*,
2: 19 or attain the paths of *l*.
3: 2 will prolong your *l* many years
3: 16 Long *l* is in her right hand;
3: 18 of *l* to those who embrace her;
3: 22 they will be *l* for you,
4: 10 the years of your *l* will be many.
4: 13 guard it well, for it is your *l*.
4: 22 for they are *l* to those who find
4: 23 for it is the wellspring of *l*.
5: 6 gives no thought to the way of *l*;
5: 11 At the end of your *l* you will groan,
6: 23 are the way to *l*,
6: 26 adulteress preys upon your very *l*.
7: 23 little knowing it will cost him his *l*.
8: 35 For whoever finds me finds *l*
9: 11 and years will be added to your *l*.
10: 11 of the righteous is a fountain of *l*,
10: 16 of the righteous bring them *l*
10: 17 discipline shows the way to *l*,
10: 27 of the LORD adds length to *l*,
11: 19 The truly righteous man attains *l*,
11: 30 of the righteous is a tree of *l*,
12: 28 of righteousness there is *l*;
13: 8 A man's riches may ransom his *l*,
13: 12 but a longing fulfilled is a tree of *l*.
13: 14 of the wise is a fountain of *l*,
14: 27 of the LORD is a fountain of *l*,
14: 30 A heart at peace gives *l* to the body
15: 4 that brings healing is a tree of *l*,
15: 24 The path of *l* leads upward
16: 15 a king's face brightens, it means *l*;
16: 22 Understanding is a fountain of *l*
16: 31 it is attained by a righteous *l*.
18: 21 The tongue has the power of *l*
19: 3 A man's own folly ruins his *l*,
19: 23 The fear of the LORD leads to *l*:
20: 2 he who angers him forfeits his *l*.
20: 7 righteous man leads a blameless *l*;
21: 21 finds *l*, prosperity and honor.
22: 4 bring wealth and honor and *l*.
23: 22 to your father, who gave you *l*,
24: 12 not he who guards your *l* know it?
28: 16 ill-gotten gain will enjoy a long *l*.
31: 12 all the days of her *l*.
Ecc 2: 17 I hated *l*, because the work that is
5: 18 days of *l* God has given him—
5: 20 reflects on the days of his *l*,
6: 12 knows what is good for a man in *l*,
7: 12 that wisdom preserves the *l*
Ecc 7: 15 In this meaningless *l*
8: 15 So I commend the enjoyment of *l*,
8: 15 the days of the *l* God has given him
9: 9 Enjoy *l* with your wife, whom you
9: 9 For this is your lot in *l*
9: 9 of this meaningless *l* that God has
10: 19 and wine makes *l* merry,
Isa 23: 15 years, the span of a king's *l*.
38: 5 I will add fifteen years to your *l*.
38: 10 I said, "In the prime of my *l*
38: 12 Like a weaver I have rolled up my *l*
38: 16 and my spirit finds *l* in them too.
42: 5 and *l* to those who walk on it:
43: 4 and people in exchange for your *l*.
53: 10 LORD makes his *l* a guilt offering,
53: 11 he will see the light of *l*
53: 12 he poured out his *l* unto death,
Jer 4: 30 they seek your *l*.
4: 31 my *l* is given over to murderers."
8: 3 evil nation will prefer death to *l*,
10: 23 that a man's *l* is not his own;
11: 21 of Anathoth who are seeking your *l*
17: 11 When his *l* is half gone, they will
20: 13 He rescues the *l* of the needy
21: 8 I am setting before you the way of *l*
21: 9 will live; he will escape with his *l*.
22: 25 you over to those who seek your *l*,
38: 2 escape with his *l*; he will live.'
38: 16 to those who are seeking your *l*."
38: 17 your *l* will be spared and this city
38: 20 with you, and your *l* will be spared.
39: 18 but will escape with your *l*,
40: 14 son of Nethaniah to take your *l*?"
40: 15 Why should he take your *l*
44: 30 over to his enemies who seek his *l*,
44: 30 the enemy who was seeking his *l*.' "
45: 5 I will let you escape with your *l*.' "
52: 33 and for the rest of his *l* ate regularly
La 3: 53 They tried to end my *l* in a pit
3: 58 you redeemed my *l*.
4: 20 anointed, our very *l* breath,
Eze 3: 18 ways in order to save his *l*,
7: 13 not one of them will preserve his *l*.
18: 27 and right, he will save his *l*.
32: 10 every moment for his *l*.
33: 4 the sword comes and takes his *l*,
33: 6 and takes the *l* of one of them,
33: 15 follows the decrees that give *l*,
37: 5 enter you, and you will come to *l*.
37: 6 in you, and you will come to *l*.
37: 10 they came to *l* and stood up
Da 5: 23 God who holds in his hand your *l*
12: 2 some to everlasting *l*, others
Am 2: 14 and the warrior will not save his *l*.
2: 15 the horseman will not save his *l*.
Jnh 1: 14 die for taking this man's *l*.
2: 6 you brought my *l* up from the pit,
2: 7 "When my *l* was ebbing away,
4: 3 Now, O LORD, take away my *l*,
Hab 2: 10 own house and forfeiting your *l*.
2: 19 says to wood, 'Come to *l*!'
Mal 2: 5 a covenant of *l* and peace,
Mt 2: 20 to take the child's *l* are dead."
6: 25 Is not *l* more important than food,
6: 25 do not worry about your *l*,
6: 27 can add a single hour to his *l*?
7: 14 and narrow the road that leads to *l*,
10: 39 Whoever finds his *l* will lose it,
10: 39 and whoever loses his *l*
13: 22 but the worries of this *l*
16: 21 and on the third day be raised to *l*.
16: 25 but whoever loses his *l*
16: 25 wants to save his *l* will lose it,
17: 23 the third day he will be raised to *l*."
18: 8 better for you to enter *l* maimed
18: 9 for you to enter *l* with one eye
19: 16 thing must I do to get eternal *l*?"
19: 17 want to enter *l*, obey
19: 29 as much and will inherit eternal *l*.
20: 19 the third day he will be raised to *l*!"
20: 28 to give his *l* as a ransom for many."
25: 46 but the righteous to eternal *l*."
27: 52 who had died were raised to *l*.
Mk 3: 4 to save *l* or to kill?" But they
4: 19 the word; but the worries of this *l*,
8: 35 but whoever loses his *l* for me
8: 35 wants to save his *l* will lose it,
9: 43 better for you to enter *l* maimed
Mk 9: 45 better for you to enter *l* crippled
10: 17 "what must I do to inherit eternal *l*
10: 30 and in the age to come, eternal *l*.
10: 45 to give his *l* as a ransom for many."
Lk 6: 9 to save *l* or to destroy it?
7: 37 a woman who had lived a sinful *l*
9: 8 of long ago had come back to *l*.
9: 19 of long ago has come back to *l*."
9: 22 and on the third day be raised to *l*."
9: 24 but whoever loses his *l*
9: 24 wants to save his *l* will lose it,
10: 25 "what must I do to inherit eternal *l*
12: 15 a man's *l* does not consist
12: 19 Take *l* easy; eat, drink
12: 20 very night your *l* will be demanded
12: 22 do not worry about your *l*,
12: 23 *L* is more than food, and the body
12: 25 can add a single hour to his *l*?
14: 26 even his own *l*— he cannot be my
17: 33 tries to keep his *l* will lose it,
17: 33 whoever loses his *l* will preserve it.
18: 18 what must I do to inherit eternal *l*
18: 30 and, in the age to come, eternal *l*."
21: 34 drunkenness and the anxieties of *l*,
Jn 1: 4 In him was *l*, and that *l* was
3: 15 believes in him may have eternal *l*.
3: 16 shall not perish but have eternal *l*.
3: 36 believes in the Son has eternal *l*,
3: 36 rejects the Son will not see *l*,
4: 14 of water welling up to eternal *l*."
4: 36 he harvests the crop for eternal *l*,
5: 21 raises the dead and gives them *l*,
5: 21 so the Son gives *l* to whom he is
5: 24 he has crossed over from death to *l*.
5: 24 him who sent me has eternal *l*
5: 26 For as the Father has *l* in himself,
5: 26 the Son to have *l* in himself.
5: 39 that by them you possess eternal *l*.
5: 40 refuse to come to me to have *l*.
6: 27 for food that endures to eternal *l*,
6: 33 down from heaven and gives *l*
6: 35 Jesus declared, "I am the bread of *l*
6: 40 believes in him shall have eternal *l*,
6: 47 he who believes has everlasting *l*.
6: 48 I am the bread of *l*.
6: 51 give for the *l* of the world."
6: 53 and drink his blood, you have no *l*
6: 54 and drinks my blood has eternal *l*,
6: 63 The Spirit gives *l*; the flesh counts
6: 63 to you are spirit and they are *l*.
6: 68 You have the words of eternal *l*
7: 1 there were waiting to take his *l*
8: 11 "Go now and leave your *l* of sin."
8: 12 but will have the light of *l*."
9: 3 of God might be displayed in his *l*.
10: 10 I have come that they may have *l*,
10: 11 lays down his *l* for the sheep.
10: 15 and I lay down my *l* for the sheep.
10: 17 loves me is that I lay down my *l*—
10: 28 I give them eternal *l*, and they shall
11: 25 "I am the resurrection and the *l*.
11: 53 day on they plotted to take his *l*.
12: 25 The man who loves his *l* will lose it,
12: 25 this world will keep it for eternal *l*.
12: 25 while the man who hates his *l*
12: 50 his command leads to eternal *l*.
13: 37 I will lay down my *l* for you."
13: 38 lay down your *l* for me?
14: 6 am the way and the truth and the *l*.
15: 13 lay down his *l* for his friends.
17: 2 people that he might give eternal *l*
17: 3 Now this is eternal *l*: that they may
20: 31 that by believing you may have *l*
Ac 2: 28 to me the paths of *l*;
2: 32 God has raised this Jesus to *l*,
3: 15 You killed the author of *l*,
5: 20 the full message of this new *l*."
8: 33 For his *l* was taken from the earth."
11: 18 the Gentiles repentance unto *l*."
13: 46 yourselves worthy of eternal *l*,
13: 48 appointed for eternal *l* believed.
17: 25 because he himself gives all men *l*
20: 24 I consider my *l* worth nothing
26: 4 of my *l* in my own country,
27: 43 centurion wanted to spare Paul's *l*
Ro 2: 7 immortality, he will give eternal *l*.
4: 17 the God who gives *l* to the dead
4: 25 was raised to *l* for our justification.

Ro 5: 10 shall we be saved through his *l!*
5: 17 the gift of righteousness reign in *l*
5: 18 was justification that brings *l*
5: 21 righteousness to bring eternal *l*
6: 4 the Father, we too may live a new *l.*
6: 10 but the *l* he lives, he lives to God.
6: 13 have been brought from death to *l;*
6: 22 holiness, and the result is eternal *l.*
6: 23 but the gift of God is eternal *l*
7: 9 came, sin sprang to *l*
7: 10 to bring *l* actually brought death.
8: 2 the law of the Spirit of *l* set me free
8: 6 mind controlled by the Spirit is *l*
8: 11 also give *l* to your mortal bodies
8: 34 more than that, who was raised to *l*
8: 38 convinced that neither death nor *l,*
11: 15 what will their acceptance be but *l*
14: 9 to *l* so that he might be the Lord
1Co 3: 22 Cephas or the world or *l* or death
4: 17 you of my way of *l* in Christ Jesus,
6: 3 How much more the things of this *l*
7: 17 in *l* that the Lord assigned to him
7: 28 will face many troubles in this *l,*
15: 19 If only for this *l* we have hope
15: 36 What you sow does not come to *l*
2Co 1: 8 so that we despaired even of *l.*
2: 16 to the other, the fragrance of *l.*
3: 6 letter kills, but the Spirit gives *l.*
4: 10 so that the *l* of Jesus may
4: 11 so that his *l* may be revealed
4: 12 at work in us, but *l* is at work in you
5: 4 is mortal may be swallowed up by *l.*
Gal 1: 13 of my previous way of *l* in Judaism,
2: 20 The *l* I live in the body, I live
3: 15 take an example from everyday *l.*
3: 21 had been given that could impart *l,*
6: 8 from the Spirit will reap eternal *l.*
Eph 4: 1 I urge you to live a *l* worthy
4: 18 and separated from the *l* of God
4: 22 with regard to your former way of *l*
5: 2 as dearly loved children and live a *l*
6: 3 and that you may enjoy long *l*
Php 1: 20 exalted in my body, whether by *l*
2: 16 as you hold out the word of *l*—
2: 30 risking his *l* to make up
4: 3 whose names are in the book of *l.*
Col 1: 10 order that you may live a *l* worthy
3: 3 your *l* is now hidden with Christ
3: 4 When Christ, who is your *l,*
3: 7 in the *l* you once lived.
1Th 4: 7 us to be impure, but to live a holy *l.*
4: 11 it your ambition to lead a quiet *l,*
4: 12 so that your daily *l* may win
1Ti 1: 16 on him and receive eternal *l.*
4: 8 for both the present *l* and the *l*
4: 12 in *l,* in love, in faith and in purity.
4: 16 Watch your *l* and doctrine closely.
6: 12 Take hold of the eternal *l*
6: 13 who gives *l* to everything,
6: 19 hold of the *l* that is truly *l.*
2Ti 1: 1 according to the promise of *l* that is
1: 9 saved us and called us to a holy *l*—
1: 10 destroyed death and has brought *l*
3: 10 my way of *l,* my purpose, faith,
3: 12 to live a godly *l* in Christ Jesus will
Tit 1: 2 resting on the hope of eternal *l,*
3: 7 heirs having the hope of eternal *l.*
Heb 5: 7 During the days of Jesus' *l* on earth
7: 3 beginning of days or end of *l,*
7: 16 of the power of an indestructible *l.*
11: 5 faith Enoch was taken from this *l,*
11: 35 back their dead, raised to *l* again.
13: 7 the outcome of their way of *l*
Jas 1: 12 crown of *l* that God has promised
1: 20 about the righteous *l* that God
3: 6 sets the whole course of his *l* on fire
3: 13 Let him show it by his good *l,*
4: 14 What is your *l?* You are a mist that
1Pe 1: 18 way of *l* handed down to you
3: 7 with you of the gracious gift of *l,*
3: 10 "Whoever would love *l*
4: 2 rest of his earthly *l* for evil human
2Pe 1: 3 given us everything we need for *l*
1Jn 1: 1 proclaim concerning the Word of *l.*
1: 2 The *l* appeared; we have seen it
1: 2 we proclaim to you the eternal *l,*
2: 25 he promised us—even eternal *l.*
3: 14 we have passed from death to *l,*
1Jn 3: 15 that no murderer has eternal *l*
3: 16 Jesus Christ laid down his *l* for us.
5: 11 has given us eternal *l,* and this *l* is
5: 12 has the Son has *l;* he who does not
5: 12 the Son of God does not have *l.*
5: 13 may know that you have eternal *l.*
5: 16 pray and God will give him *l.*
5: 20 He is the true God and eternal *l.*
Jude :21 Christ to bring you to eternal *l.*
Rev 2: 7 the right to eat from the tree of *l,*
2: 8 who died and came to *l* again.
2: 10 and I will give you the crown of *l.*
3: 5 name from the book of *l,*
11: 11 breath of *l* from God entered them,
13: 8 written in the book of *l* belonging
17: 8 in the book of *l* from the creation
20: 4 They came to *l* and reigned
20: 5 to *l* until the thousand years were
20: 12 was opened, which is the book of *l.*
20: 15 not found written in the book of *l,*
21: 6 from the spring of the water of *l.*
21: 27 written in the Lamb's book of *l.*
22: 1 me the river of the water of *l,*
22: 2 side of the river stood the tree of *l,*
22: 14 may have the right to the tree of *l*
22: 17 take the free gift of the water of *l.*
22: 19 from him his share in the tree of *l*

LIFE-GIVING (GIVE)

Pr 15: 31 He who listens to a *l* rebuke
1Co 15: 45 being"; the last Adam, a *l* spirit.

LIFE'S (LIVE)

Ps 39: 4 "Show me, O LORD, my *l* end
Lk 8: 14 way they are choked by *l* worries,

LIFEBLOOD (BLOOD)

Ge 9: 4 must not eat meat that has its *l* still
9: 5 And for your *l* I will surely demand
Jer 2: 34 the *l* of the innocent poor,

LIFEBOAT (BOAT)

Ac 27: 16 able to make the *l* secure.
27: 30 the sailors let the *l*
27: 32 cut the ropes that held the *l*

LIFELESS

Lev 26: 30 bodies on the *l* forms of your idols,
Ps 106: 28 and ate sacrifices offered to *l* gods;
Jer 16: 18 with the *l* forms of their vile images
Eze 43: 7 and the *l* idols of their kings
43: 9 and the *l* idols of their kings,
Hab 2: 19 Or to *l* stone, 'Wake up!'
1Co 14: 7 case of *l* things that make sounds,

LIFETIME (LIVE)

Nu 3: 4 as priests during the *l*
Jos 24: 31 LORD throughout the *l* of Joshua
Jdg 2: 7 LORD throughout the *l* of Joshua
8: 28 During Gideon's *l,* the land
1Sa 7: 13 Throughout Samuel's *l,* the hand
2Sa 18: 18 During his *l* Absalom had taken
1Ki 3: 13 in your *l* you will have no equal
4: 25 During Solomon's *l* Judah
11: 12 I will not do it during your *l.*
12: 6 his father Solomon during his *l.*
15: 6 Jeroboam throughout ⌞Abijah's⌟ *l.*
2Ki 20: 19 not be peace and security in my *l?"*
2Ch 10: 6 his father Solomon during his *l.*
Ps 30: 5 but his favor lasts a *l;*
Isa 39: 8 will be peace and security in my *l."*
Jer 22: 30 a man who will not prosper in his *l,*
Lk 16: 25 in your *l* you received your good

LIFT (LIFTED LIFTING LIFTS UPLIFTED)

Ge 13: 14 *L* up your eyes from where you are
21: 18 *L* the boy up and take him
40: 13 days Pharaoh will *l* up your head
40: 19 Within three days Pharaoh will *l*
41: 44 your word no one will *l* hand
Ex 40: 37 the cloud did not *l,* they did not set
Dt 28: 32 after day, powerless to *l* a hand.
32: 40 I *l* my hand to heaven and declare:
1Sa 6: 5 Perhaps he will *l* his hand from you
24: 6 or *l* my hand against him;
24: 10 'I will not *l* my hand
2Sa 1: 14 were you not afraid to *l* your hand
2Sa 18: 12 I would not *l* my hand
2Ki 6: 7 "*L* it out," he said.
Ezr 9: 6 disgraced to *l* up my face to you,
Job 10: 15 I am innocent, I cannot *l* my head,
11: 15 then you will *l* up your face
22: 26 and will *l* up your face to God.
22: 29 low and you say, '*L* them up!'
Ps 9: 13 *l* me up from the gates of death,
10: 12 Arise, LORD! *L* up your hand,
20: 5 will *l* up our banners in the name
24: 4 who does not *l* up his soul
24: 7 *L* up your heads, O you gates;
24: 9 *L* up your heads, O you gates;
24: 9 *l* them up, you ancient doors,
25: 1 To you, O LORD, I *l* up my soul;
28: 2 as I *l* up my hands
63: 4 in your name I will *l* up my hands.
75: 4 wicked, 'Do not *l* up your horns.
75: 5 Do not *l* your horns against heaven
76: 5 can *l* his hands.
86: 4 I *l* up my soul.
91: 12 they will *l* you up in their hands,
110: 7 therefore he will *l* up his head.
116: 13 I will *l* up the cup of salvation
121: 1 I *l* up my eyes to the hills—
123: 1 I *l* up my eyes to you,
134: 2 *L* up your hands in the sanctuary
142: 1 I *l* up my voice to the LORD
143: 8 for to you I *l* up my soul.
Isa 10: 24 and *l* up a club against you,
40: 9 *l* it up, do not be afraid;
40: 9 *l* up your voice with a shout,
40: 26 *L* your eyes and look
46: 7 They *l* it to their shoulders
47: 2 *L* up your skirts, bare your legs,
49: 18 *L* up your eyes and look around;
49: 22 I will *l* up my banner to the peoples
51: 6 *L* up your eyes to the heavens,
52: 8 Your watchmen *l* up their voices;
60: 4 *L* up your eyes and look about you:
Jer 13: 20 *L* up your eyes and see
25: 30 he will *l* his voice from his holy
38: 10 and *l* Jeremiah the prophet out
50: 2 *l* up a banner and proclaim it;
51: 12 *L* up a banner against the walls
51: 27 "*L* up a banner in the land!
La 2: 19 *L* up your hands to him
3: 41 Let us *l* up our hearts and our
Da 6: 23 and gave orders to *l* Daniel out
Am 5: 2 with no one to *l* her up."
Na 3: 5 "I will *l* your skirts over your face.
Mt 4: 6 they will *l* you up in their hands,
12: 11 you not take hold of it and *l* it out?
23: 4 willing to *l* a finger to move them.
Lk 4: 11 they will *l* you up in their hands,
11: 46 you yourselves will not *l* one finger
21: 28 stand up and *l* up your heads,
1Ti 2: 8 everywhere to *l* up holy hands
Jas 4: 10 the Lord, and he will *l* you up.
1Pe 5: 6 that he may *l* you up in due time.

LIFTED (LIFT)

Ge 7: 17 the waters increased they *l* the ark
40: 20 He *l* up the heads of the chief
Ex 17: 16 "For hands were *l* up to the throne
40: 36 whenever the cloud *l*
40: 37 did not set out—until the day it *l.*
Lev 9: 22 *l* his hands toward the people
Nu 9: 17 Whenever the cloud *l*
9: 21 and when it *l* in the morning,
9: 21 whenever the cloud *l,* they set out.
9: 22 but when it *l,* they would set out.
10: 11 cloud *l* from above the tabernacle
12: 10 the cloud *l* from above the Tent,
Jdg 9: 48 which he *l* to his shoulders.
16: 3 He *l* them to his shoulders
1Sa 2: 1 in the LORD my horn is *l* high.
6: 3 know why his hand has not been *l*
2Sa 18: 28 up the men who *l* their hands
20: 21 has *l* up his hand against the king,
1Ki 16: 2 "I *l* you up from the dust
2Ki 4: 20 After the servant had *l* him up
19: 22 and *l* your eyes in pride?
Ezr 6: 11 he is to be *l* up and impaled on it.
Ne 8: 6 and all the people *l* their hands
Job 5: 11 those who mourn are *l* to safety.
Ps 24: 7 be *l* up, you ancient doors,
30: 1 for you *l* me out of the depths

Ps 40: 2 He *l* me out of the slimy pit,
41: 9 has *l* up his heel against me.
75: 10 of the righteous will be *l* up.
93: 3 The seas have *l* up, O LORD,
93: 3 the seas have *l* up their pounding
93: 3 the seas have *l* up their voice;
107: 25 that *l* high the waves.
107: 41 he *l* the needy out of their affliction
112: 9 his horn will be *l* high in honor.
118: 16 The LORD's right hand is *l* high;
Isa 10: 27 In that day their burden will be *l*
26: 11 O LORD, your hand is *l* high,
33: 10 now will I be *l* up.
37: 23 and *l* your eyes in pride?
52: 13 *l* up and highly exalted.
63: 9 he *l* them up and carried them
Jer 38: 13 and *l* him out of the cistern.
Eze 3: 12 Then the Spirit *l* me up,
3: 14 The Spirit then *l* me up
8: 3 The Spirit *l* me up between earth
11: 1 Then the Spirit *l* me up
11: 24 The Spirit *l* me up and brought me
43: 5 Then the Spirit *l* me up
Da 6: 23 when Daniel was *l* from the den,
7: 4 and it was *l* from the ground
12: 7 *l* his right hand and his left hand
Hos 11: 4 I *l* the yoke from their neck
Am 5: 26 You have *l* up the shrine
Mic 5: 9 Your hand will be *l* up in triumph
Hab 3: 10 and *l* its waves on high.
Zec 1: 21 of the nations who *l* up their horns
5: 9 and they *l* up the basket
Mt 11: 23 will you be *l* up to the skies?
Mk 9: 27 by the hand and *l* him to his feet,
Lk 1: 52 but has *l* up the humble.
10: 15 will you be *l* up to the skies?
24: 50 he *l* up his hands and blessed them.
Jn 3: 14 Moses *l* up the snake in the desert,
3: 14 so the Son of Man must be *l* up,
8: 28 "When you have *l* up the Son
12: 32 when I am *l* up from the earth,
12: 34 'The Son of Man must be *l* up'?
13: 18 shares my bread has *l* up his heel
19: 29 a stalk of the hyssop plant, and *l* it
Ac 7: 43 You have *l* up the shrine of Moloch

LIFTING (LIFT)

Ps 141: 2 may the *l* up of my hands be like
Eze 31: 10 *l* its top above the thick foliage,
31: 14 *l* their tops above the thick foliage.

LIFTS (LIFT)

1Sa 2: 8 and *l* the needy from the ash heap;
Ezr 6: 12 or people who *l* a hand
Ps 3: 3 Glorious One, who *l* up my head.
46: 6 he *l* his voice, the earth melts.
113: 7 and *l* the needy from the ash heap;
145: 14 and *l* up all who are bowed down.
146: 8 LORD *l* up those who are bowed
Isa 5: 26 He *l* up a banner for the distant
10: 15 were to wield him who *l* it up,

LIGAMENT (LIGAMENTS)

Eph 4: 16 held together by every supporting *l*

LIGAMENTS (LIGAMENT)

Col 2: 19 held together by its *l* and sinews,

LIGHT (ENLIGHTEN ENLIGHTENED LIGHTED LIGHTEN LIGHTENED LIGHTER LIGHTING LIGHTS LIT SUNLIGHT)

Ge 1: 3 "Let there be *l*," and there was *l*.
1: 4 God saw that the *l* was good,
1: 4 separated the *l* from the darkness.
1: 5 God called the *l* "day"
1: 15 of the sky to give *l* on the earth."
1: 16 and the lesser *l* to govern the night.
1: 16 the greater *l* to govern the day
1: 17 of the sky to give *l* on the earth,
1: 18 and to separate *l* from darkness.
Ex 10: 23 Yet all the Israelites had *l*
13: 21 in a pillar of fire to give them *l*,
14: 20 darkness to the one side and *l*
25: 6 acacia wood; olive oil for the *l*;
25: 37 it so that they *l* the space in front
27: 20 oil of pressed olives for the *l*
35: 3 Do not *l* a fire in any
Ex 35: 8 acacia wood; olive oil for the *l*;
35: 14 and oil for the *l*; the altar of incense
35: 14 is for *l* with its accessories,
35: 28 for the *l* and for the anointing oil
39: 37 and the oil for the *l*; the gold altar,
Lev 24: 2 oil of pressed olives for the *l*
Nu 4: 9 cover the lampstand that is for *l*,
4: 16 is to have charge of the oil for the *l*,
8: 2 they are to *l* the area in front
Dt 25: 13 in your bag—one heavy, one *l*.
1Sa 29: 10 in the morning as soon as it is *l*."
2Sa 22: 29 LORD turns my darkness into *l*.
23: 4 he is like the *l* of morning at sunrise
1Ki 3: 21 at him closely in the morning *l*,
18: 25 of your god, but do not *l* the fire."
2Ch 13: 11 *l* the lamps on the gold lampstand
Ezr 9: 8 and so our God gives *l* to our eyes
Ne 4: 21 from the first *l* of dawn
9: 12 a pillar of fire to give them *l*
Job 3: 4 may no *l* shine upon it.
3: 5 may blackness overwhelm its *l*.
3: 16 like an infant who never saw the *l*
3: 20 "Why is *l* given to those in misery,
9: 7 he seals off the *l* of the stars.
10: 22 where even the *l* is like darkness."
12: 22 and brings deep shadows into the *l*.
12: 25 They grope in darkness with no *l*;
17: 12 of darkness they say, '*L* is near.'
18: 6 The *l* in his tent becomes dark;
18: 18 He is driven from *l* into darkness
22: 28 and *l* will shine on your ways.
24: 13 are those who rebel against the *l*,
24: 16 they want nothing to do with the *l*.
25: 3 Upon whom does his *l* not rise?
26: 10 for a boundary between *l*
28: 11 and brings hidden things to *l*.
29: 3 by his *l* I walked through darkness!
29: 24 the *l* of my face was precious
30: 26 looked for *l*, then came darkness.
33: 28 and I will live to enjoy the *l*.'
33: 30 that the *l* of life may shine on him.
38: 15 The wicked are denied their *l*,
38: 19 "What is the way to the abode of *l*?
41: 18 His sneezing throws out flashes of *l*
Ps 4: 6 Let the *l* of your face shine upon us
13: 3 Give *l* to my eyes, or I will sleep
18: 28 my God turns my darkness into *l*.
19: 8 giving *l* to the eyes.
27: 1 LORD is my *l* and my salvation—
36: 9 in your *l* we see *l*.
38: 10 even the *l* has gone from my eyes.
43: 3 Send forth your *l* and your truth,
44: 3 *l* of your face, for you loved them.
49: 19 who will never see the *l* ⌞of life⌟.
56: 13 God in the *l* of life.
76: 4 You are resplendent with *l*,
78: 14 and with *l* from the fire all night.
89: 15 who walk in the *l* of your presence,
90: 8 in the *l* of your presence.
97: 11 *L* is shed upon the righteous
104: 2 He wraps himself in *l*
105: 39 and a fire to give *l* at night.
112: 4 Even in darkness *l* dawns
118: 27 and he has made his *l* shine upon us
119:105 and a *l* for my path.
119:130 The entrance of your words gives *l*;
139: 11 and the *l* become night around me,
139: 12 for darkness is as *l* to you.
Pr 4: 18 till the full *l* of day.
6: 23 this teaching is a *l*,
13: 9 *l* of the righteous shines brightly,
Ecc 2: 13 just as *l* is better than darkness.
11: 7 *L* is sweet,
12: 2 before the sun and the *l*
Isa 2: 5 let us walk in the *l* of the LORD.
5: 20 and *l* for darkness,
5: 20 who put darkness for *l*
5: 30 the *l* will be darkened by the clouds
8: 20 to this word, they have no *l*
9: 2 a *l* has dawned.
9: 2 have seen a great *l*;
10: 17 The *L* of Israel will become a fire,
13: 10 and the moon will not give its *l*.
13: 10 will not show their *l*.
30: 26 like the *l* of seven full days,
42: 6 and a *l* for the Gentiles,
42: 16 the darkness into *l* before them
45: 7 I form the *l* and create darkness,
Isa 49: 6 also make you a *l* for the Gentiles,
50: 10 who has no *l*,
50: 11 But now, all you who *l* fires
50: 11 go, walk in the *l* of your fires
51: 4 my justice will become a *l*
53: 11 he will see the *l* ⌞of life⌟
57: 6 In the *l* of these things, should I
58: 8 Then your *l* will break forth like
58: 10 then your *l* will rise in the darkness
59: 9 We look for *l*, but all is darkness;
60: 1 "Arise, shine, for your *l* has come,
60: 3 Nations will come to your *l*,
60: 19 The sun will no more be your *l*
60: 19 LORD will be your everlasting *l*,
60: 20 LORD will be your everlasting *l*,
Jer 4: 23 and their *l* was gone.
7: 18 gather wood, the fathers *l* the fire,
13: 16 You hope for *l*,
25: 10 of millstones and the *l* of the lamp.
La 3: 2 walk in darkness rather than *l*;
Eze 1: 4 and surrounded by brilliant *l*.
1: 27 and brilliant *l* surrounded him.
32: 7 and the moon will not give its *l*.
Da 2: 22 and *l* dwells with him.
6: 19 At the first *l* of dawn, the king got
Am 5: 18 That day will be darkness, not *l*.
5: 20 of the LORD be darkness, not *l*—
Mic 2: 1 At morning's *l* they carry it out
7: 8 the LORD will be my *l*.
7: 9 He will bring me out into the *l*;
Zec 14: 6 On that day there will be no *l*,
14: 7 evening comes, there will be *l*.
Mal 1: 10 so that you would not *l* useless fires
Mt 4: 16 a *l* has dawned."
4: 16 have seen a great *l*;
5: 14 "You are the *l* of the world.
5: 15 Neither do people *l* a lamp
5: 15 it gives *l* to everyone in the house.
5: 16 let your *l* shine before men,
6: 22 your whole body will be full of *l*.
6: 23 If then the *l* within you is darkness,
11: 30 yoke is easy and my burden is *l*."
17: 2 his clothes became as white as the *l*
24: 29 and the moon will not give its *l*;
Mk 13: 24 and the moon will not give its *l*;
Lk 2: 32 a *l* for revelation to the Gentiles
8: 16 those who come in can see the *l*.
11: 33 those who come in may see the *l*.
11: 34 your whole body also is full of *l*.
11: 35 that the *l* within you is not
11: 36 if your whole body is full of *l*,
11: 36 when the *l* of a lamp shines on you.
15: 8 Does she not *l* a lamp, sweep
16: 8 kind than are the people of the *l*.
Jn 1: 4 and that life was the *l* of men.
1: 5 The *l* shines in the darkness,
1: 7 witness to testify concerning that *l*,
1: 8 he came only as a witness to the *l*.
1: 8 himself was not the *l*; he came only
1: 9 The true *l* that gives *l*
3: 19 but men loved darkness instead of *l*
3: 19 *L* has come into the world,
3: 20 Everyone who does evil hates the *l*,
3: 20 and will not come into the *l*
3: 21 lives by the truth comes into the *l*,
5: 35 was a lamp that burned and gave *l*,
5: 35 you chose for a time to enjoy his *l*.
8: 12 but will have the *l* of life."
8: 12 he said, "I am the *l* of the world.
9: 5 in the world, I am the *l* of the world
11: 9 for he sees by this world's *l*.
11: 10 that he stumbles, for he has no *l*."
12: 35 Walk while you have the *l*,
12: 35 going to have the *l* just a little
12: 36 so that you may become sons of *l*."
12: 36 trust in the *l* while you have it,
12: 46 I have come into the world as a *l*,
Ac 9: 3 suddenly a *l* from heaven flashed
12: 7 of the Lord appeared and a *l* shone
13: 11 unable to see the *l* of the sun."
13: 47 " 'I have made you a *l*
22: 6 suddenly a bright *l*
22: 9 My companions saw the *l*,
22: 11 brilliance of the *l* had blinded me.
26: 13 I saw a *l* from heaven, brighter
26: 18 and turn them from darkness to *l*,
26: 23 would proclaim *l* to his own people
Ro 2: 19 a *l* for those who are in the dark,

Ro 13: 12 darkness and put on the armor of *l*.
1Co 3: 13 because the Day will bring it to *l*.
4: 5 He will bring to *l* what is hidden
2Co 4: 4 so that they cannot see the *l*
4: 6 made his *l* shine in our hearts
4: 6 to give us the *l* of the knowledge
4: 6 "Let *l* shine out of darkness,"
4: 17 For our *l* and momentary troubles
6: 14 Or what fellowship can *l* have
11: 14 masquerades as an angel of *l*.
Eph 5: 8 as children of *l* (for the fruit
5: 8 but now you are *l* in the Lord.
5: 9 of the *l* consists in all goodness,
5: 13 exposed by the *l* becomes visible,
5: 14 for it is *l* that makes everything
Col 1: 12 of the saints in the kingdom of *l*.
1Th 5: 5 You are all sons of the *l*
1Ti 6: 16 and who lives in unapproachable *l*,
2Ti 1: 10 immortality to *l* through the gospel
Tit 1: 3 word to *l* through the preaching
Heb 10: 32 days after you had received the *l*,
12: 5 do not make *l* of the Lord's
1Pe 2: 9 of darkness into his wonderful *l*.
2Pe 1: 19 as to a *l* shining in a dark place,
1Jn 1: 5 God is *l*; in him there is no
1: 7 But if we walk in the *l*,
1: 7 as he is in the *l*, we have fellowship
2: 8 and the true *l* is already shining.
2: 9 Anyone who claims to be in the *l*
2: 10 loves his brother lives in the *l*,
Rev 8: 12 A third of the day was without *l*,
18: 23 The *l* of a lamp
21: 23 for the glory of God gives it *l*,
21: 24 The nations will walk by its *l*,
22: 5 for the Lord God will give them *l*.
22: 5 the *l* of a lamp or the *l* of the sun,

LIGHTED (LIGHT)

Lk 11: 36 of it dark, it will be completely *l*,

LIGHTEN (LIGHT)

1Ki 12: 4 but now *l* the harsh labor
12: 9 '*L* the yoke your father put on us'?"
2Ch 10: 4 but now *l* the harsh labor
10: 9 '*L* the yoke your father put on us'?"
Jnh 1: 5 the cargo into the sea to *l* the ship.

LIGHTENED (LIGHT)

Ac 27: 38 they *l* the ship by throwing

LIGHTER (LIGHT)

Ex 18: 22 That will make your load *l*,
1Ki 12: 10 but make our yoke *l*'— tell them,
2Ch 10: 10 but make our yoke *l*'— tell them,

LIGHTING (LIGHT)

Mt 3: 16 God descending like a dove and *l*

LIGHTNING

Ex 9: 23 and *l* flashed down to the ground.
9: 24 hail fell and *l* flashed back
19: 16 third day there was thunder and *l*,
20: 18 and *l* and heard the trumpet
2Sa 22: 13 bolts of *l* blazed forth.
22: 15 bolts of *l* and routed them.
Job 36: 30 See how he scatters his *l* about him,
36: 32 He fills his hands with *l*
37: 3 He unleashes his *l*
37: 11 he scatters his *l* through them.
37: 15 and makes his *l* flash?
38: 24 to the place where the *l* is dispersed
38: 35 Do you send the *l* bolts
Ps 18: 12 with hailstones and bolts of *l*.
18: 14 great bolts of *l* and routed them.
29: 7 with flashes of *l*.
77: 18 your *l* lit up the world;
78: 48 their livestock to bolts of *l*.
97: 4 His *l* lights up the world;
105: 32 with *l* throughout their land;
135: 7 he sends *l* with the rain
144: 6 Send forth *l* and scatter
148: 8 *l* and hail, snow and clouds,
Jer 10: 13 He sends *l* with the rain
51: 16 He sends *l* with the rain
Eze 1: 4 an immense cloud with flashing *l*
1: 13 it was bright, and *l* flashed out of it.
1: 14 back and forth like flashes of *l*.
21: 10 polished, and flashing like *l*!
Eze 21: 15 Oh! It is made to flash like *l*,
21: 28 and to flash like *l*!
Da 10: 6 his face like *l*, his eyes like flaming
Hos 6: 5 my judgments flashed like *l*
Na 2: 4 they dart about like *l*.
Hab 3: 11 at the *l* of your flashing spear.
Zec 9: 14 his arrow will flash like *l*.
Mt 24: 27 For as the *l* comes from the east
28: 3 His appearance was like *l*,
Lk 9: 29 became as bright as a flash of *l*.
10: 18 "I saw Satan fall like *l* from heaven.
17: 24 of Man in his day will be like the *l*,
24: 4 in clothes that gleamed like *l* stood
Rev 4: 5 From the throne came flashes of *l*,
8: 5 flashes of *l* and an earthquake.
11: 19 And there came flashes of *l*,
16: 18 Then there came flashes of *l*,

LIGHTS (LIGHT)

Ge 1: 14 "Let there be *l* in the expanse
1: 15 and let them be *l* in the expanse
1: 16 made two great *l*— the greater
Ex 30: 8 when he *l* the lamps at twilight
Ps 97: 4 His lightning *l* up the world;
136: 7 who made the great *l*—
Eze 32: 8 All the shining *l* in the heavens
Zec 4: 2 a bowl at the top and seven *l* on it,
4: 2 with seven channels to the *l*.
Lk 8: 16 No one *l* a lamp and hides it in a jar
11: 33 "No one *l* a lamp and puts it
17: 24 and *l* up the sky from one end
Ac 16: 29 are all here!" The jailer called for *l*,
Jas 1: 17 from the Father of the heavenly *l*,

LIKE-MINDED (MIND)

Php 2: 2 make my joy complete by being *l*,

LIKENESS

Ge 1: 26 man in our image, in our *l*,
5: 1 he made him in the *l* of God.
5: 3 son in his own *l*, in his own image;
Ps 17: 15 I will be satisfied with seeing your *l*
Isa 52: 14 his form marred beyond human *l*—
Eze 1: 28 the appearance of the *l* of the glory
10: 1 I saw the *l* of a throne of sapphire
Ro 8: 3 Son in the *l* of sinful man
8: 29 to be conformed to the *l* of his Son,
1Co 15: 49 as we have borne the *l*
15: 49 so shall we bear the *l* of the man
2Co 3: 18 his *l* with ever-increasing glory,
Php 2: 7 being made in human *l*.
Jas 3: 9 who have been made in God's *l*.

LIKHI

1Ch 7: 19 Ahian, Shechem, *L* and Aniam.

LILIES (LILY)

1Ki 7: 19 in the portico were in the shape of *l*
7: 22 on top were in the shape of *l*.
SS 2: 16 he browses among the *l*.
4: 5 that browse among the *l*.
5: 13 His lips are like *l*
6: 2 and to gather *l*.
6: 3 he browses among the *l*.
7: 2 encircled by *l*.
Mt 6: 28 See how the *l* of the field grow.
Lk 12: 27 "Consider how the *l* grow.

LILY (LILIES)

1Ki 7: 26 the rim of a cup, like a *l* blossom.
2Ch 4: 5 the rim of a cup, like a *l* blossom.
SS 2: 1 a *l* of the valleys.
2: 2 Like a *l* among thorns
Hos 14: 5 he will blossom like a *l*.

LIMB (LIMBS)

Jdg 19: 29 and cut up his concubine, *l* by *l*,

LIMBER

Ge 49: 24 his strong arms stayed *l*,

LIMBS (LIMB)

Job 18: 13 death's firstborn devours his *l*.
40: 18 his *l* like rods of iron.
41: 12 "I will not fail to speak of his *l*,

LIME

Isa 33: 12 The peoples will be burned as if to *l*
Am 2: 1 Because he burned, as if to *l*,

LIMIT (LIMITS)

Ezr 7: 22 of olive oil, and salt without *l*.
Job 15: 8 Do you *l* wisdom to yourself?
Ps 119: 96 To all perfection I see a *l*;
147: 5 his understanding has no *l*.
Isa 5: 14 and opens its mouth without *l*;
Jer 5: 28 Their evil deeds have no *l*;
Jn 3: 34 him God gives the Spirit without *l*.
1Th 2: 16 always heap up their sins to the *l*.

LIMITS (LIMIT)

Ex 19: 12 Put *l* for the people
19: 23 'Put *l* around the mountain
Nu 35: 26 outside the *l* of the city of refuge
Jos 17: 18 and its farthest *l* will be yours;
Job 11: 7 Can you probe the *l*
14: 5 and have set *l* he cannot exceed.
38: 10 when I fixed *l* for it
Ps 73: 7 of their minds know no *l*.
2Co 10: 13 will not boast beyond proper *l*,
10: 15 go beyond our *l* by boasting

LIMP (LIMPING)

Pr 26: 7 Like a lame man's legs that hang *l*
Isa 13: 7 Because of this, all hands will go *l*,
Jer 6: 24 and our hands hang *l*.
47: 3 their hands will hang *l*.
50: 43 and his hands hang *l*.
Eze 7: 17 hand will go *l*, and every knee
21: 7 heart will melt and every hand go *l*;
30: 25 but the arms of Pharaoh will fall *l*.
Zep 3: 16 do not let your hands hang *l*.

LIMPING (LIMP)

Ge 32: 31 and he was *l* because of his hip.

LINE (LINED LINES)

Ge 5: 1 is the written account of Adam's *l*.
19: 32 and preserve our family *l*
19: 34 him so we can preserve our family *l*
Nu 26: 11 *l* of Korah, however, did not die
34: 7 run a *l* from the Great Sea
34: 10 run a *l* from Hazar Enan
Dt 25: 9 not build up his brother's family *l*."
25: 10 That man's *l* shall be known
Ru 4: 4 except you, and I am next in *l*."
4: 18 This, then, is the family *l* of Perez:
1Sa 2: 31 not be an old man in your family *l*
2: 32 in your family *l* there will never be
2: 36 left in your family *l* will come
4: 12 a Benjamite ran from the battle *l*
4: 16 "I have just come from the battle *l*;
17: 2 and drew up their battle *l*
17: 8 "Why do you come out and *l* up
17: 48 toward the battle *l* to meet him.
2Sa 11: 15 "Put Uriah in the front *l*
1Ki 7: 15 and twelve cubits around, by *l*.
7: 23 It took a *l* of thirty cubits
11: 14 from the royal *l* of Edom.
2Ki 21: 13 Jerusalem the measuring *l* used
21: 13 the plumb *l* used against the house
2Ch 4: 2 It took a *l* of thirty cubits
13: 3 and Jeroboam drew up a battle *l*
Ezr 2: 6 (through the *l* of Jeshua
2: 40 and Kadmiel (through the *l*
Ne 7: 11 (through the *l* of Jeshua
7: 43 (through Kadmiel through the *l*
Job 38: 5 Who stretched a measuring *l*
Ps 89: 4 'I will establish your *l* forever
89: 29 I will establish his *l* forever,
89: 36 that his *l* will continue forever
Isa 28: 17 I will make justice the measuring *l*
28: 17 and righteousness the plumb *l*;
34: 11 and the plumb *l* of desolation.
34: 11 the measuring *l* of chaos
44: 13 The carpenter measures with a *l*
48: 1 and come from the *l* of Judah,
Jer 31: 39 The measuring *l* will stretch
33: 15 Branch sprout from David's *l*;
La 2: 8 He stretched out a measuring *l*
Eze 47: 3 with a measuring *l* in his hand,
Da 11: 7 "One from her family *l* will arise
Joel 2: 7 They all march in *l*,
Am 7: 7 with a plumb *l* in his hand.
7: 8 Amos?" "A plumb *l*," I replied.
7: 8 I am setting a plumb *l*

Zec 1:16 measuring *l* will be stretched out
2: 1 with a measuring *l* in his hand!
4:10 rejoice when they see the plumb *l*
Mt 17:27 go to the lake and throw out your *l*.
Lk 2: 4 to the house and *l* of David.
Gal 2:14 in *l* with the truth of the gospel,

LINED (LINE)

1Ki 6:15 He *l* its interior walls

LINEN (LINENS)

Ge 41:42 He dressed him in robes of fine *l*
Ex 25: 4 purple and scarlet yarn and fine *l*;
26: 1 with ten curtains of finely twisted *l*
26:31 scarlet yarn and finely twisted *l*,
26:36 scarlet yarn and finely twisted *l*—
27: 9 to have curtains of finely twisted *l*,
27:16 scarlet yarn and finely twisted *l*—
27:18 of finely twisted *l* five cubits high,
28: 5 purple and scarlet yarn, and fine *l*.
28: 6 and of finely twisted *l*— the work
28: 8 and with finely twisted *l*.
28:15 scarlet yarn, and of finely twisted *l*.
28:39 and make the turban of fine *l*.
28:39 "Weave the tunic of fine *l*
28:42 "Make *l* undergarments
35: 6 purple and scarlet yarn and fine *l*;
35:23 purple or scarlet yarn or fine *l*,
35:25 blue, purple or scarlet yarn or fine *l*
35:35 purple and scarlet yarn and fine *l*,
36: 8 with ten curtains of finely twisted *l*
36:35 scarlet yarn and finely twisted *l*,
36:37 scarlet yarn and finely twisted *l*—
38: 9 and had curtains of finely twisted *l*,
38:16 were of finely twisted *l*.
38:18 scarlet yarn and finely twisted *l*—
38:23 purple and scarlet yarn and fine *l*.)
39: 2 scarlet yarn, and of finely twisted *l*.
39: 3 purple and scarlet yarn and fine *l*—
39: 5 and with finely twisted *l*,
39: 8 scarlet yarn, and of finely twisted *l*.
39:24 finely twisted *l* around the hem
39:27 they made tunics of fine *l*—
39:28 a weaver—and the turban of fine *l*,
39:28 the *l* headbands
39:28 undergarments of finely twisted *l*
39:29 The sash was of finely twisted *l*
Lev 6:10 shall then put on his *l* clothes,
6:10 with *l* undergarments next
13:47 mildew—any woolen or *l* clothing,
13:48 or knitted material of *l* or wool,
13:52 or knitted material of wool or *l*,
13:59 by mildew in woolen or *l* clothing,
16: 4 He is to put on the sacred *l* tunic,
16: 4 around him and put on the *l* turban
16: 4 he is to tie the *l* sash around him
16: 4 with *l* undergarments next
16:23 and take off the *l* garments he put
16:32 is to put on the sacred *l* garments
Dt 22:11 of wool and *l* woven together.
Jdg 14:12 I will give you thirty *l* garments
14:13 you must give me thirty *l* garments
1Sa 2:18 LORD—a boy wearing a *l* ephod.
22:18 men who wore the *l* ephod.
2Sa 6:14 David, wearing a *l* ephod,
1Ch 4:21 the clans of the *l* workers
15:27 David also wore a *l* ephod.
15:27 was clothed in a robe of fine *l*,
2Ch 2:14 blue and crimson yarn and fine *l*.
3:14 purple and crimson yarn and fine *l*,
5:12 in fine *l* and playing cymbals,
Est 1: 6 fastened with cords of white *l*
1: 6 hangings of white and blue *l*,
8:15 and a purple robe of fine *l*.
Pr 31:22 she is clothed in fine *l* and purple.
31:24 She makes *l* garments
Isa 3:23 and the *l* garments and tiaras
19: 9 the weavers of fine *l* will lose hope.
Jer 13: 1 and buy a *l* belt and put it
Eze 9: 2 clothed in *l* who had a writing kit
9: 3 clothed in *l* who had the writing kit
9:11 the man in *l* with the writing kit
10: 2 said to the man clothed in *l*,
10: 6 LORD commanded the man in *l*,
10: 7 put it into the hands of the man in *l*
16:10 you in fine *l* and covered you
16:13 your clothes were of fine *l*
27: 7 Fine embroidered *l*
Eze 27:16 fabric, embroidered work, fine *l*,
40: 3 in the gateway with a *l* cord
44:17 they are to wear *l* clothes;
44:18 They are to wear *l* turbans
44:18 and *l* undergarments around their
Da 10: 5 before me was a man dressed in *l*,
12: 6 of them said to the man clothed in *l*
12: 7 The man clothed in *l*, who was
Hos 2: 5 my wool and my *l*, my oil
2: 9 I will take back my wool and my *l*,
Mt 27:59 wrapped it in a clean *l* cloth,
Mk 14:51 wearing nothing but a *l* garment,
15:46 So Joseph bought some *l* cloth,
15:46 down the body, wrapped it in the *l*,
Lk 16:19 fine *l* and lived in luxury every day.
23:53 wrapped it in *l* cloth and placed it
24:12 the strips of *l* lying by themselves,
Jn 11:44 and feet wrapped with strips of *l*,
19:40 with the spices, in strips of *l*.
20: 5 in at the strips of *l* lying there
20: 6 He saw the strips of *l* lying there,
20: 7 up by itself, separate from the *l*.
Rev 15: 6 shining *l* and wore golden sashes
18:12 precious stones and pearls; fine *l*,
18:16 dressed in fine *l*, purple and scarlet,
19: 8 Fine *l*, bright and clean,
19: 8 (Fine *l* stands for the righteous acts
19:14 white horses and dressed in fine *l*,

LINENS (LINEN)

Pr 7:16 bed with colored *l* from Egypt.

LINES (LINE)

Ge 10:32 according to their *l* of descent,
14: 8 drew up their battle *l* in the Valley
1Sa 17:21 drawing up their *l* facing each
17:22 ran to the battle *l* and greeted his
17:23 stepped out from his *l*
2Sa 10: 9 Joab saw that there were battle *l*
10:17 Arameans formed their battle *l*
23:16 broke through the Philistine *l*,
1Ch 11:18 broke through the Philistine *l*,
19:10 Joab saw that there were battle *l*
19:17 David formed his *l*
19:17 formed his battle *l* opposite them.
Ps 16: 6 The boundary *l* have fallen for me

LINGER (LINGERING)

Jdg 5:17 And Dan, why did he *l* by the ships
Pr 23:30 Those who *l* over wine,
Jer 51:50 leave and do not *l*!
Mic 5: 7 or *l* for mankind.
Hab 2: 3 Though it *l*, wait for it;

LINGERING (LINGER)

Dt 28:59 and severe and *l* illnesses.
2Ch 21:15 ill with a *l* disease of the bowels,

LINUS

2Ti 4:21 *L*, Claudia and all the brothers.

LION (LION'S LIONESS LIONESSES LIONS LIONS')

Ge 49: 9 Like a *l* he crouches and lies down,
Nu 23:24 they rouse themselves like a *l*
24: 9 Like a *l* they crouch and lie down,
Dt 33:20 Gad lives there like a *l*,
Jdg 14: 5 suddenly a young *l* came roaring
14: 6 power so that he tore the *l* apart
14:18 What is stronger than a *l*?"
1Sa 17:34 When a *l* or a bear came
17:36 Your servant has killed both the *l*
17:37 me from the paw of the *l*
2Sa 17:10 whose heart is like the heart of a *l*,
23:20 a pit on a snowy day and killed a *l*.
1Ki 10:19 with a *l* standing beside each
13:24 a *l* met him on the road
13:24 and the *l* standing beside it.
13:25 with the *l* standing beside the body,
13:26 LORD has given him over to the *l*,
13:28 The *l* had neither eaten the body
13:28 and the *l* standing beside it.
20:36 a *l* found him and killed him.
20:36 as you leave me a *l* will kill you."
1Ch 11:22 a pit on a snowy day and killed a *l*.
2Ch 9:18 with a *l* standing beside each
Job 4:11 The *l* perishes for lack of prey,
10:16 my head high, you stalk me like a *l*
Job 28: 8 and no *l* prowls there.
Ps 7: 2 or they will tear me like a *l*
10: 9 He lies in wait like a *l* in cover;
17:12 They are like a *l* hungry for prey,
17:12 like a great *l* crouching in cover.
91:13 You will tread upon the *l*
91:13 you will trample the great *l*
Pr 19:12 A king's rage is like the roar of a *l*,
20: 2 A king's wrath is like the roar of a *l*;
22:13 The sluggard says, "There is a *l*
26:13 The sluggard says, "There is a *l*
26:13 a fierce *l* roaming the streets!"
28: 1 but the righteous are as bold as a *l*.
28:15 Like a roaring *l* or a charging bear
30:30 a *l*, mighty among beasts,
Ecc 9: 4 a live dog is better off than a dead *l*
Isa 5:29 Their roar is like that of the *l*,
11: 6 and the *l* and the yearling together;
11: 7 and the *l* will eat straw like the ox.
15: 9 a *l* upon the fugitives of Moab
31: 4 a great *l* over his prey—
31: 4 "As a *l* growls,
35: 9 No *l* will be there,
38:13 but like a *l* he broke all my bones;
65:25 and the *l* will eat straw like the ox,
Jer 2:30 like a ravening *l*.
4: 7 A *l* has come out of his lair;
5: 6 Therefore a *l* from the forest will
12: 8 like a *l* in the forest.
25:38 Like a *l* he will leave his lair,
49:19 "Like a *l* coming up
50:44 Like a *l* coming up
51:38 they growl like *l* cubs.
La 3:10 like a *l* in hiding,
Eze 1:10 right side each had the face of a *l*,
10:14 the third the face of a *l*,
19: 3 and he became a strong *l*.
19: 5 and made him a strong *l*.
19: 6 for he was now a strong *l*.
22:25 her like a roaring *l* tearing its prey;
32: 2 You are like a *l* among the nations;
41:19 the face of a *l* toward the palm tree
Da 7: 4 "The first was like a *l*,
Hos 5:14 For I will be like a *l* to Ephraim,
5:14 like a great *l* to Judah.
11:10 he will roar like a *l*.
13: 7 So I will come upon them like a *l*,
13: 8 Like a *l* I will devour them;
Joel 1: 6 it has the teeth of a *l*,
Am 3: 4 Does a *l* roar in the thicket
3: 8 The *l* has roared—
5:19 as though a man fled from a *l*
Mic 5: 8 like a young *l* among flocks
5: 8 like a *l* among the beasts
Na 2:11 where the *l* and lioness went,
2:12 The *l* killed enough for his cubs
1Pe 5: 8 around like a roaring *l* looking
Rev 4: 7 The first living creature was like a *l*
5: 5 See, the *L* of the tribe of Judah,
10: 3 a loud shout like the roar of a *l*.
13: 2 and a mouth like that of a *l*.

LION'S (LION)

Ge 49: 9 You are a *l* cub, O Judah;
Dt 33:22 "Dan is a *l* cub,
Jdg 14: 8 aside to look at the *l* carcass.
14: 9 the honey from the *l* carcass.
Am 3:12 a shepherd saves from the *l* mouth
2Ti 4:17 I was delivered from the *l* mouth.

LIONESS (LION)

Ge 49: 9 like a *l*— who dares to rouse him?
Nu 23:24 The people rise like a *l*;
24: 9 like a *l*— who dares to rouse them?
Job 4:11 and the cubs of the *l* are scattered.
38:39 "Do you hunt the prey for the *l*
Eze 19: 2 " 'What a *l* was your mother
Joel 1: 6 the fangs of a *l*.
Na 2:11 where the lion and *l* went,

LIONESSES (LION)

Isa 30: 6 of lions and *l*,

LIONS (LION)

2Sa 1:23 they were stronger than *l*.
1Ki 7:29 Above and below the *l*
7:29 panels between the uprights were *l*,
7:36 *l* and palm trees on the surfaces

1Ki 10: 20 Twelve l stood on the six steps,
2Ki 17: 25 so he sent l among them
17: 26 He has sent l among them,
1Ch 12: 8 Their faces were the faces of l,
2Ch 9: 19 Twelve l stood on the six steps,
Job 4: 10 The l may roar and growl,
4: 10 of the great l are broken.
38: 39 and satisfy the hunger of the l
Ps 22: 13 Roaring l tearing their prey
22: 21 Rescue me from the mouth of the l;
34: 10 The l may grow weak and hungry,
35: 17 my precious life from these l.
57: 4 I am in the midst of l;
58: 6 O LORD, the fangs of the l!
104: 21 The l roar for their prey
Isa 5: 29 they roar like young l;
30: 6 of l and lionesses,
Jer 2: 15 L have roared;
50: 17 that l have chased away.
51: 38 Her people all roar like young l,
Eze 19: 2 She lay down among the young l
19: 2 mother among the l!
19: 6 He prowled among the l,
Da 6: 20 been able to rescue you from the l
6: 22 and he shut the mouths of the l.
6: 24 the l overpowered them
6: 27 Daniel from the power of the l.''
Na 2: 13 the sword will devour your young l
Zep 3: 3 Her officials are roaring l,
Zec 11: 3 Listen to the roar of the l;
Heb 11: 33 the mouths of l, quenched the fury
Rev 9: 17 horses resembled the heads of l,

LIONS' (LION)

SS 4: 8 from the l' dens
Da 6: 7 shall be thrown into the l' den.
6: 12 would be thrown into the l' den?''
6: 16 and threw him into the l' den.
6: 19 got up and hurried to the l' den.
6: 24 and thrown into the l' den,
Na 2: 11 Where now is the l' den,
Rev 9: 8 and their teeth were like l' teeth.

LIPS

Ex 6: 12 since I speak with faltering l?''
6: 30 ''Since I speak with faltering l,
13: 9 law of the LORD is to be on your l.
23: 13 do not let them be heard on your l.
Nu 30: 6 or after her l utter a rash promise
30: 12 came from her l will stand.
Dt 23: 23 Whatever your l utter you must be
1Sa 1: 13 and her l were moving
Job 6: 30 Is there any wickedness on my l?
8: 21 and your l with shouts of joy.
11: 5 that he would open his l
12: 20 He silences the l of trusted advisers
13: 6 listen to the plea of my l.
15: 6 your own l testify against you.
16: 5 from my l would bring you relief.
23: 12 from the commands of his l;
27: 4 my l will not speak wickedness,
32: 20 I must open my l and reply.
33: 3 my l sincerely speak what I know.
Ps 8: 2 From the l of children and infants
12: 2 their flattering l speak
12: 3 the LORD cut off all flattering l
12: 4 we own our l— who is our master
16: 4 or take up their names on my l.
17: 1 it does not rise from deceitful l.
17: 4 by the word of your l
21: 2 not withheld the request of his l.
31: 18 Let their lying l be silenced,
34: 1 his praise will always be on my l.
34: 13 and your l from speaking lies.
40: 9 I do not seal my l,
45: 2 and your l have been anointed
50: 16 or take my covenant on your l?
51: 15 O Lord, open my l,
59: 7 they spew out swords from their l,
59: 12 for the words of their l,
63: 3 my l will glorify you.
63: 5 with singing l my mouth will praise
66: 14 vows my l promised and my mouth
71: 23 My l will shout for joy
89: 34 or alter what my l have uttered.
106: 33 and rash words came from Moses' l
119: 13 With my l I recount
119:171 May my l overflow with praise,
Ps 120: 2 Save me, O LORD, from lying l
140: 3 the poison of vipers is on their l.
140: 9 with the trouble their l have caused
141: 3 keep watch over the door of my l.
Pr 4: 24 keep corrupt talk far from your l.
5: 2 your l may preserve knowledge.
5: 3 For the l of an adulteress drip
8: 6 I open my l to speak what is right.
8: 7 for my l detest wickedness.
10: 13 on the l of the discerning,
10: 18 who conceals his hatred has lying l,
10: 21 l of the righteous nourish many,
10: 32 l of the righteous know what is
12: 14 of his l a man is filled
12: 19 Truthful l endure forever,
12: 22 The LORD detests lying l,
13: 2 of his l a man enjoys good things,
13: 3 He who guards his l guards his soul
14: 3 but the l of the wise protect them.
14: 7 will not find knowledge on his l.
15: 7 The l of the wise spread knowledge
16: 10 The l of a king speak as an oracle,
16: 13 Kings take pleasure in honest l;
16: 23 and his l promote instruction.
16: 30 he who purses his l is bent on evil.
17: 4 A wicked man listens to evil l;
17: 7 Arrogant l are unsuited to a fool—
17: 7 how much worse lying l to a ruler!
18: 6 A fool's l bring him strife,
18: 7 and his l are a snare to his soul.
18: 20 from his l he is satisfied.
19: 1 than a fool whose l are perverse.
20: 15 l that speak knowledge are a rare
22: 18 have all of them ready on your l.
23: 16 when your l speak what is right.
24: 2 their l talk about making trouble.
24: 26 is like a kiss on the l.
24: 28 or use your l to deceive.
26: 23 are fervent l with an evil heart.
26: 24 man disguises himself with his l,
27: 2 someone else, and not your own l.
Ecc 10: 12 but a fool is consumed by his own l.
SS 4: 3 Your l are like a scarlet ribbon;
4: 11 Your l drop sweetness
5: 13 His l are like lilies
7: 9 flowing gently over l and teeth.
Isa 6: 5 For I am a man of unclean l,
6: 5 I live among a people of unclean l,
6: 7 ''See, this has touched your l;
11: 4 of his l he will slay the wicked.
28: 11 with foreign l and strange tongues
29: 13 and honor me with their l,
30: 27 his l are full of wrath,
57: 19 on the l of the mourners
59: 3 Your l have spoken lies,
Jer 7: 28 it has vanished from their l.
12: 2 You are always on their l
17: 16 What passes my l is open
Da 4: 31 still on his l when a voice came
10: 3 no meat or wine touched my l;
10: 16 looked like a man touched my l,
Hos 2: 17 of the Baals from her l;
8: 1 ''Put the trumpet to your l!
14: 2 that we may offer the fruit of our l.
Joel 1: 5 for it has been snatched from your l
Hab 3: 16 my l quivered at the sound;
Zep 3: 9 will I purify the l of the peoples,
Mal 2: 6 nothing false was found on his l.
2: 7 ''For the l of a priest ought
Mt 15: 8 These people honor me with their l
21: 16 '' 'From the l of children
Mk 7: 6 These people honor me with their l
Lk 4: 22 words that came from his l.
22: 71 We have heard it from his own l.''
Jn 19: 29 plant, and lifted it to Jesus' l.
Ac 15: 7 hear from my l the message
Ro 3: 13 ''The poison of vipers is on their l.''
1Co 14: 21 and through the l of foreigners
Col 3: 8 and filthy language from your l.
Heb 13: 15 the fruit of l that confess his name.
1Pe 3: 10 and his l from deceitful speech.

LIQUID

Ex 30: 23 shekels of l myrrh, half
Lev 11: 34 and any l that could be drunk

LIST (LISTED LISTING)

Nu 3: 40 more and make a l of their names.
Jos 17: 11 (the third in the l is Naphoth).
1Ch 11: 11 this is the l of David's mighty men:
25: 1 Here is the l of the men who
27: 1 This is the l of the Israelites—
Ezr 2: 2 The l of the men of the people
Ne 7: 7 The l of the men of Israel:
Ps 56: 8 l my tears on your scroll—
1Ti 5: 9 put on the l of widows
5: 11 do not put them on such a l.

LISTED (LIST)

Ge 25: 13 l in the order of their birth:
Nu 1: 18 twenty years old or more were l
1: 20 to serve in the army were l by name
1: 22 in the army were counted and l
1: 24 to serve in the army were l by name
1: 26 to serve in the army were l by name
1: 28 to serve in the army were l by name
1: 30 to serve in the army were l by name
1: 32 to serve in the army were l by name
1: 34 to serve in the army were l by name
1: 36 to serve in the army were l by name
1: 38 to serve in the army were l by name
1: 40 to serve in the army were l by name
1: 42 to serve in the army were l by name
3: 43 males a month old or more, l
11: 26 They were l among the elders,
26: 54 according to the number of those l.
1Ch 4: 38 men l above by name were leaders
4: 41 The men whose names were l came
5: 1 so he could not be l
5: 7 l according to their genealogical
6: 19 the clans of the Levites l according
7: 2 the descendants of Tola l
7: 5 as l in their genealogy, were 87,000
7: 7 Their genealogical record l 22,034
7: 9 genealogical record l the heads
7: 40 as l in their genealogy, was 26,000.
8: 28 chiefs as l in their genealogy,
9: 1 All Israel was l in the genealogies
9: 9 The people from Benjamin, as l
9: 34 chiefs as l in their genealogy,
2Ch 31: 18 of the whole community l
Ps 69: 28 and not be l with the righteous.
Eze 13: 9 or be l in the records of the house
48: 1 ''These are the tribes, l by name:

LISTEN (LISTENED LISTENING LISTENS)

Ge 4: 10 ''What have you done? L!
4: 23 ''Adah and Zillah, l to me;
21: 12 L to whatever Sarah tells you,
23: 6 replied to Abraham, ''Sir, l to us.
23: 8 then l to me and intercede
23: 11 ''L to me; I give you the field,
23: 13 Ephron in their hearing, ''L to me,
23: 15 Ephron answered Abraham, ''L
27: 8 l carefully and do what I tell you:
37: 6 He said to them, ''L
37: 9 ''L,'' he said, ''I had another dream,
42: 21 but we would not l; that's why this
42: 22 you wouldn't l! Now we must give
49: 2 ''Assemble and l, sons of Jacob;
49: 2 l to your father Israel.
Ex 3: 18 ''The elders of Israel will l to you.
4: 1 if they do not believe me or l to me
4: 9 do not believe these two signs or l
6: 9 but they did not l to him
6: 12 why would Pharaoh l to me,
6: 12 ''If the Israelites will not l to me,
6: 30 why would Pharaoh l to me?''
7: 4 in Egypt, he will not l to you.
7: 13 and he would not l to them,
7: 22 he would not l to Moses and Aaron
8: 15 would not l to Moses and Aaron,
8: 19 heart was hard and he would not l.
9: 12 he would not l to Moses and Aaron
11: 9 ''Pharaoh will refuse to l to you—
15: 26 ''If you l carefully to the voice
18: 19 L now to me and I will give you
20: 19 ''Speak to us yourself and we will l.
23: 21 to him and l to what he says.
23: 22 If you l carefully to what he says
Lev 26: 14 '' 'But if you will not l to me
26: 18 If after all this you will not l to me,
26: 21 toward me and refuse to l to me,
26: 27 spite of this you still do not l to me
Nu 12: 6 them stepped forward, he said, ''L

Nu 16: 8 Moses also said to Korah, "Now *l*,
20: 10 "*L*, you rebels, must we bring you
23: 18 "Arise, Balak, and *l*;
Dt 1: 43 So I told you, but you would not *l*.
3: 26 with me and would not *l* to me.
5: 27 We will *l* and obey."
5: 27 and *l* to all that the LORD our God
13: 3 you must not *l* to the words
13: 8 do not yield to him or *l* to him.
18: 14 The nations you will dispossess *l*
18: 15 You must *l* to him.
18: 19 If anyone does not *l*
21: 18 not *l* to them when they discipline
23: 5 the LORD your God would not *l*
27: 9 "Be silent, O Israel, and *l*!
30: 20 *l* to his voice, and hold fast to him.
31: 12 so they can *l* and learn
32: 1 *L*, O heavens, and I will speak;
Jos 3: 9 *l* to the words of the LORD your
8: 4 with these orders: "*L* carefully.
24: 10 But I would not *l* to Balaam,
Jdg 2: 17 Yet they would not *l* to their judges
5: 3 Hear this, you kings! *L*, you rulers!
7: 11 and *l* to what they are saying.
9: 7 so that God may *l* to you.
9: 7 "*L* to me, citizens of Shechem,
11: 17 but the king of Edom would not *l*.
19: 25 But the men would not *l* to him.
20: 13 But the Benjamites would not *l*
Ru 2: 8 to Ruth, "My daughter, *l* to me.
1Sa 2: 25 did not *l* to their father's rebuke,
8: 7 "*L* to all that the people are saying
8: 9 *l* to them; but warn them solemnly
8: 19 the people refused to *l* to Samuel.
8: 22 "*L* to them and give them a king."
15: 1 so *l* now to the message
22: 7 said to them, "*L*, men of Benjamin!
22: 12 Saul said, "*L* now, son of Ahitub."
24: 9 "Why do you *l* when men say,
26: 19 Now let my lord the king *l*
28: 22 Now please *l* to your servant
30: 24 Who will *l* to what you say?
2Sa 12: 18 to David but he would not *l* to us.
13: 14 But he refused to *l* to her,
13: 16 But he refused to *l* to her.
13: 28 Absalom ordered his men, "*L*!
20: 16 called from the city, "*L*! *L*!
20: 17 *L* to what your servant has to say."
1Ki 4: 34 came to *l* to Solomon's wisdom,
8: 52 may you *l* to them whenever they
12: 15 So the king did not *l* to the people,
12: 16 Israel saw that the king refused to *l*
20: 8 "Don't *l* to him or agree
2Ki 14: 11 Amaziah, however, would not *l*,
17: 14 But they would not *l* and were
17: 40 They would not *l*, however,
18: 31 "Do not *l* to Hezekiah.
18: 32 not death! "Do not *l* to Hezekiah,
19: 7 *L*! I am going to put such a spirit
19: 16 *l* to the words Sennacherib has sent
21: 9 But the people did not *l*.
1Ch 28: 2 "*L* to me, my brothers
2Ch 10: 15 So the king did not *l* to the people,
10: 16 Israel saw that the king refused to *l*
13: 4 "Jeroboam and all Israel, *l* to me!
15: 2 "*L* to me, Asa and all Judah
20: 15 "*L*, King Jehoshaphat
20: 20 Jehoshaphat stood and said, "*L*
24: 19 against them, they would not *l*.
25: 20 Amaziah, however, would not *l*,
28: 11 *l* to me! Send back your fellow
29: 5 on the east side and said: "*L* to me,
35: 22 He would not *l* to what Neco had
Ne 9: 17 They refused to *l* and failed
9: 29 stiff-necked and refused to *l*.
Job 13: 6 *l* to the plea of my lips.
13: 17 *L* carefully to my words;
15: 8 Do you *l* in on God's council?
15: 17 "*L* to me and I will explain to you;
21: 2 "*L* carefully to my words;
27: 9 Does God *l* to his cry
32: 10 "Therefore I say: *L* to me;
33: 1 "But now, Job, *l* to my words;
33: 31 "Pay attention, Job, and *l* to me;
33: 33 But if not, then *l* to me;
34: 2 *l* to me, you men of learning.
34: 10 *l* to me, you men of understanding.
34: 16 *l* to what I say.

Job 35: 13 God does not *l* to their empty plea;
35: 14 How much less, then, will he *l*
36: 10 He makes them *l* to correction
36: 12 But if they do not *l*,
37: 2 *L*! *L* to the roar of his voice,
37: 14 "*L* to this, Job;
42: 4 "You said, '*L* now, and I will
Ps 5: 2 *L* to my cry for help,
10: 17 you encourage them, and you *l*
17: 1 *l* to my cry.
34: 11 Come, my children, *l* to me;
39: 12 *l* to my cry for help;
45: 10 *L*, O daughter, consider
49: 1 *l*, all who live in this world,
54: 2 *l* to the words of my mouth.
55: 1 *L* to my prayer, O God,
61: 1 *l* to my prayer.
66: 16 Come and *l*, all you who fear God;
78: 1 *l* to the words of my mouth.
81: 8 if you would but *l* to me, O Israel!
81: 11 "But my people would not *l* to me;
81: 13 "If my people would but *l* to me,
84: 8 *l* to me, O God of Jacob.
85: 8 I will *l* to what God the LORD will
86: 6 *l* to my cry for mercy.
142: 6 *L* to my cry,
143: 1 *l* to my cry for mercy;
Pr 1: 5 let the wise *l* and add
1: 8 *L*, my son, to your father's
4: 1 *L*, my sons, to a father's instruction
4: 10 *L*, my son, accept what I say,
4: 20 *l* closely to my words.
5: 1 *l* well to my words of insight,
5: 7 Now then, my sons, *l* to me;
5: 13 or *l* to my instructors.
7: 24 Now then, my sons, *l* to me;
8: 6 *L*, for I have worthy things to say;
8: 32 "Now then, my sons, *l* to me;
8: 33 *L* to my instruction and be wise;
13: 1 but a mocker does not *l* to rebuke.
19: 20 *L* to advice and accept instruction,
22: 17 and *l* to the sayings of the wise;
23: 19 *L*, my son, and be wise,
23: 22 *L* to your father, who gave you life,
Ecc 5: 1 Go near to *l* rather
7: 5 than to *l* to the song of fools.
SS 2: 8 *L*! My lover!
5: 2 *L*! My lover is knocking.
Isa 1: 2 Hear, O heavens! *L*, O earth!
1: 10 *l* to the law of our God,
1: 15 I will not *l*.
8: 9 *L*, all you distant lands.
10: 30 *L*, O Laishah!
13: 4 *L*, a noise on the mountains,
13: 4 *L*, an uproar among the kingdoms,
28: 12 but they would not *l*.
28: 23 *L* and hear my voice;
30: 9 children unwilling to *l*
32: 3 the ears of those who hear will *l*.
32: 9 rise up and *l* to me;
34: 1 Come near, you nations, and *l*;
36: 16 "Do not *l* to Hezekiah.
37: 7 *L*! I am going to put a spirit in him
37: 17 *l* to all the words Sennacherib has
42: 23 Which of you will *l* to this
44: 1 "But now *l*, O Jacob, my servant,
46: 3 "*L* to me, O house of Jacob,
46: 12 *L* to me, you stubborn-hearted,
47: 8 Now then, *l*, you wanton creature,
48: 1 "*L* to this, O house of Jacob,
48: 12 "*L* to me, O Jacob,
48: 14 "Come together, all of you, and *l*:
48: 16 "Come near me and *l* to this:
49: 1 *L* to me, you islands;
50: 4 ear to *l* like one being taught.
51: 1 "*L* to me, you who pursue
51: 4 "*L* to me, my people;
52: 8 *L*! Your watchmen lift up their
55: 2 *L*, listen to me, and eat what is
55: 2 *l* to me, and eat what is good,
65: 12 I spoke but you did not *l*.
Jer 6: 10 Who will *l* to me?
6: 17 But you said, 'We will not *l*.'
6: 17 '*L* to the sound of the trumpet!'
7: 13 but you did not *l*; I called you,
7: 16 with me, for I will not *l* to you.
7: 24 But they did not *l* or pay attention;
7: 26 But they did not *l* to me

Jer 7: 27 they will not *l* to you;
8: 19 *L* to the cry of my people
10: 22 *L*! The report is coming—
11: 2 "*L* to the terms of this covenant
11: 6 '*L* to the terms of this covenant
11: 8 But they did not *l* or pay attention;
11: 10 who refused to *l* to my words.
11: 11 out to me, I will not *l* to them.
11: 14 I will not *l* when they call to me
12: 17 But if any nation does not *l*,
13: 10 who refuse to *l* to my words,
13: 17 But if you do not *l*,
14: 12 Although they fast, I will not *l*
17: 23 Yet they did not *l* or pay attention;
17: 23 would not *l* or respond to discipline
18: 19 *L* to me, O LORD;
19: 3 the God of Israel, says: *L*!
19: 15 and would not *l* to my words.' "
19: 15 the God of Israel, says: '*L*!
22: 21 but you said, 'I will not *l*!'
23: 16 "Do not *l* to what the prophets are
25: 7 "But you did not *l* to me,"
26: 3 Perhaps they will *l* and each will
26: 4 If you do not *l* to me and follow my
26: 5 and if you do not *l* to the words
27: 9 So do not *l* to your prophets,
27: 14 Do not *l* to the words
27: 16 Do not *l* to the prophets who say,
27: 17 Do not *l* to them.
28: 7 *l* to what I have to say
28: 15 "*L*, Hananiah! The LORD has not
29: 8 Do not *l* to the dreams you
29: 12 and pray to me, and I will *l* to you.
32: 33 they would not *l* or respond
34: 14 did not *l* to me or pay attention
35: 17 but they did not *l*; I called to them,
35: 17 the God of Israel, says: '*L*!
36: 25 to burn the scroll, he would not *l*
37: 14 But Irijah would not *l* to him;
37: 20 But now, my lord the king, please *l*.
38: 15 give you counsel, you would not *l*
44: 5 But they did not *l* or pay attention;
44: 16 "We will not *l* to the message you
48: 3 *L* to the cries from Horonaim,
50: 28 *L* to the fugitives and refugees
La 1: 18 *L*, all you peoples;
Eze 2: 5 And whether they *l* or fail to *l*—
2: 7 they *l* or fail to *l*, for they are
2: 8 son of man, *l* to what I say to you.
3: 7 of Israel is not willing to *l* to you
3: 7 they are not willing to *l* to me,
3: 10 *l* carefully and take
3: 11 whether they *l* or fail to *l*."
3: 27 Whoever will *l* let him *l*,
8: 18 in my ears, I will not *l* to them."
13: 19 By lying to my people, who *l* to lies
20: 8 against me and would not *l* to me;
20: 39 afterward you will surely *l* to me
33: 31 sit before you to *l* to your words,
44: 5 *l* closely and give attention
Da 9: 19 O Lord, *l*! O Lord, forgive! O Lord,
Hos 5: 1 *L*, O royal house!
Joel 1: 2 *l*, all who live in the land.
Am 5: 23 I will not *l* to the music
Mic 1: 2 *l*, O earth and all who are in it,
3: 1 "*L*, you leaders of Jacob,
6: 1 *L* to what the LORD says:
6: 2 *l*, you everlasting foundations
6: 9 *L*! The LORD is calling to the city
Hab 1: 2 but you do not *l*?
Zep 1: 14 *L*! The cry on the day
Zec 1: 4 they would not *l* or pay attention
3: 8 " '*L*, O high priest Joshua
7: 12 as flint and would not *l* to the law
7: 13 I would not *l*,' says the LORD
7: 13 they did not *l*; so when they called,
11: 3 *L* to the roar of the lions;
11: 3 *L* to the wail of the shepherds;
Mal 2: 2 If you do not *l*, and if you do not set
Mt 10: 14 If anyone will not welcome you or *l*
12: 42 earth to *l* to Solomon's wisdom,
13: 18 "*L* then to what the parable
15: 10 and said, "*L* and understand.
17: 5 *L* to him!" When the disciples
18: 16 But if he will not *l*, take one
18: 17 If he refuses to *l* to them, tell it
18: 17 if he refuses to *l* even to the church,
21: 33 "*L* to another parable: There was

Mk 4: 3 and in his teaching said: "*L!*
6: 11 any place will not welcome you or *l*
6: 20 greatly puzzled; yet he liked to *l*
7: 14 "*L* to me, everyone,
9: 7 *L* to him!" Suddenly,
15: 35 they said, "*L*, he's calling Elijah."
Lk 8: 18 consider carefully how you *l*.
9: 35 whom I have chosen; *l* to him."
9: 44 "*L* carefully to what I am about
11: 31 earth to *l* to Solomon's wisdom,
16: 29 the Prophets; let them *l* to them.'
16: 31 'If they do not *l* to Moses
18: 6 "*L* to what the unjust judge says.
Jn 9: 27 told you already and you did not *l*.
9: 31 We know that God does not *l*
10: 3 and the sheep *l* to his voice.
10: 8 but the sheep did not *l* to them.
10: 16 They too will *l* to my voice,
10: 20 Why *l* to him?" But others said,
10: 27 My sheep *l* to my voice; I know
Ac 2: 14 to you; *l* carefully to what I say.
2: 22 *l* to this: Jesus of Nazareth was
3: 22 you must *l* to everything he tells
3: 23 Anyone who does not *l*
7: 2 "Brothers and fathers, *l* to me!
10: 33 here in the presence of God to *l*
13: 16 you Gentiles who worship God, *l*
15: 13 James spoke up: "Brothers, *l* to me.
18: 14 it would be reasonable for me to *l*
22: 1 and fathers, *l* now to my defense."
26: 3 I beg you to *l* to me patiently.
28: 28 to the Gentiles, and they will *l!*"
1Co 14: 21 but even then they will not *l* to me
15: 51 *L*, I tell you a mystery: We will not
2Co 13: 11 Aim for perfection, *l* to my appeal,
Eph 4: 29 that it may benefit those who *l*.
2Ti 2: 14 and only ruins those who *l*.
Jas 1: 19 Everyone should be quick to *l*,
1: 22 Do not merely *l* to the word,
2: 5 judges with evil thoughts? *L*,
4: 13 you to judge your neighbor? Now *l*,
5: 1 Now *l*, you rich people, weep
1Jn 4: 6 not from God does not *l* to us.

LISTENED (LISTEN)

Ge 3: 17 "Because you *l* to your wife
30: 6 he has *l* to my plea and given me
30: 17 God *l* to Leah, and she became
30: 22 he *l* to her and opened her womb.
Ex 7: 16 But until now you have not *l*.
18: 24 Moses *l* to his father-in-law
Nu 21: 3 The LORD *l* to Israel's plea
Dt 9: 19 But again the LORD *l* to me.
10: 10 and the LORD *l* to me at this time
34: 9 So the Israelites *l* to him
Jos 10: 14 a day when the LORD *l* to a man.
Jdg 2: 20 for their forefathers and has not *l*
6: 10 But you have not *l* to me."
1Sa 12: 1 "I have *l* to everything you said
19: 6 Saul *l* to Jonathan and took this
28: 23 in urging him, and he *l* to them.
2Ki 13: 4 LORD's favor, and the LORD *l*
18: 12 They neither *l* to the commands
2Ch 24: 17 to the king, and he *l* to them.
25: 16 and have not *l* to my counsel."
33: 13 by his entreaty and *l* to his plea;
Ne 8: 3 And all the people *l* attentively
8: 9 as they *l* to the words of the Law.
Job 29: 21 "Men *l* to me expectantly,
32: 11 I *l* to your reasoning;
Ps 22: 24 but has *l* to his cry for help.
66: 18 the Lord would not have *l*;
66: 19 but God has surely *l*
Isa 66: 4 when I spoke, no one *l*.
Jer 6: 19 they have not *l* to my words
8: 6 I have *l* attentively,
13: 11 But they have not *l*.'
23: 18 Who has *l* and heard his word?
25: 3 and again, but you have not *l*.
25: 4 you have not *l* or paid any
25: 8 "Because you have not *l*
26: 5 and again (though you have not *l*),
29: 19 And you exiles have not *l* either,"
29: 19 For they have not *l* to my words,"
35: 15 you have not paid attention or *l*
36: 31 because they have not *l*.' "
Eze 3: 6 to them, they would have *l* to you.
9: 5 As I *l*, he said to the others,

Da 9: 6 We have not *l* to your servants
10: 9 I heard him speaking, and as I *l*
Jnh 2: 2 and you *l* to my cry.
Mal 3: 16 and the LORD *l* and heard.
Mk 12: 37 The large crowd *l* to him
Ac 14: 9 He *l* to Paul as he was speaking.
15: 12 assembly became silent as they *l*
22: 22 The crowd *l* to Paul
24: 24 He sent for Paul and *l* to him

LISTENING (LISTEN)

Ge 18: 10 Now Sarah was *l* at the entrance
27: 5 Now Rebekah was *l* as Isaac spoke
1Sa 3: 9 Speak, LORD, for your servant is *l*
3: 10 "Speak, for your servant is *l*."
2Sa 20: 17 "I'm *l*," he said.
Pr 18: 13 He who answers before *l*—
19: 27 Stop *l* to instruction, my son,
25: 12 is a wise man's rebuke to a *l* ear.
Lk 2: 46 *l* to them and asking them
5: 1 around him and *l* to the word
10: 39 at the Lord's feet *l* to what he said.
19: 11 While they were *l* to this, he went
20: 45 While all the people were *l*,
Ac 16: 14 One of those *l* was a woman named
16: 25 the other prisoners were *l* to them.
17: 21 but talking about and *l*
26: 29 but all who are *l* to me today may
27: 11 instead of *l* to what Paul said,

LISTENS (LISTEN)

Pr 1: 33 whoever *l* to me will live in safety
8: 34 Blessed is the man who *l* to me,
12: 15 but a wise man *l* to advice.
15: 31 He who *l* to a life-giving rebuke
17: 4 A wicked man *l* to evil lips;
21: 28 whoever *l* to him will be destroyed
29: 12 If a ruler *l* to lies,
Mt 18: 15 If he *l* to you, you have won your
Lk 10: 16 "He who *l* to you *l*
Jn 3: 29 attends the bridegroom waits and *l*
6: 45 Everyone who *l* to the Father
9: 31 He *l* to the godly man who does his
18: 37 on the side of truth *l* to me."
Jas 1: 23 Anyone who *l* to the word
1Jn 4: 5 of the world, and the world *l*
4: 6 and whoever knows God *l* to us;

LISTING (LIST)

Nu 1: 2 *l* every man by name, one by one.

LIT (LIGHT)

Jdg 15: 5 *l* the torches and let the foxes loose
Ps 77: 18 your lightning *l* up the world;

LITERATURE

Da 1: 4 to teach them the language and *l*
1: 17 and understanding of all kinds of *l*

LIVE (ALIVE LIFE LIFE'S LIFETIME LIVED LIVES LIVING OUTLIVED)

Ge 3: 22 tree of life and eat, and *l* forever."
4: 20 the father of those who *l* in tents
9: 27 may Japheth *l* in the tents of Shem,
12: 10 down to Egypt to *l* there for a while
12: 12 they will kill me but will let you *l*.
13: 18 and went to *l* near the great trees
16: 12 and he will *l* in hostility
17: 18 "If only Ishmael might *l*
20: 7 he will pray for you and you will *l*.
20: 15 is before you; *l* wherever you like."
24: 37 in whose land I *l*, but go
26: 2 *l* in the land where I tell you to *l*.
27: 40 You will *l* by the sword
28: 4 of the land where you now *l*
31: 32 who has your gods, he shall not *l*.
34: 10 *L* in it, trade in it, and acquire
34: 21 "Let them *l* in our land
34: 22 the men will consent to *l* with us
38: 11 *L* as a widow in your father's house
38: 11 went to *l* in her father's house.
42: 2 so that we may *l* and not die."
42: 18 and you will *l*, for I fear God:
43: 8 and our children may *l* and not die.
45: 10 You shall *l* in the region of Goshen
47: 4 "We have come to *l* here awhile,
47: 6 Let them *l* in Goshen.
47: 19 Give us seed so that we may *l*

Ge 49: 13 "Zebulun will *l* by the seashore
Ex 1: 16 kill him; but if it is a girl, let her *l*."
1: 17 them to do; they let the boys *l*.
1: 18 Why have you let the boys *l?*"
1: 22 into the river, but let every girl *l*."
2: 15 fled from Pharaoh and went to *l*
8: 22 where my people *l*; no swarms
12: 20 Wherever you *l*, you must eat
18: 20 and show them the way to *l*
19: 13 he shall not be permitted to *l*.'
20: 12 so that you may *l* long
21: 35 they are to sell the *l* one
22: 18 "Do not allow a sorceress to *l*.
23: 31 to you the people who *l* in the land
23: 33 Do not let them *l* in your land,
33: 20 for no one may see me and *l*."
34: 10 people you *l* among will see how
34: 12 to make a treaty with those who *l*
34: 15 treaty with those who *l* in the land;
Lev 3: 17 wherever you *l*: You must not eat
7: 26 wherever you *l*, you must not eat
11: 2 'Of all the animals that *l* on land,
13: 46 He must *l* alone; he must *l*
14: 4 shall order that two *l* clean birds
14: 6 He is then to take the *l* bird
14: 7 Then he is to release the *l* bird
14: 51 the scarlet yarn and the *l* bird,
14: 52 the fresh water, the *l* bird,
14: 53 Then he is to release the *l* bird
16: 20 he shall bring forward the *l* goat.
16: 21 hands on the head of the *l* goat
18: 3 do in Egypt, where you used to *l*,
18: 5 for the man who obeys them will *l*
20: 22 you to *l* may not vomit you out.
20: 23 You must not *l* according
22: 13 returns to *l* in her father's house
23: 3 wherever you *l*, it is a Sabbath
23: 14 to come, wherever you *l*.
23: 17 From wherever you *l*, bring two
23: 21 to come, wherever you *l*.
23: 31 to come, wherever you *l*.
23: 42 All native-born Israelites are to *l*
23: 42 *L* in booths for seven days:
23: 43 will know that I had the Israelites *l*
25: 6 and temporary resident who *l*
25: 18 and you will *l* safely in the land.
25: 19 and you will eat your fill and *l* there
25: 35 so he can continue to *l* among you.
25: 36 countryman may continue to *l*
26: 5 and *l* in safety in your land.
26: 32 your enemies who *l* there will be
Nu 4: 19 So that they may *l* and not die
13: 18 the people who *l* there are strong
13: 19 What kind of land do they *l* in?
13: 19 What kind of towns do they *l* in?
13: 28 the people who *l* there are powerful
13: 29 The Amalekites *l* in the Negev;
13: 29 and Amorites *l* in the hill country;
13: 29 and the Canaanites *l* near the sea
14: 21 as surely as I *l* and as surely
14: 28 as I *l*, declares the LORD,
21: 8 who is bitten can look at it and *l*."
23: 9 I see a people who *l* apart
24: 23 Ah, who can *l* when God does this?
31: 15 you allowed all the women to *l?*"
32: 17 children will *l* in fortified cities,
33: 55 trouble in the land where you will *l*.
35: 2 to give the Levites towns to *l*
35: 3 Then they will have towns to *l* in
35: 29 to come, wherever you *l*.
35: 32 *l* on his own land before the death
35: 34 Do not defile the land where you *l*
Dt 2: 4 descendants of Esau, who *l* in Seir.
2: 8 descendants of Esau, who *l* in Seir.
2: 10 (The Emites used to *l* there—
2: 12 Horites used to *l* in Seir,
2: 20 used to *l* there; but the Ammonites
2: 29 and the Moabites, who *l* in Ar,
2: 29 who *l* in Seir, and the Moabites,
4: 1 Follow them so that you may *l*
4: 9 from your heart as long as you *l*.
4: 10 as long as they *l* in the land
4: 26 You will not *l* there long
4: 40 and that you may *l* long
5: 16 so that you may *l* long
5: 24 we have seen that a man can *l*
5: 33 so that you may *l* and prosper
6: 2 as you *l* by keeping all his decrees

Dt 8: 1 so that you may *l* and increase
8: 3 to teach you that man does not *l*
11: 9 and so that you may *l* long
12: 1 as long as you *l* in the land.
12: 10 you so that you will *l* in safety.
12: 19 as long as you *l* in your land.
13: 12 to *l* in that wicked men have arisen
13: 15 to the sword all who *l* in that town.
14: 29 widows who *l* in your towns may
16: 14 the widows who *l* in your towns.
16: 20 so that you may *l* and possess
18: 1 They shall *l* on the offerings made
22: 2 If the brother does not *l* near you
23: 6 with them as long as you *l*.
23: 16 Let him *l* among you wherever he
25: 15 so that you may *l* long
28: 30 will build a house, but you will not *l*
28: 66 You will *l* in constant suspense,
30: 6 and with all your soul, and *l*.
30: 16 then you will *l* and increase,
30: 18 You will not *l* long
30: 19 that you and your children may *l*
31: 13 as you *l* in the land you are crossing
32: 40 As surely as I *l* forever,
32: 47 By them you will *l* long
33: 6 "Let Reuben *l* and not die,
33: 28 So Israel will *l* in safety alone;
Jos 2: 9 so that all who *l* in this country are
9: 7 "But perhaps you *l* near us.
9: 15 of peace with them to let them *l*,
9: 20 do to them: We will let them *l*,
9: 21 They continued, "Let them *l*,
9: 22 'We *l* a long way from you,'
9: 22 while actually you *l* near us?
13: 13 continue to *l* among the Israelites
14: 4 of the land but only towns to *l* in,
15: 63 to this day the Jebusites *l* there
16: 10 to this day the Canaanites *l*
17: 12 determined to *l* in that region.
17: 16 and all the Canaanites who *l*
20: 4 and give him a place to *l* with them.
21: 2 Moses that you give us towns to *l*
24: 13 and you *l* in them and eat
Jdg 1: 16 of Judah to *l* among the people
1: 21 to this day the Jebusites *l* there
1: 27 Canaanites were determined to *l*
1: 29 continued to *l* there among them.
6: 10 in whose land you *l*.'
8: 29 son of Joash went back home to *l*.
11: 8 head over all who *l* in Gilead."
17: 10 "*L* with me and be my father
17: 11 So the Levite agreed to *l* with him,
19: 18 country of Ephraim where I *l*.
Ru 1: 1 went to *l* for a while in the country
2: 11 to *l* with a people you did not know
1Sa 1: 22 and he will *l* there always."
1: 26 "As surely as you *l*, my lord,
10: 24 people shouted, "Long *l* the king!"
17: 55 "As surely as you *l*, O king,
20: 3 as the LORD lives and as you *l*,
20: 14 that of the LORD as long as I *l*,
25: 26 as the LORD lives and as you *l*,
25: 28 found in you as long as you *l*.
27: 5 Why should your servant *l*
27: 5 country towns, that I may *l* there.
2Sa 8: 2 the third length was allowed to *l*.
11: 11 as you *l*, I will not do such a thing!"
12: 22 gracious to me and let the child *l*.'
14: 19 As surely as you *l*, my lord the king
16: 16 "Long *l* the king! Long *l* the king!"
19: 34 "How many more years will I *l*,
1Ki 1: 25 'Long *l* King Adonijah!'
1: 31 May my lord King David *l* forever
1: 34 and shout, 'Long *l* King Solomon!'
1: 39 "Long *l* King Solomon!"
2: 4 descendants watch how they *l*,
2: 36 a house in Jerusalem and *l* there,
3: 17 this woman and I *l*
6: 13 And I will *l* among the Israelites
7: 8 And the palace in which he was to *l*
8: 36 Teach them the right way to *l*,
8: 40 they will fear you all the time they *l*
8: 61 to *l* by his decrees and obey his
20: 32 says: 'Please let me *l*.' "
2Ki 2: 2 as the LORD lives and as you *l*,
2: 4 as the LORD lives and as you *l*,
2: 6 as the LORD lives and as you *l*,
4: 7 your sons can *l* on what is left."

2Ki 4: 30 as the LORD lives and as you *l*,
6: 2 let us build a place there for us to *l*
7: 4 If they spare us, we *l*; if they kill us,
10: 19 fails to come will no longer *l*."
11: 12 and shouted, "Long *l* the king!"
17: 27 from Samaria go back to *l* there
17: 28 from Samaria came to *l* in Bethel
2Ch 2: 3 cedar to build a palace to *l* in.
6: 27 Teach them the right way to *l*,
6: 31 in your ways all the time they *l*
8: 11 "My wife must not *l* in the palace
19: 10 your fellow countrymen who *l*
20: 15 all who *l* in Judah and Jerusalem!
23: 11 and shouted, "Long *l* the king!"
34: 28 and on those who *l* here.' "
Ne 2: 3 to the king, "May the king *l* forever
8: 14 that the Israelites were to *l*
9: 29 by which a man will *l*
11: 1 out of every ten to *l* in Jerusalem,
11: 2 all the men who volunteered to *l*
Job 4: 19 how much more those who *l*
7: 16 my life; I would not *l* forever.
14: 14 If a man dies, will he *l* again?
21: 7 Why do the wicked *l* on,
26: 5 beneath the waters and all that *l*
27: 6 will not reproach me as long as I *l*.
30: 6 They were forced to *l*
33: 28 and I will *l* to enjoy the light.'
Ps 15: 1 Who may *l* on your holy hill?
22: 26 may your hearts *l* forever!
24: 1 the world, and all who *l* in it;
26: 8 I love the house where you *l*,
33: 14 all who *l* on earth—
35: 20 against those who *l* quietly
37: 27 then you will always *l* securely.
49: 1 listen, all who *l* in this world,
49: 9 that he should *l* on forever
55: 23 will not *l* out half their days.
63: 4 I will praise you as long as I *l*,
65: 4 and bring near to *l* in your courts!
68: 6 rebellious *l* in a sun-scorched land.
69: 32 who seek God, may your hearts *l*!
72: 15 Long may he *l*!
78: 10 and refused to *l* by his law
89: 48 What man can *l* and not see death,
98: 7 the world, and all who *l* in it.
102: 28 of your servants will *l*
104: 33 to my God as long as I *l*.
107: 36 there he brought the hungry to *l*,
116: 2 I will call on him as long as I *l*.
118: 17 I will not die but *l*,
119: 17 to your servant, and I will *l*;
119: 77 to me that I may *l*,
119:116 to your promise, and I will *l*;
119:144 give me understanding that I may *l*
119:175 Let me *l* that I may praise you,
120: 5 that I *l* among the tents of Kedar!
128: 6 may you *l* to see your children's
133: 1 when brothers *l* together in unity!
140: 13 and the upright will *l* before you.
146: 2 to my God as long as I *l*.
Pr 1: 33 listens to me will *l* in safety
2: 21 For the upright will *l* in the land,
4: 4 keep my commands and you will *l*.
7: 2 Keep my commands and you will *l*;
9: 6 your simple ways and you will *l*;
15: 27 but he who hates bribes will *l*.
16: 7 his enemies *l* at peace with him.
19: 10 fitting for a fool to *l* in luxury—
21: 9 Better to *l* on a corner of the roof
21: 19 Better to *l* in a desert
25: 24 Better to *l* on a corner of the roof
Ecc 3: 12 be happy and do good while they *l*.
6: 3 children and *l* many years;
9: 3 in their hearts while they *l*,
9: 4 a *l* dog is better off than a dead lion
11: 8 However many years a man may *l*,
Isa 5: 8 and you *l* alone in the land.
6: 5 I *l* among a people of unclean lips,
6: 6 flew to me with a *l* coal in his hand,
10: 24 "O my people who *l* in Zion,
11: 6 The wolf will *l* with the lamb,
18: 3 you who *l* on the earth,
20: 6 In that day the people who *l*
21: 14 you who *l* in Tema,
22: 21 a father to those who *l* in Jerusalem
23: 18 to those who *l* before the LORD,
26: 14 They are now dead, they *l* no more;

Isa 26: 19 But your dead will *l*;
30: 19 of Zion, who *l* in Jerusalem,
32: 16 righteousness *l* in the fertile field.
32: 18 people will *l* in peaceful dwelling
38: 16 Lord, by such things men *l*;
38: 16 and let me *l*.
40: 22 spreads them out like a tent to *l* in.
42: 10 you islands, and all who *l* in them.
49: 18 as I *l*," declares the LORD,
49: 20 give us more space to *l* in.'
51: 13 that you *l* in constant terror every
52: 4 went down to Egypt to *l*;
55: 3 hear me, that your soul may *l*.
57: 15 "I *l* in a high and holy place,
65: 9 and there will my servants *l*.
65: 20 man who does not *l* out his years;
65: 22 will they build houses and others *l*
Jer 1: 14 out on all who *l* in the land.
6: 8 desolate so no one can *l* in it."
6: 12 against those who *l* in the land,"
7: 3 and I will let you *l* in this place.
7: 7 then I will let you *l* in this place,
8: 16 the city and all who *l* there."
9: 6 You *l* in the midst of deception;
9: 11 Judah so no one can *l* there."
9: 26 and all who *l* in the desert
10: 17 you who *l* under siege.
10: 18 those who *l* in this land;
11: 2 and to those who *l* in Jerusalem.
11: 9 and those who *l* in Jerusalem.
12: 1 Why do all the faithless *l* at ease?
12: 4 Because those who *l*
13: 13 fill with drunkenness all who *l*
19: 12 and to those who *l* here,
20: 6 and all who *l* in your house will go
21: 6 down those who *l* in this city—
21: 9 who are besieging you will *l*;
21: 13 you who *l* above this valley
22: 23 You who *l* in 'Lebanon,'
22: 24 as I *l*," declares the LORD,
23: 6 and Israel will *l* in safety.
23: 8 Then they will *l* in their own land."
23: 14 They commit adultery and *l* a lie.
24: 8 remain in this land or *l* in Egypt.
25: 24 kings of the foreign people who *l*
25: 29 sword upon all who *l* on the earth,
25: 30 shout against all who *l* on the earth.
26: 15 on this city and on those who *l* in it,
27: 11 land to till it and to *l* there,
27: 12 and his people, and you will *l*.
27: 17 the king of Babylon, and you will *l*.
31: 24 People will *l* together in Judah
32: 37 to this place and let them *l* in safety
33: 16 and Jerusalem will *l* in safety.
34: 22 of Judah so no one can *l* there."
35: 7 Then you will *l* a long time
35: 7 but must always *l* in tents.
35: 9 houses to *l* in or had vineyards,
35: 15 you will *l* in the land I have given
38: 2 escape with his life; he will *l*.'
38: 2 goes over to the Babylonians will *l*.
38: 17 you and your family will *l*.
40: 5 and *l* with him among the people,
40: 10 *l* in the towns you have taken over
42: 14 'No, we will go and *l* in Egypt,
43: 5 back to *l* in the land of Judah
44: 8 where you have come to *l*?
44: 13 I will punish those who *l* in Egypt
44: 14 gone to *l* in Egypt will escape
44: 14 to which they long to return and *l*;
44: 28 remnant of Judah who came to *l*
46: 18 As surely as I *l*," declares the King,
46: 19 you who *l* in Egypt,
47: 2 the towns and those who *l* in them.
48: 9 with no one to *l* in them.
48: 17 Console her, all who *l* around her,
48: 19 you who *l* in Aroer.
48: 28 you who *l* in Moab.
49: 1 Why do his people *l* in its towns?
49: 8 you who *l* in Dedan,
49: 16 you who *l* in the clefts of the rocks,
49: 18 "so no one will *l* there;
49: 20 against those who *l* in Teman:
49: 30 in deep caves, you who *l* in Hazor,"
49: 31 its people *l* alone.
49: 33 No one will *l* there;
50: 3 No one will *l* in it;
50: 21 and those who *l* in Pekod.

Jer 50: 34 unrest to those who *l* in Babylon.
50: 35 "against those who *l* in Babylon
50: 39 creatures and hyenas will *l* there,
50: 40 "so no one will *l* there;
51: 13 You who *l* by many waters
51: 24 and all who *l* in Babylonia
51: 29 Babylon so that no one will *l* there.
51: 35 be on those who *l* in Babylonia,"
51: 62 that neither man nor animal will *l*
La 4: 20 we would *l* among the nations.
4: 21 you who *l* in the land of Uz.
Eze 2: 6 and you *l* among scorpions.
3: 21 he will surely *l* because he took
5: 11 I *l*, declares the Sovereign LORD,
6: 6 Wherever you *l*, the towns will be
6: 14 desert to Diblah—wherever they *l*.
7: 13 as long as both of them *l*,
12: 19 of the violence of all who *l* there.
13: 19 have spared those who should not *l*
14: 16 I *l*, declares the Sovereign LORD,
14: 18 I *l*, declares the Sovereign LORD,
14: 20 I *l*, declares the Sovereign LORD,
16: 6 "*L!*" I made you grow like a plant
16: 48 I *l*, declares the Sovereign LORD,
17: 16 I *l*, declares the Sovereign LORD,
17: 19 LORD says: As surely as I *l*,
18: 3 I *l*, declares the Sovereign LORD,
18: 9 he will surely *l*,
18: 13 Will such a man *l?* He will not!
18: 17 for his father's sin; he will surely *l*.
18: 19 all my decrees, he will surely *l*.
18: 21 he will surely *l;* he will not die.
18: 22 things he has done, he will *l*.
18: 23 turn from their ways and *l?*
18: 24 will he *l?* None of the righteous
18: 28 he will surely *l;* he will not die.
18: 32 *l!* "Take up a lament concerning
20: 3 I *l*, I will not let you inquire of me,
20: 11 for the man who obeys them will *l*
20: 13 the man who obeys them will *l*
20: 21 the man who obeys them will *l*
20: 25 and laws they could not *l* by;
20: 31 I *l*, declares the Sovereign LORD,
20: 33 I *l*, declares the Sovereign LORD,
27: 35 All who *l* in the coastlands
28: 25 Then they will *l* in their own land,
28: 26 They will *l* there in safety
28: 26 they will *l* in safety
29: 6 all who *l* in Egypt will know that I
29: 11 no one will *l* there for forty years.
32: 15 when I strike down all who *l* there,
33: 10 How then can we *l?*" ' Say to them,
33: 11 I *l*, declares the Sovereign LORD,
33: 11 turn from their ways and *l*.
33: 12 will not be allowed to *l*
33: 13 righteous man that he will surely *l*,
33: 15 he will surely *l;* he will not die.
33: 16 is just and right; he will surely *l*.
33: 19 and right, he will *l* by doing so.
33: 27 LORD says: As surely as I *l*,
34: 8 I *l*, declares the Sovereign LORD,
34: 25 so that they may *l* in the desert
34: 28 They will *l* in safety, and no one
35: 6 I *l*, declares the Sovereign LORD,
35: 11 I *l*, declares the Sovereign LORD,
36: 28 You will *l* in the land I gave your
37: 3 can these bones *l?*" I said,
37: 9 into these slain, that they may *l*.' "
37: 14 Spirit in you and you will *l*,
37: 25 They will *l* in the land I gave
37: 25 children will *l* there forever,
38: 8 and now all of them *l* in safety.
39: 6 and on those who *l* in safety
39: 9 " 'Then those who *l* in the towns
43: 7 This is where I will *l*
43: 9 and I will *l* among them forever.
44: 9 even the foreigners who *l*
45: 5 as their possession for towns to *l* in.
47: 9 living creatures will *l* wherever
47: 9 the river flows everything will *l*.
Da 2: 4 *l* forever! Tell your servants
2: 11 and they do not *l* among men."
2: 38 Wherever they *l*, he has made you
3: 9 *l* forever! You have issued a decree
4: 1 and men of every language, who *l*
4: 15 and let him *l* with the animals
4: 23 let him *l* like wild animals,
4: 25 and will *l* with the wild animals;

Da 4: 32 and will *l* with the wild animals;
5: 10 "O king, *l* forever!" she said.
6: 6 "O King Darius, *l* forever!
6: 21 answered, "O king, *l* forever!
7: 12 but were allowed to *l* for a period
Hos 3: 3 with any man, and I will *l* with you
3: 3 "You are to *l* with me many days;
3: 4 For the Israelites will *l* many days
4: 1 bring against you who *l* in the land:
4: 3 and all who *l* in it waste away;
6: 2 that we may *l* in his presence.
10: 5 The people who *l* in Samaria fear
12: 9 I will make you *l* in tents again,
Joel 1: 2 listen, all who *l* in the land.
1: 14 and all who *l* in the land
2: 1 Let all who *l* in the land tremble,
Am 5: 4 "Seek me and *l;*
5: 6 Seek the LORD and *l*,
5: 11 you will not *l* in them;
5: 14 that you may *l*.
8: 8 and all who *l* in it mourn?
9: 5 and all who *l* in it mourn—
9: 14 will rebuild the ruined cities and *l*
Ob : 3 you who *l* in the clefts of the rocks
Jnh 4: 3 for it is better for me to die than to *l*
4: 8 better for me to die than to *l*."
Mic 1: 11 Those who *l* in Zaanan
1: 11 you who *l* in Shaphir.
1: 12 Those who *l* in Maroth writhe
1: 13 You who *l* in Lachish,
1: 15 who *l* in Mareshah.
5: 4 And they will *l* securely,
Na 1: 5 the world and all who *l* in it.
Hab 2: 4 but the righteous will *l* by his faith
Zep 1: 4 and against all who *l* in Jerusalem.
1: 11 you who *l* in the market district;
1: 13 but not *l* in them;
1: 18 end of all who *l* in the earth."
2: 5 Woe to you who *l* by the sea,
2: 9 Therefore, as surely as I *l*,"
Zec 1: 5 And the prophets, do they *l* forever
2: 7 you who *l* in the Daughter
2: 10 and I will *l* among you," declares
2: 11 I will *l* among you and you will
8: 8 I will bring them back to *l*
12: 8 the LORD will shield those who *l*
Mt 4: 4 'Man does not *l* on bread alone,
9: 18 put your hand on her, and she will *l*
12: 45 and they go in and *l* there.
Mk 5: 23 so that she will be healed and *l*."
7: 5 don't your disciples *l* according
12: 44 in everything—all she had to *l* on
Lk 4: 4 'Man does not *l* on bread alone.' "
10: 28 "Do this and you will *l*."
11: 26 and they go in and *l* there.
21: 4 put in all she had to *l* on."
21: 35 upon all those who *l* on the face
Jn 4: 50 Your son will *l*."
4: 53 said to him, "Your son will *l*."
5: 25 of God and those who hear will *l*.
5: 29 who have done good will rise to *l*,
6: 51 eats of this bread, he will *l* forever.
6: 57 and I *l* because of the Father,
6: 57 so the one who feeds on me will *l*
6: 58 feeds on this bread will *l* forever."
7: 35 he go where our people *l* scattered
11: 25 He who believes in me will *l*,
14: 19 Because I *l*, you also will *l*.
Ac 2: 26 my body also will *l* in hope,
7: 48 the Most High does not *l*
17: 24 does not *l* in temples built by hands
17: 26 exact places where they should *l*.
17: 28 'For in him we *l* and move
21: 21 or *l* according to our customs.
21: 21 that you teach all the Jews who *l*
22: 22 the earth of him! He's not fit to *l!*"
25: 24 that he ought not to *l* any longer.
28: 4 Justice has not allowed him to *l*."
28: 16 Paul was allowed to *l* by himself,
Ro 1: 17 "The righteous will *l* by faith."
4: 14 For if those who *l* by law are heirs,
6: 2 how can we *l* in it any longer?
6: 4 the Father, we too may *l* a new life.
6: 8 we believe that we will also *l*
8: 4 who do not *l* according
8: 5 Those who *l* according
8: 5 but those who *l* in accordance
8: 12 to *l* according to it.

Ro 8: 13 For if you *l* according
8: 13 you will *l*, because those who are
10: 5 man who does these things will *l*
12: 16 *L* in harmony with one another.
12: 18 as it depends on you, *l* at peace
14: 8 If we *l*, we *l* to the Lord;
14: 8 we *l* or die, we belong to the Lord.
14: 11 " 'As surely as I *l*,' says the Lord,
1Co 7: 12 and she is willing to *l* with him,
7: 13 and he is willing to *l* with her,
7: 15 God has called us to *l* in peace.
7: 29 on those who have wives should *l*
7: 35 but that you may *l* in a right way
8: 6 all things came and for whom we *l;*
8: 6 and through whom we *l*.
2Co 5: 1 that if the earthly tent we *l*
5: 7 We *l* by faith, not by sight.
5: 15 that those who *l* should no longer *l*
6: 9 dying, and yet we *l* on; beaten,
6: 16 "I will *l* with them and walk
7: 3 place in our hearts that we would *l*
10: 2 some people who think that we *l*
10: 3 For though we *l* in the world,
13: 4 by God's power we will *l* with him
13: 11 be of one mind, *l* in peace.
Gal 2: 14 yet you *l* like a Gentile
2: 19 to the law so that I might *l* for God.
2: 20 The life I *l* in the body, I *l* by faith
2: 20 with Christ and I no longer *l*,
3: 11 "The righteous will *l* by faith."
3: 12 man who does these things will *l*
5: 16 *l* by the Spirit, and you will not
5: 21 that those who *l* like this will not
5: 25 Since we *l* by the Spirit, let us keep
Eph 2: 2 in which you used to *l*
4: 1 I urge you to *l* a life worthy
4: 17 that you must no longer *l*
5: 2 as dearly loved children and *l* a life
5: 8 *L* as children of light (for the fruit
5: 15 Be very careful, then, how you *l*—
Php 1: 21 to *l* is Christ and to die is gain.
3: 16 Only let us *l* up to what we have
3: 17 take note of those who *l* according
3: 18 many *l* as enemies of the cross
Col 1: 10 order that you may *l* a life worthy
2: 6 continue to *l* in him, rooted
1Th 2: 12 urging you to *l* lives worthy of God
3: 8 For now we really *l*,
4: 1 we instructed you how to *l* in order
4: 7 us to be impure, but to *l* a holy life.
5: 10 we may *l* together with him.
5: 13 *L* in peace with each other.
2Th 3: 6 and does not *l* according
1Ti 2: 2 that we may *l* peaceful
2Ti 2: 11 we will also *l* with him;
3: 12 who wants to *l* a godly life
Tit 2: 3 to be reverent in the way they *l*,
2: 12 and to *l* self-controlled, upright
3: 14 and not *l* unproductive lives.
Heb 10: 38 But my righteous one will *l* by faith
12: 9 to the Father of our spirits and *l!*
12: 14 Make every effort to *l* in peace
13: 18 desire to *l* honorably in every way.
Jas 4: 5 to *l* in us tends toward envy,
4: 15 we will *l* and do this or that."
1Pe 1: 17 *l* your lives as strangers here
2: 12 *L* such good lives
2: 16 as a cover-up for evil; *l* as servants
2: 16 *L* as free men, but do not use your
2: 24 die to sins and *l* for righteousness;
3: 7 as you *l* with your wives,
3: 8 *l* in harmony with one another;
4: 2 he does not *l* the rest
4: 6 but *l* according to God in regard
2Pe 1: 13 long as I *l* in the tent of this body,
2: 18 escaping from those who *l* in error.
3: 11 You ought to *l* holy and godly lives
1Jn 1: 6 we lie and do not *l* by the truth.
2: 6 Whoever claims to *l*
3: 24 Those who obey his commands *l*
4: 9 Son into the world that we might *l*
4: 13 We know that we *l* in him
Rev 2: 13 know where you *l*— where Satan
3: 10 to test those who *l* on the earth.
11: 10 had tormented those who *l*
13: 6 and those who *l* in heaven.
14: 6 to those who *l* on the earth—
21: 3 with men, and he will *l* with them.

LIVED (LIVE)

Ge 4: 16 from the LORD's presence and *l*
5: 3 When Adam had *l* 130 years,
5: 4 Adam *l* 800 years and had other
5: 5 Altogether, Adam *l* 930 years,
5: 6 When Seth had *l* 105 years,
5: 7 Seth *l* 807 years and had other sons
5: 8 Altogether, Seth *l* 912 years,
5: 9 When Enosh had *l* 90 years,
5: 10 Enosh *l* 815 years and had other
5: 11 Altogether, Enosh *l* 905 years,
5: 12 When Kenan had *l* 70 years,
5: 13 Kenan *l* 840 years and had other
5: 14 Altogether, Kenan *l* 910 years,
5: 15 When Mahalalel had *l* 65 years,
5: 16 Mahalalel *l* 830 years and had
5: 17 Altogether, Mahalalel *l* 895 years,
5: 18 When Jared had *l* 162 years,
5: 19 Jared *l* 800 years and had other
5: 20 Altogether, Jared *l* 962 years,
5: 21 When Enoch had *l* 65 years,
5: 23 Altogether, Enoch *l* 365 years.
5: 25 When Methuselah had *l* 187 years,
5: 26 Methuselah *l* 782 years
5: 27 Altogether, Methuselah *l* 969
5: 28 When Lamech had *l* 182 years,
5: 30 Lamech *l* 595 years and had other
5: 31 Altogether, Lamech *l* 777 years,
9: 28 After the flood Noah *l* 350 years.
9: 29 Altogether, Noah *l* 950 years,
10: 30 The region where they *l* stretched
11: 11 Shem *l* 500 years and had other
11: 12 When Arphaxad had *l* 35 years,
11: 13 Arphaxad *l* 403 years and had
11: 14 When Shelah had *l* 30 years,
11: 15 Shelah *l* 403 years and had other
11: 16 When Eber had *l* 34 years,
11: 17 Eber *l* 430 years and had other
11: 18 When Peleg had *l* 30 years,
11: 19 Peleg *l* 209 years and had other
11: 20 When Reu had *l* 32 years,
11: 21 Reu *l* 207 years and had other sons
11: 22 When Serug had *l* 30 years,
11: 23 Serug *l* 200 years and had other
11: 24 When Nahor had *l* 29 years,
11: 25 Nahor *l* 119 years and had other
11: 26 After Terah had *l* 70 years,
11: 32 Terah *l* 205 years, and he died
13: 12 Abram *l* in the land of Canaan,
13: 12 while Lot *l* among the cities
19: 29 the cities where Lot had *l*
19: 30 and his two daughters *l* in a cave.
20: 1 and *l* between Kadesh and Shur.
21: 20 He *l* in the desert and became
23: 1 Sarah *l* to be a hundred
25: 7 Abraham *l* a hundred
25: 11 blessed his son Isaac, who then *l*
25: 17 Ishmael *l* a hundred
25: 18 they *l* in hostility toward all their
35: 28 Isaac *l* a hundred and eighty years.
37: 1 Jacob *l* in the land where his father
38: 21 He asked the men who *l* there,
38: 22 Besides, the men who *l* there said,
39: 2 he *l* in the house of his Egyptian
47: 28 Jacob *l* in Egypt seventeen years,
50: 11 the Canaanites who *l* there saw
50: 22 He *l* a hundred and ten years
Ex 6: 4 the land of Canaan, where they *l*
6: 16 Levi *l* 137 years.
6: 18 Kohath *l* 133 years.
6: 20 Amram *l* 137 years.
10: 23 light in the places where they *l*.
12: 40 length of time the Israelite people *l*
Lev 18: 27 by the people who *l* in the land
26: 35 have during the sabbaths you *l* in it.
Nu 13: 22 the descendants of Anak, *l*.
14: 45 and Canaanites who *l* in that hill
20: 15 and we *l* there many years.
21: 1 king of Arad, who *l* in the Negev,
21: 9 looked at the bronze snake, he *l*.
33: 40 who *l* in the Negev of Canaan,
Dt 1: 44 The Amorites who *l*
2: 22 and have *l* in their place to this day.
2: 22 who *l* in Seir, when he destroyed
2: 23 as for the Avvites who *l* in villages
4: 25 and have *l* in the land a long time—
4: 33 *l*? Has any god ever tried to take

Dt 21: 13 After she has *l* in your house
23: 7 you *l* as an alien in his country.
26: 5 *l* there and became a great nation,
29: 16 You yourselves know how we *l*
Jos 2: 15 for the house she *l* in was part
8: 26 until he had destroyed all who *l*
8: 35 and the aliens who *l* among them.
13: 21 with Sihon—who *l* in that country.
22: 33 the Reubenites and the Gadites *l*.
24: 2 *l* beyond the River and worshiped
24: 7 you *l* in the desert for a long time.
24: 8 the land of the Amorites who *l* east
24: 18 including the Amorites, who *l*
Jdg 1: 32 of Asher *l* among the Canaanite
1: 33 the Naphtalites too *l* among
2: 18 their enemies as long as the judge *l*;
3: 5 Israelites *l* among the Canaanites,
4: 2 of his army was Sisera, who *l*
8: 31 His concubine, who *l* in Shechem,
9: 21 he *l* there because he was afraid
10: 1 He *l* in Shamir, in the hill country
11: 21 the land of the Amorites who *l*
16: 30 more when he died than while he *l*.
17: 12 young man became his priest and *l*
18: 7 *l* a long way from the Sidonians
18: 22 men who *l* near Micah were called
18: 28 they *l* a long way from Sidon
19: 1 a Levite who *l* in a remote area
Ru 1: 2 And they went to Moab and *l* there
1: 4 After they had *l* there about ten
2: 23 And she *l* with her mother-in-law.
1Sa 10: 12 A man who *l* there answered,
12: 11 so that you *l* securely
23: 29 and *l* in the strongholds of En
27: 7 David *l* in Philistine territory
27: 8 ancient times these peoples had *l*
27: 11 long as he *l* in Philistine territory.
2Sa 4: 3 have *l* there as aliens to this day.
5: 6 to attack the Jebusites, who *l* there.
9: 13 And Mephibosheth *l* in Jerusalem,
13: 20 Tamar *l* in her brother Absalom's
14: 28 Absalom *l* two years in Jerusalem
1Ki 4: 25 from Dan to Beersheba, *l* in safety,
11: 20 There Genubath *l*
11: 25 adversary as long as Solomon *l*,
12: 25 country of Ephraim and *l* there.
13: 25 in the city where the old prophet *l*.
14: 9 evil than all who *l* before you
17: 22 boy's life returned to him, and he *l*.
21: 8 and nobles who *l* in Naboth's city
21: 11 nobles who *l* in Naboth's city did
2Ki 13: 5 the Israelites *l* in their own homes
14: 17 king of Judah *l* for fifteen years
15: 5 and he *l* in a separate house.
16: 6 and have *l* there to this day.
17: 24 over Samaria and *l* in its towns.
17: 25 When they first *l* there, they did
22: 14 She *l* in Jerusalem,
25: 30 a regular allowance as long as he *l*.
1Ch 2: 55 the clans of scribes who *l* at Jabez:
4: 23 They were the potters who *l*
4: 28 They *l* in Beersheba, Moladah,
4: 40 Some Hamites had *l* there formerly
4: 43 and they have *l* there to this day.
5: 11 The Gadites *l* next to them
5: 16 The Gadites *l* in Gilead, in Bashan
7: 29 son of Israel *l* in these towns.
8: 28 listed in their genealogy, and they *l*
8: 29 the father of Gibeon *l* in Gibeon.
8: 32 They too *l* near their relatives
9: 3 Manasseh who *l* in Jerusalem were:
9: 16 who *l* in the villages
9: 34 listed in their genealogy, and they *l*
9: 35 the father of Gibeon *l* in Gibeon.
9: 38 They too *l* near their relatives
11: 4 The Jebusites who *l* there said
2Ch 11: 5 Rehoboam *l* in Jerusalem
19: 4 Jehoshaphat *l* in Jerusalem,
19: 8 And they *l* in Jerusalem.
20: 8 They have *l* in it and have built
21: 16 and of the Arabs who *l*
24: 14 as Jehoiada *l*, burnt offerings were
25: 25 king of Judah *l* for fifteen years
26: 7 the Arabs who *l* in Gur Baal
26: 21 He *l* in a separate house—
30: 25 come from Israel and those who *l*
31: 6 Judah who *l* in the towns of Judah
31: 19 who *l* on the farm lands

2Ch 34: 22 She *l* in Jerusalem,
34: 33 as he *l*, they did not fail
Ne 4: 12 the Jews who *l* near them came
8: 17 from exile built booths and *l*
9: 24 before them the Canaanites, who *l*
11: 3 of Solomon's servants *l*
11: 4 and Benjamin *l* in Jerusalem):
11: 6 The descendants of Perez who *l*
11: 21 The temple servants *l* on the hill
11: 25 people of Judah *l* in Kiriath Arba
11: 31 from Geba *l* in Micmash,
12: 27 out from where they *l*
13: 16 Men from Tyre who *l*
Job 1: 1 of Uz there *l* a man whose name
18: 19 no survivor where once he *l*.
21: 28 the tents where wicked men *l*?'
38: 21 You have *l* so many years!
42: 16 Job *l* a hundred and forty years;
Ps 49: 18 while he *l* he counted himself
105: 23 Jacob *l* as an alien in the land
107: 34 wickedness of those who *l* there.
120: 6 Too long have I *l*
Ecc 4: 15 I saw that all who *l* and walked
9: 15 Now there *l* in that city a man poor
Isa 13: 20 or *l* in through all generations;
Jer 3: 1 But you have *l* as a prostitute
35: 10 We have *l* in tents and have fully
42: 18 out on those who *l* in Jerusalem,
50: 39 *l* in from generation to generation.
52: 34 a regular allowance as long as he *l*,
La 2: 16 we have *l* to see it.''
Eze 3: 15 the exiles who *l* at Tel Aviv
16: 46 who *l* to the north of you
16: 46 who *l* to the south of you
20: 9 eyes of the nations they *l* among
26: 17 terror on all who *l* there.
31: 6 *l* in its shade.
31: 17 Those who *l* in its shade, its allies
37: 25 the land where your fathers *l*.
39: 26 toward me when they *l* in safety
Da 4: 12 the birds of the air *l* in its branches;
5: 21 he *l* with the wild donkeys
Zep 2: 15 that *l* in safety.
Mt 2: 23 and *l* in a town called Nazareth.
4: 13 he went and *l* in Capernaum,
23: 30 'If we had *l* in the days
Mk 5: 3 This man *l* in the tombs,
Lk 1: 80 he *l* in the desert until he appeared
2: 36 she had *l* with her husband seven
7: 37 a woman who had *l* a sinful life
8: 27 in a house, but had *l* in the tombs.
8: 27 this man had not worn clothes or *l*
16: 19 fine linen and *l* in luxury every day.
Jn 1: 14 and *l* for a while among us.
7: 42 the town where David *l*?''
12: 1 at Bethany, where Lazarus *l*,
Ac 7: 2 before he *l* in Haran.
9: 35 All those who *l* in Lydda
16: 1 where a disciple named Timothy *l*,
16: 3 of the Jews who *l* in that area,
17: 21 foreigners who *l* there spent their
19: 10 and Greeks who *l* in the province
20: 18 ''You know how I *l* the whole time
26: 4 Jews all know the way I have *l* ever
26: 5 the strictest sect of our religion, I *l*
Eph 2: 3 also *l* among them at one time,
Col 3: 7 in these ways, in the life you once *l*.
1Th 1: 5 You know how we *l* among you
2Ti 1: 5 which first *l* in your grandmother
Tit 3: 3 We *l* in malice and envy, being
Heb 11: 9 he *l* in tents, as did Isaac and Jacob,
Jas 5: 5 You have *l* on earth in luxury
1Pe 1: 14 had when you *l* in ignorance.
Rev 13: 14 wounded by the sword and yet *l*.

LIVELIHOOD

Dt 24: 6 that would be taking a man's *l*
Zec 13: 5 the land has been my *l*

LIVER

Ex 29: 13 covering of the *l*, and both kidneys
29: 22 the covering of the *l*, both kidneys
Lev 3: 4 of the *l*, which he will remove
3: 10 of the *l*, which he will remove
3: 15 of the *l*, which he will remove
4: 9 of the *l*, which he will remove
7: 4 and the covering of the *l*, which is
8: 16 covering of the *l*, and both kidneys

Lev 8: 25 the covering of the *l*, both kidneys
9: 10 and the covering of the *l*
9: 19 and the covering of the *l*—
Job 20: 25 the gleaming point out of his *l*.
Pr 7: 23 a noose till an arrow pierces his *l*,
Eze 21: 21 his idols, he will examine the *l*.

LIVES (LIVE)

Ge 9: 3 Everything that *l* and moves will
19: 17 "Flee for your *l!* Don't look back,
42: 13 who *l* in the land of Canaan.
42: 15 be tested: As surely as Pharaoh *l*,
42: 16 then as surely as Pharaoh *l*,
45: 5 to save *l* that God sent me ahead
45: 7 and to save your *l* by a great
47: 25 "You have saved our *l*," they said.
50: 20 being done, the saving of many *l*.
Ex 1: 14 They made their *l* bitter
30: 15 to the LORD to atone for your *l*.
30: 16 making atonement for your *l*."
Lev 19: 33 " 'When an alien *l* with you
Nu 16: 38 sinned at the cost of their *l*.
Dt 22: 19 not divorce her as long as he *l*.
22: 29 never divorce her as long as he *l*.
28: 43 The alien who *l* among you will rise
33: 20 Gad *l* there like a lion,
Jos 2: 13 a sure sign that you will spare the *l*
2: 14 "Our *l* for your *l!*" the men assured
6: 25 and she *l* among the Israelites
9: 24 we feared for our *l* because of you,
Jdg 5: 18 of Zebulun risked their very *l;*
8: 19 LORD *l*, if you had spared their
8: 19 you had spared their *l*, I would not
18: 25 you and your family will lose your *l*
Ru 3: 13 as surely as the LORD *l*, I will do it
1Sa 14: 39 as the LORD who rescues Israel *l*,
14: 45 Never! As surely as the LORD *l*,
19: 6 "As surely as the LORD *l*,
20: 3 as surely as the LORD *l* and
20: 21 surely as the LORD *l*, you are safe;
20: 31 as the son of Jesse *l* on this earth,
25: 26 as surely as the LORD *l* and
25: 29 *l* of your enemies he will hurl away
25: 34 *l*, who has kept me
26: 10 As surely as the LORD *l*," he said,
26: 16 As surely as the LORD *l*, you
28: 10 "As surely as the LORD *l*,
29: 6 "As surely as the LORD *l*,
2Sa 2: 27 as God *l*, if you had not spoken,
4: 9 "As surely as the LORD *l*,
12: 5 "As surely as the LORD *l*,
14: 11 As surely as the LORD *l*," he said,
15: 21 lord the king *l*, wherever my lord
15: 21 "As surely as the LORD *l*,
18: 8 the forest claimed more *l* that day
19: 5 daughters and the *l* of your wives
19: 5 the *l* of your sons and daughters
22: 47 "The LORD *l!* Praise be
23: 17 went at the risk of their *l?*"
1Ki 1: 29 "As surely as the LORD *l*,
2: 24 And now, as surely as the LORD *l*
17: 1 the God of Israel, *l*, whom I serve,
17: 12 As surely as the LORD your God *l*
18: 10 As surely as the LORD your God *l*
18: 15 "As the LORD Almighty *l*,
22: 14 "As surely as the LORD *l*,
2Ki 1: 13 and the *l* of these fifty men,
2: 2 as the LORD *l* and as you live,
2: 4 as the LORD *l* and as you live,
2: 6 as the LORD *l* and as you live,
3: 14 As surely as the LORD Almighty *l*
4: 30 as the LORD *l* and as you live,
5: 16 "As surely as the LORD *l*,
5: 20 as the LORD *l*, I will run after him
7: 7 as it was and ran for their *l*.
1Ch 11: 19 Because they risked their *l*
11: 19 went at the risk of their *l?*"
2Ch 18: 13 "As surely as the LORD *l*,
Job 15: 28 and houses where no one *l*,
19: 25 I know that my Redeemer *l*,
27: 2 God *l*, who has denied me justice,
38: 26 to water a land where no man *l*,
Ps 18: 46 The LORD *l!* Praise be
37: 32 seeking their very *l;*
66: 9 he has preserved our *l*
74: 19 do not forget the *l*
97: 10 for he guards the *l*
107: 5 and their *l* ebbed away.
Pr 1: 19 it takes away the *l*
3: 29 who *l* trustfully near you.
14: 25 A truthful witness saves *l*,
Ecc 2: 3 during the few days of their *l*.
6: 3 yet no matter how long he *l*,
6: 6 if he *l* a thousand years twice over
8: 12 crimes and still *l* a long time,
Isa 38: 20 all the days of our *l*
42: 11 settlements where Kedar *l* rejoice.
57: 15 he who *l* forever, whose name is
65: 20 an infant that *l* but a few days,
Jer 2: 6 where no one travels and no one *l?*'
4: 2 'As surely as the LORD *l*,'
4: 29 no one *l* in them.
5: 2 'As surely as the LORD *l*,'
12: 16 saying, 'As surely as the LORD *l*
16: 14 'As surely as the LORD *l*,
16: 15 'As surely as the LORD *l*,
17: 6 in a salt land where no one *l*.
19: 7 the hands of those who seek their *l*,
19: 9 by the enemies who seek their *l*.'
21: 7 to their enemies who seek their *l*.
23: 7 'As surely as the LORD *l*,
23: 8 'As surely as the LORD *l*,
34: 20 to their enemies who seek their *l*.
34: 21 to their enemies who seek their *l*,
38: 16 "As surely as the LORD *l*,
44: 26 As surely as the Sovereign LORD *l*
46: 26 over to those who seek their *l*,
48: 6 Flee! Run for your *l;*
49: 11 your orphans; I will protect their *l*.
49: 31 which *l* in confidence,"
49: 37 before those who seek their *l;*
51: 6 Run for your *l!*
51: 37 a place where no one *l*.
51: 43 a land where no one *l*,
51: 45 Run for your *l!*
La 2: 12 as their *l* ebb away
2: 19 him for the *l* of your children,
5: 9 We get our bread at the risk of our *l*
Eze 13: 18 Will you ensnare the *l* of my people
13: 22 their evil ways and so save their *l*,
17: 17 erected to destroy many *l*.
Da 3: 28 to give up their *l* rather than serve
4: 34 and glorified him who *l* forever.
12: 7 swear by him who *l* forever,
Hos 4: 15 'As surely as the LORD *l!*'
Am 8: 14 'As surely as the god of Beersheba *l*
8: 14 'As surely as your god *l*, O Dan,'
Mic 7: 14 which *l* by itself in a forest,
Hab 1: 16 for by his net he *l* in luxury
Jn 3: 21 But whoever *l* by the truth comes
11: 26 and whoever *l* and believes
14: 17 for he *l* with you and will be in you.
Ac 10: 32 home of Simon the tanner, who *l*
15: 26 men who have risked their *l*
27: 10 and cargo, and to our own *l* also."
27: 24 God has graciously given you the *l*
Ro 6: 10 but the life he *l*, he *l* to God.
7: 1 over a man only as long as he *l?*
7: 18 I know that nothing good *l* in me,
8: 9 if the Spirit of God *l* in you.
8: 11 through his Spirit, who *l* in you.
14: 7 For none of us *l* to himself alone
16: 4 They risked their *l* for me.
1Co 3: 16 and that God's Spirit *l* in you?
7: 39 to her husband as long as he *l*.
2Co 1: 5 of Christ flow over into our *l*,
13: 4 crucified in weakness, yet he *l*
Gal 2: 20 I no longer live, but Christ *l* in me.
Eph 2: 22 in which God *l* by his Spirit.
Col 2: 9 of the Deity *l* in bodily form,
1Th 2: 8 only the gospel of God but our *l*
2: 12 urging you to live *l* worthy of God,
1Ti 2: 2 quiet *l* in all godliness and holiness.
5: 6 pleasure is dead even while she *l*.
5: 6 widow who *l* for pleasure is dead
6: 16 and who *l* in unapproachable light,
2Ti 1: 5 I am persuaded, now *l* in you also.
1: 14 help of the Holy Spirit who *l* in us.
Tit 2: 12 and godly *l* in this present age,
3: 14 and not live unproductive *l*.
Heb 2: 15 free those who all their *l* were held
5: 13 not solid food! Anyone who *l*
7: 24 but because Jesus *l* forever,
7: 25 he always *l* to intercede for them.
13: 5 Keep your *l* free from the love
1Pe 1: 17 live your *l* as strangers here
1Pe 2: 12 Live such good *l* among the pagans
3: 2 the purity and reverence of your *l*.
2Pe 2: 7 by the filthy *l* of lawless men
3: 11 You ought to live holy and godly *l*
1Jn 1: 10 and his word has no place in our *l*.
2: 10 Whoever loves his brother *l*
2: 14 and the word of God *l* in you,
2: 17 who does the will of God *l* forever.
3: 6 No one who *l* in him keeps
3: 16 to lay down our *l* for our brothers.
3: 24 this is how we know that he *l* in us:
4: 12 God *l* in us and his love is made
4: 15 God *l* in him and he in God.
4: 16 Whoever *l* in love *l* in God,
2Jn : 2 which *l* in us and will be
Rev 2: 13 death in your city—where Satan *l*.
4: 9 and who *l* for ever and ever,
4: 10 and worship him who *l* for ever
10: 6 he swore by him who *l* for ever
12: 11 they did not love their *l* so much
15: 7 the wrath of God, who *l* for ever

LIVESTOCK

Ge 1: 24 *l*, creatures that move
1: 25 the *l* according to their kinds,
1: 26 over the *l*, over all the earth,
2: 20 So the man gave names to all the *l*,
3: 14 "Cursed are you above all the *l*
4: 20 live in tents and raise *l*.
7: 14 all *l* according to their kinds,
7: 21 on the earth perished—birds, *l*,
8: 1 the *l* that were with him in the ark,
9: 10 the *l* and all the wild animals,
13: 2 had become very wealthy in *l*
30: 29 how your *l* has fared under my care
31: 9 God has taken away your father's *l*
31: 18 and he drove all his *l* ahead of him,
33: 17 and made shelters for his *l*.
34: 5 his sons were in the fields with his *l*
34: 23 Won't their *l*, their property
36: 6 as his *l* and all his other animals
36: 7 them both because of their *l*.
46: 6 They also took with them their *l*
46: 32 The men are shepherds; they tend *l*
46: 34 'Your servants have tended *l*
47: 6 put them in charge of my own *l*."
47: 16 food in exchange for your *l*,
47: 16 "Then bring your *l*," said Joseph.
47: 17 So they brought their *l* to Joseph,
47: 17 with food in exchange for all their *l*
47: 18 money is gone and our *l* belongs
Ex 9: 3 plague on your *l* in the field—
9: 4 a distinction between the *l* of Israel
9: 6 All the *l* of the Egyptians died,
9: 19 Give an order now to bring your *l*
9: 20 to bring their slaves and their *l*
9: 21 of the LORD left their slaves and *l*
10: 26 Our *l* too must go with us;
12: 29 and the firstborn of all the *l* as well.
12: 38 as well as large droves of *l*,
13: 12 of your *l* belong to the LORD.
17: 3 our children and *l* die of thirst?"
22: 5 "If a man grazes his *l* in a field
34: 19 all the firstborn males of your *l*,
Lev 5: 2 wild animals or of unclean *l*
25: 7 as for your *l* and the wild animals
Nu 3: 41 and the *l* of the Levites in place
3: 41 firstborn of the *l* of the Israelites.
3: 45 and the *l* of the Levites in place
3: 45 of the Levites in place of their *l*.
20: 4 that we and our *l* should die here?
20: 8 so they and their *l* can drink."
20: 11 the community and their *l* drank.
20: 19 or our *l* drink any of your water,
32: 1 and Gilead were suitable for *l*.
32: 4 for *l*, and your servants have *l*.
32: 16 like to build pens here for our *l*
35: 3 flocks and all their other *l*.
Dt 2: 35 But the *l* and the plunder
3: 7 But all the *l* and the plunder
3: 19 and your *l* (I know you have much
3: 19 (I know you have much *l*) may stay
7: 14 nor any of your *l* without young.
13: 15 both its people and its *l*.
20: 14 the *l* and everything else in the city
28: 4 land and the young of your *l*—
28: 11 the young of your *l* and the crops
28: 51 will devour the young of your *l*

Lk 1:79 to shine on those *l* in darkness
2: 8 And there were shepherds *l* out
13: 4 than all the others *l* in Jerusalem?
15:13 squandered his wealth in wild *l*.
20:38 but of the *l*, for to him all are alive."
24: 5 look for the *l* among the dead?
24:18 "Are you the only one *l*
Jn 4:10 he would have given you *l* water."
4:11 Where can you get this *l* water?
4:51 with the news that his boy was *l*.
6:51 I am the *l* bread that came
6:57 Just as the *l* Father sent me
7:38 streams of *l* water will flow
14:10 Rather, it is the Father, *l* in me,
Ac 4:16 "Everybody *l* in Jerusalem knows
7: 4 to this land where you are now *l*.
7:38 he received *l* words to pass on to us
9:22 and baffled the Jews *l* in Damascus
9:31 it grew in numbers, *l* in the fear
10:42 as judge of the *l* and the dead.
11:29 help for the brothers *l* in Judea.
14:15 these worthless things to the *l* God,
19:17 known to the Jews and Greeks *l*
21:24 that you yourself are *l* in obedience
22:12 respected by all the Jews *l* there.
Ro 7:17 I myself who do it, but it is sin *l*
7:20 but it is sin *l* in me that does it.
8:11 Jesus from the dead is *l* in you,
9:26 will be called 'sons of the *l* God.' "
12: 1 to offer your bodies as *l* sacrifices,
14: 9 the Lord of both the dead and the *l*.
1Co 9: 6 Barnabas who must work for a *l*?
9:14 the gospel should receive their *l*
15: 6 most of whom are still *l*,
15:45 first man Adam became a *l* being";
2Co 3: 3 but with the Spirit of the *l* God,
6:16 For we are the temple of the *l* God.
Php 1:22 If I am to go on *l* in the body,
4:12 whether *l* in plenty or in want.
1Th 1: 9 to God from idols to serve the *l*
4: 1 to please God, as in fact you are *l*.
1Ti 3:15 which is the church of the *l* God,
4:10 we have put our hope in the *l* God,
2Ti 4: 1 who will judge the *l* and the dead,
Heb 3:12 that turns away from the *l* God.
4:12 For the word of God is *l* and active.
7: 8 by him who is declared to be *l*.
9:14 so that we may serve the *l* God!
9:17 while the one who made it is *l*.
10:20 and *l* way opened for us
10:31 to fall into the hands of the *l* God.
11:13 All these people were still *l* by faith
12:22 Jerusalem, the city of the *l* God.
1Pe 1: 3 a *l* hope through the resurrection
1:23 through the *l* and enduring word
2: 4 As you come to him, the *l* Stone—
2: 5 also, like *l* stones, are being built
4: 3 *l* in debauchery, lust, drunkenness,
4: 5 to him who is ready to judge the *l*
2Pe 2: 8 *l* among them day after day,
Rev 1:18 I am the *L* One; I was dead,
4: 6 the throne, were four *l* creatures,
4: 7 The first *l* creature was like a lion,
4: 8 of the four *l* creatures had six wings
4: 9 Whenever the *l* creatures give
5: 6 encircled by the four *l* creatures
5: 8 the four *l* creatures
5:11 and the *l* creatures and the elders.
5:14 The four *l* creatures said, "Amen,"
6: 1 one of the four *l* creatures say
6: 3 I heard the second *l* creature say,
6: 5 I heard the third *l* creature say,
6: 6 a voice among the four *l* creatures,
6: 7 voice of the fourth *l* creature say,
7: 2 having the seal of the *l* God.
7:11 the elders and the four *l* creatures.
7:17 to springs of *l* water.
8: 9 a third of the *l* creatures
14: 3 and before the four *l* creatures
15: 7 one of the four *l* creatures gave
16: 3 and every *l* thing in the sea died.
18:17 all who earn their *l* from the sea,
19: 4 and the four *l* creatures fell down

LIZARD

Lev 11:29 any kind of great *l*, the gecko,
11:30 the gecko, the monitor *l*, the wall *l*,
Pr 30:28 a *l* can be caught with the hand,

LO DEBAR

2Sa 9: 4 of Makir son of Ammiel in *L*."
9: 5 David had him brought from *L*,
17:27 and Makir son of Ammiel from *L*,
Am 6:13 rejoice in the conquest of *L* and

LO-AMMI

Hos 1: 9 Then the LORD said, "Call him *L*,

LO-RUHAMAH

Hos 1: 6 said to Hosea, "Call her *L*,
1: 8 she had weaned *L*, Gomer had

LOAD (CAMEL-LOADS LADEN LOADED LOADING LOADS SPICE-LADEN)

Ge 45:17 *L* your animals and return
Ex 18:22 That will make your *l* lighter,
23: 5 hates you fallen down under its *l*,
Ne 13:19 gates so that no *l* could be brought
Job 35: 9 under a *l* of oppression;
Isa 22:25 the *l* hanging on it will be cut down
Jer 17:21 not to carry a *l* on the Sabbath day
17:22 Do not bring a *l* out of your houses
17:24 and bring no *l* through the gates
17:27 holy by not carrying any *l*
Lk 11:46 *l* people down with burdens they
Gal 6: 5 for each one should carry his own *l*.

LOADED (LOAD)

Ge 37:25 Their camels were *l* with spices,
42:26 they *l* their grain on their donkeys
44:13 Then they all *l* their donkeys
45:23 ten donkeys *l* with the best things
45:23 ten female donkeys *l* with grain
Jos 9: 4 a delegation whose donkeys were *l*
1Sa 16:20 So Jesse took a donkey *l* with bread
17:20 *l* up and set out, as Jesse had
25:18 cakes of pressed figs, and *l* them
2Sa 16: 1 *l* with two hundred loaves of bread,
Isa 1: 4 a people *l* with guilt,
Am 2:13 as a cart crushes when *l* with grain.
2Ti 3: 6 who are *l* down with sins

LOADING (LOAD)

Ne 13:15 in grain and *l* it on donkeys,

LOADS (LOAD)

Ne 13:15 grapes, figs and all other kinds of *l*.
Job 37:11 He *l* the clouds with moisture;
Ps 144: 14 our oxen will draw heavy *l*.
La 5:13 boys stagger under *l* of wood.
Mt 23: 4 They tie up heavy *l* and put them

LOAF (LOAVES)

Ex 29:23 take a *l*, and a cake made with oil,
Lev 24: 5 two-tenths of an ephah for each *l*.
Jdg 7:13 "A round *l* of barley bread came
2Sa 6:19 he gave a *l* of bread, a cake of dates
1Ch 16: 3 he gave a *l* of bread, a cake of dates
Pr 6:26 for the prostitute reduces you to a *l*
Mk 8:14 for one *l* they had with them
1Co 10:17 Because there is one *l*, we,
10:17 for we all partake of the one *l*.

LOAN

Dt 15: 2 shall cancel the *l* he has made
24:10 When you make a *l* of any kind
24:11 are making the *l* bring the pledge
Eze 18: 7 what he took in pledge for a *l*.
18:16 or require a pledge for a *l*.
33:15 back what he took in pledge for a *l*,

LOATHE (LOATHED LOATHES LOATHING LOATHSOME)

Nu 11:20 out of your nostrils and you *l* it—
Job 10: 1 "I *l* my very life;
Eze 6: 9 They will *l* themselves
20:43 and you will *l* yourselves
36:31 you will *l* yourselves for your sins

LOATHED (LOATHE)

Ps 107: 18 They *l* all food

LOATHES (LOATHE)

Job 33:20 and his soul *l* the choicest meal.
Pr 27: 7 He who is full *l* honey,

LOATHING (LOATHE)

Ps 119:158 I look on the faithless with *l*,

LOATHSOME (LOATHE)

Job 19:17 I am *l* to my own brothers.
Ps 38: 5 My wounds fester and are *l*
Isa 66:24 and they will be *l* to all mankind."
Jer 6:15 ashamed of their *l* conduct?
8:12 ashamed of their *l* conduct?

LOAVES (LOAF)

Lev 23:17 bring two *l* made of two-tenths
24: 5 and bake twelve *l* of bread,
1Sa 10: 3 another three *l* of bread,
10: 4 and offer you two *l* of bread,
17:17 and these ten *l* of bread
21: 3 Give me five *l* of bread,
25:18 She took two hundred *l* of bread,
2Sa 16: 1 loaded with two hundred *l* of bread
1Ki 14: 3 Take ten *l* of bread with you,
2Ki 4:42 God twenty *l* of barley bread baked
Mt 14:17 "We have here only five *l* of bread
14:19 Taking the five *l* and the two fish
14:19 he gave thanks and broke the *l*.
15:34 "How many *l* do you have?"
15:36 he took the seven *l* and the fish,
16: 9 Don't you remember the five *l*
16:10 the seven *l* for the four thousand,
Mk 6:38 "How many *l* do you have?"
6:41 Taking the five *l* and the two fish
6:41 he gave thanks and broke the *l*.
6:52 had not understood about the *l*;
8: 5 "How many *l* do you have?"
8: 6 When he had taken the seven *l*
8:19 When I broke the five *l*
8:20 "And when I broke the seven *l*
Lk 9:13 "We have only five *l* of bread
9:16 Taking the five *l* and the two fish
11: 5 'Friend, lend me three *l* of bread,
Jn 6: 9 a boy with five small barley *l*
6:11 Jesus then took the *l*, gave thanks,
6:13 the pieces of the five barley *l* left
6:26 you ate the *l* and had your fill.

LOBE (LOBES)

Lev 8:23 put it on the *l* of Aaron's right ear,
14:14 and put it on the *l* of the right ear
14:17 in his palm on the *l* of the right ear
14:25 and put it on the *l* of the right ear
14:28 on the *l* of the right ear of the one
Dt 15:17 it through his ear *l* into the door,

LOBES (LOBE)

Ex 29:20 and put it on the *l* of the right ears
Lev 8:24 blood on the *l* of their right ears,

LOCAL

Mt 10:17 you over to the *l* councils
Mk 13: 9 handed over to the *l* councils

LOCATED (LOCATIONS)

Dt 19: 2 yourselves three cities centrally *l*

LOCATIONS (LOCATED)

1Ch 6:54 were the *l* of their settlements

LOCK (LOCKED)

SS 5: 5 on the handles of the *l*.

LOCKED (LOCK)

Jdg 3:23 room behind him and *l* them.
3:24 the doors of the upper room *l*.
9:51 They *l* themselves
SS 4:12 You are a garden *l* up, my sister,
Lk 3:20 to them all: He *l* John up in prison.
11: 7 door is already *l*, and my children
Jn 20:19 with the doors *l* for fear of the Jews
20:26 the doors were *l*, Jesus came
Ac 5:23 "We found the jail securely *l*,
Gal 3:23 *l* up until faith should be revealed.
Rev 20: 3 and *l* and sealed it over him,

LOCUST (LOCUSTS)

Ex 10:19 Not a *l* was left anywhere in Egypt.
Lev 11:22 Of these you may eat any kind of *l*,
Job 39:20 Do you make him leap like a *l*,
Ps 78:46 their produce to the *l*.
109: 23 I am shaken off like a *l*.

Joel 1: 4 What the *l* swarm has left
2: 25 the great *l* and the young *l*,
2: 25 the other locusts and the *l* swarm—

LOCUSTS (LOCUST)

Ex 10: 4 I will bring *l* into your country
10: 12 over Egypt so that *l* will swarm
10: 13 the wind had brought the *l*;
10: 14 had there been such a plague of *l*,
10: 19 caught up the *l* and carried them
Dt 28: 38 harvest little, because *l* will devour
28: 42 Swarms of *l* will take
Jdg 6: 5 and their tents like swarms of *l*.
7: 12 settled in the valley, thick as *l*.
1Ki 8: 37 blight or mildew, *l* or grasshoppers,
2Ch 6: 28 blight or mildew, *l* or grasshoppers,
7: 13 or command *l* to devour the land
Ps 105: 34 He spoke, and the *l* came,
Pr 30: 27 *l* have no king,
Isa 33: 4 is harvested as by young *l*;
33: 4 like a swarm of *l* men pounce on it.
Jer 46: 23 They are more numerous than *l*,
51: 14 you with men, as with a swarm of *l*,
51: 27 send up horses like a swarm of *l*.
Joel 1: 4 the great *l* have eaten;
1: 4 what the great *l* have left
1: 4 the young *l* have eaten;
1: 4 what the young *l* have left
1: 4 other *l* have eaten.
2: 25 the other *l* and the locust swarm—
2: 25 you for the years the *l* have eaten—
Am 4: 9 *L* devoured your fig and olive trees
7: 1 He was preparing swarms of *l*
Na 3: 15 multiply like *l*!
3: 16 but like *l* they strip the land
3: 17 Your guards are like *l*,
3: 17 your officials like swarms of *l*
Mt 3: 4 His food was *l* and wild honey.
Mk 1: 6 and he ate *l* and wild honey.
Rev 9: 3 And out of the smoke *l* came
9: 7 The *l* looked like horses prepared

LOD

1Ch 8: 12 *L* with its surrounding villages),
Ezr 2: 33 of Harim 320 of *L*, Hadid
Ne 7: 37 of Harim 320 of Jericho 345 of *L*,
11: 35 and Neballat, in *L* and Ono,

LODGE (LODGED LODGING)

Ps 119: 54 wherever I *l*.

LODGED (LODGE)

Ezr 4: 6 they *l* an accusation

LODGING (LODGE)

Ex 4: 24 At a *l* place on the way, the LORD
Ps 55: 15 for evil finds *l* among them.
Jer 9: 2 a *l* place for travelers,
Mic 6: 2 he is *l* a charge against Israel.
Lk 9: 12 countryside and find food and *l*,
Jas 2: 25 did when she gave *l* to the spies

LOFTINESS (LOFTY)

Ps 48: 2 It is beautiful in its *l*,

LOFTY (LOFTINESS)

Job 22: 12 And see how *l* are the highest stars
Ps 62: 4 him from his *l* place;
139: 6 too *l* for me to attain.
Isa 2: 12 store for all the proud and *l*,
2: 13 the cedars of Lebanon, tall and *l*,
2: 15 for every *l* tower
10: 33 The *l* trees will be felled,
26: 5 he lays the *l* city low;
30: 25 high mountain and every *l* hill.
57: 7 bed on a high and *l* hill;
57: 15 is what the high and *l* One says—
63: 15 from your *l* throne, holy
Jer 51: 53 and fortifies her *l* stronghold,
Eze 16: 24 and made a *l* shrine in every public
16: 25 every street you built your *l* shrines
16: 31 and made your *l* shrines
16: 39 and destroy your *l* shrines.
17: 22 plant it on a high and *l* mountain.
Am 9: 6 he who builds his *l* palace

LOG (LOGS)

Lev 14: 10 for a grain offering, and one *l* of oil.
14: 12 with the *l* of oil; he shall wave them
14: 15 priest shall then take some of the *l*
14: 21 a *l* of oil, and two doves
14: 24 together with the *l* of oil,

LOGS (LOG)

2Sa 5: 11 along with cedar *l* and carpenters
1Ki 5: 8 in providing the cedar and pine *l*.
5: 10 all the cedar and pine *l* he wanted,
1Ch 14: 1 along with cedar *l*, stonemasons
22: 4 also provided more cedar *l*
2Ch 2: 3 "Send me cedar *l* as you did
2: 8 pine and algum *l* from Lebanon,
2: 16 and we will cut all the *l*
Ezr 3: 7 so that they would bring cedar *l*
Ecc 10: 9 whoever splits *l* may be

LOINCLOTH

Job 12: 18 and ties a *l* around their waist.

LOINS

Lev 3: 4 with the fat around them near the *l*,
3: 10 with the fat around them near the *l*,
3: 15 with the fat on them near the *l*,
4: 9 with the fat on them near the *l*,
7: 4 with the fat around them near the *l*,
Dt 33: 11 Smite the *l* of those who rise up
Job 40: 16 What strength he has in his *l*,

LOIS

2Ti 1: 5 lived in your grandmother *L*

LONELY

Ps 25: 16 for I am *l* and afflicted.
68: 6 God sets the *l* in families,
Mk 1: 45 but stayed outside in *l* places.
Lk 5: 16 Jesus often withdrew to *l* places

LONG (LENGTH LENGTHEN LENGTHS LENGTHWISE LENGTHY LONGED LONGER LONGING LONGINGS LONGS)

Ge 6: 15 The ark is to be 450 feet *l*,
8: 22 "As *l* as the earth endures,
21: 34 land of the Philistines for a *l* time.
26: 8 When Isaac had been there a *l* time
38: 12 After a *l* time Judah's wife,
46: 29 his father and wept for a *l* time.
Ex 2: 23 During that *l* period, the king
10: 3 'How *l* will you refuse
10: 7 How *l* will this man be a snare to us
14: 20 went near the other all night *l*.
16: 28 "How *l* will you refuse
17: 11 As *l* as Moses held up his hands,
19: 13 horn sounds a *l* blast may they
20: 12 so that you may live *l*
25: 10 two and a half cubits *l*, a cubit
25: 17 two and a half cubits *l* and a cubit
25: 23 table of acacia wood—two cubits *l*,
26: 2 twenty-eight cubits *l* and four
26: 8 thirty cubits *l* and four cubits wide.
26: 16 Each frame is to be ten cubits *l*
27: 1 five cubits *l* and five cubits wide.
27: 9 side shall be a hundred cubits *l*
27: 11 also be a hundred cubits *l* and is
27: 14 Curtains fifteen cubits *l* are to be
27: 15 curtains fifteen cubits *l* are to be
27: 16 provide a curtain twenty cubits *l*,
27: 18 shall be a hundred cubits *l*
28: 16 a span *l* and a span wide—
30: 2 It is to be square, a cubit *l*
32: 1 *l* in coming
36: 9 twenty-eight cubits *l* and four
36: 15 thirty cubits *l* and four cubits wide.
36: 21 Each frame was ten cubits *l*
37: 1 two and a half cubits *l*, a cubit
37: 6 two and a half cubits *l* and a cubit
37: 10 table of acacia wood—two cubits *l*,
37: 25 It was square, a cubit *l*
38: 1 five cubits *l* and five cubits wide.
38: 9 south side was a hundred cubits *l*
38: 11 a hundred cubits *l* and had twenty
38: 14 Curtains fifteen cubits *l* were
38: 15 and curtains fifteen cubits *l* were
38: 18 It was twenty cubits *l* and,
39: 9 a span *l* and a span wide—
Lev 13: 46 As *l* as he has the infection he
15: 25 she will be unclean as *l*
Nu 6: 4 As *l* as he is a Nazirite, he must not
6: 5 the hair of his head grow *l*.
9: 18 As *l* as the cloud stayed
9: 19 over the tabernacle a *l* time,
14: 11 How *l* will they refuse to believe
14: 11 "How *l* will these people treat me
14: 27 "How *l* will this wicked
36: 6 may marry anyone they please as *l*
Dt 1: 6 "You have stayed *l* enough
2: 1 For a *l* time we made our way
2: 3 around this hill country *l* enough;
3: 11 and was more than thirteen feet *l*
4: 9 or let them slip from your heart as *l*
4: 10 as *l* as they live in the land
4: 25 have lived in the land a *l* time—
4: 26 You will not live there *l*
4: 32 Ask now about the former days, *l*
4: 40 and that you may live *l*
5: 16 that you may live *l* and that it may
6: 2 and so that you may enjoy *l* life.
6: 2 as *l* as you live by keeping all his
11: 9 and so that you may live *l*
12: 1 as *l* as you live in the land.
12: 19 as *l* as you live in your land.
17: 20 his descendants will reign a *l* time
20: 19 siege to a city for a *l* time,
22: 7 with you and you may have a *l* life.
22: 19 he must not divorce her as *l*
22: 29 He can never divorce her as *l*
23: 6 or good relations with them as *l*
25: 15 so that you may live *l*
30: 18 You will not live *l*
31: 13 to fear the LORD your God as *l*
32: 7 consider the generations *l* past.
32: 47 By them you will live *l*
33: 12 for he shields him all day *l*,
Jos 6: 5 you hear them sound a *l* blast
9: 13 out by the very *l* journey."
9: 22 'We live a *l* way from you,'
11: 18 against all these kings for a *l* time.
18: 3 "How *l* will you wait
22: 3 For a *l* time now—to this very day
23: 1 After a *l* time had passed
24: 2 says: '*L* ago your forefathers,
24: 7 you lived in the desert for a *l* time.
Jdg 2: 18 of the hands of their enemies as *l*
3: 16 sword about a foot and a half *l*,
5: 28 'Why is his chariot so *l* in coming?
18: 7 lived a *l* way from the Sidonians
18: 28 they lived a *l* way from Sidon
1Sa 1: 14 "How *l* will you keep
7: 2 It was a *l* time, twenty years in all,
10: 24 people shouted, "*L* live the king!"
16: 1 "How *l* will you mourn for Saul,
20: 14 kindness like that of the LORD as *l*
20: 31 As *l* as the son of Jesse lives
22: 4 and they stayed with him as *l*
25: 6 '*L* life to you! Good health to you
25: 28 no wrongdoing be found in you as *l*
27: 11 And such was his practice as *l*
2Sa 2: 26 How *l* before you order your men
3: 1 the house of David lasted a *l* time.
16: 16 "*L* live the king! *L* live the king!"
20: 18 She continued, "*L* ago they used
1Ki 1: 25 '*L* live King Adonijah!'
1: 34 and shout, '*L* live King Solomon!'
1: 39 the people shouted, "*L* live King
2: 38 stayed in Jerusalem for a *l* time.
3: 11 not for *l* life or wealth for yourself,
3: 14 father did, I will give you a *l* life."
6: 2 for the LORD was sixty cubits *l*,
6: 17 of this room was forty cubits *l*.
6: 20 sanctuary was twenty cubits *l*,
6: 24 of the first cherub was five cubits *l*,
7: 2 of Lebanon a hundred cubits *l*,
7: 6 He made a colonnade fifty cubits *l*
7: 27 each was four cubits *l*, four wide
8: 8 so *l* that their ends could be seen
11: 25 Rezon was Israel's adversary as *l*
18: 1 After a *l* time, in the third year,
18: 21 "How *l* will you waver
22: 35 All day *l* the battle raged,
2Ki 6: 25 so *l* that a donkey's head sold
9: 22 "as *l* as all the idolatry
11: 12 and shouted, "*L* live the king!"
13: 3 and for a *l* time he kept them
14: 13 a section about six hundred feet *l*.
19: 25 *L* ago I ordained it.
25: 30 Jehoiachin a regular allowance as *l*

1Ch 29: 28 having enjoyed *l* life, wealth
2Ch 1: 11 since you have not asked for a *l* life
3: 3 temple of God was sixty cubits *l*
3: 4 of the temple was twenty cubits *l*
3: 8 twenty cubits *l* and twenty cubits
3: 11 its other wing, also five cubits *l*,
3: 11 of the first cherub was five cubits *l*
3: 12 and its other wing, also five cubits *l*
3: 12 the second cherub was five cubits *l*
3: 15 ⌞together⌟ were thirty-five cubits *l*,
4: 1 a bronze altar twenty cubits *l*,
5: 9 were so *l* that their ends,
6: 13 five cubits *l*, five cubits wide
15: 3 For a *l* time Israel was
18: 34 All day *l* the battle raged,
23: 11 and shouted, "*L* live the king!"
24: 14 As *l* as Jehoiada lived, burnt
25: 23 a section about six hundred feet *l*.
26: 5 As *l* as he sought the LORD,
34: 33 As *l* as he lived, they did not fail
Ezr 4: 19 found that this city has a *l* history
Ne 2: 6 "How *l* will your journey take,
12: 46 For *l* ago, in the days of David
Est 5: 13 all this gives me no satisfaction as *l*
Job 3: 21 to those who *l* for death that does
7: 4 down I think, 'How *l*
8: 2 "How *l* will you say such things?
12: 12 Does not *l* life bring understanding
12: 19 and overthrows men *l* established.
14: 15 you will *l* for the creature your
19: 2 "How *l* will you torment me
27: 3 as *l* as I have life within me,
27: 6 will not reproach me as *l*
29: 2 "How I *l* for the months gone by,
36: 20 Do not *l* for the night
Ps 4: 2 How *l* will you love delusions
4: 2 How *l*, O men, will you turn my
6: 3 How *l*, O LORD, how *l*?
6: 6 all night *l* I flood my bed
13: 1 How *l* will you hide your face
13: 1 How *l*, O LORD? Will you forget
13: 2 How *l* must I wrestle
13: 2 How *l* will my enemy triumph
25: 5 and my hope is in you all day *l*.
32: 3 through my groaning all day *l*.
35: 17 O LORD, how *l* will you look on?
35: 28 and of your praises all day *l*.
38: 6 all day *l* I go about mourning.
38: 12 all day *l* they plot deception.
39: 1 *l* as the wicked are in my presence
42: 3 while men say to me all day *l*,
42: 10 saying to me all day *l*,
44: 1 in days *l* ago.
44: 8 In God we make our boast all day *l*,
44: 15 My disgrace is before me all day *l*,
44: 22 your sake we face death all day *l*;
52: 1 Why do you boast all day *l*,
56: 1 all day *l* they press their attack.
56: 2 My slanderers pursue me all day *l*;
56: 5 All day *l* they twist my words;
61: 4 I *l* to dwell in your tent forever
62: 3 How *l* will you assault a man?
63: 4 I will praise you as *l* as I live,
71: 8 declaring your splendor all day *l*.
71: 15 of your salvation all day *l*,
71: 24 all day *l*,
72: 5 He will endure as *l* as the sun,
72: 5 *l* as the moon, through all
72: 15 and bless him all day *l*.
72: 15 *L* may he live!
72: 17 may it continue as *l* as the sun.
73: 14 All day *l* I have been plagued;
74: 9 none of us knows how *l* this will be.
74: 10 How *l* will the enemy mock you,
74: 22 how fools mock you all day *l*.
77: 5 the years of *l* ago;
77: 11 remember your miracles of *l* ago.
79: 5 How *l* will your jealousy burn like
79: 5 How *l*, O LORD? Will you be
80: 4 how *l* will your anger smolder
82: 2 "How *l* will you defend the unjust
86: 3 for I call to you all day *l*.
88: 17 All day *l* they surround me like
89: 16 They rejoice in your name all day *l*;
89: 29 *l* as the heavens endure.
89: 46 How *l* will your wrath burn like fire
89: 46 How *l*, O LORD? Will you hide
90: 13 Relent, O LORD! How *l* will it be?
Ps 91: 16 With *l* life will I satisfy him
93: 2 Your throne was established *l* ago;
94: 3 How *l* will the wicked, O LORD,
94: 3 how *l* will the wicked be jubilant?
102: 8 All day *l* my enemies taunt me;
104: 33 I will sing praise to my God as *l*
116: 2 I will call on him as *l* as I live.
119: 40 How I *l* for your precepts!
119: 84 How *l* must your servant wait?
119: 97 I meditate on it all day *l*.
119:152 *L* ago I learned from your statutes
119:174 I *l* for your salvation, O LORD,
120: 6 Too *l* have I lived
129: 3 and made their furrows *l*.
143: 3 like those *l* dead.
143: 5 I remember the days of *l* ago;
146: 2 I will sing praise to my God as *l*
Pr 1: 22 How *l* will mockers delight
1: 22 "How *l* will you simple ones love
3: 16 *L* life is in her right hand;
6: 9 How *l* will you lie there, you
7: 19 he has gone on a *l* journey.
21: 26 All day *l* he craves for more,
28: 16 ill-gotten gain will enjoy a *l* life.
Ecc 1: 10 It was here already, *l* ago;
2: 16 the fool, will not be *l* remembered;
6: 3 yet no matter how *l* he lives,
7: 15 and a wicked man living *l*
8: 12 crimes and still lives a *l* time,
9: 6 their jealousy have *l* since vanished
SS 3: 1 All night *l* on my bed
Isa 6: 11 Then I said, "For how *l*, O Lord?"
22: 11 for the One who planned it *l* ago.
25: 1 things planned *l* ago.
30: 33 Topheth has *l* been prepared;
33: 2 we *l* for you.
37: 26 *L* ago I ordained it.
42: 14 "For a *l* time I have kept silent,
44: 8 proclaim this and foretell it *l* ago?
45: 21 Who foretold this *l* ago,
46: 9 the former things, those of *l* ago;
48: 3 I foretold the former things *l* ago,
48: 5 I told you these things *l* ago;
48: 7 are created now, and not *l* ago;
52: 5 "And all day *l*
57: 11 Is it not because I have *l* been silent
61: 4 and restore the places *l* devastated;
65: 2 All day *l* I have held out my hands
65: 22 my chosen ones will *l* enjoy
Jer 2: 20 "*L* ago you broke off your yoke
4: 14 How *l* will you harbor wicked
4: 21 How *l* must I see the battle
6: 4 and the shadows of evening grow *l*.
12: 4 How *l* will the land lie parched
13: 27 How *l* will you be unclean?"
20: 7 I am ridiculed all day *l*;
20: 8 insult and reproach all day *l*.
22: 27 back to the land you *l* to return to."
23: 26 How *l* will this continue
29: 28 to us in Babylon: It will be a *l* time.
31: 22 How *l* will you wander,
32: 14 in a clay jar so they will last a *l* time
35: 7 Then you will live a *l* time
37: 16 where he remained a *l* time.
44: 14 to which they *l* to return and live;
47: 5 how *l* will you cut yourselves?
47: 6 'how *l* till you rest?
52: 34 Jehoiachin a regular allowance as *l*
La 1: 13 faint all the day *l*.
2: 17 which he decreed *l* ago.
3: 3 again and again, all day *l*.
3: 6 like those *l* dead.
3: 14 they mock me in song all day *l*.
3: 62 and mutter against me all day *l*.
5: 20 Why do you forsake us so *l*?
Eze 7: 13 not recover the land he has sold as *l*
17: 3 *l* feathers and full plumage
26: 20 to the pit, to the people of *l* ago.
31: 5 and its branches grew *l*,
38: 8 which had *l* been desolate.
40: 5 in the man's hand was six *l* cubits,
40: 7 for the guards were one rod *l*
40: 18 and was as wide as they were *l*;
40: 21 was fifty cubits *l* and twenty-five
40: 25 was fifty cubits *l* and twenty-five
40: 29 was fifty cubits *l* and twenty-five
40: 33 was fifty cubits *l* and twenty-five
40: 36 was fifty cubits *l* and twenty-five
Eze 40: 42 each a cubit and a half *l*, a cubit
40: 43 hooks, each a handbreadth *l*,
40: 47 a hundred cubits *l* and a hundred
41: 2 was forty cubits *l* and twenty cubits
41: 8 the length of the rod, six *l* cubits.
41: 13 temple; it was a hundred cubits *l*,
41: 13 walls were also a hundred cubits *l*.
42: 2 faced north was a hundred cubits *l*
42: 4 cubits wide and a hundred cubits *l*.
42: 8 sanctuary was a hundred cubits *l*.
42: 8 to the outer court was fifty cubits *l*,
42: 20 five hundred cubits *l* and five
43: 13 of the altar in *l* cubits,
43: 16 twelve cubits *l* and twelve cubits
43: 17 fourteen cubits *l* and fourteen
44: 20 their heads or let their hair grow *l*,
45: 1 25,000 cubits *l* and 20,000
45: 3 cubits *l* and 10,000 cubits wide.
45: 5 An area 25,000 cubits *l* and 10,000
45: 6 cubits *l*, adjoining the sacred
46: 22 forty cubits *l* and thirty cubits wide
48: 9 cubits *l* and 10,000 cubits wide.
48: 10 It will be 25,000 cubits *l*
48: 10 25,000 cubits *l* on the south side.
48: 13 cubits *l* and 10,000 cubits wide.
48: 15 cubits wide and 25,000 cubits *l*,
48: 30 north side, which is 4,500 cubits *l*,
48: 32 cubits *l*, will be three gates:
48: 34 cubits *l*, will be three gates:
Da 8: 3 the canal, and the horns were *l*.
8: 13 "How *l* will it take for the vision
12: 6 *l* will it be before these astonishing
Hos 7: 13 I *l* to redeem them
8: 5 How *l* will they be incapable
Am 5: 18 Why do you *l* for the day
5: 18 Woe to you who *l*
Mic 7: 14 as in days *l* ago.
7: 20 fathers in days *l* ago.
Hab 1: 2 How *l*, O LORD, must I call
2: 6 How *l* must this go on?'
Zec 1: 12 how *l* will you withhold mercy
2: 2 to find out how wide and how *l* it is
5: 2 thirty feet *l* and fifteen feet wide."
Mt 5: 21 said to the people *l* ago,
5: 33 said to the people *l* ago,
11: 21 they would have repented *l* ago
17: 17 How *l* shall I put up with you?
17: 17 "how *l* shall I stay with you?
20: 6 here all day *l* doing nothing?'
23: 5 the tassels of their prayer shawls *l*;
24: 48 'My master is staying away a *l* time
25: 5 The bridegroom was a *l* time
25: 19 "After a *l* time the master
Mk 2: 19 so *l* as they have him with them.
6: 15 like one of the prophets of *l* ago."
8: 3 of them have come a *l* distance."
9: 19 How *l* shall I put up with you?
9: 19 "how *l* shall I stay with you?
9: 21 "How *l* has he been like this?"
Lk 1: 21 and wondering why he stayed so *l*
1: 70 through his holy prophets of *l* ago),
8: 27 For a *l* time this man had not worn
9: 8 prophets of *l* ago had come back
9: 19 prophets of *l* ago has come back
9: 41 "how *l* shall I stay with you
10: 13 they would have repented *l* ago,
12: 45 'My master is taking a *l* time
13: 16 bound for eighteen *l* years,
14: 32 while the other is still a *l* way off
15: 13 "Not *l* after that, the younger son
15: 20 "But while he was still a *l* way off,
17: 22 coming when you will *l* to see one
20: 9 and went away for a *l* time.
23: 8 for a *l* time he had been wanting
Jn 5: 6 been in this condition for a *l* time,
9: 4 As *l* as it is day, we must do
10: 24 How *l* will you keep us in suspense
14: 9 been among you such a *l* time?
14: 19 Before *l*, the world will not see me
Ac 1: 16 which the Holy Spirit spoke *l* ago
3: 21 he promised *l* ago through his holy
8: 11 them for a *l* time with his magic.
14: 28 And they stayed there a *l* time
24: 2 "We have enjoyed a *l* period
26: 5 They have known me for a *l* time
26: 29 Paul replied, "Short time or *l*—
27: 14 Before very *l*, a wind
27: 21 After the men had gone a *l* time

Ac 28: 6 but after waiting a *l* time
Ro 1: 11 I *l* to see you so that I may impart
7: 1 authority over a man only as *l*
7: 2 bound to her husband as *l*
8: 36 your sake we face death all day *l*;
10: 21 "All day *l* I have held out my
16: 25 the mystery hidden for *l* ages past,
1Co 7: 39 bound to her husband as *l*
11: 14 that if a man has *l* hair,
11: 15 For *l* hair is given to her
11: 15 but that if a woman has *l* hair,
2Co 5: 6 confident and know that as *l*
Gal 4: 1 What I am saying is that as *l*
Eph 3: 18 to grasp how wide and *l* and high
6: 3 and that you may enjoy *l* life
Php 1: 8 God can testify how I *l* for all
4: 1 you whom I love and *l* for,
1Th 3: 6 just as we also *l* to see you.
3: 6 of us and that you *l* to see us,
2Ti 1: 4 Recalling your tears, I *l* to see you,
Heb 3: 13 encourage one another daily, as *l*
4: 7 when a *l* time later he spoke
9: 8 as *l* as the first tabernacle was still
1Pe 1: 12 Even angels *l* to look
3: 20 in prison who disobeyed *l* ago
2Pe 1: 13 as *l* as I live in the tent of this body,
2: 3 condemnation has *l* been hanging
3: 5 they deliberately forget that *l* ago
Jude : 4 was written about *l* ago have
Rev 6: 10 "How *l*, Sovereign Lord, holy
9: 6 but will not find it; they will *l* to die
21: 16 and as wide and high as it is *l*.
21: 16 city was laid out like a square, as *l*

LONG-SUFFERING (SUFFER)

Jer 15: 15 You are *l*— do not take me away;

LONG-WINDED (WIND)

Job 16: 3 Will your *l* speeches never end?

LONGED (LONG)

Ge 31: 30 you *l* to return to your father's
2Sa 13: 39 of the king *l* to go to Absalom,
14: 1 knew that the king's heart *l*
23: 15 David *l* for water and said, "Oh,
1Ch 11: 17 David *l* for water and said, "Oh,
Isa 21: 4 the twilight I *l* for
Eze 23: 21 So you *l* for the lewdness
Mt 13: 17 righteous men *l* to see what you see
23: 37 how often I have *l*
Lk 13: 34 how often I have *l*
15: 16 He *l* to fill his stomach
2Ti 4: 8 to all who have *l* for his appearing.
Rev 18: 14 The fruit you *l* for is gone from you

LONGER (LONG)

Isa 62: 12 The City No *L* Deserted.

LONGING (LONG)

Dt 28: 65 with *l*, and a despairing heart.
Job 7: 2 Like a slave *l* for the evening
Ps 119: 20 My soul is consumed with *l*
119: 81 with *l* for your salvation,
119:131 *l* for your commands.
143: 7 my spirit faints with *l*.
Pr 13: 12 but a *l* fulfilled is a tree of life
13: 19 A *l* fulfilled is sweet to the soul.
Eze 23: 27 look on these things with *l*
Lk 16: 21 and *l* to eat what fell from the rich
Ro 15: 23 since I have been *l* for many years
2Co 5: 2 *l* to be clothed with our heavenly
7: 7 He told us about your *l* for me,
7: 11 what alarm, what *l*, what concern,
1Th 2: 17 out of our intense *l* we made every
Heb 11: 16 they were *l* for a better country—

LONGINGS (LONG)

Ps 38: 9 All my *l* lie open before you,
112: 10 the *l* of the wicked will come

LONGS (LONG)

Ps 63: 1 my body *l* for you,
Isa 26: 9 in the morning my spirit *l* for you.
30: 18 Yet the LORD *l* to be gracious
Php 2: 26 For he *l* for all of you and is

LOOK (FINE-LOOKING LOOKED LOOKING LOOKOUT LOOKOUTS LOOKS)

Ge 4: 5 his offering he did not *l* with favor.
13: 14 from where you are and *l* north
15: 5 "*L* up at the heavens and count
19: 8 *L*, I have two daughters who have
19: 17 "Flee for your lives! Don't *l* back,
19: 20 *L*, here is a town near enough
25: 32 "*L*, I am about to die," Esau said.
27: 6 Rebekah said to her son Jacob, "*L*,
29: 7 "*L*," he said, "the sun is still high;
31: 12 '*L* up and see that all the male
39: 14 "*L*," she said to them, "this
41: 33 now let Pharaoh *l* for a discerning
49: 18 I *l* for your deliverance, O LORD.
Ex 1: 9 "*L*," he said to his people,
3: 4 saw that he had gone over to *l*,
3: 6 because he was afraid to *l* at God.
5: 5 work!" Then Pharaoh said, "*L*,
5: 21 "May the LORD *l* upon you
Lev 13: 36 need to *l* for yellow hair;
26: 9 " 'I will *l* on you with favor
Nu 4: 20 go in to *l* at the holy things,
15: 39 You will have these tassels to *l* at
21: 8 anyone who is bitten can *l* at it
32: 8 Kadesh Barnea to *l* over the land.
Dt 3: 27 *L* at the land with your own eyes,
3: 27 *l* west and north and south and east
4: 19 And when you *l* up to the sky
4: 29 you will find him if you *l* for him
7: 16 Do not *l* on them with pity
26: 15 *L* down from heaven, your holy
Jos 2: 1 "Go, *l* over the land," he said,
2: 2 The king of Jericho was told, "*L!*
22: 28 *L* at the replica of the LORD's
Jdg 6: 36 *l*, I will place a wool fleece
9: 36 saw them, he said to Zebul, "*L*,
9: 37 But Gaal spoke up again: "*L*,
14: 8 he turned aside to *l*
19: 9 said, "Now *l*, it's almost evening.
19: 24 *L*, here is my virgin daughter,
21: 19 But *l*, there is the annual festival
Ru 1: 15 "*L*," said Naomi, "your
1Sa 1: 11 you will only *l* upon your servant's
9: 3 and go and *l* for the donkeys."
9: 6 But the servant replied, "*L*,
9: 8 "*L*," he said, "I have a quarter
10: 2 out to *l* for have been found.
14: 11 "*L!*" said the Philistines.
14: 33 Then someone said to Saul, "*L*,
16: 7 The LORD does not *l*
18: 22 to David privately and say, '*L*,
20: 2 *L*, my father doesn't do anything,
20: 5 "*L*, tomorrow is the New Moon
20: 21 '*L*, the arrows are on this side
20: 22 '*L*, the arrows are beyond you,'
21: 14 said to his servants, "*L* at the man!
23: 1 When David was told, "*L*,
24: 2 set out to *l* for David and his men
24: 11 *l* at this piece of your robe
26: 16 *L* around you.
26: 20 of Israel has come out to *l* for a flea
28: 14 "What does he *l* like?" he asked
28: 21 "*L*, your maidservant has obeyed
2Sa 2: 22 How could I *l* your brother Joab
3: 24 have you done? *L*, Abner came
13: 4 *l* so haggard morning
14: 30 Then he said to his servants, "*L*,
14: 32 Absalom said to Joab, "*L*,
15: 3 Absalom would say to him, "*L*,
18: 26 "*L*, another man running alone!"
1Ki 1: 2 "Let us *l* for a young virgin
12: 16 *L* after your own house, O David!"
17: 23 him to his mother and said, "*L*,
18: 10 master has not sent someone to *l*
18: 43 "Go and *l* toward the sea,"
20: 31 His officials said to him, "*L*,
22: 13 summon Micaiah said to him, "*L*,
2Ki 2: 16 Let them go and *l* for your master.
2: 16 "*L*," they said, "we your servants
2: 19 "*L*, our lord, this town is well
3: 14 I would not *l* at you or
4: 25 "*L!* There's the Shunammite!
6: 1 of the prophets said to Elisha, "*L*,
6: 32 *L*, when the messenger comes,
7: 2 "*L*, even if the LORD should open
2Ki 7: 6 so that they said to one another, "*L*
7: 19 said to the man of God, "*L*,
9: 2 *l* for Jehu son of Jehoshaphat,
10: 23 "*L* around and see that no servants
18: 21 that you rebel against me? *L* now,
1Ch 16: 11 *L* to the LORD and his strength;
21: 23 *L*, I will give the oxen
2Ch 10: 16 *L* after your own house, O David!"
18: 12 summon Micaiah said to him, "*L*,
Ne 2: 2 "Why does your face *l* so sad
2: 3 Why should my face not *l* sad
Est 1: 11 nobles, for she was lovely to *l* at.
Job 6: 19 The caravans of Tema *l* for water,
6: 19 of Sheba *l* in hope.
6: 28 "But now be so kind as to *l* at me.
7: 8 you will *l* for me, but I will be no
7: 19 Will you never *l* away from me,
8: 5 But if you will *l* to God
11: 18 you will *l* about you and take your
14: 6 *l* away from him and let him alone,
19: 15 they *l* upon me as an alien.
20: 9 his place will *l* on him no more.
21: 5 *L* at me and be astonished;
24: 1 Why must those who know him *l*
30: 20 I stand up, but you merely *l* at me.
31: 1 not to *l* lustfully at a girl.
35: 5 *L* up at the heavens and see;
37: 21 Now no one can *l* at the sun,
40: 11 *l* at every proud man and bring him
40: 12 *l* at every proud man and humble
40: 15 "*L* at the behemoth,
Ps 11: 2 For *l*, the wicked bend their bows;
13: 3 *L* on me and answer, O LORD my
25: 18 *L* upon my affliction and my
34: 5 Those who *l* to him are radiant;
35: 17 O LORD, how long will you *l* on?
37: 10 you *l* for them, they will not be
39: 7 "But now, Lord, what do I *l* for?
39: 13 *L* away from me, that I may rejoice
40: 4 who does not *l* to the proud,
59: 4 Arise to help me; *l* on my plight!
80: 14 *L* down from heaven and see!
84: 9 *L* upon our shield, O God;
84: 9 *l* with favor on your anointed one.
104: 27 These all *l* to you
105: 4 *L* to the LORD and his strength;
112: 8 in the end he will *l* in triumph
113: 6 who stoops down to *l*
118: 7 I will *l* in triumph on my enemies.
119:153 *L* upon my suffering and deliver
119:158 I *l* on the faithless with loathing,
123: 2 As the eyes of slaves *l* to the hand
123: 2 as the eyes of a maid *l* to the hand
123: 2 so our eyes *l* to the LORD our God
142: 4 *L* to my right and see;
145: 15 The eyes of all *l* to you,
Pr 1: 28 they will *l* for me but will not find
2: 4 and if you *l* for it as for silver
4: 25 Let your eyes *l* straight ahead,
15: 30 A cheerful *l* brings joy to the heart,
Ecc 1: 10 "*L!* This is something new"?
1: 16 "*L*, I have grown and increased
7: 27 "*L*," says the Teacher, "this is
SS 2: 8 *L!* Here he comes,
2: 9 *L!* There he stands behind our wall
3: 7 *L!* It is Solomon's carriage,
3: 11 and *l* at King Solomon wearing
6: 1 that we may *l* for him with you?
6: 11 to *l* at the new growth in the valley,
Isa 3: 9 The *l* on their faces testifies
8: 22 Then they will *l* toward the earth
10: 12 and the haughty *l* in his eyes.
13: 8 They will *l* aghast at each other,
13: 18 nor will they *l* with compassion
17: 7 In that day men will *l*
17: 8 They will not *l* to the altars,
18: 4 will *l* on from my dwelling place,
21: 9 *L*, here comes a man in a chariot
22: 11 you did not *l* to the One who made
23: 13 *L* at the land of the Babylonians,
30: 2 *l* for help to Pharaoh's protection,
31: 1 do not *l* to the Holy One of Israel,
33: 7 *L*, their brave men cry aloud
33: 20 *L* upon Zion, the city
34: 16 *L* in the scroll of the LORD
36: 6 that you rebel against me? *L* now,
38: 11 no longer will I *l* on mankind,
40: 26 Lift your eyes and *l* to the heavens:

Isa 41:27 I was the first to tell Zion, '*L*,
41:28 I *l* but there is no one—
42:18 *l*, you blind, and see!
48: 6 You have heard these things; *l*
49:18 Lift up your eyes and *l* around;
51: 1 *L* to the rock from which you were
51: 2 *l* to Abraham, your father,
51: 3 and will *l* with compassion
51: 5 The islands will *l* to me
51: 6 *l* at the earth beneath;
59: 9 We *l* for light, but all is darkness;
59:11 We *l* for justice, but find none;
60: 4 "Lift up your eyes and *l* about you:
60: 5 Then you will *l* and be radiant,
60: 9 Surely the islands *l* to me;
63:15 *L* down from heaven and see
64: 9 Oh, *l* upon us, we pray,
66:24 and *l* upon the dead bodies
Jer 2:10 over to the coasts of Kittim and *l*,
3: 2 *L* up to the barren heights and see.
3: 3 Yet you have the brazen *l*
4:13 *L!* He advances like the clouds,
5: 1 *l* around and consider,
5: 3 do not your eyes *l* for truth?
6:16 "Stand at the crossroads and *l*;
6:22 "*L*, an army is coming
7: 8 But *l*, you are trusting in deceptive
18:11 'This is what the LORD says: *L!*
25:32 "*L!* Disaster is spreading
39:12 "Take him and *l* after him;
40: 4 if you like, and I will *l* after you;
40: 4 *L*, the whole country lies
48:40 "*L!* An eagle is swooping down,
49:22 *L!* An eagle will soar and swoop
50:41 "*L!* An army is coming
La 1: 9 "*L*, O LORD, on my affliction,
1:11 "*L*, O LORD, and consider,
1:12 *L* around and see.
1:18 *l* upon my suffering.
2:20 "*L*, O LORD, and consider:
3:63 *L* at them! Sitting or standing,
5: 1 *l*, and see our disgrace.
Eze 5:11 I will not *l* on you with pity
7: 4 I will not *l* on you with pity
7: 9 I will not *l* on you with pity
8: 5 "Son of man, *l* toward the north."
8:17 *L* at them putting the branch
8:18 I will not *l* on them with pity
9:10 So I will not *l* on them with pity
18: 6 *l* to the idols of the house of Israel.
18:15 *l* to the idols of the house of Israel.
23:27 You will not *l* on these things
25: 8 'Because Moab and Seir said, "*L*,
33:25 and *l* to your idols and shed blood,
34:11 for my sheep and *l* after them.
34:12 so will I *l* after my sheep.
36: 9 and will *l* on you with favor;
40: 4 *l* with your eyes and hear
44: 5 to me, "Son of man, *l* carefully,
Da 2:13 and men were sent to *l* for Daniel
3:25 "*L!* I see four men walking
5:10 Don't be alarmed! Don't *l* so pale!
9:17 *l* with favor on your desolate
Hos 2: 2 Let her remove the adulterous *l*
2: 7 she will *l* for them but not find
Am 6: 2 Go to Calneh and *l* at it;
7: 8 "*L*, I am setting a plumb line
Ob :12 should not *l* down on your brother
:13 *l* down on them in their calamity
Jnh 2: 4 yet I will *l* again
Mic 1: 3 *L!* The LORD is coming
Na 1:15 *L*, there on the mountains,
2: 4 They *l* like flaming torches;
3:13 *L* at your troops—
Hab 1: 3 Why do you make me *l* at injustice
1: 5 "*L* at the nations and watch—
1:13 Your eyes are too pure to *l* on evil;
2: 1 I will *l* to see what he will say to me
Hag 2: 3 How does it *l* to you now?
Zec 5: 5 "*L* up and see what this is that is
6: 8 "*L*, those going toward the north
12:10 They will *l* on me, the one they
Mt 6:16 do not *l* somber as the hypocrites
6:26 than clothes? *L* at the birds
7: 3 "Why do you *l* at the speck
12: 2 saw this, they said to him, "*L!*
18:10 "See that you do not *l* down on one
18:12 go to *l* for the one that wandered

Mt 23:27 which *l* beautiful on the outside
23:38 *L*, your house is left to you desolate
24:23 time if anyone says to you, '*L*,
25:43 in prison and you did not *l* after me
26:45 you still sleeping and resting? *L*,
26:65 *L*, now you have heard
28: 1 and the other Mary went to *l*
Mk 1:36 his companions went to *l* for him,
2:24 The Pharisees said to him, "*L*,
8:24 they *l* like trees walking around."
11:21 and said to Jesus, "Rabbi, *l!*
12:15 "Bring me a denarius and let me *l*
13: 1 "*L*, Teacher! What massive stones!
13:21 '*L*, here is the Christ!' or, '*L*,
14:41 *L*, the Son of Man is betrayed
Lk 2:45 back to Jerusalem to *l* for him.
6:41 "Why do you *l* at the speck
9:38 "Teacher, I beg you to *l* at my son,
10:35 '*L* after him,' he said,
13: 6 and he went to *l* for fruit on it,
13: 7 coming to *l* for fruit on this fig tree
13:35 but you were not willing! *L*,
15:29 But he answered his father, '*L!*
18:13 He would not even *l* up to heaven,
19: 8 stood up and said to the Lord, "*L*,
21:29 "*L* at the fig tree and all the trees.
24: 5 "Why do you *l* for the living
24:39 *L* at my hands and my feet.
Jn 1:29 coming toward him and said, "*L*,
1:36 he said, "*L*, the Lamb of God!"
4:35 open your eyes and *l* at the fields!
7:34 You will *l* for me, but you will not
7:36 'You will *l* for me, but you will not
7:52 Are you from Galilee, too? *L* into it
8:21 "I am going away, and you will *l*
12:19 *L* how the whole world has gone
13:33 You will *l* for me, and just
19: 4 came out and said to the Jews, "*L*,
19:37 "They will *l* on the one they have
20:11 she bent over to *l* into the tomb
Ac 3: 4 Then Peter said, "*L* at us!"
5: 9 to test the Spirit of the Lord? *L!*
5:25 Then someone came and said, "*L!*
7:31 As he went over to *l* more closely,
7:32 with fear and did not dare to *l*.
7:56 "*L*," he said, "I see heaven open
8:36 water and the eunuch said, "*L*,
11:25 went to Tarsus to *l* for Saul,
13:41 said does not happen to you: " '*L*,
Ro 1:23 made to *l* like mortal man
14: 3 who eats everything must not *l*
14:10 why do you *l* down on your brother
1Co 1:22 miraculous signs and Greeks *l*
7:27 Are you unmarried? Do not *l*
2Co 3: 7 the Israelites could not *l* steadily
Php 2: 4 Each of you should *l* not only
1Ti 4:12 Don't let anyone *l* down on you
Jas 1:27 to *l* after orphans and widows
5: 4 *L!* The wages you failed
1Pe 1:12 long to *l* into these things.
2Pe 3:12 as you *l* forward to the day of God
Rev 1: 7 *L*, he is coming with the clouds,
5: 3 could open the scroll or even *l*
5: 4 to open the scroll or *l* inside.

LOOKED (LOOK)

Ge 4: 4 The LORD *l* with favor on Abel
13:10 Lot *l* up and saw that the whole
18: 2 Abraham *l* up and saw three men
18:16 they *l* down toward Sodom,
19:26 Lot's wife *l* back and she became
19:28 He *l* down toward Sodom
22: 4 On the third day Abraham *l* up
22:13 Abraham *l* up and there
24:63 he *l* up, he saw camels approaching
24:64 Rebekah also *l* up and saw Isaac.
26: 8 king of the Philistines *l*
31:10 I once had a dream in which I *l* up
33: 1 Jacob *l* up and there was Esau,
33: 5 Then Esau *l* up and saw the women
37:25 they *l* up and saw a caravan
41:21 they *l* just as ugly as before.
43:29 As he *l* about and saw his brother
43:30 Joseph hurried out and *l* for a place
43:33 and they *l* at each other
Ex 2:25 So God *l* on the Israelites
14:10 approached, the Israelites *l* up,
14:24 In the morning watch the LORD *l*

Ex 16:10 whole Israelite community, they *l*
24:17 of the LORD *l* like a consuming
Nu 9:15 above the tabernacle *l* like fire.
9:16 and at night it *l* like fire.
11: 7 like coriander seed and *l* like resin.
13:33 and we *l* the same to them."
17: 9 They *l* at them, and each man took
21: 9 by a snake and *l* at the bronze
24: 2 When Balaam *l* out and saw Israel
Dt 9:16 When I *l*, I saw that you had sinned
Jos 5:13 he *l* up and saw a man standing
8:20 of Ai *l* back and saw the smoke
Jdg 13: 6 He *l* like an angel of God, very
19:17 When he *l* and saw the traveler
1Sa 6:13 and when they *l* up and saw the ark
6:19 because they had *l* into the ark
9:16 I have *l* upon my people,
10:21 But when they *l* for him, he was not
17:42 He *l* David over and saw that he
24: 8 "My lord the king!" When Saul *l*
2Sa 2:20 Abner *l* behind him and asked,
13:34 Now the man standing watch *l* up
18:24 As he *l* out, he saw a man running
24:20 When Araunah *l* and saw the king
1Ki 2:15 All Israel *l* to me as their king.
3:21 But when I *l* at him closely
18:43 And he went up and *l*.
19: 6 He *l* around, and there
2Ki 2:24 *l* at them and called down a curse
3:22 the water *l* red—like blood.
6:17 he *l* and saw the hills full of horses
6:20 opened their eyes and they *l*,
6:30 the people *l*, and there, underneath
9:30 arranged her hair and *l* out
9:32 He *l* up at the window
9:32 or three eunuchs *l* down at him.
11:14 She *l* and there was the king,
23:16 Then Josiah *l* around,
1Ch 17:17 You have *l* on me as though I were
21:16 David *l* up and saw the angel
21:21 and when Araunah *l* and saw him,
2Ch 20:24 and *l* toward the vast army,
23:13 She *l*, and there was the king,
26:20 and all the other priests *l* at him,
Ne 4:14 After I *l* things over, I stood up
Est 3: 6 Instead Haman *l* for a way
Job 28:27 then he *l* at wisdom and appraised
30:26 when I *l* for light, then came
Ps 37:36 I *l* for him, he could not be found.
54: 7 my eyes have *l* in triumph
69:20 I *l* for sympathy, but there was
102:19 LORD *l* down from his sanctuary
114: 3 The sea *l* and fled,
Pr 7: 6 I *l* out through the lattice.
7:15 I *l* for you and have found you!
Ecc 4: 1 Again I *l* and saw all the oppression
SS 3: 1 I *l* for him but did not find him.
3: 1 I *l* for the one my heart loves;
3: 2 So I *l* for him but did not find him.
5: 6 I *l* for him but did not find him.
Isa 5: 2 Then he *l* for a crop of good grapes,
5: 4 When I *l* for good grapes,
5: 7 he *l* for justice, but saw bloodshed;
22: 8 And you *l* in that day
38:14 My eyes grew weak as I *l*
57: 8 and you *l* on their nakedness.
59:15 The LORD *l* and was displeased
63: 5 I *l*, but there was no one to help,
Jer 4:23 I *l* at the earth,
4:24 I *l* at the mountains,
4:25 I *l*, and there were no people;
4:26 I *l*, and the fruitful land was
31:26 At this I awoke and *l* around.
36:16 they *l* at each other in fear
La 1: 7 Her enemies *l* at her
Eze 1: 4 I *l*, and I saw a windstorm coming
1: 4 of the fire *l* like glowing metal,
1: 5 the fire was what *l* like four living
1:10 Their faces *l* like this: Each
1:15 As I *l* at the living creatures,
1:16 like chrysolite, and all four *l* alike.
1:22 creatures was what *l* like
1:26 their heads was what *l* like a throne
1:27 his waist up he *l* like glowing metal,
1:27 that from there down he *l* like fire;
2: 9 I *l*, and I saw a hand stretched out
8: 2 I *l*, and I saw a figure like that
8: 3 He stretched out what *l* like a hand

Eze 8: 5 So I *l*, and in the entrance north
8: 7 I *l*, and I saw a hole in the wall.
8: 10 and *l*, and I saw portrayed all
10: 1 I *l*, and I saw the likeness
10: 8 could be seen what *l* like the hands
10: 9 I *l*, and I saw beside the cherubim
10: 10 the four of them *l* alike;
10: 21 wings was what *l* like the hands
16: 5 No one *l* on you with pity
16: 8 when I *l* at you and saw that you
20: 17 Yet I *l* on them with pity
22: 30 "I *l* for a man among them who
23: 15 of them *l* like Babylonian chariot
34: 6 and no one searched or *l* for them.
37: 8 I *l*, and tendons and flesh appeared
40: 2 some buildings that *l* like a city.
44: 4 I *l* and saw the glory
Da 1: 15 end of the ten days they *l* healthier
2: 31 "You *l*, O king, and there
4: 10 saw while lying in my bed: I *l*,
4: 13 I *l*, and there before me was
7: 2 said: "In my vision at night I *l*,
7: 5 a second beast, which *l* like a bear.
7: 6 I *l*, and there before me was
7: 6 beast, one that *l* like a leopard.
7: 7 After that, in my vision at night I *l*,
7: 9 "As I *l*,
7: 13 "In my vision at night I *l*,
7: 20 the horn that *l* more imposing
8: 3 I *l* up, and there before me was
8: 15 me stood one who *l* like a man.
10: 5 I *l* up and there before me was
10: 16 one who *l* like a man touched my
10: 18 Again the one who *l* like a man
12: 5 *l*, and there before me stood two
Hab 3: 6 he *l*, and made the nations tremble.
Zec 1: 18 I *l* up—and there before me were
2: 1 I *l* up—and there before me was
5: 1 I *l* again—and there
5: 9 I *l* up—and there before me were
6: 1 I *l* up again—and there
Mt 17: 8 When they *l* up, they saw no one
19: 26 "Who then can be saved?" Jesus *l*
21: 46 They *l* for a way to arrest him,
25: 36 I was sick and you *l* after me,
Mk 3: 5 He *l* around at them in anger and,
3: 34 Then he *l* at those seated in a circle
7: 34 He *l* up to heaven and with a deep
8: 24 "Do you see anything?" He *l* up
8: 33 But when Jesus turned and *l*
9: 8 Suddenly, when they *l* around,
9: 26 boy *l* so much like a corpse that
10: 21 Jesus *l* at him and loved him.
10: 23 Jesus *l* around and said
10: 27 "Who then can be saved?" Jesus *l*
11: 11 He *l* around at everything,
12: 12 Then they *l* for a way to arrest him
14: 67 warming himself, she *l* closely
16: 4 But when they *l* up, they saw that
Lk 6: 10 or to destroy it?" He *l*
16: 23 he *l* up and saw Abraham far away,
18: 9 and *l* down on everybody else,
18: 24 Jesus *l* at him and said, "How hard
19: 5 Jesus reached the spot, he *l* up
20: 17 Jesus *l* directly at them and asked,
20: 19 and the chief priests *l* for a way
21: 1 As he *l* up, Jesus saw the rich
22: 56 She *l* closely at him and said,
22: 61 The Lord turned and *l* straight
Jn 1: 42 Simon to Jesus, who *l* at him
6: 5 When Jesus *l* up and saw a great
11: 41 Then Jesus *l* up and said, "Father,
17: 1 he *l* toward heaven and prayed:
20: 5 *l* in at the strips of linen lying there
Ac 3: 4 Peter *l* straight at him, as did John.
6: 15 sitting in the Sanhedrin *l* intently
7: 55 *l* up to heaven and saw the glory
11: 6 I *l* into it and saw four-footed
13: 9 *l* straight at Elymas and said,
14: 9 Paul *l* directly at him, saw that he
23: 1 Paul *l* straight at the Sanhedrin
1Jn 1: 1 which we have *l* at and our hands
Rev 4: 1 After this I *l*, and there
4: 6 throne there was what *l* like a sea
5: 11 Then I *l* and heard the voice
6: 2 I *l*, and there before me was a white
6: 5 I *l*, and there before me was a black
6: 8 I *l*, and there before me was a pale
Rev 7: 9 After this I *l* and there
9: 7 The locusts *l* like horses prepared
9: 17 riders I saw in my vision *l* like this:
11: 12 in a cloud, while their enemies *l* on
14: 1 Then I *l*, and there before me was
14: 14 I *l*, and there before me was a white
15: 2 And I saw what *l* like a sea
15: 5 After this I *l* and in heaven
16: 13 three evil spirits that *l* like frogs;

LOOKING (LOOK)

Ge 37: 15 "What are you *l* for?" He replied,
37: 16 He replied, "I'm *l* for my brothers.
42: 1 "Why do you just keep *l*
Ex 22: 10 or is taken away while no one is *l*,
25: 20 are to face each other, *l*
37: 9 The cherubim faced each other, *l*
Dt 22: 2 and keep it until he comes *l* for it.
Jdg 4: 22 I will show you the man you're *l* for
17: 9 "and I'm *l* for a place to stay."
1Sa 10: 14 "Where have you been?" "*L*
19: 2 "My father Saul is *l* for a chance
1Ki 20: 7 "See how this man is *l* for trouble!
2Ki 6: 19 you to the man you are *l* for."
Ps 69: 3 *l* for my God.
119: 82 My eyes fail, *l* for your promise;
119:123 My eyes fail, *l* for your salvation,
119:123 *l* for your righteous promise.
Ecc 12: 3 those *l* through the windows grow
SS 7: 4 *l* toward Damascus.
Isa 8: 21 become enraged and, *l* upward,
Jer 46: 5 haste without *l* back,
La 4: 17 *l* in vain for help,
Da 1: 10 Why should he see you *l* worse
7: 11 I kept *l* until the beast was slain
Mt 12: 10 *L* for a reason to accuse Jesus,
13: 45 of heaven is like a merchant *l*
14: 19 and the two fish and *l* up to heaven,
26: 59 and the whole Sanhedrin were *l*
28: 5 for I know that you are *l* for Jesus,
Mk 1: 37 they exclaimed: "Everyone is *l*
3: 2 Some of them were *l* for a reason
3: 32 and brothers are outside *l* for you."
5: 32 Jesus kept *l* around to see who had
6: 41 and the two fish and *l* up to heaven,
11: 18 and began *l* for a way to kill him,
14: 1 of the law were *l* for some sly way
14: 55 and the whole Sanhedrin were *l*
16: 6 "You are *l* for Jesus the Nazarene,
Lk 2: 38 the child to all who were *l* forward
2: 44 Then they began *l* for him
4: 42 The people were *l* for him
6: 7 of the law were *l* for a reason
6: 20 *L* at his disciples, he said:
9: 16 and the two fish and *l* up to heaven,
17: 7 of you had a servant plowing or *l*
22: 2 of the law were *l* for some way
Jn 6: 26 I tell you the truth, you are *l* for me
11: 56 They kept *l* for Jesus, and
18: 8 "If you are *l* for me, then let these
20: 15 Who is it you are *l*
Ac 1: 10 They were *l* intently up
1: 11 "why do you stand here *l*
10: 19 "Simon, three men are *l* for you.
10: 21 to the men, "I'm the one you're *l*
2Co 10: 7 You are *l* only on the surface
Php 4: 17 Not that I am *l* for a gift,
4: 17 but I am *l* for what may be credited
1Th 2: 6 We were not *l* for praise from men,
Heb 11: 10 For he was *l* forward to the city
11: 14 say such things show that they are *l*
11: 26 he was *l* ahead to his reward.
13: 14 we are *l* for the city that is to come.
Jas 1: 24 and, after *l* at himself, goes away
1Pe 5: 8 prowls around like a roaring lion *l*
2Pe 3: 13 with his promise we are *l* forward
3: 14 since you are *l* forward to this,
Rev 5: 6 I saw a Lamb, *l* as if it had been

LOOKOUT (LOOK)

2Ki 9: 17 When the *l* standing on the tower
9: 18 *l* reported, "The messenger has
9: 20 *l* reported, "He has reached them,
Isa 21: 6 "Go, post a *l*
21: 8 And the *l* shouted,

LOOKOUTS (LOOK)

1Sa 14: 16 Saul's *l* at Gibeah of Benjamin saw

LOOKS (LOOK)

Lev 14: 35 seen something that *l* like mildew
1Sa 16: 7 Man *l* at the outward appearance,
16: 7 but the LORD *l* at the heart."
16: 7 look at the things man *l* at.
Ezr 8: 22 is on everyone who *l* to him,
Job 8: 17 and *l* for a place among the stones.
41: 34 He *l* down on all that are haughty;
Ps 14: 2 The LORD *l* down from heaven
33: 13 From heaven the LORD *l* down
53: 2 God *l* down from heaven
85: 11 righteousness *l* down from heaven.
104: 32 He *l* at the earth, and it trembles;
138: 6 on high, he *l* upon the lowly,
Pr 20: 4 so at harvest time he *l*
25: 23 so a sly tongue brings angry *l*.
27: 18 he who *l* after his master will be
Ecc 11: 4 whoever *l* at the clouds will not
Isa 5: 30 And if one *l* at the land,
40: 20 He *l* for a skilled craftsman
La 3: 50 until the LORD *l* down
Eze 18: 12 He *l* to the idols.
34: 12 As a shepherd *l* after his scattered
Da 3: 25 the fourth *l* like a son of the gods."
Mt 5: 28 But I tell you that anyone who *l*
16: 4 and adulterous generation *l*
Lk 9: 62 and *l* back is fit for service
Jn 6: 40 Father's will is that everyone who *l*
9: 9 said, "No, he only *l* like him."
12: 45 When he *l* at me, he sees the one
Php 2: 21 For everyone *l* out
Jas 1: 23 do what it says is like a man who *l*
1: 24 immediately forgets what he *l* like.
1: 25 But the man who *l* intently

LOOM (LOOMS)

Jdg 16: 13 into the fabric ⌞on the *l*⌟
16: 14 and pulled up the pin and the *l*,
Isa 38: 12 and he has cut me off from the *l*;

LOOMS (LOOM)

Jer 6: 1 For disaster *l* out of the north,

LOOPS

Ex 26: 4 Make *l* of blue material
26: 5 Make fifty *l* on one curtain
26: 5 and fifty *l* on the end curtain
26: 5 with the *l* opposite each other.
26: 10 Make fifty *l* along the edge
26: 11 in the *l* to fasten the tent together
36: 11 Then they made *l* of blue material
36: 12 also made fifty *l* on one curtain
36: 12 and fifty *l* on the end curtain
36: 12 with the *l* opposite each other.
36: 17 they made fifty *l* along the edge

LOOSE (LOOSED LOOSEN LOOSENED)

Jdg 15: 5 let the foxes *l* in the standing grain
16: 3 and tore them *l*, bar and all.
Job 6: 9 to let *l* his hand and cut me off!
12: 15 if he lets them *l*, they devastate
38: 31 Can you *l* the cords of Orion?
Ps 78: 26 He let *l* the east wind
Isa 7: 25 places where cattle are turned *l*
33: 23 Your rigging hangs *l*.
58: 6 to *l* the chains of injustice
Mt 16: 19 and whatever you *l* on earth will be
18: 18 and whatever you *l* on earth will be
Ac 16: 26 and everybody's chains came *l*.
27: 40 Cutting *l* the anchors, they left

LOOSED (LOOSE)

Mt 16: 19 loose on earth will be *l* in heaven."
18: 18 loose on earth will be *l* in heaven.
Lk 1: 64 was opened and his tongue was *l*,

LOOSEN (LOOSE)

Nu 5: 18 he shall *l* her hair and place

LOOSENED (LOOSE)

Isa 5: 27 not a belt is *l* at the waist,
Mk 7: 35 his tongue was *l* and he began

LOOT (LOOTED LOOTER LOOTING)

Isa 10: 6 to seize *l* and snatch plunder,
17: 14 This is the portion of those who *l* us
21: 2 traitor betrays, the looter takes *l*.
42: 22 they have been made *l*,

Isa 42: 24 handed Jacob over to become *l*,
Eze 7: 21 and as *l* to the wicked of the earth,
26: 12 wealth and *l* your merchandise;
29: 19 He will *l* and plunder the land
38: 12 and *l* and turn my hand
38: 13 Have you gathered your hordes to *l*
39: 10 and *l* those who looted them,
Da 11: 24 *l* and wealth among his followers.
Am 3: 10 "who hoard plunder and *l*

LOOTED (LOOT)

Ge 34: 27 and *l* the city where their sister had
2Ki 21: 14 They will be *l* and plundered
Isa 13: 16 houses will be *l* and their wives
42: 22 But this is a people plundered and *l*
Eze 39: 10 and loot those who *l* them,

LOOTER (LOOT)

Isa 21: 2 The traitor betrays, the *l* takes loot.

LOOTING (LOOT)

1Sa 23: 1 and are *l* the threshing floors,"

LOP

Isa 10: 33 will *l* off the boughs

***LORD (*LORD'S LORDED LORDING LORDS)**

Ge 18: 3 my *l*, do not pass your servant by.
18: 27 been so bold as to speak to the *L*,
18: 30 he said, "May the *L* not be angry,
18: 31 been so bold as to speak to the *L*,
18: 32 he said, "May the *L* not be angry,
20: 4 "*L*, will you destroy an innocent
23: 11 "No, my *l*," he said.
23: 15 Abraham, "Listen to me, my *l*;
24: 18 my *l*," she said, and quickly
27: 29 Be *l* over your brothers,
27: 37 "I have made him *l* over you
31: 35 my *l*, that I cannot stand up
32: 5 I am sending this message to my *l*,
32: 18 They are a gift sent to my *l* Esau,
33: 8 "To find favor in your eyes, my *l*,"
33: 13 "My *l* knows that the children are
33: 14 let my *l* go on ahead of his servant,
33: 14 until I come to my *l* in Seir."
33: 15 favor in the eyes of my *l*."
42: 10 "No, my *l*," they answered.
42: 30 "The man who is *l*
42: 33 the man who is *l* over the land said
44: 7 "Why does my *l* say such things?
44: 16 "What can we say to my *l*?"
44: 18 my *l*, let your servant speak a word
44: 18 your servant speak a word to my *l*.
44: 19 My *l* asked his servants, 'Do you
44: 22 to my *l*, 'The boy cannot leave his
44: 24 we told him what my *l* had said.
45: 8 *l* of his entire household
45: 9 God has made me *l* of all Egypt.
47: 18 hide from our *l* the fact that
47: 18 there is nothing left for our *l*
47: 25 favor in the eyes of our *l*;
Ex 4: 10 "O *L*, I have never been eloquent,
4: 13 "O *L*, please send someone else
5: 22 to the LORD and said, "O *L*,
15: 17 O *L*, your hands established.
32: 22 be angry, my *l*," Aaron answered.
34: 9 he said, "then let the *L* go with us.
34: 9 "O *L*, if I have found favor
Nu 11: 28 "Moses, my *l*, stop them!"
12: 11 and he said to Moses, "Please, my *l*
16: 13 now you also want to *l* it over us?
32: 25 will do as our *l* commands.
32: 27 before the LORD, just as our *l* says
36: 2 the LORD commanded my *l*
Dt 10: 17 God of gods and *L* of lords,
Jos 3: 11 the ark of the covenant of the *L*
3: 13 the *L* of all the earth—set foot
5: 14 "What message does my *L* have
7: 8 O *L*, what can I say, now that Israel
Jdg 3: 25 There they saw their *l* fallen
4: 18 "Come, my *l*, come right in.
6: 15 Am I not sending you?" "But *L*,"
13: 8 prayed to the LORD: "O *L*,
Ru 2: 13 to find favor in your eyes, my *l*,"
1Sa 1: 15 "Not so, my *l*," Hannah replied,
1: 26 "As surely as you live, my *l*,
16: 16 Let our *l* command his servants

*See also †LORD, †LORD'S

1Sa 22: 12 "Yes, my *l*," he answered.
24: 8 My *l* the king!" When Saul looked
25: 24 My *l*, let the blame be on me alone.
25: 25 May my *l* pay no attention
26: 15 came to destroy your *l* the king.
26: 15 didn't you guard your *l* the king?
26: 17 replied, "Yes it is, my *l* the king."
26: 18 "Why is my *l* pursuing his servant?
26: 19 Now let my *l* the king listen
29: 8 the enemies of my *l* the king?"
2Sa 1: 10 have brought them here to my *l*."
3: 21 assemble all Israel for my *l* the king
4: 8 LORD has avenged my *l* the king
9: 11 do whatever my *l* the king
10: 3 nobles said to Hanun their *l*,
13: 32 "My *l* should not think that they
13: 33 My *l* the king should not be
14: 9 said to him, "My *l* the king,
14: 12 speak a word to my *l* the king."
14: 15 come to say this to my *l* the king
14: 17 for my *l* the king is like an angel
14: 17 of my *l* the king bring me rest,
14: 18 "Let my *l* the king speak,"
14: 19 As surely as you live, my *l* the king,
14: 19 from anything my *l* the king says.
14: 20 My *l* has wisdom like that
14: 22 my *l* the king, because the king has
15: 15 do whatever our *l* the king
15: 21 and as my *l* the king lives,
15: 21 wherever my *l* the king may be,
16: 4 favor in your eyes, my *l* the king."
16: 9 this dead dog curse my *l* the king?
18: 28 hands against my *l* the king."
18: 31 My *l* the king, hear the good news!
18: 32 "May the enemies of my *l* the king
19: 19 wrong on the day my *l* the king left
19: 19 "May my *l* not hold me guilty.
19: 20 down and meet my *l* the king."
19: 26 He said, "My *l* the king,
19: 27 My *l* the king is like an angel
19: 27 your servant to my *l* the king.
19: 28 but death from my *l* the king,
19: 30 now that my *l* the king has arrived
19: 35 an added burden to my *l* the king?
19: 37 cross over with my *l* the king.
24: 3 But why does my *l* the king want
24: 3 may the eyes of my *l* the king see it.
24: 21 "Why has my *l* the king come
24: 22 "Let my *l* the king take whatever
1Ki 1: 2 him so that our *l* the king may keep
1: 11 without our *l* David's knowing it?
1: 13 and say to him, 'My *l* the king,
1: 17 "My *l*, you yourself swore
1: 18 my *l* the king, do not know about it
1: 20 My *l* the king, the eyes
1: 20 throne of my *l* the king after him.
1: 21 as my *l* the king is laid to rest
1: 24 "Have you, my *l* the king,
1: 27 Is this something my *l* the king has
1: 27 throne of my *l* the king after him?"
1: 31 "May my *l* King David live forever
1: 36 the God of my *l* the king,
1: 37 than the throne of my *l* King David
1: 37 was with my *l* the king,
1: 43 "Our *l* King David has made
1: 47 to congratulate our *l* King David,
2: 38 as my *l* the king has said."
3: 10 *L* was pleased that Solomon had
3: 17 "My *l*, this woman and I live
3: 26 my *l*, give her the living baby!
12: 27 give their allegiance to their *l*,
18: 7 my *l* Elijah?" "Yes," he replied.
18: 13 my *l*, what I did while Jezebel was
20: 4 "Just as you say, my *l* the king.
20: 9 messengers, "Tell my *l* the king,
22: 6 "for the *L* will give it
2Ki 2: 19 our *l*, this town is well situated,
4: 16 "No, my *l*," she objected.
4: 28 "Did I ask you for a son, my *l*?"
6: 5 my *l*," he cried out, "it was
6: 12 "None of us, my *l* the king,"
6: 15 "Oh, my *l*, what shall we do?"
6: 26 "Help me, my *l* the king!"
7: 6 for the *L* had caused the Arameans
8: 5 "This is the woman, my *l* the king,
8: 12 "Why is my *l* weeping?" asked
19: 23 you have heaped insults on the *L*.
1Ch 21: 3 My *l* the king, are they not all my
1Ch 21: 3 Why does my *l* want to do this?
21: 23 Let my *l* the king do whatever
2Ch 2: 14 and with those of my *l*,
2: 15 let my *l* send his servants the wheat
Ezr 10: 3 with the counsel of my *l*
Ne 1: 11 O *L*, let your ear be attentive
4: 14 Remember the *L*, who is great
8: 10 This day is sacred to our *L*.
Job 28: 28 'The fear of the *L*—that is wisdom,
Ps 2: 4 the *L* scoffs at them.
8: 1 O LORD, our *L*,
8: 9 O LORD, our *L*,
16: 2 I said to the LORD, "You are my *L*
22: 30 will be told about the *L*.
30: 8 to the *L* I cried for mercy:
35: 22 Do not be far from me, O *L*.
35: 23 Contend for me, my God and *L*.
37: 13 but the *L* laughs at the wicked,
38: 9 longings lie open before you, O *L*;
38: 15 you will answer, O *L* my God.
38: 22 O *L* my Savior.
39: 7 "But now, *L*, what do I look for?
40: 17 may the *L* think of me.
44: 23 Awake, O *L*! Why do you sleep?
45: 11 honor him, for he is your *l*.
51: 15 O *L*, open my lips,
54: 4 the *L* is the one who sustains me.
55: 9 O *L*, confound their speech,
57: 9 I will praise you, O *L*,
59: 11 do not kill them, O *L* our shield,
62: 12 and that you, O *L*, are loving.
66: 18 the *L* would not have listened;
68: 11 The *L* announced the word,
68: 17 the *L* has come from Sinai
68: 19 Praise be to the *L*,
68: 22 The *L* says, "I will bring you
68: 32 sing praise to the *L*, *Selah*
69: 6 O *L*, the LORD Almighty;
73: 20 so when you arise, O *L*,
77: 2 was in distress, I sought the *L*;
77: 7 "Will the *L* reject us forever?
78: 65 Then the *L* awoke as from sleep,
79: 12 they have hurled at you, O *L*.
86: 3 Have mercy on me, O *L*,
86: 4 for to you, O *L*,
86: 5 You are kind and forgiving, O *L*,
86: 8 gods there is none like you, O *L*;
86: 9 and worship before you, O *L*;
86: 12 I will praise you, O *L* my God,
86: 15 O *L*, are a compassionate
89: 49 O *L*, where is your former great
89: 50 *L*, how your servant has been
90: 1 *L*, you have been our dwelling
90: 17 the favor of the *L* our God rest
97: 5 before the *L* of all the earth.
110: 1 The LORD says to my *L*:
110: 5 The *L* is at your right hand;
114: 7 O earth, at the presence of the *L*,
130: 2 O LORD; O *L*, hear my voice.
130: 3 O *L*, who could stand?
130: 6 My soul waits for the *L*
135: 5 that our *L* is greater than all gods.
136: 3 Give thanks to the *L* of lords:
147: 5 Great is our *L* and mighty in power
Isa 1: 24 Therefore the *L*, the LORD
3: 1 See now, the *L*,
3: 15 declares the *L*, the LORD
3: 17 Therefore the *L* will bring sores
3: 18 In that day the *L* will snatch away
4: 4 The *L* will wash away the filth
6: 1 I saw the *L* seated on a throne,
6: 8 I heard the voice of the *L* saying,
6: 11 "For how long, O *L*?"
7: 14 Therefore the *L* himself will give
7: 20 In that day the *L* will use a razor
8: 7 the *L* is about to bring against them
9: 8 The *L* has sent a message
9: 17 Therefore the *L* will take no
10: 12 When the *L* has finished all his
10: 16 the *L*, the LORD Almighty,
10: 23 The *L*, the LORD Almighty,
10: 24 is what the *L*, the LORD
10: 33 See, the *L*, the LORD Almighty,
11: 11 In that day the *L* will reach out his
19: 4 declares the *L*, the LORD
21: 6 This is what the *L* says to me:
21: 8 my *l*, I stand on the watchtower;
21: 16 This is what the *L* says to me:

Isa 22: 5 The L, the LORD Almighty,
22: 12 The L, the LORD Almighty,
22: 14 says the L, the LORD Almighty.
22: 15 is what the L, the LORD
28: 2 the L has one who is powerful
28: 22 the L, the LORD Almighty,
29: 13 The L says:
30: 20 Although the L gives you the bread
37: 24 you have heaped insults on the L.
38: 14 I am troubled; O L, come to my aid
38: 16 L, by such things men live;
49: 14 the L has forgotten me."
Jer 2: 19 declares the L, the LORD
37: 20 my l the king, please listen.
38: 9 and said to him, "My l the king,
46: 10 For the L, the LORD Almighty,
49: 5 declares the L, the LORD
50: 31 declares the L, the LORD
La 1: 14 and the L has sapped my strength.
1: 15 In his winepress the L has trampled
1: 15 "The L has rejected
2: 1 How the L has covered
2: 2 Without pity the L has swallowed
2: 5 The L is like an enemy;
2: 7 The L has rejected his altar
2: 18 cry out to the L.
2: 19 water in the presence of the L.
2: 20 killed in the sanctuary of the L?
3: 31 by the L forever.
3: 36 would not the L see such things?
3: 37 happen if the L has not decreed it?
3: 58 O L, you took up my case;
Eze 18: 25 'The way of the L is not just.'
18: 29 'The way of the L is not just.'
21: 9 and say, 'This is what the L says:
33: 17 'The way of the L is not just.'
33: 20 'The way of the L is not just.'
Da 1: 2 the L delivered Jehoiakim king
1: 10 "I am afraid of my l the king,
2: 47 and the L of kings and a revealer
4: 19 Belteshazzar answered, "My l,
4: 24 issued against my l the king:
5: 23 up against the L of heaven.
9: 3 So I turned to the L God
9: 4 "O L, the great and awesome God,
9: 7 "L, you are righteous,
9: 9 The L our God is merciful
9: 15 O L our God, who brought your
9: 16 O L, in keeping with all your
9: 17 O L, look with favor
9: 19 O L, listen! O L, forgive! O L,
10: 16 because of the vision, my l,
10: 17 your servant, talk with you, my l?
10: 19 my l, since you have given me
12: 8 "My l, what will the outcome
Hos 12: 14 his L will leave upon him the guilt
Am 3: 13 declares the L, the LORD God
5: 16 Therefore this is what the L,
7: 7 The L was standing
7: 8 L said, "Look, I am setting a plumb
9: 1 I saw the L standing by the altar,
9: 5 The L, the LORD Almighty,
Mic 1: 2 the L from his holy temple.
4: 13 their wealth to the L of all the earth
Zec 1: 9 I asked, "What are these, my l?"
4: 4 are these, my l?" He answered,
4: 5 know what these are?" "No, my l,"
4: 13 know what these are?" "No, my l,"
6: 4 my l?" The angel answered me,
6: 5 of the L of the whole world.
Mal 1: 14 a blemished animal to the L.
3: 1 suddenly the L you are seeking will
Mt 1: 20 an angel of the L appeared to him
1: 22 place to fulfill what the L had said
1: 24 angel of the L had commanded him
2: 13 angel of the L appeared to Joseph
2: 15 so was fulfilled what the L had said
2: 19 an angel of the L appeared
3: 3 'Prepare the way for the L,
4: 7 'Do not put the L your God
4: 10 'Worship the L your God,
5: 33 the oaths you have made to the L.'
7: 21 L,' will enter the kingdom
7: 21 "Not everyone who says to me, 'L,
7: 22 Many will say to me on that day, 'L
7: 22 L, did we not prophesy
8: 2 "L, if you are willing, you can
8: 6 "L," he said, "my servant lies
Mt 8: 8 The centurion replied, "L,
8: 21 one of his disciples, said to him, "L,
8: 25 L, save us! We're going to drown!"
9: 28 able to do this?" "Yes, L,"
9: 38 Ask the L of the harvest, therefore,
11: 25 Father, L of heaven and earth,
12: 8 Son of Man is L of the Sabbath."
14: 28 "L, if it's you," Peter replied,
14: 30 beginning to sink, cried out, "L,
15: 22 crying out, "L, Son of David,
15: 25 "L, help me!" she said.
15: 27 L," she said, "but even the dogs eat
16: 22 "Never, L!" he said.
17: 4 "L, it is good for us to be here.
17: 15 L, have mercy on my son," he said.
18: 21 Peter came to Jesus and asked, "L,
20: 25 of the Gentiles l it over them,
20: 30 they shouted, "L, Son of David,
20: 31 but they shouted all the louder, "L,
20: 33 "L," they answered, "we want our
21: 3 tell him that the L needs them,
21: 9 comes in the name of the L!"
21: 42 the L has done this,
22: 37 " 'Love the L your God
22: 43 calls him 'L'? For he says,
22: 44 For he says, " 'The L said to my L:
22: 45 If then David calls him 'L,'
23: 39 comes in the name of the L.' "
24: 42 on what day your L will come.
25: 37 the righteous will answer him, 'L,
25: 44 "They also will answer, 'L,
26: 22 "Surely not I, L?" Jesus replied,
27: 10 as the L commanded me."
28: 2 of the L came down from heaven
Mk 1: 3 'Prepare the way for the L,
2: 28 of Man is L even of the Sabbath."
5: 19 tell them how much the L has done
7: 28 L," she replied, "but even the dogs
10: 42 rulers of the Gentiles l it over them
11: 3 L needs it and will send it back
11: 9 comes in the name of the L!"
12: 11 the L has done this,
12: 29 the L our God, the L is one.
12: 30 Love the L your God
12: 36 " 'The L said to my L:
12: 37 David himself calls him 'L.'
13: 20 If the L had not cut short those
16: 19 After the L Jesus had spoken
16: 20 and the L worked with them
Lk 1: 9 to go into the temple of the L
1: 11 an angel of the L appeared to him,
1: 15 great in the sight of the L.
1: 16 back to the L their God.
1: 17 And he will go on before the L,
1: 17 ready a people prepared for the L."
1: 25 "The L has done this for me,"
1: 28 who are highly favored! The L is
1: 32 The L God will give him the throne
1: 43 of my L should come to me?
1: 45 believed that what the L has said
1: 46 "My soul praises the L
1: 58 heard that the L had shown her
1: 68 Praise be to the L, the God of Israel
1: 76 on before the L to prepare the way
2: 9 An angel of the L appeared to them
2: 9 glory of the L shone around them,
2: 11 born to you; he is Christ the L.
2: 15 which the L has told us about."
2: 22 Jerusalem to present him to the L
2: 23 is to be consecrated to the L),
2: 23 (as it is written in the Law of the L,
2: 24 said in the Law of the L:
2: 29 Sovereign L, as you have promised
2: 39 required by the Law of the L,
3: 4 'Prepare the way for the L,
4: 8 'Worship the L your God
4: 12 'Do not put the L your God
4: 18 "The Spirit of the L is on me,
5: 8 from me, L; I am a sinful man!"
5: 12 "L, if you are willing, you can
5: 17 the power of the L was present
6: 5 The Son of Man is L of the Sabbath
6: 46 "Why do you call me, 'L, L,'
7: 6 "L, don't trouble yourself,
7: 13 When the L saw her, his heart went
7: 19 he sent them to the L to ask,
9: 54 and John saw this, they asked, "L,
9: 59 "L, first let me go and bury my
Lk 9: 61 another said, "I will follow you, L;
10: 1 this the L appointed seventy-two
10: 2 Ask the L of the harvest, therefore,
10: 17 returned with joy and said, "L,
10: 21 Father, L of heaven and earth,
10: 27 " 'Love the L your God
10: 40 She came to him and asked, "L,
10: 41 Martha, Martha," the L answered,
11: 1 one of his disciples said to him, "L,
11: 39 Then the L said to him, "Now then
12: 41 L, are you telling this parable to us,
12: 42 or to everyone?" The L answered,
13: 15 L answered him, "You hypocrites!
13: 23 "L, are only a few people going
13: 35 comes in the name of the L.' "
17: 5 The apostles said to the L,
17: 37 "Where, L?" they asked.
18: 6 And the L said, "Listen
18: 41 "L, I want to see," he replied.
19: 8 and said to the L, "Look, L!
19: 31 tell him, 'The L needs it.' "
19: 34 They replied, "The L needs it."
19: 38 in the name of the L!"
20: 37 for he calls the L 'the God
20: 42 " 'The L said to my L:
20: 44 David calls him 'L.'
22: 25 kings of the Gentiles l it over them;
22: 33 "L, I am ready to go with you
22: 38 The disciples said, "See, L,
22: 49 L, should we strike with our swords
22: 61 The L turned and looked straight
22: 61 the word the L had spoken
24: 3 not find the body of the L Jesus.
24: 34 The L has risen and has appeared
Jn 1: 23 'Make straight the way for the L.' "
4: 3 When the L learned of this,
6: 23 bread after the L had given thanks.
6: 68 Simon Peter answered him, "L,
9: 38 Then the man said, "L, I believe,"
11: 2 one who poured perfume on the L
11: 3 "L, the one you love is sick."
11: 12 His disciples replied, "L,
11: 21 "L," Martha said to Jesus,
11: 27 Do you believe this?" "Yes, L,"
11: 32 she fell at his feet and said, "L,
11: 34 "Come and see, L," they replied.
11: 39 "But, L," said Martha, the sister
12: 13 comes in the name of the L!"
12: 38 the arm of the L been revealed?"
12: 38 "L, who has believed our message
13: 6 L, are you going to wash my feet?"
13: 9 "Then, L," Simon Peter replied,
13: 13 "You call me 'Teacher' and 'L,'
13: 14 Now that I, your L and Teacher,
13: 25 he asked him, "L, who is it?"
13: 36 "L, where are you going?"
13: 37 "L, why can't I follow you now?
14: 5 "L, we don't know where you are
14: 8 "L, show us the Father
14: 22 (not Judas Iscariot) said, "But, L,
20: 2 "They have taken the L out
20: 13 "They have taken my L away,"
20: 18 "I have seen the L!" And she told
20: 20 overjoyed when they saw the L.
20: 25 told him that they had seen the L.
20: 28 Thomas said to him, "My L
21: 7 heard him say, "It is the L,"
21: 7 said to Peter, "It is the L!"
21: 12 are you?" They knew it was the L.
21: 15 L," he said, "you know that I love
21: 16 Yes, L, you know that I love you."
21: 17 He said, "L, you know all things;
21: 20 "L, who is going to betray you?")
21: 21 he asked, "L, what about him?"
Ac 1: 6 met together, they asked him, "L,
1: 21 us the whole time the L Jesus went
1: 24 "L, you know everyone's heart.
2: 20 the great and glorious day of the L.
2: 21 on the name of the L will be saved.'
2: 25 " 'I saw the L always before me.
2: 34 " 'The L said to my L:
2: 36 whom you crucified, both L
2: 39 for all whom the L our God will
2: 47 the L added to their number daily
3: 19 of refreshing may come from the L,
3: 22 'The L your God will raise up
4: 24 "Sovereign L," they said, "you
4: 26 together against the L

Ac 4: 29 Now, *L*, consider their threats
4: 33 to the resurrection of the *L* Jesus,
5: 9 agree to test the Spirit of the *L?*
5: 14 and women believed in the *L*
5: 19 of the *L* opened the doors of the jail
7: 33 "Then the *L* said to him, 'Take
7: 49 for me? says the *L*.
7: 59 Stephen prayed, "*L* Jesus,
7: 60 *L*, do not hold this sin against them
8: 16 into the name of the *L* Jesus.
8: 22 this wickedness and pray to the *L*.
8: 24 "Pray to the *L* for me
8: 25 and proclaimed the word of the *L*,
8: 26 an angel of the *L* said to Philip,
8: 39 of the *L* suddenly took Philip away
9: 5 "Who are you, *L?*" Saul asked.
9: 10 The *L* called to him in a vision,
9: 10 "Ananias!" "Yes, *L*," he answered.
9: 11 The *L* told him, "Go to the house
9: 13 "*L*," Ananias answered, "I have
9: 15 But the *L* said to Ananias, "Go!
9: 17 "Brother Saul, the *L*— Jesus,
9: 27 Saul on his journey had seen the *L*
9: 27 and that the *L* had spoken to him,
9: 28 boldly in the name of the *L*.
9: 31 living in the fear of the *L*.
9: 35 saw him and turned to the *L*.
9: 42 and many people believed in the *L*.
10: 4 "What is it, *L?*" he asked.
10: 14 "Surely not, *L!*" Peter replied.
10: 33 everything the *L* has commanded
10: 36 through Jesus Christ, who is *L*
11: 8 *L!* Nothing impure or unclean has
11: 16 I remembered what the *L* had said,
11: 17 who believed in the *L* Jesus Christ,
11: 20 the good news about the *L* Jesus.
11: 21 believed and turned to the *L*.
11: 23 true to the *L* with all their hearts.
11: 24 of people were brought to the *L*.
12: 7 an angel of the *L* appeared
12: 11 a doubt that the *L* sent his angel
12: 17 described how the *L* had brought
12: 23 an angel of the *L* struck him down,
13: 2 While they were worshiping the *L*
13: 10 perverting the right ways of the *L?*
13: 11 the hand of the *L* is against you.
13: 12 at the teaching about the *L*.
13: 44 gathered to hear the word of the *L*.
13: 47 is what the *L* has commanded us:
13: 48 and honored the word of the *L;*
13: 49 The word of the *L* spread
14: 3 there, speaking boldly for the *L*,
14: 23 committed them to the *L*
15: 11 of our *L* Jesus that we are saved,
15: 17 remnant of men may seek the *L*,
15: 17 says the *L*, who does these things'
15: 26 for the name of our *L* Jesus Christ.
15: 35 and preached the word of the *L*.
15: 36 we preached the word of the *L*
15: 40 the brothers to the grace of the *L*.
16: 14 The *L* opened her heart to respond
16: 15 consider me a believer in the *L*,"
16: 31 replied, "Believe in the *L* Jesus,
16: 32 Then they spoke the word of the *L*
17: 24 everything in it is the *L* of heaven
18: 8 entire household believed in the *L;*
18: 9 One night the *L* spoke to Paul
18: 25 instructed in the way of the *L*,
19: 5 into the name of the *L* Jesus.
19: 10 of Asia heard the word of the *L*.
19: 13 to invoke the name of the *L* Jesus
19: 17 the name of the *L* Jesus was held
19: 20 the word of the *L* spread widely
20: 19 I served the *L* with great humility
20: 21 and have faith in our *L* Jesus.
20: 24 the task the *L* Jesus has given
20: 35 the words the *L* Jesus himself said.
21: 13 for the name of the *L* Jesus."
22: 8 " 'Who are you, *L?*' I asked.
22: 10 the *L* said, 'and go into Damascus.
22: 10 " 'What shall I do, *L?*' I asked.
22: 18 a trance and saw the *L* speaking.
22: 19 " '*L*,' I replied, 'these men know
22: 21 "Then the *L* said to me, 'Go;
23: 11 The following night the *L* stood
26: 15 'Who are you, *L?*' " 'I am Jesus,
26: 15 you are persecuting,' the *L* replied.
28: 31 taught about the *L* Jesus Christ.
Ro 1: 4 from the dead: Jesus Christ our *L*.
1: 7 and from the *L* Jesus Christ.
4: 8 whose sin the *L* will never count
4: 24 in him who raised Jesus our *L*
5: 1 God through our *L* Jesus Christ,
5: 11 in God through our *L* Jesus Christ,
5: 21 life through Jesus Christ our *L*.
6: 23 life in Christ Jesus our *L*.
7: 25 through Jesus Christ our *L!*
8: 39 of God that is in Christ Jesus our *L*.
9: 28 For the *L* will carry out
9: 29 "Unless the *L* Almighty
10: 9 with your mouth, "Jesus is *L*,"
10: 12 same *L* is *L* of all and richly blesses
10: 13 on the name of the *L* will be saved
10: 16 *L*, who has believed our message?"
11: 3 appealed to God against Israel: "*L*,
11: 34 Who has known the mind of the *L?*
12: 11 your spiritual fervor, serving the *L*.
12: 19 to avenge; I will repay," says the *L*.
13: 14 yourselves with the *L* Jesus Christ,
14: 4 for the *L* is able to make him stand.
14: 6 as special, does so to the *L*.
14: 6 does so to the *L* and gives thanks
14: 6 eats to the *L*, for he gives thanks
14: 8 and if we die, we die to the *L*.
14: 8 we live or die, we belong to the *L*.
14: 8 we live to the *L;* and if we die,
14: 9 life so that he might be the *L*
14: 11 " 'As surely as I live,' says the *L*,
14: 14 As one who is in the *L* Jesus,
15: 6 and Father of our *L* Jesus Christ.
15: 11 "Praise the *L*, all you Gentiles,
15: 30 by our *L* Jesus Christ
16: 2 her in the *L* in a way worthy
16: 8 Ampliatus, whom I love in the *L*.
16: 11 of Narcissus who are in the *L*.
16: 12 who has worked very hard in the *L*.
16: 12 women who work hard in the *L*.
16: 13 chosen in the *L*, and his mother,
16: 18 people are not serving our *L* Christ,
16: 20 The grace of our *L* Jesus be
16: 22 down this letter, greet you in the *L*.
1Co 1: 2 of our *L* Jesus Christ—their *L*
1: 3 our Father and the *L* Jesus Christ.
1: 7 wait for our *L* Jesus Christ
1: 8 on the day of our *L* Jesus Christ.
1: 9 with his Son Jesus Christ our *L*,
1: 10 in the name of our *L* Jesus Christ,
1: 31 Let him who boasts boast in the *L*."
2: 8 would not have crucified the *L*
2: 16 who has known the mind of the *L*
3: 5 the *L* has assigned to each his task.
3: 20 "The *L* knows that the thoughts
4: 4 It is the *L* who judges me.
4: 5 time; wait till the *L* comes.
4: 17 I love, who is faithful in the *L*.
4: 19 to you very soon, if the *L* is willing,
5: 4 in the name of our *L* Jesus
5: 4 the power of our *L* Jesus is present,
5: 5 his spirit saved on the day of the *L*.
6: 11 in the name of the *L* Jesus Christ
6: 13 for the *L*, and the *L* for the body.
6: 14 By his power God raised the *L*
6: 17 himself with the *L* is one with him
7: 10 the *L*): A wife must not separate
7: 12 To the rest I say this (I, not the *L*):
7: 17 in life that the *L* assigned to him
7: 22 by the *L* is the Lord's freedman;
7: 25 I have no command from the *L*,
7: 32 affairs—how he can please the *L*.
7: 34 to be devoted to the *L* in both body
7: 35 in undivided devotion to the *L*.
7: 39 but he must belong to the *L*.
8: 6 and there is but one *L*, Jesus Christ,
9: 1 Have I not seen Jesus our *L?*
9: 1 the result of my work in the *L?*
9: 2 the seal of my apostleship in the *L*.
9: 14 *L* has commanded that those who
10: 9 We should not test the *L*,
10: 21 You cannot drink the cup of the *L*
11: 11 In the *L*, however, woman is not
11: 23 For I received from the *L* what I
11: 23 The *L* Jesus, on the night he was
11: 27 against the body and blood of the *L*
11: 27 or drinks the cup of the *L*
11: 29 recognizing the body of the *L* eats
11: 32 When we are judged by the *L*,
1Co 12: 3 "Jesus is *L*," except by the Holy
12: 5 kinds of service, but the same *L*.
14: 21 says the *L*.
15: 31 over you in Christ Jesus our *L*.
15: 57 victory through our *L* Jesus Christ.
15: 58 fully to the work of the *L*,
15: 58 labor in the *L* is not in vain.
16: 7 time with you, if the *L* permits.
16: 10 carrying on the work of the *L*,
16: 19 Priscilla greet you warmly in the *L*,
16: 22 If anyone does not love the *L*—
16: 22 O *L!* The grace of the *L* Jesus be
2Co 1: 2 our Father and the *L* Jesus Christ.
1: 3 and Father of our *L* Jesus Christ,
1: 14 of you in the day of the *L* Jesus.
1: 24 Not that we *l* it over your faith,
2: 12 found that the *L* had opened a door
3: 16 whenever anyone turns to the *L*,
3: 17 Now the *L* is the Spirit,
3: 17 and where the Spirit of the *L* is,
3: 18 from the *L*, who is the Spirit.
4: 5 but Jesus Christ as *L*, and ourselves
4: 14 that the one who raised the *L* Jesus
5: 6 in the body we are away from the *L*
5: 8 and at home with the *L*.
5: 11 we know what it is to fear the *L*,
6: 17 and be separate, says the *L*.
6: 18 daughters, says the *L* Almighty."
8: 5 they gave themselves first to the *L*
8: 9 the grace of our *L* Jesus Christ,
8: 19 in order to honor the *L* himself
8: 21 not only in the eyes of the *L* but
10: 8 about the authority the *L* gave us
10: 17 Let him who boasts boast in the *L*."
10: 18 but the one whom the *L* commends
11: 17 I am not talking as the *L* would,
11: 31 The God and Father of the *L* Jesus,
12: 1 and revelations from the *L*.
12: 8 pleaded with the *L* to take it away
13: 10 the authority the *L* gave me
13: 14 May the grace of the *L* Jesus Christ
Gal 1: 3 our Father and the *L* Jesus Christ,
5: 10 in the *L* that you will take no other
6: 14 in the cross of our *L* Jesus Christ,
6: 18 The grace of our *L* Jesus Christ be
Eph 1: 2 our Father and the *L* Jesus Christ.
1: 3 and Father of our *L* Jesus Christ,
1: 15 about your faith in the *L* Jesus
1: 17 the God of our *L* Jesus Christ,
2: 21 to become a holy temple in the *L*.
3: 11 in Christ Jesus our *L*.
4: 1 As a prisoner for the *L*, then,
4: 5 one *L*, one faith, one baptism;
4: 17 it in the *L*, that you must no longer
5: 8 but now you are light in the *L*.
5: 10 and find out what pleases the *L*.
5: 19 make music in your heart to the *L*,
5: 20 in the name of our *L* Jesus Christ.
5: 22 submit to your husbands as to the *L*
6: 1 obey your parents in the *L*,
6: 4 training and instruction of the *L*.
6: 7 as if you were serving the *L*,
6: 8 know that the *L* will reward
6: 10 in the *L* and in his mighty power.
6: 21 and faithful servant in the *L*,
6: 23 the Father and the *L* Jesus Christ.
6: 24 to all who love our *L* Jesus Christ
Php 1: 2 our Father and the *L* Jesus Christ.
1: 14 in the *L* have been encouraged
2: 11 confess that Jesus Christ is *L*,
2: 19 I hope in the *L* Jesus
2: 24 in the *L* that I myself will come
2: 29 him in the *L* with great joy,
3: 1 my brothers, rejoice in the *L!*
3: 8 of knowing Christ Jesus my *L*,
3: 20 from there, the *L* Jesus Christ,
4: 1 you should stand firm in the *L*,
4: 2 to agree with each other in the *L*.
4: 4 Rejoice in the *L* always.
4: 5 The *L* is near.
4: 10 I rejoice greatly in the *L* that
4: 23 The grace of the *L* Jesus Christ be
Col 1: 3 the Father of our *L* Jesus Christ,
1: 10 you may live a life worthy of the *L*
2: 6 as you received Christ Jesus as *L*,
3: 13 Forgive as the *L* forgave you.
3: 17 do it all in the name of the *L* Jesus,
3: 18 your husbands, as is fitting in the *L*.

Col 3: 20 in everything, for this pleases the *L*
3: 22 of heart and reverence for the *L*.
3: 23 as working for the *L*, not for men,
3: 24 It is the *L* Christ you are serving.
3: 24 receive an inheritance from the *L*
4: 7 and fellow servant in the *L*.
4: 17 work you have received in the *L*.''
1Th 1: 1 the Father and the *L* Jesus Christ:
1: 3 by hope in our *L* Jesus Christ.
1: 6 imitators of us and of the *L*;
2: 15 who killed the *L* Jesus
2: 19 of our *L* Jesus when he comes?
3: 8 since you are standing firm in the *L*
3: 11 and our *L* Jesus clear the way for us
3: 12 May the *L* make your love increase
3: 13 Father when our *L* Jesus comes
4: 1 and urge you in the *L* Jesus
4: 2 you by the authority of the *L* Jesus.
4: 6 The *L* will punish men
4: 15 who are left till the coming of the *L*
4: 16 For the *L* himself will come
4: 17 so we will be with the *L* forever.
4: 17 the clouds to meet the *L* in the air.
5: 2 day of the *L* will come like a thief
5: 9 through our *L* Jesus Christ.
5: 12 who are over you in the *L*
5: 23 at the coming of our *L* Jesus Christ.
5: 27 I charge you before the *L*
5: 28 The grace of our *L* Jesus Christ be
2Th 1: 1 our Father and the *L* Jesus Christ:
1: 2 the Father and the *L* Jesus Christ.
1: 7 when the *L* Jesus is revealed
1: 8 not obey the gospel of our *L* Jesus.
1: 9 shut out from the presence of the *L*
1: 12 of our God and the *L* Jesus Christ.
1: 12 of our *L* Jesus may be glorified
2: 1 the coming of our *L* Jesus Christ
2: 2 the day of the *L* has already come.
2: 8 whom the *L* Jesus will overthrow
2: 13 for you, brothers loved by the *L*,
2: 14 in the glory of our *L* Jesus Christ.
2: 16 May our *L* Jesus Christ himself
3: 1 of the *L* may spread rapidly
3: 3 *L* is faithful, and he will strengthen
3: 4 in the *L* that you are doing
3: 5 May the *L* direct your hearts
3: 6 In the name of the *L* Jesus Christ,
3: 12 urge in the *L* Jesus Christ to settle
3: 16 The *L* be with all of you.
3: 16 may the *L* of peace himself give
3: 18 The grace of our *L* Jesus Christ be
1Ti 1: 2 the Father and Christ Jesus our *L*.
1: 12 I thank Christ Jesus our *L*,
1: 14 The grace of our *L* was poured out
6: 3 instruction of our *L* Jesus Christ
6: 14 the appearing of our *L* Jesus Christ,
6: 15 the King of kings and *L* of lords,
2Ti 1: 2 the Father and Christ Jesus our *L*.
1: 8 ashamed to testify about our *L*,
1: 16 May the *L* show mercy
1: 18 May the *L* grant that he will find
1: 18 mercy from the *L* on that day!
2: 7 for the *L* will give you insight
2: 19 the name of the *L* must turn away
2: 19 ''The *L* knows those who are his,''
2: 22 call on the *L* out of a pure heart.
3: 11 Yet the *L* rescued me from all
4: 8 which the *L*, the righteous Judge,
4: 14 The *L* will repay him
4: 17 But the *L* stood at my side
4: 18 The *L* will rescue me
4: 22 The *L* be with your spirit.
Phm : 3 our Father and the *L* Jesus Christ.
: 5 hear about your faith in the *L* Jesus
: 16 as a man and as a brother in the *L*.
: 20 benefit from you in the *L*;
: 25 The grace of the *L* Jesus Christ be
Heb 1: 10 O *L*, you laid the foundations
2: 3 which was first announced by the *L*
7: 14 For it is clear that our *L* descended
7: 21 ''The *L* has sworn
8: 2 the true tabernacle set up by the *L*,
8: 8 The time is coming, declares the *L*,
8: 9 away from them, declares the *L*.
8: 10 after that time, declares the *L*.
8: 11 his brother, saying, 'Know the *L*,'
10: 16 after that time, says the *L*.
10: 30 ''The *L* will judge his people.''
Heb 12: 6 the *L* disciplines those he loves,
12: 14 holiness no one will see the *L*.
13: 6 *L* is my helper; I will not be afraid.
13: 20 back from the dead our *L* Jesus,
Jas 1: 1 of God and of the *L* Jesus Christ,
1: 7 will receive anything from the *L*;
2: 1 in our glorious *L* Jesus Christ,
3: 9 With the tongue we praise our *L*
4: 10 Humble yourselves before the *L*,
5: 4 the ears of the *L* Almighty.
5: 10 spoke in the name of the *L*.
5: 11 The *L* is full of compassion
5: 11 seen what the *L* finally brought
5: 14 him with oil in the name of the *L*.
5: 15 person well; the *L* will raise him
1Pe 1: 3 and Father of our *L* Jesus Christ!
1: 25 the word of the *L* stands forever.''
2: 3 you have tasted that the *L* is good.
3: 12 but the face of the *L* is
3: 12 eyes of the *L* are on the righteous
3: 15 in your hearts set apart Christ as *L*.
2Pe 1: 2 of God and of Jesus our *L*.
1: 8 knowledge of our *L* Jesus Christ.
1: 11 into the eternal kingdom of our *L*
1: 14 our *L* Jesus Christ has made clear
1: 16 and coming of our *L* Jesus Christ,
2: 1 the sovereign *L* who bought
2: 9 then the *L* knows how
2: 11 beings in the presence of the *L*.
2: 20 of the world by knowing our *L*
3: 2 and the command given by our *L*
3: 8 With the *L* a day is like a thousand
3: 9 The *L* is not slow in keeping his
3: 10 day of the *L* will come like a thief.
3: 18 and knowledge of our *L* and Savior
Jude : 4 Christ our only Sovereign and *L*.
: 5 you that the *L* delivered his people
: 9 but said, ''The *L* rebuke you!''
: 14 the *L* is coming with thousands
: 17 of our *L* Jesus Christ foretold.
: 21 for the mercy of our *L* Jesus Christ
: 25 through Jesus Christ our *L*,
Rev 1: 8 says the *L* God, ''who is,
4: 8 holy, holy is the *L* God Almighty,
4: 11 ''You are worthy, our *L* and God,
6: 10 Sovereign *L*, holy and true,
11: 4 stand before the *L* of the earth.
11: 8 where also their *L* was crucified.
11: 15 has become the kingdom of our *L*
11: 17 thanks to you, *L* God Almighty,
14: 13 die in the *L* from now on.''
15: 3 *L* God Almighty.
15: 4 Who will not fear you, O *L*,
16: 7 ''Yes, *L* God Almighty,
17: 14 he is *L* of lords and King of kings—
18: 8 for mighty is the *L* God who judges
19: 6 For our *L* God Almighty reigns.
19: 16 KINGS AND *L* OF LORDS.
21: 22 because the *L* God Almighty
22: 5 for the *L* God will give them light.
22: 6 The *L*, the God of the spirits
22: 20 Come, *L* Jesus.
22: 21 The grace of the *L* Jesus be

***LORD'S (*LORD)**

Ge 44: 9 rest of us will become my *l* slaves.''
44: 16 We are now my *l* slaves—
44: 33 as my *l* slave in place of the boy,
Nu 14: 17 may the *L* strength be displayed,
2Sa 11: 11 and my *l* men are camped
21: 6 of Saul—the *L* chosen one.''
1Ki 1: 33 ''Take your *l* servants with you
3: 15 before the ark of the *L* covenant
1Ch 21: 3 are they not all my *l* subjects?
Mal 1: 12 it by saying of the *L* table,
Lk 1: 6 observing all the *L* commandments
1: 38 ''I am the *L* servant,'' Mary
1: 66 For the *L* hand was with him.
2: 26 die before he had seen the *L* Christ.
4: 19 to proclaim the year of the *L* favor
10: 39 who sat at the *L* feet listening
Ac 7: 31 he heard the *L* voice: 'I am the God
9: 1 threats against the *L* disciples.
11: 21 The *L* hand was with them,
21: 14 and said, ''The *L* will be done.''
1Co 7: 22 by the Lord is the *L* freedman;
7: 25 who by the *L* mercy is trustworthy.
7: 32 is concerned about the *L* affairs—
1Co 7: 34 is concerned about the *L* affairs:
9: 5 and the *L* brothers and Cephas?
10: 21 a part in both the *L* table
10: 22 trying to arouse the *L* jealousy?
10: 26 ''The earth is the *L*, and everything
11: 20 it is not the *L* Supper you eat,
11: 26 you proclaim the *L* death
14: 37 writing to you is the *L* command.
2Co 3: 18 faces all reflect the *L* glory,
Gal 1: 19 only James, the *L* brother.
Eph 5: 17 but understand what the *L* will is.
1Th 1: 8 The *L* message rang out
4: 15 According to the *L* own word,
2Ti 2: 24 And the *L* servant must not quarrel
Heb 12: 5 light of the *L* discipline,
Jas 4: 15 you ought to say, ''If it is the *L* will,
5: 7 then, brothers, until the *L* coming.
5: 8 because the *L* coming is near.
1Pe 2: 13 Submit yourselves for the *L* sake
2Pe 3: 15 mind that our *L* patience means
Rev 1: 10 On the *L* Day I was in the Spirit,

LORDED (*LORD)

Ne 5: 15 Their assistants also *l* it

LORDING (*LORD)

1Pe 5: 3 not *l* it over those entrusted to you,

LORDS (*LORD)

Ge 19: 2 ''My *l*,'' he said, ''please turn
19: 18 But Lot said to them, ''No, my *l*,
Dt 10: 17 God of gods and Lord of *l*,
Ps 136: 3 Give thanks to the Lord of *l*:
Ecc 8: 9 a time when a man *l* it over others
Isa 26: 13 other *l* besides you have ruled
1Co 8: 5 are many ''gods'' and many ''*l*''),
1Ti 6: 15 the King of kings and Lord of *l*,
Rev 17: 14 he is Lord of *l* and King of kings—
19: 16 KINGS AND LORD OF *L*.

†LORD (†LORD'S)

Ge 2: 4 When the *L* God made the earth
2: 5 the *L* God had not sent rain
2: 7 And the *L* God formed man
2: 8 the *L* God had planted a garden
2: 9 And the *L* God made all kinds
2: 15 The *L* God took the man
2: 16 the *L* God commanded the man,
2: 18 The *L* God said, ''It is not good
2: 19 Now the *L* God had formed out
2: 21 the *L* God caused the man to fall
2: 22 Then the *L* God made a woman
3: 1 wild animals the *L* God had made.
3: 8 and they hid from the *L* God
3: 8 wife heard the sound of the *L* God
3: 9 But the *L* God called to the man,
3: 13 Then the *L* God said to the woman
3: 14 So the *L* God said to the serpent,
3: 21 The *L* God made garments of skin
3: 22 the *L* God said, ''The man has now
3: 23 So the *L* God banished him
4: 1 of the *L* I have brought forth a man
4: 3 of the soil as an offering to the *L*.
4: 4 The *L* looked with favor on Abel
4: 6 the *L* said to Cain, ''Why are you
4: 9 the *L* said to Cain, ''Where is your
4: 10 The *L* said, ''What have you done?
4: 13 to the *L*, ''My punishment is more
4: 15 But the *L* said to him, ''Not so;
4: 15 Then the *L* put a mark on Cain
4: 26 began to call on the name of the *L*.
5: 29 by the ground the *L* has cursed.''
6: 3 *L* said, ''My Spirit will not contend
6: 5 *L* saw how great man's wickedness
6: 6 *L* was grieved that he had made
6: 7 So the *L* said, ''I will wipe mankind
6: 8 favor in the eyes of the *L*.
7: 1 The *L* then said to Noah, ''Go
7: 5 did all that the *L* commanded him.
7: 16 Then the *L* shut him in.
8: 20 Noah built an altar to the *L* and,
8: 21 The *L* smelled the pleasing aroma
9: 26 Blessed be the *L*, the God of Shem!
10: 9 a mighty hunter before the *L*.''
10: 9 was a mighty hunter before the *L*;
11: 5 the *L* came down to see the city
11: 6 *L* said, ''If as one people speaking
11: 8 So the *L* scattered them from there

†This entry represents the translation of the Hebrew name for God, *Yahweh*, always indicated in the NIV by LORD. For Lord, see the concordance entries ***LORD** and ***LORD'S**.

Ge 11: 9 From there the *L* scattered them
11: 9 there the *L* confused the language
12: 1 *L* had said to Abram, "Leave your
12: 4 Abram left, as the *L* had told him;
12: 7 So he built an altar there to the *L*,
12: 7 but the *L* appeared to Abram
12: 8 There he built an altar to the *L*
12: 8 and called on the name of the *L*.
12: 17 But the *L* inflicted serious diseases
13: 4 called on the name of the *L*.
13: 10 the garden of the *L*, like the land
13: 10 was before the *L* destroyed Sodom
13: 13 were sinning greatly against the *L*.
13: 14 The *L* said to Abram
13: 18 where he built an altar to the *L*.
14: 22 "I have raised my hand to the *L*,
15: 1 the word of the *L* came to Abram
15: 2 But Abram said, "O Sovereign *L*,
15: 4 the word of the *L* came to him:
15: 6 Abram believed the *L*,
15: 7 He also said to him, "I am the *L*,
15: 8 But Abram said, "O Sovereign *L*,
15: 9 *L* said to him, "Bring me a heifer,
15: 13 Then the *L* said to him, "Know
15: 18 On that day the *L* made a covenant
16: 2 "The *L* has kept me
16: 5 May the *L* judge between you
16: 7 The angel of the *L* found Hagar
16: 9 Then the angel of the *L* told her,
16: 11 The angel of the *L* also said to her:
16: 11 for the *L* has heard of your misery.
16: 13 name to the *L* who spoke to her:
17: 1 the *L* appeared to him and said,
18: 1 The *L* appeared to Abraham
18: 10 the *L* said, "I will surely return
18: 13 Then the *L* said to Abraham,
18: 14 Is anything too hard for the *L?*
18: 17 Then the *L* said, "Shall I hide
18: 19 so that the *L* will bring about
18: 19 way of the *L* by doing what is right
18: 20 Then the *L* said, "The outcry
18: 22 remained standing before the *L*.
18: 26 all the earth do right?" The *L* said,
18: 33 When the *L* had finished speaking
19: 13 The outcry to the *L*
19: 14 the *L* is about to destroy the city!"
19: 16 for the *L* was merciful to them.
19: 24 from the *L* out of the heavens.
19: 24 the *L* rained down burning sulfur
19: 27 where he had stood before the *L*.
20: 18 for the *L* had closed up every
21: 1 Now the *L* was gracious to Sarah
21: 1 the *L* did for Sarah what he had
21: 33 called upon the name of the *L*,
22: 11 the angel of the *L* called out to him
22: 14 of the *L* it will be provided."
22: 14 that place "The *L* will provide."
22: 15 angel of the *L* called to Abraham
22: 16 "I swear by myself, declares the *L*,
24: 1 the *L* had blessed him in every way
24: 3 I want you to swear by the *L*,
24: 7 "The *L*, the God of heaven,
24: 12 "O *L*, God of my master Abraham,
24: 21 or not the *L* had made his journey
24: 26 bowed down and worshiped the *L*,
24: 27 saying, "Praise be to the *L*,
24: 27 the *L* has led me on the journey
24: 31 you who are blessed by the *L*,"
24: 35 The *L* has blessed my master
24: 40 The *L*, before whom I have walked,
24: 42 'O *L*, God of my master Abraham,
24: 44 let her be the one the *L* has chosen
24: 48 I bowed down and worshiped the *L*
24: 48 I praised the *L*, the God
24: 50 answered, "This is from the *L;*
24: 51 son, as the *L* has directed."
24: 52 down to the ground before the *L*.
24: 56 now that the *L* has granted success
25: 21 Isaac prayed to the *L* on behalf
25: 21 The *L* answered his prayer,
25: 22 So she went to inquire of the *L*.
25: 23 The *L* said to her,
26: 2 The *L* appeared to Isaac and said,
26: 12 because the *L* blessed him.
26: 22 "Now the *L* has given us room
26: 24 That night the *L* appeared to him
26: 25 and called on the name of the *L*.
26: 28 "We saw clearly that the *L* was

Ge 26: 29 And now you are blessed by the *L*
27: 7 in the presence of the *L* before I die
27: 20 The *L* your God gave me success,"
27: 27 that the *L* has blessed.
28: 13 There above it stood the *L*,
28: 13 "I am the *L*, the God
28: 16 "Surely the *L* is in this place,
28: 21 then the *L* will be my God.
29: 31 When the *L* saw that Leah was not
29: 32 because the *L* has seen my misery.
29: 33 "Because the *L* heard that I am not
29: 35 "This time I will praise the *L*."
30: 24 May the *L* add to me another son."
30: 27 divination that the *L* has blessed
30: 30 *L* has blessed you wherever I have
31: 3 Then the *L* said to Jacob, "Go back
31: 49 "May the *L* keep watch
32: 9 God of my father Isaac, O *L*,
38: 7 so the *L* put him to death.
39: 2 The *L* was with Joseph
39: 3 and that the *L* gave him success
39: 3 his master saw that the *L* was
39: 5 The blessing of the *L* was
39: 5 the *L* blessed the household
39: 21 in the prison, the *L* was with him;
39: 23 because the *L* was with Joseph
49: 18 "I look for your deliverance, O *L*.
Ex 3: 2 the angel of the *L* appeared to him
3: 4 When the *L* saw that he had gone
3: 7 The *L* said, "I have indeed seen
3: 15 "Say to the Israelites, 'The *L*,
3: 16 'The *L*, the God of your fathers,
3: 18 'The *L*, the God of the Hebrews,
3: 18 to offer sacrifices to the *L* our God
4: 1 'The *L* did not appear to you'?"
4: 2 to you'?" Then the *L* said to him,
4: 3 The *L* said, "Throw it
4: 4 the *L* said to him, "Reach out your
4: 5 said the *L*, "is so that they may
4: 5 so that they may believe that the *L*,
4: 6 Then the *L* said, "Put your hand
4: 8 *L* said, "If they do not believe you
4: 10 Moses said to the *L*, "O Lord,
4: 11 Is it not I, the *L?* Now go;
4: 11 *L* said to him, "Who gave man his
4: 19 the *L* had said to Moses in Midian,
4: 21 *L* said to Moses, "When you return
4: 22 'This is what the *L* says: Israel is
4: 24 the *L* met Moses and was about
4: 26 So the *L* let him alone.
4: 27 The *L* said to Aaron, "Go
4: 28 Aaron everything the *L* had sent
4: 30 them everything the *L* had said
4: 31 heard that the *L* was concerned
5: 1 "This is what the *L*, the God
5: 2 I do not know the *L* and I will not
5: 2 Pharaoh said, "Who is the *L*,
5: 3 to offer sacrifices to the *L* our God,
5: 17 'Let us go and sacrifice to the *L*.'
5: 21 "May the *L* look upon you
5: 22 Moses returned to the *L* and said,
6: 1 Then the *L* said to Moses,
6: 2 also said to Moses, "I am the *L*.
6: 3 by my name the *L* I did not make
6: 6 'I am the *L* and I will bring you out
6: 7 know that I am the *L* your God,
6: 8 I am the *L*.' "
6: 10 Then the *L* said to Moses, "Go,
6: 12 to the *L*, "If the Israelites will not
6: 13 Now the *L* spoke to Moses
6: 26 and Moses to whom the *L* said,
6: 28 Now when the *L* spoke to Moses
6: 29 he said to him, "I am the *L*.
6: 30 Moses said to the *L*, "Since I speak
7: 1 Then the *L* said to Moses, "See,
7: 5 will know that I am the *L*
7: 6 as the *L* commanded them.
7: 8 The *L* said to Moses and Aaron,
7: 10 and did just as the *L* commanded.
7: 13 to them, just as the *L* had said.
7: 14 Then the *L* said to Moses,
7: 16 'The *L*, the God of the Hebrews,
7: 17 This is what the *L* says: By this you
7: 17 this you will know that I am the *L:*
7: 19 The *L* said to Moses, "Tell Aaron,
7: 20 as the *L* had commanded.
7: 22 and Aaron, just as the *L* had said.
7: 25 passed after the *L* struck the Nile.

Ex 8: 1 Then the *L* said to Moses,
8: 1 'This is what the *L* says: Let my
8: 5 Then the *L* said to Moses,
8: 8 Pray to the *L* to take the frogs away
8: 8 go to offer sacrifices to the *L*."
8: 10 there is no one like the *L* our God.
8: 12 out to the *L* about the frogs he had
8: 13 And the *L* did what Moses asked.
8: 15 and Aaron, just as the *L* had said.
8: 16 Then the *L* said to Moses,
8: 19 not listen, just as the *L* had said.
8: 20 Then the *L* said to Moses,
8: 20 'This is what the *L* says: Let my
8: 22 so that you will know that I, the *L*,
8: 24 And the *L* did this.
8: 26 we offer the *L* our God would
8: 27 to offer sacrifices to the *L* our God,
8: 28 sacrifices to the *L* your God
8: 29 as I leave you, I will pray to the *L*,
8: 29 go to offer sacrifices to the *L*."
8: 30 left Pharaoh and prayed to the *L*,
8: 31 and the *L* did what Moses asked:
9: 1 Then the *L* said to Moses,
9: 1 'This is what the *L*, the God
9: 3 of the *L* will bring a terrible plague
9: 4 But the *L* will make a distinction
9: 5 *L* set a time and said, "Tomorrow
9: 5 "Tomorrow the *L* will do this
9: 6 And the next day the *L* did it:
9: 8 Then the *L* said to Moses
9: 12 just as the *L* had said to Moses.
9: 12 the *L* hardened Pharaoh's heart
9: 13 Then the *L* said to Moses,
9: 13 'This is what the *L*, the God
9: 20 word of the *L* hurried to bring their
9: 21 the word of the *L* left their slaves
9: 22 Then the *L* said to Moses,
9: 23 So the *L* rained hail on the land
9: 23 the *L* sent thunder and hail,
9: 27 "The *L* is in the right, and I
9: 28 to the *L*, for we have had enough
9: 29 hands in prayer to the *L*.
9: 30 still do not fear the *L* God."
9: 33 spread out his hands toward the *L;*
9: 35 as the *L* had said through Moses.
10: 1 Then the *L* said to Moses,
10: 2 that you may know that I am the *L*
10: 3 "This is what the *L*, the God
10: 7 they may worship the *L* their God.
10: 8 "Go, worship the *L* your God,"
10: 9 are to celebrate a festival to the *L*."
10: 10 Pharaoh said, "The *L* be with you
10: 11 the men go; and worship the *L*,
10: 12 *L* said to Moses, "Stretch out your
10: 13 and the *L* made an east wind blow
10: 16 sinned against the *L* your God
10: 17 and pray to the *L* your God
10: 18 left Pharaoh and prayed to the *L*.
10: 19 And the *L* changed the wind
10: 20 the *L* hardened Pharaoh's heart,
10: 21 Then the *L* said to Moses,
10: 24 and said, "Go, worship the *L*.
10: 25 to present to the *L* our God.
10: 26 are to use to worship the *L*."
10: 26 them in worshiping the *L* our God,
10: 27 the *L* hardened Pharaoh's heart,
11: 1 Now the *L* had said to Moses,
11: 3 *L* made the Egyptians favorably
11: 4 said, "This is what the *L* says:
11: 7 know that the *L* makes
11: 9 *L* had said to Moses, "Pharaoh will
11: 10 but the *L* hardened Pharaoh's heart
12: 1 The *L* said to Moses and Aaron
12: 12 I am the *L*.
12: 14 celebrate it as a festival to the *L*—
12: 23 When the *L* goes through the land
12: 25 the land that the *L* will give you
12: 27 'It is the Passover sacrifice to the *L*,
12: 28 just what the *L* commanded Moses
12: 29 At midnight the *L* struck
12: 31 worship the *L* as you have
12: 36 The *L* had made the Egyptians
12: 42 Because the *L* kept vigil that night
12: 42 to honor the *L* for the generations
12: 43 The *L* said to Moses and Aaron,
12: 50 just what the *L* had commanded
12: 51 very day the *L* brought
13: 1 The *L* said to Moses, "Consecrate

Lev 2: 12 You may bring them to the *L*
2: 14 offering of firstfruits to the *L*,
2: 16 as an offering made to the *L* by fire.
3: 1 is to present before the *L* an animal
3: 3 is to bring a sacrifice made to the *L*
3: 5 an aroma pleasing to the *L*.
3: 6 as a fellowship offering to the *L*,
3: 7 he is to present it before the *L*.
3: 9 is to bring a sacrifice made to the *L*
3: 11 an offering made to the *L* by fire.
3: 12 he is to present it before the *L*.
3: 14 is to make this offering to the *L*
4: 1 The *L* said to Moses, "Say
4: 3 he must bring to the *L* a young bull
4: 4 and slaughter it before the *L*.
4: 4 to the Tent of Meeting before the *L*
4: 6 some of it seven times before the *L*,
4: 7 before the *L* in the Tent of Meeting
4: 15 on the bull's head before the *L*,
4: 15 shall be slaughtered before the *L*.
4: 17 sprinkle it before the *L* seven times
4: 18 before the *L* in the Tent of Meeting
4: 22 of the commands of the *L* his God,
4: 24 is slaughtered before the *L*.
4: 31 as an aroma pleasing to the *L*.
4: 35 top of the offerings made to the *L*
5: 6 bring to the *L* a female lamb
5: 7 or two young pigeons to the *L*
5: 12 top of the offerings made to the *L*
5: 14 *L* said to Moses: "When a person
5: 15 to bring to the *L* as a penalty a ram
5: 19 of wrongdoing against the *L*."
6: 1 *L* said to Moses: "If anyone sins
6: 2 and is unfaithful to the *L*
6: 6 that is, to the *L*, his guilt offering,
6: 7 atonement for him before the *L*,
6: 8 The *L* said to Moses: "Give Aaron
6: 14 are to bring it before the *L*,
6: 15 as an aroma pleasing to the *L*.
6: 18 to the *L* by fire for the generations
6: 19 The *L* also said to Moses, "This is
6: 20 to the *L* on the day he is anointed:
6: 21 as an aroma pleasing to the *L*.
6: 24 The *L* said to Moses, "Say
6: 25 is to be slaughtered before the *L*
7: 5 as an offering made to the *L* by fire.
7: 11 a person may present to the *L*:
7: 14 a contribution to the *L*; it belongs
7: 20 offering belonging to the *L*,
7: 21 offering belonging to the *L*,
7: 22 The *L* said to Moses, "Say
7: 25 made to the *L* must be cut
7: 28 The *L* said to Moses, "Say
7: 29 part of it as his sacrifice to the *L*.
7: 29 to the *L* is to bring part of it
7: 30 and wave the breast before the *L*
7: 30 to bring the offering made to the *L*
7: 35 they were presented to serve the *L*
7: 35 to the *L* by fire that were allotted
7: 36 *L* commanded that the Israelites
7: 38 to bring their offerings to the *L*,
7: 38 which the *L* gave Moses
8: 1 The *L* said to Moses, "Bring Aaron
8: 4 as the *L* commanded him,
8: 5 This is what the *L* has commanded
8: 9 as the *L* commanded Moses.
8: 13 as the *L* commanded Moses.
8: 17 as the *L* commanded Moses.
8: 21 an offering made to the *L* by fire,
8: 21 as the *L* commanded Moses.
8: 26 was before the *L*, he took a cake
8: 27 and waved them before the *L*
8: 28 an offering made to the *L* by fire.
8: 29 as the *L* commanded Moses.
8: 29 it before the *L* as a wave offering,
8: 34 by the *L* to make atonement
8: 35 and do what the *L* requires,
8: 36 did everything the *L* commanded
9: 2 and present them before the *L*.
9: 4 For today the *L* will appear to you
9: 4 offering to sacrifice before the *L*,
9: 5 came near and stood before the *L*.
9: 6 glory of the *L* may appear to you."
9: 6 is what the *L* has commanded you
9: 7 as the *L* has commanded."
9: 10 as the *L* commanded Moses;
9: 21 and the right thigh before the *L*
9: 23 and the glory of the *L* appeared

Lev 9: 24 out from the presence of the *L*
10: 1 unauthorized fire before the *L*,
10: 2 and they died before the *L*.
10: 2 out from the presence of the *L*
10: 3 "This is what the *L* spoke
10: 6 and the *L* will be angry
10: 6 for those the *L* has destroyed
10: 8 Then the *L* said to Aaron,
10: 11 the decrees the *L* has given them
10: 12 from the offerings made to the *L*
10: 13 share of the offerings made to the *L*
10: 15 as the *L* has commanded."
10: 15 to be waved before the *L*
10: 17 atonement for them before the *L*.
10: 19 Would the *L* have been pleased
10: 19 their burnt offering before the *L*,
11: 1 The *L* said to Moses and Aaron,
11: 44 I am the *L* your God; consecrate
11: 45 I am the *L* who brought you up out
12: 1 The *L* said to Moses, "Say
12: 7 before the *L* to make atonement
13: 1 The *L* said to Moses and Aaron,
14: 1 The *L* said to Moses, "These are
14: 11 before the *L* at the entrance
14: 12 he shall wave them before the *L*
14: 16 some of it before the *L* seven times.
14: 18 atonement for him before the *L*.
14: 23 the Tent of Meeting, before the *L*.
14: 24 and wave them before the *L*
14: 27 his palm seven times before the *L*.
14: 29 atonement for him before the *L*.
14: 31 before the *L* on behalf of the one
14: 33 The *L* said to Moses and Aaron,
15: 1 The *L* said to Moses and Aaron,
15: 14 come before the *L* to the entrance
15: 15 before the *L* for the man
15: 30 before the *L* for the uncleanness
16: 1 The *L* spoke to Moses
16: 1 died when they approached the *L*.
16: 2 *L* said to Moses: "Tell your brother
16: 7 them before the *L* at the entrance
16: 8 one lot for the *L* and the other
16: 9 the goat whose lot falls to the *L*
16: 10 alive before the *L* to be used
16: 12 coals from the altar before the *L*
16: 13 the incense on the fire before the *L*,
16: 18 out to the altar that is before the *L*
16: 30 before the *L*, you will be clean
16: 34 as the *L* commanded Moses.
17: 1 The *L* said to Moses, "Speak
17: 2 This is what the *L* has commanded:
17: 4 as an offering to the *L* in front
17: 4 in front of the tabernacle of the *L*—
17: 5 them to the priest, that is, to the *L*,
17: 5 to the *L* the sacrifices they are now
17: 6 as an aroma pleasing to the *L*.
17: 6 the altar of the *L* at the entrance
17: 9 of Meeting to sacrifice it to the *L*—
18: 1 The *L* said to Moses, "Speak
18: 2 say to them: 'I am the *L* your God.
18: 4 I am the *L* your God.
18: 5 I am the *L*.
18: 6 I am the *L*.
18: 21 I am the *L*.
18: 30 I am the *L* your God.' "
19: 1 The *L* said to Moses, "Speak
19: 2 'Be holy because I, the *L* your God,
19: 3 I am the *L* your God.
19: 4 I am the *L* your God.
19: 5 a fellowship offering to the *L*,
19: 8 desecrated what is holy to the *L*;
19: 10 I am the *L* your God.
19: 12 I am the *L*.
19: 14 I am the *L*.
19: 16 I am the *L*.
19: 18 I am the *L*.
19: 21 for a guilt offering to the *L*.
19: 22 atonement for him before the *L*
19: 24 an offering of praise to the *L*.
19: 25 I am the *L* your God.
19: 28 I am the *L*.
19: 30 I am the *L*.
19: 31 I am the *L* your God.
19: 32 I am the *L*.
19: 34 I am the *L* your God.
19: 36 I am the *L* your God, who brought
19: 37 I am the *L*.' "
20: 1 The *L* said to Moses, "Say

Lev 20: 7 because I am the *L* your God.
20: 8 I am the *L*, who makes you holy.
20: 24 I am the *L* your God, who has set
20: 26 to be holy to me because I, the *L*,
21: 1 The *L* said to Moses, "Speak
21: 6 present the offerings made to the *L*
21: 8 I the *L*, who makes you holy,
21: 12 I am the *L*.
21: 15 I am the *L*, who makes him holy.' "
21: 16 The *L* said to Moses, "Say
21: 21 present the offerings made to the *L*
21: 23 I am the *L*, who makes them holy
22: 1 The *L* said to Moses, "Tell Aaron
22: 2 I am the *L*.
22: 3 I am the *L*.
22: 3 the Israelites consecrate to the *L*,
22: 8 I am the *L*.
22: 9 I am the *L*, who makes them holy.
22: 15 present to the *L* by allowing them
22: 16 I am the *L*, who makes them holy
22: 17 The *L* said to Moses, "Speak
22: 18 a gift for a burnt offering to the *L*,
22: 21 to the *L* to fulfill a special vow
22: 22 Do not offer to the *L* the blind,
22: 22 as an offering made to the *L* by fire.
22: 24 to the *L* an animal whose testicles
22: 26 The *L* said to Moses, "When a cow
22: 27 as an offering made to the *L* by fire.
22: 29 offering of thanksgiving to the *L*,
22: 30 I am the *L*.
22: 31 I am the *L*.
22: 32 I am the *L*, who makes you holy
22: 33 I am the *L*."
23: 1 The *L* said to Moses, "Speak
23: 2 the appointed feasts of the *L*,
23: 3 you live, it is a Sabbath to the *L*.
23: 8 present an offering made to the *L*
23: 9 The *L* said to Moses, "Speak
23: 11 before the *L* so it will be accepted
23: 12 offering to the *L* a lamb a year old
23: 13 an offering made to the *L* by fire,
23: 16 an offering of new grain to the *L*.
23: 17 offering of firstfruits to the *L*.
23: 18 an aroma pleasing to the *L*.
23: 18 will be a burnt offering to the *L*,
23: 20 offering to the *L* for the priest.
23: 20 to wave the two lambs before the *L*
23: 22 I am the *L* your God.' "
23: 23 The *L* said to Moses, "Say
23: 25 present an offering made to the *L*
23: 26 *L* said to Moses, "The tenth day
23: 27 present an offering made to the *L*
23: 28 for you before the *L* your God.
23: 33 The *L* said to Moses, "Say
23: 36 present an offering made to the *L*
23: 36 present offerings made to the *L*
23: 37 bringing offerings made to the *L*
23: 38 offerings you give to the *L*.)
23: 39 the festival to the *L* for seven days;
23: 40 and rejoice before the *L* your God
23: 41 to the *L* for seven days each year.
23: 43 I am the *L* your God.' "
23: 44 the appointed feasts of the *L*.
24: 1 The *L* said to Moses, "Command
24: 3 lamps before the *L* from evening
24: 4 before the *L* must be tended
24: 6 the table of pure gold before the *L*.
24: 7 and to be an offering made to the *L*
24: 8 to be set out before the *L* regularly,
24: 9 share of the offerings made to the *L*
24: 11 the name of the *L* with a curse;
24: 12 will of the *L* should be made clear
24: 13 Then the *L* said to Moses:
24: 16 name of the *L* must be put to death.
24: 22 I am the *L* your God.' "
24: 23 as the *L* commanded Moses.
25: 1 The *L* said to Moses
25: 2 must observe a sabbath to the *L*.
25: 4 sabbath of rest, a sabbath to the *L*.
25: 17 I am the *L* your God.
25: 38 I am the *L* your God, who brought
25: 55 I am the *L* your God.
26: 1 I am the *L* your God.
26: 2 I am the *L*.
26: 13 I am the *L* your God, who brought
26: 44 I am the *L* their God.
26: 45 I am the *L*.' "
26: 46 regulations that the *L* established

Lev 27: 1 The *L* said to Moses, "Speak
27: 2 to the *L* by giving equivalent values
27: 9 acceptable as an offering to the *L*,
27: 9 given to the *L* becomes holy.
27: 11 acceptable as an offering to the *L*—
27: 14 as something holy to the *L*,
27: 16 to the *L* part of his family land,
27: 21 like a field devoted to the *L*;
27: 22 to the *L* a field he has bought,
27: 23 as something holy to the *L*.
27: 26 firstborn already belongs to the *L*;
27: 28 a man owns and devotes to the *L*—
27: 28 so devoted is most holy to the *L*.
27: 30 belongs to the *L*; it is holy
27: 30 to the LORD; it is holy to the *L*.
27: 32 rod—will be holy to the *L*.
27: 34 the commands the *L* gave Moses
Nu 1: 1 The *L* spoke to Moses in the Tent
1: 19 as the *L* commanded Moses.
1: 48 *L* had said to Moses: "You must
1: 54 as the *L* commanded Moses.
2: 1 The *L* said to Moses and Aaron:
2: 33 as the *L* commanded Moses.
2: 34 everything the *L* commanded
3: 1 at the time the *L* talked with Moses
3: 4 fell dead before the *L*
3: 5 *L* said to Moses, "Bring the tribe
3: 11 *L* also said to Moses, "I have taken
3: 13 I am the *L*."
3: 14 The *L* said to Moses in the Desert
3: 16 commanded by the word of the *L*.
3: 40 The *L* said to Moses, "Count all
3: 41 I am the *L*."
3: 42 as the *L* commanded him.
3: 44 The *L* also said to Moses, "Take
3: 45 I am the *L*.
3: 51 commanded by the word of the *L*.
4: 1 The *L* said to Moses and Aaron:
4: 17 The *L* said to Moses and Aaron,
4: 21 *L* said to Moses, "Take a census
4: 49 as the *L* commanded Moses.
5: 1 The *L* said to Moses, "Command
5: 4 as the *L* had instructed Moses.
5: 5 The *L* said to Moses, "Say
5: 6 and so is unfaithful to the *L*,
5: 8 the restitution belongs to the *L*
5: 11 Then the *L* said to Moses,
5: 16 and have her stand before the *L*.
5: 18 had the woman stand before the *L*,
5: 21 "may the *L* cause your people
5: 25 wave it before the *L* and bring it
5: 30 is to have her stand before the *L*
6: 1 The *L* said to Moses, "Speak
6: 2 a vow of separation to the *L*
6: 5 of his separation to the *L* is over;
6: 6 separation to the *L* he must not go
6: 8 he is consecrated to the *L*.
6: 12 himself to the *L* for the period
6: 14 is to present his offerings to the *L*:
6: 16 is to present them before the *L*
6: 17 as a fellowship offering to the *L*,
6: 20 shall then wave them before the *L*
6: 21 offering to the *L* in accordance
6: 22 The *L* said to Moses, "Tell Aaron
6: 24 Say to them: " ' "The *L* bless you
6: 25 the *L* make his face shine upon you
6: 26 the *L* turn his face toward you
7: 3 gifts before the *L* six covered carts
7: 4 *L* said to Moses, "Accept these
7: 11 For the *L* had said to Moses,
7: 89 of Meeting to speak with the *L*,
8: 1 The *L* said to Moses, "Speak
8: 3 just as the *L* commanded Moses.
8: 4 the pattern the *L* had shown
8: 5 *L* said to Moses: "Take the Levites
8: 10 to bring the Levites before the *L*,
8: 11 ready to do the work of the *L*.
8: 11 to present the Levites before the *L*
8: 12 the one for a sin offering to the *L*
8: 13 as a wave offering to the *L*.
8: 20 as the *L* commanded Moses.
8: 21 as a wave offering before the *L*
8: 22 as the *L* commanded Moses.
8: 23 The *L* said to Moses, "This applies
9: 1 The *L* spoke to Moses
9: 5 as the *L* commanded Moses.
9: 8 what the *L* commands concerning
9: 9 Then the *L* said to Moses,

Nu 10: 1 The *L* said to Moses: "Make two
10: 9 remembered by the *L* your God
10: 10 I am the *L* your God."
10: 29 for the *L* has promised good things
10: 29 the place about which the *L* said,
10: 32 good things the *L* gives us."
10: 33 of the *L* went before them
10: 33 out from the mountain of the *L*
10: 34 The cloud of the *L* was over them
10: 35 "Rise up, O *L*!
10: 36 "Return, O *L*,
11: 1 fire from the *L* burned among them
11: 1 hardships in the hearing of the *L*,
11: 2 he prayed to the *L* and the fire died
11: 3 because fire from the *L* had burned
11: 10 The *L* became exceedingly angry,
11: 11 He asked the *L*, "Why have you
11: 16 The *L* said to Moses: "Bring me
11: 18 Now the *L* will give you meat,
11: 18 The *L* heard you when you wailed,
11: 20 because you have rejected the *L*,
11: 23 The *L* answered Moses, "Is
11: 24 told the people what the *L* had said
11: 25 Then the *L* came down in the cloud
11: 29 and that the *L* would put his Spirit
11: 31 Now a wind went out from the *L*
11: 33 the anger of the *L* burned
12: 2 through us?" And the *L* heard this.
12: 2 "Has the *L* spoken only
12: 4 At once the *L* said to Moses,
12: 5 Then the *L* came down in a pillar
12: 6 a prophet of the *L* is among you,
12: 8 he sees the form of the *L*.
12: 9 of the *L* burned against them,
12: 13 So Moses cried out to the *L*,
12: 14 please heal her!" The *L* replied
13: 1 *L* said to Moses, "Send some men
14: 3 Why is the *L* bringing us
14: 8 If the *L* is pleased with us,
14: 9 Only do not rebel against the *L*.
14: 9 protection is gone, but the *L* is
14: 10 Then the glory of the *L* appeared
14: 11 *L* said to Moses, "How long will
14: 13 to the *L*, "Then the Egyptians will
14: 14 O *L*, have been seen face to face,
14: 14 have already heard that you, O *L*,
14: 16 'The *L* was not able
14: 18 you have declared: 'The *L* is slow
14: 20 *L* replied, "I have forgiven them,
14: 21 glory of the *L* fills the whole earth,
14: 26 The *L* said to Moses and Aaron:
14: 28 'As surely as I live, declares the *L*,
14: 35 *L*, have spoken, and I will surely do
14: 37 and died of a plague before the *L*.
14: 40 up to the place the *L* promised."
14: 42 because the *L* is not with you.
14: 43 you have turned away from the *L*,
15: 1 The *L* said to Moses, "Speak
15: 3 as an aroma pleasing to the *L*—
15: 3 present to the *L* offerings made
15: 4 to the *L* a grain offering of a tenth
15: 7 as an aroma pleasing to the *L*.
15: 8 or a fellowship offering to the *L*,
15: 10 an aroma pleasing to the *L*.
15: 13 as an aroma pleasing to the *L*.
15: 14 as an aroma pleasing to the *L*,
15: 15 shall be the same before the *L*:
15: 17 The *L* said to Moses, "Speak
15: 19 a portion as an offering to the *L*.
15: 21 offering to the *L* from the first
15: 22 commands the *L* gave Moses—
15: 23 from the day the *L* gave them
15: 24 as an aroma pleasing to the *L*,
15: 25 and they have brought to the *L*
15: 28 is to make atonement before the *L*
15: 30 or alien, blasphemes the *L*,
15: 35 Then the *L* said to Moses,
15: 36 as the *L* commanded Moses.
15: 37 The *L* said to Moses, "Speak
15: 39 all the commands of the *L*,
15: 41 I am the *L* your God, who brought
15: 41 I am the *L* your God.' "
16: 3 of them, and the *L* is with them.
16: 5 the morning the *L* will show who
16: 7 and incense in them before the *L*.
16: 7 man the *L* chooses will be the one
16: 11 It is against the *L* that you
16: 15 very angry and said to the *L*,

Nu 16: 16 to appear before the *L* tomorrow—
16: 17 and present it before the *L*.
16: 19 the glory of the *L* appeared
16: 20 The *L* said to Moses and Aaron
16: 23 Then the *L* said to Moses,
16: 28 will know that the *L* has sent me
16: 29 then the *L* has not sent me.
16: 30 But if the *L* brings about something
16: 30 that these men have treated the *L*
16: 35 And fire came out from the *L*
16: 36 *L* said to Moses, "Tell Eleazar son
16: 38 they were presented before the *L*
16: 40 come to burn incense before the *L*,
16: 40 the *L* directed him through Moses.
16: 42 and the glory of the *L* appeared.
16: 44 the Tent of Meeting, and the *L* said
16: 46 Wrath has come out from the *L*;
17: 1 The *L* said to Moses, "Speak
17: 7 the staffs before the *L* in the Tent
17: 10 *L* said to Moses, "Put back Aaron's
17: 11 as the *L* commanded him.
17: 13 near the tabernacle of the *L* will die
18: 1 The *L* said to Aaron, "You,
18: 6 dedicated to the *L* to do the work
18: 8 Then the *L* said to Aaron,
18: 12 they give the *L* as the firstfruits
18: 13 bring to the *L* will be yours.
18: 14 that is devoted to the *L* is yours.
18: 15 that is offered to the *L* is yours.
18: 17 an aroma pleasing to the *L*.
18: 19 of salt before the *L* for both you
18: 19 present to the *L* I give to you
18: 20 *L* said to Aaron, "You will have no
18: 24 present as an offering to the *L*.
18: 25 The *L* said to Moses, "Speak
18: 28 will present an offering to the *L*
19: 1 The *L* said to Moses and Aaron:
19: 2 the law that the *L* has commanded:
19: 20 has defiled the sanctuary of the *L*.
20: 3 our brothers fell dead before the *L*!
20: 6 the glory of the *L* appeared to them
20: 7 *L* said to Moses, "Take the staff,
20: 12 But the *L* said to Moses and Aaron,
20: 13 the Israelites quarreled with the *L*
20: 16 but when we cried out to the *L*,
20: 23 the *L* said to Moses and Aaron,
20: 27 Moses did as the *L* commanded:
21: 2 Then Israel made this vow to the *L*:
21: 3 The *L* listened to Israel's plea
21: 6 Then the *L* sent venomous snakes
21: 7 Pray that the *L* will take the snakes
21: 7 when we spoke against the *L*
21: 8 *L* said to Moses, "Make a snake
21: 14 the Book of the Wars of the *L* says:
21: 16 the well where the *L* said to Moses,
21: 34 *L* said to Moses, "Do not be afraid
22: 8 back the answer the *L* gives me."
22: 13 for the *L* has refused to let me go
22: 18 the command of the *L* my God.
22: 19 out what else the *L* will tell me."
22: 22 the angel of the *L* stood in the road
22: 23 angel of the *L* standing in the road
22: 24 Then the angel of the *L* stood
22: 25 the donkey saw the angel of the *L*,
22: 26 the angel of the *L* moved on ahead
22: 27 the donkey saw the angel of the *L*,
22: 28 the *L* opened the donkey's mouth,
22: 31 Then the *L* opened Balaam's eyes,
22: 31 angel of the *L* standing in the road
22: 32 The angel of the *L* asked him,
22: 34 Balaam said to the angel of the *L*,
22: 35 The angel of the *L* said to Balaam,
23: 3 Perhaps the *L* will come to meet
23: 5 The *L* put a message
23: 8 those whom the *L* has not
23: 12 "Must I not speak what the *L* puts
23: 16 The *L* met with Balaam
23: 17 asked him, "What did the *L* say?"
23: 21 The *L* their God is with them;
23: 26 I must do whatever the *L* says?"
24: 1 Balaam saw that it pleased the *L*
24: 6 like aloes planted by the *L*,
24: 11 but the *L* has kept you
24: 13 and I must say only what the *L* says
24: 13 go beyond the command of the *L*—
25: 4 The *L* said to Moses, "Take all
25: 4 in broad daylight before the *L*,
25: 10 *L* said to Moses, "Phinehas son

Nu 25: 16 The *L* said to Moses, "Treat
26: 1 After the plague the *L* said
26: 4 as the *L* commanded Moses."
26: 9 when they rebelled against the *L*.
26: 52 The *L* said to Moses, "The land is
26: 61 before the *L* with unauthorized fire
26: 65 For the *L* had told those Israelites
27: 3 who banded together against the *L*,
27: 6 before the *L* and the *L* said to him,
27: 11 as the *L* commanded Moses.' "
27: 12 Then the *L* said to Moses,
27: 15 Moses said to the *L*, "May the *L*,
27: 18 *L* said to Moses, "Take Joshua son
27: 21 inquiring of the Urim before the *L*.
27: 22 as the *L* commanded him.
27: 23 as the *L* instructed through Moses.
28: 1 The *L* said to Moses, "Give this
28: 3 are to present to the *L*:
28: 6 an offering made to the *L* by fire.
28: 7 offering to the *L* at the sanctuary.
28: 8 an aroma pleasing to the *L*.
28: 11 present to the *L* a burnt offering
28: 13 an offering made to the *L* by fire.
28: 15 is to be presented to the *L*
28: 19 Present to the *L* an offering made
28: 24 as an aroma pleasing to the *L*;
28: 26 present to the *L* an offering
28: 27 as an aroma pleasing to the *L*.
29: 2 As an aroma pleasing to the *L*,
29: 6 They are offerings made to the *L*
29: 8 pleasing to the *L* a burnt offering
29: 12 a festival to the *L* for seven days.
29: 13 as an aroma pleasing to the *L*,
29: 36 as an aroma pleasing to the *L*,
29: 39 prepare these for the *L*
29: 40 all that the *L* commanded him.
30: 1 "This is what the *L* commands:
30: 2 When a man makes a vow to the *L*
30: 3 house makes a vow to the *L*
30: 5 the *L* will release her because her
30: 8 and the *L* will release her.
30: 12 and the *L* will release her.
30: 16 the regulations the *L* gave Moses
31: 1 *L* said to Moses, "Take vengeance
31: 7 as the *L* commanded Moses,
31: 16 away from the *L* in what happened
31: 21 of the law that the *L* gave Moses:
31: 25 The *L* said to Moses, "You
31: 28 as tribute for the *L* one out
31: 31 as the *L* commanded Moses.
31: 37 the tribute for the *L* was 675;
31: 38 which the tribute for the *L* was 72;
31: 39 which the tribute for the *L* was 61;
31: 40 which the tribute for the *L* was 32.
31: 41 as the *L* commanded Moses.
31: 47 as the *L* commanded him,
31: 50 for ourselves before the *L*."
31: 50 to the *L* the gold articles each
31: 52 as a gift to the *L* weighed 16,750
31: 54 for the Israelites before the *L*.
32: 4 the land the *L* subdued
32: 7 into the land the *L* has given them?
32: 9 the land the *L* had given them.
32: 12 followed the *L* wholeheartedly.'
32: 14 and making the *L* even more angry
32: 20 yourselves before the *L* for battle,
32: 21 armed over the Jordan before the *L*
32: 22 be your possession before the *L*.
32: 22 free from your obligation to the *L*
32: 22 the land is subdued before the *L*,
32: 23 you will be sinning against the *L*;
32: 27 will cross over to fight before the *L*,
32: 29 the Jordan with you before the *L*,
32: 31 will do what the *L* has said.
32: 32 before the *L* into Canaan armed,
33: 4 for the *L* had brought judgment
33: 4 whom the *L* had struck
33: 50 from Jericho the *L* said to Moses,
34: 1 The *L* said to Moses, "Command
34: 13 The *L* has ordered that it be given
34: 16 The *L* said to Moses, "These are
34: 29 are the men the *L* commanded
35: 1 from Jericho, the *L* said to Moses,
35: 9 Then the *L* said to Moses:
35: 34 the *L*, dwell among the Israelites
36: 2 "When the *L* commanded my lord
36: 6 This is what the *L* commands
36: 10 as the *L* commanded Moses.

Nu 36: 13 and regulations the *L* gave
Dt 1: 3 all that the *L* had commanded him
1: 6 The *L* our God said to us at Horeb,
1: 8 the land that the *L* swore he would
1: 10 *L* your God has increased your
1: 11 May the *L*, the God of your fathers
1: 19 as the *L* our God commanded us,
1: 20 which the *L* our God is giving us.
1: 21 and take possession of it as the *L*,
1: 21 *L* your God has given you the land.
1: 25 a good land that the *L* our God is
1: 26 the command of the *L* your God.
1: 27 tents and said, "The *L* hates us;
1: 30 The *L* your God, who is going
1: 31 saw how the *L* your God carried
1: 32 you did not trust in the *L* your God
1: 34 When the *L* heard what you said,
1: 36 he followed the *L* wholeheartedly
1: 37 Because of you the *L* became angry
1: 41 as the *L* our God commanded us."
1: 41 "We have sinned against the *L*.
1: 42 But the *L* said to me, "Tell them,
1: 45 came back and wept before the *L*,
2: 1 Sea, as the *L* had directed me.
2: 2 *L* said to me, "You have made your
2: 7 The *L* your God has blessed you
2: 7 forty years the *L* your God has
2: 9 the *L* said to me, "Do not harass
2: 12 did in the land the *L* gave them
2: 13 And the *L* said, "Now get up
2: 14 as the *L* had sworn to them.
2: 17 the people had died, the *L* said
2: 21 The *L* destroyed them
2: 22 The *L* had done the same
2: 29 into the land the *L* our God is
2: 30 For the *L* your God had made his
2: 31 *L* said to me, "See, I have begun
2: 33 the *L* our God delivered him
2: 36 The *L* our God gave us all of them.
2: 37 the command of the *L* our God,
3: 2 The *L* said to me, "Do not be afraid
3: 3 So the *L* our God also gave
3: 18 *L* your God has given you this land
3: 20 the land that the *L* your God is
3: 20 until the *L* gives rest
3: 21 The *L* will do the same
3: 21 eyes all that the *L* your God has
3: 22 the *L* your God himself will fight
3: 24 with the *L*: "O Sovereign *L*,
3: 26 of you the *L* was angry with me
3: 26 "That is enough," the *L* said.
4: 1 possession of the land that the *L*,
4: 2 of the *L* your God that I give you.
4: 3 The *L* your God destroyed
4: 3 with your own eyes what the *L* did
4: 4 fast to the *L* your God are still alive
4: 5 as the *L* my God commanded me,
4: 7 near them the way the *L* our God is
4: 10 before the *L* your God at Horeb,
4: 12 the *L* spoke to you out of the fire.
4: 14 And the *L* directed me at that time
4: 15 of any kind the day the *L* spoke
4: 19 worshiping things the *L* your God
4: 20 *L* took you and brought you out
4: 21 The *L* was angry with me
4: 21 the good land the *L* your God is
4: 23 of anything the *L* your God has
4: 23 of the *L* your God that he made
4: 24 For the *L* your God is a consuming
4: 25 evil in the eyes of the *L* your God
4: 27 The *L* will scatter you
4: 27 to which the *L* will drive you.
4: 29 there you seek the *L* your God,
4: 30 return to the *L* your God
4: 31 For the *L* your God is a merciful
4: 34 all the things the *L* your God did
4: 35 you might know that the *L* is God;
4: 39 to heart this day that the *L* is God
4: 40 in the land the *L* your God gives
5: 2 The *L* our God made a covenant
5: 3 fathers that the *L* made this
5: 4 The *L* spoke to you face to face out
5: 5 (At that time I stood between the *L*
5: 5 to declare to you the word of the *L*,
5: 6 And he said: "I am the *L* your God,
5: 9 the *L* your God, am a jealous God,
5: 11 for the *L* will not hold anyone
5: 11 the name of the *L* your God,

Dt 5: 12 *L* your God has commanded you.
5: 14 a Sabbath to the *L* your God.
5: 15 Therefore the *L* your God has
5: 15 that the *L* your God brought you
5: 16 in the land the *L* your God is giving
5: 16 *L* your God has commanded you,
5: 22 commandments the *L* proclaimed
5: 24 *L* our God has shown us his glory
5: 25 voice of the *L* our God any longer.
5: 27 listen to all that the *L* our God says
5: 27 tell us whatever the *L* our God tells
5: 28 The *L* heard you when you spoke
5: 28 spoke to me and the *L* said to me,
5: 32 to do what the *L* your God has
5: 33 the way that the *L* your God has
6: 1 laws the *L* your God directed me
6: 2 them may fear the *L* your God
6: 3 as the *L*, the God of your fathers,
6: 4 The *L* our God, the *L* is one.
6: 5 Love the *L* your God
6: 10 When the *L* your God brings you
6: 12 that you do not forget the *L*,
6: 13 Fear the *L* your God, serve him
6: 15 for the *L* your God, who is
6: 16 Do not test the *L* your God
6: 17 the commands of the *L* your God
6: 18 the good land that the *L* promised
6: 19 enemies before you, as the *L* said.
6: 20 and laws the *L* our God has
6: 21 but the *L* brought us out of Egypt
6: 22 our eyes the *L* sent miraculous
6: 24 The *L* commanded us
6: 24 and to fear the *L* our God,
6: 25 law before the *L* our God,
7: 1 When the *L* your God brings you
7: 2 when the *L* your God has delivered
7: 6 holy to the *L* your God.
7: 6 *L* your God has chosen you out
7: 7 The *L* did not set his affection
7: 8 But it was because the *L* loved you
7: 9 that the *L* your God is God;
7: 12 then the *L* your God will keep his
7: 15 The *L* will keep you free
7: 16 the peoples the *L* your God gives
7: 18 well what the *L* your God did
7: 19 The *L* your God will do the same
7: 19 with which the *L* your God
7: 20 *L* your God will send the hornet
7: 21 for the *L* your God, who is
7: 22 *L* your God will drive out those
7: 23 the *L* your God will deliver them
7: 25 detestable to the *L* your God.
8: 1 the land that the *L* promised
8: 2 Remember how the *L* your God
8: 3 comes from the mouth of the *L*.
8: 5 so the *L* your God disciplines you.
8: 6 the commands of the *L* your God,
8: 7 For the *L* your God is bringing you
8: 10 praise the *L* your God
8: 11 you do not forget the *L* your God,
8: 14 and you will forget the *L* your God,
8: 18 But remember the *L* your God,
8: 19 If you ever forget the *L* your God
8: 20 Like the nations the *L* destroyed
8: 20 for not obeying the *L* your God.
9: 3 as the *L* has promised you.
9: 3 today that the *L* your God is
9: 4 After the *L* your God has driven
9: 4 of these nations that the *L* is going
9: 4 "The *L* has brought me here
9: 5 the *L* your God will drive them out
9: 6 righteousness that the *L* your God
9: 7 have been rebellious against the *L*.
9: 7 how you provoked the *L* your God
9: 9 the covenant that the *L* had made
9: 10 The *L* gave me two stone tablets
9: 10 commandments the *L* proclaimed
9: 11 the *L* gave me the two stone tablets
9: 12 the *L* told me, "Go down from here
9: 13 the *L* said to me, "I have seen this
9: 16 sinned against the *L* your God;
9: 16 way that the *L* had commanded
9: 18 before the *L* for forty days
9: 19 But again the *L* listened to me.
9: 19 the anger and wrath of the *L*,
9: 20 And the *L* was angry enough
9: 22 also made the *L* angry at Taberah,
9: 23 And when the *L* sent you out

Dt 9:23 the command of the *L* your God.
9:24 rebellious against the *L* ever
9:25 before the *L* those forty days
9:25 *L* had said he would destroy you.
9:26 I prayed to the *L* and said,
9:26 "O Sovereign *L*, do not destroy
9:28 'Because the *L* was not able
10: 1 At that time the *L* said to me,
10: 4 And the *L* gave them to me.
10: 4 *L* wrote on these tablets what he
10: 5 as the *L* commanded me,
10: 8 At that time the *L* set apart
10: 8 the ark of the covenant of the *L*,
10: 8 to stand before the *L* to minister
10: 9 as the *L* your God told them.)
10: 9 the *L* is their inheritance,
10: 10 the *L* listened to me at this time
10: 11 *L* said to me, "and lead the people
10: 12 but to fear the *L* your God,
10: 12 to serve the *L* your God
10: 12 what does the *L* your God ask
10: 14 To the *L* your God belong
10: 15 Yet the *L* set his affection
10: 17 For the *L* your God is God of gods
10: 20 Fear the *L* your God and serve him
10: 22 now the *L* your God has made you
11: 1 Love the *L* your God and keep his
11: 2 the discipline of the *L* your God:
11: 4 and how the *L* brought lasting ruin
11: 7 these great things the *L* has done.
11: 9 long in the land that the *L* swore
11: 12 It is a land the *L* your God cares for
11: 12 of the *L* your God are continually
11: 13 to love the *L* your God
11: 17 the good land the *L* is giving you.
11: 21 many in the land that the *L* swore
11: 22 to love the *L* your God, to walk
11: 23 then the *L* will drive out all these
11: 25 *L* your God, as he promised you,
11: 27 of the *L* your God that I am giving
11: 28 the commands of the *L* your God
11: 29 When the *L* your God has brought
11: 31 of the land the *L* your God is giving
12: 1 to follow in the land that the *L*,
12: 4 must not worship the *L* your God
12: 5 seek the place the *L* your God will
12: 7 in the presence of the *L* your God,
12: 7 the *L* your God has blessed you.
12: 9 the inheritance the *L* your God is
12: 10 in the land the *L* your God is giving
12: 11 to the place the *L* your God will
12: 11 you have vowed to the *L*.
12: 12 rejoice before the *L* your God,
12: 14 only at the place the *L* will choose
12: 15 the blessing the *L* your God gives
12: 18 at the place the *L* your God will
12: 18 in the presence of the *L* your God
12: 18 to rejoice before the *L* your God
12: 20 When the *L* your God has enlarged
12: 21 and flocks the *L* has given you,
12: 21 the place where the *L* your God
12: 25 right in the eyes of the *L*.
12: 26 go to the place the *L* will choose.
12: 27 beside the altar of the *L* your God,
12: 27 on the altar of the *L* your God,
12: 28 right in the eyes of the *L* your God.
12: 29 The *L* your God will cut
12: 31 must not worship the *L* your God
12: 31 of detestable things the *L* hates.
13: 3 The *L* your God is testing you
13: 4 It is the *L* your God you must
13: 5 rebellion against the *L* your God,
13: 5 the way the *L* your God
13: 10 away from the *L* your God,
13: 12 one of the towns the *L* your God is
13: 16 offering to the *L* your God.
13: 17 so that the *L* will turn
13: 18 because you obey the *L* your God,
14: 1 the children of the *L* your God.
14: 2 holy to the *L* your God.
14: 2 the *L* has chosen you
14: 21 holy to the *L* your God.
14: 23 in the presence of the *L* your God
14: 23 to revere the *L* your God always.
14: 24 blessed by the *L* your God
14: 24 the place where the *L* will choose
14: 25 go to the place the *L* your God will
14: 26 in the presence of the *L* your God

Dt 14: 29 so that the *L* your God may bless
15: 4 in the land the *L* your God is giving
15: 5 only you fully obey the *L* your God
15: 6 For the *L* your God will bless you
15: 7 the land that the *L* your God is
15: 9 appeal to the *L* against you,
15: 10 of this the *L* your God will bless
15: 14 as the *L* your God has blessed you.
15: 15 and the *L* your God redeemed you.
15: 18 And the *L* your God will bless you
15: 19 for the *L* your God every firstborn
15: 20 in the presence of the *L* your God
15: 21 it to the *L* your God.
16: 1 the Passover of the *L* your God,
16: 2 herd at the place the *L* will choose
16: 2 to the *L* your God an animal
16: 5 in any town the *L* your God gives
16: 7 it at the place the *L* your God will
16: 8 an assembly to the *L* your God
16: 10 Feast of Weeks to the *L* your God
16: 10 to the blessings the *L* your God has
16: 11 And rejoice before the *L* your God
16: 15 For the *L* your God will bless you
16: 15 God at the place the *L* will choose.
16: 15 the Feast to the *L* your God
16: 16 appear before the *L* empty-handed:
16: 16 appear before the *L* your God
16: 17 to the way the *L* your God has
16: 18 in every town the *L* your God is
16: 20 possess the land the *L* your God is
16: 21 build to the *L* your God,
16: 22 for these the *L* your God hates.
17: 1 sacrifice to the *L* your God an ox
17: 2 eyes of the *L* your God in violation
17: 2 one of the towns the *L* gives you is
17: 8 to the place the *L* your God will
17: 10 you at the place the *L* will choose.
17: 12 to the *L* your God must be put
17: 14 enter the land the *L* your God is
17: 15 the king the *L* your God chooses.
17: 16 for the *L* has told you, "You are
17: 19 learn to revere the *L* his God
18: 1 live on the offerings made to the *L*
18: 2 the *L* is their inheritance,
18: 5 for the *L* your God has chosen
18: 6 to the place the *L* will choose,
18: 7 of the *L* his God like all his fellow
18: 7 there in the presence of the *L*.
18: 9 enter the land the *L* your God is
18: 12 practices the *L* your God
18: 12 these things is detestable to the *L*,
18: 13 blameless before the *L* your God.
18: 14 *L* your God has not permitted you
18: 15 The *L* your God will raise up
18: 16 asked of the *L* your God at Horeb
18: 16 not hear the voice of the *L* our God
18: 17 *L* said to me: "What they say is
18: 21 has not been spoken by the *L*?"
18: 22 is a message the *L* has not spoken.
18: 22 name of the *L* does not take place
19: 1 When the *L* your God has
19: 2 in the land the *L* your God is giving
19: 3 parts the land the *L* your God is
19: 8 If the *L* your God enlarges your
19: 9 to love the *L* your God
19: 10 which the *L* your God is giving you
19: 14 in the land the *L* your God is giving
19: 17 presence of the *L* before the priests
20: 1 of them, because the *L* your God,
20: 4 For the *L* your God is the one who
20: 13 When the *L* your God delivers it
20: 14 the plunder the *L* your God gives
20: 16 of the nations the *L* your God is
20: 17 *L* your God has commanded you.
20: 18 you will sin against the *L* your God
21: 1 in the land the *L* your God is giving
21: 5 blessings in the name of the *L*.
21: 5 for the *L* your God has chosen
21: 8 whom you have redeemed, O *L*,
21: 9 right in the eyes of the *L*.
21: 10 and the *L* your God delivers them
21: 23 the land the *L* your God is
22: 5 for the *L* your God detests anyone
23: 1 may enter the assembly of the *L*.
23: 2 may enter the assembly of the *L*,
23: 3 may enter the assembly of the *L*,
23: 5 because the *L* your God loves you.
23: 5 the *L* your God would not listen

Dt 23: 8 may enter the assembly of the *L*.
23: 14 For the *L* your God moves about
23: 18 into the house of the *L* your God
23: 18 the *L* your God detests them both.
23: 20 so that the *L* your God may bless
23: 21 a vow to the *L* your God,
23: 21 for the *L* your God will certainly
23: 23 freely to the *L* your God
24: 4 detestable in the eyes of the *L*.
24: 4 sin upon the land the *L* your God is
24: 9 Remember what the *L* your God
24: 13 act in the sight of the *L* your God.
24: 15 cry to the *L* against you,
24: 18 and the *L* your God redeemed you
24: 19 so that the *L* your God may bless
25: 15 in the land the *L* your God is giving
25: 16 For the *L* your God detests anyone
25: 19 When the *L* your God gives you
26: 1 entered the land the *L* your God is
26: 2 go to the place the *L* your God will
26: 2 of the land the *L* your God is giving
26: 3 come to the land the *L* swore
26: 3 to the *L* your God that I have come
26: 4 of the altar of the *L* your God.
26: 5 declare before the *L* your God:
26: 7 Then we cried out to the *L*,
26: 7 and the *L* heard our voice
26: 8 So the *L* brought us out of Egypt
26: 10 firstfruits of the soil that you, O *L*,
26: 10 the basket before the *L* your God
26: 11 the good things the *L* your God has
26: 13 Then say to the *L* your God:
26: 14 I have obeyed the *L* my God;
26: 16 *L* your God commands you this
26: 17 this day that the *L* is your God
26: 18 *L* has declared this day that you
26: 19 holy to the *L* your God,
27: 2 into the land the *L* your God is
27: 3 as the *L*, the God of your fathers,
27: 3 enter the land the *L* your God is
27: 5 an altar to the *L* your God,
27: 6 of the *L* your God with fieldstones
27: 6 offerings on it to the *L* your God.
27: 7 in the presence of the *L* your God.
27: 9 the people of the *L* your God.
27: 10 Obey the *L* your God and follow
27: 15 a thing detestable to the *L*,
28: 1 If you fully obey the *L* your God
28: 1 the *L* your God will set you high
28: 2 you if you obey the *L* your God:
28: 7 *L* will grant that the enemies who
28: 8 The *L* will send a blessing
28: 8 The *L* your God will bless you
28: 9 The *L* will establish you
28: 9 the commands of the *L* your God
28: 10 called by the name of the *L*,
28: 11 The *L* will grant you abundant
28: 12 The *L* will open the heavens,
28: 13 The *L* will make you the head,
28: 13 of the *L* your God that I give you
28: 15 if you do not obey the *L* your God
28: 20 The *L* will send on you curses,
28: 21 The *L* will plague you with diseases
28: 22 The *L* will strike you
28: 24 The *L* will turn the rain
28: 25 The *L* will cause you to be defeated
28: 27 The *L* will afflict you with the boils
28: 28 The *L* will afflict you with madness
28: 35 The *L* will afflict your knees
28: 36 *L* will drive you and the king you
28: 37 nations where the *L* will drive you.
28: 45 you did not obey the *L* your God
28: 47 not serve the *L* your God joyfully
28: 48 will serve the enemies the *L* sends
28: 49 The *L* will bring a nation
28: 52 the land the *L* your God is
28: 53 and daughters the *L* your God has
28: 58 awesome name—the *L* your God
28: 59 the *L* will send fearful plagues
28: 61 The *L* will also bring
28: 62 you did not obey the *L* your God.
28: 63 as it pleased the *L* to make you
28: 64 Then the *L* will scatter you
28: 65 There the *L* will give you
28: 68 The *L* will send you back in ships
29: 1 covenant the *L* commanded Moses
29: 2 eyes have seen all that the *L* did
29: 4 to this day the *L* has not given you

Dt 29: 6 know that I am the *L* your God.
29: 10 in the presence of the *L* your God
29: 12 a covenant the *L* is making
29: 12 a covenant with the *L* your God,
29: 15 in the presence of the *L* our God
29: 18 away from the *L* our God to go
29: 20 The *L* will never be willing
29: 20 and the *L* will blot out his name
29: 21 The *L* will single him out
29: 22 with which the *L* has afflicted it.
29: 23 which the *L* overthrew
29: 24 "Why has the *L* done this
29: 25 abandoned the covenant of the *L*,
29: 28 in great wrath the *L* uprooted them
29: 29 things belong to the *L* our God,
30: 1 heart wherever the *L* your God
30: 2 return to the *L* your God
30: 3 then the *L* your God will restore
30: 4 from there the *L* your God will
30: 6 *L* your God will circumcise your
30: 7 *L* your God will put all these curses
30: 8 You will again obey the *L*
30: 9 The *L* will again delight in you
30: 9 *L* your God will make you most
30: 10 and turn to the *L* your God
30: 10 if you obey the *L* your God
30: 16 and the *L* your God will bless you
30: 16 today to love the *L* your God,
30: 20 For the *L* is your life, and he will
30: 20 that you may love the *L* your God,
31: 2 *L* has said to me, 'You shall not
31: 3 The *L* your God himself will cross
31: 3 over ahead of you, as the *L* said.
31: 4 the *L* will do to them what he did
31: 5 The *L* will deliver them to you,
31: 6 for the *L* your God goes with you;
31: 7 into the land that the *L* swore
31: 8 The *L* himself goes before you
31: 9 the ark of the covenant of the *L*,
31: 11 to appear before the *L* your God
31: 12 and learn to fear the *L* your God
31: 13 and learn to fear the *L* your God
31: 14 *L* said to Moses, "Now the day
31: 15 Then the *L* appeared at the Tent
31: 16 *L* said to Moses: "You are going
31: 23 The *L* gave this command
31: 25 the ark of the covenant of the *L*:
31: 26 of the covenant of the *L* your God.
31: 27 against the *L* while I am still alive
31: 29 you will do evil in the sight of the *L*
32: 3 I will proclaim the name of the *L*.
32: 6 Is this the way you repay the *L*,
32: 12 The *L* alone led him;
32: 19 The *L* saw this and rejected them
32: 27 the *L* has not done all this.' "
32: 30 unless the *L* had given them up?
32: 36 The *L* will judge his people
32: 48 On that same day the *L* told Moses
33: 2 "The *L* came from Sinai
33: 7 "Hear, O *L*, the cry of Judah;
33: 11 Bless all his skills, O *L*,
33: 12 and the one the *L* loves rests
33: 12 beloved of the *L* rest secure in him,
33: 13 "May the *L* bless his land
33: 23 abounding with the favor of the *L*
33: 29 a people saved by the *L*?
34: 1 There the *L* showed him the whole
34: 4 *L* said to him, "This is the land I
34: 5 of the *L* died there in Moab,
34: 5 there in Moab, as the *L* had said.
34: 9 did what the *L* had commanded
34: 10 whom the *L* knew face to face,
34: 11 and wonders the *L* sent him to do
Jos 1: 1 of Moses the servant of the *L*,
1: 1 the *L* said to Joshua son of Nun,
1: 9 for the *L* your God will be
1: 11 of the land the *L* your God is giving
1: 13 the servant of the *L* gave you:
1: 13 'The *L* your God is giving you rest
1: 15 the land that the *L* your God is
1: 15 the servant of the *L* gave you east
1: 15 until the *L* gives them rest,
1: 17 Only may the *L* your God be
2: 9 "I know that the *L* has given this
2: 10 have heard how the *L* dried up
2: 11 for the *L* your God is God
2: 12 me by the *L* that you will show
2: 14 when the *L* gives us the land."

Jos 2: 24 *L* has surely given the whole land
3: 3 of the covenant of the *L* your God,
3: 5 for tomorrow the *L* will do
3: 7 the *L* said to Joshua, "Today I will
3: 9 to the words of the *L* your God.
3: 13 priests who carry the ark of the *L*—
3: 17 of the covenant of the *L* stood firm
4: 1 crossing the Jordan, the *L* said
4: 5 before the ark of the *L* your God
4: 7 the ark of the covenant of the *L*.
4: 8 as the *L* had told Joshua;
4: 10 everything the *L* had commanded
4: 11 ark of the *L* and the priests came
4: 13 over before the *L* to the plains
4: 14 That day the *L* exalted Joshua
4: 15 Then the *L* said to Joshua,
4: 18 the ark of the covenant of the *L*.
4: 23 For the *L* your God dried up
4: 23 The *L* your God did
4: 24 always fear the *L* your God."
4: 24 the hand of the *L* is powerful
5: 1 heard how the *L* had dried up
5: 2 At that time the *L* said to Joshua,
5: 6 For the *L* had sworn
5: 6 since they had not obeyed the *L*.
5: 9 Then the *L* said to Joshua,
5: 14 army of the *L* I have now come."
6: 2 Then the *L* said to Joshua, "See,
6: 6 the ark of the covenant of the *L*
6: 7 ahead of the ark of the *L*."
6: 8 before the *L* went forward,
6: 11 of the *L* carried around the city,
6: 12 the priests took up the ark of the *L*.
6: 13 guard followed the ark of the *L*,
6: 13 marching before the ark of the *L*
6: 16 For the *L* has given you the city!
6: 17 is in it are to be devoted to the *L*.
6: 19 and iron are sacred to the *L*
6: 21 They devoted the city to the *L*
6: 26 before the *L* is the man who
6: 27 So the *L* was with Joshua,
7: 6 the ground before the ark of the *L*,
7: 7 And Joshua said, "Ah, Sovereign *L*
7: 10 The *L* said to Joshua, "Stand up!
7: 13 for this is what the *L*, the God
7: 14 family that the *L* takes shall come
7: 14 the clan that the *L* takes shall come
7: 14 tribe that the *L* takes shall come
7: 15 has violated the covenant of the *L*
7: 19 give glory to the *L*, the God
7: 20 I have sinned against the *L*,
7: 23 and spread them out before the *L*.
7: 25 The *L* will bring disaster
7: 26 the *L* turned from his fierce anger.
8: 1 Then the *L* said to Joshua,
8: 7 The *L* your God will give it
8: 8 Do what the *L* has commanded.
8: 18 Then the *L* said to Joshua,
8: 27 as the *L* had instructed Joshua.
8: 30 on Mount Ebal an altar to the *L*,
8: 31 offered to the *L* burnt offerings
8: 31 servant of the *L* had commanded
8: 33 of the ark of the covenant of the *L*,
8: 33 of the *L* had formerly commanded
9: 9 of the fame of the *L* your God.
9: 14 but did not inquire of the *L*.
9: 18 sworn an oath to them by the *L*,
9: 19 have given them our oath by the *L*,
9: 24 told how the *L* your God had
9: 27 and for the altar of the *L*
9: 27 at the place the *L* would choose.
10: 8 *L* said to Joshua, "Do not be afraid
10: 10 The *L* threw them into confusion
10: 11 the *L* hurled large hailstones
10: 12 Joshua said to the *L* in the presence
10: 12 the day the *L* gave the Amorites
10: 14 Surely the *L* was fighting for Israel!
10: 14 a day when the *L* listened to a man.
10: 19 for the *L* your God has given them
10: 25 This is what the *L* will do
10: 30 The *L* also gave that city
10: 32 The *L* handed Lachish
10: 40 just as the *L*, the God of Israel,
10: 42 because the *L*, the God of Israel,
11: 6 *L* said to Joshua, "Do not be afraid
11: 8 and the *L* gave them into the hand
11: 9 did to them as the *L* had directed:
11: 12 servant of the *L* had commanded.

Jos 11: 15 As the *L* commanded his servant
11: 15 of all that the *L* commanded Moses
11: 20 as the *L* had commanded Moses.
11: 20 it was the *L* himself who hardened
11: 23 just as the *L* had directed Moses,
12: 6 Moses, the servant of the *L*,
12: 6 the servant of the *L* gave their land
13: 1 *L* said to him, "You are very old,
13: 8 the servant of the *L*, had assigned it
13: 14 the offerings made by fire to the *L*,
13: 33 had given no inheritance; the *L*,
14: 2 as the *L* had commanded
14: 5 as the *L* had commanded Moses.
14: 6 "You know what the *L* said
14: 7 Moses the servant of the *L*
14: 8 followed the *L* my God
14: 9 have followed the *L* my God
14: 10 "Now then, just as the *L* promised,
14: 12 country that the *L* promised me
14: 12 *L* helping me, I will drive them out
14: 14 because he followed the *L*,
17: 4 "The *L* commanded Moses
17: 14 the *L* has blessed us abundantly."
18: 3 possession of the land that the *L*,
18: 6 in the presence of the *L* our God.
18: 7 servant of the *L* gave it to them."
18: 7 service of the *L* is their inheritance.
18: 8 at Shiloh in the presence of the *L*."
18: 10 in Shiloh in the presence of the *L*,
19: 50 as the *L* had commanded.
19: 51 presence of the *L* at the entrance
20: 1 Then the *L* said to Joshua:
21: 2 "The *L* commanded
21: 3 So, as the *L* had commanded,
21: 8 as the *L* had commanded
21: 43 the *L* gave Israel all the land he had
21: 44 The *L* gave them rest on every side
21: 44 the *L* handed all their enemies
22: 2 the servant of the *L* commanded,
22: 3 the mission the *L* your God gave
22: 4 of the *L* gave you on the other side
22: 4 that the *L* your God has given your
22: 5 the servant of the *L* gave you:
22: 5 to love the *L* your God, to walk
22: 9 command of the *L* through Moses.
22: 16 could you turn away from the *L*
22: 16 "The whole assembly of the *L* says:
22: 17 fell on the community of the *L*!
22: 18 you now turning away from the *L*?
22: 18 " 'If you rebel against the *L* today,
22: 19 But do not rebel against the *L*
22: 19 than the altar of the *L* our God.
22: 22 God, the *L*! The Mighty One, God
22: 22 The Mighty One, God, the *L*!
22: 22 or disobedience to the *L*,
22: 23 altar to turn away from the *L*
22: 23 may the *L* himself call us
22: 24 What do you have to do with the *L*,
22: 25 You have no share in the *L*.'
22: 25 ours to stop fearing the *L*.
22: 25 *L* has made the Jordan a boundary
22: 27 that we will worship the *L*
22: 27 'You have no share in the *L*.'
22: 29 altar of the *L* our God that stands
22: 29 it from us to rebel against the *L*
22: 31 toward the *L* in this matter.
22: 31 "Today we know that the *L* is
22: 34 THAT THE *L* IS GOD.
23: 1 and the *L* had given Israel rest
23: 3 it was the *L* your God who fought
23: 3 seen everything the *L* your God
23: 5 as the *L* your God promised you.
23: 5 *L* your God himself will drive them
23: 8 are to hold fast to the *L* your God,
23: 9 "The *L* has driven out
23: 10 the *L* your God fights for you,
23: 11 careful to love the *L* your God.
23: 13 be sure that the *L* your God will no
23: 13 which the *L* your God has given
23: 14 the good promises the *L* your God
23: 15 of the *L* your God has come true,
23: 15 so the *L* will bring
23: 16 the covenant of the *L* your God,
24: 2 "This is what the *L*, the God
24: 7 But they cried to the *L* for help,
24: 14 and in Egypt, and serve the *L*.
24: 14 "Now fear the *L* and serve him
24: 15 if serving the *L* seems undesirable

Jos 24: 15 my household, we will serve the *L*
24: 16 to forsake the *L* to serve other gods
24: 17 It was the *L* our God himself who
24: 18 And the *L* drove out before us all
24: 18 We too will serve the *L*,
24: 19 "You are not able to serve the *L*.
24: 20 you forsake the *L* and serve foreign
24: 21 "No! We will serve the *L*."
24: 22 you have chosen to serve the *L*."
24: 23 and yield your hearts to the *L*,
24: 24 "We will serve the *L* our God
24: 26 oak near the holy place of the *L*.
24: 27 heard all the words the *L* has said
24: 29 son of Nun, the servant of the *L*,
24: 31 Israel served the *L*
24: 31 everything the *L* had done
Jdg 1: 1 Joshua, the Israelites asked the *L*,
1: 2 The *L* answered, "Judah is to go;
1: 4 the *L* gave the Canaanites
1: 19 The *L* was with the men of Judah.
1: 22 attacked Bethel, and the *L* was
2: 1 The angel of the *L* went up
2: 4 of the *L* had spoken these things
2: 5 they offered sacrifices to the *L*.
2: 7 The people served the *L*
2: 7 all the great things the *L* had done
2: 8 son of Nun, the servant of the *L*,
2: 10 who knew neither the *L*
2: 11 evil in the eyes of the *L*
2: 12 They forsook the *L*, the God
2: 12 They provoked the *L* to anger
2: 14 against Israel the *L* handed them
2: 15 the hand of the *L* was against them
2: 16 Then the *L* raised up judges,
2: 18 Whenever the *L* raised up a judge
2: 18 for the *L* had compassion on them
2: 20 Therefore the *L* was very angry
2: 22 they will keep the way of the *L*
2: 23 The *L* had allowed those nations
3: 1 These are the nations the *L* left
3: 7 evil in the eyes of the *L*;
3: 7 they forgot the *L* their God
3: 8 anger of the *L* burned against Israel
3: 9 But when they cried out to the *L*,
3: 10 The Spirit of the *L* came upon him,
3: 10 *L* gave Cushan-Rishathaim king
3: 12 did this evil the *L* gave Eglon king
3: 12 evil in the eyes of the *L*,
3: 15 the Israelites cried out to the *L*,
3: 28 "for the *L* has given Moab,
4: 1 evil in the eyes of the *L*.
4: 2 So the *L* sold them into the hands
4: 3 they cried to the *L* for help.
4: 6 "The *L*, the God of Israel,
4: 9 for the *L* will hand Sisera
4: 14 Has not the *L* gone ahead of you?"
4: 14 is the day the *L* has given Sisera
4: 15 *L* routed Sisera and all his chariots
5: 2 praise the *L*!
5: 3 I will make music to the *L*,
5: 3 I will sing to the *L*, I will sing;
5: 4 O *L*, when you went out from Seir,
5: 5 before the *L*, the God of Israel.
5: 5 mountains quaked before the *L*,
5: 9 Praise the *L*!
5: 11 Then the people of the *L*
5: 11 recite the righteous acts of the *L*,
5: 13 the people of the *L*
5: 23 Meroz,' said the angel of the *L*.
5: 23 they did not come to help the *L*,
5: 23 to help the *L* against the mighty.'
5: 31 may all your enemies perish, O *L*!
6: 1 evil in the eyes of the *L*,
6: 6 that they cried out to the *L*
6: 7 When the Israelites cried to the *L*
6: 8 "This is what the *L*, the God
6: 10 I said to you, 'I am the *L* your God;
6: 11 The angel of the *L* came
6: 12 angel of the *L* appeared to Gideon,
6: 12 he said, "The *L* is with you,
6: 13 But now the *L* has abandoned us
6: 13 Gideon replied, "if the *L* is with us,
6: 13 'Did not the *L* bring us up out
6: 14 The *L* turned to him and said,
6: 16 The *L* answered, "I will be
6: 18 And the *L* said, "I will wait
6: 21 And the angel of the *L* disappeared
6: 21 the angel of the *L* touched the meat

Jdg 6: 22 he exclaimed, "Ah, Sovereign *L*!
6: 22 that it was the angel of the *L*,
6: 22 the angel of the *L* face to face!"
6: 23 But the *L* said to him, "Peace!
6: 24 Gideon built an altar to the *L* there
6: 24 and called it "The *L* is Peace."
6: 25 That same night the *L* said to him,
6: 26 kind of altar to the *L* your God
6: 27 servants and did as the *L* told him.
6: 34 Spirit of the *L* came upon Gideon,
7: 2 *L* said to Gideon, "You have too
7: 4 *L* said to Gideon, "There are still
7: 5 There the *L* told him, "Separate
7: 7 *L* said to Gideon, "With the three
7: 9 During that night the *L* said
7: 15 *L* has given the Midianite camp
7: 18 'For the *L* and for Gideon.'"
7: 20 "A sword for the *L* and for Gideon
7: 22 the *L* caused the men
8: 7 when the *L* has given Zebah
8: 19 the *L* lives, if you had spared their
8: 23 The *L* will rule over you."
8: 34 did not remember the *L* their God,
10: 6 because the Israelites forsook the *L*
10: 6 evil in the eyes of the *L*.
10: 10 the Israelites cried out to the *L*,
10: 11 *L* replied, "When the Egyptians,
10: 15 But the Israelites said to the *L*,
10: 16 among them and served the *L*.
11: 9 and the *L* gives them to me—
11: 10 Gilead replied, "The *L* is our
11: 11 words before the *L* in Mizpah.
11: 21 "Then the *L*, the God of Israel,
11: 23 Now since the *L*, the God of Israel,
11: 24 whatever the *L* our God has given
11: 27 Let the *L*, the Judge, decide
11: 29 of the *L* came upon Jephthah.
11: 30 And Jephthah made a vow to the *L*
11: 32 and the *L* gave them into his hands.
11: 35 vow to the *L* that I cannot break."
11: 36 now that the *L* has avenged you
11: 36 you have given your word to the *L*.
12: 3 and the *L* gave me the victory
13: 1 evil in the eyes of the *L*,
13: 1 so the *L* delivered them
13: 3 The angel of the *L* appeared to her
13: 8 Then Manoah prayed to the *L*:
13: 13 The angel of the *L* answered,
13: 15 Manoah said to the angel of the *L*,
13: 16 The angel of the *L* replied,
13: 16 a burnt offering, offer it to the *L*."
13: 16 that it was the angel of the *L*.)
13: 17 inquired of the angel of the *L*,
13: 19 And the *L* did an amazing thing
13: 19 and sacrificed it on a rock to the *L*.
13: 20 the angel of the *L* ascended
13: 21 of the *L* did not show himself again
13: 21 that it was the angel of the *L*.
13: 23 "If the *L* had meant to kill us,
13: 24 He grew and the *L* blessed him,
13: 25 the Spirit of the *L* began to stir him
14: 4 not know that this was from the *L*,
14: 6 The Spirit of the *L* came upon him
14: 19 the Spirit of the *L* came upon him
15: 14 The Spirit of the *L* came upon him
15: 18 out to the *L*, "You have given your
16: 20 not know that the *L* had left him.
16: 28 Then Samson prayed to the *L*,
16: 28 "O Sovereign *L*, remember me.
17: 2 "The *L* bless you, my son!"
17: 3 silver to the *L* for my son
17: 13 I know that the *L* will be good
19: 18 going to the house of the *L*.
20: 1 assembled before the *L* in Mizpah.
20: 18 The *L* replied, "Judah shall go first
20: 23 and they inquired of the *L*.
20: 23 our brothers?" The *L* answered,
20: 23 wept before the *L* until evening,
20: 26 and fellowship offerings to the *L*.
20: 26 there they sat weeping before the *L*
20: 27 And the Israelites inquired of the *L*
20: 28 or not?" The *L* responded, "Go,
20: 35 The *L* defeated Benjamin
21: 3 O *L*, the God of Israel," they cried,
21: 5 failed to assemble before the *L*
21: 5 failed to assemble before the *L*?"
21: 7 oath by the *L* not to give them any
21: 8 to assemble before the *L* at Mizpah

Jdg 21: 15 the *L* had made a gap in the tribes
21: 19 festival of the *L* in Shiloh,
Ru 1: 6 heard in Moab that the *L* had come
1: 8 May the *L* show kindness to you,
1: 9 May the *L* grant that each
1: 17 May the *L* deal with me, be it ever
1: 21 me Naomi? The *L* has afflicted me;
1: 21 the *L* has brought me back empty.
2: 4 *L* be with you!" "The *L* bless you!"
2: 12 May the *L* repay you
2: 12 you be richly rewarded by the *L*,
2: 20 *L* has not stopped showing his
2: 20 "The *L* bless him!" Naomi said
3: 10 "The *L* bless you, my daughter,"
3: 13 as surely as the *L* lives, I will do it.
4: 11 May the *L* make the woman who is
4: 12 the offspring the *L* gives you
4: 13 And the *L* enabled her to conceive,
4: 14 said to Naomi: "Praise be to the *L*,
1Sa 1: 3 and sacrifice to the *L* Almighty
1: 3 sons of Eli, were priests of the *L*.
1: 5 and the *L* had closed her womb.
1: 6 because the *L* had closed her womb
1: 7 up to the house of the *L*,
1: 10 wept much and prayed to the *L*.
1: 11 a vow, saying, "O *L* Almighty,
1: 11 him to the *L* for all the days
1: 12 As she kept on praying to the *L*,
1: 15 I was pouring out my soul to the *L*.
1: 19 and the *L* remembered her.
1: 19 and worshiped before the *L*
1: 20 "Because I asked the *L* for him."
1: 21 offer the annual sacrifice to the *L*
1: 22 and present him before the *L*,
1: 23 only may the *L* make good his
1: 24 him to the house of the *L* at Shiloh.
1: 26 here beside you praying to the *L*.
1: 27 the *L* has granted me what I asked
1: 28 And he worshiped the *L* there.
1: 28 So now I give him to the *L*.
1: 28 life he will be given over to the *L*."
2: 1 in the *L* my horn is lifted high.
2: 1 "My heart rejoices in the *L*;
2: 2 "There is no one holy like the *L*;
2: 3 for the *L* is a God who knows,
2: 6 The *L* brings death and makes alive
2: 7 The *L* sends poverty and wealth;
2: 10 the *L* will judge the ends
2: 10 who oppose the *L* will be shattered.
2: 11 before the *L* under Eli the priest.
2: 12 they had no regard for the *L*.
2: 18 was ministering before the *L*—
2: 20 prayed for and gave to the *L*."
2: 20 "May the *L* give you children
2: 21 And the *L* was gracious to Hannah;
2: 21 up in the presence of the *L*.
2: 25 but if a man sins against the *L*,
2: 26 in favor with the *L* and with men.
2: 27 to him, "This is what the *L* says:
2: 30 But now the *L* declares: 'Far be it
2: 30 Therefore the *L*, the God of Israel,
3: 1 days the word of the *L* was rare;
3: 1 ministered before the *L* under Eli.
3: 3 lying down in the temple of the *L*,
3: 4 Then the *L* called Samuel.
3: 6 Again the *L* called, "Samuel!"
3: 7 Samuel did not yet know the *L*:
3: 7 of the *L* had not yet been revealed
3: 8 Eli realized that the *L* was calling
3: 8 The *L* called Samuel a third time,
3: 9 *L*, for your servant is listening.'"
3: 10 The *L* came and stood there,
3: 11 And the *L* said to Samuel: "See,
3: 15 the doors of the house of the *L*.
3: 18 Then Eli said, "He is the *L*;
3: 19 The *L* was with Samuel
3: 20 was attested as a prophet of the *L*.
3: 21 The *L* continued to appear
4: 3 "Why did the *L* bring defeat
4: 4 of the covenant of the *L* Almighty,
4: 6 of the *L* had come into the camp,
5: 3 the ground before the ark of the *L*!
5: 4 the ground before the ark of the *L*!
6: 1 When the ark of the *L* had been
6: 2 do with the ark of the *L*?
6: 8 Take the ark of the *L* and put it
6: 9 *L* has brought this great disaster
6: 11 the ark of the *L* on the cart

1Sa 6: 14 as a burnt offering to the *L*.
6: 15 and made sacrifices to the *L*.
6: 15 took down the ark of the *L*,
6: 17 as a guilt offering to the *L*—
6: 18 on which they set the ark of the *L*,
6: 19 heavy blow the *L* had dealt them,
6: 19 looked into the ark of the *L*.
6: 20 in the presence of the *L*, this
6: 21 have returned the ark of the *L*.
7: 1 and took up the ark of the *L*.
7: 1 son to guard the ark of the *L*.
7: 2 mourned and sought after the *L*.
7: 3 and commit yourselves to the *L*
7: 3 to the *L* with all your hearts,
7: 4 Ashtoreths, and served the *L* only.
7: 5 I will intercede with the *L* for you."
7: 6 and poured it out before the *L*.
7: 6 "We have sinned against the *L*."
7: 8 out to the *L* our God for us,
7: 9 as a whole burnt offering to the *L*.
7: 9 behalf, and the *L* answered him.
7: 9 out to the *L* on Israel's behalf,
7: 10 But that day the *L* thundered
7: 12 "Thus far has the *L* helped us."
7: 13 the hand of the *L* was
7: 17 And he built an altar there to the *L*.
8: 6 so he prayed to the *L*.
8: 7 And the *L* told him: "Listen
8: 10 Samuel told all the words of the *L*
8: 18 and the *L* will not answer you
8: 21 he repeated it before the *L*.
8: 22 The *L* answered, "Listen to them
9: 15 the *L* had revealed this to Samuel:
9: 17 sight of Saul, the *L* said to him,
10: 1 "Has not the *L* anointed you leader
10: 6 The Spirit of the *L* will come
10: 17 people of Israel to the *L* at Mizpah
10: 18 "This is what the *L*, the God
10: 19 before the *L* by your tribes
10: 22 So they inquired further of the *L*,
10: 22 come here yet?" And the *L* said,
10: 24 you see the man the *L* has chosen?
10: 25 and deposited it before the *L*.
11: 7 Then the terror of the *L* fell
11: 13 for this day the *L* has rescued Israel
11: 15 as king in the presence of the *L*.
11: 15 fellowship offerings before the *L*,
12: 3 against me in the presence of the *L*
12: 5 "The *L* is witness against you,
12: 6 "It is the *L* who appointed Moses
12: 7 righteous acts performed by the *L*
12: 7 you with evidence before the *L*
12: 8 and the *L* sent Moses and Aaron,
12: 8 they cried to the *L* for help,
12: 9 "But they forgot the *L* their God;
12: 10 They cried out to the *L* and said,
12: 10 we have forsaken the *L*
12: 11 Then the *L* sent Jerub-Baal, Barak,
12: 12 the *L* your God was your king.
12: 13 see, the *L* has set a king over you.
12: 14 If you fear the *L* and serve
12: 14 over you follow the *L* your God—
12: 15 But if you do not obey the *L*,
12: 16 see this great thing the *L* is about
12: 17 call upon the *L* to send thunder
12: 17 the eyes of the *L* when you asked
12: 18 Then Samuel called upon the *L*,
12: 18 all the people stood in awe of the *L*
12: 18 that same day the *L* sent thunder
12: 19 "Pray to the *L* your God
12: 20 but serve the *L* with all your heart.
12: 20 yet do not turn away from the *L*,
12: 22 his great name the *L* will not reject
12: 22 the *L* was pleased to make you his
12: 23 sin against the *L* by failing to pray
12: 24 But be sure to fear the *L*
13: 13 the command the *L* your God gave
13: 14 the *L* has sought out a man
14: 6 Nothing can hinder the *L*
14: 6 Perhaps the *L* will act in our behalf.
14: 10 our sign that the *L* has given them
14: 12 the *L* has given them into the hand
14: 23 So the *L* rescued Israel that day,
14: 33 the men are sinning against the *L*
14: 34 sin against the *L* by eating meat
14: 35 Then Saul built an altar to the *L*;
14: 39 as the *L* who rescues Israel lives,
14: 41 Then Saul prayed to the *L*,

1Sa 14: 45 Never! As surely as the *L* lives,
15: 1 now to the message from the *L*.
15: 1 "I am the one the *L* sent
15: 2 This is what the *L* Almighty says:
15: 10 the word of the *L* came to Samuel:
15: 11 he cried out to the *L* all that night.
15: 13 Saul said, "The *L* bless you!
15: 15 to sacrifice to the *L* your God,
15: 16 "Let me tell you what the *L* said
15: 17 The *L* anointed you king
15: 19 Why did you not obey the *L*?
15: 19 and do evil in the eyes of the *L*?"
15: 20 on the mission the *L* assigned me.
15: 20 "But I did obey the *L*," Saul said.
15: 21 them to the *L* your God at Gilgal."
15: 22 as in obeying the voice of the *L*?
15: 22 "Does the *L* delight
15: 23 have rejected the word of the *L*,
15: 25 so that I may worship the *L*."
15: 26 and the *L* has rejected you
15: 26 have rejected the word of the *L*,
15: 28 "The *L* has torn the kingdom
15: 30 I may worship the *L* your God."
15: 31 and Saul worshiped the *L*.
15: 33 to death before the *L* at Gilgal.
15: 35 the *L* was grieved that he had made
16: 1 *L* said to Samuel, "How long will
16: 2 The *L* said, "Take a heifer with you
16: 2 'I have come to sacrifice to the *L*.'
16: 4 Samuel did what the *L* said.
16: 5 I have come to sacrifice to the *L*.
16: 6 anointed stands here before the *L*."
16: 7 The *L* does not look
16: 7 but the *L* looks at the heart."
16: 7 *L* said to Samuel, "Do not consider
16: 8 "The *L* has not chosen this one
16: 9 "Nor has the *L* chosen this one."
16: 10 "The *L* has not chosen these."
16: 12 Then the *L* said, "Rise
16: 13 Spirit of the *L* came upon David
16: 14 spirit from the *L* tormented him.
16: 14 the Spirit of the *L* had departed
16: 18 And the *L* is with him."
17: 37 The *L* who delivered me
17: 37 "Go, and the *L* be with you."
17: 45 you in the name of the *L* Almighty,
17: 46 This day the *L* will hand you
17: 47 or spear that the *L* saves;
18: 12 because the *L* was with David
18: 14 because the *L* was with him.
18: 17 and fight the battles of the *L*."
18: 28 When Saul realized that the *L* was
19: 5 The *L* won a great victory
19: 6 as the *L* lives, David will not be put
19: 9 spirit from the *L* came upon Saul
20: 3 Yet as surely as the *L* lives and
20: 8 a covenant with you before the *L*.
20: 12 "By the *L*, the God of Israel,
20: 13 May the *L* be with you
20: 13 may the *L* deal with me, be it ever
20: 14 unfailing kindness like that of the *L*
20: 15 when the *L* has cut off every one
20: 16 "May the *L* call David's enemies
20: 21 as surely as the *L* lives, you are safe
20: 22 because the *L* has sent you away.
20: 23 the *L* is witness between you
20: 42 other in the name of the *L*,
20: 42 'The *L* is witness between you
21: 6 been removed from before the *L*
21: 7 detained before the *L*; he was Doeg
22: 10 Ahimelech inquired of the *L*
22: 17 a hand to strike the priests of the *L*.
22: 17 "Turn and kill the priests of the *L*,
22: 21 Saul had killed the priests of the *L*.
23: 2 The *L* answered him, "Go,
23: 2 he inquired of the *L*, saying,
23: 4 again David inquired of the *L*,
23: 4 and the *L* answered him, "Go
23: 10 David said, "O *L*, God of Israel,
23: 11 And the *L* said, "He will."
23: 11 as your servant has heard? O *L*,
23: 12 And the *L* said, "They will."
23: 18 made a covenant before the *L*.
23: 21 "The *L* bless you for your concern
24: 4 "This is the very day the *L* spoke
24: 6 for he is the anointed of the *L*."
24: 6 "The *L* forbid that I should do such
24: 10 own eyes how the *L* delivered you

1Sa 24: 12 May the *L* judge between you
24: 12 may the *L* avenge the wrongs you
24: 15 May the *L* be our judge
24: 18 the *L* delivered me into your hands
24: 19 May the *L* reward you well
24: 21 to me by the *L* that you will not cut
25: 26 as surely as the *L* lives and
25: 26 "Now since the *L* has kept you,
25: 28 for the *L* will certainly make
25: 29 of the living by the *L* your God.
25: 30 When the *L* has done
25: 31 when the *L* has brought my master
25: 32 Praise be to the *L*, the God of Israel
25: 34 as surely as the *L*, the God of Israel
25: 38 the *L* struck Nabal and he died.
25: 39 he said, "Praise be to the *L*,
26: 10 As surely as the *L* lives," he said,
26: 10 "the *L* himself will strike him;
26: 11 *L* forbid that I should lay a hand
26: 12 because the *L* had put them
26: 16 As surely as the *L* lives, you
26: 19 If the *L* has incited you against me,
26: 19 may they be cursed before the *L*!
26: 20 far from the presence of the *L*.
26: 23 The *L* delivered you
26: 23 The *L* rewards every man
26: 24 so may the *L* value my life
28: 6 but the *L* did not answer him
28: 6 of the *L*, but the LORD did not
28: 10 Saul swore to her by the *L*,
28: 10 *L* lives, you will not be punished
28: 16 now that the *L* has turned away
28: 17 The *L* has done what he predicted
28: 17 The *L* has torn the kingdom out
28: 18 Because you did not obey the *L*
28: 18 the *L* has done this to you today.
28: 19 The *L* will also hand over the army
28: 19 The *L* will hand over both Israel
29: 6 the *L* lives, you have been reliable,
30: 6 found strength in the *L* his God.
30: 8 and David inquired of the *L*,
30: 23 that with what the *L* has given us.
2Sa 1: 12 for the army of the *L* and the house
2: 1 The *L* said, "Go up."
2: 1 of time, David inquired of the *L*.
2: 1 "To Hebron," the *L* answered.
2: 5 "The *L* bless you for showing this
2: 6 May the *L* now show you kindness
3: 9 for David what the *L* promised him
3: 18 For the *L* promised David,
3: 28 before the *L* concerning the blood
3: 39 May the *L* repay the evildoer
4: 8 This day the *L* has avenged my
4: 9 *L* lives, who has delivered me out
5: 2 *L* said to you, 'You will shepherd
5: 3 with them at Hebron before the *L*,
5: 10 the *L* God Almighty was with him.
5: 12 knew that the *L* had established
5: 19 The *L* answered him, "Go,
5: 19 so David inquired of the *L*,
5: 20 the *L* has broken out
5: 23 so David inquired of the *L*,
5: 24 that will mean the *L* has gone out
5: 25 as the *L* commanded him,
6: 2 the name of the *L* Almighty,
6: 5 with all their might before the *L*,
6: 9 David was afraid of the *L* that day
6: 9 the ark of the *L* ever come to me?"
6: 10 the ark of the *L* to be with him
6: 11 The ark of the *L* remained
6: 11 and the *L* blessed him
6: 12 "The *L* has blessed the household
6: 13 the ark of the *L* had taken six steps,
6: 14 danced before the *L*
6: 15 the ark of the *L* with shouts
6: 16 ark of the *L* was entering the City
6: 16 leaping and dancing before the *L*.
6: 17 They brought the ark of the *L*
6: 17 fellowship offerings before the *L*.
6: 18 in the name of the *L* Almighty.
6: 21 I will celebrate before the *L*.
6: 21 to Michal, "It was before the *L*,
7: 1 and the *L* had given him rest
7: 3 and do it, for the *L* is with you."
7: 4 the word of the *L* came to Nathan,
7: 5 David, 'This is what the *L* says:
7: 8 'This is what the *L* Almighty says:
7: 11 *L* declares to you that the *L* himself

2Sa 7: 18 went in and sat before the *L*,
7: 18 "Who am I, O Sovereign *L*,
7: 19 O Sovereign *L*? "What more can
7: 19 in your sight, O Sovereign *L*,
7: 20 know your servant, O Sovereign *L*.
7: 22 How great you are, O Sovereign *L*!
7: 24 O *L*, have become their God.
7: 25 *L* God, keep forever the promise
7: 26 'The *L* Almighty is God over Israel
7: 27 "O *L* Almighty, God of Israel,
7: 28 O Sovereign *L*, you are God!
7: 29 O Sovereign *L*, have spoken,
8: 6 *L* gave David victory everywhere
8: 11 dedicated these articles to the *L*,
8: 14 *L* gave David victory everywhere
10: 12 The *L* will do what is good
11: 27 David had done displeased the *L*.
12: 1 The *L* sent Nathan to David.
12: 5 as the *L* lives, the man who did this
12: 7 This is what the *L*, the God
12: 9 word of the *L* by doing what is evil
12: 11 "This is what the *L* says: 'Out
12: 13 "I have sinned against the *L*."
12: 13 "The *L* has taken away your sin.
12: 14 of the *L* show utter contempt,
12: 15 *L* struck the child that Uriah's wife
12: 20 he went into the house of the *L*
12: 22 The *L* may be gracious to me
12: 24 The *L* loved him;
12: 25 and because the *L* loved him,
14: 11 let the king invoke the *L* his God
14: 11 "As surely as the *L* lives," he said,
14: 17 May the *L* your God be with you
15: 7 and fulfill a vow I made to the *L*.
15: 8 I will worship the *L* in Hebron.'"
15: 8 If the *L* takes me back to Jerusalem
15: 21 "As surely as the *L* lives, and
15: 31 "O *L*, turn Ahithophel's counsel
16: 8 The *L* has handed the kingdom
16: 8 The *L* has repaid you
16: 10 If he is cursing because the *L* said
16: 11 for the *L* has told him to.
16: 12 may be that the *L* will see my
16: 18 chosen by the *L*, by these people,
17: 14 For the *L* had determined
18: 19 king that the *L* has delivered him
18: 28 "Praise be to the *L* your God!
18: 31 The *L* has delivered you today
19: 7 I swear by the *L* that
21: 1 The *L* said, "It is on account
21: 1 so David sought the face of the *L*.
21: 6 exposed before the *L* at Gibeah
21: 7 oath before the *L* between David
21: 9 exposed them on a hill before the *L*
22: 1 David sang to the *L* the words
22: 1 song when the *L* delivered him
22: 2 "The *L* is my rock, my fortress
22: 4 I call to the *L*, who is worthy
22: 7 In my distress I called to the *L*;
22: 14 The *L* thundered from heaven;
22: 16 bare at the rebuke of the *L*,
22: 19 but the *L* was my support.
22: 21 The *L* has dealt with me according
22: 22 For I have kept the ways of the *L*;
22: 25 The *L* has rewarded me according
22: 29 You are my lamp, O *L*;
22: 29 the *L* turns my darkness into light.
22: 31 the word of the *L* is flawless.
22: 32 For who is God besides the *L*?
22: 42 to the *L*, but he did not answer.
22: 47 The *L* lives! Praise be to my Rock!
22: 50 Therefore I will praise you, O *L*,
23: 2 Spirit of the *L* spoke through me;
23: 10 *L* brought about a great victory
23: 12 the *L* brought about a great victory
23: 16 he poured it out before the *L*.
23: 17 Far be it from me, O *L*, to do this!"
24: 1 of the *L* burned against Israel,
24: 3 "May the *L* your God multiply
24: 10 O *L*, I beg you, take away the guilt
24: 10 to the *L*, "I have sinned greatly
24: 11 the word of the *L* had come
24: 12 'This is what the *L* says: I am giving
24: 14 Let us fall into the hands of the *L*,
24: 15 So the *L* sent a plague on Israel
24: 16 The angel of the *L* was then
24: 16 the *L* was grieved
24: 17 to the *L*, "I am the one who has

2Sa 24: 18 altar to the *L* on the threshing floor
24: 19 as the *L* had commanded
24: 21 "so I can build an altar to the *L*,
24: 23 "May the *L* your God accept you."
24: 24 to the *L* my God burnt offerings
24: 25 David built an altar to the *L* there
24: 25 the *L* answered prayer in behalf
1Ki 1: 17 servant by the *L* your God:
1: 29 *L* lives, who has delivered me out
1: 30 today what I swore to you by the *L*,
1: 36 May the *L*, the God
1: 37 As the *L* was with my lord the king
1: 48 Praise be to the *L*, the God of Israel
2: 3 and observe what the *L* your God
2: 4 that the *L* may keep his promise
2: 8 to him by the *L*: 'I will not put you
2: 15 for it has come to him from the *L*.
2: 23 King Solomon swore by the *L*:
2: 24 And now, as surely as the *L* lives—
2: 26 the ark of the Sovereign *L*
2: 27 from the priesthood of the *L*,
2: 27 the word the *L* had spoken
2: 28 he fled to the tent of the *L*
2: 29 fled to the tent of the *L*
2: 30 Benaiah entered the tent of the *L*
2: 32 The *L* will repay him
2: 42 Did I not make you swear by the *L*
2: 43 did you not keep your oath to the *L*
2: 44 Now the *L* will repay you
2: 45 secure before the *L* forever."
3: 1 his palace and the temple of the *L*,
3: 2 built for the Name of the *L*.
3: 3 love for the *L* by walking according
3: 5 At Gibeon the *L* appeared
3: 7 O *L* my God, you have made your
5: 3 God until the *L* put his enemies
5: 3 for the Name of the *L* his God
5: 4 now the *L* my God has given me
5: 5 as the *L* told my father David,
5: 5 for the Name of the *L* my God,
5: 7 and said, "Praise be to the *L* today,
5: 12 The *L* gave Solomon wisdom,
6: 1 began to build the temple of the *L*.
6: 2 for the *L* was sixty cubits long,
6: 11 word of the *L* came to Solomon:
6: 19 ark of the covenant of the *L* there.
6: 37 of the temple of the *L* was laid
7: 12 the temple of the *L* with its portico.
7: 40 Solomon in the temple of the *L*:
7: 45 of the *L* were of burnished bronze.
7: 51 for the temple of the *L* was finished
8: 4 they brought up the ark of the *L*
8: 9 where the *L* made a covenant
8: 10 the cloud filled the temple of the *L*.
8: 11 the glory of the *L* filled his temple.
8: 12 The *L* has said that he would dwell
8: 15 Praise be to the *L*, the God of Israel
8: 17 a temple for the Name of the *L*,
8: 18 But the *L* said to my father David,
8: 20 just as the *L* promised,
8: 20 the temple for the Name of the *L*,
8: 20 *L* has kept the promise he made:
8: 21 the covenant of the *L* that he made
8: 22 before the altar of the *L* in front
8: 23 toward heaven and said: "O *L*,
8: 25 "Now *L*, God of Israel, keep
8: 28 his plea for mercy, O *L* my God.
8: 44 and when they pray to the *L*
8: 53 O Sovereign *L*, brought our fathers
8: 54 and supplications to the *L*,
8: 54 rose from before the altar of the *L*,
8: 56 saying: "Praise be to the *L*,
8: 57 May the *L* our God be with us
8: 59 be near to the *L* our God day
8: 59 which I have prayed before the *L*,
8: 60 earth may know that the *L* is God
8: 61 fully committed to the *L* our God,
8: 62 him offered sacrifices before the *L*.
8: 63 dedicated the temple of the *L*.
8: 63 of fellowship offerings to the *L*:
8: 64 altar before the *L* was too small
8: 64 in front of the temple of the *L*,
8: 65 it before the *L* our God
8: 66 for all the good the *L* had done
9: 1 building the temple of the *L*
9: 2 *L* appeared to him a second time,
9: 3 The *L* said to him: "I have heard
9: 8 'Why has the *L* done such a thing

1Ki 9: 9 have forsaken the *L* their God,
9: 9 that is why the *L* brought all this
9: 10 of the *L* and the royal palace—
9: 25 before the *L* along with them,
9: 25 on the altar he had built for the *L*,
10: 1 his relation to the name of the *L*,
10: 5 made at the temple of the *L*,
10: 9 Praise be to the *L* your God,
10: 12 supports for the temple of the *L*
11: 2 nations about which the *L* had told
11: 4 not fully devoted to the *L* his God,
11: 6 evil in the eyes of the *L*;
11: 6 he did not follow the *L* completely,
11: 9 The *L* became angry with Solomon
11: 9 heart had turned away from the *L*,
11: 11 So the *L* said to Solomon,
11: 14 the *L* raised up against Solomon
11: 31 for this is what the *L*, the God
12: 15 to fulfill the word the *L* had spoken
12: 15 turn of events was from the *L*,
12: 24 So they obeyed the word of the *L*
12: 24 home again, as the *L* had ordered.
12: 24 'This is what the *L* says: Do not go
12: 27 at the temple of the *L* in Jerusalem,
13: 1 By the word of the *L* a man
13: 2 altar! This is what the *L* says:
13: 2 the altar by the word of the *L*:
13: 3 This is the sign the *L* has declared:
13: 5 man of God by the word of the *L*.
13: 6 man of God interceded with the *L*,
13: 6 "Intercede with the *L* your God
13: 9 commanded by the word of the *L*:
13: 17 told by the word of the *L*:
13: 18 said to me by the word of the *L*:
13: 20 the word of the *L* came
13: 21 Judah, "This is what the *L* says:
13: 21 the command the *L* your God gave
13: 21 'You have defied the word of the *L*
13: 26 God who defied the word of the *L*.
13: 26 The *L* has given him
13: 26 the word of the *L* had warned him
13: 32 the word of the *L* against the altar
14: 5 But the *L* had told Ahijah,
14: 7 Jeroboam that this is what the *L*,
14: 11 The *L* has spoken!' "As for you,
14: 13 house of Jeroboam in whom the *L*,
14: 14 "The *L* will raise up
14: 15 And the *L* will strike Israel,
14: 15 they provoked the *L* to anger
14: 18 the *L* had said through his servant
14: 21 the city the *L* had chosen out
14: 22 Judah did evil in the eyes of the *L*.
14: 24 of the nations the *L* had driven out
14: 26 the treasures of the temple of the *L*
15: 3 not fully devoted to the *L* his God,
15: 4 David's sake the *L* his God gave
15: 5 right in the eyes of the *L*
15: 11 right in the eyes of the *L*,
15: 14 committed to the *L* all his life.
15: 15 into the temple of the *L* the silver
15: 26 He did evil in the eyes of the *L*,
15: 29 to the word of the *L* given
15: 30 and because he provoked the *L*,
15: 34 He did evil in the eyes of the *L*,
16: 1 the word of the *L* came to Jehu son
16: 7 done in the eyes of the *L*,
16: 7 the word of the *L* came
16: 12 of the *L* spoken against Baasha
16: 13 so that they provoked the *L*,
16: 19 doing evil in the eyes of the *L*
16: 25 Omri did evil in the eyes of the *L*
16: 26 so that they provoked the *L*,
16: 30 the eyes of the *L* than any of those
16: 33 and did more to provoke the *L*,
16: 34 of the *L* spoken by Joshua son
17: 1 "As the *L*, the God of Israel,
17: 2 the word of the *L* came to Elijah:
17: 5 So he did what the *L* had told him.
17: 8 the word of the *L* came to him:
17: 12 As surely as the *L* your God lives,"
17: 14 For this is what the *L*, the God
17: 14 dry until the day the *L* gives rain
17: 16 the word of the *L* spoken by Elijah.
17: 20 Then he cried out to the *L*,
17: 20 out to the LORD, "O *L* my God,
17: 21 boy three times and cried to the *L*,
17: 21 "O *L* my God, let this boy's life
17: 22 to him!" The *L* heard Elijah's cry,

1Ki 17: 24 and that the word of the L
18: 1 the word of the L came to Elijah:
18: 3 was a devout believer in the L.
18: 10 As surely as the L your God lives,
18: 12 the Spirit of the L may carry you
18: 12 your servant have worshiped the L
18: 13 was killing the prophets of the L?
18: 15 "As the L Almighty lives,
18: 21 If the L is God, follow him;
18: 24 and I will call on the name of the L.
18: 30 and he repaired the altar of the L,
18: 31 the word of the L had come,
18: 32 an altar in the name of the L,
18: 36 "O L, God of Abraham, Isaac
18: 37 Answer me, O L, answer me,
18: 37 people will know that you, O L,
18: 38 Then the fire of the L fell
18: 39 "The L— he is God! The L—
18: 46 power of the L came upon Elijah
19: 4 "I have had enough, L," he said.
19: 7 of the L came back a second time
19: 9 And the word of the L came to him
19: 10 zealous for the L God Almighty.
19: 11 The L said, "Go out and stand
19: 11 but the L was not in the earthquake
19: 11 but the L was not in the wind.
19: 11 for the L is about to pass by."
19: 11 mountain in the presence of the L,
19: 11 shattered the rocks before the L,
19: 12 but the L was not in the fire.
19: 14 zealous for the L God Almighty.
19: 15 L said to him, "Go back the way
20: 13 then you will know that I am the L
20: 13 "This is what the L says: 'Do you
20: 14 replied, "This is what the L says:
20: 28 and you will know that I am the L
20: 28 of Israel, "This is what the L says:
20: 28 the Arameans think the L is a god
20: 35 the word of the L one of the sons
20: 36 Because you have not obeyed the L
20: 42 the king, "This is what the L says:
21: 3 L forbid that I should give you
21: 17 Then the word of the L came
21: 19 Say to him, 'This is what the L says
21: 19 say to him, 'This is what the L says:
21: 20 to do evil in the eyes of the L.
21: 23 also concerning Jezebel the L says:
21: 25 to do evil in the eyes of the L,
21: 26 like the Amorites the L drove out
21: 28 Then the word of the L came
22: 5 "First seek the counsel of the L."
22: 7 of the L here whom we can inquire
22: 8 whom we can inquire of the L,
22: 11 is what the L says: 'With these
22: 12 "for the L will give it
22: 14 said, "As surely as the L lives,
22: 14 tell him only what the L tells me."
22: 15 "for the L will give it
22: 16 the truth in the name of the L?"
22: 17 the L said, 'These people have no
22: 19 I saw the L sitting on his throne
22: 19 "Therefore hear the word of the L:
22: 20 the L said, 'Who will lure Ahab
22: 21 stood before the L and said,
22: 22 succeed in luring him,' said the L.
22: 22 " 'By what means?' the L asked.
22: 23 The L has decreed disaster for you
22: 23 "So now the L has put a lying spirit
22: 24 spirit from the L go when he went
22: 28 the L has not spoken through me."
22: 38 as the word of the L had declared.
22: 43 right in the eyes of the L.
22: 52 He did evil in the eyes of the L,
22: 53 Baal and provoked the L,
2Ki 1: 3 But the angel of the L said
1: 4 Therefore this is what the L says:
1: 6 tell him, "This is what the L says:
1: 15 The angel of the L said to Elijah,
1: 16 the king, "This is what the L says:
1: 17 of the L that Elijah had spoken.
2: 1 When the L was about
2: 2 the L has sent me to Bethel."
2: 2 "As surely as the L lives and
2: 3 "Do you know that the L is going
2: 4 Elisha; the L has sent me to Jericho
2: 4 "As surely as the L lives and
2: 5 "Do you know that the L is going
2: 6 the L has sent me to the Jordan."

2Ki 2: 6 "As surely as the L lives and
2: 14 "Where now is the L, the God
2: 16 Spirit of the L has picked him up
2: 21 saying, "This is what the L says:
2: 24 curse on them in the name of the L.
3: 2 He did evil in the eyes of the L,
3: 10 "Has the L called us three kings
3: 11 inquire of the L through him?"
3: 11 "Is there no prophet of the L here,
3: 12 "The word of the L is with him."
3: 13 it was the L who called us three
3: 14 "As surely as the L Almighty lives,
3: 15 the hand of the L came upon Elisha
3: 16 "This is what the L says: Make this
3: 17 For this is what the L says:
3: 18 thing in the eyes of the L;
4: 1 you know that he revered the L.
4: 27 but the L has hidden it from me
4: 30 "As surely as the L lives and
4: 33 two of them and prayed to the L.
4: 43 For this is what the L says:
4: 44 according to the word of the L.
5: 1 through him the L had given
5: 11 call on the name of the L his God,
5: 16 as the L lives, whom I serve,
5: 17 to any other god but the L.
5: 18 But may the L forgive your servant
5: 18 may the L forgive your servant
5: 20 as the L lives, I will run after him
6: 17 And Elisha prayed, "O L,
6: 17 the L opened the servant's eyes,
6: 18 to the L, "Strike these people
6: 20 Then the L opened their eyes
6: 20 entered the city, Elisha said, "L,
6: 27 "If the L does not help you,
6: 33 wait for the L any longer?"
6: 33 "This disaster is from the L.
7: 1 This is what the L says: About this
7: 1 said, "Hear the word of the L.
7: 2 if the L should open the floodgates
7: 16 sold for a shekel, as the L had said.
7: 19 if the L should open the floodgates
8: 1 because the L has decreed a famine
8: 8 Consult the L through him;
8: 10 but the L has revealed
8: 13 "The L has shown me that you will
8: 18 He did evil in the eyes of the L.
8: 19 the L was not willing
8: 27 and did evil in the eyes of the L,
9: 3 'This is what the L says: I anoint
9: 6 "This is what the L, the God
9: 12 'This is what the L says: I anoint
9: 25 when the L made this prophecy
9: 26 declares the L, and I will surely
9: 26 plot of ground, declares the L.'
9: 26 with the word of the L."
9: 36 the word of the L that he spoke
10: 10 The L has done what he promised
10: 10 that not a word the L has spoken
10: 16 and see my zeal for the L."
10: 17 the word of the L spoken to Elijah.
10: 23 of the L are here with you—
10: 30 L said to Jehu, "Because you have
10: 31 careful to keep the law of the L,
10: 32 In those days the L began
11: 3 at the temple of the L for six years
11: 4 to him at the temple of the L.
11: 4 under oath at the temple of the L.
11: 10 that were in the temple of the L.
11: 13 to the people at the temple of the L
11: 15 to death in the temple of the L."
11: 17 made a covenant between the L
11: 18 guards at the temple of the L.
11: 19 king down from the temple of the L
12: 2 eyes of the L all the years Jehoiada
12: 4 offerings to the temple of the L—
12: 9 as one enters the temple of the L.
12: 9 brought to the temple of the L.
12: 10 brought into the temple of the L
12: 11 worked on the temple of the L—
12: 12 for the repair of the temple of the L
12: 13 or silver for the temple of the L;
12: 16 brought into the temple of the L;
12: 18 treasuries of the temple of the L
13: 2 eyes of the L by following the sins
13: 4 Lord's favor, and the L listened
13: 5 The L provided a deliverer
13: 11 He did evil in the eyes of the L

2Ki 13: 23 But the L was gracious to them
14: 3 right in the eyes of the L,
14: 6 of Moses where the L commanded:
14: 14 found in the temple of the L
14: 24 He did evil in the eyes of the L
14: 25 accordance with the word of the L,
14: 26 L had seen how bitterly everyone
14: 27 since the L had not said he would
15: 3 right in the eyes of the L,
15: 5 The L afflicted the king
15: 9 He did evil in the eyes of the L,
15: 12 So the word of the L spoken
15: 18 He did evil in the eyes of the L.
15: 24 evil in the eyes of the L.
15: 28 He did evil in the eyes of the L.
15: 34 right in the eyes of the L,
15: 35 Gate of the temple of the L.
15: 37 (In those days the L began
16: 2 right in the eyes of the L his God.
16: 3 of the nations the L had driven out
16: 8 gold found in the temple of the L
16: 14 new altar and the temple of the L—
16: 14 stood before the L he brought
16: 18 outside the temple of the L,
17: 2 He did evil in the eyes of the L,
17: 7 sinned against the L their God,
17: 8 of the nations the L had driven out
17: 9 against the L their God that were
17: 11 nations whom the L had driven out
17: 11 wicked things that provoked the L
17: 12 idols, though the L had said,
17: 13 The L warned Israel and Judah
17: 14 trust in the L their God.
17: 15 although the L had ordered them,
17: 15 the things the L had forbidden
17: 16 the commands of the L their God
17: 17 to do evil in the eyes of the L,
17: 18 So the L was very angry with Israel
17: 19 the commands of the L their God.
17: 20 Therefore the L rejected all
17: 21 away from following the L
17: 23 them until the L removed them
17: 25 they did not worship the L;
17: 28 taught them how to worship the L.
17: 32 They worshiped the L, but they
17: 33 They worshiped the L, but they
17: 34 They neither worship the L
17: 34 and commands that the L gave
17: 35 When the L made a covenant
17: 36 But the L, who brought you up out
17: 39 Rather, worship the L your God;
17: 41 people were worshiping the L,
18: 3 right in the eyes of the L,
18: 5 Hezekiah trusted in the L,
18: 6 fast to the L and did not cease
18: 6 the commands the L had given
18: 7 L was with him; he was successful
18: 12 had not obeyed the L their God,
18: 12 the servant of the L commanded.
18: 15 found in the temple of the L
18: 16 doorposts of the temple of the L,
18: 22 depending on the L our God"—
18: 25 The L himself told me to march
18: 25 place without word from the L?
18: 30 'The L will surely deliver us;
18: 30 you to trust in the L when he says,
18: 32 when he says, 'The L will deliver us
18: 35 then can the L deliver Jerusalem
19: 1 and went into the temple of the L.
19: 4 for the words the L your God has
19: 4 may be that the L your God will
19: 6 master, 'This is what the L says:
19: 14 and spread it out before the L.
19: 14 he went up to the temple of the L
19: 15 And Hezekiah prayed to the L:
19: 15 prayed to the Lord: "O L,
19: 16 O L, and hear; open your eyes,
19: 16 open your eyes, O L, and see;
19: 17 O L, that the Assyrian kings have
19: 19 Now, O L our God, deliver us
19: 19 may know that you alone, O L,
19: 20 "This is what the L, the God
19: 21 is the word that the L has spoken
19: 31 of the L Almighty will accomplish
19: 32 this is what the L says concerning
19: 33 not enter this city, declares the L.
19: 35 night the angel of the L went out
20: 1 "This is what the L says: Put your

2Ki 20: 3 prayed to the *L*, "Remember, O *L*,
20: 4 the word of the *L* came to him:
20: 5 'This is what the *L*, the God
20: 5 up to the temple of the *L*.
20: 8 be the sign that the *L* will heal me
20: 8 the temple of the *L* on the third day
20: 9 to you that the *L* will do what he
20: 11 prophet Isaiah called upon the *L*,
20: 11 *L* made the shadow go back the ten
20: 16 Hezekiah, "Hear the word of the *L*:
20: 17 Nothing will be left, says the *L*.
20: 19 of the *L* you have spoken is good,"
21: 2 He did evil in the eyes of the *L*,
21: 2 of the nations the *L* had driven out
21: 4 altars in the temple of the *L*,
21: 4 of which the *L* had said, "In
21: 5 courts of the temple of the *L*,
21: 6 evil in the eyes of the *L*,
21: 7 of which the *L* had said to David
21: 9 the nations the *L* had destroyed
21: 10 The *L* said through his servants
21: 12 Therefore this is what the *L*,
21: 16 evil in the eyes of the *L*.
21: 20 He did evil in the eyes of the *L*,
21: 22 He forsook the *L*, the God
21: 22 did not walk in the way of the *L*.
22: 2 right in the eyes of the *L*
22: 3 to the temple of the *L*.
22: 4 brought into the temple of the *L*,
22: 5 who repair the temple of the *L*
22: 8 of the Law in the temple of the *L*."
22: 9 was in the temple of the *L*
22: 13 "Go and inquire of the *L* for me
22: 15 "This is what the *L*, the God
22: 16 you to me, 'This is what the *L* says:
22: 18 'This is what the *L*, the God
22: 18 who sent you to inquire of the *L*,
22: 19 I have heard you, declares the *L*.
22: 19 you humbled yourself before the *L*
23: 2 found in the temple of the *L*.
23: 2 to the temple of the *L* with the men
23: 3 in the presence of the *L*—
23: 3 to follow the *L* and keep his
23: 4 of the *L* all the articles made
23: 6 of the *L* to the Kidron Valley
23: 7 which were in the temple of the *L*
23: 9 at the altar of the *L* in Jerusalem,
23: 11 of the *L* the horses that the kings
23: 12 courts of the temple of the *L*.
23: 16 of the *L* proclaimed by the man
23: 19 of Samaria that had provoked the *L*
23: 21 the Passover to the *L* your God,
23: 23 celebrated to the *L* in Jerusalem.
23: 24 discovered in the temple of the *L*.
23: 25 a king like him who turned to the *L*
23: 26 the *L* did not turn away
23: 27 So the *L* said, "I will remove Judah
23: 32 He did evil in the eyes of the *L*,
23: 37 And he did evil in the eyes of the *L*,
24: 2 The *L* sent Babylonian, Aramean,
24: 2 with the word of the *L* proclaimed
24: 4 and the *L* was not willing to forgive
24: 9 He did evil in the eyes of the *L*,
24: 13 As the *L* had declared,
24: 13 made for the temple of the *L*.
24: 13 treasures from the temple of the *L*
24: 19 He did evil in the eyes of the *L*,
25: 9 He set fire to the temple of the *L*,
25: 13 were at the temple of the *L*
25: 16 made for the temple of the *L*,
1Ch 2: 3 so the *L* put him to death.
6: 15 deported when the *L* sent Judah
6: 31 house of the *L* after the ark came
6: 32 the temple of the *L* in Jerusalem.
9: 19 entrance to the dwelling of the *L*.
9: 20 of the gatekeepers, and the *L* was
9: 23 the gates of the house of the *L*—
10: 13 because he was unfaithful to the *L*;
10: 13 he did not keep the word of the *L*
10: 14 So the *L* put him to death
10: 14 and did not inquire of the *L*.
11: 2 And the *L* your God said to you,
11: 3 as the *L* had promised
11: 3 with them at Hebron before the *L*,
11: 9 the *L* Almighty was with him.
11: 10 the *L* had promised—this is the list
11: 14 the *L* brought about a great victory
11: 18 he poured it out before the *L*.

1Ch 12: 23 as the *L* had said: men of Judah,
13: 2 and if it is the will of the *L* our God,
13: 6 from there the ark of God the *L*, who
13: 14 and the *L* blessed his household
14: 2 knew that the *L* had established
14: 10 The *L* answered him, "Go,
14: 17 the *L* made all the nations fear him.
15: 2 the *L* chose them to carry the ark
15: 2 them to carry the ark of the *L*
15: 3 the ark of the *L* to the place he had
15: 12 and bring up the ark of the *L*,
15: 13 first time that the *L* our God broke
15: 14 in order to bring up the ark of the *L*
15: 15 accordance with the word of the *L*.
15: 25 covenant of the *L* from the house
15: 26 the ark of the covenant of the *L*,
15: 28 the covenant of the *L* with shouts,
15: 29 of the *L* was entering the City
16: 2 the people in the name of the *L*.
16: 4 to minister before the ark of the *L*,
16: 4 to praise the *L*, the God of Israel:
16: 7 of thanks to the *L*:
16: 8 Give thanks to the *L*, call
16: 10 of those who seek the *L* rejoice.
16: 11 Look to the *L* and his strength;
16: 14 He is the *L* our God;
16: 23 Sing to the *L*, all the earth;
16: 25 For great is the *L* and most worthy
16: 26 but the *L* made the heavens.
16: 28 Ascribe to the *L*, O families
16: 28 ascribe to the *L* glory and strength,
16: 29 to the *L* the glory due his name.
16: 29 worship the *L* in the splendor
16: 31 among the nations, "The *L* reigns
16: 33 they will sing for joy before the *L*,
16: 34 Give thanks to the *L*, for he is good
16: 36 Praise be to the *L*, the God of Israel
16: 36 said "Amen" and "Praise the *L*."
16: 37 of the *L* to minister there regularly,
16: 39 of the *L* at the high place
16: 40 offerings to the *L* on the altar
16: 40 written in the Law of the *L*,
16: 41 by name to give thanks to the *L*,
17: 1 covenant of the *L* is under a tent."
17: 4 David, 'This is what the *L* says:
17: 7 'This is what the *L* Almighty says:
17: 10 to you that the *L* will build a house
17: 16 O *L* God, and what is my family,
17: 16 went in and sat before the *L*,
17: 17 the most exalted of men, O *L* God.
17: 19 For you know your servant, O *L*.
17: 20 "There is no one like you, O *L*,
17: 22 O *L*, have become their God.
17: 23 *L*, let the promise you have made
17: 24 men will say, 'The *L* Almighty,
17: 26 O *L*, you are God! You have given
17: 27 for you, O *L*, have blessed it,
18: 6 *L* gave David victory everywhere
18: 11 dedicated these articles to the *L*,
18: 13 *L* gave David victory everywhere
19: 13 The *L* will do what is good
21: 3 "May the *L* multiply his troops
21: 9 The *L* said to Gad, David's seer,
21: 10 'This is what the *L* says: I am giving
21: 11 is what the *L* says: 'Take your
21: 12 angel of the *L* ravaging every part
21: 12 or three days of the sword of the *L*
21: 13 Let me fall into the hands of the *L*,
21: 14 So the *L* sent a plague on Israel,
21: 15 angel of the *L* was then standing
21: 15 the *L* saw it and was grieved
21: 16 of the *L* standing between heaven
21: 17 have they done? O *L* my God,
21: 18 altar to the *L* on the threshing floor
21: 18 the angel of the *L* ordered Gad
21: 19 spoken in the name of the *L*.
21: 22 so I can build an altar to the *L*,
21: 24 take for the *L* what is yours,
21: 26 David built an altar to the *L* there
21: 26 and the *L* answered him with fire
21: 26 on the *L*, and the LORD answered
21: 27 Then the *L* spoke to the angel,
21: 28 saw that the *L* had answered him
21: 29 of the *L*, which Moses had made
21: 30 of the sword of the angel of the *L*.
22: 1 "The house of the *L* God is
22: 5 to be built for the *L* should be
22: 6 him to build a house for the *L*,

1Ch 22: 7 for the Name of the *L* my God.
22: 8 But this word of the *L* came to me:
22: 11 build the house of the *L* your God,
22: 11 "Now, my son, the *L* be with you,
22: 12 May the *L* give you discretion
22: 12 the law of the *L* your God.
22: 13 and laws that the *L* gave Moses
22: 14 of the *L* a hundred thousand
22: 16 Now begin the work, and the *L* be
22: 18 and the land is subject to the *L*
22: 18 "Is not the *L* your God with you?
22: 19 built for the Name of the *L*."
22: 19 soul to seeking the *L* your God.
22: 19 the ark of the covenant of the *L*
22: 19 to build the sanctuary of the *L* God
23: 4 the work of the temple of the *L*
23: 5 four thousand are to praise the *L*
23: 13 to offer sacrifices before the *L*,
23: 24 served in the temple of the *L*.
23: 25 "Since the *L*, the God of Israel,
23: 28 in the service of the temple of the *L*
23: 30 morning to thank and praise the *L*.
23: 31 presented to the *L* on Sabbaths
23: 31 to serve before the *L* regularly
23: 32 the service of the temple of the *L*.
24: 19 as the *L*, the God of Israel,
24: 19 they entered the temple of the *L*,
25: 3 in thanking and praising the *L*.
25: 6 for the music of the temple of the *L*
25: 7 and skilled in music for the *L*—
26: 12 ministering in the temple of the *L*,
26: 22 treasuries of the temple of the *L*.
26: 27 for the repair of the temple of the *L*
26: 30 the Jordan for all the work of the *L*
27: 23 the *L* had promised to make Israel
28: 2 for the ark of the covenant of the *L*,
28: 4 "Yet the *L*, the God of Israel,
28: 5 and the *L* has given me many—
28: 5 of the kingdom of the *L* over Israel.
28: 8 and of the assembly of the *L*,
28: 8 the commands of the *L* your God,
28: 9 for the *L* searches every heart
28: 10 for the *L* has chosen you
28: 12 for the courts of the temple of the *L*
28: 13 of serving in the temple of the *L*,
28: 18 the ark of the covenant of the *L*.
28: 19 the hand of the *L* was upon me,
28: 20 for the *L* God, my God, is with you
28: 20 of the temple of the *L* is finished.
29: 1 not for man but for the *L* God.
29: 5 himself today to the *L*?"
29: 8 the temple of the *L* in the custody
29: 9 and wholeheartedly to the *L*.
29: 10 David praised the *L*
29: 10 "Praise be to you, O *L*,
29: 11 O *L*, is the greatness and the power
29: 11 Yours, O *L*, is the kingdom;
29: 16 O *L* our God, as for all this
29: 18 O *L*, God of our fathers Abraham,
29: 20 So they all praised the *L*, the God
29: 20 and fell prostrate before the *L*
29: 20 "Praise the *L* your God."
29: 21 day they made sacrifices to the *L*
29: 22 him before the *L* to be ruler
29: 22 in the presence of the *L* that day,
29: 23 Solomon sat on the throne of the *L*
29: 25 The *L* highly exalted Solomon
2Ch 1: 1 for the *L* his God was with him
1: 5 in front of the tabernacle of the *L*;
1: 6 before the *L* in the Tent of Meeting
1: 9 Now, *L* God, let your promise
2: 1 a temple for the Name of the *L*
2: 4 appointed feasts of the *L* our God.
2: 4 for the Name of the *L* my God
2: 11 "Because the *L* loves his people,
2: 12 Praise be to the *L*, the God of Israel
2: 12 who will build a temple for the *L*
3: 1 the temple of the *L* in Jerusalem
3: 1 where the *L* had appeared
4: 16 of the *L* were of polished bronze.
5: 1 for the temple of the *L* was finished
5: 10 where the *L* made a covenant
5: 13 Then the temple of the *L* was filled
5: 13 their voices in praise to the *L*
5: 13 to give praise and thanks to the *L*.
5: 14 the glory of the *L* filled the temple
6: 1 The *L* has said that he would dwell
6: 4 Praise be to the *L*, the God of Israel

2Ch 6: 7 a temple for the Name of the *L*,
6: 8 But the *L* said to my father David,
6: 10 just as the *L* promised,
6: 10 the temple for the Name of the *L*,
6: 10 *L* has kept the promise he made.
6: 11 the covenant of the *L* that he made
6: 12 before the altar of the *L* in front
6: 14 He said: "O *L*, God of Israel,
6: 16 "Now *L*, God of Israel, keep
6: 17 And now, O *L*, God of Israel,
6: 19 his plea for mercy, O *L* my God.
6: 41 May your priests, O *L* God,
6: 41 O *L* God, and come
6: 42 O *L* God, do not reject your
7: 1 the glory of the *L* filled the temple.
7: 2 because the glory of the *L* filled it.
7: 2 could not enter the temple of the *L*
7: 3 and gave thanks to the *L*,
7: 3 the glory of the *L* above the temple
7: 4 offered sacrifices before the *L*.
7: 6 David had made for praising the *L*
7: 7 in front of the temple of the *L*,
7: 10 for the good things the *L* had done
7: 11 had finished the temple of the *L*
7: 11 in mind to do in the temple of the *L*
7: 12 the *L* appeared to him at night
7: 21 'Why has the *L* done such a thing
7: 22 'Because they have forsaken the *L*,
8: 1 Solomon built the temple of the *L*
8: 11 ark of the *L* has entered are holy."
8: 12 sacrificed burnt offerings to the *L*,
8: 12 the altar of the *L* that he had built
8: 16 So the temple of the *L* was finished
8: 16 of the temple of the *L* was laid
9: 4 made at the temple of the *L*,
9: 8 Praise be to the *L* your God,
9: 8 as king to rule for the *L* your God.
9: 11 steps for the temple of the *L*
10: 15 to fulfill the word the *L* had spoken
11: 2 But this word of the *L* came
11: 4 So they obeyed the words of the *L*
11: 4 'This is what the *L* says: Do not go
11: 14 rejected them as priests of the *L*.
11: 16 set their hearts on seeking the *L*,
11: 16 to offer sacrifices to the *L*,
12: 1 him abandoned the law of the *L*.
12: 2 they had been unfaithful to the *L*,
12: 5 "This is what the *L* says, 'You have
12: 6 and said, "The *L* is just."
12: 7 When the *L* saw that they humbled
12: 7 word of the *L* came to Shemaiah:
12: 9 the treasures of the temple of the *L*
12: 13 the city the *L* had chosen out
12: 14 not set his heart on seeking the *L*.
13: 5 Don't you know that the *L*,
13: 8 plan to resist the kingdom of the *L*,
13: 9 you drive out the priests of the *L*,
13: 10 priests who serve the *L* are sons
13: 10 "As for us, the *L* is our God,
13: 11 and fragrant incense to the *L*.
13: 11 the requirements of the *L* our God.
13: 12 do not fight against the *L*,
13: 14 Then they cried out to the *L*.
13: 18 because they relied on the *L*,
13: 20 And the *L* struck him down
14: 2 right in the eyes of the *L* his God.
14: 4 commanded Judah to seek the *L*,
14: 6 for the *L* gave him rest.
14: 7 we have sought the *L* our God;
14: 11 O *L* our God, for we rely on you,
14: 11 O *L*, you are our God; do not let
14: 11 Then Asa called to the *L* his God
14: 11 to the LORD his God and said, "*L*,
14: 12 The *L* struck down the Cushites
14: 13 they were crushed before the *L*
14: 14 of the *L* had fallen upon them.
15: 2 The *L* is with you when you are
15: 4 their distress they turned to the *L*,
15: 8 the altar of the *L* that was in front
15: 9 they saw that the *L* his God was
15: 11 to the *L* seven hundred head
15: 12 into a covenant to seek the *L*,
15: 13 All who would not seek the *L*,
15: 14 to the *L* with loud acclamation,
15: 15 the *L* gave them rest on every side.
15: 17 committed ⌊to the *L*⌋ all his life.
16: 7 and not on the *L* your God,
16: 8 Yet when you relied on the *L*,

2Ch 16: 9 of the *L* range throughout the earth
16: 12 he did not seek help from the *L*,
17: 3 The *L* was with Jehoshaphat
17: 5 The *L* established the kingdom
17: 6 devoted to the ways of the *L*;
17: 9 the Book of the Law of the *L*;
17: 10 The fear of the *L* fell
17: 16 himself for the service of the *L*,
18: 4 "First seek the counsel of the *L*."
18: 6 of the *L* here whom we can inquire
18: 7 whom we can inquire of the *L*,
18: 10 declared, "This is what the *L* says:
18: 11 "for the *L* will give it
18: 13 said, "As surely as the *L* lives,
18: 15 the truth in the name of the *L*?"
18: 16 the *L* said, 'These people have no
18: 18 I saw the *L* sitting on his throne
18: 18 "Therefore hear the word of the *L*:
18: 19 *L* said, 'Who will lure Ahab king
18: 20 stood before the *L* and said,
18: 20 " 'By what means?' the *L* asked.
18: 21 succeed in luring him,' said the *L*.
18: 22 The *L* has decreed disaster for you
18: 22 "So now the *L* has put a lying spirit
18: 23 spirit from the *L* go when he went
18: 27 the *L* has not spoken through me."
18: 31 cried out, and the *L* helped him.
19: 2 and love those who hate the *L*?
19: 2 the wrath of the *L* is upon you.
19: 4 and turned them back to the *L*,
19: 6 judging for man but for the *L*,
19: 7 for with the *L* our God there is no
19: 7 let the fear of the *L* be upon you.
19: 8 to administer the law of the *L*
19: 9 wholeheartedly in the fear of the *L*.
19: 10 not to sin against the *L*;
19: 11 in any matter concerning the *L*,
19: 11 may the *L* be with those who do
20: 3 resolved to inquire of the *L*,
20: 4 together to seek help from the *L*;
20: 5 at the temple of the *L* in the front
20: 6 "O *L*, God of our fathers, are you
20: 13 little ones, stood there before the *L*
20: 14 Then the Spirit of the *L* came
20: 15 This is what the *L* says to you:
20: 17 and the *L* will be with you.' "
20: 17 the deliverance the *L* will give you,
20: 18 fell down in worship before the *L*.
20: 19 stood up and praised the *L*,
20: 20 Have faith in the *L* your God
20: 21 appointed men to sing to the *L*
20: 21 "Give thanks to the *L*,
20: 22 the *L* set ambushes against the men
20: 26 Beracah, where they praised the *L*.
20: 27 for the *L* had given them cause
20: 28 to the temple of the *L* with harps
20: 29 they heard how the *L* had fought
20: 32 right in the eyes of the *L*.
20: 37 the *L* will destroy what you have
21: 6 He did evil in the eyes of the *L*.
21: 7 of the covenant the *L* had made
21: 7 the *L* was not willing
21: 10 Jehoram had forsaken the *L*,
21: 12 which said: "This is what the *L*,
21: 14 So now the *L* is about
21: 16 The *L* aroused against Jehoram
21: 18 the *L* afflicted Jehoram
22: 4 He did evil in the eyes of the *L*,
22: 7 whom the *L* had anointed
22: 9 who sought the *L* with all his heart
23: 3 as the *L* promised concerning
23: 5 courtyards of the temple of the *L*.
23: 6 is to enter the temple of the *L*
23: 6 to guard what the *L* has assigned
23: 12 to them at the temple of the *L*.
23: 14 to death at the temple of the *L*."
23: 18 of the temple of the *L* in the hands
23: 18 present the burnt offerings of the *L*
23: 20 down from the temple of the *L*.
24: 2 in the eyes of the *L* all the years
24: 4 to restore the temple of the *L*.
24: 6 by Moses the servant of the *L*
24: 8 at the gate of the temple of the *L*.
24: 9 bring to the *L* the tax that Moses
24: 12 required for the temple of the *L*.
24: 14 continually in the temple of the *L*.
24: 18 abandoned the temple of the *L*,
24: 19 Although the *L* sent prophets

2Ch 24: 20 Because you have forsaken the *L*,
24: 22 "May the *L* see this and call you
24: 24 Because Judah had forsaken the *L*,
24: 24 the *L* delivered into their hands
25: 2 right in the eyes of the *L*,
25: 4 where the *L* commanded:
25: 7 for the *L* is not with Israel—
25: 9 "The *L* can give you much more
25: 15 of the *L* burned against Amaziah,
25: 27 away from following the *L*,
26: 4 right in the eyes of the *L*,
26: 5 As long as he sought the *L*,
26: 16 He was unfaithful to the *L* his God,
26: 16 the temple of the *L* to burn incense
26: 17 priests of the *L* followed him in.
26: 18 Uzziah, to burn incense to the *L*.
26: 18 will not be honored by the *L* God."
26: 20 because the *L* had afflicted him.
26: 21 and excluded from the temple of the
27: 2 did not enter the temple of the *L*.
27: 2 right in the eyes of the *L*,
27: 3 Gate of the temple of the *L*
27: 6 steadfastly before the *L* his God.
28: 1 right in the eyes of the *L*.
28: 3 of the nations the *L* had driven out
28: 5 Therefore the *L* his God handed
28: 6 because Judah had forsaken the *L*,
28: 9 of the *L* named Oded was there,
28: 9 "Because the *L*, the God
28: 10 of sins against the *L* your God?
28: 13 "or we will be guilty before the *L*.
28: 19 The *L* had humbled Judah
28: 19 had been most unfaithful to the *L*.
28: 21 the things from the temple of the *L*
28: 22 even more unfaithful to the *L*.
28: 25 to other gods and provoked the *L*,
29: 2 right in the eyes of the *L*,
29: 3 the doors of the temple of the *L*
29: 5 and consecrate the temple of the *L*,
29: 6 evil in the eyes of the *L* our God
29: 8 the anger of the *L* has fallen
29: 10 to make a covenant with the *L*,
29: 11 for the *L* has chosen you to stand
29: 15 following the word of the *L*.
29: 15 in to purify the temple of the *L*,
29: 16 found in the temple of the *L*.
29: 16 the sanctuary of the *L* to purify it.
29: 17 the temple of the *L* itself,
29: 17 they reached the portico of the *L*.
29: 18 purified the entire temple of the *L*,
29: 20 and went up to the temple of the *L*.
29: 21 to offer these on the altar of the *L*.
29: 25 by the *L* through his prophets.
29: 25 in the temple of the *L* with cymbals
29: 27 singing to the *L* began also,
29: 30 to praise the *L* with the words
29: 31 now dedicated yourselves to the *L*.
29: 31 offerings to the temple of the *L*."
29: 32 of them for burnt offerings to the *L*.
29: 35 temple of the *L* was reestablished.
30: 1 celebrate the Passover to the *L*,
30: 1 to the temple of the *L* in Jerusalem
30: 5 celebrate the Passover to the *L*,
30: 6 return to the *L*, the God
30: 7 who were unfaithful to the *L*,
30: 8 Serve the *L* your God,
30: 8 your fathers were; submit to the *L*.
30: 9 for the *L* your God is gracious
30: 9 return to the *L*, then your brothers
30: 12 following the word of the *L*.
30: 15 offerings to the temple of the *L*.
30: 17 consecrate ⌊their lambs⌋ to the *L*.
30: 18 saying, "May the *L*, who is good,
30: 19 the *L*, the God of his fathers—
30: 20 And the *L* heard Hezekiah
30: 21 and priests sang to the *L* every day,
30: 22 of the service of the *L*.
30: 22 offerings and praised the *L*,
31: 3 as written in the Law of the *L*.
31: 4 themselves to the Law of the *L*.
31: 6 dedicated to the *L* their God,
31: 8 they praised the *L* and blessed his
31: 10 the *L* has blessed his people,
31: 10 to the temple of the *L*,
31: 11 storerooms in the temple of the *L*,
31: 14 the contributions made to the *L*
31: 16 of the *L* to perform the daily duties
31: 20 and faithful before the *L* his God.

2Ch 32: 8 with us is the *L* our God to help us
32: 11 'The *L* our God will save us
32: 16 further against the *L* God
32: 17 also wrote letters insulting the *L*,
32: 21 *L* sent an angel, who annihilated all
32: 22 So the *L* saved Hezekiah
32: 23 offerings to Jerusalem for the *L*
32: 24 prayed to the *L*, who answered him
33: 2 He did evil in the eyes of the *L*,
33: 2 of the nations the *L* had driven out
33: 4 altars in the temple of the *L*,
33: 4 of which the *L* had said, "My
33: 5 courts of the temple of the *L*,
33: 6 evil in the eyes of the *L*,
33: 9 the nations the *L* had destroyed
33: 10 The *L* spoke to Manasseh
33: 11 *L* brought against them the army
33: 12 sought the favor of the *L* his God
33: 13 Manasseh knew that the *L* is God.
33: 13 the *L* was moved by his entreaty
33: 15 the image from the temple of the *L*,
33: 16 Then he restored the altar of the *L*
33: 16 and told Judah to serve the *L*,
33: 17 but only to the *L* their God.
33: 18 spoke to him in the name of the *L*,
33: 22 He did evil in the eyes of the *L*,
33: 23 not humble himself before the *L*;
34: 2 right in the eyes of the *L*
34: 8 repair the temple of the *L* his God.
34: 14 Law of the *L* that had been given
34: 14 taken into the temple of the *L*,
34: 15 of the Law in the temple of the *L*."
34: 17 was in the temple of the *L*
34: 21 have not kept the word of the *L*;
34: 21 "Go and inquire of the *L* for me
34: 23 "This is what the *L*, the God
34: 24 you to me, 'This is what the *L* says:
34: 26 'This is what the *L*, the God
34: 26 who sent you to inquire of the *L*,
34: 27 I have heard you, declares the *L*.
34: 30 found in the temple of the *L*.
34: 30 to the temple of the *L* with the men
34: 31 in the presence of the *L*—
34: 31 to follow the *L* and keep his
34: 33 in Israel serve the *L* their God.
34: 33 they did not fail to follow the *L*.
35: 1 the Passover to the *L* in Jerusalem,
35: 3 Now serve the *L* your God
35: 3 who had been consecrated to the *L*
35: 6 doing what the *L* commanded
35: 12 of the people to offer to the *L*,
35: 16 offerings on the altar of the *L*,
35: 16 service of the *L* was carried out
35: 26 written in the Law of the *L*
36: 5 evil in the eyes of the *L* his God.
36: 7 articles from the temple of the *L*
36: 9 He did evil in the eyes of the *L*.
36: 10 of value from the temple of the *L*,
36: 12 evil in the eyes of the *L* his God
36: 12 who spoke the word of the *L*.
36: 13 and would not turn to the *L*,
36: 14 and defiling the temple of the *L*,
36: 15 The *L*, the God of their fathers,
36: 16 the wrath of the *L* was aroused
36: 21 word of the *L* spoken by Jeremiah.
36: 22 the *L* moved the heart
36: 22 word of the *L* spoken by Jeremiah,
36: 23 may the *L* his God be with him,
36: 23 " 'The *L*, the God of heaven,
Ezr 1: 1 the *L* moved the heart
1: 1 word of the *L* spoken by Jeremiah,
1: 2 " 'The *L*, the God of heaven,
1: 3 and build the temple of the *L*,
1: 5 the house of the *L* in Jerusalem.
1: 7 belonging to the temple of the *L*,
2: 68 at the house of the *L* in Jerusalem,
3: 3 burnt offerings on it to the *L*,
3: 5 as freewill offerings to the *L*.
3: 5 for all the appointed feasts of the *L*,
3: 6 to offer burnt offerings to the *L*,
3: 8 the building of the house of the *L*.
3: 10 foundation of the temple of the *L*,
3: 10 took their places to praise the *L*,
3: 11 a great shout of praise to the *L*,
3: 11 of the house of the *L* was laid.
3: 11 thanksgiving they sang to the *L*:
4: 1 were building a temple for the *L*,
4: 3 We alone will build it for the *L*,
Ezr 6: 21 neighbors in order to seek the *L*,
6: 22 the *L* had filled them with joy
7: 6 for the hand of the *L* his God was
7: 6 which the *L*, the God of Israel,
7: 10 observance of the Law of the *L*,
7: 11 and decrees of the *L* for Israel:
7: 27 Praise be to the *L*, the God
7: 27 to the house of the *L* in Jerusalem
7: 28 the hand of the *L* my God was
8: 28 articles are consecrated to the *L*.
8: 28 gold are a freewill offering to the *L*,
8: 29 of the house of the *L* in Jerusalem
8: 35 this was a burnt offering to the *L*.
9: 5 hands spread out to the *L* my God
9: 8 the *L* our God has been gracious
9: 15 O *L*, God of Israel, you are
10: 11 Now make confession to the *L*,
Ne 1: 5 Then I said: "O *L*, God of heaven,
5: 13 "Amen," and praised the *L*.
8: 1 which the *L* had commanded
8: 6 Ezra praised the *L*, the great God;
8: 6 worshiped the *L* with their faces
8: 9 sacred to the *L* your God.
8: 10 for the joy of the *L* is your strength
8: 14 which the *L* had commanded
9: 3 Book of the Law of the *L* their God
9: 3 and in worshiping the *L* their God.
9: 4 with loud voices to the *L* their God
9: 5 and praise the *L* your God,
9: 6 You alone are the *L*.
9: 7 "You are the *L* God, who chose
10: 29 and decrees of the *L* our God.
10: 34 burn on the altar of the *L* our God,
10: 35 of the *L* each year the firstfruits
Job 1: 6 to present themselves before the *L*,
1: 7 from?" Satan answered the *L*,
1: 7 *L* said to Satan, "Where have you
1: 8 the *L* said to Satan, "Have you
1: 12 The *L* said to Satan, "Very well,
1: 12 out from the presence of the *L*.
1: 21 may the name of the *L* be praised."
1: 21 *L* gave and the *L* has taken away;
2: 1 to present themselves before the *L*,
2: 2 from?" Satan answered the *L*,
2: 2 *L* said to Satan, "Where have you
2: 3 the *L* said to Satan, "Have you
2: 6 The *L* said to Satan, "Very well,
2: 7 out from the presence of the *L*
12: 9 that the hand of the *L* has done this
38: 1 the *L* answered Job out
40: 1 *L* said to Job: "Will the one who
40: 3 Then Job answered the *L*:
40: 6 the *L* spoke to Job out of the storm:
42: 1 Then Job replied to the *L*:
42: 7 After the *L* had said these things
42: 9 and the *L* accepted Job's prayer.
42: 9 did what the *L* told them;
42: 10 the *L* made him prosperous again
42: 11 all the trouble the *L* had brought
42: 12 The *L* blessed the latter part
Ps 1: 2 But his delight is in the law of the *L*
1: 6 For the *L* watches over the way
2: 2 together against the *L*
2: 7 I will proclaim the decree of the *L*:
2: 11 Serve the *L* with fear
3: 1 O *L*, how many are my foes!
3: 3 you are a shield around me, O *L*,
3: 4 To the *L* I cry aloud,
3: 5 because the *L* sustains me.
3: 7 Arise, O *L*!
3: 8 From the *L* comes deliverance.
4: 3 Know that the *L* has set apart
4: 3 the *L* will hear when I call to him.
4: 5 and trust in the *L*.
4: 6 of your face shine upon us, O *L*.
4: 8 for you alone, O *L*,
5: 1 Give ear to my words, O *L*,
5: 3 Morning by morning, O *L*,
5: 6 the *L* abhors.
5: 8 O *L*, in your righteousness
5: 12 O *L*, you bless the righteous;
6: 1 O *L*, do not rebuke me
6: 2 Be merciful to me, *L*, for I am faint;
6: 2 O *L*, heal me, for my bones are
6: 3 How long, O *L*, how long?
6: 4 Turn, O *L*, and deliver me;
6: 8 for the *L* has heard my weeping.
6: 9 The *L* has heard my cry for mercy;
Ps 6: 9 the *L* accepts my prayer.
7: 1 O *L* my God, I take refuge in you;
7: 3 O *L* my God, if I have done this
7: 6 Arise, O *L*, in your anger;
7: 8 let the *L* judge the peoples.
7: 8 *L*, according to my righteousness,
7: 17 I will give thanks to the *L*
7: 17 to the name of the *L* Most High.
8: 1 O *L*, our Lord,
8: 9 O *L*, our Lord,
9: 1 I will praise you, O *L*,
9: 7 The *L* reigns forever;
9: 9 The *L* is a refuge for the oppressed,
9: 10 *L*, have never forsaken those who
9: 11 to the *L*, enthroned in Zion;
9: 13 O *L*, see how my enemies
9: 16 The *L* is known by his justice;
9: 19 Arise, O *L*, let not man triumph;
9: 20 Strike them with terror, O *L*;
10: 1 Why, O *L*, do you stand far off?
10: 3 the greedy and reviles the *L*.
10: 12 Arise, *L*! Lift up your hand, O God
10: 16 The *L* is King for ever and ever;
10: 17 O *L*, the desire of the afflicted;
11: 1 In the *L* I take refuge.
11: 4 The *L* is in his holy temple,
11: 4 the *L* is on his heavenly throne.
11: 5 The *L* examines the righteous,
11: 7 For the *L* is righteous,
12: 1 Help, *L*, for the godly are no more;
12: 3 May the *L* cut off all flattering lips
12: 5 I will now arise," says the *L*.
12: 6 And the words of the *L* are flawless
12: 7 O *L*, you will keep us safe
13: 1 O *L*? Will you forget me forever?
13: 3 on me and answer, O *L* my God.
13: 6 I will sing to the *L*,
14: 2 The *L* looks down from heaven
14: 4 and who do not call on the *L*?
14: 6 but the *L* is their refuge.
14: 7 When the *L* restores the fortunes
15: 1 *L*, who may dwell
15: 4 but honors those who fear the *L*,
16: 2 I said to the *L*, "You are my Lord;
16: 5 *L*, you have assigned me my
16: 7 will praise the *L*, who counsels me;
16: 8 I have set the *L* always before me
17: 1 Hear, O *L*, my righteous plea;
17: 13 Rise up, O *L*, confront them,
17: 14 O *L*, by your hand save me
18: 1 I love you, O *L*, my strength.
18: 2 The *L* is my rock, my fortress
18: 3 I call to the *L*, who is worthy
18: 6 In my distress I called to the *L*;
18: 13 The *L* thundered from heaven;
18: 15 bare at your rebuke, O *L*,
18: 18 but the *L* was my support.
18: 20 The *L* has dealt with me according
18: 21 For I have kept the ways of the *L*;
18: 24 The *L* has rewarded me according
18: 28 You, O *L*, keep my lamp burning;
18: 30 the word of the *L* is flawless.
18: 31 For who is God besides the *L*?
18: 41 to the *L*, but he did not answer.
18: 46 The *L* lives! Praise be to my Rock!
18: 49 among the nations, O *L*;
19: 7 The law of the *L* is perfect,
19: 7 statutes of the *L* are trustworthy,
19: 8 The commands of the *L* are radiant
19: 8 The precepts of the *L* are right,
19: 9 The fear of the *L* is pure,
19: 9 The ordinances of the *L* are sure
19: 14 O *L*, my Rock and my Redeemer.
20: 1 May the *L* answer you
20: 5 May the *L* grant all your requests.
20: 6 know that the *L* saves his anointed;
20: 7 in the name of the *L* our God.
20: 9 O *L*, save the king!
21: 1 O *L*, the king rejoices
21: 7 For the king trusts in the *L*;
21: 9 his wrath the *L* will swallow them
21: 13 Be exalted, O *L*, in your strength;
22: 8 let the *L* rescue him.
22: 8 "He trusts in the *L*;
22: 19 But you, O *L*, be not far off;
22: 23 You who fear the *L*, praise him!
22: 26 they who seek the *L* will praise him
22: 27 will remember and turn to the *L*,

Ps 22: 28 for dominion belongs to the *L*
23: 1 The *L* is my shepherd, I shall lack
23: 6 I will dwell in the house of the *L*
24: 3 Who may ascend the hill of the *L?*
24: 5 He will receive blessing from the *L*
24: 8 The *L* strong and mighty,
24: 8 the *L* mighty in battle.
24: 10 The *L* Almighty—
25: 1 To you, O *L*, I lift up my soul
25: 4 Show me your ways, O *L*,
25: 6 O *L*, your great mercy and love,
25: 7 for you are good, O *L*.
25: 8 Good and upright is the *L;*
25: 10 All the ways of the *L* are loving
25: 11 For the sake of your name, O *L*,
25: 12 then, is the man that fears the *L?*
25: 14 *L* confides in those who fear him;
25: 15 My eyes are ever on the *L*,
26: 1 I have trusted in the *L*
26: 1 Vindicate me, O *L*,
26: 2 Test me, O *L*, and try me,
26: 6 and go about your altar, O *L*,
26: 8 love the house where you live, O *L*,
26: 12 great assembly I will praise the *L*.
27: 1 The *L* is my light and my salvation
27: 1 The *L* is the stronghold of my life
27: 4 One thing I ask of the *L*,
27: 4 dwell in the house of the *L*
27: 4 to gaze upon the beauty of the *L*
27: 6 I will sing and make music to the *L*.
27: 7 Hear my voice when I call, O *L;*
27: 8 Your face, *L*, I will seek.
27: 10 the *L* will receive me.
27: 11 Teach me your way, O *L;*
27: 13 I will see the goodness of the *L*
27: 14 Wait for the *L;*
27: 14 and wait for the *L*.
28: 1 To you I call, O *L* my Rock;
28: 5 regard for the works of the *L*
28: 6 Praise be to the *L*,
28: 7 The *L* is my strength and my shield
28: 8 The *L* is the strength of his people,
29: 1 Ascribe to the *L*, O mighty ones,
29: 1 ascribe to the *L* glory and strength.
29: 2 to the *L* the glory due his name;
29: 2 worship the *L* in the splendor
29: 3 The voice of the *L* is
29: 3 *L* thunders over the mighty waters.
29: 4 The voice of the *L* is powerful;
29: 4 the voice of the *L* is majestic.
29: 5 of the *L* breaks the cedars;
29: 5 the *L* breaks in pieces the cedars
29: 7 The voice of the *L* strikes
29: 8 of the *L* shakes the desert;
29: 8 the *L* shakes the Desert of Kadesh.
29: 9 The voice of the *L* twists the oaks
29: 10 The *L* sits enthroned over the flood
29: 10 the *L* is enthroned as King forever.
29: 11 The *L* gives strength to his people;
29: 11 the *L* blesses his people with peace.
30: 1 I will exalt you, O *L*,
30: 2 O *L* my God, I called to you
30: 3 O *L*, you brought me up
30: 4 Sing to the *L*, you saints of his;
30: 7 O *L*, when you favored me,
30: 8 To you, O *L*, I called;
30: 10 Hear, O *L*, and be merciful to me;
30: 10 O *L*, be my help."
30: 12 O *L* my God, I will give you thanks
31: 1 In you, O *L*, I have taken refuge;
31: 5 redeem me, O *L*, the God of truth.
31: 6 I trust in the *L*.
31: 9 Be merciful to me, O *L*, for I am
31: 14 But I trust in you, O *L;*
31: 17 Let me not be put to shame, O *L*,
31: 21 Praise be to the *L*,
31: 23 Love the *L*, all his saints!
31: 23 The *L* preserves the faithful,
31: 24 all you who hope in the *L*.
32: 2 whose sin the *L* does not count
32: 5 my transgressions to the *L*"—
32: 11 Rejoice in the *L* and be glad,
33: 1 joyfully to the *L*, you righteous;
33: 2 Praise the *L* with the harp;
33: 4 For the word of the *L* is right
33: 5 The *L* loves righteousness
33: 6 of the *L* were the heavens made,
33: 8 Let all the earth fear the *L;*

Ps 33: 10 The *L* foils the plans of the nations;
33: 11 of the *L* stand firm forever,
33: 12 is the nation whose God is the *L*,
33: 13 From heaven the *L* looks down
33: 18 But the eyes of the *L* are
33: 20 We wait in hope for the *L;*
33: 22 unfailing love rest upon us, O *L*,
34: 1 I will extol the *L* at all times;
34: 2 My soul will boast in the *L;*
34: 3 Glorify the *L* with me;
34: 4 I sought the *L*, and he answered me
34: 6 man called, and the *L* heard him;
34: 7 The angel of the *L* encamps
34: 8 Taste and see that the *L* is good;
34: 9 Fear the *L*, you his saints,
34: 10 those who seek the *L* lack no good
34: 11 I will teach you the fear of the *L*.
34: 15 The eyes of the *L* are
34: 16 the face of the *L* is
34: 17 cry out, and the *L* hears them;
34: 18 The *L* is close to the brokenhearted
34: 19 the *L* delivers him from them all;
34: 22 The *L* redeems his servants;
35: 1 O *L*, with those who contend
35: 5 angel of the *L* driving them away;
35: 6 the angel of the *L* pursuing them.
35: 9 Then my soul will rejoice in the *L*
35: 10 "Who is like you, O *L?*
35: 17 O *L*, how long will you look on?
35: 22 O *L*, you have seen this; be not
35: 24 in your righteousness, O *L* my God
35: 27 they always say, "The *L* be exalted,
36: 5 O *L*, reaches to the heavens,
36: 6 O *L*, you preserve both man
37: 3 Trust in the *L* and do good;
37: 4 Delight yourself in the *L*
37: 5 Commit your way to the *L;*
37: 7 still before the *L* and wait patiently
37: 9 in the *L* will inherit the land.
37: 17 but the *L* upholds the righteous.
37: 18 of the blameless are known to the *L*
37: 22 those the *L* blesses will inherit
37: 23 The *L* delights in the way
37: 24 for the *L* upholds him
37: 28 For the *L* loves the just
37: 33 but the *L* will not leave them
37: 34 Wait for the *L*
37: 39 of the righteous comes from the *L;*
37: 40 *L* helps them and delivers them;
38: 1 O *L*, do not rebuke me
38: 15 I wait for you, O *L;*
38: 21 O *L*, do not forsake me;
39: 4 "Show me, O *L*, my life's end
39: 12 "Hear my prayer, O *L*,
40: 1 I waited patiently for the *L;*
40: 3 and put their trust in the *L*.
40: 4 who makes the *L* his trust,
40: 5 Many, O *L* my God,
40: 9 as you know, O *L*.
40: 11 your mercy from me, O *L;*
40: 13 Be pleased, O *L*, to save me;
40: 13 O *L*, come quickly to help me.
40: 16 "The *L* be exalted!"
41: 1 the *L* delivers him in times
41: 2 The *L* will protect him
41: 3 The *L* will sustain him
41: 4 I said, "O *L*, have mercy on me;
41: 10 But you, O *L*, have mercy on me;
41: 13 Praise be to the *L*, the God of Israel
42: 8 By day the *L* directs his love,
46: 7 The *L* Almighty is with us;
46: 8 Come and see the works of the *L*,
46: 11 The *L* Almighty is with us;
47: 2 How awesome is the *L* Most High,
47: 5 the *L* amid the sounding
48: 1 Great is the *L*, and most worthy
48: 8 seen in the city of the *L* Almighty,
50: 1 The Mighty One, God, the *L*,
54: 6 I will praise your name, O *L*,
55: 16 and the *L* saves me.
55: 22 Cast your cares on the *L*
56: 10 in the *L*, whose word I praise—
58: 6 tear out, O *L*, the fangs of the lions!
59: 3 for no offense or sin of mine, O *L*.
59: 5 O *L* God Almighty, the God
59: 8 But you, O *L*, laugh at them;
64: 10 Let the righteous rejoice in the *L*
68: 4 his name is the *L*—

Ps 68: 16 where the *L* himself will dwell
68: 18 O *L* God, might dwell there.
68: 20 from the Sovereign *L* comes escape
68: 26 praise the *L* in the assembly
69: 6 O Lord, the *L* Almighty;
69: 13 But I pray to you, O *L*,
69: 16 O *L*, out of the goodness
69: 31 This will please the *L* more
69: 33 The *L* hears the needy
70: 1 O *L*, come quickly to help me.
70: 5 O *L*, do not delay.
71: 1 In you, O *L*, I have taken refuge;
71: 5 been my hope, O Sovereign *L*,
71: 16 your mighty acts, O Sovereign *L;*
72: 18 Praise be to the *L* God, the God
73: 28 made the Sovereign *L* my refuge;
74: 18 the enemy has mocked you, O *L*,
75: 8 In the hand of the *L* is a cup
76: 11 Make vows to the *L* your God
77: 11 I will remember the deeds of the *L;*
78: 4 the praiseworthy deeds of the *L*,
78: 21 When the *L* heard them, he was
79: 5 O *L?* Will you be angry forever?
80: 4 O *L* God Almighty,
80: 19 Restore us, O *L* God Almighty;
81: 10 I am the *L* your God,
81: 15 Those who hate the *L* would cringe
83: 16 that men will seek your name, O *L*.
83: 18 that you, whose name is the *L*—
84: 1 O *L* Almighty!
84: 2 even faints for the courts of the *L;*
84: 3 O *L* Almighty, my King
84: 8 my prayer, O *L* God Almighty;
84: 11 For the *L* God is a sun and shield;
84: 11 the *L* bestows favor and honor;
84: 12 O *L* Almighty,
85: 1 to your land, O *L;*
85: 7 Show us your unfailing love, O *L*,
85: 8 listen to what God the *L* will say;
85: 12 The *L* will indeed give what is good
86: 1 Hear, O *L*, and answer me,
86: 6 Hear my prayer, O *L;*
86: 11 Teach me your way, O *L*,
86: 17 O *L*, have helped me
87: 2 the *L* loves the gates of Zion
87: 6 The *L* will write in the register
88: 1 O *L*, the God who saves me,
88: 9 I call to you, O *L*, every day;
88: 13 But I cry to you for help, O *L;*
88: 14 Why, O *L*, do you reject me
89: 5 heavens praise your wonders, O *L*,
89: 6 above can compare with the *L?*
89: 6 is like the *L* among the heavenly
89: 8 O *L* God Almighty, who is like you
89: 8 O *L*, and your faithfulness
89: 15 in the light of your presence, O *L*.
89: 18 Indeed, our shield belongs to the *L*,
89: 46 O *L?* Will you hide yourself
89: 51 your enemies have mocked, O *L*,
89: 52 Praise be to the *L* forever!
90: 13 Relent, O *L!* How long will it be?
91: 2 I will say of the *L*, "He is my refuge
91: 9 even the *L*, who is my refuge—
91: 14 says the *L*, "I will rescue him;
92: 1 It is good to praise the *L*
92: 4 by your deeds, O *L;*
92: 5 How great are your works, O *L*,
92: 8 But you, O *L*, are exalted forever.
92: 9 For surely your enemies, O *L*,
92: 13 planted in the house of the *L*,
92: 15 proclaiming, "The *L* is upright;
93: 1 The *L* reigns, he is robed in majesty
93: 1 the *L* is robed in majesty
93: 3 The seas have lifted up, O *L*,
93: 4 the *L* on high is mighty.
93: 5 house for endless days, O *L*.
94: 1 O *L*, the God who avenges,
94: 3 How long will the wicked, O *L*,
94: 5 They crush your people, O *L;*
94: 7 They say, "The *L* does not see;
94: 11 The *L* knows the thoughts of man;
94: 12 is the man you discipline, O *L*,
94: 14 For the *L* will not reject his people;
94: 17 Unless the *L* had given me help,
94: 18 your love, O *L*, supported me.
94: 22 But the *L* has become my fortress,
94: 23 the *L* our God will destroy them.
95: 1 Come, let us sing for joy to the *L;*

Ps 95: 3 For the *L* is the great God,
95: 6 let us kneel before the *L* our Maker
96: 1 Sing to the *L* a new song;
96: 1 sing to the *L*, all the earth.
96: 2 Sing to the *L*, praise his name;
96: 4 For great is the *L* and most worthy
96: 5 but the *L* made the heavens.
96: 7 Ascribe to the *L*, O families
96: 7 ascribe to the *L* glory and strength.
96: 8 to the *L* the glory due his name;
96: 9 Worship the *L* in the splendor
96: 10 among the nations, "The *L* reigns."
96: 13 they will sing before the *L*,
97: 1 The *L* reigns, let the earth be glad;
97: 5 melt like wax before the *L*,
97: 8 because of your judgments, O *L*.
97: 9 O *L*, are the Most High
97: 10 Let those who love the *L* hate evil,
97: 12 in the *L*, you who are righteous,
98: 1 Sing to the *L* a new song,
98: 2 *L* has made his salvation known
98: 4 Shout for joy to the *L*, all the earth,
98: 5 make music to the *L* with the harp,
98: 6 shout for joy before the *L*, the King
98: 9 let them sing before the *L*,
99: 1 The *L* reigns,
99: 2 Great is the *L* in Zion;
99: 5 Exalt the *L* our God
99: 6 they called on the *L*
99: 8 O *L* our God,
99: 9 Exalt the *L* our God
99: 9 for the *L* our God is holy.
100: 1 Shout for joy to the *L*, all the earth.
100: 2 Serve the *L* with gladness;
100: 3 Know that the *L* is God.
100: 5 For the *L* is good and his love
101: 1 to you, O *L*, I will sing praise.
101: 8 evildoer from the city of the *L*.
102: 1 Hear my prayer, O *L*;
102: 12 But you, O *L*, sit enthroned forever
102: 15 nations will fear the name of the *L*,
102: 16 For the *L* will rebuild Zion
102: 18 not yet created may praise the *L*:
102: 19 *L* looked down from his sanctuary
102: 21 the name of the *L* will be declared
102: 22 assemble to worship the *L*.
103: 1 Praise the *L*, O my soul;
103: 2 Praise the *L*, O my soul,
103: 6 The *L* works righteousness
103: 8 The *L* is compassionate
103: 13 so the *L* has compassion
103: 19 The *L* has established his throne
103: 20 Praise the *L*, you his angels,
103: 21 Praise the *L*, all his heavenly hosts,
103: 22 Praise the *L*, O my soul.
103: 22 Praise the *L*, all his works
104: 1 O *L* my God, you are very great;
104: 1 Praise the *L*, O my soul.
104: 16 The trees of the *L* are well watered,
104: 24 How many are your works, O *L*!
104: 31 may the *L* rejoice in his works.
104: 31 of the *L* endure forever;
104: 33 I will sing to the *L* all my life;
104: 34 as I rejoice in the *L*.
104: 35 Praise the *L*.
104: 35 Praise the *L*, O my soul.
105: 1 Give thanks to the *L*, call
105: 3 of those who seek the *L* rejoice.
105: 4 Look to the *L* and his strength,
105: 7 He is the *L* our God;
105: 19 the word of the *L* proved him true.
105: 24 The *L* made his people very fruitful
105: 45 Praise the *L*.
106: 1 Give thanks to the *L*, for he is good
106: 1 Praise the *L*.
106: 2 proclaim the mighty acts of the *L*
106: 4 O *L*, when you show favor
106: 16 who was consecrated to the *L*.
106: 25 and did not obey the *L*.
106: 29 they provoked the *L* to anger
106: 32 of Meribah they angered the *L*,
106: 34 as the *L* had commanded them,
106: 40 Therefore the *L* was angry
106: 47 Save us, O *L* our God,
106: 48 Praise be to the *L*, the God of Israel
106: 48 Praise the *L*.
107: 1 Give thanks to the *L*, for he is good
107: 2 Let the redeemed of the *L* say this
Ps 107: 6 to the *L* in their trouble,
107: 8 to the *L* for his unfailing love
107: 13 they cried to the *L* in their trouble,
107: 15 to the *L* for his unfailing love
107: 19 they cried to the *L* in their trouble,
107: 21 to the *L* for his unfailing love
107: 24 They saw the works of the *L*,
107: 28 to the *L* in their trouble,
107: 31 to the *L* for his unfailing love
107: 43 and consider the great love of the *L*
108: 3 I will praise you, O *L*,
109: 14 be remembered before the *L*;
109: 15 sins always remain before the *L*,
109: 21 But you, O Sovereign *L*,
109: 26 Help me, O *L* my God;
109: 27 that you, O *L*, have done it.
109: 30 my mouth I will greatly extol the *L*;
110: 1 The *L* says to my Lord:
110: 2 *L* will extend your mighty scepter
110: 4 The *L* has sworn
111: 1 I will extol the *L* with all my heart
111: 1 Praise the *L*.
111: 2 Great are the works of the *L*;
111: 4 *L* is gracious and compassionate.
111: 10 The fear of the *L* is the beginning
112: 1 Blessed is the man who fears the *L*,
112: 1 Praise the *L*.
112: 7 heart is steadfast, trusting in the *L*.
113: 1 Praise the *L*.
113: 1 Praise, O servants of the *L*,
113: 1 praise the name of the *L*.
113: 2 Let the name of the *L* be praised,
113: 3 the name of the *L* is to be praised.
113: 4 *L* is exalted over all the nations,
113: 5 Who is like the *L* our God,
113: 9 Praise the *L*.
115: 1 Not to us, O *L*, not to us
115: 9 O house of Israel, trust in the *L*—
115: 10 O house of Aaron, trust in the *L*—
115: 11 You who fear him, trust in the *L*—
115: 12 *L* remembers us and will bless us:
115: 13 he will bless those who fear the *L*—
115: 14 May the *L* make you increase,
115: 15 May you be blessed by the *L*,
115: 16 highest heavens belong to the *L*,
115: 17 It is not the dead who praise the *L*,
115: 18 Praise the *L*.
115: 18 it is we who extol the *L*,
116: 1 I love the *L*, for he heard my voice;
116: 4 Then I called on the name of the *L*:
116: 4 "O *L*, save me!"
116: 5 The *L* is gracious and righteous;
116: 6 The *L* protects the simplehearted;
116: 7 for the *L* has been good to you.
116: 8 O *L*, have delivered my soul
116: 9 that I may walk before the *L*
116: 12 How can I repay the *L*
116: 13 and call on the name of the *L*.
116: 14 I will fulfill my vows to the *L*
116: 15 Precious in the sight of the *L*
116: 16 O *L*, truly I am your servant;
116: 17 and call on the name of the *L*.
116: 18 I will fulfill my vows to the *L*
116: 19 Praise the *L*.
116: 19 the courts of the house of the *L*—
117: 1 Praise the *L*, all you nations;
117: 2 Praise the *L*.
117: 2 of the *L* endures forever.
118: 1 Give thanks to the *L*, for he is good
118: 4 Let those who fear the *L* say:
118: 5 In my anguish I cried to the *L*,
118: 6 *L* is with me; I will not be afraid.
118: 7 The *L* is with me; he is my helper.
118: 8 It is better to take refuge in the *L*
118: 9 It is better to take refuge in the *L*
118: 10 in the name of the *L* I cut them off.
118: 11 in the name of the *L* I cut them off.
118: 12 in the name of the *L* I cut them off.
118: 13 but the *L* helped me.
118: 14 The *L* is my strength and my song;
118: 17 will proclaim what the *L* has done.
118: 18 The *L* has chastened me severely,
118: 19 I will enter and give thanks to the *L*
118: 20 This is the gate of the *L*
118: 23 the *L* has done this,
118: 24 This is the day the *L* has made;
118: 25 O *L*, grant us success.
118: 25 O *L*, save us;
Ps 118: 26 comes in the name of the *L*.
118: 26 of the *L* we bless you.
118: 27 The *L* is God,
118: 29 Give thanks to the *L*, for he is good
119: 1 to the law of the *L*.
119: 12 Praise be to you, O *L*;
119: 31 I hold fast to your statutes, O *L*;
119: 33 O *L*, to follow your decrees;
119: 41 unfailing love come to me, O *L*,
119: 52 I remember your ancient laws, O *L*
119: 55 night I remember your name, O *L*,
119: 57 You are my portion, O *L*;
119: 64 with your love, O *L*;
119: 65 according to your word, O *L*.
119: 75 O *L*, that your laws are righteous,
119: 89 Your word, O *L*, is eternal;
119:107 O *L*, according to your word.
119:108 O *L*, the willing praise
119:126 It is time for you to act, O *L*;
119:137 Righteous are you, O *L*,
119:145 with all my heart; answer me, O *L*,
119:149 O *L*, according to your laws.
119:151 Yet you are near, O *L*,
119:156 Your compassion is great, O *L*;
119:159 O *L*, according to your love.
119:166 I wait for your salvation, O *L*,
119:169 May my cry come before you, O *L*;
119:174 I long for your salvation, O *L*,
120: 1 I call on the *L* in my distress,
120: 2 Save me, O *L*, from lying lips
121: 2 My help comes from the *L*,
121: 5 The *L* watches over you—
121: 5 the *L* is your shade
121: 7 The *L* will keep you from all harm
121: 8 the *L* will watch over your coming
122: 1 "Let us go to the house of the *L*."
122: 4 the tribes of the *L*,
122: 4 to praise the name of the *L*
122: 9 of the house of the *L* our God,
123: 2 so our eyes look to the *L* our God,
123: 3 on us, O *L*, have mercy on us,
124: 1 If the *L* had not been on our side—
124: 2 if the *L* had not been on our side
124: 6 Praise be to the *L*,
124: 8 Our help is in the name of the *L*,
125: 1 in the *L* are like Mount Zion,
125: 2 so the *L* surrounds his people
125: 4 O *L*, to those who are good,
125: 5 the *L* will banish with the evildoers
126: 1 When the *L* brought back
126: 2 "The *L* has done great things
126: 3 The *L* has done great things for us,
126: 4 Restore our fortunes, O *L*,
127: 1 Unless the *L* builds the house,
127: 1 Unless the *L* watches over the city,
127: 3 Sons are a heritage from the *L*,
128: 1 Blessed are all who fear the *L*,
128: 4 who fears the *L*.
128: 5 May the *L* bless you from Zion
129: 4 But the *L* is righteous;
129: 8 we bless you in the name of the *L*."
129: 8 "The blessing of the *L* be upon you;
130: 1 O *L*; O Lord, hear my voice.
130: 3 If you, O *L*, kept a record of sins,
130: 5 I wait for the *L*, my soul waits,
130: 7 O Israel, put your hope in the *L*,
130: 7 for with the *L* is unfailing love
131: 1 My heart is not proud, O *L*,
131: 3 O Israel, put your hope in the *L*
132: 1 O *L*, remember David
132: 2 He swore an oath to the *L*
132: 5 till I find a place for the *L*,
132: 8 O *L*, and come to your resting
132: 11 The *L* swore an oath to David,
132: 13 For the *L* has chosen Zion,
133: 3 For there the *L* bestows his
134: 1 Praise the *L*, all you servants
134: 1 by night in the house of the *L*.
134: 1 LORD, all you servants of the *L*
134: 2 and praise the *L*.
134: 3 May the *L*, the Maker of heaven
135: 1 Praise him, you servants of the *L*,
135: 1 Praise the name of the *L*;
135: 1 Praise the *L*.
135: 2 minister in the house of the *L*,
135: 3 Praise the LORD, for the *L* is good
135: 3 Praise the *L*, for the LORD is good
135: 4 For the *L* has chosen Jacob

Ps 135: 5 I know that the *L* is great,
135: 6 The *L* does whatever pleases him,
135: 13 O *L*, through all generations.
135: 13 Your name, O *L*, endures forever,
135: 14 For the *L* will vindicate his people
135: 19 O house of Aaron, praise the *L*;
135: 19 O house of Israel, praise the *L*;
135: 20 O house of Levi, praise the *L*;
135: 20 you who fear him, praise the *L*.
135: 21 Praise be to the *L* from Zion,
135: 21 Praise the *L*.
136: 1 Give thanks to the *L*, for he is good
137: 4 How can we sing the songs of the *L*
137: 7 O *L*, what the Edomites did
138: 1 I will praise you, O *L*,
138: 4 of the earth praise you, O *L*,
138: 5 May they sing of the ways of the *L*,
138: 5 for the glory of the *L* is great.
138: 6 Though the *L* is on high, he looks
138: 8 The *L* will fulfill ⌞his purpose⌟
138: 8 your love, O *L*, endures forever—
139: 1 O *L*, you have searched me
139: 4 you know it completely, O *L*.
139: 21 I not hate those who hate you, O *L*,
140: 1 Rescue me, O *L*, from evil men;
140: 4 O *L*, from the hands of the wicked;
140: 6 Hear, O *L*, my cry for mercy.
140: 6 O *L*, I say to you, "You are
140: 7 O Sovereign *L*, my strong deliverer
140: 8 grant the wicked their desires, O *L*;
140: 12 I know that the *L* secures justice
141: 1 O *L*, I call to you; come quickly
141: 3 Set a guard over my mouth, O *L*;
141: 8 on you, O Sovereign *L*;
142: 1 I cry aloud to the *L*;
142: 1 to the *L* for mercy.
142: 5 I cry to you, O *L*;
143: 1 O *L*, hear my prayer,
143: 7 Answer me quickly, O *L*;
143: 9 Rescue me from my enemies, O *L*,
143: 11 For your name's sake, O *L*,
144: 1 Praise be to the *L*, my Rock,
144: 3 O *L*, what is man that you care
144: 5 Part your heavens, O *L*,
144: 15 are the people whose God is the *L*.
145: 3 Great is the *L* and most worthy
145: 8 *L* is gracious and compassionate,
145: 9 The *L* is good to all;
145: 10 have made will praise you, O *L*;
145: 13 The *L* is faithful to all his promises
145: 14 The *L* upholds all those who fall
145: 17 The *L* is righteous in all his ways
145: 18 The *L* is near to all who call on him
145: 20 *L* watches over all who love him,
145: 21 mouth will speak in praise of the *L*.
146: 1 Praise the *L*.
146: 1 Praise the *L*, O my soul.
146: 2 I will praise the *L* all my life;
146: 5 whose hope is in the *L* his God,
146: 6 the *L*, who remains faithful forever
146: 7 The *L* sets prisoners free,
146: 8 the *L* gives sight to the blind,
146: 8 the *L* lifts up those who are bowed
146: 8 the *L* loves the righteous.
146: 9 The *L* watches over the alien
146: 10 Praise the *L*.
146: 10 The *L* reigns forever,
147: 1 Praise the *L*.
147: 2 The *L* builds up Jerusalem;
147: 6 The *L* sustains the humble
147: 7 Sing to the *L* with thanksgiving;
147: 11 *L* delights in those who fear him,
147: 12 Extol the *L*, O Jerusalem;
147: 20 Praise the *L*.
148: 1 Praise the *L* from the heavens,
148: 1 Praise the *L*.
148: 5 Let them praise the name of the *L*,
148: 7 Praise the *L* from the earth,
148: 13 Let them praise the name of the *L*,
148: 14 Praise the *L*.
149: 1 Praise the *L*.
149: 1 Sing to the *L* a new song,
149: 4 For the *L* takes delight
149: 9 Praise the *L*.
150: 1 Praise the *L*.
150: 6 Praise the *L*.
150: 6 that has breath praise the *L*.
Pr 1: 7 The fear of the *L* is the beginning
Pr 1: 29 and did not choose to fear the *L*,
2: 5 will understand the fear of the *L*
2: 6 For the *L* gives wisdom,
3: 5 Trust in the *L* with all your heart
3: 7 fear the *L* and shun evil.
3: 9 Honor the *L* with your wealth,
3: 12 the *L* disciplines those he loves,
3: 19 By wisdom the *L* laid the earth's
3: 26 for the *L* will be your confidence
3: 32 for the *L* detests a perverse man
5: 21 are in full view of the *L*,
6: 16 There are six things the *L* hates,
8: 13 To fear the *L* is to hate evil;
8: 22 "The *L* possessed me
8: 35 and receives favor from the *L*.
9: 10 "The fear of the *L* is the beginning
10: 3 *L* does not let the righteous go
10: 22 The blessing of the *L* brings wealth,
10: 27 The fear of the *L* adds length to life
10: 29 The way of the *L* is a refuge
11: 1 The *L* abhors dishonest scales,
11: 20 The *L* detests men
12: 2 but the *L* condemns a crafty man.
12: 2 good man obtains favor from the *L*,
12: 22 The *L* detests lying lips,
14: 2 whose walk is upright fears the *L*,
14: 16 A wise man fears the *L*
14: 26 He who fears the *L* has a secure
14: 27 The fear of the *L* is a fountain
15: 3 The eyes of the *L* are everywhere,
15: 8 The *L* detests the sacrifice
15: 9 The *L* detests the way
15: 11 Destruction lie open before the *L*—
15: 16 Better a little with the fear of the *L*
15: 25 *L* tears down the proud man's
15: 26 The *L* detests the thoughts
15: 29 The *L* is far from the wicked
15: 33 of the *L* teaches a man wisdom,
16: 1 but from the *L* comes the reply
16: 2 but motives are weighed by the *L*.
16: 3 Commit to the *L* whatever you do,
16: 4 The *L* works out everything
16: 5 The *L* detests all the proud of heart
16: 6 of the *L* a man avoids evil.
16: 7 a man's ways are pleasing to the *L*,
16: 9 but the *L* determines his steps.
16: 11 balances are from the *L*;
16: 20 blessed is he who trusts in the *L*.
16: 33 but its every decision is from the *L*.
17: 3 but the *L* tests the heart.
17: 15 the *L* detests them both.
18: 10 The name of the *L* is a strong tower
18: 22 and receives favor from the *L*.
19: 3 yet his heart rages against the *L*.
19: 14 but a prudent wife is from the *L*.
19: 17 to the poor lends to the *L*,
19: 23 The fear of the *L* leads to life:
20: 10 the *L* detests them both.
20: 12 the *L* has made them both.
20: 22 for the *L*, and he will deliver you.
20: 23 The *L* detests differing weights,
20: 24 A man's steps are directed by the *L*
20: 27 of the *L* searches the spirit
21: 1 is in the hand of the *L*;
21: 2 but the *L* weighs the heart.
21: 3 to the *L* than sacrifice.
21: 30 that can succeed against the *L*.
21: 31 but victory rests with the *L*.
22: 2 The *L* is the Maker of them all.
22: 4 Humility and the fear of the *L*
22: 12 The eyes of the *L* keep watch
22: 19 So that your trust may be in the *L*,
22: 23 for the *L* will take up their case
23: 17 for the fear of the *L*.
24: 18 or the *L* will see and disapprove
24: 21 Fear the *L* and the king, my son,
25: 22 and the *L* will reward you.
28: 5 who seek the *L* understand it fully.
28: 14 is the man who always fears the *L*,
28: 25 he who trusts in the *L* will prosper.
29: 13 The *L* gives sight to the eyes
29: 25 whoever trusts in the *L* is kept safe.
29: 26 from the *L* that man gets justice.
30: 7 "Two things I ask of you, O *L*;
30: 9 and say, 'Who is the *L*?'
31: 30 a woman who fears the *L* is
Isa 1: 2 For the *L* has spoken:
1: 4 They have forsaken the *L*;
Isa 1: 9 Unless the *L* Almighty
1: 10 Hear the word of the *L*,
1: 11 what are they to me?" says the *L*.
1: 18 says the *L*.
1: 20 For the mouth of the *L* has spoken.
1: 24 the Lord, the *L* Almighty,
1: 28 those who forsake the *L* will perish.
2: 3 the word of the *L* from Jerusalem.
2: 3 up to the mountain of the *L*,
2: 5 let us walk in the light of the *L*.
2: 10 the ground from dread of the *L*
2: 11 the *L* alone will be exalted
2: 12 The *L* Almighty has a day in store
2: 17 the *L* alone will be exalted
2: 19 the ground from dread of the *L*
2: 21 crags from dread of the *L*
3: 1 the *L* Almighty,
3: 8 and deeds are against the *L*,
3: 13 The *L* takes his place in court;
3: 14 The *L* enters into judgment
3: 15 declares the Lord, the *L* Almighty.
3: 16 The *L* says,
3: 17 the *L* will make their scalps bald."
4: 2 of the *L* will be beautiful
4: 5 Then the *L* will create over all
5: 7 The vineyard of the *L* Almighty
5: 9 The *L* Almighty has declared
5: 12 regard for the deeds of the *L*,
5: 16 the *L* Almighty will be exalted
5: 24 the law of the *L* Almighty
6: 3 holy, holy is the *L* Almighty;
6: 5 seen the King, the *L* Almighty."
6: 12 until the *L* has sent everyone far
7: 3 Then the *L* said to Isaiah, "Go out,
7: 7 this is what the Sovereign *L* says:
7: 10 Again the *L* spoke to Ahaz,
7: 11 "Ask the *L* your God for a sign,
7: 12 I will not put the *L* to the test."
7: 17 The *L* will bring on you
7: 18 In that day the *L* will whistle
8: 1 *L* said to me, "Take a large scroll
8: 3 And the *L* said to me, "Name him
8: 5 *L* spoke to me again: "Because this
8: 11 The *L* spoke to me
8: 13 The *L* Almighty is the one you are
8: 17 I will wait for the *L*,
8: 18 in Israel from the *L* Almighty,
8: 18 the children the *L* has given me.
9: 7 The zeal of the *L* Almighty
9: 11 *L* has strengthened Rezin's foes
9: 13 have they sought the *L* Almighty.
9: 14 *L* will cut off from Israel both head
9: 19 By the wrath of the *L* Almighty
10: 16 the Lord, the *L* Almighty,
10: 20 but will truly rely on the *L*,
10: 23 The Lord, the *L* Almighty,
10: 24 is what the Lord, the *L* Almighty,
10: 26 The *L* Almighty will lash them
10: 33 See, the Lord, the *L* Almighty,
11: 2 The Spirit of the *L* will rest on him
11: 2 and of the fear of the *L*—
11: 3 he will delight in the fear of the *L*.
11: 9 full of the knowledge of the *L*
11: 15 The *L* will dry up
12: 1 "I will praise you, O *L*.
12: 2 The *L*, the *L*, is my strength
12: 4 "Give thanks to the *L*, call
12: 5 to the *L*, for he has done glorious
13: 4 The *L* Almighty is mustering
13: 5 the *L* and the weapons of his wrath
13: 6 Wail, for the day of the *L* is near;
13: 9 See, the day of the *L* is coming
13: 13 at the wrath of the *L* Almighty,
14: 1 The *L* will have compassion
14: 3 On the day the *L* gives you relief
14: 5 The *L* has broken the rod
14: 22 declares the *L* Almighty.
14: 22 declares the *L*.
14: 23 declares the *L* Almighty.
14: 24 The *L* Almighty has sworn,
14: 27 For the *L* Almighty has purposed,
14: 32 "The *L* has established Zion,
16: 13 the word the *L* has already spoken
16: 14 But now the *L* says: "Within three
17: 3 declares the *L* Almighty.
17: 6 declares the *L*, the God of Israel.
18: 4 This is what the *L* says to me:
18: 7 brought to the *L* Almighty

Isa 18: 7 of the Name of the *L* Almighty.
19: 1 See, the *L* rides on a swift cloud
19: 4 declares the Lord, the *L* Almighty.
19: 12 what the *L* Almighty
19: 14 The *L* has poured into them
19: 16 hand that the *L* Almighty raises
19: 17 of what the *L* Almighty is planning
19: 18 swear allegiance to the *L* Almighty
19: 19 a monument to the *L* at its border.
19: 19 altar to the *L* in the heart of Egypt,
19: 20 When they cry out to the *L*
19: 20 and witness to the *L* Almighty
19: 21 So the *L* will make himself known
19: 21 day they will acknowledge the *L*.
19: 21 they will make vows to the *L*
19: 22 The *L* will strike Egypt
19: 22 They will turn to the *L*,
19: 25 The *L* Almighty will bless them,
20: 2 at that time the *L* spoke
20: 3 Then the *L* said, "Just
21: 10 heard from the *L* Almighty,
21: 17 *L*, the God of Israel, has spoken.
22: 5 The Lord, the *L* Almighty,
22: 12 The Lord, the *L* Almighty,
22: 14 The *L* Almighty has revealed this
22: 14 says the Lord, the *L* Almighty.
22: 15 is what the Lord, the *L* Almighty,
22: 17 the *L* is about to take firm hold
22: 25 The *L* has spoken.
22: 25 day," declares the *L* Almighty,
23: 9 The *L* Almighty planned it,
23: 11 The *L* has stretched out his hand
23: 17 of seventy years, the *L* will deal
23: 18 earnings will be set apart for the *L*;
23: 18 go to those who live before the *L*,
24: 1 the *L* is going to lay waste the earth
24: 3 The *L* has spoken this word.
24: 15 in the east give glory to the *L*;
24: 15 name of the *L*, the God of Israel,
24: 21 In that day the *L* will punish
24: 23 for the *L* Almighty will reign
25: 1 O *L*, you are my God;
25: 6 this mountain the *L* Almighty will
25: 8 The Sovereign *L* will wipe away
25: 8 The *L* has spoken.
25: 9 This is the *L*, we trusted in him;
25: 10 The hand of the *L* will rest
26: 4 Trust in the *L* forever,
26: 4 for the *L*, the *L*, is the Rock eternal
26: 8 *L*, walking in the way of your laws,
26: 10 and regard not the majesty of the *L*
26: 11 O *L*, your hand is lifted high,
26: 12 *L*, you establish peace for us;
26: 13 O *L*, our God, other lords
26: 15 You have enlarged the nation, O *L*;
26: 16 *L*, they came to you
26: 17 so were we in your presence, O *L*.
26: 21 the *L* is coming out of his dwelling
27: 1 the *L* will punish with his sword,
27: 3 I, the *L*, watch over it;
27: 7 Has the *L* struck her
27: 12 In that day the *L* will thresh
27: 13 and worship the *L* on the holy
28: 5 In that day the *L* Almighty
28: 13 word of the *L* to them will become:
28: 14 Therefore hear the word of the *L*,
28: 16 this is what the Sovereign *L* says:
28: 21 The *L* will rise up as he did
28: 22 the Lord, the *L* Almighty,
28: 29 comes from the *L* Almighty,
29: 6 the *L* Almighty will come
29: 10 The *L* has brought
29: 15 to hide their plans from the *L*,
29: 19 the humble will rejoice in the *L*;
29: 22 Therefore this is what the *L*,
30: 1 declares the *L*,
30: 15 This is what the Sovereign *L*,
30: 18 For the *L* is a God of justice.
30: 18 Yet the *L* longs to be gracious
30: 26 when the *L* binds up the bruises
30: 27 the Name of the *L* comes from afar
30: 29 flutes to the mountain of the *L*,
30: 30 The *L* will cause men
30: 31 of the *L* will shatter Assyria;
30: 32 Every stroke the *L* lays on them
30: 33 the breath of the *L*,
31: 1 or seek help from the *L*.
31: 3 When the *L* stretches out his hand,

Isa 31: 4 This is what the *L* says to me:
31: 4 so the *L* Almighty will come down
31: 5 *L* Almighty will shield Jerusalem;
31: 9 declares the *L*,
32: 6 and spreads error concerning the *L*
33: 2 O *L*, be gracious to us;
33: 5 The *L* is exalted, for he dwells
33: 6 the fear of the *L* is the key
33: 10 "Now will I arise," says the *L*.
33: 21 There the *L* will be our Mighty
33: 22 For the *L* is our judge,
33: 22 the *L* is our king;
33: 22 the *L* is our lawgiver,
34: 2 The *L* is angry with all nations;
34: 6 For the *L* has a sacrifice in Bozrah
34: 6 The sword of the *L* is bathed
34: 8 For the *L* has a day of vengeance,
34: 16 Look in the scroll of the *L* and read
35: 2 they will see the glory of the *L*,
35: 10 the ransomed of the *L* will return.
36: 7 depending on the *L* our God"—
36: 10 The *L* himself told me to march
36: 10 destroy this land without the *L*?
36: 15 'The *L* will surely deliver us;
36: 15 you to trust in the *L* when he says,
36: 18 when he says, 'The *L* will deliver us
36: 20 then can the *L* deliver Jerusalem
37: 1 and went into the temple of the *L*.
37: 4 for the words the *L* your God has
37: 4 may be that the *L* your God will
37: 6 master, 'This is what the *L* says:
37: 14 and spread it out before the *L*.
37: 14 he went up to the temple of the *L*
37: 15 And Hezekiah prayed to the *L*:
37: 16 "O *L* Almighty, God of Israel,
37: 17 O *L*, and hear; open your eyes,
37: 17 open your eyes, O *L*, and see;
37: 18 O *L*, that the Assyrian kings have
37: 20 Now, O *L* our God, deliver us
37: 20 may know that you alone, O *L*,
37: 21 "This is what the *L*, the God
37: 22 this is the word the *L* has spoken
37: 32 The zeal of the *L* Almighty
37: 33 this is what the *L* says concerning
37: 34 declares the *L*.
37: 36 Then the angel of the *L* went out
38: 1 "This is what the *L* says: Put your
38: 3 prayed to the *L*, "Remember, O *L*,
38: 4 the word of the *L* came to Isaiah:
38: 5 'This is what the *L*, the God
38: 7 to you that the *L* will do what he
38: 11 I said, "I will not again see the *L*,
38: 11 the *L*, in the land of the living;
38: 20 The *L* will save me,
38: 20 lives in the temple of the *L*.
38: 22 up to the temple of the *L*?"
39: 5 "Hear the word of the *L* Almighty:
39: 6 Nothing will be left, says the *L*.
39: 8 of the *L* you have spoken is good,"
40: 3 the way for the *L*;
40: 5 For the mouth of the *L* has spoken
40: 5 the glory of the *L* will be revealed,
40: 7 the breath of the *L* blows on them.
40: 10 the Sovereign *L* comes with power,
40: 13 has understood the Spirit of the *L*,
40: 14 Whom did the *L* consult
40: 27 "My way is hidden from the *L*;
40: 28 The *L* is the everlasting God,
40: 31 but those who hope in the *L*
41: 4 I, the *L* with the first of them
41: 13 For I am the *L*, your God,
41: 14 will help you," declares the *L*,
41: 16 But you will rejoice in the *L*
41: 17 But I the *L* will answer them;
41: 20 that the hand of the *L* has done this
41: 21 "Present your case," says the *L*.
42: 5 This is what God the *L* says—
42: 6 the *L*, have called you
42: 8 "I am the *L*; that is my name!
42: 10 Sing to the *L* a new song,
42: 12 Let them give glory to the *L*
42: 13 The *L* will march out like a mighty
42: 19 blind like the servant of the *L*?
42: 21 It pleased the *L*
42: 24 Was it not the *L*,
43: 1 But now, this is what the *L* says—
43: 3 For I am the *L*, your God,
43: 10 are my witnesses," declares the *L*,

Isa 43: 11 I, even I, am the *L*,
43: 12 declares the *L*, "that I am God.
43: 14 This is what the *L* says—
43: 15 I am the *L*, your Holy One,
43: 16 This is what the *L* says—
44: 2 This is what the *L* says—
44: 5 One will say, 'I belong to the *L*';
44: 6 and Redeemer, the *L* Almighty:
44: 6 "This is what the *L* says—
44: 23 O heavens, for the *L* has done this;
44: 23 for the *L* has redeemed Jacob,
44: 24 I am the *L*,
44: 24 "This is what the *L* says—
45: 1 "This is what the *L* says
45: 3 that you may know that I am the *L*,
45: 5 I am the *L*, and there is no other;
45: 6 I am the *L*, and there is no other.
45: 7 I, the *L*, do all these things.
45: 8 I, the *L*, have created it.
45: 11 "This is what the *L* says—
45: 13 says the *L* Almighty."
45: 14 This is what the *L* says:
45: 17 But Israel will be saved by the *L*
45: 18 For this is what the *L* says—
45: 18 "I am the *L*,
45: 19 I, the *L*, speak the truth;
45: 21 Was it not I, the *L*?
45: 24 They will say of me, 'In the *L* alone
45: 25 in the *L* all the descendants
47: 4 the *L* Almighty is his name—
48: 1 oaths in the name of the *L*
48: 2 the *L* Almighty is his name:
48: 16 now the Sovereign *L* has sent me,
48: 17 This is what the *L* says—
48: 17 "I am the *L* your God,
48: 20 *L* has redeemed his servant Jacob."
48: 22 says the *L*, "for the wicked."
49: 1 Before I was born the *L* called me;
49: 5 And now the *L* says—
49: 5 honored in the eyes of the *L*
49: 7 This is what the *L* says—
49: 7 because of the *L*, who is faithful,
49: 8 This is what the *L* says:
49: 13 For the *L* comforts his people
49: 14 Zion said, "The *L* has forsaken me,
49: 18 As surely as I live," declares the *L*,
49: 22 This is what the Sovereign *L* says:
49: 23 Then you will know that I am the *L*
49: 25 But this is what the *L* says:
49: 26 that I, the *L*, am your Savior,
50: 1 This is what the *L* says:
50: 4 Sovereign *L* has given me
50: 5 Sovereign *L* has opened my ears,
50: 7 Because the Sovereign *L* helps me,
50: 9 It is the Sovereign *L* who helps me.
50: 10 Who among you fears the *L*
50: 10 trust in the name of the *L*
51: 1 and who seek the *L*:
51: 3 The *L* will surely comfort Zion
51: 3 wastelands like the garden of the *L*.
51: 9 O arm of the *L*;
51: 11 The ransomed of the *L* will return.
51: 13 that you forget the *L* your Maker,
51: 15 For I am the *L* your God,
51: 15 the *L* Almighty is his name.
51: 17 drunk from the hand of the *L*
51: 20 filled with the wrath of the *L*
51: 22 This is what your Sovereign *L* says,
52: 3 For this is what the *L* says:
52: 4 this is what the Sovereign *L* says:
52: 5 declares the *L*.
52: 5 do I have here?" declares the *L*.
52: 8 When the *L* returns to Zion,
52: 9 for the *L* has comforted his people,
52: 10 The *L* will lay bare his holy arm
52: 11 you who carry the vessels of the *L*.
52: 12 for the *L* will go before you,
53: 1 the arm of the *L* been revealed?
53: 6 and the *L* has laid on him
53: 10 and the will of the *L* will prosper
53: 10 the *L* makes his life a guilt offering,
54: 1 says the *L*.
54: 5 the *L* Almighty is his name—
54: 6 The *L* will call you back
54: 8 says the *L* your Redeemer.
54: 10 says the *L*, who has compassion
54: 13 your sons will be taught by the *L*,
54: 17 declares the *L*.

Isa 54: 17 heritage of the servants of the *L*,
55: 5 because of the *L* your God,
55: 6 Seek the *L* while he may be found;
55: 7 to the *L*, and he will have mercy
55: 8 declares the *L*.
56: 1 This is what the *L* says:
56: 3 has joined himself to the *L* say,
56: 3 "The *L* will surely exclude me
56: 4 For this is what the *L* says:
56: 6 to love the name of the *L*,
56: 6 who bind themselves to the *L*
56: 8 The Sovereign *L* declares—
57: 19 says the *L*.
58: 5 a day acceptable to the *L*?
58: 8 of the *L* will be your rear guard.
58: 9 you will call, and the *L* will answer;
58: 11 The *L* will guide you always;
58: 14 The mouth of the *L* has spoken.
58: 14 then you will find your joy in the *L*,
59: 1 the arm of the *L* is not too short
59: 13 and treachery against the *L*,
59: 15 The *L* looked and was displeased
59: 19 men will fear the name of the *L*,
59: 19 the breath of the *L* drives along.
59: 20 declares the *L*.
59: 21 covenant with them," says the *L*.
59: 21 time on and forever," says the *L*.
60: 1 the glory of the *L* rises upon you.
60: 2 but the *L* rises upon you
60: 6 and proclaiming the praise of the *L*
60: 9 to the honor of the *L* your God,
60: 14 and will call you The City of the *L*,
60: 16 Then you will know that I, the *L*,
60: 19 for the *L* will be your everlasting
60: 20 the *L* will be your everlasting light,
60: 22 I am the *L*;
61: 1 Spirit of the Sovereign *L* is on me,
61: 1 because the *L* has anointed me
61: 3 a planting of the *L*
61: 6 you will be called priests of the *L*,
61: 8 "For I, the *L*, love justice;
61: 9 are a people the *L* has blessed."
61: 10 I delight greatly in the *L*;
61: 11 so the Sovereign *L* will make
62: 2 that the mouth of the *L* will bestow
62: 4 for the *L* will take delight in you,
62: 6 You who call on the *L*,
62: 8 The *L* has sworn by his right hand
62: 9 and praise the *L*,
62: 11 The *L* has made proclamation
62: 12 The Redeemed of the *L*;
63: 7 I will tell of the kindnesses of the *L*,
63: 7 according to all the *L* has done
63: 14 rest by the Spirit of the *L*.
63: 16 you, O *L*, are our Father,
63: 17 O *L*, do you make us wander
64: 8 Yet, O *L*, you are our Father.
64: 9 beyond measure, O *L*;
64: 12 O *L*, will you hold yourself back?
65: 7 says the *L*.
65: 8 This is what the *L* says:
65: 11 "But as for you who forsake the *L*
65: 13 this is what the Sovereign *L* says:
65: 15 the Sovereign *L* will put you
65: 23 will be a people blessed by the *L*,
65: 25 says the *L*.
66: 1 This is what the *L* says:
66: 2 declares the *L*.
66: 5 Hear the word of the *L*,
66: 5 'Let the *L* be glorified,
66: 6 It is the sound of the *L*
66: 9 and not give delivery?" says the *L*.
66: 12 For this is what the *L* says:
66: 14 hand of the *L* will be made known
66: 15 See, the *L* is coming with fire,
66: 16 many will be those slain by the *L*.
66: 16 the *L* will execute judgment
66: 17 their end together," declares the *L*.
66: 20 in Jerusalem as an offering to the *L*
66: 20 of the *L* in ceremonially clean
66: 20 on mules and camels," says the *L*.
66: 21 be priests and Levites," says the *L*.
66: 22 declares the *L*, "so will your name
66: 23 bow down before me," says the *L*.
Jer 1: 2 The word of the *L* came to him
1: 4 The word of the *L* came to me,
1: 6 "Ah, Sovereign *L*," I said,
1: 7 But the *L* said to me, "Do not say,

Jer 1: 8 will rescue you," declares the *L*.
1: 9 Then the *L* reached out his hand
1: 11 The word of the *L* came to me:
1: 12 The *L* said to me, "You have seen
1: 13 The word of the *L* came
1: 14 The *L* said to me, "From the north
1: 15 kingdoms," declares the *L*.
1: 19 will rescue you," declares the *L*.
2: 1 The word of the *L* came to me:
2: 3 Israel was holy to the *L*,
2: 3 declares the *L*.
2: 4 of the *L*, O house of Jacob,
2: 5 This is what the *L* says:
2: 6 They did not ask, 'Where is the *L*,
2: 8 'Where is the *L*?'
2: 9 declares the *L*.
2: 12 declares the *L*.
2: 17 by forsaking the *L* your God
2: 19 declares the Lord, the *L* Almighty.
2: 19 when you forsake the *L* your God
2: 22 declares the Sovereign *L*.
2: 29 declares the *L*.
2: 31 consider the word of the *L*:
2: 37 for the *L* has rejected those you
3: 1 declares the *L*.
3: 6 of King Josiah, the *L* said to me,
3: 10 only in pretense," declares the *L*.
3: 11 *L* said to me, "Faithless Israel is
3: 12 faithless Israel,' declares the *L*,
3: 12 for I am merciful,' declares the *L*,
3: 13 declares the *L*.
3: 13 rebelled against the *L* your God,
3: 14 faithless people," declares the *L*,
3: 16 declares the *L*, "men will no longer
3: 16 'The ark of the covenant of the *L*.'
3: 17 Jerusalem The Throne of the *L*,
3: 17 to honor the name of the *L*.
3: 20 declares the *L*.
3: 21 and have forgotten the *L* their God
3: 22 for you are the *L* our God.
3: 23 surely in the *L* our God
3: 25 sinned against the *L* our God,
3: 25 we have not obeyed the *L* our God
4: 1 declares the *L*.
4: 2 you swear, 'As surely as the *L* lives
4: 3 This is what the *L* says to the men
4: 4 Circumcise yourselves to the *L*,
4: 8 for the fierce anger of the *L*
4: 9 "In that day," declares the *L*,
4: 10 Then I said, "Ah, Sovereign *L*,
4: 17 declares the *L*.
4: 26 before the *L*, before his fierce anger
4: 27 This is what the *L* says:
5: 2 they say, 'As surely as the *L* lives,'
5: 3 O *L*, do not your eyes look
5: 4 they do not know the way of the *L*,
5: 5 surely they know the way of the *L*,
5: 9 declares the *L*.
5: 10 people do not belong to the *L*.
5: 11 declares the *L*.
5: 12 They have lied about the *L*;
5: 14 is what the *L* God Almighty says:
5: 15 O house of Israel," declares the *L*,
5: 18 declares the *L*, "I will not destroy
5: 19 'Why has the *L* our God done all
5: 22 you not fear me?" declares the *L*.
5: 24 'Let us fear the *L* our God,
5: 29 declares the *L*.
6: 6 This is what the *L* Almighty says:
6: 9 This is what the *L* Almighty says:
6: 10 The word of the *L* is offensive
6: 11 But I am full of the wrath of the *L*,
6: 12 declares the *L*.
6: 15 says the *L*.
6: 16 This is what the *L* says:
6: 21 Therefore this is what the *L* says:
6: 22 This is what the *L* says:
6: 30 because the *L* has rejected them."
7: 1 came to Jeremiah from the *L*:
7: 2 these gates to worship the *L*.
7: 2 " 'Hear the word of the *L*,
7: 3 This is what the *L* Almighty,
7: 4 of the LORD, the temple of the *L*
7: 4 the temple of the *L*, the temple
7: 4 "This is the temple of the *L*,
7: 11 been watching! declares the *L*.
7: 13 declares the *L*, I spoke to you again
7: 19 they are provoking? declares the *L*.

Jer 7: 20 this is what the Sovereign *L* says:
7: 21 " 'This is what the *L* Almighty,
7: 28 that has not obeyed the *L* its God
7: 29 for the *L* has rejected
7: 30 evil in my eyes, declares the *L*.
7: 32 the days are coming, declares the *L*
8: 1 " 'At that time, declares the *L*,
8: 3 to life, declares the *L* Almighty.'
8: 4 to them, 'This is what the *L* says:
8: 7 the requirements of the *L*.
8: 8 for we have the law of the *L*,"
8: 9 have rejected the word of the *L*,
8: 12 says the *L*.
8: 13 away their harvest, declares the *L*.
8: 14 For the *L* our God has doomed us
8: 17 declares the *L*.
8: 19 "Is the *L* not in Zion?
9: 3 declares the *L*.
9: 6 declares the *L*.
9: 7 this is what the *L* Almighty says:
9: 9 declares the *L*.
9: 12 Who has been instructed by the *L*
9: 13 The *L* said, "It is because they have
9: 15 this is what the *L* Almighty,
9: 17 This is what the *L* Almighty says:
9: 20 O women, hear the word of the *L*;
9: 22 Say, "This is what the *L* declares:
9: 23 This is what the *L* says:
9: 24 I am the *L*, who exercises kindness,
9: 24 declares the *L*.
9: 25 days are coming," declares the *L*,
10: 1 Hear what the *L* says to you,
10: 2 This is what the *L* says:
10: 6 No one is like you, O *L*;
10: 10 But the *L* is the true God;
10: 16 the *L* Almighty is his name.
10: 18 For this is what the *L* says:
10: 21 and do not inquire of the *L*;
10: 23 O *L*, that a man's life is not his own
10: 24 Correct me, *L*, but only
11: 1 came to Jeremiah from the *L*:
11: 3 Tell them that this is what the *L*,
11: 5 I answered, "Amen, *L*."
11: 6 *L* said to me, "Proclaim all these
11: 9 Then the *L* said to me, "There is
11: 11 Therefore this is what the *L* says:
11: 16 *L* called you a thriving olive tree
11: 17 The *L* Almighty, who planted you,
11: 18 Because the *L* revealed their plot
11: 20 But, O *L* Almighty, you who judge
11: 21 prophesy in the name of the *L*
11: 21 this is what the *L* says about
11: 22 this is what the *L* Almighty says:
12: 1 You are always righteous, O *L*,
12: 3 Yet you know me, O *L*;
12: 12 for the sword of the *L* will devour
12: 14 This is what the *L* says: "As
12: 16 saying, 'As surely as the *L* lives'—
12: 17 and destroy it," declares the *L*.
13: 1 This is what the *L* said to me:
13: 2 So I bought a belt, as the *L* directed
13: 3 Then the word of the *L* came
13: 5 hid it at Perath, as the *L* told me.
13: 6 Many days later the *L* said to me,
13: 8 Then the word of the *L* came to me
13: 9 to me: "This is what the *L* says:
13: 11 declares the *L*, 'to be my people
13: 12 'This is what the *L*, the God
13: 13 tell them, 'This is what the *L* says:
13: 14 and sons alike, declares the *L*.
13: 15 for the *L* has spoken.
13: 16 Give glory to the *L* your God
13: 21 say when the *L* sets over you
13: 25 declares the *L*,
14: 1 of the *L* to Jeremiah concerning
14: 7 O *L*, do something for the sake
14: 9 You are among us, O *L*,
14: 10 So the *L* does not accept them;
14: 10 This is what the *L* says about this
14: 11 the *L* said to me, "Do not pray
14: 13 But I said, "Ah, Sovereign *L*,
14: 14 the *L* said to me, "The prophets are
14: 15 this is what the *L* says about
14: 20 O *L*, we acknowledge our
14: 22 No, it is you, O *L* our God.
15: 1 the *L* said to me: "Even if Moses
15: 2 tell them, 'This is what the *L* says:
15: 3 against them," declares the *L*,

Jer 15: 6 have rejected me," declares the *L*.
15: 9 declares the *L*.
15: 11 The *L* said,
15: 15 You understand, O *L*;
15: 16 O *L* God Almighty.
15: 19 Therefore this is what the *L* says:
15: 20 declares the *L*.
16: 1 Then the word of the *L* came to me
16: 3 this is what the *L* says about
16: 5 For this is what the *L* says:
16: 5 from this people," declares the *L*.
16: 9 For this is what the *L* Almighty,
16: 10 committed against the *L* our God?'
16: 10 'Why has the *L* decreed such
16: 11 fathers forsook me,' declares the *L*,
16: 14 days are coming," declares the *L*,
16: 14 *L* lives, who brought the Israelites
16: 15 will say, 'As surely as the *L* lives,
16: 16 declares the *L*, "and they will catch
16: 19 O *L*, my strength and my fortress,
16: 21 that my name is the *L*.
17: 5 This is what the *L* says:
17: 5 whose heart turns away from the *L*.
17: 7 is the man who trusts in the *L*,
17: 10 "I the *L* search the heart
17: 13 O *L*, the hope of Israel,
17: 13 because they have forsaken the *L*,
17: 14 Heal me, O *L*, and I will be healed;
17: 15 "Where is the word of the *L*?
17: 19 This is what the *L* said to me:
17: 20 to them, 'Hear the word of the *L*,
17: 21 This is what the *L* says: Be careful
17: 24 careful to obey me, declares the *L*,
17: 26 offerings to the house of the *L*.
18: 1 came to Jeremiah from the *L*:
18: 5 Then the word of the *L* came to me
18: 6 as this potter does?" declares the *L*.
18: 11 'This is what the *L* says: Look!
18: 13 Therefore this is what the *L* says:
18: 19 Listen to me, O *L*;
18: 23 But you know, O *L*,
19: 1 This is what the *L* says: "Go
19: 3 This is what the *L* Almighty,
19: 3 and say, 'Hear the word of the *L*,
19: 6 the days are coming, declares the *L*
19: 11 'This is what the *L* Almighty says:
19: 12 those who live here, declares the *L*.
19: 14 where the *L* had sent him
19: 15 "This is what the *L* Almighty,
20: 1 officer in the temple of the *L*,
20: 4 For this is what the *L* says:
20: 7 O *L*, you deceived me,
20: 8 the word of the *L* has brought me
20: 11 *L* is with me like a mighty warrior;
20: 12 O *L* Almighty, you who examine
20: 13 Give praise to the *L*!
20: 13 Sing to the *L*!
20: 16 the *L* overthrew without pity.
21: 1 came to Jeremiah from the *L*
21: 2 Perhaps the *L* will perform
21: 2 "Inquire now of the *L* for us
21: 4 'This is what the *L*, the God
21: 7 After that, declares the *L*,
21: 8 'This is what the *L* says: See,
21: 10 and not good, declares the *L*.
21: 11 word of the *L*, O house of David,
21: 12 of David, this is what the *L* says:
21: 13 declares the *L*—
21: 14 declares the *L*.
22: 1 This is what the *L* says: "Go
22: 2 the word of the *L*, O king of Judah,
22: 3 This is what the *L* says: Do what is
22: 5 these commands, declares the *L*,
22: 6 this is what the *L* says about
22: 8 'Why has the *L* done such a thing
22: 9 the covenant of the *L* their God
22: 11 is what the *L* says about Shallum
22: 16 declares the *L*.
22: 18 is what the *L* says about Jehoiakim
22: 24 declares the *L*, "even if you,
22: 29 hear the word of the *L*!
22: 30 This is what the *L* says:
23: 1 of my pasture!" declares the *L*.
23: 2 Therefore this is what the *L*,
23: 2 you have done," declares the *L*.
23: 4 will any be missing," declares the *L*
23: 5 days are coming," declares the *L*,
23: 6 The *L* Our Righteousness.

Jer 23: 7 days are coming," declares the *L*,
23: 7 *L* lives, who brought the Israelites
23: 8 will say, 'As surely as the *L* lives,
23: 9 because of the *L*
23: 11 declares the *L*.
23: 12 declares the *L*.
23: 15 is what the *L* Almighty says
23: 16 This is what the *L* Almighty says:
23: 16 not from the mouth of the *L*.
23: 17 'The *L* says: You will have peace.'
23: 18 stood in the council of the *L*
23: 19 See, the storm of the *L*
23: 20 anger of the *L* will not turn back
23: 23 declares the *L*,
23: 24 declares the *L*.
23: 24 declares the *L*.
23: 28 to do with grain?" declares the *L*.
23: 29 my word like fire," declares the *L*,
23: 30 "Therefore," declares the *L*,
23: 31 and yet declare, 'The *L* declares.'
23: 31 declares the *L*, "I am
23: 32 false dreams," declares the *L*.
23: 32 people in the least," declares the *L*.
23: 33 I will forsake you, declares the *L*.'
23: 33 'What is the oracle of the *L*?'
23: 34 'This is the oracle of the *L*,'
23: 35 or 'What has the *L* spoken?'
23: 36 mention 'the oracle of the *L*' again,
23: 36 the *L* Almighty, our God.
23: 37 or 'What has the *L* spoken?'
23: 38 'This is the oracle of the *L*.'
23: 38 'This is the oracle of the *L*,'
23: 38 'This is the oracle of the *L*,'
23: 38 this is what the *L* says: You used
24: 1 in front of the temple of the *L*.
24: 1 the *L* showed me two baskets
24: 3 the *L* asked me, "What do you see,
24: 4 Then the word of the *L* came to me
24: 5 "This is what the *L*, the God
24: 7 heart to know me, that I am the *L*.
24: 8 says the *L*, 'so will I deal
25: 3 the word of the *L* has come to me
25: 4 the *L* has sent you all his servants
25: 5 stay in the land the *L* gave to you
25: 7 listen to me," declares the *L*,
25: 8 Therefore the *L* Almighty says this
25: 9 declares the *L*, "and I will bring
25: 12 for their guilt," declares the *L*,
25: 15 This is what the *L*, the God
25: 27 'This is what the *L* Almighty,
25: 28 'This is what the *L* Almighty says:
25: 29 earth, declares the *L* Almighty.'
25: 30 " 'The *L* will roar from on high;
25: 31 declares the *L*.
25: 31 for the *L* will bring charges
25: 32 This is what the *L* Almighty says:
25: 33 slain by the *L* will be everywhere—
25: 36 for the *L* is destroying their pasture
25: 37 because of the fierce anger of the *L*.
26: 1 this word came from the *L*:
26: 2 LORD: "This is what the *L* says:
26: 2 to worship in the house of the *L*.
26: 4 to them, 'This is what the *L* says:
26: 7 words in the house of the *L*.
26: 8 everything the *L* had commanded
26: 9 Jeremiah in the house of the *L*.
26: 10 palace to the house of the *L*
26: 12 "The *L* sent me to prophesy
26: 13 Then the *L* will relent
26: 13 actions and obey the *L* your God.
26: 15 for in truth the *L* has sent me
26: 16 to us in the name of the *L* our God
26: 18 'This is what the *L* Almighty says:
26: 19 And did not the *L* relent,
26: 19 Did not Hezekiah fear the *L*
26: 20 prophesied in the name of the *L*;
27: 1 came to Jeremiah from the *L*:
27: 2 This is what the *L* said to me:
27: 4 'This is what the *L* Almighty,
27: 8 famine and plague, declares the *L*,
27: 11 to live there, declares the *L*." ' "
27: 13 with which the *L* has threatened
27: 15 not sent them,' declares the *L*.
27: 16 "This is what the *L* says: Do not
27: 18 and have the word of the *L*,
27: 18 plead with the *L* Almighty that
27: 18 remaining in the house of the *L*
27: 19 is what the *L* Almighty says about

Jer 27: 21 left in the house of the *L*
27: 21 yes, this is what the *L* Almighty,
27: 22 come for them,' declares the *L*.
28: 1 the house of the *L* in the presence
28: 2 "This is what the *L* Almighty,
28: 4 declares the *L*, 'for I will break
28: 5 standing in the house of the *L*.
28: 6 He said, "Amen! May the *L* do so!
28: 6 May the *L* fulfill the words you
28: 9 as one truly sent by the *L* only
28: 11 people, "This is what the *L* says:
28: 12 the word of the *L* came to Jeremiah
28: 13 'This is what the *L* says: You have
28: 14 This is what the *L* Almighty,
28: 15 Hananiah! The *L* has not sent you,
28: 16 Therefore, this is what the *L* says:
28: 16 preached rebellion against the *L*.' "
29: 4 This is what the *L* Almighty,
29: 7 Pray to the *L* for it,
29: 8 Yes, this is what the *L* Almighty,
29: 9 not sent them," declares the *L*.
29: 10 is what the *L* says: "When seventy
29: 11 declares the *L*, "plans
29: 14 declares the *L*, "and will bring you
29: 14 declares the *L*, "and will bring you
29: 15 The *L* has raised up prophets for us
29: 16 but this is what the *L* says about
29: 17 this is what the *L* Almighty says:
29: 19 not listened either," declares the *L*.
29: 19 to my words," declares the *L*,
29: 20 Therefore, hear the word of the *L*,
29: 21 This is what the *L* Almighty,
29: 22 'The *L* treat you like Zedekiah
29: 23 am a witness to it," declares the *L*.
29: 25 "This is what the *L* Almighty,
29: 26 be in charge of the house of the *L*;
29: 26 'The *L* has appointed you priest
29: 30 the word of the *L* came to Jeremiah
29: 31 is what the *L* says about Shemaiah
29: 32 declares the *L*, because he has
29: 32 this is what the *L* says: I will surely
30: 1 came to Jeremiah from the *L*:
30: 2 "This is what the *L*, the God
30: 3 days are coming,' declares the *L*,
30: 3 forefathers to possess,' says the *L*."
30: 4 the words the *L* spoke concerning
30: 5 Judah: "This is what the *L* says:
30: 8 that day,' declares the *L* Almighty,
30: 9 they will serve the *L* their God
30: 10 declares the *L*.
30: 11 declares the *L*.
30: 12 "This is what the *L* says:
30: 17 declares the *L*,
30: 18 "This is what the *L* says:
30: 21 declares the *L*.
30: 23 See, the storm of the *L*
30: 24 anger of the *L* will not turn back
31: 1 "At that time," declares the *L*,
31: 2 This is what the *L* says:
31: 3 The *L* appeared to us in the past,
31: 6 to the *L* our God.' "
31: 7 This is what the *L* says:
31: 7 'O *L*, save your people,
31: 10 Hear the word of the *L*, O nations;
31: 11 For the *L* will ransom Jacob
31: 12 rejoice in the bounty of the *L*—
31: 14 declares the *L*.
31: 15 This is what the *L* says:
31: 16 This is what the *L* says:
31: 16 declares the *L*.
31: 17 declares the *L*.
31: 18 because you are the *L* my God.
31: 20 declares the *L*.
31: 22 The *L* will create a new thing
31: 23 This is what the *L* Almighty,
31: 23 *L* bless you, O righteous dwelling,
31: 27 days are coming," declares the *L*,
31: 28 and to plant," declares the *L*.
31: 31 time is coming," declares the *L*,
31: 32 declares the *L*.
31: 33 after that time," declares the *L*.
31: 34 declares the *L*.
31: 34 his brother, saying, 'Know the *L*,'
31: 35 This is what the *L* says,
31: 35 the *L* Almighty is his name:
31: 36 declares the *L*,
31: 37 This is what the *L* says:
31: 37 declares the *L*.

Jer 31: 38 days are coming," declares the *L*,
31: 40 Horse Gate, will be holy to the *L*.
32: 1 came to Jeremiah from the *L*
32: 3 You say, 'This is what the *L* says:
32: 5 until I deal with him, declares the *L*
32: 6 "The word of the *L* came to me:
32: 8 that this was the word of the *L*;
32: 8 "Then, just as the *L* had said,
32: 14 'This is what the *L* Almighty,
32: 15 For this is what the *L* Almighty,
32: 16 to the *L*: "Ah, Sovereign LORD,
32: 17 to the LORD: "Ah, Sovereign *L*,
32: 18 whose name is the *L* Almighty,
32: 25 you, O Sovereign *L*, say to me,
32: 26 the word of the *L* came to Jeremiah
32: 27 I am the *L*, the God of all mankind.
32: 28 Therefore, this is what the *L* says:
32: 30 hands have made, declares the *L*.
32: 36 this is what the *L*, the God of Israel
32: 42 "This is what the *L* says: As I have
32: 44 their fortunes, declares the *L*."
33: 1 the word of the *L* came
33: 2 established it—the *L* is his name:
33: 2 *L* who formed it and established
33: 2 "This is what the *L* says, he who
33: 4 For this is what the *L*, the God
33: 10 "This is what the *L* says: 'You say
33: 11 as they were before,' says the *L*.
33: 11 for the *L* is good;
33: 11 offerings to the house of the *L*,
33: 11 "Give thanks to the *L* Almighty,
33: 12 "This is what the *L* Almighty says:
33: 13 one who counts them,' says the *L*.
33: 14 days are coming,' declares the *L*,
33: 16 The *L* Our Righteousness.'
33: 17 For this is what the *L* says:
33: 19 word of the *L* came to Jeremiah:
33: 20 Jeremiah: "This is what the *L* says:
33: 23 word of the *L* came to Jeremiah:
33: 24 *L* has rejected the two kingdoms he
33: 25 This is what the *L* says: 'If I have
34: 1 came to Jeremiah from the *L*:
34: 2 tell him, 'This is what the *L* says:
34: 2 "This is what the *L*, the God
34: 4 is what the *L* says concerning you:
34: 4 " 'Yet hear the promise of the *L*,
34: 5 this promise, declares the *L*.' "
34: 8 came to Jeremiah from the *L*
34: 12 the word of the *L* came to Jeremiah
34: 13 "This is what the *L*, the God
34: 17 declares the *L*— 'freedom' to fall
34: 17 "Therefore, this is what the *L* says:
34: 22 to give the order, declares the *L*,
35: 1 from the *L* during the reign
35: 2 rooms of the house of the *L*
35: 4 them into the house of the *L*,
35: 12 the word of the *L* came to Jeremiah
35: 13 obey my words?' declares the *L*.
35: 13 "This is what the *L* Almighty,
35: 17 this is what the *L* God Almighty,
35: 18 "This is what the *L* Almighty,
35: 19 this is what the *L* Almighty,
36: 1 came to Jeremiah from the *L*:
36: 4 all the words the *L* had spoken
36: 6 go to the house of the *L* on a day
36: 6 the words of the *L* that you wrote
36: 7 bring their petition before the *L*,
36: 7 people by the *L* are great."
36: 8 the words of the *L* from the scroll.
36: 9 before the *L* was proclaimed
36: 11 the words of the *L* from the scroll,
36: 26 But the *L* had hidden them.
36: 27 the word of the *L* came to Jeremiah
36: 29 is what the *L* says: You burned
36: 30 is what the *L* says about Jehoiakim
37: 2 to the words the *L* had spoken
37: 3 Please pray to the *L* our God for us
37: 6 Then the word of the *L* came
37: 7 "This is what the *L*, the God
37: 9 "This is what the *L* says: Do not
37: 17 "Is there any word from the *L*?"
38: 2 is what the *L* says: 'Whoever stays
38: 3 And this is what the *L* says:
38: 14 entrance to the temple of the *L*.
38: 16 the *L* lives, who has given us breath
38: 17 "This is what the *L* God Almighty,
38: 20 Obey the *L* by doing what I tell you
38: 21 this is what the *L* has revealed

Jer 39: 15 the word of the *L* came to him:
39: 16 'This is what the *L* Almighty,
39: 17 you on that day, declares the *L*;
39: 18 you trust in me, declares the *L*.' "
40: 1 *L* after Nebuzaradan commander
40: 2 *L* your God decreed this disaster
40: 3 now the *L* has brought it about;
40: 3 you people sinned against the *L*
41: 5 with them to the house of the *L*.
42: 2 and pray to the *L* your God
42: 3 Pray that the *L* your God will tell
42: 4 I will tell you everything the *L* says
42: 4 pray to the *L* your God
42: 5 with everything the *L* your God
42: 5 "May the *L* be a true and faithful
42: 6 for we will obey the *L* our God."
42: 6 we will obey the *L* our God,
42: 7 word of the *L* came to Jeremiah.
42: 9 "This is what the *L*, the God
42: 11 afraid of him, declares the *L*,
42: 13 and so disobey the *L* your God,
42: 15 This is what the *L* Almighty,
42: 15 then hear the word of the *L*,
42: 18 This is what the *L* Almighty,
42: 19 of Judah, the *L* has told you,
42: 20 me to the *L* your God
42: 20 'Pray to the *L* our God for us;
42: 21 have not obeyed the *L* your God
43: 1 everything the *L* had sent him
43: 1 the words of the *L* their God—
43: 2 The *L* our God has not sent you
43: 7 Egypt in disobedience to the *L*
43: 8 word of the *L* came to Jeremiah:
43: 10 'This is what the *L* Almighty,
44: 2 "This is what the *L* Almighty,
44: 7 this is what the *L* God Almighty,
44: 11 this is what the *L* Almighty,
44: 16 spoken to us in the name of the *L*!
44: 21 "Did not the *L* remember
44: 22 When the *L* could no longer
44: 23 and have sinned against the *L*
44: 24 the word of the *L*, all you people
44: 25 This is what the *L* Almighty,
44: 26 As surely as the Sovereign *L* lives."
44: 26 But hear the word of the *L*,
44: 26 by my great name,' says the *L*,
44: 29 declares the *L*, 'so that you will
44: 30 This is what the *L* says: 'I am going
45: 2 "This is what the *L*, the God
45: 3 The *L* has added sorrow to my pain
45: 4 to him: 'This is what the *L* says:
45: 4 ⌊The *L* said,⌋ "Say this to him:
45: 5 on all people, declares the *L*,
46: 1 This is the word of the *L* that came
46: 5 declares the *L*.
46: 10 But that day belongs to the *L*,
46: 10 For the Lord, the *L* Almighty,
46: 10 to the LORD, the *L* Almighty—
46: 13 This is the message the *L* spoke
46: 15 for the *L* will push them down.
46: 18 whose name is the *L* Almighty,
46: 23 declares the *L*,
46: 25 The *L* Almighty, the God of Israel,
46: 26 as in times past," declares the *L*.
46: 28 for I am with you," declares the *L*.
47: 1 This is the word of the *L* that came
47: 2 Gaza: This is what the *L* says:
47: 4 The *L* is about to destroy
47: 6 " 'Ah, sword of the *L*,' ⌊you cry,⌋
47: 7 rest when the *L* has commanded it,
48: 1 This is what the *L* Almighty,
48: 8 because the *L* has spoken.
48: 12 declares the *L*,
48: 15 whose name is the *L* Almighty.
48: 25 declares the *L*.
48: 26 for she has defied the *L*.
48: 30 declares the *L*,
48: 35 declares the *L*.
48: 38 declares the *L*.
48: 40 This is what the *L* says:
48: 42 because she defied the *L*.
48: 43 declares the *L*.
48: 44 declares the *L*.
48: 47 declares the *L*.
49: 1 This is what the *L* says:
49: 2 declares the *L*,
49: 2 says the *L*.
49: 5 declares the Lord, the *L* Almighty.

Jer 49: 6 declares the *L*.
49: 7 This is what the *L* Almighty says:
49: 12 This is what the *L* says: "If those
49: 13 I swear by myself," declares the *L*,
49: 14 I have heard a message from the *L*:
49: 16 declares the *L*.
49: 18 says the *L*,
49: 20 hear what the *L* has planned
49: 26 declares the *L* Almighty.
49: 28 attacked: This is what the *L* says:
49: 30 declares the *L*.
49: 31 declares the *L*,
49: 32 declares the *L*.
49: 34 This is the word of the *L* that came
49: 35 This is what the *L* Almighty says:
49: 37 declares the *L*.
49: 38 declares the *L*.
49: 39 declares the *L*.
50: 1 This is the word the *L* spoke
50: 4 declares the *L*,
50: 4 go in tears to seek the *L* their God.
50: 5 and bind themselves to the *L*
50: 7 for they sinned against the *L*,
50: 7 the *L*, the hope of their fathers.'
50: 10 declares the *L*.
50: 14 for she has sinned against the *L*.
50: 15 Since this is the vengeance of the *L*
50: 18 this is what the *L* Almighty,
50: 20 declares the *L*,
50: 21 declares the *L*.
50: 24 because you opposed the *L*.
50: 25 The *L* has opened his arsenal
50: 25 for the Sovereign *L* Almighty has
50: 28 how the *L* our God has taken
50: 29 For she has defied the *L*,
50: 30 declares the *L*.
50: 31 declares the Lord, the *L* Almighty,
50: 33 This is what the *L* Almighty says:
50: 34 the *L* Almighty is his name.
50: 35 declares the *L*—
50: 40 declares the *L*,
50: 45 hear what the *L* has planned
51: 1 This is what the *L* says:
51: 5 by their God, the *L* Almighty,
51: 10 what the *L* our God has done.'
51: 10 " 'The *L* has vindicated us;
51: 11 The *L* has stirred up the kings
51: 11 The *L* will take vengeance,
51: 12 The *L* will carry out his purpose,
51: 14 The *L* Almighty has sworn
51: 19 The *L* Almighty is his name.
51: 24 done in Zion," declares the *L*.
51: 25 declares the *L*.
51: 26 declares the *L*.
51: 33 This is what the *L* Almighty,
51: 36 Therefore, this is what the *L* says:
51: 39 declares the *L*.
51: 45 Run from the fierce anger of the *L*.
51: 48 declares the *L*.
51: 50 Remember the *L* in a distant land,
51: 52 days are coming," declares the *L*,
51: 53 declares the *L*.
51: 55 The *L* will destroy Babylon;
51: 56 For the *L* is a God of retribution;
51: 57 whose name is the *L* Almighty.
51: 58 This is what the *L* Almighty says:
51: 62 'O *L*, you have said you will
52: 2 He did evil in the eyes of the *L*,
52: 13 He set fire to the temple of the *L*,
52: 17 were at the temple of the *L*
52: 20 made for the temple of the *L*,
La 1: 5 The *L* has brought her grief
1: 9 "Look, O *L*, on my affliction,
1: 11 "Look, O *L*, and consider,
1: 12 that the *L* brought on me
1: 17 The *L* has decreed for Jacob
1: 18 "The *L* is righteous,
1: 20 "See, O *L*, how distressed I am!
2: 6 The *L* has made Zion forget
2: 7 a shout in the house of the *L*
2: 8 The *L* determined to tear down
2: 9 visions from the *L*.
2: 17 The *L* has done what he planned;
2: 20 "Look, O *L*, and consider:
3: 18 and all that I had hoped from the *L*
3: 24 to myself, "The *L* is my portion;
3: 25 *L* is good to those whose hope is
3: 26 quietly for the salvation of the *L*.

La 3: 28 for the *L* has laid it on him.
3: 40 and let us return to the *L*.
3: 50 until the *L* looks down
3: 55 I called on your name, O *L*,
3: 59 O *L*, the wrong done to me.
3: 61 O *L*, you have heard their insults,
3: 64 them back what they deserve, O *L*,
3: 66 from under the heavens of the *L*.
4: 11 The *L* has given full vent
4: 16 The *L* himself has scattered them;
5: 1 O *L*, what has happened to us;
5: 19 You, O *L*, reign forever;
5: 21 Restore us to yourself, O *L*,
Eze 1: 3 the hand of the *L* was upon him.
1: 3 the word of the *L* came
1: 28 of the likeness of the glory of the *L*.
2: 4 'This is what the Sovereign *L* says.'
3: 11 'This is what the Sovereign *L* says,'
3: 12 May the glory of the *L* be praised
3: 14 with the strong hand of the *L*
3: 16 the word of the *L* came to me:
3: 22 The hand of the *L* was
3: 23 glory of the *L* was standing there,
3: 27 'This is what the Sovereign *L* says.'
4: 13 The *L* said, "In this way the people
4: 14 Sovereign *L!* I have never defiled
5: 5 "This is what the Sovereign *L* says:
5: 7 this is what the Sovereign *L* says:
5: 8 this is what the Sovereign *L* says:
5: 11 as I live, declares the Sovereign *L*,
5: 13 will know that I the *L* have spoken
5: 15 I the *L* have spoken.
5: 17 I the *L* have spoken."
6: 1 The word of the *L* came to me:
6: 3 This is what the Sovereign *L* says
6: 3 hear the word of the Sovereign *L*.
6: 7 and you will know that I am the *L*.
6: 10 And they will know that I am the *L*
6: 11 This is what the Sovereign *L* says:
6: 13 And they will know that I am the *L*
6: 14 they will know that I am the *L*.' "
7: 1 The word of the *L* came to me:
7: 2 this is what the Sovereign *L* says
7: 4 Then you will know that I am the *L*
7: 5 "This is what the Sovereign *L* says:
7: 9 it is I the *L* who strikes the blow.
7: 27 they will know that I am the *L*."
8: 1 the hand of the Sovereign *L* came
8: 12 They say, 'The *L* does not see us;
8: 12 the *L* has forsaken the land.' "
8: 14 gate of the house of the *L*.
8: 16 backs toward the temple of the *L*
8: 16 court of the house of the *L*,
9: 3 the *L* called to the man clothed
9: 8 crying out, "Ah, Sovereign *L!*
9: 9 the land; the *L* does not see.'
9: 9 'The *L* has forsaken the land;
10: 2 The *L* said to the man clothed
10: 4 Then the glory of the *L* rose
10: 4 of the radiance of the glory of the *L*
10: 6 When the *L* commanded the man
10: 18 Then the glory of the *L* departed
11: 1 of the house of the *L* that faces east
11: 2 The *L* said to me, "Son of man,
11: 5 the Spirit of the *L* came upon me,
11: 5 "This is what the *L* says: That is
11: 7 this is what the Sovereign *L* says:
11: 8 you, declares the Sovereign *L*.
11: 10 Then you will know that I am the *L*
11: 12 And you will know that I am the *L*,
11: 13 Sovereign *L!* Will you completely
11: 14 The word of the *L* came to me:
11: 15 'They are far away from the *L*;
11: 16 'This is what the Sovereign *L* says:
11: 17 'This is what the Sovereign *L* says:
11: 21 declares the Sovereign *L*."
11: 23 The glory of the *L* went up
11: 25 exiles everything the *L* had shown
12: 1 The word of the *L* came to me:
12: 8 the word of the *L* came to me:
12: 10 'This is what the Sovereign *L* says:
12: 15 "They will know that I am the *L*,
12: 16 they will know that I am the *L*."
12: 17 The word of the *L* came to me:
12: 19 what the Sovereign *L* says about
12: 20 Then you will know that I am the *L*
12: 21 The word of the *L* came to me:
12: 23 'This is what the Sovereign *L* says:
Eze 12: 25 But I the *L* will speak what I will,
12: 25 declares the Sovereign *L*.' "
12: 26 The word of the *L* came to me:
12: 28 declares the Sovereign *L*.' "
12: 28 'This is what the Sovereign *L* says:
13: 1 The word of the *L* came to me:
13: 2 the word of the *L!* This is what
13: 3 This is what the Sovereign *L* says:
13: 5 in the battle on the day of the *L*.
13: 6 They say, "The *L* declares,"
13: 6 when the *L* has not sent them;
13: 7 *L* declares," though I have not
13: 8 this is what the Sovereign *L* says:
13: 8 you, declares the Sovereign *L*.
13: 9 know that I am the Sovereign *L*.
13: 13 this is what the Sovereign *L* says:
13: 14 and you will know that I am the *L*.
13: 16 declares the Sovereign *L*." '
13: 18 'This is what the Sovereign *L* says:
13: 20 this is what the Sovereign *L* says:
13: 21 then you will know that I am the *L*.
13: 23 then you will know that I am the *L*
14: 2 Then the word of the *L* came to me
14: 4 I the *L* will answer him myself
14: 4 'This is what the Sovereign *L* says:
14: 6 'This is what the Sovereign *L* says:
14: 7 I the *L* will answer him myself.
14: 8 Then you will know that I am the *L*
14: 9 I the *L* have persuaded that
14: 11 declares the Sovereign *L*.' "
14: 12 The word of the *L* came to me:
14: 14 declares the Sovereign *L*.
14: 16 as I live, declares the Sovereign *L*,
14: 18 as I live, declares the Sovereign *L*,
14: 20 declares the Sovereign *L*,
14: 21 this is what the Sovereign *L* says:
14: 23 declares the Sovereign *L*."
15: 1 The word of the *L* came to me:
15: 6 this is what the Sovereign *L* says:
15: 7 you will know that I am the *L*.
15: 8 declares the Sovereign *L*."
16: 1 The word of the *L* came to me:
16: 3 'This is what the Sovereign *L* says
16: 8 declares the Sovereign *L*.
16: 14 perfect, declares the Sovereign *L*.
16: 19 declares the Sovereign *L*.
16: 23 to you, declares the Sovereign *L*.
16: 30 declares the Sovereign *L*,
16: 35 prostitute, hear the word of the *L!*
16: 36 This is what the Sovereign *L* says:
16: 43 done, declares the Sovereign *L*.
16: 48 as I live, declares the Sovereign *L*,
16: 58 practices, declares the *L*.
16: 59 This is what the Sovereign *L* says.
16: 62 and you will know that I am the *L*.
16: 63 declares the Sovereign *L*.' "
17: 1 The word of the *L* came to me:
17: 3 'This is what the Sovereign *L* says:
17: 9 'This is what the Sovereign *L* says:
17: 11 Then the word of the *L* came to me
17: 16 declares the Sovereign *L*, he shall
17: 19 this is what the Sovereign *L* says:
17: 21 will know that I the *L* have spoken
17: 22 This is what the Sovereign *L* says:
17: 24 I the *L* have spoken, and I will do it
17: 24 field will know that I the *L* bring
18: 1 The word of the *L* came to me:
18: 3 as I live, declares the Sovereign *L*,
18: 9 declares the Sovereign *L*.
18: 23 wicked? declares the Sovereign *L*.
18: 30 his ways, declares the Sovereign *L*.
18: 32 anyone, declares the Sovereign *L*.
20: 1 of Israel came to inquire of the *L*,
20: 2 Then the word of the *L* came to me
20: 3 declares the Sovereign *L*.'
20: 3 'This is what the Sovereign *L* says:
20: 5 'This is what the Sovereign *L* says:
20: 5 to them, "I am the *L* your God."
20: 7 I am the *L* your God."
20: 12 know that I the *L* made them holy.
20: 19 I am the *L* your God; follow my
20: 20 know that I am the *L* your God."
20: 26 so they would know that I am the *L*
20: 27 'This is what the Sovereign *L* says:
20: 30 'This is what the Sovereign *L* says:
20: 31 as I live, declares the Sovereign *L*,
20: 33 as I live, declares the Sovereign *L*,
20: 36 you, declares the Sovereign *L*.
Eze 20: 38 Then you will know that I am the *L*
20: 39 this is what the Sovereign *L* says:
20: 40 of Israel, declares the Sovereign *L*,
20: 42 Then you will know that I am the *L*
20: 44 You will know that I am the *L*,
20: 44 declares the Sovereign *L*.' "
20: 45 The word of the *L* came to me:
20: 47 This is what the Sovereign *L* says:
20: 47 forest: 'Hear the word of the *L*.
20: 48 will see that I the *L* have kindled it;
20: 49 Then I said, "Ah, Sovereign *L!*
21: 1 The word of the *L* came to me:
21: 3 'This is what the *L* says: I am
21: 5 know that I the *L* have drawn my
21: 7 declares the Sovereign *L*."
21: 8 The word of the *L* came to me:
21: 13 declares the Sovereign *L*.'
21: 17 I the *L* have spoken."
21: 18 The word of the *L* came to me:
21: 24 this is what the Sovereign *L* says:
21: 26 this is what the Sovereign *L* says:
21: 28 is what the Sovereign *L* says about
21: 32 for I the *L* have spoken.' "
22: 1 The word of the *L* came to me:
22: 3 'This is what the Sovereign *L* says:
22: 12 me, declares the Sovereign *L*.
22: 14 I the *L* have spoken, and I will do it
22: 16 you will know that I am the *L*.' "
22: 17 Then the word of the *L* came to me
22: 19 this is what the Sovereign *L* says:
22: 22 know that I the *L* have poured out
22: 23 the word of the *L* came to me:
22: 28 'This is what the Sovereign *L* says
22: 28 when the *L* has not spoken.
22: 31 declares the Sovereign *L*."
23: 1 The word of the *L* came to me:
23: 22 this is what the Sovereign *L* says:
23: 28 this is what the Sovereign *L* says:
23: 32 "This is what the Sovereign *L* says:
23: 34 spoken, declares the Sovereign *L*.
23: 35 this is what the Sovereign *L* says:
23: 36 The *L* said to me: "Son of man,
23: 46 "This is what the Sovereign *L* says:
23: 49 know that I am the Sovereign *L*."
24: 1 the word of the *L* came to me:
24: 3 'This is what the Sovereign *L* says:
24: 6 this is what the Sovereign *L* says:
24: 9 this is what the Sovereign *L* says:
24: 14 declares the Sovereign *L*.' "
24: 14 " 'I the *L* have spoken.
24: 15 The word of the *L* came to me:
24: 20 "The word of the *L* came to me:
24: 21 'This is what the Sovereign *L* says:
24: 24 know that I am the Sovereign *L*.'
24: 27 and they will know that I am the *L*
25: 1 The word of the *L* came to me:
25: 3 This is what the Sovereign *L* says:
25: 3 'Hear the word of the Sovereign *L*.
25: 5 Then you will know that I am the *L*
25: 6 this is what the Sovereign *L* says:
25: 7 and you will know that I am the *L*
25: 8 "This is what the Sovereign *L* says:
25: 11 they will know that I am the *L*.' "
25: 12 "This is what the Sovereign *L* says:
25: 13 this is what the Sovereign *L* says:
25: 14 declares the Sovereign *L*.' "
25: 15 "This is what the Sovereign *L* says:
25: 16 this is what the Sovereign *L* says:
25: 17 they will know that I am the *L*,
26: 1 the word of the *L* came to me:
26: 3 this is what the Sovereign *L* says:
26: 5 spoken, declares the Sovereign *L*.
26: 6 they will know that I am the *L*.
26: 7 this is what the Sovereign *L* says:
26: 14 for I the *L* have spoken, declares
26: 14 spoken, declares the Sovereign *L*.
26: 15 "This is what the Sovereign *L* says
26: 19 "This is what the Sovereign *L* says:
26: 21 declares the Sovereign *L*."
27: 1 The word of the *L* came to me:
27: 3 'This is what the Sovereign *L* says:
28: 1 The word of the *L* came to me:
28: 2 'This is what the Sovereign *L* says:
28: 6 this is what the Sovereign *L* says:
28: 10 declares the Sovereign *L*.' "
28: 11 The word of the *L* came to me:
28: 12 'This is what the Sovereign *L* says:
28: 20 The word of the *L* came to me:

Eze 28: 22 They will know that I am the *L*,
28: 22 'This is what the Sovereign *L* says:
28: 23 they will know that I am the *L*.
28: 24 know that I am the Sovereign *L*.
28: 25 This is what the Sovereign *L* says:
28: 26 know that I am the *L* their God.' "
29: 1 the word of the *L* came to me:
29: 3 'This is what the Sovereign *L* says:
29: 6 in Egypt will know that I am the *L*.
29: 8 this is what the Sovereign *L* says:
29: 9 they will know that I am the *L*.
29: 13 this is what the Sovereign *L* says:
29: 16 know that I am the Sovereign *L*.' "
29: 17 the word of the *L* came to me:
29: 19 this is what the Sovereign *L* says:
29: 20 it for me, declares the Sovereign *L*.
29: 21 they will know that I am the *L*."
30: 1 The word of the *L* came to me:
30: 2 'This is what the Sovereign *L* says:
30: 3 the day of the *L* is near—
30: 6 declares the Sovereign *L*.
30: 6 " 'This is what the *L* says:
30: 8 they will know that I am the *L*,
30: 10 This is what the Sovereign *L* says:
30: 12 I the *L* have spoken.
30: 13 This is what the Sovereign *L* says:
30: 19 and they will know that I am the *L*
30: 20 the word of the *L* came to me:
30: 22 this is what the Sovereign *L* says:
30: 25 they will know that I am the *L*,
30: 26 they will know that I am the *L*."
31: 1 the word of the *L* came to me:
31: 10 this is what the Sovereign *L* says:
31: 15 This is what the Sovereign *L* says:
31: 18 declares the Sovereign *L*.' "
32: 1 the word of the *L* came to me:
32: 3 This is what the Sovereign *L* says:
32: 8 declares the Sovereign *L*.
32: 11 this is what the Sovereign *L* says:
32: 14 declares the Sovereign *L*.
32: 15 then they will know that I am the *L*
32: 16 declares the Sovereign *L*."
32: 17 the word of the *L* came to me:
32: 31 sword, declares the Sovereign *L*.
32: 32 declares the Sovereign *L*."
33: 1 The word of the *L* came to me:
33: 11 as I live, declares the Sovereign *L*,
33: 22 the hand of the *L* was upon me,
33: 23 Then the word of the *L* came to me
33: 25 'This is what the Sovereign *L* says:
33: 27 'This is what the Sovereign *L* says:
33: 29 they will know that I am the *L*,
33: 30 message that has come from the *L*.'
34: 1 The word of the *L* came to me:
34: 2 'This is what the Sovereign *L* says:
34: 7 hear the word of the *L*: As surely
34: 8 as I live, declares the Sovereign *L*,
34: 9 shepherds, hear the word of the *L*:
34: 10 This is what the Sovereign *L* says:
34: 11 this is what the Sovereign *L* says:
34: 15 lie down, declares the Sovereign *L*.
34: 17 this is what the Sovereign *L* says:
34: 20 this is what the Sovereign *L* says
34: 24 I the *L* have spoken.
34: 24 I the *L* will be their God,
34: 27 They will know that I am the *L*,
34: 30 people, declares the Sovereign *L*.
34: 30 will know that I, the *L* their God,
34: 31 declares the Sovereign *L*.' "
35: 1 The word of the *L* came to me:
35: 3 'This is what the Sovereign *L* says:
35: 4 Then you will know that I am the *L*
35: 6 as I live, declares the Sovereign *L*,
35: 9 Then you will know that I am the *L*
35: 10 even though I the *L* was there,
35: 11 as I live, declares the Sovereign *L*,
35: 12 know that I the *L* have heard all
35: 14 This is what the Sovereign *L* says:
35: 15 they will know that I am the *L*.' "
36: 1 of Israel, hear the word of the *L*.
36: 2 This is what the Sovereign *L* says:
36: 3 'This is what the Sovereign *L* says:
36: 4 This is what the Sovereign *L* says
36: 4 hear the word of the Sovereign *L*:
36: 5 this is what the Sovereign *L* says:
36: 6 'This is what the Sovereign *L* says:
36: 7 this is what the Sovereign *L* says:
36: 11 Then you will know that I am the *L*

Eze 36: 13 This is what the Sovereign *L* says:
36: 14 childless, declares the Sovereign *L*.
36: 15 declares the Sovereign *L*.' "
36: 16 the word of the *L* came to me:
36: 22 'This is what the Sovereign *L* says:
36: 23 declares the Sovereign *L*,
36: 23 nations will know that I am the *L*,
36: 32 sake, declares the Sovereign *L*.
36: 33 This is what the Sovereign *L* says:
36: 36 I the *L* have spoken, and I will do it
36: 36 know that I the *L* have rebuilt what
36: 37 "This is what the Sovereign *L* says:
36: 38 they will know that I am the *L*."
37: 1 The hand of the *L* was upon me,
37: 1 out by the Spirit of the *L*
37: 3 "O Sovereign *L*, you alone know."
37: 4 'Dry bones, hear the word of the *L*!
37: 5 This is what the Sovereign *L* says
37: 6 Then you will know that I am the *L*
37: 9 'This is what the Sovereign *L* says:
37: 12 'This is what the Sovereign *L* says:
37: 13 will know that I am the *L*,
37: 14 and I have done it, declares the *L*
37: 14 will know that I the *L* have spoken,
37: 15 The word of the *L* came to me:
37: 19 'This is what the Sovereign *L* says:
37: 21 'This is what the Sovereign *L* says:
37: 28 know that I the *L* make Israel holy,
38: 1 The word of the *L* came to me:
38: 3 'This is what the Sovereign *L* says:
38: 10 This is what the Sovereign *L* says:
38: 14 'This is what the Sovereign *L* says:
38: 17 This is what the Sovereign *L* says:
38: 18 aroused, declares the Sovereign *L*.
38: 21 declares the Sovereign *L*.
38: 23 they will know that I am the *L*.'
39: 1 'This is what the Sovereign *L* says:
39: 5 spoken, declares the Sovereign *L*.
39: 6 and they will know that I am the *L*.
39: 7 know that I the *L* am the Holy One
39: 8 place, declares the Sovereign *L*.
39: 10 them, declares the Sovereign *L*.
39: 13 for them, declares the Sovereign *L*.
39: 17 this is what the Sovereign *L* says:
39: 20 kind,' declares the Sovereign *L*.
39: 22 know that I am the *L* their God.
39: 25 this is what the Sovereign *L* says:
39: 28 know that I am the *L* their God,
39: 29 declares the Sovereign *L*."
40: 1 the hand of the *L* was upon me
40: 46 draw near to the *L* to minister
41: 22 This is the table that is before the *L*
42: 13 priests who approach the *L* will eat
43: 4 glory of the *L* entered the temple
43: 5 the glory of the *L* filled the temple.
43: 18 this is what the Sovereign *L* says:
43: 19 me, declares the Sovereign *L*.
43: 24 You are to offer them before the *L*,
43: 24 as a burnt offering to the *L*.
43: 27 declares the Sovereign *L*."
44: 2 It is to remain shut because the *L*,
44: 2 The *L* said to me, "This gate is
44: 3 to eat in the presence of the *L*.
44: 4 LORD filling the temple of the *L*,
44: 4 the glory of the *L* filling the temple
44: 5 The *L* said to me, "Son of man,
44: 5 regarding the temple of the *L*.
44: 6 'This is what the Sovereign *L* says:
44: 9 This is what the Sovereign *L* says:
44: 12 their sin, declares the Sovereign *L*.
44: 15 blood, declares the Sovereign *L*.
44: 27 himself, declares the Sovereign *L*.
44: 29 to the *L* will belong to them.
45: 1 are to present to the *L* a portion
45: 4 draw near to minister before the *L*.
45: 9 This is what the Sovereign *L* says:
45: 9 people, declares the Sovereign *L*.
45: 15 people, declares the Sovereign *L*.
45: 18 This is what the Sovereign *L* says:
45: 23 as a burnt offering to the *L*,
46: 1 This is what the Sovereign *L* says:
46: 3 presence of the *L* at the entrance
46: 4 to the *L* on the Sabbath day is
46: 9 before the *L* at the appointed feasts
46: 12 a freewill offering to the *L*—
46: 13 defect for a burnt offering to the *L*;
46: 14 to the *L* is a lasting ordinance.
46: 16 This is what the Sovereign *L* says:

Eze 47: 13 This is what the Sovereign *L* says:
47: 23 declares the Sovereign *L*.
48: 9 are to offer to the *L* will be 25,000
48: 10 of it will be the sanctuary of the *L*.
48: 14 because it is holy to the *L*.
48: 29 declares the Sovereign *L*.
48: 35 THE *L* IS THERE."
Da 9: 2 to the word of the *L* given
9: 4 I prayed to the *L* my God
9: 8 O *L*, we and our kings, our princes
9: 10 we have not obeyed the *L* our God
9: 13 favor of the *L* our God by turning
9: 14 The *L* did not hesitate
9: 14 for the *L* our God is righteous
9: 20 my request to the *L* my God
Hos 1: 1 The word of the *L* that came
1: 2 When the *L* began to speak
1: 2 adultery in departing from the *L*."
1: 2 through Hosea, the *L* said to him,
1: 4 Then the *L* said to Hosea,
1: 6 Then the *L* said to Hosea,
1: 7 horsemen, but by the *L* their God."
1: 9 the *L* said, "Call him Lo-Ammi,
2: 13 declares the *L*.
2: 16 "In that day," declares the *L*,
2: 20 and you will acknowledge the *L*.
2: 21 declares the *L*—
3: 1 as the *L* loves the Israelites,
3: 1 *L* said to me, "Go, show your love
3: 5 They will come trembling to the *L*
3: 5 seek the *L* their God and David
4: 1 because the *L* has a charge to bring
4: 1 the word of the *L*, you Israelites,
4: 10 because they have deserted the *L*
4: 15 swear, 'As surely as the *L* lives!'
4: 16 How then can the *L* pasture them
5: 4 they do not acknowledge the *L*.
5: 6 and herds to seek the *L*,
5: 7 They are unfaithful to the *L*;
6: 1 "Come, let us return to the *L*.
6: 3 Let us acknowledge the *L*;
7: 10 he does not return to the *L* his God
8: 1 An eagle is over the house of the *L*
8: 13 but the *L* is not pleased with them.
9: 4 come into the temple of the *L*.
9: 4 pour out wine offerings to the *L*,
9: 5 on the festival days of the *L*?
9: 14 Give them, O *L*—
10: 2 The *L* will demolish their altars
10: 3 because we did not revere the *L*.
10: 12 for it is time to seek the *L*,
11: 10 They will follow the *L*;
11: 11 declares the *L*.
12: 2 The *L* has a charge to bring
12: 5 the *L* God Almighty,
12: 5 the *L* is his name of renown!
12: 9 "I am the *L* your God,
12: 13 The *L* used a prophet
13: 4 "But I am the *L* your God,
13: 15 An east wind from the *L* will come,
14: 1 O Israel, to the *L* your God.
14: 2 and return to the *L*.
14: 9 The ways of the *L* are right;
Joel 1: 1 The word of the *L* that came
1: 9 are cut off from the house of the *L*.
1: 9 those who minister before the *L*.
1: 14 and cry out to the *L*.
1: 14 to the house of the *L* your God,
1: 15 For the day of the *L* is near;
1: 19 To you, O *L*, I call,
2: 1 for the day of the *L* is coming.
2: 11 The day of the *L* is great;
2: 11 The *L* thunders
2: 12 "Even now," declares the *L*,
2: 13 Return to the *L* your God,
2: 14 offerings for the *L* your God.
2: 17 them say, "Spare your people, O *L*.
2: 17 who minister before the *L*,
2: 18 the *L* will be jealous for his land
2: 19 The *L* will reply to them:
2: 21 Surely the *L* has done great things.
2: 23 rejoice in the *L* your God,
2: 26 the name of the *L* your God,
2: 27 that I am the *L* your God,
2: 31 the great and dreadful day of the *L*.
2: 32 as the *L* has said,
2: 32 on the name of the *L* will be saved;
2: 32 whom the *L* calls.

Joel 3: 8 The *L* has spoken.
3: 11 Bring down your warriors, O *L!*
3: 14 For the day of the *L* is near
3: 16 The *L* will roar from Zion
3: 16 the *L* will be a refuge for his people,
3: 17 will know that I, the *L* your God,
3: 21 The *L* dwells in Zion! The words
Am 1: 2 "The *L* roars from Zion
1: 3 This is what the *L* says:
1: 5 says the *L*.
1: 6 This is what the *L* says:
1: 8 says the Sovereign *L*.
1: 9 This is what the *L* says:
1: 11 This is what the *L* says:
1: 13 This is what the *L* says:
1: 15 says the *L*.
2: 1 This is what the *L* says:
2: 3 says the *L*.
2: 4 This is what the *L* says:
2: 4 they have rejected the law of the *L*
2: 6 This is what the *L* says:
2: 11 declares the *L*.
2: 16 declares the *L*.
3: 1 Hear this word the *L* has spoken
3: 6 has not the *L* caused it?
3: 7 the Sovereign *L* does nothing
3: 8 The Sovereign *L* has spoken—
3: 10 to do right," declares the *L*,
3: 11 this is what the Sovereign *L* says:
3: 12 This is what the *L* says:
3: 13 the Lord, the *L* God Almighty.
3: 15 declares the *L*.
4: 2 The Sovereign *L* has sworn
4: 3 declares the *L*.
4: 5 declares the Sovereign *L*.
4: 6 declares the *L*.
4: 8 declares the *L*.
4: 9 declares the *L*.
4: 10 declares the *L*.
4: 11 declares the *L*.
4: 13 the *L* God Almighty is his name.
5: 3 This is what the Sovereign *L* says:
5: 4 This is what the *L* says to the house
5: 6 Seek the *L* and live,
5: 8 the *L* is his name—
5: 14 Then the *L* God Almighty will be
5: 15 Perhaps the *L* God Almighty will
5: 16 the *L* God Almighty, says:
5: 17 says the *L*.
5: 18 long for the day of the *L?*
5: 18 long for the day of the *L!*
5: 20 the day of the *L* be darkness,
5: 27 says the *L*, whose name is God
6: 8 The Sovereign *L* has sworn
6: 8 the *L* God Almighty declares:
6: 10 not mention the name of the *L*."
6: 11 For the *L* has given the command,
6: 14 For the *L* God Almighty declares,
7: 1 what the Sovereign *L* showed me:
7: 2 I cried out, "Sovereign *L*, forgive!
7: 3 He is so small!" So the *L* relented.
7: 3 "This will not happen," the *L* said.
7: 4 The Sovereign *L* was calling
7: 4 what the Sovereign *L* showed me:
7: 5 "Sovereign *L*, I beg you, stop!
7: 6 He is so small!" So the *L* relented.
7: 6 either," the Sovereign *L* said.
7: 8 the *L* asked me, "What do you see,
7: 15 *L* took me from tending the flock
7: 16 Now then, hear the word of the *L*.
7: 17 "Therefore this is what the *L* says:
8: 1 what the Sovereign *L* showed me:
8: 2 the *L* said to me, "The time is ripe
8: 3 day," declares the Sovereign *L*,
8: 7 The *L* has sworn by the Pride
8: 9 day," declares the Sovereign *L*,
8: 11 coming," declares the Sovereign *L*,
8: 11 of hearing the words of the *L*.
8: 12 searching for the word of the *L*,
9: 5 The Lord, the *L* Almighty,
9: 6 the *L* is his name.
9: 7 declares the *L*.
9: 8 declares the *L*.
9: 8 "Surely the eyes of the Sovereign *L*
9: 12 declares the *L*, who will do these
9: 13 days are coming," declares the *L*,
9: 15 says the *L* your God.
Ob : 1 have heard a message from the *L*:
Ob : 1 what the Sovereign *L* says about
: 4 declares the *L*.
: 8 "In that day," declares the *L*,
: 15 "The day of the *L* is near
: 18 The *L* has spoken.
Jnh 1: 1 The word of the *L* came
1: 3 But Jonah ran away from the *L*
1: 3 for Tarshish to flee from the *L*.
1: 4 the *L* sent a great wind on the sea,
1: 9 I am a Hebrew and I worship the *L*,
1: 10 he was running away from the *L*,
1: 14 O *L*, have done as you pleased."
1: 14 Then they cried to the *L*, "O *L*,
1: 16 and they offered a sacrifice to the *L*
1: 16 this the men greatly feared the *L*,
1: 17 But the *L* provided a great fish
2: 1 fish Jonah prayed to the *L* his God.
2: 2 "In my distress I called to the *L*,
2: 6 O *L* my God.
2: 7 I remembered you, *L*,
2: 9 Salvation comes from the *L*."
2: 10 And the *L* commanded the fish,
3: 1 Then the word of the *L* came
3: 3 Jonah obeyed the word of the *L*
4: 2 He prayed to the *L*, "O *L*,
4: 3 Now, O *L*, take away my life,
4: 4 the *L* replied, "Have you any right
4: 6 Then the *L* God provided a vine
4: 10 *L* said, "You have been concerned
Mic 1: 1 The word of the *L* given to Micah
1: 2 that the Sovereign *L* may witness
1: 3 *L* is coming from his dwelling
1: 12 disaster has come from the *L*,
2: 3 Therefore, the *L* says:
2: 5 in the assembly of the *L*
2: 7 "Is the Spirit of the *L* angry?
2: 13 the *L* at their head."
3: 4 Then they will cry out to the *L*,
3: 5 This is what the *L* says:
3: 8 with the Spirit of the *L*,
3: 11 Yet they lean upon the *L* and say,
3: 11 "Is not the *L* among us?
4: 2 the word of the *L* from Jerusalem.
4: 2 up to the mountain of the *L*,
4: 4 for the *L* Almighty has spoken.
4: 5 we will walk in the name of the *L*
4: 6 "In that day," declares the *L*,
4: 7 The *L* will rule over them
4: 10 There the *L* will redeem you
4: 12 the thoughts of the *L*;
4: 13 their ill-gotten gains to the *L*,
5: 4 flock in the strength of the *L*,
5: 4 of the name of the *L* his God.
5: 7 like dew from the *L*,
5: 10 "In that day," declares the *L*,
6: 1 Listen to what the *L* says:
6: 2 For the *L* has a case
6: 5 know the righteous acts of the *L*."
6: 6 what shall I come before the *L*
6: 7 Will the *L* be pleased
6: 8 And what does the *L* require of you
6: 9 Listen! The *L* is calling to the city
7: 7 as for me, I watch in hope for the *L*,
7: 8 the *L* will be my light.
7: 10 "Where is the *L* your God?"
7: 17 turn in fear to the *L* our God
Na 1: 2 The *L* takes vengeance on his foes
1: 2 the *L* takes vengeance
1: 2 *L* is a jealous and avenging God;
1: 3 The *L* is slow to anger
1: 3 *L* will not leave the guilty
1: 7 The *L* is good,
1: 9 Whatever they plot against the *L*
1: 11 who plots evil against the *L*
1: 12 This is what the *L* says:
1: 14 *L* has given a command
2: 2 The *L* will restore the splendor
2: 13 declares the *L* Almighty.
3: 5 you," declares the *L* Almighty.
Hab 1: 2 How long, O *L*, must I call for help,
1: 12 O *L*, are you not from everlasting?
1: 12 O *L*, you have appointed them
2: 2 Then the *L* replied:
2: 13 not the *L* Almighty determined
2: 14 knowledge of the glory of the *L*,
2: 20 But the *L* is in his holy temple;
3: 2 I stand in awe of your deeds, O *L*.
3: 2 *L*, I have heard of your fame;
Hab 3: 8 angry with the rivers, O *L?*
3: 18 yet I will rejoice in the *L*,
3: 19 The Sovereign *L* is my strength;
Zep 1: 1 The word of the *L* that came
1: 2 declares the *L*.
1: 3 declares the *L*.
1: 5 bow down and swear by the *L*
1: 6 and neither seek the *L*
1: 6 back from following the *L*
1: 7 Be silent before the Sovereign *L*,
1: 7 The *L* has prepared a sacrifice;
1: 7 for the day of the *L* is near.
1: 10 "On that day," declares the *L*,
1: 12 who think, 'The *L* will do nothing,
1: 14 on the day of the *L* will be bitter,
1: 14 "The great day of the *L* is near—
1: 17 they have sinned against the *L*.
2: 2 anger of the *L* comes upon you,
2: 3 Seek the *L*, all you humble
2: 5 the word of the *L* is against you,
2: 7 The *L* their God will care for them;
2: 9 declares the *L* Almighty, the God
2: 10 of the *L* Almighty.
2: 11 The *L* will be awesome to them
3: 2 She does not trust in the *L*,
3: 5 The *L* within her is righteous;
3: 8 for me," declares the *L*,
3: 9 call on the name of the *L*
3: 12 who trust in the name of the *L*.
3: 15 The *L* has taken away your
3: 15 The *L*, the King of Israel, is
3: 17 The *L* your God is with you,
3: 20 says the *L*.
Hag 1: 1 the word of the *L* came
1: 2 This is what the *L* Almighty says:
1: 3 Then the word of the *L* came
1: 5 this is what the *L* Almighty says:
1: 7 This is what the *L* Almighty says:
1: 8 and be honored," says the *L*.
1: 9 Why?" declares the *L* Almighty.
1: 12 And the people feared the *L*.
1: 12 the voice of the *L* their God
1: 12 the *L* their God had sent him.
1: 13 message of the *L* to the people:
1: 13 "I am with you," declares the *L*.
1: 14 So the *L* stirred up the spirit
1: 14 on the house of the *L* Almighty,
2: 1 the word of the *L* came
2: 4 O Zerubbabel,' declares the *L*.
2: 4 declares the *L*, 'and work.
2: 4 with you,' declares the *L* Almighty
2: 6 "This is what the *L* Almighty says:
2: 7 with glory,' says the *L* Almighty.
2: 8 is mine,' declares the *L* Almighty.
2: 9 declares the *L* Almighty."
2: 9 house,' says the *L* Almighty.
2: 10 the word of the *L* came
2: 11 "This is what the *L* Almighty says:
2: 14 nation in my sight,' declares the *L*.
2: 17 turn to me,' declares the *L*.
2: 20 The word of the *L* came
2: 23 declares the *L* Almighty."
2: 23 son of Shealtiel,' declares the *L*,
2: 23 that day,' declares the *L* Almighty.
Zec 1: 1 the word of the *L* came
1: 2 "The *L* was very angry
1: 3 This is what the *L* Almighty says:
1: 3 to me,' declares the *L* Almighty,
1: 3 to you,' says the *L* Almighty.
1: 4 This is what the *L* Almighty says:
1: 4 pay attention to me,' declares the *L*
1: 6 'The *L* Almighty has done
1: 7 the word of the *L* came
1: 10 "They are the ones the *L* has sent
1: 11 they reported to the angel of the *L*,
1: 12 angel of the *L* said, "*L* Almighty,
1: 13 the *L* spoke kind and comforting
1: 14 This is what the *L* Almighty says:
1: 16 declares the *L* Almighty.
1: 16 "Therefore, this is what the *L* says,
1: 17 This is what the *L* Almighty says:
1: 17 and the *L* will again comfort Zion
1: 20 the *L* showed me four craftsmen.
2: 5 declares the *L*, 'and I will be its
2: 6 land of the north," declares the *L*,
2: 6 winds of heaven," declares the *L*.
2: 8 this is what the *L* Almighty says:
2: 9 know that the *L* Almighty has sent

Zec 2:10 live among you," declares the *L*.
2:11 joined with the *L* in that day
2:11 know that the *L* Almighty has sent
2:12 The *L* will inherit Judah
2:13 Be still before the *L*, all mankind,
3: 1 standing before the angel of the *L*,
3: 2 The *L*, who has chosen Jerusalem,
3: 2 *L* said to Satan, "The *L* rebuke you,
3: 5 while the angel of the *L* stood by.
3: 6 The angel of the *L* gave this charge
3: 7 "This is what the *L* Almighty says:
3: 9 on it,' says the *L* Almighty,
3:10 declares the *L* Almighty."
4: 6 by my Spirit,' says the *L* Almighty.
4: 6 the word of the *L* to Zerubbabel:
4: 8 Then the word of the *L* came to me
4: 9 know that the *L* Almighty has sent
4:10 These seven are the eyes of the *L*,
4:14 to serve the *L* of all the earth."
5: 4 The *L* Almighty declares,
6: 9 The word of the *L* came to me:
6:12 and build the temple of the *L*.
6:12 this is what the *L* Almighty says:
6:13 who will build the temple of the *L*,
6:14 a memorial in the temple of the *L*.
6:15 diligently obey the *L* your God."
6:15 help to build the temple of the *L*,
6:15 know that the *L* Almighty has sent
7: 1 word of the *L* came to Zechariah
7: 2 to entreat the *L* by asking
7: 3 of the house of the *L* Almighty
7: 4 the word of the *L* Almighty came
7: 7 not the words the *L* proclaimed
7: 8 And the word of the *L* came again
7: 9 "This is what the *L* Almighty says:
7:12 So the *L* Almighty was very angry.
7:12 the words that the *L* Almighty had
7:13 not listen,' says the *L* Almighty.
8: 1 of the *L* Almighty came to me.
8: 2 This is what the *L* Almighty says:
8: 3 This is what the *L* says: "I will
8: 3 of the *L* Almighty will be called
8: 4 This is what the *L* Almighty says:
8: 6 This is what the *L* Almighty says:
8: 6 to me?" declares the *L* Almighty.
8: 7 This is what the *L* Almighty says:
8: 9 This is what the *L* Almighty says:
8: 9 for the house of the *L* Almighty,
8:11 the past," declares the *L* Almighty.
8:14 This is what the *L* Almighty says:
8:14 says the *L* Almighty,
8:17 I hate all this," declares the *L*.
8:18 of the *L* Almighty came to me.
8:19 This is what the *L* Almighty says:
8:20 This is what the *L* Almighty says:
8:21 the *L* and seek the *L* Almighty.
8:22 Jerusalem to seek the *L* Almighty
8:23 This is what the *L* Almighty says:
9: 1 The word of the *L* is
9: 1 are on the *L*—
9: 4 *L* will take away her possessions
9:14 The Sovereign *L* will sound
9:14 Then the *L* will appear over them;
9:15 the *L* Almighty will shield them.
9:16 The *L* their God will save them
10: 1 Ask the *L* for rain in the springtime
10: 1 it is the *L* who makes the storm
10: 3 for the *L* Almighty will care
10: 5 Because the *L* is with them,
10: 6 for I am the *L* their God
10: 7 their hearts will rejoice in the *L*.
10:12 I will strengthen them in the *L*
10:12 declares the *L*.
11: 4 This is what the *L* my God says:
11: 5 who sell them say, 'Praise the *L*,
11: 6 people of the land," declares the *L*.
11:11 me knew it was the word of the *L*.
11:13 And the *L* said to me, "Throw it
11:13 into the house of the *L* to the potter
11:15 Then the *L* said to me, "Take again
12: 1 word of the *L* concerning Israel.
12: 1 *L*, who stretches out the heavens,
12: 4 with madness," declares the *L*.
12: 5 the *L* Almighty is their God.'
12: 7 "The *L* will save the dwellings
12: 8 Angel of the *L* going before them.
12: 8 On that day the *L* will shield those
13: 2 more," declares the *L* Almighty.
Zec 13: 7 declares the *L* Almighty.
13: 8 In the whole land," declares the *L*,
13: 9 they will say, 'The *L* is our God.' "
14: 1 A day of the *L* is coming
14: 3 Then the *L* will go out
14: 5 Then the *L* my God will come,
14: 7 nighttime—a day known to the *L*.
14: 9 On that day there will be one *L*,
14: 9 The *L* will be king
14:12 with which the *L* will strike all
14:13 stricken by the *L* with great panic.
14:16 the *L* Almighty, and to celebrate
14:17 *L* Almighty, they will have no rain.
14:18 *L* will bring on them the plague he
14:20 HOLY TO THE *L*
14:21 holy to the *L* Almighty,
14:21 in the house of the *L* Almighty.
Mal 1: 1 The word of the *L* to Israel
1: 2 Esau Jacob's brother?" the *L* says.
1: 2 "I have loved you," says the *L*.
1: 4 always under the wrath of the *L*.
1: 4 this is what the *L* Almighty says:
1: 5 is the *L*— even beyond the borders
1: 6 due me?" says the *L* Almighty.
1: 8 accept you?" says the *L* Almighty.
1: 9 you?"—says the *L* Almighty.
1:10 with you," says the *L* Almighty,
1:11 the nations," says the *L* Almighty.
1:13 from your hands?" says the *L*.
1:13 says the *L* Almighty.
1:14 a great king," says the *L* Almighty,
2: 2 says the *L* Almighty, "I will send
2: 4 continue," says the *L* Almighty.
2: 7 the messenger of the *L* Almighty.
2: 8 with Levi," says the *L* Almighty.
2:11 the sanctuary the *L* loves,
2:12 may the *L* cut him
2:12 offerings to the *L* Almighty.
2:14 It is because the *L* is acting
2:15 Has not the *L* made them one?
2:16 his garment," says the *L* Almighty.
2:16 "I hate divorce," says the *L* God
2:17 You have wearied the *L*
2:17 good in the eyes of the *L*,
3: 1 will come," says the *L* Almighty.
3: 3 the *L* will have men who will bring
3: 4 will be acceptable to the *L*,
3: 5 not fear me," says the *L* Almighty.
3: 6 "I the *L* do not change.
3: 7 to you," says the *L* Almighty.
3:10 me in this," says the *L* Almighty,
3:11 their fruit," says the *L* Almighty.
3:12 land," says the *L* Almighty.
3:13 things against me," says the *L*.
3:14 mourners before the *L* Almighty?
3:16 and the *L* listened and heard.
3:16 concerning those who feared the *L*
3:16 those who feared the *L* talked
3:17 will be mine," says the *L* Almighty,
4: 1 them on fire," says the *L* Almighty.
4: 3 these things," says the *L* Almighty.
4: 5 and dreadful day of the *L* comes.

†LORD'S (†LORD)

Ge 4:16 Cain went out from the *L* presence
38: 7 was wicked in the *L* sight;
38:10 he did was wicked in the *L* sight;
Ex 4:14 the *L* anger burned against Moses
9:29 may know that the earth is the *L*.
12:11 Eat it in haste; it is the *L* Passover.
12:41 all the *L* divisions left Egypt.
12:48 to celebrate the *L* Passover must
16: 3 died by the *L* hand in Egypt!
24: 3 and told the people all the *L* words
29:11 Slaughter it in the *L* presence
34:34 he entered the *L* presence
Lev 3:16 All the fat is the *L*.
4: 2 in any of the *L* commands—
4:13 in any of the *L* commands,
4:27 in any of the *L* commands,
5:15 regard to any of the *L* holy things,
5:17 in any of the *L* commands,
6:22 It is the *L* regular share
10: 7 the *L* anointing oil is on you."
23: 4 " 'These are the *L* appointed feasts,
23: 5 The *L* Passover begins at twilight
23: 6 day of that month the *L* Feast
23:34 of the seventh month the *L* Feast
Lev 23:37 These are the *L* appointed feasts,
23:38 to those for the *L* Sabbaths
27:26 a cow or a sheep, it is the *L*.
Nu 3:39 at the *L* command by Moses
4:37 to the *L* command through Moses.
4:41 according to the *L* command.
4:45 to the *L* command through Moses.
4:49 At the *L* command through Moses,
9: 7 kept from presenting the *L* offering
9:10 may still celebrate the *L* Passover.
9:13 he did not present the *L* offering
9:14 to celebrate the *L* Passover must
9:18 At the *L* command the Israelites
9:19 the Israelites obeyed the *L* order
9:20 at the *L* command they would
9:23 At the *L* command they encamped
9:23 They obeyed the *L* order,
9:23 and at the *L* command they set out.
10:13 at the *L* command through Moses.
11:23 Moses, "Is the *L* arm too short?
11:29 that all the *L* people were prophets
13: 3 So at the *L* command Moses sent
14:41 you disobeying the *L* command?
14:44 the ark of the *L* covenant moved
15:23 any of the *L* commands to you
15:31 he has despised the *L* word
16: 3 yourselves above the *L* assembly?"
16: 9 to do the work at the *L* tabernacle
16:41 "You have killed the *L* people,"
17: 9 the staffs from the *L* presence
18:26 tenth of that tithe as the *L* offering.
18:28 tithes you must give the *L* portion
18:29 present as the *L* portion the best
19:13 himself defiles the *L* tabernacle.
20: 4 did you bring the *L* community
20: 9 the staff from the *L* presence,
25: 3 the *L* anger burned against them.
25: 4 so that the *L* fierce anger may turn
27:17 so the *L* people will not be like
28:16 of the first month the *L* Passover is
31: 3 and to carry out the *L* vengeance
31:16 so that a plague struck the *L* people
31:29 to Eleazar the priest as the *L* part.
31:30 for the care of the *L* tabernacle."
31:41 to Eleazar the priest as the *L* part,
31:47 for the care of the *L* tabernacle.
32:10 The *L* anger was aroused that day
32:13 The *L* anger burned against Israel
33: 2 At the *L* command Moses
33:38 At the *L* command Aaron
36: 5 at the *L* command Moses gave this
Dt 1:43 rebelled against the *L* command
2:15 The *L* hand was against them
6:18 is right and good in the *L* sight,
7: 4 the *L* anger will burn against you
9: 8 At Horeb you aroused the *L* wrath
9:18 doing what was evil in the *L* sight
10:13 and to observe the *L* commands
11:17 the *L* anger will burn against you,
15: 2 *L* time for canceling debts has been
18: 5 and minister in the *L* name always.
29:27 Therefore the *L* anger burned
32: 9 For the *L* portion is his people,
33:21 he carried out the *L* righteous will,
Jos 5:15 commander of the *L* army replied,
6: 8 of the *L* covenant followed them.
6:24 into the treasury of the *L* house.
7: 1 the *L* anger burned against Israel.
15:13 with the *L* command to him,
17: 4 according to the *L* command.
21:45 Not one of all the *L* good promises
22:19 over to the *L* land, where the *L*
22:28 Look at the replica of the *L* altar,
22:31 the Israelites from the *L* hand."
23:16 the *L* anger will burn against you,
Jdg 2:17 of obedience to the *L* commands.
3: 4 they would obey the *L* commands,
11:31 from the Ammonites will be the *L*,
18: 6 Your journey has the *L* approval."
Ru 1:13 the *L* hand has gone out against me
1Sa 1: 9 by the doorpost of the *L* temple.
2: 8 foundations of the earth are the *L*;
2:17 men was very great in the *L* sight,
2:17 they were treating the *L* offering
2:24 spreading among the *L* people.
2:25 for it was the *L* will to put them
4: 3 ark of the *L* covenant from Shiloh,
4: 5 the ark of the *L* covenant came

†This entry represents the translation of the Hebrew name for God, *Yahweh*, always indicated in the NIV by LORD. For Lord, see the concordance entries ***LORD** and ***LORD'S**.

1Sa 5: 6 The *L* hand was heavy
5: 9 the *L* hand was against that city,
13: 12 and I have not sought the *L* favor.'
13: 14 you have not kept the *L* command
14: 3 the son of Eli, the *L* priest in Shiloh
15: 13 carried out the *L* instructions."
15: 24 I violated the *L* command
16: 6 "Surely the *L* anointed stands here
17: 47 the battle is the *L*, and he will give
24: 6 the *L* anointed, or lift my hand
24: 10 because he is the *L* anointed.'
25: 28 because he fights the *L* battles.
26: 9 a hand on the *L* anointed
26: 11 a hand on the *L* anointed.
26: 16 guard your master, the *L* anointed.
26: 19 from my share in the *L* inheritance
26: 23 a hand on the *L* anointed.
30: 26 from the plunder of the *L* enemies
2Sa 1: 14 hand to destroy the *L* anointed?"
1: 16 'I killed the *L* anointed.' "
6: 7 The *L* anger burned against Uzzah
6: 8 the *L* wrath had broken out
6: 21 ruler over the *L* people Israel—
15: 25 If I find favor in the *L* eyes,
19: 21 He cursed the *L* anointed."
20: 19 to swallow up the *L* inheritance?"
21: 3 you will bless the *L* inheritance?"
1Ki 2: 33 may there be the *L* peace forever."
7: 48 that were in the *L* temple:
7: 51 in the treasuries of the *L* temple.
8: 1 ark of the *L* covenant from Zion,
8: 6 ark of the *L* covenant to its place
9: 15 conscripted to build the *L* temple,
10: 9 Because of the *L* eternal love
11: 10 did not keep the *L* command.
14: 28 the king went to the *L* temple,
15: 5 any of the *L* commands all the days
15: 18 in the treasuries of the *L* temple
18: 4 killing off the *L* prophets,
18: 13 of the *L* prophets in two caves,
18: 18 have abandoned the *L* commands
18: 22 one of the *L* prophets left,
2Ki 9: 6 king over the *L* people Israel.
9: 7 the blood of all the *L* servants shed
11: 17 that they would be the *L* people.
13: 3 the *L* anger burned against Israel,
13: 4 Then Jehoahaz sought the *L* favor,
13: 17 "The *L* arrow of victory, the arrow
20: 9 "This is the *L* sign
22: 13 Great is the *L* anger that burns
24: 3 according to the *L* command,
24: 20 because of the *L* anger that all this
1Ch 2: 3 was wicked in the *L* sight;
13: 10 The *L* anger burned against Uzzah,
13: 11 the *L* wrath had broken out
2Ch 1: 3 which Moses the *L* servant had
5: 2 ark of the *L* covenant from Zion,
5: 7 ark of the *L* covenant to its place
7: 6 with the *L* musical instruments,
12: 11 the king went to the *L* temple,
12: 12 the *L* anger turned from him,
15: 8 front of the portico of the *L* temple.
16: 2 of the treasuries of the *L* temple
23: 16 the king would be the *L* people.
23: 19 at the gates of the *L* temple
24: 12 carpenters to restore the *L* temple,
24: 14 made articles for the *L* temple:
24: 20 do you disobey the *L* commands?
24: 21 in the courtyard of the *L* temple.
26: 19 the incense altar in the *L* temple,
28: 11 for the *L* fierce anger rests on you."
28: 24 He shut the doors of the *L* temple
29: 6 away from the *L* dwelling place
29: 16 of the *L* temple everything unclean
29: 19 They are now in front of the *L* altar
30: 21 accompanied by the *L* instruments
31: 2 at the gates of the *L* dwelling.
32: 25 therefore the *L* wrath was on him
32: 26 therefore the *L* wrath did not come
34: 10 the work on the *L* temple.
34: 21 Great is the *L* anger that is poured
35: 2 them in the service of the *L* temple.
36: 18 and the treasures of the *L* temple
Ezr 3: 6 of the *L* temple had not yet been
Ps 24: 1 The earth is the *L*, and everything
32: 10 but the *L* unfailing love
37: 20 *L* enemies will be like the beauty
89: 1 of the *L* great love forever;
Ps 103: 17 *L* love is with those who fear him,
109: 20 May this be the *L* payment
118: 15 "The *L* right hand has done mighty
118: 16 The *L* right hand is lifted high;
118: 16 the *L* right hand has done mighty
Pr 3: 11 do not despise the *L* discipline
3: 33 The *L* curse is on the house
19: 21 but it is the *L* purpose that prevails.
22: 14 is under the *L* wrath will fall
Isa 2: 2 of the *L* temple will be established
5: 25 Therefore the *L* anger burns
14: 2 and maidservants in the *L* land.
24: 14 west they acclaim the *L* majesty.
30: 9 to listen to the *L* instruction.
38: 7 " 'This is the *L* sign
40: 2 she has received from the *L* hand
44: 5 write on his hand, 'The *L*,'
48: 14 The *L* chosen ally
49: 4 Yet what is due me is in the *L* hand
53: 10 Yet it was the *L* will to crush him
55: 13 This will be for the *L* renown,
58: 13 and the *L* holy day honorable,
61: 2 to proclaim the year of the *L* favor
62: 3 of splendor in the *L* hand,
Jer 7: 2 "Stand at the gate of the *L* house
12: 13 because of the *L* fierce anger."
13: 17 the *L* flock will be taken captive.
19: 14 stood in the court of the *L* temple
20: 2 Gate of Benjamin at the *L* temple.
20: 3 The *L* name for you is not Pashhur,
23: 35 'What is the *L* answer?'
23: 37 'What is the *L* answer to you?'
25: 17 So I took the cup from the *L* hand
25: 38 and because of the *L* fierce anger.
26: 2 in the courtyard of the *L* house
26: 9 in the *L* name that this house will
26: 10 of the New Gate of the *L* house.
27: 16 from the *L* house will be brought
28: 3 the articles of the *L* house that
28: 6 bringing the articles of the *L* house
36: 5 I cannot go to the *L* temple.
36: 8 at the *L* temple he read the words
36: 10 people at the *L* temple the words
43: 4 people disobeyed the *L* command
48: 10 lax in doing the *L* work!
50: 13 of the *L* anger she will not be
51: 6 It is time for the *L* vengeance;
51: 7 was a gold cup in the *L* hand;
51: 29 for the *L* purposes
51: 51 the holy places of the *L* house."
52: 3 because of the *L* anger that all this
La 2: 22 In the day of the *L* anger
3: 22 of the *L* great love we are not
4: 20 *L* anointed, our very life breath,
Eze 7: 19 them in the day of the *L* wrath.
10: 19 to the east gate of the *L* house,
36: 20 of them, 'These are the *L* people,
Hos 9: 3 They will not remain in the *L* land;
Joel 3: 18 will flow out of the *L* house
Ob : 21 And the kingdom will be the *L*.
Mic 4: 1 of the *L* temple will be established
6: 2 O mountains, the *L* accusation;
7: 9 I will bear the *L* wrath,
Hab 2: 16 from the *L* right hand is coming
Zep 1: 8 On the day of the *L* sacrifice
1: 18 them on the day of the *L* wrath.
2: 2 of the *L* wrath comes upon you.
2: 3 sheltered on the day of the *L* anger.
Hag 1: 2 come for the *L* house to be built.' "
1: 13 Then Haggai, the *L* messenger,
2: 15 laid on another in the *L* temple.
2: 18 of the *L* temple was laid.
Zec 13: 3 you have told lies in the *L* name.'
14: 20 pots in the *L* house will be like
Mal 1: 7 saying that the *L* table is
2: 13 You flood the *L* altar with tears.

LOSE (LOSES LOSS LOSSES LOST)

Ge 26: 9 Because I thought I might *l* my life
27: 45 Why should I *l* both of you
Dt 1: 28 Our brothers have made us *l* heart.
Jdg 18: 25 and your family will *l* your lives."
1Sa 17: 32 "Let no one *l* heart on account
2Sa 22: 46 They all *l* heart;
Ps 18: 45 They all *l* heart;
Pr 25: 10 and you will never *l* your bad
Isa 7: 4 Do not *l* heart because of these two
19: 3 The Egyptians will *l* heart,
19: 9 the weavers of fine linen will *l* hope
Jer 4: 9 and the officials will *l* heart,
17: 4 Through your own fault you will *l*
51: 46 Do not *l* heart or be afraid
Da 11: 30 will oppose him, and he will *l* heart.
Zec 9: 5 Gaza will *l* her king
Mt 5: 29 for you to *l* one part of your body
5: 30 for you to *l* one part of your body
10: 39 Whoever finds his life will *l* it,
10: 42 he will certainly not *l* his reward."
16: 25 wants to save his life will *l* it,
Mk 8: 35 wants to save his life will *l* it,
9: 41 will certainly not *l* his reward.
Lk 9: 24 wants to save his life will *l* it,
9: 25 and yet *l* or forfeit his very self?
16: 4 do so that, when I *l* my job here,
17: 33 tries to keep his life will *l* it,
Jn 6: 39 that I shall *l* none of all that he has
12: 25 The man who loves his life will *l* it,
Ac 19: 27 that our trade will *l* its good name,
27: 34 Not one of you will *l* a single hair
2Co 4: 1 this ministry, we do not *l* heart.
4: 16 Therefore we do not *l* heart.
Heb 12: 3 will not grow weary and *l* heart.
12: 5 do not *l* heart when he rebukes you
2Jn : 8 that you do not *l* what you have

LOSES (LOSE)

Dt 22: 3 or his cloak or anything he *l*.
1Sa 20: 7 if he *l* his temper, you can be sure
Isa 44: 12 He gets hungry and *l* his strength;
Mt 5: 13 But if the salt *l* its saltiness,
10: 39 whoever *l* his life for my sake will
16: 25 whoever *l* his life for me will find it.
Mk 8: 35 but whoever *l* his life for me
9: 50 "Salt is good, but if it *l* its saltiness,
Lk 9: 24 whoever *l* his life for me will save it
14: 34 "Salt is good, but if it *l* its saltiness,
15: 4 you has a hundred sheep and *l* one
15: 8 has ten silver coins and *l* one.
17: 33 whoever *l* his life will preserve it.

LOSS (LOSE)

Ge 31: 39 by wild beasts; I bore the *l* myself.
Ex 21: 19 man for the *l* of his time
21: 34 owner of the pit must pay for the *l*;
22: 15 paid for the hire covers the *l*.
Isa 47: 8 or suffer the *l* of children.'
47: 9 *l* of children and widowhood.
Jer 22: 10 for the dead king or mourn his *l*;
Da 6: 2 so that the king might not suffer *l*
Jn 11: 19 them in the *l* of their brother
13: 22 at a *l* to know which
Ac 25: 20 was at a *l* how to investigate such
27: 10 and bring great *l* to ship and cargo,
27: 21 yourselves this damage and *l*.
Ro 11: 12 and their *l* means riches
1Co 3: 15 he will suffer *l*; he himself will be
Php 3: 7 was to my profit I now consider *l*
3: 8 I consider everything a *l* compared
Heb 6: 6 to their *l* they are crucifying

LOSSES (LOSE)

1Sa 4: 17 and the army has suffered heavy *l*.
23: 5 He inflicted heavy *l*
1Ki 20: 21 inflicted heavy *l* on the Arameans.
2Ch 13: 17 his men inflicted heavy *l* on them,

LOST (LOSE)

Ge 34: 19 *l* no time in doing what they said,
Ex 14: 5 and have *l* their services!"
22: 9 any other *l* property about which
Lev 6: 3 or if he finds *l* property
6: 4 or the *l* property he found,
13: 40 "When a man has *l* his hair
13: 41 If he has *l* his hair from the front
Nu 11: 6 But now we have *l* our appetite;
17: 12 "We will die! We are *l*, we are all *l*!
1Sa 4: 10 Israel *l* thirty thousand foot
9: 3 to Saul's father Kish were *l*,
9: 20 the donkeys you *l* three days ago,
25: 18 Abigail *l* no time.
2Sa 4: 1 he *l* courage, and all Israel became
1Ki 20: 25 raise an army like the one you *l*—
Ne 6: 16 our enemies *l* their self-confidence,
Ps 73: 2 I had nearly *l* my foothold.
119:176 I have strayed like a *l* sheep.
Ecc 5: 14 wealth *l* through some misfortune,

Jer 18: 18 of the law by the priest will not be *l*,
50: 6 "My people have been *l* sheep;
La 4: 1 How the gold has *l* its luster,
Eze 7: 26 of the law by the priest will be *l*,
34: 4 the strays or searched for the *l*.
34: 16 for the *l* and bring back the strays.
Zec 11: 16 the land who will not care for the *l*,
Mt 10: 6 Go rather to the *l* sheep of Israel.
15: 24 only to the *l* sheep of Israel."
18: 14 any of these little ones should be *l*.
Lk 15: 4 go after the *l* sheep until he finds it?
15: 6 with me; I have found my *l* sheep.'
15: 9 with me; I have found my *l* coin.'
15: 24 is alive again; he was *l* and is found
15: 32 is alive again; he was *l* and is found
19: 10 to seek and to save what was *l*."
Jn 17: 12 None has been *l* except the one
18: 9 "I have not *l* one of those you gave
Ac 27: 9 Much time had been *l*,
27: 22 because not one of you will be *l*;
1Co 15: 18 have fallen asleep in Christ are *l*.
Eph 4: 19 Having *l* all sensitivity, they have
Php 3: 8 for whose sake I have *l* all things.
Col 2: 19 He has *l* connection with the Head,
Rev 12: 8 and they *l* their place in heaven.

LOT (LOT'S LOTS)

Ge 11: 27 And Haran became the father of *L*.
11: 31 his grandson *L* son of Haran,
12: 4 LORD had told him; and *L* went
12: 5 took his wife Sarai, his nephew *L*,
13: 1 and everything he had, and *L* went
13: 5 Now *L*, who was moving about
13: 7 herdsmen and the herdsmen of *L*.
13: 8 said to *L*, "Let's not have any
13: 10 *L* looked up and saw that the whole
13: 11 *L* chose for himself the whole plain
13: 12 while *L* lived among the cities
13: 14 said to Abram after *L* had parted
14: 12 also carried off Abram's nephew *L*
14: 16 and brought back his relative *L*
19: 1 and *L* was sitting in the gateway
19: 5 to *L*, "Where are the men who
19: 6 *L* went outside to meet them
19: 9 They kept bringing pressure on *L*
19: 10 and pulled *L* back into the house
19: 12 to *L*, "Do you have anyone else
19: 14 So *L* went out and spoke
19: 15 the angels urged *L*, saying, "Hurry!
19: 18 But *L* said to them, "No, my lords,
19: 23 By the time *L* reached Zoar,
19: 29 he brought *L* out of the catastrophe
19: 29 the cities where *L* had lived.
19: 30 *L* and his two daughters left Zoar
Lev 16: 8 one *l* for the LORD and the other
16: 9 shall bring the goat whose *l* falls
16: 10 But the goat chosen by *l*
Nu 26: 55 that the land is distributed by *l*.
26: 56 distributed by *l* among the larger
33: 54 Distribute the land by *l*, according
33: 54 falls to them by *l* will be theirs.
34: 13 land by *l* as an inheritance.
36: 2 an inheritance to the Israelites by *l*,
Dt 2: 9 Ar to the descendants of *L*
2: 19 to the descendants of *L*."
Jos 14: 2 by *l* to the nine-and-a-half tribes,
18: 11 The *l* came up for the tribe
19: 1 The second *l* came out for the tribe
19: 10 The third *l* came up for Zebulun,
19: 17 The fourth *l* came out for Issachar,
19: 24 The fifth *l* came out for the tribe
19: 32 The sixth *l* came out for Naphtali,
19: 40 The seventh *l* came out
19: 51 of Israel assigned by *l* at Shiloh
21: 4 The first *l* came out
21: 10 because the first *l* fell to them):
Jdg 20: 9 up against it as the *l* directs.
1Sa 14: 41 Jonathan and Saul were taken by *l*,
14: 42 "Cast the *l* between me
1Ch 6: 54 because the first *l* was for them):
24: 7 The first *l* fell to Jehoiarib,
25: 9 The first *l*, which was for Asaph,
26: 14 The *l* for the East Gate fell
26: 14 the *l* for the North Gate fell to him.
26: 15 The *l* for the South Gate fell
26: 15 and the *l* for the storehouse fell
Est 3: 7 And the *l* fell on the twelfth month,
3: 7 the *l*) in the presence of Haman
Est 9: 24 the *l*) for their ruin and destruction.
Job 31: 2 For what is man's *l* from God
Ps 11: 6 a scorching wind will be their *l*.
16: 5 you have made my *l* secure.
50: 18 you throw in your *l* with adulterers
83: 8 to the descendants of *L*.
Pr 1: 14 throw in your *l* with us,
6: 33 Blows and disgrace are his *l*,
16: 33 The *l* is cast into the lap,
18: 18 Casting the *l* settles disputes
Ecc 3: 22 his work, because that is his *l*.
5: 18 has given him—for this is his *l*.
5: 19 to accept his *l* and be happy
9: 9 For this is your *l* in life
Isa 17: 14 the *l* of those who plunder us.
57: 6 they, they are your *l*.
Jer 13: 25 This is your *l*,
Eze 21: 22 Into his right hand will come the *l*
Jnh 1: 7 They cast lots and the *l* fell
Mic 2: 5 to divide the land by *l*.
Lk 1: 9 he was chosen by *l*, according
17: 28 "It was the same in the days of *L*.
17: 29 But the day *L* left Sodom,
Jn 19: 24 "Let's decide by *l* who will get it."
Ac 1: 26 Then they drew lots, and the *l* fell
2Pe 2: 7 if he rescued *L*, a righteous man,

LOT'S (LOT)

Ge 19: 26 But *L* wife looked back
19: 36 of *L* daughters became pregnant
Lk 17: 32 Remember *L* wife! Whoever tries

LOTAN (LOTAN'S)

Ge 36: 20 *L*, Shobal, Zibeon, Anah, Dishon,
36: 22 The sons of *L*: Hori and Homam.
36: 29 *L*, Shobal, Zibeon, Anah, Dishon,
1Ch 1: 38 The sons of Seir: *L*, Shobal, Zibeon
1: 39 The sons of *L*: Hori and Homam.

LOTAN'S (LOTAN)

Ge 36: 22 Timna was *L* sister.
1Ch 1: 39 Timna was *L* sister.

LOTIONS

2Sa 12: 20 put on *l* and changed his clothes,
14: 2 and don't use any cosmetic *l*.
Da 10: 3 and I used no *l* at all until the three
Am 6: 6 and use the finest *l*,

LOTS (LOT)

Lev 16: 8 He is to cast *l* for the two goats—
Jos 18: 6 I will cast *l* for you in the presence
18: 8 I will cast *l* for you here at Shiloh
18: 10 Joshua then cast *l* for them
1Ch 24: 5 them impartially by drawing *l*,
24: 31 also cast *l*, just as their brothers
25: 8 as student, cast *l* for their duties.
26: 13 *L* were cast for each gate,
26: 14 *l* were cast for his son Zechariah,
26: 16 The *l* for the West Gate
Ne 10: 34 have cast *l* to determine when each
11: 1 of the people cast *l* to bring one out
Job 6: 27 even cast *l* for the fatherless
Ps 22: 18 and cast *l* for my clothing.
Eze 21: 21 He will cast *l* with arrows,
24: 6 piece without casting *l* for them.
Joel 3: 3 They cast *l* for my people
Ob : 11 and cast *l* for Jerusalem,
Jnh 1: 7 They cast *l* and the lot fell
1: 7 let us cast *l* to find out who is
Na 3: 10 *L* were cast for her nobles,
Mt 27: 35 divided up his clothes by casting *l*.
Mk 15: 24 they cast *l* to see what each would
Lk 23: 34 divided up his clothes by casting *l*.
Jn 19: 24 and cast *l* for my clothing."
Ac 1: 26 Then they drew *l*, and the lot fell

LOTUS (LOTUSES)

Job 40: 21 Under the *l* plants he lies,

LOTUSES (LOTUS)

Job 40: 22 The *l* conceal him in their shadow;

LOUNGE (LOUNGING)

Am 6: 4 and *l* on your couches.

LOUNGING (LOUNGE)

Isa 47: 8 *l* in your security

Am 6: 7 your feasting and *l* will end.

LOVE (BELOVED LOVED LOVELY LOVER LOVER'S LOVERS LOVES LOVING LOVING-KINDNESS)

Ge 20: 13 'This is how you can show your *l*
22: 2 your only son Isaac, whom you *l*,
29: 18 Jacob was in *l* with Rachel and said
29: 20 days to him because of his *l* for her.
29: 32 Surely my husband will *l* me now."
Ex 15: 13 "In your unfailing *l* you will lead
20: 6 showing *l* to thousands who *l* me
21: 5 'I *l* my master and my wife
34: 6 abounding in *l* and faithfulness,
34: 7 maintaining *l* to thousands,
Lev 19: 18 but *l* your neighbor as yourself.
19: 34 *L* him as yourself,
Nu 14: 18 abounding in *l* and forgiving sin
14: 19 In accordance with your great *l*,
Dt 5: 10 showing *l* to thousands who *l* me
6: 5 *L* the LORD your God
7: 9 generations of those who *l* him
7: 9 keeping his covenant of *l*
7: 12 God will keep his covenant of *l*
7: 13 He will *l* you and bless you
10: 12 to walk in all his ways, to *l* him,
10: 19 you are to *l* those who are aliens,
11: 1 *L* the LORD your God
11: 13 to *l* the LORD your God
11: 22 to *l* the LORD your God,
13: 3 you *l* him with all your heart
13: 6 wife you *l*, or your closest friend
19: 9 to *l* the LORD your God
21: 15 the son of the wife he does not *l*,
21: 16 the son of the wife he does not *l*.
30: 6 so that you may *l* him
30: 16 today to *l* the LORD your God,
30: 20 and that you may *l* the LORD your
33: 3 Surely it is you who *l* the people;
Jos 22: 5 to *l* the LORD your God, to walk
23: 11 careful to *l* the LORD your God.
Jdg 5: 31 may they who *l* you be like the sun
14: 16 You hate me! You don't really *l* me
16: 4 he fell in *l* with a woman
16: 15 "How can you say, 'I *l* you,'
1Sa 18: 20 Saul's daughter Michal was in *l*
20: 17 had David reaffirm his oath out of *l*
2Sa 1: 26 Your *l* for me was wonderful,
7: 15 But my *l* will never be taken away
13: 1 son of David fell in *l* with Tamar,
13: 4 said to him, "I'm in *l* with Tamar,
16: 17 "Is this the *l* you show your friend?
19: 6 You *l* those who hate you
19: 6 hate you and hate those who *l* you.
1Ki 3: 3 Solomon showed his *l*
8: 23 you who keep your covenant of *l*
10: 9 of the LORD's eternal *l* for Israel,
11: 2 Solomon held fast to them in *l*.
1Ch 16: 34 his *l* endures forever.
16: 41 "for his *l* endures forever."
17: 13 I will never take my *l* away
2Ch 5: 13 his *l* endures forever."
6: 14 you who keep your covenant of *l*
7: 3 his *l* endures forever."
7: 6 saying, "His *l* endures forever."
9: 8 Because of the *l* of your God
19: 2 and *l* those who hate the LORD?
20: 21 for his *l* endures forever."
Ezr 3: 11 his *l* to Israel endures forever."
Ne 1: 5 covenant of *l* with those who *l* him
9: 17 slow to anger and abounding in *l*.
9: 32 who keeps his covenant of *l*,
13: 22 to me according to your great *l*.
Job 15: 34 of those who *l* bribes.
19: 19 those I *l* have turned against me.
37: 13 or to water his earth and show his *l*.
Ps 4: 2 How long will you *l* delusions
5: 11 that those who *l* your name may
6: 4 save me because of your unfailing *l*.
11: 5 wicked and those who *l* violence
13: 5 But I trust in your unfailing *l*;
17: 7 Show the wonder of your great *l*,
18: 1 I *l* you, O LORD, my strength.
21: 7 through the unfailing *l*
23: 6 Surely goodness and *l* will follow
25: 6 O LORD, your great mercy and *l*,
25: 7 according to your *l* remember me,
26: 3 for your *l* is ever before me,

Ps 26: 8 I *l* the house where you live,
31: 7 I will be glad and rejoice in your *l*,
31: 16 save me in your unfailing *l*.
31: 21 for he showed his wonderful *l*
31: 23 *L* the LORD, all his saints!
32: 10 but the LORD's unfailing *l*
33: 5 the earth is full of his unfailing *l*.
33: 18 whose hope is in his unfailing *l*,
33: 22 May your unfailing *l* rest upon us,
36: 5 Your *l*, O LORD, reaches
36: 7 How priceless is your unfailing *l*!
36: 10 Continue your *l* to those who know
40: 10 I do not conceal your *l*
40: 11 may your *l* and your truth always
40: 16 may those who *l* your salvation
42: 8 By day the LORD directs his *l*,
44: 26 of your unfailing *l*.
45: 7 You *l* righteousness and hate
48: 9 we meditate on your unfailing *l*.
51: 1 according to your unfailing *l*;
52: 3 You *l* evil rather than good,
52: 4 You *l* every harmful word,
52: 8 I trust in God's unfailing *l*
57: 3 God sends his *l* and his faithfulness
57: 10 For great is your *l*, reaching
59: 16 in the morning I will sing of your *l*;
60: 5 that those you *l* may be delivered.
61: 7 appoint your *l* and faithfulness
63: 3 Because your *l* is better than life,
66: 20 or withheld his *l* from me!
69: 13 in your great *l*, O God,
69: 16 out of the goodness of your *l*;
69: 36 and those who *l* his name will dwell
70: 4 may those who *l* your salvation
77: 8 Has his unfailing *l* vanished forever
85: 7 Show us your unfailing *l*, O LORD
85: 10 *L* and faithfulness meet together;
86: 5 abounding in *l* to all who call
86: 13 For great is your *l* toward me;
86: 15 abounding in *l* and faithfulness.
88: 11 Is your *l* declared in the grave,
89: 1 of the LORD's great *l* forever;
89: 2 declare that your *l* stands firm
89: 14 *l* and faithfulness go before you.
89: 24 My faithful *l* will be with him,
89: 28 I will maintain my *l* to him forever,
89: 33 but I will not take my *l* from him,
89: 49 where is your former great *l*,
90: 14 with your unfailing *l*,
92: 2 to proclaim your *l* in the morning
94: 18 your *l*, O LORD, supported me.
97: 10 Let those who *l* the LORD hate
98: 3 He has remembered his *l*
100: 5 is good and his *l* endures forever;
101: 1 I will sing of your *l* and justice;
103: 4 crowns me with *l* and compassion.
103: 8 slow to anger, abounding in *l*.
103: 11 so great is his *l* for those who fear
103: 17 LORD's *l* is with those who fear
106: 1 his *l* endures forever.
106: 45 and out of his great *l* he relented.
107: 1 his *l* endures forever.
107: 8 to the LORD for his unfailing *l*
107: 15 to the LORD for his unfailing *l*
107: 21 to the LORD for his unfailing *l*
107: 31 to the LORD for his unfailing *l*
107: 43 consider the great *l* of the LORD.
108: 4 For great is your *l*, higher
108: 6 that those you *l* may be delivered.
109: 21 out of the goodness of your *l*,
109: 26 save me in accordance with your *l*.
115: 1 because of your *l* and faithfulness.
116: 1 I *l* the LORD, for he heard my
117: 2 For great is his *l* toward us,
118: 1 his *l* endures forever.
118: 2 "His *l* endures forever."
118: 3 "His *l* endures forever."
118: 4 "His *l* endures forever."
118: 29 his *l* endures forever.
119: 41 May your unfailing *l* come to me,
119: 47 because I *l* them.
119: 48 for your commandments, which I *l*,
119: 64 The earth is filled with your *l*,
119: 76 May your unfailing *l* be my
119: 88 my life according to your *l*,
119: 97 Oh, how I *l* your law!
119:113 but I *l* your law.
119:119 therefore I *l* your statutes.
Ps 119:124 your servant according to your *l*
119:127 Because I *l* your commands
119:132 to those who *l* your name.
119:149 in accordance with your *l*;
119:159 O LORD, according to your *l*.
119:159 See how I *l* your precepts;
119:163 but I *l* your law.
119:165 peace have they who *l* your law,
119:167 for I *l* them greatly.
122: 6 "May those who *l* you be secure.
130: 7 for with the LORD is unfailing *l*
136: 1 *His l endures forever.*
136: 2 *His l endures forever.*
136: 3 *His l endures forever.*
136: 4 *His l endures forever.*
136: 5 *His l endures forever.*
136: 6 *His l endures forever.*
136: 7 *His l endures forever.*
136: 8 *His l endures forever.*
136: 9 *His l endures forever.*
136: 10 *His l endures forever.*
136: 11 *His l endures forever.*
136: 12 *His l endures forever.*
136: 13 *His l endures forever.*
136: 14 *His l endures forever.*
136: 15 *His l endures forever.*
136: 16 *His l endures forever.*
136: 17 *His l endures forever.*
136: 18 *His l endures forever.*
136: 19 *His l endures forever.*
136: 20 *His l endures forever.*
136: 21 *His l endures forever.*
136: 22 *His l endures forever.*
136: 23 *His l endures forever.*
136: 24 *His l endures forever.*
136: 25 *His l endures forever.*
136: 26 *His l endures forever.*
138: 2 for your *l* and your faithfulness,
138: 8 your *l*, O LORD, endures forever
143: 8 of your unfailing *l*,
143: 12 In your unfailing *l*, silence my
145: 8 slow to anger and rich in *l*.
145: 20 over all who *l* him,
147: 11 who put their hope in his unfailing *l*
Pr 1: 22 you simple ones *l* your simple
3: 3 Let *l* and faithfulness never leave
4: 6 *l* her, and she will watch over you.
5: 19 you ever be captivated by her *l*.
7: 18 let's drink deep of *l* till morning;
7: 18 let's enjoy ourselves with *l*!
8: 17 I *l* those who *l* me,
8: 21 wealth on those who *l* me
8: 36 all who hate me *l* death."
9: 8 rebuke a wise man and he will *l* you
10: 12 but *l* covers over all wrongs.
14: 22 those who plan what is good find *l*
15: 17 of vegetables where there is *l*
16: 6 Through *l* and faithfulness sin is
17: 9 over an offense promotes *l*,
18: 21 and those who *l* it will eat its fruit.
19: 22 What a man desires is unfailing *l*;
20: 6 claims to have unfailing *l*,
20: 13 Do not *l* sleep or you will grow
20: 28 *L* and faithfulness keep a king safe;
20: 28 through *l* his throne is made secure
21: 21 who pursues righteousness and *l*
27: 5 rebuke than hidden *l*.
Ecc 3: 8 a time to *l* and a time to hate,
9: 1 but no man knows whether *l*
9: 6 Their *l*, their hate
9: 9 life with your wife, whom you *l*,
SS 1: 2 for your *l* is more delightful
1: 3 No wonder the maidens *l* you!
1: 4 we will praise your *l* more
1: 7 you whom I *l*, where you graze
2: 4 and his banner over me is *l*.
2: 5 for I am faint with *l*.
2: 7 Do not arouse or awaken *l*
3: 5 Do not arouse or awaken *l*
4: 10 How delightful is your *l*, my sister,
4: 10 How much more pleasing is your *l*
5: 8 Tell him I am faint with *l*.
7: 6 O *l*, with your delights!
7: 12 there I will give you my *l*.
8: 4 Do not arouse or awaken *l*
8: 6 for *l* is as strong as death,
8: 7 Many waters cannot quench *l*;
8: 7 all the wealth of his house for *l*,
Isa 1: 23 they all *l* bribes
5: 1 I will sing for the one I *l*
16: 5 In *l* a throne will be established;
38: 17 In your *l* you kept me
43: 4 and because I *l* you,
54: 10 yet my unfailing *l* for you will not
55: 3 my faithful *l* promised to David.
56: 6 to *l* the name of the LORD,
56: 10 they *l* to sleep.
57: 8 a pact with those whose beds you *l*,
61: 8 "For I, the LORD, *l* justice;
63: 9 In his *l* and mercy he redeemed
66: 10 all you who *l* her;
Jer 2: 25 I *l* foreign gods,
2: 33 How skilled you are at pursuing *l*!
5: 31 and my people *l* it this way.
12: 7 I will give the one I *l*
14: 10 "They greatly *l* to wander;
16: 5 my *l* and my pity from this people
31: 3 you with an everlasting *l*;
32: 18 You show *l* to thousands
33: 11 his *l* endures forever."
La 3: 22 of the LORD's great *l* we are not
3: 32 so great is his unfailing *l*.
Eze 16: 8 saw that you were old enough for *l*,
23: 17 of *l*, and in their lust they defiled
33: 32 more than one who sings *l* songs
Da 9: 4 covenant of *l* with all who *l* him
Hos 1: 6 for I will no longer show *l*
1: 7 Yet I will show *l* to the house
2: 4 I will not show my *l* to her children
2: 19 in *l* and compassion.
2: 23 I will show my *l* to the one I called
3: 1 Go, show your *l* to your wife again,
3: 1 and *l* the sacred raisin cakes."
3: 1 *L* her as the LORD loves
4: 1 "There is no faithfulness, no *l*,
4: 18 their rulers dearly *l* shameful ways.
6: 4 Your *l* is like the morning mist,
9: 1 you *l* the wages of a prostitute
9: 15 I will no longer *l* them;
10: 12 reap the fruit of unfailing *l*,
11: 4 with ties of *l*;
12: 6 maintain *l* and justice,
14: 4 and *l* them freely,
Joel 2: 13 slow to anger and abounding in *l*,
Am 4: 5 for this is what you *l* to do,"
5: 15 Hate evil, *l* good;
Jnh 4: 2 slow to anger and abounding in *l*,
Mic 3: 2 you who hate good and *l* evil;
6: 8 To act justly and to *l* mercy
Zep 3: 17 he will quiet you with his *l*,
Zec 8: 17 and do not *l* to swear falsely.
8: 19 Therefore *l* truth and peace."
Mt 3: 17 "This is my Son, whom I *l*;
5: 43 '*L* your neighbor and hate your
5: 44 *L* your enemies and pray
5: 46 you *l* those who *l* you, what reward
6: 5 for they *l* to pray standing
6: 24 he will hate the one and *l* the other,
12: 18 the one I *l*, in whom I delight;
17: 5 "This is my Son, whom I *l*;
19: 19 and '*l* your neighbor as yourself.' "
22: 37 " '*L* the Lord your God
22: 39 '*L* your neighbor as yourself.'
23: 6 they *l* the place of honor
23: 7 they *l* to be greeted
24: 12 the *l* of most will grow cold,
Mk 1: 11 "You are my Son, whom I *l*;
9: 7 "This is my Son, whom I *l*.
12: 30 *L* the Lord your God
12: 31 '*L* your neighbor as yourself.'
12: 33 To *l* him with all your heart,
12: 33 and to *l* your neighbor
Lk 3: 22 "You are my Son, whom I *l*;
6: 27 you who hear me: *L* your enemies,
6: 32 Even 'sinners' *l* those who *l* them.
6: 32 you *l* those who *l* you, what credit
6: 35 *l* your enemies, do good to them,
7: 42 which of them will *l* him more?"
10: 27 and, '*L* your neighbor as yourself
10: 27 " '*L* the Lord your God
11: 42 you neglect justice and the *l* of God
11: 43 you *l* the most important seats
16: 13 he will hate the one and *l* the other,
20: 13 whom I *l*; perhaps they will respect
20: 46 *l* to be greeted in the marketplaces
Jn 5: 42 I know that you do not have the *l*

Jn 8: 42 were your Father, you would *l* me,
11: 3 "Lord, the one you *l* is sick."
13: 1 them the full extent of his *l*.
13: 34 I give you: *L* one another.
13: 34 so you must *l* one another.
13: 35 disciples if you *l* one another."
14: 15 "If you *l* me, you will obey what I
14: 21 I too will *l* him and show myself
14: 23 My Father will *l* him, and we will
14: 24 He who does not *l* me will not obey
14: 31 world must learn that I *l* the Father
15: 9 Now remain in my *l*.
15: 10 commands and remain in his *l*.
15: 10 you will remain in my *l*,
15: 12 *L* each other as I have loved you.
15: 13 Greater *l* has no one than this,
15: 17 This is my command: *L* each other.
15: 19 to the world, it would *l* you
17: 26 known in order that the *l* you have
21: 15 do you truly *l* me more than these
21: 15 he said, "you know that I *l* you."
21: 16 Yes, Lord, you know that I *l* you."
21: 16 do you truly *l* me?" He answered,
21: 17 all things; you know that I *l* you."
21: 17 "Do you *l* me?" He said, "Lord,
21: 17 "Simon son of John, do you *l* me?"
Ro 5: 5 because God has poured out his *l*
5: 8 God demonstrates his own *l* for us
8: 28 for the good of those who *l* him,
8: 35 us from the *l* of Christ?
8: 39 us from the *l* of God that is
12: 9 *L* must be sincere.
12: 10 to one another in brotherly *l*.
13: 8 continuing debt to *l* one another,
13: 9 "*L* your neighbor as yourself."
13: 10 Therefore *l* is the fulfillment
13: 10 *L* does no harm to its neighbor.
14: 15 you are no longer acting in *l*.
15: 30 and by the *l* of the Spirit,
16: 8 Greet Ampliatus, whom I *l*
1Co 2: 9 prepared for those who *l* him"—
4: 17 my son whom I *l*, who is faithful
4: 21 or in *l* and with a gentle spirit?
8: 1 Knowledge puffs up, but *l* builds up
13: 1 have not *l*, I am only a resounding
13: 2 but have not *l*, I am nothing.
13: 3 but have not *l*, I gain nothing.
13: 4 Love is patient, *l* is kind.
13: 4 *L* is patient, love is kind.
13: 6 *L* does not delight in evil
13: 8 *L* never fails.
13: 13 But the greatest of these is *l*.
13: 13 three remain: faith, hope and *l*.
14: 1 way of *l* and eagerly desire spiritual
16: 14 Do everything in *l*.
16: 22 If anyone does not *l* the Lord—
16: 24 My *l* to all of you in Christ Jesus.
2Co 2: 4 to let you know the depth of my *l*
2: 8 therefore, to reaffirm your *l* for him
5: 14 For Christ's *l* compels us,
6: 6 in the Holy Spirit and in sincere *l*;
8: 7 complete earnestness and in your *l*
8: 8 sincerity of your *l* by comparing it
8: 24 show these men the proof of your *l*
11: 11 Why? Because I do not *l* you?
12: 15 If I *l* you more, will you *l* me less?
13: 11 And the God of *l* and peace will be
13: 14 of the Lord Jesus Christ, and the *l*
Gal 5: 6 is faith expressing itself through *l*.
5: 13 rather, serve one another in *l*.
5: 14 "*L* your neighbor as yourself."
5: 22 But the fruit of the Spirit is *l*, joy,
Eph 1: 4 In *l* he predestined us
1: 15 and your *l* for all the saints,
2: 4 But because of his great *l* for us,
3: 17 being rooted and established in *l*,
3: 18 and high and deep is the *l* of Christ,
3: 19 and to know this *l* that surpasses
4: 2 bearing with one another in *l*.
4: 15 Instead, speaking the truth in *l*,
4: 16 grows and builds itself up in *l*,
5: 2 loved children and live a life of *l*,
5: 25 *l* your wives, just as Christ loved
5: 28 husbands ought to *l* their wives
5: 33 each one of you also must *l* his wife
6: 23 *l* with faith from God the Father
6: 24 Christ with an undying *l*.
6: 24 to all who *l* our Lord Jesus Christ

Php 1: 9 that your *l* may abound more
1: 16 so in *l*, knowing that I am put here
2: 1 from his *l*, if any fellowship
2: 2 having the same *l*, being one
4: 1 you whom I *l* and long for,
Col 1: 4 of the *l* you have for all the saints—
1: 5 *l* that spring from the hope that is
1: 8 also told us of your *l* in the Spirit.
2: 2 in heart and united in *l*,
3: 14 And over all these virtues put on *l*,
3: 19 *l* your wives and do not be harsh
1Th 1: 3 your labor prompted by *l*,
3: 6 good news about your faith and *l*.
3: 12 May the Lord make your *l* increase
4: 9 about brotherly *l* we do not need
4: 9 taught by God to *l* each other.
4: 10 you do *l* all the brothers
5: 8 on faith and *l* as a breastplate,
5: 13 them in the highest regard in *l*
2Th 1: 3 and the *l* every one of you has
2: 10 because they refused to *l* the truth
3: 5 direct your hearts into God's *l*
1Ti 1: 5 The goal of this command is *l*,
1: 14 and *l* that are in Christ Jesus.
2: 15 *l* and holiness with propriety.
4: 12 in life, in *l*, in faith and in purity.
6: 10 For the *l* of money is a root
6: 11 faith, *l*, endurance and gentleness.
2Ti 1: 7 of power, of *l* and of self-discipline.
1: 13 with faith and *l* in Christ Jesus.
2: 22 and pursue righteousness, faith, *l*
3: 3 unholy, without *l*, unforgiving,
3: 10 faith, patience, *l*, endurance,
Tit 2: 2 in faith, in *l* and in endurance.
2: 4 women to *l* their husbands
3: 4 and *l* of God our Savior appeared,
3: 15 Greet those who *l* us in the faith.
Phm : 5 and your *l* for all the saints.
: 7 Your *l* has given me great joy
: 9 yet I appeal to you on the basis of *l*.
Heb 6: 10 and the *l* you have shown him
10: 24 may spur one another on toward *l*
13: 5 free from the *l* of money
Jas 1: 12 promised to those who *l* him.
2: 5 he promised those who *l* him?
2: 8 "*L* your neighbor as yourself,"
1Pe 1: 8 you have not seen him, you *l* him;
1: 22 the truth so that you have sincere *l*
1: 22 *l* one another deeply,
2: 17 *L* the brotherhood of believers,
3: 8 be sympathetic, *l* as brothers,
3: 10 "Whoever would *l* life
4: 8 Above all, *l* each other deeply,
4: 8 *l* covers over a multitude of sins.
5: 14 Greet one another with a kiss of *l*.
2Pe 1: 7 and to brotherly kindness, *l*.
1: 17 "This is my Son, whom I *l*;
1Jn 2: 5 God's *l* is truly made complete
2: 15 Do not *l* the world or anything
2: 15 the *l* of the Father is not in him.
3: 1 How great is the *l* the Father has
3: 10 anyone who does not *l* his brother.
3: 11 We should *l* one another.
3: 14 Anyone who does not *l* remains
3: 14 because we *l* our brothers.
3: 16 This is how we know what *l* is:
3: 17 how can the *l* of God be in him?
3: 18 let us not *l* with words or tongue
3: 23 to *l* one another as he commanded
4: 7 Dear friends, let us *l* one another,
4: 7 for *l* comes from God.
4: 8 Whoever does not *l* does not know
4: 8 not know God, because God is *l*.
4: 9 This is how God showed his *l*
4: 10 This is *l*: not that we loved God,
4: 11 we also ought to *l* one another.
4: 12 and his *l* is made complete in us.
4: 12 seen God; but if we *l* each other,
4: 16 God is *l*.
4: 16 Whoever lives in *l* lives in God,
4: 16 and rely on the *l* God has for us.
4: 17 *L* is made complete among us
4: 18 But perfect *l* drives out fear,
4: 18 There is no fear in *l*.
4: 18 who fears is not made perfect in *l*.
4: 19 We *l* because he first loved us.
4: 20 If anyone says, "I *l* God,"
4: 20 anyone who does not *l* his brother,

1Jn 4: 20 whom he has seen, cannot *l* God.
4: 21 loves God must also *l* his brother.
5: 2 we know that we *l* the children
5: 3 This is *l* for God: to obey his
2Jn : 1 whom I *l* in the truth—
: 3 will be with us in truth and *l*.
: 5 I ask that we *l* one another.
: 6 his command is that you walk in *l*.
: 6 this is *l*: that we walk in obedience
3Jn : 1 To my dear friend Gaius, whom I *l*
: 6 have told the church about your *l*.
Jude : 2 peace and *l* be yours in abundance.
: 12 men are blemishes at your *l* feasts,
: 21 Keep yourselves in God's *l*
Rev 2: 4 You have forsaken your first *l*.
2: 19 I know your deeds, your *l* and faith
3: 19 Those whom I *l* I rebuke
12: 11 they did not *l* their lives so much

LOVED (LOVE)

Ge 24: 67 she became his wife, and he *l* her;
25: 28 *l* Esau, but Rebekah *l* Jacob.
29: 30 and he *l* Rachel more than Leah.
29: 31 the LORD saw that Leah was not *l*,
29: 33 the LORD heard that I am not *l*,
34: 3 and he *l* the girl and spoke tenderly
37: 3 Now Israel *l* Joseph more than any
37: 4 saw that their father *l* him more
Dt 4: 37 Because he *l* your forefathers
7: 8 But it was because the LORD *l* you
10: 15 on your forefathers and *l* them,
1Sa 1: 5 a double portion because he *l* her,
18: 1 in spirit with David, and he *l* him
18: 3 with David because he *l* him
18: 16 But all Israel and Judah *l* David,
18: 28 that his daughter Michal *l* David,
20: 17 because he *l* him as he *l* himself.
2Sa 1: 23 in life they were *l* and gracious,
12: 24 The LORD *l* him; and
12: 25 and because the LORD *l* him,
13: 15 hated her more than he had *l* her.
1Ki 11: 1 *l* many foreign women
2Ch 11: 21 Rehoboam *l* Maacah daughter
26: 10 in the fertile lands, for he *l* the soil.
Ne 13: 26 He was *l* by his God, and God
Ps 44: 3 light of your face, for you *l* them.
47: 4 the pride of Jacob, whom he *l*.
78: 68 Mount Zion, which he *l*.
88: 18 taken my companions and *l* ones
109: 17 He *l* to pronounce a curse—
Isa 5: 1 My *l* one had a vineyard
Jer 2: 2 how as a bride you *l* me
8: 2 which they have *l* and served
31: 3 "I have *l* you with an everlasting
Eze 16: 37 those you *l* as well as those you
Hos 2: 1 and of your sisters, 'My *l* one.'
2: 23 to the one I called 'Not my *l* one.'
3: 1 though she is *l* by another
9: 10 became as vile as the thing they *l*.
11: 1 "When Israel was a child, I *l* him,
Mal 1: 2 "But you ask, 'How have you *l* us?'
1: 2 "I have *l* you," says the LORD.
1: 2 "Yet I have *l* Jacob, but Esau I
Mk 10: 21 Jesus looked at him and *l* him.
12: 6 left to send, a son, whom he *l*.
Lk 7: 47 been forgiven—for she *l* much.
16: 14 The Pharisees, who *l* money,
Jn 3: 16 so *l* the world that he gave his one
3: 19 but men *l* darkness instead of light
11: 5 Jesus *l* Martha and her sister
11: 36 "See how he *l* him!" But some
12: 43 for they *l* praise from men more
13: 1 Having *l* his own who were
13: 23 the disciple whom Jesus *l*,
13: 34 As I have *l* you, so you must love
14: 21 He who loves me will be *l*
14: 28 If you *l* me, you would be glad that
15: 9 the Father has *l* me, so have I *l* you.
15: 12 Love each other as I have *l* you.
16: 27 loves you because you have *l* me
17: 23 have *l* them even as you have *l* me.
17: 24 you *l* me before the creation
19: 26 the disciple whom he *l* standing
20: 2 one Jesus *l*, and said, "They have
21: 7 the disciple whom Jesus *l* said
21: 20 whom Jesus *l* was following
Ro 1: 7 To all in Rome who are *l* by God
8: 37 conquerors through him who *l* us.

Ro 9: 13 "Jacob I *l*, but Esau I hated."
9: 25 her 'my *l* one' who is not my *l* one,"
11: 28 they are *l* on account
Gal 2: 20 who *l* me and gave himself for me.
Eph 5: 1 as dearly *l* children and live a life
5: 2 as Christ *l* us and gave himself up
5: 25 just as Christ *l* the church
Col 3: 12 and dearly *l*, clothe yourselves
1Th 1: 4 Brothers *l* by God, we know that
2: 8 We *l* you so much that we were
2Th 2: 13 for you, brothers *l* by the Lord,
2: 16 who *l* us and by his grace gave us
2Ti 4: 10 for Demas, because he *l* this world,
Heb 1: 9 You have *l* righteousness
2Pe 2: 15 who *l* the wages of wickedness.
1Jn 4: 10 This is love: not that we *l* God,
4: 10 but that he *l* us and sent his Son
4: 11 Dear friends, since God so *l* us,
4: 19 We love because he first *l* us.
Jude : 1 who are *l* by God the Father
Rev 3: 9 and acknowledge that I have *l* you.

LOVELY (LOVE)

Ge 29: 17 but Rachel was *l* in form,
Est 1: 11 and nobles, for she was *l* to look at.
2: 7 was *l* in form and features,
Ps 84: 1 How *l* is your dwelling place,
SS 1: 5 Dark am I, yet *l*,
2: 14 and your face is *l*.
4: 3 your mouth is *l*.
5: 16 he is altogether *l*.
6: 4 *l* as Jerusalem,
Am 8: 13 *l* young women and strong young
Php 4: 8 whatever is *l*, whatever is

LOVER (LOVE)

SS 1: 13 My *l* is to me a sachet of myrrh
1: 14 My *l* is to me a cluster
1: 16 How handsome you are, my *l*!
2: 3 is my *l* among the young men.
2: 8 Listen! My *l*!
2: 9 My *l* is like a gazelle or a young
2: 10 My *l* spoke and said to me,
2: 16 My *l* is mine and I am his;
2: 17 turn, my *l*,
4: 16 Let my *l* come into his garden
5: 2 Listen! My *l* is knocking.
5: 4 My *l* thrust his hand
5: 5 I arose to open for my *l*,
5: 6 I opened for my *l*,
5: 6 but my *l* had left; he was gone.
5: 8 if you find my *l*,
5: 10 My *l* is radiant and ruddy,
5: 16 This is my *l*, this my friend,
6: 1 Where has your *l* gone,
6: 1 Which way did your *l* turn,
6: 2 My *l* has gone
6: 3 I am my lover's and my *l* is mine;
7: 9 May the wine go straight to my *l*,
7: 10 I belong to my *l*,
7: 11 my *l*, let us go to the countryside,
7: 13 that I have stored up for you, my *l*.
8: 5 leaning on her *l*?
8: 14 Come away, my *l*,
1Ti 3: 3 not quarrelsome, not a *l* of money.

LOVER'S (LOVE)

SS 6: 3 I am my *l* and my lover is mine;

LOVERS (LOVE)

SS 5: 1 drink your fill, O *l*.
Jer 3: 1 as a prostitute with many *l*—
3: 2 the roadside you sat waiting for *l*,
4: 30 Your *l* despise you;
La 1: 2 Among all her *l*
Eze 16: 33 but you give gifts to all your *l*,
16: 36 in your promiscuity with your *l*,
16: 37 I am going to gather all your *l*,
16: 39 Then I will hand you over to your *l*,
16: 41 and you will no longer pay your *l*.
23: 5 she lusted after her *l*, the Assyrians
23: 9 I handed her over to her *l*,
23: 20 There she lusted after her *l*,
23: 22 I will stir up your *l* against you,
Hos 2: 5 She said, 'I will go after my *l*,
2: 7 She will chase after her *l*
2: 10 lewdness before the eyes of her *l*;
2: 12 she said were her pay from her *l*;
Hos 2: 13 and went after her *l*,
8: 9 Ephraim has sold herself to *l*.
2Ti 3: 2 People will be *l* of themselves,
3: 2 *l* of money, boastful, proud,
3: 3 without self-control, brutal, not *l*
3: 4 *l* of pleasure rather than *l* of God—

LOVES (LOVE)

Ge 44: 20 sons left, and his father *l* him.'
Dt 10: 18 and *l* the alien, giving him food
15: 16 because he *l* you and your family
21: 15 and he *l* one but not the other,
21: 16 son of the wife he *l* in preference
23: 5 because the LORD your God *l* you
28: 54 wife he *l* or his surviving children,
28: 56 will begrudge the husband she *l*
33: 12 and the one the LORD *l* rests
Ru 4: 15 who *l* you and who is better to you
2Ch 2: 11 "Because the LORD *l* his people,
Ps 11: 7 he *l* justice;
33: 5 The LORD *l* righteousness
34: 12 Whoever of you *l* life
37: 28 For the LORD *l* the just
87: 2 the LORD *l* the gates of Zion
91: 14 Because he *l* me," says the LORD,
99: 4 The King is mighty, he *l* justice—
119: 140 and your servant *l* them.
127: 2 for he grants sleep to those he *l*.
146: 8 the LORD *l* the righteous.
Pr 3: 12 the LORD disciplines those he *l*,
12: 1 Whoever *l* discipline *l* knowledge,
13: 24 he who *l* him is careful
15: 9 he *l* those who pursue
17: 17 A friend *l* at all times,
17: 19 He who *l* a quarrel *l* sin;
19: 8 He who gets wisdom *l* his own soul
21: 17 He who *l* pleasure will become
21: 17 whoever *l* wine and oil will never
22: 11 He who *l* a pure heart and whose
29: 3 A man who *l* wisdom brings joy
Ecc 5: 10 Whoever *l* money never has
5: 10 whoever *l* wealth is never satisfied
SS 3: 1 I looked for the one my heart *l*;
3: 2 I will search for the one my heart *l*.
3: 3 "Have you seen the one my heart *l*
3: 4 when I found the one my heart *l*.
Hos 3: 1 as the LORD *l* the Israelites,
10: 11 that *l* to thresh;
12: 7 he *l* to defraud.
Mal 2: 11 the sanctuary the LORD *l*,
Mt 10: 37 anyone who *l* his son or daughter
10: 37 "Anyone who *l* his father
Lk 7: 5 because he *l* our nation
7: 47 has been forgiven little *l* little."
Jn 3: 35 Father *l* the Son and has placed
5: 20 For the Father *l* the Son
10: 17 reason my Father *l* me is that I lay
12: 25 The man who *l* his life will lose it,
14: 21 He who *l* me will be loved
14: 21 obeys them, he is the one who *l* me.
14: 23 Jesus replied, "If anyone *l* me,
16: 27 the Father himself *l* you
Ro 13: 8 for he who *l* his fellow man has
1Co 8: 3 But the man who *l* God is known
2Co 9: 7 for God *l* a cheerful giver
Eph 1: 6 has freely given us in the One he *l*.
5: 28 He who *l* his wife *l* himself.
5: 33 must love his wife as he *l* himself,
Col 1: 13 us into the kingdom of the Son he *l*,
Tit 1: 8 one who *l* what is good, who is
Heb 12: 6 the Lord disciplines those he *l*,
1Jn 2: 10 Whoever *l* his brother lives
2: 15 If anyone *l* the world, the love
4: 7 Everyone who *l* has been born
4: 21 Whoever *l* God must also love his
5: 1 who *l* the father *l* his child
3Jn : 9 but Diotrephes, who *l* to be first,
Rev 1: 5 To him who *l* us and has freed us
20: 9 camp of God's people, the city he *l*.
22: 15 and everyone who *l* and practices

LOVING (LOVE)

Ps 25: 10 All the ways of the LORD are *l*
59: 10 my *l* God.
59: 17 O God, are my fortress, my *l* God.
62: 12 and that you, O Lord, are *l*.
144: 2 He is my *l* God and my fortress,
145: 13 and *l* toward all he has made.
Ps 145: 17 and *l* toward all he has made.
Pr 5: 19 A *l* doe, a graceful deer—
Heb 13: 1 Keep on *l* each other as brothers.
Jas 3: 17 then peace-*l*, considerate,
1Jn 5: 2 by *l* God and carrying out his

LOVING-KINDNESS (LOVE)

Jer 31: 3 I have drawn you with *l*.

LOWBORN (BEAR)

Ps 62: 9 *L* men are but a breath,

LOWER (LOWERED)

Ge 6: 16 in the side of the ark and make *l*,
Lev 13: 45 cover the *l* part of his face
Dt 28: 43 higher, but you will sink *l* and *l*.
Jos 15: 19 gave her the upper and *l* springs.
16: 3 far as the region of *L* Beth Horon
18: 13 on the hill south of *L* Beth Horon.
Jdg 1: 15 gave her the upper and *l* springs.
1Ki 9: 17 He built up *L* Beth Horon,
1Ch 7: 24 built *L* and Upper Beth Horon
2Ch 8: 5 and *L* Beth Horon as fortified
Job 41: 24 hard as a *l* millstone.
Ps 8: 5 You made him a little *l*
Isa 11: 11 from *L* Egypt, from Upper Egypt,
22: 9 water in the *L* Pool.
Jer 44: 1 all the Jews living in *L* Egypt—
44: 15 and all the people living in *L*
Eze 24: 17 do not cover the *l* part of your face
24: 22 You will not cover the *l* part
40: 18 were long; this was the *l* pavement.
40: 19 the inside of the *l* gateway to the
42: 5 them than from the rooms on the *l*
42: 6 in floor space than those on the *l*
42: 9 The *l* rooms had an entrance
43: 14 to the *l* ledge it is two cubits high
Ac 27: 30 they were going to *l* some anchors
2Co 11: 7 a sin for me to *l* myself in order
Eph 4: 9 that he also descended to the *l*,
Heb 2: 7 You made him a little *l*
2: 9 who was made a little *l*

LOWERED (LOWER)

Ge 24: 18 and quickly *l* the jar to her hands
24: 46 "She quickly *l* her jar
44: 11 Each of them quickly *l* his sack
Ex 17: 11 but whenever he *l* his hands,
Jer 38: 6 They *l* Jeremiah by ropes
Eze 1: 24 they stood still, they *l* their wings.
1: 25 as they stood with *l* wings.
Mk 2: 4 *l* the mat the paralyzed man was
Lk 5: 19 *l* him on his mat through the tiles
Ac 9: 25 and *l* him in a basket
27: 17 they *l* the sea anchor and let
2Co 11: 33 I was *l* in a basket from a window

LOWING

1Sa 6: 12 on the road and *l* all the way;
15: 14 What is this *l* of cattle that I hear?"
Jer 9: 10 and the *l* of cattle is not heard.

LOWLIEST

Eze 29: 15 It will be the *l* of kingdoms
Da 4: 17 and sets over them the *l* of men.'

LOWLY

Job 5: 11 The *l* he sets on high,
Ps 119: 141 Though I am *l* and despised,
138: 6 on high, he looks upon the *l*,
Pr 16: 19 Better to be *l* in spirit
29: 23 but a man of *l* spirit gains honor.
Isa 57: 15 also with him who is contrite and *l*
57: 15 to revive the spirit of the *l*
Eze 21: 26 *l* will be exalted and the exalted
29: 14 There they will be a *l* kingdom.
1Co 1: 28 He chose the *l* things of this world
Php 3: 21 will transform our *l* bodies

LOYAL (LOYALTY)

1Sa 22: 14 "Who of all your servants is as *l*
2Sa 3: 8 This very day I am *l* to the house
1Ki 12: 20 of Judah remained *l* to the house
1Ch 12: 29 most of whom had remained *l*
29: 18 and keep their hearts *l* to you.
Ps 78: 8 whose hearts were not *l* to God,
78: 37 their hearts were not *l* to him,
Php 4: 3 Yes, and I ask you, *l* yokefellow,

LOYALTY (LOYAL)
1Ch 12:33 to help David with undivided *l*—

LUCIUS
Ac 13: 1 Simeon called Niger, *L* of Cyrene,
Ro 16:21 as do *L*, Jason and Sosipater,

LUD (LUDITES)
Ge 10:22 Asshur, Arphaxad, *L* and Aram.
1Ch 1:17 Asshur, Arphaxad, *L* and Aram.

LUDITES (LUD)
Ge 10:13 Mizraim was the father of the *L*,
1Ch 1:11 Mizraim was the father of the *L*,

LUHITH
Isa 15: 5 They go up the way to *L*,
Jer 48: 5 They go up the way to *L*,

LUKE
Col 4:14 Our dear friend *L*, the doctor,
2Ti 4:11 Only *L* is with me.
Phm :24 Aristarchus, Demas and *L*,

LUKEWARM (WARM)
Rev 3:16 So, because you are *l*— neither hot

LUMBER
2Ch 2: 9 to provide me with plenty of *l*,

LUMP
Ro 9:21 of the same *l* of clay some pottery

LUNCHEON
Lk 14:12 "When you give a *l* or dinner,

LURE (LURED LURING)
Jdg 4: 7 I will *l* Sisera, the commander
16: 5 "See if you can *l* him
1Ki 22:20 'Who will *l* Ahab
22:21 the LORD and said, 'I will *l* him.'
2Ch 18:19 'Who will *l* Ahab king of Israel
18:20 the LORD and said, 'I will *l* him.'

LURED (LURE)
Jos 8: 6 us until we have *l* them away
8:16 and were *l* away from the city.

LURING (LURE)
1Ki 22:22 " 'You will succeed in *l* him,'
2Ch 18:21 " 'You will succeed in *l* him,'

LURK (LURKED LURKS)
Ps 56: 6 They conspire, they *l*,
Hos 13: 7 like a leopard I will *l* by the path.

LURKED (LURK)
Job 31: 9 or if I have *l* at my neighbor's door,

LURKS (LURK)
Pr 7:12 at every corner she *l*.)

LUSH
Am 5:11 you have planted *l* vineyards,
Zec 11: 3 the *l* thicket of the Jordan is ruined

LUST (LUSTED LUSTFUL LUSTS LUSTY)
Pr 6:25 Do not *l* in your heart
Isa 57: 5 You burn with *l* among the oaks
Eze 20:30 and *l* after their vile images?
23: 8 and poured out their *l* upon her.
23:11 in her *l* and prostitution she was
23:17 and in their *l* they defiled her.
Na 3: 4 because of the wanton *l* of a harlot,
Ro 1:27 and were inflamed with *l*
Eph 4:19 with a continual *l* for more.
Col 3: 5 sexual immorality, impurity, *l*,
1Th 4: 5 not in passionate *l* like the heathen,
1Pe 4: 3 in debauchery, *l*, drunkenness,
1Jn 2:16 the *l* of his eyes and the boasting

LUSTED (LUST)
Eze 6: 9 which have *l* after their idols.
20:24 and their eyes *l* after their fathers'
23: 5 she *l* after her lovers, the Assyrians
23: 7 the idols of everyone she *l* after.
23: 9 the Assyrians, for whom she *l*.
23:12 She too *l* after the Assyrians—
23:16 she *l* after them and sent
23:20 There she *l* after her lovers,
23:30 because you *l* after the nations

LUSTER
La 4: 1 How the gold has lost its *l*,

LUSTFUL (LUST)
Jer 13:27 your adulteries and *l* neighings,
Eze 16:26 the Egyptians, your *l* neighbors,
2Pe 2:18 and, by appealing to the *l* desires

LUSTS (LUST)
Nu 15:39 yourselves by going after the *l*
Ro 1:26 God gave them over to shameful *l*.

LUSTY (LUST)
Jer 5: 8 They are well-fed, *l* stallions,

LUTES
1Sa 18: 6 and with tambourines and *l*.
2Ch 20:28 of the LORD with harps and *l*

LUXURIES (LUXURY)
Rev 18: 3 rich from her excessive *l*."

LUXURIOUS (LUXURY)
Isa 13:22 jackals in her *l* palaces.

LUXURY (LUXURIES LUXURIOUS)
Pr 19:10 It is not fitting for a fool to live in *l*
Hab 1:16 for by his net he lives in *l*
Lk 7:25 and indulge in *l* are in palaces.
16:19 fine linen and lived in *l* every day.
Jas 5: 5 You have lived on earth in *l*
Rev 18: 7 as the glory and *l* she gave herself.
18: 9 and shared her *l* see the smoke

LUZ
Ge 28:19 though the city used to be called *L*.
35: 6 people with him came to *L* (that is,
48: 3 to me at *L* in the land of Canaan,
Jos 16: 2 It went on from Bethel (that is, *L*),
18:13 to the south slope of *L* (that is,
Jdg 1:23 spy out Bethel (formerly called *L*),
1:26 where he built a city and called it *L*

LYCAONIAN
Ac 14: 6 and fled to the *L* cities of Lystra
14:11 they shouted in the *L* language,

LYCIA
Ac 27: 5 Pamphylia, we landed at Myra in *L*

LYDDA
Ac 9:32 he went to visit the saints in *L*.
9:35 All those who lived in *L*
9:38 disciples heard that Peter was in *L*,
9:38 *L* was near Joppa;

LYDIA (LYDIA'S LYDIANS)
Jer 46: 9 men of *L* who draw the bow.
Eze 27:10 " 'Men of Persia, *L* and Put
30: 5 Cush and Put, *L* and all Arabia,
Ac 16:14 listening was a woman named *L*,

LYDIA'S (LYDIA)
Ac 16:40 went to *L* house, where they met

LYDIANS (LYDIA)
Isa 66:19 and *L* (famous as archers),

LYING (LIE)
Ge 28:13 the land on which you are *l*.
29: 2 with three flocks of sheep *l* near it
34: 7 in Israel by *l* with Jacob's daughter
49:14 *l* down between two saddlebags.
Ex 14:30 and Israel saw the Egyptians *l* dead
Dt 21: 1 *l* in a field in the land the LORD
22:13 If a man takes a wife and, after *l*
Jos 17: 9 to Ephraim *l* among the towns
Jdg 16:13 a fool of me and *l* to me.
Ru 3: 4 note the place where he is *l*.
3: 8 discovered a woman *l* at his feet.
1Sa 3: 2 was *l* down in his usual place.
3: 3 Samuel was *l* down in the temple
5: 4 and were *l* on the threshold;
26: 5 Saul was *l* inside the camp,
26: 7 and the soldiers were *l* around him.
26: 7 *l* asleep inside the camp
2Sa 4: 7 the house while he was *l* on the bed
12:16 spent the nights *l* on the ground.
13: 8 of her brother Amnon, who was *l*
1Ki 13:18 (But he was *l* to him.)
22:22 and be a *l* spirit in the mouths
22:23 now the LORD has put a *l* spirit
2Ki 1: 4 You will not leave the bed you are *l*
1: 6 you will not leave the bed you are *l*
1:16 will never leave the bed you are *l*
4:32 there was the boy *l* dead
2Ch 18:21 and be a *l* spirit in the mouths
18:22 now the LORD has put a *l* spirit
20:24 they saw only dead bodies *l*
Job 3:13 For now I would be *l*
3:14 built for themselves places now *l*
Ps 31:18 Let their *l* lips be silenced,
78:36 *l* to him with their tongues;
109: 2 spoken against me with *l* tongues.
120: 2 Save me, O LORD, from *l* lips
139: 3 You discern my going out and my *l*
Pr 6:17 a *l* tongue,
10:18 who conceals his hatred has *l* lips,
12:19 but a *l* tongue lasts only a moment.
12:22 The LORD detests *l* lips,
17: 7 how much worse *l* lips to a ruler!
21: 6 A fortune made by a *l* tongue
23:34 *l* on top of the rigging.
26:28 A *l* tongue hates those it hurts,
Isa 58: 5 and for *l* on sackcloth and ashes?
Jer 8: 2 will be like refuse *l* on the ground.
8: 8 when actually the *l* pen
16: 4 will be like refuse *l* on the ground.
23:26 in the hearts of these *l* prophets,
25:33 will be like refuse *l* on the ground.
43: 2 "You are *l*! The LORD our God
La 3:10 Like a bear *l* in wait,
Eze 13: 7 uttered *l* divinations when you say,
13: 8 of your false words and *l* visions,
13: 9 false visions and utter *l* divinations.
13:19 By *l* to my people, who listen to lies
21:29 and *l* divinations about you,
22:28 by false visions and *l* divinations.
29: 3 you great monster *l*
36:34 instead of *l* desolate in the sight
36:35 the cities that were *l* in ruins,
Da 2:29 "As you were *l* there, O king,
4: 5 As I was *l* in my bed, the images
4:10 These are the visions I saw while *l*
4:13 "In the visions I saw while *l*
7: 1 passed through his mind as he was *l*
Hos 4: 2 There is only cursing, *l* and murder
Mt 8:14 he saw Peter's mother-in-law *l*
9: 2 to him a paralytic, *l* on a mat.
Mk 2: 4 the mat the paralyzed man was *l*
7:30 and found her child *l* on the bed,
Lk 2:12 in strips of cloth and *l* in a manger
2:16 the baby, who was *l* in the manger.
5:25 took what he had been *l* on
24:12 the strips of linen *l* by themselves,
Jn 5: 6 When Jesus saw him *l* there
20: 5 in at the strips of linen *l* there
20: 6 He saw the strips of linen *l* there,
Ro 9: 1 I am not *l*, my conscience confirms
2Co 11:31 forever, knows that I am not *l*.
1Ti 2: 7 I am telling the truth, I am not *l*—

LYRE (LYRES)
Ps 33: 2 to him on the ten-stringed *l*.
57: 8 Awake, harp and *l*!
71:22 I will sing praise to you with the *l*,
81: 2 play the melodious harp and *l*.
92: 3 to the music of the ten-stringed *l*
108: 2 Awake, harp and *l*!
144: 9 on the ten-stringed *l* I will make
150: 3 praise him with the harp and *l*,
Da 3: 5 *l*, harp, pipes and all kinds of music
3: 7 *l*, harp and all kinds of music,
3:10 sound of the horn, flute, zither, *l*,
3:15 *l*, harp, pipes and all kinds of music

LYRES (LYRE)
1Sa 10: 5 down from the high place with *l*,
2Sa 6: 5 *l*, tambourines, sistrums
1Ki 10:12 and to make harps and *l*
1Ch 13: 8 *l*, tambourines, cymbals
15:16 by musical instruments: *l*,
15:20 to play the *l* according to *alamoth*,
15:28 and the playing of *l* and harps.

1Ch 16: 5 They were to play the *l* and harps,
25: 1 accompanied by harps, *l*
25: 6 with cymbals, *l* and harps,
2Ch 5: 12 and playing cymbals, harps and *l*.
9: 11 and to make harps and *l*
29: 25 *l* in the way prescribed by David
Ne 12: 27 the music of cymbals, harps and *l*.
Isa 5: 12 They have harps and *l*

LYSANIAS

Lk 3: 1 and *L* tetrarch of Abilene—

LYSIAS

Ac 23: 26 Claudius *L*, To His Excellency,
24: 22 "When *L* the commander comes,"

LYSTRA

Ac 14: 6 fled to the Lycaonian cities of *L*
14: 8 In *L* there sat a man crippled
14: 21 Then they returned to *L*, Iconium
16: 1 He came to Derbe and then to *L*,
16: 2 at *L* and Iconium spoke well
2Ti 3: 11 and *L*, the persecutions I endured.

MAACAH (MAACATHITE MAACATHITES)

Ge 22: 24 Tebah, Gaham, Tahash and *M*.
Jos 12: 5 of the people of Geshur and *M*,
13: 11 of the people of Geshur and *M*,
13: 13 out the people of Geshur and *M*.
2Sa 3: 3 Absalom the son of *M* daughter
10: 6 the king of *M* with a thousand men,
10: 8 and *M* were by themselves
1Ki 2: 39 ran off to Achish son of *M*,
15: 2 mother's name was *M* daughter
15: 10 name was *M* daughter
15: 13 even deposed his grandmother *M*
1Ch 2: 48 Caleb's concubine *M* was
3: 2 Absalom the son of *M* daughter
7: 15 His sister's name was *M*.
7: 16 Makir's wife *M* gave birth to a son
8: 29 His wife's name was *M*,
9: 35 His wife's name was *M*,
11: 43 son of *M*, Joshaphat the Mithnite,
19: 7 as the king of *M* with his troops,
27: 16 Shephatiah son of *M*; over Levi:
2Ch 11: 20 he married *M* daughter of Absalom
11: 21 Rehoboam loved *M* daughter
11: 22 appointed Abijah son of *M*
13: 2 His mother's name was *M*,
15: 16 also deposed his grandmother *M*

MAACATHITE (MAACAH)

2Sa 23: 34 Eliphelet son of Ahasbai the *M*,
2Ki 25: 23 Jaazaniah the son of the *M*,
1Ch 4: 19 the Garmite, and Eshtemoa the *M*.
Jer 40: 8 and Jaazaniah the son of the *M*,

MAACATHITES (MAACAH)

Dt 3: 14 of the Geshurites and the *M*;

MAADAI

Ezr 10: 34 *M*, Amram and Uel, Benaiah,

MAADIAH (MAADIAH'S)

Ne 12: 5 Abijah, Mijamin, *M*, Bilgah,

MAADIAH'S (MAADIAH)

Ne 12: 17 of Miniamin's and of *M*, Piltai;

MAAI

Ne 12: 36 Milalai, Gilalai, *M*, Nethanel,

MAARATH

Jos 15: 59 Halhul, Beth Zur, Gedor, *M*,

MAASAI

1Ch 9: 12 of Malkijah; and *M* son of Adiel,

MAASEIAH

1Ch 15: 18 Eliab, Benaiah, *M*, Mattithiah,
15: 20 *M* and Benaiah were
2Ch 23: 1 son of Obed, *M* son of Adaiah,
26: 11 *M* the officer under the direction
28: 7 warrior, killed *M* the king's
34: 8 and *M* the ruler of the city,
Ezr 10: 18 and his brothers: *M*, Eliezer,
10: 21 From the descendants of Harim: *M*
10: 22 Elioenai, *M*, Ishmael, Nethanel,
10: 30 Kelal, Benaiah, *M*, Mattaniah,
Ne 3: 23 Azariah son of *M*, the son
8: 4 Anaiah, Uriah, Hilkiah and *M*;
8: 7 Shabbethai, Hodiah, *M*, Kelita,
10: 25 Rehum, Hashabnah, *M*, Ahiah,
11: 5 of Perez; and *M* son of Baruch,
11: 7 the son of *M*, the son of Ithiel,
12: 41 Eliakim, *M*, Mijamin, Micaiah,
12: 42 and also *M*, Shemaiah, Eleazar,
Jer 21: 1 and the priest Zephaniah son of *M*.
29: 21 of Kolaiah and Zedekiah son of *M*,
29: 25 to Zephaniah son of *M* the priest,
35: 4 which was over that of *M* son
37: 3 son of *M* to Jeremiah the prophet

MAATH

Lk 3: 26 the son of *M*,

MAAZ

1Ch 2: 27 Ram the firstborn of Jerahmeel: *M*,

MAAZIAH

1Ch 24: 18 and the twenty-fourth to *M*.
Ne 10: 8 Meshullam, Abijah, Mijamin, *M*,

MACBANNAI

1Ch 12: 13 the tenth and *M* the eleventh.

MACBENAH

1Ch 2: 49 to Sheva the father of *M* and Gibea

MACEDONIA (MACEDONIAN MACEDONIANS)

Ac 16: 9 a vision of a man of *M* standing
16: 9 "Come over to *M* and help us."
16: 10 we got ready at once to leave for *M*
16: 12 the leading city of that district of *M*
18: 5 and Timothy came from *M*,
19: 21 passing through *M* and Achaia.
19: 22 Timothy and Erastus, to *M*,
19: 29 traveling companions from *M*,
20: 1 said good-by and set out for *M*.
20: 3 he decided to go back through *M*.
Ro 15: 26 For *M* and Achaia were pleased
1Co 16: 5 After I go through *M*, I will come
16: 5 for I will be going through *M*.
2Co 1: 16 and to come back to you from *M*,
1: 16 to visit you on my way to *M*
2: 13 good-by to them and went on to *M*.
7: 5 For when we came into *M*,
11: 9 from *M* supplied what I needed.
Php 4: 15 out from *M*, not one church shared
1Th 1: 7 a model to all the believers in *M*
1: 8 out from you not only in *M*
4: 10 love all the brothers throughout *M*.
1Ti 1: 3 As I urged you when I went into *M*,

MACEDONIAN (MACEDONIA)

Ac 27: 2 Aristarchus, a *M*
2Co 8: 1 God has given the *M* churches.

MACEDONIANS (MACEDONIA)

2Co 9: 2 been boasting about it to the *M*,
9: 4 For if any *M* come with me

MACHINES

2Ch 26: 15 In Jerusalem he made *m* designed

MACHPELAH

Ge 23: 9 so he will sell me the cave of *M*,
23: 17 So Ephron's field in *M* near Mamre
23: 19 field of *M* near Mamre (which is
25: 9 him in the cave of *M* near Mamre,
49: 30 cave in the field of *M*, near Mamre
50: 13 him in the cave in the field of *M*,

MACNADEBAI

Ezr 10: 40 Nathan, Adaiah, *M*, Shashai,

MAD (MADDENING MADMAN MADMEN MADNESS)

Dt 28: 34 The sights you see will drive you *m*
Jer 25: 16 they will stagger and go *m*
50: 38 idols that will go *m* with terror.
51: 7 therefore they have now gone *m*.
Jn 10: 20 is demon-possessed and raving *m*.

MADAI

Ge 10: 2 Gomer, Magog, *M*, Javan, Tubal,
1Ch 1: 5 Gomer, Magog, *M*, Javan, Tubal,

MADDENING (MAD)

Rev 14: 8 all the nations drink the *m* wine
18: 3 the *m* wine of her adulteries.

MADE (MAKE)

Ge 1: 7 So God *m* the expanse
1: 16 God *m* two great lights—
1: 16 He also *m* the stars.
1: 25 God *m* the wild animals according
1: 31 God saw all that he had *m*,
2: 3 the seventh day and *m* it holy,
2: 4 When the LORD God *m* the earth
2: 9 And the LORD God *m* all kinds
2: 22 Then the LORD God *m* a woman
3: 1 animals the LORD God had *m*.
3: 7 and *m* coverings for themselves.
3: 21 The LORD God *m* garments
5: 1 he *m* him in the likeness of God.
6: 6 was grieved that he had *m* man
6: 7 for I am grieved that I have *m* them
7: 4 every living creature I have *m*."
8: 6 opened the window he had *m*
9: 6 has God *m* man.
14: 23 able to say, 'I *m* Abram rich.'
15: 18 that day the LORD *m* a covenant
17: 5 for I have *m* you a father
21: 27 and the two men *m* a treaty.
21: 32 After the treaty had been *m*
24: 10 *m* his way to the town of Nahor.
24: 21 the LORD had *m* his journey
24: 37 my master *m* me swear an oath,
26: 30 Isaac then *m* a feast for them,
27: 17 tasty food and the bread she had *m*.
27: 37 have *m* all his relatives his servants
27: 37 "I have *m* him lord over you
28: 20 Then Jacob *m* a vow, saying,
30: 37 and *m* white stripes on them
30: 40 Thus he *m* separate flocks
30: 40 but *m* the rest face the streaked
31: 13 and where you *m* a vow to me.
33: 17 and *m* shelters for his livestock.
37: 3 and he *m* a richly ornamented robe
39: 22 and he was *m* responsible
41: 39 "Since God has *m* all this known
41: 51 God has *m* me forget all my trouble
41: 52 God has *m* me fruitful in the land
45: 1 Joseph when he *m* himself known
45: 8 He *m* me father to Pharaoh,
45: 9 God has *m* me lord of all Egypt.
46: 29 Joseph had his chariot *m* ready
50: 5 'My father *m* me swear an oath
50: 6 as he *m* you swear to do."
50: 25 And Joseph *m* the sons
Ex 1: 14 They *m* their lives bitter
2: 14 Who *m* you ruler and judge over us
5: 21 You have *m* us a stench to Pharaoh
7: 1 I have *m* you like God to Pharaoh,
8: 7 also *m* frogs come up on the land
10: 13 the LORD *m* an east wind blow
11: 3 LORD *m* the Egyptians favorably
12: 8 and bread *m* without yeast.
12: 15 are to eat bread *m* without yeast.
12: 18 are to eat bread *m* without yeast,
12: 20 Eat nothing *m* with yeast.
12: 36 The LORD had *m* the Egyptians
13: 6 For seven days eat bread *m*
13: 19 because Joseph had *m* the sons
14: 6 So he had his chariot *m* ready
14: 25 He *m* the wheels of their chariots
15: 17 O LORD, you *m* for your dwelling,
15: 25 There the LORD *m* a decree
16: 31 tasted like wafers *m* with honey.
18: 25 and *m* them leaders of the people,
20: 11 six days the LORD *m* the heavens
20: 11 the Sabbath day and *m* it holy.
23: 15 for seven days eat bread *m*
24: 8 the covenant that the LORD has *m*
24: 10 was something like a pavement *m*
27: 8 It is to be *m* just as you were shown
28: 8 with the ephod and *m* with gold,
29: 18 an offering *m* to the LORD by fire.
29: 23 and a cake *m* with oil, and a wafer.
29: 23 basket of bread *m* without yeast,
29: 25 an offering *m* to the LORD by fire.
29: 33 by which atonement was *m*
29: 41 an offering *m* to the LORD by fire.

Ex 29:42 is to be *m* regularly at the entrance
30:10 This annual atonement must be *m*
30:20 by presenting an offering *m*
31:17 six days the LORD *m* the heavens
32: 4 *m* it into an idol cast in the shape
32: 8 and have *m* themselves an idol cast
32:20 And he took the calf they had *m*
32:20 and *m* the Israelites drink it.
32:31 They have *m* themselves gods
32:35 did with the calf Aaron had *m*.
34:18 For seven days eat bread *m*
34:27 these words I have *m* a covenant
36: 8 the workmen *m* the tabernacle
36:11 Then they *m* loops of blue material
36:12 also *m* fifty loops on one curtain
36:13 Then they *m* fifty gold clasps
36:14 They *m* curtains of goat hair
36:17 they *m* fifty loops along the edge
36:18 They *m* fifty bronze clasps
36:19 Then they *m* for the tent a covering
36:20 They *m* upright frames
36:22 They *m* all the frames
36:23 They *m* twenty frames
36:24 and *m* forty silver bases to go
36:25 they *m* twenty frames
36:27 They *m* six frames for the far end,
36:28 two frames were *m* for the corners
36:29 a single ring; both were *m* alike.
36:31 also *m* crossbars of acacia wood:
36:33 They *m* the center crossbar
36:34 *m* gold rings to hold the crossbars.
36:35 They *m* the curtain of blue,
36:36 They *m* four posts of acacia wood
36:36 They *m* gold hooks for them
36:37 to the tent they *m* a curtain of blue,
36:38 and they *m* five posts with hooks
36:38 and *m* their five bases of bronze.
37: 1 Bezalel *m* the ark of acacia wood—
37: 2 and *m* a gold molding around it.
37: 4 Then he *m* poles of acacia wood
37: 6 He *m* the atonement cover
37: 7 Then he *m* two cherubim out
37: 8 He *m* one cherub on one end
37: 8 at the two ends he *m* them
37:10 They *m* the table of acacia wood—
37:11 and *m* a gold molding around it.
37:12 *m* around it a rim a handbreadth
37:15 poles for carrying the table were *m*
37:16 they *m* from pure gold the articles
37:17 They *m* the lampstand of pure gold
37:23 They *m* its seven lamps, as well
37:24 They *m* the lampstand
37:25 They *m* the altar of incense out
37:26 and *m* a gold molding around it.
37:27 They *m* two gold rings
37:28 They *m* the poles of acacia wood
37:29 also *m* the sacred anointing oil
38: 2 They *m* a horn at each
38: 3 They *m* all its utensils of bronze—
38: 4 They *m* a grating for the altar,
38: 6 They *m* the poles of acacia wood
38: 7 They *m* it hollow, out of boards.
38: 8 They *m* the bronze basin
38: 9 Next they *m* the courtyard.
38:22 *m* everything the LORD
39: 1 also *m* sacred garments for Aaron,
39: 1 yarn they *m* woven garments
39: 2 They *m* the ephod of gold,
39: 4 They *m* shoulder pieces
39: 5 with the ephod and *m* with gold,
39: 8 They *m* it like the ephod: of gold,
39:15 breastpiece they *m* braided chains
39:16 They *m* two gold filigree settings
39:19 They *m* two gold rings
39:20 Then they *m* two more gold rings
39:22 They *m* the robe of the ephod
39:24 They *m* pomegranates of blue,
39:25 And they *m* bells of pure gold
39:27 they *m* tunics of fine linen—
39:30 They *m* the plate, the sacred
Lev 1: 9 It is a burnt offering, an offering *m*
1:13 It is a burnt offering, an offering *m*
1:17 It is a burnt offering, an offering *m*
2: 2 an offering *m* by fire, an aroma
2: 3 of the offerings *m* to the LORD
2: 4 cakes *m* without yeast
2: 4 or wafers *m* without yeast
2: 5 it is to be *m* of fine flour mixed

Lev 2: 7 it is to be *m* of fine flour and oil.
2: 8 Bring the grain offering *m*
2: 9 on the altar as an offering *m* by fire,
2:10 of the offerings *m* to the LORD
2:11 bring to the LORD must be *m*
2:11 in an offering *m* to the LORD
2:16 an offering *m* to the LORD by fire.
3: 3 to bring a sacrifice *m* to the LORD
3: 5 as an offering *m* by fire, an aroma
3: 9 to bring a sacrifice *m* to the LORD
3:11 an offering *m* to the LORD by fire.
3:16 an offering *m* by fire, a pleasing
4:23 When he is *m* aware
4:28 When he is *m* aware
4:35 top of the offerings *m* to the LORD
5:12 top of the offerings *m* to the LORD
6: 7 things he did that *m* him guilty."
6:17 of the offerings *m* to me by fire.
6:18 of the offerings *m* to the LORD
7: 5 an offering *m* to the LORD by fire.
7:12 cakes of bread *m* without yeast
7:12 wafers *m* without yeast
7:13 with cakes of bread *m* with yeast.
7:25 by fire may be *m* to the LORD
7:30 is to bring the offering *m*
7:35 of the offerings *m* to the LORD
8: 2 and the basket containing bread *m*
8:21 an offering *m* to the LORD by fire,
8:26 and one *m* with oil, and a wafer;
8:26 basket of bread *m* without yeast,
8:28 an offering *m* to the LORD by fire.
10:12 from the offerings *m* to the LORD
10:13 of the offerings *m* to the LORD
10:15 portions of the offerings *m* by fire,
11:32 whether it is *m* of wood, cloth,
11:43 or be *m* unclean by them.
13:48 or anything *m* of leather—
15:32 for anyone *m* unclean
16:17 having *m* atonement for himself,
16:30 on this day atonement will be *m*
16:34 Atonement is to be *m* once a year
21: 6 they present the offerings *m*
21:21 near to present the offerings *m*
22:22 an offering *m* to the LORD by fire.
22:27 an offering *m* to the LORD by fire.
23: 6 seven days you must eat bread *m*
23: 8 seven days present an offering *m*
23:13 an offering *m* to the LORD by fire,
23:17 bring two loaves *m* of two-tenths
23:18 an offering *m* by fire, an aroma
23:25 present an offering *m* to the LORD
23:27 present an offering *m* to the LORD
23:28 when atonement is *m* for you
23:36 For seven days present offerings *m*
23:36 present an offering *m* to the LORD
23:37 assemblies for bringing offerings *m*
24: 7 to be an offering *m* to the LORD
24: 9 of the offerings *m* to the LORD
24:12 of the LORD should be *m* clear
26:41 which *m* me hostile toward them
Nu 3: 4 LORD when they *m* an offering
5: 8 to whom restitution can be *m*
5: 8 with which atonement is *m* for him
5:27 then when she is *m*
6: 3 and must not drink vinegar *m*
6:15 a basket of bread *m* without yeast
6:15 cakes *m* of fine flour mixed with oil
6:19 a wafer from the basket, both *m*
6:21 He must fulfill the vow he has *m*,
7: 2 who were counted, *m* offerings.
8: 4 It was *m* of hammered gold—
8: 4 The lampstand was *m* exactly like
8: 4 This is how the lampstand was *m*:
8:21 and *m* atonement for them
11: 8 And it tasted like something *m*
11: 8 it in a pot or *m* it into cakes.
14:36 *m* the whole community grumble
15: 3 to the LORD offerings *m* by fire,
15:10 It will be an offering *m* by fire,
15:13 way when he brings an offering *m*
15:14 among you presents an offering *m*
15:25 for their wrong an offering *m*
15:28 and when atonement has been *m*
16:47 and *m* atonement for them.
18:17 and burn their fat as an offering *m*
21: 2 Israel *m* this vow to the LORD:
21: 9 So Moses *m* a bronze snake
22:29 "You have *m* a fool of me!

Nu 25:13 *m* atonement for the Israelites."
26:61 died when they *m* an offering
28: 2 the food for my offerings *m* by fire,
28: 3 'This is the offering *m*
28: 6 an offering *m* to the LORD by fire.
28: 8 This is an offering *m* by fire,
28:13 an offering *m* to the LORD by fire.
28:14 offering to be *m* at each new moon
28:17 for seven days eat bread *m*
28:19 to the LORD an offering *m* by fire,
28:24 for the offering *m* by fire every day
29: 6 They are offerings *m* to the LORD
29:13 Present an offering *m* by fire
29:36 Present an offering *m* by fire
31:20 as well as everything *m* of leather,
32:13 and he *m* them wander
35:33 and atonement cannot be *m*
Dt 1:28 Our brothers have *m* us lose heart.
2: 1 For a long time we *m* our way
2: 3 "You have *m* your way
2:30 your God had *m* his spirit stubborn
3:11 His bed was *m* of iron and was
4:23 of the LORD your God that he *m*
4:36 From heaven he *m* you hear his
5: 2 The LORD our God *m* a covenant
5: 3 that the LORD *m* this covenant,
9: 9 covenant that the LORD had *m*
9:12 have *m* a cast idol for themselves."
9:16 you had *m* for yourselves an idol
9:21 the calf you had *m*, and burned it
9:22 *m* the LORD angry at Taberah,
10: 3 So I *m* the ark out of acacia wood
10: 5 put the tablets in the ark I had *m*,
10:22 the LORD your God has *m* you
15: 2 shall cancel the loan he has *m*
16: 3 it with bread *m* with yeast,
18: 1 on the offerings *m* to the LORD
23:23 because you *m* your vow freely
26: 6 mistreated us and *m* us suffer,
26:19 high above all the nations he has *m*
29: 1 addition to the covenant he had *m*
29:25 the covenant he *m* with them
31:16 break the covenant I *m* with them.
31:29 anger by what your hands have *m*."
32: 6 who *m* you and formed you?
32:13 He *m* him ride on the heights
32:15 He abandoned the God who *m* him
32:16 They *m* him jealous
32:21 They *m* me jealous
Jos 2:17 "This oath you *m* us swear will not
2:20 from the oath you *m* us swear."
5: 3 So Joshua *m* flint knives
7:12 because they have been *m* liable
8:28 and *m* it a permanent heap of ruins,
9:15 Then Joshua *m* a treaty of peace
9:16 Three days after they *m* the treaty
9:27 That day he *m* the Gibeonites
10: 1 of Gibeon had *m* a treaty of peace
10: 4 because it has *m* peace with Joshua
11: 5 and *m* camp together at the Waters
11:19 not one city *m* a treaty of peace
13:14 since the offerings *m* by fire
14: 8 up with me *m* the hearts
22:25 The LORD has *m* the Jordan
24:25 On that day Joshua *m* a covenant
Jdg 3:16 Ehud had *m* a double-edged sword
3:30 That day Moab was *m* subject
6:19 of flour he *m* bread without yeast.
8: 8 and *m* the same request of them,
8:27 Gideon *m* the gold into an ephod,
9:16 faith when you *m* Abimelech king,
9:18 and *m* Abimelech, the son
9:57 also *m* the men of Shechem pay
11: 4 when the Ammonites *m* war
11:11 and the people *m* him head
11:30 Jephthah *m* a vow to the LORD:
11:35 I have *m* a vow to the LORD that I
11:35 You have *m* me miserable
14:10 And Samson *m* a feast there,
15:16 I have *m* donkeys of them.
16: 2 They *m* no move during the night,
16:10 "You have *m* a fool of me;
16:15 is the third time you have *m* a fool
17: 4 who *m* them into the image
17: 5 and he *m* an ephod and some idols
18:24 "You took the gods I *m*,
18:27 Then they took what Micah had *m*,
18:31 to use the idols Micah had *m*,

Jdg 20: 34 Israel's finest men *m* a frontal
20: 37 been in ambush *m* a sudden dash
21: 15 because the LORD had *m* a gap
Ru 1: 20 Almighty has *m* my life very bitter.
1Sa 1: 11 she *m* a vow, saying, "O LORD
2: 19 Each year his mother *m* him a little
2: 28 father's house all the offerings *m*
2: 29 parts of every offering *m*
3: 13 his sons *m* themselves
6: 15 and *m* sacrifices to the LORD.
14: 29 "My father has *m* trouble
15: 11 am grieved that I have *m* Saul king,
15: 33 sword has *m* women childless,
15: 35 grieved that he had *m* Saul king
18: 3 Jonathan *m* a covenant with David
19: 10 That night David *m* good his
19: 18 David had fled and *m* his escape,
20: 6 an annual sacrifice is being *m* there
20: 16 So Jonathan *m* a covenant
23: 18 The two of them *m* a covenant
26: 3 Saul *m* his camp beside the road
30: 25 David *m* this a statute
2Sa 2: 9 He *m* him king over Gilead,
5: 3 the king *m* a compact with them
7: 21 and *m* it known to your servant.
7: 25 you have *m* concerning your
8: 2 He *m* them lie down on the ground
10: 19 they *m* peace with the Israelites
11: 13 with him, and David *m* him drunk.
12: 14 doing this you have *m* the enemies
12: 31 he *m* them work at brickmaking.
13: 8 *m* the bread in his sight
14: 15 the people have *m* me afraid.
15: 7 and fulfill a vow I *m* to the LORD.
15: 8 at Geshur in Aram, I *m* this vow:
16: 21 that you have *m* yourself a stench
19: 6 You have *m* it clear today that
22: 12 He *m* darkness his canopy
22: 40 you *m* my adversaries bow
22: 41 You *m* my enemies turn their
23: 5 Has he not *m* with me
1Ki 1: 43 King David has *m* Solomon king.
3: 1 Solomon *m* an alliance
3: 7 you have *m* your servant king
5: 12 and the two of them *m* a treaty
6: 4 He *m* narrow clerestory windows
6: 6 He *m* offset ledges around the
6: 23 In the inner sanctuary he *m* a pair
6: 31 of the inner sanctuary he *m* doors
6: 33 same way he *m* four-sided jambs
6: 34 He also *m* two pine doors,
7: 6 He *m* a colonnade fifty cubits long
7: 8 also *m* a palace like this hall
7: 9 *m* of blocks of high-grade stone
7: 16 *m* two capitals of cast bronze to set
7: 18 He *m* pomegranates
7: 23 He *m* the Sea of cast metal,
7: 27 *m* ten movable stands of bronze;
7: 28 This is how the stands were *m*:
7: 33 wheels were *m* like chariot wheels;
7: 37 This is the way he *m* the ten stands.
7: 38 He then *m* ten bronze basins,
7: 40 He also *m* the basins and shovels
7: 45 All these objects that Huram *m*
7: 48 also *m* all the furnishings that were
8: 9 where the LORD *m* a covenant
8: 20 LORD has kept the promise he *m*:
8: 21 covenant of the LORD that he *m*
8: 25 my father the promises you *m*
8: 38 or plea is *m* by any of your people
9: 3 and plea you have *m* before me;
10: 5 and the burnt offerings he *m*
10: 9 he has *m* you king,
10: 16 King Solomon *m* two hundred
10: 17 also *m* three hundred small shields
10: 18 the king *m* a great throne inlaid
10: 20 Nothing like it had ever been *m*
10: 21 Nothing was *m* of silver,
10: 27 The king *m* silver as common
11: 34 I have *m* him ruler all the days
12: 14 "My father *m* your yoke heavy;
12: 20 and *m* him king over all Israel.
12: 28 the king *m* two golden calves.
12: 32 priests at the high places he had *m*.
12: 32 sacrificing to the calves he had *m*.
14: 7 and *m* you a leader over my people
14: 9 You have *m* for yourself other gods
14: 9 for yourself other gods, idols *m*

1Ki 14: 26 the gold shields Solomon had *m*.
14: 27 King Rehoboam *m* bronze shields
15: 12 of all the idols his fathers had *m*.
15: 13 she had *m* a repulsive Asherah pole
16: 2 *m* you leader of my people Israel,
16: 33 Ahab also *m* an Asherah pole
18: 10 he *m* them swear they could not
18: 18 "I have not *m* trouble for Israel,"
18: 26 around the altar they had *m*.
20: 34 So he *m* a treaty with him,
22: 11 son of Kenaanah had *m* iron horns
2Ki 3: 2 stone of Baal that his father had *m*.
6: 6 threw it there, and *m* the iron float.
9: 25 when the LORD *m* this prophecy
11: 4 He *m* a covenant with them
11: 13 When Athaliah heard the noise *m*
11: 17 Jehoiada then *m* a covenant
11: 17 *m* a covenant between the king
13: 7 and *m* them like the dust
14: 21 and *m* him king in place
17: 15 and the covenant he had *m*
17: 16 *m* for themselves two idols cast
17: 21 they *m* Jeroboam son
17: 29 each national group *m* its own gods
17: 29 of Samaria had *m* at the high places
17: 30 Babylon *m* Succoth Benoth,
17: 30 the men from Cuthah *m* Nergal,
17: 30 the men from Hamath *m* Ashima;
17: 31 the Avvites *m* Nibhaz and Tartak,
17: 35 When the LORD *m* a covenant
17: 38 not forget the covenant I have *m*
18: 4 the bronze snake Moses had *m*,
19: 15 You have *m* heaven and earth.
20: 11 the LORD *m* the shadow go back
20: 20 and how he *m* the pool
21: 3 to Baal and *m* an Asherah pole,
21: 7 the carved Asherah pole he had *m*
21: 24 and they *m* Josiah his son king
22: 17 by all the idols their hands have *m*,
23: 4 of the LORD all the articles *m*
23: 15 the high place *m* by Jeroboam son
23: 30 *m* him king in place of his father.
23: 34 Pharaoh Neco *m* Eliakim son
24: 13 king of Israel had *m* for the temple
24: 17 He *m* Mattaniah, Jehoiachin's
25: 15 all that were *m* of gold or silver.
25: 16 which Solomon had *m*
1Ch 11: 3 he *m* a compact with them
12: 18 *m* them leaders of his raiding bands
14: 17 LORD *m* all the nations fear him.
16: 16 the covenant he *m* with Abraham,
16: 26 but the LORD *m* the heavens.
17: 19 *m* known all these great promises.
17: 22 You *m* your people Israel your
17: 23 you have *m* concerning your
19: 19 they *m* peace with David
21: 29 which Moses had *m* in the desert,
22: 5 So David *m* extensive preparations
23: 1 he *m* his son Solomon king
26: 31 of David's reign a search was *m*
28: 2 footstool of our God, and I *m* plans
29: 21 The next day they *m* sacrifices
2Ch 1: 1 and *m* him exceedingly great.
1: 3 Moses the LORD's servant had *m*
1: 5 had *m* was in Gibeon in front
1: 8 and have *m* me king in his place.
1: 9 for you have *m* me king
1: 11 over whom I have *m* you king,
1: 15 The king *m* silver and gold
2: 11 people, he has *m* you their king.
2: 12 the God of Israel, who *m* heaven
3: 10 In the Most Holy Place he *m* a pair
3: 14 He *m* the curtain of blue, purple
3: 15 of the temple he *m* two pillars,
3: 16 He also *m* a hundred pomegranates
3: 16 He *m* interwoven chains
4: 1 He *m* a bronze altar twenty cubits
4: 2 He *m* the Sea of cast metal,
4: 6 He then *m* ten basins for washing
4: 7 He *m* ten gold lampstands
4: 8 He *m* ten tables and placed them
4: 8 *m* a hundred gold sprinkling bowls.
4: 9 He *m* the courtyard of the priests,
4: 11 He also *m* the pots and shovels
4: 16 All the objects that Huram-Abi *m*
4: 18 things that Solomon *m* amounted
4: 19 also *m* all the furnishings that were
5: 10 where the LORD *m* a covenant

2Ch 6: 10 LORD has kept the promise he *m*.
6: 11 covenant of the LORD that he *m*
6: 13 Now he had *m* a bronze platform,
6: 16 my father the promises you *m*
6: 29 or plea is *m* by any of your people
7: 6 which King David had *m*
7: 7 altar he had *m* could not hold
9: 4 and the burnt offerings he *m*
9: 8 he has *m* you king over them,
9: 15 King Solomon *m* two hundred
9: 16 also *m* three hundred small shields
9: 17 the king *m* a great throne inlaid
9: 19 Nothing like it had ever been *m*
9: 20 Nothing was *m* of silver,
9: 27 The king *m* silver as common
10: 14 "My father *m* your yoke heavy;
11: 12 the cities, and *m* them very strong.
11: 15 for the goat and calf idols he had *m*
12: 9 the gold shields Solomon had *m*.
12: 10 King Rehoboam *m* bronze shields
13: 8 the golden calves that Jeroboam *m*
15: 16 she had *m* a repulsive Asherah pole
16: 14 and they *m* a huge fire in his honor.
18: 10 son of Kenaanah had *m* iron horns,
20: 35 king of Judah *m* an alliance
20: 37 will destroy what you have *m*."
20: 37 "Because you have *m* an alliance
21: 7 of the covenant the LORD had *m*
21: 19 His people *m* no fire in his honor,
22: 1 people of Jerusalem *m* Ahaziah,
23: 1 *m* a covenant
23: 3 the whole assembly *m* a covenant
23: 16 Jehoiada then *m* a covenant that he
23: 18 to whom David had *m* assignments
24: 8 a chest was *m* and placed outside,
24: 14 and with it were *m* articles
26: 1 and *m* him king in place
26: 15 Jerusalem he *m* machines designed
27: 5 Jotham *m* war on the king
28: 2 also *m* cast idols for worshiping
29: 8 he has *m* them an object of dread
30: 7 so that he *m* them an object
31: 14 distributing the contributions *m*
32: 5 also *m* large numbers of weapons
32: 27 and he *m* treasuries for his silver
32: 28 and he *m* stalls for various kinds
32: 28 *m* buildings to store the harvest
33: 3 to the Baals and *m* Asherah poles.
33: 7 He took the carved image he had *m*
33: 14 of Ophel; he also *m* it much higher.
33: 22 to all the idols Manasseh had *m*.
33: 25 and they *m* Josiah his son king
34: 25 by all that their hands have *m*,
35: 14 So the Levites *m* preparations
35: 14 they *m* preparations for themselves
35: 15 fellow Levites *m* the preparations
36: 1 *m* him king in Jerusalem in place
36: 4 The king of Egypt *m* Eliakim,
36: 10 and he *m* Jehoiachin's uncle,
36: 13 who had *m* him take an oath
Ezr 3: 13 the people *m* so much noise.
4: 15 so that a search may be *m*
4: 19 an order and a search was *m*,
5: 17 let a search be *m* in the royal
6: 11 is to be *m* a pile of rubble.
Ne 3: 4 son of Baana also *m* repairs.
3: 4 the son of Meshezabel, *m* repairs,
3: 7 repairs were *m* by men
3: 8 the perfume-makers, *m* repairs
3: 10 son of Harumaph *m* repairs
3: 10 son of Hashabneiah *m* repairs next
3: 16 *m* repairs up to a point
3: 17 the repairs were *m* by the Levites
3: 18 the repairs were *m*
3: 22 next to him were *m* by the priests
3: 23 and Hasshub *m* repairs in front
3: 23 *m* repairs beside his house.
3: 26 on the hill of Ophel *m* repairs up
3: 28 Horse Gate, the priests *m* repairs,
3: 29 Zadok son of Immer *m* repairs
3: 29 guard at the East Gate, *m* repairs.
3: 30 son of Berekiah *m* repairs
3: 31 *m* repairs as far as the house
3: 32 and merchants *m* repairs.
5: 12 the priests and *m* the nobles
8: 2 which was *m* up of men
8: 12 the words that had been *m* known
9: 6 You *m* the heavens,

Ne 9: 8 you *m* a covenant with him to give
9: 10 You *m* a name for yourself,
9: 14 You *m* known to them your holy
9: 23 You *m* their sons as numerous
13: 13 They were *m* responsible
13: 13 and *m* Hanan son of Zaccur,
13: 25 I *m* them take an oath
13: 26 and God *m* him king over all Israel,
13: 31 also *m* provision for contributions
Est 2: 2 "Let a search be *m*
2: 17 and *m* her queen instead of Vashti.
3: 14 and *m* known to the people
7: 9 He had it *m* for Mordecai,
8: 13 and *m* known to the people
9: 17 they rested and *m* it a day
9: 18 fifteenth they rested and *m* it a day
Job 4: 14 and *m* all my bones shake.
7: 20 Why have you *m* me your target?
10: 8 "Your hands shaped me and *m* me.
14: 15 for the creature your hands have *m*
16: 12 He has *m* me his target;
17: 6 "God has *m* me a byword
23: 16 God has *m* my heart faint;
27: 2 who has *m* me taste bitterness
27: 18 like a hut *m* by a watchman.
28: 26 when he *m* a decree for the rain
29: 13 I *m* the widow's heart sing.
31: 1 "I *m* a covenant with my eyes
31: 15 Did not he who *m* me
33: 4 The Spirit of God has *m* me;
37: 7 all men he has *m* may know his
38: 9 when I *m* the clouds its garment
40: 15 which I *m* along with you
42: 10 the LORD *m* him prosperous again
Ps 7: 15 falls into the pit he has *m*.
8: 5 You *m* him a little lower
8: 6 You *m* him ruler over the works
16: 5 you have *m* my lot secure.
16: 11 You have *m* known to me the path
18: 11 He *m* darkness his covering,
18: 39 you *m* my adversaries bow
18: 40 You *m* my enemies turn their
18: 43 you have *m* me the head of nations;
21: 6 *m* him glad with the joy
22: 9 you *m* me trust in you
30: 7 you *m* my mountain stand firm;
33: 6 of the LORD were the heavens *m*,
37: 23 whose steps he has *m* firm;
39: 5 You have *m* my days a mere
44: 2 and *m* our fathers flourish.
44: 10 You *m* us retreat before the enemy,
44: 13 You have *m* us a reproach
44: 14 You have *m* us a byword
44: 19 *m* us a haunt for jackals
50: 5 who *m* a covenant with me
71: 20 Though you have *m* me see
73: 28 I have *m* the Sovereign LORD my
74: 17 you *m* both summer and winter.
78: 13 he *m* the water stand firm like
78: 16 and *m* water flow down like rivers.
78: 28 *m* them come down inside their
80: 5 you have *m* them drink tears
80: 6 You have *m* us a source
86: 9 All the nations you have *m*
88: 8 and have *m* me repulsive to them.
89: 3 "I have *m* a covenant
89: 42 you have *m* all his enemies rejoice.
95: 5 The sea is his, for he *m* it,
96: 5 but the LORD *m* the heavens.
98: 2 LORD has *m* his salvation known
100: 3 It is he who *m* us, and we are his;
103: 7 He *m* known his ways to Moses,
104: 24 In wisdom you *m* them all;
105: 9 the covenant he *m* with Abraham,
105: 21 He *m* him master of his household,
105: 24 he *m* them too numerous
105: 24 LORD *m* his people very fruitful;
105: 28 sent darkness and *m* the land
106: 19 At Horeb they *m* a calf
107: 40 *m* them wander in a trackless waste
115: 4 *m* by the hands of men.
118: 24 This is the day the LORD has *m*;
118: 27 he has *m* his light shine upon us.
119: 73 Your hands *m* me and formed me;
129: 3 and *m* their furrows long.
132: 2 and *m* a vow to the Mighty One
135: 15 *m* by the hands of men.
136: 5 his understanding *m* the heavens,
Ps 136: 7 who *m* the great lights—
138: 3 you *m* me bold and stouthearted.
139: 14 I am fearfully and wonderfully *m*;
139: 15 when I was *m* in the secret place.
145: 9 he has compassion on all he has *m*.
145: 10 All you have *m* will praise you,
145: 13 and loving toward all he has *m*.
145: 17 and loving toward all he has *m*.
Pr 1: 23 and *m* my thoughts known to you.
2: 17 and ignored the covenant she *m*
8: 26 before he *m* the earth or its fields
20: 12 the LORD has *m* them both.
20: 28 through love his throne is *m* secure
21: 6 A fortune *m* by a lying tongue
21: 31 The horse is *m* ready for the day
Ecc 2: 5 I *m* gardens and parks
2: 6 I *m* reservoirs to water groves
3: 11 He has *m* everything beautiful
7: 13 what he has *m* crooked?
7: 14 God has *m* the one
7: 29 God *m* mankind upright,
10: 19 A feast is *m* for laughter,
SS 1: 6 *m* me take care of the vineyards;
3: 3 as they *m* their rounds in the city.
3: 6 *m* from all the spices
3: 9 King Solomon *m* for himself
3: 9 he *m* it of wood from Lebanon.
3: 10 Its posts he *m* of silver,
5: 7 as they *m* their rounds in the city.
Isa 2: 8 to what their fingers have *m*.
2: 20 which they *m* to worship.
14: 16 and *m* kingdoms tremble,
14: 17 the man who *m* the world a desert,
17: 8 incense altars their fingers have *m*.
22: 11 look to the One who *m* it,
23: 11 and *m* its kingdoms tremble.
23: 13 The Assyrians have *m* it
25: 2 You have *m* the city a heap
28: 15 for we have *m* a lie our refuge
28: 15 the grave we have *m* an agreement.
29: 13 is *m* up only of rules taught by men
30: 33 Its fire pit has been *m* deep
30: 33 it has been *m* ready for the king.
31: 7 and gold your sinful hands have *m*.
37: 16 You have *m* heaven and earth.
38: 12 day and night you *m* an end of me.
38: 13 day and night you *m* an end of me.
40: 4 every mountain and hill *m* low;
42: 22 they have been *m* loot,
43: 7 whom I formed and *m*."
43: 16 he who *m* a way through the sea,
44: 2 he who *m* you, who formed you
44: 14 a pine, and the rain *m* it grow.
44: 21 I have *m* you, you are my servant;
44: 24 who has *m* all things,
45: 12 It is I who *m* the earth
45: 18 he who fashioned and *m* the earth,
46: 4 I have *m* you and I will carry you;
48: 3 them and I *m* them known;
48: 21 he *m* water flow for them
49: 1 from my birth he has *m* mention
49: 2 He *m* my mouth like a sharpened
49: 2 he *m* me into a polished arrow
49: 19 you were ruined and *m* desolate
51: 2 and I blessed him and *m* him many.
51: 10 who *m* a road in the depths
51: 21 *m* drunk, but not with wine.
51: 22 the cup that *m* you stagger;
51: 23 you *m* your back like the ground,
53: 12 and *m* intercession
55: 4 I have *m* him a witness
57: 7 You have *m* your bed on a high
57: 8 you *m* a pact with those whose
62: 11 The LORD has *m* proclamation
63: 6 in my wrath I *m* them drunk
64: 7 *m* us waste away because of our
66: 2 Has not my hand *m* all these things
66: 14 of the LORD will be *m* known
Jer 1: 16 what their hands have *m*.
1: 18 Today I have *m* you a fortified city,
2: 7 and *m* my inheritance detestable.
2: 28 Where then are the gods you *m*
3: 16 nor will another one be *m*.
5: 3 They *m* their faces harder
5: 22 I *m* the sand a boundary for the sea
6: 27 "I have *m* you a tester of metals
7: 12 in Shiloh where I first *m* a dwelling
10: 9 all *m* by skilled workers.
Jer 10: 9 craftsman and goldsmith have *m*
10: 12 But God *m* the earth by his power;
11: 10 have broken the covenant I *m*
12: 11 It will be *m* a wasteland,
15: 17 never *m* merry with them;
18: 15 They *m* them walk in bypaths
18: 15 which *m* them stumble
18: 21 Let their wives be *m* childless
19: 4 and *m* this a place of foreign gods;
20: 15 who *m* him very glad, saying,
25: 6 with what your hands have *m*.
25: 7 me with what your hands have *m*,
25: 17 *m* all the nations to whom he sent
27: 5 and outstretched arm I *m* the earth
31: 32 I *m* with their forefathers
32: 17 you have *m* the heavens
32: 30 me with what their hands have *m*,
33: 2 LORD says, he who *m* the earth,
33: 14 will fulfill the gracious promise I *m*
34: 5 As people *m* a funeral fire in honor
34: 8 King Zedekiah had *m* a covenant
34: 13 *m* a covenant with your forefathers
34: 15 even *m* a covenant before me
34: 18 of the covenant they *m* before me,
37: 1 son of Josiah was *m* king of Judah
37: 15 which they had *m* into a prison.
41: 9 was the one King Asa had *m*
41: 10 Ishmael *m* captives of all the rest
42: 20 today that you *m* a fatal mistake
44: 6 *m* them the desolate ruins they are
44: 8 with what your hands have *m*,
44: 25 certainly carry out the vows we *m*
49: 37 until I have *m* an end of them.
50: 20 "search will be *m* for Israel's guilt,
51: 7 she *m* the whole earth drunk.
51: 15 "He *m* the earth by his power;
51: 34 he has *m* us an empty jar.
52: 19 all that were *m* of gold or silver.
52: 20 which King Solomon had *m*
La 1: 13 He *m* me desolate,
2: 6 The LORD has *m* Zion forget
2: 8 He *m* ramparts and walls lament;
3: 2 has driven me away and *m* me walk
3: 4 He has *m* my skin and my flesh
3: 6 He has *m* me dwell in darkness
3: 9 he has *m* my paths crooked.
3: 12 and *m* me the target for his arrows.
3: 45 You have *m* us scum and refuse
Eze 1: 16 to be *m* like a wheel intersecting
3: 17 I have *m* you a watchman
6: 6 and what you have *m* wiped out.
7: 19 for it has *m* them stumble into sin.
12: 6 for I have *m* you a sign to the house
15: 5 how much less can it be *m*
16: 7 I *m* you grow like a plant
16: 14 had given you *m* your beauty
16: 17 and you *m* for yourself male idols
16: 17 the jewelry *m* of my gold and silver
16: 24 and *m* a lofty shrine in every public
16: 31 and *m* your lofty shrines
16: 51 have *m* your sisters seem righteous
16: 52 for you have *m* your sisters appear
16: 60 I will remember the covenant I *m*
17: 13 of the royal family and *m* a treaty
19: 5 and *m* him a strong lion.
19: 12 The east wind *m* it shrivel,
20: 11 and *m* known to them my laws,
20: 12 that I the LORD *m* them holy.
20: 28 *m* offerings that provoked me
21: 11 *m* ready for the hand of the slayer.
21: 15 Oh! It is *m* to flash like lightning,
22: 4 defiled by the idols you have *m*.
22: 13 at the unjust gain you have *m*
27: 5 They *m* all your timbers
27: 6 they *m* your deck, inlaid with ivory
27: 6 they *m* your oars;
28: 13 and mountings were *m* of gold;
28: 17 I *m* a spectacle of you before kings.
28: 18 So I *m* a fire come out from you,
29: 3 I *m* it for myself."
29: 9 "The Nile is mine; I *m* it,"
29: 18 and every shoulder *m* raw.
31: 4 deep springs *m* it grow tall;
31: 9 I *m* it beautiful
31: 16 I *m* the nations tremble
32: 25 A bed is *m* for her among the slain,
33: 7 I have *m* you a watchman
33: 29 when I have *m* the land a desolate

Eze 36: 5 in their hearts they *m* my land their
44: 12 *m* the house of Israel fall into sin,
45: 21 during which you shall eat bread *m*
Da 2: 12 This *m* the king so angry
2: 23 you have *m* known
2: 23 you have *m* known to us the dream
2: 32 of the statue was *m* of pure gold,
2: 38 he has *m* you ruler over them all.
2: 48 He *m* him ruler over the entire
3: 1 King Nebuchadnezzar *m* an image
3: 15 and worship the image I *m*,
4: 5 I had a dream that *m* me afraid.
5: 7 he will be *m* the third highest ruler
5: 16 and you will be *m* the third highest
6: 2 The satraps were *m* accountable
6: 14 and *m* every effort until sundown
9: 1 was *m* ruler over the Babylonian
9: 15 and who *m* for yourself a name that
9: 16 of our fathers have *m* Jerusalem
11: 35 *m* spotless until the time of the end
12: 10 Many will be purified, *m* spotless
Hos 8: 6 This calf—a craftsman has *m* it;
14: 3 to what our own hands have *m*,
Am 2: 12 you *m* the Nazirites drink wine
5: 8 (he who *m* the Pleiades and Orion,
5: 26 which you *m* for yourselves.
Jnh 1: 9 who *m* the sea and the land.''
1: 16 to the LORD and *m* vows to him.
4: 5 There he *m* himself a shelter,
4: 6 and *m* it grow up over Jonah
Na 2: 3 on the day they are *m* ready;
Hab 1: 14 You have *m* men like fish in the sea
3: 6 and *m* the nations tremble.
Zep 2: 8 and *m* threats against their land.
Zec 7: 12 They *m* their hearts as hard as flint
7: 14 is how they *m* the pleasant land
11: 10 revoking the covenant I had *m*
Mal 2: 15 Has not ⌊the LORD⌋ *m* them one?
Mt 3: 4 John's clothes were *m*
5: 13 how can it be *m* salty again?
5: 33 but keep the oaths you have *m*
10: 26 or hidden that will not be *m* known
14: 22 Immediately Jesus *m* the disciples
15: 31 crippled *m* well, the lame walking
19: 4 the Creator '*m* them male
19: 12 others were *m* that way by men;
20: 12 'and you have *m* them equal
27: 14 But Jesus *m* no reply, not
27: 64 order for the tomb to be *m* secure
27: 66 *m* the tomb secure by putting a seal
Mk 1: 6 John wore clothing *m*
2: 4 they *m* an opening in the roof
2: 27 "The Sabbath was *m* for man,
6: 45 Immediately Jesus *m* his disciples
10: 6 of creation God '*m* them male
11: 17 But you have *m* it 'a den of robbers
14: 3 jar of very expensive perfume, *m*
14: 58 days will build another, not *m*
15: 5 But Jesus still *m* no reply,
Lk 1: 62 Then they *m* signs to his father,
3: 5 every mountain and hill *m* low.
10: 40 the preparations that had to be *m*.
11: 40 Did not the one who *m*
12: 2 or hidden that will not be *m* known
13: 22 as he *m* his way to Jerusalem.
14: 34 how can it be *m* salty again?
17: 19 your faith has *m* you well.''
19: 15 "He was *m* king, however,
19: 46 but you have *m* it 'a den of robbers
23: 26 and *m* him carry it behind Jesus.
Jn 1: 3 Through him all things were *m*;
1: 3 nothing was *m* that has been *m*.
1: 10 the world was *m* through him,
1: 18 Father's side, has *m* him known.
2: 15 So he *m* a whip out of cords,
4: 30 and *m* their way toward him.
5: 11 The man who *m* me well said to me
5: 15 it was Jesus who had *m* him well.
8: 3 They *m* her stand before the group
8: 22 This *m* the Jews ask, "Will he kill
9: 6 *m* some mud with the saliva,
9: 11 man they call Jesus *m* some mud
9: 14 day on which Jesus had *m* the mud
12: 10 So the chief priests *m* plans
15: 15 from my Father I have *m* known
17: 26 I have *m* you known to them,
18: 18 stood around a fire they had *m*
Ac 2: 13 however, *m* fun of them and said,
Ac 2: 28 You have *m* known to me the paths
2: 36 God has *m* this Jesus, whom you
3: 12 godliness we had *m* this man walk?
3: 16 you see and know was *m* strong.
3: 25 and of the covenant God *m*
4: 24 "you *m* the heaven and the earth
5: 4 What *m* you think
5: 27 they *m* them appear
7: 10 so he *m* him ruler over Egypt
7: 27 Who *m* you ruler and judge over us
7: 35 'Who *m* you ruler and judge?'
7: 41 That was the time they *m* an idol
7: 41 in honor of what their hands had *m*
7: 43 the idols you *m* to worship.
7: 44 It had been *m* as God directed
7: 48 live in houses *m* by men.
7: 50 Has not my hand *m* all these things
9: 39 other clothing that Dorcas had *m*
10: 15 impure that God has *m* clean.''
10: 26 But Peter *m* him get up.
11: 9 impure that God has *m* clean.'
12: 19 Herod had a thorough search *m*
13: 17 and *m* the people prosper
13: 22 removing Saul, he *m* David their
13: 47 " 'I have *m* you a light
14: 15 who *m* heaven and earth and sea
15: 3 This news *m* all the brothers very
15: 7 that some time ago God *m* a choice
15: 9 He *m* no distinction between us
17: 9 they *m* Jason and the others post
17: 24 "The God who *m* the world
17: 26 From one man he *m* every nation
17: 29 an image *m* by man's design
18: 12 the Jews *m* a united attack on Paul
19: 24 who *m* silver shrines of Artemis,
20: 3 Because the Jews *m* a plot
20: 13 He had *m* this arrangement
20: 28 Holy Spirit has *m* you overseers.
21: 23 men with us who have *m* a vow.
21: 26 the offering would be *m* for each
25: 8 Paul *m* his defense: "I have done
25: 21 When Paul *m* his appeal to be held
25: 25 he *m* his appeal to the Emperor I
27: 7 We *m* slow headway for many days
27: 40 to the wind and *m* for the beach.
28: 25 leave after Paul had *m* this final
Ro 1: 19 because God has *m* it plain to them
1: 20 understood from what has been *m*,
1: 23 for images *m* to look like mortal
3: 9 We have already *m* the charge that
3: 21 apart from law, has been *m* known,
4: 17 "I have *m* you a father
5: 19 man the many will be *m* righteous.
5: 19 one man the many were *m* sinners,
15: 8 to confirm the promises *m*
15: 28 and have *m* sure that they have
16: 26 *m* known through the prophetic
1Co 1: 20 Has not God *m* foolish the wisdom
3: 6 watered it, but God *m* it grow.
4: 9 We have been *m* a spectacle
7: 37 and who has *m* up his mind not
12: 12 though it is *m* up of many parts;
12: 14 the body is not *m* up of one part
15: 22 so in Christ all will be *m* alive.
15: 28 the Son himself will be *m* subject
16: 2 no collections will have to be *m*.
2Co 1: 20 how many promises God has *m*,
2: 1 I *m* up my mind that I would not
3: 6 He has *m* us competent
3: 14 But their minds were *m* dull,
4: 6 *m* his light shine in our hearts
5: 5 Now it is God who has *m* us
5: 21 God *m* him who had no sin
7: 9 not because you were *m* sorry,
8: 6 since he had earlier *m* a beginning,
9: 11 You will be *m* rich in every way
11: 6 We have *m* this perfectly clear
12: 9 for my power is *m* perfect
12: 11 I have *m* a fool of myself,
Gal 1: 11 is not something that man *m* up.
4: 7 God has *m* you also an heir.
Eph 1: 9 And he *m* known to us the mystery
2: 5 *m* us alive with Christ
2: 14 who has *m* the two one
3: 3 the mystery *m* known to me
3: 5 which was not *m* known to men
3: 10 of God should be *m* known
4: 23 to be *m* new in the attitude
Php 2: 7 being *m* in human likeness.
2: 7 but *m* himself nothing,
3: 12 or have already been *m* perfect,
Col 2: 13 God *m* you alive with Christ.
2: 15 he *m* a public spectacle of them,
1Th 2: 17 intense longing we *m* every effort
1Ti 1: 9 also know that law is *m* not
1: 18 the prophecies once *m* about you,
2: 1 thanksgiving be *m* for everyone—
6: 12 when you *m* your good confession
6: 13 before Pontius Pilate *m* the good
2Ti 2: 21 for noble purposes, *m* holy,
Heb 1: 2 through whom he *m* the universe.
2: 7 You *m* him a little lower
2: 9 who was *m* a little lower
2: 11 and those who are *m* holy are
2: 17 had to be *m* like his brothers
5: 9 he suffered and, once *m* perfect,
6: 13 When God *m* his promise
7: 19 (for the law *m* nothing perfect),
7: 28 who has been *m* perfect forever.
8: 9 I *m* with their forefathers
8: 13 he has *m* the first one obsolete;
9: 16 the death of the one who *m* it,
9: 17 while the one who *m* it is living.
10: 8 the law required them to be *m*).
10: 10 we have been *m* holy
10: 13 enemies to be *m* his footstool,
10: 14 sacrifice he has *m* perfect forever
10: 14 those who are being *m* holy.
11: 3 so that what is seen was not *m* out
11: 9 By faith he *m* his home
11: 11 faithful who had *m* the promise.
11: 40 with us would they be *m* perfect.
12: 23 spirits of righteous men *m* perfect,
Jas 2: 22 and his faith was *m* complete
3: 9 who have been *m* in God's likeness
1Pe 2: 23 when he suffered, he *m* no threats.
3: 18 death in the body but *m* alive
2Pe 1: 14 our Lord Jesus Christ has *m* clear
1: 19 of the prophets *m* more certain,
2: 3 you with stories they have *m* up.
2: 6 and *m* them an example
1Jn 2: 5 God's love is truly *m* complete
3: 2 will be has not yet been *m* known.
4: 12 and his love is *m* complete in us.
4: 17 Love is *m* complete among us
4: 18 The man who fears is not *m* perfect
5: 10 not believe God has *m* him out
Rev 1: 1 He *m* it known by sending his
1: 6 and has *m* us to be a kingdom
5: 10 You have *m* them to be a kingdom
6: 12 sun turned black like sackcloth *m*
7: 14 and *m* them white in the blood
13: 12 and *m* the earth and its inhabitants
14: 7 Worship him who *m* the heavens,
14: 8 which *m* all the nations drink
18: 12 articles of every kind *m* of ivory,
19: 7 and his bride has *m* herself ready.
21: 18 The wall was *m* of jasper,
21: 21 each gate *m* of a single pearl.

MADMAN (MAD)

1Sa 21: 13 in their hands he acted like a *m*,
2Ki 9: 11 Why did this *m* come to you?''
9: 20 of Nimshi—he drives like a *m*.''
Pr 26: 18 Like a *m* shooting
Jer 29: 26 you should put any *m* who acts like

MADMANNAH

Jos 15: 31 Hormah, Ziklag, *M*, Sansannah,
1Ch 2: 49 birth to Shaaph the father of *M*

MADMEN (MAD)

1Sa 21: 15 Am I so short of *m* that you have
Jer 48: 2 You too, O *M*, will be silenced;

MADMENAH

Isa 10: 31 *M* is in flight;

MADNESS (MAD)

Dt 28: 28 The LORD will afflict you with *m*,
Ecc 1: 17 and also of *m* and folly,
2: 12 and also *m* and folly.
7: 25 and the *m* of folly.
9: 3 and there is *m* in their hearts
10: 13 at the end they are wicked *m*—
Zec 12: 4 with panic and its rider with *m*,''

2Pe 2: 16 and restrained the prophet's *m*.

MADON

Jos 11: 1 he sent word to Jobab king of *M*,
12: 19 one the king of *M* one the king

MAGADAN

Mt 15: 39 and went to the vicinity of *M*.

MAGBISH

Ezr 2: 30 and Ai 223 of Nebo 52 of *M* 156

MAGDALA (MAGDALENE)

Jn 19: 25 the wife of Clopas, and Mary of *M*.
20: 1 Mary of *M* went to the tomb
20: 18 Mary of *M* went to the disciples

MAGDALENE (MAGDALA)

Mt 27: 56 Among them were Mary *M*,
27: 61 Mary *M* and the other Mary were
28: 1 Mary *M* and the other Mary went
Mk 15: 40 Among them were Mary *M*,
15: 47 Mary *M* and Mary the mother
16: 1 Mary *M*, Mary the mother
16: 9 he appeared first to Mary *M*,
Lk 8: 2 Mary (called *M*) from whom seven
24: 10 It was Mary *M*, Joanna, Mary

MAGDIEL

Ge 36: 43 Teman, Mibzar, *M* and Iram.
1Ch 1: 54 Teman, Mibzar, *M* and Iram.

MAGGOT (MAGGOTS)

Job 25: 6 how much less man, who is but a *m*

MAGGOTS (MAGGOT)

Ex 16: 20 it was full of *m* and began to smell.
16: 24 and it did not stink or get *m* in it.
Isa 14: 11 *m* are spread out beneath you

MAGI

Mt 2: 1 *M* from the east came to Jerusalem
2: 7 Then Herod called the *M* secretly
2: 16 he had been outwitted by the *M*,
2: 16 time he had learned from the *M*.

MAGIC (MAGICIAN MAGICIANS)

Isa 47: 12 "Keep on, then, with your *m* spells
Eze 13: 18 to the women who sew *m* charms
13: 20 I am against your *m* charms
Ac 8: 11 them for a long time with his *m*.
Rev 9: 21 their *m* arts, their sexual
18: 23 By your *m* spell all the nations
21: 8 those who practice *m* arts,
22: 15 those who practice *m* arts,

MAGICIAN (MAGIC)

Da 2: 10 ever asked such a thing of any *m*
2: 27 *m* or diviner can explain

MAGICIANS (MAGIC)

Ge 41: 8 so he sent for all the *m*
41: 24 to the *m*, but none could explain it
Ex 7: 11 the Egyptian *m* also did the same
7: 22 the Egyptian *m* did the same things
8: 7 But the *m* did the same things
8: 18 when the *m* tried to produce gnats
8: 19 The *m* said to Pharaoh, "This is
9: 11 The *m* could not stand
Da 1: 20 ten times better than all the *m*
2: 2 So the king summoned the *m*,
4: 7 When the *m*, enchanters,
4: 9 "Belteshazzar, chief of the *m*,
5: 11 appointed him chief of the *m*,

MAGISTRATE (MAGISTRATES)

Lk 12: 58 with your adversary to the *m*,

MAGISTRATES (MAGISTRATE)

Ezr 7: 25 appoint *m* and judges
Da 3: 2 *m* and all the other provincial
3: 3 *m* and all the other provincial
Ac 16: 20 They brought them before the *m*
16: 22 the *m* ordered them to be stripped
16: 35 the *m* sent their officers
16: 36 "The *m* have ordered that you
16: 38 The officers reported this to the *m*,

MAGNIFICENCE (MAGNIFY)

1Ch 22: 5 for the LORD should be of great *m*

MAGNIFICENT (MAGNIFY)

1Ki 8: 13 I have indeed built a *m* temple
2Ch 2: 9 temple I build must be large and *m*.
6: 2 I have built a *m* temple for you,
Isa 28: 29 in counsel and *m* in wisdom.
Mk 13: 1 stones! What *m* buildings!"

MAGNIFY (MAGNIFICENCE MAGNIFICENT)

Da 11: 36 and *m* himself above every god

MAGOG

Ge 10: 2 Gomer, *M*, Madai, Javan, Tubal,
1Ch 1: 5 Gomer, *M*, Madai, Javan, Tubal,
Eze 38: 2 of the land of *M*, the chief prince
39: 6 I will send fire on *M*
Rev 20: 8 and *M*— to gather them for battle.

MAGOR-MISSABIB

Jer 20: 3 for you is not Pashhur, but *M*.

MAGPIASH

Ne 10: 20 Anathoth, Nebai, *M*, Meshullam,

MAHALALEEL

Lk 3: 37 the son of Jared, the son of *M*,

MAHALALEL

Ge 5: 12 he became the father of *M*.
5: 13 after he became the father of *M*,
5: 15 When *M* had lived 65 years,
5: 16 *M* lived 830 years and had other
5: 17 Altogether, *M* lived 895 years,
1Ch 1: 2 Enosh, Kenan, *M*, Jared, Enoch,
Ne 11: 4 the son of *M*, a descendant of Perez

MAHALATH

Ge 28: 9 went to Ishmael and married *M*,
2Ch 11: 18 Rehoboam married *M*, who was

MAHANAIM

Ge 32: 2 So he named that place *M*.
Jos 13: 26 *M* to the territory of Debir; and
13: 30 The territory extending from *M*
21: 38 *M*, Heshbon and Jazer, together
2Sa 2: 8 and brought him over to *M*.
2: 12 left *M* and went to Gibeon.
2: 29 the whole Bithron and came to *M*.
17: 24 went to *M*, and Absalom crossed
17: 27 When David came to *M*, Shobi son
19: 32 for the king during his stay in *M*,
1Ki 2: 8 curses on me the day I went to *M*.
4: 14 Ahinadab son of Iddo—in *M*;
1Ch 6: 80 *M*, Heshbon and Jazer, together
SS 6: 13 as on the dance of *M*?

MAHANEH DAN

Jdg 13: 25 to stir him while he was in *M*,
18: 12 is called *M* to this day.

MAHARAI

2Sa 23: 28 the Ahohite, *M* the Netophathite,
1Ch 11: 30 the Ahohite, *M* the Netophathite,
27: 13 was *M* the Netophathite,

MAHATH

1Ch 6: 35 the son of *M*, the son of Amasai,
2Ch 29: 12 *M* son of Amasai and Joel son
31: 13 *M* and Benaiah were supervisors

MAHAVITE

1Ch 11: 46 Joha the Tizite, Eliel the *M*,

MAHAZIOTH

1Ch 25: 4 Mallothi, Hothir and *M*.
25: 30 12 the twenty-third to *M*, his sons

MAHER-SHALAL-HASH-BAZ

Isa 8: 1 write on it with an ordinary pen: *M*
8: 3 said to me, "Name him *M*.

MAHLAH (MAHLITE MAHLITES)

Nu 26: 33 whose names were *M*, Noah,
27: 1 names of the daughters were *M*,
36: 11 Zelophehad's daughters—*M*,
Jos 17: 3 whose names were *M*, Noah,
1Ch 7: 18 birth to Ishhod, Abiezer and *M*.

MAHLI

Ex 6: 19 The sons of Merari were *M*
Nu 3: 20 The Merarite clans: *M* and Mushi.
1Ch 6: 19 The sons of Merari: *M* and Mushi.
6: 29 The descendants of Merari: *M*,
6: 47 the son of *M*, the son of Mushi,
23: 21 The sons of Merari: *M* and Mushi.
23: 21 The sons of *M*: Eleazar and Kish.
23: 23 The sons of Mushi: *M*, Eder
24: 26 The sons of Merari: *M* and Mushi.
24: 28 From *M*: Eleazar, who had no sons
24: 30 And the sons of Mushi: *M*,
Ezr 8: 18 from the descendants of *M* son

MAHLITE (MAHLAH)

Nu 26: 58 the Hebronite clan, the *M* clan,

MAHLITES (MAHLAH)

Nu 3: 33 Merari belonged the clans of the *M*

MAHLON (MAHLON'S)

Ru 1: 2 the names of his two sons were *M*
1: 5 both *M* and Kilion also died,
4: 9 of Elimelech, Kilion and *M*.

MAHLON'S (MAHLON)

Ru 4: 10 Ruth the Moabitess, *M* widow,

MAHOL

1Ki 4: 31 Calcol and Darda, the sons of *M*.

MAHSEIAH

Jer 32: 12 son of Neriah, the son of *M*,
51: 59 son of Neriah, the son of *M*,

MAID (MAIDEN MAIDENS MAIDS)

Ps 123: 2 as the eyes of a *m* look to the hand
Isa 24: 2 for mistress as for *m*,

MAIDEN (MAID)

Ge 24: 43 if a *m* comes out to draw water
Pr 30: 19 and the way of a man with a *m*.
Isa 62: 5 As a young man marries a *m*,
Jer 2: 32 Does a *m* forget her jewelry,
51: 22 you I shatter young man and *m*,

MAIDENS (MAID)

Ps 68: 25 are the *m* playing tambourines.
78: 63 and their *m* had no wedding songs;
148: 12 young men and *m*,
SS 1: 3 No wonder the *m* love you!
2: 2 is my darling among the *m*.
6: 9 *m* saw her and called her blessed;
Jer 31: 13 Then *m* will dance and be glad,
La 1: 4 her *m* grieve,
1: 18 My young men and *m*
2: 21 my young men and *m*
Eze 9: 6 young men and *m*, women

MAIDS (MAID)

Ge 24: 61 Then Rebekah and her *m* got ready
1Sa 25: 42 and, attended by her five *m*, went
Est 2: 9 and her *m* into the best place
2: 9 assigned to her seven *m* selected
4: 4 When Esther's *m* and eunuchs
4: 16 I and my *m* will fast as you do.
Pr 9: 3 She has sent out her *m*,

MAIDSERVANT (SERVANT)

Ge 16: 1 had an Egyptian *m* named Hagar;
16: 2 with my *m*; perhaps I can build
16: 3 wife took her Egyptian *m* Hagar
21: 12 about the boy and your *m*.
21: 13 the son of the *m* into a nation
25: 12 whom Sarah's *m*, Hagar
29: 24 Zilpah to his daughter as her *m*.
29: 29 to his daughter Rachel as her *m*.
30: 3 she said, "Here is Bilhah, my *m*.
30: 9 she took her *m* Zilpah
30: 18 for giving my *m* to my husband."
35: 25 The sons of Rachel's *m* Bilhah:
35: 26 The sons of Leah's *m* Zilpah:
Ex 20: 10 nor your manservant or *m*,
20: 17 or his manservant or *m*, his ox
21: 26 or *m* in the eye and destroys it,

Ex 21:27 the tooth of a manservant or *m*,
Lev 25: 6 yourself, your manservant and *m*,
Dt 5:14 nor your manservant or *m*,
5:14 your manservant and *m* may rest,
5:21 his manservant or *m*, his ox
15:17 Do the same for your *m*.
Jdg 19:19 your *m*, and the young man with us
1Sa 25:41 Here is your *m*, ready to serve you
28:21 "Look, your *m* has obeyed you.
Ps 86:16 and save the son of your *m*.
116:16 am your servant, the son of your *m*;
Pr 30:23 and a *m* who displaces her mistress

MAIDSERVANTS (SERVANT)

Ge 12:16 menservants and *m*, and camels.
24:35 menservants and *m*, and camels
30:43 and *m* and menservants,
31:33 and into the tent of the two *m*,
32: 5 and goats, menservants and *m*.
32:22 his two *m* and his eleven sons
33: 1 Leah, Rachel and the two *m*.
33: 2 He put the *m* and their children
33: 6 *m* and their children approached
Dt 12:12 your menservants and *m*,
12:18 your menservants and *m*,
16:11 and *m*, the Levites in your towns,
16:14 your menservants and *m*,
1Sa 8:16 Your menservants and *m*
2Ki 5:26 herds, or menservants and *m*?
Ezr 2:65 their 7,337 menservants and *m*;
Ne 7:67 their 7,337 menservants and *m*;
Job 19:15 my *m* count me a stranger;
31:13 justice to my menservants and *m*
Isa 14: 2 and *m* in the LORD's land.

MAIMED

Lev 22:22 or the *m*, or anything with warts
Mt 18: 8 It is better for you to enter life *m*
Mk 9:43 to enter life *m* than with two hands

MAIN

Nu 20:19 "We will go along the *m* road,
Dt 2:27 We will stay on the *m* road;
1Ki 6: 3 portico at the front of the *m* hall
6: 5 Against the walls of the *m* hall
6:17 The *m* hall in front
6:33 for the entrance to the *m* hall.
7:50 doors of the *m* hall of the temple.
2Ch 3: 5 He paneled the *m* hall with pine
3:13 on their feet, facing the *m* hall.
4:22 and the doors of the *m* hall.
Eze 19:14 from one of its *m* branches

MAINLAND

Eze 26: 6 on the *m* will be ravaged
26: 8 on the *m* with the sword;

MAINSTAY

Jer 49:35 the *m* of their might.

MAINTAIN (MAINTAINED MAINTAINING MAINTAINS)

Ru 4: 5 in order to *m* the name of the dead
4:10 in order to *m* the name of the dead
1Ki 10: 9 to *m* justice and righteousness."
2Ki 8:19 He had promised to *m* a lamp
2Ch 9: 8 to *m* justice and righteousness."
21: 7 He had promised to *m* a lamp
Job 27: 6 I will *m* my righteousness
Ps 82: 3 *m* the rights of the poor
89:28 I will *m* my love to him forever,
106: 3 Blessed are they who *m* justice,
Pr 5: 2 that you may *m* discretion
Isa 56: 1 "*M* justice
Da 11:20 collector to *m* the royal splendor.
Hos 12: 6 *m* love and justice,
Am 5:15 *m* justice in the courts.
Ro 3:28 For we *m* that a man is justified

MAINTAINED (MAINTAIN)

Rev 6: 9 and the testimony they had *m*.

MAINTAINING (MAINTAIN)

Ex 34: 7 faithfulness, *m* love to thousands,

MAINTAINS (MAINTAIN)

Job 2: 3 And he still *m* his integrity,
Pr 28: 2 and knowledge *m* order.

Na 1: 2 *m* his wrath against his enemies.

MAJESTIC (MAJESTY)

Ex 15: 6 was *m* in power.
15:11 *m* in holiness,
Job 37: 4 he thunders with his *m* voice.
Ps 8: 1 how *m* is your name in all the earth
8: 9 how *m* is your name in all the earth
29: 4 the voice of the LORD is *m*.
68:15 of Bashan are *m* mountains;
76: 4 more *m* than mountains rich
111: 3 Glorious and *m* are his deeds,
SS 6: 4 *m* as troops with banners.
6:10 *m* as the stars in procession?
Isa 30:30 men to hear his *m* voice
Eze 31: 7 It was *m* in beauty,
2Pe 1:17 came to him from the *M* Glory,

MAJESTY (MAJESTIC)

Ex 15: 7 In the greatness of your *m*
Dt 5:24 has shown us his glory and his *m*,
11: 2 his *m*, his mighty hand, his
33:17 In *m* he is like a firstborn bull;
33:26 and on the clouds in his *m*.
1Ch 16:27 Splendor and *m* are before him;
29:11 and the *m* and the splendor,
Est 1: 4 the splendor and glory of his *m*.
7: 3 if it pleases your *m*, grant me my
Job 37:22 God comes in awesome *m*.
40:10 and clothe yourself in honor and *m*
Ps 21: 5 on him splendor and *m*.
45: 3 with splendor and *m*.
45: 4 In your *m* ride forth victoriously
68:34 whose *m* is over Israel,
93: 1 The LORD reigns, he is robed in *m*
93: 1 the LORD is robed in *m*
96: 6 Splendor and *m* are before him;
104: 1 clothed with splendor and *m*.
110: 3 Arrayed in holy *m*,
145: 5 of the glorious splendor of your *m*,
Isa 2:10 and the splendor of his *m*!
2:19 and the splendor of his *m*,
2:21 and the splendor of his *m*,
24:14 west they acclaim the LORD's *m*.
26:10 and regard not the *m* of the LORD.
53: 2 or *m* to attract us to him,
Eze 31: 2 can be compared with you in *m*?
31:18 with you in splendor and *m*?
Da 4:30 and for the glory of my *m*?"
Mic 5: 4 in the *m* of the name
Zec 6:13 and he will be clothed with *m*
Ac 19:27 will be robbed of her divine *m*."
25:26 to write to His *M* about him.
2Th 1: 9 and from the *m* of his power
Heb 1: 3 hand of the *M* in heaven.
8: 1 of the throne of the *M* in heaven,
2Pe 1:16 but we were eyewitnesses of his *m*.
Jude :25 only God our Savior be glory, *m*,

MAJOR

2Ki 3:19 fortified city and every *m* town.

MAJORITY

Ac 27:12 the *m* decided that we should sail
2Co 2: 6 on him by the *m* is sufficient

MAKAZ

1Ki 4: 9 Ben-Deker—in *M*, Shaalbim,

MAKE (MADE MAKER MAKERS MAKES MAKING MAN-MADE)

Ge 1:26 "Let us *m* man in our image,
2:18 I will *m* a helper suitable for him."
6:14 *m* rooms in it and coat it with pitch
6:14 *m* yourself an ark of cypress wood;
6:16 in the side of the ark and *m* lower,
6:16 *M* a roof for it and finish the ark
11: 3 let's *m* bricks and bake them
11: 4 so that we may *m* a name
12: 2 I will *m* your name great,
12: 2 "I will *m* you into a great nation
13:16 I will *m* your offspring like the dust
17: 6 I will *m* you very fruitful; I will
17: 6 you very fruitful; I will *m* nations
17:20 I will *m* him fruitful and will
17:20 and I will *m* him into a great nation
21:13 I will *m* the son of the maidservant
21:18 for I will *m* him into a great nation

Ge 22:17 *m* your descendants as numerous
24: 6 "*M* sure that you do not take my
24:40 and *m* your journey a success,
26: 4 I will *m* your descendants
26:28 Let us *m* a treaty with you that you
28: 3 bless you and *m* you fruitful
31:44 Come now, let's *m* a covenant,
32: 9 relatives, and I will *m* you prosper,'
32:12 and will *m* your descendants like
32:12 'I will surely *m* you prosper
34:12 *M* the price for the bride
39:14 brought to us to *m* sport of us!
39:17 came to me to *m* sport of me.
41:43 men shouted before him, "*M* way
46: 3 for I will *m* you into a great nation
48: 4 I will *m* you a community
48: 4 'I am going to *m* you fruitful
48:20 'May God *m* you like Ephraim
Ex 3:21 I will *m* the Egyptians favorably
5: 8 them to *m* the same number
5: 9 *M* the work harder for the men
5:16 yet we are told, '*M* bricks!'
6: 3 LORD I did not *m* myself known
8: 5 and *m* frogs come up on the land
8:23 I will *m* a distinction
9: 4 But the LORD will *m* a distinction
10:28 *M* sure you do not appear
17: 3 bring us up out of Egypt to *m* us
17:14 and *m* sure that Joshua hears it,
18:22 That will *m* your load lighter,
20: 4 You shall not *m* for yourself an idol
20:23 Do not *m* any gods to be
20:23 do not *m* for yourselves gods
20:24 " '*M* an altar of earth for me
20:25 If you *m* an altar of stones for me,
22: 3 thief must certainly *m* restitution,
22: 5 he must *m* restitution from the best
22: 6 started the fire must *m* restitution.
22:12 he must *m* restitution to the owner.
22:14 not present, he must *m* restitution.
23:27 I will *m* all your enemies turn their
23:32 Do not *m* a covenant with them
25: 8 have them *m* a sanctuary for me,
25: 9 *M* this tabernacle and all its
25:10 "Have them *m* a chest
25:11 and *m* a gold molding around it.
25:13 Then *m* poles of acacia wood
25:17 *M* an atonement cover of pure gold
25:18 And *m* two cherubim out
25:19 *M* one cherub on one end
25:19 *m* the cherubim of one piece
25:23 "*M* a table of acacia wood—
25:24 and *m* a gold molding around it.
25:25 *m* around it a rim a handbreadth
25:26 *M* four gold rings for the table
25:28 *M* the poles of acacia wood,
25:29 *m* its plates and ladles of pure gold,
25:31 "*M* a lampstand of pure gold
25:37 "Then *m* its seven lamps
25:40 See that you *m* them according
26: 1 *M* the tabernacle with ten curtains
26: 4 *M* loops of blue material
26: 5 *M* fifty loops on one curtain
26: 6 Then *m* fifty gold clasps
26: 7 *M* curtains of goat hair for the tent
26:10 *M* fifty loops along the edge
26:11 Then *m* fifty bronze clasps
26:14 *M* for the tent a covering
26:15 "*M* upright frames of acacia wood
26:17 *M* all the frames of the tabernacle
26:18 *M* twenty frames for the south side
26:19 and *m* forty silver bases to go
26:20 *m* twenty frames and forty silver
26:22 *M* six frames for the far end, that is,
26:23 and *m* two frames for the corners
26:26 "Also *m* crossbars of acacia wood:
26:29 *m* gold rings to hold the crossbars.
26:31 "*M* a curtain of blue, purple
26:36 to the tent *m* a curtain of blue,
26:37 *M* gold hooks for this curtain
27: 2 *M* a horn at each of the four
27: 3 *M* all its utensils of bronze—
27: 4 and *m* a bronze ring at each
27: 4 *M* a grating for it, a bronze network
27: 6 *M* poles of acacia wood
27: 8 *M* the altar hollow, out of boards.
27: 9 "*M* a courtyard for the tabernacle.
28: 2 *M* sacred garments

Ex 28: 3 are to *m* garments for Aaron,
28: 4 are the garments they are to *m*:
28: 4 are to *m* these sacred garments
28: 6 "*M* the ephod of gold, and of blue,
28: 13 *M* gold filigree settings
28: 15 *M* it like the ephod: of gold,
28: 22 the breastpiece *m* braided chains
28: 23 *M* two gold rings for it
28: 26 *M* two gold rings and attach them
28: 27 *M* two more gold rings
28: 31 "*M* the robe of the ephod entirely
28: 33 *M* pomegranates of blue, purple
28: 36 "*M* a plate of pure gold
28: 39 and *m* the turban of fine linen.
28: 40 *M* tunics, sashes and headbands
28: 42 "*M* linen undergarments
29: 2 *m* bread, and cakes mixed with oil,
29: 28 are to *m* to the LORD
29: 36 as a sin offering to *m* atonement.
29: 37 For seven days *m* atonement
30: 1 "*M* an altar of acacia wood
30: 3 and *m* a gold molding around it.
30: 4 *M* two gold rings for the altar
30: 5 *M* the poles of acacia wood
30: 10 a year Aaron shall *m* atonement
30: 15 less when you *m* the offering
30: 18 said to Moses, "*M* a bronze basin,
30: 25 *M* these into a sacred anointing oil,
30: 32 and do not *m* any oil with the same
30: 35 and *m* a fragrant blend of incense,
30: 37 Do not *m* any incense
31: 4 to *m* artistic designs for work
31: 6 craftsmen to *m* everything I have
31: 11 They are to *m* them just
32: 1 *m* us gods who will go before us.
32: 10 I will *m* you into a great nation."
32: 13 'I will *m* your descendants
32: 23 '*M* us gods who will go before us.
32: 30 perhaps I can *m* atonement
34: 12 Be careful not to *m* a treaty
34: 15 "Be careful not to *m* a treaty
34: 17 "Do not *m* cast idols.
35: 10 and *m* everything the LORD has
35: 32 to *m* artistic designs for work
36: 6 or woman is to *m* anything else
38: 28 of the posts, and to *m* their bands.
38: 28 shekels to *m* the hooks
38: 30 They used it to *m* the bases
Lev 1: 4 behalf to *m* atonement for him.
3: 14 is to *m* this offering to the LORD
4: 20 way the priest will *m* atonement
4: 26 way the priest will *m* atonement
4: 31 way the priest will *m* atonement
4: 35 way the priest will *m* atonement
5: 3 that would *m* him unclean—
5: 6 and the priest shall *m* atonement
5: 10 and *m* atonement for him
5: 13 way the priest will *m* atonement
5: 16 He must *m* restitution
5: 16 who will *m* atonement for him
5: 18 way the priest will *m* atonement
6: 5 He must *m* restitution in full,
6: 7 way the priest will *m* atonement
6: 30 Tent of Meeting to *m* atonement
8: 15 it to *m* atonement for it.
8: 34 LORD to *m* atonement for you.
9: 7 and *m* atonement for them,
9: 7 and *m* atonement for yourself
11: 24 " 'You will *m* yourselves unclean
11: 43 Do not *m* yourselves unclean
11: 44 Do not *m* yourselves unclean
12: 7 the LORD to *m* atonement for her,
12: 8 way the priest will *m* atonement
14: 18 and *m* atonement for him
14: 19 and *m* atonement for the one
14: 20 and *m* atonement for him,
14: 21 waved to *m* atonement for him,
14: 29 to *m* atonement for him
14: 31 way the priest will *m* atonement
14: 53 In this way he will *m* atonement
15: 3 is blocked, it will *m* him unclean.
15: 15 In this way he will *m* atonement
15: 30 In this way he will *m* atonement
15: 31 from things that *m* them unclean,
16: 6 to *m* atonement for himself
16: 11 to *m* atonement for himself
16: 16 In this way he will *m* atonement
16: 17 goes in to *m* atonement
Lev 16: 18 the LORD and *m* atonement
16: 24 to *m* atonement for himself
16: 27 Most Holy Place to *m* atonement,
16: 32 as high priest is to *m* atonement.
16: 33 *m* atonement for the Most Holy
17: 11 it to you to *m* atonement
19: 4 *m* gods of cast metal for yourselves
19: 22 is to *m* atonement for him
20: 25 *m* a distinction between clean
21: 1 must not *m* himself ceremonially
21: 3 for her he may *m* himself unclean.
21: 4 He must not *m* himself unclean
21: 11 He must not *m* himself unclean,
22: 14 he must *m* restitution to the priest
24: 18 animal must *m* restitution—
24: 21 kills an animal must *m* restitution,
25: 39 do not *m* him work as a slave.
25: 46 and can *m* them slaves for life,
26: 1 Do not *m* idols or set up an image
26: 6 and no one will *m* you afraid.
26: 9 *m* you fruitful and increase your
26: 10 out to *m* room for the new.
26: 19 and *m* the sky above you like iron
26: 22 *m* you so few in number that your
26: 36 I will *m* their hearts so fearful
27: 33 If he does *m* a substitution,
27: 33 from the bad or *m* any substitution.
Nu 3: 40 or more and *m* a list of their names.
5: 7 He must *m* full restitution
6: 2 woman wants to *m* a special vow,
6: 7 must not *m* himself ceremonially
6: 11 offering to *m* atonement for him
6: 16 *m* the sin offering and the burnt
6: 25 the LORD *m* his face shine
8: 6 and *m* them ceremonially clean.
8: 12 to *m* atonement for the Levites.
8: 19 and to *m* atonement for them
10: 2 "*M* two trumpets of hammered
14: 12 I will *m* you into a nation greater
14: 30 with uplifted hand to *m* your home
15: 25 The priest is to *m* atonement
15: 28 The priest is to *m* atonement
15: 38 are to *m* tassels on the corners
16: 46 assembly to *m* atonement for them.
21: 8 "*M* a snake and put it up on a pole;
22: 28 to *m* you beat me these three times
28: 9 *m* an offering of two lambs a year
28: 22 offering to *m* atonement for you.
28: 30 goat to *m* atonement for you.
29: 5 offering to *m* atonement for you.
31: 50 to *m* atonement for ourselves
32: 5 Do not *m* us cross the Jordan."
Dt 4: 16 and *m* for yourselves an idol,
4: 23 do not *m* for yourselves an idol
4: 25 become corrupt and *m* any kind
5: 8 You shall not *m* for yourself an idol
7: 2 *M* no treaty with them,
9: 14 I will *m* you into a nation stronger
10: 1 Also *m* a wooden chest.
17: 16 or *m* the people return to Egypt
19: 18 The judges must *m* a thorough
20: 10 *m* its people an offer of peace.
20: 12 If they refuse to *m* peace
22: 8 *m* a parapet around your roof
22: 12 *M* tassels on the four corners
23: 21 If you *m* a vow to the LORD your
24: 10 When you *m* a loan of any kind
25: 2 the judge shall *m* him lie down
28: 13 The LORD will *m* you the head,
28: 63 the LORD to *m* you prosper
28: 68 I said you should never *m* again.
29: 1 to *m* with the Israelites in Moab,
29: 18 *M* sure there is no man or woman,
29: 18 *m* sure there is no root
30: 5 He will *m* you more prosperous
30: 9 in you and *m* you prosperous,
30: 9 your God will *m* you most
32: 21 I will *m* them angry
32: 21 I will *m* them envious
32: 25 the sword will *m* them childless;
32: 42 I will *m* my arrows drunk
32: 43 and *m* atonement for his land
Jos 5: 2 "*M* flint knives and circumcise
6: 18 Otherwise you will *m* the camp
9: 2 together to *m* war against Joshua
9: 6 from a distant country; *m* a treaty
9: 7 How then can we *m* a treaty
9: 11 "We are your servants; *m* a treaty
Jos 18: 4 out to *m* a survey of the land
18: 8 "Go and *m* a survey of the land
24: 20 on you and *m* an end of you,
Jdg 2: 2 and you shall not *m* a covenant
5: 3 I will *m* music to the LORD,
6: 39 Let me *m* just one more request.
6: 39 This time *m* the fleece dry
17: 3 for my son to *m* a carved image
Ru 4: 11 May the LORD *m* the woman who
1Sa 1: 23 may the LORD *m* good his word."
3: 11 in Israel that will *m* the ears
6: 5 *M* models of the tumors
8: 11 and *m* them serve with his chariots
8: 12 still others to *m* weapons of war
11: 1 said to him, "*M* a treaty with us,
11: 2 "I will *m* a treaty with you only
12: 3 a bribe to *m* me shut my eyes?
12: 3 any of these, I will *m* it right."
12: 22 was pleased to *m* you his own.
13: 19 the Hebrews will *m* swords
15: 18 *m* war on them until you have
20: 26 to *m* him ceremonially unclean—
22: 7 Will he *m* all of you commanders
23: 22 Go and *m* further preparation.
25: 28 LORD will certainly *m* a lasting
28: 2 I will *m* you my bodyguard for life
2Sa 3: 12 "Whose land is it? *M* an agreement
3: 13 "I will *m* an agreement with you.
3: 17 wanted to *m* David your king.
3: 21 so that they may *m* a compact
7: 9 Now I will *m* your name great,
7: 23 and to *m* a name for himself,
13: 6 *m* some special bread in my sight,
15: 20 today shall I *m* you wander about
19: 28 have to *m* any more appeals
21: 3 How shall I *m* amends
22: 36 you stoop down to *m* me great.
1Ki 1: 37 be with Solomon to *m* his throne
1: 47 'May your God *m* Solomon's name
2: 16 I have one request to *m* of you.
2: 16 "You may *m* it," she said.
2: 20 The king replied, "*M* it, my mother
2: 20 "I have one small request to *m*
2: 42 "Did I not *m* you swear
9: 22 Solomon did not *m* slaves of any
10: 12 and to *m* harps and lyres
10: 12 to *m* supports for the temple
12: 1 had gone there to *m* him king.
12: 10 but *m* our yoke lighter'—tell them,
12: 11 laid on you a heavy yoke; I will *m* it
12: 14 made your yoke heavy; I will *m* it
12: 21 to *m* war against the house of Israel
12: 33 went up to the altar to *m* offerings.
13: 1 by the altar to *m* an offering.
13: 2 places who now *m* offerings here,
16: 3 and I will *m* your house like that
17: 12 *m* a meal for myself and my son,
17: 13 and then *m* something for yourself
17: 13 first *m* a small cake of bread for me
19: 2 tomorrow I do not *m* your life like
21: 22 I will *m* your house like that
22: 16 many times must I *m* you swear
2Ki 2: 21 or *m* the land unproductive.' "
3: 16 *M* this valley full of ditches.
4: 10 Let's *m* a small room on the roof
5: 17 will never again *m* burnt offerings
9: 9 I will *m* the house of Ahab like
9: 26 and I will surely *m* you pay for it
10: 24 So they went in to *m* sacrifices
18: 23 *m* a bargain with my master,
18: 31 *M* peace with me and come out
19: 28 and I will *m* you return
21: 8 I will not again *m* the feet
1Ch 12: 31 name to come and *m* David king—
12: 38 also of one mind to *m* David king
12: 38 fully determined to *m* David king
16: 4 to *m* petition, to give thanks,
16: 8 *m* known among the nations what
17: 8 I will *m* your name like the names
17: 21 and to *m* a name for yourself,
18: 8 used to *m* the bronze Sea,
22: 3 of iron to *m* nails for the doors
22: 5 Therefore I will *m* preparations
27: 23 LORD had promised to *m* Israel
28: 4 to *m* me king over all Israel.
2Ch 7: 20 I will *m* it a byword and an object
8: 9 But Solomon did not *m* slaves
9: 11 and to *m* harps and lyres

2Ch 9: 11 to *m* steps for the temple
10: 1 had gone there to *m* him king.
10: 10 but *m* our yoke lighter'—tell them,
10: 11 laid on you a heavy yoke; I will *m* it
10: 14 made your yoke heavy; I will *m* it
11: 1 to *m* war against Israel
11: 22 in order to *m* him king.
13: 9 and *m* priests of your own
17: 10 so that they did not *m* war
18: 15 many times must I *m* you swear
20: 1 came to *m* war on Jehoshaphat.
28: 10 And now you intend to *m* the men
29: 10 Now I intend to *m* a covenant
32: 2 intended to *m* war on Jerusalem,
32: 18 and *m* them afraid in order
33: 8 I will not again *m* the feet
36: 22 king of Persia to *m* a proclamation
Ezr 1: 1 king of Persia to *m* a proclamation
4: 4 *m* them afraid to go on building.
10: 3 let us *m* a covenant before our God
10: 11 Now *m* confession to the LORD,
Ne 2: 8 timber to *m* beams for the gates
6: 7 to *m* this proclamation about you
8: 15 palms and shade trees, to *m* booths
10: 33 to *m* atonement for Israel;
Job 7: 17 "What is man that you *m* so much
11: 19 with no one to *m* you afraid,
13: 26 *m* me inherit the sins of my youth.
16: 4 I could *m* fine speeches against you
20: 10 His children must *m* amends
20: 15 God will *m* his stomach vomit
21: 12 they *m* merry to the sound
24: 17 they *m* friends with the terrors
31: 15 me in the womb *m* them?
36: 33 the cattle *m* known its approach.
38: 27 and *m* it sprout with grass?
39: 20 Do you *m* him leap like a locust,
41: 4 Will he *m* an agreement with you
41: 5 Can you *m* a pet of him like a bird
41: 28 Arrows do not *m* him flee;
Ps 2: 8 and I will *m* the nations your
4: 8 *m* me dwell in safety.
5: 8 *m* straight your way before me.
7: 5 and *m* me sleep in the dust.
7: 9 and *m* the righteous secure.
18: 35 you stoop down to *m* me great.
20: 4 and *m* all your plans succeed.
21: 9 you will *m* them like a fiery furnace
21: 12 for you will *m* them turn their
27: 6 and *m* music to the LORD.
33: 2 *m* music to him on the ten-stringed
37: 6 He will *m* your righteousness shine
39: 8 do not *m* me the scorn of fools.
44: 8 In God we *m* our boast all day long
45: 16 you will *m* them princes
46: 4 river whose streams *m* glad the city
51: 18 good pleasure *m* Zion prosper;
52: 7 who did not *m* God his stronghold
57: 7 I will sing and *m* music.
59: 11 In your might *m* them wander
67: 1 and *m* his face shine upon us; *Selah*
69: 11 people *m* sport of me.
76: 11 *M* vows to the LORD your God
79: 10 *m* known among the nations
80: 3 *m* your face shine upon us,
80: 7 *m* your face shine upon us,
80: 19 *m* your face shine upon us,
83: 11 *M* their nobles like Oreb and Zeeb,
83: 13 *M* them like tumbleweed,
84: 6 they *m* it a place of springs;
87: 7 As they *m* music they will sing,
89: 1 mouth I will *m* your faithfulness
89: 4 and *m* your throne firm
90: 15 *M* us glad for as many days
91: 9 If you *m* the Most High your
92: 1 and *m* music to your name,
92: 4 For you *m* me glad by your deeds,
98: 5 *m* music to the LORD
104: 15 oil to *m* his face shine,
104: 17 There the birds *m* their nests;
105: 1 *m* known among the nations what
106: 8 to *m* his mighty power known.
106: 26 that he would *m* them fall
106: 27 *m* their descendants fall
108: 1 *m* music with all my soul.
110: 1 hand until I *m* your enemies
115: 8 Those who *m* them will be like
115: 14 May the LORD *m* you increase,

Ps 119: 98 Your commands *m* me wiser
119:135 *M* your face shine
119:165 and nothing can *m* them stumble.
132: 17 "Here I will *m* a horn grow
135: 18 Those who *m* them will be like
139: 8 if I *m* my bed in the depths,
140: 3 They *m* their tongues as sharp
144: 9 the ten-stringed lyre I will *m* music
147: 7 *m* music to our God on the harp.
149: 3 *m* music to him with tambourine
Pr 3: 6 and he will *m* your paths straight.
4: 16 of slumber till they *m* someone fall.
4: 26 *M* level paths for your feet
8: 15 and rulers *m* laws that are just;
10: 4 Lazy hands *m* a man poor,
11: 14 but many advisers *m* victory sure.
20: 18 *M* plans by seeking advice;
22: 24 not *m* friends with a hot-tempered
30: 26 yet they *m* their home in the crags;
Ecc 5: 4 When you *m* a vow to God,
5: 5 not to vow than to *m* a vow
SS 1: 11 We will *m* you earrings of gold,
Isa 1: 16 wash and *m* yourselves clean.
3: 4 I will *m* boys their officials;
3: 7 do not *m* me the leader
3: 17 the LORD will *m* their scalps bald
5: 6 I will *m* it a wasteland,
6: 10 *M* the heart of this people
6: 10 *m* their ears dull
7: 6 *m* the son of Tabeel king over it."
10: 1 Woe to those who *m* unjust laws,
12: 4 *m* known among the nations what
13: 9 to *m* the land desolate
13: 12 I will *m* man scarcer than pure gold
13: 13 Therefore I will *m* the heavens
14: 2 They will *m* captives
14: 14 I will *m* myself like the Most High
16: 3 *M* your shadow like night—
17: 2 with no one to *m* them afraid.
17: 11 set them out, you *m* them grow,
19: 12 Let them show you and *m* known
19: 14 they *m* Egypt stagger
19: 21 the LORD will *m* himself known
19: 21 they will *m* vows to the LORD
26: 7 you *m* the way of the righteous
27: 5 let them *m* peace with me,
27: 5 yes, let them *m* peace with me."
27: 11 women come and *m* fires
28: 17 I will *m* justice the measuring line
28: 28 Grain must be ground to *m* bread;
29: 16 "He did not *m* me"?
29: 21 those who with a word *m* a man out
30: 30 will *m* them see his arm coming
36: 8 *m* a bargain with my master,
36: 16 *M* peace with me and come out
37: 29 and I will *m* you return
38: 8 I will *m* the shadow cast
40: 3 *m* straight in the wilderness
41: 15 I will *m* you into a threshing sledge
41: 18 I will *m* rivers flow
42: 6 I will keep you and will *m* you
42: 16 and *m* the rough places smooth.
42: 21 to *m* his law great and glorious.
44: 9 All who *m* idols are nothing,
44: 19 Shall I *m* a detestable thing
45: 13 I will *m* all his ways straight.
46: 6 they hire a goldsmith to *m* it
46: 10 I *m* known the end
47: 13 stargazers who *m* predictions
49: 6 also *m* you a light for the Gentiles,
49: 8 I will keep you and will *m* you
49: 26 I will *m* your oppressors eat their
50: 3 and *m* sackcloth its covering."
51: 3 he will *m* her deserts like Eden,
54: 12 I will *m* your battlements of rubies,
55: 3 I will *m* an everlasting covenant
59: 6 with what they *m*.
60: 15 I will *m* you the everlasting pride
60: 17 I will *m* peace your governor
61: 8 and *m* an everlasting covenant
61: 11 LORD will *m* righteousness
63: 14 to *m* for yourself a glorious name.
63: 17 do you *m* us wander
64: 2 come down to *m* your name known
66: 22 the new earth that I *m* will endure
Jer 5: 14 I will *m* my words
6: 8 and *m* your land desolate
7: 18 and *m* cakes of bread for the Queen

Jer 9: 3 "They *m* ready their tongue
9: 11 "I will *m* Jerusalem a heap of ruins,
9: 15 I will *m* this people eat bitter food
10: 11 who did not *m* the heavens
10: 22 It will *m* the towns
15: 4 I will *m* them abhorrent
15: 8 I will *m* their widows more
15: 11 surely I will *m* your enemies plead
15: 20 I will *m* you a wall to this people,
16: 20 Do men *m* their own gods?
18: 18 let's *m* plans against Jeremiah;
19: 3 on this place that will *m* the ears
19: 7 I will *m* them fall by the sword
19: 8 and *m* it an object of scorn;
19: 9 I will *m* them eat the flesh
19: 12 I will *m* this city like Topheth.
20: 4 'I will *m* you a terror to yourself
22: 6 I will surely *m* you like a desert,
22: 15 "Does it *m* you a king
23: 15 "I will *m* them eat bitter food
23: 27 one another will *m* my people
24: 9 I will *m* them abhorrent
25: 9 and *m* them an object of horror
25: 12 "and will *m* it desolate forever.
25: 15 *m* all the nations to whom I send
25: 18 to *m* them a ruin and an object
26: 6 then I will *m* this house like Shiloh
27: 2 "*M* a yoke out of straps
27: 6 I will *m* even the wild animals
28: 14 to *m* them serve Nebuchadnezzar
29: 17 I will *m* them like poor figs that are
29: 18 and will *m* them abhorrent
30: 10 and no one will *m* him afraid.
30: 16 all who *m* spoil of you I will despoil
31: 7 *M* your praises heard, and say,
31: 31 "when I will *m* a new covenant
31: 33 "This is the covenant I will *m*
32: 35 thing and so *m* Judah sin.
32: 40 I will *m* an everlasting covenant
33: 15 I will *m* a righteous Branch sprout
33: 22 I will *m* the descendants
34: 5 O master!" I myself *m* this promise
34: 5 so they will *m* a fire in your honor
34: 17 I will *m* you abhorrent
44: 8 *m* yourselves an object of cursing
46: 27 and no one will *m* him afraid.
48: 26 "*M* her drunk,
48: 35 an end to those who *m* offerings
49: 15 *m* you small among the nations,
51: 25 and *m* you a burned-out mountain.
51: 36 and *m* her springs dry.
51: 39 and *m* them drunk,
51: 44 *m* him spew out what he has
51: 57 I will *m* her officials and wise men
Eze 3: 8 But I will *m* you as unyielding
3: 9 I will *m* your forehead like
3: 26 I will *m* your tongue stick
4: 9 use them to *m* bread for yourself.
5: 14 "I will *m* you a ruin and a reproach
6: 14 and *m* the land a desolate waste
7: 20 used it to *m* their detestable idols
13: 18 and *m* veils of various lengths
14: 8 *m* him an example and a byword.
15: 3 Do they *m* pegs from it
15: 3 taken from it to *m* anything useful?
15: 8 I will *m* the land desolate
16: 4 washed with water to *m* you clean,
16: 16 garments to *m* gaudy high places,
16: 63 Then, when I *m* atonement for you
17: 24 and *m* the dry tree flourish.
17: 24 and *m* the low tree grow tall.
21: 19 *M* a signpost where the road
21: 27 A ruin! A ruin! I will *m* it a ruin!
22: 4 Therefore I will *m* you an object
22: 12 *m* unjust gain from your neighbors
22: 25 and *m* many widows within her.
22: 27 and kill people to *m* unjust gain.
26: 4 away her rubble and *m* her a bare
26: 14 I will *m* you a bare rock,
26: 19 When I *m* you a desolate city,
26: 20 I will *m* you dwell in the earth
27: 5 Lebanon to *m* a mast for you.
28: 23 and *m* blood flow in her streets.
29: 4 *m* the fish of your streams stick
29: 10 I will *m* the land of Egypt a ruin
29: 12 I will *m* the land of Egypt desolate
29: 15 I will *m* it so weak that it will never
29: 21 "On that day I will *m* a horn grow

Eze 30: 22 and *m* the sword fall from his hand.
32: 14 and *m* her streams flow like oil,
32: 15 When I *m* Egypt desolate
33: 2 and *m* him their watchman,
33: 28 I will *m* the land a desolate waste,
34: 25 " 'I will *m* a covenant of peace
34: 28 and no one will *m* them afraid.
35: 3 and *m* you a desolate waste.
35: 7 I will *m* Mount Seir a desolate
35: 9 I will *m* you desolate forever;
35: 11 I will *m* myself known among them
35: 14 rejoices, I will *m* you desolate.
36: 11 and will *m* you prosper more
36: 14 or *m* your nation childless,
36: 15 No longer will I *m* you hear
36: 29 call for the grain and *m* it plentiful
36: 37 I will *m* their people as numerous
37: 5 I will *m* breath enter you,
37: 6 and *m* flesh come upon you
37: 22 I will *m* them one nation
37: 26 I will *m* a covenant of peace
37: 28 that I the LORD *m* Israel holy,
38: 23 I will *m* myself known in the sight
39: 3 and *m* your arrows drop
39: 7 " 'I will *m* known my holy name
39: 26 land with no one to *m* them afraid.
43: 11 *m* known to them the design
43: 20 purify the altar and *m* atonement
43: 26 are to *m* atonement for the altar
45: 15 offerings to *m* atonement
45: 17 offerings to *m* atonement
45: 20 so you are to *m* atonement
45: 25 he is to *m* the same provision
Da 9: 18 We do not *m* requests of you
11: 6 king of the North to *m* an alliance,
11: 17 and will *m* an alliance with the king
11: 39 He will *m* them rulers
Hos 2: 3 I will *m* her like a desert,
2: 3 *m* her as bare as on the day she was
2: 12 I will *m* them a thicket,
2: 15 will *m* the Valley of Achor a door
2: 18 In that day I will *m* a covenant
8: 4 they *m* idols for themselves
10: 4 They *m* many promises,
10: 4 and *m* agreements;
11: 8 How can I *m* you like Zeboiim?
12: 9 I will *m* you live in tents again,
13: 2 they *m* idols for themselves
Joel 2: 17 Do not *m* your inheritance
2: 19 never again will I *m* you
Am 8: 9 "I will *m* the sun go down at noon
8: 10 I will *m* all of you wear sackcloth
8: 10 I will *m* that time like mourning
9: 14 they will *m* gardens and eat their
Ob : 2 *m* you small among the nations;
: 3 and *m* your home on the heights,
: 4 and *m* your nest among the stars,
Jnh 1: 11 do to you to *m* the sea calm
2: 9 What I have vowed I will *m* good.
4: 10 you did not tend it or *m* it grow.
Mic 1: 6 "Therefore I will *m* Samaria a heap
1: 16 *m* yourselves as bald as the vulture,
4: 4 and no one will *m* them afraid,
4: 7 I will *m* the lame a remnant,
Na 1: 8 he will *m* an end of ⌊Nineveh⌋;
3: 6 and *m* you a spectacle.
Hab 1: 3 Why do you *m* me look at injustice
2: 2 and *m* it plain on tablets
2: 7 not wake up and *m* you tremble?
3: 2 in our time *m* them known;
Zep 1: 18 for he will *m* a sudden end
3: 13 and no one will *m* them afraid."
Hag 2: 23 and I will *m* you like my signet ring
Zec 6: 11 the silver and gold and *m* a crown,
9: 13 and *m* you like a warrior's sword
9: 17 Grain will *m* the young men thrive,
10: 3 *m* them like a proud horse in battle.
12: 2 to *m* Jerusalem a cup that sends all
12: 3 I will *m* Jerusalem an immovable
12: 6 "On that day I will *m* the leaders
Mal 3: 17 the day when I *m* up my treasured
Mt 2: 8 *m* a careful search for the child.
3: 3 *m* straight paths for him.' "
4: 19 "and I will *m* you fishers of men."
5: 36 for you cannot *m* even one hair
8: 2 are willing, you can *m* me clean."
12: 33 *m* a tree bad and its fruit will be bad
12: 33 "*M* a tree good and its fruit will be
Mt 15: 11 mouth does not *m* him 'unclean,'
15: 18 and these *m* a man 'unclean.'
15: 20 These are what *m* a man 'unclean';
15: 20 hands does not *m* him 'unclean.' "
23: 5 They *m* their phylacteries wide
23: 15 you *m* him twice as much a son
26: 17 us to *m* preparations for you
27: 65 *m* the tomb as secure as you know
28: 19 and *m* disciples of all nations,
Mk 1: 3 *m* straight paths for him.' "
1: 17 "and I will *m* you fishers of men."
1: 40 are willing, you can *m* me clean."
7: 15 outside a man can *m* him 'unclean'
7: 18 the outside can *m* him 'unclean'?
7: 23 from inside and *m* a man 'unclean
9: 50 how can you *m* it salty again?
12: 40 and for a show *m* lengthy prayers.
14: 12 and *m* preparations for you
14: 15 *M* preparations for us there."
Lk 1: 17 to *m* ready a people prepared
3: 4 *m* straight paths for him.
5: 12 are willing, you can *m* me clean."
5: 34 "Can you *m* the guests
11: 40 the outside *m* the inside
13: 24 "*M* every effort to enter
14: 18 they all alike began to *m* excuses.
14: 23 country lanes and *m* them come in,
15: 19 *m* me like one of your hired men.'
16: 6 sit down quickly, and *m* it four
16: 7 your bill and *m* it eight hundred.'
20: 43 hand until I *m* your enemies
20: 47 and for a show *m* lengthy prayers.
21: 14 But *m* up your mind not
22: 8 and *m* preparations for us
22: 12 *M* preparations there."
Jn 1: 23 '*M* straight the way for the Lord.' "
5: 44 yet *m* no effort to obtain the praise
6: 15 to come and *m* him king by force,
7: 24 mere appearances, and *m* a right
11: 52 them together and *m* them one.
14: 23 and *m* our home with him.
16: 15 from what is mine and *m* it known
17: 26 and will continue to *m* you known
Ac 2: 35 hand until I *m* your enemies
5: 28 and are determined to *m* us guilty
7: 40 '*M* us gods who will go before us.
15: 19 that we should not *m* it difficult
19: 33 for silence in order to *m* a defense
24: 10 so I gladly *m* my defense.
26: 2 as I *m* my defense against all
27: 16 able to *m* the lifeboat secure.
Ro 1: 11 gift to *m* you strong—
9: 20 'Why did you *m* me like this?' "
9: 21 the right to *m* out of the same lump
9: 22 his wrath and *m* his power known,
9: 23 What if he did this to *m* the riches
10: 19 I will *m* you angry
10: 19 "I will *m* you envious
11: 11 to the Gentiles to *m* Israel envious.
11: 13 I *m* much of my ministry
14: 4 for the Lord is able to *m* him stand.
14: 13 *m* up your mind not
14: 19 *m* every effort to do what leads
15: 26 pleased to *m* a contribution
1Co 4: 4 but that does not *m* me innocent.
9: 18 and so not *m* use of my rights
9: 19 I *m* myself a slave to everyone,
9: 27 and *m* it my slave so that
14: 7 of lifeless things that *m* sounds,
16: 7 and *m* only a passing visit;
2Co 1: 17 Or do I *m* my plans in a worldly
2: 1 I would not *m* another painful visit
2: 2 who is left to *m* me glad
2: 3 those who ought to *m* me rejoice.
5: 9 So we *m* it our goal to please him,
7: 2 *M* room for us in your hearts.
9: 8 God is able to *m* all grace abound
10: 5 thought to *m* it obedient to Christ.
Gal 2: 4 in Christ Jesus and to *m* us slaves.
6: 12 to *m* a good impression outwardly
Eph 3: 9 and to *m* plain to everyone
4: 3 *M* every effort to keep the unity
5: 19 *m* music in your heart to the Lord,
5: 26 up for her to *m* her holy,
6: 19 I will fearlessly *m* known
Php 2: 2 then *m* my joy complete
2: 30 risking his life to *m* up
3: 15 that too God will *m* clear to you.
Col 1: 27 them God has chosen to *m* known
4: 5 *m* the most of every opportunity.
1Th 2: 3 the appeal we *m* does not spring
3: 12 May the Lord *m* your love increase
4: 11 *M* it your ambition
5: 15 *M* sure that nobody pays back
2Th 3: 9 but in order to *m* ourselves a model
2Ti 3: 15 which are able to *m* you wise
Tit 2: 10 way they will *m* the teaching about
Heb 1: 13 hand until I *m* your enemies
2: 10 should *m* the author
2: 17 and that he might *m* atonement
4: 11 *m* every effort to enter that rest,
6: 11 in order to *m* your hope sure.
6: 17 to *m* the unchanging nature
8: 5 it that you *m* everything according
8: 8 when I will *m* a new covenant
8: 10 This is the covenant I will *m*
10: 1 *m* perfect those who draw
10: 16 "This is the covenant I will *m*
12: 5 do not *m* light of the Lord's
12: 13 "*M* level paths for your feet,"
12: 14 *M* every effort to live in peace
13: 12 gate to *m* the people holy
Jas 3: 3 of horses to *m* them obey us,
4: 13 carry on business and *m* money."
5: 15 in faith will *m* the sick person well;
1Pe 3: 5 used to *m* themselves beautiful.
5: 10 restore you and *m* you strong,
2Pe 1: 5 *m* every effort to add
1: 10 all the more eager to *m* your calling
1: 15 I will *m* every effort to see that
3: 14 *m* every effort to be found spotless,
1Jn 1: 4 this to *m* our joy complete.
1: 10 we *m* him out to be a liar
2: 10 nothing in him to *m* him stumble.
Rev 2: 22 and I will *m* those who commit
3: 9 I will *m* them come and fall
3: 9 I will *m* those who are
3: 12 who overcomes I will *m* a pillar
6: 4 and to *m* men slay each other.
12: 17 went off to *m* war against the rest
13: 4 Who can *m* war against him?"
13: 7 power to *m* war against the saints
17: 14 They will *m* war against the Lamb,
19: 19 together to *m* war against the rider

MAKER (MAKE)

Job 4: 17 Can a man be more pure than his *M*
9: 9 He is the *M* of the Bear and Orion,
32: 22 my *M* would soon take me away.
35: 10 no one says, 'Where is God my *M*,
36: 3 I will ascribe justice to my *M*.
40: 19 yet his *M* can approach him
Ps 95: 6 kneel before the LORD our *M*;
115: 15 the *M* of heaven and earth.
121: 2 the *M* of heaven and earth.
124: 8 the *M* of heaven and earth.
134: 3 the *M* of heaven and earth,
146: 6 the *M* of heaven and earth,
149: 2 Let Israel rejoice in their *M*;
Pr 14: 31 poor shows contempt for their *M*,
17: 5 poor shows contempt for their *M*;
22: 2 The LORD is the *M* of them all.
Ecc 11: 5 the *M* of all things.
Isa 17: 7 that day men will look to their *M*
27: 11 so their *M* has no compassion
45: 9 to him who quarrels with his *M*,
45: 11 the Holy One of Israel, and its *M*:
51: 13 that you forget the LORD your *M*,
54: 5 For your *M* is your husband—
Jer 10: 16 for he is the *M* of all things,
51: 19 for he is the *M* of all things,
Hos 8: 14 Israel has forgotten his *M*

MAKERS (MAKE)

Isa 45: 16 All the *m* of idols will be put

MAKES (MAKE)

Ex 4: 11 Who *m* him deaf or dumb?
4: 11 gives him sight or *m* him blind?
11: 7 that the LORD *m* a distinction
30: 33 Whoever *m* perfume like it
30: 38 Whoever *m* any like it
31: 13 I am the LORD, who *m* you holy.
Lev 7: 7 to the priest who *m* atonement
17: 11 it is the blood that *m* atonement
20: 8 I am the LORD, who *m* you holy.

Lev 21: 8 who *m* you holy, am holy.
21: 15 I am the LORD, who *m* him holy
21: 23 I am the LORD, who *m* them holy
22: 5 crawling thing that *m* him unclean,
22: 5 or any person who *m* him unclean,
22: 9 I am the LORD, who *m* them holy.
22: 16 I am the LORD, who *m* them holy
22: 32 who *m* you holy and who brought
27: 2 'If anyone *m* a special vow
Nu 30: 2 When a man *m* a vow to the LORD
30: 3 living in her father's house *m* a vow
30: 6 "If she marries after she *m* a vow
30: 10 living with her husband *m* a vow
30: 13 or nullify any vow she *m*
1Sa 2: 6 LORD brings death and *m* alive;
22: 8 me when my son *m* a covenant
2Sa 22: 33 and *m* my way perfect.
22: 34 He *m* my feet like the feet of a deer
Job 6: 7 such food *m* me ill.
9: 6 and *m* its pillars tremble.
12: 17 and *m* fools of judges.
12: 23 He *m* nations great, and destroys
12: 25 he *m* them stagger like drunkards.
35: 11 *m* us wiser than the birds of the air
36: 10 He *m* them listen to correction
37: 15 and *m* his lightning flash?
41: 31 He *m* the depths churn like
Ps 7: 13 he *m* ready his flaming arrows.
18: 32 and *m* my way perfect.
18: 33 He *m* my feet like the feet of a deer
19: 6 and *m* its circuit to the other;
23: 2 *m* me lie down in green pastures,
25: 14 he *m* his covenant known to them.
29: 6 He *m* Lebanon skip like a calf,
40: 4 who *m* the LORD his trust,
45: 8 the music of the strings *m* you glad.
46: 9 He *m* wars cease to the ends
48: 8 God *m* her secure forever.
60: 3 given us wine that *m* us stagger.
104: 3 He *m* the clouds his chariot
104: 4 He *m* winds his messengers,
104: 10 He *m* springs pour water
104: 14 He *m* grass grow for the cattle,
135: 7 He *m* clouds rise from the ends
143: 3 he *m* me dwell in darkness
147: 8 and *m* grass grow on the hills.
Pr 1: 21 of the city she *m* her speech:
4: 19 do not know what *m* them stumble.
11: 5 of the blameless *m* a straight way
13: 11 by little *m* it grow.
13: 12 Hope deferred *m* the heart sick,
15: 13 A happy heart *m* the face cheerful,
16: 7 he *m* even his enemies live at peace
31: 22 She *m* coverings for her bed;
31: 24 She *m* linen garments
Ecc 7: 19 Wisdom *m* one wise man more
10: 19 and wine *m* life merry,
Isa 8: 14 and a rock that *m* them fall.
14: 9 it *m* them rise from their thrones—
21: 4 fear *m* me tremble;
26: 1 God *m* salvation
27: 9 When he *m* all the altar stones
32: 7 he *m* up evil schemes
32: 8 But the noble man *m* noble plans,
44: 13 and *m* an outline with a marker;
44: 15 he *m* an idol and bows down to it.
44: 17 From the rest he *m* a god, his idol;
44: 25 and *m* fools of diviners,
51: 17 the goblet that *m* men stagger.
53: 10 LORD *m* his life a guilt offering,
57: 13 But the man who *m* me his refuge
61: 11 as the soil *m* the sprout come up
62: 7 and *m* her the praise of the earth.
66: 3 whoever *m* a grain offering
Jer 10: 13 he *m* clouds rise from the ends
22: 14 So he *m* large windows in it,
48: 28 Be like a dove that *m* its nest
51: 16 he *m* clouds rise from the ends
Eze 44: 18 anything that *m* them perspire.
46: 16 If the prince *m* a gift
46: 17 he *m* a gift from his inheritance
47: 9 and *m* the salt water fresh;
Hos 12: 1 He *m* a treaty with Assyria
Na 1: 4 he *m* all the rivers run dry.
Hab 2: 6 *m* himself wealthy by extortion!
2: 18 For he who *m* it trusts
2: 18 he *m* idols that cannot speak.
3: 19 he *m* my feet like the feet of a deer,
Zec 10: 1 the LORD who *m* the storm
Mt 15: 11 that is what *m* him 'unclean.' "
23: 17 the temple that *m* the gold sacred?
23: 19 or the altar that *m* the gift sacred?
Mk 7: 15 of a man that *m* him 'unclean.' "
7: 20 of a man is what *m* him 'unclean.'
7: 37 "He even *m* the deaf hear
Jn 16: 30 This *m* us believe that you came
Ro 8: 15 receive a spirit that *m* you a slave
9: 33 and a rock that *m* them fall,
1Co 2: 15 spiritual man *m* judgments about
3: 7 but only God, who *m* things grow.
4: 7 For who *m* you different
2Co 1: 21 Now it is God who *m* both us
Gal 2: 6 they were *m* no difference
Eph 5: 14 it is light that *m* everything visible.
Heb 1: 7 "He *m* his angels winds,
2: 11 Both the one who *m* men holy
Jas 3: 5 of the body, but it *m* great boasts.
1Pe 2: 8 and a rock that *m* them fall."
Rev 19: 11 With justice he judges and *m* war.

MAKHELOTH

Nu 33: 25 left Haradah and camped at *M*.
33: 26 They left *M* and camped at Tahath.

MAKI

Nu 13: 15 the tribe of Gad, Geuel son of *M*.

MAKING (MAKE)

Ge 9: 12 the sign of the covenant I am *m*
34: 30 trouble on me by *m* me a stench
Ex 5: 7 the people with straw for *m* bricks;
28: 15 a breastpiece for *m* decisions—
28: 30 of *m* decisions for the Israelites
29: 36 the altar by *m* atonement for it,
30: 16 *m* atonement for your lives."
34: 10 "I am *m* a covenant with you.
Lev 10: 17 by *m* atonement for them
16: 10 LORD to be used for *m* atonement
16: 20 Aaron has finished *m* atonement
17: 5 the sacrifices they are now *m*
19: 29 daughter by *m* her a prostitute,
27: 8 If anyone *m* the vow is too poor
27: 8 to what the man *m* the vow can
Nu 25: 12 tell him I am *m* my covenant
32: 14 and *m* the LORD even more angry
Dt 23: 22 But if you refrain from *m* a vow,
24: 11 to whom you are *m* the loan bring
29: 12 a covenant the LORD is *m*
29: 14 I am *m* this covenant, with its oath,
Jdg 16: 13 you have been *m* a fool of me
1Sa 13: 10 Just as he finished *m* the offering,
21: 13 *m* marks on the doors of the gate
1Ki 8: 33 and *m* supplication to you
14: 15 to anger by *m* Asherah poles.
15: 4 and by *m* Jerusalem strong.
2Ki 10: 25 as Jehu had finished *m* the burnt
12: 13 spent for *m* silver basins,
1Ch 6: 49 *m* atonement for Israel,
2Ch 2: 4 and for *m* burnt offerings every
6: 24 and *m* supplication before you
Ezr 5: 8 and is *m* rapid progress
Ne 6: 8 you are just *m* it up out
8: 8 *m* it clear and giving the meaning
9: 38 we are *m* a binding agreement,
Ps 19: 7 *m* wise the simple.
Pr 8: 21 and *m* their treasuries full.
14: 9 Fools mock at *m* amends for sin,
16: 11 in the bag are of his *m*.
24: 2 and their lips talk about *m* trouble.
Ecc 12: 12 Of *m* many books there is no end,
Isa 10: 2 *m* widows their prey
43: 19 I am *m* a way in the desert
45: 9 'What are you *m*?'
55: 10 and *m* it bud and flourish,
Jer 22: 13 *m* his countrymen work
44: 19 that we were *m* cakes like her
Eze 22: 3 and defiles herself by *m* idols,
37: 19 *m* them a single stick of wood,
Da 9: 20 *m* my request to the LORD my
Jnh 1: 8 responsible for *m* all this trouble
Mt 9: 16 from the garment, *m* the tear worse
13: 22 of wealth choke it, *m* it unfruitful.
21: 13 but you are *m* it a 'den of robbers
Mk 2: 21 from the old, *m* the tear worse.
4: 19 choke the word, *m* it unfruitful.
Lk 1: 22 for he kept *m* signs to them
Jn 5: 18 *m* himself equal with God.
16: 14 from what is mine and *m* it known
Ac 16: 19 hope of *m* money was gone,
18: 14 you Jews were *m* a complaint
24: 13 to you the charges they are now *m*
Ro 7: 23 *m* me a prisoner of the law of sin
2Co 5: 20 God were *m* his appeal through us.
6: 10 yet *m* many rich; having nothing,
Eph 2: 15 out of the two, thus *m* peace,
5: 16 *m* the most of every opportunity,
Col 1: 20 by *m* peace through his blood,
Rev 21: 5 "I am *m* everything new!"

MAKIR (MAKIR'S MAKIRITE MAKIRITES)

Ge 50: 23 Also the children of *M* son
Nu 26: 29 of Manasseh: through *M*,
26: 29 the Makirite clan (*M* was the father
27: 1 the son of *M*, the son of Manasseh,
32: 39 The descendants of *M* son
36: 1 of the clan of Gilead son of *M*,
Dt 3: 15 And I gave Gilead to *M*.
Jos 13: 31 half of the sons of *M*, clan by clan.
13: 31 of *M* son of Manasseh—
17: 1 *M* was the ancestor
17: 1 that is, for *M*, Manasseh's firstborn
17: 3 the son of *M*, the son of Manasseh,
Jdg 5: 14 From *M* captains came down,
2Sa 9: 4 is at the house of *M* son of Ammiel
9: 5 the house of *M* son of Ammiel.
17: 27 and *M* son of Ammiel from Lo
1Ch 2: 21 with the daughter of *M* the father
2: 23 of *M* the father of Gilead.
7: 14 She gave birth to *M* the father
7: 15 *M* took a wife
7: 17 the sons of Gilead son of *M*,

MAKIR'S (MAKIR)

1Ch 7: 16 *M* wife Maacah gave birth to a son

MAKIRITE (MAKIR)

Nu 26: 29 the *M* clan (Makir was the father

MAKIRITES (MAKIR)

Nu 32: 40 So Moses gave Gilead to the *M*,
Jos 17: 1 because the *M* were great soldiers.

MAKKEDAH

Jos 10: 10 down all the way to Azekah and *M*.
10: 16 and hidden in the cave at *M*.
10: 17 been found hiding in the cave at *M*,
10: 21 safely to Joshua in the camp at *M*,
10: 28 And he did to the king of *M*
10: 28 That day Joshua took *M*.
10: 29 moved on from *M* to Libnah
12: 16 one the king of *M* one the king
15: 41 Beth Dagon, Naamah and *M*—

MALACHI

Mal 1: 1 of the LORD to Israel through *M*.

MALCAM

1Ch 8: 9 *M*, Jeuz, Sakia and Mirmah.

MALCHUS

Jn 18: 10 (The servant's name was *M*.)

MALE (MALES)

Ge 1: 27 *m* and female he created them.
5: 2 He created them *m* and female;
6: 19 *m* and female, to keep them alive
7: 2 kind of unclean animal, a *m*
7: 2 of every kind of clean animal, a *m*
7: 3 also seven of every kind of bird, *m*
7: 9 *m* and female, came to Noah
7: 16 The animals going in were *m*
12: 16 and cattle, *m* and female donkeys,
17: 10 Every *m* among you shall be
17: 12 the generations to come every *m*
17: 14 Any uncircumcised *m*, who has
17: 23 every *m* in his household,
17: 27 every *m* in Abraham's household,
20: 14 and cattle and *m* and female slaves
30: 35 removed all the *m* goats that were
31: 10 and saw that the *m* goats mating
31: 12 and see that all the *m* goats mating
32: 14 female goats and twenty *m* goats,
32: 15 donkeys and ten *m* donkeys.

Ge 34: 24 and every *m* in the city was
34: 25 unsuspecting city, killing every *m*.
Ex 12: 48 No uncircumcised *m* may eat of it.
13: 2 to me every firstborn *m*.
13: 15 to the LORD the first *m* offspring
21: 20 If a man beats his *m* or female slave
21: 32 If the bull gores a *m* or female slave
Lev 1: 3 he is to offer a *m* without defect.
1: 10 he is to offer a *m* without defect.
3: 1 animal from the herd, whether *m*
3: 6 is to offer a *m* or female
4: 23 his offering a *m* goat without defect
6: 18 Any *m* descendant
6: 29 Any *m* in a priest's family may eat
7: 6 Any *m* in a priest's family may eat
9: 3 'Take a *m* goat for a sin offering,
14: 10 day he must bring two *m* lambs
14: 12 is to take one of the *m* lambs
14: 21 he must take one *m* lamb
16: 5 is to take two *m* goats
22: 19 you must present a *m*
23: 18 with this bread seven *m* lambs,
23: 19 Then sacrifice one *m* goat
25: 44 " 'Your *m* and female slaves are
27: 3 the value of a *m* between the ages
27: 5 the value of a *m* at twenty shekels
27: 6 set the value of a *m* at five shekels
27: 7 the value of a *m* at fifteen shekels
Nu 3: 12 in place of the first *m* offspring
3: 15 Count every *m* a month old
3: 39 including every *m* a month old
5: 3 Send away *m* and female alike;
6: 12 and must bring a year-old *m* lamb
6: 14 a year-old *m* lamb without defect
7: 15 one ram and one *m* lamb a year old
7: 16 one *m* goat for a sin offering;
7: 17 five *m* goats and five *m* lambs
7: 21 one ram and one *m* lamb a year old
7: 22 one *m* goat for a sin offering;
7: 23 five *m* goats and five *m* lambs
7: 27 one ram and one *m* lamb a year old
7: 28 one *m* goat for a sin offering;
7: 29 five *m* goats and five *m* lambs
7: 33 one ram and one *m* lamb a year old
7: 34 one *m* goat for a sin offering;
7: 35 five *m* goats and five *m* lambs
7: 39 one ram and one *m* lamb a year old
7: 40 one *m* goat for a sin offering;
7: 41 five *m* goats and five *m* lambs
7: 45 one ram and one *m* lamb a year old
7: 46 one *m* goat for a sin offering;
7: 47 five *m* goats and five *m* lambs
7: 51 one ram and one *m* lamb a year old
7: 52 one *m* goat for a sin offering;
7: 53 five *m* goats and five *m* lambs
7: 57 one ram and one *m* lamb a year old
7: 58 one *m* goat for a sin offering;
7: 59 five *m* goats and five *m* lambs
7: 63 one ram and one *m* lamb a year old
7: 64 one *m* goat for a sin offering;
7: 65 five *m* goats and five *m* lambs
7: 69 one ram and one *m* lamb a year old
7: 70 one *m* goat for a sin offering;
7: 71 five *m* goats and five *m* lambs
7: 75 one ram and one *m* lamb a year old
7: 76 one *m* goat for a sin offering;
7: 77 five *m* goats and five *m* lambs
7: 81 one ram and one *m* lamb a year old
7: 82 one *m* goat for a sin offering;
7: 83 five *m* goats and five *m* lambs
7: 87 Twelve *m* goats were used
7: 87 and twelve *m* lambs a year old,
7: 88 sixty *m* goats and sixty *m* lambs
8: 16 the first *m* offspring
8: 17 Every firstborn *m* in Israel,
15: 24 and a *m* goat for a sin offering.
18: 10 most holy; every *m* shall eat it.
18: 15 firstborn *m* of unclean animals.
26: 62 All the *m* Levites a month old
28: 11 and seven *m* lambs a year old,
28: 15 one *m* goat is to be presented
28: 19 and seven *m* lambs a year old,
28: 22 Include one *m* goat as a sin offering
28: 27 and seven *m* lambs a year old
28: 30 Include one *m* goat
29: 2 and seven *m* lambs a year old,
29: 5 Include one *m* goat as a sin offering
29: 8 and seven *m* lambs a year old,
Nu 29: 11 Include one *m* goat as a sin offering
29: 13 and fourteen *m* lambs a year old,
29: 16 Include one *m* goat as a sin offering
29: 17 and fourteen *m* lambs a year old,
29: 19 Include one *m* goat as a sin offering
29: 20 and fourteen *m* lambs a year old,
29: 22 Include one *m* goat as a sin offering
29: 23 and fourteen *m* lambs a year old,
29: 25 Include one *m* goat as a sin offering
29: 26 and fourteen *m* lambs a year old,
29: 28 Include one *m* goat as a sin offering
29: 29 and fourteen *m* lambs a year old,
29: 31 Include one *m* goat as a sin offering
29: 32 and fourteen *m* lambs a year old,
29: 34 Include one *m* goat as a sin offering
29: 36 and seven *m* lambs a year old,
29: 38 Include one *m* goat as a sin offering
Dt 15: 19 LORD your God every firstborn *m*
23: 18 or of a *m* prostitute into the house
28: 68 for sale to your enemies as *m*
Jos 17: 2 These are the other *m* descendants
Jdg 21: 11 "Kill every *m* and every woman
1Sa 25: 22 if by morning I leave alive one *m*
25: 34 not one *m* belonging
2Sa 21: 6 of his *m* descendants be given
1Ki 14: 10 off from Jeroboam every last *m*
14: 24 *m* shrine prostitutes in the land;
15: 12 expelled the *m* shrine prostitutes
16: 11 He did not spare a single *m*,
21: 21 off from Ahab every last *m* in Israel
22: 46 rest of the *m* shrine prostitutes who
2Ki 9: 8 off from Ahab every last *m* in Israel
23: 7 of the *m* shrine prostitutes,
1Ch 29: 21 rams and a thousand *m* lambs,
2Ch 29: 21 seven *m* lambs and seven *m* goats
29: 32 and two hundred *m* lambs—
31: 19 portions to every *m* among them
Ezr 6: 9 *m* lambs for burnt offerings
6: 17 for all Israel, twelve *m* goats,
6: 17 four hundred *m* lambs and,
7: 17 and *m* lambs, together
8: 35 as a sin offering, twelve *m* goats.
8: 35 rams, seventy-seven *m* lambs,
Est 7: 4 If we had merely been sold as *m*
Job 36: 14 among *m* prostitutes of the shrines.
Ecc 2: 7 I bought *m* and female slaves
Jer 34: 9 to free his Hebrew slaves, both *m*
34: 10 agreed that they would free their *m*
34: 16 each of you has taken back the *m*
Eze 16: 17 and you made for yourself *m* idols
43: 22 are to offer a *m* goat without defect
43: 25 are to provide a *m* goat daily
45: 23 and a *m* goat for a sin offering.
46: 4 Sabbath day is to be six *m* lambs
Mal 1: 14 the cheat who has an acceptable *m*
Mt 19: 4 the Creator 'made them *m*
Mk 10: 6 of creation God 'made them *m*
Lk 2: 23 "Every firstborn *m* is
1Co 6: 9 nor adulterers nor *m* prostitutes
Gal 3: 28 slave nor free, *m* nor female,
Rev 12: 5 She gave birth to a son, a *m* child,
12: 13 who had given birth to the *m* child.

MALES (MALE)

Ge 34: 15 us by circumcising all your *m*.
34: 22 that our *m* be circumcised,
Ex 12: 5 you choose must be year-old *m*
12: 48 Passover must have all the *m*
13: 12 All the firstborn *m*
34: 19 including all the firstborn *m*
Nu 3: 22 number of all the *m* a month old
3: 28 number of all the *m* a month old
3: 34 number of all the *m* a month old
3: 40 all the firstborn Israelite *m* who are
3: 43 number of firstborn *m* a month old
2Ch 31: 16 distributed to the *m* three years old
Jer 2: 24 Any *m* that pursue her need not

MALICE (MALICIOUS)

Nu 35: 20 with *m* aforethought shoves
Dt 4: 42 neighbor without *m* aforethought.
19: 4 without *m* aforethought.
19: 6 neighbor without *m* aforethought.
Jos 20: 5 and without *m* aforethought.
Job 6: 30 Can my mouth not discern *m?*
Ps 28: 3 but harbor *m* in their hearts.
41: 5 My enemies say of me in *m*,
55: 10 *m* and abuse are within it.
Ps 73: 8 They scoff, and speak with *m;*
Pr 26: 26 His *m* may be concealed
Eze 25: 6 with all the *m* of your heart
25: 15 took revenge with *m* in their hearts
36: 5 with *m* in their hearts they made
Mk 7: 22 adultery, greed, *m*, deceit,
Ro 1: 29 murder, strife, deceit and *m*.
1Co 5: 8 the yeast of *m* and wickedness,
Eph 4: 31 along with every form of *m*.
Col 3: 8 *m*, slander, and filthy language
Tit 3: 3 lived in *m* and envy, being hated
1Pe 2: 1 rid yourselves of all *m*

MALICIOUS (MALICE)

Ex 23: 1 man by being a *m* witness.
Dt 19: 16 If a *m* witness takes the stand
Pr 17: 4 a liar pays attention to a *m* tongue.
26: 24 A *m* man disguises himself
Isa 58: 9 with the pointing finger and *m* talk,
Eze 28: 24 of Israel have *m* neighbors who are
36: 3 and the object of people's *m* talk
1Ti 3: 11 not *m* talkers but temperate
6: 4 *m* talk, evil suspicions

MALIGN (MALIGNED)

Ps 12: 5 from those who *m* them."
Tit 2: 5 so that no one will *m* the word

MALIGNED (MALIGN)

Eze 28: 26 on all their neighbors who *m* them.
Ac 19: 9 to believe and publicly *m* the Way.

MALKI-SHUA

1Sa 14: 49 sons were Jonathan, Ishvi and *M*.
31: 2 sons Jonathan, Abinadab and *M*.
1Ch 8: 33 *M*, Abinadab and Esh-Baal.
9: 39 *M*, Abinadab and Esh-Baal.
10: 2 sons Jonathan, Abinadab and *M*.

MALKIEL (MALKIELITE)

Ge 46: 17 The sons of Beriah: Heber and *M*.
Nu 26: 45 through *M*, the Malkielite clan.
1Ch 7: 31 The sons of Beriah: Heber and *M*,

MALKIELITE (MALKIEL)

Nu 26: 45 through Malkiel, the *M* clan.

MALKIJAH

1Ch 6: 40 the son of *M*, the son of Ethni,
9: 12 the son of *M;* and Maasai son
24: 9 the fifth to *M*, the sixth to Mijamin,
Ezr 10: 25 Mijamin, Eleazar, *M* and Benaiah.
10: 25 Ramiah, Izziah, *M*, Mijamin,
10: 31 Eliezer, Ishijah, *M*, Shemaiah,
Ne 3: 11 *M* son of Harim and Hasshub son
3: 14 repaired by *M* son of Recab,
3: 31 Next to him, *M*, one
8: 4 *M*, Hashum, Hashbaddanah,
10: 3 Pashhur, Amariah, *M*, Hattush,
11: 12 the son of *M*, and his associates,
12: 42 Eleazar, Uzzi, Jehohanan, *M*,
Jer 21: 1 sent to him Pashhur son of *M*
38: 1 son of *M* heard what Jeremiah was
38: 6 and put him into the cistern of *M*,

MALKIRAM

1Ch 3: 18 Shealtiel his son, *M*, Pedaiah,

MALLOTHI

1Ch 25: 4 *M*, Hothir and Mahazioth.
25: 26 12 the nineteenth to *M*, his sons

MALLUCH (MALLUCH'S)

1Ch 6: 44 the son of *M*, the son of Hashabiah,
Ezr 10: 29 Meshullam, *M*, Adaiah, Jashub,
10: 32 Benjamin, *M* and Shemariah.
Ne 10: 4 Hattush, Shebaniah, *M*, Harim,
10: 27 Anan, *M*, Harim and Baanah.
12: 2 Ezra, Amariah, *M*, Hattush,

MALLUCH'S (MALLUCH)

Ne 12: 14 Jehohanan; of *M*, Jonathan;

MALTA

Ac 28: 1 out that the island was called *M*.

MAMRE

Ge 13: 18 near the great trees of *M* at Hebron
14: 13 trees of *M* the Amorite,

Ge 14:24 with me—to Aner, Eshcol and *M*.
18: 1 trees of *M* while he was sitting
23:17 field in Machpelah near *M*—
23:19 of Machpelah near *M* (which is
25: 9 in the cave of Machpelah near *M*,
35:27 home to his father Isaac in *M*,
49:30 of Machpelah, near *M* in Canaan,
50:13 near *M*, which Abraham had

MAN-MADE (MAKE)

Dt 4:28 There you will worship *m* gods
Mk 14:58 'I will destroy this *m* temple
Ac 19:26 He says that *m* gods are no gods
Heb 9:11 perfect tabernacle that is not *m*,
9:24 not enter a *m* sanctuary that was

MANAEN

Ac 13: 1 *M* (who had been brought up

MANAGE (MANAGED MANAGEMENT MANAGER)

Jer 12: 5 how will you *m* in the thickets
1Ti 3: 4 He must *m* his own family well
3: 5 how to *m* his own family,
3:12 one wife and must *m* his children
5:14 to *m* their homes and to give

MANAGED (MANAGE)

1Ki 12:18 *m* to get into his chariot
2Ch 10:18 *m* to get into his chariot

MANAGEMENT (MANAGE)

Lk 16: 2 Give an account of your *m*,

MANAGER (MANAGE)

Lk 8: 3 the *m* of Herod's household;
12:42 Who then is the faithful and wise *m*
16: 1 a rich man whose *m* was accused
16: 2 you cannot be *m* any longer.'
16: 3 *m* said to himself, 'What shall I do
16: 6 "The *m* told him, 'Take your bill,
16: 8 commended the dishonest *m*

MANAHATH (MANAHATHITES)

Ge 36:23 Alvan, *M*, Ebal, Shepho and Onam
1Ch 1:40 Alvan, *M*, Ebal, Shepho and Onam
8: 6 in Geba and were deported to *M*:

MANAHATHITES (MANAHATH)

1Ch 2:52 half the *M*, and the clans
2:54 Atroth Beth Joab, half the *M*,

MANASSEH (MANASSEH'S MANASSITES)

Ge 41:51 Joseph named his firstborn *M*
46:20 *M* and Ephraim were born
48: 1 So he took his two sons *M*
48: 5 Ephraim and *M* will be mine,
48:13 *M* on his left toward Israel's right
48:14 even though *M* was the firstborn.
48:20 So he put Ephraim ahead of *M*.
48:20 make you like Ephraim and *M*.' "
50:23 of Makir son of *M* were placed
Nu 1:10 from *M*, Gamaliel son of Pedahzur;
1:34 From the descendants of *M*:
1:35 from the tribe of *M* was 32,200.
2:20 The tribe of *M* will be next to them.
2:20 of the people of *M* is Gamaliel son
7:54 the leader of the people of *M*,
10:23 over the division of the tribe of *M*,
13:11 from the tribe of *M* (a tribe
26:28 of Joseph by their clans through *M*
26:29 descendants of *M*: through Makir,
26:34 These were the clans of *M*;
27: 1 the son of Makir, the son of *M*,
27: 1 to the clans of *M* son of Joseph.
32:33 and the half-tribe of *M* son
32:39 of Makir son of *M* went to Gilead,
32:40 the descendants of *M*,
32:41 of *M*, captured their settlements
34:14 half-tribe of *M* have received their
34:23 from the tribe of *M* son of Joseph;
36: 1 the son of *M*, who were
36:12 descendants of *M* son of Joseph,
Dt 3:13 I gave to the half tribe of *M*.
3:14 of *M*, took the whole region
29: 8 the Gadites and the half-tribe of *M*.
33:17 such are the thousands of *M*."
Dt 34: 2 the territory of Ephraim and *M*,
Jos 1:12 the Gadites and the half-tribe of *M*,
4:12 the half-tribe of *M* crossed over,
12: 6 and the half-tribe of *M*
13: 7 and half of the tribe of *M*."
13: 8 half of *M*, the Reubenites
13:29 given to the half-tribe of *M*,
13:29 the family of the descendants of *M*,
13:31 descendants of Makir son of *M*—
14: 4 Joseph had become two tribes—*M*
16: 4 *M* and Ephraim, the descendants
17: 1 was the allotment for the tribe of *M*
17: 2 for the rest of the people of *M*—
17: 2 of *M* son of Joseph by their clans.
17: 3 the son of *M*, had no sons
17: 6 to the rest of the descendants of *M*.
17: 6 tribe of *M* received an inheritance
17: 7 The territory of *M* extended
17: 8 on the boundary of *M*, belonged
17: 8 (*M* had the land of Tappuah,
17: 9 lying among the towns of *M*,
17: 9 of *M* was the northern side
17:10 The territory of *M* reached the sea
17:10 to Ephraim, on the north to *M*.
17:11 and Asher, *M* also had Beth Shan,
17:17 and *M*—"You are numerous
18: 7 of *M* have already received their
20: 8 Golan in Bashan in the tribe of *M*.
21: 5 of Ephraim, Dan and half of *M*.
21: 6 and the half-tribe of *M* in Bashan.
21:25 tribe of *M* they received Taanach
21:27 from the half-tribe of *M*,
22: 1 the half-tribe of *M* and said to them
22: 7 (To the half-tribe of *M*
22: 9 half-tribe of *M* left the Israelites
22:10 of *M* built an imposing altar there
22:13 Gad and the half-tribe of *M*.
22:15 Gad and the half-tribe of *M*—
22:21 and the half-tribe of *M* replied
22:30 what Reuben, Gad and *M* had
22:31 said to Reuben, Gad and *M*,
Jdg 1:27 But *M* did not drive out the people
6:15 My clan is the weakest in *M*,
6:35 He sent messengers throughout *M*,
7:23 Asher and all *M* were called out,
11:29 He crossed Gilead and *M*,
12: 4 renegades from Ephraim and *M*."
1Ki 4:13 Jair son of *M* in Gilead were his, as
2Ki 10:33 and *M*), from Aroer by the Arnon
20:21 And *M* his son succeeded him
21: 1 *M* was twelve years old
21: 9 *M* led them astray,
21:11 "*M* king of Judah has committed
21:16 *M* also shed so much innocent
21:18 *M* rested with his fathers
21:20 as his father *M* had done.
23:12 and the altars *M* had built
23:26 because of all that *M* had done
24: 3 of the sins of *M* and all he had done
1Ch 3:13 Hezekiah his son, *M* his son,
5:18 and the half-tribe of *M* had 44,760
5:23 the half-tribe of *M* were numerous;
5:26 and the half-tribe of *M* into exile.
6:61 from the clans of half the tribe of *M*
6:62 of the tribe of *M* that is in Bashan,
6:70 tribe of *M* the Israelites gave Aner
6:71 of *M* they received Golan
7:14 of *M*: Asriel was his descendant
7:17 son of Makir, the son of *M*.
7:29 Along the borders of *M*
9: 3 *M* who lived in Jerusalem were:
12:19 of the men of *M* defected to David
12:20 leaders of units of a thousand in *M*.
12:20 the men of *M* who defected to him:
12:31 men of half the tribe of *M*,
12:37 Gad and the half-tribe of *M*,
26:32 and the half-tribe of *M*
27:20 the tribe of *M*: Joel son of Pedaiah;
27:21 over the half-tribe of *M* in Gilead:
2Ch 15: 9 *M* and Simeon who had settled
30: 1 wrote letters to Ephraim and *M*,
30:10 town to town in Ephraim and *M*,
30:11 *M* and Zebulun humbled
30:18 *M*, Issachar and Zebulun had not
31: 1 Benjamin and in Ephraim and *M*.
32:33 And *M* his son succeeded him
33: 1 *M* was twelve years old
33: 9 But *M* led Judah and the people
2Ch 33:10 The LORD spoke to *M*
33:11 who took *M* prisoner, put a hook
33:13 *M* knew that the LORD is God.
33:20 *M* rested with his fathers
33:22 as his father *M* had done.
33:22 to all the idols *M* had made.
33:23 But unlike his father *M*, he did not
34: 6 In the towns of *M*, Ephraim
34: 9 collected from the people of *M*,
Ezr 10:30 Mattaniah, Bezalel, Binnui and *M*.
10:33 Eliphelet, Jeremai, *M* and Shimei.
Ps 60: 7 Gilead is mine, and *M* is mine;
80: 2 before Ephraim, Benjamin and *M*.
108: 8 Gilead is mine, *M* is mine;
Isa 9:21 *M* will feed on Ephraim,
9:21 on Ephraim, and Ephraim on *M*;
Jer 15: 4 of what *M* son of Hezekiah king
Eze 48: 4 "*M* will have one portion;
48: 5 territory of *M* from east to west.
Mt 1:10 father of *M*, *M* the father of Amon,
Rev 7: 6 from the tribe of *M* 12,000,

MANASSEH'S (MANASSEH)

Ge 48:14 he put his left hand on *M* head,
48:17 it from Ephraim's head to *M* head.
Jos 17: 1 that is, for Makir, *M* firstborn.
17: 5 *M* share consisted of ten tracts
2Ki 21:17 As for the other events of *M* reign,
2Ch 33:18 The other events of *M* reign,

MANASSITES (MANASSEH)

Dt 4:43 and Golan in Bashan, for the *M*.
Jos 16: 9 within the inheritance of the *M*
17:12 Yet the *M* were not able

MANDRAKE (MANDRAKES)

Ge 30:14 the fields and found some *m* plants,

MANDRAKES (MANDRAKE)

Ge 30:14 give me some of your son's *m*."
30:15 Will you take my son's *m* too?"
30:15 tonight in return for your son's *m*."
30:16 I have hired you with my son's *m*."
SS 7:13 The *m* send out their fragrance,

MANE

Job 39:19 or clothe his neck with a flowing *m*

MANGER

Job 39: 9 Will he stay by your *m* at night?
Pr 14: 4 there are no oxen, the *m* is empty,
Isa 1: 3 the donkey his owner's *m*,
Lk 2: 7 in cloths and placed him in a *m*,
2:12 in strips of cloth and lying in a *m*."
2:16 the baby, who was lying in the *m*.

MANGLED (MANGLES)

La 3:11 me from the path and *m* me

MANGLES (MANGLED)

Mic 5: 8 which mauls and *m* as it goes,

MANIAC

Hos 9: 7 the inspired man a *m*.

MANIFESTATION

1Co 12: 7 to each one the *m* of the Spirit is

MANKIND

Ge 6: 7 I will wipe *m*, whom I have created
7:21 swarm over the earth, and all *m*.
Nu 16:22 "O God, God of the spirits of all *m*,
27:16 the God of the spirits of all *m*,
Dt 32: 8 when he divided all *m*,
32:26 and erase their memory from *m*,
Job 12:10 and the breath of all *m*.
34:15 all *m* would perish together
36:25 All *m* has seen it;
36:28 and abundant showers fall on *m*.
Ps 21:10 their posterity from *m*.
33:13 and sees all *m*;
64: 9 All *m* will fear;
Pr 8: 4 I raise my voice to all *m*.
8:31 and delighting in *m*.
30:14 the needy from among *m*.
Ecc 7:29 God made *m* upright,
Isa 2: 9 and *m* humbled—
5:15 and *m* humbled,

Isa 38: 11 no longer will I look on *m*,
40: 5 and all *m* together will see it.
45: 12 and created *m* upon it.
49: 26 Then all *m* will know
66: 23 all *m* will come and bow
66: 24 and they will be loathsome to all *m*
Jer 25: 31 he will bring judgment on all *m*
32: 20 both in Israel and among all *m*,
32: 27 "I am the LORD, the God of all *m*.
Da 2: 38 in your hands he has placed *m*
Joel 1: 12 Surely the joy of *m*
Mic 5: 7 or linger for *m*.
Zec 2: 13 Be still before the LORD, all *m*,
Lk 3: 6 And all *m* will see God's salvation
Rev 9: 15 released to kill a third of *m*.
9: 18 A third of *m* was killed
9: 20 The rest of *m* that were not killed

MANNA

Ex 16: 31 people of Israel called the bread *m*.
16: 32 'Take an omer of *m* and keep it
16: 33 and put an omer of *m* in it.
16: 34 Aaron put the *m* in front
16: 35 The Israelites ate *m* forty years,
16: 35 they ate *m* until they reached
Nu 11: 6 we never see anything but this *m*!"
11: 7 The *m* was like coriander seed
11: 9 settled on the camp at night, the *m*
Dt 8: 3 and then feeding you with *m*,
8: 16 He gave you *m* to eat in the desert,
Jos 5: 12 The *m* stopped the day
5: 12 there was no longer any *m*
Ne 9: 20 You did not withhold your *m*
Ps 78: 24 he rained down *m* for the people
Jn 6: 31 Our forefathers ate the *m*
6: 49 Your forefathers ate the *m*
6: 58 Our forefathers ate *m* and died,
Heb 9: 4 ark contained the gold jar of *m*,
Rev 2: 17 I will give some of the hidden *m*.

MANNER

Nu 15: 11 is to be prepared in this *m*.
Jos 6: 15 the city seven times in the same *m*,
1Ki 21: 26 in the vilest *m* by going after idols,
1Co 11: 27 in an unworthy *m* will be guilty
2Co 1: 17 plans in a worldly *m* so that
Php 1: 27 conduct yourselves in a *m* worthy
3Jn : 6 on their way in a *m* worthy of God.

MANOAH

Jdg 13: 2 A certain man of Zorah, named *M*,
13: 8 Then *M* prayed to the LORD:
13: 9 God heard *M*, and the angel
13: 9 her husband *M* was not with her.
13: 11 *M* got up and followed his wife.
13: 12 *M* asked him, "When your words
13: 15 *M* said to the angel of the LORD,
13: 16 (*M* did not realize that it was
13: 17 Then *M* inquired of the angel
13: 19 Then *M* took a young goat,
13: 19 did an amazing thing while *M*
13: 20 *M* and his wife fell with their faces
13: 21 did not show himself again to *M*
13: 21 *M* realized that it was the angel
16: 31 Eshtaol in the tomb of *M* his father.

MANSERVANT (SERVANT)

Ex 20: 10 nor your *m* or maidservant,
20: 17 or his *m* or maidservant, his ox
21: 26 "If a man hits a *m* or maidservant
21: 27 if he knocks out the tooth of a *m*
Lev 25: 6 yourself, your *m* and maidservant,
Dt 5: 14 nor your *m* or maidservant,
5: 14 so that your *m* and maidservant
5: 21 his *m* or maidservant, his ox

MANSIONS

Ps 49: 14 far from their princely *m*.
Isa 5: 9 the fine *m* left without occupants.
Am 3: 15 and the *m* will be demolished,"
5: 11 though you have built stone *m*,

MANTLE (MANTLED)

Ps 89: 45 with a *m* of shame.

MANTLED (MANTLE)

Ps 65: 13 and the valleys are *m* with grain;

MANURE

Isa 25: 10 as straw is trampled down in the *m*.
Eze 4: 15 bread over cow *m* instead
Lk 14: 35 for the soil nor for the *m* pile;

MAOCH

1Sa 27: 2 to Achish son of *M* king of Gath.

MAON (MAONITES)

Jos 15: 55 *M*, Carmel, Ziph, Juttah, Jezreel,
1Sa 23: 24 his men were in the Desert of *M*,
23: 25 and stayed in the Desert of *M*.
23: 25 into the Desert of *M* in pursuit
25: 1 moved down into the Desert of *M*.
25: 2 man in *M*, who had property there
1Ch 2: 45 The son of Shammai was *M*,
2: 45 *M* was the father of Beth Zur.

MAONITES (MAON)

Jdg 10: 12 and the *M* oppressed you

MAP

Jos 18: 8 on their way to *m* out the land,

MARA

Ru 1: 20 "Call me *M*, because the Almighty

MARAH

Ex 15: 23 (That is why the place is called *M*.)
15: 23 to *M*, they could not drink its water
Nu 33: 8 of Etham, they camped at *M*.
33: 9 They left *M* and went to Elim,

MARALAH

Jos 19: 11 ran to *M*, touched Dabbesheth,

MARAUDERS (MARAUDING)

Job 12: 6 The tents of *m* are undisturbed,
15: 21 when all seems well, *m* attack him.
Hos 6: 9 As *m* lie in ambush for a man,

MARAUDING (MARAUDERS)

Zec 9: 8 against *m* forces.

MARBLE

1Ch 29: 2 and all kinds of fine stone and *m*—
Est 1: 6 material to silver rings on *m* pillars.
1: 6 *m*, mother-of-pearl and other
SS 5: 15 His legs are pillars of *m*
Rev 18: 12 costly wood, bronze, iron and *m*;

MARCH (MARCHED MARCHES MARCHING)

Nu 10: 28 of *m* for the Israelite divisions
20: 18 we will *m* out and attack you
Dt 20: 10 When you *m* up to attack a city,
Jos 6: 3 *M* around the city once
6: 4 *m* around the city seven times,
6: 7 "Advance! *M* around the city,
10: 9 After an all-night *m* from Gilgal,
Jdg 5: 21 *M* on, my soul; be strong!
2Sa 15: 22 said to Ittai, "Go ahead, *m* on."
18: 2 I myself will surely *m* out with you
2Ki 3: 9 After a roundabout *m*
18: 25 me to *m* against this country
24: 7 The king of Egypt did not *m* out
2Ch 20: 16 Tomorrow *m* down against them.
25: 7 from Israel must not *m* with you,
Isa 27: 4 I would *m* against them in battle;
36: 10 me to *m* against this country
42: 13 LORD will *m* out like a mighty
Jer 46: 3 and *m* out for battle!
46: 9 *M* on, O warriors—
Da 11: 11 of the South will *m* out in a rage
Joel 2: 7 They all *m* in line,
Ob : 13 You should not *m*
Zec 9: 14 he will *m* in the storms of the south

MARCHED (MARCH)

Ge 14: 8 Zoar) *m* out and drew up their
Nu 21: 23 *m* out into the desert against Israel.
21: 33 his whole army *m* out to meet them
33: 3 They *m* out boldly in full view
Dt 1: 43 and in your arrogance you *m* up
3: 1 Bashan with his whole army *m* out
Jos 6: 9 The armed guard *m* ahead
6: 14 So on the second day they *m*
6: 15 and *m* around the city seven times

Jos 8: 10 the leaders of Israel *m* before them
8: 11 entire force that was with him *m* up
10: 7 So Joshua *m* up from Gilgal
15: 15 From there he *m* against the people
Jdg 5: 4 when you *m* from the land
1Sa 29: 2 As the Philistine rulers *m*
2Sa 2: 29 his men *m* through the Arabah.
2: 32 Then Joab and his men *m* all night
5: 6 and his men *m* to Jerusalem
15: 18 All his men *m* past him,
15: 18 him from Gath *m* before the king.
15: 22 So Ittai the Gittite *m*
18: 4 while all the men *m* out in units
18: 6 The army *m* into the field
20: 7 They *m* out from Jerusalem
1Ki 20: 19 the provincial commanders *m* out
20: 27 and given provisions, they *m* out
2Ki 6: 24 and *m* up and laid siege to Samaria.
16: 5 king of Israel *m* up to fight
17: 5 *m* against Samaria and laid siege
18: 9 king of Assyria *m* against Samaria
23: 29 King Josiah *m* out to meet him
25: 1 of Babylon *m* against Jerusalem
1Ch 11: 4 all the Israelites *m* to Jerusalem,
2Ch 14: 9 Zerah the Cushite *m* out
24: 23 the army of Aram *m* against Joash;
35: 20 Josiah *m* out to meet him in battle.
Job 18: 14 and *m* off to the king of terrors.
Ps 68: 7 when you *m* through the wasteland
Isa 7: 1 king of Israel *m* up to fight
Jer 37: 5 Pharaoh's army had *m* out
37: 7 which has *m* out to support you,
39: 1 of Babylon *m* against Jerusalem
52: 4 of Babylon *m* against Jerusalem
Heb 11: 30 after the people had *m*
Rev 20: 9 They *m* across the breadth

MARCHES (MARCH)

Joel 2: 8 each *m* straight ahead.
Am 5: 3 city that *m* out a thousand strong
5: 3 town that *m* out a hundred strong
Mic 5: 5 and *m* through our fortresses,
5: 6 and *m* into our borders.

MARCHING (MARCH)

Ex 14: 8 Israelites, who were *m* out boldly.
14: 10 and there were the Egyptians, *m*
Jos 6: 13 *m* before the ark of the LORD
1Sa 29: 2 and his men were *m* at the rear
2Sa 5: 24 you hear the sound of *m* in the tops
2Ki 19: 9 was *m* out to fight against him.
1Ch 14: 15 you hear the sound of *m* in the tops
2Ch 11: 4 back from *m* against Jeroboam.
Isa 37: 9 was *m* out to fight against him.

MARDUK

Jer 50: 2 *M* filled with terror.

MARE

SS 1: 9 I liken you, my darling, to a *m*

MARESHAH

Jos 15: 44 Nezib, Keilah, Aczib and *M*—
1Ch 2: 42 and his son *M*, who was the father
4: 21 Laadah the father of *M*
2Ch 11: 8 Adullam, Gath, *M*, Ziph, Adoraim,
14: 9 chariots, and came as far as *M*.
14: 10 in the Valley of Zephathah near *M*.
20: 37 son of Dodavahu of *M* prophesied
Mic 1: 15 who live in *M*.

MARINERS (MARITIME)

Eze 27: 27 your *m*, seamen and shipwrights,
27: 29 the *m* and all the seamen

MARITAL (MARRY)

Ex 21: 10 of her food, clothing and *m* rights.
Mt 5: 32 except for *m* unfaithfulness,
19: 9 except for *m* unfaithfulness,
1Co 7: 3 husband should fulfill his *m* duty

MARITIME (MARINERS)

Ge 10: 5 (From these the *m* peoples spread

MARK (MARKED MARKER MARKS)

Ge 1: 14 as signs to *m* seasons and days
4: 15 Then the LORD put a *m* on Cain
1Ki 22: 28 Then he added, "*M* my words,

2Ch 18:27 Then he added, "*M* my words,
Job 36:32 and commands it to strike its *m*.
Isa 59: 7 ruin and destruction *m* their ways.
Eze 9: 4 and put a *m* on the foreheads
9: 6 not touch anyone who has the *m*.
21:19 *m* out two roads for the sword
21:20 *M* out one road for the sword
Ac 12:12 called *M*, where many people had
12:25 with them John, also called *M*.
15:37 wanted to take John, also called *M*,
15:39 Barnabas took *M* and sailed
Ro 3:16 ruin and misery *m* their ways,
2Co 12:12 The things that *m* an apostle—
Gal 5: 2 *M* my words! I, Paul, tell you that
Col 4:10 as does *M*, the cousin of Barnabas.
2Th 3:17 which is the distinguishing *m*
2Ti 3: 1 *m* this: There will be terrible times
4:11 Get *M* and bring him with you,
Phm :24 And so do *M*, Aristarchus,
1Pe 5:13 and so does my son *M*.
Rev 13:16 to receive a *m* on his right hand
13:17 or sell unless he had the *m*,
14: 9 and receives his *m* on the forehead
14:11 or for anyone who receives the *m*
16: 2 out on the people who had the *m*
19:20 those who had received the *m*
20: 4 and had not received his *m*

MARKED (MARK)

Jos 18:20 the boundaries that *m* out
Job 15:22 he is *m* for the sword.
38: 5 Who *m* off its dimensions?
Pr 8:27 when he *m* out the horizon
8:29 and when he *m* out the foundations
Isa 40:12 of his hand *m* off the heavens?
Zec 11: 4 "Pasture the flock *m* for slaughter.
11: 7 I pastured the flock *m* for slaughter
Eph 1:13 you were *m* in him with a seal,
Heb 12: 1 with perseverance the race *m* out

MARKER (MARK)

Isa 44:13 and makes an outline with a *m*;
Eze 39:15 he will set up a *m* beside it

MARKET (MARKETPLACE MARKETPLACES)

1Ki 20:34 "You may set up your own *m* areas
Am 8: 5 that we may *m* wheat?"—
Zep 1:11 you who live in the *m* district;
Jn 2:16 turn my Father's house into a *m*!"
1Co 10:25 meat *m* without raising questions

MARKETPLACE (MARKET)

Isa 23: 3 she became the *m* of the nations.
Eze 27:24 In your *m* they traded
Mt 20: 3 standing in the *m* doing nothing.
Mk 7: 4 come from the *m* they do not eat
Lk 7:32 are like children sitting in the *m*
Ac 16:19 and dragged them into the *m*
17: 5 some bad characters from the *m*,
17:17 as in the *m* day by day

MARKETPLACES (MARKET)

Mt 11:16 are like children sitting in the *m*
23: 7 they love to be greeted in the *m*
Mk 6:56 they placed the sick in the *m*.
12:38 robes and be greeted in the *m*,
Lk 11:43 synagogues and greetings in the *m*.
20:46 and love to be greeted in the *m*

MARKS (MARK)

Ge 35:20 day that pillar *m* Rachel's tomb.
Lev 19:28 or put tattoo *m* on yourselves.
1Sa 21:13 making *m* on the doors of the gate
2Ki 23:17 "It *m* the tomb of the man
Job 13:27 paths by putting *m* on the soles
26:10 He *m* out the horizon on the face
Ps 104:19 The moon *m* off the seasons,
Isa 44:13 and *m* it with compasses.
Jn 20:25 Unless I see the nail *m* in his hands
Gal 6:17 bear on my body the *m* of Jesus.

MAROTH

Mic 1:12 Those who live in *M* writhe in pain,

MARRED

Isa 52:14 his form *m* beyond human likeness
Jer 18: 4 from the clay was *m* in his hands;

MARRIAGE (MARRY)

Ge 29:26 daughter in *m* before the older one.
Ex 2:21 daughter Zipporah to Moses in *m*.
Lev 21: 4 for people related to him by *m*,
Dt 22:16 "I gave my daughter in *m*
23: 2 No one born of a forbidden *m*
Jos 15:16 Acsah in *m* to the man who attacks
15:17 his daughter Acsah to him in *m*.
Jdg 1:12 Acsah in *m* to the man who attacks
1:13 his daughter Acsah to him in *m*.
3: 6 They took their daughters in *m*
12: 9 away in *m* to those outside his clan,
21: 1 daughter in *m* to a Benjamite."
21: 7 any of our daughters in *m*?"
1Sa 17:25 also give him his daughter in *m*
18:17 I will give her to you in *m*;
18:19 she was given in *m* to Adriel
18:27 gave him his daughter Michal in *m*.
1Ki 2:21 in *m* to your brother Adonijah."
11:19 own wife, Queen Tahpenes, in *m*.
2Ki 8:27 related by *m* to Ahab's family.
14: 9 Give your daughter to my son in *m*
1Ch 2:35 daughter in *m* to his servant Jarha,
5: 1 when he defiled his father's *m* bed,
2Ch 18: 1 he allied himself with Ahab by *m*.
25:18 Give your daughter to my son in *m*
Ezr 9:12 do not give your daughters in *m*
Ne 10:30 daughters in *m* to the peoples
13:25 daughters in *m* for your sons
13:25 daughters in *m* to their sons,
Jer 29: 6 and give your daughters in *m*,
Da 11:17 in *m* in order to overthrow
Mal 2:14 the wife of your *m* covenant
Mt 19:12 and others have renounced *m*
22:30 neither marry nor be given in *m*;
24:38 marrying and giving in *m*,
Mk 12:25 neither marry nor be given in *m*;
Lk 2:36 husband seven years after her *m*,
17:27 and being given in *m* up
20:34 this age marry and are given in *m*.
20:35 neither marry nor be given in *m*,
Ro 7: 2 she is released from the law of *m*.
Heb 13: 4 by all, and the *m* bed kept pure,
13: 4 *M* should be honored by all,

MARRIAGES (MARRY)

Ne 13:26 of *m* like these that Solomon king

MARRIED (MARRY)

Ge 4:19 Lamech *m* two women, one named
6: 2 and they *m* any of them they chose
11:29 Abram and Nahor both *m*.
20: 3 have taken; she is a *m* woman."
24:67 mother Sarah, and he *m* Rebekah.
25:20 old when he *m* Rebekah daughter
26:34 he *m* Judith daughter
28: 9 went to Ishmael and *m* Mahalath,
38: 2 He *m* her and lay with her;
Ex 2: 1 house of Levi *m* a Levite woman,
6:20 Amram *m* his father's sister
6:23 Aaron *m* Elisheba, daughter
6:25 Eleazar son of Aaron *m* one
22:16 a virgin who is not pledged to be *m*
Nu 5:19 and become impure while *m*
5:20 astray while *m* to your husband
5:29 and defiles herself while *m*
12: 1 for he had *m* a Cushite.
36:11 *m* their cousins on their father's
36:12 They *m* within the clans
Dt 20: 7 to a woman and not *m* her?
22:14 *m* this woman, but when I
22:23 in a town a virgin pledged to be *m*
22:25 to meet a girl pledged to be *m*
22:28 a virgin who is not pledged to be *m*
24: 5 a man has recently *m*, he must not
24: 5 happiness to the wife he has *m*.
28:30 pledged to be *m* to a woman,
Ru 1: 4 They *m* Moabite women, one
1Sa 25:43 also *m* Ahinoam of Jezreel,
2Sa 13:13 me from being *m* to you."
17:25 an Israelite who had *m* Abigail,
1Ki 3: 1 king of Egypt and *m* his daughter.
4:11 in Naphoth Dor (he was *m*
4:15 (he had *m* Basemath daughter
7: 8 daughter, whom he had *m*.
16:31 *m* Jezebel daughter of Ethbaal king
2Ki 8:18 for he *m* a daughter of Ahab.
1Ch 2:19 Azubah died, Caleb *m* Ephrath,
2:21 the father of Gilead (he had *m* her
4:18 Bithiah, whom Mered had *m*.
23:22 cousins, the sons of Kish, *m* them.
2Ch 11:18 Rehoboam *m* Mahalath, who was
11:20 he *m* Maacah daughter of Absalom
13:21 He *m* fourteen wives and had
21: 6 for he *m* a daughter of Ahab.
Ezr 2:61 (a man who had *m* a daughter
10:10 you have *m* foreign women,
10:14 towns who has *m* a foreign woman
10:17 men who had *m* foreign women.
10:18 following had *m* foreign women:
10:44 All these had *m* foreign women,
Ne 6:18 son Jehohanan had *m* the daughter
7:63 (a man who had *m* a daughter
13:23 men of Judah who had *m* women
Pr 30:23 an unloved woman who is *m*,
Isa 54: 6 a wife who *m* young,
62: 4 and your land will be *m*.
Hos 1: 3 he *m* Gomer daughter of Diblaim,
Mt 1:18 pledged to be *m* to Joseph,
22:25 The first one *m* and died,
22:28 since all of them were *m* to her?"
Mk 6:17 Philip's wife, whom he had *m*.
12:20 The first one *m* and died
12:21 The second one *m* the widow,
12:23 since the seven were *m* to her?"
Lk 1:27 to be *m* to a man named Joseph,
2: 5 who was pledged to be *m* to him
14:20 'I just got *m*, so I can't come.'
20:29 The first one *m* a woman
20:31 second and then the third *m* her,
20:33 since the seven were *m* to her?"
Ro 7: 2 by law a *m* woman is bound
1Co 7:10 To the *m* I give this command (not
7:27 Are you *m*? Do not seek a divorce.
7:33 But a *m* man is concerned about
7:34 But a *m* woman is concerned about
7:36 They should get *m*.

MARRIES (MARRY)

Ex 21:10 If he *m* another woman, he must
Lev 20:14 " 'If a man *m* both a woman
20:17 If a man *m* his sister, the daughter
20:21 " 'If a man *m* his brother's wife,
21:13 The woman he *m* must be a virgin.
22:12 a priest's daughter *m* anyone other
Nu 30: 6 "If she *m* after she makes a vow
Dt 24: 1 If a man *m* a woman who becomes
Isa 62: 5 As a young man *m* a maiden,
Jer 3: 1 she leaves him and *m* another man,
Mt 5:32 and anyone who *m* a woman
19: 9 and *m* another woman commits
Mk 10:11 and *m* another woman commits
10:12 her husband and *m* another man,
Lk 16:18 and *m* another woman commits
16:18 the man who *m* a divorced woman
Ro 7: 3 even though she *m* another man.
7: 3 if she *m* another man
1Co 7:28 if a virgin *m*, she has not sinned.
7:38 he who *m* the virgin does right,

MARROW

Job 21:24 his bones rich with *m*,
Heb 4:12 joints and *m*; it judges the thoughts

MARRY (INTERMARRY MARITAL MARRIAGE MARRIAGES MARRIED MARRIES MARRYING)

Ge 19:14 pledged to *m* his daughters.
28: 1 "Do not *m* a Canaanite woman.
28: 6 "Do not *m* a Canaanite woman,"
34:21 We can *m* their daughters
34:21 daughters and they can *m* ours.
Lev 21: 7 " 'They must not *m* women defiled
21:14 He must not *m* a widow, a divorced
Nu 36: 3 Now suppose they *m* men
36: 3 to that of the tribe they *m* into.
36: 4 that of the tribe into which they *m*,
36: 6 They may *m* anyone they please
36: 6 as they *m* within the tribal clan
36: 8 any Israelite tribe must *m* someone
Dt 20: 7 in battle and someone else *m* her."
22:29 He must *m* the girl,
22:30 A man is not to *m* his father's wife;
24: 4 is not allowed to *m* her again
25: 5 brother shall take her and *m* her

Dt 25: 5 his widow must not *m*
25: 7 want to *m* his brother's wife,
25: 8 in saying, "I do not want to *m* her,"
Jdg 11: 37 friends, because I will never *m*."
11: 38 wept because she would never *m*.
14: 8 when he went back to *m* her,
Isa 62: 5 so will your sons *m* you;
Jer 16: 2 "You must not *m* and have sons
29: 6 *M* and have sons and daughters;
Eze 44: 22 They must not *m* widows
44: 22 they may *m* only virgins
Mt 19: 10 and wife, it is better not to *m*."
22: 24 his brother must *m* the widow
22: 30 resurrection people will neither *m*
Mk 12: 19 the man must *m* the widow
12: 25 they will neither *m* nor be given
Lk 20: 28 the man must *m* the widow
20: 34 "The people of this age *m*
20: 35 from the dead will neither *m*
1Co 7: 1 It is good for a man not to *m*.
7: 9 control themselves, they should *m*,
7: 9 for it is better to *m* than to burn
7: 28 But those who *m* will face many
7: 28 if you do *m*, you have not sinned;
7: 36 and he feels he ought to *m*,
7: 37 up his mind not to *m* the virgin—
7: 38 but he who does not *m* her does
7: 39 she is free to *m* anyone she wishes,
1Ti 4: 3 They forbid people to *m*
5: 11 to Christ, they want to *m*.
5: 14 So I counsel younger widows to *m*,

MARRYING (MARRY)

Ezr 10: 2 to our God by *m* foreign women
Ne 13: 27 to our God by *m* foreign women?"
Mal 2: 11 by *m* the daughter of a foreign god.
Mt 24: 38 drinking, *m* and giving in marriage,
Lk 17: 27 *m* and being given in marriage up

MARSENA

Est 1: 14 Tarshish, Meres, *M* and Memucan,

MARSH

Job 8: 11 grow tall where there is no *m?*
40: 21 hidden among the reeds in the *m*.

MARSHAL (MARSHALED)

Mic 5: 1 *M* your troops, O city of troops,
Na 2: 1 *m* all your strength!

MARSHALED (MARSHAL)

2Ch 25: 11 Amaziah then *m* his strength
Job 6: 4 God's terrors are *m* against me.
32: 14 Job has not *m* his words against me
Isa 45: 12 I *m* their starry hosts.

MARSHES

Jer 51: 32 the *m* set on fire,
Eze 47: 11 and *m* will not become fresh;

MARTHA

Lk 10: 38 a woman named *M* opened her
10: 40 But *M* was distracted by all
10: 41 *"M, M,"* the Lord answered,
Jn 11: 1 village of Mary and her sister *M*.
11: 5 Jesus loved *M* and her sister
11: 19 and many Jews had come to *M*
11: 20 When *M* heard that Jesus was
11: 21 *M* said to Jesus, "if you had been
11: 24 *M* answered, "I know he will rise
11: 30 at the place where *M* had met him.
11: 39 said *M*, the sister of the dead man,
12: 2 *M* served, while Lazarus was

MARTYR

Ac 22: 20 blood of your *m* Stephen was shed,

MARVELED (MARVELOUS)

Lk 2: 33 mother *m* at what was said about
2Th 1: 10 and to be *m* at among all those who

MARVELING (MARVELOUS)

Lk 9: 43 While everyone was *m*

MARVELOUS (MARVELED MARVELING)

1Ch 16: 24 his *m* deeds among all peoples.
Job 37: 5 God's voice thunders in *m* ways;
Ps 71: 17 to this day I declare your *m* deeds.
72: 18 who alone does *m* deeds.
86: 10 For you are great and do *m* deeds;
96: 3 his *m* deeds among all peoples.
98: 1 for he has done *m* things;
118: 23 and it is *m* in our eyes.
Isa 25: 1 you have done *m* things,
Zec 8: 6 but will it seem *m* to me?"
8: 6 "It may seem *m* to the remnant
Mt 21: 42 and it is *m* in our eyes'?
Mk 12: 11 and it is *m* in our eyes'?"
Rev 15: 1 in heaven another great and *m* sign
15: 3 "Great and *m* are your deeds,

MARY (MARY'S)

Mt 1: 16 the husband of *M*,
1: 18 His mother *M* was pledged
1: 20 do not be afraid to take *M* home
1: 24 and took *M* home as his wife.
2: 11 the child with his mother *M*,
13: 55 Isn't his mother's name *M*,
27: 56 Among them were *M* Magdalene,
27: 56 *M* the mother of James and Joseph,
27: 61 *M* Magdalene and the other *M*
28: 1 *M* Magdalene and the other *M*
Mk 15: 40 Among them were *M* Magdalene,
15: 40 *M* the mother of James
15: 47 *M* Magdalene and *M* the mother
16: 1 *M* Magdalene, *M* the mother
16: 9 he appeared first to *M* Magdalene,
Lk 1: 27 The virgin's name was *M*.
1: 29 *M* was greatly troubled
1: 30 *M*, you have found favor with God.
1: 34 will this be," *M* asked the angel,
1: 38 the Lord's servant," *M* answered.
1: 39 At that time *M* got ready
1: 46 be accomplished!" And *M* said:
1: 56 *M* stayed with Elizabeth
2: 5 He went there to register with *M*,
2: 16 So they hurried off and found *M*
2: 19 But *M* treasured up all these things
2: 22 and *M* took him to Jerusalem
2: 34 Simeon blessed them and said to *M*
2: 39 *M* had done everything required
8: 2 *M* (called Magdalene)
10: 39 She had a sister called *M*, who sat
10: 42 *M* has chosen what is better,
24: 10 It was *M* Magdalene, Joanna,
24: 10 Joanna, *M* the mother of James,
Jn 11: 1 village of *M* and her sister Martha.
11: 2 This *M*, whose brother Lazarus
11: 19 and *M* to comfort them in the loss
11: 20 to meet him, but *M* stayed at home.
11: 28 and called her sister *M* aside.
11: 29 When *M* heard this, she got up
11: 31 been with *M* in the house,
11: 32 When *M* reached the place where
11: 45 the Jews who had come to visit *M*,
12: 3 *M* took about a pint of pure nard,
19: 25 his mother's sister, *M* the wife
19: 25 wife of Clopas, and *M* of Magdala.
20: 1 *M* of Magdala went to the tomb
20: 11 *M* stood outside the tomb crying.
20: 16 Jesus said to her, *"M."*
20: 18 *M* of Magdala went to the disciples
Ac 1: 14 and *M* the mother of Jesus,
12: 12 went to the house of *M* the mother
Ro 16: 6 Greet *M*, who worked very hard

MARY'S (MARY)

Mk 6: 3 Isn't this *M* son and the brother
Lk 1: 41 When Elizabeth heard *M* greeting,

MASH

Isa 30: 24 work the soil will eat fodder and *m*,

MASHAL

1Ch 6: 74 the tribe of Asher they received *M*,

MASK

1Th 2: 5 put on a *m* to cover up greed—

MASONS

2Ki 12: 12 builders, the *m* and stonecutters.
22: 6 carpenters, the builders and the *m*.
1Ch 22: 15 stonecutters, *m* and carpenters,
2Ch 24: 12 They hired *m* and carpenters
Ezr 3: 7 Then they gave money to the *m*

MASQUERADE (MASQUERADES MASQUERADING)

2Co 11: 15 if his servants *m* as servants

MASQUERADES (MASQUERADE)

2Co 11: 14 for Satan himself *m* as an angel

MASQUERADING (MASQUERADE)

2Co 11: 13 deceitful workmen, *m*

MASREKAH

Ge 36: 36 Samlah from *M* succeeded him
1Ch 1: 47 Samlah from *M* succeeded him

MASSA

Ge 25: 14 Mishma, Dumah, *M*, Hadad, Tema
1Ch 1: 30 Mishma, Dumah, *M*, Hadad, Tema

MASSACRE

Hos 1: 4 house of Jehu for the *m* at Jezreel,

MASSAH

Ex 17: 7 he called the place *M* and Meribah
Dt 6: 16 LORD your God as you did at *M*.
9: 22 the LORD angry at Taberah, at *M*
33: 8 You tested him at *M;*
Ps 95: 8 you did that day at *M* in the desert,

MASSES (MASSING)

Isa 5: 13 their *m* will be parched with thirst.
5: 14 it will descend their nobles and *m*

MASSING (MASSES)

Isa 13: 4 like nations *m* together!

MASSIVE

Mk 13: 1 "Look, Teacher! What *m* stones!

MAST

Isa 33: 23 The *m* is not held secure,
Eze 27: 5 Lebanon to make a *m* for you.

MASTER (MASTER'S MASTERED MASTERS MASTERS' MASTERY)

Ge 4: 7 to have you, but you must *m* it."
18: 12 I am worn out and my *m* is old,
24: 9 under the thigh of his *m* Abraham
24: 10 kinds of good things from his *m*.
24: 12 O LORD, God of my *m* Abraham,
24: 12 show kindness to my *m* Abraham.
24: 14 have shown kindness to my *m*."
24: 27 kindness and faithfulness to my *m*.
24: 27 the God of my *m* Abraham,
24: 35 has blessed my *m* abundantly,
24: 37 And my *m* made me swear an oath,
24: 39 "Then I asked my *m*, 'What
24: 42 God of my *m* Abraham, if you will,
24: 48 the God of my *m* Abraham,
24: 49 kindness and faithfulness to my *m*,
24: 54 "Send me on my way to my *m*."
24: 56 on my way so I may go to my *m*."
24: 65 He is my *m*," the servant answered
32: 4 are to say to my *m* Esau:
39: 2 in the house of his Egyptian *m*.
39: 3 When his *m* saw that the LORD
39: 8 "my *m* does not concern himself
39: 9 My *m* has withheld nothing
39: 16 beside her until his *m* came home.
39: 19 When his *m* heard the story his
39: 20 Joseph's *m* took him and put him
40: 1 the king of Egypt offended their *m*,
44: 5 Isn't this the cup my *m* drinks from
Ex 21: 4 If his *m* gives him a wife
21: 4 her children shall belong to her *m*,
21: 5 'I love my *m* and my wife
21: 6 then his *m* must take him
21: 8 not please the *m* who has selected
21: 32 of silver to the *m* of the slave,
35: 35 all of them *m* craftsmen
Dt 23: 15 do not hand him over to his *m*.
Jdg 19: 11 the servant said to his *m*, "Come,
19: 12 His *m* replied, "No.
19: 26 the house where her *m* was staying,
19: 27 When her *m* got up in the morning
1Sa 20: 38 up the arrow and returned to his *m*.
24: 6 I should do such a thing to my *m*,
24: 10 will not lift my hand against my *m*,
25: 14 desert to give our *m* his greetings,

1Sa 25: 17 disaster is hanging over our *m*
25: 25 I did not see the men my *m* sent.
25: 26 intend to harm my *m* be like Nabal.
25: 26 the LORD has kept you, my *m*,
25: 27 your servant has brought to my *m*,
25: 28 make a lasting dynasty for my *m*,
25: 29 life of my *m* will be bound securely
25: 30 done for my *m* every good thing he
25: 31 LORD has brought my *m* success,
25: 31 my *m* will not have
26: 16 because you did not guard your *m*,
30: 13 My *m* abandoned me
30: 15 or hand me over to my *m*,
2Sa 2: 5 to Saul your *m* by burying him.
2: 7 and brave, for Saul your *m* is dead,
9: 10 Mephibosheth, grandson of your *m*
11: 11 my *m* Joab and my lord's men are
1Ki 11: 23 fled from his *m*, Hadadezer king
18: 8 "Go tell your *m*, 'Elijah is here.' "
18: 10 kingdom where my *m* has not sent
18: 11 But now you tell me to go to my *m*
18: 14 And now you tell me to go to my *m*
22: 17 said, 'These people have no *m*.
2Ki 2: 3 to take your *m* from you today?"
2: 5 to take your *m* from you today?"
2: 16 Let them go and look for your *m*.
5: 1 man in the sight of his *m*
5: 3 "If only my *m* would see
5: 4 Naaman went to his *m*
5: 18 When my *m* enters the temple
5: 20 "My *m* was too easy on Naaman,
5: 22 "My *m* sent me to say, 'Two young
5: 25 and stood before his *m* Elisha.
6: 22 drink and then go back to their *m*."
6: 23 and they returned to their *m*.
8: 14 left Elisha and returned to his *m*.
9: 7 destroy the house of Ahab your *m*,
9: 31 Zimri, you murderer of your *m?"*
10: 9 was I who conspired against my *m*
18: 23 make a bargain with my *m*,
18: 27 and you that my *m* sent me
18: 27 "Was it only to your *m*
19: 4 whom his *m*, the king of Assyria,
19: 6 Isaiah said to them, "Tell your *m*,
1Ch 12: 19 heads if he deserts to his *m* Saul.")
2Ch 13: 6 of David, rebelled against his *m*.
18: 16 said, 'These people have no *m*.
Job 3: 19 and the slave is freed from his *m*.
Ps 12: 4 we own our lips—who is our *m?"*
105: 21 He made him *m* of his household,
123: 2 look to the hand of their *m*,
Pr 27: 18 after his *m* will be honored.
30: 10 "Do not slander a servant to his *m*,
Isa 1: 3 The ox knows his *m*,
19: 4 over to the power of a cruel *m*,
24: 2 for *m* as for servant,
36: 8 make a bargain with my *m*,
36: 12 and you that my *m* sent me
36: 12 "Was it only to your *m*
37: 4 whom his *m*, the king of Assyria,
37: 6 Isaiah said to them, "Tell your *m*,
Jer 22: 18 'Alas, my *m!* Alas, his splendor!'
34: 5 O *m!"* I myself make this promise,
Da 8: 23 a stern-faced king, a *m* of intrigue,
Hos 2: 16 you will no longer call me 'my *m*.'
Mal 1: 6 If I am a *m*, where is the respect
1: 6 his father, and a servant his *m*.
Mt 10: 24 nor a servant above his *m*.
10: 25 and the servant like his *m*
18: 25 the *m* ordered that he and his wife
18: 27 The servant's *m* took pity on him,
18: 31 told their *m* everything that had
18: 32 "Then the *m* called the servant in.
18: 34 In anger his *m* turned him
23: 8 for you have only one *M*
24: 45 whom the *m* has put in charge
24: 46 that servant whose *m* finds him
24: 48 'My *m* is staying away a long time,'
24: 50 The *m* of that servant will come
25: 19 "After a long time the *m*
25: 20 *'M,'* he said, 'you entrusted me
25: 21 "His *m* replied, 'Well done,
25: 22 *'M,'* he said, 'you entrusted me
25: 23 "His *m* replied, 'Well done,
25: 24 *'M,'* he said, 'I knew that you are
25: 26 "His *m* replied, 'You wicked,
Lk 5: 5 *"M,* we've worked hard all night
7: 2 whom his *m* valued highly,
Lk 8: 24 *"M, M,* we're going to drown!"
8: 45 they all denied it, Peter said, *"M,*
9: 33 *"M,* it is good for us to be here.
9: 49 *"M,"* said John, "we saw a man
12: 36 waiting for their *m* to return
12: 37 those servants whose *m* finds them
12: 38 those servants whose *m* finds them
12: 42 whom the *m* puts in charge
12: 43 servant whom the *m* finds doing
12: 45 'My *m* is taking a long time
12: 46 The *m* of that servant will come
12: 47 not do what his *m* wants will be
14: 21 and reported this to his *m*.
14: 23 "Then the *m* told his servant,
16: 3 My *m* is taking away my job.
16: 5 'How much do you owe my *m?'*
16: 8 "The *m* commended the dishonest
17: 13 "Jesus, *M,* have pity on us!"
19: 17 my good servant!' his *m* replied.
19: 19 His *m* answered, 'You take charge
19: 22 "His *m* replied, 'I will judge you
Jn 2: 8 take it to the *m* of the banquet."
2: 9 *m* of the banquet tasted the water
13: 16 no servant is greater than his *m*,
15: 20 'No servant is greater than his *m*.'
Ro 6: 14 For sin shall not be your *m*,
14: 4 To his own *m* he stands or falls.
Eph 6: 9 know that he who is both their *M*
Col 4: 1 you know that you also have a *M*
2Ti 2: 21 useful to the *M* and prepared
1Pe 3: 6 Abraham and called him her *m*.

MASTER'S (MASTER)

Ge 24: 10 servant took ten of his *m* camels
24: 27 to the house of my *m* relatives."
24: 36 My *m* wife Sarah has borne him
24: 44 LORD has chosen for my *m* son.'
24: 48 of my *m* brother for his son.
24: 51 her become the wife of your *m* son,
39: 7 after a while his *m* wife took notice
40: 7 in custody with him in his *m* house,
44: 8 or gold from your *m* house?
1Sa 25: 41 wash the feet of my *m* servants."
29: 4 better could he regain his *m* favor
29: 10 with your *m* servants who have
2Sa 9: 9 given your *m* grandson everything
9: 10 so that your *m* grandson may be
11: 9 to the palace with all his *m* servants
11: 13 on his mat among his *m* servants;
12: 8 I gave your *m* house to you,
12: 8 and your *m* wives into your arms.
16: 3 "Where is your *m* grandson?"
20: 6 Take your *m* men and pursue him,
2Ki 6: 32 of his *m* footsteps behind him?"
10: 2 since your *m* sons are with you
10: 3 Then fight for your *m* house."
10: 3 and most worthy of your *m* sons
10: 6 take the heads of your *m* sons
18: 24 of the least of my *m* officials,
Isa 22: 18 you disgrace to your *m* house!
36: 9 of the least of my *m* officials,
Mt 25: 18 in the ground and hid his *m* money.
25: 21 Come and share your *m* happiness
25: 23 Come and share your *m* happiness
Lk 12: 47 That servant who knows his *m* will
16: 5 called in each one of his *m* debtors.
Jn 15: 15 does not know his *m* business.

MASTERED (MASTER)

1Co 6: 12 but I will not be *m* by anything.
2Pe 2: 19 a slave to whatever has *m* him.

MASTERS (MASTER)

Ex 1: 11 So they put slave *m* over them
1Sa 25: 10 away from their *m* these days.
Pr 25: 13 he refreshes the spirit of his *m*.
Jer 27: 4 Give them a message for their *m*
27: 4 says: "Tell this to your *m:*
La 1: 5 Her foes have become her *m;*
Mt 6: 24 "No one can serve two *m*.
Lk 16: 13 "No servant can serve two *m*.
Eph 6: 5 obey your earthly *m* with respect
6: 9 And *m*, treat your slaves
Col 3: 22 obey your earthly *m* in everything;
4: 1 *M,* provide your slaves
1Ti 6: 1 should consider their *m* worthy
6: 2 who have believing *m* are not
Tit 2: 9 subject to their *m* in everything,
1Pe 2: 18 to your *m* with all respect,

MASTERS' (MASTER)

Mt 15: 27 fall from their *m'* table."

MASTERY (MASTER)

Ro 6: 9 death no longer has *m* over him.

MAT (MATS)

2Sa 11: 13 sleep on his *m* among his master's
Mt 9: 2 to him a paralytic, lying on a *m*.
9: 6 Get up, take your *m* and go home."
Mk 2: 4 lowered the *m* the paralyzed man
2: 9 'Get up, take your *m* and walk'?
2: 11 get up, take your *m* and go home."
2: 12 took his *m* and walked out
Lk 5: 18 came carrying a paralytic on a *m*
5: 19 him on his *m* through the tiles
5: 24 get up, take your *m* and go home."
Jn 5: 8 Get up! Pick up your *m* and walk."
5: 9 he picked up his *m* and walked.
5: 10 the law forbids you to carry your *m*
5: 11 'Pick up your *m* and walk.' "
Ac 9: 34 Get up and take care of your *m*."

MATCH (MATCHED MATCHING)

1Ch 12: 14 the least was a *m* for a hundred,
Eze 31: 8 could *m* its beauty.
Lk 5: 36 from the new will not *m* the old.

MATCHED (MATCH)

2Co 8: 11 do it may be *m* by your completion

MATCHING (MATCH)

Ezr 1: 10 gold bowls 30 *m* silver bowls 410

MATE (MATED MATING)

Ge 7: 2 and its *m*, and two of every kind
7: 2 its *m*, and also seven of every kind
30: 41 so they would *m* near the branches,
Lev 19: 19 " 'Do not *m* different kinds
Isa 34: 15 each with its *m*.
34: 16 not one will lack her *m*.
Na 2: 12 and strangled the prey for his *m*,

MATED (MATE)

Ge 30: 39 they *m* in front of the branches.

MATING (MATE)

Ge 31: 10 and saw that the male goats *m*
31: 12 and see that all the male goats *m*
Jer 2: 24 at *m* time they will find her.

MATRED

Ge 36: 39 was Mehetabel daughter of *M*,
1Ch 1: 50 was Mehetabel daughter of *M*,

MATRI'S

1Sa 10: 21 by clan, and *M* clan was chosen

MATS (MAT)

Mk 6: 55 and carried the sick on *m*
Ac 5: 15 *m* so that at least Peter's shadow

MATTAN

2Ki 11: 18 killed *M* the priest of Baal in front
2Ch 23: 17 killed *M* the priest of Baal in front
Jer 38: 1 Shephatiah son of *M*, Gedaliah son

MATTANAH

Nu 21: 18 they went from the desert to *M*,
21: 19 from *M* to Nahaliel, from Nahaliel

MATTANIAH

2Ki 24: 17 He made *M*, Jehoiachin's uncle,
1Ch 9: 15 Heresh, Galal and *M* son of Mica,
25: 4 from his sons: Bukkiah, *M*, Uzziel,
25: 16 12 the ninth to *M*, his sons
2Ch 20: 14 son of *M*, a Levite and descendant
29: 13 *M;* from the descendants of Heman
Ezr 10: 26 *M*, Zechariah, Jehiel, Abdi,
10: 27 Elioenai, Eliashib, *M*, Jeremoth,
10: 30 Benaiah, Maaseiah, *M*, Bezalel,
10: 37 Vaniah, Meremoth, Eliashib, *M*,
Ne 11: 17 *M* son of Mica, the son of Zabdi,
11: 22 the son of *M*, the son of Mica.
12: 8 Sherebiah, Judah, and also *M*, who,
12: 25 *M*, Bakbukiah, Obadiah,
12: 35 the son of *M*, the son of Micaiah,

Ne 13: 13 the son of *M*, their assistant,

MATTATHA

Lk 3: 31 the son of *M*, the son of Nathan,

MATTATHIAS

Lk 3: 25 the son of *M*, the son of Amos,
3: 26 the son of *M*, the son of Semein,

MATTATTAH

Ezr 10: 33 Mattenai, *M*, Zabad, Eliphelet,

MATTENAI

Ezr 10: 33 *M*, Mattattah, Zabad, Eliphelet,
10: 37 Eliashib, Mattaniah, *M* and Jaasu.
Ne 12: 19 of Joiarib's, *M;* of Jedaiah's,

MATTHAN

Mt 1: 15 father of *M*, *M* the father of Jacob,

MATTHAT

Lk 3: 24 the son of *M*,
3: 29 the son of Jorim, the son of *M*,

MATTHEW (MATTHEW'S)

Mt 9: 9 and *M* got up and followed him.
9: 9 he saw a man named *M* sitting
10: 3 Thomas and *M* the tax collector;
Mk 3: 18 Philip, Bartholomew, *M*, Thomas,
Lk 6: 15 Philip, Bartholomew, *M*, Thomas,
Ac 1: 13 and Thomas, Bartholomew and *M;*

MATTHEW'S (MATTHEW)

Mt 9: 10 was having dinner at *M* house,

MATTHIAS

Ac 1: 23 (also known as Justus) and *M*.
1: 26 the lot fell to *M;* so he was added

MATTITHIAH

1Ch 9: 31 Levite named *M*, the firstborn son
15: 18 Benaiah, Maaseiah, *M*, Eliphelehu,
15: 21 and *M*, Eliphelehu, Mikneiah,
16: 5 Shemiramoth, Jehiel, *M*, Eliab,
25: 3 Shimei, Hashabiah and *M*, six in all
25: 21 12 the fourteenth to *M*, his sons
Ezr 10: 43 Jeiel, *M*, Zabad, Zebina, Jaddai,
Ne 8: 4 Beside him on his right stood *M*,

MATTOCKS

1Sa 13: 20 *m*, axes and sickles sharpened.
13: 21 for sharpening plowshares and *m*,

MATURE (MATURITY)

Lk 8: 14 and pleasures, and they do not *m*.
1Co 2: 6 a message of wisdom among the *m*,
Eph 4: 13 of the Son of God and become *m*,
Php 3: 15 of us who are *m* should take such
Col 4: 12 firm in all the will of God, *m*
Heb 5: 14 But solid food is for the *m*,
Jas 1: 4 work so that you may be *m*

MATURITY (MATURE)

Heb 6: 1 about Christ and go on to *m*,

MAULED (MAULS)

1Ki 13: 26 which has *m* him and killed him,
13: 28 eaten the body nor *m* the donkey.
2Ki 2: 24 and *m* forty-two of the youths.

MAULS (MAULED)

Mic 5: 8 which *m* and mangles as it goes,

MAXIMS

Job 13: 12 Your *m* are proverbs of ashes;

ME JARKON

Jos 19: 46 Gath Rimmon, *M* and Rakkon,

ME-ZAHAB

Ge 36: 39 of Matred, the daughter of *M*.
1Ch 1: 50 of Matred, the daughter of *M*.

MEADOW (MEADOWS)

Isa 44: 4 will spring up like grass in a *m*,
Hos 4: 16 like lambs in a *m?*

MEADOWS (MEADOW)

Ps 65: 13 The *m* are covered with flocks
Isa 30: 23 your cattle will graze in broad *m*.
Jer 25: 37 The peaceful *m* will be laid waste

MEAL (MEALTIME)

Ge 19: 3 He prepared a *m* for them,
31: 54 and invited his relatives to a *m*.
37: 25 As they sat down to eat their *m*,
Nu 15: 20 from the first of your ground *m*
15: 21 from the first of your ground *m*.
1Sa 20: 27 the son of Jesse come to the *m*,
2Sa 12: 4 or cattle to prepare a *m*
1Ki 4: 22 of fine flour and sixty cors of *m*,
17: 12 make a *m* for myself and my son,
2Ki 4: 8 who urged him to stay for a *m*.
Ne 10: 37 first of our ground *m*, of our ⌊grain⌋
Job 33: 20 and his soul loathes the choicest *m*.
Pr 15: 17 Better a *m* of vegetables where
Isa 44: 16 over it he prepares his *m*,
Jer 16: 5 a house where there is a funeral *m;*
Eze 44: 30 of your ground *m* so that a blessing
Lk 11: 38 did not first wash before the *m*,
Jn 13: 2 The evening *m* was being served,
13: 4 up from the *m*, took off his outer
13: 28 at the *m* understood why Jesus said
Ac 10: 10 while the *m* was being prepared,
16: 34 them into his house and set a *m*
1Co 10: 27 some unbeliever invites you to a *m*
10: 30 part in the *m* with thankfulness,
Heb 12: 16 for a single *m* sold his inheritance

MEALTIME (MEAL)

Ru 2: 14 At *m* Boaz said to her, "Come

MEAN (MEANING MEANS MEANT)

Ge 33: 8 "What do you *m* by all these
Ex 12: 26 What does this ceremony *m* to you
13: 14 'What does this *m?*' say to him,
Jos 4: 6 'What do these stones *m?*'
4: 21 What do these stones *m?*' tell them
1Sa 1: 8 Don't I *m* more to you
25: 3 was surly and *m* in his dealings.
2Sa 5: 24 that will *m* the LORD has gone out
17: 3 the man you seek will *m* the return
19: 6 and their men *m* nothing to you.
1Ch 14: 15 that will *m* God has gone out
Job 6: 26 Do you *m* to correct what I say,
Isa 3: 15 What do you *m* by crushing my
Eze 17: 12 not know what these things *m?*'
18: 2 "What do you people *m*
37: 18 'Won't you tell us what you *m*
Da 5: 26 "This is what these words *m:*
Mt 12: 7 had known what these words *m*,
Jn 7: 36 What did he *m* when he said,
7: 47 "You *m* he has deceived you also?"
16: 17 "What does he *m* by saying,
16: 18 "What does he *m* by 'a little while'?
Ac 2: 12 "What does this *m?*" Some,
17: 20 and we want to know what they *m*
1Co 1: 12 What I *m* is this: One of you says,
7: 29 What I *m*, brothers, is that the time
10: 19 Do I *m* then that a sacrifice offered
10: 29 the other man's conscience, I *m*,
15: 31 I die every day—I *m* that, brothers
Gal 2: 17 does that *m* that Christ promotes
3: 17 What I *m* is this: The law,
Eph 4: 9 (What does "he ascended" *m*
Php 1: 22 this will *m* fruitful labor for me.

MEANING (MEAN)

Ge 21: 29 "What is the *m* of these seven ewe
40: 5 and each dream had a *m* of its own.
41: 11 and each dream had a *m* of its own.
Dt 6: 20 "What is the *m* of the stipulations,
1Sa 4: 14 "What is the *m* of this uproar?"
1Ki 1: 41 "What's the *m* of all the noise
Ne 8: 8 and giving the *m* so that the people
Job 7: 16 Let me alone; my days have no *m*.
Ecc 6: 4 It comes without *m*, it departs
6: 11 the less the *m*,
8: 17 man cannot discover its *m*
Da 2: 45 This is the *m* of the vision
4: 19 and its *m* to your adversaries!
4: 19 let the dream or its *m* alarm you."
7: 16 asked him the true *m* of all this.
7: 19 wanted to know the true *m*
8: 16 tell this man the *m* of the vision."
Lk 8: 11 "This is the *m* of the parable:
18: 34 Its *m* was hidden from them,
Lk 20: 17 what is the *m* of that which is
Ac 10: 17 Peter was wondering about the *m*
1Co 4: 6 learn from us the *m* of the saying,
5: 10 not at all *m* the people
14: 10 yet none of them is without *m*.
14: 11 If then I do not grasp the *m*
Gal 3: 16 *m* many people, but
3: 16 "and to your seed," *m* one person,

MEANINGLESS

Job 27: 12 Why then this *m* talk?
Ecc 1: 2 Everything is *m*."
1: 2 "Utterly *m!*
1: 2 *"M! M!"* says the Teacher.
1: 14 all of them are *m*, a chasing
2: 1 But that also proved to be *m*.
2: 11 everything was *m*, a chasing
2: 15 "This too is *m*."
2: 17 All of it is *m*, a chasing
2: 19 This too is *m*.
2: 21 This too is *m* and a great
2: 23 This too is *m*.
2: 26 This too is *m*, a chasing
3: 19 Everything is *m*.
4: 4 This too is *m*, a chasing
4: 7 Again I saw something *m*
4: 8 This too is *m*—
4: 16 This too is *m*, a chasing
5: 7 dreaming and many words are *m*.
5: 10 This too is *m*.
6: 2 This is *m*, a grievous evil.
6: 9 This too is *m*,
6: 12 and *m* days he passes through like
7: 6 This too is *m*.
7: 15 In this *m* life of mine I have seen
8: 10 This too is *m*.
8: 14 This too, I say, is *m*.
8: 14 is something else *m* that occurs
9: 9 of this *m* life that God has given
9: 9 under the sun—all your *m* days.
11: 8 Everything to come is *m*.
11: 10 for youth and vigor are *m*.
12: 8 "Everything is *m!*"
12: 8 *"M! M!"* says the Teacher.
Isa 1: 13 Stop bringing *m* offerings!
1Ti 1: 6 from these and turned to *m* talk.

MEANS (MEAN)

Ge 40: 12 "This is what it *m*," Joseph said
40: 18 "This is what it *m*," Joseph said.
Ex 28: 30 Thus Aaron will always bear the *m*
Lev 11: 43 not make yourselves unclean by *m*
25: 26 acquires sufficient *m* to redeem it,
25: 28 But if he does not acquire the *m*
Nu 31: 16 were the *m* of turning the Israelites
1Sa 6: 3 by all *m* send a guilt offering to him
2Sa 15: 21 whether it *m* life or death,
1Ki 22: 22 " 'By what *m?*' the LORD asked.
2Ki 5: 5 "By all *m*, go," the king
5: 23 "By all *m*, take two talents,"
2Ch 18: 20 " 'By what *m?*' the LORD asked.
Pr 16: 15 a king's face brightens, it *m* life;
22: 27 if you lack the *m* to pay,
Jer 17: 11 man who gains riches by unjust *m*.
22: 16 Is that not what it *m* to know me?"
Eze 44: 19 the people by *m* of their garments.
Da 2: 3 and I want to know what it *m*."
2: 25 tell the king what his dream *m*."
4: 18 Belteshazzar, tell me what it *m*,
4: 26 with its roots *m* that your kingdom
5: 7 tells me what it *m* will be clothed
5: 12 he will tell you what the writing *m*
5: 15 this writing and tell me what it *m*,
5: 16 this writing and tell me what it *m*,
5: 17 for the king and tell him what it *m*.
Hos 11: 7 he will by no *m* exalt them.
Mt 1: 23 call him Immanuel"—which *m*,
2: 6 are by no *m* least among the rulers
5: 18 will by any *m* disappear
9: 13 But go and learn what this *m:*
13: 18 to what the parable of the sower *m:*
23: 16 swears by the temple, it *m* nothing;
23: 18 swears by the altar, it *m* nothing;
27: 33 Golgotha (which *m* The Place
27: 46 lama *sabachthani?"*—which *m*,
Mk 3: 17 which *m* Sons of Thunder);
5: 41 *"Talitha koum!"* (which *m*,
7: 34 (which *m*, "Be opened!").

Mk 15:22 Golgotha (which *m* The Place
15:34 lama *sabachthani?*"—which *m*,
Lk 8: 3 to support them out of their own *m*
Jn 1:38 "Rabbi" (which *m* Teacher),
8:54 myself, my glory *m* nothing.
9: 7 of Siloam" (this word *m* Sent).
13:24 "Ask him which one he *m*."
20:16 "Rabboni!" (which *m* Teacher).
Ac 4:36 called Barnabas (which *m* Son
13: 8 is what his name *m*) opposed them
Ro 6: 2 that grace may increase? By no *m!*
6:15 but under grace? By no *m!*
7:13 become death to me? By no *m!*
11: 1 By no *m!* I am an Israelite myself,
11:12 But if their transgression *m* riches
11:12 their loss *m* riches for the Gentiles,
1Co 6: 7 among you *m* you have been
9:22 by all possible *m* I might save some
12: 8 the message of knowledge by *m*
2Co 8:11 of it, according to your *m*.
Gal 6:15 nor uncircumcision *m* anything;
1Ti 6: 5 and who think that godliness is a *m*
Heb 7: 2 his name *m* "king of righteousness
7: 2 "king of Salem" *m* "king of peace."
9:12 He did not enter by *m* of the blood
2Pe 3:15 our Lord's patience *m* salvation,

MEANT (MEAN)

Jdg 13:23 "If the LORD had *m* to kill us,
Da 5: 8 or tell the king what it *m*.
Mk 4:22 For whatever is hidden is *m*
4:22 and whatever is concealed is *m*
9:10 "rising from the dead" *m*.
9:32 they did not understand what he *m*
Lk 8: 9 asked him what this parable *m*.
9:45 did not understand what this *m*.
Jn 1:30 This is the one I *m* when I said,
6:71 (He *m* Judas, the son of Simon
7:39 By this he *m* the Spirit, whom
11:13 thought he *m* natural sleep.
12: 7 "It was *m* that she should save this
13:22 a loss to know which of them he *m*.
16:19 you asking one another what I *m*
1Co 6:13 The body is not *m*

MEASURE (MEASURED MEASUREMENT MEASUREMENTS MEASURES MEASURING)

Ge 15:16 has not yet reached its full *m*."
41:49 records because it was beyond *m*.
Nu 35: 5 *m* three thousand feet
Dt 21: 2 and *m* the distance from the body
1Ki 7:23 line of thirty cubits to *m* around it.
2Ch 4: 2 line of thirty cubits to *m* around it.
Job 11: 9 Their *m* is longer than the earth
Ps 60: 6 and *m* off the Valley of Succoth.
71:15 though I know not its *m*.
108: 7 and *m* off the Valley of Succoth.
Isa 34:17 his hand distributes them by *m*.
47: 9 They will come upon you in full *m*,
64: 9 Do not be angry beyond *m*,
64:12 silent and punish us beyond *m?*
65: 7 I will *m* into their laps
La 5:22 and are angry with us beyond *m*.
Eze 4:11 Also *m* out a sixth of a hin of water
45: 3 In the sacred district, *m*
45:11 is to be the standard *m* for both.
Am 8: 5 skimping the *m*,
Zec 2: 2 He answered me, "To *m* Jerusalem
Mt 7: 2 and with the *m* you use,
23:32 the *m* of the sin of your forefathers!
Mk 4:24 "With the *m* you use, it will be
Lk 6:38 A good *m*, pressed
6:38 For with the *m* you use, it will be
Jn 17:13 so that they may have the full *m*
Ro 12: 3 in accordance with the *m*
15:29 come in the full *m* of the blessing
2Co 10:12 When they *m* themselves
Eph 3:19 to the *m* of all the fullness of God.
4:13 to the whole *m* of the fullness
2Pe 1: 8 these qualities in increasing *m*,
Rev 11: 1 "Go and *m* the temple of God
11: 2 exclude the outer court; do not *m* it
21:15 rod of gold to *m* the city,

MEASURED (MEASURE)

Ex 16:18 And when they *m* it by the omer,
2Sa 8: 2 *m* them off with a length of cord.
1Ki 6:25 second cherub also *m* ten cubits,
7:31 and with its basework it *m* a cubit
Job 28:25 and *m* out the waters,
Isa 40:12 Who has *m* the waters
Jer 31:37 if the heavens above can be *m*
Eze 40: 5 He *m* the wall; it was one
40: 6 and *m* the threshold of the gate;
40: 8 he *m* the portico of the gateway;
40:11 he *m* the width of the entrance
40:13 he *m* the gateway from the top
40:14 He *m* along the faces
40:19 Then he *m* the distance from the
40:20 Then he *m* the length and width
40:23 He *m* from one gate to
40:24 He *m* its jambs and its portico,
40:27 and he *m* from this gate
40:28 and he *m* the south gate; it had
40:32 he *m* the gateway; it had the same
40:35 me to the north gate and *m* it.
40:47 Then he *m* the court: It was square
40:48 and *m* the jambs of the portico;
41: 1 outer sanctuary and *m* the jambs;
41: 2 He also *m* the outer sanctuary;
41: 3 and *m* the jambs of the entrance;
41: 4 And he *m* the length of the inner
41: 5 Then he *m* the wall of the temple;
41:13 he *m* the temple; it was a hundred
41:15 he *m* the length of the building
42:15 and *m* the area all around:
42:16 He *m* the east side
42:17 He *m* the north side; it was five
42:18 He *m* the south side; it was five
42:19 he turned to the west side and *m*:
42:20 So he *m* the area on all four sides.
45:14 portion of oil, *m* by the bath,
47: 3 he *m* off a thousand cubits
47: 4 He *m* off another thousand
47: 4 He *m* off another thousand cubits
47: 5 He *m* off another thousand,
Hos 1:10 which cannot be *m* or counted.
Am 7:17 Your land will be *m* and divided up
Mt 7: 2 the measure you use, it will be *m*
Mk 4:24 it will be *m* to you—and
Lk 6:38 the measure you use, it will be *m*
Rev 21:16 He *m* the city with the rod
21:17 He *m* its wall and it was 144 cubits

MEASURELESS

1Ki 4:29 a breadth of understanding as *m*
Jer 33:22 as *m* as the sand on the seashore.' "

MEASUREMENT (MEASURE)

Eze 40:14 The *m* was up to the portico facing
Rev 21:17 by man's *m*, which the angel was

MEASUREMENTS (MEASURE)

1Ch 23:29 and all *m* of quantity and size.
Eze 40:10 the three had the same *m*,
40:10 walls on each side had the same *m*.
40:21 and its portico had the same *m*
40:22 tree decorations had the same *m*
40:24 they had the same *m* as the others.
40:28 it had the same *m* as the others.
40:29 and its portico had the same *m*
40:32 it had the same *m* as the others.
40:33 and its portico had the same *m*
40:35 It had the same *m* as the others,
43:13 "These are the *m* of the altar
48:16 center of it and will have these *m*:

MEASURES (MEASURE)

Dt 25:14 Do not have two differing *m*
25:15 and honest weights and *m*,
Ru 3:15 he poured into it six *m* of barley
3:17 "He gave me these six *m* of barley,
Pr 20:10 Differing weights and differing *m*
Isa 44:13 The carpenter *m* with a line
Eze 48:33 "On the south side, which *m* 4,500
Hag 2:16 came to a heap of twenty *m*,
2:16 went to a wine vat to draw fifty *m*,

MEASURING (MEASURE)

Lev 19:35 standards when *m* length,
1Ki 7:10 some *m* ten cubits and some eight.
7:23 *m* ten cubits from rim to rim
7:38 forty baths and *m* four cubits
2Ki 21:13 out over Jerusalem the *m* line used
2Ch 3:15 with a capital on top *m* five cubits.
2Ch 4: 2 *m* ten cubits from rim to rim
Job 38: 5 Who stretched a *m* line across it?
Isa 28:17 I will make justice the *m* line
34:11 the *m* line of chaos
Jer 31:39 The *m* line will stretch
La 2: 8 He stretched out a *m* line
Eze 40: 3 with a linen cord and a *m* rod
40: 5 The length of the *m* rod
40: 5 it was one *m* rod thick
42:15 When he had finished *m* what was
42:16 the east side with the *m* rod;
42:17 five hundred cubits by the *m* rod.
42:18 five hundred cubits by the *m* rod.
42:19 five hundred cubits by the *m* rod.
47: 3 eastward with a *m* line in his hand,
Zec 1:16 the *m* line will be stretched out
2: 1 a man with a *m* line in his hand!
5: 6 He replied, "It is a *m* basket."
Rev 11: 1 I was given a reed like a *m* rod
21:15 talked with me had a *m* rod of gold

MEAT (MEATS)

Ge 9: 4 you must not eat *m* that has its
Ex 12: 8 to eat the *m* roasted over the fire,
12: 9 Do not eat the *m* raw or cooked
12:46 none of the *m* outside the house.
16: 3 There we sat around pots of *m*
16: 8 LORD when he gives you *m* to eat
16:12 'At twilight you will eat *m*,
21:28 and its *m* must not be eaten.
22:31 do not eat the *m* of an animal torn
27: 3 sprinkling bowls, *m* forks
29:31 and cook the *m* in a sacred place.
29:32 his sons are to eat the *m* of the ram
29:34 any of the *m* of the ordination ram
38: 3 sprinkling bowls, *m* forks
Lev 6:28 The clay pot the *m* is cooked
7:15 The *m* of his fellowship offering
7:17 Any *m* of the sacrifice left
7:18 If any *m* of the fellowship offering
7:19 for other *m*, anyone ceremonially
7:19 " '*M* that touches anything
7:20 anyone who is unclean eats any *m*
7:21 and then eats any of the *m*
8:31 "Cook the *m* at the entrance
8:32 Then burn up the rest of the *m*
11: 8 You must not eat their *m*
11:11 you must not eat their *m*
19:26 " 'Do not eat any *m*
Nu 4:14 including the firepans, *m* forks,
11: 4 and said, "If only we had *m* to eat!
11:13 Where can I get *m*
11:13 wailing to me, 'Give us *m* to eat!'
11:18 Now the LORD will give you *m*,
11:18 for tomorrow, when you will eat *m*.
11:18 "If only we had *m*
11:21 'I will give them *m* to eat
11:33 But while the *m* was still
18:18 Their *m* is to be yours, just
Dt 12:15 eat as much of the *m* as you want,
12:20 and say, "I would like some *m*,"
12:20 you crave *m* and say, "I would like
12:23 you must not eat the life with the *m*
12:27 both the *m* and the blood.
12:27 your God, but you may eat the *m*.
14: 8 You are not to eat their *m*
16: 4 any of the *m* you sacrifice
Jdg 6:19 Putting the *m* in a basket
6:20 "Take the *m* and the unleavened
6:21 angel of the LORD touched the *m*
6:21 consuming the *m* and the bread.
1Sa 1: 4 of the *m* to his wife Peninnah
2:13 and while the *m* was being boiled,
2:15 he won't accept boiled *m* from you,
2:15 "Give the priest some *m* to roast;
9:23 "Bring the piece of *m* I gave you,
14:33 LORD by eating *m* that has blood
14:34 LORD by eating *m* with blood still
25:11 and the *m* I have slaughtered
1Ki 17: 6 and bread and *m* in the evening,
17: 6 and *m* in the morning and bread
19:21 plowing equipment to cook the *m*
2Ch 4:16 *m* forks and all related articles.
Job 31:31 'Who has not had his fill of Job's *m*
Ps 78:20 Can he supply *m* for his people?"
78:27 He rained *m* down on them like
Pr 9: 2 She has prepared her *m*
23:20 or gorge themselves on *m*,

Isa 22: 13 eating of *m* and drinking of wine!
44: 16 he roasts his *m* and eats his fill.
44: 19 I roasted *m* and I ate.
65: 4 pots hold broth of unclean *m;*
Jer 7: 21 and eat the *m* yourselves!
11: 15 Can consecrated *m* avert your
Eze 4: 14 No unclean *m* has ever entered my
11: 3 is a cooking pot, and we are the *m.'*
11: 7 you have thrown there are the *m*
11: 11 nor will you be the *m* in it;
24: 4 Put into it the pieces of *m,*
24: 10 Cook the *m* well,
33: 25 Since you eat *m* with the blood still
Da 10: 3 no *m* or wine touched my lips;
Hos 8: 13 and they eat the *m,*
Mic 3: 3 who chop them up like *m*
Hag 2: 12 If a person carries consecrated *m*
Zec 11: 16 will eat the *m* of the choice sheep,
Ac 15: 20 from the *m* of strangled animals
15: 29 from the *m* of strangled animals
21: 25 from the *m* of strangled animals
Ro 14: 6 He who eats *m,* eats to the Lord,
14: 21 It is better not to eat *m*
1Co 8: 13 I will never eat *m* again,
10: 25 *m* market without raising questions

MEATS (MEAT)
Isa 25: 6 the best of *m* and the finest

MEBUNNAI
2Sa 23: 27 from Anathoth, *M* the Hushathite,

MECONAH
Ne 11: 28 in Ziklag, in *M* and its settlements,

MEDAD
Nu 11: 26 whose names were Eldad and *M,*
11: 27 *M* are prophesying in the camp.''

MEDAN
Ge 25: 2 *M,* Midian, Ishbak and Shuah.
1Ch 1: 32 Zimran, Jokshan, *M,* Midian,

MEDDLER (MEDDLES)
1Pe 4: 15 kind of criminal, or even as a *m.*

MEDDLES (MEDDLER)
Pr 26: 17 is a passer-by who *m*

MEDE (MEDIA)
Da 5: 31 and Darius the *M* took
9: 1 son of Xerxes (a *M* by descent),
11: 1 in the first year of Darius the *M,*

MEDEBA
Nu 21: 30 which extends to *M.''*
Jos 13: 9 included the whole plateau of *M*
13: 16 and the whole plateau past *M*
1Ch 19: 7 who came and camped near *M,*
Isa 15: 2 Moab wails over Nebo and *M.*

MEDES (MEDIA)
2Ki 17: 6 and in the towns of the *M.*
18: 11 and in towns of the *M.*
Isa 13: 17 I will stir up against them the *M,*
Jer 51: 11 has stirred up the kings of the *M,*
51: 28 the kings of the *M,*
Da 5: 28 and given to the *M* and Persians.''
6: 8 accordance with the laws of the *M*
6: 12 accordance with the laws of the *M*
6: 15 that according to the law of the *M*
Ac 2: 9 Parthians, *M* and Elamites;

MEDIA (MEDE MEDES MEDIAN)
Ezr 6: 2 of Ecbatana in the province of *M,*
Est 1: 3 military leaders of Persia and *M,*
1: 14 and *M* who had special access
1: 19 written in the laws of Persia and *M,*
10: 2 of the annals of the kings of *M*
Isa 21: 2 Elam, attack! *M,* lay siege!
Jer 25: 25 all the kings of Zimri, Elam and *M;*
Da 8: 20 you saw represents the kings of *M*

MEDIAN (MEDIA)
Est 1: 18 *M* women of the nobility who have

MEDIATE (MEDIATOR)
1Sa 2: 25 against another man, God may *m*

MEDIATOR (MEDIATE)
Job 33: 23 as a *m,* one out of a thousand,
Gal 3: 19 into effect through angels by a *m.*
3: 20 A *m,* however, does not represent
1Ti 2: 5 and one *m* between God and men,
Heb 8: 6 of which he is *m* is superior
9: 15 For this reason Christ is the *m*
12: 24 to Jesus the *m* of a new covenant,

MEDICINE
Pr 17: 22 A cheerful heart is good *m,*

MEDITATE (MEDITATED MEDITATES MEDITATION)
Ge 24: 63 out to the field one evening to *m,*
Jos 1: 8 from your mouth; *m* on it day
Ps 48: 9 we *m* on your unfailing love.
77: 12 I will *m* on all your works
119: 15 I *m* on your precepts
119: 23 your servant will *m*
119: 27 then I will *m* on your wonders.
119: 48 and I *m* on your decrees.
119: 78 but I will *m* on your precepts.
119: 97 I *m* on it all day long.
119: 99 for I *m* on your statutes.
119:148 that I may *m* on your promises.
143: 5 I *m* on all your works
145: 5 I will *m* on your wonderful works.

MEDITATED (MEDITATE)
Ps 39: 3 and as I *m,* the fire burned;

MEDITATES (MEDITATE)
Ps 1: 2 and on his law he *m* day and night.

MEDITATION (MEDITATE)
Ps 19: 14 of my mouth and the *m* of my heart
104: 34 May my *m* be pleasing to him,

MEDIUM (MEDIUMS)
Lev 20: 27 '' 'A man or woman who is a *m*
Dt 18: 11 or who is a *m* or spiritist
1Sa 28: 7 ''Find me a woman who is a *m,*
1Ch 10: 13 even consulted a *m* for guidance,

MEDIUMS (MEDIUM)
Lev 19: 31 turn to *m* or seek out spiritists,
20: 6 against the person who turns to *m*
1Sa 28: 3 Saul had expelled the *m*
28: 9 He has cut off the *m* and spiritists
2Ki 21: 6 and consulted *m* and spiritists.
23: 24 Josiah got rid of the *m*
2Ch 33: 6 and consulted *m* and spiritists.
Isa 8: 19 When men tell you to consult *m*
19: 3 the *m* and the spiritists.
Jer 27: 9 your *m* or your sorcerers who tell

MEEK (MEEKNESS)
Ps 37: 11 But the *m* will inherit the land
Zep 3: 12 the *m* and humble,
Mt 5: 5 Blessed are the *m,*

MEEKNESS (MEEK)
2Co 10: 1 By the *m* and gentleness of Christ,

MEET (MEETING MEETINGS MEETS MET)
Ge 14: 17 out to *m* him in the Valley
18: 2 the entrance of his tent to *m* them
19: 1 he got up to *m* them and bowed
19: 6 Lot went outside to *m* them
24: 17 The servant hurried to *m* her
24: 65 man in the field coming to *m* us?''
29: 13 his sister's son, he hurried to *m* him
30: 16 evening, Leah went out to *m* him.
32: 6 and now he is coming to *m* you,
32: 19 thing to Esau when you *m* him.
33: 4 But Esau ran to *m* Jacob
46: 29 to Goshen to *m* his father Israel.
Ex 4: 14 He is already on his way to *m* you,
4: 27 ''Go into the desert to *m* Moses.''
5: 20 and Aaron waiting to *m* them,
7: 15 on the bank of the Nile to *m* him,
18: 7 out to *m* his father-in-law
19: 17 out of the camp to *m* with God,
25: 22 I will *m* with you and give you all
29: 42 There I will *m* you and speak
29: 43 also I will *m* with the Israelites,
Ex 30: 6 the Testimony—where I will *m*
30: 36 Tent of Meeting, where I will *m*
Nu 14: 35 They will *m* their end in this desert
17: 4 front of the Testimony, where I *m*
21: 33 out to *m* them in battle at Edrei.
22: 36 he went out to *m* him
23: 3 Perhaps the LORD will come to *m*
23: 15 while I *m* with him over there.''
31: 13 went to *m* them outside the camp.
Dt 2: 32 out to *m* us in battle at Jahaz,
3: 1 out to *m* us in battle at Edrei.
22: 23 If a man happens to *m*
22: 25 to *m* a girl pledged to be married
22: 28 to *m* a virgin who is not pledged
23: 4 come to *m* you with bread
Jos 8: 14 in the morning to *m* Israel in battle
9: 11 go and *m* them and say to them,
Jdg 4: 18 Jael went out to *m* Sisera
4: 22 and Jael went out to *m* him.
6: 35 so that they too went up to *m* them.
11: 31 of my house to *m* me when I return
11: 34 who should come out to *m* him
20: 31 Benjamites came out to *m* them
1Sa 4: 2 deployed their forces to *m* Israel,
10: 2 you will *m* two men
10: 3 to God at Bethel will *m* you there.
10: 5 you will *m* a procession
15: 12 Samuel got up and went to *m* Saul,
17: 2 line to *m* the Philistines.
17: 48 toward the battle line to *m* him.
17: 55 out to *m* the Philistine,
18: 6 the towns of Israel to *m* King Saul
21: 2 I have told them to *m* me
23: 28 and went to *m* the Philistines.
25: 32 who has sent you today to *m* me.
25: 34 you had not come quickly to *m* me,
30: 21 They came out to *m* David
2Sa 6: 20 of Saul came out to *m* him
10: 5 he sent messengers to *m* the men,
10: 17 their battle lines to *m* David
15: 32 the Arkite was there to *m* him,
16: 1 of Mephibosheth, waiting to *m* him
18: 9 happened to *m* David's men.
19: 15 and *m* the king and bring him
19: 16 the men of Judah to *m* King David.
19: 20 down and *m* my lord the king.''
19: 24 also went down to *m* the king.
19: 25 from Jerusalem to *m* the king,
20: 8 in Gibeon, Amasa came to *m* them.
1Ki 2: 8 came down to *m* me at the Jordan,
2: 19 the king stood up to *m* her,
18: 16 So Obadiah went to *m* Ahab
18: 16 and Ahab went to *m* Elijah.
18: 19 all over Israel to *m* me
20: 9 but this demand I cannot *m.'* ''
20: 27 they marched out to *m* them.
21: 18 Go down to *m* Ahab king of Israel,
2Ki 1: 3 and *m* the messengers of the king
1: 6 A man came to *m* us,'' they replied.
1: 7 of man was it who came to *m* you
2: 15 And they went to *m* him
4: 26 Run to *m* her and ask her,
4: 29 If you *m* anyone, do not greet him,
4: 31 So Gehazi went back to *m* Elisha
5: 21 down from the chariot to *m* him.
5: 26 down from his chariot to *m* you?
6: 1 the place where we *m*
8: 8 and go to *m* the man of God.
8: 9 illness?' '' Hazael went to *m* Elisha,
9: 17 ''Send him to *m* them and ask,
9: 18 The horseman rode off to *m* Jehu
9: 21 each in his own chariot, to *m* Jehu.
10: 15 who was on his way to *m* him.
14: 8 ''Come, *m* me face to face.''
16: 10 to *m* Tiglath-Pileser king
23: 29 out to *m* him in battle,
1Ch 12: 17 David went out to *m* them
14: 8 about it and went out to *m* them.
19: 5 he sent messengers to *m* them,
19: 17 lines to *m* the Arameans in battle,
2Ch 14: 10 Asa went out to *m* him,
15: 2 He went out to *m* Asa
19: 2 went out to *m* him and said
22: 7 out with Joram to *m* Jehu son
25: 17 ''Come, *m* me face to face.''
28: 9 and he went out to *m* the army
35: 20 out to *m* him in battle.
Ne 4: 9 and night to *m* this threat.

Ne 6: 2 let us *m* together in one
6: 10 "Let us *m* in the house of God,
Ps 42: 2 When can I go and *m* with God?
79: 8 your mercy come quickly to *m* us,
85: 10 Love and faithfulness *m* together;
Pr 7: 10 Then out came a woman to *m* him,
7: 15 So I came out to *m* you;
8: 2 where the paths *m*, she takes her
17: 12 Better to *m* a bear robbed
Isa 1: 12 When you come to *m* with me,
7: 3 to *m* Ahaz at the end
14: 9 astir to *m* you at your coming;
34: 14 Desert creatures will *m*
41: 1 let us *m* together at the place
66: 17 they will *m* their end together,"
Jer 41: 6 out from Mizpah to *m* them,
Am 4: 12 prepare to *m* your God, O Israel."
5: 19 only to *m* a bear,
9: 10 Disaster will not overtake or *m* us.'
Zec 2: 3 and another angel came to *m* him
Mt 8: 34 whole town went out to *m* Jesus.
25: 1 and went out to *m* the bridegroom.
25: 6 bridegroom! Come out to *m* him!'
Mk 5: 2 came from the tombs to *m* him.
14: 13 a jar of water will *m* you.
Lk 22: 10 a jar of water will *m* you.
Jn 11: 20 she went out to *m* him,
12: 13 branches and went out to *m* him,
12: 18 sign, went out to *m* him.
Ac 2: 46 day they continued to *m* together
5: 12 *m* together in Solomon's
28: 15 and the Three Taverns to *m* us.
28: 23 They arranged to *m* Paul
1Co 11: 34 when you *m* together it may not
Php 4: 19 And my God will *m* all your needs
1Th 4: 17 them in the clouds to *m* the Lord

MEETING (MEET)

Ex 27: 21 of *M*, outside the curtain that is
28: 43 whenever they enter the Tent of *M*
29: 4 to the entrance to the Tent of *M*
29: 10 bull to the front of the Tent of *M*,
29: 11 at the entrance to the Tent of *M*.
29: 30 comes to the Tent of *M* to minister
29: 32 At the entrance to the Tent of *M*,
29: 42 to the Tent of *M* before the LORD.
29: 44 "So I will consecrate the Tent of *M*
30: 16 it for the service of the Tent of *M*.
30: 18 Place it between the Tent of *M*
30: 20 they enter the Tent of *M*,
30: 26 Then use it to anoint the Tent of *M*,
30: 36 of the Testimony in the Tent of *M*,
31: 7 the Tent of *M*, the ark
33: 7 away, calling it the "tent of *m*."
33: 7 to the tent of *m* outside the camp
35: 21 for the work on the Tent of *M*,
38: 8 at the entrance to the Tent of *M*.
38: 30 for the entrance to the Tent of *M*,
39: 32 the Tent of *M*, was completed.
39: 40 for the tabernacle, the Tent of *M*;
40: 2 up the tabernacle, the Tent of *M*,
40: 6 the Tent of *M*; place the basin
40: 7 the basin between the Tent of *M*
40: 12 to the entrance to the Tent of *M*
40: 22 in the Tent of *M* on the north side
40: 24 in the Tent of *M* opposite the table
40: 26 altar in the Tent of *M* in front
40: 29 the Tent of *M*, and offered
40: 30 the basin between the Tent of *M*
40: 32 they entered the Tent of *M*
40: 34 the cloud covered the Tent of *M*,
40: 35 could not enter the Tent of *M*
Lev 1: 1 spoke to him from the Tent of *M*.
1: 3 of *M* so that it will be acceptable
1: 5 at the entrance to the Tent of *M*.
3: 2 it at the entrance to the Tent of *M*.
3: 8 it in front of the Tent of *M*.
3: 13 it in front of the Tent of *M*.
4: 4 to the Tent of *M* before the LORD.
4: 5 and carry it into the Tent of *M*.
4: 7 at the entrance to the Tent of *M*.
4: 7 before the LORD in the Tent of *M*.
4: 14 and present it before the Tent of *M*.
4: 16 blood into the Tent of *M*.
4: 18 at the entrance to the Tent of *M*.
4: 18 before the LORD in the Tent of *M*.
6: 16 it in the courtyard of the Tent of *M*.
6: 26 in the courtyard of the Tent of *M*.
Lev 6: 30 the Tent of *M* to make atonement
8: 3 at the entrance to the Tent of *M*."
8: 4 at the entrance to the Tent of *M*.
8: 31 at the entrance to the Tent of *M*
8: 33 to the Tent of *M* for seven days,
8: 35 the entrance to the Tent of *M* day
9: 5 to the front of the Tent of *M*,
9: 23 went into the Tent of *M*.
10: 7 leave the entrance to the Tent of *M*
10: 9 go into the Tent of *M*,
12: 6 to the Tent of *M* a year-old lamb
14: 11 at the entrance to the Tent of *M*.
14: 23 at the entrance to the Tent of *M*,
15: 14 to the entrance to the Tent of *M*
15: 29 at the entrance to the Tent of *M*.
16: 7 at the entrance to the Tent of *M*.
16: 16 is to do the same for the Tent of *M*,
16: 17 of *M* from the time Aaron goes
16: 20 the Tent of *M* and the altar,
16: 23 Aaron is to go into the Tent of *M*
16: 33 for the Tent of *M* and the altar,
17: 4 to the Tent of *M* to present it
17: 5 at the entrance to the Tent of *M*
17: 6 at the entrance to the Tent of *M*
17: 9 to the Tent of *M* to sacrifice it
19: 21 to the Tent of *M* for a guilt offering
24: 3 of the Testimony in the Tent of *M*,
Nu 1: 1 in the Tent of *M* in the Desert
2: 2 the Tent of *M* some distance
2: 17 Then the Tent of *M* and the camp
3: 7 at the Tent of *M* by doing the work
3: 8 all the furnishings of the Tent of *M*,
3: 25 Tent of *M* the Gershonites were
3: 25 at the entrance to the Tent of *M*,
3: 38 in front of the Tent of *M*.
4: 3 serve in the work in the Tent of *M*.
4: 4 of the Kohathites in the Tent of *M*:
4: 15 things that are in the Tent of *M*.
4: 23 serve in the work at the Tent of *M*.
4: 25 for the entrance to the Tent of *M*,
4: 25 the Tent of *M*, its covering
4: 28 Gershonite clans at the Tent of *M*.
4: 30 serve in the work at the Tent of *M*.
4: 31 perform service at the Tent of *M*:
4: 33 the Tent of *M* under the direction
4: 35 serve in the work in the Tent of *M*,
4: 37 clans who served in the Tent of *M*.
4: 39 serve in the work at the Tent of *M*,
4: 41 clans who served at the Tent of *M*.
4: 43 serve in the work at the Tent of *M*,
4: 47 the Tent of *M* numbered 8,580.
6: 10 at the entrance to the Tent of *M*
6: 13 to the entrance to the Tent of *M*.
6: 18 at the entrance to the Tent of *M*,
7: 5 used in the work at the Tent of *M*.
7: 89 of *M* to speak with the LORD,
8: 9 to the front of the Tent of *M*
8: 15 to do their work at the Tent of *M*.
8: 19 the work at the Tent of *M* on behalf
8: 22 Tent of *M* under the supervision
8: 24 part in the work at the Tent of *M*,
8: 26 their duties at the Tent of *M*,
10: 3 at the entrance to the Tent of *M*.
11: 16 Have them come to the Tent of *M*,
12: 4 "Come out to the Tent of *M*,
14: 10 at the Tent of *M* to all the Israelites
16: 18 at the entrance to the Tent of *M*.
16: 19 at the entrance to the Tent of *M*,
16: 42 and turned toward the Tent of *M*,
16: 43 went to the front of the Tent of *M*,
16: 50 at the entrance to the Tent of *M*,
17: 4 them in the Tent of *M* in front
18: 4 for the care of the Tent of *M*—
18: 6 to do the work at the Tent of *M*.
18: 21 do while serving at the Tent of *M*.
18: 22 go near the Tent of *M*,
18: 23 are to do the work at the Tent of *M*
18: 31 for your work at the Tent of *M*.
19: 4 toward the front of the Tent of *M*.
20: 6 to the entrance to the Tent of *M*
25: 6 at the entrance to the Tent of *M*.
27: 2 the entrance to the Tent of *M*
31: 54 and brought it into the Tent of *M*
Dt 31: 14 present yourselves at the Tent of *M*
31: 14 themselves at the Tent of *M*.
Jos 18: 1 and set up the Tent of *M* there.
19: 51 at the entrance to the Tent of *M*.
22: 32 from their *m* with the Reubenites
1Sa 2: 22 at the entrance to the Tent of *M*.
20: 35 to the field for his *m* with David.
1Ki 8: 4 of *M* and all the sacred furnishings
2Ki 4: 38 of the prophets was *m* with him,
1Ch 6: 32 the tabernacle—the Tent of *M*—
9: 21 at the entrance to the Tent of *M*.
23: 32 responsibilities for the Tent of *M*,
2Ch 1: 3 for God's Tent of *M* was there,
1: 6 before the LORD in the Tent of *M*
1: 13 from before the Tent of *M*.
5: 5 of *M* and all the sacred furnishings
Ne 5: 7 I called together a large *m* to deal
La 2: 6 he has destroyed his place of *m*.
Jn 11: 47 and the Pharisees called a *m*
Ac 4: 31 where they were *m* was shaken.
17: 19 him to a *m* of the Areopagus,
17: 22 up in the *m* of the Areopagus
20: 8 upstairs room where we were *m*.
Heb 10: 25 Let us not give up *m* together,
Jas 2: 2 into your *m* wearing a gold ring

MEETINGS (MEET)

1Co 11: 17 for your *m* do more harm

MEETS (MEET)

Ge 32: 17 "When my brother Esau *m* you
Nu 35: 19 when he *m* him, he shall put him
35: 21 murderer to death when he *m* him.
Ro 16: 5 the church that *m* at their house.
1Co 16: 19 and so does the church that *m*
Phm : 2 to the church that *m* in your home:
Heb 7: 26 Such a high priest *m* our need—

MEGIDDO

Jos 12: 21 one the king of *M* one the king
17: 11 of Dor, Endor, Taanach and *M*,
Jdg 1: 27 or *M* and their surrounding
5: 19 at Taanach by the waters of *M*,
1Ki 4: 12 son of Ahilud—in Taanach and *M*,
9: 15 wall of Jerusalem, and Hazor, *M*
2Ki 9: 27 but he escaped to *M* and died there
23: 29 faced him and killed him at *M*.
23: 30 in a chariot from *M* to Jerusalem
1Ch 7: 29 *M* and Dor, together
2Ch 35: 22 went to fight him on the plain of *M*.
Zec 12: 11 Hadad Rimmon in the plain of *M*,

MEHETABEL

Ge 36: 39 his wife's name was *M* daughter
1Ch 1: 50 his wife's name was *M* daughter
Ne 6: 10 the son of *M*, who was shut

MEHIDA

Ezr 2: 52 Harhur, Bazluth, *M*, Harsha,
Ne 7: 54 Harhur, Bazluth, *M*, Harsha,

MEHIR

1Ch 4: 11 brother, was the father of *M*,

MEHOLAH

1Sa 18: 19 given in marriage to Adriel of *M*.

MEHOLATHITE

2Sa 21: 8 to Adriel son of Barzillai the *M*.

MEHUJAEL

Ge 4: 18 and Irad was the father of *M*,
4: 18 *M* was the father of Methushael,

MEHUMAN

Est 1: 10 *M*, Biztha, Harbona, Bigtha,

MEKERATHITE

1Ch 11: 36 Hepher the *M*, Ahijah the Pelonite,

MELATIAH

Ne 3: 7 *M* of Gibeon and Jadon

MELCHIZEDEK

Ge 14: 18 *M* king of Salem brought out bread
Ps 110: 4 in the order of *M*."
Heb 5: 6 in the order of *M*."
5: 10 to be high priest in the order of *M*.
6: 20 priest forever, in the order of *M*.
7: 1 This *M* was king of Salem
7: 10 because when *M* met Abraham,
7: 11 in the order of *M*, not in the order
7: 15 if another priest like *M* appears,
7: 17 in the order of *M*."

MELEA

Lk 3: 31 the son of *M*, the son of Menna,

MELECH

1Ch 8: 35 Pithon, *M*, Tarea and Ahaz.
9: 41 Pithon, *M*, Tahrea and Ahaz.

MELKI

Lk 3: 24 the son of Levi, the son of *M*,
3: 28 the son of *M*,

MELODIOUS (MELODY)

Ps 81: 2 play the *m* harp and lyre.

MELODY (MELODIOUS)

Ps 92: 3 and the *m* of the harp.

MELON (MELONS)

Jer 10: 5 Like a scarecrow in a *m* patch,

MELONS (MELON)

Nu 11: 5 also the cucumbers, *m*, leeks,
Isa 1: 8 like a hut in a field of *m*,

MELT (MELTED MELTING MELTS)

Ex 15: 15 the people of Canaan will *m* away;
Jos 14: 8 hearts of the people *m* with fear.
2Sa 17: 10 the heart of a lion, will *m* with fear,
Ps 97: 5 The mountains *m* like wax
Isa 13: 7 every man's heart will *m*.
14: 31 *M* away, all you Philistines!
19: 1 of the Egyptians *m* within them.
Eze 21: 7 Every heart will *m* and every hand
21: 15 So that hearts may *m*
22: 20 and tin into a furnace to *m* it
22: 20 put you inside the city and *m* you.
Mic 1: 4 The mountains *m* beneath him
Na 1: 5 and the hills *m* away.
2: 10 Hearts *m*, knees give way,
2Pe 3: 12 and the elements will *m* in the heat.

MELTED (MELT)

Ex 16: 21 when the sun grew hot, it *m* away.
Jos 7: 5 At this the hearts of the people *m*
Job 24: 19 drought snatch away the *m* snow,
Ps 22: 14 it has *m* away within me.
107: 26 in their peril their courage *m* away.
Eze 22: 21 and you will be *m* inside her.
22: 22 As silver is *m* in a furnace,
22: 22 so you will be *m* inside her,
24: 11 glows so its impurities may be *m*

MELTING (MELT)

Jos 2: 9 live in this country are *m* in fear
2: 24 all the people are *m* in fear
1Sa 14: 16 of Benjamin saw the army *m* away
Job 6: 16 and swollen with *m* snow,
Ps 58: 8 Like a slug *m* away as it moves

MELTS (MELT)

Ps 46: 6 he lifts his voice, the earth *m*.
68: 2 as wax *m* before the fire,
147: 18 He sends his word and *m* them;
Am 9: 5 he who touches the earth and it *m*,

MEMBER (MEMBERS)

Lev 4: 27 " 'If a *m* of the community sins
25: 47 or to a *m* of the alien's clan,
Eze 17: 13 he took a *m* of the royal family
Mk 15: 43 a prominent *m* of the Council,
Lk 23: 50 was a man named Joseph, a *m*
Jn 3: 1 a *m* of the Jewish ruling council.
Ac 17: 34 Among them was Dionysius, a *m*
Ro 12: 5 each *m* belongs to all the others.

MEMBERS (MEMBER)

Ge 36: 6 and all the *m* of his household,
46: 27 *m* of Jacob's family, which went
50: 8 all the *m* of Joseph's household
Lev 25: 45 and *m* of their clans born
Nu 16: 2 leaders who had been appointed *m*
2Sa 9: 12 all the *m* of Ziba's household were
2Ch 21: 13 murdered your own brothers, *m*
Mic 7: 6 a man's enemies are the *m*
Mt 10: 25 how much more the *m*
10: 36 a man's enemies will be the *m*
Ac 5: 17 who were *m* of the party
6: 9 from *m* of the Synagogue
16: 15 *m* of her household were baptized,
Ro 7: 23 law at work in the *m* of my body,
7: 23 the law of sin at work within my *m*.
12: 4 of us has one body with many *m*,
12: 4 these *m* do not all have the same
1Co 6: 15 Shall I then take the *m* of Christ
6: 15 not know that your bodies are *m*
12: 24 But God has combined the *m*
Eph 2: 19 and *m* of God's household,
3: 6 *m* together of one body,
4: 25 for we are all *m* of one body.
5: 30 for we are *m* of his body.
Col 3: 15 as *m* of one body you were called

MEMORABLE (MEMORY)

Eze 39: 13 day I am glorified will be a *m* day

MEMORANDUM

Ezr 6: 2 and this was written on it: *M*:

MEMORIAL (MEMORY)

Ex 28: 12 as a *m* before the LORD.
28: 12 as *m* stones for the sons of Israel.
28: 29 a continuing *m* before the LORD.
30: 16 It will be a *m* for the Israelites
39: 7 as *m* stones for the sons of Israel,
Lev 2: 2 burn this as a *m* portion on the altar
2: 9 He shall take out the *m* portion
2: 16 The priest shall burn the *m* portion
5: 12 a handful of it as a *m* portion
6: 15 and burn the *m* portion on the altar
24: 7 a *m* portion to represent the bread
Nu 5: 26 a *m* offering and burn it on the altar
10: 10 and they will be a *m* for you
31: 54 as a *m* for the Israelites
Jos 4: 7 are to be a *m* to the people
Isa 56: 5 a *m* and a name
66: 3 and whoever burns *m* incense,
Zec 6: 14 as a *m* in the temple of the LORD.

MEMORIES (MEMORY)

1Th 3: 6 us that you always have pleasant *m*

MEMORY (MEMORABLE MEMORIAL MEMORIES)

Ex 17: 14 I will completely erase the *m*
Dt 25: 19 you shall blot out the *m* of Amalek
32: 26 and erase their *m* from mankind,
2Sa 18: 18 son to carry on the *m* of my name."
Est 9: 28 nor should the *m* of them die out
Job 18: 17 The *m* of him perishes
Ps 9: 6 even the *m* of them has perished.
34: 16 to cut off the *m* of them
45: 17 I will perpetuate your *m*
109: 15 off the *m* of them from the earth.
Pr 10: 7 *m* of the righteous will be
Ecc 9: 5 even the *m* of them is forgotten.
Isa 26: 14 you wiped out all *m* of them.
Mt 26: 13 she has done will also be told, in *m*
Mk 14: 9 she has done will also be told, in *m*
2Pe 1: 13 I think it is right to refresh your *m*

MEMPHIS

Isa 19: 13 the leaders of *M* are deceived;
Jer 2: 16 Also, the men of *M* and Tahpanhes
44: 1 in Migdol, Tahpanhes and *M*—
46: 14 also in *M* and Tahpanhes:
46: 19 for *M* will be laid waste
Eze 30: 13 and put an end to the images in *M*.
30: 16 *M* will be in constant distress.
Hos 9: 6 and *M* will bury them.

MEMUCAN

Est 1: 14 Tarshish, Meres, Marsena and *M*,
1: 16 Then *M* replied in the presence
1: 21 so the king did as *M* proposed.

MENAHEM (MENAHEM'S)

2Ki 15: 14 *M* son of Gadi went from Tirzah up
15: 16 At that time *M*, starting out
15: 17 *M* son of Gadi became king
15: 19 and *M* gave him a thousand talents
15: 20 *M* exacted this money from Israel.
15: 22 of Israel? *M* rested with his fathers.
15: 23 Pekahiah son of *M* became king

MENAHEM'S (MENAHEM)

2Ki 15: 21 As for the other events of *M* reign,

MEND (MENDED)

Ps 60: 2 *m* its fractures, for it is quaking.
Ecc 3: 7 a time to tear and a time to *m*,

MENDED (MEND)

Jos 9: 4 and old wineskins, cracked and *m*.

MENE

Da 5: 25 that was written: *M, M*,
5: 26 is what these words mean: *M*:

MENNA

Lk 3: 31 the son of Melea, the son of *M*,

MENSERVANTS (SERVANT)

Ge 12: 16 and female donkeys, *m*
24: 35 and gold, *m* and maidservants,
30: 43 maidservants and *m*, and camels
32: 5 and goats, *m* and maidservants.
Ex 21: 7 she is not to go free as *m* do.
Dt 12: 12 your *m* and maidservants,
12: 18 your *m* and maidservants,
16: 11 your *m* and maidservants,
16: 14 your *m* and maidservants,
1Sa 8: 16 Your *m* and maidservants
2Ki 5: 26 herds, or *m* and maidservants?
Ezr 2: 65 their 7,337 *m* and maidservants;
Ne 7: 67 their 7,337 *m* and maidservants;
Job 31: 13 "If I have denied justice to my *m*
Isa 14: 2 as *m* and maidservants
Lk 12: 45 and he then begins to beat the *m*

MENSTRUAL

Isa 30: 22 throw them away like a *m* cloth

MENTION (MENTIONED MENTIONING)

Ge 40: 14 *m* me to Pharaoh and get me out
Job 28: 18 jasper are not worthy of *m*;
Isa 49: 1 from my birth he has made *m*
Jer 19: 5 something I did not command or *m*
20: 9 But if I say, "I will not *m* him
23: 36 But you must not *m* 'the oracle
Eze 16: 56 *m* your sister Sodom in the day
Am 6: 10 We must not *m* the name
Jn 5: 34 but I *m* it that you may be saved.
Eph 5: 12 even to *m* what the disobedient do
Phm : 19 to *m* that you owe me your very

MENTIONED (MENTION)

Ru 4: 1 kinsman-redeemer he had *m* came
1Sa 4: 18 When he *m* the ark of God,
Isa 14: 20 will never be *m* again.
19: 17 whom Judah is *m* will be terrified,

MENTIONING (MENTION)

1Th 1: 2 for all of you, *m* you in our prayers.

MEONOTHAI

1Ch 4: 13 sons of Othniel: Hathath and *M*.
4: 14 *M* was the father of Ophrah.

MEPHAATH

Jos 13: 18 *M*, Kiriathaim, Sibmah, Zereth
21: 37 Bezer, Jahaz, Kedemoth and *M*,
1Ch 6: 79 Jahzah, Kedemoth and *M*,
Jer 48: 21 to Holon, Jahzah and *M*,

MEPHIBOSHETH

2Sa 4: 4 His name was *M*.)
9: 6 David said, "*M*!" "Your servant,"
9: 6 When *M* son of Jonathan,
9: 8 *M* bowed down and said, "What is
9: 10 And *M*, grandson of your master,
9: 11 So *M* ate at David's table like one
9: 12 household were servants of *M*.
9: 12 *M* had a young son named Mica,
9: 13 And *M* lived in Jerusalem,
16: 1 the steward of *M*, waiting
16: 4 belonged to *M* is now yours."
19: 24 *M*, Saul's grandson, also went
19: 25 "Why didn't you go with me, *M*?"
19: 30 *M* said to the king, "Let him take
21: 7 The king spared *M* son of Jonathan
21: 8 But the king took Armoni and *M*,

MERAB

1Sa 14: 49 name of his older daughter was *M*,
18: 17 "Here is my older daughter *M*.

1Sa 18: 19 So when the time came for *M*,
2Sa 21: 8 sons of Saul's daughter *M*,

MERAIAH

Ne 12: 12 of Seraiah's family, *M*,

MERAIOTH

1Ch 6: 7 of *M*, *M* the father of Amariah,
6: 52 *M* his son, Amariah his son,
9: 11 the son of *M*, the son of Ahitub,
Ezr 7: 3 the son of *M*, the son of Zerahiah,
Ne 11: 11 the son of *M*, the son of Ahitub,

MERARI (MERARITE MERARITES)

Ge 46: 11 of Levi: Gershon, Kohath and *M*.
Ex 6: 16 records: Gershon, Kohath and *M*.
6: 19 The sons of *M* were Mahli
Nu 3: 17 of Levi: Gershon, Kohath and *M*.
3: 33 To *M* belonged the clans
26: 57 through *M*, the Merarite clan.
Jos 21: 7 The descendants of *M*, clan by clan
1Ch 6: 1 of Levi: Gershon, Kohath and *M*.
6: 16 of Levi: Gershon, Kohath and *M*.
6: 19 The sons of *M*: Mahli and Mushi.
6: 29 The descendants of *M*: Mahli,
6: 47 the son of *M*, the son of Levi.
6: 63 The descendants of *M*, clan by clan
15: 6 from the descendants of *M*,
23: 6 of Levi: Gershon, Kohath and *M*.
23: 21 The sons of *M*: Mahli and Mushi.
24: 26 The sons of *M*: Mahli and Mushi.
24: 27 The sons of *M*: from Jaaziah: Beno,
26: 19 were descendants of Korah and *M*.
2Ch 34: 12 Levites descended from *M*,
Ezr 8: 19 from the descendants of *M*.

MERARITE (MERARI)

Nu 3: 20 The *M* clans: Mahli and Mushi.
3: 33 Mushites; these were the *M* clans.
3: 35 of the *M* clans was Zuriel son
4: 33 This is the service of the *M* clans
4: 45 the total of those in the *M* clans.
26: 57 through Merari, the *M* clan.
Jos 21: 34 The *M* clans (the rest
21: 40 the towns allotted to the *M* clans,
1Ch 9: 14 the son of Hashabiah, a *M*;
26: 10 Hosah the *M* had sons: Shimri

MERARITES (MERARI)

Nu 3: 36 The *M* were appointed to take care
4: 29 "Count the *M* by their clans
4: 42 The *M* were counted by their clans
7: 8 four carts and eight oxen to the *M*,
10: 17 and the Gershonites and *M*,
1Ch 6: 44 and from their associates, the *M*,
6: 77 *M* (the rest of the Levites) received
15: 17 and from their brothers the *M*,
2Ch 29: 12 from the *M*, Kish son of Abdi

MERATHAIM

Jer 50: 21 "Attack the land of *M*

MERCENARIES

Jer 46: 21 The *m* in her ranks

MERCHANDISE

Ne 10: 31 the neighboring peoples bring *m*
13: 16 and all kinds of *m* and selling them
Isa 45: 14 of Egypt and the *m* of Cush,
Eze 26: 12 your wealth and loot your *m*;
27: 12 iron, tin and lead for your *m*.
27: 14 war horses and mules for your *m*.
27: 16 coral and rubies for your *m*.
27: 19 Greeks from Uzal bought your *m*;
27: 22 for your *m* they exchanged
27: 27 Your wealth, *m* and wares,
27: 33 When your *m* went out on the seas,
Mk 11: 16 to carry *m* through the temple

MERCHANT (MERCHANTS)

Pr 31: 14 She is like the *m* ships,
SS 3: 6 made from all the spices of the *m*?
Eze 27: 3 *m* of peoples on many coasts,
Hos 12: 7 The *m* uses dishonest scales;
Mt 13: 45 of heaven is like a *m* looking

MERCHANTS (MERCHANT)

Ge 23: 16 to the weight current among the *m*.
Ge 37: 28 So when the Midianite *m* came by,
1Ki 10: 15 not including the revenues from *m*
10: 28 the royal *m* purchased them
2Ch 1: 16 the royal *m* purchased them
9: 14 the revenues brought in by *m*
Ne 3: 31 of the temple servants and the *m*,
3: 32 goldsmiths and *m* made repairs.
13: 20 twice the *m* and sellers of all kinds
Job 6: 19 the traveling *m* of Sheba look
41: 6 they divide him up among the *m*?
Ps 107: 23 they were *m* on the mighty waters.
Pr 31: 24 and supplies the *m* with sashes.
Isa 23: 2 and you *m* of Sidon,
23: 8 whose *m* are princes,
Eze 16: 29 of *m*, but even with this you were
17: 4 and carried it away to a land of *m*,
27: 22 *m* of Sheba and Raamah traded
27: 23 Canneh and Eden and *m* of Sheba,
27: 27 your *m* and all your soldiers,
27: 36 The *m* among the nations hiss
38: 13 and Dedan and the *m* of Tarshish
Na 3: 16 increased the number of your *m*
Zep 1: 11 all your *m* will be wiped out,
Rev 18: 3 and the *m* of the earth grew rich
18: 11 "The *m* of the earth will weep
18: 15 The *m* who sold these things
18: 23 Your *m* were the world's great men

MERCIFUL (MERCY)

Ge 19: 16 for the LORD was *m* to them.
Dt 4: 31 the LORD your God is a *m* God;
1Ki 20: 31 kings of the house of Israel are *m*.
Ne 9: 31 for you are a gracious and *m* God.
Ps 4: 1 be *m* to me and hear my prayer.
6: 2 Be *m* to me, LORD, for I am faint;
26: 11 redeem me and be *m* to me.
27: 7 be *m* to me and answer me.
30: 10 Hear, O LORD, and be *m* to me;
31: 9 Be *m* to me, O LORD, for I am
56: 1 Be *m* to me, O God,
77: 9 Has God forgotten to be *m*?
78: 38 Yet he was *m*;
Jer 3: 12 for I am *m*,' declares the LORD,
Da 9: 9 The Lord our God is *m*
Mt 5: 7 Blessed are the *m*,
Lk 1: 54 remembering to be *m*
6: 36 Be *m*, just as your Father is *m*.
Heb 2: 17 in order that he might become a *m*
Jas 2: 13 to anyone who has not been *m*.
Jude : 22 Be *m* to those who doubt; snatch

MERCILESS

Pr 17: 11 a *m* official will be sent against him

MERCY (MERCIFUL)

Ge 43: 14 may God Almighty grant you *m*
Ex 33: 19 *m* on whom I will have *m*,
Dt 7: 2 with them, and show them no *m*.
13: 17 will show you *m*, have compassion
Jos 11: 20 exterminating them without *m*,
2Sa 24: 14 of the LORD, for his *m* is great;
1Ki 8: 28 servant's prayer and his plea for *m*,
8: 50 their conquerors to show them *m*;
1Ch 21: 13 for his *m* is very great;
2Ch 6: 19 servant's prayer and his plea for *m*,
Ne 9: 31 But in your great *m* you did not put
13: 22 and show *m* to me according
Est 4: 8 the king's presence to beg for *m*
Job 9: 15 plead with my Judge for *m*.
27: 22 against him without *m*
41: 3 Will he keep begging you for *m*?
Ps 5: 7 But I, by your great *m*,
6: 9 The LORD has heard my cry for *m*
9: 13 Have *m* and lift me up
25: 6 O LORD, your great *m* and love,
28: 2 Hear my cry for *m*
28: 6 for he has heard my cry for *m*.
30: 8 to the Lord I cried for *m*:
31: 22 Yet you heard my cry for *m*
40: 11 Do not withhold your *m* from me,
41: 4 I said, "O LORD, have *m* on me;
41: 10 But you, O LORD, have *m* on me;
51: 1 Have *m* on me, O God,
57: 1 Have *m* on me, O God, have *m*
59: 5 show no *m* to wicked traitors.
69: 16 in your great *m* turn to me.
79: 8 may your *m* come quickly
86: 3 Have *m* on me, O Lord,
Ps 86: 6 listen to my cry for *m*.
86: 16 Turn to me and have *m* on me;
116: 1 he heard my cry for *m*.
119: 132 Turn to me and have *m* on me,
123: 2 till he shows us his *m*.
123: 3 Have *m* on us, O LORD, have
123: 3 on us, O LORD, have *m* on us,
130: 2 attentive to my cry for *m*.
140: 6 Hear, O LORD, my cry for *m*.
142: 1 to the LORD for *m*.
143: 1 listen to my cry for *m*;
Pr 6: 34 and he will show no *m*
18: 23 A poor man pleads for *m*,
21: 10 his neighbor gets no *m* from him.
28: 13 renounces them finds *m*.
Isa 13: 18 they will have no *m* on infants
47: 6 and you showed them no *m*.
55: 7 and he will have *m* on him,
63: 9 and *m* he redeemed them;
Jer 6: 23 they are cruel and show no *m*.
13: 14 I will allow no pity or *m*
21: 7 he will show them no *m* or pity
50: 42 they are cruel and without *m*.
Da 2: 18 them to plead for *m* from the God
9: 18 but because of your great *m*.
Hos 6: 6 For I desire *m*, not sacrifice,
Am 5: 15 LORD God Almighty will have *m*
Mic 6: 8 To act justly and to love *m*
7: 18 but delight to show *m*.
7: 20 and show *m* to Abraham,
Hab 1: 17 destroying nations without *m*?
3: 2 in wrath remember *m*.
Zec 1: 12 how long will you withhold *m*
1: 16 'I will return to Jerusalem with *m*,
7: 9 show *m* and compassion
Mt 5: 7 for they will be shown *m*.
9: 13 learn what this means: 'I desire *m*,
9: 27 calling out, "Have *m* on us,
12: 7 'I desire *m*, not sacrifice,' you
15: 22 Lord, Son of David, have *m* on me!
17: 15 "Lord, have *m* on my son," he said.
18: 33 Shouldn't you have had *m*
20: 30 "Lord, Son of David, have *m* on us
20: 31 "Lord, Son of David, have *m* on us
23: 23 justice, *m* and faithfulness.
Mk 5: 19 and how he has had *m* on you."
10: 47 Jesus, Son of David, have *m* on me
10: 48 "Son of David, have *m* on me!"
Lk 1: 50 His *m* extends to those who fear
1: 58 the Lord had shown her great *m*,
1: 72 to show *m* to our fathers
1: 78 because of the tender *m* of our God
10: 37 "The one who had *m* on him."
18: 13 'God, have *m* on me, a sinner.'
18: 38 Jesus, Son of David, have *m* on me
18: 39 "Son of David, have *m* on me!"
Ro 9: 15 "I will have *m* on whom I have *m*,
9: 16 or effort, but on God's *m*.
9: 18 Therefore God has *m*
9: 18 on whom he wants to have *m*,
9: 23 known to the objects of his *m*,
11: 30 to God have now received *m*
11: 31 as a result of God's *m* to you.
11: 31 that they too may now receive *m*
11: 32 so that he may have *m* on them all.
12: 1 brothers, in view of God's *m*,
12: 8 if it is showing *m*, let him do it
15: 9 may glorify God for his *m*,
1Co 7: 25 by the Lord's *m* is trustworthy.
2Co 4: 1 through God's *m* we have this
Gal 6: 16 and *m* to all who follow this rule,
Eph 2: 4 who is rich in *m*, made us alive
Php 2: 27 But God had *m* on him,
1Ti 1: 2 *m* and peace from God the Father
1: 13 I was shown *m* because I acted
1: 16 for that very reason I was shown *m*
2Ti 1: 2 *m* and peace from God the Father
1: 16 May the Lord show *m*
1: 18 the Lord grant that he will find *m*
Tit 3: 5 we had done, but because of his *m*.
Heb 4: 16 so that we may receive *m*
10: 28 died without *m* on the testimony
Jas 2: 13 judgment without *m* will be shown
2: 13 *M* triumphs over judgment!
3: 17 submissive, full of *m* and good fruit
5: 11 full of compassion and *m*.
1Pe 1: 3 In his great *m* he has given us new
2: 10 but now you have received *m*.

1Pe 2: 10 once you had not received *m*,
2Jn : 3 *m* and peace from God the Father
Jude : 2 *M*, peace and love be yours
: 21 as you wait for the *m*
: 23 to others show *m*, mixed with fear

MERED (MERED'S)

1Ch 4: 17 Jether, *M*, Epher and Jalon.
4: 18 Bithiah, whom *M* had married.

MERED'S (MERED)

1Ch 4: 17 One of *M* wives gave birth

MEREMOTH (MEREMOTH'S)

Ezr 8: 33 into the hands of *M* son of Uriah,
10: 36 Keluhi, Vaniah, *M*, Eliashib,
Ne 3: 4 *M* son of Uriah, the son of Hakkoz,
3: 21 Next to him, *M* son of Uriah,
10: 5 Malluch, Harim, *M*, Obadiah,
12: 3 Shecaniah, Rehum, *M*, Iddo,

MEREMOTH'S (MEREMOTH)

Ne 12: 15 Adna; of *M*, Helkai; of Iddo's,

MERES

Est 1: 14 Shethar, Admatha, Tarshish, *M*,

MERIB-BAAL

1Ch 8: 34 *M*, who was the father of Micah.
9: 40 *M*, who was the father of Micah.

MERIBAH

Ex 17: 7 *M* because the Israelites quarreled
Nu 20: 13 These were the waters of *M*,
20: 24 command at the waters of *M*.
27: 14 (These were the waters of *M*
Dt 33: 8 with him at the waters of *M*.
Ps 81: 7 I tested you at the waters of *M*.
95: 8 harden your hearts as you did at *M*,
106: 32 of *M* they angered the LORD,

MERIBAH KADESH

Dt 32: 51 waters of *M* in the Desert of Zin
Eze 47: 19 as far as the waters of *M*,
48: 28 from Tamar to the waters of *M*,

MERODACH-BALADAN

2Ki 20: 12 At that time *M* son of Baladan king
Isa 39: 1 At that time *M* son of Baladan king

MEROM

Jos 11: 5 together at the Waters of *M*,
11: 7 suddenly at the Waters of *M*

MERONOTH (MERONOTHITE)

Ne 3: 7 of Gibeon and Jadon of *M*—

MERONOTHITE (MERONOTH)

1Ch 27: 30 Jehdeiah the *M* was in charge

MEROZ

Jdg 5: 23 'Curse *M*,' said the angel

MERRIMENT (MERRY)

Isa 32: 13 yes, mourn for all houses of *m*

MERRY (MERRIMENT MERRYMAKERS)

Job 21: 12 they make *m* to the sound
Ecc 10: 19 and wine makes life *m*,
Jer 15: 17 never made *m* with them;
Lk 12: 19 Take life easy; eat, drink and be *m*

MERRYMAKERS (MERRY)

Isa 24: 7 all the *m* groan.

MESH

Job 18: 8 and he wanders into its *m*.

MESHA

Ge 10: 30 stretched from *M* toward Sephar,
2Ki 3: 4 Now *M* king of Moab raised sheep,
1Ch 2: 42 of Jerahmeel: *M* his firstborn,
8: 9 *M*, Malcam, Jeuz, Sakia

MESHACH

Da 1: 7 to Mishael, *M*; and to Azariah,
2: 49 *M* and Abednego administrators
3: 12 Shadrach, *M* and Abednego—
3: 13 summoned Shadrach, *M*
3: 14 Shadrach, *M* and Abednego,
3: 16 *M* and Abednego replied
3: 19 furious with Shadrach, *M*
3: 20 *M* and Abednego and throw them
3: 22 *M* and Abednego, and these three
3: 26 *M* and Abednego came out
3: 26 "Shadrach, *M* and Abednego,
3: 28 be to the God of Shadrach, *M*
3: 29 *M* and Abednego be cut into pieces
3: 30 *M* and Abednego in the province

MESHECH

Ge 10: 2 Madai, Javan, Tubal, *M* and Tiras.
10: 23 of Aram: Uz, Hul, Gether and *M*.
1Ch 1: 5 Madai, Javan, Tubal, *M* and Tiras.
1: 17 of Aram: Uz, Hul, Gether and *M*.
Ps 120: 5 Woe to me that I dwell in *M*,
Eze 27: 13 Tubal and *M* traded with you;
32: 26 "*M* and Tubal are there,
38: 2 the chief prince of *M* and Tubal;
38: 3 chief prince of *M* and Tubal.
39: 1 chief prince of *M* and Tubal.

MESHELEMIAH

1Ch 9: 21 son of *M* was the gatekeeper
26: 1 From the Korahites: *M* son of Kore
26: 2 *M* had sons: Zechariah
26: 9 *M* had sons and relatives, who

MESHEZABEL

Ne 3: 4 the son of *M*, made repairs,
10: 21 Meshullam, Hezir, *M*, Zadok,
11: 24 Pethahiah son of *M*, one

MESHILLEMITH

1Ch 9: 12 the son of *M*, the son of Immer.

MESHILLEMOTH

2Ch 28: 12 Berekiah son of *M*, Jehizkiah son
Ne 11: 13 the son of *M*, the son of Immer,

MESHOBAB

1Ch 4: 34 *M*, Jamlech, Joshah son

MESHULLAM

2Ki 22: 3 the son of *M*, to the temple
1Ch 3: 19 The sons of Zerubbabel: *M*
5: 13 were: Michael, *M*, Sheba, Jorai,
8: 17 Zebadiah, *M*, Hizki, Heber,
9: 7 Sallu son of *M*, the son
9: 8 of Micri; and *M* son of Shephatiah,
9: 11 the son of *M*, the son of Zadok,
9: 12 the son of *M*, the son
2Ch 34: 12 and *M*, descended from Kohath.
Ezr 8: 16 Nathan, Zechariah and *M*,
10: 15 by *M* and Shabbethai the Levite,
10: 29 *M*, Malluch, Adaiah, Jashub,
Ne 3: 4 Next to him *M* son of Berekiah,
3: 6 of Paseah and *M* son of Besodeiah.
3: 30 *M* son of Berekiah made repairs
6: 18 the daughter of *M* son of Berekiah.
8: 4 Hashbaddanah, Zechariah and *M*.
10: 7 Ginnethon, Baruch, *M*, Abijah,
10: 20 Nebai, Magpiash, *M*, Hezir,
11: 7 Sallu son of *M*, the son of Joed,
11: 11 the son of *M*, the son of Zadok,
12: 13 of Ezra's, *M*; of Amariah's,
12: 16 of Ginnethon's, *M*; of Abijah's,
12: 25 Bakbukiah, Obadiah, *M*,
12: 33 Ezra, *M*, Judah, Benjamin,

MESHULLEMETH

2Ki 21: 19 mother's name was *M* daughter

MESOPOTAMIA

Ac 2: 9 of *M*, Judea and Cappadocia,
7: 2 Abraham while he was still in *M*,

MESSAGE (MESSENGER MESSENGERS)

Ge 32: 5 I am sending this *m* to my lord,
38: 25 she sent a *m* to her father-in-law.
50: 17 When their *m* came to him,
Nu 22: 10 king of Moab, sent me this *m*:
23: 5 The LORD put a *m*
23: 5 back to Balak and give him this *m*."
23: 16 and put a *m* in his mouth and said,
23: 16 back to Balak and give him this *m*."
Dt 18: 21 when a *m* has not been spoken
18: 22 that is a *m* the LORD has not
Jos 2: 3 of Jericho sent this *m* to Rahab,
5: 14 "What *m* does my Lord have
Jdg 3: 19 I have a secret *m* for you, O king."
3: 20 "I have a *m* from God for you."
11: 28 to the *m* Jephthah sent him.
1Sa 9: 27 so that I may give you a *m*
15: 1 now to the *m* from the LORD.
25: 9 they gave Nabal this *m*
2Sa 17: 16 Now send a *m* immediately
19: 11 King David sent this *m* to Zadok
1Ki 5: 2 Solomon sent back this *m* to Hiram
5: 7 When Hiram heard Solomon's *m*,
5: 8 "I have received the *m* you sent me
13: 32 For the *m* he declared by the word
20: 10 Then Ben-Hadad sent another *m*
20: 12 Ben-Hadad heard this *m* while he
2Ki 3: 7 sent this *m* to Jehoshaphat king
5: 8 he sent him this *m*: "Why have you
9: 5 "I have a *m* for you, commander,"
10: 5 the guardians sent this *m* to Jehu:
14: 9 in Lebanon sent a *m* to a cedar
18: 14 of Judah sent this *m* to the king
19: 20 son of Amoz sent a *m* to Hezekiah:
2Ch 2: 3 Solomon sent this *m* to Hiram king
25: 18 in Lebanon sent a *m* to a cedar
32: 9 with this *m* for Hezekiah king
Ezr 4: 14 we are sending this *m*
Ne 6: 2 and Geshem sent me this *m*:
6: 4 times they sent me the same *m*,
6: 5 aide to me with the same *m*,
Pr 26: 6 is the sending of a *m* by the hand
Isa 9: 8 The Lord has sent a *m*
28: 9 To whom is he explaining his *m*?
28: 19 The understanding of this *m*
30: 12 "Because you have rejected this *m*,
37: 21 son of Amoz sent a *m* to Hezekiah:
53: 1 Who has believed our *m*
Jer 3: 12 proclaim this *m* toward the north:
7: 2 and there proclaim this *m*:
18: 2 and there I will give you my *m*."
22: 1 and proclaim this *m* there:
23: 21 yet they have run with their *m*;
27: 4 Give them a *m* for their masters
27: 12 I gave the same *m* to Zedekiah king
29: 28 He has sent this *m* to us in Babylon
29: 31 "Send this *m* to all the exiles:
37: 3 Jeremiah the prophet with this *m*:
44: 16 to the *m* you have spoken to us
46: 2 This is the *m* against the army
46: 13 This is the *m* the LORD spoke
49: 14 I have heard a *m* from the LORD:
51: 59 This is the *m* Jeremiah gave
Eze 33: 30 and hear the *m* that has come
Da 9: 23 consider the *m* and understand
10: 1 Its *m* was true and it concerned
10: 1 of the *m* came to him
Am 7: 10 the priest of Bethel sent a *m*
Ob : 1 We have heard a *m*
Jnh 3: 2 proclaim to it the *m* I give you."
Hag 1: 12 and the *m* of the prophet Haggai,
1: 13 gave this *m* of the LORD
Mt 10: 7 preach this *m*: 'The kingdom
13: 19 anyone hears the *m* about
27: 19 sent him this *m*: "Don't have
Mk 1: 7 And this was his *m*: "After me will
Lk 4: 32 because his *m* had authority.
Jn 12: 38 "Lord, who has believed our *m*
17: 20 believe in me through their *m*,
Ac 2: 41 who accepted his *m* were baptized,
4: 4 many who heard the *m* believed,
5: 20 "and tell the people the full *m*
10: 36 This is the *m* God sent
10: 44 came on all who heard the *m*.
11: 14 He will bring you a *m*
11: 19 telling the *m* only to Jews.
13: 15 if you have a *m* of encouragement
13: 26 is to us that this *m* of salvation has
14: 3 who confirmed the *m* of his grace
15: 7 from my lips the *m* of the gospel
15: 31 were glad for its encouraging *m*.
16: 14 heart to respond to Paul's *m*.
17: 11 for they received the *m*
19: 31 sent him a *m* begging him not
Ro 10: 16 who has believed our *m*?"
10: 17 faith comes from hearing the *m*,
10: 17 the *m* is heard through the word
1Co 1: 18 For the *m* of the cross is

1Co 2: 4 My *m* and my preaching were not
2: 6 speak a *m* of wisdom
12: 8 through the Spirit the *m* of wisdom
12: 8 to another the *m* of knowledge
2Co 1: 18 our *m* to you is not "Yes" and "No
5: 19 to us the *m* of reconciliation.
Gal 2: 6 those men added nothing to my *m*.
Col 4: 3 God may open a door for our *m*,
1Th 1: 6 you welcomed the *m*
1: 8 The Lord's *m* rang out
2Th 3: 1 pray for us that the *m*
1Ti 4: 14 you through a prophetic *m*
2Ti 4: 15 because he strongly opposed our *m*
4: 17 through me the *m* might be fully
Tit 1: 9 firmly to the trustworthy *m*
Heb 2: 2 For if the *m* spoken
4: 2 the *m* they heard was of no value
1Pe 2: 8 because they disobey the *m*—
1Jn 1: 5 This is the *m* we have heard
2: 7 command is the *m* you have heard.
3: 11 This is the *m* you heard

MESSENGER (MESSAGE)

1Sa 23: 27 a *m* came to Saul, saying, "Come
2Sa 11: 19 He instructed the *m*: "When you
11: 22 *m* set out, and when he arrived he
11: 23 The *m* said to David, "The men
11: 25 David told the *m*, "Say this to Joab
15: 13 A *m* came and told David,
1Ki 19: 2 So Jezebel sent a *m* to Elijah to say,
22: 13 The *m* who had gone
2Ki 5: 10 Elisha sent a *m* to say to him, "Go,
6: 32 Look, when the *m* comes,
6: 32 The king sent a *m* ahead,
6: 33 to them, the *m* came down to him.
9: 18 "The *m* has reached them,
10: 8 When the *m* arrived, he told Jehu,
2Ch 18: 12 The *m* who had gone
Job 1: 14 *m* came to Job and said, "The oxen
1: 16 another *m* came and said,
1: 17 another *m* came and said,
1: 18 yet another *m* came and said,
Pr 13: 17 A wicked *m* falls into trouble,
16: 14 A king's wrath is a *m* of death,
25: 13 is a trustworthy *m*
Ecc 5: 6 do not protest to the temple *m*,
Isa 41: 27 to Jerusalem a *m* of good tidings.
42: 19 and deaf like the *m* I send?
Jer 51: 31 and *m* follows *m*
Da 4: 13 and there before me was a *m*,
4: 23 "You, O king, saw a *m*, a holy one,
Hag 1: 13 Then Haggai, the LORD's *m*,
Mal 2: 7 he is the *m* of the LORD Almighty
3: 1 I will send my *m*, who will prepare
3: 1 the *m* of the covenant, whom you
Mt 11: 10 " 'I will send my *m* ahead of you,
Mk 1: 2 "I will send my *m* ahead of you,
Lk 7: 27 " 'I will send my *m* ahead of you,
Jn 13: 16 nor is a *m* greater than the one who
2Co 12: 7 a *m* of Satan, to torment me.
Php 2: 25 fellow soldier, who is also your *m*,

MESSENGERS (MESSAGE)

Ge 32: 3 Jacob sent *m* ahead of him
32: 6 When the *m* returned to Jacob,
Nu 20: 14 Moses sent *m* from Kadesh
21: 21 Israel sent *m* to say to Sihon king
22: 5 sent *m* to summon Balaam son
24: 12 "Did I not tell the *m* you sent me,
Dt 2: 26 the desert of Kedemoth I sent *m*
Jos 7: 22 So Joshua sent *m*, and they ran
Jdg 6: 35 He sent *m* throughout Manasseh,
7: 24 Gideon sent *m* throughout the hill
9: 31 Under cover he sent *m*
11: 12 Jephthah sent *m* to the Ammonite
11: 13 answered Jephthah's *m*,
11: 14 Jephthah sent back *m*
11: 17 Israel sent *m* to the king of Edom,
11: 19 "Then Israel sent *m* to Sihon king
1Sa 6: 21 *m* to the people of Kiriath Jearim,
11: 3 so we can send *m* throughout Israel
11: 4 When the *m* came to Gibeah
11: 7 the pieces by *m* throughout Israel,
11: 9 They told the *m* who had come,
11: 9 When the *m* went and reported
16: 19 Then Saul sent *m* to Jesse and said,
25: 14 "David sent *m* from the desert
25: 42 with David's *m* and became his
1Sa 31: 9 they sent *m* throughout the land
2Sa 2: 5 *m* to the men of Jabesh Gilead
3: 12 Abner sent *m* on his behalf to say
3: 14 David sent *m* to Ish-Bosheth son
3: 26 Joab then left David and sent *m*
5: 11 king of Tyre sent *m* to David,
10: 5 he sent *m* to meet the men,
11: 4 Then David sent *m* to get her.
12: 27 Joab then sent *m* to David, saying,
15: 10 Then Absalom sent secret *m*
1Ki 20: 2 He sent *m* into the city
20: 5 The *m* came again and said,
20: 9 So he replied to Ben-Hadad's *m*,
2Ki 1: 2 So he sent *m*, saying to them,
1: 3 meet the *m* of the king of Samaria
1: 5 When the *m* returned to the king,
1: 16 to consult that you have sent *m*
7: 15 So the *m* returned and reported
14: 8 Amaziah sent *m* to Jehoash son
16: 7 Ahaz sent *m* to say
19: 9 So he again sent *m* to Hezekiah
19: 14 received the letter from the *m*
19: 23 By your *m*
20: 13 Hezekiah received the *m*
1Ch 10: 9 and sent *m* throughout the land
14: 1 king of Tyre sent *m* to David,
19: 5 he sent *m* to meet them,
19: 16 they sent *m* and had Arameans
2Ch 35: 21 But Neco sent *m* to him, saying,
36: 15 word to them through his *m* again
36: 16 But they mocked God's *m*,
Ne 6: 3 so I sent *m* to them with this reply:
Job 33: 22 and his life to the *m* of death.
Ps 104: 4 He makes winds his *m*,
Isa 18: 2 Go, swift *m*,
37: 9 he sent *m* to Hezekiah
37: 14 received the letter from the *m*
37: 24 By your *m*
44: 26 and fulfills the predictions of his *m*,
Eze 23: 16 and sent *m* to them in Chaldea.
23: 40 even sent *m* for men who came
30: 9 On that day *m* will go out from me
Da 4: 17 " 'The decision is announced by *m*;
Na 2: 13 The voices of your *m*
Lk 7: 22 So he replied to the *m*, "Go back
7: 24 After John's *m* left, Jesus began
9: 52 out for Jerusalem, and he sent *m*

MESSIAH

Jn 1: 41 "We have found the *M*" (that is,
4: 25 "I know that *M*" (called Christ) "is

MET (MEET)

Ge 32: 1 and the angels of God *m* him.
33: 8 mean by all these droves I *m*?"
38: 2 There Judah *m* the daughter
Ex 3: 18 of the Hebrews, has *m* with us.
4: 24 the LORD *m* Moses and was about
4: 27 So he *m* Moses at the mountain
5: 3 God of the Hebrews has *m* with us.
5: 14 "Why haven't you *m* your quota
18: 8 about all the hardships they had *m*
Nu 23: 4 God *m* with him, and Balaam said,
23: 16 The LORD *m* with Balaam
Dt 25: 18 they *m* you on your journey
1Sa 9: 11 they *m* some girls coming out
10: 10 a procession of prophets *m* him;
16: 4 trembled when they *m* him.
18: 30 David *m* with more success
21: 1 trembled when he *m* him,
25: 20 toward her, and she *m* them.
2Sa 2: 13 and *m* them at the pool of Gibeon.
1Ki 11: 29 of Shiloh *m* him on the way,
13: 24 a lion *m* him on the road
18: 7 walking along, Elijah *m* him.
2Ki 9: 21 They *m* him at the plot
10: 13 he *m* some relatives
12: 12 and *m* all the other expenses
Ne 13: 2 they had not *m* the Israelites
Job 2: 11 and *m* together by agreement to go
Ps 74: 4 in the place where you *m* with us;
Jer 41: 6 When he *m* them, he said,
Mt 8: 28 coming from the tombs *m* him.
27: 32 they *m* a man from Cyrene,
28: 9 Suddenly Jesus *m* them.
28: 12 When the chief priests had *m*
Lk 8: 27 he was *m* by a demon-possessed
9: 37 mountain, a large crowd *m* him.
Lk 17: 12 ten men who had leprosy *m* him.
22: 66 *m* together, and Jesus was led
Jn 4: 51 his servants *m* him
11: 30 place where Martha had *m* him.
18: 2 because Jesus had often *m* there
Ac 1: 6 So when they *m* together,
4: 5 teachers of the law *m* in Jerusalem.
4: 27 and Pontius Pilate *m* together
8: 27 his way he *m* an Ethiopian eunuch,
10: 25 Cornelius *m* him and fell at his feet
11: 26 and Saul *m* with the church
13: 6 There they *m* a Jewish sorcerer
15: 6 elders *m* to consider this question.
16: 16 we were *m* by a slave girl who had
16: 40 where they *m* with the brothers
18: 2 There he *m* a Jew named Aquila,
20: 14 When he *m* us at Assos, we took
Ro 8: 4 of the law might be fully *m* in us,
Col 2: 1 all who have not *m* me personally.
Heb 7: 1 He *m* Abraham returning
7: 10 when Melchizedek *m* Abraham,

METAL (METALS)

Lev 19: 4 make gods of cast *m* for yourselves.
1Ki 7: 23 He made the Sea of cast *m*,
7: 33 spokes and hubs were all of cast *m*.
14: 9 other gods, idols made of *m*;
2Ch 4: 2 He made the Sea of cast *m*,
Ps 106: 19 and worshiped an idol cast from *m*.
Isa 48: 5 and *m* god ordained them.'
Eze 1: 4 of the fire looked like glowing *m*,
1: 27 waist up he looked like glowing *m*,
8: 2 was as bright as glowing *m*.
Da 11: 8 their *m* images and their valuable
Na 2: 3 The *m* on the chariots flashes

METALS (METAL)

Jer 6: 27 "I have made you a tester of *m*

METALWORKER

2Ti 4: 14 Alexander the *m* did me a great

METE

Ps 58: 2 and your hands *m* out violence

METHEG AMMAH

2Sa 8: 1 and he took *M* from the control of

METHOD (METHODS)

Ru 4: 7 the *m* of legalizing transactions

METHODS (METHOD)

Isa 32: 7 The scoundrel's *m* are wicked,

METHUSELAH

Ge 5: 21 he became the father of *M*.
5: 22 after he became the father of *M*,
5: 25 When *M* had lived 187 years,
5: 26 *M* lived 782 years and had other
5: 27 Altogether, *M* lived 969 years,
1Ch 1: 3 Jared, Enoch, *M*, Lamech, Noah.
Lk 3: 37 the son of *M*, the son of Enoch,

METHUSHAEL

Ge 4: 18 and Mehujael was the father of *M*,
4: 18 and *M* was the father of Lamech.

MEUNIM

Ezr 2: 50 Besai, Asnah, *M*, Nephussim,
Ne 7: 52 Paseah, Besai, *M*, Nephussim

MEUNITES

1Ch 4: 41 and also the *M* who were there
2Ch 20: 1 with some of the *M* came
26: 7 in Gur Baal and against the *M*.

MEZOBAITE

1Ch 11: 47 Eliel, Obed and Jaasiel the *M*.

MIBHAR

1Ch 11: 38 brother of Nathan, *M* son of Hagri,

MIBSAM

Ge 25: 13 Kedar, Adbeel, *M*, Mishma,
1Ch 1: 29 Kedar, Adbeel, *M*, Mishma,
4: 25 *M* his son and Mishma his son.

MIBZAR

Ge 36: 42 Pinon, Kenaz, Teman, *M*,

1Ch 1: 53 Pinon, Kenaz, Teman, *M*,

MICA

2Sa 9: 12 had a young son named *M*,
1Ch 9: 15 Galal and Mattaniah son of *M*,
Ne 10: 11 Pelaiah, Hanan, *M*, Rehob,
11: 17 Mattaniah son of *M*, the son
11: 22 the son of Mattaniah, the son of *M*.

MICAH (MICAH'S)

Jdg 17: 1 Now a man named *M* from the hill
17: 5 Now this man *M* had a shrine,
17: 9 *M* asked him, "Where are you from
17: 10 Then *M* said to him, "Live with me
17: 12 Then *M* installed the Levite,
17: 13 And *M* said, "Now I know that
18: 2 and came to the house of *M*,
18: 4 He told them what *M* had done
18: 22 lived near *M* were called together
18: 23 the Danites turned and said to *M*,
18: 26 the Danites went their way, and *M*,
18: 27 Then they took what *M* had made,
18: 31 to use the idols *M* had made,
1Ch 5: 5 Shimei his son, *M* his son,
8: 34 who was the father of *M*.
8: 35 The sons of *M:* Pithon, Melech,
9: 40 who was the father of *M*.
9: 41 The sons of *M:* Pithon, Melech,
23: 20 *M* the first and Isshiah the second.
24: 24 *M;* from the sons of *M:* Shamir.
24: 25 The brother of *M:* Isshiah;
2Ch 34: 20 son of Shaphan, Abdon son of *M*,
Jer 26: 18 "*M* of Moresheth prophesied
Mic 1: 1 given to *M* of Moresheth

MICAH'S (MICAH)

Jdg 17: 4 And they were put in *M* house.
17: 8 came to *M* house in the hill country
18: 3 When they were near *M* house,
18: 13 of Ephraim and came to *M* house.
18: 15 of the young Levite at *M* place
18: 18 these men went into *M* house
18: 22 gone some distance from *M* house,

MICAIAH

1Ki 22: 8 He is *M* son of Imlah."
22: 9 "Bring *M* son of Imlah at once."
22: 13 gone to summon *M* said to him,
22: 14 But *M* said, "As surely
22: 15 he arrived, the king asked him, "*M*,
22: 17 Then *M* answered, "I saw all Israel
22: 19 but only bad?" *M* continued,
22: 24 and slapped *M* in the face.
22: 25 *M* replied, "You will find out
22: 26 "Take *M* and send him back
22: 28 *M* declared, "If you ever return
2Ki 22: 12 son of Shaphan, Acbor son of *M*,
2Ch 17: 7 *M* to teach in the towns of Judah.
18: 7 He is *M* son of Imlah."
18: 8 "Bring *M* son of Imlah at once."
18: 12 gone to summon *M* said to him,
18: 13 But *M* said, "As surely
18: 14 he arrived, the king asked him, "*M*,
18: 16 Then *M* answered, "I saw all Israel
18: 18 but only bad?" *M* continued,
18: 23 and slapped *M* in the face.
18: 24 *M* replied, "You will find out
18: 25 "Take *M* and send him back
18: 27 *M* declared, "If you ever return
Ne 12: 35 the son of *M*, the son of Zaccur,
12: 41 Maaseiah, Mijamin, *M*, Elioenai,
Jer 36: 11 When *M* son of Gemariah,
36: 13 After *M* told them everything he

MICHAEL

Nu 13: 13 Sethur son of *M;* from the tribe
1Ch 5: 13 were: *M*, Meshullam, Sheba,
5: 14 the son of *M*, the son of Jeshishai,
6: 40 the son of *M*, the son of Baaseiah,
7: 3 The sons of Izrahiah: *M*, Obadiah,
8: 16 Zebadiah, Arad, Eder, *M*,
12: 20 Jozabad, Jediael, *M*, Jozabad,
27: 18 Omri son of *M;* over Zebulun:
2Ch 21: 2 Azariahu, *M* and Shephatiah.
Ezr 8: 8 Zebadiah son of *M*,
Da 10: 13 Then *M*, one of the chief princes,
10: 21 me against them except *M*,
12: 1 "At that time *M*, the great prince
Jude : 9 But even the archangel *M*,
Rev 12: 7 *M* and his angels fought

MICHAL

1Sa 14: 49 and that of the younger was *M*.
18: 20 Now Saul's daughter *M* was in love
18: 27 Then Saul gave him his daughter *M*
18: 28 that his daughter *M* loved David,
19: 11 But *M*, David's wife, warned him,
19: 12 So *M* let David
19: 13 Then *M* took an idol and laid it
19: 14 the men to capture David, *M* said,
19: 17 *M* told him, "He said to me,
19: 17 to *M*, "Why did you deceive me
25: 44 But Saul had given his daughter *M*,
2Sa 3: 13 you bring *M* daughter of Saul
3: 14 demanding, "Give me my wife *M*,
6: 16 *M* daughter of Saul watched
6: 20 *M* daughter of Saul came out
6: 21 David said to *M*, "It was
6: 23 *M* daughter of Saul had no children
1Ch 15: 29 *M* daughter of Saul watched

MICMASH

1Sa 13: 2 two thousand were with him at *M*
13: 5 They went up and camped at *M*,
13: 11 Philistines were assembling at *M*,
13: 16 while the Philistines camped at *M*.
13: 23 had gone out to the pass at *M*.
14: 5 stood to the north toward *M*,
14: 31 the Philistines from *M* to Aijalon,
Ezr 2: 27 and Geba 621 of *M* 122 of Bethel
Ne 7: 31 and Geba 621 of *M* 122 of Bethel
11: 31 Benjamites from Geba lived in *M*,
Isa 10: 28 they store supplies at *M*.

MICMETHATH

Jos 16: 6 From *M* on the north it curved
17: 7 from Asher to *M* east of Shechem.

MICRI

1Ch 9: 8 the son of *M;* and Meshullam son

MIDAIR (AIR)

2Sa 18: 9 He was left hanging in *m*,
Rev 8: 13 flying in *m* call out in a loud voice:
14: 6 I saw another angel flying in *m*,
19: 17 voice to all the birds flying in *m*,

MIDDAY (DAY)

Dt 28: 29 At *m* you will grope about like
1Ki 18: 29 *M* passed, and they continued their
Ps 91: 6 nor the plague that destroys at *m*.
SS 1: 7 and where you rest your sheep at *m*
Isa 59: 10 At *m* we stumble as if it were
Jer 15: 8 At *m* I will bring a destroyer
Zep 2: 4 At *m* Ashdod will be emptied

MIDDIN

Jos 15: 61 Beth Arabah, *M*, Secacah,

MIDIAN (MIDIAN'S MIDIANITE MIDIANITES)

Ge 25: 2 Medan, *M*, Ishbak and Shuah.
25: 4 The sons of *M* were Ephah, Epher,
36: 35 who defeated *M* in the country
Ex 2: 15 Pharaoh and went to live in *M*,
2: 16 a priest of *M* had seven daughters,
3: 1 his father-in-law, the priest of *M*,
4: 19 the LORD had said to Moses in *M*,
18: 1 the priest of *M* and father-in-law
Nu 22: 4 said to the elders of *M*,
22: 7 The elders of Moab and *M* left,
31: 7 They fought against *M*,
31: 8 Hur and Reba—the five kings of *M*
Jdg 6: 2 the power of *M* was so oppressive,
6: 6 *M* so impoverished the Israelites
6: 7 cried to the LORD because of *M*,
6: 13 and put us into the hand of *M*."
7: 1 The camp of *M* was north of them
7: 2 me to deliver *M* into their hands.
7: 8 Now the camp of *M* lay below him
8: 1 us when you went to fight *M?*"
8: 5 and Zalmunna, the kings of *M*."
8: 12 and Zalmunna, the two kings of *M*,
8: 22 out of the hand of *M*."
8: 26 garments worn by the kings of *M*
8: 28 Thus *M* was subdued
Jdg 9: 17 to rescue you from the hand of *M*
1Ki 11: 18 They set out from *M* and went
1Ch 1: 32 Zimran, Jokshan, Medan, *M*,
1: 33 The sons of *M:* Ephah, Epher,
1: 46 who defeated *M* in the country
Ps 83: 9 Do to them as you did to *M*,
Isa 10: 26 when he struck down *M* at the rock
60: 6 young camels of *M* and Ephah.
Hab 3: 7 the dwellings of *M* in anguish.
Ac 7: 29 Moses heard this, he fled to *M*,

MIDIAN'S (MIDIAN)

Jdg 6: 14 and save Israel out of *M* hand.
Isa 9: 4 For as in the day of *M* defeat,

MIDIANITE (MIDIAN)

Ge 37: 28 So when the *M* merchants came by
Nu 10: 29 said to Hobab son of Reuel the *M*,
25: 6 to his family a *M* woman right
25: 14 with the *M* woman was Zimri son
25: 15 a tribal chief of a *M* family.
25: 15 name of the *M* woman who was put
25: 18 the daughter of a *M* leader,
31: 9 Israelites captured the *M* women
31: 9 children and took all the *M* herds,
Jos 13: 21 had defeated him and the *M* chiefs,
Jdg 7: 13 came tumbling into the *M* camp.
7: 15 The LORD has given the *M* camp
7: 25 also captured two of the *M* leaders,
8: 3 the *M* leaders, into your hands.

MIDIANITES (MIDIAN)

Ge 37: 36 the *M* sold Joseph in Egypt
Nu 25: 17 "Treat the *M* as enemies
31: 2 on the *M* for the Israelites.
31: 3 men to go to war against the *M*
31: 10 the towns where the *M* had settled,
Jdg 6: 1 them into the hands of the *M*.
6: 3 planted their crops, the *M*,
6: 11 a winepress to keep it from the *M*.
6: 16 and you will strike down the *M*
6: 33 Now all the *M*, Amalekites
7: 7 and give the *M* into your hands.
7: 12 The *M*, the Amalekites
7: 14 God has given the *M* and the whole
7: 21 all the *M* ran, crying out
7: 23 called out, and they pursued the *M*.
7: 24 "Come down against the *M*
7: 25 They pursued the *M* and brought

MIDNIGHT (NIGHT)

Ex 11: 4 'About *m* I will go
12: 29 At *m* the LORD struck
Ps 119: 62 At *m* I rise to give you thanks
Mt 25: 6 "At *m* the cry rang out: 'Here's
Mk 13: 35 or at *m*, or when the rooster crows,
Lk 11: 5 and he goes to him at *m* and says,
Ac 16: 25 About *m* Paul and Silas were
20: 7 kept on talking until *m*.
27: 27 when about *m* the sailors sensed

MIDWIFE (MIDWIVES)

Ge 35: 17 the *m* said to her, "Don't be afraid,
38: 28 so the *m* took a scarlet thread

MIDWIVES (MIDWIFE)

Ex 1: 15 of Egypt said to the Hebrew *m*,
1: 17 The *m*, however, feared God
1: 18 the king of Egypt summoned the *m*
1: 19 The *m* answered Pharaoh,
1: 19 and give birth before the *m* arrive."
1: 20 So God was kind to the *m*
1: 21 And because the *m* feared God,

MIGDAL EDER

Ge 35: 21 and pitched his tent beyond *M*.

MIGDAL EL

Jos 19: 38 Iron, *M*, Horeim

MIGDAL GAD

Jos 15: 37 Zenan, Hadashah, *M*, Dilean,

MIGDOL

Ex 14: 2 near Pi Hahiroth, between *M*
Nu 33: 7 Baal Zephon, and camped near *M*.
Jer 44: 1 in *M*, Tahpanhes and Memphis—
46: 14 this in Egypt, and proclaim it in *M;*

Eze 29: 10 a desolate waste from *M* to Aswan,
30: 6 From *M* to Aswan

MIGHT (ALMIGHTY MIGHTIER MIGHTIEST MIGHTY)

Ge 49: 3 my *m*, the first sign of my strength,
Jdg 16: 30 Then he pushed with all his *m*,
2Sa 6: 5 with all their *m* before the LORD,
6: 14 before the LORD with all his *m*,
1Ch 13: 8 with all their *m* before God,
2Ch 6: 41 you and the ark of your *m*.
20: 6 Power and *m* are in your hand,
Est 10: 2 And all his acts of power and *m*,
Job 30: 21 with the *m* of your hand you attack
Ps 21: 13 we will sing and praise your *m*.
54: 1 vindicate me by your *m*.
59: 11 In your *m* make them wander
71: 18 your *m* to all who are to come.
78: 61 of his *m* into captivity,
80: 2 Awaken your *m*;
132: 8 you and the ark of your *m*.
145: 11 and speak of your *m*,
Ecc 9: 10 it with all your *m*, for in the grave,
Isa 44: 12 he forges it with the *m* of his arm.
63: 15 Where are your zeal and your *m*?
Jer 16: 21 my power and *m*.
49: 35 the mainstay of their *m*.
Da 2: 37 and power and *m* and glory;
11: 17 determine to come with the *m*
Mic 3: 8 and with justice and *m*,
Zec 4: 6 'Not by *m* nor by power,
Col 1: 11 power according to his glorious *m*
1Ti 6: 16 To him be honor and *m* forever

MIGHTIER (MIGHT)

Ps 93: 4 *M* than the thunder
93: 4 *m* than the breakers of the sea—

MIGHTIEST (MIGHT)

Da 11: 39 He will attack the *m* fortresses

MIGHTY (MIGHT)

Ge 10: 8 to be a *m* warrior on the earth.
10: 9 He was a *m* hunter
10: 9 a *m* hunter before the LORD."
23: 6 You are a *m* prince among us.
49: 24 of the hand of the *M* One of Jacob,
Ex 3: 19 unless a *m* hand compels him
6: 1 of my *m* hand he will drive them
6: 1 of my *m* hand he will let them go;
6: 6 and with *m* acts of judgment.
7: 4 with *m* acts of judgment I will bring
13: 3 out of it with a *m* hand.
13: 9 out of Egypt with his *m* hand.
13: 14 'With a *m* hand the LORD brought
13: 16 out of Egypt with his *m* hand."
15: 10 lead in the *m* waters.
32: 11 with great power and a *m* hand?
Dt 3: 24 do the deeds and *m* works you do?
4: 34 by a *m* hand and an outstretched
5: 15 out of there with a *m* hand
6: 21 out of Egypt with a *m* hand.
7: 8 he brought you out with a *m* hand
7: 19 the *m* hand and outstretched arm,
9: 26 out of Egypt with a *m* hand.
10: 17 the great God, *m* and awesome,
11: 2 his *m* hand, his outstretched arm;
26: 8 out of Egypt with a *m* hand
34: 12 one has ever shown the *m* power
Jos 22: 22 God, the LORD! The *M* One, God
22: 22 "The *M* One, God, the LORD!
Jdg 5: 13 came to me with the *m*.
5: 22 galloping, galloping go his *m* steeds
5: 23 to help the LORD against the *m*.'
6: 12 "The LORD is with you, *m* warrior
11: 1 the Gileadite was a *m* warrior.
1Sa 4: 8 us from the hand of these *m* gods?
14: 52 and whenever Saul saw a *m*
2Sa 1: 19 How the *m* have fallen!
1: 21 the shield of the *m* was defiled,
1: 22 from the flesh of the *m*,
1: 25 "How the *m* have fallen in battle!
1: 27 "How the *m* have fallen!
20: 7 and all the *m* warriors went out
23: 8 the names of David's *m* men:
23: 9 As one of the three *m* men,
23: 16 So the three *m* men broke
23: 17 the exploits of the three *m* men.
2Sa 23: 22 as famous as the three *m* men.
1Ki 8: 42 and your *m* hand and your
2Ki 17: 36 out of Egypt with *m* power
1Ch 1: 10 grew to be a *m* warrior on earth.
11: 10 the chiefs of David's *m* men—
11: 11 this is the list of David's *m* men:
11: 12 one of the three *m* men.
11: 19 the exploits of the three *m* men.
11: 24 as famous as the three *m* men.
11: 26 *m* men were: Asahel the brother
12: 4 a *m* man among the Thirty,
12: 22 until he had a great and *m* army.
27: 6 was the Benaiah who was a *m* man
28: 1 *m* men and all the brave warriors.
29: 24 All the officers and *m* men,
2Ch 6: 32 and your *m* hand and your
14: 11 to help the powerless against the *m*
16: 8 and Libyans a *m* army
Ne 1: 10 great strength and your *m* hand.
9: 11 like a stone into *m* waters.
9: 32 the great, *m* and awesome God,
Job 1: 19 when suddenly a *m* wind swept
9: 19 If it is a matter of strength, he is *m*!
12: 21 and disarms the *m*.
24: 22 God drags away the *m*
34: 17 you condemn the just and *m* One?
34: 20 the *m* are removed
34: 24 Without inquiry he shatters the *m*
36: 5 God is *m*, but does not despise men
36: 5 he is *m*, and firm in his purpose.
36: 19 or even all your *m* efforts
37: 6 rain shower, 'Be a *m* downpour.'
41: 25 he rises up, the *m* are terrified;
Ps 24: 8 The LORD strong and *m*,
24: 8 the LORD *m* in battle.
29: 1 Ascribe to the LORD, O *m* ones,
29: 3 thunders over the *m* waters.
32: 6 surely when the *m* waters rise,
36: 6 is like the *m* mountains,
45: 3 upon your side, O *m* one;
50: 1 The *M* One, God, the LORD,
52: 1 boast of evil, you *m* man?
62: 7 he is my *m* rock, my refuge.
68: 33 who thunders with *m* voice.
71: 16 proclaim your *m* acts,
77: 12 and consider all your *m* deeds.
77: 15 With your *m* arm you redeemed
77: 19 your way through the *m* waters,
80: 10 the *m* cedars with its branches.
89: 8 You are *m*, O LORD,
93: 4 the LORD on high is *m*.
99: 4 The King is *m*, he loves justice—
103: 20 you *m* ones who do his bidding,
106: 2 Who can proclaim the *m* acts
106: 8 to make his *m* power known.
107: 23 were merchants on the *m* waters.
110: 2 LORD will extend your *m* scepter
112: 2 His children will be *m* in the land;
118: 15 right hand has done *m* things!
118: 16 right hand has done *m* things!"
132: 2 made a vow to the *M* One of Jacob:
132: 5 a dwelling for the *M* One of Jacob
135: 10 and killed *m* kings—
136: 12 with a *m* hand and outstretched
136: 18 and killed *m* kings—
144: 7 me from the *m* waters,
145: 4 they will tell of your *m* acts.
145: 12 all men may know of your *m* acts
147: 5 Great is our Lord and *m* in power;
150: 1 praise him in his *m* heavens.
Pr 7: 26 her slain are a *m* throng.
21: 22 wise man attacks the city of the *m*
30: 30 a lion, *m* among beasts,
SS 8: 6 like a *m* flame.
Isa 1: 24 the *M* One of Israel, declares:
1: 31 The *m* man will become tinder
8: 7 the *m* flood waters of the River—
9: 6 Wonderful Counselor, *M* God,
10: 13 like a *m* one I subdued their kings.
10: 21 will return to the *M* God.
10: 34 Lebanon will fall before the *M* One
22: 17 and hurl you away, O you *m* man.
33: 21 no *m* ship will sail them.
33: 21 the LORD will be our *M* One.
40: 26 of his great power and *m* strength,
42: 13 will march out like a *m* man,
43: 16 a path through the *m* waters,
49: 26 your Redeemer, the *M* One
Isa 56: 11 They are dogs with *m* appetites;
60: 16 your Redeemer, the *M* One
60: 22 the smallest a *m* nation.
62: 8 and by his *m* arm:
63: 1 *m* to save."
Jer 5: 16 all of them are *m* warriors.
10: 6 and your name is *m* in power.
11: 16 But with the roar of a *m* storm
20: 11 with me like a *m* warrior;
21: 5 and a *m* arm in anger and fury
25: 32 a *m* storm is rising
32: 19 your purposes and *m* are your
32: 21 by a *m* hand and an outstretched
48: 17 say, 'How broken is the *m* scepter,
Eze 7: 24 an end to the pride of the *m*,
17: 17 Pharaoh with his *m* army
20: 33 I will rule over you with a *m* hand
20: 34 with a *m* hand and an outstretched
32: 12 fall by the swords of *m* men—
32: 18 and the daughters of *m* nations,
32: 21 the grave the *m* leaders will say
38: 15 on horses, a great horde, a *m* army.
39: 18 You will eat the flesh of *m* men
39: 20 *m* men and soldiers of every kind,'
Da 2: 10 No king, however great and *m*,
4: 3 how *m* his wonders!
4: 30 by my *m* power and for the glory
8: 24 He will destroy the *m* men
9: 15 out of Egypt with a *m* hand
11: 3 Then a *m* king will appear,
Hos 8: 10 under the oppression of the *m* king.
Joel 2: 2 a large and *m* army comes,
2: 5 like a *m* army drawn up for battle.
2: 11 and *m* are those who obey his
Zep 3: 17 he is *m* to save.
Zec 4: 7 "What are you, O *m* mountain?
10: 5 Together they will be like *m* men
10: 7 will become like *m* men,
Mt 26: 64 at the right hand of the *M* One
Mk 14: 62 at the right hand of the *M* One
Lk 1: 49 for the *M* One has done great
1: 51 He has performed *m* deeds
22: 69 at the right hand of the *m* God."
Ac 13: 17 With *m* power he led them out
Eph 1: 19 like the working of his *m* strength,
6: 10 in the Lord and in his *m* power.
1Pe 5: 6 therefore, under God's *m* hand,
Rev 5: 2 And I saw a *m* angel proclaiming
6: 15 the generals, the rich, the *m*,
10: 1 I saw another *m* angel coming
18: 2 With a *m* voice he shouted:
18: 8 for *m* is the Lord God who judges
18: 21 a *m* angel picked up a boulder
19: 18 *m* men, of horses and their riders,

MIGRATION

Jer 8: 7 observe the time of their *m*.

MIGRON

1Sa 14: 2 under a pomegranate tree in *M*.
Isa 10: 28 they pass through *M*;

MIJAMIN

1Ch 24: 9 the sixth to *M*, the seventh
Ezr 10: 25 Izziah, Malkijah, *M*, Eleazar,
Ne 10: 7 Meshullam, Abijah, *M*, Maaziah,
12: 5 Ginnethon, Abijah, *M*, Maadiah,
12: 41 Eliakim, Maaseiah, *M*, Micaiah,

MIKLOTH

1Ch 8: 32 Nadab, Gedor, Ahio, Zeker and *M*,
9: 37 Gedor, Ahio, Zechariah and *M*.
9: 38 *M* was the father of Shimeam.
27: 4 *M* was the leader of his division.

MIKNEIAH

1Ch 15: 18 Mattithiah, Eliphelehu, *M*,
15: 21 Eliphelehu, *M*, Obed-Edom,

MILALAI

Ne 12: 36 Shemaiah, Azarel, *M*, Gilalai,

MILCAH

Ge 11: 29 the father of both *M* and Iscah.
11: 29 the name of Nahor's wife was *M*;
22: 20 time later Abraham was told, "*M* is
22: 23 *M* bore these eight sons
24: 15 the daughter of Bethuel son of *M*,

Ge 24:24 the son that *M* bore to Nahor.''
24:47 of Nahor, whom *M* bore to him.'
Nu 26:33 Noah, Hoglah, *M* and Tirzah.)
27:1 Noah, Hoglah, *M* and Tirzah.
36:11 Tirzah, Hoglah, *M* and Noah—
Jos 17:3 Noah, Hoglah, *M* and Tirzah.

MILDEW

Lev 13:47 clothing is contaminated with *m*—
13:49 it is a spreading *m* and must be
13:50 The priest is to examine the *m*
13:51 if the *m* has spread in the clothing,
13:51 it is a destructive *m;* the article is
13:52 because the *m* is destructive;
13:53 the *m* has not spread
13:55 and if the *m* has not changed its
13:55 the *m* has affected one side
13:56 the *m* has faded after the article has
13:57 whatever has the *m* must be burned
13:58 been washed and is rid of the *m,*
13:59 concerning contamination by *m*
14:34 and I put a spreading *m* in a house
14:35 seen something that looks like *m*
14:36 before he goes in to examine the *m,*
14:37 He is to examine the *m* on the walls
14:39 If the *m* has spread on the walls,
14:43 ''If the *m* reappears in the house
14:44 if the *m* has spread in the house,
14:44 it is a destructive *m;* the house is
14:48 and the *m* has not spread
14:48 house clean, because the *m* is gone.
14:55 for *m* in clothing or in a house,
14:57 for infectious skin diseases and *m.*
Dt 28:22 and *m,* which will plague you
1Ki 8:37 or blight or *m,* locusts
2Ch 6:28 or blight or *m,* locusts
Am 4:9 I struck them with blight and *m.*
Hag 2:17 *m* and hail, yet you did not turn

MILE (MILES)

Mt 5:41 If someone forces you to go one *m,*

MILES (MILE)

Mt 5:41 to go one mile, go with him two *m.*
Lk 24:13 about seven *m* from Jerusalem.
Jn 6:19 rowed three or three and a half *m,*
11:18 less than two *m* from Jerusalem,

MILETUS

Ac 20:15 on the following day arrived at *M.*
20:17 From *M,* Paul sent to Ephesus
2Ti 4:20 and I left Trophimus sick in *M.*

MILITARY

Jos 5:4 of Egypt—all the men of *m* age—
5:6 until all the men who were of *m* age
2Sa 5:2 Israel on their *m* campaigns.
20:8 Joab was wearing his *m* tunic,
1Ki 22:45 he achieved and his *m* exploits,
2Ki 14:28 all he did, and his *m* achievements,
18:20 have strategy and *m* strength—
1Ch 5:18 men ready for *m* service—
11:2 Israel on their *m* campaigns.
2Ch 25:5 thousand men ready for *m* service,
32:3 *m* staff about blocking off the water
32:6 He appointed *m* officers
33:14 He stationed *m* commanders
Est 1:3 The *m* leaders of Persia and Media,
Isa 36:5 have strategy and *m* strength—
Mk 6:21 *m* commanders and the leading

MILK

Ge 18:8 He then brought some curds and *m*
49:12 his teeth whiter than *m.*
Ex 3:8 a land flowing with *m* and honey—
3:17 a land flowing with *m* and honey.'
13:5 a land flowing with *m* and honey—
23:19 a young goat in its mother's *m.*
33:3 Go up to the land flowing with *m*
34:26 goat in its mother's *m.*''
Lev 20:24 a land flowing with *m* and honey.''
Nu 13:27 and it does flow with *m* and honey!
14:8 a land flowing with *m* and honey,
16:13 out of a land flowing with *m*
16:14 us into a land flowing with *m*
Dt 6:3 greatly in a land flowing with *m*
11:9 a land flowing with *m* and honey.
14:21 a young goat in its mother's *m.*
Dt 26:9 a land flowing with *m* and honey;
26:15 a land flowing with *m* and honey.''
27:3 a land flowing with *m* and honey,
31:20 them into the land flowing with *m*
32:14 with curds and *m* from herd
Jos 5:6 a land flowing with *m* and honey.
Jdg 4:19 a skin of *m,* gave him a drink,
5:25 for water, and she gave him *m;*
5:25 nobles she brought him curdled *m.*
2Sa 17:29 and cheese from cows' *m* for David
Job 10:10 Did you not pour me out like *m*
Pr 27:27 You will have plenty of goats' *m*
30:33 as churning the *m* produces butter,
SS 4:11 *m* and honey are under your
5:1 I have drunk my wine and my *m.*
5:12 washed in *m,*
Isa 7:22 the abundance of the *m* they give,
28:9 To children weaned from their *m,*
55:1 Come, buy wine and *m*
60:16 You will drink the *m* of nations
Jer 11:5 to give them a land flowing with *m*
32:22 a land flowing with *m* and honey.
La 4:7 and whiter than *m,*
Eze 20:6 a land flowing with *m* and honey,
20:15 a land flowing with *m* and honey,
25:4 eat your fruit and drink your *m.*
Joel 3:18 and the hills will flow with *m;*
1Co 3:2 I gave you *m,* not solid food,
9:7 and does not drink of the *m?*
Heb 5:12 You need *m,* not solid food!
5:13 lives on *m,* being still an infant,
1Pe 2:2 babies, crave pure spiritual *m,*

MILL (HANDMILL)

Ex 11:5 at her hand *m,* and all the firstborn
Joel 1:18 The herds *m* about
Mt 24:41 will be grinding with a hand *m;*

MILLET

Eze 4:9 beans and lentils, *m* and spelt;

MILLION

1Ch 21:5 there were one *m* one hundred
22:14 a *m* talents of silver, quantities
Rev 9:16 troops was two hundred *m.*

MILLSTONE (STONE)

Jdg 9:53 a woman dropped an upper *m*
2Sa 11:21 Didn't a woman throw an upper *m*
Job 41:24 hard as a lower *m.*
Mt 18:6 him to have a large *m* hung
Mk 9:42 with a large *m* tied around his neck
Lk 17:2 sea with a *m* tied around his neck
Rev 18:21 up a boulder the size of a large *m*
18:22 The sound of a *m*

MILLSTONES (STONE)

Dt 24:6 Do not take a pair of *m*— not
Isa 47:2 Take *m* and grind flour;
Jer 25:10 the sound of *m* and the light
La 5:13 Young men toil at the *m;*

MINA (MINAS)

Eze 45:12 plus fifteen shekels equal one *m.*
Lk 19:16 'Sir, your *m* has earned ten more.'
19:18 'Sir, your *m* has earned five more.'
19:20 and said, 'Sir, here is your *m;*
19:24 'Take his *m* away from him

MINAS (MINA)

1Ki 10:17 with three *m* of gold in each shield.
Ezr 2:69 *m* of silver and 100 priestly
Ne 7:71 of gold and 2,200 *m* of silver.
7:72 *m* of silver and 67 garments
Lk 19:13 his servants and gave them ten *m.*
19:24 give it to the one who has ten *m.*'

MINCING

Isa 3:16 tripping along with *m* steps,

MIND (DOUBLE-MINDED LIKE-MINDED MINDED MINDFUL MINDS)

Ge 37:11 but his father kept the matter in *m.*
41:8 In the morning his *m* was troubled,
45:20 Never *m* about your belongings,
Ex 16:29 in *m* that the LORD has given you
Nu 23:19 that he should change his *m.*
Dt 28:28 blindness and confusion of *m.*
Dt 28:65 LORD will give you an anxious *m,*
29:4 not given you a *m* that understands
1Sa 2:35 to what is in my heart and *m.*
14:7 ''Do all that you have in *m,*''
15:29 Israel does not lie or change his *m;*
15:29 that he should change his *m.*''
2Sa 7:3 ''Whatever you have in *m,*
19:19 May the king put it out of his *m.*
1Ki 10:2 about all that she had on her *m.*
2Ki 10:30 house of Ahab all I had in *m* to do,
24:1 But then he changed his *m*
1Ch 12:38 also of one *m* to make David king.
17:2 ''Whatever you have in *m,* do it,
28:9 devotion and with a willing *m,*
28:12 put in his *m* for the courts
2Ch 7:11 had in *m* to do in the temple
9:1 him about all she had on her *m.*
30:12 the people to give them unity of *m*
Ne 5:7 I pondered them in my *m*
Job 10:13 and I know that this was in your *m:*
12:3 But I have a *m* as well as you;
38:36 or gave understanding to the *m?*
Ps 26:2 examine my heart and my *m;*
64:6 Surely the *m* and heart
83:5 With one *m* they plot together;
110:4 and will not change his *m:*
Pr 23:33 your *m* imagine confusing things.
Ecc 2:3 my *m* still guiding me with wisdom
2:23 even at night his *m* does not rest.
7:25 So I turned my *m* to understand,
8:9 I applied my *m* to everything done
8:16 When I applied my *m*
Isa 10:7 this is not what he has in *m;*
26:3 him whose *m* is steadfast,
32:4 The *m* of the rash will know
32:6 his *m* is busy with evil:
46:8 ''Remember this, fix it in *m,*
65:17 nor will they come to *m.*
Jer 7:31 command nor did it enter my *m.*
11:20 and test the heart and *m,*
17:10 and examine the *m,*
19:5 or mention, nor did it enter my *m.*
20:12 and probe the heart and *m,*
32:35 nor did it enter my *m,*
La 3:21 Yet this I call to *m*
Eze 11:5 what is going through your *m.*
20:32 have in *m* will never happen.
21:24 have brought to *m* your guilt
38:10 thoughts will come into your *m*
Da 2:1 his *m* was troubled and he could
2:28 visions that passed through your *m*
2:29 your *m* turned to things to come,
2:30 what went through your *m.*
4:5 passed through my *m* terrified me.
4:16 Let his *m* be changed from that
4:16 let him be given the *m* of an animal
5:12 was found to have a keen *m*
5:21 and given the *m* of an animal;
7:1 and visions passed through his *m*
7:15 through my *m* disturbed me.
10:12 the first day that you set your *m*
Mt 1:19 he had in *m* to divorce her quietly.
16:23 have in *m* the things of God,
21:29 later he changed his *m* and went.
22:37 all your soul and with all your *m.*'
Mk 3:21 for they said, ''He is out of his *m.*''
5:15 dressed and in his right *m;*
8:33 have in *m* the things of God,
12:30 with all your *m* and with all your
Lk 8:35 dressed and in his right *m;*
10:27 your strength and with all your *m*';
21:14 But make up your *m* not
Jn 6:6 had in *m* what he was going
15:18 keep in *m* that it hated me first.
Ac 4:32 believers were one in heart and *m.*
12:15 out of your *m,*'' they told her.
26:24 ''You are out of your *m,* Paul!''
Ro 1:28 he gave them over to a depraved *m*
7:23 war against the law of my *m*
7:25 I myself in my *m* am a slave
8:6 The *m* of sinful man is death,
8:6 the *m* controlled by the Spirit is life
8:7 the sinful *m* is hostile to God.
8:27 searches our hearts knows the *m*
11:34 Who has known the *m* of the Lord?
12:2 by the renewing of your *m.*
14:5 be fully convinced in his own *m.*
14:13 make up your *m* not

1Co 1: 10 you may be perfectly united in *m*
2: 9 no *m* has conceived
2: 16 But we have the *m* of Christ.
2: 16 "For who has known the *m*
7: 37 and who has made up his *m* not
7: 37 has settled the matter in his own *m*,
14: 14 spirit prays, but my *m* is unfruitful.
14: 15 but I will also pray with my *m*;
14: 15 but I will also sing with my *m*.
14: 23 not say that you are out of your *m*?
2Co 2: 1 I made up my *m* that I would not
2: 13 I still had no peace of *m*,
5: 13 if we are in our right *m*, it is for you
5: 13 out of our *m*, it is for the sake
11: 23 (I am out of my *m* to talk like this.)
13: 11 be of one *m*, live in peace.
Eph 6: 18 With this in *m*, be alert
Php 3: 19 Their *m* is on earthly things.
Col 2: 18 and his unspiritual *m* puffs him up
1Th 4: 11 to *m* your own business
2Th 1: 11 With this in *m*, we constantly pray
1Ti 6: 5 friction between men of corrupt *m*,
Heb 7: 21 and will not change his *m*:
12: 17 could bring about no change of *m*,
2Pe 3: 15 Bear in *m* that our Lord's patience
Rev 17: 9 "This calls for a *m* with wisdom.

MINDED (MIND)

1Pe 4: 7 be clear *m* and self-controlled

MINDFUL (MIND)

Ps 8: 4 what is man that you are *m* of him,
Lk 1: 48 God my Savior, for he has been *m*
Heb 2: 6 What is man that you are *m* of him,

MINDS (MIND)

Ex 13: 17 they might change their *m*
14: 5 changed their *m* about them
Dt 11: 18 of mine in your hearts and *m*;
Job 17: 4 You have closed their *m*
Ps 7: 9 who searches *m* and hearts,
73: 7 of their *m* know no limits.
Pr 12: 8 men with warped *m* are despised.
Isa 44: 18 and their *m* closed so they cannot
Jer 3: 16 It will never enter their *m*
14: 14 and the delusions of their own *m*.
23: 16 visions from their own *m*,
23: 26 the delusions of their own *m*?
31: 33 "I will put my law in their *m*
34: 11 afterward they changed their *m*
Lk 24: 38 and why do doubts rise in your *m*?
24: 45 Then he opened their *m*
Ac 14: 2 their *m* against the brothers.
15: 24 troubling your *m* by what they said
28: 6 they changed their *m* and said he
Ro 8: 5 to the sinful nature have their *m* set
8: 5 with the Spirit have their *m* set
16: 18 and flattery they deceive the *m*
2Co 3: 14 But their *m* were made dull,
4: 4 god of this age has blinded the *m*
11: 3 your *m* may somehow be led astray
Eph 4: 23 new in the attitude of your *m*;
Php 4: 7 and your *m* in Christ Jesus.
Col 1: 21 and were enemies in your *m*
3: 2 Set your *m* on things above,
2Ti 3: 8 men of depraved *m*, who, as far
Tit 1: 15 both their *m* and consciences are
Heb 8: 10 I will put my laws in their *m*
10: 16 and I will write them on their *m*."
1Pe 1: 13 prepare your *m* for action;
Rev 2: 23 I am he who searches hearts and *m*,

MINE

Job 28: 1 "There is a *m* for silver

MINGLE (MINGLED)

Ps 102: 9 and *m* my drink with tears

MINGLED (MINGLE)

Ezr 9: 2 and have *m* the holy race
Ps 106: 35 but they *m* with the nations

MINIAMIN (MINIAMIN'S)

2Ch 31: 15 Eden, *M*, Jeshua, Shemaiah,

MINIAMIN'S (MINIAMIN)

Ne 12: 17 Zicri; of *M* and of Maadiah's,

MINISTER (MINISTERED MINISTERING MINISTERS MINISTRY)

Ex 28: 43 or approach the altar to *m*
29: 30 Meeting to *m* in the Holy Place is
30: 20 altar to *m* by presenting an offering
Nu 16: 9 stand before the community and *m*
18: 2 and your sons *m* before the Tent
Dt 10: 8 to stand before the LORD to *m*
18: 5 *m* in the LORD's name always.
18: 7 he may *m* in the name
21: 5 your God has chosen them to *m*
1Sa 2: 30 and your father's house would *m*
2: 35 he will *m* before my anointed one
1Ch 15: 2 and to *m* before him forever."
16: 4 of the Levites to *m* before the ark
16: 37 of the LORD to *m* there regularly,
16: 38 and his sixty-eight associates to *m*
23: 13 *m* before him and to pronounce
2Ch 29: 11 *m* before him and to burn incense."
31: 2 and fellowship offerings, to *m*,
Ps 101: 6 will *m* to me.
134: 1 who *m* by night in the house
135: 2 you who *m* in the house
Jer 33: 22 and the Levites who *m* before me
Eze 40: 46 near to the LORD to *m* before him
42: 14 the garments in which they *m*,
43: 19 who come near to *m* before me,
44: 15 are to come near to *m* before me;
44: 16 come near my table to *m* before me
44: 27 sanctuary to *m* in the sanctuary,
45: 4 draw near to *m* before the LORD.
45: 4 who *m* in the sanctuary
46: 24 the kitchens where those who *m*
Joel 1: 9 those who *m* before the LORD.
1: 13 wail, you who *m* before the altar.
1: 13 you who *m* before my God;
2: 17 who *m* before the LORD,
Ro 15: 16 me to be a *m* of Christ Jesus
Col 1: 7 who is a faithful *m* of Christ
4: 7 a faithful *m* and fellow servant
1Ti 4: 6 you will be a good *m*
Heb 13: 10 an altar from which those who *m*

MINISTERED (MINISTER)

1Sa 2: 11 but the boy *m* before the LORD
3: 1 The boy Samuel *m*
1Ch 6: 32 They *m* with music

MINISTERING (MINISTER)

Ex 35: 19 worn for *m* in the sanctuary—
39: 1 garments for *m* in the sanctuary.
39: 26 hem of the robe to be worn for *m*,
39: 41 worn for *m* in the sanctuary,
Nu 3: 31 articles of the sanctuary used in *m*,
4: 12 used for *m* in the sanctuary,
4: 14 on it all the utensils used for *m*
Dt 17: 12 for the priest who stands *m* there
Jdg 20: 28 the son of Aaron, *m* before it.)
1Sa 2: 18 Samuel was *m* before the LORD—
1Ch 9: 13 responsible for *m* in the house
24: 3 for their appointed order of *m*.
24: 19 of *m* when they entered the temple
26: 12 had duties for *m* in the temple
Ezr 2: 63 food until there was a priest *m*
Ne 7: 65 until there should be a priest *m*
10: 36 of our God, to the priests *m* there.
10: 39 are kept and where the *m* priests,
12: 44 pleased with the *m* priests
Jer 33: 21 with the Levites who are priests *m*
Eze 44: 17 garment while *m* at the gates
44: 19 off the clothes they have been *m* in
Heb 1: 14 Are not all angels *m* spirits sent

MINISTERS (MINISTER)

Ex 28: 35 Aaron must wear it when he *m*.
2Ki 10: 19 all his *m* and all his priests.
10: 19 in order to destroy the *m* of Baal.
10: 21 and all the *m* of Baal came;
10: 22 "Bring robes for all the *m* of Baal."
10: 23 Jehu said to the *m* of Baal,
10: 23 here with you—only *m* of Baal."
Isa 61: 6 you will be named *m* of our God.
2Co 3: 6 as *m* of a new covenant—

MINISTRY (MINISTER)

1Ch 25: 1 Jeduthun for the *m* of prophesying,
25: 6 for the *m* at the house of God.
Lk 3: 23 old when he began his *m*.
Ac 1: 17 of our number and shared in this *m*
1: 25 to take over this apostolic *m*,
6: 2 for us to neglect the *m* of the word
6: 4 to prayer and the *m* of the word."
8: 21 You have no part or share in this *m*
21: 19 among the Gentiles through his *m*.
Ro 11: 13 I make much of my *m*
2Co 3: 3 the result of our *m*, written not
3: 7 Now if the *m* that brought death,
3: 8 will not the *m* of the Spirit be
3: 9 If the *m* that condemns men is
3: 9 glorious is the *m* that brings
4: 1 God's mercy we have this *m*,
5: 18 gave us the *m* of reconciliation:
6: 3 so that our *m* will not be
Gal 2: 8 was also at work in my *m*
2: 8 who was at work in the *m* of Peter
2Ti 4: 5 discharge all the duties of your *m*.
4: 11 because he is helpful to me in my *m*
Heb 8: 6 But the *m* Jesus has received is
9: 6 room to carry on their *m*.

MINNI

Jer 51: 27 Ararat, *M* and Ashkenaz.

MINNITH

Jdg 11: 33 from Aroer to the vicinity of *M*,
Eze 27: 17 they exchanged wheat from *M*

MINT

Mt 23: 23 a tenth of your spices—*m*,
Lk 11: 42 you give God a tenth of your *m*,

MINUS

2Co 11: 24 the Jews the forty lashes *m* one.

MIRACLE (MIRACLES MIRACULOUS)

Ex 7: 9 'Perform a *m*,' then say to Aaron,
Mk 9: 39 "No one who does a *m*
Lk 23: 8 hoped to see him perform some *m*.
Jn 7: 21 "I did one *m*, and you are all
Ac 4: 16 they have done an outstanding *m*.

MIRACLES (MIRACLE)

1Ch 16: 12 his *m*, and the judgments he
Ne 9: 17 to remember the *m* you performed
Job 5: 9 *m* that cannot be counted.
9: 10 *m* that cannot be numbered.
Ps 77: 11 I will remember your *m* of long ago
77: 14 You are the God who performs *m*;
78: 12 He did *m* in the sight
105: 5 his *m*, and the judgments he
106: 7 they gave no thought to your *m*;
106: 22 *m* in the land of Ham
Mt 7: 22 out demons and perform many *m*?'
11: 20 most of his *m* had been performed,
11: 21 If the *m* that were performed
11: 23 If the *m* that were performed
13: 58 And he did not do many *m* there
24: 24 and perform great signs and *m*
Mk 6: 2 does *m*! Isn't this the carpenter?
6: 5 He could not do any *m* there,
13: 22 and *m* to deceive the elect—
Lk 10: 13 For if the *m* that were performed
19: 37 for all the *m* they had seen:
Jn 7: 3 disciples may see the *m* you do.
10: 25 *m* I do in my Father's name speak
10: 32 "I have shown you many great *m*
10: 38 do not believe me, believe the *m*,
14: 11 the evidence of the *m* themselves.
15: 24 But now they have seen these *m*,
Ac 2: 22 accredited by God to you by *m*,
8: 13 by the great signs and *m* he saw.
19: 11 God did extraordinary *m*
Ro 15: 19 by the power of signs and *m*,
1Co 12: 28 third teachers, then workers of *m*,
12: 29 Are all teachers? Do all work *m*?
2Co 12: 12 and *m*— were done among you
Gal 3: 5 work *m* among you because you
2Th 2: 9 in all kinds of counterfeit *m*,
Heb 2: 4 it by signs, wonders and various *m*,

MIRACULOUS (MIRACLE)

Ex 4: 8 or pay attention to the first *m* sign,
4: 17 so you can perform *m* signs with it
4: 28 also about all the *m* signs he had
7: 3 and though I multiply my *m* signs
8: 23 This *m* sign will occur tomorrow

Ex 10: 1 that I may perform these *m* signs
Nu 14: 11 of all the *m* signs I have performed
14: 22 the *m* signs I performed in Egypt
Dt 4: 34 by testings, by *m* signs
6: 22 our eyes the LORD sent *m* signs
7: 19 *m* signs and wonders, the mighty
13: 1 and announces to you a *m* sign
26: 8 and with *m* signs and wonders.
29: 3 those *m* signs and great wonders.
34: 11 who did all those *m* signs
2Ch 32: 24 him and gave him a *m* sign.
32: 31 ask him about the *m* sign that had
Ne 9: 10 You sent *m* signs and wonders
Ps 74: 9 We are given no *m* signs;
78: 43 the day he displayed his *m* signs
105: 27 They performed his *m* signs
Jer 32: 20 You performed *m* signs
Da 4: 2 to tell you about the *m* signs
Mt 12: 38 we want to see a *m* sign from you."
12: 39 generation asks for a *m* sign!
13: 54 this wisdom and these *m* powers?"
14: 2 That is why *m* powers are at work
16: 4 generation looks for a *m* sign,
Mk 6: 14 that is why *m* powers are at work
8: 12 this generation ask for a *m* sign?
Lk 11: 29 for a *m* sign, but none will be given
Jn 2: 11 This, the first of his *m* signs,
2: 18 "What *m* sign can you show us
2: 23 people saw the *m* signs he was
3: 2 could perform the *m* signs you are
4: 48 "Unless you people see *m* signs
4: 54 was the second *m* sign that Jesus
6: 2 they saw the *m* signs he had
6: 14 people saw the *m* sign that Jesus
6: 26 not because you saw *m* signs but
6: 30 "What *m* sign then will you give
7: 31 will he do more *m* signs
9: 16 "How can a sinner do such *m* signs
10: 41 John never performed a *m* sign,
11: 47 this man performing many *m* signs.
12: 18 heard that he had given this *m* sign,
12: 37 Jesus had done all these *m* signs
20: 30 Jesus did many other *m* signs
Ac 2: 43 *m* signs were done by the apostles.
4: 30 hand to heal and perform *m* signs
5: 12 apostles performed many *m* signs
6: 8 and *m* signs among the people.
7: 36 did wonders and *m* signs in Egypt,
8: 6 and saw the *m* signs he did,
14: 3 by enabling them to do *m* signs
15: 12 and Paul telling about the *m* signs
1Co 1: 22 Jews demand *m* signs and Greeks
12: 10 to another *m* powers,
Rev 13: 13 he performed great and *m* signs,
16: 14 of demons performing *m* signs,
19: 20 who had performed the *m* signs

MIRE (MIRY)

Ps 40: 2 out of the mud and *m;*
69: 14 Rescue me from the *m,*
Isa 57: 20 whose waves cast up *m* and mud.
Mic 7: 10 like *m* in the streets.

MIRIAM

Ex 15: 20 *M* the prophetess, Aaron's sister,
15: 21 *M* sang to them:
Nu 12: 1 *M* and Aaron began to talk
12: 4 and *M,* "Come out to the Tent
12: 5 and summoned Aaron and *M.*
12: 10 there stood *M*— leprous, like snow
12: 15 *M* was confined outside the camp
20: 1 There *M* died and was buried.
26: 59 Aaron, Moses and their sister *M.*
Dt 24: 9 did to *M* along the way
1Ch 4: 17 of Mered's wives gave birth to *M,*
6: 3 of Amram: Aaron, Moses and *M.*
Mic 6: 4 also Aaron and *M.*

MIRMAH

1Ch 8: 10 Malcam, Jeuz, Sakia and *M.*

MIRROR (MIRRORS)

Job 37: 18 hard as a *m* of cast bronze?
Jas 1: 23 a man who looks at his face in a *m*

MIRRORS (MIRROR)

Ex 38: 8 and its bronze stand from the *m*
Isa 3: 23 and *m,* and the linen garments

MIRTH

Job 20: 5 that the *m* of the wicked is brief,

MIRY (MIRE)

Ps 69: 2 I sink in the *m* depths,
140: 10 into *m* pits, never to rise.

MISCARRIED (MISCARRY)

Ge 31: 38 Your sheep and goats have not *m,*

MISCARRY (MISCARRIED)

Ex 23: 26 and none will *m* or be barren
Job 21: 10 their cows calve and do not *m.*
Hos 9: 14 Give them wombs that *m*

MISDEEDS

Ps 99: 8 though you punished their *m.*
Ro 8: 13 put to death the *m* of the body,

MISDEMEANOR

Ac 18: 14 making a complaint about some *m*

MISERABLE (MISERY)

Nu 21: 5 And we detest this *m* food!"
Jdg 11: 35 You have made me *m*
Job 16: 2 *m* comforters are you all!
Ecc 4: 8 a *m* business!
Gal 4: 9 to those weak and *m* principles?

MISERY (MISERABLE)

Ge 16: 11 for the LORD has heard of your *m.*
29: 32 because the LORD has seen my *m.*
44: 29 head down to the grave in *m.*'
44: 34 let me see the *m* that would come
Ex 3: 7 "I have indeed seen the *m*
3: 17 of your *m* in Egypt into the land
4: 31 about them and had seen their *m,*
Nu 23: 21 no *m* observed in Israel.
Dt 26: 7 heard our voice and saw our *m,*
Jdg 10: 16 he could bear Israel's *m* no longer.
1Sa 1: 11 look upon your servant's *m*
Job 3: 20 "Why is light given to those in *m,*
6: 2 all my *m* be placed on the scales!
7: 3 and nights of *m* have been assigned
9: 18 but would overwhelm me with *m.*
20: 22 the full force of *m* will come
Ps 44: 24 and forget our *m* and oppression?
94: 20 one that brings on *m* by its decrees
Pr 31: 7 and remember their *m* no more.
Ecc 8: 6 a man's *m* weighs heavily
Hos 5: 15 in their *m* they will earnestly seek
Mic 7: 1 What *m* is mine!
Ro 3: 16 ruin and *m* mark their ways,
Jas 5: 1 of the *m* that is coming upon you.

MISFORTUNE

Nu 23: 21 "No *m* is seen in Jacob,
Ru 1: 21 the Almighty has brought *m*
1Ch 7: 23 there had been *m* in his family.
Job 12: 5 Men at ease have contempt for *m*
31: 29 I have rejoiced at my enemy's *m*
Pr 13: 21 *M* pursues the sinner,
Ecc 2: 21 too is meaningless and a great *m.*
5: 14 or wealth lost through some *m,*
Isa 65: 23 or bear children doomed to *m;*
Ob : 12 brother in the day of his *m,*

MISHAEL

Ex 6: 22 The sons of Uzziel were *M,*
Lev 10: 4 Moses summoned *M* and Elzaphan
Ne 8: 4 *M,* Malkijah, Hashum,
Da 1: 6 Daniel, Hananiah, *M* and Azariah.
1: 7 Shadrach; to *M,* Meshach;
1: 11 Hananiah, *M* and Azariah,
1: 19 Hananiah, *M* and Azariah;
2: 17 matter to his friends Hananiah, *M*

MISHAL

Jos 19: 26 Allammelech, Amad and *M.*
21: 30 *M,* Abdon, Helkath and Rehob,

MISHAM

1Ch 8: 12 The sons of Elpaal: Eber, *M,*

MISHMA

Ge 25: 14 Adbeel, Mibsam, *M,* Dumah,
1Ch 1: 30 Adbeel, Mibsam, *M,* Dumah,
4: 25 Mibsam his son and *M* his son.
1Ch 4: 26 of *M:* Hammuel his son,

MISHMANNAH

1Ch 12: 10 Eliab the third, *M* the fourth,

MISHRAITES

1Ch 2: 53 Puthites, Shumathites and *M.*

MISLEAD (MISLEADING MISLEADS MISLED)

2Ki 4: 16 "Don't *m* your servant, O man
2Ch 32: 15 deceive you and *m* you like this.
Isa 9: 16 who guide this people *m* them,
36: 18 "Do not let Hezekiah *m* you
47: 10 wisdom and knowledge *m* you

MISLEADING (MISLEAD)

2Ki 18: 32 for he is *m* you when he says,
2Ch 32: 11 he is *m* you, to let you die
La 2: 14 were false and *m.*
Da 2: 9 You have conspired to tell me *m*

MISLEADS (MISLEAD)

Isa 44: 20 on ashes, a deluded heart *m* him;
Rev 2: 20 By her teaching she *m* my servants

MISLED (MISLEAD)

Jer 38: 22 They *m* you and overcame you—
1Co 15: 33 Do not be *m:* "Bad company

MISPAR

Ezr 2: 2 Mordecai, Bilshan, *M,* Bigvai,

MISPERETH

Ne 7: 7 Mordecai, Bilshan, *M,* Bigvai,

MISREPHOTH MAIM

Jos 11: 8 to *M,* and to the Valley of Mizpah
13: 6 regions from Lebanon to *M,*

MISS (MISSED MISSES MISSING)

Jdg 20: 16 a stone at a hair and not *m.*
Pr 19: 2 nor to be hasty and *m* the way.

MISSED (MISS)

1Sa 20: 18 You will be *m,* because your seat
Jer 3: 16 it will not be *m,* nor will another
46: 17 he has *m* his opportunity.'

MISSES (MISS)

1Sa 20: 6 If your father *m* me at all, tell him,
Heb 12: 15 See to it that no one *m* the grace

MISSING (MISS)

Nu 31: 49 our command, and not one is *m.*
Jdg 21: 3 Why should one tribe be *m*
1Sa 25: 7 at Carmel nothing of theirs was *m.*
25: 15 fields near them nothing was *m.*
25: 21 desert so that nothing of his was *m.*
30: 19 Nothing was *m:* young or old,
2Sa 2: 30 of David's men were found *m.*
1Ki 20: 39 If he is *m,* it will be your life
2Ki 10: 19 that no one is *m,* because I am
Job 5: 24 your property and find nothing *m.*
Isa 34: 16 None of these will be *m,*
40: 26 not one of them is *m.*
Jer 23: 4 will any be *m,*" declares the LORD

MISSION (MISSIONS)

Jos 22: 3 carried out the *m* the LORD your
1Sa 15: 18 And he sent you on a *m,* saying,
15: 20 on the *m* the LORD assigned me.
21: 2 is to know anything about your *m*
Isa 48: 15 and he will succeed in his *m.*
Ac 12: 25 and Saul had finished their *m,*

MISSIONS (MISSION)

1Sa 21: 5 even on *m* that are not holy.

MIST (MISTS)

Isa 44: 22 your sins like the morning *m.*
Hos 6: 4 Your love is like the morning *m,*
13: 3 they will be like the morning *m,*
Ac 13: 11 Immediately *m* and darkness came
Jas 4: 14 You are a *m* that appears for a little

MISTAKE (MISTAKEN)

Ge 43: 12 Perhaps it was a *m.*
Lev 22: 14 anyone eats a sacred offering by *m,*

Jdg 9:36 "You *m* the shadows
Ecc 5:6 messenger, "My vow was a *m*."
Jer 42:20 you today that you made a fatal *m*

MISTAKEN (MISTAKE)

Mk 12:27 You are badly *m*!" One

MISTREAT (MISTREATED MISTREATING)

Ge 31:50 If you *m* my daughters
Ex 22:21 "Do not *m* an alien or oppress him,
Lev 19:33 you in your land, do not *m* him.
1Sa 25:7 were with us, we did not *m* them,
25:15 They did not *m* us, and the whole
Jer 38:19 over to them and they will *m* me."
Eze 22:29 and needy and *m* the alien,
Lk 6:28 pray for those who *m* you.
Ac 14:5 to *m* them and stone them.

MISTREATED (MISTREAT)

Ge 15:13 and *m* four hundred years.
16:6 Sarai *m* Hagar; so she fled from her
Nu 20:15 Egyptians *m* us and our fathers,
Dt 26:6 But the Egyptians *m* us
Jer 13:22 and your body *m*.
Eze 22:7 *m* the fatherless and the widow.
Mt 22:6 rest seized his servants, *m* them
Ac 7:6 and *m* four hundred years.
7:24 of them being *m* by an Egyptian,
Heb 11:25 to be *m* along with the people
11:37 destitute, persecuted and *m*—
13:3 who are *m* as if you yourselves

MISTREATING (MISTREAT)

Ac 7:27 man who was *m* the other pushed

MISTRESS

Ge 16:4 she began to despise her *m*.
16:8 I'm running away from my *m* Sarai
16:9 "Go back to your *m* and submit
2Ki 5:3 to her *m*, "If only my master would
Ps 123:2 of a maid look to the hand of her *m*,
Pr 30:23 a maidservant who displaces her *m*
Isa 24:2 for *m* as for maid,
Na 3:4 alluring, the *m* of sorceries,

MISTS (MIST)

2Pe 2:17 without water and *m* driven

MISUNDERSTAND

Dt 32:27 lest the adversary *m*

MISUSE (MISUSES)

Ex 20:7 "You shall not *m* the name
Dt 5:11 "You shall not *m* the name
Ps 139:20 your adversaries *m* your name.

MISUSES (MISUSE)

Ex 20:7 anyone guiltless who *m* his name.
Dt 5:11 anyone guiltless who *m* his name.

MITHCAH

Nu 33:28 They left Terah and camped at *M*.
33:29 They left *M* and camped

MITHNITE

1Ch 11:43 Joshaphat the *M*, Uzzia

MITHREDATH

Ezr 1:8 brought by *M* the treasurer,
4:7 king of Persia, Bishlam, *M*,

MITYLENE

Ac 20:14 took him aboard and went on to *M*.

MIX (MIXED MIXES MIXING MIXTURE WELL-MIXED)

Rev 18:6 *M* her a double portion

MIXED (MIX)

Ex 29:2 make bread, and cakes *m* with oil,
29:40 ephah of fine flour *m* with a fourth
Lev 2:4 made without yeast and *m* with oil,
2:5 to be made of fine flour *m* with oil,
7:10 whether *m* with oil or dry,
7:12 made without yeast and *m* with oil,
7:12 of fine flour well-kneaded and *m*
9:4 with a grain offering *m* with oil.
14:10 of an ephah of fine flour *m* with oil
Lev 14:21 of an ephah of fine flour *m* with oil
23:13 of an ephah of fine flour *m* with oil
Nu 6:15 cakes made of fine flour *m* with oil,
7:13 filled with fine flour *m* with oil
7:19 filled with fine flour *m* with oil
7:25 filled with fine flour *m* with oil
7:31 filled with fine flour *m* with oil
7:37 filled with fine flour *m* with oil
7:43 filled with fine flour *m* with oil
7:49 filled with fine flour *m* with oil
7:55 filled with fine flour *m* with oil
7:61 filled with fine flour *m* with oil
7:67 filled with fine flour *m* with oil
7:73 filled with fine flour *m* with oil
7:79 filled with fine flour *m* with oil
8:8 offering of fine flour *m* with oil;
15:4 ephah of fine flour *m* with a fourth
15:6 ephah of fine flour *m* with a third
15:9 of fine flour *m* with half a hin
28:5 ephah of fine flour *m* with a fourth
28:9 of an ephah of fine flour *m* with oil.
28:12 of an ephah of fine flour *m* with oil;
28:12 of an ephah of fine flour *m* with oil;
28:13 of an ephah of fine flour *m* with oil.
28:20 of an ephah of fine flour *m* with oil;
28:28 of an ephah of fine flour *m* with oil;
29:3 of an ephah of fine flour *m* with oil;
29:9 of an ephah of fine flour *m* with oil;
29:14 of an ephah of fine flour *m* with oil;
Ps 75:8 full of foaming wine *m* with spices;
Pr 9:2 prepared her meat and *m* her wine;
9:5 and drink the wine I have *m*.
23:30 who go to sample bowls of *m* wine.
Isa 65:11 fill bowls of *m* wine for Destiny,
Da 2:41 even as you saw iron *m* with clay.
2:43 you saw the iron *m* with baked clay
Mt 13:33 and *m* into a large amount of flour
27:34 *m* with gall; but after tasting it,
Mk 15:23 Then they offered him wine *m*
Lk 13:1 whose blood Pilate had *m*
13:21 and *m* into a large amount of flour
Jude :23 to others show mercy, *m* with fear
Rev 8:7 and there came hail and fire *m*
15:2 a sea of glass *m* with fire

MIXES (MIX)

Da 2:43 any more than iron *m* with clay.
Hos 7:8 "Ephraim *m* with the nations;

MIXING (MIX)

1Ch 9:30 priests took care of *m* the spices.
23:29 wafers, the baking and the *m*,
Isa 5:22 and champions at *m* drinks,
Eze 24:10 *m* in the spices;

MIXTURE (MIX)

Da 2:43 so the people will be a *m*
Jn 19:39 Nicodemus brought a *m* of myrrh

MIZAR

Ps 42:6 of Hermon—from Mount *M*.

MIZPAH

Ge 31:49 also called *M*, because he said,
Jos 11:3 below Hermon in the region of *M*.
11:8 and to the Valley of *M* on the east,
15:38 Dilean, *M*, Joktheel, Lachish,
18:26 Ramah, Beeroth, *M*, Kephirah,
Jdg 10:17 assembled and camped at *M*.
11:11 words before the LORD in *M*.
11:29 passed through *M* of Gilead,
11:34 returned to his home in *M*,
20:1 assembled before the LORD in *M*.
20:3 the Israelites had gone up to *M*.)
21:1 of Israel had taken an oath at *M*:
21:5 at *M* should certainly be put
21:8 to assemble before the LORD at *M*
1Sa 7:5 "Assemble all Israel at *M*
7:6 Samuel was leader of Israel at *M*.
7:6 When they had assembled at *M*,
7:7 that Israel had assembled at *M*,
7:11 The men of Israel rushed out of *M*
7:12 and set it up between *M* and Shen.
7:16 circuit from Bethel to Gilgal to *M*,
10:17 people of Israel to the LORD at *M*
22:3 From there David went to *M*
1Ki 15:22 Geba in Benjamin, and also *M*.
2Ki 25:23 they came to Gedaliah at *M*—
2Ki 25:25 who were with him at *M*.
2Ch 16:6 With them he built up Geba and *M*.
Ne 3:7 by men from Gibeon and *M*—
3:15 ruler of the district of *M*.
3:19 of *M*, repaired another section,
Jer 40:6 to Gedaliah son of Ahikam at *M*
40:8 they came to Gedaliah at *M*—
40:10 stay at *M* to represent you
40:12 at *M*, from all the countries where
40:13 country came to Gedaliah at *M*
40:15 said privately to Gedaliah in *M*,
41:1 to Gedaliah son of Ahikam at *M*.
41:3 were with Gedaliah at *M*,
41:6 out from *M* to meet them,
41:10 rest of the people who were in *M*—
41:14 had taken captive at *M* turned
41:16 from *M* whom he had recovered
Hos 5:1 You have been a snare at *M*,

MIZRAIM

Ge 10:6 Cush, *M*, Put and Canaan.
10:13 *M* was the father of the Ludites,
1Ch 1:8 Cush, *M*, Put and Canaan.
1:11 *M* was the father of the Ludites,

MIZZAH

Ge 36:13 Nahath, Zerah, Shammah and *M*.
36:17 Nahath, Zerah, Shammah and *M*.
1Ch 1:37 Nahath, Zerah, Shammah and *M*.

MNASON

Ac 21:16 and brought us to the home of *M*,

MOAB (MOAB'S MOABITE MOABITES MOABITESS)

Ge 19:37 she named him *M*; he is the father
36:35 Midian in the country of *M*,
Ex 15:15 the leaders of *M* will be seized
Nu 21:11 in the desert that faces *M*
21:13 The Arnon is the border of *M*,
21:13 between *M* and the Amorites.
21:15 and lie along the border of *M*."
21:20 to the valley in *M* where the top
21:26 against the former king of *M*
21:28 It consumed Ar of *M*,
21:29 Woe to you, O *M*!
22:1 traveled to the plains of *M*
22:3 *M* was filled with dread
22:3 *M* was terrified because there were
22:4 who was king of *M* at that time,
22:7 The elders of *M* and Midian left,
22:10 king of *M*, sent me this message:
22:21 and went with the princes of *M*.
23:6 with all the princes of *M*.
23:7 of *M* from the eastern mountains.
23:17 with the princes of *M*.
24:17 He will crush the foreheads of *M*,
26:3 So on the plains of *M* by the Jordan
26:63 on the plains of *M* by the Jordan
31:12 at their camp on the plains of *M*,
33:44 at Iye Abarim, on the border of *M*.
33:48 on the plains of *M* by the Jordan
33:49 on the plains of *M* they camped
33:50 On the plains of *M* by the Jordan
35:1 On the plains of *M* by the Jordan
36:13 on the plains of *M* by the Jordan
Dt 1:5 of the Jordan in the territory of *M*,
2:8 traveled along the desert road of *M*
2:18 to pass by the region of *M* at Ar.
29:1 to make with the Israelites in *M*,
32:49 Range to Mount Nebo in *M*,
34:1 from the plains of *M* to the top
34:5 of the LORD died there in *M*,
34:6 He buried him in *M*, in the valley
34:8 in the plains of *M* thirty days,
Jos 13:32 plains of *M* across the Jordan east
24:9 the king of *M*, prepared to fight
Jdg 3:12 king of *M* power over Israel.
3:14 king of *M* for eighteen years.
3:15 with tribute to Eglon king of *M*.
3:17 the tribute to Eglon king of *M*,
3:28 fords of the Jordan that led to *M*,
3:28 "for the LORD has given *M*,
3:30 That day *M* was made subject
10:6 the gods of Sidon, the gods of *M*,
11:15 Israel did not take the land of *M*
11:17 They sent also to the king of *M*,
11:18 did not enter the territory of *M*,

Jdg 11:18 side of the country of *M*,
11:18 skirted the lands of Edom and *M*,
11:25 than Balak son of Zippor, king of *M*
Ru 1: 1 live for a while in the country of *M*.
1: 2 they went to *M* and lived there.
1: 6 in *M* that the LORD had come
1:22 returned from *M* accompanied
2: 6 back from *M* with Naomi.
4: 3 who has come back from *M*,
1Sa 12: 9 of the Philistines and the king of *M*
14:47 *M*, the Ammonites, Edom,
22: 3 in *M* and said to the king of *M*,
22: 4 So he left them with the king of *M*,
2Sa 8:12 Edom and *M*, the Ammonites
1Ki 11: 7 Chemosh the detestable god of *M*,
2Ki 1: 1 After Ahab's death, *M* rebelled
3: 4 Now Mesha king of *M* raised sheep
3: 5 the king of *M* rebelled
3: 7 go with me to fight against *M*?"
3: 7 "The king of *M* has rebelled
3:10 only to hand us over to *M*?"
3:13 together to hand us over to *M*."
3:18 he will also hand *M* over to you.
3:23 *M*!" But when the Moabites came
3:26 of *M* saw that the battle had gone
23:13 for Chemosh the vile god of *M*,
1Ch 1:46 Midian in the country of *M*,
4:22 ruled in *M* and Jashubi Lehem.
8: 8 Sons were born to Shaharaim in *M*
18:11 Edom and *M*, the Ammonites
2Ch 20:10 now here are men from Ammon, *M*
20:22 and *M* and Mount Seir who were
20:23 and *M* rose up against the men
Ne 13:23 from Ashdod, Ammon and *M*.
Ps 60: 8 *M* is my washbasin,
83: 6 of *M* and the descendants of Hagar
108: 9 *M* is my washbasin,
Isa 11:14 will lay hands on Edom and *M*,
15: 1 An oracle concerning *M*:
15: 1 Ar in *M* is ruined,
15: 1 Kir in *M* is ruined,
15: 2 *M* wails over Nebo and Medeba.
15: 4 the armed men of *M* cry out,
15: 5 My heart cries out over *M*;
15: 8 echoes along the border of *M*;
15: 9 a lion upon the fugitives of *M*
16: 2 so are the women of *M*
16: 7 they wail together for *M*.
16:11 My heart laments for *M* like a harp,
16:12 When *M* appears at her high place,
16:13 has already spoken concerning *M*.
25:10 but *M* will be trampled under him
Jer 9:26 *M* and all who live in the desert
25:21 left at Ashdod); Edom, *M*
27: 3 send word to the kings of Edom, *M*
40:11 When all the Jews in *M*, Ammon,
48: 1 Concerning *M*: This is what
48: 2 *M* will be praised no more;
48: 4 *M* will be broken;
48: 9 Put salt on *M*,
48:11 "*M* has been at rest from youth,
48:13 *M* will be ashamed of Chemosh,
48:15 *M* will be destroyed and her towns
48:16 "The fall of *M* is at hand;
48:18 for he who destroys *M*
48:20 *M* is disgraced for she is shattered.
48:20 that *M* is destroyed.
48:24 to all the towns of *M*, far and near.
48:26 Let *M* wallow in her vomit;
48:28 you who live in *M*.
48:31 Therefore I wail over *M*,
48:31 for all *M* I cry out,
48:33 from the orchards and fields of *M*.
48:35 In *M* I will put an end
48:36 my heart laments for *M* like a flute;
48:38 On all the housetops in *M*
48:38 for I have broken *M*
48:39 How *M* turns her back in shame!
48:39 *M* has become an object of ridicule,
48:40 spreading its wings over *M*.
48:42 *M* will be destroyed as a nation
48:43 O people of *M*,"
48:44 for I will bring upon *M*
48:45 it burns the foreheads of *M*,
48:46 Woe to you, O *M*!
48:47 Here ends the judgment on *M*.
48:47 I will restore the fortunes of *M*
Eze 25: 8 'Because *M* and Seir said, "Look,
25: 9 I will expose the flank of *M*,
25:10 give *M* along with the Ammonites
25:11 and I will inflict punishment on *M*.
Da 11:41 *M* and the leaders
Am 2: 1 "For three sins of *M*,
2: 2 I will send fire upon *M*
2: 2 *M* will go down in great tumult
Mic 6: 5 king of *M* counseled
Zep 2: 8 "I have heard the insults of *M*
2: 9 "surely *M* will become like Sodom,

MOAB'S (MOAB)

2Sa 23:20 He struck down two of *M* best men
1Ch 11:22 He struck down two of *M* best men
Isa 16: 6 We have heard of *M* pride—
16:14 *M* splendor and all her many
Jer 48:25 *M* horn is cut off;
48:29 "We have heard of *M* pride—
48:41 that day the hearts of *M* warriors

MOABITE (MOAB)

Nu 22: 8 So the *M* princes stayed with him.
22:14 So the *M* princes returned to Balak
22:36 out to meet him at the *M* town
25: 1 sexual immorality with *M* women,
Dt 23: 3 or *M* or any of his descendants may
Ru 1: 4 They married *M* women, one
2Ki 13:20 *M* raiders used to enter the country
24: 2 *M* and Ammonite raiders
1Ch 11:46 Ithmah the *M*, Eliel, Obed
2Ch 24:26 son of Shimrith a *M* woman.
Ne 13: 1 or *M* should ever be admitted
Isa 16: 4 Let the *M* fugitives stay with you;

MOABITES (MOAB)

Ge 19:37 he is the father of the *M* of today.
Nu 22: 4 The *M* said to the elders of Midian,
Dt 2: 9 not harass the *M* or provoke them
2:11 but the *M* called them Emites.
2:29 and the *M*, who live in Ar,
Jdg 3:29 down about ten thousand *M*,
2Sa 8: 2 David also defeated the *M*.
8: 2 So the *M* became subject to David
1Ki 11: 1 *M*, Ammonites, Edomites,
11:33 Chemosh the god of the *M*,
2Ki 3:21 all the *M* had heard that the kings
3:22 To the *M* across the way, the water
3:24 But when the *M* came to the camp
3:24 the land and slaughtered the *M*.
1Ch 18: 2 David also defeated the *M*,
2Ch 20: 1 the *M* and Ammonites with some
Ezr 9: 1 Jebusites, Ammonites, *M*,
Isa 16: 7 Therefore the *M* wail,

MOABITESS (MOAB)

Ru 1:22 accompanied by Ruth the *M*,
2: 2 And Ruth the *M* said to Naomi,
2: 6 "She is the *M* who came back
2:21 Then Ruth the *M* said, "He
4: 5 from Naomi and from Ruth the *M*,
4:10 I have also acquired Ruth the *M*,

MOAN (MOANED MOANING)

Ps 90: 9 we finish our years with a *m*.
Isa 59:11 we *m* mournfully like doves.
Jer 48:31 I *m* for the men of Kir Hareseth.
Joel 1:18 How the cattle *m*!
Mic 1: 8 and *m* like an owl.
Na 2: 7 Its slave girls *m* like doves

MOANED (MOAN)

Isa 38:14 I *m* like a mourning dove.

MOANING (MOAN)

Jer 31:18 "I have surely heard Ephraim's *m*:
Eze 7:16 *m* like doves of the valleys,

MOB

Eze 16:40 They will bring a *m* against you,
23:46 Bring a *m* against them
23:47 The *m* will stone them
Jn 7:49 But this *m* that knows nothing
Ac 17: 5 formed a *m* and started a riot
21:35 the violence of the *m* was

MOBILIZED

Jdg 20:15 the Benjamites *m* twenty-six
2Ki 3: 6 out from Samaria and *m* all Israel.
2Ki 6:24 king of Aram *m* his entire army

MOCK (MOCKED MOCKER MOCKERS MOCKERY MOCKING MOCKS)

Job 11: 3 no one rebuke you when you *m*?
21: 3 and after I have spoken, *m* on.
22:19 the innocent *m* them, saying,
30: 1 "But now they *m* me,
30: 9 "And now their sons *m* me in song;
Ps 22: 7 All who see me *m* me;
69:12 Those who sit at the gate *m* me,
74:10 How long will the enemy *m* you,
74:22 remember how fools *m* you all day
80: 6 and our enemies *m* us.
119:51 The arrogant *m* me
Pr 1:26 I will *m* when calamity overtakes
14: 9 Fools *m* at making amends for sin,
Isa 52: 5 and those who rule them *m*,"
La 3:14 they *m* me in song all day long.
3:63 they *m* me in their songs.
Eze 22: 5 those who are far away will *m* you,
Mk 10:34 who will *m* him and spit on him,
Lk 18:32 They will *m* him, insult him,

MOCKED (MOCK)

2Ch 36:16 But they *m* God's messengers,
Ne 2:19 the Arab heard about it, they *m*
Ps 35:16 the ungodly they maliciously *m*;
74:18 how the enemy has *m* you,
89:50 Lord, how your servant has been *m*
89:51 with which they have *m* every step
89:51 with which your enemies have *m*,
Mt 20:19 him over to the Gentiles to be *m*
27:29 knelt in front of him and *m* him.
27:31 After they had *m* him, they took
27:41 of the law and the elders *m* him.
Mk 15:20 And when they had *m* him,
15:31 and the teachers of the law *m* him
Lk 23:11 his soldiers ridiculed and *m* him.
23:36 soldiers also came up and *m* him.
Gal 6: 7 not be deceived: God cannot be *m*.

MOCKER (MOCK)

Pr 9: 7 corrects a *m* invites insult;
9: 8 Do not rebuke a *m* or he will hate
9:12 if you are a *m*, you alone will suffer
13: 1 but a *m* does not listen to rebuke.
14: 6 *m* seeks wisdom and finds none,
15:12 A *m* resents correction;
19:25 Flog a *m*, and the simple will learn
20: 1 Wine is a *m* and beer a brawler;
21:11 When a *m* is punished, the simple
21:24 arrogant man—"*M*" is his name;
22:10 Drive out the *m*, and out goes strife
24: 9 and men detest a *m*.

MOCKERS (MOCK)

Job 17: 2 Surely *m* surround me;
Ps 1: 1 or sit in the seat of *m*.
Pr 1:22 How long will *m* delight
3:34 He mocks proud *m*
19:29 Penalties are prepared for *m*,
29: 8 *M* stir up a city,
Isa 29:20 the *m* will disappear,
Hos 7: 5 and he joins hands with the *m*.

MOCKERY (MOCK)

Pr 1:22 long will mockers delight in *m*
Jer 10:15 are worthless, the objects of *m*;
51:18 are worthless, the objects of *m*;

MOCKING (MOCK)

Ge 21: 9 borne to Abraham was *m*,
Isa 28:22 Now stop your *m*,
50: 6 face from *m* and spitting.
57: 4 Whom are you *m*?
Zep 2:10 *m* the people of the LORD
Lk 22:63 who were guarding Jesus began *m*

MOCKS (MOCK)

2Ki 19:21 despises you and *m* you.
Job 9:23 he *m* the despair of the innocent.
Pr 3:34 He *m* proud mockers
17: 5 He who *m* the poor shows
19:28 A corrupt witness *m* at justice,
30:17 "The eye that *m* a father,
Isa 37:22 despises and *m* you.
Jer 20: 7 everyone *m* me.

MODEL (MODELS)
Eze 28: 12 " 'You were the *m* of perfection,
1Th 1: 7 And so you became a *m*
2Th 3: 9 to make ourselves a *m* for you

MODELS (MODEL)
1Sa 6: 5 Make *m* of the tumors
6: 11 containing the gold rats and the *m*

MODESTY
1Co 12: 23 are treated with special *m*,

MOISTEN (MOISTURE)
Eze 46: 14 a third of a hin of oil to *m* the flour.

MOISTURE (MOISTEN)
Job 36: 28 the clouds pour down their *m*
37: 11 He loads the clouds with *m;*
Lk 8: 6 withered because they had no *m*.

MOLADAH
Jos 15: 26 Hazor), Amam, Shema, *M*,
19: 2 Beersheba (or Sheba), *M*,
1Ch 4: 28 They lived in Beersheba, *M*,
Ne 11: 26 in Jeshua, in *M*, in Beth Pelet,

MOLDED (MOLDS)
Job 10: 9 Remember that you *m* me like clay

MOLDING (MOLDS)
Ex 25: 11 and make a gold *m* around it.
25: 24 and make a gold *m* around it.
25: 25 and put a gold *m* on the rim.
30: 3 and make a gold *m* around it.
30: 4 rings for the altar below the *m*
37: 2 and made a gold *m* around it.
37: 11 and made a gold *m* around it.
37: 12 and put a gold *m* on the rim.
37: 26 and made a gold *m* around it.
37: 27 made two gold rings below the *m*—

MOLDS (MOLDED MOLDING MOLDY)
1Ki 7: 37 They were all cast in the same *m*
7: 46 in clay *m* in the plain of the Jordan
2Ch 4: 17 in clay *m* in the plain of the Jordan

MOLDY (MOLDS)
Jos 9: 5 of their food supply was dry and *m*.
9: 12 But now see how dry and *m* it is.

MOLECH
Lev 18: 21 children to be sacrificed to *M*,
20: 2 of his children to *M* must be put
20: 3 for by giving his children to *M*,
20: 4 one of his children to *M*
20: 5 in prostituting themselves to *M*.
1Ki 11: 5 and *M* the detestable god
11: 7 and for *M* the detestable god
11: 33 and *M* the god of the Ammonites,
2Ki 23: 10 or daughter in the fire to *M*.
23: 13 and for *M* the detestable god
Isa 57: 9 You went to *M* with olive oil
Jer 32: 35 their sons and daughters to *M*,
49: 1 Why then has *M* taken possession
49: 3 for *M* will go into exile,
Zep 1: 5 and who also swear by *M*,

MOLEST (MOLESTS)
Ge 26: 29 just as we did not *m* you
Est 7: 8 *m* the queen while she is with me

MOLESTS (MOLEST)
Ge 26: 11 "Anyone who *m* this man

MOLID
1Ch 2: 29 who bore him Ahban and *M*.

MOLOCH
Ac 7: 43 You have lifted up the shrine of *M*

MOMENT (MOMENT'S MOMENTARY)
Ex 33: 5 were to go with you even for a *m*,
Nu 4: 20 even for a *m*, or they will die."
Ezr 9: 8 for a brief *m*, the LORD our God
Job 7: 18 and test him every *m?*
20: 5 the joy of the godless lasts but a *m*.
Ps 2: 12 for his wrath can flare up in a *m*.
30: 5 For his anger lasts only a *m*,
Pr 12: 19 but a lying tongue lasts only a *m*.
Isa 47: 9 you in a *m*, on a single day:
54: 7 "For a brief *m* I abandoned you,
54: 8 I hid my face from you for a *m*,
66: 8 or a nation be brought forth in a *m!*
66: 9 Do I bring to the *m* of birth
Jer 4: 20 my shelter in a *m*.
La 4: 6 which was overthrown in a *m*
Eze 26: 16 trembling every *m*, appalled at you
32: 10 every *m* for his life.
Mt 3: 16 At that *m* heaven was opened,
9: 22 the woman was healed from that *m*
17: 18 and he was healed from that *m*.
27: 51 At that *m* the curtain
Mk 9: 39 can in the next *m* say anything bad
Lk 2: 38 Coming up to them at that very *m*,
6: 49 *m* the torrent struck that house,
Jn 18: 27 at that *m* a rooster began to crow.
Ac 5: 10 At that *m* she fell down at his feet
16: 18 At that *m* the spirit left her.
22: 13 at that very *m* I was able to see him
1Co 4: 13 to this *m* we have become the scum
Gal 2: 5 We did not give in to them for a *m*,
Rev 12: 4 devour her child the *m* it was born.

MOMENT'S (MOMENT)
Job 10: 20 away from me so I can have a *m* joy

MOMENTARY (MOMENT)
2Co 4: 17 and *m* troubles are achieving

MONEY
Ge 17: 12 bought with *m* from a foreigner—
17: 13 household or bought with your *m*,
17: 23 household or bought with his *m*,
42: 35 their father saw the *m* pouches,
47: 14 Joseph collected all the *m* that was
47: 15 When the *m* of the people of Egypt
47: 15 before your eyes? Our *m* is used up
47: 16 since your *m* is gone."
47: 18 that since our *m* is gone
Ex 21: 11 without any payment of *m*.
21: 35 and divide both the *m* and the dead
22: 15 *m* paid for the hire covers the loss.
22: 25 "If you lend *m* to one of my people
30: 16 Receive the atonement *m*
Lev 22: 11 But if a priest buys a slave with *m*,
25: 37 You must not lend him *m*
Nu 3: 48 Give the *m* for the redemption
3: 49 Moses collected the redemption *m*
3: 51 Moses gave the redemption *m*
Dt 18: 8 he has received *m* from the sale
23: 19 on *m* or food or anything else that
2Ki 5: 26 Is this the time to take *m*,
12: 4 and the *m* brought voluntarily
12: 4 the *m* collected in the census,
12: 4 the *m* received from personal vows
12: 4 "Collect all the *m* that is brought
12: 5 Let every priest receive the *m*
12: 7 no more *m* from your treasurers,
12: 8 they would not collect any more *m*
12: 9 chest all the *m* that was brought
12: 10 counted the *m* that had been
12: 10 that there was a large amount of *m*
12: 11 they gave the *m* to the men
12: 13 *m* brought into the temple was not
12: 15 those to whom they gave the *m*
12: 16 The *m* from the guilt offerings
15: 20 Menahem exacted this *m*
22: 4 him get ready the *m* that has been
22: 7 for the *m* entrusted to them,
22: 9 have paid out the *m* that was
2Ch 24: 5 and collect the *m* due annually
24: 11 and collected a great amount of *m*.
24: 11 that there was a large amount of *m*,
24: 14 the rest of the *m* to the king
34: 9 and gave him the *m* that had been
34: 11 They also gave *m* to the carpenters
34: 14 bringing out the *m* that had been
34: 17 They have paid out the *m* that was
Ezr 3: 7 Then they gave *m* to the masons
7: 17 With this *m* be sure to buy bulls,
Ne 5: 4 "We have had to borrow *m*
5: 10 lending the people *m* and grain.
5: 11 the hundredth part of the *m*, grain,
Est 3: 11 "Keep the *m*," the king said
4: 7 amount of *m* Haman had promised
Ps 15: 5 who lends his *m* without usury
Pr 7: 20 He took his purse filled with *m*
13: 11 Dishonest *m* dwindles away,
13: 11 he who gathers *m* little
17: 16 Of what use is *m* in the hand
Ecc 5: 10 Whoever loves *m* never has *m*
7: 12 as *m* is a shelter,
10: 19 but *m* is the answer for everything.
Isa 52: 3 without *m* you will be redeemed."
55: 1 and you who have no *m*,
55: 1 milk without *m* and without cost.
55: 2 Why spend *m* on what is not bread,
Mic 3: 11 her prophets tell fortunes for *m*.
Mt 6: 24 You cannot serve both God and *M*.
20: 15 to do what I want with my own *m?*
21: 12 the tables of the *m* changers
25: 15 To one he gave five talents of *m*,
25: 16 put his *m* to work and gained five
25: 18 the ground and hid his master's *m*.
25: 27 you should have put my *m*
26: 9 and the *m* given to the poor."
27: 5 Judas threw the *m* into the temple
27: 6 since it is blood *m*."
27: 7 So they decided to use the *m*
28: 12 gave the soldiers a large sum of *m*,
28: 15 So the soldiers took the *m* and did
Mk 6: 8 no bag, no *m* in your belts.
11: 15 the tables of the *m* changers
12: 41 watched the crowd putting their *m*
14: 5 and the *m* given to the poor."
14: 11 and promised to give him *m*.
Lk 3: 14 "Don't extort *m* and don't accuse
7: 41 "Two men owed *m*
7: 42 of them had the *m* to pay him back,
9: 3 no bread, no *m*, no extra tunic.
14: 28 if he has enough *m* to complete it?
16: 13 You cannot serve both God and *M*
16: 14 The Pharisees, who loved *m*,
19: 13 'Put this *m* to work,' he said,
19: 15 to whom he had given the *m*,
19: 23 Why then didn't you put my *m*
22: 5 and agreed to give him *m*.
Jn 2: 14 sitting at tables exchanging *m*.
2: 15 the coins of the *m* changers
12: 5 and the *m* given to the poor?
12: 6 as keeper of the *m* bag, he used
13: 29 Since Judas had charge of the *m*,
Ac 3: 3 to enter, he asked them for *m*.
4: 34 brought the *m* from the sales
4: 37 and brought the *m* and put it
5: 2 part of the *m* for himself,
5: 3 some of the *m* you received
5: 4 wasn't the *m* at your disposal?
7: 16 at Shechem for a certain sum of *m*.
8: 18 he offered them *m* and said,
8: 20 could buy the gift of God with *m!*
8: 20 "May your *m* perish with you,
16: 16 deal of *m* for her owners
16: 19 hope of making *m* was gone,
1Co 16: 2 set aside a sum of *m* in keeping
1Ti 3: 3 not quarrelsome, not a lover of *m*.
6: 10 For the love of *m* is a root
6: 10 Some people, eager for *m*,
2Ti 3: 2 lovers of *m*, boastful, proud,
Heb 13: 5 free from the love of *m*
Jas 4: 13 carry on business and make *m*."
1Pe 5: 2 not greedy for *m*, but eager to serve

MONEYLENDER (LEND)
Ex 22: 25 not be like a *m;* charge him no
Lk 7: 41 men owed money to a certain *m*.

MONITOR
Lev 11: 30 the *m* lizard, the wall lizard,

MONSTER
Job 7: 12 Am I the sea, or the *m* of the deep,
Ps 74: 13 of the *m* in the waters.
Isa 27: 1 he will slay the *m* of the sea.
51: 9 who pierced that *m* through?
Eze 29: 3 great *m* lying among your streams.
32: 2 you are like a *m* in the seas

MONTH (MONTHLY MONTHS MONTHS')
Ge 7: 11 day of the second *m*—
8: 4 day of the seventh *m* the ark came
8: 5 day of the tenth *m* the tops
8: 5 to recede until the tenth *m*,

Ge 8: 13 of the first *m* of Noah's six hundred
8: 14 day of the second *m* the earth was
29: 14 stayed with him for a whole *m*,
Ex 12: 2 be for you the first *m*, the first *m*
12: 2 "This *m* is to be for you the first
12: 3 day of this *m* each man is
12: 6 until the fourteenth day of the *m*,
12: 18 In the first *m* you are
13: 4 in the *m* of Abib, you are leaving.
13: 5 to observe this ceremony in this *m*:
16: 1 day of the second *m* after they had
19: 1 In the third *m* after the Israelites
23: 15 for in that *m* you came out
23: 15 this at the appointed time in the *m*
34: 18 for in that *m* you came out
34: 18 this at the appointed time in the *m*
40: 2 on the first day of the first *m*.
40: 17 of the first *m* in the second year.
Lev 16: 29 of the seventh *m* you must deny
23: 5 on the fourteenth day of the first *m*
23: 6 day of that *m* the LORD's Feast
23: 24 day of the seventh *m* you are
23: 27 day of this seventh *m* is the Day
23: 32 evening of the ninth day of the *m*
23: 34 day of the seventh *m* the LORD's
23: 39 the fifteenth day of the seventh *m*,
23: 41 celebrate it in the seventh *m*.
25: 9 on the tenth day of the seventh *m*;
27: 6 If it is a person between one *m*
Nu 1: 1 of the second *m* of the second year
1: 18 on the first day of the second *m*.
3: 15 Count every male a *m* old or more
3: 22 number of all the males a *m* old
3: 28 number of all the males a *m* old
3: 34 number of all the males a *m* old
3: 39 including every male a *m* old
3: 40 Israelite males who are a *m* old
3: 43 number of firstborn males a *m* old
9: 1 in the first *m* of the second year
9: 3 on the fourteenth day of this *m*,
9: 5 on the fourteenth day of the first *m*
9: 11 day of the second *m* at twilight.
9: 22 the tabernacle for two days or a *m*
10: 11 of the second *m* of the second year,
11: 20 twenty days, but for a whole *m*—
11: 21 meat to eat for a whole *m*!'
18: 16 When they are a *m* old, you must
20: 1 In the first *m* the whole Israelite
26: 62 All the male Levites a *m* old
28: 11 " 'On the first of every *m*,
28: 16 of the first *m* the LORD's Passover
28: 17 the fifteenth day of this *m* there is
29: 1 day of the seventh *m* hold a sacred
29: 7 day of this seventh *m* hold a sacred
29: 12 the fifteenth day of the seventh *m*,
33: 3 on the fifteenth day of the first *m*,
33: 38 of the fifth *m* of the fortieth year
Dt 1: 3 on the first day of the eleventh *m*,
16: 1 Observe the *m* of Abib
16: 1 in the *m* of Abib he brought you
21: 13 her father and mother for a full *m*,
Jos 4: 19 of the first *m* the people went up
5: 10 of the fourteenth day of the *m*,
1Sa 20: 27 of the *m*, David's place was empty
20: 34 day of the *m* he did not eat,
1Ki 4: 7 supplies for one *m* in the year.
4: 27 The district officers, each in his *m*,
5: 14 in shifts of ten thousand a *m*,
5: 14 so that they spent one *m*
6: 1 in the *m* of Ziv, the second *m*,
6: 37 in the fourth year, in the *m* of Ziv.
6: 38 year in the *m* of Bul, the eighth *m*,
8: 2 in the *m* of Ethanim, the seventh *m*
12: 32 on the fifteenth day of the eighth *m*
12: 33 day of the eighth *m*, a *m*
2Ki 15: 13 and he reigned in Samaria one *m*.
25: 1 on the tenth day of the tenth *m*,
25: 3 day of the ⌊fourth⌋ *m* the famine
25: 8 On the seventh day of the fifth *m*,
25: 25 In the seventh *m*, however,
25: 27 day of the twelfth *m*.
1Ch 12: 15 Jordan in the first *m* when it was
27: 1 duty *m* by *m* throughout the year.
27: 2 for the first *m*, was Jashobeam son
27: 3 all the army officers for the first *m*.
27: 4 for the second *m* was Dodai
27: 5 army commander, for the third *m*,
27: 7 The fourth, for the fourth *m*,
1Ch 27: 8 for the fifth *m*, was the commander
27: 9 The sixth, for the sixth *m*,
27: 10 for the seventh *m*, was Helez
27: 11 for the eighth *m*, was Sibbecai
27: 12 for the ninth *m*, was Abiezer
27: 13 for the tenth *m*, was Maharai
27: 14 for the eleventh *m*, was Benaiah
27: 15 for the twelfth *m*, was Heldai
2Ch 3: 2 of the second *m* in the fourth year
5: 3 of the festival in the seventh *m*.
7: 10 of the seventh *m* he sent the people
15: 10 in the third *m* of the fifteenth year
29: 3 In the first *m* of the first year
29: 17 of the *m* they reached the portico
29: 17 on the first day of the first *m*,
29: 17 on the sixteenth day of the first *m*.
30: 2 the Passover in the second *m*.
30: 13 Bread in the second *m*.
30: 15 fourteenth day of the second *m*.
31: 7 and finished in the seventh *m*.
31: 7 began doing this in the third *m*
35: 1 on the fourteenth day of the first *m*
Ezr 3: 1 When the seventh *m* came
3: 6 day of the seventh *m* they began
3: 8 In the second *m* of the second year
6: 15 on the third day of the *m* Adar,
6: 19 the fourteenth day of the first *m*,
7: 8 in the fifth *m* of the seventh year
7: 9 on the first day of the fifth *m*,
7: 9 on the first day of the first *m*,
8: 31 day of the first *m* we set out
10: 9 on the twentieth day of the ninth *m*
10: 16 day of the tenth *m* they sat
10: 17 of the first *m* they finished dealing
Ne 1: 1 In the *m* of Kislev
2: 1 In the *m* of Nisan in the twentieth
7: 73 When the seventh *m* came
8: 2 of the seventh *m* Ezra the priest
8: 13 On the second day of the *m*,
8: 14 during the feast of the seventh *m*
9: 1 twenty-fourth day of the same *m*,
Est 2: 16 the royal residence in the tenth *m*,
2: 16 *m* of Tebeth, in the seventh year
3: 7 in the first *m*, the *m* of Nisan,
3: 7 of Haman to select a day and *m*.
3: 7 on the twelfth *m*, the *m* of Adar.
3: 12 of the first *m* the royal secretaries
3: 13 the thirteenth day of the twelfth *m*,
3: 13 the *m* of Adar, and to plunder their
8: 9 day of the third *m*, the *m* of Sivan.
8: 12 of the twelfth *m*, the *m* of Adar.
9: 1 of the twelfth *m*, the *m* of Adar,
9: 15 on the fourteenth day of the *m*
9: 17 on the thirteenth day of the *m*
9: 19 observe the fourteenth of the *m*
9: 21 and fifteenth days of the *m* of Adar
9: 22 *m* when their sorrow was turned
Isa 47: 13 who make predictions *m* by *m*,
Jer 1: 3 down to the fifth *m*
28: 1 In the fifth *m* of that same year,
28: 17 In the seventh *m* of that same year,
36: 9 In the ninth *m* of the fifth year
36: 22 It was the ninth *m* and the king was
39: 1 king of Judah, in the tenth *m*,
39: 2 fourth *m* of Zedekiah's eleventh
41: 1 In the seventh *m* Ishmael son
52: 4 on the tenth day of the tenth *m*,
52: 6 day of the fourth *m* the famine
52: 12 On the tenth day of the fifth *m*,
52: 31 twenty-fifth day of the twelfth *m*.
Eze 1: 1 in the fourth *m* on the fifth day,
1: 2 fifth of the *m*— it was the fifth year
8: 1 in the sixth *m* on the fifth day,
20: 1 in the fifth *m* on the tenth day,
24: 1 in the tenth *m* on the tenth day,
26: 1 on the first day of the *m*, the word
29: 1 in the tenth *m* on the twelfth day,
29: 17 in the first *m* on the first day,
30: 20 in the first *m* on the seventh day,
31: 1 in the third *m* on the first day,
32: 1 in the twelfth *m* on the first day,
32: 17 on the fifteenth day of the *m*,
33: 21 in the tenth *m* on the fifth day,
40: 1 of the *m*, in the fourteenth year
45: 18 In the first *m* on the first day you
45: 20 day of the *m* for anyone who sins
45: 21 " 'In the first *m* on the fourteenth
45: 25 in the seventh *m* on the fifteenth
Eze 47: 12 Every *m* they will bear,
Da 10: 4 twenty-fourth day of the first *m*,
Hag 1: 1 on the first day of the sixth *m*,
1: 15 of the sixth *m* in the second year
2: 1 twenty-first day of the seventh *m*,
2: 10 twenty-fourth day of the ninth *m*,
2: 18 twenty-fourth day of the ninth *m*,
2: 20 on the twenty-fourth day of the *m*:
Zec 1: 1 In the eighth *m* of the second year
1: 7 day of the eleventh *m*,
1: 7 the *m* of Shebat, in the second year
7: 1 day of the ninth *m*, the *m* of Kislev.
7: 3 I mourn and fast in the fifth *m*,
11: 8 In one *m* I got rid of the three
Lk 1: 26 In the sixth *m*, God sent the angel
1: 36 said to be barren is in her sixth *m*.
Rev 9: 15 and *m* and year were released
22: 2 of fruit, yielding its fruit every *m*.

MONTHLY (MONTH)

Lev 12: 2 she is unclean during her *m* period.
15: 19 of her *m* period will last seven days
15: 24 and her *m* flow touches him,
15: 25 at a time other than her *m* period
15: 26 as is her bed during her *m* period,
15: 33 for a woman in her *m* period,
18: 19 the uncleanness of her *m* period.
20: 18 with a woman during her *m* period
Nu 28: 14 This is the *m* burnt offering
29: 6 These are in addition to the *m*
Eze 36: 17 was like a woman's *m* uncleanness

MONTHS (MONTH)

Ge 38: 24 About three *m* later Judah was told
Ex 2: 2 fine child, she hid him for three *m*.
Jdg 11: 37 "Give me two *m* to roam the hills
11: 38 And he let her go for two *m*.
11: 39 After the two *m*, she returned
19: 2 After she had been there four *m*,
20: 47 where they stayed four *m*.
1Sa 6: 1 in Philistine territory seven *m*,
27: 7 territory a year and four *m*.
2Sa 2: 11 of Judah was seven years and six *m*
5: 5 over Judah seven years and six *m*,
6: 11 the Gittite for three *m*,
24: 8 to Jerusalem at the end of nine *m*
24: 13 *m* of fleeing from your enemies
1Ki 5: 14 in Lebanon and two *m* at home.
11: 16 Israelites stayed there for six *m*,
2Ki 15: 8 in Samaria, and he reigned six *m*.
23: 31 he reigned in Jerusalem three *m*.
24: 8 he reigned in Jerusalem three *m*.
1Ch 3: 4 he reigned seven years and six *m*.
13: 14 in his house for three *m*,
21: 12 three *m* of being swept away
2Ch 36: 2 he reigned in Jerusalem three *m*.
36: 9 he reigned in Jerusalem three *m*
Est 2: 12 had to complete twelve *m*
2: 12 six *m* with oil of myrrh
Job 3: 6 nor be entered in any of the *m*.
7: 3 so I have been allotted *m* of futility,
14: 5 have decreed the number of his *m*
21: 21 when his allotted *m* come to an end
29: 2 "How I long for the *m* gone by,
39: 2 Do you count the *m* till they bear?
Eze 39: 12 " 'For seven *m* the house
39: 14 of the seven *m* they will begin their
Da 4: 29 Twelve *m* later, as the king was
Am 4: 7 the harvest was still three *m* away.
Zec 7: 5 and seventh *m* for the past seventy
8: 19 and tenth *m* will become joyful
Mk 6: 37 "That would take eight *m*
Lk 1: 24 for five *m* remained in seclusion.
1: 56 with Elizabeth for about three *m*
Jn 4: 35 'Four *m* more and then the harvest
Ac 7: 20 For three *m* he was cared
19: 8 and spoke boldly there for three *m*,
20: 3 in Greece, where he stayed three *m*
28: 11 After three *m* we put out to sea
Gal 4: 10 and *m* and seasons and years!
Heb 11: 23 him for three *m* after he was born,
Rev 9: 5 but only to torture them for five *m*.
9: 10 to torment people for five *m*.
11: 2 trample on the holy city for 42 *m*.
13: 5 his authority for forty-two *m*.

MONTHS' (MONTH)

Jn 6: 7 "Eight *m*' wages would not buy

MONUMENT

1Sa 15: 12 There he has set up a *m*
2Sa 18: 18 it in the King's Valley as a *m*
18: 18 it is called Absalom's *M* to this day.
Isa 19: 19 and a *m* to the LORD at its border.

MOON (MOONS)

Ge 37: 9 and this time the sun and *m*
Nu 10: 10 feasts and New *M* festivals—
28: 14 at each new *m* during the year.
Dt 4: 19 *m* and the stars—all the heavenly
17: 3 or the *m* or the stars of the sky,
33: 14 and the finest the *m* can yield;
Jos 10: 12 O *m*, over the Valley of Aijalon."
10: 13 and the *m* stopped,
1Sa 20: 5 tomorrow is the New *M* festival,
20: 18 "Tomorrow is the New *M* festival.
20: 24 and when the New *M* festival came
2Ki 4: 23 "It's not the New *M* or the Sabbath
23: 5 and *m*, to the constellations
1Ch 23: 31 and at New *M* festivals
Ezr 3: 5 New *M* sacrifices and the sacrifices
Ne 10: 33 New *M* festivals and appointed
Job 25: 5 If even the *m* is not bright
26: 9 He covers the face of the full *m*,
31: 26 or the *m* moving in splendor,
Ps 8: 3 the *m* and the stars,
72: 5 the *m*, through all generations.
72: 7 till the *m* is no more.
74: 16 you established the sun and *m*.
81: 3 and when the *m* is full, on the day
81: 3 the ram's horn at the New *M*,
89: 37 be established forever like the *m*,
104: 19 The *m* marks off the seasons,
121: 6 nor the *m* by night.
136: 9 the *m* and stars to govern the night;
148: 3 Praise him, sun and *m*,
Pr 7: 20 and will not be home till full *m*."
Ecc 12: 2 and the *m* and the stars grow dark,
SS 6: 10 fair as the *m*, bright as the sun,
Isa 1: 14 Your New *M* festivals
13: 10 and the *m* will not give its light.
24: 23 The *m* will be abashed, the sun
30: 26 The *m* will shine like the sun,
60: 19 brightness of the *m* shine on you,
60: 20 and your *m* will wane no more;
66: 23 From one New *M* to another
Jer 8: 2 and the *m* and all the stars
31: 35 who decrees the *m* and stars
Eze 32: 7 and the *m* will not give its light.
46: 1 of the New *M* it is to be opened.
46: 6 On the day of the New *M* he is
Hos 5: 7 Now their New *M* festivals
Joel 2: 10 the sun and *m* are darkened,
2: 31 and the *m* to blood
3: 15 The sun and *m* will be darkened,
Am 8: 5 "When will the New *M* be over
Hab 3: 11 and *m* stood still in the heavens
Mt 24: 29 and the *m* will not give its light;
Mk 13: 24 and the *m* will not give its light;
Lk 21: 25 "There will be signs in the sun, *m*
Ac 2: 20 and the *m* to blood
1Co 15: 41 *m* another and the stars another;
Col 2: 16 a New *M* celebration or a Sabbath
Rev 6: 12 the whole *m* turned blood red,
8: 12 a third of the *m*, and a third
12: 1 with the *m* under her feet
21: 23 city does not need the sun or the *m*

MOONS (MOON)

2Ch 2: 4 and on Sabbaths and New *M*
8: 13 New *M* and the three annual feasts
31: 3 New *M* and appointed feasts
Isa 1: 13 New *M*, Sabbaths
Eze 45: 17 the New *M* and the Sabbaths—
46: 3 New *M* the people of the land are
Hos 2: 11 her yearly festivals, her New *M*,

MORAL

Jas 1: 21 rid of all *m* filth and the evil that is

MORDECAI (MORDECAI'S)

Ezr 2: 2 Seraiah, Reelaiah, *M*, Bilshan,
Ne 7: 7 Raamiah, Nahamani, *M*, Bilshan,
Est 2: 5 named *M* son of Jair, the son
2: 7 and *M* had taken her as his own
2: 7 *M* had a cousin named Hadassah,
2: 10 *M* had forbidden her to do so.
Est 2: 15 for Esther (the girl *M* had adopted,
2: 19 *M* was sitting at the king's gate.
2: 20 nationality just as *M* had told her
2: 21 During the time *M* was sitting
2: 22 But *M* found out about the plot
2: 22 it to the king, giving credit to *M*.
3: 2 But *M* would not kneel down
3: 3 officials at the king's gate asked *M*,
3: 5 Haman saw that *M* would not
3: 6 scorned the idea of killing only *M*.
4: 1 When *M* learned of all that had
4: 4 came and told her about *M*,
4: 5 to find out what was troubling *M*
4: 6 So Hathach went out to *M*
4: 7 *M* told him everything that had
4: 9 reported to Esther what *M* had said
4: 10 she instructed him to say to *M*,
4: 12 Esther's words were reported to *M*,
4: 15 Then Esther sent this reply to *M*:
4: 17 So *M* went away and carried out all
5: 9 he was filled with rage against *M*.
5: 9 when he saw *M* at the king's gate
5: 13 as I see that Jew *M* sitting
5: 14 morning to have *M* hanged on it.
6: 2 recorded there that *M* had exposed
6: 3 recognition has *M* received for this
6: 4 speak to the king about hanging *M*
6: 10 you have suggested for *M* the Jew,
6: 11 He robed *M*, and led him
6: 12 Afterward *M* returned
6: 13 "Since *M*, before whom your
7: 9 made for *M*, who spoke up
7: 10 the gallows he had prepared for *M*.
8: 1 And *M* came into the presence
8: 2 from Haman, and presented it to *M*
8: 7 to Queen Esther and to *M* the Jew,
8: 10 *M* wrote in the name
8: 15 *M* left the king's presence wearing
9: 3 because fear of *M* had seized them.
9: 4 *M* was prominent in the palace;
9: 20 *M* recorded these events,
9: 23 doing what *M* had written to them.
9: 29 of Abihail, along with *M* the Jew,
9: 30 And *M* sent letters to all the Jews
9: 31 *M* the Jew and Queen Esther had
10: 2 account of the greatness of *M*
10: 3 *M* the Jew was second in rank

MORDECAI'S (MORDECAI)

Est 2: 20 continued to follow *M* instructions
3: 4 *M* behavior would be tolerated,
3: 6 for a way to destroy all *M* people,
3: 6 learned who *M* people were,
8: 9 They wrote out all *M* orders

MOREH

Ge 12: 6 of the great tree of *M* at Shechem.
Dt 11: 30 near the great trees of *M*,
Jdg 7: 1 in the valley near the hill of *M*.

MORESHETH

Jer 26: 18 Micah of *M* prophesied in the days
Mic 1: 1 to Micah of *M* during the reigns

MORESHETH GATH

Mic 1: 14 give parting gifts to *M*.

MORIAH

Ge 22: 2 and go to the region of *M*.
2Ch 3: 1 LORD in Jerusalem on Mount *M*,

MORNING (MORNING'S MORNINGS)

Ge 1: 5 and there was *m*— the first day.
1: 8 and there was *m*— the second day.
1: 13 and there was *m*— the third day.
1: 19 and there was *m*— the fourth day.
1: 23 and there was *m*— the fifth day.
1: 31 and there was *m*— the sixth day.
19: 2 then go on your way early in the *m*
19: 27 Early the next *m* Abraham got up
20: 8 the next *m* Abimelech summoned
21: 14 Early the next *m* Abraham took
22: 3 Early the next *m* Abraham got up
24: 54 When they got up the next *m*,
26: 31 Early the next *m* the men swore
28: 18 Early the next *m* Jacob took
29: 25 When *m* came, there was Leah!
31: 55 Early the next *m* Laban kissed his
Ge 40: 6 came to them the next *m*,
41: 8 In the *m* his mind was troubled,
44: 3 As *m* dawned, the men were sent
49: 27 in the *m* he devours the prey,
Ex 7: 15 Go to Pharaoh in the *m*
8: 20 "Get up early in the *m*
9: 13 early in the *m*, confront Pharaoh
10: 13 By *m* the wind had brought
12: 10 Do not leave any of it till *m*;
12: 10 left till *m*, you must burn it.
12: 22 the door of his house until *m*.
14: 24 In the *m* watch the LORD looked
16: 7 and in the *m* you will see the glory
16: 8 all the bread you want in the *m*,
16: 12 and in the *m* you will be filled
16: 13 in the *m* there was a layer of dew
16: 19 "No one is to keep any of it until *m*
16: 20 they kept part of it until *m*,
16: 21 Each *m* everyone gathered
16: 23 is left and keep it until *m*.' "
16: 24 it until *m*, as Moses commanded,
18: 13 around him from *m* till evening.
18: 14 around you from *m* till evening?"
19: 16 On the *m* of the third day there was
23: 18 offerings must not be kept until *m*.
24: 4 He got up early the next *m*
27: 21 the LORD from evening till *m*.
29: 34 or any bread is left over till *m*,
29: 39 Offer one in the *m* and the other
29: 41 and its drink offering as in the *m*—
30: 7 incense on the altar every *m*
34: 2 ready in the *m*, and then come up
34: 4 went up Mount Sinai early in the *m*
34: 25 the Passover Feast remain until *m*.
36: 3 bring freewill offerings *m* after *m*.
Lev 6: 9 till *m*, and the fire must be kept
6: 12 Every *m* the priest is
6: 20 half of it in the *m* and half
7: 15 he must leave none of it till *m*.
22: 30 same day; leave none of it till *m*.
24: 3 the LORD from evening till *m*,
Nu 9: 12 They must not leave any of it till *m*
9: 15 From evening till *m* the cloud
9: 21 and when it lifted in the *m*,
9: 21 only from evening till *m*,
14: 40 Early the next *m* they went up
16: 5 "In the *m* the LORD will show
22: 13 The next *m* Balaam got up
22: 21 up in the *m*, saddled his donkey
22: 41 The next *m* Balak took Balaam up
28: 4 Prepare one lamb in the *m*
28: 8 offering that you prepare in the *m*.
28: 23 to the regular *m* burnt offering.
Dt 16: 4 of the first day remain until *m*.
16: 7 Then in the *m* return to your tents.
28: 67 In the *m* you will say, "If only it
28: 67 in the evening, "If only it were *m*
Jos 3: 1 Early in the *m* Joshua
6: 12 Joshua got up early the next *m*
7: 14 In the *m*, present yourselves tribe
7: 16 Early the next *m* Joshua had Israel
8: 10 Early the next *m* Joshua mustered
8: 14 out early in the *m* to meet Israel
Jdg 6: 28 In the *m* when the men
6: 31 for him shall be put to death by *m*!
7: 1 Early in the *m*, Jerub-Baal (that is,
9: 33 In the *m* at sunrise, advance
19: 8 On the *m* of the fifth day,
19: 9 Early tomorrow *m* you can get up
19: 27 When her master got up in the *m*
20: 19 The next *m* the Israelites got up
Ru 2: 7 and has worked steadily from *m*
3: 13 Lie here until *m*."
3: 13 and in the *m* if he wants to redeem,
3: 14 So she lay at his feet until *m*,
1Sa 1: 19 Early the next *m* they arose
3: 15 Samuel lay down until *m*
5: 4 the following *m* when they rose,
9: 19 and in the *m* I will let you go
15: 12 Early in the *m* Samuel got up
17: 16 Philistine came forward every *m*
17: 20 Early in the *m* David left the flock
19: 2 Be on your guard tomorrow *m*;
19: 11 to watch it and to kill him in the *m*.
20: 35 In the *m* Jonathan went out
25: 22 if by *m* I leave alive one male
25: 37 in the *m*, when Nabal was sober,
29: 10 and leave in the *m* as soon

1Sa 29: 11 up early in the *m* to go back
2Sa 2: 27 pursuit of their brothers until *m*.''
11: 14 In the *m* David wrote a letter
13: 4 look so haggard *m* after *m?*
23: 4 he is like the light of *m* at sunrise
23: 4 sunrise on a cloudless *m*,
24: 11 Before David got up the next *m*,
24: 15 on Israel from that *m* until the end
1Ki 3: 21 The next *m*, I got up
3: 21 at him closely in the *m* light,
17: 6 and meat in the *m* and bread
18: 26 the name of Baal from *m* till noon.
2Ki 3: 20 The next *m*, about the time
3: 22 When they got up early in the *m*,
6: 15 and went out early the next *m*,
10: 8 entrance of the city gate until *m*.''
10: 9 The next *m* Jehu went out.
16: 15 offer the *m* burnt offering
19: 35 When the people got up the next *m*
1Ch 9: 27 of the key for opening it each *m*.
16: 40 *m* and evening, in accordance
23: 30 also to stand every *m* to thank
2Ch 2: 4 for making burnt offerings every *m*
13: 11 Every *m* and evening they present
20: 20 Early in the *m* they left
29: 20 Early the next *m* King Hezekiah
31: 3 from his own possessions for the *m*
Ezr 3: 3 both the *m* and evening sacrifices.
Est 2: 14 and in the *m* return to another part
5: 14 in the *m* to have Mordecai hanged
Job 1: 5 in the *m* he would sacrifice a burnt
3: 9 May its *m* stars become dark;
7: 18 that you examine him every *m*
11: 17 and darkness will become like *m*.
24: 17 of them, deep darkness is their *m;*
38: 7 while the *m* stars sang together
38: 12 you ever given orders to the *m*,
Ps 5: 3 *M* by *m*, O LORD,
5: 3 *m* by *m* I lay my requests
30: 5 but rejoicing comes in the *m*.
49: 14 rule over them in the *m;*
55: 17 Evening, *m* and noon
59: 16 in the *m* I will sing of your love;
65: 8 where *m* dawns and evening fades
73: 14 I have been punished every *m*.
88: 13 in the *m* my prayer comes
90: 5 they are like the new grass of the *m*
90: 6 though in the *m* it springs up new,
90: 14 Satisfy us in the *m*
92: 2 to proclaim your love in the *m*
101: 8 Every *m* I will put to silence
130: 6 than watchmen wait for the *m*,
130: 6 than watchmen wait for the *m*.
143: 8 Let the *m* bring me word
Pr 7: 18 let's drink deep of love till *m;*
27: 14 blesses his neighbor early in the *m*,
Ecc 10: 16 and whose princes feast in the *m*.
11: 6 Sow your seed in the *m*,
Isa 5: 11 to those who rise early in the *m*
14: 12 O *m* star, son of the dawn!
17: 11 and on the *m* when you plant them,
17: 14 Before the *m*, they are gone!
21: 12 ''*M* is coming, but also the night.
26: 9 in the *m* my spirit longs for you.
26: 19 Your dew is like the dew of the *m;*
28: 19 *m* after *m*, by day and by night,
33: 2 Be our strength every *m*,
37: 36 When the people got up the next *m*
44: 22 your sins like the *m* mist.
50: 4 He wakens me *m* by *m*,
Jer 20: 16 May he hear wailing in the *m*,
21: 12 '' 'Administer justice every *m;*
La 3: 23 They are new every *m;*
Eze 12: 8 In the *m* the word
24: 18 So I spoke to the people in the *m*,
24: 18 The next *m* I did as I had been
33: 22 the man came to me in the *m*.
46: 13 *m* by *m* you shall provide it.
46: 14 with it *m* by *m* a grain offering,
46: 15 and the oil shall be provided *m*
46: 15 by *m* for a regular burnt offering.
Hos 6: 4 Your love is like the *m* mist,
7: 6 in the *m* it blazes like a flaming fire.
13: 3 they will be like the *m* mist,
Am 4: 4 Bring your sacrifices every *m*,
Zep 3: 3 who leave nothing for the *m*.
3: 5 *M* by *m* he dispenses his justice,
Mt 16: 3 in the *m*, 'Today it will be stormy,
Mt 20: 1 early in the *m* to hire men to work
21: 18 Early in the *m*, as he was
27: 1 Early in the *m*, all the chief priests
Mk 1: 35 Very early in the *m*,
11: 20 In the *m*, as they went along,
15: 1 early in the *m*, the chief priests,
Lk 6: 13 When *m* came, he called his
21: 38 came early in the *m* to hear him
24: 1 of the week, very early in the *m*,
24: 22 They went to the tomb early this *m*
Jn 18: 28 By now it was early *m*,
21: 4 Early in the *m*, Jesus stood
Ac 2: 15 It's only nine in the *m!* No,
12: 18 In the *m*, there was a great
23: 12 The next *m* the Jews formed
28: 23 From *m* till evening he explained
2Pe 1: 19 and the *m* star rises in your hearts.
Rev 2: 28 I will also give him the *m* star.
22: 16 of David, and the bright *M* Star.''

MORNING'S (MORNING)

Lev 9: 17 in addition to the *m* burnt offering.
Mic 2: 1 At *m* light they carry it out

MORNINGS (MORNING)

Da 8: 14 ''It will take 2,300 evenings and *m;*
8: 26 *m* that has been given you is true,

MORSELS

Pr 18: 8 of a gossip are like choice *m;*
26: 22 of a gossip are like choice *m;*

MORTAL (MORTALLY MORTALS)

Ge 6: 3 for he is *m;* his days will be
Dt 5: 26 For what *m* man has ever heard
Job 4: 17 'Can a *m* be more righteous
9: 2 But how can a *m* be righteous
10: 4 Do you see as a *m* sees?
10: 5 Are your days like those of a *m*
Ps 17: 9 from my *m* enemies who surround
42: 10 My bones suffer *m* agony
56: 4 What can *m* man do to me?
146: 3 in *m* men, who cannot save.
Isa 51: 12 Who are you that you fear *m* men,
Eze 31: 14 for the earth below, among *m* men,
Ro 1: 23 made to look like *m* man
6: 12 do not let sin reign in your *m* body
8: 11 also give life to your *m* bodies
1Co 15: 53 and the *m* with immortality.
15: 54 and the *m* with immortality,
2Co 4: 11 life may be revealed in our *m* body.
5: 4 that what is *m* may be swallowed

MORTALLY (MORTAL)

Eze 30: 24 before him like a *m* wounded man.

MORTALS (MORTAL)

Isa 31: 8 not of *m*, will devour them.

MORTAR

Ge 11: 3 of stone, and tar instead of *m*.
Ex 1: 14 and *m* and with all kinds of work
Nu 11: 8 it in a handmill or crushed it in a *m*.
Pr 27: 22 Though you grind a fool in a *m*,
Isa 41: 25 treads on rulers as if they were *m*,
Na 3: 14 tread the *m*,

MORTGAGING

Ne 5: 3 were saying, ''We are *m* our fields,

MOSAIC

Est 1: 6 and silver on a *m* pavement

MOSERAH

Dt 10: 6 the wells of the Jaakanites to *M*.

MOSEROTH

Nu 33: 30 left Hashmonah and camped at *M*.
33: 31 left *M* and camped at Bene Jaakan.

MOSES (MOSES')

Ex 2: 10 She named him *M*, saying,
2: 11 One day, after *M* had grown up,
2: 14 Then *M* was afraid and thought,
2: 15 but *M* fled from Pharaoh
2: 15 heard of this, he tried to kill *M*,
2: 17 *M* got up and came to their rescue
2: 21 gave his daughter Zipporah to *M*
Ex 2: 21 *M* agreed to stay with the man,
2: 22 and *M* named him Gershom,
3: 1 Now *M* was tending the flock
3: 2 *M* saw that though the bush was
3: 3 So *M* thought, ''I will go over
3: 4 ''*M, M!*'' And *M* said, ''Here I am.''
3: 6 *M* hid his face, because he was
3: 11 But *M* said to God, ''Who am I,
3: 13 *M* said to God, ''Suppose I go
3: 14 God said to *M*, ''I am who I am.
3: 15 said to *M*, ''Say to the Israelites,
4: 1 *M* answered, ''What
4: 3 *M* threw it on the ground
4: 4 So *M* reached out and took hold
4: 6 So *M* put his hand into his cloak,
4: 7 *M* put his hand back into his cloak,
4: 10 *M* said to the LORD, ''O Lord,
4: 13 But *M* said, ''O Lord, please send
4: 14 LORD's anger burned against *M*
4: 18 Then *M* went back to Jethro his
4: 19 the LORD had said to *M* in Midian
4: 20 So *M* took his wife and sons,
4: 21 said to *M*, ''When you return
4: 24 the LORD met *M* and was about
4: 27 he met *M* at the mountain of God
4: 27 ''Go into the desert to meet *M*.''
4: 28 Then *M* told Aaron everything
4: 29 *M* and Aaron brought together all
4: 30 the LORD had said to *M*.
5: 1 Afterward *M* and Aaron went
5: 4 But the king of Egypt said, ''*M*
5: 20 they found *M* and Aaron waiting
5: 22 *M* returned to the LORD and said,
6: 1 Then the LORD said to *M*,
6: 2 also said to *M*, ''I am the LORD.
6: 9 *M* reported this to the Israelites,
6: 10 Then the LORD said to *M*, ''Go,
6: 12 But *M* said to the LORD, ''If
6: 13 Now the LORD spoke to *M*
6: 20 who bore him Aaron and *M*.
6: 26 and *M* to whom the LORD said,
6: 27 It was the same *M* and Aaron.
6: 28 Now when the LORD spoke to *M*
6: 30 But *M* said to the LORD, ''Since I
7: 1 Then the LORD said to *M*, ''See,
7: 6 *M* and Aaron did just as the LORD
7: 7 *M* was eighty years old
7: 8 The LORD said to *M* and Aaron,
7: 10 *M* and Aaron went to Pharaoh
7: 14 Then the LORD said to *M*,
7: 19 The LORD said to *M*, ''Tell Aaron,
7: 20 *M* and Aaron did just as the LORD
7: 22 he would not listen to *M*
8: 1 Then the LORD said to *M*,
8: 5 Then the LORD said to *M*,
8: 8 Pharaoh summoned *M* and Aaron
8: 9 *M* said to Pharaoh, ''I leave
8: 10 *M* replied, ''It will be as you say,
8: 12 After *M* and Aaron left Pharaoh,
8: 12 *M* cried out to the LORD about
8: 13 And the LORD did what *M* asked.
8: 15 would not listen to *M* and Aaron,
8: 16 Then the LORD said to *M*,
8: 20 Then the LORD said to *M*,
8: 25 Pharaoh summoned *M* and Aaron
8: 26 *M* said, ''That would not be right.
8: 29 *M* answered, ''As soon
8: 30 Then *M* left Pharaoh and prayed
8: 31 and the LORD did what *M* asked:
9: 1 Then the LORD said to *M*,
9: 8 and have *M* toss it into the air
9: 8 the LORD said to *M* and Aaron,
9: 10 *M* tossed it into the air,
9: 11 could not stand before *M*
9: 12 and he would not listen to *M*
9: 12 just as the LORD had said to *M*.
9: 13 Then the LORD said to *M*,
9: 22 Then the LORD said to *M*,
9: 23 When *M* stretched out his staff
9: 27 Pharaoh summoned *M* and Aaron.
9: 29 *M* replied, ''When I have gone out
9: 33 Then *M* left Pharaoh and went out
9: 35 as the LORD had said through *M*.
10: 1 Then the LORD said to *M*,
10: 3 So *M* and Aaron went to Pharaoh
10: 6 Then *M* turned and left Pharaoh.
10: 8 *M* and Aaron were brought back
10: 9 who will be going?'' *M* answered,

Ex 10: 11 *M* and Aaron were driven out
10: 12 And the LORD said to *M*,
10: 13 So *M* stretched out his staff
10: 16 Pharaoh quickly summoned *M*
10: 18 *M* then left Pharaoh and prayed
10: 21 Then the LORD said to *M*,
10: 22 So *M* stretched out his hand
10: 24 Pharaoh summoned *M* and said,
10: 25 But *M* said, "You must allow us
10: 28 Pharaoh said to *M*, "Get out
10: 29 "Just as you say," *M* replied,
11: 1 Now the LORD had said to *M*,
11: 3 and *M* himself was highly regarded
11: 4 *M* said, "This is what the LORD
11: 8 *M*, hot with anger, left Pharaoh.
11: 9 The LORD had said to *M*,
11: 10 *M* and Aaron performed all these
12: 1 The LORD said to *M* and Aaron
12: 21 Then *M* summoned all the elders
12: 28 what the LORD commanded *M*
12: 31 the night Pharaoh summoned *M*
12: 35 The Israelites did as *M* instructed
12: 43 The LORD said to *M* and Aaron,
12: 50 the LORD had commanded *M*
13: 1 The LORD said to *M*, "Consecrate
13: 3 Then *M* said to the people,
13: 19 *M* took the bones of Joseph
14: 1 Then the LORD said to *M*,
14: 11 They said to *M*, "Was it
14: 13 *M* answered the people, "Do not
14: 15 Then the LORD said to *M*,
14: 21 Then *M* stretched out his hand
14: 26 Then the LORD said to *M*,
14: 27 *M* stretched out his hand
14: 31 trust in him and in *M* his servant.
15: 1 *M* and the Israelites sang this song
15: 22 *M* led Israel from the Red Sea
15: 24 So the people grumbled against *M*,
15: 25 Then *M* cried out to the LORD,
16: 2 community grumbled against *M*
16: 4 Then the LORD said to *M*,
16: 6 So *M* and Aaron said
16: 8 you should grumble against us?" *M*
16: 9 Then *M* told Aaron, "Say
16: 11 to *M*, "I have heard the grumbling
16: 15 *M* said to them, "It is the bread
16: 19 Then *M* said to them, "No one is
16: 20 So *M* was angry with them.
16: 20 of them paid no attention to *M*;
16: 22 came and reported this to *M*.
16: 24 it until morning, as *M* commanded,
16: 25 *M* said, "because today is
16: 28 Then the LORD said to *M*,
16: 32 *M* said, "This is what the LORD
16: 33 So *M* said to Aaron, "Take a jar
16: 34 As the LORD commanded *M*,
17: 2 So they quarreled with *M* and said,
17: 2 *M* replied, "Why do you quarrel
17: 3 and they grumbled against *M*.
17: 4 Then *M* cried out to the LORD,
17: 5 The LORD answered *M*, "Walk
17: 6 *M* did this in the sight of the elders
17: 9 *M* said to Joshua, "Choose some
17: 10 as *M* had ordered, and *M*,
17: 11 As long as *M* held up his hands,
17: 14 Then the LORD said to *M*,
17: 15 *M* built an altar and called it
18: 1 of Midian and father-in-law of *M*,
18: 1 of everything God had done for *M*
18: 2 After *M* had sent away his wife
18: 3 was named Gershom, for *M* said,
18: 7 So *M* went out to meet his
18: 8 *M* told his father-in-law about
18: 13 The next day *M* took his seat
18: 14 saw all that *M* was doing
18: 15 till evening?" *M* answered him,
18: 24 *M* listened to his father-in-law
18: 26 difficult cases they brought to *M*,
18: 27 *M* sent his father-in-law on his way
19: 3 Then *M* went up to God,
19: 7 So *M* went back and summoned
19: 8 So *M* brought their answer back
19: 9 The LORD said to *M*, "I am going
19: 9 *M* told the LORD what the people
19: 10 And the LORD said to *M*,
19: 14 After *M* had gone
19: 17 *M* led the people out of the camp
19: 19 Then *M* spoke and the voice

Ex 19: 20 So *M* went up and the LORD said
19: 20 called *M* to the top of the mountain
19: 23 *M* said to the LORD, "The people
19: 25 So *M* went down to the people
20: 19 stayed at a distance and said to *M*,
20: 20 *M* said to the people, "Do not be
20: 21 while *M* approached the thick
20: 22 Then the LORD said to *M*,
24: 1 Then he said to *M*, "Come up
24: 2 *M* alone is to approach the LORD;
24: 3 When *M* went and told the people
24: 4 *M* then wrote down everything
24: 6 *M* took half of the blood
24: 8 *M* then took the blood, sprinkled it
24: 9 *M* and Aaron, Nadab and Abihu,
24: 12 The LORD said to *M*, "Come up
24: 13 *M* set out with Joshua his aide,
24: 13 *M* went up on the mountain of God
24: 15 When *M* went up on the mountain,
24: 16 called to *M* from within the cloud.
24: 18 Then *M* entered the cloud
25: 1 said to *M*, "Tell the Israelites
30: 11 Then the LORD said to *M*,
30: 17 Then the LORD said to *M*,
30: 22 Then the LORD said to *M*,
30: 34 Then the LORD said to *M*,
31: 1 Then the LORD said to *M*, "See,
31: 12 Then the LORD said to *M*,
31: 18 speaking to *M* on Mount Sinai,
32: 1 When the people saw that *M* was
32: 1 for this fellow *M* who brought us
32: 7 Then the LORD said to *M*,
32: 9 to *M*, "and they are a stiff-necked
32: 11 But *M* sought the favor
32: 15 *M* turned and went
32: 17 he said to *M*, "There is the sound
32: 18 *M* replied:
32: 19 When *M* approached the camp
32: 23 for this fellow *M* who brought us
32: 25 *M* saw that the people were
32: 28 The Levites did as *M* commanded,
32: 29 *M* said, "You have been set apart
32: 30 The next day *M* said to the people,
32: 31 So *M* went back to the LORD
32: 33 replied to *M*, "Whoever has sinned
33: 1 Then the LORD said to *M*,
33: 5 For the LORD had said to *M*,
33: 7 Now *M* used to take a tent
33: 8 watching *M* until he entered
33: 8 whenever *M* went out to the tent,
33: 9 As *M* went into the tent, the pillar
33: 9 while the LORD spoke with *M*
33: 11 The LORD would speak to *M* face
33: 11 Then *M* would return to the camp,
33: 12 *M* said to the LORD, "You have
33: 15 *M* said to him, "If your Presence
33: 17 And the LORD said to *M*,
33: 18 *M* said, "Now show me your glory
34: 1 to *M*, "Chisel out two stone tablets
34: 4 So *M* chiseled out two stone tablets
34: 6 And he passed in front of *M*,
34: 8 *M* bowed to the ground at once
34: 27 Then the LORD said to *M*,
34: 28 *M* was there with the LORD forty
34: 29 *M* came down from Mount Sinai
34: 30 and all the Israelites saw *M*,
34: 31 But *M* called to them; so Aaron
34: 33 When *M* finished speaking to them
34: 35 Then *M* would put the veil back
35: 1 *M* assembled the whole Israelite
35: 4 *M* said to the whole Israelite
35: 29 through *M* had commanded them
35: 30 Then *M* said to the Israelites, "See,
36: 2 Then *M* summoned Bezalel
36: 3 received from *M* all the offerings
36: 5 left their work and said to *M*,
36: 6 Then *M* gave an order
38: 22 the LORD commanded *M*;
39: 1 as the LORD commanded *M*.
39: 5 as the LORD commanded *M*.
39: 7 as the LORD commanded *M*.
39: 21 as the LORD commanded *M*.
39: 26 as the LORD commanded *M*.
39: 29 as the LORD commanded *M*.
39: 31 as the LORD commanded *M*.
39: 32 as the LORD commanded *M*.
39: 33 they brought the tabernacle to *M*:
39: 42 as the LORD had commanded *M*.

Ex 39: 43 So *M* blessed them.
39: 43 *M* inspected the work
40: 1 Then the LORD said to *M*:
40: 16 *M* did everything just
40: 18 When *M* set up the tabernacle,
40: 22 *M* placed the table in the Tent
40: 26 *M* placed the gold altar in the Tent
40: 31 *M* and Aaron and his sons used it
40: 32 as the LORD commanded *M*.
40: 33 And so *M* finished the work.
40: 33 Then *M* set up the courtyard
40: 35 *M* could not enter the Tent
Lev 1: 1 The LORD called to *M*
4: 1 The LORD said to *M*, "Say
5: 14 to *M*: "When a person commits
6: 1 said to *M*: "If anyone sins
6: 8 said to *M*: "Give Aaron
6: 19 The LORD also said to *M*,
6: 24 said to *M*, "Say to Aaron
7: 22 The LORD said to *M*, "Say
7: 28 The LORD said to *M*, "Say
7: 38 which the LORD gave *M*
8: 1 said to *M*, "Bring Aaron
8: 4 *M* did as the LORD commanded
8: 5 *M* said to the assembly, "This is
8: 6 Then *M* brought Aaron
8: 9 as the LORD commanded *M*.
8: 10 Then *M* took the anointing oil
8: 13 as the LORD commanded *M*.
8: 15 *M* slaughtered the bull
8: 16 *M* also took all the fat
8: 17 as the LORD commanded *M*.
8: 19 Then *M* slaughtered the ram
8: 21 as the LORD commanded *M*.
8: 23 *M* slaughtered the ram
8: 24 *M* also brought Aaron's sons
8: 28 *M* took them from their hands
8: 29 as the LORD commanded *M*.
8: 30 *M* took some of the anointing oil
8: 31 *M* then said to Aaron and his sons,
8: 36 LORD commanded through *M*.
9: 1 eighth day *M* summoned Aaron
9: 5 took the things *M* commanded
9: 6 *M* said, "This is what the LORD
9: 7 *M* said to Aaron, "Come
9: 10 as the LORD commanded *M*;
9: 21 a wave offering, as *M* commanded.
9: 23 *M* and Aaron then went
10: 3 *M* then said to Aaron, "This is
10: 4 *M* summoned Mishael
10: 5 outside the camp, as *M* ordered.
10: 6 Then *M* said to Aaron
10: 7 So they did as *M* said.
10: 11 has given them through *M*."
10: 12 *M* said to Aaron and his remaining
10: 16 When *M* inquired about the goat
10: 19 to *M*, "Today they sacrificed their
10: 20 When *M* heard this, he was
11: 1 The LORD said to *M* and Aaron,
12: 1 The LORD said to *M*, "Say
13: 1 The LORD said to *M* and Aaron,
14: 1 to *M*, "These are the regulations
14: 33 The LORD said to *M* and Aaron,
15: 1 The LORD said to *M* and Aaron,
16: 1 spoke to *M* after the death
16: 2 to *M*: "Tell your brother Aaron not
16: 34 as the LORD commanded *M*.
17: 1 said to *M*, "Speak to Aaron
18: 1 The LORD said to *M*, "Speak
19: 1 The LORD said to *M*, "Speak
20: 1 The LORD said to *M*, "Say
21: 1 The LORD said to *M*, "Speak
21: 16 said to *M*, "Say to Aaron:
21: 24 So *M* told this to Aaron
22: 1 The LORD said to *M*, "Tell Aaron
22: 17 said to *M*, "Speak to Aaron
22: 26 said to *M*, "When a cow,
23: 1 The LORD said to *M*, "Speak
23: 9 The LORD said to *M*, "Speak
23: 23 The LORD said to *M*, "Say
23: 26 said to *M*, "The tenth day
23: 33 The LORD said to *M*, "Say
23: 44 So *M* announced to the Israelites
24: 1 to *M*, "Command the Israelites
24: 11 so they brought him to *M*.
24: 13 Then the LORD said to *M*:
24: 23 Then *M* spoke to the Israelites,
24: 23 as the LORD commanded *M*.

Lev 25: 1 said to *M* on Mount Sinai,
26: 46 and the Israelites through *M*.
27: 1 The LORD said to *M*, "Speak
27: 34 the commands the LORD gave *M*
Nu 1: 1 The LORD spoke to *M* in the Tent
1: 17 *M* and Aaron took these men
1: 19 as the LORD commanded *M*.
1: 44 These were the men counted by *M*
1: 48 The LORD had said to *M*:
1: 54 as the LORD commanded *M*.
2: 1 The LORD said to *M* and Aaron:
2: 33 as the LORD commanded *M*.
2: 34 the LORD commanded *M*;
3: 1 *M* at the time the LORD talked
3: 1 talked with *M* on Mount Sinai.
3: 5 said to *M*, "Bring the tribe
3: 11 The LORD also said to *M*,
3: 14 The LORD said to *M* in the Desert
3: 16 So *M* counted them, as he was
3: 38 *M* and Aaron and his sons were
3: 39 at the LORD's command by *M*
3: 40 said to *M*, "Count all the firstborn
3: 42 So *M* counted all the firstborn
3: 44 The LORD also said to *M*,
3: 49 *M* collected the redemption money
3: 51 *M* gave the redemption money
4: 1 The LORD said to *M* and Aaron:
4: 17 The LORD said to *M* and Aaron,
4: 21 said to *M*, "Take a census
4: 34 *M*, Aaron and the leaders
4: 37 *M* and Aaron counted them
4: 37 the LORD's command through *M*.
4: 41 *M* and Aaron counted them
4: 45 *M* and Aaron counted them
4: 45 the LORD's command through *M*.
4: 46 So *M*, Aaron and the leaders
4: 49 as the LORD commanded *M*.
4: 49 the LORD's command through *M*,
5: 1 to *M*, "Command the Israelites
5: 4 as the LORD had instructed *M*.
5: 5 The LORD said to *M*, "Say
5: 11 Then the LORD said to *M*,
6: 1 The LORD said to *M*, "Speak
6: 22 The LORD said to *M*, "Tell Aaron
7: 1 When *M* finished setting up
7: 4 said to *M*, "Accept these
7: 6 So *M* took the carts and oxen
7: 9 But *M* did not give any
7: 11 For the LORD had said to *M*,
7: 89 When *M* entered the Tent
8: 1 said to *M*, "Speak to Aaron
8: 3 just as the LORD commanded *M*.
8: 4 pattern the LORD had shown *M*.
8: 5 said to *M*: "Take the Levites
8: 20 as the LORD commanded *M*.
8: 20 *M*, Aaron and the whole Israelite
8: 22 as the LORD commanded *M*.
8: 23 said to *M*, "This applies
9: 1 spoke to *M* in the Desert
9: 4 So *M* told the Israelites
9: 5 as the LORD commanded *M*.
9: 6 to *M* and Aaron that same day
9: 7 Aaron that same day and said to *M*
9: 8 *M* answered them, "Wait
9: 9 Then the LORD said to *M*,
9: 23 with his command through *M*.
10: 1 said to *M*: "Make two trumpets
10: 13 the LORD's command through *M*.
10: 29 Now *M* said to Hobab son
10: 31 But *M* said, "Please do not leave us
10: 35 Whenever the ark set out, *M* said,
11: 2 When the people cried out to *M*,
11: 10 angry, and *M* was troubled.
11: 10 *M* heard the people
11: 16 said to *M*: "Bring me seventy
11: 21 ever leave Egypt?" ' " But *M* said,
11: 23 The LORD answered *M*, "Is
11: 24 So *M* went out and told the people
11: 27 A young man ran and told *M*,
11: 28 spoke up and said, "*M*, my lord,
11: 29 my lord, stop them!" But *M* replied
11: 30 *M* and the elders of Israel returned
12: 1 and Aaron began to talk against *M*
12: 2 LORD spoken only through *M*?"
12: 3 (Now *M* was a very humble man,
12: 4 At once the LORD said to *M*,
12: 7 But this is not true of my servant *M*
12: 8 to speak against my servant *M*?"
Nu 12: 11 and he said to *M*, "Please, my lord,
12: 13 So *M* cried out to the LORD,
12: 14 her!" The LORD replied to *M*,
13: 1 said to *M*, "Send some men
13: 3 LORD's command *M* sent them
13: 16 the names of the men *M* sent
13: 16 (*M* gave Hoshea son
13: 17 When *M* sent them
13: 26 They came back to *M* and Aaron
13: 27 They gave *M* this account:
13: 30 Caleb silenced the people before *M*
14: 2 the Israelites grumbled against *M*
14: 5 *M* and Aaron fell facedown in front
14: 11 to *M*, "How long will these people
14: 13 *M* said to the LORD,
14: 26 The LORD said to *M* and Aaron:
14: 36 So the men *M* had sent
14: 39 When *M* reported this
14: 41 *M* said, "Why are you disobeying
14: 44 though neither *M* nor the ark
15: 1 The LORD said to *M*, "Speak
15: 17 The LORD said to *M*, "Speak
15: 22 commands the LORD gave *M*—
15: 33 gathering wood brought him to *M*
15: 35 Then the LORD said to *M*,
15: 36 as the LORD commanded *M*.
15: 37 The LORD said to *M*, "Speak
16: 2 insolent and rose up against *M*.
16: 3 as a group to oppose *M* and Aaron
16: 4 When *M* heard this, he fell
16: 8 You Levites have gone too far!" *M*
16: 12 Then *M* summoned Dathan
16: 15 Then *M* became very angry
16: 16 *M* said to Korah, "You
16: 18 and stood with *M* and Aaron
16: 20 The LORD said to *M* and Aaron,
16: 22 But *M* and Aaron fell facedown
16: 23 Then the LORD said to *M*,
16: 25 *M* got up and went to Dathan
16: 28 *M* said, "This is how you will know
16: 36 said to *M*, "Tell Eleazar son
16: 40 LORD directed him through *M*.
16: 41 community grumbled against *M*
16: 42 gathered in opposition to *M*
16: 43 *M* and Aaron went to the front
16: 44 the LORD said to *M*, "Get away
16: 46 Then *M* said to Aaron, "Take your
16: 47 So Aaron did as *M* said,
16: 50 Then Aaron returned to *M*
17: 1 The LORD said to *M*, "Speak
17: 6 So *M* spoke to the Israelites,
17: 7 *M* placed the staffs
17: 8 The next day *M* entered the Tent
17: 9 Then *M* brought out all the staffs
17: 10 said to *M*, "Put back Aaron's staff
17: 11 *M* did just as the LORD
17: 12 said to *M*, "We will die!
18: 25 The LORD said to *M*, "Speak
19: 1 The LORD said to *M* and Aaron:
20: 2 gathered in opposition to *M*
20: 3 They quarreled with *M* and said,
20: 6 *M* and Aaron went
20: 7 said to *M*, "Take the staff,
20: 9 *M* took the staff from the LORD's
20: 10 of the rock and *M* said to them,
20: 11 Then *M* raised his arm
20: 12 the LORD said to *M* and Aaron,
20: 14 *M* sent messengers from Kadesh
20: 23 the LORD said to *M* and Aaron,
20: 27 *M* did as the LORD commanded:
20: 28 Then *M* and Eleazar came
20: 28 *M* removed Aaron's garments
21: 5 spoke against God and against *M*,
21: 7 So *M* prayed for the people.
21: 7 The people came to *M* and said,
21: 8 said to *M*, "Make a snake
21: 9 So *M* made a bronze snake
21: 16 well where the LORD said to *M*,
21: 32 After *M* had sent spies to Jazer,
21: 34 said to *M*, "Do not be afraid
25: 4 said to *M*, "Take all the leaders
25: 5 So *M* said to Israel's judges,
25: 6 right before the eyes of *M*
25: 10 said to *M*, "Phinehas son
25: 16 said to *M*, "Treat the Midianites
26: 1 the plague the LORD said to *M*
26: 3 *M* and Eleazar the priest spoke
26: 4 as the LORD commanded *M*."
Nu 26: 9 officials who rebelled against *M*
26: 52 The LORD said to *M*, "The land is
26: 59 *M* and their sister Miriam.
26: 63 These are the ones counted by *M*
26: 64 was among those counted by *M*
27: 2 of Meeting and stood before *M*,
27: 5 So *M* brought their case
27: 11 as the LORD commanded *M*.' "
27: 12 Then the LORD said to *M*,
27: 15 *M* said to the LORD, "May
27: 18 said to *M*, "Take Joshua son
27: 22 *M* did as the LORD commanded
27: 23 the LORD instructed through *M*.
28: 1 said to *M*, "Give this command
29: 40 *M* told the Israelites all that
30: 1 *M* said to the heads of the tribes
30: 16 the LORD gave *M* concerning
31: 1 said to *M*, "Take vengeance
31: 3 *M* said to the people, "Arm some
31: 6 *M* sent them into battle, a thousand
31: 7 as the LORD commanded *M*,
31: 12 spoils and plunder to *M*
31: 13 *M*, Eleazar the priest and all
31: 14 *M* was angry with the officers
31: 21 of the law that the LORD gave *M*:
31: 25 The LORD said to *M*, "You
31: 31 So *M* and Eleazar the priest did
31: 31 as the LORD commanded *M*.
31: 41 as the LORD commanded *M*.
31: 41 *M* gave the tribute
31: 42 which *M* set apart from that
31: 47 *M* selected one out
31: 48 went to *M* and said to him,
31: 51 *M* and Eleazar the priest accepted
31: 52 commanders of hundreds that *M*
31: 54 *M* and Eleazar the priest accepted
32: 2 came to *M* and Eleazar the priest
32: 6 *M* said to the Gadites
32: 20 *M* said to them, "If you will do this
32: 25 and Reubenites said to *M*,
32: 28 Then *M* gave orders about them
32: 33 Then *M* gave to the Gadites,
32: 40 So *M* gave Gilead to the Makirites,
33: 1 divisions under the leadership of *M*
33: 2 the LORD's command *M* recorded
33: 50 from Jericho the LORD said to *M*,
34: 1 to *M*, "Command the Israelites
34: 13 *M* commanded the Israelites:
34: 16 said to *M*, "These are the names
35: 1 from Jericho, the LORD said to *M*,
35: 9 Then the LORD said to *M*:
36: 1 spoke before *M* and the leaders,
36: 5 the LORD's command *M* gave this
36: 10 as the LORD commanded *M*.
36: 13 gave through *M* to the Israelites
Dt 1: 1 These are the words *M* spoke
1: 3 *M* proclaimed to the Israelites all
1: 5 *M* began to expound this law,
4: 41 Then *M* set aside three cities east
4: 44 This is the law *M* set
4: 45 and laws *M* gave them
4: 46 defeated by *M* and the Israelites
5: 1 *M* summoned all Israel and said:
27: 1 *M* and the elders of Israel
27: 9 *M* and the priests, who are Levites,
27: 11 the same day *M* commanded
29: 1 the LORD commanded *M*
29: 2 *M* summoned all the Israelites
31: 1 *M* went out and spoke these words
31: 7 Then *M* summoned Joshua
31: 9 So *M* wrote down this law
31: 10 Then *M* commanded them:
31: 14 So *M* and Joshua came
31: 14 The LORD said to *M*,
31: 16 And the LORD said to *M*:
31: 22 *M* wrote down this song that day
31: 24 After *M* finished writing
31: 30 *M* recited the words of this song
32: 44 *M* came with Joshua son of Nun
32: 45 When *M* finished reciting all these
32: 48 that same day the LORD told *M*,
33: 1 This is the blessing that *M* the man
33: 4 the law that *M* gave us,
34: 1 Then *M* climbed Mount Nebo
34: 5 *M* the servant of the LORD died
34: 7 *M* was a hundred and twenty years
34: 8 grieved for *M* in the plains
34: 9 *M* had laid his hands on him.

Dt 34: 9 the LORD had commanded *M*.
34: 10 prophet has risen in Israel like *M*,
34: 12 the awesome deeds that *M* did
Jos 1: 1 After the death of *M* the servant
1: 2 "*M* my servant is dead.
1: 3 you set your foot, as I promised *M*.
1: 5 As I was with *M*, so I will be
1: 7 all the law my servant *M* gave you;
1: 13 the command that *M* the servant
1: 14 in the land that *M* gave you east
1: 15 which *M* the servant
1: 17 Just as we fully obeyed *M*,
1: 17 be with you as he was with *M*.
3: 7 am with you as I was with *M*.
4: 10 just as *M* had directed Joshua.
4: 12 the Israelites, as *M* had directed
4: 14 just as they had revered *M*.
8: 31 as *M* the servant of the LORD had
8: 31 in the Book of the Law of *M*—
8: 32 copied on stones the law of *M*,
8: 33 as *M* the servant of the LORD had
8: 35 of all that *M* had commanded that
9: 24 had commanded his servant *M*
11: 12 as *M* the servant of the LORD had
11: 15 all that the LORD commanded *M*.
11: 15 LORD commanded his servant *M*,
11: 15 so *M* commanded Joshua,
11: 20 as the LORD had commanded *M*.
11: 23 just as the LORD had directed *M*,
12: 6 *M* the servant of the LORD gave
12: 6 *M*, the servant of the LORD,
13: 8 the inheritance that *M* had given
13: 12 *M* had defeated them and taken
13: 15 This is what *M* had given
13: 21 *M* had defeated him
13: 24 This is what *M* had given
13: 29 This is what *M* had given
13: 32 This is the inheritance *M* had given
13: 33 *M* had given no inheritance;
14: 2 had commanded through *M*.
14: 3 *M* had granted the two-and-a-half
14: 5 as the LORD had commanded *M*.
14: 6 said to *M* the man of God
14: 7 old when *M* the servant
14: 9 So on that day *M* swore to me,
14: 10 since the time he said this to *M*,
14: 11 as the day *M* sent me out;
17: 4 "The LORD commanded *M*
18: 7 *M* the servant of the LORD gave it
20: 2 as I instructed you through *M*,
21: 2 through *M* that you give us towns
21: 8 had commanded through *M*.
22: 2 have done all that *M* the servant
22: 4 in the land that *M* the servant
22: 5 and the law that *M* the servant
22: 7 Manasseh *M* had given land
22: 9 of the LORD through *M*.
23: 6 in the Book of the Law of *M*,
24: 5 " 'Then I sent *M* and Aaron,
Jdg 1: 20 As *M* had promised, Hebron was
3: 4 given their forefathers through *M*.
18: 30 son of Gershom, the son of *M*,
1Sa 12: 6 "It is the LORD who appointed *M*
12: 8 and the LORD sent *M* and Aaron,
1Ki 2: 3 as written in the Law of *M*,
8: 9 stone tablets that *M* had placed
8: 53 through your servant *M* when you,
8: 56 gave through his servant *M*.
2Ki 14: 6 the Law of *M* where the LORD
18: 4 the bronze snake *M* had made,
18: 6 the LORD had given *M*.
18: 12 all that *M* the servant
21: 8 that my servant *M* gave them."
23: 25 accordance with all the Law of *M*.
1Ch 6: 3 The children of Amram: Aaron, *M*
6: 49 with all that *M* the servant
15: 15 *M* had commanded in accordance
21: 29 which *M* had made in the desert,
22: 13 and laws that the LORD gave *M*
23: 13 The sons of Amram: Aaron and *M*.
23: 14 The sons of *M* the man
23: 15 The sons of *M*: Gershom
26: 24 a descendant of Gershom son of *M*
2Ch 1: 3 which *M* the LORD's servant had
5: 10 the two tablets that *M* had placed
8: 13 commanded by *M* for Sabbaths,
23: 18 as written in the Law of *M*,
24: 6 the tax imposed by *M* the servant
2Ch 24: 9 LORD the tax that *M* the servant
25: 4 the Book of *M*, where the LORD
30: 16 in the Law of *M* the man of God.
33: 8 and ordinances given through *M*."
34: 14 that had been given through *M*.
35: 6 LORD commanded through *M*."
35: 12 as is written in the Book of *M*.
Ezr 3: 2 in the Law of *M* the man of God.
6: 18 to what is written in the Book of *M*.
7: 6 well versed in the Law of *M*,
Ne 1: 7 and laws you gave your servant *M*.
1: 8 you gave your servant *M*,
8: 1 out the Book of the Law of *M*,
8: 14 had commanded through *M*,
9: 14 and laws through your servant *M*.
10: 29 given through *M* the servant
13: 1 the Book of *M* was read aloud
Ps 77: 20 by the hand of *M* and Aaron.
99: 6 *M* and Aaron were
103: 7 He made known his ways to *M*,
105: 26 He sent *M* his servant,
106: 16 the camp they grew envious of *M*
106: 23 had not *M*, his chosen one,
106: 32 trouble came to *M* because of them
Isa 63: 11 the days of *M* and his people—
Jer 15: 1 "Even if *M* and Samuel were
Da 9: 11 judgments written in the Law of *M*,
9: 13 Just as it is written in the Law of *M*,
Mic 6: 4 I sent *M* to lead you,
Mal 4: 4 the law of my servant *M*,
Mt 8: 4 and offer the gift *M* commanded,
17: 3 then there appeared before them *M*
17: 4 one for *M* and one for Elijah."
19: 7 "did *M* command that a man give
19: 8 "*M* permitted you
22: 24 "*M* told us that if a man dies
Mk 1: 44 the sacrifices that *M* commanded
7: 10 For *M* said, 'Honor your father
9: 4 before them Elijah and *M*,
9: 5 one for *M* and one for Elijah."
10: 3 "What did *M* command you?"
10: 4 "*M* permitted a man
10: 5 were hard that *M* wrote you this
12: 19 "*M* wrote for us that
12: 26 have you not read in the book of *M*,
Lk 2: 22 the Law of *M* had been completed,
5: 14 the sacrifices that *M* commanded
9: 30 *M* and Elijah, appeared
9: 33 one for *M* and one for Elijah."
16: 29 'They have *M* and the Prophets;
16: 31 'If they do not listen to *M*
20: 28 "*M* wrote for us that
20: 37 even *M* showed that the dead rise,
24: 27 And beginning with *M*
24: 44 written about me in the Law of *M*,
Jn 1: 17 For the law was given through *M*;
1: 45 have found the one *M* wrote about
3: 14 *M* lifted up the snake in the desert,
5: 45 Your accuser is *M*,
5: 46 If you believed *M*, you would
6: 32 it is not *M* who has given you
7: 19 Has not *M* given you the law?
7: 22 actually it did not come from *M*,
7: 22 because *M* gave you circumcision
7: 23 the law of *M* may not be broken,
8: 5 In the Law *M* commanded us
9: 28 of *M*! We know that God spoke
9: 29 We know that God spoke to *M*,
Ac 3: 22 For *M* said, 'The Lord your God
6: 11 words of blasphemy against *M*
6: 14 and change the customs *M* handed
7: 20 "At that time *M* was born,
7: 22 *M* was educated in all the wisdom
7: 23 "When *M* was forty years old,
7: 25 *M* thought that his own people
7: 26 The next day *M* came
7: 27 mistreating the other pushed *M*
7: 29 When *M* heard this, he fled
7: 30 appeared to *M* in the flames
7: 32 *M* trembled with fear and did not
7: 35 is the same *M* whom they had
7: 37 This is that *M* who told
7: 40 As for this fellow *M* who led us out
7: 44 had been made as God directed *M*,
13: 39 justified from by the law of *M*.
15: 1 to the custom taught by *M*,
15: 5 required to obey the law of *M*."
15: 21 For *M* has been preached
Ac 21: 21 the Gentiles to turn away from *M*,
26: 22 and *M* said would happen—
28: 23 Jesus from the Law of *M*
Ro 5: 14 the time of Adam to the time of *M*,
9: 15 Not at all! For he says to *M*,
10: 5 *M* describes in this way
10: 19 not understand? First, *M* says,
1Co 9: 9 For it is written in the Law of *M*:
10: 2 baptized into *M* in the cloud
2Co 3: 7 not look steadily at the face of *M*
3: 13 We are not like *M*, who would put
3: 15 Even to this day when *M* is read,
2Ti 3: 8 as Jannes and Jambres opposed *M*,
Heb 3: 2 *M* was faithful in all God's house.
3: 3 worthy of greater honor than *M*,
3: 5 *M* was faithful as a servant
3: 16 Were they not all those *M* led out
7: 14 to that tribe *M* said nothing about
8: 5 This is why *M* was warned
9: 19 When *M* had proclaimed every
10: 28 the law of *M* died without mercy
11: 24 By faith *M*, when he had grown up,
12: 21 was so terrifying that *M* said,
Jude : 9 with the devil about the body of *M*,
Rev 15: 3 and sang the song of *M* the servant

MOSES' (MOSES)

Ex 4: 25 and touched *M'* feet with it.
17: 12 When *M'* hands grew tired,
18: 5 *M'* father-in-law, together
18: 5 together with *M'* sons and wife,
18: 12 Then Jethro, *M'* father-in-law,
18: 12 to eat bread with *M'* father-in-law
18: 17 *M'* father-in-law replied, "What
35: 20 withdrew from *M'* presence,
38: 21 were recorded at *M'* command
Lev 8: 29 *M'* share of the ordination ram—
Nu 10: 29 the Midianite, *M'* father-in-law,
11: 28 who had been *M'* aide since youth,
Jos 1: 1 Joshua son of Nun, *M'* aide:
Jdg 1: 16 descendants of *M'* father-in-law,
4: 11 of Hobab, *M'* brother-in-law,
Ps 106: 33 and rash words came from *M'* lips.
Isa 63: 12 power to be at *M'* right hand,
Mt 23: 2 and the Pharisees sit in *M'* seat.
Heb 11: 23 By faith *M'* parents hid him

MOTH

Job 4: 19 are crushed more readily than a *m*!
Ps 39: 11 you consume their wealth like a *m*
Isa 51: 8 For the *m* will eat them up like
Hos 5: 12 I am like a *m* to Ephraim,
Mt 6: 19 where *m* and rust destroy,
6: 20 where *m* and rust do not destroy,
Lk 12: 33 comes near and no *m* destroys.

MOTH'S (MOTHS)

Job 27: 18 house he builds is like a *m* cocoon,

MOTHER (GRANDMOTHER GRANDMOTHER'S MOTHER-IN-LAW MOTHER'S MOTHERS MOTHERS')

Ge 2: 24 and *m* and be united to his wife,
3: 20 because she would become the *m*
17: 16 so that she will be the *m* of nations;
20: 12 of my father though not of my *m*;
21: 21 his *m* got a wife for him from Egypt
22: 20 also a *m*; she has borne sons
24: 53 gifts to her brother and to her *m*.
24: 55 But her brother and her *m* replied,
24: 67 her into the tent of his *m* Sarah,
27: 11 Jacob said to Rebekah his *m*,
27: 13 His *m* said to him, "My son,
27: 14 and brought them to his *m*,
27: 29 sons of your *m* bow down to you.
28: 5 who was the *m* of Jacob and Esau.
28: 7 and *m* and had gone to Paddan
30: 14 which he brought to his *m* Leah.
37: 10 Will your *m* and I and your
Ex 2: 8 the girl went and got the baby's *m*.
20: 12 "Honor your father and your *m*,
21: 15 or his *m* must be put to death.
21: 17 or *m* must be put to death.
Lev 18: 7 She is your *m*; do not have
18: 7 sexual relations with your *m*.
19: 3 " 'Each of you must respect his *m*
20: 9 He has cursed his father or his *m*,
20: 9 " 'If anyone curses his father or *m*,

Lev 20: 14 marries both a woman and her *m*,
20: 17 of either his father or his *m*,
20: 19 either your *m* or your father,
21: 2 such as his *m* or father, his son
21: 11 even for his father or *m*,
22: 27 to remain with its *m* for seven days.
24: 10 Now the son of an Israelite *m*
Nu 6: 7 or *m* or brother or sister dies,
Dt 5: 16 "Honor your father and your *m*,
21: 13 and mourned her father and *m*
21: 18 who does not obey his father and *m*
21: 19 and *m* shall take hold of him
22: 6 and the *m* is sitting on the young
22: 6 do not take the *m* with the young.
22: 7 but be sure to let the *m* go,
22: 15 *m* shall bring proof that she was
27: 16 who dishonors his father or his *m*."
27: 22 or the daughter of his *m*."
33: 9 He said of his father and *m*,
Jos 2: 13 the lives of my father and *m*,
2: 18 have brought your father and *m*,
6: 23 her father and *m* and brothers
Jdg 5: 7 arose a *m* in Israel.
5: 28 the window peered Sisera's *m*;
8: 19 brothers, the sons of my own *m*.
11: 1 was Gilead; his *m* was a prostitute.
14: 2 he said to his father and *m*,
14: 3 and *m* replied, "Isn't there
14: 5 together with his father and *m*.
14: 6 nor his *m* what he had done.
14: 16 explained it to my father or *m*,"
17: 2 country of Ephraim said to his *m*,
17: 2 his *m* said, "The LORD bless you,
17: 3 hundred shekels of silver to his *m*,
17: 4 So he returned the silver to his *m*,
Ru 2: 11 and *m* and your homeland
1Sa 2: 19 Each year his *m* made him a little
15: 33 so will your *m* be childless
20: 30 the shame of the *m* who bore you?
22: 3 you let my father and *m* come
2Sa 17: 25 and sister of Zeruiah the *m* of Joab.
19: 37 near the tomb of my father and *m*.
20: 19 to destroy a city that is a *m* in Israel
1Ki 1: 5 Adonijah, whose *m* was Haggith,
1: 11 asked Bathsheba, Solomon's *m*,
2: 13 went to Bathsheba, Solomon's *m*.
2: 19 a throne brought for the king's *m*,
2: 20 my *m*; I will not refuse you."
2: 22 King Solomon answered his *m*,
3: 27 Do not kill him; she is his *m*."
7: 14 whose *m* was a widow
11: 26 his *m* was a widow named Zeruah.
15: 13 from her position as queen *m*,
17: 23 He gave him to his *m* and said,
19: 20 me kiss my father and *m* good-by,"
22: 52 in the ways of his father and *m*
2Ki 3: 2 not as his father and *m* had done.
3: 13 and the prophets of your *m*."
4: 19 a servant, "Carry him to his *m*."
4: 20 him up and carried him to his *m*,
4: 30 But the child's *m* said, "As surely
9: 22 of your *m* Jezebel abound?"
10: 13 of the king and of the queen *m*."
11: 1 When Athaliah the *m*
24: 12 Jehoiachin king of Judah, his *m*,
24: 15 Jerusalem to Babylon the king's *m*,
1Ch 2: 17 Abigail was the *m* of Amasa,
2: 26 name was Atarah; she was the *m*
2: 46 concubine Ephah was the *m*
2: 48 concubine Maacah was the *m*
4: 9 His *m* had named him Jabez,
2Ch 2: 14 whose *m* was from Dan
15: 16 from her position as queen *m*,
22: 3 for his *m* encouraged him
22: 10 When Athaliah the *m*
Est 2: 7 she had neither father nor *m*.
2: 7 when her father and *m* died.
Job 17: 14 to the worm, 'My *m*' or 'My sister,'
Ps 27: 10 my father and *m* forsake me,
35: 14 as though weeping for my *m*.
51: 5 from the time my *m* conceived me.
109: 14 of his *m* never be blotted out.
113: 9 as a happy *m* of children.
131: 2 like a weaned child with its *m*,
Pr 4: 3 and an only child of my *m*,
10: 1 but a foolish son grief to his *m*.
15: 20 but a foolish man despises his *m*.
19: 26 robs his father and drives out his *m*
Pr 20: 20 If a man curses his father or *m*,
23: 22 do not despise your *m*
23: 25 May your father and *m* be glad;
28: 24 He who robs his father or *m*
29: 15 a child left to itself disgraces his *m*.
30: 17 that scorns obedience to a *m*,
31: 1 an oracle his *m* taught him:
SS 3: 11 with which his *m* crowned him
6: 9 the only daughter of her *m*,
8: 5 there your *m* conceived you,
Isa 8: 4 how to say 'My father' or 'My *m*,'
45: 10 or to his *m*,
49: 15 "Can a *m* forget the baby
50: 1 transgressions your *m* was sent
66: 13 As a *m* comforts her child,
Jer 13: 18 Say to the king and to the queen *m*,
15: 9 The *m* of seven will grow faint
15: 10 Alas, my *m*, that you gave me birth
16: 7 not even for a father or a *m*—
20: 14 May the day my *m* bore me not be
20: 17 with my *m* as my grave,
22: 26 and the *m* who gave you birth
29: 2 King Jehoiachin and the queen *m*,
50: 12 your *m* will be greatly ashamed;
Eze 16: 3 an Amorite and your *m* a Hittite.
16: 44 this proverb about you: "Like *m*,
16: 45 You are a true daughter of your *m*,
16: 45 Your *m* was a Hittite and your
19: 2 " 'What a lioness was your *m*
19: 10 " 'Your *m* was like a vine
22: 7 you they have treated father and *m*
23: 2 women, daughters of the same *m*.
44: 25 dead person was his father or *m*,
Hos 2: 2 "Rebuke your *m*, rebuke her,
2: 5 Their *m* has been unfaithful
4: 5 So I will destroy your *m*—
Mic 7: 6 a daughter rises up against her *m*,
Zec 13: 3 and *m*, to whom he was born,
Mt 1: 3 whose *m* was Tamar, Perez
1: 5 father of Obed, whose *m* was Ruth,
1: 5 of Boaz, whose *m* was Rahab,
1: 6 whose *m* had been Uriah's wife,
1: 18 His *m* Mary was pledged
2: 11 they saw the child with his *m* Mary
2: 13 and his *m* and escape to Egypt.
2: 14 and his *m* during the night
2: 20 take the child and his *m*
2: 21 took the child and his *m*
10: 35 a daughter against her *m*,
10: 37 or *m* more than me is not worthy
12: 46 his *m* and brothers stood outside,
12: 47 "Your *m* and brothers are standing
12: 48 He replied, "Who is my *m*,
12: 49 "Here are my *m* and my brothers.
12: 50 is my brother and sister and *m*."
14: 8 Prompted by her *m*, she said,
14: 11 to the girl, who carried it to her *m*.
15: 4 'Honor your father and *m*'
15: 4 or *m* must be put to death.'
15: 5 that if a man says to his father or *m*,
19: 5 and *m* and be united to his wife,
19: 19 honor your father and *m*,'
19: 29 or sisters or father or *m* or children
20: 20 the *m* of Zebedee's sons came
27: 56 Mary the *m* of James and Joseph,
27: 56 and the *m* of Zebedee's sons.
Mk 3: 31 Then Jesus' *m* and brothers arrived
3: 32 "Your *m* and brothers are
3: 33 "Who are my *m* and my brothers?"
3: 34 "Here are my *m* and my brothers!
3: 35 is my brother and sister and *m*."
5: 40 he took the child's father and *m*
6: 24 She went out and said to her *m*,
6: 28 to the girl, and she gave it to her *m*.
7: 10 'Honor your father and *m*,' and,
7: 10 or *m* must be put to death.'
7: 11 that if a man says to his father or *m*:
7: 12 anything for his father or *m*.
10: 7 and *m* and be united to his wife,
10: 19 honor your father and *m*.' "
10: 29 or brothers or sisters or *m* or father
15: 40 Mary the *m* of James the younger
15: 47 Mary the *m* of Joses saw where he
16: 1 Mary Magdalene, Mary the *m*
Lk 1: 43 that the *m* of my Lord should come
1: 60 but his *m* spoke up and said, "No!
2: 33 *m* marveled at what was said about
2: 34 them and said to Mary, his *m*:
Lk 2: 48 His *m* said to him, "Son, why have
2: 51 But his *m* treasured all these things
7: 12 son of his *m*, and she was a widow.
7: 15 and Jesus gave him back to his *m*.
8: 19 Now Jesus' *m* and brothers came
8: 20 "Your *m* and brothers are standing
8: 21 "My *m* and brothers are those who
8: 51 and the child's father and *m*.
11: 27 "Blessed is the *m* who gave you
12: 53 daughter and daughter against *m*,
12: 53 *m* against daughter and daughter
14: 26 and does not hate his father and *m*,
18: 20 honor your father and *m*.' "
24: 10 Joanna, Mary the *m* of James,
Jn 2: 1 Jesus' *m* was there, and Jesus
2: 3 the wine was gone, Jesus' *m* said
2: 5 His *m* said to the servants,
2: 12 down to Capernaum with his *m*
6: 42 whose father and *m* we know?
19: 25 Near the cross of Jesus stood his *m*
19: 26 When Jesus saw his *m* there,
19: 26 he said to his *m*, "Dear woman,
19: 27 to the disciple, "Here is your *m*."
Ac 1: 14 with the women and Mary the *m*
12: 12 to the house of Mary the *m* of John
16: 1 whose *m* was a Jewess
Ro 16: 13 chosen in the Lord, and his *m*,
16: 13 who has been a *m* to me, too.
Gal 4: 26 is above is free, and she is our *m*.
Eph 5: 31 and *m* and be united to his wife,
6: 2 "Honor your father and *m*"—
1Th 2: 7 like a *m* caring for her little
2Ti 1: 5 and in your *m* Eunice and,
Heb 7: 3 or *m*, without genealogy,
Rev 17: 5 THE *M* OF PROSTITUTES

MOTHER-IN-LAW (MOTHER)

Dt 27: 23 is the man who sleeps with his *m*."
Ru 1: 14 Then Orpah kissed her *m* good-by,
2: 11 done for your *m* since the death
2: 18 and her *m* saw how much she had
2: 19 Her *m* asked her, "Where did you
2: 19 Ruth told her *m* about the one
2: 23 And she lived with her *m*.
3: 1 One day Naomi her *m* said to her,
3: 6 did everything her *m* told her to do
3: 16 When Ruth came to her *m*,
3: 17 back to your *m* empty-handed.' "
Mic 7: 6 a daughter-in-law against her *m*—
Mt 8: 14 he saw Peter's *m* lying in bed
10: 35 a daughter-in-law against her *m*—
Mk 1: 30 Simon's *m* was in bed with a fever,
Lk 4: 38 Now Simon's *m* was suffering
12: 53 and daughter-in-law against *m*."
12: 53 *m* against daughter-in-law

MOTHER-OF-PEARL (PEARL)

Est 1: 6 marble, *m* and other costly stones.

MOTHER'S (MOTHER)

Ge 24: 28 told her *m* household about these
24: 67 was comforted after his *m* death.
28: 2 of Laban, your *m* brother.
28: 2 the house of your *m* father Bethuel.
29: 10 his *m* brother, and Laban's sheep,
43: 29 his own *m* son, he asked, "Is this
44: 20 he is the only one of his *m* sons left,
Ex 23: 19 cook a young goat in its *m* milk.
34: 26 cook a young goat in its *m* milk."
Lev 18: 9 daughter or your *m* daughter,
18: 13 because she is your *m* close relative
18: 13 relations with your *m* sister,
24: 11 (His *m* name was Shelomith,
Nu 12: 12 from its *m* womb with its flesh half
Dt 14: 21 cook a young goat in its *m* milk.
Jdg 9: 1 said to them and to all his *m* clan,
9: 1 went to his *m* brothers in Shechem
Ru 1: 8 each of you, to your *m* home.
1Ki 14: 21 His *m* name was Naamah;
14: 31 His *m* name was Naamah;
15: 2 His *m* name was Maacah daughter
22: 42 His *m* name was Azubah daughter
2Ki 8: 26 His *m* name was Athaliah,
12: 1 His *m* name was Zibiah; she was
14: 2 His *m* name was Jehoaddin;
15: 2 His *m* name was Jecoliah;
15: 33 His *m* name was Jerusha daughter
18: 2 His *m* name was Abijah daughter

2Ki 21: 1 His *m* name was Hephzibah.
21: 19 His *m* name was Meshullemeth
22: 1 His *m* name was Jedidah daughter
23: 31 His *m* name was Hamutal daughter
23: 36 His *m* name was Zebidah daughter
24: 8 His *m* name was Nehushta
24: 18 His *m* name was Hamutal daughter
2Ch 12: 13 His *m* name was Naamah;
13: 2 His *m* name was Maacah,
20: 31 His *m* name was Azubah daughter
22: 2 His *m* name was Athaliah,
24: 1 His *m* name was Zibiah; she was
25: 1 His *m* name was Jehoaddin;
26: 3 His *m* name was Jecoliah;
27: 1 His *m* name was Jerusha daughter
29: 1 His *m* name was Abijah daughter
Job 1: 21 "Naked I came from my *m* womb,
Ps 22: 9 even at my *m* breast.
22: 10 from my *m* womb you have been
50: 20 and slander your own *m* son.
69: 8 an alien to my own *m* sons;
71: 6 from my *m* womb.
139: 13 knit me together in my *m* womb.
Pr 1: 8 and do not forsake your *m* teaching
6: 20 and do not forsake your *m* teaching
Ecc 5: 15 from his *m* womb,
11: 5 the body is formed in a *m* womb,
SS 1: 6 My *m* sons were angry with me
3: 4 I had brought him to my *m* house,
8: 1 who was nursed at my *m* breasts!
8: 2 and bring you to my *m* house—
Isa 50: 1 "Where is your *m* certificate
Jer 52: 1 His *m* name was Hamutal daughter
Mt 13: 55 son? Isn't his *m* name Mary,
Jn 3: 4 time into his *m* womb to be born!"
19: 25 his *m* sister, Mary the wife

MOTHERS (MOTHER)

Ge 32: 11 and also the *m* with their children.
Ex 22: 30 stay with their *m* for seven days,
Job 31: 15 one form us both within our *m?*
Pr 30: 11 and do not bless their *m;*
Isa 49: 23 and their queens your nursing *m*.
Jer 15: 8 against the *m* of their young men;
16: 3 about the women who are their *m*
31: 8 expectant *m* and women in labor;
La 2: 12 They say to their *m*,
5: 3 our *m* like widows.
Hos 10: 14 when *m* were dashed to the ground
Mt 24: 19 for pregnant women and nursing *m*
Mk 10: 30 sisters, *m*, children and fields—
13: 17 for pregnant women and nursing *m*
Lk 21: 23 for pregnant women and nursing *m*
1Ti 1: 9 for those who kill their fathers or *m*
5: 2 as *m*, and younger women

MOTHERS' (MOTHER)

La 2: 12 away in their *m'* arms.

MOTHS

Job 13: 28 like a garment eaten by *m*.
Isa 50: 9 the *m* will eat them up.
Jas 5: 2 and *m* have eaten your clothes.

MOTIONED (MOTIONS)

Jn 13: 24 Simon Peter *m* to this disciple
Ac 12: 17 Peter *m* with his hand for them
13: 16 Paul *m* with his hand and said:
19: 33 He *m* for silence in order
21: 40 on the steps and *m* to the crowd.
24: 10 When the governor *m* for him
26: 1 So Paul *m* with his hand

MOTIONS (MOTIONED)

Pr 6: 13 and *m* with his fingers,

MOTIVE (MOTIVES)

1Ch 28: 9 and understands every *m*

MOTIVES (MOTIVE)

Pr 16: 2 but *m* are weighed by the LORD.
1Co 4: 5 will expose the *m* of men's hearts.
Php 1: 18 whether from false *m* or true,
1Th 2: 3 spring from error or impure *m*,
Jas 4: 3 because you ask with wrong *m*,

MOUND (MOUNDS)

SS 7: 2 Your waist is a *m* of wheat
Jer 26: 18 the temple hill a *m* overgrown
49: 2 it will become a *m* of ruins,
Eze 16: 24 you built a *m* for yourself
Mic 3: 12 the temple hill a *m* overgrown

MOUNDS (MOUND)

Jos 11: 13 any of the cities built on their *m*—
Eze 16: 31 When you built your *m* at the head
16: 39 and they will tear down your *m*

MOUNT (MOUNTAIN MOUNTAINS MOUNTAINSIDE MOUNTAINTOP MOUNTAINTOPS MOUNTED MOUNTINGS MOUNTS)

Ex 19: 11 come down on *M* Sinai in the sight
19: 18 *M* Sinai was covered with smoke,
19: 20 descended to the top of *M* Sinai
19: 23 people cannot come up *M* Sinai,
24: 16 of the LORD settled on *M* Sinai.
28: 11 Then *m* the stones in gold filigree
28: 17 *m* four rows of precious stones
28: 20 *M* them in gold filigree settings.
31: 18 speaking to Moses on *M* Sinai,
33: 6 off their ornaments at *M* Horeb.
34: 2 and then come up on *M* Sinai.
34: 4 up *M* Sinai early in the morning,
34: 29 came down from *M* Sinai
34: 32 LORD had given him on *M* Sinai.
Lev 7: 38 the LORD gave Moses on *M* Sinai
25: 1 said to Moses on *M* Sinai,
26: 46 on *M* Sinai between himself
27: 34 Moses on *M* Sinai for the Israelites.
Nu 3: 1 talked with Moses on *M* Sinai.
20: 22 from Kadesh and came to *M* Hor.
20: 23 At *M* Hor, near the border
20: 25 Eleazar and take them up *M* Hor.
20: 27 They went up *M* Hor in the sight
21: 4 They traveled from *M* Hor
28: 6 burnt offering instituted at *M* Sinai
33: 23 and camped at *M* Shepher.
33: 24 They left *M* Shepher and camped
33: 37 left Kadesh and camped at *M* Hor,
33: 38 Aaron the priest went up *M* Hor,
33: 39 old when he died on *M* Hor.
33: 41 They left *M* Hor and camped
34: 7 a line from the Great Sea to *M* Hor
34: 8 from *M* Hor to Lebo Hamath.
Dt 1: 2 by the *M* Seir road.)
3: 8 Arnon Gorge as far as *M* Hermon.
4: 48 Gorge to *M* Siyon (that is,
11: 29 and on *M* Ebal the curses.
11: 29 on *M* Gerizim the blessings,
27: 4 set up these stones on *M* Ebal,
27: 12 tribes shall stand on *M* Gerizim
27: 13 on *M* Ebal to pronounce curses:
32: 49 Range to *M* Nebo in Moab,
32: 50 your brother Aaron died on *M* Hor
33: 2 he shone forth from *M* Paran.
34: 1 Then Moses climbed *M* Nebo
Jos 8: 30 Joshua built on *M* Ebal an altar
8: 33 and half of them in front of *M* Ebal,
8: 33 stood in front of *M* Gerizim
11: 17 from *M* Halak, which rises
11: 17 of Lebanon below *M* Hermon.
12: 1 the Arnon Gorge to *M* Hermon,
12: 5 He ruled over *M* Hermon, Salecah,
12: 7 the Valley of Lebanon to *M* Halak,
13: 5 below *M* Hermon to Lebo Hamath
13: 11 all of *M* Hermon and all Bashan
15: 9 came out at the towns of *M* Ephron
15: 10 slope of *M* Jearim (that is,
15: 10 westward from Baalah to *M* Seir,
15: 11 passed along to *M* Baalah
24: 30 of Ephraim, north of *M* Gaash.
Jdg 1: 35 also to hold out in *M* Heres,
2: 9 of Ephraim, north of *M* Gaash.
3: 3 mountains from *M* Baal Hermon
4: 6 and lead the way to *M* Tabor.
4: 12 Abinoam had gone up to *M* Tabor,
4: 14 So Barak went down *M* Tabor,
7: 3 turn back and leave *M* Gilead.' "
9: 7 up on the top of *M* Gerizim
9: 48 and all his men went up *M* Zalmon.
1Sa 31: 1 and many fell slain on *M* Gilboa.
31: 8 his three sons fallen on *M* Gilboa.
2Sa 1: 6 "I happened to be on *M* Gilboa,"
15: 30 But David continued up the *M*
1Ki 18: 19 Israel to meet me on *M* Carmel.
1Ki 18: 20 the prophets on *M* Carmel.
2Ki 2: 25 And he went on to *M* Carmel
4: 25 to the man of God at *M* Carmel.
19: 31 out of *M* Zion a band of survivors
1Ch 5: 23 that is, to Senir (*M* Hermon).
10: 1 and many fell slain on *M* Gilboa.
10: 8 and his sons fallen on *M* Gilboa.
2Ch 3: 1 LORD in Jerusalem on *M* Moriah,
13: 4 Abijah stood on *M* Zemaraim,
20: 10 from Ammon, Moab and *M* Seir,
20: 22 *M* Seir who were invading Judah,
20: 23 the men from *M* Seir to destroy
Ne 2: 14 room for my *m* to get through;
9: 13 "You came down on *M* Sinai;
Ps 42: 6 of Hermon—from *M* Mizar.
48: 2 heights of Zaphon is *M* Zion.
48: 11 *M* Zion rejoices,
74: 2 *M* Zion, where you dwelt.
78: 68 *M* Zion, which he loved.
89: 9 when its waves *m* up, you still them
125: 1 in the LORD are like *M* Zion,
133: 3 were falling on *M* Zion.
SS 4: 1 descending from *M* Gilead.
7: 5 head crowns you like *M* Carmel.
Isa 4: 5 create over all of *M* Zion
8: 18 Almighty, who dwells on *M* Zion.
10: 12 all his work against *M* Zion
10: 32 at the *m* of the Daughter of Zion,
14: 13 enthroned on the *m* of assembly,
16: 1 to the *m* of the Daughter of Zion.
18: 7 the gifts will be brought to *M* Zion,
24: 23 reign on *M* Zion and in Jerusalem,
28: 21 will rise up as he did at *M* Perazim,
29: 8 that fight against *M* Zion.
31: 4 down to do battle on *M* Zion
37: 32 out of *M* Zion a band of survivors.
Jer 46: 4 *m* the steeds!
La 5: 18 for *M* Zion, which lies desolate,
Eze 28: 14 You were on the holy *m* of God;
28: 16 you in disgrace from the *m* of God,
35: 2 set your face against *M* Seir;
35: 3 am against you, *M* Seir,
35: 7 I will make *M* Seir a desolate waste
35: 15 You will be desolate, O *M* Seir,
Hos 14: 3 we will not *m* war-horses.
Joel 2: 32 for on *M* Zion and in Jerusalem
Am 4: 1 you cows of Bashan on *M* Samaria,
6: 1 you who feel secure on *M* Samaria,
Ob : 17 But on *M* Zion will be deliverance;
: 21 Deliverers will go up on *M* Zion
Mic 4: 7 rule over them in *M* Zion
Hab 3: 3 the Holy One from *M* Paran.
Zec 14: 4 stand on the *M* of Olives,
14: 4 the *M* of Olives will be split in two
Mt 21: 1 to Bethphage on the *M* of Olives,
24: 3 sitting on the *M* of Olives,
26: 30 they went out to the *M* of Olives.
Mk 11: 1 and Bethany at the *M* of Olives,
13: 3 sitting on the *M* of Olives
14: 26 they went out to the *M* of Olives.
Lk 19: 29 at the hill called the *M* of Olives,
19: 37 down the *M* of Olives,
21: 37 on the hill called the *M* of Olives,
22: 39 as usual to the *M* of Olives,
Jn 8: 1 But Jesus went to the *M* of Olives.
Ac 1: 12 from the hill called the *M* of Olives
7: 30 bush in the desert near *M* Sinai.
7: 38 spoke to him on *M* Sinai;
Gal 4: 24 One covenant is from *M* Sinai
4: 25 Hagar stands for *M* Sinai in Arabia
Heb 12: 22 But you have come to *M* Zion,
Rev 14: 1 standing on *M* Zion,

MOUNTAIN (MOUNT)

Ge 22: 14 "On the *m* of the LORD it will be
Ex 3: 1 and came to Horeb, the *m* of God.
3: 12 you will worship God on this *m*."
4: 27 So he met Moses at the *m* of God
15: 17 on the *m* of your inheritance—
18: 5 camped near the *m* of God.
19: 2 in the desert in front of the *m*.
19: 3 called to him from the *m*
19: 12 careful that you do not go up the *m*
19: 12 limits for the people around the *m*
19: 12 touches the *m* shall surely
19: 13 blast may they go up to the *m*."
19: 14 gone down the *m* to the people,
19: 16 with a thick cloud over the *m*,

Ex 19: 17 and they stood at the foot of the *m*.
19: 18 the whole *m* trembled violently,
19: 20 called Moses to the top of the *m*.
19: 23 'Put limits around the *m*
20: 18 heard the trumpet and saw the *m*
24: 4 built an altar at the foot of the *m*
24: 12 "Come up to me on the *m*
24: 13 Moses went up on the *m* of God.
24: 15 When Moses went up on the *m*,
24: 16 six days the cloud covered the *m*,
24: 17 a consuming fire on top of the *m*.
24: 18 And he stayed on the *m* forty days
24: 18 the cloud as he went on up the *m*.
25: 40 to the pattern shown you on the *m*.
26: 30 to the plan shown you on the *m*.
27: 8 as you were shown on the *m*.
32: 1 so long in coming down from the *m*
32: 15 down the *m* with the two tablets
32: 19 them to pieces at the foot of the *m*.
34: 2 to me there on top of the *m*.
34: 3 herds may graze in front of the *m*."
34: 3 or be seen anywhere on the *m;*
Nu 10: 33 out from the *m* of the LORD
20: 28 Aaron died there on top of the *m*.
20: 28 Eleazar came down from the *m*,
27: 12 "Go up this *m* in the Abarim range
Dt 1: 6 have stayed long enough at this *m*.
4: 11 at the foot of the *m* while it blazed
5: 4 face to face out of the fire on the *m*.
5: 5 of the fire and did not go up the *m.)*
5: 22 there on the *m* from out of the fire,
5: 23 while the *m* was ablaze with fire,
9: 9 I stayed on the *m* forty days
9: 9 up on the *m* to receive the tablets
9: 10 to you on the *m* out of the fire,
9: 15 and went down from the *m*
9: 21 a stream that flowed down the *m*.
10: 1 and come up to me on the *m*.
10: 3 up on the *m* with the two tablets
10: 4 he had proclaimed to you on the *m*,
10: 5 Then I came back down the *m*
10: 10 I had stayed on the *m* forty days
14: 5 the antelope and the *m* sheep.
32: 50 on the *m* that you have climbed
33: 2 from the south, from his *m* slopes.
33: 19 will summon peoples to the *m*
Jos 10: 40 western foothills and the *m* slopes,
12: 8 foothills, the Arabah, the *m* slopes,
13: 6 of the *m* regions from Lebanon
Jdg 6: 2 shelters for themselves in *m* clefts,
1Sa 23: 26 going along one side of the *m*,
25: 20 riding her donkey into a *m* ravine,
1Ki 19: 8 until he reached Horeb, the *m*
19: 11 and stand on the *m* in the presence
2Ki 2: 16 and set him down on some *m*
4: 27 reached the man of God at the *m*,
Job 14: 18 "But as a *m* erodes and crumbles
24: 8 They are drenched by *m* rains
39: 1 know when the *m* goats give birth?
Ps 11: 1 "Flee like a bird to your *m*.
30: 7 you made my *m* stand firm;
43: 3 let them bring me to your holy *m*,
48: 1 in the city of our God, his holy *m*.
68: 16 at the *m* where God chooses
87: 1 set his foundation on the holy *m;*
95: 4 and the *m* peaks belong to him.
99: 9 and worship at his holy *m*,
SS 4: 6 I will go to the *m* of myrrh
4: 8 and the *m* haunts of the leopards.
Isa 2: 2 *m* of the LORD's temple will be
2: 3 let us go up to the *m* of the LORD,
11: 9 nor destroy on all my holy *m*,
14: 13 the utmost heights of the sacred *m*.
18: 6 left to the *m* birds of prey
25: 6 On this *m* the LORD Almighty
25: 7 On this *m* he will destroy
25: 10 of the LORD will rest on this *m;*
27: 13 LORD on the holy *m* in Jerusalem.
30: 25 of water will flow on every high *m*
30: 29 flutes to the *m* of the LORD,
33: 16 whose refuge will be the *m* fortress.
40: 4 every *m* and hill made low;
40: 9 go up on a high *m*.
56: 7 these I will bring to my holy *m*
57: 13 and possess my holy *m*."
65: 11 and forget my holy *m*,
65: 25 nor destroy in all my holy *m*,"
66: 20 to my holy *m* in Jerusalem
Jer 16: 16 will hunt them down on every *m*
17: 3 My *m* in the land
31: 23 O righteous dwelling, O sacred *m*.'
50: 6 They wandered over *m* and hill
51: 25 and make you a burned-out *m*.
51: 25 "I am against you, O destroying *m*,
Eze 11: 23 and stopped above the *m* east of it.
17: 22 and plant it on a high and lofty *m*.
17: 23 On the *m* heights of Israel I will
18: 6 He does not eat at the *m* shrines
18: 11 "He eats at the *m* shrines.
18: 15 "He does not eat at the *m* shrines
20: 40 For on my holy *m*, the high *m*
22: 9 are those who eat at the *m* shrines
34: 14 the *m* heights of Israel will be their
40: 2 and set me on a very high *m*,
43: 12 on top of the *m* will be most holy.
Da 2: 35 struck the statue became a huge *m*
2: 45 vision of the rock cut out of a *m*,
11: 45 the seas at the beautiful holy *m*.
Mic 4: 1 *m* of the LORD's temple will be
4: 2 let us go up to the *m* of the LORD,
7: 12 and from *m* to *m*.
Zec 4: 7 "What are you, O mighty *m?*
8: 3 will be called The Holy *M*."
8: 3 *m* of the LORD Almighty will be
14: 4 with half of the *m* moving north
14: 5 You will flee by my *m* valley,
Mt 4: 8 the devil took him to a very high *m*
17: 1 and led them up a high *m*
17: 9 As they were coming down the *m*,
17: 20 say to this *m*, 'Move from here
21: 21 but also you can say to this *m*, 'Go,
28: 16 to the *m* where Jesus had told them
Mk 9: 2 with him and led them up a high *m*,
9: 9 As they were coming down the *m*,
11: 23 if anyone says to this *m*, 'Go,
Lk 3: 5 every *m* and hill made low.
9: 28 and went up onto a *m* to pray.
9: 37 when they came down from the *m*,
Jn 4: 20 Our fathers worshiped on this *m*,
4: 21 the Father neither on this *m*
Heb 8: 5 to the pattern shown you on the *m*
12: 18 come to a *m* that can be touched
12: 20 "If even an animal touches the *m*,
2Pe 1: 18 were with him on the sacred *m*.
Rev 6: 14 every *m* and island was removed
8: 8 and something like a huge *m*,
21: 10 away in the Spirit to a *m* great

MOUNTAINS (MOUNT)

Ge 7: 19 and all the high *m* under the entire
7: 20 covered the *m* to a depth of more
8: 4 came to rest on the *m* of Ararat.
8: 5 the tops of the *m* became visible.
19: 17 to the *m* or you will be swept away
19: 19 to the *m;* this disaster will overtake
19: 30 left Zoar and settled in the *m*,
22: 2 on one of the *m* I will tell you about
49: 26 than the blessings of the ancient *m*,
Ex 32: 12 them in the *m* and to wipe them
Nu 23: 7 king of Moab from the eastern *m*.
33: 47 and camped in the *m* of Abarim,
33: 48 They left the *m* of Abarim
Dt 1: 7 in the *m*, in the western foothills,
11: 11 to take possession of is a land of *m*
11: 30 these *m* are across the Jordan,
12: 2 all the places on the high *m*
32: 22 set afire the foundations of the *m*.
33: 15 the choicest gifts of the ancient *m*
Jos 11: 2 northern kings who were in the *m*,
11: 16 the *m* of Israel with their foothills,
Jdg 3: 3 living in the Lebanon *m*
5: 5 The *m* quaked before the LORD,
9: 36 down from the tops of the *m!*"
9: 36 the shadows of the *m* for men."
1Sa 26: 20 as one hunts a partridge in the *m*."
2Sa 1: 21 "O *m* of Gilboa,
1Ki 19: 11 and powerful wind tore the *m* apart
2Ki 19: 23 ascended the heights of the *m*,
1Ch 12: 8 as swift as gazelles in the *m*.
Job 9: 5 moves *m* without their knowing
28: 9 and lays bare the roots of the *m*.
Ps 18: 7 and the foundations of the *m* shook
36: 6 righteousness is like the mighty *m*,
46: 2 the *m* fall into the heart of the sea,
46: 3 and the *m* quake with their surging.
50: 11 I know every bird in the *m*,
Ps 65: 6 who formed the *m* by your power,
68: 15 of Bashan are majestic *m;*
68: 15 rugged are the *m* of Bashan.
68: 15 *m* of Bashan are majestic
68: 16 Why gaze in envy, O rugged *m*,
72: 3 The *m* will bring prosperity
76: 4 more majestic than *m* rich
78: 69 built his sanctuary like the high *m*,
80: 10 The *m* were covered with its shade,
83: 14 or a flame sets the *m* ablaze,
90: 2 Before the *m* were born
97: 5 The *m* melt like wax
98: 8 let the *m* sing together for joy;
104: 6 the waters stood above the *m*.
104: 8 they flowed over the *m*,
104: 10 it flows between the *m*.
104: 13 He waters the *m* from his upper
104: 18 The high *m* belong
104: 32 he touches the *m*, and they smoke.
114: 4 the *m* skipped like rams,
114: 6 you *m*, that you skipped like rams,
125: 2 As the *m* surround Jerusalem,
144: 5 touch the *m*, so that they smoke.
148: 9 you *m* and all hills,
Pr 8: 25 before the *m* were settled in place,
SS 2: 8 leaping across the *m*,
8: 14 stag on the spice-laden *m*.
Isa 2: 2 as chief among the *m;*
2: 14 for all the towering *m*
5: 25 The *m* shake,
13: 4 Listen, a noise on the *m*,
14: 25 on my *m* I will trample him down.
18: 3 when a banner is raised on the *m*,
22: 5 and of crying out to the *m*.
34: 3 the *m* will be soaked
37: 24 ascended the heights of the *m*,
40: 12 or weighed the *m* on the scales
41: 15 will thresh the *m* and crush them,
42: 15 I will lay waste the *m* and hills
44: 23 Burst into song, you *m*,
45: 2 and will level the *m;*
49: 11 I will turn all my *m* into roads,
49: 13 burst into song, O *m!*
52: 7 How beautiful on the *m*
54: 10 Though the *m* be shaken
55: 12 the *m* and hills
64: 1 that the *m* would tremble
64: 3 and the *m* trembled before you.
65: 7 they burned sacrifices on the *m*
65: 9 those who will possess my *m;*
Jer 3: 23 and *m* is a deception;
4: 24 I looked at the *m*,
9: 10 I will weep and wail for the *m*
46: 18 who is like Tabor among the *m*,
50: 6 and caused them to roam on the *m*.
La 4: 19 they chased us over the *m*
Eze 6: 2 set your face against the *m* of Israel
6: 3 against them and say: 'O *m*
6: 3 the Sovereign LORD says to the *m*
7: 7 there is panic, not joy, upon the *m*.
7: 16 and escape will be in the *m*,
19: 9 longer on the *m* of Israel.
31: 12 Its boughs fell on the *m*
32: 5 I will spread your flesh on the *m*
32: 6 all the way to the *m*,
33: 28 *m* of Israel will become desolate
34: 6 My sheep wandered over all the *m*
34: 13 them on the *m* of Israel,
34: 14 in a rich pasture on the *m* of Israel.
35: 8 I will fill your *m* with the slain;
35: 12 said against the *m* of Israel.
36: 1 'O *m* of Israel, hear the word
36: 1 prophesy to the *m* of Israel and say
36: 4 O *m* of Israel, hear the word
36: 4 the Sovereign LORD says to the *m*
36: 6 and say to the *m* and hills,
36: 8 O *m* of Israel, will produce
37: 22 in the land, on the *m* of Israel.
38: 8 from many nations to the *m*
38: 20 The *m* will be overturned,
38: 21 a sword against Gog on all my *m*,
39: 2 send you against the *m* of Israel.
39: 4 On the *m* of Israel you will fall,
39: 17 sacrifice on the *m* of Israel.
Hos 10: 8 Then they will say to the *m*,
Joel 2: 2 Like dawn spreading across the *m*
3: 18 "In that day the *m* will drip new
Am 3: 9 yourselves on the *m* of Samaria;

Am 4:13 He who forms the *m*,
9:13 New wine will drip from the *m*
Ob :8 of understanding in the *m* of Esau?
:9 and everyone in Esau's *m*
:19 the *m* of Esau,
:21 to govern the *m* of Esau.
Jnh 2:6 To the roots of the *m* I sank down;
Mic 1:4 The *m* melt beneath him
4:1 as chief among the *m;*
6:1 plead your case before the *m;*
6:2 O *m*, the LORD's accusation;
Na 1:5 The *m* quake before him
1:15 Look, there on the *m*,
3:18 Your people are scattered on the *m*
Hab 3:6 The ancient *m* crumbled
3:10 the *m* saw you and writhed.
Hag 1:8 Go up into the *m* and bring
1:11 a drought on the fields and the *m*,
Zec 6:1 out from between two *m*—
6:1 *m* of bronze! The first chariot had
Mal 1:3 and I have turned his *m*
Mt 24:16 are in Judea flee to the *m*.
Mk 13:14 are in Judea flee to the *m*.
Lk 21:21 are in Judea flee to the *m*,
23:30 they will say to the *m*, "Fall on us!"
1Co 13:2 if I have a faith that can move *m*,
Heb 11:38 They wandered in deserts and *m*,
Rev 6:15 and among the rocks of the *m*.
6:16 They called to the *m* and the rocks,
16:20 and the *m* could not be found.

MOUNTAINSIDE (MOUNT)

SS 2:14 in the hiding places on the *m*,
Mt 5:1 he went up on a *m* and sat down.
8:1 When he came down from the *m*,

MOUNTAINTOP (MOUNT)

Isa 30:17 like a flagstaff on a *m*,

MOUNTAINTOPS (MOUNT)

Isa 42:11 let them shout from the *m*.
Eze 6:13 on every high hill and on all the *m*,
Hos 4:13 They sacrifice on the *m*
Joel 2:5 they leap over the *m*,

MOUNTED (MOUNT)

Ge 24:61 got ready and *m* their camels
Ex 25:7 other gems to be *m* on the ephod
35:9 other gems to be *m* on the ephod
35:27 other gems to be *m* on the ephod
39:6 They *m* the onyx stones
39:10 *m* four rows of precious stones
39:13 They were *m* in gold filigree
2Sa 13:29 king's sons got up, *m* their mules
22:11 He *m* the cherubim and flew;
1Ki 13:13 he *m* it and rode after the man
Est 8:10 and sent them by *m* couriers,
Ps 18:10 He *m* the cherubim and flew;
107:26 They *m* up to the heavens
SS 5:12 *m* like jewels.
Eze 23:6 young men, and *m* horsemen.
23:12 warriors in full dress, *m* horsemen,
23:23 men of high rank, all *m* on horses.
Rev 9:16 of the *m* troops was two hundred

MOUNTINGS (MOUNT)

Eze 28:13 Your settings and *m* were made

MOUNTS (MOUNT)

Ne 2:12 There were no *m* with me
Ac 23:24 Provide *m* for Paul

MOURN (MOURNED MOURNERS MOURNFUL MOURNING MOURNS)

Ge 23:2 and Abraham went to *m* for Sarah
Ex 33:4 they began to *m* and no one put
Lev 10:6 may *m* for those the LORD has
1Sa 16:1 "How long will you *m* for Saul,
1Ki 13:29 back to his own city to *m* for him
14:13 All Israel will *m* for him
Ezr 10:6 because he continued to *m*
Ne 8:9 Do not *m* or weep."
Job 5:11 those who *m* are lifted to safety.
Ecc 3:4 a time to *m* and a time to dance,
Isa 3:26 of Zion will lament and *m;*
29:2 she will *m* and lament,
32:13 yes, *m* for all houses of merriment
61:2 to comfort all who *m*,
66:10 all you who *m* over her.
Jer 4:28 Therefore the earth will *m*
6:26 *m* with bitter wailing
8:21 I *m*, and horror grips me.
15:5 Who will *m* for you?
16:5 do not go to *m* or show sympathy,
16:7 food to comfort those who *m*
22:10 for the dead ⌊king⌋ or *m* his loss;
22:18 They will not *m* for him:
22:18 "They will not *m* for him:
49:3 Put on sackcloth and *m;*
La 1:4 The roads to Zion *m*,
Eze 7:27 The king will *m*, the prince will be
24:17 Groan quietly; do not *m*
24:23 You will not *m* or weep
27:32 As they wail and *m* over you,
Hos 10:5 Its people will *m* over it,
Joel 1:8 *M* like a virgin in sackcloth
1:13 Put on sackcloth, O priests, and *m;*
Am 8:8 and all who live in it *m?*
9:5 and all who live in it *m*—
Na 3:7 is in ruins—who will *m* for her?'
Zec 7:3 "Should I *m* and fast
12:10 and they will *m* for him
12:12 The land will *m*, each clan by itself,
Mt 5:4 Blessed are those who *m*,
9:15 of the bridegroom *m* while he is
11:17 and you did not *m*.'
24:30 all the nations of the earth will *m*.
Lk 6:25 for you will *m* and weep.
Jn 11:31 going to the tomb to *m* there.
16:20 and *m* while the world rejoices.
Ro 12:15 *m* with those who *m*.
1Co 7:30 those who *m*, as if they did not;
Jas 4:9 Grieve, *m* and wail.
Rev 1:7 all the peoples of the earth will *m*
18:7 and I will never *m*.'
18:9 they will weep and *m* over her.
18:11 of the earth will weep and *m*
18:15 They will weep and *m* and cry out:

MOURNED (MOURN)

Ge 37:34 and *m* for his son many days.
50:3 Egyptians *m* for him seventy days.
Nu 14:39 to all the Israelites, they *m* bitterly.
20:29 of Israel *m* for him thirty days
Dt 21:13 in your house and *m* her father
1Sa 6:19 The people *m* because of the heavy
7:2 and all the people of Israel *m*
15:35 though Samuel *m* for him.
25:1 all Israel assembled and *m* for him;
28:3 and all Israel had *m* for him
2Sa 1:12 They *m* and wept and fasted
11:26 that her husband was dead, she *m*
13:37 King David *m* for his son every day
1Ki 13:30 and they *m* over him and said, "Oh
14:18 They buried him, and all Israel *m*
1Ch 7:22 Their father Ephraim *m*
2Ch 35:24 all Judah and Jerusalem *m* for him.
Ne 1:4 For some days I *m* and fasted
Jer 16:4 They will not be *m* or buried
16:6 They will not be buried or *m*,
25:33 They will not be *m* or gathered up
Da 10:2 Daniel, *m* for three weeks.
Zec 7:5 'When you fasted and *m* in the fifth
Lk 23:27 including women who *m*
Ac 8:2 men buried Stephen and *m* deeply

MOURNERS (MOURN)

Job 29:25 I was like one who comforts *m*.
Ecc 12:5 and *m* go about the streets.
Isa 57:19 on the lips of the *m* in Israel.
Eze 24:17 or eat the customary food ⌊of *m*⌋."
24:22 or eat the customary food ⌊of *m*⌋.
Hos 9:4 be to them like the bread of *m;*
Am 5:16 and the *m* to wail.
Mal 3:14 and going about like *m*

MOURNFUL (MOURN)

Mic 2:4 will taunt you with this *m* song:

MOURNING (MOURN)

Ge 27:41 "The days of *m* for my father are
37:35 "in *m* will I go down to the grave
50:4 When the days of *m* had passed,
50:10 period of *m* for his father.
50:11 holding a solemn ceremony of *m*."
50:11 who lived there saw the *m*
Dt 26:14 sacred portion while I was in *m*,
34:8 time of weeping and *m* was over.
2Sa 3:31 and walk in *m* in front of Abner."
11:27 After the time of *m* was over,
14:2 in *m* clothes, and don't use any
14:2 said to her, "Pretend you are in *m*.
19:1 "The king is weeping and *m*
19:2 victory that day was turned into *m*,
Est 4:3 there was great *m* among the Jews,
9:22 their *m* into a day of celebration.
Job 30:31 My harp is tuned to *m*,
Ps 35:14 I went about *m*
38:6 all day long I go about *m*.
42:9 Why must I go about *m*,
43:2 Why must I go about *m*,
Ecc 7:2 It is better to go to a house of *m*
7:4 of the wise is in the house of *m*,
Isa 38:14 I moaned like a *m* dove.
61:3 instead of *m*,
Jer 31:13 I will turn their *m* into gladness;
31:15 *m* and great weeping,
47:5 Gaza will shave her head in *m;*
48:38 there is nothing but *m*,
La 2:5 has multiplied *m* and lamentation
5:15 our dancing has turned to *m*.
Eze 2:10 written words of lament and *m*
8:14 and I saw women sitting there, *m*
27:31 and with bitter *m*.
31:15 I covered the deep springs with *m*
Joel 1:9 The priests are in *m*,
2:12 with fasting and weeping and *m*."
Am 8:10 I will make that time like *m*
8:10 turn your religious feasts into *m*
Mic 1:11 Beth Ezel is in *m;*
1:16 Shave your heads in *m*
Mt 2:18 weeping and great *m*,
Mk 16:10 and who were *m* and weeping.
Lk 8:52 all the people were wailing and *m*
Jas 4:9 Change your laughter to *m*
Rev 18:8 death, *m* and famine.
18:19 and with weeping and *m* cry out:
21:4 There will be no more death or *m*

MOURNS (MOURN)

Job 14:22 and *m* only for himself."
Isa 33:9 The land *m* and wastes away,
Jer 14:2 concerning the drought: "Judah *m*,
Hos 4:3 Because of this the land *m*,
Zec 12:10 as one *m* for an only child,

MOUTH (MOUTHS)

Ge 4:11 which opened its *m*
29:2 The stone over the *m*
29:3 the stone away from the well's *m*
29:3 to its place over the *m* of the well.
29:8 away from the *m* of the well.
29:10 away from the *m* of the well
42:27 silver in the *m* of his sack.
43:21 in the *m* of his sack.
44:1 silver in the *m* of his sack.
44:2 in the *m* of the youngest one's sack,
Ex 4:11 gave man his *m?* Who makes him
4:15 to him and put words in his *m;*
4:16 it will be as if he were your *m* and
Nu 16:30 the earth opens its *m* and swallows
16:32 and the earth opened its *m*
22:28 the LORD opened the donkey's *m*,
22:38 only what God puts in my *m*."
23:5 put a message in Balaam's *m*
23:12 what the LORD puts in my *m?*"
23:16 put a message in his *m* and said,
26:10 The earth opened its *m*
Dt 8:3 comes from the *m* of the LORD.
11:6 when the earth opened its *m* right
18:18 I will put my words in his *m*,
23:23 your God with your own *m*.
30:14 it is in your *m* and in your heart
32:1 hear, O earth, the words of my *m*.
Jos 1:8 of the Law depart from your *m;*
10:18 up to the *m* of the cave,
10:22 "Open the *m* of the cave
10:27 At the *m* of the cave they placed
15:5 as far as the *m* of the Jordan.
15:5 of the sea at the *m* of the Jordan,
18:19 at the *m* of the Jordan in the south.
1Sa 1:12 to the LORD, Eli observed her *m*.
2:1 My *m* boasts over my enemies,
2:3 or let your *m* speak such arrogance

1Sa 14: 26 yet no one put his hand to his *m*,
14: 27 He raised his hand to his *m*,
17: 35 and rescued the sheep from its *m*.
2Sa 1: 16 Your own *m* testified against you
14: 3 And Joab put the words in her *m*.
14: 19 words into the *m* of your servant.
22: 9 consuming fire came from his *m*,
1Ki 8: 15 with his own *m* to my father David.
8: 24 with your *m* you have promised
17: 24 LORD from your *m* is the truth.''
19: 13 and stood at the *m* of the cave.
2Ki 4: 34 *m* to *m*, eyes to eyes, hands
19: 28 and my bit in your *m*,
2Ch 6: 4 with his *m* to my father David.
6: 15 with your *m* you have promised
Est 7: 8 as the word left the king's *m*,
Job 3: 1 Job opened his *m* and cursed
5: 15 from the sword in their *m*;
5: 16 and injustice shuts its *m*.
6: 30 Can my *m* not discern malice?
8: 21 He will yet fill your *m*
9: 20 my *m* would condemn me;
15: 5 Your sin prompts your *m*;
15: 6 Your own *m* condemns you,
15: 13 pour out such words from your *m*?
15: 30 of God's *m* will carry him away.
16: 5 But my *m* would encourage you;
19: 16 though I beg him with my own *m*.
20: 12 ''Though evil is sweet in his *m*
20: 13 and keeps it in his *m*,
21: 5 clap your hand over your *m*.
22: 22 Accept instruction from his *m*
23: 4 and fill my *m* with arguments.
23: 12 of his *m* more than my daily bread.
26: 4 whose spirit spoke from your *m*?
31: 30 I have not allowed my *m* to sin
33: 2 I am about to open my *m*;
35: 16 So Job opens his *m* with empty talk
37: 2 rumbling that comes from his *m*.
40: 4 I put my hand over my *m*.
40: 23 Jordan should surge against his *m*.
41: 14 Who dares open the doors of his *m*,
41: 19 Firebrands stream from his *m*;
41: 21 and flames dart from his *m*.
Ps 5: 9 from their *m* can be trusted;
10: 7 His *m* is full of curses and lies
17: 3 resolved that my *m* will not sin.
18: 8 consuming fire came from his *m*,
19: 14 May the words of my *m*
22: 15 sticks to the roof of my *m*;
22: 21 Rescue me from the *m* of the lions;
33: 6 by the breath of his *m*.
36: 3 The words of his *m* are wicked
37: 30 *m* of the righteous man utters
38: 13 like a mute, who cannot open his *m*
38: 14 whose *m* can offer no reply.
39: 1 I will put a muzzle on my *m*
39: 9 was silent; I would not open my *m*,
40: 3 He put a new song in my *m*,
49: 3 My *m* will speak words of wisdom;
50: 19 You use your *m* for evil
51: 15 and my *m* will declare your praise.
54: 2 listen to the words of my *m*.
63: 5 singing lips my *m* will praise you.
66: 14 my lips promised and my *m* spoke
66: 17 I cried out to him with my *m*;
69: 15 or the pit close its *m* over me.
71: 8 My *m* is filled with your praise,
71: 15 *m* will tell of your righteousness,
78: 1 listen to the words of my *m*.
78: 2 I will open my *m* in parables,
81: 10 Open wide your *m* and I will fill it.
89: 1 with my *m* I will make your
109: 30 With my *m* I will greatly extol
119: 13 all the laws that come from your *m*.
119: 43 of truth from my *m*,
119: 72 from your *m* is more precious
119: 88 I will obey the statutes of your *m*.
119:103 sweeter than honey to my *m*!
119:108 the willing praise of my *m*,
119:131 I open my *m* and pant,
137: 6 cling to the roof of my *m*
138: 4 they hear the words of your *m*.
141: 3 Set a guard over my *m*, O LORD;
141: 7 at the *m* of the grave.''
145: 21 My *m* will speak in praise
Pr 2: 6 and from his *m* come knowledge
4: 24 Put away perversity from your *m*;
Pr 6: 2 ensnared by the words of your *m*,
6: 12 who goes about with a corrupt *m*,
8: 7 My *m* speaks what is true,
8: 8 All the words of my *m* are just;
10: 6 violence overwhelms the *m*
10: 11 The *m* of the righteous is a fountain
10: 11 violence overwhelms the *m*
10: 14 but the *m* of a fool invites ruin.
10: 31 *m* of the righteous brings forth
10: 32 *m* of the wicked only what is
11: 9 With his *m* the godless destroys his
11: 11 by the *m* of the wicked it is
15: 2 but the *m* of the fool gushes folly.
15: 14 but the *m* of a fool feeds on folly.
15: 28 but the *m* of the wicked gushes evil
16: 10 and his *m* should not betray justice.
16: 23 A wise man's heart guides his *m*,
18: 4 of a man's *m* are deep waters,
18: 6 and his *m* invites a beating.
18: 7 A fool's *m* is his undoing,
18: 20 of his *m* a man's stomach is filled;
19: 24 even bring it back to his *m*!
19: 28 the *m* of the wicked gulps
20: 17 he ends up with a *m* full of gravel.
21: 23 who guards his *m* and his tongue
22: 14 The *m* of an adulteress is a deep pit
26: 7 is a proverb in the *m* of a fool.
26: 9 is a proverb in the *m* of a fool.
26: 15 to bring it back to his *m*.
26: 28 and a flattering *m* works ruin.
27: 2 praise you, and not your own *m*;
30: 20 She eats and wipes her *m*
30: 32 clap your hand over your *m*!
Ecc 5: 2 Do not be quick with your *m*,
5: 6 Do not let your *m* lead you into sin.
6: 7 All man's efforts are for his *m*,
10: 12 from a wise man's *m* are gracious,
SS 1: 2 with the kisses of his *m*—
4: 3 your *m* is lovely.
5: 16 His *m* is sweetness itself;
7: 9 and your *m* like the best wine.
Isa 1: 20 For the *m* of the LORD has spoken
5: 14 and opens its *m* without limit;
6: 7 With it he touched my *m* and said,
9: 12 have devoured Israel with open *m*.
9: 17 every *m* speaks vileness.
10: 14 or opened its *m* to chirp.' ''
11: 4 the earth with the rod of his *m*;
19: 7 at the *m* of the river.
29: 13 come near to me with their *m*
34: 16 For it is his *m* that has given
37: 29 and my bit in your *m*,
40: 5 For the *m* of the LORD has spoken
45: 23 my *m* has uttered in all integrity
48: 3 my *m* announced them
49: 2 He made my *m* like a sharpened
51: 16 I have put my words in your *m*
53: 7 so he did not open his *m*.
53: 7 yet he did not open his *m*;
53: 9 nor was any deceit in his *m*.
55: 11 my word that goes out from my *m*:
58: 14 The *m* of the LORD has spoken.
59: 21 *m* will not depart from your *m*,
62: 2 that the *m* of the LORD will
Jer 1: 9 I have put my words in your *m*.
1: 9 and touched my *m* and said to me,
5: 14 make my words in your *m* a fire
9: 8 With his *m* each speaks cordially
9: 20 to the words of his *m*.
23: 16 not from the *m* of the LORD.
48: 28 nest at the *m* of a cave.
La 3: 38 not from the *m* of the Most High
4: 4 sticks to the roof of its *m*;
Eze 2: 8 open your *m* and eat what I give
3: 2 So I opened my *m*, and he gave me
3: 3 it tasted as sweet as honey in my *m*
3: 26 stick to the roof of your *m*
3: 27 I will open your *m* and you shall
4: 14 meat has ever entered my *m*.''
16: 63 and never again open your *m*
24: 27 At that time your *m* will be opened
29: 21 I will open your *m* among them.
33: 22 So my *m* was opened and I was no
33: 22 he opened my *m* before the man
Da 6: 17 and placed over the *m* of the den,
7: 5 ribs in its *m* between its teeth.
7: 8 and a *m* that spoke boastfully.
7: 20 and a *m* that spoke boastfully.
Da 10: 16 I opened my *m* and began to speak.
Hos 6: 5 you with the words of my *m*;
Am 3: 12 a shepherd saves from the lion's *m*
Na 3: 12 the figs fall into the *m* of the eater.
Zec 5: 8 the lead cover down over its *m*.
Mal 2: 6 True instruction was in his *m*
2: 7 and from his *m* men should seek
Mt 4: 4 comes from the *m* of God.' ''
12: 34 overflow of the heart the *m* speaks.
13: 35 ''I will open my *m* in parables,
15: 11 but what comes out of his *m*,
15: 11 into a man's *m* does not make him
15: 17 that whatever enters the *m* goes
15: 18 out of the *m* come from the heart,
17: 27 open its *m* and you will find
Mk 9: 18 foams at the *m*, gnashes his teeth
9: 20 rolled around, foaming at the *m*.
Lk 1: 64 Immediately his *m* was opened
6: 45 overflow of his heart his *m* speaks.
9: 39 so that he foams at the *m*.
Ac 1: 16 through the *m* of David concerning
4: 25 through the *m* of your servant,
8: 32 so he did not open his *m*.
11: 8 or unclean has ever entered my *m*.'
15: 27 by word of *m* what we are writing.
22: 14 and to hear words from his *m*.
23: 2 near Paul to strike him on the *m*.
Ro 3: 19 so that every *m* may be silenced
10: 8 it is in your *m* and in your heart,''
10: 9 That if you confess with your *m*,
10: 10 it is with your *m* that you confess
15: 6 and *m* you may glorify the God
Eph 6: 19 that whenever I open my *m*,
2Th 2: 8 overthrow with the breath of his *m*
2: 15 whether by word of *m* or by letter.
2Ti 4: 17 I was delivered from the lion's *m*.
Jas 3: 10 Out of the same *m* come praise
1Pe 2: 22 and no deceit was found in his *m*.''
2Pe 2: 18 For they *m* empty, boastful words
Rev 1: 16 and out of his *m* came a sharp
2: 16 them with the sword of my *m*.
3: 16 I am about to spit you out of my *m*.
10: 9 but in your *m* it will be as sweet
10: 10 It tasted as sweet as honey in my *m*
12: 15 from his *m* the serpent spewed
12: 16 dragon had spewed out of his *m*.
12: 16 the woman by opening its *m*
13: 2 of a bear and a *m* like that of a lion.
13: 5 The beast was given a *m*
13: 6 opened his *m* to blaspheme God,
16: 13 out of the *m* of the beast
16: 13 out of the *m* of the dragon,
16: 13 out of the *m* of the false prophet.
19: 15 Out of his *m* comes a sharp sword
19: 21 of the *m* of the rider on the horse,

MOUTHS (MOUTH)

Ge 43: 12 back into the *m* of your sacks.
44: 8 found inside the *m* of our sacks.
Jdg 7: 6 lapped with their hands to their *m*.
1Ki 19: 18 all whose *m* have not kissed him.''
22: 22 spirit in the *m* of all his prophets,'
22: 23 spirit in the *m* of all these prophets
2Ch 18: 21 spirit in the *m* of all his prophets,'
18: 22 in the *m* of these prophets of yours.
Ne 9: 20 withhold your manna from their *m*,
Job 16: 10 Men open their *m* to jeer at me;
29: 9 covered their *m* with their hands;
29: 10 stuck to the roof of their *m*.
Ps 17: 10 and their *m* speak with arrogance.
22: 13 open their *m* wide against me.
58: 6 Break the teeth in their *m*, O God;
59: 7 See what they spew from their *m*—
59: 12 For the sins of their *m*,
62: 4 With their *m* they bless,
63: 11 while the *m* of liars will be silenced.
73: 9 Their *m* lay claim to heaven,
78: 30 even while it was still in their *m*,
78: 36 would flatter him with their *m*,
107: 42 but all the wicked shut their *m*.
109: 2 have opened their *m* against me;
115: 5 They have *m*, but cannot speak,
126: 2 Our *m* were filled with laughter,
135: 16 They have *m*, but cannot speak,
135: 17 nor is there breath in their *m*.
144: 8 whose *m* are full of lies,
144: 11 whose *m* are full of lies,
149: 6 the praise of God be in their *m*

Isa 52: 15 and kings will shut their *m*
59: 21 or from the *m* of their descendants
59: 21 or from the *m* of your children,
La 2: 16 All your enemies open their *m*
3: 46 our enemies have opened their *m*
Eze 33: 31 With their *m* they express devotion
34: 10 I will rescue my flock from their *m*,
Da 6: 22 and he shut the *m* of the lions.
Mic 7: 16 will lay their hands on their *m*
Zep 3: 13 nor will deceit be found in their *m*.
Zec 9: 7 I will take the blood from their *m*,
14: 12 and their tongues will rot in their *m*
Ro 3: 14 "Their *m* are full of cursing
Eph 4: 29 talk come out of your *m*,
Heb 11: 33 was promised; who shut the *m*
Jas 3: 3 bits into the *m* of horses
Rev 9: 17 and out of their *m* came fire,
9: 18 and sulfur that came out of their *m*.
9: 19 power of the horses was in their *m*
11: 5 fire comes from their *m*
14: 5 No lie was found in their *m*;

MOVABLE (MOVE)

1Ki 7: 27 also made ten *m* stands of bronze;
2Ki 16: 17 the basins from the *m* stands.
25: 13 *m* stands and the bronze Sea that
25: 16 pillars, the Sea and the *m* stands,
Jer 27: 19 *m* stands and the other furnishings
52: 17 *m* stands and the bronze Sea that
52: 20 bulls under it, and the *m* stands,

MOVE (MOVABLE MOVED MOVEMENTS MOVES MOVING)

Ge 1: 24 creatures that *m* along the ground,
1: 25 and all the creatures that *m*
1: 26 and over all the creatures that *m*
1: 30 and all the creatures that *m*
6: 7 creatures that *m* along the ground,
7: 8 and of all creatures that *m*
7: 23 and the creatures that *m*
8: 17 and all the creatures that *m*
8: 19 and all the creatures that *m*
26: 16 said to Isaac, "*M* away from us;
33: 14 while I *m* along slowly at the pace
48: 17 hand to *m* it from Ephraim's head
Ex 14: 15 Tell the Israelites to *m* on.
Lev 5: 2 or of unclean creatures that *m*
11: 29 " 'Of the animals that *m* about
11: 31 Of all those that *m*
26: 10 when you will have to *m* it out
Nu 1: 51 Whenever the tabernacle is to *m*,
4: 5 When the camp is to *m*, Aaron
4: 15 and when the camp is ready to *m*,
12: 15 and the people did not *m*
16: 24 '*M* away from the tents of Korah,
16: 26 "*M* back from the tents
Dt 19: 14 Do not *m* your neighbor's
Jos 3: 3 are to *m* out from your positions
Jdg 16: 2 They made no *m* during the night,
2Sa 5: 24 tops of the balsam trees, *m* quickly,
15: 14 or he will *m* quickly to overtake us
1Ch 14: 15 of the balsam trees, *m* out to battle,
Job 24: 2 Men *m* boundary stones;
Ps 69: 34 the seas and all that *m* in them,
Pr 22: 28 Do not *m* an ancient boundary
23: 10 Do not *m* an ancient boundary
30: 29 four that *m* with stately bearing:
Isa 46: 7 From that spot it cannot *m*.
Jer 31: 24 and those who *m* about
Eze 36: 27 and *m* you to follow my decrees
Hos 2: 18 and the creatures that *m*
5: 10 who *m* boundary stones.
Zec 12: 3 try to *m* it will injure themselves.
Mt 17: 20 from here to there' and it will *m*.
17: 20 '*M* from here to there'
23: 4 willing to lift a finger to *m* them.
Lk 10: 7 Do not *m* around from house
14: 10 'Friend, *m* up to a better place.'
Ac 17: 28 and *m* and have our being.'
27: 41 bow stuck fast and would not *m*,
1Co 13: 2 have a faith that can *m* mountains,
15: 58 Let nothing *m* you.
2Co 11: 26 I have been constantly on the *m*.

MOVED (MOVE)

Ge 7: 21 Every living thing that *m*
11: 2 As men *m* eastward, they found
13: 18 Abram *m* his tents and went to live
19: 9 *m* forward to break down the door.
20: 1 Now Abraham *m* on from there
26: 17 So Isaac *m* away from there
26: 22 He *m* on from there and dug
35: 16 Then they *m* on from Bethel.
35: 21 Israel *m* on again and pitched his
36: 6 and *m* to a land some distance
37: 17 "They have *m* on from here,"
43: 30 Deeply *m* at the sight of his brother
Ex 14: 19 pillar of cloud also *m* from in front
35: 21 and whose heart *m* him came
Nu 14: 44 the ark of the LORD's covenant *m*
16: 27 So they *m* away from the tents
21: 10 The Israelites *m* on and camped
21: 12 From there they *m* on
22: 26 the angel of the LORD *m* on ahead
Jos 5: 6 The Israelites had *m* about
8: 3 the whole army *m* out to attack Ai.
10: 5 They *m* up with all their troops
10: 29 with him *m* on from Makkedah
10: 31 Israel with him *m* on from Libnah
10: 34 Israel with him *m* on from Lachish
14: 10 while Israel *m* about in the desert.
Jdg 9: 26 son of Ebed *m* with his brothers
20: 33 men of Israel *m* from their places
1Sa 5: 8 ark of the god of Israel *m* to Gath."
5: 8 they *m* the ark of the God of Israel.
5: 9 after they had *m* it, the LORD's
14: 23 battle *m* on beyond Beth Aven.
15: 6 So the Kenites *m* away
17: 48 As the Philistine *m* closer
25: 1 David *m* down into the Desert
2Sa 7: 7 Wherever I have *m*
15: 23 the people *m* on toward the desert.
2Ki 16: 6 Edomites then *m* into Elath
1Ch 13: 7 They *m* the ark of God
16: 30 firmly established; it cannot be *m*.
17: 5 I have *m* from one tent site
17: 6 Wherever I have *m*
19: 7 from their towns and *m* out
2Ch 33: 13 the LORD was *m* by his entreaty
33: 19 how God was *m* by his entreaty,
36: 22 the LORD *m* the heart
Ezr 1: 1 the LORD *m* the heart
1: 5 everyone whose heart God had *m*
Ne 2: 14 I *m* on toward the Fountain Gate
Est 2: 9 and *m* her and her maids
Job 14: 18 and as a rock is *m* from its place,
18: 4 Or must the rocks be *m*
Ps 93: 1 it cannot be *m*.
96: 10 firmly established, it cannot be *m*;
104: 5 it can never be *m*.
Isa 33: 20 abode, a tent that will not be *m*;
Eze 1: 9 they did not turn as they *m*.
1: 13 Fire *m* back and forth
1: 17 As they *m*, they would go
1: 19 When the living creatures *m*,
1: 19 the wheels beside them *m*;
1: 21 When the creatures *m*, they
1: 21 *m*; when the creatures stood still,
1: 24 When the creatures *m*, I heard
9: 3 *m* to the threshold of the temple.
10: 4 *m* to the threshold of the temple.
10: 11 As they *m*, they would go
10: 16 When the cherubim *m*, the wheels
10: 16 the wheels beside them *m*;
Mt 13: 53 had finished these parables, he *m*
Lk 2: 27 *M* by the Spirit, he went
Jn 11: 33 he was deeply *m* in spirit
11: 38 Jesus, once more deeply *m*,
11: 54 Jesus no longer *m* about publicly
Ac 9: 28 and *m* about freely in Jerusalem,
27: 8 We *m* along the coast
Col 1: 23 not *m* from the hope held out

MOVEMENTS (MOVE)

2Sa 3: 25 and observe your *m* and find out

MOVES (MOVE)

Ge 1: 28 over every living creature that *m*
6: 20 kind of creature that *m*
7: 14 every creature that *m*
8: 19 everything that *m* on the earth—
9: 2 upon every creature that *m*
9: 3 and *m* will be food for you.
Lev 11: 41 " 'Every creature that *m* about
11: 42 to eat any creature that *m* about
11: 42 whether it *m* on its belly
11: 44 by any creature that *m* about
11: 46 and every creature that *m* about
11: 46 every living thing that *m*
20: 25 anything that *m* along the ground
Dt 4: 18 or like any creature that *m*
18: 6 If a Levite *m* from one
23: 14 For the LORD your God *m* about
27: 17 the man who *m* his neighbor's
Job 9: 5 *m* mountains without their
Ps 58: 8 Like a slug melting away as it *m*
102: 14 her very dust *m* them to pity.
Isa 41: 3 He pursues them and *m*
Eze 38: 20 every creature that *m*

MOVING (MOVE)

Ge 1: 21 and *m* thing with which the water
13: 5 who was *m* about with Abram,
1Sa 1: 13 her lips were *m* but her voice was
12: 12 king of the Ammonites was *m*
23: 13 and kept *m* from place to place.
2Sa 7: 6 I have been *m* from place to place
Job 31: 26 or the moon *m* in splendor,
Zec 14: 4 *m* north and half *m* south.

MOWED (MOWN)

Jas 5: 4 the workmen who *m* your fields are

MOWN (MOWED)

Ps 72: 6 will be like rain falling on a *m* field,

MOZA

1Ch 2: 46 Ephah was the mother of Haran, *M*
8: 36 and Zimri was the father of *M*.
8: 37 *M* was the father of Binea;
9: 42 and Zimri was the father of *M*.
9: 43 *M* was the father of Binea;

MOZAH

Jos 18: 26 Mizpah, Kephirah, *M*, Rekem,

MUD (MUDDIED MUDDY MUDDYING)

2Sa 22: 43 trampled them like *m* in the streets
Job 30: 19 He throws me into the *m*,
41: 30 in the *m* like a threshing sledge.
Ps 18: 42 I poured them out like *m*
40: 2 out of the *m* and mire;
Isa 10: 6 them down like *m* in the streets.
57: 20 whose waves cast up mire and *m*.
Jer 38: 6 Jeremiah sank down into the *m*.
38: 6 it had no water in it, only *m*,
38: 22 Your feet are sunk in the *m*;
Jn 9: 6 made some *m* with the saliva,
9: 11 man they call Jesus made some *m*
9: 14 on which Jesus had made the *m*
9: 15 "He put *m* on my eyes," the man
2Pe 2: 22 back to her wallowing in the *m*."

MUDDIED (MUD)

Pr 25: 26 Like a *m* spring or a polluted well
Eze 32: 13 or *m* by the hoofs of cattle.
34: 19 and drink what you have *m*

MUDDY (MUD)

Eze 34: 18 also *m* the rest with your feet?
Zec 10: 5 trampling the *m* streets in battle.

MUDDYING (MUD)

Eze 32: 2 and *m* the streams.

MULBERRY

Lk 17: 6 you can say to this *m* tree,

MULE (MULES)

2Sa 18: 9 He was riding his *m*, and
18: 9 while the *m* he was riding kept
18: 9 *m* went under the thick branches
1Ki 1: 33 set Solomon my son on my own *m*
1: 38 put Solomon on King David's *m*
1: 44 they have put him on the king's *m*,
Ps 32: 9 Do not be like the horse or the *m*,

MULES (MULE)

2Sa 13: 29 mounted their *m* and fled.
1Ki 10: 25 and spices, and horses and *m*.
18: 5 and *m* alive so we will not have
2Ki 5: 17 much earth as a pair of *m* can carry
1Ch 12: 40 food on donkeys, camels, *m*
2Ch 9: 24 and spices, and horses and *m*.

Ezr 2:66 horses 245 *m*, 435 camels
Ne 7:68 horses 245 *m*, 435 camels
Isa 66:20 on *m* and camels," says the LORD.
Eze 27:14 and *m* for your merchandise.
Zec 14:15 plague will strike the horses and *m*,

MULTICOLORED

Eze 27:24 and *m* rugs with cords twisted

MULTIPLIED (MULTIPLY)

Ex 1: 7 were fruitful and *m* greatly
1:12 the more they *m* and spread;
11: 9 so that my wonders may be *m*
Dt 8:13 gold increase and all you have is *m*,
Jdg 16:24 and *m* our slain."
Ps 25:17 The troubles of my heart have *m*;
La 2: 5 He has *m* mourning

MULTIPLIES (MULTIPLY)

Job 34:37 and *m* his words against God."
35:16 without knowledge he *m* words."
Pr 23:28 and *m* the unfaithful among men.
Ecc 10:14 and the fool *m* words.
Hos 12: 1 and *m* lies and violence.

MULTIPLY (MULTIPLIED MULTIPLIES MULTIPLYING)

Ge 8:17 so they can *m* on the earth
9: 7 *m* on the earth and increase upon it
Ex 7: 3 though I *m* my miraculous signs
Lev 26:21 I will *m* your afflictions seven
Dt 7:22 the wild animals will *m* around you
2Sa 24: 3 the LORD your God *m* the troops
1Ch 21: 3 "May the LORD *m* his troops
Job 9:17 and *m* my wounds for no reason.
Jer 46:11 But you *m* remedies in vain;
Eze 36:10 and I will *m* the number of people
Na 3:15 *M* like grasshoppers,
3:15 *m* like locusts!

MULTIPLYING (MULTIPLY)

Mk 4: 8 grew and produced a crop, *m* thirty

MULTITUDE (MULTITUDES)

Ps 42: 4 how I used to go with the *m*,
Isa 1:11 "The *m* of your sacrifices—
13: 4 like that of a great *m*!
31: 1 who trust in the *m* of their chariots
Da 10: 6 and his voice like the sound of a *m*.
Jas 5:20 and cover over a *m* of sins.
1Pe 4: 8 love covers over a *m* of sins.
Rev 7: 9 me was a great *m* that no one could
19: 1 of a great *m* in heaven shouting:
19: 6 heard what sounded like a great *m*,

MULTITUDES (MULTITUDE)

Ne 9: 6 and the *m* of heaven worship you.
Da 12: 2 *M* who sleep in the dust
Joel 3:14 *M*, *m* in the valley of decision!
Rev 17:15 *m*, nations and languages.

MUMBLE

Isa 29: 4 your speech will *m* out of the dust.

MUPPIM

Ge 46:21 Ehi, Rosh, *M*, Huppim and Ard.

MURDER (MURDERED MURDERER MURDERERS MURDERING MURDEROUS MURDERS)

Ex 20:13 "You shall not *m*.
Nu 35:12 a person accused of *m* may not die
35:25 of *m* from the avenger of blood
35:27 accused without being guilty of *m*.
Dt 5:17 "You shall not *m*.
Jos 21:13 of refuge for one accused of *m*),
21:21 city of refuge for one accused of *m*)
21:27 city of refuge for one accused of *m*)
21:32 of refuge for one accused of *m*),
21:38 of refuge for one accused of *m*),
Jdg 9:24 who had helped him *m* his brothers
2Sa 3:37 part in the *m* of Abner son of Ner.
Ps 94: 6 they *m* the fatherless.
Pr 28:17 A man tormented by the guilt of *m*
Isa 33:15 stops his ears against plots of *m*
Jer 7: 9 you steal and *m*, commit adultery
Hos 4: 2 There is only cursing, lying and *m*,
6: 9 they *m* on the road to Shechem,
Mt 5:21 'Do not *m*, and anyone who
15:19 *m*, adultery, sexual immorality,
19:18 Jesus replied, " 'Do not *m*,
Mk 7:21 sexual immorality, theft, *m*,
10:19 Do not *m*, do not commit adultery,
15: 7 who had committed *m*
Lk 18:20 Do not commit adultery, do not *m*,
23:19 insurrection in the city, and for *m*.)
23:25 into prison for insurrection and *m*,
Ro 1:29 *m*, strife, deceit and malice.
13: 9 "Do not *m*," "Do not steal,"
Jas 2:11 adultery," also said, "Do not *m*."
2:11 commit adultery but do commit *m*,
1Jn 3:12 why did he *m* him? Because his

MURDERED (MURDER)

Jdg 9: 5 and on one stone *m* his seventy
9:18 *m* his seventy sons
20: 4 the husband of the *m* woman, said,
2Sa 3:30 and his brother Abishai *m* Abner
1Ki 16:16 plotted against the king and *m* him,
21:19 Have you not *m* a man
2Ki 11: 2 princes who were about to be *m*.
12:21 officials who *m* him were Jozabad
14: 5 the officials who had *m* his father
2Ch 21:13 You have also *m* your own
22:11 princes who were about to be *m*
25: 3 the officials who had *m* his father
Pr 22:13 or, "I will be *m* in the streets!"
Mt 23:31 of those who *m* the prophets.
23:35 whom you *m* between the temple
Ac 7:52 now you have betrayed and *m* him
Jas 5: 6 condemned and *m* innocent men,
1Jn 3:12 to the evil one and *m* his brother.

MURDERER (MURDER)

Nu 35:16 he is a *m*; the *m* shall be put
35:17 he is a *m*; the *m* shall be put
35:18 he is a *m*; the *m* shall be put
35:19 of blood shall put the *m* to death;
35:21 of blood shall put the *m* to death
35:21 put to death; he is a *m*.
35:30 as a *m* only on the testimony
35:31 accept a ransom for the life of a *m*,
2Ki 6:32 see how this *m* is sending someone
9:31 Zimri, you *m* of your master?"
Job 24:14 daylight is gone, the *m* rises up
Jn 8:44 He was a *m* from the beginning,
Ac 3:14 asked that a *m* be released to you.
28: 4 "This man must be a *m*; for
1Pe 4:15 it should not be as a *m* or thief
1Jn 3:15 who hates his brother is a *m*,
3:15 you know that no *m* has eternal life

MURDERERS (MURDER)

Isa 1:21 but now *m*!
Jer 4:31 my life is given over to *m*."
Mt 22: 7 and destroyed those *m* and burned
1Ti 1: 9 for *m*, for adulterers and perverts,
Rev 21: 8 the *m*, the sexually immoral,
22:15 the sexually immoral, the *m*,

MURDERING (MURDER)

Jdg 9:56 father by *m* his seventy brothers.
2Ch 24:25 against him for *m* the son

MURDEROUS (MURDER)

Ac 9: 1 was still breathing out *m* threats

MURDERS (MURDER)

Dt 22:26 who attacks and *m* his neighbor,
Ps 10: 8 from ambush he *m* the innocent,
Mt 5:21 and anyone who *m* will be subject
Rev 9:21 Nor did they repent of their *m*,

MUSCLES

Job 40:16 what power in the *m* of his belly!

MUSED

Ps 77: 3 I *m*, and my spirit grew faint.
77: 6 My heart *m* and my spirit inquired:

MUSHI (MUSHITE MUSHITES)

Ex 6:19 sons of Merari were Mahli and *M*.
Nu 3:20 The Merarite clans: Mahli and *M*.
1Ch 6:19 The sons of Merari: Mahli and *M*.
6:47 the son of *M*, the son of Merari,
23:21 The sons of Merari: Mahli and *M*.
1Ch 23:23 The sons of *M*: Mahli, Eder
24:26 The sons of Merari: Mahli and *M*.
24:30 And the sons of *M*: Mahli,

MUSHITE (MUSHI)

Nu 26:58 the Mahlite clan, the *M* clan,

MUSHITES (MUSHI)

Nu 3:33 clans of the Mahlites and the *M*;

MUSIC (MUSICAL MUSICIAN MUSICIANS)

Ge 31:27 singing to the *m* of tambourines
Jdg 5: 3 I will make *m* to the LORD,
1Ch 6:31 put in charge of the *m* in the house
6:32 They ministered with *m*
25: 6 fathers for the *m* of the temple
25: 7 and skilled in *m* for the LORD—
Ne 12:27 and with the *m* of cymbals,
Job 21:12 They sing to the *m* of tambourine
Ps 27: 6 and make *m* to the LORD.
33: 2 make *m* to him on the ten-stringed
45: 8 the *m* of the strings makes you glad
57: 7 I will sing and make *m*.
81: 2 Begin the *m*, strike the tambourine,
87: 7 As they make *m* they will sing,
92: 1 and make *m* to your name,
92: 3 to the *m* of the ten-stringed lyre
95: 2 and extol him with *m* and song.
98: 4 burst into jubilant song with *m*;
98: 5 make *m* to the LORD
108: 1 make *m* with all my soul.
144: 9 the ten-stringed lyre I will make *m*
147: 7 make *m* to our God on the harp.
149: 3 make *m* to him with tambourine
Isa 30:32 will be to the *m* of tambourines
La 5:14 young men have stopped their *m*.
Eze 26:13 *m* of your harps will be heard no
Da 3: 5 lyre, harp, pipes and all kinds of *m*,
3: 7 and all kinds of *m*, all the peoples,
3:10 and all kinds of *m* must fall down
3:15 lyre, harp, pipes and all kinds of *m*,
Am 5:23 to the *m* of your harps.
Hab 3:19 For the director of *m*.
Lk 15:25 came near the house, he heard *m*
Eph 5:19 make *m* in your heart to the Lord,
Rev 18:22 The *m* of harpists and musicians,

MUSICAL (MUSIC)

1Ch 15:16 accompanied by *m* instruments:
23: 5 with the *m* instruments I have
2Ch 7: 6 with the LORD's *m* instruments,
23:13 with *m* instruments were leading
34:12 skilled in playing *m* instruments—
Ne 12:36 with *m* instruments prescribed
Am 6: 5 and improvise on *m* instruments.

MUSICIAN (MUSIC)

1Ch 6:33 Heman, the *m*, the son of Joel,

MUSICIANS (MUSIC)

1Ki 10:12 to make harps and lyres for the *m*.
1Ch 9:33 Those who were *m*, heads
15:19 The *m* Heman, Asaph
2Ch 5:12 All the Levites who were *m*—
9:11 to make harps and lyres for the *m*.
35:15 The *m*, the descendants of Asaph,
Ps 68:25 are the singers, after them the *m*;
Rev 18:22 The music of harpists and *m*,

MUSTACHE

2Sa 19:24 care of his feet or trimmed his *m*

MUSTARD

Mt 13:31 kingdom of heaven is like a *m* seed,
17:20 you have faith as small as a *m* seed,
Mk 4:31 It is like a *m* seed, which is
Lk 13:19 it to? It is like a *m* seed,
17: 6 you have faith as small as a *m* seed,

MUSTER (MUSTERED MUSTERING)

1Sa 14:17 "*M* the forces and see who has left
2Sa 12:28 Now *m* the rest of the troops
Da 11:13 of the North will *m* another army,
Am 2:14 the strong will not *m* their strength

MUSTERED (MUSTER)

Nu 21:23 He *m* his entire army and marched

Jos 8: 10 next morning Joshua *m* his men,
Jdg 11: 20 He *m* all his men and encamped
20: 17 *m* four hundred thousand
1Sa 11: 8 When Saul *m* them at Bezek,
15: 4 summoned the men and *m* them
2Sa 12: 29 So David *m* the entire army
18: 1 David *m* the men who were
1Ki 12: 21 he *m* the whole house of Judah
20: 1 king of Aram *m* his entire army.
20: 26 spring Ben-Hadad *m*
20: 27 also *m* and given provisions,
1Ch 19: 7 while the Ammonites were *m*
2Ch 11: 1 he *m* the house of Judah
25: 5 He then *m* those twenty years old
26: 11 as *m* by Jeiel the secretary

MUSTERING (MUSTER)

Isa 13: 4 The LORD Almighty is *m*

MUTE

Ps 38: 13 like a *m*, who cannot open his
Isa 56: 10 they are all *m* dogs,
Mt 12: 22 man who was blind and *m*,
Lk 11: 14 driving out a demon that was *m*.

MUTILATORS

Php 3: 2 those men who do evil, those *m*

MUTTER (MUTTERED MUTTERS)

Isa 8: 19 and *m*, should not a people inquire
La 3: 62 what my enemies whisper and *m*
Lk 19: 7 the people saw this and began to *m*,

MUTTERED (MUTTER)

Lk 15: 2 and the teachers of the law *m*,

MUTTERS (MUTTER)

Isa 59: 3 and your tongue *m* wicked things.

MUTUAL (MUTUALLY)

Ro 14: 19 leads to peace and to *m* edification.
1Co 7: 5 by *m* consent and for a time,

MUTUALLY (MUTUAL)

Ro 1: 12 and I may be *m* encouraged

MUZZLE

Dt 25: 4 Do not *m* an ox while it is treading
Ps 39: 1 I will put a *m* on my mouth
1Co 9: 9 "Do not *m* an ox while it is
1Ti 5: 18 "Do not *m* the ox while it is

MYRA

Ac 27: 5 and Pamphylia, we landed at *M*

MYRIADS

Dt 33: 2 He came with *m* of holy ones

MYRRH

Ge 37: 25 loaded with spices, balm and *m*,
43: 11 and *m*, some pistachio nuts
Ex 30: 23 shekels of liquid *m*, half
Est 2: 12 six months with oil of *m*
Ps 45: 8 All your robes are fragrant with *m*
Pr 7: 17 with *m*, aloes and cinnamon.
SS 1: 13 My lover is to me a sachet of *m*
3: 6 perfumed with *m* and incense
4: 6 I will go to the mountain of *m*
4: 14 with *m* and aloes
5: 1 I have gathered my *m*
5: 5 and my hands dripped with *m*,
5: 5 my fingers with flowing *m*,
5: 13 dripping with *m*.
Mt 2: 11 of gold and of incense and of *m*.
Mk 15: 23 offered him wine mixed with *m*,
Jn 19: 39 Nicodemus brought a mixture of *m*
Rev 18: 13 of incense, *m* and frankincense,

MYRTLE (MYRTLES)

Isa 41: 19 the acacia, the *m* and the olive.
55: 13 instead of briers the *m* will grow.
Zec 1: 8 among the *m* trees in a ravine.
1: 10 among the *m* trees explained,
1: 11 standing among the *m* trees,

MYRTLES (MYRTLE)

Ne 8: 15 and from *m*, palms and shade trees,

MYSIA

Ac 16: 7 came to the border of *M*,
16: 8 So they passed by *M* and went

MYSTERIES (MYSTERY)

Job 11: 7 "Can you fathom the *m* of God?
Da 2: 28 a God in heaven who reveals *m*.
2: 29 of *m* showed you what is going
2: 47 Lord of kings and a revealer of *m*,
1Co 13: 2 can fathom all *m* and all knowledge
14: 2 he utters *m* with his spirit.

MYSTERY (MYSTERIES)

Da 2: 18 God of heaven concerning this *m*,
2: 19 the night the *m* was revealed
2: 27 to the king the *m* he has asked
2: 30 this *m* has been revealed to me,
2: 47 for you were able to reveal this *m*."
4: 9 and no *m* is too difficult for you.
Ro 11: 25 you to be ignorant of this *m*,
16: 25 to the revelation of the *m* hidden
1Co 15: 51 I tell you a *m*: We will not all sleep,
Eph 1: 9 to us the *m* of his will according
3: 3 the *m* made known to me
3: 4 insight into the *m* of Christ,
3: 6 This *m* is that through the gospel
3: 9 the administration of this *m*,
5: 32 This is a profound *m*—
6: 19 I will fearlessly make known the *m*
Col 1: 26 the *m* that has been kept hidden
1: 27 the glorious riches of this *m*,
2: 2 in order that they may know the *m*
4: 3 so that we may proclaim the *m*
1Ti 3: 16 the *m* of godliness is great:
Rev 1: 20 *m* of the seven stars that you saw
10: 7 the *m* of God will be accomplished,
17: 5 written on her forehead:
17: 7 explain to you the *m* of the woman

MYTHS

1Ti 1: 4 nor to devote themselves to *m*
4: 7 Have nothing to do with godless *m*
2Ti 4: 4 from the truth and turn aside to *m*.
Tit 1: 14 will pay no attention to Jewish *m*

NAAM

1Ch 4: 15 son of Jephunneh: Iru, Elah and *N*.

NAAMAH

Ge 4: 22 Tubal-Cain's sister was *N*.
Jos 15: 41 Gederoth, Beth Dagon, *N*
1Ki 14: 21 His mother's name was *N*;
14: 31 His mother's name was *N*;
2Ch 12: 13 His mother's name was *N*;

NAAMAN (NAAMAN'S NAAMITE)

Ge 46: 21 Beker, Ashbel, Gera, *N*, Ehi, Rosh,
Nu 26: 40 of Bela through Ard and *N* were:
26: 40 through *N*, the Naamite clan.
2Ki 5: 1 *N* was commander of the army
5: 4 *N* went to his master and told him
5: 5 *N* left, taking with him ten talents
5: 6 letter I am sending my servant *N*
5: 9 So *N* went with his horses
5: 11 But *N* went away angry and said,
5: 15 *N* and all his attendants went back
5: 16 And even though *N* urged him,
5: 17 will not," said *N*, "please let me,
5: 19 After *N* had traveled some distance
5: 20 "My master was too easy on *N*,
5: 21 So Gehazi hurried after *N*.
5: 21 When *N* saw him running
5: 23 means, take two talents," said *N*.
1Ch 8: 4 Abihud, Abishua, *N*, Ahoah, Gera,
8: 7 were deported to Manahath: *N*,
Lk 4: 27 was cleansed—only *N* the Syrian."

NAAMAN'S (NAAMAN)

2Ki 5: 2 from Israel, and she served *N* wife.
5: 13 *N* servants went to him and said,
5: 27 *N* leprosy will cling to you

NAAMATHITE

Job 2: 11 the Shuhite and Zophar the *N*,
11: 1 Then Zophar the *N* replied:
20: 1 Then Zophar the *N* replied:
42: 9 Zophar the *N* did what the LORD

NAAMITE (NAAMAN)

Nu 26: 40 through Naaman, the *N* clan.

NAARAH

Jos 16: 7 from Janoah to Ataroth and *N*,
1Ch 4: 5 Tekoa had two wives, Helah and *N*.
4: 6 These were the descendants of *N*.
4: 6 *N* bore him Ahuzzam, Hepher,

NAARAI

1Ch 11: 37 Hezro the Carmelite, *N* son

NAARAN

1Ch 7: 28 and its surrounding villages, *N*

NABAL (NABAL'S)

1Sa 25: 3 His name was *N* and his wife's
25: 4 he heard that *N* was shearing sheep
25: 5 "Go up to *N* at Carmel
25: 9 they gave *N* this message
25: 10 *N* answered David's servants,
25: 19 But she did not tell her husband *N*.
25: 25 attention to that wicked man *N*.
25: 26 to harm my master be like *N*.
25: 34 to *N* would have been left alive
25: 36 When Abigail went to *N*, he was
25: 37 in the morning, when *N* was sober,
25: 38 the LORD struck *N* and he died.
25: 39 David heard that *N* was dead,
25: 39 cause against *N* for treating me
27: 3 Abigail of Carmel, the widow of *N*.
30: 5 the widow of *N* of Carmel.
2Sa 2: 2 the widow of *N* of Carmel.
3: 3 the son of Abigail the widow of *N*

NABAL'S (NABAL)

1Sa 25: 14 of the servants told *N* wife Abigail:
25: 39 and has brought *N* wrongdoing

NABOTH (NABOTH'S)

1Ki 21: 1 belonging to *N* the Jezreelite.
21: 2 to *N*, "Let me have your vineyard
21: 3 *N* replied, "The LORD forbid that
21: 4 because *N* the Jezreelite had said,
21: 6 "Because I said to *N* the Jezreelite,
21: 7 the vineyard of *N* the Jezreelite."
21: 9 and seat *N* in a prominent place
21: 12 and seated *N* in a prominent place
21: 13 and brought charges against *N*
21: 13 "*N* has cursed both God
21: 14 "*N* has been stoned and is dead."
21: 15 as Jezebel heard that *N* had been
21: 15 of *N* the Jezreelite that he refused
21: 16 When Ahab heard that *N* was dead
2Ki 9: 21 belonged to *N* the Jezreelite.
9: 25 belonged to *N* the Jezreelite.
9: 26 'Yesterday I saw the blood of *N*

NABOTH'S (NABOTH)

1Ki 21: 8 nobles who lived in *N* city with him
21: 11 and nobles who lived in *N* city did
21: 16 to take possession of *N* vineyard.
21: 18 in *N* vineyard, where he has gone
21: 19 where dogs licked up *N* blood,

NACON

2Sa 6: 6 came to the threshing floor of *N*,

NADAB (NADAB'S)

Ex 6: 23 and she bore him *N* and Abihu,
24: 1 you and Aaron, *N* and Abihu,
24: 9 Moses and Aaron, *N* and Abihu,
28: 1 along with his sons *N* and Abihu,
Lev 10: 1 Aaron's sons *N* and Abihu took
Nu 3: 2 sons of Aaron were *N* the firstborn
3: 4 *N* and Abihu, however, fell dead
26: 60 Aaron was the father of *N*
26: 61 *N* and Abihu died when they made
1Ki 14: 20 And *N* his son succeeded him
15: 25 *N* son of Jeroboam became king
15: 27 while *N* and all Israel were
15: 28 Baasha killed *N* in the third year
1Ch 2: 28 The sons of Shammai: *N*
2: 30 The sons of *N*: Seled and Appaim.
6: 3 The sons of Aaron: *N*, Abihu,
8: 30 Kish, Baal, Ner, *N*, Gedor, Ahio,
9: 36 Kish, Baal, Ner, *N*, Gedor, Ahio,
24: 1 The sons of Aaron were *N*, Abihu,

1Ch 24: 2 But *N* and Abihu died before their

NADAB'S (NADAB)

1Ki 15: 31 As for the other events of *N* reign,

NAGGAI

Lk 3: 25 the son of *N*,

NAGGING

Jdg 16: 16 With such *n* she prodded him day

NAHALAL

Jos 19: 15 Included were Kattath, *N*, Shimron
21: 35 Jokneam, Kartah, Dimnah and *N*,

NAHALIEL

Nu 21: 19 Mattanah to *N*, from *N* to Bamoth,

NAHALOL

Jdg 1: 30 Canaanites living in Kitron or *N*,

NAHAM

1Ch 4: 19 the sister of *N*: the father

NAHAMANI

Ne 7: 7 Azariah, Raamiah, *N*, Mordecai,

NAHARAI

2Sa 23: 37 the Ammonite, *N* the Beerothite,
1Ch 11: 39 the Ammonite, *N* the Berothite,

NAHASH

1Sa 11: 1 *N* the Ammonite went up
11: 2 But *N* the Ammonite replied,
12: 12 "But when you saw that *N* king
2Sa 10: 2 kindness to Hanun son of *N*,
17: 25 the daughter of *N* and sister
17: 27 Shobi son of *N* from Rabbah
1Ch 19: 1 *N* king of the Ammonites died,
19: 2 kindness to Hanun son of *N*,

NAHATH

Ge 36: 13 The sons of Reuel: *N*, Zerah,
36: 17 Chiefs *N*, Zerah, Shammah
1Ch 1: 37 The sons of Reuel: *N*, Zerah,
6: 26 Zophai his son, *N* his son, Eliab his
2Ch 31: 13 Jehiel, Azaziah, *N*, Asahel,

NAHBI

Nu 13: 14 tribe of Naphtali, *N* son of Vophsi;

NAHOR (NAHOR'S)

Ge 11: 22 he became the father of *N*.
11: 23 after he became the father of *N*,
11: 24 When *N* had lived 29 years,
11: 25 *N* lived 119 years and had other
11: 26 he became the father of Abram, *N*
11: 27 became the father of Abram, *N*
11: 29 Abram and *N* both married.
22: 20 sons to your brother *N*:
22: 23 sons to Abraham's brother *N*.
24: 10 and made his way to the town of *N*.
24: 15 the wife of Abraham's brother *N*.
24: 24 the son that Milcah bore to *N*."
24: 47 'The daughter of Bethuel son of *N*,
31: 53 of Abraham and the God of *N*,
Jos 24: 2 the father of Abraham and *N*,
1Ch 1: 26 Shelah, Eber, Peleg, Reu, Serug, *N*,
Lk 3: 34 the son of Terah, the son of *N*,

NAHOR'S (NAHOR)

Ge 11: 29 and the name of *N* wife was Milcah
29: 5 Do you know Laban, *N* grandson?"

NAHSHON

Ex 6: 23 of Amminadab and sister of *N*,
Nu 1: 7 from Judah, *N* son of Amminadab;
2: 3 of Judah is *N* son of Amminadab.
7: 12 offering on the first day was *N* son
7: 17 offering of *N* son of Amminadab.
10: 14 *N* son of Amminadab was
Ru 4: 20 father of *N*, *N* the father of Salmon,
1Ch 2: 10 and Amminadab the father of *N*,
2: 11 *N* was the father of Salmon,
Mt 1: 4 father of *N*, *N* the father of Salmon,
Lk 3: 32 the son of Salmon, the son of *N*,

NAHUM

Na 1: 1 of the vision of *N* the Elkoshite.

Lk 3: 25 the son of *N*, the son of Esli,

NAIL (NAILING NAILS)

Jn 20: 25 "Unless I see the *n* marks

NAILING (NAIL)

Ac 2: 23 him to death by *n* him to the cross.
Col 2: 14 he took it away, *n* it to the cross.

NAILS (NAIL)

Dt 21: 12 trim her *n* and put
1Ch 22: 3 of iron to make *n* for the doors
2Ch 3: 9 The gold *n* weighed fifty shekels.
Ecc 12: 11 sayings like firmly embedded *n*—
Isa 41: 7 He *n* down the idol
Jer 10: 4 they fasten it with hammer and *n*
Da 4: 33 and his *n* like the claws of a bird.
Jn 20: 25 put my finger where the *n* were,

NAIN

Lk 7: 11 Jesus went to a town called *N*,

NAIOTH

1Sa 19: 18 Samuel went to *N* and stayed there.
19: 19 "David is in *N* at Ramah";
19: 22 "Over in *N* at Ramah," they said.
19: 23 So Saul went to *N* at Ramah.
19: 23 prophesying until he came to *N*.
20: 1 Then David fled from *N* at Ramah

NAIVE

Ro 16: 18 they deceive the minds of *n* people.

NAKED (NAKEDNESS)

Ge 2: 25 The man and his wife were both *n*,
3: 7 and they realized they were *n*;
3: 10 and I was afraid because I was *n*;
3: 11 "Who told you that you were *n*?
2Ch 28: 15 they clothed all who were *n*.
Job 1: 21 and *n* I will depart.
1: 21 *N* I came from my mother's womb,
22: 6 of their clothing, leaving them *n*.
24: 7 clothes, they spend the night *n*;
24: 10 Lacking clothes, they go about *n*;
26: 6 Death is *n* before God;
Ecc 5: 15 *N* a man comes from his mother's
Isa 58: 7 when you see the *n*, to clothe him,
La 4: 21 you will be drunk and stripped *n*.
Eze 16: 7 you who were *n* and bare.
16: 22 when you were *n* and bare,
16: 39 your fine jewelry and leave you *n*
18: 7 and provides clothing for the *n*.
18: 16 and provides clothing for the *n*.
23: 10 They stripped her *n*, took away her
23: 29 They will leave you *n* and bare,
Hos 2: 3 Otherwise I will strip her *n*
Am 2: 16 will flee *n* on that day,"
Mic 1: 8 I will go about barefoot and *n*.
Hab 2: 15 that he can gaze on their *n* bodies.
Mk 14: 52 he fled *n*, leaving his garment
Ac 19: 16 that they ran out of the house *n*
2Co 5: 3 are clothed, we will not be found *n*.
11: 27 food; I have been cold and *n*.
Rev 3: 17 pitiful, poor, blind and *n*.
16: 15 so that he may not go *n*
17: 16 her to ruin and leave her *n*;

NAKEDNESS (NAKED)

Ge 9: 22 saw his father's *n* and told his two
9: 23 and covered their father's *n*.
9: 23 they would not see their father's *n*.
Ex 20: 26 lest your *n* be exposed on it.'
Dt 28: 48 and thirst, in *n* and dire poverty,
Isa 47: 3 Your *n* will be exposed
57: 8 and you looked on their *n*.
La 1: 8 for they have seen her *n*;
Eze 16: 8 over you and covered your *n*.
16: 36 your *n* in your promiscuity
16: 37 and they will see all your *n*.
23: 18 openly and exposed her *n*,
Hos 2: 9 intended to cover her *n*.
Mic 1: 11 Pass on in *n* and shame,
Na 3: 5 I will show the nations your *n*
Ro 8: 35 or persecution or famine or *n*
Rev 3: 18 so you can cover your shameful *n*;

NAME (NAME'S NAMED NAMELESS NAMES)

Ge 2: 11 The *n* of the first is the Pishon;
2: 13 *n* of the second river is the Gihon;
2: 14 The *n* of the third river is the Tigris
2: 19 each living creature, that was its *n*.
2: 19 man to see what he would *n* them;
4: 21 His brother's *n* was Jubal;
4: 26 to call on the *n* of the LORD.
11: 4 so that we may make a *n*
11: 29 The *n* of Abram's wife was Sarai,
11: 29 the *n* of Nahor's wife was Milcah;
12: 2 I will make your *n* great,
12: 8 and called on the *n* of the LORD.
13: 4 called on the *n* of the LORD.
16: 11 You shall *n* him Ishmael,
16: 13 She gave this *n* to the LORD who
16: 15 and Abram gave the *n* Ishmael
17: 5 called Abram; your *n* will be
17: 15 to call her Sarai; her *n* will be Sarah
21: 3 Abraham gave the *n* Isaac
21: 33 called upon the *n* of the LORD,
22: 24 concubine, whose *n* was Reumah,
25: 1 wife, whose *n* was Keturah.
26: 25 and called on the *n* of the LORD.
26: 33 to this day the *n* of the town has
29: 16 the *n* of the older was Leah,
29: 16 the *n* of the younger was Rachel.
30: 28 He added, "*N* your wages,
31: 53 an oath in the *n* of the Fear
32: 27 "What is your *n*?" "Jacob,"
32: 28 "Your *n* will no longer be Jacob,
32: 29 Jacob said, "Please tell me your *n*."
32: 29 "Why do you ask my *n*?"
35: 10 God said to him, "Your *n* is Jacob,
35: 10 called Jacob; your *n* will be Israel."
36: 39 and his wife's *n* was Mehetabel
36: 40 by *n*, according to their clans
38: 6 his firstborn, and her *n* was Tamar.
38: 30 and he was given the *n* Zerah.
41: 45 Joseph the *n* Zaphenath-Paneah
48: 16 May they be called by my *n*
48: 20 "In your *n* will Israel pronounce
Ex 3: 13 'What is his *n*?' Then what shall I
3: 15 This is my *n* forever, the *n*
5: 23 to Pharaoh to speak in your *n*,
6: 3 by my *n* the LORD I did not make
9: 16 and that my *n* might be proclaimed
15: 3 the LORD is his *n*.
20: 7 anyone guiltless who misuses his *n*.
20: 7 "You shall not misuse the *n*
20: 24 Wherever I cause my *n*
23: 21 since my *N* is in him.
28: 21 seal with the *n* of one of the twelve
33: 12 you by *n* and you have found favor
33: 17 with you and I know you by *n*."
33: 19 I will proclaim my *n*, the LORD,
34: 5 with him and proclaimed his *n*,
34: 14 for the LORD, whose *n* is Jealous,
39: 14 seal with the *n* of one of the twelve
Lev 18: 21 for you must not profane the *n*
19: 12 and so profane the *n* of your God.
19: 12 " 'Do not swear falsely by my *n*
20: 3 sanctuary and profaned my holy *n*.
21: 6 and must not profane the *n*
22: 2 so they will not profane my holy *n*.
22: 32 Do not profane my holy *n*.
24: 11 Israelite woman blasphemed the *n*
24: 11 (His mother's *n* was Shelomith,
24: 16 anyone who blasphemes the *n*
24: 16 when he blasphemes the *N*,
Nu 1: 2 listing every man by *n*, one by one.
1: 18 or more were listed by *n*,
1: 20 serve in the army were listed by *n*,
1: 22 army were counted and listed by *n*,
1: 24 serve in the army were listed by *n*,
1: 26 serve in the army were listed by *n*,
1: 28 serve in the army were listed by *n*,
1: 30 serve in the army were listed by *n*,
1: 32 serve in the army were listed by *n*,
1: 34 serve in the army were listed by *n*,
1: 36 serve in the army were listed by *n*,
1: 38 serve in the army were listed by *n*,
1: 40 serve in the army were listed by *n*,
1: 42 serve in the army were listed by *n*,
3: 43 a month old or more, listed by *n*,
6: 27 they will put my *n* on the Israelites,

Nu 13: 16 son of Nun the *n* Joshua.)
17: 2 Write the *n* of each man on his staff
17: 3 the staff of Levi write Aaron's *n*,
25: 14 *n* of the Israelite who was killed
25: 15 *n* of the Midianite woman who was
26: 59 *n* of Amram's wife was Jochebed,
27: 4 should our father's *n* disappear
Dt 5: 11 anyone guiltless who misuses his *n*.
5: 11 "You shall not misuse the *n*
6: 13 and take your oaths in his *n*.
9: 14 blot out their *n* from under heaven.
10: 8 to pronounce blessings in his *n*,
10: 20 and take your oaths in his *n*.
12: 5 to put his *N* there for his dwelling.
12: 11 choose as a dwelling for his *N*—
12: 21 chooses to put his *N* is too far away
14: 23 will choose as a dwelling for his *N*,
14: 24 choose to put his *N* is so far away),
16: 2 will choose as a dwelling for his *N*.
16: 6 will choose as a dwelling for his *N*.
16: 11 choose as a dwelling for his *N*—
18: 5 minister in the LORD's *n* always.
18: 7 he may minister in the *n*
18: 19 that the prophet speaks in my *n*,
18: 20 speak in my *n* anything I have not
18: 20 speaks in the *n* of other gods,
18: 22 what a prophet proclaims in the *n*
21: 5 blessings in the *n* of the LORD
22: 14 slanders her and gives her a bad *n*,
22: 19 given an Israelite virgin a bad *n*.
25: 6 carry on the *n* of the dead brother
25: 6 so that his *n* will not be blotted out
25: 7 to carry on his brother's *n* in Israel.
26: 2 as a dwelling for his *N* and say
28: 10 called by the *n* of the LORD,
28: 58 this glorious and awesome *n*—
29: 20 and the LORD will blot out his *n*
32: 3 I will proclaim the *n* of the LORD.
Jos 7: 9 and wipe out our *n* from the earth.
7: 9 do for your own great *n*?"
21: 9 by *n* (these towns were assigned
22: 34 the Gadites gave the altar this *n*:
Jdg 1: 26 and called it Luz, which is its *n*
13: 6 and he didn't tell me his *n*.
13: 17 "What is your *n*, so that we may
13: 18 "Why do you ask my *n*? It is
16: 4 of Sorek whose *n* was Delilah.
Ru 1: 2 The man's *n* was Elimelech,
1: 2 was Elimelech, his wife's *n* Naomi,
2: 1 of standing, whose *n* was Boaz.
2: 19 "The *n* of the man I worked
4: 5 order to maintain the *n* of the dead
4: 10 order to maintain the *n* of the dead
4: 10 so that his *n* will not disappear
1Sa 1: 1 whose *n* was Elkanah son
8: 2 The *n* of his firstborn was Joel
8: 2 and the *n* of his second was Abijah,
9: 1 whose *n* was Kish son of Abiel,
12: 22 of his great *n* the LORD will not
14: 49 *n* of his older daughter was Merab,
14: 50 His wife's *n* was Ahinoam
14: 50 The *n* of the commander
17: 45 come against you in the *n*
18: 30 and his *n* became well known.
20: 42 other in the *n* of the LORD,
24: 21 or wipe out my *n* from my father's
25: 3 His *n* was Nabal and his wife's
25: 3 and his wife's *n* was Abigail.
25: 5 at Carmel and greet him in my *n*.
25: 9 Nabal this message in David's *n*.
25: 25 He is just like his *n*— his *n* is Fool,
28: 8 "and bring up for me the one I *n*."
2Sa 4: 4 His *n* was Mephibosheth.)
6: 2 the *n* of the LORD Almighty,
6: 2 which is called by the *N*, the name
6: 18 in the *n* of the LORD Almighty.
7: 9 Now I will make your *n* great,
7: 13 who will build a house for my *N*,
7: 23 and to make a *n* for himself,
7: 26 so that your *n* will be great forever.
12: 25 the prophet to *n* him Jedidiah.
14: 7 leaving my husband neither *n*
14: 27 The daughter's *n* was Tamar,
16: 5 His *n* was Shimei son of Gera,
18: 18 to carry on the memory of my *n*."
22: 50 I will sing praises to your *n*.
1Ki 1: 47 make Solomon's *n* more famous
3: 2 built for the *N* of the LORD.

1Ki 5: 3 for the *N* of the LORD his God
5: 5 for the *N* of the LORD my God,
5: 5 will build the temple for my *N*.'
8: 16 built for my *N* to be there,
8: 17 a temple for the *N* of the LORD,
8: 18 heart to build a temple for my *N*,
8: 19 will build the temple for my *N*.'
8: 20 the temple for the *N* of the LORD,
8: 29 you said, 'My *N* shall be there,'
8: 33 back to you and confess your *n*,
8: 35 and confess your *n* and turn
8: 41 a distant land because of your *n*—
8: 42 for men will hear of your great *n*
8: 43 house I have built bears your *N*.
8: 43 of the earth may know your *n*
8: 44 the temple I have built for your *N*,
8: 48 the temple I have built for your *N*;
9: 3 by putting my *N* there forever.
9: 7 I have consecrated for my *N*.
9: 13 of Cabul, a *n* they have to this day.
10: 1 his relation to the *n* of the LORD,
11: 36 the city where I chose to put my *N*.
14: 21 His mother's *n* was Naamah;
14: 21 of Israel in which to put his *N*.
14: 31 His mother's *n* was Naamah;
15: 2 His mother's *n* was Maacah
15: 10 His grandmother's *n* was Maacah
16: 24 the *n* of the former owner
18: 24 I will call on the *n* of the LORD.
18: 24 Then you call on the *n* of your god,
18: 25 Call on the *n* of your god,
18: 26 Then they called on the *n* of Baal
18: 31 saying, "Your *n* shall be Israel."
18: 32 an altar in the *n* of the LORD,
21: 8 So she wrote letters in Ahab's *n*,
22: 16 the truth in the *n* of the LORD?"
22: 42 His mother's *n* was Azubah
2Ki 2: 24 on them in the *n* of the LORD.
5: 11 call on the *n* of the LORD his God,
8: 26 His mother's *n* was Athaliah,
12: 1 His mother's *n* was Zibiah;
14: 2 His mother's *n* was Jehoaddin;
14: 7 calling it Joktheel, the *n* it has
14: 27 not said he would blot out the *n*
15: 2 His mother's *n* was Jecoliah;
15: 33 His mother's *n* was Jerusha
18: 2 His mother's *n* was Abijah
21: 1 His mother's *n* was Hephzibah
21: 4 "In Jerusalem I will put my *N*."
21: 7 of Israel, I will put my *N* forever.
21: 19 His mother's *n* was Meshullemeth
22: 1 His mother's *n* was Jedidah
23: 27 I said, 'There shall my *N* be.'"
23: 31 His mother's *n* was Hamutal
23: 34 changed Eliakim's *n* to Jehoiakim.
23: 36 His mother's *n* was Zebidah
24: 8 His mother's *n* was Nehushta
24: 17 and changed his *n* to Zedekiah.
24: 18 His mother's *n* was Hamutal
1Ch 1: 50 and his wife's *n* was Mehetabel
2: 26 another wife, whose *n* was Atarah;
4: 38 listed above by *n* were leaders
7: 15 His sister's *n* was Maacah.
8: 29 His wife's *n* was Maacah,
9: 35 His wife's *n* was Maacah.
12: 31 designated by *n* to come
13: 6 the ark that is called by the *N*.
16: 2 the people in the *n* of the LORD.
16: 8 to the LORD, call on his *n*;
16: 10 Glory in his holy *n*;
16: 29 to the LORD the glory due his *n*.
16: 35 we may give thanks to your holy *n*,
16: 41 and designated by *n* to give thanks
17: 8 I will make your *n* like the names
17: 21 and to make a *n* for yourself,
17: 24 that your *n* will be great forever.
21: 19 spoken in the *n* of the LORD.
22: 7 for the *N* of the LORD my God.
22: 8 not to build a house for my *N*,
22: 9 His *n* will be Solomon,
22: 10 who will build a house for my *N*.
22: 19 built for the *N* of the LORD."
23: 13 blessings in his *n* forever.
28: 3 not to build a house for my *N*,
29: 13 and praise your glorious *n*.
29: 16 you a temple for your Holy *N*,
2Ch 2: 1 a temple for the *N* of the LORD
2: 4 for the *N* of the LORD my God

2Ch 6: 5 built for my *N* to be there,
6: 6 Jerusalem for my *N* to be there,
6: 7 a temple for the *N* of the LORD,
6: 8 heart to build a temple for my *N*,
6: 9 will build the temple for my *N*.'
6: 10 the temple for the *N* of the LORD,
6: 20 said you would put your *N* there.
6: 24 they turn back and confess your *n*,
6: 26 and confess your *n* and turn
6: 32 of your great *n* and your mighty
6: 33 house I have built bears your *N*.
6: 33 of the earth may know your *n*
6: 34 the temple I have built for your *N*,
6: 38 the temple I have built for your *N*;
7: 14 my people, who are called by my *n*,
7: 16 so that my *N* may be there forever.
7: 20 I have consecrated for my *N*.
12: 13 His mother's *n* was Naamah;
12: 13 of Israel in which to put his *N*.
13: 2 His mother's *n* was Maacah,
14: 11 and in your *n* we have come
18: 15 the truth in the *n* of the LORD?"
20: 8 built in it a sanctuary for your *N*,
20: 9 this temple that bears your *N*
20: 31 His mother's *n* was Azubah
22: 2 His mother's *n* was Athaliah,
24: 1 His mother's *n* was Zibiah;
25: 1 His mother's *n* was Jehoaddin;
26: 3 His mother's *n* was Jecoliah;
27: 1 His mother's *n* was Jerusha
28: 15 designated by *n* took the prisoners,
29: 1 His mother's *n* was Abijah
31: 19 by *n* to distribute portions
33: 4 "My *N* will remain
33: 7 of Israel, I will put my *N* forever.
33: 18 to him in the *n* of the LORD,
36: 4 changed Eliakim's *n* to Jehoiakim.
36: 13 made him take an oath in God's *n*.
Ezr 2: 61 Gileadite and was called by that *n*).
5: 1 and Jerusalem in the *n* of the God
6: 12 who has caused his *N*
8: 20 All were registered by *n*.
10: 16 and all of them designated by *n*.
Ne 1: 9 chosen as a dwelling for my *N*.'
1: 11 delight in revering your *n*.
6: 13 then they would give me a bad *n*
7: 63 Gileadite and was called by that *n*).
9: 5 "Blessed be your glorious *n*,
9: 10 You made a *n* for yourself,
13: 25 made them take an oath in God's *n*
Est 2: 14 with her and summoned her by *n*.
3: 12 In the *n* of King Xerxes himself
8: 8 document written in the king's *n*
8: 8 in the king's *n* in behalf of the Jews
8: 10 wrote in the *n* of King Xerxes,
Job 1: 1 there lived a man whose *n* was Job.
1: 21 may the *n* of the LORD be praised
18: 17 he has no *n* in the land.
Ps 5: 11 those who love your *n* may rejoice
7: 17 will sing praise to the *n*
8: 1 how majestic is your *n*
8: 9 how majestic is your *n*
9: 2 I will sing praise to your *n*,
9: 5 you have blotted out their *n*
9: 10 Those who know your *n* will trust
18: 49 I will sing praises to your *n*.
20: 1 may the *n* of the God
20: 5 in the *n* of our God.
20: 7 in the *n* of the LORD our God.
22: 22 I will declare your *n* to my brothers
25: 11 For the sake of your *n*, O LORD,
29: 2 to the LORD the glory due his *n*;
30: 4 praise his holy *n*.
31: 3 for the sake of your *n* lead
33: 21 for we trust in his holy *n*.
34: 3 let us exalt his *n* together.
41: 5 When will he die and his *n* perish?"
44: 5 through your *n* we trample our foes
44: 8 and we will praise your *n* forever.
44: 20 If we had forgotten the *n*
48: 10 Like your *n*, O God,
52: 9 for your *n* is good.
52: 9 in your *n* I will hope,
54: 1 Save me, O God, by your *n*;
54: 6 I will praise your *n*, O LORD,
61: 5 of those who fear your *n*.
61: 8 will I ever sing praise to your *n*
63: 4 in your *n* I will lift up my hands.

Ps 63: 11 swear by God's *n* will praise him,
66: 2 Sing to the glory of his *n;*
66: 4 they sing praise to your *n*.''
68: 4 Sing to God, sing praise to his *n*,
68: 4 his *n* is the LORD—
69: 30 I will praise God's *n* in song
69: 36 who love his *n* will dwell there.
72: 17 May his *n* endure forever;
72: 19 Praise be to his glorious *n* forever;
74: 7 the dwelling place of your *N*.
74: 10 Will the foe revile your *n* forever?
74: 18 foolish people have reviled your *n*.
74: 21 the poor and needy praise your *n*.
75: 1 we give thanks, for your *N* is near;
76: 1 his *n* is great in Israel.
79: 6 that do not call on your *n;*
79: 9 for the glory of your *n;*
80: 18 and we will call on your *n*.
83: 4 that the *n* of Israel be remembered
83: 16 so that men will seek your *n*,
83: 18 that you, whose *n* is the LORD—
86: 9 they will bring glory to your *n*.
86: 11 that I may fear your *n*.
86: 12 I will glorify your *n* forever.
89: 12 Hermon sing for joy at your *n*.
89: 16 They rejoice in your *n* all day long;
89: 24 through my *n* his horn will be
91: 14 for he acknowledges my *n*.
92: 1 and make music to your *n*,
96: 2 Sing to the LORD, praise his *n;*
96: 8 to the LORD the glory due his *n;*
97: 12 and praise his holy *n*.
99: 3 praise your great and awesome *n*—
99: 6 among those who called on his *n;*
100: 4 give thanks to him and praise his *n*.
102: 8 those who rail against me use my *n*
102: 15 The nations will fear the *n*
102: 21 the *n* of the LORD will be declared
103: 1 my inmost being, praise his holy *n*.
105: 1 to the LORD, call on his *n;*
105: 3 Glory in his holy *n;*
106: 47 we may give thanks to your holy *n*
111: 9 holy and awesome is his *n*.
113: 1 praise the *n* of the LORD.
113: 2 Let the *n* of the LORD be praised,
113: 3 the *n* of the LORD is to be praised.
115: 1 but to your *n* be the glory,
116: 4 I called on the *n* of the LORD:
116: 13 and call on the *n* of the LORD.
116: 17 and call on the *n* of the LORD.
118: 10 in the *n* of the LORD I cut them
118: 11 in the *n* of the LORD I cut them
118: 12 in the *n* of the LORD I cut them
118: 26 comes in the *n* of the LORD.
119: 55 In the night I remember your *n*,
119:132 to those who love your *n*.
122: 4 to praise the *n* of the LORD
124: 8 Our help is in the *n* of the LORD,
129: 8 we bless you in the *n* of the LORD
135: 1 Praise the *n* of the LORD;
135: 3 sing praise to his *n*,
135: 13 Your *n*, O LORD, endures forever,
138: 2 and will praise your *n*
138: 2 your *n* and your word.
139: 20 your adversaries misuse your *n*.
140: 13 the righteous will praise your *n*
142: 7 that I may praise your *n*.
145: 1 I will praise your *n* for ever
145: 2 and extol your *n* for ever and ever.
145: 21 Let every creature praise his holy *n*
147: 4 and calls them each by *n*.
148: 5 Let them praise the *n* of the LORD
148: 13 Let them praise the *n* of the LORD
148: 13 for his *n* alone is exalted;
149: 3 Let them praise his *n* with dancing
Pr 3: 4 you will win favor and a good *n*
10: 7 but the *n* of the wicked will rot.
18: 10 *n* of the LORD is a strong tower;
21: 24 arrogant man—''Mocker'' is his *n;*
22: 1 A good *n* is more desirable
30: 4 What is his *n*, and the *n* of his son?
30: 9 and so dishonor the *n* of my God.
Ecc 6: 4 and in darkness its *n* is shrouded.
7: 1 A good *n* is better
SS 1: 3 your *n* is like perfume poured out.
Isa 4: 1 only let us be called by your *n*.
8: 3 ''*N* him Maher-Shalal-Hash-Baz.
12: 4 and proclaim that his *n* is exalted.

Isa 12: 4 thanks to the LORD, call on his *n;*
14: 22 ''I will cut off from Babylon her *n*
18: 7 of the *N* of the LORD Almighty.
24: 15 exalt the *n* of the LORD, the God
25: 1 I will exalt you and praise your *n*,
26: 8 your *n* and renown
26: 13 but your *n* alone do we honor.
29: 23 they will keep my *n* holy;
30: 27 the *N* of the LORD comes
40: 26 and calls them each by *n*.
41: 25 the rising sun who calls on my *n*.
42: 8 ''I am the LORD; that is my *n!*
43: 1 you by *n;* you are mine.
43: 7 everyone who is called by my *n*,
44: 5 and will take the *n* Israel.
44: 5 another will call himself by the *n*
45: 3 God of Israel, who calls you by *n*.
45: 4 I call you by *n*
47: 4 the LORD Almighty is his *n*—
48: 1 oaths in the *n* of the LORD
48: 1 you who are called by the *n*
48: 2 the LORD Almighty is his *n:*
48: 19 their *n* would never be cut off
49: 1 birth he has made mention of my *n*.
50: 10 trust in the *n* of the LORD
51: 15 the LORD Almighty is his *n*.
52: 5 my *n* is constantly blasphemed.
52: 6 my people will know my *n;*
54: 5 the LORD Almighty is his *n*—
56: 5 I will give them an everlasting *n*
56: 5 a memorial and a *n*
56: 6 to love the *n* of the LORD,
57: 15 who lives forever, whose *n* is holy:
59: 19 men will fear the *n* of the LORD,
62: 2 you will be called by a new *n*
62: 4 or *n* your land Desolate.
63: 14 to make for yourself a glorious *n*.
63: 16 our Redeemer from of old is your *n*
63: 19 have not been called by your *n*.
64: 2 come down to make your *n* known
64: 7 No one calls on your *n*
65: 1 a nation that did not call on my *n*,
65: 15 You will leave your *n*
65: 15 his servants he will give another *n*.
66: 5 and exclude you because of my *n*,
66: 22 ''so will your *n* and descendants
Jer 3: 17 to honor the *n* of the LORD.
7: 10 which bears my *N*, and say,
7: 11 Has this house, which bears my *N*,
7: 12 I first made a dwelling for my *N*,
7: 14 do to the house that bears my *N*,
7: 30 idols in the house that bears my *N*
10: 6 and your *n* is mighty in power.
10: 16 the LORD Almighty is his *n*.
10: 25 peoples who do not call on your *n*.
11: 19 that his *n* be remembered no more
11: 21 prophesy in the *n* of the LORD
12: 16 of my people and swear by my *n*,
14: 7 do something for the sake of your *n*
14: 9 and we bear your *n;*
14: 14 are prophesying lies in my *n*.
14: 15 who are prophesying in my *n:*
14: 21 of your *n* do not despise us;
15: 16 for I bear your *n*,
16: 21 that my *n* is the LORD.
20: 3 LORD's *n* for you is not Pashhur,
20: 9 or speak any more in his *n*,''
23: 6 This is the *n* by which he will be
23: 25 say who prophesy lies in my *n*.
23: 27 as their fathers forgot my *n*
23: 27 will make my people forget my *n*,
25: 29 on the city that bears my *N*,
26: 9 in the LORD's *n* that this house
26: 16 us in the *n* of the LORD our God.''
26: 20 prophesied in the *n* of the LORD;
27: 15 'They are prophesying lies in my *n*.
29: 9 prophesying lies to you in my *n*.
29: 21 prophesying lies to you in my *n:*
29: 23 and in my *n* have spoken lies,
29: 25 in your own *n* to all the people
31: 35 the LORD Almighty is his *n:*
32: 18 whose *n* is the LORD Almighty,
32: 34 idols in the house that bears my *N*
33: 2 established it—the LORD is his *n:*
33: 16 This is the *n* by which it will be
34: 15 me in the house that bears my *N*.
34: 16 turned around and profaned my *n;*
37: 13 whose *n* was Irijah son

Jer 44: 16 spoken to us in the *n* of the LORD!
44: 26 Egypt will ever again invoke my *n*
44: 26 by my great *n*,' says the LORD,
46: 18 whose *n* is the LORD Almighty,
48: 15 whose *n* is the LORD Almighty.
50: 34 the LORD Almighty is his *n*.
51: 19 The LORD Almighty is his *n*.
51: 57 whose *n* is the LORD Almighty.
52: 1 His mother's *n* was Hamutal
La 3: 55 I called on your *n*, O LORD,
Eze 20: 9 of my *n* I did what would keep it
20: 14 of my *n* I did what would keep it
20: 22 of my *n* I did what would keep it
20: 39 and no longer profane my holy *n*
36: 20 nations they profaned my holy *n*,
36: 21 I had concern for my holy *n*,
36: 22 but for the sake of my holy *n*,
36: 23 show the holiness of my great *n*,
36: 23 the *n* you have profaned
39: 7 longer let my holy *n* be profaned,
39: 7 '' 'I will make known my holy *n*
39: 25 and I will be zealous for my holy *n*.
43: 7 will never again defile my holy *n*—
43: 8 they defiled my holy *n*
48: 1 by *n:* At the northern frontier,
48: 35 the *n* of the city from that time
Da 1: 7 to Daniel, the *n* Belteshazzar;
2: 20 ''Praise be to the *n* of God for ever
4: 8 after the *n* of my god,
9: 6 who spoke in your *n* to our kings,
9: 15 made for yourself a *n* that endures
9: 18 of the city that bears your *N*.
9: 19 and your people bear your *N*.''
12: 1 everyone whose *n* is found written
Hos 12: 5 the LORD is his *n* of renown!
Joel 2: 26 and you will praise the *n*
2: 32 on the *n* of the LORD will be saved
Am 2: 7 and so profane my holy *n*.
4: 13 the LORD God Almighty is his *n*.
5: 8 the LORD is his *n*—
5: 27 whose *n* is God Almighty.
6: 10 We must not mention the *n*
9: 6 the LORD is his *n*.
9: 12 and all the nations that bear my *n*,''
Mic 4: 5 walk in the *n* of their gods;
4: 5 we will walk in the *n* of the LORD
5: 4 in the majesty of the *n*
6: 9 and to fear your *n* is wisdom—
Na 1: 14 no descendants to bear your *n*.
Zep 3: 9 call on the *n* of the LORD
3: 12 who trust in the *n* of the LORD.
Zec 5: 4 of him who swears falsely by my *n*.
6: 12 is the man whose *n* is the Branch,
10: 12 and in his *n* they will walk,''
13: 3 you have told lies in the LORD's *n*
13: 9 They will call on my *n*
14: 9 one LORD, and his *n* the only *n*.
Mal 1: 6 O priests, who despise my *n*.
1: 6 'How have we despised your *n?*'
1: 11 My *n* will be great
1: 11 because my *n* will be great
1: 11 offerings will be brought to my *n*,
1: 14 ''and my *n* is to be feared
2: 2 not set your heart to honor my *n*,''
2: 5 me and stood in awe of my *n*.
3: 16 the LORD and honored his *n*.
4: 2 But for you who revere my *n*,
Mt 1: 21 and you are to give him the *n* Jesus,
1: 25 And he gave him the *n* Jesus.
6: 9 hallowed be your *n*,
7: 22 and in your *n* drive out demons
7: 22 did we not prophesy in your *n*,
12: 21 In his *n* the nations will put their
13: 55 Isn't his mother's *n* Mary,
18: 5 this in my *n* welcomes me.
18: 20 or three come together in my *n*,
21: 9 comes in the *n* of the Lord!''
23: 39 comes in the *n* of the Lord.' ''
24: 5 For many will come in my *n*,
26: 3 whose *n* was Caiaphas,
28: 19 them in the *n* of the Father
Mk 3: 16 (to whom he gave the *n* Peter);
3: 17 (to them he gave the *n* Boanerges,
5: 9 ''What is your *n?*'' ''My *n* is Legion
6: 14 for Jesus' *n* had become well
9: 37 children in my *n* welcomes me;
9: 38 man driving out demons in your *n*
9: 39 who does a miracle in my *n* can

Mk 9: 41 gives you a cup of water in my *n*
11: 9 comes in the *n* of the Lord!''
13: 6 Many will come in my *n*, claiming,
16: 17 In my *n* they will drive out demons
Lk 1: 13 and you are to give him the *n* John.
1: 27 The virgin's *n* was Mary.
1: 31 and you are to give him the *n* Jesus.
1: 49 holy is his *n*.
1: 59 and they were going to *n* him
1: 61 your relatives who has that *n*.''
1: 62 what he would like to *n* the child.
1: 63 he wrote, ''His *n* is John.''
2: 21 the *n* the angel had given him
5: 27 collector by the *n* of Levi sitting
6: 22 and reject your *n* as evil,
8: 30 ''What is your *n*?'' ''Legion,''
9: 48 child in my *n* welcomes me;
9: 49 man driving out demons in your *n*
10: 17 the demons submit to us in your *n*
11: 2 hallowed be your *n*,
13: 35 comes in the *n* of the Lord.' ''
19: 2 there by the *n* of Zacchaeus;
19: 38 in the *n* of the Lord!''
21: 8 For many will come in my *n*,
21: 12 and all on account of my *n*.
24: 47 preached in his *n* to all nations,
Jn 1: 6 sent from God; his *n* was John.
1: 12 to those who believed in his *n*,
2: 23 he was doing and believed in his *n*.
3: 18 believed in the *n* of God's one
5: 43 I have come in my Father's *n*,
5: 43 if someone else comes in his own *n*,
10: 3 He calls his own sheep by *n*
10: 25 do in my Father's *n* speak for me,
12: 13 comes in the *n* of the Lord!''
12: 28 glorify your *n*!'' Then a voice came
14: 13 I will do whatever you ask in my *n*,
14: 14 me for anything in my *n*,
14: 26 whom the Father will send in my *n*,
15: 16 give you whatever you ask in my *n*.
15: 21 treat you this way because of my *n*,
16: 23 give you whatever you ask in my *n*.
16: 24 asked for anything in my *n*.
16: 26 In that day you will ask in my *n*.
17: 11 of your *n*— the *n* you gave me—
17: 12 safe by that *n* you gave me.
18: 10 (The servant's *n* was Malchus.)
20: 31 you may have life in his *n*.
Ac 2: 21 on the *n* of the Lord will be saved.'
2: 38 in the *n* of Jesus Christ
3: 6 In the *n* of Jesus Christ
3: 16 It is Jesus' *n* and the faith that
3: 16 in the *n* of Jesus, this man whom
4: 7 or what *n* did you do this?''
4: 10 It is by the *n* of Jesus Christ
4: 12 for there is no other *n*
4: 17 longer to anyone in this *n*.''
4: 18 or teach at all in the *n* of Jesus.
4: 30 and wonders through the *n*
5: 28 not to teach in this *n*,''
5: 40 not to speak in the *n* of Jesus,
5: 41 of suffering disgrace for the *N*.
8: 12 of God and the *n* of Jesus Christ,
8: 16 into the *n* of the Lord Jesus.
9: 14 to arrest all who call on your *n*.''
9: 15 to carry my *n* before the Gentiles
9: 16 much he must suffer for my *n*.''
9: 21 among those who call on this *n*?
9: 27 he had preached fearlessly in the *n*
9: 28 boldly in the *n* of the Lord.
10: 43 forgiveness of sins through his *n*.''
10: 48 baptized in the *n* of Jesus Christ.
13: 8 is what his *n* means) opposed them
15: 17 and all the Gentiles who bear my *n*,
15: 26 for the *n* of our Lord Jesus Christ.
16: 18 ''In the *n* of Jesus Christ I
19: 5 into the *n* of the Lord Jesus.
19: 13 They would say, ''In the *n* of Jesus,
19: 13 to invoke the *n* of the Lord Jesus
19: 17 the *n* of the Lord Jesus was held
19: 27 that our trade will lose its good *n*,
21: 13 die in Jerusalem for the *n*
22: 16 your sins away, calling on his *n*.'
26: 9 possible to oppose the *n* of Jesus
Ro 2: 24 ''God's *n* is blasphemed
9: 17 and that my *n* might be proclaimed
10: 13 ''Everyone who calls on the *n*
15: 9 I will sing hymns to your *n*.''
1Co 1: 2 on the *n* of our Lord Jesus Christ—
1: 10 in the *n* of our Lord Jesus Christ,
1: 13 baptized into the *n* of Paul?
1: 15 that you were baptized into my *n*.
5: 4 in the *n* of our Lord Jesus
6: 11 you were justified in the *n*
Eph 3: 15 in heaven and on earth derives its *n*
5: 20 in the *n* of our Lord Jesus Christ.
Php 2: 9 him the *n* that is above every *n*,
2: 10 at the *n* of Jesus every knee should
Col 3: 17 do it all in the *n* of the Lord Jesus,
2Th 1: 12 We pray this so that the *n*
3: 6 In the *n* of the Lord Jesus Christ,
1Ti 6: 1 so that God's *n* and our teaching
2Ti 2: 19 ''Everyone who confesses the *n*
Heb 1: 4 as the *n* he has inherited is superior
2: 12 I will declare your *n* to my brothers
7: 2 his *n* means ''king of righteousness
13: 15 the fruit of lips that confess his *n*.
Jas 2: 7 who are slandering the noble *n*
5: 10 spoke in the *n* of the Lord.
5: 14 him with oil in the *n* of the Lord.
1Pe 4: 14 If you are insulted because of the *n*
4: 16 but praise God that you bear that *n*
1Jn 2: 12 on account of his *n*.
3: 23 to believe in the *n* of his Son,
5: 13 believe in the *n* of the Son of God
3Jn : 7 sake of the *N* that they went out,
: 14 Greet the friends there by *n*.
Rev 2: 3 have endured hardships for my *n*,
2: 13 Yet you remain true to my *n*.
2: 17 stone with a new *n* written on it,
3: 5 I will never erase his *n*
3: 5 but will acknowledge his *n*
3: 8 and have not denied my *n*
3: 12 I will also write on him my new *n*.
3: 12 I will write on him the *n* of my God
3: 12 and the *n* of the city of my God,
8: 11 the *n* of the star is Wormwood.
9: 11 whose *n* in Hebrew is Abaddon,
11: 18 and those who reverence your *n*,
13: 1 and on each head a blasphemous *n*.
13: 6 to slander his *n* and his dwelling
13: 17 of the beast or the number of his *n*.
13: 17 which is the *n* of the beast
14: 1 and his Father's *n* written
14: 1 who had his *n* and his Father's
14: 11 who receives the mark of his *n*.''
15: 2 and over the number of his *n*.
15: 4 and bring glory to your *n*?
16: 9 and they cursed the *n* of God,
19: 12 He has a *n* written
19: 13 and his *n* is the Word of God.
19: 16 on his thigh he has this *n* written:
20: 15 If anyone's *n* was not found written
22: 4 and his *n* will be on their foreheads.

NAME'S (NAME)

Ps 23: 3 righteousness for his *n* sake.
79: 9 sins for your *n* sake.
106: 8 Yet he saved them for his *n* sake,
109: 21 deal well with me for your *n* sake;
143: 11 For your *n* sake, O LORD,
Isa 48: 9 For my own *n* sake I delay my
Eze 20: 44 when I deal with you for my *n* sake
Ro 1: 5 Through him and for his *n* sake,

NAMED (NAME)

Ge 3: 20 Adam *n* his wife Eve, because she
4: 17 and he *n* it after his son Enoch.
4: 19 one *n* Adah and the other Zillah.
4: 25 birth to a son and *n* him Seth,
4: 26 had a son, and he *n* him Enosh.
5: 3 his own image; and he *n* him Seth.
5: 29 He *n* him Noah and said, ''He will
10: 25 born to Eber: One was *n* Peleg,
10: 25 divided; his brother was *n* Joktan.
16: 1 an Egyptian maidservant *n* Hagar;
19: 37 had a son, and she *n* him Moab;
19: 38 and she *n* him Ben-Ammi;
23: 16 out for him the price he had *n*
24: 29 Rebekah had a brother *n* Laban,
25: 25 so they *n* him Esau.
25: 26 so he was *n* Jacob.
26: 20 is ours!'' So he *n* the well Esek,
26: 21 over that one also; so he *n* it Sitnah.
26: 22 He *n* it Rehoboth, saying,
27: 36 Esau said, ''Isn't he rightly *n* Jacob
Ge 29: 32 She *n* him Reuben, for she said,
29: 33 So she *n* him Simeon.
29: 34 So he was *n* Levi.
29: 35 So she *n* him Judah.
30: 6 Because of this she *n* him Dan.
30: 8 So she *n* him Naphtali.
30: 11 good fortune!'' So she *n* him Gad.
30: 13 So she *n* him Asher.
30: 18 So she *n* him Issachar.
30: 20 So she *n* him Zebulun.
30: 21 to a daughter and *n* her Dinah.
30: 24 She *n* him Joseph, and said,
32: 2 So he *n* that place Mahanaim.
35: 8 So it was *n* Allon Bacuth.
35: 10 So he *n* him Israel.
35: 15 Jacob *n* the place where God had
35: 18 But his father *n* him Benjamin.
35: 18 was dying—she *n* her son
36: 12 also had a concubine *n* Timna,
36: 32 His city was *n* Dinhabah.
36: 35 His city was *n* Avith.
36: 39 His city was *n* Pau, and his wife's
38: 1 with a man of Adullam *n* Hirah.
38: 2 of a Canaanite man *n* Shua.
38: 3 gave birth to a son, who was *n* Er.
38: 4 gave birth to a son and *n* him Onan
38: 5 still another son and *n* him Shelah.
38: 29 broken out!'' And he was *n* Perez.
41: 51 Joseph *n* his firstborn Manasseh
41: 52 The second son he *n* Ephraim
Ex 2: 10 She *n* him Moses, saying, ''I drew
2: 22 and Moses *n* him Gershom, saying,
18: 3 One son was *n* Gershom,
18: 4 and the other was *n* Eliezer,
Nu 11: 34 the place was *n* Kibroth Hattaavah,
21: 3 so the place was *n* Hormah.
26: 46 (Asher had a daughter *n* Serah.)
Dt 3: 14 it was *n* after him, so that
Jos 2: 1 the house of a prostitute *n* Rahab
19: 47 and *n* it Dan after their forefather.)
Jdg 8: 31 him a son, whom he *n* Abimelech.
13: 2 A certain man of Zorah, *n* Manoah
13: 24 birth to a boy and *n* him Samson.
17: 1 man *n* Micah from the hill country
18: 29 They *n* it Dan after their forefather
Ru 1: 4 one *n* Orpah and the other Ruth.
4: 17 And they *n* him Obed.
1Sa 1: 20 She *n* him Samuel, saying,
4: 21 She *n* the boy Ichabod, saying,
7: 12 He *n* it Ebenezer, saying, ''Thus far
9: 2 He had a son *n* Saul, an impressive
17: 4 A champion *n* Goliath, who was
17: 12 the son of an Ephrathite *n* Jesse,
2Sa 3: 7 a concubine *n* Rizpah daughter
4: 2 One was *n* Baanah and the other
9: 2 servant of Saul's household *n* Ziba
9: 12 had a young son *n* Mica,
12: 24 to a son, and they *n* him Solomon.
12: 28 I will take the city, and it will be *n*
13: 3 Amnon had a friend *n* Jonadab son
17: 25 the son of a man *n* Jether,
18: 18 He *n* the pillar after himself,
20: 1 Now a troublemaker *n* Sheba son
20: 21 A man *n* Sheba son of Bicri,
1Ki 7: 21 The pillar to the south he *n* Jakin
11: 20 bore him a son *n* Genubath,
11: 26 his mother was a widow *n* Zeruah.
13: 2 'A son *n* Josiah will be born
2Ki 17: 34 of Jacob, whom he *n* Israel.
23: 11 of an official *n* Nathan-Melech.
1Ch 1: 19 born to Eber: One was *n* Peleg,
1: 19 divided; his brother was *n* Joktan.
1: 43 whose city was *n* Dinhabah.
1: 46 His city was *n* Avith.
1: 50 His city was *n* Pau, and his wife's
2: 29 Abishur's wife was *n* Abihail,
2: 34 had an Egyptian servant *n* Jarha.
4: 3 Their sister was *n* Hazzelelponi.
4: 9 His mother had *n* him Jabez,
6: 65 allotted the previously *n* towns.
7: 15 descendant was *n* Zelophehad,
7: 16 His brother was *n* Sheresh,
7: 16 birth to a son and *n* him Peresh.
7: 23 He *n* him Beriah, because there
9: 31 Levite *n* Mattithiah, the firstborn
2Ch 3: 17 The one to the south he *n* Jakin
28: 9 of the LORD *n* Oded was there,
Ezr 5: 14 them to a man *n* Sheshbazzar,

Ne 9: 7 Chaldeans and *n* him Abraham.
13: 13 and a Levite *n* Pedaiah in charge
Est 2: 5 *n* Mordecai son of Jair, the son
2: 7 Mordecai had a cousin *n* Hadassah
Job 42: 14 The first daughter he *n* Jemimah,
Ps 49: 11 they had *n* lands after themselves.
Ecc 6: 10 Whatever exists has already been *n*
Isa 61: 6 you will be *n* ministers of our God.
Eze 23: 4 The older was *n* Oholah,
48: 31 of the city will be *n* after the tribes
Mt 9: 9 he saw a man *n* Matthew sitting
27: 32 a man from Cyrene, *n* Simon,
27: 57 man from Arimathea, *n* Joseph,
Mk 5: 22 of the synagogue rulers, *n* Jairus,
Lk 1: 5 there was a priest *n* Zechariah,
1: 27 to be married to a man *n* Joseph,
2: 21 to circumcise him, he was *n* Jesus,
6: 14 Simon (whom he *n* Peter),
8: 41 Just then a man *n* Jairus, a ruler
10: 38 where a woman *n* Martha opened
16: 20 gate was laid a beggar *n* Lazarus,
23: 50 Now there was a man *n* Joseph,
24: 18 One of them, *n* Cleopas, asked him
Jn 3: 1 of the Pharisees *n* Nicodemus,
11: 1 Now a man *n* Lazarus was sick.
11: 49 Then one of them, *n* Caiaphas,
Ac 5: 1 Now a man *n* Ananias, together
5: 34 But a Pharisee *n* Gamaliel,
7: 58 at the feet of a young man *n* Saul.
8: 9 time a man *n* Simon had practiced
9: 10 there was a disciple *n* Ananias.
9: 11 ask for a man from Tarsus *n* Saul,
9: 12 he has seen a man *n* Ananias come
9: 33 There he found a man *n* Aeneas,
9: 36 was a disciple *n* Tabitha (which,
9: 43 time with a tanner *n* Simon.
10: 1 there was a man *n* Cornelius,
10: 5 bring back a man *n* Simon who is
11: 28 *n* Agabus, stood up
12: 13 and a servant girl *n* Rhoda came
13: 6 and false prophet *n* Bar-Jesus,
16: 1 where a disciple *n* Timothy lived,
16: 14 listening was a woman *n* Lydia,
17: 34 also a woman *n* Damaris,
18: 2 There he met a Jew *n* Aquila,
18: 24 Meanwhile a Jew *n* Apollos,
19: 24 A silversmith *n* Demetrius,
20: 9 was a young man *n* Eutychus,
21: 10 a prophet *n* Agabus came
22: 12 "A man *n* Ananias came to see me.
24: 1 the elders and a lawyer *n* Tertullus,
25: 19 about a dead man *n* Jesus who Paul
27: 1 over to a centurion *n* Julius,
Rev 6: 8 Its rider was *n* Death, and Hades

NAMELESS (NAME)

Job 30: 8 A base and *n* brood,

NAMES (NAME)

Ge 2: 20 the man gave *n* to all the livestock,
25: 13 These are the *n* of the sons
25: 16 these are the *n* of the twelve tribal
26: 18 them the same *n* his father had
36: 10 These are the *n* of Esau's sons:
46: 8 These are the *n* of the Israelites
48: 6 under the *n* of their brothers.
48: 16 and the *n* of my fathers Abraham
Ex 1: 1 These are the *n* of the sons
1: 15 whose *n* were Shiphrah and Puah,
6: 16 These were the *n* of the sons
23: 13 Do not invoke the *n* of other gods;
28: 9 engrave on them the *n* of the sons
28: 10 six *n* on one stone
28: 11 Engrave the *n* of the sons of Israel
28: 12 is to bear the *n* on his shoulders
28: 21 one for each of the *n* of the sons
28: 29 he will bear the *n* of the sons
39: 6 seal with the *n* of the sons of Israel.
39: 14 one for each of the *n* of the sons
Nu 1: 5 These are the *n* of the men who are
1: 17 these men whose *n* had been given,
3: 2 *n* of the sons of Aaron were Nadab
3: 3 Those were the *n* of Aaron's sons,
3: 17 These were the *n* of the sons
3: 18 These were the *n* of the Gershonite
3: 40 or more and make a list of their *n*.
11: 26 whose *n* were Eldad and Medad,
13: 4 These are their *n*: from the tribe
Nu 13: 16 These are the *n* of the men Moses
26: 33 whose *n* were Mahlah, Noah,
26: 53 based on the number of *n*.
26: 55 to the *n* for its ancestral tribe.
27: 1 *n* of the daughters were Mahlah,
32: 38 Baal Meon (these *n* were changed)
32: 38 They gave *n* to the cities they
34: 17 These are the *n* of the men who are
34: 19 These are their *n*: Caleb son
Dt 7: 24 and you will wipe out their *n*
12: 3 wipe out their *n* from those places.
Jos 17: 3 whose *n* were Mahlah, Noah,
23: 7 do not invoke the *n* of their gods
Jdg 8: 14 wrote down for him the *n*
Ru 1: 2 the *n* of his two sons were Mahlon
2Sa 5: 14 These are the *n* of the children
7: 9 like the *n* of the greatest men
23: 8 These are the *n* of David's mighty
1Ki 4: 8 These are their *n*: Ben-Hur—
1Ch 4: 41 The men whose *n* were listed came
6: 17 These are the *n* of the sons
8: 38 and these were their *n*: Azrikam,
9: 44 and these were their *n*: Azrikam,
14: 4 These are the *n* of the children
17: 8 I will make your name like the *n*
23: 24 they were registered under their *n*
24: 6 recorded their *n* in the presence
2Ch 31: 16 or more whose *n* were
Ezr 5: 4 "What are the *n* of the men
5: 10 We also asked them their *n*,
5: 10 write down the *n* of their leaders
8: 13 last ones, whose *n* were Eliphelet,
Ps 16: 4 or take up their *n* on my lips.
109: 13 their *n* blotted out
Da 1: 7 The chief official gave them new *n*:
Hos 2: 17 I will remove the *n* of the Baals
2: 17 no longer will their *n* be invoked.
Zep 1: 4 *n* of the pagan and the idolatrous
Zec 13: 2 I will banish the *n* of the idols
Mt 10: 2 These are the *n* of the twelve
Lk 10: 20 but rejoice that your *n* are written
Ac 18: 15 and *n* and your own law—
Php 4: 3 whose *n* are in the book of life.
Heb 12: 23 whose *n* are written in heaven.
Rev 13: 8 all whose *n* have not been written
17: 3 covered with blasphemous *n*
17: 8 of the earth whose *n* have not been
21: 12 On the gates were written the *n*
21: 14 and on them were the *n*
21: 27 but only those whose *n* are written

NAOMI (NAOMI'S)

Ru 1: 2 was Elimelech, his wife's name *N*,
1: 5 *N* was left without her two sons
1: 6 *N* and her daughters-in-law
1: 8 *N* said to her two daughters-in-law,
1: 11 But *N* said, "Return home,
1: 15 said *N*, "your sister-in-law is going
1: 18 When *N* realized that Ruth was
1: 19 "Can this be *N*?" "Don't call me
1: 20 "Don't call me *N*," she told them.
1: 21 Why call me *N*? The LORD has
1: 22 So *N* returned from Moab
2: 1 *N* had a relative on her husband's
2: 2 And Ruth the Moabitess said to *N*,
2: 2 *N* said to her, "Go ahead, my
2: 6 back from Moab with *N*.
2: 20 *N* said to her daughter-in-law.
2: 22 *N* said to Ruth her daughter-in-law
3: 1 One day *N* her mother-in-law said
3: 16 to her mother-in-law, *N* asked,
3: 18 Then *N* said, "Wait, my daughter,
4: 3 said to the kinsman-redeemer, "*N*,
4: 5 the day you buy the land from *N*
4: 9 bought from *N* all the property
4: 14 The women said to *N*: "Praise be
4: 16 *N* took the child, laid him in her lap
4: 17 living there said, "*N* has a son."

NAOMI'S (NAOMI)

Ru 1: 3 Now Elimelech, *N* husband, died,

NAPHISH

Ge 25: 15 Tema, Jetur, *N* and Kedemah.
1Ch 1: 31 Tema, Jetur, *N* and Kedemah.
5: 19 war against the Hagrites, Jetur, *N*

NAPHOTH

Jos 17: 11 (the third in the list is *N*).

NAPHOTH DOR

Jos 11: 2 in the western foothills and in *N*
12: 23 one the king of Dor (in *N*)
1Ki 4: 11 in *N* (he was married to

NAPHTALI (NAPHTALITES)

Ge 30: 8 So she named him *N*.
35: 25 maidservant Bilhah: Dan and *N*.
46: 24 The sons of *N*: Jahziel, Guni,
49: 21 "*N* is a doe set free
Ex 1: 4 Dan and *N*; Gad and Asher.
Nu 1: 15 from *N*, Ahira son of Enan."
1: 42 From the descendants of *N*:
1: 43 from the tribe of *N* was 53,400.
2: 29 The tribe of *N* will be next.
2: 29 of the people of *N* is Ahira son
7: 78 the leader of the people of *N*,
10: 27 over the division of the tribe of *N*.
13: 14 from the tribe of *N*, Nahbi son
26: 48 The descendants of *N*
26: 50 These were the clans of *N*;
34: 28 the leader from the tribe of *N*."
Dt 27: 13 Gad, Asher, Zebulun, Dan and *N*.
33: 23 About *N* he said:
33: 23 "*N* is abounding with the favor
34: 2 from Gilead to Dan, all of *N*,
Jos 19: 32 The sixth lot came out for *N*,
19: 39 the inheritance of the tribe of *N*,
20: 7 in Galilee in the hill country of *N*,
21: 6 *N* and the half-tribe of Manasseh
21: 32 four towns; from the tribe of *N*,
Jdg 1: 33 Neither did *N* drive out those
4: 6 son of Abinoam from Kedesh in *N*
4: 6 with you ten thousand men of *N*
4: 10 he summoned Zebulun and *N*.
5: 18 so did *N* on the heights of the field.
6: 35 and also into Asher, Zebulun and *N*
7: 23 Israelites from *N*, Asher
1Ki 4: 15 in *N* (he had married Basemath
7: 14 a widow from the tribe of *N*
15: 20 and all Kinnereth in addition to *N*.
2Ki 15: 29 of *N*— and deported the people
1Ch 2: 2 Dan, Joseph, Benjamin, *N*,
6: 62 the tribes of Issachar, Asher and *N*,
6: 76 the tribe of *N* they received Kedesh
7: 13 The sons of *N*: Jahziel, Guni,
12: 34 men of *N*— 1,000 officers,
12: 40 *N* came bringing food on donkeys,
27: 19 over *N*: Jerimoth son of Azriel;
2Ch 16: 4 and all the store cities of *N*.
34: 6 Ephraim and Simeon, as far as *N*,
Ps 68: 27 the princes of Zebulun and of *N*.
Isa 9: 1 land of Zebulun and the land of *N*,
Eze 48: 3 "*N* will have one portion; it will
48: 4 the territory of *N* from east to west.
48: 34 the gate of Asher and the gate of *N*.
Mt 4: 13 lake in the area of Zebulun and *N*—
4: 15 "Land of Zebulun and land of *N*,
Rev 7: 6 from the tribe of *N* 12,000,

NAPHTALITES (NAPHTALI)

Jdg 1: 33 *N* too lived among the Canaanite

NAPHTUHITES

Ge 10: 13 Lehabites, *N*, Pathrusites,
1Ch 1: 11 Lehabites, *N*, Pathrusites,

NARCISSUS

Ro 16: 11 in the household of *N* who are

NARD

SS 4: 13 with henna and *n*,
4: 14 *n* and saffron,
Mk 14: 3 perfume, made of pure *n*.
Jn 12: 3 Mary took about a pint of pure *n*,

NARROW (NARROWER)

Nu 22: 24 in a *n* path between two vineyards,
22: 26 in a *n* place where there was no
1Ki 6: 4 He made *n* clerestory windows
Pr 23: 27 and a wayward wife is a *n* well.
Isa 28: 20 the blanket too *n* to wrap
Eze 40: 16 by *n* parapet openings all around,
40: 25 and its portico had *n* openings all
41: 16 the thresholds and the *n* windows

Eze 41: 26 of the portico were *n* windows
Mt 7: 13 "Enter through the *n* gate.
7: 14 and *n* the road that leads to life,
Lk 13: 24 effort to enter through the *n* door,

NARROWER (NARROW)

Eze 42: 5 Now the upper rooms were *n*,

NATHAN

2Sa 5: 14 Shammua, Shobab, *N*, Solomon,
7: 2 said to *N* the prophet, "Here I am,
7: 3 *N* replied to the king, "Whatever
7: 4 the word of the LORD came to *N*,
7: 17 *N* reported to David all the words
12: 1 The LORD sent *N* to David.
12: 5 against the man and said to *N*,
12: 7 *N* said to David, "You are the man!
12: 13 David said to *N*, "I have sinned
12: 13 *N* replied, "The LORD has taken
12: 15 After *N* had gone home,
12: 25 word through *N* the prophet
23: 36 Paarai the Arbite, Igal son of *N*
1Ki 1: 8 son of Jehoiada, *N* the prophet,
1: 10 but he did not invite *N* the prophet
1: 11 *N* asked Bathsheba, Solomon's
1: 22 with the king, *N* the prophet
1: 23 told the king, "*N* the prophet is
1: 24 *N* said, "Have you, my lord
1: 32 *N* the prophet and Benaiah son
1: 34 and *N* the prophet anoint him king
1: 38 So Zadok the priest, *N* the prophet,
1: 44 *N* the prophet, Benaiah son
1: 45 *N* the prophet have anointed him
4: 5 Zabud son of *N*—a priest
4: 5 priests; Azariah son of *N*—
1Ch 2: 36 father of *N*, *N* the father of Zabad,
3: 5 Shammua, Shobab, *N* and Solomon
11: 38 Joel the brother of *N*, Mibhar son
14: 4 Shammua, Shobab, *N*, Solomon,
17: 1 said to *N* the prophet, "Here I am,
17: 2 *N* replied to David, "Whatever you
17: 3 the word of God came to *N*,
17: 15 *N* reported to David all the words
29: 29 the records of *N* the prophet
2Ch 9: 29 in the records of *N* the prophet,
29: 25 the king's seer and *N* the prophet;
Ezr 8: 16 Elnathan, Jarib, Elnathan, *N*,
10: 39 Shimei, Shelemiah, *N*, Adaiah,
Zec 12: 12 the clan of the house of *N*
Lk 3: 31 the son of Mattatha, the son of *N*,

NATHAN-MELECH

2Ki 23: 11 the room of an official named *N*.

NATHANAEL

Jn 1: 45 Philip found *N* and told him,
1: 46 come from there?" *N* asked.
1: 47 When Jesus saw *N* approaching,
1: 48 "How do you know me?" *N* asked.
1: 49 Then *N* declared, "Rabbi,
21: 2 Thomas (called Didymus), *N*

NATION (NATIONAL NATIONALITIES NATIONALITY NATIONS NATIONS')

Ge 12: 2 "I will make you into a great *n*
15: 14 But I will punish the *n* they serve
17: 20 and I will make him into a great *n*.
18: 18 become a great and powerful *n*,
20: 4 will you destroy an innocent *n*?
21: 13 the son of the maidservant into a *n*
21: 18 for I will make him into a great *n*."
35: 11 A *n* and a community
46: 3 you into a great *n* there.
Ex 9: 24 of Egypt since it had become a *n*.
19: 6 a kingdom of priests and a holy *n*.'
23: 27 confusion every *n* you encounter.
32: 10 Then I will make you into a great *n*
33: 13 Remember that this *n* is your
34: 10 never before done in any *n*
Nu 14: 12 but I will make you into a *n* greater
Dt 4: 6 "Surely this great *n* is a wise
4: 7 What other *n* is so great
4: 8 And what other *n* is so great
4: 34 for himself one *n* out of another *n*,
9: 14 I will make you into a *n* stronger
26: 5 lived there and became a great *n*,
28: 32 will be given to another *n*,
28: 36 set over you to a *n* unknown to you
Dt 28: 49 The LORD will bring a *n*
28: 49 a *n* whose language you will not
28: 50 a fierce-looking *n* without respect
32: 21 by a *n* that has no understanding.
32: 28 They are a *n* without sense,
Jos 3: 17 by until the whole *n* had completed
4: 1 When the whole *n* had finished
5: 8 And after the whole *n* had been
10: 13 till the *n* avenged itself
Jdg 2: 20 "Because this *n* has violated
2Sa 7: 23 one *n* on earth that God went out
1Ki 5: 7 son to rule over this great *n*."
18: 10 there is not a *n* or kingdom where
18: 10 whenever a *n* or kingdom claimed
2Ki 18: 33 of any *n* ever delivered his land
1Ch 16: 20 they wandered from *n* to *n*,
17: 21 one *n* on earth whose God went
2Ch 15: 6 One *n* was being crushed
32: 15 of any *n* or kingdom has been able
Job 34: 29 Yet he is over man and *n* alike,
Ps 33: 12 Blessed is the *n* whose God is
43: 1 cause against an ungodly *n*;
83: 4 "let us destroy them as a *n*,
105: 13 they wandered from *n* to *n*,
106: 5 share in the joy of your *n*
147: 20 He has done this for no other *n*;
Pr 11: 14 For lack of guidance a *n* falls,
14: 34 Righteousness exalts a *n*,
Isa 1: 4 Ah, sinful *n*,
2: 4 *N* will not take up sword
2: 4 will not take up sword against *n*,
9: 3 You have enlarged the *n*
10: 6 I send him against a godless *n*,
14: 32 given to the envoys of that *n*?
18: 2 an aggressive *n* of strange speech,
18: 7 an aggressive *n* of strange speech,
26: 2 that the righteous *n* may enter,
26: 2 the *n* that keeps faith.
26: 15 You have enlarged the *n*, O LORD
26: 15 you have enlarged the *n*.
30: 6 to that unprofitable *n*,
36: 18 of any *n* ever delivered his land
49: 7 despised and abhorred by the *n*,
51: 4 hear me, my *n*;
58: 2 as if they were a *n* that does what is
60: 12 For the *n* or kingdom that will not
60: 22 the smallest a mighty *n*.
65: 1 To a *n* that did not call on my name
66: 8 a *n* be brought forth in a moment?
Jer 2: 11 Has a *n* ever changed its gods?
3: 19 beautiful inheritance of any *n*.'
5: 9 myself on such a *n* as this?
5: 15 an ancient and enduring *n*,
5: 15 "I am bringing a distant *n*
5: 29 myself on such a *n* as this?
6: 22 a great *n* is being stirred up
7: 28 'This is the *n* that has not obeyed
8: 3 of this evil *n* will prefer death to life
9: 9 myself on such a *n* as this?"
12: 17 But if any *n* does not listen,
18: 7 If at any time I announce that a *n*
18: 8 if that *n* I warned repents of its evil,
18: 9 at another time I announce that a *n*
19: 11 I will smash this *n* and this city just
25: 12 the king of Babylon and his *n*,
25: 32 spreading from *n* to *n*;
27: 8 I will punish that *n* with the sword,
27: 8 any *n* or kingdom will not serve
27: 11 But if any *n* will bow its neck
27: 11 I will let that *n* remain
27: 13 has threatened any *n* that will not
28: 15 yet you have persuaded this *n*
31: 36 cease to be a *n* before me."
33: 24 and no longer regard them as a *n*.
48: 2 'Come, let us put an end to that *n*.'
48: 42 Moab will be destroyed as a *n*
49: 31 "Arise and attack a *n* at ease,
49: 31 "a *n* that has neither gates nor bars;
49: 36 and there will not be a *n*
50: 3 A *n* from the north will attack her
50: 41 a great *n* and many kings
La 4: 17 for a *n* that could not save us.
Eze 2: 3 to a rebellious *n* that has rebelled
36: 13 and deprive your *n* of its children,"
36: 14 or make your *n* childless,
36: 15 of the peoples or cause your *n*
37: 22 I will make them one *n* in the land,
Da 3: 29 I decree that the people of any *n*
Da 8: 22 that will emerge from his *n*
Joel 1: 6 A *n* has invaded my land,
3: 8 them to the Sabeans, a *n* far away."
Am 6: 1 you notable men of the foremost *n*,
6: 14 "I will stir up a *n* against you,
Mic 4: 3 *N* will not take up sword
4: 3 will not take up sword against *n*,
4: 7 those driven away a strong *n*.
Hab 3: 16 to come on the *n* invading us.
Zep 2: 1 O shameful *n*,
2: 9 of my *n* will inherit their land."
Hag 2: 14 is with this people and this *n*
Mal 3: 9 under a curse—the whole *n* of you
Mt 24: 7 *N* will rise against *n*,
Mk 13: 8 *N* will rise against *n*,
Lk 7: 5 because he loves our *n*
21: 10 "*N* will rise against *n*,
23: 2 found this man subverting our *n*.
Jn 11: 48 take away both our place and our *n*
11: 50 than that the whole *n* perish."
11: 51 Jesus would die for the Jewish *n*,
11: 52 and not only for that *n* but
Ac 2: 5 Jews from every *n* under heaven.
7: 7 But I will punish the *n* they serve
10: 35 men from every *n* who fear him
17: 26 From one man he made every *n*
24: 2 brought about reforms in this *n*.
24: 10 you have been a judge over this *n*;
Ro 10: 19 by a *n* that has no understanding."
10: 19 envious by those who are not a *n*;
1Pe 2: 9 a royal priesthood, a holy *n*,
Rev 5: 9 and language and people and *n*.
7: 9 from every *n*, tribe, people
11: 9 and *n* will gaze on their bodies
13: 7 tribe, people, language and *n*.
14: 6 to every *n*, tribe, language

NATIONAL (NATION)

2Ki 17: 29 each *n* group made its own gods

NATIONALITIES (NATION)

Est 8: 17 people of other *n* became Jews
9: 2 people of all the other *n* were afraid

NATIONALITY (NATION)

Est 2: 10 Esther had not revealed her *n*
2: 20 her family background and *n* just
3: 14 known to the people of every *n*
8: 11 any armed force of any *n*
8: 13 known to the people of every *n*

NATIONS (NATION)

Ge 10: 5 by their clans within their *n*,
10: 20 languages, in their territories and *n*
10: 31 languages, in their territories and *n*
10: 32 From these the *n* spread out
10: 32 lines of descent, within their *n*.
17: 4 You will be the father of many *n*.
17: 5 have made you a father of many *n*.
17: 6 I will make *n* of you, and kings will
17: 16 so that she will be the mother of *n*;
18: 18 and all *n* on earth will be blessed
22: 18 and through your offspring all *n*
25: 23 "Two *n* are in your womb,
26: 4 and through your offspring all *n*
27: 29 May *n* serve you
35: 11 and a community of *n* will come
48: 19 will become a group of *n*."
49: 10 and the obedience of the *n* is his.
Ex 15: 14 The *n* will hear and tremble;
19: 5 of all *n* you will be my treasured
34: 24 I will drive out *n* before you
Lev 18: 24 this is how the *n* that I am going
18: 28 as it vomited out the *n* that were
20: 23 to the customs of the *n* I am going
20: 24 who has set you apart from the *n*.
20: 26 apart from the *n* to be my own.
25: 44 are to come from the *n* around you;
26: 33 I will scatter you among the *n*
26: 38 You will perish among the *n*;
26: 45 in the sight of the *n* to be their God
Nu 14: 15 *n* who have heard this report about
23: 9 consider themselves one of the *n*.
24: 8 They devour hostile *n*
24: 20 "Amalek was first among the *n*,
Dt 2: 25 of you on all the *n* under heaven.
4: 6 and understanding to the *n*,
4: 19 to all the *n* under heaven.

Dt 4:27 few of you will survive among the *n*
4:38 to drive out before you *n* greater
7: 1 drives out before you many *n*—
7: 1 seven *n* larger and stronger
7:17 "These *n* are stronger than we are.
7:22 your God will drive out those *n*
8:20 Like the *n* the LORD destroyed
9: 1 dispossess *n* greater and stronger
9: 4 of these *n* that the LORD is going
9: 5 of the wickedness of these *n*,
10:15 above all the *n*, as it is today.
11:23 and you will dispossess *n* larger
11:23 the LORD will drive out all these *n*
12: 2 tree where the *n* you are
12:29 off before you the *n* you are about
12:30 "How do these *n* serve their gods?
15: 6 You will rule over many *n*
15: 6 and you will lend to many *n*
17:14 over us like all the *n* around us,"
18: 9 the detestable ways of the *n* there.
18:12 your God will drive out those *n*
18:14 The *n* you will dispossess listen
19: 1 has destroyed the *n* whose land he
20:15 and do not belong to the *n* nearby.
20:16 of the *n* the LORD your God is
26:19 high above all the *n* he has made
28: 1 high above all the *n* on earth.
28:12 You will lend to many *n*
28:37 to all the *n* where the LORD will
28:64 will scatter you among all *n*,
28:65 Among those *n* you will find no
29:18 and worship the gods of those *n*;
29:24 All the *n* will ask: "Why has
30: 1 God disperses you among the *n*,
30: 3 from all the *n* where he scattered
31: 3 He will destroy these *n* before you,
32: 8 High gave the *n* their inheritance,
32:43 Rejoice, O *n*, with his people,
33:17 with them he will gore the *n*,
Jos 23: 3 done to all these *n* for your sake;
23: 4 the land of the *n* that remain—
23: 4 the *n* I conquered—
23: 7 associate with these *n* that remain
23: 9 before you great and powerful *n*;
23:12 of these *n* that remain among you
23:13 will no longer drive out these *n*
24:17 among all the *n* through which we
24:18 out before us all the *n*,
Jdg 2:21 any of the *n* Joshua left
2:23 The LORD had allowed those *n*
3: 1 These are the *n* the LORD left
1Sa 8: 5 such as all the other *n* have."
8:20 Then we will be like all the other *n*,
2Sa 7:23 awesome wonders by driving out *n*
8:11 gold from all the *n* he had subdued:
22:44 preserved me as the head of *n*.
22:48 who puts the *n* under me,
22:50 praise you, O LORD, among the *n*;
1Ki 4:31 spread to all the surrounding *n*.
4:34 Men of all *n* came to listen
8:53 out from all the *n* of the world
11: 2 from *n* about which the LORD had
14:24 of the *n* the LORD had driven out
2Ki 16: 3 of the *n* the LORD had driven out
17: 8 of the *n* the LORD had driven out
17:11 *n* whom the LORD had driven out
17:15 They imitated the *n* around them
17:33 with the customs of the *n*
19:12 gods of the *n* that were destroyed
19:17 kings have laid waste these *n*
21: 2 of the *n* the LORD had driven out
21: 9 evil than the *n* the LORD had
1Ch 14:17 the LORD made all the *n* fear him.
16: 8 among the *n* what he has done.
16:24 Declare his glory among the *n*,
16:26 For all the gods of the *n* are idols,
16:28 to the LORD, O families of *n*,
16:31 let them say among the *n*,
16:35 gather us and deliver us from the *n*,
17:21 out *n* from before your people,
18:11 gold he had taken from all these *n*:
22: 5 splendor in the sight of all the *n*.
2Ch 20: 6 rule over all the kingdoms of the *n*.
28: 3 of the *n* the LORD had driven out
32:13 Were the gods of those *n* ever able
32:14 the gods of these *n* that my fathers
32:23 he was highly regarded by all the *n*.
33: 2 of the *n* the LORD had driven out

2Ch 33: 9 evil than the *n* the LORD had
36:14 all the detestable practices of the *n*
Ne 1: 8 I will scatter you among the *n*,
5:17 came to us from the surrounding *n*.
6: 6 "It is reported among the *n*—
6:16 and all the surrounding *n* saw it,
9:22 "You gave them kingdoms and *n*,
13:26 Among the many *n* there was no
Job 12:23 He makes *n* great, and destroys
12:23 he enlarges *n*, and disperses them.
36:31 This is the way he governs the *n*
Ps 2: 1 Why do the *n* rage
2: 8 I will make the *n* your inheritance,
9: 5 You have rebuked the *n*
9:11 among the *n* what he has done.
9:15 *n* have fallen into the pit they have
9:17 all the *n* that forget God.
9:19 let the *n* be judged in your presence
9:20 let the *n* know they are but men.
10:16 the *n* will perish from his land.
18:43 you have made me the head of *n*;
18:47 who subdues *n* under me,
18:49 I will praise you among the *n*,
22:27 and all the families of the *n*
22:28 and he rules over the *n*.
33:10 The LORD foils the plans of the *n*;
44: 2 your hand you drove out the *n*
44:11 and have scattered us among the *n*.
44:14 made us a byword among the *n*;
45: 5 let the *n* fall beneath your feet.
45:17 the *n* will praise you for ever
46: 6 *N* are in uproar, kingdoms fall;
46:10 I will be exalted among the *n*,
47: 1 Clap your hands, all you *n*;
47: 3 He subdued *n* under us,
47: 8 God reigns over the *n*;
47: 9 The nobles of the *n* assemble
56: 7 O God, bring down the *n*.
57: 9 praise you, O Lord, among the *n*;
59: 5 rouse yourself to punish all the *n*;
59: 8 you scoff at all those *n*.
65: 7 and the turmoil of the *n*.
66: 7 his eyes watch the *n*—
67: 2 your salvation among all *n*.
67: 4 May the *n* be glad and sing for joy,
67: 4 and guide the *n* of the earth.
68:30 Scatter the *n* who delight in war.
68:30 of bulls among the calves of the *n*.
72:11 and all *n* will serve him.
72:17 All *n* will be blessed through him,
78:55 He drove out *n* before them
79: 1 *n* have invaded your inheritance;
79: 6 Pour out your wrath on the *n*
79:10 Why should the *n* say,
79:10 make known among the *n*
80: 8 you drove out the *n* and planted it.
82: 8 for all the *n* are your inheritance.
86: 9 All the *n* you have made
89:50 in my heart the taunts of all the *n*,
94:10 he who disciplines *n* not punish?
96: 3 Declare his glory among the *n*,
96: 5 For all the gods of the *n* are idols,
96: 7 to the LORD, O families of *n*,
96:10 among the *n*, "The LORD reigns."
98: 2 revealed his righteousness to the *n*.
99: 1 let the *n* tremble;
99: 2 he is exalted over all the *n*.
102: 15 The *n* will fear the name
105: 1 among the *n* what he has done.
105: 44 he gave them the lands of the *n*,
106: 27 their descendants fall among the *n*
106: 35 but they mingled with the *n*
106: 41 He handed them over to the *n*,
106: 47 and gather us from the *n*,
108: 3 praise you, O LORD, among the *n*;
110: 6 He will judge the *n*, heaping up
111: 6 giving them the lands of other *n*.
113: 4 The LORD is exalted over all the *n*
115: 2 Why do the *n* say,
117: 1 Praise the LORD, all you *n*;
118: 10 All the *n* surrounded me,
126: 2 Then it was said among the *n*,
135: 10 He struck down many *n*
135: 15 The idols of the *n* are silver
148: 11 kings of the earth and all *n*,
149: 7 to inflict vengeance on the *n*
Pr 24:24 curse him and *n* denounce him.
Isa 2: 2 and all *n* will stream to it.

Isa 2: 4 He will judge between the *n*
5:26 lifts up a banner for the distant *n*,
8: 9 Raise the war cry, you *n*,
10: 7 to put an end to many *n*.
10:13 I removed the boundaries of *n*,
10:14 reached for the wealth of the *n*;
11:10 the *n* will rally to him,
11:12 He will raise a banner for the *n*
12: 4 among the *n* what he has done,
13: 4 like *n* massing together!
14: 2 house of Israel will possess the *n*
14: 2 *N* will take them
14: 6 and in fury subdued *n*
14: 9 all those who were kings over the *n*
14:12 you who once laid low the *n*!
14:18 All the kings of the *n* lie in state,
14:26 is the hand stretched out over all *n*.
16: 8 The rulers of the *n*
17:12 Oh, the raging of many *n*—
23: 3 became the marketplace of the *n*.
24:13 and among the *n*,
25: 3 cities of ruthless *n* will revere you.
25: 7 the sheet that covers all *n*;
29: 7 of all the *n* that fight against Ariel,
29: 8 be with the hordes of all the *n*
30:28 He shakes the *n* in the sieve
33: 3 when you rise up, the *n* scatter.
33: 4 *n*, is harvested as by young locusts;
34: 1 Come near, you *n*, and listen;
34: 2 The LORD is angry with all *n*;
37:12 gods of the *n* that were destroyed
40:15 Surely the *n* are like a drop
40:17 Before him all the *n* are as nothing;
41: 1 Let the *n* renew their strength!
41: 2 He hands *n* over to him
42: 1 and he will bring justice to the *n*.
43: 9 All the *n* gather together
45: 1 of to subdue *n* before him
45:20 assemble, you fugitives from the *n*.
49: 1 hear this you distant *n*:
51: 4 justice will become a light to the *n*.
51: 5 my arm will bring justice to the *n*.
52:10 arm in the sight of all the *n*,
52:15 so will he sprinkle many *n*,
54: 3 your descendants will dispossess *n*
55: 5 you will summon *n* you know not,
55: 5 *n* that do not know you will hasten
56: 7 a house of prayer for all *n*."
60: 3 *N* will come to your light,
60: 5 to you the riches of the *n* will come
60:11 bring you the wealth of the *n*—
60:16 You will drink the milk of *n*
61: 6 You will feed on the wealth of *n*,
61: 9 will be known among the *n*
61:11 spring up before all *n*.
62: 2 The *n* will see your righteousness,
62:10 Raise a banner for the *n*.
63: 3 from the *n* no one was with me.
63: 6 I trampled the *n* in my anger;
64: 2 cause the *n* to quake before you!
66:12 wealth of *n* like a flooding stream;
66:18 and gather all *n* and tongues,
66:19 of those who survive to the *n*—
66:19 proclaim my glory among the *n*.
66:20 all your brothers, from all the *n*,
Jer 1: 5 you as a prophet to the *n*."
1:10 today I appoint you over *n*
3:17 and all *n* will gather in Jerusalem
4: 2 then the *n* will be blessed by him
4: 7 a destroyer of *n* has set out.
4:16 "Tell this to the *n*,
6:18 Therefore hear, O *n*;
9:16 them among *n* that neither they
9:26 For all these *n* are really
10: 2 though the *n* are terrified by them.
10: 2 "Do not learn the ways of the *n*
10: 7 Among all the wise men of the *n*
10: 7 O King of the *n*?
10:10 the *n* cannot endure his wrath.
10:25 Pour out your wrath on the *n*
14:22 idols of the *n* bring rain?
16:19 to you the *n* will come
18:13 "Inquire among the *n*:
22: 8 "People from many *n* will pass
25: 9 and against all the surrounding *n*.
25:11 and these *n* will serve the king
25:13 by Jeremiah against all the *n*.
25:14 will be enslaved by many *n*

Jer 25: 15 make all the *n* to whom I send you
25: 17 made all the *n* to whom he sent me
25: 31 will bring charges against the *n;*
26: 6 among all the *n* of the earth.' "
27: 7 All *n* will serve him and his son
27: 7 then many *n* and great kings will
28: 11 of all the *n* within two years.' "
28: 14 yoke on the necks of all these *n*
29: 14 I will gather you from all the *n*
29: 18 among all the *n* where I drive them
30: 11 I completely destroy all the *n*
31: 7 shout for the greatest of the *n.*
31: 10 "Hear the word of the LORD, O *n;*
33: 9 and honor before all *n*
36: 2 and all the other *n* from the time I
43: 5 from all the *n* where they had been
44: 8 reproach among all the *n* on earth.
46: 1 the prophet concerning the *n:*
46: 12 The *n* will hear of your shame;
46: 28 I completely destroy all the *n*
49: 14 An envoy was sent to the *n* to say,
49: 15 I will make you small among the *n,*
50: 2 and proclaim among the *n,*
50: 9 an alliance of great *n* from the land
50: 12 She will be the least of the *n—*
50: 23 Babylon among the *n!*
50: 46 its cry will resound among the *n.*
51: 7 The *n* drank her wine;
51: 20 with you I shatter *n,*
51: 27 Blow the trumpet among the *n!*
51: 27 Prepare the *n* for battle against her;
51: 28 Prepare the *n* for battle against her
51: 41 be among the *n!*
51: 44 The *n* will no longer stream to him.
La 1: 1 who once was great among the *n!*
1: 3 She dwells among the *n;*
1: 10 she saw pagan *n*
2: 9 her princes are exiled among the *n,*
3: 45 among the *n.*
4: 15 people among the *n* say,
4: 20 we would live among the *n.*
Eze 4: 13 among the *n* where I will drive
5: 5 set in the center of the *n,*
5: 6 and decrees more than the *n*
5: 7 the standards of the *n* around you.
5: 7 unruly than the *n* around you
5: 8 on you in the sight of the *n.*
5: 14 reproach among the *n* around you,
5: 15 of horror to the *n* around you
6: 8 scattered among the lands and *n.*
6: 9 in the *n* where they have been
7: 24 wicked of the *n* to take possession
11: 12 standards of the *n* around you."
11: 16 I sent them far away among the *n*
11: 17 I will gather you from the *n*
12: 15 when I disperse them among the *n*
12: 16 in the *n* where they go they may
16: 14 spread among the *n* on account
19: 4 The *n* heard about him,
19: 8 Then the *n* came against him,
20: 9 the eyes of the *n* they lived among
20: 14 profaned in the eyes of the *n*
20: 22 profaned in the eyes of the *n*
20: 23 I would disperse them among the *n*
20: 32 "We want to be like the *n,*
20: 34 I will bring you from the *n*
20: 35 you into the desert of the *n*
20: 41 among you in the sight of the *n.*
20: 41 when I bring you out from the *n*
22: 4 you an object of scorn to the *n*
22: 15 I will disperse you among the *n*
22: 16 defiled in the eyes of the *n,*
23: 30 because you lusted after the *n*
25: 7 I will cut you off from the *n*
25: 7 and give you as plunder to the *n.*
25: 8 has become like all the other *n,*"
25: 10 not be remembered among the *n;*
26: 2 'Aha! The gate to the *n* is broken,
26: 3 and I will bring many *n* against you
26: 5 She will become plunder for the *n,*
27: 33 you satisfied many *n;*
27: 36 merchants among the *n* hiss at you;
28: 7 the most ruthless of *n;*
28: 19 All the *n* who knew you
28: 25 among them in the sight of the *n.*
28: 25 from the *n* where they have been
29: 12 the Egyptians among the *n*
29: 13 from the *n* where they were

Eze 29: 15 it will never again rule over the *n.*
29: 15 itself above the other *n.*
30: 3 a time of doom for the *n.*
30: 11 his army—the most ruthless of *n—*
30: 23 the Egyptians among the *n*
30: 26 the Egyptians among the *n*
31: 6 all the great *n*
31: 11 it over to the ruler of the *n,*
31: 12 All the *n* of the earth came out
31: 12 ruthless of foreign *n* cut it down
31: 16 I made the *n* tremble at the sound
31: 17 its allies among the *n,* had
32: 2 " 'You are like a lion among the *n;*
32: 9 your destruction among the *n,*
32: 12 the most ruthless of all *n.*
32: 16 The daughters of the *n* will chant it
32: 18 and the daughters of mighty *n,*
34: 13 I will bring them out from the *n*
34: 28 no longer be plundered by the *n,*
34: 29 or bear the scorn of the *n.*
35: 10 "These two *n* and countries will be
36: 3 the possession of the rest of the *n*
36: 4 by the rest of the *n* around you—
36: 5 spoken against the rest of the *n,*
36: 6 have suffered the scorn of the *n.*
36: 7 swear with uplifted hand that the *n*
36: 15 I make you hear the taunts of the *n,*
36: 19 I dispersed them among the *n,*
36: 20 among the *n* they profaned my
36: 21 among the *n* where they had gone.
36: 22 among the *n* where you have gone.
36: 23 has been profaned among the *n,*
36: 23 *n* will know that I am the LORD,
36: 24 " 'For I will take you out of the *n;*
36: 30 longer suffer disgrace among the *n*
36: 36 the *n* around you that remain will
37: 21 out of the *n* where they have gone.
37: 22 and they will never again be two *n*
37: 28 *n* will know that I the LORD make
38: 6 with all its troops—the many *n*
38: 8 from many *n* to the mountains
38: 8 had been brought out from the *n,*
38: 9 the many *n* with you will go up,
38: 12 the people gathered from the *n,*
38: 15 you and many *n* with you,
38: 16 so that the *n* may know me
38: 22 and on the many *n* with him.
38: 23 known in the sight of many *n.*
39: 4 all your troops and the *n* with you.
39: 7 *n* will know that I the LORD am
39: 21 I will display my glory among the *n*
39: 21 all the *n* will see the punishment I
39: 23 the *n* will know that the people
39: 27 have brought them back from the *n*
39: 27 them in the sight of many *n.*
39: 28 I sent them into exile among the *n,*
Da 3: 4 *n* and men of every language:
3: 7 *n* and men of every language fell
4: 1 *n* and men of every language,
5: 19 and *n* and men of every language
6: 25 *n* and men of every language
7: 14 *n* and men of every language
12: 1 from the beginning of *n* until then.
Hos 7: 8 "Ephraim mixes with the *n;*
8: 8 now she is among the *n*
8: 10 have sold themselves among the *n,*
9: 1 do not be jubilant like the other *n.*
9: 17 will be wanderers among the *n.*
10: 10 *n* will be gathered against them
Joel 2: 6 of them, *n* are in anguish;
2: 17 a byword among the *n.*
2: 19 an object of scorn to the *n.*
3: 2 I will gather all *n*
3: 2 scattered my people among the *n*
3: 9 Proclaim this among the *n:*
3: 11 Come quickly, all you *n*
3: 12 sit to judge all the *n* on every side.
3: 12 "Let the *n* be roused;
Am 9: 9 Israel among all the *n*
9: 12 and all the *n* that bear my name,"
Ob : 1 An envoy was sent to the *n* to say,
: 2 I will make you small among the *n;*
: 15 for all *n.*
: 16 so all the *n* will drink continually;
Mic 4: 2 Many *n* will come and say,
4: 3 will settle disputes for strong *n* far
4: 5 All the *n* may walk
4: 11 But now many *n*

Mic 4: 13 you will break to pieces many *n.*"
5: 8 of Jacob will be among the *n,*
5: 15 upon the *n* that have not obeyed
6: 16 you will bear the scorn of the *n.*"
7: 16 *N* will see and be ashamed,
Na 3: 4 who enslaved *n* by her prostitution
3: 5 I will show the *n* your nakedness
Hab 1: 5 "Look at the *n* and watch—
1: 17 destroying *n* without mercy?
2: 5 he gathers to himself all the *n*
2: 8 you have plundered many *n,*
2: 13 that the *n* exhaust themselves
3: 6 he looked, and made the *n* tremble.
3: 12 and in anger you threshed the *n.*
Zep 2: 11 *n* on every shore will worship him,
3: 6 "I have cut off *n;*
3: 8 I have decided to assemble the *n,*
Hag 2: 7 I will shake all *n,* and the desired
2: 7 and the desired of all *n* will come,
Zec 1: 15 angry with the *n* that feel secure.
1: 21 of the *n* who lifted up their horns
2: 8 against the *n* that have plundered
2: 11 "Many *n* will be joined
7: 14 with a whirlwind among all the *n,*
8: 13 an object of cursing among the *n,*
8: 22 powerful *n* will come to Jerusalem
8: 23 *n* will take firm hold of one Jew
9: 10 He will proclaim peace to the *n.*
11: 10 covenant I had made with all the *n.*
12: 3 an immovable rock for all the *n.*
12: 3 when all the *n* of the earth are
12: 4 I will blind all the horses of the *n.*
12: 9 destroy all the *n* that attack
14: 2 I will gather all the *n* to Jerusalem
14: 3 go out and fight against those *n,*
14: 12 will strike all the *n* that fought
14: 14 all the surrounding *n* will be
14: 16 from all the *n* that have attacked
14: 18 inflicts on the *n* that do not go up
14: 19 of all the *n* that do not go up
Mal 1: 11 My name will be great among the *n*
1: 11 my name will be great among the *n*
1: 14 is to be feared among the *n.*
3: 12 Then all the *n* will call you blessed,
Mt 12: 18 he will proclaim justice to the *n.*
12: 21 In his name the *n* will put their
24: 9 and you will be hated by all *n*
24: 14 whole world as a testimony to all *n,*
24: 30 all the *n* of the earth will mourn.
25: 32 All the *n* will be gathered
28: 19 and make disciples of all *n,*
Mk 11: 17 a house of prayer for all *n'?*
13: 10 must first be preached to all *n.*
Lk 21: 24 be taken as prisoners to all the *n.*
21: 25 *n* will be in anguish and perplexity
24: 47 preached in his name to all *n,*
Ac 4: 25 " 'Why do the *n* rage
7: 45 the land from the *n* God drove out
13: 19 He overthrew seven *n* in Canaan
14: 16 he let all *n* go their own way.
Ro 4: 17 I have made you a father of many *n*
4: 18 so became the father of many *n,*
15: 12 who will arise to rule over the *n;*
16: 26 so that all *n* might believe
Gal 3: 8 All *n* will be blessed through you."
1Ti 3: 16 was preached among the *n,*
Jas 1: 1 tribes scattered among the *n:*
Rev 2: 26 I will give authority over the *n—*
10: 11 again about many peoples, *n,*
11: 18 The *n* were angry;
12: 5 who will rule all the *n*
14: 8 made all the *n* drink
15: 4 All *n* will come
16: 19 and the cities of the *n* collapsed.
17: 15 multitudes, *n* and languages.
18: 3 For all the *n* have drunk
18: 23 spell all the *n* were led astray.
19: 15 with which to strike down the *n.*
20: 3 him from deceiving the *n* any more
20: 8 to deceive the *n* in the four corners
21: 24 The *n* will walk by its light,
21: 26 and honor of the *n* will be brought
22: 2 are for the healing of the *n.*

NATIONS' (NATION)

Jer 51: 58 the *n'* labor is only fuel

NATIVE (NATIVES)

Ge 24: 7 my *n* land and who spoke to me
31: 13 and go back to your *n* land.' "
Nu 22: 5 near the River, in his *n* land.
Ps 37: 35 like a green tree in its *n* soil,
Isa 13: 14 each will flee to his *n* land.
Jer 22: 10 nor see his *n* land again.
46: 16 to our own people and our *n* lands,
Am 7: 11 away from their *n* land.' "
7: 17 away from their *n* land.' "
Jn 8: 44 he lies, he speaks his *n* language,
Ac 2: 8 them in his own *n* language?
18: 2 he met a Jew named Aquila, a *n*
18: 24 a *n* of Alexandria, came to Ephesus

NATIVE-BORN (BEAR)

Ex 12: 19 whether he is an alien or *n*.
12: 49 The same law applies to the *n*
Lev 16: 29 *n* or an alien living among you—
17: 15 " 'Anyone, whether *n* or alien,
18: 26 The *n* and the aliens living
19: 34 must be treated as one of your *n*.
23: 42 All *n* Israelites are to live in booths
24: 16 *n*, when he blasphemes the Name,
24: 22 law for the alien and the *n*.
Nu 9: 14 for the alien and the *n*.' "
15: 13 " 'Everyone who is *n* must do these
15: 29 whether he is a *n* Israelite
15: 30 *n* or alien, blasphemes the LORD,
1Ch 7: 21 killed by the *n* men of Gath,
Eze 47: 22 are to consider them as *n* Israelites;

NATIVES (NATIVE)

Eze 23: 15 like Babylonian chariot officers, *n*

NATURAL (NATURE)

Nu 16: 29 If these men die a *n* death
19: 16 someone who has died a *n* death,
19: 18 someone who has died a *n* death.
Jn 1: 13 children born not of *n* descent,
11: 13 disciples thought he meant *n* sleep.
Ro 1: 26 their women exchanged *n* relations
1: 27 abandoned *n* relations with women
6: 19 you are weak in your *n* selves.
9: 8 it is not the *n* children who are
11: 21 if God did not spare the *n* branches
11: 24 readily will these, the *n* branches,
1Co 15: 44 If there is a *n* body, there is
15: 44 it is sown a *n* body, it is raised
15: 46 the *n*, and after that the spiritual.
Jude : 19 who follow mere *n* instincts

NATURE (NATURAL)

Ro 1: 3 as to his human *n* was a descendant
1: 20 his eternal power and divine *n*—
2: 14 do by *n* things required by the law,
7: 5 we were controlled by the sinful *n*,
7: 18 lives in me, that is, in my sinful *n*.
7: 25 but in the sinful *n* a slave to the law
8: 3 it was weakened by the sinful *n*,
8: 4 do not live according to the sinful *n*
8: 5 set on what that *n* desires;
8: 5 to the sinful *n* have their minds set
8: 8 by the sinful *n* cannot please God.
8: 9 are controlled not by the sinful *n*
8: 12 but it is not to the sinful *n*,
8: 13 if you live according to the sinful *n*,
11: 24 and contrary to *n* were grafted
11: 24 of an olive tree that is wild by *n*,
13: 14 to gratify the desires of the sinful *n*.
1Co 5: 5 that the sinful *n* may be destroyed
11: 14 Does not the very *n*
Gal 4: 8 to those who by *n* are not gods.
5: 13 freedom to indulge the sinful *n*;
5: 16 gratify the desires of the sinful *n*.
5: 17 For the sinful *n* desires what is
5: 17 what is contrary to the sinful *n*.
5: 19 The acts of the sinful *n* are obvious:
5: 24 Jesus have crucified the sinful *n*
6: 8 from that *n* will reap destruction;
6: 8 sows to please his sinful *n*,
Eph 2: 3 the cravings of our sinful *n*
2: 3 we were by *n* objects of wrath.
Php 2: 6 Who, being in very *n* God,
2: 7 taking the very *n* of a servant,
Col 2: 11 in the putting off of the sinful *n*,
2: 13 uncircumcision of your sinful *n*,
3: 5 whatever belongs to your earthly *n*
Heb 6: 17 wanted to make the unchanging *n*
2Pe 1: 4 you may participate in the divine *n*
2: 10 the corrupt desire of the sinful *n*
2: 18 desires of sinful human *n*,

NAVEL

SS 7: 2 Your *n* is a rounded goblet

NAZARENE (NAZARETH)

Mt 2: 23 prophets: "He will be called a *N*."
Mk 14: 67 "You also were with that *N*, Jesus,"
16: 6 "You are looking for Jesus the *N*,
Ac 24: 5 He is a ringleader of the *N* sect and

NAZARETH (NAZARETH)

Mt 2: 23 and lived in a town called *N*.
4: 13 Leaving *N*, he went and lived
21: 11 the prophet from *N* in Galilee."
26: 71 "This fellow was with Jesus of *N*."
Mk 1: 9 At that time Jesus came from *N*
1: 24 Jesus of *N*? Have you come
10: 47 he heard that it was Jesus of *N*,
Lk 1: 26 God sent the angel Gabriel to *N*,
2: 4 up from the town of *N* in Galilee
2: 39 to Galilee to their own town of *N*.
2: 51 Then he went down to *N* with them
4: 16 to *N*, where he had been brought
4: 34 Jesus of *N*? Have you come
18: 37 "Jesus of *N* is passing by."
24: 19 "About Jesus of *N*," they replied.
Jn 1: 45 Jesus of *N*, the son of Joseph."
1: 46 "*N*! Can anything good come
18: 5 "Jesus of *N*," they replied.
18: 7 And they said, "Jesus of *N*."
19: 19 It read, JESUS OF *N*,
Ac 2: 22 Jesus of *N* was a man accredited
3: 6 In the name of Jesus Christ of *N*,
4: 10 is by the name of Jesus Christ of *N*,
6: 14 Jesus of *N* will destroy this place
10: 38 Jesus of *N* with the Holy Spirit
22: 8 of *N*, whom you are persecuting,'
26: 9 to oppose the name of Jesus of *N*.

NAZIRITE (NAZIRITES)

Nu 6: 2 of separation to the LORD as a *N*,
6: 4 he is a *N*, he must not eat anything
6: 13 the law for the *N* when the period
6: 18 *N* must shave off the hair that he
6: 19 After the *N* has shaved off the hair
6: 20 After that, the *N* may drink wine.
6: 21 according to the law of the *N*.' "
6: 21 law of the *N* who vows his offering
Jdg 13: 5 because the boy is to be a *N*,
13: 7 because the boy will be a *N* of God
16: 17 I have been a *N* set apart to God

NAZIRITES (NAZIRITE)

Am 2: 11 *N* from among your young men.
2: 12 "But you made the *N* drink wine

NEAH

Jos 19: 13 at Rimmon and turned toward *N*.

NEAPOLIS

Ac 16: 11 and the next day on to *N*.

NEARIAH

1Ch 3: 22 Igal, Bariah, *N* and Shaphat—
3: 23 The sons of *N*: Elioenai, Hizkiah
4: 42 led by Pelatiah, *N*, Rephaiah

NEARSIGHTED

2Pe 1: 9 anyone does not have them, he is *n*

NEBAI

Ne 10: 19 Hariph, Anathoth, *N*, Magpiash,

NEBAIOTH

Ge 25: 13 *N* the firstborn of Ishmael, Kedar,
28: 9 the sister of *N* and daughter
36: 3 of Ishmael and sister of *N*.
1Ch 1: 29 *N* the firstborn of Ishmael,
Isa 60: 7 the rams of *N* will serve you;

NEBALLAT

Ne 11: 34 Zeboim and *N*, in Lod and Ono,

NEBAT

1Ki 11: 26 Also, Jeroboam son of *N* rebelled
1Ki 12: 2 son of *N* heard this (he was still
12: 15 spoken to Jeroboam son of *N*
15: 1 of the reign of Jeroboam son of *N*,
16: 3 that of Jeroboam son of *N*.
16: 26 the ways of Jeroboam son of *N*
16: 31 the sins of Jeroboam son of *N*,
21: 22 that of Jeroboam son of *N*
22: 52 in the ways of Jeroboam son of *N*,
2Ki 3: 3 to the sins of Jeroboam son of *N*,
9: 9 the house of Jeroboam son of *N*
10: 29 from the sins of Jeroboam son of *N*,
13: 2 the sins of Jeroboam son of *N*,
13: 11 of the sins of Jeroboam son of *N*,
14: 24 of the sins of Jeroboam son of *N*,
15: 9 from the sins of Jeroboam son of *N*,
15: 18 from the sins of Jeroboam son of *N*,
15: 24 from the sins of Jeroboam son of *N*,
15: 28 from the sins of Jeroboam son of *N*,
17: 21 Jeroboam son of *N* their king.
23: 15 made by Jeroboam son of *N*,
2Ch 9: 29 concerning Jeroboam son of *N*?
10: 2 son of *N* heard this (he was
10: 15 spoken to Jeroboam son of *N*
13: 6 Yet Jeroboam son of *N*, an official

NEBO

Nu 32: 3 Elealeh, Sebam, *N* and Beon—
32: 38 as well as *N* and Baal Meon
33: 47 in the mountains of Abarim, near *N*
Dt 32: 49 Range to Mount *N* in Moab,
34: 1 Then Moses climbed Mount *N*
1Ch 5: 8 settled in the area from Aroer to *N*
Ezr 2: 29 and Ai 223 of *N* 52 of Magbish 156
10: 43 From the descendants of *N*: Jeiel,
Ne 7: 33 and Ai 123 of the other *N* 52
Isa 15: 2 Moab wails over *N* and Medeba.
46: 1 Bel bows down, *N* stoops low;
Jer 48: 1 "Woe to *N*, for it will be ruined.
48: 22 to Dibon, *N* and Beth Diblathaim,

NEBO-SARSEKIM

Jer 39: 3 of Samgar, *N* a chief officer,

NEBUCHADNEZZAR (NEBUCHADNEZZAR'S)

2Ki 24: 1 his mind and rebelled against *N*.
24: 1 *N* king of Babylon invaded the land
24: 10 of *N* king of Babylon advanced
24: 11 and *N* himself came up to the city
24: 13 *N* removed all the treasures
24: 15 *N* took Jehoiachin captive
25: 1 *N* king of Babylon marched
25: 8 year of *N* king of Babylon,
25: 22 *N* king of Babylon appointed
1Ch 6: 15 into exile by the hand of *N*.
2Ch 36: 6 *N* king of Babylon attacked him
36: 7 *N* also took to Babylon articles
36: 10 King *N* sent for him and brought
36: 13 He also rebelled against King *N*,
36: 17 God handed all of them over to *N*.
Ezr 1: 7 which *N* had carried away
2: 1 whom *N* king of Babylon had taken
5: 12 them over to *N* the Chaldean,
5: 14 which *N* had taken from the temple
6: 5 which *N* took from the temple
Ne 7: 6 captivity of the exiles whom *N* king
Est 2: 6 exile from Jerusalem by *N* king
Jer 21: 2 *N* king of Babylon is attacking us.
21: 7 to *N* king of Babylon
22: 25 to *N* king of Babylon
24: 1 to Babylon by *N* king of Babylon,
25: 1 year of *N* king of Babylon.
25: 9 my servant *N* king of Babylon,"
27: 6 to my servant *N* king of Babylon;
27: 8 or kingdom will not serve *N* king
27: 20 which *N* king of Babylon did not
28: 3 of the LORD's house that *N* king
28: 11 of *N* king of Babylon off the neck
28: 14 nations to make them serve *N* king
29: 1 all the other people *N* had carried
29: 3 of Judah sent to King *N* in Babylon.
29: 21 them over to *N* king of Babylon,
32: 1 which was the eighteenth year of *N*
32: 28 and to *N* king of Babylon,
34: 1 While *N* king of Babylon
35: 11 when *N* king of Babylon invaded
37: 1 of Judah by *N* king of Babylon;
39: 1 *N* king of Babylon marched

Jer 39: 5 and took him to *N* king of Babylon
39: 11 *N* king of Babylon had given these
43: 10 for my servant *N* king of Babylon,
44: 30 of Judah over to *N* king of Babylon,
46: 2 River by *N* king of Babylon
46: 13 the coming of *N* king of Babylon
46: 26 to *N* king of Babylon and his
49: 28 which *N* king of Babylon attacked:
49: 30 "*N* king of Babylon has plotted
50: 17 was *N* king of Babylon."
51: 34 *N* king of Babylon has devoured us,
52: 4 *N* king of Babylon marched
52: 12 year of *N* king of Babylon,
52: 28 of the people *N* carried into exile:
Eze 26: 7 against Tyre *N* king of Babylon,
29: 18 *N* king of Babylon drove his army
29: 19 to give Egypt to *N* king of Babylon,
30: 10 by the hand of *N* king of Babylon.
Da 1: 1 *N* king of Babylon came
1: 18 chief official presented them to *N*.
2: 1 year of his reign, *N* had dreams;
2: 28 has shown King *N* what will
2: 46 King *N* fell prostrate before Daniel
3: 1 King *N* made an image of gold,
3: 3 of the image that King *N* had set up
3: 5 of gold that King *N* has set up.
3: 7 of gold that King *N* had set up.
3: 9 They said to King *N*, "O king,
3: 13 with rage, *N* summoned Shadrach,
3: 14 and *N* said to them, "Is it true,
3: 16 replied to the king, "O *N*,
3: 19 Then *N* was furious with Shadrach,
3: 24 Then King *N* leaped to his feet
3: 26 *N* then approached the opening
3: 28 Then *N* said, "Praise be to the God
4: 1 King *N*, To the peoples, nations
4: 4 I, *N*, was at home in my palace,
4: 18 "This is the dream that I, King *N*,
4: 28 All this happened to King *N*.
4: 31 is what is decreed for you, King *N*:
4: 33 had been said about *N* was fulfilled.
4: 34 I, *N*, raised my eyes toward heaven
4: 37 *N*, praise and exalt and glorify
5: 2 silver goblets that *N* his father had
5: 11 King *N* your father—your father
5: 18 gave your father *N* sovereignty

NEBUCHADNEZZAR'S (NEBUCHADNEZZAR)

Jer 52: 29 3,023 Jews; in *N* eighteenth year,

NEBUSHAZBAN

Jer 39: 13 of the guard, *N* a chief officer,

NEBUZARADAN

2Ki 25: 8 *N* commander of the imperial
25: 11 *N* the commander
25: 20 *N* the commander took them all
Jer 39: 9 *N* commander of the imperial
39: 10 *N* the commander of the guard left
39: 11 Jeremiah through *N* commander
39: 13 So *N* the commander of the guard,
40: 1 the LORD after *N* commander
40: 5 Jeremiah turned to go, *N* added,
41: 10 over whom *N* commander
43: 6 daughters whom *N* commander
52: 12 *N* commander of the imperial
52: 15 *N* the commander
52: 16 But *N* left behind the rest
52: 26 *N* the commander took them all
52: 30 into exile by *N* the commander

NECESSARY (NECESSITIES)

Ac 1: 21 Therefore it is *n* to choose one
Ro 13: 5 it is *n* to submit to the authorities,
2Co 9: 5 I thought it *n* to urge the brothers
Php 1: 24 it is more *n* for you that I remain
2: 25 But I think it is *n* to send back
Heb 8: 3 and so it was *n* for this one
9: 16 it is *n* to prove the death
9: 23 It was *n*, then, for the copies

NECESSITIES (NECESSARY)

Tit 3: 14 that they may provide for daily *n*

NECK (NECKS STIFF-NECKED)

Ge 27: 16 part of his *n* with the goatskins.
27: 40 yoke from off your *n*."
33: 4 he threw his arms around his *n*
41: 42 and put a gold chain around his *n*.
49: 8 be on the *n* of your enemies;
Ex 13: 13 if you do not redeem it, break its *n*.
34: 20 if you do not redeem it, break its *n*.
Lev 5: 8 He is to wring its head from its *n*,
Dt 21: 4 are to break the heifer's *n*.
21: 6 over the heifer whose *n* was broken
28: 48 on your *n* until he has destroyed
Jdg 5: 30 embroidered garments for my *n*—
1Sa 4: 18 His *n* was broken and he died,
Job 16: 12 by the *n* and crushed me.
30: 18 he binds me like the *n*
39: 19 or clothe his *n* with a flowing mane
41: 22 Strength resides in his *n*;
Ps 69: 1 the waters have come up to my *n*.
75: 5 do not speak with outstretched *n*
105: 18 his *n* was put in irons,
Pr 1: 9 and a chain to adorn your *n*.
3: 3 bind them around your *n*,
3: 22 an ornament to grace your *n*.
6: 21 fasten them around your *n*.
SS 1: 10 your *n* with strings of jewels.
4: 4 Your *n* is like the tower of David,
7: 4 Your *n* is like an ivory tower.
Isa 8: 8 through it and reaching up to the *n*.
10: 27 their yoke from your *n*;
30: 28 rising up to the *n*.
48: 4 the sinews of your *n* were iron,
52: 2 yourself from the chains on your *n*,
66: 3 like one who breaks a dog's *n*;
Jer 27: 2 and crossbars and put it on your *n*.
27: 8 or bow its *n* under his yoke,
27: 11 But if any nation will bow its *n*
27: 12 "Bow your *n* under the yoke
28: 10 off the *n* of the prophet Jeremiah
28: 11 king of Babylon off the *n*
28: 12 off the *n* of the prophet Jeremiah,
La 1: 14 They have come upon my *n*
Eze 16: 11 and a necklace around your *n*,
Da 5: 7 a gold chain placed around his *n*,
5: 16 a gold chain placed around your *n*,
5: 29 chain was placed around his *n*,
Hos 10: 11 a yoke on her fair *n*.
11: 4 I lifted the yoke from their *n*
Na 1: 13 I will break their yoke from your *n*
Mt 18: 6 a large millstone hung around his *n*
Mk 9: 42 a large millstone tied around his *n*.
Lk 17: 2 tied around his *n* than for him

NECK-IRONS (IRON)

Jer 29: 26 a prophet into the stocks and *n*.

NECKLACE (NECKLACES)

Ps 73: 6 Therefore pride is their *n*;
SS 4: 9 with one jewel of your *n*.
Eze 16: 11 and a *n* around your neck,

NECKLACES (NECKLACE)

Nu 31: 50 signet rings, earrings and *n*—
Isa 3: 18 and headbands and crescent *n*,

NECKS (NECK)

Jos 10: 24 and placed their feet on their *n*.
10: 24 feet on the *n* of these kings."
Jdg 8: 21 the ornaments off their camels' *n*.
8: 26 were on their camels' *n*.
Isa 3: 16 walking along with outstretched *n*,
Jer 28: 14 yoke on the *n* of all these nations
30: 8 'I will break the yoke off their *n*
Eze 21: 29 it will be laid on the *n*
Ac 15: 10 try to test God by putting on the *n*

NECO

2Ki 23: 29 Pharaoh *N* king of Egypt
23: 29 but *N* faced him and killed him
23: 33 Pharaoh *N* put him in chains
23: 34 Pharaoh *N* made Eliakim son
23: 35 Jehoiakim paid Pharaoh *N*
2Ch 35: 20 *N* king of Egypt went up to fight
35: 21 But *N* sent messengers to him,
35: 22 listen to what *N* had said
36: 4 *N* took Eliakim's brother Jehoahaz
Jer 46: 2 Pharaoh *N* king of Egypt,

NECTAR

SS 8: 2 the *n* of my pomegranates.

NEDABIAH

1Ch 3: 18 Jekamiah, Hoshama and *N*.

NEED (NEEDED NEEDING NEEDLESS NEEDS NEEDY)

Ge 33: 11 gracious to me and I have all I *n*."
Ex 14: 14 for you; you *n* only to be still."
Lev 13: 36 the priest does not *n* to look
Jdg 19: 19 We don't *n* anything."
19: 20 "Let me supply whatever you *n*.
1Ki 8: 59 Israel according to each day's *n*,
2Ki 22: 7 But they *n* not account
1Ch 23: 26 the Levites no longer *n*
2Ch 2: 16 the logs from Lebanon that you *n*
35: 15 gatekeepers at each gate did not *n*
Job 5: 21 *n* not fear when destruction comes.
5: 22 *n* not fear the beasts of the earth.
34: 23 God has no *n* to examine men
Ps 50: 9 I have no *n* of a bull from your stall
79: 8 for we are in desperate *n*.
116: 6 when I was in great *n*, he saved me.
142: 6 for I am in desperate *n*;
Pr 24: 6 for waging war you *n* guidance,
Jer 2: 24 that pursue her *n* not tire
Eze 39: 10 They will not *n* to gather wood
Da 3: 16 we do not *n* to defend ourselves
Hos 7: 4 whose fire the baker *n* not stir
Mt 3: 14 saying, "I *n* to be baptized by you,
6: 8 for your Father knows what you *n*
6: 32 Father knows that you *n* them.
9: 12 It is not the healthy who *n* a doctor
14: 16 "They do not *n* to go away.
26: 65 Why do we *n* any more witnesses?
Mk 2: 17 It is not the healthy who *n* a doctor
2: 25 companions were hungry and in *n*?
14: 63 "Why do we *n* any more witnesses
Lk 5: 31 It is not the healthy who *n* a doctor
12: 30 your Father knows that you *n* them
15: 7 righteous persons who do not *n*
15: 14 country, and he began to be in *n*.
22: 71 Why do we *n* any more testimony?
Jn 2: 25 He did not *n* man's testimony
16: 30 *n* to have anyone ask you questions
Ac 2: 45 they gave to anyone as he had *n*.
4: 35 distributed to anyone as he had *n*.
10: 2 he gave generously to those in *n*
27: 34 You *n* it to survive.
Ro 12: 13 with God's people who are in *n*.
16: 2 and to give her any help she may *n*
1Co 12: 21 say to the hand, "I don't *n* you!"
12: 21 "I don't *n* you!" On the contrary,
12: 24 our presentable parts *n* no special
2Co 3: 1 Or do we *n*, like some people,
8: 14 plenty will supply what they *n*,
8: 14 their plenty will supply what you *n*.
9: 1 There is no *n* for me to write
9: 8 all that you *n*, you will abound
Eph 4: 28 something to share with those in *n*.
Php 4: 11 not saying this because I am in *n*,
4: 12 I know what it is to be in *n*,
4: 16 and again when I was in *n*.
1Th 1: 8 Therefore we do not *n*
4: 9 about brotherly love we do not *n*
5: 1 dates we do not *n* to write to you,
1Ti 5: 3 to those widows who are really in *n*
5: 5 The widow who is really in *n*
5: 16 those widows who are really in *n*.
2Ti 2: 15 a workman who does not *n*
Tit 3: 13 that they have everything they *n*.
Heb 4: 16 grace to help us in our time of *n*.
5: 12 You *n* milk, not solid food!
5: 12 you *n* someone to teach you
7: 11 why was there still *n*
7: 26 Such a high priest meets our *n*—
7: 27 he does not *n* to offer sacrifices day
10: 36 You *n* to persevere so that
2Pe 1: 3 has given us everything we *n*
1Jn 2: 27 you do not *n* anyone to teach you.
3: 17 sees his brother in *n* but has no pity
Rev 3: 17 wealth and do not *n* a thing.'
21: 23 The city does not *n* the sun
22: 5 They will not *n* the light of a lamp

NEEDED (NEED)

Ex 12: 4 amount of lamb *n* in accordance
16: 18 Each one gathered as much as he *n*
16: 21 gathered as much as he *n*,

Jos 19: 9 portion was more than they *n*.
Ezr 6: 9 Whatever is *n*— young bulls, rams,
7: 20 And anything else *n* for the temple
Ecc 10: 10 more strength is *n*
Mt 25: 36 I *n* clothes and you clothed me,
25: 43 I *n* clothes and you did not clothe
Lk 9: 11 and healed those who *n* healing.
10: 42 things, but only one thing is *n*.
Jn 13: 29 to buy what was *n* for the Feast,
Ac 17: 25 human hands, as if he *n* anything,
28: 10 us with the supplies we *n*.
2Co 11: 9 from Macedonia supplied what I *n*.
11: 9 was with you and *n* something,

NEEDING (NEED)

Mt 25: 38 or *n* clothes and clothe you?
25: 44 or a stranger or *n* clothes or sick

NEEDLE

Mt 19: 24 go through the eye of a *n*
Mk 10: 25 go through the eye of a *n*
Lk 18: 25 go through the eye of a *n*

NEEDLESS (NEED)

1Sa 25: 31 staggering burden of *n* bloodshed
Pr 23: 29 Who has *n* bruises? Who has

NEEDS (NEED)

Ex 16: 16 is to gather as much as he *n*.
Nu 4: 26 are to do all that *n* to be done
Dt 15: 8 and freely lend him whatever he *n*.
Pr 12: 10 for the *n* of his animal,
Isa 58: 10 and satisfy the *n* of the oppressed,
58: 11 he will satisfy your *n*
Jer 5: 7 I supplied all their *n*,
Mt 21: 3 tell him that the Lord *n* them,
27: 55 Jesus from Galilee to care for his *n*.
Mk 11: 3 Lord *n* it and will send it back here
15: 41 followed him and cared for his *n*.
Lk 11: 8 and give him as much as he *n*.
19: 31 tell him, 'The Lord *n* it.' "
19: 34 They replied, "The Lord *n* it."
Jn 13: 10 person who has had a bath *n* only
Ac 20: 34 and the *n* of my companions.
20: 34 of mine have supplied my own *n*
24: 23 friends to take care of his *n*.
27: 3 so they might provide for his *n*.
Ro 12: 8 if it is contributing to the *n*
2Co 9: 12 perform is not only supplying the *n*
Eph 4: 29 others up according to their *n*,
Php 2: 25 sent to take care of my *n*.
4: 19 God will meet all your *n* according
Jas 2: 16 does nothing about his physical *n*,

NEEDY (NEED)

Ex 22: 25 of my people among you who is *n*,
Dt 15: 9 will toward your *n* brother
15: 11 toward the poor and *n* in your land.
24: 14 of a hired man who is poor and *n*,
1Sa 2: 8 and lifts the *n* from the ash heap;
Job 5: 15 He saves the *n* from the sword
24: 4 They thrust the *n* from the path
24: 14 and kills the poor and *n*;
29: 16 I was a father to the *n*;
31: 19 or a *n* man without a garment,
34: 28 so that he heard the cry of the *n*.
Ps 9: 18 the *n* will not always be forgotten,
12: 5 and the groaning of the *n*,
35: 10 and *n* from those who rob them."
37: 14 bow to bring down the poor and *n*,
40: 17 Yet I am poor and *n*;
69: 33 The LORD hears the *n*
70: 5 Yet I am poor and *n*;
72: 4 and save the children of the *n*;
72: 12 he will deliver the *n* who cry out,
72: 13 and save the *n* from death.
72: 13 on the weak and the *n*
74: 21 the poor and *n* praise your name.
82: 4 Rescue the weak and *n*;
86: 1 for I am poor and *n*.
107: 41 he lifted the *n* out of their affliction
109: 16 and the *n* and the brokenhearted.
109: 22 For I am poor and *n*,
109: 31 at the right hand of the *n* one,
113: 7 and lifts the *n* from the ash heap;
140: 12 and upholds the cause of the *n*.
Pr 14: 21 blessed is he who is kind to the *n*.
14: 31 to the *n* honors God.
Pr 22: 22 and do not crush the *n* in court,
30: 14 the *n* from among mankind.
31: 9 defend the rights of the poor and *n*
31: 20 and extends her hands to the *n*.
Isa 11: 4 righteousness he will judge the *n*,
14: 30 and the *n* will lie down in safety.
25: 4 a refuge for the *n* in his distress,
29: 19 the *n* will rejoice in the Holy One
32: 7 even when the plea of the *n* is just.
41: 17 "The poor and *n* search for water,
Jer 20: 13 He rescues the life of the *n*
22: 16 the cause of the poor and *n*,
Eze 16: 49 they did not help the poor and *n*.
18: 12 He oppresses the poor and *n*.
22: 29 and *n* and mistreat the alien,
Am 2: 6 and the *n* for a pair of sandals.
4: 1 oppress the poor and crush the *n*
8: 4 Hear this, you who trample the *n*
8: 6 and the *n* for a pair of sandals,
Mt 6: 2 "So when you give to the *n*,
6: 3 But when you give to the *n*,
Ac 4: 34 There were no *n* persons

NEGEV

Ge 12: 9 and continued toward the *N*.
13: 1 up from Egypt to the *N*,
13: 3 From the *N* he went from place
20: 1 from there into the region of the *N*
24: 62 for he was living in the *N*.
Nu 13: 17 "Go up through the *N*
13: 22 They went up through the *N*
13: 29 The Amalekites live in the *N*;
21: 1 king of Arad, who lived in the *N*,
33: 40 who lived in the *N* of Canaan,
Dt 1: 7 in the *N* and along the seacoast,
34: 3 the *N* and the whole region
Jos 10: 40 including the hill country, the *N*,
11: 16 all the *N*, the whole region
12: 8 the *N*— the lands of the Hittites,
15: 19 you have given me land in the *N*,
15: 21 in the *N* toward the boundary
19: 8 Baalath Beer (Ramah in the *N*).
Jdg 1: 9 the *N* and the western foothills.
1: 15 you have given me land in the *N*,
1: 16 of Judah in the *N* near Arad.
1Sa 27: 10 or "Against the *N* of Jerahmeel"
27: 10 or "Against the *N* of the Kenites."
27: 10 "Against the *N* of Judah"
30: 1 the Amalekites had raided the *N*
30: 14 We raided the *N* of the Kerethites
30: 14 to Judah and the *N* of Caleb.
2Sa 24: 7 on to Beersheba in the *N* of Judah.
2Ch 28: 18 towns in the foothills and in the *N*
Ps 126: 4 like streams in the *N*.
Isa 30: 6 concerning the animals of the *N*:
Jer 13: 19 The cities in the *N* will be shut up,
17: 26 from the hill country and the *N*,
32: 44 the western foothills and of the *N*,
33: 13 the western foothills and of the *N*,
Ob : 19 People from the *N* will occupy
: 20 will possess the towns of the *N*.
Zec 7: 7 *N* and the western foothills were

NEGLECT (NEGLECTED NEGLECTING NEGLIGENT)

Dt 12: 19 Be careful not to *n* the Levites
14: 27 And do not *n* the Levites living
Ezr 4: 22 Be careful not to *n* this matter.
Ne 10: 39 We will not *n* the house of our God
Est 6: 10 Do not *n* anything you have
Ps 119: 16 I will not *n* your word.
Lk 11: 42 you *n* justice and the love of God.
Ac 6: 2 for us to *n* the ministry of the word
1Ti 4: 14 Do not *n* your gift, which was

NEGLECTED (NEGLECT)

Ne 13: 11 "Why is the house of God *n*?"
SS 1: 6 my own vineyard I have *n*.
Mt 23: 23 But you have *n* the more important

NEGLECTING (NEGLECT)

Mt 23: 23 without *n* the former.

NEGLIGENT (NEGLECT)

2Ch 29: 11 My sons, do not be *n* now,
Da 6: 4 and neither corrupt nor *n*.

NEHELAMITE

Jer 29: 24 Tell Shemaiah the *N*, "This is what
29: 31 LORD says about Shemaiah the *N*:
29: 32 I will surely punish Shemaiah the *N*

NEHEMIAH

Ezr 2: 2 Jeshua, *N*, Seraiah, Reelaiah,
Ne 1: 1 The words of *N* son of Hacaliah:
3: 16 Beyond him, *N* son of Azbuk,
7: 7 Jeshua, *N*, Azariah, Raamiah,
8: 9 *N* the governor, Ezra the priest
8: 10 *N* said, "Go and enjoy choice food
10: 1 who sealed it were: *N* the governor,
12: 26 and in the days of *N* the governor
12: 47 in the days of Zerubbabel and of *N*,

NEHUM

Ne 7: 7 Mispereth, Bigvai, *N* and Baanah):

NEHUSHTA

2Ki 24: 8 His mother's name was *N* daughter

NEHUSHTAN

2Ki 18: 4 (It was called *N*.)

NEIEL

Jos 19: 27 went north to Beth Emek and *N*,

NEIGH (NEIGHING NEIGHINGS)

Jer 50: 11 and *n* like stallions,

NEIGHBOR (NEIGHBOR'S NEIGHBORING NEIGHBORS NEIGHBORS')

Ex 3: 22 Every woman is to ask her *n*
12: 4 one with their nearest *n*,
20: 16 give false testimony against your *n*.
20: 17 or anything that belongs to your *n*
22: 7 "If a man gives his *n* silver
22: 9 must pay back double to his *n*.
22: 10 animal to his *n* for safekeeping
22: 11 the LORD that the *n* did not lay
22: 12 if the animal was stolen from the *n*,
22: 14 man borrows an animal from his *n*
32: 27 his brother and friend and *n*.' "
Lev 6: 2 by deceiving his *n* about something
19: 13 Do not defraud your *n* or rob him.
19: 15 to the great, but judge your *n* fairly.
19: 17 Rebuke your *n* frankly
19: 18 but love your *n* as yourself.
20: 10 wife of his *n*— both the adulterer
24: 19 anyone injures his *n*, whatever he
Dt 4: 42 he had unintentionally killed his *n*
5: 20 give false testimony against your *n*.
5: 21 or anything that belongs to your *n*
19: 4 one who kills his *n* unintentionally,
19: 5 the forest with his *n* to cut wood,
19: 5 the head may fly off and hit his *n*
19: 6 his *n* without malice aforethought.
19: 11 But if a man hates his *n*
22: 26 who attacks and murders his *n*,
24: 10 a loan of any kind to your *n*,
27: 24 is the man who kills his *n* secretly."
Jos 20: 5 he killed his *n* unintentionally
1Ki 8: 31 "When a man wrongs his *n*
2Ch 6: 22 "When a man wrongs his *n*
Ps 12: 2 Everyone lies to his *n*;
15: 3 who does his *n* no wrong
101: 5 Whoever slanders his *n* in secret,
Pr 3: 28 Do not say to your *n*,
3: 29 Do not plot harm against your *n*,
6: 1 have put up security for your *n*,
6: 3 press your plea with your *n*!
11: 9 mouth the godless destroys his *n*,
11: 12 who lacks judgment derides his *n*,
14: 21 He who despises his *n* sins,
16: 29 A violent man entices his *n*
17: 18 and puts up security for his *n*.
21: 10 his *n* gets no mercy from him.
24: 28 against your *n* without cause,
25: 8 end if your *n* puts you to shame?
25: 9 If you argue your case with a *n*,
25: 18 gives false testimony against his *n*.
26: 19 is a man who deceives his *n*
27: 10 better a *n* nearby than a brother far
27: 14 If a man loudly blesses his *n*
29: 5 Whoever flatters his *n*
Ecc 4: 4 spring from man's envy of his *n*.

Isa 3: 5 man against man, *n* against *n*.
19: 2 *n* against *n*,
Jer 9: 8 each speaks cordially to his *n*,
31: 34 No longer will a man teach his *n*,
Mic 7: 5 Do not trust a *n*;
Zec 3: 10 each of you will invite his *n* to sit
8: 10 turned every man against his *n*.
8: 17 do not plot evil against your *n*,
11: 6 "I will hand everyone over to his *n*
Mt 5: 43 Love your *n* and hate your enemy.'
19: 19 and 'love your *n* as yourself.' "
22: 39 the second is like it: 'Love your *n*
Mk 12: 31 The second is this: 'Love your *n*
12: 33 to love your *n* as yourself is more
Lk 10: 27 and, 'Love your *n* as yourself.' "
10: 29 who is my *n*?" In reply Jesus said:
10: 36 of these three do you think was a *n*
Ro 13: 9 "Love your *n* as yourself."
13: 10 Love does no harm to its *n*.
15: 2 Each of us should please his *n*
Gal 5: 14 "Love your *n* as yourself."
Eph 4: 25 and speak truthfully to his *n*,
Heb 8: 11 No longer will a man teach his *n*,
Jas 2: 8 "Love your *n* as yourself,"
4: 12 who are you to judge your *n*?

NEIGHBOR'S (NEIGHBOR)

Ex 20: 17 You shall not covet your *n* wife,
20: 17 "You shall not covet your *n* house.
22: 7 they are stolen from the *n* house,
22: 26 If you take your *n* cloak as a pledge
Lev 18: 20 have intercourse with your *n* wife
19: 16 that endangers your *n* life.
Dt 5: 21 not set your desire on your *n* house
5: 21 "You shall not covet your *n* wife.
19: 14 not move your *n* boundary stone
23: 24 If you enter your *n* vineyard,
23: 25 If you enter your *n* grainfield,
27: 17 who moves his *n* boundary stone."
Job 31: 9 or if I have lurked at my *n* door,
Pr 6: 3 fallen into your *n* hands:
25: 17 Seldom set foot in your *n* house—
Eze 18: 6 He does not defile his *n* wife
18: 11 He defiles his *n* wife.
18: 15 He does not defile his *n* wife.
22: 11 a detestable offense with his *n* wife,
33: 26 and each of you defiles his *n* wife.

NEIGHBORING (NEIGHBOR)

Dt 1: 7 go to all the *n* peoples
21: 2 from the body to the *n* towns.
1Sa 7: 14 and Israel delivered the *n* territory
Ezr 9: 1 separate from the *n* peoples
Ne 9: 30 them over to the *n* peoples.
10: 28 from the *n* peoples for the sake
10: 31 "When the *n* peoples bring
Ps 76: 11 let all the *n* lands
Jer 49: 18 along with their *n* towns,"
50: 40 along with their *n* towns,"

NEIGHBORS (NEIGHBOR)

Ex 11: 2 to ask their *n* for articles of silver
Jos 9: 16 Israelites heard that they were *n*,
1Sa 15: 28 and has given it to one of your *n*—
28: 17 and given it to one of your *n*—
2Ki 4: 3 and ask all your *n* for empty jars.
1Ch 12: 40 their *n* from as far away as Issachar
Ezr 1: 6 All their *n* assisted them
6: 21 practices of their Gentile *n* in order
Ps 28: 3 who speak cordially with their *n*
31: 11 I am the utter contempt of my *n*;
38: 11 my *n* stay far away.
44: 13 have made us a reproach to our *n*,
79: 4 We are objects of reproach to our *n*
79: 12 into the laps of our *n* seven times
80: 6 of contention to our *n*,
89: 41 he has become the scorn of his *n*.
Pr 14: 20 poor are shunned even by their *n*,
Jer 6: 21 *n* and friends will perish."
12: 14 "As for all my wicked *n* who seize
49: 10 relatives and *n* will perish,
La 1: 17 that his *n* become his foes;
Eze 16: 26 with the Egyptians, your lustful *n*,
16: 57 and all her *n* and the daughters
22: 12 gain from your *n* by extortion.
28: 24 Israel have malicious *n* who are
28: 26 on all their *n* who maligned them.
Hab 2: 15 to him who gives drink to his *n*,

Lk 1: 58 Her *n* and relatives heard that
1: 65 The *n* were all filled with awe,
14: 12 or relatives, or your rich *n*;
15: 6 he calls his friends and *n* together
15: 9 she calls her friends and *n* together
Jn 9: 8 His *n* and those who had formerly

NEIGHBORS' (NEIGHBOR)

Jer 29: 23 adultery with their *n'* wives

NEIGHING (NEIGH)

Jer 5: 8 each *n* for another man's wife.
8: 16 at the *n* of their stallions

NEIGHINGS (NEIGH)

Jer 13: 27 your adulteries and lustful *n*,

NEKODA

Ezr 2: 48 Reaiah, Rezin, *N*, Gazzam, Uzza,
2: 60 *N* 652 And from among the priests:
Ne 7: 50 Reaiah, Rezin, *N*, Gazzam, Uzza,
7: 62 *N* 642 And from among the priests:

NEMUEL (NEMUELITE)

Nu 26: 9 and the sons of Eliab were *N*,
26: 12 through *N*, the Nemuelite clan;
1Ch 4: 24 The descendants of Simeon: *N*,

NEMUELITE (NEMUEL)

Nu 26: 12 through Nemuel, the *N* clan;

NEPHEG

Ex 6: 21 The sons of Izhar were Korah, *N*
2Sa 5: 15 Ibhar, Elishua, *N*, Japhia, Elishama
1Ch 3: 7 Eliphelet, Nogah, *N*, Japhia,
14: 6 Elpelet, Nogah, *N*, Japhia,

NEPHEW (NEPHEWS)

Ge 12: 5 He took his wife Sarai, his *n* Lot,
14: 12 also carried off Abram's *n* Lot

NEPHEWS (NEPHEW)

Ezr 8: 19 and his brothers and *n*, 20 men.

NEPHILIM

Ge 6: 4 The *N* were on the earth
Nu 13: 33 We saw the *N* there
13: 33 of Anak come from the *N*).

NEPHTOAH

Jos 15: 9 the spring of the Waters of *N*,
18: 15 at the spring of the Waters of *N*.

NEPHUSSIM

Ezr 2: 50 Asnah, Meunim, *N*, Bakbuk,
Ne 7: 52 Besai, Meunim, *N*, Bakbuk,

NER

1Sa 14: 50 son of *N*, and *N* was Saul's uncle.
14: 51 and Abner's father *N* were sons
26: 5 where Saul and Abner son of *N*,
26: 14 to the army and to Abner son of *N*,
2Sa 2: 8 Meanwhile, Abner son of *N*,
2: 12 Abner son of *N*, together
3: 23 son of *N* had come to the king
3: 25 You know Abner son of *N*;
3: 28 the blood of Abner son of *N*.
3: 37 in the murder of Abner son of *N*.
1Ki 2: 5 Abner son of *N* and Amasa son
2: 32 Abner son of *N*, commander
1Ch 8: 30 Kish, Baal, *N*, Nadab, Gedor, Ahio
8: 33 *N* was the father of Kish, Kish
9: 36 Kish, Baal, *N*, Nadab, Gedor, Ahio
9: 39 *N* was the father of Kish, Kish
26: 28 Abner son of *N* and Joab son

NEREUS

Ro 16: 15 Greet Philologus, Julia, *N*

NERGAL

2Ki 17: 30 the men from Cuthah made *N*,

NERGAL-SHAREZER

Jer 39: 3 *N* a high official and all the other
39: 3 *N* of Samgar, Nebo-Sarsekim
39: 13 *N* a high official and all the other

NERI

Lk 3: 27 the son of *N*,

NERIAH

Jer 32: 12 I gave this deed to Baruch son of *N*,
32: 16 of purchase to Baruch son of *N*,
36: 4 So Jeremiah called Baruch son of *N*
36: 8 son of *N* did everything Jeremiah
36: 14 So Baruch son of *N* went to them
36: 32 it to the scribe Baruch son of *N*,
43: 3 But Baruch son of *N* is inciting you
43: 6 the prophet and Baruch son of *N*.
45: 1 son of *N* in the fourth year
51: 59 to the staff officer Seraiah son of *N*,

NEST (NESTED NESTING NESTS)

Nu 24: 21 your *n* is set in a rock;
Dt 22: 6 across a bird's *n* beside the road,
32: 11 like an eagle that stirs up its *n*
Job 39: 27 and build his *n* on high?
Ps 84: 3 and the swallow a *n* for herself,
104: 12 The birds of the air *n* by the waters;
Pr 27: 8 Like a bird that strays from its *n*
Isa 10: 14 As one reaches into a *n*,
11: 8 put his hand into the viper's *n*.
16: 2 pushed from the *n*,
34: 11 the raven will *n* there.
34: 15 The owl will *n* there and lay eggs,
Jer 48: 28 Be like a dove that makes its *n*
49: 16 Though you build your *n* as high
Eze 17: 23 Birds of every kind will *n* in it;
Ob : 4 and make your *n* among the stars,
Hab 2: 9 gain to set his *n* on high,

NESTED (NEST)

Eze 31: 6 *n* in its boughs,

NESTING (NEST)

Da 4: 21 and having *n* places in its branches

NESTLED

Jer 22: 23 who are *n* in cedar buildings,

NESTS (NEST)

Ps 104: 17 There the birds make their *n*;
Isa 60: 8 like doves to their *n*?
Mt 8: 20 and birds of the air have *n*,
Lk 9: 58 and birds of the air have *n*,

NET (DRAGNET FISHNETS NETS)

Job 18: 8 His feet thrust him into a *n*
19: 6 and drawn his *n* around me.
Ps 9: 15 in the *n* they have hidden.
10: 9 and drags them off in his *n*.
35: 7 Since they hid their *n* for me
35: 8 may the *n* they hid entangle them,
57: 6 They spread a *n* for my feet—
140: 5 have spread out the cords of their *n*
Pr 1: 17 How useless to spread a *n*
29: 5 is spreading a *n* for his feet.
Ecc 9: 12 As fish are caught in a cruel *n*,
Isa 51: 20 like antelope caught in a *n*.
La 1: 13 He spread a *n* for my feet
Eze 12: 13 I will spread my *n* for him,
17: 20 I will spread my *n* for him,
19: 8 They spread their *n* for him,
32: 3 I will cast my *n* over you,
32: 3 and they will haul you up in my *n*.
Hos 5: 1 a *n* spread out on Tabor.
7: 12 I will throw my *n* over them;
Mic 7: 2 each hunts his brother with a *n*.
Hab 1: 15 he catches them in his *n*,
1: 16 Therefore he sacrifices to his *n*
1: 16 for by his *n* he lives in luxury
1: 17 Is he to keep on emptying his *n*,
Mt 4: 18 They were casting a *n* into the lake,
13: 47 of heaven is like a *n* that was let
Mk 1: 16 and his brother Andrew casting a *n*
Jn 21: 6 they were unable to haul the *n* in
21: 6 "Throw your *n* on the right side
21: 8 in the boat, towing the *n* full of fish,
21: 11 aboard and dragged the *n* ashore.
21: 11 with so many the *n* was not torn.

NETAIM

1Ch 4: 23 were the potters who lived at *N*

NETHANEL

Nu 1: 8 from Issachar, *N* son of Zuar;
2: 5 people of Issachar is *N* son of Zuar.
7: 18 On the second day *N* son of Zuar,

Nu 7: 23 This was the offering of *N* son
10: 15 *N* son of Zuar was over the division
1Ch 2: 14 the fourth *N*, the fifth Raddai,
15: 24 Shebaniah, Joshaphat, *N*, Amasai,
24: 6 The scribe Shemaiah son of *N*,
26: 4 Sacar the fourth, *N* the fifth,
2Ch 17: 7 *N* and Micaiah to teach
35: 9 along with Shemaiah and *N*,
Ezr 10: 22 Elioenai, Maaseiah, Ishmael, *N*,
Ne 12: 21 Hashabiah; of Jedaiah's, *N*.
12: 36 Maai, *N*, Judah and Hanani—

NETHANIAH

2Ki 25: 23 Ishmael son of *N*, Johanan son
25: 25 however, Ishmael son of *N*,
1Ch 25: 2 Zaccur, Joseph, *N* and Asarelah.
25: 12 12 the fifth to *N*, his sons
2Ch 17: 8 Shemaiah, *N*, Zebadiah, Asahel,
Jer 36: 14 all the officials sent Jehudi son of *N*
40: 8 Ishmael son of *N*, Johanan
40: 14 son of *N* to take your life?"
40: 15 Let me go and kill Ishmael son of *N*
41: 1 seventh month Ishmael son of *N*,
41: 2 son of *N* and the ten men who were
41: 6 Ishmael son of *N* went out
41: 7 son of *N* and the men who were
41: 9 Ishmael son of *N* filled it
41: 10 Ishmael son of *N* took them captive
41: 11 son of *N* had committed,
41: 12 and went to fight Ishmael son of *N*.
41: 15 But Ishmael son of *N* and eight
41: 16 recovered from Ishmael son of *N*
41: 18 son of *N* had killed Gedaliah son

NETOPHAH (NETOPHATHITE NETOPHATHITES)

Ezr 2: 22 the men of Bethlehem 123 of *N* 56
Ne 7: 26 of Bethlehem and *N*

NETOPHATHITE (NETOPHAH NETOPHATHITES)

2Sa 23: 28 the Ahohite, Maharai the *N*,
23: 29 Heled son of Baanah the *N*,
2Ki 25: 23 Seraiah son of Tanhumeth the *N*,
1Ch 11: 30 Heled son of Baanah the *N*,
11: 30 Ilai the Ahohite, Maharai the *N*,
27: 13 was Maharai the *N*, a Zerahite.
27: 15 was Heldai the *N*, from the family
Jer 40: 8 the sons of Ephai the *N*,

NETOPHATHITES (NETOPHAH NETOPHATHITE)

1Ch 2: 54 of Salma: Bethlehem, the *N*,
9: 16 who lived in the villages of the *N*.
Ne 12: 28 from the villages of the *N*,

NETS (NET)

Ps 141: 10 Let the wicked fall into their own *n*
Isa 19: 8 those who throw *n* on the water
Eze 47: 10 there will be places for spreading *n*.
Mt 4: 20 At once they left their *n*
4: 21 father Zebedee, preparing their *n*.
Mk 1: 18 At once they left their *n*
1: 19 John in a boat, preparing their *n*.
Lk 5: 2 who were washing their *n*.
5: 4 and let down the *n* for a catch."
5: 5 you say so, I will let down the *n*."
5: 6 of fish that their *n* began to break.

NETTLES

Isa 34: 13 *n* and brambles her strongholds.

NETWORK

Ex 27: 4 Make a grating for it, a bronze *n*,
27: 4 at each of the four corners of the *n*.
38: 4 a bronze *n*, to be under its ledge,
1Ki 7: 17 *n* of interwoven chains festooned
7: 18 in two rows encircling each *n*
7: 20 the bowl-shaped part next to the *n*,
7: 41 sets of *n* decorating the two
7: 42 of *n* (two rows of pomegranates
7: 42 rows of pomegranates for each *n*,
2Ki 25: 17 The other pillar, with its *n*,
25: 17 and was decorated with a *n*
2Ch 4: 12 sets of *n* decorating the two
4: 13 of *n* (two rows of pomegranates
4: 13 rows of pomegranates for each *n*,
Jer 52: 22 and was decorated with a *n*
52: 23 above the surrounding *n* was

NEVER-FAILING

Am 5: 24 righteousness like a *n* stream!

NEW

Ge 27: 28 an abundance of grain and *n* wine.
27: 37 him with grain and *n* wine.
45: 22 To each of them he gave *n* clothing
Ex 1: 8 a *n* king, who did not know about
Lev 2: 14 crushed heads of *n* grain roasted
14: 42 take *n* clay and plaster the house.
23: 14 any bread, or roasted or *n* grain,
23: 16 offering of *n* grain to the LORD.
26: 10 out to make room for the *n*.
Nu 10: 10 feasts and *N* Moon festivals—
16: 30 brings about something totally *n*,
18: 12 all the finest *n* wine and grain they
28: 14 at each *n* moon during the year.
28: 26 offering of *n* grain during the Feast
Dt 7: 13 your grain, *n* wine and oil—
11: 14 gather in your grain, *n* wine
12: 17 the tithe of your grain and *n* wine
14: 23 Eat the tithe of your grain, *n* wine
18: 4 the firstfruits of your grain, *n* wine
20: 5 "Has anyone built a *n* house
22: 8 When you build a *n* house,
28: 51 will leave you no grain, *n* wine
32: 2 like showers on *n* grass,
33: 28 in a land of grain and *n* wine,
Jos 9: 13 wineskins that we filled were *n*,
Jdg 5: 8 When they chose *n* gods,
15: 13 they bound him with two *n* ropes
16: 11 with *n* ropes that have never been
16: 12 So Delilah took *n* ropes
1Sa 6: 7 "Now then, get a *n* cart ready,
20: 5 tomorrow is the *N* Moon festival,
20: 18 "Tomorrow is the *N* Moon festival.
20: 24 when the *N* Moon festival came,
2Sa 6: 3 They set the ark of God on a *n* cart
6: 3 were guiding the *n* cart
21: 16 who was armed with a *n* ⌊sword⌋,
1Ki 11: 29 him on the way, wearing a *n* cloak.
11: 30 hold of the *n* cloak he was wearing
2Ki 2: 20 "Bring me a *n* bowl," he said,
4: 23 It's not the *N* Moon or the Sabbath
4: 42 along with some heads of *n* grain.
16: 14 from between the *n* altar
16: 14 it on the north side of the *n* altar.
16: 15 "On the large *n* altar, offer
18: 32 a land of grain and *n* wine,
1Ch 13: 7 from Abinadab's house on a *n* cart,
23: 31 and at *N* Moon festivals
2Ch 2: 4 and on Sabbaths and *N* Moons
8: 13 *N* Moons and the three annual
20: 5 in the front of the *n* courtyard
31: 3 *N* Moons and appointed feasts
31: 5 the firstfruits of their grain, *n* wine,
32: 28 to store the harvest of grain, *n* wine
Ezr 3: 5 the *N* Moon sacrifices
9: 9 He has granted us *n* life
Ne 5: 11 part of the money, grain, *n* wine
10: 33 *N* Moon festivals and appointed
10: 37 of all our trees and of our *n* wine
10: 39 *n* wine and oil to the storerooms
13: 5 *n* wine and oil prescribed
13: 12 *n* wine and oil into the storerooms.
Job 10: 17 You bring *n* witnesses against me
14: 7 and its *n* shoots will not fail.
29: 20 the bow ever *n* in my hand.'
32: 19 like *n* wineskins ready to burst.
Ps 4: 7 their grain and *n* wine abound.
33: 3 Sing to him a *n* song;
40: 3 He put a *n* song in my mouth,
81: 3 the ram's horn at the *N* Moon,
90: 5 they are like the *n* grass
90: 6 in the morning it springs up *n*,
96: 1 Sing to the LORD a *n* song;
98: 1 Sing to the LORD a *n* song,
144: 9 I will sing a *n* song to you, O God;
149: 1 Sing to the LORD a *n* song,
Pr 3: 10 vats will brim over with *n* wine.
27: 25 is removed and *n* growth appears
Ecc 1: 9 there is nothing *n* under the sun.
1: 10 "Look! This is something *n*"?
SS 6: 11 trees to look at the *n* growth
7: 13 both *n* and old,
Isa 1: 13 *N* Moons, Sabbaths
1: 14 Your *N* Moon festivals
Isa 24: 7 *n* wine dries up and the vine
36: 17 a land of grain and *n* wine,
41: 15 *n* and sharp, with many teeth.
42: 9 and *n* things I declare;
42: 10 Sing to the LORD a *n* song,
43: 19 See, I am doing a *n* thing!
48: 6 now on I will tell you of *n* things,
62: 2 you will be called by a *n* name
62: 8 will foreigners drink the *n* wine
65: 17 *n* heavens and a *n* earth.
66: 22 "As the *n* heavens and the *n* earth
66: 23 From one *N* Moon to another
Jer 8: 10 and their fields to *n* owners.
26: 10 at the entrance of the *N* Gate
31: 12 the grain, the *n* wine and the oil,
31: 22 The LORD will create a *n* thing
31: 31 "when I will make a *n* covenant
36: 10 of the *N* Gate of the temple,
La 3: 23 They are *n* every morning;
Eze 11: 19 undivided heart and put a *n* spirit
17: 9 All its *n* growth will wither.
18: 31 and get a *n* heart and a *n* spirit.
36: 26 give you a *n* heart and put a *n* spirit
45: 17 the *N* Moons and the Sabbaths—
46: 1 and on the day of the *N* Moon it is
46: 3 *N* Moons the people of the land are
46: 6 On the day of the *N* Moon he is
Da 1: 7 chief official gave them *n* names:
Hos 2: 8 who gave her the grain, the *n* wine
2: 9 and my *n* wine when it is ready.
2: 11 her yearly festivals, her *N* Moons,
2: 22 the *n* wine and oil,
4: 11 to old wine and *n*,
5: 7 Now their *N* Moon festivals
7: 14 together for grain and *n* wine
9: 2 the *n* wine will fail them.
Joel 1: 10 the *n* wine is dried up,
2: 19 "I am sending you grain, *n* wine
2: 24 the vats will overflow with *n* wine
3: 18 day the mountains will drip *n* wine,
Am 8: 5 "When will the *N* Moon be over
9: 13 *N* wine will drip
Zep 1: 10 wailing from the *N* Quarter,
3: 5 and every *n* day he does not fail,
Hag 1: 11 the *n* wine, the oil and whatever
Zec 9: 17 and *n* wine the young women.
Mt 9: 17 Neither do men pour *n* wine
9: 17 they pour *n* wine into *n* wineskins,
13: 52 out of his storeroom *n* treasures
27: 60 it in his own *n* tomb that he had cut
Mk 1: 27 "What is this? A *n* teaching—
2: 21 the *n* piece will pull away
2: 22 And no one pours *n* wine
2: 22 he pours *n* wine into *n* wineskins."
16: 17 they will speak in *n* tongues;
Lk 5: 36 from the *n* will not match the old.
5: 36 he will have torn the *n* garment,
5: 36 one tears a patch from a *n* garment
5: 37 And no one pours *n* wine
5: 37 the *n* wine will burst the skins,
5: 38 must be poured into *n* wineskins.
5: 38 *n* wine must be poured
5: 39 after drinking old wine wants the *n*
22: 20 "This cup is the *n* covenant
Jn 13: 34 "A *n* commandment I give you:
19: 41 and in the garden a *n* tomb,
Ac 5: 20 the full message of this *n* life."
17: 19 know what this *n* teaching is that
Ro 6: 4 the Father, we too may live a *n* life.
7: 6 serve in the *n* way of the Spirit,
1Co 5: 7 old yeast that you may be a *n* batch
11: 25 "This cup is the *n* covenant
2Co 3: 6 as ministers of a *n* covenant—
5: 17 he is a *n* creation; the old has gone,
5: 17 the old has gone, the *n* has come!
Gal 6: 15 what counts is a *n* creation.
Eph 2: 15 to create in himself one *n* man out
4: 23 to be made *n* in the attitude
4: 24 and to put on the *n* self, created
Col 2: 16 a *N* Moon celebration
3: 10 and have put on the *n* self,
Heb 8: 8 when I will make a *n* covenant
8: 13 By calling this covenant "*n*,"
9: 10 until the time of the *n* order.
9: 15 is the mediator of a *n* covenant,
10: 20 by a *n* and living way opened for us
12: 24 Jesus the mediator of a *n* covenant,
1Pe 1: 3 great mercy he has given us *n* birth

2Pe 3:13 to a *n* heaven and a *n* earth,
1Jn 2: 7 I am not writing you a *n* command
2: 8 Yet I am writing you a *n* command;
2Jn : 5 I am not writing you a *n* command
Rev 2:17 stone with a *n* name written on it,
3:12 I will also write on him my *n* name.
3:12 the *n* Jerusalem, which is coming
5: 9 And they sang a *n* song:
14: 3 And they sang a *n* song
21: 1 I saw a *n* heaven and a *n* earth,
21: 2 the Holy City, the *n* Jerusalem,
21: 5 "I am making everything *n*!"

NEWBORN (BEAR)

Jer 14: 5 deserts her *n* fawn
Ac 7:19 them to throw out their *n* babies
1Pe 2: 2 Like *n* babies, crave pure spiritual

NEWS

Ge 29:13 as Laban heard the *n* about Jacob,
45:16 When the *n* reached Pharaoh's
1Sa 4:17 The man who brought the *n* replied
4:19 When she heard the *n* that the ark
13: 4 Israel heard the *n*: "Saul has
31: 9 to proclaim the *n* in the temple
2Sa 4: 4 old when the *n* about Saul
4:10 the reward I gave him for his *n*!
4:10 thought he was bringing good *n*,
18:19 and take the *n* to the king that
18:20 the one to take the *n* today,"
18:20 "You may take the *n* another time,
18:22 don't have any *n* that will bring
18:25 If he is alone, he must have good *n*
18:26 "He must be bringing good *n*, too."
18:27 "He comes with good *n*."
18:31 My lord the king, hear the good *n*!
1Ki 1:42 like you must be bringing good *n*."
2:28 When the *n* reached Joab,
14: 6 I have been sent to you with bad *n*.
2Ki 7: 9 This is a day of good *n*
7:11 The gatekeepers shouted the *n*,
9:15 city to go and tell the *n* in Jezreel."
1Ch 10: 9 to proclaim the *n* among their idols
Ps 112: 7 He will have no fear of bad *n*;
Pr 15:30 good *n* gives health to the bones.
25:25 is good *n* from a distant land.
Isa 52: 7 the feet of those who bring good *n*,
61: 1 me to preach good *n* to the poor
Jer 20:15 man who brought my father the *n*,
49:23 for they have heard bad *n*.
Eze 21: 7 'Because of the *n* that is coming.
24:26 fugitive will come to tell you the *n*.
Jnh 3: 6 When the *n* reached the king
Na 1:15 the feet of one who brings good *n*,
3:19 who hears the *n* about you
Mt 4:23 preaching the good *n*
4:24 *N* about him spread all over Syria,
9:26 *N* of this spread through all that
9:31 and spread the *n* about him all
9:35 preaching the good *n*
11: 5 the good *n* is preached to the poor.
Mk 1:14 proclaiming the good *n* of God.
1:15 Repent and believe the good *n*!"
1:28 *N* about him spread quickly
1:45 to talk freely, spreading the *n*.
16:15 preach the good *n* to all creation.
Lk 1:19 and to tell you this good *n*.
2:10 I bring you good *n*
3:18 and preached the good *n* to them.
4:14 and *n* about him spread
4:18 me to preach good *n* to the poor.
4:37 And the *n* about him spread
4:43 "I must preach the good *n*
5:15 Yet the *n* about him spread all
7:17 This *n* about Jesus spread
7:22 the good *n* is preached to the poor.
8: 1 proclaiming the good *n*
16:16 the good *n* of the kingdom
Jn 4:51 with the *n* that his boy was living.
20:18 went to the disciples with the *n*:
Ac 5:42 proclaiming the good *n* that Jesus
8:12 as he preached the good *n*
8:35 told him the good *n* about Jesus.
10:36 telling the good *n* of peace
11:20 them the good *n* about the Lord
11:22 *N* of this reached the ears
13:32 you the good *n*: What God
14: 7 continued to preach the good *n*.
Ac 14:15 We are bringing you good *n*,
14:21 They preached the good *n*
15: 3 This *n* made all the brothers very
17:18 preaching the good *n* about Jesus
21:31 *n* reached the commander
Ro 10:15 feet of those who bring good *n*!"
10:16 the Israelites accepted the good *n*.
Php 2:19 when I receive *n* about you.
Col 4: 7 will tell you all the *n* about me.
1Th 3: 6 and has brought good *n* about your

NEZIAH

Ezr 2:54 *N* and Hatipha The descendants
Ne 7:56 *N* and Hatipha The descendants

NEZIB

Jos 15:43 Ashan, Iphtah, Ashnah, *N*, Keilah,

NIBHAZ

2Ki 17:31 the Avvites made *N* and Tartak,

NIBSHAN

Jos 15:62 Beth Arabah, Middin, Secacah, *N*,

NICANOR

Ac 6: 5 Procorus, *N*, Timon, Parmenas,

NICODEMUS

Jn 3: 1 a man of the Pharisees named *N*,
3: 4 born when he is old?" *N* asked.
3: 9 "How can this be?" *N* asked.
7:50 *N*, who had gone to Jesus earlier
19:39 He was accompanied by *N*,
19:39 *N* brought a mixture of myrrh

NICOLAITANS

Rev 2: 6 You hate the practices of the *N*,
2:15 hold to the teaching of the *N*.

NICOLAS

Ac 6: 5 Parmenas, and *N* from Antioch,

NICOPOLIS

Tit 3:12 do your best to come to me at *N*,

NIGER

Ac 13: 1 Barnabas, Simeon called *N*,

NIGHT (ALL-NIGHT MIDNIGHT NIGHTFALL NIGHTS NIGHTTIME OVERNIGHT)

Ge 1: 5 and the darkness he called "*n*."
1:14 sky to separate the day from the *n*,
1:16 and the lesser light to govern the *n*.
1:18 to govern the day and the *n*,
8:22 day and *n*
14:15 During the *n* Abram divided his
19: 2 can wash your feet and spend the *n*
19: 2 we will spend the *n* in the square."
19:33 That *n* they got their father
19:34 "Last *n* I lay with my father.
19:35 father to drink wine that *n*
20: 3 to Abimelech in a dream one *n*
24:23 house for us to spend the *n*?"
24:25 well as room for you to spend the *n*
24:54 and drank and spent the *n* there.
26:24 That *n* the LORD appeared to him
28:11 for the *n* because the sun had set.
30:16 So he slept with her that *n*.
31:24 Laban the Aramean in a dream at *n*
31:29 last *n* the God of your father said
31:39 for whatever was stolen by day or *n*
31:40 in the daytime and the cold at *n*,
31:42 and last *n* he rebuked you."
31:54 had eaten, they spent the *n* there.
32:13 He spent the *n* there,
32:21 he himself spent the *n* in the camp.
32:22 That *n* Jacob got up and took his
40: 5 had a dream the same *n*,
41:11 Each of us had a dream the same *n*,
42:27 for the *n* one of them opened his
43:21 for the *n* we opened our sacks
46: 2 God spoke to Israel in a vision at *n*
Ex 10:13 the land all that day and all that *n*.
12: 8 That same *n* they are
12:12 "On that same *n* I will pass
12:30 the Egyptians got up during the *n*,
12:31 During the *n* Pharaoh summoned
Ex 12:42 on this *n* all the Israelites are
12:42 the LORD kept vigil that *n*
13:21 and by *n* in a pillar of fire
13:21 that they could travel by day or *n*.
13:22 the pillar of fire by *n* left its place
14:20 Throughout the *n* the cloud
14:20 went near the other all *n* long.
14:21 all that *n* the LORD drove the sea
40:38 and fire was in the cloud by *n*,
Lev 6: 9 the altar hearth throughout the *n*,
8:35 and *n* for seven days and do what
Nu 9:16 and at *n* it looked like fire.
9:21 or by *n*, whenever the cloud lifted,
11: 9 the dew settled on the camp at *n*,
11:32 *n* and all the next day the people
14: 1 That *n* all the people
14:14 by day and a pillar of fire by *n*.
22: 8 "Spend the *n* here," Balaam said
22:20 That *n* God came to Balaam
Dt 1:33 in fire by *n* and in a cloud by day,
16: 1 he brought you out of Egypt by *n*.
28:66 filled with dread both *n* and day,
Jos 1: 8 and *n*, so that you may be careful
2: 8 Before the spies lay down for the *n*,
6:11 to camp and spent the *n* there.
8: 3 out at *n* with these orders:
8: 9 Joshua spent that *n* with the people
8:13 That *n* Joshua went into the valley.
Jdg 6:25 That same *n* the LORD said to him
6:27 he did it at *n* rather
6:40 That *n* God did so.
7: 9 During that *n* the LORD said
9:32 during the *n* you and your men
9:34 and all his troops set out by *n*
16: 1 He went in to spend the *n* with her.
16: 2 They made no move during the *n*,
16: 2 in wait for him all *n* at the city gate.
16: 3 only until the middle of the *n*.
18: 2 of Micah, where they spent the *n*.
19: 7 so he stayed there that *n*.
19: 9 Spend the *n* here; the day is nearly
19:10 But, unwilling to stay another *n*,
19:11 of the Jebusites and spend the *n*."
19:13 spend the *n* in one of those places."
19:15 There they stopped to spend the *n*.
19:15 them into his home for the *n*.
19:20 Only don't spend the *n*
19:25 and abused her throughout the *n*,
20: 4 Gibeah in Benjamin to spend the *n*.
20: 5 During the *n* the men
Ru 3: 8 middle of the *n* something startled
3:13 Stay here for the *n*,
1Sa 3: 2 One *n* Eli, whose eyes were
11:11 of the *n* they broke into the camp
14:34 So everyone brought his ox that *n*
14:36 go down after the Philistines by *n*
15:11 he cried out to the LORD all that *n*
15:16 what the LORD said to me last *n*."
19:10 That *n* David made good his
19:24 He lay that way all that day and *n*.
25:16 *N* and day they were a wall
26: 7 and Abishai went to the army by *n*,
28: 8 and at *n* he and two men went
28:20 eaten nothing all that day and *n*.
28:25 That same *n* they got up and left.
31:12 through the *n* to Beth Shan.
2Sa 2:29 All that *n* Abner and his men
2:32 Joab and his men marched all *n*
4: 7 they traveled all *n* by way
7: 4 That *n* the word of the LORD
17: 8 he will not spend the *n*
17:16 'Do not spend the *n* at the fords
21:10 or the wild animals by *n*.
1Ki 3: 5 to Solomon during the *n* in a dream
3:19 "During the *n* this woman's son
3:20 So she got up in the middle of the *n*
8:29 open toward this temple *n*
8:59 to the LORD our God day and *n*,
19: 9 went into a cave and spent the *n*.
2Ki 6:14 went by *n* and surrounded the city.
7:12 The king got up in the *n*
8:21 he rose up and broke through by *n*;
19:35 That *n* the angel of the LORD
25: 4 fled at *n* through the gate
1Ch 9:27 They would spend the *n* stationed
9:33 responsible for the work day and *n*.
17: 3 That *n* the word of God came
2Ch 1: 7 That *n* God appeared to Solomon

2Ch 6: 20 open toward this temple day and *n*,
7: 12 the LORD appeared to him at *n*
21: 9 he rose up and broke through by *n*.
Ne 1: 6 praying before you day and *n*
2: 12 out during the *n* with a few men.
2: 13 By *n* I went out through the Valley
2: 15 so I went up the valley by *n*,
4: 9 and posted a guard day and *n*
4: 22 guards by *n* and workmen by day."
4: 22 stay inside Jerusalem at *n*,
6: 10 by *n* they are coming to kill you."
9: 12 and by *n* with a pillar of fire
9: 19 nor the pillar of fire by *n* to shine
13: 20 kinds of goods spent the *n*
13: 21 "Why do you spend the *n*
Est 4: 16 or drink for three days, *n* or day.
6: 1 That *n* the king could not sleep;
Job 3: 3 and the *n* it was said, 'A boy is born
3: 6 That *n*— may thick darkness seize
3: 7 May that *n* be barren;
4: 13 Amid disquieting dreams in the *n*,
5: 14 at noon they grope as in the *n*.
7: 4 The *n* drags on, and I toss till dawn.
10: 22 to the land of deepest *n*,
17: 12 These men turn *n* into day;
20: 8 banished like a vision of the *n*.
24: 7 clothes, they spend the *n* naked;
24: 14 in the *n* he steals forth like a thief.
27: 20 snatches him away in the *n*.
29: 19 the dew will lie all *n*
30: 3 land in desolate wastelands at *n*.
30: 17 *N* pierces my bones;
31: 32 had to spend the *n* in the street,
33: 15 In a dream, in a vision of the *n*,
34: 20 in an instant, in the middle of the *n*;
34: 25 he overthrows them in the *n*
35: 10 who gives songs in the *n*,
36: 20 Do not long for the *n*
39: 9 Will he stay by your manger at *n*?
39: 28 on a cliff and stays there at *n*;
Ps 1: 2 on his law he meditates day and *n*.
6: 6 all *n* long I flood my bed
16: 7 even at *n* my heart instructs me.
17: 3 my heart and examine me at *n*,
19: 2 *n* after *n* they display knowledge.
22: 2 by *n*, and am not silent.
30: 5 weeping may remain for a *n*,
32: 4 For day and *n*
42: 3 day and *n*,
42: 8 at *n* his song is with me—
55: 10 *n* they prowl about on its walls;
63: 6 of you through the watches of the *n*
74: 16 day is yours, and yours also the *n*;
77: 2 at *n* I stretched out untiring hands
77: 6 I remembered my songs in the *n*.
78: 14 and with light from the fire all *n*.
88: 1 day and *n* I cry out before you.
90: 4 or like a watch in the *n*.
91: 5 You will not fear the terror of *n*,
92: 2 and your faithfulness at *n*,
104: 20 You bring darkness, it becomes *n*,
105: 39 and a fire to give light at *n*.
119: 55 In the *n* I remember your name,
119:148 through the watches of the *n*,
121: 6 nor the moon by *n*.
134: 1 who minister by *n* in the house
136: 9 the moon and stars to govern the *n*;
139: 11 and the light become *n* around me
139: 12 the *n* will shine like the day,
Pr 7: 9 as the dark of *n* set in.
31: 18 and her lamp does not go out at *n*.
Ecc 2: 23 even at *n* his mind does not rest.
8: 16 his eyes not seeing sleep day or *n*—
SS 3: 1 All *n* long on my bed
3: 8 prepared for the terrors of the *n*.
5: 2 my hair with the dampness of the *n*
7: 11 let us spend the *n* in the villages.
Isa 4: 5 and a glow of flaming fire by *n*;
5: 11 who stay up late at *n*
15: 1 destroyed in a *n*!
15: 1 destroyed in a *n*!
16: 3 Make your shadow like *n*—
21: 8 every *n* I stay at my post.
21: 11 Watchman, what is left of the *n*?"
21: 11 "Watchman, what is left of the *n*?
21: 12 "Morning is coming, but also the *n*.
26: 9 My soul yearns for you in the *n*;
27: 3 I guard it day and *n*

Isa 28: 19 after morning, by day and by *n*,
29: 7 with a vision in the *n*—
30: 29 as on the *n* you celebrate a holy
34: 10 It will not be quenched *n* and day;
34: 14 there the *n* creatures will
38: 12 day and *n* you made an end of me.
38: 13 day and *n* you made an end of me.
58: 10 and your *n* will become like
60: 11 they will never be shut, day or *n*,
62: 6 they will never be silent day or *n*.
Jer 6: 5 So arise, let us attack at *n*
9: 1 I would weep day and *n*
14: 8 like a traveler who stays only a *n*?
14: 17 *n* and day without ceasing;
16: 13 will serve other gods day and *n*,
31: 35 and stars to shine by *n*,
33: 20 and my covenant with the *n*,
33: 20 and *n* no longer come at their
33: 25 and *n* and the fixed laws of heaven
36: 30 the heat by day and the frost by *n*.
39: 4 they left the city at *n* by way
49: 9 If thieves came during the *n*,
52: 7 the city at *n* through the gate
La 1: 2 Bitterly she weeps at *n*,
2: 18 day and *n*;
2: 19 Arise, cry out in the *n*,
2: 19 as the watches of the *n* begin;
Da 2: 19 During the *n* the mystery was
5: 30 That very *n* Belshazzar, king
6: 18 and spent the *n* without eating
7: 2 "In my vision at *n* I looked,
7: 7 in my vision at *n* I looked,
7: 13 "In my vision at *n* I looked,
Hos 4: 5 You stumble day and *n*,
7: 6 Their passion smolders all *n*;
Joel 1: 13 Come, spend the *n* in sackcloth,
Am 5: 8 and darkens day into *n*,
Ob : 5 if robbers in the *n*—
Mic 3: 6 Therefore *n* will come over you,
Zec 1: 8 During the *n* I had a vision—
Mt 2: 14 and his mother during the *n*
14: 25 of the *n* Jesus went out to them,
21: 17 to Bethany, where he spent the *n*.
24: 43 time of *n* the thief was coming,
26: 31 "This very *n* you will all fall away
26: 34 Jesus answered, "this very *n*,
28: 13 'His disciples came during the *n*
Mk 4: 27 *N* and day, whether he sleeps
5: 5 *N* and day among the tombs
6: 48 watch of the *n* he went out to them,
Lk 2: 8 watch over their flocks at *n*.
2: 37 left the temple but worshiped *n*
5: 5 we've worked hard all *n*
6: 12 and spent the *n* praying to God.
12: 20 This very *n* your life will be
12: 38 the second or third watch of the *n*.
17: 34 on that *n* two people will be
18: 7 who cry out to him day and *n*?
21: 37 out to spend the *n* on the hill called
Jn 3: 2 He came to Jesus at *n* and said,
9: 4 *N* is coming, when no one can work
11: 10 walks by *n* that he stumbles,
13: 30 And it was *n*.
19: 39 who earlier had visited Jesus at *n*.
21: 3 but that *n* they caught nothing.
Ac 5: 19 But during the *n* an angel
9: 24 and *n* they kept close watch
9: 25 But his followers took him by *n*
12: 6 The *n* before Herod was
16: 9 During the *n* Paul had a vision
16: 33 hour of the *n* the jailer took them
17: 10 as it was *n*, the brothers sent Paul
18: 9 One *n* the Lord spoke to Paul
20: 31 stopped warning each of you *n*
23: 11 The following *n* the Lord stood
23: 31 took Paul with them during the *n*
26: 7 earnestly serve God day and *n*.
27: 23 Last *n* an angel of the God whose I
27: 27 On the fourteenth *n* we were still
Ro 13: 12 *n* is nearly over; the day is almost
1Co 11: 23 on the *n* he was betrayed,
2Co 11: 25 I spent a *n* and a day
1Th 2: 9 we worked *n* and day in order not
3: 10 *N* and day we pray most earnestly
5: 2 Lord will come like a thief in the *n*.
5: 5 We do not belong to the *n*
5: 7 sleep at *n*, and those who get drunk
5: 7 who get drunk, get drunk at *n*.

2Th 3: 8 On the contrary, we worked *n*
1Ti 5: 5 and continues *n* and day to pray
2Ti 1: 3 *n* and day I constantly remember
Rev 4: 8 Day and *n* they never stop saying:
7: 15 serve him day and *n* in his temple;
8: 12 light, and also a third of the *n*.
12: 10 them before our God day and *n*,
14: 11 *n* for those who worship the beast
20: 10 They will be tormented day and *n*
21: 25 for there will be no *n* there.
22: 5 There will be no more *n*.

NIGHTFALL (NIGHT)

2Sa 19: 7 not a man will be left with you by *n*
2Ch 35: 14 and the fat portions until *n*.

NIGHTS (NIGHT)

Ge 7: 4 the earth for forty days and forty *n*,
7: 12 on the earth forty days and forty *n*.
Ex 24: 18 mountain forty days and forty *n*.
34: 28 and forty *n* without eating bread
Dt 9: 9 mountain forty days and forty *n*;
9: 11 end of the forty days and forty *n*,
9: 18 LORD for forty days and forty *n*;
9: 25 and forty *n* because the LORD had
10: 10 on the mountain forty days and *n*,
1Sa 30: 12 water for three days and three *n*.
2Sa 12: 16 spent the *n* lying on the ground.
1Ki 19: 8 and forty *n* until he reached Horeb,
Job 2: 13 him for seven days and seven *n*.
7: 3 and *n* of misery have been assigned
Isa 65: 4 spend their *n* keeping secret vigil;
Jnh 1: 17 the fish three days and three *n*.
Mt 4: 2 After fasting forty days and forty *n*
12: 40 three *n* in the belly of a huge fish,
12: 40 three *n* in the heart of the earth.
2Co 6: 5 in hard work, sleepless *n*

NIGHTTIME (NIGHT)

Zec 14: 7 or *n*— a day known to the LORD.

NILE

Ge 41: 1 He was standing by the *N*,
41: 3 out of the *N* and stood beside those
41: 17 standing on the bank of the *N*,
Ex 2: 3 the reeds along the bank of the *N*.
2: 5 went down to the *N* to bathe,
4: 9 take some water from the *N*
7: 15 on the bank of the *N* to meet him,
7: 17 I will strike the water of the *N*,
7: 18 The fish in the *N* will die,
7: 20 and struck the water of the *N*,
7: 21 The fish in the *N* died,
7: 24 along the *N* to get drinking water,
7: 25 after the LORD struck the *N*.
8: 3 The *N* will teem with frogs.
8: 9 for those that remain in the *N*."
8: 11 they will remain only in the *N*."
17: 5 staff with which you struck the *N*,
Isa 19: 7 Every sown field along the *N*
19: 7 also the plants along the *N*,
19: 8 all who cast hooks into the *N*;
23: 3 harvest of the *N* was the revenue
23: 10 Daughter of Tarshish, like the *N*,
Jer 46: 7 "Who is this that rises like the *N*,
46: 8 Egypt rises like the *N*,
Eze 29: 3 You say, "The *N* is mine;
29: 9 Because you said, "The *N* is mine;
30: 12 I will dry up the streams of the *N*
Am 8: 8 The whole land will rise like the *N*;
9: 5 the whole land rises like the *N*,
Na 3: 8 situated on the *N*,
Zec 10: 11 all the depths of the *N* will dry up.

NIMRAH

Nu 32: 3 Dibon, Jazer, *N*, Heshbon, Elealeh,

NIMRIM

Isa 15: 6 The waters of *N* are dried up
Jer 48: 34 even the waters of *N* are dried up.

NIMROD

Ge 10: 8 Cush was the father of *N*, who grew
10: 9 "Like *N*, a mighty hunter
1Ch 1: 10 Cush was the father of *N*, who grew
Mic 5: 6 the land of *N* with drawn sword.

NIMSHI
1Ki 19: 16 son of *N* king over Israel,
2Ki 9: 2 son of Jehoshaphat, the son of *N*.
9: 14 the son of *N*, conspired
9: 20 that of Jehu son of *N*—
2Ch 22: 7 with Joram to meet Jehu son of *N*,

NINEVEH (NINEVITES)
Ge 10: 11 where he built *N*, Rehoboth Ir,
10: 12 is between *N* and Calah; that
2Ki 19: 36 He returned to *N* and stayed there.
Isa 37: 37 He returned to *N* and stayed there.
Jnh 1: 2 "Go to the great city of *N*
3: 2 "Go to the great city of *N*
3: 3 Now *N* was a very large city;
3: 3 word of the LORD and went to *N*.
3: 4 more days and *N* will be
3: 6 the news reached the king of *N*,
3: 7 Then he issued a proclamation in *N*
4: 11 But *N* has more than a hundred
Na 1: 1 An oracle concerning *N*.
1: 8 he will make an end of ⌊*N*⌋;
1: 11 From you, ⌊O *N*,⌋ has one come
1: 14 a command concerning you, ⌊*N*⌋:
2: 1 attacker advances against you, ⌊*N*⌋.
2: 8 *N* is like a pool,
3: 7 '*N* is in ruins—who will mourn
Zep 2: 13 leaving *N* utterly desolate
Mt 12: 41 The men of *N* will stand up
Lk 11: 32 The men of *N* will stand up

NINEVITES (NINEVEH)
Jnh 3: 5 The *N* believed God.
Lk 11: 30 For as Jonah was a sign to the *N*,

NISAN
Ne 2: 1 In the month of *N*
Est 3: 7 of *N*, they cast the *pur* (that is,

NISROCH
2Ki 19: 37 in the temple of his god *N*,
Isa 37: 38 in the temple of his god *N*,

NOADIAH
Ezr 8: 33 son of Jeshua and *N* son of Binnui.
Ne 6: 14 remember also the prophetess *N*

NOAH (NOAH'S)
Ge 5: 29 He named him *N* and said,
5: 30 After *N* was born, Lamech lived
5: 32 After *N* was 500 years old,
6: 8 But *N* found favor in the eyes
6: 9 This is the account of *N*.
6: 9 *N* was a righteous man, blameless
6: 10 *N* had three sons: Shem, Ham
6: 13 So God said to *N*, "I am going
6: 22 *N* did everything just as God
7: 1 The LORD then said to *N*,
7: 5 And *N* did all that the LORD
7: 6 *N* was six hundred years old
7: 7 And *N* and his sons and his wife
7: 9 as God had commanded *N*.
7: 9 came to *N* and entered the ark,
7: 13 On that very day *N* and his sons,
7: 15 the breath of life in them came to *N*
7: 16 as God had commanded *N*.
7: 23 Only *N* was left, and those
8: 1 But God remembered *N*
8: 6 After forty days *N* opened
8: 9 so it returned to *N* in the ark.
8: 11 *N* knew that the water had receded
8: 13 *N* then removed the covering
8: 15 Then God said to *N*, "Come out
8: 18 *N* came out, together with his sons
8: 20 Then *N* built an altar to the LORD
9: 1 Then God blessed *N* and his sons,
9: 8 Then God said to *N* and to his sons
9: 17 So God said to *N*, "This is the sign
9: 18 The sons of *N* who came out
9: 19 These were the three sons of *N*,
9: 20 *N*, a man of the soil, proceeded
9: 24 When *N* awoke from his wine
9: 28 After the flood *N* lived 350 years.
9: 29 Altogether, *N* lived 950 years,
Nu 26: 33 whose names were Mahlah, *N*,
27: 1 *N*, Hoglah, Milcah and Tirzah.
36: 11 Tirzah, Hoglah, Milcah and *N*—
Jos 17: 3 whose names were Mahlah, *N*,
1Ch 1: 3 Enoch, Methuselah, Lamech, *N*.
1: 4 The sons of *N*: Shem, Ham
Isa 54: 9 of *N* would never again cover
54: 9 "To me this is like the days of *N*,
Eze 14: 14 even if these three men—*N*,
14: 20 the Sovereign LORD, even if *N*,
Mt 24: 37 As it was in the days of *N*,
24: 38 up to the day *N* entered the ark;
Lk 3: 36 the son of *N*, the son of Lamech,
17: 26 "Just as it was in the days of *N*,
17: 27 up to the day *N* entered the ark.
Heb 11: 7 By faith *N*, when warned about
1Pe 3: 20 of *N* while the ark was being built.
2Pe 2: 5 but protected *N*, a preacher

NOAH'S (NOAH)
Ge 7: 11 In the six hundredth year of *N* life,
8: 13 of the first month of *N* six hundred
10: 1 Ham and Japheth, *N* sons,
10: 32 These are the clans of *N* sons,

NOB
1Sa 21: 1 went to *N*, to Ahimelech the priest.
22: 9 to Ahimelech son of Ahitub at *N*.
22: 11 who were the priests at *N*,
22: 19 He also put to the sword *N*,
Ne 11: 32 in Anathoth, *N* and Ananiah,
Isa 10: 32 This day they will halt at *N*;

NOBAH
Nu 32: 42 And *N* captured Kenath
32: 42 and called it *N* after himself.
Jdg 8: 11 the route of the nomads east of *N*

NOBILITY (NOBLE)
Est 1: 18 of the *n* who have heard about
Da 1: 3 from the royal family and the *n*—

NOBLE (NOBILITY NOBLEMAN NOBLES NOBLEST)
Ru 3: 11 you are a woman of *n* character.
Est 6: 9 to one of the king's most *n* princes.
Ps 45: 1 My heart is stirred by a *n* theme
Pr 12: 4 of *n* character is her husband's
31: 10 A wife of *n* character who can find?
31: 29 "Many women do *n* things,
Ecc 10: 17 O land whose king is of *n* birth
Isa 32: 5 No longer will the fool be called *n*
32: 8 But the *n* man makes *n* plans,
32: 8 and by *n* deeds he stands.
Lk 8: 15 good soil stands for those with a *n*
19: 12 "A man of *n* birth went
Ac 17: 11 were of more *n* character
Ro 9: 21 of clay some pottery for *n* purposes
1Co 1: 26 not many were of *n* birth.
Php 4: 8 whatever is *n*, whatever is right,
1Ti 3: 1 an overseer, he desires a *n* task.
2Ti 2: 20 some are for *n* purposes
2: 21 be an instrument for *n* purposes,
Jas 2: 7 who are slandering the *n* name

NOBLEMAN (NOBLE)
Pr 25: 7 for him to humiliate you before a *n*.

NOBLES (NOBLE)
Nu 21: 18 that the *n* of the people sank—
21: 18 the *n* with scepters and staffs."
Jdg 5: 13 came down to the *n*;
5: 25 for *n* she brought him curdled milk.
2Sa 10: 3 the Ammonite *n* said
1Ki 21: 8 and *n* who lived in Naboth's city
21: 11 *n* who lived in Naboth's city did
2Ki 24: 12 his *n* and his officials all
1Ch 19: 3 the Ammonite *n* said to Hanun,
2Ch 23: 20 commanders of hundreds, the *n*,
Ne 2: 16 or the priests or *n* or officials
3: 5 but their *n* would not put their
4: 14 I stood up and said to the *n*,
4: 19 Then I said to the *n*, the officials
5: 7 then accused the *n* and officials.
5: 12 the priests and made the *n*
6: 17 Also, in those days the *n*
7: 5 it into my heart to assemble the *n*,
10: 29 these now join their brothers the *n*,
13: 17 I rebuked the *n* of Judah
Est 1: 3 reign he gave a banquet for all his *n*
1: 3 the *n* of the provinces were present
1: 11 beauty to the people and *n*,
Est 1: 14 seven *n* of Persia and Media who
1: 16 the king but also against all the *n*
1: 16 the presence of the king and the *n*,
1: 18 to all the king's *n* in the same way.
1: 21 his *n* were pleased with this advice,
2: 18 Esther's banquet, for all his *n*
3: 1 higher than that of all the other *n*.
3: 12 and the *n* of the various peoples.
5: 11 had elevated him above the other *n*
8: 9 *n* of the 127 provinces stretching
9: 3 And all the *n* of the provinces,
Job 12: 21 He pours contempt on *n*
29: 10 the voices of the *n* were hushed,
34: 18 and to *n*, 'You are wicked,'
Ps 47: 9 The *n* of the nations assemble
83: 11 Make their *n* like Oreb and Zeeb,
107: 40 he who pours contempt on *n*
149: 8 their *n* with shackles of iron,
Pr 8: 16 and all *n* who rule on earth.
Isa 5: 14 into it will descend their *n*
13: 2 them to enter the gates of the *n*.
34: 12 Her *n* will have nothing there
Jer 14: 3 The *n* send their servants for water;
27: 20 along with all the *n* of Judah
39: 6 and also killed all the *n* of Judah.
Eze 17: 12 and carried off her king and her *n*,
Da 4: 36 My advisers and *n* sought me out,
5: 1 banquet for a thousand of his *n*
5: 2 so that the king and his *n*, his wives
5: 3 and the king and his *n*, his wives
5: 9 His *n* were baffled.
5: 10 the voices of the king and his *n*,
5: 23 and you and your *n*, your wives
6: 17 and with the rings of his *n*,
Jnh 3: 7 By the decree of the king and his *n*:
Na 3: 10 Lots were cast for her *n*,
3: 18 your *n* lie down to rest.

NOBLEST (NOBLE)
SS 3: 7 the *n* of Israel,

NOCTURNAL
Dt 23: 10 is unclean because of a *n* emission,

NOD
Ge 4: 16 presence and lived in the land of *N*,

NODAB
1Ch 5: 19 Hagrites, Jetur, Naphish and *N*.

NOGAH
1Ch 3: 7 Elishua, Eliphelet, *N*, Nepheg,
14: 6 Elishua, Elpelet, *N*, Nepheg,

NOHAH
1Ch 8: 2 *N* the fourth and Rapha the fifth.

NOISE (NOISY)
Ex 32: 17 When Joshua heard the *n*
1Ki 1: 41 meaning of all the *n* in the city?"
1: 45 That's the *n* you hear.
2Ki 11: 13 When Athaliah heard the *n* made
2Ch 23: 12 When Athaliah heard the *n*
Ezr 3: 13 the people made so much *n*.
Isa 13: 4 Listen, a *n* on the mountains,
14: 11 along with the *n* of your harps;
24: 8 the *n* of the revelers has stopped,
29: 6 and earthquake and great *n*,
66: 6 hear that *n* from the temple!
Jer 46: 17 king of Egypt is only a loud *n*;
47: 3 at the *n* of enemy chariots
50: 22 The *n* of battle is in the land,
50: 22 the *n* of great destruction!
Eze 23: 42 "The *n* of a carefree crowd was
26: 10 tremble at the *n* of the war horses,
37: 7 there was a *n*, a rattling sound,
Joel 2: 5 With a *n* like that of chariots
Am 5: 23 Away with the *n* of your songs!

NOISY (NOISE)
Ps 64: 2 from that *n* crowd of evildoers,
Pr 1: 21 head of the *n* streets she cries out,
Isa 32: 14 the *n* city deserted;
Jer 48: 45 the skulls of the *n* boasters.
51: 55 he will silence her *n* din.
Eze 26: 13 I will put an end to your *n* songs,
Mt 9: 23 the flute players and the *n* crowd,

NOMAD (NOMADS)

Jer 3: 2 sat like a *n* in the desert.

NOMADS (NOMAD)

Jdg 8: 11 by the route of the *n* east of Nobah
Jer 35: 7 time in the land where you are *n*.'

NON-GREEKS

Ro 1: 14 am obligated both to Greeks and *n*,

NONSENSE

Job 21: 34 can you console me with your *n?*
Isa 44: 25 and turns it into *n*,
Lk 24: 11 their words seemed to them like *n*.

NOON (NOONDAY)

Ge 43: 16 they are to eat with me at *n*.''
43: 25 gifts for Joseph's arrival at *n*,
1Ki 18: 26 name of Baal from morning till *n*.
18: 27 At *n* Elijah began to taunt them.
20: 16 They set out at *n* while Ben-Hadad
2Ki 4: 20 the boy sat on her lap until *n*,
Ne 8: 3 aloud from daybreak till *n*
Job 5: 14 at *n* they grope as in the night.
Ps 55: 17 Evening, morning and *n*
Isa 16: 3 at high *n*.
Jer 6: 4 Arise, let us attack at *n!*
20: 16 a battle cry at *n*.
Am 8: 9 ''I will make the sun go down at *n*
Ac 10: 9 About *n* the following day
22: 6 About *n* as I came near Damascus,
26: 13 About *n*, O king, as I was

NOONDAY (NOON)

2Sa 4: 5 day while he was taking his *n* rest.
Job 11: 17 Life will be brighter than *n*,
Ps 37: 6 justice of your cause like the *n* sun.
Isa 58: 10 your night will become like the *n*.

NOOSE

Job 18: 10 A *n* is hidden for him
Pr 7: 22 like a deer stepping into a *n*

NOPHAH

Nu 21: 30 have demolished them as far as *N*,

NORTH (NORTHERN NORTHWARD)

Ge 13: 14 from where you are and look *n*
14: 15 as far as Hobah, *n* of Damascus.
28: 14 to the *n* and to the south.
Ex 26: 20 the *n* side of the tabernacle,
26: 35 on the *n* side of the tabernacle
27: 11 The *n* side shall also be a hundred
36: 25 the *n* side of the tabernacle,
38: 11 *n* side was also a hundred cubits
40: 22 the Tent of Meeting on the *n* side
Lev 1: 11 it at the *n* side of the altar
Nu 2: 25 On the *n* will be the divisions
3: 35 were to camp on the *n* side
34: 9 will be your boundary on the *n*.
35: 5 and three thousand on the *n*,
Dt 2: 3 country long enough; now turn *n*.
3: 12 and the Gadites the territory *n*
3: 27 look west and *n* and south and east.
Jos 8: 11 They set up camp *n* of Ai,
8: 13 in the camp to the *n* of the city
13: 3 to the territory of Ekron on the *n*,
15: 6 continued *n* of Beth Arabah
15: 7 of Achor and turned *n* to Gilgal,
16: 6 on the *n* it curved eastward
17: 10 and bordered Asher on the *n*
17: 10 to Ephraim, on the *n* to Manasseh.
18: 5 of Joseph in its territory on the *n*.
18: 12 On the *n* side their boundary began
18: 16 *n* of the Valley of Rephaim.
18: 17 curved *n*, went to En Shemesh,
19: 14 around on the *n* to Hannathon
19: 27 went *n* to Beth Emek and Neiel,
24: 30 of Ephraim, *n* of Mount Gaash.
Jdg 2: 9 of Ephraim, *n* of Mount Gaash.
7: 1 The camp of Midian was *n* of them
21: 19 in Shiloh, to the *n* of Bethel,
1Sa 14: 5 stood to the *n* toward Micmash,
1Ki 7: 21 and the one to the *n* Boaz.
7: 25 three facing *n*, three facing west,
7: 39 of the temple and five on the *n*.
2Ki 11: 11 side to the *n* side of the temple.
16: 14 put it on the *n* side of the new altar.
1Ch 9: 24 were on the four sides: east, west, *n*
26: 14 the lot for the *N* Gate fell to him.
26: 17 day on the east, four a day on the *n*,
2Ch 3: 17 and the one to the *n* Boaz.
3: 17 one to the south and one to the *n*.
4: 4 three facing *n*, three facing west,
4: 6 on the south side and five on the *n*.
4: 7 on the south side and five on the *n*.
4: 8 on the south side and five on the *n*.
23: 10 side to the *n* side of the temple.
Job 23: 9 When he is at work in the *n*,
37: 22 Out of the *n* he comes
Ps 89: 12 You created the *n* and the south;
107: 3 and west, from *n* and south.
Pr 25: 23 As a *n* wind brings rain,
Ecc 1: 6 and turns to the *n;*
11: 3 falls to the south or to the *n*,
SS 4: 16 Awake, *n* wind,
Isa 14: 31 cloud of smoke comes from the *n*,
41: 25 ''I have stirred up one from the *n*,
43: 6 I will say to the *n*, 'Give them up!'
49: 12 some from the *n*, some
Jer 1: 13 away from the *n*,'' I answered.
1: 14 ''From the *n* disaster will be
3: 12 proclaim this message toward the *n*
4: 6 I am bringing disaster from the *n*,
6: 1 For disaster looms out of the *n*,
6: 22 coming from the land of the *n;*
10: 22 commotion from the land of the *n!*
13: 20 those who are coming from the *n*.
15: 12 iron from the *n*— or bronze?
16: 15 out of the land of the *n*
23: 8 of Israel up out of the land of the *n*
25: 9 summon all the peoples of the *n*
25: 26 all the kings of the *n*, near and far,
31: 8 from the land of the *n*
46: 6 In the *n* by the River Euphrates
46: 10 in the land of the *n* by the River
46: 20 coming against her from the *n*.
46: 24 handed over to the people of the *n*
47: 2 how the waters are rising in the *n;*
50: 3 A nation from the *n* will attack her
50: 9 and from the *n* she will be captured
50: 9 from the land of the *n*.
50: 41 An army is coming from the *n;*
51: 48 for out of the *n*
Eze 1: 4 a windstorm coming out of the *n*—
8: 3 to the entrance to the *n* gate
8: 5 and in the entrance *n* of the gate
8: 5 ''Son of man, look toward the *n*.''
8: 14 entrance to the *n* gate of the house
9: 2 which faces *n*, each
16: 46 who lived to the *n* of you
20: 47 from south to *n* will be scorched
21: 4 against everyone from south to *n*.
26: 7 From the *n* I am going to bring
32: 30 ''All the princes of the *n*
38: 6 from the far *n* with all its troops—
38: 15 come from your place in the far *n*,
39: 2 I will bring you from the far *n*
40: 19 on the east side as well as on the *n*.
40: 20 and width of the gate facing *n*,
40: 23 to the inner court facing the *n* gate,
40: 35 Then he brought me to the *n* gate
40: 40 to the *n* gateway were two tables,
40: 44 one at the side of the *n* gate
40: 44 side of the south gate and facing *n*.
40: 46 and the room facing *n* is
41: 11 one on the *n* and another
42: 1 the outer wall on the *n* side.
42: 2 whose door faced *n* was a hundred
42: 4 Their doors were on the *n*.
42: 11 These were like the rooms on the *n*
42: 11 on the *n* were the doorways
42: 13 ''The *n* and south rooms facing
42: 17 He measured the *n* side; it was five
44: 4 me by way of the *n* gate to the front
46: 9 is to go out the *n* gate.
46: 9 whoever enters by the *n* gate
46: 19 gate to the sacred rooms facing *n*,
47: 2 out through the *n* gate
47: 15 ''On the *n* side it will run
47: 17 This will be the *n* boundary.
47: 17 with the border of Hamath to the *n*
48: 10 cubits long on the *n* side, 10,000
48: 16 *n* side 4,500 cubits, the south side
48: 17 the city will be 250 cubits on the *n*,
48: 30 on the *n* side, which is 4,500
Eze 48: 31 gates on the *n* side will be the gate
Da 8: 4 charged toward the west and the *n*
11: 6 king of the *N* to make an alliance,
11: 7 the forces of the king of the *N*
11: 8 will leave the king of the *N* alone.
11: 9 king of the *N* will invade the realm
11: 11 and fight against the king of the *N*,
11: 13 of the *N* will muster another army,
11: 15 Then the king of the *N* will come
11: 28 The king of the *N* will return
11: 40 and the king of the *N* will storm out
11: 44 the east and the *n* will alarm him,
Am 8: 12 and wander from *n* to east,
Zep 2: 13 stretch out his hand against the *n*
Zec 2: 6 Flee from the land of the *n*,''
6: 6 going toward the *n* country,
6: 8 rest in the land of the *n*.''
6: 8 toward the *n* country have given
14: 4 with half of the mountain moving *n*
Lk 13: 29 and west and *n* and south,
Rev 21: 13 three on the *n*, three on the south

NORTHEASTER (EAST)

Ac 27: 14 called the ''*N*,'' swept

NORTHERN (NORTH)

Nu 34: 7 '' 'For your *n* boundary, run a line
Jos 11: 2 and to the *n* kings who were
15: 5 The *n* boundary started
15: 8 Valley at the *n* end of the Valley
15: 10 ran along the *n* slope
15: 11 It went to the *n* slope of Ekron,
17: 9 of Manasseh was the *n* side
18: 12 passed the *n* slope of Jericho
18: 18 to the *n* slope of Beth Arabah
18: 19 and came out at the *n* bay
18: 19 to the *n* slope of Beth Hoglah
Job 26: 7 He spreads out the *n* ⌞skies⌟
Jer 1: 15 the peoples of the *n* kingdoms,''
3: 18 they will come from a *n* land
Eze 47: 17 along the *n* border of Damascus,
48: 1 and the *n* border of Damascus next
48: 1 listed by name: At the *n* frontier,
Joel 2: 20 I will drive the *n* army far from you

NORTHWARD (NORTH)

Eze 42: 1 man led me *n* into the outer court

NORTHWEST (WEST)

Ac 27: 12 facing both southwest and *n*.

NOSE (NOSES)

Ge 24: 22 took out a gold *n* ring weighing
24: 30 As soon as he had seen the *n* ring,
24: 47 the ring in her *n* and the bracelets
2Ki 19: 28 I will put my hook in your *n*
2Ch 33: 11 prisoner, put a hook in his *n*,
Job 40: 24 or trap him and pierce his *n?*
41: 2 Can you put a cord through his *n*
Pr 30: 33 as twisting the *n* produces blood,
SS 7: 4 Your *n* is like the tower of Lebanon
Isa 3: 21 the signet rings and *n* rings,
37: 29 I will put my hook in your *n*
Eze 8: 17 them putting the branch to their *n!*
16: 12 and I put a ring on your *n*,

NOSES (NOSE)

Ps 115: 6 *n*, but they cannot smell;
Eze 23: 25 They will cut off your *n*

NOSTRILS

Ge 2: 7 and breathed into his *n* the breath
7: 22 the breath of life in its *n* died.
Ex 15: 8 By the blast of your *n*
Nu 11: 20 until it comes out of your *n*
2Sa 10: 6 had become a stench in David's *n*,
16: 21 yourself a stench in your father's *n*,
22: 9 Smoke rose from his *n;*
22: 16 at the blast of breath from his *n*.
1Ch 19: 6 had become a stench in David's *n*,
Job 27: 3 the breath of God in my *n*,
41: 20 Smoke pours from his *n*
Ps 18: 8 Smoke rose from his *n;*
18: 15 at the blast of breath from your *n*.
Isa 2: 22 who has but a breath in his *n*.
65: 5 Such people are smoke in my *n*,
Am 4: 10 I filled your *n* with the stench

NOTABLE (NOTE)
Am 6: 1 you *n* men of the foremost nation,

NOTE (ANNOTATIONS NOTABLE NOTES)
Ru 3: 4 *n* the place where he is lying.
2Sa 3: 36 the people took *n* and were
Job 11: 11 he sees evil, does he not take *n?*
34: 25 Because he takes *n* of their deeds,
Ps 106: 44 But he took *n* of their distress
Pr 21: 12 The Righteous One takes *n*
23: 1 *n* well what is before you,
Jer 31: 21 Take *n* of the highway,
Eze 20: 37 I will take *n* of you as you pass
Ac 4: 13 and they took *n* that these men had
Php 3: 17 take *n* of those who live according
2Th 3: 14 in this letter, take special *n* of him.
Jas 1: 19 My dear brothers, take *n* of this:

NOTES (NOTE)
1Co 14: 7 there is a distinction in the *n?*

NOTICE (NOTICED NOTICING)
Ge 39: 7 a while his master's wife took *n*
Dt 21: 11 if you *n* among the captives
Ru 2: 10 favor in your eyes that you *n* me—
2: 19 Blessed be the man who took *n*
2Sa 9: 8 that you should *n* a dead dog like
2Ki 3: 14 look at you or even *n* you.
Job 35: 15 and he does not take the least *n*
Eze 38: 14 in safety, will you not take *n* of it?
Hos 7: 9 but he does not *n*.
Jnh 1: 6 Maybe he will take *n* of us,
Mk 15: 26 The written *n* of the charge
Lk 23: 38 There was a written *n* above him,
Jn 19: 19 Pilate had a *n* prepared
Ac 21: 26 to the temple to give *n* of the date
26: 26 none of this has escaped his *n*,

NOTICED (NOTICE)
Ge 31: 2 And Jacob *n* that Laban's attitude
2Sa 12: 19 David *n* that his servants were
1Ki 21: 29 "Have you *n* how Ahab has
Pr 7: 7 I *n* among the young men,
Isa 58: 3 and you have not *n?*'
Jer 33: 24 "Have you not *n* that these people
Mt 22: 11 he *n* a man there who was not
Lk 14: 7 When he *n* how the guests picked
Jn 11: 31 *n* how quickly she got up

NOTICING (NOTICE)
Mk 12: 28 *N* that Jesus had given them a good
Lk 11: 38 *n* that Jesus did not first wash

NOTIONS
Job 15: 2 a wise man answer with empty *n*
Col 2: 18 mind puffs him up with idle *n*.

NOTORIOUS
Mt 27: 16 At that time they had a *n* prisoner,

NOURISH (NOURISHED NOURISHING NOURISHMENT WELL-NOURISHED)
Pr 10: 21 The lips of the righteous *n* many,
27: 27 and to *n* your servant girls.

NOURISHED (NOURISH)
Dt 32: 13 He *n* him with honey from the rock
Job 21: 24 his body well *n*,
Eze 31: 4 The waters *n* it,
Da 1: 15 better *n* than any of the young men

NOURISHING (NOURISH)
Ro 11: 17 and now share in the *n* sap

NOURISHMENT (NOURISH)
Pr 3: 8 and *n* to your bones.

NUBIANS
Da 11: 43 with the Libyans and *N*

NUGGETS
Job 22: 24 and assign your *n* to the dust,
28: 6 and its dust contains *n* of gold.

NULLIFIED (NULLIFY)
Nu 30: 12 Her husband has *n* them,

NULLIFIES (NULLIFY)
Nu 30: 8 he *n* the vow that obligates her
30: 12 But if her husband *n* them
30: 15 he *n* them some time

NULLIFY (NULLIFIED NULLIFIES)
Nu 30: 13 may confirm or *n* any vow she
Mt 15: 6 Thus you *n* the word of God
Mk 7: 13 Thus you *n* the word of God
Ro 3: 3 lack of faith *n* God's faithfulness?
3: 31 Do we, then, *n* the law by this faith
1Co 1: 28 to *n* the things that are,

NUN
Ex 33: 11 son of *N* did not leave the tent.
Nu 11: 28 of *N*, who had been Moses' aide
13: 8 Hoshea son of *N*; from the tribe
13: 16 son of *N* the name Joshua.)
14: 6 Joshua son of *N* and Caleb son
14: 30 of Jephunneh and Joshua son of *N*.
14: 38 only Joshua son of *N* and Caleb son
26: 65 of Jephunneh and Joshua son of *N*.
27: 18 "Take Joshua son of *N*, a man
32: 12 the Kenizzite and Joshua son of *N*,
32: 28 son of *N* and to the family heads
34: 17 the priest and Joshua son of *N*.
Dt 1: 38 Joshua son of *N*, will enter it.
31: 23 command to Joshua son of *N*:
32: 44 Moses came with Joshua son of *N*
34: 9 Now Joshua son of *N* was filled
Jos 1: 1 the LORD said to Joshua son of *N*,
2: 1 son of *N* secretly sent two spies
2: 23 and came to Joshua son of *N*
6: 6 Joshua son of *N* called the priests
14: 1 Joshua son of *N* and the heads
17: 4 Joshua son of *N*, and the leaders
19: 49 of *N* an inheritance among them,
19: 51 Joshua son of *N* and the heads
21: 1 Eleazar the priest, Joshua son of *N*,
24: 29 Joshua son of *N*, the servant
Jdg 2: 8 Joshua son of *N*, the servant
1Ki 16: 34 spoken by Joshua son of *N*.
1Ch 7: 27 *N* his son and Joshua his son.
Ne 8: 17 of Joshua son of *N* until that day,

NURSE (NURSED NURSING)
Ge 21: 7 that Sarah would *n* children?
24: 59 with her *n* and Abraham's servant
35: 8 Now Deborah, Rebekah's *n*,
Ex 2: 7 women to *n* the baby for you?"
2: 9 "Take this baby and *n* him for me,
Nu 11: 12 in my arms, as a *n* carries an infant,
2Sa 4: 4 His *n* picked him up and fled,
1Ki 3: 21 I got up to *n* my son—
2Ki 11: 2 and his *n* in a bedroom to hide him
11: 3 hidden with his *n* at the temple
2Ch 22: 11 put him and his *n* in a bedroom.
Isa 66: 11 For you will *n* and be satisfied
66: 12 you will *n* and be carried
La 4: 3 breasts to *n* their young,

NURSED (NURSE)
Ex 2: 9 woman took the baby and *n* him.
1Sa 1: 23 *n* her son until she had weaned him
Job 3: 12 and breasts that I might be *n?*
SS 8: 1 who was *n* at my mother's breasts!
Isa 60: 16 and be *n* at royal breasts.
Mk 6: 19 Herodias *n* a grudge against John
Lk 11: 27 who gave you birth and *n* you."
23: 29 and the breasts that never *n!*'

NURSING (NURSE)
Ge 33: 13 and cows that are *n* their young.
Isa 49: 23 and their queens your *n* mothers.
Joel 2: 16 those *n* at the breast.
Mt 24: 19 for pregnant women and *n* mothers
Mk 13: 17 for pregnant women and *n* mothers
Lk 21: 23 for pregnant women and *n* mothers

NURTURED (WELL-NURTURED)
La 4: 5 Those *n* in purple

NUT (NUTS)
SS 6: 11 I went down to the grove of *n* trees

NUTS (NUT)
Ge 43: 11 some pistachio *n* and almonds.

NYMPHA
Col 4: 15 to *N* and the church in her house.

OAK (OAKS)
Ge 35: 4 them under the *o* at Shechem.
35: 8 buried under the *o* below Bethel.
Jos 24: 26 under the *o* near the holy place
Jdg 6: 11 and sat down under the *o*
6: 19 offered them to him under the *o*.
2Sa 18: 9 the thick branches of a large *o*,
18: 10 saw Absalom hanging in an *o* tree."
18: 14 was still alive in the *o* tree.
1Ki 13: 14 found him sitting under an *o* tree
Isa 1: 30 You will be like an *o*
6: 13 But as the terebinth and *o*
44: 14 or perhaps took a cypress or *o*.
Eze 6: 13 spreading tree and every leafy *o*—
Hos 4: 13 under *o*, poplar and terebinth,

OAKS (OAK)
Ps 29: 9 of the LORD twists the *o*
Isa 1: 29 be ashamed because of the sacred *o*
2: 13 and all the *o* of Bashan,
57: 5 You burn with lust among the *o*
61: 3 They will be called *o*
Eze 27: 6 Of *o* from Bashan
Am 2: 9 and strong as the *o*.
Zec 11: 2 Wail, *o* of Bashan;

OARS (OARSMEN)
Isa 33: 21 No galley with *o* will ride them,
Eze 27: 6 they made your *o*;
27: 29 All who handle the *o*
Mk 6: 48 saw the disciples straining at the *o*,

OARSMEN (OARS)
Eze 27: 8 of Sidon and Arvad were your *o*;
27: 26 Your *o* take you

OATH (OATHS)
Ge 14: 22 have taken an *o* that I will accept
21: 31 the two men swore an *o* there.
24: 7 spoke to me and promised me on *o*,
24: 8 released from this *o* of mine.
24: 9 swore an *o* to him concerning this
24: 37 my master made me swear an *o*,
24: 41 you will be released from my *o*
24: 41 you will be released from my *o*.'
25: 33 So he swore an *o* to him, selling his
26: 3 and will confirm the *o* I swore
26: 31 next morning the men swore an *o*
31: 53 So Jacob took an *o* in the name
50: 5 'My father made me swear an *o*
50: 24 land to the land he promised on *o*
50: 25 the sons of Israel swear an *o*
Ex 13: 11 as he promised on *o* to you
13: 19 the sons of Israel swear an *o*.
22: 11 settled by the taking of an *o*
33: 1 up to the land I promised on *o*
Lev 5: 4 if a person thoughtlessly takes an *o*
Nu 5: 19 priest shall put the woman under *o*
5: 21 woman under this curse of the *o*—
11: 12 promised on *o* to their forefathers?
14: 16 the land he promised them on *o*;
14: 23 promised on *o* to their forefathers.
30: 2 or takes an *o* to obligate himself
30: 10 herself by a pledge under *o*
32: 10 that day and he swore this *o*:
32: 11 will see the land I promised on *o*
Dt 4: 31 which he confirmed to them by *o*.
6: 18 promised on *o* to your forefathers,
6: 23 promised on *o* to our forefathers.
7: 8 and kept the *o* he swore
8: 1 promised on *o* to your forefathers.
13: 17 promised on *o* to your forefathers,
19: 8 promised on *o* to your forefathers,
26: 15 as you promised on *o*
28: 9 as he promised you on *o*,
29: 12 you this day and sealing with an *o*,
29: 14 making this covenant, with its *o*,
29: 19 a person hears the words of this *o*,
31: 20 promised on *o* to their forefathers,
31: 21 into the land I promised them on *o*
31: 23 into the land I promised them on *o*,
34: 4 "This is the land I promised on *o*
Jos 2: 17 "This *o* you made us swear will not
2: 20 from the *o* you made us swear."
6: 22 in accordance with your *o* to her."

Jos 6: 26 Joshua pronounced this solemn *o:*
9: 15 of the assembly ratified it by *o.*
9: 18 of the assembly had sworn an *o*
9: 19 "We have given them our *o*
9: 20 us for breaking the *o* we swore
Jdg 21: 1 of Israel had taken an *o* at Mizpah:
21: 5 taken a solemn *o* that anyone who
21: 7 since we have taken an *o*
21: 18 we Israelites have taken this *o:*
1Sa 14: 24 had bound the people under an *o,*
14: 26 because they feared the *o.*
14: 27 had bound the people with the *o,*
14: 28 bound the army under a strict *o,*
19: 6 to Jonathan and took this *o:*
20: 3 But David took an *o* and said,
20: 17 had David reaffirm his *o* out
24: 22 So David gave his *o* to Saul.
2Sa 3: 9 the LORD promised him on *o*
3: 35 but David took an *o,* saying,
19: 23 And the king promised him on *o.*
21: 7 because of the *o* before the LORD
1Ki 1: 29 king then took an *o:* "As surely
2: 43 Why then did you not keep your *o*
8: 31 and is required to take an *o*
8: 31 and swears the *o* before your altar
2Ki 11: 4 and put them under *o* at the temple
25: 24 Gedaliah took an *o*
1Ch 16: 16 the *o* he swore to Isaac.
2Ch 6: 22 and is required to take an *o*
6: 22 and swears the *o* before your altar
15: 14 They took an *o* to the LORD
15: 15 All Judah rejoiced about the *o*
36: 13 who had made him take an *o*
Ezr 10: 5 And they took the *o.*
10: 5 Israel under *o* to do what had been
Ne 5: 12 officials take an *o* to do what they
6: 18 in Judah were under *o* to him,
10: 29 and an *o* to follow the Law
13: 25 I made them take an *o*
Ps 15: 4 who keeps his *o*
95: 11 So I declared on *o* in my anger,
105: 9 the *o* he swore to Isaac.
119: 106 I have taken an *o* and confirmed it,
132: 2 He swore an *o* to the LORD
132: 11 The LORD swore an *o* to David,
132: 11 a sure *o* that he will not revoke:
Pr 29: 24 under *o* and dare not testify.
Ecc 8: 2 because you took an *o* before God.
Isa 65: 16 he who takes an *o* in the land
Jer 11: 5 Then I will fulfill the *o* I swore
38: 16 Zedekiah swore this *o* secretly
40: 9 took an *o* to reassure them
Eze 16: 8 I gave you my solemn *o*
16: 59 because you have despised my *o*
17: 13 with him, putting him under *o.*
17: 16 whose *o* he despised and whose
17: 18 He despised the *o* by breaking
17: 19 on his head my *o* that he despised
Mic 7: 20 as you pledged on *o* to our fathers
Mt 5: 33 'Do not break your *o,* but keep
14: 7 with an *o* to give her whatever she
23: 16 of the temple, he is bound by his *o.*'
23: 18 the gift on it, he is bound by his *o.*'
26: 63 "I charge you under *o*
26: 72 with an *o:* "I don't know the man!"
Mk 6: 23 And he promised her with an *o,*
Lk 1: 73 *o* he swore to our father Abraham:
Ac 2: 30 him on *o* that he would place one
23: 12 themselves with an *o* not to eat
23: 14 "We have taken a solemn *o* not
23: 21 They have taken an *o* not to eat
Heb 3: 11 So I declared on *o* in my anger,
4: 3 "So I declared on *o* in my anger,
6: 16 and the *o* confirms what is said
6: 17 he confirmed it with an *o.*
7: 20 And it was not without an *o!*
7: 20 became priests without any *o,*
7: 21 with an *o* when God said to him:
7: 22 Because of this *o,* Jesus has become
7: 28 but the *o,* which came after the law,

OATHS (OATH)

Dt 6: 13 and take your *o* in his name.
10: 20 and take your *o* in his name.
Ecc 9: 2 as it is with those who take *o,*
Isa 48: 1 you who take *o* in the name
Hos 10: 4 take false *o*
Mt 5: 33 but keep the *o* you have made
Mt 14: 9 of his *o* and his dinner guests,
Mk 6: 26 of his *o* and his dinner guests,

OBADIAH

1Ki 18: 3 and Ahab had summoned *O,*
18: 3 *(O* was a devout believer
18: 4 *O* had taken a hundred prophets
18: 5 Ahab had said to *O,* "Go
18: 6 in one direction and *O* in another.
18: 7 As *O* was walking
18: 7 *O* recognized him, bowed
18: 9 What have I done wrong," asked *O*
18: 16 So *O* went to meet Ahab
1Ch 3: 21 of Arnan, of *O* and of Shecaniah.
7: 3 Michael, *O,* Joel and Isshiah.
8: 38 Ishmael, Sheariah, *O* and Hanan.
9: 16 son of Asaph; *O* son of Shemaiah,
9: 44 Ishmael, Sheariah, *O* and Hanan.
12: 9 *O* the second in command,
27: 19 Ishmaiah son of *O;* over Naphtali:
2Ch 17: 7 *O,* Zechariah, Nethanel
34: 12 to direct them were Jahath and *O,*
Ezr 8: 9 of Joab, *O* son of Jehiel,
Ne 10: 5 Harim, Meremoth, *O,* Daniel,
12: 25 Bakbukiah, *O,* Meshullam,
Ob : 1 The vision of *O.*

OBAL

Ge 10: 28 Uzal, Diklah, *O,* Abimael, Sheba,
1Ch 1: 22 Uzal, Diklah, *O,* Abimael, Sheba,

OBED

Ru 4: 17 And they named him *O.*
4: 21 father of *O, O* the father of Jesse,
1Ch 2: 12 of *O* and *O* the father of Jesse.
2: 38 father of *O, O* the father of Jehu,
11: 47 Eliel, *O* and Jaasiel the Mezobaite.
26: 7 Othni, Rephael, *O* and Elzabad;
2Ch 23: 1 Azariah son of *O,* Maaseiah son
Mt 1: 5 mother was Ruth, *O* the father
1: 5 of *O,* whose mother was Ruth,
Lk 3: 32 the son of *O,* the son of Boaz,

OBED-EDOM

2Sa 6: 10 aside to the house of *O* the Gittite.
6: 11 in the house of *O* the Gittite
6: 12 from the house of *O* to the City
6: 12 has blessed the household of *O*
1Ch 13: 13 aside to the house of *O* the Gittite.
13: 14 with the family of *O* in his house
15: 18 Eliphelehu, Mikneiah, *O* and Jeiel,
15: 21 Eliphelehu, Mikneiah, *O,*
15: 24 *O* and Jehiah were
15: 25 of the LORD from the house of *O,*
16: 5 Eliab, Benaiah, *O* and Jeiel.
16: 38 left *O* and his sixty-eight associates
16: 38 *O* son of Jeduthun, and also Hosah,
26: 4 *O* also had sons: Shemaiah
26: 5 (For God had blessed *O.)*
26: 8 All these were descendants of *O;*
26: 8 descendants of *O,* 62 in all.
26: 15 The lot for the South Gate fell to *O,*
2Ch 25: 24 God that had been in the care of *O,*

OBEDIENCE (OBEY)

Ge 49: 10 and the *o* of the nations is his.
Jdg 2: 17 of *o* to the LORD's commands.
1Ch 21: 19 So David went up in *o*
2Ch 31: 21 in *o* to the law and the commands,
Pr 30: 17 that scorns *o* to a mother,
Lk 23: 56 Sabbath in *o* to the commandment.
Ac 21: 24 but that you yourself are living in *o*
Ro 1: 5 to the *o* that comes from faith.
5: 19 also through the *o* of the one man
6: 16 to *o,* which leads to righteousness?
16: 19 Everyone has heard about your *o,*
2Co 9: 13 for the *o* that accompanies your
10: 6 once your *o* is complete.
Phm : 21 Confident of your *o,* I write to you,
Heb 5: 8 he learned *o* from what he suffered
1Pe 1: 2 for *o* to Jesus Christ and sprinkling
2Jn : 6 that we walk in *o* to his commands.

OBEDIENT (OBEY)

Dt 30: 17 heart turns away and you are not *o,*
Isa 1: 19 If you are willing and *o,*
Lk 2: 51 with them and was *o* to them.
Ac 6: 7 of priests became *o* to the faith.
2Co 2: 9 if you would stand the test and be *o*
7: 15 he remembers that you were all *o,*
10: 5 thought to make it *o* to Christ.
Php 2: 8 and became *o* to death—
Tit 3: 1 to be *o,* to be ready
1Pe 1: 14 As *o* children, do not conform

OBEY (OBEDIENCE OBEDIENT OBEYED OBEYING OBEYS)

Ex 5: 2 that I should *o* him and let Israel go
12: 24 "*O* these instructions as a lasting
19: 5 Now if you *o* me fully and keep my
24: 7 the LORD has said; we will *o.*"
34: 11 *O* what I command you today.
Lev 18: 4 You must *o* my laws and be careful
25: 18 and be careful to *o* my laws,
26: 3 and are careful to *o* my commands,
Nu 15: 39 that you may *o* them and not
15: 40 remember to *o* all my commands
27: 20 Israelite community will *o* him.
Dt 4: 30 to the LORD your God and *o* him.
5: 27 We will listen and *o.*"
6: 3 careful to *o* so that it may go well
6: 24 us to *o* all these decrees
6: 25 if we are careful to *o* all this law
9: 23 You did not trust him or *o* him.
11: 13 if you faithfully *o* the commands I
11: 27 the blessing if you *o* the commands
11: 32 be sure that you *o* all the decrees
12: 28 to *o* all these regulations I am
13: 4 Keep his commands and *o* him;
13: 18 you *o* the LORD your God,
15: 5 if only you fully *o* the LORD your
21: 18 son who does not *o* his father
21: 20 He will not *o* us.
26: 17 and laws, and that you will *o* him.
27: 10 *O* the LORD your God
28: 1 If you fully *o* the LORD your God
28: 2 you if you *o* the LORD your God:
28: 15 if you do not *o* the LORD your
28: 45 you did not *o* the LORD your God
28: 62 you did not *o* the LORD your God
30: 2 and *o* him with all your heart
30: 8 You will again *o* the LORD
30: 10 if you *o* the LORD your God
30: 12 proclaim it to us so we may *o* it?"
30: 13 proclaim it to us so we may *o* it?"
30: 14 and in your heart so you may *o* it.
32: 46 children to *o* carefully all the words
Jos 1: 7 to *o* all the law my servant Moses
1: 17 obeyed Moses, so we will *o* you.
1: 18 and does not *o* your words,
22: 5 in all his ways, to *o* his commands,
23: 6 be careful to *o* all that is written
24: 24 the LORD our God and *o* him."
Jdg 3: 4 whether they would *o* the LORD's
1Sa 12: 14 the LORD and serve and *o* him
12: 15 But if you do not *o* the LORD,
15: 19 Why did you not *o* the LORD?
15: 20 "But I did *o* the LORD," Saul said.
15: 22 To *o* is better than sacrifice,
28: 18 Because you did not *o* the LORD
2Sa 22: 45 as soon as they hear me, they *o* me.
1Ki 2: 42 I will *o.*'
2: 43 and *o* the command I gave you?"
3: 14 and *o* my statutes and commands
6: 12 keep all my commands and *o* them,
8: 61 by his decrees and *o* his commands
2Ki 10: 6 If you are on my side and will *o* me,
17: 13 that I commanded your fathers to *o*
1Ch 28: 21 the people will *o* your every
2Ch 14: 4 and to *o* his laws and commands.
34: 31 and to *o* the words of the covenant
Ezr 7: 26 Whoever does not *o* the law
Ne 1: 5 who love him and *o* his commands,
1: 9 return to me and *o* my commands,
9: 16 and did not *o* your commands.
10: 29 to *o* carefully all the commands,
Est 3: 8 and they do not *o* the king's laws;
Job 36: 11 If they *o* and serve him,
Ps 18: 44 As soon as they hear me, they *o* me
103: 18 and remember to *o* his precepts.
103: 20 who *o* his word.
106: 25 and did not *o* the LORD.
119: 8 I will *o* your decrees;
119: 17 I will *o* your word.
119: 34 and *o* it with all my heart.
119: 44 I will always *o* your law,

Ps 119: 56 I *o* your precepts.
119: 57 I have promised to *o* your words.
119: 60 to *o* your commands.
119: 67 but now I *o* your word.
119: 88 I will *o* the statutes of your mouth.
119:100 for I *o* your precepts.
119:101 so that I might *o* your word.
119:129 therefore I *o* them.
119:134 that I may *o* your precepts.
119:145 and I will *o* your decrees.
119:158 for they do not *o* your word.
119:167 I *o* your statutes,
119:168 I *o* your precepts and your statutes,
Pr 5: 13 I would not *o* my teachers
Ecc 8: 2 *O* the king's command, I say,
Isa 42: 24 they did not *o* his law.
Jer 7: 23 I gave them this command: *O* me,
11: 3 the man who does not *o* the terms
11: 4 '*O* me and do everything I
11: 7 and again, saying, "*O* me."
17: 24 But if you are careful to *o* me,
17: 27 But if you do not *o* me
18: 10 evil in my sight and does not *o* me,
22: 5 if you do not *o* these commands,
26: 13 and *o* the LORD your God.
32: 23 but they did not *o* you
35: 13 not learn a lesson and *o* my words?'
35: 14 they *o* their forefather's command.
38: 20 "*O* the LORD by doing what I tell
40: 3 the LORD and did not *o* him.
42: 6 for we will *o* the LORD our God."
42: 6 we will *o* the LORD our God,
Da 7: 27 all rulers will worship and *o* him.'
9: 4 who love him and *o* his commands,
9: 11 and turned away, refusing to *o* you.
Joel 2: 11 are those who *o* his command.
Zec 6: 15 if you diligently *o* the LORD your
Mt 8: 27 the winds and the waves *o* him!"
19: 17 to enter life, *o* the commandments
23: 3 So you must *o* them and do
28: 20 to *o* everything I have commanded
Mk 1: 27 to evil spirits and they *o* him."
4: 41 Even the wind and the waves *o* him
Lk 8: 25 and the water, and they *o* him."
11: 28 hear the word of God and *o* it."
17: 6 planted in the sea,' and it will *o* you
Jn 14: 15 you will *o* what I command.
14: 23 loves me, he will *o* my teaching.
14: 24 not love me will not *o* my teaching.
15: 10 If you *o* my commands, you will
15: 20 my teaching, they will *o* yours
Ac 4: 19 right in God's sight to *o* you rather
5: 29 "We must *o* God rather than men!
5: 32 given to those who *o* him."
7: 39 "But our fathers refused to *o* him.
15: 5 required to *o* the law of Moses."
16: 4 in Jerusalem for the people to *o*.
Ro 2: 13 it is those who *o* the law who will
6: 12 body so that you *o* its evil desires.
6: 16 slaves to the one whom you *o*—
6: 16 yourselves to someone to *o* him
15: 18 in leading the Gentiles to *o* God
16: 26 nations might believe and *o* him—
Gal 5: 3 obligated to *o* the whole law.
6: 13 who are circumcised *o* the law,
Eph 6: 1 *o* your parents in the Lord,
6: 5 just as you would *o* Christ.
6: 5 *o* your earthly masters with respect
6: 6 *O* them not only to win their favor
Col 3: 20 *o* your parents in everything,
3: 22 *o* your earthly masters
2Th 1: 8 and do not *o* the gospel
3: 14 anyone does not *o* our instruction
1Ti 3: 4 and see that his children *o* him
Heb 5: 9 eternal salvation for all who *o* him
13: 17 *O* them so that their work will be
13: 17 *O* your leaders and submit
Jas 3: 3 of horses to make them *o* us,
1Pe 4: 17 for those who do not *o* the gospel
1Jn 2: 3 to know him if we *o* his commands.
3: 22 because we *o* his commands
3: 24 Those who *o* his commands live
5: 3 love for God: to *o* his commands.
Rev 3: 3 you have received and heard; *o* it,
12: 17 those who *o* God's commandments
14: 12 the saints who *o* God's

OBEYED (OBEY)

Ge 22: 18 blessed, because you have *o* me."
26: 5 because Abraham *o* me
28: 7 and that Jacob had *o* his father
Nu 9: 19 the Israelites *o* the LORD's order
9: 23 They *o* the LORD's order,
Dt 26: 14 I have *o* the LORD my God;
Jos 1: 17 we fully *o* Moses, so we will obey
5: 6 since they had not *o* the LORD.
22: 2 and you have *o* me in everything I
1Sa 28: 21 Look, your maidservant has *o* you.
1Ki 12: 24 So they *o* the word of the LORD
20: 36 Because you have not *o* the LORD
2Ki 18: 12 they had not *o* the LORD their
22: 13 our fathers have not *o* the words
1Ch 29: 23 He prospered and all Israel *o* him.
2Ch 11: 4 So they *o* the words of the LORD
Ne 1: 7 We have not *o* the commands,
Est 1: 15 "She has not *o* the command
Ps 119: 4 that are to be fully *o*.
119:136 for your law is not *o*.
Jer 3: 13 and have not *o* me,' "
3: 25 we have not *o* the LORD our God
7: 28 nation that has not *o* the LORD its
9: 13 they have not *o* me or followed my
22: 21 you have not *o* me.
34: 17 LORD says: You have not *o* me;
35: 8 We have *o* everything our
35: 10 and have fully *o* everything our
35: 14 and again, yet you have not *o* me.
35: 16 but these people have not *o* me.'
35: 18 'You have *o* the command
42: 21 still have not *o* the LORD your
44: 23 have not *o* him or followed his law
Eze 20: 24 because they had not *o* my laws
Da 9: 10 we have not *o* the LORD our God
9: 14 he does; yet we have not *o* him.
Hos 9: 17 because they have not *o* him;
Jnh 3: 3 Jonah *o* the word of the LORD
Mic 5: 15 the nations that have not *o* me."
Hag 1: 12 remnant of the people *o* the voice
Jn 15: 10 as I have *o* my Father's commands
15: 20 If they *o* my teaching, they will
17: 6 and they have *o* your word.
Ac 7: 53 through angels but have not *o* it."
Ro 6: 17 you wholeheartedly *o* the form
Php 2: 12 as you have always *o*— not only
Heb 11: 8 *o* and went, even though he did not
1Pe 3: 6 who *o* Abraham and called him her

OBEYING (OBEY)

Dt 8: 20 for not *o* the LORD your God.
1Sa 15: 22 as in *o* the voice of the LORD?
Ps 119: 5 steadfast in *o* your decrees!
Jer 16: 12 of his evil heart instead of *o* me.
Gal 5: 7 and kept you from *o* the truth?
1Pe 1: 22 purified yourselves by *o* the truth

OBEYS (OBEY)

Lev 18: 5 for the man who *o* them will live
Ne 9: 29 which a man will live if he *o* them.
Pr 19: 16 He who *o* instructions guards his
Ecc 8: 5 Whoever *o* his command will come
Isa 50: 10 and *o* the word of his servant?
Eze 20: 11 for the man who *o* them will live
20: 13 the man who *o* them will live
20: 21 the man who *o* them will live
Zep 3: 2 She *o* no one,
Jn 14: 21 has my commands and *o* them,
Ro 2: 27 and yet *o* the law will condemn you
1Jn 2: 5 if anyone *o* his word, God's love is

OBIL

1Ch 27: 30 *O* the Ishmaelite was in charge

OBJECT (OBJECTED OBJECTION OBJECTIONS OBJECTS)

Nu 35: 16 with an iron *o* so that he dies,
35: 18 Or if anyone has a wooden *o*
Dt 28: 37 a thing of horror and an *o* of scorn
1Ki 9: 7 an *o* of ridicule among all peoples.
2Ch 7: 20 an *o* of ridicule among all peoples.
29: 8 he has made them an *o* of dread
30: 7 so that he made them an *o*
Ps 109: 25 I am an *o* of scorn to my accusers;
Jer 18: 16 an *o* of lasting scorn;
19: 8 devastate this city and make it an *o*
22: 28 an *o* no one wants?
Jer 24: 9 an *o* of ridicule and cursing,
25: 9 and make them an *o* of horror
25: 18 and an *o* of horror and scorn
26: 6 and this city an *o* of cursing
29: 18 and an *o* of cursing and horror,
42: 18 You will be an *o* of cursing
44: 8 make yourselves an *o* of cursing
44: 12 They will become an *o* of cursing
44: 22 your land became an *o* of cursing
48: 26 let her be an *o* of ridicule.
48: 27 Was not Israel the *o*
48: 39 Moab has become an *o* of ridicule,
48: 39 an *o* of horror to all those
49: 13 Bozrah will become a ruin and an *o*
49: 17 "Edom will become an *o* of horror;
51: 37 an *o* of horror and scorn,
Eze 5: 15 and an *o* of horror to the nations
22: 4 Therefore I will make you an *o*
24: 21 of your eyes, the *o* of your affection
36: 3 and the *o* of people's malicious talk
Da 9: 16 and your people an *o* of scorn
Joel 2: 17 Do not make your inheritance an *o*
2: 19 an *o* of scorn to the nations.
Zec 8: 13 As you have been an *o* of cursing

OBJECTED (OBJECT)

2Ki 4: 16 "No, my lord," she *o*.
Jn 12: 4 who was later to betray him, *o*,
18: 31 to execute anyone," the Jews *o*.
Ac 28: 19 when the Jews *o*, I was compelled

OBJECTION (OBJECT)

Ac 10: 29 I came without raising any *o*.

OBJECTIONS (OBJECT)

Ac 11: 18 had no further *o* and praised God,

OBJECTS (OBJECT)

1Sa 6: 8 it put the gold *o* you are sending
6: 15 the chest containing the gold *o*,
1Ki 7: 45 All these *o* that Huram made
2Ki 12: 18 took all the sacred *o* dedicated
2Ch 4: 16 All the *o* that Huram-Abi made
24: 7 even its sacred *o* for the Baals.
24: 14 and also ladles and other *o* of gold
Ps 79: 4 We are *o* of reproach
Jer 10: 15 They are worthless, the *o*
51: 18 They are worthless, the *o*
Ac 17: 23 and observed your *o* of worship,
Ro 9: 22 bore with great patience the *o*
9: 23 known to the *o* of his mercy,
Eph 2: 3 we were by nature *o* of wrath.

OBLIGATE (OBLIGATED OBLIGATES OBLIGATION OBLIGATIONS)

Nu 30: 2 or takes an oath to *o* himself

OBLIGATED (OBLIGATE)

Nu 30: 4 by which she *o* herself will stand.
30: 5 by which she *o* herself will stand;
30: 7 by which she *o* herself will stand.
30: 11 by which she *o* herself will stand.
Ro 1: 14 I am *o* both to Greeks
Gal 5: 3 himself be circumcised that he is *o*

OBLIGATES (OBLIGATE)

Nu 30: 3 *o* herself by a pledge and her father
30: 6 promise by which she *o* herself
30: 8 he nullifies the vow that *o* her
30: 8 promise by which she *o* herself,
30: 10 or *o* herself by a pledge under oath

OBLIGATION (OBLIGATE)

Nu 30: 9 "Any vow or *o* taken by a widow
32: 22 be free from your *o* to the LORD
Ezr 4: 14 since we are under *o* to the palace
Ro 4: 4 to him as a gift, but as an *o*.
8: 12 Therefore, brothers, we have an *o*

OBLIGATIONS (OBLIGATE)

Nu 3: 8 fulfilling the *o* of the Israelites
1Ki 9: 25 and so fulfilled the temple *o*.

OBLIVION

Ps 88: 12 righteous deeds in the land of *o*?

OBOTH

Nu 21: 10 moved on and camped at *O*.

Nu 21: 11 they set out from *O* and camped
33: 43 They left Punon and camped at *O*.
33: 44 left *O* and camped at Iye Abarim,

OBSCENITY

Eph 5: 4 Nor should there be *o*, foolish talk

OBSCURE (OBSCURES)

Pr 22: 29 he will not serve before *o* men.
Isa 33: 19 those people of an *o* speech,
Eze 3: 5 sent to a people of *o* speech
3: 6 not to many peoples of *o* speech

OBSCURES (OBSCURE)

Job 42: 3 'Who is this that *o* my counsel

OBSERVANCE (OBSERVE)

Ex 13: 9 This *o* will be for you like a sign
Ezr 7: 10 and *o* of the Law of the LORD,

OBSERVE (OBSERVANCE OBSERVED OBSERVER OBSERVES OBSERVING)

Ex 1: 16 and *o* them on the delivery stool,
12: 25 as he promised, *o* this ceremony.
13: 5 you are to *o* this ceremony
31: 13 'You must *o* my Sabbaths.
31: 14 " '*O* the Sabbath, because it is holy
31: 16 The Israelites are to *o* the Sabbath,
Lev 19: 3 and you must *o* my Sabbaths.
19: 30 *O* my Sabbaths and have reverence
23: 32 are to *o* your sabbath."
25: 2 the land itself must *o* a sabbath
26: 2 *O* my Sabbaths and have reverence
Dt 4: 6 *O* them carefully, for this will show
5: 12 "*O* the Sabbath day
5: 15 you to *o* the Sabbath day.
6: 1 you to *o* in the land that you are
8: 6 *O* the commands of the LORD
8: 11 failing to *o* his commands,
10: 13 and to *o* the LORD's commands
11: 8 *O* therefore all the commands I am
11: 22 If you carefully *o* all these
12: 14 there *o* everything I command you.
16: 1 *O* the month of Abib and celebrate
26: 16 carefully *o* them with all your heart
28: 45 *o* the commands and decrees he
2Sa 3: 25 you and *o* your movements
1Ki 2: 3 and *o* what the LORD your God
9: 4 and *o* my decrees and laws,
9: 6 and do not *o* the commands
2Ki 17: 13 *O* my commands and decrees,
1Ch 22: 13 if you are careful to *o* the decrees
2Ch 7: 17 and *o* my decrees and laws,
Est 9: 19 *o* the fourteenth of the month
9: 22 He wrote them to *o* the days
9: 27 without fail *o* these two days every
Ps 37: 37 the blameless, *o* the upright;
91: 8 You will only *o* with your eyes
105: 45 and *o* his laws.
Ecc 8: 16 and to *o* man's labor on earth—
Jer 2: 10 send to Kedar and *o* closely;
6: 18 *o*, O witnesses,
6: 27 that you may *o*
8: 7 *o* the time of their migration.
Eze 45: 21 day you are to *o* the Passover,
Mk 7: 4 And they *o* many other traditions,
7: 9 in order to *o* your own traditions!
Ro 2: 25 has value if you *o* the law,
Gal 3: 5 among you because you *o* the law,

OBSERVED (OBSERVE)

Ge 50: 10 there Joseph *o* a seven-day period
Nu 23: 21 no misery *o* in Israel.
1Sa 1: 12 to the LORD, Eli *o* her mouth.
1Ki 8: 65 Solomon *o* the festival at that time,
11: 34 who *o* my commands and statutes.
2Ki 23: 22 had any such Passover been *o*.
2Ch 7: 8 Solomon *o* the festival at that time
35: 17 *o* the Feast of Unleavened Bread
35: 18 Passover had not been *o* like this
Est 5: 9 king's gate and *o* that he neither
9: 28 and *o* in every generation
Job 4: 8 As I have *o*, those who plow evil
Pr 24: 32 I applied my heart to what I *o*
Mic 6: 16 You have *o* the statutes of Omri
Ac 17: 23 and *o* your objects of worship,

OBSERVER (OBSERVE)

Ac 22: 12 He was a devout *o* of the law

OBSERVES (OBSERVE)

Ps 11: 4 He *o* the sons of men;

OBSERVING (OBSERVE)

1Sa 20: 29 because our family is *o* a sacrifice
2Ch 13: 11 We are *o* the requirements
Lk 1: 6 *o* all the Lord's commandments
Ro 3: 20 righteous in his sight by *o* the law;
3: 27 principle? On that of *o* the law?
3: 28 by faith apart from *o* the law.
Gal 2: 16 a man is not justified by *o* the law,
2: 16 by *o* the law no one will be justified
2: 16 faith in Christ and not by *o* the law,
3: 2 you receive the Spirit by *o* the law,
3: 10 All who rely on *o* the law are
4: 10 You are *o* special days and months

OBSESSION

Ac 26: 11 In my *o* against them, I

OBSOLETE

Heb 8: 13 and what is *o* and aging will soon
8: 13 he has made the first one *o*;

OBSTACLE (OBSTACLES)

Ro 14: 13 or *o* in your brother's way.

OBSTACLES (OBSTACLE)

Isa 57: 14 Remove the *o* out of the way
Jer 6: 21 "I will put *o* before this people.
Ro 16: 17 put *o* in your way that are contrary

OBSTINATE

Dt 2: 30 and his heart *o* in order to give him
Isa 30: 1 "Woe to the *o* children,"
65: 2 hands to an *o* people,
Eze 2: 4 to whom I am sending you are *o*
3: 7 house of Israel is hardened and *o*.
Ac 19: 9 But some of them became *o*;
Ro 10: 21 to a disobedient and *o* people."

OBTAIN (OBTAINED OBTAINS)

Nu 27: 21 who will *o* decisions for him
Ezr 7: 16 gold you may *o* from the province
Pr 20: 18 if you wage war, *o* guidance.
Jn 5: 44 effort to *o* the praise that comes
Ro 11: 7 sought so earnestly it did not *o*,
2Ti 2: 10 they too may *o* the salvation that

OBTAINED (OBTAIN)

Ex 38: 25 The silver *o* from those
Ac 22: 5 even *o* letters from them
27: 13 thought they had *o* what they
Ro 9: 30 not pursue righteousness, have *o* it,
Php 3: 12 Not that I have already *o* all this,
Heb 9: 12 having *o* eternal redemption.

OBTAINS (OBTAIN)

Pr 12: 2 A good man *o* favor

OBVIOUS

Mt 6: 18 so that it will not be *o*
Gal 5: 19 The acts of the sinful nature are *o*:
1Ti 5: 24 The sins of some men are *o*,
5: 25 In the same way, good deeds are *o*,

OCCASION (OCCASIONS)

Jdg 14: 4 who was seeking an *o*
1Sa 9: 24 it was set aside for you for this *o*,
2Ch 13: 18 of Israel were subdued on that *o*,
Ezr 7: 20 of your God that you may have *o*
10: 9 greatly distressed by the *o* and
Ne 8: 4 wooden platform built for the *o*.
Mk 4: 1 On another *o* Jesus began to teach
Lk 10: 25 On one *o* an expert
Ac 1: 4 On one *o*, while he was eating
2Co 9: 11 you can be generous on every *o*,

OCCASIONS (OCCASION)

Zec 8: 19 and glad *o* and happy festivals
Eph 6: 18 in the Spirit on all *o* with all kinds

OCCUPANTS (OCCUPY)

Isa 5: 9 the fine mansions left without *o*.

OCCUPATION

Ge 46: 33 'What is your *o*?' you should
47: 3 "What is your *o*?" "Your servants

OCCUPIED (OCCUPY)

Ge 36: 43 settlements in the land they *o*.
Nu 21: 25 cities of the Amorites and *o* them,
Jos 19: 47 took it, put it to the sword and *o* it.
Jdg 11: 26 hundred years Israel *o* Heshbon,
1Sa 17: 3 The Philistines *o* one hill
31: 7 the Philistines came and *o* them.
1Ch 5: 9 To the east they *o* the land up
5: 10 they *o* the dwellings
5: 22 And they *o* the land until the exile.
10: 7 the Philistines came and *o* them.
2Ch 28: 18 captured and *o* Beth Shemesh,
Ecc 5: 20 God keeps him *o* with gladness

OCCUPY (OCCUPANTS OCCUPIED)

Jos 1: 15 may go back and *o* your own land,
17: 12 were not able to *o* these towns,
Ne 2: 8 and for the residence I will *o*?"
Ecc 10: 6 while the rich *o* the low ones.
Jer 49: 16 who *o* the heights of the hill.
Ob : 19 People from the Negev will *o*
: 19 They will *o* the fields of Ephraim
Zec 9: 6 Foreigners will *o* Ashdod,

OCCUR (OCCURRED OCCURS)

Ex 8: 23 miraculous sign will *o* tomorrow.' "
Eze 16: 16 not happen, nor should they ever *o*.
1Co 5: 1 and of a kind that does not *o*

OCCURRED (OCCUR)

2Ch 32: 31 the miraculous sign that had *o*
1Co 10: 6 Now these things *o* as examples,
Rev 16: 18 No earthquake like it has ever *o*

OCCURS (OCCUR)

Ecc 8: 14 something else meaningless that *o*
2Th 2: 3 until the rebellion *o*

OCEAN (OCEANS)

Ps 148: 7 great sea creatures and all *o* depths,
Eze 26: 19 when I bring the *o* depths over you

OCEANS (OCEAN)

Pr 8: 24 When there were no *o*, I was given

OCRAN

Nu 1: 13 Pagiel son of *O*; from Gad,
2: 27 people of Asher is Pagiel son of *O*.
7: 72 the eleventh day Pagiel son of *O*,
7: 77 the offering of Pagiel son of *O*.
10: 26 Pagiel son of *O* was

ODED

2Ch 15: 1 came upon Azariah son of *O*.
15: 8 of Azariah son of *O* the prophet,
28: 9 of the LORD named *O* was there,

ODIOUS

1Sa 27: 12 "He has become so *o* to his people,

ODOR

Jn 11: 39 "by this time there is a bad *o*,

OFFAL

Ex 29: 14 its hide and its *o* outside the camp.
Lev 4: 11 the inner parts and *o*—that is,
8: 17 its *o* he burned up outside the camp
16: 27 flesh and *o* are to be burned up.
Nu 19: 5 its hide, flesh, blood and *o*.
Mal 2: 3 spread on your faces the *o*

OFFEND (OFFENDED OFFENDER OFFENDERS OFFENSE OFFENSES OFFENSIVE)

Job 34: 31 'I am guilty but will *o* no more.
Mt 17: 27 "But so that we may not *o* them,
Jn 6: 61 said to them, "Does this *o* you?

OFFENDED (OFFEND)

Ge 40: 1 of the king of Egypt *o* their master,
Pr 18: 19 An *o* brother is more unyielding
Mt 15: 12 you know that the Pharisees were *o*

OFFENDER (OFFEND)
Ex 21:22 the *o* must be fined whatever

OFFENDERS (OFFEND)
1Co 6: 9 nor homosexual *o* nor thieves

OFFENSE (OFFEND)
Ge 20:16 This is to cover the *o* against you
Dt 19:15 or *o* he may have committed.
21:22 guilty of a capital *o* is put to death
1Sa 25:28 Please forgive your servant's *o*,
2Sa 3: 8 me of an *o* involving this woman!
Job 10:14 would not let my *o* go unpunished.
13:23 Show me my *o* and my sin.
Ps 59: 3 for no *o* or sin of mine, O LORD.
Pr 17: 9 over an *o* promotes love,
19:11 it is to his glory to overlook an *o*.
Jer 24: 9 and an *o* to all the kingdoms
Eze 22:11 one man commits a detestable *o*
Mt 13:57 all these things?" And they took *o*
Mk 6: 3 with us?" And they took *o* at him.
Gal 5:11 In that case the *o* of the cross has

OFFENSES (OFFEND)
Nu 18: 1 for *o* against the priesthood.
18: 1 for *o* against the sanctuary,
18:23 and bear the responsibility for *o*
1Ki 8:50 forgive all the *o* they have
Job 7:21 Why do you not pardon my *o*
14:17 My *o* will be sealed up in a bag;
Isa 43:24 and wearied me with your *o*.
44:22 swept away your *o* like a cloud,
59:12 For our *o* are many in your sight,
59:12 Our *o* are ever with us,
Eze 18:22 of the *o* he has committed will be
18:28 considers all the *o* he has
18:30 Repent! Turn away from all your *o*;
18:31 of all the *o* you have committed,
33:10 "Our *o* and sins weigh us down,
37:23 vile images or with any of their *o*,
39:24 to their uncleanness and their *o*,
Am 5:12 For I know how many are your *o*

OFFENSIVE (OFFEND)
Job 19:17 My breath is *o* to my wife;
Ps 139:24 See if there is any *o* way in me,
Jer 6:10 word of the LORD is *o* to them;

OFFER (OFFERED OFFERING OFFERINGS OFFERS)
Ex 3:18 into the desert to *o* sacrifices
5: 3 into the desert to *o* sacrifices
8: 8 go to *o* sacrifices to the LORD."
8:26 if we *o* sacrifices that are detestable
8:26 sacrifices we *o* the LORD our God
8:27 into the desert to *o* sacrifices
8:28 "I will let you go to *o* sacrifices
8:29 go to *o* sacrifices to the LORD."
23:18 "Do not *o* the blood of a sacrifice
29:38 "This is what you are to *o*
29:39 *O* one in the morning and the other
29:40 With the first lamb *o* a tenth
30: 9 Do not *o* on this altar any other
34:25 "Do not *o* the blood of a sacrifice
Lev 1: 3 he is to *o* a male without defect.
1:10 he is to *o* a male without defect.
1:14 he is to *o* a dove or a young pigeon.
2:14 *o* crushed heads of new grain
3: 6 he is to *o* a male or female
5: 8 who shall first *o* the one
5:10 The priest shall then *o* the other
7:12 is to *o* cakes of bread made
12: 7 He shall *o* them before the LORD
14:12 one of the male lambs and *o* it
14:20 slaughter the burnt offering and *o* it
16: 6 "Aaron is to *o* the bull
17: 7 They must no longer *o* any
21: 8 they *o* up the food of your God.
21:17 come near to *o* the food of his God.
21:21 come near to *o* the food of his God.
22:22 Do not *o* to the LORD the blind,
22:24 You must not *o* to the LORD
22:25 *o* them as the food of your God.
Nu 6:11 is to *o* one as a sin offering
15: 7 *O* it as an aroma pleasing
15:24 community is to *o* a young bull
Dt 12:14 *O* them only at the place
20:10 make its people an *o* of peace.
Dt 27: 6 and *o* burnt offerings on it
28:68 There you will *o* yourselves for sale
33:19 there *o* sacrifices of righteousness;
Jos 22:23 and to *o* burnt offerings and grain
Jdg 5: 2 people willingly *o* themselves—
6:26 *o* the second bull as a burnt
13:16 if you prepare a burnt offering, *o* it
16:23 assembled to *o* a great sacrifice
21:13 the assembly sent an *o* of peace
1Sa 1:21 family to *o* the annual sacrifice
2:19 husband to *o* the annual sacrifice.
10: 4 and *o* you two loaves of bread,
13:12 compelled to *o* the burnt offering."
2Sa 7:27 courage to *o* you this prayer.
24:22 whatever pleases him and *o* it up.
1Ki 3: 4 went to Gibeon to *o* sacrifices,
12:27 up to *o* sacrifices at the temple
22:43 the people continued to *o* sacrifices
2Ki 12: 3 the people continued to *o* sacrifices
14: 4 the people continued to *o* sacrifices
15: 4 the people continued to *o* sacrifices
15:35 the people continued to *o* sacrifices
16:15 *o* the morning burnt offering
17:36 bow down and to him *o* sacrifices.
1Ch 23:13 to *o* sacrifices before the LORD,
2Ch 11:16 Levites to Jerusalem to *o* sacrifices
29:21 to *o* these on the altar of the LORD
31: 2 to *o* burnt offerings and fellowship
35:12 of the people to *o* to the LORD,
Ezr 3: 6 to *o* burnt offerings to the LORD,
6:10 that they may *o* sacrifices pleasing
Ne 4: 2 their wall? Will they *o* sacrifices?
Ps 4: 5 *O* right sacrifices
38:14 whose mouth can *o* no reply.
66: 2 *o* him glory and praise!
66:15 I will *o* bulls and goats.
Ecc 5: 1 than to *o* the sacrifice of fools,
9: 2 those who *o* sacrifices
Isa 1:15 even if you *o* many prayers,
57: 7 up to *o* your sacrifices.
Jer 7:16 nor *o* any plea or petition for them;
11:14 nor *o* any plea or petition for them,
14:12 though they *o* burnt offerings
16: 7 No one will *o* food
33:18 continually to *o* burnt offerings,
46:10 LORD Almighty, will *o* sacrifice
La 3:30 Let him *o* his cheek
4: 3 Even jackals *o* their breasts
Eze 20:31 When you *o* your gifts—
43:22 are to *o* a male goat without defect
43:23 you are to *o* a young bull
43:24 You are to *o* them
44:15 before me to *o* sacrifices of fat
44:27 he is to *o* a sin offering for himself,
45:13 This is the special gift you are to *o*:
46: 6 New Moon he is to *o* a young bull,
46:12 He shall *o* his burnt offering
48: 9 "The special portion you are to *o*
Hos 8:13 They *o* sacrifices given to me
13: 2 "They *o* human sacrifice
14: 2 that we may *o* the fruit of our lips.
Mic 6: 7 Shall I *o* my firstborn
Hag 2:14 whatever they *o* there is defiled.
Mal 1:13 or diseased animals and *o* them
Mt 5:24 then come and *o* your gift.
8: 4 and *o* the gift Moses commanded,
Mk 1:44 and *o* the sacrifices that Moses
Lk 2:24 and to *o* a sacrifice in keeping
5:14 and *o* the sacrifices that Moses
Ac 14:13 wanted to *o* sacrifices to them.
24:26 that Paul would *o* him a bribe,
Ro 6:13 Do not *o* the parts of your body
6:13 and *o* the parts of your body to him
6:13 but rather *o* yourselves to God,
6:16 when you *o* yourselves to someone
6:19 as you used to *o* the parts
6:19 so now *o* them in slavery
12: 1 to *o* your bodies as living sacrifices,
1Co 9:18 preaching the gospel I may *o* it free
Heb 5: 1 to *o* gifts and sacrifices for sins.
5: 3 has to *o* sacrifices for his own sins,
7:27 need to *o* sacrifices day after day,
8: 3 also to have something to *o*.
8: 3 priest is appointed to *o* both gifts
8: 4 already men who *o* the gifts
9:25 he enter heaven to *o* himself again
13:15 therefore, let us continually *o*
1Pe 4: 9 *O* hospitality to one another
Rev 8: 3 He was given much incense to *o*,

OFFERED (OFFER)
Ge 31:54 He *o* a sacrifice there
46: 1 he *o* sacrifices to the God
Ex 24: 5 and they *o* burnt offerings
40:29 and *o* on it burnt offerings
Lev 2:12 but they are not to be *o* on the altar
7: 3 All its fat shall be *o*: the fat tail
7:15 must be eaten on the day it is *o*;
7:18 credited to the one who *o* it,
9:15 and slaughtered it and *o* it
9:16 and *o* it in the prescribed way.
10: 1 and they *o* unauthorized fire
Nu 16:47 but Aaron *o* the incense
18:15 that is *o* to the LORD is yours.
23: 2 and the two of them *o* a bull
23: 4 and on each altar I have *o* a bull
23:14 he built seven altars and *o* a bull
23:30 and *o* a bull and a ram on each altar
Dt 26:14 nor have I *o* any of it to the dead.
Jos 8:31 On it they *o* to the LORD burnt
Jdg 2: 5 There they *o* sacrifices
6:19 and *o* them to him under the oak.
Ru 2:14 he *o* her some roasted grain.
1Sa 2:13 that whenever anyone *o* a sacrifice
6:15 Beth Shemesh *o* burnt offerings
7: 9 took a suckling lamb and *o* it up
13: 9 And Saul *o* up the burnt offering.
2Sa 15:24 and Abiathar *o* sacrifices
1Ki 3: 3 except that he *o* sacrifices
3: 4 and Solomon *o* a thousand burnt
8:62 and all Israel with him *o* sacrifices
8:63 Solomon *o* a sacrifice
8:64 and there he *o* burnt offerings,
11: 8 and *o* sacrifices to their gods.
12:32 and *o* sacrifices on the altar.
12:33 he *o* sacrifices on the altar he had
20:34 from your father," Ben-Hadad *o*.
2Ki 3:27 *o* him as a sacrifice on the city wall.
16: 4 He *o* sacrifices and burned incense
16:13 He *o* up his burnt offering
1Ch 21:28 the Jebusite, he *o* sacrifices there.
2Ch 1: 6 *o* a thousand burnt offerings on it.
6:40 to the prayers *o* in this place.
7: 4 and all the people *o* sacrifices
7: 5 And King Solomon *o* a sacrifice
7: 7 and there he *o* burnt offerings
7:15 to the prayers *o* in this place.
28: 4 He *o* sacrifices and burned incense
28:23 He *o* sacrifices to the gods
30:22 *o* fellowship offerings and praised
33:22 and *o* sacrifices to all the idols
Ezr 6:17 of God they *o* a hundred bulls,
Ne 12:43 on that day they *o* great sacrifices,
Job 26: 3 What advice you have *o* to one
31:27 my hand *o* them a kiss of homage,
Ps 51:19 then bulls will be *o* on your altar.
106:28 and ate sacrifices *o* to lifeless gods;
Isa 50: 6 I *o* my back to those who beat me,
57: 6 and *o* grain offerings.
Eze 6:13 where they *o* fragrant incense
16:18 and you *o* my oil and incense
16:19 you *o* as fragrant incense
20:28 there they *o* their sacrifices,
44: 7 temple while you *o* me food,
Jnh 1:16 and they *o* a sacrifice to the LORD
Mt 26:27 gave thanks and *o* it to them,
27:34 There they *o* him wine to drink,
27:48 on a stick, and *o* it to Jesus to drink
Mk 14:23 gave thanks and *o* it to them,
15:23 they *o* him wine mixed with myrrh,
15:36 on a stick, and *o* it to Jesus to drink
Lk 23:36 They *o* him wine vinegar and said,
Ac 8:18 he *o* them money and said,
Ro 11:16 If the part of the dough *o*
1Co 9:13 share in what is *o* on the altar?
10:19 Do I mean then that a sacrifice *o*
10:20 of pagans are *o* to demons,
10:28 "This has been *o* in sacrifice,"
Heb 5: 7 he *o* up prayers and petitions
6:18 fled to take hold of the hope *o*
7:27 once for all when he *o* himself.
9: 7 which he *o* for himself
9: 9 and sacrifices being *o* were not able
9:14 the eternal Spirit *o* himself
10: 2 they not have stopped being *o*?
10:12 But when this priest had *o*

Heb 11: 4 By faith Abel *o* God a better
11: 17 when God tested him, *o* Isaac
Jas 2: 21 did when he *o* his son Isaac
5: 15 prayer *o* in faith will make the sick
Rev 14: 4 purchased from among men and *o*

OFFERING (OFFER)

Ge 4: 3 of the soil as an *o* to the LORD.
4: 4 with favor on Abel and his *o*,
4: 5 his *o* he did not look with favor.
22: 2 a burnt *o* on one of the mountains I
22: 3 cut enough wood for the burnt *o*,
22: 6 took the wood for the burnt *o*
22: 7 where is the lamb for the burnt *o*?''
22: 8 provide the lamb for the burnt *o*,
22: 13 as a burnt *o* instead of his son.
35: 14 and he poured out a drink *o* on it;
Ex 18: 12 brought a burnt *o* and other
25: 2 Tell the Israelites to bring me an *o*.
25: 2 You are to receive the *o* for me
29: 14 It is a sin *o*.
29: 18 It is a burnt *o* to the LORD,
29: 18 an *o* made to the LORD by fire.
29: 24 before the LORD as a wave *o*.
29: 25 an *o* made to the LORD by fire.
29: 25 the altar along with the burnt *o*
29: 26 it before the LORD as a wave *o*,
29: 36 as a sin *o* to make atonement.
29: 40 fourth of a hin of wine as a drink *o*.
29: 41 an *o* made to the LORD by fire.
29: 41 and its drink *o* as in the morning—
29: 41 at twilight with the same grain *o*
29: 42 generations to come this burnt *o* is
30: 9 and do not pour a drink *o* on it.
30: 9 or any burnt *o* or grain *o*,
30: 10 the blood of the atoning sin *o*
30: 13 This half shekel is an *o*
30: 14 are to give an *o* to the LORD.
30: 15 when you make the *o* to the LORD
30: 20 minister by presenting an *o* made
30: 28 altar of burnt *o* and all its utensils,
31: 9 altar of burnt *o* and all its utensils,
35: 5 From what you have, take an *o*
35: 5 to bring to the LORD an *o* of gold,
35: 16 the altar of burnt *o*
35: 21 and brought an *o* to the LORD
35: 22 as a wave *o* to the LORD.
35: 24 Those presenting an *o* of silver
35: 24 or bronze brought it as an *o*
36: 6 as an *o* for the sanctuary.''
38: 1 the altar of burnt *o* of acacia wood,
38: 24 the gold from the wave *o* used
38: 29 from the wave *o* was 70 talents
40: 6 ''Place the altar of burnt *o* in front
40: 10 Then anoint the altar of burnt *o*
40: 29 altar of burnt *o* near the entrance
Lev 1: 2 bring as your *o* an animal from
1: 2 of you brings an *o* to the LORD,
1: 3 If the *o* is a burnt *o* from the herd,
1: 4 hand on the head of the burnt *o*,
1: 6 He is to skin the burnt *o*
1: 9 It is a burnt *o*, an *o* made by fire,
1: 10 If the *o* is a burnt *o* from the flock,
1: 13 It is a burnt *o*, an *o* made by fire,
1: 14 to the LORD is a burnt *o* of birds,
1: 14 '' 'If the *o* to the LORD is a burnt
1: 17 It is a burnt *o*, an *o* made by fire,
2: 1 *o* to the LORD, his *o* is to be
2: 2 *o* made by fire, an aroma pleasing
2: 3 rest of the grain *o* belongs to Aaron
2: 4 '' 'If you bring a grain *o* baked
2: 5 If your grain *o* is prepared
2: 6 and pour oil on it; it is a grain *o*.
2: 7 If your grain *o* is cooked in a pan,
2: 8 Bring the grain *o* made
2: 9 it on the altar as an *o* made by fire,
2: 9 memorial portion from the grain *o*
2: 10 rest of the grain *o* belongs to Aaron
2: 11 honey in an *o* made to the LORD
2: 11 '' 'Every grain *o* you bring
2: 12 them to the LORD as an *o*
2: 14 If you bring a grain *o* of firstfruits
2: 15 and incense on it; it is a grain *o*.
2: 16 as an *o* made to the LORD by fire.
3: 1 '' 'If someone's *o* is a fellowship *o*,
3: 2 to lay his hand on the head of his *o*
3: 3 From the fellowship *o* he is
3: 5 altar on top of the burnt *o* that is
Lev 3: 5 *o* made by fire, an aroma pleasing
3: 6 as a fellowship *o* to the LORD,
3: 8 to lay his hand on the head of his *o*
3: 9 From the fellowship *o* he is
3: 11 an *o* made to the LORD by fire.
3: 12 If his *o* is a goat, he is to present it
3: 14 to make this *o* to the LORD by fire
3: 16 an *o* made by fire, a pleasing aroma
4: 3 a sin *o* for the sin he has committed
4: 7 the altar of burnt *o* at the entrance
4: 8 the fat from the bull of the sin *o*—
4: 10 cow sacrificed as a fellowship *o*.
4: 10 them on the altar of burnt *o*.
4: 14 as a sin *o* and present it
4: 18 the altar of burnt *o* at the entrance
4: 20 as he did with the bull for the sin *o*.
4: 21 This is the sin *o* for the community.
4: 23 as his *o* a male goat without defect.
4: 24 It is a sin *o*.
4: 24 where the burnt *o* is slaughtered
4: 25 blood of the sin *o* with his finger
4: 25 on the horns of the altar of burnt *o*
4: 26 the fat of the fellowship *o*.
4: 28 as his *o* for the sin he committed
4: 29 hand on the head of the sin *o*
4: 29 it at the place of the burnt *o*.
4: 30 on the horns of the altar of burnt *o*
4: 31 removed from the fellowship *o*,
4: 32 '' 'If he brings a lamb as his sin *o*,
4: 33 and slaughter it for a sin *o*
4: 33 where the burnt *o* is slaughtered.
4: 34 blood of the sin *o* with his finger
4: 34 on the horns of the altar of burnt *o*
4: 35 from the lamb of the fellowship *o*,
5: 6 or goat from the flock as a sin *o*;
5: 7 and the other for a burnt *o*.
5: 7 one for a sin *o* and the other
5: 8 shall first offer the one for the sin *o*.
5: 9 It is a sin *o*.
5: 9 blood of the sin *o* against the side
5: 10 as a burnt *o* in the prescribed way
5: 11 an *o* for his sin a tenth of an ephah
5: 11 incense on it, because it is a sin *o*.
5: 11 of an ephah of fine flour for a sin *o*.
5: 12 It is a sin *o*.
5: 13 The rest of the *o* will belong
5: 13 as in the case of the grain *o*.' ''
5: 15 It is a guilt *o*.
5: 16 for him with the ram as a guilt *o*,
5: 18 as a guilt *o* a ram from the flock,
5: 19 It is a guilt *o*; he has been guilty
6: 5 on the day he presents his guilt *o*.
6: 6 his guilt *o*, a ram from the flock,
6: 9 The burnt *o* is to remain
6: 9 are the regulations for the burnt *o*:
6: 10 of the burnt *o* that the fire has
6: 12 and arrange the burnt *o* on the fire
6: 14 are the regulations for the grain *o*:
6: 15 with all the incense on the grain *o*,
6: 17 Like the sin *o* and the guilt *o*,
6: 20 This is the *o* Aaron and his sons are
6: 20 of fine flour as a regular grain *o*,
6: 21 present the grain *o* broken in pieces
6: 23 Every grain *o* of a priest shall be
6: 25 The sin *o* is to be slaughtered
6: 25 are the regulations for the sin *o*:
6: 25 place the burnt *o* is slaughtered;
6: 30 any sin *o* whose blood is brought
7: 1 are the regulations for the guilt *o*,
7: 2 The guilt *o* is to be slaughtered
7: 2 where the burnt *o* is slaughtered,
7: 5 It is a guilt *o*.
7: 5 as an *o* made to the LORD by fire.
7: 7 to both the sin *o* and the guilt *o*:
7: 8 The priest who offers a burnt *o*
7: 9 Every grain *o* baked in an oven
7: 10 and every grain *o*, whether mixed
7: 11 for the fellowship *o* a person may
7: 13 Along with his fellowship *o*
7: 13 is to present an *o* with cakes
7: 14 is to bring one of each kind as an *o*,
7: 15 The meat of his fellowship *o*
7: 16 his *o* is the result of a vow
7: 16 the result of a vow or is a freewill *o*,
7: 18 meat of the fellowship *o* is eaten
7: 20 meat of the fellowship *o* belonging
7: 21 meat of the fellowship *o* belonging
7: 25 from which an *o* by fire may be
Lev 7: 29 'Anyone who brings a fellowship *o*
7: 30 before the LORD as a wave *o*.
7: 30 is to bring the *o* made to the LORD
7: 33 fat of the fellowship *o* shall have
7: 37 are the regulations for the burnt *o*,
7: 37 ordination *o* and the fellowship *o*,
7: 37 the grain *o*, the sin *o*, the guilt *o*,
8: 2 anointing oil, the bull for the sin *o*,
8: 14 presented the bull for the sin *o*,
8: 18 presented the ram for the burnt *o*,
8: 21 an *o* made to the LORD by fire,
8: 21 ram on the altar as a burnt *o*,
8: 27 before the LORD as a wave *o*.
8: 28 an *o* made to the LORD by fire.
8: 28 of the burnt *o* as an ordination *o*,
8: 29 it before the LORD as a wave *o*,
9: 2 and a ram for your burnt *o*,
9: 2 ''Take a bull calf for your sin *o*
9: 3 and without defect—for a burnt *o*,
9: 3 'Take a male goat for a sin *o*,
9: 4 a ram for a fellowship *o* to sacrifice
9: 4 with a grain *o* mixed with oil.
9: 7 sacrifice the *o* that is for the people
9: 7 sacrifice your sin *o* and your burnt
9: 7 your burnt *o* and make atonement
9: 8 and slaughtered the calf as a sin *o*
9: 10 covering of the liver from the sin *o*,
9: 12 Then he slaughtered the burnt *o*.
9: 13 They handed him the burnt *o* piece
9: 14 on top of the burnt *o* on the altar.
9: 15 Aaron then brought the *o* that was
9: 15 and offered it for a sin *o* as he did
9: 15 the goat for the people's sin *o*
9: 16 He brought the burnt *o*
9: 17 He also brought the grain *o*,
9: 17 addition to the morning's burnt *o*.
9: 18 as the fellowship *o* for the people.
9: 21 before the LORD as a wave *o*,
9: 22 And having sacrificed the sin *o*,
9: 22 the burnt *o* and the fellowship *o*,
9: 24 and consumed the burnt *o*
10: 12 ''Take the grain *o* left
10: 15 before the LORD as a wave *o*.
10: 16 inquired about the goat of the sin *o*
10: 17 ''Why didn't you eat the sin *o*
10: 19 if I had eaten the sin *o* today?''
10: 19 their burnt *o* before the LORD,
10: 19 ''Today they sacrificed their sin *o*
12: 6 a year-old lamb for a burnt *o*
12: 6 a young pigeon or a dove for a sin *o*
12: 8 a burnt *o* and the other for a sin *o*.
14: 10 mixed with oil for a grain *o*,
14: 12 before the LORD as a wave *o*.
14: 12 male lambs and offer it as a guilt *o*,
14: 13 Like the sin *o*, the guilt *o* belongs
14: 13 and the burnt *o* are slaughtered.
14: 13 in the holy place where the sin *o*
14: 14 some of the blood of the guilt *o*
14: 17 on top of the blood of the guilt *o*.
14: 19 priest shall slaughter the burnt *o*
14: 19 the priest is to sacrifice the sin *o*
14: 20 together with the grain *o*,
14: 21 as a guilt *o* to be waved
14: 21 mixed with oil for a grain *o*,
14: 22 and the other for a burnt *o*.
14: 22 one for a sin *o* and the other
14: 24 before the LORD as a wave *o*.
14: 24 is to take the lamb for the guilt *o*,
14: 25 slaughter the lamb for the guilt *o*
14: 28 he put the blood of the guilt *o*—
14: 31 a burnt *o*, together with the grain *o*.
14: 31 as a sin *o* and the other as a burnt *o*,
15: 15 and the other for a burnt *o*.
15: 15 the one for a sin *o* and the other
15: 30 and the other for a burnt *o*.
15: 30 is to sacrifice one for a sin *o*
16: 3 for a sin *o* and a ram for a burnt *o*.
16: 5 for a sin *o* and a ram for a burnt *o*.
16: 6 his own sin *o* to make atonement
16: 9 LORD and sacrifice it for a sin *o*.
16: 11 his own sin *o* to make atonement
16: 11 slaughter the bull for his own sin *o*.
16: 15 the goat for the sin *o* for the people
16: 24 and the burnt *o* for the people,
16: 24 sacrifice the burnt *o* for himself
16: 25 burn the fat of the sin *o* on the altar
17: 4 as an *o* to the LORD in front
17: 8 among them who offers a burnt *o*

Lev 19: 5 When you sacrifice a fellowship *o*
19: 21 Meeting for a guilt *o* to the LORD.
19: 22 the ram of the guilt *o* the priest is
19: 24 an *o* of praise to the LORD.
22: 16 family may eat the sacred *o*,
22: 14 restitution to the priest for the *o*
22: 14 " 'If anyone eats a sacred *o*
22: 18 a gift for a burnt *o* to the LORD,
22: 18 to fulfill a vow or as a freewill *o*,
22: 21 a special vow or as a freewill *o*,
22: 21 flock a fellowship *o* to the LORD
22: 22 as an *o* made to the LORD by fire.
22: 23 present as a freewill *o* a cow
22: 27 as an *o* made to the LORD by fire.
22: 29 "When you sacrifice an *o*
23: 8 For seven days present an *o* made
23: 12 burnt *o* to the LORD a lamb a year
23: 13 an *o* made to the LORD by fire,
23: 13 and its drink *o* of a fourth of a hin
23: 13 with its grain *o* of two-tenths
23: 14 until the very day you bring this *o*
23: 15 brought the sheaf of the wave *o*,
23: 16 and then present an *o* of new grain
23: 17 a wave *o* of firstfruits to the LORD
23: 18 They will be a burnt *o*
23: 18 drink offerings—an *o* made by fire,
23: 19 each a year old, for a fellowship *o*.
23: 19 sacrifice one male goat for a sin *o*
23: 20 They are a sacred *o* to the LORD
23: 20 before the LORD as a wave *o*,
23: 25 present an *o* made to the LORD
23: 27 present an *o* made to the LORD
23: 36 present an *o* made to the LORD
24: 7 and to be an *o* made to the LORD
27: 9 an animal that is acceptable as an *o*
27: 11 one that is not acceptable as an *o*
Nu 3: 4 the LORD when they made an *o*
4: 16 regular grain *o* and the anointing
5: 15 a reminder *o* to draw attention
5: 15 because it is a grain *o* for jealousy,
5: 15 take an *o* of a tenth of an ephah
5: 18 place in her hands the reminder *o*,
5: 18 the grain *o* for jealousy,
5: 25 take from her hands the grain *o*
5: 26 as a memorial *o* and burn it
5: 26 then to take a handful of the grain *o*
6: 11 The priest is to offer one as a sin *o*
6: 11 as a burnt *o* to make atonement
6: 12 a year-old male lamb as a guilt *o*.
6: 14 lamb without defect for a burnt *o*,
6: 14 lamb without defect for a sin *o*,
6: 14 without defect for a fellowship *o*,
6: 16 and make the sin *o* and the burnt *o*.
6: 17 as a fellowship *o* to the LORD,
6: 17 with its grain *o* and drink *o*.
6: 18 the sacrifice of the fellowship *o*.
6: 20 before the LORD as a wave *o*;
6: 21 law of the Nazirite who vows his *o*
7: 11 is to bring his *o* for the dedication
7: 12 The one who brought his *o*
7: 13 His *o* was one silver plate weighing
7: 13 mixed with oil as a grain *o*;
7: 15 for a burnt *o*; one male goat
7: 16 one male goat for a sin *o*;
7: 17 This was the *o* of Nahshon son
7: 17 to be sacrificed as a fellowship *o*.
7: 18 leader of Issachar, brought his *o*.
7: 19 mixed with oil as a grain *o*;
7: 19 *o* he brought was one silver plate
7: 21 for a burnt *o*; one male goat
7: 22 one male goat for a sin *o*;
7: 23 This was the *o* of Nethanel son
7: 23 to be sacrificed as a fellowship *o*.
7: 24 people of Zebulun, brought his *o*.
7: 25 His *o* was one silver plate weighing
7: 25 mixed with oil as a grain *o*;
7: 27 for a burnt *o*; one male goat
7: 28 one male goat for a sin *o*;
7: 29 This was the *o* of Eliab son
7: 29 to be sacrificed as a fellowship *o*.
7: 30 people of Reuben, brought his *o*.
7: 31 His *o* was one silver plate weighing
7: 31 mixed with oil as a grain *o*;
7: 33 for a burnt *o*; one male goat
7: 34 one male goat for a sin *o*;
7: 35 This was the *o* of Elizur son
7: 35 to be sacrificed as a fellowship *o*.
7: 36 people of Simeon, brought his *o*.

Nu 7: 37 His *o* was one silver plate weighing
7: 37 mixed with oil as a grain *o*;
7: 39 for a burnt *o*; one male goat
7: 40 one male goat for a sin *o*;
7: 41 This was the *o* of Shelumiel son
7: 41 to be sacrificed as a fellowship *o*.
7: 42 of the people of Gad, brought his *o*.
7: 43 His *o* was one silver plate weighing
7: 43 mixed with oil as a grain *o*;
7: 45 for a burnt *o*; one male goat
7: 46 one male goat for a sin *o*;
7: 47 This was the *o* of Eliasaph son
7: 47 to be sacrificed as a fellowship *o*.
7: 48 people of Ephraim, brought his *o*.
7: 49 His *o* was one silver plate weighing
7: 49 mixed with oil as a grain *o*;
7: 51 for a burnt *o*; one male goat
7: 52 one male goat for a sin *o*;
7: 53 This was the *o* of Elishama son
7: 53 to be sacrificed as a fellowship *o*.
7: 54 people of Manasseh, brought his *o*.
7: 55 His *o* was one silver plate weighing
7: 55 mixed with oil as a grain *o*;
7: 57 for a burnt *o*; one male goat
7: 58 one male goat for a sin *o*;
7: 59 This was the *o* of Gamaliel son
7: 59 to be sacrificed as a fellowship *o*.
7: 60 people of Benjamin, brought his *o*.
7: 61 His *o* was one silver plate weighing
7: 61 mixed with oil as a grain *o*;
7: 63 for a burnt *o*; one male goat
7: 64 one male goat for a sin *o*;
7: 65 This was the *o* of Abidan son
7: 65 to be sacrificed as a fellowship *o*.
7: 66 of the people of Dan, brought his *o*.
7: 67 His *o* was one silver plate weighing
7: 67 mixed with oil as a grain *o*;
7: 69 for a burnt *o*; one male goat
7: 70 one male goat for a sin *o*;
7: 71 This was the *o* of Ahiezer son
7: 71 to be sacrificed as a fellowship *o*.
7: 72 the people of Asher, brought his *o*.
7: 73 His *o* was one silver plate weighing
7: 73 mixed with oil as a grain *o*;
7: 75 for a burnt *o*; one male goat
7: 76 one male goat for a sin *o*;
7: 77 This was the *o* of Pagiel son
7: 77 to be sacrificed as a fellowship *o*.
7: 78 people of Naphtali, brought his *o*.
7: 79 His *o* was one silver plate weighing
7: 79 mixed with oil as a grain *o*;
7: 81 for a burnt *o*; one male goat
7: 82 one male goat for a sin *o*;
7: 83 This was the *o* of Ahira son
7: 83 to be sacrificed as a fellowship *o*.
7: 87 male goats were used for the sin *o*.
7: 87 of animals for the burnt *o* came
7: 87 together with their grain *o*.
7: 88 sacrifice of the fellowship *o* came
8: 8 take a second young bull for a sin *o*.
8: 8 with its grain *o* of fine flour mixed
8: 11 as a wave *o* from the Israelites,
8: 12 and the other for a burnt *o*,
8: 12 use the one for a sin *o* to the LORD
8: 13 as a wave *o* to the LORD.
8: 15 and presented them as a wave *o*,
8: 21 as a wave *o* before the LORD
9: 7 from presenting the LORD's *o*
9: 13 he did not present the LORD's *o*
15: 4 one who brings his *o* shall present
15: 4 to the LORD a grain *o* of a tenth
15: 5 With each lamb for the burnt *o*
15: 5 fourth of a hin of wine as a drink *o*.
15: 6 " 'With a ram prepare a grain *o*
15: 7 a third of a hin of wine as a drink *o*.
15: 8 or a fellowship *o* to the LORD,
15: 8 prepare a young bull as a burnt *o*
15: 9 bring with the bull a grain *o*
15: 10 It will be an *o* made by fire,
15: 10 bring half a hin of wine as a drink *o*.
15: 13 when he brings an *o* made by fire
15: 14 among you presents an *o* made
15: 19 present a portion as an *o*
15: 20 as an *o* from the threshing floor.
15: 21 are to give this *o* to the LORD
15: 24 and a male goat for a sin *o*.
15: 24 is to offer a young bull for a burnt *o*
15: 24 its prescribed grain *o* and drink *o*,

Nu 15: 25 for their wrong an *o* made by fire
15: 25 made by fire and a sin *o*.
15: 27 a year-old female goat for a sin *o*.
16: 15 the LORD, "Do not accept their *o*.
16: 35 250 men who were *o* the incense.
18: 17 burn their fat as an *o* made by fire,
18: 18 as the breast of the wave *o*
18: 24 that the Israelites present as an *o*
18: 26 of that tithe as the LORD's *o*.
18: 27 Your *o* will be reckoned to you
18: 28 also will present an *o* to the LORD
19: 17 from the burned purification *o*
23: 3 "Stay here beside your *o* while I go
23: 6 found him standing beside his *o*,
23: 15 here beside your *o* while I meet
23: 17 found him standing beside his *o*,
26: 61 died when they made an *o*
28: 3 as a regular burnt *o* each day.
28: 3 'This is the *o* made
28: 5 together with a grain *o* of a tenth
28: 6 an *o* made to the LORD by fire.
28: 6 is the regular burnt *o* instituted
28: 7 Pour out the drink *o* to the LORD
28: 7 The accompanying drink *o* is
28: 8 This is an *o* made by fire, an aroma
28: 8 along with the same kind of grain *o*
28: 8 and drink *o* that you prepare
28: 9 a grain *o* of two-tenths of an ephah
28: 9 make an *o* of two lambs a year old
28: 9 together with its drink *o*
28: 10 This is the burnt *o*
28: 10 the regular burnt *o* and its drink *o*.
28: 11 present to the LORD a burnt *o*
28: 12 a grain *o* of two-tenths of an ephah
28: 12 is to be a grain *o* of three-tenths
28: 13 a grain *o* of a tenth of an ephah
28: 13 an *o* made to the LORD by fire.
28: 13 is for a burnt *o*, a pleasing aroma,
28: 14 This is the monthly burnt *o*
28: 14 to be a drink *o* of half a hin of wine,
28: 15 presented to the LORD as a sin *o*.
28: 15 the regular burnt *o* with its drink *o*,
28: 19 a burnt *o* of two young bulls,
28: 19 to the LORD an *o* made by fire,
28: 20 With each bull prepare a grain *o*
28: 22 a sin *o* to make atonement for you.
28: 23 to the regular morning burnt *o*.
28: 24 for the *o* made by fire every day
28: 24 the regular burnt *o* and its drink *o*.
28: 26 to the LORD an *o* of new grain
28: 27 Present a burnt *o* of two young
28: 28 is to be a grain *o* of three-tenths
28: 31 the regular burnt *o* and its grain *o*.
29: 2 prepare a burnt *o* of one young bull
29: 3 With the bull prepare a grain *o*
29: 5 a sin *o* to make atonement for you.
29: 8 pleasing to the LORD a burnt *o*
29: 9 With the bull prepare a grain *o*
29: 11 Include one male goat as a sin *o*,
29: 11 addition to the sin *o* for atonement
29: 11 the regular burnt *o* with its grain *o*,
29: 13 Present an *o* made by fire
29: 13 a burnt *o* of thirteen young bulls,
29: 14 the thirteen bulls prepare a grain *o*
29: 16 Include one male goat as a sin *o*,
29: 16 addition to the regular burnt *o*
29: 16 with its grain *o* and drink *o*.
29: 19 Include one male goat as a sin *o*,
29: 19 the regular burnt *o* with its grain *o*,
29: 22 Include one male goat as a sin *o*,
29: 22 addition to the regular burnt *o*
29: 22 with its grain *o* and drink *o*.
29: 25 Include one male goat as a sin *o*,
29: 25 addition to the regular burnt *o*
29: 25 with its grain *o* and drink *o*.
29: 28 Include one male goat as a sin *o*,
29: 28 addition to the regular burnt *o*
29: 28 with its grain *o* and drink *o*.
29: 31 Include one male goat as a sin *o*,
29: 31 addition to the regular burnt *o*
29: 31 with its grain *o* and drink *o*.
29: 34 Include one male goat as a sin *o*,
29: 34 addition to the regular burnt *o*
29: 34 with its grain *o* and drink *o*.
29: 36 Present an *o* made by fire
29: 36 a burnt *o* of one bull, one ram
29: 38 Include one male goat as a sin *o*,
29: 38 addition to the regular burnt *o*

Nu 29: 38 with its grain *o* and drink *o*.
31: 50 an *o* to the LORD the gold articles
Dt 2: 26 to Sihon king of Heshbon *o* peace
13: 16 a whole burnt *o* to the LORD your
16: 10 by giving a freewill *o* in proportion
24: 10 go into his house to get what he is *o*
Jdg 6: 18 bring my *o* and set it before you."
6: 26 offer the second bull as a burnt *o*."
11: 31 and I will sacrifice it as a burnt *o*."
13: 16 But if you prepare a burnt *o*,
13: 19 together with the grain *o*,
13: 23 and grain *o* from our hands,
13: 23 would not have accepted a burnt *o*
1Sa 2: 17 they were treating the LORD's *o*
2: 29 parts of every *o* made by my people
2: 29 *o* that I prescribed for my dwelling
3: 14 atoned for by sacrifice or *o*.' "
6: 3 by all means send a guilt *o* to him.
6: 4 What guilt *o* should we send to him
6: 8 back to him as a guilt *o*.
6: 14 as a burnt *o* to the LORD.
6: 17 as a guilt *o* to the LORD—
7: 9 as a whole burnt *o* to the LORD.
7: 10 Samuel was sacrificing the burnt *o*,
13: 9 And Saul offered up the burnt *o*.
13: 9 "Bring me the burnt *o*
13: 10 Just as he finished making the *o*,
13: 12 I felt compelled to offer the burnt *o*
26: 19 me, then may he accept an *o*.
2Sa 15: 12 While Absalom was *o* sacrifices,
24: 22 Here are oxen for the burnt *o*,
1Ki 13: 1 standing by the altar to make an *o*.
18: 33 pour it on the *o* and on the wood."
2Ki 3: 20 about the time for *o* the sacrifice,
10: 25 had finished making the burnt *o*,
16: 13 offered up his burnt *o* and grain *o*,
16: 13 poured out his drink *o*,
16: 15 and the burnt *o* of all the people
16: 15 and their grain *o* and their drink *o*.
16: 15 burnt *o* and the evening grain *o*,
16: 15 the king's burnt *o* and his grain *o*,
1Ch 6: 49 offerings on the altar of burnt *o*
9: 31 for baking the *o* bread.
16: 29 Bring an *o* and come before him;
16: 40 on the altar of burnt *o* regularly,
21: 23 and the wheat for the grain *o*.
21: 24 or sacrifice a burnt *o* that costs me
21: 26 from heaven on the altar of burnt *o*.
21: 29 and the altar of burnt *o* were
22: 1 also the altar of burnt *o* for Israel."
2Ch 7: 1 and consumed the burnt *o*
29: 18 the altar of burnt *o*
29: 21 as a sin *o* for the kingdom,
29: 23 goats for the sin *o* were brought
29: 24 for a sin *o* to atone for all Israel,
29: 24 ordered the burnt *o* and the sin *o*
29: 27 As the *o* began, singing
29: 27 to sacrifice the burnt *o* on the altar.
29: 28 of the burnt *o* was completed.
35: 16 the *o* of burnt offerings on the altar
Ezr 6: 17 as a sin *o* for all Israel, twelve male
8: 25 out to them the *o* of silver
8: 28 gold are a freewill *o* to the LORD,
8: 35 All this was a burnt *o* to the LORD
8: 35 and as a sin *o*, twelve male goats.
10: 19 a ram from the flock as a guilt *o*.)
Job 1: 5 he would sacrifice a burnt *o*
42: 8 sacrifice a burnt *o* for yourselves.
Ps 40: 6 Sacrifice and *o* you did not desire,
54: 6 I will sacrifice a freewill *o* to you;
66: 15 and an *o* of rams;
96: 8 bring an *o* and come into his courts
116: 17 I will sacrifice a thank *o* to you
Isa 40: 20 to present such an *o*
53: 10 the LORD makes his life a guilt *o*,
65: 3 *o* sacrifices in gardens
66: 3 whoever makes a grain *o*
66: 20 in Jerusalem as an *o* to the LORD
Eze 16: 25 *o* your body with increasing
43: 19 are to give a young bull as a sin *o*
43: 21 are to take the bull for the sin *o*
43: 22 goat without defect for a sin *o*,
43: 24 as a burnt *o* to the LORD.
43: 25 a male goat daily for a sin *o*;
44: 27 he is to offer a sin *o* for himself,
45: 19 some of the blood of the sin *o*
45: 22 as a sin *o* for himself and for all
45: 23 and a male goat for a sin *o*.
Eze 45: 23 as a burnt *o* to the LORD,
45: 24 as a grain *o* an ephah for each bull
46: 2 are to sacrifice his burnt *o*
46: 4 The burnt *o* the prince brings
46: 5 The grain *o* given with the ram is
46: 5 the grain *o* with the lambs is to be
46: 7 a grain *o* one ephah with the bull,
46: 11 the grain *o* is to be an ephah
46: 12 He shall offer his burnt *o*
46: 12 a burnt *o* or fellowship offerings—
46: 12 the prince provides a freewill *o*
46: 13 defect for a burnt *o* to the LORD;
46: 14 The presenting of this grain *o*
46: 14 morning by morning a grain *o*,
46: 15 So the lamb and the grain *o*
46: 15 by morning for a regular burnt *o*.
46: 20 and the sin *o* and bake the grain *o*,
46: 20 the priests will cook the guilt *o*
Da 2: 46 ordered that an *o* and incense be
9: 27 will put an end to sacrifice and *o*.
Am 4: 5 Burn leavened bread as a thank *o*
Mal 1: 8 Try *o* them to your governor!
1: 10 I will accept no *o* from your hands.
Mt 5: 23 if you are *o* your gift at the altar
Jn 16: 2 kills you will think he is *o* a service
Ac 21: 26 and the *o* would be made for each
Ro 8: 3 likeness of sinful man to be a sin *o*.
15: 16 might become an *o* acceptable
2Co 8: 19 to accompany us as we carry the *o*,
Eph 5: 2 as a fragrant *o* and sacrifice to God.
Php 2: 17 I am being poured out like a drink *o*
4: 18 are a fragrant *o*, an acceptable
2Ti 4: 6 being poured out like a drink *o*,
Heb 10: 5 "Sacrifice and *o* you did not desire,
13: 11 into the Most Holy Place as a sin *o*,
1Pe 2: 5 *o* spiritual sacrifices acceptable

OFFERINGS (OFFER)

Ge 8: 20 he sacrificed burnt *o* on it.
Ex 10: 25 and burnt *o* to present
20: 24 on it your burnt *o* and fellowship *o*,
22: 29 "Do not hold back *o*
23: 18 of my festival *o* must not be kept
24: 5 and they offered burnt *o*
24: 5 as fellowship *o* to the LORD.
25: 3 These are the *o* you are to receive
25: 29 and bowls for the pouring out of *o*.
29: 28 the LORD from their fellowship *o*.
29: 33 They are to eat these *o*
32: 6 and presented fellowship *o*.
32: 6 sacrificed burnt *o* and presented
35: 29 brought to the LORD freewill *o*
36: 3 Moses all the *o* the Israelites had
36: 3 to bring freewill *o* morning
37: 16 for the pouring out of drink *o*.
40: 29 offered on it burnt *o* and grain *o*,
Lev 2: 3 of the *o* made to the LORD by fire.
2: 10 of the *o* made to the LORD by fire.
2: 13 Season all your grain *o* with salt.
2: 13 your grain *o*; add salt to all your *o*.
4: 35 on top of the *o* made to the LORD
5: 12 on top of the *o* made to the LORD
6: 12 the fat of the fellowship *o* on it.
6: 17 as their share of the *o* made to me
6: 18 of the *o* made to the LORD by fire
7: 14 the blood of the fellowship *o*.
7: 32 of your fellowship *o* to the priest
7: 34 From the fellowship *o*
7: 35 of the *o* made to the LORD
7: 38 to bring their *o* to the LORD,
8: 31 from the basket of ordination *o*,
10: 12 over from the *o* made to the LORD
10: 13 share of the *o* made to the LORD
10: 14 share of the Israelites' fellowship *o*.
10: 15 portions of the *o* made by fire,
14: 11 and his *o* before the LORD
14: 32 who cannot afford the regular *o*
16: 27 The bull and the goat for the sin *o*,
17: 5 and sacrifice them as fellowship *o*.
21: 6 Because they present the *o* made
21: 21 come near to present the *o* made
22: 2 respect the sacred *o* the Israelites
22: 3 near the sacred *o* that the Israelites
22: 4 he may not eat the sacred *o*
22: 6 He must not eat any of the sacred *o*
22: 7 after that he may eat the sacred *o*,
22: 15 the sacred *o* the Israelites
22: 16 them to eat the sacred *o*
Lev 23: 18 with their grain *o* and drink *o*—
23: 36 For seven days present *o* made
23: 37 and drink *o* required for each day.
23: 37 assemblies for bringing *o* made
23: 37 the burnt *o* and grain *o*, sacrifices
23: 38 These *o* are in addition to those
23: 38 and all the freewill *o* you give
24: 9 share of the *o* made to the LORD
26: 31 in the pleasing aroma of your *o*.
Nu 4: 7 and bowls, and the jars for drink *o*;
6: 14 is to present his *o* to the LORD:
6: 15 with their grain *o* and drink *o*,
7: 2 of those who were counted, made *o*
7: 10 the leaders brought their *o*
7: 84 These were the *o* of the Israelite
7: 88 These were the *o* for the dedication
10: 10 over your burnt *o* and fellowship *o*,
15: 3 or freewill *o* or festival *o*—
15: 3 to the LORD *o* made by fire,
15: 3 whether burnt *o* or sacrifices,
18: 8 all the holy *o* the Israelites give me
18: 8 in charge of the *o* presented to me;
18: 9 gifts they bring me as most holy *o*,
18: 9 part of the most holy *o* that is kept
18: 9 whether grain or sin or guilt *o*,
18: 11 of all the wave *o* of the Israelites.
18: 19 aside from the holy *o* the Israelites
18: 32 then you will not defile the holy *o*
28: 2 the food for my *o* made by fire,
28: 31 together with their drink *o*,
29: 6 They are *o* made to the LORD
29: 6 and daily burnt *o* with their grain
29: 6 with their grain *o* and drink *o*
29: 11 its grain offering, and their drink *o*.
29: 18 drink *o* according to the number
29: 18 prepare their grain *o* and drink
29: 19 its grain offering, and their drink *o*.
29: 21 drink *o* according to the number
29: 21 prepare their grain *o* and drink
29: 24 drink *o* according to the number
29: 24 prepare their grain *o* and drink
29: 27 drink *o* according to the number
29: 27 prepare their grain *o* and drink
29: 30 drink *o* according to the number
29: 30 prepare their grain *o* and drink
29: 33 drink *o* according to the number
29: 33 prepare their grain *o* and drink
29: 37 drink *o* according to the number
29: 37 prepare their grain *o* and drink
29: 39 drink *o* and fellowship *o*.' "
29: 39 what you vow and your freewill *o*,
29: 39 your burnt *o*, grain *o*, drink
Dt 12: 6 there bring your burnt *o*
12: 6 vowed to give and your freewill *o*,
12: 11 your burnt *o* and sacrifices,
12: 13 your burnt *o* anywhere you
12: 17 or your freewill *o* or special gifts.
12: 27 Present your burnt *o* on the altar
18: 1 live on the *o* made to the LORD
27: 6 offer burnt *o* on it to the LORD
27: 7 Sacrifice fellowship *o* there,
32: 38 and drank the wine of their drink *o*
33: 10 and whole burnt *o* on your altar.
Jos 8: 31 and sacrificed fellowship *o*.
8: 31 offered to the LORD burnt *o*
13: 14 since the *o* made by fire
22: 23 and to offer burnt *o* and grain *o*,
22: 23 or to sacrifice fellowship *o* on it,
22: 26 but not for burnt *o* or sacrifices.'
22: 27 at his sanctuary with our burnt *o*,
22: 27 sacrifices and fellowship *o*.
22: 28 not for burnt *o* and sacrifices,
22: 29 by building an altar for burnt *o*,
22: 29 grain *o* and sacrifices, other
Jdg 20: 26 and fellowship *o* to the LORD.
20: 26 presented burnt *o* and fellowship
21: 4 presented burnt *o* and fellowship *o*.
1Sa 2: 28 your father's house all the *o* made
6: 15 Beth Shemesh offered burnt *o*
10: 8 sacrifice burnt *o* and fellowship *o*,
11: 15 There they sacrificed fellowship *o*
13: 9 offering and the fellowship *o*."
15: 22 Does the LORD delight in burnt *o*
2Sa 1: 21 nor fields that yield *o* of grain.
6: 17 and David sacrificed burnt *o*
6: 17 and fellowship *o* before the LORD.
6: 18 the burnt *o* and fellowship *o*,
24: 24 my God burnt *o* that cost me

OFFERS (OFFER)

OFFICE (OFFICER OFFICERS OFFICIAL OFFICIALS OFFICIATE)

OFFICER (OFFICE)

OFFICERS (OFFICE)

Nu 31: 48 Then the *o* who were over the units
Dt 20: 5 The *o* shall say to the army:
20: 8 the *o* shall add, "Is any man afraid
20: 9 When the *o* have finished speaking
Jos 1: 10 Joshua ordered the *o* of the people:
3: 2 After three days the *o* went
1Sa 18: 5 pleased all the people, and Saul's *o*
18: 30 success than the rest of Saul's *o*,
2Sa 8: 7 belonged to the *o* of Hadadezer
1Ki 4: 5 charge of the district *o;* Zabud son
4: 27 The district *o*, each in his month,
9: 22 his government officials, his *o*,
20: 14 'The young *o* of the provincial
20: 15 So Ahab summoned the young *o*
20: 17 The young *o* of the provincial
20: 19 The young *o* of the provincial
20: 24 and replace them with other *o*.
2Ki 6: 8 After conferring with his *o*, he said,
6: 11 He summoned his *o* and demanded
6: 12 said one of his *o*, "but Elisha,
7: 12 up in the night and said to his *o*,
7: 13 of his *o* answered, "Have some
9: 5 found the army *o* sitting together.
9: 11 When Jehu went out to his fellow *o*
10: 25 and *o* threw the bodies out
10: 25 he ordered the guards and *o:*
11: 14 The *o* and the trumpeters were
15: 25 One of his chief *o*, Pekah son
24: 10 time the *o* of Nebuchadnezzar king
24: 11 city while his *o* were besieging it.
24: 14 all the *o* and fighting men,
25: 23 When all the army *o* and their men
25: 26 with the army *o*, fled to Egypt
1Ch 11: 11 a Hacmonite, was chief of the *o;*
12: 28 with 22 *o* from his family;
12: 34 men of Naphtali—1,000 *o*,
13: 1 David conferred with each of his *o*,
18: 7 carried by the *o* of Hadadezer
27: 1 of hundreds, and their *o*,
27: 3 of all the army *o* for the first month
27: 16 The *o* over the tribes of Israel:
27: 22 These were the *o* over the tribes
28: 1 at Jerusalem: the *o* over the tribes,
29: 6 the *o* of the tribes of Israel,
29: 24 All the *o* and mighty men,
2Ch 8: 18 ships commanded by his own *o*,
21: 9 So Jehoram went there with his *o*
23: 13 The *o* and the trumpeters were
32: 6 He appointed military *o*
32: 9 he sent his *o* to Jerusalem
32: 16 Sennacherib's *o* spoke further
32: 21 *o* in the camp of the Assyrian king.
35: 23 and he told his *o*, "Take me away;
Ne 2: 9 sent army *o* and cavalry with me.
4: 16 The *o* posted themselves
Est 2: 21 two of the king's *o* who guarded
6: 2 two of the king's *o*, who guarded
Isa 21: 5 Get up, you *o*,
Jer 26: 21 and all his *o* and officials heard his
38: 17 If you surrender to the *o* of the king
38: 18 to the *o* of the king of Babylon,
39: 13 and all the other *o* of the king
40: 7 When all the army *o* and their men
40: 13 and all the army *o* still
41: 1 and had been one of the king's *o*,
41: 11 and all the army *o* who were
41: 13 and the army *o* who were with him,
41: 16 and all the army *o* who were
42: 1 all the army *o*, including Johanan
42: 8 all the army *o* who were with him
43: 4 son of Kareah and all the army *o*
43: 5 and all the army *o* led away all
46: 26 king of Babylon and his *o*.
51: 57 her governors, *o* and warriors
Eze 23: 15 looked like Babylonian chariot *o*,
23: 23 chariot *o* and men of high rank,
Lk 22: 4 and the *o* of the temple guard
22: 52 the *o* of the temple guard,
Ac 5: 22 the *o* did not find them there.
5: 26 the captain went with his *o*
16: 35 the magistrates sent their *o*
16: 37 to the *o:* "They beat us publicly
16: 38 The *o* reported this
21: 32 He at once took some *o*
25: 23 room with the high ranking *o*

OFFICIAL (OFFICE)

2Ki 8: 6 Then he assigned an *o* to her case
2Ki 23: 11 of an *o* named Nathan-Melech.
25: 8 an *o* of the king of Babylon,
1Ch 9: 11 the *o* in charge of the house of God
2Ch 13: 6 an *o* of Solomon son of David,
31: 13 and Azariah the *o* in charge
Ne 2: 10 the Ammonite *o* heard about
2: 19 Tobiah the Ammonite *o*
Pr 17: 11 a merciless *o* will be sent
Ecc 5: 8 for one *o* is eyed by a higher one,
Jer 38: 7 a Cushite, an *o* in the royal palace,
39: 3 Nergal-Sharezer a high *o*
39: 13 Nergal-Sharezer a high *o*
Da 1: 7 The chief *o* gave them new names:
1: 8 and he asked the chief *o*
1: 9 Now God had caused the *o*
1: 10 but the *o* told Daniel, "I am afraid
1: 11 whom the chief *o* had appointed
1: 18 the chief *o* presented them
Jn 4: 46 was a certain royal *o* whose son lay
4: 49 The royal *o* said, "Sir, come
Ac 8: 27 an important *o* in charge
28: 7 to Publius, the chief *o* of the island.

OFFICIALS (OFFICE)

Ge 12: 15 And when Pharaoh's *o* saw her,
20: 8 Abimelech summoned all his *o*,
37: 36 one of Pharaoh's *o*, the captain
39: 1 who was one of Pharaoh's *o*,
40: 2 Pharaoh was angry with his two *o*,
40: 7 So he asked Pharaoh's *o* who were
40: 20 and he gave a feast for all his *o*.
40: 20 baker in the presence of his *o:*
41: 37 good to Pharaoh and to all his *o*.
45: 16 Pharaoh and all his *o* were pleased.
50: 7 All Pharaoh's *o* accompanied him
Ex 7: 10 down in front of Pharaoh and his *o*,
7: 20 and his *o* and struck the water
8: 3 into the houses of your *o*
8: 4 and your people and all your *o*.' "
8: 9 your *o* and your people that you
8: 11 and your houses, your *o* and your
8: 21 swarms of flies on you and your *o*,
8: 24 and into the houses of his *o*,
8: 29 flies will leave Pharaoh and his *o*
8: 31 The flies left Pharaoh and his *o*
9: 14 against your *o* and your people,
9: 20 Those *o* of Pharaoh who feared
9: 30 your *o* still do not fear the LORD
9: 34 He and his *o* hardened their hearts.
10: 1 of his *o* so that I may perform these
10: 6 of all your *o* and all the Egyptians
10: 7 Pharaoh's *o* said to him, "How
11: 3 regarded in Egypt by Pharaoh's *o*
11: 8 All these *o* of yours will come
12: 30 all his *o* and all the Egyptians got
14: 5 his *o* changed their minds about
18: 21 appoint them as *o* over thousands,
18: 25 *o* over thousands, hundreds,
Nu 11: 16 as leaders and *o* among the people.
26: 9 the community *o* who rebelled
Dt 1: 15 of fifties and of tens and as tribal *o*.
16: 18 and *o* for each of your tribes
29: 2 to all his *o* and to all his land.
29: 10 *o*, and all the other men of Israel,
31: 28 elders of your tribes and all your *o*,
34: 11 to all his *o* and to his whole land.
Jos 8: 33 with their elders, *o* and judges,
23: 2 judges and *o*— and said to them:
24: 1 leaders, judges and *o* of Israel,
Jdg 8: 6 *o* of Succoth said, "Do you already
8: 14 of the seventy-seven *o* of Succoth,
1Sa 8: 15 and give it to his *o* and attendants.
22: 6 with all his *o* standing around him.
22: 9 who was standing with Saul's *o*,
22: 17 But the king's *o* were not willing
2Sa 13: 24 the king and his *o* please join me?"
15: 14 said to all his *o* who were with him
15: 15 The king's *o* answered him,
16: 6 and all the king's *o* with stones,
16: 11 said to Abishai and all his *o*,
1Ki 1: 9 men of Judah who were royal *o*,
1: 47 Also, the royal *o* have come
4: 2 And these were his chief *o:*
9: 22 his government *o*, his officers,
9: 23 projects—550 *o* supervising
9: 23 also the chief *o* in charge
10: 5 of his *o*, the attending servants
10: 8 men must be! How happy your *o*,
1Ki 11: 17 with some Edomite *o* who had
11: 26 He was one of Solomon's *o*,
15: 18 He entrusted it to his *o*
16: 9 one of his *o*, who had command
20: 6 palace and the houses of your *o*.
20: 6 to send my *o* to search your palace
20: 23 *o* of the king of Aram advised him,
20: 31 His *o* said to him, "Look, we have
22: 3 The king of Israel had said to his *o*,
22: 9 the king of Israel called one of his *o*
2Ki 10: 1 to Samaria: to the *o* of Jezreel,
12: 20 His *o* conspired against him
12: 21 *o* who murdered him were Jozabad
14: 5 he executed the *o* who had
18: 24 of the least of my master's *o*,
19: 5 When King Hezekiah's *o* came
21: 23 Amon's *o* conspired against him
22: 9 "Your *o* have paid out the money
24: 12 and his *o* all surrendered to him.
24: 15 his *o* and the leading men
25: 24 afraid of the Babylonian *o*,"
1Ch 18: 17 and David's sons were chief *o*
23: 4 six thousand are to be *o* and judges.
24: 5 for there were *o* of the sanctuary
24: 5 *o* of God among the descendants
24: 6 presence of the king and of the *o:*
26: 29 as *o* and judges over Israel.
27: 31 All these were the *o* in charge
28: 1 David summoned all the *o* of Israel
28: 1 the *o* in charge of all the property
28: 1 together with the palace *o*,
28: 21 *o* and all the people will obey your
29: 6 *o* in charge of the king's work gave
2Ch 8: 10 also King Solomon's chief *o*—
8: 10 and fifty *o* supervising the men.
9: 4 of his *o*, the attending servants
9: 7 men must be! How happy your *o*,
17: 7 of his reign he sent his *o* Ben-Hail,
18: 8 the king of Israel called one of his *o*
19: 11 and the Levites will serve as *o*
24: 10 All the *o* and all the people brought
24: 11 in by the Levites to the king's *o*
24: 17 *o* of Judah came and paid homage
24: 25 His *o* conspired against him
25: 3 he executed the *o* who had
26: 11 of Hananiah, one of the royal *o*.
28: 14 plunder in the presence of the *o*
29: 20 gathered the city *o* together
29: 30 and his *o* ordered the Levites
30: 2 and his *o* and the whole assembly
30: 6 from the king and from his *o*,
30: 12 the king and his *o* had ordered,
30: 24 and the *o* provided them
31: 8 When Hezekiah and his *o* came
32: 3 he consulted with his *o*
33: 24 Amon's *o* conspired against him
34: 16 "Your *o* are doing everything that
35: 8 His *o* also contributed voluntarily
36: 18 the treasures of the king and his *o*.
Ezr 4: 9 and *o* over the men from Tripolis,
5: 6 the *o* of Trans-Euphrates,
6: 6 their fellow *o* of that province,
7: 28 and all the king's powerful *o*.
8: 20 and the *o* had established
8: 25 his *o* and all Israel present there
9: 2 and *o* have led the way
10: 8 with the decision of the *o*
10: 14 Let our *o* act for the whole
Ne 2: 16 or the priests or nobles or *o*
2: 16 *o* did not know where I had gone
4: 14 the *o* and the rest of the people,
4: 19 the *o* and the rest of the people,
5: 7 and then accused the nobles and *o*.
5: 12 *o* take an oath to do what they had
5: 17 fifty Jews and *o* ate at my table,
7: 5 the *o* and the common people
9: 10 against all his *o* and all the people
12: 40 together with half the *o*, as well
13: 11 So I rebuked the *o* and asked them,
Est 1: 3 a banquet for all his nobles and *o*.
2: 18 for all his nobles and *o*.
2: 23 the two *o* were hanged on a gallows
3: 2 All the royal *o* at the king's gate
3: 3 the royal *o* at the king's gate asked
4: 11 "All the king's *o* and the people
5: 11 him above the other nobles and *o*.
Pr 17: 26 or to flog *o* for their integrity.
29: 12 all his *o* become wicked.

Isa 3: 4 I will make boys their *o*;
19: 11 The *o* of Zoan are nothing but fools
19: 13 The *o* of Zoan have become fools,
30: 4 Though they have *o* in Zoan,
36: 9 of the least of my master's *o*,
37: 5 When King Hezekiah's *o* came
Jer 1: 18 against the kings of Judah, its *o*,
2: 26 they, their kings and their *o*,
4: 9 "the king and the *o* will lose heart,
8: 1 bones of the kings and *o* of Judah,
17: 25 the gates of this city with their *o*.
17: 25 their *o* will come riding in chariots
21: 7 his *o* and the people
22: 2 your *o* and your people who come
22: 4 accompanied by their *o*
24: 1 king of Judah and the *o*,
24: 8 his *o* and the survivors
25: 18 the towns of Judah, its kings and *o*,
25: 19 his attendants, his *o* and all his
26: 10 When the *o* of Judah heard about
26: 11 and the prophets said to the *o*
26: 12 Then Jeremiah said to all the *o*
26: 16 Then the *o* and all the people said
26: 21 his officers and *o* heard his words,
29: 2 the court *o* and the leaders
32: 32 their kings and *o*, their priests
34: 10 all the *o* and people who entered
34: 19 and Jerusalem, the court *o*,
34: 21 and his *o* over to their enemies who
35: 4 It was next to the room of the *o*,
36: 12 of Hananiah, and all the other *o*.
36: 12 where all the *o* were sitting:
36: 14 all the *o* sent Jehudi son
36: 19 Then the *o* said to Baruch,
36: 21 and all the *o* standing beside him.
37: 14 Jeremiah and brought him to the *o*.
37: 18 committed against you or your *o*
38: 4 Then the *o* said to the king,
38: 22 out to the *o* of the king of Babylon.
38: 25 If the *o* hear that I talked with you,
38: 27 All the *o* did come to Jeremiah
39: 3 Then all the *o* of the king
39: 3 and all the other *o* of the king
41: 16 and court *o* he had brought
44: 17 and our *o* did in the towns of Judah
44: 21 your kings and your *o*
48: 7 together with his priests and *o*.
49: 3 together with his priests and *o*.
49: 38 and destroy her king and *o*,"
50: 35 and against her *o* and wise men!
51: 23 with you I shatter governors and *o*.
51: 28 their governors and all their *o*,
51: 57 I will make her *o* and wise men
52: 10 he also killed all the *o* of Judah.
Eze 22: 27 Her *o* within her are like wolves
Da 1: 3 Ashpenaz, chief of his court *o*,
3: 2 all the other provincial *o* to come
3: 3 the other provincial *o* assembled
Am 1: 15 he and his *o* together,"
2: 3 and kill all her *o* with him,"
Na 3: 17 your *o* like swarms of locusts
Zep 3: 3 Her *o* are roaring lions,
Mt 20: 25 and their high *o* exercise authority
Mk 6: 21 Herod gave a banquet for his high *o*
10: 42 and their high *o* exercise authority
Jn 18: 3 and some *o* from the chief priests
18: 12 and the Jewish *o* arrested Jesus.
18: 18 and *o* stood around a fire they had
18: 22 one of the *o* nearby struck him
19: 6 chief priests and their *o* saw him,
Ac 17: 6 other brothers before the city *o*,
17: 8 the city *o* were thrown into turmoil
19: 31 Even some of the *o* of the province,

OFFICIATE (OFFICE)

2Ki 17: 32 of their own people to *o* for them

OFFSET

1Ki 6: 6 He made *o* ledges around the

OFFSHOOTS

Isa 22: 24 and *o*— all its lesser vessels,

OFFSPRING

Ge 3: 15 and between your *o* and hers;
12: 7 "To your *o* I will give this land."
13: 15 give to you and your *o* forever.
13: 16 I will make your *o* like the dust
Ge 13: 16 then your *o* could be counted.
15: 5 he said to him, "So shall your *o* be
17: 12 those who are not your *o*.
21: 12 Isaac that your *o* will be reckoned.
21: 13 also, because he is your *o*."
22: 18 and through your *o* all nations
24: 7 'To your *o* I will give this land'—
24: 60 may your *o* possess
26: 4 and through your *o* all nations
28: 14 blessed through you and your *o*.
38: 8 to produce *o* for your brother."
38: 9 Onan knew that the *o* would not be
38: 9 from producing *o* for his brother.
46: 6 Jacob and all his *o* went to Egypt.
46: 7 and granddaughters—all his *o*.
Ex 13: 2 The first *o* of every womb
13: 12 over to the LORD the first *o*
13: 15 to the LORD the first male *o*
34: 19 "The first *o* of every womb belongs
Lev 21: 15 so he will not defile his *o*
Nu 3: 12 of the first male *o* of every Israelite
8: 16 the first male *o* from every Israelite
18: 15 The first *o* of every womb,
18: 19 LORD for both you and your *o*."
Ru 4: 12 Through the *o* the LORD gives
2Sa 4: 8 the king against Saul and his *o*."
7: 12 I will raise up your *o*
1Ch 17: 11 I will raise up your *o*
Job 18: 19 He has no *o* or descendants
21: 8 their *o* before their eyes.
27: 14 his *o* will never have enough to eat.
Ps 37: 28 the *o* of the wicked will be cut off;
Isa 9: 20 feed on the flesh of his own *o*:
14: 20 The *o* of the wicked
14: 22 her *o* and descendants,"
22: 24 its *o* and offshoots—all its lesser
44: 3 I will pour out my Spirit on your *o*,
53: 10 he will see his *o* and prolong his
57: 3 you *o* of adulterers and prostitutes!
57: 4 the *o* of liars?
61: 9 and their *o* among the peoples.
Jer 22: 30 for none of his *o* will prosper,
31: 27 house of Judah with the *o* of men
La 2: 20 Should women eat their *o*,
Hos 9: 16 I will slay their cherished *o*."
Mal 2: 15 Because he was seeking godly *o*.
Ac 3: 25 'Through your *o* all peoples
17: 28 own poets have said, 'We are his *o*.'
17: 29 "Therefore since we are God's *o*,
Ro 4: 13 his *o* received the promise that he
4: 16 guaranteed to all Abraham's *o*—
4: 18 said to him, "So shall your *o* be."
9: 7 Isaac that your *o* will be
9: 8 who are regarded as Abraham's *o*.
Heb 11: 18 Isaac that your *o* will be
Rev 12: 17 war against the rest of her *o*—
22: 16 I am the Root and the *O* of David,

OG (OG'S)

Nu 21: 33 *O* king of Bashan and his whole
32: 33 the kingdom of *O* king of Bashan—
Dt 1: 4 and at Edrei had defeated *O* king
3: 1 *O* king of Bashan with his whole
3: 3 into our hands *O* king of Bashan
3: 11 (Only *O* king of Bashan was left
3: 13 the kingdom of *O*, I gave
4: 47 and the land of *O* king of Bashan,
29: 7 *O* king of Bashan came out to fight
31: 4 to them what he did to Sihon and *O*
Jos 2: 10 and what you did to Sihon and *O*,
9: 10 of Heshbon, and *O* king of Bashan,
12: 4 the territory of *O* king of Bashan,
13: 12 the whole kingdom of *O* in Bashan,
13: 30 realm of *O* king of Bashan—
13: 31 and Edrei (the royal cities of *O*
1Ki 4: 19 the country of *O* king of Bashan).
Ne 9: 22 the country of *O* king of Bashan.
Ps 135: 11 *O* king of Bashan
136: 20 and *O* king of Bashan—

OG'S (OG)

Dt 3: 4 of Argob, *O* kingdom in Bashan.
3: 10 towns of *O* kingdom in Bashan.

OHAD

Ge 46: 10 sons of Simeon: Jemuel, Jamin, *O*,
Ex 6: 15 of Simeon were Jemuel, Jamin, *O*,

OHEL

1Ch 3: 20 *O*, Berekiah, Hasadiah

OHOLAH

Eze 23: 4 The older was named *O*,
23: 4 *O* is Samaria, and Oholibah is
23: 5 "*O* engaged in prostitution
23: 36 will you judge *O* and Oholibah?
23: 44 slept with those lewd women, *O*

OHOLIAB

Ex 31: 6 I have appointed *O* son
35: 34 he has given both him and *O* son
36: 1 *O* and every skilled person
36: 2 Moses summoned Bezalel and *O*
38: 23 with him was *O* son of Ahisamach,

OHOLIBAH

Eze 23: 4 Oholah, and her sister was *O*.
23: 4 is Samaria, and *O* is Jerusalem.
23: 11 Her sister *O* saw this, yet in her lust
23: 22 *O*, this is what the Sovereign
23: 36 will you judge Oholah and *O*?
23: 44 those lewd women, Oholah and *O*.

OHOLIBAMAH

Ge 36: 2 and *O* daughter of Anah
36: 5 bore Reuel, and *O* bore Jeush,
36: 14 of Esau's wife *O* daughter of Anah
36: 18 The sons of Esau's wife *O*:
36: 18 from Esau's wife *O* daughter
36: 25 Dishon and *O* daughter of Anah.
36: 41 Alvah, Jetheth, *O*, Elah, Pinon,
1Ch 1: 52 Alvah, Jetheth, *O*, Elah, Pinon,

OIL (OILS)

Ge 28: 18 as a pillar and poured *o* on top of it.
35: 14 on it; he also poured *o* on it.
Ex 25: 6 acacia wood; olive *o* for the light;
25: 6 spices for the anointing *o*
27: 20 the Israelites to bring you clear *o*
29: 2 with *o*, and wafers spread with *o*.
29: 7 Take the anointing *o* and anoint
29: 21 and some of the anointing *o*
29: 23 a cake made with *o*, and a wafer.
29: 40 of a hin of *o* from pressed olives,
30: 24 shekel—and a hin of olive *o*.
30: 25 It will be the sacred anointing *o*.
30: 25 these into a sacred anointing *o*,
30: 31 is to be my sacred anointing *o*
30: 32 and do not make any *o*
31: 11 anointing *o* and fragrant incense
35: 8 acacia wood; olive *o* for the light;
35: 8 spices for the anointing *o*
35: 14 *o* for the light; the altar of incense
35: 15 the anointing *o* and the fragrant
35: 28 also brought spices and olive *o*
35: 28 and for the anointing *o*
37: 29 also made the sacred anointing *o*
39: 37 the *o* for the light; the gold altar,
39: 38 anointing *o*, the fragrant incense,
40: 9 "Take the anointing *o*
Lev 2: 1 He is to pour *o* on it, put incense
2: 2 a handful of the fine flour and *o*,
2: 4 without yeast and mixed with *o*,
2: 4 without yeast and spread with *o*.
2: 5 made of fine flour mixed with *o*,
2: 6 Crumble it and pour *o* on it;
2: 7 it is to be made of fine flour and *o*.
2: 15 Put *o* and incense on it; it is a grain
2: 16 of the crushed grain and the *o*,
5: 11 He must not put *o* or incense on it,
6: 15 to take a handful of fine flour and *o*
6: 21 Prepare it with *o* on a griddle;
7: 10 whether mixed with *o* or dry,
7: 12 well-kneaded and mixed with *o*.
7: 12 without yeast and mixed with *o*,
7: 12 without yeast and spread with *o*,
8: 2 their garments, the anointing *o*,
8: 10 Then Moses took the anointing *o*
8: 11 He sprinkled some of the *o*
8: 12 of the anointing *o* on Aaron's head
8: 26 and one made with *o*, and a wafer;
8: 30 took some of the anointing *o*
9: 4 with a grain offering mixed with *o*.
10: 7 the LORD's anointing *o* is on you
14: 10 a grain offering, and one log of *o*.
14: 10 mixed with *o* for a grain offering,

Lev 14: 12 the log of *o;* he shall wave them
14: 15 shall then take some of the log of *o,*
14: 16 forefinger into the *o* in his palm,
14: 17 some of the *o* remaining in his palm
14: 18 of the *o* in his palm the priest shall
14: 21 a log of *o,* and two doves
14: 21 mixed with *o* for a grain offering,
14: 24 together with the log of *o,*
14: 26 to pour some of the *o* into the palm
14: 27 of the *o* from his palm seven times
14: 28 Some of the *o* in his palm he is
14: 29 of the *o* in his palm the priest shall
21: 10 has had the anointing *o* poured
21: 12 by the anointing *o* of his God.
23: 13 ephah of fine flour mixed with *o*—
24: 2 the Israelites to bring you clear *o*
Nu 4: 9 all its jars for the *o* used to supply it
4: 16 grain offering and the anointing *o.*
4: 16 to have charge of the *o* for the light,
5: 15 He must not pour *o* on it
6: 15 with *o,* and wafers spread with *o.*
7: 13 filled with fine flour mixed with *o*
7: 19 filled with fine flour mixed with *o*
7: 25 filled with fine flour mixed with *o*
7: 31 filled with fine flour mixed with *o*
7: 37 filled with fine flour mixed with *o*
7: 43 filled with fine flour mixed with *o*
7: 49 filled with fine flour mixed with *o*
7: 55 filled with fine flour mixed with *o*
7: 61 filled with fine flour mixed with *o*
7: 67 filled with fine flour mixed with *o*
7: 73 filled with fine flour mixed with *o*
7: 79 filled with fine flour mixed with *o*
8: 8 offering of fine flour mixed with *o;*
11: 8 like something made with olive *o.*
15: 4 mixed with a fourth of a hin of *o.*
15: 6 mixed with a third of a hin of *o,*
15: 9 mixed with half a hin of *o.*
18: 12 "I give you all the finest olive *o*
28: 5 of a hin of *o* from pressed olives.
28: 9 an ephah of fine flour mixed with *o.*
28: 12 an ephah of fine flour mixed with *o;*
28: 12 an ephah of fine flour mixed with *o;*
28: 13 an ephah of fine flour mixed with *o.*
28: 20 an ephah of fine flour mixed with *o;*
28: 28 an ephah of fine flour mixed with *o;*
29: 3 an ephah of fine flour mixed with *o;*
29: 9 an ephah of fine flour mixed with *o;*
29: 14 an ephah of fine flour mixed with *o;*
35: 25 who was anointed with the holy *o.*
Dt 7: 13 your grain, new wine and *o*—
8: 8 pomegranates, olive *o* and honey;
11: 14 in your grain, new wine and *o.*
12: 17 of your grain and new wine and *o,*
14: 23 tithe of your grain, new wine and *o,*
18: 4 and *o,* and the first wool
28: 40 but you will not use the *o,*
28: 51 leave you no grain, new wine or *o,*
32: 13 and with *o* from the flinty crag,
33: 24 and let him bathe his feet in *o.*
Jdg 9: 9 'Should I give up my *o,*
1Sa 10: 1 Then Samuel took a flask of *o*
16: 1 Fill your horn with *o* and be
16: 13 So Samuel took the horn of *o*
2Sa 1: 21 of Saul—no longer rubbed with *o.*
1Ki 1: 39 the horn of *o* from the sacred tent
5: 11 baths of pressed olive *o.*
17: 12 of flour in a jar and a little *o* in a jug
17: 14 and the jug of *o* will not run dry
17: 16 and the jug of *o* did not run dry,
2Ki 4: 2 she said, "except a little *o.*"
4: 4 Pour *o* into all the jars, and
4: 6 Then the *o* stopped flowing.
4: 7 "Go, sell the *o* and pay your debts.
9: 1 take this flask of *o* with you
9: 3 pour the *o* on his head and declare,
9: 6 Then the prophet poured the *o*
20: 13 the gold, the spices and the fine *o*
1Ch 9: 29 and the *o,* incense and spices.
12: 40 raisin cakes, wine, *o,* cattle
27: 28 in charge of the supplies of olive *o.*
2Ch 2: 10 twenty thousand baths of olive *o.*"
2: 15 the olive *o* and wine he promised,
11: 11 with supplies of food, olive *o*
31: 5 *o* and honey and all that the fields
32: 28 and *o;* and he made stalls
Ezr 3: 7 drink and *o* to the people of Sidon
6: 9 and wheat, salt, wine and *o,*
Ezr 7: 22 a hundred baths of olive *o,*
Ne 5: 11 the money, grain, new wine and *o.*"
10: 37 and of our new wine and *o.*
10: 39 and *o* to the storerooms where
13: 5 and *o* prescribed for the Levites,
13: 12 and *o* into the storerooms.
Est 2: 12 six months with *o* of myrrh
Job 29: 6 out for me streams of olive *o.*
Ps 23: 5 You anoint my head with *o;*
45: 7 by anointing you with the *o* of joy.
55: 21 his words are more soothing than *o*
89: 20 with my sacred *o* I have anointed
104: 15 *o* to make his face shine,
109: 18 into his bones like *o.*
133: 2 It is like precious *o* poured
141: 5 let him rebuke me—it is *o*
Pr 5: 3 and her speech is smoother than *o;*
21: 17 loves wine and *o* will never be
21: 20 of choice food and *o,*
27: 16 or grasping *o* with the hand.
Ecc 9: 8 and always anoint your head with *o*
Isa 1: 6 or soothed with *o.*
21: 5 *o* the shields!
39: 2 the gold, the spices, the fine *o,*
57: 9 You went to Molech with olive *o*
61: 3 the *o* of gladness
Jer 31: 12 the grain, the new wine and the *o,*
40: 10 *o,* and put them in your storage jars
41: 8 We have wheat and barley, *o*
Eze 16: 13 was fine flour, honey and olive *o.*
16: 18 and you offered my *o* and incense
16: 19 olive *o* and honey I gave you to eat
23: 41 and *o* that belonged to me.
27: 17 honey, *o* and balm for your wares.
32: 14 and make her streams flow like *o,*
45: 14 The prescribed portion of *o,*
45: 24 along with a hin of *o* for each ephah
45: 25 offerings, grain offerings and *o.*
46: 5 along with a hin of *o* for each ephah
46: 7 with a hin of *o* with each ephah.
46: 11 along with a hin of *o* for each ephah
46: 14 of a hin of *o* to moisten the flour.
46: 15 the *o* shall be provided morning
Hos 2: 5 and my linen, my *o* and my drink.'
2: 8 her the grain, the new wine and *o,*
2: 22 the new wine and *o,*
12: 1 and sends olive *o* to Egypt.
Joel 1: 10 the *o* fails.
2: 19 sending you grain, new wine and *o,*
2: 24 with new wine and *o.*
Mic 6: 7 with ten thousand rivers of *o?*
6: 15 but not use the *o* on yourselves,
Hag 1: 11 the *o* and whatever the ground
2: 12 some wine, *o* or other food,
Zec 4: 12 gold pipes that pour out golden *o?*"
Mt 6: 17 put *o* on your head and wash your
25: 3 but did not take any *o* with them.
25: 4 *o* in jars along with their lamps.
25: 8 of your *o;* our lamps are going out.'
25: 9 to those who sell *o* and buy some
25: 10 were on their way to buy the *o,*
Mk 6: 13 anointed many sick people with *o*
Lk 7: 46 You did not put *o* on my head,
10: 34 bandaged his wounds, pouring on *o*
16: 6 Eight hundred gallons of olive *o,*'
Heb 1: 9 by anointing you with the *o* of joy."
Jas 5: 14 and anoint him with *o* in the name
Rev 6: 6 do not damage the *o* and the wine
18: 13 of wine and olive *o,* of fine flour

OILS (OIL)

Ps 92: 10 fine *o* have been poured upon me.

OINTMENT (OINTMENTS)

Job 41: 31 and stirs up the sea like a pot of *o.*

OINTMENTS (OINTMENT)

Eze 16: 9 blood from you and put *o* on you.

OLIVE (OLIVES)

Ge 8: 11 beak was a freshly plucked *o* leaf!
Ex 23: 11 your vineyard and your *o* grove.
25: 6 acacia wood; *o* oil for the light;
30: 24 shekel—and a hin of *o* oil.
35: 8 acacia wood; *o* oil for the light;
35: 28 also brought spices and *o* oil
Nu 11: 8 like something made with *o* oil.
18: 12 "I give you all the finest *o* oil
Dt 6: 11 and *o* groves you did not plant—
8: 8 pomegranates, *o* oil and honey;
28: 40 You will have *o* trees
Jos 24: 13 *o* groves that you did not plant.'
Jdg 9: 8 said to the *o* tree, 'Be our king.'
9: 9 *o* tree answered, 'Should I give up
15: 5 with the vineyards and *o* groves.
1Sa 8: 14 and vineyards and *o* groves
1Ki 5: 11 thousand baths of pressed *o* oil.
6: 23 a pair of cherubim of *o* wood,
6: 31 of *o* wood with five-sided jambs.
6: 32 on the two *o* wood doors he carved
6: 33 jambs of *o* wood for the entrance
2Ki 5: 26 *o* groves, vineyards, flocks,
18: 32 a land of *o* trees and honey.
1Ch 27: 28 in charge of the supplies of *o* oil.
27: 28 the Gederite was in charge of the *o*
2Ch 2: 10 twenty thousand baths of *o* oil."
2: 15 and the *o* oil and wine he promised,
11: 11 with supplies of food, *o* oil
Ezr 7: 22 a hundred baths of *o* oil,
Ne 5: 11 vineyards, *o* groves and houses,
8: 15 branches from *o* and wild *o* trees,
9: 25 *o* groves and fruit trees
Job 15: 33 like an *o* tree shedding its blossoms
29: 6 out for me streams of *o* oil.
Ps 52: 8 But I am like an *o* tree
128: 3 your sons will be like *o* shoots
Isa 17: 6 as when an *o* tree is beaten,
24: 13 as when an *o* tree is beaten,
41: 19 the acacia, the myrtle and the *o.*
57: 9 You went to Molech with *o* oil
Jer 11: 16 LORD called you a thriving *o* tree
Eze 16: 13 was fine flour, honey and *o* oil.
16: 19 *o* oil and honey I gave you to eat—
Hos 12: 1 and sends *o* oil to Egypt.
14: 6 His splendor will be like an *o* tree,
Am 4: 9 devoured your fig and *o* trees,
Hab 3: 17 though the *o* crop fails
Hag 2: 19 and the *o* tree have not borne fruit.
Zec 4: 3 Also there are two *o* trees by it,
4: 11 "What are these two *o* trees
4: 12 "What are these two *o* branches
Lk 16: 6 " 'Eight hundred gallons of *o* oil,'
Jn 18: 1 the other side there was an *o* grove,
18: 26 you with him in the *o* grove?"
Ro 11: 17 and you, though a wild *o* shoot,
11: 17 the nourishing sap from the *o* root,
11: 24 be grafted into their own *o* tree!
11: 24 grafted into a cultivated *o* tree,
11: 24 of an *o* tree that is wild by nature,
Rev 11: 4 These are the two *o* trees
18: 13 and frankincense, of wine and *o* oil,

OLIVES (OLIVE)

Ex 27: 20 oil of pressed *o* for the light
29: 40 of a hin of oil from pressed *o,*
Lev 24: 2 oil of pressed *o* for the light
Nu 28: 5 of a hin of oil from pressed *o.*
Dt 24: 20 When you beat the *o*
28: 40 because the *o* will drop off.
2Sa 15: 30 continued up the Mount of *O,*
Job 24: 11 They crush *o* among the terraces;
Isa 17: 6 three *o* on the topmost branches,
Mic 6: 15 you will press *o* but not use the oil
Zec 14: 4 stand on the Mount of *O,*
14: 4 the Mount of *O* will be split in two
Mt 21: 1 to Bethphage on the Mount of *O,*
24: 3 sitting on the Mount of *O,*
26: 30 they went out to the Mount of *O.*
Mk 11: 1 and Bethany at the Mount of *O,*
13: 3 Mount of *O* opposite the temple,
14: 26 they went out to the Mount of *O.*
Lk 19: 29 at the hill called the Mount of *O,*
19: 37 down the Mount of *O,*
21: 37 on the hill called the Mount of *O,*
22: 39 as usual to the Mount of *O,*
Jn 8: 1 But Jesus went to the Mount of *O.*
Ac 1: 12 from the hill called the Mount of *O*
Jas 3: 12 a fig tree bear *o,* or a grapevine bear

OLYMPAS

Ro 16: 15 and *O* and all the saints with them.

OMAR

Ge 36: 11 *O,* Zepho, Gatam and Kenaz.
36: 15 Chiefs Teman, *O,* Zepho, Kenaz,
1Ch 1: 36 *O,* Zepho, Gatam and Kenaz;

OMEGA

Rev 1: 8 "I am the Alpha and the *O*,"
21: 6 I am the Alpha and the *O*,
22: 13 I am the Alpha and the *O*,

OMEN (OMENS)

Eze 21: 21 to seek an *o*: He will cast lots
21: 23 It will seem like a false *o*

OMENS (OMEN)

Dt 18: 10 interprets *o*, engages in witchcraft,

OMER (OMERS)

Ex 16: 16 Take an *o* for each person you have
16: 18 when they measured it by the *o*,
16: 32 'Take an *o* of manna and keep it
16: 33 and put an *o* of manna in it.
16: 36 (An *o* is one tenth of an ephah.)

OMERS (OMER)

Ex 16: 22 as much—two *o* for each person—

OMIT

Jer 26: 2 I command you; do not *o* a word.

OMRI (OMRI'S)

1Ki 16: 16 they proclaimed *O*,
16: 17 Then *O* and all the Israelites
16: 21 and the other half supported *O*.
16: 22 So Tibni died and *O* became king.
16: 23 of Judah, *O* became king of Israel,
16: 25 *O* did evil in the eyes of the LORD
16: 28 *O* rested with his fathers
16: 29 Ahab son of *O* became king
16: 30 Ahab son of *O* did more evil
2Ki 8: 26 a granddaughter of *O* king of Israel.
1Ch 7: 8 Eliezer, Elioenai, *O*, Jeremoth,
9: 4 the son of *O*, the son of Imri,
27: 18 over Issachar: *O* son of Michael;
2Ch 22: 2 Athaliah, a granddaughter of *O*.
Mic 6: 16 have observed the statutes of *O*

OMRI'S (OMRI)

1Ki 16: 22 But *O* followers proved stronger
16: 27 As for the other events of *O* reign,

ON

Ge 41: 45 daughter of Potiphera, priest of *O*,
41: 50 daughter of Potiphera, priest of *O*.
46: 20 daughter of Potiphera, priest of *O*.
Nu 16: 1 sons of Eliab, and *O* son of Peleth

ONAM

Ge 36: 23 Manahath, Ebal, Shepho and *O*.
1Ch 1: 40 Manahath, Ebal, Shepho and *O*.
2: 26 Atarah; she was the mother of *O*.
2: 28 The sons of *O*: Shammai and Jada.

ONAN

Ge 38: 4 birth to a son and named him *O*.
38: 8 Then Judah said to *O*, "Lie
38: 9 *O* knew that the offspring would
46: 12 The sons of Judah: Er, *O*, Shelah,
46: 12 *O* had died in the land of Canaan).
Nu 26: 19 Er and *O* were sons of Judah,
1Ch 2: 3 The sons of Judah: Er, *O*

ONE-TENTH (TEN)

Nu 28: 21 and with each of the seven lambs, *o*
28: 29 and with each of the seven lambs, *o*
29: 4 and with each of the seven lambs, *o*
29: 10 and with each of the seven lambs, *o*
29: 15 with each of the fourteen lambs, *o*.

ONESIMUS

Col 4: 9 He is coming with *O*, our faithful
Phm : 10 I appeal to you for my son *O*,

ONESIPHORUS

2Ti 1: 16 mercy to the household of *O*,
4: 19 Aquila and the household of *O*.

ONIONS

Nu 11: 5 melons, leeks, *o* and garlic.

ONO

1Ch 8: 12 Shemed (who built *O* and Lod
Ezr 2: 33 and *O* 725 of Jericho 345
Ne 6: 2 of the villages on the plain of *O*."
7: 37 Hadid and *O* 721 of Senaah 3,930
11: 35 and Neballat, in Lod and *O*,

ONYCHA

Ex 30: 34 gum resin, *o* and galbanum—

ONYX

Ge 2: 12 aromatic resin and *o* are also there
Ex 25: 7 and *o* stones and other gems
28: 9 "Take two *o* stones and engrave
28: 20 in the fourth row a chrysolite, an *o*
35: 9 and *o* stones and other gems
35: 27 The leaders brought *o* stones
39: 6 They mounted the *o* stones
39: 13 in the fourth row a chrysolite, an *o*
1Ch 29: 2 as well as *o* for the settings,
Job 28: 16 with precious *o* or sapphires.
Eze 28: 13 chrysolite, *o* and jasper,

OOZING

1Sa 14: 26 woods, they saw the honey *o* out,

OPENHANDED (HAND)

Dt 15: 8 Rather be *o* and freely lend him
15: 11 you to be *o* toward your brothers

OPHEL

2Ch 27: 3 work on the wall at the hill of *O*.
33: 14 and encircling the hill of *O*;
Ne 3: 26 on the hill of *O* made repairs up
3: 27 projecting tower to the wall of *O*.
11: 21 servants lived on the hill of *O*,

OPHIR

Ge 10: 29 Sheba, *O*, Havilah and Jobab.
1Ki 9: 28 to *O* and brought back 420 talents
10: 11 Hiram's ships brought gold from *O*;
22: 48 of trading ships to go to *O* for gold,
1Ch 1: 23 Sheba, *O*, Havilah and Jobab.
29: 4 talents of gold (gold of *O*)
2Ch 8: 18 sailed to *O* and brought back four
9: 10 of Solomon brought gold from *O*;
Job 22: 24 your gold of *O* to the rocks
28: 16 with the gold of *O*,
Ps 45: 9 hand is the royal bride in gold of *O*.
Isa 13: 12 more rare than the gold of *O*.

OPHNI

Jos 18: 24 Kephar Ammoni, *O* and Geba—

OPHRAH

Jos 18: 23 Parah, *O*, Kephar Ammoni,
Jdg 6: 11 under the oak in *O* that belonged
6: 24 stands in *O* of the Abiezrites.
8: 27 which he placed in *O*, his town.
8: 32 Joash in *O* of the Abiezrites.
9: 5 He went to his father's home in *O*
1Sa 13: 17 One turned toward *O*
1Ch 4: 14 Meonothai was the father of *O*.

OPINION (OPINIONS)

2Sa 17: 6 he says? If not, give us your *o*."
Mt 22: 17 Tell us then, what is your *o*?

OPINIONS (OPINION)

1Ki 18: 21 will you waver between two *o*?
Pr 18: 2 but delights in airing his own *o*.

OPPONENT (OPPOSE)

2Sa 2: 16 each man grabbed his *o* by the head
1Ki 20: 20 and each one struck down his *o*.
Job 16: 9 my *o* fastens on me his piercing

OPPONENT'S (OPPOSE)

2Sa 2: 16 thrust his dagger into his *o* side,

OPPONENTS (OPPOSE)

Pr 18: 18 and keeps strong *o* apart.
Lk 13: 17 said this, all his *o* were humiliated,

OPPORTUNE (OPPORTUNITY)

Mk 6: 21 Finally the *o* time came.
Lk 4: 13 he left him until an *o* time.

OPPORTUNITY (OPPORTUNE)

1Sa 18: 21 "Now you have a second *o*
Jer 46: 17 he has missed his *o*.'
Mt 26: 16 watched for an *o* to hand him over.
Mk 14: 11 So he watched for an *o* to hand him
Lk 22: 6 and watched for an *o* to hand Jesus
Ac 25: 16 and has had an *o* to defend himself
Ro 7: 8 seizing the *o* afforded
7: 11 seizing the *o* afforded
1Co 16: 12 but he will go when he has the *o*.
2Co 5: 12 are giving you an *o* to take pride
11: 12 from under those who want an *o*
Gal 6: 10 as we have *o*, let us do good
Eph 5: 16 making the most of every *o*,
Php 4: 10 but you had no *o* to show it.
Col 4: 5 make the most of every *o*.
1Ti 5: 14 to give the enemy no *o* for slander.
Heb 11: 15 they would have had *o* to return.

OPPOSE (OPPONENT OPPONENT'S OPPONENTS OPPOSED OPPOSES OPPOSING OPPOSITION)

Ex 23: 22 and will *o* those who *o* you.
Nu 16: 3 as a group to *o* Moses and Aaron
22: 22 stood in the road to *o* him.
22: 32 I have come here to *o* you
22: 34 standing in the road to *o* me.
Jdg 20: 25 out from Gibeah to *o* them,
1Sa 2: 10 those who *o* the LORD will be
Job 11: 10 convenes a court, who can *o* him?
23: 6 Would he *o* me with great power?
23: 13 he stands alone, and who can *o* him
Ps 55: 18 even though many *o* me.
109: 6 Appoint an evil man to *o* him;
Isa 41: 11 those who *o* you
Jer 38: 5 The king can do nothing to *o* you."
51: 2 they will *o* her on every side
Da 11: 30 the western coastlands will *o* him,
Lk 11: 53 of the law began to *o* him fiercely
14: 31 men to *o* the one coming
Ac 11: 17 I to think that I could *o* God!"
26: 9 to *o* the name of Jesus of Nazareth.
1Co 16: 9 and there are many who *o* me.
Php 1: 28 in any way by those who *o* you.
2Ti 2: 25 Those who *o* him he must gently
3: 8 so also these men *o* the truth—
Tit 1: 9 doctrine and refute those who *o* it.
2: 8 so that those who *o* you may be

OPPOSED (OPPOSE)

Ex 15: 7 you threw down those who *o* you.
2Ch 13: 7 and *o* Rehoboam son of Solomon
Ezr 10: 15 and Shabbethai the Levite, *o* this.
Jer 50: 24 because you *o* the LORD.
Ac 13: 8 is what his name means) *o* them
18: 6 But when the Jews *o* Paul
Gal 2: 11 to Antioch, I *o* him to his face,
3: 21 therefore, *o* to the promises of God
Col 2: 14 against us and that stood *o* to us;
2Ti 3: 8 as Jannes and Jambres *o* Moses,
4: 15 because he strongly *o* our message.

OPPOSES (OPPOSE)

Mk 3: 26 And if Satan *o* himself
Lk 23: 2 He *o* payment of taxes to Caesar
Jn 19: 12 claims to be a king *o* Caesar."
2Th 2: 4 He *o* and exalts himself
Jas 4: 6 "God *o* the proud
1Pe 5: 5 because, "God *o* the proud

OPPOSING (OPPOSE)

2Ch 35: 21 so stop *o* God, who is with me,
1Ti 6: 20 the *o* ideas of what is falsely called
Jas 5: 6 innocent men, who were not *o* you.

OPPOSITION (OPPOSE)

Nu 16: 19 in *o* to them at the entrance
16: 42 when the assembly gathered in *o*
20: 2 the people gathered in *o* to Moses
Jdg 9: 25 In *o* to him these citizens
Ac 6: 9 *O* arose, however, from members
1Th 2: 2 gospel in spite of strong *o*.
Heb 12: 3 Consider him who endured such *o*

OPPRESS (OPPRESSED OPPRESSES OPPRESSING OPPRESSION OPPRESSIVE OPPRESSOR OPPRESSORS)

Ex 1: 11 masters over them to *o* them
22: 21 "Do not mistreat an alien or *o* him,
23: 9 "Do not *o* an alien; you yourselves
Dt 23: 16 Do not *o* him.
2Sa 7: 10 people will not *o* them anymore,

1Ch 16: 21 He allowed no man to *o* them;
17: 9 people will not *o* them anymore,
Job 10: 3 Does it please you to *o* me,
37: 23 great righteousness, he does not *o*.
Ps 89: 22 no wicked man will *o* him.
94: 5 they *o* your inheritance.
105: 14 He allowed no one to *o* them;
119:122 let not the arrogant *o* me.
Isa 3: 5 People will *o* each other—
3: 12 Youths *o* my people,
Jer 7: 6 if you do not *o* the alien,
30: 20 I will punish all who *o* them.
Eze 18: 7 He does not *o* anyone,
18: 16 He does not *o* anyone
22: 29 they *o* the poor and needy
45: 8 princes will no longer *o* my people
Da 7: 25 the Most High and *o* his saints
Am 4: 1 you women who *o* the poor
5: 12 You *o* the righteous and take bribes
6: 14 that will *o* you all the way
Zec 7: 10 Do not *o* the widow
11: 6 They will *o* the land, and I will not
Mal 3: 5 who *o* the widows

OPPRESSED (OPPRESS)

Ex 1: 12 But the more they were *o*,
Dt 28: 29 day after day you will be *o*
Jdg 2: 18 as they groaned under those who *o*
4: 3 and had cruelly *o* the Israelites
10: 8 eighteen years they *o* all
10: 12 and the Maonites *o* you
1Sa 10: 18 and all the kingdoms that *o* you.'
12: 3 have I cheated? Whom have I *o?*
12: 4 "You have not cheated or *o* us,"
2Ki 13: 22 Hazael king of Aram *o* Israel
2Ch 16: 10 the same time Asa brutally *o* some
Ne 9: 27 over to their enemies, who *o* them.
9: 27 when they were *o* they cried out
Job 20: 19 For he has *o* the poor and left them
Ps 9: 9 The LORD is a refuge for the *o*,
10: 18 defending the fatherless and the *o*,
42: 9 *o* by the enemy?"
43: 2 *o* by the enemy?
74: 21 Do not let the *o* retreat in disgrace;
82: 3 the rights of the poor and *o*.
103: 6 and justice for all the *o*.
106: 42 Their enemies *o* them
129: 1 They have greatly *o* me
129: 2 they have greatly *o* me
146: 7 He upholds the cause of the *o*
Pr 15: 15 All the days of the *o* are wretched,
16: 19 in spirit and among the *o*
31: 5 and deprive all the *o* of their rights.
Ecc 4: 1 I saw the tears of the *o*—
5: 8 If you see the poor *o* in a district,
Isa 1: 17 encourage the *o*.
10: 2 and rob my *o* people of justice,
26: 6 the feet of the *o*,
52: 4 lately, Assyria has *o* them.
53: 7 He was *o* and afflicted,
58: 6 to set the *o* free
58: 10 and satisfy the needs of the *o*,
Jer 50: 33 "The people of Israel are *o*,
Eze 22: 7 in you they have *o* the alien
Da 4: 27 wickedness by being kind to the *o*.
Hos 5: 11 Ephraim is *o*,
Am 2: 7 and deny justice to the *o*.
Zep 3: 19 deal with all who *o* you;
Zec 10: 2 *o* for lack of a shepherd.
11: 7 particularly the *o* of the flock.
Lk 4: 18 to release the *o*,
Ac 7: 19 *o* our forefathers by forcing them

OPPRESSES (OPPRESS)

Pr 14: 31 He who *o* the poor shows contempt
22: 16 He who *o* the poor
28: 3 A ruler who *o* the poor
Eze 18: 12 He *o* the poor and needy.

OPPRESSING (OPPRESS)

Ex 3: 9 the way the Egyptians are *o* them.
Nu 10: 9 against an enemy who is *o* you,
2Ki 13: 4 the king of Aram was *o* Israel.

OPPRESSION (OPPRESS)

Dt 26: 7 and saw our misery, toil and *o*.
28: 33 nothing but cruel *o* all your days.
Job 35: 9 "Men cry out under a load of *o;*
Ps 12: 5 "Because of the *o* of the weak
44: 24 and forget our misery and *o?*
72: 14 He will rescue them from *o*
73: 8 in their arrogance they threaten *o*.
107: 39 by *o*, calamity and sorrow;
119:134 Redeem me from the *o* of men,
Ecc 4: 1 saw all the *o* that was taking place
Isa 30: 12 relied on *o*
53: 8 By *o* and judgment, he was taken
58: 9 "If you do away with the yoke of *o*,
59: 13 fomenting *o* and revolt,
Jer 6: 6 it is filled with *o*.
22: 17 and on *o* and extortion."
Eze 45: 9 Give up your violence and *o*
Hos 8: 10 under the *o* of the mighty king.
Am 3: 9 and the *o* among her people."
Ac 7: 34 I have indeed seen the *o*

OPPRESSIVE (OPPRESS)

Jdg 6: 2 the power of Midian was so *o*,
Ps 73: 16 it was *o* to me
Isa 10: 1 to those who issue *o* decrees,

OPPRESSOR (OPPRESS)

Ps 72: 4 he will crush the *o*.
78: 42 day he redeemed them from the *o*,
Pr 29: 13 the *o* have this in common:
Isa 9: 4 the rod of their *o*.
14: 4 How the *o* has come to an end!
16: 4 The *o* will come to an end,
51: 13 For where is the wrath of the *o?*
51: 13 because of the wrath of the *o*,
Jer 21: 12 rescue from the hand of his *o*
22: 3 hand of his *o* the one who has been
25: 38 because of the sword of the *o*
46: 16 away from the sword of the *o*.'
50: 16 Because of the sword of the *o*
Zec 9: 8 again will an *o* overrun my people,

OPPRESSORS (OPPRESS)

Jdg 6: 9 and from the hand of all your *o*.
Ps 27: 11 because of my *o*.
119:121 do not leave me to my *o*.
Ecc 4: 1 power was on the side of their *o*—
Isa 14: 2 and rule over their *o*.
19: 20 to the LORD because of their *o*,
49: 26 I will make your *o* eat their own
60: 14 sons of your *o* will come bowing
Zep 3: 1 Woe to the city of *o*,

OPTIONS

2Sa 24: 12 says: I am giving you three *o*.
1Ch 21: 10 says: I am giving you three *o*.

ORACLE (ORACLES)

Nu 23: 7 Then Balaam uttered his *o:*
23: 18 say?" Then he uttered his *o:*
24: 3 the *o* of one whose eye sees clearly,
24: 3 upon him and he uttered his *o:*
24: 3 "The *o* of Balaam son of Beor,
24: 4 the *o* of one who hears the words
24: 15 Then he uttered his *o:*
24: 15 the *o* of one whose eye sees clearly,
24: 15 "The *o* of Balaam son of Beor,
24: 16 the *o* of one who hears the words
24: 20 saw Amalek and uttered his *o:*
24: 21 saw the Kenites and uttered his *o:*
24: 23 Then he uttered his *o:*
2Sa 23: 1 the *o* of the man exalted
23: 1 "The *o* of David son of Jesse,
Ps 36: 1 An *o* is within my heart
Pr 16: 10 The lips of a king speak as an *o*,
30: 1 of Agur son of Jakeh—an *o:*
31: 1 an *o* his mother taught him:
Isa 13: 1 *o* concerning Babylon that Isaiah
14: 28 This *o* came in the year King Ahaz
15: 1 An *o* concerning Moab:
17: 1 An *o* concerning Damascus:
19: 1 An *o* concerning Egypt:
21: 1 An *o* concerning the Desert
21: 11 An *o* concerning Dumah:
21: 13 An *o* concerning Arabia:
22: 1 An *o* concerning the Valley
23: 1 An *o* concerning Tyre:
30: 6 An *o* concerning the animals
Jer 23: 33 'What is the *o* of the LORD?'
23: 33 'What *o?* I will forsake you,
23: 34 'This is the *o* of the LORD,'
Jer 23: 36 But you must not mention 'the *o*
23: 36 man's own word becomes his *o*
23: 38 'This is the *o* of the LORD.'
23: 38 'This is the *o* of the LORD,'
23: 38 'This is the *o* of the LORD,'
Eze 12: 10 This *o* concerns the prince
Na 1: 1 An *o* concerning Nineveh.
Hab 1: 1 The *o* that Habakkuk the prophet
Zec 8: 23 An *O*
11: 17 An *O* This is the word
Mal 1: 1 An *o:* The word of the LORD

ORACLES (ORACLE)

La 2: 14 The *o* they gave you

ORCHARD (ORCHARDS)

SS 4: 13 Your plants are an *o*

ORCHARDS (ORCHARD)

Isa 16: 10 gladness are taken away from the *o*
Jer 48: 33 from the *o* and fields of Moab.

ORDAIN (ORDAINED ORDINATION)

Ex 28: 41 and his sons, anoint and *o* them.
29: 9 In this way you shall *o* Aaron
29: 35 taking seven days to *o* them.

ORDAINED (ORDAIN)

Ex 29: 29 so that they can be anointed and *o*
Lev 16: 32 and *o* to succeed his father
21: 10 who has been *o* to wear the priestly
Nu 3: 3 who were *o* to serve as priests.
2Ki 19: 25 Long ago I *o* it.
Ps 8: 2 you have *o* praise
65: 9 for so you have *o* it.
111: 9 he *o* his covenant forever—
139: 16 All the days *o* for me
Isa 37: 26 Long ago I *o* it.
48: 5 image and metal god *o* them.'
Eze 28: 14 for so I *o* you.
Hab 1: 12 you have *o* them to punish.
Mt 21: 16 you have *o* praise'?"

ORDER (ORDERED ORDERLY ORDERS)

Ge 25: 13 listed in the *o* of their birth:
38: 20 in *o* to get his pledge back
43: 33 before him in the *o* of their ages,
Ex 1: 22 Then Pharaoh gave this *o*
5: 6 That same day Pharaoh gave this *o*
9: 19 Give an *o* now to bring your
28: 10 of Israel in the *o* of their birth—
36: 6 Then Moses gave an *o*
Lev 13: 54 he shall *o* that the contaminated
14: 4 the priest shall *o* that two live clean
14: 5 Then the priest shall *o* that one
14: 36 The priest is to *o* the house
14: 40 to *o* that the contaminated stones
22: 19 goats in *o* that it may be accepted
Nu 2: 17 They will set out in the same *o*
9: 19 Israelites obeyed the LORD's *o*
9: 23 They obeyed the LORD's *o*,
10: 28 This was the *o* of march
36: 5 command Moses gave this *o*
Dt 2: 30 his heart obstinate in *o* to give him
8: 2 to test you in *o* to know what was
29: 12 You are standing here in *o* to enter
Jos 10: 27 At sunset Joshua gave the *o*
Jdg 7: 2 In *o* that Israel may not boast
9: 24 God did this in *o* that the crime
Ru 4: 5 in *o* to maintain the name
4: 10 in *o* to maintain the name
1Sa 1: 6 her in *o* to irritate her.
15: 21 in *o* to sacrifice them
2Sa 2: 26 How long before you *o* your men
4: 12 So David gave an *o* to his men,
13: 28 Have not I given you this *o?*
14: 8 and I will issue an *o* in your behalf
14: 29 sent for Joab in *o* to send him
17: 14 of Ahithophel in *o* to bring disaster
17: 23 in *o* and then hanged himself.
19: 29 I *o* you and Ziba to divide the fields
1Ki 2: 46 the king gave the *o* to Benaiah son
3: 25 He then gave an *o:* "Cut the living
15: 22 King Asa issued an *o* to all Judah—
2Ki 10: 19 in *o* to destroy the ministers
17: 27 the king of Assyria gave this *o:*
20: 1 house in *o*, because you will die;
23: 21 The king gave this *o*

2Ki 23: 35 In *o* to do so, he taxed the land
24: 3 in *o* to remove them
1Ch 15: 14 consecrated themselves in *o*
24: 3 for their appointed *o* of ministering
24: 19 This was their appointed *o*
2Ch 11: 22 prince among his brothers, in *o*
24: 21 by *o* of the king they stoned him
29: 27 Hezekiah gave the *o*
31: 5 As soon as the *o* went out,
32: 18 and make them afraid in *o*
35: 20 when Josiah had set the temple in *o*
36: 22 in *o* to fulfill the word
Ezr 1: 1 in *o* to fulfill the word
4: 19 I issued an *o* and a search was
4: 21 Now issue an *o* to these men
4: 21 city will not be rebuilt until I so *o*.
6: 1 King Darius then issued an *o*,
6: 21 neighbors in *o* to seek the LORD,
7: 21 *o* all the treasurers
Ne 5: 2 in *o* for us to eat and stay alive,
9: 17 in *o* to return to their slavery.
9: 26 them in *o* to turn them back
13: 22 and guard the gates in *o*
Est 1: 11 in *o* to display her beauty
2: 8 When the king's *o* and edict had
3: 13 provinces with the *o* to destroy,
4: 3 province to which the edict and *o*
8: 5 let an *o* be written overruling
Job 25: 2 he establishes *o* in the heights
Ps 10: 18 in *o* that man, who is of the earth,
110: 4 in the *o* of Melchizedek.''
Pr 28: 2 knowledge maintains *o*.
Ecc 12: 9 and set in *o* many proverbs.
Isa 23: 11 given an *o* concerning Phoenicia
34: 16 it is his mouth that has given the *o*,
38: 1 house in *o*, because you are going
Jer 34: 22 to give the *o*, declares the LORD,
Eze 3: 18 ways in *o* to save his life,
13: 18 heads in *o* to ensnare people.
39: 12 them in *o* to cleanse the land.
Da 6: 16 king gave the *o*, and they brought
11: 17 in *o* to overthrow the kingdom,
Am 1: 13 Gilead in *o* to extend his borders,
Zec 13: 4 garment of hair in *o* to deceive.
Mt 12: 44 swept clean and put in *o*.
27: 64 So give the *o* for the tomb
Mk 7: 9 in *o* to observe your own traditions
Lk 4: 29 in *o* to throw him down the cliff.
8: 31 him repeatedly not to *o* them
11: 25 the house swept clean and put in *o*.
19: 15 in *o* to find out what they had
Jn 8: 6 in *o* to have a basis
17: 26 known in *o* that the love you have
Ac 6: 2 word of God in *o* to wait on tables
9: 24 on the city gates in *o* to kill him.
16: 35 officers to the jailer with the *o*:
17: 5 and Silas in *o* to bring them out
19: 33 for silence in *o* to make a defense
20: 30 and distort the truth in *o*
22: 24 in *o* to find out why the people
24: 4 But in *o* not to weary you further,
Ro 1: 13 in *o* that I might have a harvest
4: 11 in *o* that righteousness might be
6: 4 baptism into death in *o* that,
7: 4 in *o* that we might bear fruit to God
7: 13 in *o* that sin might be recognized
8: 4 in *o* that the righteous
8: 17 in his sufferings in *o* that we may
9: 11 in *o* that God's purpose
11: 31 in *o* that they too may now receive
15: 7 in *o* to bring praise to God.
2Co 1: 23 as my witness that it was in *o*
2: 11 in *o* that Satan might not outwit us.
8: 19 which we administer in *o*
9: 3 in *o* that our boasting about you
11: 7 to lower myself in *o* to elevate you
11: 12 doing in *o* to cut the ground
11: 32 of the Damascenes guarded in *o*
Gal 3: 14 us in *o* that the blessing given
Eph 1: 12 in *o* that we, who were the first
1: 18 in *o* that you may know the hope
2: 7 in *o* that in the coming ages he
4: 10 in *o* to fill the whole universe.)
Php 2: 16 in *o* that I may boast on the day
Col 1: 10 in *o* that you may live a life worthy
2: 2 in *o* that they may know
1Th 2: 9 and day in *o* not to be a burden
4: 1 how to live in *o* to please God,
2Th 3: 9 but in *o* to make ourselves a model
3: 14 in *o* that he may feel ashamed.
1Ti 4: 3 and *o* them to abstain from certain
Tit 3: 14 in *o* that they may provide
Phm : 8 *o* you to do what you ought to do,
Heb 2: 17 in *o* that he might become
5: 6 in the *o* of Melchizedek.''
5: 10 priest in the *o* of Melchizedek.
6: 11 in *o* to make your hope sure.
6: 20 in the *o* of Melchizedek.
7: 11 not in the *o* of Aaron?
7: 11 one in the *o* of Melchizedek,
7: 17 in the *o* of Melchizedek.''
9: 10 until the time of the new *o*.
Rev 21: 4 for the old *o* of things has passed

ORDERED (ORDER)

Ex 17: 10 the Amalekites as Moses had *o*,
Lev 10: 5 outside the camp, as Moses *o*.
Nu 34: 13 The LORD has *o* that it be given
36: 2 he *o* you to give the inheritance
Jos 1: 10 Joshua *o* the officers of the people:
6: 7 And he *o* the people, ''Advance!
8: 29 Joshua *o* them to take his body
Jdg 3: 28 he *o*, ''for the LORD has given
9: 48 He *o* the men with him, ''Quick!
1Sa 18: 22 Then Saul *o* his attendants:
20: 29 my brother has *o* me to be there.
22: 17 the king *o* the guards at his side:
22: 18 The king then *o* Doeg, ''You turn
2Sa 1: 18 *o* that the men of Judah be taught
13: 28 Absalom *o* his men, ''Listen!
13: 29 to Amnon what Absalom had *o*.
1Ki 2: 29 Then Solomon *o* Benaiah son
12: 24 home again, as the LORD had *o*.
17: 4 and I have *o* the ravens
18: 34 ''Do it a third time,'' he *o*,
20: 12 he *o* his men: ''Prepare to attack.''
22: 26 of Israel then *o*, ''Take Micaiah
22: 31 king of Aram had *o* his thirty-two
2Ki 6: 13 find out where he is,'' the king *o*,
9: 17 ''Get a horseman,'' Joram *o*.
9: 21 ''Hitch up my chariot,'' Joram *o*.
10: 8 Jehu *o*, ''Put them in two piles
10: 14 ''Take them alive!'' he *o*.
10: 25 he *o* the guards and officers:
11: 9 did just as Jehoiada the priest *o*.
11: 15 the priest *o* the commanders
16: 16 priest did just as King Ahaz had *o*.
17: 15 although the LORD had *o* them,
23: 4 The king *o* Hilkiah the high priest,
1Ch 21: 17 Was it not I who *o* the fighting men
21: 18 of the LORD *o* Gad to tell David
22: 17 David *o* all the leaders of Israel
2Ch 8: 14 what David the man of God had *o*.
18: 25 of Israel then *o*, ''Take Micaiah
18: 30 the king of Aram had *o* his chariot
23: 8 did just as Jehoiada the priest *o*.
23: 18 and singing, as David had *o*.
29: 15 the king had *o*, following the word
29: 24 the king had *o* the burnt offering
29: 30 and his officials *o* the Levites
30: 12 the king and his officials had *o*,
31: 4 He *o* the people living in Jerusalem
35: 10 in their divisions as the king had *o*.
35: 16 of the LORD, as King Josiah had *o*
Ezr 2: 63 The governor *o* them not to eat any
Ne 7: 65 therefore, *o* them not to eat any
13: 19 I *o* the doors to be shut
Est 4: 5 and *o* him to find out what was
6: 1 so he *o* the book of the chronicles,
6: 5 ''Bring him in,'' the king *o*.
Jer 35: 14 son of Recab *o* his sons not
35: 18 and have done everything he *o*.'
38: 27 everything the king had *o* him
47: 7 when he has *o* it
Da 1: 3 Then the king *o* Ashpenaz,
2: 12 and furious that he *o* the execution
2: 46 him honor and *o* that an offering
3: 19 He *o* the furnace heated seven
Mt 14: 9 he *o* that her request be granted
18: 25 the master *o* that he and his wife
27: 58 and Pilate *o* that it be given to him.
Lk 5: 14 Jesus *o* him, ''Don't tell anyone,
8: 56 he *o* them not to tell anyone what
14: 21 became angry and *o* his servant,
14: 22 'what you *o* has been done,
18: 40 *o* the man to be brought to him.
Ac 4: 15 So they *o* them to withdraw
5: 34 and *o* that the men be put
5: 40 Then they *o* them not to speak
8: 38 And he *o* the chariot to stop.
10: 48 So he *o* that they be baptized
12: 19 and *o* that they be executed.
16: 22 and the magistrates *o* them
16: 36 ''The magistrates have *o* that you
18: 2 because Claudius had *o* all the Jews
21: 33 *o* him to be bound with two chains.
21: 34 he *o* that Paul be taken
22: 24 the commander *o* Paul to be taken
22: 30 released him and *o* the chief priests
23: 2 priest Ananias *o* those standing
23: 10 He *o* the troops to go down
23: 23 two of his centurions and *o* them,
23: 30 also *o* his accusers to present
23: 35 he *o* that Paul be kept under guard
24: 23 He *o* the centurion to keep Paul
25: 6 *o* that Paul be brought before him.
25: 17 and *o* the man to be brought in.
25: 21 I *o* him held until I could send him
27: 43 He *o* those who could swim
Rev 13: 14 He *o* them to set up an image

ORDERLY (ORDER)

Lk 1: 3 to me to write an *o* account for you,
1Co 14: 40 done in a fitting and *o* way.
Col 2: 5 and delight to see how *o* you are

ORDERS (ORDER)

Ge 12: 20 Then Pharaoh gave *o* about Abram
26: 11 Abimelech gave *o* to all the people:
41: 40 are to submit to your *o*.
42: 25 Joseph gave *o* to fill their bags
Nu 32: 28 Then Moses gave *o* about them
Dt 2: 4 the people these *o*: 'You are about
Jos 3: 3 throughout the camp, giving *o*
8: 4 sent them out at night with these *o*:
8: 8 See to it; you have my *o*.''
Ru 2: 15 to glean, Boaz gave *o* to his men,
2Sa 3: 15 So Ish-Bosheth gave *o*
18: 5 king giving *o* concerning Absalom
1Ki 2: 25 So King Solomon gave *o*
5: 6 give *o* that cedars of Lebanon be
2Ki 16: 15 King Ahaz then gave these *o*
22: 12 He gave these *o* to Hilkiah
1Ch 14: 12 and David gave *o* to burn them
22: 2 David gave *o* to assemble the aliens
2Ch 2: 1 Solomon gave *o* to build a temple
19: 9 gave them these *o*: ''You must
31: 11 gave *o* to prepare storerooms
34: 20 He gave these *o* to Hilkiah,
Ezr 8: 36 also delivered the king's *o*
Ne 11: 23 The singers were under the king's *o*
13: 9 I gave *o* to purify the rooms,
Est 3: 12 of each people all Haman's *o*
8: 9 These *o* were written in the script
8: 9 They wrote out all Mordecai's *o*
9: 25 he issued written *o* that the evil
Job 38: 12 ''Have you ever given *o*
Isa 45: 11 or give me *o* about the work
Jer 37: 21 King Zedekiah then gave *o*
39: 11 had given these *o* about Jeremiah
Da 5: 2 he gave *o* to bring in the gold
6: 23 gave *o* to lift Daniel out of the den.
Mt 2: 16 and he gave *o* to kill all the boys
8: 18 he gave *o* to cross to the other side
Mk 1: 27 He even gives *o* to evil spirits
3: 12 But he gave them strict *o* not
5: 43 He gave strict *o* not
6: 17 For Herod himself had given *o*
6: 27 with *o* to bring John's head.
9: 9 Jesus gave them *o* not
Lk 4: 36 and power he gives *o* to evil spirits
15: 29 and never disobeyed your *o*.
Jn 11: 57 and Pharisees had given *o* that
Ac 5: 28 ''We gave you strict *o* not to teach
16: 24 Upon receiving such *o*, he put
23: 31 So the soldiers, carrying out their *o*

ORDINANCE (ORDINANCES)

Ex 12: 14 festival to the LORD—a lasting *o*.
12: 17 as a lasting *o* for the generations
12: 24 as a lasting *o* for you and your
13: 10 You must keep this *o*
27: 21 be a lasting *o* among the Israelites
28: 43 ''This is to be a lasting *o* for Aaron

Ex 29: 9 priesthood is theirs by a lasting *o*.
30: 21 This is to be a lasting *o* for Aaron
Lev 3: 17 " 'This is a lasting *o*
10: 9 is a lasting *o* for the generations
16: 29 "This is to be a lasting *o* for you:
16: 31 deny yourselves; it is a lasting *o*.
16: 34 "This is to be a lasting *o* for you:
17: 7 This is to be a lasting *o* for them
23: 14 to be a lasting *o* for the generations
23: 21 to be a lasting *o* for the generations
23: 31 to be a lasting *o* for the generations
23: 41 to be a lasting *o* for the generations
24: 3 to be a lasting *o* for the generations
Nu 10: 8 This is to be a lasting *o* for you
15: 15 is a lasting *o* for the generations
18: 23 is a lasting *o* for the generations
19: 10 This will be a lasting *o* both
19: 21 This is a lasting *o* for them.
1Sa 30: 25 *o* for Israel from that day to this.
2Ch 2: 4 This is a lasting *o* for Israel.
8: 14 Following the *o* of his father David
Ps 81: 4 an *o* of the God of Jacob.
Eze 46: 14 offering to the LORD is a lasting *o*.

ORDINANCES (ORDINANCE)

2Ki 17: 34 nor adhere to the decrees and *o*,
17: 37 careful to keep the decrees and *o*,
2Ch 19: 10 commands, decrees or *o*—
33: 8 decrees and *o* given through Moses
Ne 9: 29 They sinned against your *o*,
Ps 19: 9 The *o* of the LORD are sure
Eze 44: 24 and decide it according to my *o*.

ORDINARY

1Sa 21: 4 "I don't have any *o* bread on hand;
Isa 8: 1 and write on it with an *o* pen:
Ac 4: 13 that they were unschooled, *o* men,
7: 20 was born, and he was no *o* child.
21: 39 in Cilicia, a citizen of no *o* city.
Gal 4: 23 woman was born in the *o* way;
4: 29 in the *o* way persecuted the son
Heb 11: 23 because they saw he was no *o* child

ORDINATION (ORDAIN)

Ex 29: 22 (This is the ram for the *o*.)
29: 26 the breast of the ram for Aaron's *o*,
29: 27 parts of the *o* ram that belong
29: 31 "Take the ram for the *o*
29: 33 atonement was made for their *o*
29: 34 And if any of the meat of the *o* ram
Lev 7: 37 the *o* offering and the fellowship
8: 22 the other ram, the ram for the *o*,
8: 28 the burnt offering as an *o* offering,
8: 29 Moses' share of the *o* ram—
8: 31 from the basket of *o* offerings,
8: 33 for your *o* will last seven days.
8: 33 the days of your *o* are completed,

ORE

Job 28: 2 and copper is smelted from *o*.
28: 3 for *o* in the blackest darkness.
Jer 6: 27 and my people the *o*,

OREB

Jdg 7: 25 They killed *O* at the rock of *O*,
7: 25 and brought the heads of *O*
7: 25 two of the Midianite leaders, *O*
8: 3 God gave *O* and Zeeb,
Ps 83: 11 Make their nobles like *O* and Zeeb,
Isa 10: 26 down Midian at the rock of *O*;

OREN

1Ch 2: 25 Bunah, *O*, Ozem and Ahijah.

ORGIES

Ro 13: 13 not in *o* and drunkenness,
Gal 5: 21 drunkenness, *o*, and the like.
1Pe 4: 3 *o*, carousing and detestable

ORIGIN (ORIGINAL ORIGINATE ORIGINS)

Est 6: 13 is of Jewish *o*, you cannot stand
Ac 5: 38 or activity is of human *o*,
2Pe 1: 21 For prophecy never had its *o*

ORIGINAL (ORIGIN)

2Ch 24: 13 of God according to its *o* design

ORIGINATE (ORIGIN)

1Co 14: 36 Did the word of God *o* with you?

ORIGINS (ORIGIN)

Mic 5: 2 whose *o* are from of old,

ORION

Job 9: 9 He is the Maker of the Bear and *O*,
38: 31 Can you loose the cords of *O*?
Am 5: 8 (he who made the Pleiades and *O*,

ORNAMENT (ORNAMENTED ORNAMENTS)

Pr 3: 22 an *o* to grace your neck.
25: 12 of gold or an *o* of fine gold

ORNAMENTED (ORNAMENT)

Ge 37: 3 and he made a richly *o* robe for him
37: 23 the richly *o* robe he was wearing—
37: 32 They took the *o* robe back
2Sa 13: 18 She was wearing a richly *o* robe,
13: 19 tore the *o* robe she was wearing.

ORNAMENTS (ORNAMENT)

Ex 33: 4 to mourn and no one put on any *o*.
33: 5 off your *o* and I will decide what
33: 6 off their *o* at Mount Horeb.
35: 22 brooches, earrings, rings and *o*.
Jdg 8: 21 took the *o* off their camels' necks.
8: 26 shekels, not counting the *o*,
2Sa 1: 24 who adorned your garments with *o*
Isa 3: 16 with *o* jingling on their ankles.
49: 18 "you will wear them all as *o*;
Jer 2: 32 a bride her wedding *o*?

ORPAH

Ru 1: 4 one named *O* and the other Ruth.
1: 14 Then *O* kissed her mother-in-law

ORPHAN (ORPHAN'S ORPHANS)

Ex 22: 22 advantage of a widow or an *o*.

ORPHAN'S (ORPHAN)

Job 24: 3 They drive away the *o* donkey

ORPHANS (ORPHAN)

Jer 49: 11 Leave your *o*; I will protect their
La 5: 3 We have become *o* and fatherless,
Jn 14: 18 will not leave you as *o*; I will come
Jas 1: 27 to look after *o* and widows

OSPREY

Lev 11: 18 the desert owl, the *o*, the stork,
Dt 14: 17 desert owl, the *o*, the cormorant,

OSTRICH (OSTRICHES)

Job 39: 13 "The wings of the *o* flap joyfully,

OSTRICHES (OSTRICH)

La 4: 3 like *o* in the desert.

OTHNI

1Ch 26: 7 The sons of Shemaiah: *O*, Rephael,

OTHNIEL

Jos 15: 17 *O* son of Kenaz, Caleb's brother,
15: 18 One day when she came to *O*,
Jdg 1: 13 *O* son of Kenaz, Caleb's younger
1: 14 One day when she came to *O*,
3: 9 *O* son of Kenaz, Caleb's younger
3: 10 king of Aram into the hands of *O*,
3: 11 until *O* son of Kenaz died.
1Ch 4: 13 The sons of Kenaz: *O* and Seraiah.
4: 13 The sons of *O*: Hathath
27: 15 from the family of *O*.

OUSTED

Isa 22: 19 you will be *o* from your position.

OUTBREAK

1Sa 5: 9 and old, with an *o* of tumors.

OUTBURSTS

2Co 12: 20 jealousy, *o* of anger, factions,

OUTCAST (CAST)

Jer 30: 17 'because you are called an *o*,

OUTCOME

Isa 41: 22 and know their final *o*.
Da 11: 29 but this time the *o* will be different
12: 8 what will the *o* of all this be?"
Mt 26: 58 down with the guards to see the *o*.
Heb 13: 7 Consider the *o* of their way of life
1Pe 4: 17 what will the *o* be for those who do

OUTCRY

Ge 18: 20 "The *o* against Sodom
18: 21 as bad as the *o* that has reached me.
19: 13 The *o* to the LORD
1Sa 4: 14 Eli heard the *o* and asked,
5: 12 the *o* of the city went up to heaven.
Ne 5: 1 and their wives raised a great *o*
5: 6 I heard their *o* and these charges,
Isa 15: 8 Their *o* echoes along the border

OUTLAW

Pr 24: 15 in wait like an *o* against a righteous

OUTLET

2Ch 32: 30 Hezekiah who blocked the upper *o*

OUTLINE

Isa 44: 13 and makes an *o* with a marker;

OUTLIVED (LIVE)

Jos 24: 31 and of the elders who *o* him
Jdg 2: 7 and of the elders who *o* him

OUTLYING

1Ch 5: 16 in Bashan and its *o* villages,
27: 25 of the storehouses in the *o* districts,

OUTNUMBER

Ps 69: 4 *o* the hairs of my head;
139: 18 they would *o* the grains of sand.

OUTPOST (OUTPOSTS)

1Sa 10: 5 where there is a Philistine *o*.
13: 3 Jonathan attacked the Philistine *o*
13: 4 "Saul has attacked the Philistine *o*,
14: 1 go over to the Philistine *o*
14: 4 to reach the Philistine *o* was a cliff;
14: 6 to the *o* of those uncircumcised
14: 11 themselves to the Philistine *o*.
14: 12 men of the *o* shouted to Jonathan

OUTPOSTS (OUTPOST)

Jdg 7: 11 went down to the *o* of the camp.
1Sa 14: 15 those in the *o* and raiding parties—

OUTPOURED (POUR)

Ps 79: 10 that you avenge the *o* blood
Eze 20: 33 outstretched arm and with *o* wrath.
20: 34 outstretched arm and with *o* wrath.

OUTPOURING (POUR)

Eze 9: 8 of Israel in this *o* of your wrath

OUTRAGEOUS (RAGE)

Jer 29: 23 For they have done *o* things

OUTRAN (RUN)

2Sa 18: 23 way of the plain and *o* the Cushite.
Jn 20: 4 but the other disciple *o* Peter

OUTSIDERS

Col 4: 5 wise in the way you act toward *o*;
1Th 4: 12 daily life may win the respect of *o*
1Ti 3: 7 also have a good reputation with *o*,

OUTSKIRTS

Nu 11: 1 some of the *o* of the camp.
Jos 18: 15 The southern side began at the *o*
1Sa 14: 2 Saul was staying on the *o* of Gibeah
1Ch 4: 39 and they went to the *o* of Gedor

OUTSPREAD

Isa 8: 8 Its *o* wings will cover the breadth

OUTSTANDING

1Ch 7: 40 brave warriors and *o* leaders.
SS 5: 10 *o* among ten thousand.
Da 5: 14 intelligence and *o* wisdom.
Ac 4: 16 they have done an *o* miracle,
Ro 13: 8 no debt remain *o*,
16: 7 They are *o* among the apostles,

OUTSTRETCHED (STRETCH)
Ex 6: 6 and will redeem you with an *o* arm
Dt 4: 34 by a mighty hand and an *o* arm,
5: 15 with a mighty hand and an *o* arm.
7: 19 the mighty hand and *o* arm,
9: 29 your great power and your *o* arm."
11: 2 his mighty hand, his *o* arm;
26: 8 with a mighty hand and an *o* arm,
1Ki 8: 42 your mighty hand and your *o* arm
2Ki 17: 36 with mighty power and *o* arm,
2Ch 6: 32 your mighty hand and your *o* arm
Ps 75: 5 do not speak with *o* neck.' "
136: 12 with a mighty hand and *o* arm;
Isa 3: 16 walking along with *o* necks,
Jer 21: 5 fight against you with an *o* hand
27: 5 and *o* arm I made the earth
32: 17 by your great power and *o* arm.
32: 21 and an *o* arm and with great terror.
Eze 20: 33 an *o* arm and with outpoured wrath
20: 34 an *o* arm and with outpoured wrath

OUTWEIGH (WEIGH)
Job 6: 3 It would surely *o* the sand

OUTWEIGHS (WEIGH)
Ecc 10: 1 so a little folly *o* wisdom and honor
2Co 4: 17 an eternal glory that far *o* them all.

OUTWIT (OUTWITTED)
2Co 2: 11 in order that Satan might not *o* us.

OUTWITTED (OUTWIT)
Mt 2: 16 Herod realized that he had been *o*

OVEN (OVENS)
Lev 2: 4 bring a grain offering baked in an *o*,
7: 9 Every grain offering baked in an *o*
11: 35 an *o* or cooking pot must be broken
26: 26 able to bake your bread in one *o*,
La 5: 10 Our skin is hot as an *o*,
Hos 7: 4 burning like an *o*
7: 6 Their hearts are like an *o*;
7: 7 All of them are hot as an *o*;

OVENS (OVEN)
Ex 8: 3 into your *o* and kneading troughs.
Ne 3: 11 section and the Tower of the *O*.
12: 38 Tower of the *O* to the Broad Wall,

OVERAWED (AWE)
Ps 49: 16 Do not be *o* when a man grows rich

OVERBEARING
Tit 1: 7 not *o*, not quick-tempered,

OVERBOARD
Jnh 1: 15 they took Jonah and threw him *o*,
Ac 27: 18 began to throw the cargo *o*.
27: 19 they threw the ship's tackle *o*
27: 43 who could swim to jump *o* first

OVERCAME (OVERCOME)
Ex 17: 13 So Joshua *o* the Amalekite army
Jer 38: 22 " 'They misled you and *o* you—
Hos 12: 4 with the angel and *o* him;
Rev 3: 21 as I *o* and sat down with my Father
12: 11 They *o* him

OVERCAST
Mt 16: 3 for the sky is red and *o*.'

OVERCOME (OVERCAME OVERCOMES)
Ge 32: 28 and with men and have *o*."
1Sa 4: 19 but was *o* by her labor pains.
17: 9 but if I *o* him and kill him,
Ps 13: 4 my enemy will say, "I have *o* him,"
39: 10 I am *o* by the blow of your hand.
116: 3 I was *o* by trouble and sorrow.
Jer 1: 19 fight against you but will not *o* you,
15: 20 but will not *o* you,
23: 9 like a man *o* by wine,
Da 10: 16 "I am *o* with anguish
Zec 9: 15 and *o* with slingstones.
Mt 16: 18 and the gates of Hades will not *o* it.
Mk 9: 24 I do believe; help me *o* my unbelief
Lk 8: 37 because they were *o* with fear.
10: 19 to *o* all the power of the enemy;
Jn 16: 33 But take heart! I have *o* the world."
Ro 12: 21 Do not be *o* by evil, but *o* evil
1Ti 5: 11 sensual desires *o* their dedication
2Pe 2: 20 and are again entangled in it and *o*,
1Jn 2: 13 because you have *o* the evil one.
2: 14 and you have *o* the evil one.
4: 4 are from God and have *o* them,
5: 4 is the victory that has *o* the world,
Rev 17: 14 but the Lamb will *o* them

OVERCOMES (OVERCOME)
1Jn 5: 4 born of God *o* the world.
5: 5 Who is it that *o* the world?
Rev 2: 7 To him who *o*, I will give the right
2: 11 He who *o* will not be hurt at all
2: 17 To him who *o*, I will give some
2: 26 To him who *o* and does my will
3: 5 He who *o* will, like them, be
3: 12 Him who *o* I will make a pillar
3: 21 To him who *o*, I will give the right
21: 7 He who *o* will inherit all this,

OVERFED (FEED)
Eze 16: 49 and her daughters were arrogant, *o*

OVERFLOW (OVERFLOWING OVERFLOWS)
Job 6: 15 as the streams that *o*
Ps 65: 11 and your carts *o* with abundance.
65: 12 The grasslands of the desert *o*;
119: 171 May my lips *o* with praise,
Pr 5: 16 Should your springs *o* in the streets
Isa 8: 7 It will *o* all its channels,
28: 17 and water will *o* your hiding place.
Jer 9: 18 us till our eyes *o* with tears
14: 17 " 'Let my eyes *o* with tears
47: 2 They will *o* the land
La 1: 16 and my eyes *o* with tears.
Joel 2: 24 the vats will *o* with new wine
3: 13 and the vats *o*—
Zec 1: 17 'My towns will again *o*
Mt 12: 34 out of the *o* of the heart the mouth
Lk 6: 45 out of the *o* of his heart his mouth
Ro 5: 15 Jesus Christ, *o* to the many! Again,
15: 13 so that you may *o* with hope
2Co 4: 15 to *o* to the glory of God.
Php 1: 26 in Christ Jesus will *o* on account
1Th 3: 12 *o* for each other and for everyone

OVERFLOWING (OVERFLOW)
1Ch 12: 15 month when it was *o* all its banks,
Pr 3: 10 then your barns will be filled to *o*,
Isa 66: 11 and delight in her *o* abundance."
Jer 13: 17 *o* with tears,
47: 2 they will become an *o* torrent.
2Co 8: 2 their *o* joy and their extreme
9: 12 *o* in many expressions of thanks
Col 2: 7 as you were taught, and *o*

OVERFLOWS (OVERFLOW)
Ps 23: 5 my cup *o*.
2Co 1: 5 also through Christ our comfort *o*.

OVERGROWN (GROW)
Isa 32: 13 a land *o* with thorns and briers—
Jer 26: 18 the temple hill a mound *o*
Mic 3: 12 the temple hill a mound *o*

OVERHANG (HANG)
Eze 41: 25 there was a wooden *o* on the front

OVERHANGING (HANG)
1Ki 7: 6 of that were pillars and an *o* roof.
Isa 2: 21 and to the *o* crags
57: 5 and under the *o* crags.

OVERHANGS (HANG)
Eze 41: 26 rooms of the temple also had *o*.

OVERHEAD
Isa 31: 5 Like birds hovering *o*,

OVERHEARD (HEAR)
Ge 27: 6 I *o* your father say
1Sa 17: 31 What David said was *o*

OVERJOYED (JOY)
Da 6: 23 The king was *o* and gave orders
Mt 2: 10 they saw the star, they were *o*.
Jn 20: 20 The disciples were *o*
Ac 12: 14 she was so *o* she ran back
1Pe 4: 13 so that you may be *o*

OVERLAID (OVERLAY)
Ex 26: 32 posts of acacia wood *o* with gold
26: 37 posts of acacia wood *o* with gold.
36: 34 They also *o* the crossbars with gold
36: 34 They *o* the frames with gold
36: 36 wood for it and *o* them with gold.
36: 38 They *o* the tops of the posts
37: 2 He *o* it with pure gold, both inside
37: 4 poles of acacia wood and *o* them
37: 11 Then they *o* it with pure gold
37: 15 made of acacia wood and were *o*
37: 26 They *o* the top and all the sides
37: 28 poles of acacia wood and *o* them
38: 2 and they *o* the altar with bronze.
38: 6 poles of acacia wood and *o* them
38: 17 and their tops were *o* with silver;
38: 19 and their tops were *o* with silver.
1Ki 6: 20 He *o* the inside with pure gold,
6: 20 and he also *o* the altar of cedar.
6: 21 of the inner sanctuary, which was *o*
6: 22 he *o* the whole interior with gold.
6: 22 *o* with gold the altar that belonged
6: 28 He *o* the cherubim with gold.
6: 32 and *o* the cherubim and palm trees
6: 35 and *o* them with gold hammered
10: 18 with ivory and *o* with fine gold.
2Ch 3: 4 He *o* the inside with pure gold.
3: 7 He *o* the ceiling beams, doorframes
3: 8 He *o* the inside with six hundred
3: 9 He also *o* the upper parts with gold.
3: 10 of sculptured cherubim and *o* them
4: 9 and *o* the doors with bronze.
9: 17 with ivory and *o* with pure gold.
Isa 30: 22 Then you will defile your idols *o*

OVERLAY (OVERLAID OVERLAYING OVERLAYS)
Ex 25: 11 *O* it with pure gold, both inside
25: 13 poles of acacia wood and *o* them
25: 24 *O* it with pure gold and make a gold
25: 28 *o* them with gold and carry
26: 29 Also *o* the crossbars with gold.
26: 29 *O* the frames with gold
27: 2 and *o* the altar with bronze.
27: 6 wood for the altar and *o* them
30: 3 *O* the top and all the sides
30: 5 poles of acacia wood and *o* them
38: 28 hooks for the posts, to *o* the tops
Nu 16: 38 censers into sheets to *o* the altar,
16: 39 them hammered out to *o* the altar,

OVERLAYING (OVERLAY)
1Ch 29: 4 for the *o* of the walls

OVERLAYS (OVERLAY)
Isa 40: 19 and a goldsmith *o* it with gold

OVERLOOK (OVERLOOKED OVERLOOKING OVERLOOKS)
Dt 9: 27 *O* the stubbornness of this people,
24: 19 in your field and you *o* a sheaf,
Pr 19: 11 it is to his glory to *o* an offense.

OVERLOOKED (OVERLOOK)
Ac 6: 1 because their widows were being *o*
17: 30 In the past God *o* such ignorance,

OVERLOOKING (OVERLOOK)
Nu 23: 28 to the top of Peor, *o* the wasteland.
Jos 8: 14 at a certain place *o* the Arabah.
1Sa 13: 18 the borderland *o* the Valley of

OVERLOOKS (OVERLOOK)
Nu 21: 20 the top of Pisgah *o* the wasteland.
2Ch 20: 24 came to the place that *o* the desert
Pr 12: 16 but a prudent man *o* an insult.

OVERNIGHT (NIGHT)
Lev 19: 13 back the wages of a hired man *o*.
Dt 21: 23 not leave his body on the tree *o*.
Isa 10: 29 "We will camp *o* at Geba."
Jnh 4: 10 It sprang up *o* and died *o*.

OVERPOWER (POWER)

Ge 32: 25 man saw that he could not *o* him,
43: 18 He wants to attack us and *o* us
Jdg 16: 5 and how we can *o* him
2Ki 16: 5 Ahaz, but they could not *o* him.
Est 9: 1 of the Jews had hoped to *o* them,
Job 14: 20 You *o* him once for all,
Isa 7: 1 Jerusalem, but they could not *o* it.
Ob : 7 your friends will deceive and *o* you
Rev 11: 7 the Abyss will attack them, and *o*

OVERPOWERED (POWER)

Jdg 3: 10 the hands of Othniel, who *o* him.
2Sa 11: 23 "The men *o* us and came out
1Ki 20: 21 and *o* the horses and chariots
2Ki 10: 32 Hazael *o* the Israelites
Ecc 4: 12 Though one may be *o*,
Jer 20: 7 you *o* me and prevailed.
Da 6: 24 lions *o* them and crushed all their
Ac 19: 16 jumped on them and *o* them all.

OVERPOWERING (POWER)

Job 41: 9 the mere sight of him is *o*.

OVERPOWERS (POWER)

Lk 11: 22 stronger attacks and *o* him,

OVERRAN (OVERRUN)

Jdg 20: 43 and easily *o* them in the vicinity

OVERRIGHTEOUS (RIGHTEOUS)

Ecc 7: 16 Do not be *o*,

OVERRULED (OVERRULING)

2Sa 24: 4 *o* Joab and the army commanders;
1Ch 21: 4 The king's word, however, *o* Joab;

OVERRULING (OVERRULED)

Est 8: 5 order be written *o* the dispatches

OVERRUN (OVERRAN)

Isa 34: 13 Thorns will *o* her citadels,
Hos 9: 6 and thorns will *o* their tents.
Am 3: 11 "An enemy will *o* the land;
Zec 9: 8 will an oppressor *o* my people,

OVERSEER (OVERSEERS OVERSIGHT)

Pr 6: 7 no *o* or ruler,
1Ti 3: 1 anyone sets his heart on being an *o*,
3: 2 Now the *o* must be above reproach,
Tit 1: 7 Since an *o* is entrusted
1Pe 2: 25 returned to the Shepherd and *O*

OVERSEERS (OVERSEER)

Ac 20: 28 the Holy Spirit has made you *o*.
Php 1: 1 together with the *o* and deacons:
1Pe 5: 2 as *o*— not because you must,

OVERSHADOW (OVERSHADOWED OVERSHADOWING)

Lk 1: 35 power of the Most High will *o* you.

OVERSHADOWED (OVERSHADOW)

1Ki 8: 7 *o* the ark and its carrying poles.

OVERSHADOWING (OVERSHADOW)

Ex 25: 20 wings spread upward, *o* the cover
37: 9 wings spread upward, *o* the cover
Eze 31: 3 with beautiful branches *o* the forest
Heb 9: 5 cherubim of the Glory, *o* the place

OVERSIGHT (OVERSEER)

2Ch 23: 18 Jehoiada placed the *o* of the temple

OVERSTEP (STEP)

Pr 8: 29 waters would not *o* his command,

OVERTAKE (OVERTAKEN OVERTAKES OVERTAKING OVERTOOK)

Ge 19: 19 this disaster will *o* me, and I'll die.
Ex 15: 9 'I will pursue, I will *o* them.
Dt 19: 6 *o* him if the distance is too great,
28: 15 come upon you and *o* you:
28: 45 and *o* you until you are destroyed,
1Sa 30: 8 Will I *o* them?" "Pursue them,"
30: 8 "You will certainly *o* them
2Sa 15: 14 or he will move quickly to *o* us
2Ki 7: 9 until daylight, punishment will *o* us
Job 20: 22 of his plenty, distress will *o* him;
27: 20 Terrors *o* him like a flood;
Ps 7: 5 let my enemy pursue and *o* me;
35: 8 may ruin *o* them by surprise—
69: 24 let your fierce anger *o* them.
Pr 6: 15 Therefore disaster will *o* him
10: 24 What the wicked dreads will *o* him;
Ecc 2: 15 "The fate of the fool will *o* me also.
Isa 35: 10 Gladness and joy will *o* them,
47: 9 Both of these will *o* you
51: 11 Gladness and joy will *o* them,
Jer 42: 16 the sword you fear will *o* you there,
Hos 10: 9 Did not war *o*
Am 9: 10 'Disaster will not *o* or meet us.'
Mic 2: 6 disgrace will not *o* us."
Zec 1: 6 the prophets, *o* your forefathers?
Rev 12: 15 to *o* the woman and sweep her
18: 8 in one day her plagues will *o* her:

OVERTAKEN (OVERTAKE)

Ps 9: 6 Endless ruin has *o* the enemy,
40: 12 my sins have *o* me, and I cannot
La 1: 3 All who pursue her have *o* her
Am 9: 13 "when the reaper will be *o*

OVERTAKES (OVERTAKE)

Pr 1: 26 I will mock when calamity *o* you—
1: 27 when calamity *o* you like a storm,
3: 25 or of the ruin that *o* the wicked,
Ecc 2: 14 that the same fate *o* them both.
9: 3 the sun: The same destiny *o* all.
Jn 12: 35 before darkness *o* you.

OVERTAKING (OVERTAKE)

1Ch 21: 12 with their swords *o* you,

OVERTHREW (OVERTHROW)

Ge 19: 25 Thus he *o* those cities
19: 29 the catastrophe that *o* the cities
Dt 29: 23 which the LORD *o* in fierce anger.
Isa 14: 17 who *o* its cities
Jer 20: 16 the LORD *o* without pity.
50: 40 As God *o* Sodom and Gomorrah
Am 4: 11 as I *o* Sodom and Gomorrah.
4: 11 "I *o* some of you
Ac 13: 19 He *o* seven nations in Canaan

OVERTHROW (OVERTHREW OVERTHROWN OVERTHROWS)

Ge 19: 21 I will not *o* the town you speak of.
2Sa 10: 3 the city and spy it out and *o* it?"
2Ki 3: 19 You will *o* every fortified city
1Ch 19: 3 and spy out the country and *o* it?"
2Ch 25: 8 God has the power to help or to *o*."
25: 8 God will *o* you before the enemy,
Ezr 6: 12 *o* any king or people who lifts
Jer 1: 10 to destroy and *o*, to build
31: 28 and to *o*, destroy and bring disaster
45: 4 I will *o* what I have built
Da 11: 17 in order to *o* the kingdom,
11: 24 He will plot the *o* of fortresses—
Hag 2: 22 I will *o* chariots and their drivers;
Zec 10: 5 they will fight and *o* the horsemen.
2Th 2: 8 whom the Lord Jesus will *o*

OVERTHROWN (OVERTHROW)

Nu 21: 30 "But we have *o* them;
Pr 12: 7 Wicked men are *o* and are no more
Isa 1: 7 laid waste as when *o* by strangers.
13: 19 will be *o* by God
Jer 18: 23 Let them be *o* before you;
49: 18 As Sodom and Gomorrah were *o*,
La 2: 17 He has *o* you without pity,
4: 6 which was *o* in a moment
Eze 32: 12 and all her hordes will be *o*.

OVERTHROWS (OVERTHROW)

Job 12: 19 and *o* men long established.
34: 25 he *o* them in the night
Pr 13: 6 but wickedness *o* the sinner.
Isa 44: 25 who *o* the learning of the wise

OVERTOOK (OVERTAKE)

Ge 31: 25 of Gilead when Laban *o* him,
Ex 14: 9 pursued the Israelites and *o* them
Jdg 18: 22 called together and *o* the Danites.
1Sa 31: 3 and when the archers *o* him,
2Ki 25: 5 and *o* him in the plains of Jericho.
1Ch 10: 3 and when the archers *o* him,
Ps 18: 37 I pursued my enemies and *o* them;
Jer 2: 3 and disaster *o* them,' "
39: 5 *o* Zedekiah in the plains of Jericho.
52: 8 and *o* him in the plains of Jericho.

OVERTURN (OVERTURNED OVERTURNS)

Hag 2: 22 I will *o* royal thrones and shatter

OVERTURNED (OVERTURN)

Jdg 7: 13 tent with such force that the tent *o*
Eze 38: 20 mountains will be *o*, the cliffs will
Mt 21: 12 He *o* the tables of the money
Mk 11: 15 He *o* the tables of the money
Jn 2: 15 money changers and *o* their tables.

OVERTURNS (OVERTURN)

Job 9: 5 and *o* them in his anger.

OVERWEENING

Pr 21: 24 he behaves with *o* pride.
Isa 16: 6 her *o* pride and conceit,
Jer 48: 29 her *o* pride and conceit,

OVERWHELM (OVERWHELMED OVERWHELMING OVERWHELMS)

Job 3: 5 may blackness *o* its light.
9: 18 but would *o* me with misery.
15: 24 they *o* him, like a king poised
30: 15 Terrors *o* me;
Pr 1: 27 when distress and troubles *o* you.
SS 6: 5 they *o* me.
Hab 2: 17 to Lebanon will *o* you,

OVERWHELMED (OVERWHELM)

Dt 11: 4 how he *o* them with the waters
2Sa 22: 5 the torrents of destruction *o* me.
1Ki 10: 5 temple of the LORD, she was *o*.
2Ch 9: 4 temple of the LORD, she was *o*.
Ps 14: 5 There they are, *o* with dread,
18: 4 the torrents of destruction *o* me.
38: 4 My guilt has *o* me
53: 5 There they were, *o* with dread,
55: 5 horror has *o* me.
65: 3 When we were *o* by sins,
88: 7 you have *o* me with all your waves.
Eze 3: 15 sat among them for seven days—*o*.
Da 10: 7 such terror *o* them that they fled
Mt 26: 38 "My soul is *o* with sorrow
Mk 7: 37 People were *o* with amazement.
9: 15 they were *o* with wonder
14: 34 "My soul is *o* with sorrow
2Co 2: 7 so that he will not be *o*

OVERWHELMING (OVERWHELM)

Pr 27: 4 Anger is cruel and fury *o*,
Isa 10: 22 *o* and righteous.
28: 15 When an *o* scourge sweeps by,
28: 18 When the *o* scourge sweeps by,
Da 11: 22 Then an *o* army will be swept away
Na 1: 8 but with an *o* flood

OVERWHELMS (OVERWHELM)

Pr 10: 6 violence *o* the mouth of the wicked
10: 11 violence *o* the mouth of the wicked

OVERWICKED (WICKED)

Ecc 7: 17 Do not be *o*,

OVERWISE (WISE)

Ecc 7: 16 neither be *o*—

OWE (OWED OWES)

Mt 18: 28 'Pay back what you *o* me!'
Lk 16: 5 'How much do you *o* my master?'
16: 7 'And how much do you *o*?'
Ro 13: 7 Give everyone what you *o* him:
13: 7 If you *o* taxes, pay taxes; if revenue
15: 27 and indeed they *o* it to them.
15: 27 they *o* it to the Jews to share
Phm : 19 to mention that you *o* me your very

OWED (OWE)

Mt 18: 24 a man who *o* him ten thousand
18: 28 fellow servants who *o* him
18: 34 until he should pay back all he *o*.
Lk 7: 41 One *o* him five hundred denarii,

Lk 7: 41 "Two men *o* money

OWES (OWE)

Dt 15: 3 any debt your brother *o* you.
Phm 1: 18 you any wrong or *o* you anything,

OWL (OWLS)

Lev 11: 16 the horned *o*, the screech *o*,
11: 17 the little *o*, the cormorant,
11: 18 great *o*, the white *o*, the desert *o*,
Dt 14: 15 the horned *o*, the screech *o*,
14: 16 any kind of hawk, the little *o*,
14: 16 great *o*, the white *o*, the desert *o*,
Ps 102: 6 I am like a desert *o*,
102: 6 like an *o* among the ruins.
Isa 34: 11 desert *o* and screech *o* will possess
34: 11 great *o* and the raven will nest
34: 15 The *o* will nest there and lay eggs,
Jer 50: 39 and there the *o* will dwell.
Mic 1: 8 and moan like an *o*.
Zep 2: 14 The desert *o* and the screech *o*

OWLS (OWL)

Job 30: 29 a companion of *o*.
Isa 13: 21 there the *o* will dwell,
14: 23 "I will turn her into a place for *o*
34: 13 a home for *o*.
43: 20 the jackals and the *o*,

OWN (OWNED OWNER OWNER'S OWNERS OWNERSHIP OWNING OWNS)

Ge 30: 43 and came to *o* large flocks,
46: 32 and herds and everything they *o*.'
47: 1 and herds and everything they *o*,
Ps 12: 4 we *o* our lips—who is our master?"

OWNED (OWN)

Ge 25: 5 Abraham left everything he *o*
31: 1 has taken everything our father *o*
39: 4 to his care everything he *o*.
39: 5 of his household and of all that he *o*
Nu 16: 33 with everything they *o*; the earth
Jdg 19: 22 to the old man who *o* the house,
1Ki 17: 17 the woman who *o* the house
Job 1: 3 and he *o* seven thousand sheep,
Ecc 2: 7 also *o* more herds and flocks
Jer 39: 10 who *o* nothing; and at that time he
Ac 4: 34 time to time those who *o* lands
4: 37 sold a field he *o* and brought

OWNER (OWN)

Ex 21: 28 But the *o* of the bull will not be held
21: 29 and the *o* also must be put to death.
21: 29 and the *o* has been warned
21: 32 the *o* must pay thirty shekels
21: 34 he must pay its *o*, and the dead
21: 34 the *o* of the pit must pay
21: 36 the *o* must pay, animal for animal,
21: 36 yet the *o* did not keep it penned up,
22: 8 the *o* of the house must appear
22: 11 The *o* is to accept this,
22: 12 he must make restitution to the *o*.
22: 14 or dies while the *o* is not present,
22: 15 But if the *o* is with the animal,
Lev 6: 5 to the *o* on the day he presents his
14: 35 the *o* of the house must go
25: 53 see to it that his *o* does not rule
27: 13 If the *o* wishes to redeem
Jdg 19: 23 The *o* of the house went outside
1Ki 16: 24 the name of the former *o* of the hill.
Ecc 5: 11 And what benefit are they to the *o*
5: 13 wealth hoarded to the harm of its *o*
Mt 13: 52 the kingdom of heaven is like the *o*
20: 8 the *o* of the vineyard said
21: 40 when the *o* of the vineyard comes,
24: 43 If the *o* of the house had known
Mk 12: 9 "What then will the *o*
13: 35 you do not know when the *o*
14: 14 Say to the *o* of the house he enters,
Lk 12: 39 If the *o* of the house had known
13: 25 Once the *o* of the house gets up
14: 21 the *o* of the house became angry
20: 13 "Then the *o* of the vineyard said,
20: 15 "What then will the *o*
22: 11 and say to the *o* of the house,
Ac 21: 11 Jews of Jerusalem will bind the *o*
27: 11 of the pilot and of the *o* of the ship.

OWNER'S (OWN)

Isa 1: 3 the donkey his *o* manger,
Mt 13: 27 "The *o* servants came to him

OWNERS (OWN)

Jer 8: 10 and their fields to new *o*.
Lk 19: 33 untying the colt, its *o* asked them,
Ac 16: 16 money for her *o* by fortune-telling.
16: 19 When the *o* of the slave girl

OWNERSHIP (OWN)

2Co 1: 22 He anointed us, set his seal of *o*

OWNING (OWN)

Job 22: 8 you were a powerful man, *o* land—

OWNS (OWN)

Ge 24: 36 he has given him everything he *o*.
32: 17 and who *o* all these animals in front
38: 25 pregnant by the man who *o* these,"
39: 8 everything he *o* he has entrusted
Lev 27: 28 " 'But nothing that a man *o*
Ecc 2: 21 and then he must leave all he *o*
Mt 18: 12 If a man *o* a hundred sheep,
Jn 10: 12 not the shepherd who *o* the sheep.
Gal 4: 1 although he *o* the whole estate.

OX (OXEN)

Ex 20: 17 or maidservant, his *o* or donkey,
21: 33 and fails to cover it and an *o*
22: 1 back five head of cattle for the *o*
22: 1 "If a man steals an *o* or a sheep
22: 4 whether *o* or donkey or sheep—
22: 9 cases of illegal possession of an *o*,
22: 10 "If a man gives a donkey, an *o*,
23: 4 If you come across your enemy's *o*
23: 12 so that your *o* and your donkey
Nu 7: 3 an *o* from each leader and a cart
18: 17 not redeem the firstborn of an *o*,
22: 4 as an *o* licks up the grass of the field
23: 22 they have the strength of a wild *o*.
24: 8 they have the strength of a wild *o*.
Dt 5: 14 or maidservant, nor your *o*,
5: 21 or maidservant, his *o* or donkey,
14: 4 the *o*, the sheep, the goat, the deer,
17: 1 to the LORD your God an *o*
22: 1 If you see your brother's *o*
22: 4 or his *o* fallen on the road,
22: 10 Do not plow with an *o*
25: 4 Do not muzzle an *o*
28: 31 Your *o* will be slaughtered
33: 17 his horns are the horns of a wild *o*.
1Sa 12: 3 Whose *o* have I taken? Whose
14: 34 everyone brought his *o* that night
2Sa 24: 22 are threshing sledges and *o* yokes
Ne 5: 18 Each day one *o*, six choice sheep
Job 6: 5 or an *o* bellow when it has fodder?
24: 3 and take the widow's *o* in pledge.
39: 9 "Will the wild *o* consent
40: 15 and which feeds on grass like an *o*.
Ps 29: 6 Sirion like a young wild *o*.
69: 31 please the LORD more than an *o*,
92: 10 my horn like that of a wild *o*;
Pr 7: 22 like an *o* going to the slaughter,
14: 4 of an *o* comes an abundant harvest.
Isa 1: 3 The *o* knows his master,
11: 7 and the lion will eat straw like the *o*
65: 25 and the lion will eat straw like the *o*
Eze 1: 10 and on the left the face of an *o*;
Lk 13: 15 of you on the Sabbath untie his *o*
14: 5 or an *o* that falls into a well
1Co 9: 9 "Do not muzzle an *o*
1Ti 5: 18 "Do not muzzle the *o*
Rev 4: 7 second was like an *o*, the third had

OXEN (OX)

Ge 49: 6 and hamstrung *o* as they pleased.
Nu 7: 3 six covered carts and twelve *o*—
7: 6 So Moses took the carts and *o*
7: 7 and four *o* to the Gershonites,
7: 8 and eight *o* to the Merarites,
7: 17 goat for a sin offering; and two *o*,
7: 23 goat for a sin offering; and two *o*,
7: 29 goat for a sin offering; and two *o*,
7: 35 goat for a sin offering; and two *o*,
7: 41 goat for a sin offering; and two *o*,
7: 47 goat for a sin offering; and two *o*,
7: 53 goat for a sin offering; and two *o*,
Nu 7: 59 goat for a sin offering; and two *o*,
7: 65 goat for a sin offering; and two *o*,
7: 71 goat for a sin offering; and two *o*,
7: 77 goat for a sin offering; and two *o*,
7: 83 goat for a sin offering; and two *o*,
7: 88 offering came to twenty-four *o*.
Dt 15: 19 the firstborn of your *o* to work,
1Sa 11: 5 behind his *o*, and he asked,
11: 7 a pair of *o*, cut them into pieces,
11: 7 to the *o* of anyone who does not
2Sa 6: 6 of God, because the *o* stumbled.
24: 22 Here are *o* for the burnt offering,
24: 24 the threshing floor and the *o*
1Ki 19: 19 plowing with twelve yoke of *o*,
19: 20 Elisha then left his *o* and ran
19: 21 yoke of *o* and slaughtered them.
1Ch 12: 40 on donkeys, camels, mules and *o*.
13: 9 the ark, because the *o* stumbled.
21: 23 I will give the *o* for the burnt
Job 1: 3 five hundred yoke of *o*
1: 14 *o* were plowing and the donkeys
42: 12 yoke of *o* and a thousand donkeys.
Ps 22: 21 from the horns of the wild *o*.
144: 14 our *o* will draw heavy loads.
Pr 14: 4 there are no *o*, the manger is
Isa 30: 24 *o* and donkeys that work the soil
32: 20 letting your *o* and donkeys range
34: 7 And the wild *o* will fall with them,
Jer 51: 23 with you I shatter farmer and *o*,
Am 6: 12 Does one plow there with *o*?
Mt 22: 4 My *o* and fattened cattle have been
Lk 14: 19 'I have just bought five yoke of *o*,
1Co 9: 9 Is it about *o* that God is concerned?

OXGOAD

Jdg 3: 31 six hundred Philistines with an *o*.

OZEM

1Ch 2: 15 the sixth *O* and the seventh David.
2: 25 Bunah, Oren, *O* and Ahijah.

OZNI (OZNITE)

Nu 26: 16 through *O*, the Oznite clan;

OZNITE (OZNI)

Nu 26: 16 through Ozni, the *O* clan;

PAARAI

2Sa 23: 35 Hezro the Carmelite, *P* the Arbite,

PACE

Ge 33: 14 along slowly at the *p* of the droves

PACIFIES (PEACE)

Pr 21: 14 in the cloak *p* great wrath.

PACIFY (PEACE)

Ge 32: 20 "I will *p* him with these gifts I am

PACK (PACKED)

Jer 46: 19 *P* your belongings for exile,
Eze 12: 3 *p* your belongings for exile

PACKED (PACK)

Jos 9: 12 warm when we *p* it at home
Eze 12: 4 bring out your belongings *p*
12: 7 the day I brought out my things *p*

PACT

Isa 57: 8 you made a *p* with those whose

PAD

Jer 38: 12 under your arms to *p* the ropes."

PADDAN

Ge 48: 7 As I was returning from *P*,

PADDAN ARAM

Ge 25: 20 Bethuel the Aramean from *P*
28: 2 Go at once to *P*, to the house of
28: 5 and he went to *P*, to Laban son of
28: 6 had sent him to *P* to take a wife
28: 7 and mother and had gone to *P*.
31: 18 the goods he had accumulated in *P*,
33: 18 came from *P*, he arrived safely at
35: 9 After Jacob returned from *P*,
35: 26 who were born to him in *P*.
46: 15 the sons Leah bore to Jacob in *P*,

PADON

Ezr 2:44 Keros, Siaha, *P*, Lebanah, Hagabah
Ne 7:47 Keros, Sia, *P*, Lebana, Hagaba,

PAGAN (PAGANS)

2Ki 23: 5 away with the *p* priests appointed
Isa 57: 8 you have put your *p* symbols.
La 1:10 she saw *p* nations
Am 7:17 you yourself will die in a *p* country.
Zep 1: 4 of the *p* and the idolatrous priests
Mt 18:17 as you would a *p* or a tax collector.
Lk 12:30 For the *p* world runs
1Co 10: 7 and got up to indulge in *p* revelry."

PAGANS (PAGAN)

Isa 2: 6 and clasp hands with *p*.
Mt 5:47 Do not even *p* do that? Be perfect,
6: 7 do not keep on babbling like *p*,
6:32 For the *p* run after all these things,
1Co 5: 1 that does not occur even among *p*:
10:20 but the sacrifices of *p* are offered
12: 2 You know that when you were *p*,
1Pe 2:12 such good lives among the *p* that,
4: 3 in the past doing what *p* choose
3Jn : 7 receiving no help from the *p*.

PAGIEL

Nu 1:13 from Asher, *P* son of Ocran;
2:27 people of Asher is *P* son of Ocran.
7:72 On the eleventh day *P* son
7:77 the offering of *P* son of Ocran.
10:26 *P* son of Ocran was

PAHATH-MOAB

Ezr 2: 6 of Arah 775 of *P* (through the line
8: 4 descendants of *P*, Eliehoenai son
10:30 From the descendants of *P*: Adna,
Ne 3:11 son of *P* repaired another section
7:11 of Arah 652 of *P* (through the line
10:14 Parosh, *P*, Elam, Zattu, Bani,

PAID (PAY)

Ge 30:33 check on the wages you have *p* me.
31:15 he has used up what was *p* for us.
39:23 The warden *p* no attention
Ex 16:20 some of them *p* no attention
22:15 the money *p* for the hire covers
Lev 25:50 based on the rate *p* to a hired man
25:51 share of the price *p* for him.
Dt 1:45 he *p* no attention to your weeping
Jdg 1: 7 God has *p* me back for what I did
11:28 *p* no attention to the message
1Sa 25:21 He has *p* me back evil for good.
2Sa 24:24 *p* fifty shekels of silver for them.
1Ki 18:29 one answered, no one *p* attention.
2Ki 12:11 With it they *p* those who worked
12:14 it was *p* to the workmen, who used
17: 3 vassal and had *p* him tribute.
17: 4 he no longer *p* tribute to the king
22: 9 "Your officials have *p* out
23:35 Jehoiakim *p* Pharaoh Neco
1Ch 21:25 So David *p* Araunah six hundred
2Ch 24:17 of Judah came and *p* homage
25: 9 what about the hundred talents I *p*
27: 5 year the Ammonites *p* him
33:10 his people, but they *p* no attention.
34:10 These men *p* the workers who
34:17 They have *p* out the money that
Ezr 4:13 tribute or duty will be *p*,
4:20 tribute and duty were *p* to them.
6: 4 are to be *p* by the royal treasury.
6: 8 are to be fully *p* out of the royal
Ne 9:30 Yet they *p* no attention,
Est 3: 2 knelt down and *p* honor to Haman,
Job 15:32 Before his time he will be *p* in full,
21:29 Have you *p* no regard
Isa 3:11 They will be *p* back
40: 2 that her sin has been *p* for,
42:20 things, but have *p* no attention;
48:18 If only you had *p* attention
Jer 25: 4 not listened or *p* any attention.
35:15 But you have not *p* attention
37: 2 people of the land *p* any attention
Eze 27:15 they *p* you with ivory tusks
Da 2:46 before Daniel and *p* him honor
Zec 11:12 So they *p* me thirty pieces of silver.
Mt 5:26 out until you have *p* the last penny.
22: 5 "But they *p* no attention
Lk 12:59 until you have *p* the last penny."
Ac 8: 6 they all *p* close attention
Heb 7: 9 *p* the tenth through Abraham,
2Pe 2:13 They will be *p* back with harm

PAIN (PAINFUL PAINS)

Ge 3:16 with *p* you will give birth
6: 6 and his heart was filled with *p*.
34:25 while all of them were still in *p*,
1Ch 4: 9 saying, "I gave birth to him in *p*."
4:10 harm so that I will be free from *p*."
2Ch 21:19 the disease, and he died in great *p*.
Job 6:10 my joy in unrelenting *p*—
14:22 He feels but the *p* of his own body
16: 6 Yet if I speak, my *p* is not relieved;
33:19 may be chastened on a bed of *p*
Ps 38: 7 My back is filled with searing *p*;
38:17 and my *p* is ever with me.
48: 6 *p* like that of a woman in labor.
69:26 talk about the *p* of those you hurt.
69:29 I am in *p* and distress;
Ecc 2:23 All his days his work is *p* and grief;
Isa 13: 8 *p* and anguish will grip them;
17:11 the day of disease and incurable *p*.
21: 3 At this my body is racked with *p*,
26:17 writhes and cries out in her *p*,
26:18 with child, we writhed in *p*,
Jer 4:19 I writhe in *p*.
5: 3 You struck them, but they felt no *p*;
6:24 *p* like that of a woman in labor.
13:21 Will not *p* grip you
15:18 Why is my *p* unending
22:23 *p* like that of a woman in labor!
30:15 your *p* that has no cure?
45: 3 LORD has added sorrow to my *p*;
49:24 anguish and *p* have seized her,
49:24 *p* like that of a woman in labor.
50:43 *p* like that of a woman in labor.
51: 8 Get balm for her *p*;
Mic 1:12 live in Maroth writhe in *p*,
4: 9 that *p* seizes you like that
Mt 4:24 suffering severe *p*,
Jn 16:21 woman giving birth to a child has *p*
1Pe 2:19 up under the *p* of unjust suffering
Rev 12: 2 She was pregnant and cried out in *p*
21: 4 or mourning or crying or *p*,

PAINFUL (PAIN)

Ge 3:17 through *p* toil you will eat of it
5:29 and *p* toil of our hands caused
Dt 28:35 with *p* boils that cannot be cured,
Job 2: 7 and afflicted Job with *p* sores
6:25 How *p* are honest words!
Eze 28:24 neighbors who are *p* briers
2Co 2: 1 I would not make another *p* visit
Heb 12:11 seems pleasant at the time, but *p*.
1Pe 4:12 at the *p* trial you are suffering,
Rev 16: 2 and *p* sores broke out on the people

PAINS (PAIN)

Ge 3:16 "I will greatly increase your *p*
1Sa 4:19 but was overcome by her labor *p*.
1Ch 22:14 "I have taken great *p* to provide
2Ch 6:29 aware of his afflictions and *p*,
Job 30:17 my gnawing *p* never rest.
39: 3 their labor *p* are ended.
Isa 66: 7 before the *p* come upon her,
Hos 13:13 *P* as of a woman in childbirth come
Mt 24: 8 these are the beginning of birth *p*.
Mk 13: 8 These are the beginning of birth *p*.
Ro 8:22 as in the *p* of childbirth right up
2Co 8:21 For we are taking *p*
Gal 4:19 again in the *p* of childbirth
4:27 you who have no labor *p*;
1Th 5: 3 as labor *p* on a pregnant woman,
Rev 16:11 because of their *p* and their sores,

PAINT (PAINTED)

Jer 4:30 Why shade your eyes with *p*?

PAINTED (PAINT)

2Ki 9:30 heard about it, she *p* her eyes,
Eze 23:40 *p* your eyes and put

PAIR (PAIRS)

Ex 25:35 a second bud under the second *p*,
25:35 and a third bud under the third *p*—
25:35 the first *p* of branches extending
37:21 a second bud under the second *p*,
37:21 and a third bud under the third *p*—
37:21 the first *p* of branches extending
Dt 24: 6 Do not take a *p* of millstones—
Jdg 15: 4 He then fastened a torch to every *p*
1Sa 11: 7 He took a *p* of oxen, cut them
1Ki 6:23 In the inner sanctuary he made a *p*
19:19 himself was driving the twelfth *p*.
2Ki 5:17 as a *p* of mules can carry,
2Ch 3:10 the Most Holy Place he made a *p*
Am 2: 6 and the needy for a *p* of sandals.
8: 6 and the needy for a *p* of sandals,
Lk 2:24 "a *p* of doves or two young pigeons
Rev 6: 5 Its rider was holding a *p* of scales

PAIRS (PAIR)

Ge 7: 8 *P* of clean and unclean animals,
7:15 *P* of all creatures that have
Jdg 15: 4 and tied them tail to tail in *p*.

PALACE (PALACES PALATIAL)

Ge 12:15 and she was taken into his *p*.
41:40 You shall be in charge of my *p*,
45:16 reached Pharaoh's *p* that Joseph's
47:14 and he brought it to Pharaoh's *p*.
Ex 7:23 he turned and went into his *p*,
8: 3 They will come up into your *p*
8:24 of flies poured into Pharaoh's *p*
Nu 22:18 "Even if Balak gave me his *p* filled
24:13 'Even if Balak gave me his *p* filled
Jdg 3:20 in the upper room of his summer *p*
2Sa 5: 8 and lame' will not enter the *p*."
5:11 and they built a *p* for David.
7: 1 After the king was settled in his *p*
7: 2 "Here I am, living in a *p* of cedar,
11: 2 walked around on the roof of the *p*.
11: 8 So Uriah left the *p*, and a gift
11: 9 slept at the entrance to the *p*
13: 7 David sent word to Tamar at the *p*:
15:16 concubines to take care of the *p*.
15:35 anything you hear in the king's *p*.
16:21 left to take care of the *p*.
19:11 last to bring the king back to his *p*,
20: 3 left to take care of the *p*
20: 3 returned to his *p* in Jerusalem,
1Ki 3: 1 until he finished building his *p*
4: 6 in charge of the *p*; Adoniram son
7: 1 complete the construction of his *p*.
7: 2 He built the *P* of the Forest
7: 8 And the *p* in which he was to live,
7: 8 also made a *p* like this hall
9: 1 of the LORD and the royal *p*,
9:10 of the LORD and the royal *p*—
9:15 his own *p*, the supporting terraces,
9:24 David to the *p* Solomon had built
10: 4 of Solomon and the *p* he had built,
10:12 of the LORD and for the royal *p*,
10:17 in the *P* of the Forest of Lebanon.
10:21 articles in the *P* of the Forest
11:20 brought up in the royal *p*.
14:26 and the treasures of the royal *p*.
14:27 duty at the entrance to the royal *p*.
15:18 LORD's temple and of his own *p*.
16: 9 the man in charge of the *p* at Tirzah
16:18 and set the *p* on fire around him.
16:18 went into the citadel of the royal *p*
18: 3 who was in charge of his *p*.
20: 6 send my officials to search your *p*
20:43 of Israel went to his *p* in Samaria.
21: 1 close to the *p* of Ahab king
21: 2 since it is close to my *p*.
22:39 the *p* he built and inlaid with ivory,
2Ki 7: 9 and report this to the royal *p*."
7:11 and it was reported within the *p*.
10: 5 *p* administrator, the city governor,
11: 5 a third of you guarding the royal *p*,
11:16 the horses enter the *p* grounds,
11:19 of the LORD and went into the *p*,
11:20 slain with the sword at the *p*.
12:18 of the LORD and of the royal *p*,
14:14 and in the treasuries of the royal *p*.
15: 5 the king's son had charge of the *p*
15:25 citadel of the royal *p* at Samaria.
16: 8 and in the treasuries of the royal *p*
18:15 and in the treasuries of the royal *p*.
18:18 son of Hilkiah the *p* administrator,
18:37 son of Hilkiah the *p* administrator,
19: 2 sent Eliakim the *p* administrator,

2Ki 20: 13 There was nothing in his *p*
20: 15 "They saw everything in my *p*,"
20: 15 "What did they see in your *p*?"
20: 17 come when everything in your *p*,
20: 18 in the *p* of the king of Babylon."
21: 18 and was buried in his *p* garden,
21: 23 and assassinated the king in his *p*.
24: 13 of the LORD and from the royal *p*,
25: 9 the royal *p* and all the houses
1Ch 14: 1 and carpenters to build a *p* for him.
17: 1 After David was settled in his *p*,
17: 1 "Here I am, living in a *p* of cedar,
28: 1 together with the *p* officials,
2Ch 2: 1 Name of the LORD and a royal *p*
2: 3 cedar to build a *p* to live in.
2: 12 for the LORD and a *p* for himself.
7: 11 of the LORD and in his own *p*,
7: 11 of the LORD and the royal *p*,
8: 1 of the LORD and his own *p*,
8: 11 City of David to the *p* he had built
8: 11 live in the *p* of David king of Israel,
9: 3 as well as the *p* he had built,
9: 11 of the LORD and for the royal *p*,
9: 16 in the *P* of the Forest of Lebanon.
9: 20 articles in the *P* of the Forest
12: 9 and the treasures of the royal *p*.
12: 10 duty at the entrance to the royal *p*.
16: 2 and of his own *p* and sent it
19: 1 safely to his *p* in Jerusalem,
21: 17 all the goods found in the king's *p*,
23: 5 a third of you at the royal *p*
23: 15 of the Horse Gate on the *p* grounds
23: 20 They went into the *p*
25: 24 together with the *p* treasures
26: 21 Jotham his son had charge of the *p*
28: 7 the officer in charge of the *p*,
28: 21 the royal *p* and from the princes
33: 20 his fathers and was buried in his *p*.
33: 24 and assassinated him in his *p*.
Ezr 4: 14 are under obligation to the *p*
Ne 3: 25 from the upper *p* near the court
Est 1: 5 the enclosed garden of the king's *p*,
1: 9 in the royal *p* of King Xerxes.
2: 8 also was taken to the king's *p*
2: 9 maids selected from the king's *p*
2: 13 her from the harem to the king's *p*.
5: 1 stood in the inner court of the *p*,
6: 4 of the *p* to speak to the king about
7: 7 and went out into the *p* garden.
7: 8 returned from the *p* garden
9: 4 Mordecai was prominent in the *p*;
Ps 45: 15 they enter the *p* of the king.
144: 12 carved to adorn a *p*.
Isa 22: 8 the weapons in the *P* of the Forest;
22: 15 to Shebna, who is in charge of the *p*
36: 3 son of Hilkiah the *p* administrator,
36: 22 son of Hilkiah the *p* administrator,
37: 2 sent Eliakim the *p* administrator,
39: 2 There was nothing in his *p*
39: 4 "They saw everything in my *p*,"
39: 4 "What did they see in your *p*?"
39: 6 come when everything in your *p*,
39: 7 in the *p* of the king of Babylon."
Jer 22: 1 "Go down to the *p* of the king
22: 4 come through the gates of this *p*,
22: 5 by myself that this *p* will become
22: 6 is what the LORD says about the *p*
22: 13 "Woe to him who builds his *p*
22: 14 'I will build myself a great *p*
26: 10 up from the royal *p* to the house
27: 18 and in the *p* of the king of Judah
27: 21 and in the *p* of the king of Judah
30: 18 the *p* will stand in its proper place.
32: 2 of the guard in the royal *p* of Judah.
36: 12 the secretary's room in the royal *p*,
37: 17 and had him brought to the *p*,
38: 7 a Cushite, an official in the royal *p*,
38: 8 Ebed-Melech went out of the *p*
38: 11 a room under the treasury in the *p*.
38: 22 left in the *p* of the king
39: 8 Babylonians set fire to the royal *p*
43: 9 to Pharaoh's *p* in Tahpanhes.
52: 13 the royal *p* and all the houses
Da 1: 4 qualified to serve in the king's *p*.
4: 4 was at home in my *p*, contented
4: 29 the roof of the royal *p* of Babylon,
5: 5 near the lampstand in the royal *p*.
6: 18 Then the king returned to his *p*

Am 9: 6 he who builds his lofty *p*
Na 2: 6 and the *p* collapses.
Mt 26: 3 in the *p* of the high priest,
Mk 15: 16 led Jesus away into the *p* (that is,
Jn 18: 28 Jesus from Caiaphas to the *p*
18: 28 the Jews did not enter the *p*;
18: 33 Pilate then went back inside the *p*,
19: 9 and he went back inside the *p*.
Ac 7: 10 ruler over Egypt and all his *p*.
23: 35 kept under guard in Herod's *p*.
Php 1: 13 clear throughout the whole *p* guard

PALACES (PALACE)

2Ch 36: 19 burned all the *p* and destroyed
Ps 45: 8 from *p* adorned with ivory
Pr 30: 28 yet it is found in kings' *p*.
Isa 13: 22 jackals in her luxurious *p*.
Jer 33: 4 the royal *p* of Judah that have been
La 2: 5 He has swallowed up all her *p*
2: 7 the walls of her *p*;
Hos 8: 14 and built *p*;
Mt 11: 8 wear fine clothes are in kings' *p*.
Lk 7: 25 and indulge in luxury are in *p*.

PALAL

Ne 3: 25 and *P* son of Uzai worked

PALATIAL (PALACE)

1Ch 29: 1 this *p* structure is not for man
29: 19 everything to build the *p* structure

PALE

Isa 29: 22 no longer will their faces grow *p*.
Jer 30: 6 every face turned deathly *p*?
Da 5: 6 His face turned *p* and he was
5: 9 terrified and his face grew more *p*.
5: 10 Don't be alarmed! Don't look so *p*!
7: 28 and my face turned *p*, but I kept
10: 8 my face turned deathly *p*
Joel 2: 6 every face turns *p*.
Na 2: 10 bodies tremble, every face grows *p*.
Rev 6: 8 and there before me was a *p* horse!

PALLU (PALLUITE)

Ge 46: 9 Hanoch, *P*, Hezron and Carmi.
Ex 6: 14 son of Israel were Hanoch and *P*,
Nu 26: 5 through *P*, the Palluite clan;
26: 8 The son of *P* was Eliab,
1Ch 5: 3 Hanoch, *P*, Hezron and Carmi.

PALLUITE (PALLU)

Nu 26: 5 the *P* clan; through Hezron,

PALM (PALMS)

Ex 15: 27 twelve springs and seventy *p* trees,
Lev 14: 15 pour it in the *p* of his own left hand,
14: 16 forefinger into the oil in his *p*,
14: 17 remaining in his *p* on the lobe
14: 18 of the oil in his *p* the priest shall put
14: 26 some of the oil into the *p*
14: 27 of the oil from his *p* seven times
14: 28 Some of the oil in his *p* he is to put
14: 29 of the oil in his *p* the priest shall put
23: 40 and *p* fronds, leafy branches
Nu 33: 9 twelve springs and seventy *p* trees,
Jdg 4: 5 court under the *P* of Deborah
1Ki 6: 29 he carved cherubim, *p* trees
6: 32 and *p* trees with beaten gold.
6: 32 doors he carved cherubim, *p* trees
6: 35 *p* trees and open flowers on them
7: 36 and *p* trees on the surfaces
2Ch 3: 5 and decorated it with *p* tree
Ps 92: 12 righteous will flourish like a *p* tree,
SS 7: 7 Your stature is like that of the *p*,
7: 8 I said, "I will climb the *p* tree;
Isa 9: 14 both *p* branch and reed
19: 15 head or tail, *p* branch or reed.
Eze 40: 16 walls were decorated with *p* trees.
40: 22 its *p* tree decorations had the same
40: 26 it had *p* tree decorations
40: 31 *p* trees decorated its jambs,
40: 34 *p* trees decorated the jambs on
40: 37 *p* trees decorated the jambs on
41: 18 *P* trees alternated with cherubim.
41: 18 were carved cherubim and *p* trees.
41: 19 a man toward the *p* tree on one side
41: 19 lion toward the *p* tree on the other.
41: 20 and *p* trees were carved on the wall

Eze 41: 25 and *p* trees like those carved
41: 26 with *p* trees carved on each side.
Joel 1: 12 the *p* and the apple tree—
Jn 12: 13 They took *p* branches and went out
Rev 7: 9 and were holding *p* branches

PALMS (PALM)

Dt 34: 3 the City of *P*, as far as Zoar.
Jdg 1: 16 up from the City of *P* with the men
3: 13 took possession of the City of *P*.
2Ch 28: 15 the City of *P*, and returned
Ne 8: 15 from myrtles, *p* and shade trees,
Isa 49: 16 you on the *p* of my hands;

PALTI

Nu 13: 9 tribe of Benjamin, *P* son of Raphu;

PALTIEL

Nu 34: 26 tribe of Zebulun; *P* son of Azzan,
1Sa 25: 44 David's wife, to *P* son of Laish,
2Sa 3: 15 from her husband *P* son of Laish.

PALTITE

2Sa 23: 26 Elika the Harodite, Helez the *P*,

PAMPERS

Pr 29: 21 If a man *p* his servant from youth,

PAMPHYLIA

Ac 2: 10 Pontus and Asia, Phrygia and *P*,
13: 13 his companions sailed to Perga in *P*
14: 24 through Pisidia, they came into *P*,
15: 38 because he had deserted them in *P*
27: 5 sea off the coast of Cilicia and *P*,

PAN (PANS)

Lev 2: 7 your grain offering is cooked in a *p*,
7: 9 baked in an oven or cooked in a *p*
1Sa 2: 14 He would plunge it into the *p*
2Sa 13: 9 she took the *p* and served him
Eze 4: 3 Then take an iron *p*, place it
Mic 3: 3 chop them up like meat for the *p*,

PANELED (PANELING PANELS)

2Ch 3: 5 He *p* the main hall with pine
Hag 1: 4 to be living in your *p* houses,

PANELING (PANELED)

1Ki 6: 15 *p* them from the floor of the temple
Ps 74: 6 They smashed all the carved *p*

PANELS (PANELED)

1Ki 7: 28 They had side *p* attached
7: 29 On the *p* between the uprights
7: 31 The *p* of the stands were square,
7: 32 The four wheels were under the *p*,
7: 35 and *p* were attached to the top
7: 36 of the supports and on the *p*,
2Ki 16: 17 King Ahaz took away the side *p*
SS 8: 9 we will enclose her with *p* of cedar.
Jer 22: 14 *p* it with cedar

PANGS

Isa 21: 3 *p* seize me, like those of a woman
Jer 22: 23 groan when *p* come upon you,

PANIC

Dt 20: 3 or give way to *p* before them.
1Sa 5: 9 that city, throwing it into a great *p*.
5: 11 For death had filled the city with *p*;
7: 10 into such a *p* that they were routed
14: 15 It was a *p* sent by God.
14: 15 Then *p* struck the whole army—
Isa 31: 9 their commanders will *p*,"
Jer 49: 24 and *p* has gripped her;
Eze 7: 7 there is *p*, not joy,
Zec 12: 4 day I will strike every horse with *p*
14: 13 by the LORD with great *p*.

PANS (PAN)

2Ch 35: 13 and *p* and served them quickly
Ezr 1: 9 silver *p* 29 gold bowls 30 matching

PANT (PANTS)

Job 5: 5 and the thirsty *p* after his wealth.
Ps 119:131 I open my mouth and *p*,
Isa 42: 14 I cry out, I gasp and *p*.
Jer 14: 6 and *p* like jackals;
Joel 1: 20 Even the wild animals *p* for you;

PANTS (PANT)
Ps 42: 1 As the deer *p* for streams of water,
42: 1 so my soul *p* for you, O God.

PAPER
2Jn : 12 but I do not want to use *p* and ink.

PAPHOS
Ac 13: 6 island until they came to *P*.
13: 13 From *P*, Paul and his companions

PAPYRUS
Ex 2: 3 she got a *p* basket for him
Job 8: 11 Can *p* grow tall where there is no
9: 26 They skim past like boats of *p*,
Isa 18: 2 sea in *p* boats over the water.
35: 7 grass and reeds and *p* will grow.

PARABLE (PARABLES)
Eze 17: 2 and tell the house of Israel a *p*.
24: 3 Tell this rebellious house a *p*
Mt 13: 18 to what the *p* of the sower means:
13: 24 Jesus told them another *p:*
13: 31 them another *p:* "The kingdom
13: 33 He told them still another *p:*
13: 34 anything to them without using a *p*.
13: 36 "Explain to us the *p* of the weeds
15: 15 Peter said, "Explain the *p* to us."
21: 33 "Listen to another *p:* There was
Mk 4: 13 then will you understand any *p?*
4: 13 "Don't you understand this *p?*
4: 30 or what *p* shall we use to describe it
4: 34 anything to them without using a *p*.
7: 17 his disciples asked him about this *p*
12: 12 they knew he had spoken the *p*
Lk 5: 36 He told them this *p:* "No one tears
6: 39 told them this *p:* "Can a blind man
8: 4 he told this *p:* "A farmer went out
8: 9 asked him what this *p* meant.
8: 11 "This is the meaning of the *p:*
12: 16 he told them this *p:* "The ground
12: 41 "Lord, are you telling this *p* to us,
13: 6 he told this *p:* "A man had a fig tree
14: 7 told them this *p:* "When someone
15: 3 Then Jesus told them this *p:*
18: 1 Then Jesus told his disciples a *p*
18: 9 Jesus told this *p:* "Two men went
19: 11 he went on to tell them a *p*,
20: 9 He went on to tell the people this *p:*
20: 19 they knew he had spoken this *p*
21: 29 He told them this *p:* "Look

PARABLES (PARABLE)
Ps 78: 2 I will open my mouth in *p*,
Pr 1: 6 for understanding proverbs and *p*,
Eze 20: 49 'Isn't he just telling *p?'* " The word
Hos 12: 10 and told *p* through them."
Mt 13: 3 he told them many things in *p*,
13: 10 speak to the people in *p?"*
13: 13 This is why I speak to them in *p:*
13: 34 all these things to the crowd in *p;*
13: 35 "I will open my mouth in *p*,
13: 53 When Jesus had finished these *p*,
21: 45 and the Pharisees heard Jesus' *p*,
22: 1 Jesus spoke to them again in *p*,
Mk 3: 23 called them and spoke to them in *p:*
4: 2 He taught them many things by *p*,
4: 10 around him asked him about the *p*.
4: 11 the outside everything is said in *p*
4: 33 With many similar *p* Jesus spoke
12: 1 began to speak to them in *p:*
Lk 8: 10 but to others I speak in *p*, so that,

PARADE
Isa 3: 9 they *p* their sin like Sodom;

PARADISE
Lk 23: 43 today you will be with me in *p*."
2Co 12: 4 God knows—was caught up to *P*.
Rev 2: 7 of life, which is in the *p* of God.

PARAH
Jos 18: 23 Avvim, *P*, Ophrah,

PARALLEL
Ex 26: 17 with two projections set *p*
36: 22 with two projections set *p*
Eze 42: 7 There was an outer wall *p*
42: 12 of the passageway that was *p*
45: 7 to the eastern border *p* to one

PARALYTIC (PARALYZED)
Mt 9: 2 Some men brought to him a *p*,
9: 2 he said to the *p*, "Take heart, son;
9: 6 Then he said to the *p*, "Get up,
Mk 2: 3 bringing to him a *p*, carried by four
2: 5 said to the *p*, "Son, your sins are
2: 9 to the *p*, 'Your sins are forgiven,'
2: 10 He said to the *p*, "I tell you, get up,
Lk 5: 18 Some men came carrying a *p*
Ac 9: 33 a *p* who had been bedridden

PARALYTICS (PARALYZED)
Mt 4: 24 the epileptics and the *p*,
Ac 8: 7 many *p* and cripples were healed.

PARALYZED (PARALYTIC PARALYTICS)
Hab 1: 4 Therefore the law is *p*,
Mt 8: 6 "my servant lies at home *p*
Mk 2: 4 the mat the *p* man was lying
Lk 5: 24 He said to the *p* man, "I tell you,
Jn 5: 3 to lie—the blind, the lame, the *p*.

PARAN
Ge 21: 21 living in the Desert of *P*,
Nu 10: 12 came to rest in the Desert of *P*.
12: 16 and encamped in the Desert of *P*.
13: 3 out from the Desert of *P*.
13: 26 at Kadesh in the Desert of *P*.
Dt 1: 1 opposite Suph, between *P*
33: 2 he shone forth from Mount *P*.
1Ki 11: 18 Then taking men from *P* with them
11: 18 out from Midian and went to *P*.
Hab 3: 3 the Holy One from Mount *P*.

PARAPET
Dt 22: 8 make a *p* around your roof
Eze 40: 13 cubits from one *p* opening to
40: 16 by narrow *p* openings all around,

PARCEL (PARCELED)
Ps 60: 6 "In triumph I will *p* out Shechem
108: 7 "In triumph I will *p* out Shechem

PARCELED (PARCEL)
Da 11: 4 and *p* out toward the four winds

PARCHED
Job 14: 11 or a riverbed becomes *p* and dry,
30: 3 they roamed the *p* land
Ps 69: 3 my throat is *p*.
107: 35 the *p* ground into flowing springs;
143: 6 my soul thirsts for you like a *p* land.
Isa 5: 13 their masses will be *p* with thirst.
19: 5 and the riverbed will be *p* and dry.
19: 7 will become *p*, will blow away
35: 1 and the *p* land will be glad;
41: 17 their tongues are *p* with thirst.
41: 18 and the *p* ground into springs.
Jer 12: 4 How long will the land lie *p*
12: 11 *p* and desolate before me;
17: 6 dwell in the *p* places of the desert,
23: 10 because of the curse the land lies *p*
48: 18 and sit on the *p* ground,
Hos 2: 3 turn her into a *p* land,
Joel 2: 20 pushing it into a *p* and barren land,

PARCHMENTS
2Ti 4: 13 and my scrolls, especially the *p*.

PARDON (PARDONED PARDONS)
2Ch 30: 18 *p* everyone who sets his heart
Job 7: 21 Why do you not *p* my offenses
Isa 55: 7 and to our God, for he will freely *p*.
Joel 3: 21 I will *p*."

PARDONED (PARDON)
Nu 14: 19 as you have *p* them from the time
Joel 3: 21 bloodguilt, which I have not *p*,

PARDONS (PARDON)
Mic 7: 18 who *p* sin and forgives

PARENTS (GRANDPARENTS)
Dt 22: 17 Then her *p* shall display the cloth
Jdg 14: 4 (His *p* did not know that this was
Jdg 14: 9 he rejoined his *p*, he gave them
Pr 17: 6 and *p* are the pride of their children
19: 14 wealth are inherited from *p*,
Zec 13: 3 prophesies, his own *p* will stab him.
Mt 10: 21 children will rebel against their *p*
Mk 13: 12 Children will rebel against their *p*
Lk 2: 27 When the *p* brought
2: 41 Every year his *p* went to Jerusalem
2: 43 while his *p* were returning home,
2: 48 When his *p* saw him, they were
8: 56 Her *p* were astonished,
18: 29 left home or wife or brothers or *p*
21: 16 You will be betrayed by *p*, brothers
Jn 9: 2 or his *p*, that he was born blind?"
9: 3 Neither this man nor his *p* sinned,"
9: 18 until they sent for the man's *p*.
9: 20 he is our son," the *p* answered,
9: 22 His *p* said this because they were
9: 23 That was why his *p* said, "He is
Ro 1: 30 they disobey their *p;* they are
2Co 12: 14 for their *p*, but *p* for their children.
Eph 6: 1 Children, obey your *p* in the Lord,
Col 3: 20 obey your *p* in everything,
1Ti 5: 4 repaying their *p* and grandparents,
2Ti 3: 2 disobedient to their *p*, ungrateful,
Heb 11: 23 By faith Moses' *p* hid him

PARKS
Ecc 2: 5 I made gardens and *p*

PARMASHTA
Est 9: 9 Adalia, Aridatha, *P*, Arisai,

PARMENAS
Ac 6: 5 Procorus, Nicanor, Timon, *P*,

PARNACH
Nu 34: 25 Elizaphan son of *P*, the leader

PAROSH
Ezr 2: 3 the descendants of *P* 2,172
8: 3 of the descendants of *P*, Zechariah,
10: 25 From the descendants of *P:*
Ne 3: 25 of *P* and the temple servants living
7: 8 the descendants of *P* 2,172
10: 14 *P*, Pahath-Moab, Elam, Zattu,

PARSHANDATHA
Est 9: 7 They also killed *P*, Dalphon,

PARSIN
Da 5: 25 MENE, MENE, TEKEL, *P*

PARTAKE
1Co 10: 17 for we all *p* of the one loaf.

PARTHIANS
Ac 2: 9 *P*, Medes and Elamites; residents

PARTIAL (PARTIALITY)
Pr 18: 5 It is not good to be *p* to the wicked

PARTIALITY (PARTIAL)
Lev 19: 15 do not show *p* to the poor
Dt 1: 17 Do not show *p* in judging;
10: 17 who shows no *p* and accepts no
16: 19 Do not pervert justice or show *p*.
2Ch 19: 7 our God there is no injustice or *p*
Job 13: 8 Will you show him *p?*
13: 10 you if you secretly showed *p*.
32: 21 I will show *p* to no one,
34: 19 who shows no *p* to princes
Ps 82: 2 and show *p* to the wicked? *Selah*
Pr 24: 23 To show *p* in judging is not good:
28: 21 To show *p* is not good—
Mal 2: 9 have shown *p* in matters of the law
Lk 20: 21 and that you do not show *p*
1Ti 5: 21 keep these instructions without *p*,

PARTICIPANTS (PARTICIPATE)
1Co 10: 20 you to be *p* with demons.

PARTICIPATE (PARTICIPANTS PARTICIPATION)
Eze 45: 16 of the land will *p* in this special gift
1Co 10: 18 not those who eat the sacrifices *p*
1Pe 4: 13 rejoice that you *p* in the sufferings
2Pe 1: 4 that through them you may *p*

PARTICIPATION (PARTICIPATE)
1Co 10: 16 for which we give thanks a *p*
10: 16 is not the bread that we break a *p*

PARTIES (PARTY)
Ex 18: 16 and I decide between the *p*
22: 9 both *p* are to bring their cases
1Sa 13: 17 Raiding *p* went out
14: 15 those in the outposts and raiding *p*
Job 1: 17 Chaldeans formed three raiding *p*

PARTING
Mic 1: 14 Therefore you will give *p* gifts

PARTITIONED
1Ki 6: 16 He *p* off twenty cubits at the rear

PARTNER (PARTNERS PARTNERSHIP)
Pr 2: 17 who has left the *p* of her youth
28: 24 he is *p* to him who destroys.
Mal 2: 14 though she is your *p*, the wife
2Co 8: 23 he is my *p* and fellow worker
Phm : 17 you consider me a *p*, welcome him
1Pe 3: 7 them with respect as the weaker *p*

PARTNERS (PARTNER)
Lk 5: 7 So they signaled their *p*
5: 10 the sons of Zebedee, Simon's *p*.
Eph 5: 7 Therefore do not be *p* with them.

PARTNERSHIP (PARTNER)
Php 1: 5 because of your *p* in the gospel

PARTRIDGE
1Sa 26: 20 as one hunts a *p* in the mountains."
Jer 17: 11 Like a *p* that hatches eggs it did not

PARTY (PARTIES)
Ru 4: 7 one *p* took off his sandal
1Sa 30: 8 "Shall I pursue this raiding *p?*
30: 15 me down to this raiding *p?*"
Pr 19: 18 do not be a willing *p* to his death.
Ac 5: 17 members of the *p* of the Sadducees,
15: 5 to the *p* of the Pharisees stood up
2Co 7: 12 did the wrong or of the injured *p*,
Gal 3: 20 does not represent just one *p*,

PARUAH
1Ki 4: 17 Jehoshaphat son of *P*— in Issachar

PARVAIM
2Ch 3: 6 And the gold he used was gold of *P*

PAS DAMMIM
2Sa 23: 9 the Philistines gathered ⌊at *P*⌋
1Ch 11: 13 He was with David at *P* when

PASACH
1Ch 7: 33 The sons of Japhlet: *P*, Bimhal

PASEAH
1Ch 4: 12 *P* and Tehinnah the father
Ezr 2: 49 Gazzam, Uzza, *P*, Besai, Asnah,
Ne 3: 6 repaired by Joiada son of *P*
7: 51 Gazzam, Uzza, *P*, Besai, Meunim,

PASHHUR
1Ch 9: 12 the son of *P*, the son of Malkijah;
Ezr 2: 38 of *P* 1,247 of Harim 1,017
10: 22 From the descendants of *P*:
Ne 7: 41 of *P* 1,247 of Harim 1,017
10: 3 Azariah, Jeremiah, *P*, Amariah,
11: 12 the son of *P*, the son of Malkijah,
Jer 20: 1 When the priest *P* son of Immer,
20: 3 The LORD's name for you is not *P*
20: 3 when *P* released him
20: 6 *P*, and all who live
21: 1 sent to him *P* son of Malkijah
38: 1 Gedaliah son of *P*, Jehucal son
38: 1 and *P* son of Malkijah heard what

PASS (PASSED PASSER-BY PASSES PASSING)
Ge 18: 3 my lord, do not *p* your servant by.
Ex 12: 12 "On that same night I will *p*
12: 13 and when I see the blood, I will *p*
12: 23 and will *p* over that doorway,
15: 16 until the people you bought *p* by.
Ex 15: 16 until your people *p* by, O LORD,
33: 19 goodness to *p* in front of you,
Lev 26: 6 and the sword will not *p*
Nu 20: 17 let us *p* through your country.
20: 18 "You may not *p* through here;
20: 19 We only want to *p* through on foot
20: 20 "You may not *p* through."
21: 22 "Let us *p* through your country.
21: 23 But Sihon would not let Israel *p*
34: 4 cross south of Scorpion *P*,
36: 7 in Israel is to *p* from tribe to tribe,
36: 9 No inheritance may *p* from tribe
Dt 2: 4 about to *p* through the territory
2: 18 "Today you are to *p* by the region
2: 27 "Let us *p* through your country.
2: 28 Only let us *p* through on foot—
2: 30 refused to let us *p* through.
Jos 15: 3 crossed south of Scorpion *P*,
15: 7 faces the *P* of Adummim south
18: 17 which faces the *P* of Adummim,
Jdg 1: 36 was from Scorpion *P* to Sela
8: 13 from the battle by the *P* of Heres.
11: 19 'Let us *p* through your country
11: 20 Israel to *p* through his territory.
1Sa 13: 23 out to the *p* at Micmash.
14: 4 of the *p* that Jonathan intended
16: 8 and had him *p* in front of Samuel.
16: 9 Jesse then had Shammah *p* by,
16: 10 seven of his sons *p* before Samuel,
1Ki 9: 8 all who *p* by will be appalled
19: 11 for the LORD is about to *p* by."
2Ki 19: 25 now I have brought it to *p*,
1Ch 28: 8 may possess this good land and *p* it
2Ch 7: 21 all who *p* by will be appalled
20: 16 They will be climbing up by the *P*
Job 16: 22 "Only a few years will *p*
19: 8 has blocked my way so I cannot *p*;
34: 20 people are shaken and they *p* away;
41: 16 that no air can *p* between.
Ps 80: 12 so that all who *p* by pick its grapes?
84: 6 As they *p* through the Valley
89: 41 All who *p* by have plundered him;
90: 9 All our days *p* away
90: 10 for they quickly *p*, and we fly away.
105: 19 till what he foretold came to *p*,
129: 8 May those who *p* by not say,
141: 10 while I *p* by in safety.
148: 6 a decree that will never *p* away.
Pr 9: 15 calling out to those who *p* by,
Isa 10: 28 they *p* through Migron;
10: 29 They go over the *p*, and say,
31: 5 he will '*p* over' it and will rescue it
34: 10 no one will ever *p* through it again.
37: 26 now I have brought it to *p*,
43: 2 When you *p* through the waters,
43: 2 and when you *p* through the rivers,
48: 3 I acted, and they came to *p*.
62: 10 *P* through, *p* through the gates!
Jer 2: 35 But I will *p* judgment on you
6: 9 *p* your hand over the branches
18: 16 all who *p* by will be appalled
19: 8 all who *p* by will be appalled
22: 8 "People from many nations will *p*
33: 13 flocks will again *p* under the hand
49: 17 all who *p* by will be appalled
50: 13 All who *p* Babylon will be horrified
La 1: 12 to you, all you who *p* by?
2: 15 All who *p* your way
Eze 5: 14 in the sight of all who *p* by.
14: 15 so that no one can *p* through it
14: 17 the sword *p* throughout the land,'
20: 37 of you as you *p* under my staff,
29: 11 or animal will *p* through it;
36: 34 in the sight of all who *p* through it.
48: 14 and must not *p* into other hands,
Da 4: 16 till seven times *p* by for him.
4: 23 until seven times *p* by for him.'
4: 25 Seven times will *p* by for you
4: 32 Seven times will *p* by for you
7: 14 dominion that will not *p* away,
Am 5: 17 for I will *p* through your midst,"
Mic 1: 11 *P* on in nakedness and shame,
2: 8 from those who *p* by without a care
2: 13 king will *p* through before them,
Na 1: 12 they will be cut down and *p* away.
Zep 2: 15 All who *p* by her scoff
Zec 10: 11 They will *p* through the sea
10: 11 and Egypt's scepter will *p* away.
Mt 8: 28 that no one could *p* that way.
24: 34 will certainly not *p* away
24: 35 Heaven and earth will *p* away,
24: 35 but my words will never *p* away.
Mk 6: 48 He was about to *p* by them,
13: 30 will certainly not *p* away
13: 31 Heaven and earth will *p* away,
13: 31 but my words will never *p* away.
14: 35 that if possible the hour might *p*
Lk 21: 32 will certainly not *p* away
21: 33 Heaven and earth will *p* away,
21: 33 but my words will never *p* away.
Jn 8: 15 by human standards; I *p* judgment
Ac 7: 38 and he received living words to *p*
Ro 2: 1 you who *p* judgment
2: 1 you who *p* judgment do the same
2: 3 *p* judgment on them and yet do
1Co 13: 8 there is knowledge, it will *p* away.
Jas 1: 10 he will *p* away like a wild flower.
1Jn 2: 17 The world and its desires *p* away,

PASSAGE (PASSAGEWAY)
Ac 8: 32 The eunuch was reading this *p*
8: 35 began with that very *p* of Scripture
Ro 11: 2 says in the *p* about Elijah—
Heb 4: 5 And again in the *p* above he says,

PASSAGEWAY (PASSAGE)
Eze 42: 4 was an inner *p* ten cubits wide
42: 11 were rooms with a *p* in front
42: 12 beginning of the *p* that was parallel

PASSED (PASS)
Ge 15: 17 a blazing torch appeared and *p*
32: 31 rose above him as he *p* Peniel,
41: 1 When two full years had *p*,
50: 4 When the days of mourning had *p*,
Ex 7: 25 Seven days *p* after the LORD
12: 27 who *p* over the houses
33: 22 you with my hand until I have *p* by.
34: 6 And he *p* in front of Moses,
Lev 25: 30 redeemed before a full year has *p*,
Nu 14: 7 "The land we *p* through
20: 17 we have *p* through your territory."
21: 22 we have *p* through your territory."
33: 8 *p* through the sea into the desert,
Dt 2: 14 Thirty-eight years *p*
29: 16 how we *p* through the countries
Jos 3: 17 while all Israel *p* by until the whole
15: 4 It then *p* along to Azmon
15: 11 *p* along to Mount Baalah
18: 12 *p* the northern slope of Jericho
23: 1 After a long time had *p*
Jdg 3: 26 He *p* by the idols and escaped
9: 25 and rob everyone who *p* by,
11: 18 *p* along the eastern side
11: 29 *p* through Mizpah of Gilead,
1Sa 9: 4 So he *p* through the hill country
9: 4 Then he *p* through the territory
2Sa 15: 23 wept aloud as all the people *p*
20: 14 Sheba *p* through all the tribes
1Ki 13: 25 Some people who *p*
18: 29 Midday *p*, and they continued
20: 39 As the king *p* by, the prophet called
2Ch 21: 20 He *p* away, to no one's regret,
Ne 9: 11 so that they *p* through it
12: 37 and *p* above the house of David
Est 4: 11 But thirty days have *p*
Job 14: 13 conceal me till your anger has *p*!
15: 19 when no alien *p* among them):
17: 11 My days have *p*, my plans are
Ps 37: 36 he soon *p* away and was no more;
57: 1 wings until the disaster has *p*.
66: 6 they *p* through the river on foot—
SS 3: 4 Scarcely had I *p* them
Isa 26: 20 while until his wrath has *p* by.
La 4: 21 But to you also the cup will be *p*;
Eze 16: 6 I *p* by and saw you kicking about
16: 8 " 'Later I *p* by, and when I looked
16: 15 favors on anyone who *p* by
16: 25 promiscuity to anyone who *p* by.
Da 2: 28 visions that *p* through your mind
4: 5 visions that *p* through my mind
7: 1 and visions *p* through his mind
7: 15 the visions that *p* through my mind
Mt 27: 39 Those who *p* by hurled insults
Mk 9: 30 They left that place and *p*
15: 29 Those who *p* by hurled insults

PASTURELANDS (PASTURE)

Nu 35: 2 And give them *p* around the towns.
35: 3 to live in and *p* for their cattle,
35: 4 *p* around the towns that you give
35: 7 towns, together with their *p*.
Jos 14: 4 with *p* for their flocks and herds.
21: 2 to live in, with *p* for our livestock."
21: 3 and *p* out of their own inheritance:
21: 8 the Levites these towns and their *p*,
21: 16 together with their *p*— nine towns
21: 18 together with their *p*— four towns.
21: 19 were thirteen, together with their *p*
21: 22 together with their *p*— four towns.
21: 24 together with their *p*— four towns.
21: 25 together with their *p*— two towns.
21: 26 and their *p* were given to the rest
21: 27 together with their *p*— two towns;
21: 29 together with their *p*— four towns;
21: 31 together with their *p*— four towns;
21: 32 together with their *p*— three towns
21: 33 thirteen, together with their *p*.
21: 35 together with their *p*— four towns;
21: 37 together with their *p*— four towns;
21: 39 together with their *p*— four towns
21: 41 in all, together with their *p*.
21: 42 of these towns had *p* surrounding it
1Ch 5: 16 and on all the *p* of Sharon as far
6: 55 in Judah with its surrounding *p*.
6: 59 together with their *p*.
6: 60 Anathoth, together with their *p*.
6: 64 the Levites these towns and their *p*.
6: 69 together with their *p*.
6: 70 together with their *p*, to the rest
6: 71 together with their *p*; from the tribe
6: 73 and Anem, together with their *p*;
6: 75 and Rehob, together with their *p*;
6: 76 Kiriathaim, together with their *p*.
6: 77 and Tabor, together with their *p*;
6: 79 Mephaath, together with their *p*;
6: 81 and Jazer, together with their *p*.
13: 2 are with them in their towns and *p*,
2Ch 11: 14 abandoned their *p* and property,
Ps 83: 12 possession of the *p* of God."
Mic 7: 14 in fertile *p*.

PASTURES (PASTURE)

Ps 23: 2 He makes me lie down in green *p*,
Jer 9: 10 a lament concerning the desert *p*.
23: 10 and the *p* in the desert are withered
33: 12 in all its towns there will again be *p*
Eze 45: 15 from the well-watered *p* of Israel.
Joel 1: 19 for fire has devoured the open *p*
1: 20 and fire has devoured the open *p*.
2: 22 for the open *p* are becoming green.
Am 1: 2 the *p* of the shepherds dry up,
Zec 11: 3 their rich *p* are destroyed!

PATARA

Ac 21: 1 to Rhodes and from there to *P*.

PATCH (PATCHED)

Jer 10: 5 Like a scarecrow in a melon *p*,
Mt 9: 16 No one sews a *p* of unshrunk cloth
9: 16 for the *p* will pull away
Mk 2: 21 No one sews a *p* of unshrunk cloth
Lk 5: 36 the *p* from the new will not match
5: 36 "No one tears a *p* from a new

PATCHED (PATCH)

Jos 9: 5 and *p* sandals on their feet

PATH (BYPATHS PATHS)

Ge 49: 17 a viper along the *p*,
Nu 22: 24 a narrow *p* between two vineyards,
22: 32 your *p* is a reckless one before me.
2Sa 22: 37 You broaden the *p* beneath me,
Ne 9: 19 cease to guide them on their *p*,
Job 18: 10 a trap lies in his *p*.
22: 15 Will you keep to the old *p*
24: 4 They thrust the needy from the *p*
28: 7 of prey knows that hidden *p*,
28: 26 and a *p* for the thunderstorm,
29: 6 when my *p* was drenched
31: 7 if my steps have turned from the *p*,
38: 25 and a *p* for the thunderstorm,
Ps 16: 11 known to me the *p* of life;
18: 36 You broaden the *p* beneath me,
27: 11 lead me in a straight *p*
Ps 35: 6 may their *p* be dark and slippery,
44: 18 feet had not strayed from your *p*.
57: 6 They dug a pit in my *p*—
77: 19 Your *p* led through the sea,
78: 50 He prepared a *p* for his anger;
119: 32 I run in the *p* of your commands,
119: 35 in the *p* of your commands,
119:101 have kept my feet from every evil *p*
119:104 therefore I hate every wrong *p*.
119:105 and a light for my *p*.
119:128 I hate every wrong *p*.
140: 5 have set traps for me along my *p*.
142: 3 In the *p* where I walk
Pr 2: 9 and fair—every good *p*.
4: 14 on the *p* of the wicked
4: 18 *p* of the righteous is like the first
5: 8 Keep to a *p* far from her,
12: 28 along that *p* is immortality.
15: 10 awaits him who leaves the *p*;
15: 19 the *p* of the upright is a highway.
15: 24 The *p* of life leads upward
16: 29 leads him down a *p* that is not good
21: 16 from the *p* of understanding
23: 19 and keep your heart on the right *p*.
28: 10 leads the upright along an evil *p*
Ecc 11: 5 As you do not know the *p*
Isa 3: 12 they turn you from the *p*.
26: 7 The *p* of the righteous is level;
30: 11 get off this *p*,
40: 14 showed him the *p* of understanding
41: 3 by a *p* his feet have not traveled
43: 16 a *p* through the mighty waters,
Jer 23: 12 "Therefore their *p* will become
31: 9 on a level *p* where they will not
La 3: 11 he dragged me from the *p*
Hos 2: 6 Therefore I will block her *p*
13: 7 like a leopard I will lurk by the *p*.
Mt 13: 4 fell along the *p*, and the birds came
13: 19 This is the seed sown along the *p*.
Mk 4: 4 fell along the *p*, and the birds came
4: 15 people are like seed along the *p*,
Lk 1: 79 to guide our feet into the *p* of peace
8: 5 fell along the *p*; it was trampled
8: 12 along the *p* are the ones who hear,
2Co 6: 3 no stumbling block in anyone's *p*,

PATHROS

Eze 29: 14 captivity and return them to *P*,
30: 14 I will lay *P* waste,

PATHRUSITES

Ge 10: 14 Lehabites, Naphtuhites, *P*,
1Ch 1: 12 Lehabites, Naphtuhites, *P*,

PATHS (PATH)

Jdg 5: 6 travelers took to winding *p*.
Job 13: 27 you keep close watch on all my *p*
19: 8 he has shrouded my *p* in darkness.
24: 13 or stay in its *p*.
33: 11 he keeps close watch on all my *p*.'
38: 20 Do you know the *p*
Ps 8: 8 all that swim the *p* of the seas.
17: 5 My steps have held to your *p*;
23: 3 He guides me in *p* of righteousness
25: 4 teach me your *p*;
Pr 1: 15 do not set foot on their *p*;
2: 13 who leave the straight *p*
2: 15 whose *p* are crooked
2: 18 and her *p* to the spirits of the dead.
2: 19 or attain the *p* of life.
2: 20 and keep to the *p* of the righteous.
3: 6 and he will make your *p* straight.
3: 17 and all her *p* are peace.
4: 11 and lead you along straight *p*.
4: 26 Make level *p* for your feet
5: 6 her *p* are crooked, but she knows it
5: 21 and he examines all his *p*.
7: 25 or stray into her *p*.
8: 2 where the *p* meet, she takes her
8: 20 along the *p* of justice,
10: 9 who takes crooked *p* will be found
22: 5 In the *p* of the wicked lie thorns
Isa 2: 3 so that we may walk in his *p*."
42: 16 along unfamiliar *p* I will guide
59: 8 there is no justice in their *p*.
Jer 6: 16 ask for the ancient *p*,
18: 15 and in the ancient *p*.
La 3: 9 he has made my *p* crooked.
Hos 9: 8 yet snares await him on all his *p*,
Mic 4: 2 so that we may walk in his *p*."
Mt 3: 3 make straight *p* for him.' "
Mk 1: 3 make straight *p* for him.' "
Lk 3: 4 make straight *p* for him.
Ac 2: 28 to me the *p* of life;
Ro 11: 33 and his *p* beyond tracing out!
Heb 12: 13 "Make level *p* for your feet,"

PATIENCE (PATIENT)

Pr 19: 11 A man's wisdom gives him *p*;
25: 15 Through *p* a ruler can be persuaded
Ecc 7: 8 and *p* is better than pride.
Isa 7: 13 Is it not enough to try the *p* of men?
7: 13 Will you try the *p* of my God also?
Ro 2: 4 and *p*, not realizing that God's
9: 22 bore with great *p* the objects
2Co 6: 6 understanding, *p* and kindness;
Gal 5: 22 joy, peace, *p*, kindness, goodness,
Col 1: 11 may have great endurance and *p*,
3: 12 humility, gentleness and *p*.
1Ti 1: 16 Jesus might display his unlimited *p*
2Ti 3: 10 my purpose, faith, *p*, love,
4: 2 with great *p* and careful instruction
Heb 6: 12 *p* inherit what has been promised.
Jas 5: 10 as an example of *p* in the face
2Pe 3: 15 that our Lord's *p* means salvation,

PATIENT (PATIENCE PATIENTLY)

Ne 9: 30 For many years you were *p*
Job 6: 11 What prospects, that I should be *p*?
Pr 14: 29 A *p* man has great understanding,
15: 18 but a *p* man calms a quarrel.
16: 32 Better a *p* man than a warrior,
Mt 18: 26 'Be *p* with me,' he begged,
18: 29 'Be *p* with me, and I will pay you
Ro 12: 12 Be joyful in hope, *p* in affliction,
1Co 13: 4 Love is *p*, love is kind.
2Co 1: 6 produces in you *p* endurance
Eph 4: 2 humble and gentle; be *p*,
1Th 5: 14 help the weak, be *p* with everyone.
Jas 5: 7 Be *p*, then, brothers,
5: 7 and how *p* he is for the autumn
5: 8 You too, be *p* and stand firm,
2Pe 3: 9 He is *p* with you, not wanting
Rev 1: 9 *p* endurance that are ours in Jesus,
13: 10 This calls for *p* endurance
14: 12 This calls for *p* endurance

PATIENTLY (PATIENT)

Ps 37: 7 still before the LORD and wait *p*
40: 1 I waited *p* for the LORD;
Isa 38: 13 I waited *p* till dawn,
Hab 3: 16 Yet I will wait *p* for the day
Ac 26: 3 I beg you to listen to me *p*.
Ro 8: 25 we do not yet have, we wait for it *p*.
Heb 6: 15 after waiting *p*, Abraham received
1Pe 3: 20 ago when God waited *p* in the days
Rev 3: 10 kept my command to endure *p*,

PATMOS

Rev 1: 9 the island of *P* because of the word

PATRIARCH (PATRIARCHS)

Ac 2: 29 confidently that the *p* David died
Heb 7: 4 Even the *p* Abraham gave him

PATRIARCHS (PATRIARCH)

Jn 7: 22 from the *p*), you circumcise a child
Ac 7: 8 became the father of the twelve *p*.
7: 9 "Because the *p* were jealous
Ro 9: 5 Theirs are the *p*, and from them is
11: 28 they are loved on account of the *p*,
15: 8 confirm the promises made to the *p*

PATROBAS

Ro 16: 14 Asyncritus, Phlegon, Hermes, *P*,

PATTERN

Ex 25: 9 exactly like the *p* I will show
25: 40 according to the *p* shown you
Nu 8: 4 exactly like the *p* the LORD had
Ac 7: 44 according to the *p* he had seen.
Ro 5: 14 who was a *p* of the one to come.
12: 2 longer to the *p* of this world,
Php 3: 17 according to the *p* we gave you
2Ti 1: 13 keep as the *p* of sound teaching,
Heb 8: 5 according to the *p* shown you

PAU

Ge 36: 39 His city was named *P*,
1Ch 1: 50 His city was named *P*,

PAUL (PAUL'S)

Ac 13: 9 called *P*, filled with the Holy Spirit,
13: 13 *P* and his companions sailed
13: 16 *P* motioned with his hand and said:
13: 42 As *P* and Barnabas were leaving
13: 43 converts to Judaism followed *P*
13: 45 against what *P* was saying.
13: 46 *P* and Barnabas answered them
13: 50 stirred up persecution against *P*
14: 1 At Iconium *P* and Barnabas went
14: 3 *P* and Barnabas spent considerable
14: 9 He listened to *P* as he was speaking
14: 9 *P* looked directly at him, saw that
14: 11 the crowd saw what *P* had done,
14: 12 and *P* they called Hermes
14: 14 the apostles Barnabas and *P* heard
14: 19 They stoned *P* and dragged him
14: 23 *P* and Barnabas appointed elders
15: 2 So *P* and Barnabas were appointed,
15: 2 This brought *P* and Barnabas
15: 12 and *P* telling about the miraculous
15: 22 and send them to Antioch with *P*
15: 25 our dear friends Barnabas and *P*—
15: 35 But *P* and Barnabas remained
15: 36 Some time later *P* said to Barnabas,
15: 38 *P* did not think it wise to take him,
15: 40 sailed for Cyprus, but *P* chose Silas
16: 3 *P* wanted to take him
16: 6 *P* and his companions traveled
16: 9 During the night *P* had a vision
16: 10 After *P* had seen the vision,
16: 17 This girl followed *P* and the rest
16: 18 Finally *P* became so troubled that
16: 19 they seized *P* and Silas
16: 22 joined in the attack against *P*
16: 25 About midnight *P* and Silas were
16: 28 *P* shouted, "Don't harm yourself!
16: 29 fell trembling before *P* and Silas.
16: 36 jailer told *P*, "The magistrates have
16: 37 *P* said to the officers: "They beat us
16: 38 and when they heard that *P*
16: 40 After *P* and Silas came out
17: 2 *P* went into the synagogue,
17: 4 Jews were persuaded and joined *P*
17: 5 to Jason's house in search of *P*
17: 10 the brothers sent *P* and Silas away
17: 11 day to see if what *P* said was true.
17: 13 learned that *P* was preaching
17: 14 The brothers immediately sent *P*
17: 15 who accompanied *P* brought him
17: 16 While *P* was waiting for them
17: 18 *P* was preaching the good news
17: 22 *P* then stood up in the meeting
17: 33 At that, *P* left the Council.
17: 34 A few men became followers of *P*
18: 1 *P* left Athens and went to Corinth.
18: 2 *P* went to see them, and
18: 5 *P* devoted himself exclusively
18: 6 But when the Jews opposed *P*
18: 7 Then *P* left the synagogue
18: 9 One night the Lord spoke to *P*
18: 11 So *P* stayed for a year and a half,
18: 12 the Jews made a united attack on *P*
18: 14 Just as *P* was about to speak,
18: 18 *P* stayed on in Corinth
18: 19 where *P* left Priscilla and Aquila.
18: 23 *P* set out from there and traveled
19: 1 *P* took the road
19: 3 *P* asked, "Then what baptism did
19: 4 *P* said, "John's baptism was
19: 6 When *P* placed his hands on them,
19: 8 *P* entered the synagogue
19: 9 So *P* left them.
19: 11 extraordinary miracles through *P*.
19: 13 name of Jesus, whom *P* preaches,
19: 15 "Jesus I know and *P* I know about,
19: 21 *P* decided to go to Jerusalem,
19: 26 how this fellow *P* has convinced
19: 30 *P* wanted to appear
19: 31 of the province, friends of *P*,
20: 1 *P* sent for the disciples and,
20: 7 *P* spoke to the people and,
20: 9 into a deep sleep as *P* talked on
Ac 20: 10 *P* went down, threw himself
20: 13 we were going to take *P* aboard.
20: 16 *P* had decided to sail past Ephesus
20: 17 *P* sent to Ephesus for the elders
21: 4 the Spirit they urged *P* not
21: 12 pleaded with *P* not to go up
21: 13 Then *P* answered, "Why are you
21: 18 The next day *P* and the rest
21: 19 *P* greeted them and reported
21: 20 Then they said to *P*: "You see,
21: 26 The next day *P* took the men
21: 27 of Asia saw *P* at the temple.
21: 29 assumed that *P* had brought him
21: 29 the Ephesian in the city with *P*
21: 30 Seizing *P*, they dragged him
21: 32 his soldiers, they stopped beating *P*
21: 34 he ordered that *P* be taken
21: 35 When *P* reached the steps,
21: 37 about to take *P* into the barracks,
21: 39 *P* answered, "I am a Jew,
21: 40 *P* stood on the steps and motioned
22: 2 *P* said: "I am a Jew, born in Tarsus
22: 22 The crowd listened to *P*
22: 24 the commander ordered *P*
22: 25 *P* said to the centurion standing
22: 27 The commander went to *P*
22: 28 But I was born a citizen," *P* replied.
22: 29 when he realized that he had put *P*,
22: 30 he brought *P* and had him stand
22: 30 out exactly why *P* was being
23: 1 *P* looked straight at the Sanhedrin
23: 2 near *P* to strike him on the mouth.
23: 3 *P* said to him, "God will strike you,
23: 4 who were standing near *P* said,
23: 5 God's high priest?" *P* replied,
23: 6 Then *P*, knowing that some
23: 10 commander was afraid *P* would be
23: 11 night the Lord stood near *P*
23: 12 or drink until they had killed *P*.
23: 14 anything until we have killed *P*.
23: 16 went into the barracks and told *P*.
23: 17 *P* called one of the centurions
23: 18 centurion said, "*P*, the prisoner,
23: 20 to bring *P* before the Sanhedrin
23: 24 Provide mounts for *P*
23: 31 took *P* with them during the night
23: 33 and handed *P* over to him.
23: 35 Then he ordered that *P* be kept
24: 1 against *P* before the governor.
24: 2 When *P* was called
24: 10 for him to speak, *P* replied:
24: 23 centurion to keep *P* under guard
24: 24 He sent for *P* and listened to him
24: 25 As *P* discoursed on righteousness,
24: 26 was hoping that *P* would offer him
24: 27 to the Jews, he left *P* in prison.
25: 2 presented the charges against *P*.
25: 3 to have *P* transferred to Jerusalem,
25: 4 "*P* is being held at Caesarea,
25: 6 and ordered that *P* be brought
25: 7 When *P* appeared, the Jews who
25: 8 *P* made his defense: "I have done
25: 9 to do the Jews a favor, said to *P*,
25: 10 *P* answered: "I am now standing
25: 19 named Jesus who *P* claimed was
25: 21 When *P* made his appeal to be held
25: 23 of Festus, *P* was brought in.
26: 1 So *P* motioned with his hand
26: 1 said to *P*, "You have permission
26: 24 "You are out of your mind, *P*!"
26: 25 most excellent Festus," *P* replied.
26: 28 said to *P*, "Do you think that
26: 29 *P* replied, "Short time or long—
27: 1 *P* and some other prisoners were
27: 3 and Julius, in kindness to *P*,
27: 9 So *P* warned them, "Men,
27: 11 instead of listening to what *P* said,
27: 21 *P* stood up before them and said:
27: 24 and said, 'Do not be afraid, *P*.
27: 31 Then *P* said to the centurion
27: 33 Just before dawn *P* urged them all
28: 3 *P* gathered a pile of brushwood and
28: 5 *P* shook the snake off into the fire
28: 8 *P* went in to see him
28: 15 sight of these men *P* thanked God
28: 16 *P* was allowed to live by himself,
28: 17 When they had assembled, *P* said
28: 23 They arranged to meet *P*
Ac 28: 25 leave after *P* had made this final
28: 30 For two whole years *P* stayed there
Ro 1: 1 *P*, a servant of Christ Jesus,
1Co 1: 1 *P*, called to be an apostle
1: 12 "I follow *P*"; another, "I follow
1: 13 Is Christ divided? Was *P* crucified
1: 13 baptized into the name of *P*?
3: 4 "I follow *P*," and another,
3: 5 And what is *P*? Only servants,
3: 22 whether *P* or Apollos or Cephas
16: 21 *P*, write this greeting
2Co 1: 1 *P*, an apostle of Christ Jesus
10: 1 *P*, who am "timid" when face
Gal 1: 1 *P*, an apostle—sent not from men
5: 2 *P*, tell you that if you let yourselves
Eph 1: 1 *P*, an apostle of Christ Jesus
3: 1 *P*, the prisoner of Christ Jesus
Php 1: 1 *P* and Timothy, servants
Col 1: 1 *P*, an apostle of Christ Jesus
1: 23 *P*, have become a servant.
4: 18 *P*, write this greeting
1Th 1: 1 *P*, Silas and Timothy, To
2: 18 certainly I, *P*, did, again and again
2Th 1: 1 *P*, Silas and Timothy, To
3: 17 *P*, write this greeting
1Ti 1: 1 *P*, an apostle of Christ Jesus
2Ti 1: 1 *P*, an apostle of Christ Jesus
Tit 1: 1 *P*, a servant of God and an apostle
Phm : 1 *P*, a prisoner of Christ Jesus,
: 9 as *P*— an old man and now
: 19 *P*, am writing this with my own
2Pe 3: 15 just as our dear brother *P*

PAUL'S (PAUL)

Ac 16: 14 heart to respond to *P* message.
19: 29 *P* traveling companions
21: 11 Coming over to us, he took *P* belt,
23: 16 But when the son of *P* sister heard
25: 14 Festus discussed *P* case
26: 24 point Festus interrupted *P* defense.
27: 43 centurion wanted to spare *P* life

PAVEMENT

Ex 24: 10 feet was something like a *p* made
2Ch 7: 3 they knelt on the *p* with their faces
Est 1: 6 silver on a mosaic *p* of porphyry,
Jer 43: 9 clay in the brick *p* at the entrance
Eze 40: 17 a *p* that had been constructed all
40: 17 there were thirty rooms along the *p*
40: 18 were long; this was the lower *p*.
42: 3 opposite the *p* of the outer court,
Jn 19: 13 as The Stone *P* (which

PAVILION

Job 36: 29 how he thunders from his *p*?
Ps 19: 5 coming forth from his *p*,

PAW (PAWS)

1Sa 17: 37 me from the *p* of the lion
17: 37 the *p* of the bear will deliver me

PAWS (PAW)

Lev 11: 27 walk on their *p* are unclean for you;
Job 39: 21 He *p* fiercely, rejoicing

PAY (PAID PAYING PAYMENT PAYS REPAID REPAY REPAYING REPAYMENT REPAYS)

Ge 23: 13 I will *p* the price of the field.
30: 28 your wages, and I will *p* them."
34: 12 and I'll *p* whatever you ask me.
43: 28 they bowed low to *p* him honor.
Ex 2: 9 nurse him for me, and I will *p* you."
4: 8 *p* attention to the first miraculous
5: 9 and *p* no attention to lies."
15: 26 if you *p* attention to his commands
21: 19 he must *p* the injured man
21: 32 the owner must *p* thirty shekels
21: 34 he must *p* its owner, and the dead
21: 34 owner of the pit must *p* for the loss;
21: 36 the owner must *p*, animal
22: 1 he must *p* back five head of cattle
22: 3 he must be sold to *p* for his theft.
22: 4 or sheep—he must *p* back double.
22: 7 if he is caught, must *p* back double.
22: 9 declare guilty must *p* back double
22: 13 required to *p* for the torn animal.
22: 15 the borrower will not have to *p*.

Ex 22:16 he must *p* the bride-price,
22:17 he must still *p* the bride-price
23:21 *P* attention to him and listen
30:12 each one must *p* the LORD
Lev 25:51 he must *p* for his redemption
25:52 *p* for his redemption accordingly.
26:41 hearts are humbled and they *p*
26:43 They will *p* for their sins
27:8 poor to *p* the specified amount,
27:23 and the man must *p* its value
Nu 20:19 any of your water, we will *p* for it.
Dt 2:6 You are to *p* them in silver
7:12 If you *p* attention to these laws
22:29 he shall *p* the girl's father fifty
23:18 the LORD your God to *p* any vow,
23:21 your God, do not be slow to *p* it,
24:15 *P* him his wages each day
28:13 If you *p* attention to the commands
Jdg 9:57 the men of Shechem *p* for all their
1Sa 4:20 did not respond or *p* any attention.
6:5 and *p* honor to Israel's god.
25:25 May my lord *p* no attention
2Sa 1:2 he fell to the ground to *p* him honor
9:6 he bowed down to *p* him honor.
12:6 He must *p* for that lamb four times
14:4 face to the ground to *p* him honor,
14:22 face to the ground to *p* him honor,
1Ki 2:23 if Adonijah does not *p* with his life
5:6 I will *p* you for your men whatever
20:39 or you must *p* a talent of silver.'
21:2 I will *p* you whatever it is worth."
2Ki 4:7 "Go, sell the oil and *p* your debts.
9:26 and I will surely make you *p* for it
12:15 gave the money to *p* the workers,
18:14 and I will *p* whatever you demand
22:5 have these men *p* the workers who
Ne 5:4 to borrow money to *p* the king's tax
9:34 they did not *p* attention
Est 3:2 kneel down or *p* him honor.
3:5 kneel down or *p* him honor,
4:7 to *p* into the royal treasury
Job 6:22 *p* a ransom for me
33:1 *p* attention to everything I say.
33:31 "*P* attention, Job, and listen to me;
41:11 a claim against me that I must *p*?
Ps 79:12 *P* back into the laps
94:2 *p* back to the proud what they
Pr 4:1 *p* attention and gain understanding
4:20 My son, *p* attention to what I say;
5:1 My son, *p* attention to my wisdom,
6:31 if he is caught, he must *p* sevenfold,
7:24 *p* attention to what I say.
13:13 He who scorns instruction will *p*
19:19 man must *p* the penalty;
20:22 "I'll *p* you back for this wrong!"
22:17 *P* attention and listen
22:27 if you lack the means to *p*,
24:29 I'll *p* that man back for what he did
30:10 he will curse you, and you will *p*
Ecc 7:21 Do not *p* attention
Isa 28:23 *p* attention and hear what I say.
34:1 *p* attention, you peoples!
42:23 or *p* close attention in time to come
65:6 I will not keep silent but will *p* back
65:6 I will *p* it back into their laps—
Jer 7:24 they did not listen or *p* attention,
7:26 listen to me or *p* attention.
11:8 they did not listen or *p* attention;
13:15 Hear and *p* attention,
17:23 they did not listen or *p* attention;
18:18 *p* no attention to anything he says
34:14 listen to me or *p* attention to me.
44:5 they did not listen or *p* attention;
51:6 he will *p* her what she deserves.
La 3:64 *P* them back what they deserve,
Eze 16:41 you will no longer *p* your lovers.
29:19 plunder the land as *p* for his army.
40:4 and *p* attention to everything I am
Da 3:12 who *p* no attention to you,
Hos 2:12 which she said were her *p*
5:1 *P* attention, you Israelites!
12:12 and to *p* for her he tended sheep.
Zec 1:4 they would not listen or *p* attention
7:11 "But they refused to *p* attention;
11:12 give me my *p*; but if not, keep it."
Mt 7:3 and *p* no attention to the plank
17:24 "Doesn't your teacher *p* the temple
18:25 Since he was not able to *p*,
Mt 18:26 'and I will *p* back everything.'
18:28 '*P* back what you owe me!'
18:29 with me, and I will *p* you back.'
18:30 prison until he could *p* the debt.
18:34 until he should *p* back all he owed.
20:2 He agreed to *p* them a denarius
20:4 and I will *p* you whatever is right.'
20:8 the workers and *p* them their
20:14 to work for a denarius? Take your *p*
22:16 you *p* no attention to who they are.
22:17 Is it right to *p* taxes to Caesar
Mk 12:14 Is it right to *p* taxes to Caesar
12:14 you *p* no attention to who they are;
12:15 Should we *p* or shouldn't we?"
Lk 3:14 falsely—be content with your *p*."
6:41 and *p* no attention to the plank
7:42 them had the money to *p* him back,
19:8 I will *p* back four times the amount
20:22 Is it right for us to *p* taxes to Caesar
Ac 21:24 rites and *p* their expenses,
22:28 "I had to *p* a big price
25:13 at Caesarea to *p* their respects
Ro 13:6 This is also why you *p* taxes,
13:7 If you owe taxes, *p* taxes; if revenue
Gal 5:10 into confusion will *p* the penalty,
2Th 1:6 He will *p* back trouble
Tit 1:14 will *p* no attention to Jewish myths
Phm :19 I will *p* it back—not
Heb 2:1 We must *p* more careful attention,
Jas 5:4 to *p* the workmen who mowed
2Pe 1:19 you will do well to *p* attention to it,
Rev 18:6 *p* her back double for what she has

PAYING (PAY)

Ex 21:2 he shall go free, without *p* anything
21:30 life by *p* whatever is demanded.
2Sa 24:24 "No, I insist on *p* you for it.
1Ch 21:24 "No, I insist on *p* the full price.
Jer 22:13 not *p* them for their labor.
Joel 3:4 I have done? If you are *p* me back,
Jnh 1:3 After *p* the fare, he went aboard
Mt 22:19 Show me the coin used for *p* the tax
2Th 3:8 did we eat anyone's food without *p*

PAYMENT (PAY)

Ge 31:39 And you demanded *p* from me
47:14 in *p* for the grain they were buying,
Ex 21:11 to go free, without any *p* of money.
21:30 However, if *p* is demanded of him,
Lev 22:16 bring upon them guilt requiring *p*.
Dt 15:2 He shall not require *p*
15:3 You may require *p* from a foreigner
Job 31:39 I have devoured its yield without *p*
Ps 49:8 no *p* is ever enough—
109:20 May this be the LORD's *p*
Isa 65:7 the full *p* for their former deeds."
Eze 16:31 prostitute, because you scorned *p*.
16:34 for you give *p* and none is given
Lk 23:2 He opposes *p* of taxes to Caesar
Php 4:18 I have received full *p* and

PAYS (PAY)

Ge 50:15 *p* us back for all the wrongs we did
Job 35:13 the Almighty *p* no attention to it.
Ps 31:23 but the proud he *p* back in full.
94:7 the God of Jacob *p* no heed."
Pr 17:4 liar *p* attention to a malicious
17:13 If a man *p* back evil for good,
Da 6:13 *p* no attention to you, O king,
Mal 2:13 because he no longer *p* attention
1Th 5:15 sure that nobody *p* back wrong

PEACE (PACIFIES PACIFY PEACEABLE PEACEFUL PEACEMAKERS PEACETIME)

Ge 15:15 will go to your fathers in *p*
26:29 you well and sent you away in *p*.
26:31 on their way, and they left him in *p*.
44:17 go back to your father in *p*."
Lev 26:6 " 'I will grant *p* in the land,
Nu 6:26 and give you *p*." '
25:12 him I am making my covenant of *p*
Dt 2:26 king of Heshbon offering *p*
20:10 make its people an offer of *p*.
20:12 If they refuse to make *p*
23:6 Do not seek *p* or good relations
Jos 9:15 Then Joshua made a treaty of *p*
10:1 of Gibeon had made a treaty of *p*
Jos 10:4 "because it has made *p* with Joshua
11:19 a treaty of *p* with the Israelites,
Jdg 3:11 So the land had *p* for forty years,
3:30 and the land had *p* for eighty years.
5:31 Then the land had *p* forty years.
6:23 But the LORD said to him, "*P*!
6:24 and called it "The LORD is *P*."
8:28 the land enjoyed *p* forty years.
18:6 priest answered them, "Go in *p*.
21:13 an offer of *p* to the Benjamites
1Sa 1:17 "Go in *p*, and may the God
7:14 And there was *p* between Israel
16:4 come in *p*?" Samuel replied,
16:5 Samuel replied, "Yes, in *p*;
20:42 Jonathan said to David, "Go in *p*,
25:35 him and said, "Go home in *p*.
29:7 and go in *p*; do nothing
2Sa 3:21 sent Abner away, and he went in *p*.
3:22 him away, and he had gone in *p*.
3:23 away and that he had gone in *p*.
10:19 they made *p* with the Israelites
15:9 The king said to him, "Go in *p*."
15:27 city in *p*, with your son Ahimaaz
1Ki 2:6 go down to the grave in *p*.
2:33 may there be the LORD's *p* forever
4:24 to Gaza, and had *p* on all sides.
5:4 the LORD my God has given me *p*
20:18 "If they have come out for *p*,
22:17 Let each one go home in *p*.' "
22:44 also at *p* with the king of Israel
2Ki 5:19 "Go in *p*," Elisha said.
9:17 come in *p*?' " The horseman rode
9:18 come in *p*?' " "What do you have
9:18 "What do you have to do with *p*?"
9:19 'Do you come in *p*?' " Jehu replied,
9:19 "What do you have to do with *p*?
9:22 How can there be *p*," Jehu replied,
9:22 "Have you come in *p*, Jehu?"
9:31 "Have you come in *p*, Zimri,
18:31 Make *p* with me and come out
20:19 "Will there not be *p* and security
22:20 and you will be buried in *p*.
1Ch 12:17 "If you have come to me in *p*,
19:19 they made *p* with David
22:9 and I will grant Israel *p*
22:9 have a son who will be a man of *p*
2Ch 14:1 and in his days the country was at *p*
14:5 the kingdom was at *p* under him.
14:6 of Judah, since the land was at *p*.
18:16 Let each one go home in *p*.' "
20:30 kingdom of Jehoshaphat was at *p*,
34:28 and you will be buried in *p*.
Job 3:13 For now I would be lying down in *p*
3:26 I have no *p*, no quietness;
5:23 the wild animals will be at *p*
21:13 and go down to the grave in *p*.
22:21 to God and be at *p* with him;
Ps 4:8 I will lie down and sleep in *p*,
7:4 evil to him who is at *p* with me
29:11 LORD blesses his people with *p*.
34:14 seek *p* and pursue it.
37:11 and enjoy great *p*.
37:37 there is a future for the man of *p*.
85:8 he promises *p* to his people,
85:10 righteousness and *p* kiss each other
119:165 Great *p* have they who love your
120:6 lived among those who hate *p*.
120:7 I am a man of *p*;
122:6 Pray for the *p* of Jerusalem:
122:7 May there be *p* within your walls
122:8 I will say, "*P* be within you."
125:5 *P* be upon Israel.
128:6 *P* be upon Israel.
147:14 He grants *p* to your borders
Pr 3:17 and all her paths are *p*.
12:20 but joy for those who promote *p*.
14:30 A heart at *p* gives life to the body,
16:7 his enemies live at *p* with him.
17:1 Better a dry crust with *p* and quiet
29:9 scoffs, and there is no *p*.
29:17 your son, and he will give you *p*;
Ecc 3:8 a time for war and a time for *p*.
Isa 9:6 Everlasting Father, Prince of *P*.
9:7 of his government and *p*
14:7 All the lands are at rest and at *p*;
26:3 You will keep in perfect *p*
26:12 LORD, you establish *p* for us;
27:5 let them make *p* with me,

Isa 27: 5 yes, let them make *p* with me."
32: 17 The fruit of righteousness will be *p;*
33: 7 the envoys of *p* weep bitterly.
36: 16 Make *p* with me and come out
39: 8 "There will be *p* and security
48: 18 your *p* would have been like a river,
48: 22 "There is no *p,*" says the LORD,
52: 7 who proclaim *p,*
53: 5 punishment that brought us *p* was
54: 10 nor my covenant of *p* be removed,"
54: 13 and great will be your children's *p.*
55: 12 and be led forth in *p;*
57: 2 enter into *p;*
57: 19 *P, p,* to those far and near,"
57: 21 "There is no *p,*" says my God,
59: 8 The way of *p* they do not know;
59: 8 walks in them will know *p.*
60: 17 I will make *p* your governor
66: 12 "I will extend *p* to her like a river,
Jer 4: 10 You will have *p,*' when the sword is
6: 14 *'P, p,'* they say,
6: 14 when there is no *p.*
8: 11 *"P, p,"* . . . there is no *p.*
8: 15 We hoped for *p*
14: 13 I will give you lasting *p* in this place
14: 19 We hoped for *p*
23: 17 'The LORD says: You will have *p.*'
28: 9 prophet who prophesies *p* will be
29: 7 Also, seek the *p* and prosperity
30: 5 terror, not *p.*
30: 10 Jacob will again have *p*
33: 6 and will let them enjoy abundant *p*
33: 9 prosperity and *p* I provide
46: 27 Jacob will again have *p*
La 3: 17 I have been deprived of *p;*
Eze 7: 25 they will seek *p,* but there will be
13: 10 *"P,"* when there is no *p,*
13: 16 of *p* for her when there was no *p,*
34: 25 " 'I will make a covenant of *p*
37: 26 I will make a covenant of *p*
Da 10: 19 *"P!* Be strong now; be strong."
Mic 3: 5 they proclaim *'p';*
5: 5 And he will be their *p.*
Na 1: 15 who proclaims *p!*
Hag 2: 9 'And in this place I will grant *p,*'
Zec 1: 11 the whole world at rest and in *p.*"
8: 19 Therefore love truth and *p.*"
9: 10 He will proclaim *p* to the nations.
Mal 2: 5 a covenant of life and *p,*
2: 6 He walked with me in *p*
Mt 10: 13 home is deserving, let your *p* rest
10: 13 if it is not, let your *p* return to you.
10: 34 I did not come to bring *p,*
10: 34 come to bring *p* to the earth.
Mk 5: 34 Go in *p* and be freed
9: 50 and be at *p* with each other."
Lk 1: 79 to guide our feet into the path of *p*
2: 14 on earth *p* to men on whom his
2: 29 you now dismiss your servant in *p.*
7: 50 Your faith has saved you; go in *p.*"
8: 48 Go in *p.*"
10: 5 you enter a house, first say, *'P*
10: 6 a man of *p* is there, your *p* will rest
12: 51 came to bring *p* on earth?
14: 32 and will ask for terms of *p.*
19: 38 *"P* in heaven and glory
19: 42 on this day what would bring you *p*
24: 36 and said to them, *"P* be with you."
Jn 14: 27 *P* I leave with you; my *p*
16: 33 so that in me you may have *p.*
20: 19 *"P* be with you!" After he said this,
20: 21 Again Jesus said, *"P* be with you!
20: 26 and said, *"P* be with you!"
Ac 9: 31 and Samaria enjoyed a time of *p.*
10: 36 news of *p* through Jesus Christ,
12: 20 of the king, they asked for *p,*
15: 33 with the blessing of *p* to return
16: 36 Go in *p.*"
24: 2 We have enjoyed a long period of *p*
Ro 1: 7 and *p* to you from God our Father
2: 10 and *p* for everyone who does good:
3: 17 and the way of *p* they do not know
5: 1 we have *p* with God
8: 6 by the Spirit is life and *p;*
12: 18 on you, live at *p* with everyone.
14: 17 *p* and joy in the Holy Spirit,
14: 19 effort to do what leads to *p*
15: 13 of hope fill you with all joy and *p*
Ro 15: 33 The God of *p* be with you all.
16: 20 The God of *p* will soon crush Satan
1Co 1: 3 and *p* to you from God our Father
7: 15 God has called us to live in *p.*
14: 33 a God of disorder but of *p.*
16: 11 way in *p* so that he may return
2Co 1: 2 and *p* to you from God our Father
2: 13 I still had no *p* of mind,
13: 11 God of love and *p* will be with you.
13: 11 be of one mind, live in *p.*
Gal 1: 3 and *p* to you from God our Father
5: 22 joy, *p,* patience, kindness,
6: 16 *P* and mercy to all who follow this
Eph 1: 2 and *p* to you from God our Father
2: 14 he himself is our *p,* who has made
2: 15 thus making *p,* and in this one body
2: 17 and *p* to those who were near.
2: 17 preached *p* to you who were far
4: 3 of the Spirit through the bond of *p.*
6: 15 comes from the gospel of *p.*
6: 23 *P* to the brothers, and love
Php 1: 2 and *p* to you from God our Father
4: 7 the *p* of God, which transcends all
4: 9 And the God of *p* will be with you.
Col 1: 2 and *p* to you from God our Father.
1: 20 by making *p* through his blood,
3: 15 Let the *p* of Christ rule
3: 15 of one body you were called to *p.*
1Th 1: 1 the Lord Jesus Christ: Grace and *p*
5: 3 While people are saying, *"P*
5: 13 Live in *p* with each other.
5: 23 the God of *p,* sanctify you through
2Th 1: 2 and *p* to you from God the Father
3: 16 the Lord of *p* himself give you *p*
1Ti 1: 2 mercy and *p* from God the Father
2Ti 1: 2 mercy and *p* from God the Father
2: 22 righteousness, faith, love and *p,*
Tit 1: 4 Grace and *p* from God the Father
Phm : 3 and *p* from God our Father
Heb 7: 2 "king of Salem" means "king of *p.*"
12: 11 *p* for those who have been trained
12: 14 effort to live in *p* with all men
13: 20 May the God of *p,* who
Jas 3: 17 then *p* loving, considerate,
3: 18 sow in *p* raise a harvest
1Pe 1: 2 Grace and *p* be yours in abundance
3: 11 he must seek *p* and pursue it.
5: 14 *P* to all of you who are in Christ.
2Pe 1: 2 and *p* be yours in abundance
3: 14 blameless and at *p* with him.
2Jn : 3 mercy and *p* from God the Father
3Jn : 14 *P* to you.
Jude : 2 *p* and love be yours in abundance.
Rev 1: 4 and *p* to you from him who is,
6: 4 power to take *p* from the earth

PEACEABLE (PEACE)

Tit 3: 2 to slander no one, to be *p*

PEACEFUL (PEACE)

Jdg 18: 27 against a *p* and unsuspecting
2Sa 20: 19 We are the *p* and faithful in Israel.
1Ki 5: 12 There were *p* relations
1Ch 4: 40 the land was spacious, *p* and quiet.
Isa 32: 18 live in *p* dwelling places,
33: 20 a *p* abode, a tent that will not be
Jer 25: 37 The *p* meadows will be laid waste
Eze 38: 11 will attack a *p* and unsuspecting
1Ti 2: 2 that we may live *p* and quiet lives

PEACEMAKERS (PEACE)

Mt 5: 9 Blessed are the *p,*
Jas 3: 18 *P* who sow in peace raise a harvest

PEACETIME (PEACE)

1Ki 2: 5 shedding their blood in *p*

PEAKS

Nu 23: 9 From the rocky *p* I see them,
Ps 95: 4 and the mountain *p* belong to him.

PEAL (PEALS)

Rev 14: 2 and like a loud *p* of thunder.

PEALS (PEAL)

Rev 4: 5 rumblings and *p* of thunder.
8: 5 and there came *p* of thunder,
11: 19 flashes of lightning, rumblings, *p*
Rev 16: 18 *p* of thunder and a severe
19: 6 and like loud *p* of thunder,

PEARL (MOTHER-OF-PEARL PEARLS)

Rev 21: 21 each gate made of a single *p.*

PEARLS (PEARL)

Mt 7: 6 do not throw your *p* to pigs.
13: 45 like a merchant looking for fine *p.*
1Ti 2: 9 or gold or *p* or expensive clothes,
Rev 17: 4 with gold, precious stones and *p.*
18: 12 precious stones and *p;* fine linen,
18: 16 with gold, precious stones and *p!*
21: 21 The twelve gates were twelve *p,*

PEBBLES

Ps 147: 17 He hurls down his hail like *p.*

PECKED

Pr 30: 17 will be *p* out by the ravens

PEDAHEL

Nu 34: 28 tribe of Asher; *P* son of Ammihud,

PEDAHZUR

Nu 1: 10 Gamaliel son of *P;* from Benjamin,
2: 20 of Manasseh is Gamaliel son of *P.*
7: 54 the eighth day Gamaliel son of *P,*
7: 59 the offering of Gamaliel son of *P.*
10: 23 Gamaliel son of *P* was

PEDAIAH

2Ki 23: 36 name was Zebidah daughter of *P;*
1Ch 3: 18 Malkiram, *P,* Shenazzar, Jekamiah
3: 19 The sons of *P:* Zerubbabel
27: 20 Joel son of *P;* over the half-tribe
Ne 3: 25 *P* son of Parosh and the temple
8: 4 and on his left were *P,* Mishael,
11: 7 the son of *P,* the son of Kolaiah,
13: 13 and a Levite named *P* in charge

PEDDLE

2Co 2: 17 we do not *p* the word of God

PEDESTAL

Am 5: 26 the *p* of your idols,

PEELED (PEELING PEELS)

Ge 30: 38 Then he placed the *p* branches

PEELING (PEELED)

Ge 30: 37 stripes on them by *p* the bark

PEELS (PEELED)

Job 30: 30 My skin grows black and *p;*

PEERED (PEERING)

Jdg 5: 28 the window *p* Sisera's mother;

PEERING (PEERED)

SS 2: 9 *p* through the lattice.

PEG (PEGS)

Jdg 4: 21 She drove the *p* through his temple
4: 21 picked up a tent *p* and a hammer
4: 22 with the tent *p* through his temple
5: 26 Her hand reached for the tent *p,*
Isa 22: 23 I will drive him like a *p*
22: 25 *p* driven into the firm place will
Zec 10: 4 from him the tent *p,*

PEGS (PEG)

Ex 27: 19 including all the tent *p* for it
35: 18 the tent *p* for the tabernacle
38: 20 All the tent *p* of the tabernacle
38: 31 and all the tent *p* for the tabernacle
39: 40 and tent *p* for the courtyard;
Nu 3: 37 courtyard with their bases, tent *p*
4: 32 tent *p,* ropes, all their equipment
Eze 15: 3 Do they make *p* from it

PEKAH (PEKAH'S)

2Ki 15: 25 One of his chief officers, *P* son
15: 25 *P* killed Pekahiah and succeeded
15: 27 *P* son of Remaliah became king
15: 29 In the time of *P* king of Israel,
15: 30 against *P* son of Remaliah.
15: 32 year of *P* son of Remaliah king
15: 37 *P* son of Remaliah against Judah.)

2Ki 16: 1 year of *P* son of Remaliah,
16: 5 and *P* son of Remaliah king
2Ch 28: 6 one day *P* son of Remaliah killed
Isa 7: 1 and *P* son of Remaliah king

PEKAH'S (PEKAH)

2Ki 15:31 As for the other events of *P* reign,

PEKAHIAH (PEKAHIAH'S)

2Ki 15:22 And *P* his son succeeded him
15:23 *P* son of Menahem became king
15:24 *P* did evil in the eyes of the LORD.
15:25 Pekah killed *P* and succeeded him
15:25 he assassinated *P*,

PEKAHIAH'S (PEKAHIAH)

2Ki 15:26 The other events of *P* reign,

PEKOD

Jer 50:21 and those who live in *P*.
Eze 23:23 the men of *P* and Shoa and Koa,

PELAIAH

1Ch 3:24 Hodaviah, Eliashib, *P*, Akkub,
Ne 8: 7 Azariah, Jozabad, Hanan and *P*—
10:10 Hodiah, Kelita, *P*, Hanan, Mica,

PELALIAH

Ne 11:12 the son of *P*, the son of Amzi,

PELATIAH

1Ch 3:21 The descendants of Hananiah: *P*
4:42 led by *P*, Neariah, Rephaiah
Ne 10:22 Zadok, Jaddua, *P*, Hanan, Anaiah,
Eze 11: 1 son of Azzur and *P* son of Benaiah,
11:13 Now as I was prophesying, *P* son

PELEG

Ge 10:25 One was named *P*,
11:16 he became the father of *P*.
11:17 after he became the father of *P*,
11:18 When *P* had lived 30 years,
11:19 *P* lived 209 years and had other
1Ch 1:19 One was named *P*,
1:25 Shelah, Eber, *P*, Reu, Serug,
Lk 3:35 the son of *P*, the son of Eber,

PELET

1Ch 2:47 Regem, Jotham, Geshan, *P*,
12: 3 Jeziel and *P* the sons of Azmaveth;

PELETH (PELETHITES)

Nu 16: 1 sons of Eliab, and On son of *P*—
1Ch 2:33 The sons of Jonathan: *P* and Zaza.

PELETHITES (PELETH)

2Sa 8:18 was over the Kerethites and *P*;
15:18 along with all the Kerethites and *P*;
20: 7 men and the Kerethites and *P*
20:23 was over the Kerethites and *P*;
1Ki 1:38 the Kerethites and the *P* went
1:44 Jehoiada, the Kerethites and the *P*,
1Ch 18:17 was over the Kerethites and *P*;

PELONITE

1Ch 11:27 the Harorite, Helez the *P*,
11:36 Ahijah the *P*, Hezro the Carmelite,
27:10 was Helez the *P*, an Ephraimite.

PELT (PELTED)

Na 3: 6 I will *p* you with filth,

PELTED (PELT)

2Sa 16: 6 He *p* David and all the king's

PELUSIUM

Eze 30:15 I will pour out my wrath on *P*,
30:16 *P* will writhe in agony.

PEN (PENNED PENS PENT-UP)

1Sa 6: 7 their calves away and *p* them up.
Ps 45: 1 my tongue is the *p*
Isa 8: 1 and write on it with an ordinary *p*:
Jer 8: 8 when actually the lying *p*
Mic 2:12 them together like sheep in a *p*,
Hab 3:17 though there are no sheep in the *p*
Mt 5:18 letter, not the least stroke of a *p*,
Lk 16:17 than for the least stroke of a *p*
Jn 10: 1 who does not enter the sheep *p*
10:16 sheep that are not of this sheep *p*.
3Jn :13 but I do not want to do so with *p*

PENALTIES (PENALTY)

Pr 19:29 *P* are prepared for mockers,

PENALTY (PENALTIES)

Lev 5: 6 as a *p* for the sin he has committed,
5: 7 to the LORD as a *p* for his sin—
5:15 as a *p* a ram from the flock,
6: 6 as a *p* he must bring to the priest,
Job 8: 4 them over to the *p* of their sin.
Pr 19:19 hot-tempered man must pay the *p*;
Eze 23:49 You will suffer the *p*
Da 2: 9 there is just one *p* for you.
Lk 23:22 in him no grounds for the death *p*.
Ro 1:27 received in themselves the due *p*
Gal 5:10 you into confusion will pay the *p*,

PENDANTS

Jdg 8:26 *p* and the purple garments worn

PENETRATES

Heb 4:12 it *p* even to dividing soul and spirit,

PENIEL (PENUEL)

Ge 32:30 So Jacob called the place *P*, saying,
32:31 rose above him as he passed *P*,
Jdg 8: 8 From there he went up to *P*
8: 9 So he said to the men of *P*,
8:17 He also pulled down the tower of *P*
1Ki 12:25 there he went out and built up *P*.

PENINNAH

1Sa 1: 2 *P* had children, but Hannah had
1: 2 was called Hannah and the other *P*.
1: 4 portions of the meat to his wife *P*

PENITENT (REPENT)

Isa 1:27 her *p* ones with righteousness.

PENNED (PEN)

Ex 21:29 but has not kept it *p* up and it kills
21:36 yet the owner did not keep it *p* up,
1Sa 6:10 to the cart and *p* up their calves.

PENNIES (PENNY)

Lk 12: 6 not five sparrows sold for two *p*?

PENNY (PENNIES)

Mt 5:26 out until you have paid the last *p*.
10:29 Are not two sparrows sold for a *p*?
Mk 12:42 worth only a fraction of a *p*.
Lk 12:59 out until you have paid the last *p*."

PENS (PEN)

Nu 32:16 like to build *p* here for our livestock
32:24 and children, and *p* for your flocks,
32:36 and built *p* for their flocks.
1Sa 24: 3 came to the sheep *p* along the way;
2Ch 32:28 kinds of cattle, and *p* for the flocks.
Ps 50: 9 or of goats from your *p*,
78:70 and took him from the sheep *p*;
Zep 2: 6 for shepherds and sheep *p*.

PENT-UP (PEN)

Isa 59:19 For he will come like a *p* flood

PENTECOST

Ac 2: 1 of *P* came, they were all together
20:16 if possible, by the day of *P*.
1Co 16: 8 I will stay on at Ephesus until *P*,

PENUEL (PENIEL)

1Ch 4: 4 *P* was the father of Gedor,
8:25 and *P* were the sons of Shashak.

PEOR

Nu 23:28 Balak took Balaam to the top of *P*,
25: 3 joined in worshiping the Baal of *P*.
25: 5 in worshiping the Baal of *P*."
25:18 the plague came as a result of *P*."
25:18 they deceived you in the affair of *P*
31:16 the LORD in what happened at *P*,
Dt 4: 3 who followed the Baal of *P*,
Jos 22:17 Was not the sin of *P* enough for us?
Ps 106: 28 yoked themselves to the Baal of *P*

PERATH

Jer 13: 4 and go now to *P* and hide it there
13: 5 hid it at *P*, as the LORD told me.
13: 6 now to *P* and get the belt I told you
13: 7 So I went to *P* and dug up the belt

PERAZIM

Isa 28:21 will rise up as he did at Mount *P*,

PERCEIVE (PERCEIVED PERCEIVING)

Job 9:11 when he goes by, I cannot *p* him.
33:14 though man may not *p* it.
Ps 139: 2 you *p* my thoughts from afar.
Pr 24:12 not he who weighs the heart *p* it?
Isa 43:19 Now it springs up; do you not *p* it?

PERCEIVED (PERCEIVE)

Isa 64: 4 no ear has *p*,

PERCEIVING (PERCEIVE)

Isa 6: 9 be ever seeing, but never *p*.'
Mt 13:14 you will be ever seeing but never *p*.
Mk 4:12 may be ever seeing but never *p*,
Ac 28:26 you will be ever seeing but never *p*

PERCH (PERCHED)

Mt 13:32 the birds of the air come and *p*
Mk 4:32 birds of the air can *p* in its shade."

PERCHED (PERCH)

Lk 13:19 the birds of the air *p* in its branches

PERES

Da 5:28 *P*: Your kingdom is divided

PERESH

1Ch 7:16 birth to a son and named him *P*.

PEREZ (PEREZITE)

Ge 38:29 broken out!" And he was named *P*.
46:12 The sons of *P*: Hezron and Hamul.
46:12 *P* and Zerah (but Er and Onan had
Nu 26:20 through *P*, the Perezite clan;
26:21 The descendants of *P* were:
Ru 4:12 may your family be like that of *P*,
4:18 *P* was the father of Hezron,
4:18 then, is the family line of *P*:
1Ch 2: 4 daughter-in-law, bore him *P*
2: 5 The sons of *P*: Hezron and Hamul.
4: 1 The descendants of Judah: *P*,
9: 4 a descendant of *P* son of Judah.
27: 3 He was a descendant of *P*
Ne 11: 4 descendant of *P*; and Maaseiah son
11: 6 The descendants of *P* who lived
Mt 1: 3 Judah the father of *P* and Zerah,
1: 3 mother was Tamar, *P* the father
Lk 3:33 the son of Hezron, the son of *P*,

PEREZ UZZAH

2Sa 6: 8 to this day that place is called *P*.
1Ch 13:11 to this day that place is called *P*.

PEREZITE (PEREZ)

Nu 26:20 through Perez, the *P* clan;

PERFECT (PERFECTER PERFECTING PERFECTION)

Dt 32: 4 He is the Rock, his works are *p*,
2Sa 22:31 "As for God, his way is *p*,
22:33 and makes my way *p*.
Job 36: 4 one *p* in knowledge is with you.
37:16 of him who is *p* in knowledge?
Ps 18:30 As for God, his way is *p*;
18:32 and makes my way *p*.
19: 7 The law of the LORD is *p*,
50: 2 From Zion, *p* in beauty,
64: 6 "We have devised a *p* plan!"
SS 6: 9 but my dove, my *p* one, is unique,
Isa 25: 1 for in *p* faithfulness
26: 3 You will keep in *p* peace
Eze 16:14 had given you made your beauty *p*,
27: 3 "I am *p* in beauty."
28:12 full of wisdom and *p* in beauty.
Mt 5:48 Do not even pagans do that? Be *p*,
5:48 as your heavenly Father is *p*.
19:21 answered, "If you want to be *p*,
Ro 12: 2 his good, pleasing and *p* will.
2Co 12: 9 for my power is made *p*

Php 3: 12 or have already been made *p*,
Col 1: 28 so that we may present everyone *p*
3: 14 binds them all together in *p* unity.
Heb 2: 10 the author of their salvation *p*
5: 9 what he suffered and, once made *p*,
7: 19 useless (for the law made nothing *p*
7: 28 who has been made *p* forever.
9: 11 and more *p* tabernacle that is not
10: 1 make *p* those who draw
10: 14 he has made *p* forever those who
11: 40 with us would they be made *p*.
12: 23 spirits of righteous men made *p*,
Jas 1: 17 Every good and *p* gift is from above
1: 25 into the *p* law that gives freedom,
3: 2 he is a *p* man, able
1Jn 4: 18 But *p* love drives out fear,
4: 18 The man who fears is not made *p*

PERFECTER (PERFECT)

Heb 12: 2 the author and *p* of our faith,

PERFECTING (PERFECT)

2Co 7: 1 *p* holiness out of reverence for God

PERFECTION (PERFECT)

Ps 119: 96 To all *p* I see a limit;
La 2: 15 the *p* of beauty,
Eze 27: 4 builders brought your beauty to *p*.
27: 11 they brought your beauty to *p*.
28: 12 " 'You were the model of *p*,
1Co 13: 10 but when *p* comes, the imperfect
2Co 13: 9 and our prayer is for your *p*.
13: 11 Aim for *p*, listen to my appeal,
Heb 7: 11 If *p* could have been attained

PERFORM (PERFORMANCE PERFORMED PERFORMING PERFORMS)

Ex 3: 20 with all the wonders that I will *p*
4: 17 hand so you can *p* miraculous signs
4: 21 see that you *p* before Pharaoh all
4: 28 signs he had commanded him to *p*.
7: 9 says to you, '*P* a miracle,'
10: 1 that I may *p* these miraculous signs
18: 20 and the duties they are to *p*.
Nu 3: 7 They are to *p* duties for him
4: 31 as they *p* service at the Tent
18: 3 are to *p* all the duties of the Tent,
Jdg 16: 27 and women watching Samson *p*.
2Sa 7: 23 to *p* great and awesome wonders
1Ki 8: 11 the priests could not *p* their service
1Ch 17: 21 to *p* great and awesome wonders
2Ch 5: 14 the priests could not *p* their service
31: 16 of the LORD to *p* the daily duties
Isa 28: 21 and *p* his task, his alien task.
Jer 21: 2 Perhaps the LORD will *p* wonders
Eze 44: 16 before me and *p* my service.
Mt 7: 22 out demons and *p* many miracles?'
24: 24 will appear and *p* great signs
Mk 13: 22 prophets will appear and *p* signs
Lk 23: 8 hoped to see him *p* some miracle.
Jn 3: 2 no one could *p* the miraculous
Ac 4: 30 to heal and *p* miraculous signs
2Co 9: 12 This service that you *p* is not only

PERFORMANCE (PERFORM)

1Ch 23: 28 the *p* of other duties at the house

PERFORMED (PERFORM)

Ex 4: 30 also *p* the signs before the people,
10: 2 and how I *p* my signs among them,
11: 10 and Aaron *p* all these wonders
Nu 14: 11 of all the miraculous signs I have *p*
14: 22 the miraculous signs I *p* in Egypt
Dt 10: 21 who *p* for you those great
11: 3 the signs he *p* and the things he did
34: 12 or *p* the awesome deeds that Moses
Jos 24: 17 *p* those great signs before our eyes.
Jdg 16: 25 of the prison, and he *p* for them.
1Sa 12: 7 as to all the righteous acts *p*
2Sa 23: 20 from Kabzeel, who *p* great exploits.
1Ch 6: 32 They *p* their duties according
11: 22 from Kabzeel, who *p* great exploits.
25: 1 list of the men who *p* this service:
Ne 9: 17 to remember the miracles you *p*
12: 45 They *p* the service of their God
Ps 105: 27 They *p* his miraculous signs
Jer 32: 20 You *p* miraculous signs
Da 4: 2 that the Most High God has *p*
Mt 11: 20 most of his miracles had been *p*,
11: 21 If the miracles that were *p*
11: 21 in you had been *p* in Tyre
11: 23 If the miracles that were *p*
11: 23 in you had been *p* in Sodom,
Lk 1: 51 He has *p* mighty deeds
10: 13 For if the miracles that were *p*
10: 13 in you had been *p* in Tyre
Jn 2: 11 Jesus *p* in Cana of Galilee.
4: 54 miraculous sign that Jesus *p*,
6: 2 saw the miraculous signs he had *p*
10: 41 John never *p* a miraculous
Ac 5: 12 apostles *p* many miraculous signs
Rev 13: 13 he *p* great and miraculous signs,
19: 20 prophet who had *p* the miraculous

PERFORMING (PERFORM)

Nu 8: 26 in *p* their duties at the Tent
Jn 11: 47 is this man *p* many miraculous
Rev 16: 14 of demons *p* miraculous signs,

PERFORMS (PERFORM)

Job 5: 9 He *p* wonders that cannot be
9: 10 He *p* wonders that cannot be
Ps 77: 14 You are the God who *p* miracles;
Da 6: 27 he *p* signs and wonders
Heb 10: 11 priest stands and *p* his religious

PERFUME (PERFUME-MAKERS PERFUMED PERFUMER PERFUMERS PERFUMES)

Ex 30: 33 Whoever makes *p* like it
Ru 3: 3 and *p* yourself, and put
Pr 27: 9 *P* and incense bring joy to the heart
Ecc 7: 1 A good name is better than fine *p*,
10: 1 As dead flies give *p* a bad smell,
SS 1: 3 your name is like *p* poured out.
1: 12 my *p* spread its fragrance.
4: 10 fragrance of your *p* than any spice!
5: 13 yielding *p*.
Isa 3: 20 sashes, the *p* bottles and charms,
Mt 26: 7 jar of very expensive *p*,
26: 9 "This *p* could have been sold
26: 12 When she poured this *p*
Mk 14: 3 and poured the *p* on his head.
14: 3 jar of very expensive *p*,
14: 4 one another, "Why this waste of *p*?
14: 8 She poured *p* on my body
Lk 7: 37 she brought an alabaster jar of *p*,
7: 38 kissed them and poured *p* on them.
7: 46 but she has poured *p* on my feet.
Jn 11: 2 was the same one who poured *p*
12: 3 a pint of pure nard, an expensive *p*;
12: 3 filled with the fragrance of the *p*.
12: 5 "Why wasn't this *p* sold
12: 7 meant that she should save this *p*

PERFUME-MAKERS (PERFUME)

Ne 3: 8 and Hananiah, one of the *p*,

PERFUMED (PERFUME)

Pr 7: 17 I have *p* my bed
SS 3: 6 *p* with myrrh and incense

PERFUMER (PERFUME)

Ex 30: 25 a fragrant blend, the work of a *p*.
30: 35 blend of incense, the work of a *p*.
37: 29 fragrant incense—the work of a *p*.

PERFUMERS (PERFUME)

1Sa 8: 13 He will take your daughters to be *p*

PERFUMES (PERFUME)

2Ch 16: 14 with spices and various blended *p*,
Est 2: 12 and six with *p* and cosmetics.
SS 1: 3 Pleasing is the fragrance of your *p*;
Isa 57: 9 and increased your *p*.
Lk 23: 56 and prepared spices and *p*.

PERGA

Ac 13: 13 sailed to *P* in Pamphylia,
13: 14 From *P* they went on
14: 25 they had preached the word in *P*,

PERGAMUM

Rev 1: 11 Smyrna, *P*, Thyatira, Sardis,
2: 12 the angel of the church in *P* write:

PERIDA

Ne 7: 57 Sophereth, *P*, Jaala, Darkon,

PERIL

Job 22: 10 why sudden *p* terrifies you,
Ps 107: 26 in their *p* their courage melted
2Co 1: 10 us from such a deadly *p*,

PERIOD (PERIODS)

Ge 31: 35 in your presence; I'm having my *p*
50: 10 Joseph observed a seven-day *p*
Ex 2: 23 During that long *p*, the king
Lev 12: 2 unclean during her monthly *p*.
12: 5 woman will be unclean, as in her *p*.
15: 19 of her monthly *p* will last seven
15: 20 lies on during her *p* will be unclean,
15: 25 at a time other than her monthly *p*
15: 25 just as in the days of her *p*.
15: 25 that continues beyond her *p*,
15: 26 as is her bed during her monthly *p*,
15: 26 on will be unclean, as during her *p*.
15: 33 for a woman in her monthly *p*,
18: 19 the uncleanness of her monthly *p*.
20: 18 a woman during her monthly *p*
25: 8 amount to a *p* of forty-nine years.
Nu 6: 5 holy until the *p* of his separation
6: 5 " 'During the entire *p* of his vow
6: 6 Throughout the *p* of his separation
6: 8 Throughout the *p* of his separation
6: 12 LORD for the *p* of his separation
6: 13 when the *p* of his separation is
Job 1: 5 When a *p* of feasting had run its
Eze 18: 6 or lie with a woman during her *p*.
22: 10 during their *p* when they are
Da 7: 12 were allowed to live for a *p* of time
Ac 1: 3 to them over a *p* of forty days
24: 2 We have enjoyed a long *p* of peace

PERIODS (PERIOD)

1Ch 9: 25 share their duties for seven-day *p*.

PERISH (PERISHABLE PERISHED PERISHES PERISHING)

Ge 6: 17 Everything on earth will *p*.
47: 19 Why should we *p* before your eyes
Ex 19: 21 the LORD and many of them *p*.
Lev 26: 38 You will *p* among the nations;
Dt 4: 26 you this day that you will quickly *p*
11: 17 you will soon *p* from the good land
28: 22 which will plague you until you *p*.
32: 25 men and young women will *p*,
Jos 23: 13 until you *p* from this good land,
23: 16 you will quickly *p* from the good
Jdg 5: 31 "So may all your enemies *p*,
1Sa 26: 10 or he will go into battle and *p*.
2Ki 9: 8 The whole house of Ahab will *p*.
Est 4: 14 you and your father's family will *p*.
4: 16 And if I *p*, I *p*."
Job 3: 3 "May the day of my birth *p*,
3: 11 "Why did I not *p* at birth,
4: 9 at the blast of his anger they *p*.
4: 20 unnoticed, they *p* forever.
6: 18 they go up into the wasteland and *p*
20: 7 he will *p* forever, like his own dung;
34: 15 all mankind would *p* together
36: 12 they will *p* by the sword
Ps 1: 6 but the way of the wicked will *p*.
9: 3 they stumble and *p* before you.
9: 18 nor the hope of the afflicted ever *p*.
10: 16 the nations will *p* from his land.
37: 20 But the wicked will *p*:
41: 5 When will he die and his name *p*?"
49: 10 the foolish and the senseless alike *p*
49: 12 he is like the beasts that *p*.
49: 20 is like the beasts that *p*.
68: 2 may the wicked *p* before God.
71: 13 May my accusers *p* in shame;
73: 27 Those who are far from you will *p*;
80: 16 at your rebuke your people *p*.
83: 17 may they *p* in disgrace.
92: 9 surely your enemies will *p*;
102: 26 They will *p*, but you remain;
Pr 11: 10 when the wicked *p*, there are
19: 9 and he who pours out lies will *p*.
21: 28 A false witness will *p*,
28: 28 when the wicked *p*, the righteous
Isa 1: 28 who forsake the LORD will *p*.
29: 14 the wisdom of the wise will *p*,

Isa 31: 3 both will *p* together.
41: 11 will be as nothing and *p*.
57: 1 The righteous *p*,
60: 12 that will not serve you will *p*;
Jer 6: 21 neighbors and friends will *p*.''
8: 14 and *p* there!
8: 14 our God has doomed us to *p*
10: 11 will *p* from the earth and
10: 15 their judgment comes, they will *p*.
14: 15 Those same prophets will *p*
16: 4 They will *p* by sword and famine,
27: 10 I will banish you and you will *p*.
27: 15 I will banish you and you will *p*,
40: 15 and the remnant of Judah to *p*?''
44: 12 They will all *p* in Egypt; they will
44: 27 the Jews in Egypt will *p* by sword
49: 10 relatives and neighbors will *p*,
51: 18 their judgment comes, they will *p*.
Eze 5: 12 or *p* by famine inside you;
Jnh 1: 6 notice of us, and we will not *p*.''
3: 9 anger so that we will not *p*.''
Zec 11: 9 the dying die, and the perishing *p*.
13: 8 will be struck down and *p*;
Lk 13: 3 unless you repent, you too will all *p*
13: 5 unless you repent, you too will all *p*
21: 18 But not a hair of your head will *p*.
Jn 3: 16 whoever believes in him shall not *p*
10: 28 eternal life, and they shall never *p*;
11: 50 than that the whole nation *p*.''
Ac 8: 20 ''May your money *p* with you,
13: 41 wonder and *p*,
Ro 2: 12 apart from the law will also *p* apart
Col 2: 22 These are all destined to *p* with use,
2Th 2: 10 They *p* because they refused
Heb 1: 11 They will *p*, but you remain;
1Pe 1: 4 into an inheritance that can never *p*
2Pe 2: 12 and like beasts they too will *p*.
3: 9 not wanting anyone to *p*,

PERISHABLE (PERISH)

1Co 15: 42 The body that is sown is *p*,
15: 50 does the *p* inherit the imperishable.
15: 53 For the *p* must clothe itself
15: 54 When the *p* has been clothed
1Pe 1: 18 not with *p* things such
1: 23 not of *p* seed, but of imperishable,

PERISHED (PERISH)

Ge 7: 21 thing that moved on the earth *p*—
Nu 16: 33 and they *p* and were gone
Dt 2: 14 generation of fighting men had *p*
7: 20 who hide from you have *p*.
2Sa 1: 27 The weapons of war have *p*!''
Job 4: 7 Who, being innocent, has ever *p*?
Ps 9: 6 even the memory of them has *p*.
83: 10 who *p* at Endor
119: 92 I would have *p* in my affliction.
Jer 7: 28 Truth has *p*; it has vanished
12: 4 the animals and birds have *p*.
49: 7 Has counsel *p* from the prudent?
La 1: 19 *p* in the city
Mic 4: 9 Has your counselor *p*,

PERISHES (PERISH)

Job 4: 11 The lion *p* for lack of prey,
8: 13 so *p* the hope of the godless.
18: 17 of him *p* from the earth;
Pr 11: 7 a wicked man dies, his hope *p*;
1Pe 1: 7 which *p* even though refined by fire

PERISHING (PERISH)

Job 31: 19 if I have seen anyone *p* for lack
33: 18 his life from *p* by the sword.
Pr 31: 6 Give beer to those who are *p*,
Ecc 7: 15 man *p* in his righteousness,
Isa 27: 13 Those who were *p* in Assyria
Jer 44: 18 have been *p* by sword and famine.''
Zec 11: 9 Let the dying die, and the *p* perish.
1Co 1: 18 foolishness to those who are *p*,
2Co 2: 15 being saved and those who are *p*.
4: 3 it is veiled to those who are *p*.
2Th 2: 10 evil that deceives those who are *p*.

PERIZZITES

Ge 13: 7 The Canaanites and *P* were
15: 20 Kadmonites, Hittites, *P*, Rephaites
34: 30 a stench to the Canaanites and *P*,
Ex 3: 8 Amorites, *P*, Hivites and Jebusites.
3: 17 Amorites, *P*, Hivites and Jebusites
23: 23 *P*, Canaanites, Hivites
33: 2 Hittites, *P*, Hivites and Jebusites.
34: 11 Hittites, *P*, Hivites and Jebusites.
Dt 7: 1 Amorites, Canaanites, *P*,
20: 17 *P*, Hivites and Jebusites—
Jos 3: 10 Hittites, Hivites, *P*, Girgashites,
9: 1 *P*, Hivites and Jebusites)—
11: 3 *P* and Jebusites in the hill country;
12: 8 Canaanites, *P*, Hivites
17: 15 there in the land of the *P*
24: 11 *P*, Canaanites, Hittites, Girgashites
Jdg 1: 4 LORD gave the Canaanites and *P*
1: 5 to rout the Canaanites and *P*.
3: 5 Amorites, *P*, Hivites and Jebusites.
1Ki 9: 20 left from the Amorites, Hittites, *P*,
2Ch 8: 7 left from the Hittites, Amorites, *P*,
Ezr 9: 1 Hittites, *P*, Jebusites, Ammonites,
Ne 9: 8 *P*, Jebusites and Girgashites.

PERJURERS (PERJURY)

Mal 3: 5 and *p*, against those who defraud
1Ti 1: 10 for slave traders and liars and *p*—

PERJURY (PERJURERS)

Jer 7: 9 murder, commit adultery and *p*,

PERMANENT

Lev 25: 34 not be sold; it is their *p* possession
Jos 8: 28 and made it a *p* heap of ruins,
Jn 8: 35 a slave has no *p* place in the family,
Heb 7: 24 lives forever, he has a *p* priesthood.

PERMISSIBLE (PERMIT)

1Co 6: 12 ''Everything is *p* for me''—
6: 12 ''Everything is *p* for me''—
10: 23 ''Everything is *p*''—but not
10: 23 ''Everything is *p*''—but not

PERMISSION (PERMIT)

Jdg 11: 17 us *p* to go through your country,'
1Sa 20: 6 'David earnestly asked my *p*
20: 28 me for *p* to go to Bethlehem.
Ne 13: 6 Some time later I asked his *p*
Est 9: 13 ''give the Jews in Susa *p*
Isa 22: 16 you doing here and who gave you *p*
Da 1: 8 he asked the chief official for *p* not
Mk 5: 13 He gave them *p*, and the evil spirits
Lk 8: 32 go into them, and he gave them *p*.
Jn 19: 38 With Pilate's *p*, he came
Ac 21: 40 received the commander's *p*,
26: 1 ''You have *p* to speak for yourself.''

PERMIT (PERMISSIBLE PERMISSION PERMITS PERMITTED PERMITTING)

Ex 12: 23 and he will not *p* the destroyer
Hos 5: 4 ''Their deeds do not *p* them
Ac 24: 23 and *p* his friends to take care
1Ti 2: 12 I do not *p* a woman to teach

PERMITS (PERMIT)

Ecc 5: 12 *p* him no sleep.
1Co 16: 7 time with you, if the Lord *p*.

PERMITTED (PERMIT)

Ex 19: 13 or animal, he shall not be *p* to live.'
Dt 18: 14 the LORD your God has not *p* you
Mt 19: 8 Moses *p* you to divorce your wives
Mk 10: 4 Moses *p* a man to write a certificate
2Co 12: 4 things that man is not *p* to tell.

PERMITTING (PERMIT)

Heb 6: 3 And God *p*, we will do so.

PERPETUATE

Ps 45: 17 I will *p* your memory

PERPLEXED (PERPLEXITY)

Da 4: 19 called Belteshazzar) was greatly *p*
Lk 9: 7 And he was *p*, because some were
Ac 2: 12 and *p*, they asked one another,
2Co 4: 8 not crushed; *p*, but not in despair;
Gal 4: 20 because I am *p* about you! Tell me,

PERPLEXITY (PERPLEXED)

Lk 21: 25 be in anguish and *p* at the roaring

PERSECUTE (PERSECUTED PERSECUTING PERSECUTION PERSECUTIONS PERSECUTOR PERSECUTORS)

Dt 30: 7 your enemies who hate and *p* you.
Ps 9: 13 see how my enemies *p* me!
69: 26 For they *p* those you wound
119: 86 for men *p* me without cause.
119:157 Many are the foes who *p* me,
119:161 Rulers *p* me without cause,
Mt 5: 11 *p* you and falsely say all kinds
5: 44 and pray for those who *p* you,
Lk 11: 49 will kill and others they will *p*.'
21: 12 will lay hands on you and *p* you.
Jn 15: 20 they persecuted me, they will *p* you
Ac 7: 52 a prophet your fathers did not *p*?
9: 4 why do you *p* me?'' ''Who are you,
12: 1 to the church, intending to *p* them.
22: 7 Why do you *p* me?' '' 'Who are you
26: 11 went to foreign cities to *p* them.
26: 14 'Saul, Saul, why do you *p* me?
Ro 12: 14 Bless those who *p* you; bless

PERSECUTED (PERSECUTE)

Mt 5: 10 Blessed are those who are *p*
5: 12 same way they *p* the prophets who
10: 23 When you are *p* in one place,
24: 9 you will be handed over to be *p*
Jn 5: 16 on the Sabbath, the Jews *p* him.
15: 20 If they *p* me, they will persecute
Ac 22: 4 I *p* the followers of this Way
1Co 4: 12 when we are *p*, we endure it;
15: 9 because I *p* the church of God.
2Co 4: 9 in despair; *p*, but not abandoned;
Gal 1: 13 how intensely I *p* the church
1: 23 man who formerly *p* us is now
4: 29 in the ordinary way *p* the son born
5: 11 why am I still being *p*?
6: 12 is to avoid being *p* for the cross
1Th 3: 4 kept telling you that we would be *p*.
2Ti 3: 12 life in Christ Jesus will be *p*,
Heb 11: 37 destitute, *p* and mistreated—

PERSECUTING (PERSECUTE)

Ac 9: 5 whom you are *p*,'' he replied.
22: 8 whom you are *p*,' he replied.
26: 15 whom you are *p*,' the Lord replied.
Php 3: 6 a Pharisee; as for zeal, *p* the church

PERSECUTION (PERSECUTE)

Mt 13: 21 When trouble or *p* comes
Mk 4: 17 When trouble or *p* comes
Ac 8: 1 On that day a great *p* broke out
11: 19 scattered by the *p* in connection
13: 50 They stirred up *p* against Paul
Ro 8: 35 or hardship or *p* or famine
1Th 3: 7 *p* we were encouraged about you
Heb 10: 33 publicly exposed to insult and *p*;
Rev 2: 10 and you will suffer *p* for ten days.

PERSECUTIONS (PERSECUTE)

Mk 10: 30 and with them, *p*) and in the age
2Co 12: 10 in hardships, in *p*, in difficulties.
2Th 1: 4 faith in all the *p* and trials you are
2Ti 3: 11 and Lystra, the *p* I endured.
3: 11 love, endurance, *p*, sufferings—

PERSECUTOR (PERSECUTE)

1Ti 1: 13 and a *p* and a violent man,

PERSECUTORS (PERSECUTE)

Ps 119: 84 When will you punish my *p*?
Jer 15: 15 Avenge me on my *p*.
17: 18 Let my *p* be put to shame,
20: 11 so my *p* will stumble and not

PERSEVERANCE (PERSEVERE)

Ro 5: 3 we know that suffering produces *p*;
5: 4 *p*, character; and character, hope.
2Co 12: 12 were done among you with great *p*.
2Th 1: 4 churches we boast about your *p*
3: 5 into God's love and Christ's *p*.
Heb 12: 1 run with *p* the race marked out
Jas 1: 3 the testing of your faith develops *p*.
1: 4 *P* must finish its work
5: 11 You have heard of Job's *p*
2Pe 1: 6 *p*; and to *p*, godliness;
Rev 2: 2 your hard work and your *p*.

Rev 2: 19 and faith, your service and *p*,

PERSEVERE (PERSEVERANCE PERSEVERED PERSEVERES PERSEVERING)

1Ti 4: 16 *P* in them, because if you do,
Heb 10: 36 You need to *p* so that

PERSEVERED (PERSEVERE)

Heb 11: 27 he *p* because he saw him who is
Jas 5: 11 consider blessed those who have *p*.
Rev 2: 3 You have *p* and have endured

PERSEVERES (PERSEVERE)

1Co 13: 7 trusts, always hopes, always *p*.
Jas 1: 12 Blessed is the man who *p*

PERSEVERING (PERSEVERE)

Lk 8: 15 retain it, and by *p* produce a crop.

PERSIA (PERSIAN PERSIANS)

2Ch 36: 20 the kingdom of *P* came to power.
36: 22 In the first year of Cyrus king of *P*,
36: 22 the heart of Cyrus king of *P*
36: 23 "This is what Cyrus king of *P* says:
Ezr 1: 1 In the first year of Cyrus king of *P*,
1: 1 the heart of Cyrus king of *P*
1: 2 "This is what Cyrus king of *P* says:
1: 8 Cyrus king of *P* had them brought
3: 7 as authorized by Cyrus king of *P*.
4: 3 the king of *P*, commanded us."
4: 5 reign of Cyrus king of *P*
4: 5 to the reign of Darius king of *P*.
4: 7 in the days of Artaxerxes king of *P*,
4: 9 *P*, Erech and Babylon,
4: 24 of the reign of Darius king of *P*.
6: 14 Darius and Artaxerxes, kings of *P*.
7: 1 the reign of Artaxerxes king of *P*,
9: 9 in the sight of the kings of *P*:
Est 1: 3 The military leaders of *P*
1: 14 of *P* and Media who had special
1: 19 and let it be written in the laws of *P*
10: 2 of the kings of Media and *P*?
Eze 27: 10 " 'Men of *P*, Lydia and Put
38: 5 *P*, Cush and Put will be with them,
Da 8: 20 the kings of Media and *P*.
10: 1 In the third year of Cyrus king of *P*,
10: 13 there with the king of *P*.
10: 20 to fight against the prince of *P*,
11: 2 Three more kings will appear in *P*,

PERSIAN (PERSIA)

Ne 12: 22 in the reign of Darius the *P*.
Est 1: 18 very day the *P* and Median women
Da 6: 28 and the reign of Cyrus the *P*.
10: 13 of the *P* kingdom resisted me

PERSIANS (PERSIA)

Da 5: 28 and given to the Medes and *P*."
6: 8 with the laws of the Medes and *P*,
6: 12 with the laws of the Medes and *P*,
6: 15 law of the Medes and *P* no decree

PERSIS

Ro 16: 12 my dear friend *P*, another woman

PERSIST (PERSISTED PERSISTENCE PERSISTS)

Dt 29: 19 though I *p* in going my own way."
1Sa 12: 25 Yet if you *p* in doing evil, both you
2Ki 17: 34 To this day they *p*
Isa 1: 5 Why do you *p* in rebellion?
Ro 11: 23 And if they do not *p* in unbelief,

PERSISTED (PERSIST)

2Ki 2: 17 they *p* until he was too ashamed
17: 22 The Israelites *p* in all the sins
17: 40 but *p* in their former practices.

PERSISTENCE (PERSIST)

Lk 11: 8 of the man's *p* he will get up
Ro 2: 7 To those who by *p*

PERSISTS (PERSIST)

Dt 25: 8 If he *p* in saying, "I do not want

PERSPIRE

Eze 44: 18 wear anything that makes them *p*.

PERSUADE (PERSUADED PERSUADING PERSUASION PERSUASIVE)

Jdg 19: 3 went to her to *p* her to return.
2Ki 18: 30 Do not let Hezekiah *p* you to trust
Isa 36: 15 Do not let Hezekiah *p* you to trust
Ac 18: 4 trying to *p* Jews and Greeks.
26: 28 in such a short time you can *p* me
2Co 5: 11 is to fear the Lord, we try to *p* men.

PERSUADED (PERSUADE)

Jdg 19: 7 his father-in-law *p* him,
Pr 25: 15 Through patience a ruler can be *p*,
Jer 28: 15 yet you have *p* this nation to trust
Eze 14: 9 I the LORD have *p* that prophet,
14: 9 " 'And if the prophet is *p* to utter
Mt 27: 20 and the elders *p* the crowd to ask
Lk 20: 6 they are *p* that John was a prophet
Ac 5: 40 His speech *p* them.
6: 11 they secretly *p* some men to say,
16: 15 And she *p* us.
17: 4 Some of the Jews were *p*
Ro 4: 21 being fully *p* that God had power
2Ti 1: 5 and, I am *p*, now lives in you also.

PERSUADING (PERSUADE)

Ac 18: 13 "is *p* the people to worship God

PERSUASION (PERSUADE)

Gal 5: 8 That kind of *p* does not come

PERSUASIVE (PERSUADE)

Pr 7: 21 With *p* words she led him astray;
1Co 2: 4 not with wise and *p* words,

PERUDA

Ezr 2: 55 Hassophereth, *P*, Jaala, Darkon,

PERVERSE (PERVERT)

Dt 32: 20 for they are a *p* generation,
1Sa 20: 30 son of a *p* and rebellious woman!
Ps 101: 4 Men of *p* heart shall be far from me
Pr 2: 12 from men whose words are *p*,
3: 32 for the LORD detests a *p* man
8: 8 none of them is crooked or *p*.
8: 13 evil behavior and *p* speech.
10: 31 but a *p* tongue will be cut out.
10: 32 of the wicked only what is *p*.
11: 20 The LORD detests men of *p* heart
16: 28 A *p* man stirs up dissension,
17: 20 A man of *p* heart does not prosper;
19: 1 than a fool whose lips are *p*.
28: 6 than a rich man whose ways are *p*.
28: 18 whose ways are *p* will suddenly
Mt 17: 17 "O unbelieving and *p* generation,"
Lk 9: 41 "O unbelieving and *p* generation,"

PERVERSENESS (PERVERT)

Pr 2: 14 and rejoice in the *p* of evil,

PERVERSION (PERVERT)

Lev 18: 23 sexual relations with it; that is a *p*.
20: 12 What they have done is a *p*;
Ro 1: 27 the due penalty for their *p*.
Jude : 7 up to sexual immorality and *p*.

PERVERSITY (PERVERT)

Pr 4: 24 Put away *p* from your mouth;
16: 30 with his eye is plotting *p*;

PERVERT (PERVERSE PERVERSENESS PERVERSION PERVERSITY PERVERTED PERVERTING PERVERTS)

Ex 23: 2 do not *p* justice by siding
Lev 19: 15 " 'Do not *p* justice; do not show
Dt 16: 19 Do not *p* justice or show partiality
Job 8: 3 Does God *p* justice?
8: 3 Does the Almighty *p* what is right?
34: 12 that the Almighty would *p* justice.
Pr 17: 23 to *p* the course of justice.
Gal 1: 7 are trying to *p* the gospel of Christ.

PERVERTED (PERVERT)

1Sa 8: 3 and accepted bribes and *p* justice.
Job 33: 27 'I sinned, and *p* what was right,
Jer 3: 21 because they have *p* their ways
Hab 1: 4 so that justice is *p*.

PERVERTING (PERVERT)

Ac 13: 10 you never stop *p* the right ways

PERVERTS (PERVERT)

1Ti 1: 10 for murderers, for adulterers and *p*,

PESTILENCE (PESTILENCES)

Dt 32: 24 consuming *p* and deadly plague;
Ps 91: 3 and from the deadly *p*.
91: 6 nor the *p* that stalks in the darkness
Hab 3: 5 *p* followed his steps.

PESTILENCES (PESTILENCE)

Lk 21: 11 famines and *p* in various places,

PESTLE

Pr 27: 22 grinding him like grain with a *p*,

PESTS

Mal 3: 11 will prevent *p* from devouring your

PET

Job 41: 5 Can you make a *p* of him like a bird

PETER (PETER'S SIMON PETER)

Mt 4: 18 Simon called *P* and his brother
10: 2 Simon (who is called *P*)
14: 28 "Lord, if it's you," *P* replied,
14: 29 Then *P* got down out of the boat
15: 15 *P* said, "Explain the parable to us."
16: 18 And I tell you that you are *P*,
16: 22 *P* took him aside and began
16: 23 Jesus turned and said to *P*,
17: 1 six days Jesus took with him *P*,
17: 4 *P* said to Jesus, "Lord, it is good
17: 24 of the two-drachma tax came to *P*
17: 25 When *P* came into the house,
17: 26 "From others," *P* answered.
18: 21 Then *P* came to Jesus and asked,
19: 27 *P* answered him, "We have left
26: 33 *P* replied, "Even if all fall away
26: 35 *P* declared, "Even if I have to die
26: 37 He took *P* and the two sons
26: 40 with me for one hour?" he asked *P*.
26: 58 But *P* followed him at a distance,
26: 69 *P* was sitting out in the courtyard,
26: 73 those standing there went up to *P*
26: 75 *P* remembered the word Jesus had
Mk 3: 16 (to whom he gave the name *P*);
5: 37 not let anyone follow him except *P*,
8: 29 *P* answered, "You are the Christ."
8: 32 and *P* took him aside and began
8: 33 at his disciples, he rebuked *P*.
9: 2 After six days Jesus took *P*,
9: 5 *P* said to Jesus, "Rabbi, it is good
10: 28 *P* said to him, "We have left
11: 21 *P* remembered and said to Jesus,
13: 3 *P*, James, John and Andrew asked
14: 29 *P* declared, "Even if all fall away,
14: 31 But *P* insisted emphatically,
14: 33 He took *P*, James and John
14: 37 he said to *P*, "are you asleep?
14: 54 *P* followed him at a distance,
14: 66 *P* was below in the courtyard,
14: 67 When she saw *P* warming himself,
14: 70 those standing near said to *P*,
14: 72 *P* remembered the word Jesus had
16: 7 But go, tell his disciples and *P*,
Lk 6: 14 Simon (whom he named *P*),
8: 45 When they all denied it, *P* said,
8: 51 go in with him except *P*,
9: 20 *P* answered, "The Christ of God."
9: 28 after Jesus said this, he took *P*,
9: 32 *P* and his companions were very
9: 33 the men were leaving Jesus, *P* said
12: 41 *P* asked, "Lord, are you telling this
18: 28 *P* said to him, "We have left all we
22: 8 Jesus sent *P* and John, saying,
22: 34 Jesus answered, "I tell you, *P*,
22: 54 *P* followed at a distance.
22: 55 and had sat down together, *P* sat
22: 58 "Man, I am not!" *P* replied.
22: 60 *P* replied, "Man, I don't know
22: 61 *P* remembered the word the Lord
22: 61 turned and looked straight at *P*.
24: 12 *P*, however, got up and ran
Jn 1: 42 when translated, is *P*).
1: 44 Philip, like Andrew and *P*,

Jn 13: 8 said *P*, "you shall never wash my
13: 37 *P* asked, "Lord, why can't I follow
18: 11 Jesus commanded *P*, "Put your
18: 16 girl on duty there and brought *P* in.
18: 16 *P* had to wait outside at the door.
18: 17 the girl at the door asked *P*.
18: 18 *P* also was standing with them,
18: 26 of the man whose ear *P* had cut off,
18: 27 olive grove?" Again *P* denied it,
20: 3 So *P* and the other disciple started
20: 4 but the other disciple outran *P*
21: 7 whom Jesus loved said to *P*,
21: 17 *P* was hurt because Jesus asked
21: 19 by which *P* would glorify God.
21: 20 *P* turned and saw that the disciple
21: 21 When *P* saw him, he asked, "Lord,
Ac 1: 13 Those present were *P*, John,
1: 15 In those days *P* stood up
1: 20 said *P*, "it is written in the book
2: 14 Then *P* stood up with the Eleven,
2: 37 said to *P* and the other apostles,
2: 38 what shall we do?" *P* replied,
3: 1 One day *P* and John were going up
3: 3 When he saw *P* and John about
3: 4 Then *P* said, "Look at us!"
3: 4 *P* looked straight at him,
3: 6 *P* said, "Silver or gold I do not have
3: 11 While the beggar held on to *P*
3: 12 When *P* saw this, he said to them:
4: 1 and the Sadducees came up to *P*
4: 3 They seized *P* and John, and
4: 7 They had *P* and John brought
4: 8 Then *P*, filled with the Holy Spirit,
4: 13 When they saw the courage of *P*
4: 19 But *P* and John replied, "Judge
4: 23 *P* and John went back
5: 3 *P* said, "Ananias, how is it that
5: 8 *P* asked her, "Tell me, is this
5: 9 *P* said to her, "How could you
5: 29 *P* and the other apostles replied:
8: 14 they sent *P* and John to them.
8: 17 *P* and John placed their hands
8: 20 *P* answered: "May your money
8: 25 *P* and John returned to Jerusalem,
9: 32 As *P* traveled about the country,
9: 34 *P* said to him, "Jesus Christ heals
9: 38 the disciples heard that *P* was
9: 39 come at once!" *P* went with them,
9: 40 her eyes, and seeing *P* she sat up.
9: 40 *P* sent them all out of the room;
9: 43 *P* stayed in Joppa for some time
10: 5 man named Simon who is called *P*.
10: 9 *P* went up on the roof to pray.
10: 13 Then a voice told him, "Get up, *P*.
10: 14 "Surely not, Lord!" *P* replied.
10: 17 While *P* was wondering about
10: 18 was known as *P* was staying there.
10: 19 While *P* was still thinking about
10: 21 *P* went down and said to the men,
10: 23 The next day *P* started out
10: 23 *P* invited the men into the house
10: 25 As *P* entered the house, Cornelius
10: 26 But *P* made him get up.
10: 27 *P* went inside and found a large
10: 32 to Joppa for Simon who is called *P*,
10: 34 *P* began to speak: "I now realize
10: 44 While *P* was still speaking these
10: 45 with *P* were astonished that the gift
10: 46 *P* said, "Can anyone keep these
10: 48 they asked *P* to stay with them
11: 2 So when *P* went up to Jerusalem,
11: 4 *P* began and explained everything
11: 7 a voice telling me, 'Get up, *P*.
11: 13 to Joppa for Simon who is called *P*.
12: 3 he proceeded to seize *P* also.
12: 5 So *P* was kept in prison,
12: 6 *P* was sleeping between two
12: 7 He struck *P* on the side
12: 8 And *P* did so.
12: 9 *P* followed him out of the prison,
12: 11 Then *P* came to himself and said,
12: 13 *P* knocked at the outer entrance,
12: 14 "*P* is at the door!" "You're out
12: 16 But *P* kept on knocking,
12: 17 *P* motioned with his hand for them
12: 18 What could have happened to *P*?"
15: 7 *P* got up and addressed them:
1Co 15: 5 and that he appeared to *P*,
Gal 1: 18 Jerusalem to get acquainted with *P*
2: 7 as *P* had been given the task
2: 8 was at work in the ministry of *P*
2: 9 *P* and John, those reputed
2: 11 When *P* came to Antioch,
2: 14 I said to *P* in front of them all,
1Pe 1: 1 *P*, an apostle of Jesus Christ,

PETER'S (PETER)

Mt 8: 14 When Jesus came into *P* house,
8: 14 he saw *P* mother-in-law lying
Jn 1: 40 Andrew, Simon *P* brother,
6: 8 Andrew, Simon *P* brother,
Ac 5: 15 so that at least *P* shadow might fall
12: 7 and the chains fell off *P* wrists.
12: 14 When she recognized *P* voice,

PETHAHIAH

1Ch 24: 16 the nineteenth to *P*, the twentieth
Ezr 10: 23 Kelaiah (that is Kelita), *P*,
Ne 9: 5 Hodiah, Shebaniah and *P*— said:
11: 24 *P* son of Meshezabel, one

PETHOR

Nu 22: 5 who was at *P*, near the River,
Dt 23: 4 from *P* in Aram Naharaim

PETHUEL

Joel 1: 1 LORD that came to Joel son of *P*.

PETITION (PETITIONED PETITIONS)

1Ch 16: 4 to make *p*, to give thanks,
Est 5: 6 what is your *p*? It will be given you.
5: 7 "My *p* and my request is this:
5: 8 if it pleases the king to grant my *p*
7: 2 "Queen Esther, what is your *p*?
7: 3 grant me my life—this is my *p*.
9: 12 what is your *p*? It will be given you.
Jer 7: 16 nor offer any plea or *p* for them;
11: 14 nor offer any plea or *p* for them,
36: 7 Perhaps they will bring their *p*
37: 20 Let me bring my *p* before you:
42: 2 "Please hear our *p* and pray
42: 9 you sent me to present your *p*,
Da 9: 3 pleaded with him in prayer and *p*,
Ac 23: 15 the Sanhedrin *p* the commander
Php 4: 6 by prayer and *p*, with thanksgiving,

PETITIONED (PETITION)

Ezr 8: 23 we fasted and *p* our God about this,
Ac 25: 24 Jewish community has *p* me about

PETITIONS (PETITION)

Da 9: 17 hear the prayers and *p*
Heb 5: 7 he offered up prayers and *p*

PEULLETHAI

1Ch 26: 5 the seventh and *P* the eighth.

PHANTOM

Ps 39: 6 Man is a mere *p* as he goes to

PHANUEL

Lk 2: 36 the daughter of *P*, of the tribe

PHARAOH (PHARAOH'S)

Ge 12: 15 her to *P*, and she was taken
12: 17 inflicted serious diseases on *P*
12: 18 So *P* summoned Abram.
12: 20 Then *P* gave orders about Abram
40: 2 *P* was angry with his two officials,
40: 13 Within three days *P* will lift up
40: 14 mention me to *P* and get me out
40: 17 kinds of baked goods for *P*,
40: 19 Within three days *P* will lift
41: 1 years had passed, *P* had a dream:
41: 4 Then *P* woke up.
41: 7 *P* woke up; it had been a dream.
41: 8 *P* told them his dreams,
41: 9 Then the chief cupbearer said to *P*,
41: 10 *P* was once angry with his servants,
41: 14 So *P* sent for Joseph, and he was
41: 14 his clothes, he came before *P*.
41: 15 *P* said to Joseph, "I had a dream,
41: 16 I cannot do it," Joseph replied to *P*,
41: 16 "but God will give *P* the answer he
41: 17 *P* said to Joseph, "In my dream I
41: 25 Joseph said to *P*, "The dreams
Ge 41: 25 revealed to *P* what he is about
41: 25 "The dreams of *P* are one
41: 28 to *P*: God has shown *P* what he is
41: 32 reason the dream was given to *P*
41: 33 And now let *P* look for a discerning
41: 34 Let *P* appoint commissioners
41: 35 the grain under the authority of *P*,
41: 37 The plan seemed good to *P*
41: 38 So *P* asked them, "Can we find
41: 39 of God?" Then *P* said to Joseph,
41: 41 *P* said to Joseph, "I hereby put you
41: 42 Then *P* took his signet ring
41: 44 Then *P* said to Joseph, "I am *P*,
41: 45 *P* gave Joseph the name
41: 46 the service of *P* king of Egypt.
41: 55 Then *P* told all the Egyptians,
41: 55 the people cried to *P* for food.
42: 15 will be tested: As surely as *P* lives,
42: 16 as surely as *P* lives, you are spies!"
44: 18 though you are equal to *P* himself.
45: 8 He made me father to *P*, lord
45: 16 *P* and all his officials were pleased.
45: 17 *P* said to Joseph, "Tell your
45: 21 them carts, as *P* had commanded,
46: 5 wives in the carts that *P* had sent
46: 31 and speak to *P* and will say to him,
46: 33 When *P* calls you in and asks,
47: 1 went and told *P*, "My father
47: 2 and presented them before *P*.
47: 3 *P* asked the brothers, "What is
47: 3 they replied to *P*, "just
47: 5 *P* said to Joseph, "Your father
47: 7 After Jacob blessed *P*,
47: 7 and presented him before *P*.
47: 8 *P* asked him, "How old are you?"
47: 9 old are you?" And Jacob said to *P*,
47: 10 Then Jacob blessed *P* and went out
47: 11 district of Rameses, as *P* directed.
47: 19 our land will be in bondage to *P*.
47: 20 bought all the land in Egypt for *P*.
47: 22 a regular allotment from *P*
47: 22 from the allotment *P* gave them.
47: 23 and your land today for *P*,
47: 24 comes in, give a fifth of it to *P*.
47: 25 we will be in bondage to *P*."
47: 26 a fifth of the produce belongs to *P*.
50: 4 in your eyes, speak to *P* for me.
50: 6 *P* said, "Go up and bury your
Ex 1: 11 and Rameses as store cities for *P*.
1: 19 The midwives answered *P*,
1: 22 *P* gave this order to all his people:
2: 15 When *P* heard of this, he tried
2: 15 but Moses fled from *P*
3: 10 I am sending you to *P*
3: 11 go to *P* and bring the Israelites out
4: 21 before *P* all the wonders I have
4: 22 to *P*, 'This is what the LORD says:
5: 1 and Aaron went to *P* and said,
5: 2 *P* said, "Who is the LORD,
5: 5 back to your work!" Then *P* said,
5: 6 That same day *P* gave this order
5: 10 "This is what *P* says: 'I will not give
5: 15 foremen went and appealed to *P*:
5: 17 *P* said, "Lazy, that's what you are
5: 20 When they left *P*, they found
5: 21 You have made us a stench to *P*
5: 23 Ever since I went to *P* to speak
6: 1 you will see what I will do to *P*:
6: 11 tell *P* king of Egypt
6: 12 why would *P* listen to me,
6: 13 about the Israelites and *P* king
6: 27 were the ones who spoke to *P* king
6: 29 Tell *P* king of Egypt everything I
6: 30 why would *P* listen to me?"
7: 1 See, I have made you like God to *P*
7: 2 and your brother Aaron is to tell *P*
7: 7 eighty-three when they spoke to *P*.
7: 9 and throw it down before *P*,'
7: 9 "When *P* says to you, 'Perform
7: 10 and Aaron went to *P* and did just
7: 10 staff down in front of *P*
7: 11 *P* then summoned wise men
7: 15 Go to *P* in the morning
7: 20 staff in the presence of *P*
8: 1 the LORD said to Moses, "Go to *P*
8: 8 *P* summoned Moses and Aaron
8: 9 Moses said to *P*, "I leave
8: 10 "Tomorrow," *P* said.

PHARAOH'S (PHARAOH)

PHARISEE (PHARISEE'S PHARISEES)

PHARISEE'S (PHARISEE)

PHARISEES (PHARISEE)

PHARPAR
2Ki 5:12 and *P*, the rivers of Damascus,

PHICOL
Ge 21:22 *P* the commander of his forces said
21:32 and *P* the commander
26:26 and *P* the commander of his forces.

PHILADELPHIA
Rev 1:11 Thyatira, Sardis, *P* and Laodicea."
3:7 the angel of the church in *P* write:

PHILEMON
Phm :1 To *P* our dear friend and fellow

PHILETUS
2Ti 2:17 them are Hymenaeus and *P*,

PHILIP (PHILIP'S)
Mt 10:3 brother John; *P* and Bartholomew;
Mk 3:18 Andrew, *P*, Bartholomew,
Lk 3:1 his brother *P* tetrarch of Iturea
6:14 James, John, *P*, Bartholomew,
Jn 1:43 Finding *P*, he said to him,
1:44 *P*, like Andrew and Peter,
1:45 *P* found Nathanael and told him,
1:46 "Come and see," said *P*.
1:48 tree before *P* called you."
6:5 to *P*, "Where shall we buy bread
6:7 *P* answered him, "Eight months'
12:21 They came to *P*, who was
12:22 Andrew and *P* in turn told Jesus.
12:22 *P* went to tell Andrew; Andrew
14:0 *P* said, "Lord, show us the Father
14:9 answered: "Don't you know me, *P*,
Ac 1:13 James and Andrew; *P* and Thomas,
6:5 also *P*, Procorus, Nicanor, Timon,
8:5 *P* went down to a city in Samaria
8:6 When the crowds heard *P*
8:12 But when they believed *P*
8:13 And he followed *P* everywhere,
8:26 Now an angel of the Lord said to *P*,
8:29 The Spirit told *P*, "Go
8:30 Then *P* ran up to the chariot
8:30 what you are reading?" *P* asked.
8:31 So he invited *P* to come up
8:34 The eunuch asked *P*, "Tell me,
8:35 *P* began with that very passage
8:38 Then both *P* and the eunuch went
8:38 into the water and *P* baptized him.
8:39 of the Lord suddenly took *P* away,
8:40 *P*, however, appeared at Azotus
21:8 at the house of *P* the evangelist,

PHILIP'S (PHILIP)
Mt 14:3 his brother *P* wife,
Mk 6:17 his brother *P* wife, whom he had

PHILIPPI (PHILIPPIANS)
Ac 16:12 From there we traveled to *P*,
20:6 we sailed from *P* after the Feast
Php 1:1 To all the saints in Christ Jesus at *P*
1Th 2:2 suffered and been insulted in *P*,

PHILIPPIANS (PHILIPPI)
Php 4:15 Moreover, as you *P* know,

PHILISTIA (PHILISTINE)
Ex 15:14 anguish will grip the people of *P*.
Ps 60:8 over *P* I shout in triumph."
83:7 *P*, with the people of Tyre.
87:4 *P* too, and Tyre, along with Cush—
108:9 over *P* I shout in triumph."
Isa 11:14 down on the slopes of *P* to the west
Joel 3:4 and Sidon and all you regions of *P*?
Am 6:2 and then go down to Gath in *P*.

PHILISTINE (PHILISTIA PHILISTINE'S PHILISTINES)
Ex 13:17 on the road through the *P* country,
Jos 13:3 of the five *P* rulers in Gaza,
Jdg 14:1 and saw there a young *P* woman.
14:2 "I have seen a *P* woman in Timnah;
1Sa 6:1 been in *P* territory seven months,
6:4 to the number of the *P* rulers,
6:18 the number of *P* towns belonging
10:5 where there is a *P* outpost.
13:3 Jonathan attacked the *P* outpost
13:4 "Saul has attacked the *P* outpost,
13:17 the *P* camp in three detachments.
14:1 let's go over to the *P* outpost
14:4 to reach the *P* outpost was a cliff;
14:11 themselves to the *P* outpost.
14:19 in the *P* camp increased more
17:4 from Gath, came out of the *P* camp
17:8 Am I not a *P*, and are you not
17:10 *P* said, "This day I defy the ranks
17:16 forty days the *P* came forward
17:23 the *P* champion from Gath,
17:26 done for the man who kills this *P*
17:26 is this uncircumcised *P* that he
17:32 heart on account of this *P*;
17:33 able to go out against this *P*
17:36 this uncircumcised *P* will be like
17:37 me from the hand of this *P*."
17:40 in his hand, approached the *P*.
17:41 the *P*, with his shield bearer
17:43 the *P* cursed David by his gods.
17:45 David said to the *P*, "You come
17:46 of the *P* army to the birds of the air
17:48 As the *P* moved closer
17:49 and struck the *P* on the forehead.
17:50 in his hand he struck down the *P*
17:50 triumphed over the *P* with a sling
17:55 David going out to meet the *P*,
17:57 David returned from killing the *P*,
18:6 home after David had killed the *P*,
18:25 bride than a hundred *P* foreskins,
18:30 The *P* commanders continued
19:5 in his hands when he killed the *P*.
21:9 "The sword of Goliath the *P*,
22:10 and the sword of Goliath the *P*."
23:3 go to Keilah against the *P* forces!"
27:7 David lived in *P* territory a year
27:11 as long as he lived in *P* territory.
28:5 When Saul saw the *P* army,
29:2 As the *P* rulers marched
29:4 But the *P* commanders were angry
29:7 do nothing to displease the *P* rulers
29:9 the *P* commanders have said,
2Sa 3:14 price of a hundred *P* foreskins."
5:24 in front of you to strike the *P* army
21:17 he struck the *P* down and killed
23:14 the *P* garrison was at Bethlehem.
23:16 broke through the *P* lines,
1Ki 15:27 him down at Gibbethon, a *P* town,
16:15 near Gibbethon, a *P* town.
1Ch 11:16 the *P* garrison was at Bethlehem.
11:18 broke through the *P* lines,
14:15 in front of you to strike the *P* army
14:16 and they struck down the *P* army,

PHILISTINE'S (PHILISTINE)
1Sa 17:11 On hearing the *P* words, Saul
17:51 He took hold of the *P* sword
17:54 David took the *P* head
17:54 and he put the *P* weapons
17:57 with David still holding the *P* head.

PHILISTINES (PHILISTINE)
Ge 10:14 Casluhites (from whom the *P* came
21:32 returned to the land of the *P*.
21:34 in the land of the *P* for a long time.
26:1 went to Abimelech king of the *P*
26:8 Abimelech king of the *P* looked
26:14 and servants that the *P* envied him.
26:15 the *P* stopped up, filling them
26:18 which the *P* had stopped up
Ex 23:31 Sea to the Sea of the *P*,
Jos 13:2 all the regions of the *P*
Jdg 3:3 rulers of the *P*, all the Canaanites,
3:31 struck down six hundred *P*
10:6 Ammonites and the gods of the *P*.
10:7 them into the hands of the *P*
10:11 Ammonites, the *P*, the Sidonians,
13:1 the hands of the *P* for forty years.
13:5 of Israel from the hands of the *P*."
14:3 go to the uncircumcised *P*
14:4 an occasion to confront the *P*;
15:3 a right to get even with the *P*;
15:5 loose in the standing grain of the *P*.
15:6 So the *P* went up and burned her
15:6 When the *P* asked, "Who did this
15:9 The *P* went up and camped
15:11 you realize that the *P* are rulers
15:12 and hand you over to the *P*."
Jdg 15:14 the *P* came toward him shouting.
15:20 years in the days of the *P*.
16:5 The rulers of the *P* went to her
16:8 of the *P* brought her seven fresh
16:9 "Samson, the *P* are upon you!"
16:12 "Samson, the *P* are upon you!"
16:14 "Samson, the *P* are upon you!"
16:18 So the rulers of the *P* returned
16:18 she sent word to the rulers of the *P*,
16:20 "Samson, the *P* are upon you!"
16:21 *P* seized him, gouged out his eyes
16:23 Now the rulers of the *P* assembled
16:27 all the rulers of the *P* were there,
16:28 revenge on the *P* for my two eyes."
16:30 said, "Let me die with the *P*!"
1Sa 4:1 at Ebenezer, and the *P* at Aphek.
4:1 out to fight against the *P*.
4:2 Israel was defeated by the *P*,
4:2 The *P* deployed their forces
4:3 defeat upon us today before the *P*?
4:6 Hearing the uproar, the *P* asked,
4:7 into the camp, the *P* were afraid.
4:9 *P*! Be men, or you will be subject
4:10 and fight!" So the *P* fought,
4:17 "Israel fled before the *P*,
5:1 After the *P* had captured the ark
5:8 together all the rulers of the *P*
5:11 together all the rulers of the *P*
6:2 the *P* called for the priests
6:4 The *P* asked, "What guilt offering
6:12 The rulers of the *P* followed them
6:16 The five rulers of the *P* saw all this
6:17 are the gold tumors the *P* sent
6:21 "The *P* have returned the ark
7:3 out of the hand of the *P*."
7:7 When the *P* heard that Israel had
7:7 the rulers of the *P* came up
7:7 they were afraid because of the *P*.
7:8 us from the hand of the *P*."
7:10 the *P* drew near to engage Israel
7:10 with loud thunder against the *P*
7:11 out of Mizpah and pursued the *P*,
7:13 So the *P* were subdued
7:13 of the LORD was against the *P*.
7:14 territory from the power of the *P*.
7:14 to Gath that the *P* had captured
9:16 people from the hand of the *P*.
12:9 and into the hands of the *P*
13:3 at Geba, and the *P* heard about it.
13:4 has become a stench to the *P*."
13:5 The *P* assembled to fight Israel,
13:11 and that the *P* were assembling
13:12 the *P* will come down against me
13:16 while the *P* camped at Micmash.
13:19 because the *P* had said, "Otherwise
13:20 to the *P* to have their plowshares,
13:23 a detachment of *P* had gone out
14:11 "Look!" said the *P*.
14:13 The *P* fell before Jonathan,
14:20 They found the *P* in total confusion
14:21 had previously been with the *P*
14:22 of Ephraim heard that the *P* were
14:30 the slaughter of the *P* have been
14:31 struck down the *P* from Micmash
14:36 Let us go down after the *P* by night
14:37 "Shall I go down after the *P*?
14:46 Then Saul stopped pursuing the *P*,
14:47 the kings of Zobah, and the *P*.
14:52 there was bitter war with the *P*,
17:1 the *P* gathered their forces for war
17:2 up their battle line to meet the *P*.
17:3 The *P* occupied one hill
17:19 of Elah, fighting against the *P*."
17:21 the *P* were drawing up their lines
17:51 When the *P* saw that their hero was
17:52 and pursued the *P* to the entrance
17:53 returned from chasing the *P*,
18:17 Let the *P* do that!" But David said
18:21 hand of the *P* may be against him."
18:25 fall by the hands of the *P*.
18:27 went out and killed two hundred *P*.
19:8 David went out and fought the *P*.
23:1 the *P* are fighting against Keilah
23:2 Go, attack the *P* and save Keilah."
23:2 "Shall I go and attack these *P*?"
23:4 to give the *P* into your hand."
23:5 He inflicted heavy losses on the *P*
23:5 fought the *P* and carried

1Sa 23: 27 The *P* are raiding the land.''
23: 28 of David and went to meet the *P*.
24: 1 returned from pursuing the *P*,
27: 1 is to escape to the land of the *P*.
28: 1 those days the *P* gathered their
28: 4 The *P* assembled and came
28: 15 ''The *P* are fighting against me,
28: 19 over both Israel and you to the *P*,
28: 19 over the army of Israel to the *P*.''
29: 1 The *P* gathered all their forces
29: 3 The commanders of the *P* asked,
29: 11 and the *P* went up to Jezreel.
29: 11 to go back to the land of the *P*,
30: 16 taken from the land of the *P*
31: 1 Now the *P* fought against Israel;
31: 2 The *P* pressed hard after Saul
31: 7 the *P* came and occupied them.
31: 8 when the *P* came to strip the dead,
31: 9 land of the *P* to proclaim the news
31: 11 of what the *P* had done to Saul,
2Sa 1: 20 lest the daughters of the *P* be glad,
3: 18 Israel from the hand of the *P*
5: 17 When the *P* heard that David had
5: 18 the *P* had come and spread out
5: 19 for I will surely hand the *P*
5: 19 ''Shall I go and attack the *P?*
5: 21 The *P* abandoned their idols there,
5: 22 Once more the *P* came up
5: 25 he struck down the *P* all the way
8: 1 David defeated the *P* and subdued
8: 1 from the control of the *P*.
8: 12 the Ammonites and the *P*,
19: 9 us from the hand of the *P*.
21: 12 Shan, where the *P* had hung them
21: 15 there was a battle between the *P*
21: 15 with his men to fight against the *P*,
21: 18 there was another battle with the *P*
21: 19 In another battle with the *P* at Gob
23: 9 when they taunted the *P* gathered
23: 10 and struck down the *P*
23: 11 When the *P* banded together
23: 12 He defended it and struck the *P*
23: 13 while a band of *P* was encamped
1Ki 4: 21 from the River to the land of the *P*,
2Ki 8: 2 in the land of the *P* seven years.
8: 3 back from the land of the *P*
18: 8 he defeated the *P*, as far as Gaza
1Ch 1: 12 Casluhites (from whom the *P* came
10: 1 Now the *P* fought against Israel;
10: 2 The *P* pressed hard after Saul
10: 7 the *P* came and occupied them.
10: 8 when the *P* came to strip the dead,
10: 9 land of the *P* to proclaim the news
10: 11 heard of everything the *P* had done
11: 13 *P* gathered there for battle.
11: 13 the troops fled from the *P*.
11: 14 They defended it and struck the *P*
11: 15 while a band of *P* was encamped
12: 19 his men did not help the *P* because,
12: 19 with the *P* to fight against Saul.
14: 8 When the *P* heard that David had
14: 9 *P* had come and raided the Valley
14: 10 ''Shall I go and attack the *P?*
14: 12 *P* had abandoned their gods there,
14: 13 Once more the *P* raided the valley;
18: 1 David defeated the *P* and subdued
18: 1 villages from the control of the *P*.
18: 11 the Ammonites and the *P*,
20: 4 and the *P* were subjugated.
20: 4 war broke out with the *P*, at Gezer.
20: 5 In another battle with the *P*,
2Ch 9: 26 from the River to the land of the *P*,
17: 11 Some *P* brought Jehoshaphat gifts
21: 16 Jehoram the hostility of the *P*
26: 6 He went to war against the *P*
26: 6 and elsewhere among the *P*.
26: 7 God helped him against the *P*
28: 18 while the *P* had raided towns
Isa 2: 6 they practice divination like the *P*
9: 12 from the east and *P* from the west
14: 29 died: Do not rejoice, all you *P*,
14: 31 Melt away, all you *P!*
Jer 25: 20 kings of the *P* (those of Ashkelon,
47: 1 the prophet concerning the *P*
47: 4 come to destroy all the *P*
47: 4 LORD is about to destroy the *P*,
Eze 16: 27 of the *P*, who were shocked
16: 57 and the daughters of the *P*—
25: 15 'Because the *P* acted in vengeance
25: 16 stretch out my hand against the *P*,
Am 1: 8 Ekron till the last of the *P* is dead,''
9: 7 the *P* from Caphtor
Ob : 19 the land of the *P*.
Zep 2: 5 O Canaan, land of the *P*.
Zec 9: 6 and I will cut off the pride of the *P*.

PHILOLOGUS

Ro 16: 15 Greet *P*, Julia, Nereus

PHILOSOPHER (PHILOSOPHY)

1Co 1: 20 Where is the *p* of this age?

PHILOSOPHERS (PHILOSOPHY)

Ac 17: 18 Stoic *p* began to dispute with him.

PHILOSOPHY (PHILOSOPHER PHILOSOPHERS)

Col 2: 8 through hollow and deceptive *p*,

PHINEHAS

Ex 6: 25 of Putiel, and she bore him *P*.
Nu 25: 7 When *P* son of Eleazar, the son
25: 11 said to Moses, ''*P* son of Eleazar,
31: 6 along with *P* son of Eleazar,
Jos 22: 13 the Israelites sent *P* son of Eleazar,
22: 30 When *P* the priest and the leaders
22: 31 And *P* son of Eleazar, the priest,
22: 32 Then *P* son of Eleazar, the priest,
24: 33 to his son *P* in the hill country
Jdg 20: 28 with *P* son of Eleazar, the son
1Sa 1: 3 where Hophni and *P*, the two sons
2: 34 Hophni and *P*, will be a sign to you
4: 4 And Eli's two sons, Hophni and *P*,
4: 11 and Eli's two sons, Hophni and *P*,
4: 17 Also your two sons, Hophni and *P*,
4: 19 His daughter-in-law, the wife of *P*,
14: 3 Ichabod's brother Ahitub son of *P*,
1Ch 6: 4 father of *P*, *P* the father of Abishua,
6: 50 Eleazar his son, *P* his son,
9: 20 In earlier times *P* son
Ezr 7: 5 the son of *P*, the son of Eleazar,
8: 2 of the descendants of *P*, Gershom;
8: 33 Eleazar son of *P* was with him,
Ps 106: 30 But *P* stood up and intervened,

PHLEGON

Ro 16: 14 Greet Asyncritus, *P*, Hermes,

PHOEBE

Ro 16: 1 I commend to you our sister *P*,

PHOENICIA

Isa 23: 11 has given an order concerning *P*
Mk 7: 26 was a Greek, born in Syrian *P*.
Ac 11: 19 with Stephen traveled as far as *P*,
15: 3 and as they traveled through *P*
21: 2 We found a ship crossing over to *P*,

PHOENIX

Ac 27: 12 hoping to reach *P* and winter there.

PHRYGIA

Ac 2: 10 Pontus and Asia, *P* and Pamphylia,
16: 6 traveled throughout the region of *P*
18: 23 the region of Galatia and *P*,

PHYGELUS

2Ti 1: 15 including *P* and Hermogenes.

PHYLACTERIES

Mt 23: 5 They make their *p* wide

PHYSICAL (PHYSICALLY)

Da 1: 4 young men without any *p* defect,
Ro 2: 28 merely outward and *p*.
Col 1: 22 by Christ's *p* body through death
1Ti 4: 8 For *p* training is of some value,
Jas 2: 16 but does nothing about his *p* needs,

PHYSICALLY (PHYSICAL)

Ro 2: 27 The one who is not circumcised *p*
1Co 5: 3 Even though I am not *p* present,

PHYSICIAN (PHYSICIANS)

Jer 8: 22 Is there no *p* there?
Lk 4: 23 will quote this proverb to me: '*P*,

PHYSICIANS (PHYSICIAN)

Ge 50: 2 Joseph directed the *p* in his service
50: 2 *p* embalmed him, taking a full forty
2Ch 16: 12 the LORD, but only from the *p*.
Job 13: 4 you are worthless *p*, all of you!

PI HAHIROTH

Ex 14: 2 to turn back and encamp near *P*,
14: 9 as they camped by the sea near *P*,
Nu 33: 7 They left Etham, turned back to *P*,
33: 8 They left *P* and passed through

PICK (PICKED PICKERS PICKS)

Lev 19: 10 or *p* up the grapes that have fallen.
27: 33 He must not *p* out the good
Dt 23: 25 you may *p* kernels with your hands
Ru 2: 2 and *p* up the leftover grain
2: 16 and leave them for her to *p* up,
1Ki 20: 33 and were quick to *p* up his word.
2Ki 5: 7 trying to *p* a quarrel with me!''
9: 25 ''*P* him up and throw him
9: 26 *p* him up and throw him
Ps 74: 3 *P* your way through these
80: 12 so that all who pass by *p* its grapes?
Isa 41: 16 them, the wind will *p* them up,
Eze 24: 5 take the *p* of the flock.
Jnh 1: 12 *P* me up and throw me into the sea
Mt 7: 16 Do people *p* grapes
12: 1 and began to *p* some heads of grain
Mk 2: 23 they began to *p* some heads
8: 19 basketfuls of pieces did you *p* up?''
8: 20 basketfuls of pieces did you *p* up?''
16: 18 they will *p* up snakes
Lk 6: 1 his disciples began to *p* some heads
6: 44 People do not *p* figs
Jn 5: 8 ''Get up! *P* up your mat and walk.''
5: 11 '*P* up your mat and walk.' ''
5: 12 is this fellow who told you to *p* it up

PICKED (PICK)

Jdg 1: 7 big toes cut off have *p* up scraps
4: 21 *p* up a tent peg and a hammer
1Sa 20: 38 The boy *p* up the arrow
2Sa 4: 4 His nurse *p* him up and fled,
1Ki 13: 29 So the prophet *p* up the body
17: 23 Elijah *p* up the child and carried
2Ki 2: 13 He *p* up the cloak that had fallen
2: 16 Spirit of the LORD has *p* him up
Eze 29: 5 and not be gathered or *p* up.
Na 2: 5 He summons his *p* troops,
Mt 14: 20 the disciples *p* up twelve basketfuls
15: 37 Afterward the disciples *p* up seven
27: 6 The chief priests *p* up the coins
Mk 6: 43 the disciples *p* up twelve basketfuls
8: 8 Afterward the disciples *p* up seven
Lk 9: 17 the disciples *p* up twelve basketfuls
14: 7 noticed how the guests *p* the places
Jn 5: 9 he *p* up his mat and walked.
8: 59 they *p* up stones to stone him,
10: 31 Again the Jews *p* up stones
15: 6 such branches are *p* up, thrown
Ac 20: 9 the third story and was *p* up dead.
Rev 18: 21 Then a mighty angel *p* up a boulder

PICKERS (PICK)

Jer 49: 9 If grape *p* came to you,
Ob : 5 If grape *p* came to you,

PICKS (PICK)

Lev 11: 25 Whoever *p* up one
11: 28 Anyone who *p* up their carcasses
11: 40 Anyone who *p* up the carcass must
15: 10 whoever *p* up those things must
2Sa 12: 31 to labor with saws and with iron *p*
1Ch 20: 3 to labor with saws and with iron *p*

PIECE (PIECES)

Ex 15: 25 and the LORD showed him a *p*
25: 19 cherubim of one *p* with the cover,
25: 31 blossoms shall be of one *p* with it.
25: 36 be of one *p* with the lampstand,
27: 2 the horns and the altar are of one *p*,
28: 8 of one *p* with the ephod
30: 2 two cubits high—its horns of one *p*
37: 8 them of one *p* with the cover.
37: 17 and blossoms were of one *p* with it.
37: 22 all of one *p* with the lampstand,
37: 25 two cubits high—its horns of one *p*

Ex 38: 2 and the altar were of one *p*,
39: 5 of one *p* with the ephod
Lev 9: 13 him the burnt offering *p* by *p*,
Jdg 16: 9 as a *p* of string snaps when it comes
20: 6 and sent one *p* to each region
Ru 4: 3 is selling the *p* of land that
1Sa 2: 36 down before him for a *p* of silver
9: 23 "Bring the *p* of meat I gave you,
24: 11 look at this *p* of your robe
2Sa 17: 13 even a *p* of it can be found."
1Ki 7: 24 in two rows in one *p* with the Sea.
17: 11 "And bring me, please, a *p* of bread
2Ch 4: 3 in two rows in one *p* with the Sea.
Job 2: 8 Job took a *p* of broken pottery
41: 29 to him but a *p* of straw;
42: 11 and each one gave him a *p* of silver
Pr 28: 21 yet a man will do wrong for a *p*
Eze 24: 6 Empty it *p* by *p*
Am 3: 12 only two leg bones or a *p* of an ear,
Mk 2: 21 the new *p* will pull away
Lk 19: 20 I have kept it laid away in a *p*
24: 42 They gave him a *p* of broiled fish,
Jn 13: 26 Then, dipping the *p* of bread,
13: 26 to whom I will give this *p* of bread
19: 23 woven in one *p* from top to bottom.
Ac 5: 1 with his wife Sapphira, also sold a *p*

PIECES (PIECE)

Ge 15: 17 and passed between the *p*.
33: 19 For a hundred *p* of silver, he
37: 33 Joseph has surely been torn to *p*."
44: 28 "He has surely been torn to *p*."
Ex 22: 13 If it was torn to *p* by a wild animal,
23: 24 and break their sacred stones to *p*.
28: 7 is to have two shoulder *p* attached
28: 12 on the shoulder *p* of the ephod
28: 25 to the shoulder *p* of the ephod
28: 27 of the shoulder *p* on the front
29: 17 ram into *p* and wash the inner parts
29: 17 with the head and the other *p*.
32: 19 breaking them to *p* at the foot
39: 4 They made shoulder *p*
39: 7 on the shoulder *p* of the ephod
39: 18 to the shoulder *p* of the ephod
39: 20 of the shoulder *p* on the front
Lev 1: 6 the burnt offering and cut it into *p*.
1: 8 sons the priests shall arrange the *p*,
1: 12 into *p*, and the priest shall arrange
6: 21 the grain offering broken in *p*
8: 20 burned the head, the *p* and the fat.
8: 20 ram into *p* and burned the head,
Nu 24: 8 and break their bones in *p*;
Dt 9: 17 breaking them to *p*
Jos 24: 32 bought for a hundred *p* of silver
Jdg 20: 6 cut her into *p* and sent one piece
1Sa 11: 7 cut them into *p*, and sent the *p*
1Ki 11: 30 wearing and tore it into twelve *p*.
11: 31 said to Jeroboam, "Take ten *p*
18: 23 and let them cut it into *p*
18: 33 cut the bull into *p* and laid it
2Ki 11: 18 smashed the altars and idols to *p*
18: 4 into *p* the bronze snake Moses had
23: 12 them to *p* and threw the rubble
2Ch 25: 12 down so that all were dashed to *p*.
34: 4 These he broke to *p* and scattered
34: 4 cut to *p* the incense altars that were
34: 7 and cut to *p* all the incense altars
Job 4: 20 and dusk they are broken to *p*;
18: 4 yourself to *p* in your anger,
26: 12 by his wisdom he cut Rahab to *p*.
Ps 2: 9 you will dash them to *p* like pottery
7: 2 and rip me to *p* with no one
29: 5 the LORD breaks in *p* the cedars
50: 22 you to *p*, with none to rescue:
119: 72 than thousands of *p* of silver
Isa 13: 16 to *p* before their eyes;
24: 12 its gate is battered to *p*.
27: 9 to be like chalk stones crushed to *p*,
30: 14 It will break in *p* like pottery,
30: 14 among its *p* not a fragment will be
51: 9 Was it not you who cut Rahab to *p*,
Jer 5: 6 to tear to *p* any who venture out,
23: 29 a hammer that breaks a rock in *p*?
34: 18 and then walked between its *p*.
34: 19 walked between the *p* of the calf,
Eze 16: 40 hack you to *p* with their swords.
23: 34 you will dash it to *p*
24: 4 Put into it the *p* of meat,
Eze 24: 4 all the choice *p*— the leg
27: 26 the east wind will break you to *p*
Da 2: 5 I will have you cut into *p*
2: 35 broken to *p* at the same time
2: 40 and as iron breaks things to *p*,
2: 45 the clay, the silver and the gold to *p*
3: 29 and Abednego be cut into *p*
Hos 5: 14 I will tear them to *p* and go away;
6: 1 He has torn us to *p*
6: 5 you in *p* with my prophets,
8: 6 It will be broken in *p*,
Am 6: 11 he will smash the great house into *p*
Mic 1: 7 All her idols will be broken to *p*;
3: 3 and break their bones in *p*;
4: 13 you will break to *p* many nations."
Na 3: 10 Her infants were dashed to *p*
Zec 11: 12 So they paid me thirty *p* of silver.
11: 13 So I took the thirty *p* of silver
Mt 7: 6 and then turn and tear you to *p*.
14: 20 of broken *p* that were left over.
15: 37 of broken *p* that were left over.
21: 44 on this stone will be broken to *p*,
24: 51 him to *p* and assign him a place
Mk 6: 43 basketfuls of broken *p* of bread
8: 8 of broken *p* that were left over.
8: 19 basketfuls of *p* did you pick up?"
8: 20 basketfuls of *p* did you pick up?"
Lk 9: 17 of broken *p* that were left over.
12: 46 him to *p* and assign him a place
20: 18 on that stone will be broken to *p*,
Jn 6: 12 "Gather the *p* that are left over.
6: 13 and filled twelve baskets with the *p*
Ac 23: 10 was afraid Paul would be torn to *p*
27: 41 broken to *p* by the pounding
27: 44 there on planks or on *p* of the ship.
Rev 2: 27 he will dash them to *p* like pottery

PIERCE (PIERCED PIERCES PIERCING)

Ex 21: 6 and *p* his ear with an awl.
Nu 24: 8 with their arrows they *p* them.
Job 40: 24 or trap him and *p* his nose?
41: 2 or *p* his jaw with a hook?
Ps 37: 15 their swords will *p* their own hearts
45: 5 Let your sharp arrows *p* the hearts
Pr 12: 18 Reckless words *p* like a sword,
Eze 28: 7 and *p* your shining splendor.
Lk 2: 35 a sword will *p* your own soul too."

PIERCED (PIERCE)

Jdg 5: 26 she shattered and *p* his temple.
2Ki 9: 24 arrow *p* his heart and he slumped
Job 26: 13 his hand *p* the gliding serpent.
Ps 22: 16 they have *p* my hands and my feet.
38: 2 For your arrows have *p* me,
40: 6 but my ears you have *p*;
Isa 14: 19 with those *p* by the sword,
51: 9 who *p* that monster through?
53: 5 But he was *p* for our transgressions,
La 3: 13 He *p* my heart
Hab 3: 14 With his own spear you *p* his head
Zec 12: 10 look on me, the one they have *p*,
Jn 19: 34 one of the soldiers *p* Jesus' side
19: 37 look on the one they have *p*."
1Ti 6: 10 and *p* themselves with many griefs.
Rev 1: 7 even those who *p* him;

PIERCES (PIERCE)

2Ki 18: 21 which *p* a man's hand and wounds
Job 16: 13 Without pity, he *p* my kidneys
20: 24 a bronze-tipped arrow *p* him.
30: 17 Night *p* my bones;
Pr 7: 23 a noose till an arrow *p* his liver,
Isa 36: 6 which *p* a man's hand and wounds
Jer 4: 18 How it *p* to the heart!"

PIERCING (PIERCE)

Job 16: 9 opponent fastens on me his *p* eyes.

PIETY

Job 4: 6 Should not your *p* be your
15: 4 But you even undermine *p*
22: 4 "Is it for your *p* that he rebukes you

PIG (PIG'S PIGS)

Lev 11: 7 the *p*, though it has a split hoof
Dt 14: 8 *p* is also unclean; although it has

PIG'S (PIG)

Pr 11: 22 Like a gold ring in a *p* snout
Isa 66: 3 is like one who presents *p* blood,

PIGEON (PIGEONS)

Ge 15: 9 along with a dove and a young *p*."
Lev 1: 14 he is to offer a dove or a young *p*.
12: 6 and a young *p* or a dove

PIGEONS (PIGEON)

Lev 5: 7 or two young *p* to the LORD
5: 11 afford two doves or two young *p*,
12: 8 to bring two doves or two young *p*,
14: 22 and two doves or two young *p*,
14: 30 sacrifice the doves or the young *p*,
15: 14 take two doves or two young *p*
15: 29 take two doves or two young *p*
Nu 6: 10 or two young *p* to the priest
Lk 2: 24 "a pair of doves or two young *p*."

PIGS (PIG)

Isa 65: 4 who eat the flesh of *p*,
66: 17 of those who eat the flesh of *p*
Mt 7: 6 do not throw your pearls to *p*.
8: 30 them a large herd of *p* was feeding.
8: 31 send us into the herd of *p*."
8: 32 they came out and went into the *p*,
8: 33 Those tending the *p* ran off,
Mk 5: 11 A large herd of *p* was feeding on
5: 12 Send us among the *p*; allow us to go
5: 13 came out and went into the *p*.
5: 14 Those tending the *p* ran off
5: 16 and told about the *p* as well.
Lk 8: 32 A large herd of *p* was feeding there
8: 33 of the man, they went into the *p*,
8: 34 those tending the *p* saw what had
15: 15 who sent him to his fields to feed *p*
15: 16 the pods that the *p* were eating,

PILATE (PILATE'S)

Mt 27: 2 and handed him over to *P*,
27: 13 *P* asked him, "Don't you hear how
27: 17 crowd had gathered, *P* asked them,
27: 19 While *P* was sitting
27: 22 who is called Christ?" *P* asked.
27: 23 crime has he committed?" asked *P*.
27: 24 When *P* saw that he was getting
27: 58 Going to *P*, he asked
27: 58 *P* ordered that it be given to him.
27: 62 and the Pharisees went to *P*.
27: 65 "Take a guard," *P* answered.
Mk 15: 1 and handed him over to *P*.
15: 2 the king of the Jews?" asked *P*.
15: 4 So again *P* asked him, "Aren't you
15: 5 made no reply, and *P* was amazed.
15: 8 and asked *P* to do for them what he
15: 9 the king of the Jews?" asked *P*,
15: 11 to have *P* release Barabbas instead.
15: 12 king of the Jews?" *P* asked them.
15: 14 crime has he committed?" asked *P*.
15: 15 *P* released Barabbas to them.
15: 43 went boldly to *P* and asked
15: 44 *P* was surprised to hear that he was
Lk 3: 1 when Pontius *P* was governor
13: 1 whose blood *P* had mixed
23: 1 assembly rose and led him off to *P*.
23: 3 *P* asked Jesus, "Are you the king
23: 4 *P* announced to the chief priests
23: 6 *P* asked if the man was a Galilean.
23: 11 robe, they sent him back to *P*.
23: 12 day Herod and *P* became friends—
23: 13 *P* called together the chief priests,
23: 20 *P* appealed to them again.
23: 24 So *P* decided to grant their demand
23: 52 Going to *P*, he asked
Jn 18: 29 So *P* came out to them and asked,
18: 31 *P* said, "Take him yourselves
18: 33 *P* then went back inside the palace,
18: 35 you think I am a Jew?" *P* replied.
18: 37 "You are a king, then!" said *P*.
18: 38 "What is truth?" *P* asked.
19: 1 *P* took Jesus and had him flogged.
19: 4 Once more *P* came out
19: 5 *P* said to them, "Here is the man!"
19: 6 Crucify! Crucify!" But *P* answered
19: 8 When *P* heard this, he was
19: 10 refuse to speak to me?" *P* said.
19: 12 From then on, *P* tried

Jn 19: 13 When *P* heard this, he brought
19: 14 "Here is your king," *P* said
19: 15 Shall I crucify your king?" *P* asked.
19: 16 Finally *P* handed him over to them
19: 19 *P* had a notice prepared
19: 21 priests of the Jews protested to *P*,
19: 22 *P* answered, "What I have written,
19: 31 they asked *P* to have the legs
19: 38 of Arimathea asked *P* for the body
Ac 3: 13 and you disowned him before *P*,
4: 27 and Pontius *P* met together
13: 28 they asked *P* to have him executed.
1Ti 6: 13 before Pontius *P* made the good

PILATE'S (PILATE)

Jn 19: 38 With *P* permission, he came

PILDASH

Ge 22: 22 Hazo, *P*, Jidlaph and Bethuel."

PILE (PILED PILES)

Lev 26: 30 and *p* your dead bodies
Jos 7: 26 Achan they heaped up a large *p*
8: 29 they raised a large *p* of rocks over it
Ru 3: 7 down at the far end of the grain *p*.
Ezr 6: 11 is to be made a *p* of rubble.
Job 8: 17 roots around a *p* of rocks
Jer 50: 26 *p* her up like heaps of grain.
Eze 24: 5 *P* wood beneath it for the bones;
24: 9 I, too, will *p* the wood high.
Lk 14: 35 for the soil nor for the manure *p*;
Ac 28: 3 Paul gathered a *p* of brushwood

PILED (PILE)

Ge 31: 46 So they took stones and *p* them
Ex 8: 14 They were *p* into heaps,
15: 8 the waters *p* up.
Jos 3: 16 It *p* up in a heap a great distance
Jdg 9: 49 *p* them against the stronghold
2Sa 18: 17 *p* up a large heap of rocks over him.
2Ch 31: 6 LORD their God, and they *p* them
Rev 18: 5 for her sins are *p* up to heaven,

PILES (PILE)

2Ki 10: 8 "Put them in two *p* at the entrance
19: 25 cities into *p* of stone.
Job 27: 16 and clothes like *p* of clay,
Isa 37: 26 cities into *p* of stone.
Da 2: 5 your houses turned into *p* of rubble
3: 29 and their houses be turned into *p*
Hos 12: 11 Their altars will be like *p* of stones
Na 3: 3 *p* of dead,
Hab 2: 6 to him who *p* up stolen goods

PILGRIMAGE

Ge 47: 9 the years of the *p* of my fathers."
47: 9 "The years of my *p* are a hundred
Ps 84: 5 who have set their hearts on *p*.

PILHA

Ne 10: 24 Hasshub, Hallohesh, *P*, Shobek,

PILLAGE (PILLAGED)

Ezr 9: 7 to *p* and humiliation at the hand
Jer 50: 11 you who *p* my inheritance,

PILLAGED (PILLAGE)

Ob : 6 his hidden treasures *p*!
Na 2: 10 She is *p*, plundered, stripped!

PILLAR (PILLARS)

Ge 19: 26 and she became a *p* of salt.
28: 18 as a *p* and poured oil on top of it.
28: 22 as a *p* will be God's house,
31: 13 where you anointed a *p*
31: 45 took a stone and set it up as a *p*.
31: 51 and here is this *p* I have set up
31: 52 and *p* to my side to harm me.
31: 52 is a witness, and this *p* is a witness,
35: 14 Jacob set up a stone *p*
35: 20 Over her tomb Jacob set up a *p*,
35: 20 this day that *p* marks Rachel's
Ex 13: 21 ahead of them in a *p* of cloud
13: 21 and by night in a *p* of fire
13: 22 Neither the *p* of cloud by day
13: 22 the *p* of fire by night left its place
14: 19 The *p* of cloud also moved
14: 24 looked down from the *p* of fire
Ex 33: 9 the *p* of cloud would come down
33: 10 Whenever the people saw the *p*
Nu 12: 5 came down in a *p* of cloud;
14: 14 before them in a *p* of cloud by day
14: 14 by day and a *p* of fire by night.
Dt 31: 15 at the Tent in a *p* of cloud,
Jdg 9: 6 tree at the *p* in Shechem
2Sa 18: 18 He named the *p* after himself,
18: 18 his lifetime Absalom had taken a *p*
1Ki 7: 21 The *p* to the south he named Jakin
2Ki 11: 14 by the *p*, as the custom was.
23: 3 The king stood by the *p*
25: 17 Each *p* was twenty-seven feet high.
25: 17 The other *p*, with its network,
25: 17 capital on top of one *p* was four
2Ch 23: 13 standing by his *p* at the entrance.
34: 31 The king stood by his *p*
Ne 9: 12 By day you led them with a *p*
9: 12 and by night with a *p* of fire
9: 19 By day the *p* of cloud did not cease
9: 19 nor the *p* of fire by night to shine
Ps 99: 7 to them from the *p* of cloud;
Jer 1: 18 an iron *p* and a bronze wall to stand
52: 22 The other *p*, with its pomegranates,
52: 22 of the one *p* was five cubits high
1Ti 3: 15 the *p* and foundation of the truth.
Rev 3: 12 who overcomes I will make a *p*

PILLARS (PILLAR)

Ex 24: 4 up twelve stone *p* representing
Jdg 16: 25 When they stood him among the *p*,
16: 26 I can feel the *p* that support
16: 29 reached toward the two central *p*
1Ki 7: 6 of that were *p* and an overhanging
7: 15 cast two bronze *p*, each eighteen
7: 16 bronze to set on the tops of the *p*;
7: 17 the capitals on top of the *p*,
7: 18 the capitals on top of the *p*.
7: 19 on top of the *p* in the portico were
7: 20 On the capitals of both *p*,
7: 21 He erected the *p* at the portico
7: 22 the work on the *p* was completed.
7: 41 capitals on top of the *p*;
7: 41 capitals on top of the *p*;
7: 41 the two *p*; the two bowl-shaped
7: 42 capitals on top of the *p*);
2Ki 25: 13 Babylonians broke up the bronze *p*,
25: 16 The bronze from the two *p*,
1Ch 18: 8 the *p* and various bronze articles.
2Ch 3: 15 front of the temple he made two *p*,
3: 16 and put them on top of the *p*.
3: 17 He erected the *p* in the front
4: 12 capitals on top of the *p*;
4: 12 capitals on top of the *p*;
4: 12 the two *p*; the two bowl-shaped
4: 13 capitals on top of the *p*);
Est 1: 6 material to silver rings on marble *p*.
Job 9: 6 and makes its *p* tremble.
26: 11 The *p* of the heavens quake,
Ps 75: 3 it is I who hold its *p* firm.
144: 12 and our daughters will be like *p*
Pr 9: 1 she has hewn out its seven *p*.
SS 5: 15 His legs are *p* of marble
Jer 27: 19 LORD Almighty says about the *p*,
43: 13 he will demolish the sacred *p*
52: 17 Babylonians broke up the bronze *p*,
52: 20 The bronze from the two *p*,
52: 21 of the *p* was eighteen cubits high
Eze 26: 11 your strong *p* will fall to the ground
40: 49 and there were *p* on each side
42: 6 rooms on the third floor had no *p*,
Am 9: 1 "Strike the tops of the *p*
Gal 2: 9 and John, those reputed to be *p*,
Rev 10: 1 and his legs were like fiery *p*.

PILOT

Ac 27: 11 followed the advice of the *p*
Jas 3: 4 small rudder wherever the *p* wants

PILTAI

Ne 12: 17 of Miniamin's and of Maadiah's, *P*;

PIN

Jdg 16: 13 and tighten it with the *p*,
16: 14 and pulled up the *p* and the loom,
16: 14 and tightened it with the *p*.
1Sa 18: 11 saying to himself, "I'll *p* David
19: 10 Saul tried to *p* him to the wall
1Sa 26: 8 Now let me *p* him to the ground

PINE (PINES)

1Ki 5: 8 in providing the cedar and *p* logs.
5: 10 all the cedar and *p* logs he wanted,
6: 15 floor of the temple with planks of *p*.
6: 34 He also made two *p* doors,
9: 11 and *p* and gold he wanted.
2Ch 2: 8 *p* and algum logs from Lebanon,
3: 5 He paneled the main hall with *p*
Ps 104: 17 the stork has its home in the *p* trees
Isa 14: 8 Even the *p* trees and the cedars
19: 8 will *p* away.
44: 14 or planted a *p*, and the rain made it
55: 13 the thornbush will grow the *p* tree,
60: 13 *p*, the fir and the cypress together,
Eze 27: 5 timbers of *p* trees from Senir;
31: 8 nor could the *p* trees
Hos 14: 8 I am like a green *p* tree;
Na 2: 3 the spears of *p* are brandished.
Zec 11: 2 O *p* tree, for the cedar has fallen;

PINES (PINE)

1Sa 2: 5 she who has had many sons *p* away
2Ki 19: 23 the choicest of its *p*.
Isa 37: 24 the choicest of its *p*.
41: 19 I will set *p* in the wasteland,

PINIONS

Dt 32: 11 and carries them on its *p*.
Job 39: 13 they cannot compare with the *p*

PINON

Ge 36: 41 Oholibamah, Elah, *P*, Kenaz,
1Ch 1: 52 Oholibamah, Elah, *P*, Kenaz,

PINT

Jn 12: 3 Mary took about a *p* of pure nard,

PIPES

Da 3: 5 lyre, harp, *p* and all kinds of music,
3: 10 *p* and all kinds of music must fall
3: 15 lyre, harp, *p* and all kinds of music,
Zec 4: 12 beside the two gold *p* that pour out

PIRAM

Jos 10: 3 king of Hebron, *P* king of Jarmuth,

PIRATHON (PIRATHONITE)

Jdg 12: 13 Abdon son of Hillel, from *P*,
12: 15 and was buried at *P* in Ephraim,

PIRATHONITE (PIRATHON)

2Sa 23: 30 Benaiah the *P*, Hiddai
1Ch 11: 31 Benaiah the *P*, Hurai
27: 14 was Benaiah the *P*, an Ephraimite.

PISGAH

Nu 21: 20 top of *P* overlooks the wasteland.
23: 14 the field of Zophim on the top of *P*,
Dt 3: 17 below the slopes of *P*.
3: 27 Go up to the top of *P* and look west
4: 49 below the slopes of *P*.
34: 1 the plains of Moab to the top of *P*,
Jos 12: 3 southward below the slopes of *P*.
13: 20 Beth Peor, the slopes of *P*,

PISHON

Ge 2: 11 The name of the first is the *P*;

PISIDIA

Ac 14: 24 After going through *P*, they came

PISIDIAN ANTIOCH

Ac 13: 14 From Perga they went on to *P*.

PISPAH

1Ch 7: 38 The sons of Jether: Jephunneh, *P*

PISTACHIO

Ge 43: 11 some *p* nuts and almonds.

PIT (PITS)

Ex 21: 33 "If a man uncovers a *p* or digs one
21: 34 the owner of the *p* must pay
2Sa 18: 17 threw him into a big *p* in the forest
23: 20 went down into a *p* on a snowy day
1Ch 11: 22 went down into a *p* on a snowy day
Job 9: 31 you would plunge me into a slime *p*

Job 33: 18 to preserve his soul from the *p*,
33: 22 His soul draws near to the *p*,
33: 24 him from going down to the *p*;
33: 28 from going down to the *p*,
33: 30 to turn back his soul from the *p*,
Ps 7: 15 falls into the *p* he has made.
9: 15 into the *p* they have dug;
28: 1 who have gone down to the *p*.
30: 3 from going down into the *p*.
30: 9 in my going down into the *p*?
35: 7 and without cause dug a *p* for me,
35: 8 fall into the *p*, to their ruin.
40: 2 He lifted me out of the slimy *p*,
55: 23 the wicked into the *p* of corruption;
57: 6 They dug a *p* in my path—
69: 15 or the *p* close its mouth over me.
88: 4 among those who go down to the *p*;
88: 6 You have put me in the lowest *p*,
94: 13 till a *p* is dug for the wicked.
103: 4 he redeems my life from the *p*
143: 7 be like those who go down to the *p*.
Pr 1: 12 like those who go down to the *p*;
22: 14 mouth of an adulteress is a deep *p*;
23: 27 for a prostitute is a deep *p*
26: 27 If a man digs a *p*, he will fall into it;
Ecc 10: 8 Whoever digs a *p* may fall into it;
Isa 14: 15 to the depths of the *p*.
14: 19 descend to the stones of the *p*.
24: 17 Terror and *p* and snare await you,
24: 18 whoever climbs out of the *p*
24: 18 will fall into a *p*;
30: 33 Its fire *p* has been made deep
38: 17 me from the *p* of destruction;
38: 18 those who go down to the *p*
Jer 18: 20 Yet they have dug a *p* for me.
18: 22 for they have dug a *p* to capture me
48: 43 Terror and *p* and snare await you,
48: 44 whoever climbs out of the *p*
48: 44 will fall into a *p*,
La 3: 53 They tried to end my life in a *p*
3: 55 from the depths of the *p*.
Eze 19: 4 and he was trapped in their *p*.
19: 8 and he was trapped in their *p*.
26: 20 with those who go down to the *p*,
26: 20 with those who go down to the *p*,
28: 8 They will bring you down to the *p*,
31: 14 with those who go down to the *p*.
31: 16 with those who go down to the *p*
32: 18 with those who go down to the *p*.
32: 23 are in the depths of the *p*
32: 24 with those who go down to the *p*.
32: 25 with those who go down to the *p*;
32: 29 with those who go down to the *p*.
32: 30 with those who go down to the *p*.
Jnh 2: 6 you brought my life up from the *p*,
Zec 9: 11 from the waterless *p*.
Mt 12: 11 and it falls into a *p* on the Sabbath,
15: 14 a blind man, both will fall into a *p*."
Mk 12: 1 dug a *p* for the winepress
Lk 6: 39 Will they not both fall into a *p*?

PITCH (PITCHED)

Ge 6: 14 and coat it with *p* inside and out.
Ex 2: 3 and coated it with tar and *p*.
33: 7 and *p* it outside the camp some
Pr 20: 20 will be snuffed out in *p* darkness.
Isa 13: 20 no Arab will *p* his tent there,
34: 9 her land will become blazing *p*!
34: 9 streams will be turned into *p*,
Jer 6: 3 they will *p* their tents around her,
10: 20 no one is left now to *p* my tent
Eze 25: 4 and *p* their tents among you;
Da 11: 45 He will *p* his royal tents

PITCH-DARK (DARK)

Am 5: 20 *p*, without a ray of brightness?

PITCHED (PITCH)

Ge 12: 8 east of Bethel and *p* his tent,
13: 12 and *p* his tents near Sodom.
26: 25 There he *p* his tent, and there his
31: 25 Jacob had *p* his tent
33: 19 plot of ground where he *p* his tent.
35: 21 and *p* his tent beyond Migdal
Jdg 4: 11 and *p* his tent by the great tree
20: 19 the Israelites got up and *p* camp
1Sa 17: 1 They *p* camp at Ephes Dammim,
2Sa 6: 17 inside the tent that David had *p*
2Sa 16: 22 So they *p* a tent for Absalom
1Ch 15: 1 for the ark of God and *p* a tent for it
16: 1 it inside the tent that David had *p*
2Ch 1: 4 he had *p* a tent for it in Jerusalem.
Ps 19: 4 In the heavens he has *p* a tent

PITCHER (PITCHERS)

Ecc 12: 6 before the *p* is shattered

PITCHERS (PITCHER)

Ex 25: 29 its *p* and bowls for the pouring out
37: 16 and its *p* for the pouring out
1Ch 28: 17 and *p*; the weight of gold
Mk 7: 4 the washing of cups, *p* and kettles.)

PITFALLS

Ps 119: 85 The arrogant dig *p* for me,
La 3: 47 We have suffered terror and *p*,

PITHOM

Ex 1: 11 and they built *P* and Rameses

PITHON

1Ch 8: 35 The sons of Micah: *P*, Melech,
9: 41 The sons of Micah: *P*, Melech,

PITIED (PITY)

Ps 106: 46 He caused them to be *p*
1Co 15: 19 we are to be *p* more than all men.

PITIFUL (PITY)

Rev 3: 17 realize that you are wretched, *p*,

PITS (PIT)

Ge 14: 10 Valley of Siddim was full of tar *p*,
1Sa 13: 6 among the rocks, and in *p*
Ps 140: 10 into miry *p*, never to rise.
Isa 42: 22 all of them trapped in *p*
Zep 2: 9 a place of weeds and salt *p*,

PITTANCE

Ps 44: 12 You sold your people for a *p*,

PITY (PITIED PITIFUL)

Dt 7: 16 Do not look on them with *p*
13: 8 Show him no *p*
19: 13 Show him no *p*.
19: 21 Show no *p*: life for life, eye for eye,
25: 12 Show her no *p*.
28: 50 for the old or *p* for the young.
2Sa 12: 6 he did such a thing and had no *p*."
2Ch 36: 15 because he had *p* on his people
Job 16: 13 Without *p*, he pierces my kidneys
19: 21 on me, my friends, have *p*,
19: 21 "Have *p* on me, my friends,
Ps 72: 13 He will take *p* on the weak
102: 14 her very dust moves them to *p*.
109: 12 or take *p* on his fatherless children.
Ecc 4: 10 But *p* the man who falls
Isa 9: 17 nor will he *p* the fatherless
Jer 13: 14 I will allow no *p* or mercy
15: 5 "Who will have *p* on you, O
16: 5 my love and my *p* from this people
20: 16 the LORD overthrew without *p*.
21: 7 he will show them no mercy or *p*
La 2: 2 Without *p* the Lord has swallowed
2: 17 He has overthrown you without *p*,
2: 21 have slaughtered them without *p*.
3: 43 you have slain without *p*.
Eze 5: 11 I will not look on you with *p*
7: 4 I will not look on you with *p*
7: 9 I will not look on you with *p*
8: 18 I will not look on them with *p*
9: 5 without showing *p* or compassion.
9: 10 So I will not look on them with *p*
16: 5 No one looked on you with *p*
20: 17 Yet I looked on them with *p*
24: 14 I will not have *p*, nor will I relent.
Joel 2: 14 knows? He may turn and have *p*
2: 18 and take *p* on his people.
Zec 8: 14 and showed no *p* when your fathers
11: 6 For I will no longer have *p*
Mt 18: 27 The servant's master took *p* on him
Mk 9: 22 if you can do anything, take *p* on us
Lk 10: 33 when he saw him, he took *p* on him
16: 24 have *p* on me and send Lazarus
17: 13 "Jesus, Master, have *p* on us!"
1Jn 3: 17 in need but has no *p* on him,

PLACING

Ac 9: 17 *P* his hands on Saul, he said,

PLAGUE (PLAGUED PLAGUES)

Ex 8: 2 I will *p* your whole country
9: 3 of the LORD will bring a terrible *p*
9: 15 with a *p* that would have wiped you
10: 14 before had there been such a *p*
10: 17 to take this deadly *p* away from me
11: 1 I will bring one more *p* on Pharaoh
12: 13 No destructive *p* will touch you
30: 12 Then no *p* will come on them
32: 35 LORD struck the people with a *p*
Lev 26: 25 I will send a *p* among you,
Nu 8: 19 so that no *p* will strike the Israelites
11: 33 and he struck them with a severe *p*.
14: 12 I will strike them down with a *p*
14: 37 and died of a *p* before the LORD.
16: 46 from the LORD; the *p* has started
16: 47 The *p* had already started
16: 48 and the dead, and the *p* stopped.
16: 49 But 14,700 people died from the *p*,
16: 50 of Meeting, for the *p* had stopped.
25: 8 the *p* against the Israelites was
25: 9 died in the *p* numbered 24,000.
25: 18 who was killed when the *p* came
26: 1 After the *p* the LORD said
31: 16 so that a *p* struck the LORD's
Dt 28: 21 The LORD will *p* you
28: 22 which will *p* you until you perish.
32: 24 consuming pestilence and deadly *p*
Jos 22: 17 though a *p* fell on the community
1Sa 6: 4 the same *p* has struck both you
2Sa 24: 13 Or three days of *p* in your land?
24: 15 So the LORD sent a *p* on Israel
24: 21 that the *p* on the people may be
24: 25 and the *p* on Israel was stopped.
1Ki 8: 37 "When famine or *p* comes
1Ch 21: 12 sword of the LORD—days of *p*
21: 14 So the LORD sent a *p* on Israel,
21: 17 but do not let this *p* remain
21: 22 that the *p* on the people may be
2Ch 6: 28 "When famine or *p* comes
7: 13 or send a *p* among my people,
20: 9 the sword of judgment, or *p*
Job 27: 15 *p* will bury those who survive him,
Ps 78: 50 but gave them over to the *p*.
91: 6 nor the *p* that destroys at midday.
106: 29 and a *p* broke out among them.
106: 30 and the *p* was checked.
Isa 19: 22 LORD will strike Egypt with a *p*;
Jer 14: 12 with the sword, famine and *p*."
21: 6 and they will die of a terrible *p*.
21: 7 in this city who survive the *p*,
21: 9 die by the sword, famine or *p*.
24: 10 and *p* against them until they are
27: 8 famine and *p*, declares the LORD,
27: 13 and *p* with which the LORD has
28: 8 and *p* against many countries
29: 17 famine and *p* against them
29: 18 *p* and will make them abhorrent
32: 24 Because of the sword, famine and *p*
32: 36 *p* it will be handed over to the king
34: 17 'freedom' to fall by the sword, *p*
38: 2 or *p*, but whoever goes
42: 17 and *p*; not one of them will survive
42: 22 *p* in the place where you want to go
44: 13 and *p*, as I punished Jerusalem.
Eze 5: 12 of your people will die of the *p*
5: 17 *P* and bloodshed will sweep
6: 11 fall by the sword, famine and *p*.
6: 12 He that is far away will die of the *p*,
7: 15 will be devoured by famine and *p*.
7: 15 "Outside is the sword, inside are *p*
12: 16 from the sword, famine and *p*,
14: 19 "Or if I send a *p* into that land
14: 21 and famine and wild beasts and *p*—
28: 23 I will send a *p* upon her
33: 27 and caves will die of a *p*.
38: 22 execute judgment upon him with *p*
Hab 3: 5 *P* went before him,
Zec 14: 12 This is the *p* with which the LORD
14: 15 A similar *p* will strike the horses
14: 18 bring on them the *p* he inflicts
Rev 6: 8 and *p*, and by the wild beasts
11: 6 the earth with every kind of *p*
16: 21 God on account of the *p* of hail,

Rev 16: 21 because the *p* was so terrible.

PLAGUED (PLAGUE)

Ps 73: 5 they are not *p* by human ills.
73: 14 All day long I have been *p;*

PLAGUES (PLAGUE)

Ex 5: 3 or he may strike us with *p*
9: 14 force of my *p* against you
Dt 28: 59 the LORD will send fearful *p*
1Sa 4: 8 with all kinds of *p* in the desert.
Hos 13: 14 Where, O death, are your *p?*
Am 4: 10 "I sent *p* among you
Rev 9: 18 killed by the three *p* of fire,
9: 20 killed by these *p* still did not repent
15: 1 seven angels with the seven last *p*
15: 6 the seven angels with the seven *p.*
15: 8 until the seven *p* of the seven
16: 9 who had control over these *p,*
18: 4 you will not receive any of her *p;*
18: 8 in one day her *p* will overtake her:
21: 9 full of the seven last *p* came
22: 18 to him the *p* described in this book.

PLAIN (PLAINS)

Ge 11: 2 they found a *p* in Shinar
13: 10 and saw that the whole *p*
13: 11 chose for himself the whole *p*
13: 12 lived among the cities of the *p*
19: 17 and don't stop anywhere in the *p!*
19: 25 those cities and the entire *p,*
19: 28 toward all the land of the *p,*
19: 29 God destroyed the cities of the *p,*
Jos 17: 16 live in the *p* have iron chariots,
Jdg 1: 34 them to come down into the *p.*
2Sa 18: 23 Then Ahimaaz ran by way of the *p*
1Ki 7: 46 in clay molds in the *p* of the Jordan
2Ch 4: 17 in clay molds in the *p* of the Jordan
26: 10 in the foothills and in the *p.*
35: 22 to fight him on the *p* of Megiddo.
Ne 6: 2 of the villages on the *p* of Ono."
Isa 40: 4 the rugged places a *p.*
63: 14 like cattle that go down to the *p,*
Jer 47: 5 O remnant on the *p,*
Eze 3: 22 "Get up and go out to the *p,*
3: 23 So I got up and went out to the *p.*
8: 4 as in the vision I had seen in the *p.*
Da 3: 1 and set it up on the *p* of Dura
Hab 2: 2 and make it *p* on tablets
Zec 12: 11 in the *p* of Megiddo.
Ro 1: 19 because God has made it *p* to them.
1: 19 what may be known about God is *p*
2Co 5: 11 What we are is *p* to God,
5: 11 hope it is also *p* to your conscience.
Eph 3: 9 and to make *p* to everyone

PLAINS (PLAIN)

Nu 22: 1 the Israelites traveled to the *p*
26: 3 So on the *p* of Moab by the Jordan
26: 63 on the *p* of Moab by the Jordan
31: 12 at their camp on the *p* of Moab,
33: 48 and camped on the *p* of Moab
33: 49 on the *p* of Moab they camped
33: 50 On the *p* of Moab by the Jordan
35: 1 On the *p* of Moab by the Jordan
36: 13 to the Israelites on the *p* of Moab
Dt 34: 1 from the *p* of Moab to the top
34: 8 grieved for Moses in the *p*
Jos 4: 13 LORD to the *p* of Jericho for war.
5: 10 at Gilgal on the *p* of Jericho,
13: 32 when he was in the *p* of Moab
Jdg 1: 19 to drive the people from the *p,*
1Ki 20: 23 But if we fight them on the *p,*
20: 25 so we can fight Israel on the *p.*
2Ki 25: 5 overtook him in the *p* of Jericho.
Jer 39: 5 Zedekiah in the *p* of Jericho.
52: 8 overtook him in the *p* of Jericho.

PLAN (PLANNED PLANNING PLANS)

Ge 11: 6 then nothing they *p*
41: 37 The *p* seemed good to Pharaoh
Ex 26: 30 according to the *p* shown you
Nu 33: 56 do to you what I *p* to do to them.' "
1Sa 18: 25 Saul's *p* was to have David fall
2Sa 17: 4 This *p* seemed good to Absalom
1Ch 28: 18 also gave him the *p* for the chariot,
28: 19 in all the details of the *p.*"
2Ch 13: 8 now you *p* to resist the kingdom
2Ch 30: 4 The *p* seemed right both to the king
Est 8: 3 to the evil *p* of Haman the Agagite,
Job 42: 2 no *p* of yours can be thwarted.
Ps 64: 6 "We have devised a perfect *p!*"
140: 4 who *p* to trip my feet.
Pr 14: 22 those who *p* what is good find love
21: 30 is no wisdom, no insight, no *p*
Isa 5: 19 let the *p* of the Holy One
8: 10 propose your *p,* but it will not stand
14: 26 This is the *p* determined
Jer 18: 11 and devising a *p* against you.
36: 3 Judah hear about every disaster I *p*
49: 30 he has devised a *p* against you.
Eze 43: 10 Let them consider the *p,*
Am 3: 7 nothing without revealing his *p*
Mic 2: 1 Woe to those who *p* iniquity,
4: 12 they do not understand his *p,*
Mt 28: 12 with the elders and devised a *p,*
Ac 9: 24 but Saul learned of their *p.*
27: 43 kept them from carrying out their *p*
Ro 15: 24 I *p* to do so when I go to Spain.
Eph 1: 11 predestined according to the *p*

PLANE

Ge 30: 37 and *p* trees and made white stripes
Eze 31: 8 nor could the *p* trees

PLANK (PLANKS)

Mt 7: 3 attention to the *p* in your own eye?
7: 4 when all the time there is a *p*
7: 5 first take the *p* out of your own eye,
Lk 6: 41 attention to the *p* in your own eye?
6: 42 fail to see the *p* in your own eye?
6: 42 first take the *p* out of your eye,

PLANKS (PLANK)

1Ki 6: 9 roofing it with beams and cedar *p.*
6: 15 floor of the temple with *p* of pine.
Ac 27: 44 The rest were to get there on *p*

PLANNED (PLAN)

2Ki 19: 25 In days of old I *p* it;
Ps 40: 5 The things you *p* for us
Pr 30: 32 or if you have *p* evil,
Isa 14: 24 "Surely, as I have *p,* so it will be,
19: 12 has *p* against Egypt.
22: 11 for the One who *p* it long ago.
23: 8 Who *p* this against Tyre,
23: 9 The LORD Almighty *p* it,
25: 1 things *p* long ago.
37: 26 In days of old I *p* it;
46: 11 what I have *p,* that will I do.
Jer 18: 8 not inflict on it the disaster I had *p.*
49: 20 hear what the LORD has *p*
50: 45 hear what the LORD has *p*
La 2: 17 The LORD has done what he *p;*
Da 6: 3 qualities that the king *p*
Ac 27: 42 The soldiers *p* to kill the prisoners
Ro 1: 13 that I *p* many times to come to you
2Co 1: 15 I *p* to visit you first
1: 16 I *p* to visit you on my way
1: 17 When I *p* this, did I do it lightly?
Heb 11: 40 God had *p* something better for us

PLANNING (PLAN)

Ecc 9: 10 nor *p* nor knowledge nor wisdom.
Isa 19: 17 of what the LORD Almighty is *p*
Jer 26: 3 bring on them the disaster I was *p*
Mic 2: 3 "I am *p* disaster against this people,

PLANS (PLAN)

1Sa 23: 10 has heard definitely that Saul *p*
2Ki 16: 10 with detailed *p* for its construction.
16: 11 with all the *p* that King Ahaz had
1Ch 28: 2 of our God, and I made *p* to build it
28: 11 David gave his son Solomon the *p*
28: 12 He gave him the *p*
Ezr 4: 5 frustrate their *p* during the entire
Job 5: 12 He thwarts the *p* of the crafty,
17: 11 have passed, my *p* are shattered,
23: 14 many such *p* he still has in store.
Ps 14: 6 You evildoers frustrate the *p*
20: 4 and make all your *p* succeed.
33: 10 The LORD foils the *p*
33: 11 *p* of the LORD stand firm forever,
64: 5 encourage each other in evil *p,*
140: 2 who devise evil *p* in their hearts
140: 8 do not let their *p* succeed,
Ps 146: 4 on that very day their *p* come
Pr 12: 5 The *p* of the righteous are just,
15: 22 *P* fail for lack of counsel,
16: 1 To man belong the *p* of the heart,
16: 3 and your *p* will succeed.
16: 9 In his heart a man *p* his course,
19: 21 Many are the *p* in a man's heart,
20: 18 Make *p* by seeking advice;
21: 5 The *p* of the diligent lead to profit
Isa 19: 3 and I will bring their *p* to nothing;
29: 15 to hide their *p* from the LORD,
30: 1 those who carry out *p* that are not
32: 8 But the noble man makes noble *p,*
Jer 18: 12 We will continue with our own *p;*
18: 18 let's make *p* against Jeremiah;
19: 7 " 'In this place I will ruin the *p*
29: 11 For I know the *p* I have for you,"
29: 11 *p* to give you hope and a future.
29: 11 "*p* to prosper you and not
Da 11: 17 but his *p* will not succeed
Hos 11: 6 and put an end to their *p.*
Mt 22: 15 and laid *p* to trap him in his words.
Jn 12: 10 So the chief priests made *p*
2Co 1: 17 Or do I make my *p* in a worldly

PLANT (PLANTED PLANTER PLANTING PLANTS REPLANTED TRANSPLANTED)

Ge 1: 29 "I give you every seed-bearing *p*
1: 30 I give every green *p* for food."
2: 5 no *p* of the field had yet sprung up;
9: 20 proceeded to *p* a vineyard.
47: 23 for you so you can *p* the ground.
Ex 10: 15 or *p* in all the land of Egypt.
15: 17 You will bring them in and *p* them
Lev 19: 19 Do not *p* your field with two kinds
19: 23 and *p* any kind of fruit tree,
25: 20 in the seventh year if we do not *p*
25: 22 While you *p* during the eighth year,
26: 16 You will *p* seed in vain,
Dt 6: 11 and olive groves you did not *p*—
22: 9 Do not *p* two kinds of seed
22: 9 not only the crops you *p* but
28: 30 You will *p* a vineyard,
28: 39 You will *p* vineyards and cultivate
Jos 24: 13 olive groves that you did not *p.*'
2Sa 7: 10 will *p* them so that they can have
1Ki 4: 33 He described *p* life, from the cedar
2Ki 19: 29 *p* vineyards and eat their fruit.
1Ch 17: 9 will *p* them so that they can have
Job 8: 16 He is like a well-watered *p*
14: 9 and put forth shoots like a *p.*
Ecc 3: 2 a time to *p* and a time to uproot,
11: 4 watches the wind will not *p;*
Isa 17: 10 and *p* imported vines,
17: 11 on the morning when you *p* them,
28: 25 Does he not *p* wheat in its place,
37: 30 *p* vineyards and eat their fruit.
65: 21 they will *p* vineyards and eat their
65: 22 or *p* and others eat.
Jer 1: 10 and overthrow, to build and to *p.*"
24: 6 I will *p* them and not uproot them.
29: 5 *p* gardens and eat what they
29: 28 *p* gardens and eat what they
31: 5 Again you will *p* vineyards
31: 5 the farmers will *p* them
31: 27 "when I will *p* the house of Israel
31: 28 watch over them to build and to *p,*"
32: 41 will assuredly *p* them in this land
35: 7 houses, sow seed or *p* vineyards;
42: 10 I will *p* you and not uproot you,
Eze 16: 7 I made you grow like a *p*
17: 22 top of a cedar and *p* it;
17: 22 *p* it on a high and lofty mountain.
17: 23 heights of Israel I will *p* it;
28: 26 will build houses and *p* vineyards;
Hos 2: 23 I will *p* her for myself in the land;
Am 9: 14 They will *p* vineyards and drink
9: 15 I will *p* Israel in their own land,
Mic 6: 15 You will *p* but not harvest;
Zep 1: 13 they will *p* vineyards
Mt 15: 13 "Every *p* that my heavenly Father
Mk 4: 31 which is the smallest seed you *p*
Jn 19: 29 sponge on a stalk of the hyssop *p,*
1Co 15: 37 you do not *p* the body that will be,
Jas 1: 11 scorching heat and withers the *p;*
Rev 9: 4 the grass of the earth or any *p*

PLANTED (PLANT)

Ge 2: 8 the LORD God had *p* a garden
21: 33 Abraham *p* a tamarisk tree
26: 12 Isaac *p* crops in that land
Lev 11: 37 falls on any seeds that are to be *p*,
Nu 24: 6 like aloes *p* by the LORD,
Dt 11: 10 where you *p* your seed
20: 6 Has anyone *p* a vineyard
21: 4 or *p* and where there is a flowing
29: 23 nothing *p*, nothing sprouting,
Jdg 6: 3 the Israelites *p* their crops,
Ps 1: 3 He is like a tree *p* by streams
44: 2 and *p* our fathers;
80: 8 you drove out the nations and *p* it.
80: 15 the root your right hand has *p*,
92: 13 *p* in the house of the LORD,
104: 16 the cedars of Lebanon that he *p*.
107: 37 They sowed fields and *p* vineyards
Ecc 2: 4 houses for myself and *p* vineyards.
2: 5 *p* all kinds of fruit trees in them.
Isa 5: 2 and *p* it with the choicest vines.
40: 24 No sooner are they *p*,
44: 14 *p* a pine, and the rain made it grow.
60: 21 They are the shoot I have *p*,
Jer 2: 21 I had *p* you like a choice vine
11: 17 The LORD Almighty, who *p* you,
12: 2 You have *p* them, and they have
17: 8 He will be like a tree *p* by the water
18: 9 or kingdom is to be built up and *p*,
45: 4 built and uproot what I have *p*,
Eze 17: 4 where he *p* it in a city of traders.
17: 5 He *p* it like a willow
17: 7 him from the plot where it was *p*
17: 8 It had been *p* in good soil
19: 10 *p* by the water;
19: 13 Now it is *p* in the desert,
Hos 9: 13 *p* in a pleasant place.
10: 13 But you have *p* wickedness,
Am 5: 11 though you have *p* lush vineyards,
Hag 1: 6 You have *p* much, but have
Mt 13: 31 which a man took and *p* in his field.
15: 13 Father has not *p* will be pulled
21: 33 was a landowner who *p* a vineyard.
Mk 4: 32 Yet when *p*, it grows and becomes
12: 1 in parables: "A man *p* a vineyard.
Lk 13: 6 "A man had a fig tree, *p*
13: 19 which a man took and *p*
17: 6 'Be uprooted and *p* in the sea,'
20: 9 this parable: "A man *p* a vineyard,
1Co 3: 6 I *p* the seed, Apollos watered it,
Jas 1: 21 humbly accept the word *p* in you,
Rev 10: 2 He *p* his right foot on the sea

PLANTER (PLANT)

Am 9: 13 the *p* by the one treading grapes.

PLANTING (PLANT)

Lev 26: 5 grape harvest will continue until *p*,
Isa 28: 24 When a farmer plows for *p*,
61: 3 a *p* of the LORD
Mic 1: 6 a place for *p* vineyards.
Lk 17: 28 buying and selling, *p* and building.

PLANTS (PLANT)

Ge 1: 11 seed-bearing *p* and trees
1: 12 *p* bearing seed according
3: 18 and you will eat the *p* of the field.
9: 3 Just as I gave you the green *p*,
30: 14 and found some mandrake *p*,
Dt 32: 2 like abundant rain on tender *p*.
2Ki 19: 26 They are like *p* in the field,
Job 8: 19 and from the soil other *p* grow.
40: 21 Under the lotus *p* he lies,
Ps 37: 2 like green *p* they will soon die away
104: 14 and *p* for man to cultivate—
144: 12 will be like well nurtured *p*,
Pr 31: 16 out of her earnings she *p* a vineyard
SS 4: 13 Your *p* are an orchard
Isa 17: 10 though you set out the finest *p*
19: 7 also the *p* along the Nile,
37: 27 They are like *p* in the field,
Da 4: 15 animals among the *p* of the earth.
Zec 10: 1 and *p* of the field to everyone.
Mt 13: 6 sun came up, the *p* were scorched,
13: 7 which grew up and choked the *p*.
13: 32 it is the largest of garden *p*
Mk 4: 6 sun came up, the *p* were scorched,
4: 7 which grew up and choked the *p*,
4: 32 becomes the largest of all garden *p*,
Lk 8: 6 the *p* withered because they had no
8: 7 up with it and choked the *p*.
1Co 3: 7 So neither he who *p* nor he who
3: 8 The man who *p* and the man who
9: 7 Who *p* a vineyard and does not eat

PLASTER (PLASTERED)

Lev 14: 42 and take new clay and *p* the house.
14: 45 its stones, timbers and all the *p*—
Dt 27: 2 large stones and coat them with *p*.
27: 4 you today, and coat them with *p*.
Da 5: 5 and wrote on the *p* of the wall,

PLASTERED (PLASTER)

Lev 14: 43 and the house scraped and *p*,
14: 48 spread after the house has been *p*,
Isa 44: 18 their eyes are *p* over so they cannot

PLATE (PLATES PLATTER)

Ex 28: 36 "Make a *p* of pure gold
39: 30 They made the *p*, the sacred
Lev 8: 9 on Aaron's head and set the gold *p*,
Nu 7: 13 was one silver *p* weighing
7: 19 was one silver *p* weighing
7: 25 was one silver *p* weighing
7: 31 was one silver *p* weighing
7: 37 was one silver *p* weighing
7: 43 was one silver *p* weighing
7: 49 was one silver *p* weighing
7: 55 was one silver *p* weighing
7: 61 was one silver *p* weighing
7: 67 was one silver *p* weighing
7: 73 was one silver *p* weighing
7: 79 was one silver *p* weighing
7: 85 Each silver *p* weighed a hundred

PLATEAU

Dt 3: 10 We took all the towns on the *p*,
4: 43 in the desert *p*, for the Reubenites;
Jos 13: 9 included the whole *p* of Medeba
13: 16 and the whole *p* past Medeba
13: 17 Heshbon and all its towns on the *p*,
13: 21 the towns on the *p* and the entire
20: 8 in the desert on the *p* in the tribe
Jer 21: 13 valley on the rocky *p*,
48: 8 and the *p* destroyed,
48: 21 Judgment has come to the *p*—

PLATES (PLATE)

Ex 25: 29 make its *p* and ladles of pure gold,
37: 16 its *p* and ladles and bowls
Nu 4: 7 a blue cloth and put on it the *p*,
7: 84 twelve silver *p*, twelve silver

PLATFORM

2Ch 6: 13 He stood on the *p* and then knelt
6: 13 Now he had made a bronze *p*,
Ne 8: 4 stood on a high wooden *p* built

PLATTER (PLATE)

Mt 14: 8 "Give me here on a *p* the head
14: 11 His head was brought in on a *p*
Mk 6: 25 head of John the Baptist on a *p*."
6: 28 and brought back his head on a *p*.

PLAY (PLAYED PLAYERS PLAYING PLAYS)

Ge 4: 21 the father of all who *p* the harp
19: 9 and now he wants to *p* the judge!
1Sa 16: 16 He will *p* when the evil spirit
16: 16 for someone who can *p* the harp.
16: 18 who knows how to *p* the harp.
16: 23 David would take his harp and *p*.
1Ch 15: 20 were to *p* the lyres according
15: 21 and Azaziah were to *p* the harps,
16: 5 They were to *p* the lyres and harps,
Job 40: 20 and all the wild animals *p* nearby.
Ps 33: 3 *p* skillfully, and shout for joy.
81: 2 *p* the melodious harp and lyre.
Isa 11: 8 The infant will *p* near the hole
23: 16 *p* the harp well, sing many a song,

PLAYED (PLAY)

1Sa 10: 5 and harps being *p* before them,
2Ch 29: 28 singers sang and the trumpeters *p*.
Pr 30: 32 "If you have *p* the fool
Mt 11: 17 to others: " 'We *p* the flute for you,
Lk 7: 32 " 'We *p* the flute for you,
1Co 14: 7 anyone know what tune is being *p*

PLAYERS (PLAY)

Mt 9: 23 saw the flute *p* and the noisy crowd
Rev 18: 22 musicians, flute *p* and trumpeters,

PLAYING (PLAY)

1Sa 18: 10 while David was *p* the harp,
19: 9 While David was *p* the harp,
1Ki 1: 40 *p* flutes and rejoicing greatly,
2Ki 3: 15 While the harpist was *p*, the hand
1Ch 15: 28 and the *p* of lyres and harps.
16: 42 for the *p* of the other instruments
2Ch 5: 12 dressed in fine linen and *p* cymbals,
34: 12 skilled in *p* musical instruments—
Ps 68: 25 are the maidens *p* tambourines.
Zec 8: 5 filled with boys and girls *p* there."
Rev 14: 2 that of harpists *p* their harps.

PLAYS (PLAY)

1Sa 16: 17 "Find someone who *p* well
Eze 33: 32 beautiful voice and *p* an instrument

PLEA (PLEAD PLEADED PLEADING PLEADS PLEAS)

Ge 30: 6 he has listened to my *p*
Nu 21: 3 The LORD listened to Israel's *p*
1Ki 8: 28 to your servant's prayer and his *p*
8: 38 or *p* is made by any of your people
8: 45 heaven their prayer and their *p*,
8: 49 hear their prayer and their *p*,
8: 52 and to the *p* of your people Israel,
8: 52 open to your servant's *p*
9: 3 and *p* you have made before me;
2Ch 6: 19 to your servant's prayer and his *p*
6: 29 or *p* is made by any of your people
6: 35 heaven their prayer and their *p*,
33: 13 by his entreaty and listened to his *p*
Job 13: 6 listen to the *p* of my lips.
35: 13 does not listen to their empty *p*;
Ps 17: 1 Hear, O LORD, my righteous *p*;
55: 1 do not ignore my *p*;
102: 17 he will not despise their *p*.
Pr 6: 3 press your *p* with your neighbor!
Isa 32: 7 even when the *p* of the needy is just
Jer 7: 16 nor offer any *p* or petition for them;
11: 14 nor offer any *p* or petition for them,
La 3: 56 You heard my *p*: "Do not close
Eze 36: 37 yield to the *p* of the house of Israel
Lk 18: 3 who kept coming to him with the *p*,

PLEAD (PLEA)

Jdg 6: 31 "Are you going to *p* Baal's cause?
1Sa 2: 36 and a crust of bread and *p*,
1Ki 8: 47 and *p* with you in the land
2Ch 6: 37 and *p* with you in the land
Est 4: 8 and *p* with him for her people.
Job 8: 5 and *p* with the Almighty,
9: 15 I could only *p* with my Judge
35: 9 they *p* for relief from the arm
Ps 43: 1 and *p* my cause against an ungodly
Isa 1: 17 *p* the case of the widow.
45: 14 and *p* with you, saying,
Jer 5: 28 they do not *p* the case
7: 16 do not *p* with me, for I will not
15: 11 surely I will make your enemies *p*
27: 18 let them *p* with the LORD
30: 13 There is no one to *p* your cause,
Da 2: 18 He urged them to *p* for mercy
Mic 6: 1 *p* your case before the mountains;
Mk 5: 17 the people began to *p* with Jesus
Gal 4: 12 I *p* with you, brothers, become like
Php 4: 2 I *p* with Euodia and I *p*

PLEADED (PLEA)

Ge 42: 21 was when he *p* with us for his life,
Dt 3: 23 At that time I *p* with the LORD:
2Sa 12: 16 David *p* with God for the child.
Est 8: 3 Esther again *p* with the king,
Da 9: 3 *p* with him in prayer and petition,
Mt 8: 34 they *p* with him to leave their
Mk 5: 23 at his feet and *p* earnestly with him,
Lk 7: 4 they *p* earnestly with him,
15: 28 his father went out and *p* with him.
Ac 2: 40 he *p* with them, "Save yourselves
21: 12 the people there *p* with Paul not

2Co 8: 4 they urgently *p* with us
12: 8 Three times I *p* with the Lord

PLEADING (PLEA)

Pr 19: 7 Though he pursues them with *p*,
Jer 3: 21 and *p* of the people of Israel,
38: 26 'I was *p* with the king not
Lk 8: 41 *p* with him to come to his house
13: 25 stand outside knocking and *p*,

PLEADS (PLEA)

Job 16: 21 as a man *p* for his friend.
16: 21 on behalf of a man he *p* with God
Pr 18: 23 A poor man *p* for mercy,
Isa 59: 4 no one *p* his case with integrity.
Mic 7: 9 until he *p* my case

PLEAS (PLEA)

2Ch 6: 39 hear their prayer and their *p*,
Isa 19: 22 and he will respond to their *p*

PLEASANT (PLEASE)

Ge 49: 15 and how *p* is his land,
Ps 16: 6 for me in *p* places;
106: 24 Then they despised the *p* land;
133: 1 How good and *p* it is
135: 3 sing praise to his name, for that is *p*
147: 1 how *p* and fitting to praise him!
Pr 2: 10 knowledge will be *p* to your soul.
3: 17 Her ways are *p* ways,
16: 21 and *p* words promote instruction.
16: 24 *P* words are a honeycomb,
Isa 30: 10 Tell us *p* things,
32: 12 Beat your breasts for the *p* fields,
Jer 12: 10 they will turn my *p* field
31: 26 My sleep had been *p* to me.
Hos 4: 13 where the shade is *p*.
9: 13 planted in a *p* place.
Mic 2: 9 from their *p* homes.
Zec 7: 14 they made the *p* land desolate.' "
1Th 3: 6 that you always have *p* memories
Heb 12: 11 No discipline seems *p* at the time,

PLEASANTNESS (PLEASE)

Pr 27: 9 the *p* of one's friend springs

PLEASE (PLEASANT PLEASANTNESS PLEASED PLEASES PLEASING PLEASURE PLEASURES)

Ge 19: 2 *p* turn aside to your servant's house
19: 18 Lot said to them, "No, my lords, *p!*
24: 14 '*P* let down your jar that I may
24: 17 "*P* give me a little water
24: 23 Whose daughter are you? *P* tell me,
24: 42 *p* grant success to the journey
24: 43 "*P* let me drink a little water
24: 45 and I said to her, '*P* give me a drink
27: 19 *P* sit up and eat some of my game
30: 14 "*P* give me some of your son's
30: 27 favor in your eyes, *p* stay.
32: 29 Jacob said, "*P* tell me your name."
33: 10 "No, *p!*" said Jacob.
33: 11 *P* accept the present that was
34: 8 *P* give her to him as his wife.
43: 20 "*P*, sir," they said, "we came
44: 18 Judah went up to him and said: "*P*,
44: 33 *p* let your servant remain here
47: 4 *p* let your servants settle in Goshen
50: 17 *p* forgive the sins of the servants
Ex 4: 13 *p* send someone else to do it."
21: 8 If she does not *p* the master who
32: 32 But now, *p* forgive their sin—
Nu 10: 31 But Moses said, "*P* do not leave us.
12: 11 and he said to Moses, "*P*, my lord,
12: 13 *p* heal her!" The LORD replied
20: 17 *P* let us pass through your country.
23: 27 Perhaps it will *p* God
36: 6 They may marry anyone they *p*
Dt 12: 13 burnt offerings anywhere you *p*.
28: 63 so it will *p* him to ruin and destroy
Jos 2: 12 *p* swear to me by the LORD that
Jdg 4: 19 "*P* give me some water."
6: 18 *P* do not go away until I come back
10: 15 think best, but *p* rescue us now."
16: 28 *p* strengthen me just once more,
18: 5 "*P* inquire of God to learn
19: 6 *P* stay tonight and enjoy yourself."
Ru 2: 7 '*P* let me glean and gather
1Sa 9: 18 "Would you *p* tell me where
15: 30 But *p* honor me before the elders
25: 8 *P* give your servants and your son
25: 24 *P* let your servant speak to you;
25: 28 *P* forgive your servant's offense,
28: 22 Now *p* listen to your servant
2Sa 13: 13 *P* speak to the king; he will not
13: 24 and his officials *p* join me?"
13: 26 *p* let my brother Amnon come
18: 22 *p* let me run behind the Cushite."
1Ki 2: 17 So he continued, "*P* ask King
3: 26 *P*, my lord, give her the living baby
17: 11 And bring me, *p*, a piece of bread."
20: 32 servant Ben-Hadad says: '*P* let me
20: 37 man and said, "Strike me, *p*."
2Ki 1: 13 "*p* have respect for my life
4: 22 "*P* send me one of the servants
5: 15 *P* accept now a gift
5: 17 said Naaman, "*p* let me, your
5: 22 *P* give them a talent of silver
6: 3 "Won't you *p* come
18: 26 "*P* speak to your servants
2Ch 10: 7 *p* them and give them a favorable
Ne 9: 37 our bodies and our cattle as they *p*.
Est 3: 11 "and do with the people as you *p*."
Job 10: 3 Does it *p* you to oppress me,
34: 9 when he tries to *p* God.'
Ps 69: 31 This will *p* the LORD more
Pr 20: 23 and dishonest scales do not *p* him.
Isa 29: 11 "Read this, *p*," he will answer,
29: 12 "Read this, *p*," he will answer,
36: 11 "*P* speak to your servants
44: 28 and will accomplish all that I *p*;
46: 10 and I will do all that I *p*.
58: 3 day of your fasting, you do as you *p*
58: 13 as you *p* on my holy day,
58: 13 as you *p* or speaking idle words,
Jer 6: 20 your sacrifices do not *p* me."
27: 5 and I give it to anyone I *p*.
36: 15 "Sit down, *p*, and read it to us."
37: 3 "*P* pray to the LORD our God
37: 20 But now, my lord the king, *p* listen.
40: 4 before you; go wherever you *p*."
40: 5 or go anywhere else you *p*."
42: 2 "*P* hear our petition and pray
Da 1: 12 "*P* test your servants for ten days:
Hos 9: 4 nor will their sacrifices *p* him.
10: 10 When I *p*, I will punish them;
Jnh 1: 14 *p* do not let us die for taking this
Mk 5: 23 *P* come and put your hands on her
Lk 14: 18 *P* excuse me.'
14: 19 *P* excuse me.'
Jn 5: 30 for I seek not to *p* myself
Ac 8: 34 eunuch asked Philip, "Tell me, *p*,
9: 38 "*P* come at once!" Peter went
13: 15 for the people, *p* speak."
21: 39 *P* let me speak to the people."
Ro 8: 8 by the sinful nature cannot *p* God.
15: 1 of the weak and not to *p* ourselves.
15: 2 Each of us should *p* his neighbor
15: 3 even Christ did not *p* himself but,
1Co 7: 32 affairs—how he can *p* the Lord.
7: 33 how he can *p* his wife—
7: 34 how she can *p* her husband.
10: 33 I try to *p* everybody in every way.
2Co 5: 9 So we make it our goal to *p* him,
Gal 1: 10 If I were still trying to *p* men,
1: 10 or of God? Or am I trying to *p* men
6: 8 sows to *p* his sinful nature,
6: 8 the one who sows to *p* the Spirit,
Col 1: 10 and may *p* him in every way:
1Th 2: 4 We are not trying to *p* men
4: 1 how to live in order to *p* God,
2Ti 2: 4 wants to *p* his commanding officer.
Tit 2: 9 to try to *p* them, not to talk back
Heb 11: 6 faith it is impossible to *p* God,

PLEASED (PLEASE)

Ge 45: 16 Pharaoh and all his officials were *p*.
49: 6 and hamstrung oxen as they *p*.
Ex 33: 16 will anyone know that you are *p*
33: 17 because I am *p* with you
Lev 10: 19 Would the LORD have been *p*
Nu 14: 8 If the LORD is *p* with us, he will
24: 1 Balaam saw that it *p* the LORD
Dt 21: 14 If you are not *p* with her, let her go
28: 63 as it *p* the LORD to make you
33: 11 and be *p* with the work of his hands
Jos 22: 30 Manasseh had to say, they were *p*.
1Sa 12: 22 LORD was *p* to make you his own.
16: 22 in my service, for I am *p* with him."
18: 5 This *p* all the people, and Saul's
18: 20 they told Saul about it, he was *p*.
18: 22 'Look, the king is *p* with you,
18: 26 he was *p* to become the king's
29: 6 and I would be *p* to have you serve
2Sa 3: 36 everything the king did *p* them.
3: 36 the people took note and were *p*;
7: 29 Now be *p* to bless the house
15: 26 'I am not *p* with you,' then I am
19: 6 I see that you would be *p*
1Ki 3: 10 The Lord was *p* that Solomon had
5: 7 message, he was greatly *p*
9: 12 had given him, he was not *p*
11: 19 so *p* with Hadad that he gave him
1Ch 17: 27 you have been *p* to bless the house
28: 4 and from my father's sons he was *p*
29: 17 that you test the heart and are *p*
Ne 2: 6 will you get back?" It *p* the king
9: 24 to deal with them as they *p*.
12: 44 Judah was *p* with the ministering
Est 1: 21 his nobles were *p* with this advice,
2: 9 The girl *p* him and won his favor.
2: 14 he was *p* with her and summoned
5: 2 he was *p* with her and held out
8: 5 if he is *p* with me, let an order be
9: 5 and they did what they *p*
Ps 40: 13 Be *p*, O LORD, to save me;
41: 11 I know that you are *p* with me,
105: 22 to discipline his princes as he *p*
Ecc 4: 16 those who came later were not *p*
Isa 42: 21 It *p* the LORD
Eze 18: 23 am I not *p* when they turn
Da 4: 27 O king, be *p* to accept my advice:
6: 1 It *p* Darius to appoint 120 satraps
8: 4 He did as he *p* and became great.
Hos 8: 13 but the LORD is not *p* with them.
Jnh 1: 14 O LORD, have done as you *p*."
Mic 6: 7 Will the LORD be *p*
Mal 1: 8 Would he be *p* with you? Would he
1: 10 I am not *p* with you," says
2: 17 and he is *p* with them"
Mt 3: 17 whom I love; with him I am well *p*
14: 6 *p* Herod so much that he promised
17: 5 whom I love; with him I am well *p*.
Mk 1: 11 whom I love; with you I am well *p*
6: 22 she *p* Herod and his dinner guests.
Lk 3: 22 whom I love; with you I am well *p*
12: 32 for your Father has been *p*
23: 8 Herod saw Jesus, he was greatly *p*,
Jn 5: 21 life to whom he is *p* to give it.
Ac 6: 5 This proposal *p* the whole group.
12: 3 When he saw that this *p* the Jews,
Ro 15: 26 and Achaia were *p* to make
15: 27 They were *p* to do it, and indeed
1Co 1: 21 God was *p* through the foolishness
10: 5 God was not *p* with most of them;
Gal 1: 15 was *p* to reveal his Son in me
Col 1: 19 For God was *p* to have all his
Heb 10: 6 you were not *p*.
10: 8 nor were you *p* with them"
10: 38 I will not be *p* with him."
11: 5 commended as one who *p* God.
13: 16 for with such sacrifices God is *p*.
2Pe 1: 17 whom I love; with him I am well *p*

PLEASES (PLEASE)

1Sa 23: 20 down whenever it *p* you to do
2Sa 19: 27 of God; so do whatever *p* you.
19: 37 Do for him whatever *p* you."
19: 38 I will do for him whatever *p* you.
24: 22 lord the king take whatever *p* him
1Ch 21: 23 lord the king do whatever *p* him.
Ezr 5: 17 if it *p* the king, let a search be made
Ne 2: 5 "If it *p* the king and if your servant
2: 7 I also said to him, "If it *p* the king,
Est 1: 19 "Therefore, if it *p* the king,
2: 4 let the girl who *p* the king be queen
3: 9 If it *p* the king, let a decree be
5: 4 "If it *p* the king," replied Esther,
5: 8 if it *p* the king to grant my petition
7: 3 O king, and if it *p* your majesty,
8: 5 "If it *p* the king," she said,
9: 13 "If it *p* the king," Esther answered,
Job 23: 13 He does whatever he *p*.
Ps 115: 3 he does whatever *p* him.

Ps 135: 6 The LORD does whatever *p* him,
Pr 15: 8 but the prayer of the upright *p* him.
21: 1 it like a watercourse wherever he *p*.
Ecc 2: 26 To the man who *p* him, God gives
2: 26 it over to the one who *p* God.
7: 26 man who *p* God will escape her,
8: 3 for he will do whatever he *p*.
11: 7 and it *p* the eyes to see the sun.
Isa 56: 4 who choose what *p* me
Eze 46: 5 is to be as much as he *p*,
46: 11 with the lambs as much as one *p*,
Da 4: 35 He does as he *p*
11: 3 with great power and do as he *p*.
11: 16 The invader will do as he *p*;
11: 36 "The king will do as he *p*.
Jn 3: 8 The wind blows wherever it *p*.
8: 29 for I always do what *p* him."
Eph 5: 10 truth) and find out what *p* the Lord
Col 3: 20 in everything, for this *p* the Lord.
1Ti 2: 3 This is good, and *p* God our Savior,
1Jn 3: 22 his commands and do what *p* him.

PLEASING (PLEASE)

Ge 2: 9 trees that were *p* to the eye
3: 6 good for food and *p* to the eye,
8: 21 The LORD smelled the *p* aroma
Ex 29: 18 offering to the LORD, a *p* aroma,
29: 25 for a *p* aroma to the LORD,
29: 41 a *p* aroma, an offering made
Lev 1: 9 an aroma *p* to the LORD.
1: 13 an aroma *p* to the LORD.
1: 17 an aroma *p* to the LORD.
2: 2 an aroma *p* to the LORD.
2: 9 an aroma *p* to the LORD.
2: 12 offered on the altar as a *p* aroma.
3: 5 an aroma *p* to the LORD.
3: 16 an offering made by fire, a *p* aroma.
4: 31 as an aroma *p* to the LORD.
6: 15 as an aroma *p* to the LORD.
6: 21 as an aroma *p* to the LORD.
8: 21 a *p* aroma, an offering made
8: 28 a *p* aroma, an offering made
17: 6 as an aroma *p* to the LORD.
23: 13 to the LORD by fire, a *p* aroma—
23: 18 an aroma *p* to the LORD.
26: 31 in the *p* aroma of your offerings.
Nu 15: 3 as an aroma *p* to the LORD—
15: 7 Offer it as an aroma *p* to the LORD
15: 10 an aroma *p* to the LORD.
15: 13 as an aroma *p* to the LORD.
15: 14 as an aroma *p* to the LORD,
15: 24 as an aroma *p* to the LORD,
18: 17 an aroma *p* to the LORD.
28: 2 made by fire, as an aroma *p* to me.'
28: 6 at Mount Sinai as a *p* aroma,
28: 8 an aroma *p* to the LORD.
28: 13 is for a burnt offering, a *p* aroma,
28: 24 as an aroma *p* to the LORD;
28: 27 as an aroma *p* to the LORD.
29: 2 As an aroma *p* to the LORD,
29: 6 to the LORD by fire—a *p* aroma.
29: 8 as an aroma *p* to the LORD a burnt
29: 13 as an aroma *p* to the LORD,
29: 36 as an aroma *p* to the LORD,
1Sa 29: 9 "I know that you have been as *p*
Ezr 6: 10 so that they may offer sacrifices *p*
Ps 19: 14 be *p* in your sight,
104: 34 May my meditation be *p* to him,
Pr 15: 26 but those of the pure are *p* to him.
16: 7 When a man's ways are *p*
22: 18 for it is *p* when you keep them
SS 1: 3 *P* is the fragrance of your perfumes
4: 10 How much more *p* is your love
7: 6 How beautiful you are and how *p*,
La 2: 4 all who were *p* to the eye;
Ro 12: 1 *p* to God—which is your spiritual
12: 2 his good, *p* and perfect will.
14: 18 Christ in this way is *p* to God
Php 4: 18 an acceptable sacrifice, *p* to God.
1Ti 5: 4 grandparents, for this is *p* to God.
Heb 13: 21 may he work in us what is *p* to him,

PLEASURE (PLEASE)

Ge 18: 12 will I now have this *p*?"
Job 22: 3 What *p* would it give the Almighty
Ps 5: 4 You are not a God who takes *p*
51: 16 you do not take *p* in burnt offerings
51: 18 In your good *p* make Zion prosper;
Ps 109: 17 he found no *p* in blessing—
147: 10 His *p* is not in the strength
Pr 10: 23 A fool finds *p* in evil conduct,
16: 13 Kings take *p* in honest lips;
18: 2 A fool finds no *p* in understanding
21: 17 He who loves *p* will become poor;
Ecc 2: 1 I will test you with *p*
2: 2 And what does *p* accomplish?"
2: 10 I refused my heart no *p*.
5: 4 He has no *p* in fools; fulfill your
7: 4 of fools is in the house of *p*.
12: 1 "I find no *p* in them"—
Isa 1: 11 I have no *p*
9: 17 Therefore the Lord will take no *p*
Jer 6: 10 they find no *p* in it.
Eze 16: 37 whom you found *p*, those you
18: 23 Do I take any *p* in the death
18: 32 For I take no *p* in the death
33: 11 I take no *p* in the death
Da 4: 2 It is my *p* to tell you about
Hag 1: 8 so that I may take *p* in it
Mal 2: 13 or accepts them with *p*
Mt 11: 26 Father, for this was your good *p*.
Lk 10: 21 Father, for this was your good *p*.
Eph 1: 5 in accordance with his *p* and will—
1: 9 of his will according to his good *p*,
1Ti 5: 6 the widow who lives for *p* is dead
2Ti 3: 4 lovers of *p* rather than lovers
2Pe 2: 13 Their idea of *p* is to carouse

PLEASURES (PLEASE)

Ps 16: 11 with eternal *p* at your right hand.
Lk 8: 14 and *p*, and they do not mature.
Tit 3: 3 by all kinds of passions and *p*.
Heb 11: 25 rather than to enjoy the *p* of sin
Jas 4: 3 may spend what you get on your *p*.
2Pe 2: 13 reveling in their *p* while they feast

PLEDGE (PLEDGED PLEDGES)

Ge 38: 17 "Will you give me something as a *p*
38: 18 He said, "What *p* should I give you
38: 20 to get his *p* back from the woman,
Ex 22: 26 take your neighbor's cloak as a *p*,
Nu 30: 2 an oath to obligate himself by a *p*,
30: 3 or obligates herself by a *p*
30: 4 and every *p* by which she obligated
30: 4 or *p* but says nothing to her,
30: 10 obligates herself by a *p* under oath
30: 13 or any sworn *p* to deny herself.
Dt 24: 10 to get what he is offering as a *p*.
24: 11 are making the loan bring the *p* out
24: 12 sleep with his *p* in your possession.
24: 17 take the cloak of the widow as a *p*.
2Ch 34: 32 and Benjamin *p* themselves to it;
Ezr 10: 19 hands in *p* to put away their wives,
Job 17: 3 O God, the *p* you demand.
24: 3 and take the widow's ox in *p*.
Pr 6: 1 if you have struck hands in *p*
11: 15 to strike hands in *p* is safe.
17: 18 in judgment strikes hands in *p*
20: 16 hold it in *p* if he does it
22: 26 not be a man who strikes hands in *p*
27: 13 hold it in *p* if he does it
Eze 17: 18 Because he had given his hand in *p*
18: 7 returns what he took in *p* for a loan.
18: 12 does not return what he took in *p*.
18: 16 or require a *p* for a loan.
33: 15 if he gives back what he took in *p*
Am 2: 8 on garments taken in *p*.
1Ti 5: 12 they have broken their first *p*.
1Pe 3: 21 but the *p* of a good conscience

PLEDGED (PLEDGE)

Ge 19: 14 who were *p* to marry his daughters.
Ex 22: 16 a man seduces a virgin who is not *p*
Dt 20: 7 Has anyone become *p* to a woman
22: 23 in a town a virgin *p* to be married
22: 25 to meet a girl *p* to be married
22: 28 to meet a virgin who is not *p*
28: 30 You will be *p* to be married
2Ki 23: 3 Then all the people *p* themselves
1Ch 29: 24 *p* their submission
Mic 7: 20 as you *p* on oath to our fathers
Mt 1: 18 His mother Mary was *p*
Lk 1: 27 to a virgin *p* to be married
2: 5 who was *p* to be married to him

PLEDGES (PLEDGE)

Nu 30: 5 *p* by which she obligated herself
30: 7 *p* by which she obligated herself
30: 11 *p* by which she obligated herself
30: 12 *p* that came from her lips will stand
30: 14 all her vows or the *p* binding

PLEIADES

Job 9: 9 the *P* and the constellations
38: 31 "Can you bind the beautiful *P*?
Am 5: 8 (he who made the *P* and Orion,

PLENTIFUL (PLENTY)

1Ki 10: 27 as *p* as sycamore-fig trees
1Ch 12: 40 There were *p* supplies of flour,
2Ch 1: 15 as *p* as sycamore-fig trees
9: 27 as *p* as sycamore-fig trees
Isa 30: 23 from the land will be rich and *p*.
Eze 36: 29 make it *p* and will not bring famine
Mt 9: 37 harvest is *p* but the workers are
Lk 10: 2 harvest is *p*, but the workers are

PLENTY (PLENTIFUL)

Ge 24: 25 "We have *p* of straw and fodder,
33: 9 "I already have *p*, my brother.
34: 21 the land has *p* of room for them.
2Ch 2: 9 to provide me with *p* of lumber,
31: 10 enough to eat and *p* to spare,
32: 4 of Assyria come and find *p* of water
Job 20: 22 of his *p*, distress will overtake him;
Ps 17: 14 their sons have *p*,
37: 19 in days of famine they will enjoy *p*.
Pr 27: 27 You will have *p* of goats' milk
Jer 44: 17 At that time we had *p* of food
Joel 2: 26 You will have *p* to eat,
Mic 2: 11 'I will prophesy for you *p* of wine
Lk 12: 19 "You have *p* of good things laid up
Jn 3: 23 because there was *p* of water,
6: 10 There was *p* of grass in that place,
Ac 14: 17 he provides you with *p* of food
2Co 8: 14 in turn their *p* will supply what you
8: 14 the present time your *p* will supply
Php 4: 12 and I know what it is to have *p*.
4: 12 whether living in *p* or in want.

PLIED (PLY)

Lk 23: 9 He *p* him with many questions,

PLIGHT

2Ki 7: 13 Their *p* will be like that
Ps 59: 4 Arise to help me; look on my *p*!

PLOT (PLOTS PLOTTED PLOTTING)

Ge 33: 19 *p* of ground where he pitched his
2Ki 9: 10 her on the *p* of ground at Jezreel,
9: 21 They met him at the *p*
9: 26 him up and throw him on that *p*,
9: 26 pay for it on this *p* of ground,
9: 36 On the *p* of ground
9: 37 on the ground in the *p* at Jezreel,
Ne 4: 15 heard that we were aware of their *p*
Est 2: 22 Mordecai found out about the *p*
9: 25 But when the *p* came to the king's
Ps 2: 1 and the peoples *p* in vain?
21: 11 Though they *p* evil against you
31: 13 and *p* to take my life.
35: 4 may those who *p* my ruin
37: 12 The wicked *p* against the righteous
38: 12 all day long they *p* deception.
64: 6 They *p* injustice and say,
83: 3 they *p* against those you cherish.
83: 5 With one mind they *p* together;
Pr 3: 29 not *p* harm against your neighbor,
12: 20 in the hearts of those who *p* evil,
14: 22 Do not those who *p* evil go astray?
24: 2 for their hearts *p* violence,
Isa 28: 25 barley in its *p*,
Jer 11: 18 the LORD revealed their *p*
48: 2 Heshbon men will *p* her downfall:
Eze 17: 7 from the *p* where it was planted
17: 10 wither away in the *p* where it grew
Da 11: 24 He will *p* the overthrow
Hos 7: 15 but they *p* evil against me.
Mic 2: 1 to those who *p* evil on their beds!
Na 1: 9 they *p* against the LORD
Zec 8: 17 do not *p* evil against your neighbor,
Mk 3: 6 to *p* with the Herodians how they
Jn 4: 5 near the *p* of ground Jacob had

Ac 4:25 and the peoples *p* in vain?
14: 5 There was a *p* afoot
20: 3 Because the Jews made a *p*
23:13 forty men were involved in this *p*.
23:16 son of Paul's sister heard of this *p*,
23:30 informed of a *p* to be carried out

PLOTS (PLOT)

Ps 36: 4 Even on his bed he *p* evil;
52: 2 Your tongue *p* destruction;
Pr 6:14 who *p* evil with deceit in his heart
16:27 A scoundrel *p* evil,
24: 8 He who *p* evil
Isa 33:15 ears against *p* of murder
Jer 18:23 all their *p* to kill me.
La 3:60 all their *p* against me.
3:61 all their *p* against me—
Da 11:25 of the *p* devised against him.
Na 1:11 who *p* evil against the LORD
Ac 20:19 tested by the *p* of the Jews.

PLOTTED (PLOT)

Ge 37:18 and before he reached them, they *p*
2Sa 21: 5 *p* against us so that we have been
1Ki 15:27 the house of Issachar *p* against him,
16: 9 of half his chariots, *p* against him.
16:16 in the camp heard that Zimri had *p*
2Ki 21:24 of the land killed all who had *p*
2Ch 24:21 But they *p* against him,
33:25 of the land killed all who had *p*
Ne 4: 8 They all *p* together to come
Est 9:24 had *p* against the Jews
Isa 7: 5 Remaliah's son have *p* your ruin,
Jer 11:19 I did not realize that they had *p*
49:30 king of Babylon has *p* against you;
Hab 2:10 You have *p* the ruin
Mt 12:14 and *p* how they might kill Jesus.
26: 4 and they *p* to arrest Jesus
Jn 11:53 day on they *p* to take his life.

PLOTTING (PLOT)

1Sa 23: 9 David learned that Saul was *p*
Ne 6: 6 and the Jews are *p* to revolt,
Ps 56: 5 they are always *p* to harm me.
Pr 16:30 with his eye is *p* perversity;
Eze 11: 2 these are the men who are *p* evil

PLOW (PLOWED PLOWING PLOWMAN PLOWMEN PLOWS PLOWSHARES)

Dt 22:10 Do not *p* with an ox and a donkey
1Sa 8:12 and others to *p* his ground
Job 4: 8 I have observed, those who *p* evil
Pr 20: 4 A sluggard does not *p* in season;
Isa 28:24 for planting, does he *p* continually?
Hos 10:11 Judah must *p*,
Am 6:12 Does one *p* there with oxen?
Lk 9:62 "No one who puts his hand to the *p*

PLOWED (PLOW)

Dt 21: 4 to a valley that has not been *p*
Jdg 14:18 "If you had not *p* with my heifer,
Ps 129: 3 Plowmen have *p* my back
Jer 26:18 " 'Zion will be *p* like a field,
Eze 36: 9 you will be *p* and sown,
Hos 10: 4 like poisonous weeds in a *p* field.
12:11 stones on a *p* field.
Mic 3:12 Zion will be *p* like a field,

PLOWING (PLOW)

Ge 45: 6 next five years there will not be *p*
Ex 34:21 even during the *p* season
1Ki 19:19 He was *p* with twelve yoke of oxen,
19:21 He burned the *p* equipment
Job 1:14 oxen were *p* and the donkeys were
Lk 17: 7 Suppose one of you had a servant *p*

PLOWMAN (PLOW)

Am 9:13 reaper will be overtaken by the *p*
1Co 9:10 because when the *p* plows

PLOWMEN (PLOW)

Ps 129: 3 *P* have plowed my back

PLOWS (PLOW)

Ps 141: 7 "As one *p* and breaks up the earth,
Isa 28:24 When a farmer *p* for planting,
1Co 9:10 because when the plowman *p*

PLOWSHARES (PLOW)

1Sa 13:20 to the Philistines to have their *p*,
13:21 thirds of a shekel for sharpening *p*
Isa 2: 4 They will beat their swords into *p*
Joel 3:10 Beat your *p* into swords
Mic 4: 3 They will beat their swords into *p*

PLUCK (PLUCKED)

Mk 9:47 your eye causes you to sin, *p* it out.

PLUCKED (PLUCK)

Ge 8:11 in its beak was a freshly *p* olive leaf

PLUMAGE

Eze 17: 3 and full *p* of varied colors came
17: 7 with powerful wings and full *p*.

PLUMB

2Ki 21:13 the *p* line used against the house
Isa 28:17 and righteousness the *p* line;
34:11 and the *p* line of desolation.
Am 7: 7 true to *p*, with a *p* line in his hand.
7: 8 Amos?" "A *p* line," I replied.
7: 8 I am setting a *p* line
Zec 4:10 rejoice when they see the *p* line

PLUNDER (PLUNDERED PLUNDERERS)

Ge 34:29 as *p* everything in the houses.
49:27 in the evening he divides the *p*."
Ex 3:22 And so you will *p* the Egyptians."
Nu 14: 3 and children will be taken as *p*.
14:31 that you said would be taken as *p*,
31: 9 herds, flocks and goods as *p*.
31:11 They took all the *p* and spoils,
31:12 *p* to Moses and Eleazar the priest
31:32 *p* remaining from the spoils that
31:53 Each soldier had taken *p*
Dt 2:35 *p* from the towns we had captured
3: 7 the *p* from their cities we carried
13:16 Gather all the *p* of the town
13:16 burn the town and all its *p*
20:14 you may take these as *p*
20:14 you may use the *p* the LORD your
Jos 7:21 saw in the *p* a beautiful robe
8: 2 that you may carry off their *p*
8:27 for themselves the livestock and *p*
11:14 carried off for themselves all the *p*
22: 8 and divide with your brothers the *p*
Jdg 5:19 but they carried off no silver, no *p*.
5:30 all this as *p*?'
5:30 colorful garments as *p* for Sisera,
8:24 earring from your share of the *p*."
8:25 each man threw a ring from his *p*
1Sa 14:30 the *p* they took from their enemies.
14:32 They pounced on the *p* and,
14:36 by night and *p* them till dawn,
15:19 Why did you pounce on the *p*
15:21 took sheep and cattle from the *p*,
30:16 amount of *p* they had taken
30:19 *p* or anything else they had taken.
30:20 saying, "This is David's *p*."
30:22 with them the *p* we recovered.
30:26 a present for you from the *p*
30:26 he sent some of the *p* to the elders
2Sa 3:22 brought with them a great deal of *p*.
8:12 also dedicated the *p* taken
12:30 He took a great quantity of *p*
2Ki 3:23 Now to the *p*, Moab!"
1Ch 20: 2 He took a great quantity of *p*
26:27 Some of the *p* taken
2Ch 14:13 carried off a large amount of *p*.
15:11 from the *p* they had brought back.
20:25 his men went to carry off their *p*,
20:25 so much *p* that it took three days
24:23 They sent all the *p* to their king
25:13 carried off great quantities of *p*.
28: 8 They also took a great deal of *p*,
28:14 *p* in the presence of the officials
28:15 and from the *p* they clothed all who
Ne 4: 4 as *p* in a land of captivity.
Est 3:13 of Adar, and to *p* their goods.
8:11 to *p* the property of their enemies.
9:10 did not lay their hands on the *p*.
9:15 did not lay their hands on the *p*.
9:16 but did not lay their hands on the *p*.
Ps 68:12 in the camps men divide the *p*.
109:11 may strangers *p* the fruits
Pr 1:13 and fill our houses with *p*;
12:12 The wicked desire the *p* of evil men
16:19 than to share *p* with the proud.
22:23 and will *p* those who *p* them.
Isa 3:14 the *p* from the poor is
8: 4 and the *p* of Samaria will be carried
9: 3 rejoice when dividing the *p*.
10: 6 to seize loot and snatch *p*,
11:14 together they will *p* the people
17:14 the lot of those who *p* us.
33: 4 Your *p*, O nations, is harvested
33:23 and even the lame will carry off *p*.
42:22 They have become *p*,
49:24 Can *p* be taken from warriors,
49:25 and *p* retrieved from the fierce;
Jer 2:14 Why then has he become *p*?
15:13 I will give as *p*, without charge,
17: 3 I will give away as *p*,
20: 5 They will take it away as *p*
30:16 Those who *p* you will be plundered
49:32 Their camels will become *p*,
50:10 all who *p* her will have their fill,"
Eze 7:21 all over as *p* to foreigners
23:46 and give them over to terror and *p*.
25: 7 and give you as *p* to the nations.
26: 5 She will become *p* for the nations,
26:12 They will *p* your wealth
29:19 He will loot and *p* the land
36: 5 so that they might *p* its pastureland
38:12 I will *p* and loot and turn my hand
38:13 and goods and to seize much *p*?" '
38:13 to *p*? Have you gathered your
39:10 they will *p* those who plundered
Da 11:24 He will distribute *p*, loot
Am 3:10 "who hoard *p* and loot
3:11 and *p* your fortresses."
Na 2: 9 *P* the gold!
2: 9 *P* the silver!
3: 1 full of *p*,
Hab 2: 8 the peoples who are left will *p* you.
Zep 2: 9 remnant of my people will *p* them;
Zec 2: 9 so that their slaves will *p* them.
14: 1 when your *p* will be divided
Heb 7: 4 gave him a tenth of the *p*!

PLUNDERED (PLUNDER)

Ex 12:36 asked for; so they *p* the Egyptians.
Jdg 2:14 them over to raiders who *p* them.
1Sa 14:48 the hands of those who had *p* them.
17:53 the Philistines, they *p* their camp.
2Ki 7:16 and *p* the camp of the Arameans.
21:14 They will be looted and *p*
2Ch 14:14 They *p* all these villages,
Ps 44:10 and our adversaries have *p* us.
76: 5 Valiant men lie *p*,
89:41 All who pass by have *p* him;
Isa 10:13 I *p* their treasures;
24: 3 and totally *p*.
42:22 But this is a people *p* and looted,
Jer 30:16 Those who plunder you will be *p*;
50:10 So Babylonia will be *p*;
50:37 They will be *p*.
Eze 34: 8 lacks a shepherd and so has been *p*
34:22 and they will no longer be *p*.
34:28 They will no longer be *p*
36: 4 deserted towns that have been *p*
39:10 they will plunder those who *p* them
Da 11:33 or be burned or captured or *p*.
Hos 13:15 His storehouse will be *p*
Na 2:10 She is pillaged, *p*, stripped!
Hab 2: 8 Because you have *p* many nations,
Zep 1:13 Their wealth will be *p*,
Zec 2: 8 against the nations that have *p* you

PLUNDERERS (PLUNDER)

2Ki 17:20 and gave them into the hands of *p*,
Isa 42:24 and Israel to the *p*?

PLUNGE (PLUNGED)

1Sa 2:14 He would *p* it into the pan or kettle
Job 9:31 you would *p* me into a slime pit
Ps 68:23 that you may *p* your feet
Joel 2: 8 They *p* through defenses
1Ti 6: 9 and harmful desires that *p* men
1Pe 4: 4 think it strange that you do not *p*

PLUNGED (PLUNGE)

Jdg 3:21 and *p* it into the king's belly.
2Sa 18:14 and *p* them into Absalom's heart

2Sa 20: 10 and Joab *p* it into his belly,
Rev 16: 10 his kingdom was *p* into darkness.

PLUS

Eze 45: 12 Twenty shekels *p* twenty-five
45: 12 twenty-five shekels *p* fifteen

PLY (PLIED)

Isa 23: 17 and will *p* her trade with all

POCKET

1Sa 25: 29 as from the *p* of a sling.

PODS

2Ki 6: 25 of a cab of seed *p* for five shekels.
Lk 15: 16 with the *p* that the pigs were eating,

POETS

Nu 21: 27 That is why the *p* say:
Ac 17: 28 As some of your own *p* have said,

POINT (POINTED POINTING POINTS)

Jdg 3: 25 waited to the *p* of embarrassment,
1Sa 7: 11 along the way to a *p* below Beth
17: 7 and its iron *p* weighed six hundred
2Sa 13: 2 to the *p* of illness on account
2Ki 19: 3 as when children come to the *p*
20: 1 became ill and was at the *p*
2Ch 32: 24 became ill and was at the *p*
Ne 3: 16 a *p* opposite the tombs of David, as
3: 19 from a *p* facing the ascent
3: 26 up to a *p* opposite the Water Gate
Job 20: 25 the gleaming *p* out of his liver.
Pr 9: 3 from the highest *p* of the city.
9: 14 on a seat at the highest *p* of the city
Isa 37: 3 as when children come to the *p*
38: 1 became ill and was at the *p*
Jer 17: 1 inscribed with a flint *p*,
Eze 47: 20 to a *p* opposite Lebo Hamath.
Mt 4: 5 on the highest *p* of the temple.
26: 38 with sorrow to the *p* of death.
Mk 14: 34 with sorrow to the *p* of death,"
Lk 4: 9 on the highest *p* of the temple.
Jn 7: 25 At that *p* some of the people
Ac 26: 24 At this *p* Festus interrupted Paul's
Ro 2: 1 at whatever *p* you judge the other,
1Co 9: 8 merely from a human *p* of view?
2Co 5: 16 one from a worldly *p* of view.
7: 11 At every *p* you have proved
Php 3: 15 if on some *p* you think differently,
1Ti 4: 6 If you *p* these things out
2Ti 2: 9 even to the *p* of being chained like
Heb 8: 1 The *p* of what we are saying is this:
12: 4 to the *p* of shedding your blood.
Jas 2: 10 yet stumbles at just one *p* is guilty
Rev 2: 10 Be faithful, even to the *p* of death,

POINTED (POINT)

Jn 4: 44 (Now Jesus himself had *p* out that

POINTING (POINT)

Isa 58: 9 with the *p* finger and malicious talk
Mt 12: 49 and who are my brothers?" *P*
1Pe 1: 11 the Spirit of Christ in them was *p*

POINTS (POINT)

Ne 4: 13 behind the lowest *p* of the wall
Ac 25: 19 they had some *p* of dispute
Ro 15: 15 written you quite boldly on some *p*,

POISED

Job 15: 24 they overwhelm him, like a king *p*
37: 16 you know how the clouds hang *p*,

POISON (POISONED POISONOUS POISONS)

Dt 29: 18 you that produces such bitter *p*.
32: 32 Their grapes are filled with *p*,
32: 33 the deadly *p* of cobras.
Job 6: 4 my spirit drinks in their *p*;
20: 16 He will suck the *p* of serpents;
Ps 140: 3 the *p* of vipers is on their lips.
Am 6: 12 But you have turned justice into *p*
Mk 16: 18 and when they drink deadly *p*,
Ro 3: 13 "The *p* of vipers is on their lips."
Jas 3: 8 It is a restless evil, full of deadly *p*.

POISONED (POISON)

Jer 8: 14 and given us *p* water to drink,
9: 15 eat bitter food and drink *p* water.
23: 15 and drink *p* water,
Ac 14: 2 *p* their minds against the brothers.

POISONOUS (POISON)

Hos 10: 4 like *p* weeds in a plowed field.

POISONS (POISON)

Pr 23: 32 and *p* like a viper.

POKERETH-HAZZEBAIM

Ezr 2: 57 *P* and Ami The temple servants
Ne 7: 59 *P* and Amon The temple servants

POLE (POLES)

Nu 13: 23 it on a *p* between them,
21: 8 "Make a snake and put it up on a *p*;
21: 9 a bronze snake and put it up on a *p*.
Dt 16: 21 not set up any wooden Asherah *p*
Jdg 6: 25 cut down the Asherah *p* beside it.
6: 26 of the Asherah *p* that you cut down
6: 28 with the Asherah *p* beside it cut
6: 30 cut down the Asherah *p* beside it."
1Ki 15: 13 Asa cut the *p* down and burned it
15: 13 had made a repulsive Asherah *p*.
16: 33 Ahab also made an Asherah *p*
2Ki 6: 2 where each of us can get a *p*;
13: 6 the Asherah *p* remained standing
17: 16 shape of calves, and an Asherah *p*.
21: 3 to Baal and made an Asherah *p*,
21: 7 the carved Asherah *p* he had made
23: 6 He took the Asherah *p*
23: 15 and burned the Asherah *p* also.
2Ch 15: 16 Asa cut the *p* down, broke it up
15: 16 had made a repulsive Asherah *p*.

POLES (POLE)

Ex 25: 13 Then make *p* of acacia wood
25: 14 Insert the *p* into the rings
25: 15 The *p* are to remain in the rings
25: 27 rim to hold the *p* used in carrying
25: 28 Make the *p* of acacia wood,
27: 6 Make *p* of acacia wood for the altar
27: 7 The *p* are to be inserted
30: 4 to hold the *p* used to carry it.
30: 5 Make the *p* of acacia wood
34: 13 and cut down their Asherah *p*.
35: 12 with its *p* and the atonement cover
35: 13 table with its *p* and all its articles
35: 15 the altar of incense with its *p*,
35: 16 with its bronze grating, its *p*
37: 4 Then he made *p* of acacia wood
37: 5 And he inserted the *p* into the rings
37: 14 rim to hold the *p* used in carrying
37: 15 *p* for carrying the table were made
37: 27 to hold the *p* used to carry it.
37: 28 They made the *p* of acacia wood
38: 5 to hold the *p* for the four corners
38: 6 They made the *p* of acacia wood
38: 7 They inserted the *p* into the rings
39: 35 the ark of the Testimony with its *p*
39: 39 altar with its bronze grating, its *p*
40: 20 attached the *p* to the ark
Nu 4: 6 over that and put the *p* in place.
4: 8 of sea cows and put its *p* in place.
4: 11 of sea cows and put its *p* in place.
4: 14 of sea cows and put its *p* in place.
Dt 7: 5 cut down their Asherah *p*
12: 3 burn their Asherah *p* in the fire;
1Ki 8: 7 the ark and its carrying *p*.
8: 8 These *p* were so long that their
14: 15 to anger by making Asherah *p*.
14: 23 and Asherah *p* on every high hill
2Ki 17: 10 and Asherah *p* on every high hill
18: 4 and cut down the Asherah *p*.
23: 14 and cut down the Asherah *p*
1Ch 15: 15 God with the *p* on their shoulders,
2Ch 5: 8 covered the ark and its carrying *p*.
5: 9 These *p* were so long that their
14: 3 and cut down the Asherah *p*.
17: 6 and the Asherah *p* from Judah.
19: 3 have rid the land of the Asherah *p*
24: 18 and worshiped Asherah *p* and idols
31: 1 and cut down the Asherah *p*.
33: 3 to the Baals and made Asherah *p*.
33: 19 and set up Asherah *p* and idols
2Ch 34: 3 Asherah *p*, carved idols
34: 4 and smashed the Asherah *p*,
34: 7 Asherah *p* and crushed the idols
Isa 17: 8 have no regard for the Asherah *p*
27: 9 no Asherah *p* or incense altars
Jer 17: 2 their altars and Asherah *p*
Mic 5: 14 from among you your Asherah *p*

POLISH (POLISHED)

Jer 46: 4 *P* your spears,

POLISHED (POLISH)

2Ch 4: 16 of the LORD were of *p* bronze.
Ezr 8: 27 and two fine articles of *p* bronze,
SS 5: 14 His body is like *p* ivory
Isa 49: 2 he made me into a *p* arrow
Eze 21: 9 sharpened and *p*—
21: 10 *p*, and flashing like lightning!
21: 11 it is sharpened and *p*,
21: 11 " 'The sword is appointed to be *p*,
21: 28 *p* to consume

POLLUTE (POLLUTED POLLUTES)

Nu 35: 33 " 'Do not *p* the land where you are.
Jude : 8 these dreamers *p* their own bodies,

POLLUTED (POLLUTE)

Ezr 9: 11 entering to possess is a land *p*
Pr 25: 26 Like a muddied spring or a *p* well
Ac 15: 20 to abstain from food *p* by idols,
Jas 1: 27 oneself from being *p* by the world.

POLLUTES (POLLUTE)

Nu 35: 33 Bloodshed *p* the land,

POLLUX

Ac 28: 11 of the twin gods Castor and *P*.

POMEGRANATE (POMEGRANATES)

1Sa 14: 2 of Gibeah under a *p* tree in Migron.
SS 4: 3 are like the halves of a *p*.
6: 7 are like the halves of a *p*.
Joel 1: 12 the *p*, the palm and the apple tree
Hag 2: 19 *p* and the olive tree have not borne

POMEGRANATES (POMEGRANATE)

Ex 28: 33 Make *p* of blue, purple
28: 34 and the *p* are to alternate
39: 24 They made *p* of blue, purple
39: 25 around the hem between the *p*.
39: 26 and *p* alternated around the hem
Nu 13: 23 along with some *p* and figs.
20: 5 no grain or figs, grapevines or *p*.
Dt 8: 8 vines and fig trees, *p*, olive oil
1Ki 7: 18 He made *p* in two rows encircling
7: 20 were the two hundred *p* in rows all
7: 42 rows of *p* for each network,
7: 42 the four hundred *p* for the two sets
2Ki 25: 17 and *p* of bronze all around.
2Ch 3: 16 He also made a hundred *p*
4: 13 rows of *p* for each network,
4: 13 the four hundred *p* for the two sets
SS 4: 13 Your plants are an orchard of *p*
6: 11 or the *p* were in bloom.
7: 12 and if the *p* are in bloom—
8: 2 the nectar of my *p*.
Jer 52: 22 The other pillar, with its *p*,
52: 22 and *p* of bronze all around.
52: 23 There were ninety-six *p*
52: 23 the total number of *p*

POMP

Isa 8: 7 the king of Assyria with all his *p*.
10: 16 under his *p* a fire will be kindled
14: 11 All your *p* has been brought
21: 16 all the *p* of Kedar will come
Ac 25: 23 and Bernice came with great *p*

PONDER (PONDERED PONDERS)

Ps 64: 9 and *p* what he has done.
119: 95 but I will *p* your statutes.
Isa 14: 16 they *p* your fate:
33: 18 thoughts you will *p* the former

PONDERED (PONDER)

Ne 5: 7 I *p* them in my mind and then
Ps 111: 2 they are *p* by all who delight
Ecc 12: 9 He *p* and searched out

Isa 57: 11 nor *p* this in your hearts?
Lk 2: 19 up all these things and *p* them

PONDERS (PONDER)

Isa 57: 1 and no one *p* it in his heart;

PONDS

Ex 7: 19 over the *p* and all the reservoirs'—
8: 5 over the streams and canals and *p*,

PONTIUS

Lk 3: 1 when *P* Pilate was governor
Ac 4: 27 and *P* Pilate met together
1Ti 6: 13 before *P* Pilate made the good

PONTUS

Ac 2: 9 Judea and Cappadocia, *P* and Asia,
18: 2 a Jew named Aquila, a native of *P*,
1Pe 1: 1 scattered throughout *P*, Galatia,

POOL (POOLS)

2Sa 2: 13 and met them at the *p* of Gibeon.
2: 13 sat down on one side of the *p*
4: 12 hung the bodies by the *p* in Hebron
1Ki 22: 38 They washed the chariot at a *p*
2Ki 18: 17 at the aqueduct of the Upper *P*,
20: 20 and how he made the *p*
Ne 2: 14 Fountain Gate and the King's *P*,
3: 15 repaired the wall of the *P* of Siloam
3: 16 as far as the artificial *p*
Ps 114: 8 who turned the rock into a *p*,
Isa 7: 3 of the aqueduct of the Upper *P*,
22: 9 water in the Lower *P*.
22: 11 walls for the water of the Old *P*,
35: 7 The burning sand will become a *p*,
36: 2 at the aqueduct of the Upper *P*,
Jer 41: 12 him near the great *p* in Gibeon.
Na 2: 8 Nineveh is like a *p*,
Jn 5: 2 Jerusalem near the Sheep Gate a *p*,
5: 7 one to help me into the *p*
9: 7 in the *p* of Siloam" (this word

POOLS (POOL)

Dt 8: 7 a land with streams and *p* of water,
Ps 84: 6 autumn rains also cover it with *p*.
107: 35 He turned the desert into *p*
SS 7: 4 Your eyes are the *p* of Heshbon
Isa 41: 18 I will turn the desert into *p* of water
42: 15 and dry up the *p*.

POOR (POOREST POVERTY)

Ex 23: 3 favoritism to a *p* man in his lawsuit.
23: 6 to your *p* people in their lawsuits.
23: 11 *p* among your people may get food
30: 15 and the *p* are not to give less
Lev 14: 21 he is *p* and cannot afford these,
19: 10 Leave them for the *p* and the alien.
19: 15 do not show partiality to the *p*
23: 22 Leave them for the *p* and the alien.
25: 25 one of your countrymen becomes *p*
25: 35 one of your countrymen becomes *p*
25: 39 one of your countrymen becomes *p*
25: 47 one of your countrymen becomes *p*
27: 8 If anyone making the vow is too *p*
Nu 13: 20 or *p*? Are there trees on it
Dt 15: 4 there should be no *p* among you,
15: 7 is a *p* man among your brothers
15: 7 tightfisted toward your *p* brother.
15: 11 There will always be *p* people
15: 11 and toward the *p* and needy
24: 12 If the man is *p*, do not go to sleep
24: 14 advantage of a hired man who is *p*
24: 15 because he is *p* and is counting on it
Ru 3: 10 younger men, whether rich or *p*.
1Sa 2: 8 He raises the *p* from the dust
18: 23 I'm only a *p* man and little known."
2Sa 12: 1 town, one rich and the other *p*.
12: 3 but the *p* man had nothing
12: 4 lamb that belonged to the *p* man
Est 9: 22 to one another and gifts to the *p*.
Job 5: 16 So the *p* have hope,
20: 10 must make amends to the *p*;
20: 19 For he has oppressed the *p*
24: 4 force all the *p* of the land
24: 5 the *p* go about their labor
24: 9 the infant of the *p* is seized
24: 14 and kills the *p* and needy;
29: 12 I rescued the *p* who cried for help,
30: 25 Has not my soul grieved for the *p*?
31: 16 I have denied the desires of the *p*
34: 19 does not favor the rich over the *p*,
34: 28 of the *p* to come before him,
Ps 14: 6 frustrate the plans of the *p*,
22: 26 The *p* will eat and be satisfied;
34: 6 This *p* man called, and the LORD
35: 10 You rescue the *p* from those too
35: 10 *p* and needy from those who rob
37: 14 to bring down the *p* and needy,
40: 17 Yet I am *p* and needy;
49: 2 rich and *p* alike:
68: 10 O God, you provided for the *p*.
69: 32 The *p* will see and be glad—
70: 5 Yet I am *p* and needy;
74: 21 may the *p* and needy praise your
82: 3 maintain the rights of the *p*
86: 1 for I am *p* and needy.
109: 16 but hounded to death the *p*
109: 22 For I am *p* and needy,
112: 9 scattered abroad his gifts to the *p*,
113: 7 He raises the *p* from the dust
132: 15 her *p* will I satisfy with food.
140: 12 the LORD secures justice for the *p*
Pr 10: 4 Lazy hands make a man *p*,
10: 15 but poverty is the ruin of the *p*.
13: 7 to be *p*, yet has great wealth.
13: 8 but a *p* man hears no threat.
13: 23 *p* man's field may produce
14: 20 The *p* are shunned
14: 31 oppresses the *p* shows contempt
17: 5 who mocks the *p* shows contempt
18: 23 A *p* man pleads for mercy,
19: 1 Better a *p* man whose walk is
19: 4 but a *p* man's friend deserts him.
19: 7 A *p* man is shunned
19: 17 to the *p* lends to the LORD,
19: 22 better to be *p* than a liar.
20: 13 not love sleep or you will grow *p*;
21: 13 to the cry of the *p*,
21: 17 who loves pleasure will become *p*;
22: 2 Rich and *p* have this in common:
22: 7 The rich rule over the *p*,
22: 9 for he shares his food with the *p*.
22: 16 He who oppresses the *p*
22: 22 not exploit the *p* because they are *p*
23: 21 drunkards and gluttons become *p*,
28: 3 A ruler who oppresses the *p*
28: 6 Better a *p* man whose walk is
28: 8 another, who will be kind to the *p*.
28: 11 a *p* man who has discernment sees
28: 27 to the *p* will lack nothing,
29: 7 care about justice for the *p*,
29: 13 *p* man and the oppressor have this
29: 14 If a king judges the *p* with fairness,
30: 9 Or I may become *p* and steal,
30: 14 to devour the *p* from the earth,
31: 9 defend the rights of the *p*
31: 20 She opens her arms to the *p*
Ecc 4: 13 Better a *p* but wise youth
5: 8 If you see the *p* oppressed
6: 8 What does a *p* man gain
9: 15 nobody remembered that *p* man.
9: 15 there lived in that city a man *p*
9: 16 But the *p* man's wisdom is despised
Isa 3: 14 the plunder from the *p* is
3: 15 and grinding the faces of the *p*?"
10: 2 to deprive the *p* of their rights
10: 30 *P* Anathoth!
11: 4 decisions for the *p* of the earth.
14: 30 of the *p* will find pasture,
25: 4 You have been a refuge for the *p*,
26: 6 the footsteps of the *p*.
32: 7 schemes to destroy the *p* with lies,
40: 20 man too *p* to present such
41: 17 "The *p* and needy search for water,
58: 7 and to provide the *p* wanderer
61: 1 me to preach good news to the *p*.
Jer 2: 34 the lifeblood of the innocent *p*,
5: 4 I thought, "These are only the *p*;
5: 28 do not defend the rights of the *p*.
22: 16 He defended the cause of the *p*
24: 2 the other basket had very *p* figs,
24: 3 *p* ones are so bad they cannot be
24: 8 " 'But like the *p* figs, which are
29: 17 I will make them like *p* figs that are
39: 10 land of Judah some of the *p* people,
Eze 16: 49 they did not help the *p* and needy.
Eze 18: 12 He oppresses the *p* and needy.
22: 29 they oppress the *p* and needy
Am 2: 7 They trample on the heads of the *p*
4: 1 you women who oppress the *p*
5: 11 You trample on the *p*
5: 12 and you deprive the *p* of justice
8: 4 and do away with the *p* of the land,
8: 6 buying the *p* with silver
Zec 7: 10 or the fatherless, the alien or the *p*.
Mt 5: 3 saying: "Blessed are the *p* in spirit,
11: 5 the good news is preached to the *p*.
19: 21 your possessions and give to the *p*,
26: 9 and the money given to the *p*."
26: 11 The *p* you will always have
Mk 10: 21 you have and give to the *p*,
12: 42 But a *p* widow came and put
12: 43 this *p* widow has put more
14: 5 and the money given to the *p*."
14: 7 The *p* you will always have
Lk 4: 18 me to preach good news to the *p*.
6: 20 "Blessed are you who are *p*,
7: 22 the good news is preached to the *p*.
11: 41 is inside ⌊the dish⌋ to the *p*,
12: 33 your possessions and give to the *p*.
14: 13 invite the *p*, the crippled, the lame,
14: 21 of the town and bring in the *p*,
18: 22 you have and give to the *p*,
19: 8 half of my possessions to the *p*,
21: 2 also saw a *p* widow put
21: 3 "this *p* widow has put in more
Jn 12: 5 and the money given to the *p*?
12: 6 because he cared about the *p* but
12: 8 You will always have the *p*
13: 29 or to give something to the *p*.
Ac 9: 36 doing good and helping the *p*.
10: 4 and gifts to the *p* have come up
10: 31 remembered your gifts to the *p*.
24: 17 to bring my people gifts for the *p*
Ro 15: 26 for the *p* among the saints
1Co 13: 3 If I give all I possess to the *p*
13: 12 Now we see but a *p* reflection;
2Co 6: 10 sorrowful, yet always rejoicing; *p*,
8: 9 yet for your sakes he became *p*,
9: 9 scattered abroad his gifts to the *p*;
Gal 2: 10 continue to remember the *p*,
Jas 2: 2 and a *p* man in shabby clothes
2: 3 seat for you," but say to the *p* man,
2: 5 not God chosen those who are *p*
2: 6 But you have insulted the *p*.
Rev 3: 17 pitiful, *p*, blind and naked.
13: 16 small and great, rich and *p*,

POOREST (POOR)

2Ki 24: 14 Only the *p* people
25: 12 left behind some of the *p* people
Isa 14: 30 The *p* of the poor will find pasture,
Jer 40: 7 children who were the *p* in the land
52: 15 into exile some of the *p* people
52: 16 the rest of the *p* people of the land

POPLAR (POPLARS)

Ge 30: 37 took fresh-cut branches from *p*,
Isa 44: 4 like *p* trees by flowing streams.
Hos 4: 13 under oak, *p* and terebinth,

POPLARS (POPLAR)

Lev 23: 40 palm fronds, leafy branches and *p*,
Job 40: 22 the *p* by the stream surround him.
Ps 137: 2 There on the *p*
Isa 15: 7 over the Ravine of the *P*.

POPULACE (POPULATION)

2Ki 25: 11 along with the rest of the *p*

POPULATION (POPULACE)

Pr 14: 28 A large *p* is a king's glory,

PORATHA

Est 9: 8 Dalphon, Aspatha, *P*, Adalia,

PORCH (PORTICO PORTICOES)

Jdg 3: 23 Then Ehud went out to the *p*;
Joel 2: 17 weep between the temple *p*

PORCIUS FESTUS

Ac 24: 27 Felix was succeeded by *P*,

PORPHYRY

Est 1: 6 silver on a mosaic pavement of *p*,

PORT

Jnh 1: 3 he found a ship bound for that *p*.

PORTENT

Ps 71: 7 I have become like a *p* to many,
Isa 20: 3 as a sign and *p* against Egypt

PORTICO (PORCH)

1Ki 6: 3 The *p* at the front of the main hall
7: 6 In front of it was a *p*, and in front
7: 12 the temple of the LORD with its *p*.
7: 19 pillars in the *p* were in the shape
7: 21 the pillars at the *p* of the temple.
1Ch 28: 11 the plans for the *p* of the temple,
2Ch 3: 4 The *p* at the front of the temple was
8: 12 that he had built in front of the *p*,
15: 8 of the *p* of the LORD's temple.
29: 7 also shut the doors of the *p*
29: 17 of the month they reached the *p*
Eze 8: 16 between the *p* and the altar,
40: 7 to the *p* facing the temple was one
40: 8 he measured the *p* of the gateway;
40: 9 *p* of the gateway faced the temple.
40: 14 up to the *p* facing the courtyard.
40: 15 end of its *p* was fifty cubits.
40: 16 as was the *p*; the openings all
40: 21 its *p* had the same measurements
40: 22 its *p* and its palm tree decorations
40: 22 up to it, with its *p* opposite them.
40: 24 He measured its jambs and its *p*,
40: 25 and its *p* had narrow openings all
40: 26 up to it, with its *p* opposite them;
40: 29 and its *p* had openings all around.
40: 29 its *p* had the same measurements
40: 31 Its *p* faced the outer court;
40: 33 and its *p* had openings all around.
40: 33 its *p* had the same measurements
40: 34 Its *p* faced the outer court;
40: 36 its projecting walls and its *p*,
40: 37 Its *p* faced the outer court;
40: 38 room with a doorway was by the *p*
40: 39 In the *p* of the gateway were two
40: 40 outside wall of the *p* of the gateway
40: 48 and measured the jambs of the *p*,
40: 48 me to the *p* of the temple
40: 49 The *p* was twenty cubits wide,
41: 15 and the *p* facing the court,
41: 25 overhang on the front of the *p*.
41: 26 of the *p* were narrow windows
44: 3 by way of the *p* of the gateway
46: 2 the outside through the *p*
46: 8 go in through the *p* of the gateway,

PORTICOES (PORCH)

Eze 40: 30 (The *p* of the gateways

PORTION (PORTIONS)

Ge 43: 34 Benjamin's *p* was five times
Lev 2: 2 as a memorial *p* on the altar,
2: 9 He shall take out the memorial *p*
2: 16 priest shall burn the memorial *p*
5: 12 a handful of it as a memorial *p*
6: 15 burn the memorial *p* on the altar
7: 35 This is the *p* of the offerings made
24: 7 memorial *p* to represent the bread
Nu 15: 19 present a *p* as an offering
18: 8 as your *p* and regular share.
18: 28 tithes you must give the LORD's *p*
18: 29 as the LORD's *p* the best
Dt 26: 13 from my house the sacred *p*
26: 14 any of the sacred *p* while I was
32: 9 For the LORD's *p* is his people,
33: 21 the leader's *p* was kept for him.
Jos 15: 13 son of Jephunneh a *p* in Judah—
17: 14 and one *p* for an inheritance?
18: 7 however, do not get a *p* among you,
19: 9 because Judah's *p* was more
1Sa 1: 5 But to Hannah he gave a double *p*
2Ki 2: 9 "Let me inherit a double *p*
1Ch 16: 18 as the *p* you will inherit."
2Ch 30: 22 days they ate their assigned *p*
31: 4 to give the *p* due the priests
Ne 12: 47 set aside the *p* for the descendants
12: 47 set aside the *p* for the other Levites
Job 24: 18 their *p* of the land is cursed,
Ps 16: 5 you have assigned me my *p*
73: 26 and my *p* forever.
105: 11 as the *p* you will inherit."
119: 57 You are my *p*, O LORD;
142: 5 my *p* in the land of the living."
Isa 17: 14 This is the *p* of those who loot us,
53: 12 Therefore I will give him a *p*
57: 6 of the ravines are your *p*;
61: 7 and so they will inherit a double *p*
61: 7 my people will receive a double *p*,
Jer 6: 3 each tending his own *p*."
10: 16 He who is the *P* of Jacob is not like
13: 25 the *p* I have decreed for you,"
51: 19 He who is the *P* of Jacob is not like
La 3: 24 to myself, "The LORD is my *p*;
Eze 44: 30 are to give them the first *p*
45: 1 to the LORD a *p* of the land
45: 4 It will be the sacred *p* of the land
45: 6 cubits long, adjoining the sacred *p*;
45: 14 The prescribed *p* of oil, measured
48: 1 frontier, Dan will have one *p*;
48: 2 will have one *p*; it will border
48: 3 "Naphtali will have one *p*;
48: 4 "Manasseh will have one *p*;
48: 5 "Ephraim will have one *p*;
48: 6 will have one *p*; it will border
48: 7 will have one *p*; it will border
48: 8 east to west will be the *p* you are
48: 9 "The special *p* you are to offer
48: 10 This will be the sacred *p*
48: 12 a most holy *p*, bordering
48: 12 them from the sacred *p* of the land,
48: 18 bordering on the sacred *p*
48: 20 The entire *p* will be a square,
48: 20 set aside the sacred *p*,
48: 21 cubits of the sacred *p*
48: 21 of the area formed by the sacred *p*
48: 21 sacred *p* with the temple sanctuary
48: 23 Benjamin will have one *p*;
48: 24 will have one *p*; it will border
48: 25 "Issachar will have one *p*;
48: 26 "Zebulun will have one *p*;
48: 27 "Gad will have one *p*; it will border
Zec 2: 12 LORD will inherit Judah as his *p*
Rev 18: 6 Mix her a double *p*

PORTIONS (PORTION)

Ge 4: 4 But Abel brought fat *p* from some
43: 34 When *p* were served to them
Lev 8: 26 he put these on the fat *p*
9: 19 But the fat *p* of the cow
9: 24 the burnt offering and the fat *p*
10: 15 with the fat *p* of the offerings made
Jos 19: 49 dividing the land into its allotted *p*,
1Sa 1: 4 he would give *p* of the meat
2Ch 7: 7 the grain offerings and the fat *p*.
31: 19 name to distribute *p* to every male
35: 14 and the fat *p* until nightfall.
Ne 8: 12 to send *p* of food and to celebrate
12: 44 into the storerooms the *p* required
12: 47 all Israel contributed the daily *p*
13: 10 also learned that the *p* assigned
Pr 31: 15 and *p* for her servant girls.
Ecc 11: 2 Give *p* to seven, yes to eight,
Isa 34: 17 He allots their *p*;
Eze 45: 7 parallel to one of the tribal *p*.
47: 13 of Israel, with two *p* for Joseph.
48: 8 to west will equal one of the tribal *p*
48: 21 the length of the tribal *p* will belong
48: 29 will be their *p*," declares

PORTRAIT

Mt 22: 20 he asked them, "Whose *p* is this?
Mk 12: 16 he asked them, "Whose *p* is this?
Lk 20: 24 Whose *p* and inscription are on it?"

PORTRAYED

Eze 8: 10 I saw *p* all over the walls all kinds
23: 14 She saw men *p* on a wall, figures
23: 14 figures of Chaldeans *p* in red,
Gal 3: 1 very eyes Jesus Christ was clearly *p*

PORTS

Ac 27: 2 about to sail for *p* along the coast

POSES

Jer 29: 27 who *p* as a prophet among you?

POSITION (POSITIONS)

Ge 40: 13 head and restore you to your *p*,
40: 21 the chief cupbearer to his *p*,
41: 13 I was restored to my *p*,
Jos 8: 19 ambush rose quickly from their *p*
Jdg 7: 21 While each man held his *p*
9: 44 forward to a *p* at the entrance
2Sa 3: 6 had been strengthening his own *p*
1Ki 2: 35 Jehoiada over the army in Joab's *p*
15: 13 grandmother Maacah from her *p*
20: 22 "Strengthen your *p* and see what
2Ch 12: 1 After Rehoboam's *p* as king was
15: 16 grandmother Maacah from her *p*
Est 1: 19 Also let the king give her royal *p*
4: 14 come to royal *p* for such a time
Isa 22: 19 and you will be ousted from your *p*.
Da 2: 48 the king placed Daniel in a high *p*
5: 19 Because of the high *p* he gave him,
Ro 12: 16 to associate with people of low *p*.
Jas 1: 9 ought to take pride in his high *p*.
1: 10 rich should take pride in his low *p*,
2Pe 3: 17 and fall from your secure *p*.

POSITIONS (POSITION)

Jos 3: 3 you are to move out from your *p*
8: 13 had the soldiers take up their *p*—
10: 5 and took up *p* against Gibeon
10: 31 he took up *p* against it
10: 34 they took up *p* against it
Jdg 9: 34 took up concealed *p* near Shechem
20: 20 and took up battle *p* against them
20: 22 took up their *p* where they had
20: 30 and took up *p* against Gibeah
20: 33 from their places and took up *p*
1Sa 17: 20 army was going out to its battle *p*,
1Ch 9: 22 to their *p* of trust by David
2Ch 7: 6 The priests took their *p*,
14: 10 they took up battle *p* in the Valley
20: 17 Take up your *p*; stand firm
30: 16 Then they took up their regular *p*
Ecc 10: 6 Fools are put in many high *p*,
Jer 46: 4 Take your *p*
46: 14 'Take your *p* and get ready,
50: 9 They will take up their *p*
50: 14 "Take up your *p* around Babylon,
Eze 23: 24 they will take up *p* against you
Jude : 6 the angels who did not keep their *p*

POSSESS (POSSESSED POSSESSING POSSESSION POSSESSIONS POSSESSOR)

Ge 24: 60 may your offspring *p*
Lev 20: 24 I said to you, "You will *p* their land
25: 32 the Levitical towns, which they *p*.
Nu 27: 11 relative in his clan, that he may *p* it.
33: 53 for I have given you the land to *p*.
35: 2 the inheritance the Israelites will *p*.
35: 8 from the land the Israelites *p* are
36: 8 Israelite will *p* the inheritance
Dt 2: 31 begin to conquer and *p* his land."
4: 14 you are crossing the Jordan to *p*.
4: 26 you are crossing the Jordan to *p*.
5: 31 in the land I am giving them to *p*."
5: 33 days in the land that you will *p*.
6: 1 you are crossing the Jordan to *p*,
7: 1 into the land you are entering to *p*
8: 1 and *p* the land that the LORD
9: 6 is giving you this good land to *p*,
10: 11 and *p* the land that I swore
11: 8 you are crossing the Jordan to *p*,
11: 29 into the land you are entering to *p*,
12: 1 has given you to *p*— as long
15: 4 LORD your God is giving you to *p*
16: 20 *p* the land the LORD your God is
19: 2 LORD your God is giving you to *p*.
19: 14 LORD your God is giving you to *p*.
21: 1 LORD your God is giving you to *p*,
23: 20 to in the land you are entering to *p*.
25: 19 you in the land he is giving you to *p*
28: 21 from the land you are entering to *p*.
28: 63 from the land you are entering to *p*.
30: 16 in the land you are entering to *p*,
30: 18 crossing the Jordan to enter and *p*.
31: 13 you are crossing the Jordan to *p*."
32: 47 you are crossing the Jordan to *p*."
Jos 22: 19 If the land you *p* is defiled,
Jdg 11: 24 our God has given us, we will *p*.
1Ch 28: 8 that you may *p* this good land

Ezr 7: 25 wisdom of your God, which you *p*,
9: 11 entering to *p* is a land polluted
Ne 9: 23 told their fathers to enter and *p*.
Ps 37: 34 He will exalt you to *p* the land;
69: 35 people will settle there and *p* it;
Pr 8: 12 I *p* knowledge and discretion.
Isa 14: 2 house of Israel will *p* the nations
34: 11 desert owl and screech owl will *p* it;
34: 17 They will *p* it forever
57: 13 and *p* my holy mountain."
60: 21 and they will *p* the land forever.
65: 9 those who will *p* my mountains;
Jer 11: 5 honey'—the land you *p* today."
30: 3 land I gave their forefathers to *p*,'
32: 8 right to redeem it and *p* it,
Eze 33: 25 should you then *p* the land?
33: 26 Should you then *p* the land?'
36: 12 They will *p* you, and you will be
45: 8 of Israel to *p* the land according
Da 7: 18 the kingdom and will *p* it forever—
Am 9: 12 so that they may *p* the remnant
Ob : 17 will *p* its inheritance.
: 19 and Benjamin will *p* Gilead.
: 19 and people from the foothills will *p*
: 20 will *p* the towns of the Negev.
: 20 will *p* ⌊the land⌋ as far as Zarephath;
Jn 5: 39 that by them you *p* eternal life.
Ac 7: 5 after him would *p* the land,
1Co 8: 1 We know that we all *p* knowledge.
13: 3 If I give all I *p* to the poor
2Pe 1: 8 For if you *p* these qualities

POSSESSED (POSSESS)

Ps 105: 21 ruler over all he *p*,
Pr 8: 22 "The LORD *p* me at the beginning
Isa 63: 18 while your people *p* your holy
Jer 16: 19 "Our fathers *p* nothing
Eze 33: 24 only one man, yet he *p* the land.
Da 7: 22 came when they *p* the kingdom.
Mk 1: 23 man in their synagogue who was *p*
3: 22 "He is *p* by Beelzebub! By
5: 15 they saw the man who had been *p*
7: 25 woman whose little daughter was *p*
9: 17 who is *p* by a spirit that has robbed
Lk 4: 33 In the synagogue there was a man *p*
Jn 8: 49 I am not *p* by a demon," said Jesus,
10: 21 the sayings of a man *p* by a demon.

POSSESSING (POSSESS)

2Co 6: 10 nothing, and yet *p* everything.

POSSESSION (POSSESS)

Ge 15: 7 to give you this land to take *p* of it
15: 8 how can I know that I will gain *p*
17: 8 I will give as an everlasting *p* to you
22: 17 Your descendants will take *p*
28: 4 so that you may take *p*
30: 33 goat in my *p* that is not speckled
48: 4 everlasting *p* to your descendants
Ex 6: 8 I will give it to you as a *p*.
19: 5 nations you will be my treasured *p*.
22: 4 animal is found alive in his *p*—
22: 9 In all cases of illegal *p* of an ox,
23: 30 enough to take *p* of the land.
Lev 14: 34 which I am giving you as your *p*,
25: 24 the country that you hold as a *p*,
25: 28 in the *p* of the buyer until the Year
25: 34 not be sold; it is their permanent *p*.
Nu 13: 30 "We should go up and take *p*
21: 35 And they took *p* of his land.
32: 5 given to your servants as our *p*.
32: 22 And this land will be your *p*
32: 29 the land of Gilead as their *p*.
32: 30 they must accept their *p* with you
33: 53 Take *p* of the land and settle in it,
Dt 1: 8 take *p* of the land that the LORD
1: 21 Go up and take *p* of it as the LORD
1: 39 it to them and they will take *p* of it.
2: 9 to the descendants of Lot as a *p*."
2: 12 the LORD gave them as their *p*.)
2: 19 as a *p* to the descendants of Lot."
2: 19 for I will not give you *p*
2: 24 to take *p* of it and engage him
3: 18 has given you this land to take *p*
3: 20 back to the *p* I have given you."
4: 1 take *p* of the land that the LORD,
4: 5 the land you are entering to take *p*
4: 22 and take *p* of that good land.
Dt 4: 47 They took *p* of his land
7: 6 to be his people, his treasured *p*.
9: 4 here to take *p* of this land
9: 5 going in to take *p* of their land;
9: 23 take *p* of the land I have given you
11: 11 to take *p* of is a land of mountains
11: 31 take *p* of the land the LORD your
14: 2 you to be his treasured *p*.
16: 4 found in your *p* in all your land
17: 14 have taken *p* of it and settled in it,
24: 12 to sleep with his pledge in your *p*.
26: 1 as an inheritance and have taken *p*
26: 18 his treasured *p* as he promised,
30: 5 to your fathers, and you will take *p*
31: 3 and you will take *p* of their land.
32: 49 giving the Israelites as their own *p*.
33: 4 the *p* of the assembly of Jacob.
Jos 1: 11 take *p* of the land the LORD your
1: 15 and until they too have taken *p*
12: 6 of Manasseh to be their *p*.
18: 3 wait before you begin to take *p*
19: 47 the Danites had difficulty taking *p*
21: 12 to Caleb son of Jephunneh as his *p*.
21: 43 they took *p* of it and settled there.
23: 5 and you will take *p* of their land,
24: 8 and you took *p* of their land.
Jdg 1: 19 They took *p* of the hill country,
2: 6 they went to take *p* of the land,
3: 13 they took *p* of the City of Palms.
3: 28 and, taking *p* of the fords
8: 6 of Zebah and Zalmunna in your *p*?
8: 15 of Zebah and Zalmunna in your *p*?
1Ki 21: 15 and take *p* of the vineyard
21: 16 to take *p* of Naboth's vineyard.
21: 18 where he has gone to take *p* of it.
2Ch 20: 11 to drive us out of the *p* you gave us
Ne 9: 15 take *p* of the land you had sworn
9: 24 went in and took *p* of the land.
9: 25 they took *p* of houses filled
Ps 2: 8 the ends of the earth your *p*.
73: 9 their tongues take *p* of the earth.
83: 12 who said, "Let us take *p*
135: 4 Israel to be his treasured *p*.
Jer 32: 23 They came in and took *p* of it,
49: 1 Why then has Molech taken *p*
Eze 7: 24 nations to take *p* of their houses;
11: 15 this land was given to us as our *p*.'
25: 4 you to the people of the East as a *p*.
25: 10 to the people of the East as a *p*,
33: 24 land has been given to us as our *p*.'
35: 10 and we will take *p* of them,"
36: 2 heights have become our *p*." '
36: 3 so that you became the *p* of the rest
36: 5 they made my land their own *p*
44: 28 You are to give them no *p* in Israel;
44: 28 in Israel; I will be their *p*.
45: 5 as their *p* for towns to live in.
45: 8 This land will be his *p* in Israel.
Mic 2: 4 my people's *p* is divided up.
Mal 3: 17 when I make up my treasured *p*.
Eph 1: 14 of those who are God's *p*—

POSSESSIONS (POSSESS)

Ge 12: 5 all the *p* they had accumulated
13: 6 for their *p* were so great that they
14: 12 off Abram's nephew Lot and his *p*,
14: 16 back his relative Lot and his *p*,
15: 14 they will come out with great *p*.
32: 23 the stream, he sent over all his *p*.
36: 7 Their *p* were too great for them
46: 6 the *p* they had acquired in Canaan,
Nu 16: 32 and all Korah's men and all their *p*.
Dt 12: 11 all the choice *p* you have vowed
18: 8 money from the sale of family *p*.
Jos 7: 11 have put them with their own *p*.
Jdg 18: 21 and their *p* in front of them,
1Ki 13: 8 if you were to give me half your *p*,
2Ch 31: 3 from his own *p* for the morning
35: 7 all from the king's own *p*.
Ezr 8: 21 and our children, with all our *p*.
Ne 5: 13 *p* every man who does not keep
Job 15: 29 nor will his *p* spread over the land.
Pr 12: 27 but the diligent man prizes his *p*.
Ecc 5: 19 God gives any man wealth and *p*,
6: 2 God gives a man wealth, *p*
Zec 9: 4 But the LORD will take away her *p*
Mt 12: 29 carry off his *p* unless he first ties up
19: 21 go, sell your *p* and give to the poor,
Mt 24: 47 he will put him in charge of all his *p*
Mk 3: 27 carry off his *p* unless he first ties up
Lk 11: 21 guards his own house, his *p* are safe
12: 15 consist in the abundance of his *p*."
12: 33 Sell your *p* and give to the poor.
12: 44 he will put him in charge of all his *p*
16: 1 was accused of wasting his *p*.
19: 8 now I give half of my *p* to the poor,
Ac 2: 45 Selling their *p* and goods, they gave
4: 32 any of his *p* was his own,
2Co 12: 14 what I want is not your *p* but you.
Heb 10: 34 yourselves had better and lasting *p*.
1Jn 3: 17 If anyone has material *p*

POSSESSOR (POSSESS)

Ecc 7: 12 wisdom preserves the life of its *p*.

POSSIBLE

Ne 5: 8 *p*, we have bought back our Jewish
Mt 19: 26 but with God all things are *p*."
24: 24 even the elect—if that were *p*.
26: 39 if it is *p*, may this cup be taken
26: 42 if it is not *p* for this cup
Mk 9: 23 "Everything is *p* for him who
10: 27 all things are *p* with God."
13: 22 to deceive the elect—if that were *p*
14: 35 prayed that if *p* the hour might pass
14: 36 he said, "everything is *p* for you.
Lk 18: 27 with men is *p* with God."
Ac 17: 15 Timothy to join him as soon as *p*.
20: 16 if *p*, by the day of Pentecost.
26: 9 ought to do all that was *p*
Ro 12: 18 If it is *p*, as far as it depends on you,
13: 5 because of *p* punishment but also
1Co 6: 5 Is it *p* that there is nobody
9: 19 to everyone, to win as many as *p*.
9: 22 by all *p* means I might save some.

POST (POSTED POSTING POSTS)

Jos 10: 18 and *p* some men there to guard it.
Ecc 10: 4 do not leave your *p*;
Isa 21: 6 "Go, *p* a lookout
21: 8 every night I stay at my *p*.
Ac 17: 9 the others *p* bond and let them go.

POSTED (POST)

2Ki 10: 24 Now Jehu had *p* eighty men
11: 18 Then Jehoiada the priest *p* guards
Ne 4: 9 to our God and *p* a guard day
4: 16 The officers *p* themselves
Isa 22: 7 horsemen are *p* at the city gates;
62: 6 I have *p* watchmen on your walls,

POSTERITY

Ps 21: 10 their *p* from mankind.
22: 30 *P* will serve him;

POSTING (POST)

Ne 4: 13 *p* them by families,
Mt 27: 66 a seal on the stone and *p* the guard.

POSTS (POST)

Ex 26: 32 on four *p* of acacia wood overlaid
26: 37 and five *p* of acacia wood overlaid
27: 10 silver hooks and bands on the *p*.
27: 10 with twenty *p* and twenty bronze
27: 11 silver hooks and bands on the *p*.
27: 11 with twenty *p* and twenty bronze
27: 12 and have curtains, with ten *p*
27: 14 with three *p* and three bases.
27: 15 with three *p* and three bases.
27: 16 with four *p* and four bases.
27: 17 All the *p* around the courtyard are
35: 11 frames, crossbars, *p* and bases;
35: 17 curtains of the courtyard with its *p*
36: 36 They made four *p* of acacia wood
36: 38 They overlaid the tops of the *p*
36: 38 and they made five *p* with hooks
38: 10 silver hooks and bands on the *p*.
38: 10 with twenty *p* and twenty bronze
38: 11 had twenty *p* and twenty bronze
38: 11 silver hooks and bands on the *p*.
38: 12 silver hooks and bands on the *p*.
38: 12 with ten *p* and ten bases,
38: 14 with three *p* and three bases,
38: 15 with three *p* and three bases.
38: 17 The bases for the *p* were bronze.
38: 17 and bands on the *p* were silver,

Ex 38: 17 so all the *p* of the courtyard had
38: 19 with four *p* and four bronze bases.
38: 28 shekels to make the hooks for the *p*
38: 28 to overlay the tops of the *p*,
39: 33 frames, crossbars, *p* and bases;
39: 40 curtains of the courtyard with its *p*
40: 18 the crossbars and set up the *p*.
Nu 3: 36 *p*, bases, all its equipment,
3: 37 the *p* of the surrounding courtyard
4: 31 of the tabernacle, its crossbars, *p*
4: 32 the *p* of the surrounding courtyard
Jdg 16: 3 together with the two *p*,
2Ch 35: 15 gate did not need to leave their *p*,
Ne 7: 3 some at their *p* and some
13: 11 and stationed them at their *p*.
SS 3: 10 Its *p* he made of silver,

POT (POTS POTSHERD POTSHERDS POTTER POTTER'S POTTERS POTTERY)

Ge 15: 17 smoking fire *p* with a blazing torch
Lev 6: 28 The clay *p* the meat is cooked
6: 28 but if it is cooked in a bronze *p*,
6: 28 the *p* is to be scoured and rinsed
11: 33 If one of them falls into a clay *p*,
11: 33 and you must break the *p*.
11: 34 on it from such a *p* is unclean,
11: 35 or cooking *p* must be broken up.
14: 5 killed over fresh water in a clay *p*.
14: 50 birds over fresh water in a clay *p*.
15: 12 clay *p* that the man touches must
Nu 11: 8 They cooked it in a *p* or made it
Jdg 6: 19 in a basket and its broth in a *p*,
1Sa 2: 14 the pan or kettle or caldron or *p*,
2Ki 4: 38 on the large *p* and cook some stew
4: 39 he cut them up into the *p* of stew,
4: 40 there is death in the *p*!"
4: 41 He put it into the *p* and said,
4: 41 there was nothing harmful in the *p*.
Job 41: 20 from a boiling *p* over a fire of reeds.
41: 31 stirs up the sea like a *p* of ointment.
Ecc 7: 6 of thorns under the *p*,
Isa 29: 16 Can the *p* say of the potter,
Jer 1: 13 "I see a boiling *p*, tilting away
18: 4 But the *p* he was shaping
18: 4 the potter formed it into another *p*,
22: 28 Jehoiachin a despised, broken *p*,
Eze 11: 3 This city is a cooking *p*,
11: 7 are the meat and this city is the *p*,
11: 11 This city will not be a *p* for you,
24: 3 " 'Put on the cooking *p*; put it on
24: 6 to the *p* now encrusted,
24: 11 Then set the empty *p* on the coals
Mic 3: 3 like flesh for the *p*?"
Zec 14: 21 Every *p* in Jerusalem and Judah

POTENT

Isa 47: 9 and all your *p* spells.

POTIPHAR

Ge 37: 36 sold Joseph in Egypt to *P*,
39: 1 *P*, an Egyptian who was one
39: 4 *P* put him in charge
39: 5 was on everything *P* had,

POTIPHERA

Ge 41: 45 gave him Asenath daughter of *P*,
41: 50 Joseph by Asenath daughter of *P*,
46: 20 Joseph by Asenath daughter of *P*,

POTS (POT)

Ex 16: 3 There we sat around *p* of meat
27: 3 utensils of bronze—its *p* to remove
38: 3 its *p*, shovels, sprinkling bowls,
1Ki 7: 45 the *p*, shovels and sprinkling bowls.
2Ki 25: 14 They also took away the *p*, shovels,
2Ch 4: 11 He also made the *p* and shovels
4: 16 the *p*, shovels, meat forks
35: 13 and boiled the holy offerings in *p*,
Ps 58: 9 Before your *p* can feel the heat
Isa 65: 4 and whose *p* hold broth
Jer 52: 18 They also took away the *p*, shovels,
52: 19 sprinkling bowls, *p*, lampstands,
La 4: 2 are now considered as *p* of clay,
Zec 14: 20 the cooking *p* in the LORD's house
14: 21 to sacrifice will take some of the *p*

POTSHERD (POT)

Ps 22: 15 My strength is dried up like a *p*,
Isa 45: 9 a *p* among the potsherds
Jer 19: 2 near the entrance of the *P* Gate.

POTSHERDS (POT)

Job 41: 30 His undersides are jagged *p*,
Isa 45: 9 among the *p* on the ground.

POTTER (POT)

Isa 29: 16 Can the pot say of the *p*,
29: 16 as if the *p* were thought
41: 25 as if he were a *p* treading the clay.
45: 9 Does the clay say to the *p*,
64: 8 We are the clay, you are the *p*;
Jer 18: 4 so the *p* formed it into another pot,
18: 6 can I not do with you as this *p* does
18: 6 "Like clay in the hand of the *p*,
19: 1 "Go and buy a clay jar from a *p*.
Zec 11: 13 it to the *p*"— the handsome price
11: 13 the house of the LORD to the *p*.
Ro 9: 21 Does not the *p* have the right

POTTER'S (POT)

Jer 18: 2 "Go down to the *p* house,
18: 3 So I went down to the *p* house,
19: 11 this city just as this *p* jar is smashed
La 4: 2 the work of a *p* hands!
Mt 27: 7 to use the money to buy the *p* field
27: 10 they used them to buy the *p* field,

POTTERS (POT)

1Ch 4: 23 They were the *p* who lived

POTTERY (POT)

2Sa 17: 28 and bowls and articles of *p*.
Job 2: 8 Then Job took a piece of broken *p*
Ps 2: 9 you will dash them to pieces like *p*
31: 12 I have become like broken *p*.
Isa 30: 14 It will break in pieces like *p*,
Jer 25: 34 and be shattered like fine *p*.
Ro 9: 21 of clay some *p* for noble purposes
Rev 2: 27 he will dash them to pieces like *p*

POUCH (POUCHES)

Ge 42: 35 there in each man's sack was his *p*
1Sa 17: 40 them in the *p* of his shepherd's bag

POUCHES (POUCH)

Ge 42: 35 and their father saw the money *p*,

POULTICE

2Ki 20: 7 Isaiah said, "Prepare a *p* of figs."
Isa 38: 21 "Prepare a *p* of figs and apply it

POULTRY

Ne 5: 18 and some *p* were prepared for me,

POUNCE (POUNCED)

1Sa 15: 19 Why did you *p* on the plunder
Isa 33: 4 like a swarm of locusts men *p* on it.

POUNCED (POUNCE)

1Sa 14: 32 They *p* on the plunder and,

POUND (POUNDED POUNDING POUNDS)

SS 5: 4 my heart began to *p* for him.

POUNDED (POUND)

2Sa 22: 43 I *p* and trampled them like mud
Hab 3: 16 I heard and my heart *p*,

POUNDING (POUND)

Jdg 19: 22 *P* on the door, they shouted
Ps 93: 3 seas have lifted up their *p* waves.
Ac 27: 41 to pieces by the *p* of the surf.

POUNDS (POUND)

Job 37: 1 "At this my heart *p*
Ps 38: 10 My heart *p*, my strength fails me;
Jer 4: 19 My heart *p* within me,
Jn 19: 39 and aloes, about seventy-five *p*.
Rev 16: 21 of about a hundred *p* each fell

POUR (DOWNPOUR OUTPOURED OUTPOURING POURED POURING POURS)

Ex 4: 9 and *p* it on the dry ground.
29: 12 and *p* out the rest of it at the base
30: 9 and do not *p* a drink offering on it.
30: 32 Do not *p* it on men's bodies
Lev 2: 1 He is to *p* oil on it, put incense on it
2: 6 and *p* oil on it; it is a grain offering.
4: 7 of the bull's blood he shall *p* out
4: 18 The rest of the blood he shall *p* out
4: 25 and *p* out the rest of the blood
4: 30 and *p* out the rest of the blood
4: 34 and *p* out the rest of the blood
14: 15 *p* it in the palm of his own left hand
14: 26 The priest is to *p* some of the oil
Nu 5: 15 He must not *p* oil on it
19: 17 and *p* fresh water over them.
20: 8 their eyes and it will *p* out its water.
28: 7 *P* out the drink offering
Dt 12: 16 *p* it out on the ground like water.
12: 24 *p* it out on the ground like water.
15: 23 *p* it out on the ground like water.
Jdg 6: 20 on this rock, and *p* out the broth."
1Ki 18: 33 with water and *p* it on the offering
2Ki 3: 11 He used to *p* water on the hands
4: 4 *P* oil into all the jars, and
9: 3 Then take the flask and *p* the oil
Job 3: 24 my groans *p* out like water.
10: 10 Did you not *p* me out like milk
15: 13 *p* out such words from your mouth
16: 20 as my eyes *p* out tears to God;
36: 28 the clouds *p* down their moisture
Ps 16: 4 I will not *p* out their libations
19: 2 Day after day they *p* forth speech;
42: 4 as I *p* out my soul:
62: 8 *p* out your hearts to him,
69: 24 *P* out your wrath on them;
79: 6 *P* out your wrath on the nations
94: 4 They *p* out arrogant words;
104: 10 He makes springs *p* water
142: 2 I *p* out my complaint before him;
Ecc 11: 3 they *p* rain upon the earth.
Isa 44: 3 For I will *p* water on the thirsty
44: 3 I will *p* out my Spirit
46: 6 Some *p* out gold from their bags
Jer 6: 11 "*P* it out on the children
7: 18 They *p* out drink offerings
10: 25 *P* out your wrath on the nations
14: 16 I will *p* out on them the calamity
44: 17 will *p* out drink offerings to her just
44: 25 *p* out drink offerings to the Queen
48: 12 and they will *p* her out;
48: 12 "when I will send men who *p*
La 2: 19 *p* out your heart like water
Eze 7: 8 I am about to *p* out my wrath
14: 19 and *p* out my wrath upon it
20: 8 So I said I would *p* out my wrath
20: 13 So I said I would *p* out my wrath
20: 21 So I said I would *p* out my wrath
21: 31 I will *p* out my wrath upon you
22: 31 So I will *p* out my wrath on them
24: 3 and *p* water into it.
24: 7 she did not *p* it on the ground,
30: 15 I will *p* out my wrath on Pelusium,
38: 22 I will *p* down torrents of rain,
39: 29 for I will *p* out my Spirit
Hos 5: 10 I will *p* out my wrath on them
9: 4 They will not *p* out wine offerings
Joel 2: 28 I will *p* out my Spirit on all people.
2: 29 I will *p* out my Spirit in those days.
Mic 1: 6 I will *p* her stones into the valley
Zep 3: 8 and to *p* out my wrath on them—
Zec 4: 12 gold pipes that *p* out golden oil?"
12: 10 I will *p* out on the house of David
Mal 3: 10 *p* out so much blessing that you
Mt 9: 17 Neither do men *p* new wine
9: 17 *p* new wine into new wineskins,
Ac 2: 17 I will *p* out my Spirit on all people.
2: 18 I will *p* out my Spirit in those days,
Rev 16: 1 *p* out the seven bowls

POURED (POUR)

Ge 28: 18 as a pillar and *p* oil on top of it.
35: 14 and he *p* out a drink offering on it;
35: 14 offering on it; he also *p* oil on it.
Ex 8: 24 of flies *p* into Pharaoh's palace
9: 33 and the rain no longer *p*
Lev 8: 12 He *p* some of the anointing oil
8: 15 He *p* out the rest of the blood
9: 9 of the blood he *p* out at the base
21: 10 who has had the anointing oil *p*
Dt 12: 27 blood of your sacrifices must be *p*
Jdg 5: 4 the clouds *p* down water.
5: 4 the earth shook, the heavens *p*,

Ru 3: 15 he *p* into it six measures of barley
1Sa 7: 6 and *p* it out before the LORD.
10: 1 a flask of oil and *p* it on Saul's head
2Sa 21: 10 the rain *p* down from the heavens
23: 16 he *p* it out before the LORD.
1Ki 13: 3 and the ashes on it will be *p* out."
13: 5 and its ashes *p* out according
2Ki 4: 40 The stew was *p* out for the men,
9: 6 the prophet *p* the oil on Jehu's head
16: 13 and grain offering, *p* out his drink
1Ch 11: 18 he *p* it out before the LORD.
2Ch 12: 7 My wrath will not be *p* out
34: 21 is the LORD's anger that is *p* out
34: 25 my anger will be *p* out on this place
Job 29: 6 and the rock *p* out for me streams
Ps 18: 42 I *p* them out like mud in the streets.
22: 14 I am *p* out like water,
68: 8 the heavens *p* down rain,
77: 17 The clouds *p* down water,
79: 3 They have *p* out blood like water
92: 10 fine oils have been *p* upon me.
133: 2 It is like precious oil *p* on the head,
Pr 1: 23 I would have *p* out my heart to you
25: 20 or like vinegar *p* on soda,
Ecc 2: 19 work into which I have *p* my effort
SS 1: 3 your name is like perfume *p* out.
Isa 19: 14 The LORD has *p* into them
32: 15 till the Spirit is *p* upon us
42: 25 he *p* out on them his burning anger,
53: 12 because he *p* out his life unto death,
57: 6 them you have *p* out drink
63: 6 and *p* their blood on the ground."
Jer 1: 14 the north disaster will be *p* out
7: 20 my wrath will be *p* out on this place
19: 13 *p* out drink offerings to other gods
42: 18 and wrath have been *p* out
42: 18 so will my wrath be *p* out on you
44: 6 my fierce anger was *p* out;
44: 19 and *p* out drink offerings to her,
48: 11 not *p* from one jar to another—
La 2: 4 he has *p* out his wrath like fire
2: 11 my heart is *p* out on the ground
4: 11 he has *p* out his fierce anger.
Eze 16: 36 Because you *p* out your wealth
20: 28 and *p* out their drink offerings.
22: 22 I the LORD have *p* out my wrath
23: 8 and *p* out their lust upon her.
24: 7 She *p* it on the bare rock;
36: 18 So I *p* out my wrath on them
Da 9: 11 of God, have been *p* out on us,
9: 27 until the end that is decreed is *p* out
Na 1: 6 His wrath is *p* out like fire;
Zep 1: 17 Their blood will be *p* out like dust
Mt 26: 7 which she *p* on his head
26: 12 When she *p* this perfume
26: 28 which is *p* out for many
Mk 14: 3 and *p* the perfume on his head.
14: 8 She *p* perfume on my body
14: 24 which is *p* out for many," he said
Lk 5: 38 new wine must be *p*
6: 38 over, will be *p* into your lap.
7: 38 kissed them and *p* perfume
7: 46 but she has *p* perfume on my feet.
22: 20 in my blood, which is *p* out for you.
Jn 11: 2 was the same one who *p* perfume
12: 3 she *p* it on Jesus' feet and wiped his
13: 5 he *p* water into a basin
Ac 2: 33 and has *p* out what you now see
10: 45 of the Holy Spirit had been *p* out
Ro 5: 5 because God has *p* out his love
Php 2: 17 even if I am being *p* out like a drink
1Ti 1: 14 The grace of our Lord was *p* out
2Ti 4: 6 I am already being *p* out like
Tit 3: 6 whom he *p* out on us generously
Rev 14: 10 which has been *p* full strength
16: 2 and *p* out his bowl on the land,
16: 3 The second angel *p* out his bowl
16: 4 The third angel *p* out his bowl
16: 8 The fourth angel *p* out his bowl
16: 10 The fifth angel *p* out his bowl
16: 12 The sixth angel *p* out his bowl
16: 17 The seventh angel *p* out his bowl

POURING (POUR)

Ex 25: 29 and bowls for the *p* out of offerings.
29: 7 and anoint him by *p* it on his head.
37: 16 and its pitchers for the *p* out
1Sa 1: 15 I was *p* out my soul to the LORD.
2Ki 4: 5 the jars to her and she kept *p*.
Jer 32: 29 and by *p* out drink offerings
44: 18 and *p* out drink offerings to her,
44: 19 and *p* out drink offerings to her?"
Hab 2: 15 *p* it from the wineskin
Lk 10: 34 and bandaged his wounds, *p* on oil

POURS (POUR)

Job 12: 21 He *p* contempt on nobles
41: 20 Smoke *p* from his nostrils
Ps 75: 8 he *p* it out, and all the wicked
107: 40 he who *p* contempt on nobles
Pr 6: 19 a false witness who *p* out lies
14: 5 but a false witness *p* out lies.
19: 5 he who *p* out lies will not go free.
19: 9 and he who *p* out lies will perish.
Jer 6: 7 As a well *p* out its water,
6: 7 so she *p* out her wickedness.
Am 5: 8 *p* them out over the face of the land
9: 6 *p* them out over the face of the land
Mk 2: 22 And no one *p* new wine
2: 22 he *p* new wine into new wineskins
Lk 5: 37 And no one *p* new wine

POVERTY (POOR)

Dt 28: 48 and thirst, in nakedness and dire *p*,
1Sa 2: 7 The LORD sends *p* and wealth;
Pr 6: 11 *p* will come on you like a bandit
10: 15 but *p* is the ruin of the poor.
11: 24 withholds unduly, but comes to *p*.
13: 18 who ignores discipline comes to *p*
14: 23 but mere talk leads only to *p*.
21: 5 as surely as haste leads to *p*.
22: 16 to the rich—both come to *p*.
24: 34 *p* will come on you like a bandit
28: 19 fantasies will have his fill of *p*.
28: 22 and is unaware that *p* awaits him.
30: 8 give me neither *p* nor riches,
31: 7 let them drink and forget their *p*
Ecc 4: 14 born in *p* within his kingdom.
Mk 12: 44 out of her *p*, put in everything—
Lk 21: 4 she out of her *p* put in all she had
2Co 8: 2 and their extreme *p* welled up
8: 9 through his *p* might become rich.
Rev 2: 9 I know your afflictions and your *p*

POWDER

Ex 30: 36 Grind some of it to *p* and place it
32: 20 then he ground it to *p*, scattered it
Dt 9: 21 and ground it to *p* as fine as dust
28: 24 of your country into dust and *p*;
2Ki 23: 6 it to *p* and scattered the dust
23: 15 the high place and ground it to *p*,
2Ch 34: 7 poles and crushed the idols to *p*

POWER (OVERPOWER OVERPOWERED OVERPOWERING OVERPOWERS POWERFUL POWERS)

Ge 31: 29 I have the *p* to harm you;
49: 3 excelling in honor, excelling in *p*.
Ex 1: 8 not know about Joseph, came to *p*
4: 21 the wonders I have given you the *p*
9: 16 that I might show you my *p*
14: 31 saw the great *p* the LORD
15: 6 was majestic in *p*.
15: 16 By the *p* of your arm
32: 11 out of Egypt with great *p*
Nu 14: 13 By your *p* you brought these
Dt 7: 8 from the *p* of Pharaoh king
8: 17 "My *p* and the strength
9: 26 that you redeemed by your great *p*
9: 29 you brought out by your great *p*
34: 12 one has ever shown the mighty *p*
Jdg 1: 35 but when the *p* of the house
3: 12 king of Moab *p* over Israel.
6: 2 Because the *p* of Midian was
6: 9 I snatched you from the *p* of Egypt
14: 6 of the LORD came upon him in *p*
14: 19 of the LORD came upon him in *p*.
15: 14 of the LORD came upon him in *p*.
1Sa 7: 14 from the *p* of the Philistines.
10: 6 LORD will come upon you in *p*,
10: 10 Spirit of God came upon him in *p*,
10: 18 I delivered you from the *p* of Egypt
11: 6 Spirit of God came upon him in *p*,
16: 13 the LORD came upon David in *p*.
1Ki 18: 46 The *p* of the LORD came
2Ki 13: 3 under the *p* of Hazael king of Aram
2Ki 13: 5 they escaped from the *p* of Aram.
17: 7 from under the *p* of Pharaoh king
17: 36 out of Egypt with mighty *p*
19: 26 Their people, drained of *p*,
1Ch 29: 11 LORD, is the greatness and the *p*
29: 12 In your hands are strength and *p*
29: 30 with the details of his reign and *p*,
2Ch 13: 20 Jeroboam did not regain *p*
20: 6 *P* and might are in your hand,
20: 12 For we have no *p* to face this vast
25: 8 for God has the *p* to help
32: 7 for there is a greater *p* with us
36: 20 the kingdom of Persia came to *p*.
Est 10: 2 And all his acts of *p* and might,
Job 6: 13 Do I have any *p* to help myself,
9: 4 wisdom is profound, his *p* is vast.
10: 16 again display your awesome *p*
12: 13 "To God belong wisdom and *p*;
21: 7 growing old and increasing in *p*?
23: 6 Would he oppose me with great *p*?
24: 22 drags away the mighty by his *p*;
26: 12 By his *p* he churned up the sea;
26: 14 understand the thunder of his *p*?"
27: 11 I will teach you about the *p* of God;
27: 22 as he flees headlong from its *p*.
30: 18 In his great *p* ⌊God⌋ becomes like
36: 22 "God is exalted in his *p*.
37: 23 beyond our reach and exalted in *p*;
40: 16 what *p* in the muscles of his belly!
Ps 20: 6 with the saving *p* of his right hand.
22: 20 from the *p* of the dogs.
37: 17 for the *p* of the wicked will be
37: 33 will not leave them in their *p*
63: 2 and beheld your *p* and your glory.
65: 6 formed the mountains by your *p*,
66: 3 So great is your *p*
66: 7 He rules forever by his *p*,
68: 28 Summon your *p*, O God;
68: 34 Proclaim the *p* of God,
68: 34 whose *p* is in the skies.
68: 35 the God of Israel gives *p*
71: 18 till I declare your *p*
74: 13 who split open the sea by your *p*;
77: 14 you display your *p*
78: 4 his *p*, and the wonders he has done.
78: 26 led forth the south wind by his *p*.
78: 42 They did not remember his *p*—
89: 13 Your arm is endued with *p*;
89: 48 save himself from the *p* of the grave
90: 11 Who knows the *p* of your anger?
106: 8 to make his mighty *p* known.
106: 42 and subjected them to their *p*.
111: 6 He has shown his people the *p*
145: 6 of the *p* of your awesome works,
147: 5 Great is our Lord and mighty in *p*;
150: 2 Praise him for his acts of *p*;
Pr 3: 27 when it is in your *p* to act.
8: 14 I have understanding and *p*.
11: 7 from his *p* comes to nothing.
18: 21 The tongue has the *p* of life
24: 5 A wise man has great *p*,
28: 12 but when the wicked rise to *p*,
28: 28 When the wicked rise to *p*,
30: 26 conies are creatures of little *p*,
Ecc 4: 1 *p* was on the side of their
8: 8 No man has *p* over the wind
8: 8 so no one has *p* over the day
Isa 10: 33 will lop off the boughs with great *p*.
11: 2 the Spirit of counsel and of *p*,
17: 3 and royal *p* from Damascus;
19: 4 over to the *p* of a cruel master,
33: 13 are near, acknowledge my *p*!
37: 27 Their people, drained of *p*,
40: 10 the Sovereign LORD comes with *p*
40: 26 of his great *p* and mighty strength,
40: 29 and increases the *p* of the weak.
47: 14 themselves from the *p* of the flame.
63: 12 who sent his glorious arm of *p*
Jer 10: 6 and your name is mighty in *p*.
10: 12 But God made the earth by his *p*;
16: 21 my *p* and might.
18: 21 over to the *p* of the sword.
23: 10 and use their *p* unjustly.
27: 5 With my great *p* and outstretched
32: 17 and the earth by your great *p*
51: 15 "He made the earth by his *p*;
Eze 13: 21 will no longer fall prey to your *p*;
22: 6 are in you uses his *p* to shed blood.

Eze 26: 17 You were a *p* on the seas,
32: 29 and all her princes; despite their *p*,
32: 30 despite the terror caused by their *p*.
Da 2: 20 wisdom and *p* are his.
2: 23 You have given me wisdom and *p*,
2: 37 and *p* and might and glory;
4: 30 by my mighty *p* and for the glory
6: 27 Daniel from the *p* of the lions.''
7: 14 glory and sovereign *p*; all peoples,
7: 26 and his *p* will be taken away
7: 27 *p* and greatness of the kingdoms
8: 4 and none could rescue from his *p*.
8: 7 could rescue the ram from his *p*.
8: 8 of his *p* his large horn was broken
8: 9 which started small but grew in *p*
8: 22 but will not have the same *p*.
8: 24 very strong, but not by his own *p*.
8: 25 be destroyed, but not by human *p*.
11: 2 When he has gained *p*
11: 3 who will rule with great *p* and do
11: 4 nor will it have the *p* he exercised,
11: 5 rule his own kingdom with great *p*.
11: 6 and he and his *p* will not last.
11: 6 but she will not retain her *p*,
11: 16 and will have the *p* to destroy it.
11: 23 only a few people he will rise to *p*.
11: 42 He will extend his *p*
12: 7 When the *p* of the holy people has
Hos 13: 14 from the *p* of the grave;
Mic 2: 1 because it is in their *p* to do it.
3: 8 But as for me, I am filled with *p*,
7: 16 deprived of all their *p*.
Na 1: 3 to anger and great in *p*;
Hab 3: 4 where his *p* was hidden.
Hag 2: 22 and shatter the *p* of the foreign
Zec 4: 6 not by *p*, but by my Spirit,'
9: 4 and destroy her *p* on the sea,
Mt 22: 29 do not know the Scriptures or the *p*
24: 30 on the clouds of the sky, with *p*
Mk 5: 30 Jesus realized that *p* had gone out
9: 1 the kingdom of God come with *p*.''
12: 24 do not know the Scriptures or the *p*
13: 26 coming in clouds with great *p*
Lk 1: 17 in the spirit and *p* of Elijah,
1: 35 and the *p* of the Most High will
4: 14 to Galilee in the *p* of the Spirit,
4: 36 and *p* he gives orders to evil spirits
5: 17 And the *p* of the Lord was present
6: 19 because *p* was coming from him
8: 46 I know that *p* has gone out from me
9: 1 he gave them *p* and authority
10: 19 to overcome all the *p* of the enemy;
12: 5 has *p* to throw you into hell.
20: 20 they might hand him over to the *p*
21: 27 of Man coming in a cloud with *p*
24: 49 clothed with *p* from on high.''
Jn 13: 3 had put all things under his *p*,
17: 11 protect them by the *p* of your name
19: 10 ''Don't you realize I have *p*
19: 11 ''You would have no *p* over me
Ac 1: 8 you will receive *p* when the Holy
3: 12 if by our own *p* or godliness we had
4: 7 ''By what *p* or what name did you
4: 28 They did what your *p* and will had
4: 33 With great *p* the apostles
6: 8 a man full of God's grace and *p*,
8: 10 power known as the Great *P*.''
8: 10 ''This man is the divine *p* known
10: 38 were under the *p* of the devil,
10: 38 with the Holy Spirit and *p*,
13: 17 With mighty *p* he led them out
19: 20 Lord spread widely and grew in *p*.
26: 18 and from the *p* of Satan to God,
Ro 1: 4 declared with *p* to be the Son
1: 16 it is the *p* of God for the salvation
1: 20 his eternal *p* and divine nature—
4: 21 fully persuaded that God had *p*
9: 17 that I might display my *p* in you
9: 22 his wrath and make his *p* known,
15: 13 overflow with hope by the *p*
15: 19 by the *p* of signs and miracles,
15: 19 through the *p* of the Spirit.
1Co 1: 17 cross of Christ be emptied of its *p*
1: 18 to us who are being saved it is the *p*
1: 24 Christ the *p* of God
2: 4 a demonstration of the Spirit's *p*,
2: 5 on men's wisdom, but on God's *p*.
4: 19 are talking, but what *p* they have.
4: 20 God is not a matter of talk but of *p*.
5: 4 the *p* of our Lord Jesus is present,
6: 14 By his *p* God raised the Lord
15: 24 all dominion, authority and *p*.
15: 43 in *p*; it is sown a natural body,
15: 56 of death is sin, and the *p*
2Co 4: 7 to show that this all-surpassing *p* is
6: 7 in truthful speech and in the *p*
10: 4 they have divine *p*
12: 9 for my *p* is made perfect
12: 9 so that Christ's *p* may rest on me.
13: 4 weakness, yet he lives by God's *p*.
13: 4 yet by God's *p* we will live
Gal 4: 29 born by the *p* of the Spirit.
Eph 1: 19 That *p* is like the working
1: 19 and his incomparably great *p*
1: 21 and authority, *p* and dominion,
3: 7 me through the working of his *p*.
3: 16 you with *p* through his Spirit
3: 18 may have *p*, together
3: 20 according to his *p* that is at work
6: 10 in the Lord and in his mighty *p*.
Php 3: 10 and the *p* of his resurrection
3: 21 by the *p* that enables him
Col 1: 11 strengthened with all *p* according
2: 10 who is the head over every *p*
2: 12 through your faith in the *p* of God,
1Th 1: 5 also with *p*, with the Holy Spirit
2Th 1: 9 and from the majesty of his *p*
1: 11 by his *p* he may fulfill every good
2: 7 For the secret *p* of lawlessness is
2Ti 1: 7 but a spirit of *p*, of love
1: 8 for the gospel, by the *p* of God,
3: 5 form of godliness but denying its *p*.
Heb 2: 14 might destroy him who holds the *p*
7: 16 of the *p* of an indestructible life.
1Pe 1: 5 by God's *p* until the coming
4: 11 and the *p* for ever and ever.
5: 11 To him be the *p* for ever and ever.
2Pe 1: 3 His divine *p* has given us
1: 16 when we told you about the *p*
Jude : 25 *p* and authority, through Jesus
Rev 1: 6 to him be glory and *p* for ever
4: 11 to receive glory and honor and *p*,
5: 12 to receive *p* and wealth
5: 13 and honor and glory and *p*,
6: 4 Its rider was given *p* to take peace
6: 8 They were given *p* over a fourth
7: 2 four angels who had been given *p*
7: 12 and *p* and strength
9: 3 were given *p* like that of scorpions
9: 5 They were not given *p* to kill them,
9: 10 and in their tails they had *p*
9: 19 The *p* of the horses was
11: 3 I will give *p* to my two witnesses,
11: 6 These men have *p*
11: 6 and they have *p* to turn the waters
11: 17 you have taken your great *p*
12: 10 have come the salvation and the *p*
13: 2 The dragon gave the beast his *p*
13: 7 He was given *p* to make war
13: 14 of the signs he was given *p* to do
13: 15 He was given *p* to give breath
15: 8 the glory of God and from his *p*,
16: 8 and the sun was given *p*
17: 13 and will give their *p* and authority
17: 17 to give the beast their *p* to rule,
18: 10 O Babylon, city of *p*!
19: 1 and glory and *p* belong to our God,
20: 6 The second death has no *p*

POWERFUL (POWER)

Ge 18: 18 surely become a great and *p* nation,
26: 16 you have become too *p* for us.''
Nu 13: 28 But the people who live there are *p*,
20: 20 them with a large and *p* army.
22: 6 because they are too *p* for me.
Dt 26: 5 and became a great nation, *p*
Jos 4: 24 that the hand of the LORD is *p*
17: 17 ''You are numerous and very *p*.
23: 9 out before you great and *p* nations;
2Sa 5: 10 And he became more and more *p*,
22: 18 He rescued me from my *p* enemy,
1Ki 19: 11 *p* wind tore the mountains apart
1Ch 11: 9 David became more and more *p*,
2Ch 17: 12 became more and more *p*;
22: 9 in the house of Ahaziah *p* enough
26: 8 because he had become very *p*.
2Ch 26: 13 a *p* force to support the king
26: 15 helped until he became *p*.
26: 16 But after Uzziah became *p*,
27: 6 Jotham grew *p* because he walked
Ezr 4: 20 Jerusalem has had *p* kings ruling
7: 28 and all the king's *p* officials.
Est 9: 4 and he became more and more *p*.
Job 5: 15 from the clutches of the *p*.
22: 8 though you were a *p* man,
35: 9 for relief from the arm of the *p*.
Ps 18: 17 He rescued me from my *p* enemy,
29: 4 The voice of the LORD is *p*;
Ecc 7: 19 makes one wise man more *p*
9: 14 And a *p* king came against it,
Isa 27: 1 his fierce, great and *p* sword,
28: 2 the Lord has one who is *p*
Jer 5: 27 they have become rich and *p*
32: 18 *p* God, whose name is the LORD
Eze 17: 3 A great eagle with *p* wings,
17: 7 another great eagle with *p* wings
Da 7: 7 and frightening and very *p*.
11: 25 war with a large and very *p* army,
Joel 1: 6 *p* and without number;
Mic 7: 3 the *p* dictate what they desire—
Zec 6: 3 the fourth dappled—all of them *p*.
6: 7 When the *p* horses went out,
8: 22 *p* nations will come to Jerusalem
Mt 3: 11 me will come one who is more *p*
Mk 1: 7 ''After me will come one more *p*
Lk 3: 16 But one more *p* than I will come,
24: 19 *p* in word and deed before God
Ac 7: 22 and was *p* in speech and action.
9: 22 Yet Saul grew more and more *p*
2Co 13: 3 with you, but is *p* among you.
2Th 1: 7 in blazing fire with his *p* angels.
2: 11 God sends them a *p* delusion
Heb 1: 3 sustaining all things by his *p* word.
11: 34 and who became *p* in battle
Jas 5: 16 The prayer of a righteous man is *p*
2Pe 2: 11 they are stronger and more *p*,

POWERLESS

Dt 28: 32 day after day, *p* to lift a hand.
2Ch 14: 11 to help the *p* against the mighty.
Ne 5: 5 but we are *p*, because our fields
Job 26: 2 ''How you have helped the *p*!
Jer 14: 9 like a warrior *p* to save?
Da 8: 7 The ram was *p* to stand against him
11: 15 of the South will be *p* to resist;
Ro 5: 6 when we were still *p*, Christ died
6: 6 body of sin might be rendered *p*,
8: 3 For what the law was *p* to do

POWERS (POWER)

Isa 24: 21 the *p* in the heavens above
Da 4: 35 pleases with the *p* of heaven
Mt 13: 54 wisdom and these miraculous *p*?''
14: 2 That is why miraculous *p* are
Mk 6: 14 and that is why miraculous *p* are
Ro 8: 38 nor any *p*, neither height nor depth
1Co 12: 10 to another miraculous *p*,
Eph 6: 12 against the *p* of this dark world
Col 1: 16 whether thrones or *p* or rulers
2: 15 And having disarmed the *p*
Heb 6: 5 and the *p* of the coming age,
1Pe 3: 22 and *p* in submission to him.

PRACTICE (PRACTICED PRACTICES)

Lev 19: 26 '' 'Do not *p* divination or sorcery.
Dt 18: 14 listen to those who *p* sorcery
1Sa 2: 13 Now it was the *p* of the priests
27: 11 And such was his *p* as long
Ps 52: 2 you who *p* deceit.
119: 56 This has been my *p*:
Ecc 8: 8 will not release those who *p* it.
Isa 2: 6 they *p* divination like
Jer 6: 13 all *p* deceit.
8: 10 all *p* deceit.
Eze 13: 23 see false visions or *p* divination.
22: 29 The people of the land *p* extortion
33: 31 but they do not put them into *p*.
33: 32 but do not put them into *p*,
Hos 7: 1 They *p* deceit,
Mt 7: 24 into *p* is like a wise man who built
7: 26 into *p* is like a foolish man who
23: 3 for they do not *p* what they preach.
Lk 6: 47 my words and puts them into *p*.
6: 49 them into *p* is like a man who built

Lk 8:21 hear God's word and put it into *p*."
Ac 16:21 for us Romans to accept or *p*."
Ro 1:32 also approve of those who *p* them.
3:13 their tongues *p* deceit."
12:13 *P* hospitality.
1Co 11:16 we have no other *p*— nor do
Php 4:9 or seen in me—put it into *p*.
1Ti 5:4 to put their religion into *p* by caring
Jas 3:16 you find disorder and every evil *p*.
Rev 21:8 immoral, those who *p* magic arts,
22:15 those who *p* magic arts,

PRACTICED (PRACTICE)

Lev 18:30 the detestable customs that were *p*
Jos 13:22 son of Beor, who *p* divination.
2Ki 17:17 They *p* divination and sorcery
21:6 son in the fire, *p* sorcery
2Ch 33:6 *p* sorcery, divination
Eze 18:18 his own sin, because he *p* extortion,
Mt 23:23 You should have *p* the latter,
Lk 11:42 You should have *p* the latter
Ac 8:9 a man named Simon had *p* sorcery
19:19 number who had *p* sorcery brought

PRACTICES (PRACTICE)

Ex 23:24 or worship them or follow their *p*.
Lev 18:3 Do not follow their *p*.
Dt 18:10 who *p* divination or sorcery,
18:12 of these detestable *p* the LORD
Jdg 2:19 They refused to give up their evil *p*
1Ki 14:24 engaged in all the detestable *p*
2Ki 17:8 and followed the *p* of the nations
17:8 as the *p* which the kings
17:19 They followed the *p* Israel had
17:34 day they persist in their former *p*.
17:40 but persisted in their former *p*.
21:2 following the detestable *p*
2Ch 17:4 rather than the *p* of Israel.
27:2 however, continued their corrupt *p*
33:2 following the detestable *p*
36:14 following all the detestable *p*
Ezr 6:21 themselves from the unclean *p*
9:1 peoples with their detestable *p*,
9:11 By their detestable *p* they have
9:14 who commit such detestable *p*?
Ps 101:7 No one who *p* deceit
Isa 32:6 He *p* ungodliness
Jer 25:5 from your evil ways and your evil *p*
Eze 5:11 your vile images and detestable *p*,
6:9 and for all their detestable *p*.
6:11 detestable *p* of the house of Israel,
7:3 repay you for all your detestable *p*.
7:4 and the detestable *p* among you.
7:8 repay you for all your detestable *p*.
7:9 and the detestable *p* among you.
12:16 acknowledge all their detestable *p*.
14:6 and renounce all your detestable *p*!
16:2 Jerusalem with her detestable *p*
16:22 In all your detestable *p*
16:43 to all your other detestable *p*?
16:47 and copied their detestable *p*,
16:58 lewdness and your detestable *p*,
20:4 them with the detestable *p*
20:44 your evil ways and your corrupt *p*,
22:2 her with all her detestable *p*
23:36 them with their detestable *p*,
36:31 for your sins and detestable *p*.
43:8 name by their detestable *p*.
44:6 Enough of your detestable *p*,
44:7 to all your other detestable *p*,
44:13 the shame of their detestable *p*.
Mic 6:16 and all the *p* of Ahab's house,
Zec 1:4 from your evil ways and your evil *p*
1:6 to us what our ways and *p* deserve,
Mt 5:19 but whoever *p* and teaches these
Col 3:9 taken off your old self with its *p*
Rev 2:6 You hate the *p* of the Nicolaitans,
22:15 who loves and *p* falsehood.

PRAETORIUM

Mt 27:27 soldiers took Jesus into the *P*
Mk 15:16 *P*) and called together the whole

PRAISE (PRAISED PRAISES PRAISEWORTHY PRAISING)

Ge 24:27 saying, "*P* be to the LORD,
29:35 "This time I will *p* the LORD."
49:8 "Judah, your brothers will *p* you;
Ex 15:2 He is my God, and I will *p* him,
18:10 He said, "*P* be to the LORD,
Lev 19:24 an offering of *p* to the LORD.
Dt 8:10 *p* the LORD your God
10:21 He is your *p*; he is your God,
26:19 declared that he will set you in *p*,
32:3 Oh, *p* the greatness of our God!
Jos 7:19 God of Israel, and give him the *p*.
Jdg 5:2 *p* the LORD!
5:9 *P* the LORD!
Ru 4:14 said to Naomi: "*P* be to the LORD,
1Sa 25:32 David said to Abigail, "*P* be
25:39 he said, "*P* be to the LORD,
2Sa 18:28 "*P* be to the LORD your God!
22:4 to the LORD, who is worthy of *p*,
22:47 The LORD lives! *P* be to my Rock
22:50 Therefore I will *p* you, O LORD,
1Ki 1:48 '*P* be to the LORD, the God
5:7 "*P* be to the LORD today,
8:15 Then he said: "*P* be to the LORD,
8:56 saying: "*P* be to the LORD,
10:9 *P* be to the LORD your God,
1Ch 16:4 to give thanks, and to *p* the LORD,
16:9 Sing to him, sing *p* to him;
16:25 is the LORD and most worthy of *p*;
16:35 that we may glory in your *p*."
16:36 *P* be to the LORD, the God
16:36 said "Amen" and "*P* the LORD."
23:5 four thousand are to *p* the LORD
23:30 to thank and *p* the LORD.
29:10 "*P* be to you, O LORD,
29:13 and *p* your glorious name.
29:20 "*P* the LORD your God."
2Ch 2:12 Hiram added: "*P* be to the LORD,
5:13 they raised their voices in *p*
5:13 to give *p* and thanks to the LORD.
6:4 Then he said: "*P* be to the LORD,
8:14 and the Levites to lead the *p*
9:8 *P* be to the LORD your God,
20:21 and to *p* him for the splendor
20:22 As they began to sing and *p*,
29:30 to *p* the LORD with the words
30:21 by the LORD's instruments of *p*.
Ezr 3:10 took their places to *p* the LORD,
3:11 With *p* and thanksgiving they sang
3:11 shout of *p* to the LORD,
7:27 *P* be to the LORD, the God
Ne 9:5 and *p* the LORD your God,
9:5 exalted above all blessing and *p*.
12:24 who stood opposite them to give *p*
12:46 for the songs of *p* and thanksgiving
Ps 7:17 will sing *p* to the name
8:2 you have ordained *p*
9:1 I will *p* you, O LORD,
9:2 I will sing *p* to your name,
16:7 I will *p* the LORD, who counsels
18:3 to the LORD, who is worthy of *p*,
18:46 The LORD lives! *P* be to my Rock
18:49 Therefore I will *p* you
21:13 we will sing and *p* your might.
22:3 you are the *p* of Israel.
22:22 in the congregation I will *p* you.
22:23 You who fear the LORD, *p* him!
22:25 From you comes my *p*
22:26 who seek the LORD will *p* him—
26:7 proclaiming aloud your *p*
26:12 great assembly I will *p* the LORD.
28:6 *P* be to the LORD,
30:4 *p* his holy name.
30:9 Will the dust *p* you?
31:21 *P* be to the LORD,
33:1 it is fitting for the upright to *p* him.
33:2 *P* the LORD with the harp;
34:1 his *p* will always be on my lips.
35:18 of people I will *p* you.
40:3 a hymn of *p* to our God.
41:13 *P* be to the LORD, the God
42:5 for I will yet *p* him,
42:11 for I will yet *p* him,
43:4 I will *p* you with the harp,
43:5 for I will yet *p* him,
44:8 and we will *p* your name forever.
45:17 the nations will *p* you for ever
47:7 sing to him a psalm of *p*.
48:1 the LORD, and most worthy of *p*,
48:10 your *p* reaches to the ends
49:18 and men *p* you when you prosper
51:15 and my mouth will declare your *p*.
Ps 52:9 I will *p* you forever
52:9 I will *p* you in the presence
54:6 I will *p* your name, O LORD,
56:4 In God, whose word I *p*,
56:10 In God, whose word I *p*,
56:10 in the LORD, whose word I *p*—
57:9 I will *p* you, O Lord,
59:17 O my Strength, I sing *p* to you;
61:8 will I ever sing *p* to your name
63:4 I will *p* you as long as I live,
63:5 singing lips my mouth will *p* you.
63:11 swear by God's name will *p* him,
64:10 let all the upright in heart *p* him!
65:1 *P* awaits you, O God, in Zion;
66:2 offer him glory and *p*!
66:4 they sing *p* to you,
66:4 they sing *p* to your name."
66:8 let the sound of his *p* be heard;
66:8 *P* our God, O peoples,
66:17 his *p* was on my tongue.
66:20 *P* be to God,
67:3 May the peoples *p* you, O God;
67:3 may all the peoples *p* you.
67:5 May the peoples *p* you, O God;
67:5 may all the peoples *p* you.
68:4 Sing to God, sing *p* to his name,
68:19 *P* be to the Lord, to God our Savior
68:26 *P* God in the great congregation;
68:26 *p* the LORD in the assembly
68:32 sing *p* to the Lord, *Selah*
68:35 *P* be to God!
69:30 I will *p* God's name in song
69:34 Let heaven and earth *p* him,
71:6 I will ever *p* you.
71:8 My mouth is filled with your *p*,
71:14 I will *p* you more and more.
71:22 I will sing *p* to you with the lyre,
71:22 I will *p* you with the harp
71:23 joy when I sing *p* to you—
72:18 *P* be to the LORD God, the God
72:19 *P* be to his glorious name forever;
74:21 the poor and needy *p* your name.
75:9 I will sing *p* to the God of Jacob.
76:10 against men brings you *p*,
79:13 we will recount your *p*.
79:13 will *p* you forever;
86:12 I will *p* you, O Lord my God,
88:10 who are dead rise up and *p* you?
89:5 The heavens *p* your wonders,
89:52 *P* be to the LORD forever!
92:1 It is good to *p* the LORD
96:2 Sing to the LORD, *p* his name;
96:4 is the LORD and most worthy of *p*;
97:12 and *p* his holy name.
99:3 Let them *p* your great
100:4 and his courts with *p*;
100:4 give thanks to him and *p* his name.
101:1 to you, O LORD, I will sing *p*.
102:18 not yet created may *p* the LORD:
102:21 and his *p* in Jerusalem
103:1 my inmost being, *p* his holy name.
103:1 *P* the LORD, O my soul;
103:2 *P* the LORD, O my soul,
103:20 *P* the LORD, you his angels,
103:21 *P* the LORD, all his heavenly hosts
103:22 *P* the LORD, O my soul.
103:22 *P* the LORD, all his works
104:1 *P* the LORD, O my soul.
104:33 I will sing *p* to my God as long
104:35 *P* the LORD.
104:35 *P* the LORD, O my soul.
105:2 Sing to him, sing *p* to him;
105:45 *P* the LORD.
106:1 *P* the LORD.
106:2 or fully declare his *p*?
106:5 join your inheritance in giving *p*.
106:12 and sang his *p*.
106:47 and glory in your *p*.
106:48 *P* be to the LORD, the God
106:48 *P* the LORD.
107:32 *p* him in the council of the elders.
108:3 I will *p* you, O LORD,
109:1 O God, whom I *p*,
109:30 in the great throng I will *p* him.
111:1 *P* the LORD.
111:10 To him belongs eternal *p*.
112:1 *P* the LORD.
113:1 *P* the LORD.

Ps 113: 1 *P*, O servants of the LORD,
113: 1 *p* the name of the LORD.
113: 9 *P* the LORD.
115: 17 It is not the dead who *p* the LORD,
115: 18 *P* the LORD.
116: 19 *P* the LORD.
117: 1 *P* the LORD, all you nations;
117: 2 *P* the LORD.
119: 7 I will *p* you with an upright heart
119: 12 *P* be to you, O LORD;
119:108 the willing *p* of my mouth,
119:164 Seven times a day I *p* you
119:171 May my lips overflow with *p*,
119:175 Let me live that I may *p* you,
122: 4 to *p* the name of the LORD
124: 6 *P* be to the LORD,
134: 1 *P* the LORD, all you servants
134: 2 and *p* the LORD.
135: 1 *P* him, you servants of the LORD,
135: 1 *P* the LORD.
135: 1 *P* the name of the LORD;
135: 3 *P* the LORD, for the LORD is
135: 3 sing *p* to his name,
135: 19 O house of Aaron, *p* the LORD;
135: 19 O house of Israel, *p* the LORD;
135: 20 O house of Levi, *p* the LORD;
135: 20 you who fear him, *p* the LORD.
135: 21 *P* be to the LORD from Zion,
135: 21 *P* the LORD.
138: 1 I will *p* you, O LORD,
138: 1 before the "gods" I will sing your *p*.
138: 2 and will *p* your name
138: 4 May all the kings of the earth *p* you
139: 14 I *p* you because I am fearfully
140: 13 the righteous will *p* your name
142: 7 that I may *p* your name.
144: 1 *P* be to the LORD, my Rock,
145: 1 I will *p* your name for ever and ever
145: 2 Every day I will *p* you
145: 3 is the LORD and most worthy of *p*;
145: 10 All you have made will *p* you,
145: 21 Let every creature *p* his holy name
145: 21 speak in *p* of the LORD.
146: 1 *P* the LORD.
146: 1 *P* the LORD, O my soul.
146: 2 I will sing *p* to my God as long
146: 2 I will *p* the LORD all my life;
146: 10 *P* the LORD.
147: 1 how pleasant and fitting to *p* him!
147: 1 *P* the LORD.
147: 12 *p* your God, O Zion,
147: 20 *P* the LORD.
148: 1 *P* the LORD from the heavens,
148: 1 *P* the LORD.
148: 1 *p* him in the heights above.
148: 2 *P* him, all his angels,
148: 2 *p* him, all his heavenly hosts.
148: 3 *P* him, sun and moon,
148: 3 *p* him, all you shining stars.
148: 4 *P* him, you highest heavens
148: 5 Let them *p* the name of the LORD,
148: 7 *P* the LORD from the earth,
148: 13 Let them *p* the name of the LORD,
148: 14 *P* the LORD.
148: 14 the *p* of all his saints,
149: 1 his *p* in the assembly of the saints.
149: 1 *P* the LORD.
149: 3 Let them *p* his name with dancing
149: 6 May the *p* of God be
149: 9 *P* the LORD.
150: 1 *P* God in his sanctuary;
150: 1 *P* the LORD.
150: 1 *p* him in his mighty heavens.
150: 2 *P* him for his acts of power;
150: 2 *p* him for his surpassing greatness.
150: 3 *P* him with the sounding
150: 3 *p* him with the harp and lyre,
150: 4 *p* him with tambourine
150: 4 *p* him with the strings and flute,
150: 5 *p* him with resounding cymbals,
150: 5 *p* him with the clash of cymbals,
150: 6 *P* the LORD.
150: 6 that has breath *p* the LORD.
Pr 27: 2 Let another *p* you, and not your
27: 21 man is tested by the *p* he receives.
28: 4 who forsake the law *p* the wicked,
31: 31 let her works bring her *p*
Ecc 8: 10 receive *p* in the city where they did
SS 1: 4 we will *p* your love more than wine
Isa 12: 1 "I will *p* you, O LORD.
25: 1 I will exalt you and *p* your name,
38: 18 For the grave cannot *p* you,
38: 18 death cannot sing your *p*;
38: 19 The living, the living—they *p* you,
42: 8 or my *p* to idols.
42: 10 his *p* from the ends of the earth,
42: 12 and proclaim his *p* in the islands.
43: 21 that they may proclaim my *p*.
48: 9 for the sake of my *p* I hold it back
57: 19 creating *p* on the lips
60: 6 proclaiming the *p* of the LORD.
60: 18 and your gates *P*.
61: 3 and a garment of *p*
61: 11 will make righteousness and *p*
62: 7 and makes her the *p* of the earth.
62: 9 and *p* the LORD,
Jer 13: 11 people for my renown and *p*
17: 14 for you are the one I *p*.
20: 13 Give *p* to the LORD!
33: 9 *p* and honor before all nations
Da 2: 20 "*P* be to the name of God for ever
2: 23 and *p* you, O God of my fathers:
3: 28 "*P* be to the God of Shadrach,
4: 37 *p* and exalt and glorify the King
Joel 2: 26 and you will *p* the name
Hab 3: 3 and his *p* filled the earth.
Zep 3: 19 I will give them *p* and honor
3: 20 I will give you honor and *p*
Zec 11: 5 who sell them say, '*P* the LORD,
Mt 5: 16 and *p* your Father in heaven.
11: 25 At that time Jesus said, "I *p* you,
21: 16 you have ordained *p*'?"
Lk 1: 68 *P* be to the Lord, the God of Israel,
5: 26 Everyone was amazed and gave *p*
10: 21 "I *p* you, Father, Lord of heaven
17: 18 give *p* to God except this foreigner
19: 37 to *p* God in loud voices
Jn 5: 41 "I do not accept *p* from men,
5: 44 effort to obtain the *p* that comes
5: 44 if you accept *p* from one another,
12: 43 for they loved *p* from men more
12: 43 from men more than *p* from God.
Ac 12: 23 Herod did not give *p* to God,
Ro 2: 29 Such a man's *p* is not from men,
15: 7 in order to bring *p* to God.
15: 9 "Therefore I will *p* you
15: 11 "*P* the Lord, all you Gentiles,
1Co 4: 5 At that time each will receive his *p*
11: 2 I *p* you for remembering me
11: 17 the following directives I have no *p*
11: 22 Shall I *p* you for this? Certainly not
2Co 1: 3 *P* be to the God and Father
9: 13 men will *p* God for the obedience
Eph 1: 3 *P* be to the God and Father
1: 6 to the *p* of his glorious grace,
1: 12 might be for the *p* of his glory.
1: 14 to the *p* of his glory.
Php 1: 11 to the glory and *p* of God.
1Th 2: 6 We were not looking for *p*
Heb 13: 15 offer to God a sacrifice of *p*—
Jas 3: 9 With the tongue we *p* our Lord
3: 10 Out of the same mouth come *p*
5: 13 happy? Let him sing songs of *p*.
1Pe 1: 3 *P* be to the God and Father
1: 7 genuine and may result in *p*,
4: 16 but *p* God that you bear that name.
Rev 5: 12 and honor and glory and *p*!"
5: 13 be *p* and honor and glory
7: 12 *P* and glory
19: 5 "*P* our God,

PRAISED (PRAISE)

Ge 12: 15 officials saw her, they *p* her
24: 48 I *p* the LORD, the God
Jos 22: 33 glad to hear the report and *p* God.
Jdg 16: 24 people saw him, they *p* their god,
2Sa 14: 25 a man so highly *p* for his handsome
1Ch 29: 10 David *p* the LORD in the presence
29: 20 So they all *p* the LORD, the God
2Ch 20: 19 stood up and *p* the LORD,
20: 26 Beracah, where they *p* the LORD.
30: 22 offerings and *p* the LORD,
31: 8 they *p* the LORD and blessed his
Ne 5: 13 "Amen," and *p* the LORD.
8: 6 Ezra *p* the LORD, the great God;
Job 1: 21 may the name of the LORD be *p*."
Job 36: 24 which men have *p* in song.
Ps 113: 2 Let the name of the LORD be *p*,
113: 3 the name of the LORD is to be *p*.
Pr 12: 8 A man is *p* according to his wisdom
31: 30 who fears the LORD is to be *p*.
SS 6: 9 the queens and concubines *p* her.
Isa 63: 7 the deeds for which he is to be *p*,
64: 11 temple, where our fathers *p* you,
Jer 48: 2 Moab will be *p* no more;
Eze 3: 12 the glory of the LORD be *p*
Da 2: 19 Then Daniel *p* the God of heaven
4: 34 Then I *p* the Most High; I honored
5: 4 they *p* the gods of gold and silver,
5: 23 You *p* the gods of silver and gold,
Mt 9: 8 filled with awe; and they *p* God,
15: 31 And they *p* the God of Israel.
Mk 2: 12 amazed everyone and they *p* God,
Lk 2: 28 in his arms and *p* God,
4: 15 synagogues, and everyone *p* him.
7: 16 filled with awe and *p* God.
13: 13 she straightened up and *p* God.
18: 43 the people saw it, they also *p* God.
23: 47 seeing what had happened, *p* God
Ac 11: 18 no further objections and *p* God,
21: 20 When they heard this, they *p* God.
Ro 1: 25 than the Creator—who is forever *p*
9: 5 who is God over all, forever *p*!
2Co 8: 18 along with him the brother who is *p*
11: 31 to be *p* forever, knows that I am not
Gal 1: 24 And they *p* God because of me.
1Pe 4: 11 that in all things God may be *p*

PRAISES (PRAISE)

2Sa 22: 50 I will sing *p* to your name.
2Ch 23: 13 instruments were leading the *p*.
29: 30 So they sang *p* with gladness
31: 2 and to sing *p* at the gates
Ps 6: 5 Who *p* you from the grave?
9: 11 Sing *p* to the LORD, enthroned
9: 14 that I may declare your *p*
18: 49 I will sing *p* to your name.
35: 28 and of your *p* all day long.
47: 6 Sing *p* to God, sing *p*;
47: 6 sing *p* to our King, sing *p*.
147: 1 How good it is to sing *p* to our God,
Pr 31: 28 her husband also, and he *p* her:
Jer 31: 7 Make your *p* heard, and say,
Lk 1: 46 "My soul *p* the Lord
Ro 15: 11 and sing *p* to him, all you peoples."
Heb 2: 12 congregation I will sing your *p*."
1Pe 2: 9 that you may declare the *p*

PRAISEWORTHY (PRAISE)

Ps 78: 4 the *p* deeds of the LORD,
Php 4: 8 if anything is excellent or *p*—

PRAISING (PRAISE)

1Ch 25: 3 harp in thanking and *p* the LORD.
2Ch 7: 6 David had made for *p* the LORD
Ps 84: 4 they are ever *p* you.
Lk 1: 64 and he began to speak, *p* God.
2: 13 *p* God and saying, "Glory to God
2: 20 *p* God for all the things they had
5: 25 lying on and went home *p* God.
17: 15 came back, *p* God in a loud voice.
18: 43 and followed Jesus, *p* God.
24: 53 continually at the temple, *p* God.
Ac 2: 47 *p* God and enjoying the favor
3: 8 walking and jumping, and *p* God.
3: 9 saw him walking and *p* God,
4: 21 because all the people were *p* God
10: 46 speaking in tongues and *p* God.
1Co 14: 16 If you are *p* God with your spirit,

PRAY (PRAYED PRAYER PRAYERS PRAYING PRAYS)

Ge 20: 7 he will *p* for you and you will live.
32: 11 I *p*, from the hand
Ex 8: 8 "*P* to the LORD to take the frogs
8: 9 the time for me to *p* for you
8: 28 Now *p* for me."
8: 29 I leave you, I will *p* to the LORD,
9: 28 *P* to the LORD, for we have had
10: 17 and *p* to the LORD your God
Nu 21: 7 *P* that the LORD will take
Dt 4: 7 is near us whenever we *p* to him?
1Sa 12: 19 "*P* to the LORD your God
12: 23 the LORD by failing to *p* for you.

1Ki 8: 30 when they *p* toward this place.
8: 35 and when they *p* toward this place
8: 44 and when they *p* to the LORD
8: 48 *p* to you toward the land you gave
13: 6 and *p* for me that my hand may be
2Ki 19: 4 Therefore *p* for the remnant that
1Ch 17: 25 servant has found courage to *p*
2Ch 6: 21 when they *p* toward this place.
6: 26 and when they *p* toward this place
6: 34 and when they *p* to you
6: 38 *p* toward the land you gave their
7: 14 will humble themselves and *p*
Ezr 6: 10 and *p* for the well-being of the king
Job 22: 27 You will *p* to him, and he will hear
42: 8 My servant Job will *p* for you,
Ps 5: 2 for to you I *p*.
32: 6 let everyone who is godly *p*
69: 13 But I *p* to you, O LORD,
72: 15 May people ever *p* for him
122: 6 *P* for the peace of Jerusalem:
Isa 16: 12 when she goes to her shrine to *p*,
37: 4 Therefore *p* for the remnant that
45: 20 who *p* to gods that cannot save.
64: 9 Oh, look upon us, we *p*,
Jer 7: 16 "So do not *p* for this people
11: 14 "Do not *p* for this people
14: 11 "Do not *p* for the well-being
29: 7 *P* to the LORD for it,
29: 12 upon me and come and *p* to me,
31: 9 they will *p* as I bring them back.
37: 3 "Please *p* to the LORD our God
42: 2 and *p* to the LORD your God
42: 3 *P* that the LORD your God will
42: 4 "I will certainly *p* to the LORD
42: 20 '*P* to the LORD our God for us;
Da 9: 23 As soon as you began to *p*,
Mt 5: 44 and *p* for those who persecute you,
6: 5 for they love to *p* standing
6: 5 "But when you *p*, do not be like
6: 6 When you *p*, go into your room,
6: 6 close the door and *p* to your Father
6: 7 And when you *p*, do not keep
6: 9 "This is how you should *p*:
14: 23 up into the hills by himself to *p*.
19: 13 hands on them and *p* for them.
24: 20 *P* that your flight will not take
26: 36 Sit here while I go over there and *p*
26: 41 and *p* so that you will not fall
Mk 6: 46 he went into the hills to *p*.
13: 18 *P* that this will not take place
14: 32 to his disciples, "Sit here while I *p*
14: 38 and *p* so that you will not fall
Lk 5: 33 "John's disciples often fast and *p*,
6: 12 Jesus went out into the hills to *p*,
6: 28 *p* for those who mistreat you.
9: 28 and went up onto a mountain to *p*.
11: 1 us to *p*, just as John taught his
11: 2 He said to them, "When you *p*, say:
18: 1 them that they should always *p*
18: 10 up to the temple to *p*,
21: 36 and *p* that you may be able
22: 40 "*P* that you will not fall
22: 46 and *p* so that you will not fall
Jn 17: 9 I *p* for them.
17: 20 I *p* also for those who will believe
Ac 8: 22 Repent of this wickedness and *p*
8: 24 "*P* to the Lord for me
10: 9 Peter went up on the roof to *p*.
21: 5 there on the beach we knelt to *p*.
26: 29 I *p* God that not only you
Ro 1: 10 and I *p* that now at last
8: 26 do not know what we ought to *p*,
15: 31 *P* that I may be rescued
1Co 11: 13 proper for a woman to *p* to God
14: 13 in a tongue should *p* that he may
14: 14 if I *p* in a tongue, my spirit prays,
14: 15 So what shall I do? I will *p*
14: 15 but I will also *p* with my mind;
2Co 13: 7 we *p* to God that you will not do
Eph 1: 18 I *p* also that the eyes
3: 16 I *p* that out of his glorious riches he
3: 17 And I *p* that you, being rooted
6: 18 And *p* in the Spirit on all occasions
6: 19 *P* also for me, that whenever I open
6: 20 *P* that I may declare it fearlessly,
Php 1: 4 I always *p* with joy
Col 1: 3 when we *p* for you,
1: 10 we *p* this in order that you may live
Col 4: 3 *p* for us, too, that God may open
4: 4 *P* that I may proclaim it clearly,
1Th 3: 10 day we *p* most earnestly that we
5: 17 Be joyful always; *p* continually;
5: 25 Brothers, *p* for us.
2Th 1: 11 in mind, we constantly *p* for you,
1: 12 We *p* this so that the name
3: 1 *p* for us that the message
3: 2 And *p* that we may be delivered
1Ti 5: 5 and continues night and day to *p*
Phm : 6 I *p* that you may be active
Heb 13: 18 *P* for us.
13: 19 I particularly urge you to *p*
Jas 5: 13 one of you in trouble? He should *p*.
5: 14 elders of the church to *p* over him
5: 16 *p* for each other so that you may be
1Pe 4: 7 self-controlled so that you can *p*.
1Jn 5: 16 he should *p* and God will give him
5: 16 saying that he should *p* about that.
3Jn : 2 I *p* that you may enjoy good health
Jude : 20 up in your most holy faith and *p*

PRAYED (PRAY)

Ge 20: 17 Then Abraham *p* to God,
24: 12 Then he *p*, "O LORD, God
25: 21 Isaac *p* to the LORD on behalf
32: 9 Then Jacob *p*, "O God of my father
Ex 8: 30 Then Moses left Pharaoh and *p*
10: 18 Moses then left Pharaoh and *p*
Nu 11: 2 he *p* to the LORD and the fire died
21: 7 So Moses *p* for the people.
Dt 9: 20 but at that time I *p* for Aaron too.
9: 26 I *p* to the LORD and said,
Jdg 13: 8 Then Manoah *p* to the LORD:
16: 28 Then Samson *p* to the LORD,
1Sa 1: 10 of soul Hannah wept much and *p*
1: 27 I *p* for this child, and the LORD
2: 1 Then Hannah *p* and said:
2: 20 the place of the one she *p* for
8: 6 so he *p* to the LORD.
14: 41 Then Saul *p* to the LORD,
2Sa 15: 31 So David *p*, "O LORD, turn
1Ki 8: 59 which I have *p* before the LORD,
18: 36 Elijah stepped forward and *p*:
19: 4 under it and *p* that he might die.
2Ki 4: 33 two of them and *p* to the LORD.
6: 17 And Elisha *p*, "O LORD,
6: 18 toward him, Elisha *p* to the LORD,
19: 15 And Hezekiah *p* to the LORD:
20: 2 to the wall and *p* to the LORD,
2Ch 30: 18 But Hezekiah *p* for them, saying,
32: 24 He *p* to the LORD, who answered
33: 13 when he *p* to him, the LORD was
Ezr 9: 6 out to the LORD my God and *p*:
Ne 1: 4 and *p* before the God of heaven.
2: 4 Then I *p* to the God of heaven,
4: 9 we *p* to our God and posted a guard
6: 9 I *p*, "Now strengthen my hands."
Job 42: 10 After Job had *p* for his friends,
Isa 37: 15 And Hezekiah *p* to the LORD:
37: 21 Because you have *p*
38: 2 to the wall and *p* to the LORD,
Jer 32: 16 I *p* to the LORD: "Ah, Sovereign
Da 6: 10 got down on his knees and *p*,
9: 4 I *p* to the LORD my God
Jnh 2: 1 From inside the fish Jonah *p*
4: 2 He *p* to the LORD, "O LORD,
Mt 26: 39 with his face to the ground and *p*,
26: 42 He went away a second time and *p*,
26: 44 once more and *p* the third time,
Mk 1: 35 off to a solitary place, where he *p*.
14: 35 *p* that if possible the hour might
14: 39 he went away and *p* the same thing.
Lk 5: 16 withdrew to lonely places and *p*.
18: 11 stood up and *p* about himself;
22: 32 But I have *p* for you, Simon,
22: 41 knelt down and *p*, "Father,
22: 44 in anguish, he *p* more earnestly,
Jn 17: 1 he looked toward heaven and *p*:
Ac 1: 24 Then they *p*, "Lord, you know
4: 31 After they *p*, the place where they
6: 6 who *p* and laid their hands on them
7: 59 Stephen *p*, "Lord Jesus, receive my
8: 15 they *p* for them that they might
9: 40 got down on his knees and *p*.
10: 2 in need and *p* to God regularly.
13: 3 So after they had fasted and *p*,
20: 36 knelt down with all of them and *p*.
Ac 27: 29 from the stern and *p* for daylight.
Jas 5: 17 He *p* earnestly that it would not
5: 18 Again he *p*, and the heavens gave

PRAYER (PRAY)

Ge 25: 21 The LORD answered his *p*,
Ex 9: 29 hands in *p* to the LORD.
2Sa 7: 27 courage to offer you this *p*.
21: 14 God answered *p* in behalf
24: 25 the LORD answered *p* in behalf
1Ki 8: 28 attention to your servant's *p*
8: 28 the *p* that your servant is praying
8: 29 will hear the *p* your servant prays
8: 38 when a *p* or plea is made by any
8: 45 then hear from heaven their *p*
8: 49 hear their *p* and their plea,
9: 3 "I have heard the *p* and plea you
2Ki 19: 20 heard your *p* concerning
20: 5 I have heard your *p* and seen your
2Ch 6: 19 attention to your servant's *p*
6: 19 the *p* that your servant is praying
6: 20 you hear the *p* your servant prays
6: 29 when a *p* or plea is made by any
6: 35 then hear from heaven their *p*
6: 39 hear their *p* and their pleas,
7: 12 have heard your *p* and have chosen
30: 27 for their *p* reached heaven,
32: 20 out in *p* to heaven about this.
33: 18 including his *p* to his God
33: 19 His *p* and how God was moved
Ezr 8: 23 about this, and he answered our *p*.
Ne 1: 6 open to hear the *p* your servant is
1: 11 and to the *p* of your servants who
1: 11 to the *p* of this your servant
11: 17 led in thanksgiving and *p*;
Job 16: 17 and my *p* is pure.
42: 8 and I will accept his *p* and not deal
42: 9 and the LORD accepted Job's *p*.
Ps 4: 1 be merciful to me and hear my *p*.
6: 9 the LORD accepts my *p*.
17: 1 Give ear to my *p*—
17: 6 give ear to me and hear my *p*.
39: 12 "Hear my *p*, O LORD,
42: 8 a *p* to the God of my life.
54: 2 Hear my *p*, O God;
55: 1 Listen to my *p*, O God,
61: 1 listen to my *p*.
65: 2 O you who hear *p*,
66: 19 and heard my voice in *p*.
66: 20 who has not rejected my *p*
84: 8 Hear my *p*, O LORD God
86: 6 Hear my *p*, O LORD;
88: 2 May my *p* come before you;
88: 13 in the morning my *p* comes
102: 1 Hear my *p*, O LORD;
102: 17 to the *p* of the destitute;
109: 4 but I am a man of *p*.
141: 2 May my *p* be set before you like
141: 5 Yet my *p* is ever against the deeds
143: 1 O LORD, hear my *p*,
Pr 15: 8 but the *p* of the upright pleases him
15: 29 but he hears the *p* of the righteous.
Isa 1: 15 you spread out your hands in *p*,
26: 16 they could barely whisper a *p*.
38: 5 I have heard your *p* and seen your
56: 7 a house of *p* for all nations."
56: 7 and give them joy in my house of *p*.
La 3: 8 he shuts out my *p*.
3: 44 so that no *p* can get through.
Da 9: 3 pleaded with him in *p* and petition,
9: 21 while I was still in *p*, Gabriel,
Jnh 2: 7 and my *p* rose to you,
Hab 3: 1 A *p* of Habakkuk the prophet.
Mt 21: 13 house will be called a house of *p*,'
21: 22 receive whatever you ask for in *p*."
23: 5 the tassels of their *p* shawls long;
Mk 9: 29 This kind can come out only by *p*."
11: 17 a house of *p* for all nations'?
11: 24 whatever you ask for in *p*,
Lk 1: 13 Zechariah; your *p* has been heard.
19: 46 " 'My house will be a house of *p*';
22: 45 rose from *p* and went back
Jn 17: 15 My *p* is not that you take them out
17: 20 "My *p* is not for them alone.
Ac 1: 14 all joined together constantly in *p*,
2: 42 to the breaking of bread and to *p*.
3: 1 up to the temple at the time of *p*—
4: 24 raised their voices together in *p*

Ac 6: 4 and will give our attention to *p*
10: 31 has heard your *p* and remembered
14: 23 for them in each church and, with *p*
16: 13 expected to find a place of *p*.
16: 16 we were going to the place of *p*,
28: 8 Paul went in to see him and, after *p*
Ro 10: 1 *p* to God for the Israelites is that
12: 12 patient in affliction, faithful in *p*.
1Co 7: 5 you may devote yourselves to *p*.
2Co 13: 9 and our *p* is for your perfection.
Php 1: 9 this is my *p*: that your love may
4: 6 but in everything, by *p* and petition
Col 4: 2 yourselves to *p*, being watchful
4: 12 He is always wrestling in *p* for you,
1Ti 2: 8 to lift up holy hands in *p*,
4: 5 by the word of God and *p*.
Jas 5: 15 *p* offered in faith will make the sick
5: 16 *p* of a righteous man is powerful
1Pe 3: 12 and his ears are attentive to their *p*,

PRAYERS (PRAY)

1Ki 8: 54 Solomon had finished all these *p*
1Ch 5: 20 He answered their *p*, because they
2Ch 6: 40 to the *p* offered in this place.
7: 15 to the *p* offered in this place.
Ps 35: 13 When my *p* returned
72: 20 This concludes the *p* of David son
80: 4 against the *p* of your people?
109: 7 and may his *p* condemn him.
Pr 28: 9 even his *p* are detestable.
Isa 1: 15 even if you offer many *p*,
Da 9: 17 hear the *p* and petitions
Mk 12: 40 and for a show make lengthy *p*.
Lk 20: 47 and for a show make lengthy *p*.
Ac 10: 4 "Your *p* and gifts to the poor have
Ro 1: 10 you in my *p* at all times;
2Co 1: 11 as you help us by your *p*.
1: 11 us in answer to the *p* of many.
9: 14 in their *p* for you their hearts will
Eph 1: 16 remembering you in my *p*.
6: 18 on all occasions with all kinds of *p*
Php 1: 4 In all my *p* for all of you, I always
1: 19 for I know that through your *p*
1Th 1: 2 all of you, mentioning you in our *p*.
1Ti 2: 1 then, first of all, that requests, *p*,
2Ti 1: 3 constantly remember you in my *p*.
Phm : 4 as I remember you in my *p*,
: 22 restored to you in answer to your *p*.
Heb 5: 7 he offered up *p* and petitions
1Pe 3: 7 so that nothing will hinder your *p*.
Rev 5: 8 which are the *p* of the saints.
8: 3 with the *p* of all the saints,
8: 4 together with the *p* of the saints,

PRAYING (PRAY)

Ge 24: 15 he had finished *p*, Rebekah came
24: 45 "Before I finished *p* in my heart,
1Sa 1: 12 As she kept on *p* to the LORD,
1: 13 Hannah was *p* in her heart,
1: 16 I have been *p* here out
1: 26 here beside you *p* to the LORD.
1Ki 8: 28 the prayer that your servant is *p*
8: 33 *p* and making supplication to you
2Ch 6: 19 the prayer that your servant is *p*
6: 24 *p* and making supplication
7: 1 When Solomon finished *p*,
Ezr 10: 1 While Ezra was *p* and confessing,
Ne 1: 6 to hear the prayer your servant is *p*
Job 21: 15 What would we gain by *p* to him?'
Da 6: 11 as a group and found Daniel *p*.
9: 20 While I was speaking and *p*,
Mk 11: 25 And when you stand *p*,
Lk 1: 10 the assembled worshipers were *p*
2: 37 night and day, fasting and *p*.
3: 21 as he was *p*, heaven was opened
6: 12 and spent the night *p* to God.
9: 18 Once when Jesus was *p* in private
9: 29 As he was *p*, the appearance
11: 1 One day Jesus was *p*
Jn 17: 9 I am not *p* for the world,
18: 1 When he had finished *p*, Jesus left
Ac 9: 11 from Tarsus named Saul, for he is *p*
10: 30 was in my house *p* at this hour.
11: 5 "I was in the city of Joppa *p*,
12: 5 the church was earnestly *p* to God
12: 12 people had gathered and were *p*.
16: 25 and Silas were *p* and singing hymns
22: 17 returned to Jerusalem and was *p*
Ro 15: 30 in my struggle by *p* to God for me.
Eph 6: 18 always keep on *p* for all the saints.
Col 1: 9 we have not stopped *p* for you

PRAYS (PRAY)

1Ki 8: 29 will hear the prayer your servant *p*
8: 42 when he comes and *p*
2Ch 6: 20 you hear the prayer your servant *p*
6: 32 when he comes and *p*
Job 33: 26 He *p* to God and finds favor
Isa 44: 17 He *p* to it and says,
Da 6: 7 the decree that anyone who *p*
6: 12 the next thirty days anyone who *p*
6: 13 He still *p* three times a day."
1Co 11: 4 Every man who *p* or prophesies
11: 5 And every woman who *p*
14: 14 my spirit *p*, but my mind is

PREACH (PREACHED PREACHER PREACHES PREACHING)

Isa 61: 1 me to *p* good news to the poor.
Eze 20: 46 *p* against the south and prophesy
21: 2 and *p* against the sanctuary.
Jnh 1: 2 city of Nineveh and *p* against it,
Mt 4: 17 From that time on Jesus began to *p*,
10: 7 As you go, *p* this message:
11: 1 and *p* in the towns of Galilee.
23: 3 they do not practice what they *p*.
Mk 1: 38 nearby villages—so I can *p* there
3: 14 that he might send them out to *p*
16: 15 and *p* the good news to all creation.
Lk 4: 18 me to *p* good news to the poor.
4: 43 "I must *p* the good news
9: 2 out to *p* the kingdom of God
Ac 9: 20 At once he began to *p*
10: 42 He commanded us to *p*
14: 7 continued to *p* the good news.
16: 10 us to *p* the gospel to them.
20: 20 to *p* anything that would be helpful
Ro 1: 15 am so eager to *p* the gospel
2: 21 You who *p* against stealing,
10: 15 how can they *p* unless they are sent
15: 20 to *p* the gospel where Christ was
1Co 1: 17 to *p* the gospel—not with words
1: 23 wisdom, but we *p* Christ crucified:
9: 14 that those who *p* the gospel should
9: 16 Woe to me if I do not *p* the gospel!
9: 16 for I am compelled to *p*.
9: 16 when I *p* the gospel, I cannot boast,
9: 17 If I *p* voluntarily, I have a reward;
15: 11 this is what we *p*, and this is what
2Co 2: 12 to Troas to *p* the gospel of Christ
4: 5 For we do not *p* ourselves,
10: 16 so that we can *p* the gospel
Gal 1: 8 from heaven should *p* a gospel
1: 16 me so that I might *p* him
2: 2 set before them the gospel that I *p*
Eph 3: 8 to *p* to the Gentiles
Php 1: 15 It is true that some *p* Christ out
1: 17 The former *p* Christ out
2Ti 4: 2 I give you this charge: *P* the Word;

PREACHED (PREACH)

Dt 13: 5 he *p* rebellion against the LORD
Jer 28: 16 because you have *p* rebellion
29: 32 he has *p* rebellion against me.' "
Mt 11: 5 and the good news is *p* to the poor.
24: 14 gospel of the kingdom will be *p*
26: 13 wherever this gospel is *p*
Mk 2: 2 and he *p* the word to them.
6: 12 and *p* that people should repent.
13: 10 And the gospel must first be *p*
14: 9 wherever the gospel is *p*
16: 20 went out and *p* everywhere,
Lk 3: 18 and *p* the good news to them.
7: 22 and the good news is *p* to the poor.
16: 16 of the kingdom of God is being *p*,
24: 47 of sins will be *p* in his name
Ac 8: 4 had been scattered *p* the word
8: 12 he *p* the good news of the kingdom
9: 27 in Damascus he had *p* fearlessly
10: 37 after the baptism that John *p*—
13: 24 John *p* repentance and baptism
14: 21 They *p* the good news in that city
14: 25 when they had *p* the word in Perga,
15: 21 For Moses has been *p* in every city
15: 35 and *p* the word of the Lord.
15: 36 all the towns where we *p* the word
Ac 26: 20 also, I *p* that they should repent
28: 31 hindrance he *p* the kingdom
1Co 1: 21 of what was *p* to save those who
9: 27 so that after I have *p* to others,
15: 1 you of the gospel I *p* to you,
15: 2 firmly to the word I *p* to you.
15: 12 if it is *p* that Christ has been raised
2Co 1: 19 who was *p* among you by me
11: 4 other than the Jesus we *p*,
Gal 1: 8 other than the one we *p* to you,
1: 11 that the gospel I *p* is not something
4: 13 of an illness that I first *p* the gospel
Eph 2: 17 *p* peace to you who were far away
Php 1: 18 false motives or true, Christ is *p*.
1Th 2: 9 to anyone while we *p* the gospel
1Ti 3: 16 was *p* among the nations,
Heb 4: 2 also have had the gospel *p* to us,
4: 6 who formerly had the gospel *p*
1Pe 1: 12 you by those who have *p* the gospel
1: 25 this is the word that was *p* to you.
3: 19 and *p* to the spirits in prison who
4: 6 this is the reason the gospel was *p*

PREACHER (PREACH)

2Pe 2: 5 but protected Noah, a *p*

PREACHES (PREACH)

Ac 19: 13 whom Paul *p*, I command you
2Co 11: 4 *p* a Jesus other than the Jesus we

PREACHING (PREACH)

Ezr 6: 14 and prosper under the *p*
Am 7: 16 stop *p* against the house of Isaac.'
Mt 3: 1 *p* in the Desert of Judea and saying
4: 23 *p* the good news of the kingdom,
9: 35 *p* the good news of the kingdom
12: 41 for they repented at the *p* of Jonah,
Mk 1: 4 and *p* a baptism of repentance
1: 39 *p* in their synagogues and driving
Lk 3: 3 *p* a baptism of repentance
4: 44 he kept on *p* in the synagogues
9: 6 *p* the gospel and healing people
11: 32 for they repented at the *p* of Jonah,
20: 1 the temple courts and *p* the gospel,
Ac 8: 25 *p* the gospel in many Samaritan
8: 40 *p* the gospel in all the towns
16: 6 by the Holy Spirit from *p* the word
17: 13 learned that Paul was *p* the word
17: 18 Paul was *p* the good news about
18: 5 devoted himself exclusively to *p*,
20: 25 have gone about *p* the kingdom
Ro 1: 9 with my whole heart in *p* the gospel
10: 14 hear without someone *p* to them?
1Co 2: 4 and my *p* were not with wise
9: 18 in *p* the gospel I may offer it free
9: 18 so not make use of my rights in *p* it.
15: 14 our *p* is useless and so is your faith.
2Co 11: 7 order to elevate you by *p* the gospel
Gal 1: 9 If anybody is *p* to you a gospel
1: 23 persecuted us is now *p* the faith he
2: 7 task of *p* the gospel to the Gentiles,
2: 7 the task of *p* the gospel to the Jews.
5: 11 if I am still *p* circumcision,
1Ti 4: 13 the public reading of Scripture, to *p*
5: 17 especially those whose work is *p*
Tit 1: 3 light through the *p* entrusted to me

PRECEDE (PRECEDED PRECEDING)

1Th 4: 15 will certainly not *p* those who have

PRECEDED (PRECEDE)

2Ki 17: 2 the kings of Israel who *p* him.
21: 11 evil than the Amorites who *p* him
Jer 28: 8 early times the prophets who *p* you
34: 5 the former kings who *p* you,

PRECEDING (PRECEDE)

Ne 5: 15 the earlier governors—those *p* me

PRECEPTS

Dt 33: 10 He teaches your *p* to Jacob
Ps 19: 8 The *p* of the LORD are right,
103: 18 and remember to obey his *p*.
105: 45 that they might keep his *p*
111: 7 all his *p* are trustworthy.
111: 10 who follow his *p* have good
119: 4 You have laid down *p*
119: 15 I meditate on your *p*

Ps 119: 27 understand the teaching of your *p;*
119: 40 How I long for your *p!*
119: 45 for I have sought out your *p*.
119: 56 I obey your *p*.
119: 63 to all who follow your *p*.
119: 69 I keep your *p* with all my heart.
119: 78 but I will meditate on your *p*.
119: 87 but I have not forsaken your *p*.
119: 93 I will never forget your *p*,
119: 94 I have sought out your *p*.
119:100 for I obey your *p*.
119:104 I gain understanding from your *p;*
119:110 but I have not strayed from your *p*.
119:128 because I consider all your *p* right,
119:134 that I may obey your *p*.
119:141 I do not forget your *p*.
119:159 See how I love your *p;*
119:168 I obey your *p* and your statutes,
119:173 for I have chosen your *p*.

PRECINCTS

Eze 42: 14 Once the priests enter the holy *p*,

PRECIOUS

Ge 30: 20 God has presented me with a *p* gift.
Ex 28: 17 mount four rows of *p* stones on it.
39: 10 they mounted four rows of *p* stones
Dt 33: 13 with the *p* dew from heaven above
1Sa 26: 21 you considered my life *p* today,
2Sa 12: 30 and it was set with *p* stones—
1Ki 10: 2 quantities of gold, and *p* stones—
10: 10 quantities of spices, and *p* stones.
10: 11 of almugwood and *p* stones.
1Ch 20: 2 and it was set with *p* stones—
29: 8 Any who had *p* stones gave them
2Ch 3: 6 adorned the temple with *p* stones.
9: 1 quantities of gold, and *p* stones—
9: 9 quantities of spices, and *p* stones.
9: 10 brought algumwood and *p* stones.
32: 27 and gold and for his *p* stones,
Ezr 8: 27 articles of polished bronze, as *p*
Job 28: 16 with *p* onyx or sapphires.
29: 24 the light of my face was *p* to them.
Ps 19: 10 They are more *p* than gold,
22: 20 my *p* life from the power
35: 17 my *p* life from these lions.
72: 14 for *p* is their blood in his sight.
116: 15 *P* in the sight of the LORD
119: 72 from your mouth is more *p* to me
133: 2 It is like *p* oil poured on the head,
139: 17 How *p* to me are your thoughts,
Pr 3: 15 She is more *p* than rubies;
8: 11 for wisdom is more *p* than rubies,
Isa 28: 16 a *p* cornerstone for a sure
43: 4 Since you are *p* and honored
54: 12 and all your walls of *p* stones.
La 4: 2 How the *p* sons of Zion,
Eze 22: 25 take treasures and *p* things
27: 22 of all kinds of spices and *p* stones,
28: 13 every *p* stone adorned you:
Da 11: 38 with *p* stones and costly gifts.
1Pe 1: 19 but with the *p* blood of Christ,
2: 4 but chosen by God and *p* to him—
2: 6 a chosen and *p* cornerstone,
2: 7 to you who believe, this stone is *p*.
2Pe 1: 1 Christ have received a faith as *p*
1: 4 us his very great and *p* promises,
Rev 17: 4 was glittering with gold, *p* stones
18: 12 silver, *p* stones and pearls;
18: 16 and glittering with gold, *p* stones
21: 11 was like that of a very *p* jewel,
21: 19 with every kind of *p* stone.

PREDECESSOR (PREDECESSORS)

1Ch 17: 13 as I took it away from your *p*.

PREDECESSORS (PREDECESSOR)

Dt 19: 14 up by your *p* in the inheritance you
Ezr 4: 15 made in the archives of your *p*.

PREDESTINED (DESTINE)

Ro 8: 29 *p* to be conformed to the likeness
8: 30 And those he *p*, he also called;
Eph 1: 5 In love he *p* us to be adopted
1: 11 having been *p* according

PREDICTED (PREDICTION)

1Sa 28: 17 The LORD has done what he *p*
Ac 7: 52 killed those who *p* the coming
11: 28 through the Spirit *p* that a severe
16: 16 a spirit by which she *p* the future.
1Pe 1: 11 when he *p* the sufferings of Christ

PREDICTING (PREDICTION)

1Ki 22: 13 the other prophets are *p* success
2Ch 18: 12 the other prophets are *p* success

PREDICTION (PREDICTED PREDICTING PREDICTIONS)

Jer 28: 9 only if his *p* comes true."

PREDICTIONS (PREDICTION)

Isa 44: 26 and fulfills the *p* of his messengers,
47: 13 stargazers who make *p* month

PREEMINENT

Est 10: 3 to King Xerxes, *p* among the Jews,

PREFECTS

Da 3: 2 *p*, governors, advisers, treasurers,
3: 3 So the satraps, *p*, governors,
3: 27 *p*, governors and royal advisers
6: 7 The royal administrators, *p*,

PREFER (PREFERENCE)

1Ki 21: 2 if you *p*, I will pay you whatever it
21: 6 'Sell me your vineyard; or if you *p*,
Job 7: 15 so that I *p* strangling and death,
36: 21 which you seem to *p* to affliction.
Jer 8: 3 of this evil nation will *p* death
Eze 16: 32 You *p* strangers to your own
1Co 4: 21 What do you *p?* Shall I come
2Co 5: 8 would *p* to be away from the body

PREFERENCE (PREFER)

Dt 21: 16 loves in *p* to his actual firstborn,

PREGNANCY (PREGNANT)

Hos 9: 11 no birth, no *p*, no conception.

PREGNANT (PREGNANCY)

Ge 4: 17 and she became *p* and gave birth
16: 4 When she knew she was *p*,
16: 5 and now that she knows she is *p*,
19: 36 both of Lot's daughters became *p*
21: 2 Sarah became *p* and bore a son
25: 21 and his wife Rebekah became *p*.
29: 32 Leah became *p* and gave birth
30: 5 she became *p* and bore him a son.
30: 17 she became *p* and bore Jacob a fifth
30: 23 She became *p* and gave birth
38: 3 she became *p* and gave birth
38: 18 with her, and she became *p* by him.
38: 24 and as a result she is now *p*."
38: 25 "I am *p* by the man who owns these
Ex 2: 2 and she became *p* and gave birth
21: 22 who are fighting hit a *p* woman
Lev 12: 2 'A woman who becomes *p*
1Sa 4: 19 was *p* and near the time of delivery.
2Sa 11: 5 sent word to David, saying, "I am *p*
2Ki 4: 17 But the woman became *p*,
8: 12 and rip open their *p* women."
15: 16 and ripped open all the *p* women.
1Ch 7: 23 and she became *p* and gave birth
Ps 7: 14 He who is *p* with evil
Hos 13: 16 their *p* women ripped open."
Am 1: 13 he ripped open the *p* women
Mt 24: 19 be in those days for *p* women
Mk 13: 17 be in those days for *p* women
Lk 1: 24 this his wife Elizabeth became *p*
21: 23 be in those days for *p* women
1Th 5: 3 as labor pains on a *p* woman,
Rev 12: 2 She was *p* and cried out in pain

PREPARATION (PREPARE)

Nu 11: 18 yourselves in *p* for tomorrow,
Jos 7: 13 yourselves in *p* for tomorrow;
1Sa 23: 22 Go and make further *p*.
Mt 27: 62 The next day, the one after *P* Day,
Mk 15: 42 It was *P* Day (that is, the day
Lk 23: 54 It was *P* Day, and the Sabbath was
Jn 19: 14 the day of *P* of Passover Week,
19: 31 Now it was the day of *P*,
19: 42 Because it was the Jewish day of *P*

PREPARATIONS (PREPARE)

1Ch 22: 5 So David made extensive *p*
22: 5 Therefore I will make *p* for it."
2Ch 35: 14 the Levites made *p* for themselves
35: 14 they made *p* for themselves
35: 15 their fellow Levites made the *p*
Mt 26: 17 us to make *p* for you to eat
Mk 14: 12 make *p* for you to eat the Passover
14: 15 Make *p* for us there."
Lk 10: 40 by all the *p* that had to be made.
22: 8 make *p* for us to eat the Passover."
22: 12 Make *p* there."

PREPARE (PREPARATION PREPARATIONS PREPARED PREPARES PREPARING)

Ge 18: 7 it to a servant, who hurried to *p* it.
27: 4 *P* me the kind of tasty food I like
27: 7 and *p* me some tasty food to eat,
27: 9 so I can *p* some tasty food
43: 16 slaughter an animal and *p* dinner;
Ex 12: 16 except to *p* food for everyone to eat
12: 39 time to *p* food for themselves.
16: 5 are to *p* what they bring in,
19: 15 "*P* yourselves for the third day.
Lev 6: 21 *P* it with oil on a griddle; bring it
6: 22 as anointed priest shall *p* it.
Nu 15: 5 *p* a fourth of a hin of wine
15: 6 " 'With a ram *p* a grain offering
15: 8 " 'When you *p* a young bull
15: 12 for each one, for as many as you *p*.
23: 1 and *p* seven bulls and seven rams
23: 29 and *p* seven bulls and seven rams
28: 4 *P* one lamb in the morning
28: 8 and drink offering that you *p*
28: 8 *P* the second lamb at twilight,
28: 20 With each bull *p* a grain offering
28: 23 *P* these in addition
28: 24 In this way *p* the food
28: 31 *P* these together with their drink
29: 2 *p* a burnt offering of one young bull
29: 3 With the bull *p* a grain offering
29: 9 With the bull *p* a grain offering
29: 14 the thirteen bulls *p* a grain offering
29: 17 the second day *p* twelve young
29: 18 *p* their grain offerings and drink
29: 20 " 'On the third day *p* eleven bulls,
29: 21 *p* their grain offerings and drink
29: 23 " 'On the fourth day *p* ten bulls,
29: 24 *p* their grain offerings and drink
29: 26 " 'On the fifth day *p* nine bulls,
29: 27 *p* their grain offerings and drink
29: 29 " 'On the sixth day *p* eight bulls,
29: 30 *p* their grain offerings and drink
29: 32 On the seventh day *p* seven bulls,
29: 33 *p* their grain offerings and drink
29: 37 *p* their grain offerings and drink
29: 39 *p* these for the LORD
Jdg 13: 15 you to stay until we *p* a young goat
13: 16 But if you *p* a burnt offering,
2Sa 12: 4 to *p* a meal for the traveler who had
13: 5 Let her *p* the food in my sight
13: 7 and *p* some food for him."
1Ki 18: 23 I will *p* the other bull and put it
18: 25 one of the bulls and *p* it first,
20: 12 he ordered his men: "*P* to attack."
2Ki 20: 7 Isaiah said, "*P* a poultice of figs."
1Ch 22: 2 stonecutters to *p* dressed stone
2Ch 31: 11 gave orders to *p* storerooms
35: 4 *P* yourselves by families
35: 6 and *p* the lambs, for your fellow
Est 5: 8 to the banquet I will *p* for them.
Job 33: 5 *p* yourself and confront me.
Ps 23: 5 You *p* a table before me
Isa 8: 9 *P* for battle, and be shattered!
8: 9 *P* for battle, and be shattered!
14: 21 *P* a place to slaughter his sons
25: 6 the LORD Almighty will *p*
38: 21 "*P* a poultice of figs and apply it
40: 3 "In the desert *p*
57: 14 "Build up, build up, *p* the road!
62: 10 *P* the way for the people.
Jer 6: 4 "*P* for battle against her!
46: 3 *P* your shields, both large and small
51: 12 *p* an ambush!
51: 27 *P* the nations for battle against her;
51: 28 *P* the nations for battle against her

Eze 7: 23 "*P* chains, because the land is full
Da 11: 10 His sons will *p* for war
Joel 3: 9 *P* for war!
Am 4: 12 *p* to meet your God, O Israel."
Mic 3: 5 they *p* to wage war against him.
Na 1: 14 I will *p* your grave,
Mal 3: 1 who will *p* the way before me.
Mt 3: 3 '*P* the way for the Lord,
11: 10 who will *p* your way before you.'
26: 12 she did it to *p* me for burial.
Mk 1: 2 who will *p* your way"—
1: 3 '*P* the way for the Lord,
14: 8 beforehand to *p* for my burial.
Lk 1: 76 on before the Lord to *p* the way
3: 4 '*P* the way for the Lord,
7: 27 who will *p* your way before you.'
17: 8 he not rather say, '*P* my supper,
22: 9 "Where do you want us to *p* for it?"
Jn 14: 2 there to *p* a place for you.
14: 3 And if I go and *p* a place for you,
Eph 4: 12 to *p* God's people for works
Phm : 22 one thing more: *P* a guest room
1Pe 1: 13 Therefore, *p* your minds for action;
Rev 16: 12 up to *p* the way for the kings

PREPARED (PREPARE)

Ge 18: 8 milk and the calf that had been *p*,
19: 3 He *p* a meal for them, baking bread
24: 31 I have *p* the house and a place
27: 14 and she *p* some tasty food,
27: 31 He too *p* some tasty food
43: 25 *p* their gifts for Joseph's arrival
Ex 23: 20 to bring you to the place I have *p*.
Lev 2: 5 If your grain offering is *p*
10: 12 and eat it *p* without yeast
Nu 15: 11 is to be *p* in this manner.
23: 4 Balaam said, "I have *p* seven altars,
28: 24 it is to be *p* in addition
Jos 24: 9 the king of Moab, *p* to fight
Jdg 6: 2 the Israelites *p* shelters
6: 19 Gideon went in, *p* a young goat,
19: 5 up early and he *p* to leave,
Ru 1: 6 and her daughters-in-law *p*
2Sa 3: 20 David *p* a feast for him and his men
12: 4 and *p* it for the one who had come
13: 10 Tamar took the bread she had *p*
1Ki 5: 18 men of Gebal cut and *p* the timber
6: 19 He *p* the inner sanctuary
18: 26 took the bull given them and *p* it.
20: 12 So they *p* to attack the city.
2Ki 6: 23 So he *p* a great feast for them,
1Ch 12: 33 experienced soldiers *p* for battle
12: 36 experienced soldiers *p* for battle—
15: 1 he *p* a place for the ark of God
15: 3 LORD to the place he had *p* for it.
15: 12 to the place I have *p* for it.
2Ch 1: 4 to the place he had *p* for it,
29: 19 We have *p* and consecrated all
Ezr 1: 5 *p* to go up and build the house
Ne 5: 18 and some poultry were *p* for me,
8: 10 some to those who have nothing *p*.
Est 5: 4 to a banquet I have *p* for him."
5: 5 went to the banquet Esther had *p*.
6: 14 away to the banquet Esther had *p*.
7: 10 Haman on the gallows he had *p*
Job 13: 18 Now that I have *p* my case,
Ps 7: 13 He has *p* his deadly weapons;
78: 50 He *p* a path for his anger;
Pr 9: 2 She has *p* her meat and mixed her
19: 29 Penalties are *p* for mockers,
SS 3: 8 *p* for the terrors of the night.
Isa 30: 33 Topheth has long been *p*;
Eze 28: 13 day you were created they were *p*.
38: 7 be *p*, you and all the hordes
Zep 1: 7 The LORD has *p* a sacrifice;
Mt 20: 23 those for whom they have been *p*
22: 2 a king who *p* a wedding banquet
22: 4 invited that I have *p* my dinner:
25: 34 the kingdom *p* for you
25: 41 into the eternal fire *p* for the devil
26: 19 directed them and *p* the Passover.
Mk 10: 40 those for whom they have been *p*."
14: 16 So they *p* the Passover
Lk 1: 17 to make ready a people *p*
2: 31 which you have *p* in the sight
12: 20 Then who will get what you have *p*
22: 13 So they *p* the Passover.
23: 56 and *p* spices and perfumes.
Lk 24: 1 women took the spices they had *p*
Jn 19: 19 Pilate had a notice *p* and fastened
Ac 10: 10 and while the meal was being *p*,
Ro 9: 22 of his wrath—*p* for destruction?
9: 23 whom he *p* in advance for glory—
1Co 2: 9 what God has *p* for those who love
Eph 2: 10 which God *p* in advance for us
2Ti 2: 21 and *p* to do any good work.
4: 2 be *p* in season and out of season;
Heb 10: 5 but a body you *p* for me;
11: 16 for he has *p* a city for them.
1Pe 3: 15 Always be *p* to give an answer
Rev 8: 6 who had the seven trumpets *p*
9: 7 The locusts looked like horses *p*
12: 6 desert to a place *p* for her by God,
12: 14 to the place *p* for her in the desert,
21: 2 *p* as a bride beautifully dressed

PREPARES (PREPARE)

Ps 50: 23 and he *p* the way
85: 13 and *p* the way for his steps.
Isa 44: 16 over it he *p* his meal,

PREPARING (PREPARE)

1Ch 9: 32 of *p* for every Sabbath the bread set
Jer 18: 11 I am *p* a disaster for you
Eze 39: 17 to the sacrifice I am *p* for you,
39: 19 At the sacrifice I am *p* for you,
Am 7: 1 He was *p* swarms of locusts
Mt 4: 21 their father Zebedee, *p* their nets.
Mk 1: 19 John in a boat, *p* their nets.
Lk 14: 16 certain man was *p* a great banquet
Ac 25: 3 for they were *p* an ambush

PRESCRIBED

Lev 5: 10 as a burnt offering in the *p* way
9: 16 and offered it in the *p* way.
Nu 15: 24 along with its *p* grain offering
1Sa 2: 29 offering that I *p* for my dwelling?
1Ch 15: 13 how to do it in the *p* way."
23: 31 and in the way *p* for them.
24: 19 to the regulations *p* for them
2Ch 4: 20 in front of the inner sanctuary as *p*;
29: 25 and lyres in the way *p* by David
30: 16 as *p* in the Law of Moses the man
35: 13 Passover animals over the fire as *p*,
35: 15 were in the places *p* by David,
Ezr 3: 4 of burnt offerings *p* for each day.
3: 10 as *p* by David king of Israel.
7: 23 Whatever the God of heaven has *p*,
Ne 12: 24 as *p* by David the man of God.
12: 36 with musical instruments *p*
13: 5 new wine and oil *p* for the Levites,
Est 2: 12 months of beauty treatments *p*
9: 27 in the way *p* and at the time
Job 36: 23 Who has *p* his ways for him,
Eze 45: 14 The *p* portion of oil, measured
Heb 8: 4 already men who offer the gifts *p*

PRESENCE (PRESENT)

Ge 4: 14 and I will be hidden from your *p*;
4: 16 Cain went out from the LORD's *p*
23: 11 it to you in the *p* of my people.
23: 18 as his property in the *p*
27: 7 in the *p* of the LORD before I die.'
27: 30 had scarcely left his father's *p*,
31: 32 In the *p* of our relatives, see
31: 35 that I cannot stand up in your *p*;
40: 20 baker in the *p* of his officials:
41: 46 Joseph went out from Pharaoh's *p*
45: 1 "Have everyone leave my *p*!"
45: 3 because they were terrified at his *p*.
47: 10 Pharaoh and went out from his *p*.
Ex 7: 20 staff in the *p* of Pharaoh
9: 8 it into the air in the *p* of Pharaoh.
10: 11 were driven out of Pharaoh's *p*.
18: 12 with Moses' father-in-law in the *p*
25: 30 Put the bread of the *P* on this table
28: 30 heart whenever he enters the *p*
29: 11 it in the LORD's *p* at the entrance
33: 14 The LORD replied, "My *P* will go
33: 15 "If your *P* does not go with us,
33: 19 my name, the LORD, in your *p*.
34: 34 he entered the LORD's *p*
35: 13 its articles and the bread of the *P*;
35: 20 withdrew from Moses' *p*,
39: 36 its articles and the bread of the *P*;
Lev 9: 24 out from the *p* of the LORD
Lev 10: 2 out from the *p* of the LORD
19: 32 " 'Rise in the *p* of the aged,
22: 3 person must be cut off from my *p*.
Nu 4: 7 "Over the table of the *P* they are
6: 9 If someone dies suddenly in his *p*,
6: 11 by being in the *p* of the dead body.
17: 9 the staffs from the LORD's *p*
19: 3 the camp and slaughtered in his *p*.
20: 9 the staff from the LORD's *p*,
27: 19 and commission him in their *p*.
Dt 4: 37 brought you out of Egypt by his *P*
12: 7 in the *p* of the LORD your God,
12: 18 are to eat them in the *p*
14: 23 in the *p* of the LORD your God
14: 26 in the *p* of the LORD your God
15: 20 are to eat them in the *p*
18: 7 there in the *p* of the LORD.
19: 17 stand in the *p* of the LORD
25: 2 flogged in his *p* with the number
25: 9 up to him in the *p* of the elders,
27: 7 in the *p* of the LORD your God.
29: 10 in the *p* of the LORD your God—
29: 15 here with us today in the *p*
31: 7 and said to him in the *p* of all Israel,
32: 51 with me in the *p* of the Israelites
Jos 8: 32 There in the *p* of the Israelites,
10: 12 said to the LORD in the *p* of Israel:
18: 6 you in the *p* of the LORD our God.
18: 8 at Shiloh in the *p* of the LORD."
18: 10 in Shiloh in the *p* of the LORD,
19: 51 lot at Shiloh in the *p* of the LORD
Ru 4: 4 in the *p* of the elders of my people.
4: 4 it in the *p* of these seated here
1Sa 2: 21 up in the *p* of the LORD.
2: 28 and to wear an ephod in my *p*.
6: 20 in the *p* of the LORD, this
11: 15 as king in the *p* of the LORD.
12: 3 against me in the *p* of the LORD
16: 13 him in the *p* of his brothers,
19: 24 and also prophesied in Samuel's *p*.
21: 6 of the *P* that had been removed
21: 13 So he feigned insanity in their *p*;
26: 20 far from the *p* of the LORD.
2Sa 3: 13 Do not come into my *p*
22: 13 Out of the brightness of his *p*
24: 4 so they left the *p* of the king
1Ki 1: 28 So she came into the king's *p*
7: 48 on which was the bread of the *P*;
8: 1 into his *p* at Jerusalem the elders
8: 28 praying in your *p* this day.
19: 11 mountain in the *p* of the LORD,
2Ki 3: 14 for the *p* of Jehoshaphat king
5: 27 Then Gehazi went from Elisha's *p*
13: 23 or banish them from his *p*.
17: 18 and removed them from his *p*.
17: 20 until he thrust them from his *p*.
17: 23 LORD removed them from his *p*,
22: 10 read from it in the *p* of the king.
22: 19 tore your robes and wept in my *p*,
23: 3 covenant in the *p* of the LORD—
23: 27 also from my *p* as I removed Israel,
24: 3 in order to remove them from his *p*
24: 20 the end he thrust them from his *p*.
1Ch 12: 1 banished from the *p* of Saul son
24: 6 names in the *p* of the king
24: 31 in the *p* of King David
29: 10 in the *p* of the whole assembly,
29: 22 and drank with great joy in the *p*
2Ch 4: 19 on which was the bread of the *P*;
6: 19 your servant is praying in your *p*.
20: 9 we will stand in your *p*
26: 19 in their *p* before the incense altar
28: 14 and plunder in the *p* of the officials
34: 18 read from it in the *p* of the king.
34: 24 read in the *p* of the king of Judah.
34: 27 tore your robes and wept in my *p*,
34: 31 covenant in the *p* of the LORD—
Ezr 4: 18 been read and translated in my *p*.
9: 15 one of us can stand in your *p*."
Ne 1: 11 favor in the *p* of this man."
2: 1 I had not been sad in his *p* before;
4: 2 and in the *p* of his associates
8: 3 Gate in the *p* of the men,
Est 1: 16 replied in the *p* of the king
1: 19 again to enter the *p* of King Xerxes.
2: 23 of the annals in the *p* of the king.
3: 7 the lot) in the *p* of Haman
4: 8 into the king's *p* to beg for mercy

Est 5: 9 rose nor showed fear in his *p*,
8: 1 came into the *p* of the king,
8: 15 left the king's *p* wearing royal
Job 1: 12 out from the *p* of the LORD.
2: 7 out from the *p* of the LORD
30: 11 they throw off restraint in my *p*.
Ps 5: 5 arrogant cannot stand in your *p*;
9: 19 let the nations be judged in your *p*.
16: 11 you will fill me with joy in your *p*,
18: 12 of his *p* clouds advanced,
21: 6 with the joy of your *p*.
23: 5 in the *p* of my enemies.
31: 20 the shelter of your *p* you hide them
39: 1 as long as the wicked are in my *p*."
41: 12 and set me in your *p* forever.
51: 11 Do not cast me from your *p*
52: 9 in the *p* of your saints.
61: 7 in God's *p* forever;
89: 15 who walk in the light of your *p*,
90: 8 our secret sins in the light of your *p*
101: 7 will stand in my *p*.
102: 28 of your servants will live in your *p*;
114: 7 O earth, at the *p* of the Lord,
114: 7 at the *p* of the God of Jacob,
116: 14 in the *p* of all his people.
116: 18 LORD in the *p* of all his people,
139: 7 Where can I flee from your *p*?
Pr 8: 30 rejoicing always in his *p*,
14: 19 down in the *p* of the good,
18: 16 ushers him into the *p* of the great.
25: 5 the wicked from the king's *p*,
25: 6 not exalt yourself in the king's *p*,
Ecc 8: 3 be in a hurry to leave the king's *p*.
Isa 3: 8 defying his glorious *p*.
26: 17 so were we in your *p*, O LORD.
63: 9 and the angel of his *p* saved them.
Jer 5: 22 "Should you not tremble in my *p*?
7: 15 I will thrust you from my *p*,
15: 1 Send them away from my *p*!
23: 39 and cast you out of my *p*
28: 1 of the LORD in the *p* of the priests
32: 12 in the *p* of my cousin Hanamel
32: 13 "In their *p* I gave Baruch these
52: 3 the end he thrust them from his *p*.
La 2: 19 water in the *p* of the Lord.
Eze 28: 9 in the *p* of those who kill you?
38: 20 of the earth will tremble at my *p*.
44: 3 to eat in the *p* of the LORD.
44: 12 them in the *p* of their idols
46: 3 to worship in the *p* of the LORD
Da 4: 8 Daniel came into my *p*
7: 13 of Days and was led into his *p*.
Hos 6: 2 that we may live in his *p*.
Na 1: 5 The earth trembles at his *p*,
Zec 6: 5 from standing in the *p* of the Lord
Mal 3: 16 in his *p* concerning those who
Mk 7: 24 yet he could not keep his *p* secret.
Lk 1: 19 I stand in the *p* of God,
8: 47 In the *p* of all the people, she told
14: 10 in the *p* of all your fellow guests.
15: 10 rejoicing in the *p* of the angels
23: 14 I have examined him in your *p*
24: 43 and he took it and ate it in their *p*.
Jn 8: 38 what I have seen in the Father's *p*,
12: 37 these miraculous signs in their *p*,
17: 5 glorify me in your *p*
20: 30 signs in the *p* of his disciples,
Ac 2: 28 you will fill me with joy in your *p*.'
10: 33 here in the *p* of God to listen
24: 21 thing I shouted as I stood in their *p*:
2Co 4: 14 and present us with you in his *p*.
Php 2: 12 only in my *p*, but now much more
1Th 2: 19 glory in the *p* of our Lord Jesus
3: 9 have in the *p* of our God
3: 13 and holy in the *p* of our God
2Th 1: 9 and shut out from the *p* of the Lord
1Ti 6: 12 in the *p* of many witnesses.
2Ti 2: 2 in the *p* of many witnesses entrust
4: 1 In the *p* of God and of Christ Jesus,
Heb 2: 12 in the *p* of the congregation I will
9: 24 now to appear for us in God's *p*.
2Pe 2: 11 beings in the *p* of the Lord.
1Jn 3: 19 rest in his *p* whenever our hearts
Jude : 24 before his glorious *p* without fault
Rev 14: 10 sulfur in the *p* of the holy angels
20: 11 Earth and sky fled from his *p*,

PRESENT (PRESENCE PRESENTABLE PRESENTED PRESENTING PRESENTS)

Ge 33: 11 Please accept the *p* that was
Ex 10: 25 and burnt offerings to *p*
22: 14 or dies while the owner is not *p*,
29: 3 them in a basket and *p* them in it—
34: 2 *P* yourself to me there on top
Lev 1: 3 He must *p* it at the entrance
2: 8 to the LORD; *p* it to the priest,
3: 1 is to *p* before the LORD an animal
3: 7 he is to *p* it before the LORD.
3: 12 he is to *p* it before the LORD.
4: 4 He is to *p* the bull at the entrance
4: 14 *p* it before the Tent of Meeting.
6: 21 and *p* the grain offering broken
7: 11 fellowship offering a person may *p*
7: 13 is to *p* an offering with cakes
9: 2 and *p* them before the LORD.
13: 19 he must *p* himself to the priest.
14: 11 him clean shall *p* both the one
16: 7 and *p* them before the LORD
17: 4 to the Tent of Meeting to *p* it
18: 23 A woman must not *p* herself
21: 6 Because they *p* the offerings made
21: 21 come near to *p* the offerings made
22: 15 the sacred offerings the Israelites *p*
22: 19 you must *p* a male without defect
22: 23 *p* as a freewill offering a cow
23: 8 For seven days *p* an offering made
23: 16 and then *p* an offering of new grain
23: 18 *P* with this bread seven male lambs
23: 25 *p* an offering made to the LORD
23: 27 *p* an offering made to the LORD
23: 36 For seven days *p* offerings made
23: 36 *p* an offering made to the LORD
27: 8 he is to *p* the person to the priest,
Nu 3: 6 and *p* them to Aaron the priest
6: 14 There he is to *p* his offerings
6: 16 " 'The priest is to *p* them
6: 17 He is to *p* the basket
8: 11 Aaron is to *p* the Levites
8: 13 and his sons and then *p* them
9: 13 he did not *p* the LORD's offering
15: 3 you *p* to the LORD offerings made
15: 4 one who brings his offering shall *p*
15: 19 *p* a portion as an offering
15: 20 and *p* it as an offering
15: 20 *P* a cake from the first
16: 17 Aaron are to *p* your censers also."
16: 17 and *p* it before the LORD.
18: 19 the holy offerings the Israelites *p*
18: 24 the tithes that the Israelites *p*
18: 26 you must *p* a tenth of that tithe
18: 28 also will *p* an offering to the LORD
18: 29 You must *p* as the LORD's portion
18: 30 'When you *p* the best part,
28: 2 'See that you *p* to me
28: 3 are to *p* to the LORD:
28: 11 *p* to the LORD a burnt offering
28: 19 *P* to the LORD an offering made
28: 26 when you *p* to the LORD
28: 27 *P* a burnt offering of two young
29: 8 *P* as an aroma pleasing
29: 13 *P* an offering made by fire
29: 36 *P* an offering made by fire
Dt 12: 27 *P* your burnt offerings on the altar
31: 14 *p* yourselves at the Tent of Meeting
Jos 7: 14 *p* yourselves tribe by tribe.
1Sa 1: 22 and *p* him before the LORD,
10: 19 *p* yourselves before the LORD
30: 26 "Here is a *p* for you
2Sa 14: 20 this to change the *p* situation.
1Ki 18: 1 "Go and *p* yourself to Ahab,
18: 2 So Elijah went to *p* himself to Ahab
18: 15 I will surely *p* myself
1Ch 9: 18 Gate on the east, up to the *p* time.
16: 40 in Gibeon to *p* burnt offerings
2Ch 13: 11 and evening they *p* burnt offerings
23: 18 to *p* the burnt offerings
29: 7 or *p* any burnt offerings
29: 29 everyone *p* with him knelt down
30: 21 The Israelites who were *p*
34: 33 and he had all who were *p*
35: 17 Israelites who were *p* celebrated
Ezr 5: 16 From that day to the *p* it has been
6: 3 be rebuilt as a place to *p* sacrifices,
8: 25 and all Israel *p* there had donated

Est 1: 3 the nobles of the provinces were *p*.
Job 1: 6 to *p* themselves before the LORD,
2: 1 to *p* themselves before the LORD,
2: 1 with them to *p* himself before him.
23: 7 an upright man could *p* his case
Ps 14: 5 for God is *p* in the company
46: 1 an ever *p* help in trouble.
56: 12 I will *p* my thank offerings to you.
72: 10 will *p* him gifts.
Pr 4: 9 and *p* you with a crown of splendor
18: 17 The first to *p* his case seems right,
Isa 40: 20 to *p* such an offering
41: 21 "*P* your case," says the LORD.
45: 21 Declare what is to be, *p* it—
Jer 33: 18 offerings and to *p* sacrifices.' "
40: 5 gave him provisions and a *p*
42: 9 me to *p* your petition,
44: 15 with all the women who were *p*—
Eze 43: 27 are to *p* your burnt offerings
45: 1 you are to *p* to the LORD a portion
48: 8 will be the portion you are to *p*
Hag 2: 9 glory of this *p* house will be greater
Mk 8: 9 About four thousand men were *p*.
10: 30 as much in this *p* age (homes,
14: 4 of those *p* were saying indignantly
Lk 2: 22 to Jerusalem to *p* him to the Lord
5: 17 power of the Lord was *p* for him
12: 56 how to interpret this *p* time?
13: 1 Now there were some *p*
22: 6 over to them when no crowd was *p*.
Ac 1: 13 Those *p* were Peter, John,
5: 38 in the *p* case I advise you:
21: 18 James, and all the elders were *p*.
23: 30 also ordered his accusers to *p*
24: 17 gifts for the poor and to *p* offerings.
25: 24 "King Agrippa, and all who are *p*
Ro 3: 26 his justice at the *p* time,
8: 18 consider that our *p* sufferings are
8: 22 of childbirth right up to the *p* time.
8: 38 neither the *p* nor the future,
11: 5 at the *p* time there is a remnant
13: 11 understanding the *p* time.
1Co 3: 22 life or death or the *p* or the future—
5: 3 Even though I am not physically *p*,
5: 3 one who did this, just as if I were *p*.
5: 4 the power of our Lord Jesus is *p*,
7: 26 of the *p* crisis, I think that it is good
7: 31 world in its *p* form is passing away.
2Co 4: 14 and *p* us with you in his presence.
8: 14 At the *p* time your plenty will
10: 11 be in our actions when we are *p*.
11: 2 so that I might *p* you as a pure
Gal 1: 4 to rescue us from the *p* evil age,
4: 25 and corresponds to the *p* city
Eph 1: 21 not only in the *p* age but
5: 27 and to *p* her to himself
Php 4: 6 with thanksgiving, *p* your requests
Col 1: 22 body through death to *p* you holy
1: 25 me to *p* to you the word of God
1: 28 so that we may *p* everyone perfect
2: 5 I am *p* with you in spirit
1Ti 4: 8 holding promise for both the *p* life
6: 17 in this *p* world not to be arrogant
2Ti 2: 15 Do your best to *p* yourself to God
Tit 2: 12 upright and godly lives in this *p* age
Heb 2: 8 Yet at *p* we do not see everything
9: 9 This is an illustration for the *p* time
2Pe 3: 7 By the same word the *p* heavens
Jude : 24 and to *p* you before his glorious

PRESENTABLE (PRESENT)

1Co 12: 24 while our *p* parts need no special

PRESENTED (PRESENT)

Ge 30: 20 "God has *p* me with a precious gift.
43: 15 and *p* themselves to Joseph.
43: 26 they *p* to him the gifts they had
47: 2 and *p* them before Pharaoh.
47: 7 and *p* him before Pharaoh.
Ex 29: 27 waved and the thigh that was *p*.
32: 6 and *p* fellowship offerings.
35: 22 They all *p* their gold as a wave
Lev 7: 34 thigh that is *p* and have given them
7: 35 sons on the day they were *p*
8: 14 He then *p* the bull
8: 18 He then *p* the ram
8: 22 He then *p* the other ram, the ram
10: 14 waved and the thigh that was *p*.

Lev 10: 15 thigh that was *p* and the breast that
16: 10 as the scapegoat shall be *p* alive
27: 11 the animal must be *p* to the priest,
Nu 6: 20 waved and the thigh that was *p*.
7: 3 These they *p* before the tabernacle.
7: 10 and *p* them before the altar.
8: 15 and *p* them as a wave offering,
8: 21 Aaron *p* them as a wave offering
16: 38 for they were *p* before the LORD
18: 8 in charge of the offerings *p* to me;
28: 15 is to be *p* to the LORD
31: 52 hundreds that Moses and Eleazar *p*
Dt 31: 14 and *p* themselves at the Tent
Jos 24: 1 and they *p* themselves before God.
Jdg 3: 17 He *p* the tribute to Eglon king
3: 18 After Ehud had *p* the tribute,
20: 26 until evening and *p* burnt offerings
21: 4 *p* burnt offerings and fellowship
1Sa 18: 27 and *p* the full number to the king
2Ki 11: 12 he *p* him with a copy
16: 12 he approached it and *p* offerings
1Ch 6: 49 were the ones who *p* offerings
16: 1 and they *p* burnt offerings
23: 31 whenever burnt offerings were *p*
29: 21 and *p* burnt offerings to him:
2Ch 23: 11 they *p* him with a copy
24: 14 burnt offerings were *p* continually
28: 21 and *p* them to the king of Assyria,
29: 24 and *p* their blood on the altar
Ezr 3: 5 they *p* the regular burnt offerings,
10: 19 for their guilt they each *p* a ram
Est 8: 2 from Haman, and *p* it to Mordecai.
Eze 20: 28 *p* their fragrant incense
Da 1: 18 the chief official *p* them
2: 46 that an offering and incense be *p*
Mt 2: 11 and *p* him with gifts of gold
Mk 6: 28 He *p* it to the girl, and she gave it
Ac 6: 6 They *p* these men to the apostles,
9: 41 the widows and *p* her to them alive.
24: 2 Tertullus *p* his case before Felix:
25: 2 and *p* the charges against Paul.
Ro 3: 25 God *p* him as a sacrifice

PRESENTING (PRESENT)

Ex 30: 20 to minister by *p* an offering made
35: 24 Those *p* an offering of silver
Nu 9: 7 kept from *p* the LORD's offering
18: 32 By *p* the best part of it you will not
Eze 46: 14 The *p* of this grain offering
Ac 17: 19 this new teaching is that you are *p*?

PRESENTS (PRESENT)

Lev 6: 5 on the day he *p* his guilt offering.
22: 18 *p* a gift for a burnt offering
Nu 15: 14 among you *p* an offering made
Est 9: 19 a day for giving *p* to each other.
9: 22 and giving *p* of food to one another
Isa 66: 3 is like one who *p* pig's blood,

PRESERVE (PRESERVED PRESERVES)

Ge 19: 32 *p* our family line through our father
19: 34 him so we can *p* our family line
45: 7 ahead of you to *p* for you a remnant
Job 33: 18 to *p* his soul from the pit,
Ps 36: 6 you *p* both man and beast.
41: 2 will protect him and *p* his life;
79: 11 *p* those condemned to die.
119: 88 *P* my life according to your love,
119:159 *p* my life, O LORD, according
138: 7 you *p* my life;
143: 11 name's sake, O LORD, *p* my life;
Pr 3: 21 *p* sound judgment and discernment
5: 2 and your lips may *p* knowledge.
Eze 7: 13 not one of them will *p* his life.
13: 18 lives of my people but *p* your own?
Mal 2: 7 of a priest ought to *p* knowledge,
Lk 17: 33 and whoever loses his life will *p* it.

PRESERVED (PRESERVE)

2Sa 22: 44 you have *p* me as the head
Ps 66: 9 he has *p* our lives
Mt 9: 17 into new wineskins, and both are *p*

PRESERVES (PRESERVE)

Ps 31: 23 The LORD *p* the faithful,
Ecc 7: 12 that wisdom *p* the life

PRESIDES

Ps 82: 1 God *p* in the great assembly;

PRESS (PRESSED PRESSES PRESSING PRESSURE)

Jdg 14: 17 because she continued to *p* him.
2Sa 11: 25 *P* the attack against the city
Job 23: 6 he would not *p* charges against me.
Ps 56: 1 all day long they *p* their attack.
Pr 6: 3 *p* your plea with your neighbor!
Hos 6: 3 let us *p* on to acknowledge him.
Mic 6: 15 you will *p* olives but not use the oil
Ac 19: 38 They can *p* charges.
25: 5 *p* charges against the man there,
Php 3: 12 but I *p* on to take hold of that
3: 14 I *p* on toward the goal
Rev 14: 20 and blood flowed out of the *p*,

PRESSED (PRESS)

Ex 27: 20 oil of *p* olives for the light
29: 40 a fourth of a hin of oil from *p* olives,
Lev 24: 2 oil of *p* olives for the light
Nu 22: 25 she *p* close to the wall, crushing
28: 5 a fourth of a hin of oil from *p* olives.
Jdg 1: 28 they *p* the Canaanites
1: 35 they too were *p* into forced labor.
9: 45 All that day Abimelech *p* his attack
1Sa 13: 6 and that their army was hard *p*,
25: 18 and two hundred cakes of *p* figs,
30: 12 of a cake of *p* figs and two cakes
31: 2 The Philistines *p* hard after Saul
1Ki 5: 11 thousand baths of *p* olive oil.
1Ch 10: 2 The Philistines *p* hard after Saul
Mk 5: 24 A large crowd followed and *p*
Lk 6: 38 *p* down, shaken together
2Co 4: 8 We are hard *p* on every side,
8: 13 relieved while you are hard *p*,

PRESSES (PRESS)

Isa 16: 10 no one treads out wine at the *p*,
Jer 48: 33 the flow of wine from the *p*;

PRESSING (PRESS)

Ex 5: 13 The slave drivers kept *p* them,
Jdg 20: 45 They kept *p* after the Benjamites
Lk 8: 45 the people are crowding and *p*

PRESSURE (PRESS)

Ge 19: 9 They kept bringing *p* on Lot
2Co 1: 8 We were under great *p*, far
11: 28 I face daily the *p* of my concern

PRESUME (PRESUMES PRESUMPTION)

Jas 3: 1 of you should *p* to be teachers,

PRESUMES (PRESUME)

Dt 18: 20 But a prophet who *p* to speak

PRESUMPTION (PRESUME)

Nu 14: 44 in their *p* they went up

PRETEND (PRETENDED PRETENDING PRETENDS PRETENSE PRETENSION)

2Sa 13: 5 "Go to bed and *p* to be ill,"
14: 2 He said to her, "*P* you are
1Ki 14: 5 she will *p* to be someone else."
Pr 12: 9 than *p* to be somebody

PRETENDED (PRETEND)

Ge 42: 7 but he *p* to be a stranger
2Sa 13: 6 So Amnon lay down and *p* to be ill.
Lk 20: 20 they sent spies, who *p* to be honest.

PRETENDING (PRETEND)

Ac 27: 30 *p* they were going to lower some

PRETENDS (PRETEND)

Pr 13: 7 One man *p* to be rich, yet has
13: 7 another *p* to be poor, yet has great

PRETENSE (PRETEND)

1Ki 14: 6 Why this *p*? I have been sent
Jer 3: 10 but only in *p*," declares the LORD.

PRETENSION (PRETEND)

2Co 10: 5 and every *p* that sets itself up

PRETEXT

Ac 23: 15 to bring him before you on the *p*
23: 20 the Sanhedrin tomorrow on the *p*

PREVAIL (PREVAILED PREVAILS PREVALENT)

2Ch 14: 11 do not let man *p* against you."
Isa 54: 17 forged against you will *p*,
Jer 5: 22 waves may roll, but they cannot *p*;
20: 10 then we will *p* over him
20: 11 persecutors will stumble and not *p*.
Ro 3: 4 and *p* in your judging."

PREVAILED (PREVAIL)

Jdg 19: 4 the girl's father, *p* upon him to stay;
Jer 20: 7 you overpowered me and *p*.
La 1: 16 because the enemy has *p*."
Lk 23: 23 he be crucified, and their shouts *p*.

PREVAILS (PREVAIL)

1Sa 2: 9 "It is not by strength that one *p*;
Pr 19: 21 but it is the LORD's purpose that *p*
Hab 1: 4 and justice never *p*.

PREVALENT (PREVAIL)

Jas 1: 21 moral filth and the evil that is so *p*,

PREVENT (PREVENTED)

2Sa 14: 11 God to *p* the avenger of blood
1Ki 15: 17 and fortified Ramah to *p* anyone
2Ch 16: 1 and fortified Ramah to *p* anyone
Mal 3: 11 I will *p* pests from devouring your
Jn 18: 36 servants would fight to *p* my arrest
Ac 27: 42 to kill the prisoners to *p* any
Rev 7: 1 winds of the earth to *p* any wind

PREVENTED (PREVENT)

Ro 1: 13 (but have been *p* from doing
Heb 7: 23 since death *p* them

PREVIOUS

Nu 6: 12 The *p* days do not count,
Jdg 3: 2 had not had *p* battle experience):
Gal 1: 13 of my *p* way of life in Judaism,

PREY (PREYS)

Ge 15: 11 of *p* came down on the carcasses,
49: 9 you return from the *p*, my son
49: 27 in the morning he devours the *p*,
Nu 23: 24 rest till he devours his *p*
Job 4: 11 The lion perishes for lack of *p*,
9: 26 eagles swooping down on their *p*.
24: 21 They *p* on the barren and childless
28: 7 of *p* knows that hidden path,
38: 39 "Do you hunt the *p* for the lioness
Ps 17: 12 They are like a lion hungry for *p*,
22: 13 Roaring lions tearing their *p*
104: 21 The lions roar for their *p*
Isa 5: 29 they growl as they seize their *p*
10: 2 making widows their *p*
18: 6 left to the mountain birds of *p*
31: 4 a great lion over his *p*—
46: 11 From the east I summon a bird of *p*
59: 15 whoever shuns evil becomes a *p*.
Jer 12: 9 like a speckled bird of *p*
12: 9 that other birds of *p* surround
Eze 13: 21 and they will no longer fall *p*
19: 3 He learned to tear the *p*
19: 6 He learned to tear the *p*
22: 25 her like a roaring lion tearing its *p*;
22: 27 her are like wolves tearing their *p*;
Am 3: 4 the thicket when he has no *p*?
Na 2: 12 and his dens with the *p*,
2: 12 and strangled the *p* for his mate,
2: 13 I will leave you no *p* on the earth.

PREYS (PREY)

Pr 6: 26 the adulteress *p* upon your very life

PRICE (PRICED PRICELESS)

Ge 23: 9 him to sell it to me for the full *p*
23: 13 I will pay the *p* of the field.
23: 16 out for him the *p* he had named
34: 12 Make the *p* for the bride
Lev 25: 16 are few, you are to decrease the *p*,
25: 16 you are to increase the *p*,
25: 50 The *p* for his release is to be based
25: 51 share of the *p* paid for him.

Nu 18: 16 them at the redemption *p* set
Dt 2: 28 water to drink for their *p* in silver.
1Sa 13: 21 The *p* was two thirds of a shekel
18: 25 'The king wants no other *p*
2Sa 3: 14 betrothed to myself for the *p*
1Ch 21: 22 Sell it to me at the full *p*.''
21: 24 ''No, I insist on paying the full *p*.
Job 28: 15 nor can its *p* be weighed in silver.
28: 18 the *p* of wisdom is beyond rubies.
Pr 27: 26 and the goats with the *p* of a field.
Isa 45: 13 but not for a *p* or reward,
La 5: 4 our wood can be had only at a *p*.
Da 11: 39 and will distribute the land at a *p*.
Am 8: 5 boosting the *p*
Mic 3: 11 her priests teach for a *p*,
Zec 11: 13 handsome *p* at which they priced
Mt 26: 9 could have been sold at a high *p*
27: 9 the *p* set on him by the people
Ac 5: 8 is this the *p* you and Ananias got
5: 8 ''Yes,'' she said, ''that is the *p*.''
22: 28 to pay a big *p* for my citizenship.''
1Co 6: 20 your own; you were bought at a *p*.
7: 23 bought at a *p*; do not become slaves

PRICED (PRICE)

Zec 11: 13 price at which they *p* me!

PRICELESS (PRICE)

Ps 36: 7 How *p* is your unfailing love!

PRIDE (PROUD)

Lev 26: 19 I will break down your stubborn *p*
2Ki 19: 22 and lifted your eyes in *p*?
2Ch 26: 16 Uzziah became powerful, his *p* led
32: 26 repented of the *p* of his heart,
Job 20: 6 Though his *p* reaches
33: 17 and keep him from *p*,
Ps 10: 4 In his *p* the wicked does not seek
31: 18 for with *p* and contempt
47: 4 the *p* of Jacob, whom he loved.
56: 2 many are attacking me in their *p*.
59: 12 let them be caught in their *p*.
62: 10 or take *p* in stolen goods;
73: 6 Therefore *p* is their necklace;
Pr 8: 13 I hate *p* and arrogance,
11: 2 When *p* comes, then comes
13: 10 *P* only breeds quarrels,
16: 18 *P* goes before destruction,
17: 6 parents are the *p* of their children.
21: 24 he behaves with overweening *p*.
29: 23 A man's *p* brings him low,
Ecc 7: 8 and patience is better than *p*.
Isa 2: 11 and the *p* of men brought low;
2: 17 and the *p* of men humbled;
4: 2 the fruit of the land will be the *p*
9: 9 who say with *p*
10: 12 Assyria for the willful *p* of his heart
13: 11 will humble the *p* of the ruthless.
13: 19 the glory of the Babylonians' *p*,
16: 6 We have heard of Moab's *p*—
16: 6 her overweening *p* and conceit,
16: 6 her *p* and her insolence—
23: 9 to bring low the *p* of all glory
25: 11 God will bring down their *p*
28: 1 the *p* of Ephraim's drunkards,
28: 1 the *p* of those laid low by wine!
28: 3 the *p* of Ephraim's drunkards,
37: 23 and lifted your eyes in *p*?
43: 14 in the ships in which they took *p*.
60: 15 I will make you the everlasting *p*
Jer 13: 9 and the great *p* of Jerusalem.
13: 9 'In the same way I will ruin the *p*
13: 17 because of your *p*;
48: 29 her overweening *p* and conceit,
48: 29 her *p* and arrogance
48: 29 ''We have heard of Moab's *p*—
49: 16 *p* of your heart have deceived you,
Eze 7: 24 an end to the *p* of the mighty,
16: 56 Sodom in the day of your *p*,
24: 21 the stronghold in which you take *p*,
28: 2 '' 'In the *p* of your heart
32: 12 They will shatter the *p* of Egypt,
Da 4: 37 And those who walk in *p* he is able
5: 20 arrogant and hardened with *p*,
11: 12 of the South will be filled with *p*
Am 6: 8 ''I abhor the *p* of Jacob
8: 7 The LORD has sworn by the *P*
Ob : 3 *p* of your heart has deceived you,
Zep 2: 10 in return for their *p*,
3: 11 those who rejoice in their *p*.
Zec 9: 6 I will cut off the *p* of the Philistines.
10: 11 Assyria's *p* will be brought down
1Co 4: 6 you will not take *p* in one man
2Co 5: 12 giving you an opportunity to take *p*
5: 12 you can answer those who take *p*
7: 4 in you; I take great *p* in you.
8: 24 and the reason for our *p* in you,
Gal 6: 4 Then he can take *p* in himself,
Jas 1: 9 ought to take *p* in his high position.
1: 10 the one who is rich should take *p*

PRIEST (PRIEST'S PRIESTHOOD PRIESTLY PRIESTS PRIESTS')

Ge 14: 18 He was *p* of God Most High,
41: 45 daughter of Potiphera, *p* of On,
41: 50 daughter of Potiphera, *p* of On.
46: 20 daughter of Potiphera, *p* of On.
Ex 2: 16 a *p* of Midian had seven daughters,
3: 1 of Jethro his father-in-law, the *p*
18: 1 the *p* of Midian and father-in-law
28: 3 so he may serve me as *p*.
29: 30 The son who succeeds him as *p*
30: 33 other than a *p* must be cut
31: 10 sacred garments for Aaron the *p*
35: 19 sacred garments for Aaron the *p*
38: 21 of Ithamar son of Aaron, the *p*.
39: 41 sacred garments for Aaron the *p*
40: 13 him so he may serve me as *p*.
Lev 1: 7 sons of Aaron the *p* are to put fire
1: 9 the *p* is to burn all of it on the altar.
1: 12 and the *p* shall arrange them,
1: 13 and the *p* is to bring all of it
1: 15 The *p* shall bring it to the altar,
1: 17 and then the *p* shall burn it
2: 2 The *p* shall take a handful
2: 8 present it to the *p*, who shall take it
2: 16 *p* shall burn the memorial portion
3: 11 The *p* shall burn them on the altar
3: 16 The *p* shall burn them on the altar
4: 3 If the anointed *p* sins, bringing guilt
4: 5 the anointed *p* shall take some
4: 7 The *p* shall then put some
4: 10 the *p* shall burn them on the altar
4: 16 Then the anointed *p* is to take some
4: 20 this way the *p* will make atonement
4: 25 the *p* shall take some of the blood
4: 26 this way the *p* will make atonement
4: 30 the *p* is to take some of the blood
4: 31 and the *p* shall burn it on the altar
4: 31 this way the *p* will make atonement
4: 34 the *p* shall take some of the blood
4: 35 and the *p* shall burn it on the altar
4: 35 this way the *p* will make atonement
5: 6 the *p* shall make atonement for him
5: 8 He is to bring them to the *p*,
5: 10 The *p* shall then offer the other
5: 12 it to the *p*, who shall take a handful
5: 13 of the offering will belong to the *p*,
5: 13 this way the *p* will make atonement
5: 16 value to that and give it all to the *p*,
5: 18 this way the *p* will make atonement
5: 18 to the *p* as a guilt offering a ram
6: 6 as a penalty he must bring to the *p*,
6: 7 this way the *p* will make atonement
6: 10 The *p* shall then put
6: 12 Every morning the *p* is
6: 15 The *p* is to take a handful
6: 22 as anointed *p* shall prepare it.
6: 23 of a *p* shall be burned completely;
6: 26 The *p* who offers it shall eat it;
7: 5 The *p* shall burn them on the altar
7: 7 to the *p* who makes atonement
7: 8 The *p* who offers a burnt offering
7: 9 belongs to the *p* who offers it,
7: 14 to the *p* who sprinkles the blood
7: 31 The *p* shall burn the fat on the altar
7: 32 your fellowship offerings to the *p*
7: 34 have given them to Aaron the *p*
12: 6 is to bring to the *p* at the entrance
12: 8 this way the *p* will make atonement
13: 2 he must be brought to Aaron the *p*
13: 2 or to one of his sons who is a *p*.
13: 3 The *p* is to examine the sore
13: 3 When the *p* examines him,
13: 4 the *p* is to put the infected person
13: 5 On the seventh day the *p* is
Lev 13: 6 On the seventh day the *p* is
13: 6 the *p* shall pronounce him clean;
13: 7 he must appear before the *p* again.
13: 7 to the *p* to be pronounced clean,
13: 8 The *p* is to examine him,
13: 9 he must be brought to the *p*.
13: 10 The *p* is to examine him,
13: 11 the *p* shall pronounce him unclean.
13: 12 and, so far as the *p* can see,
13: 13 the *p* is to examine him,
13: 15 When the *p* sees the raw flesh,
13: 16 and turn white, he must go to the *p*.
13: 17 The *p* is to examine him,
13: 17 the *p* shall pronounce the infected
13: 19 he must present himself to the *p*.
13: 20 The *p* is to examine it,
13: 20 the *p* shall pronounce him unclean.
13: 21 But if, when the *p* examines it,
13: 21 then the *p* is to put him in isolation
13: 22 the *p* shall pronounce him unclean;
13: 23 the *p* shall pronounce him clean.
13: 25 The *p* shall pronounce him unclean
13: 25 the *p* is to examine the spot,
13: 26 But if the *p* examines it
13: 26 then the *p* is to put him in isolation
13: 27 On the seventh day the *p* is
13: 27 the *p* shall pronounce him unclean;
13: 28 the *p* shall pronounce him clean;
13: 30 the *p* is to examine the sore,
13: 30 the *p* shall pronounce that person
13: 31 then the *p* is to put the infected
13: 31 when the *p* examines this kind
13: 32 On the seventh day the *p* is
13: 33 and the *p* is to keep him
13: 34 On the seventh day the *p* is
13: 34 the *p* shall pronounce him clean.
13: 36 the *p* does not need to look
13: 36 the *p* is to examine him,
13: 37 the *p* shall pronounce him clean.
13: 39 the *p* is to examine them,
13: 43 The *p* is to examine him and,
13: 44 The *p* shall pronounce him unclean
13: 49 and must be shown to the *p*.
13: 50 The *p* is to examine the mildew
13: 53 ''But if, when the *p* examines it,
13: 55 article has been washed, the *p* is
13: 56 If, when the *p* examines it,
14: 2 when he is brought to the *p*:
14: 3 The *p* is to go outside the camp
14: 4 the *p* shall order that two live clean
14: 5 Then the *p* shall order that one
14: 11 *p* who pronounces him clean shall
14: 12 ''Then the *p* is to take one
14: 13 the guilt offering belongs to the *p*;
14: 14 The *p* is to take some of the blood
14: 15 The *p* shall then take some
14: 17 The *p* is to put some
14: 18 the oil in his palm the *p* shall put
14: 19 the *p* is to sacrifice the sin offering
14: 19 *p* shall slaughter the burnt offering
14: 23 cleansing to the *p* at the entrance
14: 24 The *p* is to take the lamb
14: 26 The *p* is to pour some of the oil
14: 29 the oil in his palm the *p* shall put
14: 31 this way the *p* will make atonement
14: 35 of the house must go and tell the *p*,
14: 36 After this the *p* is to go in
14: 36 The *p* is to order the house
14: 38 the *p* shall go out of the house
14: 39 the seventh day the *p* shall return
14: 44 the *p* is to go and examine it and,
14: 48 ''But if the *p* comes to examine it
15: 14 of Meeting and give them to the *p*.
15: 15 The *p* is to sacrifice them, the one
15: 29 bring them to the *p* at the entrance
15: 30 The *p* is to sacrifice one
16: 32 The *p* who is anointed
16: 32 as high *p* is to make atonement.
17: 5 They must bring them to the *p*,
17: 6 The *p* is to sprinkle the blood
19: 22 the ram of the guilt offering the *p* is
21: 1 'A *p* must not make himself
21: 10 '' 'The high *p*, the one
21: 21 of Aaron the *p* who has any defect
22: 10 nor may the guest of a *p*
22: 11 But if a *p* buys a slave with money,
22: 12 marries anyone other than a *p*,
22: 14 restitution to the *p* for the offering

Lev 23: 10 bring to the *p* a sheaf
23: 11 the *p* is to wave it on the day
23: 20 The *p* is to wave the two lambs
23: 20 offering to the LORD for the *p*.
27: 8 he is to present the person to the *p*,
27: 11 animal must be presented to the *p*,
27: 12 Whatever value the *p* then sets,
27: 14 Whatever value the *p* then sets,
27: 14 the *p* will judge its quality as good
27: 18 the *p* will determine the value
27: 23 the *p* will determine its value up
Nu 3: 6 them to Aaron the *p* to assist him.
3: 32 was Eleazar son of Aaron, the *p*.
4: 16 "Eleazar son of Aaron, the *p*,
4: 28 of Ithamar son of Aaron, the *p*.
4: 33 of Ithamar son of Aaron, the *p*."
5: 8 and must be given to the *p*,
5: 9 bring to a *p* will belong to him.
5: 10 to the *p* will belong to the *p*.' "
5: 15 then he is to take his wife to the *p*.
5: 16 " 'The *p* shall bring her
5: 18 After the *p* has had the woman
5: 19 Then the *p* shall put the woman
5: 21 here the *p* is to put the woman
5: 23 " 'The *p* is to write these curses
5: 25 The *p* is to take from her hands
5: 26 The *p* is then to take a handful
5: 30 The *p* is to have her stand
6: 10 pigeons to the *p* at the entrance
6: 11 *p* is to offer one as a sin offering
6: 16 " 'The *p* is to present them
6: 19 *p* is to place in his hands a boiled
6: 20 The *p* shall then wave them
6: 20 they are holy and belong to the *p*;
7: 8 of Ithamar son of Aaron, the *p*.
15: 25 The *p* is to make atonement
15: 28 The *p* is to make atonement
16: 37 "Tell Eleazar son of Aaron, the *p*,
16: 39 Eleazar the *p* collected the bronze
18: 28 LORD's portion to Aaron the *p*.
19: 3 Give it to Eleazar the *p*; it is
19: 4 Then Eleazar the *p* is to take some
19: 6 The *p* is to take some cedar wood,
19: 7 the *p* must wash his clothes
25: 7 the son of Aaron, the *p*, saw this,
25: 11 the *p*, has turned my anger away
26: 1 the *p*, "Take a census
26: 3 and Eleazar the *p* spoke with them
26: 63 Eleazar the *p* when they counted
26: 64 Aaron the *p* when they counted
27: 2 Eleazar the *p*, the leaders
27: 19 stand before Eleazar the *p*
27: 21 He is to stand before Eleazar the *p*,
27: 22 had him stand before Eleazar the *p*
31: 6 with Phinehas son of Eleazar, the *p*
31: 12 plunder to Moses and Eleazar the *p*
31: 13 Eleazar the *p* and all the leaders
31: 21 Eleazar the *p* said to the soldiers
31: 26 "You and Eleazar the *p*
31: 29 and give it to Eleazar the *p*
31: 31 So Moses and Eleazar the *p* did
31: 41 gave the tribute to Eleazar the *p*
31: 51 and Eleazar the *p* accepted
31: 54 Eleazar the *p* accepted the gold
32: 2 came to Moses and Eleazar the *p*
32: 28 orders about them to Eleazar the *p*
33: 38 command Aaron the *p* went up
34: 17 Eleazar the *p* and Joshua son
35: 25 there until the death of the high *p*,
35: 28 death of the high *p* may he return
35: 28 refuge until the death of the high *p*;
35: 32 land before the death of the high *p*.
Dt 10: 6 Eleazar his son succeeded him as *p*.
17: 12 or for the *p* who stands ministering
20: 2 the *p* shall come forward
26: 3 say to the *p* in office at the time,
26: 4 The *p* shall take the basket
Jos 14: 1 which Eleazar the *p*, Joshua son
17: 4 They went to Eleazar the *p*,
19: 51 the territories that Eleazar the *p*,
20: 6 death of the high *p* who is serving
21: 1 Levites approached Eleazar the *p*,
21: 4 of Aaron the *p* were allotted
21: 13 of Aaron the *p* they gave Hebron
22: 13 the *p*, to the land of Gilead—
22: 30 When Phinehas the *p*
22: 31 And Phinehas son of Eleazar, the *p*
22: 32 Phinehas son of Eleazar, the *p*,

Jdg 17: 5 installed one of his sons as his *p*.
17: 10 with me and be my father and *p*,
17: 12 and the young man became his *p*
17: 13 since this Levite has become my *p*
18: 4 "He has hired me and I am his *p*."
18: 6 The *p* answered them, "Go
18: 17 and the cast idol while the *p*
18: 18 the *p* said to them, "What are you
18: 19 as *p* rather than just one man's
18: 19 with us, and be our father and *p*.
18: 20 household?" Then the *p* was glad.
18: 24 and my *p*, and went away.
18: 27 and his *p*, and went on to Laish,
1Sa 1: 9 Now Eli the *p* was sitting on a chair
2: 11 before the LORD under Eli the *p*.
2: 13 the servant of the *p* would come
2: 14 *p* would take for himself whatever
2: 15 the servant of the *p* would come
2: 15 "Give the *p* some meat to roast;
2: 28 of all the tribes of Israel to be my *p*,
2: 35 I will raise up for myself a faithful *p*
14: 3 son of Eli, the LORD's *p* in Shiloh.
14: 19 While Saul was talking to the *p*,
14: 19 to the *p*, "Withdraw your hand."
14: 36 But the *p* said, "Let us inquire
21: 1 went to Nob, to Ahimelech the *p*.
21: 2 David answered Ahimelech the *p*,
21: 4 But the *p* answered David,
21: 6 *p* gave him the consecrated bread,
21: 9 The *p* replied, "The sword
22: 11 for the *p* Ahimelech son of Ahitub
23: 9 said to Abiathar the *p*, "Bring
30: 7 Then David said to Abiathar the *p*,
2Sa 15: 27 The king also said to Zadok the *p*,
20: 26 and Ira the Jairite was David's *p*.
1Ki 1: 7 of Zeruiah and with Abiathar the *p*,
1: 8 But Zadok the *p*, Benaiah son
1: 19 Abiathar the *p* and Joab
1: 25 of the army and Abiathar the *p*.
1: 26 and Zadok the *p*, and Benaiah son
1: 32 David said, "Call in Zadok the *p*,
1: 34 There have Zadok the *p*
1: 38 Zadok the *p*, Nathan the prophet,
1: 39 Zadok the *p* took the horn of oil
1: 42 son of Abiathar the *p* arrived.
1: 44 sent with him Zadok the *p*,
1: 45 and Zadok the *p* and Nathan
2: 22 for Abiathar the *p* and Joab son
2: 26 To Abiathar the *p* the king said,
2: 35 Abiathar with Zadok the *p*.
4: 2 the *p*; Elihoreph and Ahijah,
4: 5 a *p* and personal adviser to the king
13: 33 to become a *p* he consecrated
2Ki 11: 9 and came to Jehoiada the *p*
11: 9 as Jehoiada the *p* ordered.
11: 15 For the *p* had said, "She must not
11: 15 Jehoiada the *p* ordered
11: 18 Then Jehoiada the *p* posted guards
11: 18 killed Mattan the *p* of Baal in front
12: 2 Jehoiada the *p* instructed him.
12: 5 Let every *p* receive the money
12: 7 Joash summoned Jehoiada the *p*
12: 9 Jehoiada the *p* took a chest
12: 10 secretary and the high *p* came,
16: 10 and sent to Uriah the *p* a sketch
16: 11 So Uriah the *p* built an altar
16: 15 gave these orders to Uriah the *p*:
16: 16 And Uriah the *p* did just
22: 4 "Go up to Hilkiah the high *p*
22: 8 Hilkiah the high *p* said
22: 10 "Hilkiah the *p* has given me a book
22: 12 gave these orders to Hilkiah the *p*,
22: 14 Hilkiah the *p*, Ahikam, Acbor,
23: 4 king ordered Hilkiah the high *p*,
23: 24 that Hilkiah the *p* had discovered
25: 18 Zephaniah the *p* next in rank
25: 18 as prisoners Seraiah the chief *p*,
1Ch 6: 10 as *p* in the temple Solomon built
16: 39 David left Zadok the *p*
24: 6 and of the officials: Zadok the *p*,
27: 5 was Benaiah son of Jehoiada the *p*.
29: 22 to be ruler and Zadok to be *p*.
2Ch 13: 9 and seven rams may become a *p*
15: 3 without a *p* to teach
19: 11 "Amariah the chief *p* will be
22: 11 and wife of the *p* Jehoiada,
23: 8 as Jehoiada the *p* ordered.
23: 8 for Jehoiada the *p* had not released

2Ch 23: 14 For the *p* had said, "Do not put her
23: 14 Jehoiada the *p* sent out
23: 17 killed Mattan the *p* of Baal in front
24: 2 all the years of Jehoiada the *p*.
24: 6 summoned Jehoiada the chief *p*
24: 11 officer of the chief *p* would come
24: 20 Zechariah son of Jehoiada the *p*.
24: 25 the son of Jehoiada the *p*,
26: 17 Azariah the *p* with eighty other
26: 20 When Azariah the chief *p*
31: 10 and Azariah the chief *p*,
34: 9 They went to Hilkiah the high *p*
34: 14 Hilkiah the *p* found the Book
34: 18 "Hilkiah the *p* has given me a book
Ezr 2: 63 food until there was a *p* ministering
7: 5 the son of Aaron the chief *p*—
7: 11 Artaxerxes had given to Ezra the *p*
7: 12 king of kings, To Ezra the *p*,
7: 21 with diligence whatever Ezra the *p*,
8: 33 of Meremoth son of Uriah, the *p*.
10: 10 Then Ezra the *p* stood up
10: 16 Ezra the *p* selected men who were
Ne 3: 1 Eliashib the high *p* and his fellow
3: 20 of the house of Eliashib the high *p*.
7: 65 there should be a *p* ministering
8: 2 month Ezra the *p* brought the Law
8: 9 Nehemiah the governor, Ezra the *p*
10: 38 A *p* descended from Aaron is
12: 26 and of Ezra the *p* and scribe.
13: 4 Eliashib the *p* had been put
13: 13 put Shelemiah the *p*, Zadok
13: 28 Eliashib the high *p* was son-in-law
Ps 110: 4 "You are a *p* forever,
Isa 8: 2 And I will call in Uriah the *p*
24: 2 the same for *p* as for people,
61: 10 adorns his head like a *p*,
Jer 14: 18 Both prophet and *p*
18: 18 of the law by the *p* will not be lost,
20: 1 When the *p* Pashhur son of Immer,
21: 1 the *p* Zephaniah son of Maaseiah.
23: 11 "Both prophet and *p* are godless;
23: 33 or a prophet or a *p*, ask you,
23: 34 or a *p* or anyone else claims,
29: 25 son of Maaseiah the *p*,
29: 26 'The LORD has appointed you *p*
29: 29 Zephaniah the *p*, however,
37: 3 with the *p* Zephaniah son
52: 24 Zephaniah the *p* next in rank
52: 24 as prisoners Seraiah the chief *p*,
La 2: 6 both king and *p*.
2: 20 Should *p* and prophet be killed
Eze 1: 3 of the LORD came to Ezekiel the *p*
7: 26 of the law by the *p* will be lost,
44: 21 No *p* is to drink wine
44: 25 " 'A *p* must not defile himself
45: 19 The *p* is to take some of the blood
Hos 4: 4 who bring charges against a *p*.
Am 7: 10 Then Amaziah the *p* of Bethel sent
Hag 1: 1 the high *p*: This is what the LORD
1: 12 son of Jehozadak, the high *p*,
1: 14 son of Jehozadak, the high *p*,
2: 2 son of Jehozadak, the high *p*,
2: 4 son of Jehozadak, the high *p*.
Zec 3: 1 me Joshua the high *p* standing
3: 8 O high *p* Joshua and your
6: 11 and set it on the head of the high *p*,
6: 13 And he will be a *p* on his throne.
Mal 2: 7 of a *p* ought to preserve knowledge,
Mt 8: 4 show yourself to the *p*
26: 3 in the palace of the high *p*,
26: 51 struck the servant of the high *p*,
26: 57 him to Caiaphas, the high *p*,
26: 58 up to the courtyard of the high *p*.
26: 62 Then the high *p* stood up
26: 63 high *p* said to him, "I charge you
26: 65 Then the high *p* tore his clothes
Mk 1: 44 show yourself to the *p*
2: 26 In the days of Abiathar the high *p*,
14: 47 struck the servant of the high *p*,
14: 53 They took Jesus to the high *p*,
14: 54 into the courtyard of the high *p*.
14: 60 the high *p* stood up before them
14: 61 Again the high *p* asked him,
14: 63 The high *p* tore his clothes.
14: 66 girls of the high *p* came by.
Lk 1: 5 there was a *p* named Zechariah,
1: 8 he was serving as *p* before God,
5: 14 show yourself to the *p*

Lk 10: 31 A *p* happened to be going
22: 50 struck the servant of the high *p*.
22: 54 him into the house of the high *p*.
Jn 11: 49 who was high *p* that year, spoke up,
11: 51 high *p* that year he prophesied that
18: 13 of Caiaphas, the high *p* that year.
18: 15 disciple was known to the high *p*,
18: 16 who was known to the high *p*,
18: 19 high *p* questioned Jesus about his
18: 22 way to answer the high *p*?"
18: 24 still bound, to Caiaphas the high *p*.
Ac 4: 6 Annas the high *p* was there,
5: 17 the high *p* and all his associates,
5: 21 When the high *p* and his associates
5: 27 to be questioned by the high *p*.
7: 1 Then the high *p* asked him,
9: 1 went to the high *p* and asked him
14: 13 *p* of Zeus, whose temple was just
19: 14 a Jewish chief *p*, were doing this.
22: 5 the high *p* and all the council can
23: 2 this the high *p* Ananias ordered
23: 4 "You dare to insult God's high *p*?"
23: 5 not realize that he was the high *p*;
24: 1 days later the high *p* Ananias went
Heb 2: 17 faithful high *p* in service to God,
3: 1 and high *p* whom we confess.
4: 14 have a great high *p* who has gone
4: 15 do not have a high *p* who is unable
5: 1 Every high *p* is selected
5: 5 the glory of becoming a high *p*.
5: 6 "You are a *p* forever,
5: 10 by God to be high *p* in the order
6: 20 He has become a high *p* forever,
7: 1 of Salem and *p* of God Most High.
7: 3 Son of God he remains a *p* forever.
7: 11 need for another *p* to come—
7: 15 clear if another *p* like Melchizedek
7: 16 one who has become a *p* not
7: 17 "You are a *p* forever,
7: 21 but he became a *p* with an oath
7: 21 'You are a *p* forever.' "
7: 26 Such a high *p* meets our need—
8: 1 We do have such a high *p*,
8: 3 Every high *p* is appointed
8: 4 were on earth, he would not be a *p*,
9: 7 only the high *p* entered the inner
9: 11 as high *p* of the good things that are
9: 25 the way the high *p* enters the Most
10: 11 Day after day every *p* stands
10: 12 But when this *p* had offered
10: 21 and since we have a great *p*
13: 11 The high *p* carries the blood

PRIEST'S (PRIEST)

Lev 6: 29 Any male in a *p* family may eat it;
7: 6 Any male in a *p* family may eat it,
21: 9 " 'If a *p* daughter defiles herself
22: 10 one outside a *p* family may eat
22: 12 If a *p* daughter marries anyone
22: 13 if a *p* daughter becomes a widow
Jn 18: 10 and struck the high *p* servant,
18: 15 Jesus into the high *p* courtyard,
18: 26 One of the high *p* servants,
Ac 4: 6 the other men of the high *p* family.

PRIESTHOOD (PRIEST)

Ex 29: 9 *p* is theirs by a lasting ordinance.
40: 15 be to a *p* that will continue
Nu 16: 10 now you are trying to get the *p* too.
18: 1 for offenses against the *p*.
18: 7 I am giving you the service of the *p*
25: 13 will have a covenant of a lasting *p*,
1Ki 2: 27 Abiathar from the *p* of the LORD,
Ezr 2: 62 and so were excluded from the *p*
Ne 7: 64 and so were excluded from the *p*
13: 29 and the covenant of the *p*
Lk 1: 9 according to the custom of the *p*,
3: 2 during the high *p* of Annas
Heb 7: 11 attained through the Levitical *p*
7: 12 For when there is a change of the *p*,
7: 24 lives forever, he has a permanent *p*.
1Pe 2: 5 into a spiritual house to be a holy *p*,
2: 9 you are a chosen people, a royal *p*,

PRIESTLY (PRIEST)

Lev 21: 10 ordained to wear the *p* garments,
Jos 18: 7 the *p* service of the LORD is their
1Sa 2: 36 "Appoint me to some *p* office
Ezr 2: 69 minas of silver and 100 *p* garments.
Ne 12: 12 were the heads of the *p* families:
13: 29 because they defiled the *p* office
Lk 1: 5 to the *p* division of Abijah;
Ro 15: 16 to the Gentiles with the *p* duty

PRIESTS (PRIEST)

Ge 47: 22 he did not buy the land of the *p*,
47: 26 land of the *p* that did not become
Ex 19: 6 you will be for me a kingdom of *p*
19: 22 Even the *p*, who approach
19: 24 the *p* and the people must not force
28: 1 so they may serve me as *p*.
28: 4 so they may serve me as *p*.
28: 41 them so they may serve me as *p*.
29: 1 so they may serve me as *p*:
29: 44 and his sons to serve me as *p*.
30: 30 them so they may serve me as *p*.
31: 10 for his sons when they serve as *p*,
35: 19 for his sons when they serve as *p*."
39: 41 for his sons when serving as *p*.
40: 15 so they may serve me as *p*.
Lev 1: 5 then Aaron's sons the *p* shall bring
1: 8 Aaron's sons the *p* shall arrange
1: 11 Aaron's sons the *p* shall sprinkle its
2: 2 and take it to Aaron's sons the *p*.
3: 2 Aaron's sons the *p* shall sprinkle
7: 35 presented to serve the LORD as *p*.
16: 33 and for the *p* and all the people
21: 1 "Speak to the *p*, the sons of Aaron,
21: 5 " '*P* must not shave their heads
21: 7 because *p* are holy to their God.
22: 9 The *p* are to keep my requirements
22: 15 *p* must not desecrate the sacred
27: 21 it will become the property of the *p*
Nu 3: 3 the anointed *p*, who were ordained
3: 3 who were ordained to serve as *p*.
3: 4 as *p* during the lifetime
3: 10 Aaron and his sons to serve as *p*;
10: 8 "The sons of Aaron, the *p*,
18: 7 as *p* in connection with everything
Dt 17: 9 Go to the *p*, who are Levites,
17: 18 from that of the *p*, who are Levites.
18: 1 The *p*, who are Levites—indeed
18: 3 This is the share due the *p*
19: 17 presence of the LORD before the *p*
21: 5 The *p*, the sons of Levi, shall step
24: 8 careful to do exactly as the *p*,
27: 9 Moses and the *p*, who are Levites,
31: 9 down this law and gave it to the *p*,
Jos 3: 3 and the *p*, who are Levites,
3: 6 said to the *p*, "Take up the ark
3: 8 Tell the *p* who carry the ark
3: 13 as the *p* who carry the ark
3: 14 the *p* carrying the ark
3: 15 the *p* who carried the ark reached
3: 17 The *p* who carried the ark
4: 3 from right where the *p* stood
4: 9 the spot where the *p* who carried
4: 10 the *p* who carried the ark remained
4: 11 and the *p* came to the other side
4: 16 "Command the *p* carrying the ark
4: 17 So Joshua commanded the *p*,
4: 18 *p* came up out of the river carrying
6: 4 Have seven *p* carry trumpets
6: 4 with the *p* blowing the trumpets.
6: 6 So Joshua son of Nun called the *p*
6: 6 and have seven *p* carry trumpets
6: 8 the seven *p* carrying the seven
6: 9 of the *p* who blew the trumpets,
6: 12 the *p* took up the ark of the LORD.
6: 13 The seven *p* carrying the seven
6: 16 when the *p* sounded the trumpet
8: 33 facing those who carried it—the *p*,
21: 19 for the *p*, the descendants of Aaron
Jdg 18: 30 his sons were *p* for the tribe of Dan
1Sa 1: 3 sons of Eli, were *p* of the LORD.
2: 13 Now it was the practice of the *p*
5: 5 to this day neither the *p* of Dagon
6: 2 the Philistines called for the *p*
22: 11 who were the *p* at Nob,
22: 17 a hand to strike the *p* of the LORD.
22: 17 "Turn and kill the *p* of the LORD,
22: 18 "You turn and strike down the *p*."
22: 19 the town of the *p*, with its men
22: 21 David that Saul had killed the *p*
2Sa 8: 17 Ahimelech son of Abiathar were *p*;
15: 35 Won't the *p* Zadok and Abiathar be
2Sa 17: 15 told Zadok and Abiathar, the *p*,
19: 11 the *p*: "Ask the elders of Judah,
20: 25 Zadok and Abiathar were *p*;
1Ki 4: 4 *p*; Azariah son of Nathan—
8: 3 Israel had arrived, the *p* took up
8: 4 The *p* and Levites carried them up,
8: 6 The *p* then brought the ark
8: 10 When the *p* withdrew
8: 11 *p* could not perform their service
12: 31 appointed *p* from all sorts of people
12: 32 installed *p* at the high places he had
13: 2 On you he will sacrifice the *p*
13: 33 but once more appointed *p*
2Ki 10: 11 his close friends and his *p*,
10: 19 all his ministers and all his *p*.
12: 4 to the *p*, "Collect all the money
12: 6 of King Joash the *p* still had not
12: 7 and the other *p* and asked them,
12: 8 The *p* agreed that they would not
12: 9 *p* who guarded the entrance put
12: 16 of the LORD; it belonged to the *p*.
17: 27 Have one of the *p* you took captive
17: 28 one of the *p* who had been exiled
17: 32 *p* in the shrines at the high places
19: 2 the secretary and the leading *p*,
23: 2 the people of Jerusalem, the *p*
23: 4 *p* next in rank and the doorkeepers
23: 5 away with the pagan *p* appointed
23: 8 Josiah brought all the *p*
23: 8 where the *p* had burned incense.
23: 9 Although the *p* of the high places
23: 9 bread with their fellow *p*.
23: 20 Josiah slaughtered all the *p*
1Ch 9: 2 *p*, Levites and temple servants.
9: 10 Of the *p*: Jedaiah; Jehoiarib; Jakin;
9: 13 The *p*, who were heads of families,
9: 30 But some of the *p* took care
13: 2 also to the *p* and Levites who are
15: 11 Zadok and Abiathar the *p*,
15: 14 So the *p* and Levites consecrated
15: 24 and Eliezer the *p* were
16: 6 and Jahaziel the *p* were
16: 39 his fellow *p* before the tabernacle
18: 16 Ahimelech son of Abiathar were *p*;
23: 2 as well as the *p* and Levites.
24: 2 and Ithamar served as the *p*.
24: 6 and the heads of families of the *p*
24: 31 and the heads of families of the *p*
28: 13 for the divisions of the *p*
28: 21 of the *p* and Levites are ready
2Ch 4: 6 to be used by the *p* for washing.
4: 9 He made the courtyard of the *p*,
5: 5 *p*, who were Levites, carried them
5: 7 The *p* then brought the ark
5: 11 All the *p* who were there had
5: 11 The *p* then withdrew
5: 12 by 120 *p* sounding trumpets.
5: 14 *p* could not perform their service
6: 41 May your *p*, O LORD God,
7: 2 The *p* could not enter the temple
7: 6 The *p* took their positions,
7: 6 the *p* blew their trumpets,
8: 14 and to assist the *p* according
8: 14 divisions of the *p* for their duties,
8: 15 from the king's commands to the *p*
11: 13 The *p* and Levites
11: 14 and his sons had rejected them as *p*
11: 15 And he appointed his own *p*
13: 9 But didn't you drive out the *p*
13: 9 and make *p* of your own
13: 10 *p* who serve the LORD are sons
13: 12 His *p* with their trumpets will
13: 14 The *p* blew their trumpets
17: 8 and the *p* Elishama and Jehoram.
19: 8 *p* and heads of Israelite families
23: 4 of you *p* and Levites who are going
23: 6 except the *p* and Levites on duty;
23: 18 of the LORD in the hands of the *p*,
24: 5 He called together the *p*
26: 17 with eighty other courageous *p*
26: 18 That is for the *p*, the descendants
26: 19 raging at the *p* in their presence
26: 20 and all the other *p* looked at him,
29: 4 He brought in the *p* and the Levites
29: 16 The *p* went into the sanctuary
29: 21 The king commanded the *p*,
29: 22 and the *p* took the blood
29: 24 The *p* then slaughtered the goats

2Ch 29: 26 and the *p* with their trumpets.
29: 34 The *p*, however, were too few
29: 34 themselves than the *p* had been.
29: 34 until other *p* had been consecrated,
30: 3 not enough *p* had consecrated
30: 15 *p* and the Levites were ashamed
30: 16 The *p* sprinkled the blood handed
30: 21 and *p* sang to the LORD every day,
30: 24 of *p* consecrated themselves.
30: 25 along with the *p* and Levites
30: 27 The *p* and the Levites stood
31: 2 Hezekiah assigned the *p*
31: 2 according to their duties as *p*
31: 4 to give the portion due the *p*
31: 9 Hezekiah asked the *p* and Levites
31: 15 faithfully in the towns of the *p*,
31: 15 to their fellow *p* according
31: 17 they distributed to the *p* enrolled
31: 19 As for the *p*, the descendants
34: 5 the bones of the *p* on their altars,
34: 30 the people of Jerusalem, the *p*
35: 2 He appointed the *p* to their duties
35: 8 gave the *p* twenty-six hundred
35: 8 voluntarily to the people and the *p*
35: 10 and the *p* stood in their places
35: 11 the *p* sprinkled the blood handed
35: 14 for themselves and for the *p*,
35: 14 the *p*, the descendants of Aaron,
35: 14 themselves and for the Aaronic *p*.
35: 18 with the *p*, the Levites
36: 14 all the leaders of the *p*
Ezr 1: 5 *p* and Levites—everyone whose
2: 36 The *p*:
2: 61 And from among the *p*:
2: 70 The *p*, the Levites, the singers,
3: 2 his fellow *p* and Zerubbabel son
3: 8 and the rest of their brothers (the *p*
3: 10 the *p* in their vestments
3: 12 many of the older *p* and Levites
6: 9 as requested by the *p* in Jerusalem
6: 16 Then the people of Israel—the *p*,
6: 18 And they installed the *p*
6: 20 The *p* and Levites had purified
6: 20 for their brothers the *p*
7: 7 including *p*, Levites, singers,
7: 13 including *p* and Levites, who wish
7: 16 and *p* for the temple of their God
7: 24 tribute or duty on any of the *p*,
8: 15 among the people and the *p*,
8: 24 I set apart twelve of the leading *p*,
8: 29 in Jerusalem before the leading *p*
8: 30 *p* and Levites received the silver
9: 1 including the *p* and the Levites,
9: 7 and our *p* have been subjected
10: 5 and put the leading *p* and Levites
10: 18 Among the descendants of the *p*,
Ne 2: 16 or the *p* or nobles or officials
3: 1 and his fellow *p* went to work
3: 22 by the *p* from the surrounding
3: 28 Horse Gate, the *p* made repairs,
5: 12 Then I summoned the *p*
7: 39 Ono 721 of Senaah 3,930 The *p*:
7: 63 And from among the *p*:
7: 70 bowls and 530 garments for *p*.
7: 72 of silver and 67 garments for *p*.
7: 73 The *p*, the Levites, the gatekeepers,
8: 13 along with the *p* and the Levites,
9: 32 leaders, upon our *p* and prophets,
9: 34 our *p* and our fathers did not follow
9: 38 our *p* are affixing their seals to it."
10: 8 These were the *p*.
10: 28 *p*, Levites, gatekeepers, singers,
10: 34 the *p*, the Levites and the people—
10: 36 to the *p* ministering there.
10: 37 to the *p*, the first of our ground
10: 39 and where the ministering *p*,
11: 3 Jerusalem (now some Israelites, *p*,
11: 10 From the *p*: Jedaiah; the son
11: 20 The rest of the Israelites, with the *p*
12: 1 These were the *p* and Levites who
12: 7 These were the leaders of the *p*
12: 22 Jaddua, as well as those of the *p*,
12: 30 When the *p* and Levites had
12: 35 as well as some *p* with trumpets,
12: 41 as well as the *p*— Eliakim,
12: 42 pleased with the ministering *p*
12: 44 required by the Law for the *p*
13: 5 well as the contributions for the *p*.
Ne 13: 30 So I purified the *p* and the Levites
Job 12: 19 He leads *p* away stripped
Ps 78: 64 their *p* were put to the sword,
99: 6 and Aaron were among his *p*,
132: 9 May your *p* be clothed
132: 16 I will clothe her *p* with salvation,
Isa 28: 7 *P* and prophets stagger from beer
37: 2 the leading *p*, all wearing sackcloth
61: 6 you will be called *p* of the LORD,
66: 21 some of them also to be *p*
Jer 1: 1 one of the *p* at Anathoth
1: 18 its *p* and the people of the land.
2: 8 The *p* did not ask,
2: 26 their *p* and their prophets.
4: 9 the *p* will be horrified,
5: 31 the *p* rule by their own authority,
6: 13 prophets and *p* alike,
8: 1 the bones of the *p* and prophets,
8: 10 prophets and *p* alike,
13: 13 *p*, the prophets and all those living
19: 1 of the *p* and go out to the Valley
26: 7 *p*, the prophets and all the people
26: 8 *p*, the prophets and all the people
26: 11 Then the *p* and the prophets said
26: 16 and all the people said to the *p*
27: 16 I said to the *p* and all these people,
28: 1 the LORD in the presence of the *p*
28: 5 the prophet Hananiah before the *p*
29: 1 among the exiles and to the *p*,
29: 25 the priest, and to all the other *p*.
31: 14 I will satisfy the *p* with abundance,
32: 32 and officials, their *p* and prophets,
33: 18 nor will the *p*, who are Levites,
33: 21 the Levites who are *p* ministering
34: 19 the *p* and all the people
48: 7 together with his *p* and officials.
49: 3 together with his *p* and officials.
La 1: 4 her *p* groan,
1: 19 My *p* and my elders
4: 13 and the iniquities of her *p*,
4: 16 The *p* are shown no honor,
Eze 22: 26 Her *p* do violence to my law
40: 45 is for the *p* who have charge
40: 46 is for the *p* who have charge
42: 13 where the *p* who approach
42: 14 Once the *p* enter the holy precincts
43: 19 young bull as a sin offering to the *p*,
43: 24 the *p* are to sprinkle salt on them
43: 27 the *p* are to present your burnt
44: 13 as *p* or come near any
44: 15 " 'But the *p*, who are Levites
44: 22 of Israelite descent or widows of *p*.
44: 24 the *p* are to serve as judges
44: 28 be the only inheritance the *p* have.
44: 30 special gifts will belong to the *p*.
44: 31 The *p* must not eat anything,
45: 4 portion of the land for the *p*,
46: 2 *p* are to sacrifice his burnt offering
46: 19 which belonged to the *p*,
46: 20 the place where the *p* will cook
48: 10 will be the sacred portion for the *p*.
48: 11 This will be for the consecrated *p*,
48: 13 "Alongside the territory of the *p*,
Hos 4: 6 I also reject you as my *p*;
4: 7 The more the *p* increased,
4: 9 And it will be: Like people, like *p*.
5: 1 "Hear this, you *p*!
6: 9 so do bands of *p*;
10: 5 and so will its idolatrous *p*,
Joel 1: 9 The *p* are in mourning,
1: 13 Put on sackcloth, O *p*, and mourn;
2: 17 Let the *p*, who minister
Mic 3: 11 her *p* teach for a price,
Zep 1: 4 of the pagan and the idolatrous *p*—
3: 4 Her *p* profane the sanctuary
Hag 2: 11 'Ask the *p* what the law says:
2: 12 consecrated?' " The *p* answered,
2: 13 the *p* replied, "it becomes defiled."
Zec 7: 3 LORD by asking the *p* of the house
7: 5 the people of the land and the *p*,
Mal 1: 6 O *p*, who despise my name.
2: 1 now this admonition is for you, O *p*
Mt 2: 4 together all the people's chief *p*
12: 4 for them to do, but only for the *p*.
12: 5 that on the Sabbath the *p*
16: 21 chief *p* and teachers of the law,
20: 18 Man will be betrayed to the chief *p*
21: 15 when the chief *p* and the teachers
Mt 21: 23 the chief *p* and the elders
21: 45 When the chief *p* and the Pharisees
26: 3 Then the chief *p* and the elders
26: 14 went to the chief *p* and asked,
26: 47 sent from the chief *p* and the elders
26: 59 chief *p* and the whole Sanhedrin
27: 1 all the chief *p* and the elders
27: 3 the thirty silver coins to the chief *p*
27: 6 The chief *p* picked up the coins
27: 12 he was accused by the chief *p*
27: 20 chief *p* and the elders persuaded
27: 41 In the same way the chief *p*,
27: 62 the chief *p* and the Pharisees went
28: 11 to the chief *p* everything that had
28: 12 When the chief *p* had met
Mk 2: 26 which is lawful only for *p* to eat.
8: 31 chief *p* and teachers of the law,
10: 33 Man will be betrayed to the chief *p*
11: 18 The chief *p* and the teachers
11: 27 in the temple courts, the chief *p*,
14: 1 and the chief *p* and the teachers
14: 10 went to the chief *p* to betray Jesus
14: 43 sent from the chief *p*, the teachers
14: 53 and all the chief *p*, elders
14: 55 chief *p* and the whole Sanhedrin
15: 1 the chief *p*, with the elders,
15: 3 The chief *p* accused him
15: 10 that the chief *p* had handed Jesus
15: 11 But the chief *p* stirred up the crowd
15: 31 In the same way the chief *p*
Lk 6: 4 he ate what is lawful only for *p*
9: 22 chief *p* and teachers of the law,
17: 14 "Go, show yourselves to the *p*."
19: 47 the chief *p*, the teachers of the law
20: 1 the chief *p* and the teachers
20: 19 and the chief *p* looked for a way
22: 2 and the chief *p* and the teachers
22: 4 And Judas went to the chief *p*
22: 52 Then Jesus said to the chief *p*,
22: 66 both the chief *p* and teachers
23: 4 Pilate announced to the chief *p*
23: 10 The chief *p* and the teachers
23: 13 Pilate called together the chief *p*,
24: 20 chief *p* and our rulers handed him
Jn 1: 19 when the Jews of Jerusalem sent *p*
7: 32 the chief *p* and the Pharisees sent
7: 45 guards went back to the chief *p*
11: 47 the chief *p* and the Pharisees called
11: 57 the chief *p* and Pharisees had given
12: 10 So the chief *p* made plans
18: 3 and some officials from the chief *p*
18: 35 and your chief *p* who handed you
19: 6 chief *p* and their officials saw him,
19: 15 but Caesar," the chief *p* answered.
19: 21 The chief *p* of the Jews protested
Ac 4: 1 The *p* and the captain
4: 23 and reported all that the chief *p*
5: 24 and the chief *p* were puzzled,
6: 7 number of *p* became obedient
9: 14 with authority from the chief *p*
9: 21 as prisoners to the chief *p*?"
22: 30 and ordered the chief *p* and all
23: 14 They went to the chief *p* and elders
25: 2 where the chief *p* and Jewish
25: 15 the chief *p* and elders
26: 10 authority of the chief *p* I put many
26: 12 and commission of the chief *p*.
Heb 7: 5 descendants of Levi who become *p*
7: 14 tribe Moses said nothing about *p*.
7: 20 Others became *p* without any oath,
7: 23 Now there were many of those *p*,
7: 27 the other high *p*, he does not
7: 28 as high *p* men who are weak;
9: 6 the *p* entered regularly
Rev 1: 6 *p* to serve his God and Father—
5: 10 to be a kingdom and *p*
20: 6 but they will be *p* of God

PRIESTS' (PRIEST)

Eze 41: 10 *p'* rooms was twenty cubits wide
42: 13 temple courtyard are the *p'* rooms,

PRIME

1Sa 2: 33 your descendants will die in the *p*
Job 29: 4 for the days when I was in my *p*,
Isa 38: 10 recovery: I said, "In the *p* of my life

PRINCE (PRINCE'S PRINCELY PRINCES PRINCESS)
Ge 23: 6 You are a mighty *p* among us.
49: 26 brow of the *p* among his brothers.
Dt 33: 16 brow of the *p* among his brothers.
Jdg 8: 18 "each one with the bearing of a *p*."
2Sa 3: 38 "Do you not realize that a *p*
2Ch 11: 22 be the chief *p* among his brothers,
Ezr 1: 8 out to Sheshbazzar the *p* of Judah.
Job 31: 37 like a *p* I would approach him.)—
Pr 14: 28 but without subjects a *p* is ruined.
Isa 9: 6 Everlasting Father, *P* of Peace.
Eze 7: 27 the *p* will be clothed with despair,
12: 10 This oracle concerns the *p*
12: 12 *p* among them will put his things
21: 25 O profane and wicked *p* of Israel,
30: 13 No longer will there be a *p* in Egypt
34: 24 and my servant David will be *p*
37: 25 my servant will be their *p* forever.
38: 2 the chief *p* of Meshech and Tubal;
38: 3 chief *p* of Meshech and Tubal.
39: 1 chief *p* of Meshech and Tubal.
44: 3 *p* himself is the only one who may
45: 7 *p* will have the land bordering each
45: 16 gift for the use of the *p* in Israel.
45: 17 duty of the *p* to provide the burnt
45: 22 On that day the *p* is
46: 2 The *p* is to enter from the
46: 4 The burnt offering the *p* brings
46: 8 When the *p* enters, he is to go
46: 10 The *p* is to be among them,
46: 12 When the *p* provides a freewill
46: 16 If the *p* makes a gift
46: 17 then it will revert to the *p*.
46: 18 The *p* must not take any
48: 21 city property will belong to the *p*.
48: 21 tribal portions will belong to the *p*,
48: 22 The area belonging to the *p* will lie
48: 22 of the area that belongs to the *p*.
Da 8: 11 as great as the *P* of the host;
8: 25 stand against the *P* of princes.
10: 13 *p* of the Persian kingdom resisted
10: 20 the *p* of Greece will come;
10: 20 to fight against the *p* of Persia,
10: 21 them except Michael, your *p*.
11: 22 and a *p* of the covenant will be
12: 1 great *p* who protects your people,
Hos 3: 4 live many days without king or *p*,
Mt 9: 34 is by the *p* of demons that he drives
12: 24 by Beelzebub, the *p* of demons,
Mk 3: 22 By the *p* of demons he is driving
Lk 11: 15 "By Beelzebub, the *p* of demons,
Jn 12: 31 now the *p* of this world will be
14: 30 for the *p* of this world is coming.
16: 11 the *p* of this world now stands
Ac 5: 31 as *P* and Savior that he might give

PRINCE'S (PRINCE)
SS 7: 1 O *p* daughter!

PRINCELY (PRINCE)
Ps 49: 14 far from their *p* mansions.

PRINCES (PRINCE)
Nu 21: 18 about the well that the *p* dug,
22: 8 So the Moabite *p* stayed with him.
22: 13 got up and said to Balak's *p*,
22: 14 So the Moabite *p* returned to Balak
22: 15 Balak sent other *p*, more numerous
22: 21 and went with the *p* of Moab.
22: 35 So Balaam went with the *p* of Balak
22: 40 and the *p* who were with him.
23: 6 with all the *p* of Moab.
23: 17 with the *p* of Moab.
Jos 13: 21 and Reba—*p* allied with Sihon—
Jdg 5: 2 "When the *p* in Israel take the lead,
5: 9 My heart is with Israel's *p*,
5: 15 The *p* of Issachar were
1Sa 2: 8 he seats them with *p*
2Sa 13: 32 not think that they killed all the *p*;
2Ki 10: 6 Now the royal *p*, seventy of them,
10: 7 men took the *p* and slaughtered all
10: 8 have brought the heads of the *p*."
11: 2 among the royal *p* who were about
2Ch 21: 4 along with some of the *p* of Israel.
22: 8 he found the *p* of Judah
22: 11 among the royal *p* who were about
2Ch 28: 21 the royal palace and from the *p*
Est 1: 3 leaders of Persia and Media, the *p*,
6: 9 to one of the king's most noble *p*.
Job 34: 19 who shows no partiality to *p*
Ps 45: 16 you will make them *p*
68: 27 and there the *p* of Zebulun
68: 27 there the great throng of Judah's *p*,
83: 11 all their *p* like Zebah
105: 22 to discipline his *p* as he pleased
113: 8 he seats them with *p*,
113: 8 with the *p* of their people.
118: 9 than to trust in *p*.
119: 23 Though *p* sit together and slander
146: 3 Do not put your trust in *p*,
148: 11 you *p* and all rulers on earth,
Pr 8: 16 by me *p* govern,
19: 10 worse for a slave to rule over *p*!
Ecc 10: 7 while *p* go on foot like slaves.
10: 16 and whose *p* feast in the morning.
10: 17 and whose *p* eat at a proper time—
Isa 23: 8 whose merchants are *p*,
34: 12 all her *p* will vanish away.
40: 23 He brings *p* to naught
49: 7 *p* will see and bow down,
La 1: 6 Her *p* are like deer
2: 2 has brought her kingdom and its *p*
2: 9 her *p* are exiled among the nations,
4: 7 Their *p* were brighter than snow
5: 12 *P* have been hung up by their hands
Eze 19: 1 Take up a lament concerning the *p*
21: 12 it is against all the *p* of Israel.
22: 6 each of the *p* of Israel who are
22: 25 There is a conspiracy of her *p*
26: 16 all the *p* of the seacoast will step
27: 21 and all the *p* of Kedar were your
32: 29 and all her *p*; despite their power,
32: 30 "All the *p* of the north
39: 18 drink the blood of the *p* of the earth
45: 8 my *p* will no longer oppress my
45: 9 You have gone far enough, O *p*
Da 8: 25 stand against the Prince of *p*.
9: 6 in your name to our kings, our *p*
9: 8 our *p* and our fathers are covered
10: 13 one of the chief *p*, came to help me,
Hos 7: 3 the *p* with their lies.
7: 5 the *p* become inflamed with wine,
8: 4 they choose *p* without my approval
13: 10 'Give me a king and *p*'?
Zep 1: 8 I will punish the *p*
Rev 6: 15 the *p*, the generals, the rich,

PRINCESS (PRINCE)
Ps 45: 13 All glorious is the *p*

PRINCIPAL
1Ch 9: 26 But the four *p* gatekeepers,

PRINCIPLE (PRINCIPLES)
Ro 3: 27 On what *p*? On that

PRINCIPLES (PRINCIPLE)
Gal 4: 3 under the basic *p* of the world.
4: 9 to those weak and miserable *p*?
Col 2: 8 and the basic *p* of this world rather
2: 20 Christ to the basic *p* of this world,

PRISCILLA
Ac 18: 2 come from Italy with his wife *P*,
18: 18 accompanied by *P* and Aquila.
18: 19 where Paul left *P* and Aquila.
18: 26 When *P* and Aquila heard him,
Ro 16: 3 Greet *P* and Aquila, my fellow
1Co 16: 19 *P* greet you warmly in the Lord,
2Ti 4: 19 Greet *P* and Aquila

PRISON (IMPRISON IMPRISONED IMPRISONMENT IMPRISONMENTS IMPRISONS PRISONER PRISONERS PRISONS)
Ge 39: 20 But while Joseph was there in the *p*
39: 20 master took him and put him in *p*,
39: 21 favor in the eyes of the *p* warden.
39: 22 in charge of all those held in the *p*,
40: 3 in the same *p* where Joseph was
40: 5 who were being held in *p*—
40: 14 to Pharaoh and get me out of this *p*.
42: 16 the rest of you will be kept in *p*,
42: 19 one of your brothers stay here in *p*,
Jdg 16: 21 they set him to grinding in the *p*.
16: 25 So they called Samson out of the *p*,
1Ki 22: 27 fellow in *p* and give him nothing
2Ki 17: 4 seized him and put him in *p*.
25: 27 he released Jehoiachin from *p*
25: 29 Jehoiachin put aside his *p* clothes
2Ch 16: 10 so enraged that he put him in *p*.
18: 26 fellow in *p* and give him nothing
Job 11: 10 comes along and confines you in *p*
Ps 66: 11 You brought us into *p*
142: 7 Set me free from my *p*,
Ecc 4: 14 come from *p* to the kingship,
Isa 24: 22 they will be shut up in *p*
42: 7 to free captives from *p*
Jer 37: 4 for he had not yet been put in *p*.
37: 15 which they had made into a *p*.
37: 18 that you have put me in *p*?
52: 11 where he put him in *p* till the day
52: 31 him from *p* on the twenty-fifth day
52: 33 Jehoiachin put aside his *p* clothes
Eze 19: 9 They put him in *p*,
Mt 4: 12 heard that John had been put in *p*,
5: 25 and you may be thrown into *p*.
11: 2 heard in *p* what Christ was doing,
14: 3 put him in *p* because of Herodias,
14: 10 and had John beheaded in the *p*.
18: 30 and had the man thrown into *p*
25: 36 I was in *p* and you came to visit me
25: 39 or in *p* and go to visit you?'
25: 43 in *p* and you did not look after me.'
25: 44 or needing clothes or sick or in *p*,
Mk 1: 14 put in *p*, Jesus went into Galilee,
6: 17 and he had him bound and put in *p*.
6: 27 man went, beheaded John in the *p*,
15: 7 A man called Barabbas was in *p*
Lk 3: 20 to them all: He locked John up in *p*.
12: 58 and the officer throw you into *p*.
22: 33 I am ready to go with you to *p*
23: 19 thrown into *p* for an insurrection
23: 25 thrown into *p* for insurrection
Jn 3: 24 This was before John was put in *p*.)
Ac 8: 3 and women and put them in *p*.
12: 4 After arresting him, he put him in *p*
12: 5 So Peter was kept in *p*,
12: 9 Peter followed him out of the *p*,
12: 17 the Lord had brought him out of *p*.
16: 23 they were thrown into *p*,
16: 26 At once all the *p* doors flew open,
16: 26 foundations of the *p* were shaken.
16: 27 and when he saw the *p* doors open,
16: 37 citizens, and threw us into *p*.
16: 39 and escorted them from the *p*,
16: 40 and Silas came out of the *p*,
20: 23 the Holy Spirit warns me that *p*
22: 4 women and throwing them into *p*,
24: 27 to the Jews, he left Paul in *p*.
26: 10 priests I put many of the saints in *p*,
Ro 16: 7 my relatives who have been in *p*
2Co 11: 23 been in *p* more frequently,
Heb 10: 34 You sympathized with those in *p*
11: 36 others were chained and put in *p*.
13: 3 Remember those in *p*
1Pe 3: 19 spirits in *p* who disobeyed long ago
Rev 2: 10 some of you in *p* to test you,
20: 7 Satan will be released from his *p*

PRISONER (PRISON)
Ex 12: 29 to the firstborn of the *p*, who was
Jdg 15: 10 "We have come to take Samson *p*,"
2Ki 24: 12 of Babylon, he took Jehoiachin *p*.
2Ch 33: 11 who took Manasseh *p*, put a hook
Isa 22: 3 were caught were taken *p* together,
Mt 27: 15 to release a *p* chosen by the crowd.
27: 16 At that time they had a notorious *p*
Mk 15: 6 to release a *p* whom the people
Jn 18: 39 to release to you one *p* at the time
Ac 23: 18 The centurion said, "Paul, the *p*,
25: 14 a man here whom Felix left as a *p*.
25: 27 send on a *p* without specifying
Ro 7: 23 and making me a *p* of the law of sin
Gal 3: 22 declares that the whole world is a *p*
Eph 3: 1 the *p* of Christ Jesus for the sake
4: 1 As a *p* for the Lord, then, I urge
Col 4: 10 My fellow *p* Aristarchus sends you
2Ti 1: 8 our Lord, or ashamed of me his *p*.
Phm : 1 *p* of Christ Jesus, and Timothy our
: 9 and now also a *p* of Christ Jesus—
: 23 my fellow *p* for Christ Jesus,

PRISONERS (PRISON)

Ge 39: 20 where the king's *p* were confined.
2Ki 25: 18 as *p* Seraiah the chief priest,
2Ch 28: 5 *p* and brought them to Damascus.
28: 11 countrymen you have taken as *p*,
28: 13 "You must not bring those *p* here,"
28: 14 So the soldiers gave up the *p*
28: 15 designated by name took the *p*,
28: 17 attacked Judah and carried away *p*,
Ps 68: 6 he leads forth the *p* with singing;
79: 11 groans of the *p* come before you;
102: 20 to hear the groans of the *p*
107: 10 *p* suffering in iron chains,
146: 7 The LORD sets *p* free,
Isa 24: 22 like *p* bound in a dungeon;
51: 14 cowering *p* will soon be set free;
61: 1 and release for the *p*,
Jer 52: 24 as *p* Seraiah the chief priest,
La 3: 34 all *p* in the land,
Hab 1: 9 and gather *p* like sand.
Zec 9: 11 I will free your *p* from the waterless
9: 12 to your fortress, O *p* of hope;
Lk 4: 18 me to proclaim freedom for the *p*
21: 24 will be taken as *p* to all the nations.
Ac 9: 2 he might take them as *p*
9: 21 as *p* to the chief priests?"
16: 25 the other *p* were listening to them.
16: 27 he thought the *p* had escaped.
22: 5 as *p* to Jerusalem to be punished.
27: 1 and some other *p* were handed
27: 42 to kill the *p* to prevent any of them
Gal 3: 23 we were held *p* by the law,
Heb 13: 3 as if you were their fellow *p*,

PRISONS (PRISON)

Isa 42: 22 or hidden away in *p*.
Lk 21: 12 you to synagogues and *p*,

PRIVATE

Ge 43: 30 He went into his *p* room
Dt 25: 11 and seizes him by his *p* parts,
Mt 17: 19 the disciples came to Jesus in *p*
Lk 9: 18 Once when Jesus was praying in *p*

PRIVILEGE

2Co 8: 4 pleaded with us for the *p* of sharing

PRIZE (PRIZES)

1Co 9: 24 Run in such a way as to get the *p*.
9: 24 but only one gets the *p*? Run
9: 27 will not be disqualified for the *p*.
Php 3: 14 on toward the goal to win the *p*
Col 2: 18 of angels disqualify you for the *p*.

PRIZES (PRIZE)

Pr 12: 27 the diligent man *p* his possessions.

PROBE

Dt 13: 14 *p* and investigate it thoroughly.
Job 10: 6 and *p* after my sin—
11: 7 Can you *p* the limits
Ps 17: 3 Though you *p* my heart
Jer 20: 12 and *p* the heart and mind,

PROBLEMS

Dt 1: 12 can I bear your *p* and your burdens
Da 5: 12 explain riddles and solve difficult *p*
5: 16 and to solve difficult *p*.

PROCEDURE (PROCEED)

Ecc 8: 5 will know the proper time and *p*.
8: 6 For there is a proper time and *p*

PROCEED (PROCEDURE PROCEEDED PROCEEDINGS PROCESSION)

Ne 12: 31 One was to *p* on top of the wall

PROCEEDED (PROCEED)

Ge 9: 20 of the soil, *p* to plant a vineyard.
42: 20 This they *p* to do.
44: 12 Then the steward *p* to search,
2Ki 8: 2 The woman *p* to do as the man
11: 1 she *p* to destroy the whole royal
2Ch 22: 10 she *p* to destroy the whole royal
Ne 12: 38 The second choir *p* in
Ac 12: 3 saw that this pleased the Jews, he *p*

PROCEEDINGS (PROCEED)

Ac 24: 22 with the Way, adjourned the *p*.

PROCESSION (PROCEED)

1Sa 10: 5 will meet a *p* of prophets coming
10: 10 at Gibeah, a *p* of prophets met him;
Ne 12: 36 Ezra the scribe led the *p*.
Ps 42: 4 leading the *p* to the house of God,
68: 24 Your *p* has come into view, O God,
68: 24 the *p* of my God and King
118: 27 boughs in hand, join in the festal *p*
SS 6: 10 majestic as the stars in *p*?
Isa 60: 11 their kings led in triumphal *p*.
1Co 4: 9 on display at the end of the *p*,
2Co 2: 14 us in triumphal *p* in Christ

PROCLAIM (PROCLAIMED PROCLAIMING PROCLAIMS PROCLAMATION)

Ex 33: 19 and I will *p* my name, the LORD,
Lev 23: 2 are to *p* as sacred assemblies.
23: 4 are to *p* at their appointed times:
23: 21 are to *p* a sacred assembly
23: 37 are to *p* as sacred assemblies
25: 10 and *p* liberty throughout the land
Dt 11: 29 are to *p* on Mount Gerizim
30: 12 and *p* it to us so we may obey it?"
30: 13 and *p* it to us so we may obey it?"
32: 3 I will *p* the name of the LORD.
1Sa 31: 9 land of the Philistines to *p* the news
2Sa 1: 20 *p* it not in the streets of Ashkelon,
1Ki 21: 9 "*P* a day of fasting and seat Naboth
1Ch 10: 9 land of the Philistines to *p* the news
16: 23 *p* his salvation day after day.
Ne 8: 15 and that they should *p* this word
Ps 2: 7 I will *p* the decree of the LORD:
9: 11 *p* among the nations what he has
19: 1 the skies *p* the work of his hands.
22: 31 They will *p* his righteousness
30: 9 Will it *p* your faithfulness?
40: 9 I *p* righteousness in the great
50: 6 the heavens *p* his righteousness,
64: 9 they will *p* the works of God
68: 34 *P* the power of God,
71: 16 I will come and *p* your mighty acts,
71: 16 I will *p* your righteousness,
92: 2 to *p* your love in the morning
96: 2 *p* his salvation day after day.
97: 6 The heavens *p* his righteousness,
106: 2 Who can *p* the mighty acts
118: 17 will *p* what the LORD has done.
145: 6 and I will *p* your great deeds.
Isa 12: 4 and *p* that his name is exalted.
40: 2 and *p* to her
42: 12 and *p* his praise in the islands.
43: 21 that they may *p* my praise.
44: 7 Who then is like me? Let him *p* it.
44: 8 Did I not *p* this and foretell it long
48: 20 and *p* it.
52: 7 who *p* peace,
52: 7 who *p* salvation,
61: 1 to *p* freedom for the captives
61: 2 to *p* the year of the LORD's favor
66: 19 They will *p* my glory
Jer 2: 2 and *p* in the hearing of Jerusalem:
3: 12 *p* this message toward the north:
4: 5 in Judah and *p* in Jerusalem
4: 16 *p* it to Jerusalem:
5: 20 and *p* it in Judah:
7: 2 house and there *p* this message:
11: 6 "*P* all these words in the towns
19: 2 There *p* the words I tell you,
22: 1 of Judah and *p* this message there:
31: 10 *p* it in distant coastlands:
34: 8 people in Jerusalem to *p* freedom
34: 17 So I now *p* 'freedom' for you,
46: 14 this in Egypt, and *p* it in Migdol;
46: 14 *p* it also in Memphis
50: 2 lift up a banner and *p* it;
50: 2 "Announce and *p*
Hos 5: 9 I *p* what is certain.
Joel 3: 9 *P* this among the nations:
Am 3: 9 *P* to the fortresses of Ashdod
Jnh 3: 2 and *p* to it the message I give you."
Mic 3: 5 they *p* 'peace';
Zec 1: 14 speaking to me said, "*P* this word:
1: 17 "*P* further: This is what the LORD
Zec 9: 10 He will *p* peace to the nations.
Mt 10: 27 in your ear, *p* from the housetops.
12: 18 and he will *p* justice to the nations.
Lk 4: 18 me to *p* freedom for the prisoners
4: 19 to *p* the year of the Lord's favor."
9: 60 you go and *p* the kingdom of God."
Ac 17: 23 unknown I am going to *p*
20: 27 hesitated to *p* to you the whole will
26: 23 would *p* light to his own people
1Co 11: 26 you *p* the Lord's death
Col 1: 28 We *p* him, admonishing
4: 3 so that we may *p* the mystery
4: 4 Pray that I may *p* it clearly,
1Jn 1: 1 this we *p* concerning the Word
1: 2 and we *p* to you the eternal life,
1: 3 We *p* to you what we have seen
Rev 14: 6 gospel to *p* to those who live

PROCLAIMED (PROCLAIM)

Ex 9: 16 and that my name might be *p*
34: 5 there with him and *p* his name,
Dt 1: 3 Moses *p* to the Israelites all that
5: 22 the commandments the LORD *p*
9: 10 the commandments the LORD *p*
10: 4 The Ten Commandments he had *p*
15: 2 for canceling debts has been *p*.
1Ki 16: 16 they *p* Omri, the commander
21: 12 They *p* a fast and seated Naboth
2Ki 10: 20 So they *p* it.
11: 12 of the covenant and *p* him king.
23: 16 word of the LORD *p* by the man
24: 2 of the LORD *p* by his servants
2Ch 20: 3 and he *p* a fast for all Judah.
23: 11 of the covenant and *p* him king.
Ezr 8: 21 by the Ahava Canal, I *p* a fast,
Est 1: 20 Then when the king's edict is *p*
2: 8 king's order and edict had been *p*,
2: 18 *p* a holiday
Ps 68: 11 was the company of those who *p* it:
Isa 43: 9 and *p* to us the former things?
43: 12 I have revealed and saved and *p*—
Jer 23: 22 they would have *p* my words
34: 15 Each of you *p* freedom
34: 17 you have not *p* freedom
36: 9 fasting before the LORD was *p*
Da 3: 4 herald loudly *p*, "This is what you
5: 29 and he was *p* the third highest ruler
Jnh 3: 4 going a day's journey, and he *p*:
Zec 1: 4 to whom the earlier prophets *p*:
7: 7 these not the words the LORD *p*
Lk 12: 3 the ear in the inner rooms will be *p*
16: 16 and the Prophets were *p* until John.
Ac 8: 5 in Samaria and *p* the Christ there.
8: 25 and *p* the word of the Lord,
13: 5 they *p* the word of God
13: 38 Jesus the forgiveness of sins is *p*
Ro 9: 17 and that my name might be *p*
15: 19 I have fully *p* the gospel of Christ.
1Co 2: 1 I *p* to you the testimony about God
Col 1: 23 that has been *p* to every creature
2Ti 4: 17 me the message might be fully *p*
Heb 9: 19 Moses had *p* every commandment

PROCLAIMING (PROCLAIM)

Ex 34: 6 *p*, "The LORD, the LORD,
1Sa 11: 7 by messengers throughout Israel, *p*
Est 1: 22 *p* in each people's tongue that
6: 9 the horse through the city streets, *p*
6: 11 through the city streets, *p*
Ps 26: 7 *p* aloud your praise
92: 15 *p*, "The LORD is upright;
Isa 60: 6 and *p* the praise of the LORD.
Jer 4: 15 *p* disaster from the hills of Ephraim
20: 8 *p* violence and destruction.
Mk 1: 14 went into Galilee, *p* the good news
Lk 8: 1 *p* the good news of the kingdom
Ac 4: 2 and *p* in Jesus the resurrection
5: 42 and *p* the good news that Jesus is
17: 3 "This Jesus I am *p*
Ro 10: 8 the word of faith we are *p*:
15: 16 duty of *p* the gospel of God,
2Th 2: 4 up in God's temple, *p* himself
Rev 5: 2 And I saw a mighty angel *p*

PROCLAIMS (PROCLAIM)

Dt 18: 22 If what a prophet *p* in the name
Na 1: 15 who *p* peace!

PROCLAMATION (PROCLAIM)

2Ch 24: 9 A *p* was then issued in Judah
30: 5 to send a *p* throughout Israel,
36: 22 to make a *p* throughout his realm
Ezr 1: 1 to make a *p* throughout his realm
10: 7 A *p* was then issued
Ne 6: 7 prophets to make this *p* about you
Isa 62: 11 The LORD has made *p*
Jnh 3: 7 Then he issued a *p* in Nineveh:
Ro 16: 25 you by my gospel and the *p*

PROCONSUL (PROCONSULS)

Ac 13: 7 The *p*, an intelligent man, sent
13: 7 who was an attendant of the *p*,
13: 8 tried to turn the *p* from the faith.
13: 12 When the *p* saw what had
18: 12 While Gallio was *p* of Achaia,

PROCONSULS (PROCONSUL)

Ac 19: 38 the courts are open and there are *p*.

PROCORUS

Ac 6: 5 also Philip, *P*, Nicanor, Timon,

PRODDED

Jdg 16: 16 With such nagging she *p* him day

PRODUCE (PRODUCED PRODUCES PRODUCING PRODUCT PRODUCTS)

Ge 1: 11 "Let the land *p* vegetation:
1: 24 "Let the land *p* living creatures
3: 18 It will *p* thorns and thistles for you,
38: 8 as a brother-in-law to *p* offspring
47: 26 a fifth of the *p* belongs to Pharaoh.
Ex 5: 18 yet you must *p* your full quota
8: 18 when the magicians tried to *p* gnats
Dt 8: 18 gives you the ability to *p* wealth,
11: 17 and the ground will yield no *p*,
14: 22 of all that your fields *p* each year.
14: 28 bring all the tithes of that year's *p*
16: 13 days after you have gathered the *p*
26: 2 of all that you *p* from the soil
26: 12 tenth of all your *p* in the third year,
28: 33 will eat what your land and labor *p*,
Jos 5: 11 they ate some of the *p* of the land:
5: 12 ate of the *p* of Canaan.
1Ch 27: 27 in charge of the *p* of the vineyards
Job 40: 20 The hills bring him their *p*,
Ps 78: 46 their *p* to the locust.
105: 35 ate up the *p* of their soil.
Pr 13: 23 man's field may *p* abundant food,
Isa 5: 10 ten-acre vineyard will *p* only a bath
Jer 2: 7 land to eat its fruit and rich *p*.
29: 5 plant gardens and eat what they *p*.
29: 28 plant gardens and eat what they *p*
Eze 17: 8 water so that it would *p* branches,
17: 23 it will *p* branches and bear fruit
36: 8 will *p* branches and fruit
48: 18 Its *p* will supply food
Hos 8: 7 it will *p* no flour.
Hab 3: 17 and the fields *p* no food,
Zec 8: 12 the ground will *p* its crops,
Mt 3: 8 *P* fruit in keeping with repentance.
3: 10 tree that does not *p* good fruit will
21: 43 given to a people who will *p* its fruit
Mk 4: 20 accept it, and *p* a crop—thirty,
Lk 3: 8 *P* fruit in keeping with repentance.
3: 9 tree that does not *p* good fruit will
8: 15 and by persevering *p* a crop.
2Ti 2: 23 because you know they *p* quarrels.
Jas 3: 12 can a salt spring *p* fresh water.

PRODUCED (PRODUCE)

Ge 1: 12 land *p* vegetation: plants bearing
41: 47 of abundance the land *p* plentifully.
41: 48 Joseph collected all the food *p*
Nu 17: 8 blossomed and *p* almonds.
Dt 8: 17 of my hands have *p* this wealth
2Ch 31: 5 and honey and all that the fields *p*.
Eze 17: 6 So it became a vine and *p* branches
Mt 13: 8 where it *p* a crop—a hundred,
Mk 4: 8 and *p* a crop, multiplying thirty,
Lk 12: 16 of a certain rich man *p* a good crop.
Ac 6: 13 They *p* false witnesses, who
Ro 7: 8 *p* in me every kind
7: 13 it *p* death in me through what was
2Co 7: 11 See what this godly sorrow has *p*
1Th 1: 3 and Father your work *p* by faith,
Jas 5: 18 gave rain, and the earth *p* its crops.

PRODUCES (PRODUCE)

Lev 25: 7 Whatever the land *p* may be eaten.
Dt 29: 18 root among you that *p* such bitter
Ne 9: 36 and the other good things it *p*.
Job 37: 10 The breath of God *p* ice,
Pr 30: 33 For as churning the milk *p* butter,
30: 33 and as twisting the nose *p* blood,
30: 33 so stirring up anger *p* strife."
Hag 1: 11 the oil and whatever the ground *p*,
Mt 13: 23 He *p* a crop, yielding a hundred,
Mk 4: 28 All by itself the soil *p* grain—
Jn 12: 24 But if it dies, it *p* many seeds.
Ro 5: 3 that suffering *p* perseverance;
2Co 1: 6 which *p* in you patient endurance
Heb 6: 7 and that *p* a crop useful to those
6: 8 But land that *p* thorns
12: 11 it *p* a harvest of righteousness

PRODUCING (PRODUCE)

Ge 38: 9 the ground to keep from *p* offspring
Col 1: 6 over the world this gospel is *p* fruit

PRODUCT (PRODUCE)

Nu 18: 30 as the *p* of the threshing floor

PRODUCTS (PRODUCE)

Ge 43: 11 Put some of the best *p* of the land
Isa 45: 14 *p* of Egypt and the merchandise
Jer 20: 5 all its *p*, all its valuables
Eze 27: 16 with you because of your many *p*;
27: 18 because of your many *p*

PROFANE (PROFANED)

Lev 10: 10 between the holy and the *p*,
18: 21 for you must not *p* the name
19: 12 and so *p* the name of your God.
21: 6 must not *p* the name of their God.
22: 2 so they will not *p* my holy name.
22: 32 Do not *p* my holy name.
Eze 20: 39 and no longer *p* my holy name
21: 25 " 'O *p* and wicked prince of Israel,
22: 26 to my law and *p* my holy things;
Am 2: 7 and so *p* my holy name.
Zep 3: 4 Her priests *p* the sanctuary
Mal 1: 12 you *p* it by saying of the Lord's
2: 10 Why do we *p* the covenant

PROFANED (PROFANE)

Lev 20: 3 my sanctuary and *p* my holy name.
Jer 34: 16 turned around and *p* my name;
Eze 13: 19 You have *p* me among my people
20: 9 it from being *p* in the eyes
20: 14 it from being *p* in the eyes
20: 22 it from being *p* in the eyes
22: 26 so that I am *p* among them.
36: 20 the nations they *p* my holy name,
36: 21 which the house of Israel *p*
36: 22 you have *p* among the nations
36: 23 has been *p* among the nations,
36: 23 the name you have *p* among them.
39: 7 no longer let my holy name be *p*,

PROFESS (PROFESSED)

1Ti 2: 10 for women who *p* to worship God.
Heb 4: 14 let us hold firmly to the faith we *p*.
10: 23 unswervingly to the hope we *p*,

PROFESSED (PROFESS)

1Ti 6: 21 which some have *p* and

PROFIT (PROFITABLE PROFITS)

Lev 25: 37 at interest or sell him food at a *p*.
Job 20: 18 he will not enjoy the *p*
35: 3 Yet you ask him, 'What *p* is it to me
Pr 14: 23 All hard work brings a *p*,
21: 5 The plans of the diligent lead to *p*
Ecc 6: 11 and how does that *p* anyone?
10: 11 there is no *p* for the charmer.
Isa 23: 18 Yet her *p* and her earnings will be
44: 10 which can *p* him nothing?
2Co 2: 17 not peddle the word of God for *p*.
Php 3: 7 was to my *p* I now consider loss
Jude : 11 rushed for *p* into Balaam's error;

PROFITABLE (PROFIT)

Pr 3: 14 for she is more *p* than silver
31: 18 She sees that her trading is *p*,
Tit 3: 8 These things are excellent and *p*

PROFITS (PROFIT)

Job 34: 9 For he says, 'It *p* a man nothing
Ecc 5: 9 the king himself *p* from the fields.
Isa 23: 18 Her *p* will go to those who live

PROFLIGATE

Dt 21: 20 He is a *p* and a drunkard."

PROFOUND

Job 9: 4 His wisdom is *p*, his power is vast.
Ps 92: 5 how *p* your thoughts!
Ecc 7: 24 it is far off and most *p*—
Ac 24: 3 acknowledge this with *p* gratitude.
Eph 5: 32 This is a *p* mystery—but I am

PROFUSE

Pr 27: 6 The kisses of an enemy may be *p*.

PROGRESS (PROGRESSED)

Ezr 5: 8 rapid *p* under their direction.
Php 1: 25 continue with all of you for your *p*
1Ti 4: 15 so that everyone may see your *p*.

PROGRESSED (PROGRESS)

2Ch 24: 13 and the repairs *p* under them.

PROJECT (PROJECTED PROJECTING PROJECTION PROJECTIONS PROJECTS)

1Ki 5: 16 foremen who supervised the *p*
Ne 6: 3 "I am carrying on a great *p*
Eze 43: 15 and four horns *p* upward

PROJECTED (PROJECT)

1Ki 6: 3 and *p* ten cubits from the front

PROJECTING (PROJECT)

1Ki 7: 34 on each corner, *p* from the stand.
Ne 3: 25 the tower *p* from the upper palace
3: 26 toward the east and the *p* tower.
3: 27 from the great *p* tower to the wall
Eze 40: 7 *p* walls between the alcoves were
40: 10 and the faces of the *p* walls
40: 14 faces of the *p* walls all around the
40: 16 faces of the *p* walls were decorated
40: 16 the *p* walls inside the gateway were
40: 21 its *p* walls and its portico had
40: 26 faces of the *p* walls on each side.
40: 29 its *p* walls and its portico had
40: 33 its *p* walls and its portico had
40: 36 as did its alcoves, its *p* walls
40: 48 its *p* walls were three cubits wide

PROJECTION (PROJECT)

Ex 26: 19 for each frame, one under each *p*.
36: 24 for each frame, one under each *p*.

PROJECTIONS (PROJECT)

Ex 26: 17 with two *p* set parallel
36: 22 with two *p* set parallel

PROJECTS (PROJECT)

1Ki 9: 23 officials in charge of Solomon's *p*—
Ecc 2: 4 I undertook great *p*: I built houses

PROLONG (PROLONGED)

Dt 5: 33 *p* your days in the land that you
Ps 85: 5 Will you *p* your anger
Pr 3: 2 for they will *p* your life many years
Isa 53: 10 will see his offspring and *p* his days,
La 4: 22 he will not *p* your exile.

PROLONGED (PROLONG)

Dt 28: 59 harsh and *p* disasters, and severe
Isa 13: 22 and her days will not be *p*.

PROMINENT

1Ki 21: 9 and seat Naboth in a *p* place
21: 12 and seated Naboth in a *p* place
Est 9: 4 Mordecai was *p* in the palace;
Isa 9: 15 the elders and *p* men are the head,
Da 8: 5 suddenly a goat with a *p* horn
8: 8 in its place four *p* horns grew up
Mk 15: 43 a *p* member of the Council,
Lk 14: 1 to eat in the house of a *p* Pharisee,
Ac 17: 4 Greeks and not a few *p* women.
17: 12 also a number of *p* Greek women

PROMISCUITY (PROMISCUOUS)

Eze 16: 25 with increasing *p* to anyone who
16: 26 me to anger with your increasing *p*.
16: 29 Then you increased your *p*
16: 36 In your *p* with your lovers,
23: 29 and *p* have brought this upon you,

PROMISCUOUS (PROMISCUITY)

Dt 22: 21 thing in Israel by being *p* while still
Eze 23: 19 Yet she became more and more *p*

PROMISE (PROMISED PROMISES)

Ge 47: 29 *p* that you will show me kindness
Nu 23: 19 Does he *p* and not fulfill?
30: 6 or after her lips utter a rash *p*
30: 8 or the rash *p* by which she obligates
Jos 9: 21 So the leaders' *p* to them was kept.
23: 14 Every *p* has been fulfilled;
23: 15 as every good *p* of the LORD your
2Sa 7: 25 keep forever the *p* you have made
7: 28 and you have given this good *p*
1Ki 2: 4 and that the LORD may keep his *p*
6: 12 fulfill through you the *p* I gave
8: 20 The LORD has kept the *p* he made
8: 24 You have kept your *p*
1Ch 17: 23 let the *p* you have made
17: 26 You have given this good *p*
2Ch 1: 9 let your *p* to my father David be
6: 10 The LORD has kept the *p* he made
6: 15 You have kept your *p*
Ne 5: 13 man who does not keep this *p*.
9: 8 have kept your *p* because you are
10: 30 "We *p* not to give our daughters
Ps 77: 8 Has his *p* failed for all time?
105: 42 For he remembered his holy *p*
106: 24 they did not believe his *p*.
119: 38 Fulfill your *p* to your servant,
119: 41 your salvation according to your *p*;
119: 50 Your *p* renews my life.
119: 58 to me according to your *p*.
119: 76 according to your *p* to your servant
119: 82 My eyes fail, looking for your *p*;
119:116 Sustain me according to your *p*,
119:123 looking for your righteous *p*.
119:154 renew my life according to your *p*.
119:162 I rejoice in your *p*
119:170 deliver me according to your *p*.
Jer 29: 10 and fulfill my gracious *p*
33: 14 I will fulfill the gracious *p* I made
34: 4 " 'Yet hear the *p* of the LORD,
34: 5 myself make this *p*, declares
Ac 2: 39 The *p* is for you and your children
7: 17 for God to fulfill his *p* to Abraham,
26: 7 This is the *p* our twelve tribes are
Ro 4: 13 offspring received the *p* that he
4: 14 has no value and the *p* is worthless,
4: 16 Therefore, the *p* comes by faith,
4: 20 unbelief regarding the *p* of God,
9: 8 children of the *p* who are regarded
9: 9 For this was how the *p* was stated:
Gal 3: 14 that by faith we might receive the *p*
3: 17 and thus do away with the *p*.
3: 18 it to Abraham through a *p*.
3: 18 then it no longer depends on a *p*;
3: 19 to whom the *p* referred had come
3: 29 and heirs according to the *p*.
4: 23 was born as the result of a *p*.
4: 28 like Isaac, are children of *p*.
Eph 2: 12 foreigners to the covenants of the *p*
3: 6 together in the *p* in Christ Jesus.
6: 2 the first commandment with a *p*—
1Ti 4: 8 holding *p* for both the present life
2Ti 1: 1 according to the *p* of life that is
Heb 4: 1 since the *p* of entering his rest still
6: 13 When God made his *p* to Abraham
11: 9 heirs with him of the same *p*.
11: 11 him faithful who had made the *p*.
2Pe 2: 19 They *p* them freedom,
3: 9 Lord is not slow in keeping his *p*,
3: 13 with his *p* we are looking forward

PROMISED (PROMISE)

Ge 18: 19 for Abraham what he has *p* him."
21: 1 did for Sarah what he had *p*.
21: 2 at the very time God had *p* him.
24: 7 who spoke to me and *p* me on oath,
28: 15 until I have done what I have *p* you
50: 24 land to the land he *p* on oath
Ex 3: 17 And I have *p* to bring you up out
12: 25 the LORD will give you as he *p*,
13: 11 as he *p* on oath to you and your
32: 13 descendants all this land I *p* them,
33: 1 to the land I *p* on oath to Abraham,
Lev 19: 20 with a woman who is a slave girl *p*
Nu 10: 29 for the LORD has *p* good things
11: 12 to the land you *p* on oath
14: 16 into the land he *p* them on oath;
14: 23 of them will ever see the land I *p*
14: 40 up to the place the LORD *p*."
32: 11 out of Egypt will see the land I *p*
32: 24 flocks, but do what you have *p*."
Dt 1: 11 times and bless you as he has *p*!
6: 3 the God of your fathers, *p* you.
6: 18 the good land that the LORD *p*
6: 23 give us the land that he *p* on oath
8: 1 possess the land that the LORD *p*
9: 3 quickly, as the LORD has *p* you.
9: 28 them into the land he had *p* them,
11: 25 The LORD your God, as he *p* you,
12: 20 enlarged your territory as he *p* you,
13: 17 as he *p* on oath to your forefathers,
15: 6 your God will bless you as he has *p*,
18: 2 is their inheritance, as he *p* them.
19: 8 as he *p* on oath to your forefathers,
19: 8 gives you the whole land he *p* them
26: 15 as you *p* on oath to our forefathers,
26: 18 his treasured possession as he *p*.
26: 19 to the LORD your God, as he *p*.
27: 3 the God of your fathers, *p* you.
28: 9 his holy people, as he *p* you on oath
29: 13 he may be your God as he *p* you
31: 20 the land I *p* on oath
31: 21 into the land I *p* them on oath."
31: 23 into the land I *p* them on oath,
34: 4 "This is the land I *p* on oath
Jos 1: 3 you set your foot, as I *p* Moses.
5: 6 that he had solemnly *p* their fathers
13: 14 are their inheritance, as he *p* them.
13: 33 is their inheritance, as he *p* them.
14: 10 "Now then, just as the LORD *p*,
14: 12 that the LORD *p* me that day.
22: 4 given your brothers rest as he *p*,
23: 5 as the LORD your God *p* you.
23: 10 fights for you, just as he *p*.
Jdg 1: 20 As Moses had *p*, Hebron was given
6: 36 Israel by my hand as you have *p*—
11: 36 as you *p*, now that the LORD has
1Sa 2: 30 'I *p* that your house and your
25: 30 good thing he *p* concerning him
2Sa 3: 9 for David what the LORD *p* him
3: 18 Now do it! For the LORD *p* David
7: 25 as you *p*, so that your name will be
19: 23 And the king *p* him on oath.
1Ki 2: 24 founded a dynasty for me as he *p*—
5: 12 wisdom, just as he had *p* him.
8: 15 own hand has fulfilled what he *p*
8: 20 as the LORD *p*, and I have built
8: 24 with your mouth you have *p*
8: 26 word that you *p* your servant
8: 56 rest to his people Israel just as he *p*.
9: 5 I *p* David your father when I said,
2Ki 8: 19 He had *p* to maintain a lamp
10: 10 The LORD has done what he *p*
20: 9 the LORD will do what he has *p*:
1Ch 11: 3 the LORD had *p* through Samuel.
11: 10 as the LORD had *p*— this is the list
17: 23 you *p*, so that it will be established
27: 23 the LORD had *p* to make Israel
2Ch 2: 15 and the olive oil and wine he *p*,
6: 4 his hands has fulfilled what he *p*
6: 10 as the LORD *p*, and I have built
6: 15 with your mouth you have *p*
6: 17 word that you *p* your servant
6: 42 Remember the kindnesses *p*
21: 7 He had *p* to maintain a lamp
23: 3 as the LORD *p* concerning
Ne 5: 12 an oath to do what they had *p*.
5: 13 And the people did as they had *p*.
Est 4: 7 of money Haman had *p* to pay
Ps 66: 14 vows my lips *p* and my mouth
119: 57 I have *p* to obey your words.
Isa 38: 7 the LORD will do what he has *p*:
55: 3 my faithful love *p* to David.
Jer 32: 42 all the prosperity I have *p* them.
44: 25 do what you *p*! Keep your vows!
Jer 44: 25 shown by your actions what you *p*
Mt 14: 7 so much that he *p* with an oath
Mk 6: 23 And he *p* her with an oath,
14: 11 to hear this and *p* to give him
Lk 2: 29 "Sovereign Lord, as you have *p*,
24: 49 to send you what my Father has *p*;
Ac 1: 4 but wait for the gift my Father *p*,
2: 30 and knew that God had *p* him
2: 33 from the Father the *p* Holy Spirit
3: 21 as he *p* long ago through his holy
7: 5 But God *p* him that he
13: 23 to Israel the Savior Jesus, as he *p*.
13: 32 What God *p* our fathers he has
13: 34 sure blessings *p* to David.'
18: 21 he *p*, "I will come back
26: 6 in what God has *p* our fathers that I
Ro 1: 2 the gospel he *p* beforehand
4: 21 power to do what he had *p*.
2Co 9: 5 for the generous gift you had *p*.
11: 2 I *p* you to one husband, to Christ,
Gal 3: 22 so that what was *p*, being given
Eph 1: 13 in him with a seal, the *p* Holy Spirit
Tit 1: 2 *p* before the beginning of time,
Heb 6: 12 patience inherit what has been *p*.
6: 15 Abraham received what was *p*.
6: 17 clear to the heirs of what was *p*,
9: 15 receive the *p* eternal inheritance—
10: 23 for he who *p* is faithful.
10: 36 you will receive what he has *p*.
11: 9 home in the *p* land like a stranger
11: 13 They did not receive the things *p*;
11: 33 justice, and gained what was *p*;
11: 39 of them received what had been *p*.
12: 26 shook the earth, but now he has *p*,
Jas 1: 12 the crown of life that God has *p*
2: 5 the kingdom he *p* those who love
2Pe 3: 4 "Where is this 'coming' he *p*?
1Jn 2: 25 And this is what he *p* us—

PROMISES (PROMISE)

Jos 21: 45 one of all the LORD's good *p*
23: 14 of all the good *p* the LORD your
1Ki 8: 25 David my father the *p* you made
8: 56 failed of all the good *p* he gave
1Ch 17: 19 and made known all these great *p*.
25: 5 through the *p* of God to exalt him.
2Ch 6: 16 David my father the *p* you made
Ps 85: 8 he *p* peace to his people, his saints
106: 12 Then they believed his *p*
119:103 How sweet are your *p* to my taste,
119:140 Your *p* have been thoroughly
119:148 that I may meditate on your *p*.
145: 13 The LORD is faithful to all his *p*
Hos 10: 4 They make many *p*,
Ro 9: 4 the temple worship and the *p*.
15: 8 to confirm the *p* made
2Co 1: 20 matter how many *p* God has made,
7: 1 Since we have these *p*, dear friends,
Gal 3: 16 The *p* were spoken to Abraham
3: 21 therefore, opposed to the *p* of God?
Heb 7: 6 and blessed him who had the *p*.
8: 6 and it is founded on better *p*.
11: 17 who had received the *p* was about
2Pe 1: 4 us his very great and precious *p*,

PROMOTE (PROMOTED PROMOTES)

Ne 2: 10 to *p* the welfare of the Israelites.
Pr 12: 20 but joy for those who *p* peace.
16: 21 and pleasant words *p* instruction.
16: 23 and his lips *p* instruction.
Da 5: 19 those he wanted to *p*, he promoted;
Hab 1: 7 and *p* their own honor.
1Ti 1: 4 These *p* controversies rather

PROMOTED (PROMOTE)

2Ch 28: 19 for he had *p* wickedness in Judah
Da 3: 30 Then the king *p* Shadrach,
5: 19 those he wanted to promote, he *p*;

PROMOTES (PROMOTE)

Pr 17: 9 over an offense *p* love,
Gal 2: 17 does that mean that Christ *p* sin?

PROMPT (PROMPTED PROMPTS)

Job 20: 2 "My troubled thoughts *p* me

PROMPTED (PROMPT)

Mt 14: 8 *P* by her mother, she said,

Jn 13: 2 devil had already *p* Judas Iscariot,
1Th 1: 3 your labor *p* by love, and your
2Th 1: 11 and every act *p* by your faith.

PROMPTS (PROMPT)

Ex 25: 2 from each man whose heart *p* him
Job 15: 5 Your sin *p* your mouth;

PRONE

Ex 32: 22 "You know how *p* these people are

PRONOUNCE (PRONOUNCED PRONOUNCES PRONOUNCING)

Ge 48: 20 name will Israel *p* this blessing:
Lev 13: 3 he shall *p* him ceremonially
13: 6 the priest shall *p* him clean;
13: 8 he shall *p* him unclean; it is
13: 11 and the priest shall *p* him unclean.
13: 13 he shall *p* that person clean.
13: 15 raw flesh, he shall *p* him unclean.
13: 17 priest shall *p* the infected person
13: 20 the priest shall *p* him unclean.
13: 22 the priest shall *p* him unclean;
13: 23 and the priest shall *p* him clean.
13: 25 The priest shall *p* him unclean;
13: 27 the priest shall *p* him unclean;
13: 28 and the priest shall *p* him clean;
13: 30 priest shall *p* that person unclean;
13: 34 the priest shall *p* him clean.
13: 37 and the priest shall *p* him clean.
13: 44 The priest shall *p* him unclean
14: 7 infectious disease and *p* him clean.
14: 48 he shall *p* the house clean,
Dt 10: 8 and to *p* blessings in his name,
21: 5 and to *p* blessings in the name
23: 4 to *p* a curse on you.
27: 13 stand on Mount Ebal to *p* curses:
Jdg 12: 6 he could not *p* the word correctly,
1Ch 23: 13 to *p* blessings in his name forever.
Job 9: 20 blameless, it would *p* me guilty.
Ps 109: 17 He loved to *p* a curse—
Jer 1: 16 I will *p* my judgments
4: 12 I *p* my judgments against them."

PRONOUNCED (PRONOUNCE)

Lev 13: 7 himself to the priest to be *p* clean,
13: 35 in the skin after he is *p* clean,
14: 36 in the house will be *p* unclean.
Dt 33: 1 the man of God *p* on the Israelites
Jos 6: 26 that time Joshua *p* this solemn
1Ki 20: 40 "You have *p* it yourself."
2Ki 23: 17 and *p* against the altar of Bethel
25: 6 where sentence was *p* on him.
1Ch 16: 12 miracles, and the judgments he *p*,
Ps 76: 8 From heaven you *p* judgment,
105: 5 miracles, and the judgments he *p*,
Jer 19: 15 villages around it every disaster I *p*
26: 13 and not bring the disaster he has *p*
26: 19 he did not bring the disaster he *p*
35: 17 in Jerusalem every disaster I *p*
36: 7 and wrath *p* against this people
36: 31 people of Judah every disaster I *p*
39: 5 where he *p* sentence on him.
52: 9 where he *p* sentence on him.
Da 7: 22 *p* judgment in favor of the saints

PRONOUNCES (PRONOUNCE)

Lev 14: 11 The priest who *p* him clean shall

PRONOUNCING (PRONOUNCE)

Lev 13: 59 for *p* them clean or unclean.

PROOF (PROVE)

Dt 22: 14 I did not find *p* of her virginity,"
22: 15 mother shall bring *p* that she was
22: 17 But here is the *p* of my daughter's
22: 20 no *p* of the girl's virginity can be
Ac 17: 31 He has given *p* of this to all men
2Co 8: 24 Therefore show these men the *p*
13: 3 you are demanding *p* that Christ is

PROOFS (PROVE)

Ac 1: 3 gave many convincing *p* that he

PROPER

Lev 5: 15 and of the *p* value in silver,
5: 18 without defect and of the *p* value.
6: 6 without defect and of the *p* value.
Jdg 6: 26 Then build a *p* kind of altar
2Sa 15: 3 "Look, your claims are valid and *p*,
1Ki 4: 28 brought to the *p* place their quotas
1Ch 23: 31 LORD regularly in the *p* number
Ezr 4: 14 and it is not *p* for us to see the king
Ps 104: 27 give them their food at the *p* time.
145: 15 give them their food at the *p* time.
Ecc 5: 18 Then I realized that it is good and *p*
6: 3 and does not receive *p* burial,
8: 5 the wise heart will know the *p* time
8: 6 For there is a *p* time and procedure
10: 17 and whose princes eat at a *p* time—
Jer 30: 18 the palace will stand in its *p* place.
Mt 3: 15 it is *p* for us to do this
24: 45 give them their food at the *p* time?
Lk 1: 20 which will come true at their *p* time
12: 42 their food allowance at the *p* time?
Ac 13: 28 Though they found no *p* ground
1Co 11: 13 Is it *p* for a woman to pray to God
2Co 10: 13 will not boast beyond *p* limits,
Gal 6: 9 at the *p* time we will reap a harvest
2Th 2: 6 he may be revealed at the *p* time.
1Ti 2: 6 the testimony given in its *p* time.
3: 4 children obey him with *p* respect.
5: 3 Give *p* recognition
1Pe 2: 17 Show *p* respect to everyone:

PROPERTY

Ge 23: 4 Sell me some *p* for a burial site here
23: 18 as his *p* in the presence
34: 10 trade in it, and acquire *p* in it."
34: 23 their *p* and all their other animals
47: 11 and gave them *p* in the best part
47: 27 They acquired *p* there
Ex 21: 21 or two, since the slave is his *p*.
22: 8 hands on the other man's *p*.
22: 9 or any other lost *p* about which
22: 11 hands on the other person's *p*.
Lev 6: 3 or if he finds lost *p* and lies about it,
6: 4 to him, or the lost *p* he found,
25: 10 of you is to return to his family *p*
25: 13 is to return to his own *p*.
25: 25 poor and sells some of his *p*,
25: 27 he can then go back to his own *p*.
25: 28 and he can then go back to his *p*.
25: 33 the towns of the Levites are their *p*
25: 33 the *p* of the Levites is redeemable
25: 41 and to the *p* of his forefathers.
25: 45 and they will become your *p*.
25: 46 as inherited *p* and can make them
27: 21 it will become the *p* of the priests.
Nu 27: 4 Give us *p* among our father's
27: 7 You must certainly give them *p*
32: 32 the *p* we inherit will be on this side
35: 28 priest may he return to his own *p*.
36: 4 and their *p* will be taken
Dt 21: 16 when he wills his *p* to his sons,
Ru 4: 5 the name of the dead with his *p*."
4: 7 and transfer of *p* to become final,
4: 9 from Naomi all the *p* of Elimelech,
4: 10 the name of the dead with his *p*,
1Sa 25: 2 who had *p* there at Carmel,
25: 21 over this fellow's *p* in the desert
1Ki 21: 19 murdered a man and seized his *p*?'
1Ch 9: 2 the first to resettle on their own *p*
27: 31 in charge of King David's *p*.
28: 1 the officials in charge of all the *p*
2Ch 11: 14 their pasturelands and *p*,
31: 1 their own towns and to their own *p*.
Ezr 7: 26 confiscation of *p*, or imprisonment.
10: 8 three days would forfeit all his *p*,
Ne 11: 3 on his own *p* in the various towns,
11: 20 of Judah, each on his ancestral *p*.
Est 8: 11 to plunder the *p* of their enemies.
Job 5: 24 you will take stock of your *p*
Jer 37: 12 of the *p* among the people there.
Eze 45: 6 give the city as its *p* an area 5,000
45: 7 by the sacred district and the *p*
46: 16 it is to be their *p* by inheritance.
46: 18 the people, driving them off their *p*.
46: 18 their inheritance out of his own *p*,
46: 18 will be separated from his *p*.' "
48: 20 along with the *p* of the city.
48: 21 the city *p* will belong to the prince.
48: 22 So the *p* of the Levites
48: 22 and the *p* of the city will lie
Mt 25: 14 and entrusted his *p* to them.
Lk 15: 12 So he divided his *p* between them.
15: 30 yours who has squandered your *p*
16: 12 trustworthy with someone else's *p*,
16: 12 who will give you *p* of your own?
Ac 5: 1 Sapphira, also sold a piece of *p*.
Heb 10: 34 the confiscation of your *p*,

PROPHECIES (PROPHESY)

2Ch 24: 27 of his sons, the many *p* about him,
1Co 13: 8 where there are *p*, they will cease;
1Th 5: 20 do not treat *p* with contempt.
1Ti 1: 18 with the *p* once made about you,

PROPHECY (PROPHESY)

2Ki 9: 25 the LORD made this *p* about him:
2Ch 9: 29 in the *p* of Ahijah the Shilonite
15: 8 and the *p* of Azariah son
Eze 14: 9 prophet is persuaded to utter a *p*,
Da 9: 24 to seal up vision and *p*
Mt 13: 14 In them is fulfilled the *p* of Isaiah:
1Co 12: 10 miraculous powers, to another *p*,
13: 2 of *p* and can fathom all mysteries
14: 1 gifts, especially the gift of *p*.
14: 6 or *p* or word of instruction?
14: 22 *p*, however, is for believers,
2Th 2: 2 unsettled or alarmed by some *p*,
2Pe 1: 20 you must understand that no *p*
1: 21 For *p* never had its origin
Rev 1: 3 one who reads the words of this *p*,
19: 10 of Jesus is the spirit of *p*."
22: 7 the words of the *p* in this book."
22: 10 the words of the *p* of this book,
22: 18 the words of the *p* of this book:
22: 19 away from this book of *p*,

PROPHESIED (PROPHESY)

Nu 11: 25 the Spirit rested on them, they *p*,
11: 26 on them, and they *p* in the camp.
1Sa 19: 20 upon Saul's men and they also *p*.
19: 21 he sent more men, and they *p* too.
19: 21 men a third time, and they also *p*.
19: 24 and also *p* in Samuel's presence.
1Ch 25: 2 who *p* under the king's supervision.
25: 3 of their father Jeduthun, who *p*,
2Ch 20: 37 of Mareshah *p* against Jehoshaphat
Ezr 5: 1 *p* to the Jews in Judah
Ne 6: 12 but that he had *p* against me
Jer 2: 8 The prophets *p* by Baal,
20: 6 friends to whom you have *p* lies.' "
23: 13 They *p* by Baal
23: 21 yet they have *p*.
25: 13 and *p* by Jeremiah against all
26: 11 because he has *p* against this city.
26: 18 "Micah of Moresheth *p* in the days
26: 20 he *p* the same things
26: 20 was another man who *p*
28: 6 LORD fulfill the words you have *p*
28: 8 preceded you and me have *p* war,
29: 31 Because Shemaiah has *p* to you,
37: 19 Where are your prophets who *p*
Eze 13: 16 of Israel who *p* to Jerusalem
37: 7 So I *p* as I was commanded.
37: 10 So I *p* as he commanded me,
38: 17 At that time they *p*
Mt 11: 13 For all the Prophets and the Law *p*
15: 7 when he *p* about you:
Mk 7: 6 when he *p* about you hypocrites;
Lk 1: 67 with the Holy Spirit and *p*:
Jn 11: 51 that year he *p* that Jesus would
Ac 19: 6 and they spoke in tongues and *p*.
21: 9 four unmarried daughters who *p*.
Jude : 14 from Adam, *p* about these men:

PROPHESIES (PROPHESY)

1Ki 22: 8 he never *p* anything good about me
22: 18 that he never *p* anything good
2Ch 18: 7 he never *p* anything good about me
18: 17 that he never *p* anything good
Jer 28: 9 the prophet who *p* peace will be
Eze 12: 27 and he *p* about the distant future.'
Zec 13: 3 And if anyone still *p*, his father
13: 3 When he *p*, his own parents will
1Co 11: 4 *p* with his head covered dishonors
11: 5 or *p* with her head uncovered
14: 3 But everyone who *p* speaks to men
14: 4 but he who *p* edifies the church.
14: 5 He who *p* is greater

PROPHESY (PROPHECIES PROPHECY PROPHESIED PROPHESIES PROPHESYING PROPHET PROPHET'S PROPHETESS PROPHETIC PROPHETS)

1Sa 10: 6 and you will *p* with them;
Isa 30: 10 *p* illusions.
Jer 5: 31 The prophets *p* lies,
11: 21 Do not *p* in the name of the LORD
19: 14 where the LORD had sent him to *p*
23: 25 what the prophets say who *p* lies
23: 26 who *p* the delusions
23: 32 against those who *p* false dreams,''
25: 30 *p* all these words against them
26: 9 Why do you *p* in the LORD's
26: 12 me to *p* against this house
27: 10 They *p* lies to you that will only
27: 15 and the prophets who *p* to you.' ''
32: 3 saying, ''Why do you *p* as you do?
Eze 4: 7 and with bared arm *p* against her.
6: 2 mountains of Israel; *p* against them
11: 4 Therefore *p* against them; *p*,
13: 2 Say to those who *p* out
13: 2 *p* against the prophets
13: 17 daughters of your people who *p* out
13: 17 *P* against them and say, 'This is
20: 46 and *p* against the forest
21: 2 *P* against the land of Israel
21: 9 *p* and say, 'This is what the Lord
21: 14 ''So *p*, son of man,
21: 28 ''And you, son of man, *p* and say,
25: 2 face against the Ammonites and *p*
28: 21 face against Sidon; *p* against her
29: 2 *p* against him and against all Egypt.
30: 2 *p* and say: 'This is what
34: 2 against the shepherds of Israel; *p*
34: 2 *p* against the shepherds of Israel;
35: 2 against Mount Seir; *p* against it
36: 1 *p* to the mountains of Israel and say
36: 3 Therefore *p* and say, 'This is what
36: 6 Therefore *p* concerning the land
37: 4 ''*P* to these bones and say to them,
37: 9 ''*P* to the breath; *p*,
37: 12 Therefore *p* and say to them:
38: 2 and Tubal; *p* against him and say:
38: 14 son of man, *p* and say to Gog:
39: 1 Son of man, *p* against Gog and say:
Joel 2: 28 Your sons and daughters will *p*,
Am 2: 12 commanded the prophets not to *p*.
3: 8 who can but *p*?
7: 13 Don't *p* anymore at Bethel,
7: 15 'Go, *p* to my people Israel.'
7: 16 '' 'Do not *p* against Israel,
Mic 2: 6 ''Do not *p* about these things;
2: 6 ''Do not *p*,'' their prophets say.
2: 11 'I will *p* for you plenty of wine
Mt 7: 22 Lord, did we not *p* in your name,
26: 68 Others slapped him and said, ''*P*
Mk 14: 65 him with their fists, and said, ''*P*!''
Lk 22: 64 him and demanded, ''*P*!
Ac 2: 17 Your sons and daughters will *p*,
2: 18 and they will *p*.
1Co 13: 9 know in part and we *p* in part,
14: 5 but I would rather have you *p*.
14: 31 For you can all *p* in turn
14: 39 my brothers, be eager to *p*,
Rev 10: 11 ''You must *p* again about many
11: 3 and they will *p* for 1,260 days,

PROPHESYING (PROPHESY)

Nu 11: 27 and Medad are *p* in the camp.''
1Sa 10: 5 before them, and they will be *p*.
10: 10 in power, and he joined in their *p*.
10: 11 had formerly known him saw him *p*
10: 13 After Saul stopped *p*, he went
18: 10 He was *p* in his house,
19: 20 they saw a group of prophets *p*,
19: 23 he walked along *p* until he came
1Ki 18: 29 and they continued their frantic *p*
22: 10 with all the prophets *p* before them
22: 12 the other prophets were *p* the same
1Ch 25: 1 and Jeduthun for the ministry of *p*,
2Ch 18: 9 with all the prophets *p* before them
18: 11 the other prophets were *p* the same
Jer 14: 14 The prophets are *p* lies in my name.
14: 14 They are *p* to you false visions,
14: 15 says about the prophets who are *p*
14: 16 And the people they are *p*
Jer 20: 1 heard Jeremiah *p* these things,
23: 16 to what the prophets are *p* to you;
27: 14 for they are *p* lies to you.
27: 15 'They are *p* lies in my name.
27: 16 They are *p* lies to you.
29: 9 They are *p* lies to you in my name.
29: 21 who are *p* lies to you in my name:
Eze 11: 13 Now as I was *p*, Pelatiah son
13: 2 prophets of Israel who are now *p*.
37: 7 And as I was *p*, there was a noise,
Am 7: 12 bread there and do your *p* there.
Ro 12: 6 If a man's gift is *p*, let him use it
1Co 14: 24 comes in while everybody is *p*,
Rev 11: 6 rain during the time they are *p*;

PROPHET (PROPHESY)

Ge 20: 7 return the man's wife, for he is a *p*,
Ex 7: 1 your brother Aaron will be your *p*.
Nu 12: 6 ''When a *p* of the LORD is
Dt 13: 1 If a *p*, or one who foretells
13: 3 listen to the words of that *p*
13: 5 That *p* or dreamer must be put
18: 15 up for you a *p* like me
18: 18 up for them a *p* like you
18: 19 to my words that the *p* speaks
18: 20 But a *p* who presumes to speak
18: 20 or a *p* who speaks in the name
18: 22 If what a *p* proclaims in the name
18: 22 That *p* has spoken presumptuously.
34: 10 no *p* has risen in Israel like Moses,
Jdg 6: 8 he sent them a *p*, who said,
1Sa 3: 20 that Samuel was attested as a *p*
9: 9 because the *p* of today used
22: 5 But the *p* Gad said to David,
2Sa 7: 2 said to Nathan the *p*, ''Here I am,
12: 25 word through Nathan the *p*
24: 11 the LORD had come to Gad the *p*,
1Ki 1: 8 son of Jehoiada, Nathan the *p*,
1: 10 but he did not invite Nathan the *p*
1: 22 with the king, Nathan the *p* arrived
1: 23 the king, ''Nathan the *p* is here.''
1: 32 Nathan the *p* and Benaiah son
1: 34 and Nathan the *p* anoint him king
1: 38 Nathan the *p*, Benaiah son
1: 44 Nathan the *p*, Benaiah son
1: 45 Nathan the *p* have anointed him
11: 29 and Ahijah the *p* of Shiloh met him
13: 11 there was a certain old *p* living
13: 13 So the *p* said to him, ''Come home
13: 18 The old *p* answered, ''I too am a *p*,
13: 20 to the old *p* who had brought him
13: 23 the *p* who had brought him back
13: 25 it in the city where the old *p* lived.
13: 26 When the *p* who had brought him
13: 27 The *p* said to his sons, ''Saddle
13: 29 So the *p* picked up the body
14: 2 Ahijah the *p* is there — the one who
14: 18 through his servant the *p* Ahijah.
16: 7 through the *p* Jehu son of Hanani
16: 12 against Baasha through the *p* Jehu
18: 36 the *p* Elijah stepped forward
19: 16 to succeed you as *p*.
20: 13 Meanwhile a *p* came to Ahab king
20: 14 The *p* answered, ''You will.''
20: 14 *p* replied, ''This is what the LORD
20: 22 the *p* came to the king of Israel
20: 36 the *p* said, ''Because you have not
20: 37 The *p* found another man and said,
20: 38 Then the *p* went and stood
20: 39 passed by, the *p* called out to him,
20: 41 *p* quickly removed the headband
22: 7 ''Is there not a *p* of the LORD here
2Ki 3: 11 ''Is there no *p* of the LORD here,
5: 3 my master would see the *p* who is
5: 8 and he will know that there is a *p*
5: 13 if the *p* had told you
5: 16 The *p* answered, ''As surely
6: 12 ''but Elisha, the *p* who is in Israel,
6: 16 ''Don't be afraid,'' the *p* answered.
9: 1 The *p* Elisha summoned a man
9: 4 So the young man, the *p*, went
9: 6 the *p* poured the oil on Jehu's head
14: 25 the *p* from Gath Hepher.
19: 2 to the *p* Isaiah son of Amoz.
20: 1 The *p* Isaiah son of Amoz went
20: 11 the *p* Isaiah called upon the LORD
20: 14 Isaiah the *p* went to King Hezekiah
20: 15 The *p* asked, ''What did they see
2Ki 23: 18 and those of the *p* who had come
1Ch 17: 1 said to Nathan the *p*, ''Here I am,
29: 29 the records of Nathan the *p*
2Ch 9: 29 in the records of Nathan the *p*,
12: 5 the *p* Shemaiah came to Rehoboam
12: 15 in the records of Shemaiah the *p*
13: 22 in the annotations of the *p* Iddo.
15: 8 of Azariah son of Oded the *p*,
18: 6 ''Is there not a *p* of the LORD here
21: 12 received a letter from Elijah the *p*,
25: 15 and he sent a *p* to him, who said,
25: 16 So the *p* stopped but said,
26: 22 are recorded by the *p* Isaiah son
28: 9 a *p* of the LORD named Oded was
29: 25 the king's seer and Nathan the *p*;
32: 20 the *p* Isaiah son of Amoz cried out
32: 32 vision of the *p* Isaiah son of Amoz
35: 18 since the days of the *p* Samuel;
36: 12 himself before Jeremiah the *p*,
Ezr 5: 1 Haggai the *p* and Zechariah the *p*,
6: 14 the preaching of Haggai the *p*
Isa 3: 2 the judge and *p*,
37: 2 to the *p* Isaiah son of Amoz.
38: 1 The *p* Isaiah son of Amoz went
39: 3 Isaiah the *p* went to King Hezekiah
39: 4 The *p* asked, ''What did they see
Jer 1: 5 I appointed you as a *p*
14: 18 Both *p* and priest
20: 2 he had Jeremiah the *p* beaten
23: 11 ''Both *p* and priest are godless;
23: 28 Let the *p* who has a dream tell his
23: 33 ''When these people, or a *p*
23: 34 If a *p* or a priest or anyone else
23: 37 This is what you keep saying to a *p*:
25: 2 So Jeremiah the *p* said
28: 1 the *p* Hananiah son of Azzur,
28: 5 Then the *p* Jeremiah replied
28: 5 replied to the *p* Hananiah
28: 9 the *p* who prophesies peace will be
28: 10 Then the *p* Hananiah took the yoke
28: 10 yoke off the neck of the *p* Jeremiah
28: 11 the *p* Jeremiah went on his way.
28: 12 after the *p* Hananiah had broken
28: 12 off the neck of the *p* Jeremiah,
28: 15 Then the *p* Jeremiah said
28: 15 said to Hananiah the *p*,
28: 17 same year, Hananiah the *p* died.
29: 1 the letter that the *p* Jeremiah sent
29: 26 put any madman who acts like a *p*
29: 27 who poses as a *p* among you?
29: 29 read the letter to Jeremiah the *p*.
32: 2 and Jeremiah the *p* was confined
34: 6 Then Jeremiah the *p* told all this
36: 8 everything Jeremiah the *p* told him
36: 26 the scribe and Jeremiah the *p*.
37: 2 spoken through Jeremiah the *p*.
37: 3 to Jeremiah the *p* with this message
37: 6 came to Jeremiah the *p*:
38: 9 done to Jeremiah the *p*.
38: 10 and lift Jeremiah the *p* out
38: 14 sent for Jeremiah the *p*
42: 2 approached Jeremiah the *p*
42: 4 heard you,'' replied Jeremiah the *p*.
43: 6 and Jeremiah the *p* and Baruch son
45: 1 what Jeremiah the *p* told Baruch
46: 1 came to Jeremiah the *p* concerning
46: 13 to Jeremiah the *p* about the coming
47: 1 came to Jeremiah the *p* concerning
49: 34 to Jeremiah the *p* concerning Elam
50: 1 Jeremiah the *p* concerning
La 2: 20 Should priest and *p* be killed
Eze 2: 5 they will know that a *p* has been
7: 26 try to get a vision from the *p*;
14: 4 before his face and then goes to a *p*,
14: 7 then goes to a *p* to inquire of me,
14: 9 I the LORD have persuaded that *p*,
14: 9 '' 'And if the *p* is persuaded
14: 10 *p* will be as guilty as the one who
33: 33 they will know that a *p* has been
Da 9: 2 given to Jeremiah the *p*,
Hos 9: 7 the *p* is considered a fool,
9: 8 The *p*, along with my God,
12: 13 The LORD used a *p*
12: 13 by a *p* he cared for him.
Am 7: 14 ''I was neither a *p* nor a prophet's
Mic 2: 11 he would be just the *p*
Hab 1: 1 that Habakkuk the *p* received.
3: 1 A prayer of Habakkuk the *p*.

Hag 1: 1 came through the p Haggai
1: 3 came through the p Haggai:
1: 12 and the message of the p Haggai,
2: 1 came through the p Haggai:
2: 10 of the LORD came to the p Haggai
Zec 1: 1 to the p Zechariah son of Berekiah,
1: 7 to the p Zechariah son of Berekiah,
13: 4 that day every p will be ashamed
13: 5 He will say, 'I am not a p.
Mal 4: 5 I will send you the p Elijah
Mt 1: 22 the Lord had said through the p:
2: 5 "for this is what the p has written:
2: 15 the Lord had said through the p:
2: 17 said through the p Jeremiah was
3: 3 spoken of through the p Isaiah:
4: 14 said through the p Isaiah:
8: 17 spoken through the p Isaiah:
10: 41 Anyone who receives a p
10: 41 he is a p will receive a prophet's
11: 9 Yes, I tell you, and more than a p.
11: 9 what did you go out to see? A p?
12: 17 spoken through the p Isaiah:
12: 39 except the sign of the p Jonah.
13: 35 what was spoken through the p:
13: 57 and in his own house is a p
14: 5 because they considered him a p.
21: 4 what was spoken through the p:
21: 11 the p from Nazareth in Galilee."
21: 26 for they all hold that John was a p."
21: 46 the people held that he was a p.
24: 15 spoken of through the p Daniel—
27: 9 by Jeremiah the p was fulfilled:
Mk 1: 2 It is written in Isaiah the p:
6: 4 and in his own house is a p
6: 15 And still others claimed, "He is a p,
11: 32 held that John really was a p.)
Lk 1: 76 will be called a p of the Most High;
3: 4 book of the words of Isaiah the p:
4: 17 scroll of the p Isaiah was handed
4: 24 "no p is accepted in his home town.
4: 27 leprosy in the time of Elisha the p,
7: 16 A great p has appeared among us,"
7: 26 But what did you go out to see? A p
7: 26 Yes, I tell you, and more than a p.
7: 39 to himself, "If this man were a p,
13: 33 for surely no p can die
20: 6 are persuaded that John was a p."
24: 19 "He was a p, powerful in word
Jn 1: 21 "Are you the P?" He answered,
1: 23 replied in the words of Isaiah the p,
1: 25 nor the P?" "I baptize with water,"
4: 19 "I can see that you are a p.
4: 44 pointed out that a p has no honor
6: 14 "Surely this is the P who is to come
7: 40 "Surely this man is the P."
7: 52 will find that a p does not come out
9: 17 The man replied, "He is a p."
12: 38 to fulfill the word of Isaiah the p:
Ac 2: 16 is what was spoken by the p Joel:
2: 30 he was a p and knew that God had
3: 22 up for you a p like me
7: 37 'God will send you a p like me
7: 48 As the p says: " 'Heaven is my
7: 52 Was there ever a p your fathers did
8: 28 reading the book of Isaiah the p.
8: 30 heard the man reading Isaiah the p.
8: 34 please, who is the p talking about,
13: 6 and false p named Bar-Jesus,
13: 20 until the time of Samuel the p.
21: 10 a p named Agabus came
28: 25 when he said through Isaiah the p:
1Co 14: 37 If anybody thinks he is a p
Rev 16: 13 and out of the mouth of the false p.
19: 20 him the false p who had performed
20: 10 and the false p had been thrown.

PROPHET'S (PROPHESY)

Am 7: 14 I was neither a prophet nor a p son,
Zec 13: 4 put on a p garment of hair in order
Mt 10: 41 is a prophet will receive a p reward,
2Pe 1: 20 about by the p own interpretation.
2: 16 and restrained the p madness.

PROPHETESS (PROPHESY)

Ex 15: 20 Then Miriam the p, Aaron's sister,
Jdg 4: 4 a p, the wife of Lappidoth,
2Ki 22: 14 went to speak to the p Huldah,
2Ch 34: 22 went to speak to the p Huldah,
Ne 6: 14 remember also the p Noadiah
Isa 8: 3 I went to the p, and she conceived
Lk 2: 36 a p, Anna, the daughter of Phanuel,
Rev 2: 20 Jezebel, who calls herself a p.

PROPHETIC (PROPHESY)

Zec 13: 4 will be ashamed of his p vision.
Ro 16: 26 known through the p writings
1Ti 4: 14 you through a p message

PROPHETS (PROPHESY)

Nu 11: 29 that all the LORD's people were p
1Sa 10: 5 will meet a procession of p coming
10: 10 a procession of p met him;
10: 11 Is Saul also among the p?"
10: 11 saw him prophesying with the p,
10: 12 "Is Saul also among the p?"
19: 20 they saw a group of p prophesying,
19: 24 "Is Saul also among the p?"
28: 6 him by dreams or Urim or p.
28: 15 no longer answers me, either by p
1Ki 18: 4 Obadiah had taken a hundred p
18: 4 killing off the LORD's p,
18: 13 did while Jezebel was killing the p
18: 13 of the LORD's p in two caves,
18: 19 and the four hundred p of Asherah,
18: 19 bring the four hundred and fifty p
18: 20 assembled the p on Mount Carmel.
18: 22 Baal has four hundred and fifty p.
18: 22 one of the LORD's p left,
18: 25 Elijah said to the p of Baal,
18: 40 commanded them, "Seize the p
19: 1 and how he had killed all the p
19: 10 put your p to death with the sword.
19: 14 put your p to death with the sword.
20: 35 sons of the p said to his companion,
20: 41 recognized him as one of the p.
22: 6 of Israel brought together the p—
22: 10 with all the p prophesying
22: 12 All the other p were prophesying
22: 13 man the other p are predicting
22: 22 spirit in the mouths of all his p,'
22: 23 in the mouths of all these p of yours
2Ki 2: 3 The company of the p
2: 5 The company of the p
2: 7 men of the company of the p went
2: 15 The company of the p from Jericho
3: 13 Go to the p of your father
3: 13 and the p of your mother."
4: 1 of the p cried out to Elisha,
4: 38 of the p was meeting with him,
5: 22 company of the p have just come
6: 1 company of the p said to Elisha,
9: 1 a man from the company of the p
9: 7 the blood of my servants the p
10: 19 Now summon all the p of Baal,
17: 13 Judah through all his p and seers:
17: 13 to you through my servants the p."
17: 23 through all his servants the p.
21: 10 said through his servants the p:
23: 2 of Jerusalem, the priests and the p
24: 2 proclaimed by his servants the p.
1Ch 16: 22 do my p no harm."
2Ch 18: 5 of Israel brought together the p—
18: 9 with all the p prophesying
18: 11 All the other p were prophesying
18: 12 man the other p are predicting
18: 21 spirit in the mouths of all his p,'
18: 22 in the mouths of these p of yours.
20: 20 in his p and you will be successful."
24: 19 Although the LORD sent p
29: 25 by the LORD through his p.
36: 16 and scoffed at his p until the wrath
Ezr 5: 2 And the p of God were with them,
9: 11 gave through your servants the p
Ne 6: 7 even appointed p to make this
6: 14 rest of the p who have been trying
9: 26 They killed your p, who had
9: 30 admonished them through your p.
9: 32 upon our priests and p,
Ps 74: 9 no p are left,
105: 15 do my p no harm."
Isa 9: 15 the p who teach lies are the tail.
28: 7 Priests and p stagger from beer
29: 10 He has sealed your eyes (the p);
30: 10 and to the p,
44: 25 who foils the signs of false p
Jer 2: 8 The p prophesied by Baal,
2: 26 their priests and their p.
2: 30 Your sword has devoured your p
4: 9 and the p will be appalled."
5: 13 The p are but wind
5: 31 The p prophesy lies,
6: 13 p and priests alike,
7: 25 again I sent you my servants the p.
8: 1 the bones of the priests and p,
8: 10 p and priests alike,
13: 13 the p and all those living
14: 13 LORD, the p keep telling
14: 14 "The p are prophesying lies
14: 15 Those same p will perish by sword
14: 15 says about the p who are
18: 18 the wise, nor the word from the p.
23: 9 Concerning the p:
23: 10 The p follow an evil course
23: 13 "Among the p of Samaria
23: 14 And among the p of Jerusalem
23: 15 Almighty says concerning the p:
23: 15 because from the p of Jerusalem
23: 16 to what the p are prophesying
23: 21 I did not send these p,
23: 25 heard what the p say who prophesy
23: 26 in the hearts of these lying p,
23: 30 "I am against the p who steal
23: 31 against the p who wag their own
25: 4 sent you all his servants the p again
26: 5 to the words of my servants the p,
26: 7 p and all the people heard Jeremiah
26: 8 the p and all the people seized him
26: 11 and the p said to the officials
26: 16 said to the priests and the p,
27: 9 listen to your p, your diviners,
27: 14 the words of the p who say to you,
27: 15 and the p who prophesy to you.' "
27: 16 Do not listen to the p who say,
27: 18 If they are p and have the word
28: 8 early times the p who preceded you
29: 1 the p and all the other people
29: 8 "Do not let the p and diviners
29: 15 "The LORD has raised up p for us
29: 19 and again by my servants the p.
32: 32 and officials, their priests and p,
35: 15 again I sent all my servants the p
37: 19 Where are your p who prophesied
44: 4 and again I sent my servants the p,
50: 36 A sword against her false p!
La 2: 9 and her p no longer find
2: 14 The visions of your p
4: 13 because of the sins of her p
Eze 13: 2 prophesy against the p
13: 3 to the foolish p who follow their
13: 4 Your p, O Israel, are like jackals
13: 9 against the p who see false visions
13: 16 those p of Israel who prophesied
22: 28 Her p whitewash these deeds
38: 17 days by my servants the p of Israel?
Da 9: 6 listened to your servants the p,
9: 10 us through his servants the p.
Hos 4: 5 and the p stumble with you.
6: 5 you in pieces with my p,
12: 10 I spoke to the p,
Am 2: 11 raised up p from among your sons
2: 12 commanded the p not to prophesy.
3: 7 plan to his servants the p.
Mic 2: 6 "Do not prophesy," their p say.
3: 5 "As for the p
3: 6 The sun will set for the p,
3: 11 and her p tell fortunes for money.
Zep 3: 4 Her p are arrogant;
Zec 1: 4 to whom the earlier p proclaimed:
1: 5 And the p, do they live forever?
1: 6 I commanded my servants the p,
7: 3 of the LORD Almighty and the p,
7: 7 proclaimed through the earlier p
7: 12 by his Spirit through the earlier p.
8: 9 spoken by the p who were there
13: 2 "I will remove both the p
Mt 2: 23 what was said through the p:
5: 12 they persecuted the p who were
5: 17 come to abolish the Law or the P;
7: 12 for this sums up the Law and the P.
7: 15 "Watch out for false p.
11: 13 For all the P and the Law
13: 17 many p and righteous men longed
16: 14 Jeremiah or one of the p."
22: 40 and the P hang on these two

Mt 23: 29 You build tombs for the *p*
23: 30 in shedding the blood of the *p*.'
23: 31 of those who murdered the *p*.
23: 34 Therefore I am sending you *p*
23: 37 you who kill the *p* and stone those
24: 11 and many false *p* will appear
24: 24 false Christs and false *p* will appear
26: 56 of the *p* might be fulfilled.''
Mk 6: 15 like one of the *p* of long ago.''
8: 28 and still others, one of the *p*.''
13: 22 false Christs and false *p* will appear
Lk 1: 70 through his holy *p* of long ago),
6: 23 is how their fathers treated the *p*.
6: 26 their fathers treated the false *p*.
9: 8 and still others that one of the *p*
9: 19 of the *p* of long ago has come back
10: 24 For I tell you that many *p*
11: 47 because you build tombs for the *p*,
11: 48 they killed the *p*, and you build
11: 49 'I will send them *p* and apostles,
11: 50 of all the *p* that has been shed
13: 28 all the *p* in the kingdom of God,
13: 34 you who kill the *p* and stone those
16: 16 the *P* were proclaimed until John.
16: 29 'They have Moses and the *P*;
16: 31 listen to Moses and the *P*,
18: 31 written by the *p* about the Son
24: 25 believe all that the *p* have spoken!
24: 27 beginning with Moses and all the *P*
24: 44 me in the Law of Moses, the *P*
Jn 1: 45 and about whom the *p* also wrote—
6: 45 in the *P*: 'They will all be taught
8: 52 Abraham died and so did the *p*,
8: 53 He died, and so did the *p*.
Ac 3: 18 he had foretold through all the *p*,
3: 21 ago through his holy *p*.
3: 24 "Indeed, all the *p* from Samuel on,
3: 25 And you are heirs of the *p*
7: 42 written in the book of the *p*:
10: 43 All the *p* testify about him that
11: 27 During this time some *p* came
13: 1 the church at Antioch there were *p*
13: 15 reading from the Law and the *P*,
13: 27 of the *p* that are read every Sabbath
13: 40 care that what the *p* have said does
15: 15 of the *p* are in agreement
15: 32 and Silas, who themselves were *p*,
24: 14 and that is written in the *P*,
26: 22 nothing beyond what the *p*
26: 27 do you believe the *p*? I know you
28: 23 the Law of Moses and from the *P*.
Ro 1: 2 through his *p* in the Holy
3: 21 to which the Law and the *P* testify.
11: 3 they have killed your *p*
1Co 12: 28 second *p*, third teachers, then
12: 29 Are all *p*? Are all teachers?
14: 29 Two or three *p* should speak,
14: 32 The spirits of *p* are subject
14: 32 subject to the control of *p*.
Eph 2: 20 foundation of the apostles and *p*,
3: 5 Spirit to God's holy apostles and *p*.
4: 11 some to be *p*, some
1Th 2: 15 and the *p* and also drove us out.
Tit 1: 12 Even one of their own *p* has said,
Heb 1: 1 through the *p* at many times
11: 32 Jephthah, David, Samuel and the *p*
Jas 5: 10 take the *p* who spoke in the name
1Pe 1: 10 Concerning this salvation, the *p*,
2Pe 1: 19 word of the *p* made more certain,
2: 1 also false *p* among the people,
3: 2 spoken in the past by the holy *p*
1Jn 4: 1 because many false *p* have gone out
Rev 10: 7 he announced to his servants the *p*
11: 10 these two *p* had tormented those
11: 18 for rewarding your servants the *p*
16: 6 the blood of your saints and *p*,
18: 20 Rejoice, saints and apostles and *p*!
18: 24 In her was found the blood of *p*
22: 6 the God of the spirits of the *p*,
22: 9 and with your brothers the *p*

PROPORTION

Nu 35: 8 to be given in *p* to the inheritance
Dt 16: 10 by giving a freewill offering in *p*
16: 17 Each of you must bring a gift in *p*
Ro 12: 6 let him use it in *p* to his faith.

PROPOSAL (PROPOSE)

Ge 34: 18 Their *p* seemed good to Hamor
Ac 6: 5 This *p* pleased the whole group.

PROPOSE (PROPOSAL PROPOSED)

Dt 1: 14 "What you *p* to do is good."
Isa 8: 10 *p* your plan, but it will not stand,

PROPOSED (PROPOSE)

Ezr 10: 16 So the exiles did as was *p*.
Est 1: 21 so the king did as Memucan *p*.
2: 2 the king's personal attendants *p*,
Ac 1: 23 So they *p* two men: Joseph called

PROPPED

1Ki 22: 35 king was *p* up in his chariot facing
2Ch 18: 34 and the king of Israel *p* himself up

PROPRIETY

1Ti 2: 9 with decency and *p*,
2: 15 in faith, love and holiness with *p*.

PROSPECT (PROSPECTS)

Pr 10: 28 The *p* of the righteous is joy,

PROSPECTS (PROSPECT)

Job 6: 11 What *p*, that I should be patient?

PROSPER (PROSPERED PROSPERITY PROSPEROUS PROSPERS)

Ge 32: 9 relatives, and I will make you *p*,'
32: 12 'I will surely make you *p*
Dt 5: 33 so that you may live and *p*
6: 24 so that we might always *p*
28: 63 pleased the LORD to make you *p*
29: 9 that you may *p* in everything you
1Ki 2: 3 so that you may *p* in all you do
2Ch 24: 20 commands? You will not *p*.
Ezr 6: 14 and *p* under the preaching
Ps 49: 18 and men praise you when you *p*—
51: 18 In your good pleasure make Zion *p*;
Pr 11: 10 When the righteous *p*, the city
11: 25 A generous man will *p*;
17: 20 A man of perverse heart does not *p*
28: 13 who conceals his sins does not *p*,
28: 25 he who trusts in the LORD will *p*.
Isa 53: 10 of the LORD will *p* in his hand.
Jer 10: 21 so they do not *p*
12: 1 Why does the way of the wicked *p*?
22: 30 a man who will not *p* in his lifetime,
22: 30 for none of his offspring will *p*,
29: 7 if it prospers, you too will *p*."
29: 11 plans to *p* you and not to harm you,
Eze 26: 2 now that she lies in ruins I will *p*,'
36: 11 will make you *p* more than before.
Da 4: 1 in all the world: May you *p* greatly!
6: 25 the land: "May you *p* greatly!
8: 25 He will cause deceit to *p*,
Mal 3: 15 Certainly the evildoers *p*, and
Ac 13: 17 made the people *p* during their stay

PROSPERED (PROSPER)

Ge 39: 2 was with Joseph and he *p*,
1Ch 29: 23 He *p* and all Israel obeyed him.
2Ch 14: 7 So they built and *p*.
31: 21 And so he *p*.
Da 6: 28 Daniel *p* during the reign of Darius
8: 12 It *p* in everything it did,
Hos 10: 1 as his land *p*,

PROSPERITY (PROSPER)

Dt 28: 11 will grant you abundant *p*—
28: 47 and gladly in the time of *p*,
30: 15 I set before you today life and *p*,
Ezr 9: 12 Do not further their welfare or *p*
Job 20: 21 his *p* will not endure.
21: 13 They spend their years in *p*
21: 16 their *p* is not in their own hands,
22: 21 in this way *p* will come to you.
36: 11 will spend the rest of their days in *p*
Ps 25: 13 He will spend his days in *p*,
72: 3 The mountains will bring *p*
72: 7 *p* will abound till the moon is no
73: 3 when I saw the *p* of the wicked.
106: 5 that I may enjoy the *p*
122: 9 I will seek your *p*.
128: 2 blessings and *p* will be yours.
128: 5 may you see the *p* of Jerusalem,
Pr 3: 2 and bring you *p*.
8: 18 enduring wealth and *p*.
13: 21 but *p* is the reward of the righteous.
21: 21 finds life, *p* and honor.
Ecc 6: 3 if he cannot enjoy his *p*
6: 6 twice over but fails to enjoy his *p*.
Isa 45: 7 I bring *p* and create disaster;
Jer 17: 6 he will not see *p* when it comes.
29: 7 *p* of the city to which I have carried
32: 42 give them all the *p* I have promised
33: 9 and will tremble at the abundant *p*
39: 16 city through disaster, not *p*.
La 3: 17 I have forgotten what *p* is.
Da 4: 27 be that then your *p* will continue."
Zec 1: 17 towns will again overflow with *p*,

PROSPEROUS (PROSPER)

Ge 30: 43 way the man grew exceedingly *p*
Dt 30: 5 He will make you more *p*
30: 9 delight in you and make you *p*,
30: 9 your God will make you most *p*
Jos 1: 8 Then you will be *p* and successful.
Jdg 18: 7 land lacked nothing, they were *p*.
Job 8: 7 so *p* will your future be.
42: 10 the LORD made him *p* again
Ps 10: 5 His ways are always *p*;
Da 4: 4 in my palace, contented and *p*.
Zec 7: 7 towns were at rest and *p*,

PROSPERS (PROSPER)

Lev 25: 26 he himself *p* and acquires sufficient
25: 49 Or if he *p*, he may redeem himself.
Ps 1: 3 Whatever he does *p*.
Pr 16: 20 gives heed to instruction *p*,
19: 8 he who cherishes understanding *p*.
Jer 29: 7 because if it *p*, you too will prosper

PROSTITUTE (PROSTITUTE'S PROSTITUTED PROSTITUTES PROSTITUTING PROSTITUTION)

Ge 34: 31 he have treated our sister like a *p*?"
38: 15 he thought she was a *p*,
38: 21 hasn't been any shrine *p* here,"
38: 21 "Where is the shrine *p* who was
38: 22 hasn't been any shrine *p* here.' "
Ex 34: 15 for when they *p* themselves
34: 16 and those daughters *p* themselves
Lev 17: 7 idols to whom they *p* themselves.
19: 29 daughter by making her a *p*,
20: 6 and spiritists to *p* himself
21: 9 defiles herself by becoming a *p*,
Nu 15: 39 and not *p* yourselves by going
Dt 23: 17 or woman is to become a temple *p*.
23: 18 not bring the earnings of a female *p*
23: 18 or of a male *p* into the house
31: 16 people will soon *p* themselves
Jos 2: 1 the house of a *p* named Rahab
6: 17 Only Rahab the *p* and all who are
6: 25 But Joshua spared Rahab the *p*,
Jdg 11: 1 was Gilead; his mother was a *p*.
16: 1 went to Gaza, where he saw a *p*.
2Ch 21: 11 of Jerusalem to *p* themselves
21: 13 of Jerusalem to *p* themselves,
Pr 6: 26 for the *p* reduces you to a loaf
7: 10 like a *p* and with crafty intent.
23: 27 for a *p* is a deep pit
Isa 23: 15 to Tyre as in the song of the *p*:
23: 16 O *p* forgotten;
23: 17 She will return to her hire as a *p*
Jer 2: 20 you lay down as a *p*.
3: 1 as a *p* with many lovers—
3: 3 Yet you have the brazen look of a *p*
Eze 16: 15 and used your fame to become a *p*.
16: 30 these things, acting like a brazen *p*!
16: 31 were unlike a *p*, because you
16: 33 own husband! Every *p* receives
16: 35 you *p*, hear the word of the LORD!
23: 7 a *p* to all the elite of the Assyrians
23: 19 when she was a *p* in Egypt.
23: 43 'Now let them use her as a *p*,
23: 44 As men sleep with a *p*, so they slept
Hos 3: 3 you must not be a *p* or be intimate
9: 1 you love the wages of a *p*
Am 7: 17 " 'Your wife will become a *p*
1Co 6: 15 of Christ and unite them with a *p*?
6: 16 with a *p* is one with her in body?
Heb 11: 31 By faith the *p* Rahab, because she
Jas 2: 25 Rahab the *p* considered righteous

Rev 17: 1 you the punishment of the great *p*,
17: 15 where the *p* sits, are peoples,
17: 16 ten horns you saw will hate the *p*.
19: 2 He has condemned the great *p*

PROSTITUTE'S (PROSTITUTE)

Jos 6: 22 into the *p* house and bring her out

PROSTITUTED (PROSTITUTE)

Jdg 2: 17 but *p* themselves to other gods
8: 27 All Israel *p* themselves
8: 33 the Israelites again *p* themselves
1Ch 5: 25 and *p* themselves to the gods
Ps 106: 39 by their deeds they *p* themselves.

PROSTITUTES (PROSTITUTE)

1Ki 3: 16 Now two *p* came to the king
14: 24 even male shrine *p* in the land;
15: 12 He expelled the male shrine *p*
22: 38 in Samaria (where the *p* bathed)
22: 46 the male shrine *p* who remained
2Ki 23: 7 the quarters of the male shrine *p*,
Job 36: 14 among male *p* of the shrines.
Pr 29: 3 of *p* squanders his wealth.
Isa 57: 3 you offspring of adulterers and *p!*
Jer 5: 7 and thronged to the houses of *p*.
Eze 23: 3 They became *p* in Egypt, engaging
Hos 4: 14 and sacrifice with temple *p*—
Joel 3: 3 and traded boys for *p*;
Mic 1: 7 gifts from the wages of *p*,
1: 7 wages of *p* they will again be used."
Mt 21: 31 and the *p* are entering the kingdom
21: 32 but the tax collectors and the *p* did.
Lk 15: 30 property with *p* comes home,
1Co 6: 9 male *p* nor homosexual offenders
Rev 17: 5 THE MOTHER OF P

PROSTITUTING (PROSTITUTE)

Lev 20: 5 him in *p* themselves to Molech.

PROSTITUTION (PROSTITUTE)

Ge 38: 24 Tamar is guilty of *p*,
Lev 19: 29 the land will turn to *p* and be filled
21: 7 not marry women defiled by *p*
21: 14 or a woman defiled by *p*,
Jer 3: 2 land with your *p* and wickedness.
13: 27 your shameless *p!*
Eze 16: 16 where you carried on your *p*.
16: 17 and engaged in *p* with them.
16: 20 Was your *p* not enough? You
16: 22 and your *p* you did not remember
16: 26 engaged in *p* with the Egyptians,
16: 28 in *p* with the Assyrians too,
16: 34 So in your *p* you are the
16: 41 I will put a stop to your *p*,
23: 3 engaging in *p* from their youth.
23: 5 "Oholah engaged in *p*
23: 8 She did not give up the *p* she began
23: 11 and *p* she was more depraved
23: 14 "But she carried her *p* still further.
23: 18 When she carried on her *p* openly
23: 27 and *p* you began in Egypt.
23: 29 the shame of your *p* will be exposed
23: 35 of your lewdness and *p*."
43: 7 by their *p* and the lifeless idols
43: 9 let them put away from me their *p*
Hos 4: 10 engage in *p* but not increase,
4: 11 themselves to *p*,
4: 12 A spirit of *p* leads them astray;
4: 13 Therefore your daughters turn to *p*
4: 14 daughters when they turn to *p*,
4: 18 they continue their *p*;
5: 3 you have now turned to *p*;
5: 4 A spirit of *p* is in their heart;
6: 10 There Ephraim is given to *p*
Na 3: 4 who enslaved nations by her *p*

PROSTRATE (PROSTRATED)

Nu 24: 4 who falls *p*, and whose eyes are
24: 16 who falls *p*, and whose eyes are
Dt 9: 18 again I fell *p* before the LORD
9: 25 I lay *p* before the LORD those
2Sa 19: 18 he fell *p* before the king
1Ki 18: 39 they fell *p* and cried, "The LORD
1Ch 29: 20 and fell *p* before the LORD
Isa 15: 3 *p* with weeping.
51: 23 'Fall *p* that we may walk over you.'
Da 2: 46 Then King Nebuchadnezzar fell *p*
Da 8: 17 standing, I was terrified and fell *p*.

PROSTRATED (PROSTRATE)

1Sa 24: 8 and *p* himself with his face
28: 14 and *p* himself with his face

PROTECT (PROTECTED PROTECTION PROTECTIVE PROTECTS)

Nu 35: 25 assembly must *p* the one accused
Dt 23: 14 about in your camp to *p* you
2Sa 18: 12 '*P* the young man Absalom
Ezr 8: 22 and horsemen to *p* us from enemies
Est 8: 11 right to assemble and *p* themselves;
9: 16 also assembled to *p* themselves
Ps 12: 5 "I will *p* them from those who
12: 7 and *p* us from such people forever.
20: 1 of the God of Jacob *p* you.
25: 21 integrity and uprightness *p* me,
32: 7 you will *p* me from trouble
40: 11 your truth always *p* me.
41: 2 The LORD will *p* him
59: 1 *p* me from those who rise up
61: 7 your love and faithfulness to *p* him.
64: 1 *p* my life from the threat
69: 29 may your salvation, O God, *p* me.
91: 14 I will *p* him, for he acknowledges
140: 1 *p* me from men of violence,
140: 4 *p* me from men of violence
Pr 2: 11 Discretion will *p* you,
4: 6 forsake wisdom, and she will *p* you;
14: 3 but the lips of the wise *p* them.
Jer 49: 11 your orphans; I will *p* their lives.
Da 11: 1 stand to support and *p* him.)
Jn 17: 11 *p* them by the power of your name
17: 15 that you *p* them from the evil one.
2Th 3: 3 and *p* you from the evil one.

PROTECTED (PROTECT)

Jos 24: 17 He *p* us on our entire journey
1Sa 30: 23 He has *p* us and handed
Ezr 8: 31 and he *p* us from enemies
Job 5: 21 You will be *p* from the lash
Ps 37: 28 They will be *p* forever,
Mk 6: 20 Herod feared John and *p* him,
Jn 17: 12 I *p* them and kept them safe
2Pe 2: 5 but *p* Noah, a preacher

PROTECTION (PROTECT)

Ge 19: 8 come under the *p* of my roof."
Nu 14: 9 Their *p* is gone, but the LORD is
32: 17 for *p* from the inhabitants
Jos 20: 3 find *p* from the avenger of blood.
Ezr 9: 9 he has given us a wall of *p* in Judah
Ps 5: 11 Spread your *p* over them,
Isa 30: 2 who look for help to Pharaoh's *p*,
30: 3 Pharaoh's *p* will be to your shame,
Mic 1: 11 its *p* is taken from you.

PROTECTIVE (PROTECT)

Na 2: 5 the *p* shield is put in place.

PROTECTS (PROTECT)

Ps 34: 20 he *p* all his bones,
116: 6 The LORD *p* the simplehearted;
Pr 2: 8 and *p* the way of his faithful ones.
Da 12: 1 the great prince who *p* your people,
1Co 13: 7 It always *p*, always trusts,

PROTEST (PROTESTED)

Ecc 5: 6 do not *p* to the ⌊temple⌋ messenger,
Ac 13: 51 from their feet in *p* against them
18: 6 he shook out his clothes in *p*

PROTESTED (PROTEST)

Jn 8: 41 not illegitimate children," they *p*.
19: 21 priests of the Jews *p* to Pilate,

PROUD (PRIDE)

Dt 8: 14 then your heart will become *p*
2Ch 25: 19 and now you are arrogant and *p*.
32: 25 But Hezekiah's heart was *p*
Job 28: 8 *P* beasts do not set foot on it,
38: 11 here is where your *p* waves halt'?
39: 20 striking terror with his *p* snorting?
40: 11 at every *p* man and bring him low,
40: 12 at every *p* man and humble him,
41: 34 he is king over all that are *p*."
Ps 31: 23 but the *p* he pays back in full.
Ps 36: 11 of the *p* not come against me,
40: 4 who does not look to the *p*,
94: 2 to the *p* what they deserve.
101: 5 has haughty eyes and a *p* heart,
123: 4 endured much ridicule from the *p*,
131: 1 My heart is not *p*, O LORD,
138: 6 but the *p* he knows from afar.
140: 5 *P* men have hidden a snare for me;
140: 8 or they will become *p*.
Pr 3: 34 He mocks *p* mockers
15: 25 down the *p* man's house
16: 5 The LORD detests all the *p*
16: 19 than to share plunder with the *p*.
18: 12 his downfall a man's heart is *p*,
21: 4 Haughty eyes and a *p* heart,
21: 24 The *p* and arrogant man—
Isa 2: 12 store for all the *p* and lofty,
Eze 7: 20 They were *p* of their beautiful
28: 5 your heart has grown *p*.
28: 17 Your heart became *p*
30: 6 and her *p* strength will fail.
30: 18 there her *p* strength will come
31: 10 and because it was *p* of its height,
33: 28 her *p* strength will come to an end,
Hos 13: 6 they were satisfied, they became *p*;
Zec 10: 3 make them like a *p* horse in battle.
Lk 1: 51 he has scattered those who are *p*
Ro 12: 16 Do not be *p*, but be willing
1Co 5: 2 you are *p!* Shouldn't you rather
13: 4 it does not boast, it is not *p*.
2Ti 3: 2 lovers of money, boastful, *p*,
Jas 4: 6 "God opposes the *p*
1Pe 5: 5 because, "God opposes the *p*
Rev 13: 5 was given a mouth to utter *p* words

PROVE (PROOF PROOFS PROVED PROVES PROVING)

Ge 44: 16 How can we *p* our innocence?
Job 6: 25 But what do your arguments *p?*
24: 25 not so, who can *p* me false
Pr 29: 25 Fear of man will *p* to be a snare,
30: 6 he will rebuke you and *p* you a liar.
Isa 43: 9 witnesses to *p* they were right,
Jer 17: 11 and in the end he will *p* to be a fool.
Mic 1: 14 The town of Aczib will *p* deceptive
Hab 2: 3 and will not *p* false.
Jn 2: 18 to *p* your authority to do all this?"
8: 46 Can any of you *p* me guilty of sin?
Ac 24: 13 they cannot *p* to you the charges
25: 7 him, which they could not *p*.
26: 20 *p* their repentance by their deeds.
1Co 4: 2 been given a trust must *p* faithful.
2Co 9: 3 in this matter should not *p* hollow,
Gal 2: 18 I *p* that I am a lawbreaker.
Heb 9: 16 it is necessary to *p* the death

PROVED (PROVE)

Dt 13: 14 it has been *p* that this detestable
17: 4 it has been *p* that this detestable
1Ki 16: 22 But Omri's followers *p* stronger
Job 6: 21 you too have *p* to be of no help;
32: 12 But not one of you has *p* Job wrong
Ps 51: 4 so that you are *p* right
105: 19 the word of the LORD *p* him true.
Ecc 2: 1 But that also *p* to be meaningless.
Mt 11: 19 wisdom is *p* right by her actions."
Lk 7: 35 But wisdom is *p* right by all her
Ro 3: 4 "So that you may be *p* right
2Co 7: 11 every point you have *p* yourselves
7: 14 you to Titus has *p* to be true
8: 22 them our brother who has often *p*
9: 13 by which you have *p* yourselves,
Php 2: 22 know that Timothy has *p* himself,
Col 4: 11 and they have *p* a comfort to me.
1Pe 1: 7 may be *p* genuine and may result

PROVERB (PROVERBS)

Ps 49: 4 I will turn my ear to a *p*;
Pr 26: 7 is a *p* in the mouth of a fool.
26: 9 is a *p* in the mouth of a fool.
Eze 12: 22 what is this *p* you have in the land
12: 23 I am going to put an end to this *p*,
16: 44 will quote this *p* about you:
18: 2 by quoting this *p* about the land
18: 3 you will no longer quote this *p*
Lk 4: 23 "Surely you will quote this *p* to me:

PROVERBS (PROVERB)
1Ki 4:32 He spoke three thousand *p*
Job 13:12 Your maxims are *p* of ashes;
Pr 1: 1 The *p* of Solomon son of David,
1: 6 for understanding *p* and parables,
10: 1 The *p* of Solomon:
25: 1 These are more *p* of Solomon,
Ecc 12: 9 out and set in order many *p*.
Eze 16:44 who quotes *p* will quote
2Pe 2:22 Of them the *p* are true: "A dog

PROVES (PROVE)
Dt 19:18 and if the witness *p* to be a liar,

PROVIDE (PROVIDED PROVIDES PROVIDING PROVISION PROVISIONS)
Ge 22: 8 "God himself will *p* the lamb
22:14 that place "The LORD will *p*."
45:11 I will *p* for you there, because five
49:16 "Dan will *p* justice for his people
49:20 he will *p* delicacies fit for a king.
50:21 I will *p* for you and your children."
Ex 21:11 If he does not *p* her
27:16 *p* a curtain twenty cubits long,
Lev 25:24 you must *p* for the redemption
Dt 6:11 kinds of good things you did not *p*,
11:15 I will *p* grass in the fields
Jdg 21: 7 "How can we *p* wives
21:16 how shall we *p* wives
2Sa 7:10 I will *p* a place for my people Israel
19:33 in Jerusalem, and I will *p* for you."
1Ki 4: 7 Each one had to *p* supplies
5:17 of quality stone to *p* a foundation
1Ch 17: 9 I will *p* a place for my people Israel
22:14 pains to *p* for the temple
2Ch 2: 9 with yours to *p* me with plenty
Ezr 1: 4 are to *p* him with silver
7:20 you may *p* from the royal treasury.
7:21 treasurers of Trans-Euphrates to *p*
Ne 2: 7 so that they will *p* me safe-conduct
Ps 65: 9 water to *p* the people with grain,
Pr 27:26 the lambs will *p* you with clothing,
Isa 4: 1 and *p* our own clothes;
43:20 because I *p* water in the desert
50:11 *p* yourselves with flaming torches,
58: 7 to *p* the poor wanderer with shelter
61: 3 and *p* for those who grieve in Zion
Jer 33: 9 abundant prosperity and peace I *p*
Eze 34:29 I will *p* for them a land renowned
43:25 are to *p* a male goat daily
43:25 you are also to *p* a young bull
45:17 He will *p* the sin offerings,
45:17 the prince to *p* the burnt offerings,
45:22 On that day the prince is to *p* a bull
45:23 of the Feast he is to *p* seven bulls
45:24 is to *p* as a grain offering an ephah
46: 7 is to *p* as a grain offering one ephah
46:13 are to *p* a year-old lamb
46:13 morning by morning you shall *p* it.
46:14 also to *p* with it morning
Lk 12:33 *P* purses for yourselves that will
Ac 7:46 that he might *p* a dwelling place
11:29 to *p* help for the brothers living
23:24 *P* mounts for Paul
27: 3 so they might *p* for his needs.
1Co 10:13 *p* a way out so that you can stand
Col 4: 1 *p* your slaves with what is right
1Ti 5: 8 If anyone does not *p*
Tit 3:14 in order that they may *p*

PROVIDED (PROVIDE)
Ge 22:14 of the LORD it will be *p*."
43:24 and *p* fodder for their donkeys.
47:12 Joseph also *p* his father
Ru 3: 1 where you will be well *p* for?
1Sa 21: 4 *p* the men have kept themselves
2Sa 9:10 your master's grandson may be *p*
15: 1 Absalom *p* himself with a chariot
19:32 He had *p* for the king
20: 3 He *p* for them, but did not lie
1Ki 8:21 I have *p* a place there for the ark,
11:18 and land and *p* him with food.
2Ki 13: 5 The LORD *p* a deliverer for Israel,
1Ch 22: 3 He *p* a large amount of iron
22: 4 *p* more cedar logs than could be
23: 5 the musical instruments I have *p*
29: 2 With all my resources I have *p*
1Ch 29: 3 and above everything I have *p*
29:16 all this abundance that we have *p*
29:19 structure for which I have *p*."
2Ch 2: 7 whom my father David *p*.
3: 1 Araunah the Jebusite, the place *p*
26:14 Uzziah *p* shields, spears, helmets,
28:15 They *p* them with clothes
30:24 and the officials *p* them
30:24 king of Judah *p* a thousand bulls
35: 7 Josiah *p* for all the lay people who
35: 9 *p* five thousand Passover offerings
Ne 13: 5 and he had *p* him with a large room
Est 2: 9 Immediately he *p* her
Ps 68:10 O God, you *p* for the poor.
111: 9 He *p* redemption for his people;
Eze 16:19 Also the food I *p* for you—
46:15 and the oil shall be *p* morning
Jnh 1:17 But the LORD *p* a great fish
4: 6 Then the LORD God *p* a vine
4: 7 dawn the next day God *p* a worm,
4: 8 God *p* a scorching east wind,
Ro 11:22 *p* that you continue in his kindness.
Gal 4:18 to be zealous, *p* the purpose is good
Heb 1: 3 After he had *p* purification for sins,

PROVIDENCE
Job 10:12 in your *p* watched over my spirit.

PROVIDES (PROVIDE)
Job 24: 5 the wasteland *p* food
36:31 and *p* food in abundance.
38:41 Who *p* food for the raven
Ps 111: 5 He *p* food for those who fear him;
147: 9 He *p* food for the cattle
Pr 31:15 she *p* food for her family
Eze 18: 7 and *p* clothing for the naked.
18:16 and *p* clothing for the naked.
46:12 When the prince *p* a freewill
Ac 14:17 he *p* you with plenty of food
1Ti 6:17 who richly *p* us with everything
1Pe 4:11 it with the strength God *p*,

PROVIDING (PROVIDE)
Ru 1: 6 of his people by *p* food for them,
1Ki 5: 8 will do all you want in *p* the cedar
5: 9 are to grant my wish by *p* food
Ne 13: 7 in *p* Tobiah a room in the courts
Da 4:21 and abundant fruit, *p* food for all,

PROVINCE (PROVINCES PROVINCIAL)
Ezr 2: 1 the people of the *p* who came up
6: 2 of Ecbatana in the *p* of Media,
6: 6 their fellow officials of that *p*,
7:16 obtain from the *p* of Babylon,
Ne 1: 3 and are back in the *p* are
7: 6 the people of the *p* who came up
Est 1:22 to each *p* in its own script
2: 3 in every *p* of his realm
3:12 out in the script of each *p*
3:14 was to be issued as law in every *p*
4: 3 In every *p* to which the edict
8: 9 written in the script of each *p*
8:11 or *p* that might attack them
8:13 was to be issued as law in every *p*
8:17 In every *p* and in every city,
9:28 and in every *p* and in every city.
Da 2:48 ruler over the entire *p* of Babylon
2:49 over the *p* of Babylon,
3: 1 plain of Dura in the *p* of Babylon.
3:12 over the affairs of the *p* of Babylon
3:30 and Abednego in the *p* of Babylon.
8: 2 the citadel of Susa in the *p* of Elam;
Ac 16: 6 from preaching the word in the *p*
19:10 and Greeks who lived in the *p*
19:22 while he stayed in the *p*
19:26 in practically the whole *p* of Asia.
19:27 throughout the *p* of Asia
19:31 Even some of the officials of the *p*,
20: 4 and from the *p* of Asia Tychicus
20:16 to avoid spending time in the *p*
20:18 from the first day I came into the *p*
21:27 some Jews from the *p*
23:34 and asked what *p* he was from.
24:19 Jews from the *p* of Asia,
25: 1 Three days after arriving in the *p*,
27: 2 along the coast of the *p* of Asia,
Ro 16: 5 convert to Christ in the *p* of Asia.
1Co 16:19 The churches in the *p*
2Co 1: 8 the hardships we suffered in the *p*
2Ti 1:15 in the *p* of Asia has deserted me,
Rev 1: 4 To the seven churches in the *p*

PROVINCES (PROVINCE)
Ezr 4:15 troublesome to kings and *p*,
Est 1: 1 over 127 *p* stretching from India
1: 3 the nobles of the *p* were present.
1:16 peoples of all the *p* of King Xerxes.
2:18 a holiday throughout the *p*
3: 8 among the peoples in all the *p*
3:12 the governors of the various *p*
3:13 to all the king's *p* with the order
4:11 the people of the royal *p* know that
8: 5 destroy the Jews in all the king's *p*.
8: 9 of the 127 *p* stretching from India
8:12 the Jews to do this in all the *p*
9: 2 cities in all the *p* of King Xerxes
9: 3 And all the nobles of the *p*,
9: 4 spread throughout the *p*,
9:12 done in the rest of the king's *p*?
9:16 the Jews who were in the king's *p*
9:20 throughout the *p* of King Xerxes,
9:30 Jews in the 127 *p* of the kingdom
Ecc 2: 8 and the treasure of kings and *p*.
La 1: 1 She who was queen among the *p*
Da 11:24 When the richest *p* feel secure,
Ac 6: 9 as well as the *p* of Cilicia and Asia.

PROVINCIAL (PROVINCE)
1Ki 20:14 of the *p* commanders will do it.' "
20:15 officers of the *p* commanders,
20:17 of the *p* commanders went out first
20:19 of the *p* commanders marched out
Ne 11: 3 These are the *p* leaders who settled
Da 3: 2 and all the other *p* officials to come
3: 3 all the other *p* officials assembled

PROVING (PROVE)
Ac 9:22 by *p* that Jesus is the Christ.
17: 3 and *p* that the Christ had to suffer
18:28 *p* from the Scriptures that Jesus

PROVISION (PROVIDE)
Ne 13:31 made *p* for contributions of wood
Ps 144: 13 with every kind of *p*.
Eze 45:25 to make the same *p* for sin offerings
Ro 5:17 who receive God's abundant *p*

PROVISIONS (PROVIDE)
Ge 42:25 and to give them *p* for their journey
45:21 also gave them *p* for their journey.
45:23 bread and other *p* for his journey.
Jos 9:11 'Take *p* for your journey; go
9:14 The men of Israel sampled their *p*
Jdg 7: 8 who took over the *p* and trumpets
20:10 to get *p* for the army.
1Sa 22:10 also gave him *p* and the sword
2Sa 19:42 Have we eaten any of the king's *p*?
1Ki 4: 7 who supplied *p* for the king
4:22 Solomon's daily *p* were thirty cors
4:27 supplied *p* for King Solomon
20:27 also mustered and given *p*,
1Ch 12:39 for their families had supplied *p*
2Ch 11:23 He gave them abundant *p*
Ps 132: 15 I will bless her with abundant *p*;
Pr 6: 8 yet it stores its *p* in summer
Jer 40: 5 Then the commander gave him *p*
Da 11:26 eat from the king's *p* will try

PROVOCATION (PROVOKE)
Pr 27: 3 but *p* by a fool is heavier than both.

PROVOKE (PROVOCATION PROVOKED PROVOKES PROVOKING)
Dt 2: 5 Do not *p* them to war,
2: 9 not harass the Moabites or *p* them
2:19 do not harass them or *p* them
31:29 *p* him to anger by what your hands
1Ki 16: 2 and to *p* me to anger by their sins.
16:33 and did more to *p* the LORD,
2Ki 23:26 that Manasseh had done to *p* him
Job 12: 6 and those who *p* God are secure—
Isa 65: 3 a people who continually *p* me
Jer 7:18 to other gods to *p* me to anger.
25: 6 do not *p* me to anger
32:30 *p* me with what their hands have
44: 8 Why *p* me to anger

Eze 8: 17 and continually *p* me to anger?

PROVOKED (PROVOKE)

Dt 9: 7 forget how you *p* the LORD your
Jdg 2: 12 They *p* the LORD to anger
1Sa 1: 7 her rival *p* her till she wept
1Ki 14: 9 you have *p* me to anger
14: 15 because they *p* the LORD to anger
15: 30 and because he *p* the LORD,
16: 13 so that they *p* the LORD, the God
16: 26 so that they *p* the LORD, the God
21: 22 because you have *p* me to anger
22: 53 worshiped Baal and *p* the LORD,
2Ki 17: 11 did wicked things that *p* the LORD
21: 15 and have *p* me to anger
22: 17 *p* me to anger by all the idols their
23: 19 of Samaria that had *p* the LORD
2Ch 28: 25 to other gods and *p* the LORD,
34: 25 and *p* me to anger by all that their
Ps 106: 29 they *p* the LORD to anger
Ecc 7: 9 Do not be quickly *p* in your spirit,
Jer 8: 19 "Why have they *p* me to anger
11: 17 *p* me to anger by burning incense
25: 7 you have *p* me with what your
32: 29 the houses where the people *p* me
32: 32 Judah have *p* me by all the evil they
44: 3 They *p* me to anger
Eze 16: 26 *p* me to anger with your increasing
20: 28 made offerings that *p* me to anger,
Hos 12: 14 But Ephraim has bitterly *p* him

PROVOKES (PROVOKE)

Eze 8: 3 where the idol that *p*

PROVOKING (PROVOKE)

Dt 4: 25 of the LORD your God and *p* him
9: 18 in the LORD's sight and so *p* him
1Sa 1: 6 her rival kept *p* her in order
1Ki 16: 7 *p* him to anger by the things he did,
2Ki 17: 17 eyes of the LORD, *p* him to anger.
21: 6 eyes of the LORD, *p* him to anger.
2Ch 33: 6 eyes of the LORD, *p* him to anger.
Jer 7: 19 But am I the one they are *p?*
Gal 5: 26 *p* and envying each other.

PROWL (PROWLED PROWLING PROWLS)

Ps 55: 10 night they *p* about on its walls;
59: 6 and *p* about the city.
59: 14 and *p* about the city.
104: 20 and all the beasts of the forest *p*.

PROWLED (PROWL)

Eze 19: 6 He *p* among the lions,

PROWLING (PROWL)

La 5: 18 with jackals *p* over it.

PROWLS (PROWL)

Job 28: 8 and no lion *p* there.
1Pe 5: 8 Your enemy the devil *p*

PRUDENCE (PRUDENT)

Pr 1: 4 for giving *p* to the simple,
8: 5 You who are simple, gain *p;*
8: 12 "I, wisdom, dwell together with *p;*
15: 5 whoever heeds correction shows *p*.
19: 25 and the simple will learn *p;*

PRUDENT (PRUDENCE)

Pr 1: 3 acquiring a disciplined and *p* life,
12: 16 but a *p* man overlooks an insult.
12: 23 A *p* man keeps his knowledge
13: 16 Every *p* man acts out of knowledge
14: 8 The wisdom of the *p* is
14: 15 a *p* man gives thought to his steps.
14: 18 the *p* are crowned with knowledge.
19: 14 but a *p* wife is from the LORD.
22: 3 *p* man sees danger and takes
27: 12 The *p* see danger and take refuge,
Jer 49: 7 Has counsel perished from the *p?*
Am 5: 13 Therefore the *p* man keeps quiet

PRUNE (PRUNED PRUNING)

Lev 25: 3 and for six years *p* your vineyards
25: 4 your fields or *p* your vineyards.

PRUNED (PRUNE)

Isa 5: 6 neither *p* nor cultivated,

PRUNING (PRUNE)

Isa 2: 4 and their spears into *p* hooks.
18: 5 cut off the shoots with *p* knives,
Joel 3: 10 and your *p* hooks into spears.
Mic 4: 3 and their spears into *p* hooks.

PSALM (PSALMS)

1Ch 16: 7 his associates this *p* of thanks
Ps 47: 7 sing to him a *p* of praise.
Ac 13: 33 As it is written in the second *P:*

PSALMS (PSALM)

Lk 20: 42 himself declares in the Book of *P:*
24: 44 of Moses, the Prophets and the *P*."
Ac 1: 20 "it is written in the book of *P*,
Eph 5: 19 Speak to one another with *p*,
Col 3: 16 and as you sing *p*, hymns

PTOLEMAIS

Ac 21: 7 voyage from Tyre and landed at *P*,

PUAH (PUITE)

Ge 46: 13 Tola, *P*, Jashub and Shimron.
Ex 1: 15 whose names were Shiphrah and *P*,
Nu 26: 23 the Tolaite clan; through *P*,
Jdg 10: 1 Tola son of *P*, the son of Dodo,
1Ch 7: 1 Tola, *P*, Jashub and Shimron—

PUBLIC (PUBLICLY)

Lev 5: 1 when he hears a *p* charge to testify
Dt 13: 16 into the middle of the *p* square
2Sa 21: 12 secretly from the *p* square at Beth
Job 29: 7 and took my seat in the *p* square,
Pr 1: 20 she raises her voice in the *p* squares
5: 16 streams of water in the *p* squares?
Isa 15: 3 on the roofs and in the *p* squares
Jer 9: 21 the young men from the *p* squares.
48: 38 and in the *p* squares
Eze 16: 24 a lofty shrine in every *p* square.
16: 31 lofty shrines in every *p* square,
Am 5: 16 cries of anguish in every *p* square.
Mt 1: 19 want to expose her to *p* disgrace,
Lk 20: 26 him in what he had said there in *p*.
Jn 7: 4 to become a *p* figure acts in secret.
Ac 5: 18 apostles and put them in the *p* jail.
12: 4 out for *p* trial after the Passover.
12: 21 delivered a *p* address to the people.
18: 28 refuted the Jews in *p* debate,
Ro 16: 23 who is the city's director of *p* works
Col 2: 15 he made a *p* spectacle of them,
1Ti 4: 13 to the *p* reading of Scripture,
Heb 6: 6 and subjecting him to *p* disgrace.

PUBLICLY (PUBLIC)

Lk 1: 80 desert until he appeared *p* to Israel.
Jn 7: 10 he went also, not *p*, but in secret.
7: 13 would say anything *p* about him
7: 26 speaking *p*, and they are not saying
11: 54 Jesus no longer moved about *p*
Ac 16: 37 "They beat us *p* without a trial,
19: 9 to believe and *p* maligned the Way.
19: 19 scrolls together and burned them *p*.
20: 20 have taught you *p* and from house
1Ti 5: 20 Those who sin are to be rebuked *p*,
Heb 10: 33 Sometimes you were *p* exposed

PUBLISH (PUBLISHED)

Da 6: 12 "Did you not *p* a decree that

PUBLISHED (PUBLISH)

Est 4: 8 which had been *p* in Susa,
Da 6: 10 learned that the decree had been *p*,

PUBLIUS

Ac 28: 7 estate nearby that belonged to *P*,

PUDENS

2Ti 4: 21 Eubulus greets you, and so do *P*,

PUFFED (PUFFS)

Hab 2: 4 "See, he is *p* up;

PUFFS (PUFFED)

1Co 8: 1 Knowledge *p* up, but love builds up
Col 2: 18 and his unspiritual mind *p* him up

PUITE (PUAH)

Nu 26: 23 the *P* clan; through Jashub,

PUL

2Ki 15: 19 *P* king of Assyria invaded the land,
1Ch 5: 26 spirit of *P* king of Assyria (that is,

PULL (PULLED PULLING PULLS)

Jdg 3: 22 Ehud did not *p* the sword out,
Ru 2: 16 *p* out some stalks for her
1Ki 13: 4 so that he could not *p* it back.
Job 41: 1 "Can you *p* in the leviathan
Jer 13: 26 I will *p* up your skirts
22: 24 my right hand, I would still *p* you
Eze 17: 9 many people to *p* it up by the roots.
26: 4 of Tyre and *p* down her towers;
29: 4 *p* you out from among your
Hos 7: 12 I will *p* them down like birds
Am 3: 11 he will *p* down your strongholds
Mt 9: 16 for the patch will *p* away
13: 28 us to go and *p* them up?'
Mk 2: 21 the new piece will *p* away
Lk 14: 5 will you not immediately *p* him out

PULLED (PULL)

Ge 19: 10 and *p* Lot back into the house
37: 28 his brothers *p* Joseph up out
Jdg 8: 17 He also *p* down the tower of Peniel
16: 14 from his sleep and *p* up the pin
1Ki 19: 13 he *p* his cloak over his face
2Ki 23: 12 He *p* down the altars the kings
Ezr 6: 11 a beam is to be *p* from his house
9: 3 *p* hair from my head and beard
Ne 13: 25 of the men and *p* out their hair.
Job 4: 21 Are not the cords of their tent *p* up,
Isa 33: 20 its stakes will never be *p* up,
38: 12 has been *p* down and taken
50: 6 to those who *p* out my beard;
Jer 38: 13 and they *p* him up with the ropes
Eze 19: 9 With hooks they *p* him into a cage
Mt 13: 40 "As the weeds are *p* up
13: 48 the fishermen *p* it up on the shore.
15: 13 Father has not planted will be *p* up
Lk 5: 11 So they *p* their boats up on shore,
Ac 11: 10 then it was all *p* up to heaven again.

PULLING (PULL)

Mt 13: 29 'because while you are *p* the weeds,
2Co 10: 8 building you up rather than *p* you

PULLS (PULL)

Job 20: 25 He *p* it out of his back,
Pr 21: 22 *p* down the stronghold
Hab 1: 15 The wicked foe *p* all of them up

PUNISH (PUNISHED PUNISHES PUNISHING PUNISHMENT PUNISHMENTS)

Ge 15: 14 But I will *p* the nation they serve
Ex 32: 34 I will *p* them for their sin."
32: 34 when the time comes for me to *p*,
Lev 26: 18 I will *p* you for your sins seven
26: 28 and I myself will *p* you
Dt 22: 18 shall take the man and *p* him.
1Sa 15: 2 'I will *p* the Amalekites
2Sa 7: 14 I will *p* him with the rod of men,
Job 37: 13 He brings the clouds to *p* men,
Ps 59: 5 rouse yourself to *p* all the nations;
89: 32 I will *p* their sin with the rod,
94: 10 he who disciplines nations not *p?*
119: 84 When will you *p* my persecutors?
120: 4 He will *p* you with a warrior's sharp
Pr 17: 26 It is not good to *p* an innocent man,
23: 13 if you *p* him with the rod, he will
23: 14 *P* him with the rod
Isa 10: 12 "I will *p* the king of Assyria
13: 11 I will *p* the world for its evil,
24: 21 In that day the LORD will *p*
26: 21 to *p* the people of the earth
27: 1 the LORD will *p* with his sword,
64: 12 and *p* us beyond measure?
Jer 2: 19 Your wickedness will *p* you;
5: 9 Should I not *p* them for this?"
5: 29 Should I not *p* them for this?"
6: 15 brought down when I *p* them,"
9: 9 Should I not *p* them for this?"
9: 25 "when I will *p* all who are
11: 22 Almighty says: 'I will *p* them.

Jer 14: 10 and *p* them for their sins.''
21: 14 I will *p* you as your deeds deserve,
23: 34 I will *p* that man and his household
25: 12 I will *p* the king of Babylon
27: 8 I will *p* that nation with the sword,
29: 32 I will surely *p* Shemaiah
30: 20 I will *p* all who oppress them.
36: 31 I will *p* him and his children
44: 13 I will *p* those who live in Egypt
44: 29 to you that I will *p* you in this place
49: 8 Esau at the time I *p* him.
50: 18 ''I will *p* the king of Babylon
51: 44 I will *p* Bel in Babylon
51: 47 when I will *p* the idols of Babylon;
51: 52 ''when I will *p* her idols,
La 4: 22 of Edom, he will *p* your sin
Eze 7: 11 grown into a rod to *p* wickedness;
23: 24 and they will *p* you according
25: 17 on them and *p* them in my wrath.
Hos 1: 4 I will soon *p* the house of Jehu
2: 13 I will *p* her for the days
4: 9 I will *p* both of them for their ways
4: 14 ''I will not *p* your daughters
8: 13 and *p* their sins:
9: 9 and *p* them for their sins.
10: 10 When I please, I will *p* them;
12: 2 he will *p* Jacob according
Am 3: 2 therefore I will *p* you
3: 14 ''On the day I *p* Israel for her sins,
Hab 1: 12 you have ordained them to *p*.
Zep 1: 8 I will *p* the princes
1: 9 On that day I will *p*
1: 12 and *p* those who are complacent,
Zec 10: 3 and I will *p* the leaders;
Lk 23: 16 I will *p* him and then release him.''
Ac 4: 21 could not decide how to *p* them,
7: 7 But I will *p* the nation they serve
2Co 10: 6 to *p* every act of disobedience,
1Th 4: 6 The Lord will *p* men
2Th 1: 8 He will *p* those who do not know
1Pe 2: 14 by him to *p* those who do wrong

PUNISHED (PUNISH)

Ge 19: 15 away when the city is *p*.''
42: 21 ''Surely we are being *p*
Ex 21: 20 he must be *p*, but he is not
21: 21 he is not to be *p* if the slave gets up
Lev 18: 25 Even the land was defiled; so I *p* it
1Sa 28: 10 you will not be *p* for this.''
1Ch 21: 7 in the sight of God; so he *p* Israel.
Ezr 7: 26 the law of the king must surely be *p*
9: 13 you have *p* us less than our sins
Ps 73: 14 I have been *p* every morning.
99: 8 though you *p* their misdeeds.
Pr 21: 11 a mocker is *p*, the simple gain
Isa 24: 22 and be *p* after many days.
26: 14 You *p* them and brought them
57: 17 I *p* him, and hid my face in anger,
Jer 2: 30 ''In vain I *p* your people;
6: 6 This city must be *p*;
8: 12 brought down when they are *p*,
23: 12 them in the year they are *p*,''
30: 14 and *p* you as would the cruel,
44: 13 famine and plague, as I *p* Jerusalem
46: 21 the time for them to be *p*.
50: 18 as I *p* the king of Assyria.
50: 27 the time for them to be *p*.
50: 31 the time for you to be *p*.
La 3: 39 complain when *p* for his sins?
Mk 12: 40 Such men will be *p* most severely.''
Lk 20: 47 Such men will be *p* most severely.''
23: 22 Therefore I will have him *p*
23: 41 the same sentence? We are *p* justly,
Ac 22: 5 as prisoners to Jerusalem to be *p*.
26: 11 to another to have them *p*,
2Th 1: 9 be *p* with everlasting destruction
Heb 10: 29 to be *p* who has trampled the Son

PUNISHES (PUNISH)

Ex 34: 7 he *p* the children and their children
Nu 14: 18 he *p* the children for the sin
Job 34: 26 He *p* them for their wickedness
35: 15 and further, that his anger never *p*
Heb 12: 6 and he *p* everyone he accepts

PUNISHING (PUNISH)

Ex 20: 5 *p* the children for the sin
Dt 5: 9 *p* the children for the sin
Jdg 8: 16 lesson by *p* them with desert thorns
Isa 30: 32 them with his *p* rod

PUNISHMENT (PUNISH)

Ge 4: 13 ''My *p* is more than I can bear.
Lev 19: 20 her freedom, there must be due *p*.
1Sa 14: 47 Wherever he turned, he inflicted *p*
2Ki 7: 9 until daylight, *p* will overtake us.
Job 19: 29 for wrath will bring *p* by the sword,
21: 19 'God stores up a man's *p*
Ps 81: 15 and their *p* would last forever.
91: 8 and see the *p* of the wicked.
149: 7 and *p* on the peoples,
Pr 10: 16 of the wicked brings them *p*.
16: 22 but folly brings *p* to fools.
Isa 53: 5 the *p* that brought us peace was
Jer 4: 18 This is your *p*.
11: 15 consecrated meat avert ⌊your *p*⌋?
11: 23 of Anathoth in the year of their *p*
23: 2 I will bestow *p* on you
32: 18 but bring the *p* for the fathers' sins
46: 25 I am about to bring *p* on Amon god
48: 44 the year of her *p*,''
La 4: 6 The *p* of my people
4: 22 of Zion, your *p* will end;
5: 7 and we bear their *p*.
Eze 5: 8 I will inflict *p* on you in the sight
5: 10 I will inflict *p* on you and will
5: 15 you when I inflict *p* on you in anger
11: 9 to foreigners and inflict *p* on you.
16: 38 you to the *p* of women who commit
16: 41 and inflict *p* on you in the sight
21: 25 time of *p* has reached its climax,
21: 29 time of *p* has reached its climax.
23: 10 and *p* was inflicted on her.
23: 24 I will turn you over to them for *p*,
23: 45 to the *p* of women who commit
25: 11 and I will inflict *p* on Moab.
28: 22 when I inflict *p* on her
28: 26 live in safety when I inflict *p*
30: 14 and inflict *p* on Thebes.
30: 19 So I will inflict *p* on Egypt,
32: 27 The *p* for their sins rested
35: 5 the time their *p* reached its climax,
39: 21 all the nations will see the *p* I inflict
Hos 9: 7 The days of *p* are coming,
Zep 3: 15 The LORD has taken away your *p*,
Zec 14: 19 This will be the *p* of Egypt
14: 19 *p* of all the nations that do not go
Mt 25: 46 Then they will go away to eternal *p*
Lk 12: 48 and does things deserving *p* will be
21: 22 For this is the time of *p*
Ro 13: 4 wrath to bring *p* on the wrongdoer.
13: 5 not only because of possible *p* but
2Co 2: 6 The *p* inflicted on him
Heb 2: 2 disobedience received its just *p*,
2Pe 2: 9 while continuing their *p*.
1Jn 4: 18 because fear has to do with *p*.
Jude : 7 example of those who suffer the *p*
Rev 17: 1 I will show you the *p*

PUNISHMENTS (PUNISH)

Zep 3: 7 nor all my *p* come upon her.

PUNON

Nu 33: 42 left Zalmonah and camped at *P*.
33: 43 They left *P* and camped at Oboth.

PUR

Est 3: 7 of Nisan, they cast the *p* (that is,
9: 24 and had cast the *p* (that is,
9: 26 called Purim, from the word *p*.)

PURAH

Jdg 7: 10 to the camp with your servant *P*
7: 11 and *P* his servant went

PURCHASE (PURCHASED)

2Ki 22: 6 Also have them *p* timber
2Ch 34: 11 and builders to *p* dressed stone,
Pr 20: 14 off he goes and boasts about his *p*.
Jer 32: 11 of *p*— the sealed copy containing
32: 14 unsealed copies of the deed of *p*,
32: 16 deed of *p* to Baruch son of Neriah,

PURCHASED (PURCHASE)

1Ki 10: 28 the royal merchants *p* them
2Ki 12: 12 They *p* timber and dressed stone
2Ch 1: 16 the royal merchants *p* them
Ps 74: 2 Remember the people you *p* of old,
Rev 5: 9 with your blood you *p* men for God
14: 4 They were *p* from among men

PURE (PUREST PURIFICATION PURIFIED PURIFIER PURIFIES PURIFY PURIFYING PURITY)

Ex 25: 11 Overlay it with *p* gold, both inside
25: 17 Make an atonement cover of *p* gold
25: 24 Overlay it with *p* gold
25: 29 make its plates and ladles of *p* gold,
25: 31 ''Make a lampstand of *p* gold
25: 36 hammered out of *p* gold.
25: 38 and trays are to be of *p* gold.
25: 39 A talent of *p* gold is to be used
28: 14 and two braided chains of *p* gold,
28: 22 make braided chains of *p* gold,
28: 36 ''Make a plate of *p* gold
30: 3 and the horns with *p* gold,
30: 34 galbanum—and *p* frankincense,
30: 35 It is to be salted and *p* and sacred.
31: 8 the *p* gold lampstand and all its
37: 2 He overlaid it with *p* gold,
37: 6 the atonement cover of *p* gold—
37: 11 Then they overlaid it with *p* gold
37: 16 they made from *p* gold the articles
37: 17 They made the lampstand of *p* gold
37: 22 hammered out of *p* gold.
37: 23 wick trimmers and trays, of *p* gold.
37: 24 from one talent of *p* gold.
37: 26 and the horns with *p* gold,
37: 29 the sacred anointing oil and the *p*,
39: 15 they made braided chains of *p* gold,
39: 25 And they made bells of *p* gold
39: 30 out of *p* gold and engraved on it,
39: 37 the *p* gold lampstand with its row
Lev 24: 4 The lamps on the *p* gold lampstand
24: 6 on the table of *p* gold
24: 7 Along each row put some *p* incense
2Sa 22: 27 to the *p* you show yourself *p*,
1Ki 6: 20 He overlaid the inside with *p* gold,
6: 21 inside of the temple with *p* gold,
7: 49 the lampstands of *p* gold (five
7: 50 the *p* gold dishes, wick trimmers,
10: 21 the Forest of Lebanon were *p* gold.
1Ch 28: 17 the weight of *p* gold for the forks,
2Ch 3: 4 He overlaid the inside with *p* gold.
4: 20 the lampstands of *p* gold
4: 22 *p* gold wick trimmers, sprinkling
9: 17 with ivory and overlaid with *p* gold
9: 20 the Forest of Lebanon were *p* gold.
Job 4: 17 Can a man be more *p*
8: 6 if you are *p* and upright,
11: 4 and I am *p* in your sight.'
14: 4 Who can bring what is *p*
15: 14 ''What is man, that he could be *p*,
15: 15 the heavens are not *p* in his eyes,
16: 17 and my prayer is *p*.
25: 4 How can one born of woman be *p*?
25: 5 and the stars are not *p* in his eyes,
28: 19 it cannot be bought with *p* gold.
31: 24 said to *p* gold, 'You are my security
33: 9 'I am *p* and without sin;
Ps 18: 26 to the *p* you show yourself *p*,
19: 9 The fear of the LORD is *p*,
19: 10 than much *p* gold;
21: 3 placed a crown of *p* gold
24: 4 who has clean hands and a *p* heart,
51: 10 Create in me a *p* heart, O God,
73: 1 to those who are *p* in heart.
73: 13 in vain have I kept my heart *p*;
119: 9 can a young man keep his way *p*?
119:127 more than gold, more than *p* gold,
Pr 15: 26 those of the *p* are pleasing to him.
20: 9 can say, ''I have kept my heart *p*;
20: 11 his conduct is *p* and right.
22: 11 He who loves a *p* heart
30: 12 those who are *p* in their own eyes
SS 5: 15 set on bases of *p* gold.
Isa 13: 12 I will make man scarcer than *p* gold
52: 11 Come out from it and be *p*,
Da 2: 32 of the statue was made of *p* gold,
Hab 1: 13 Your eyes are too *p* to look on evil;
Mal 1: 11 and *p* offerings will be brought
Mt 5: 8 Blessed are the *p* in heart,
Mk 14: 3 perfume, made of *p* nard.
Jn 12: 3 Mary took about a pint of *p* nard,

2Co 11: 2 I might present you as a *p* virgin
11: 3 from your sincere and *p* devotion
Php 1: 10 and may be *p* and blameless
2: 15 you may become blameless and *p*,
4: 8 whatever is *p*, whatever is lovely,
1Ti 1: 5 which comes from a *p* heart
5: 22 Keep yourself *p*.
2Ti 2: 22 call on the Lord out of a *p* heart.
Tit 1: 15 To the *p*, all things are *p*,
1: 15 and do not believe, nothing is *p*.
2: 5 to be self-controlled and *p*,
Heb 7: 26 blameless, *p*, set apart from sinners
10: 22 our bodies washed with *p* water.
13: 4 and the marriage bed kept *p*,
Jas 1: 2 Consider it *p* joy, my brothers,
1: 27 that God our Father accepts as *p*
3: 17 comes from heaven is first of all *p*;
1Pe 2: 2 babies, crave *p* spiritual milk,
1Jn 3: 3 him purifies himself, just as he is *p*.
Rev 14: 4 for they kept themselves *p*.
21: 18 and the city of *p* gold, as *p* as glass.
21: 21 The street of the city was of *p* gold,

PUREST (PURE)

SS 5: 11 His head is *p* gold;

PURGE (PURGED)

Dt 13: 5 You must *p* the evil
17: 7 You must *p* the evil
17: 12 You must *p* the evil from Israel.
19: 13 You must *p* from Israel the guilt
19: 19 You must *p* the evil
21: 9 you will *p* from yourselves the guilt
21: 21 You must *p* the evil
22: 21 You must *p* the evil
22: 22 You must *p* the evil from Israel.
22: 24 You must *p* the evil
24: 7 You must *p* the evil
Jdg 20: 13 and *p* the evil from Israel."
2Ch 34: 3 twelfth year he began to *p* Judah
Pr 20: 30 and beatings *p* the inmost being.
Isa 1: 25 I will thoroughly *p* away your dross
Eze 20: 38 I will *p* you of those who revolt

PURGED (PURGE)

2Ch 34: 5 and so he *p* Judah and Jerusalem.
Jer 6: 29 the wicked are not *p* out.

PURIFICATION (PURE)

Lev 12: 4 until the days of her *p* are over.
12: 6 " 'When the days of her *p* for a son
Nu 19: 9 of cleansing; it is for *p* from sin.
19: 17 ashes from the burned *p* offering
1Ch 23: 28 the *p* of all sacred things
Ne 12: 45 of their God and the service of *p*,
Lk 2: 22 of their *p* according to the Law
Ac 21: 24 join in their *p* rites and pay their
21: 26 date when the days of *p* would end
Heb 1: 3 After he had provided *p* for sins,

PURIFIED (PURE)

Lev 12: 4 days to be *p* from her bleeding.
12: 5 days to be *p* from her bleeding.
Nu 8: 15 "After you have *p* the Levites
8: 21 The Levites *p* themselves
31: 23 be *p* with the water of cleansing.
2Sa 11: 4 (She had *p* herself
2Ch 29: 18 "We have *p* the entire temple
30: 18 and Zebulun had not *p* themselves,
Ezr 6: 20 and Levites had *p* themselves
Ne 12: 30 and Levites had *p* themselves
12: 30 they *p* the people, the gates
13: 30 So I *p* the priests and the Levites
Job 1: 5 Job would send and have them *p*.
Ps 12: 6 *p* seven times.
Eze 43: 22 is to be *p* as it was *p* with the bull.
Da 11: 35 *p* and made spotless until the time
12: 10 Many will be *p*, made spotless
Ac 15: 9 for he *p* their hearts by faith.
21: 26 and *p* himself along with them.
Heb 9: 23 things to be *p* with these sacrifices,
1Pe 1: 22 Now that you have *p* yourselves

PURIFIER (PURE)

Mal 3: 3 as a refiner and *p* of silver;

PURIFIES (PURE)

1Jn 1: 7 of Jesus, his Son, *p* us from all sin.
1Jn 3: 3 who has this hope in him *p* himself,

PURIFY (PURE)

Ge 35: 2 and *p* yourselves and change your
Ex 29: 36 *P* the altar by making atonement
Lev 8: 15 the horns of the altar to *p* the altar.
14: 49 To *p* the house he is
14: 52 He shall *p* the house
Nu 8: 7 To *p* them, do this: Sprinkle
8: 7 their clothes, and so *p* themselves.
8: 21 atonement for them to *p* them.
19: 12 He must *p* himself with the water
19: 12 if he does not *p* himself on the third
19: 13 to *p* himself defiles the LORD's
19: 19 on the seventh day he is to *p* him.
19: 20 who is unclean does not *p* himself,
31: 19 days you must *p* yourselves
31: 20 *P* every garment as well
2Ch 29: 15 they went in to *p* the temple
29: 16 the sanctuary of the LORD to *p* it.
34: 8 to *p* the land and the temple,
Ne 13: 9 I gave orders to *p* the rooms,
13: 22 the Levites to *p* themselves
Isa 66: 17 *p* themselves to go into the gardens
Eze 43: 20 so *p* the altar and make atonement
45: 18 without defect and *p* the sanctuary.
Zep 3: 9 Then will I *p* the lips of the peoples,
Mal 3: 3 he will *p* the Levites and refine
2Co 7: 1 us *p* ourselves from everything that
Tit 2: 14 to *p* for himself a people that are
Jas 4: 8 you sinners, and *p* your hearts,
1Jn 1: 9 and *p* us from all unrighteousness.

PURIFYING (PURE)

Eze 43: 23 When you have finished *p* it,

PURIM

Est 9: 26 Therefore these days were called *P*
9: 28 these days of *P* should never cease
9: 29 this second letter concerning *P*.
9: 31 days of *P* at their designated times,
9: 32 these regulations about *P*,

PURITY (PURE)

Hos 8: 5 long will they be incapable of *p*?
2Co 6: 6 in *p*, understanding, patience
1Ti 4: 12 in life, in love, in faith and in *p*.
5: 2 as sisters, with absolute *p*.
1Pe 3: 2 when they see the *p* and reverence

PURPLE

Ex 25: 4 *p* and scarlet yarn and fine linen;
26: 1 and blue, *p* and scarlet yarn,
26: 31 *p* and scarlet yarn and finely
26: 36 *p* and scarlet yarn and finely
27: 16 *p* and scarlet yarn and finely
28: 5 and blue, *p* and scarlet yarn,
28: 6 and of blue, *p* and scarlet yarn,
28: 8 and with blue, *p* and scarlet yarn,
28: 15 and of blue, *p* and scarlet yarn,
28: 33 *p* and scarlet yarn around the hem
35: 6 *p* and scarlet yarn and fine linen;
35: 23 *p* or scarlet yarn or fine linen,
35: 25 blue, *p* or scarlet yarn or fine linen.
35: 35 *p* and scarlet yarn and fine linen,
36: 8 *p* and scarlet yarn,
36: 35 *p* and scarlet yarn and finely
36: 37 *p* and scarlet yarn and finely
38: 18 *p* and scarlet yarn and finely
38: 23 *p* and scarlet yarn and fine linen.)
39: 1 *p* and scarlet yarn they made
39: 2 and of blue, *p* and scarlet yarn,
39: 3 *p* and scarlet yarn and fine linen—
39: 5 and with blue, *p* and scarlet yarn,
39: 8 and of blue, *p* and scarlet yarn,
39: 24 *p* and scarlet yarn and finely
39: 29 *p* and scarlet yarn—the work
Nu 4: 13 and spread a *p* cloth over it.
Jdg 8: 26 the *p* garments worn by the kings
2Ch 2: 7 and in *p*, crimson and blue yarn,
2: 14 with *p* and blue and crimson yarn
3: 14 *p* and crimson yarn and fine linen,
Est 1: 6 and *p* material to silver rings
8: 15 of gold and a *p* robe of fine linen.
Pr 31: 22 she is clothed in fine linen and *p*.
SS 3: 10 Its seat was upholstered with *p*,
Jer 10: 9 is then dressed in blue and *p*—
La 4: 5 Those nurtured in *p*
Eze 27: 7 your awnings were of blue and *p*
27: 16 they exchanged turquoise, *p* fabric,
Da 5: 7 what it means will be clothed in *p*
5: 16 you will be clothed in *p*
5: 29 command, Daniel was clothed in *p*,
Mk 15: 17 They put a *p* robe on him, then
15: 20 they took off the *p* robe
Lk 16: 19 a rich man who was dressed in *p*
Jn 19: 2 They clothed him in a *p* robe
19: 5 the crown of thorns and the *p* robe,
Ac 16: 14 a dealer in *p* cloth from the city
Rev 17: 4 The woman was dressed in *p*
18: 12 fine linen, *p*, silk and scarlet cloth;
18: 16 dressed in fine linen, *p* and scarlet,

PURPOSE (PURPOSED PURPOSES)

Ex 9: 16 I have raised you up for this very *p*,
Lev 7: 24 may be used for any other *p*,
1Ch 23: 5 I have provided for that *p*."
Job 36: 5 he is mighty, and firm in his *p*.
Ps 57: 2 to God, who fulfills ⌊his *p*⌋ for me.
138: 8 The LORD will fulfill ⌊his *p*⌋ for me
Pr 19: 21 but it is the LORD's *p* that prevails
Isa 10: 7 his *p* is to destroy,
46: 10 I say: My *p* will stand,
46: 11 a far-off land, a man to fulfill my *p*.
48: 14 will carry out his *p* against Babylon
49: 4 But I said, "I have labored to no *p*;
55: 11 and achieve the *p* for which I sent it
Jer 15: 11 I will deliver you for a good *p*;
51: 11 because his *p* is to destroy Babylon.
51: 12 The LORD will carry out his *p*,
Lk 7: 30 experts in the law rejected God's *p*
Ac 2: 23 handed over to you by God's set *p*
5: 38 For if their *p* or activity is
13: 36 when David had served God's *p*
Ro 8: 28 have been called according to his *p*.
9: 11 in order that God's *p*
9: 17 "I raised you up for this very *p*,
1Co 3: 8 the man who waters have one *p*,
2Co 5: 5 who has made us for this very *p*
Gal 3: 19 What, then, was the *p* of the law?
4: 18 be zealous, provided the *p* is good,
Eph 1: 11 in conformity with the *p* of his will,
2: 15 His *p* was to create
3: 11 according to his eternal *p* which he
6: 22 him to you for this very *p*,
Php 2: 2 love, being one in spirit and *p*.
2: 13 and to act according to his good *p*.
Col 2: 2 My *p* is that they may be
4: 8 you for the express *p* that you may
2Th 1: 11 power he may fulfill every good *p*
1Ti 2: 7 for this *p* I was appointed a herald
2Ti 1: 9 but because of his own *p* and grace.
3: 10 my *p*, faith, patience, love,
Heb 6: 17 of his *p* very clear to the heirs
Rev 17: 13 They have one *p* and will give their
17: 17 to accomplish his *p* by agreeing

PURPOSED (PURPOSE)

Isa 14: 24 and as I have *p*, so it will stand.
14: 27 For the LORD Almighty has *p*,
Jer 49: 20 what he has *p* against those who
50: 45 what he has *p* against the land
Eph 1: 9 which he *p* in Christ, to be put

PURPOSES (PURPOSE)

Ps 33: 10 he thwarts the *p* of the peoples.
33: 11 *p* of his heart through all
Pr 20: 5 *p* of a man's heart are deep waters,
Jer 23: 20 the *p* of his heart.
30: 24 the *p* of his heart.
32: 19 great are your *p* and mighty are
51: 29 LORD's *p* against Babylon stand—
Ro 9: 21 of clay some pottery for noble *p*
2Ti 2: 20 some are for noble *p* and some
2: 21 he will be an instrument for noble *p*

PURSE (PURSES)

Pr 1: 14 and we will share a common *p*"—
7: 20 He took his *p* filled with money
Hag 1: 6 to put them in a *p* with holes in it."
Lk 10: 4 Do not take a *p* or bag or sandals;
22: 35 "When I sent you without *p*,
22: 36 "But now if you have a *p*, take it,

PURSES (PURSE)

Pr 16: 30 he who *p* his lips is bent on evil.

Isa 3: 22 and cloaks, the *p* and mirrors,
Lk 12: 33 Provide *p* for yourselves that will

PURSUE (PURSUED PURSUER PURSUERS PURSUES PURSUING PURSUIT)

Ex 14: 4 heart, and he will *p* them.
15: 9 'I will *p*, I will overtake them.
Lev 26: 7 You will *p* your enemies,
26: 33 will draw out my sword and *p* you.
Dt 19: 6 of blood might *p* him in a rage,
28: 45 They will *p* you and overtake you
Jos 8: 6 They will *p* us until we have lured
8: 16 men of Ai were called to *p* them,
10: 19 But don't stop! *P* your enemies,
1Sa 30: 8 Will I overtake them?" "*P* them,"
30: 8 "Shall I *p* this raiding party?
2Sa 20: 6 Take your master's men and *p* him,
20: 7 out from Jerusalem to *p* Sheba son
20: 13 went on with Joab to *p* Sheba son
24: 13 your enemies while they *p* you?
Job 19: 22 Why do you *p* me as God does?
Ps 7: 1 and deliver me from all who *p* me,
7: 5 let my enemy *p* and overtake me;
31: 15 and from those who *p* me.
34: 14 seek peace and *p* it.
35: 3 against those who *p* me.
56: 1 O God, for men hotly *p* me;
56: 2 My slanderers *p* me all day long;
57: 3 rebuking those who hotly *p* me;
71: 11 *p* him and seize him,
83: 15 so *p* them with your tempest
142: 6 rescue me from those who *p* me,
Pr 15: 9 he loves those who *p* righteousness
Isa 51: 1 to me, you who *p* righteousness
Jer 2: 24 Any males that *p* her need not tire
9: 16 and I will *p* them with the sword
29: 18 I will *p* them with the sword,
48: 2 the sword will *p* you.
49: 37 "I will *p* them with the sword
50: 21 *P*, kill and completely destroy
La 1: 3 All who *p* her have overtaken her
3: 66 *P* them in anger and destroy them
5: 5 Those who *p* us are at our heels;
Eze 5: 2 For I will *p* them with drawn sword
5: 12 scatter to the winds and *p*
12: 14 and I will *p* them with drawn sword
35: 6 bloodshed, bloodshed will *p* you.
35: 6 over to bloodshed and it will *p* you.
Hos 8: 3 an enemy will *p* him.
Na 1: 8 he will *p* his foes into darkness.
Mt 23: 34 flog in your synagogues and *p*
Ro 9: 30 who did not *p* righteousness,
1Ti 6: 11 and *p* righteousness, godliness,
2Ti 2: 22 and *p* righteousness, faith,
1Pe 3: 11 he must seek peace and *p* it.

PURSUED (PURSUE)

Ge 31: 23 he *p* Jacob for seven days
35: 5 around them so that no one *p* them.
Ex 14: 8 so that he *p* the Israelites, who
14: 9 *p* the Israelites and overtook them
14: 23 The Egyptians *p* them,
Jos 8: 16 they *p* Joshua and were lured away
10: 10 Israel *p* them along the road going
11: 8 and *p* them all the way
24: 6 the Egyptians *p* them with chariots
Jdg 4: 16 But Barak *p* the chariots and army
7: 23 and they *p* the Midianites.
7: 25 They *p* the Midianites
8: 12 but he *p* them and captured them,
1Sa 7: 11 of Mizpah and *p* the Philistines,
17: 52 *p* the Philistines to the entrance
2Sa 2: 19 nor to the left as he *p* him.
2: 24 But Joab and Abishai *p* Abner,
2: 28 they no longer *p* Israel,
20: 10 his brother Abishai *p* Sheba son
22: 38 "I *p* my enemies and crushed them;
2Ki 25: 5 but the Babylonian army *p* the king
2Ch 13: 19 Abijah *p* Jeroboam and took
14: 13 and Asa and his army *p* them as far
Ps 18: 37 I *p* my enemies and overtook them;
Jer 39: 5 But the Babylonian army *p* them
52: 8 Babylonian army *p* King Zedekiah
La 3: 43 with anger and *p* us;
Am 1: 11 Because he *p* his brother
Ro 9: 31 who *p* a law of righteousness,
9: 32 Because they *p* it not by faith but
Rev 12: 13 he *p* the woman who had given

PURSUER (PURSUE)

La 1: 6 fled before the *p*.

PURSUERS (PURSUE)

Jos 2: 7 and as soon as the *p* had gone out,
2: 16 the hills so the *p* will not find you.
2: 22 until the *p* had searched all
8: 20 had turned back against their *p*.
Ne 9: 11 you hurled their *p* into the depths,
Isa 30: 16 Therefore your *p* will be swift!
La 4: 19 Our *p* were swifter

PURSUES (PURSUE)

Jos 20: 5 If the avenger of blood *p* him,
Ps 143: 3 The enemy *p* me,
Pr 11: 19 but he who *p* evil goes to his death.
13: 21 Misfortune *p* the sinner,
18: 1 An unfriendly man *p* selfish ends;
19: 7 Though he *p* them with pleading,
21: 21 He who *p* righteousness and love
28: 1 wicked man flees though no one *p*,
Isa 41: 3 He *p* them and moves
Jer 8: 6 Each *p* his own course
Hos 12: 1 he *p* the east wind all day

PURSUING (PURSUE)

Ge 14: 15 *p* them as far as Hobah, north
Lev 26: 17 even when no one is *p* you.
26: 36 even though no one is *p* them.
26: 37 even though no one is *p* them.
Dt 11: 4 of the Red Sea as they were *p* you,
Jdg 8: 5 I am still *p* Zebah and Zalmunna,
1Sa 14: 46 Then Saul stopped *p* the Philistines
24: 1 returned from *p* the Philistines,
24: 14 Whom are you *p*? A dead dog?
25: 29 someone is *p* you to take your life,
26: 18 "Why is my lord *p* his servant?
2Sa 2: 26 men to stop *p* their brothers?"
2: 30 Then Joab returned from *p* Abner
18: 16 and the troops stopped *p* Israel,
1Ki 22: 33 king of Israel and stopped *p* him.
2Ch 18: 32 king of Israel, they stopped *p* him.
Ps 35: 6 the angel of the LORD *p* them
Isa 65: 2 *p* their own imaginations—
Jer 2: 33 How skilled you are at *p* love!
Hos 5: 11 intent on *p* idols.
1Ti 3: 8 wine, and not *p* dishonest gain.
Tit 1: 7 not violent, not *p* dishonest gain.

PURSUIT (PURSUE)

Ge 14: 14 and went in *p* as far as Dan.
Jos 2: 7 So the men set out in *p* of the spies
8: 17 left the city open and went in *p*
Jdg 4: 22 Barak came by in *p* of Sisera,
8: 4 exhausted yet keeping up the *p*,
1Sa 14: 22 they joined the battle in hot *p*.
23: 25 the Desert of Maon in *p* of David.
23: 28 Then Saul broke off his *p* of David
30: 10 four hundred men continued the *p*.
2Sa 2: 23 But Asahel refused to give up the *p*;
2: 27 men would have continued the *p*
17: 1 and set out tonight in *p* of David.
1Ki 20: 20 with the Israelites in *p*.

PUSH (PUSHED PUSHES PUSHING)

Dt 15: 17 and *p* it through his ear lobe
Jos 23: 5 He will *p* them out before you,
2Ki 4: 27 Gehazi came over to *p* her away,
Ps 44: 5 Through you we *p* back our
Jer 46: 15 for the LORD will *p* them down.

PUSHED (PUSH)

Jdg 16: 30 Then he *p* with all his might,
Ps 118: 13 I was *p* back and about to fall,
Isa 16: 2 *p* from the nest,
Zec 5: 8 and he *p* her back into the basket
5: 8 and *p* the lead cover down over its
Ac 7: 27 was mistreating the other *p* Moses
19: 33 The Jews *p* Alexander to the front,

PUSHES (PUSH)

2Co 11: 20 of you or *p* himself forward

PUSHING (PUSH)

Joel 2: 20 *p* it into a parched and barren land,
Mk 3: 10 those with diseases were *p* forward

PUT

Ge 10: 6 Cush, Mizraim, *P* and Canaan.
1Ch 1: 8 Cush, Mizraim, *P* and Canaan.
Jer 46: 9 of Cush and *P* who carry shields,
Eze 27: 10 " 'Men of Persia, Lydia and *P*
30: 5 Cush and *P*, Lydia and all Arabia,
38: 5 Cush and *P* will be with them,
Na 3: 9 *P* and Libya were among her allies.

PUTEOLI

Ac 28: 13 on the following day we reached *P*.

PUTHITES

1Ch 2: 53 *P*, Shumathites and Mishraites.

PUTIEL

Ex 6: 25 one of the daughters of *P*,

PUZZLED

Mk 6: 20 heard John, he was greatly *p*;
Ac 5: 24 and the chief priests were *p*,

PYRRHUS

Ac 20: 4 by Sopater son of *P* from Berea,

QUAIL

Ex 16: 13 That evening *q* came and covered
Nu 11: 31 and drove *q* in from the sea.
11: 32 people went out and gathered *q*.
Ps 105: 40 They asked, and he brought them *q*

QUAKE (EARTHQUAKE EARTHQUAKES QUAKED QUAKING)

Job 26: 11 The pillars of the heavens *q*,
Ps 46: 3 the mountains *q* with their surging.
75: 3 When the earth and all its people *q*,
Isa 64: 2 cause the nations to *q* before you!
Eze 27: 28 The shorelands will *q*
Na 1: 5 The mountains *q* before him
Rev 16: 18 on earth, so tremendous was the *q*.

QUAKED (QUAKE)

Jdg 5: 5 The mountains *q* before the LORD
2Sa 22: 8 "The earth trembled and *q*,
Ps 18: 7 The earth trembled and *q*,
77: 18 the earth trembled and *q*.

QUAKING (QUAKE)

1Sa 13: 7 troops with him were *q* with fear.
Ps 60: 2 mend its fractures, for it is *q*.
Jer 4: 24 and they were *q*;

QUALIFIED

Da 1: 4 and *q* to serve in the king's palace.
Col 1: 12 who has *q* you to share
2Ti 2: 2 to reliable men who will also be *q*

QUALITIES (QUALITY)

Da 6: 3 by his exceptional *q* that the king
Ro 1: 20 of the world God's invisible *q*—
2Pe 1: 8 For if you possess these *q*

QUALITY (QUALITIES)

Lev 27: 12 who will judge its *q* as good or bad.
27: 14 the priest will judge its *q* as good
1Ki 5: 17 of *q* stone to provide a foundation
7: 10 laid with large stones of good *q*,
1Co 3: 13 and the fire will test the *q*

QUALM

Jude : 12 with you without the slightest *q*—

QUANTITIES (QUANTITY)

Ge 41: 49 Joseph stored up huge *q* of grain,
1Ki 10: 2 with camels carrying spices, large *q*
10: 10 large *q* of spices, and precious
1Ch 22: 14 *q* of bronze and iron too great
29: 2 and marble—all of these in large *q*.
2Ch 9: 1 with camels carrying spices, large *q*
9: 9 large *q* of spices, and precious
25: 13 and carried off great *q* of plunder.
Zec 14: 14 great *q* of gold and silver

QUANTITY (QUANTITIES)

Lev 19: 35 measuring length, weight or *q*.
Jos 22: 8 and a great *q* of clothing—
2Sa 8: 8 King David took a great *q*
12: 30 He took a great *q* of plunder

1Ch 18: 8 David took a great *q* of bronze,
20: 2 He took a great *q* of plunder
23: 29 and all measurements of *q* and size.

QUARREL (QUARRELED QUARRELING QUARRELS QUARRELSOME)

Ge 45: 24 to them, "Don't *q* on the way!"
Ex 17: 2 Moses replied, "Why do you *q*
21: 18 "If men *q* and one hits the other
Jdg 11: 25 Did he ever *q* with Israel
2Ki 5: 7 trying to pick a *q* with me!"
2Ch 35: 21 "What *q* is there between you
Pr 15: 18 but a patient man calms a *q*.
17: 14 Starting a *q* is like breaching a dam;
17: 19 He who loves a *q* loves sin;
20: 3 but every fool is quick to *q*.
26: 17 in a *q* not his own.
26: 20 without gossip a *q* dies down.
Mt 12: 19 He will not *q* or cry out;
2Ti 2: 24 And the Lord's servant must not *q;*
Jas 4: 2 You *q* and fight.

QUARRELED (QUARREL)

Ge 26: 20 of Gerar *q* with Isaac's herdsmen
26: 21 but they *q* over that one also;
26: 22 and dug another well, and no one *q*
Ex 17: 2 So they *q* with Moses and said,
17: 7 Meribah because the Israelites *q*
Nu 20: 3 They *q* with Moses and said,
20: 13 where the Israelites *q*

QUARRELING (QUARREL)

Ge 13: 7 And *q* arose between Abram's
13: 8 "Let's not have any *q* between you
Isa 58: 4 Your fasting ends in *q* and strife,
Ac 12: 20 He had been *q* with the people
1Co 3: 3 For since there is jealousy and *q*
2Co 12: 20 I fear that there may be *q*, jealousy,
1Ti 6: 4 *q*, malicious talk, evil suspicions
2Ti 2: 14 before God against *q* about words;

QUARRELS (QUARREL)

Pr 13: 10 Pride only breeds *q*,
22: 10 *q* and insults are ended.
Isa 45: 9 Woe to him who *q* with his Maker,
1Co 1: 11 have informed me that there are *q*
2Ti 2: 23 because you know they produce *q*.
Tit 3: 9 and arguments and *q* about the law,
Jas 4: 1 What causes fights and *q*

QUARRELSOME (QUARREL)

Pr 19: 13 a *q* wife is like a constant dripping.
21: 9 than share a house with a *q* wife.
21: 19 than with a *q* and ill-tempered wife.
25: 24 than share a house with a *q* wife.
26: 21 so is a *q* man for kindling strife.
27: 15 A *q* wife is like
1Ti 3: 3 not violent but gentle, not *q*,

QUARRIES (QUARRY)

Jos 7: 5 as the stone *q* and struck them
Ecc 10: 9 Whoever *q* stones may be injured

QUARRY (QUARRIES)

1Ki 5: 17 removed from the *q* large blocks
6: 7 dressed at the *q* were used,
Isa 51: 1 to the *q* from which you were hewn

QUART (QUARTS)

Rev 6: 6 "A *q* of wheat for a day's wages,

QUARTER (QUARTERS)

1Sa 9: 8 "I have a *q* of a shekel of silver.
Zep 1: 10 wailing from the New *Q*,

QUARTERS (QUARTER)

2Sa 19: 11 Israel has reached the king at his *q?*
2Ki 23: 7 tore down the *q* of the male shrine
Ne 3: 30 repairs opposite his living *q*
Isa 11: 12 Judah from the four *q* of the earth.
Jer 49: 36 from the four *q* of the heavens;

QUARTS (QUART)

Rev 6: 6 three *q* of barley for a day's wages,

QUARTUS

Ro 16: 23 and our brother *Q* send you their

QUEEN (QUEEN'S QUEENS)

1Ki 10: 1 When the *q* of Sheba heard about
10: 4 When the *q* of Sheba saw all
10: 10 as those the *q* of Sheba gave
10: 13 King Solomon gave the *q*
11: 19 sister of his own wife, *Q* Tahpenes,
15: 13 from her position as *q* mother,
2Ki 10: 13 of the king and of the *q* mother."
2Ch 9: 1 When the *q* of Sheba heard
9: 3 When the *q* of Sheba saw
9: 9 as those the *q* of Sheba gave
9: 12 King Solomon gave the *q*
15: 16 from her position as *q* mother,
Ne 2: 6 with the *q* sitting beside him,
Est 1: 9 *Q* Vashti also gave a banquet
1: 11 to bring before him *Q* Vashti,
1: 12 *Q* Vashti refused to come.
1: 15 what must be done to *Q* Vashti?"
1: 16 "*Q* Vashti has done wrong,
1: 17 King Xerxes commanded *Q* Vashti
2: 4 who pleases the king be *q* instead
2: 17 and made her *q* instead of Vashti.
2: 22 about the plot and told *Q* Esther,
5: 2 When he saw *Q* Esther standing
5: 3 *Q* Esther? What is your request?
5: 12 the only person *Q* Esther invited
7: 1 Haman went to dine with *Q* Esther
7: 2 the king again asked, "*Q* Esther,
7: 3 *Q* Esther answered, "If I have
7: 5 King Xerxes asked *Q* Esther,
7: 6 terrified before the king and *q*.
7: 7 stayed behind to beg *Q* Esther
7: 8 molest the *q* while she is with me
8: 1 King Xerxes gave *Q* Esther
8: 7 King Xerxes replied to *Q* Esther
9: 12 The king said to *Q* Esther,
9: 29 So *Q* Esther, daughter of Abihail,
9: 31 *Q* Esther had decreed for them,
Isa 47: 5 *q* of kingdoms.
47: 7 the eternal *q!*"
Jer 7: 18 cakes of bread for the *Q* of Heaven.
13: 18 Say to the king and to the *q* mother
29: 2 King Jehoiachin and the *q* mother,
44: 17 incense to the *Q* of Heaven
44: 18 incense to the *Q* of Heaven
44: 19 incense to the *Q* of Heaven
44: 25 offerings to the *Q* of Heaven.'
La 1: 1 who was *q* among the provinces
Eze 16: 13 very beautiful and rose to be a *q*.
Da 5: 10 The *q*, hearing the voices
Mt 12: 42 The *Q* of the South will rise
Lk 11: 31 The *Q* of the South will rise
Ac 8: 27 of Candace, *q* of the Ethiopians.
Rev 18: 7 'I sit as *q;* I am not a widow,

QUEEN'S (QUEEN)

Est 1: 17 For the *q* conduct will become
1: 18 heard about the *q* conduct will

QUEENS (QUEEN)

SS 6: 8 Sixty *q* there may be,
6: 9 the *q* and concubines praised her.
Isa 49: 23 and their *q* your nursing mothers.
Jer 44: 9 and by the kings and *q* of Judah

QUENCH (QUENCHED)

Ps 104: 11 the wild donkeys *q* their thirst.
SS 8: 7 Many waters cannot *q* love;
Isa 1: 31 with no one to *q* the fire."
Jer 4: 4 burn with no one to *q* it.
21: 12 burn with no one to *q* it.
Am 5: 6 and Bethel will have no one to *q* it.

QUENCHED (QUENCH)

2Ki 22: 17 against this place and will not be *q*.'
2Ch 34: 25 out on this place and will not be *q*.'
Isa 34: 10 It will not be *q* night and day;
66: 24 nor will their fire be *q*,
Jer 7: 20 and it will burn and not be *q*.
46: 10 till it has *q* its thirst with blood.
Eze 20: 47 The blazing flame will not be *q*,
20: 48 have kindled it; it will not be *q*.' "
Mk 9: 48 and the fire is not *q*.'
Heb 11: 34 of lions, *q* the fury of the flames,

QUESTION (QUESTIONED QUESTIONING QUESTIONS)

Jdg 11: 12 to the Ammonite king with the *q:*
Est 5: 8 Then I will answer the king's *q*."
Job 38: 3 I will *q* you,
40: 7 I will *q* you,
42: 4 I will *q* you,
Ps 35: 11 they *q* me on things I know nothing
Isa 45: 11 do you *q* me about my children,
Jer 38: 27 come to Jeremiah and *q* him,
Mt 21: 24 replied, "I will also ask you one *q*.
22: 23 resurrection, came to him with a *q*.
22: 35 tested him with this *q:* "Teacher,
Mk 8: 11 came and began to *q* Jesus.
11: 29 Jesus replied, "I will ask you one *q*.
12: 18 resurrection, came to him with a *q*.
Lk 20: 3 He replied, "I will also ask you a *q*.
20: 27 came to Jesus with a *q*.
22: 23 to *q* among themselves which
Jn 8: 6 They were using this *q* as a trap,
18: 21 Why *q* me? Ask those who heard
Ac 4: 7 before them and began to *q* them:
15: 2 the apostles and elders about this *q*.
15: 6 and elders met to consider this *q*.
22: 29 to *q* him withdrew immediately.
1Ti 3: 16 Beyond all *q*, the mystery

QUESTIONED (QUESTION)

Ge 43: 7 man *q* us closely about ourselves
Jdg 8: 14 man of Succoth and *q* him,
Ezr 5: 9 We *q* the elders and asked them,
Ne 1: 2 I *q* them about the Jewish remnant
Job 21: 29 Have you never *q* those who travel
Da 1: 20 about which the king *q* them,
Lk 20: 21 So the spies *q* him: "Teacher,
Jn 1: 25 Pharisees who had been sent *q* him,
18: 19 the high priest *q* Jesus about his
Ac 5: 27 to be *q* by the high priest.
22: 24 and *q* in order to find out why

QUESTIONING (QUESTION)

Jn 8: 7 When they kept on *q* him,

QUESTIONS (QUESTION)

Ge 43: 7 We simply answered his *q*.
1Ki 10: 1 she came to test him with hard *q*.
10: 3 Solomon answered all her *q;*
2Ch 9: 1 Jerusalem to test him with hard *q*.
9: 2 Solomon answered all her *q;*
Pr 18: 17 another comes forward and *q* him.
Ecc 7: 10 For it is not wise to ask such *q*.
Mt 22: 46 dared to ask him any more *q*.
Mk 12: 34 no one dared ask him any more *q*.
Lk 2: 46 to them and asking them *q*.
11: 53 and to besiege him with *q*,
20: 40 dared to ask him any more *q*.
23: 9 He plied him with many *q*,
Jn 16: 30 need to have anyone ask you *q*.
Ac 18: 15 But since it involves *q* about words
23: 29 had to do with *q* about their law,
1Co 10: 25 without raising *q* of conscience,
10: 27 without raising *q* of conscience.

QUICK-TEMPERED (TEMPER)

Pr 14: 17 A *q* man does foolish things,
14: 29 but a *q* man displays folly.
Tit 1: 7 not *q*, not given to much wine,

QUIET (QUIETED QUIETNESS)

Ge 25: 27 while Jacob was a *q* man, staying
34: 5 so he kept *q* about it
Jdg 3: 19 *Q!*" And all his attendants left him.
18: 19 They answered him, "Be *q!*
2Sa 13: 20 been with you? Be *q* now, my sister
2Ki 11: 20 city was *q*, because Athaliah had
1Ch 4: 40 land was spacious, peaceful and *q*.
22: 9 and I will grant Israel peace and *q*
2Ch 23: 21 city was *q*, because Athaliah had
Ne 5: 8 They kept *q*, because they could
Est 7: 4 would have kept *q*, because no
Job 6: 24 "Teach me, and I will be *q;*
Ps 23: 2 he leads me beside *q* waters,
76: 8 and the land feared and was *q*—
83: 1 be not *q*, O God, be not still.
Pr 17: 1 Better a dry crust with peace and *q*
Ecc 9: 17 The *q* words of the wise are more
Isa 18: 4 "I will remain *q* and will look
42: 14 I have been *q* and held myself back.

Isa 62: 1 sake I will not remain *q*,
Am 5: 13 Therefore the prudent man keeps *q*
Zep 3: 17 he will *q* you with his love,
Mt 20: 31 them and told them to be *q*,
Mk 1: 25 "Be *q*!" said Jesus sternly.
4: 39 and said to the waves, "*Q*!
6: 31 with me by yourselves to a *q* place
9: 34 But they kept *q* because on the way
10: 48 rebuked him and told him to be *q*,
Lk 4: 35 "Be *q*!" Jesus said sternly.
18: 39 rebuked him and told him to be *q*,
19: 40 he replied, "if they keep *q*,
Ac 12: 17 with his hand for them to be *q*
19: 36 to be *q* and not do anything rash.
22: 2 in Aramaic, they became very *q*.
1Co 14: 28 the speaker should keep *q*
1Th 4: 11 it your ambition to lead a *q* life,
1Ti 2: 2 we may live peaceful and *q* lives
1Pe 3: 4 beauty of a gentle and *q* spirit,

QUIETED (QUIET)

Ps 131: 2 But I have stilled and *q* my soul;
Ac 19: 35 The city clerk *q* the crowd and said

QUIETNESS (QUIET)

Job 3: 26 I have no peace, no *q*;
Isa 30: 15 in *q* and trust is your strength,
32: 17 the effect of righteousness will be *q*
1Ti 2: 11 A woman should learn in *q*

QUIRINIUS

Lk 2: 2 while *Q* was governor of Syria.)

QUIVER (QUIVERED QUIVERS)

Ge 27: 3 get your weapons—your *q*
Job 39: 23 The *q* rattles against his side,
Ps 127: 5 whose *q* is full of them.
Isa 22: 6 Elam takes up the *q*,
49: 2 and concealed me in his *q*.
La 3: 13 with arrows from his *q*.

QUIVERED (QUIVER)

Hab 3: 16 my lips *q* at the sound;

QUIVERS (QUIVER)

Jer 5: 16 Their *q* are like an open grave;

QUOTA (QUOTAS)

Ex 5: 8 as before; don't reduce the *q*
5: 14 "Why haven't you met your *q*
5: 18 yet you must produce your full *q*

QUOTAS (QUOTA)

1Ki 4: 28 to the proper place their *q* of barley

QUOTE (QUOTES QUOTING)

Eze 12: 23 and they will no longer *q* it in Israel
16: 44 quotes proverbs will *q* this proverb
18: 3 you will no longer *q* this proverb
Lk 4: 23 "Surely you will *q* this proverb

QUOTES (QUOTE)

Eze 16: 44 " 'Everyone who *q* proverbs will

QUOTING (QUOTE)

Eze 18: 2 by *q* this proverb about the land

RAAMAH

Ge 10: 7 Havilah, Sabtah, *R* and Sabtecah.
10: 7 The sons of *R*: Sheba and Dedan.
1Ch 1: 9 Havilah, Sabta, *R* and Sabteca.
1: 9 The sons of *R*: Sheba and Dedan.
Eze 27: 22 of Sheba and *R* traded with you;

RAAMIAH

Ne 7: 7 Nehemiah, Azariah, *R*, Nahamani,

RABBAH

Dt 3: 11 It is still in *R* of the Ammonites.)
Jos 13: 25 near *R*; and from Heshbon
15: 60 Kiriath Jearim) and *R*— two towns
2Sa 11: 1 the Ammonites and besieged *R*.
12: 26 fought against *R* of the Ammonites
12: 27 "I have fought against *R*
12: 29 the entire army and went to *R*,
17: 27 son of Nahash from *R*
1Ch 20: 1 Joab attacked *R* and left it in ruins.
20: 1 and went to *R* and besieged it,
Jer 49: 2 cry against *R* of the Ammonites;
49: 3 Cry out, O inhabitants of *R*!
Eze 21: 20 the sword to come against *R*
25: 5 I will turn *R* into a pasture
Am 1: 14 I will set fire to the walls of *R*

RABBI (RABBONI)

Mt 23: 7 and to have men call them '*R*.'
23: 8 "But you are not to be called '*R*,'
26: 25 "Surely not I, *R*?" Jesus answered,
26: 49 Judas said, "Greetings, *R*!"
Mk 9: 5 "*R*, it is good for us to be here.
10: 51 The blind man said, "*R*, I want
11: 21 remembered and said to Jesus, "*R*,
14: 45 Judas said, "*R*!" and kissed him.
Jn 1: 38 "*R*" (which means Teacher),
1: 49 Then Nathanael declared, "*R*,
3: 2 came to Jesus at night and said, "*R*,
3: 26 came to John and said to him, "*R*,
4: 31 his disciples urged him, "*R*,
6: 25 "*R*, when did you get here?"
9: 2 His disciples asked him, "*R*,
11: 8 "But *R*," they said, "a short

RABBIT

Lev 11: 6 The *r*, though it chews the cud,
Dt 14: 7 you may not eat the camel, the *r*

RABBITH

Jos 19: 20 Shion, Anaharath, *R*, Kishion,

RABBLE

Nu 11: 4 The *r* with them began
Eze 23: 42 desert along with men from the *r*

RABBONI (RABBI)

Jn 20: 16 "*R*!" (which means Teacher).

RACA

Mt 5: 22 '*R*,' is answerable to the Sanhedrin.

RACAL

1Sa 30: 29 Siphmoth, Eshtemoa and *R*;

RACE (RACED)

Ezr 9: 2 and have mingled the holy *r*
Ecc 9: 11 The *r* is not to the swift
Ac 20: 24 if only I may finish the *r*
Ro 9: 3 those of my own *r*, the people
1Co 9: 24 that in a *r* all the runners run,
Gal 2: 2 that I was running or had run my *r*
5: 7 You were running a good *r*.
2Ti 4: 7 I have finished the *r*, I have kept
Heb 12: 1 perseverance the *r* marked out

RACED (RACE)

Est 8: 14 riding the royal horses, *r* out,
Jer 12: 5 "If you have *r* with men on foot

RACHEL (RACHEL'S)

Ge 29: 6 "and here comes his daughter *R*
29: 9 *R* came with her father's sheep,
29: 10 When Jacob saw *R* daughter
29: 11 Then Jacob kissed *R* and began
29: 12 He had told *R* that he was
29: 16 and the name of the younger was *R*
29: 17 had weak eyes, but *R* was lovely
29: 18 Jacob was in love with *R* and said,
29: 18 for your younger daughter *R*."
29: 20 Jacob served seven years to get *R*,
29: 25 I served you for *R*, didn't I?
29: 28 Laban gave him his daughter *R*
29: 29 girl Bilhah to his daughter *R*
29: 30 Jacob lay with *R* also,
29: 30 and he loved *R* more than Leah.
29: 31 her womb, but *R* was barren.
30: 1 When *R* saw that she was not
30: 6 *R* said, "God has vindicated me;
30: 8 *R* said, "I have had a great struggle
30: 14 *R* said to Leah, "Please give me
30: 15 too?" "Very well," *R* said,
30: 22 Then God remembered *R*;
30: 25 After *R* gave birth to Joseph,
31: 4 So Jacob sent word to *R*
31: 14 Then *R* and Leah replied,
31: 19 *R* stole her father's household gods
31: 32 did not know that *R* had stolen
31: 34 *R* had taken the household gods
31: 35 *R* said to her father, "Don't be
Ge 33: 1 *R* and the two maidservants.
33: 2 and *R* and Joseph in the rear.
33: 7 Last of all came Joseph and *R*,
35: 16 *R* began to give birth and had great
35: 19 *R* died and was buried on the way
35: 24 The sons of *R*: Joseph
46: 19 The sons of Jacob's wife *R*:
46: 22 the sons of *R* who were born
46: 25 given to his daughter *R*—
48: 7 to my sorrow *R* died in the land
Ru 4: 11 coming into your home like *R*
Jer 31: 15 *R* weeping for her children
Mt 2: 18 *R* weeping for her children

RACHEL'S (RACHEL)

Ge 30: 7 *R* servant Bilhah conceived again
31: 33 of Leah's tent, he entered *R* tent.
35: 20 this day that pillar marks *R* tomb.
35: 25 The sons of *R* maidservant Bilhah:
1Sa 10: 2 will meet two men near *R* tomb,

RACKED

Isa 21: 3 At this my body is *r* with pain,
La 4: 9 *r* with hunger, they waste away

RADDAI

1Ch 2: 14 the fourth Nethanel, the fifth *R*,

RADIANCE (RADIANT)

Job 31: 26 if I have regarded the sun in its *r*
Eze 1: 28 so was the *r* around him.
10: 4 full of the *r* of the glory
2Co 3: 13 at it while the *r* was fading away.
Heb 1: 3 The Son is the *r* of God's glory

RADIANT (RADIANCE)

Ex 34: 29 he was not aware that his face was *r*
34: 30 his face was *r*, and they were afraid
34: 35 they saw that his face was *r*.
Ps 19: 8 The commands of the LORD are *r*,
34: 5 Those who look to him are *r*;
SS 5: 10 My lover is *r* and ruddy,
Isa 60: 5 Then you will look and be *r*,
Eze 43: 2 and the land was *r* with his glory.
Eph 5: 27 her to himself as a *r* church,

RAFTERS

Ecc 10: 18 If a man is lazy, the *r* sag,
SS 1: 17 our *r* are firs.

RAFTS

1Ki 5: 9 and I will float them in *r* by sea
2Ch 2: 16 and will float them in *r* by sea

RAGE (ENRAGED OUTRAGEOUS RAGED RAGES RAGING)

Dt 19: 6 of blood might pursue him in a *r*,
2Ki 5: 12 So he turned and went off in a *r*.
19: 27 and how you *r* against me.
19: 28 Because you *r* against me
2Ch 25: 10 and left for home in a great *r*.
28: 9 them in a *r* that reaches to heaven.
Est 5: 9 filled with *r* against Mordecai.
7: 7 The king got up in a *r*, left his wine
Job 15: 13 so that you vent your *r* against God
Ps 2: 1 Why do the nations *r*
7: 6 rise up against the *r* of my enemies.
Pr 19: 12 A king's *r* is like the roar of a lion,
Isa 17: 12 they *r* like the raging sea!
37: 28 and how you *r* against me.
37: 29 Because you *r* against me
41: 11 "All who *r* against you
Jer 51: 55 of enemies will *r* like great waters;
Da 3: 13 Furious with *r*, Nebuchadnezzar
8: 6 and charged at him in great *r*.
11: 11 of the South will march out in a *r*
11: 44 out in a great *r* to destroy
Hab 3: 8 Did you *r* against the sea
Ac 4: 25 " 'Why do the nations *r*
Gal 5: 20 jealousy, fits of *r*, selfish ambition,
Eph 4: 31 Get rid of all bitterness, *r*
Col 3: 8 *r*, malice, slander, and filthy

RAGED (RAGE)

1Ki 22: 35 All day long the battle *r*,
2Ch 18: 34 All day long the battle *r*,
Isa 45: 24 All who have *r* against him
Jer 44: 6 it *r* against the towns of Judah

Am 1: 11 because his anger *r* continually

RAGES (RAGE)

Job 40: 23 When the river *r*, he is not alarmed;
Ps 50: 3 and around him a tempest *r*.
Pr 19: 3 yet his heart *r* against the LORD.
29: 9 fool *r* and scoffs, and there is no

RAGING (RAGE)

2Ch 26: 19 While he was *r* at the priests
Ps 124: 5 the *r* waters would have swept us
Isa 17: 12 Oh, the *r* of many nations—
17: 12 they rage like the *r* sea!
30: 30 with *r* anger and consuming fire,
Jnh 1: 15 overboard, and the *r* sea grew
Lk 8: 24 rebuked the wind and the *r* waters;
Ac 27: 20 and the storm continued *r*,
Heb 10: 27 and of *r* fire that will consume

RAGS

Pr 23: 21 and drowsiness clothes them in *r*.
Isa 64: 6 our righteous acts are like filthy *r*;
Jer 38: 11 took some old *r* and worn-out
38: 12 "Put these old *r* and worn-out
1Co 4: 11 we are in *r*, we are brutally treated,

RAHAB

Jos 2: 1 the house of a prostitute named *R*
2: 3 of Jericho sent this message to *R*,
6: 17 Only *R* the prostitute and all who
6: 23 went in and brought out *R*,
6: 25 But Joshua spared *R* the prostitute,
Job 9: 13 the cohorts of *R* cowered at his feet
26: 12 by his wisdom he cut *R* to pieces.
Ps 87: 4 "I will record *R* and Babylon
89: 10 You crushed *R* like one of the slain
Isa 30: 7 *R* the Do-Nothing.
51: 9 Was it not you who cut *R* to pieces,
Mt 1: 5 whose mother was *R*, Boaz
Heb 11: 31 By faith the prostitute *R*,
Jas 2: 25 even *R* the prostitute considered

RAHAM

1Ch 2: 44 Shema was the father of *R*,
2: 44 and *R* the father of Jorkeam.

RAID (RAIDED RAIDERS RAIDING)

2Sa 3: 22 and Joab returned from a *r*
Pr 24: 15 do not *r* his dwelling place;

RAIDED (RAID)

1Sa 27: 8 men went up and *r* the Geshurites,
30: 1 the Amalekites had *r* the Negev
30: 14 We *r* the Negev of the Kerethites
1Ch 14: 9 and *r* the Valley of Rephaim;
14: 13 more the Philistines *r* the valley;
2Ch 25: 13 part in the war *r* Judean towns
28: 18 while the Philistines had *r* towns

RAIDERS (RAID)

Ge 49: 19 Gad will be attacked by a band of *r*,
Jdg 2: 14 over to *r* who plundered them.
2: 16 out of the hands of these *r*.
2Ki 13: 20 Now Moabite *r* used to enter
13: 21 suddenly they saw a band of *r*;
24: 2 and Ammonite *r* against him.
2Ch 22: 1 king in his place, since the *r*,

RAIDING (RAID)

1Sa 13: 17 *R* parties went out
14: 15 those in the outposts and *r* parties
23: 27 The Philistines are *r* the land."
27: 10 "Where did you go *r* today?"
30: 8 "Shall I pursue this *r* party?
30: 15 me down to this *r* party?"
2Sa 4: 2 men who were leaders of *r* bands.
2Ki 6: 23 Aram stopped *r* Israel's territory.
1Ch 12: 18 made them leaders of his *r* bands.
12: 21 They helped David against *r* bands
Job 1: 17 Chaldeans formed three *r* parties

RAIL

Ps 102: 8 those who *r* against me use my

RAIN (RAINBOW RAINED RAINING RAINS RAINY)

Ge 2: 5 the LORD God had not sent *r*
7: 4 from now I will send *r* on the earth
7: 12 And *r* fell on the earth forty days
8: 2 and the *r* had stopped falling
Ex 9: 33 and the *r* no longer poured
9: 34 When Pharaoh saw that the *r*
16: 4 "I will *r* down bread from heaven
Lev 26: 4 I will send you *r* in its season,
Dt 11: 11 valleys that drinks *r* from heaven.
11: 14 then I will send *r* on your land
11: 17 the heavens so that it will not *r*
28: 12 to send *r* on your land in season
28: 24 The LORD will turn the *r*
32: 2 Let my teaching fall like *r*
32: 2 like abundant *r* on tender plants.
1Sa 12: 17 the LORD to send thunder and *r*.
12: 18 day the LORD sent thunder and *r*.
2Sa 1: 21 may you have neither dew nor *r*,
21: 10 of the harvest till the *r* poured
22: 12 the dark *r* clouds of the sky.
23: 4 like the brightness after *r*
1Ki 8: 35 there is no *r* because your people
8: 36 send *r* on the land you gave your
17: 1 nor *r* in the next few years
17: 7 there had been no *r* in the land.
17: 14 dry until the day the LORD gives *r*
18: 1 and I will send *r* on the land."
18: 41 for there is the sound of a heavy *r*."
18: 44 go down before the *r* stops you.' "
18: 45 a heavy *r* came on and Ahab rode
2Ki 3: 17 You will see neither wind nor *r*,
2Ch 6: 26 there is no *r* because your people
6: 27 send *r* on the land you gave your
7: 13 the heavens so that there is no *r*,
Ezr 10: 9 the occasion and because of the *r*.
Job 5: 10 He bestows *r* on the earth;
20: 23 and *r* down his blows upon him.
28: 26 when he made a decree for the *r*
29: 23 drank in my words as the spring *r*.
36: 27 which distill as *r* to the streams;
37: 6 to the *r* shower, 'Be a mighty
38: 25 a channel for the torrents of *r*,
38: 28 Does the *r* have a father?
Ps 11: 6 On the wicked he will *r*
18: 11 the dark *r* clouds of the sky.
68: 8 the heavens poured down *r*,
72: 6 He will be like *r* falling
105: 32 He turned their *r* into hail,
135: 7 he sends lightning with the *r*
147: 8 he supplies the earth with *r*
Pr 16: 15 his favor is like a *r* cloud in spring.
25: 14 Like clouds and wind without *r*
25: 23 As a north wind brings *r*,
26: 1 snow in summer or *r* in harvest,
28: 3 is like a driving *r* that leaves no
Ecc 11: 3 they pour *r* upon the earth.
12: 2 and the clouds return after the *r*;
Isa 4: 6 hiding place from the storm and *r*.
5: 6 not to *r* on it."
28: 2 like a driving *r* and a flooding
30: 23 send you *r* for the seed you sow
44: 14 a pine, and the *r* made it grow.
45: 8 above, *r* down righteousness;
55: 10 As the *r* and the snow
Jer 10: 13 He sends lightning with the *r*
14: 4 because there is no *r* in the land;
14: 22 idols of the nations bring *r*?
51: 16 He sends lightning with the *r*
Eze 13: 11 *R* will come in torrents,
13: 13 and torrents of *r* will fall
22: 24 'You are a land that has had no *r*
38: 22 I will pour down torrents of *r*,
Am 4: 7 I sent *r* on one town,
4: 7 One field had *r*;
4: 7 "I also withheld *r* from you
Zec 10: 1 He gives showers of *r* to men,
10: 1 the LORD for *r* in the springtime;
14: 17 Almighty, they will have no *r*.
14. 18 and take part, they will have no *r*.
Mt 5: 45 and sends *r* on the righteous
7: 25 The *r* came down, the streams rose,
7: 27 The *r* came down, the streams rose,
Lk 12: 54 'It's going to *r*,' and it does.
Ac 14: 17 by giving you *r* from heaven
Heb 6: 7 drinks in the *r* often falling on it
Jas 5: 17 earnestly that it would not *r*,
5: 17 it did not *r* on the land for three
5: 18 and the heavens gave *r*,
Jude : 12 They are clouds without *r*,
Rev 11: 6 the sky so that it will not *r*

RAINBOW (RAIN)

Ge 9: 13 I have set my *r* in the clouds,
9: 14 and the *r* appears in the clouds,
9: 16 Whenever the *r* appears
Eze 1: 28 the appearance of a *r* in the clouds
Rev 4: 3 A *r*, resembling an emerald,
10: 1 in a cloud, with a *r* above his head;

RAINED (RAIN)

Ge 19: 24 the LORD *r* down burning sulfur
Ex 9: 23 So the LORD *r* hail on the land
Ps 78: 24 he *r* down manna for the people
78: 27 He *r* meat down on them like dust,
Lk 17: 29 fire and sulfur *r* down from heaven

RAINING (RAIN)

Ac 28: 2 welcomed us all because it was *r*

RAINS (RAIN)

Dt 11: 14 both autumn and spring *r*,
Job 24: 8 They are drenched by mountain *r*
Ps 84: 6 the autumn *r* also cover it
SS 2: 11 the *r* are over and gone.
Jer 3: 3 and no spring *r* have fallen.
5: 24 who gives autumn and spring *r*
Hos 6: 3 he will come to us like the winter *r*,
6: 3 like the spring *r* that water
Joel 2: 23 both autumn and spring *r*, as before
Jas 5: 7 is for the autumn and spring *r*.

RAINY (RAIN)

Ezr 10: 13 people here and it is the *r* season;
Pr 27: 15 a constant dripping on a *r* day;
Eze 1: 28 a rainbow in the clouds on a *r* day,

RAISE (RISE)

Ge 4: 20 live in tents and *r* livestock.
Ex 14: 16 *R* your staff and stretch out your
24: 11 But God did not *r* his hand
Dt 18: 15 The LORD your God will *r* up
18: 18 I will *r* up for them a prophet like
Jos 6: 10 a war cry, do not *r* your voices,
Jdg 8: 28 and did not *r* its head again.
1Sa 2: 35 I will *r* up for myself a faithful
18: 17 "I will not *r* a hand against him.
22: 17 to *r* a hand to strike the priests
2Sa 7: 12 I will *r* up your offspring
1Ki 14: 14 "The LORD will *r* up
20: 25 *r* an army like the one you lost—
2Ki 4: 28 Didn't I tell you, 'Don't *r* my hopes
1Ch 17: 11 I will *r* up your offspring
Job 38: 34 "Can you *r* your voice
Ps 41: 10 *r* me up, that I may repay them.
Pr 8: 1 not understanding *r* her voice?
8: 4 I *r* my voice to all mankind.
Isa 8: 9 *R* the war cry, you nations,
10: 15 Does the ax *r* itself
10: 26 he will *r* his rod over the waters,
11: 12 He will *r* a banner for the nations
13: 2 *R* a banner on a bare hilltop,
14: 13 I will *r* my throne
24: 14 They *r* their voices, they shout
42: 2 or *r* his voice in the streets.
42: 11 its towns *r* their voices;
42: 13 with a shout he will *r* the battle cry
45: 13 *r* up Cyrus in my righteousness:
58: 1 *R* your voice like a trumpet.
58: 12 will *r* up the age-old foundations;
62: 10 *R* a banner for the nations.
Jer 4: 6 *R* the signal to go to Zion!
6: 1 *R* the signal over Beth Hakkerem!
23: 5 "when I will *r* up to David
30: 9 whom I will *r* up for them.
Eze 26: 8 and *r* his shields against you.
27: 30 They will *r* their voice
Da 11: 11 who will *r* a large army,
Hos 5: 8 *R* the battle cry in Beth Aven;
Mic 5: 5 we will *r* against him seven
Zec 1: 21 so that no one could *r* his head,
2: 9 I will surely *r* my hand
11: 16 For I am going to *r* up a shepherd
Mt 3: 9 these stones God can *r* up children
10: 8 *r* the dead, cleanse those who have
Lk 3: 8 these stones God can *r* up children
Jn 2: 19 and I will *r* it again in three days."
2: 20 you are going to *r* it in three days?"
6: 39 but *r* them up at the last day.
6: 40 and I will *r* him up at the last day."

Jn 6:44 and I will *r* him up at the last day.
6:54 and I will *r* him up at the last day.
Ac 3:22 'The Lord your God will *r* up
1Co 6:14 from the dead, and he will *r* us
15:15 he did not *r* him if in fact the dead
2Co 4:14 also *r* us with Jesus and present us
Heb 11:19 that God could *r* the dead,
Jas 3:18 sow in peace *r* a harvest
5:15 person well; the Lord will *r* him up.

RAISED (RISE)

Ge 14:22 "I have *r* my hand to the LORD,
Ex 7:20 He *r* his staff in the presence
9:16 But I have *r* you up for this very
Nu 14:1 of the community *r* their voices
20:11 Then Moses *r* his arm
Jos 5:7 So he *r* up their sons in their place,
8:29 they *r* a large pile of rocks over it,
Jdg 2:16 Then the LORD *r* up judges,
2:18 Whenever the LORD *r* up a judge
3:9 he *r* up for them a deliverer,
1Sa 4:5 all Israel *r* such a great shout that
14:27 He *r* his hand to his mouth,
2Sa 12:3 He *r* it, and it grew up with him
23:8 he *r* his spear against eight hundred
23:18 *r* his spear against three hundred
1Ki 11:14 the LORD *r* up against Solomon
11:23 God *r* up against Solomon another
14:7 'I *r* you up from among the people
2Ki 3:4 Now Mesha king of Moab *r* sheep,
19:22 whom have you *r* your voice
1Ch 11:11 *r* his spear against three hundred
11:20 *r* his spear against three hundred
2Ch 5:13 they *r* their voices in praise
13:15 the men of Judah *r* the battle cry.
Ne 5:1 and their wives *r* a great outcry
Est 10:2 to which the king had *r* him,
Job 31:21 if I have *r* my hand
Ps 60:4 who fear you, you have *r* a banner
80:15 the son you have *r* up for yourself.
80:17 of man you have *r* up for yourself.
148:14 He has *r* up for his people a horn,
Isa 2:2 it will be *r* above the hills,
5:25 his hand is *r* and he strikes them
18:3 when a banner is *r*
23:13 they *r* up their siege towers,
37:23 whom have you *r* your voice
40:4 Every valley shall be *r* up,
49:11 and my highways will be *r* up.
52:13 he will be *r* and lifted up
Jer 12:6 they have *r* a loud cry against you.
29:15 "The LORD has *r* up prophets
La 2:7 they have *r* a shout in the house
Eze 2:2 came into me and *r* me to my feet,
3:24 came into me and *r* me to my feet.
41:8 saw that the temple had a *r* base all
Da 4:34 *r* my eyes toward heaven,
7:5 It was *r* up on one of its sides,
8:18 he touched me and *r* me to my feet.
Am 2:11 *r* up prophets from among your
Mic 4:1 it will be *r* above the hills,
Zec 5:7 Then the cover of lead was *r*,
14:10 But Jerusalem will be *r* up
Mt 11:5 the deaf hear, the dead are *r*,
16:21 and on the third day be *r* to life.
17:9 of Man has been *r* from the dead."
17:23 on the third day he will be *r* to life
20:19 On the third day he will be *r* to life
27:52 holy people who had died were *r*
27:64 tell the people that he has been *r*
Mk 6:14 "John the Baptist has been *r*
6:16 has been *r* from the dead!"
Lk 1:69 He has *r* up a horn of salvation
7:22 the deaf hear, the dead are *r*,
9:7 were saying that John had been *r*
9:22 and on the third day be *r* to life."
24:7 and on the third day be *r* again.' "
Jn 2:22 After he was *r* from the dead,
12:1 whom Jesus had *r* from the dead.
12:9 whom he had *r* from the dead.
21:14 after he was *r* from the dead.
Ac 2:14 *r* his voice and addressed
2:24 But God *r* him from the dead,
2:32 God has *r* this Jesus to life,
3:15 but God *r* him from the dead.
3:26 When God *r* up his servant,
4:10 but whom God *r* from the dead,
4:24 they *r* their voices together
5:30 of our fathers *r* Jesus from the dead
9:21 "Isn't he the man who *r* havoc
10:40 but God *r* him from the dead
13:30 But God *r* him from the dead,
13:34 The fact that God *r* him
13:37 But the one whom God *r*
22:22 Then they *r* their voices
Ro 4:24 in him who *r* Jesus our Lord
4:25 was *r* to life for our justification.
6:4 as Christ was *r* from the dead
6:9 since Christ was *r* from the dead,
7:4 to him who was *r* from the dead,
8:11 And if the Spirit of him who *r* Jesus
8:11 he who *r* Christ from the dead will
8:34 more than that, who was *r* to life—
9:17 "I *r* you up for this very purpose,
10:9 in your heart that God *r* him
1Co 6:14 By his power God *r* the Lord
15:4 that he was *r* on the third day
15:12 it is preached that Christ has been *r*
15:13 then not even Christ has been *r*.
15:14 And if Christ has not been *r*,
15:15 him if in fact the dead are not *r*.
15:15 testified about God that he *r* Christ
15:16 the dead are not *r*, then Christ has
15:16 then Christ has not been *r* either.
15:17 And if Christ has not been *r*,
15:20 But Christ has indeed been *r*
15:29 If the dead are not *r* at all,
15:32 have I gained? If the dead are not *r*,
15:35 may ask, "How are the dead *r?*
15:42 it is *r* imperishable; it is sown
15:43 sown in dishonor, it is *r* in glory;
15:43 sown in weakness, it is *r* in power;
15:44 natural body, it is *r* a spiritual body.
15:52 the dead will be *r* imperishable,
2Co 4:14 that the one who *r* the Lord Jesus
5:15 died for them and was *r* again.
Gal 1:1 who *r* him from the dead—
Eph 1:20 exerted in Christ when he *r* him
2:6 And God *r* us up with Christ
Col 2:12 and *r* with him through your faith
2:12 of God, who *r* him from the dead.
3:1 then, you have been *r* with Christ,
1Th 1:10 whom he *r* from the dead—Jesus,
2Ti 2:8 Remember Jesus Christ, *r*
Heb 11:35 Women received back their dead, *r*
1Pe 1:21 who *r* him from the dead
Rev 10:5 and on the land *r* his right hand

RAISES (RISE)

1Sa 2:6 down to the grave and *r* up.
2:8 He *r* the poor from the dust
Ps 113:7 He *r* the poor from the dust
Pr 1:20 she *r* her voice in the public
Isa 19:16 hand that the LORD Almighty *r*
Jn 5:21 For just as the Father *r* the dead
Ac 26:8 it incredible that God *r* the dead?
2Co 1:9 but on God, who *r* the dead.

RAISIN (RAISINS)

1Ch 12:40 fig cakes, *r* cakes, wine, oil,
Isa 16:7 for the *r* cakes of Kir Hareseth.

RAISIN-CAKES (CAKE)

Hos 3:1 to other gods and love the sacred *r*

RAISING (RISE)

Jdg 21:2 *r* their voices and weeping bitterly.
1Ki 15:4 a lamp in Jerusalem by *r* up a son
Ps 55:12 if a foe were *r* himself against me,
Jer 4:16 *r* a war cry against the cities
Am 7:10 Amos is *r* a conspiracy against you
Hab 1:6 I am *r* up the Babylonians,
Jn 12:17 from the tomb, *r* him from the dead
Ac 10:29 I came without *r* any objection.
13:33 their children, by *r* up Jesus.
17:31 to all men by *r* him from the dead."
1Co 10:25 without *r* questions of conscience,
10:27 put before you without *r* questions

RAISINS (RAISIN)

Nu 6:3 drink grape juice or eat grapes or *r*.
1Sa 25:18 cakes of *r* and two hundred cakes
30:12 of pressed figs and two cakes of *r*.
2Sa 6:19 and a cake of *r* to each person
16:1 cakes of *r*, a hundred cakes
1Ch 16:3 a cake of *r* to each Israelite man

SS 2:5 Strengthen me with *r*,

RAKEM

1Ch 7:16 and his sons were Ulam and *R*.

RAKKATH

Jos 19:35 Zer, Hammath, *R*, Kinnereth,

RAKKON

Jos 19:46 and *R*, with the area facing Joppa.

RALLIED (RALLY)

Ge 48:2 Israel *r* his strength and sat up
Ex 32:26 And all the Levites *r* to him.
2Sa 2:25 men of Benjamin *r* behind Abner.
Ac 5:36 about four hundred men *r* to him.

RALLY (RALLIED)

Isa 11:10 the nations will *r* to him,

RAM (RAM'S RAMS RAMS')

Ge 15:9 a goat and a *r*, each three years old,
22:13 and took the *r* and sacrificed it
22:13 there in a thicket he saw a *r* caught
Ex 25:5 *r* skins dyed red and hides
26:14 a covering of *r* skins dyed red,
29:17 Cut the *r* into pieces and wash
29:18 Then burn the entire *r* on the altar.
29:19 "Take the other *r*, and Aaron
29:22 Take from this *r* the fat, the fat tail,
29:22 (This is the *r* for the ordination.)
29:26 of the *r* for Aaron's ordination,
29:27 of the ordination *r* that belong
29:31 "Take the *r* for the ordination
29:32 his sons are to eat the meat of the *r*
29:34 any of the meat of the ordination *r*
35:7 *r* skins dyed red and hides
35:23 *r* skins dyed red or hides
36:19 a covering of *r* skins dyed red,
39:34 the covering of *r* skins dyed red,
Lev 5:15 as a penalty a *r* from the flock,
5:16 make atonement for him with the *r*
5:18 a guilt offering a *r* from the flock,
6:6 his guilt offering, a *r* from the flock,
8:18 He then presented the *r*
8:19 Then Moses slaughtered the *r*
8:20 He cut the *r* into pieces
8:21 and burned the whole *r* on the altar
8:22 He then presented the other *r*, the *r*
8:23 Moses slaughtered the *r*
8:29 Moses' share of the ordination *r*—
9:2 and a *r* for your burnt offering,
9:4 and a *r* for a fellowship offering
9:18 He slaughtered the cow and the *r*
9:19 portions of the cow and the *r*—
16:3 and a *r* for a burnt offering.
16:5 and a *r* for a burnt offering.
19:21 must bring a *r* to the entrance
19:22 With the *r* of the guilt offering
Nu 5:8 with the *r* with which atonement is
6:14 a *r* without defect for a fellowship
6:17 is to sacrifice the *r* as a fellowship
6:19 his hands a boiled shoulder of the *r*,
7:15 one *r* and one male lamb a year old,
7:21 one *r* and one male lamb a year old,
7:27 one *r* and one male lamb a year old,
7:33 one *r* and one male lamb a year old,
7:39 one *r* and one male lamb a year old,
7:45 one *r* and one male lamb a year old,
7:51 one *r* and one male lamb a year old,
7:57 one *r* and one male lamb a year old,
7:63 one *r* and one male lamb a year old,
7:69 one *r* and one male lamb a year old,
7:75 one *r* and one male lamb a year old,
7:81 one *r* and one male lamb a year old,
15:6 " 'With a *r* prepare a grain offering
15:11 Each bull or *r*, each lamb
23:2 two of them offered a bull and a *r*
23:4 altar I have offered a bull and a *r*."
23:14 offered a bull and a *r* on each altar.
23:30 offered a bull and a *r* on each altar.
28:11 one *r* and seven male lambs a year
28:12 with the *r*, a grain offering
28:14 with the *r*, a third of a hin;
28:19 one *r* and seven male lambs a year
28:20 with the *r*, two-tenths;
28:27 one *r* and seven male lambs a year
28:28 with the *r*, two-tenths;

Nu 29: 2 one *r* and seven male lambs a year
29: 3 with the *r*, two-tenths;
29: 8 one *r* and seven male lambs a year
29: 9 with the *r*, two-tenths;
29: 36 one *r* and seven male lambs a year
29: 37 With the bull, the *r* and the lambs,
Ru 4: 19 the father of *R*, *R* the father
1Ch 2: 9 born to Hezron were: Jerahmeel, *R*
2: 10 *R* was the father of Amminadab,
2: 25 *R* his firstborn, Bunah, Oren,
2: 27 The sons of *R* the firstborn
Ezr 10: 19 their guilt they each presented a *r*
Job 32: 2 of the family of *R*,
Eze 43: 23 are to offer a young bull and a *r*
43: 25 also to provide a young bull and a *r*
45: 24 each bull and an ephah for each *r*,
46: 4 is to be six male lambs and a *r*,
46: 5 given with the *r* is to be an ephah,
46: 6 six lambs and a *r*, all without defect
46: 7 one ephah with the *r*,
46: 11 an ephah with a *r*,
Da 8: 3 before me was a *r* with two horns,
8: 4 I watched the *r* as he charged
8: 6 toward the two-horned *r* I had seen
8: 7 I saw him attack the *r* furiously,
8: 7 The *r* was powerless to stand
8: 7 and none could rescue the *r*
8: 7 striking the *r* and shattering his
8: 20 The two-horned *r* that you saw
Mt 1: 3 the father of *R*, *R* the father
Lk 3: 33 son of Amminadab, the son of *R*,

RAM'S (RAM)

Ex 19: 13 when the *r* horn sounds a long blast
Ps 81: 3 Sound the *r* horn at the New Moon
98: 6 and the blast of the *r* horn—

RAMAH

Jos 18: 25 Gibeon, *R*, Beeroth, Mizpah,
19: 8 Baalath Beer (*R* in the Negev).
19: 29 then turned back toward *R*
19: 36 Kinnereth, Adamah, *R*, Hazor,
Jdg 4: 5 the Palm of Deborah between *R*
19: 13 let's try to reach Gibeah or *R*
1Sa 1: 19 then went back to their home at *R*.
2: 11 Then Elkanah went home to *R*,
7: 17 But he always went back to *R*,
8: 4 together and came to Samuel at *R*.
15: 34 Then Samuel left for *R*,
16: 13 Samuel then went to *R*.
19: 18 he went to Samuel at *R*
19: 19 "David is in Naioth at *R*";
19: 22 he himself left for *R* and went
19: 22 "Over in Naioth at *R*," they said.
19: 23 So Saul went to Naioth at *R*.
20: 1 Then David fled from Naioth at *R*
25: 1 they buried him at his home in *R*.
28: 3 buried him in his own town of *R*.
1Ki 15: 17 and fortified *R* to prevent anyone
15: 21 he stopped building *R*
15: 22 away from *R* the stones
2Ch 16: 1 and fortified *R* to prevent anyone
16: 5 he stopped building *R*
16: 6 away from *R* the stones
Ezr 2: 26 Kephirah and Beeroth 743 of *R*
Ne 7: 30 of *R* and Geba
11: 33 in Hazor, *R* and Gittaim, in Hadid,
Isa 10: 29 *R* trembles;
Jer 31: 15 "A voice is heard in *R*,
40: 1 guard had released him at *R*.
Hos 5: 8 the horn in *R*.
Mt 2: 18 fulfilled: "A voice is heard in *R*,

RAMATH LEHI

Jdg 15: 17 and the place was called *R*.

RAMATH MIZPAH

Jos 13: 26 from Heshbon to *R* and Betonim,

RAMATHAIM

1Sa 1: 1 There was a certain man from *R*,

RAMATHITE

1Ch 27: 27 Shimei the *R* was in charge

RAMESES

Ge 47: 11 district of *R*, as Pharaoh directed.
Ex 1: 11 and they built Pithom and *R*
Ex 12: 37 journeyed from *R* to Succoth.
Nu 33: 3 out from *R* on the fifteenth day
33: 5 The Israelites left *R* and camped

RAMIAH

Ezr 10: 25 *R*, Izziah, Malkijah, Mijamin,

RAMOTH

Dt 4: 43 for the Reubenites; *R* in Gilead,
Jos 20: 8 *R* in Gilead in the tribe of Gad,
21: 38 *R* in Gilead (a city of refuge
2Ki 8: 29 inflicted on him at *R* in his battle
1Ch 6: 73 *R* and Anem, together
6: 80 of Gad they received *R* in Gilead,
2Ch 22: 6 inflicted on him at *R* in his battle

RAMOTH GILEAD

1Ki 4: 13 in *R* (the settlements of Jair
22: 3 "Don't you know that *R* belongs to
22: 4 go with me to fight against *R*?"
22: 6 "Shall I go to war against *R*,
22: 12 "Attack *R* and be victorious," they
22: 15 shall we go to war against *R*,
22: 20 will lure Ahab into attacking *R* and
22: 29 king of Judah went up to *R*.
2Ki 8: 28 against Hazael king of Aram at *R*.
9: 1 flask of oil with you and go to *R*.
9: 4 man, the prophet, went to *R*.
9: 14 and all Israel had been defending *R*
2Ch 18: 2 and urged him to attack *R*.
18: 3 "Will you go with me against *R*?"
18: 5 "Shall we go to war against *R*,
18: 11 "Attack *R* and be victorious,"
18: 14 shall we go to war against *R*,
18: 19 king of Israel into attacking *R*
18: 28 king of Judah went up to *R*.
22: 5 against Hazael king of Aram at *R*.

RAMOTH NEGEV

1Sa 30: 27 *R* and Jattir; to those in Aroer,

RAMP (RAMPS)

2Sa 20: 15 They built a siege *r* up to the city,
2Ki 19: 32 or build a siege *r* against it.
Job 19: 12 they build a siege *r* against me
Isa 37: 33 or build a siege *r* against it.
Eze 4: 2 works against it, build a *r* up to it,
21: 22 to build a *r* and to erect siege works
26: 8 build a *r* up to your walls

RAMPART (RAMPARTS)

Ps 91: 4 will be your shield and *r*.

RAMPARTS (RAMPART)

Ps 48: 13 consider well her *r*,
Isa 26: 1 its walls and *r*.
La 2: 8 He made *r* and walls lament;
Hab 2: 1 and station myself on the *r*;

RAMPS (RAMP)

Job 30: 12 they build their siege *r* against me.
Jer 6: 6 and build siege *r* against Jerusalem.
32: 24 "See how the siege *r* are built up
33: 4 down to be used against the siege *r*
Eze 17: 17 when *r* are built and siege works
Da 11: 15 build up siege *r* and will capture
Hab 1: 10 they build earthen *r* and capture

RAMS (RAM)

Ge 31: 38 nor have I eaten *r* from your flocks.
32: 14 two hundred ewes and twenty *r*,
Ex 29: 1 Take a young bull and two *r*
29: 3 along with the bull and the two *r*.
29: 15 "Take one of the *r*, and Aaron
Lev 8: 2 the two *r* and the basket containing
23: 18 defect, one young bull and two *r*.
Nu 7: 17 five *r*, five male goats and five male
7: 23 five *r*, five male goats and five male
7: 29 five *r*, five male goats and five male
7: 35 five *r*, five male goats and five male
7: 41 five *r*, five male goats and five male
7: 47 five *r*, five male goats and five male
7: 53 five *r*, five male goats and five male
7: 59 five *r*, five male goats and five male
7: 65 five *r*, five male goats and five male
7: 71 five *r*, five male goats and five male
7: 77 five *r*, five male goats and five male
7: 83 five *r*, five male goats and five male
Nu 7: 87 twelve *r* and twelve male lambs
7: 88 sixty *r*, sixty male goats
23: 1 and prepare seven bulls and seven *r*
23: 29 and prepare seven bulls and seven *r*
29: 13 two *r* and fourteen male lambs
29: 14 with each of the two *r*, two-tenths;
29: 17 two *r* and fourteen male lambs
29: 18 With the bulls, *r* and lambs,
29: 20 two *r* and fourteen male lambs
29: 21 With the bulls, *r* and lambs,
29: 23 two *r* and fourteen male lambs
29: 24 With the bulls, *r* and lambs,
29: 26 two *r* and fourteen male lambs
29: 27 With the bulls, *r* and lambs,
29: 29 two *r* and fourteen male lambs
29: 30 With the bulls, *r* and lambs,
29: 32 two *r* and fourteen male lambs
29: 33 With the bulls, *r* and lambs,
Dt 32: 14 with choice *r* of Bashan
1Sa 15: 22 to heed is better than the fat of *r*.
2Ki 3: 4 the wool of a hundred thousand *r*.
1Ch 15: 26 and seven *r* were sacrificed.
29: 21 a thousand *r* and a thousand male
2Ch 13: 9 and seven *r* may become a priest
17: 11 seven thousand seven hundred *r*
29: 21 They brought seven bulls, seven *r*,
29: 22 next they slaughtered the *r*
29: 32 a hundred *r* and two hundred male
Ezr 6: 9 is needed—young bulls, *r*,
6: 17 two hundred *r*, four hundred male
7: 17 this money be sure to buy bulls, *r*
8: 35 ninety-six *r*, seventy-seven male
Job 42: 8 now take seven bulls and seven *r*
Ps 66: 15 and an offering of *r*;
114: 4 the mountains skipped like *r*,
114: 6 mountains, that you skipped like *r*,
Isa 1: 11 of *r* and the fat of fattened animals;
34: 6 fat from the kidneys of *r*.
60: 7 the *r* of Nebaioth will serve you;
Jer 51: 40 like *r* and goats.
Eze 4: 2 and put battering *r* around it.
21: 22 to set battering *r* against the gates,
21: 22 where he is to set up battering *r*,
26: 9 of his battering *r* against your walls
27: 21 business with you in lambs, *r*
34: 17 another, and between *r* and goats.
39: 18 as if they were *r* and lambs,
45: 23 and seven *r* without defect
Mic 6: 7 pleased with thousands of *r*,

RAMS' (RAM)

Jos 6: 4 trumpets of *r*' horns in front
1Ch 15: 28 with the sounding of *r*' horns

RAN (RUN)

Ge 18: 7 Then he *r* to the herd and selected
24: 20 *r* back to the well to draw more
24: 28 The girl *r* and told her mother's
29: 12 So she *r* and told her father.
33: 4 But Esau *r* to meet Jacob
39: 12 in her hand and *r* out of the house.
39: 15 beside me and *r* out of the house."
39: 18 beside me and *r* out of the house."
Ex 4: 3 it became a snake, and he *r* from it.
Nu 11: 27 A young man *r* and told Moses,
16: 47 *r* into the midst of the assembly.
Jos 4: 18 and *r* at flood stage as before.
7: 22 Joshua sent messengers, and they *r*
15: 3 Then it *r* past Hezron up to Addar
15: 8 it *r* up the Valley of Ben Hinnom
15: 10 *r* along the northern slope
17: 7 The boundary *r* southward
18: 17 *r* down to the Stone of Bohan son
19: 11 Going west it *r* to Maralah,
19: 34 The boundary *r* west
Jdg 7: 21 all the Midianites *r*, crying out
9: 54 So his servant *r* him through,
1Sa 3: 5 he *r* to Eli and said, "Here I am;
4: 12 That same day a Benjamite *r*
10: 23 They *r* and brought him out,
17: 22 *r* to the battle lines and greeted his
17: 24 they all *r* from him in great fear.
17: 48 David *r* quickly toward the battle
17: 51 David *r* and stood over him.
17: 51 hero was dead, they turned and *r*.
20: 36 As the boy *r*, he shot an arrow
2Sa 18: 21 bowed down before Joab and *r* off.
18: 23 Ahimaaz *r* by way of the plain

1Ki 2:39 two of Shimei's slaves *r*
18:35 The water *r* down around the altar
18:46 he *r* ahead of Ahab all the way
19:3 Elijah was afraid and *r* for his life.
19:20 Elisha then left his oxen and *r*
22:35 from his wound *r* onto the floor
2Ki 7:7 as it was and *r* for their lives.
9:10 Then he opened the door and *r*.
Jnh 1:3 But Jonah *r* away from the LORD
Mt 8:33 Those tending the pigs *r* off,
27:48 Immediately one of them *r*
28:8 with joy, and *r* to tell his disciples.
Mk 5:6 he *r* and fell on his knees in front
5:14 Those tending the pigs *r* off
6:33 and *r* on foot from all the towns
6:55 They *r* throughout that whole
9:15 with wonder and *r* to greet him.
10:17 a man *r* up to him and fell
15:36 One man *r*, filled a sponge
Lk 8:34 they *r* off and reported this
15:20 he *r* to his son, threw his arms
19:4 So he *r* ahead and climbed
24:12 however, got up and *r* to the tomb.
Ac 8:30 Then Philip *r* up to the chariot
12:14 was so overjoyed she *r* back
19:16 them such a beating that they *r* out
21:32 soldiers and *r* down to the crowd.
27:41 struck a sandbar and *r* aground.

RANDOM

1Ki 22:34 But someone drew his bow at *r*
2Ch 18:33 But someone drew his bow at *r*
Pr 26:10 Like an archer who wounds at *r*

RANG (RING)

Mt 25:6 "At midnight the cry *r* out:
1Th 1:8 The Lord's message *r* out

RANGE (RANGES)

Nu 27:12 up this mountain in the Abarim *r*
Dt 32:49 into the Abarim *R* to Mount Nebo
2Ch 16:9 the LORD *r* throughout the earth
Isa 32:20 your oxen and donkeys *r* free.
Zec 4:10 which *r* throughout the earth.)"

RANGES (RANGE)

Job 39:8 He *r* the hills for his pasture

RANK (RANKING RANKS)

1Sa 18:5 that Saul gave him a high *r*
2Ki 23:4 next in *r* and the doorkeepers
25:18 Zephaniah the priest next in *r*
1Ch 15:18 with them their brothers next in *r*:
2Ch 31:12 his brother Shimei was next in *r*.
Est 10:3 second in *r* to King Xerxes,
Isa 3:3 the captain of fifty and man of *r*,
5:13 their men of *r* will die of hunger
Jer 52:24 Zephaniah the priest next in *r*
Eze 23:23 chariot officers and men of high *r*,

RANKING (RANK)

Ac 25:23 room with the high *r* officers

RANKS (RANK)

1Sa 17:8 and shouted to the *r* of Israel,
17:10 "This day I defy the *r* of Israel!
2Ki 11:8 who approaches your *r* must be put
11:15 "Bring her out between the *r*
1Ch 12:38 who volunteered to serve in the *r*.
2Ch 23:14 "Bring her out between the *r*
Job 40:19 He *r* first among the works of God,
Pr 30:27 yet they advance together in *r*;
Isa 14:31 and there is not a straggler in its *r*.
Jer 46:21 The mercenaries in her *r*
50:37 and all the foreigners in her *r*!
Joel 2:8 defenses without breaking *r*.
Gal 2:4 false brothers had infiltrated our *r*

RANSACKED

Ob :6 But how Esau will be *r*,
Zec 14:2 the houses *r*, and the women raped.

RANSOM (RANSOMED RANSOMS)

Ex 30:12 each one must pay the LORD a *r*
Nu 35:31 " 'Do not accept a *r* for the life
35:32 " 'Do not accept a *r*
Job 5:20 In famine he will *r* you from death,
6:22 pay a *r* for me from your wealth,
6:23 *r* me from the clutches
33:24 I have found a *r* for him'—
Ps 49:7 or give to God a *r* for him—
49:8 the *r* for a life is costly,
Pr 13:8 A man's riches may *r* his life,
21:18 The wicked become a *r*
Isa 43:3 I give Egypt for your *r*,
47:11 that you cannot ward off with a *r*;
50:2 Was my arm too short to *r* you?
Jer 31:11 For the LORD will *r* Jacob
Hos 13:14 "I will *r* them from the power
Mt 20:28 and to give his life as a *r* for many."
Mk 10:45 and to give his life as a *r* for many."
1Ti 2:6 who gave himself as a *r* for all men
Heb 9:15 as a *r* to set them free

RANSOMED (RANSOM)

Lev 19:20 but who has not been *r* or given her
27:29 devoted to destruction may be *r*;
Isa 35:10 and the *r* of the LORD will return.
51:11 The *r* of the LORD will return.

RANSOMS (RANSOM)

Ps 55:18 He *r* me unharmed

RAPED (RAPES)

Jdg 19:25 and they *r* her and abused her
20:5 They *r* my concubine, and she died
2Sa 13:14 stronger than she, he *r* her.
13:32 the day Amnon *r* his sister Tamar.
Zec 14:2 ransacked, and the women *r*.

RAPES (RAPED)

Dt 22:25 pledged to be married and *r* her,
22:28 and *r* her and they are discovered,

RAPHA

2Sa 21:16 one of the descendants of *R*,
21:18 one of the descendants of *R*.
21:20 He also was descended from *R*.
21:22 These four were descendants of *R*
1Ch 8:2 Nohah the fourth and *R* the fifth.
20:6 He also was descended from *R*.
20:8 These were descendants of *R*

RAPHAH

1Ch 8:37 the father of Binea; *R* was his son,

RAPHU

Nu 13:9 Palti son of *R*; from the tribe

RAPID

Ezr 5:8 and is making *r* progress

RARE

1Sa 3:1 the word of the LORD was *r*;
Pr 20:15 that speak knowledge are a *r* jewel.
24:4 with *r* and beautiful treasures.
Isa 13:12 more *r* than the gold of Ophir.

RASH

Lev 13:2 "When anyone has a swelling or a *r*
13:6 pronounce him clean; it is only a *r*.
13:7 But if the *r* does spread in his skin
13:8 and if the *r* has spread in the skin,
13:39 it is a harmless *r* that has broken
14:56 for a swelling, a *r* or a bright spot,
Nu 30:6 or after her lips utter a *r* promise
30:8 *r* promise by which she obligates
Ps 106:33 and *r* words came from Moses' lips
Isa 32:4 The mind of the *r* will know
Ac 19:36 to be quiet and not do anything *r*.
2Ti 3:4 treacherous, *r*, conceited,

RAT (RATS)

Lev 11:29 the *r*, any kind of great lizard,

RATE

Lev 25:50 is to be based on the *r* paid

RATIFIED

Jos 9:15 leaders of the assembly *r* it by oath.

RATIONED

Eze 4:16 The people will eat *r* food
4:16 and drink *r* water in despair,

RATS (RAT)

1Sa 6:4 "Five gold tumors and five gold *r*,
6:5 and of the *r* that are destroying
6:11 it the chest containing the gold *r*
6:18 number of the gold *r* was according
Isa 66:17 *r* and other abominable things—

RATTLES (RATTLING)

Job 39:23 The quiver *r* against his side,

RATTLING (RATTLES)

Job 41:29 he laughs at the *r* of the lance.
Eze 37:7 there was a noise, a *r* sound,

RAVAGE (RAVAGED RAVAGES RAVAGING)

Ge 41:30 and the famine will *r* the land.
Jdg 6:5 they invaded the land to *r* it.
Ps 80:13 Boars from the forest *r* it
Jer 5:6 a wolf from the desert will *r* them,
5:10 through her vineyards and *r* them,
Eze 26:8 He will *r* your settlements

RAVAGED (RAVAGE)

Isa 6:11 and the fields ruined and *r*,
Eze 26:6 on the mainland will be *r*
36:3 Because they *r* and hounded you

RAVAGES (RAVAGE)

Ps 35:17 Rescue my life from their *r*,
Jer 14:18 I see the *r* of famine.

RAVAGING (RAVAGE)

1Ch 21:12 of the LORD *r* every part of Israel

RAVEN (RAVENS)

Ge 8:7 made in the ark and sent out a *r*,
Lev 11:15 any kind of *r*, the horned owl,
Dt 14:14 any kind of *r*, the horned owl,
Job 38:41 Who provides food for the *r*
SS 5:11 and black as a *r*.
Isa 34:11 great owl and the *r* will nest there.

RAVENING (RAVENOUS)

Jer 2:30 like a *r* lion.

RAVENOUS (RAVENING)

Ge 49:27 "Benjamin is a *r* wolf;
Ps 57:4 I lie among *r* beasts—

RAVENS (RAVEN)

1Ki 17:4 and I have ordered the *r*
17:6 The *r* brought him bread
Ps 147:9 and for the young *r* when they call.
Pr 30:17 out by the *r* of the valley,
Lk 12:24 Consider the *r*: They do not sow

RAVINE (RAVINES)

Jos 16:8 border went west to the Kanah *R*
17:9 continued south to the Kanah *R*
17:9 was the northern side of the *r*
19:11 extended to the *r* near Jokneam.
1Sa 15:5 and set an ambush in the *r*.
25:20 donkey into a mountain *r*,
30:9 *R*, where some stayed behind,
30:10 were too exhausted to cross the *r*.
30:21 left behind at the Besor *R*
1Ki 17:3 eastward and hide in the Kerith *R*,
17:5 to the Kerith *R*, east of the Jordan,
Isa 15:7 over the *R* of the Poplars.
Zec 1:8 among the myrtle trees in a *r*.

RAVINES (RAVINE)

Nu 21:14 ". . . Waheb in Suphah
21:15 and the slopes of the *r*
2Sa 23:30 Hiddai from the *r* of Gaash,
1Ch 11:32 Hurai from the *r* of Gaash,
Job 22:24 gold of Ophir to the rocks in the *r*,
Ps 104:10 springs pour water into the *r*;
Isa 7:19 and settle in the steep *r*
57:5 you sacrifice your children in the *r*
57:6 of the *r* are your portion;
Eze 6:3 to the *r* and valleys: I am about
31:12 broken in all the *r* of the land.
32:6 the *r* will be filled with your flesh.
34:13 in the *r* and in all the settlements
35:8 in your valleys and in all your *r*.
36:4 and hills, to the *r* and valleys,
36:6 to the *r* and valleys: 'This is what
Joel 3:18 all the *r* of Judah will run

RAVING

Jn 10:20 He is demon-possessed and *r* mad.

RAVISH (RAVISHED)

Dt 28:30 but another will take her and *r* her.

RAVISHED (RAVISH)

Isa 13:16 will be looted and their wives *r*.
Jer 3: 2 place where you have not been *r?*
La 5:11 Women have been *r* in Zion,

RAW

Ex 12: 9 Do not eat the meat *r* or cooked
Lev 13:10 if there is *r* flesh in the swelling,
13:14 whenever *r* flesh appears on him,
13:15 The *r* flesh is unclean; he has
13:15 When the priest sees the *r* flesh,
13:16 Should the *r* flesh change
13:24 appears in the *r* flesh of the burn,
1Sa 2:15 meat from you, but only *r*."
Eze 29:18 and every shoulder made *r*.

RAWBONED

Ge 49:14 "Issachar is a *r* donkey

RAY (RAYS)

Am 5:20 without a *r* of brightness?

RAYS (RAY)

Job 3: 9 and not see the first *r* of dawn,
41:18 his eyes are like the *r* of dawn.
Hab 3: 4 *r* flashed from his hand,

RAZOR

Nu 6: 5 vow of separation no *r* may be used
Jdg 13: 5 No *r* may be used on his head,
16:17 "No *r* has ever been used
1Sa 1:11 no *r* will ever be used on his head."
Ps 52: 2 it is like a sharpened *r*,
Isa 7:20 that day the Lord will use a *r* hired
Eze 5: 1 as a barber's *r* to shave your head

READ (READER READING READS)

Ex 24: 7 the Book of the Covenant and *r* it
Dt 17:19 he is to *r* it all the days of his life
31:11 you shall *r* this law before them
Jos 8:34 Joshua *r* all the words of the law—
8:35 commanded that Joshua did not *r*
2Ki 5: 6 took to the king of Israel *r:*
5: 7 as the king of Israel *r* the letter,
19:14 letter from the messengers and *r* it.
22: 8 He gave it to Shaphan, who *r* it.
22:10 Shaphan *r* from it in the presence
22:16 in the book the king of Judah has *r*.
23: 2 He *r* in their hearing all the words
2Ch 30: 6 which *r:* "People of Israel,
34:18 Shaphan *r* from it in the presence
34:24 written in the book that has been *r*
34:30 He *r* in their hearing all the words
Ezr 4:18 The letter you sent us has been *r*
4:23 of King Artaxerxes was *r* to Rehum
5: 7 The report they sent him *r*
Ne 8: 3 He *r* it aloud from daybreak
8: 8 They *r* from the Book of the Law
8: 8 could understand what was being *r*.
8:18 Ezra *r* from the Book of the Law
9: 3 and *r* from the Book of the Law
13: 1 of Moses was *r* aloud in the hearing
Est 6: 1 to be brought in and *r* to him.
Isa 29:11 and say to him, "*R* this, please,"
29:11 the scroll to someone who can *r*,
29:12 answer, "I don't know how to *r*."
29:12 scroll to someone who cannot *r*,
29:12 "*R* this, please," he will answer,
34:16 in the scroll of the LORD and *r:*
37:14 letter from the messengers and *r* it.
Jer 29:29 *r* the letter to Jeremiah the prophet
36: 6 and *r* to the people from the scroll
36: 6 *R* them to all the people
36: 8 the LORD's temple he *r* the words
36:10 Baruch *r* to all the people
36:13 everything he had heard Baruch *r*
36:14 the scroll from which you have *r*
36:15 So Baruch *r* it to them.
36:15 "Sit down, please, and *r* it to us."
36:21 of Elishama the secretary and *r* it
36:23 Whenever Jehudi had *r* three
51:61 see that you *r* all these words aloud
Da 5: 8 but they could not *r* the writing
5:15 brought before me to *r* this writing
5:16 If you can *r* this writing
5:17 I will *r* the writing for the king
Mt 12: 3 "Haven't you *r* what David did
12: 5 Or haven't you *r* in the Law that
19: 4 "Haven't you *r*," he replied,
21:16 replied Jesus, "have you never *r*,
21:42 Have you never *r* in the Scriptures:
22:31 have you not *r* what God said
Mk 2:25 "Have you never *r* what David did
12:10 Haven't you *r* this scripture:
12:26 have you not *r* in the book
15:26 notice of the charge against him *r:*
Lk 4:16 And he stood up to *r*.
6: 3 "Have you never *r* what David did
10:26 "How do you *r* it?" He answered:
23:38 notice above him, which *r:*
Jn 19:19 It *r*, JESUS OF NAZARETH,
19:20 Many of the Jews *r* this sign,
Ac 13:27 prophets that are *r* every Sabbath.
15:21 and is *r* in the synagogues
15:31 The people *r* it and were glad
23:34 The governor *r* the letter
2Co 1:13 write you anything you cannot *r*
3: 2 known and *r* by everybody.
3:14 when the old covenant is *r*.
3:15 Even to this day when Moses is *r*,
Col 4:16 After this letter has been *r* to you,
4:16 and that you in turn *r* the letter
4:16 *r* in the church of the Laodiceans
1Th 5:27 the Lord to have this letter *r*

READER (READ)

Mt 24:15 Daniel—let the *r* understand—
Mk 13:14 let the *r* understand—then let

READINESS

2Co 7:11 what *r* to see justice done.
Eph 6:15 fitted with the *r* that comes

READING (READ)

Jer 51:63 When you finish *r* this scroll,
Ac 8:28 sitting in his chariot *r* the book
8:30 Do you understand what you are *r*
8:30 heard the man *r* Isaiah the prophet.
8:32 The eunuch was *r* this passage
13:15 After the *r* from the Law
Eph 3: 4 In *r* this, then, you will be able
1Ti 4:13 to the public *r* of Scripture,

READS (READ)

Da 5: 7 "Whoever *r* this writing
Rev 1: 3 Blessed is the one who *r* the words

REAFFIRM (AFFIRM)

1Sa 11:14 to Gilgal and there *r* the kingship."
20:17 Jonathan had David *r* his oath out
2Co 2: 8 therefore, to *r* your love for him.

REAIAH

1Ch 4: 2 *R* son of Shobal was the father
5: 5 Micah his son, *R* his son, Baal his
Ezr 2:47 Giddel, Gahar, *R*, Rezin, Nekoda,
Ne 7:50 Giddel, Gaher, *R*, Rezin, Nekoda,

REAL (REALITIES REALITY)

Jn 6:55 is *r* food and my blood is *r* drink.
1Jn 2:27 all things and as that anointing is *r*,

REALITIES (REAL)

Heb 10: 1 are coming—not the *r* themselves.

REALITY (REAL)

Col 2:17 the *r*, however, is found in Christ.

REALIZE (REALIZED REALIZING)

Ge 42:23 They did not *r* that Joseph could
Ex 10: 7 Do you not yet *r* that Egypt is
Nu 22:34 I did not *r* you were standing
Jdg 13:16 (Manoah did not *r* that it was
15:11 "Don't you *r* that the Philistines
20:34 that the Benjamites did not *r* how
1Sa 12:17 you will *r* what an evil thing you
2Sa 2:26 Don't you *r* that this will end
3:38 "Do you not *r* that a prince
Ecc 2:14 but I came to *r*
Jer 2:19 Consider then and *r*
Jer 11:19 I did not *r* that they had plotted
Da 2: 8 you *r* that this is what I have firmly
Hos 7: 2 but they do not *r*
7: 9 but he does not *r* it.
11: 3 but they did not *r*
14: 9 Who is wise? He will *r* these things.
Jn 2: 9 He did not *r* where it had come
11:50 You do not *r* that it is better
12:16 glorified did they *r* that these
13: 7 You do not *r* now what I am doing,
14:20 On that day you will *r* that I am
19:10 "Don't you *r* I have power
20:14 but she did not *r* that it was Jesus.
21: 4 disciples did not *r* that it was Jesus.
Ac 7:25 own people would *r* that God was
10:34 "I now *r* how true it is that God
23: 5 I did not *r* that he was the high
1Co 11: 3 Now I want you to *r* that the head
2Co 10:11 Such people should *r* that what we
13: 5 Do you not *r* that Christ Jesus is
Rev 3:17 you do not *r* that you are wretched,

REALIZED (REALIZE)

Ge 3: 7 and they *r* they were naked;
28: 8 Esau then *r* how displeasing
Ex 5:19 The Israelite foremen *r* they were
Jdg 6:22 When Gideon *r* that it was
13:21 Manoah *r* that it was the angel
20:41 they *r* that disaster had come
Ru 1:18 When Naomi *r* that Ruth was
1Sa 3: 8 Eli *r* that the LORD was calling
18:28 When Saul *r* that the LORD was
2Sa 10: 6 When the Ammonites *r* that they
12:19 and he *r* the child was dead.
20:12 When he *r* that everyone who
1Ki 3:15 and he *r* it had been a dream.
1Ch 19: 6 When the Ammonites *r* that they
Ne 6:12 I *r* that God had not sent him,
6:16 they *r* that this work had been done
Ecc 5:18 Then I *r* that it is good
SS 6:12 Before I *r* it,
Eze 10:20 and I *r* that they were cherubim.
Mt 2:16 When Herod *r* that he had been
Mk 5:30 At once Jesus *r* that power had
Lk 1:22 They *r* he had seen a vision
Jn 4:53 father *r* that this was the exact time
6:22 of the lake *r* that only one boat had
6:24 Once the crowd *r* that neither
Ac 4:13 and *r* that they were unschooled,
16:19 of the slave girl *r* that their hope
19:34 But when they *r* he was a Jew,
22:29 when he *r* that he had put Paul,

REALIZING (REALIZE)

Ge 38:16 Not *r* that she was his
Est 7: 7 *r* that the king had already decided
Ro 2: 4 not *r* that God's kindness leads you

REALM (REALMS)

Dt 32:22 to the *r* of death below.
Jos 13:21 and the entire *r* of Sihon king
13:27 with the rest of the *r* of Sihon king
13:30 the entire *r* of Og king of Bashan—
2Ch 36:22 a proclamation throughout his *r*
Ezr 1: 1 a proclamation throughout his *r*
7:23 wrath against the *r* of the king
Est 1:20 throughout all his vast *r*,
2: 3 in every province of his *r*
Da 11: 9 king of the North will invade the *r*
Hab 2: 9 "Woe to him who builds his *r*

REALMS (REALM)

Eph 1: 3 the heavenly *r* with every spiritual
1:20 at his right hand in the heavenly *r*,
2: 6 in the heavenly *r* in Christ Jesus,
3:10 and authorities in the heavenly *r*,
6:12 forces of evil in the heavenly *r*.

REAP (REAPED REAPER REAPERS REAPING REAPS)

Lev 19: 9 do not *r* to the very edges
19: 9 " 'When you *r* the harvest
23:10 to give you and you *r* its harvest,
23:22 do not *r* to the very edges
23:22 " 'When you *r* the harvest
25: 5 Do not *r* what grows of itself
25:11 and do not *r* what grows of itself
1Sa 8:12 plow his ground and *r* his harvest,

2Ki 19: 29 But in the third year sow and *r*,
Job 4: 8 and those who sow trouble *r* it.
Ps 126: 5 will *r* with songs of joy.
Ecc 11: 4 at the clouds will not *r*.
Isa 37: 30 But in the third year sow and *r*,
Jer 12: 13 They will sow wheat but *r* thorns;
Hos 8: 7 and *r* the whirlwind.
10: 12 *r* the fruit of unfailing love,
Mt 6: 26 or *r* or store away in barns,
Lk 12: 24 or *r*, they have no storeroom
19: 21 and *r* what you did not sow.'
Jn 4: 38 you to *r* what you have not worked
Ro 6: 21 What benefit did you *r* at that time
6: 22 the benefit you *r* leads to holiness,
1Co 9: 11 if we *r* a material harvest from you?
2Co 9: 6 generously will also *r* generously.
9: 6 sows sparingly will also *r* sparingly,
Gal 6: 8 from that nature will *r* destruction;
6: 8 from the Spirit will *r* eternal life.
6: 9 the proper time we will *r* a harvest
Rev 14: 15 because the time to *r* has come,
14: 15 "Take your sickle and *r*,

REAPED (REAP)

Ge 26: 12 and the same year *r* a hundredfold,
Hos 10: 13 you have *r* evil,
Jn 4: 38 and you have *r* the benefits

REAPER (REAP)

Ps 129: 7 with it the *r* cannot fill his hands,
Isa 17: 5 when a *r* gathers the standing grain
Jer 9: 22 like cut grain behind the *r*,
50: 16 and the *r* with his sickle at harvest.
Am 9: 13 "when the *r* will be overtaken
Jn 4: 36 Even now the *r* draws his wages,
4: 36 and the *r* may be glad together.

REAPERS (REAP)

2Ki 4: 18 to his father, who was with the *r*.

REAPING (REAP)

Ge 45: 6 there will not be plowing and *r*.
Lk 19: 22 put in, and *r* what I did not sow?

REAPPEARS (APPEAR)

Lev 13: 57 But if it *r* in the clothing,
14: 43 "If the mildew *r* in the house

REAPS (REAP)

Pr 11: 18 who sows righteousness *r* a sure
22: 8 He who sows wickedness *r* trouble,
Jn 4: 37 'One sows and another *r*' is true.
Gal 6: 7 A man *r* what he sows.

REASON (REASONABLE REASONED REASONING REASONS)

Ge 2: 24 For this *r* a man will leave his
20: 10 "What was your *r* for doing this?"
41: 32 The *r* the dream was given
1Sa 19: 5 David by killing him for no *r*?"
Job 2: 3 him to ruin him without any *r*."
9: 17 and multiply my wounds for no *r*.
12: 24 of the earth of their *r*;
22: 6 from your brothers for no *r*;
Ps 35: 19 not those who hate me without *r*
38: 19 without *r* are numerous.
69: 4 Those who hate me without *r*
Pr 3: 30 Do not accuse a man for no *r*—
Isa 1: 18 "Come now, let us *r* together,"
Mt 12: 10 Looking for a *r* to accuse Jesus,
19: 3 wife for any and every *r*?"
19: 5 'For this *r* a man will leave his
Mk 3: 2 looking for a *r* to accuse Jesus,
10: 7 'For this *r* a man will leave his
Lk 6: 7 looking for a *r* to accuse Jesus,
Jn 1: 31 but the *r* I came baptizing
5: 18 For this *r* the Jews tried all
8: 47 *r* you do not hear is that you do not
10: 17 *r* my Father loves me is that I lay
12: 27 it was for this very *r* I came
12: 39 For this *r* they could not believe,
15: 25 'They hated me without *r*.'
18: 37 In fact, for this *r* I was born,
Ac 19: 40 since there is no *r* for it."
28: 20 For this *r* I have asked to see you
Ro 14: 9 For this very *r*, Christ died
1Co 4: 17 For this *r* I am sending
11: 10 this *r*, and because of the angels,
1Co 12: 15 not for that *r* cease to be part
12: 16 not for that *r* cease to be part
14: 13 For this *r* the man who speaks
2Co 2: 9 The *r* I wrote you was to see
8: 24 and the *r* for our pride in you,
Gal 6: 12 The only *r* they do this is
Eph 1: 15 For this *r*, ever since I heard about
3: 1 For this *r* I, Paul, the prisoner
3: 14 For this *r* I kneel before the Father,
5: 31 "For this *r* a man will leave his
Col 1: 9 For this *r*, since the day we heard
1Th 3: 5 For this *r*, when I could stand it no
2Th 2: 11 For this *r* God sends them
1Ti 1: 16 for that very *r* I was shown mercy
2Ti 1: 6 For this *r* I remind you to fan
Tit 1: 5 *r* I left you in Crete was that you
Phm : 15 Perhaps the *r* he was separated
Heb 2: 17 For this *r* he had to be made like
9: 15 For this *r* Christ is the mediator
10: 1 For this *r* it can never,
Jas 4: 5 without *r* that the spirit he caused
1Pe 3: 15 to give the *r* for the hope that you
4: 6 For this is the *r* the gospel was
2Pe 1: 5 For this very *r*, make every effort
1Jn 3: 1 The *r* the world does not know us is
3: 8 The *r* the Son of God appeared was

REASONABLE (REASON)

Ac 18: 14 it would be *r* for me to listen to you
26: 25 "What I am saying is true and *r*.

REASONED (REASON)

Ac 17: 2 and on three Sabbath days he *r*
17: 17 he *r* in the synagogue with the Jews
18: 4 Every Sabbath he *r*
18: 19 went into the synagogue and *r*
1Co 13: 11 thought like a child, I *r* like a child.
Heb 11: 19 Abraham *r* that God could raise

REASONING (REASON)

Job 32: 11 I listened to your *r*;

REASONS (REASON)

1Co 15: 32 in Ephesus for merely human *r*,
Php 3: 4 I myself have *r* for such confidence
3: 4 If anyone else thinks he has *r*

REASSIGN (ASSIGN)

Isa 49: 8 and to *r* its desolate inheritances,

REASSURE (ASSURE)

2Ki 25: 24 Gedaliah took an oath to *r* them
Jer 40: 9 took an oath to *r* them

REASSURED (ASSURE)

Ge 50: 21 And he *r* them and spoke kindly

REBA

Nu 31: 8 Rekem, Zur, Hur and *R*—
Jos 13: 21 Rekem, Zur, Hur and *R*—

REBECCA'S (REBEKAH)

Ro 9: 10 but *R* children had one

REBEKAH (REBECCA'S REBEKAH'S)

Ge 22: 23 Bethuel became the father of *R*.
24: 15 *R* came out with her jar
24: 29 Now *R* had a brother named Laban
24: 30 had heard *R* tell what the man said
24: 45 praying in my heart, *R* came out,
24: 51 Here is *R*; take her and go,
24: 53 of clothing and gave them to *R*;
24: 58 So they called *R* and asked her,
24: 59 they sent their sister *R* on her way,
24: 60 And they blessed *R* and said to her,
24: 61 So the servant took *R* and left.
24: 61 Then *R* and her maids got ready
24: 64 *R* also looked up and saw Isaac.
24: 67 mother Sarah, and he married *R*.
25: 20 old when he married *R* daughter
25: 21 and his wife *R* became pregnant.
25: 26 old when *R* gave birth to them.
25: 28 loved Esau, but *R* loved Jacob.
26: 7 might kill me on account of *R*,
26: 8 and saw Isaac caressing his wife *R*.
26: 35 a source of grief to Isaac and *R*.
27: 5 Now *R* was listening as Isaac spoke
27: 6 *R* said to her son Jacob, "Look,
Ge 27: 11 Jacob said to *R* his mother,
27: 15 Then *R* took the best clothes
27: 42 When *R* was told what her older
27: 46 in one day?" Then *R* said to Isaac,
28: 5 brother of *R*, who was the mother
29: 12 of her father and a son of *R*.
49: 31 and his wife *R* were buried,

REBEKAH'S (REBEKAH)

Ge 35: 8 *R* nurse, died and was buried

REBEL (REBELLED REBELLING REBELLION REBELLIOUS REBELS)

Ex 23: 21 Do not *r* against him; he will not
Nu 14: 9 Only do not *r* against the LORD.
Dt 31: 27 how much more will you *r*
Jos 22: 18 If you *r* against the LORD today,
22: 19 But do not *r* against the LORD
22: 29 it from us to *r* against the LORD
1Sa 12: 14 and do not *r* against his commands,
12: 15 and if you *r* against his commands,
2Ki 18: 20 that you *r* against me? Look now,
Job 24: 13 "There are those who *r*
Isa 1: 20 but if you resist and *r*,
36: 5 that you *r* against me? Look now,
48: 8 you were called a *r* from birth.
Eze 2: 8 Do not *r* like that rebellious house;
20: 38 you of those who revolt and *r*
Da 11: 14 men among your own people will *r*
Mt 10: 21 children will *r* against their parents
Mk 13: 12 will *r* against their parents

REBELLED (REBEL)

Ge 14: 4 but in the thirteenth year they *r*.
Nu 20: 24 both of you *r* against my command
26: 9 the community officials who *r*
26: 9 when they *r* against the LORD.
27: 14 for when the community *r*
Dt 1: 26 you *r* against the command
1: 43 You *r* against the LORD's
9: 23 But you *r* against the command
1Sa 22: 13 so that he has *r* against me
1Ki 11: 26 son of Nebat *r* against the king.
11: 27 of how he *r* against the king:
2Ki 1: 1 After Ahab's death, Moab *r*
3: 5 the king of Moab *r* against the king
3: 7 The king of Moab has *r* against me.
8: 20 Edom *r* against Judah
18: 7 He *r* against the king of Assyria
24: 1 and *r* against Nebuchadnezzar.
24: 20 Now Zedekiah *r* against the king
2Ch 13: 6 son of David, *r* against his master.
21: 8 Edom *r* against Judah
36: 13 *r* against King Nebuchadnezzar,
Ne 9: 26 "But they were disobedient and *r*
Ps 5: 10 for they have *r* against you.
78: 40 How often they *r* against him
78: 56 and *r* against the Most High;
105: 28 for had they not *r* against his words
106: 7 and they *r* by the sea, the Red Sea.
106: 33 for they *r* against the Spirit of God,
107: 11 for they had *r* against the words
Isa 1: 2 but they have *r* against me.
43: 27 your spokesmen *r* against me.
63: 10 Yet they *r*
66: 24 bodies of those who *r* against me;
Jer 2: 8 the leaders *r* against me.
2: 29 You have all *r* against me,"
3: 13 you have *r* against the LORD your
4: 17 because she has *r* against me,' "
52: 3 Now Zedekiah *r* against the king
La 1: 18 yet I *r* against his command.
3: 42 "We have sinned and *r*
Eze 2: 3 to a rebellious nation that has *r*
5: 6 Yet in her wickedness she has *r*
17: 15 But the king *r* against him
20: 8 " 'But they *r* against me
20: 13 the people of Israel *r* against me
20: 21 " 'But the children *r* against me:
Da 9: 5 We have been wicked and have *r*;
9: 9 even though we have *r* against him;
Hos 7: 13 because they have *r* against me!
8: 1 and *r* against my law.
13: 16 they have *r* against their God.
Heb 3: 16 Who were they who heard and *r*?

REBELLING (REBEL)

Ne 2: 19 "Are you *r* against the king?"

Ps 78: 17 *r* in the desert against the Most
Ro 13: 2 rebels against the authority is *r*

REBELLION (REBEL)

Ex 23: 21 he will not forgive your *r*,
34: 7 and forgiving wickedness, *r* and sin
Lev 16: 16 because of the uncleanness and *r*
16: 21 over it all the wickedness and *r*
Nu 14: 18 in love and forgiving sin and *r*.
Dt 13: 5 he preached *r* against the LORD
Jos 22: 16 an altar in *r* against him now?
22: 22 If this has been in *r* or disobedience
24: 19 He will not forgive your *r*
1Sa 15: 23 For *r* is like the sin of divination,
24: 11 guilty of wrongdoing or *r*.
1Ki 12: 19 been in *r* against the house
16: 20 reign, and the *r* he carried out,
2Ki 8: 22 been in *r* against Judah.
2Ch 10: 19 been in *r* against the house
21: 10 been in *r* against Judah.
Ezr 4: 15 a place of *r* from ancient times.
4: 19 has been a place of *r* and sedition.
Ne 9: 17 and in their *r* appointed a leader
Job 34: 37 To his sin he adds *r*;
Ps 106: 43 but they were bent on *r*
Pr 17: 11 An evil man is bent only on *r*;
Isa 1: 5 Why do you persist in *r*?
24: 20 so heavy upon it is the guilt of its *r*
58: 1 Declare to my people their *r*
59: 13 *r* and treachery against the LORD,
Jer 5: 6 for their *r* is great
28: 16 because you have preached *r*
29: 32 he has preached *r* against me.' "
33: 8 and will forgive all their sins of *r*
Eze 21: 24 to mind your guilt by your open *r*,
Da 8: 12 Because of *r*, the host ⌊of the saints⌋
8: 13 the *r* that causes desolation,
Mt 26: 55 to the crowd, "Am I leading a *r*,
Mk 14: 48 "Am I leading a *r*," said Jesus,
Lk 22: 52 "Am I leading a *r*, that you have
23: 14 who was inciting the people to *r*.
Jn 18: 40 Now Barabbas had taken part in a *r*
2Th 2: 3 will not come⌋ until the *r* occurs
Heb 3: 8 as you did in the *r*,
3: 15 as you did in the *r*."
Jude : 11 have been destroyed in Korah's *r*.

REBELLIOUS (REBEL)

Nu 17: 10 to be kept as a sign to the *r*.
Dt 9: 7 you have been *r* against the LORD
9: 24 You have been *r* against the LORD
21: 18 *r* son who does not obey his father
21: 20 "This son of ours is stubborn and *r*.
31: 27 I know how *r* and stiff-necked you
31: 27 If you have been *r*
1Sa 20: 30 You son of a perverse and *r* woman
Ezr 4: 12 are rebuilding that *r* and wicked
4: 15 will find that this city is a *r* city,
Ps 25: 7 and my *r* ways;
66: 7 let not the *r* rise up against him.
68: 6 the *r* live in a sun-scorched land.
68: 18 even from the *r*—
78: 8 a stubborn and *r* generation,
107: 17 through their *r* ways
Pr 24: 21 and do not join with the *r*,
28: 2 When a country is *r*, it has many
Isa 30: 9 These are *r* people, deceitful
50: 5 and I have not been *r*;
Jer 5: 23 people have stubborn and *r* hearts;
La 1: 20 for I have been most *r*.
Eze 2: 3 to a *r* nation that has rebelled
2: 5 for they are a *r* house—they will
2: 6 though they are a *r* house.
2: 7 or fail to listen, for they are *r*.
2: 8 Do not rebel like that *r* house;
3: 9 though they are a *r* house."
3: 26 though they are a *r* house.
3: 27 for they are a *r* house.
12: 2 do not hear, for they are a *r* people.
12: 2 you are living among a *r* people.
12: 3 though they are a *r* house.
12: 9 did not that *r* house
12: 25 For in your days, you *r* house,
17: 12 to this *r* house, 'Do you not know
24: 3 Tell this *r* house a parable
44: 6 Say to the *r* house of Israel,
Hos 9: 15 all their leaders are *r*.
14: 9 but the *r* stumble in them.

Zep 3: 1 *r* and defiled!
Tit 1: 10 For there are many *r* people,

REBELS (REBEL)

Nu 20: 10 you *r*, must we bring you water out
Jos 1: 18 Whoever *r* against your word
1Ki 11: 24 a band of *r* when David destroyed
11: 24 *r* went to Damascus, where they
Isa 1: 23 Your rulers are *r*,
1: 28 *r* and sinners will both be broken
46: 8 take it to heart, you *r*.
57: 4 Are you not a brood of *r*,
Jer 6: 28 They are all hardened *r*,
Da 8: 23 when *r* have become completely
Hos 5: 2 The *r* are deep in slaughter.
Ro 13: 2 he who *r* against the authority is
1Ti 1: 9 but for lawbreakers and *r*,

REBIRTH (BEAR)

Tit 3: 5 us through the washing of *r*

REBUILD (BUILD)

Jos 6: 26 man who undertakes to *r* this city,
Ezr 5: 2 set to work to *r* the house of God
5: 3 authorized you to *r* this temple
5: 9 authorized you to *r* this temple
5: 13 a decree to *r* this house of God.
5: 15 And *r* the house of God on its site.'
5: 17 a decree to *r* this house of God
6: 7 and the Jewish elders *r* this house
9: 9 life to *r* the house of our God
Ne 2: 5 are buried so that I can *r* it."
2: 17 let us *r* the wall of Jerusalem,
4: 10 rubble that we cannot *r* the wall."
Ps 69: 35 and *r* the cities of Judah.
102: 16 For the LORD will *r* Zion
Isa 9: 10 but we will *r* with dressed stone;
45: 13 He will *r* my city
58: 12 Your people will *r* the ancient ruins
60: 10 "Foreigners will *r* your walls,
61: 4 They will *r* the ancient ruins
Jer 33: 7 will *r* them as they were before.
Da 9: 25 and *r* Jerusalem until the Anointed
Am 9: 14 they will *r* the ruined cities
Mal 1: 4 been crushed, we will *r* the ruins."
Mt 26: 61 of God and *r* it in three days.' "
Ac 15: 16 Its ruins I will *r*,
15: 16 and *r* David's fallen tent.
Gal 2: 18 not! If I *r* what I destroyed,

REBUILDING (BUILD)

Ezr 2: 68 toward the *r* of the house of God
4: 12 are *r* that rebellious and wicked
5: 11 we are *r* the temple that was built
Ne 2: 18 They replied, "Let us start *r*."
2: 20 We his servants will start *r*,
4: 1 heard that we were *r* the wall,

REBUILT (BUILD)

Nu 21: 27 "Come to Heshbon and let it be *r*;
32: 37 And the Reubenites *r* Heshbon,
32: 38 names to the cities they *r*.
Dt 13: 16 remain a ruin forever, never to be *r*.
Jdg 18: 28 The Danites *r* the city
21: 23 to their inheritance and *r* the towns
1Ki 9: 17 And Solomon *r* Gezer.)
16: 34 Hiel of Bethel *r* Jericho.
2Ki 14: 22 He was the one who *r* Elath
15: 35 Jotham *r* the Upper Gate
21: 3 He *r* the high places his father
2Ch 8: 2 Solomon *r* the villages that Hiram
8: 5 He *r* Upper Beth Horon
24: 13 They *r* the temple
26: 2 He was the one who *r* Elath
26: 6 He then *r* towns near Ashdod
27: 3 Jotham *r* the Upper Gate
33: 3 He *r* the high places his father
33: 14 Afterward he *r* the outer wall
Ezr 4: 21 so that this city will not be *r* until I
6: 3 Let the temple be *r* as a place
Ne 3: 1 went to work and *r* the Sheep Gate.
3: 3 The Fish Gate was *r* by the sons
3: 13 They *r* it and put its doors and bolts
3: 14 He *r* it and put its doors and bolts
3: 15 He *r* it, roofing it over
4: 6 So we *r* the wall till all
6: 1 of our enemies that I had *r* the wall
7: 1 After the wall had been *r*

Ne 7: 4 and the houses had not yet been *r*.
Job 12: 14 What he tears down cannot be *r*;
Isa 25: 2 it will never be *r*.
44: 28 say of Jerusalem, "Let it be *r*,"
Jer 30: 18 the city will be *r* on her ruins,
31: 4 and you will be *r*, O Virgin Israel.
31: 38 "when this city will be *r* for me
Eze 26: 14 You will never be *r*,
36: 10 will be inhabited and the ruins *r*.
36: 33 your towns, and the ruins will be *r*.
36: 36 the LORD have *r* what was
Da 9: 25 It will be *r* with streets and a trench
Zec 1: 16 and there my house will be *r*.

REBUKE (REBUKED REBUKES REBUKING)

Lev 19: 17 *R* your neighbor frankly
Dt 28: 20 *r* in everything you put your hand
Ru 2: 16 for her to pick up, and don't *r* her."
1Sa 2: 25 did not listen to their father's *r*,
2Sa 22: 16 bare at the *r* of the LORD,
2Ki 19: 3 This day is a day of distress and *r*
19: 4 and that he will *r* him for the words
Job 11: 3 Will no one *r* you when you mock?
13: 10 He would surely *r* you
20: 3 I hear a *r* that dishonors me,
26: 11 aghast at his *r*.
Ps 6: 1 O LORD, do not *r* me
18: 15 bare at your *r*, O LORD,
38: 1 O LORD, do not *r* me
39: 11 You *r* and discipline men
50: 8 I do not *r* you for your sacrifices
50: 21 But I will *r* you
68: 30 *R* the beast among the reeds,
76: 6 At your *r*, O God of Jacob,
80: 16 at your *r* your people perish.
104: 7 But at your *r* the waters fled,
119: 21 You *r* the arrogant, who are cursed
141: 5 let him *r* me—it is oil on my head.
Pr 1: 23 If you had responded to my *r*,
1: 25 and would not accept my *r*,
1: 30 and spurned my *r*,
3: 11 and do not resent his *r*,
9: 8 Do not *r* a mocker or he will hate
9: 8 *r* a wise man and he will love you.
13: 1 but a mocker does not listen to *r*.
15: 31 He who listens to a life-giving *r*
17: 10 A *r* impresses a man
19: 25 *r* a discerning man, and he will gain
25: 12 is a wise man's *r* to a listening ear.
27: 5 Better is open *r*
30: 6 or he will *r* you and prove you a liar
Ecc 7: 5 It is better to heed a wise man's *r*
Isa 37: 3 This day is a day of distress and *r*
37: 4 and that he will *r* him for the words
50: 2 By a mere *r* I dry up the sea,
51: 20 and the *r* of your God.
54: 9 never to *r* you again.
66: 15 and his *r* with flames of fire.
Jer 2: 19 your backsliding will *r* you.
Eze 3: 26 will be silent and unable to *r* them,
5: 15 and in wrath and with stinging *r*.
Hos 2: 2 "*R* your mother, *r* her,
Zec 3: 2 who has chosen Jerusalem, *r* you!
3: 2 "The LORD *r* you, Satan!
Mal 2: 3 of you I will *r* your descendants;
Mt 16: 22 him aside and began to *r* him.
Mk 8: 32 him aside and began to *r* him.
Lk 17: 3 "If your brother sins, *r* him,
19: 39 "Teacher, *r* your disciples!"
1Ti 5: 1 Do not *r* an older man harshly,
2Ti 4: 2 correct, *r* and encourage—
Tit 1: 13 Therefore, *r* them sharply,
2: 15 Encourage and *r* with all authority.
Jude : 9 but said, "The Lord *r* you!"
Rev 3: 19 Those whom I love I *r*

REBUKED (REBUKE)

Ge 31: 42 my hands, and last night he *r* you."
37: 10 his father *r* him and said, "What is
1Sa 24: 7 With these words David *r* his men
1Ch 16: 21 for their sake he *r* kings:
Ne 13: 11 So I *r* the officials and asked them,
13: 17 I *r* the nobles of Judah
13: 25 I *r* them and called curses
Ps 9: 5 You have *r* the nations
105: 14 for their sake he *r* kings:
106: 9 He *r* the Red Sea, and it dried up;

Mt 8: 26 Then he got up and *r* the winds
17: 18 Jesus *r* the demon, and it came out
19: 13 the disciples *r* those who brought
20: 31 The crowd *r* them and told them
Mk 4: 39 *r* the wind and said to the waves,
8: 33 looked at his disciples, he *r* Peter.
9: 25 to the scene, he *r* the evil spirit.
10: 13 them, but the disciples *r* them.
10: 48 Many *r* him and told him
14: 5 And they *r* her harshly.
16: 14 he *r* them for their lack of faith
Lk 3: 19 when John *r* Herod the tetrarch
4: 39 So he bent over her and *r* the fever,
4: 41 But he *r* them and would not allow
8: 24 He got up and *r* the wind
9: 42 But Jesus *r* the evil spirit, healed
9: 55 But Jesus turned and *r* them,
18: 15 the disciples saw this, they *r* them.
18: 39 Those who led the way *r* him
23: 40 But the other criminal *r* him.
1Ti 5: 20 Those who sin are to be *r* publicly,
2Pe 2: 16 But he was *r* for his wrongdoing

REBUKES (REBUKE)

Job 22: 4 "Is it for your piety that he *r* you
Ps 2: 5 Then he *r* them in his anger
Pr 9: 7 whoever *r* a wicked man incurs
28: 23 He who *r* a man will
29: 1 remains stiff-necked after many *r*
Isa 17: 13 when he *r* them they flee far away,
Na 1: 4 He *r* the sea and dries it up;
Heb 12: 5 do not lose heart when he *r* you,

REBUKING (REBUKE)

Ps 57: 3 *r* those who hotly pursue me; *Selah*
2Ti 3: 16 *r*, correcting and training

RECAB (RECABITE RECABITES)

2Sa 4: 2 named Baanah and the other *R*;
4: 5 Now *R* and Baanah, the sons
4: 6 *R* and his brother Baanah slipped
4: 9 David answered *R* and his brother
2Ki 10: 15 he came upon Jehonadab son of *R*,
10: 23 and Jehonadab son of *R* went
1Ch 2: 55 the father of the house of *R*.
Ne 3: 14 repaired by Malkijah son of *R*.
Jer 35: 6 son of *R* gave us this command:
35: 8 son of *R* commanded us.
35: 14 son of *R* ordered his sons not
35: 16 of *R* have carried out the command
35: 19 'Jonadab son of *R* will never fail

RECABITE (RECAB)

Jer 35: 2 Go to the *R* family and invite them
35: 5 before the men of the *R* family

RECABITES (RECAB)

Jer 35: 3 the whole family of the *R*.
35: 18 said to the family of the *R*,

RECAH

1Ch 4: 12 These were the men of *R*.

RECALL (RECALLED RECALLING)

2Pe 3: 2 I want you to *r* the words spoken

RECALLED (RECALL)

Isa 63: 11 Then his people *r* the days of old,
Eze 23: 19 as she *r* the days of her youth,
Jn 2: 22 his disciples *r* what he had said.

RECALLING (RECALL)

Job 11: 16 *r* it only as waters gone by.
2Ti 1: 4 *R* your tears, I long to see you,

RECAPTURE (CAPTURE)

Eze 14: 5 I will do this to *r* the hearts

RECAPTURED (CAPTURE)

2Ki 13: 25 of Jehoahaz *r* from Ben-Hadad son

RECEDE (RECEDED)

Ge 8: 5 The waters continued to *r*

RECEDED (RECEDE)

Ge 8: 1 over the earth and the waters *r*.
8: 3 The water *r* steadily from the earth
8: 8 if the water had *r* from the surface
8: 11 Noah knew that the water had *r*

Rev 6: 14 The sky *r* like a scroll, rolling up,

RECEIVE (RECEIVED RECEIVES RECEIVING RECEPTION)

Ge 4: 11 mouth to *r* your brother's blood
32: 20 I see him, perhaps he will *r* me."
Ex 25: 2 You are to *r* the offering for me
25: 3 These are the offerings you are to *r*
30: 16 *R* the atonement money
Nu 18: 23 They will *r* no inheritance
18: 26 'When you *r* from the Israelites
18: 28 the LORD from all the tithes you *r*
26: 54 is to *r* its inheritance according
32: 19 We will not *r* any inheritance
Dt 9: 9 up on the mountain to *r* the tablets
19: 14 in the inheritance you *r*
33: 3 and from you *r* instruction,
2Ki 12: 5 Let every priest *r* the money
Ne 10: 38 the Levites when they *r* the tithes,
Job 3: 12 Why were there knees to *r* me
35: 7 or what does he *r* from your hand?
Ps 24: 5 He will *r* blessing from the LORD
27: 10 the LORD will *r* me.
110: 3 you will *r* the dew of your youth.
Pr 11: 31 If the righteous *r* their due on earth
28: 10 blameless will *r* a good inheritance.
Ecc 6: 3 and does not *r* proper burial,
8: 10 *r* praise in the city where they did
Isa 50: 11 This is what you shall *r*
61: 7 my people will *r* a double portion,
Eze 16: 61 ashamed when you *r* your sisters,
Da 2: 6 you will *r* from me gifts
7: 18 the Most High will *r* the kingdom
11: 34 they fall, they will *r* a little help,
12: 13 rise to *r* your allotted inheritance."
Hos 14: 2 and *r* us graciously,
Mt 10: 41 a prophet will *r* a prophet's reward,
10: 41 a righteous man will *r* a righteous
11: 5 The blind *r* sight, the lame walk,
19: 29 for my sake will *r* a hundred times
20: 10 first, they expected to *r* more.
21: 22 you will *r* whatever you ask
Mk 4: 16 and at once *r* it with joy.
10: 15 anyone who will not *r* the kingdom
10: 30 fail to *r* a hundred times
Lk 7: 22 The blind *r* sight, the lame walk
8: 13 rock are the ones who *r* the word
18: 17 anyone who will not *r* the kingdom
18: 30 of God will fail to *r* many times
18: 42 Jesus said to him, "*R* your sight;
Jn 1: 11 but his own did not *r* him.
3: 27 A man can *r* only what is given him
7: 39 believed in him were later to *r*.
16: 24 and you will *r*, and your joy will be
20: 22 and said, "*R* the Holy Spirit.
Ac 1: 8 you will *r* power when the Holy
2: 38 you will *r* the gift of the Holy Spirit
7: 59 prayed, "Lord Jesus, *r* my spirit."
8: 15 that they might *r* the Holy Spirit,
8: 19 my hands may *r* the Holy Spirit."
19: 2 "Did you *r* the Holy Spirit
19: 3 "Then what baptism did you *r?*"
19: 25 you know we *r* a good income
20: 35 'It is more blessed to give than to *r*
22: 13 'Brother Saul, *r* your sight!'
26: 18 so that they may *r* forgiveness
Ro 5: 17 will those who *r* God's abundant
8: 15 For you did not *r* a spirit that
11: 31 that they too may now *r* mercy
16: 2 I ask you to *r* her in the Lord
1Co 3: 14 built survives, he will *r* his reward.
4: 5 At that time each will *r* his praise
4: 7 do you have that you did not *r?*
4: 7 if you did *r* it, why do you boast
9: 14 the gospel should *r* their living
2Co 5: 10 that each one may *r* what is due
6: 1 not to *r* God's grace in vain.
6: 17 and I will *r* you."
11: 4 or if you *r* a different spirit
11: 16 then *r* me just as you would a fool,
Gal 1: 12 I did not *r* it from any man,
3: 2 Did you *r* the Spirit
3: 14 by faith we might *r* the promise
4: 5 that we might *r* the full rights
Php 2: 19 cheered when I *r* news about you.
Col 3: 24 know that you will *r* an inheritance
1Th 5: 9 but to *r* salvation through our Lord
1Ti 1: 16 believe on him and *r* eternal life.

2Ti 2: 5 he does not *r* the victor's crown
2: 6 the first to *r* a share of the crops.
Heb 4: 16 so that we may *r* mercy
9: 15 are called may *r* the promised
10: 36 you will *r* what he has promised.
11: 8 to go to a place he would later *r*
11: 13 They did not *r* the things promised;
11: 19 he did *r* Isaac back from death.
Jas 1: 7 should not think he will *r* anything
1: 12 he will *r* the crown
4: 3 When you ask, you do not *r*,
1Pe 2: 20 it to your credit if you *r* a beating
5: 4 you will *r* the crown
2Pe 1: 11 and you will *r* a rich welcome
1Jn 3: 22 and *r* from him anything we ask,
Rev 4: 11 to *r* glory and honor and power,
5: 12 to *r* power and wealth and wisdom
13: 16 to *r* a mark on his right hand
17: 12 who for one hour will *r* authority
18: 4 so that you will not *r* any

RECEIVED (RECEIVE)

Ge 33: 10 now that you have *r* me favorably.
43: 23 in your sacks; I *r* your silver."
47: 22 because they *r* a regular allotment
Ex 18: 2 his father-in-law Jethro *r* her
36: 3 They *r* from Moses all the offerings
Nu 23: 20 I have *r* a command to bless;
26: 62 they *r* no inheritance among them.
32: 18 Israelite has *r* his inheritance.
34: 14 Manasseh have *r* their inheritance.
34: 15 half tribes have *r* their inheritance
Dt 18: 8 he has *r* money from the sale
Jos 13: 8 Gadites had *r* the inheritance that
14: 1 these are the areas the Israelites *r*
14: 4 The Levites *r* no share of the land
16: 4 of Joseph, *r* their inheritance.
17: 1 who had *r* Gilead and Bashan
17: 6 tribe of Manasseh *r* an inheritance
18: 2 had not yet *r* their inheritance.
18: 7 have already *r* their inheritance
19: 9 the Simeonites *r* their inheritance
21: 7 *r* twelve towns from the tribes
21: 23 the tribe of Dan they *r* Eltekeh,
21: 25 tribe of Manasseh they *r* Taanach
1Ki 5: 8 "I have *r* the message you sent me
10: 14 gold that Solomon *r* yearly was 666
2Ki 12: 4 the money *r* from personal vows
19: 9 Now Sennacherib *r* a report that
19: 14 Hezekiah *r* the letter
20: 13 Hezekiah *r* the messengers
1Ch 6: 71 The Gershonites *r* the following:
6: 71 of Manasseh they *r* Golan
6: 72 the tribe of Issachar they *r* Kedesh,
6: 74 the tribe of Asher they *r* Mashal,
6: 76 the tribe of Naphtali they *r* Kedesh
6: 77 rest of the Levites) *r* the following:
6: 77 tribe of Zebulun they *r* Jokneam,
6: 78 east of Jericho they *r* Bezer
6: 80 of Gad they *r* Ramoth in Gilead,
11: 6 and so he *r* the command.
12: 18 So David *r* them and made them
2Ch 9: 13 gold that Solomon *r* yearly was 666
21: 12 Jehoram *r* a letter from Elijah
Ezr 5: 5 to Darius and his written reply be *r*
8: 30 the priests and Levites *r* the silver
Est 6: 3 recognition has Mordecai *r* for this
Job 15: 18 hiding nothing *r* from their fathers
Ps 68: 18 you *r* gifts from men,
Isa 37: 9 Now Sennacherib *r* a report that
37: 14 Hezekiah *r* the letter
39: 2 Hezekiah *r* the envoys gladly
40: 2 that she has *r* from the LORD's
47: 13 counsel you have *r* has only worn
Hab 1: 1 that Habakkuk the prophet *r*.
Mt 6: 2 they have *r* their reward in full.
6: 5 they have *r* their reward in full.
6: 16 they have *r* their reward in full.
10: 8 Freely you have *r*, freely give.
15: 5 help you might otherwise have *r*
20: 9 hour came and each *r* a denarius.
20: 10 each one of them also *r* a denarius.
20: 11 When they *r* it, they began
20: 34 Immediately they *r* their sight
25: 16 The man who had *r* the five talents
25: 18 man who had *r* the one talent went
25: 20 The man who had *r* the five talents
25: 24 the man who had *r* the one talent

RECEIVES (RECEIVE)

RECEIVING (RECEIVE)

RECEPTION (RECEIVE)

RECESSES

RECITE (RECITED RECITING)

RECITED (RECITE)

RECITING (RECITE)

RECKLESS

RECKONED (RECKONING)

RECKONING (RECKONED)

RECLAIM (CLAIM)

RECLAIMED (CLAIM)

RECLINE (RECLINED RECLINING)

RECLINED (RECLINE)

RECLINING (RECLINE)

RECOGNITION (RECOGNIZE)

RECOGNIZE (RECOGNITION RECOGNIZED RECOGNIZES RECOGNIZING)

RECOGNIZED (RECOGNIZE)

RECOGNIZES (RECOGNIZE)

RECOGNIZING (RECOGNIZE)

RECOIL (RECOILS)

RECOILS (RECOIL)

RECOMMENDATION (RECOMMENDED)

RECOMMENDED (RECOMMENDATION)

RECOMPENSE

RECONCILE (RECONCILED RECONCILIATION RECONCILING)

RECONCILED (RECONCILE)

RECONCILIATION (RECONCILE)

2Co 5: 18 and gave us the ministry of *r:*
5: 19 committed to us the message of *r.*

RECONCILING (RECONCILE)
2Co 5: 19 that God was *r* the world to himself

RECONSECRATED (CONSECRATE)
Da 8: 14 then the sanctuary will be *r.*''

RECONSIDER (CONSIDER)
Job 6: 29 *r,* for my integrity is at stake.
Jer 18: 10 then I will *r* the good I had

RECORD (RECORDED RECORDER RECORDS)
1Ch 4: 33 And they kept a genealogical *r.*
5: 1 in the genealogical *r* in accordance
7: 7 Their genealogical *r* listed 22,034
7: 9 Their genealogical *r* listed
2Ch 24: 27 and the *r* of the restoration
Ne 7: 5 I found the genealogical *r*
Est 6: 1 of the chronicles, the *r* of his reign,
Ps 56: 8 are they not in your *r?*
56: 8 *R* my lament;
87: 4 "I will *r* Rahab and Babylon
130: 3 If you, O LORD, kept a *r* of sins,
Jer 22: 30 "*R* this man as if childless,
Eze 24: 2 of man, *r* this date, this very date,
Hos 13: 12 his sins are kept on *r.*
Mt 1: 1 A *r* of the genealogy
1Co 13: 5 is not easily angered, it keeps no *r*

RECORDED (RECORD)
Ex 38: 21 which were *r* at Moses' command
Nu 33: 2 command Moses *r* the stages
Dt 28: 61 and disaster not *r* in this Book
Jos 24: 26 Joshua *r* these things in the Book
1Ki 8: 5 and cattle that they could not be *r*
1Ch 9: 1 in the genealogies *r* in the book
24: 6 *r* their names in the presence
2Ch 5: 6 and cattle that they could not be *r*
20: 34 which are *r* in the book of the kings
26: 22 are *r* by the prophet Isaiah son
31: 19 to all who were *r* in the genealogies
Ezr 8: 34 the entire weight was *r* at that time.
Ne 12: 22 were *r* in the reign
12: 23 son of Eliashib were *r* in the book
Est 2: 23 All this was *r* in the book
6: 2 It was found *r* there that Mordecai
9: 20 Mordecai *r* these events,
Job 19: 23 "Oh, that my words were *r,*
Isa 4: 3 all who are *r* among the living
Jer 51: 60 had been *r* concerning Babylon.
Jn 20: 30 which are not *r* in this book.
Rev 20: 12 to what they had done as *r*

RECORDER (RECORD)
2Sa 8: 16 Jehoshaphat son of Ahilud was *r;*
20: 24 Jehoshaphat son of Ahilud was *r;*
1Ki 4: 3 Jehoshaphat son of Ahilud—*r;*
2Ki 18: 18 of Asaph the *r* went out to them.
18: 37 of Asaph the *r* went to Hezekiah,
1Ch 18: 15 Jehoshaphat son of Ahilud was *r;*
2Ch 34: 8 with Joah son of Joahaz, the *r,*
Isa 36: 3 son of Asaph the *r* went out to him.
36: 22 of Asaph the *r* went to Hezekiah,

RECORDS (RECORD)
Ge 41: 49 so much that he stopped keeping *r*
Ex 6: 16 sons of Levi according to their *r:*
6: 19 clans of Levi according to their *r.*
Nu 1: 20 according to the *r* of their clans
1: 22 according to the *r* of their clans
1: 24 according to the *r* of their clans
1: 26 according to the *r* of their clans
1: 28 according to the *r* of their clans
1: 30 according to the *r* of their clans
1: 32 according to the *r* of their clans
1: 34 according to the *r* of their clans
1: 36 according to the *r* of their clans
1: 38 according to the *r* of their clans
1: 40 according to the *r* of their clans
1: 42 according to the *r* of their clans
Ru 4: 10 his family or from the town *r.*
1Ch 4: 22 (These *r* are from ancient times.)
5: 7 according to their genealogical *r:*
5: 17 entered in the genealogical *r*
26: 31 according to the genealogical *r*
1Ch 26: 31 reign a search was made in the *r,*
29: 29 of Nathan the prophet and the *r*
29: 29 the *r* of Nathan the prophet
29: 29 written in the *r* of Samuel the seer,
2Ch 9: 29 in the *r* of Nathan the prophet,
12: 15 in the *r* of Shemaiah the prophet
31: 16 were in the genealogical *r*—
31: 17 families in the genealogical *r*
31: 18 listed in these genealogical *r.*
33: 19 all are written in the *r* of the seers.
Ezr 2: 62 These searched for their family *r,*
4: 15 In these *r* you will find that this
Ne 7: 64 These searched for their family *r,*
Est 9: 32 and it was written down in the *r.*
Eze 13: 9 or be listed in the *r* of the house

RECOUNT (RECOUNTED)
Ps 40: 5 no one can *r* to you;
79: 13 we will *r* your praise.
119: 13 With my lips I *r*

RECOUNTED (RECOUNT)
Ps 119: 26 I *r* my ways and you answered me;

RECOVER (RECOVERED RECOVERY)
2Ki 1: 2 to see if I will *r* from this injury."
8: 8 ask him, 'Will I *r* from this illness
8: 9 'Will I *r* from this illness?' "
8: 10 say to him, 'You will certainly *r*';
8: 14 me that you would certainly *r.*"
8: 29 King Joram returned to Jezreel to *r*
9: 15 Joram had returned to Jezreel to *r*
20: 1 because you will die; you will not *r*
2Ch 14: 13 Cushites fell that they could not *r;*
22: 6 so he returned to Jezreel to *r*
Isa 38: 1 you are going to die; you will not *r*
38: 21 apply it to the boil, and he will *r.*"
Eze 7: 13 seller will not *r* the land he has sold

RECOVERED (RECOVER)
Ge 14: 16 He *r* all the goods and brought
38: 12 When Judah had *r* from his grief,
1Sa 30: 18 David *r* everything the Amalekites
30: 22 share with them the plunder we *r.*
2Sa 14: 14 which cannot be *r,* so we must die.
2Ki 13: 25 and so he *r* the Israelite towns.
14: 28 including how he *r*
16: 6 king of Aram *r* Elath for Aram
20: 7 and applied it to the boil, and he *r.*
Jer 41: 16 from Mizpah whom he had *r*
Eze 38: 8 you will invade a land that has *r*
Rev 18: 14 have vanished, never to be *r.*'

RECOVERY (RECOVER)
Isa 38: 9 king of Judah after his illness and *r:*
39: 1 he had heard of his illness and *r.*
Lk 4: 18 and *r* of sight for the blind,
Ro 11: 11 stumble so as to fall beyond *r?*

RECTANGULAR
1Ki 7: 5 All the doorways had *r* frames;
Eze 41: 21 outer sanctuary had a *r* doorframe,

RED (REDDISH)
Ge 25: 25 The first to come out was *r,*
25: 30 let me have some of that *r* stew!
Ex 10: 19 and carried them into the *R*
13: 18 by the desert road toward the *R*
15: 4 are drowned in the *R* Sea.
15: 22 Moses led Israel from the *R* Sea
23: 31 borders from the *R* Sea to the Sea
25: 5 ram skins dyed *r* and hides
26: 14 a covering of ram skins dyed *r,*
35: 7 ram skins dyed *r* and hides
35: 23 ram skins dyed *r* or hides
36: 19 a covering of ram skins dyed *r,*
39: 34 the covering of ram skins dyed *r,*
Lev 11: 14 the black vulture, the *r* kite,
Nu 14: 25 the desert along the route to the *R*
19: 2 the Israelites to bring you a *r* heifer
21: 4 Hor along the route to the *R*
33: 10 left Elim and camped by the *R*
33: 11 They left the *R* Sea and camped
Dt 1: 40 the desert along the route to the *R*
2: 1 the desert along the route to the *R*
11: 4 them with the waters of the *R* Sea
14: 13 the black vulture, the *r* kite,
32: 14 You drank the *r* blood of the grape.
Jos 2: 10 the water of the *R* Sea for you
4: 23 to the *R* Sea when he dried it up
24: 6 and horsemen as far as the *R*
Jdg 11: 16 through the desert to the *R* Sea
1Ki 9: 26 in Edom, on the shore of the *R*
2Ki 3: 22 the water looked *r*— like blood.
Ne 9: 9 you heard their cry at the *R* Sea.
Job 16: 16 My face is *r* with weeping,
Ps 106: 7 and they rebelled by the sea, the *R*
106: 9 He rebuked the *R* Sea,
106: 22 and awesome deeds by the *R* Sea.
136: 13 him who divided the *R* Sea asunder
136: 15 Pharaoh and his army into the *R*
Pr 23: 31 Do not gaze at wine when it is *r,*
Isa 1: 18 though they are *r* as crimson,
63: 2 Why are your garments *r,*
Jer 22: 14 and decorates it in *r.*
49: 21 their cry will resound to the *R* Sea.
Eze 23: 14 figures of Chaldeans portrayed in *r*
Na 2: 3 The shields of his soldiers are *r;*
Zec 1: 8 Behind him were *r,* brown
1: 8 me was a man riding a *r* horse!
6: 2 The first chariot had *r* horses,
Mt 16: 2 for the sky is *r,*' and in the morning
16: 3 for the sky is *r* and overcast.'
Ac 7: 36 at the *R* Sea and for forty years
Heb 11: 29 passed through the *R* Sea
Rev 6: 4 horse came out, a fiery *r* one.
6: 12 the whole moon turned blood *r,*
9: 17 Their breastplates were fiery *r,*
12: 3 an enormous *r* dragon

REDDISH (RED)
Lev 13: 49 any leather article, is greenish or *r,*
14: 37 or *r* depressions that appear

REDDISH-WHITE (WHITE)
Lev 13: 19 a white swelling or *r* spot appears,
13: 24 a burn on his skin and a *r*
13: 42 if he has a *r* sore on his bald head
13: 43 forehead is *r* like an infectious skin

REDEEM (KINSMAN-REDEEMER KINSMAN-REDEEMERS REDEEMABLE REDEEMED REDEEMER REDEEMS REDEMPTION)
Ex 6: 6 will *r* you with an outstretched arm
13: 13 but if you do not *r* it, break its neck.
13: 13 *R* every firstborn among your sons.
13: 13 *R* with a lamb every firstborn
13: 15 and *r* each of my firstborn sons.'
21: 30 may *r* his life by paying whatever
34: 20 but if you do not *r* it, break its neck.
34: 20 *R* all your firstborn sons.
34: 20 *R* the firstborn donkey with a lamb
Lev 25: 25 *r* what his countryman has sold.
25: 26 a man has no one to *r* it for him
25: 26 acquires sufficient means to *r* it,
25: 29 During that time he may *r* it.
25: 32 to *r* their houses in the Levitical
25: 48 One of his relatives may *r* him:
25: 49 Or if he prospers, he may *r* himself.
25: 49 relative in his clan may *r* him.
27: 13 If the owner wishes to *r* the animal,
27: 19 dedicates the field wishes to *r* it,
27: 20 If, however, he does not *r* the field,
27: 27 If he does not *r* it, it is to be sold
Nu 3: 46 To *r* the 273 firstborn Israelites
18: 15 But you must *r* every firstborn son
18: 16 you must *r* them at the redemption
18: 17 "But you must not *r* the firstborn
Ru 3: 13 if he wants to *r,* good; let him *r.*
4: 4 If you will *r* it, do so.
4: 4 "I will *r* it," he said.
4: 6 You *r* it yourself.
4: 6 "Then I cannot *r* it because I might
2Sa 7: 23 on earth that God went out to *r*
1Ch 17: 21 out to *r* a people for himself,
Ps 25: 22 *R* Israel, O God,
26: 11 *r* me and be merciful to me.
31: 5 *r* me, O LORD, the God of truth.
44: 26 *r* us because of your unfailing love.
49: 7 No man can *r* the life of another
49: 15 God will *r* my soul from the grave;
69: 18 *r* me because of my foes.
119:134 *R* me from the oppression of men,
119:154 Defend my cause and *r* me;
130: 8 He himself will *r* Israel

Jer 15: 21 *r* you from the grasp of the cruel.''
31: 11 *r* them from the hand
32: 8 Since it is your right to *r* it
Hos 7: 13 I long to *r* them
13: 14 I will *r* them from death.
Mic 4: 10 There the LORD will *r* you
Zec 10: 8 Surely I will *r* them;
Lk 24: 21 the one who was going to *r* Israel.
Gal 4: 5 under law, to *r* those under law,
Tit 2: 14 for us to *r* us from all wickedness

REDEEMABLE (REDEEM)

Lev 25: 33 So the property of the Levites is *r*

REDEEMED (REDEEM)

Ex 15: 13 the people you have *r*.
21: 8 for himself, he must let her be *r*.
Lev 25: 30 If it is not *r* before a full year has
25: 31 They can be *r*, and they are
25: 54 '' 'Even if he is not *r* in any
27: 20 to someone else, it can never be *r*.
27: 28 or *r*; everything so devoted is most
27: 33 become holy and cannot be *r*.' ''
Nu 3: 49 those who exceeded the number *r*
Dt 7: 8 and *r* you from the land of slavery,
9: 26 your own inheritance that you *r*
13: 5 and *r* you from the land of slavery;
15: 15 and the LORD your God *r* you.
21: 8 whom you have *r*, O LORD,
24: 18 and the LORD your God *r* you
2Sa 7: 23 whom you *r* from Egypt? You have
1Ch 17: 21 whom you *r* from Egypt? You
Ne 1: 10 whom you *r* by your great strength
Job 33: 28 He *r* my soul from going
Ps 71: 23 I, whom you have *r*.
74: 2 the tribe you *r* as your inheritance
77: 15 mighty arm you *r* your people,
78: 42 day he *r* them from the oppressor,
106: 10 of the enemy he *r* them.
107: 2 Let the *r* of the LORD say this—
107: 2 those he *r* from the hand of the foe,
Isa 1: 27 Zion will be *r* with justice,
29: 22 what the LORD, who *r* Abraham,
35: 9 But only the *r* will walk there,
43: 1 ''Fear not, for I have *r* you;
44: 22 for I have *r* you.''
44: 23 for the LORD has *r* Jacob,
48: 20 The LORD has *r* his servant Jacob
51: 10 sea so that the *r* might cross over?
52: 3 and without money you will be *r*.''
52: 9 he has *r* Jerusalem.
62: 12 The *R* of the LORD;
63: 9 In his love and mercy he *r* them;
La 3: 58 you *r* my life.
Mic 6: 4 and *r* you from the land of slavery.
Lk 1: 68 he has come and has *r* his people.
Gal 3: 13 Christ *r* us from the curse
3: 14 He *r* us in order that the blessing
1Pe 1: 18 or gold that you were *r*
Rev 14: 3 who had been *r* from the earth.

REDEEMER (REDEEM)

Job 19: 25 I know that my *R* lives,
Ps 19: 14 O LORD, my Rock and my *R*.
78: 35 that God Most High was their *R*.
Isa 41: 14 your *R*, the Holy One of Israel.
43: 14 your *R*, the Holy One of Israel:
44: 6 and *R*, the LORD Almighty:
44: 24 your *R*, who formed you
47: 4 Our *R*— the LORD Almighty is
48: 17 your *R*, the Holy One of Israel:
49: 7 the *R* and Holy One of Israel—
49: 26 your *R*, the Mighty One of Jacob.''
54: 5 the Holy One of Israel is your *R*;
54: 8 says the LORD your *R*.
59: 20 ''The *R* will come to Zion,
60: 16 your *R*, the Mighty One of Jacob.
63: 16 our *R* from of old is your name.
Jer 50: 34 Yet their *R* is strong;

REDEEMS (REDEEM)

Lev 27: 15 man who dedicates his house *r* it,
27: 31 If a man *r* any of his tithe, he must
Ps 34: 22 The LORD *r* his servants;
103: 4 he *r* my life from the pit

REDEMPTION (REDEEM)

Lev 25: 24 provide for the *r* of the land.
25: 29 he retains the right of *r* a full year
25: 48 he retains the right of *r*
25: 51 he must pay for his *r* a larger share
25: 52 and pay for his *r* accordingly.
Nu 3: 48 for the *r* of the additional Israelites
3: 49 So Moses collected the *r* money
3: 51 Moses gave the *r* money to Aaron
18: 16 at the *r* price set at five shekels
Ru 4: 7 for the *r* and transfer of property
Ps 111: 9 He provided *r* for his people;
130: 7 and with him is full *r*.
Isa 63: 4 and the year of my *r* has come.
Lk 2: 38 forward to the *r* of Jerusalem.
21: 28 because your *r* is drawing near.''
Ro 3: 24 grace through the *r* that came
8: 23 as sons, the *r* of our bodies.
1Co 1: 30 our righteousness, holiness and *r*.
Eph 1: 7 In him we have *r* through his blood
1: 14 until the *r* of those who are God's
4: 30 you were sealed for the day of *r*.
Col 1: 14 in whom we have *r*, the forgiveness
Heb 9: 12 having obtained eternal *r*.

REDUCE (REDUCED REDUCES)

Ex 5: 8 as before; don't *r* the quota.
5: 19 ''You are not to *r* the number
2Ki 10: 32 began to *r* the size of Israel.
Job 11: 3 Will your idle talk *r* men to silence?
24: 25 and *r* my words to nothing?''
Isa 41: 15 and *r* the hills to chaff.
Jer 10: 24 lest you *r* me to nothing.

REDUCED (REDUCE)

Ge 47: 21 Joseph *r* the people to servitude,
Ex 5: 11 but your work will not be *r* at all.' ''
Lev 27: 18 of Jubilee, and its set value will be *r*
Job 30: 19 and I am *r* to dust and ashes.
Ps 79: 1 they have *r* Jerusalem to rubble.
89: 40 and *r* his strongholds to ruins.
102: 5 I am *r* to skin and bones.
Isa 25: 5 heat is *r* by the shadow of a cloud,
Eze 16: 27 against you and *r* your territory;
28: 18 and I *r* you to ashes on the ground
Am 5: 5 and Bethel will be *r* to nothing.''

REDUCES (REDUCE)

Pr 6: 26 for the prostitute *r* you to a loaf
Isa 40: 23 *r* the rulers of this world to nothing

REED (REEDS)

1Ki 14: 15 so that it will be like a *r* swaying
2Ki 18: 21 that splintered *r* of a staff,
Isa 9: 14 both palm branch and *r*
19: 15 head or tail, palm branch or *r*.
36: 6 that splintered *r* of a staff,
42: 3 A bruised *r* he will not break,
58: 5 only for bowing one's head like a *r*
Eze 29: 6 a staff of *r* for the house of Israel.
Mt 11: 7 A *r* swayed by the wind? If not,
12: 20 A bruised *r* he will not break,
Lk 7: 24 A *r* swayed by the wind? If not,
Rev 11: 1 I was given a *r* like a measuring rod

REEDS (REED)

Ge 41: 2 and they grazed among the *r*.
41: 18 and they grazed among the *r*.
Ex 2: 3 put it among the *r* along the bank
2: 5 She saw the basket among the *r*
Job 8: 11 Can *r* thrive without water?
40: 21 hidden among the *r* in the marsh.
41: 20 as from a boiling pot over a fire of *r*.
Ps 68: 30 Rebuke the beast among the *r*,
Isa 19: 6 The *r* and rushes will wither,
35: 7 grass and *r* and papyrus will grow.

REEKED

Ex 8: 14 into heaps, and the land *r* of them.

REEL (REELED REELING REELS)

Isa 28: 7 and *r* from beer:
28: 7 they *r* from beer,

REELAIAH

Ezr 2: 2 Nehemiah, Seraiah, *R*, Mordecai,

REELED (REEL)

Ps 107: 27 They *r* and staggered like drunken

REELING (REEL)

Zec 12: 2 sends all the surrounding peoples *r*.

REELS (REEL)

Isa 24: 20 The earth *r* like a drunkard,

REENTERED (ENTER)

Ne 2: 15 I turned back and *r*

REESTABLISHED (ESTABLISH)

2Ch 29: 35 of the temple of the LORD was *r*.

REFER (REFERRED REFERRING)

1Jn 5: 16 I *r* to those whose sin does not lead

REFERRED (REFER)

Gal 3: 19 to whom the promise *r* had come.

REFERRING (REFER)

Ex 4: 26 of blood,'' *r* to circumcision.)
Jn 13: 18 ''I am not *r* to all of you; I know

REFINE (REFINED REFINER REFINER'S REFINING)

Jer 9: 7 ''See, I will *r* and test them,
Zec 13: 9 I will *r* them like silver
Mal 3: 3 and *r* them like gold and silver.

REFINED (REFINE)

1Ch 28: 18 the weight of the *r* gold for the altar
29: 4 seven thousand talents of *r* silver,
Job 28: 1 and a place where gold is *r*.
Ps 12: 6 like silver *r* in a furnace of clay,
66: 10 you *r* us like silver.
Isa 48: 10 I have *r* you, though not as silver;
Da 11: 35 so that they may be *r*, purified
12: 10 be purified, made spotless and *r*,
1Pe 1: 7 which perishes even though *r*
Rev 3: 18 to buy from me gold *r* in the fire,

REFINER (REFINE)

Mal 3: 3 as a *r* and purifier of silver;

REFINER'S (REFINE)

Mal 3: 2 For he will be like a *r* fire

REFINING (REFINE)

Jer 6: 29 but the *r* goes on in vain;

REFLECT (REFLECTED REFLECTION REFLECTS)

Isa 47: 7 or *r* on what might happen.
2Co 3: 18 unveiled faces all *r* the Lord's
2Ti 2: 7 *R* on what I am saying,

REFLECTED (REFLECT)

Ecc 9: 1 So I *r* on all this and concluded that

REFLECTION (REFLECT)

1Co 13: 12 but a poor *r*; then we shall see face

REFLECTS (REFLECT)

Pr 27: 19 As water *r* a face,
27: 19 so a man's heart *r* the man.
Ecc 5: 20 He seldom *r* on the days of his life,

REFORM (REFORMS)

Jer 7: 3 says: *R* your ways and your actions
18: 11 and *r* your ways and your actions.'
26: 13 Now *r* your ways and your actions
35: 15 wicked ways and *r* your actions;

REFORMS (REFORM)

Ac 24: 2 your foresight has brought about *r*

REFRAIN (REFRAINED)

Dt 23: 22 But if you *r* from making a vow,
1Sa 18: 8 was very angry; this *r* galled him.
1Ki 22: 6 or shall I *r*?'' ''Go,'' they answered,
22: 15 or shall I *r*?'' ''Attack and be
2Ch 18: 5 or shall I *r*?'' ''Go,'' they answered,
18: 14 or shall I *r*?'' ''Attack and be
Job 16: 6 and if I *r*, it does not go away.
Ps 37: 8 *R* from anger and turn from wrath;
Ecc 3: 5 a time to embrace and a time to *r*,
2Co 12: 6 I *r*, so no one will think more of me

REFRAINED (REFRAIN)

2Sa 12: 4 but the rich man *r* from taking one

Job 29: 9 the chief men *r* from speaking

REFRESH (REFRESHED REFRESHES REFRESHING)

Jdg 19: 5 "*R* yourself with something to eat;
19: 8 the girl's father said, "*R* yourself.
2Sa 16: 2 to *r* those who become exhausted
SS 2: 5 *r* me with apples,
Jer 31: 25 I will *r* the weary and satisfy
Phm : 20 in the Lord; *r* my heart in Christ.
2Pe 1: 13 I think it is right to *r* your memory

REFRESHED (REFRESH)

Ge 18: 5 so you can be *r* and then go
Ex 23: 12 and the alien as well, may be *r*.
2Sa 16: 14 And there he *r* himself.
Ps 68: 9 you *r* your weary inheritance.
Pr 11: 25 refreshes others will himself be *r*.
Ro 15: 32 and together with you be *r*.
1Co 16: 18 For they *r* my spirit and yours also.
2Co 7: 13 his spirit has been *r* by all of you.
2Ti 1: 16 because he often *r* me
Phm : 7 have *r* the hearts of the saints.

REFRESHES (REFRESH)

Pr 11: 25 he who *r* others will himself be
25: 13 he *r* the spirit of his masters.

REFRESHING (REFRESH)

Ac 3: 19 that times of *r* may come

REFUGE (REFUGEES)

Nu 35: 6 give the Levites will be cities of *r*,
35: 11 towns to be your cities of *r*,
35: 12 places of *r* from the avenger,
35: 13 you give will be your cities of *r*.
35: 14 and three in Canaan as cities of *r*.
35: 15 These six towns will be a place of *r*
35: 25 to the city of *r* to which he fled.
35: 26 of the city of *r* to which he has fled
35: 28 stay in his city of *r* until the death
35: 32 anyone who has fled to a city of *r*
Dt 23: 15 If a slave has taken *r* with you,
32: 37 the rock they took *r* in,
33: 27 The eternal God is your *r*,
Jos 20: 2 to designate the cities of *r*,
21: 13 of *r* for one accused of murder),
21: 21 city of *r* for one accused of murder)
21: 27 (a city of *r* for one accused
21: 32 (a city of *r* for one accused
21: 38 (a city of *r* for one accused
Jdg 9: 15 come and take *r* in my shade;
Ru 2: 12 wings you have come to take *r*."
2Sa 22: 3 God is my rock, in whom I take *r*,
22: 3 He is my stronghold, my *r*
22: 31 a shield for all who take *r* in him.
1Ch 6: 57 were given Hebron (a city of *r*),
6: 67 were given Shechem (a city of *r*),
Ps 2: 12 Blessed are all who take *r* in him.
5: 11 But let all who take *r* in you be glad
7: 1 O LORD my God, I take *r* in you;
9: 9 The LORD is a *r* for the oppressed,
11: 1 In the LORD I take *r*.
14: 6 but the LORD is their *r*.
16: 1 for in you I take *r*.
17: 7 those who take *r* in you
18: 2 God is my rock, in whom I take *r*.
18: 30 a shield for all who take *r* in him.
25: 20 for I take *r* in you.
31: 1 In you, O LORD, I have taken *r*;
31: 2 be my rock of *r*,
31: 4 for you are my *r*.
31: 19 men on those who take *r* in you.
34: 8 blessed is the man who takes *r*
34: 22 no one who takes *r*
36: 7 find *r* in the shadow of your wings.
37: 40 because they take *r* in him.
46: 1 God is our *r* and strength,
57: 1 I will take *r* in the shadow
57: 1 for in you my soul takes *r*.
59: 16 my *r* in times of trouble.
61: 3 For you have been my *r*,
61: 4 take *r* in the shelter of your wings.
62: 7 he is my mighty rock, my *r*.
62: 8 for God is our *r*.
64: 10 and take *r* in him;
71: 1 In you, O LORD, I have taken *r*;
71: 3 Be my rock of *r*,
Ps 71: 7 but you are my strong *r*.
73: 28 made the Sovereign LORD my *r*;
91: 2 "He is my *r* and my fortress,
91: 4 and under his wings you will find *r*;
91: 9 even the LORD, who is my *r*—
94: 22 my God the rock in whom I take *r*.
104: 18 the crags are a *r* for the coneys.
118: 8 It is better to take *r* in the LORD
118: 9 It is better to take *r* in the LORD
119: 114 You are my *r* and my shield;
141: 8 in you I take *r*— do not give me
142: 4 I have no *r*;
142: 5 I say, "You are my *r*,
144: 2 my shield, in whom I take *r*,
Pr 10: 29 of the LORD is a *r*
14: 26 and for his children it will be a *r*.
14: 32 in death the righteous have a *r*.
22: 3 man sees danger and takes *r*,
27: 12 The prudent see danger and take *r*,
30: 5 a shield to those who take *r* in him.
Isa 4: 6 a *r* and hiding place from the storm
14: 32 in her his afflicted people will find *r*
25: 4 You have been a *r* for the poor,
25: 4 a *r* for the needy in his distress,
27: 5 Or else let them come to me for *r*;
28: 15 for we have made a lie our *r*
28: 17 hail will sweep away your *r*, the lie,
30: 2 to Egypt's shade for *r*.
32: 2 and a *r* from the storm,
33: 16 whose *r* will be the mountain
57: 13 But the man who makes me his *r*
Jer 16: 19 my *r* in time of distress,
17: 17 you are my *r* in the day of disaster.
21: 13 Who can enter our *r*?"
Joel 3: 16 the LORD will be a *r* for his people
Na 1: 7 a *r* in times of trouble.
3: 11 and seek *r* from the enemy.

REFUGEES (REFUGE)

Isa 16: 3 do not betray the *r*.
Jer 50: 28 to the fugitives and *r* from Babylon

REFUND

Lev 25: 27 and *r* the balance to the man

REFUSAL (REFUSE)

Mk 16: 14 their stubborn *r* to believe those

REFUSE (REFUSAL REFUSED REFUSES REFUSING)

Ge 23: 6 None of us will *r* you his tomb
24: 41 even if they *r* to give her to you—
Ex 8: 2 If you *r* to let them go, I will plague
9: 2 If you *r* to let them go and continue
10: 3 'How long will you *r*
10: 4 If you *r* to let them go, I will bring
11: 9 "Pharaoh will *r* to listen to you—
16: 28 "How long will you *r*
Lev 26: 21 toward me and *r* to listen to me,
Nu 14: 11 How long will they *r* to believe
Dt 20: 12 If they *r* to make peace
1Ki 2: 16 Do not *r* me."
2: 17 Solomon—he will not *r* you—
2: 20 my mother; I will not *r* you."
2: 20 "Do not *r* me."
20: 7 and my gold, I did not *r* him."
2Ki 2: 17 until he was too ashamed to *r*.
9: 37 Jezebel's body will be like *r*
Job 6: 7 I *r* to touch it;
34: 33 when you *r* to repent?
Ps 26: 5 and *r* to sit with the wicked.
83: 10 and became like *r* on the ground.
141: 5 My head will not *r* it.
Pr 6: 35 he will *r* the bribe, however great it
21: 7 for they *r* to do what is right.
21: 25 because his hands *r* to work.
30: 7 do not *r* me before I die:
Isa 5: 25 and the dead bodies are like *r*
Jer 3: 3 you *r* to blush with shame.
8: 2 will be like *r* lying on the ground.
8: 5 they *r* to return.
9: 6 in their deceit they *r*
9: 22 like *r* on the open field,
13: 10 who *r* to listen to my words,
16: 4 will be like *r* lying on the ground.
25: 28 But if they *r* to take the cup
25: 33 will be like *r* lying on the ground.
38: 21 if you *r* to surrender, this is what
La 3: 45 You have made us scum and *r*
Eze 3: 27 and whoever will *r* let him *r*;
Hos 11: 5 because they *r* to repent?
Mk 6: 26 guests, he did not want to *r* her.
Jn 5: 40 yet you *r* to come to me to have life
19: 10 "Do you *r* to speak to me?"
Ac 25: 11 deserving death, I do not *r*
1Co 4: 13 of the earth, the *r* of the world.
16: 11 then, should *r* to accept him.
Heb 12: 25 that you do not *r* him who speaks.
Rev 11: 9 on their bodies and *r* them burial.

REFUSED (REFUSE)

Ge 37: 35 came to comfort him, but he *r*
39: 8 "Come to bed with me!" But he *r*.
39: 10 he *r* to go to bed with her or
48: 19 But his father *r* and said, "I know,
Ex 4: 23 But you *r* to let him go;
13: 15 When Pharaoh stubbornly *r*
Nu 20: 21 Since Edom *r* to let them go
22: 13 for the LORD has *r* to let me go
22: 14 "Balaam *r* to come with us."
Dt 2: 30 But Sihon king of Heshbon *r*
Jdg 2: 19 They *r* to give up their evil
11: 17 also to the king of Moab, and he *r*.
1Sa 8: 19 But the people *r* to listen to Samuel
28: 23 He *r* and said, "I will not eat."
2Sa 2: 23 But Asahel *r* to give up the pursuit;
12: 17 he *r*, and he would not eat any food
13: 9 and served him the bread, but he *r*
13: 14 But he *r* to listen to her,
13: 16 But he *r* to listen to her.
13: 25 Absalom urged him, he still *r*
14: 29 So he sent a second time, but he *r*
14: 29 but Joab *r* to come to him.
23: 16 But he *r* to drink it; instead,
1Ki 12: 16 When all Israel saw that the king *r*
20: 35 with your weapon," but the man *r*.
21: 4 lay on his bed sulking and *r* to eat.
21: 15 of Naboth the Jezreelite that he *r*
22: 49 with your men," but Jehoshaphat *r*
2Ki 5: 16 though Naaman urged him, he *r*.
15: 16 because they *r* to open their gates.
1Ch 11: 18 But he *r* to drink it; instead,
2Ch 10: 16 When all Israel saw that the king *r*
Ne 9: 17 They *r* to listen and failed
9: 29 became stiff-necked and *r* to listen.
Est 1: 12 king's command, Queen Vashti *r*
3: 4 spoke to him but he *r* to comply.
Ps 77: 2 and my soul *r* to be comforted.
78: 10 and *r* to live by his law,
Ecc 2: 10 I *r* my heart no pleasure.
Jer 5: 3 and *r* to repent.
5: 3 them, but they *r* correction
11: 10 who *r* to listen to my words.
Zec 7: 11 "But they *r* to pay attention;
Mt 18: 30 "But he *r*.
22: 3 them to come, but they *r* to come.
27: 34 but after tasting it, he *r* to drink it.
Lk 15: 28 older brother became angry and *r*
18: 4 "For some time he *r*.
Ac 7: 39 "But our fathers *r* to obey him.
14: 2 the Jews who *r* to believe stirred up
19: 9 they *r* to believe and publicly
2Th 2: 10 because they *r* to love the truth
Heb 11: 24 *r* to be known as the son
11: 35 Others were tortured and *r*
12: 25 when they *r* him who warned them
Rev 13: 15 and cause all who *r* to worship
16: 9 but they *r* to repent and glorify him
16: 11 they *r* to repent of what they had

REFUSES (REFUSE)

Ex 7: 14 "Pharaoh's heart is unyielding; he *r*
22: 17 If her father absolutely *r* to give her
Dt 25: 7 "My husband's brother *r* to carry
Pr 11: 15 whoever *r* to strike hands
Mt 18: 17 If he *r* to listen to them, tell it
18: 17 if he *r* to listen even to the church,
3Jn : 10 he *r* to welcome the brothers.

REFUSING (REFUSE)

Jer 31: 15 and *r* to be comforted,
50: 33 *r* to let them go.
Da 9: 11 and turned away, *r* to obey you.
Mt 2: 18 and *r* to be comforted,

REFUTE (REFUTED)

Job 32: 3 they had found no way to r Job,
32: 13 let God r him, not man.'
Isa 54: 17 and you will r every tongue that
Tit 1: 9 and r those who oppose it.

REFUTED (REFUTE)

Ac 18: 28 For he vigorously r the Jews

REGAIN (GAIN)

1Sa 29: 4 better could he r his master's favor
1Ki 12: 21 r the kingdom for Rehoboam son
2Ch 11: 1 to r the kingdom for Rehoboam.
13: 20 Jeroboam did not r power
Job 9: 18 He would not let me r my breath

REGAINED (GAIN)

Ac 9: 19 taking some food, he r his strength.

REGARD (REGARDED REGARDS)

Ge 31: 15 Does he not r us as foreigners?
Lev 5: 15 and sins unintentionally in r to any
5: 16 failed to do in r to the holy things,
11: 35 and you are to r them as unclean.
19: 23 kind of fruit tree, r its fruit
21: 8 R them as holy, because they offer
Nu 18: 10 You must r it as holy.
Dt 33: 9 'I have no r for them.'
Jos 7: 1 in r to the devoted things;
1Sa 2: 12 they had no r for the LORD.
Ezr 7: 14 and Jerusalem with r to the Law
Est 9: 31 and their descendants in r
Job 21: 29 Have you paid no r
34: 27 and had no r for any of his ways.
37: 24 for does he not have r
Ps 28: 5 Since they show no r for the works
41: 1 Blessed is he who has r
54: 3 men without r for God.
74: 20 Have r for your covenant,
86: 14 men without r for you.
119:117 I will always have r
Isa 5: 12 but they have no r for the deeds
8: 13 Almighty is the one you are to r
17: 8 and they will have no r
22: 11 have r for the One who planned it
26: 10 and r not the majesty of the LORD
Jer 24: 5 I r as good the exiles from Judah,
33: 24 and no longer r them as a nation.
Eze 44: 8 duty in r to my holy things,
Da 11: 37 He will show no r for the gods
11: 37 nor will he r any god, but will exalt
Am 5: 22 I will have no r for them.
Jn 16: 8 will convict the world of guilt in r
16: 9 in r to sin, because men do not
16: 10 believe in me; in r to righteousness,
16: 11 you can see me no longer; and in r
1Co 4: 1 men ought to r us as servants
14: 20 In r to evil be infants,
2Co 5: 16 So from now on we r no one
Eph 4: 22 with r to your former way of life,
Php 3: 5 of Hebrews; in r to the law,
Col 1: 24 lacking in r to Christ's afflictions,
2: 16 or with r to a religious festival,
1Th 5: 13 Hold them in the highest r in love
2Th 3: 15 Yet do not r him as an enemy,
Heb 7: 14 and in r to that tribe Moses said
11: 20 and Esau in r to their future.
1Pe 4: 6 according to God in r to the spirit.
4: 6 according to men in r to the body,
5: 12 whom I r as a faithful brother,

REGARDED (REGARD)

Ex 11: 3 and Moses himself was highly r
Dt 24: 13 and it will be r as a righteous act
2Sa 16: 23 r all of Ahithophel's advice.
2Ki 5: 1 the sight of his master and highly r,
2Ch 32: 23 then on he was highly r
Job 18: 3 Why are we r as cattle
31: 26 if I have r the sun in its radiance
Isa 40: 15 they are r as dust on the scales,
40: 17 they are r by him as worthless
Da 4: 35 are r as nothing.
Hos 8: 12 but they r them as something alien.
Mk 10: 42 "You know that those who are r
Ac 5: 13 they were highly r by the people.
Ro 2: 26 will they not be r as though they
9: 8 children of the promise who are r
2Co 5: 16 Though we once r Christ
6: 8 genuine, yet r as impostors; known
6: 9 known, yet r as unknown; dying,
Heb 11: 26 He r disgrace for the sake of Christ

REGARDS (REGARD)

Est 5: 8 If the king r me with favor
8: 5 "and if he r me with favor
Ro 14: 6 He who r one day as special,
14: 14 But if anyone r something

REGEM

1Ch 2: 47 R, Jotham, Geshan, Pelet,

REGEM-MELECH

Zec 7: 2 of Bethel had sent Sharezer and R,

REGIMENT

Ac 10: 1 in what was known as the Italian R.
27: 1 who belonged to the Imperial R.

REGISTER (REGISTERED REGISTRATION)

Ps 87: 6 in the r of the peoples:
Lk 2: 3 everyone went to his own town to r
2: 5 He went there to r with Mary,

REGISTERED (REGISTER)

1Ch 9: 22 They were r by genealogy
23: 24 as they were r under their names
Ezr 8: 1 those r with them who came up
8: 3 and with him were r 150 men;
8: 20 All were r by name.

REGISTRATION (REGISTER)

Ne 7: 5 and the common people for r

REGRET

2Ch 21: 20 He passed away, to no one's r,
2Co 7: 8 Though I did r it—I see that my
7: 8 sorrow by my letter, I do not r it.
7: 10 leads to salvation and leaves no r,

REGROUPED (GROUP)

2Sa 10: 15 had been routed by Israel, they r.

REGULAR

Ge 47: 22 because they received a r allotment
Ex 29: 28 to be the r share from the Israelites
Lev 6: 18 It is his r share of the offerings
6: 20 of fine flour as a r grain offering,
6: 22 It is the LORD's r share
7: 34 their r share from the Israelites.' "
7: 36 as their r share for the generations
10: 15 This will be the r share for you
14: 32 who cannot afford the r offerings
15: 19 " 'When a woman has her r flow
16: 24 and put on his r garments.
23: 7 sacred assembly and do no r work.
23: 8 assembly and do no r work.' "
23: 21 sacred assembly and do no r work.
23: 25 Do no r work, but present
23: 35 is a sacred assembly; do no r work.
23: 36 the closing assembly; do no r work.
24: 9 part of their r share of the offerings
Nu 4: 16 r grain offering and the anointing
8: 25 retire from their r service
18: 8 as your portion and r share.
18: 11 and daughters as your r share.
18: 19 and daughters as your r share.
28: 3 as a r burnt offering each day.
28: 6 This is the r burnt offering
28: 10 in addition to the r burnt offering
28: 15 Besides the r burnt offering
28: 18 sacred assembly and do no r work.
28: 23 to the r morning burnt offering.
28: 24 in addition to the r burnt offering
28: 25 sacred assembly and do no r work
28: 26 sacred assembly and do no r work.
28: 31 in addition to the r burnt offering
29: 1 sacred assembly and do no r work.
29: 11 and the r burnt offering
29: 12 sacred assembly and do no r work.
29: 16 in addition to the r burnt offering
29: 19 in addition to the r burnt offering
29: 22 in addition to the r burnt offering
29: 25 in addition to the r burnt offering
29: 28 in addition to the r burnt offering
29: 31 in addition to the r burnt offering
29: 34 in addition to the r burnt offering
29: 35 hold an assembly and do no r work.
29: 38 in addition to the r burnt offering
2Ki 25: 30 king gave Jehoiachin a r allowance
2Ch 30: 3 able to celebrate it at the r time
30: 16 Then they took up their r positions
Ezr 3: 5 presented the r burnt offerings,
Ne 10: 33 for the r grain offerings
Job 1: 5 This was Job's r custom.
Jer 5: 24 us of the r weeks of harvest.'
52: 34 gave Jehoiachin a r allowance
Eze 41: 17 and on the walls at r intervals all
46: 15 by morning for a r burnt offering.

REGULATED (REGULATION)

Ne 11: 23 which r their daily activity.

REGULATION (REGULATED REGULATIONS)

Ne 8: 18 with the r, there was an assembly.
Heb 7: 16 a priest not on the basis of a r
7: 18 The former r is set aside

REGULATIONS (REGULATION)

Ex 12: 43 "These are the r for the Passover:
Lev 6: 9 'These are the r for the burnt
6: 14 " 'These are the r for the grain
6: 25 'These are the r for the sin offering:
7: 1 " 'These are the r for the guilt
7: 11 " 'These are the r for the fellowship
7: 37 are the r for the burnt offering,
11: 46 These are the r concerning animals
12: 7 These are the r for the woman who
13: 59 are the r concerning
14: 2 "These are the r for the diseased
14: 32 These are the r for anyone who has
14: 54 These are the r for any infectious
14: 57 These are the r for infectious skin
15: 32 These are the r for a man
26: 46 the r that the LORD established
Nu 9: 3 accordance with all its rules and r."
9: 12 they must follow all the r.
9: 14 You must have the same r
9: 14 in accordance with its rules and r.
15: 16 and r will apply both to you
30: 16 These are the r the LORD gave
35: 24 of blood according to these r.
36: 13 r the LORD gave through Moses
Dt 12: 28 to obey all these r I am giving you,
1Sa 10: 25 to the people the r of the kingship.
1Ki 6: 12 carry out my r and keep all my
8: 58 decrees and r he gave our fathers.
2Ki 23: 3 r and decrees with all his heart
1Ch 6: 32 to the r laid down for them.
24: 19 according to the r prescribed
2Ch 34: 31 r and decrees with all his heart
Ne 9: 13 You gave them r and laws that are
10: 29 r and decrees of the LORD our
Est 9: 32 confirmed these r about Purim,
Eze 43: 11 its whole design and all its r
43: 11 to its design and follow all its r.
43: 18 These will be the r
44: 5 I tell you concerning all the r
Lk 1: 6 commandments and r blamelessly.
Eph 2: 15 law with its commandments and r.
Col 2: 14 the written code, with its r,
2: 23 Such r indeed have an appearance
Heb 9: 1 the first covenant had r for worship
9: 10 external r applying until the time

REHABIAH

1Ch 23: 17 of Eliezer: R was the first.
23: 17 the sons of R were very numerous.
24: 21 As for R, from his sons: Isshiah was
26: 25 through Eliezer: R his son,

REHOB

Nu 13: 21 from the Desert of Zin as far as R,
Jos 19: 28 It went to Abdon, R, Hammon
19: 30 of Aczib, Ummah, Aphek and R.
21: 31 Mishal, Abdon, Helkath and R,
Jdg 1: 31 or Aczib or Helbah or Aphek or R,
2Sa 8: 3 David fought Hadadezer son of R,
8: 12 taken from Hadadezer son of R,
10: 8 and R and the men of Tob
1Ch 6: 75 R, together with their pasturelands
Ne 10: 11 Hanan, Mica, R, Hashabiah,

REHOBOAM (REHOBOAM'S)

1Ki 11: 43 And *R* his son succeeded him
12: 1 *R* went to Shechem,
12: 3 assembly of Israel went to *R*
12: 5 *R* answered, "Go away
12: 6 King *R* consulted the elders who
12: 8 *R* rejected the advice the elders
12: 12 and all the people returned to *R*,
12: 17 of Judah, *R* still ruled over them.
12: 18 King *R* sent out Adoniram,
12: 18 King *R*, however, managed to get
12: 21 When *R* arrived in Jerusalem,
12: 21 the kingdom for *R* son of Solomon.
12: 23 "Say to *R* son of Solomon king
12: 27 to their lord, *R* king of Judah.
12: 27 will kill me and return to King *R*."
14: 21 *R* son of Solomon was king
14: 25 In the fifth year of King *R*,
14: 27 So King *R* made bronze shields
14: 30 was continual warfare between *R*
14: 31 And *R* rested with his fathers
15: 6 There was war between *R*
1Ch 3: 10 Solomon's son was *R*, Abijah his
2Ch 9: 31 And *R* his son succeeded him
10: 1 *R* went to Shechem,
10: 3 all Israel went to *R* and said to him:
10: 5 *R* answered, "Come back to me
10: 6 King *R* consulted the elders who
10: 8 *R* rejected the advice the elders
10: 12 and all the people returned to *R*,
10: 17 of Judah, *R* still ruled over them.
10: 18 King *R* sent out Adoniram,
10: 18 King *R*, however, managed to get
11: 1 When *R* arrived in Jerusalem,
11: 1 and to regain the kingdom for *R*.
11: 3 "Say to *R* son of Solomon king
11: 5 *R* lived in Jerusalem and built up
11: 17 supported *R* son of Solomon three
11: 18 *R* married Mahalath, who was
11: 21 *R* loved Maacah daughter
11: 22 *R* appointed Abijah son of Maacah
12: 2 in the fifth year of King *R*.
12: 5 the prophet Shemaiah came to *R*
12: 10 So King *R* made bronze shields
12: 12 Because *R* humbled himself,
12: 13 King *R* established himself firmly
12: 15 was continual warfare between *R*
12: 16 *R* rested with his fathers
13: 7 and opposed *R* son of Solomon
Mt 1: 7 father of *R*, *R* the father of Abijah,

REHOBOAM'S (REHOBOAM)

1Ki 14: 29 As for the other events of *R* reign,
2Ch 12: 1 After *R* position as king was
12: 15 As for the events of *R* reign,

REHOBOTH

Ge 26: 22 He named it *R*, saying,
36: 37 from *R* on the river succeeded him
1Ch 1: 48 from *R* on the river succeeded him

REHOBOTH IR

Ge 10: 11 where he built Nineveh, *R*,

REHUM

Ezr 2: 2 Mispar, Bigvai, *R* and Baanah):
4: 8 *R* the commanding officer
4: 9 *R* the commanding officer
4: 17 To *R* the commanding officer,
4: 23 of King Artaxerxes was read to *R*
Ne 3: 17 by the Levites under *R* son of Bani.
10: 25 Pilha, Shobek, *R*, Hashabnah,
12: 3 Hattush, Shecaniah, *R*, Meremoth,

REI

1Ki 1: 8 *R* and David's special guard did

REIGN (REIGNED REIGNING REIGNS)

Ge 37: 8 "Do you intend to *r* over us?
Ex 15: 18 The LORD will *r*
Dt 17: 20 his descendants will *r* a long time
32: 25 in their homes terror will *r*.
1Sa 8: 9 know what the king who will *r*
8: 11 "This is what the king who will *r*
11: 12 Who was it that asked, 'Shall Saul *r*
2Sa 21: 1 During the *r* of David, there was
1Ki 1: 35 sit on my throne and *r* in my place.
6: 1 year of Solomon's *r* over Israel,
1Ki 11: 41 for the other events of Solomon's *r*
14: 19 The other events of Jeroboam's *r*,
14: 29 the other events of Rehoboam's *r*,
15: 1 of the *r* of Jeroboam son of Nebat,
15: 7 for the other events of Abijah's *r*,
15: 23 for all the other events of Asa's *r*,
15: 29 to *r*, he killed Jeroboam's whole
15: 31 for the other events of Nadab's *r*,
16: 5 for the other events of Baasha's *r*,
16: 11 As soon as he began to *r*
16: 14 As for the other events of Elah's *r*,
16: 20 As for the other events of Zimri's *r*,
16: 27 As for the other events of Omri's *r*,
22: 39 As for the other events of Ahab's *r*,
22: 45 events of Jehoshaphat's *r*,
22: 46 even after the *r* of his father Asa.
2Ki 1: 18 all the other events of Ahaziah's *r*,
8: 16 son of Jehoshaphat began his *r*
8: 23 for the other events of Jehoram's *r*,
8: 25 king of Judah began to *r*.
10: 34 As for the other events of Jehu's *r*,
11: 21 old when he began to *r*.
12: 19 As for the other events of the *r*
13: 8 events of the *r* of Jehoahaz,
13: 12 events of the *r* of Jehoash,
13: 22 throughout the *r* of Jehoahaz.
14: 1 of Joash king of Judah began to *r*.
14: 15 events of the *r* of Jehoash,
14: 18 for the other events of Amaziah's *r*,
14: 28 the other events of Jeroboam's *r*,
15: 1 king of Judah began to *r*.
15: 6 for the other events of Azariah's *r*,
15: 11 events of Zechariah's *r* are written
15: 15 The other events of Shallum's *r*,
15: 18 During his entire *r* he did not turn
15: 21 the other events of Menahem's *r*,
15: 26 The other events of Pekahiah's *r*,
15: 31 As for the other events of Pekah's *r*
15: 32 of Uzziah king of Judah began to *r*.
15: 36 for the other events of Jotham's *r*,
16: 1 of Jotham king of Judah began to *r*
16: 19 As for the other events of the *r*
18: 1 of Ahaz king of Judah began to *r*.
18: 13 year of King Hezekiah's *r*,
20: 20 for the other events of Hezekiah's *r*
21: 17 the other events of Manasseh's *r*,
21: 25 As for the other events of Amon's *r*
22: 3 In the eighteenth year of his *r*,
23: 28 As for the other events of Josiah's *r*
23: 33 so that he might not *r* in Jerusalem,
24: 1 Jehoiakim's *r*, Nebuchadnezzar
24: 5 the other events of Jehoiakim's *r*,
24: 12 year of the *r* of the king of Babylon,
25: 1 So in the ninth year of Zedekiah's *r*
1Ch 4: 31 towns until the *r* of David.
5: 10 During Saul's *r* they waged war
7: 2 During the *r* of David,
13: 3 inquire of it during the *r* of Saul."
22: 9 Israel peace and quiet during his *r*.
26: 31 of David's *r* a search was made
29: 29 As for the events of King David's *r*,
29: 30 together with the details of his *r*
2Ch 3: 2 month in the fourth year of his *r*.
9: 29 for the other events of Solomon's *r*,
12: 15 As for the events of Rehoboam's *r*,
13: 1 year of the *r* of Jeroboam,
13: 22 The other events of Abijah's *r*,
15: 10 of the fifteenth year of Asa's *r*.
15: 19 until the thirty-fifth year of Asa's *r*.
16: 1 year of Asa's *r* Baasha king
16: 11 events of Asa's *r*, from beginning
16: 12 year of his *r* Asa was afflicted
16: 13 the forty-first year of his *r* Asa died
17: 7 year of his *r* he sent his officials
20: 34 events of Jehoshaphat's *r*,
22: 1 king of Judah began to *r*.
23: 3 to them, "The king's son shall *r*,
25: 26 for the other events of Amaziah's *r*,
26: 22 The other events of Uzziah's *r*,
27: 7 The other events in Jotham's *r*,
28: 26 The other events of his *r*
29: 3 month of the first year of his *r*,
32: 32 The other events of Hezekiah's *r*
33: 18 The other events of Manasseh's *r*,
34: 3 In the eighth year of his *r*,
34: 8 In the eighteenth year of Josiah's *r*,
35: 19 in the eighteenth year of Josiah's *r*.
35: 26 The other events of Josiah's *r*
2Ch 36: 8 The other events of Jehoiakim's *r*,
Ezr 4: 5 and down to the *r* of Darius king
4: 5 during the entire *r* of Cyrus king
4: 6 At the beginning of the *r* of Xerxes,
4: 24 of the *r* of Darius king of Persia.
6: 15 year of the *r* of King Darius.
7: 1 during the *r* of Artaxerxes king
8: 1 during the *r* of King Artaxerxes:
Ne 12: 22 were recorded in the *r*
Est 1: 3 year of his *r* he gave a banquet
2: 16 in the seventh year of his *r*.
6: 1 the record of his *r*, to be brought in
Ps 68: 16 mountain where God chooses to *r*,
Pr 8: 15 By me kings *r*
Isa 9: 7 He will *r* on David's throne
24: 23 for the LORD Almighty will *r*
32: 1 See, a king will *r* in righteousness
36: 1 year of King Hezekiah's *r*,
Jer 1: 2 year of the *r* of Josiah son
1: 3 and through the *r* of Jehoiakim son
3: 6 During the *r* of King Josiah,
23: 5 a King who will *r* wisely
26: 1 Early in the *r* of Jehoiakim son
27: 1 Early in the *r* of Zedekiah son
28: 1 early in the *r* of Zedekiah king
33: 21 a descendant to *r* on his throne.
35: 1 during the *r* of Jehoiakim son
36: 2 to you in the *r* of Josiah till now.
49: 34 early in the *r* of Zedekiah king
51: 59 of Judah in the fourth year of his *r*.
52: 4 So in the ninth year of Zedekiah's *r*
La 5: 19 You, O LORD, *r* forever;
Da 1: 1 of the *r* of Jehoiakim king of Judah,
2: 1 In the second year of his *r*,
5: 26 has numbered the days of your *r*
6: 28 and the *r* of Cyrus the Persian.
6: 28 prospered during the *r* of Darius
8: 1 year of King Belshazzar's *r*,
8: 23 "In the latter part of their *r*,
9: 2 in the first year of his *r*, I, Daniel,
Hos 1: 1 and during the *r* of Jeroboam son
Am 6: 3 and bring near a *r* of terror.
Zep 1: 1 during the *r* of Josiah son
Lk 1: 33 and he will *r* over the house
3: 1 year of the *r* of Tiberius Caesar—
Ac 11: 28 during the *r* of Claudius.)
Ro 5: 17 of the gift of righteousness *r* in life
5: 21 also grace might *r*
6: 12 Therefore do not let sin *r*
1Co 15: 25 For he must *r* until he has put all
2Ti 2: 12 we will also *r* with him.
Rev 5: 10 and they will *r* on the earth."
11: 15 and he will *r* for ever and ever."
11: 17 and have begun to *r*.
20: 6 will *r* with him for a thousand years
22: 5 And they will *r* for ever and ever.

REIGNED (REIGN)

Ge 36: 31 These were the kings who *r*
36: 31 in Edom before any Israelite king *r*
Nu 21: 34 of the Amorites, who *r* in Heshbon
Dt 1: 4 of Bashan, who *r* in Ashtaroth.
1: 4 who *r* in Heshbon,
3: 2 of the Amorites, who *r* in Heshbon
4: 46 who *r* in Heshbon and was
Jos 9: 10 of Bashan, who *r* in Ashtaroth.
12: 2 of the Amorites, who *r* in Heshbon.
12: 4 who *r* in Ashtaroth and Edrei.
13: 12 who had *r* in Ashtaroth and Edrei
Jdg 4: 2 a king of Canaan, who *r* in Hazor.
1Sa 13: 1 *r* over Israel forty- two years.
2Sa 2: 10 over Israel, and he *r* two years.
5: 4 became king, and he *r* forty years.
5: 5 In Hebron he *r* over Judah seven
5: 5 and in Jerusalem he *r* over all Israel
8: 15 David *r* over all Israel, doing what
16: 8 in whose place you have *r*.
1Ki 2: 11 He had *r* forty years over Israel—
11: 42 Solomon *r* in Jerusalem
14: 20 He *r* for twenty-two years
14: 21 he *r* seventeen years in Jerusalem,
15: 2 and he *r* in Jerusalem three years.
15: 10 he *r* in Jerusalem forty-one years.
15: 25 and he *r* over Israel two years.
15: 33 and he *r* twenty-four years.
16: 8 and he *r* in Tirzah two years.
16: 15 Zimri *r* in Tirzah seven days.
16: 23 of Israel, and he *r* twelve years,

1Ki 16: 29 *r* in Samaria over Israel
22: 42 he *r* in Jerusalem twenty-five years
22: 51 and he *r* over Israel two years.
2Ki 3: 1 of Judah, and he *r* twelve years.
8: 17 and he *r* in Jerusalem eight years.
8: 26 and he *r* in Jerusalem one year.
10: 36 The time that Jehu *r* over Israel
12: 1 and he *r* in Jerusalem forty years.
13: 1 Samaria, and he *r* seventeen years.
13: 10 in Samaria, and he *r* sixteen years.
14: 2 and he *r* in Jerusalem twenty-nine
14: 23 Samaria, and he *r* forty-one years.
15: 2 he *r* in Jerusalem fifty-two years.
15: 8 in Samaria, and he *r* six months.
15: 13 and he *r* in Samaria one month.
15: 17 and he *r* in Samaria ten years.
15: 23 in Samaria, and he *r* two years.
15: 27 in Samaria, and he *r* twenty years.
15: 33 and he *r* in Jerusalem sixteen years.
16: 2 and he *r* in Jerusalem sixteen years.
17: 1 in Samaria, and he *r* nine years.
18: 2 and he *r* in Jerusalem twenty-nine
21: 1 he *r* in Jerusalem fifty-five years.
21: 19 and he *r* in Jerusalem two years.
22: 1 he *r* in Jerusalem thirty-one years.
23: 31 and he *r* in Jerusalem three months
23: 36 and he *r* in Jerusalem eleven years.
24: 8 and he *r* in Jerusalem three months
24: 18 and he *r* in Jerusalem eleven years.
1Ch 1: 43 These were the kings who *r*
1: 43 in Edom before any Israelite king *r*
3: 4 David *r* in Jerusalem thirty-three
3: 4 where he *r* seven years
18: 14 David *r* over all Israel, doing what
2Ch 1: 13 And he *r* over Israel.
9: 30 Solomon *r* in Jerusalem
12: 13 he *r* seventeen years in Jerusalem,
13: 2 and he *r* in Jerusalem three years.
20: 31 So Jehoshaphat *r* over Judah.
20: 31 he *r* in Jerusalem twenty-five years
21: 5 and he *r* in Jerusalem eight years.
21: 20 and he *r* in Jerusalem eight years.
22: 2 and he *r* in Jerusalem one year.
24: 1 and he *r* in Jerusalem forty years.
25: 1 and he *r* in Jerusalem twenty-nine
26: 3 he *r* in Jerusalem fifty-two years.
27: 1 and he *r* in Jerusalem sixteen years.
27: 8 and he *r* in Jerusalem sixteen years.
28: 1 and he *r* in Jerusalem sixteen years.
29: 1 and he *r* in Jerusalem twenty-nine
33: 1 he *r* in Jerusalem fifty-five years.
33: 21 and he *r* in Jerusalem two years.
34: 1 he *r* in Jerusalem thirty-one years.
36: 2 and he *r* in Jerusalem three months
36: 5 and he *r* in Jerusalem eleven years.
36: 9 and he *r* in Jerusalem three months
36: 11 and he *r* in Jerusalem eleven years.
Est 1: 2 At that time King Xerxes *r*
Jer 37: 1 he *r* in place of Jehoiachin son
52: 1 and he *r* in Jerusalem eleven years.
Ro 5: 14 death *r* from the time of Adam
5: 17 death *r* through that one man,
5: 21 so that, just as sin *r* in death,
Rev 20: 4 and *r* with Christ a thousand years.

REIGNING (REIGN)

Mt 2: 22 he heard that Archelaus was *r*

REIGNS (REIGN)

1Sa 12: 14 and the king who *r* over you follow
1Ki 15: 16 king of Israel throughout their *r*.
15: 32 king of Israel throughout their *r*.
1Ch 5: 17 records during the *r* of Jotham king
16: 31 among the nations, "The LORD *r*
Ps 9: 7 The LORD *r* forever;
47: 8 God *r* over the nations;
93: 1 The LORD *r*, he is robed
96: 10 among the nations, "The LORD *r*
97: 1 The LORD *r*, let the earth be glad;
99: 1 The LORD *r*,
146: 10 The LORD *r* forever,
Isa 1: 1 saw during the *r* of Uzziah,
52: 7 "Your God *r*!"
Hos 1: 1 son of Beeri during the *r* of Uzziah,
Mic 1: 1 Moresheth during the *r* of Jotham,
Lk 22: 53 when darkness *r*."
Rev 19: 6 For our Lord God Almighty *r*.

REIMBURSE

Lk 10: 35 I will *r* you for any extra expense

REIN

Job 10: 1 I will give free *r* to my complaint
Jas 1: 26 and yet does not keep a tight *r*

REINFORCE (REINFORCED REINFORCEMENTS)

Jer 51: 12 *R* the guard,

REINFORCED (REINFORCE)

2Ch 24: 13 to its original design and *r* it.
32: 5 and *r* the supporting terraces

REINFORCEMENTS (REINFORCE)

Isa 43: 17 the army and *r* together,

REJECT (REJECTED REJECTING REJECTION REJECTS)

Lev 26: 15 and if you *r* my decrees
26: 44 I will not *r* them or abhor them so
1Sa 12: 22 the LORD will not *r* his people,
1Ki 9: 7 and will *r* this temple I have
2Ki 23: 27 I will *r* Jerusalem, the city I chose,
1Ch 28: 9 forsake him, he will *r* you forever.
2Ch 6: 42 do not *r* your anointed one.
7: 20 and will *r* this temple I have
Job 8: 20 God does not *r* a blameless man
Ps 27: 9 Do not *r* me or forsake me,
36: 4 and does not *r* what is wrong.
44: 23 Rouse yourself! Do not *r* us forever
77: 7 "Will the Lord *r* us forever?
88: 14 Why, O LORD, do you *r* me
94: 14 For the LORD will not *r* his people
119: 118 You *r* all who stray
132: 10 do not *r* your anointed one.
Isa 7: 15 he knows enough to *r* the wrong
7: 16 boy knows enough to *r* the wrong
31: 7 one of you will *r* the idols of silver
Jer 31: 37 will I *r* all the descendants of Israel
33: 26 then I will *r* the descendants
Hos 4: 6 I also *r* you as my priests;
9: 17 My God will *r* them
Lk 6: 22 and *r* your name as evil,
Ac 13: 46 Since you *r* it and do not consider
Ro 2: 8 and who *r* the truth and follow evil,
11: 1 I ask then, Did God *r* his people?
11: 2 God did not *r* his people, whom he
1Th 4: 8 this instruction does not *r* man
Tit 1: 14 of those who *r* the truth.
Jude : 8 *r* authority and slander celestial

REJECTED (REJECT)

Lev 26: 43 they *r* my laws and abhorred my
Nu 11: 20 because you have *r* the LORD,
14: 31 in to enjoy the land you have *r*.
Dt 32: 15 and *r* the Rock his Savior.
32: 19 The LORD saw this and *r* them
1Sa 8: 7 it is not you they have *r*
10: 19 But you have now *r* your God,
15: 23 Because you have *r* the word
15: 23 he has *r* you as king."
15: 26 You have *r* the word of the LORD,
15: 26 and the LORD has *r* you
16: 1 since I have *r* him as king
16: 7 or his height, for I have *r* him.
1Ki 12: 8 Rehoboam *r* the advice the elders
19: 10 The Israelites have *r* your covenant
19: 14 The Israelites have *r* your covenant
2Ki 17: 15 They *r* his decrees
17: 20 Therefore the LORD *r* all
2Ch 10: 8 Rehoboam *r* the advice the elders
11: 14 Jeroboam and his sons had *r* them
Ps 43: 2 Why have you *r* me?
44: 9 now you have *r* and humbled us;
60: 1 You have *r* us, O God,
60: 10 O God, you who have *r* us
66: 20 who has not *r* my prayer
74: 1 Why have you *r* us forever, O God
78: 59 he *r* Israel completely.
78: 67 Then he *r* the tents of Joseph,
89: 38 But you have *r*, you have spurned,
108: 11 O God, you who have *r* us
118: 22 The stone the builders *r*
Pr 1: 24 But since you *r* me when I called
Isa 5: 24 for they have *r* the law
8: 6 "Because this people has *r*
14: 19 like a *r* branch;
30: 12 "Because you have *r* this message,
41: 9 chosen you and have not *r* you.
49: 21 I was exiled and *r*.
53: 3 He was despised and *r* by men,
54: 6 only to be *r*," says your God.
Jer 2: 37 for the LORD has *r* those you trust
6: 19 and have *r* my law.
6: 30 They are called *r* silver,
6: 30 because the LORD has *r* them."
7: 29 the LORD has *r* and abandoned
8: 9 Since they have *r* the word
14: 19 Have you *r* Judah completely?
15: 6 You have *r* me," declares
33: 24 LORD has *r* the two kingdoms he
La 1: 15 "The Lord has *r*
2: 7 The Lord has *r* his altar
5: 22 unless you have utterly *r* us
Eze 5: 6 She has *r* my laws and has not
20: 13 follow my decrees but *r* my laws—
20: 16 because they *r* my laws
20: 24 had *r* my decrees and desecrated
Hos 4: 6 "Because you have *r* knowledge,
8: 3 But Israel has *r* what is good;
Am 2: 4 Because they have *r* the law
Zec 10: 6 as though I had not *r* them,
Mt 21: 42 " 'The stone the builders *r*
Mk 8: 31 must suffer many things and be *r*
9: 12 of Man must suffer much and be *r?*
12: 10 " 'The stone the builders *r*
Lk 7: 30 experts in the law *r* God's purpose
9: 22 must suffer many things and be *r*
17: 25 and be *r* by this generation.
20: 17 " 'The stone the builders *r*
Ac 4: 11 " 'the stone you builders *r*,
7: 35 the same Moses whom they had *r*
7: 39 they *r* him and in their hearts
1Ti 1: 19 Some have *r* these
4: 4 nothing is to be *r* if it is received
2Ti 3: 8 far as the faith is concerned, are *r*.
Heb 10: 28 Anyone who *r* the law
12: 17 to inherit this blessing, he was *r*.
1Pe 2: 4 *r* by men but chosen by God
2: 7 "The stone the builders *r*

REJECTING (REJECT)

Dt 31: 20 *r* me and breaking my covenant.
1Ki 12: 13 *R* the advice given him
2Ch 10: 13 *R* the advice of the elders,

REJECTION (REJECT)

Ro 11: 15 For if their *r* is the reconciliation

REJECTS (REJECT)

Isa 33: 15 who *r* gain from extortion
Lk 10: 16 but he who *r* me *r* him who sent me
10: 16 listens to me; he who *r* you *r* me;
Jn 3: 36 whoever *r* the Son will not see life,
12: 48 a judge for the one who *r* me
1Th 4: 8 he who *r* this instruction does not

REJOICE (JOY)

Lev 23: 40 and *r* before the LORD your God
Dt 12: 7 shall *r* in everything you have put
12: 12 there *r* before the LORD your God
12: 18 to *r* before the LORD your God
14: 26 of the LORD your God and *r*.
16: 11 And *r* before the LORD your God
26: 11 and the aliens among you shall *r*
32: 43 *R*, O nations, with his people,
33: 18 "*R*, Zebulun, in your going out,
2Sa 1: 20 daughters of the uncircumcised *r*.
1Ch 16: 10 of those who seek the LORD *r*.
16: 31 Let the heavens *r*, let the earth be
2Ch 6: 41 may your saints *r* in your goodness.
20: 27 cause to *r* over their enemies.
Job 3: 22 and *r* when they reach the grave?
22: 19 "The righteous see their ruin and *r*;
Ps 2: 11 and *r* with trembling.
5: 11 those who love your name may *r*
9: 2 I will be glad and *r* in you;
9: 14 and there *r* in your salvation.
13: 4 and my foes will *r* when I fall.
14: 7 let Jacob *r* and Israel be glad!
31: 7 I will be glad and *r* in your love,
32: 11 *R* in the LORD and be glad,
33: 21 In him our hearts *r*,
34: 2 let the afflicted hear and *r*.

Ps 35: 9 Then my soul will *r* in the LORD
39: 13 from me, that I may *r* again
40: 16 *r* and be glad in you;
51: 8 let the bones you have crushed *r*.
53: 6 let Jacob *r* and Israel be glad!
63: 11 But the king will *r* in God;
64: 10 Let the righteous *r* in the LORD
66: 6 come, let us *r* in him.
68: 3 and *r* before God;
68: 4 and *r* before him.
70: 4 *r* and be glad in you;
85: 6 that your people may *r* in you?
89: 16 They *r* in your name all day long;
89: 42 you have made all his enemies *r*.
96: 11 Let the heavens *r*, let the earth be
97: 1 let the distant shores *r*.
97: 12 *R* in the LORD, you who are
104: 31 may the LORD *r* in his works.
104: 34 as I *r* in the LORD.
105: 3 of those who seek the LORD *r*.
107: 42 The upright see and *r*,
109: 28 but your servant will *r*.
118: 24 let us *r* and be glad in it.
119: 14 I *r* in following your statutes
119: 74 May they who fear you *r*
119:162 I *r* in your promise
149: 2 Let Israel *r* in their Maker;
149: 5 Let the saints *r* in this honor
Pr 2: 14 and *r* in the perverseness of evil,
5: 18 may you *r* in the wife of your youth
23: 16 my inmost being will *r*
23: 25 may she who gave you birth *r!*
24: 17 stumbles, do not let your heart *r*,
29: 2 the righteous thrive, the people *r;*
SS 1: 4 We *r* and delight in you;
Isa 9: 3 as men *r*
9: 3 as people *r* at the harvest,
9: 3 they *r* before you
13: 3 those who *r* in my triumph.
14: 29 Do not *r*, all you Philistines,
25: 9 let us *r* and be glad in his salvation
29: 19 Once more the humble will *r*
29: 19 the needy will *r* in the Holy One
30: 29 your hearts will *r*
35: 1 the wilderness will *r* and blossom.
35: 2 it will *r* greatly and shout for joy.
41: 16 But you will *r* in the LORD
42: 11 settlements where Kedar lives *r*.
49: 13 *r*, O earth;
61: 7 they will *r* in their inheritance;
62: 5 so will your God *r* over you.
65: 13 my servants will *r*,
65: 18 But be glad and *r* forever
65: 19 I will *r* over Jerusalem
66: 10 *r* greatly with her,
66: 10 "*R* with Jerusalem and be glad
66: 14 you see this, your heart will *r*
Jer 11: 15 then you *r*."
31: 12 they will *r* in the bounty
32: 41 I will *r* in doing them good
50: 11 "Because you *r* and are glad,
La 1: 21 they *r* at what you have done.
4: 21 *R* and be glad, O Daughter
Eze 7: 12 Let not the buyer *r* nor the seller
Hos 9: 1 Do not *r*, O Israel;
Joel 2: 21 be glad and *r*.
2: 23 *r* in the LORD your God,
Am 6: 13 *r* in the conquest of Lo Debar
Ob : 12 nor *r* over the people of Judah
Hab 3: 18 yet I will *r* in the LORD,
Zep 3: 11 those who *r* in their pride.
3: 14 Be glad and *r* with all your heart,
3: 17 he will *r* over you with singing."
Zec 4: 10 Men will *r* when they see
9: 9 *R* greatly, O Daughter of Zion!
10: 7 their hearts will *r* in the LORD.
Mt 5: 12 *R* and be glad, because great is
Lk 1: 14 and many will *r* because of his birth
6: 23 "*R* in that day and leap for joy,
10: 20 but *r* that your names are written
10: 20 do not *r* that the spirits submit
15: 6 '*R* with me; I have found my lost
15: 9 '*R* with me; I have found my lost
Jn 16: 22 I will see you again and you will *r*,
Ro 5: 2 And we *r* in the hope of the glory
5: 3 but we also *r* in our sufferings,
5: 11 *r* in God through our Lord Jesus
12: 15 Rejoice with those who *r;* mourn
Ro 12: 15 *R* with those who rejoice; mourn
15: 10 "*R*, O Gentiles, with his people."
2Co 2: 3 by those who ought to make me *r*.
Php 1: 18 And because of this I *r*.
1: 18 Yes, and I will continue to *r*,
2: 17 I am glad and *r* with all of you.
2: 18 So you too should be glad and *r*
3: 1 Finally, my brothers, *r* in the Lord!
4: 4 *R* in the Lord always.
4: 4 *R!* Let your gentleness be evident
4: 10 I *r* greatly in the Lord that
Col 1: 24 I *r* in what was suffered for you,
1Pe 1: 6 In this you greatly *r*, though now
4: 13 But *r* that you participate
Rev 12: 12 Therefore *r*, you heavens
18: 20 *R* over her, O heaven!
18: 20 *R*, saints and apostles and prophets
19: 7 Let us *r* and be glad

REJOICED (JOY)

1Sa 6: 13 and saw the ark, they *r* at the sight.
2Ki 11: 20 and all the people of the land *r*.
1Ch 29: 9 David the king also *r* greatly.
29: 9 people *r* at the willing response
2Ch 15: 15 All Judah *r* about the oath
23: 21 and all the people of the land *r*.
29: 36 all the people *r* at what God had
30: 25 The entire assembly of Judah *r*,
Ne 12: 43 The women and children also *r*.
Job 31: 25 if I have *r* over my great wealth,
31: 29 "If I have *r* at my enemy's
Ps 122: 1 I *r* with those who said to me,
SS 3: 11 the day his heart *r*.
Eze 35: 15 you *r* when the inheritance
Hos 10: 5 those who had *r* over its splendor,
Jn 8: 56 Your father Abraham *r*

REJOICES (JOY)

1Sa 2: 1 "My heart *r* in the LORD;
Ps 13: 5 my heart *r* in your salvation.
16: 9 my heart is glad and my tongue *r;*
21: 1 the king *r* in your strength.
48: 11 Mount Zion *r*,
97: 8 Zion hears and *r*
119: 14 as one *r* in great riches.
Pr 11: 10 the righteous prosper, the city *r;*
Isa 8: 6 and *r* over Rezin
61: 10 my soul *r* in my God.
62: 5 as a bridegroom *r* over his bride,
Eze 35: 14 the whole earth *r*, I will make
Hab 1: 15 and so he *r* and is glad.
Lk 1: 47 and my spirit *r* in God my Savior,
Jn 16: 20 and mourn while the world *r*.
Ac 2: 26 my heart is glad and my tongue *r;*
1Co 12: 26 if one part is honored, every part *r*
13: 6 delight in evil but *r* with the truth.

REJOICING (JOY)

Nu 10: 10 times of *r*— your appointed feasts
Dt 27: 7 and *r* in the presence of the LORD
2Sa 6: 12 to the City of David with *r*.
1Ki 1: 40 playing flutes and *r* greatly,
2Ki 11: 14 all the people of the land were *r*
1Ch 15: 25 the house of Obed-Edom, with *r*.
2Ch 23: 13 all the people of the land were *r*
23: 18 with *r* and singing, as David had
30: 21 Bread for seven days with great *r*,
Ne 12: 43 of *r* in Jerusalem could be heard far
12: 43 *r* because God had given them
Job 39: 21 He paws fiercely, *r* in his strength,
Ps 19: 5 like a champion *r* to run his course.
30: 5 but *r* comes in the morning.
105: 43 He brought out his people with *r*,
Pr 8: 30 *r* always in his presence,
8: 31 *r* in his whole world
Jer 30: 19 and the sound of *r*.
Eze 25: 6 *r* with all the malice of your heart
Lk 15: 7 in the same way there is more *r*
15: 10 there is *r* in the presence
Ac 5: 41 *r* because they had been counted
8: 39 him again, but went on his way *r*.
2Co 6: 10 sorrowful, yet always *r;* poor,

REJOINED (JOIN)

Jdg 14: 9 When he *r* his parents, he gave

REKEM

Nu 31: 8 Among their victims were Evi, *R*,
Jos 13: 21 Evi, *R*, Zur, Hur and Reba—
18: 27 Kephirah, Mozah, *R*, Irpeel,
1Ch 2: 43 Korah, Tappuah, *R* and Shema.
2: 44 *R* was the father of Shammai.

RELATED (RELATING RELATION RELATIONS RELATIONSHIP RELATIONSHIPS RELATIVE RELATIVES)

Lev 21: 4 for people *r* to him by marriage,
Nu 3: 26 and everything *r* to their use.
3: 31 and everything *r* to their use.
3: 36 and everything *r* to their use,
4: 32 and everything *r* to their use.
2Sa 19: 42 because the king is closely *r* to us.
2Ki 8: 27 for he was *r* by marriage
2Ch 4: 16 meat forks and all *r* articles.
Est 8: 1 for Esther had told how he was *r*
Ac 19: 25 along with the workmen in *r* trades
Heb 5: 1 them in matters *r* to God,

RELATING (RELATED)

Ne 11: 24 agent in all affairs *r* to the people.

RELATION (RELATED)

1Ki 10: 1 his *r* to the name of the LORD,

RELATIONS (RELATED)

Ex 19: 15 Abstain from sexual *r*."
22: 19 "Anyone who has sexual *r*
Lev 18: 6 any close relative to have sexual *r*.
18: 7 She is your mother; do not have *r*
18: 7 father by having sexual *r*
18: 8 " 'Do not have sexual *r*
18: 9 " 'Do not have sexual *r*
18: 10 " 'Do not have sexual *r*
18: 11 " 'Do not have sexual *r*
18: 12 " 'Do not have sexual *r*
18: 13 " 'Do not have sexual *r*
18: 14 his wife to have sexual *r;*
18: 15 is your son's wife; do not have *r*
18: 15 " 'Do not have sexual *r*
18: 16 " 'Do not have sexual *r*
18: 17 Do not have sexual *r* with
18: 17 " 'Do not have sexual *r*
18: 18 and have sexual *r* with her
18: 19 sexual *r* during the uncleanness
18: 23 to an animal to have sexual *r* with it
18: 23 " 'Do not have sexual *r*
20: 15 " 'If a man has sexual *r*
20: 16 an animal to have sexual *r* with it,
20: 17 they have sexual *r*, it is a disgrace.
20: 18 monthly period and has sexual *r*
20: 19 Do not have sexual *r* with the sister
Dt 23: 6 or good *r* with them as long
27: 21 Cursed is the man who has sexual *r*
Jdg 4: 17 because there were friendly *r*
1Ki 1: 4 the king had no intimate *r* with her.
5: 12 There were peaceful *r*
Ro 1: 26 their women exchanged natural *r*
1: 27 abandoned natural *r* with women
2Co 1: 12 and especially in our *r* with you,

RELATIONSHIP (RELATED)

Jdg 18: 7 and had no *r* with anyone else.
18: 28 and had no *r* with anyone else.
Ro 2: 17 and brag about your *r* to God;

RELATIONSHIPS (RELATED)

Nu 30: 16 LORD gave Moses concerning *r*

RELATIVE (RELATED)

Ge 14: 14 heard that his *r* had been taken
14: 16 and brought back his *r* Lot
29: 12 He had told Rachel that he was a *r*
29: 15 "Just because you are a *r* of mine,
Lev 18: 6 is to approach any close *r*
18: 12 she is your father's close *r*.
18: 13 she is your mother's close *r*.
20: 19 for that would dishonor a close *r;*
21: 2 except for a close *r*, such
25: 25 his nearest *r* is to come
25: 49 any blood *r* in his clan may redeem
Nu 5: 8 But if that person has no close *r*
27: 11 to the nearest *r* in his clan,
Ru 2: 1 Naomi had a *r* on her husband's
2: 20 "That man is our close *r;* he is one
1Ki 16: 11 not spare a single male, whether *r*

Jer 23: 35 keeps on saying to his friend or *r*:
32: 7 because as nearest *r* it is your right
Am 6: 10 And if a *r* who is to burn the bodies
Lk 1: 36 Even Elizabeth your *r* is going
Jn 18: 26 a *r* of the man whose ear Peter had
Ro 16: 11 Greet Herodion, my *r*.

RELATIVES (RELATED)

Ge 24: 4 go to my country and my own *r*
24: 27 to the house of my master's *r*."
27: 37 have made all his *r* his servants,
31: 3 land of your fathers and to your *r*,
31: 23 Taking his *r* with him, he pursued
31: 25 Laban and his *r* camped there too.
31: 32 presence of our *r*, see for yourself
31: 37 Put it here in front of your *r*
31: 46 to his *r*, "Gather some stones."
31: 54 and invited his *r* to a meal.
32: 9 back to your country and your *r*,
Lev 10: 6 But your *r*, all the house of Israel,
18: 17 daughter; they are her close *r*.
25: 48 One of his *r* may redeem him:
Nu 27: 4 property among our father's *r*."
27: 7 inheritance among their father's *r*
Jdg 14: 3 acceptable woman among your *r*
2Ki 10: 13 They said, "We are *r* of Ahaziah,
10: 13 met some *r* of Ahaziah king of
1Ch 5: 7 Their *r* by clans, listed according
5: 13 Their *r*, by families, were: Michael,
7: 5 *r* who were fighting men belonging
7: 22 and his *r* came to comfort him.
8: 32 lived near their *r* in Jerusalem.
9: 38 lived near their *r* in Jerusalem.
12: 32 all their *r* under their command;
15: 5 Uriel the leader and 120 *r*;
15: 6 Asaiah the leader and 220 *r*;
15: 7 and 130 *r*; from the descendants
15: 8 Shemaiah the leader and 200 *r*;
15: 9 and 80 *r*; from the descendants
15: 10 Amminadab the leader and 112 *r*.
25: 7 Along with their *r*— all
25: 9 Joseph, his sons and *r*, 12
25: 9 Gedaliah, he and his *r*, and sons,
25: 10 Zaccur, his sons and *r*, 12
25: 11 Izri, his sons and *r*, 12
25: 12 Nethaniah, his sons and *r*, 12
25: 13 Bukkiah, his sons and *r*, 12
25: 14 Jesarelah, his sons and *r*, 12
25: 15 Jeshaiah, his sons and *r*, 12
25: 16 Mattaniah, his sons and *r*, 12
25: 17 Shimei, his sons and *r*, 12
25: 18 Azarel, his sons and *r*, 12
25: 19 Hashabiah, his sons and *r*, 12
25: 20 Shubael, his sons and *r*, 12
25: 21 Mattithiah, his sons and *r*, 12
25: 22 Jerimoth, his sons and *r*, 12
25: 23 Hananiah, his sons and *r*, 12
25: 24 Joshbakashah, his sons and *r*, 12
25: 25 Hanani, his sons and *r*, 12
25: 26 Mallothi, his sons and *r*, 12
25: 27 Eliathah, his sons and *r*, 12
25: 28 Hothir, his sons and *r*, 12
25: 29 Giddalti, his sons and *r*, 12
25: 30 Mahazioth, his sons and *r*, 12
25: 31 Romamti-Ezer, his sons and *r*, 12
26: 7 his *r* Elihu and Semakiah were
26: 8 and their *r* were capable men
26: 9 Meshelemiah had sons and *r*,
26: 11 and *r* of Hosah were 13 in all.
26: 12 of the LORD, just as their *r* had.
26: 25 His *r* through Eliezer: Rehabiah his
26: 26 and his *r* were in charge
26: 28 in the care of Shelomith and his *r*.
26: 30 and his *r*— seventeen hundred able
26: 32 Jeriah had twenty-seven hundred *r*
2Ch 5: 12 Jeduthun and their sons and *r*—
22: 8 and the sons of Ahaziah's *r*,
Pr 19: 7 A poor man is shunned by all his *r*
Jer 49: 10 *r* and neighbors will perish,
Eze 11: 15 your brothers who are your blood *r*
Mk 6: 4 among his *r* and in his own house is
Lk 1: 58 *r* heard that the Lord had shown
1: 61 among your *r* who has that name."
2: 44 looking for him among their *r*
14: 12 or *r*, or your rich neighbors;
21: 16 betrayed by parents, brothers, *r*
Ac 10: 24 and had called together his *r*
Ro 16: 7 my *r* who have been in prison
Ro 16: 21 Jason and Sosipater, my *r*.
1Ti 5: 8 If anyone does not provide for his *r*

RELEASE (RELEASED RELEASES)

Lev 14: 7 Then he is to *r* the live bird
14: 53 Then he is to *r* the live bird
16: 22 and the man shall *r* it in the desert.
25: 50 The price for his *r* is to be based
Nu 30: 5 the LORD will *r* her because her
30: 8 herself, and the LORD will *r* her.
30: 12 them, and the LORD will *r* her.
Dt 15: 13 when you *r* him, do not send him
Ps 25: 15 for only he will *r* my feet
102: 20 and *r* those condemned to death."
Ecc 8: 8 wickedness will not *r* those who
Isa 42: 7 to *r* from the dungeon those who
61: 1 and *r* for the prisoners,
Mt 27: 15 at the Feast to *r* a prisoner chosen
27: 17 "Which one do you want me to *r*
27: 21 of the two do you want me to *r*
Mk 15: 6 to *r* a prisoner whom the people
15: 9 me to *r* to you the king
15: 11 to have Pilate *r* Barabbas instead.
Lk 4: 18 to *r* the oppressed,
23: 16 I will punish him and then *r* him."
23: 18 with this man! *R* Barabbas to us!"
23: 20 Wanting to *r* Jesus, Pilate appealed
23: 22 him punished and then *r* him."
Jn 18: 39 Do you want me to *r* 'the king
18: 39 for me to *r* to you one prisoner
Ac 4: 23 On their *r*, Peter and John went
16: 35 with the order: "*R* those men."
28: 18 examined me and wanted to *r* me,
Rev 9: 14 "*R* the four angels who are bound

RELEASED (RELEASE)

Ge 24: 8 then you will be *r* from this oath
24: 41 you will be *r* from my oath
24: 41 you will be *r* from my oath.'
Lev 25: 41 Then he and his children are to be *r*
25: 54 his children are to be *r* in the Year
27: 21 When the field is *r* in the Jubilee,
Jos 2: 20 we will be *r* from the oath you
2Ki 25: 27 he *r* Jehoiachin from prison
2Ch 23: 8 Jehoiada the priest had not *r* any
Job 12: 14 the man he imprisons cannot be *r*.
Ps 105: 20 The king sent and *r* him,
Jer 20: 3 when Pashhur *r* him
40: 1 of the imperial guard had *r* him
52: 31 he *r* Jehoiachin king of Judah
Mal 4: 2 and leap like calves *r* from the stall.
Mt 27: 26 Then he *r* Barabbas to them.
Mk 15: 15 Pilate *r* Barabbas to them.
Lk 23: 25 He *r* the man who had been thrown
Ac 3: 14 asked that a murderer be *r* to you.
16: 36 ordered that you and Silas be *r*.
22: 30 he *r* him and ordered the chief
Ro 7: 2 she is *r* from the law of marriage.
7: 3 she is *r* from that law and is not
7: 6 we have been *r* from the law
Heb 11: 35 were tortured and refused to be *r*,
13: 23 our brother Timothy has been *r*.
Rev 9: 15 and year were *r* to kill a third
20: 7 Satan will be *r* from his prison

RELEASES (RELEASE)

Lev 16: 26 "The man who *r* the goat

RELENT (RELENTED RELENTS)

Ex 32: 12 *r* and do not bring disaster
Job 6: 29 *R*, do not be unjust;
Ps 7: 12 If he does not *r*,
90: 13 *R*, O LORD! How long will it be?
Isa 57: 6 the light of these things, should I *r*?
Jer 4: 28 I have spoken and will not *r*,
18: 8 then I will *r* and not inflict
26: 3 Then I will *r* and not bring
26: 13 Then the LORD will *r*
26. 19 And did not the LORD *r*,
Eze 24: 14 I will not have pity, nor will I *r*.
Jnh 3: 9 yet *r* and with compassion turn

RELENTED (RELENT)

Ex 32: 14 the LORD *r* and did not bring
Ps 106: 45 and out of his great love he *r*.
Am 7: 3 He is so small!" So the LORD *r*.
7: 6 He is so small!" So the LORD *r*.

RELENTLESS

Isa 14: 6 nations with *r* aggression.

RELENTS (RELENT)

Joel 2: 13 and he *r* from sending calamity.
Jnh 4: 2 a God who *r* from sending calamity

RELIABLE (RELY)

1Sa 29: 6 the LORD lives, you have been *r*,
Pr 22: 21 teaching you true and *r* words,
Isa 8: 2 of Jeberekiah as *r* witnesses for me
Jer 2: 21 of sound and *r* stock.
Jn 8: 26 But he who sent me is *r*,
2Ti 2: 2 witnesses entrust to *r* men who will

RELIANCE (RELY)

Pr 25: 19 is *r* on the unfaithful in times

RELIED (RELY)

Jdg 20: 36 they *r* on the ambush they had set
2Ch 13: 18 were victorious because they *r*
16: 7 Because you *r* on the king of Aram
16: 8 Yet when you *r* on the LORD,
Ps 71: 6 From birth I have *r* on you;
Isa 20: 6 what has happened to those we *r*
30: 12 *r* on oppression

RELIEF (RELIEVE)

Ex 8: 15 when Pharaoh saw that there was *r*
1Sa 8: 18 you will cry out for *r*
16: 23 Then *r* would come to Saul;
Ezr 9: 8 and a little *r* in our bondage.
Est 4: 14 *r* and deliverance for the Jews will
9: 16 and get *r* from their enemies.
9: 22 as the time when the Jews got *r*
Job 16: 5 from my lips would bring you *r*.
32: 20 I must speak and find *r*;
35: 9 they plead for *r* from the arm
Ps 4: 1 Give me *r* from my distress;
94: 13 you grant him *r* from days
143: 1 come to my *r*.
Isa 1: 24 "Ah, I will get *r* from my foes
14: 3 On the day the LORD gives you *r*
La 2: 18 give yourself no *r*,
3: 49 without *r*,
3: 56 to my cry for *r*."
Mic 1: 12 waiting for *r*,
2Th 1: 7 and give *r* to you who are troubled,

RELIES (RELY)

Job 8: 14 what he *r* on is a spider's web.

RELIEVE (RELIEF RELIEVED RELIEVING)

Dt 23: 12 where you can go to *r* yourself.
23: 13 and when you *r* yourself, dig a hole
1Sa 24: 3 and Saul went in to *r* himself.

RELIEVED (RELIEVE)

Job 16: 6 "Yet if I speak, my pain is not *r*;
2Co 8: 13 desire is not that others might be *r*

RELIEVING (RELIEVE)

Jdg 3: 24 "He must be *r* himself

RELIGION (RELIGIOUS)

Ac 25: 19 dispute with him about their own *r*
26: 5 to the strictest sect of our *r*,
1Ti 5: 4 all to put their *r* into practice
Jas 1: 26 himself and his *r* is worthless.
1: 27 *R* that God our Father accepts

RELIGIOUS (RELIGION)

Am 5: 21 "I hate, I despise your *r* feasts;
8: 10 I will turn your *r* feasts
Ac 17: 22 that in every way you are very *r*.
Col 2: 16 or with regard to a *r* festival,
Heb 10: 11 stands and performs his *r* duties;
Jas 1: 26 If anyone considers himself *r*

RELISH

Hos 4: 8 and *r* their wickedness.

RELY (RELIABLE RELIANCE RELIED RELIES)

2Ch 14: 11 O LORD our God, for we *r* on you,
Job 39: 11 Will you *r* on him for his great
Isa 10: 20 but will truly *r* on the LORD,

Isa 10: 20 will no longer *r* on him
31: 1 who *r* on horses,
48: 2 and *r* on the God of Israel—
50: 10 and *r* on his God.
59: 4 They *r* on empty arguments
Jer 46: 25 and on those who *r* on Pharaoh.
Eze 33: 26 you then possess the land? You *r*
Ro 2: 17 if you *r* on the law and brag about
2Co 1: 9 this happened that we might not *r*
Gal 3: 10 All who *r* on observing the law are
1Jn 4: 16 and *r* on the love God has for us.

REMAIN (REMAINDER REMAINED REMAINING REMAINS)

Ge 15: 2 can you give me since I *r* childless
24: 55 Let the girl *r* with us ten days or so;
36: 7 great for them to *r* together;
44: 33 please let your servant *r* here
Ex 8: 9 except for those that *r* in the Nile."
8: 11 they will *r* only in the Nile."
25: 15 The poles are to *r* in the rings
34: 25 sacrifice from the Passover Feast *r*
Lev 6: 9 is to *r* on the altar hearth
11: 37 are to be planted, they *r* clean.
22: 27 it is to *r* with its mother
25: 28 what he sold will *r*
25: 51 If many years *r*, he must pay
25: 52 If only a few years *r* until the Year
26: 21 " 'If you *r* hostile toward me
27: 14 the priest then sets, so it will *r*.
27: 18 of years that *r* until the next Year
Nu 4: 7 that is continually there is to *r*
9: 22 the Israelites would *r* in camp
32: 26 and herds will *r* here in the cities
33: 55 allow to *r* will become barbs
Dt 13: 16 It is to *r* a ruin forever, never
16: 4 of the first day *r* until morning.
31: 26 There it will *r* as a witness
Jos 18: 5 Judah is to *r* in its territory
23: 4 the land of the nations that *r*—
23: 7 associate with these nations that *r*
23: 12 of these nations that *r* among you
Jdg 2: 23 had allowed those nations to *r*;
Ru 1: 13 Would you *r* unmarried for them?
1Sa 16: 22 "Allow David to *r* in my service,
2Sa 14: 14 person may not *r* estranged
16: 18 his I will be, and I will *r* with him.
1Ki 2: 45 and David's throne will *r* secure
1Ch 21: 17 but do not let this plague *r*
2Ch 32: 10 that you *r* in Jerusalem under siege
33: 4 Name will *r* in Jerusalem forever."
Est 4: 14 For if you *r* silent at this time,
Job 29: 20 My glory will *r* fresh in me,
37: 8 they *r* in their dens.
Ps 28: 1 For if you *r* silent,
30: 5 weeping may *r* for a night,
49: 11 Their tombs will *r* their houses
102: 26 They will perish, but you *r*;
102: 27 But you *r* the same,
109: 1 do not *r* silent,
109: 15 May their sins always *r*
125: 3 The scepter of the wicked will not *r*
Pr 2: 21 and the blameless will *r* in it;
10: 30 but the wicked will not *r* in the land
Isa 4: 3 who *r* in Jerusalem, will be called
7: 22 All who *r* in the land will eat curds
10: 4 Nothing will *r* but to cringe
15: 9 and upon those who *r* in the land.
17: 6 Yet some gleanings will *r*,
18: 4 "I will *r* quiet and will look
22: 18 there your splendid chariots will *r*
46: 3 all you who *r* of the house of Israel,
62: 1 Jerusalem's sake I will not *r* quiet,
Jer 24: 8 whether they *r* in this land
27: 11 I will let that nation *r*
27: 22 and there they will *r* until the day I
29: 16 all the people who *r* in this city,
32: 5 where he will *r* until I deal
51: 30 they *r* in their strongholds.
Eze 36: 36 around you that *r* will know that I
39: 14 others will bury those that *r*
44: 2 It is to *r* shut because the LORD,
44: 2 said to me, "This gate is to *r* shut.
Da 2: 43 be a mixture and will not *r* united,
4: 15 and bronze, *r* in the ground,
4: 23 while its roots *r* in the ground.
11: 12 yet he will not *r* triumphant.
Hos 9: 3 They will not *r* in the LORD's land
Zec 5: 4 It will *r* in his house and destroy it,
12: 6 Jerusalem will *r* intact in her place.
14: 10 Jerusalem will be raised up and *r*
Jn 1: 32 from heaven as a dove and *r* on him
1: 33 and *r* is he who will baptize
12: 34 Law that the Christ will *r* forever,
15: 4 *R* in me, and I will *r* in you.
15: 4 can you bear fruit unless you *r*
15: 4 fruit by itself; it must *r* in the vine.
15: 6 If anyone does not *r* in me,
15: 7 If you *r* in me and my words
15: 7 in me and my words *r* in you,
15: 9 Now *r* in my love.
15: 10 my Father's commands and *r*
15: 10 you obey my commands, you will *r*
17: 11 I will *r* in the world no longer,
21: 22 him to *r* alive until I return,
21: 23 him to *r* alive until I return,
Ac 3: 21 He must *r* in heaven
11: 23 and encouraged them all to *r* true
14: 22 and encouraging them to *r* true
Ro 13: 8 Let no debt *r* outstanding,
1Co 7: 11 she must *r* unmarried or else be
7: 20 Each one should *r*
7: 24 should *r* in the situation God called
7: 26 I think that it is good for you to *r*
13: 13 And now these three *r*: faith,
14: 34 women should *r* silent
Gal 2: 5 of the gospel might *r* with you.
Php 1: 24 for you that I *r* in the body.
1: 25 of this, I know that I will *r*,
2Ti 2: 13 he will *r* faithful,
Heb 1: 11 They will perish, but you *r*;
1: 12 But you *r* the same,
8: 9 because they did not *r* faithful
12: 27 that what cannot be shaken may *r*.
1Jn 2: 24 you also will *r* in the Son
2: 27 just as it has taught you, *r* in him.
Rev 2: 13 Yet you *r* true to my name.
14: 12 commandments and *r* faithful
17: 10 he must *r* for a little while.

REMAINDER (REMAIN)

Est 9: 16 the *r* of the Jews who were

REMAINED (REMAIN)

Ge 18: 22 but Abraham *r* standing
32: 4 with Laban and have *r* there
49: 24 But his bow *r* steady,
Ex 8: 31 officials and his people; not a fly *r*.
10: 15 Nothing green *r* on tree
17: 12 so that his hands *r* steady till sunset
20: 21 The people *r* at a distance,
Lev 10: 3 Aaron *r* silent.
Nu 9: 18 over the tabernacle, they *r* in camp.
9: 19 the cloud *r* over the tabernacle
11: 26 and Medad, had *r* in the camp.
36: 12 and their inheritance *r*
Jos 4: 10 who carried the ark *r* standing
5: 8 they *r* where they were in camp
8: 17 Not a man *r* in Ai or Bethel who
Jdg 1: 30 who *r* among them; but they did
5: 17 Asher *r* on the seacoast
7: 3 while ten thousand *r*.
13: 2 who was sterile and *r* childless.
19: 4 so he *r* with him three days,
1Sa 5: 4 on the threshold; only his body *r*.
7: 2 years in all, that the ark *r* at Kiriath
13: 7 Saul *r* at Gilgal, and all the troops
18: 29 he *r* his enemy the rest of his days.
23: 18 Jonathan went home, but David *r*
2Sa 6: 11 ark of the LORD *r* in the house
11: 1 But David *r* in Jerusalem.
11: 12 So Uriah *r* in Jerusalem that day
1Ki 12: 20 tribe of Judah *r* loyal to the house
22: 46 male shrine prostitutes who *r* there
2Ki 2: 22 And the water has *r* wholesome
10: 11 in Jezreel who *r* of the house
11: 3 He *r* hidden with his nurse
13: 6 Also, the Asherah pole *r* standing
18: 36 But the people *r* silent
25: 11 carried into exile the people who *r*
1Ch 12: 29 most of whom had *r* loyal
13: 14 The ark of God *r* with the family
20: 1 and besieged it, but David *r*
2Ch 22: 12 He *r* hidden with them
Isa 36: 21 But the people *r* silent
Jer 35: 11 So we have *r* in Jerusalem."
Jer 37: 16 a dungeon, where he *r* a long time.
37: 21 So Jeremiah *r* in the courtyard
38: 13 And Jeremiah *r* in the courtyard
38: 28 And Jeremiah *r* in the courtyard
39: 9 exile to Babylon the people who *r*
39: 14 So he *r* among his own people.
52: 15 and those who *r* in the city,
Eze 17: 6 toward him, but its roots *r* under it.
Da 1: 21 Daniel *r* there until the first year
2: 49 while Daniel himself *r*
Hos 10: 9 and there you have *r*.
Mt 11: 23 it would have *r* to this day.
26: 63 against you?" But Jesus *r* silent.
Mk 3: 4 or to kill?" But they *r* silent.
14: 61 Jesus *r* silent and gave no answer.
Lk 1: 22 signs to them but *r* unable to speak.
1: 24 and for five months *r* in seclusion.
14: 4 or not?" But they *r* silent.
Ac 7: 45 It *r* in the land until the time
15: 35 Paul and Barnabas *r* in Antioch,
1Jn 2: 19 they would have *r* with us;

REMAINING (REMAIN)

Ex 28: 10 names on one stone and the *r* six
Lev 10: 12 Moses said to Aaron and his *r* sons,
10: 16 Aaron's *r* sons, and asked,
14: 17 to put some of the oil *r* in his palm
Nu 31: 32 The plunder *r* from the spoils that
Jos 7: 6 of the LORD, *r* there till evening.
1Ki 9: 21 their descendants *r* in the land,
1Ch 4: 43 They killed the *r* Amalekites who
2Ch 8: 8 their descendants *r* in the land,
Ne 11: 1 while the *r* nine were to stay
Isa 10: 19 the *r* trees of his forests will be
Jer 27: 18 Almighty that the furnishings *r*
Eze 25: 16 destroy those *r* along the seacoast.
48: 15 "The *r* area, 5,000 cubits wide
Jn 19: 23 of them, with the undergarment *r*.

REMAINS (REMAIN)

Ex 22: 13 he shall bring in the *r* as evidence
Lev 11: 36 cistern for collecting water *r* clean,
13: 46 he has the infection he *r* unclean.
27: 17 the value that has been set *r*.
Nu 15: 31 cut off; his guilt *r* on him.' "
16: 37 out of the smoldering *r*
19: 13 he is unclean; his uncleanness *r*
Dt 24: 20 Leave what *r* for the alien,
24: 21 Leave what *r* for the alien,
Jos 7: 26 pile of rocks, which *r* to this day.
8: 29 of rocks over it, which *r* to this day.
13: 2 is the land that *r*: all the regions
2Sa 7: 2 while the ark of God *r* in a tent."
1Ki 20: 10 if enough dust *r* in Samaria
2Ki 6: 31 of Shaphat *r* on his shoulders today
Ne 9: 10 for yourself, which *r* to this day.
Job 19: 4 my error *r* my concern alone.
34: 29 But if he *r* silent, who can condemn
Ps 146: 6 the LORD, who *r* faithful forever.
Pr 29: 1 A man who *r* stiff-necked
Ecc 1: 4 but the earth *r* forever.
Isa 6: 13 And though a tenth *r* in the land,
29: 8 but he awakens, and his hunger *r*;
Eze 32: 5 and fill the valleys with your *r*.
48: 18 What *r* of the area, bordering
48: 21 "What *r* on both sides
Mic 7: 2 not one upright man *r*.
Hag 1: 4 while this house *r* a ruin?"
1: 9 of my house, which *r* a ruin,
2: 5 And my Spirit *r* among you.
Jn 3: 36 for God's wrath *r* on him."
6: 56 and drinks my blood *r* in me,
9: 41 you claim you can see, your guilt *r*.
12: 24 and dies, it *r* only a single seed.
15: 5 If a man *r* in me and I in him,
1Co 11: 21 One *r* hungry, another gets drunk.
2Co 3: 14 for to this day the same veil *r*
Heb 4: 6 It still *r* that some will enter that
4: 9 There *r*, then, a Sabbath-rest
7: 3 Son of God he *r* a priest forever.
1Jn 2: 24 heard from the beginning *r* in you.
2: 27 received from him *r* in you,
3: 9 because God's seed *r* in him;
3: 14 Anyone who does not love *r*
Rev 3: 2 Strengthen what *r* and is about

REMALIAH (REMALIAH'S)

2Ki 15: 25 Pekah son of *R*, conspired

2Ki 15:27 Pekah son of *R* became king
15:30 conspired against Pekah son of *R*.
15:32 of Pekah son of *R* king of Israel,
15:37 and Pekah son of *R* against Judah.)
16: 1 year of Pekah son of *R*,
16: 5 and Pekah son of *R* king
2Ch 28: 6 son of *R* killed a hundred
Isa 7: 1 and Pekah son of *R* king
7: 4 and Aram and of the son of *R*.
8: 6 and the son of *R*,

REMALIAH'S (REMALIAH)

Isa 7: 5 and *R* son have plotted your ruin,
7: 9 the head of Samaria is only *R* son.

REMARKABLE

Lk 5:26 "We have seen *r* things today."
Jn 9:30 The man answered, "Now that is *r!*

REMARKED (REMARKING)

Ac 17:18 Others *r*, "He seems

REMARKING (REMARKED)

Lk 21: 5 of his disciples were *r* about how

REMEDIES (REMEDY)

Jer 46:11 But you multiply *r* in vain;

REMEDY (REMEDIES)

2Ch 36:16 his people and there was no *r*.
Pr 6:15 suddenly be destroyed—without *r*.
29: 1 suddenly be destroyed—without *r*.
Isa 3: 7 "I have no *r*.
Jer 30:13 no *r* for your sore,
Mic 2:10 it is ruined, beyond all *r*.

REMEMBER (REMEMBERED REMEMBERING REMEMBERS REMEMBRANCE)

Ge 9:15 I will *r* my covenant between me
9:16 and *r* the everlasting covenant
31:50 *r* that God is a witness
40:14 *r* me and show me kindness;
40:23 however, did not *r* Joseph;
Ex 20: 8 "*R* the Sabbath day
32:13 *R* your servants Abraham,
33:13 *R* that this nation is your people."
Lev 26:42 I will *r* my covenant with Jacob
26:42 with Abraham, and I will *r* the land
26:45 for their sake I will *r* the covenant
Nu 11: 5 We *r* the fish we ate in Egypt
15:39 and so you will *r* all the commands
15:40 Then you will *r* to obey all my
Dt 4:10 *R* the day you stood
5:15 *R* that you were slaves in Egypt
7:18 *r* well what the LORD your God
8: 2 *R* how the LORD your God led
8:18 But *r* the LORD your God,
9: 7 *R* this and never forget how you
9:27 *R* your servants Abraham,
11: 2 *R* today that your children were
15:15 *R* that you were slaves in Egypt
16: 3 days of your life you may *r* the time
16:12 *R* that you were slaves in Egypt,
24: 9 *R* what the LORD your God did
24:18 *R* that you were slaves in Egypt
24:22 *R* that you were slaves in Egypt.
25:17 *R* what the Amalekites did to you
32: 7 *R* the days of old;
Jos 1:13 "*R* the command that Moses
23: 4 *R* how I have allotted
Jdg 8:34 and did not *r* the LORD their God,
9: 2 *R*, I am your flesh and blood."
16:28 "O Sovereign LORD, *r* me.
1Sa 1:11 your servant's misery and *r* me,
20:23 the matter you and I discussed—*r*,
25:31 master success, *r* your servant."
2Sa 19:19 Do not *r* how your servant did
1Ki 2: 8 *r*, you have with you Shimei son
2Ki 9:25 *R* how you and I were riding
20: 3 and prayed to the LORD, "*R*,
1Ch 16:12 *R* the wonders he has done,
2Ch 6:42 *R* the kindnesses promised
24:22 Joash did not *r* the kindness
Ne 1: 8 "*R* the instruction you gave your
4:14 *R* the Lord, who is great
5:19 *R* me with favor, O my God,
6:14 *R* Tobiah and Sanballat, O my God
Ne 6:14 *r* also the prophetess Noadiah
9:17 to *r* the miracles you performed
13:14 *R* me for this, O my God,
13:22 *R* me for this also, O my God,
13:29 *R* them, O my God, because they
13:31 *R* me with favor, O my God.
Job 7: 7 *R*, O God, that my life is
10: 9 *R* that you molded me like clay.
14:13 and then *r* me!
36:24 *R* to extol his work,
41: 8 you will *r* the struggle
Ps 20: 3 May he *r* all your sacrifices
22:27 will *r* and turn to the LORD,
25: 6 *R*, O LORD, your great mercy
25: 7 according to your love *r* me,
25: 7 *R* not the sins of my youth
42: 4 These things I *r*
42: 6 therefore I will *r* you
63: 6 On my bed I *r* you;
74: 2 *R* the people you purchased of old,
74:18 *R* how the enemy has mocked you,
74:22 *r* how fools mock you all day long.
77:11 I will *r* the deeds of the LORD;
77:11 I will *r* your miracles of long ago.
78:42 They did not *r* his power—
88: 5 whom you *r* no more,
89:47 *R* how fleeting is my life.
89:50 *R*, Lord, how your servant has
103: 18 and *r* to obey his precepts.
105: 5 *R* the wonders he has done,
106: 4 *R* me, O LORD, when you show
106: 7 they did not *r* your many
119: 49 *R* your word to your servant,
119: 52 I *r* your ancient laws, O LORD,
119: 55 In the night I *r* your name,
132: 1 O LORD, *r* David
137: 6 mouth if I do not *r* you,
137: 7 *R*, O LORD, what the Edomites
143: 5 I *r* the days of long ago;
Pr 31: 7 and *r* their misery no more.
Ecc 11: 8 But let him *r* the days of darkness,
12: 1 *R* your Creator
12: 6 *R* him—before the silver cord is
Isa 38: 3 and prayed to the LORD, "*R*,
44:21 "*R* these things, O Jacob,
46: 8 "*R* this, fix it in mind,
46: 9 *R* the former things, those
54: 4 and *r* no more the reproach
64: 5 who *r* your ways.
64: 9 do not *r* our sins forever.
Jer 2: 2 " 'I *r* the devotion of your youth,
14:10 he will now *r* their wickedness
14:21 *R* your covenant with us
15:15 *r* me and care for me.
17: 2 Even their children *r*
18:20 *R* that I stood before you
31:20 I still *r* him.
31:34 and will *r* their sins no more."
44:21 "Did not the LORD *r*
51:50 *R* the LORD in a distant land,
La 3:19 I *r* my affliction and my wandering
3:20 I well *r* them,
5: 1 *R*, O LORD, what has happened
Eze 6: 9 those who escape will *r* me—
16:22 prostitution you did not *r* the days
16:43 " 'Because you did not *r* the days
16:60 Yet I will *r* the covenant I made
16:61 Then you will *r* your ways
16:63 you will *r* and be ashamed
20:43 There you will *r* your conduct
23:27 with longing or *r* Egypt anymore.
36:31 Then you will *r* your evil ways
Da 6:15 to the king and said to him, "*R*,
Hos 7: 2 that I *r* all their evil deeds.
8:13 Now he will *r* their wickedness
9: 9 God will *r* their wickedness
Mic 6: 5 My people, *r* what Balak
6: 5 *R* ⌊your journey⌋ from Shittim
Hab 3: 2 in wrath *r* mercy.
Zec 10: 9 yet in distant lands they will *r* me.
Mal 4: 4 "*R* the law of my servant Moses,
Mt 5:23 and there *r* that your brother has
16: 9 Don't you *r* the five loaves
27:63 "we *r* that while he was still alive
Mk 8:18 but fail to hear? And don't you *r?*
Lk 1:72 and to *r* his holy covenant,
16:25 *r* that in your lifetime you received
17:32 *R* Lot's wife! Whoever tries
Lk 23:42 *r* me when you come
24: 6 he has risen! *R* how he told you,
Jn 15:20 *R* the words I spoke to you:
16: 4 time comes you will *r* that I warned
Ac 20:31 *R* that for three years I never
Ro 1: 9 my witness how constantly I *r* you
1Co 1:16 I don't *r* if I baptized anyone else.)
2Co 9: 6 *R* this: Whoever sows sparingly
Gal 2:10 we should continue to *r* the poor,
Eph 2:11 *r* that formerly you who are
2:12 *r* that at that time you were
Php 1: 3 I thank my God every time I *r* you.
Col 4:18 *R* my chains.
1Th 1: 3 We continually *r* before our God
2: 9 Surely you *r*, brothers, our toil
2Th 2: 5 Don't you *r* that when I was
2Ti 1: 3 and day I constantly *r* you
2: 8 *R* Jesus Christ, raised
Phm : 4 I always thank my God as I *r* you
Heb 8:12 and will *r* their sins no more."
10:17 I will *r* no more."
10:32 *R* those earlier days
13: 3 *R* those in prison as if you were
13: 7 *R* your leaders, who spoke
Jas 5:20 should bring him back, *r* this:
2Pe 1:15 always be able to *r* these things.
Jude : 17 *r* what the apostles
Rev 2: 5 *R* the height from which you have
3: 3 *R*, therefore, what you have

REMEMBERED (REMEMBER)

Ge 8: 1 But God *r* Noah and all the wild
19:29 cities of the plain, he *r* Abraham,
30:22 God *r* Rachel; he listened to her
41:31 abundance in the land will not be *r*,
42: 9 Then he *r* his dreams about them
Ex 2:24 he *r* his covenant with Abraham,
3:15 am to be *r* from generation
6: 5 and I have *r* my covenant.
17:14 to be *r* and make sure that Joshua
Nu 10: 9 you will be *r* by the LORD your
1Sa 1:19 his wife, and the LORD *r* her.
Est 2: 1 he *r* Vashti and what she had done
9:28 These days should be *r*
Job 24:20 evil men are no longer *r*
Ps 77: 3 I *r* you, O God, and I groaned;
77: 6 I *r* my songs in the night.
78:35 They *r* that God was their Rock,
78:39 He *r* that they were but flesh,
83: 4 of Israel be *r* no more."
98: 3 He has *r* his love
105: 42 For he *r* his holy promise
106: 45 for their sake he *r* his covenant
109: 14 his fathers be *r* before the LORD;
111: 4 He has caused his wonders to be *r;*
112: 6 a righteous man will be *r* forever.
136: 23 to the One who *r* us
137: 1 when we *r* Zion.
Ecc 1:11 will not be *r*
2:16 like the fool, will not be long *r;*
9:15 But nobody *r* that poor man.
Isa 17:10 you have not *r* the Rock, your
23:16 so that you will be *r*."
57:11 and have neither *r* me
65:17 The former things will not be *r*,
Jer 3:16 will never enter their minds or be *r;*
11:19 that his name be *r* no more."
La 2: 1 he has not *r* his footstool
Eze 3:20 things he did will not be *r*,
18:22 offenses he has committed will be *r*
18:24 things he has done will be *r*.
21:32 you will be *r* no more;
25:10 so that the Ammonites will not be *r*
33:13 things he has done will be *r;*
33:16 the sins he has committed will be *r*
Jnh 2: 7 I *r* you, LORD,
Zec 13: 2 and they will be *r* no more,"
Mt 26:75 Peter *r* the word Jesus had spoken:
Mk 11:21 Peter *r* and said to Jesus, "Rabbi,
14:72 Peter *r* the word Jesus had spoken
Lk 22:61 Peter *r* the word the Lord had
24: 8 Then they *r* his words.
Jn 2:17 His disciples *r* that it is written:
Ac 10:31 and *r* your gifts to the poor.
11:16 Then I *r* what the Lord had said,
Rev 16:19 God *r* Babylon the Great
18: 5 and God has *r* her crimes.

REMEMBERING (REMEMBER)

Lk 1: 54 *r* to be merciful
Ac 20: 35 *r* the words the Lord Jesus himself
1Co 11: 2 I praise you for *r* me in everything
Eph 1: 16 for you, *r* you in my prayers.

REMEMBERS (REMEMBER)

1Ch 16: 15 He *r* his covenant forever,
Ps 6: 5 No one *r* you when he is dead.
9: 12 For he who avenges blood *r*;
103: 14 he *r* that we are dust.
103: 16 and its place *r* it no more.
105: 8 He *r* his covenant forever,
111: 5 he *r* his covenant forever.
115: 12 The LORD *r* us and will bless us:
Isa 43: 25 and *r* your sins no more.
La 1: 7 Jerusalem *r* all the treasures
2Co 7: 15 greater when he *r* that you were all

REMEMBRANCE (REMEMBER)

Ecc 1: 11 There is no *r* of men of old,
Mal 3: 16 A scroll of *r* was written
Lk 22: 19 given for you; do this in *r* of me."
Ac 10: 4 to the poor have come up as a *r*
1Co 11: 24 which is for you; do this in *r* of me
11: 25 whenever you drink it, in *r* of me."

REMETH

Jos 19: 21 Rabbith, Kishion, Ebez, *R*,

REMIND (REMINDED REMINDER REMINDERS REMINDING)

Nu 16: 40 was to *r* the Israelites that no one
1Ki 17: 18 Did you come to *r* me of my sin
Eze 21: 23 but he will *r* them of their guilt
Jn 14: 26 will *r* you of everything I have said
Ro 15: 15 as if to *r* you of them again,
1Co 4: 17 He will *r* you of my way of life
15: 1 to *r* you of the gospel I preached
2Ti 1: 6 For this reason I *r* you to fan
Tit 3: 1 *R* the people to be subject to rulers
2Pe 1: 12 I will always *r* you of these things,
Jude : 5 to *r* you that the Lord delivered his

REMINDED (REMIND)

Ge 41: 9 "Today I am *r* of my shortcomings.
2Ti 1: 5 I have been *r* of your sincere faith,

REMINDER (REMIND)

Ex 13: 9 a *r* on your forehead that the law
Nu 5: 15 a *r* offering to draw attention
5: 18 place in her hands the *r* offering,
Eze 29: 16 but will be a *r* of their sin in turning
Heb 10: 3 But those sacrifices are an annual *r*

REMINDERS (REMIND)

2Pe 3: 1 as *r* to stimulate you to wholesome

REMINDING (REMIND)

2Ti 2: 14 Keep *r* them of these things.

REMNANT

Ge 45: 7 you to preserve for you a *r* on earth
Dt 3: 11 left of the *r* of the Rephaites.
2Ki 19: 4 pray for the *r* that still survives."
19: 30 Once more a *r* of the house
19: 31 For out of Jerusalem will come a *r*,
21: 14 I will forsake the *r*
2Ch 34: 9 Ephraim and the entire *r* of Israel
34: 21 for me and for the *r* in Israel
36: 20 carried into exile to Babylon the *r*,
Ezr 9: 8 has been gracious in leaving us a *r*
9: 13 and have given us a *r* like this.
9: 14 leaving us no *r* or survivor?
9: 15 We are left this day as a *r*.
Ne 1: 2 about the Jewish *r* that survived
Isa 10: 20 In that day the *r* of Israel,
10: 21 A *r* will return, a *r* of Jacob
10: 22 only a *r* will return.
11: 11 time to reclaim the *r* that is left
11: 16 a highway for the *r* of his people
17: 3 the *r* of Aram will be
28: 5 wreath for the *r* of his people.
37: 4 pray for the *r* that still survives."
37: 31 Once more a *r* of the house
37: 32 For out of Jerusalem will come a *r*,
Jer 6: 9 "Let them glean the *r* of Israel
11: 23 Not even a *r* will be left to them,
Jer 23: 3 "I myself will gather the *r*
31: 7 the *r* of Israel.'
40: 11 of Babylon had left a *r* in Judah
40: 15 and the *r* of Judah to perish?"
42: 2 LORD your God for this entire *r*.
42: 15 word of the LORD, O *r* of Judah.
42: 19 "O *r* of Judah, the LORD has told
43: 5 the army officers led away all the *r*
44: 7 and so leave yourselves without a *r*
44: 12 I will take away the *r*
44: 14 of the *r* of Judah who have gone
44: 28 the whole *r* of Judah who came
47: 4 the *r* from the coasts of Caphtor.
47: 5 O *r* on the plain,
50: 20 for I will forgive the *r* I spare.
50: 26 and leave her no *r*.
Eze 9: 8 to destroy the entire *r* of Israel
11: 13 Will you completely destroy the *r*
Am 5: 15 mercy on the *r* of Joseph.
9: 12 so that they may possess the *r*
Mic 2: 12 I will surely bring together the *r*
4: 7 I will make the lame a *r*,
5: 7 The *r* of Jacob will be
5: 8 The *r* of Jacob will be
7: 18 of the *r* of his inheritance?
Zep 1: 4 off from this place every *r* of Baal,
2: 7 It will belong to the *r* of the house
2: 9 *r* of my people will plunder them;
3: 13 The *r* of Israel will do no wrong;
Hag 1: 12 the whole *r* of the people obeyed
1: 14 spirit of the whole *r* of the people.
2: 2 and to the *r* of the people.
Zec 8: 6 marvelous to the *r* of this people
8: 11 deal with the *r* of this people
8: 12 inheritance to the *r* of this people.
Ac 15: 17 that the *r* of men may seek
Ro 9: 27 only the *r* will be saved.
11: 5 the present time there is a *r* chosen

REMORSE

Mt 27: 3 with *r* and returned the thirty silver

REMOTE (REMOTEST)

Jdg 19: 1 lived in a *r* area in the hill country
19: 18 Bethlehem in Judah to a *r* area
Mt 14: 15 "This is a *r* place, and it's already
15: 33 in this *r* place to feed such a crowd
Mk 6: 35 "This is a *r* place," they said.
8: 4 in this *r* place can anyone get
Lk 9: 12 because we are in a *r* place here."

REMOTEST (REMOTE)

2Ki 19: 23 I have reached its *r* parts,
Ne 9: 22 to them even the *r* frontiers.
Isa 37: 24 I have reached its *r* heights,

REMOVAL (REMOVE)

Isa 27: 9 this will be the full fruitage of the *r*
1Pe 3: 21 not the *r* of dirt from the body

REMOVE (REMOVAL REMOVED REMOVES REMOVING)

Ge 30: 32 and *r* from them every speckled
Ex 12: 15 On the first day *r* the yeast
27: 3 pots to *r* the ashes, and its shovels,
33: 23 I will *r* my hand and you will see
Lev 1: 16 He is to *r* the crop with its contents
3: 4 which he will *r* with the kidneys.
3: 10 which he will *r* with the kidneys.
3: 15 which he will *r* with the kidneys.
4: 8 He shall *r* all the fat from the bull
4: 9 which he will *r* with the kidneys—
4: 19 He shall *r* all the fat from it
4: 31 He shall *r* all the fat, just
4: 35 He shall *r* all the fat, just
6: 10 and shall *r* the ashes of the burnt
26: 6 I will *r* savage beasts from the land,
Nu 4: 13 "They are to *r* the ashes
20: 26 *R* Aaron's garments and put them
Jos 7: 13 against your enemies until you *r* it.
1Ki 15: 14 he did not *r* the high places,
20: 24 *R* all the kings from their
2Ki 23: 4 and the doorkeepers to *r*
23: 27 will *r* Judah also from my presence
24: 3 order to *r* them from his presence
2Ch 15: 17 he did not *r* the high places
29: 5 *R* all defilement
32: 12 not Hezekiah himself *r* this god's
Job 9: 34 someone to *r* God's rod from me,
22: 23 If you *r* wickedness far
Ps 39: 10 *R* your scourge from me;
119: 22 *R* from me scorn and contempt,
Pr 25: 4 *R* the dross from the silver,
25: 5 *r* the wicked from the king's
27: 22 you will not *r* his folly from him.
Isa 1: 25 and *r* your impurities.
25: 8 he will *r* the disgrace of his people
57: 14 *R* the obstacles out of the way
62: 10 *R* the stones.
Jer 27: 10 serve to *r* you far from your lands;
28: 16 'I am about to *r* you from the face
32: 31 wrath that I must *r* it from my sight
Eze 11: 18 return to it and *r* all its vile images
11: 19 I will *r* from them their heart
21: 26 Take off the turban, *r* the crown.
34: 10 I will *r* them from tending the flock
36: 26 I will *r* from you your heart
Hos 2: 2 Let her *r* the adulterous look
2: 17 I will *r* the names of the Baals
Zep 3: 11 because I will *r* from this city
3: 18 I will *r* from you;
Zec 3: 9 'and I will *r* the sin of this land
13: 2 "I will *r* both the prophets
Mt 7: 5 you will see clearly to *r* the speck
Lk 6: 42 you will see clearly to *r* the speck
Rev 2: 5 *r* your lampstand from its place.

REMOVED (REMOVE)

Ge 8: 13 Noah then *r* the covering
30: 35 That same day he *r* all the male
48: 12 Joseph *r* them from Israel's knees
Ex 25: 15 of this ark; they are not to be *r*.
34: 34 he *r* the veil until he came out.
Lev 4: 10 the fat is *r* from the cow sacrificed
4: 31 fat is *r* from the fellowship offering,
4: 35 as the fat is *r* from the lamb
7: 4 which is to be *r* with the kidneys.
Nu 20: 28 Moses *r* Aaron's garments
Dt 26: 13 "I have *r* from my house the sacred
26: 14 nor have I *r* any of it while I was
Ru 4: 8 And he *r* his sandal.
1Sa 21: 6 of the Presence that had been *r*
2Sa 7: 15 whom I *r* from before you.
20: 13 After Amasa had been *r*
1Ki 2: 27 So Solomon *r* Abiathar
5: 17 At the king's command they *r*
20: 41 the prophet quickly *r* the headband
22: 43 high places, however, were not *r*,
2Ki 12: 3 high places, however, were not *r*;
14: 4 high places, however, were not *r*;
15: 4 high places, however, were not *r*;
15: 35 high places, however, were not *r*;
16: 17 He *r* the Sea from the bronze bulls
16: 17 and *r* the basins from the movable
16: 18 and *r* the royal entryway
17: 18 and *r* them from his presence.
17: 23 them until the LORD *r* them
18: 4 He *r* the high places, smashed
18: 22 high places and altars Hezekiah *r*,
23: 11 He *r* from the entrance
23: 12 He *r* them from there, smashed
23: 16 he had the bones *r* from them
23: 19 Josiah *r* and defiled all the shrines
23: 27 also from my presence as I *r* Israel,
24: 13 Nebuchadnezzar *r* all the treasures
2Ch 14: 3 He *r* the foreign altars
14: 5 He *r* the high places and incense
15: 8 He *r* the detestable idols
17: 6 furthermore, he *r* the high places
20: 33 high places, however, were not *r*,
29: 19 all the articles that King Ahaz *r*
30: 14 They *r* the altars in Jerusalem
33: 15 and *r* the image from the temple
34: 33 Josiah *r* all the detestable idols
Ezr 5: 14 even *r* from the temple of Babylon
Job 19: 9 and *r* the crown from my head.
34: 20 mighty are *r* without human hand.
Ps 30: 11 you *r* my sackcloth and clothed me
81: 6 I *r* the burden from their shoulders;
103: 12 so far has he *r* our transgressions
Pr 27: 25 When the hay is *r* and new growth
Isa 10: 13 I *r* the boundaries of nations,
14: 25 his burden *r* from their shoulders."
36: 7 high places and altars Hezekiah *r*,
54: 10 and the hills be *r*,
54: 10 nor my covenant of peace be *r*,"

Isa 54: 14 Terror will be far *r;*
Jer 8: 1 the people of Jerusalem will be *r*
28: 3 king of Babylon *r* from here
Eze 24: 12 its heavy deposit has not been *r,*
Jn 20: 1 and saw that the stone had been *r*
2Co 3: 14 It has not been *r,* because only
Rev 6: 14 and island was *r* from its place.

REMOVES (REMOVE)

1Sa 17: 26 and *r* this disgrace from Israel?

REMOVING (REMOVE)

Ac 13: 22 After *r* Saul, he made David their
Heb 12: 27 words "once more" indicate the *r*

REND

Isa 64: 1 that you would *r* the heavens
Joel 2: 13 *R* your heart

RENDER (RENDERED RENDERING)

Isa 16: 3 *r* a decision.
Zec 8: 16 and *r* true and sound judgment

RENDERED (RENDER)

Ro 6: 6 body of sin might be *r* powerless,

RENDERING (RENDER)

Isa 28: 7 they stumble when *r* decisions.

RENEGADES

Jdg 12: 4 You Gileadites are *r* from Ephraim

RENEW (RENEWAL RENEWED RENEWING RENEWS)

Ru 4: 15 He will *r* your life and sustain you
Ps 51: 10 and *r* a steadfast spirit within me.
104: 30 and you *r* the face of the earth.
119: 25 *r* my life according to your word.
119: 37 *r* my life according to your word.
119: 40 *R* my life in your righteousness.
119:107 *r* my life, O LORD, according
119:149 *r* my life, O LORD, according
119:154 *r* my life according to your promise
119:156 *r* my life according to your laws.
Isa 40: 31 will *r* their strength.
41: 1 Let the nations *r* their strength!
61: 4 they will *r* the ruined cities
La 5: 21 *r* our days as of old
Hab 3: 2 *R* them in our day,

RENEWAL (RENEW)

Job 14: 14 I will wait for my *r* to come.
Isa 57: 10 You found *r* of your strength,
Mt 19: 28 at the *r* of all things,
Tit 3: 5 of rebirth and *r* by the Holy Spirit,

RENEWED (RENEW)

2Ki 23: 3 and *r* the covenant in the presence
2Ch 34: 31 and *r* the covenant in the presence
Job 33: 25 then his flesh is *r* like a child's;
Ps 103: 5 that my youth is *r* like the eagle's.
119: 93 for by them you have *r* my life.
2Co 4: 16 yet inwardly we are being *r* day
Php 4: 10 that at last you have *r* your concern
Col 3: 10 which is being *r* in knowledge

RENEWING (RENEW)

Ro 12: 2 transformed by the *r* of your mind.

RENEWS (RENEW)

Ps 119: 50 Your promise *r* my life.

RENOUNCE (RENOUNCED RENOUNCES)

Eze 14: 6 and *r* all your detestable practices!
Da 4: 27 *R* your sins by doing what is right,
Rev 2: 13 You did not *r* your faith in me,

RENOUNCED (RENOUNCE)

Ps 89: 39 You have *r* the covenant
Mt 19: 12 and others have *r* marriage
2Co 4: 2 we have *r* secret and shameful

RENOUNCES (RENOUNCE)

Pr 28: 13 confesses and *r* them finds

RENOWN (RENOWNED)

Ge 6: 4 were the heroes of old, men of *r.*
Ps 102: 12 *r* endures through all generations.
135: 13 *r,* O LORD, through all
Isa 26: 8 your name and *r*
55: 13 This will be for the LORD's *r,*
63: 12 to gain for himself everlasting *r,*
Jer 13: 11 to be my people for my *r* and praise
32: 20 have gained the *r* that is still yours.
33: 9 Then this city will bring me *r,* joy,
49: 25 the city of *r* not been abandoned,
Eze 26: 17 How you are destroyed, O city of *r,*
Hos 12: 5 the LORD is his name of *r!*

RENOWNED (RENOWN)

Isa 23: 8 whose traders are *r* in the earth?
23: 9 and to humble all who are *r*
Eze 34: 29 for them a land *r* for its crops,

RENT (RENTED)

Mt 21: 41 "and he will *r* the vineyard

RENTED (RENT)

Mt 21: 33 he *r* the vineyard to some farmers
Mk 12: 1 he *r* the vineyard to some farmers
Lk 20: 9 *r* it to some farmers and went away
Ac 28: 30 there in his own *r* house

REPAID (PAY)

Ge 44: 4 'Why have you *r* good with evil?
Jdg 9: 56 Thus God *r* the wickedness that
2Sa 16: 8 The LORD has *r* you
Pr 14: 14 The faithless will be fully *r*
Jer 18: 20 Should good be *r* with evil?
Lk 6: 34 to 'sinners,' expecting to be *r* in full
14: 12 you back and so you will be *r.*
14: 14 you will be *r* at the resurrection
Col 3: 25 Anyone who does wrong will be *r*

REPAIR (REPAIRED REPAIRER REPAIRING REPAIRS)

2Ki 12: 5 used to *r* whatever damage is found
12: 8 they would not *r* the temple
12: 12 stone for the *r* of the temple
12: 14 who used it to *r* the temple.
22: 5 pay the workers who *r* the temple
22: 6 and dressed stone to *r* the temple.
1Ch 26: 27 dedicated for the *r* of the temple
2Ch 24: 5 to *r* the temple of your God.
24: 12 and bronze to *r* the temple.
34: 8 to *r* the temple of the LORD his
Ezr 9: 9 house of our God and *r* its ruins,
Eze 13: 5 in the wall to *r* it for the house
Am 9: 11 I will *r* its broken places,
Na 3: 14 *r* the brickwork!

REPAIRED (REPAIR)

1Ki 18: 30 and he *r* the altar of the LORD,
2Ki 12: 6 priests still had not *r* the temple.
2Ch 15: 8 He *r* the altar of the LORD that
29: 3 temple of the LORD and *r* them.
34: 10 These men paid the workers who *r*
Ne 3: 4 son of Hakkoz, *r* the next section.
3: 5 The next section was *r* by the men
3: 6 The Jeshanah Gate was *r*
3: 8 one of the goldsmiths, *r* the next
3: 9 of Jerusalem, *r* the next section.
3: 11 of Pahath-Moab *r* another section
3: 12 *r* the next section with the help
3: 13 The Valley Gate was *r* by Hanun
3: 13 *r* five hundred yards of the wall
3: 14 The Dung Gate was *r*
3: 15 The Fountain Gate was *r*
3: 15 *r* the wall of the Pool of Siloam,
3: 19 ruler of Mizpah, *r* another section,
3: 20 Zabbai zealously *r* another section,
3: 21 son of Hakkoz, *r* another section,
3: 24 son of Henadad *r* another section,
3: 27 the men of Tekoa *r* another section
3: 30 son of Zalaph, *r* another section.
Jer 19: 11 jar is smashed and cannot be *r.*

REPAIRER (REPAIR)

Isa 58: 12 you will be called *R*

REPAIRING (REPAIR)

2Ki 12: 7 Why aren't you *r* the damage done
12: 7 but hand it over for *r* the temple."
2Ch 32: 5 he worked hard *r* all the broken
Ezr 4: 12 the walls and *r* the foundations.

REPAIRS (REPAIR)

2Ch 24: 13 and the *r* progressed under them.
Ne 3: 4 son of Baana also made *r.*
3: 4 the son of Meshezabel, made *r,*
3: 7 *r* were made by men from Gibeon
3: 8 the perfume-makers, made *r* next
3: 10 of Hashabneiah made *r* next to him
3: 10 son of Harumaph made *r*
3: 16 made *r* up to a point
3: 17 carried out *r* for his district.
3: 17 the *r* were made by the Levites
3: 18 *r* were made by their countrymen
3: 22 The *r* next to him were made
3: 23 and Hasshub made *r* in front
3: 23 the son of Ananiah, made *r*
3: 26 hill of Ophel made *r* up to a point
3: 28 the Horse Gate, the priests made *r,*
3: 29 Immer made *r* opposite his house.
3: 29 the guard at the East Gate, made *r.*
3: 30 son of Berekiah made *r*
3: 31 made *r* as far as the house
3: 32 goldsmiths and merchants made *r.*
4: 7 the men of Ashdod heard that the *r*

REPAY (PAY)

Lev 25: 28 not acquire the means to *r* him,
Dt 7: 10 But those who hate him he will *r*
7: 10 he will not be slow to *r*
32: 6 Is this the way you *r* the LORD,
32: 35 It is mine to avenge; I will *r.*
32: 41 and *r* those who hate me.
Ru 2: 12 May the LORD *r* you
2Sa 3: 39 May the LORD *r* the evildoer
16: 12 *r* me with good for the cursing I am
1Ki 2: 32 The LORD will *r* him
2: 44 Now the LORD will *r* you
Job 21: 19 Let him *r* the man himself,
Ps 28: 4 *R* them for their deeds
28: 4 *r* them for what their hands have
35: 12 They *r* me evil for good
37: 21 The wicked borrow and do not *r,*
38: 20 Those who *r* my good with evil
41: 10 raise me up, that I may *r* them.
94: 23 He will *r* them for their sins
103: 10 or *r* us according to our iniquities.
109: 5 They *r* me evil for good,
116: 12 How can I *r* the LORD
Pr 24: 12 Will he not *r* each person
Isa 59: 18 he will *r* the islands their due.
59: 18 so will he *r*
Jer 16: 18 I will *r* them double
25: 14 I will *r* them according
50: 29 *R* her for her deeds;
51: 24 "Before your eyes I will *r* Babylon
51: 56 he will *r* in full.
Eze 7: 3 and *r* you for all your detestable
7: 4 I will surely *r* you for your conduct
7: 8 and *r* you for all your detestable
7: 9 I will *r* you in accordance
Hos 4: 9 and *r* them for their deeds.
12: 2 and *r* him according to his deeds.
12: 14 and will *r* him for his contempt.
Joel 2: 25 "I will *r* you for the years
Mt 18: 25 all that he had be sold to *r* the debt.
Lk 14: 14 Although they cannot *r* you,
Ro 11: 35 that God should *r* him?"
12: 17 Do not *r* anyone evil for evil.
12: 19 "It is mine to avenge; I will *r,*"
2Ti 4: 14 The Lord will *r* him
Heb 10: 30 "It is mine to avenge; I will *r,*"
1Pe 3: 9 Do not *r* evil with evil
Rev 2: 23 and I will *r* each of you according

REPAYING (PAY)

2Ch 6: 23 *r* the guilty by bringing
20: 11 See how they are *r* us by coming
Isa 66: 6 *r* his enemies all they deserve.
Joel 3: 4 Are you *r* me for something I have
1Ti 5: 4 so *r* their parents and grandparents

REPAYMENT (PAY)

Lk 6: 34 to those from whom you expect *r,*

REPAYS (PAY)

Job 21: 31 Who *r* him for what he has done?
34: 11 He *r* a man for what he has done;
Ps 137: 8 happy is he who *r* you

REPEALED
Est 1: 19 which cannot be *r*, that Vashti is

REPEAT (REPEATED REPEATS)
2Co 11: 16 I *r*: Let no one take me for a fool.
13: 2 I now *r* it while absent: On my

REPEATED (REPEAT)
Ge 44: 6 up with them, he *r* these words
Jdg 9: 3 When the brothers *r* all this
11: 11 he *r* all his words before the LORD
1Sa 8: 21 all that the people said, he *r* it
11: 5 Then they *r* to him what the men
17: 27 They *r* to him what they had been
18: 23 They *r* these words to David.
Heb 10: 1 the same sacrifices *r* endlessly year

REPEATS (REPEAT)
Pr 17: 9 whoever *r* the matter separates
26: 11 so a fool *r* his folly.

REPENT (PENITENT REPENTANCE REPENTED REPENTS)
1Ki 8: 47 *r* and plead with you in the land
2Ch 6: 37 *r* and plead with you in the land
Job 34: 33 when you refuse to *r*?
36: 10 commands them to *r* of their evil.
42: 6 and *r* in dust and ashes."
Isa 59: 20 to those in Jacob who *r* of their sins
Jer 5: 3 and refused to *r*.
15: 19 "If you *r*, I will restore you
Eze 14: 6 the Sovereign LORD says: *R!*
18: 30 *R!* Turn away from all your
18: 32 *R* and live! "Take up a lament
Hos 11: 5 because they refuse to *r*?
Mt 3: 2 "*R*, for the kingdom of heaven is
4: 17 "*R*, for the kingdom of heaven is
11: 20 performed, because they did not *r*.
21: 32 you did not *r* and believe him.
Mk 1: 15 *R* and believe the good news!"
6: 12 and preached that people should *r*.
Lk 13: 3 unless you *r*, you too will all perish.
13: 5 unless you *r*, you too will all perish
15: 7 persons who do not need to *r*.
16: 30 goes to them, they will *r*.'
17: 4 back to you and says, 'I *r*,'
Ac 2: 38 Peter replied, "*R* and be baptized,
3: 19 *R*, then, and turn to God,
8: 22 *R* of this wickedness and pray
17: 30 all people everywhere to *r*.
26: 20 also, I preached that they should *r*
Rev 2: 5 If you do not *r*, I will come to you
2: 5 *R* and do the things you did at first.
2: 16 *R* therefore! Otherwise, I will soon
2: 21 time to *r* of her immorality,
2: 22 her suffer intensely, unless they *r*
3: 3 received and heard; obey it, and *r*.
3: 19 So be earnest, and *r*.
9: 20 by these plagues still did not *r*
9: 21 Nor did they *r* of their murders,
16: 9 they refused to *r* and glorify him.
16: 11 refused to *r* of what they had done.

REPENTANCE (REPENT)
Isa 30: 15 "In *r* and rest is your salvation,
Mt 3: 8 Produce fruit in keeping with *r*.
3: 11 "I baptize you with water for *r*.
Mk 1: 4 a baptism of *r* for the forgiveness
Lk 3: 3 a baptism of *r* for the forgiveness
3: 8 Produce fruit in keeping with *r*.
5: 32 call the righteous, but sinners to *r*."
24: 47 and *r* and forgiveness of sins will be
Ac 5: 31 and Savior that he might give *r*
11: 18 granted the Gentiles *r* unto life."
13: 24 John preached *r* and baptism
19: 4 "John's baptism was a baptism of *r*.
20: 21 that they must turn to God in *r*
26: 20 and prove their *r* by their deeds.
Ro 2: 4 kindness leads you toward *r*?
2Co 7: 9 because your sorrow led you to *r*.
7: 10 Godly sorrow brings *r* that leads
2Ti 2: 25 God will grant them *r* leading them
Heb 6: 1 foundation of *r* from acts that lead
6: 6 to be brought back to *r*,
2Pe 3: 9 but everyone to come to *r*.

REPENTED (REPENT)
2Ch 32: 26 Hezekiah *r* of the pride of his heart,
Jer 31: 19 I *r*;
34: 15 Recently you *r* and did what is
Zec 1: 6 your forefathers? "Then they *r*
Mt 11: 21 they would have *r* long ago
12: 41 for they *r* at the preaching of Jonah
Lk 10: 13 they would have *r* long ago,
11: 32 for they *r* at the preaching of Jonah
2Co 12: 21 and have not *r* of the impurity,

REPENTS (REPENT)
Jer 8: 6 No one *r* of his wickedness,
18: 8 if that nation I warned *r* of its evil,
Lk 15: 7 in heaven over one sinner who *r*
15: 10 of God over one sinner who *r*."
17: 3 rebuke him, and if he *r*, forgive him

REPHAEL
1Ch 26: 7 Othni, *R*, Obed and Elzabad;

REPHAH
1Ch 7: 25 *R* was his son, Resheph his son,

REPHAIAH
1Ch 3: 21 and the sons of *R*, of Arnan,
4: 42 led by Pelatiah, Neariah, *R*
7: 2 The sons of Tola: Uzzi, *R*, Jeriel,
9: 43 the father of Binea; *R* was his son,
Ne 3: 9 *R* son of Hur, ruler of a half-district

REPHAIM
Jos 15: 8 end of the Valley of *R*.
18: 16 Hinnom, north of the Valley of *R*.
2Sa 5: 18 and spread out in the Valley of *R*;
5: 22 and spread out in the Valley of *R*;
23: 13 encamped in the Valley of *R*.
1Ch 11: 15 encamped in the Valley of *R*.
14: 9 and raided the Valley of *R*;
Isa 17: 5 grain in the Valley of *R*.

REPHAITES
Ge 14: 5 and defeated the *R* in Ashteroth
15: 20 Hittites, Perizzites, *R*, Amorites,
Dt 2: 11 they too were considered *R*,
2: 20 too was considered a land of the *R*,
3: 11 left of the remnant of the *R*.
3: 13 to be known as a land of the *R*.)
Jos 12: 4 of the *R*, who reigned in Ashtaroth
13: 12 as one of the last of the *R*.
17: 15 in the land of the Perizzites and *R*
1Ch 20: 4 one of the descendants of the *R*,

REPHAN
Ac 7: 43 and the star of your god *R*,

REPHIDIM
Ex 17: 1 at *R*, but there was no water
17: 8 and attacked the Israelites at *R*.
19: 2 After they set out from *R*,
Nu 33: 14 They left Alush and camped at *R*,
33: 15 They left *R* and camped

REPLACE (REPLACED)
Lev 14: 42 are to take other stones to *r* these
1Ki 14: 27 made bronze shields to *r* them
20: 24 and *r* them with other officers.
2Ki 17: 24 towns of Samaria to *r* the Israelites.
2Ch 12: 10 made bronze shields to *r* them
Isa 9: 10 but we will *r* them with cedars."

REPLACED (REPLACE)
1Sa 21: 6 *r* by hot bread on the day it was
1Ki 2: 35 *r* Abiathar with Zadok the priest.
Da 8: 22 four horns that *r* the one that was

REPLANTED (PLANT)
Eze 36: 36 and have *r* what was desolate.

REPLICA
Jos 22: 28 Look at the *r* of the LORD's altar,

REPOINTING
1Sa 13: 21 forks and axes and for *r* goads.

REPORT (REPORTED REPORTING REPORTS)
Ge 37: 2 their father a bad *r* about them.
Nu 13: 32 the Israelites a bad *r* about the land
14: 15 have heard this *r* about you will
14: 36 him by spreading a bad *r* about it—
14: 37 spreading the bad *r* about the land
Dt 1: 22 bring back a *r* about the route we
Jos 14: 7 I brought him back a *r* according
22: 33 They were glad to hear the *r*
1Sa 2: 24 is not a good *r* that I hear spreading
2Sa 1: 5 young man who brought him the *r*,
1: 13 young man who brought him the *r*,
13: 30 on their way, the *r* came to David:
13: 33 be concerned about the *r* that all
1Ki 10: 6 *r* I heard in my own country about
10: 7 have far exceeded the *r* I heard.
2Ki 6: 13 The *r* came back: "He is in Dothan
7: 9 and *r* this to the royal palace."
19: 7 that when he hears a certain *r*,
19: 9 received a *r* that Tirhakah,
1Ch 21: 2 *r* back to me so that I may know
2Ch 9: 5 *r* I heard in my own country about
9: 6 you have far exceeded the *r* I heard
Ezr 5: 5 stopped until a *r* could go to Darius
5: 7 The *r* they sent him read as follows
Ne 6: 7 Now this *r* will get back to the king
Est 2: 23 And when the *r* was investigated
Job 38: 35 Do they *r* to you, 'Here we are'?
Ecc 10: 20 on the wing may *r* what you say.
Isa 21: 6 and have him *r* what he sees.
23: 5 in anguish at the *r* from Tyre.
37: 7 so that when he hears a certain *r*,
37: 9 received a *r* that Tirhakah,
Jer 10: 22 Listen! The *r* is coming—
20: 10 Report him! Let's *r* him!"
20: 10 *R* him! Let's report him!"
36: 16 "We must *r* all these words
37: 5 Jerusalem heard the *r* about them,
Mt 2: 8 As soon as you find him, *r* to me,
11: 4 and *r* to John what you hear
28: 14 If this *r* gets to the governor,
Lk 7: 22 and *r* to John what you have seen
Jn 11: 57 he should *r* it so that they might
Ac 5: 24 On hearing this *r*, the captain
2Co 6: 8 bad *r* and good *r*; genuine,
Gal 1: 23 only heard the *r*: "The man who
1Th 1: 9 for they themselves *r* what kind
2Th 2: 2 *r* or letter supposed to have come

REPORTED (REPORT)
Ge 14: 13 and *r* this to Abram the Hebrew.
Ex 6: 9 Moses *r* this to the Israelites,
16: 22 of the community came and *r* this
Nu 13: 26 There they *r* to them
14: 39 When Moses *r* this
Dt 1: 25 they brought it down to us and *r*,
Jos 22: 32 in Gilead and *r* to the Israelites.
Jdg 9: 25 and this was *r* to Abimelech.
9: 42 and this was *r* to Abimelech.
1Sa 11: 4 and *r* these terms to the people,
11: 9 and *r* this to the men of Jabesh,
17: 31 David said was overheard and *r*
25: 12 they arrived, they *r* every word.
2Sa 7: 17 Nathan *r* to David all the words
18: 25 out to the king and *r* it.
24: 9 Joab *r* the number
1Ki 2: 30 Benaiah *r* to the king, "This is how
13: 25 and *r* it in the city where the old
18: 44 The seventh time the servant *r*,
20: 17 who *r*, "Men are advancing
2Ki 7: 11 and it was *r* within the palace.
7: 15 So the messengers returned and *r*
9: 18 The lookout *r*, "The messenger has
9: 20 lookout *r*, "He has reached them,
17: 26 It was *r* to the king of Assyria:
22: 9 went to the king and *r* to him:
1Ch 17: 15 Nathan *r* to David all the words
21: 5 Joab *r* the number
2Ch 29: 18 went in to King Hezekiah and *r*:
34: 16 the book to the king and *r* to him:
Ne 6: 6 "It is *r* among the nations—
Est 2: 22 who in turn *r* it to the king,
4: 9 *r* to Esther what Mordecai had said
4: 12 When Esther's words were *r*
9: 11 slain in the citadel of Susa was *r*
Jer 36: 20 in the courtyard and *r* everything
Zec 1: 11 they *r* to the angel of the LORD,
Mt 8: 33 went into the town and *r* all this,
28: 11 *r* to the chief priests everything
Mk 5: 14 *r* this in the town and countryside,
6: 30 and *r* to him all they had done
16: 13 These returned and *r* it to the rest;
Lk 8: 34 they ran off and *r* this in the town

Lk 9:10 they *r* to Jesus what they had done.
14:21 "The servant came back and *r* this
Ac 4:23 and *r* all that the chief priests
5:22 and *r*, "We found the jail securely
14:27 and *r* all that God had done
15: 4 to whom they *r* everything God
16:38 officers *r* this to the magistrates,
21:19 and *r* in detail what God had done
22:26 he went to the commander and *r* it.
23:22 tell anyone that you have *r* this
28:21 who has come from there has *r*
Ro 1: 8 because your faith is being *r* all
3: 8 as we are being slanderously *r*
1Co 5: 1 It is actually *r* that there is sexual

REPORTING (REPORT)

Ne 6:19 they kept *r* to me his good deeds

REPORTS (REPORT)

Ex 23: 1 "Do not spread false *r*.
Dt 2:25 They will hear *r* of you
Jos 9: 9 For we have heard *r* of him:
Ne 6: 6 according to these *r* you are about
Jer 6:24 We have heard *r* about them,
50:43 of Babylon has heard *r* about them,
Da 11:44 *r* from the east and the north will
Mt 14: 1 tetrarch heard the *r* about Jesus,
Ac 9:13 I have heard many *r* about this man
21:24 truth in these *r* about you,

REPOSE (REPOSES)

Dt 28:65 those nations you will find no *r*,
Isa 28:12 and, "This is the place of *r*"—
34:14 there the night creatures will also *r*

REPOSES (REPOSE)

Pr 14:33 Wisdom *r* in the heart

REPRESENT (REPRESENTATION REPRESENTATIVE REPRESENTATIVES REPRESENTED REPRESENTING REPRESENTS)

Lev 24: 7 a memorial portion to *r* the bread
Jer 40:10 stay at Mizpah to *r* you
Da 8:22 off *r* four kingdoms that will
Gal 3:20 however, does not *r* just one party;
4:24 for the women *r* two covenants.
Heb 5: 1 and is appointed to *r* them

REPRESENTATION (REPRESENT)

Heb 1: 3 and the exact *r* of his being,

REPRESENTATIVE (REPRESENT)

Ex 18:19 You must be the people's *r*
2Sa 15: 3 there is no *r* of the king to hear you

REPRESENTATIVES (REPRESENT)

2Co 8:23 they are *r* of the churches

REPRESENTED (REPRESENT)

Nu 17: 8 which *r* the house of Levi,
Jdg 18: 2 These men *r* all their clans.

REPRESENTING (REPRESENT)

Ex 24: 4 twelve stone pillars *r* the twelve
Nu 1:44 of Israel, each one *r* his family.

REPRESENTS (REPRESENT)

Da 8:20 ram that you saw *r* the kings

REPRIMANDED

Jer 29:27 So why have you not *r* Jeremiah

REPROACH (REPROACHED)

Jos 5: 9 "Today I have rolled away the *r*
Ne 5: 9 God to avoid the *r* of our Gentile
Job 27: 6 my conscience will not *r* me
Ps 44:13 You have made us a *r*
44:16 shame at the taunts of those who *r*
79: 4 of *r* to our neighbors,
79:12 the *r* they have hurled at you,
Isa 51: 7 Do not fear the *r* of men
54: 4 and remember no more the *r*
Jer 15:15 think of how I suffer *r* for your sake
20: 8 insult and *r* all day long.
24: 9 a *r* and a byword, an object
29:18 *r*, among all the nations where I
42:18 and *r*; you will never see this place
44: 8 *r* among all the nations on earth.
44:12 and horror, of condemnation and *r*.
49:13 and an object of horror, of *r*
Eze 5:14 a *r* among the nations around you,
5:15 You will be a *r* and a taunt,
Zep 3:18 they are a burden and a *r* to you.
1Ti 3: 2 Now the overseer must be above *r*,

REPROACHED (REPROACH)

Job 19: 3 Ten times now you have *r* me;

REPROVES

Am 5:10 you hate the one who *r* in court

REPTILES

1Ki 4:33 taught about animals and birds, *r*
Ac 10:12 as well as *r* of the earth
11: 6 wild beasts, *r*, and birds of the air.
Ro 1:23 and birds and animals and *r*.
Jas 3: 7 *r* and creatures of the sea are being

REPULSE (REPULSIVE)

2Ki 18:24 How can you *r* one officer
Isa 36: 9 How then can you *r* one officer

REPULSIVE (REPULSE)

1Ki 15:13 she had made a *r* Asherah pole.
1Ch 21: 6 the king's command was *r* to him.
2Ch 15:16 she had made a *r* Asherah pole.
Job 33:20 so that his very being finds food *r*
Ps 88: 8 and have made me *r* to them.
Jer 23:13 I saw this *r* thing:

REPUTATION (REPUTED)

Est 9: 4 *r* spread throughout the provinces,
Pr 25:10 and you will never lose your bad *r*.
1Ti 3: 7 also have a good *r* with outsiders,
Rev 3: 1 you have a *r* of being alive,

REPUTED (REPUTATION)

Gal 2: 9 Peter and John, those *r* to be pillars

REQUEST (REQUESTED REQUESTING REQUESTS)

Ge 19:21 "Very well, I will grant this *r* too;
Jdg 6:39 Let me make just one more *r*.
8: 8 and made the same *r* of them,
8:24 And he said, "I do have one *r*,
11:37 But grant me this one *r*," she said.
1Sa 25:35 your words and granted your *r*."
2Sa 12:20 and at his *r* they served him food,
14:22 the king has granted his servant's *r*
1Ki 2:16 Now I have one *r* to make of you.
2:20 I have one small *r* to make of you,"
2:22 as well *r* the kingdom for him—
2:22 "Why do you *r* Abishag
2:23 pay with his life for this *r*!
1Ch 4:10 And God granted his *r*.
Est 5: 3 Queen Esther? What is your *r*?
5: 6 And what is your *r*? Even up
5: 7 "My petition and my *r* is this:
5: 8 to grant my petition and fulfill my *r*
7: 2 What is your *r*? Even up
7: 3 And spare my people—this is my *r*
9:12 What is your *r*? It will
Job 6: 8 "Oh, that I might have my *r*,
Ps 21: 2 have not withheld the *r* of his lips.
Da 2:49 at Daniel's *r* the king appointed
9:20 and making my *r* to the LORD my
Mt 14: 9 he ordered that her *r* be granted
15:28 great faith! Your *r* is granted."
Mk 6:25 hurried in to the king with the *r*:
Jn 12:21 from Bethsaida in Galilee, with a *r*.
Ac 23:21 waiting for your consent to their *r*
24: 4 I would *r* that you be kind enough

REQUESTED (REQUEST)

Ex 12:31 worship the LORD as you have *r*.
Ezr 6: 9 as *r* by the priests in Jerusalem—
Jer 42: 4 the LORD your God as you have *r*;
Mk 15: 6 a prisoner whom the people *r*.
Ac 25: 3 They urgently *r* Festus,

REQUESTING (REQUEST)

Ac 16:39 them from the prison, *r* them

REQUESTS (REQUEST)

Ne 2: 8 upon me, the king granted my *r*.
Ps 5: 3 by morning I lay my *r* before you
20: 5 May the LORD grant all your *r*.
Da 9:18 We do not make *r* of you
Eph 6:18 with all kinds of prayers and *r*.
Php 4: 6 with thanksgiving, present your *r*
1Ti 2: 1 then, first of all, that *r*, prayers,

REQUIRE (REQUIRED REQUIREMENT REQUIREMENTS REQUIRES REQUIRING)

Ex 5: 8 *r* them to make the same number
Dt 15: 2 He shall not *r* payment
15: 3 You may *r* payment
2Ki 12:15 They did not *r* an accounting
Ps 40: 6 you did not *r*.
Eze 18:16 or *r* a pledge for a loan.
20:40 There I will *r* your offerings
Mic 6: 8 And what does the LORD *r* of you

REQUIRED (REQUIRE)

Ge 50: 3 for that was the time *r*
Ex 5:13 "Complete the work *r* of you
5:19 of bricks *r* of you for each day."
22:11 accept this, and no restitution is *r*.
22:13 and he will not be *r* to pay
Lev 23:37 and drink offerings *r* for each day.
27:16 to the amount of seed *r* for it—
Nu 7: 7 their work *r*, and he gave four carts
7: 8 to the Merarites, as their work *r*.
Jos 16:10 but are *r* to do forced labor.
1Ki 8:31 is *r* to take an oath and he comes
2Ch 6:22 is *r* to take an oath and he comes
24: 6 "Why haven't you *r* the Levites
24: 9 of God had *r* of Israel in the desert.
24:12 the men who carried out the work *r*
Ezr 3: 4 of Tabernacles with the *r* number
Ne 12:44 into the storerooms the portions *r*
Lk 2:27 him what the custom of the Law *r*,
2:39 and Mary had done everything *r*
3:13 more than you are *r* to,"
Ac 15: 5 and *r* to obey the law of Moses."
Ro 2:14 do by nature things *r* by the law,
1Co 4: 2 it is *r* that those who have been
Heb 10: 8 the law *r* them to be made).

REQUIREMENT (REQUIRE)

Nu 19: 2 "This is a *r* of the law that
27:11 is to be a legal *r* for the Israelites,
31:21 "This is the *r* of the law that
2Ch 8:13 daily *r* for offerings commanded
8:14 priests according to each day's *r*.

REQUIREMENTS (REQUIRE)

Ge 26: 5 Abraham obeyed me and kept my *r*
Lev 18:30 Keep my *r* and do not follow any
22: 9 " 'The priests are to keep my *r*
Nu 35:29 " 'These are to be legal *r* for you
Dt 11: 1 LORD your God and keep his *r*,
1Ki 2: 3 *r*, as written in the Law of Moses,
2Ki 23:24 did to fulfill the *r* of the law written
1Ch 16:37 according to each day's *r*.
29:19 *r* and decrees and to do everything
2Ch 13:11 We are observing the *r*
Jer 5: 4 the *r* of their God.
5: 5 the *r* of their God."
8: 7 the *r* of the LORD.
Zec 3: 7 walk in my ways and keep my *r*,
Mal 3:14 gain by carrying out his *r*
Ac 15:28 anything beyond the following *r*:
Ro 2:15 since they show that the *r*
2:26 not circumcised keep the law's *r*,
8: 4 in order that the righteous *r*

REQUIRES (REQUIRE)

Lev 8:35 days and do what the LORD *r*,
Nu 7: 5 to the Levites as each man's work *r*
1Ki 2: 3 what the LORD your God *r*:
2Ki 17:26 the people do not know what he *r*."
17:26 what the god of that country *r*.
17:27 people what the god of the land *r*."
Jn 6:28 do to do the works God *r*?"
Heb 7: 5 Now the law *r* the descendants
9:22 the law *r* that nearly everything be

REQUIRING (REQUIRE)

Lev 22:16 so bring upon them guilt *r* payment

RESCUE (RESCUED RESCUES RESCUING)
Ge 37:21 he tried to *r* him from their hands.
37:22 this to *r* him from them
Ex 2:17 to their *r* and watered their flock.
3: 8 down to *r* them from the hand
Dt 22:27 there was no one to *r* her.
25:11 of them comes to *r* her husband
28:29 and robbed, with no one to *r* you.
28:31 enemies, and no one will *r* them.
Jdg 9:17 risked his life to *r* you
10:15 think best, but please *r* us now."
18:28 There was no one to *r* them
1Sa 7: 8 that he may *r* us from the hand
11: 3 comes to *r* us, we will surrender
12:21 can they *r* you, because they are
30: 8 them and succeed in the *r*."
2Sa 3:18 David I will *r* my people Israel
10:11 for you, then I will come to *r* you.
10:11 then you are to come to my *r*;
21:17 son of Zeruiah came to David's *r*;
1Ch 19:12 strong for you, then I will *r* you.
19:12 then you are to *r* me;
2Ch 32:17 of Hezekiah will not *r* his people
32:17 other lands did not *r* their people
Job 5:19 From six calamities he will *r* you;
10: 7 and that no one can *r* me
Ps 7: 2 me to pieces with no one to *r* me.
17:13 *r* me from the wicked
22: 8 let the LORD *r* him.
22:21 *R* me from the mouth of the lions;
25:20 Guard my life and *r* me;
31: 2 come quickly to my *r*;
35:10 You *r* the poor from those too
35:17 *R* my life from their ravages,
43: 1 *r* me from deceitful and wicked
50:22 you to pieces, with none to *r*:
69:14 *R* me from the mire,
69:18 Come near and *r* me;
71: 2 *R* me and deliver me
71:11 for no one will *r* him."
72:14 He will *r* them from oppression
82: 4 *R* the weak and needy;
91:14 says the LORD, "I will *r* him;
140: 1 *R* me, O LORD, from evil men;
142: 6 *r* me from those who pursue me,
143: 9 *R* me from my enemies, O LORD,
144: 7 deliver me and *r* me
144:11 Deliver me and *r* me
Pr 19:19 if you *r* him, you will have
24:11 *R* those being led away to death;
Isa 5:29 and carry it off with no one to *r*.
19:20 and defender, and he will *r* them.
31: 5 he will 'pass over' it and will *r* it."
42:22 with no one to *r* them;
46: 2 unable to *r* the burden,
46: 4 I will sustain you and I will *r* you.
50: 2 Do I lack the strength to *r* you?
Jer 1: 8 for I am with you and will *r* you,"
1:19 for I am with you and will *r* you,"
15:20 you to *r* and save you,"
21:12 *r* from the hand of his oppressor
22: 3 *R* from the hand of his oppressor
39:17 But I will *r* you on that day,
Eze 34:10 I will *r* my flock from their mouths,
34:12 I will *r* them from all the places
34:27 and *r* them from the hands
Da 3:15 able to *r* you from my hand?"
3:17 and he will *r* us from your hand,
6:14 he was determined to *r* Daniel
6:16 whom you serve continually, *r* you
6:20 been able to *r* you from the lions?"
8: 4 and none could *r* from his power.
8: 7 and none could *r* the ram
Hos 5:14 them off, with no one to *r* them.
Mic 5: 8 and no one can *r*.
Zep 3:19 I will *r* the lame
Zec 11: 6 I will not *r* them from their hands."
Mt 27:43 Let God *r* him now if he wants him
Lk 1:74 to *r* us from the hand
Ac 7:25 that God was using him to *r* them,
26:17 I will *r* you from your own people
Ro 7:24 Who will *r* me from this body
Gal 1: 4 himself for our sins to *r* us
2Ti 4:18 The Lord will *r* me
2Pe 2: 9 how to *r* godly men from trials

RESCUED (RESCUE)
Ex 2:19 "An Egyptian *r* us
5:23 you have not *r* your people at all."
18:10 who *r* the people from the hand
18:10 who *r* you from the hand
Nu 10: 9 by the LORD your God and *r*
Jos 22:31 Now you have *r* the Israelites
Jdg 8:34 who had *r* them from the hands
1Sa 11:13 for this day the LORD has *r* Israel
14:23 So the LORD *r* Israel that day,
14:45 So the men *r* Jonathan,
17:35 and *r* the sheep from its mouth.
2Sa 19: 9 he is the one who *r* us
22:18 He *r* me from my powerful enemy,
22:20 he *r* me because he delighted in me
22:49 from violent men you *r* me.
2Ki 18:34 Have they *r* Samaria from my hand
Ne 9:27 who *r* them from the hand
Job 29:12 I *r* the poor who cried for help,
Ps 18:17 He *r* me from my powerful enemy,
18:19 he *r* me because he delighted in me
18:48 from violent men you *r* me.
81: 7 distress you called and I *r* you,
107: 20 he *r* them from the grave.
Pr 11: 8 The righteous man is *r*
Isa 36:19 Have they *r* Samaria from my hand
49:24 or captives *r* from the fierce?
Da 3:28 sent his angel and *r* his servants!
6:27 He has *r* Daniel
Mic 4:10 there you will be *r*.
Ac 7:10 and *r* him from all his troubles.
12:11 and *r* me from Herod's clutches
23:27 I came with my troops and *r* him.
Ro 15:31 Pray that I may be *r*
Col 1:13 For he has *r* us from the dominion
2Ti 3:11 Yet the Lord *r* me from all of them.
2Pe 2: 7 and if he *r* Lot, a righteous man,

RESCUES (RESCUE)
1Sa 14:39 as the LORD who *r* Israel lives,
Pr 12: 6 the speech of the upright *r* them.
Jer 20:13 He *r* the life of the needy
Da 6:27 He *r* and he saves;
1Th 1:10 who *r* us from the coming wrath.

RESCUING (RESCUE)
Ex 18: 9 for Israel in *r* them from the hand

RESEMBLED (RESEMBLING)
Rev 9: 7 and their faces *r* human faces.
9:17 of the horses *r* the heads of lions,
13: 2 The beast I saw *r* a leopard,

RESEMBLING (RESEMBLED)
Rev 4: 3 *r* an emerald, encircled the throne.

RESEN
Ge 10:12 and *R*, which is between Nineveh

RESENT (RESENTFUL RESENTMENT RESENTS)
Pr 3:11 and do not *r* his rebuke,

RESENTFUL (RESENT)
2Ti 2:24 to everyone, able to teach, not *r*.

RESENTMENT (RESENT)
Jdg 8: 3 their *r* against him subsided.
Job 5: 2 *R* kills a fool,
36:13 "The godless in heart harbor *r*;

RESENTS (RESENT)
Pr 15:12 A mocker *r* correction;

RESERVE (RESERVED)
Ge 41:36 held in *r* for the country,
Dt 32:34 "Have I not kept this in *r*
1Ki 19:18 Yet I *r* seven thousand in Israel—
Job 38:23 which I *r* for times of trouble,

RESERVED (RESERVE)
Ge 27:36 "Haven't you *r* any blessing for me
Isa 26:11 let the fire *r* for your enemies
Ro 11: 4 "I have *r* for myself seven
2Pe 2:17 Blackest darkness is *r* for them.
3: 7 the present heavens and earth are *r*
Jude :13 darkness has been *r* forever.

RESERVOIR (RESERVOIRS)
Isa 22:11 You built a *r* between the two walls

RESERVOIRS (RESERVOIR)
Ex 7:19 over the ponds and all the *r*'—
Ecc 2: 6 I made *r* to water groves

RESETTLE (SETTLE)
1Ch 9: 2 the first to *r* on their own property
Eze 36:33 I will *r* your towns, and the ruins

RESETTLED (SETTLE)
2Ki 17:26 *r* in the towns of Samaria do not
Eze 38:12 turn my hand against the *r* ruins

RESHEPH
1Ch 7:25 Rephah was his son, *R* his son,

RESIDE (RESIDENCE RESIDENT RESIDENTS RESIDES)
Job 38:19 And where does darkness *r*?

RESIDENCE (RESIDE)
2Sa 5: 9 David then took up *r* in the fortress
1Ch 11: 7 David then took up *r* in the fortress
Ne 2: 8 and for the *r* I will occupy?"
Est 2:16 in the royal *r* in the tenth month,
Da 4:30 Babylon I have built as the royal *r*,

RESIDENT (RESIDE)
Ex 12:45 a temporary *r* and a hired worker
Lev 25: 6 temporary *r* who live among you,
25:35 would an alien or a temporary *r*,
25:40 or a temporary *r* among you;
25:47 a temporary *r* among you becomes

RESIDENTS (RESIDE)
Lev 25:45 some of the temporary *r* living
Ne 3:13 by Hanun and the *r* of Zanoah.
7: 3 Also appoint *r* of Jerusalem
Ac 2: 9 and Elamites; *r* of Mesopotamia,

RESIDES (RESIDE)
Job 18:15 Fire *r* in his tent;
41:22 Strength *r* in his neck;
Ecc 7: 9 for anger *r* in the lap of fools.

RESIN
Ge 2:12 aromatic *r* and onyx are also there
Ex 30:34 gum *r*, onycha and galbanum—
Nu 11: 7 coriander seed and looked like *r*.

RESIST (RESISTED RESISTS)
Jdg 2:14 whom they were no longer able to *r*
2Ki 10: 4 "If two kings could not *r* him,
2Ch 13: 7 and not strong enough to *r* them.
13: 8 now you plan to *r* the kingdom
Pr 28: 4 but those who keep the law *r* them.
Isa 1:20 but if you *r* and rebel,
Da 11:15 of the South will be powerless to *r*;
11:32 know their God will firmly *r* him.
Mt 5:39 I tell you, Do not *r* an evil person.
Lk 21:15 of your adversaries will be able to *r*
Ac 7:51 You always *r* the Holy Spirit!
Jas 4: 7 *R* the devil, and he will flee
1Pe 5: 9 *R* him, standing firm in the faith,

RESISTED (RESIST)
Job 9: 4 Who has *r* him and come out
Da 10:13 Persian kingdom *r* me twenty-one
Heb 12: 4 you have not yet *r* to the point

RESISTS (RESIST)
Ro 9:19 For who *r* his will?" But who are

RESOLVED
2Ch 20: 3 Jehoshaphat *r* to inquire
Ps 17: 3 I have *r* that my mouth will not sin.
Da 1: 8 But Daniel *r* not to defile himself
1Co 2: 2 For I *r* to know nothing while I was

RESORT (RESORTED)
Nu 24: 1 he did not *r* to sorcery

RESORTED (RESORT)
Jos 9: 4 to Jericho and Ai, they *r* to a ruse:

RESOUND (RESOUNDED RESOUNDING RESOUNDS)
1Ch 16:32 Let the sea *r*, and all that is in it;
Ps 96:11 let the sea *r*, and all that is in it;
98:7 Let the sea *r*, and everything in it,
118:15 *r* in the tents of the righteous:
Jer 6:7 Violence and destruction *r* in her;
25:31 The tumult will *r* to the ends
49:21 their cry will *r* to the Red Sea.
50:46 its cry will *r* among the nations.
51:55 the roar of their voices will *r*.

RESOUNDED (RESOUND)
2Sa 22:14 the voice of the Most High *r*.
Ps 18:13 the voice of the Most High *r*.
77:17 the skies *r* with thunder;

RESOUNDING (RESOUND)
Ps 150:5 praise him with *r* cymbals.
1Co 13:1 I am only a *r* gong or a clanging

RESOUNDS (RESOUND)
1Ki 1:45 gone up cheering, and the city *r*
Job 37:4 When his voice *r*,

RESOURCES
1Ch 29:2 With all my *r* I have provided

RESPECT (RESPECTABLE RESPECTED RESPECTS)
Ge 41:40 Only with *r* to the throne will I be
Lev 19:3 " 'Each of you must *r* his mother
19:32 show *r* for the elderly and revere
22:2 treat with *r* the sacred offerings
Dt 28:50 nation without *r* for the old
2Ki 1:13 "please have *r* for my life
1:14 But now have *r* for my life!"
3:14 if I did not have *r* for the presence
Est 1:20 all the women will *r* their husbands
Pr 11:16 A kindhearted woman gains *r*,
Isa 5:12 no *r* for the work of his hands.
La 5:12 elders are shown no *r*.
Mal 1:6 where is the *r* due me?" says
Mt 21:37 'They will *r* my son,' he said.
Mk 12:6 saying, 'They will *r* my son.'
Lk 20:13 I love; perhaps they will *r* him.'
Ro 13:7 if *r*, then *r*; if honor, then honor.
Eph 5:33 and the wife must *r* her husband.
6:5 obey your earthly masters with *r*
1Th 4:12 so that your daily life may win the *r*
5:12 to *r* those who work hard
1Ti 3:4 children obey him with proper *r*.
3:8 are to be men worthy of *r*, sincere,
3:11 are to be women worthy of *r*,
6:1 their masters worthy of full *r*,
6:2 not to show less *r* for them
Tit 2:2 worthy of *r*, self-controlled,
1Pe 2:17 Show proper *r* to everyone:
2:18 to your masters with all *r*,
3:7 them with *r* as the weaker partner
3:15 But do this with gentleness and *r*,

RESPECTABLE (RESPECT)
1Ti 3:2 self-controlled, *r*, hospitable,

RESPECTED (RESPECT)
Dt 1:13 and *r* men from each of your tribes,
1:15 and *r* men, and appointed them
1Sa 9:6 he is highly *r*, and everything he
22:14 and highly *r* in your household?
Pr 31:23 Her husband is *r* at the city gate,
Isa 32:5 nor the scoundrel be highly *r*.
33:8 no one is *r*.
Ac 10:22 who is *r* by all the Jewish people.
22:12 highly *r* by all the Jews living there.
Heb 12:9 who disciplined us and we *r* them

RESPECTS (RESPECT)
Pr 13:13 he who *r* a command is rewarded.
Ac 25:13 at Caesarea to pay their *r* to Festus.

RESPITE
Job 20:20 "Surely he will have no *r*

RESPLENDENT
Ps 76:4 You are *r* with light,
132:18 but the crown on his head will be *r*

RESPOND (RESPONDED RESPONDING RESPONSE RESPONSIVE)
1Sa 4:20 she did not *r* or pay any attention.
2Ch 32:25 he did not *r* to the kindness shown
Est 1:18 about the queen's conduct will *r*
Ps 102:17 He will *r* to the prayer
Pr 29:19 he understands, he will not *r*.
Isa 14:10 They will all *r*,
19:22 and he will *r* to their pleas
Jer 2:30 they did not *r* to correction.
17:23 would not listen or *r* to discipline.
32:33 they would not listen or *r*
Hos 2:21 and they will *r* to the earth;
2:21 "I will *r* to the skies,
2:21 "In that day I will *r*,"
2:22 and the earth will *r* to the grain,
2:22 and they will *r* to Jezreel.
Ac 16:14 heart to *r* to Paul's message.
Rev 16:7 And I heard the altar *r*:

RESPONDED (RESPOND)
Ex 19:8 people all *r* together, "We will do
24:3 they *r* with one voice, "Everything
24:7 They *r*, "We will do everything
Jdg 7:14 His friend *r*, "This can be nothing
20:28 or not?" The LORD *r*, "Go,
2Sa 19:43 But the men of Judah *r*
Ezr 10:12 The whole assembly *r*
Ne 8:6 the people lifted their hands and *r*,
Job 9:16 Even if I summoned him and he *r*,
Pr 1:23 If you had *r* to my rebuke,
Jer 7:28 not obeyed the LORD its God or *r*
Lk 20:39 Some of the teachers of the law *r*,

RESPONDING (RESPOND)
Ne 12:24 one section *r* to the other,

RESPONSE (RESPOND)
1Ki 18:26 there was no *r*; no one answered.
18:29 there was no *r*, no one answered,
2Ki 4:31 but there was no sound or *r*.
1Ch 29:9 at the willing *r* of their leaders,
Job 19:7 'I've been wronged!' I get no *r*;
Da 10:12 and I have come in *r* to them.
Ro 8:31 What, then, shall we say in *r* to this
Gal 2:2 I went in *r* to a revelation

RESPONSIBILITIES (RESPONSIBLE)
Nu 8:26 are to assign the *r* of the Levites."
1Ch 23:32 so the Levites carried out their *r*
2Ch 31:16 to their *r* and their divisions.
31:17 to their *r* and their divisions.

RESPONSIBILITY (RESPONSIBLE)
Nu 4:27 as their *r* all they are to carry.
18:1 are to bear the *r* for offenses
18:1 are to bear the *r* for offenses
18:23 bear the *r* for offenses against it.
1Ch 9:26 entrusted with the *r* for the rooms
9:31 was entrusted with the *r*
15:22 that was his *r* because he was
Ne 10:32 "We assume the *r*
10:35 assume *r* for bringing to the house
Mt 27:4 "That's your *r*."
27:24 "It is your *r*!" All the people
Ac 6:3 We will turn this *r* over to them
18:6 your own heads! I am clear of my *r*.

RESPONSIBLE (RESPONSIBILITIES RESPONSIBILITY)
Ge 16:5 "You are *r* for the wrong I am
39:22 he was made *r* for all that was done
43:9 you can hold me personally *r*
Ex 21:19 struck the blow will not be held *r*
21:28 owner of the bull will not be held *r*.
Lev 5:1 or learned about, he will be held *r*.
5:17 he is guilty and will be held *r*.
7:18 any of it will be held *r*.
17:16 bathe himself, he will be held *r*.' "
19:8 Whoever eats it will be held *r*
20:17 his sister and will be held *r*.
20:19 both of you would be held *r*.
20:20 They will be held *r*; they will die
24:15 curses his God, he will be held *r*;
Nu 1:53 The Levites are to be *r* for the care
3:25 of Meeting the Gershonites were *r*
3:28 The Kohathites were *r* for the care
3:31 They were *r* for the care of the ark,
3:32 over those who were *r* for the care
3:38 They were *r* for the care
7:9 for which they were *r*.
14:37 these men *r* for spreading the bad
18:3 They are to be *r* to you
18:4 and be *r* for the care of the Tent
18:5 "You are to be *r* for the care
30:15 he hears about them, then he is *r*
31:30 who are *r* for the care
31:47 who were *r* for the care
Jos 2:19 on his own head; we will not be *r*.
1Sa 22:22 I am *r* for the death
23:20 and we will be *r* for handing him
1Ch 9:13 *r* for ministering in the house
9:19 as their fathers had been *r*
9:19 his family (the Korahites) were *r*
9:33 they were *r* for the work day
16:42 Jeduthun were *r* for the sounding
26:30 were *r* in Israel west of the Jordan
Ne 11:22 who were the singers *r*
13:10 singers *r* for the service had gone
13:13 They were made *r*
Jnh 1:7 lots to find out who is *r*
1:8 who is *r* for making all this trouble
Lk 11:50 this generation will be held *r*
11:51 this generation will be held *r*
1Co 7:24 Brothers, each man, as *r* to God,

RESPONSIVE (RESPOND)
2Ki 22:19 Because your heart was *r*
2Ch 34:27 Because your heart was *r*

REST (RESTED RESTING RESTS SABBATH-REST)
Ge 8:4 to *r* on the mountains of Ararat.
14:10 into them and the *r* fled to the hills.
18:4 you may all wash your feet and *r*
30:36 to tend the *r* of Laban's flocks.
30:40 but made the *r* face the streaked
42:16 the *r* of you will be kept in prison,
42:19 while the *r* of you go and take grain
44:9 the *r* of us will become my lord's
44:10 the *r* of you will be free from blame
44:17 The *r* of you, go back to your father
47:30 but when I *r* with my fathers,
49:26 Let all these *r* on the head
Ex 4:7 it was restored, like the *r*
16:23 'Tomorrow is to be a day of *r*,
23:12 your donkey may *r* and the slave
29:12 and pour out the *r* of it at the base
31:15 the seventh day is a Sabbath of *r*,
33:14 go with you, and I will give you *r*."
34:21 but on the seventh day you shall *r*;
34:21 season and harvest you must *r*.
35:2 a Sabbath of *r* to the LORD.
Lev 2:3 The *r* of the grain offering belongs
2:10 The *r* of the grain offering belongs
4:7 *r* of the bull's blood he shall pour
4:12 that is, all the *r* of the bull—
4:18 The *r* of the blood he shall pour out
4:25 and pour out the *r* of the blood
4:30 and pour out the *r* of the blood
4:34 and pour out the *r* of the blood
5:9 *r* of the blood must be drained out
5:13 The *r* of the offering will belong
6:16 and his sons shall eat the *r* of it,
8:15 He poured out the *r* of the blood
8:32 Then burn up the *r* of the meat
9:9 the *r* of the blood he poured out
14:9 his eyebrows and the *r* of his hair.
14:18 *r* of the oil in his palm the priest
14:29 *r* of the oil in his palm the priest
16:31 of *r*, and you must deny yourselves
23:3 the seventh day is a Sabbath of *r*,
23:24 month you are to have a day of *r*,
23:32 It is a sabbath of *r* for you,
23:39 and the eighth day also is a day of *r*
23:39 the first day is a day of *r*,
25:4 is to have a sabbath of *r*,
25:5 The land is to have a year of *r*.
26:34 then the land will *r* and enjoy its
26:35 land will have the *r* it did not have
Nu 10:12 place until the cloud came to *r*
10:33 days to find them a place to *r*.
10:36 Whenever it came to *r*, he said,
16:9 you from the *r* of the Israelite
18:31 and your households may eat the *r*
23:24 that does not *r* till he devours his

Nu 31: 27 and the *r* of the community.
Dt 3: 13 The *r* of Gilead and also all
3: 20 until the LORD gives *r*
5: 14 and maidservant may *r*,
12: 10 and he will give you *r* from all your
19: 20 The *r* of the people will hear of this
25: 19 the LORD your God gives you *r*
31: 16 going to *r* with your fathers,
33: 12 of the LORD *r* secure in him,
33: 16 Let all these *r* on the head
Jos 1: 13 LORD your God is giving you *r*
1: 15 until the LORD gives them *r*,
7: 25 and after they had stoned the *r*,
11: 23 Then the land had *r* from war.
13: 27 Zaphon with the *r* of the realm of
14: 3 an inheritance among the *r*,
14: 15 Then the land had *r* from war.
17: 2 was for the *r* of the people
17: 6 to the *r* of the descendants
21: 5 *r* of Kohath's descendants were
21: 20 The *r* of the Kohathite clans
21: 26 to the *r* of the Kohathite clans.
21: 34 The Merarite clans (the *r*
21: 40 who were the *r* of the Levites,
21: 44 The LORD gave them *r*
22: 4 your God has given your brothers *r*
23: 1 and the LORD had given Israel *r*
Jdg 7: 6 All the *r* got down on their knees
7: 8 Gideon sent the *r* of the Israelites
Ru 1: 9 each of you will find *r* in the home
2: 7 except for a short *r* in the shelter.''
3: 18 For the man will not *r*
1Sa 13: 2 The *r* of the men he sent back
15: 15 but we totally destroyed the *r*.''
18: 29 and he remained his enemy the *r*
18: 30 success than the *r* of Saul's officers,
2Sa 4: 5 while he was taking his noonday *r*.
7: 1 and the LORD had given him *r*
7: 11 give you *r* from all your enemies.
7: 12 and you *r* with your fathers,
10: 10 He put the *r* of the men
12: 28 Now muster the *r* of the troops
13: 27 and the *r* of the king's sons.
14: 9 let the blame *r* on me
14: 17 of my lord the king bring me *r*,
1Ki 1: 21 laid to *r* with his fathers,
2: 33 of their blood *r* on the head of Joab
8: 56 who has given *r* to his people Israel
12: 23 to the *r* of the people, 'This is what
20: 15 he assembled the *r* of the Israelites,
20: 30 The *r* of them escaped to the city
22: 46 He rid the land of the *r*
2Ki 13: 7 king of Aram had destroyed the *r*
25: 11 along with the *r* of the populace
25: 29 and for the *r* of his life ate regularly
1Ch 6: 31 after the ark came to *r* there.
6: 61 *r* of Kohath's descendants were
6: 70 to the *r* of the Kohathite clans.
6: 77 The Merarites (the *r*
11: 8 while Joab restored the *r* of the city
12: 38 All the *r* of the Israelites were
13: 2 and wide to the *r* of our brothers
16: 41 Jeduthun and the *r* of those chosen
19: 11 He put the *r* of the men
22: 9 and I will give him *r* from all his
22: 9 who will be a man of peace and *r*,
22: 18 And has he not granted you *r*
23: 25 has granted *r* to his people
24: 20 As for the *r* of the descendants
28: 2 as a place of *r* for the ark
2Ch 14: 6 for the LORD gave him *r*.
14: 7 he has given us *r* on every side.''
15: 15 So the LORD gave them *r*
20: 30 for his God had given him *r*
24: 14 they brought the *r* of the money
Ezr 2: 70 and the *r* of the Israelites settled
3: 8 the *r* of their brothers (the priests
4: 3 the *r* of the heads of the families
4: 7 the *r* of his associates wrote a letter
4: 9 together with the *r*
4: 17 and the *r* of their associates living
6: 16 the Levites and the *r* of the exiles—
7: 18 best with the *r* of the silver
Ne 4: 14 the officials and the *r* of the people,
4: 19 the officials and the *r* of the people,
6: 1 *r* of our enemies that I had rebuilt
6: 14 *r* of the prophets who have been
7: 72 The total given by the *r*
Ne 7: 73 certain of the people and the *r*
9: 28 "But as soon as they were at *r*,
10: 28 "The *r* of the people—priests,
11: 1 and the *r* of the people cast lots
11: 20 The *r* of the Israelites,
Est 9: 12 in the *r* of the king's provinces?
Job 3: 13 I would be asleep and at *r*
3: 17 and there the weary are at *r*.
3: 26 I have no *r*, but only turmoil.''
11: 18 will look about you and take your *r*
16: 18 may my cry never be laid to *r*!
24: 23 He may let them *r* in a feeling
30: 17 my gnawing pains never *r*.
36: 11 they will spend the *r* of their days
Ps 16: 9 my body also will *r* secure,
33: 22 May your unfailing love *r* upon us,
55: 6 I would fly away and be at *r*—
62: 1 My soul finds *r* in God alone;
62: 5 Find *r*, O my soul, in God alone;
80: 17 Let your hand *r* on the man
90: 17 of the Lord our God *r* upon us;
91: 1 will *r* in the shadow
95: 11 "They shall never enter my *r*.''
116: 7 Be at *r* once more, O my soul,
Pr 6: 10 a little folding of the hands to *r*—
21: 16 comes to *r* in the company
24: 33 a little folding of the hands to *r*—
26: 2 curse does not come to *r*.
Ecc 2: 23 even at night his mind does not *r*.
6: 5 it has more *r* than does that man—
10: 4 calmness can lay great errors to *r*.
SS 1: 7 where you *r* your sheep at midday.
Isa 11: 2 Spirit of the LORD will *r* on him—
11: 10 and his place of *r* will be glorious.
13: 20 no shepherd will *r* his flocks there.
14: 7 All the lands are at *r* and at peace;
23: 12 even there you will find no *r*.''
25: 10 The hand of the LORD will *r*
28: 12 the resting place, let the weary *r*'';
30: 15 "In repentance and *r* is your
32: 18 in undisturbed places of *r*.
34: 14 and find for themselves places of *r*.
38: 10 and be robbed of the *r* of my years
44: 17 From the *r* he makes a god, his idol
57: 2 they find *r* as they lie in death.
57: 20 which cannot *r*,
62: 6 give yourselves no *r*,
62: 7 and give him no *r* till he establishes
63: 14 they were given *r* by the Spirit
Jer 6: 16 and you will find *r* for your souls.
31: 2 I will come to give *r* to Israel.''
33: 12 for shepherds to *r* their flocks.
39: 9 over to him, and the *r* of the people
41: 10 of all the *r* of the people who were
45: 3 out with groaning and find no *r*.' ''
47: 6 'how long till you *r*?
47: 7 But how can it *r*
48: 11 "Moab has been at *r* from youth,
50: 34 so that he may bring *r* to their land,
52: 15 along with the *r* of the craftsmen
52: 16 But Nebuzaradan left behind the *r*
52: 33 and for the *r* of his life ate regularly
La 2: 18 your eyes no *r*.
5: 5 we are weary and find no *r*.
Eze 34: 18 also muddy the *r* with your feet?
34: 18 also trample the *r* of your pasture
36: 3 possession of the *r* of the nations
36: 4 ridiculed by the *r* of the nations
36: 5 spoken against the *r* of the nations,
44: 30 meal so that a blessing may *r*
48: 23 "As for the *r* of the tribes:
Da 2: 18 executed with the *r* of the wise men
12: 13 You will *r*, and then at the end
Mic 5: 3 and the *r* of his brothers return
Na 3: 18 your nobles lie down to *r*.
Hab 2: 5 he is arrogant and never at *r*.
Zec 1: 11 and found the whole world at *r*
6: 8 country have given my Spirit *r*
7: 7 and its surrounding towns were at *r*
9: 1 and will *r* upon Damascus—
12: 14 and all the *r* of the clans
14: 2 the *r* of the people will not be taken
Mt 10: 13 let your peace *r* on it; if it is not,
11: 28 and burdened, and I will give you *r*.
11: 29 and you will find *r* for your souls.
12: 43 goes through arid places seeking *r*
22: 6 *r* seized his servants, mistreated
27: 49 But the *r* said, "Leave him alone.
Mk 6: 31 to a quiet place and get some *r*.''
16: 13 returned and reported it to the *r*;
Lk 10: 6 your peace will *r* on him; if not,
11: 24 goes through arid places seeking *r*
12: 26 why do you worry about the *r*?
Jn 11: 16 said to the *r* of the disciples,
Ac 2: 3 and came to *r* on each of them.
5: 2 but brought the *r* and put it
16: 17 This girl followed Paul and the *r*
21: 18 and the *r* of us went to see James,
27: 44 The *r* were to get there on planks
28: 9 the *r* of the sick on the island came
1Co 2: 5 so that your faith might not *r*
7: 12 To the *r* I say this (I, not the Lord):
2Co 7: 5 this body of ours had no *r*,
12: 9 so that Christ's power may *r* on me
Eph 2: 3 Like the *r*, we were
Php 4: 3 and the *r* of my fellow workers,
1Th 4: 13 or to grieve like the *r* of men,
Heb 3: 11 'They shall never enter my *r*.' ''
3: 18 that they would never enter his *r*
4: 1 of entering his *r* still stands,
4: 3 'They shall never enter my *r*.' ''
4: 3 we who have believed enter that *r*,
4: 5 "They shall never enter my *r*.''
4: 6 remains that some will enter that *r*,
4: 8 For if Joshua had given them *r*,
4: 10 for anyone who enters God's *r*
4: 11 make every effort to enter that *r*,
1Pe 4: 2 he does not live the *r*
1Jn 3: 19 and how we set our hearts at *r*
Rev 2: 24 I say to the *r* of you in Thyatira,
9: 20 *r* of mankind that were not killed
12: 17 war against the *r* of her offspring—
14: 11 There is no *r* day or night
14: 13 "they will *r* from their labor,
19: 21 The *r* of them were killed
20: 5 (The *r* of the dead did not come

RESTED (REST)

Ge 2: 2 so on the seventh day he *r*
2: 3 because on it he *r* from all the work
Ex 16: 30 So the people *r* on the seventh day.
20: 11 but he *r* on the seventh day.
31: 17 abstained from work and *r*.' ''
Nu 11: 25 When the Spirit *r* on them,
11: 26 Yet the Spirit also *r* on them,
1Ki 2: 10 Then David *r* with his fathers
7: 3 cedar above the beams that *r*
7: 25 The Sea *r* on top of them,
11: 21 Hadad heard that David *r*
11: 43 Then he *r* with his fathers
14: 20 and then *r* with his fathers.
14: 31 And Rehoboam *r* with his fathers
15: 8 And Abijah *r* with his fathers
15: 24 Then Asa *r* with his fathers
16: 6 Baasha *r* with his fathers
16: 28 Omri *r* with his fathers
22: 40 of Israel? Ahab *r* with his fathers.
22: 50 Jehoshaphat *r* with his fathers
2Ki 8: 24 Jehoram *r* with his fathers
10: 35 Jehu *r* with his fathers
13: 9 Jehoahaz *r* with his fathers
13: 13 Jehoash *r* with his fathers,
14: 16 Jehoash *r* with his fathers
14: 22 after Amaziah *r* with his fathers.
14: 29 Jeroboam *r* with his fathers,
15: 7 Azariah *r* with his fathers
15: 22 Menahem *r* with his fathers.
15: 38 Jotham *r* with his fathers
16: 20 Ahaz *r* with his fathers
20: 21 Hezekiah *r* with his fathers.
21: 18 Manasseh *r* with his fathers
24: 6 Jehoiakim *r* with his fathers.
2Ch 4: 4 The Sea *r* on top of them,
9: 31 Then he *r* with his fathers
12: 16 Rehoboam *r* with his fathers
14: 1 And Abijah *r* with his fathers
16: 13 year of his reign Asa died and *r*
21: 1 Jehoshaphat *r* with his fathers
26: 2 after Amaziah *r* with his fathers.
26: 23 Uzziah *r* with his fathers
27: 9 Jotham *r* with his fathers
28: 27 Ahaz *r* with his fathers
32: 33 Hezekiah *r* with his fathers
33: 20 Manasseh *r* with his fathers
36: 21 all the time of its desolation it *r*,
Ezr 8: 32 Jerusalem, where we *r* three days.

Est 9: 17 and on the fourteenth they *r*
9: 18 and then on the fifteenth they *r*
Eze 32: 27 for their sins *r* on their bones,
Am 5: 19 and *r* his hand on the wall
Lk 23: 56 they *r* on the Sabbath in obedience
Heb 4: 4 "And on the seventh day God *r*

RESTING (REST)

Ge 28: 12 dream in which he saw a stairway *r*
49: 15 he sees how good is his *r* place
Dt 12: 9 have not yet reached the *r* place
28: 65 no *r* place for the sole of your foot.
1Ki 7: 30 each had a basin *r* on four supports,
2Ki 2: 15 "The spirit of Elijah is *r* on Elisha."
9: 16 because Joram was *r* there
2Ch 6: 41 God, and come to your *r* place,
Ps 132: 8 LORD, and come to your *r* place,
132: 14 This is my *r* place for ever and ever
SS 1: 13 *r* between my breasts.
Isa 22: 16 chiseling your *r* place in the rock?
28: 12 "This is the *r* place, let the weary
65: 10 Valley of Achor a *r* place for herds,
66: 1 Where will my *r* place be?
Jer 50: 6 and forgot their own *r* place.
La 1: 3 she finds no *r* place.
Eze 25: 5 Ammon into a *r* place for sheep.
Mic 2: 10 For this is not your *r* place,
Mt 26: 45 Are you still sleeping and *r?* Look,
Mk 14: 41 "Are you still sleeping and *r?*
Ac 7: 49 Or where will my *r* place be?
Tit 1: 2 and knowledge *r* on the hope

RESTITUTION

Ex 22: 3 "A thief must certainly make *r*,
22: 5 he must make *r* from the best
22: 6 who started the fire must make *r*.
22: 11 to accept this, and no *r* is required.
22: 12 he must make *r* to the owner.
22: 14 is not present, he must make *r*.
Lev 5: 16 He must make *r* for what he has
6: 5 He must make *r* in full, add a fifth
22: 14 he must make *r* to the priest
24: 18 of someone's animal must make *r*
24: 21 kills an animal must make *r*,
Nu 5: 7 He must make full *r* for his wrong,
5: 8 relative to whom *r* can be made
5: 8 the *r* belongs to the LORD

RESTLESS

Ge 4: 12 You will be a *r* wanderer
4: 14 I will be a *r* wanderer on the earth,
27: 40 But when you grow *r*,
Jer 49: 23 troubled like the *r* sea.
Jas 3: 8 It is a *r* evil, full of deadly poison.

RESTORATION (RESTORE)

2Ch 24: 27 the record of the *r* of the temple

RESTORE (RESTORATION RESTORED RESTORER RESTORES RESTORING)

Ge 40: 13 and *r* you to your position,
Dt 30: 3 your God will *r* your fortunes
2Sa 8: 3 when he went to *r* his control
9: 7 I will *r* to you all the land that
2Ch 24: 4 to *r* the temple of the LORD.
24: 12 carpenters to *r* the LORD's temple
Ezr 5: 3 this temple and *r* this structure?"
5: 9 this temple and *r* this structure?"
Ne 4: 2 Will they *r* their wall? Will they
Job 8: 6 and *r* you to your rightful place.
Ps 41: 3 and *r* him from his bed of illness.
51: 12 *R* to me the joy of your salvation
60: 1 you have been angry—now *r* us!
69: 4 I am forced to *r*
71: 20 you will *r* my life again;
80: 3 *R* us, O God;
80: 7 *R* us, O God Almighty;
80: 19 *R* us, O LORD God Almighty;
85: 4 *R* us again, O God our Savior,
126: 4 *R* our fortunes, O LORD,
Isa 1: 26 I will *r* your judges as in days of old
44: 26 and of their ruins, 'I will *r* them,'
49: 6 servant to *r* the tribes of Jacob
49: 8 to *r* the land
57: 18 I will guide him and *r* comfort
61: 4 and *r* the places long devastated;
Jer 15: 19 "If you repent, I will *r* you
16: 15 For I will *r* them to the land I gave
27: 22 and *r* them to this place.' "
30: 3 and *r* them to the land I gave their
30: 17 But I will *r* you to health
30: 18 " 'I will *r* the fortunes
31: 18 *R* me, and I will return,
32: 44 because I will *r* their fortunes,
33: 11 For I will *r* the fortunes of the land
33: 26 For I will *r* their fortunes
42: 12 on you and *r* you to your land.'
48: 47 "Yet I will *r* the fortunes of Moab
49: 6 I will *r* the fortunes
49: 39 "Yet I will *r* the fortunes of Elam
La 1: 16 no one to *r* my spirit.
5: 21 *R* us to yourself, O LORD,
Eze 16: 53 I will *r* the fortunes of Sodom
Da 9: 25 From the issuing of the decree to *r*
Hos 6: 2 on the third day he will *r* us,
7: 1 "Whenever I would *r* the fortunes
Joel 3: 1 when I *r* the fortunes of Judah
Am 9: 11 "In that day I will *r*
9: 11 *r* its ruins,
Na 2: 2 The LORD will *r* the splendor
Zep 2: 7 he will *r* their fortunes.
3: 20 the earth when I *r* your fortunes
Zec 9: 12 now I announce that I will *r* twice
10: 6 I will *r* them
Mt 17: 11 Elijah comes and will *r* all things.
Ac 1: 6 going to *r* the kingdom to Israel?"
3: 21 comes for God to *r* everything,
9: 12 hands on him to *r* his sight."
15: 16 and I will *r* it,
Gal 6: 1 are spiritual should *r* him gently.
1Pe 5: 10 will himself *r* you and make you

RESTORED (RESTORE)

Ge 40: 21 He *r* the chief cupbearer
41: 13 I was *r* to my position,
Ex 4: 7 it was *r*, like the rest of his flesh.
Nu 21: 27 let Sihon's city be *r*.
1Sa 7: 14 captured from Israel were *r* to her,
1Ki 13: 6 pray for me that my hand may be *r*
13: 6 the king's hand was *r* and became
2Ki 5: 10 and your flesh will be *r*
5: 14 his flesh was *r* and became clean
8: 1 to the woman whose son he had *r*
8: 5 the king how Elisha had *r* the dead
8: 5 this is her son whom Elisha *r* to life
14: 22 *r* it to Judah after Amaziah rested
14: 25 was the one who *r* the boundaries
1Ch 11: 8 while Joab *r* the rest of the city.
2Ch 26: 2 *r* it to Judah after Amaziah rested
33: 16 Then he *r* the altar of the LORD
34: 10 who repaired and *r* the temple.
Ezr 4: 13 if this city is built and its walls are *r*
4: 16 if this city is built and its walls are *r*
Ne 3: 8 They *r* Jerusalem as far
Job 22: 23 to the Almighty, you will be *r*:
33: 25 it is *r* as in the days of his youth.
33: 26 he is *r* by God to his righteous state
Ps 85: 1 you *r* the fortunes of Jacob.
Isa 38: 16 You *r* me to health
Eze 21: 27 It will not be *r* until he comes
Da 4: 26 means that your kingdom will be *r*
4: 34 heaven, and my sanity was *r*.
4: 36 and I was *r* to my throne
4: 36 the same time that my sanity was *r*,
Mic 4: 8 the former dominion will be *r*
Mt 9: 30 done to you"; and their sight was *r*.
12: 13 it out and it was completely *r*,
Mk 3: 5 and his hand was completely *r*.
8: 25 his sight was *r*, and he saw
Lk 6: 10 and his hand was completely *r*.
Phm : 22 I hope to be *r* to you in answer
Heb 13: 19 pray so that I may be *r* to you soon.

RESTORER (RESTORE)

Isa 58. 12 *R* of Streets with Dwellings.

RESTORES (RESTORE)

Ps 14: 7 When the LORD *r* the fortunes
23: 3 he *r* my soul.
53: 6 When God *r* the fortunes
Mk 9: 12 does come first, and *r* all things.

RESTORING (RESTORE)

2Ki 12: 12 the other expenses of *r* the temple.
Ezr 4: 12 They are *r* the walls and repairing

RESTRAIN (RESTRAINED RESTRAINING RESTRAINT)

1Sa 3: 13 and he failed to *r* them.
Job 9: 13 God does not *r* his anger;
Jer 2: 24 in her heat who can *r* her?
14: 10 they do not *r* their feet.
31: 16 "*R* your voice from weeping

RESTRAINED (RESTRAIN)

Ex 36: 6 And so the people were *r*
Est 5: 10 Haman *r* himself and went home.
Ps 76: 10 the survivors of your wrath are *r*.
78: 38 Time after time he *r* his anger
Eze 31: 15 and its abundant waters were *r*.
2Pe 2: 16 and *r* the prophet's madness.

RESTRAINING (RESTRAIN)

Pr 27: 16 *r* her is like *r* the wind
Col 2: 23 value in *r* sensual indulgence.

RESTRAINT (RESTRAIN)

Job 30: 11 they throw off *r* in my presence.
Ps 119: 51 The arrogant mock me without *r*,
Pr 17: 27 of knowledge uses words with *r*,
23: 4 have the wisdom to show *r*.
29: 18 no revelation, the people cast off *r*;
Eze 35: 13 and spoke against me without *r*,

RESTRICT (RESTRICTED RESTRICTION)

1Co 7: 35 for your own good, not to *r* you,

RESTRICTED (RESTRICT)

Jer 36: 5 Jeremiah told Baruch, "I am *r*;

RESTRICTION (RESTRICT)

Job 36: 16 to a spacious place free from *r*,

RESTS (REST)

Dt 33: 12 and the one the LORD loves *r*
2Ch 28: 11 for the LORD's fierce anger *r*
28: 13 and his fierce anger *r* on Israel."
36: 21 The land enjoyed its Sabbath *r*;
Pr 19: 23 one *r* content, untouched
21: 31 but victory *r* with the LORD.
Lk 2: 14 to men on whom his favor *r*."
Heb 4: 10 who enters God's rest also *r*
1Pe 4: 14 Spirit of glory and of God *r* on you.

RESULT

Ge 38: 24 and as a *r* she is now pregnant."
Ex 21: 20 and the slave dies as a direct *r*,
Lev 7: 16 his offering is the *r* of a vow
Nu 25: 18 killed when the plague came as a *r*
Ezr 9: 13 to us is a *r* of our evil deeds
Mic 7: 13 as the *r* of their deeds.
Mk 1: 45 As a *r*, Jesus could no longer enter
Lk 21: 13 This will *r* in your being witnesses
Ac 5: 15 As a *r*, people brought the sick
25: 26 a *r* of this investigation I may have
Ro 3: 8 "Let us do evil that good may *r*"?
5: 16 the gift of God is not like the *r*
5: 18 as the *r* of one trespass was
5: 18 *r* of one act of righteousness was
6: 21 of? Those things *r* in death!
6: 22 to holiness, and the *r* is eternal life.
11: 30 as a *r* of their disobedience,
11: 31 as a *r* of God's mercy to you.
1Co 9: 1 Are you not the *r* of my work
11: 34 you meet together it may not *r*
2Co 3: 3 from Christ, the *r* of our ministry,
9: 11 through us your generosity will *r*
Gal 4: 23 the free woman was born as the *r*
Php 1: 13 As a *r*, it has become clear
2Th 1: 5 as a *r* you will be counted worthy
1Ti 6: 4 and arguments that *r* in envy,
1Pe 1: 7 may be proved genuine and may *r*
4: 2 As a *r*, he does not live the rest

RESURRECTION

Mt 22: 23 who say there is no *r*, came to him
22: 28 at the *r*, whose wife will she be
22: 30 At the *r* people will neither marry
22: 31 But about the *r* of the dead—
27: 53 and after Jesus' *r* they went
Mk 12: 18 who say there is no *r*, came to him
12: 23 At the *r* whose wife will she be,
Lk 14: 14 repaid at the *r* of the righteous."
20: 27 who say there is no *r*, came to Jesus

Lk 20:33 at the *r* whose wife will she be,
20:35 in the *r* from the dead will neither
20:36 since they are children of the *r*.
Jn 11:24 again in the *r* at the last day."
11:25 Jesus said to her, "I am the *r*
Ac 1:22 become a witness with us of his *r*."
2:31 he spoke of the *r* of the Christ,
4: 2 in Jesus the *r* of the dead.
4:33 to testify to the *r* of the Lord Jesus,
17:18 good news about Jesus and the *r*.
17:32 When they heard about the *r*
23: 6 of my hope in the *r* of the dead."
23: 8 Sadducees say that there is no *r*,
24:15 that there will be a *r*
24:21 'It is concerning the *r*
Ro 1: 4 Son of God by his *r* from the dead:
6: 5 also be united with him in his *r*.
1Co 15:12 some of you say that there is no *r*
15:13 If there is no *r* of the dead,
15:21 the *r* of the dead comes
15:29 if there is no *r*, what will those do
15:42 So will it be with the *r* of the dead.
Php 3:10 power of his *r* and the fellowship
3:11 to attain to the *r* from the dead.
2Ti 2:18 say that the *r* has already taken
Heb 6: 2 on of hands, the *r* of the dead,
11:35 so that they might gain a better *r*.
1Pe 1: 3 hope through the *r* of Jesus Christ
3:21 It saves you by the *r* of Jesus Christ
Rev 20: 5 This is the first *r*.
20: 6 those who have part in the first *r*.

RETAIN (RETAINS)

2Ch 22: 9 powerful enough to *r* the kingdom.
Da 11: 6 but she will not *r* her power,
Lk 8:15 *r* it, and by persevering produce
Ro 1:28 to *r* the knowledge of God,
1Co 7:17 each one should *r* the place

RETAINS (RETAIN)

Lev 25:29 he *r* the right of redemption a full
25:48 he *r* the right of redemption

RETAKE (TAKE)

Jdg 11:26 Why didn't you *r* them
1Ki 22: 3 nothing to *r* it from the king

RETALIATE

1Pe 2:23 he did not *r*; when he suffered,

RETINUE

1Ki 10:13 and returned with her *r*
2Ch 9:12 and returned with her *r*

RETIRE

Nu 8:25 they must *r* from their regular

RETORTED

Jn 7:47 you also?" the Pharisees *r*.

RETREAT (RETREATED RETREATING RETREATS)

Jdg 20:32 "Let's *r* and draw them away
Job 41:25 they *r* before his thrashing.
Ps 44:10 You made us *r* before the enemy,
74:21 Do not let the oppressed *r*
Da 11: 9 but will *r* to his own country.

RETREATED (RETREAT)

2Sa 23: 9 Then the men of Israel *r*,

RETREATING (RETREAT)

Jer 46: 5 they are *r*,

RETREATS (RETREAT)

Pr 30:30 who *r* before nothing;

RETRIBUTION

Ps 69:22 may it become *r* and a trap.
Isa 34: 8 a year of *r*, to uphold Zion's cause.
35: 4 with divine *r*
59:18 and *r* to his foes;
Jer 51:56 For the LORD is a God of *r*;
Ro 11: 9 a stumbling block and a *r* for them.

RETRIEVED

Isa 49:25 and plunder *r* from the fierce;

RETURN (RETURNED RETURNING RETURNS)

Ge 3:19 and to dust you will *r*."
3:19 food until you *r* to the ground,
8:12 but this time it did not *r* to him.
18:10 "I will surely *r* to you about this
18:14 I will *r* to you at the appointed time
20: 7 if you do not *r* her, you may be sure
20: 7 *r* the man's wife, for he is a prophet
28:21 clothes to wear so that I *r* safely
29: 3 they would *r* the stone to its place
29:18 work for you seven years in *r*
29:27 in *r* for another seven years of work
30:15 sleep with you tonight in *r*
31:30 longed to *r* to your father's house.
43:12 for you must *r* the silver that was
44:33 and let the boy *r* with his brothers.
45:17 and *r* to the land of Canaan,
49: 9 you *r* from the prey, my son.
50: 5 and bury my father; then I will *r*.' "
Ex 4:21 to Moses, "When you *r* to Egypt,
13:17 might change their minds and *r*
22:26 as a pledge, *r* it to him by sunset,
33:11 Then Moses would *r* to the camp,
Lev 6: 4 he must *r* what he has stolen
14:39 the seventh day the priest shall *r*
25:10 of you is to *r* to his family property
25:13 is to *r* to his own property.
Nu 10:36 "*R*, O LORD,
18:21 as their inheritance in *r*
32:18 We will not *r* to our homes
32:22 you may *r* and be free
35:28 death of the high priest may he *r*
Dt 4:30 then in later days you will *r*
5:30 "Go, tell them to *r* to their tents.
16: 7 Then in the morning *r* to your tents
17:16 or make the people *r* to Egypt
23:11 and at sunset he may *r* to the camp.
24:13 *R* his cloak to him by sunset
30: 2 your children *r* to the LORD your
Jos 2:16 there three days until they *r*,
18: 4 Then they will *r* to me.
18: 8 Then *r* to me, and I will cast lots
22: 4 *r* to your homes in the land that
22: 8 "*R* to your homes
22: 9 at Shiloh in Canaan to *r* to Gilead,
Jdg 6:18 said, "I will wait until you *r*."
8: 9 "When I *r* in triumph, I will tear
11:31 to meet me when I *r* in triumph
19: 3 went to her to persuade her to *r*.
20: 8 not one of us will *r* to his house.
Ru 1: 6 prepared to *r* home from there.
1:11 But Naomi said, "*R* home,
1:12 become your husbands? *R* home,
1Sa 6: 3 If you *r* the ark of the god of Israel,
18: 2 and did not let him *r* to his father's
29: 4 that he may *r* to the place you
2Sa 1:22 sword of Saul did not *r* unsatisfied.
12:23 go to him, but he will not *r* to me."
15:34 But if you *r* to the city
17: 3 of the man you seek will mean the *r*
19:14 "*R*, you and all your men."
19:37 me in this way? Let your servant *r*,
1Ki 11:21 that I may *r* to my own country."
12:27 and *r* to King Rehoboam."
13: 9 or *r* by the way you came.' "
13:10 did not *r* by the way he had come
13:17 or *r* by the way you came.' "
17:21 let this boy's life *r* to him!"
20:34 "I will *r* the cities my father took
22:27 bread and water until I *r* safely.' "
22:28 declared, "If you ever *r* safely,
2Ki 4:22 to the man of God quickly and *r*."
19: 7 he will *r* to his own country,
19:28 and I will make you *r*
19:33 By the way that he came he will *r*;
2Ch 18:26 bread and water until I *r* safely.' "
18:27 declared, "If you ever *r* safely,
30: 6 that he may *r* to you who are left,
30: 6 "People of Israel, *r* to the LORD,
30: 9 If you *r* to the LORD, then your
30: 9 face from you if you *r* to him."
Ne 1: 9 but if you *r* to me and obey my
7: 5 of those who had been the first to *r*.
9:17 leader in order to *r* to their slavery.
9:29 You warned them to *r* to your law,
Est 2:14 She would not *r* to the king
2:14 in the morning *r* to another part
Job 7: 9 down to the grave does not *r*.
10:21 joy before I go to the place of no *r*,
15:31 for he will get nothing in *r*.
16:22 before I go on the journey of no *r*.
22:23 If you *r* to the Almighty, you will
34:15 and man would *r* to the dust.
39: 4 they leave and do not *r*.
Ps 9:17 The wicked *r* to the grave,
59: 6 They *r* at evening,
59:14 They *r* at evening,
78:39 a passing breeze that does not *r*.
80:14 *R* to us, O God Almighty!
85: 8 but let them not *r* to folly.
90: 3 saying, "*R* to dust, O sons of men."
104:22 they *r* and lie down in their dens.
104:29 they die and *r* to the dust.
109: 4 In *r* for my friendship they accuse
126: 6 will *r* with songs of joy,
146: 4 When their spirit departs, they *r*
Pr 2:19 None who go to her *r*
Ecc 1: 7 there they *r* again.
3:20 all come from dust, and to dust all *r*
4: 9 they have a good *r* for their work:
12: 2 and the clouds *r* after the rain;
Isa 10:21 A remnant will *r*, a remnant
10:21 will *r* to the Mighty God.
10:22 only a remnant will *r*.
13:14 each will *r* to his own people,
23:17 She will *r* to her hire as a prostitute
31: 6 *R* to him you have
35:10 the ransomed of the LORD will *r*.
37: 7 he will *r* to his own country,
37:29 and I will make you *r*
37:34 By the way that he came he will *r*;
44:22 *R* to me,
51:11 The ransomed of the LORD will *r*.
55:10 and do not *r* to it
55:11 It will not *r* to me empty,
63:17 *R* for the sake of your servants,
Jer 3: 1 should he *r* to her again?
3: 1 would you now *r* to me?"
3: 7 she had done all this she would *r*
3:10 her unfaithful sister Judah did not *r*
3:12 " '*R*, faithless Israel,' declares
3:14 "*R*, faithless people," declares
3:22 "*R*, faithless people;
4: 1 "If you will *r*, O Israel,
4: 1 *r* to me,"
8: 4 a man turns away, does he not *r*?
8: 5 they refuse to *r*.
14: 3 They *r* with their jars unfilled;
22:10 because he will never *r*
22:11 from this place: "He will never *r*.
22:27 back to the land you long to *r* to."
24: 7 for they will *r* to me
31: 8 a great throng will *r*.
31:16 "They will *r* from the land
31:17 "Your children will *r*
31:18 Restore me, and I will *r*,
31:21 *R*, O Virgin Israel,
31:21 *r* to your towns.
37: 8 Then the Babylonians will *r*
44:14 none will *r* except a few fugitives."
44:14 or survive to *r* to the land of Judah,
44:14 to which they long to *r* and live;
44:28 and *r* to the land of Judah
47: 6 *R* to your scabbard;
50: 9 who do not *r* empty-handed.
50:16 let everyone *r* to his own people,
La 3:40 and let us *r* to the LORD.
5:21 yourself, O LORD, that we may *r*;
Eze 11:18 "They will *r* to it and remove all its
16:55 and your daughters will *r*
16:55 will *r* to what they were before;
18:12 He does not *r* what he took
21: 5 from its scabbard; it will not *r* again
21:30 *R* the sword to its scabbard.
26:20 you will not *r* or take your place
29:14 back from captivity and *r* them
46: 9 No one is to *r* through the gate
Da 10:20 Soon I will *r* to fight
11:28 The king of the North will *r*
11:28 and then *r* to his own country.
11:30 He will *r* and show favor
Hos 3: 5 Afterward the Israelites will *r*
5: 4 to *r* to their God.
6: 1 "Come, let us *r* to the LORD.

Hos 7: 10 he does not r to the LORD his God
8: 13 They will r to Egypt.
9: 3 Ephraim will r to Egypt
11: 5 "Will they not r to Egypt
12: 6 But you must r to your God;
14: 1 R, O Israel, to the LORD your
14: 2 and r to the LORD.
Joel 2: 12 "r to me with all your heart,
2: 13 R to the LORD your God,
3: 4 speedily r on your own heads what
3: 7 I will r on your own heads what
Ob : 15 your deeds will r upon your own
Mic 5: 3 and the rest of his brothers r
Zep 2: 10 in r for their pride,
Zec 1: 3 I will r to you,' says the LORD
1: 3 'R to me,' declares the LORD
1: 16 'I will r to Jerusalem with mercy,
8: 3 "I will r to Zion and dwell
9: 12 R to your fortress, O prisoners
10: 9 and they will r.
Mal 3: 7 R to me, and I will r to you,"
3: 7 'How are we to r?'
Mt 10: 13 if it is not, let your peace r to you.
12: 44 'I will r to the house I left.'
Lk 8: 39 "R home and tell how much God
10: 6 rest on him; if not, it will r to you.
10: 35 after him,' he said, 'and when I r,
11: 24 'I will r to the house I left.'
12: 36 waiting for their master to r
17: 18 Was no one found to r
19: 12 appointed king and then to r.
Jn 21: 22 him to remain alive until I r,
21: 23 him to remain alive until I r,
Ac 13: 13 where John left them to r
15: 16 as it is written: " 'After this I will r
15: 33 with the blessing of peace to r
Ro 9: 9 "At the appointed time I will r,
1Co 16: 11 in peace so that he may r to me.
2Co 1: 23 order to spare you that I did not r
13: 2 On my r I will not spare those who
1Th 3: 9 for you in r for all the joy we have
Heb 11: 15 would have had opportunity to r.

RETURNED (RETURN)

Ge 8: 9 surface of the earth; so it r to Noah
8: 11 When the dove r to him
14: 17 r from defeating Kedorlaomer
18: 33 he left, and Abraham r home.
19: 27 r to the place where he had stood
20: 14 and he r Sarah his wife to him.
21: 32 of his forces r to the land
22: 19 Then Abraham r to his servants,
31: 55 Then he left and r home.
32: 6 When the messengers r to Jacob,
35: 9 After Jacob r from Paddan Aram,
37: 29 When Reuben r to the cistern
42: 28 "My silver has been r," he said
43: 10 we could have gone and r twice."
44: 13 they all loaded their donkeys and r
50: 14 After burying his father, Joseph r
Ex 2: 18 When the girls r to Reuel their
2: 18 "Why have you r so early today?"
5: 22 Moses r to the LORD and said,
18: 27 and he r to his own country.
Lev 25: 28 It will be r in the Jubilee,
25: 30 It is not to be r in the Jubilee.
25: 31 and they are to be r in the Jubilee.
25: 33 and is to be r in the Jubilee,
Nu 11: 30 the elders of Israel r to the camp.
13: 25 the end of forty days they r
14: 36 who r and made the whole
16: 50 Aaron r to Moses at the entrance
22: 14 So the Moabite princes r to Balak
24: 25 Then Balaam got up and r home
31: 14 commanders of hundreds—who r
Dt 28: 31 taken from you and will not be r.
Jos 2: 22 and r without finding them.
4: 18 waters of the Jordan r to their place
6: 11 Then the people r to camp
6: 14 around the city once and r
7: 3 When they r to Joshua, they said,
8: 24 all the Israelites r to Ai
10: 15 Joshua r with all Israel to the camp
10: 21 The whole army then r safely
10: 43 Joshua r with all Israel to the camp
18: 9 r to Joshua in the camp at Shiloh.
22: 32 and the leaders r to Canaan
Jdg 2: 19 people r to ways even more corrupt
Jdg 7: 15 He r to the camp of Israel
8: 13 son of Joash then r from the battle
11: 34 When Jephthah r to his home
11: 39 she r to her father and he did to her
14: 2 When he r, he said to his father
15: 19 his strength r and he revived.
16: 18 of the Philistines r with the silver
17: 3 When he r the eleven hundred
17: 4 So he r the silver to his mother,
18: 8 When they r to Zorah and Eshtaol,
21: 14 So the Benjamites r at that time
21: 23 Then they r to their inheritance
Ru 1: 22 Naomi r from Moab accompanied
1Sa 4: 3 When the soldiers r to camp,
6: 16 and then r that same day to Ekron.
6: 21 "The Philistines have r the ark
17: 53 When the Israelites r
17: 57 David r from killing the Philistine,
20: 38 The boy picked up the arrow and r
24: 1 After Saul r from pursuing
24: 22 Then Saul r home, but David
26: 25 went on his way, and Saul r home.
27: 9 Then he r to Achish.
2Sa 1: 1 David r from defeating
2: 30 Then Joab r from pursuing Abner
3: 22 Just then David's men and Joab r
3: 27 Now when Abner r to Hebron,
6: 20 When David r home
8: 13 famous after he r from striking
10: 14 So Joab r from fighting
12: 31 and his entire army r to Jerusalem.
17: 20 so they r to Jerusalem.
19: 15 Then the king r and went as far
19: 24 left until the day he r safely.
19: 39 and Barzillai r to his home.
20: 3 When David r to his palace
23: 10 The troops r to Eleazar,
1Ki 2: 41 from Jerusalem to Gath and had r,
3: 15 He r to Jerusalem, stood
10: 13 and r with her retinue to her own
10: 22 every three years it r carrying gold,
12: 2 fled from King Solomon), he r
12: 12 and all the people r to Rehoboam,
12: 20 heard that Jeroboam had r,
13: 19 the man of God r with him and ate
14: 28 and afterward they r them
17: 22 and the boy's life r to him,
2Ki 1: 5 When the messengers r to the king,
2: 18 When they r to Elisha, who was
2: 25 and from there r to Samaria.
3: 27 they withdrew and r
4: 38 Elisha r to Gilgal and there was
4: 39 When he r, he cut them up
6: 23 and they r to their master.
7: 8 They r and entered another tent
7: 15 So the messengers r and reported
8: 14 Then Hazael left Elisha and r
8: 29 so King Joram r to Jezreel
9: 15 but King Joram had r to Jezreel
14: 14 took hostages and r to Samaria.
16: 11 and finished it before King Ahaz r.
19: 36 He r to Nineveh and stayed there.
1Ch 16: 43 David r home to bless his family.
20: 3 and his entire army r to Jerusalem.
2Ch 9: 12 and r with her retinue to her own
9: 21 Once every three years it r,
10: 2 fled from King Solomon), he r
10: 12 and all the people r to Rehoboam,
12: 11 and afterward they r them
14: 15 Then they r to Jerusalem.
19: 1 king of Judah r safely to his palace
20: 27 Jerusalem r joyfully to Jerusalem,
22: 6 so he r to Jezreel to recover
25: 14 When Amaziah r
25: 24 and the hostages, and r to Samaria.
28: 9 the army when it r to Samaria.
28: 15 the City of Palms, and r to Samaria
31: 1 the Israelites r to their own towns
Ezr 2: 1 to Babylon (they r to Jerusalem
3: 8 all who had r from the captivity
6: 5 are to be r to their places
6: 21 So the Israelites who had r
8: 35 Then the exiles who had r
Ne 4: 15 we all r to the wall, each
7: 6 Babylon had taken captive (they r
8: 17 The whole company that had r
12: 1 Levites who r with Zerubbabel son
13: 6 king of Babylon I had r to the king.
Est 6: 12 Afterward Mordecai r
7: 8 the king r from the palace garden
Ps 35: 13 When my prayers r
Isa 9: 13 the people have not r
37: 37 He r to Nineveh and stayed there.
Jer 11: 10 They have r to the sins
19: 14 Jeremiah then r from Topheth,
Da 2: 17 Then Daniel r to his house
4: 36 splendor were r to me for the glory
6: 18 Then the king r to his palace
Am 4: 6 yet you have not r to me,"
4: 8 yet you have not r to me,"
4: 9 yet you have not r to me,"
4: 10 yet you have not r to me,"
4: 11 yet you have not r to me,"
Zec 4: 1 the angel who talked with me r
Mt 2: 12 they r to their country
4: 12 put in prison, he r to Galilee.
25: 19 the master of those servants r
25: 27 when I r I would have received it
26: 40 Then he r to his disciples
26: 45 Then he r to the disciples
27: 3 and r the thirty silver coins
Mk 14: 37 Then he r to his disciples
16: 13 These r and reported it to the rest;
Lk 1: 23 service was completed, he r home.
1: 56 three months and then r home.
2: 20 The shepherds r, glorifying
2: 39 they r to Galilee to their own town
4: 1 r from the Jordan and was led
4: 14 Jesus r to Galilee in the power
7: 10 Then the men who had been sent r
8: 40 when Jesus r, a crowd welcomed
8: 55 "My child, get up!" Her spirit r,
9: 10 When the apostles r, they reported
10: 17 The seventy-two r with joy
19: 15 made king, however, and r home.
24: 33 and r at once to Jerusalem.
24: 52 and r to Jerusalem with great joy.
Jn 4: 27 Just then his disciples r
13: 12 on his clothes and r to his place.
20: 17 for I have not yet r to the Father.
Ac 1: 12 Then they r to Jerusalem
8: 25 Peter and John r to Jerusalem,
12: 25 they r from Jerusalem, taking
14: 21 Then they r to Lystra, Iconium
21: 6 aboard the ship, and they r home.
22: 17 "When I r to Jerusalem
23: 32 while they r to the barracks.
Ro 14: 9 and r to life so that he might be
Gal 1: 17 into Arabia and later r
1Pe 2: 25 now you have r to the Shepherd

RETURNING (RETURN)

Ge 48: 7 As I was r from Paddan,
1Sa 7: 3 "If you are r to the LORD
11: 5 Just then Saul was r from the fields,
18: 6 When the men were r home
2Sa 20: 22 from the city, each r to his home.
Ecc 1: 6 ever r on its course.
Mic 2: 8 like men r from battle.
Mk 14: 41 R the third time, he said to them,
Lk 2: 43 while his parents were r home,
Jn 13: 3 come from God and was r to God;
20: 17 'I am r to my Father and your
Heb 7: 1 He met Abraham r from the defeat

RETURNS (RETURN)

Lev 22: 13 she r to live in her father's house
Pr 3: 14 and yields better r than gold.
26: 11 As a dog r to its vomit,
Ecc 12: 7 and the spirit r to God who gave it.
12: 7 the dust r to the ground it came
Isa 52: 8 When the LORD r to Zion,
Eze 18: 7 r what he took in pledge for a loan.
33: 15 r what he has stolen, follows
Mt 24: 46 finds him doing so when he r.
Lk 12: 43 master finds doing so when he r.
2Pe 2: 22 "A dog r to its vomit," and,

REU

Ge 11: 18 he became the father of R.
11: 19 after he became the father of R,
11: 20 When R had lived 32 years,
11: 21 R lived 207 years and had other
1Ch 1: 25 Eber, Peleg, R, Serug, Nahor,
Lk 3: 35 the son of Serug, the son of R,

REUBEN (REUBENITE REUBENITES)

Ge 29: 32 She named him *R*, for she said,
30: 14 *R* went out into the fields
35: 22 *R* went in and slept
35: 23 The sons of Leah: *R* the firstborn
37: 21 When *R* heard this, he tried
37: 22 *R* said this to rescue him
37: 29 When *R* returned to the cistern
42: 22 *R* replied, "Didn't I tell you not
42: 37 is against me!" Then *R* said
46: 8 to Egypt: *R* the firstborn of Jacob.
46: 9 The sons of *R*: Hanoch, Pallu,
48: 5 just as *R* and Simeon are mine.
49: 3 "*R*, you are my firstborn,
Ex 1: 2 each with his family: *R*, Simeon,
6: 14 The sons of *R* the firstborn son
6: 14 These were the clans of *R*.
Nu 1: 5 from *R*, Elizur son of Shedeur;
1: 20 descendants of *R* the firstborn son
1: 21 from the tribe of *R* was 46,500.
2: 10 camp of *R* under their standard.
2: 10 of the people of *R* is Elizur son
2: 16 the men assigned to the camp of *R*,
7: 30 the leader of the people of *R*,
10: 18 of the camp of *R* went next,
13: 4 from the tribe of *R*, Shammua son
26: 5 descendants of *R*, the firstborn son
26: 7 These were the clans of *R*;
34: 14 the families of the tribe of *R*,
Dt 27: 13 *R*, Gad, Asher, Zebulun, Dan
33: 6 "Let *R* live and not die,
Jos 4: 12 men of *R*, Gad and the half-tribe
13: 15 Moses had given to the tribe of *R*,
15: 6 to the Stone of Bohan son of *R*.
18: 7 *R* and the half-tribe
18: 17 to the Stone of Bohan son of *R*.
20: 8 on the plateau in the tribe of *R*,
21: 7 towns from the tribes of *R*,
21: 36 from the tribe of *R*, Bezer, Jahaz,
22: 13 to the land of Gilead—to *R*,
22: 15 When they went to Gilead—to *R*,
22: 21 Then *R*, Gad and the half-tribe
22: 30 heard what *R*, Gad and Manasseh
22: 31 said to *R*, Gad and Manasseh,
Jdg 5: 15 In the districts of *R*
5: 16 In the districts of *R*
2Ki 10: 33 *R* and Manasseh), from Aroer
1Ch 2: 1 *R*, Simeon, Levi, Judah, Issachar,
5: 1 The sons of *R* the firstborn
5: 3 the sons of *R* the firstborn of Israel:
6: 63 towns from the tribes of *R*,
6: 78 from the tribe of *R*
12: 37 men of *R*, Gad and the half-tribe
Eze 48: 6 "*R* will have one portion; it will
48: 7 the territory of *R* from east to west.
48: 31 the north side will be the gate of *R*,
Rev 7: 5 from the tribe of *R* 12,000,

REUBENITE (REUBEN)

Dt 11: 6 and Abiram, sons of Eliab the *R*,
1Ch 11: 42 son of Shiza the *R*, who was chief

REUBENITES (REUBEN)

Nu 16: 1 and certain *R*— Dathan
32: 1 *R* and Gadites, who had very large
32: 6 Moses said to the Gadites and *R*,
32: 25 The Gadites and *R* said to Moses,
32: 29 and *R*, every man armed for battle,
32: 31 The Gadites and *R* answered,
32: 33 the *R* and the half-tribe
32: 37 And the *R* rebuilt Heshbon,
Dt 3: 12 I gave the *R* and the Gadites
3: 16 But to the *R* and the Gadites I gave
4: 43 for the *R*; Ramoth in Gilead,
29: 8 gave it as an inheritance to the *R*,
Jos 1: 12 But to the *R*, the Gadites
12: 6 the LORD gave their land to the *R*,
13: 8 the *R* and the Gadites had received
13: 23 boundary of the *R* was the bank
13: 23 were the inheritance of the *R*,
22: 1 Then Joshua summoned the *R*,
22: 9 *R*, the Gadites and the half-tribe
22: 10 in the land of Canaan, the *R*,
22: 25 you *R* and Gadites! You have no
22: 32 from their meeting with the *R*
22: 33 devastate the country where the *R*
22: 34 *R* and the Gadites gave the altar
1Ch 5: 6 Beerah was a leader of the *R*.
5: 18 *R*, the Gadites and the half-tribe
5: 26 king of Assyria), who took the *R*,
11: 42 who was chief of the *R*,
26: 32 them in charge of the *R*,
27: 16 over the *R*: Eliezer son of Zicri;

REUEL

Ge 36: 4 Basemath bore *R*, and Oholibamah
36: 10 *R*, the son of Esau's wife Basemath
36: 13 The sons of *R*: Nahath, Zerah,
36: 17 of Esau's son *R*: Chiefs Nahath,
36: 17 were the chiefs descended from *R*
Ex 2: 18 the girls returned to *R* their father,
Nu 10: 29 to Hobab son of *R* the Midianite,
1Ch 1: 35 *R*, Jeush, Jalam and Korah.
1: 37 The sons of *R*: Nahath, Zerah,
9: 8 the son of *R*, the son of Ibnijah.

REUMAH

Ge 22: 24 whose name was *R*, also had sons:

REUNITED (UNITE)

Hos 1: 11 and the people of Israel will be *r*,

REVEAL (REVEALED REVEALER REVEALING REVEALS REVELATION REVELATIONS)

Nu 12: 6 I *r* myself to him in visions,
1Sa 2: 27 'Did I not clearly *r* myself
Da 2: 11 No one can *r* it to the king
2: 47 for you were able to *r* this mystery
Mt 11: 27 to whom the Son chooses to *r* him.
Lk 10: 22 to whom the Son chooses to *r* him
Gal 1: 16 was pleased to *r* his Son in me

REVEALED (REVEAL)

Ge 35: 7 it was there that God *r* himself
41: 25 God has *r* to Pharaoh what he is
Dt 29: 29 but the things *r* belong to us
1Sa 3: 7 of the LORD had not yet been *r*
3: 21 and there he *r* himself to Samuel
9: 15 the LORD had *r* this to Samuel:
2Sa 7: 27 you have *r* this to your servant,
2Ki 8: 10 the LORD has *r* to me that he will
1Ch 17: 25 have *r* to your servant that you will
Est 2: 10 Esther had not *r* her nationality
Ps 98: 2 *r* his righteousness to the nations.
147: 19 He has *r* his word to Jacob,
Isa 22: 14 The LORD Almighty has *r* this
40: 5 the glory of the LORD will be *r*,
43: 12 I have *r* and saved and proclaimed
53: 1 the arm of the LORD been *r*?
56: 1 my righteousness will soon be *r*.
65: 1 I *r* myself to those who did not ask
Jer 11: 18 Because the LORD *r* their plot
38: 21 this is what the LORD has *r* to me:
Eze 20: 5 and *r* myself to them in Egypt.
20: 9 and in whose sight I had *r* myself
Da 2: 19 During the night the mystery was *r*
2: 30 this mystery has been *r* to me,
Hos 7: 1 and the crimes of Samaria *r*.
Mt 11: 25 and *r* them to little children.
16: 17 for this was not *r* to you by man,
Lk 2: 26 It had been *r* to him
2: 35 thoughts of many hearts will be *r*.
10: 21 and *r* them to little children.
17: 30 this on the day the Son of Man is *r*.
Jn 1: 31 with water was that he might be *r*
2: 11 *r* his glory, and his disciples put
12: 38 the arm of the Lord been *r*?"
17: 6 "I have *r* you to those whom you
Ro 1: 17 a righteousness from God is *r*,
1: 18 of God is being *r* from heaven
2: 5 his righteous judgment will be *r*.
8: 18 with the glory that will be *r* in us.
8: 19 for the sons of God to be *r*.
10: 20 I *r* myself to those who did not ask
16: 26 but now *r* and made known
1Co 1: 7 for our Lord Jesus Christ to be *r*.
2: 10 but God has *r* it to us by his Spirit.
3: 13 It will be *r* with fire, and the fire
2Co 4: 10 of Jesus may also be *r* in our body.
4: 11 so that his life may be *r*
Gal 3: 23 locked up until faith should be *r*.
Eph 3: 5 as it has now been *r* by the Spirit
2Th 1: 7 happen when the Lord Jesus is *r*
2: 3 and the man of lawlessness is *r*,
2Th 2: 6 so that he may be *r*
2: 8 And then the lawless one will be *r*,
2Ti 1: 10 now been *r* through the appearing
1Pe 1: 5 ready to be *r* in the last time.
1: 7 and honor when Jesus Christ is *r*.
1: 12 It was *r* to them that they were not
1: 13 you when Jesus Christ is *r*.
1: 20 but was *r* in these last times
4: 13 overjoyed when his glory is *r*.
5: 1 also will share in the glory to be *r*:
Rev 15: 4 for your righteous acts have been *r*

REVEALER (REVEAL)

Da 2: 29 *r* of mysteries showed you what is
2: 47 Lord of kings and a *r* of mysteries,

REVEALING (REVEAL)

Eze 21: 24 *r* your sins in all that you do—
Am 3: 7 nothing without *r* his plan

REVEALS (REVEAL)

Nu 23: 3 Whatever he *r* to me I will tell you
Job 12: 22 He *r* the deep things of darkness
Da 2: 22 He *r* deep and hidden things;
2: 28 a God in heaven who *r* mysteries.
Am 4: 13 and *r* his thoughts to man,

REVELATION (REVEAL)

2Sa 7: 17 David all the words of this entire *r*.
1Ch 17: 15 David all the words of this entire *r*.
Pr 29: 18 Where there is no *r*, the people cast
Da 10: 1 a *r* was given to Daniel (who was
Hab 2: 2 "Write down the *r*
2: 3 For the *r* awaits an appointed time;
Lk 2: 32 a light for *r* to the Gentiles
Ro 16: 25 according to the *r*
1Co 14: 6 I bring you some *r* or knowledge
14: 26 a *r*, a tongue or an interpretation.
14: 30 And if a *r* comes to someone who is
Gal 1: 12 I received it by *r* from Jesus Christ.
2: 2 I went in response to a *r*
Eph 1: 17 you the Spirit of wisdom and *r*,
3: 3 mystery made known to me by *r*,
Rev 1: 1 *r* of Jesus Christ, which God gave

REVELATIONS (REVEAL)

2Co 12: 1 on to visions and *r* from the Lord.
12: 7 of these surpassingly great *r*.

REVELED (REVELRY)

Ne 9: 25 they *r* in your great goodness.

REVELERS (REVELRY)

Isa 5: 14 with all their brawlers and *r*.
24: 8 the noise of the *r* has stopped,
Jer 15: 17 I never sat in the company of *r*,

REVELING (REVELRY)

1Sa 30: 16 and *r* because of the great amount
Isa 23: 12 He said, "No more of your *r*,
2Pe 2: 13 *r* in their pleasures while they feast

REVELRY (REVELED REVELERS REVELING)

Ex 32: 6 drink and got up to indulge in *r*.
Isa 22: 2 O city of tumult and *r*?
22: 13 But see, there is joy and *r*,
23: 7 Is this your city of *r*,
32: 13 and for this city of *r*.
1Co 10: 7 and got up to indulge in pagan *r*."

REVENGE (VENGEANCE)

Lev 19: 18 " 'Do not seek *r* or bear a grudge
Jdg 15: 7 I won't stop until I get my *r* on you
16: 28 me with one blow get *r*
1Sa 18: 25 to take *r* on his enemies.' "
Ps 44: 16 of the enemy, who is bent on *r*.
Pr 6: 34 show no mercy when he takes *r*.
Jer 20: 10 and take our *r* on him."
Eze 24: 8 To stir up wrath and take *r*
25: 12 'Because Edom took *r* on the house
25: 15 took *r* with malice in their hearts,
Ro 12: 19 Do not take *r*, my friends,

REVENUE (REVENUES)

Isa 23: 3 of the Nile was the *r* of Tyre,
33: 18 Where is the one who took the *r*?
Ro 13: 7 if *r*, then *r*; if respect, then respect;

REVENUES (REVENUE)

1Ki 10: 15 not including the *r* from merchants
2Ch 9: 14 not including the *r* brought
Ezr 4: 13 and the royal *r* will suffer.
6: 8 from the *r* of Trans-Euphrates,

REVERE (REVERED REVERENCE REVERENT REVERING)

Lev 19: 32 for the elderly and *r* your God.
Dt 4: 10 so that they may learn to *r* me
13: 4 must follow, and him you must *r*.
14: 23 to *r* the LORD your God always.
17: 19 learn to *r* the LORD his God
28: 58 and do not *r* this glorious
Job 37: 24 Therefore, men *r* him,
Ps 22: 23 *R* him, all you descendants
33: 8 let all the people of the world *r* him
102: 15 of the earth will *r* your glory.
Ecc 3: 14 God does it, so men will *r* him.
Isa 25: 3 cities of ruthless nations will *r* you.
59: 19 of the sun, they will *r* his glory.
63: 17 hearts so we do not *r* you?
Jer 10: 7 Who should not *r* you,
Hos 10: 3 because we did not *r* the LORD.
Mal 4: 2 But for you who *r* my name,

REVERED (REVERE)

Jos 4: 14 of his life, just as they had *r* Moses.
4: 14 they *r* him all the days of his life,
2Ki 4: 1 and you know that he *r* the LORD.
Mal 2: 5 called for reverence and he *r* me

REVERENCE (REVERE)

Lev 19: 30 and have *r* for my sanctuary.
26: 2 and have *r* for my sanctuary.
Jos 5: 14 facedown to the ground in *r*,
Ne 5: 15 of *r* for God I did not act like that.
Ps 5: 7 in *r* will I bow down
Jer 44: 10 humbled themselves or shown *r*,
Da 6: 26 people must fear and *r* the God
Mal 2: 5 this called for *r* and he revered me
Ac 10: 25 met him and fell at his feet in *r*.
2Co 7: 1 perfecting holiness out of *r* for God
Eph 5: 21 to one another out of *r* for Christ.
Col 3: 22 of heart and *r* for the Lord.
Heb 12: 28 so worship God acceptably with *r*
1Pe 3: 2 when they see the purity and *r*
Rev 11: 18 and those who *r* your name,

REVERENT (REVERE)

Ecc 8: 12 with God-fearing men, who are *r*
Tit 2: 3 women to be *r* in the way they live,
Heb 5: 7 because of his *r* submission.
1Pe 1: 17 as strangers here in *r* fear.

REVERING (REVERE)

Dt 8: 6 walking in his ways and *r* him.
Ne 1: 11 who delight in *r* your name.

REVERSE (REVERSED)

Isa 43: 13 When I act, who can *r* it?''

REVERSED (REVERSE)

Eze 7: 13 the whole crowd will not be *r*.

REVERT

Lev 27: 24 the Year of Jubilee the field will *r*
1Ki 12: 26 ''The kingdom will now likely *r*
Eze 46: 17 then it will *r* to the prince.

REVIEW

Isa 43: 26 *R* the past for me,

REVILE (REVILED REVILES)

Ps 10: 13 Why does the wicked man *r* God?
44: 16 of those who reproach and *r* me,
55: 3 and *r* me in their anger.
74: 10 Will the foe *r* your name forever?
Ecc 10: 20 *r* the king even in your thoughts,

REVILED (REVILE)

Ps 74: 18 foolish people have *r* your name.

REVILES (REVILE)

Ps 10: 3 the greedy and *r* the LORD.

REVIVE (REVIVED REVIVING)

Ps 80: 18 *r* us, and we will call on your name.
85: 6 Will you not *r* us again,
Isa 57: 15 and to *r* the heart of the contrite.
57: 15 to *r* the spirit of the lowly
Hos 6: 2 After two days he will *r* us;

REVIVED (REVIVE)

Ge 45: 27 the spirit of their father Jacob *r*.
Jdg 15: 19 his strength returned and he *r*.
1Sa 30: 12 and was *r*, for he had not eaten any

REVIVING (REVIVE)

Ps 19: 7 *r* the soul.

REVOKE (REVOKED REVOKING)

Ps 132: 11 a sure oath that he will not *r*:

REVOKED (REVOKE)

Est 8: 8 and sealed with his ring can be *r*.''
Isa 45: 23 a word that will not be *r*:
Zec 11: 11 It was *r* on that day,

REVOKING (REVOKE)

Zec 11: 10 *r* the covenant I had made

REVOLT (REVOLTED REVOLUTIONS)

Ezr 4: 19 that this city has a long history of *r*
Ne 6: 6 and the Jews are plotting to *r*,
Isa 59: 13 fomenting oppression and *r*,
Eze 2: 3 and their fathers have been in *r*
20: 38 I will purge you of those who *r*
Ac 5: 37 and led a band of people in *r*.
21: 38 you the Egyptian who started a *r*

REVOLTED (REVOLT)

Jdg 9: 18 you have *r* against my father's
2Ki 8: 22 Libnah *r* at the same time.
2Ch 21: 10 Libnah *r* at the same time,
Isa 31: 6 to him you have so greatly *r* against

REVOLUTIONS (REVOLT)

Lk 21: 9 When you hear of wars and *r*,

REWARD (REWARDED REWARDING REWARDS)

Ge 15: 1 your very great *r*.''
Nu 22: 17 because I will *r* you handsomely
22: 37 Am I really not able to *r* you?''
24: 11 I said I would *r* you handsomely,
1Sa 24: 19 May the LORD *r* you well
2Sa 4: 10 That was the *r* I gave him
18: 22 any news that will bring you a *r*.''
19: 36 but why should the king *r* me
Job 17: 5 If a man denounces his friends for *r*
34: 33 Should God then *r* you
Ps 17: 14 of this world whose *r* is in this life.
19: 11 in keeping them there is great *r*.
62: 12 Surely you will *r* each person
127: 3 children a *r* from him.
Pr 9: 12 are wise, your wisdom will *r* you;
11: 18 sows righteousness reaps a sure *r*.
13: 21 prosperity is the *r* of the righteous.
19: 17 he will *r* him for what he has done.
25: 22 and the LORD will *r* you.
31: 31 Give her the *r* she has earned,
Ecc 2: 10 and this was the *r* for all my labor.
9: 5 they have no further *r*,
Isa 40: 10 See, his *r* is with him,
45: 13 but not for a price or *r*,
49: 4 and my *r* is with my God.''
61: 8 In my faithfulness I will *r* them
62: 11 See, his *r* is with him,
Jer 17: 10 to *r* a man according to his conduct
32: 19 you *r* everyone according
Eze 29: 18 army got no *r* from the campaign
29: 20 as a *r* for his efforts because he
Mt 5: 12 because great is your *r* in heaven,
5: 46 who love you, what *r* will you get?
6: 1 you will have no *r*
6: 2 they have received their *r* in full.
6: 4 done in secret, will *r* you.
6: 5 they have received their *r* in full.
6: 6 done in secret, will *r* you.
6: 16 they have received their *r* in full.
6: 18 done in secret, will *r* you.
10: 41 a prophet will receive a prophet's *r*,
10: 41 will receive a righteous man's *r*.
10: 42 he will certainly not lose his *r*.''
16: 27 and then he will *r* each person
Mk 9: 41 Christ will certainly not lose his *r*.
Lk 6: 23 because great is your *r* in heaven.
6: 35 Then your *r* will be great,
Ac 1: 18 (With the *r* he got
1Co 3: 14 built survives, he will receive his *r*.
9: 17 I have a *r*; if not voluntarily,
9: 18 What then is my *r*? Just this:
Eph 6: 8 know that the Lord will *r* everyone
Col 3: 24 an inheritance from the Lord as a *r*.
Heb 11: 26 he was looking ahead to his *r*.
Rev 22: 12 I am coming soon! My *r* is with me

REWARDED (REWARD)

Ge 30: 18 ''God has *r* me for giving my
Nu 24: 11 LORD has kept you from being *r*.''
Ru 2: 12 May you be richly *r* by the LORD,
2Sa 22: 21 of my hands he has *r* me.
22: 25 The LORD has *r* me according
2Ch 15: 7 for your work will be *r*.''
Ps 18: 20 of my hands he has *r* me.
18: 24 The LORD has *r* me according
58: 11 ''Surely the righteous still are *r*;
Pr 13: 13 he who respects a command is *r*.
14: 14 and the good man *r* for his.
Jer 31: 16 for your work will be *r*,''
1Co 3: 8 and each will be *r* according
Heb 10: 35 your confidence; it will be richly *r*.
2Jn : 8 but that you may be *r* fully.

REWARDING (REWARD)

Rev 11: 18 for *r* your servants the prophets

REWARDS (REWARD)

1Sa 26: 23 The LORD *r* every man
Pr 12: 14 the work of his hands *r* him.
Da 2: 6 you will receive from me gifts and *r*
5: 17 and give your *r* to someone else.
Heb 11: 6 that he *r* those who earnestly seek

REZEPH

2Ki 19: 12 *R* and the people of Eden who
Isa 37: 12 *R* and the people of Eden who

REZIN (REZIN'S)

2Ki 15: 37 began to send *R* king of Aram
16: 5 *R* king of Aram and Pekah son
16: 6 *R* king of Aram recovered Elath
16: 9 to Kir and put *R* to death.
Ezr 2: 48 Gahar, Reaiah, *R*, Nekoda,
Ne 7: 50 Gaher, Reaiah, *R*, Nekoda,
Isa 7: 1 King *R* of Aram and Pekah son
7: 4 of the fierce anger of *R* and Aram
7: 8 the head of Damascus is only *R*.
8: 6 and rejoices over *R*

REZIN'S (REZIN)

Isa 9: 11 the LORD has strengthened *R* foes

REZON

1Ki 11: 23 Solomon another adversary, *R* son
11: 25 So *R* ruled in Aram and was hostile
11: 25 *R* was Israel's adversary as long

RHEGIUM

Ac 28: 13 there we set sail and arrived at *R*.

RHESA

Lk 3: 27 the son of Joanan, the son of *R*,

RHODA

Ac 12: 13 and a servant girl named *R* came

RHODES

Eze 27: 15 '' 'The men of *R* traded with you,
Ac 21: 1 The next day we went to *R*

RIB (RIBS)

Ge 2: 22 woman from the *r* he had taken out

RIBAI

2Sa 23: 29 Ithai son of *R* from Gibeah
1Ch 11: 31 Ithai son of *R* from Gibeah

RIBBON

SS 4: 3 Your lips are like a scarlet *r*;

RIBLAH

Nu 34: 11 go down from Shepham to *R*
2Ki 23: 33 him in chains at *R* in the land
25: 6 taken to the king of Babylon at *R*,
25: 20 them to the king of Babylon at *R*.
25: 21 There at *R*, in the land of Hamath,
Jer 39: 5 king of Babylon at *R* in the land
39: 6 There at *R* the king
52: 9 the king of Babylon at *R* in the land
52: 10 There at *R* the king
52: 26 them to the king of Babylon at *R*.
52: 27 There at *R*, in the land of Hamath,

RIBS (RIB)

Ge 2: 21 he took one of the man's *r*
Da 7: 5 and it had three *r* in its mouth

RICH (ENRICH ENRICHED RICHER RICHES RICHEST RICHNESS)

Ge 14: 23 able to say, 'I made Abram *r*.'
26: 13 The man became *r*, and his wealth
49: 20 "Asher's food will be *r*;
Ex 30: 15 The *r* are not to give more
Lev 25: 47 resident among you becomes *r*
Ru 3: 10 after the younger men, whether *r*
2Sa 12: 1 men in a certain town, one *r*
12: 2 The *r* man had a very large number
12: 4 but the *r* man refrained
12: 4 "Now a traveler came to the *r* man,
1Ch 4: 40 They found *r*, good pasture,
Job 15: 29 will no longer be *r* and his wealth
21: 24 his bones *r* with marrow.
34: 19 does not favor the *r* over the poor,
Ps 21: 3 welcomed him with *r* blessings
22: 29 All the *r* of the earth will feast
49: 2 *r* and poor alike:
49: 16 overawed when a man grows *r*,
76: 4 than mountains *r* with game.
145: 8 slow to anger and *r* in love.
Pr 10: 15 of the *r* is their fortified city,
13: 7 One man pretends to be *r*,
14: 20 but the *r* have many friends.
18: 11 of the *r* is their fortified city;
18: 23 but a *r* man answers harshly.
21: 17 loves wine and oil will never be *r*.
22: 2 *R* and poor have this in common:
22: 7 The *r* rule over the poor,
22: 16 and he who gives gifts to the *r*—
23: 4 Do not wear yourself out to get *r*;
24: 25 and *r* blessing will come upon them
28: 6 than a *r* man whose ways are
28: 11 A *r* man may be wise
28: 20 to get *r* will not go unpunished.
28: 22 A stingy man is eager to get *r*
Ecc 5: 12 but the abundance of a *r* man
10: 6 while the *r* occupy the low ones.
10: 20 or curse the *r* in your bedroom,
Isa 5: 17 among the ruins of the *r*.
25: 6 a feast of *r* food for all peoples,
30: 23 comes from the land will be *r*
33: 6 a *r* store of salvation and wisdom
53: 9 and with the *r* in his death,
Jer 2: 7 land to eat its fruit and *r* produce.
5: 27 they have become *r* and powerful
9: 23 or the *r* man boast of his riches,
49: 19 thickets to a *r* pastureland,
50: 44 thickets to a *r* pastureland,
51: 13 and are *r* in treasures,
Eze 34: 14 in a *r* pasture on the mountains
38: 12 *r* in livestock and goods, living
Hos 12: 8 I am very *r*; I have become wealthy
Mic 2: 8 You strip off the *r* robe
6: 12 Her *r* men are violent;
Zec 3: 4 and I will put *r* garments on you."
11: 3 their *r* pastures are destroyed!
11: 5 'Praise the LORD, I am *r*!'
Mt 19: 23 it is hard for a *r* man
19: 24 for a *r* man to enter the kingdom
27: 57 there came a *r* man
Mk 10: 23 is for the *r* to enter the kingdom
10: 25 for a *r* man to enter the kingdom
12: 41 Many *r* people threw
Lk 1: 53 but has sent the *r* away empty.
6: 24 "But woe to you who are *r*,
12: 16 of a certain *r* man produced a good
12: 21 for himself but is not *r* toward God
14: 12 or your *r* neighbors; if you do,
Lk 16: 1 "There was a *r* man whose
16: 19 "There was a *r* man who was
16: 21 fell from the *r* man's table.
16: 22 The *r* man also died and was buried
18: 24 is for the *r* to enter the kingdom
18: 25 for a *r* man to enter the kingdom
21: 1 Jesus saw the *r* putting their gifts
1Co 4: 8 Already you have become *r*!
2Co 6: 10 yet making many *r*; having nothing
8: 2 poverty welled up in *r* generosity.
8: 9 he was *r*, yet for your sakes he
8: 9 his poverty might become *r*.
9: 11 You will be made *r* in every way
Eph 2: 4 love for us, God, who is *r* in mercy,
1Ti 6: 9 want to get *r* fall into temptation
6: 17 Command those who are *r*
6: 18 to do good, to be *r* in good deeds,
Jas 1: 10 the one who is *r* should take pride
1: 11 the *r* man will fade away
2: 5 the eyes of the world to be *r* in faith
2: 6 Is it not the *r* who are exploiting
5: 1 you *r* people, weep and wail
2Pe 1: 11 and you will receive a *r* welcome
Rev 2: 9 and your poverty—yet you are *r*!
3: 17 'I am *r*; I have acquired wealth
3: 18 you can become *r*; and white
6: 15 the generals, the *r*, the mighty,
13: 16 small and great, *r* and poor,
18: 3 the merchants of the earth grew *r*
18: 19 became *r* through her wealth!

RICHER (RICH)

Da 11: 2 who will be far *r* than all the others.

RICHES (RICH)

1Ki 3: 13 you have not asked for—both *r*
10: 23 King Solomon was greater in *r*
2Ch 1: 11 *r* or honor, nor for the death
1: 12 also give you wealth, *r* and honor,
9: 22 King Solomon was greater in *r*
32: 27 Hezekiah had very great *r*
32: 29 for God had given him very great *r*.
Job 20: 15 He will spit out the *r* he swallowed;
36: 18 that no one entices you by *r*;
Ps 49: 6 and boast of their great *r*?
49: 12 despite his *r*, does not endure;
49: 20 who has *r* without understanding
62: 10 though your *r* increase,
112: 3 Wealth and *r* are in his house,
119: 14 as one rejoices in great *r*.
Pr 3: 16 in her left hand are *r* and honor.
8: 18 With me are *r* and honor,
11: 28 Whoever trusts in his *r* will fall,
13: 8 A man's *r* may ransom his life,
22: 1 is more desirable than great *r*;
23: 5 but a glance at *r*, and they are gone,
27: 24 for *r* do not endure forever,
30: 8 give me neither poverty nor *r*,
Isa 10: 3 Where will you leave your *r*?
30: 6 the envoys carry their *r*
45: 3 *r* stored in secret places,
60: 5 to you the *r* of the nations will
61: 6 and in their *r* you will boast.
Jer 9: 23 or the rich man boast of his *r*,
17: 11 is the man who gains *r*
48: 7 Since you trust in your deeds and *r*,
49: 4 you trust in your *r* and say,
Da 11: 43 and silver and all the *r* of Egypt,
Joel 2: 22 fig tree and the vine yield their *r*.
Lk 8: 14 *r* and pleasures, and they do not
16: 11 who will trust you with true *r*?
Ro 2: 4 contempt for the *r* of his kindness,
9: 23 to make the *r* of his glory known
11: 12 But if their transgression means *r*
11: 12 how much greater *r* will their
11: 12 their loss means *r* for the Gentiles,
11: 33 the depth of the *r* of the wisdom
Eph 1: 7 in accordance with the *r*
1: 18 the *r* of his glorious inheritance
2: 7 he might show the incomparable *r*
3: 8 to the Gentiles the unsearchable *r*
3: 16 of his glorious *r* he may strengthen
Php 4: 19 to his glorious *r* in Christ Jesus.
Col 1: 27 among the Gentiles the glorious *r*
2: 2 so that they may have the full *r*
Rev 18: 14 All your *r* and splendor have

RICHEST (RICH)

Ps 63: 5 with the *r* of foods;
Isa 55: 2 and your soul will delight in the *r*
Da 11: 24 When the *r* provinces feel secure,

RICHNESS (RICH)

Ge 27: 28 and of earth's *r*—
27: 39 away from the earth's *r*,

RID

Ge 21: 10 "Get *r* of that slave woman
35: 2 "Get *r* of the foreign gods you have
Ex 8: 9 your houses may be *r* of the frogs,
Lev 13: 58 that has been washed and is *r*
Nu 17: 5 and I will *r* myself of this constant
Jdg 9: 29 Then I would get *r* of him.
10: 16 Then they got *r* of the foreign gods
1Sa 1: 14 keep on getting drunk? Get *r*
7: 3 then *r* yourselves of the foreign
2Sa 4: 11 from your hand and *r* the earth
13: 13 Where could I get *r* of my disgrace?
14: 7 then we will get *r* of the heir as well
1Ki 15: 12 got *r* of all the idols his fathers had
22: 46 He *r* the land of the rest
2Ki 3: 2 He got *r* of the sacred stone
23: 24 Josiah got *r* of the mediums
2Ch 19: 3 for you have *r* the land
33: 15 He got *r* of the foreign gods
Eze 18: 31 *R* yourselves of all the offenses you
20: 7 get *r* of the vile images you have set
20: 8 they did not get *r* of the vile images
34: 25 and *r* the land of wild beasts
Zec 11: 8 In one month I got *r*
Lk 22: 2 for some way to get *r* of Jesus,
Ac 16: 37 want to get *r* of us quietly?
22: 22 and shouted, "*R* the earth of him!
1Co 5: 7 Get *r* of the old yeast that you may
Gal 4: 30 "Get *r* of the slave woman
Eph 4: 31 Get *r* of all bitterness, rage
Col 3: 8 But now you must *r* yourselves
Jas 1: 21 get *r* of all moral filth and the evil
1Pe 2: 1 *r* yourselves of all malice

RIDDEN (RIDE)

Nu 22: 30 which you have always *r*,
Est 6: 8 and a horse the king has *r*,
Mk 11: 2 tied there, which no one has ever *r*.
Lk 19: 30 tied there, which no one has ever *r*.

RIDDLE (RIDDLES)

Jdg 14: 12 "Let me tell you a *r*," Samson said
14: 13 "Tell us your *r*," they said.
14: 15 into explaining the *r* for us,
14: 16 You've given my people a *r*,
14: 17 She in turn explained the *r*
14: 18 you would not have solved my *r*."
14: 19 to those who had explained the *r*.
Ps 49: 4 with the harp I will expound my *r*:

RIDDLES (RIDDLE)

Nu 12: 8 clearly and not in *r*;
Pr 1: 6 the sayings and *r* of the wise.
Da 5: 12 explain *r* and solve difficult

RIDE (RIDDEN RIDER RIDERS RIDES RIDING RODE)

Ge 41: 43 He had him *r* in a chariot
Dt 32: 13 He made him *r* on the heights
Jdg 5: 10 "You who *r* on white donkeys,
2Sa 16: 2 are for the king's household to *r* on,
19: 26 have my donkey saddled and will *r*
2Ki 10: 16 he had him *r* along in his chariot.
Ps 45: 4 In your majesty *r* forth victoriously
66: 12 You let men *r* over our heads;
Isa 30: 16 'We will *r* off on swift horses.'
33: 21 No galley with oars will *r* them,
58: 14 I will cause you to *r* on the heights
Jer 6: 23 as they *r* on their horses;
50: 42 as they *r* on their horses;

RIDER (RIDE)

Ge 49: 17 so that its *r* tumbles backward.
Ex 15: 1 The horse and its *r*
15: 21 The horse and its *r*
Job 39: 18 she laughs at horse and *r*.
Jer 51: 21 with you I shatter horse and *r*,
Zec 12: 4 with panic and its *r* with madness,"
Rev 6: 2 was a white horse! Its *r* held a bow,

Rev 6: 4 Its *r* was given power to take peace
6: 5 Its *r* was holding a pair of scales
6: 8 pale horse! Its *r* was named Death,
19: 11 whose *r* is called Faithful and True.
19: 19 war against the *r* on the horse
19: 21 of the mouth of the *r* on the horse,

RIDERS (RIDE)

2Sa 1: 6 with the chariots and *r* almost
2Ki 18: 23 if you can put *r* on them.
Isa 21: 7 or *r* on camels,
21: 7 *r* on donkeys
36: 8 if you can put *r* on them.
Eze 39: 20 will eat your fill of horses and *r*,
Hag 2: 22 horses and their *r* will fall,
Rev 9: 17 *r* I saw in my vision looked like this
19: 18 their *r*, and the flesh of all people,

RIDES (RIDE)

Dt 33: 26 who *r* on the heavens to help you
Ps 68: 4 extol him who *r* on the clouds—
68: 33 to him who *r* the ancient skies
104: 3 and *r* on the wings of the wind.
Isa 19: 1 See, the LORD *r* on a swift cloud
Rev 17: 7 of the woman and of the beast she *r*

RIDGE (RIDGES)

Ge 48: 22 I give the *r* of land I took

RIDGES (RIDGE)

Ps 65: 10 and level its *r*;

RIDICULE (RIDICULED)

Dt 28: 37 and *r* to all the nations where
1Ki 9: 7 an object of *r* among all peoples.
2Ki 19: 4 has sent to *r* the living God,
2Ch 7: 20 an object of *r* among all peoples.
Job 19: 18 when I appear, they *r* me.
Ps 123: 4 We have endured much *r*
Isa 37: 4 has sent to *r* the living God,
Jer 24: 9 an object of *r* and cursing,
48: 26 let her be an object of *r*.
48: 27 Was not Israel the object of your *r?*
48: 39 Moab has become an object of *r*,
Mic 2: 4 In that day men will *r* you;
Hab 2: 6 all of them taunt him with *r*
Lk 14: 29 everyone who sees it will *r* him,

RIDICULED (RIDICULE)

Jdg 9: 38 Aren't these the men you *r?*
2Ch 30: 10 but the people scorned and *r* them.
Ne 2: 19 about it, they mocked and *r* us.
4: 1 He *r* the Jews, and in the presence
Jer 20: 7 I am *r* all day long;
Eze 36: 4 and *r* by the rest of the nations
Hos 7: 16 For this they will be *r*
Lk 23: 11 and his soldiers *r* and mocked him.

RIDING (RIDE)

Lev 15: 9 sits on when *r* will be unclean,
Nu 22: 22 Balaam was *r* on his donkey,
1Sa 25: 20 As she came *r* her donkey
2Sa 18: 9 He was *r* his mule, and
18: 9 while the mule he was *r* kept
2Ki 9: 25 and I were *r* together in chariots
Ne 2: 12 with me except the one I was *r* on.
Est 8: 14 The couriers, *r* the royal horses,
Jer 17: 25 and their officials will come *r*
22: 4 *r* in chariots and on horses,
Eze 38: 15 of them *r* on horses, a great horde,
Zec 1: 8 before me was a man *r* a red horse!
9: 9 gentle and *r* on a donkey,
Mt 21: 5 gentle and *r* on a donkey,
Rev 19: 14 *r* on white horses and dressed

RIFTS

Jer 2: 6 through a land of deserts and *r*,

RIGGING

Pr 23: 34 lying on top of the *r*.
Isa 33: 23 Your *r* hangs loose:

RIGHT (ARIGHT RIGHTFUL RIGHTS)

Ge 4: 7 But if you do not do what is *r*,
4: 7 If you do what is *r*, will you not be
13: 9 I'll go to the *r*; if you go to the *r*,
18: 19 of the LORD by doing what is *r*
18: 25 the Judge of all the earth do *r?*''
24: 48 me on the *r* road to get
43: 23 "It's all *r*," he said.
48: 13 on his left toward Israel's *r* hand,
48: 13 on his *r* toward Israel's left hand
48: 14 But Israel reached out his *r* hand
48: 17 saw his father placing his *r* hand
48: 18 put your *r* hand on his head."
Ex 8: 26 Moses said, "That would not be *r*.
9: 27 "The LORD is in the *r*, and I
14: 22 with a wall of water on their *r*
14: 29 with a wall of water on their *r*
15: 6 Your *r* hand, O LORD,
15: 6 "Your *r* hand, O LORD,
15: 12 You stretched out your *r* hand
15: 26 and do what is *r* in his eyes,
21: 8 He has no *r* to sell her to foreigners
29: 20 and on the big toes of their *r* feet.
29: 20 on the lobes of the *r* ears of Aaron
29: 20 on the thumbs of their *r* hands,
29: 22 fat around them, and the *r* thigh.
Lev 7: 32 You are to give the *r* thigh
7: 33 offering shall have the *r* thigh
8: 23 and on the big toe of his *r* foot.
8: 23 on the thumb of his *r* hand
8: 23 put it on the lobe of Aaron's *r* ear,
8: 24 and on the big toes of their *r* feet.
8: 24 blood on the lobes of their *r* ears,
8: 24 on the thumbs of their *r* hands
8: 25 and their fat and the *r* thigh.
8: 26 the fat portions and on the *r* thigh.
9: 21 and the *r* thigh before the LORD
14: 14 and on the big toe of his *r* foot.
14: 14 it on the lobe of the *r* ear of the one
14: 14 on the thumb of his *r* hand
14: 16 dip his *r* forefinger into the oil
14: 17 and on the big toe of his *r* foot,
14: 17 on the lobe of the *r* ear of the one
14: 17 on the thumb of his *r* hand
14: 25 and on the big toe of his *r* foot.
14: 25 it on the lobe of the *r* ear of the one
14: 25 on the thumb of his *r* hand
14: 27 with his *r* forefinger sprinkle some
14: 28 and on the big toe of his *r* foot.
14: 28 on the lobe of the *r* ear of the one
14: 28 on the thumb of his *r* hand
25: 29 he retains the *r* of redemption a full
25: 32 " 'The Levites always have the *r*
25: 48 he retains the *r* of redemption
Nu 11: 15 put me to death *r* now—
18: 18 offering and the *r* thigh are yours.
20: 17 and not turn to the *r* or to the left
22: 26 either to the *r* or to the left.
22: 29 in my hand, I would kill you *r* now
25: 6 to his family a Midianite woman *r*
27: 7 daughters are saying is *r*.
36: 5 of Joseph is saying is *r*.
Dt 2: 27 we will not turn aside to the *r*
5: 32 do not turn aside to the *r*
6: 18 Do what is *r* and good
11: 6 when the earth opened its mouth *r*
12: 25 because you will be doing what is *r*
12: 28 *r* in the eyes of the LORD your
13: 18 and doing what is *r* in his eyes.
17: 11 from what they tell you, to the *r*
17: 20 and turn from the law to the *r*
21: 9 since you have done what is *r*
21: 17 The *r* of the firstborn belongs
28: 14 to the *r* or to the left, following
Jos 1: 7 do not turn from it to the *r*
4: 3 from *r* where the priests stood
9: 25 to us whatever seems good and *r*
23: 6 without turning aside to the *r*
Jdg 3: 16 to his *r* thigh under his clothing.
3: 21 drew the sword from his *r* thigh
4: 18 "Come, my lord, come *r* in.
5: 26 her *r* hand for the workman's
7: 20 in their *r* hands the trumpets they
11: 23 what *r* have you to take it over?
12: 6 they said, "All *r*, say 'Shibboleth
14: 3 She's the *r* one for me."
15: 3 "This time I have a *r* to get
16: 29 his *r* hand on the one and his left
Ru 4: 4 For no one has the *r* to do it
1Sa 6: 12 they did not turn to the *r*
11: 2 condition that I gouge out the *r* eye
12: 3 any of these, I will make it *r*."
12: 23 you the way that is good and *r*.
14: 13 with his armor-bearer *r* behind him
1Sa 14: 41 of Israel, "Give me the *r* answer."
2Sa 2: 14 "All *r*, let them do it," Joab said.
2: 19 turning neither to the *r*
2: 21 "Turn aside to the *r* or to the left;
8: 15 doing what was just and *r*
14: 19 no one can turn to the *r*
16: 6 the special guard were on David's *r*
18: 11 him to the ground *r* there?
19: 28 what *r* do I have to make any more
20: 9 beard with his *r* hand to kiss him.
21: 4 nor do we have the *r* to put anyone
21: 4 "We have no *r* to demand silver
23: 5 "Is not my house *r* with God?
1Ki 1: 25 *R* now they are eating
2: 19 and she sat down at his *r* hand.
3: 9 to distinguish between *r* and wrong
7: 49 of pure gold (five on the *r*
8: 36 Teach them the *r* way to live,
11: 33 nor done what is *r* in my eyes,
11: 38 and do what is *r* in my eyes
14: 8 doing only what was *r* in my eyes.
15: 5 For David had done what was *r*
15: 11 Asa did what was *r* in the eyes
22: 19 standing around him on his *r*
22: 43 he did what was *r* in the eyes
2Ki 2: 8 The water divided to the *r*
2: 14 it divided to the *r* and to the left,
4: 23 "It's all *r*," she said.
4: 26 Is your husband all *r?* Is your child
4: 26 'Are you all *r?* Is your husband all
4: 26 your child all *r?*' " "Everything is
4: 26 "Everything is all *r*," she said.
5: 21 "Is everything all *r?*" he asked.
5: 22 is all *r*," Gehazi answered.
7: 9 to each other, "We're not doing *r*.
9: 11 "Is everything all *r?* Why did this
10: 30 well in accomplishing what is *r*
12: 2 Joash did what was *r* in the eyes
12: 9 on the *r* side as one enters
14: 3 He did what was *r* in the eyes
15: 3 He did what was *r* in the eyes
15: 34 He did what was *r* in the eyes
16: 2 he did not do what was *r*
17: 9 LORD their God that were not *r*.
18: 3 He did what was *r* in the eyes
22: 2 He did what was *r* in the eyes
22: 2 not turning aside to the *r*
1Ch 6: 39 served at his *r* hand: Asaph son
13: 4 it seemed *r* to all the people.
18: 14 doing what was just and *r*
2Ch 6: 27 Teach them the *r* way to live,
14: 2 *r* in the eyes of the LORD his God.
18: 18 the host of heaven standing on his *r*
20: 32 he did what was *r* in the eyes
24: 2 Joash did what was *r* in the eyes
25: 2 He did what was *r* in the eyes
26: 4 He did what was *r* in the eyes
26: 18 "It is not *r* for you, Uzziah,
27: 2 He did what was *r* in the eyes
28: 1 he did not do what was *r*
29: 2 He did what was *r* in the eyes
30: 4 The plan seemed *r* both to the king
31: 20 doing what was good and *r*
34: 2 He did what was *r* in the eyes
34: 2 not turning aside to the *r*
Ezr 10: 12 "You are *r!* We must do as you say.
Ne 2: 20 or any claim or historic *r* to it."
4: 11 we will be *r* there among them
5: 9 "What you are doing is not *r*.
8: 4 him on his *r* stood Mattithiah,
9: 13 and laws that are just and *r*,
12: 31 proceed on top of the wall to the *r*,
Est 8: 5 and thinks it the *r* thing to do,
8: 11 Jews in every city the *r* to assemble
Job 8: 3 the Almighty pervert what is *r?*
27: 5 I will never admit you are in the *r*;
30: 12 On my *r* the tribe attacks;
32: 9 the aged who understand what is *r*.
33: 12 "But I tell you, in this you are not *r*,
33: 23 to tell a man what is *r* for him,
33: 27 and perverted what was *r*,
34: 4 for ourselves what is *r*;
34: 6 Although I am *r*,
40: 14 that your own *r* hand can save you.
42: 7 have not spoken of me what is *r*,
42: 8 have not spoken of me what is *r*,
Ps 4: 5 Offer *r* sacrifices
9: 4 For you have upheld my *r*

Ps 16: 8 Because he is at my *r* hand,
16: 11 eternal pleasures at your *r* hand.
17: 2 may your eyes see what is *r*.
17: 7 you who save by your *r* hand
18: 35 and your *r* hand sustains me;
19: 8 The precepts of the LORD are *r*,
20: 6 with the saving power of his *r* hand
21: 8 your *r* hand will seize your foes.
25: 9 He guides the humble in what is *r*
26: 10 whose *r* hands are full of bribes.
33: 4 For the word of the LORD is *r*
44: 3 it was your *r* hand, your arm,
45: 4 let your *r* hand display awesome
45: 9 at your *r* hand is the royal bride
48: 10 your *r* hand is filled
50: 16 "What *r* have you to recite my laws
51: 4 so that you are proved *r*
60: 5 help us with your *r* hand,
63: 8 your *r* hand upholds me.
73: 23 you hold me by my *r* hand.
74: 11 hold back your hand, your *r* hand?
77: 10 the years of the *r* hand
78: 54 hill country his *r* hand had taken.
80: 15 the root your *r* hand has planted,
80: 17 on the man at your *r* hand,
89: 13 hand is strong, your *r* hand exalted.
89: 25 his *r* hand over the rivers.
89: 42 You have exalted the *r* hand
91: 7 ten thousand at your *r* hand,
98: 1 his *r* hand and his holy arm
99: 4 what is just and *r*.
106: 3 who constantly do what is *r*.
108: 6 help us with your *r* hand,
109: 6 let an accuser stand at his *r* hand.
109: 31 For he stands at the *r* hand
110: 1 "Sit at my *r* hand
110: 5 The Lord is at your *r* hand;
118: 15 LORD's *r* hand has done mighty
118: 16 The LORD's *r* hand is lifted high;
118: 16 LORD's *r* hand has done mighty
119:128 I consider all your precepts *r*,
119:137 and your laws are *r*.
119:144 Your statutes are forever *r*;
121: 5 is your shade at your *r* hand;
137: 5 may my *r* hand forget ⌊its skill⌋.
138: 7 with your *r* hand you save me.
139: 10 your *r* hand will hold me fast.
142: 4 Look to my *r* and see;
144: 8 whose *r* hands are deceitful.
144: 11 whose *r* hands are deceitful.
Pr 1: 3 doing what is *r* and just and fair;
2: 9 you will understand what is *r*
3: 16 Long life is in her *r* hand;
4: 27 Do not swerve to the *r* or the left;
8: 6 I open my lips to speak what is *r*.
8: 9 To the discerning all of them are *r*;
12: 15 The way of a fool seems *r* to him,
14: 12 There is a way that seems *r*
16: 25 There is a way that seems *r*
18: 17 The first to present his case seems *r*
20: 11 his conduct is pure and *r*.
21: 2 All a man's ways seem *r* to him,
21: 3 To do what is *r* and just
21: 7 for they refuse to do what is *r*.
23: 16 when your lips speak what is *r*.
23: 19 and keep your heart on the *r* path.
Ecc 7: 20 who does what is *r* and never sins.
10: 2 of the wise inclines to the *r*,
12: 10 searched to find just the *r* words,
SS 1: 4 How *r* they are to adore you!
2: 6 and his *r* arm embraces me.
8: 3 and his *r* arm embraces me.
Isa 1: 7 *r* before you,
1: 17 learn to do *r*!
7: 15 reject the wrong and choose the *r*.
7: 16 reject the wrong and choose the *r*,
9: 20 On the *r* they will devour,
28: 26 and teaches him the *r* way.
30: 10 us no more visions of what is *r*!
30: 21 Whether you turn to the *r*
33: 15 and speaks what is *r*,
40: 14 and who taught him the *r* way?
41: 10 you with my righteous *r* hand.
41: 13 who takes hold of your *r* hand
41: 26 so we could say, 'He was *r*'?
43: 9 witnesses to prove they were *r*,
44: 20 "Is not this thing in my *r* hand a lie
45: 1 whose *r* hand I take hold of

Isa 45: 19 I declare what is *r*.
48: 13 my *r* hand spread out the heavens;
51: 7 "Hear me, you who know what is *r*,
54: 3 For you will spread out to the *r*
56: 1 and do what is *r*,
58: 2 were a nation that does what is *r*
62: 8 LORD has sworn by his *r* hand
63: 12 power to be at Moses' *r* hand,
64: 5 to the help of those who gladly do *r*
Jer 8: 6 but they do not say what is *r*.
22: 3 LORD says: Do what is just and *r*.
22: 15 He did what was *r* and just,
22: 24 were a signet ring on my *r* hand,
23: 5 and do what is just and *r* in the land
26: 14 whatever you think is good and *r*.
32: 7 as nearest relative it is your *r*
32: 8 Since it is your *r* to redeem it
33: 15 he will do what is just and *r*
34: 15 and did what is *r* in my sight:
La 2: 3 He has withdrawn his *r* hand
2: 4 his *r* hand is ready.
Eze 1: 10 and on the *r* side each had the face
4: 6 again, this time on your *r* side,
18: 5 who does what is just and *r*.
18: 19 the son has done what is just and *r*
18: 21 and does what is just and *r*,
18: 27 and does what is just and *r*,
21: 16 O sword, slash to the *r*,
21: 22 Into his *r* hand will come the lot
33: 14 and does what is just and *r*—
33: 16 He has done what is just and *r*;
33: 19 and does what is just and *r*,
39: 3 arrows drop from your *r* hand.
45: 9 and do what is just and *r*.
Da 4: 27 sins by doing what is *r*.
4: 37 because everything he does is *r*
12: 7 lifted his *r* hand and his left hand
Hos 14: 9 The ways of the LORD are *r*;
Am 3: 10 "They do not know how to do *r*,"
Jnh 4: 4 "Have you any *r* to be angry?"
4: 9 "Do you have a *r* to be angry about
4: 11 people who cannot tell their *r* hand
Mic 3: 9 and distort all that is *r*;
7: 9 and establishes my *r*.
Hab 2: 16 from the LORD's *r* hand is coming
Zec 3: 1 and Satan standing at his *r* side
4: 3 one on the *r* of the bowl
4: 11 are these two olive trees on the *r*
11: 17 his *r* eye totally blinded!"
11: 17 sword strike his arm and his *r* eye!
12: 6 They will consume *r* and left all
Mt 5: 29 If your *r* eye causes you to sin,
5: 30 if your *r* hand causes you to sin,
5: 39 strikes you on the *r* cheek,
6: 3 know what your *r* hand is doing,
11: 19 wisdom is proved *r* by her actions."
15: 7 Isaiah was *r* when he prophesied
15: 26 "It is not *r* to take the children's
20: 4 and I will pay you whatever is *r*.'
20: 15 Don't I have the *r*
20: 21 sons of mine may sit at your *r*
20: 23 to sit at my *r* or left is not for me
21: 3 and he will send them *r* away."
22: 17 Is it *r* to pay taxes to Caesar or not
22: 26 and third brother, *r* on
22: 44 "Sit at my *r* hand
24: 33 is near, *r* at the door.
25: 33 He will put the sheep on his *r*
25: 34 the King will say to those on his *r*,
26: 58 *r* up to the courtyard
26: 64 the Son of Man sitting at the *r* hand
27: 29 They put a staff in his *r* hand
27: 38 one on his *r* and one on his left.
Mk 5: 15 dressed and in his *r* mind;
6: 25 you to give me *r* now the head
7: 6 "Isaiah was *r* when he prophesied
7: 27 "for it is not *r* to take the children's
10: 37 "Let one of us sit at your *r*
10: 40 to sit at my *r* or left is not for me
12: 14 Is it *r* to pay taxes to Caesar or not?
12: 32 You are *r* in saying that God is one
12: 36 "Sit at my *r* hand
13: 29 is near, *r* at the door.
14: 54 *r* into the courtyard
14: 62 the Son of Man sitting at the *r* hand
15: 27 one on his *r* and one on his left.
16: 5 in a white robe sitting on the *r* side,
16: 19 and he sat at the *r* hand of God.

Lk 1: 11 standing at the *r* side of the altar
4: 30 But he walked *r* through the crowd
5: 19 of the crowd, *r* in front of Jesus.
6: 6 was there whose *r* hand was
7: 29 that God's way was *r*,
7: 35 But wisdom is proved *r*
8: 35 dressed and in his *r* mind;
12: 57 judge for yourselves what is *r*?
20: 21 that you speak and teach what is *r*,
20: 22 Is it *r* for us to pay taxes to Caesar
20: 42 "Sit at my *r* hand
21: 9 but the end will not come *r* away."
22: 50 the high priest, cutting off his *r* ear.
22: 69 at the *r* hand of the mighty God."
22: 70 "You are *r* in saying I am."
23: 33 one on his *r*, the other on his left.
Jn 1: 12 he gave the *r* to become children
4: 17 "You are *r* when you say you have
7: 6 The *r* time for me has not yet come
7: 6 for you any time is *r*.
7: 8 for me the *r* time has not yet come
7: 24 and make a *r* judgment."
8: 16 my decisions are *r*, because I am
8: 48 "Aren't we *r* in saying that you are
18: 10 servant, cutting off his *r* ear.
18: 31 we have no *r* to execute anyone,"
18: 37 "You are *r* in saying I am a king.
21: 6 net on the *r* side of the boat
Ac 2: 25 Because he is at my *r* hand,
2: 33 Exalted to the *r* hand of God,
2: 34 "Sit at my *r* hand
3: 7 Taking him by the *r* hand,
4: 19 whether it is *r* in God's sight
5: 31 God exalted him to his own *r* hand
6: 2 "It would not be *r* for us
7: 55 Jesus standing at the *r* hand of God
7: 56 standing at the *r* hand of God."
8: 21 your heart is not *r* before God.
10: 35 who fear him and do what is *r*.
11: 11 "*R* then three men who had been
13: 10 an enemy of everything that is *r*!
13: 10 never stop perverting the *r* ways
25: 11 no one has the *r* to hand me
Ro 3: 4 "So that you may be proved *r*
5: 6 You see, at just the *r* time,
7: 21 to do good, evil is *r* there with me.
8: 22 as in the pains of childbirth *r* up
8: 34 is at the *r* hand of God and is
9: 21 Does not the potter have the *r*
12: 17 careful to do what is *r* in the eyes
13: 3 do what is *r* and he will commend
13: 3 terror for those who do *r*.
1Co 7: 35 in a *r* way in undivided devotion
7: 37 this man also does the *r* thing.
7: 38 he who marries the virgin does *r*,
9: 4 Don't we have the *r* to food
9: 5 Don't we have the *r*
9: 12 If others have this *r* of support
9: 12 the more? But we did not use this *r*.
2Co 5: 13 if we are in our *r* mind, it is for you.
6: 7 of righteousness in the *r* hand
8: 21 we are taking pains to do what is *r*,
13: 7 but that you will do what is *r* even
Gal 2: 9 Barnabas the *r* hand of fellowship
Eph 1: 20 and seated him at his *r* hand
6: 1 parents in the Lord, for this is *r*.
Php 1: 7 It is *r* for me to feel this way about
4: 8 whatever is *r*, whatever is pure,
Col 3: 1 seated at the *r* hand of God.
4: 1 provide your slaves with what is *r*
2Th 1: 5 evidence that God's judgment is *r*,
3: 9 we do not have the *r* to such help,
3: 13 never tire of doing what is *r*.
Heb 1: 3 down at the *r* hand of the Majesty
1: 13 "Sit at my *r* hand
8: 1 down at the *r* hand of the throne
10: 12 he sat down at the *r* hand of God.
12: 2 and sat down at the *r* hand
13: 10 at the tabernacle have no *r* to eat.
Jas 2: 8 as yourself," you are doing *r*.
1Pe 2: 14 and to commend those who do *r*.
3: 6 daughters if you do what is *r*
3: 14 if you should suffer for what is *r*,
3: 22 into heaven and is at God's *r* hand
2Pe 1: 13 I think it is *r* to refresh your
1Jn 2: 29 who does what is *r* has been born
3: 7 He who does what is *r* is righteous,
3: 10 does not do what is *r* is not a child

Rev 1:16 In his *r* hand he held seven stars,
1:17 Then he placed his *r* hand on me
1:20 stars that you saw in my *r* hand
2: 1 holds the seven stars in his *r* hand
2: 7 I will give the *r* to eat from the tree
3:21 I will give the *r* to sit with me
5: 1 I saw in the *r* hand of him who sat
5: 7 and took the scroll from the *r* hand
10: 2 He planted his *r* foot on the sea
10: 5 and on the land raised his *r* hand
13:16 to receive a mark on his *r* hand
22:11 let him who does *r* continue to do *r*
22:14 that they may have the *r* to the tree

RIGHT-HANDED (HAND)

1Ch 12: 2 or to sling stones *r* or left-handed;

RIGHTEOUS (OVERRIGHTEOUS RIGHTEOUSLY RIGHTEOUSNESS)

Ge 6: 9 Noah was a *r* man, blameless
7: 1 because I have found you *r*
18:23 "Will you sweep away the *r*
18:24 if there are fifty *r* people in the city
18:24 the sake of the fifty *r* people in it?
18:25 to kill the *r* with the wicked,
18:25 treating the *r* and the wicked alike.
18:26 "If I find fifty *r* people in the city
18:28 if the number of the *r* is five less
38:26 and said, "She is more *r* than I,
Ex 23: 8 and twists the words of the *r*.
Nu 23:10 Let me die the death of the *r*,
Dt 4: 8 as to have such *r* decrees and laws
16:19 and twists the words of the *r*.
24:13 *r* act in the sight of the LORD your
33:21 he carried out the LORD's *r* will,
Jdg 5:11 They recite the *r* acts of the LORD
5:11 the *r* acts of his warriors in Israel.
1Sa 12: 7 as to all the *r* acts performed
24:17 "You are more *r* than I," he said.
1Ki 3: 6 and *r* and upright in heart.
Ezr 9:15 O LORD, God of Israel, you are *r!*
Ne 9: 8 your promise because you are *r*.
Job 4:17 'Can a mortal be more *r* than God?
9: 2 how can a mortal be *r* before God?
12: 4 a mere laughingstock, though *r*
15:14 born of woman, that he could be *r?*
17: 9 the *r* will hold to their ways,
22: 3 it give the Almighty if you were *r?*
22:19 "The *r* see their ruin and rejoice;
25: 4 How then can a man be *r*
27:17 what he lays up the *r* will wear,
32: 1 because he was *r* in his own eyes.
33:26 he is restored by God to his *r* state.
35: 7 If you are *r*, what do you give
36: 7 He does not take his eyes off the *r;*
Ps 1: 5 nor sinners in the assembly of the *r*.
1: 6 over the way of the *r*,
4: 1 O my *r* God.
5:12 O LORD, you bless the *r;*
7: 9 O *r* God,
7: 9 and make the *r* secure.
7:11 God is a *r* judge,
11: 3 what can the *r* do?"
11: 5 The LORD examines the *r*,
11: 7 For the LORD is *r*,
14: 5 present in the company of the *r*.
15: 2 and who does what is *r*,
17: 1 Hear, O LORD, my *r* plea;
19: 9 and altogether *r*.
31:18 they speak arrogantly against the *r*.
32:11 in the LORD and be glad, you *r;*
33: 1 Sing joyfully to the LORD, you *r;*
34:15 The eyes of the LORD are on the *r*
34:17 *r* cry out, and the LORD hears
34:19 A *r* man may have many troubles,
34:21 the foes of the *r* will be condemned
37:12 The wicked plot against the *r*
37:16 Better the little that the *r* have
37:17 but the LORD upholds the *r*.
37:21 but the *r* give generously;
37:25 yet I have never seen the *r* forsaken
37:29 the *r* will inherit the land
37:30 of the *r* man utters wisdom,
37:32 The wicked lie in wait for the *r*,
37:39 The salvation of the *r* comes
51:19 Then there will be *r* sacrifices,
52: 6 The *r* will see and fear;
Ps 55:22 he will never let the *r* fall.
58:10 *r* will be glad when they are
58:11 "Surely the *r* still are rewarded;
64:10 Let the *r* rejoice in the LORD
68: 3 But may the *r* be glad
69:28 and not be listed with the *r*.
71:24 My tongue will tell of your *r* acts
72: 7 In his days the *r* will flourish;
75:10 the horns of the *r* will be lifted up.
88:12 your *r* deeds in the land of oblivion
92:12 The *r* will flourish like a palm tree,
94:21 They band together against the *r*
97:11 Light is shed upon the *r*
97:12 in the LORD, you who are *r*,
112: 4 compassionate and *r* man.
112: 6 *r* man will be remembered forever.
116: 5 The LORD is gracious and *r;*
118: 15 resound in the tents of the *r:*
118: 20 through which the *r* may enter.
119: 7 as I learn your *r* laws.
119: 62 for your *r* laws.
119: 75 O LORD, that your laws are *r*,
119:106 that I will follow your *r* laws.
119:121 I have done what is *r* and just;
119:123 looking for your *r* promise.
119:137 *R* are you, O LORD,
119:138 statutes you have laid down are *r;*
119:160 all your *r* laws are eternal.
119:164 for your *r* laws.
119:172 for all your commands are *r*.
125: 3 for then the *r* might use
125: 3 over the land allotted to the *r*,
129: 4 But the LORD is *r;*
140: 13 Surely the *r* will praise your name
141: 5 Let a *r* man strike me—it is
142: 7 Then the *r* will gather about me
143: 2 for no one living is *r* before you.
145: 17 The LORD is *r* in all his ways
146: 8 the LORD loves the *r*.
Pr 2:20 and keep to the paths of the *r*.
3:33 but he blesses the home of the *r*.
4:18 of the *r* is like the first gleam
9: 9 teach a *r* man and he will add
10: 3 LORD does not let the *r* go hungry
10: 6 Blessings crown the head of the *r*,
10: 7 of the *r* will be a blessing,
10:11 The mouth of the *r* is a fountain
10:16 The wages of the *r* bring them life
10:20 The tongue of the *r* is choice silver,
10:21 The lips of the *r* nourish many,
10:24 what the *r* desire will be granted.
10:25 but the *r* stand firm forever.
10:28 The prospect of the *r* is joy,
10:29 of the LORD is a refuge for the *r*,
10:30 The *r* will never be uprooted,
10:31 of the *r* brings forth wisdom,
10:32 of the *r* know what is fitting,
11: 8 The *r* man is rescued from trouble,
11: 9 through knowledge the *r* escape.
11:10 When the *r* prosper, the city
11:19 The truly *r* man attains life,
11:21 but those who are *r* will go free.
11:23 The desire of the *r* ends only
11:28 but the *r* will thrive like a green leaf
11:30 The fruit of the *r* is a tree of life,
11:31 If the *r* receive their due on earth,
12: 3 but the *r* cannot be uprooted.
12: 5 The plans of the *r* are just,
12: 7 but the house of the *r* stands firm.
12:10 A *r* man cares for the needs
12:12 but the root of the *r* flourishes.
12:13 but a *r* man escapes trouble.
12:21 No harm befalls the *r*,
12:26 A *r* man is cautious in friendship,
13: 5 The *r* hate what is false,
13: 9 The light of the *r* shines brightly,
13:21 but prosperity is the reward of the *r*
13:22 wealth is stored up for the *r*.
13:25 The *r* eat to their hearts' content,
14:19 and the wicked at the gates of the *r*.
14:32 even in death the *r* have a refuge.
15: 6 of the *r* contains great treasure,
15:28 of the *r* weighs its answers,
15:29 but he hears the prayer of the *r*.
16:31 it is attained by a *r* life.
18:10 the *r* run to it and are safe.
20: 7 The *r* man leads a blameless life;
21:12 The *R* One takes note of the house
Pr 21:15 justice is done, it brings joy to the *r*
21:18 wicked become a ransom for the *r*,
21:26 but the *r* give without sparing.
23:24 The father of a *r* man has great joy;
24:15 an outlaw against a *r* man's house,
24:16 for though a *r* man falls seven times
25:26 is a *r* man who gives way
28: 1 but the *r* are as bold as a lion.
28:12 When the *r* triumph, there is great
28:28 the wicked perish, the *r* thrive.
29: 2 When the *r* thrive, the people
29: 6 but a *r* one can sing and be glad.
29: 7 The *r* care about justice
29:16 but the *r* will see their downfall.
29:27 The *r* detest the dishonest;
Ecc 3:17 both the *r* and the wicked,
7:15 a *r* man perishing in his
7:20 There is not a *r* man on earth
8:14 men who get what the *r* deserve.
8:14 *r* men who get what the wicked
9: 1 concluded that the *r* and the wise
9: 2 share a common destiny—the *r*
Isa 3:10 Tell the *r* it will be well with them,
10:22 overwhelming and *r*.
24:16 "Glory to the *R* One."
26: 2 that the *r* nation may enter,
26: 7 The path of the *r* is level;
26: 7 you make the way of the *r* smooth.
41:10 you with my *r* right hand.
45:21 a *r* God and a Savior;
45:25 will be found *r* and will exult.
53:11 his knowledge my *r* servant will
57: 1 The *r* perish,
57: 1 that the *r* are taken away
60:21 Then will all your people be *r*
64: 6 and all our *r* acts are like filthy rags
Jer 3:11 "Faithless Israel is more *r*
4: 2 and if in a truthful, just and *r* way
12: 1 You are always *r*, O LORD,
20:12 Almighty, you who examine the *r*
23: 5 up to David a *r* Branch,
31:23 O *r* dwelling, O sacred mountain.'
33:15 I will make a *r* Branch sprout
La 1:18 "The LORD is *r*,
4:13 the blood of the *r*.
Eze 3:20 The *r* things he did will not be
3:20 when a *r* man turns
3:21 if you do warn the *r* man not to sin
13:22 Because you disheartened the *r*
16:51 and have made your sisters seem *r*
16:52 have made your sisters appear *r*.
16:52 they appear more *r* than you.
18: 5 "Suppose there is a *r* man
18: 9 That man is *r;*
18:20 of the *r* man will be credited
18:22 Because of the *r* things he has done
18:24 of the *r* things he has done will be
18:24 *r* man turns from his righteousness
18:26 *r* man turns from his righteousness
21: 3 and cut off from you both the *r*
21: 4 Because I am going to cut off the *r*
23:45 But *r* men will sentence them
33:12 The *r* man, if he sins, will not be
33:12 of the *r* man will not save him
33:13 If I tell the *r* man that he will surely
33:13 of the *r* things he has done will be
33:18 *r* man turns from his righteousness
Da 9: 7 you are *r*, but this day we are
9:14 for the LORD our God is *r*
9:16 in keeping with all your *r* acts,
9:18 requests of you because we are *r*,
Hos 14: 9 the *r* walk in them,
Am 2: 6 They sell the *r* for silver,
5:12 You oppress the *r* and take bribes
Mic 6: 5 that you may know the *r* acts
Hab 1: 4 The wicked hem in the *r*,
1:13 swallow up those more *r*
2: 4 but the *r* will live by his faith—
Zep 3: 5 The LORD within her is *r;*
Zec 8: 8 and I will be faithful and *r* to them
9: 9 *r* and having salvation,
Mal 3:18 see the distinction between the *r*
Mt 1:19 Joseph her husband was a *r* man
5:45 rain on the *r* and the unrighteous.
9:13 For I have not come to call the *r*,
10:41 and anyone who receives a *r* man
10:41 because he is a *r* man will receive
10:41 man will receive a *r* man's reward.

Mt 13: 17 *r* men longed to see what you see
13: 43 Then the *r* will shine like the sun
13: 49 and separate the wicked from the *r*
23: 28 outside you appear to people as *r*
23: 29 and decorate the graves of the *r*.
23: 35 from the blood of *r* Abel
23: 35 will come all the *r* blood that has
25: 37 "Then the *r* will answer him, 'Lord,
25: 46 to eternal punishment, but the *r*
Mk 2: 17 I have not come to call the *r*,
6: 20 him to be a *r* and holy man.
Lk 1: 17 to the wisdom of the *r*—
2: 25 called Simeon, who was *r*
5: 32 I have not come to call the *r*,
14: 14 repaid at the resurrection of the *r*."
15: 7 over ninety-nine *r* persons who do
23: 47 "Surely this was a *r* man."
Jn 17: 25 "*R* Father, though the world does
Ac 3: 14 You disowned the Holy and *R* One
7: 52 predicted the coming of the *R* One.
10: 22 He is a *r* and God-fearing man,
22: 14 to see the *R* One and to hear words
24: 15 will be a resurrection of both the *r*
Ro 1: 17 as it is written: "The *r* will live
1: 32 they know God's *r* decree that
2: 5 when his *r* judgment will be
2: 13 the law who will be declared *r*.
2: 13 those who hear the law who are *r*
3: 10 "There is no one *r*, not even one;
3: 20 Therefore no one will be declared *r*
5: 7 rarely will anyone die for a *r* man,
5: 19 one man the many will be made *r*.
7: 12 and the commandment is holy, *r*
8: 4 in order that the *r* requirements
Gal 3: 11 because, "The *r* will live by faith."
1Th 2: 10 *r* and blameless we were
2Ti 4: 8 which the Lord, the *r* Judge,
Tit 3: 5 because of *r* things we had done,
Heb 10: 38 But my *r* one will live by faith.
11: 4 he was commended as a *r* man,
12: 23 to the spirits of *r* men made perfect
Jas 1: 20 not bring about the *r* life that God
2: 21 ancestor Abraham considered *r*
2: 25 Rahab the prostitute considered *r*
5: 16 The prayer of a *r* man is powerful
1Pe 3: 12 the eyes of the Lord are on the *r*
3: 18 the *r* for the unrighteous,
4: 18 "If it is hard for the *r* to be saved,
2Pe 2: 7 and if he rescued Lot, a *r* man,
2: 8 of lawless men (for that *r* man,
2: 8 was tormented in his *r* soul
1Jn 2: 1 defense—Jesus Christ, the *R* One.
2: 29 know that he is *r*, you know that
3: 7 does what is right is *r*, just as he is *r*.
3: 12 were evil and his brother's were *r*.
Rev 15: 4 for your *r* acts have been revealed
19: 8 stands for the *r* acts of the saints.)

RIGHTEOUSLY (RIGHTEOUS)

Ps 9: 4 on your throne, judging *r*.
Isa 33: 15 He who walks *r*
Jer 11: 20 LORD Almighty, you who judge *r*

RIGHTEOUSNESS (RIGHTEOUS)

Ge 15: 6 and he credited it to him as *r*.
Dt 6: 25 commanded us, that will be our *r*."
9: 4 of this land because of my *r*."
9: 5 It is not because of your *r*
9: 6 of your *r* that the LORD your God
33: 19 and there offer sacrifices of *r*;
1Sa 26: 23 LORD rewards every man for his *r*
2Sa 22: 21 with me according to my *r*;
22: 25 rewarded me according to my *r*,
23: 3 'When one rules over men in *r*,
1Ki 10: 9 to maintain justice and *r*."
2Ch 9: 8 to maintain justice and *r*."
Job 27: 6 I will maintain my *r* and never let
29: 14 I put on *r* as my clothing;
35: 8 and your *r* only the sons of men.
37: 23 great *r*, he does not oppress.
Ps 5: 8 Lead me, O LORD, in your *r*
7: 8 O LORD, according to my *r*,
7: 17 to the LORD because of his *r*
9: 8 He will judge the world in *r*;
17: 15 And I—in *r* I will see your face;
18: 20 with me according to my *r*;
18: 24 rewarded me according to my *r*,
22: 31 They will proclaim his *r*
Ps 23: 3 He guides me in paths of *r*
31: 1 deliver me in your *r*.
33: 5 The LORD loves *r* and justice;
35: 24 in your *r*, O LORD my God;
35: 28 My tongue will speak of your *r*
36: 6 Your *r* is like the mighty
36: 10 your *r* to the upright in heart.
37: 6 He will make your *r* shine like
40: 9 I proclaim *r* in the great assembly;
40: 10 I do not hide your *r* in my heart;
45: 4 in behalf of truth, humility and *r*;
45: 7 You love *r* and hate wickedness;
48: 10 your right hand is filled with *r*.
50: 6 And the heavens proclaim his *r*,
51: 14 and my tongue will sing of your *r*.
65: 5 us with awesome deeds of *r*,
71: 2 Rescue me and deliver me in your *r*
71: 15 My mouth will tell of your *r*,
71: 16 I will proclaim your *r*, yours alone.
71: 19 Your *r* reaches to the skies, O God,
72: 1 the royal son with your *r*.
72: 2 He will judge your people in *r*,
72: 3 the hills the fruit of *r*.
85: 10 *r* and peace kiss each other.
85: 11 and *r* looks down from heaven.
85: 13 *R* goes before him
89: 14 *R* and justice are the foundation
89: 16 they exult in your *r*.
94: 15 will again be founded on *r*,
96: 13 He will judge the world in *r*
97: 2 *r* and justice are the foundation
97: 6 The heavens proclaim his *r*,
98: 2 and revealed his *r* to the nations.
98: 9 He will judge the world in *r*
103: 6 The LORD works *r*
103: 17 his *r* with their children's children
106: 31 This was credited to him as *r*
111: 3 and his *r* endures forever.
112: 3 and his *r* endures forever.
112: 9 his *r* endures forever;
118: 19 Open for me the gates of *r*;
119: 40 Renew my life in your *r*.
119:142 Your *r* is everlasting
132: 9 May your priests be clothed with *r*;
143: 1 in your faithfulness and *r*
143: 11 in your *r*, bring me out of trouble.
145: 7 and joyfully sing of your *r*.
Pr 8: 20 I walk in the way of *r*,
10: 2 but *r* delivers from death.
11: 4 but *r* delivers from death.
11: 5 *r* of the blameless makes a straight
11: 6 The *r* of the upright delivers them,
11: 18 he who sows *r* reaps a sure reward.
12: 28 In the way of *r* there is life;
13: 6 *R* guards the man of integrity,
14: 34 *R* exalts a nation,
15: 9 but he loves those who pursue *r*.
16: 8 Better a little with *r*
16: 12 a throne is established through *r*.
21: 21 He who pursues *r* and love
25: 5 will be established through *r*.
Ecc 7: 15 a righteous man perishing in his *r*,
Isa 1: 21 *r* used to dwell in her—
1: 26 The City of *R*,
1: 27 her penitent ones with *r*.
5: 7 for *r*, but heard cries of distress.
5: 16 will show himself holy by his *r*.
9: 7 it with justice and *r*
11: 4 but with *r* he will judge the needy,
11: 5 *R* will be his belt
16: 5 and speeds the cause of *r*.
26: 9 the people of the world learn *r*.
26: 10 they do not learn *r*;
28: 17 and *r* the plumb line;
32: 1 See, a king will reign in *r*
32: 16 and *r* live in the fertile field.
32: 17 The fruit of *r* will be peace;
32: 17 the effect of *r* will be quietness
33: 5 he will fill Zion with justice and *r*.
41: 2 calling him in *r* to his service?
42: 6 "I, the LORD, have called you in *r*;
42: 21 the LORD for the sake of his *r*
45: 8 let *r* grow with it,
45: 8 "You heavens above, rain down *r*;
45: 13 I will raise up Cyrus in my *r*:
45: 24 are *r* and strength.' "
46: 12 you who are far from *r*.
46: 13 I am bringing my *r* near,
Isa 48: 1 but not in truth or *r*—
48: 18 your *r* like the waves of the sea.
51: 1 "Listen to me, you who pursue *r*
51: 5 My *r* draws near speedily,
51: 6 my *r* will never fail.
51: 8 But my *r* will last forever,
54: 14 In *r* you will be established:
56: 1 and my *r* will soon be revealed.
57: 12 I will expose your *r* and your works
58: 8 then your *r* will go before you,
59: 9 and *r* does not reach us.
59: 14 and *r* stands at a distance;
59: 16 and his own *r* sustained him.
59: 17 He put on *r* as his breastplate,
60: 17 and *r* your ruler.
61: 3 They will be called oaks of *r*,
61: 10 and arrayed me in a robe of *r*,
61: 11 the Sovereign LORD will make *r*
62: 1 till her *r* shines out like the dawn,
62: 2 The nations will see your *r*,
63: 1 "It is I, speaking in *r*,
Jer 9: 24 justice and *r* on earth,
23: 6 The LORD Our *R*.
33: 16 The LORD Our *R*.'
Eze 3: 20 a righteous man turns from his *r*
14: 14 save only themselves by their *r*,
14: 20 save only themselves by their *r*.
18: 20 The *r* of the righteous man will be
18: 24 if a righteous man turns from his *r*
18: 26 If a righteous man turns from his *r*
33: 12 to live because of his former *r*.'
33: 12 *r* of the righteous man will not save
33: 13 then he trusts in his *r* and does evil,
33: 18 If a righteous man turns from his *r*
Da 9: 24 to bring in everlasting *r*,
12: 3 and those who lead many to *r*,
Hos 2: 19 I will betroth you in *r* and justice,
10: 12 Sow for yourselves *r*,
10: 12 and showers *r* on you.
Joel 2: 23 a teacher for *r*.
Am 5: 7 and cast *r* to the ground
5: 24 *r* like a never-failing stream!
6: 12 and the fruit of *r* into bitterness—
Zep 2: 3 Seek *r*, seek humility;
Mal 3: 3 men who will bring offerings in *r*,
4: 2 the sun of *r* will rise with healing
Mt 3: 15 for us to do this to fulfill all *r*."
5: 6 those who hunger and thirst for *r*,
5: 10 who are persecuted because of *r*,
5: 20 unless your *r* surpasses that
6: 1 to do your 'acts of *r*' before men,
6: 33 But seek first his kingdom and his *r*
21: 32 to you to show you the way of *r*,
Lk 1: 75 and *r* before him all our days.
18: 9 who were confident of their own *r*
Jn 16: 8 world of guilt in regard to sin and *r*
16: 10 in regard to *r*, because I am going
Ac 24: 25 Paul discoursed on *r*, self-control
Ro 1: 17 For in the gospel a *r* from God is
1: 17 a *r* that is by faith from first to last,
3: 5 brings out God's *r* more clearly,
3: 21 now a *r* from God, apart from law,
3: 22 This *r* from God comes
4: 3 and it was credited to him as *r*."
4: 5 wicked, his faith is credited as *r*.
4: 6 man to whom God credits *r* apart
4: 9 faith was credited to him as *r*.
4: 11 a seal of the *r* that he had by faith
4: 11 in order that *r* might be credited
4: 13 through the *r* that comes by faith.
4: 22 why "it was credited to him as *r*."
4: 24 to whom God will credit *r*—
5: 17 and of the gift of *r* reign in life
5: 18 of *r* was justification that brings life
5: 21 also grace might reign through *r*
6: 13 body to him as instruments of *r*.
6: 16 or to obedience, which leads to *r*?
6: 18 and have become slaves to *r*.
6: 19 in slavery to *r* leading to holiness.
6: 20 you were free from the control of *r*.
8: 10 yet your spirit is alive because of *r*.
9: 30 did not pursue *r*, have obtained it,
9: 30 have obtained it, a *r* that is by faith;
9: 31 a law of *r*, has not attained it.
10: 3 they did not know the *r* that comes
10: 3 they did not submit to God's *r*.
10: 4 the law so that there may be *r*
10: 5 in this way the *r* that is by the law:

Ro 10: 6 But the *r* that is by faith says:
14: 17 but of *r*, peace and joy
1Co 1: 30 our *r*, holiness and redemption.
2Co 3: 9 is the ministry that brings *r!*
5: 21 that in him we might become the *r*
6: 7 with weapons of *r* in the right hand
6: 14 For what do *r* and wickedness have
9: 9 his *r* endures forever."
9: 10 will enlarge the harvest of your *r*.
11: 15 masquerade as servants of *r*.
Gal 2: 21 for if *r* could be gained
3: 6 and it was credited to him as *r*."
3: 21 then *r* would certainly have come
5: 5 await through the Spirit the *r*
Eph 4: 24 created to be like God in true *r*
5: 9 *r* and truth) and find out what
6: 14 with the breastplate of *r* in place,
Php 1: 11 filled with the fruit of *r* that comes
3: 6 as for legalistic *r*, faultless.
3: 9 not having a *r* of my own that
3: 9 the *r* that comes from God
1Ti 6: 11 and pursue *r*, godliness, faith, love,
2Ti 2: 22 and pursue *r*, faith, love and peace,
3: 16 correcting and training in *r*,
4: 8 is in store for me the crown of *r*,
Heb 1: 8 and *r* will be the scepter
1: 9 You have loved *r* and hated
5: 13 with the teaching about *r*.
7: 2 his name means "king of *r*";
11: 7 became heir of the *r* that comes
12: 11 it produces a harvest of *r*
Jas 2: 23 and it was credited to him as *r*,"
3: 18 sow in peace raise a harvest of *r*.
1Pe 2: 24 die to sins and live for *r*;
2Pe 1: 1 who through the *r* of our God
2: 5 a preacher of *r*, and seven others;
2: 21 not to have known the way of *r*,
3: 13 and a new earth, the home of *r*.

RIGHTFUL (RIGHT)

Job 8: 6 and restore you to your *r* place.

RIGHTS (RIGHT)

Ex 21: 9 he must grant her the *r*
21: 10 of her food, clothing and marital *r*.
Dt 21: 16 he must not give the *r*
1Ch 5: 1 his *r* as firstborn were given
5: 2 the *r* of the firstborn belonged
Job 36: 6 but gives the afflicted their *r*.
Ps 82: 3 maintain the *r* of the poor
Pr 31: 5 deprive all the oppressed of their *r*.
31: 8 for the *r* of all who are destitute.
31: 9 defend the *r* of the poor and needy
Ecc 5: 8 and *r* denied, do not be surprised
Isa 10: 2 to deprive the poor of their *r*
Jer 5: 28 they do not defend the *r*
La 3: 35 to deny a man his *r*
1Co 9: 15 But I have not used any of these *r*.
9: 18 use of my *r* in preaching it.
Gal 4: 5 that we might receive the full *r*
Heb 12: 16 a single meal sold his inheritance *r*

RIGID

Mk 9: 18 gnashes his teeth and becomes *r*.

RIM (RIMS)

Ex 25: 25 and put a gold molding on the *r*.
25: 25 around it a *r* a handbreadth wide
25: 27 are to be close to the *r*
37: 12 and put a gold molding on the *r*.
37: 12 around it a *r* a handbreadth wide
37: 14 close to the *r* to hold the poles used
Dt 2: 36 From Aroer on the *r* of the Arnon
4: 48 extended from Aroer on the *r*
Jos 12: 2 from Aroer on the *r* of the Arnon
13: 9 from Aroer on the *r* of the Arnon
13: 16 from Aroer on the *r* of the Arnon
1Ki 7: 23 measuring ten cubits from *r* to *r*
7: 24 Below the *r*, gourds encircled it—
7: 26 and its *r* was like the *r* of a cup,
2Ch 4: 2 measuring ten cubits from *r* to *r*
4: 3 Below the *r*, figures
4: 5 and its *r* was like the *r* of a cup,
Eze 43: 13 with a *r* of one span
43: 17 with a *r* of half a cubit and a gutter
43: 20 upper ledge and all around the *r*,

RIMMON

Jos 15: 32 Lebaoth, Shilhim, Ain and *R*—
19: 7 Ain, *R*, Ether and Ashan—
19: 13 out at *R* and turned toward Neah.
Jdg 20: 45 toward the desert to the rock of *R*,
20: 47 fled into the desert to the rock of *R*
21: 13 to the Benjamites at the rock of *R*.
2Sa 4: 2 they were sons of *R* the Beerothite
4: 5 the sons of *R* the Beerothite,
4: 9 the sons of *R* the Beerothite,
2Ki 5: 18 bow down in the temple of *R*,
5: 18 my master enters the temple of *R*
1Ch 4: 32 Ain, *R*, Token and Ashan—
Zec 14: 10 from Geba to *R*, south

RIMMON PEREZ

Nu 33: 19 left Rithmah and camped at *R*.
33: 20 They left *R* and camped at Libnah.

RIMMONO

1Ch 6: 77 *R* and Tabor, together

RIMS (RIM)

1Ki 7: 33 *r*, spokes and hubs were all
Eze 1: 18 Their *r* were high and awesome,
1: 18 and all four *r* were full of eyes all

RING (RANG RINGED RINGS)

Ge 24: 22 out a gold nose *r* weighing a beka
24: 30 As soon as he had seen the nose *r*,
24: 47 "Then I put the *r* in her nose
41: 42 Then Pharaoh took his signet *r*
Ex 26: 24 into a single *r*; both shall be like
27: 4 and make a bronze *r* at each
36: 29 to the top and fitted into a single *r*;
Jdg 8: 25 and each man threw a *r*
Est 3: 10 So the king took the signet *r*
3: 12 himself and sealed with his own *r*.
8: 2 The king took off his signet *r*,
8: 8 and seal it with the king's signet *r*
8: 8 sealed with his *r* can be revoked."
8: 10 dispatches with the king's signet *r*,
Job 16: 16 deep shadows *r* my eyes;
42: 11 a piece of silver and a gold *r*.
Pr 11: 22 Like a gold *r* in a pig's snout
Jer 22: 24 were a signet *r* on my right hand,
Eze 16: 12 and I put a *r* on your nose,
Da 6: 17 it with his own signet *r*
Hag 2: 23 I will make you like my signet *r*,
Lk 15: 22 Put a *r* on his finger and sandals
Jas 2: 2 into your meeting wearing a gold *r*

RINGED (RING)

Job 41: 14 *r* about with his fearsome teeth?

RINGLEADER (LEAD)

Ac 24: 5 He is a *r* of the Nazarene sect and

RINGS (RING)

Ge 35: 4 the foreign gods they had and the *r*
Ex 25: 12 Cast four gold *r* for it and fasten
25: 12 on one side and two *r* on the other.
25: 12 with two *r* on one side
25: 14 the poles into the *r* on the sides
25: 15 are to remain in the *r* of this ark;
25: 26 Make four gold *r* for the table
25: 27 The *r* are to be close to the rim
26: 29 make gold *r* to hold the crossbars.
27: 7 inserted into the *r* so they will be
28: 23 Make two gold *r* for it
28: 24 chains to the *r* at the corners
28: 26 Make two gold *r* and attach them
28: 27 Make two more gold *r*
28: 28 The *r* of the breastpiece are
28: 28 are to be tied to the *r* of the ephod
30: 4 Make two gold *r* for the altar
35: 22 earrings, *r* and ornaments.
36: 34 made gold *r* to hold the crossbars.
37: 3 He cast four gold *r* for it
37: 3 on one side and two *r* on the other.
37: 3 with two *r* on one side
37: 5 the poles into the *r* on the sides
37: 13 They cast four gold *r* for the table
37: 14 The *r* were put close to the rim
37: 27 They made two gold *r*
38: 5 They cast bronze *r*
38: 7 poles into the *r* so they would be
39: 16 fastened the *r* to two of the corners

Ex 39: 16 filigree settings and two gold *r*,
39: 17 chains to the *r* at the corners
39: 19 They made two gold *r*
39: 20 Then they made two more gold *r*
39: 21 They tied the *r* of the breastpiece
39: 21 breastpiece to the *r* of the ephod
Nu 31: 50 armlets, bracelets, signet *r*,
Jdg 8: 26 of the gold *r* he asked for came
Est 1: 6 to silver *r* on marble pillars.
Isa 3: 21 signet *r* and nose *r*, the fine robes
Da 6: 17 and with the *r* of his nobles,
Hos 2: 13 she decked herself with *r*

RINNAH

1Ch 4: 20 Amnon, *R*, Ben-Hanan and Tilon.

RINSED (RINSING)

Lev 6: 28 is to be scoured and *r* with water.
15: 12 is to be *r* with water.
2Ch 4: 6 used for the burnt offerings were *r*,

RINSING (RINSED)

Lev 15: 11 touches without *r* his hands

RIOT (RIOTERS RIOTING RIOTS)

Mt 26: 5 there may be a *r* among the people
Mk 14: 2 they said, "or the people may *r*."
Ac 17: 5 formed a mob and started a *r*

RIOTERS (RIOT)

Ac 21: 32 When the *r* saw the commander

RIOTING (RIOT)

Ac 19: 40 in danger of being charged with *r*

RIOTS (RIOT)

Ac 24: 5 stirring up *r* among the Jews all
2Co 6: 5 imprisonments and *r*; in hard work,

RIP (RIPPED)

2Ki 8: 12 and *r* open their pregnant women."
Ps 7: 2 and *r* me to pieces with no one
Hos 13: 8 I will attack them and *r* them open.

RIPE (RIPEN RIPENED RIPENING RIPENS)

Nu 13: 20 the season for the first *r* grapes.)
2Ki 4: 42 baked from the first *r* grain,
Isa 28: 4 will be like a fig *r* before harvest—
Joel 3: 13 for the harvest is *r*.
Am 8: 1 showed me: a basket of *r* fruit.
8: 2 "A basket of *r* fruit," I answered.
8: 2 "The time is *r* for my people Israel;
Na 3: 12 trees with their first *r* fruit;
Zec 8: 4 and women of *r* old age will sit
Mk 4: 29 the grain is *r*, he puts the sickle to it
Jn 4: 35 at the fields! They are *r* for harvest.
Rev 14: 15 for the harvest of the earth is *r*."
14: 18 vine, because its grapes are *r*."

RIPEN (RIPE)

Ex 9: 32 destroyed, because they *r* later.)
Jer 24: 2 like those that *r* early; the other

RIPENED (RIPE)

Ge 40: 10 and its clusters *r* into grapes.
Isa 16: 9 The shouts of joy over your *r* fruit
Jer 48: 32 fallen on your *r* fruit and grapes.

RIPENING (RIPE)

Isa 18: 5 and the flower becomes a *r* grape,

RIPENS (RIPE)

Hos 2: 9 I will take away my grain when it *r*,

RIPHATH

Ge 10: 3 Ashkenaz, *R* and Togarmah.
1Ch 1: 6 Ashkenaz, *R* and Togarmah.

RIPPED (RIP)

2Ki 15: 16 and *r* open all the pregnant women.
Hos 13: 16 their pregnant women *r* open."
Am 1: 13 Because he *r* open the pregnant

RISE (ARISE ARISEN ARISES AROSE RAISE RAISED RAISES RAISING RISEN RISES RISING ROSE UPRAISED UPRISING)

Lev 19: 32 " '*R* in the presence of the aged,

Nu 10: 35 "*R* up, O LORD!
23: 24 The people *r* like a lioness;
24: 17 a scepter will *r* out of Israel.
Dt 28: 7 grant that the enemies who *r* up
28: 43 among you will *r* above you higher
32: 38 Let them *r* up to help you!
33: 11 loins of those who *r* up against him;
33: 11 strike his foes till they *r* no more."
Jos 8: 7 you are to *r* up from ambush
Jdg 20: 40 of smoke began to *r* from the city,
1Sa 16: 12 the LORD said, "*R* and anoint him
2Sa 18: 32 all who *r* up to harm you be like
22: 39 completely, and they could not *r;*
Ezr 10: 4 *R* up; this matter is in your hands.
Job 14: 12 so man lies down and does not *r;*
20: 27 the earth will *r* up against him.
24: 12 of the dying *r* from the city,
25: 3 Upon whom does his light not *r?*
Ps 3: 1 How many *r* up against me!
7: 6 *r* up against the rage of my enemies
17: 1 it does not *r* from deceitful lips.
17: 13 *R* up, O LORD, confront them,
18: 38 so that they could not *r;*
20: 8 but we *r* up and stand firm.
27: 12 for false witnesses *r* up against me,
32: 6 surely when the mighty waters *r,*
35: 23 Awake, and *r* to my defense!
36: 12 thrown down, not able to *r!*
44: 26 *R* up and help us;
59: 1 from those who *r* up against me.
66: 7 let not the rebellious *r* up
74: 22 *R* up, O God, and defend your
82: 8 *R* up, O God, judge the earth,
88: 10 Do those who are dead *r* up
94: 2 *R* up, O Judge of the earth;
94: 16 Who will *r* up for me
119: 62 At midnight I *r* to give you thanks
119:147 I *r* before dawn and cry for help;
127: 2 In vain you *r* early
135: 7 He makes clouds *r* from the ends
139: 2 You know when I sit and when I *r;*
139: 9 If I *r* on the wings of the dawn,
139: 21 abhor those who *r* up against you?
140: 10 into miry pits, never to *r.*
Pr 28: 12 but when the wicked *r* to power,
28: 28 When the wicked *r* to power,
Ecc 12: 4 when men *r* up at the sound
Isa 3: 5 The young will *r* up against the old,
5: 11 Woe to those who *r*
14: 9 it makes them *r* from their thrones
14: 21 they are not to *r* to inherit the land
14: 22 "I will *r* up against them,"
24: 20 that it falls—never to *r* again.
26: 14 those departed spirits do not *r.*
26: 19 their bodies will *r.*
28: 21 The LORD will *r* up as he did
31: 2 He will *r* up against the house
32: 9 *r* up and listen to me;
33: 3 when you *r* up, the nations scatter.
34: 10 its smoke will *r* forever.
43: 17 and they lay there, never to *r* again,
49: 7 "Kings will see you and *r* up,
51: 17 *R* up, O Jerusalem,
52: 2 *r* up, sit enthroned, O Jerusalem.
58: 10 then your light will *r*
Jer 10: 13 he makes clouds *r* from the ends
25: 27 to *r* no more because of the sword I
46: 8 'I will *r* and cover the earth;
49: 14 *R* up for battle!"
51: 16 he makes clouds *r* from the ends
51: 42 The sea will *r* over Babylon;
51: 64 'So will Babylon sink to *r* no more
Eze 1: 20 and the wheels would *r*
10: 16 wings to *r* from the ground,
17: 14 unable to *r* again, surviving only
Da 2: 39 another kingdom will *r,* inferior
7: 17 beasts are four kingdoms that will *r*
11: 14 "In those times many will *r*
11: 23 and with only a few people he will *r*
11: 31 "His armed forces will *r* up
12: 13 the end of the days you will *r*
Hos 10: 14 of battle will *r* against your people,
Joel 2: 20 its smell will *r.*"
Am 5: 2 never to *r* again,
7: 9 with my sword I will *r*
8: 8 The whole land will *r* like the Nile;
8: 14 never to *r* again."
Ob : 1 "*R,* and let us go against her
Mic 4: 13 *R* and thresh, O Daughter of Zion,
7: 8 Though I have fallen, I will *r.*
Mal 4: 2 of righteousness will *r* with healing
Mt 5: 45 He causes his sun to *r* on the evil
12: 42 of the South will *r* at the judgment
24: 7 Nation will *r* against nation,
26: 46 *R,* let us go! Here comes my
27: 63 'After three days I will *r* again.'
Mk 8: 31 and after three days *r* again.
9: 31 and after three days he will *r.*"
10: 34 Three days later he will *r.*"
12: 25 When the dead *r,* they will neither
13: 8 Nation will *r* against nation,
14: 42 *R!* Let us go! Here comes my
Lk 11: 31 of the South will *r* at the judgment
17: 19 Then he said to him, "*R* and go;
18: 33 On the third day he will *r* again."
20: 37 even Moses showed that the dead *r*
21: 10 "Nation will *r* against nation,
24: 38 and why do doubts *r* in your minds
24: 46 *r* from the dead on the third day,
Jn 5: 29 and those who have done evil will *r*
5: 29 those who have done good will *r*
11: 23 "Your brother will *r* again."
11: 24 "I know he will *r* again
20: 9 had to *r* from the dead.)
Ac 17: 3 had to suffer and *r* from the dead.
26: 23 and, as the first to *r* from the dead,
Eph 5: 14 *r* from the dead,
1Th 4: 16 and the dead in Christ will *r* first.

RISEN (RISE)

Ge 19: 23 the sun had *r* over the land.
Dt 34: 10 no prophet has *r* in Israel like
2Sa 14: 7 Now the whole clan has *r* up
Eze 47: 5 because the water had *r*
Mic 2: 8 Lately my people have *r* up
Mt 11: 11 there has not *r* anyone greater
14: 2 "This is John the Baptist; he has *r*
26: 32 after I have *r,* I will go ahead of you
28: 6 He is not here; he has *r,* just
28: 7 'He has *r* from the dead
Mk 9: 9 Son of Man had *r* from the dead.
14: 28 after I have *r,* I will go ahead of you
16: 6 He has *r!* He is not here.
16: 14 who had seen him after he had *r.*
Lk 24: 6 he has *r!* Remember how he told
24: 34 The Lord has *r* and has appeared

RISES (RISE)

Jos 11: 17 from Mount Halak, which *r*
12: 7 which *r* toward Seir (their lands
Jdg 5: 31 the sun when it *r* in its strength."
Job 16: 8 my gauntness *r* up and testifies
24: 14 daylight is gone, the murderer *r* up
41: 25 When he *r* up, the mighty are
Ps 19: 6 It *r* at one end of the heavens
74: 23 your enemies, which *r* continually.
104: 22 The sun *r,* and they steal away;
Pr 24: 16 man falls seven times, he *r* again,
Ecc 1: 5 The sun *r* and the sun sets,
1: 5 and hurries back to where it *r.*
3: 21 knows if the spirit of man *r* upward
10: 4 If a ruler's anger *r* against you,
Isa 2: 19 when he *r* to shake the earth.
2: 21 when he *r* to shake the earth.
3: 13 he *r* to judge the people.
30: 18 he *r* to show you compassion.
60: 1 the glory of the LORD *r* upon you.
60: 2 but the LORD *r* upon you
Jer 46: 7 "Who is this that *r* like the Nile,
46: 8 Egypt *r* like the Nile,
48: 34 "The sound of their cry *r*
51: 9 it *r* as high as the clouds.'
Hos 6: 3 As surely as the sun *r,*
7: 4 the kneading of the dough till it *r.*
Am 9: 5 the whole land *r* like the Nile,
Mic 7: 6 a daughter *r* up against her mother,
Lk 16: 31 even if someone *r* from the dead.' "
Eph 2: 21 and *r* to become a holy temple
Jas 1: 11 For the sun *r* with scorching heat
2Pe 1: 19 the morning star *r* in your hearts.
Rev 14: 11 smoke of their torment *r* for ever

RISING (RISE)

Ge 19: 28 and he saw dense smoke *r*
Jos 8: 20 smoke of the city *r* against the sky,
1Ki 18: 44 as a man's hand is *r* from the sea."
Ps 50: 1 the earth from the *r* of the sun
113: 3 From the *r* of the sun
Isa 13: 10 The *r* sun will be darkened
30: 28 *r* up to the neck.
41: 25 one from the *r* sun who calls
45: 6 so that from the *r* of the sun
59: 19 from the *r* of the sun, they will
Jer 25: 32 a mighty storm is *r*
47: 2 "See how the waters are *r*
Eze 8: 11 a fragrant cloud of incense was *r.*
Mal 1: 11 from the *r* to the setting of the sun.
Mk 9: 10 discussing what "*r*
12: 26 about the dead *r*—have you not
Lk 1: 78 by which the *r* sun will come to us
2: 34 to cause the falling and *r* of many
12: 54 When you see a cloud *r* in the west,
Rev 14: 20 *r* as high as the horses' bridles

RISK (RISKED RISKING)

2Sa 17: 17 they could not *r* being seen
23: 17 went at the *r* of their lives?"
1Ch 11: 19 went at the *r* of their lives?"
La 5: 9 at the *r* of our lives

RISKED (RISK)

Jdg 5: 18 of Zebulun *r* their very lives;
9: 17 *r* his life to rescue you
1Ch 11: 19 Because they *r* their lives
Ac 15: 26 men who have *r* their lives
Ro 16: 4 They *r* their lives for me.

RISKING (RISK)

Php 2: 30 *r* his life to make up

RISSAH

Nu 33: 21 They left Libnah and camped at *R.*
33: 22 They left *R* and camped

RITES

Ac 21: 24 join in their purification *r*

RITHMAH

Nu 33: 18 left Hazeroth and camped at *R.*
33: 19 They left *R* and camped

RIVAL (RIVALRY)

Lev 18: 18 take your wife's sister as a *r* wife
1Sa 1: 6 her *r* kept provoking her in order
1: 7 her *r* provoked her till she wept
Eze 31: 8 could not *r* it,

RIVALRY (RIVAL)

Php 1: 15 preach Christ out of envy and *r,*

RIVER (RIVERBANK RIVERBED RIVERS)

Ge 2: 10 A *r* watering the garden flowed
2: 13 name of the second *r* is the Gihon;
2: 14 And the fourth *r* is the Euphrates.
2: 14 The name of the third *r* is the Tigris
15: 18 from the *r* of Egypt to the great *r,*
31: 21 and crossing the *R,* he headed
36: 37 Rehoboth on the *r* succeeded him
41: 2 of the *r* there came up seven cows,
41: 18 of the *r* there came up seven cows,
Ex 1: 22 is born you must throw into the *r,*
2: 5 were walking along the *r* bank
4: 9 take from the *r* will become blood
7: 18 Nile will die, and the *r* will stink;
7: 21 *r* smelled so bad that the Egyptians
7: 24 could not drink the water of the *r.*
23: 31 and from the desert to the *R.*
Nu 22: 5 near the *R,* in his native land.
24: 6 like gardens beside a *r,*
Dt 1: 7 as far as the great *r,* the Euphrates.
3: 16 and out to the Jabbok *R,*
11: 24 and from the Euphrates *R*
Jos 1: 2 get ready to cross the Jordan *R,*
1: 4 and from Lebanon to the great *r,*
2: 23 forded the *r* and came
3: 8 waters, go and stand in the *r.*' "
4: 18 out of the *r* carrying the ark
12: 2 of the gorge—to the Jabbok *R,*
13: 3 from the Shihor *R* on the east
24: 2 beyond the *R* and worshiped other
24: 3 from the land beyond the *R*
24: 14 worshiped beyond the *R*
24: 15 forefathers served beyond the *R,*

Jdg 4: 7 and his troops to the Kishon R
4: 13 to the Kishon R.
5: 21 The r Kishon swept them away,
5: 21 the age-old r, the r Kishon.
2Sa 8: 3 control along the Euphrates R.
10: 16 brought from beyond the R;
17: 21 "Set out and cross the r at once;
1Ki 4: 21 kingdoms from the R to the land
4: 24 over all the kingdoms west of the R
14: 15 and scatter them beyond the R,
2Ki 17: 6 in Gozan on the Habor R
18: 11 in Gozan on the Habor R
23: 29 the Euphrates R to help the king of
24: 7 Wadi of Egypt to the Euphrates R.
1Ch 1: 48 Rehoboth on the r succeeded him
5: 9 extends to the Euphrates R,
5: 26 Habor, Hara and the r of Gozan,
13: 5 from the Shihor R in Egypt
18: 3 control along the Euphrates R.
19: 16 brought from beyond the R,
2Ch 9: 26 the kings from the R to the land
Job 40: 23 When the r rages, he is not alarmed
Ps 36: 8 from your r of delights.
46: 4 There is a r whose streams make
66: 6 they passed through the r on foot
72: 8 from the R to the ends of the earth.
80: 11 its shoots as far as the R.
83: 9 to Sisera and Jabin at the r Kishon,
105: 41 like a r it flowed in the desert.
Isa 7: 20 hired from beyond the R—
8: 7 the mighty flood waters of the R—
11: 15 hand over the Euphrates R.
19: 5 The waters of the r will dry up,
19: 7 at the mouth of the r.
48: 18 peace would have been like a r,
66: 12 "I will extend peace to her like a r,
Jer 2: 18 Assyria to drink water from the R?
46: 2 Carchemish on the Euphrates R
46: 6 In the north by the R Euphrates
46: 10 the north by the R Euphrates.
51: 32 the r crossings seized,
La 2: 18 let your tears flow like a r
Eze 1: 1 among the exiles by the Kebar R,
1: 3 by the Kebar R in the land
3: 15 Tel Aviv near the Kebar R.
3: 23 glory I had seen by the Kebar R,
10: 15 I had seen by the Kebar R.
10: 20 the God of Israel by the Kebar R,
10: 22 as those I had seen by the Kebar R.
43: 3 visions I had seen by the Kebar R,
47: 5 a r that no one could cross.
47: 5 now it was a r that I could not cross
47: 6 he led me back to the bank of the r.
47: 7 of trees on each side of the r.
47: 9 so where the r flows everything
47: 9 will live wherever the r flows.
47: 12 grow on both banks of the r.
Da 7: 10 A r of fire was flowing,
10: 4 standing on the bank of the great r,
12: 5 one on this bank of the r
12: 6 who was above the waters of the r,
12: 7 who was above the waters of the r,
Am 5: 24 But let justice roll on like a r,
8: 8 like the r of Egypt.
9: 5 then sinks like the r of Egypt—
Na 2: 6 The r gates are thrown open
3: 8 The r was her defense,
Zec 9: 10 from the R to the ends of the earth.
Mt 3: 6 baptized by him in the Jordan R.
Mk 1: 5 baptized by him in the Jordan R.
Ac 16: 13 went outside the city gate to the r,
Rev 9: 14 bound at the great r Euphrates."
12: 15 the serpent spewed water like a r,
12: 16 swallowing the r that the dragon
16: 12 bowl on the great r Euphrates,
22: 1 Then the angel showed me the r
22: 2 On each side of the r stood the tree

RIVERBANK (RIVER)

Ge 41: 3 and stood beside those on the r.

RIVERBED (RIVER)

Job 14: 11 or a r becomes parched and dry,
Isa 19: 5 and the r will be parched and dry.

RIVERS (RIVER)

2Ki 5: 12 and Pharpar, the r of Damascus,
Job 20: 17 the r flowing with honey
Job 28: 11 He searches the sources of the r
Ps 74: 15 you dried up the ever flowing r.
78: 16 and made water flow down like r.
78: 44 He turned their r to blood;
89: 25 his right hand over the r.
98: 8 Let the r clap their hands,
107: 33 He turned r into a desert,
137: 1 By the r of Babylon we sat
SS 8: 7 r cannot wash it away.
Isa 18: 1 wings along the r of Cush,
18: 2 whose land is divided by r.
18: 7 whose land is divided by r—
33: 21 It will be like a place of broad r
41: 18 I will make r flow on barren heights
42: 15 I will turn r into islands
43: 2 and when you pass through the r,
50: 2 I turn r into a desert;
Jer 46: 7 like r of surging waters?
46: 8 like r of surging waters.
Mic 6: 7 with ten thousand r of oil?
Na 1: 4 he makes all the r run dry.
Hab 3: 8 Were you angry with the r,
3: 9 You split the earth with r;
Zep 3: 10 From beyond the r of Cush
2Co 11: 26 I have been in danger from r,
Rev 8: 10 fell from the sky on a third of the r
16: 4 angel poured out his bowl on the r

RIZIA

1Ch 7: 39 sons of Ulla: Arah, Hanniel and R.

RIZPAH

2Sa 3: 7 a concubine named R daughter
21: 8 the two sons of Aiah's daughter R,
21: 10 R daughter of Aiah took sackcloth
21: 11 was told what Aiah's daughter R,

ROAD (CROSSROADS ROADS ROADSIDE)

Ge 16: 7 is beside the r to Shur.
24: 48 me on the right r to get
38: 14 which is on the r to Timnah.
38: 21 was beside the r at Enaim?"
48: 7 beside the r to Ephrath" (that is,
Ex 13: 17 on the r through the Philistine
13: 18 by the desert r toward the Red
Nu 20: 19 "We will go along the main r,
21: 1 coming along the r to Atharim,
21: 33 went up along the r toward Bashan,
22: 22 stood in the r to oppose him.
22: 23 her to get her back on the r.
22: 23 in the r with a drawn sword
22: 23 she turned off the r into a field.
22: 31 in the r with his sword drawn.
22: 34 standing in the r to oppose me.
Dt 1: 2 by the Mount Seir r.)
2: 8 We turned from the Arabah r,
2: 8 traveled along the desert r of Moab
2: 27 We will stay on the main r;
3: 1 went up along the r toward Bashan,
6: 7 and when you walk along the r,
11: 19 and when you walk along the r,
11: 30 of the r, toward the setting sun,
22: 4 donkey or his ox fallen on the r,
22: 6 across a bird's nest beside the r,
27: 18 leads the blind astray on the r."
Jos 2: 7 of the spies on the r that leads
2: 22 had searched all along the r
10: 10 them along the r going up
10: 11 fled before Israel on the r
Jdg 5: 10 and you who walk along the r,
21: 19 east of the r that goes from Bethel
Ru 1: 7 on the r that would take them back
1Sa 4: 13 on his chair by the side of the r,
6: 12 on the r and lowing all the way;
17: 52 along the Shaaraim r to Gath
26: 3 camp beside the r on the hill
2Sa 13: 34 people on the r west of him,
15: 2 stand by the side of the r leading
16: 13 along the r while Shimei was going
20: 12 him from the r into a field
20: 12 in his blood in the middle of the r,
20: 13 had been removed from the r,
1Ki 13: 10 So he took another r and did not
13: 12 sons showed him which r the man
13: 24 a lion met him on the r
13: 24 his body was thrown down on the r
13: 28 the body thrown down on the r,
1Ki 20: 38 stood by the r waiting for the king.
2Ki 2: 23 As he was walking along the r,
6: 19 "This is not the r and this is not
7: 15 and they found the whole r strewn
9: 27 had happened, he fled up the r
12: 20 Beth Millo, on the r down to Silla.
18: 17 on the r to the Washerman's Field.
1Ch 26: 16 Gate on the upper r fell to Shuppim
26: 18 there were four at the r
Ezr 8: 22 to protect us from enemies on the r
Job 30: 13 They break up my r;
Pr 26: 13 says, "There is a lion in the r,
Ecc 10: 3 Even as he walks along the r,
Isa 7: 3 on the r to the Washerman's Field.
15: 5 on the r to Horonaim
36: 2 on the r to the Washerman's Field,
51: 10 who made a r in the depths
57: 14 "Build up, build up, prepare the r!
Jer 31: 21 the r that you take.
31: 21 "Set up r signs;
48: 5 on the r down to Horonaim
48: 19 Stand by the r and watch,
Eze 21: 19 a signpost where the r branches
21: 20 Mark out one r for the sword
21: 21 stop at the fork in the r,
47: 15 Great Sea by the Hethlon r
48: 1 the Hethlon r to Lebo Hamath;
Hos 6: 9 they murder on the r to Shechem,
Na 2: 1 watch the r,
Mt 7: 13 and broad is the r that leads
7: 14 and narrow the r that leads to life,
21: 8 crowd spread their cloaks on the r,
21: 8 the trees and spread them on the r.
21: 19 tree by the r, he went up to it
Mk 9: 33 were you arguing about on the r?"
10: 52 and followed Jesus along the r.
11: 8 people spread their cloaks on the r,
Lk 9: 57 As they were walking along the r,
10: 4 and do not greet anyone on the r.
10: 31 to be going down the same r,
19: 36 people spread their cloaks on the r.
19: 37 near the place where the r goes
24: 32 us while he talked with us on the r
Ac 8: 26 "Go south to the r— the desert r—
8: 36 As they traveled along the r,
9: 17 who appeared to you on the r
19: 1 Paul took the r through the interior
26: 13 as I was on the r, I saw a light

ROADS (ROAD)

Lev 26: 22 number that your r will be
Dt 19: 3 Build r to them and divide
Jdg 5: 6 days of Jael, the r were abandoned;
20: 31 fell in the open field and on the r—
20: 32 away from the city to the r."
20: 45 five thousand men along the r.
Isa 33: 8 no travelers are on the r.
49: 9 "They will feed beside the r
49: 11 I will turn all my mountains into r,
59: 8 have turned them into crooked r;
Jer 6: 25 or walk on the r,
18: 15 and on r not built up.
La 1: 4 The r to Zion mourn,
Eze 21: 19 mark out two r for the sword
21: 21 at the junction of the two r,
Lk 3: 5 crooked r shall become straight,
14: 23 'Go out to the r and country lanes

ROADSIDE (ROAD)

Ge 38: 16 he went over to her by the r
49: 17 Dan will be a serpent by the r,
Jer 3: 2 By the r you sat waiting for lovers,
Mt 20: 30 blind men were sitting by the r,
Mk 10: 46 was sitting by the r begging.
Lk 18: 35 man was sitting by the r begging.

ROAM (ROAMED ROAMING)

Jdg 11: 37 "Give me two months to r the hills
Isa 8: 21 they will r through the land;
Jer 2: 31 do my people say, 'We are free to r;
50: 6 caused them to r on the mountains.

ROAMED (ROAM)

1Sa 30: 31 where David and his men had r.
Job 30: 3 they r the parched land

ROAMING (ROAM)

Job 1: 7 "From r through the earth

Job 2: 2 "From *r* through the earth
Pr 26: 13 a fierce lion *r* the streets!"

ROAR (ROARED ROARING ROARS)

Job 4: 10 The lions may *r* and growl,
37: 2 Listen! Listen to the *r* of his voice,
37: 4 After that comes the sound of his *r;*
Ps 42: 7 deep in the *r* of your waterfalls;
46: 3 though its waters *r* and foam
104: 21 The lions *r* for their prey
Pr 19: 12 A king's rage is like the *r* of a lion,
20: 2 A king's wrath is like the *r* of a lion;
Isa 5: 29 Their *r* is like that of the lion,
5: 29 they *r* like young lions;
5: 30 In that day they will *r* over it
17: 12 they *r* like the roaring
17: 13 Although the peoples *r* like the *r*
51: 15 the sea so that its waves *r*—
Jer 5: 22 they may *r*, but they cannot cross it
10: 13 the waters in the heavens *r;*
11: 16 But with the *r* of a mighty storm
25: 30 and *r* mightily against his land.
25: 30 " 'The LORD will *r* from on high;
31: 35 the sea so that its waves *r*—
51: 16 the waters in the heavens *r;*
51: 38 Her people all *r* like young lions,
51: 55 the *r* of their voices will resound.
Eze 1: 24 like the *r* of rushing waters,
19: 9 so his *r* was heard no longer
43: 2 His voice was like the *r*
Hos 10: 14 the *r* of battle will rise
11: 10 he will *r* like a lion.
Joel 3: 16 The LORD will *r* from Zion
Am 3: 4 Does a lion *r* in the thicket
Zec 9: 15 They will drink and *r* as with wine;
11: 3 Listen to the *r* of the lions;
2Pe 3: 10 The heavens will disappear with a *r*
Rev 10: 3 and he gave a loud shout like the *r*
14: 2 a sound from heaven like the *r*
19: 1 this I heard what sounded like the *r*
19: 6 like the *r* of rushing waters

ROARED (ROAR)

Ps 74: 4 Your foes *r* in the place where you
Jer 2: 15 Lions have *r;*
Am 3: 8 The lion has *r*—
Hab 3: 10 the deep *r*

ROARING (ROAR)

Jdg 14: 5 suddenly a young lion came *r*
Ps 22: 13 *R* lions tearing their prey
65: 7 the *r* of their waves,
65: 7 who stilled the *r* of the seas,
Pr 28: 15 Like a *r* lion or a charging bear
Isa 5: 30 like the *r* of the sea.
17: 12 they roar like the *r* of great waters!
Jer 6: 23 They sound like the *r* sea
50: 42 They sound like the *r* sea
51: 42 its *r* waves will cover her.
Eze 19: 7 were terrified by his *r*.
22: 25 within her like a *r* lion tearing its
Zep 3: 3 Her officials are *r* lions,
Lk 21: 25 and perplexity at the *r* and tossing
1Pe 5: 8 prowls around like a *r* lion looking

ROARS (ROAR)

Jer 12: 8 She *r* at me;
Hos 11: 10 When he *r*,
Am 1: 2 "The LORD *r* from Zion

ROAST (ROASTED ROASTS)

Ex 12: 9 but *r* it over the fire—head,
Dt 16: 7 *R* it and eat it at the place
1Sa 2: 15 "Give the priest some meat to *r;*
Pr 12: 27 The lazy man does not *r* his game,

ROASTED (ROAST)

Ex 12: 8 are to eat the meat *r* over the fire,
Lev 2: 14 heads of new grain *r* in the fire.
23: 14 You must not eat any bread, or *r*
Jos 5: 11 unleavened bread and *r* grain.
Ru 2: 14 he offered her some *r* grain.
1Sa 17: 17 "Take this ephah of *r* grain
25: 18 dressed sheep, five seahs of *r* grain,
2Sa 17: 28 flour and *r* grain, beans and lentils,
2Ch 35: 13 They *r* the Passover animals
Isa 44: 19 I *r* meat and I ate.

ROASTS (ROAST)

Isa 44: 16 he *r* his meat and eats his fill.

ROB (ROBBED ROBBER ROBBERS ROBBERY ROBBING ROBS)

Lev 19: 13 defraud your neighbor or *r* him.
26: 22 and they will *r* you of your children
Jdg 9: 25 and *r* everyone who passed by,
14: 15 Did you invite us here to *r* us?"
Ps 35: 10 needy from those who *r* them."
Isa 10: 2 *r* my oppressed people of justice,
Hos 7: 1 bandits *r* in the streets;
Mal 3: 8 'How do we *r* you?' "In tithes
3: 8 "Will a man *r* God? Yet you *r* me.
Mt 12: 29 man? Then he can *r* his house.
Mk 3: 27 Then he can *r* his house.
Ro 2: 22 who abhor idols, do you *r* temples?

ROBBED (ROB)

Dt 28: 29 day you will be oppressed and *r*,
2Sa 17: 8 as fierce as a wild bear *r* of her cubs
Ps 7: 4 or without cause have *r* my foe—
Pr 4: 16 they are *r* of slumber
17: 12 Better to meet a bear *r* of her cubs
Isa 38: 10 and be *r* of the rest of my years?"
Jer 21: 12 the one who has been *r*,
22: 3 oppressor the one who has been *r*.
Eze 18: 18 *r* his brother and did what was
Hos 13: 8 Like a bear *r* of her cubs,
Mk 9: 17 by a spirit that has *r* him of speech.
Ac 19: 27 will be *r* of her divine majesty."
19: 37 though they have neither *r* temples
2Co 11: 8 I *r* other churches
1Ti 6: 5 who have been *r* of the truth

ROBBER (ROB)

Jn 10: 1 some other way, is a thief and a *r*.

ROBBERS (ROB)

Jer 7: 11 become a den of *r* to you?
Eze 7: 22 *r* will enter it and desecrate it.
Ob : 5 if *r* in the night—
Mt 21: 13 but you are making it a 'den of *r*.' "
27: 38 Two *r* were crucified with him,
27: 44 same way the *r* who were crucified
Mk 11: 17 But you have made it 'a den of *r*.' "
15: 27 They crucified two *r* with him,
Lk 10: 30 when he fell into the hands of *r*.
10: 36 fell into the hands of *r?*"
18: 11 *r*, evildoers, adulterers—or
19: 46 but you have made it 'a den of *r*.' "
Jn 10: 8 came before me were thieves and *r*,

ROBBERY (ROB)

Isa 61: 8 I hate *r* and iniquity.
Eze 18: 7 He does not commit *r*
18: 12 He commits *r*.
18: 16 He does not commit *r*
22: 29 practice extortion and commit *r;*

ROBBING (ROB)

Isa 10: 2 and *r* the fatherless.
Mal 3: 9 of you—because you are *r* me.

ROBE (ROBED ROBES)

Ge 37: 3 and he made a richly ornamented *r*
37: 23 the richly ornamented *r* he was
37: 23 they stripped him of his *r*—
37: 31 and dipped the *r* in the blood.
37: 31 now?" Then they got Joseph's *r*,
37: 32 They took the ornamented *r* back
37: 32 it to see whether it is your son's *r*."
37: 33 is my son's *r!* Some ferocious
Ex 28: 4 an ephod, a *r*, a woven tunic,
28: 31 "Make the *r* of the ephod entirely
28: 33 yarn around the hem of the *r*,
28: 34 alternate around the hem of the *r*.
29: 5 the *r* of the ephod, the ephod itself
39: 22 They made the *r* of the ephod
39: 23 the center of the *r* like the opening
39: 24 linen around the hem of the *r*.
39: 26 around the hem of the *r* to be worn
Lev 8: 7 clothed him with the *r*
Jos 7: 21 saw in the plunder a beautiful *r*
7: 24 the silver, the *r*, the gold wedge,
1Sa 2: 19 year his mother made him a little *r*
15: 27 hold of the edge of his *r*,
18: 4 took off the *r* he was wearing
1Sa 24: 4 and cut off a corner of Saul's *r*.
24: 5 for having cut off a corner of his *r*.
24: 11 I cut off the corner of your *r*
24: 11 at this piece of your *r* in my hand!
28: 14 old man wearing a *r* is coming up,"
2Sa 13: 18 was wearing a richly ornamented *r*,
13: 19 and tore the ornamented *r* she was
15: 32 his *r* torn and dust on his head.
1Ch 15: 27 clothed in a *r* of fine linen,
Ne 5: 13 also shook out the folds of my *r*
Est 6: 8 them bring a royal *r* the king has
6: 9 Let them *r* the man the king
6: 9 let the *r* and horse be entrusted
6: 10 Get the *r* and the horse and do just
6: 11 So Haman got the *r* and the horse.
8: 15 and a purple *r* of fine linen.
Job 1: 20 and tore his *r* and shaved his head.
29: 14 justice was my *r* and my turban.
SS 5: 3 I have taken off my *r*—
Isa 6: 1 the train of his *r* filled the temple.
22: 21 I will clothe him with your *r*
61: 10 arrayed me in a *r* of righteousness,
Mic 2: 8 You strip off the rich *r*
Zec 8: 23 hold of one Jew by the edge of his *r*
Mt 27: 28 and put a scarlet *r* on him,
27: 31 off the *r* and put his own clothes
Mk 15: 17 They put a purple *r* on him,
15: 20 they took off the purple *r*
16: 5 in a white *r* sitting on the right side,
Lk 15: 22 Bring the best *r* and put it on him.
23: 11 Dressing him in an elegant *r*,
Jn 19: 2 They clothed him in a purple *r*
19: 5 crown of thorns and the purple *r*,
Heb 1: 12 You will roll them up like a *r;*
Rev 1: 13 dressed in a *r* reaching
6: 11 each of them was given a white *r*,
19: 13 He is dressed in a *r* dipped in blood
19: 16 On his *r* and on his thigh he has

ROBED (ROBE)

Est 6: 11 He *r* Mordecai, and led him
Ps 93: 1 The LORD reigns, he is *r*
93: 1 the LORD is *r* in majesty
Isa 63: 1 Who is this, *r* in splendor,
Rev 10: 1 He was *r* in a cloud, with a rainbow

ROBES (ROBE)

Ge 41: 42 He dressed him in *r* of fine linen
49: 11 his *r* in the blood of grapes.
1Sa 19: 24 He stripped off his *r* and
1Ki 10: 5 the attending servants in their *r*,
10: 25 articles of silver and gold, *r*,
22: 10 Dressed in their royal *r*, the king
22: 30 but you wear your royal *r*."
2Ki 5: 7 he tore his *r* and said, "Am I God?
5: 8 the king of Israel had torn his *r*,
5: 8 "Why have you torn your *r?*
6: 30 the woman's words, he tore his *r*.
10: 22 Bring *r* for all the ministers of Baal
10: 22 So he brought out *r* for them.
11: 14 Athaliah tore her *r* and called out,
22: 11 the Book of the Law, he tore his *r*.
22: 19 and because you tore your *r*
2Ch 9: 4 the attending servants in their *r*,
9: 4 the cupbearers in their *r*
9: 24 and *r*, weapons and spices,
18: 9 Dressed in their royal *r*, the king
18: 29 but you wear your royal *r*."
23: 13 Athaliah tore her *r* and shouted,
34: 19 the words of the Law, he tore his *r*.
34: 27 and tore your *r* and wept
Est 5: 1 third day Esther put on her royal *r*
Job 2: 12 they tore their *r* and sprinkled dust
Ps 45: 8 All your *r* are fragrant with myrrh
133: 2 down upon the collar of his *r*.
Isa 3: 22 the fine *r* and the capes and cloaks,
Eze 26: 16 and lay aside their *r* and take
Da 3: 21 So these men, wearing their *r*,
3: 27 their *r* were not scorched,
Jnh 3: 6 from his throne, took off his royal *r*
Mk 12: 38 like to walk around in flowing *r*
Lk 20: 46 like to walk around in flowing *r*
Ac 9: 39 crying and showing him the *r*
12: 21 day Herod, wearing his royal *r*,
Rev 7: 9 They were wearing white *r*
7: 13 "These in white *r*—who are they,
7: 14 they have washed their *r*
22: 14 Blessed are those who wash their *r*,

ROBS (ROB)
Pr 19: 26 He who *r* his father and drives out
28: 24 He who *r* his father or mother

ROCK (ROCKS ROCKY)
Ge 49: 24 of the Shepherd, the *R* of Israel,
Ex 17: 6 Strike the *r*, and water will come
17: 6 there before you by the *r* at Horeb.
33: 21 me where you may stand on a *r*.
33: 22 I will put you in a cleft in the *r*
Nu 20: 8 Speak to that *r* before their eyes
20: 8 of the *r* for the community so they
20: 10 assembly together in front of the *r*
20: 10 we bring you water out of this *r?''*
20: 11 struck the *r* twice with his staff.
24: 21 your nest is set in a *r;*
Dt 8: 15 He brought you water out of hard *r*
32: 4 He is the *R*, his works are perfect,
32: 13 him with honey from the *r*,
32: 15 and rejected the *R* his Savior.
32: 18 You deserted the *R*, who fathered
32: 30 unless their *R* had sold them,
32: 31 For their rock is not like our *R*,
32: 31 For their *r* is not like our Rock,
32: 37 the *r* they took refuge in,
Jdg 6: 20 on this *r*, and pour out the broth."
6: 21 from the *r*, consuming the meat
7: 25 They killed Oreb at the *r* of Oreb,
13: 19 sacrificed it on a *r* to the LORD.
15: 8 stayed in a cave in the *r* of Etam.
15: 11 down to the cave in the *r* of Etam
15: 13 and led him up from the *r*.
20: 45 the desert to the *r* of Rimmon,
20: 47 into the desert to the *r* of Rimmon,
21: 13 the Benjamites at the *r* of Rimmon.
1Sa 2: 2 there is no *R* like our God.
6: 14 there it stopped beside a large *r*.
6: 15 and placed them on the large *r*.
6: 18 large *r*, on which they set the ark
23: 25 he went down to the *r*
2Sa 20: 8 were at the great *r* in Gibeon,
21: 10 and spread it out for herself on a *r*.
22: 2 "The LORD is my *r*, my fortress
22: 3 my God is my *r*, in whom I take
22: 32 And who is the *R* except our God?
22: 47 Exalted be God, the *R*, my Savior!
22: 47 LORD lives! Praise be to my *R!*
23: 3 the *R* of Israel said to me:
1Ch 11: 15 down to David to the *r* at the cave
Ne 9: 15 you brought them water from the *r;*
Job 14: 18 and as a *r* is moved from its place,
19: 24 or engraved in *r* forever!
28: 9 Man's hand assaults the flinty *r*
28: 10 He tunnels through the *r;*
29: 6 the *r* poured out for me streams
41: 24 His chest is hard as *r*,
Ps 18: 2 The LORD is my *r*, my fortress
18: 2 my God is my *r*, in whom I take
18: 31 And who is the *R* except our God?
18: 46 LORD lives! Praise be to my *R!*
19: 14 O LORD, my *R* and my Redeemer
27: 5 and set me high upon a *r*.
28: 1 To you I call, O LORD my *R;*
31: 2 be my *r* of refuge,
31: 3 Since you are my *r* and my fortress,
40: 2 he set my feet on a *r*
42: 9 I say to God my *R*,
61: 2 lead me to the *r* that is higher
62: 2 He alone is my *r* and my salvation;
62: 6 He alone is my *r* and my salvation;
62: 7 he is my mighty *r*, my refuge.
71: 3 Be my *r* of refuge,
71: 3 for you are my *r* and my fortress.
78: 20 he struck the *r*, water gushed out,
78: 35 remembered that God was their *R*,
81: 16 from the *r* I would satisfy you."
89: 26 my God, the *R* my Savior.'
92: 15 he is my *R*, and there is no
94: 22 my God the *r* in whom I take
95: 1 to the *R* of our salvation.
105: 41 He opened the *r*, and water gushed
114: 8 the hard *r* into springs of water.
114: 8 who turned the *r* into a pool,
144: 1 Praise be to the LORD, my *R*,
Pr 30: 19 the way of a snake on a *r*,
SS 2: 14 My dove in the clefts of the *r*
Isa 8: 14 and a *r* that makes them fall.
Isa 10: 26 down Midian at the *r* of Oreb;
17: 10 you have not remembered the *R*,
22: 16 chiseling your resting place in the *r*
26: 4 the LORD, is the *R* eternal.
30: 29 to the *R* of Israel.
32: 2 of a great *r* in a thirsty land.
44: 8 there is no other *R;* I know not one
48: 21 flow for them from the *r;*
48: 21 he split the *r*
51: 1 to the *r* from which you were cut
Jer 23: 29 "and like a hammer that breaks a *r*
51: 26 No *r* will be taken from you
Eze 24: 7 She poured it on the bare *r;*
24: 8 I put her blood on the bare *r*,
26: 4 her rubble and make her a bare *r*.
26: 14 I will make you a bare *r*,
Da 2: 34 you were watching, a *r* was cut out,
2: 35 the *r* that struck the statue became
2: 45 by human hands—a *r* that broke
2: 45 of the vision of the *r* cut out
Hab 1: 12 O *R*, you have ordained them
Zec 12: 3 make Jerusalem an immovable *r*
Mt 7: 24 man who built his house on the *r*.
7: 25 it had its foundation on the *r*.
16: 18 and on this *r* I will build my church
27: 60 tomb that he had cut out of the *r*.
Mk 15: 46 and placed it in a tomb cut out of *r*.
Lk 6: 48 and laid the foundation on *r*.
8: 6 fell on *r*, and when it came up,
8: 13 on the *r* are the ones who receive
23: 53 and placed it in a tomb cut in the *r*,
Ro 9: 33 and a *r* that makes them fall,
1Co 10: 4 the spiritual *r* that accompanied
10: 4 them, and that *r* was Christ.
1Pe 2: 8 and a *r* that makes them fall."

ROCKS (ROCK)
Dt 8: 9 a land where the *r* are iron
Jos 7: 26 they heaped up a large pile of *r*,
8: 29 they raised a large pile of *r* over it,
10: 18 "Roll large *r* up to the mouth
10: 27 of the cave they placed large *r*,
1Sa 13: 6 among the *r*, and in pits
2Sa 18: 17 piled up a large heap of *r* over him.
1Ki 19: 11 shattered the *r* before the LORD,
Job 8: 17 entwines its roots around a pile of *r*
18: 4 Or must the *r* be moved
22: 24 of Ophir to the *r* in the ravines,
24: 8 and hug the *r* for lack of shelter.
28: 6 sapphires come from its *r*,
30: 6 among the *r* and in holes
Ps 78: 15 He split the *r* in the desert
137: 9 and dashes them against the *r*.
Isa 2: 10 Go into the *r*,
2: 19 Men will flee to caves in the *r*
2: 21 They will flee to caverns in the *r*
7: 19 and in the crevices in the *r*,
Jer 4: 29 some climb up among the *r*.
13: 4 hide it there in a crevice in the *r*."
16: 16 hill and from the crevices of the *r*.
48: 28 your towns and dwell among the *r*,
49: 16 you who live in the clefts of the *r*,
Ob : 3 you who live in the clefts of the *r*
Na 1: 6 the *r* are shattered before him.
Mt 27: 51 The earth shook and the *r* split.
Ac 27: 29 we would be dashed against the *r*,
Rev 6: 15 and among the *r* of the mountains.
6: 16 called to the mountains and the *r*,

ROCKY (ROCK)
Nu 23: 9 From the *r* peaks I see them,
Job 39: 28 a *r* crag is his stronghold.
Ps 78: 16 he brought streams out of a *r* crag
Jer 18: 14 ever vanish from its *r* slopes?
21: 13 valley on the *r* plateau,
Am 6: 12 Do horses run on the *r* crags?
Mt 13: 5 on *r* places, where it did not have
13: 20 on *r* places is the man who hears
Mk 4: 5 on *r* places, where it did not have
4: 16 Others, like seed sown on *r* places,

ROD (RODS)
Ex 21: 20 slave with a *r* and the slave dies
Lev 27: 32 passes under the shepherd's *r*—
1Sa 17: 7 spear shaft was like a weaver's *r*,
2Sa 7: 14 I will punish him with the *r* of men,
21: 19 spear with a shaft like a weaver's *r*.
1Ch 11: 23 had a spear like a weaver's *r*
1Ch 20: 5 spear with a shaft like a weaver's *r*.
Job 9: 34 to remove God's *r* from me,
21: 9 the *r* of God is not upon them.
Ps 23: 4 your *r* and your staff,
89: 32 I will punish their sin with the *r*,
Pr 10: 13 *r* is for the back of him who lacks
13: 24 He who spares the *r* hates his son,
14: 3 A fool's talk brings a *r* to his back,
22: 8 the *r* of his fury will be destroyed.
22: 15 the *r* of discipline will drive it far
23: 13 if you punish him with the *r*,
23: 14 Punish him with the *r*
26: 3 and a *r* for the backs of fools!
29: 15 *r* of correction imparts wisdom,
Isa 9: 4 the *r* of their oppressor.
10: 5 to the Assyrian, the *r* of my anger,
10: 15 if a *r* were to wield him who lifts it
10: 24 who beat you with a *r*
10: 26 he will raise his *r* over the waters,
11: 4 the earth with the *r* of his mouth;
14: 5 The LORD has broken the *r*
14: 29 that the *r* that struck you is broken;
28: 27 caraway is beaten out with a *r*,
30: 32 them with his punishing *r*
La 3: 1 affliction by the *r* of his wrath.
Eze 7: 10 has burst forth, the *r* has budded,
7: 11 into a *r* to punish wickedness;
21: 10 have despised the *r* and all advice.
21: 13 is it that you have despised the *r?*
40: 3 and a measuring *r* in his hand.
40: 5 The length of the measuring *r*
40: 5 measuring *r* thick and one *r* high.
40: 6 of the gate; it was one *r* deep.
40: 7 facing the temple was one *r* deep.
40: 7 were one *r* long and one *r* wide,
41: 8 the length of the *r*, six long cubits.
42: 16 side with the measuring *r;*
42: 17 cubits by the measuring *r*.
42: 18 cubits by the measuring *r*.
42: 19 cubits by the measuring *r*.
Mic 5: 1 ruler on the cheek with a *r*.
6: 9 "Heed the *r* and the One who
Heb 9: 4 Aaron's *r* that had budded,
Rev 11: 1 was given a reed like a measuring *r*
21: 15 with me had a measuring *r* of gold
21: 16 He measured the city with the *r*

RODANIM
Ge 10: 4 Tarshish, the Kittim and the *R*.
1Ch 1: 7 Tarshish, the Kittim and the *R*.

RODE (RIDE)
Jdg 10: 4 thirty sons, who *r* thirty donkeys.
12: 14 who *r* on seventy donkeys.
1Sa 30: 17 four hundred young men who *r*
1Ki 13: 14 and *r* after the man of God.
18: 45 came on and Ahab *r* off to Jezreel.
2Ki 9: 16 got into his chariot and *r* to Jezreel,
9: 18 The horseman *r* off to meet Jehu
9: 21 and Ahaziah king of Judah *r* out,
Est 8: 10 who *r* fast horses especially bred
Hab 3: 8 sea when you *r* with your horses
Rev 6: 2 and he *r* out as a conqueror bent

RODENTS
Isa 2: 20 away to the *r* and bats

RODS (ROD)
Job 40: 18 his limbs like *r* of iron.
SS 5: 14 His arms are *r* of gold
2Co 11: 25 Three times I was beaten with *r*,

ROE (ROEBUCKS)
Dt 14: 5 gazelle, the *r* deer, the wild goat,

ROEBUCKS (ROE)
1Ki 4: 23 gazelles, *r* and choice fowl.

ROGELIM
2Sa 17: 27 Gileadite from *R* brought bedding
19: 31 also came down from *R*

ROHGAH
1Ch 7: 34 Ahi, *R*, Hubbah and Aram.

ROLL (ROLLED ROLLING ROLLS)
Ge 29: 3 shepherds would *r* the stone away
Jos 10: 18 "*R* large rocks up to the mouth

1Sa 14: 33 *R* a large stone over here at once.''
Pr 26: 27 if a man rolls a stone, it will *r* back
Isa 22: 18 He will *r* you up tightly like a ball
Jer 5: 22 The waves may *r*, but they cannot
6: 26 and *r* in ashes;
25: 34 *r* in the dust, you leaders
51: 25 *r* you off the cliffs,
Eze 27: 30 and *r* in ashes.
Am 5: 24 But let justice *r* on like a river,
Mic 1: 10 *r* in the dust.
Mk 16: 3 ''Who will *r* the stone away
Heb 1: 12 You will *r* them up like a robe;

ROLLED (ROLL)

Ge 29: 8 and the stone has been *r* away
29: 10 *r* the stone away from the mouth
Jos 5: 9 ''Today I have *r* away the reproach
2Ki 2: 8 *r* it up and struck the water with it.
Isa 9: 5 and every garment *r* in blood
28: 27 nor is a cartwheel *r* over cummin;
34: 4 and the sky *r* up like a scroll;
38: 12 Like a weaver I have *r* up my life,
Mt 27: 60 He *r* a big stone in front
28: 2 *r* back the stone and sat on it.
Mk 9: 20 He fell to the ground and *r* around,
15: 46 he *r* a stone against the entrance
16: 4 was very large, had been *r* away.
Lk 4: 20 Then he *r* up the scroll, gave it back
24: 2 They found the stone *r* away

ROLLING (ROLL)

Job 30: 14 amid the ruins they come *r* in.
Rev 6: 14 The sky receded like a scroll, *r* up,

ROLLS (ROLL)

Pr 26: 27 if a man *r* a stone, it will roll back
Isa 9: 18 so that it *r* upward in a column

ROMAMTI-EZER

1Ch 25: 4 Giddalti and *R*; Joshbekashah,
25: 31 12 the twenty-fourth to *R*,

ROMAN (ROME)

Lk 2: 1 taken of the entire *R* world.
Jn 18: 28 to the palace of the *R* governor.
Ac 11: 28 spread over the entire *R* world.
16: 12 a *R* colony and the leading city
16: 37 even though we are *R* citizens,
16: 38 that Paul and Silas were *R* citizens,
21: 31 of the *R* troops that the whole city
22: 25 you to flog a *R* citizen who hasn't
22: 26 ''This man is a *R* citizen.''
22: 27 are you a *R* citizen?'' ''Yes, I am,''
22: 29 that he had put Paul, a *R* citizen,
23: 27 I had learned that he is a *R* citizen.
25: 16 them that it is not the *R* custom

ROMANS (ROME)

Jn 11: 48 and then the *R* will come
Ac 16: 21 customs unlawful for us *R*
28: 17 and handed over to the *R*.

ROME (ROMAN ROMANS)

Ac 2: 10 visitors from *R* (both Jews
18: 2 had ordered all the Jews to leave *R*.
19: 21 he said, ''I must visit *R* also.''
23: 11 so you must also testify in *R*.''
25: 25 I decided to send him to *R*.
28: 14 And so we went to *R*.
28: 16 got to *R*, Paul was allowed
Ro 1: 7 To all in *R* who are loved by God
1: 15 also to you who are at *R*.
2Ti 1: 17 On the contrary, when he was in *R*,

ROOF (ROOFED ROOFING ROOFS)

Ge 6: 16 Make a *r* for it and finish the ark
19: 8 under the protection of my *r*.''
Dt 22: 8 house if someone falls from the *r*.
22: 8 make a parapet around your *r*
Jos 2: 6 (But she had taken them up to the *r*
2: 6 of flax she had laid out on the *r*.)
2: 8 up on the *r* and said to them,
Jdg 9: 51 and climbed up on the tower *r*.
16: 27 on the *r* were about three thousand
1Sa 9: 25 with Saul on the *r* of his house.
9: 26 and Samuel called to Saul on the *r*,
2Sa 11: 2 From the *r* he saw a woman
11: 2 around on the *r* of the palace.
2Sa 16: 22 a tent for Absalom on the *r*,
18: 24 up to the *r* of the gateway
1Ki 7: 6 were pillars and an overhanging *r*.
2Ki 4: 10 Let's make a small room on the *r*
23: 12 on the *r* near the upper room
Job 29: 10 stuck to the *r* of their mouths.
Ps 22: 15 sticks to the *r* of my mouth;
137: 6 cling to the *r* of my mouth
Pr 21: 9 Better to live on a corner of the *r*
25: 24 Better to live on a corner of the *r*
La 4: 4 sticks to the *r* of its mouth;
Eze 3: 26 stick to the *r* of your mouth
Da 4: 29 walking on the *r* of the royal palace
Mt 8: 8 to have you come under my *r*.
24: 17 Let no one on the *r* of his house go
Mk 2: 4 an opening in the *r* above Jesus
13: 15 Let no one on the *r* of his house go
Lk 5: 19 up on the *r* and lowered him
7: 6 to have you come under my *r*.
17: 31 is on the *r* of his house,
Ac 10: 9 Peter went up on the *r* to pray.

ROOFED (ROOF)

1Ki 7: 3 It was *r* with cedar

ROOFING (ROOF)

1Ki 6: 9 *r* it with beams and cedar planks.
Ne 3: 15 *r* it over and putting its doors

ROOFS (ROOF)

Ne 8: 16 themselves booths on their own *r*,
Isa 15: 3 on the *r* and in the public squares
Jer 19: 13 on the *r* to all the starry hosts
32: 29 by burning incense on the *r* to Baal

ROOM (ROOMS STOREROOM STOREROOMS)

Ge 24: 23 is there *r* in your father's house
24: 25 well as *r* for you to spend the night
26: 22 ''Now the Lord has given us *r*
34: 21 the land has plenty of *r* for them.
43: 30 He went into his private *r*
Lev 26: 10 out to make *r* for the new.
Nu 22: 26 narrow place where there was no *r*
Jdg 3: 20 in the upper *r* of his summer palace
3: 23 the doors of the upper *r* behind him
3: 24 himself in the inner *r* of the house.''
3: 24 the doors of the upper *r* locked.
3: 25 he did not open the doors of the *r*,
15: 1 He said, ''I'm going to my wife's *r*.''
16: 9 With men hidden in the *r*,
16: 12 hidden in the *r*, she called to him,
2Sa 18: 33 up to the *r* over the gateway
1Ki 1: 15 went to see the aged king in his *r*,
6: 17 front of this *r* was forty cubits long.
6: 27 cherubim inside the innermost *r*
6: 27 other in the middle of the *r*.
7: 50 for the doors of the innermost *r*,
17: 19 to the upper *r* where he was staying
17: 23 down from the *r* into the house.
20: 30 to the city and hid in an inner *r*.
22: 25 go to hide in an inner *r*.''
2Ki 1: 2 the lattice of his upper *r* in Samaria
4: 10 Let's make a small *r* on the roof
4: 11 up to his *r* and lay down there.
4: 35 and walked back and forth in the *r*
9: 2 and take him into an inner *r*.
23: 11 were in the court near the *r*
23: 12 the roof near the upper *r* of Ahaz,
2Ch 18: 24 go to hide in an inner *r*.''
Ezr 10: 6 and went to the *r* of Jehohanan son
Ne 2: 14 but there was not enough *r*
3: 31 and as far as the *r* above the corner;
3: 32 and between the *r* above the corner
13: 5 him with a large *r* formerly used
13: 7 done in providing Tobiah a *r*
13: 8 household goods out of the *r*.
Ps 10: 4 in all his thoughts there is no *r*
SS 3: 4 to the *r* of the one who conceived
Jer 7: 32 in Topheth until there is no more *r*.
19: 11 in Topheth until there is no more *r*.
35: 4 It was next to the *r* of the officials,
35: 4 into the *r* of the sons of Hanan son
36: 10 From the *r* of Gemariah son
36: 12 went down to the secretary's *r*
36: 20 in the *r* of Elishama the secretary,
36: 21 it from the *r* of Elishama
38: 11 and went to a *r* under the treasury
Eze 40: 38 A *r* with a doorway was
40: 45 ''The *r* facing south is
40: 46 and the *r* facing north is
41: 5 each side *r* around the temple was
Da 6: 10 to his upstairs *r* where the windows
Joel 2: 16 Let the bridegroom leave his *r*
Zec 10: 10 there will not be *r* enough for them.
Mal 3: 10 that you will not have *r* enough
Mt 6: 6 When you pray, go into your *r*,
Mk 2: 2 gathered that there was no *r* left,
14: 14 Teacher asks: Where is my guest *r*,
14: 15 He will show you a large upper *r*,
Lk 2: 7 there was no *r* for them in the inn.
14: 22 has been done, but there is still *r*.'
22: 11 Teacher asks: Where is the guest *r*,
22: 12 He will show you a large upper *r*,
Jn 8: 37 because you have no *r* for my word
21: 25 the whole world would not have *r*
Ac 1: 13 to the *r* where they were staying.
9: 37 and placed in an upstairs *r*.
9: 39 he was taken upstairs to the *r*.
9: 40 Peter sent them all out of the *r*;
20: 8 in the upstairs *r* where we were
25: 23 and entered the audience *r*
26: 31 They left the *r*, and while talking
Ro 12: 19 but leave *r* for God's wrath,
2Co 7: 2 Make *r* for us in your hearts.
Phm : 22 one thing more: Prepare a guest *r*
Heb 9: 2 In its first *r* were the lampstand,
9: 3 curtain was a *r* called the Most
9: 6 regularly into the outer *r* to carry
9: 7 the high priest entered the inner *r*,

ROOMS (ROOM)

Ge 6: 14 make *r* in it and coat it with pitch
1Ki 6: 5 in which there were side *r*.
6: 10 And he built the side *r* all
6: 29 in both the inner and outer *r*,
6: 30 and outer *r* of the temple with gold.
1Ch 9: 26 with the responsibility for the *r*
9: 33 stayed in the *r* of the temple
23: 28 charge of the courtyards, the side *r*,
28: 11 its inner *r* and the place
28: 12 Lord and all the surrounding *r*,
Ne 13: 9 I gave orders to purify the *r*,
Pr 24: 4 through knowledge its *r* are filled
Isa 26: 20 Go, my people, enter your *r*
Jer 22: 13 his upper *r* by injustice,
22: 14 with spacious upper *r*.'
35: 2 to one of the side *r* of the house
Eze 40: 17 There I saw some *r* and a pavement
40: 17 there were thirty *r*
40: 44 within the inner court, were two *r*,
41: 6 The side *r* were on three levels,
41: 6 as supports for the side *r*,
41: 7 side *r* all around the temple were
41: 7 so that the *r* widened as one went
41: 8 the foundation of the side *r*.
41: 9 between the side *r* of the temple
41: 9 of the side *r* was five cubits thick.
41: 10 ⌊priests'⌋ *r* was twenty cubits wide
41: 11 to the side *r* from the open area,
41: 26 The side *r* of the temple
42: 1 and brought me to the *r*
42: 4 of the *r* was an inner passageway
42: 5 Now the upper *r* were narrower,
42: 5 them than from the *r* on the lower
42: 6 *r* on the third floor had no pillars,
42: 7 in front of the *r* for fifty cubits.
42: 7 was an outer wall parallel to the *r*
42: 8 While the row of *r* on the side next
42: 9 The lower *r* had an entrance
42: 10 were *r* with a passageway in front
42: 11 These were like the *r* on the north;
42: 12 by which one enters the *r*.
42: 12 the doorways of the *r* on the south.
42: 13 south *r* facing the temple courtyard
42: 13 temple courtyard are the priests' *r*,
44: 19 are to leave them in the sacred *r*,
46: 19 gate to the sacred *r* facing north,
Mt 24: 26 in the inner *r*,' do not believe it.
Lk 12: 3 in the inner *r* will be proclaimed
Jn 14: 2 In my Father's house are many *r*;

ROOST

Zep 2: 14 will *r* on her columns.

ROOSTER
Pr 30: 31 a strutting *r*, a he-goat,
Mt 26: 34 this very night, before the *r* crows,
26: 74 the man!" Immediately a *r* crowed.
26: 75 "Before the *r* crows, you will
Mk 13: 35 or when the *r* crows, or at dawn.
14: 30 before the *r* crows twice you
14: 72 Immediately the *r* crowed
14: 72 "Before the *r* crows twice you will
Lk 22: 34 Peter, before the *r* crows today,
22: 60 as he was speaking, the *r* crowed.
22: 61 "Before the *r* crows today,
Jn 13: 38 before the *r* crows,
18: 27 at that moment a *r* began to crow.

ROOT (ROOTED ROOTS)
Dt 29: 18 make sure there is no *r*
2Ki 19: 30 will take *r* below and bear fruit
Job 5: 3 I myself have seen a fool taking *r*,
19: 28 since the *r* of the trouble lies in him
30: 4 their food was the *r*
Ps 80: 9 and it took *r* and filled the land.
80: 15 the *r* your right hand has planted,
Pr 12: 12 but the *r* of the righteous flourishes
Isa 11: 10 In that day the *R* of Jesse will stand
14: 29 from the *r* of that snake will spring
14: 30 But your *r* I will destroy by famine;
27: 6 In days to come Jacob will take *r*,
37: 31 will take *r* below and bear fruit
40: 24 no sooner do they take *r*
53: 2 and like a *r* out of dry ground.
Jer 12: 2 them, and they have taken *r*;
Hos 9: 16 their *r* is withered,
Mal 4: 1 "Not a *r* or a branch will be left
Mt 3: 10 already at the *r* of the trees,
13: 6 withered because they had no *r*.
13: 21 But since he has no *r*, he lasts only
13: 29 you may *r* up the wheat with them.
Mk 4: 6 withered because they had no *r*.
4: 17 since they have no *r*, they last only
Lk 3: 9 already at the *r* of the trees,
8: 13 they hear it, but they have no *r*.
Ro 11: 16 if the *r* is holy, so are the branches.
11: 17 the nourishing sap from the olive *r*,
11: 18 the *r*, but the *r* supports you.
15: 12 "The *r* of Jesse will spring up,
1Ti 6: 10 of money is a *r* of all kinds of evil.
Heb 12: 15 and that no bitter *r* grows up
Rev 5: 5 the *R* of David, has triumphed.
22: 16 I am the *R* and the Offspring

ROOTED (ROOT)
Eph 3: 17 being *r* and established in love,
Col 2: 7 continue to live in him, *r*

ROOTS (ROOT)
Jdg 5: 14 from Ephraim, whose *r* were
Job 8: 17 it entwines its *r* around a pile
14: 8 Its *r* may grow old in the ground
18: 16 His *r* dry up below
28: 9 lays bare the *r* of the mountains.
29: 19 My *r* will reach to the water,
Isa 5: 24 so their *r* will decay
11: 1 from his *r* a Branch will bear fruit.
Jer 17: 8 that sends out its *r* by the stream.
Eze 17: 6 but its *r* remained under it.
17: 7 The vine now sent out its *r*
17: 9 many people to pull it up by the *r*.
31: 7 for its *r* went down
Da 4: 15 But let the stump and its *r*,
4: 23 while its *r* remain in the ground.
4: 26 with its *r* means that your kingdom
Hos 14: 5 he will send down his *r*;
Am 2: 9 and his *r* below.
Jnh 2: 6 To the *r* of the mountains I sank
Mt 15: 13 planted will be pulled up by the *r*.
Mk 11: 20 the fig tree withered from the *r*.

ROPE (ROPES)
Ex 28: 14 like a *r*, and attach the chains
28: 22 chains of pure gold, like a *r*.
39: 15 chains of pure gold, like a *r*.
Jos 2: 15 down by a *r* through the window,
Job 41: 1 or tie down his tongue with a *r*?
Isa 3: 24 instead of a sash, a *r*;

ROPES (ROPE)
Ex 35: 18 their *r*; the woven garments worn
39: 40 the *r* and tent pegs
Nu 3: 26 and the *r*— and everything related
3: 37 with their bases, tent pegs and *r*.
4: 26 the *r* and all the equipment used
4: 32 *r*, all their equipment
Jdg 15: 13 So they bound him with two new *r*
15: 14 *r* on his arms became like charred
16: 11 with new *r* that have never been
16: 12 But he snapped the *r* off his arms
16: 12 So Delilah took new *r*
2Sa 17: 13 then all Israel will bring *r*
1Ki 20: 31 sackcloth around our waists and *r*
20: 32 sackcloth around their waists and *r*
Job 39: 5 Who untied his *r*?
Ps 119: 61 Though the wicked bind me with *r*,
Isa 5: 18 and wickedness as with cart *r*,
33: 20 nor any of its *r* broken.
Jer 10: 20 all its *r* are snapped.
38: 6 Jeremiah by *r* into the cistern;
38: 11 let them down with *r* to Jeremiah
38: 12 under your arms to pad the *r*."
38: 13 and they pulled him up with the *r*
Eze 3: 25 son of man, they will tie with *r*;
4: 8 up with *r* so that you cannot turn
Ac 27: 17 they passed *r* under the ship itself
27: 32 So the soldiers cut the *r* that held
27: 40 same time untied the *r* that held

ROSE (RISE)
Ge 7: 18 The waters *r* and increased greatly
7: 19 They *r* greatly on the earth,
7: 20 The waters *r* and covered
23: 3 Abraham *r* from beside his dead
23: 7 Then Abraham *r* and bowed
32: 31 The sun *r* above him as he passed
37: 7 the field when suddenly my sheaf *r*
Ex 32: 6 So the next day the people *r* early
33: 8 all the people *r* and stood
Nu 16: 2 became insolent and *r* up
Jos 8: 19 the men in the ambush *r* quickly
Jdg 3: 20 As the king *r* from his seat,
6: 38 Gideon *r* early the next day;
9: 43 out of the city, he *r* to attack them.
10: 1 the son of Dodo, *r* to save Israel.
19: 8 when he *r* to go, the girl's father
20: 8 All the people *r* as one man,
1Sa 5: 3 of Ashdod *r* early the next day,
5: 4 the following morning when they *r*,
9: 26 They *r* about daybreak
2Sa 18: 31 from all who *r* up against you."
22: 9 Smoke *r* from his nostrils;
1Ki 1: 49 all Adonijah's guests *r* in alarm
8: 54 he *r* from before the altar
18: 45 black with clouds, the wind *r*,
2Ki 3: 24 the Israelites *r* up and fought them
8: 21 he *r* up and broke through by night;
1Ch 21: 1 Satan *r* up against Israel
28: 2 King David *r* to his feet and said:
2Ch 20: 23 and Moab *r* up against the men
21: 9 he *r* up and broke through by night.
Ezr 9: 5 I *r* from my self-abasement,
10: 5 So Ezra *r* up and put the leading
Est 5: 9 and observed that he neither *r*
Job 29: 8 and the old men *r* to their feet;
Ps 18: 8 Smoke *r* from his nostrils;
76: 9 when you, O God, *r* up to judge,
78: 21 and his wrath *r* against Israel,
78: 31 God's anger *r* against them;
SS 2: 1 I am a *r* of Sharon,
Eze 1: 19 and when the living creatures *r*
1: 19 from the ground, the wheels also *r*.
1: 21 and when the creatures *r*
1: 21 the wheels *r* along with them,
10: 4 LORD *r* from above the cherubim
10: 15 Then the cherubim *r* upward.
10: 17 and when the cherubim *r*, they *r*
10: 19 cherubim spread their wings and *r*
16: 13 You became very beautiful and *r*
Jnh 2: 7 and my prayer *r* to you,
3: 6 he *r* from his throne, took
4: 8 When the sun *r*, God provided
Mt 7: 25 The rain came down, the streams *r*,
7: 27 The rain came down, the streams *r*,
Mk 16: 9 When Jesus *r* early on the first day
Lk 22: 45 When he *r* from prayer
23: 1 Then the whole assembly *r*
Ac 10: 41 with him after he *r* from the dead.
26: 30 king *r*, and with him the governor
1Th 4: 14 believe that Jesus died and *r* again
Rev 9: 2 smoke *r* from it like the smoke

ROSH
Ge 46: 21 Gera, Naaman, Ehi, *R*, Muppim,

ROT (ROTS ROTTED ROTTEN)
Pr 10: 7 but the name of the wicked will *r*.
Isa 40: 20 selects wood that will not *r*.
50: 2 their fish *r* for lack of water
Hos 5: 12 like *r* to the people of Judah.
Zec 14: 12 Their flesh will *r* while they are still
14: 12 their eyes will *r* in their sockets,
14: 12 their tongues will *r* in their mouths.

ROTS (ROT)
Pr 14: 30 but envy *r* the bones.

ROTTED (ROT)
Jas 5: 2 Your wealth has *r*, and moths have

ROTTEN (ROT)
Job 13: 28 man wastes away like something *r*,
41: 27 and bronze like *r* wood.

ROUGH (ROUGHER ROUGHS)
Isa 40: 4 the *r* ground shall become level,
42: 16 and make the *r* places smooth.
Lk 3: 5 the *r* ways smooth.
Jn 6: 18 was blowing and the waters grew *r*.

ROUGHER (ROUGH)
Jnh 1: 11 The sea was getting *r* and *r*.

ROUGHS (ROUGH)
Isa 44: 13 he *r* it out with chisels

ROUND (ROUNDED ROUNDS)
Jdg 7: 13 "A *r* loaf of barley bread came
1Ki 7: 31 This opening was *r*,
7: 31 of the stands were square, not *r*.
Ecc 1: 6 *r* and *r* it goes,
Eze 19: 8 those from regions *r* about.

ROUNDED (ROUND)
1Ki 10: 19 six steps, and its back had a *r* top.
SS 7: 2 Your navel is a *r* goblet
Ac 17: 5 so they *r* up some bad characters

ROUNDS (ROUND)
SS 3: 3 as they made their *r* in the city.
5: 7 as they made their *r* in the city.

ROUSE (AROUSE AROUSED AROUSES ROUSED ROUSES)
Ge 49: 9 like a lioness—who dares to *r* him?
Nu 23: 24 they *r* themselves like a lion
24: 9 a lioness—who dares to *r* them?
Job 3: 8 those who are ready to *r* Leviathan
8: 6 even now he will *r* himself
41: 10 No one is fierce enough to *r* him.
Ps 44: 23 *R* yourself! Do not reject us
59: 5 *r* yourself to punish all the nations;
Isa 28: 21 he will *r* himself as in the Valley
Joel 3: 7 I am going to *r* them out
3: 9 *R* the warriors!
Zec 9: 13 I will *r* your sons, O Zion,

ROUSED (ROUSE)
Job 14: 12 or be *r* from their sleep.
SS 8: 5 Under the apple tree I *r* you;
Eze 7: 6 The end has come! It has *r* itself
Joel 3: 12 "Let the nations be *r*;
Zec 2: 13 he has *r* himself from his holy

ROUSES (ROUSE)
Isa 14: 9 it *r* the spirits of the departed

ROUT (ROUTED ROUTING ROUTS)
Jdg 1: 5 putting to *r* the Canaanites
Ps 92: 11 my ears have heard the *r*
144: 6 shoot your arrows and *r* them.

ROUTE (ROUTES)
Nu 14: 25 the desert along the *r* to the Red
21: 4 Hor along the *r* to the Red
Dt 1: 22 back a report about the *r* we are
1: 40 the desert along the *r* to the Red
2: 1 the desert along the *r* to the Red

Jdg 8: 11 up by the *r* of the nomads east
2Ki 3: 8 "By what *r* shall we attack?"
Mt 2: 12 to their country by another *r*.

ROUTED (ROUT)

Ge 14: 15 men to attack them and he *r* them,
Jos 7: 4 but they were *r* by the men of Ai,
7: 8 now that Israel has been *r*
Jdg 4: 15 LORD *r* Sisera and all his chariots
1Sa 7: 10 into such a panic that they were *r*
2Sa 10: 15 Arameans saw that they had been *r*
22: 15 bolts of lightning and *r* them.
2Ki 14: 12 Judah was *r* by Israel, and every
1Ch 19: 16 Arameans saw that they had been *r*
2Ch 13: 15 God *r* Jeroboam and all Israel
25: 22 Judah was *r* by Israel, and every
Ps 18: 14 great bolts of lightning and *r* them.
Heb 11: 34 in battle and *r* foreign armies.

ROUTES (ROUTE)

Job 6: 18 Caravans turn aside from their *r*;

ROUTING (ROUT)

Jdg 8: 12 captured them, *r* their entire army.

ROUTS (ROUT)

Jos 23: 10 One of you *r* a thousand,

ROVING

Ecc 6: 9 sees than the *r* of the appetite.

ROW (ROWED ROWS)

Ex 28: 17 In the first *r* there shall be a ruby,
28: 18 in the second *r* a turquoise,
28: 19 in the third *r* a jacinth, an agate
28: 20 in the fourth *r* a chrysolite,
39: 10 In the first *r* there was a ruby,
39: 11 in the second *r* a turquoise,
39: 12 in the third *r* a jacinth, an agate
39: 13 in the fourth *r* a chrysolite,
39: 37 lampstand with its *r* of lamps
Lev 24: 6 Set them in two rows, six in each *r*,
24: 7 Along each *r* put some pure
1Ki 7: 3 forty-five beams, fifteen to a *r*.
Eze 42: 8 While the *r* of rooms
42: 8 *r* on the side nearest the sanctuary
Jnh 1: 13 the men did their best to *r* back

ROWED (ROW)

Jn 6: 19 When they had *r* three or three

ROWS (ROW)

Ex 28: 17 mount four *r* of precious stones
39. 10 Then they mounted four *r*
Lev 24: 6 Set them in two *r*, six in each row,
1Ki 7: 2 with four *r* of cedar columns
7: 18 in two *r* encircling each network
7: 20 two hundred pomegranates in *r* all
7: 24 cast in two *r* in one piece
7: 42 of network (two *r* of pomegranates
2Ch 4: 3 cast in two *r* in one piece
4: 13 of network (two *r* of pomegranates
Job 41: 15 His back has *r* of shields

ROYAL (ROYALTY)

Jos 10: 2 like one of the *r* cities; it was larger
11: 12 Joshua took all these *r* cities
13: 31 Edrei (the *r* cities of Og in Bashan).
1Sa 27: 5 live in the *r* city with you?"
2Sa 8: 18 and David's sons were *r* advisers.
12: 26 and captured the *r* citadel.
14: 26 hundred shekels by the *r* standard.
1Ki 1: 9 men of Judah who were *r* officials,
1: 46 has taken his seat on the *r* throne.
1: 47 Also, the *r* officials have come
4: 7 for the king and the *r* household.
5: 9 food for my *r* household."
9: 1 of the LORD and the *r* palace,
9: 5 I will establish your *r* throne
9: 10 of the LORD and the *r* palace—
10: 12 of the LORD and for the *r* palace,
10: 13 had given her out of his *r* bounty.
10: 28 the *r* merchants purchased them
11: 3 had seven hundred wives of *r* birth
11: 14 from the *r* line of Edom.
11: 20 brought up in the *r* palace.
14: 26 and the treasures of the *r* palace.
14: 27 duty at the entrance to the *r* palace.
1Ki 16: 18 went into the citadel of the *r* palace
22: 10 Dressed in their *r* robes, the king
22: 30 but you wear your *r* robes."
2Ki 7: 9 and report this to the *r* palace."
10: 6 Now the *r* princes, seventy of them
11: 1 to destroy the whole *r* family.
11: 2 among the *r* princes who were
11: 5 a third of you guarding the *r* palace
11: 19 then took his place on the *r* throne,
12: 10 the *r* secretary and the high priest
12: 18 of the LORD and of the *r* palace,
14: 14 in the treasuries of the *r* palace.
15: 25 citadel of the *r* palace at Samaria.
16: 8 and in the treasuries of the *r* palace
16: 18 and removed the *r* entryway
18: 15 in the treasuries of the *r* palace.
24: 13 of the LORD and from the *r* palace
25: 9 the *r* palace and all the houses
25: 19 fighting men and five *r* advisers.
25: 25 of Elishama, who was of *r* blood,
1Ch 27: 25 was in charge of the *r* storehouses.
27: 34 was the commander of the *r* army.
29: 25 bestowed on him *r* splendor such
2Ch 1: 16 the *r* merchants purchased them
2: 1 Name of the LORD and a *r* palace
7: 11 of the LORD and the *r* palace,
7: 18 I will establish your *r* throne,
9: 11 of the LORD and for the *r* palace,
12: 9 and the treasures of the *r* palace.
12: 10 duty at the entrance to the *r* palace.
18: 9 Dressed in their *r* robes, the king
18: 29 but you wear your *r* robes."
22: 10 to destroy the whole *r* family
22: 11 among the *r* princes who were
23: 5 a third of you at the *r* palace
23: 20 and seated the king on the *r* throne,
24: 11 the *r* secretary and the officer
26: 11 of Hananiah, one of the *r* officials.
28: 21 the *r* palace and from the princes
Ezr 4: 13 and the *r* revenues will suffer.
4: 22 to the detriment of the *r* interests?
5: 17 in the *r* archives of Babylon to see
6: 4 are to be paid by the *r* treasury.
6: 8 to be fully paid out of the *r* treasury
7: 20 provide from the *r* treasury.
8: 36 the king's orders to the *r* satraps
Est 1: 2 from his *r* throne in the citadel
1: 7 and the *r* wine was abundant,
1: 9 in the *r* palace of King Xerxes.
1: 11 Vashti, wearing her *r* crown,
1: 19 Also let the king give her *r* position
1: 19 let him issue a *r* decree
2: 16 to King Xerxes in the *r* residence
2: 17 So he set a *r* crown on her head
2: 18 distributed gifts with *r* liberality.
3: 2 All the *r* officials at the king's gate
3: 3 *r* officials at the king's gate asked
3: 9 talents of silver into the *r* treasury
3: 12 first month the *r* secretaries were
4: 7 promised to pay into the *r* treasury
4: 11 people of the *r* provinces know that
4: 14 that you have come to *r* position
5: 1 sitting on his *r* throne in the hall,
5: 1 third day Esther put on her *r* robes
6: 8 have them bring a *r* robe the king
6: 8 one with a *r* crest placed
8: 9 At once the *r* secretaries were
8: 14 riding the *r* horses, raced out,
8: 15 king's presence wearing *r* garments
Ps 45: 9 at your right hand is the *r* bride
72: 1 the *r* son with your righteousness.
SS 6: 12 among the *r* chariots of my people.
7: 5 Your hair is like *r* tapestry;
Isa 17: 3 and *r* power from Damascus;
60: 16 and be nursed at *r* breasts.
62: 3 a *r* diadem in the hand of your God
Jer 21: 11 say to the *r* house of Judah,
26: 10 up from the *r* palace to the house
32: 2 the guard in the *r* palace of Judah.
33: 4 *r* palaces of Judah that have been
36: 12 secretary's room in the *r* palace,
38: 7 a Cushite, an official in the *r* palace
39: 8 Babylonians set fire to the *r* palace
41: 1 was of *r* blood and had been one
43: 10 he will spread his *r* canopy
52: 13 the *r* palace and all the houses
52: 25 fighting men, and seven *r* advisers.
Eze 17: 13 he took a member of the *r* family
Da 1: 3 of the Israelites from the *r* family
1: 8 not to defile himself with the *r* food
1: 13 the young men who eat the *r* food,
1: 15 the young men who ate the *r* food.
2: 49 himself remained at the *r* court.
3: 27 *r* advisers crowded around them.
4: 29 the roof of the *r* palace of Babylon,
4: 30 I have built as the *r* residence,
4: 31 Your *r* authority has been taken
5: 5 near the lampstand in the *r* palace.
5: 20 he was deposed from his *r* throne
6: 7 The *r* administrators, prefects,
6: 12 spoke to him about his *r* decree:
11: 6 together with her *r* escort
11: 20 to maintain the *r* splendor.
11: 45 He will pitch his *r* tents
Hos 5: 1 Listen, O *r* house!
Jnh 3: 6 from his throne, took off his *r* robes
Hag 2: 22 I will overturn *r* thrones
Zec 14: 10 of Hananel to the *r* winepresses.
Jn 4: 46 was a certain *r* official whose son
4: 49 The *r* official said, "Sir, come
Ac 12: 21 day Herod, wearing his *r* robes,
Jas 2: 8 If you really keep the *r* law found
1Pe 2: 9 a *r* priesthood, a holy nation,

ROYALTY (ROYAL)

Da 11: 21 has not been given the honor of *r*.

RUB (RUBBED)

Lk 6: 1 *r* them in their hands and eat

RUBBED (RUB)

2Sa 1: 21 of Saul—no longer *r* with oil.
Eze 16: 4 nor were you *r* with salt
29: 18 every head was *r* bare and every

RUBBISH (RUBBLE)

Php 3: 8 I consider them *r*, that I may gain

RUBBLE (RUBBISH)

2Ki 23: 12 threw the *r* into the Kidron Valley.
Ezr 6: 11 is to be made a pile of *r*.
Ne 4: 2 back to life from those heaps of *r*—
4: 10 is so much *r* that we cannot rebuild
Job 15: 28 houses crumbling to *r*
Ps 79: 1 they have reduced Jerusalem to *r*.
Isa 25: 2 You have made the city a heap of *r*,
Jer 26: 18 Jerusalem will become a heap of *r*,
Eze 26: 4 I will scrape away her *r*
26: 12 throw your stones, timber and *r*
Da 2: 5 your houses turned into piles of *r*.
3: 29 houses be turned into piles of *r*,
Mic 1: 6 I will make Samaria a heap of *r*,
3: 12 Jerusalem will become a heap of *r*,
Zep 1: 3 wicked will have only heaps of *r*
2: 14 *r* will be in the doorways,

RUBIES (RUBY)

Job 28: 18 the price of wisdom is beyond *r*.
Pr 3: 15 She is more precious than *r*;
8: 11 for wisdom is more precious than *r*,
20: 15 Gold there is, and *r* in abundance,
31: 10 She is worth far more than *r*.
Isa 54: 12 I will make your battlements of *r*,
La 4: 7 their bodies more ruddy than *r*,
Eze 27: 16 coral and *r* for your merchandise.

RUBY (RUBIES)

Ex 28: 17 In the first row there shall be a *r*,
39: 10 In the first row there was a *r*,
Eze 28: 13 *r*, topaz and emerald,

RUDDER (RUDDERS)

Jas 3: 4 by a very small *r* wherever the pilot

RUDDERS (RUDDER)

Ac 27: 40 untied the ropes that held the *r*.

RUDDY

1Sa 16: 12 He was *r*, with a fine appearance
17: 42 *r* and handsome, and he despised
SS 5: 10 My lover is radiant and *r*,
La 4: 7 their bodies more *r* than rubies,

RUDE

1Co 13: 5 It is not *r*, it is not self-seeking,

RUE
Lk 11:42 *r* and all other kinds

RUFUS
Mk 15:21 the father of Alexander and *R*,
Ro 16:13 Greet *R*, chosen in the Lord,

RUGGED
Ps 68:15 *r* are the mountains of Bashan.
68:16 Why gaze in envy, O *r* mountains,
SS 2:17 stag on the *r* hills.
Isa 40: 4 the *r* places a plain.

RUGS
Isa 21: 5 they spread the *r*,
Eze 27:24 multicolored *r* with cords twisted

RUIN (RUINED RUINING RUINS)
Nu 11:15 and do not let me face my own *r*."
24:20 but he will come to *r* at last."
24:24 but they too will come to *r*."
Dt 11: 4 how the LORD brought lasting *r*
13:16 It is to remain a *r* forever, never
28:20 destroyed and come to sudden *r*
28:63 so it will please him to *r*
2Sa 15:14 to overtake us and bring *r* upon us
16: 8 come to *r* because you are a man
2Ki 3:19 and *r* every good field with stones
2Ch 34:11 of Judah had allowed to fall into *r*.
Est 6:13 you will surely come to *r*!"
9:24 the lot) for their *r* and destruction.
Job 2: 3 me against him to *r* him
22:19 "The righteous see their *r*
31: 3 Is it not *r* for the wicked,
Ps 9: 6 Endless *r* has overtaken the enemy
35: 4 may those who plot my *r*
35: 8 may they fall into the pit, to their *r*.
35: 8 may *r* overtake them by surprise—
38:12 who would harm me talk of my *r*;
40:14 may all who desire my *r*
52: 5 you down to everlasting *r*:
64: 8 and bring them to *r*;
70: 2 may all who desire my *r*
73:18 you cast them down to *r*.
Pr 3:25 of the *r* that overtakes the wicked,
5:14 I have come to the brink of utter *r*
10: 8 but a chattering fool comes to *r*.
10:10 and a chattering fool comes to *r*.
10:14 but the mouth of a fool invites *r*.
10:15 but poverty is the *r* of the poor.
10:29 but it is the *r* of those who do evil.
13: 3 he who speaks rashly will come to *r*
18:24 many companions may come to *r*,
19:13 A foolish son is his father's *r*,
21:12 and brings the wicked to *r*.
26:28 and a flattering mouth works *r*.
31: 3 your vigor on those who *r* kings.
SS 2:15 that *r* the vineyards,
Isa 7: 5 Remaliah's son have plotted your *r*
23:13 and turned it into a *r*.
24: 1 he will *r* its face
25: 2 the fortified town a *r*,
26:14 them and brought them to *r*;
51:19 *r* and destruction, famine
59: 7 *r* and destruction mark their ways.
60:18 nor *r* or destruction within your
Jer 12:10 shepherds will *r* my vineyard
13: 9 'In the same way I will *r* the pride
19: 7 " 'In this place I will *r* the plans
22: 5 that this palace will become a *r*.' "
25: 9 and scorn, and an everlasting *r*.
25:18 to make them a *r* and an object
27:17 Why should this city become a *r*?
38: 4 good of these people but their *r*."
48:18 and *r* your fortified cities.
49:13 "that Bozrah will become a *r*
La 3:47 *r* and destruction."
Eze 5:14 "I will make you a *r* and a reproach
21:27 A *r*! A *r*! I will make it a *r*!
23:33 the cup of *r* and desolation,
29:10 I will make the land of Egypt a *r*
Hos 2:12 I will *r* her vines and her fig trees,
4:14 understanding will come to *r*!
Am 5: 9 and brings the fortified city to *r*),
6: 6 grieve over the *r* of Joseph.
Mic 6:13 to *r* you because of your sins.
6:16 Therefore I will give you over to *r*
Hab 2: 9 to escape the clutches of *r*!
Hab 2:10 You have plotted the *r*
Zep 1:15 a day of trouble and *r*,
2:15 What a *r* she has become,
Hag 1: 4 while this house remains a *r*?"
1: 9 of my house, which remains a *r*,
Ro 3:16 *r* and misery mark their ways,
1Ti 6: 9 desires that plunge men into *r*
Rev 17:16 They will bring her to *r*
18:17 wealth has been brought to *r*!'
18:19 one hour she has been brought to *r*!

RUINED (RUIN)
Ge 41:36 so that the country may not be *r*
Ex 8:24 throughout Egypt the land was *r*
10: 7 not yet realize that Egypt is *r*?"
Dt 28:24 down from the skies until you are *r*.
28:51 lambs of your flocks until you are *r*.
Jdg 6: 4 and *r* the crops all the way to Gaza
Job 15:28 he will inhabit *r* towns
Ps 109:10 from their *r* homes.
Pr 14:28 but without subjects a prince is *r*.
Isa 3:14 "It is you who have *r* my vineyard;
6: 5 "I am *r*! For I am a man
6:11 and the fields *r* and ravaged,
6:11 "Until the cities lie *r*
15: 1 Ar in Moab is *r*,
15: 1 Kir in Moab is *r*,
24:10 The *r* city lies desolate;
49:19 "Though you were *r* and made
60:12 it will be utterly *r*.
61: 4 they will renew the *r* cities
Jer 4:13 Woe to us! We are *r*!
4:27 "The whole land will be *r*,
9:12 Why has the land been *r*
9:19 'How *r* we are!
13: 7 but now it was *r* and completely
48: 1 "Woe to Nebo, for it will be *r*.
48: 8 The valley will be *r*
Eze 6: 6 your idols smashed and *r*,
29:12 desolate forty years among *r* cities.
30: 7 lie among *r* cities.
36:38 will the *r* cities be filled with flocks
Joel 1: 7 and *r* my fig trees.
1:10 The fields are *r*,
Am 7: 9 the sanctuaries of Israel will be *r*;
9:14 they will rebuild the *r* cities
Mic 2: 4 'We are utterly *r*;
2:10 it is *r*, beyond all remedy.
Na 2: 2 and have *r* their vines.
Zep 1:11 all who trade with silver will be *r*.
Zec 11: 2 the stately trees are *r*!
11: 3 the lush thicket of the Jordan is *r*!
Mt 9:17 and the wineskins will be *r*.
12:25 divided against itself will be *r*,
Mk 2:22 and the wineskins will be *r*.
Lk 5:37 and the wineskins will be *r*.
11:17 divided against itself will be *r*,

RUINING (RUIN)
Tit 1:11 they are *r* whole households

RUINS (RUIN)
Lev 26:31 I will turn your cities into *r*
26:33 and your cities will lie in *r*.
Jos 8:28 and made it a permanent heap of *r*,
1Ki 18:30 altar of the LORD, which was in *r*.
1Ch 20: 1 attacked Rabbah and left it in *r*.
2Ch 34: 6 Naphtali, and in the *r* around them
Ezr 9: 9 house of our God and repair its *r*,
Ne 2: 3 my fathers are buried lies in *r*,
2:17 in *r*, and its gates have been burned
Job 3:14 themselves places now lying in *r*,
30:14 amid the *r* they come rolling in.
Ps 74: 3 through these everlasting *r*,
89:40 and reduced his strongholds to *r*.
102: 6 like an owl among the *r*.
Pr 19: 3 A man's own folly *r* his life,
24:31 and the stone wall was in *r*.
Ecc 4: 5 and *r* himself.
Isa 3: 6 take charge of this heap of *r*!"
5:17 among the *r* of the rich.
17: 1 but will become a heap of *r*.
24:12 The city is left in *r*,
44:26 and of their *r*, 'I will restore them,'
51: 3 look with compassion on all her *r*;
52: 9 you *r* of Jerusalem,
58:12 people will rebuild the ancient *r*
61: 4 They will rebuild the ancient *r*
Isa 64:11 and all that we treasured lies in *r*.
Jer 4: 7 Your towns will lie in *r*
4:20 the whole land lies in *r*.
4:26 all its towns lay in *r*
9:11 "I will make Jerusalem a heap of *r*,
9:19 because our houses are in *r*.' "
30:18 the city will be rebuilt on her *r*,
44: 2 Today they lie deserted and in *r*
44: 6 them the desolate *r* they are today.
46:19 and lie in *r* without inhabitant.
49: 2 it will become a mound of *r*,
49:13 and all its towns will be in *r* forever
51:37 Babylon will be a heap of *r*,
Eze 13: 4 O Israel, are like jackals among *r*.
26: 2 now that she lies in *r* I will prosper
26:20 as in ancient *r*, with those who go
33:24 living in those *r* in the land
33:27 left in the *r* will fall by the sword,
35: 4 I will turn your towns into *r*
36: 4 to the desolate *r* and the deserted
36:10 will be inhabited and the *r* rebuilt.
36:33 towns, and the *r* will be rebuilt.
36:35 the cities that were lying in *r*,
38:12 hand against the resettled *r*
Joel 1:17 The storehouses are in *r*,
Am 9:11 restore its *r*,
Na 3: 7 'Nineveh is in *r*— who will mourn
Zep 2: 4 and Ashkelon left in *r*.
Mal 1: 4 crushed, we will rebuild the *r*."
Ac 15:16 Its *r* I will rebuild,
2Ti 2:14 and only *r* those who listen.

RULE (RULED RULER RULER'S RULERS RULES RULING)
Ge 1:26 let them *r* over the fish of the sea
1:28 *R* over the fish of the sea
3:16 and he will *r* over you."
37: 8 over us? Will you actually *r* us?"
Lev 25:43 Do not *r* over them ruthlessly,
25:46 but you must not *r* over your fellow
25:53 see to it that his owner does not *r*
26:17 those who hate you will *r* over you,
Dt 15: 6 You will *r* over many nations
15: 6 over many nations but none will *r*
19: 4 This is the *r* concerning the man
Jdg 8:22 said to Gideon, "*R* over us—
8:23 But Gideon told them, "I will not *r*
8:23 The LORD will *r* over you."
8:23 nor will my son *r* over you.
9: 2 of Jerub-Baal's sons *r* over you,
13:12 what is to be the *r* for the boy's life
1Sa 12:12 'No, we want a king to *r* over us'—
14:47 After Saul had assumed *r*
2Sa 3:21 that you may *r* over all that your
19:10 whom we anointed to *r* over us,
1Ki 2:12 and his *r* was firmly established.
5: 7 son to *r* over this great nation."
8:16 David to *r* my people Israel.'
11:37 you will *r* over all that your heart
2Ch 6: 6 David to *r* my people Israel.'
7:18 fail to have a man to *r* over Israel.'
9: 8 king to *r* for the LORD your God.
20: 6 You *r* over all the kingdoms
Ne 9:37 They *r* over our bodies
Ps 2: 9 You will *r* them with an iron
7: 7 *R* over them from on high;
19:13 may they not *r* over me.
49:14 The upright will *r* over them
67: 4 for you *r* the peoples justly
72: 8 He will *r* from sea to sea
89: 9 You *r* over the surging sea;
110: 2 you will *r* in the midst
119:133 let no sin *r* over me.
Pr 8:16 and all nobles who *r* on earth.
12:24 Diligent hands will *r*,
17: 2 A wise servant will *r*
19:10 worse for a slave to *r* over princes!
22: 7 The rich *r* over the poor,
29: 2 when the wicked *r*, the people
Isa 3:12 women *r* over them.
14: 2 and *r* over their oppressors.
19: 4 and a fierce king will *r* over them,"
28:10 *r* on *r*, *r* on *r*;
28:13 *r* on *r*, *r* on *r*;
28:14 who *r* this people in Jerusalem.
32: 1 and rulers will *r* with justice.
52: 5 and those who *r* them mock,"
Jer 5:31 the priests *r* by their own authority,

Jer 22: 30 or *r* anymore in Judah.''
33: 26 sons to *r* over the descendants
51: 28 and all the countries they *r*.
La 5: 8 Slaves *r* over us,
Eze 20: 33 I will *r* over you with a mighty
29: 15 it so weak that it will never again *r*
Da 2: 39 will *r* over the whole earth.
6: 1 to *r* throughout the kingdom,
7: 6 and it was given authority to *r*.
11: 3 who will *r* with great power and do
11: 5 and will *r* his own kingdom
Hos 11: 5 and will not Assyria *r* over them
Mic 4: 7 The LORD will *r* over them
5: 6 They will *r* the land of Assyria
Zec 6: 13 and will sit and *r* on his throne.
9: 10 His *r* will extend from sea to sea
Ro 13: 9 are summed up in this one *r*:
15: 12 arise to *r* over the nations;
1Co 7: 17 This is the *r* I lay down in all
Gal 6: 16 and mercy to all who follow this *r*,
Eph 1: 21 far above all *r* and authority,
Col 3: 15 the peace of Christ *r* in your hearts,
2Th 3: 10 we gave you this *r*: ''If a man will
Rev 2: 27 He will *r* them with an iron scepter;
12: 5 who will *r* all the nations
17: 17 to give the beast their power to *r*,
19: 15 He will *r* them with an iron scepter

RULED (RULE)

Jos 12: 2 He *r* from Aroer on the rim
12: 3 also *r* over the eastern Arabah
12: 5 He *r* over Mount Hermon, Salecah
13: 10 who *r* in Heshbon, out
13: 21 of the Amorites, who *r* at Heshbon.
Jdg 11: 19 who *r* in Heshbon, and said to him,
Ru 1: 1 In the days when the judges *r*,
1Ki 4: 1 So King Solomon *r* over all Israel.
4: 21 Solomon *r* over all the kingdoms
4: 24 For he *r* over all the kingdoms west
9: 19 throughout all the territory he *r*.
11: 25 Rezon *r* in Aram and was hostile
12: 17 Rehoboam still *r* over them.
14: 19 reign, his wars and how he *r*,
22: 47 king in Edom; a deputy *r*.
2Ki 11: 3 years while Athaliah *r* the land.
1Ch 4: 22 who *r* in Moab and Jashubi Lehem.
29: 27 He *r* over Israel forty years—
2Ch 8: 6 throughout all the territory he *r*.
9: 26 He *r* over all the kings
10: 17 Rehoboam still *r* over them.
22: 12 years while Athaliah *r* the land.
Ne 9: 28 enemies so that they *r* over them.
Est 1: 1 Xerxes who *r* over 127 provinces
Ps 106: 41 and their foes *r* over them.
Ecc 1: 16 more than anyone who has *r*
Isa 26: 13 besides you have *r* over us,
63: 19 but you have not *r* over them,
Jer 34: 1 in the empire he *r* were fighting
Eze 34: 4 You have *r* them harshly
Ac 13: 21 of Benjamin, who *r* forty years.

RULER (RULE)

Ge 34: 2 the *r* of that area, saw her,
45: 8 lord of his entire household and *r*
45: 26 In fact, he is *r* of all Egypt.''
Ex 2: 14 Who made you *r* and judge over us
22: 28 or curse the *r* of your people.
Nu 24: 19 A *r* will come out of Jacob
2Sa 5: 2 and you will become their *r*.' ''
6: 21 house when he appointed me *r*
7: 8 flock to be *r* over my people Israel.
1Ki 1: 35 I have appointed him *r* over Israel
11: 34 I have made him *r* all the days
22: 26 back to Amon the *r* of the city
1Ch 5: 2 of his brothers and a *r* came
11: 2 and you will become their *r*.' ''
17: 7 to be *r* over my people Israel.
29: 12 you are the *r* of all things.
29: 22 him before the LORD to be *r*
2Ch 18: 25 back to Amon the *r* of the city
34: 8 and Maaseiah the *r* of the city,
Ne 3: 9 *r* of a half-district of Jerusalem,
3: 12 *r* of a half-district of Jerusalem,
3: 14 son of Recab, *r* of the district
3: 15 *r* of the district of Mizpah.
3: 16 son of Azbuk, *r* of a half-district
3: 17 *r* of half the district of Keilah,
3: 18 *r* of the other half-district of Keilah
Ne 3: 19 Ezer son of Jeshua, *r* of Mizpah,
Est 1: 22 tongue that every man should be *r*
Ps 8: 6 You made him *r* over the works
82: 7 you will fall like every other *r*.''
105: 20 the *r* of peoples set him free.
105: 21 *r* over all he possessed,
Pr 6: 7 no overseer or *r*,
17: 7 how much worse lying lips to a *r*!
19: 6 Many curry favor with a *r*,
23: 1 When you sit to dine with a *r*,
25: 15 Through patience a *r* can be
28: 3 A *r* who oppresses the poor
28: 16 A tyrannical *r* lacks judgment,
29: 12 If a *r* listens to lies,
29: 26 Many seek an audience with a *r*,
Ecc 9: 17 than the shouts of a *r* of fools.
10: 5 the sort of error that arises from a *r*
Isa 16: 1 as tribute to the *r* of the land,
60: 17 and righteousness your *r*.
Jer 30: 21 their *r* will arise from among them.
51: 46 and of *r* against *r*.
Eze 28: 2 ''Son of man, say to the *r* of Tyre,
31: 11 it over to the *r* of the nations,
Da 2: 38 he has made you *r* over them all.
2: 48 He made him *r* over the entire
5: 7 he will be made the third highest *r*
5: 16 you will be made the third highest *r*
5: 29 was proclaimed the third highest *r*
9: 1 was made *r* over the Babylonian
9: 25 the *r*, comes, there will be seven
9: 26 of the *r* who will come will destroy
Am 2: 3 I will destroy her *r*
Mic 5: 1 They will strike Israel's *r*
5: 2 one who will be *r* over Israel,
7: 3 the *r* demands gifts,
Hab 1: 14 like sea creatures that have no *r*.
Zec 10: 4 from him every *r*.
Mt 2: 6 for out of you will come a *r*
9: 18 a *r* came and knelt before him
Mk 5: 35 house of Jairus, the synagogue *r*.
5: 36 Jesus told the synagogue *r*,
5: 38 to the home of the synagogue *r*,
Lk 8: 41 Just then a man named Jairus, a *r*
8: 49 house of Jairus, the synagogue *r*.
13: 14 the synagogue *r* said to the people,
18: 18 A certain *r* asked him, ''Good
Ac 7: 10 so he made him *r* over Egypt
7: 18 nothing about Joseph, became *r*
7: 27 'Who made you *r* and judge over us
7: 35 He was sent to be their *r*
7: 35 'Who made you *r* and judge?'
18: 8 the synagogue *r*, and his entire
18: 17 on Sosthenes the synagogue *r*
23: 5 'Do not speak evil about the *r*
Eph 2: 2 of the *r* of the kingdom of the air,
1Ti 6: 15 God, the blessed and only *R*,
Rev 1: 5 and the *r* of the kings of the earth.
3: 14 and true witness, the *r*

RULER'S (RULE)

Ge 49: 10 the *r* staff from between his feet,
Ecc 10: 4 If a *r* anger rises against you,
Eze 19: 11 fit for a *r* scepter.
19: 14 fit for a *r* scepter.'
Mt 9: 23 When Jesus entered the *r* house

RULERS (RULE)

Ge 17: 20 He will be the father of twelve *r*,
25: 16 of the twelve tribal *r* according
Jos 13: 3 of the five Philistine *r* in Gaza,
Jdg 3: 3 the five *r* of the Philistines,
5: 3 Hear this, you kings! Listen, you *r*!
15: 11 you realize that the Philistines are *r*
16: 5 The *r* of the Philistines went to her
16: 8 the *r* of the Philistines brought her
16: 18 So the *r* of the Philistines returned
16: 18 word to the *r* of the Philistines,
16: 23 the *r* of the Philistines assembled
16: 27 all the *r* of the Philistines were
16: 30 and down came the temple on the *r*
1Sa 5: 8 So they called together all the *r*
5: 11 So they called together all the *r*
6: 4 has struck both you and your *r*.
6: 4 to the number of the Philistine *r*,
6: 12 *r* of the Philistines followed them
6: 16 five *r* of the Philistines saw all this
6: 18 towns belonging to the five *r*—
7: 7 the *r* of the Philistines came up
1Sa 29: 2 As the Philistine *r* marched
29: 6 but the *r* don't approve of you.
29: 7 to displease the Philistine *r*.''
2Sa 7: 7 any of their *r* whom I commanded
1Ch 12: 19 after consultation, their *r* sent him
2Ch 23: 20 *r* of the people and all the people
32: 31 sent by the *r* of Babylon
Job 3: 15 with *r* who had gold,
Ps 2: 2 and the *r* gather together
2: 10 be warned, you *r* of the earth.
58: 1 Do you *r* indeed speak justly?
76: 12 He breaks the spirit of *r*;
105: 30 into the bedrooms of their *r*.
110: 6 crushing the *r* of the whole earth.
119:161 *R* persecute me without cause,
141: 6 their *r* will be thrown
148: 11 you princes and all *r* on earth,
Pr 8: 15 and *r* make laws that are just;
28: 2 country is rebellious, it has many *r*,
31: 4 not for *r* to crave beer,
Ecc 7: 19 than ten *r* in a city.
Isa 1: 10 you *r* of Sodom;
1: 23 Your *r* are rebels,
14: 5 the scepter of the *r*,
16: 8 The *r* of the nations
32: 1 and *r* will rule with justice.
40: 23 reduces the *r* of this world
41: 25 treads on *r* as if they were mortar,
49: 7 to the servant of *r*:
Da 7: 27 and all *r* will worship and obey him
9: 12 and against our *r* by bringing
11: 39 He will make them *r*
Hos 4: 18 their *r* dearly love shameful ways.
7: 7 they devour their *r*.
13: 10 Where are your *r* in all your towns,
Mic 3: 1 you *r* of the house of Israel.
3: 9 you *r* of the house of Israel,
Hab 1: 10 and scoff at *r*.
Zep 3: 3 her *r* are evening wolves,
Mt 2: 6 least among the *r* of Judah;
20: 25 ''You know that the *r*
Mk 5: 22 of the synagogue *r*, named Jairus,
10: 42 *r* of the Gentiles lord it over them,
Lk 1: 52 down *r* from their thrones
12: 11 brought before synagogues, *r*
23: 13 together the chief priests, the *r*
23: 35 and the *r* even sneered at him.
24: 20 *r* handed him over to be sentenced
Jn 7: 48 of the *r* or of the Pharisees believed
Ac 4: 5 The next day the *r*, elders
4: 8 ''*R* and elders of the people!
4: 26 and the *r* gather together
13: 15 the synagogue *r* sent word to them,
13: 27 and their *r* did not recognize Jesus,
Ro 13: 3 For *r* hold no terror
1Co 2: 6 of this age or of the *r* of this age,
2: 8 of the *r* of this age understood it,
Eph 3: 10 should be made known to the *r*
6: 12 the *r*, against the authorities,
Col 1: 16 or powers or *r* or authorities;
Tit 3: 1 the people to be subject to *r*

RULES (RULE)

Nu 9: 3 in accordance with all its *r*
9: 14 do so in accordance with its *r*
15: 15 is to have the same *r* for you
2Sa 23: 3 when he *r* in the fear of God,
23: 3 'When one *r* over men
1Ki 21: 18 king of Israel, who *r* in Samaria.
2Ch 30: 19 to the *r* of the sanctuary.''
Ps 22: 28 and he *r* over the nations.
59: 13 that God *r* over Jacob.
66: 7 He *r* forever by his power,
103: 19 and his kingdom *r* over all.
Isa 29: 13 is made up only of *r* taught by men.
40: 10 and his arm *r* for him.
Da 4: 26 you acknowledge that Heaven *r*.
Mt 15: 9 their teachings are but *r* taught
Mk 7: 7 their teachings are but *r* taught
Lk 22: 26 one who *r* like the one who serves.
Col 2: 20 submit to its *r*: ''Do not handle!
2Ti 2: 5 he competes according to the *r*.
Rev 17: 18 you saw is the great city that *r*

RULING (RULE)

Jdg 14: 4 at that time they were *r* over Israel
1Ki 3: 27 the king gave his *r*: ''Give the living
15: 18 of Aram, who was *r* in Damascus.

2Ch 16: 2 of Aram, who was *r* in Damascus.
Ezr 4: 20 Jerusalem has had powerful kings *r*
Job 34: 30 to keep a godless man from *r*,
Pr 28: 15 is a wicked man *r* over a helpless
Jn 3: 1 a member of the Jewish *r* council.

RUMAH

2Ki 23: 36 of Pedaiah; she was from *R*.

RUMBLE (RUMBLING RUMBLINGS)

Jer 47: 3 and the *r* of their wheels.

RUMBLING (RUMBLE)

Job 37: 2 to the *r* that comes from his mouth.

RUMBLINGS (RUMBLE)

Rev 4: 5 throne came flashes of lightning, *r*
8: 5 and there came peals of thunder, *r*,
11: 19 there came flashes of lightning, *r*,
16: 18 there came flashes of lightning, *r*,

RUMOR (RUMORS)

Job 28: 22 'Only a *r* of it has reached our ears.'
Jer 51: 46 one *r* comes this year, another
Eze 7: 26 calamity will come, and *r* upon *r*.
Jn 21: 23 *r* spread among the brothers that

RUMORS (RUMOR)

Jer 51: 46 afraid when *r* are heard in the land;
51: 46 *r* of violence in the land
Mt 24: 6 You will hear of wars and *r* of wars,
Mk 13: 7 hear of wars and *r* of wars,

RUN (OUTRAN OVERRAN OVERRUN RAN RUNNER RUNNERS RUNNING RUNS)

Ge 19: 20 here is a town near enough to *r* to,
31: 27 Why did you *r* off secretly
39: 13 and had *r* out of the house,
Ex 23: 27 enemies turn their backs and *r*.
Lev 26: 36 They will *r* as though fleeing
Nu 34: 7 *r* a line from the Great Sea
34: 10 *r* a line from Hazar Enan
Jos 7: 12 they turn their backs and *r*
Ru 3: 10 You have not *r* after the younger
1Sa 8: 11 they will *r* in front of his chariots.
14: 22 that the Philistines were on the *r*,
19: 11 "If you don't *r* for your life tonight,
20: 36 "*R* and find the arrows I shoot."
21: 13 and letting saliva *r* down his beard.
31: 4 Draw your sword and *r* me through
31: 4 and *r* me through and abuse me."
2Sa 15: 1 with fifty men to *r* ahead of him.
18: 19 "Let me *r* and take the news
18: 22 please let me *r* behind the Cushite
18: 23 "Come what may, I want to *r*."
18: 23 "*R*!" Then Ahimaaz ran by way
1Ki 1: 5 with fifty men to *r* ahead of him.
17: 14 and the jug of oil will not *r* dry
17: 16 and the jug of oil did not *r* dry,
2Ki 4: 26 *R* to meet her and ask her,
4: 29 take my staff in your hand and *r*.
5: 20 I will *r* after him and get something
9: 3 Then open the door and *r*;
1Ch 10: 4 Draw your sword and *r* me through
Ne 6: 11 "Should a man like me *r* away?
Job 1: 5 a period of feasting had *r* its course,
39: 18 when she spreads her feathers to *r*,
Ps 16: 4 who *r* after other gods.
19: 5 champion rejoicing to *r* his course.
119: 32 I *r* in the path of your commands,
Pr 4: 12 when you *r*, you will not stumble.
18: 10 the righteous *r* to it and are safe.
Isa 5: 11 the morning to *r* after their drinks,
7: 25 are turned loose and where sheep *r*.
8: 7 *r* over all its banks
10: 3 To whom will you *r* for help?
40: 31 they will *r* and not grow weary,
Jer 2: 23 I have not *r* after the Baals'?
2: 25 Do not *r* until your feet are bare
17: 16 I have not *r* away from being your
23: 21 yet they have *r* with their message;
48: 6 Flee! *R* for your lives;
51: 6 *R* for your lives!
51: 45 *R* for your lives!
51: 45 *R* from the fierce anger
Eze 47: 15 "On the north side it will *r*
47: 18 the east side the boundary will *r*
47: 19 "On the south side it will *r*
Eze 48: 28 of Gad will *r* south from Tamar
Joel 2: 9 they *r* along the wall.
3: 18 ravines of Judah will *r* with water.
Am 6: 12 Do horses *r* on the rocky crags?
Na 1: 4 he makes all the rivers *r* dry.
Hab 2: 2 so that a herald may *r* with it.
Zec 2: 4 to meet him and said to him: "*R*,
Mt 6: 32 For the pagans *r* after all these
9: 17 wine will *r* out and the wineskins
Lk 5: 37 wine will *r* out and the wineskins
Jn 10: 5 they will *r* away from him
Ac 27: 17 Fearing that they would *r* aground
27: 26 we must *r* aground on some island
27: 39 decided to *r* the ship aground
1Co 9: 24 *R* in such a way as to get the prize.
9: 24 that in a race all the runners *r*,
9: 26 Therefore I do not *r* like a man
Gal 2: 2 that I was running or had *r* my race
Php 2: 16 on the day of Christ that I did not *r*
Heb 12: 1 let us *r* with perseverance the race

RUNNER (RUN)

Job 9: 25 "My days are swifter than a *r*;

RUNNERS (RUN)

1Co 9: 24 that in a race all the *r* run,

RUNNING (RUN)

Ge 16: 8 "I'm *r* away from my mistress Sarai
31: 20 by not telling him he was *r* away.
Ex 32: 25 saw that the people were *r* wild
Lev 21: 20 or who has festering or *r* sores
22: 22 with warts or festering or *r* sores.
Jos 8: 6 'They are *r* away from us
2Sa 3: 29 without someone who has a *r* sore
18: 24 looked out, he saw a man *r* alone.
18: 26 the watchman saw another man *r*,
18: 26 "Look, another man *r* alone!"
2Ki 5: 21 When Naaman saw him *r*
2Ch 23: 12 heard the noise of the people *r*
Ps 133: 2 *r* down on Aaron's beard,
133: 2 *r* down on the beard,
Pr 5: 15 *r* water from your own well.
Jer 2: 23 *r* here and there,
Eze 45: 7 *r* lengthwise from the western
48: 18 the sacred portion and *r* the length
48: 21 Both these areas *r* the length
Jnh 1: 10 (They knew he was *r* away
Mk 9: 25 When Jesus saw that a crowd was *r*
Lk 6: 38 shaken together and *r* over,
17: 23 Do not go *r* off after them.
Jn 20: 2 So she came *r* to Simon Peter
20: 4 Both were *r*, but the other disciple
Ac 3: 11 came *r* to them in the place called
21: 30 and the people came *r*
1Co 9: 26 I do not run like a man *r* aimlessly;
Gal 2: 2 for fear that I was *r* or had run my
5: 7 You were *r* a good race.

RUNS (RUN)

Ge 2: 14 it *r* along the east side of Asshur.
2Sa 18: 27 the first one *r* like Ahimaaz son
Ps 147: 15 his word *r* swiftly.
Eze 16: 34 no one *r* after you for your favors.
Lk 12: 30 For the pagan world *r*
Jn 10: 12 he abandons the sheep and *r* away.
10: 13 man *r* away because he is a hired
2Jn : 9 Anyone who *r* ahead and does not

RURAL

Est 9: 19 That is why *r* Jews—those living

RUSE

Jos 9: 4 they resorted to a *r*: They went

RUSH (RUSHED RUSHES RUSHING)

Jdg 21: 21 then *r* from the vineyards
Pr 1: 16 for their feet *r* into sin,
6: 18 feet that are quick to *r* into evil,
Isa 59: 7 Their feet *r* into sin;
Jer 49: 3 *r* here and there inside the walls,
Joel 2: 9 They *r* upon the city;

RUSHED (RUSH)

Jos 8: 19 from their position and *r* forward.
Jdg 9: 44 Then two companies *r* upon those
9: 44 the companies with him *r* forward
1Sa 7: 11 The men of Israel *r* out of Mizpah
2Sa 19: 17 They *r* to the Jordan, where
Est 6: 12 But Haman *r* home, with his head
Mt 8: 32 whole herd *r* down the steep bank
Mk 5: 13 *r* down the steep bank into the lake
Lk 8: 33 and the herd *r* down the steep bank
Ac 7: 57 top of their voices, they all *r* at him,
14: 14 they tore their clothes and *r* out
16: 29 *r* in and fell trembling before Paul
17: 5 They *r* to Jason's house in search
19: 29 and *r* as one man into the theater.
Jude : 11 they have *r* for profit

RUSHES (RUSH)

Dt 32: 35 and their doom *r* upon them."
Job 16: 14 he *r* at me like a warrior.
Isa 19: 6 The reeds and *r* will wither,

RUSHING (RUSH)

Jdg 5: 15 *r* after him into the valley.
Job 20: 28 *r* waters on the day of God's wrath.
Isa 30: 28 His breath is like a *r* torrent,
Eze 1: 24 the roar of *r* waters, like the voice
3: 12 I heard behind me a loud *r* sound—
3: 13 wheels beside them, a loud *r* sound.
43: 2 voice was like the roar of *r* waters,
Mic 1: 4 like water *r* down a slope.
Na 2: 4 *r* back and forth
Rev 1: 15 was like the sound of *r* waters.
9: 9 of many horses and chariots *r*
14: 2 heaven like the roar of *r* waters
19: 6 like the roar of *r* waters

RUST

Mt 6: 19 where moth and *r* destroy,
6: 20 where moth and *r* do not destroy,

RUTH

Ru 1: 4 one named Orpah and the other *R*.
1: 14 good-by, but *R* clung
1: 16 But *R* replied, "Don't urge me
1: 18 realized that *R* was determined
1: 22 accompanied by *R* the Moabitess,
2: 2 *R* the Moabitess said to Naomi,
2: 8 So Boaz said to *R*, "My daughter,
2: 17 *R* gleaned in the field until evening
2: 18 *R* also brought out and gave her
2: 19 *R* told her mother-in-law about
2: 21 Then *R* the Moabitess said,
2: 22 said to *R* her daughter-in-law,
2: 23 *R* stayed close to the servant girls
3: 5 do whatever you say," *R* answered.
3: 7 *R* approached quietly, uncovered
3: 9 "I am your servant *R*," she said.
3: 16 *R* came to her mother-in-law,
4: 5 and from *R* the Moabitess,
4: 10 also acquired *R* the Moabitess,
4: 13 So Boaz took *R* and she became his
Mt 1: 5 whose mother was *R*, Obed

RUTHLESS

Job 6: 23 me from the clutches of the *r*'?
15: 20 *r* through all the years stored up
27: 13 the heritage a *r* man receives
Ps 35: 11 *R* witnesses come forward;
37: 35 I have seen a wicked and *r* man
54: 3 *r* men seek my life—
86: 14 a band of *r* men seeks my life—
Pr 11: 16 but *r* men gain only wealth.
Isa 13: 11 and will humble the pride of the *r*.
25: 3 cities of *r* nations will revere you.
25: 4 For the breath of the *r*
25: 5 so the song of the *r* is stilled.
29: 5 the *r* hordes like blown chaff.
29: 20 The *r* will vanish,
Eze 28: 7 the most *r* of nations;
30: 11 his army—the most *r* of nations—
31: 12 the most *r* of foreign nations cut it
32: 12 the most *r* of all nations.
Hab 1: 6 that *r* and impetuous people,
Ro 1: 31 are senseless, faithless, heartless, *r*.

SABACHTHANI

Mt 27: 46 *Eloi, lama s?*"— which means,
Mk 15: 34 *Eloi, lama s?*"— which means,

SABBATH (SABBATHS)

Ex 16: 23 day of rest, a holy *S* to the LORD.
16: 25 because today is a *S* to the LORD.

Ex 16: 26 the *S*, there will not be any.''
16: 29 the LORD has given you the *S*;
20: 8 ''Remember the *S* day
20: 10 but the seventh day is a *S*
20: 11 the LORD blessed the *S* day
31: 14 '' 'Observe the *S*, because it is holy
31: 15 but the seventh day is a *S* of rest,
31: 15 work on the *S* day must be put
31: 16 The Israelites are to observe the *S*,
35: 2 day shall be your holy day, a *S*
35: 3 of your dwellings on the *S* day.''
Lev 16: 31 It is a *s* of rest, and you must deny
23: 3 but the seventh day is a *S* of rest,
23: 3 wherever you live, it is a *S*
23: 11 is to wave it on the day after the *S*.
23: 15 '' 'From the day after the *S*,
23: 16 up to the day after the seventh *S*,
23: 32 It is a *s* of rest for you,
23: 32 are to observe your *s*.''
24: 8 *S* after *S*, on behalf of the Israelites,
25: 2 the land itself must observe a *s*
25: 4 to have a *s* of rest, a *s* to the LORD.
25: 6 yields during the *s* year will be food
26: 34 the land will enjoy its *s* years all
Nu 15: 32 gathering wood on the *S* day.
28: 9 '' 'On the *S* day, make an offering
28: 10 is the burnt offering for every *S*,
Dt 5: 12 ''Observe the *S* day
5: 14 but the seventh day is a *S*
5: 15 you to observe the *S* day.
2Ki 4: 23 ''It's not the New Moon or the *S*.''
11: 5 going on duty on the *S*—
11: 7 go off *S* duty are all to guard
11: 9 who were going on duty on the *S*
16: 18 took away the *S* canopy that had
1Ch 9: 32 for every *S* the bread set out
2Ch 23: 4 on duty on the *S* are to keep watch
23: 8 who were going on duty on the *S*
36: 21 The land enjoyed its *S* rests;
Ne 9: 14 known to them your holy *S*
10: 31 or grain to sell on the *S*,
10: 31 we will not buy from them on the *S*
13: 15 this into Jerusalem on the *S*.
13: 15 treading winepresses on the *S*
13: 16 in Jerusalem on the *S* to the people
13: 17 desecrating the *S* day? Didn't your
13: 18 against Israel by desecrating the *S*
13: 19 could be brought in on the *S* day.
13: 19 not opened until the *S* was over.
13: 19 the gates of Jerusalem before the *S*,
13: 21 on they no longer came on the *S*.
13: 22 in order to keep the *S* day holy.
Isa 56: 2 keeps the *S* without desecrating it,
56: 6 all who keep the *S*
58: 13 feet from breaking the *S*
58: 13 if you call the *S* a delight
66: 23 and from one *S* to another,
Jer 17: 21 not to carry a load on the *S* day
17: 22 but keep the *S* day holy,
17: 22 houses or do any work on the *S*,
17: 24 but keep the *S* day holy
17: 24 the gates of this city on the *S*,
17: 27 gates of Jerusalem on the *S* day,
17: 27 me to keep the *S* day holy
Eze 46: 1 but on the *S* day and on the day
46: 4 brings to the LORD on the *S* day is
46: 12 offerings as he does on the *S* day.
Hos 2: 11 her *S* days—all her appointed
Am 8: 5 and the *S* be ended
Mt 12: 1 through the grainfields on the *S*.
12: 2 doing what is unlawful on the *S*.''
12: 5 in the Law that on the *S* the priests
12: 8 For the Son of Man is Lord of the *S*
12: 10 ''Is it lawful to heal on the *S*?''
12: 11 and it falls into a pit on the *S*,
12: 12 lawful to do good on the *S*.''
24: 20 place in winter or on the *S*.
28: 1 After the *S*, at dawn
Mk 1: 21 Capernaum, and when the *S* came,
2: 23 One *S* Jesus was going
2: 24 doing what is unlawful on the *S*?''
2: 27 made for man, not man for the *S*
2: 27 ''The *S* was made for man,
2: 28 Son of Man is Lord even of the *S*.''
3: 2 to see if he would heal him on the *S*
3: 4 ''Which is lawful on the *S*:
6: 2 When the *S* came, he began
15: 42 Day (that is, the day before the *S*).
Mk 16: 1 the *S* was over, Mary Magdalene,
Lk 4: 16 and on the *S* day he went
4: 31 on the *S* began to teach the people.
6: 1 One *S* Jesus was going
6: 2 doing what is unlawful on the *S*?''
6: 5 ''The Son of Man is Lord of the *S*.''
6: 6 On another *S* he went
6: 7 to see if he would heal on the *S*.
6: 9 which is lawful on the *S*: to do good
13: 10 On a *S* Jesus was teaching in one
13: 14 because Jesus had healed on the *S*,
13: 14 on those days, not on the *S*.''
13: 15 each of you on the *S* untie his ox
13: 16 be set free on the *S* day
14: 1 One *S*, when Jesus went to eat
14: 3 Is it lawful to heal on the *S* or not?''
14: 5 falls into a well on the *S* day,
23: 54 and the *S* was about to begin.
23: 56 they rested on the *S* in obedience
Jn 5: 9 on which this took place was a *S*,
5: 10 ''It is the *S*; the law forbids you
5: 16 was doing these things on the *S*,
5: 18 not only was he breaking the *S*,
7: 22 you circumcise a child on the *S*.
7: 23 for healing the whole man on the *S*
7: 23 on the *S* so that the law
9: 14 and opened the man's eyes was a *S*.
9: 16 for he does not keep the *S*.''
19: 31 left on the crosses during the *S*,
19: 31 the next day was to be a special *S*.
Ac 1: 12 a *S* day's walk from the city.
13: 14 On the *S* they entered
13: 27 the prophets that are read every *S*.
13: 42 about these things on the next *S*.
13: 44 On the next *S* almost the whole
15: 21 in the synagogues on every *S*.''
16: 13 On the *S* we went outside the city
17: 2 and on three *S* days he reasoned
18: 4 Every *S* he reasoned
Col 2: 16 a New Moon celebration or a *S* day

SABBATH-REST (REST)

Heb 4: 9 then, a *S* for the people of God;

SABBATHS (SABBATH)

Ex 31: 13 Israelites, 'You must observe my *S*.
Lev 19: 3 and you must observe my *S*.
19: 30 Observe my *S* and have reverence
23: 38 addition to those for the LORD's *S*
25: 8 so that the seven *s* of years amount
25: 8 '' 'Count off seven *s* of years—
26: 2 Observe my *S* and have reverence
26: 34 the land will rest and enjoy its *s*.
26: 35 have during the *s* you lived in it.
26: 43 will enjoy its *s* while it lies desolate
1Ch 23: 31 presented to the LORD on *S*
2Ch 2: 4 evening and on *S* and New Moons
8: 13 commanded by Moses for *S*,
31: 3 for the burnt offerings on the *S*,
Ne 10: 33 on the *S*, New Moon festivals
Isa 1: 13 New Moons, *S* and convocations
56: 4 ''To the eunuchs who keep my *S*,
La 2: 6 her appointed feasts and her *S*;
Eze 20: 12 Also I gave them my *S*
20: 13 and they utterly desecrated my *S*.
20: 16 my decrees and desecrated my *S*.
20: 20 Keep my *S* holy, that they may be
20: 21 and they desecrated my *S*.
20: 24 my decrees and desecrated my *S*,
22: 8 holy things and desecrated my *S*.
22: 26 eyes to the keeping of my *S*,
23: 38 my sanctuary and desecrated my *S*.
44: 24 and they are to keep my *S* holy.
45: 17 the New Moons and the *S*—
46: 3 On the *S* and New Moons

SABEANS

Job 1: 15 the *S* attacked and carried them off
Isa 45: 14 and those tall *S*—
Eze 23: 42 *S* were brought from the desert
Joel 3: 8 and they will sell them to the *S*,

SABTA

1Ch 1: 9 Havilah, *S*, Raamah and Sabteca.

SABTAH

Ge 10: 7 Havilah, *S*, Raamah and Sabtecah.

SABTECA

1Ch 1: 9 Havilah, Sabta, Raamah and *S*.

SABTECAH

Ge 10: 7 Havilah, Sabtah, Raamah and *S*.

SACAR

1Ch 11: 35 Ahiam son of *S* the Hararite,
26: 4 Joah the third, *S* the fourth,

SACHET

SS 1: 13 My lover is to me a *s* of myrrh

SACK (SACKED SACKS)

Ge 42: 25 put each man's silver back in his *s*,
42: 27 of them opened his *s* to get feed
42: 27 silver in the mouth of his *s*.
42: 28 ''Here it is in my *s*.''
42: 35 there in each man's *s* was his pouch
43: 21 in the mouth of his *s*.
44: 1 silver in the mouth of his *s*.
44: 2 the mouth of the youngest one's *s*,
44: 11 Each of them quickly lowered his *s*
44: 12 the cup was found in Benjamin's *s*.

SACKCLOTH

Ge 37: 34 put on *s* and mourned
Lev 11: 32 it is made of wood, cloth, hide or *s*.
2Sa 3: 31 ''Tear your clothes and put on *s*
21: 10 Rizpah daughter of Aiah took *s*
1Ki 20: 31 of Israel with *s* around our waists
20: 32 Wearing *s* around their waists
21: 27 He lay in *s* and went
21: 27 he tore his clothes, put on *s*
2Ki 6: 30 underneath, he had *s* on his body.
19: 1 he tore his clothes and put on *s*
19: 2 all wearing *s*, to the prophet Isaiah
1Ch 21: 16 clothed in *s*, fell facedown.
Ne 9: 1 and wearing *s* and having dust
Est 4: 1 he tore his clothes, put on *s*
4: 2 no one clothed in *s* was allowed
4: 3 Many lay on *s* and ashes.
4: 4 for him to put on instead of his *s*,
Job 16: 15 ''I have sewed *s* over my skin
Ps 30: 11 you removed my *s* and clothed me
35: 13 Yet when they were ill, I put on *s*
69: 11 when I put on *s*,
Isa 3: 24 instead of fine clothing, *s*;
15: 3 In the streets they wear *s*;
20: 2 ''Take off the *s* from your body
22: 12 to tear out your hair and put on *s*.
32: 11 put *s* around your waists.
37: 1 he tore his clothes and put on *s*
37: 2 the leading priests, all wearing *s*,
50: 3 and make *s* its covering.''
58: 5 and for lying on *s* and ashes?
Jer 4: 8 So put on *s*,
6: 26 O my people, put on *s*
48: 37 and every waist is covered with *s*.
49: 3 Put on *s* and mourn;
La 2: 10 and put on *s*.
Eze 7: 18 They will put on *s* and be clothed
27: 31 and will put on *s*.
Da 9: 3 in fasting, and in *s* and ashes.
Joel 1: 8 Mourn like a virgin in *s*
1: 13 Come, spend the night in *s*,
1: 13 Put on *s*, O priests, and mourn;
Am 8: 10 I will make all of you wear *s*
Jnh 3: 5 the greatest to the least, put on *s*
3: 6 covered himself with *s*
3: 8 let man and beast be covered with *s*
Mt 11: 21 would have repented long ago in *s*
Lk 10: 13 have repented long ago, sitting in *s*
Rev 6: 12 The sun turned black like *s* made
11: 3 for 1,260 days, clothed in *s*.''

SACKED (SACK)

2Ki 15: 16 He *s* Tiphsah and ripped open all

SACKS (SACK)

Ge 42: 35 As they were emptying their *s*,
43: 12 back into the mouths of your *s*
43: 18 back into our *s* the first time.
43: 21 for the night we opened our *s*
43: 22 know who put our silver in our *s*.''
43: 23 has given you treasure in your *s*;
44: 1 ''Fill the men's *s* with as much food
44: 8 found inside the mouths of our *s*.

Jos 9: 4 were loaded with worn-out *s*
1Sa 9: 7 the man? The food in our *s* is gone.

SACRED

Ex 12: 16 On the first day hold a *s* assembly,
23: 24 and break their *s* stones to pieces.
28: 2 Make *s* garments for your brother
28: 4 They are to make these *s* garments
28: 38 involved in the *s* gifts the Israelites
29: 6 attach the *s* diadem to the turban.
29: 29 "Aaron's *s* garments will belong
29: 31 and cook the meat in a *s* place.
29: 33 may eat them, because they are *s*.
29: 34 It must not be eaten, because it is *s*.
30: 25 It will be the *s* anointing oil.
30: 25 Make these into a *s* anointing oil,
30: 31 'This is to be my *s* anointing oil
30: 32 It is *s*, and you are
30: 32 and you are to consider it *s*.
30: 35 It is to be salted and pure and *s*.
31: 10 both the *s* garments
34: 13 smash their *s* stones and cut
35: 19 both the *s* garments
35: 21 and for the *s* garments.
37: 29 They also made the *s* anointing oil
39: 1 also made *s* garments for Aaron,
39: 30 They made the plate, the *s* diadem,
39: 41 both the *s* garments
40: 13 dress Aaron in the *s* garments,
Lev 8: 9 the *s* diadem, on the front of it,
12: 4 She must not touch anything *s*
16: 4 He is to put on the *s* linen tunic,
16: 4 These are *s* garments;
16: 32 He is to put on the *s* linen garments
22: 2 treat with respect the *s* offerings
22: 3 comes near the *s* offerings that
22: 4 he may not eat the *s* offerings
22: 6 must not eat any of the *s* offerings
22: 7 after that he may eat the *s* offerings
22: 10 family may eat the *s* offering,
22: 12 any of the *s* contributions.
22: 14 " 'If anyone eats a *s* offering
22: 15 not desecrate the *s* offerings
22: 16 them to eat the *s* offerings
23: 2 are to proclaim as *s* assemblies.
23: 3 of rest, a day of *s* assembly.
23: 4 the *s* assemblies you are
23: 7 On the first day hold a *s* assembly
23: 8 the seventh day hold a *s* assembly
23: 20 They are a *s* offering to the LORD
23: 21 are to proclaim a *s* assembly
23: 24 a *s* assembly commemorated
23: 27 Hold a *s* assembly and deny
23: 35 The first day is a *s* assembly;
23: 36 on the eighth day hold a *s* assembly
23: 37 *s* assemblies for bringing offerings
26: 1 or a *s* stone for yourselves,
Nu 5: 9 All the *s* contributions
5: 10 Each man's *s* gifts are his own,
28: 18 On the first day hold a *s* assembly
28: 25 the seventh day hold a *s* assembly
28: 26 hold a *s* assembly and do no regular
29: 1 seventh month hold a *s* assembly
29: 7 seventh month hold a *s* assembly.
29: 12 hold a *s* assembly and do no regular
Dt 7: 5 their altars, smash their *s* stones,
12: 3 smash their *s* stones and burn their
16: 22 and do not erect a *s* stone,
26: 13 from my house the *s* portion
26: 14 any of the *s* portion while I was
Jos 6: 19 and iron are *s* to the LORD
1Ki 1: 39 the horn of oil from the *s* tent
8: 4 and all the *s* furnishings in it.
14: 23 *s* stones and Asherah poles
2Ki 3: 2 He got rid of the *s* stone
10: 26 They brought the *s* stone out
10: 27 They demolished the *s* stone
12: 4 as *s* offerings to the temple
12: 18 took all the *s* objects dedicated
17: 10 They set up *s* stones and Asherah
18: 4 smashed the *s* stones and cut
23: 14 Josiah smashed the *s* stones
1Ch 16: 42 of the other instruments for *s* song.
22: 19 and the *s* articles belonging to God
23: 28 the purification of all *s* things
2Ch 5: 5 and all the *s* furnishings in it.
14: 3 smashed the *s* stones and cut
24: 7 even its *s* objects for the Baals.
2Ch 31: 1 smashed the *s* stones and cut
35: 3 "Put the *s* ark in the temple that
Ezr 2: 63 not to eat any of the most *s* food
8: 30 *s* articles that had been weighed
8: 33 and the *s* articles into the hands
Ne 7: 65 not to eat any of the most *s* food
8: 9 "This day is *s* to the LORD your
8: 10 This day is *s* to our Lord.
8: 11 saying, "Be still, for this is a *s* day.
Ps 89: 20 with my *s* oil I have anointed him.
Isa 1: 29 be ashamed because of the *s* oaks
14: 13 heights of the *s* mountain.
64: 10 Your *s* cities have become a desert;
65: 5 for I am too *s* for you!'
Jer 31: 23 righteous dwelling, O *s* mountain.'
43: 13 Egypt he will demolish the *s* pillars
La 4: 1 The *s* gems are scattered
Eze 44: 19 are to leave them in the *s* rooms,
45: 1 a portion of the land as a *s* district,
45: 3 In the *s* district, measure
45: 4 It will be the *s* portion of the land
45: 6 cubits long, adjoining the *s* portion;
45: 7 of the area formed by the *s* district
46: 19 gate to the *s* rooms facing north,
48: 10 This will be the *s* portion
48: 12 gift to them from the *s* portion
48: 18 bordering on the *s* portion
48: 20 set aside the *s* portion,
48: 21 and the *s* portion with the temple
48: 21 cubits of the *s* portion
48: 21 of the area formed by the *s* portion
Hos 3: 1 and love the *s* raisin-cakes."
3: 4 without sacrifice or *s* stones,
10: 1 he adorned his *s* stones.
10: 2 and destroy their *s* stones.
Joel 1: 14 call a *s* assembly.
2: 15 call a *s* assembly.
Mic 5: 13 and your *s* stones from among you;
Zec 14: 20 house will be like the *s* bowls
Mt 7: 6 "Do not give dogs what is *s*;
23: 17 or the temple that makes the gold *s*
23: 19 or the altar that makes the gift *s*?
Ro 14: 5 One man considers one day more *s*
1Co 3: 17 for God's temple is *s*, and you are
2Pe 1: 18 were with him on the *s* mountain.
2: 21 on the *s* commandment that was

SACRIFICE (SACRIFICED SACRIFICES SACRIFICING)

Ge 22: 2 *S* him there as a burnt offering
31: 54 He offered a *s* there
Ex 5: 8 'Let us go and *s* to our God.'
5: 17 'Let us go and *s* to the LORD.'
8: 25 "Go, *s* to your God here in the land
12: 27 'It is the Passover *s* to the LORD,
13: 15 This is why I *s* to the LORD
20: 24 and *s* on it your burnt offerings
23: 18 "Do not offer the blood of a *s* to me
29: 36 *S* a bull each day as a sin offering
29: 41 *S* the other lamb at twilight
34: 15 to their gods and *s* to them,
34: 25 of the *s* from the Passover Feast
34: 25 "Do not offer the blood of a *s* to me
Lev 3: 3 is to bring a *s* made to the LORD
3: 9 is to bring a *s* made to the LORD
7: 12 then along with this *s*
7: 16 the *s* shall be eaten
7: 17 Any meat of the *s* left
7: 29 part of it as his *s* to the LORD.
9: 4 offering to *s* before the LORD,
9: 7 to the altar and *s* your sin offering
9: 7 *s* the offering that is for the people
14: 19 the priest is to *s* the sin offering
14: 30 Then he shall *s* the doves
15: 15 The priest is to *s* them, the one
15: 30 The priest is to *s* one
16: 9 falls to the LORD and *s* it
16: 24 and *s* the burnt offering for himself
17: 5 and *s* them as fellowship offerings.
17: 8 who offers a burnt offering or *s*
17: 9 of Meeting to *s* it to the LORD—
19: 5 *s* it in such a way that it will be
19: 5 " 'When you *s* a fellowship offering
19: 6 It shall be eaten on the day you *s* it
22: 29 *s* it in such a way that it will be
22: 29 "When you *s* an offering
23: 12 you must *s* as a burnt offering
23: 19 *s* one male goat for a sin offering
Nu 6: 17 to *s* the ram as a fellowship offering
6: 18 is under the *s* of the fellowship
7: 88 number of animals for the *s*
15: 5 lamb for the burnt offering or the *s*,
15: 8 young bull as a burnt offering or *s*,
Dt 12: 13 to *s* your burnt offerings anywhere
15: 21 you must not *s* it to the LORD
16: 2 *S* as the Passover to the LORD
16: 4 of the meat you *s* on the evening
16: 5 You must not *s* the Passover
16: 6 There you must *s* the Passover
17: 1 Do not *s* to the LORD your God
18: 3 priests from the people who *s* a bull
27: 7 *S* fellowship offerings there,
Jos 22: 23 or to *s* fellowship offerings on it,
Jdg 11: 31 and I will *s* it as a burnt offering."
16: 23 to offer a great *s* to Dagon their god
1Sa 1: 3 *s* to the LORD Almighty at Shiloh,
1: 4 the day came for Elkanah to *s*,
1: 21 to offer the annual *s* to the LORD
2: 13 that whenever anyone offered a *s*
2: 19 husband to offer the annual *s*.
2: 29 Why do you scorn my *s*
3: 14 house will never be atoned for by *s*
9: 12 for the people have a *s*
9: 13 because he must bless the *s*;
10: 8 down to you to *s* burnt offerings
15: 15 cattle to *s* to the LORD your God,
15: 21 to *s* them to the LORD your God
15: 22 To obey is better than *s*,
16: 2 'I have come to *s* to the LORD.'
16: 3 to the *s*, and I will show you what
16: 5 I have come to *s* to the LORD.
16: 5 and come to the *s* with me."
16: 5 his sons and invited them to the *s*.
20: 6 an annual *s* is being made there
20: 29 because our family is observing a *s*
2Sa 24: 24 I will not *s* to the LORD my God
1Ki 8: 63 Solomon offered a *s*
13: 2 On you he will *s* the priests
18: 29 until the time for the evening *s*.
18: 36 of *s*, the prophet Elijah stepped
18: 38 the LORD fell and burned up the *s*,
2Ki 3: 20 about the time for offering the *s*,
3: 27 offered him as a *s* on the city wall.
10: 19 I am going to hold a great *s* for Baal
17: 35 to them, serve them or *s* to them.
23: 10 so no one could use it to *s* his son
1Ch 21: 24 or *s* a burnt offering that costs me
2Ch 7: 5 And King Solomon offered a *s*
28: 23 I will *s* to them so they will help me
29: 27 the order to *s* the burnt offering
29: 28 All this continued until the *s*
33: 17 continued to *s* at the high places,
Ezr 3: 2 of Israel to *s* burnt offerings on it,
7: 17 *s* them on the altar of the temple
9: 4 appalled until the evening *s*.
9: 5 Then, at the evening *s*, I rose
Job 1: 5 the morning he would *s* a burnt
42: 8 *s* a burnt offering for yourselves.
Ps 27: 6 at his tabernacle will I *s* with shouts
40: 6 *S* and offering you did not desire,
50: 5 who made a covenant with me by *s*
50: 14 *S* thank offerings to God,
51: 16 You do not delight in *s*,
54: 6 I will *s* a freewill offering to you;
66: 15 I will *s* fat animals to you
107: 22 Let them *s* thank offerings
116: 17 I will *s* a thank offering to you
141: 2 of my hands be like the evening *s*.
Pr 15: 8 The LORD detests the *s*
21: 3 to the LORD than *s*.
21: 27 The *s* of the wicked is detestable—
Ecc 5: 1 rather than to offer the *s* of fools,
Isa 34: 6 For the LORD has a *s* in Bozrah
57: 5 you *s* your children in the ravines
Jer 32: 35 of Ben Hinnom to *s* their sons
46: 10 the LORD Almighty, will offer *s*
Eze 20: 26 defiled through their gifts—the *s*
20: 31 the *s* of your sons in the fire—
39: 17 all around to the *s* I am preparing
39: 17 the great *s* on the mountains
39: 19 At the *s* I am preparing for you,
43: 24 and *s* them as a burnt offering
46: 2 are to *s* his burnt offering
Da 8: 11 it took away the daily *s* from him,
8: 12 the daily *s* were given over to it.
8: 13 the vision concerning the daily *s*,

Da 9: 21 about the time of the evening *s*.
9: 27 that 'seven' he will put an end to *s*
11: 31 and will abolish the daily *s*.
12: 11 time that the daily *s* is abolished
Hos 3: 4 without *s* or sacred stones,
4: 13 They *s* on the mountaintops
4: 14 and *s* with temple prostitutes—
6: 6 For I desire mercy, not *s*,
12: 11 Do they *s* bulls in Gilgal?
13: 2 "They offer human *s*
Jnh 1: 16 and they offered a *s* to the LORD
2: 9 will *s* to you.
Zep 1: 7 The LORD has prepared a *s*;
1: 8 On the day of the LORD's *s*
Zec 14: 21 all who come to *s* will take some
Mal 1: 8 When you bring blind animals for *s*
1: 8 When you *s* crippled or diseased
Mt 9: 13 this means: 'I desire mercy, not *s*.'
12: 7 not *s*,' you would not have
Mk 14: 12 customary to *s* the Passover lamb,
Lk 2: 24 and to offer a *s* in keeping
Ro 3: 25 God presented him as a *s*
1Co 10: 19 Do I mean then that a *s* offered
10: 28 "This has been offered in *s*,"
Eph 5: 2 as a fragrant offering and *s* to God.
Php 2: 17 out like a drink offering on the *s*
4: 18 an acceptable *s*, pleasing to God.
Heb 9: 26 away with sin by the *s* of himself.
10: 5 "*S* and offering you did not desire,
10: 10 holy through the *s* of the body
10: 12 offered for all time one *s* for sins,
10: 14 by one *s* he has made perfect
10: 18 there is no longer any *s* for sin.
10: 26 of the truth, no *s* for sins is left,
11: 4 faith Abel offered God a better *s*
11: 17 tested him, offered Isaac as a *s*.
11: 17 the promises was about to *s* his one
13: 15 offer to God a *s* of praise—
1Jn 2: 2 He is the atoning *s* for our sins,
4: 10 as an atoning *s* for our sins.

SACRIFICED (SACRIFICE)

Ge 8: 20 clean birds, he *s* burnt offerings
22: 13 went over and took the ram and *s* it
Ex 24: 5 burnt offerings and *s* young bulls
32: 6 and *s* burnt offerings and presented
32: 8 bowed down to it and *s* to it
Lev 4: 10 the fat is removed from the cow *s*
9: 22 And having *s* the sin offering,
10: 19 "Today they *s* their sin offering
18: 21 of your children to be *s* to Molech,
Nu 7: 17 to be *s* as a fellowship offering.
7: 23 to be *s* as a fellowship offering.
7: 29 to be *s* as a fellowship offering.
7: 35 to be *s* as a fellowship offering.
7: 41 to be *s* as a fellowship offering.
7: 47 to be *s* as a fellowship offering.
7: 53 to be *s* as a fellowship offering.
7: 59 to be *s* as a fellowship offering.
7: 65 to be *s* as a fellowship offering.
7: 71 to be *s* as a fellowship offering.
7: 77 to be *s* as a fellowship offering.
7: 83 to be *s* as a fellowship offering.
22: 40 Balak *s* cattle and sheep,
Dt 32: 17 They *s* to demons, which are not
Jos 8: 31 and *s* fellowship offerings.
Jdg 6: 28 the second bull *s* on the newly built
13: 19 and *s* it on a rock to the LORD.
1Sa 6: 14 and *s* the cows as a burnt offering
11: 15 There they *s* fellowship offerings
2Sa 6: 13 he *s* a bull and a fattened calf.
6: 17 and David *s* burnt offerings
24: 25 *s* burnt offerings and fellowship
1Ki 1: 9 Adonijah then *s* sheep, cattle
1: 19 He has *s* great numbers of cattle,
1: 25 and *s* great numbers of cattle,
3: 15 *s* burnt offerings and fellowship
9: 25 a year Solomon *s* burnt offerings
2Ki 16: 3 and even *s* his son in the fire,
17: 17 They *s* their sons and daughters
21: 6 He *s* his own son in the fire,
1Ch 15: 26 seven bulls and seven rams were *s*.
21: 26 *s* burnt offerings and fellowship
2Ch 8: 12 Solomon *s* burnt offerings
15: 11 At that time they *s*
28: 3 of Ben Hinnom and *s* his sons
33: 6 He *s* his sons in the fire
33: 16 *s* fellowship and thank offerings
2Ch 34: 4 graves of those who had *s* to them.
Ezr 3: 3 *s* burnt offerings on it to the LORD
8: 35 from captivity *s* burnt offerings
Ps 106: 37 They *s* their sons
106: 38 whom they *s* to the idols of Canaan
Eze 16: 20 and *s* them as food to the idols.
16: 21 my children and *s* them
23: 37 they even *s* their children,
23: 39 the very day they *s* their children
Hos 11: 2 They *s* to the Baals
Lk 22: 7 the Passover lamb had to be *s*.
Ac 15: 29 are to abstain from food *s* to idols,
21: 25 abstain from food *s* to idols,
1Co 5: 7 our Passover lamb, has been *s*.
8: 1 Now about food *s* to idols:
8: 4 about eating food *s* to idols:
8: 7 as having been *s* to an idol,
8: 10 to eat what has been *s* to idols?
Heb 7: 27 He *s* for their sins once for all
9: 28 so Christ was *s* once
Rev 2: 14 to sin by eating food *s* to idols
2: 20 and the eating of food *s* to idols.

SACRIFICES (SACRIFICE)

Ge 46: 1 he offered *s* to the God
Ex 3: 18 journey into the desert to offer *s*
5: 3 journey into the desert to offer *s*
8: 8 go to offer *s* to the LORD."
8: 26 And if we offer *s* that are detestable
8: 26 The *s* we offer the LORD our God
8: 27 journey into the desert to offer *s*
8: 28 to offer *s* to the LORD your God
8: 29 go to offer *s* to the LORD."
10: 25 "You must allow us to have *s*
18: 12 a burnt offering and other *s*
22: 20 "Whoever *s* to any god other
34: 15 invite you and you will eat their *s*.
Lev 17: 3 Any Israelite who *s* a cow,
17: 5 to the LORD the *s* they are now
17: 7 any of their *s* to the goat idols
23: 37 *s* and drink offerings required
Nu 15: 3 whether burnt offerings or *s*,
25: 2 them to the *s* to their gods.
Dt 12: 6 bring your burnt offerings and *s*,
12: 11 your burnt offerings and *s*,
12: 27 The blood of your *s* must be poured
12: 31 in the fire as *s* to their gods.
18: 10 found among you who *s* his son
32: 38 the gods who ate the fat of their *s*
33: 19 and there offer *s* of righteousness;
Jos 22: 26 but not for burnt offerings or *s*.'
22: 27 *s* and fellowship offerings.
22: 28 not for burnt offerings and *s*,
22: 29 and *s*, other than the altar
Jdg 2: 5 There they offered *s* to the LORD.
1Sa 6: 15 offered burnt offerings and made *s*
15: 22 delight in burnt offerings and *s*
2Sa 15: 12 While Absalom was offering *s*,
15: 24 and Abiathar offered *s*
1Ki 3: 3 except that he offered *s*
3: 4 The king went to Gibeon to offer *s*,
8: 62 Israel with him offered *s*
11: 8 and offered *s* to their gods.
12: 27 up to offer *s* at the temple
12: 32 in Judah, and offered *s* on the altar.
12: 33 he offered *s* on the altar he had
22: 43 and the people continued to offer *s*
2Ki 5: 17 *s* to any other god but the LORD.
10: 24 So they went in to make *s*
12: 3 the people continued to offer *s*
14: 4 the people continued to offer *s*
15: 4 the people continued to offer *s*
15: 35 the people continued to offer *s*
16: 4 He offered *s* and burned incense
16: 15 blood of the burnt offerings and *s*.
17: 31 as *s* to Adrammelech
17: 36 bow down and to him offer *s*.
1Ch 21: 28 the Jebusite, he offered *s* there.
23: 13 to offer *s* before the LORD,
29: 21 The next day they made *s*
29: 21 other *s* in abundance for all Israel.
2Ch 2: 6 as a place to burn *s* before him?
7: 1 the burnt offering and the *s*,
7: 4 and all the people offered *s*
7: 12 place for myself as a temple for *s*.
11: 16 Jerusalem to offer *s* to the LORD,
25: 14 to them and burned *s* to them.
28: 3 He burned *s* in the Valley
2Ch 28: 4 He offered *s* and burned incense
28: 23 He offered *s* to the gods
28: 25 places to burn *s* to other gods
29: 31 So the assembly brought *s*
29: 31 and bring *s* and thank offerings
29: 33 as *s* amounted to six hundred bulls
32: 12 before one altar and burn *s* on it'?
33: 22 offered *s* to all the idols Manasseh
Ezr 3: 3 both the morning and evening *s*.
3: 5 the New Moon *s* and the *s*
6: 3 be rebuilt as a place to present *s*,
6: 10 so that they may offer *s* pleasing
Ne 4: 2 Will they offer *s*? Will they finish
12: 43 on that day they offered great *s*,
Ps 4: 5 Offer right *s*
20: 3 May he remember all your *s*
50: 8 I do not rebuke you for your *s*
50: 23 He who *s* thank offerings honors
51: 17 The *s* of God are a broken spirit;
51: 19 Then there will be righteous *s*,
106: 28 and ate *s* offered to lifeless gods;
Ecc 9: 2 those who offer *s* and those who do
Isa 1: 11 "The multitude of your *s*—
19: 21 They will worship with *s*
43: 23 nor honored me with your *s*.
43: 24 or lavished on me the fat of your *s*.
56: 7 Their burnt offerings and *s*
57: 7 there you went up to offer your *s*.
65: 3 offering *s* in gardens
65: 7 "Because they burned *s*
66: 3 But whoever *s* a bull
Jer 6: 20 your *s* do not please me."
7: 21 your burnt offerings to your other *s*
7: 22 about burnt offerings and *s*,
17: 26 bringing burnt offerings and *s*,
19: 4 they have burned *s* in it
33: 18 grain offerings and to present *s*.' "
Eze 20: 28 they offered their *s*, made offerings
20: 40 along with all your holy *s*.
40: 41 on which the *s* were slaughtered.
40: 42 the burnt offerings and the other *s*.
44: 11 slaughter the burnt offerings and *s*
44: 15 to stand before me to offer *s* of fat
46: 24 at the temple will cook the *s*
Hos 4: 19 and their *s* will bring them shame.
8: 13 They offer *s* given to me
9: 4 Such *s* will be to them like
9: 4 nor will their *s* please him.
Am 4: 4 Bring your *s* every morning,
5: 25 "Did you bring me *s* and offerings
Hab 1: 16 Therefore he *s* to his net
Mal 1: 13 animals and offer them as *s*,
1: 14 but then *s* a blemished animal
2: 3 the offal from your festival *s*,
Mk 1: 44 offer the *s* that Moses commanded
12: 33 than all burnt offerings and *s*."
Lk 5: 14 offer the *s* that Moses commanded
13: 1 blood Pilate had mixed with their *s*.
Ac 7: 41 They brought *s* to it and held
7: 42 " 'Did you bring me *s* and offerings
14: 13 and the crowd wanted to offer *s*
Ro 12: 1 to offer your bodies as living *s*,
1Co 10: 18 not those who eat the *s* participate
10: 20 but the *s* of pagans are offered
Heb 5: 1 to offer gifts and *s* for sins.
5: 3 has to offer *s* for his own sins,
7: 27 need to offer *s* day after day,
8: 3 appointed to offer both gifts and *s*,
9: 9 and *s* being offered were not able
9: 23 things to be purified with these *s*,
9: 23 with better *s* than these.
10: 1 by the same *s* repeated endlessly
10: 3 But those *s* are an annual reminder
10: 8 First he said, "*S* and offerings,
10: 11 and again he offers the same *s*,
13: 16 for with such *s* God is pleased.
1Pe 2: 5 offering spiritual *s* acceptable

SACRIFICING (SACRIFICE)

1Sa 2: 15 and say to the man who was *s*,
7: 10 While Samuel was *s* the burnt
2Sa 6: 18 he had finished *s* the burnt
1Ki 3: 2 were still *s* at the high places,
8: 5 *s* so many sheep and cattle that
12: 32 *s* to the calves he had made.
1Ch 16: 2 David had finished *s* the burnt
2Ch 5: 6 *s* so many sheep and cattle that
35: 14 were *s* the burnt offerings

Ezr 4: 2 have been *s* to him since the time
Eze 43: 18 the regulations for *s* burnt offerings
Ac 14: 18 difficulty keeping the crowd from *s*

SAD (SADDENED SADNESS)

Ge 40: 7 "Why are your faces so *s* today?"
Ne 2: 1 I had not been *s* in his presence
2: 2 look so *s* when you are not ill?
2: 3 Why should my face not look *s*
Ecc 7: 3 a *s* face is good for the heart.
Mt 19: 22 he went away *s*, because he had
26: 22 They were very *s* and began to say
Mk 10: 22 He went away *s*, because he had
Lk 18: 23 he heard this, he became very *s*,

SADDENED (SAD)

Mk 14: 19 They were *s*, and one

SADDLE (SADDLEBAGS SADDLED)

Ge 31: 34 and put them inside her camel's *s*
Jdg 5: 10 sitting on your *s* blankets,
1Ki 13: 13 to his sons, "*S* the donkey for me."
13: 27 to his sons, "*S* the donkey for me,"
Eze 27: 20 " 'Dedan traded in *s* blankets

SADDLEBAGS (SADDLE)

Ge 49: 14 lying down between two *s*.

SADDLED (SADDLE)

Ge 22: 3 Abraham got up and *s* his donkey.
Nu 22: 21 *s* his donkey and went
Jdg 19: 10 with his two *s* donkeys
2Sa 16: 1 He had a string of donkeys *s*
17: 23 he *s* his donkey and set out
19: 26 'I will have my donkey *s*
1Ki 2: 40 he *s* his donkey and went to Achish
13: 13 And when they had *s* the donkey
13: 23 had brought him back *s* his donkey
2Ki 4: 24 She *s* the donkey and said

SADDUCEES

Mt 3: 7 and *S* coming to where he was
16: 1 The Pharisees and *S* came to Jesus
16: 6 the yeast of the Pharisees and *S*."
16: 11 the yeast of the Pharisees and *S*."
16: 12 the teaching of the Pharisees and *S*.
22: 23 That same day the *S*, who say there
22: 34 that Jesus had silenced the *S*,
Mk 12: 18 *S*, who say there is no resurrection,
Lk 20: 27 Some of the *S*, who say there is no
Ac 4: 1 and the *S* came up to Peter
5: 17 members of the party of the *S*,
23: 6 knowing that some of them were *S*
23: 7 between the Pharisees and the *S*,
23: 8 *S* say that there is no resurrection,

SADNESS (SAD)

Ne 2: 2 This can be nothing but *s* of heart."

SAFE (SAVE)

Dt 29: 19 "I will be *s*, even though I persist
1Sa 20: 7 'Very well,' then your servant is *s*.
20: 21 you are *s*; there is no danger.
22: 23 You will be *s* with me."
2Sa 18: 29 "Is the young man Absalom *s*?"
18: 32 "Is the young man Absalom *s*?"
2Ch 15: 5 In those days it was not *s*
Ezr 8: 21 and ask him for a *s* journey for us
Job 21: 9 Their homes are *s* and free
Ps 12: 7 O LORD, you will keep us *s*
16: 1 Keep me *s*, O God,
27: 5 he will keep me *s* in his dwelling;
31: 20 in your dwelling you keep them *s*
37: 3 in the land and enjoy *s* pasture.
Pr 11: 15 to strike hands in pledge is *s*.
18: 10 the righteous run to it and are *s*.
20: 28 Love and faithfulness keep a king *s*;
28: 18 whose walk is blameless is kept *s*,
28: 26 he who walks in wisdom is kept *s*.
29: 25 in the LORD is kept *s*.
Jer 7: 10 "We are *s*"—*s* to do all these
12: 5 If you stumble in *s* country,
12: 12 no one will be *s*.
Lk 11: 21 own house, his possessions are *s*.
15: 27 he has him back *s* and sound.'
Jn 17: 12 kept them *s* by that name you gave
1Ti 2: 15 But women will be kept *s*
1Jn 5: 18 born of God keeps him *s*,

SAFE-CONDUCT (CONDUCT)

Ne 2: 7 so that they will provide me *s*

SAFEGUARD (GUARD)

Php 3: 1 to you again, and it is a *s* for you.

SAFEKEEPING (KEEP)

Ex 22: 7 or goods for *s* and they are stolen
22: 10 animal to his neighbor for *s*

SAFETY (SAVE)

Ge 43: 9 I myself will guarantee his *s*;
44: 32 servant guaranteed the boy's *s*
Lev 25: 19 will eat your fill and live there in *s*.
26: 5 all the food you want and live in *s*
Dt 12: 10 around you so that you will live in *s*
33: 28 So Israel will live in *s* alone;
Jdg 18: 7 saw that the people were living in *s*,
1Ki 4: 25 from Dan to Beersheba, lived in *s*,
Job 5: 4 His children are far from *s*,
5: 11 and those who mourn are lifted to *s*
11: 18 about you and take your rest in *s*.
30: 15 my *s* vanishes like a cloud.
Ps 4: 8 make me dwell in *s*.
141: 10 while I pass by in *s*.
Pr 1: 33 whoever listens to me will live in *s*
3: 23 Then you will go on your way in *s*,
Isa 14: 30 and the needy will lie down in *s*.
Jer 4: 6 Flee for *s* without delay!
6: 1 "Flee for *s*, people of Benjamin!
23: 6 and Israel will live in *s*.
32: 37 to this place and let them live in *s*.
33: 16 and Jerusalem will live in *s*.
Eze 28: 26 They will live there in *s*
28: 26 live in *s* when I inflict punishment
34: 25 and sleep in the forests in *s*.
34: 28 in *s*, and no one will make them
38: 8 and now all of them live in *s*.
38: 14 my people Israel are living in *s*,
39: 6 live in *s* in the coastlands,
39: 26 when they lived in *s* in their land
Hos 2: 18 so that all may lie down in *s*.
Zep 2: 15 that lived in *s*.
Ac 27: 44 way everyone reached land in *s*.
1Th 5: 3 people are saying, "Peace and *s*,"

SAFFRON

SS 4: 14 nard and *s*,

SAG

Ecc 10: 18 If a man is lazy, the rafters *s*;

SAIL (FORESAIL SAILED SAILING SAILORS)

1Ki 22: 48 but they never set *s*— they were
22: 49 "Let my men *s* with your men,"
2Ch 20: 37 and were not able to set *s* to trade.
Isa 33: 21 no mighty ship will *s* them.
33: 23 the *s* is not spread.
Eze 27: 7 linen from Egypt was your *s*
Ac 18: 21 Then he set *s* from Ephesus.
20: 3 as he was about to *s* for Syria,
20: 15 The next day we set *s* from there
20: 16 Paul had decided to *s* past Ephesus
21: 2 went on board and set *s*.
27: 1 it was decided that we would *s*
27: 2 ship from Adramyttium about to *s*
27: 12 majority decided that we should *s*
27: 21 have taken my advice not to *s*
27: 24 the lives of all who *s* with you.'
28: 10 and when we were ready to *s*,
28: 13 From there we set *s* and arrived

SAILED (SAIL)

1Ki 9: 28 They *s* to Ophir and brought back
2Ch 8: 18 *s* to Ophir and brought back four
Jnh 1: 3 and *s* for Tarshish to flee
Lk 8: 23 As they *s*, he fell asleep.
8: 26 They *s* to the region
Ac 13: 4 and *s* from there to Cyprus.
13: 13 and his companions *s* to Perga
14: 26 From Attalia they *s* back
15: 39 Barnabas took Mark and *s*
16: 11 and *s* straight for Samothrace,
18: 18 Before he *s*, he had his hair cut
18: 18 he left the brothers and *s* for Syria,
20: 6 we *s* from Philippi after the Feast
20: 13 ahead to the ship and *s* for Assos,
Ac 21: 1 out to sea and *s* straight to Cos.
21: 3 to the south of it, we *s* on to Syria.
27: 5 When we had *s* across the open sea
27: 7 we *s* to the lee of Crete,
27: 13 and *s* along the shore of Crete.

SAILING (SAIL)

Ac 27: 6 found an Alexandrian ship *s*
27: 9 *s* had already become dangerous

SAILORS (SAIL)

1Ki 9: 27 Hiram sent his men—*s* who knew
Eze 27: 9 All the ships of the sea and their *s*
Jnh 1: 5 All the *s* were afraid and each cried
1: 7 Then the *s* said to each other,
Ac 27: 27 about midnight the *s* sensed they
27: 30 the *s* let the lifeboat
Rev 18: 17 and all who travel by ship, the *s*,

SAINTS

1Sa 2: 9 He will guard the feet of his *s*,
2Ch 6: 41 may your *s* rejoice
Ps 16: 3 As for the *s* who are in the land,
30: 4 Sing to the LORD, you *s* of his;
31: 23 Love the LORD, all his *s*!
34: 9 Fear the LORD, you his *s*,
52: 9 in the presence of your *s*.
79: 2 the flesh of your *s* to the beasts
85: 8 peace to his people, his *s*—
116: 15 is the death of his *s*.
132: 9 may your *s* sing for joy."
132: 16 and her *s* will ever sing for joy.
145: 10 your *s* will extol you.
148: 14 the praise of all his *s*,
149: 1 his praise in the assembly of the *s*.
149: 5 Let the *s* rejoice in this honor
149: 9 This is the glory of all his *s*.
Da 7: 18 the *s* of the Most High will receive
7: 21 horn was waging war against the *s*
7: 22 in favor of the *s* of the Most High,
7: 25 The *s* will be handed over to him
7: 25 and oppress his *s* and try
7: 27 will be handed over to the *s*,
8: 12 of the *s* and the daily sacrifice
Ac 9: 13 done to your *s* in Jerusalem.
9: 32 he went to visit the *s* in Lydda.
26: 10 the chief priests I put many of the *s*
Ro 1: 7 loved by God and called to be *s*:
8: 27 intercedes for the *s* in accordance
15: 25 in the service of the *s* there.
15: 26 the poor among the *s* in Jerusalem.
15: 31 may be acceptable to the *s* there,
16: 2 in the Lord in a way worthy of the *s*
16: 15 Olympas and all the *s* with them.
1Co 6: 1 for judgment instead of before the *s*
6: 2 not know that the *s* will judge
14: 33 As in all the congregations of the *s*,
16: 15 themselves to the service of the *s*.
2Co 1: 1 with all the *s* throughout Achaia:
8: 4 of sharing in this service to the *s*.
9: 1 to you about this service to the *s*.
13: 13 All the *s* send their greetings.
Eph 1: 1 To the *s* in Ephesus, the faithful
1: 15 Jesus and your love for all the *s*,
1: 18 of his glorious inheritance in the *s*,
3: 18 have power, together with all the *s*,
6: 18 always keep on praying for all the *s*
Php 1: 1 To all the *s* in Christ Jesus
4: 21 Greet all the *s* in Christ Jesus.
4: 22 All the *s* send you greetings,
Col 1: 4 of the love you have for all the *s*—
1: 12 inheritance of the *s* in the kingdom
1: 26 but is now disclosed to the *s*.
1Ti 5: 10 washing the feet of the *s*,
Phm : 5 Jesus and your love for all the *s*.
: 7 have refreshed the hearts of the *s*.
Jude : 3 once for all entrusted to the *s*.
Rev 5: 8 which are the prayers of the *s*.
8: 3 with the prayers of all the *s*,
8: 4 together with the prayers of the *s*,
11: 18 your *s* and those who reverence
13: 7 power to make war against the *s*
13: 10 faithfulness on the part of the *s*.
14: 12 the part of the *s* who obey God's
16: 6 they have shed the blood of your *s*
17: 6 drunk with the blood of the *s*,
18: 20 *s* and apostles and prophets!
18: 24 of prophets and of the *s*,

Rev 19: 8 for the righteous acts of the *s*.)

SAKE (SAKES)

Ge 12: 13 that I will be treated well for your *s*
12: 16 He treated Abram well for her *s*,
18: 24 place for the *s* of the fifty righteous
18: 26 spare the whole place for their *s*."
18: 29 He said, "For the *s* of forty,
18: 31 He said, "For the *s* of twenty,
18: 32 He answered, "For the *s* of ten,
26: 24 for the *s* of my servant Abraham."
Ex 18: 8 and the Egyptians for Israel's *s*
Lev 26: 45 But for their *s* I will remember
Nu 11: 29 "Are you jealous for my *s*?
Jos 23: 3 done to all these nations for your *s*;
1Sa 12: 22 For the *s* of his great name
2Sa 5: 12 for the *s* of his people Israel.
7: 21 For the *s* of your word
9: 1 kindness for Jonathan's *s*?"
9: 7 for the *s* of your father Jonathan.
18: 5 the young man Absalom for my *s*."
18: 12 the young man Absalom for my *s*.'
1Ki 11: 12 for the *s* of David your father,
11: 13 and for the *s* of Jerusalem,
11: 13 tribe for the *s* of David my servant
11: 32 But for the *s* of my servant David
11: 34 life for the *s* of David my servant,
15: 4 for David's *s* the LORD his God
2Ki 8: 19 for the *s* of his servant David,
19: 34 for my *s* and for the *s*
20: 6 I will defend this city for my *s*
20: 6 for the *s* of my servant David.' "
1Ch 14: 2 for the *s* of his people Israel.
16: 21 for their *s* he rebuked kings:
17: 19 For the *s* of your servant
Ne 10: 28 for the *s* of the Law of God,
Job 18: 4 earth to be abandoned for your *s*?
Ps 23: 3 righteousness for his name's *s*.
25: 11 For the *s* of your name, O LORD,
31: 3 for the *s* of your name lead
44: 22 Yet for your *s* we face death all day
69: 7 For I endure scorn for your *s*,
79: 9 sins for your name's *s*.
105: 14 for their *s* he rebuked kings:
106: 8 Yet he saved them for his name's *s*,
106: 45 for their *s* he remembered his
109: 21 deal well with me for your name's *s*
122: 8 For the *s* of my brothers
122: 9 For the *s* of the house
132: 10 For the *s* of David your servant,
143: 11 For your name's *s*, O LORD,
Isa 37: 35 for my *s* and for the *s* of David
42: 21 for the *s* of his righteousness
43: 14 "For your *s* I will send to Babylon
43: 25 your transgressions, for my own *s*,
45: 4 For the *s* of Jacob my servant,
48: 9 For my own name's *s* I delay my
48: 9 for the *s* of my praise I hold it back
48: 11 For my own *s*, for my own *s*,
62: 1 For Zion's *s* I will not keep silent,
62: 1 for Jerusalem's *s* I will not remain
63: 17 Return for the *s* of your servants,
Jer 14: 7 for the *s* of your name.
14: 21 For the *s* of your name do not
15: 15 of how I suffer reproach for your *s*.
Eze 20: 9 But for the *s* of my name I did what
20: 14 But for the *s* of my name I did what
20: 22 and for the *s* of my name I did what
20: 44 deal with you for my name's *s*
36: 22 but for the *s* of my holy name,
36: 22 not for your *s*, O house of Israel,
36: 32 that I am not doing this for your *s*,
Da 9: 17 For your *s*, O Lord, look with favor
9: 19 and act! For your *s*, O my God,
Mt 10: 39 life for my *s* will find it.
15: 3 of God for the *s* of your tradition?
15: 6 of God for the *s* of your tradition.
19: 29 for my *s* will receive a hundred
24: 22 for the *s* of the elect those days will
Mk 13: 20 for the *s* of the elect, whom he has
Lk 18: 29 or children for the *s* of the kingdom
Jn 11: 15 for your *s* I am glad I was not there,
Ro 1: 5 Through him and for his name's *s*,
8: 36 "For your *s* we face death all day
9: 3 from Christ for the *s* of my brothers
14: 20 the work of God for the *s* of food.
1Co 9: 23 I do all this for the *s* of the gospel,
10: 28 and for conscience' *s*—
1Co 10: 28 for the *s* of the man who told you
2Co 2: 10 in the sight of Christ for your *s*,
4: 5 as your servants for Jesus' *s*.
4: 11 given over to death for Jesus' *s*,
5: 13 it is for the *s* of God; if we are
12: 10 for Christ's *s*, I delight
Eph 3: 1 Jesus for the *s* of you Gentiles—
Php 3: 7 loss for the *s* of Christ.
3: 8 for whose *s* I have lost all things.
Col 1: 24 for the *s* of his body, which is
1Th 1: 5 lived among you for your *s*.
2Ti 2: 10 everything for the *s* of the elect,
Tit 1: 11 and that for the *s* of dishonest gain.
Heb 11: 26 He regarded disgrace for the *s*
1Pe 1: 20 in these last times for your *s*.
2: 13 for the Lord's *s* to every authority
3Jn : 7 was for the *s* of the Name that they

SAKES (SAKE)

2Co 8: 9 yet for your *s* he became poor,

SAKIA

1Ch 8: 10 Malcam, Jeuz, *S* and Mirmah.

SALAMIS

Ac 13: 5 at *S*, they proclaimed the word

SALE (SELL)

Lev 25: 29 of redemption a full year after its *s*.
Dt 18: 8 from the *s* of family possessions.
28: 68 yourselves for *s* to your enemies
Ps 44: 12 gaining nothing from their *s*.

SALECAH

Dt 3: 10 and all Bashan as far as *S* and Edrei
Jos 12: 5 He ruled over Mount Hermon, *S*,
13: 11 and all Bashan as far as *S*—
1Ch 5: 11 as far as *S*: Joel was the chief,

SALEM

Ge 14: 18 king of *S* brought out bread
Ps 76: 2 His tent is in *S*,
Heb 7: 1 This Melchizedek was king of *S*
7: 2 "king of *S*" means "king of peace."

SALES (SELL)

Ac 4: 34 brought the money from the *s*

SALIM

Jn 3: 23 also was baptizing at Aenon near *S*,

SALIVA

1Sa 21: 13 and letting *s* run down his beard.
Jn 9: 6 made some mud with the *s*,

SALLAI

Ne 11: 8 and his followers, Gabbai and *S*—

SALLU (SALLU'S)

1Ch 9: 7 Of the Benjamites: *S* son
Ne 11: 7 of Benjamin: *S* son of Meshullam,
12: 7 Joiarib, Jedaiah, *S*, Amok,

SALLU'S (SALLU)

Ne 12: 20 Uzzi; of *S*, Kallai; of Amok's,

SALMA

1Ch 2: 51 *S* the father of Bethlehem,
2: 54 The descendants of *S*: Bethlehem,

SALMON

Ru 4: 20 the father of *S*, *S* the father of Boaz,
1Ch 2: 11 the father of *S*, *S* the father of Boaz,
Mt 1: 5 the father of *S*, *S* the father of Boaz,
Lk 3: 32 the son of *S*, the son of Nahshon,

SALMONE

Ac 27: 7 to the lee of Crete, opposite *S*.

SALOME

Mk 15: 40 the younger and of Joses, and *S*.
16: 1 *S* bought spices so that they might

SALT (SALTED SALTINESS SALTY)

Ge 14: 3 in the Valley of Siddim (the *S* Sea).
19: 26 and she became a pillar of *s*.
Lev 2: 13 Do not leave the *s* of the covenant
2: 13 add *s* to all your offerings.
2: 13 all your grain offerings with *s*.
Nu 18: 19 covenant of *s* before the LORD
34: 3 start from the end of the *S* Sea,
34: 12 the Jordan and end at the *S* Sea.
Dt 3: 17 to the Sea of the Arabah (the *S* Sea
29: 23 land will be a burning waste of *s*
Jos 3: 16 the Arabah (the *S* Sea) was
12: 3 to the Sea of the Arabah (the *S* Sea
15: 2 at the southern end of the *S* Sea,
15: 5 The eastern boundary is the *S* Sea
15: 62 Nibshan, the City of *S*
18: 19 at the northern bay of the *S* Sea,
Jdg 9: 45 destroyed the city and scattered *s*
2Sa 8: 13 Edomites in the Valley of *S*.
2Ki 2: 20 me a new bowl," he said, "and put *s*
2: 21 to the spring and threw the *s* into it,
14: 7 Edomites in the Valley of *S*
1Ch 18: 12 Edomites in the Valley of *S*.
2Ch 13: 5 forever by a covenant of *s*?
25: 11 and led his army to the Valley of *S*,
Ezr 6: 9 and wheat, *s*, wine and oil,
7: 22 of olive oil, and *s* without limit.
Job 6: 6 Is tasteless food eaten without *s*,
30: 4 In the brush they gathered *s* herbs,
39: 6 the *s* flats as his habitat.
Ps 107: 34 and fruitful land into a *s* waste,
Jer 17: 6 in a *s* land where no one lives.
48: 9 Put *s* on Moab,
Eze 16: 4 nor were you rubbed with *s*
43: 24 the priests are to sprinkle *s* on them
47: 9 and makes the *s* water fresh;
47: 11 become fresh; they will be left for *s*.
Zep 2: 9 a place of weeds and *s* pits,
Mt 5: 13 But if the *s* loses its saltiness,
5: 13 "You are the *s* of the earth.
Mk 9: 50 can you make it salty again? Have *s*
9: 50 *S* is good, but if it loses its saltiness,
Lk 14: 34 *S* is good, but if it loses its saltiness,
Col 4: 6 with *s*, so that you may know how
Jas 3: 11 *s* water flow from the same spring?
3: 12 Neither can a *s* spring produce

SALTED (SALT)

Ex 30: 35 It is to be *s* and pure and sacred.
Mk 9: 49 Everyone will be *s* with fire.

SALTINESS (SALT)

Mt 5: 13 if the salt loses its *s*, how can it be
Mk 9: 50 if it loses its *s*, how can you make it
Lk 14: 34 if it loses its *s*, how can it be made

SALTY (SALT)

Mt 5: 13 how can it be made *s* again?
Mk 9: 50 how can you make it *s* again?
Lk 14: 34 how can it be made *s* again?

SALU

Nu 25: 14 woman was Zimri son of *S*,

SALVATION (SAVE)

Ex 15: 2 he has become my *s*.
2Sa 22: 3 my shield and the horn of my *s*.
23: 5 Will he not bring to fruition my *s*
1Ch 16: 23 proclaim his *s* day after day.
2Ch 6: 41 O LORD God, be clothed with *s*,
Ps 9: 14 and there rejoice in your *s*.
13: 5 my heart rejoices in your *s*.
14: 7 that *s* for Israel would come out
18: 2 is my shield and the horn of my *s*,
27: 1 The LORD is my light and my *s*—
28: 8 a fortress of *s* for his anointed one.
35: 3 "I am your *s*."
35: 9 and delight in his *s*.
37: 39 The *s* of the righteous comes
40: 10 I speak of your faithfulness and *s*.
40: 16 those who love your *s* always say,
50: 23 way so that I may show him the *s*
51: 12 Restore to me the joy of your *s*
53: 6 that *s* for Israel would come out
62: 1 my *s* comes from him.
62: 2 He alone is my rock and my *s*;
62: 6 He alone is my rock and my *s*;
62: 7 My *s* and my honor depend
67: 2 your *s* among all nations.
69: 13 answer me with your sure *s*.
69: 27 do not let them share in your *s*.
69: 29 may your *s*, O God, protect me.
70: 4 those who love your *s* always say,
71: 15 of your *s* all day long,

Ps 74: 12 you bring *s* upon the earth.
85: 7 and grant us your *s*.
85: 9 Surely his *s* is near those who fear
91: 16 and show him my *s*."
95: 1 to the Rock of our *s*.
96: 2 proclaim his *s* day after day.
98: 1 have worked *s* for him.
98: 2 The LORD has made his *s* known
98: 3 the *s* of our God.
116: 13 I will lift up the cup of *s*
118: 14 he has become my *s*.
118: 21 you have become my *s*.
119: 41 your *s* according to your promise;
119: 81 with longing for your *s*,
119:123 My eyes fail, looking for your *s*,
119:155 *S* is far from the wicked,
119:166 I wait for your *s*, O LORD,
119:174 I long for your *s*, O LORD,
132: 16 I will clothe her priests with *s*,
149: 4 he crowns the humble with *s*.
Isa 12: 2 Surely God is my *s*;
12: 2 he has become my *s*."
12: 3 from the wells of *s*.
25: 9 let us rejoice and be glad in his *s*."
26: 1 God makes *s*
26: 18 We have not brought *s* to the earth;
30: 15 "In repentance and rest is your *s*,
33: 2 our *s* in time of distress.
33: 6 a rich store of *s* and wisdom
45: 8 let *s* spring up,
45: 17 the LORD with an everlasting *s*;
46: 13 I will grant *s* to Zion,
46: 13 and my *s* will not be delayed.
49: 6 that you may bring my *s*
49: 8 and in the day of *s* I will help you;
51: 5 my *s* is on the way,
51: 6 But my *s* will last forever,
51: 8 my *s* through all generations."
52: 7 who proclaim *s*,
52: 10 the *s* of our God.
56: 1 for my *s* is close at hand
59: 16 so his own arm worked *s* for him,
59: 17 and the helmet of *s* on his head;
60: 18 but you will call your walls *S*
61: 10 me with garments of *s*
62: 1 her *s* like a blazing torch.
63: 5 so my own arm worked *s* for me,
Jer 3: 23 is the *s* of Israel.
La 3: 26 quietly for the *s* of the LORD.
Jnh 2: 9 *S* comes from the LORD."
Zec 9: 9 righteous and having *s*,
Lk 1: 69 He has raised up a horn of *s* for us
1: 71 of long ago), *s* from our enemies
1: 77 give his people the knowledge of *s*
2: 30 For my eyes have seen your *s*,
3: 6 And all mankind will see God's *s*
19: 9 "Today *s* has come to this house,
Jn 4: 22 for *s* is from the Jews.
Ac 4: 12 *S* is found in no one else,
13: 26 message of *s* has been sent.
13: 47 that you may bring *s* to the ends
28: 28 to know that God's *s* has been sent
Ro 1: 16 for the *s* of everyone who believes:
11: 11 *s* has come to the Gentiles
13: 11 because our *s* is nearer now
2Co 1: 6 it is for your comfort and *s*;
6: 2 and in the day of *s* I helped you."
6: 2 of God's favor, now is the day of *s*.
7: 10 brings repentance that leads to *s*
Eph 1: 13 word of truth, the gospel of your *s*.
6: 17 Take the helmet of *s* and the sword
Php 2: 12 to work out your *s* with fear
1Th 5: 8 and the hope of *s* as a helmet.
5: 9 to receive *s* through our Lord Jesus
2Ti 2: 10 they too may obtain the *s* that is
3: 15 wise for *s* through faith
Tit 2: 11 of God that brings *s* has appeared
Heb 1: 14 to serve those who will inherit *s*?
2: 3 This *s*, which was first announced
2: 3 escape if we ignore such a great *s*?
2: 10 of their *s* perfect through suffering.
5: 9 of eternal *s* for all who obey him
6: 9 case—things that accompany *s*.
9: 28 to bring *s* to those who are waiting
1Pe 1: 5 the coming of the *s* that is ready
1: 9 of your faith, the *s* of your souls.
1: 10 Concerning this *s*, the prophets,
2: 2 by it you may grow up in your *s*,
2Pe 3: 15 that our Lord's patience means *s*,
Jude : 3 to write to you about the *s* we share
Rev 7: 10 "*S* belongs to our God,
12: 10 have come the *s* and the power
19: 1 *S* and glory and power belong

SALVE

Rev 3: 18 your shameful nakedness; and *s*

SAMARIA (SAMARITAN SAMARITANS)

1Ki 13: 32 of *S* will certainly come true."
16: 24 He bought the hill of *S*
16: 24 calling it *S*, after Shemer, the name
16: 28 with his fathers and was buried in *S*
16: 29 in *S* over Israel twenty-two years.
16: 32 temple of Baal that he built in *S*.
18: 2 Now the famine was severe in *S*,
20: 1 and besieged *S* and attacked it.
20: 10 if enough dust remains in *S*
20: 17 "Men are advancing from *S*."
20: 34 in Damascus, as my father did in *S*
20: 43 of Israel went to his palace in *S*.
21: 1 to the palace of Ahab king of *S*.
21: 18 king of Israel, who rules in *S*.
22: 10 by the entrance of the gate of *S*,
22: 37 the king died and was brought to *S*,
22: 38 in *S* (where the prostitutes bathed)
22: 51 Israel in *S* in the seventeenth year
2Ki 1: 2 the lattice of his upper room in *S*
1: 3 the messengers of the king of *S*
2: 25 and from there returned to *S*.
3: 1 of Israel in *S* in the eighteenth year
3: 6 time King Joram set out from *S*
5: 3 would see the prophet who is in *S*!
6: 19 And he led them to *S*.
6: 20 and there they were, inside *S*.
6: 24 and marched up and laid siege to *S*.
7: 1 barley for a shekel at the gate of *S*."
7: 18 barley for a shekel at the gate of *S*."
10: 1 Now there were in *S* seventy sons
10: 1 wrote letters and sent them to *S*:
10: 12 then set out and went toward *S*.
10: 17 to *S*, he killed all who were left
10: 35 with his fathers and was buried in *S*
10: 36 Israel in *S* was twenty-eight years.
13: 1 of Jehu became king of Israel in *S*,
13: 6 pole remained standing in *S*.
13: 9 with his fathers and was buried in *S*
13: 10 became king of Israel in *S*,
13: 13 buried in *S* with the kings
14: 14 took hostages and returned to *S*.
14: 16 and was buried in *S* with the kings
14: 23 king of Israel became king in *S*,
15: 8 became king of Israel in *S*,
15: 13 and he reigned in *S* one month.
15: 14 Shallum son of Jabesh in *S*,
15: 14 of Gadi went from Tirzah up to *S*.
15: 17 and he reigned in *S* ten years.
15: 23 became king of Israel in *S*,
15: 25 the citadel of the royal palace at *S*.
15: 27 became king of Israel in *S*,
17: 1 of Elah became king of Israel in *S*,
17: 5 marched against *S* and laid siege
17: 6 the king of Assyria captured *S*
17: 24 They took over *S* and lived
17: 24 towns of *S* to replace the Israelites.
17: 26 of *S* do not know what the god
17: 27 captive from *S* go back to live there
17: 28 exiled from *S* came to live in Bethel
17: 29 shrines the people of *S* had made
18: 9 king of Assyria marched against *S*
18: 10 *S* was captured in Hezekiah's sixth
18: 34 Have they rescued *S* from my hand
21: 13 the measuring line used against *S*
23: 18 the prophet who had come from *S*.
23: 19 of *S* that had provoked the LORD
2Ch 18: 2 went down to visit Ahab in *S*.
18: 9 by the entrance to the gate of *S*,
22: 9 him while he was hiding in *S*.
25: 13 war raided Judean towns from *S*
25: 24 the hostages, and returned to *S*.
28: 8 which they carried back to *S*.
28: 9 the army when it returned to *S*.
28: 15 City of Palms, and returned to *S*.
Ezr 4: 10 in the city of *S* and elsewhere
4: 17 rest of their associates living in *S*
Ne 4: 2 of his associates and the army of *S*,
Isa 7: 9 The head of Ephraim is *S*,
Isa 7: 9 of *S* is only Remaliah's son.
8: 4 and the plunder of *S* will be carried
9: 9 Ephraim and the inhabitants of *S*—
10: 9 and *S* like Damascus?
10: 10 those of Jerusalem and *S*—
10: 11 as I dealt with *S* and her idols?' "
36: 19 Have they rescued *S* from my hand
Jer 23: 13 "Among the prophets of *S*
31: 5 vineyards on the hills of *S*;
41: 5 came from Shechem, Shiloh and *S*,
Eze 16: 46 Your older sister was *S*, who lived
16: 51 *S* did not commit half the sins you
16: 53 and of *S* and her daughters,
16: 55 Sodom with her daughters and *S*
23: 4 Oholah is *S*, and Oholibah is
23: 33 the cup of your sister *S*.
Hos 7: 1 and the crimes of *S* revealed.
8: 5 Throw out your calf-idol, O *S*!
8: 6 that calf of *S*.
10: 5 The people who live in *S* fear
10: 7 *S* and its king will float away
13: 16 of *S* must bear their guilt,
Am 3: 9 yourselves on the mountains of *S*;
3: 12 those who sit in *S*
4: 1 you cows of Bashan on Mount *S*,
6: 1 to you who feel secure on Mount *S*,
8: 14 They who swear by the shame of *S*,
Ob : 19 the fields of Ephraim and *S*,
Mic 1: 1 the vision he saw concerning *S*
1: 5 Is it not *S*?
1: 6 "Therefore I will make *S* a heap
Lk 17: 11 along the border between *S*
Jn 4: 4 Now he had to go through *S*.
4: 5 came to a town in *S* called Sychar,
Ac 1: 8 and in all Judea and *S*,
8: 1 scattered throughout Judea and *S*.
8: 5 Philip went down to a city in *S*
8: 9 and amazed all the people of *S*.
8: 14 heard that *S* had accepted
9: 31 and *S* enjoyed a time of peace.
15: 3 traveled through Phoenicia and *S*,

SAMARITAN (SAMARIA)

Lk 9: 52 They went into a *S* village
10: 33 But a *S*, as he traveled, came where
17: 16 and thanked him—and he was a *S*.
Jn 4: 7 When a *S* woman came
4: 9 The *S* woman said to him,
4: 9 You are a Jew and I am a *S* woman.
8: 48 right in saying that you are a *S*
Ac 8: 25 the gospel in many *S* villages.

SAMARITANS (SAMARIA)

Mt 10: 5 or enter any town of the *S*.
Jn 4: 9 (For Jews do not associate with *S*.)
4: 22 You *S* worship what you do not
4: 39 of the *S* from that town believed
4: 40 So when the *S* came to him,

SAMGAR

Jer 39: 3 of *S*, Nebo-Sarsekim a chief officer

SAMLAH

Ge 36: 36 *S* from Masrekah succeeded him
36: 37 When *S* died, Shaul
1Ch 1: 47 *S* from Masrekah succeeded him
1: 48 When *S* died, Shaul

SAMOS

Ac 20: 15 day after that we crossed over to *S*,

SAMOTHRACE

Ac 16: 11 out to sea and sailed straight for *S*,

SAMPLE (SAMPLED)

Pr 23: 30 who go to *s* bowls of mixed wine.

SAMPLED (SAMPLE)

Jos 9: 14 The men of Israel *s* their provisions

SAMSON (SAMSON'S)

Jdg 13: 24 birth to a boy and named him *S*.
14: 1 *S* went down to Timnah
14: 3 *S* said to his father, "Get her for me
14: 5 *S* went down to Timnah together
14: 10 And *S* made a feast there,
14: 12 "Let me tell you a riddle," *S* said
14: 18 *S* said to them,

Jdg 15: 1 *S* took a young goat and went
15: 3 *S* said to them, "This time I have
15: 6 "*S*, the Timnite's son-in-law,
15: 7 *S* said to them, "Since you've acted
15: 10 We have come to take *S* prisoner,"
15: 11 in the rock of Etam and said to *S*,
15: 12 *S* said, "Swear to me that you
15: 16 Then *S* said,
15: 19 When *S* drank, his strength
15: 20 *S* led Israel for twenty years
16: 1 One day *S* went to Gaza, where he
16: 2 of Gaza were told, "*S* is here!"
16: 3 *S* lay there only until the middle
16: 6 said to *S*, "Tell me the secret
16: 7 *S* answered her, "If anyone ties me
16: 9 "*S*, the Philistines are upon you!"
16: 10 said to *S*, "You have made a fool
16: 12 "*S*, the Philistines are upon you!"
16: 13 Delilah then said to *S*, "Until now,
16: 14 Again she called to him, "*S*,
16: 20 "*S*, the Philistines are upon you!"
16: 23 "Our god has delivered *S*,
16: 25 So they called *S* out of the prison,
16: 25 "Bring out *S* to entertain us."
16: 26 *S* said to the servant who held his
16: 27 and women watching *S* perform.
16: 28 Then *S* prayed to the LORD,
16: 29 *S* reached toward the two central
16: 30 *S* said, "Let me die
Heb 11: 32 Barak, *S*, Jephthah, David,

SAMSON'S (SAMSON)

Jdg 14: 15 the fourth day, they said to *S* wife,
14: 16 Then *S* wife threw herself on him,
14: 20 *S* wife was given to the friend who

SAMUEL (SAMUEL'S)

1Sa 1: 20 named him *S*, saying, "Because
2: 18 But *S* was ministering
2: 21 the boy *S* grew up in the presence
2: 26 And the boy *S* continued to grow
3: 1 The boy *S* ministered
3: 3 and *S* was lying down in the temple
3: 4 Then the LORD called *S*.
3: 4 *S* answered, "Here I am."
3: 6 Again the LORD called, "*S*!"
3: 6 And *S* got up and went to Eli
3: 7 *S* did not yet know the LORD:
3: 8 The LORD called *S* a third time,
3: 8 and *S* got up and went to Eli
3: 9 So Eli told *S*, "Go and lie down,
3: 9 So *S* went and lay down in his place
3: 10 "*S*! *S*!" Then *S* said, "Speak,
3: 11 And the LORD said to *S*. "See,
3: 15 *S* lay down until morning
3: 16 but Eli called him and said, "*S*,
3: 16 *S* answered, "Here I am."
3: 18 So *S* told him everything, hiding
3: 19 The LORD was with *S*
3: 20 recognized that *S* was attested
3: 21 himself to *S* through his word.
7: 3 *S* said to the whole house of Israel,
7: 5 Then *S* said, "Assemble all Israel
7: 6 *S* was leader of Israel at Mizpah.
7: 8 said to *S*, "Do not stop crying out
7: 9 Then *S* took a suckling lamb
7: 10 While *S* was sacrificing the burnt
7: 12 Then *S* took a stone and set it up
7: 15 *S* continued as judge
8: 1 When *S* grew old, he appointed his
8: 4 gathered together and came to *S*
8: 6 this displeased *S*; so he prayed
8: 10 *S* told all the words of the LORD
8: 19 But the people refused to listen to *S*
8: 21 When *S* heard all that the people
8: 22 Then *S* said to the men of Israel,
9: 14 they were entering it, there was *S*,
9: 15 the LORD had revealed this to *S*:
9: 17 When *S* caught sight of Saul,
9: 18 Saul approached *S* in the gateway
9: 19 "I am the seer," *S* replied.
9: 22 *S* brought Saul and his servant
9: 23 *S* said to the cook, "Bring the piece
9: 24 And Saul dined with *S* that day.
9: 24 *S* said, "Here is what has been kept
9: 25 *S* talked with Saul on the roof
9: 26 and *S* called to Saul on the roof,
9: 26 he and *S* went outside together.
1Sa 9: 27 the edge of the town, *S* said to Saul,
10: 1 Then *S* took a flask of oil
10: 9 As Saul turned to leave *S*,
10: 14 not to be found, we went to *S*."
10: 15 "Tell me what *S* said to you."
10: 16 tell his uncle what *S* had said about
10: 17 *S* summoned the people of Israel
10: 20 When *S* brought all the tribes
10: 24 *S* said to all the people, "Do you
10: 25 Then *S* dismissed the people,
10: 25 *S* explained to the people
11: 7 who does not follow Saul and *S*."
11: 12 The people then said to *S*,
11: 14 Then *S* said to the people, "Come,
12: 1 *S* said to all Israel, "I have listened
12: 5 *S* said to them, "The LORD is
12: 6 Then *S* said to the people,
12: 11 Jerub-Baal, Barak, Jephthah and *S*,
12: 18 Then *S* called upon the LORD,
12: 18 in awe of the LORD and of *S*.
12: 19 The people all said to *S*, "Pray
12: 20 "Do not be afraid," *S* replied.
13: 8 set by *S*; but *S* did not come
13: 10 making the offering, *S* arrived,
13: 11 "What have you done?" asked *S*.
13: 13 "You acted foolishly," *S* said.
13: 15 *S* left Gilgal and went up to Gibeah
15: 1 *S* said to Saul, "I am the one
15: 10 the word of the LORD came to *S*:
15: 11 *S* was troubled, and he cried out
15: 12 Early in the morning *S* got up
15: 13 When *S* reached him, Saul said,
15: 14 *S* said, "What then is this bleating
15: 16 "Stop!" *S* said to Saul.
15: 17 *S* said, "Although you were once
15: 22 But *S* replied:
15: 24 Then Saul said to *S*, "I have sinned.
15: 26 *S* said to him, "I will not go back
15: 27 over Israel!" As *S* turned to leave,
15: 28 *S* said to him, "The LORD has
15: 31 So *S* went back with Saul,
15: 32 Then *S* said, "Bring me Agag king
15: 33 And *S* put Agag to death
15: 33 But *S* said,
15: 34 Then *S* left for Ramah,
15: 35 Until the day *S* died, he did not go
15: 35 though *S* mourned for him.
16: 1 to *S*, "How long will you mourn
16: 2 But *S* said, "How can I go?
16: 4 *S* did what the LORD said.
16: 5 Do you come in peace?" *S* replied,
16: 6 When they arrived, *S* saw Eliab
16: 7 said to *S*, "Do not consider his
16: 8 and had him pass in front of *S*.
16: 8 *S* said, "The LORD has not chosen
16: 9 had Shammah pass by, but *S* said,
16: 10 *S* said to him, "The LORD has not
16: 10 seven of his sons pass before *S*,
16: 11 *S* said, "Send for him; we will not
16: 13 So *S* took the horn of oil
16: 13 *S* then went to Ramah.
19: 18 Then he and *S* went to Naioth
19: 18 he went to *S* at Ramah
19: 20 with *S* standing there as their
19: 22 "Where are *S* and David?"
25: 1 *S* died, and all Israel assembled
28: 3 Now *S* was dead, and all Israel had
28: 11 up for you?" "Bring up *S*,"
28: 12 the woman saw *S*, she cried out
28: 14 Saul knew it was *S*, and he bowed
28: 15 *S* said to Saul, "Why have you
28: 16 *S* said, "Why do you consult me,
1Ch 6: 27 Elkanah his son and *S* his son.
6: 28 The sons of *S*: Joel the firstborn
6: 33 the son of *S*, the son of Elkanah,
7: 2 Jeriel, Jahmai, Ibsam and *S*—
9: 22 of trust by David and *S* the seer.
11: 3 LORD had promised through *S*.
26: 28 everything dedicated by *S* the seer
29: 29 written in the records of *S* the seer,
2Ch 35: 18 since the days of the prophet *S*;
Ps 99: 6 *S* was among those who called
Jer 15: 1 and *S* were to stand before me,
Ac 3: 24 Indeed, all the prophets from *S* on,
13: 20 until the time of *S* the prophet.
Heb 11: 32 David, *S* and the prophets,

SAMUEL'S (SAMUEL)

1Sa 4: 1 And *S* word came to all Israel.
7: 13 Throughout *S* lifetime, the hand
19: 24 and also prophesied in *S* presence.
28: 20 filled with fear because of *S* words.

SANBALLAT

Ne 2: 10 When *S* the Horonite and Tobiah
2: 19 But when *S* the Horonite, Tobiah
4: 1 When *S* heard that we were
4: 7 But when *S*, Tobiah, the Arabs,
6: 1 When word came to *S*, Tobiah,
6: 2 *S* and Geshem sent me this
6: 5 *S* sent his aide to me
6: 12 Tobiah and *S* had hired him.
6: 14 Remember Tobiah and *S*, O my
13: 28 son-in-law to *S* the Horonite.

SANCTIFIED (SANCTIFY)

Jn 17: 19 that they too may be truly *s*.
Ac 20: 32 among all those who are *s*.
26: 18 among those who are *s* by faith
Ro 15: 16 to God, *s* by the Holy Spirit.
1Co 1: 2 to those *s* in Christ Jesus
6: 11 But you were washed, you were *s*,
7: 14 and the unbelieving wife has been *s*
7: 14 the unbelieving husband has been *s*
Heb 10: 29 blood of the covenant that *s* him,

SANCTIFY (SANCTIFIED SANCTIFYING)

Jn 17: 17 *S* them by the truth; your word is
17: 19 For them I *s* myself, that they too
1Th 5: 23 *s* you through and through.
Heb 9: 13 are ceremonially unclean *s* them

SANCTIFYING (SANCTIFY)

2Th 2: 13 through the *s* work of the Spirit
1Pe 1: 2 through the *s* work of the Spirit,

SANCTUARIES (SANCTUARY)

Lev 26: 31 into ruins and lay waste your *s*,
Eze 7: 24 and their *s* will be desecrated.
28: 18 you have desecrated your *s*.
Am 7: 9 and the *s* of Israel will be ruined;

SANCTUARY (SANCTUARIES)

Ex 15: 17 *s*, O Lord, your hands established.
25: 8 "Then have them make a *s* for me,
30: 13 to the *s* shekel, which weighs
30: 24 all according to the *s* shekel—
35: 19 worn for ministering in the *s*—
36: 1 the work of constructing the *s* are
36: 3 the work of constructing the *s*.
36: 4 the work on the *s* left their work
36: 6 else as an offering for the *s*."
38: 24 shekels, according to the *s* shekel.
38: 24 the work on the *s* was 29 talents
38: 25 shekels, according to the *s* shekel
38: 26 a shekel, according to the *s* shekel,
38: 27 used to cast the bases for the *s*
39: 1 garments for ministering in the *s*.
39: 41 worn for ministering in the *s*,
Lev 4: 6 in front of the curtain of the *s*.
5: 15 in silver, according to the *s* shekel.
10: 4 away from the front of the *s*."
10: 17 eat the sin offering in the *s* area?
10: 18 have eaten the goat in the *s* area,
12: 4 or go to the *s* until the days
16: 3 is to enter the *s* area:
19: 30 and have reverence for my *s*.
20: 3 has defiled my *s* and profaned my
21: 12 nor leave the *s* of his God
21: 23 and so desecrate my *s*.
26: 2 and have reverence for my *s*.
27: 3 according to the *s* shekel;
27: 25 to be set according to the *s* shekel,
Nu 3: 10 who approaches the *s* must be put
3: 28 responsible for the care of the *s*.
3: 31 articles of the *s* used in ministering,
3: 32 responsible for the care of the *s*.
3: 38 else who approached the *s* was
3: 38 for the care of the *s* on behalf
3: 47 to the *s* shekel, which weighs
3: 50 shekels, according to the *s* shekel.
4: 12 used for ministering in the *s*,
4: 19 and his sons are to go into the *s*
7: 13 both according to the *s* shekel,
7: 19 both according to the *s* shekel,

Nu 7: 25 both according to the *s* shekel,
7: 31 both according to the *s* shekel,
7: 37 both according to the *s* shekel,
7: 43 both according to the *s* shekel,
7: 49 both according to the *s* shekel,
7: 55 both according to the *s* shekel,
7: 61 both according to the *s* shekel,
7: 67 both according to the *s* shekel,
7: 73 both according to the *s* shekel,
7: 79 both according to the *s* shekel,
7: 85 shekels, according to the *s* shekel.
7: 86 each, according to the *s* shekel.
8: 19 Israelites when they go near the *s*.''
18: 1 for offenses against the *s*,
18: 3 go near the furnishings of the *s*
18: 5 responsible for the care of the *s*
18: 7 near the *s* must be put to death.''
18: 16 to the *s* shekel, which weighs
19: 20 he has defiled the *s* of the LORD.
28: 7 offering to the LORD at the *s*.
31: 6 took with him articles from the *s*
Jos 22: 27 at his *s* with our burnt offerings,
1Ki 6: 5 and inner *s* he built a structure
6: 16 form within the temple an inner *s*,
6: 19 He prepared the inner *s*
6: 20 The inner *s* was twenty cubits long,
6: 21 across the front of the inner *s*,
6: 22 altar that belonged to the inner *s*.
6: 23 In the inner *s* he made a pair
6: 31 of the inner *s* he made doors
7: 49 of the inner *s*); the gold floral work
8: 6 place in the inner *s* of the temple,
8: 8 Place in front of the inner *s*,
1Ch 9: 29 and all the other articles of the *s*,
22: 19 Begin to build the *s*
24: 5 for there were officials of the *s*
28: 10 you to build a temple as a *s*.
2Ch 4: 20 to burn in front of the inner *s*
5: 7 place in the inner *s* of the temple,
5: 9 seen from in front of the inner *s*,
20: 8 have built in it a *s* for your Name,
26: 18 Leave the *s*, for you have been
29: 5 Remove all defilement from the *s*.
29: 7 at the *s* to the God of Israel.
29: 16 went into the *s* of the LORD
29: 21 offering for the kingdom, for the *s*
30: 8 to the *s*, which he has consecrated
30: 19 according to the rules of the *s*.''
36: 17 men with the sword in the *s*,
Ezr 9: 8 and giving us a firm place in his *s*,
Ne 10: 39 where the articles for the *s* are kept
Ps 15: 1 LORD, who may dwell in your *s*?
20: 2 May he send you help from the *s*
60: 6 God has spoken from his *s*:
63: 2 I have seen you in the *s*
68: 17 from Sinai into his *s*.
68: 24 of my God and King into the *s*.
68: 35 are awesome, O God, in your *s*;
73: 17 me till I entered the *s* of God;
74: 3 the enemy has brought on the *s*.
74: 7 They burned your *s* to the ground;
78: 69 He built his *s* like the high
96: 6 strength and glory are in his *s*.
102: 19 looked down from his *s* on high,
108: 7 God has spoken from his *s*:
114: 2 Judah became God's *s*,
134: 2 Lift up your hands in the *s*
150: 1 Praise God in his *s*;
Isa 8: 14 and he will be a *s*;
60: 13 to adorn the place of my *s*;
62: 9 it in the courts of my *s*.''
63: 18 have trampled down your *s*.
Jer 17: 12 is the place of our *s*.
La 1: 10 enter her *s*—
2: 7 and abandoned his *s*.
2: 20 killed in the *s* of the Lord?
Eze 5: 11 because you have defiled my *s*
8: 6 that will drive me far from my *s*?
9: 6 Begin at my *s*.''
11: 16 little while I have been a *s* for them
21: 2 Jerusalem and preach against the *s*.
23: 38 that same time they defiled my *s*
23: 39 they entered my *s* and desecrated
24: 21 I am about to desecrate my *s*—
25: 3 over my *s* when it was desecrated
37: 26 I will put my *s* among them forever
37: 28 when my *s* is among them forever
41: 1 the man brought me to the outer *s*
Eze 41: 2 He also measured the outer *s*;
41: 3 Then he went into the inner *s*
41: 4 cubits across the end of the outer *s*.
41: 4 measured the length of the inner *s*;
41: 15 The outer *s*, the inner *s*
41: 17 and outer *s* were carved cherubim
41: 17 of the entrance to the inner *s*
41: 20 carved on the wall of the outer *s*.
41: 21 The outer *s* had a rectangular
41: 23 Both the outer *s* and the Most Holy
41: 25 doors of the outer *s* were carved
42: 8 side nearest the *s* was a hundred
43: 21 of the temple area outside the *s*.
44: 1 back to the outer gate of the *s*,
44: 5 the temple and all the exits of the *s*.
44: 7 in heart and flesh into my *s*,
44: 8 you put others in charge of my *s*.
44: 9 in heart and flesh is to enter my *s*,
44: 11 serve in my *s*, having charge
44: 15 of my *s* when the Israelites went
44: 16 They alone are to enter my *s*;
44: 27 court of the *s* to minister in the *s*,
45: 2 cubits square is to be for the *s*,
45: 3 it will be the *s*, the Most Holy
45: 4 as well as a holy place for the *s*.
45: 4 who minister in the *s* and who draw
45: 18 without defect and purify the *s*.
47: 12 the water from the *s* flows to them.
48: 8 the *s* will be in the center of it.
48: 10 of it will be the *s* of the LORD.
48: 21 portion with the temple *s* will be
Da 8: 11 the place of his *s* was brought low.
8: 13 and the surrender of the *s*
8: 14 then the *s* will be reconsecrated.''
9: 17 look with favor on your desolate *s*.
9: 26 will destroy the city and the *s*.
Am 7: 13 because this is the king's *s*
Zep 3: 4 Her priests profane the *s*
Mal 2: 11 has desecrated the *s* the LORD
Lk 11: 51 killed between the altar and the *s*.
Heb 6: 19 It enters the inner *s*
8: 2 in the *s*, the true tabernacle set up
8: 5 They serve at a *s* that is a copy
9: 1 for worship and also an earthly *s*.
9: 24 enter a man-made *s* that was only

SAND (SANDY)

Ge 22: 17 and as the *s* on the seashore.
32: 12 make your descendants like the *s*
41: 49 of grain, like the *s* of the sea;
Ex 2: 12 the Egyptian and hid him in the *s*.
Dt 33: 19 on the treasures hidden in the *s*.''
Jos 11: 4 numerous as the *s* on the seashore.
Jdg 7: 12 counted than the *s* on the seashore.
1Sa 13: 5 numerous as the *s* on the seashore.
2Sa 17: 11 numerous as the *s* on the seashore
1Ki 4: 20 numerous as the *s* on the seashore;
4: 29 as measureless as the *s*
Job 6: 3 It would surely outweigh the *s*
29: 18 numerous as the grains of *s*.
39: 14 and lets them warm in the *s*,
Ps 78: 27 flying birds like *s* on the seashore.
139: 18 would outnumber the grains of *s*.
Pr 27: 3 Stone is heavy and *s* a burden,
Isa 10: 22 O Israel, be like the *s* by the sea,
35: 7 The burning *s* will become a pool,
48: 19 would have been like the *s*,
Jer 5: 22 I made the *s* a boundary for the sea,
15: 8 than the *s* of the sea.
33: 22 as the *s* on the seashore.' ''
Hos 1: 10 ''Yet the Israelites will be like the *s*
Hab 1: 9 and gather prisoners like *s*.
Mt 7: 26 man who built his house on *s*.
Ro 9: 27 of the Israelites be like the *s*
Heb 11: 12 countless as the *s* on the seashore.
Rev 20: 8 In number they are like the *s*

SANDAL (SANDALED SANDALS)

Ge 14: 23 even a thread or the thong of a *s*,
Ru 4: 7 one party took off his *s*
4: 8 And he removed his *s*.
Ps 60: 8 upon Edom I toss my *s*;
108: 9 upon Edom I toss my *s*;
Isa 5: 27 not a *s* thong is broken.

SANDALED (SANDAL)

SS 7: 1 How beautiful your *s* feet,

SANDALS (SANDAL)

Ex 3: 5 off your *s*, for the place where you
12: 11 your *s* on your feet and your staff
Dt 25: 9 take off one of his *s*, spit in his face
29: 5 did not wear out, nor did the *s*
Jos 5: 15 off your *s*, for the place where you
9: 5 and patched *s* on their feet
9: 13 and *s* are worn out by the very long
1Ki 2: 5 the belt around his waist and the *s*
2Ch 28: 15 them with clothes and *s*,
Isa 11: 15 so that men can cross over in *s*.
20: 2 sackcloth from your body and the *s*
Eze 16: 10 dress and put leather *s*
24: 17 your turban fastened and your *s*
24: 23 turbans on your heads and your *s*
Am 2: 6 and the needy for a pair of *s*.
8: 6 and the needy for a pair of *s*,
Mt 3: 11 whose *s* I am not fit to carry.
10: 10 or extra tunic, or *s* or a staff;
Mk 1: 7 thongs of whose *s* I am not worthy
6: 9 Wear *s* but not an extra tunic.
Lk 3: 16 thongs of whose *s* I am not worthy
10: 4 Do not take a purse or bag or *s*;
15: 22 ring on his finger and *s* on his feet.
22: 35 bag or *s*, did you lack anything?''
Jn 1: 27 thongs of whose *s* I am not worthy
Ac 7: 33 said to him, 'Take off your *s*;
12: 8 ''Put on your clothes and *s*.''
13: 25 whose *s* I am not worthy to untie.'

SANDBAR (SANDBARS)

Ac 27: 41 the ship struck a *s* and ran aground.

SANDBARS (SANDBAR)

Ac 27: 17 they would run aground on the *s*

SANDY (SAND)

Ac 27: 39 but they saw a bay with a *s* beach,

SANG (SING)

Ex 15: 1 and the Israelites *s* this song
15: 21 Miriam *s* to them:
Nu 21: 17 Then Israel *s* this song:
Jdg 5: 1 Barak son of Abinoam *s* this song:
1Sa 18: 7 As they danced, they *s*:
29: 5 Isn't this the David they *s* about
2Sa 3: 33 The king *s* this lament for Abner:
22: 1 David *s* to the LORD the words
2Ch 5: 13 in praise to the LORD and *s*:
29: 28 while the singers *s*
29: 30 So they *s* praises with gladness
30: 21 priests *s* to the LORD every day,
Ezr 3: 11 thanksgiving they *s* to the LORD:
Ne 12: 42 The choirs *s* under the direction
Job 38: 7 while the morning stars *s* together
Ps 106: 12 and *s* his praise.
Mt 11: 17 we *s* a dirge,
Lk 7: 32 we *s* a dirge,
Rev 5: 9 And they *s* a new song:
5: 12 In a loud voice they *s*:
14: 3 they *s* a new song before the throne
15: 3 and *s* the song of Moses the servant

SANHEDRIN

Mt 5: 22 'Raca,' is answerable to the *S*.
26: 59 and the whole *S* were looking
Mk 14: 55 and the whole *S* were looking
15: 1 of the law and the whole *S*,
Jn 11: 47 Pharisees called a meeting of the *S*.
Ac 4: 15 them to withdraw from the *S*
5: 21 they called together the *S*—
5: 27 before the *S* to be questioned
5: 34 in the *S* and ordered that the men
5: 41 The apostles left the *S*, rejoicing
6: 12 and brought him before the *S*.
6: 15 in the *S* looked intently at Stephen,
22: 30 the chief priests and all the *S*
23: 1 Paul looked straight at the *S*
23: 6 called out in the *S*, ''My brothers,
23: 15 and the *S* petition the commander
23: 20 Paul before the *S* tomorrow
23: 28 so I brought him to their *S*.
24: 20 in me when I stood before the *S*—

SANITY

Da 4: 34 heaven, and my *s* was restored.
4: 36 same time that my *s* was restored,

SANK (SINK)

Ge 42:28 Their hearts *s* and they turned
Ex 15: 5 they *s* to the depths like a stone.
15:10 They *s* like lead
Nu 21:18 that the nobles of the people *s*—
Jos 2:11 our hearts *s* and everyone's
5: 1 their hearts *s* and they no longer
Jdg 3:22 Even the handle *s* in after the blade
5:27 At her feet he *s*,
5:27 At her feet he *s*, he fell;
5:27 where he *s*, there he fell—dead.
1Sa 17:49 The stone *s* into his forehead,
Jer 38: 6 and Jeremiah *s* down into the mud.
Jnh 2: 6 of the mountains I *s* down;

SANSANNAH

Jos 15:31 Ziklag, Madmannah, *S*, Lebaoth,

SAP (SAPPED)

Hos 7: 9 Foreigners *s* his strength,
Ro 11:17 share in the nourishing *s*

SAPH

2Sa 21:18 Sibbecai the Hushathite killed *S*,

SAPPED (SAP)

Ps 32: 4 my strength was *s*
La 1:14 and the Lord has *s* my strength.

SAPPHIRA

Ac 5: 1 together with his wife *S*,

SAPPHIRE (SAPPHIRES)

Ex 24:10 like a pavement made of *s*,
28:18 in the second row a turquoise, a *s*
39:11 in the second row a turquoise, a *s*
Eze 1:26 was what looked like a throne of *s*,
10: 1 of *s* above the expanse that was
28:13 *s*, turquoise and beryl.
Rev 21:19 the second *s*, the third chalcedony,

SAPPHIRES (SAPPHIRE)

Job 28: 6 *s* come from its rocks,
28:16 with precious onyx or *s*.
SS 5:14 decorated with *s*.
Isa 54:11 your foundations with *s*.
La 4: 7 their appearance like *s*.

SARAH (SARAH'S SARAI)

Ge 17:15 to call her Sarai; her name will be *S*
17:17 Will *S* bear a child at the age
17:19 but your wife *S* will bear you a son,
17:21 whom *S* will bear to you
18: 6 Abraham hurried into the tent to *S*.
18: 9 is your wife *S*?'' they asked him.
18:10 and *S* your wife will have a son.''
18:10 *S* was listening at the entrance
18:11 Abraham and *S* were already old
18:11 *S* was past the age of childbearing.
18:12 So *S* laughed to herself
18:13 ''Why did *S* laugh and say,
18:14 time next year and *S* will have
18:15 *S* was afraid, so she lied and said,
20: 2 Abimelech king of Gerar sent for *S*
20: 2 there Abraham said of his wife *S*,
20:14 and he returned *S* his wife to him.
20:16 To *S* he said, ''I am giving your
20:18 because of Abraham's wife *S*.
21: 1 Now the LORD was gracious to *S*
21: 1 did for *S* what he had promised.
21: 2 *S* became pregnant and bore a son
21: 3 Isaac to the son *S* bore him.
21: 6 *S* said, ''God has brought me
21: 7 to Abraham that *S* would nurse
21: 9 *S* saw that the son whom Hagar
21:12 Listen to whatever *S* tells you,
23: 1 *S* lived to be a hundred
23: 2 and Abraham went to mourn for *S*
23:19 Abraham buried his wife *S*
24:36 My master's wife *S* has borne him
24:67 her into the tent of his mother *S*,
25:10 was buried with his wife *S*.
49:31 and his wife *S* were buried,
Isa 51: 2 and to *S*, who gave you birth.
Ro 9: 9 I will return, and *S* will have
Heb 11:11 and *S* herself was barren—
1Pe 3: 6 to their own husbands, like *S*,

SARAH'S (SARAH)

Ge 25:12 whom *S* maidservant, Hagar
Ro 4:19 and that *S* womb was also dead.

SARAI (SARAH)

Ge 11:29 The name of Abram's wife was *S*,
11:30 *S* was barren; she had no children.
11:31 and his daughter-in-law *S*,
12: 5 He took his wife *S*, his nephew Lot,
12:11 said to his wife *S*, ''I know what
12:17 because of Abram's wife *S*.
16: 1 *S*, Abram's wife, had borne him no
16: 2 Abram agreed to what *S* said.
16: 3 *S* his wife took her Egyptian
16: 5 Then *S* said to Abram, ''You are
16: 6 Then *S* mistreated Hagar;
16: 8 away from my mistress *S*,''
16: 8 servant of *S*, where have you come
17:15 to Abraham, ''As for *S* your wife,
17:15 you are no longer to call her *S*;

SARAPH

1Ch 4:22 Joash and *S*, who ruled in Moab

SARDIS

Rev 1:11 Smyrna, Pergamum, Thyatira, *S*,
3: 1 the angel of the church in *S* write:
3: 4 in *S* who have not soiled their

SARDONYX

Rev 21:20 the fifth *s*, the sixth carnelian,

SARGON

Isa 20: 1 sent by *S* king of Assyria,

SARID

Jos 19:10 of their inheritance went as far as *S*
19:12 east from *S* toward the sunrise

SASH (SASHES)

Ex 28: 4 a woven tunic, a turban and a *s*.
28:39 The *s* is to be the work
39:29 The *s* was of finely twisted linen
Lev 8: 7 on Aaron, tied the *s* around him,
16: 4 he is to tie the linen *s* around him
Isa 3:24 instead of a *s*, a rope;
11: 5 faithfulness the *s* around his waist.
22:21 and fasten your *s* around him
Rev 1:13 with a golden *s* around his chest.

SASHES (SASH)

Ex 28:40 *s* and headbands for Aaron's sons,
29: 9 Then tie *s* on Aaron and his sons.
Lev 8:13 tied *s* around them and put
Pr 31:24 and supplies the merchants with *s*.
Isa 3:20 and ankle chains and *s*,
Rev 15: 6 wore golden *s* around their chests.

SAT (SIT)

Ge 21:16 And as she *s* there nearby,
21:16 she went off and *s* down nearby,
37:25 As they *s* down to eat their meal,
38:14 and then *s* down at the entrance
48: 2 Israel rallied his strength and *s* up
Ex 2:15 where he *s* down by a well.
12:29 of Pharaoh, who *s* on the throne,
16: 3 There we *s* around pots of meat
17:12 and put it under him and he *s* on it.
32: 6 Afterward they *s* down to eat
Lev 15: 6 with a discharge *s* on must wash his
Jdg 6:11 and *s* down under the oak
19: 6 So the two of them *s* down to eat
19:15 They went and *s* in the city square,
20:26 and there they *s* weeping
21: 2 where they *s* before God
Ru 2:14 she *s* down with the harvesters,
4: 1 So he went over and *s* down.
4: 1 up to the town gate and *s* there.
1Sa 20:24 Moon festival came, the king *s*
20:25 He *s* in his customary place
20:25 *s* opposite him, and Abner *s* next
28:23 from the ground and *s* on the couch
2Sa 2:13 One group *s* down on one side
7:18 went in and *s* before the LORD,
19:28 among those who *s* at your table.
1Ki 2:12 So Solomon *s* on the throne
2:19 and she *s* down at his right hand.
2:19 to her and *s* down on his throne.
1Ki 19: 4 *s* down under it and prayed that he
21:13 Then two scoundrels came and *s*
2Ki 4:20 the boy *s* on her lap until noon,
1Ch 17:16 went in and *s* before the LORD,
29:23 So Solomon *s* on the throne
Ezr 9: 3 and beard and *s* down appalled.
9: 4 I *s* there appalled until the evening
10:16 day of the tenth month they *s*
Ne 1: 4 When I heard these things, I *s*
Est 3:15 and Haman *s* down to drink,
Job 2: 8 with it as he *s* among the ashes.
2:13 they *s* on the ground with him
29:25 I chose the way for them and *s*
Ps 9: 4 you have *s* on your throne,
107: 10 Some *s* in darkness and the deepest
137: 1 By the rivers of Babylon we *s*
Jer 3: 2 By the roadside you *s* waiting
3: 2 *s* like a nomad in the desert.
15:17 I never *s* in the company
15:17 I *s* alone because your hand was
Eze 3:15 I *s* among them for seven days—
14: 1 and *s* down in front of me.
20: 1 and they *s* down in front of me.
23:41 You *s* on an elegant couch,
Jnh 3: 6 himself with sackcloth and *s*
4: 5 *s* down at a place east of the city.
4: 5 *s* in its shade and waited
Zec 5: 7 and there in the basket *s* a woman!
Mt 5: 1 up on a mountainside and *s* down.
13: 1 out of the house and *s* by the lake.
13: 2 got into a boat and *s* in it,
13:48 they *s* down and collected the good
15:29 up into the hills and *s* down.
21: 7 on them, and Jesus *s* on them.
26:55 Every day I *s* in the temple courts
26:58 and *s* down with the guards
28: 2 rolled back the stone and *s* on it.
Mk 4: 1 got into a boat and *s* in it out
6:40 they *s* down in groups of hundreds
11: 7 threw their cloaks over it, he *s* on it
12:41 Jesus *s* down opposite the place
14:54 There he *s* with the guards
16:19 and he *s* at the right hand of God.
Lk 4:20 back to the attendant and *s* down.
5: 3 he *s* down and taught the people
7:15 The dead man *s* up and began
9:15 did so, and everybody *s* down.
10:39 who *s* at the Lord's feet listening
22:55 *s* down together, Peter *s*
Jn 4: 6 was from the journey, *s*
6: 3 and *s* down with his disciples.
6:10 men *s* down, about five thousand
8: 2 and he *s* down to teach them.
12:14 Jesus found a young donkey and *s*
19:13 and *s* down on the judge's seat
Ac 9:40 her eyes, and seeing Peter she *s* up.
12:21 *s* on his throne and delivered
13:14 they entered the synagogue and *s*
14: 8 In Lystra there *s* a man crippled
16:13 We *s* down and began to speak
1Co 10: 7 The people *s* down to eat and drink
Heb 1: 3 he *s* down at the right hand
8: 1 who *s* down at the right hand
10:12 he *s* down at the right hand of God.
12: 2 and *s* down at the right hand
Rev 3:21 and *s* down with my Father
4: 3 And the one who *s* there had
5: 1 of him who *s* on the throne a scroll
5: 7 hand of him who *s* on the throne.

SATAN (SATAN'S)

1Ch 21: 1 *S* rose up against Israel
Job 1: 6 and *S* also came with them.
1: 7 from?'' *S* answered the LORD,
1: 7 said to *S*, ''Where have you come
1: 8 Then the LORD said to *S*,
1: 9 God for nothing?'' *S* replied.
1:12 The LORD said to *S*, ''Very well,
1:12 Then *S* went out from the presence
2: 1 and *S* also came with them
2: 2 from?'' *S* answered the LORD,
2: 2 said to *S*, ''Where have you come
2: 3 Then the LORD said to *S*,
2: 4 ''Skin for skin!'' *S* replied.
2: 6 The LORD said to *S*, ''Very well,
2: 7 So *S* went out from the presence
Zec 3: 1 and *S* standing at his right side
3: 2 said to *S*, ''The LORD rebuke you,

Zec 3: 2 "The LORD rebuke you, *S!*
Mt 4: 10 Away from me, *S!* For it is written:
12: 26 If *S* drives out *S*, he is divided
16: 23 *S!* You are a stumbling block to me
Mk 1: 13 forty days, being tempted by *S*.
3: 23 can *S* drive out *S?* If a kingdom is
3: 26 And if *S* opposes himself
4: 15 *S* comes and takes away the word
8: 33 "Out of my sight, *S!*" he said.
Lk 10: 18 "I saw *S* fall like lightning
11: 18 If *S* is divided against himself,
13: 16 whom *S* has kept bound
22: 3 *S* entered Judas, called Iscariot,
22: 31 *S* has asked to sift you as wheat.
Jn 13: 27 as Judas took the bread, *S* entered
Ac 5: 3 how is it that *S* has
26: 18 and from the power of *S* to God,
Ro 16: 20 The God of peace will soon crush *S*
1Co 5: 5 is present, hand this man over to *S*,
7: 5 again so that *S* will not tempt you
2Co 2: 11 in order that *S* might not outwit us.
11: 14 for *S* himself masquerades
12: 7 a messenger of *S*, to torment me.
1Th 2: 18 again and again—but *S* stopped us.
2Th 2: 9 with the work of *S* displayed
1Ti 1: 20 handed over to *S* to be taught not
5: 15 already turned away to follow *S*.
Rev 2: 9 are not, but are a synagogue of *S*.
2: 13 death in your city—where *S* lives.
2: 13 you live—where *S* has his throne.
3: 9 are of the synagogue of *S*,
12: 9 serpent called the devil or *S*,
20: 2 or *S*, and bound him for a thousand
20: 7 *S* will be released from his prison

SATAN'S (SATAN)

Rev 2: 24 have not learned *S* so-called deep

SATED (SATISFY)

La 3: 15 and *s* me with gall.

SATISFACTION (SATISFY)

Est 5: 13 But all this gives me no *s* as long
Ecc 2: 24 and drink and find *s* in his work.
3: 13 drink, and find *s* in all his toil—
5: 18 and to find *s* in his toilsome labor

SATISFIED (SATISFY)

Ex 18: 23 and all these people will go home *s*
Lev 10: 20 When Moses heard this, he was *s*.
26: 26 You will eat, but you will not be *s*.
Dt 6: 11 then when you eat and are *s*,
8: 10 When you have eaten and are *s*,
8: 12 Otherwise, when you eat and are *s*,
11: 15 cattle, and you will eat and be *s*.
14: 29 towns may come and eat and be *s*,
26: 12 eat in your towns and be *s*.
Ps 17: 15 I will be *s* with seeing your likeness
22: 26 The poor will eat and be *s*;
59: 15 and howl if not *s*.
63: 5 My soul will be *s* as with the richest
104: 13 the earth is *s* by the fruit
104: 28 they are *s* with good things.
105: 40 *s* them with the bread of heaven.
Pr 13: 4 the desires of the diligent are fully *s*
18: 20 with the harvest from his lips he is *s*
27: 20 Death and Destruction are never *s*,
30: 15 are three things that are never *s*,
30: 16 land, which is never *s* with water,
Ecc 5: 10 whoever loves wealth is never *s*
6: 7 yet his appetite is never *s*.
Isa 9: 20 but not be *s*.
53: 11 he will see the light ⌊of life⌋ and be *s*
66: 11 For you will nurse and be *s*
Jer 46: 10 The sword will devour till it is *s*,
50: 19 his appetite will be *s*
Eze 16: 28 even after that, you still were not *s*.
16: 29 but even with this you were not *s*.
27: 33 you *s* many nations;
Hos 13: 6 When I fed them, they were *s*;
13: 6 when they were *s*, they became
Mic 6: 14 You will eat but not be *s*;
Hab 2: 5 and like death is never *s*,
Mt 14: 20 They all ate and were *s*,
15: 37 They all ate and were *s*.
Mk 6: 42 They all ate and were *s*,
8: 8 The people ate and were *s*.
Lk 6: 21 for you will be *s*.
9: 17 They all ate and were *s*,
3Jn : 10 Not *s* with that, he refuses

SATISFIES (SATISFY)

Ps 103: 5 He *s* my desires with good things,
107: 9 for he *s* the thirsty
147: 14 and *s* you with the finest of wheat.

SATISFY (SATED SATISFACTION SATISFIED SATISFIES)

Job 38: 27 to *s* a desolate wasteland
38: 39 and *s* the hunger of the lions
Ps 81: 16 from the rock I would *s* you."
90: 14 *S* us in the morning
91: 16 With long life will I *s* him
132: 15 her poor will I *s* with food.
145: 16 *s* the desires of every living thing.
Pr 5: 19 may her breasts *s* you always,
6: 30 to *s* his hunger when he is starving.
Isa 55: 2 and your labor on what does not *s?*
58: 10 and *s* the needs of the oppressed,
58: 11 he will *s* your needs
Jer 31: 14 I will *s* the priests with abundance,
31: 25 refresh the weary and *s* the faint."
Eze 7: 19 They will not *s* their hunger
Joel 2: 19 enough to *s* you fully;
Mt 28: 14 we will *s* him and keep you out
Mk 15: 15 him!" Wanting to *s* the crowd,

SATRAPS

Ezr 8: 36 the king's orders to the royal *s*
Est 3: 12 all Haman's orders to the king's *s*,
8: 9 orders to the Jews, and to the *s*,
9: 3 the nobles of the provinces, the *s*,
Da 3: 2 He then summoned the *s*, prefects,
3: 3 So the *s*, prefects, governors,
3: 27 and the *s*, prefects, governors
6: 1 Darius to appoint 120 *s* to rule
6: 2 The *s* were made accountable
6: 3 *s* by his exceptional qualities that
6: 4 and the *s* tried to find grounds
6: 6 the administrators and the *s* went
6: 7 royal administrators, prefects, *s*,

SAUL (SAUL'S)

1Sa 9: 2 a son named *S*, an impressive
9: 3 and Kish said to his son *S*,
9: 5 *S* said to the servant who was
9: 7 *S* said to his servant, "If we go,
9: 10 "Good," *S* said to his servant.
9: 15 Now the day before *S* came,
9: 17 When Samuel caught sight of *S*,
9: 18 *S* approached Samuel
9: 21 *S* answered, "But am I not
9: 22 Then Samuel brought *S*
9: 24 And *S* dined with Samuel that day.
9: 24 was on it and set it in front of *S*.
9: 25 Samuel talked with *S* on the roof
9: 26 When *S* got ready, he and Samuel
9: 26 and Samuel called to *S* on the roof,
9: 27 Samuel said to *S*, "Tell the servant
10: 9 As *S* turned to leave Samuel,
10: 11 Is *S* also among the prophets?"
10: 12 "Is *S* also among the prophets?"
10: 13 After *S* stopped prophesying,
10: 16 *S* replied, "He assured us that
10: 21 Finally *S* son of Kish was chosen.
10: 26 *S* also went to his home in Gibeah,
10: 27 But *S* kept silent.
11: 4 messengers came to Gibeah of *S*
11: 5 Just then *S* was returning
11: 6 When *S* heard their words,
11: 7 of anyone who does not follow *S*
11: 8 When *S* mustered them at Bezek,
11: 11 The next day *S* separated his men
11: 12 was it that asked, 'Shall *S* reign
11: 13 But *S* said, "No one shall be put
11: 15 *S* and all the Israelites held a great
11: 15 went to Gilgal and confirmed *S*
13: 1 *S* was ⌊thirty⌋ years old
13: 2 *S* chose three thousand men
13: 3 Then *S* had the trumpet blown
13: 4 summoned to join *S* at Gilgal.
13: 4 "*S* has attacked the Philistine
13: 7 *S* remained at Gilgal, and all
13: 9 And *S* offered up the burnt offering
13: 10 and *S* went out to greet him.
13: 11 *S* replied, "When I saw that
1Sa 13: 15 and *S* counted the men who were
13: 16 *S* and his son Jonathan
13: 22 of the battle not a soldier with *S*
13: 22 only *S* and his son Jonathan had
14: 1 One day Jonathan son of *S* said
14: 2 *S* was staying on the outskirts
14: 17 Then *S* said to the men who were
14: 18 *S* said to Ahijah, "Bring the ark
14: 19 So *S* said to the priest, "Withdraw
14: 19 While *S* was talking to the priest,
14: 20 Then *S* and all his men assembled
14: 21 to the Israelites who were with *S*
14: 24 because *S* had bound the people
14: 33 Then someone said to *S*, "Look,
14: 35 Then *S* built an altar to the LORD;
14: 36 *S* said, "Let us go
14: 37 So *S* asked God, "Shall I go
14: 38 *S* therefore said, "Come here,
14: 40 *S* then said to all the Israelites,
14: 41 Jonathan and *S* were taken by lot,
14: 41 Then *S* prayed to the LORD,
14: 42 *S* said, "Cast the lot between me
14: 43 *S* said to Jonathan, "Tell me what
14: 44 And now must I die?" *S* said,
14: 45 said to *S*, "Should Jonathan die—
14: 46 *S* stopped pursuing the Philistines,
14: 47 After *S* had assumed rule
14: 52 and whenever *S* saw a mighty
14: 52 the days of *S* there was bitter war
15: 1 to *S*, "I am the one the LORD sent
15: 4 So *S* summoned the men
15: 5 *S* went to the city of Amalek
15: 7 Then *S* attacked the Amalekites all
15: 9 But *S* and the army spared Agag
15: 11 grieved that I have made *S* king,
15: 12 Samuel got up and went to meet *S*,
15: 12 he was told, "*S* has gone to Carmel.
15: 13 When Samuel reached him, *S* said,
15: 15 *S* answered, "The soldiers brought
15: 16 "Stop!" Samuel said to *S*.
15: 16 "Tell me," *S* replied.
15: 20 But I did obey the LORD," *S* said.
15: 24 *S* said to Samuel, "I have sinned.
15: 27 *S* caught hold of the edge
15: 30 *S* replied, "I have sinned.
15: 31 So Samuel went back with *S*,
15: 31 and *S* worshiped the LORD.
15: 34 *S* went up to his home in Gibeah
15: 34 up to his home in Gibeah of *S*.
15: 35 grieved that he had made *S* king
15: 35 he did not go to see *S* again,
16: 1 "How long will you mourn for *S*,
16: 2 *S* will hear about it and kill me."
16: 14 of the LORD had departed from *S*,
16: 17 So *S* said to his attendants,
16: 19 Then *S* sent messengers to Jesse
16: 20 sent them with his son David to *S*.
16: 21 came to *S* and entered his service.
16: 21 *S* liked him very much,
16: 22 Then *S* sent word to Jesse, saying,
16: 23 Then relief would come to *S*;
16: 23 the spirit from God came upon *S*,
17: 2 *S* and the Israelites assembled
17: 8 and are you not the servants of *S?*
17: 11 *S* and all the Israelites were
17: 13 three oldest sons had followed *S*
17: 14 The three oldest followed *S*,
17: 15 from *S* to tend his father's sheep
17: 19 They are with *S* and all the men
17: 31 reported to *S*, and *S* sent for him.
17: 32 said to *S*, "Let no one lose heart
17: 33 *S* replied, "You are not able
17: 34 said to *S*, "Your servant has been
17: 37 *S* said to David, "Go,
17: 38 *S* dressed David in his own tunic.
17: 39 said to *S*, "because I am not used
17: 55 As *S* watched David going out
17: 57 and brought him before *S*,
17: 58 young man?" *S* asked him.
18: 1 David had finished talking with *S*,
18: 2 From that day *S* kept David
18: 5 Whatever *S* sent him to do,
18: 5 it so successfully that *S* gave him
18: 6 Israel to meet King *S* with singing
18: 7 "*S* has slain his thousands,
18: 8 *S* was very angry; this refrain
18: 9 time on *S* kept a jealous eye
18: 10 from God came forcefully upon *S*.

1Sa 18: 10 S had a spear in his hand
18: 12 S was afraid of David,
18: 12 was with David but had left S.
18: 15 When S saw how successful he was
18: 17 For S said to himself, "I will not
18: 17 S said to David, "Here is my older
18: 18 But David said to S, "Who am I,
18: 20 and when they told S about it,
18: 21 So S said to David, "Now you have
18: 22 Then S ordered his attendants:
18: 25 what David had said, S replied,
18: 27 S gave him his daughter Michal
18: 28 When S realized that the LORD
18: 29 S became still more afraid of him,
19: 1 S told his son Jonathan
19: 2 My father S is looking for a chance
19: 4 well of David to S his father
19: 6 S listened to Jonathan
19: 7 and David was with S as before.
19: 7 him to S, and David was
19: 9 spirit from the LORD came upon S
19: 10 as S drove the spear into the wall.
19: 10 S tried to pin him to the wall
19: 11 S sent men to David's house
19: 14 When S sent the men
19: 15 S sent the men back to see David
19: 17 S said to Michal, "Why did you
19: 18 told him all that S had done to him.
19: 19 Word came to S: "David is
19: 21 S sent men a third time, and they
19: 21 S was told about it, and he sent
19: 23 So S went to Naioth at Ramah.
19: 24 "Is S also among the prophets?"
20: 25 and Abner sat next to S,
20: 26 S said nothing that day,
20: 27 Then S said to his son Jonathan,
20: 33 S hurled his spear at him to kill him
21: 10 That day David fled from S
21: 11 " 'S has slain his thousands,
22: 6 And S, spear in hand, was seated
22: 6 Now S heard that David
22: 7 S said to them, "Listen, men
22: 12 S said, "Listen now, son of Ahitub
22: 13 S said to him, "Why have you
22: 21 He told David that S had killed
22: 22 I knew he would be sure to tell S.
23: 7 S was told that David had gone
23: 8 S called up all his forces for battle,
23: 9 David learned that S was plotting
23: 10 has heard definitely that S plans
23: 11 Will S come down, as your servant
23: 12 surrender me and my men to S?"
23: 13 When S was told that David had
23: 14 Day after day S searched for him,
23: 15 he learned that S had come out
23: 17 Even my father S knows this."
23: 17 "My father S will not lay a hand
23: 19 The Ziphites went up to S
23: 21 S replied, "The LORD bless you
23: 24 and went to Ziph ahead of S.
23: 25 When S heard this, he went
23: 25 S and his men began the search,
23: 26 As S and his forces were closing
23: 26 hurrying to get away from S.
23: 26 S was going along one side
23: 27 a messenger came to S, saying,
23: 28 S broke off his pursuit of David
24: 1 After S returned from pursuing
24: 2 S took three thousand chosen men
24: 3 and S went in to relieve himself.
24: 7 and did not allow them to attack S.
24: 7 S left the cave and went his way.
24: 8 When S looked behind him,
24: 8 out of the cave and called out to S,
24: 9 He said to S, "Why do you listen
24: 16 David finished saying this, S asked,
24: 22 So David gave his oath to S.
24: 22 Then S returned home, but David
25: 44 S had given his daughter Michal,
26: 1 The Ziphites went to S at Gibeah
26: 2 S went down to the Desert of Ziph,
26: 3 he saw that S had followed him
26: 3 S made his camp beside the road
26: 4 and learned that S had definitely
26: 5 He saw where S and Abner son
26: 5 S was lying inside the camp,
26: 5 to the place where S had camped.
26: 6 down into the camp with me to S?"
1Sa 26: 7 the army by night, and there was S,
26: 17 S recognized David's voice
26: 21 Then S said, "I have sinned.
26: 25 Then S said to David, "May you be
26: 25 on his way, and S returned home.
27: 1 Then S will give up searching
27: 1 will be destroyed by the hand of S.
27: 4 When S was told that David had
28: 3 S had expelled the mediums
28: 4 while S gathered all the Israelites
28: 5 When S saw the Philistine army,
28: 7 S then said to his attendants,
28: 8 So S disguised himself, putting
28: 9 "Surely you know what S has done.
28: 10 S swore to her by the LORD,
28: 12 You are S!" The king said to her,
28: 12 at the top of her voice and said to S,
28: 14 Then S knew it was Samuel,
28: 15 to S, "Why have you disturbed me
28: 15 "I am in great distress," S said.
28: 20 Immediately S fell full length
28: 21 When the woman came to S
28: 25 she set it before S and his men,
29: 3 an officer of S king of Israel?
29: 3 from the day he left S until now,
29: 5 " 'S has slain his thousands,
31: 2 The Philistines pressed hard after S
31: 3 The fighting grew fierce around S,
31: 4 S said to his armor-bearer,
31: 4 so S took his own sword
31: 5 armor-bearer saw that S was dead,
31: 6 So S and three of his sons
31: 7 and that S and his sons had died,
31: 8 they found S and his three sons
31: 11 the Philistines had done to S, all
31: 12 They took down the bodies of S
2Sa 1: 1 the death of S, David returned
1: 4 S and his son Jonathan are dead."
1: 5 "How do you know that S
1: 6 there was S, leaning on his spear,
1: 12 and fasted till evening for S
1: 17 took up this lament concerning S
1: 21 the shield of S— no longer rubbed
1: 22 of S did not return unsatisfied.
1: 23 "S and Jonathan—
1: 24 weep for S,
2: 4 Jabesh Gilead who had buried S,
2: 5 this kindness to S your master
2: 7 brave, for S your master is dead,
2: 8 had taken Ish-Bosheth son of S
2: 10 son of S was forty years old
2: 12 the men of Ish-Bosheth son of S,
2: 15 and Ish-Bosheth son of S,
3: 1 The war between the house of S
3: 1 while the house of S grew weaker
3: 6 his own position in the house of S
3: 6 the war between the house of S
3: 7 Now S had had a concubine named
3: 8 loyal to the house of your father S
3: 10 the kingdom from the house of S
3: 13 daughter of S when you come
3: 14 to Ish-Bosheth son of S,
4: 1 son of S heard that Abner had died
4: 4 old when the news about S
4: 4 son of S had a son who was lame
4: 8 avenged my lord the king against S
4: 8 the head of Ish-Bosheth son of S,
4: 10 when a man told me, 'S is dead,'
5: 2 In the past, while S was king
6: 16 Michal daughter of S watched
6: 20 Michal daughter of S came out
6: 23 daughter of S had no children
7: 15 away from S, whom I removed
9: 1 of S to whom I can show kindness
9: 3 of S to whom I can show God's
9: 6 the son of S, came to David,
9: 7 belonged to your grandfather S,
9: 9 everything that belonged to S
12: 7 I delivered you from the hand of S.
16: 8 shed in the household of S,
21: 1 of S and his blood-stained house;
21: 2 but S in his zeal for Israel
21: 4 or gold from S or his family,
21: 6 before the LORD at Gibeah of S—
21: 7 David and Jonathan son of S.
21: 7 son of Jonathan, the son of S,
21: 8 whom she had borne to S,
21: 12 after they struck S down on Gilboa
2Sa 21: 12 he went and took the bones of S
21: 13 David brought the bones of S
21: 14 They buried the bones of S
22: 1 and from the hand of S.
1Ch 8: 33 the father of S, and S the father
9: 39 the father of S, and S the father
10: 2 The Philistines pressed hard after S
10: 3 The fighting grew fierce around S,
10: 4 S said to his armor-bearer,
10: 4 so S took his own sword
10: 5 armor-bearer saw that S was dead,
10: 6 So S and three of his sons died,
10: 7 and that S and his sons had died,
10: 8 they found S and his sons fallen
10: 11 Philistines had done to S, all
10: 12 took the bodies of S and his sons
10: 13 S died because he was unfaithful
11: 2 In the past, even while S was king,
12: 1 from the presence of S son
12: 2 kinsmen of S from the tribe
12: 19 if he deserts to his master S.")
12: 19 the Philistines to fight against S.
13: 3 inquire of it during the reign of S."
15: 29 Michal daughter of S watched
26: 28 by Samuel the seer and by S son
Isa 10: 29 Gibeah of S flees.
Ac 7: 58 at the feet of a young man named S
8: 1 And S was there, giving approval
8: 3 But S began to destroy the church.
9: 1 S was still breathing out murderous
9: 4 "S, S, why do you persecute me?"
9: 5 "Who are you, Lord?" S asked.
9: 7 with S stood there speechless;
9: 8 S got up from the ground,
9: 11 ask for a man from Tarsus named S
9: 17 Placing his hands on S, he said,
9: 17 he said, "Brother S, the Lord—
9: 19 S spent several days
9: 22 Yet S grew more and more
9: 24 but S learned of their plan.
9: 27 He told them how S
9: 28 So S stayed with them
11: 25 went to Tarsus to look for S,
11: 26 and S met with the church
11: 30 to the elders by Barnabas and S.
12: 25 and S had finished their mission,
13: 1 up with Herod the tetrarch) and S.
13: 2 and S for the work to which I have
13: 7 sent for Barnabas and S
13: 9 Then S, who was also called Paul,
13: 21 and he gave them S son of Kish,
13: 22 After removing S, he made David
22: 7 'S! S! Why do you persecute me?'
22: 13 'Brother S, receive your sight!'
26: 14 'S, S, why do you persecute me?

SAUL'S (SAUL)

1Sa 9: 3 to S father Kish were lost,
10: 1 poured it on S head and kissed him,
10: 9 Samuel, God changed S heart,
10: 14 Now S uncle asked him
10: 15 S uncle said, "Tell me what Samuel
13: 8 and S men began to scatter.
14: 16 S lookouts at Gibeah
14: 49 S sons were Jonathan, Ishvi
14: 50 of S army was Abner son
14: 50 son of Ner, and Ner was S uncle.
14: 51 S father Kish and Abner's father
16: 15 S attendants said to him, "See,
17: 12 and in S time he was old
18: 5 all the people, and S officers
18: 19 S daughter, to be given to David,
18: 20 S daughter Michal was in love
18: 24 When S servants told him what
18: 25 S plan was to have David fall
18: 30 success than the rest of S officers,
19: 20 the Spirit of God came upon S men
20: 30 S anger flared up at Jonathan
21: 7 of S servants was there that day,
21: 7 the Edomite, S head shepherd.
22: 9 who was standing with S officials,
23: 16 And S son Jonathan went to David
24: 4 and cut off a corner of S robe.
26: 12 and water jug near S head,
2Sa 1: 2 day a man arrived from S camp,
2: 8 the commander of S army,
4: 2 Now S son had two men who were
9: 2 of S household named Ziba.

2Sa 9: 9 the king summoned Ziba, *S* servant
16: 5 as *S* family came out from there.
19: 17 the steward of *S* household,
19: 24 Mephibosheth, *S* grandson,
21: 8 sons of *S* daughter Merab,
21: 11 daughter Rizpah, *S* concubine,
21: 14 in the tomb of *S* father Kish,
1Ch 5: 10 During *S* reign they waged war
12: 23 at Hebron to turn *S* kingdom
12: 29 loyal to *S* house until then;
12: 29 men of Benjamin, *S* kinsmen—
Ac 9: 18 like scales fell from *S* eyes,

SAVAGE

Lev 26: 6 I will remove *s* beasts from the land
Ac 20: 29 *s* wolves will come in among you

SAVE (SAFE SAFETY SALVATION SAVED SAVES SAVING SAVIOR)

Ge 32: 11 *S* me, I pray, from the hand
45: 5 to *s* lives that God sent me ahead
45: 7 and to *s* your lives by a great
Ex 16: 23 *S* whatever is left and keep it
Nu 31: 18 *s* for yourselves every girl who has
Dt 4: 42 into one of these cities and *s* his life
19: 4 and flees there to *s* his life—
19: 5 to one of these cities and *s* his life.
Jos 2: 13 and that you will *s* us from death.''
10: 6 Come up to us quickly and *s* us!
Jdg 6: 14 and *s* Israel out of Midian's hand.
6: 15 Gideon asked, ''how can I *s* Israel?
6: 31 cause? Are you trying to *s* him?
6: 36 ''If you will *s* Israel by my hand
6: 37 I will know that you will *s* Israel
7: 7 men that lapped I will *s* you
10: 1 the son of Dodo, rose to *s* Israel.
10: 12 did I not *s* you from their hands?
10: 13 so I will no longer *s* you.
10: 14 Let them *s* you when you are
12: 2 you didn't *s* me out of their hands.
1Sa 4: 3 *s* us from the hand of our enemies.''
10: 27 ''How can this fellow *s* us?''
23: 2 attack the Philistines and *s* Keilah
2Sa 22: 3 from violent men you *s* me.
22: 28 You *s* the humble,
22: 42 but there was no one to *s* them—
1Ki 1: 12 you how you can *s* your own life
2Ki 16: 7 *s* me out of the hand of the king
18: 35 able to *s* his land from me?
19: 34 I will defend this city and *s* it,
1Ch 16: 35 Cry out, ''*S* us, O God our Savior;
2Ch 20: 9 and you will hear us and *s* us.'
25: 15 which could not *s* their own people
32: 11 'The LORD our God will *s* us
32: 14 able to *s* his people from me?
Ne 6: 11 go into the temple to *s* his life?
Job 20: 20 he cannot *s* himself by his treasure.
22: 29 then he will *s* the downcast.
40: 14 that your own right hand can *s* you.
Ps 6: 4 *s* me because of your unfailing love
7: 1 *s* and deliver me from all who
17: 7 you who *s* by your right hand
17: 14 by your hand *s* me from such men,
18: 27 You *s* the humble
18: 41 but there was no one to *s* them—
20: 9 O LORD, *s* the king!
22: 21 *s* me from the horns
28: 9 *S* your people and bless your
31: 2 a strong fortress to *s* me.
31: 16 *s* me in your unfailing love.
33: 17 all its great strength it cannot *s*.
39: 8 *S* me from all my transgressions;
40: 13 Be pleased, O LORD, to *s* me;
51: 14 *S* me from bloodguilt, O God,
54: 1 *S* me, O God, by your name;
59: 2 and *s* me from bloodthirsty men.
60: 5 *S* us and help us with your right
69: 1 *S* me, O God,
69: 35 for God will *s* Zion
70: 1 Hasten, O God, to *s* me;
71: 2 turn your ear to me and *s* me.
71: 3 give the command to *s* me,
72: 4 and *s* the children of the needy;
72: 13 and *s* the needy from death.
76: 9 to *s* all the afflicted of the land.
80: 2 come and *s* us.
86: 2 You are my God; *s* your servant
86: 16 and *s* the son of your maidservant.
Ps 89: 48 or *s* himself from the power
91: 3 Surely he will *s* you
106: 4 come to my aid when you *s* them,
106: 47 *S* us, O LORD our God,
108: 6 *S* us and help us with your right
109: 26 *s* me in accordance with your love.
109: 31 to *s* his life from those who
116: 4 ''O LORD, *s* me!''
118: 25 O LORD, *s* us;
119: 94 *S* me, for I am yours;
119: 146 I call out to you; *s* me
120: 2 *S* me, O LORD, from lying lips
138: 7 with your right hand you *s* me.
146: 3 in mortal men, who cannot *s*.
Pr 2: 12 Wisdom will *s* you from the ways
2: 16 will *s* you also from the adulteress,
23: 14 and *s* his soul from death.
Isa 33: 22 it is he who will *s* us.
35: 4 he will come to *s* you.''
36: 20 able to *s* his land from me?
37: 35 ''I will defend this city and *s* it,
38: 20 The LORD will *s* me,
44: 17 ''*S* me; you are my god.''
44: 20 he cannot *s* himself, or say,
45: 20 who pray to gods that cannot *s*.
46: 7 it cannot *s* him from his troubles.
47: 13 let them *s* you from what is coming
47: 14 They cannot even *s* themselves
47: 15 there is not one that can *s* you.
49: 25 and your children I will *s*.
57: 13 let your collection of idols *s* you!
59: 1 of the LORD is not too short to *s*,
63: 1 mighty to *s*.''
Jer 2: 27 'Come and *s* us!'
2: 28 Let them come if they can *s* you
14: 9 like a warrior powerless to *s*?
15: 20 you to rescue and *s* you,''
15: 21 ''I will *s* you from the hands
17: 14 *s* me and I will be saved,
30: 10 'I will surely *s* you out
30: 11 I am with you and will *s* you,'
31: 7 'O LORD, *s* your people,
39: 18 I will *s* you; you will not fall
42: 11 for I am with you and will *s* you
46: 27 I will surely *s* you out
La 4: 17 for a nation that could not *s* us.
Eze 3: 18 ways in order to *s* his life,
7: 19 able to *s* them in the day
13: 21 and *s* my people from your hands,
13: 22 their evil ways and so *s* their lives,
13: 23 I will *s* my people from your hands.
14: 14 they could *s* only themselves
14: 16 they could not *s* their own sons
14: 18 they could not *s* their own sons
14: 20 They would *s* only themselves
14: 20 they could *s* neither son
18: 27 and right, he will *s* his life.
33: 12 of the righteous man will not *s* him
34: 22 I will *s* my flock, and they will no
36: 29 I will *s* you from all your
37: 23 for I will *s* them from all their sinful
Da 3: 17 the God we serve is able to *s* us
3: 29 for no other god can *s* in this way.''
6: 14 effort until sundown to *s* him.
Hos 1: 7 and I will *s* them—not by bow,
13: 10 is your king, that he may *s* you?
14: 3 Assyria cannot *s* us;
Am 2: 14 and the warrior will not *s* his life.
2: 15 and the horseman will not *s* his life.
Mic 2: 3 which you cannot *s* yourselves.
6: 14 You will store up but *s* nothing,
6: 14 what you *s* I will give to the sword.
Hab 1: 2 but you do not *s*?
3: 13 to *s* your anointed one.
Zep 1: 18 will be able to *s* them
3: 17 he is mighty to *s*.
Zec 8: 7 ''I will *s* my people
8: 13 O Judah and Israel, so will I *s* you,
9: 16 The LORD their God will *s* them
10: 6 and *s* the house of Joseph.
12: 7 ''The LORD will *s* the dwellings
Mt 1: 21 he will *s* his people from their sins
8: 25 Lord, *s* us! We're going to drown!''
14: 30 to sink, cried out, ''Lord, *s* me!''
16: 25 wants to *s* his life will lose it,
27: 40 *s* yourself! Come
27: 42 they said, ''but he can't *s* himself!
27: 49 Let's see if Elijah comes to *s* him.''
Mk 3: 4 or to do evil, to *s* life or to kill?''
8: 35 and for the gospel will *s* it.
8: 35 wants to *s* his life will lose it,
15: 30 down from the cross and *s* yourself
15: 31 he can't *s* himself! Let this Christ,
Lk 6: 9 to do evil, to *s* life or to destroy it?''
9: 24 loses his life for me will *s* it.
9: 24 wants to *s* his life will lose it,
19: 10 to seek and to *s* what was lost.''
21: 19 standing firm you will *s* yourselves.
23: 35 let him *s* himself if he is the Christ
23: 37 the king of the Jews, *s* yourself.''
23: 39 ''Aren't you the Christ? *S* yourself
Jn 3: 17 but to *s* the world through him.
12: 7 that she should *s* this perfume
12: 27 'Father, *s* me from this hour'? No,
12: 47 come to judge the world, but to *s* it.
Ac 2: 40 ''*S* yourselves from this corrupt
Ro 11: 14 people to envy and *s* some of them.
1Co 1: 21 preached to *s* those who believe.
7: 16 whether you will *s* your husband?
7: 16 whether you will *s* your wife?
9: 22 all possible means I might *s* some.
2Co 12: 14 have to *s* up for their parents,
1Ti 1: 15 came into the world to *s* sinners—
4: 16 you will *s* both yourself
Heb 5: 7 tears to the one who could *s* him
7: 25 to *s* completely those who come
11: 7 fear built an ark to *s* his family.
Jas 1: 21 planted in you, which can *s* you.
2: 14 Can such faith *s* him? Suppose
4: 12 the one who is able to *s* and destroy
5: 20 of his way will *s* him from death
Jude : 23 others from the fire and *s* them;

SAVED (SAVE)

Ge 47: 25 ''You have *s* our lives,'' they said.
Ex 14: 30 That day the LORD *s* Israel
16: 24 So they *s* it until morning,
18: 4 he *s* me from the sword of Pharaoh
18: 8 and how the LORD had *s* them.
Dt 33: 29 a people *s* by the LORD?
Jos 9: 26 Joshua *s* them from the Israelites,
Jdg 2: 16 who *s* them out of the hands
2: 18 and *s* them out of the hands
3: 9 younger brother, who *s* them.
3: 31 He too *s* Israel.
7: 2 me that her own strength has *s* her,
8: 22 you have *s* us out of the hand
1Sa 23: 5 and *s* the people of Keilah.
2Sa 19: 5 who have just *s* your life
22: 4 and I am *s* from my enemies.
2Ki 14: 27 he *s* them by the hand
2Ch 32: 22 So the LORD *s* Hezekiah
Job 26: 2 How you have *s* the arm that is
Ps 18: 3 and I am *s* from my enemies.
22: 5 They cried to you and were *s*;
33: 16 No king is *s* by the size of his army;
34: 6 he *s* him out of all his troubles.
80: 3 that we may be *s*.
80: 7 that we may be *s*.
80: 19 that we may be *s*.
106: 8 Yet he *s* them for his name's sake,
106: 10 He *s* them from the hand of the foe;
106: 21 They forgot the God who *s* them,
107: 13 and he *s* them from their distress.
107: 19 and he *s* them from their distress.
116: 6 when I was in great need, he *s* me.
Ecc 9: 15 and he *s* the city by his wisdom.
Isa 25: 9 we trusted in him, and he *s* us.
43: 12 revealed and *s* and proclaimed—
45: 17 But Israel will be *s* by the LORD
45: 22 ''Turn to me and be *s*,
63: 9 the angel of his presence *s* them.
64: 5 How then can we be *s*?
Jer 4: 14 from your heart and be *s*.
8: 20 and we are not *s*.''
17: 14 save me and I will be *s*,
23: 6 In his days Judah will be *s*
30: 7 but he will be *s* out of it.
33: 16 In those days Judah will be *s*
Eze 3: 19 but you will have *s* yourself.
3: 21 and you will have *s* yourself.''
14: 16 They alone would be *s*,
14: 18 They alone would be *s*.
33: 5 warning, he would have *s* himself.
33: 9 but you will have *s* yourself.
Joel 2: 32 on the name of the LORD will be *s*;

Am 3: 12 so will the Israelites be s,
Mt 10: 22 firm to the end will be s.
19: 25 "Who then can be s?" Jesus looked
24: 13 firm to the end will be s.
27: 42 "He s others," they said,
Mk 10: 26 "Who then can be s?" Jesus looked
13: 13 firm to the end will be s.
15: 31 "He s others," they said,
16: 16 believes and is baptized will be s,
Lk 7: 50 "Your faith has s you; go in peace."
8: 12 so that they cannot believe and be s
13: 23 are only a few people going to be s
18: 26 Who then can be s?" Jesus replied,
23: 35 "He s others; let him save himself
Jn 2: 10 but you have s the best till now."
5: 34 but I mention it that you may be s.
10: 9 enters through me will be s.
Ac 2: 21 on the name of the Lord will be s.'
2: 47 daily those who were being s.
4: 12 to men by which we must be s."
11: 14 and all your household will be s.'
15: 1 taught by Moses, you cannot be s."
15: 11 of our Lord Jesus that we are s,
16: 17 who are telling you the way to be s
16: 30 do to be s?" They replied,
16: 31 and you will be s— you
27: 20 finally gave up all hope of being s.
27: 31 with the ship, you cannot be s."
Ro 5: 9 how much more shall we be s
5: 10 shall we be s through his life!
8: 24 For in this hope we were s.
9: 27 only the remnant will be s.
10: 1 the Israelites is that they may be s.
10: 9 him from the dead, you will be s.
10: 10 mouth that you confess and are s.
10: 13 on the name of the Lord will be s."
11: 26 so all Israel will be s, as it is written:
1Co 1: 18 to us who are being s it is the power
3: 15 will suffer loss; he himself will be s,
5: 5 his spirit s on the day of the Lord.
10: 33 of many, so that they may be s.
15: 2 By this gospel you are s,
2Co 2: 15 among those who are being s
Eph 2: 5 it is by grace you have been s.
2: 8 For it is by grace you have been s,
Php 1: 28 but that you will be s— and that
1Th 2: 16 the Gentiles so that they may be s.
2Th 2: 10 to love the truth and so be s.
2: 13 you to be s through the sanctifying
1Ti 2: 4 who wants all men to be s
2Ti 1: 9 who has s us and called us
Tit 3: 5 He s us through the washing
3: 5 s us, not because of righteous
Heb 10: 39 but of those who believe and are s.
1Pe 3: 20 eight in all, were s through water,
4: 18 If it is hard for the righteous to be s,

SAVES (SAVE)

1Sa 10: 19 who s you out of all your calamities
17: 47 or spear that the LORD s;
Job 5: 15 He s the needy from the sword
5: 15 he s them from the clutches
Ps 7: 10 who s the upright in heart.
18: 48 who s me from my enemies.
20: 6 that the LORD s his anointed;
34: 18 s those who are crushed in spirit.
37: 40 them from the wicked and s them,
51: 14 the God who s me,
55: 16 and the LORD s me.
57: 3 He sends from heaven and s me,
68: 20 Our God is a God who s;
88: 1 O LORD, the God who s me,
145: 19 he hears their cry and s them.
Pr 14: 25 A truthful witness s lives,
Da 6: 27 He rescues and he s;
Am 3: 12 "As a shepherd s from the lion's
1Pe 3: 21 It s you by the resurrection
3: 21 symbolizes baptism that now s you

SAVING (SAVE)

Ge 50: 20 what is now being done, the s
1Sa 14: 6 can hinder the LORD from s,
Ps 20: 6 with the s power of his right hand.
22: 1 Why are you so far from s me,
1Co 16: 2 s it up, so that when I come no

SAVIOR (SAVE)

Dt 32: 15 and rejected the Rock his S.
2Sa 22: 3 stronghold, my refuge and my s—
22: 47 Exalted be God, the Rock, my S!
1Ch 16: 35 Cry out, "Save us, O God our S;
Ps 18: 46 Exalted be God my S!
24: 5 and vindication from God his S.
25: 5 for you are God my S,
27: 9 O God my S.
38: 22 O Lord my S.
42: 5 my S and
42: 11 my S and my God.
43: 5 my S and my God.
65: 5 O God our S,
68: 19 Praise be to the Lord, to God our S,
79: 9 Help us, O God our S,
85: 4 Restore us again, O God our S,
89: 26 my God, the Rock my S.'
Isa 17: 10 You have forgotten God your S;
19: 20 he will send them a s and defender,
43: 3 the Holy One of Israel, your S;
43: 11 and apart from me there is no s.
45: 15 O God and S of Israel.
45: 21 a righteous God and a S;
49: 26 that I, the LORD, am your S,
60: 16 know that I, the LORD, am your S,
62: 11 'See, your S comes!
63: 8 and so he became their S.
Jer 14: 8 its S in times of distress,
Hos 13: 4 no S except me.
Mic 7: 7 I wait for God my S;
Hab 3: 18 I will be joyful in God my S.
Lk 1: 47 and my spirit rejoices in God my S,
2: 11 of David a S has been born to you;
Jn 4: 42 know that this man really is the S
Ac 5: 31 S that he might give repentance
13: 23 God has brought to Israel the S
Eph 5: 23 his body, of which he is the S.
Php 3: 20 we eagerly await a S from there,
1Ti 1: 1 by the command of God our S
2: 3 This is good, and pleases God our S
4: 10 who is the S of all men,
2Ti 1: 10 through the appearing of our S,
Tit 1: 3 me by the command of God our S,
1: 4 the Father and Christ Jesus our S.
2: 10 about God our S attractive.
2: 13 appearing of our great God and S,
3: 4 and love of God our S appeared,
3: 6 through Jesus Christ our S,
2Pe 1: 1 S Jesus Christ have received a faith
1: 11 eternal kingdom of our Lord and S
2: 20 and S Jesus Christ and are again
3: 2 and S through your apostles.
3: 18 and knowledge of our Lord and S
1Jn 4: 14 Son to be the S of the world.
Jude : 25 to the only God our S be glory,

SAWDUST

Mt 7: 3 the speck of s in your brother's eye
Lk 6: 41 the speck of s in your brother's eye

SAWED (SAWS)

Heb 11: 37 They were stoned; they were s

SAWS (SAWED)

2Sa 12: 31 consigning them to labor with s
1Ch 20: 3 consigning them to labor with s

SCABBARD

1Sa 17: 51 sword and drew it from the s.
Jer 47: 6 Return to your s;
Eze 21: 3 I will draw my sword from its s
21: 5 have drawn my sword from its s;
21: 30 Return the sword to its s.

SCABS

Job 7: 5 with worms and s,

SCALE (SCALES)

1Sa 17: 5 and wore a coat of s armor
2Sa 22: 30 with my God I can s a wall.
Ps 18: 29 with my God I can s a wall.
Joel 2: 7 they s walls like soldiers.

SCALES (SCALE)

Lev 11: 9 may eat any that have fins and s.
11: 10 streams that do not have fins and s
11: 12 and s is to be detestable to you.
19: 36 Use honest s and honest weights,
Dt 14: 9 you may eat any that has fins and s.
Dt 14: 10 not have fins and s you may not
Job 6: 2 all my misery be placed on the s!
31: 6 let God weigh me in honest s
Pr 11: 1 The LORD abhors dishonest s,
16: 11 Honest s and balances are
20: 23 and dishonest s do not please him.
Isa 40: 12 or weighed the mountains on the s
40: 15 they are regarded as dust on the s;
46: 6 and weigh out silver on the s;
Jer 32: 10 and weighed out the silver on the s.
Eze 5: 1 a set of s and divide up the hair.
29: 4 of your streams stick to your s.
29: 4 with all the fish sticking to your s.
45: 10 are to use accurate s, an accurate
Da 5: 27 You have been weighed on the s
Hos 12: 7 The merchant uses dishonest s;
Am 8: 5 and cheating with dishonest s,
Mic 6: 11 I acquit a man with dishonest s,
Ac 9: 18 something like s fell
Rev 6: 5 Its rider was holding a pair of s

SCALP (SCALPS)

Lev 13: 41 hair from the front of his s

SCALPS (SCALP)

Isa 3: 17 the LORD will make their s bald."

SCAPEGOAT (GOAT)

Lev 16: 8 the LORD and the other for the s.
16: 10 as the s shall be presented alive
16: 10 by sending it into the desert as a s.
16: 26 as a s must wash his clothes

SCAR

Lev 13: 23 it is only a s from the boil,
13: 28 it is only a s from the burn.

SCARCE (SCARCER SCARCITY)

Dt 8: 9 a land where bread will not be s
Eze 4: 17 for food and water will be s.

SCARCER (SCARCE)

Isa 13: 12 I will make man s than pure gold,

SCARCITY (SCARCE)

Pr 6: 11 and s like an armed man.
24: 34 and s like an armed man.

SCARECROW

Jer 10: 5 Like a s in a melon patch,

SCARLET

Ge 38: 28 so the midwife took a s thread
38: 30 who had the s thread on his wrist,
Ex 25: 4 purple and s yarn and fine linen;
26: 1 and s yarn, with cherubim worked
26: 31 and s yarn and finely twisted linen,
26: 36 s yarn and finely twisted linen—
27: 16 s yarn and finely twisted linen—
28: 5 and blue, purple and s yarn,
28: 6 and of blue, purple and s yarn,
28: 8 and with blue, purple and s yarn,
28: 15 and of blue, purple and s yarn,
28: 33 s yarn around the hem of the robe,
35: 6 purple and s yarn and fine linen;
35: 23 purple or s yarn or fine linen,
35: 25 blue, purple or s yarn or fine linen.
35: 35 purple and s yarn and fine linen,
36: 8 and s yarn, with cherubim worked
36: 35 and s yarn and finely twisted linen,
36: 37 s yarn and finely twisted linen—
38: 18 s yarn and finely twisted linen—
38: 23 purple and s yarn and fine linen.)
39: 1 s yarn they made woven garments
39: 2 and of blue, purple and s yarn,
39: 3 purple and s yarn and fine linen—
39: 5 and with blue, purple and s yarn,
39: 8 and of blue, purple and s yarn,
39: 24 and s yarn and finely twisted linen
39: 29 and s yarn—the work
Lev 14: 4 s yarn and hyssop be brought
14: 6 the s yarn and the hyssop,
14: 49 and some cedar wood, s yarn
14: 51 the s yarn and the live bird,
14: 52 the hyssop and the s yarn.
Nu 4: 8 are to spread a s cloth,
19: 6 and s wool and throw them
Jos 2: 18 you have tied this s cord

Jos 2:21 she tied the *s* cord in the window.
2Sa 1:24 who clothed you in *s* and finery,
Pr 31:21 for all of them are clothed in *s*.
SS 4:3 Your lips are like a *s* ribbon;
Isa 1:18 "Though your sins are like *s*,
Jer 4:30 Why dress yourself in *s*
Na 2:3 the warriors are clad in *s*.
Mt 27:28 They stripped him and put a *s* robe
Heb 9:19 *s* wool and branches of hyssop,
Rev 17:3 on a *s* beast that was covered
17:4 was dressed in purple and *s*,
18:12 fine linen, purple, silk and *s* cloth;
18:16 dressed in fine linen, purple and *s*,

SCATTER (SCATTERED SCATTERING SCATTERS)

Ge 49:7 I will *s* them in Jacob
Lev 26:33 I will *s* you among the nations
Nu 16:37 *s* the coals some distance away,
Dt 4:27 The LORD will *s* you
28:64 Then the LORD will *s* you
32:26 I said I would *s* them
1Sa 13:8 and Saul's men began to *s*.
1Ki 14:15 and *s* them beyond the River,
Ne 1:8 I will *s* you among the nations,
Ps 68:30 *S* the nations who delight in war.
106:27 and *s* them throughout the lands.
144:6 forth lightning and *s* ⌞the enemies⌟;
Ecc 3:5 a time to *s* stones and a time
Isa 24:1 and *s* its inhabitants—
28:25 he not sow caraway and *s* cummin?
33:3 when you rise up, the nations *s*.
Jer 9:16 I will *s* them among nations that
13:24 "I will *s* you like chaff
18:17 I will *s* them before their enemies;
30:11 the nations among which I *s* you,
46:28 the nations among which I *s* you,
49:32 I will *s* to the winds those who are
49:36 I will *s* them to the four winds,
Eze 5:2 And *s* a third to the wind.
5:10 and will *s* all your survivors
5:12 and a third I will *s* to the winds
6:5 and I will *s* your bones
10:2 among the cherubim and *s* them
12:14 I will *s* to the winds all those
12:15 and *s* them through the countries.
20:23 and *s* them through the countries,
22:15 and *s* you through the countries;
29:12 and *s* them through the countries.
30:23 and *s* them through the countries.
30:26 and *s* them through the countries.
Da 4:14 strip off its leaves and *s* its fruit.
Hab 3:14 his warriors stormed out to *s* us,
Zec 1:21 the land of Judah to *s* its people."
10:9 I *s* them among the peoples,

SCATTERED (SCATTER)

Ge 9:19 them came the people who were *s*
10:18 Later the Canaanite clans *s*
11:4 and not be *s* over the face
11:8 So the LORD *s* them from there
11:9 From there the LORD *s* them
Ex 5:12 So the people *s* all over Egypt
32:20 *s* it on the water and made
Nu 10:35 May your enemies be *s*;
Dt 30:3 from all the nations where he *s* you.
Jdg 9:45 he destroyed the city and *s* salt
1Sa 11:11 Those who survived were *s*,
30:16 they were, *s* over the countryside,
2Sa 17:19 of the well and *s* grain over it.
22:15 He shot arrows and *s*
1Ki 22:17 "I saw all Israel *s* on the hills like
2Ki 23:6 and *s* the dust over the graves
25:5 were separated from him and *s*,
2Ch 18:16 "I saw all Israel *s* on the hills like
34:4 *s* over the graves of those who had
Est 3:8 and *s* among the peoples
Job 4:11 and the cubs of the lioness are *s*.
18:15 burning sulfur is *s* over his dwelling
38:24 place where the east winds are *s*
Ps 18:14 shot his arrows and *s* ⌞the enemies⌟,
44:11 and have *s* us among the nations.
53:5 God *s* the bones of those who
68:1 God arise, may his enemies be *s*;
68:14 When the Almighty *s* the kings
89:10 strong arm you *s* your enemies.
92:9 all evildoers will be *s*.
112:9 He has *s* abroad his gifts
Ps 141:7 so our bones have been *s*
Isa 11:12 he will assemble the *s* people
Jer 3:13 you have *s* your favors
10:21 and all their flock is *s*.
23:2 "Because you have *s* my flock
31:10 'He who *s* Israel will gather them
40:12 countries where they had been *s*.
40:15 gathered around you to be *s*
43:5 the nations where they had been *s*.
50:17 "Israel is a *s* flock
52:8 were separated from him and *s*,
La 4:1 The sacred gems are *s*
4:16 The LORD himself has *s* them;
Eze 6:8 when you are *s* among the lands
11:16 and *s* them among the countries,
11:17 countries where you have been *s*,
17:21 the survivors will be *s* to the winds.
20:34 countries where you have been *s*—
20:41 countries where you have been *s*,
28:25 nations where they have been *s*,
29:13 from the nations where they were *s*
34:5 and when they were *s* they became
34:5 they were *s* because there was no
34:6 They were *s* over the whole earth,
34:12 all the places where they were *s*
34:12 looks after his *s* flock when he is
36:19 they were *s* through the countries;
Da 9:7 the countries where you have *s* us
Joel 3:2 for they *s* my people
Na 3:18 people are *s* on the mountains
Zep 3:10 my worshipers, my *s* people,
3:19 and gather those who have been *s*.
Zec 1:19 "These are the horns that *s* Judah,
1:21 "These are the horns that *s* Judah
2:6 "for I have *s* you to the four winds
7:14 'I *s* them with a whirlwind
13:7 and the sheep will be *s*,
Mt 25:24 where you have not *s* seed.
25:26 and gather where I have not *s* seed?
26:31 and the sheep of the flock will be *s*.'
Mk 14:27 and the sheep will be *s*.'
Lk 1:51 he has *s* those who are proud
Jn 2:15 he *s* the coins of the money
7:35 Will he go where our people live *s*
11:52 but also for the *s* children of God,
16:32 when you will be *s*, each
Ac 5:37 and all his followers were *s*.
8:1 except the apostles were *s*
8:4 who had been *s* preached the word
11:19 Now those who had been *s*
1Co 10:5 their bodies were *s* over the desert.
2Co 9:9 "He has *s* abroad his gifts
Jas 1:1 To the twelve tribes *s*
1Pe 1:1 *s* throughout Pontus, Galatia,

SCATTERING (SCATTER)

1Sa 13:11 "When I saw that the men were *s*,
Jer 23:1 and *s* the sheep of my pasture!"
Mt 13:4 As he was *s* the seed, some fell
Mk 4:4 As he was *s* the seed, some fell
Lk 8:5 As he was *s* the seed, some fell

SCATTERS (SCATTER)

Job 36:30 See how he *s* his lightning about
37:11 he *s* his lightning through them.
Ps 147:16 and *s* the frost like ashes.
Mt 12:30 he who does not gather with me *s*.
Mk 4:26 A man *s* seed on the ground.
Lk 11:23 he who does not gather with me, *s*.
Jn 10:12 the wolf attacks the flock and *s* it.

SCENE

Mk 9:25 that a crowd was running to the *s*,

SCENT

Job 14:9 yet at the *s* of water it will bud
39:25 He catches the *s* of battle from afar,

SCEPTER (SCEPTERS)

Ge 49:10 The *s* will not depart from Judah,
Nu 24:17 a *s* will rise out of Israel.
Est 4:11 the king to extend the gold *s* to him
5:2 and touched the tip of the *s*.
5:2 out to her the gold *s* that was
8:4 Then the king extended the gold *s*
Ps 2:9 You will rule them with an iron *s*;
45:6 a *s* of justice will be the *s*
60:7 Judah my *s*.
Ps 108:8 Judah my *s*.
110:2 LORD will extend your mighty *s*
125:3 The *s* of the wicked will not remain
Isa 14:5 the *s* of the rulers,
30:31 with his *s* he will strike them down.
Jer 48:17 say, 'How broken is the mighty *s*,
Eze 19:11 fit for a ruler's *s*.
19:14 fit for a ruler's *s*.'
Am 1:5 who holds the *s* in Beth Eden.
1:8 the one who holds the *s*
Zec 10:11 and Egypt's *s* will pass away.
Heb 1:8 and righteousness will be the *s*
Rev 2:27 'He will rule them with an iron *s*;
12:5 rule all the nations with an iron *s*.
19:15 "He will rule them with an iron *s*."

SCEPTERS (SCEPTER)

Nu 21:18 the nobles with *s* and staffs."

SCEVA

Ac 19:14 sons of *S*, a Jewish chief priest,

SCHEME (SCHEMER SCHEMES SCHEMING)

Est 9:25 that the evil *s* Haman had devised
Ecc 7:25 and to search out wisdom and the *s*
7:27 to discover the *s* of things—
Eze 38:10 and you will devise an evil *s*.

SCHEMER (SCHEME)

Pr 24:8 will be known as a *s*.

SCHEMES (SCHEME)

Ex 21:14 if a man *s* and kills another man
Job 5:13 the *s* of the wily are swept away.
10:3 smile on the *s* of the wicked?
18:7 his own *s* throw him down.
21:27 *s* by which you would wrong me.
Ps 10:2 who are caught in the *s* he devises.
21:11 and devise wicked *s*, they cannot
26:10 in whose hands are wicked *s*,
37:7 when they carry out their wicked *s*.
119:150 Those who devise wicked *s* are
Pr 1:31 and be filled with the fruit of their *s*
6:18 a heart that devises wicked *s*,
24:9 The *s* of folly are sin,
Ecc 7:29 men have gone in search of many *s*
8:11 filled with *s* to do wrong.
Isa 32:7 he makes up evil *s*
Jer 6:19 the fruit of their *s*,
11:15 she works out her evil *s* with many?
2Co 2:11 For we are not unaware of his *s*.
Eph 6:11 stand against the devil's *s*.

SCHEMING (SCHEME)

Ne 6:2 But they were *s* to harm me;
Eph 4:14 of men in their deceitful *s*.

SCHOLAR

1Co 1:20 Where is the *s*? Where is

SCOFF (SCOFFED SCOFFERS SCOFFING SCOFFS)

1Ki 9:8 pass by will be appalled and will *s*
Ps 59:8 you *s* at all those nations.
73:8 They *s*, and speak with malice;
Jer 19:8 and will *s* because of all its wounds.
49:17 pass by will be appalled and will *s*
50:13 pass Babylon will be horrified and *s*
La 2:15 they *s* and shake their heads
2:16 they *s* and gnash their teeth
Hab 1:10 and *s* at rulers.
Zep 2:15 All who pass by her *s*

SCOFFED (SCOFF)

2Ch 36:16 *s* at his prophets until the wrath

SCOFFERS (SCOFF)

Isa 28:14 of the LORD, you *s*
Ac 13:41 happen to you: " 'Look, you *s*,
2Pe 3:3 that in the last days *s* will come,
Jude :18 there will be *s* who will follow

SCOFFING (SCOFF)

2Pe 3:3 *s* and following their own evil

SCOFFS (SCOFF)

Ps 2:4 the Lord *s* at them.

Pr 29: 9 *s*, and there is no peace.

SCOOP (SCOOPED SCOOPING SCOOPS)

Pr 6: 27 Can a man *s* fire into his lap

SCOOPED (SCOOP)

Jdg 14: 9 which he *s* out with his hands

SCOOPING (SCOOP)

Isa 30: 14 or *s* water out of a cistern."

SCOOPS (SCOOP)

Ps 7: 15 He who digs a hole and *s* it out

SCORCH (SCORCHED SCORCHING SUN-SCORCHED)

Rev 16: 8 power to *s* people with fire.

SCORCHED (SCORCH)

Ge 41: 6 thin and *s* by the east wind.
41: 23 and thin and *s* by the east wind.
41: 27 heads of grain *s* by the east wind:
2Ki 19: 26 *s* before it grows up.
Pr 6: 28 coals without his feet being *s*?
Isa 9: 19 the land will be *s*
37: 27 *s* before it grows up.
Eze 20: 47 from south to north will be *s* by it.
Da 3: 27 their robes were not *s*,
Mt 13: 6 plants were *s*, and they withered
Mk 4: 6 plants were *s*, and they withered

SCORCHING (SCORCH)

Dt 28: 22 and inflammation, with *s* heat
Ps 11: 6 a *s* wind will be their lot.
Pr 16: 27 and his speech is like a *s* fire.
Isa 11: 15 with a *s* wind he will sweep his
Jer 4: 11 "A *s* wind from the barren heights
Jnh 4: 8 God provided a *s* east wind,
Jas 1: 11 For the sun rises with *s* heat
Rev 7: 16 nor any *s* heat.

SCORN (SCORNED SCORNING SCORNS)

Dt 28: 37 a thing of horror and an object of *s*
1Sa 2: 29 Why do you *s* my sacrifice
2Ch 29: 8 an object of dread and horror and *s*,
Job 16: 10 they strike my cheek in *s*
19: 18 Even the little boys *s* me;
34: 7 who drinks *s* like water?
Ps 39: 8 do not make me the *s* of fools.
44: 13 the *s* and derision of those
64: 8 them will shake their heads in *s*.
69: 7 For I endure *s* for your sake,
69: 10 I must endure *s*;
69: 20 *S* has broken my heart
71: 13 be covered with *s* and disgrace.
79: 4 of *s* and derision to those around us
89: 41 he has become the *s*
109: 25 I am an object of *s* to my accusers;
119: 22 Remove from me *s* and contempt,
Pr 23: 9 for he will *s* the wisdom
Isa 43: 28 and Israel to *s*.
Jer 18: 16 an object of lasting *s*;
19: 8 this city and make it an object of *s*;
25: 9 them an object of horror and *s*,
25: 18 and an object of horror and *s*
29: 18 of *s* and reproach,
48: 27 that you shake your head in *s*
51: 37 an object of horror and *s*,
Eze 22: 4 I will make you an object of *s*
23: 32 it will bring *s* and derision,
34: 29 or bear the *s* of the nations.
36: 6 because you have suffered the *s*
36: 7 around you will also suffer *s*.
36: 15 and no longer will you suffer the *s*
Da 9: 16 and your people an object of *s*
Joel 2: 17 your inheritance an object of *s*,
2: 19 an object of *s* to the nations.
Mic 6: 16 you will bear the *s* of the nations."
Hab 2: 6 him with ridicule and *s*,
Gal 4: 14 me with contempt or *s*.

SCORNED (SCORN)

2Ch 30: 10 but the people *s* and ridiculed them
Est 3: 6 he *s* the idea of killing only
Ps 22: 6 *s* by men and despised
69: 19 You know how I am *s*, disgraced
SS 8: 7 it would be utterly *s*.
Eze 16: 31 prostitute, because you *s* payment.
16: 57 you are now *s* by the daughters

SCORNING (SCORN)

Heb 12: 2 him endured the cross, *s* its shame,

SCORNS (SCORN)

Pr 13: 13 He who *s* instruction will pay for it,
30: 17 that *s* obedience to a mother,

SCORPION (SCORPIONS)

Nu 34: 4 cross south of *S* Pass, continue
Jos 15: 3 crossed south of *S* Pass, continued
Jdg 1: 36 was from *S* Pass to Sela
Lk 11: 12 will give him a *s*? If you then,
Rev 9: 5 sting of a *s* when it strikes a man.

SCORPIONS (SCORPION)

Dt 8: 15 with its venomous snakes and *s*.
1Ki 12: 11 I will scourge you with *s*.' "
12: 14 I will scourge you with *s*."
2Ch 10: 11 I will scourge you with *s*.' "
10: 14 I will scourge you with *s*."
Eze 2: 6 around you and you live among *s*.
Lk 10: 19 *s* and to overcome all the power
Rev 9: 3 and were given power like that of *s*
9: 10 They had tails and stings like *s*,

SCOUNDREL (SCOUNDREL'S SCOUNDRELS)

2Sa 16: 7 get out, you man of blood, you *s*!
Pr 6: 12 A *s* and villain,
16: 27 A *s* plots evil,
Isa 32: 5 nor the *s* be highly respected.

SCOUNDREL'S (SCOUNDREL)

Isa 32: 7 The *s* methods are wicked,

SCOUNDRELS (SCOUNDREL)

1Ki 21: 10 But seat two *s* opposite him
21: 13 two *s* came and sat opposite him
2Ch 13: 7 Some worthless *s* gathered

SCOURED

Lev 6: 28 is to be *s* and rinsed with water.

SCOURGE (SCOURGED)

1Ki 12: 11 I will *s* you with scorpions.' "
12: 14 I will *s* you with scorpions."
2Ch 10: 11 I will *s* you with scorpions.' "
10: 14 I will *s* you with scorpions."
Job 9: 23 When a *s* brings sudden death,
Ps 39: 10 Remove your *s* from me;
Isa 28: 15 When an overwhelming *s* sweeps
28: 18 When the overwhelming *s* sweeps

SCOURGED (SCOURGE)

1Ki 12: 11 My father *s* you with whips;
12: 14 My father *s* you with whips;
2Ch 10: 11 My father *s* you with whips;
10: 14 My father *s* you with whips;

SCOUTS

1Sa 26: 4 he sent out *s* and learned that Saul
1Ki 20: 17 Now Ben-Hadad had dispatched *s*,

SCRAPE (SCRAPED)

Eze 26: 4 I will *s* away her rubble

SCRAPED (SCRAPE)

Lev 14: 41 the inside walls of the house *s*
14: 41 the material that is *s* off dumped
14: 43 and the house *s* and plastered,
Job 2: 8 of broken pottery and *s* himself

SCRAPS

Jdg 1: 7 off have picked up *s* under my table
Eze 13: 19 handfuls of barley and *s* of bread.

SCRAWNY

Ge 41: 19 seven other cows came up—*s*

SCREAM (SCREAMED SCREAMS)

Ge 39: 15 When he heard me *s* for help,
Dt 22: 24 in a town and did not *s* for help,

SCREAMED (SCREAM)

Ge 39: 14 in here to sleep with me, but I *s*.
39: 18 But as soon as I *s* for help,
Dt 22: 27 and though the betrothed girl *s*,

SCREAMS (SCREAM)

Lk 9: 39 spirit seizes him and he suddenly *s*;

SCREECH

Lev 11: 16 the horned owl, the *s* owl, the gull,
Dt 14: 15 the horned owl, the *s* owl, the gull,
Isa 34: 11 desert owl and *s* owl will possess it;
Zep 2: 14 The desert owl and the *s* owl

SCRIBE (SCRIBE'S SCRIBES)

1Ch 24: 6 The *s* Shemaiah son of Nethanel,
27: 32 counselor, a man of insight and a *s*.
Ne 8: 1 They told Ezra the *s*
8: 4 Ezra the *s* stood on a high wooden
8: 9 the governor, Ezra the priest and *s*,
8: 13 around Ezra the *s* to give attention
12: 26 and of Ezra the priest and *s*.
12: 36 Ezra the *s* led the procession.
13: 13 Shelemiah the priest, Zadok the *s*,
Jer 36: 26 of Abdeel to arrest Baruch the *s*
36: 32 and gave it to the *s* Baruch son

SCRIBE'S (SCRIBE)

Jer 36: 23 the king cut them off with a *s* knife

SCRIBES (SCRIBE)

1Ch 2: 55 the clans of *s* who lived at Jabez:
2Ch 34: 13 of the Levites were secretaries, *s*
Jer 8: 8 when actually the lying pen of the *s*

SCRIPT

Ezr 4: 7 The letter was written in Aramaic *s*
Est 1: 22 to each province in its own *s*
3: 12 out in the *s* of each province
8: 9 and also to the Jews in their own *s*
8: 9 written in the *s* of each province

SCRIPTURE (SCRIPTURES)

Mk 12: 10 Haven't you read this *s*:
Lk 4: 21 "Today this *s* is fulfilled
Jn 2: 22 Then they believed the *S*
7: 38 believes in me, as the *S* has said,
7: 42 Does not the *S* say that the Christ
10: 35 and the *S* cannot be broken—
13: 18 is to fulfill the *s*: 'He who shares my
17: 12 so that *S* would be fulfilled.
19: 24 happened that the *S* might be
19: 28 and so that the *S* would be fulfilled,
19: 36 so that the *S* would be fulfilled:
19: 37 as another *S* says, "They will look
20: 9 from *S* that Jesus had to rise
Ac 1: 16 *S* had to be fulfilled which the Holy
8: 32 was reading this passage of *S*:
8: 35 began with that very passage of *S*
Ro 4: 3 What does the *S* say? "Abraham
9: 17 For the *S* says to Pharaoh:
10: 11 As the *S* says, "Everyone who
11: 2 Don't you know what the *S* says
Gal 3: 8 *S* foresaw that God would justify
3: 16 The *S* does not say "and to seeds,"
3: 22 *S* declares that the whole world is
4: 30 But what does the *S* say? "Get rid
1Ti 4: 13 yourself to the public reading of *S*,
5: 18 For the *S* says, "Do not muzzle
2Ti 3: 16 All *S* is God-breathed
Jas 2: 8 keep the royal law found in *S*,
2: 23 And the *s* was fulfilled that says,
4: 5 Or do you think *S* says
4: 6 us more grace? That is why *S* says:
1Pe 2: 6 For in *S* it says:
2Pe 1: 20 that no prophecy of *S* came about

SCRIPTURES (SCRIPTURE)

Da 9: 2 I, Daniel, understood from the *S*,
Mt 21: 42 "Have you never read in the *S*:
22: 29 because you do not know the *S*
26: 54 then would the *S* be fulfilled that
Mk 12: 24 because you do not know the *S*
14: 49 But the *S* must be fulfilled."
Lk 24: 27 said in all the *S* concerning himself.
24: 32 on the road and opened the *S* to us
24: 45 so they could understand the *S*.
Jn 5: 39 These are the *S* that testify about
5: 39 You diligently study the *S*
Ac 17: 2 reasoned with them from the *S*,
17: 11 examined the *S* every day to see
18: 24 a thorough knowledge of the *S*.
18: 28 proving from the *S* that Jesus was

Ro 1: 2 in the Holy *S* regarding his Son,
15: 4 of the *S* we might have hope.
1Co 15: 3 died for our sins according to the *S*,
15: 4 on the third day according to the *S*,
2Ti 3: 15 you have known the holy *S*,
2Pe 3: 16 as they do the other *S*,

SCROLL (SCROLLS)

Ex 17: 14 "Write this on a *s* as something
Nu 5: 23 is to write these curses on a *s*
Dt 17: 18 for himself on a *s* a copy of this law,
Jos 18: 9 They wrote its description on a *s*,
1Sa 10: 25 He wrote them down on a *s*
Ezr 6: 2 A *s* was found in the citadel
Job 19: 23 that they were written on a *s*,
Ps 40: 7 it is written about me in the *s*.
56: 8 list my tears on your *s*—
Isa 8: 1 "Take a large *s* and write on it
29: 11 if you give the *s* to someone who
29: 11 is nothing but words sealed in a *s*.
29: 12 if you give the *s* to someone who
29: 18 deaf will hear the words of the *s*,
30: 8 inscribe it on a *s*,
34: 4 and the sky rolled up like a *s*;
34: 16 Look in the *s* of the LORD
Jer 36: 2 "Take a *s* and write
36: 4 Baruch wrote them on the *s*.
36: 6 to the people from the *s* the words
36: 8 the words of the LORD from the *s*.
36: 10 the words of Jeremiah from the *s*.
36: 11 the words of the LORD from the *s*,
36: 13 read to the people from the *s*,
36: 14 went to them with the *s* in his hand.
36: 14 "Bring the *s* from which you have
36: 18 and I wrote them in ink on the *s*."
36: 20 After they put the *s* in the room
36: 21 The king sent Jehudi to get the *s*,
36: 23 read three or four columns of the *s*,
36: 23 until the entire *s* was burned
36: 25 urged the king not to burn the *s*,
36: 27 the king burned the *s* containing
36: 28 the words that were on the first *s*,
36: 28 "Take another *s* and write
36: 29 You burned that *s* and said,
36: 32 So Jeremiah took another *s*
36: 32 words of the *s* that Jehoiakim king
45: 1 on a *s* the words Jeremiah was then
51: 60 on a *s* about all the disasters that
51: 63 When you finish reading this *s*,
Eze 2: 9 In it was a *s*, which he unrolled
3: 1 eat what is before you, eat this *s*;
3: 2 and he gave me the *s* to eat.
3: 3 eat this *s* I am giving you
Da 12: 4 the words of the *s* until the time
Zec 5: 1 and there before me was a flying *s*!
5: 2 I answered, "I see a flying *s*,
Mal 3: 16 A *s* of remembrance was written
Lk 4: 17 *s* of the prophet Isaiah was handed
4: 20 he rolled up the *s*, gave it back
Heb 9: 19 sprinkled the *s* and all the people.
10: 7 it is written about me in the *s*—
Rev 1: 11 "Write on a *s* what you see
5: 1 sat on the throne a *s* with writing
5: 2 to break the seals and open the *s*?"
5: 3 under the earth could open the *s* or
5: 4 who was worthy to open the *s*
5: 5 He is able to open the *s*
5: 7 and took the *s* from the right hand
5: 9 "You are worthy to take the *s*
6: 14 The sky receded like a *s*, rolling up,
10: 2 holding a little *s*, which lay open
10: 8 take the *s* that lies open in the hand
10: 9 asked him to give me the little *s*.
10: 10 I took the little *s* from the angel's

SCROLLS (SCROLL)

Ac 19: 19 sorcery brought their *s* together
19: 19 they calculated the value of the *s*,
2Ti 4: 13 my *s*, especially the parchments.

SCULPTURED

2Ch 3: 10 Place he made a pair of *s* cherubim

SCUM

La 3: 45 You have made us *s* and refuse
1Co 4: 13 this moment we have become the *s*

SCYTHIAN

Col 3: 11 barbarian, *S*, slave or free,

SEA (SEAFARERS SEAMEN SEAS SEASHORE)

Ge 1: 21 created the great creatures of the *s*
1: 26 let them rule over the fish of the *s*
1: 28 Rule over the fish of the *s*
9: 2 and upon all the fish of the *s*;
14: 3 in the Valley of Siddim (the Salt *S*).
32: 12 descendants like the sand of the *s*,
41: 49 of grain, like the sand of the *s*;
Ex 10: 19 and carried them into the Red *S*.
13: 18 road toward the Red *S*.
14: 2 They are to encamp by the *s*,
14: 2 between Migdol and the *s*.
14: 9 near Pi Hahiroth, opposite Baal
14: 16 go through the *s* on dry ground.
14: 16 hand over the *s* to divide the water
14: 21 night the LORD drove the *s* back
14: 21 stretched out his hand over the *s*,
14: 22 went through the *s* on dry ground,
14: 23 horsemen followed them into the *s*.
14: 26 "Stretch out your hand over the *s*
14: 27 and at daybreak the *s* went back
14: 27 stretched out his hand over the *s*,
14: 27 the LORD swept them into the *s*.
14: 28 followed the Israelites into the *s*.
14: 29 went through the *s* on dry ground,
15: 1 he has hurled into the *s*.
15: 4 are drowned in the Red *S*.
15: 4 he has hurled into the *s*.
15: 8 congealed in the heart of the *s*.
15: 10 and the *s* covered them.
15: 19 and horsemen went into the *s*,
15: 19 the waters of the *s* back over them,
15: 19 through the *s* on dry ground.
15: 21 he has hurled into the *s*."
15: 22 Moses led Israel from the Red *S*
20: 11 the *s*, and all that is in them,
23: 31 borders from the Red *S* to the *S*
25: 5 skins dyed red and hides of *s* cows;
26: 14 a covering of hides of *s* cows.
35: 7 skins dyed red and hides of *s* cows;
35: 23 or hides of *s* cows brought them.
36: 19 a covering of hides of *s* cows.
39: 34 the covering of hides of *s* cows
Nu 4: 6 to cover this with hides of *s* cows,
4: 8 cover that with hides of *s* cows
4: 10 in a covering of hides of *s* cows
4: 11 and cover that with hides of *s* cows
4: 12 cover that with hides of *s* cows
4: 14 spread a covering of hides of *s* cows
4: 25 covering of hides of *s* cows,
11: 22 fish in the *s* were caught for them?"
11: 31 and drove quail in from the *s*.
13: 29 and the Canaanites live near the *s*
14: 25 along the route to the Red *S*."
21: 4 Hor along the route to the Red *S*,
33: 8 passed through the *s* into the desert
33: 10 and camped by the Red *S*.
33: 11 They left the Red *S* and camped
34: 3 start from the end of the Salt *S*,
34: 5 the Wadi of Egypt and end at the *S*.
34: 6 will be the coast of the Great *S*.
34: 7 from the Great *S* to Mount Hor
34: 11 east of the *S* of Kinnereth.
34: 12 the Jordan and end at the Salt *S*.
Dt 1: 40 along the route to the Red *S*."
2: 1 *S*, as the LORD had directed me.
3: 17 to the *S* of the Arabah (the Salt *S*),
4: 49 as far as the *S* of the Arabah,
11: 4 them with the waters of the Red *S*
11: 24 Euphrates River to the western *s*.
30: 13 it beyond the *s*, so that you have
30: 13 "Who will cross the *s* to get it
34: 2 of Judah as far as the western *s*,
Jos 1: 4 and to the Great *S* on the west.
2: 10 the water of the Red *S* for you
3: 16 Arabah (the Salt *S*) was completely
3: 16 the water flowing down to the *S*
4: 23 to the Red *S* when he dried it up
9: 1 the entire coast of the Great *S*
12: 3 Arabah from the *S* of Kinnereth
12: 3 to the *S* of the Arabah (the Salt *S*),
13: 27 to the end of the *S* of Kinnereth).
15: 2 at the southern end of the Salt *S*,
Jos 15: 4 the Wadi of Egypt, ending at the *s*.
15: 5 The eastern boundary is the Salt *S*
15: 5 from the bay of the *s* at the mouth
15: 11 The boundary ended at the *s*.
15: 12 is the coastline of the Great *S*.
15: 47 and the coastline of the Great *S*.
16: 3 and on to Gezer, ending at the *s*.
16: 6 and continued to the *s*.
16: 8 Kanah Ravine and ended at the *s*.
17: 9 of the ravine and ended at the *s*.
17: 10 of Manasseh reached the *s*
18: 19 the northern bay of the Salt *S*, at
19: 29 and came out at the *s* in the region
23: 4 and the Great *S* in the west.
24: 6 and horsemen as far as the Red *S*.
24: 6 out of Egypt, you came to the *s*,
24: 7 he brought the *s* over them
Jdg 11: 16 through the desert to the Red *S*
2Sa 22: 16 The valleys of the *s* were exposed
1Ki 5: 9 in rafts by *s* to the place you specify
5: 9 them down from Lebanon to the *s*,
7: 23 He made the *S* of cast metal,
7: 24 in two rows in one piece with the *S*.
7: 25 The *S* rested on top of them,
7: 25 The *S* stood on twelve bulls,
7: 39 He placed the *S* on the south side,
7: 44 the *S* and the twelve bulls under it;
9: 26 on the shore of the Red *S*.
9: 27 sailors who knew the *s*— to serve
10: 22 a fleet of trading ships at *s*
18: 43 "Go and look toward the *s*,"
18: 44 a man's hand is rising from the *s*."
2Ki 14: 25 to the *S* of the Arabah,
16: 17 He removed the *S*
25: 13 and the bronze *S* that were
25: 16 the *S* and the movable stands,
1Ch 16: 32 Let the *s* resound, and all that is
18: 8 used to make the bronze *S*,
2Ch 2: 16 them in rafts by *s* down to Joppa.
4: 2 He made the *S* of cast metal,
4: 3 in two rows in one piece with the *S*.
4: 4 The *S* rested on top of them,
4: 4 The *S* stood on twelve bulls,
4: 6 the *S* was to be used by the priests
4: 10 He placed the *S* on the south side,
4: 15 the *S* and the twelve bulls under it;
8: 18 own officers, men who knew the *s*.
20: 2 from the other side of the *S*.
Ezr 3: 7 logs by *s* from Lebanon to Joppa,
Ne 9: 9 you heard their cry at the Red *S*.
9: 11 You divided the *s* before them,
Job 7: 12 Am I the *s*, or the monster
9: 8 and treads on the waves of the *s*.
11: 9 and wider than the *s*.
12: 8 or let the fish of the *s* inform you.
14: 11 As water disappears from the *s*
26: 12 By his power he churned up the *s*;
28: 14 the *s* says, 'It is not with me.'
36: 30 bathing the depths of the *s*.
38: 8 "Who shut up the *s* behind doors
38: 16 journeyed to the springs of the *s*
41: 31 stirs up the *s* like a pot of ointment.
Ps 8: 8 and the fish of the *s*,
18: 15 The valleys of the *s* were exposed
33: 7 He gathers the waters of the *s*
46: 2 fall into the heart of the *s*,
66: 6 He turned the *s* into dry land,
68: 22 you from the depths of the *s*,
72: 8 He will rule from *s* to *s*
74: 13 It was you who split open the *s*
77: 19 Your path led through the *s*,
78: 13 He divided the *s* and led them
78: 53 but the *s* engulfed their enemies.
80: 11 It sent out its boughs to the *S*,
89: 9 You rule over the surging *s*;
89: 25 I will set his hand over the *s*,
93: 4 mightier than the breakers of the *s*
95: 5 The *s* is his, for he made it,
96: 11 let the *s* resound, and all that is in it
98: 7 Let the *s* resound, and everything
104: 25 There is the *s*, vast and spacious,
106: 7 and they rebelled by the *s*, the Red
106: 7 they rebelled by the sea, the Red *S*.
106: 9 He rebuked the Red *S*,
106: 22 and awesome deeds by the Red *S*.
107: 23 Others went out on the *s* in ships;
107: 29 the waves of the *s* were hushed.
114: 3 The *s* looked and fled,

Ps 114: 5 Why was it, O *s*, that you fled,
136: 13 who divided the Red *S* asunder
136: 15 his army into the Red *S*;
139: 9 if I settle on the far side of the *s*,
146: 6 the *s*, and everything in them—
148: 7 you great *s* creatures and all ocean
Pr 8: 29 when he gave the *s* its boundary
Ecc 1: 7 All streams flow into the *s*,
1: 7 yet the *s* is never full.
Isa 5: 30 like the roaring of the *s*.
9: 1 way of the *s*, along the Jordan—
10: 22 O Israel, be like the sand by the *s*,
11: 9 as the waters cover the *s*.
11: 11 and from the islands of the *s*.
11: 15 the gulf of the Egyptian *s*;
16: 8 and went as far as the *s*.
17: 12 they rage like the raging *s*!
18: 2 which sends envoys by *s*
21: 1 concerning the Desert by the *S*:
23: 4 and you, O fortress of the *s*,
23: 4 for the *s* has spoken:
23: 11 stretched out his hand over the *s*
24: 15 in the islands of the *s*.
27: 1 he will slay the monster of the *s*.
42: 10 you who go down to the *s*,
43: 16 he who made a way through the *s*,
48: 18 like the waves of the *s*.
50: 2 By a mere rebuke I dry up the *s*,
51: 10 Was it not you who dried up the *s*,
51: 10 a road in the depths of the *s*
51: 15 who churns up the *s*
57: 20 the wicked are like the tossing *s*,
63: 11 who brought them through the *s*,
Jer 5: 22 made the sand a boundary for the *s*,
6: 23 They sound like the roaring *s*
15: 8 than the sand of the *s*.
25: 22 kings of the coastlands across the *s*;
27: 19 says about the pillars, the *S*,
31: 35 who stirs up the *s*
46: 18 like Carmel by the *s*.
48: 32 branches spread as far as the *s*;
48: 32 they reached as far as the *s* of Jazer
49: 21 their cry will resound to the Red *S*.
49: 23 troubled like the restless *s*.
50: 42 They sound like the roaring *s*
51: 36 I will dry up her *s*
51: 42 The *s* will rise over Babylon;
52: 17 and the bronze *S* that were
52: 20 the *S* and the twelve bronze bulls
La 2: 13 Your wound is as deep as the *s*.
Eze 26: 3 like the *s* casting up its waves.
26: 5 Out in the *s* she will become a place
26: 12 timber and rubble into the *s*.
26: 17 peopled by men of the *s*!
26: 18 the islands in the *s*
27: 3 situated at the gateway to the *s*,
27: 9 the ships of the *s* and their sailors
27: 25 cargo in the heart of the *s*.
27: 26 pieces in the heart of the *s*.
27: 27 will sink into the heart of the *s*
27: 32 surrounded by the *s*?''
27: 34 Now you are shattered by the *s*
38: 20 The fish of the *s*, the birds of the air
39: 11 those who travel east toward the *S*.
47: 8 When it empties into the *S*,
47: 8 the Arabah, where it enters the *S*.
47: 10 like the fish of the Great *S*.
47: 15 from the Great *S* by the Hethlon
47: 17 extend from the *s* to Hazar Enan,
47: 18 to the eastern *s* and as far as Tamar.
47: 19 the Wadi ⌞of Egypt⌟ to the Great *S*.
47: 20 the Great *S* will be the boundary
48: 28 the Wadi ⌞of Egypt⌟ to the Great *S*.
Da 7: 2 of heaven churning up the great *s*.
7: 3 the others, came up out of the *s*.
Hos 4: 3 and the fish of the *s* are dying.
Joel 2: 20 columns going into the eastern *s*
2: 20 those in the rear into the western *s*.
Am 5: 8 who calls for the waters of the *s*
8: 12 Men will stagger from *s* to *s*
9: 3 from me at the bottom of the *s*,
9: 6 who calls for the waters of the *s*
Jnh 1: 4 LORD sent a great wind on the *s*,
1: 5 cargo into the *s* to lighten the ship.
1: 9 who made the *s* and the land.''
1: 11 The *s* was getting rougher
1: 11 to make the *s* calm down for us?''
1: 12 Pick me up and throw me into the *s*
Jnh 1: 13 for the *s* grew even wilder
1: 15 and the raging *s* grew calm.
Mic 7: 12 and from *s* to *s*
7: 19 iniquities into the depths of the *s*.
Na 1: 4 He rebukes the *s* and dries it up;
Hab 1: 14 have made men like fish in the *s*,
1: 14 like *s* creatures that have no ruler.
2: 14 as the waters cover the *s*.
3: 8 Did you rage against the *s*
3: 15 You trampled the *s*
Zep 1: 3 and the fish of the *s*.
2: 5 Woe to you who live by the *s*,
2: 6 by the *s*, where the Kerethites
Hag 2: 6 the earth, the *s* and the dry land.
Zec 9: 4 and destroy her power on the *s*,
9: 10 His rule will extend from *s* to *s*
10: 11 pass through the *s* of trouble;
10: 11 the surging *s* will be subdued
14: 8 eastern *s* and half to the western *s*,
Mt 4: 15 the way to the *s*, along the Jordan,
4: 18 walking beside the *S* of Galilee,
15: 29 and went along the *S* of Galilee.
18: 6 drowned in the depths of the *s*.
21: 21 'Go, throw yourself into the *s*,'
23: 15 and *s* to win a single convert,
Mk 1: 16 walked beside the *S* of Galilee,
7: 31 down to the *S* of Galilee
9: 42 him to be thrown into the *s*
11: 23 'Go, throw yourself into the *s*,'
Lk 17: 2 into the *s* with a millstone tied
17: 6 'Be uprooted and planted in the *s*,'
21: 25 at the roaring and tossing of the *s*.
Jn 6: 1 of Galilee (that is, the *S* of Tiberias
6: 1 shore of the *S* of Galilee (that is,
21: 1 to his disciples by the *S* of Tiberias.
Ac 4: 24 the heaven and the earth and the *s*,
7: 36 at the Red *S* and for forty years
10: 6 tanner, whose house is by the *s*.''
10: 32 the tanner, who lives by the *s*.'
14: 15 earth and *s* and everything in them.
16: 11 From Troas we put out to *s*
21: 1 we put out to *s* and sailed straight
27: 2 of Asia, and we put out to *s*.
27: 4 From there we put out to *s* again
27: 5 across the open *s* off the coast
27: 17 they lowered the *s* anchor
27: 27 *S*, when about midnight the sailors
27: 30 let the lifeboat down into the *s*,
27: 38 by throwing the grain into the *s*.
27: 40 they left them in the *s*
28: 4 for though he escaped from the *s*,
28: 11 out to *s* in a ship that had wintered
Ro 9: 27 Israelites be like the sand by the *s*,
1Co 10: 1 that they all passed through the *s*.
10: 2 into Moses in the cloud and in the *s*
2Co 11: 25 a night and a day in the open *s*,
11: 26 in danger at *s*; and in danger
Heb 11: 29 passed through the Red *S*
Jas 1: 6 who doubts is like a wave of the *s*,
3: 7 creatures of the *s* are being tamed
Jude : 13 They are wild waves of the *s*,
Rev 4: 6 there was what looked like a *s*
5: 13 and under the earth and on the *s*,
7: 1 or on the *s* or on any tree.
7: 2 power to harm the land and the *s*:
7: 3 "Do not harm the land or the *s*
8: 8 A third of the *s* turned into blood,
8: 8 all ablaze, was thrown into the *s*.
8: 9 of the living creatures in the *s* died,
10: 2 He planted his right foot on the *s*
10: 5 angel I had seen standing on the *s*
10: 6 and the *s* and all that is in it,
10: 8 the angel who is standing on the *s*
12: 12 But woe to the earth and the *s*,
13: 1 I saw a beast coming out of the *s*.
13: 1 stood on the shore of the *s*.
14: 7 the *s* and the springs of water.''
15: 2 And I saw what looked like a *s*
15: 2 with fire and, standing beside the *s*,
16: 3 and every living thing in the *s* died.
16: 3 angel poured out his bowl on the *s*,
18: 17 Every *s* captain, and all who travel
18: 17 all who earn their living from the *s*,
18: 19 where all who had ships on the *s*
18: 21 millstone and threw it into the *s*,
20: 13 The *s* gave up the dead that were
21: 1 and there was no longer any *s*.

SEACOAST (COAST)

Dt 1: 7 in the Negev and along the *s*,
Jos 5: 1 along the *s* heard how the LORD
Jdg 5: 17 Asher remained on the *s*
2Ch 8: 17 and Elath on the *s* of Edom.
Jer 47: 7 it to attack Ashkelon and the *s*?''
Eze 25: 16 those remaining along the *s*.
26: 16 all the princes of the *s* will step
Lk 6: 17 and from the *s* of Tyre and Sidon,

SEAFARERS (SEA)

Isa 23: 2 whom the *s* have enriched.

SEAH (SEAHS)

2Ki 7: 1 a *s* of flour will sell for a shekel
7: 16 So a *s* of flour sold for a shekel,
7: 18 a *s* of flour will sell for a shekel

SEAHS (SEAH)

Ge 18: 6 get three *s* of fine flour and knead it
1Sa 25: 18 five dressed sheep, five *s*
1Ki 18: 32 enough to hold two *s* of seed.
2Ki 7: 1 and two *s* of barley for a shekel
7: 16 and two *s* of barley sold for a shekel
7: 18 and two *s* of barley for a shekel

SEAL (SEALED SEALING SEALS)

Ge 38: 18 pledge should I give you?'' "Your *s*
38: 25 "See if you recognize whose *s*
Ex 28: 11 the way a gem cutter engraves a *s*.
28: 21 each engraved like a *s*
28: 36 and engrave on it as on a *s*:
39: 6 and engraved them like a *s*
39: 14 each engraved like a *s*
39: 30 an inscription on a *s*: HOLY
1Ki 21: 8 letters in Ahab's name, placed his *s*
Est 8: 8 and *s* it with the king's signet ring
Job 38: 14 takes shape like clay under a *s*;
Ps 40: 9 I do not *s* my lips,
SS 8: 6 Place me like a *s* over your heart,
8: 6 like a *s* over your arm;
Isa 8: 16 *s* up the law among my disciples.
Da 8: 26 but *s* up the vision, for it concerns
9: 24 to *s* up vision and prophecy
12: 4 and *s* the words of the scroll
Mt 27: 66 secure by putting a *s* on the stone
Jn 6: 27 God the Father has placed his *s*
Ro 4: 11 a *s* of the righteousness that he had
1Co 9: 2 For you are the *s* of my apostleship
2Co 1: 22 set his *s* of ownership on us,
Eph 1: 13 you were marked in him with a *s*,
Rev 6: 3 the Lamb opened the second *s*,
6: 5 When the Lamb opened the third *s*,
6: 7 the Lamb opened the fourth *s*,
6: 9 When he opened the fifth *s*,
6: 12 I watched as he opened the sixth *s*.
7: 2 having the *s* of the living God.
7: 3 until we put a *s* on the foreheads
8: 1 When he opened the seventh *s*,
9: 4 people who did not have the *s*
10: 4 "*S* up what the seven thunders
22: 10 "Do not *s* up the words

SEALED (SEAL)

Dt 32: 34 and *s* it in my vaults?
Ne 10: 1 Those who *s* it were: Nehemiah
Est 3: 12 name of King Xerxes himself and *s*
8: 8 *s* with his ring can be revoked.''
8: 10 *s* the dispatches with the king's
Job 14: 17 My offenses will be *s* up in a bag;
41: 15 tightly *s* together;
SS 4: 12 are a spring enclosed, a *s* fountain.
Isa 29: 10 He has *s* your eyes (the prophets);
29: 11 he will answer, "I can't; it is *s*.''
29: 11 whole vision is nothing but words *s*
Jer 32: 10 and *s* the deed, had it witnessed,
32: 11 the *s* copy containing the terms
32: 14 both the *s* and unsealed copies
32: 44 *s* and witnessed in the territory
Da 6: 17 king *s* it with his own signet ring
12: 9 and *s* until the time of the end.
Eph 4: 30 with whom you were *s* for the day
2Ti 2: 19 solid foundation stands firm, *s*
Rev 5: 1 on both sides and *s* with seven seals
7: 4 the number of those who were *s*:
7: 5 the tribe of Judah 12,000 were *s*,
20: 3 and locked and *s* it over him,

SEALING (SEAL)

Dt 29: 12 making with you this day and *s*

SEALS (SEAL)

Ne 9: 38 our priests are affixing their *s* to it."
Job 9: 7 he *s* off the light of the stars.
Rev 5: 1 both sides and sealed with seven *s*.
5: 2 "Who is worthy to break the *s*
5: 5 to open the scroll and its seven *s*."
5: 9 and to open its *s*,
6: 1 opened the first of the seven *s*.

SEAM (SEAMS)

Ex 28: 27 to the *s* just above the waistband
39: 20 to the *s* just above the waistband

SEAMEN (SEA)

Eze 27: 8 O Tyre, were aboard as your *s*.
27: 27 your mariners, *s* and shipwrights,
27: 28 when your *s* cry out.
27: 29 the mariners and all the *s*

SEAMLESS

Jn 19: 23 This garment was *s*, woven

SEAMS (SEAM)

Eze 27: 9 as shipwrights to caulk your *s*.

SEARCH (SEARCHED SEARCHES SEARCHING)

Ge 44: 12 Then the steward proceeded to *s*,
Dt 1: 33 to *s* out places for you to camp
Jdg 17: 8 town in *s* of some other place
1Sa 16: 16 here to *s* for someone who can play
23: 25 Saul and his men began the *s*,
26: 2 men of Israel, to *s* there for David.
2Sa 5: 17 up in full force to *s* for him,
1Ki 2: 40 to Achish at Gath in *s* of his slaves.
20: 6 send my officials to *s* your palace
1Ch 4: 39 the east of the valley in *s* of pasture
14: 8 up in full force to *s* for him,
26: 31 year of David's reign a *s* was made
2Ch 22: 9 He then went in *s* of Ahaziah,
Ezr 4: 15 so that a *s* may be made
4: 19 I issued an order and a *s* was made,
5: 17 let a *s* be made in the royal archives
Est 2: 2 a *s* be made for beautiful young
Job 3: 21 *s* for it more than for hidden
7: 21 you will *s* for me, but I will be no
10: 6 that you must *s* out my faults
Ps 4: 4 *s* your hearts and be silent.
139: 23 *S* me, O God, and know my heart;
Pr 2: 4 and *s* for it as for hidden treasure,
25: 2 to *s* out a matter is the glory
Ecc 3: 6 a time to *s* and a time to give up,
7: 25 to investigate and to *s* out wisdom
7: 29 gone in *s* of many schemes."
8: 17 Despite all his efforts to *s* it out,
SS 3: 2 I will *s* for the one my heart loves.
Isa 41: 12 Though you *s* for your enemies,
41: 17 "The poor and needy *s* for water,
Jer 5: 1 *s* through her squares.
17: 10 "I the LORD *s* the heart
50: 20 "*s* will be made for Israel's guilt,
La 1: 11 as they *s* for bread;
Eze 34: 8 because my shepherds did not *s*
34: 11 I myself will *s* for my sheep
34: 16 I will *s* for the lost and bring back
39: 14 months they will begin their *s*.
Hos 7: 10 or *s* for him.
Zep 1: 12 At that time I will *s* Jerusalem
Mt 2: 8 and make a careful *s* for the child.
2: 13 for Herod is going to *s* for the child
10: 11 *s* for some worthy person there
Lk 15: 8 and *s* carefully until she finds it?
Jn 6: 24 went to Capernaum in *s* of Jesus.
Ac 12: 19 Herod had a thorough *s* made
17: 5 rushed to Jason's house in *s* of Paul

SEARCHED (SEARCH)

Ge 31: 34 Laban *s* through everything
31: 35 So he *s* but could not find
31: 37 that you have *s* through all my
Jos 2: 22 until the pursuers had *s* all
1Sa 23: 14 Day after day Saul *s* for him,
27: 4 to Gath, he no longer *s* for him.
2Sa 17: 20 The men *s* but found no one,
1Ki 1: 3 Then they *s* throughout Israel
2Ki 2: 17 who *s* for three days but did not
Ezr 2: 62 These *s* for their family records,
6: 1 and they *s* in the archives stored
Ne 7: 64 These *s* for their family records,
Ps 139: 1 O LORD, you have *s* me
Ecc 12: 9 He pondered and *s* out
12: 10 The Teacher *s* to find just the right
Jer 31: 37 of the earth below be *s* out
La 1: 19 the city while they *s* for food
Eze 20: 6 into a land I had *s* out for them,
34: 4 not brought back the strays or *s*
34: 6 and no one *s* or looked for them.
2Ti 1: 17 he *s* hard for me until he found me.
1Pe 1: 10 *s* intently and with the greatest

SEARCHES (SEARCH)

1Ch 28: 9 for the LORD *s* every heart
Job 28: 3 he *s* the farthest recesses
28: 11 He *s* the sources of the rivers
39: 8 and *s* for any green thing.
Ps 7: 9 who *s* minds and hearts,
Pr 11: 27 but evil comes to him who *s* for it.
20: 27 The lamp of the LORD *s* the spirit
20: 27 it *s* out his inmost being.
Ro 8: 27 And he who *s* our hearts knows
1Co 2: 10 The Spirit *s* all things,
Rev 2: 23 will know that I am he who *s* hearts

SEARCHING (SEARCH)

Jdg 5: 15 there was much *s* of heart.
5: 16 there was much *s* of heart.
1Sa 27: 1 Saul will give up *s* for me anywhere
Job 32: 11 while you were *s* for words,
Ecc 7: 28 while I was still *s*
Am 8: 12 *s* for the word of the LORD,
Lk 2: 48 I have been anxiously *s* for you."
2: 49 Why were you *s* for me?" he asked.

SEARED (SEARING)

1Ti 4: 2 whose consciences have been *s*
Rev 16: 9 They were *s* by the intense heat

SEARING (SEARED)

Ps 38: 7 My back is filled with *s* pain;

SEAS (SEA)

Ge 1: 10 the gathered waters he called "*s*."
1: 22 in number and fill the water in the *s*
Lev 11: 9 living in the water of the *s*
11: 10 But all creatures in the *s*
Dt 33: 19 feast on the abundance of the *s*,
Ne 9: 6 the *s* and all that is in them.
Job 6: 3 surely outweigh the sand of the *s*—
Ps 8: 8 all that swim the paths of the *s*.
24: 2 for he founded it upon the *s*
65: 5 and of the farthest *s*,
65: 7 who stilled the roaring of the *s*,
69: 34 the *s* and all that move in them,
78: 15 them water as abundant as the *s*;
93: 3 The *s* have lifted up, O LORD,
93: 3 the *s* have lifted up their pounding
93: 3 the *s* have lifted up their voice;
135: 6 in the *s* and all their depths.
Pr 23: 34 be like one sleeping on the high *s*,
30: 19 the way of a ship on the high *s*,
Isa 60: 5 the wealth on the *s* will be brought
Eze 26: 17 You were a power on the *s*,
27: 4 Your domain was on the high *s*;
27: 26 out to the high *s*.
27: 33 merchandise went out on the *s*,
28: 2 a god in the heart of the *s*."
28: 8 death in the heart of the *s*.
32: 2 you are like a monster in the *s*
Da 11: 45 between the *s* at the beautiful holy
Jnh 2: 3 into the very heart of the *s*,

SEASHORE (SEA)

Ge 22: 17 in the sky and as the sand on the *s*.
49: 13 "Zebulun will live by the *s*
Jos 11: 4 as numerous as the sand on the *s*.
Jdg 7: 12 counted than the sand on the *s*.
1Sa 13: 5 as numerous as the sand on the *s*.
2Sa 17: 11 as numerous as the sand on the *s*—
1Ki 4: 20 as numerous as the sand on the *s*;
4: 29 as measureless as the sand on the *s*.
Ps 78: 27 flying birds like sand on the *s*.
Jer 33: 22 as measureless as the sand on the *s*
Hos 1: 10 will be like the sand on the *s*,
Heb 11: 12 as countless as the sand on the *s*.
Rev 20: 8 they are like the sand on the *s*.

SEASON (SEASONED SEASONS)

Ge 31: 10 "In breeding *s* I once had a dream
Ex 34: 21 even during the plowing *s*
Lev 2: 13 *S* all your grain offerings with salt.
26: 4 I will send you rain in its *s*,
Nu 13: 20 (It was the *s* for the first ripe grapes
Dt 11: 14 rain on your land in its *s*,
28: 12 to send rain on your land in *s*
Ezr 10: 13 people here and it is the rainy *s*;
Job 5: 26 like sheaves gathered in *s*.
6: 17 but that cease to flow in the dry *s*,
Ps 1: 3 which yields its fruit in *s*
Pr 20: 4 A sluggard does not plow in *s*;
Ecc 3: 1 a *s* for every activity under heaven:
SS 2: 12 the *s* of singing has come,
Jer 5: 24 gives autumn and spring rains in *s*,
Eze 34: 26 I will send down showers in *s*;
Mk 11: 13 because it was not the *s* for figs.
2Ti 4: 2 be prepared in *s* and out of *s*;
Tit 1: 3 at his appointed *s* he brought his

SEASONED (SEASON)

Col 4: 6 full of grace, *s* with salt,

SEASONS (SEASON)

Ge 1: 14 signs to mark *s* and days and years,
Job 38: 32 forth the constellations in their *s*
Ps 104: 19 The moon marks off the *s*,
Jer 8: 7 knows her appointed *s*,
Da 2: 21 He changes times and *s*;
Ac 14: 17 from heaven and crops in their *s*;
Gal 4: 10 and months and *s* and years!

SEAT (SEATED SEATING SEATS)

Ex 18: 13 The next day Moses took his *s*
Jdg 3: 20 As the king rose from his *s*,
1Sa 20: 18 because your *s* will be empty.
2Sa 19: 8 and took his *s* in the gateway.
1Ki 1: 46 Solomon has taken his *s*
10: 19 sides of the *s* were armrests,
21: 9 and *s* Naboth in a prominent place
21: 10 But *s* two scoundrels opposite him
2Ki 25: 28 and gave him a *s* of honor higher
2Ch 9: 18 sides of the *s* were armrests,
Est 3: 1 and giving him a *s* of honor higher
Job 29: 7 and took my *s* in the public square,
Ps 1: 1 or sit in the *s* of mockers.
Pr 9: 14 on a *s* at the highest point
31: 23 where he takes his *s*
SS 3: 10 Its *s* was upholstered with purple,
Isa 22: 23 he will be a *s* of honor for the house
Jer 52: 32 and gave him a *s* of honor higher
Da 7: 9 and the Ancient of Days took his *s*.
Mt 23: 2 and the Pharisees sit in Moses' *s*.
27: 19 Pilate was sitting on the judge's *s*,
Lk 14: 9 say to you, 'Give this man your *s*.'
Jn 19: 13 and sat down on the judge's *s*
Ro 14: 10 stand before God's judgment *s*.
2Co 5: 10 before the judgment *s* of Christ,
Jas 2: 3 "Here's a good *s* for you,"

SEATED (SEAT)

Ge 43: 33 The men had been *s* before him
Ru 4: 4 it in the presence of these *s* here
1Sa 9: 22 and *s* them at the head
22: 6 was *s* under the tamarisk tree
1Ki 16: 11 to reign and was *s* on the throne,
21: 12 and *s* Naboth in a prominent place
2Ch 23: 20 and *s* the king on the royal throne,
Ps 47: 8 God is *s* on his holy throne.
Isa 6: 1 I saw the Lord *s* on a throne,
Da 7: 10 The court was *s*,
Zec 3: 8 and your associates *s* before you,
Mk 3: 34 he looked at those *s* in a circle
Lk 22: 56 A servant girl saw him *s* there
22: 69 of Man will be *s* at the right hand
Jn 6: 11 and distributed to those who were *s*
12: 15 *s* on a donkey's colt."
20: 12 *s* where Jesus' body had been,
Ac 20: 9 *S* in a window was a young man
Eph 1: 20 and *s* him at his right hand
2: 6 and *s* us with him in the heavenly
Col 3: 1 where Christ is *s* at the right hand
Rev 4: 4 *s* on them were twenty-four elders.
11: 16 who were *s* on their thrones

Rev 14: 14 *s* on the cloud was one "like a son
14: 16 he that was *s* on the cloud swung
19: 4 and worshiped God, who was *s*
20: 4 on which were *s* those who had
20: 11 white throne and him who was *s*
21: 5 He who was *s* on the throne said,

SEATING (SEAT)

1Ki 10: 5 on his table, the *s* of his officials,
2Ch 9: 4 on his table, the *s* of his officials,

SEATS (SEAT)

1Sa 2: 8 he *s* them with princes
Ps 113: 8 he *s* them with princes,
Jer 39: 3 and took *s* in the Middle Gate:
Mt 23: 6 and the most important *s*
Mk 12: 39 and have the most important *s*
Lk 11: 43 you love the most important *s*
20: 46 and have the most important *s*

SEAWEED (WEED)

Jnh 2: 5 *s* was wrapped around my head.

SEBA

Ge 10: 7 The sons of Cush: *S*, Havilah,
1Ch 1: 9 The sons of Cush: *S*, Havilah, Sabta
Ps 72: 10 the kings of Sheba and *S*
Isa 43: 3 Cush and *S* in your stead.

SEBAM

Nu 32: 3 Nimrah, Heshbon, Elealeh, *S*,

SECACAH

Jos 15: 61 Beth Arabah, Middin, *S*, Nibshan,

SECLUSION

Lk 1: 24 and for five months remained in *s*.

SECOND-IN-COMMAND (COMMAND)

Ge 41: 43 He had him ride in a chariot as his *s*

SECRET (SECRETLY SECRETS)

Ex 7: 11 did the same things by their *s* arts:
7: 22 did the same things by their *s* arts,
8: 7 did the same things by their *s* arts;
8: 18 to produce gnats by their *s* arts,
Dt 27: 15 hands—and sets it up in *s*."
29: 29 The *s* things belong
Jdg 3: 19 "I have a *s* message for you, O king
16: 5 him into showing you the *s*
16: 6 Tell me the *s* of your great strength
16: 9 So the *s* of his strength was not
16: 15 and haven't told me the *s*
2Sa 12: 12 it in *s*, but I will do this thing
15: 10 Then Absalom sent *s* messengers
Est 2: 20 But Esther had kept *s* her family
Ps 10: 8 watching in *s* for his victims.
90: 8 our *s* sins in the light
101: 5 Whoever slanders his neighbor in *s*
139: 15 when I was made in the *s* place.
Pr 9: 17 food eaten in *s* is delicious!"
11: 13 but a trustworthy man keeps a *s*.
17: 23 A wicked man accepts a bribe in *s*
21: 14 A gift given in *s* soothes anger,
Isa 45: 3 riches stored in *s* places,
45: 19 I have not spoken in *s*,
48: 16 I have not spoken in *s*,
65: 4 spend their nights keeping *s* vigil,
Jer 13: 17 I will weep in *s*
23: 24 Can anyone hide in *s* places
Eze 28: 3 Is no *s* hidden from you?
Mt 6: 4 so that your giving may be in *s*.
6: 4 who sees what is done in *s*,
6: 6 who sees what is done in *s*,
6: 18 who sees what is done in *s*,
Mk 4: 11 "The *s* of the kingdom
7: 24 he could not keep his presence *s*.
Jn 7: 4 to become a public figure acts in *s*.
7: 10 he went also, not publicly, but in *s*.
18: 20 I said nothing in *s*.
1Co 2: 7 No, we speak of God's *s* wisdom,
4: 1 entrusted with the *s* things of God.
2Co 4: 2 we have renounced *s* and shameful
Eph 5: 12 what the disobedient do in *s*.
Php 4: 12 I have learned the *s*
2Th 2: 7 For the *s* power of lawlessness is

SECRETARIES (SECRETARY)

1Ki 4: 3 *s*; Jehoshaphat son of Ahilud—
2Ch 34: 13 Some of the Levites were *s*,
Est 3: 12 month the royal *s* were summoned.
8: 9 once the royal *s* were summoned—

SECRETARY (SECRETARIES SECRETARY'S)

2Sa 8: 17 Seraiah was *s*; Benaiah son
20: 25 Sheva was *s*; Zadok and Abiathar
2Ki 12: 10 the royal *s* and the high priest came
18: 18 palace administrator, Shebna the *s*,
18: 37 Shebna the *s* and Joah son
19: 2 Shebna the *s* and the leading
22: 3 Josiah sent the *s*, Shaphan son
22: 8 high priest said to Shaphan the *s*,
22: 9 Shaphan the *s* went to the king
22: 10 Shaphan the *s* informed the king,
22: 12 Shaphan the *s* and Asaiah
25: 19 took the *s* who was chief officer
1Ch 18: 16 Shavsha was *s*; Benaiah son
2Ch 24: 11 the royal *s* and the officer
26: 11 as mustered by Jeiel the *s*
34: 15 Hilkiah said to Shaphan the *s*,
34: 18 Shaphan the *s* informed the king,
34: 20 Shaphan the *s* and Asaiah
Ezr 4: 8 and Shimshai the *s* wrote a letter
4: 9 officer and Shimshai the *s*,
4: 17 Shimshai the *s* and the rest
4: 23 Shimshai the *s* and their associates,
Isa 36: 3 palace administrator, Shebna the *s*,
36: 22 palace administrator, Shebna the *s*,
37: 2 Shebna the *s*, and the leading
Jer 36: 10 of Gemariah son of Shaphan the *s*,
36: 12 Elishama the *s*, Delaiah son
36: 20 in the room of Elishama the *s*,
36: 21 it from the room of Elishama the *s*
37: 15 in the house of Jonathan the *s*,
37: 20 to the house of Jonathan the *s*,
52: 25 took the *s* who was chief officer

SECRETARY'S (SECRETARY)

Jer 36: 12 he went down to the *s* room

SECRETLY (SECRET)

Ge 31: 27 run off *s* and deceive me?
Dt 13: 6 or your closest friend *s* entices you,
27: 24 the man who kills his neighbor *s*."
28: 57 to eat them *s* during the siege
Jos 2: 1 Joshua son of Nun *s* sent two spies
2Sa 21: 12 (They had taken them *s*
2Ki 17: 9 The Israelites *s* did things
Job 4: 12 "A word was *s* brought to me,
13: 10 you if you *s* showed partiality.
31: 27 so that my heart was *s* enticed
Jer 38: 16 King Zedekiah swore this oath *s*
Mt 2: 7 Then Herod called the Magi *s*
Jn 19: 38 but *s* because he feared the Jews.
Ac 6: 11 they *s* persuaded some men to say,
2Pe 2: 1 They will *s* introduce destructive
Jude : 4 about long ago have *s* slipped

SECRETS (SECRET)

Job 11: 6 and disclose to you the *s* of wisdom
Ps 44: 21 since he knows the *s* of the heart?
Mt 13: 11 knowledge of the *s* of the kingdom
Lk 8: 10 knowledge of the *s* of the kingdom
Ro 2: 16 day when God will judge men's *s*
1Co 14: 25 the *s* of his heart will be laid bare.
Rev 2: 24 Satan's so-called deep *s* (I will not

SECT

Lk 5: 30 belonged to their *s* complained
Ac 24: 5 is a ringleader of the Nazarene *s*
24: 14 of the Way, which they call a *s*.
26: 5 to the strictest *s* of our religion,
28: 22 are talking against this *s*."

SECTION (SECTIONS)

2Ki 14: 13 a *s* about six hundred feet long.
2Ch 25: 23 a *s* about six hundred feet long.
Ne 3: 2 of Jericho built the adjoining *s*,
3: 4 son of Hakkoz, repaired the next *s*.
3: 5 The next *s* was repaired by the men
3: 8 repaired the next *s*; and Hananiah,
3: 9 of Jerusalem, repaired the next *s*.
3: 11 of Pahath-Moab repaired another *s*
3: 12 repaired the next *s* with the help
Ne 3: 19 ruler of Mizpah, repaired another *s*
3: 20 zealously repaired another *s*,
3: 21 son of Hakkoz, repaired another *s*,
3: 24 son of Henadad repaired another *s*,
3: 27 men of Tekoa repaired another *s*,
3: 30 son of Zalaph, repaired another *s*.
12: 24 one *s* responding to the other,
Eze 42: 3 Both in the *s* twenty cubits
42: 3 and in the *s* opposite the pavement
45: 2 a *s* 500 cubits square is to be
45: 3 measure off a *s* 25,000 cubits long

SECTIONS (SECTION)

1Ki 22: 34 of Israel between the *s* of his armor.
2Ch 18: 33 of Israel between the *s* of his armor.
32: 5 hard repairing all the broken *s*

SECU

1Sa 19: 22 and went to the great cistern at *S*.

SECUNDUS

Ac 20: 4 Aristarchus and *S*

SECURE (SECURED SECURES SECURITY)

Nu 24: 21 "Your dwelling place is *s*,
Dt 33: 12 beloved of the LORD rest *s* in him,
33: 28 Jacob's spring is *s*
Jdg 18: 7 the Sidonians, unsuspecting and *s*.
1Ki 2: 45 and David's throne will remain *s*
Job 5: 24 You will know that your tent is *s*;
11: 18 You will be *s*, because there is hope
12: 6 and those who provoke God are *s*
21: 23 completely *s* and at ease,
40: 23 he is *s*, though the Jordan should
Ps 7: 9 and make the righteous *s*.
16: 5 you have made my lot *s*.
16: 9 my body also will rest *s*,
30: 6 When I felt *s*, I said,
48: 8 God makes her *s* forever.
112: 8 His heart is *s*, he will have no fear;
122: 6 "May those who love you be *s*.
Pr 14: 26 fears the LORD has a *s* fortress,
20: 28 through love his throne is made *s*.
27: 24 a crown is not *s* for all generations.
29: 14 his throne will always be *s*
Isa 32: 9 you daughters who feel *s*,
32: 10 you who feel *s* will tremble;
32: 11 shudder, you daughters who feel *s*!
32: 18 in *s* homes,
33: 23 The mast is not held *s*,
Jer 22: 21 I warned you when you felt *s*,
Eze 34: 27 the people will be *s* in their land.
Da 8: 25 When they feel *s*, he will destroy
11: 21 the kingdom when its people feel *s*,
11: 24 When the richest provinces feel *s*,
Am 6: 1 you who feel *s* on Mount Samaria,
Zec 1: 15 angry with the nations that feel *s*.
14: 11 Jerusalem will be *s*.
Mt 27: 64 to be made *s* until the third day.
27: 65 make the tomb as *s* as you know
27: 66 made the tomb *s* by putting a seal
Ac 27: 16 able to make the lifeboat *s*.
Heb 6: 19 an anchor for the soul, firm and *s*.
2Pe 3: 17 and fall from your *s* position.

SECURED (SECURE)

2Sa 23: 5 arranged and *s* in every part?
Ac 12: 20 Having *s* the support of Blastus,

SECURES (SECURE)

Ps 140: 12 I know that the LORD *s* justice

SECURITY (SECURE)

Dt 24: 6 be taking a man's livelihood as *s*.
24: 6 the upper one—as *s* for a debt,
2Ki 20: 19 "Will there not be peace and *s*
Job 17: 3 Who else will put up *s* for me?
18: 14 He is torn from the *s* of his tent
22: 6 demanded *s* from your brothers
24: 23 may let them rest in a feeling of *s*,
31: 24 or said to pure gold, 'You are my *s*,'
Ps 122: 7 and *s* within your citadels."
Pr 6: 1 if you have put up *s*
11: 15 He who puts up *s* for another will
17: 18 and puts up *s* for his neighbor.
20: 16 of one who puts up *s* for a stranger;
22: 26 or puts up *s* for debts;

Pr 27: 13 of one who puts up *s* for a stranger;
Isa 39: 8 "There will be peace and *s*
47: 8 lounging in your *s*
Jer 30: 10 Jacob will again have peace and *s*,
33: 6 them enjoy abundant peace and *s*.
46: 27 Jacob will again have peace and *s*,

SEDITION

Ezr 4: 19 has been a place of rebellion and *s*.

SEDUCE (SEDUCED SEDUCES SEDUCTIVE)

2Pe 2: 14 stop sinning; they *s* the unstable;

SEDUCED (SEDUCE)

Pr 7: 21 she *s* him with her smooth talk.

SEDUCES (SEDUCE)

Ex 22: 16 "If a man *s* a virgin who is not

SEDUCTIVE (SEDUCE)

Pr 2: 16 the wayward wife with her *s* words,
7: 5 the wayward wife with her *s* words.

SEED (SEED-BEARING SEEDS SEEDTIME)

Ge 1: 11 on the land that bear fruit with *s*
1: 12 fruit with *s* in it according
1: 12 plants bearing *s* according
1: 29 every tree that has fruit with *s* in it.
38: 9 he spilled his *s* on the ground
47: 19 Give us *s* so that we may live
47: 23 here is *s* for you so you can plant
47: 24 other four-fifths you may keep as *s*
Ex 16: 31 It was white like coriander *s*
Lev 11: 38 But if water has been put on the *s*
19: 19 field with two kinds of *s*.
26: 16 You will plant *s* in vain,
27: 16 of silver to a homer of barley *s*.
27: 16 to the amount of *s* required for it—
Nu 11: 7 The manna was like coriander *s*
24: 7 their *s* will have abundant water.
Dt 11: 10 where you planted your *s*
22: 9 kinds of *s* in your vineyard;
28: 38 You will sow much *s* in the field
1Ki 18: 32 enough to hold two seahs of *s*.
2Ki 6: 25 of a cab of *s* pods for five shekels.
Ps 126: 6 carrying *s* to sow,
Ecc 11: 6 Sow your *s* in the morning,
Isa 5: 10 a homer of *s* only an ephah of grain
6: 13 so the holy *s* will be the stump
30: 23 also send you rain for the *s* you sow
32: 20 sowing your *s* by every stream,
55: 10 so that it yields *s* for the sower
Jer 35: 7 you must never build houses, sow *s*
Eze 17: 5 He took some of the *s* of your land
Hag 2: 19 Is there yet any *s* left in the barn?
Zec 8: 12 *s* will grow well, the vine will yield
Mt 13: 3 "A farmer went out to sow his *s*.
13: 4 As he was scattering the *s*,
13: 7 Other *s* fell among thorns,
13: 8 Still other *s* fell on good soil,
13: 19 This is the *s* sown along the path.
13: 24 is like a man who sowed good *s*
13: 27 didn't you sow good *s* in your field?
13: 31 of heaven is like a mustard *s*,
13: 37 who sowed the good *s* is the Son
13: 38 and the good *s* stands for the sons
17: 20 have faith as small as a mustard *s*,
25: 24 where you have not scattered *s*.
25: 26 gather where I have not scattered *s*
Mk 4: 3 A farmer went out to sow his *s*.
4: 4 As he was scattering the *s*,
4: 7 Other *s* fell among thorns,
4: 8 Still other *s* fell on good soil.
4: 15 Some people are like *s*
4: 16 Others, like *s* sown on rocky places
4: 18 like *s* sown among thorns,
4: 20 Others, like *s* sown on good soil,
4: 26 A man scatters *s* on the ground.
4: 27 or gets up, the *s* sprouts and grows,
4: 31 is like a mustard *s*, which is
4: 31 which is the smallest *s* you plant
Lk 8: 5 As he was scattering the *s*,
8: 5 "A farmer went out to sow his *s*.
8: 7 Other *s* fell among thorns,
8: 8 Still other *s* fell on good soil.
8: 11 of the parable: The *s* is the word
Lk 8: 14 The *s* that fell among thorns stands
8: 15 the *s* on good soil stands for those
13: 19 is like a mustard *s*, which a man
17: 6 have faith as small as a mustard *s*,
Jn 12: 24 and dies, it remains only a single *s*.
1Co 3: 6 I planted the *s*, Apollos watered it,
9: 11 If we have sown spiritual *s*
15: 37 but just a *s*, perhaps of wheat
15: 38 kind of *s* he gives its own body.
2Co 9: 10 he who supplies *s* to the sower
9: 10 supply and increase your store of *s*
Gal 3: 16 spoken to Abraham and to his *s*.
3: 16 to your *s*," meaning one person,
3: 19 of transgressions until the *S*
3: 29 then you are Abraham's *s*,
1Pe 1: 23 not of perishable *s*,
1Jn 3: 9 because God's *s* remains in him;

SEED-BEARING (SEED)

Ge 1: 11 *s* plants and trees on the land that
1: 29 I give you every *s* plant on the face

SEEDS (SEED)

Lev 11: 37 falls on any *s* that are to be planted,
Nu 6: 4 from the grapevine, not even the *s*
Isa 61: 11 and a garden causes *s* to grow,
Joel 1: 17 The *s* are shriveled
Mt 13: 32 it is the smallest of all your *s*,
Jn 12: 24 But if it dies, it produces many *s*.
Gal 3: 16 Scripture does not say "and to *s*,"

SEEDTIME (SEED)

Ge 8: 22 *s* and harvest,

SEEK (SEEKING SEEKS SELF-SEEKING SOUGHT)

Ex 18: 15 come to me to *s* God's will.
Lev 19: 18 Do not *s* revenge or bear a grudge
19: 31 turn to mediums or *s* out spiritists,
Dt 4: 29 if from there you *s* the LORD your
12: 5 to *s* the place the LORD your God
23: 6 Do not *s* peace or good relations
2Sa 17: 3 death of the man you *s* will mean
1Ki 22: 5 "First *s* the counsel of the LORD."
1Ch 16: 10 of those who *s* the LORD rejoice.
16: 11 *s* his face always.
28: 9 If you *s* him, he will be found
2Ch 7: 14 themselves and pray and *s* my face
14: 4 commanded Judah to *s* the LORD,
15: 2 If you *s* him, he will be found
15: 12 into a covenant to *s* the LORD,
15: 13 All who would not *s* the LORD,
16: 12 even in his illness he did not *s* help
18: 4 "First *s* the counsel of the LORD."
20: 4 from every town in Judah to *s* him.
20: 4 together to *s* help from the LORD;
34: 3 he began to *s* the God
Ezr 4: 2 we *s* your God and have been
6: 21 neighbors in order to *s* the LORD,
Ps 4: 2 love delusions and *s* false gods?
9: 10 never forsaken those who *s* you.
10: 4 pride the wicked does not *s* him;
14: 2 any who *s* God.
22: 26 they who *s* the LORD will praise
24: 6 of those who *s* him,
24: 6 who *s* your face, O God of Jacob.
27: 4 and to *s* him in his temple.
27: 4 this is what I *s*:
27: 8 My heart says of you, "*S* his face!"
27: 8 Your face, LORD, I will *s*.
34: 10 those who *s* the LORD lack no
34: 14 *s* peace and pursue it.
35: 4 May those who *s* my life
38: 12 Those who *s* my life set their traps,
38: 20 slander me when I *s* what is good.
40: 14 May all who *s* to take my life
40: 16 But may all who *s* you
45: 12 men of wealth will *s* your favor.
53: 2 any who *s* God.
54: 3 ruthless men *s* my life—
63: 1 earnestly I *s* you;
63: 9 They who *s* my life will be
69: 4 those who *s* to destroy me.
69: 6 may those who *s* you
69: 32 you who *s* God, may your hearts
70: 2 May those who *s* my life
70: 4 But may all who *s* you
78: 34 God slew them, they would *s* him;
Ps 83: 16 so that men will *s* your name,
104: 21 and *s* their food from God.
105: 3 of those who *s* the LORD rejoice.
105: 4 *s* his face always.
119: 2 and *s* him with all their heart.
119: 10 I *s* you with all my heart;
119:155 for they do not *s* out your decrees.
119:176 *S* your servant,
122: 9 I will *s* your prosperity.
Pr 8: 17 and those who *s* me find me.
18: 15 the ears of the wise *s* it out.
25: 27 is it honorable to *s* one's own honor
28: 5 those who *s* the LORD understand
29: 10 and *s* to kill the upright.
29: 26 Many *s* an audience with a ruler,
Isa 1: 17 *S* justice,
31: 1 or *s* help from the LORD.
45: 19 '*S* me in vain.'
51: 1 and who *s* the LORD:
55: 6 *S* the LORD while he may be
58: 2 For day after day they *s* me out;
65: 1 found by those who did not *s* me.
65: 10 for my people who *s* me.
Jer 4: 30 they *s* your life.
19: 7 the hands of those who *s* their lives,
19: 9 by the enemies who *s* their lives.'
21: 7 to their enemies who *s* their lives.
22: 25 you over to those who *s* your life,
26: 19 fear the LORD and *s* his favor?
29: 7 Also, *s* the peace and prosperity
29: 13 You will *s* me and find me
29: 13 and find me when you *s* me
34: 20 to their enemies who *s* their lives.
34: 21 to their enemies who *s* their lives,
44: 30 over to his enemies who *s* his life,
45: 5 Should you then *s* great things
45: 5 things for yourself? *S* them not.
46: 26 over to those who *s* their lives,
49: 37 before those who *s* their lives;
50: 4 in tears to *s* the LORD their God.
Eze 7: 25 terror comes, they will *s* peace,
21: 21 of the two roads, to *s* an omen:
Hos 3: 5 and *s* the LORD their God
5: 6 and herds to *s* the LORD,
5: 15 And they will *s* my face;
5: 15 misery they will earnestly *s* me."
10: 12 for it is time to *s* the LORD,
Am 5: 4 "*S* me and live;
5: 5 do not *s* Bethel,
5: 6 *S* the LORD and live,
5: 14 *S* good, not evil,
Na 3: 11 and *s* refuge from the enemy.
Zep 1: 6 and neither *s* the LORD
2: 3 *S* righteousness, *s* humility;
2: 3 *S* the LORD, all you humble
Zec 8: 21 and *s* the LORD Almighty.
8: 22 to *s* the LORD Almighty
11: 16 or *s* the young, or heal the injured,
Mal 2: 7 mouth men should *s* instruction—
Mt 6: 33 But *s* first his kingdom
7: 7 and it will be given to you; *s*
Lk 11: 9 and it will be given to you; *s*
12: 31 *s* his kingdom, and these things will
19: 10 For the Son of Man came to *s*
Jn 5: 30 for I *s* not to please myself
Ac 15: 17 remnant of men may *s* the Lord,
17: 27 this so that men would *s* him
Ro 2: 7 persistence in doing good *s* glory,
10: 20 found by those who did not *s* me;
1Co 7: 27 you married? Do not *s* a divorce.
10: 24 Nobody should *s* his own good,
Gal 2: 17 while we *s* to be justified in Christ,
Heb 11: 6 rewards those who earnestly *s* him.
1Pe 3: 11 he must *s* peace and pursue it.
Rev 9: 6 During those days men will *s* death

SEEKING (SEEK)

Jdg 14: 4 who was *s* an occasion
18: 1 tribe of the Danites was *s* a place
1Sa 22: 23 the man who is *s* your life is *s* mine
1Ki 12: 28 After *s* advice, the king made two
2Ki 16: 15 the bronze altar for *s* guidance."
1Ch 22: 19 and soul to *s* the LORD your God.
2Ch 11: 16 set their hearts on *s* the LORD,
12: 14 not set his heart on *s* the LORD.
19: 3 and have set your heart on *s* God."
30: 19 who sets his heart on *s* God—
Est 9: 2 to attack those *s* their destruction.

Ps 37: 32 *s* their very lives;
Pr 20: 18 Make plans by *s* advice;
Jer 11: 21 of Anathoth who are *s* your life
38: 4 This man is not *s* the good
38: 16 over to those who are *s* your life.''
44: 30 the enemy who was *s* his life.' ''
Mal 2: 15 Because he was *s* godly offspring.
3: 1 the Lord you are *s* will come
Mt 12: 43 it goes through arid places *s* rest
Lk 11: 24 it goes through arid places *s* rest
Jn 8: 50 I am not *s* glory for myself;
Ac 13: 11 *s* someone to lead him by the hand.
1Co 10: 33 For I am not *s* my own good

SEEKS (SEEK)

Job 39: 29 From there he *s* out his food;
Ps 86: 14 a band of ruthless men *s* my life—
Pr 11: 27 He who *s* good finds good will,
14: 6 The mocker *s* wisdom
15: 14 The discerning heart *s* knowledge,
Isa 16: 5 one who in judging *s* justice
56: 11 each *s* his own gain.
Jer 5: 1 who deals honestly and *s* the truth,
La 3: 25 to the one who *s* him;
Mt 7: 8 he who *s* finds; and to him who
Lk 11: 10 he who *s* finds; and to him who
Jn 4: 23 the kind of worshipers the Father *s*.
8: 50 but there is one who *s* it,
Ro 3: 11 no one who *s* God.

SEER (SEER'S SEERS)

1Sa 9: 9 of today used to be called a *s*.)
9: 9 ''Come, let us go to the *s*,''
9: 11 ''Is the *s* here?'' ''He is,'' they
9: 19 ''I am the *s*,'' Samuel replied.
2Sa 15: 27 Aren't you a *s*? Go back to the city
24: 11 David's *s*: ''Go and tell David,
1Ch 9: 22 of trust by David and Samuel the *s*.
21: 9 David's *s*, ''Go and tell David,
25: 5 sons of Heman the king's *s*.
26: 28 dedicated by Samuel the *s*
29: 29 and the records of Gad the *s*,
29: 29 in the records of Samuel the *s*,
2Ch 9: 29 of Iddo the *s* concerning Jeroboam
12: 15 and of Iddo the *s* that deal
16: 7 At that time Hanani the *s* came
16: 10 Asa was angry with the *s*
19: 2 Jehu the *s*, the son of Hanani,
29: 25 and Gad the king's *s* and Nathan
29: 30 words of David and of Asaph the *s*.
35: 15 Heman and Jeduthun the king's *s*.
Am 7: 12 you *s*! Go back to the land of Judah

SEER'S (SEER)

1Sa 9: 18 tell me where the *s* house is?''

SEERS (SEER)

2Ki 17: 13 through all his prophets and *s*:
2Ch 33: 18 and the words the *s* spoke to him
33: 19 written in the records of the *s*.
Isa 29: 10 he has covered your heads (the *s*).
30: 10 They say to the *s*,
Mic 3: 7 The *s* will be ashamed

SEGUB

1Ki 16: 34 at the cost of his youngest son *S*,
1Ch 2: 21 years old), and she bore him *S*.
2: 22 *S* was the father of Jair, who

SEIR

Ge 14: 6 the Horites in the hill country of *S*,
32: 3 to his brother Esau in the land of *S*,
33: 14 until I come to my lord in *S*.''
33: 16 started on his way back to *S*.
36: 8 settled in the hill country of *S*.
36: 9 Edomites in the hill country of *S*.
36: 20 These were the sons of *S* the Horite,
36: 21 of *S* in Edom were Horite chiefs.
36: 30 to their divisions, in the land of *S*.
Nu 24: 18 *S*, his enemy, will be conquered,
Dt 1: 2 by the Mount *S* road.)
1: 44 beat you down from *S* all the way
2: 1 way around the hill country of *S*.
2: 4 descendants of Esau, who live in *S*.
2: 5 given Esau the hill country of *S*
2: 8 descendants of Esau, who live in *S*.
2: 12 Horites used to live in *S*,
2: 22 lived in *S*, when he destroyed
2: 29 who live in *S*, and the Moabites,
33: 2 and dawned over them from *S*;
Jos 11: 17 Halak, which rises toward *S*,
12: 7 toward *S* (their lands Joshua gave
15: 10 westward from Baalah to Mount *S*,
24: 4 I assigned the hill country of *S*
Jdg 5: 4 when you went out from *S*,
1Ch 1: 38 The sons of *S*: Lotan, Shobal,
4: 42 invaded the hill country of *S*.
2Ch 20: 10 from Ammon, Moab and Mount *S*,
20: 22 Mount *S* who were invading Judah
20: 23 slaughtering the men from *S*,
20: 23 the men from Mount *S* to destroy
25: 11 he killed ten thousand men of *S*.
25: 14 the gods of the people of *S*.
Isa 21: 11 Someone calls to me from *S*,
Eze 25: 8 'Because Moab and *S* said, ''Look,
35: 2 set your face against Mount *S*;
35: 3 I am against you, Mount *S*,
35: 7 will make Mount *S* a desolate
35: 15 O Mount *S*, you and all of Edom.

SEIRAH

Jdg 3: 26 by the idols and escaped to *S*.

SEIZE (SEIZED SEIZES SEIZING)

Ge 43: 18 and overpower us and *s* us as slaves
Jdg 7: 24 *s* the waters of the Jordan ahead
21: 21 each of you *s* a wife from the girls
1Ki 13: 4 from the altar and said, ''*S* him!''
18: 40 commanded them, ''*S* the prophets
20: 6 They will *s* everything you value
1Ch 7: 21 went down to *s* their livestock.
Job 3: 6 night—may thick darkness *s* it;
Ps 21: 8 your right hand will *s* your foes.
71: 11 pursue him and *s* him,
109: 11 May a creditor *s* all he has;
Isa 3: 6 A man will *s* one of his brothers
5: 29 they growl as they *s* their prey
10: 6 to *s* loot and snatch plunder,
13: 8 Terror will *s* them,
21: 3 pangs *s* me, like those of a woman
Jer 12: 14 neighbors who *s* the inheritance
Eze 38: 13 goods and to *s* much plunder?'' '
Da 11: 8 *s* their gods, their metal images
11: 21 and he will *s* it through intrigue.
Am 9: 3 I will hunt them down and *s* them.
Ob : 13 nor *s* their wealth
Mic 2: 2 They covet fields and *s* them,
Hab 1: 6 to *s* dwelling places not their own.
Zec 14: 13 Each man will *s* the hand
Jn 7: 30 At this they tried to *s* him,
7: 44 Some wanted to *s* him,
10: 39 Again they tried to *s* him,
Ac 12: 3 he proceeded to *s* Peter also.

SEIZED (SEIZE)

Ge 14: 11 The four kings *s* all the goods
21: 25 that Abimelech's servants had *s*.
34: 28 They *s* their flocks and herds
Ex 15: 15 of Moab will be *s* with trembling,
Jdg 12: 6 they *s* him and killed him
16: 21 Then the Philistines *s* him,
1Sa 17: 35 turned on me, I *s* it by its hair,
2Sa 4: 10 I *s* him and put him to death
10: 4 So Hanun *s* David's men, shaved
1Ki 18: 40 let anyone get away!'' They *s* them,
21: 19 a man and *s* his property?'
2Ki 11: 16 they *s* her as she reached the place
17: 4 Therefore Shalmaneser *s* him
1Ch 5: 21 They *s* the livestock of the Hagrites
19: 4 So Hanun *s* David's men, shaved
2Ch 23: 15 So they *s* her as she reached
Est 8: 17 fear of the Jews had *s* them.
9: 3 fear of Mordecai had *s* them.
Job 4: 14 fear and trembling *s* me
16: 12 he *s* me by the neck and crushed
18: 20 men of the east are *s* with horror.
20: 19 he has *s* houses he did not build.
24: 9 the infant of the poor is *s* for a debt.
Ps 48: 6 Trembling *s* them there,
Isa 10: 10 As my hand *s* the kingdoms
Jer 26: 8 and all the people *s* him and said,
49: 24 anguish and pain have *s* her,
51: 32 the river crossings *s*,
51: 41 the boast of the whole earth *s*!
Mt 21: 35 ''The tenants *s* his servants;
22: 6 rest *s* his servants, mistreated them
26: 50 the men stepped forward, *s* Jesus
27: 3 he was *s* with remorse
Mk 12: 3 But they *s* him, beat him
14: 46 The men *s* Jesus and arrested him.
14: 51 When they *s* him, he fled naked,
Lk 8: 29 Many times it had *s* him, and
23: 26 they *s* Simon from Cyrene,
Jn 8: 20 Yet no one *s* him, because his time
Ac 4: 3 They *s* Peter and John, and
5: 5 great fear *s* all who heard what had
5: 11 Great fear *s* the whole church
6: 12 They *s* Stephen and brought him
16: 19 they *s* Paul and Silas and dragged
19: 17 they were all *s* with fear,
19: 29 people *s* Gaius and Aristarchus,
21: 27 up the whole crowd and *s* him,
23: 27 This man was *s* by the Jews
24: 6 desecrate the temple; so we *s* him.
26: 21 That is why the Jews *s* me
1Co 10: 13 No temptation has *s* you
Rev 20: 2 He *s* the dragon, that ancient

SEIZES (SEIZE)

Dt 25: 11 and *s* him by his private parts,
Job 18: 9 A trap *s* him by the heel;
21: 6 trembling *s* my body.
Ps 137: 9 he who *s* your infants
Pr 26: 17 Like one who *s* a dog by the ears
Mic 4: 9 that pain *s* you like that of a woman
Mk 9: 18 Whenever it *s* him, it throws him
Lk 9: 39 A spirit *s* him and he suddenly

SEIZING (SEIZE)

Lk 22: 54 Then *s* him, they led him away
Ac 21: 30 *S* Paul, they dragged him
Ro 7: 8 *s* the opportunity afforded
7: 11 *s* the opportunity afforded

SELA

Jdg 1: 36 was from Scorpion Pass to *S*
2Ki 14: 7 of Salt and captured *S* in battle,
Isa 16: 1 from *S*, across the desert,
42: 11 Let the people of *S* sing for joy;

SELA HAMMAHLEKOTH

1Sa 23: 28 That is why they call this place *S*.

SELAH

Ps 3:2,4,8; 4:2,4; 7:5; 9:16,20; 20:3; 21:2; 24:6,10; 32:4,5,7; 39:5,11; 44:8; 46:3,7,11; 47:4; 48:8; 49:13,15; 50:6; 52:3,5; 54:3; 55:7,19; 57:3,6; 59:5,13; 60:4; 61:4; 62:4,8; 66:4,7,15; 67:1,4; 68:7,19,32; 75:3; 76:3,9; 77:3,9,15; 81:7; 82:2; 83:8; 84:4,8; 85:2; 87:3,6; 88:7,10; 89:4,37,45,48; 140:3,5,8; 143:6; Hab 3:3,9,13

SELECT (SELECTED SELECTS)

Ex 12: 21 and *s* the animals for your families
18: 21 *s* capable men from all the people
Nu 31: 30 From the Israelites' half, *s* one out
35: 11 *s* some towns to be your cities
Est 3: 7 in the presence of Haman to *s* a day
Isa 66: 21 And I will *s* some of them

SELECTED (SELECT)

Ge 18: 7 he ran to the herd and *s* a choice,
32: 13 had with him he *s* a gift
Ex 21: 8 not please the master who has *s* her
Nu 18: 6 I myself have *s* your fellow Levites
31: 47 Moses *s* one out of every fifty
Dt 1: 23 good to me; so I *s* twelve of you,
2Sa 10: 9 so he *s* some of the best troops
2Ki 7: 14 So they *s* two chariots
1Ch 19: 10 so he *s* some of the best troops
Ezr 10: 16 Ezra the priest *s* men who were
Est 2: 9 assigned to her seven maids *s*
Heb 5: 1 Every high priest is *s*

SELECTS (SELECT)

Ex 21: 9 If he *s* her for his son, he must grant
Pr 31: 13 She *s* wool and flax
Isa 40: 20 *s* wood that will not rot.

SELED

1Ch 2: 30 The sons of Nadab: *S* and Appaim.
2: 30 *S* died without children.

SELEUCIA

Ac 13: 4 went down to *S* and sailed

SELF-ABASEMENT

Ezr 9: 5 I rose from my *s*, with my tunic

SELF-CONDEMNED (CONDEMN)

Tit 3: 11 a man is warped and sinful; he is *s*.

SELF-CONFIDENCE (CONFIDENCE)

Ne 6: 16 our enemies lost their *s*,

SELF-CONFIDENT (CONFIDENCE)

2Co 11: 17 In this *s* boasting I am not talking

SELF-CONTROL (CONTROL)

Pr 25: 28 is a man who lacks *s*.
Ac 24: 25 *s* and the judgment to come,
1Co 7: 5 you because of your lack of *s*.
Gal 5: 23 faithfulness, gentleness and *s*.
2Ti 3: 3 slanderous, without *s*, brutal,
2Pe 1: 6 and to knowledge, *s*; and to *s*,

SELF-CONTROLLED (CONTROL)

1Th 5: 6 are asleep, but let us be alert and *s*.
5: 8 let us be *s*, putting on faith and love
1Ti 3: 2 *s*, respectable, hospitable,
Tit 1: 8 who is *s*, upright, holy
2: 2 worthy of respect, *s*, and sound
2: 5 to be *s* and pure, to be busy at home
2: 6 encourage the young men to be *s*.
2: 12 to live *s*, upright and godly lives
1Pe 1: 13 prepare your minds for action; be *s*;
4: 7 and *s* so that you can pray.
5: 8 Be *s* and alert.

SELF-DISCIPLINE (DISCIPLINE)

2Ti 1: 7 a spirit of power, of love and of *s*.

SELF-IMPOSED (IMPOSE)

Col 2: 23 of wisdom, with their *s* worship,

SELF-INDULGENCE (INDULGE)

Mt 23: 25 inside they are full of greed and *s*.
Jas 5: 5 lived on earth in luxury and *s*.

SELF-SEEKING (SEEK)

Ro 2: 8 But for those who are *s*
1Co 13: 5 it is not *s*, it is not easily angered,

SELFISH

Ps 119: 36 and not toward *s* gain.
Pr 18: 1 An unfriendly man pursues *s* ends;
Gal 5: 20 fits of rage, *s* ambition, dissensions,
Php 1: 17 preach Christ out of *s* ambition,
2: 3 Do nothing out of *s* ambition
Jas 3: 14 and *s* ambition in your hearts,
3: 16 you have envy and *s* ambition,

SELL (SALE SALES SELLER SELLERS SELLING SELLS SOLD)

Ge 23: 4 *S* me some property
23: 9 Ask him to *s* it to me
23: 9 behalf so he will *s* me the cave
25: 31 "First *s* me your birthright."
37: 27 let's *s* him to the Ishmaelites
47: 16 "I will *s* you food in exchange
47: 22 is why they did not *s* their land.
Ex 21: 8 right to *s* her to foreigners,
21: 35 they are to *s* the live one
Lev 25: 14 " 'If you *s* land to one
25: 15 And he is to *s* to you on the basis
25: 37 at interest or *s* him food at a profit.
Dt 2: 28 *S* us food to eat and water to drink
14: 21 or you may *s* it to a foreigner.
21: 14 You must not *s* her or treat her
1Ki 21: 6 Naboth the Jezreelite, '*S* me your
21: 15 Jezreelite that he refused to *s* you.
2Ki 4: 7 "Go, *s* the oil and pay your debts.
7: 1 a seah of flour will *s* for a shekel
7: 18 a seah of flour will *s* for a shekel
1Ch 21: 22 *S* it to me at the full price."
Ne 10: 31 or grain to *s* on the Sabbath,
Pr 11: 26 crowns him who is willing to *s*.
23: 23 Buy the truth and do not *s* it;
Isa 50: 1 did I *s* you?
Eze 30: 12 and *s* the land to evil men;
48: 14 They must not *s* or exchange any
Joel 3: 8 I will *s* your sons and daughters
3: 8 and they will *s* them to the Sabeans
Am 2: 6 They *s* the righteous for silver,
8: 5 that we may *s* grain,
Zec 11: 5 Those who *s* them say, 'Praise
Mt 19: 21 *s* your possessions and give
25: 9 go to those who *s* oil and buy some
Mk 10: 21 *s* everything you have
Lk 12: 33 *S* your possessions and give
18: 22 *S* everything you have
22: 36 don't have a sword, *s* your cloak
Rev 13: 17 or *s* unless he had the mark,

SELLER (SELL)

Isa 24: 2 for *s* as for buyer,
Eze 7: 12 the buyer rejoice nor the *s* grieve,
7: 13 *s* will not recover the land he has

SELLERS (SELL)

Ne 13: 20 and *s* of all kinds of goods spent

SELLING (SELL)

Ge 25: 33 to him, *s* his birthright to Jacob.
45: 5 with yourselves for *s* me here,
Lev 25: 16 because what he is really *s* you is
Ru 4: 3 is *s* the piece of land that belonged
Ne 5: 8 Now you are *s* your brothers,
13: 15 them against *s* food on that day.
13: 16 *s* them in Jerusalem on the Sabbath
Am 8: 6 *s* even the sweepings
Mt 21: 12 all who were buying and *s* there.
21: 12 and the benches of those *s* doves.
Mk 11: 15 and the benches of those *s* doves,
11: 15 those who were buying and *s* there.
Lk 17: 28 buying and *s*, planting and building
19: 45 began driving out those who were *s*
Jn 2: 14 courts he found men *s* cattle,
Ac 2: 45 *S* their possessions and goods,

SELLS (SELL)

Ex 21: 7 If a man *s* his daughter as a servant,
21: 16 kidnaps another and either *s* him
22: 1 or a sheep and slaughters it or *s* it,
Lev 25: 25 and *s* some of his property,
25: 29 If a man *s* a house in a walled city,
25: 39 among you and *s* himself to you,
25: 47 and *s* himself to the alien living
Dt 24: 7 and treats him as a slave or *s* him,
Pr 31: 24 makes linen garments and *s* them,

SEMAKIAH

1Ch 26: 7 his relatives Elihu and *S* were

SEMEIN

Lk 3: 26 the son of Mattathias, the son of *S*,

SEMEN

Lev 15: 16 When a man has an emission of *s*,
15: 17 or leather that has *s* on it must be
15: 18 and there is an emission of *s*,
15: 32 unclean by an emission of *s*,
22: 4 by anyone who has an emission of *s*

SENAAH

Ezr 2: 35 Ono 725 of Jericho 345 of *S* 3,630
Ne 7: 38 Hadid and Ono 721 of *S* 3,930

SEND (SENDING SENDS SENT)

Ge 7: 4 from now I will *s* rain on the earth
24: 7 he will *s* his angel before you
24: 40 will *s* his angel with you
24: 54 "*S* me on my way to my master."
24: 56 *S* me on my way so I may go
27: 45 I'll *s* word for you to come back
30: 25 "*S* me on my way so I can go back
31: 27 so I could *s* you away with joy
37: 13 I am going to *s* you to them."
38: 17 as a pledge until you *s* it?"
38: 17 "I'll *s* you a young goat
38: 23 After all, I did *s* her this young goat
42: 4 But Jacob did not *s* Benjamin,
42: 16 *S* one of your number
43: 4 If you will *s* our brother
43: 5 if you will not *s* him, we will not go
43: 8 "*S* the boy along with me
Ex 4: 13 please *s* someone else to do it."
8: 21 I will *s* swarms of flies on you
9: 14 or this time I will *s* the full force
Ex 9: 18 tomorrow I will *s* the worst
23: 27 "I will *s* my terror ahead of you
23: 28 I will *s* the hornet ahead of you
33: 2 I will *s* an angel before you
33: 12 not let me know whom you will *s*
33: 15 with us, do not *s* us up from here.
Lev 16: 21 He shall *s* the goat away
25: 21 I will *s* you such a blessing
26: 4 I will *s* you rain in its season,
26: 22 I will *s* wild animals against you,
26: 25 I will *s* a plague among you,
Nu 5: 2 "Command the Israelites to *s* away
5: 3 *S* away male and female alike;
5: 3 *s* them outside the camp
13: 2 From each ancestral tribe *s* one
13: 2 "*S* some men to explore the land
22: 37 Did I not *s* you an urgent summons
31: 4 *S* into battle a thousand men
35: 25 and *s* him back to the city of refuge
Dt 1: 22 "Let us *s* men ahead
7: 20 LORD your God will *s* the hornet
11: 14 then I will *s* rain on your land
15: 13 do not *s* him away empty-handed.
19: 12 elders of his town shall *s* for him,
28: 8 The LORD will *s* a blessing
28: 12 to *s* rain on your land in season
28: 20 The LORD will *s* on you curses,
28: 59 the LORD will *s* fearful plagues
28: 68 The LORD will *s* you back in ships
32: 24 I will *s* against them the fangs
32: 24 I will *s* wasting famine
Jos 1: 16 and wherever you *s* us we will go.
7: 3 *S* two or three thousand men
18: 4 I will *s* them out to make a survey
Jdg 20: 38 that they should *s* up a great
1Sa 5: 11 *S* the ark of the god of Israel away;
6: 2 Tell us how we should *s* it back
6: 3 but by all means *s* a guilt offering
6: 3 of Israel, do not *s* it away empty,
6: 4 "What guilt offering should we *s*
6: 6 did they not *s* the Israelites out
6: 8 *S* it on its way, but keep watching it
9: 16 time tomorrow I will *s* you a man
9: 26 and I will *s* you on your way."
11: 3 days so we can *s* messengers
12: 17 call upon the LORD to *s* thunder
16: 11 "*S* for him; we will not sit
16: 19 and said, "*S* me your son David,
19: 17 and *s* my enemy away so that he
20: 12 will I not *s* you word and let you
20: 13 you know and *s* you away safely.
20: 21 Then I will *s* a boy and say, 'Go,
20: 31 Now *s* and bring him to me,
29: 4 and said, "*S* the man back,
2Sa 11: 6 to Joab: "*S* me Uriah the Hittite."
11: 12 and tomorrow I will *s* you back."
13: 9 "*S* everyone out of here," Amnon
14: 29 Joab in order to *s* him to the king,
14: 32 here so I can *s* you to the king
15: 36 *S* them to me with anything you
17: 16 Now *s* a message immediately
18: 29 about to *s* the king's servant
19: 31 and to *s* him on his way from there.
1Ki 8: 36 *s* rain on the land you gave your
8: 44 enemies, wherever you *s* them,
18: 1 and I will *s* rain on the land."
20: 6 to *s* my officials to search your
22: 26 and *s* him back to Amon the ruler
2Ki 2: 16 Elisha replied, "do not *s* them."
2: 17 So he said, "*S* them."
4: 22 "Please *s* me one of the servants
5: 5 "I will *s* a letter to the king of Israel
5: 7 Why does this fellow *s* someone
6: 13 "so I can *s* men and capture him."
7: 13 So let us *s* them to find out what
9: 17 "*S* him to meet them and ask,
15: 37 began to *s* Rezin king of Aram
1Ch 13: 2 let us *s* word far and wide
2Ch 2: 3 "*S* me cedar logs as you did
2: 7 sacrifices before him? "*S* me,
2: 8 "*S* me also cedar, pine
2: 15 let my lord *s* his servants the wheat
6: 27 *s* rain on the land you gave your
6: 34 enemies, wherever you *s* them,
7: 13 or *s* a plague among my people,
18: 25 and *s* him back to Amon the ruler
28: 11 *S* back your fellow countrymen
30: 5 They decided to *s* a proclamation

Ezr 5:17 Then let the king *s* us his decision
10:3 God to *s* away all these women
Ne 2:5 let him *s* me to the city
2:6 It pleased the king to *s* me;
8:10 *s* some to those who have nothing
8:12 to *s* portions of food
Job 1:5 Job would *s* and have them purified
14:20 his countenance and *s* him away.
21:11 They *s* forth their children
38:35 Do you *s* the lightning bolts
Ps 20:2 May he *s* you help
43:3 *S* forth your light and your truth,
104:30 When you *s* your Spirit,
144:6 *S* forth lightning and scatter
Pr 10:26 so is a sluggard to those who *s* him.
24:22 those two will *s* sudden destruction
25:13 messenger to those who *s* him;
SS 7:13 mandrakes *s* out their fragrance,
Isa 6:8 *S* me!" He said, "Go and tell this
6:8 "Whom shall I *s?* And who will go
10:6 I *s* him against a godless nation,
10:16 will *s* a wasting disease
16:1 *S* lambs as tribute
19:20 he will *s* them a savior
30:23 also *s* you rain for the seed you sow
34:3 their dead bodies will *s* up a stench;
42:19 and deaf like the messenger I *s?*
42:22 with no one to say, "*S* them back."
43:14 "For your sake I will *s* to Babylon
48:20 *S* it out to the ends of the earth;
66:19 I will *s* some of those who survive
Jer 1:7 You must go to everyone I *s* you to
2:10 *s* to Kedar and observe closely;
8:17 I will *s* venomous snakes
9:17 *s* for the most skillful of them.
14:3 The nobles *s* their servants
14:15 I did not *s* them, yet they are
14:22 Do the skies themselves *s*
15:1 *S* them away from my presence!
15:3 "I will *s* four kinds of destroyers
16:16 After that I will *s* for many hunters,
16:16 now I will *s* for many fishermen,"
22:7 I will *s* destroyers against you,
23:21 I did not *s* these prophets,
23:32 yet I did not *s* or appoint them.
24:10 I will *s* the sword, famine
25:15 nations to whom I *s* you drink it.
25:16 of the sword I will *s* among them."
25:27 of the sword I will *s* among you.'
27:3 Then *s* word to the kings of Edom,
29:17 Almighty says: "I will *s* the sword,
29:31 even though I did not *s* him,
29:31 "*S* this message to all the exiles:
37:20 Do not *s* me back to the house
38:26 with the king not to *s* me back
43:10 I will *s* for my servant
48:12 "when I will *s* men who pour
51:2 I will *s* foreigners to Babylon
51:27 *s* up horses like a swarm of locusts.
51:53 I will *s* destroyers against her,"
Eze 5:17 I will *s* famine and wild beasts
13:11 I will *s* hailstones hurtling down,
14:13 *s* famine upon it and kill its men
14:15 I *s* wild beasts through that country
14:19 "Or if I *s* a plague into that land
14:21 when I *s* against Jerusalem my four
28:23 I will *s* a plague upon her
34:26 I will *s* down showers in season;
39:2 and *s* you against the mountains
39:6 I will *s* fire on Magog
Da 11:20 "His successor will *s* out a tax
Hos 8:14 But I will *s* fire upon their cities
14:5 he will *s* down his roots;
Joel 3:6 that you might *s* them far
Am 1:4 I will *s* fire upon the house
1:7 I will *s* fire upon the walls of Gaza
1:10 I will *s* fire upon the walls of Tyre
1:12 I will *s* fire upon Teman
2:2 I will *s* fire upon Moab
2:5 I will *s* fire upon Judah
5:27 Therefore I will *s* you into exile
8:11 "when I will *s* a famine
Zec 5:4 Almighty declares, 'I will *s* it out,
Mal 2:2 "I will *s* a curse upon you,
3:1 "See, I will *s* my messenger,
4:5 I will *s* you the prophet Elijah
Mt 8:31 *s* us into the herd of pigs."
9:38 to *s* out workers into his harvest
Mt 11:10 I will *s* my messenger ahead of you,
13:41 Son of Man will *s* out his angels,
14:15 *S* the crowds away, so they can go
15:23 and urged him, "*S* her away,
15:32 want to *s* them away hungry,
19:7 of divorce and *s* her away?"
21:3 and he will *s* them right away."
24:31 And he will *s* his angels
Mk 1:2 I will *s* my messenger ahead of you,
3:14 that he might *s* them out to preach
5:10 again not to *s* them out of the area.
5:12 The demons begged Jesus, "*S* us
6:36 *S* the people away so they can go
8:3 If I *s* them home hungry, they will
10:4 of divorce and *s* her away."
11:3 and will *s* it back here shortly.' "
12:6 "He had one left to *s*, a son,
13:27 And he will *s* his angels
Lk 7:27 I will *s* my messenger ahead of you,
9:12 "*S* the crowd away so they can go
10:2 to *s* out workers into his harvest
11:49 I will *s* them prophets and apostles,
14:32 he will *s* a delegation
16:24 *s* Lazarus to dip the tip of his finger
16:27 *s* Lazarus to my father's house,
20:13 I will *s* my son, whom I love;
24:49 going to *s* you what my Father has
Jn 3:17 For God did not *s* his Son
13:20 accepts anyone I *s* accepts me;
14:26 whom the Father will *s* in my name
15:26 whom I will *s* to you
16:7 but if I go, I will *s* him to you.
Ac 3:20 and that he may *s* the Christ,
7:34 I will *s* you back to Egypt.'
7:37 'God will *s* you a prophet like me
7:43 Therefore I will *s* you into exile'
10:5 *s* men to Joppa to bring back a man
10:32 *S* to Joppa for Simon who is called
11:13 '*S* to Joppa for Simon who is called
15:22 and *s* them to Antioch with Paul
15:25 *s* them to you with our dear friends
22:21 I will *s* you far away to the Gentiles
24:25 When I find it convenient, I will *s*
25:21 held until I could *s* him to Caesar."
25:25 to the Emperor I decided to *s* him
25:27 For I think it is unreasonable to *s*
Ro 16:16 the churches of Christ *s* greetings.
16:23 and our brother Quartus *s* you their
1Co 1:17 For Christ did not *s* me to baptize,
16:3 *s* them with your gift to Jerusalem.
16:11 *S* him on his way in peace
16:19 province of Asia *s* you greetings.
16:20 the brothers here *s* you greetings.
2Co 1:16 then to have you *s* me on my way
13:13 All the saints *s* their greetings.
Php 2:19 Jesus to *s* Timothy to you soon,
2:23 to *s* him as soon as I see how things
2:25 to *s* back to you Epaphroditus,
2:28 I am all the more eager to *s* him,
4:21 are with me *s* greetings.
4:22 All the saints *s* you greetings,
Col 4:14 the doctor, and Demas *s* greetings.
Tit 3:12 As soon as I *s* Artemas
Heb 13:24 from Italy *s* you their greetings.
2Jn :13 your chosen sister *s* their greetings.
3Jn :6 well to *s* them on their way
:14 The friends here *s* their greetings.
Rev 1:11 and *s* it to the seven churches:

SENDING (SEND)

Ge 32:5 Now I am *s* this message to my lord
32:20 with these gifts I am *s* on ahead;
Ex 3:10 I am *s* you to Pharaoh
23:20 I am *s* an angel ahead of you
Lev 16:10 used for making atonement by *s* it
Jdg 6:14 Am I not *s* you?" "But Lord,"
1Sa 6:8 put the gold objects you are *s* back
16:1 I am *s* you to Jesse of Bethlehem.
2Sa 10:3 *s* men to you to express sympathy?
13:16 "*S* me away would be a greater
1Ki 15:19 I am *s* you a gift of silver and gold.
2Ki 1:6 God in Israel that you are *s* men
5:6 letter I am *s* my servant Naaman
6:32 see how this murderer is *s* someone
1Ch 19:3 *s* men to you to express sympathy?
2Ch 2:13 "I am *s* you Huram-Abi, a man
16:3 See, I am *s* you silver and gold.
Ezr 4:14 we are *s* this message
Ne 6:17 nobles of Judah were *s* many letters
Pr 26:6 is the *s* of a message by the hand
Jer 42:6 to whom we are *s* you,
Eze 2:3 I am *s* you to the Israelites,
2:4 to whom I am *s* you are obstinate
17:15 against him by *s* his envoys
Joel 2:13 and he relents from *s* calamity.
2:19 I am *s* you grain, new wine and oil,
Jnh 4:2 a God who relents from *s* calamity.
Mt 10:16 "I am *s* you out like sheep
23:34 Therefore I am *s* you prophets
Lk 10:3 I am *s* you out like lambs
Jn 20:21 Father has sent me, I am *s* you."
Ac 11:30 *s* their gift to the elders
15:27 Therefore we are *s* Judas
26:17 I am *s* you to open their eyes
Ro 8:3 God did by *s* his own Son
1Co 4:17 For this reason I am *s*
2Co 8:18 we are *s* along with him the brother
8:22 we are *s* with them our brother who
9:3 But I am *s* the brothers
Eph 6:22 I am *s* him to you for this very
Col 4:8 I am *s* him to you for the express
Phm :12 I am *s* him—who is my very heart
Rev 1:1 He made it known by *s* his angel
11:10 will celebrate by *s* each other gifts,

SENDS (SEND)

Dt 24:1 it to her and *s* her from his house,
24:3 it to her and *s* her from his house,
28:48 will serve the enemies the LORD *s*
1Sa 2:7 The LORD *s* poverty and wealth;
Job 5:10 he *s* water upon the countryside.
12:24 he *s* them wandering
37:3 and *s* it to the ends of the earth.
Ps 57:3 God *s* his love and his faithfulness.
57:3 He *s* from heaven and saves me,
135:7 he *s* lightning with the rain
147:15 He *s* his command to the earth;
147:18 He *s* his word and melts them;
Isa 18:2 which *s* envoys by sea
Jer 10:13 He *s* lightning with the rain
17:8 that *s* out its roots by the stream.
42:5 the LORD your God *s* you
51:16 He *s* lightning with the rain
Hos 12:1 and *s* olive oil to Egypt.
Joel 2:23 He *s* you abundant showers,
Zec 12:2 a cup that *s* all the surrounding
Mt 5:45 and *s* rain on the righteous
Ro 16:21 my fellow worker, *s* his greetings
16:23 church here enjoy, *s* you his
Col 4:10 prisoner Aristarchus *s* you his
4:11 is called Justus, also *s* greetings.
4:12 servant of Christ Jesus, *s* greetings.
2Th 2:11 this reason God *s* them a powerful
Tit 3:15 Everyone with me *s* you greetings.
Phm :23 for Christ Jesus, *s* you greetings.
1Pe 5:13 with you, *s* you her greetings,

SENEH

1Sa 14:4 was called Bozez, and the other *S.*

SENIR

Dt 3:9 Sidonians; the Amorites call it *S.)*
1Ch 5:23 that is, to *S* (Mount Hermon).
SS 4:8 from the top of *S*, the summit
Eze 27:5 timbers of pine trees from *S;*

SENNACHERIB (SENNACHERIB'S)

2Ki 18:13 *S* king of Assyria attacked all
19:9 *S* received a report that Tirhakah,
19:16 listen to the words *S* has sent
19:20 your prayer concerning *S* king
19:36 So *S* king of Assyria broke camp
2Ch 32:1 *S* king of Assyria came
32:2 Hezekiah saw that *S* had come
32:9 when *S* king of Assyria
32:10 This is what *S* king of Assyria says:
32:22 from the hand of *S* king of Assyria
Isa 36:1 *S* king of Assyria attacked all
37:9 *S* received a report that Tirhakah,
37:17 listen to all the words *S* has sent
37:21 to me concerning *S* king of Assyria
37:37 So *S* king of Assyria broke camp

SENNACHERIB'S (SENNACHERIB)

2Ch 32:16 *S* officers spoke further

SENSE (SENSED SENSES SENSIBLE SENSITIVE SENSITIVITY)

Dt 32: 28 They are a nation without *s*,
Job 39: 17 or give her a share of good *s*.
Ecc 10: 3 the fool lacks *s*
1Co 12: 17 where would the *s* of hearing be?
12: 17 where would the *s* of smell be?

SENSED (SENSE)

Ac 27: 27 midnight the sailors *s* they were

SENSELESS

Ps 49: 10 the foolish and the *s* alike perish
73: 22 I was *s* and ignorant;
92: 6 The *s* man does not know,
94: 8 you *s* ones among the people;
Isa 19: 11 of Pharaoh give *s* advice.
Jer 4: 22 They are *s* children;
5: 21 Hear this, you foolish and *s* people,
10: 8 They are all *s* and foolish;
10: 14 Everyone is *s*
10: 21 The shepherds are *s*
51: 17 "Every man is *s*
Hos 7: 11 easily deceived and *s*—
Ro 1: 31 they are *s*, faithless, heartless,

SENSES (SENSE)

Lk 15: 17 "When he came to his *s*, he said,
1Co 15: 34 Come back to your *s* as you ought,
2Ti 2: 26 and that they will come to their *s*

SENSIBLE (SENSE)

Job 18: 2 Be *s*, and then we can talk.
1Co 10: 15 I speak to *s* people; judge

SENSITIVE (SENSE)

Dt 28: 54 and *s* man among you will have no
28: 56 and *s* woman among you—
28: 56 so *s* and gentle that she would not

SENSITIVITY (SENSE)

Eph 4: 19 Having lost all *s*, they have given

SENSUAL (SENSUALITY)

Col 2: 23 value in restraining *s* indulgence.
1Ti 5: 11 For when their *s* desires overcome

SENSUALITY (SENSUAL)

Eph 4: 19 have given themselves over to *s*

SENT (SEND)

Ge 2: 5 the LORD God had not *s* rain
8: 1 and he *s* a wind over the earth
8: 7 made in the ark and *s* out a raven,
8: 8 Then he *s* out a dove to see
8: 10 again *s* out the dove from the ark.
8: 12 seven more days and *s* the dove out
12: 20 and they *s* him on his way,
19: 13 is so great that he has *s* us
20: 2 king of Gerar *s* for Sarah
21: 14 and then *s* her off with the boy.
24: 59 So they *s* their sister Rebekah
25: 6 and *s* them away from his son Isaac
26: 27 hostile to me and *s* me away?"
26: 29 treated you well and *s* you away
26: 31 Then Isaac *s* them on their way,
27: 42 she *s* for her younger son Jacob
28: 5 Then Isaac *s* Jacob on his way,
28: 6 and had *s* him to Paddan Aram
31: 4 So Jacob *s* word to Rachel
31: 42 would surely have *s* me away
32: 3 Jacob *s* messengers ahead of him
32: 18 They are a gift *s* to my lord Esau,
32: 23 After he had *s* them
32: 23 he *s* over all his possessions.
37: 14 So he *s* him off from the Valley
38: 20 Meanwhile Judah *s* the young goat
38: 25 she *s* a message to her father-in-law
41: 8 so he *s* for all the magicians
41: 14 So Pharaoh *s* for Joseph,
44: 3 the men were *s* on their way
45: 5 to save lives that God *s* me ahead
45: 7 God *s* me ahead of you to preserve
45: 8 it was not you who *s* me here,
45: 23 And this is what he *s* to his father:
45: 24 Then he *s* his brothers away,
45: 27 when he saw the carts Joseph had *s*
46: 5 in the carts that Pharaoh had *s*
46: 28 Now Jacob *s* Judah ahead of him
50: 16 So they *s* word to Joseph, saying,
Ex 2: 5 and *s* her slave girl to get it.
3: 12 to you that it is I who have *s* you:
3: 13 of your fathers has *s* me to you,'
3: 14 to the Israelites: 'I AM has *s* me
3: 15 the God of Jacob—has *s* me to you
4: 28 everything the LORD had *s* him
5: 22 this people? Is this why you *s* me?
7: 16 of the Hebrews, has *s* me to say
9: 7 Pharaoh *s* men to investigate
9: 23 the LORD *s* thunder and hail,
18: 2 After Moses had *s* away his wife
18: 6 Jethro had *s* word to him, "I,
18: 27 Then Moses *s* his father-in-law
24: 5 Then he *s* young Israelite men,
36: 6 *s* this word throughout the camp:
Lev 26: 41 them so that I *s* them into the land
Nu 5: 4 they *s* them outside the camp.
13: 3 command Moses *s* them out
13: 16 the names of the men Moses *s*
13: 17 When Moses *s* them
13: 27 into the land to which you *s* us,
14: 36 So the men Moses had *s*
16: 28 will know that the LORD has *s* me
16: 29 then the LORD has not *s* me.
20: 14 Moses *s* messengers from Kadesh
20: 16 he heard our cry and *s* an angel
21: 6 the LORD *s* venomous snakes
21: 21 Israel *s* messengers to say
21: 32 After Moses had *s* spies to Jazer,
22: 5 *s* messengers to summon Balaam
22: 10 king of Moab, *s* me this message:
22: 15 Then Balak *s* other princes,
24: 12 I not tell the messengers you *s* me,
31: 6 Moses *s* them into battle,
32: 8 I *s* them from Kadesh Barnea
Dt 2: 26 desert of Kedemoth I *s* messengers
6: 22 eyes the LORD *s* miraculous signs
9: 23 And when the LORD *s* you out
24: 5 he must not be *s* to war
34: 11 wonders the LORD *s* him to do
Jos 2: 1 son of Nun secretly *s* two spies
2: 3 the king of Jericho *s* this message
2: 21 she *s* them away and they departed
6: 17 because she hid the spies we *s*.
6: 25 she hid the men Joshua had *s*
7: 2 Joshua *s* men from Jericho to Ai,
7: 22 So Joshua *s* messengers,
8: 3 and *s* them out at night
8: 9 Then Joshua *s* them off,
10: 6 The Gibeonites then *s* word
11: 1 he *s* word to Jobab king of Madon,
14: 7 *s* me from Kadesh Barnea
14: 11 as the day Moses *s* me out;
22: 6 blessed them and *s* them away,
22: 7 When Joshua *s* them home,
22: 13 So the Israelites *s* Phinehas son
22: 14 With him they *s* ten
24: 5 " 'Then I *s* Moses and Aaron,
24: 9 he *s* for Balaam son of Beor
24: 12 I *s* the hornet ahead of you,
24: 28 Then Joshua *s* the people away,
Jdg 1: 23 When they *s* men to spy out Bethel
3: 15 The Israelites *s* him with tribute
3: 18 he *s* on their way the men who had
4: 6 She *s* for Barak son of Abinoam
6: 8 he *s* them a prophet, who said,
6: 35 He *s* messengers
7: 8 Gideon *s* the rest of the Israelites
7: 24 Gideon *s* messengers
9: 23 God *s* an evil spirit
9: 31 Under cover he *s* messengers
11: 12 Then Jephthah *s* messengers
11: 14 Jephthah *s* back messengers
11: 17 Israel *s* messengers to the king
11: 17 They *s* also to the king of Moab,
11: 19 Israel *s* messengers to Sihon king
11: 28 to the message Jephthah *s* him.
13: 8 man of God you *s* to us come again
16: 18 she *s* word to the rulers
18: 2 So the Danites *s* five warriors
19: 25 man took his concubine and *s* her
19: 29 *s* them into all the areas of Israel.
20: 6 and *s* one piece to each region
20: 12 The tribes of Israel *s* men
21: 10 So the assembly *s* twelve thousand
21: 13 the assembly *s* an offer of peace
1Sa 4: 4 So the people *s* men to Shiloh,
4: 13 the whole town *s* up a cry.
5: 10 So they *s* the ark of God to Ekron.
6: 17 the gold tumors the Philistines *s*
6: 21 they *s* messengers to the people
11: 7 and *s* the pieces by messengers
12: 8 and the LORD *s* Moses and Aaron
12: 11 Then the LORD *s* Jerub-Baal,
12: 18 that same day the LORD *s* thunder
13: 2 of the men he *s* back to their homes
14: 15 It was a panic *s* by God.
15: 1 "I am the one the LORD *s*
15: 18 And he *s* you on a mission, saying,
16: 12 So he *s* and had him brought in.
16: 19 Then Saul *s* messengers to Jesse
16: 20 *s* them with his son David to Saul.
16: 22 Then Saul *s* word to Jesse, saying,
17: 31 reported to Saul, and Saul *s* for him
18: 5 Whatever Saul *s* him to do,
18: 13 So he *s* David away from him
19: 11 Saul *s* men to David's house
19: 14 When Saul *s* the men
19: 15 Saul *s* the men back to see David
19: 20 so he *s* men to capture him.
19: 21 Saul *s* men a third time, and they
19: 21 and he *s* more men, and they
20: 22 because the LORD has *s* you away.
22: 11 king *s* for the priest Ahimelech son
25: 5 So he *s* ten young men
25: 14 "David *s* messengers
25: 25 I did not see the men my master *s*.
25: 32 who has *s* you today to meet me.
25: 39 Then David *s* word to Abigail,
25: 40 "David has *s* us to you to take you
26: 4 he *s* out scouts and learned that
30: 26 he *s* some of the plunder
30: 27 He *s* it to those who were in Bethel,
31: 9 and they *s* messengers
2Sa 2: 5 *s* messengers to the men of
3: 12 Abner *s* messengers on his behalf
3: 14 Then David *s* messengers
3: 21 So David *s* Abner away,
3: 22 because David had *s* him away,
3: 23 and that the king had *s* him away
3: 26 and *s* messengers after Abner,
5: 11 of Tyre *s* messengers to David,
8: 10 he *s* his son Joram to King David
10: 2 So David *s* a delegation
10: 3 Hasn't David *s* them to you
10: 4 at the buttocks, and *s* them away.
10: 5 he *s* messengers to meet the men,
10: 7 David *s* Joab out with the entire
11: 1 David *s* Joab out with the king's
11: 3 David *s* someone to find out about
11: 4 David *s* messengers to get her.
11: 5 The woman conceived and *s* word
11: 6 And Joab *s* him to David.
11: 6 So David *s* this word to Joab:
11: 8 a gift from the king was *s* after him.
11: 14 a letter to Joab and *s* it with Uriah.
11: 18 Joab *s* David a full account
11: 22 David everything Joab had *s* him
12: 1 The LORD *s* Nathan to David.
12: 25 he *s* word through Nathan
12: 27 Joab then *s* messengers to David,
13: 7 David *s* word to Tamar
13: 27 so he *s* with him Amnon
14: 2 So Joab *s* someone to Tekoa
14: 29 So he *s* a second time,
14: 29 Then Absalom *s* for Joab in order
14: 32 "Look, I *s* word to you and said,
15: 10 Then Absalom *s* secret messengers
15: 12 also *s* for Ahithophel the Gilonite,
18: 2 David *s* the troops out—a third
19: 11 King David *s* this message
19: 14 They *s* word to the king, "Return,
24: 13 I should answer the one who *s* me."
24: 15 So the LORD *s* a plague on Israel
1Ki 1: 44 The king has *s* with him Zadok
1: 53 Then King Solomon *s* men,
2: 36 Then the king *s* for Shimei
4: 34 *s* by all the kings of the world,
5: 1 he *s* his envoys to Solomon,
5: 2 Solomon *s* back this message
5: 8 So Hiram *s* word to Solomon:
5: 8 received the message you *s* me
5: 14 He *s* them off to Lebanon in shifts
7: 13 King Solomon *s* to Tyre

1Ki 8:66 following day he *s* the people away.
9:14 Hiram had *s* to the king 120 talents
9:27 Hiram *s* his men—sailors who
12: 3 So they *s* for Jeroboam, and he
12:18 King Rehoboam *s* out Adoniram,
12:20 they *s* and called him
14: 6 I have been *s* to you with bad news.
15:18 and *s* them to Ben-Hadad son
15:20 and *s* the commanders of his forces
18:10 my master has not *s* someone
18:20 Ahab *s* word throughout all Israel
19: 2 So Jezebel *s* a messenger to Elijah
20: 2 He *s* messengers into the city
20: 5 'I *s* to demand your silver and gold,
20: 7 When he *s* for my wives
20:10 Ben-Hadad *s* another message
21: 8 and *s* them to the elders
21:14 Then they *s* word to Jezebel:
2Ki 1: 2 So he *s* messengers, saying to them
1: 6 'Go back to the king who *s* you
1: 9 Then he *s* to Elijah a captain
1:11 At this the king *s* to Elijah another
1:13 So the king *s* a third captain
1:16 consult that you have *s* messengers
2: 2 the LORD has *s* me to Bethel."
2: 4 the LORD has *s* me to Jericho."
2: 6 the LORD has *s* me to the Jordan."
2:17 they *s* fifty men, who searched
3: 7 *s* this message to Jehoshaphat king
5: 8 he *s* him this message: "Why have
5:10 Elisha *s* a messenger to say to him,
5:22 "My master *s* me to say, 'Two
5:24 He *s* the men away and they left.
6: 9 The man of God *s* word to the king
6:14 Then he *s* horses and chariots
6:23 he *s* them away, and they returned
6:32 The king *s* a messenger ahead,
7:14 the king *s* them after the Aramean
8: 9 king of Aram has *s* me to ask,
9:19 the king *s* out a second horseman.
10: 1 So Jehu wrote letters and *s* them
10: 5 and the guardians *s* this message
10: 7 and *s* them to Jehu in Jezreel.
10:21 Then he *s* word throughout Israel,
11: 4 In the seventh year Jehoiada *s*
12:18 he *s* them to Hazael king of Aram,
14: 8 Then Amaziah *s* messengers
14: 9 "A thistle in Lebanon *s* a message
14:19 but they *s* men after him to Lachish
16: 7 Ahaz *s* messengers to say
16: 8 of the royal palace and *s* it
16:10 and *s* to Uriah the priest a sketch
16:11 all the plans that King Ahaz had *s*
17: 4 for he had *s* envoys to
17:25 so he *s* lions among them
17:26 He has *s* lions among them,
18:14 king of Judah *s* this message
18:17 The king of Assyria *s* his supreme
18:27 and you that my master *s* me
19: 2 He *s* Eliakim the palace
19: 4 has *s* to ridicule the living God,
19: 9 he again *s* messengers to Hezekiah
19:16 to the words Sennacherib has *s*
19:20 Isaiah son of Amoz *s* a message
20:12 king of Babylon *s* Hezekiah letters
22: 3 King Josiah *s* the secretary,
22:15 says: Tell the man who *s* you to me,
22:18 who *s* you to inquire of the LORD,
24: 2 He *s* them to destroy Judah,
24: 2 The LORD *s* Babylonian,
1Ch 6:15 deported when the LORD *s* Judah
10: 9 *s* messengers throughout the land
12:19 their rulers *s* him away.
14: 1 of Tyre *s* messengers to David,
18:10 he *s* his son Hadoram
19: 2 So David *s* a delegation
19: 4 at the buttocks, and *s* them away.
19: 5 he *s* messengers to meet them,
19: 6 Ammonites *s* a thousand talents
19: 8 David *s* Joab out with the entire
19:16 they *s* messengers and had
21:12 I should answer the one who *s* me."
21:14 So the LORD *s* a plague on Israel,
21:15 *s* an angel to destroy Jerusalem.
2Ch 2: 3 David when you *s* him cedar
2: 3 Solomon *s* this message
7:10 the seventh month he *s* the people
8:18 Hiram *s* him ships commanded
2Ch 10: 3 So they *s* for Jeroboam, and he
10:18 King Rehoboam *s* out Adoniram,
13:13 Now Jeroboam had *s* troops
16: 2 *s* it to Ben-Hadad king of Aram,
16: 4 and *s* the commanders of his forces
17: 7 his reign he *s* his officials Ben-Hail,
23:14 Jehoiada the priest *s* out
24:19 Although the LORD *s* prophets
24:23 They *s* all the plunder to their king
25:10 from Ephraim and *s* them home.
25:13 the troops that Amaziah had *s* back
25:15 and he *s* a prophet to him, who said
25:17 he *s* this challenge to Jehoash son
25:18 "A thistle in Lebanon *s* a message
25:27 but they *s* men after him to Lachish
28:16 At that time King Ahaz *s*
30: 1 Hezekiah *s* word to all Israel
32: 9 he *s* his officers to Jerusalem
32:21 And the LORD *s* an angel,
32:31 when envoys were *s* by the rulers
34: 8 he *s* Shaphan son of Azaliah
34:22 those the king had *s* with him went
34:23 says: Tell the man who *s* you to me,
34:26 who *s* you to inquire of the LORD,
35:21 But Neco *s* messengers to him,
36:10 King Nebuchadnezzar *s* for him
36:15 *s* word to them through his
Ezr 4:11 a copy of the letter they *s* him.)
4:17 The king *s* this reply: To Rehum
4:18 The letter you *s* us has been read
5: 6 the officials of Trans-Euphrates, *s*
5: 7 The report they *s* him read
6:13 of the decree King Darius had *s*,
7:14 You are *s* by the king and his seven
8:17 of learning, and I *s* them to Iddo,
Ne 2: 9 The king had also *s* army officers
6: 2 and Geshem *s* me this message:
6: 3 so I *s* messengers to them
6: 4 Four times they *s* me the same
6: 5 Sanballat *s* his aide to me
6: 8 I *s* him this reply: "Nothing like
6:12 I realized that God had not *s* him,
6:19 Tobiah *s* letters to intimidate me.
9:10 You *s* miraculous signs
Est 1:22 He *s* dispatches to all parts
3:13 Dispatches were *s* by couriers
4: 4 She *s* clothes for him to put
4:13 to Mordecai, he *s* back this answer:
4:15 Esther *s* this reply to Mordecai:
8:10 and *s* them by mounted couriers,
9:20 and he *s* letters to all the Jews
9:30 Mordecai *s* letters to all the Jews
Job 22: 9 you *s* widows away empty-handed
Ps 78:25 he *s* them all the food they could
78:45 He *s* swarms of flies that devoured
78:61 He *s* the ark of his might
80:11 It *s* out its boughs to the Sea,
105: 17 and he *s* a man before them—
105: 20 The king *s* and released him,
105: 26 He *s* Moses his servant,
105: 28 He *s* darkness and made the land
106: 15 but *s* a wasting disease upon them.
107: 20 He *s* forth his word and healed
135: 9 He *s* his signs and wonders
Pr 9: 3 She has *s* out her maids,
17:11 a merciless official will be *s*
22:21 answers to him who *s* you?
Isa 6:12 the LORD has *s* everyone far away
9: 8 The Lord has *s* a message
20: 1 *s* by Sargon king of Assyria,
36: 2 of Assyria *s* his field commander
36:12 and you that my master *s* me
37: 2 He *s* Eliakim the palace
37: 4 has *s* to ridicule the living God,
37: 9 he *s* messengers to Hezekiah
37:17 to all the words Sennacherib has *s*
37:21 Isaiah son of Amoz *s* a message
39: 1 king of Babylon *s* Hezekiah letters
48:16 now the Sovereign LORD has *s* me
50: 1 divorce with which I *s* her away?
50: 1 your mother was *s* away.
55:11 achieve the purpose for which I *s* it.
57: 9 You *s* your ambassadors far away;
61: 1 He has *s* me to bind up
63:12 who *s* his glorious arm of power
Jer 3: 8 and *s* her away because of all her
7:25 and again I *s* you my servants
14:14 I have not *s* them or appointed
Jer 19:14 where the LORD had *s* him
21: 1 the LORD when King Zedekiah *s*
24: 5 whom I *s* away from this place
25: 4 LORD has *s* you all his servants
25:17 nations to whom he *s* me drink it:
26: 5 whom I have *s* to you again
26:12 "The LORD *s* me to prophesy
26:15 in truth the LORD has *s* me to you
26:22 *s* Elnathan son of Acbor to Egypt,
27:15 'I have not *s* them,' declares
28: 9 as one truly *s* by the LORD only
28:15 The LORD has not *s* you,
29: 1 letter that the prophet Jeremiah *s*
29: 3 Judah *s* to King Nebuchadnezzar
29: 9 I have not *s* them," declares
29:19 "words that I *s* to them again
29:20 all you exiles whom I have *s* away
29:25 You *s* letters in your own name
29:28 He has *s* this message to us
35:15 and again I *s* all my servants
36:14 all the officials *s* Jehudi
36:21 The king *s* Jehudi to get the scroll,
37: 3 *s* Jehucal son of Shelemiah
37: 7 who *s* you to inquire of me,
37:17 Then King Zedekiah *s* for him
38:14 Then King Zedekiah *s* for Jeremiah
39:14 officers of the king of Babylon *s*
40:14 the Ammonites has *s* Ishmael son
42: 9 to whom you *s* me
42:20 when you *s* me to the LORD your
42:21 God in all he *s* me to tell you.
43: 1 everything the LORD had *s* him
43: 2 The LORD our God has not *s* you
44: 4 again I *s* my servants the prophets,
49:14 An envoy was *s* to the nations
La 1:13 "From on high he *s* fire,
1:13 *s* it down into my bones.
Eze 3: 5 You are not being *s* to a people
3: 6 Surely if I had *s* you to them,
11:16 Although I *s* them far away
13: 6 when the LORD has not *s* them;
17: 7 The vine now *s* out its roots
23:16 *s* messengers to them in Chaldea.
23:40 *s* messengers for men who came
31: 4 and *s* their channels
39:28 though I *s* them into exile
Da 2:13 and men were *s* to look for Daniel
3:28 who has *s* his angel and rescued his
5:24 Therefore he *s* the hand that wrote
6:22 live forever! My God *s* his angel,
10:11 for I have now been *s* to you."
Hos 5:13 and *s* to the great king for help.
Joel 2:25 my great army that I *s* among you.
Am 4: 7 I *s* rain on one town,
4:10 "I *s* plagues among you
7:10 the priest of Bethel *s* a message
Ob : 1 An envoy was *s* to the nations
Jnh 1: 4 Then the LORD *s* a great wind
Mic 6: 4 I *s* Moses to lead you,
Hag 1:12 the LORD their God had *s* him.
Zec 1:10 They are the ones the LORD has *s*
2: 8 has *s* me against the nations that
2: 9 that the LORD Almighty has *s* me.
2:11 that the LORD Almighty has *s* me
4: 9 that the LORD Almighty has *s* me
6:15 that the LORD Almighty has *s* me
7: 2 people of Bethel had *s* Sharezer
7:12 that the LORD Almighty had *s*
Mal 2: 4 that I have *s* you this admonition
Mt 2: 8 He *s* them to Bethlehem and said,
10: 5 These twelve Jesus *s* out
10:40 me receives the one who *s* me.
11: 2 he *s* his disciples to ask him,
14:35 they *s* word to all the surrounding
15:24 "I was *s* only to the lost sheep
15:39 After Jesus had *s* the crowd away,
20: 2 and *s* them into his vineyard.
21: 1 Jesus *s* two disciples, saying
21:34 he *s* his servants to the tenants
21:36 Then he *s* other servants to them,
21:37 Last of all, he *s* his son to them.
22: 3 He *s* his servants to those who had
22: 4 "Then he *s* some more servants
22: 7 He *s* his army and destroyed those
22:16 They *s* their disciples to him
23:37 kill the prophets and stone those *s*
26:47 *s* from the chief priests
27:19 his wife *s* him this message:

Mk 1: 12 At once the Spirit *s* him out
1: 43 Jesus *s* him away at once
3: 31 they *s* someone in to call him.
6: 7 he *s* them out two by two
6: 27 he immediately *s* an executioner
8: 9 And having *s* them away, he got
8: 26 Jesus *s* him home, saying, "Don't
9: 37 me but the one who *s* me."
11: 1 Jesus *s* two of his disciples,
12: 2 At harvest time he *s* a servant
12: 3 and *s* him away empty-handed.
12: 4 Then he *s* another servant to them;
12: 5 He *s* many others; some
12: 5 He *s* still another, and that one
12: 6 He *s* him last of all, saying,
12: 13 Later they *s* some of the Pharisees
14: 13 So he *s* two of his disciples,
14: 43 *s* from the chief priests,
Lk 1: 19 and I have been *s* to speak to you
1: 26 God *s* the angel Gabriel
1: 53 but has *s* the rich away empty.
4: 18 He has *s* me to proclaim freedom
4: 26 Yet Elijah was not *s* to any of them,
4: 43 also, because that is why I was *s*."
7: 3 *s* some elders of the Jews to him,
7: 6 when the centurion *s* friends to say
7: 10 the men who had been *s* returned
7: 19 he *s* them to the Lord to ask,
7: 20 John the Baptist *s* us to you to ask,
8: 38 but Jesus *s* him away, saying,
9: 2 and he *s* them out to preach
9: 48 me welcomes the one who *s* me.
9: 52 and he *s* messengers on ahead.
10: 1 *s* them two by two ahead of him
10: 16 rejects me rejects him who *s* me."
13: 34 kill the prophets and stone those *s*
14: 4 he healed him and *s* him away.
14: 17 time of the banquet he *s* his servant
15: 15 who *s* him to his fields to feed pigs.
19: 14 and *s* a delegation after him to say,
19: 15 Then he *s* for the servants
19: 29 he *s* two of his disciples, saying
19: 32 Those who were *s* ahead went
20: 10 At harvest time he *s* a servant
20: 10 and *s* him away empty-handed.
20: 11 He *s* another servant, but that one
20: 11 and *s* away empty-handed.
20: 12 He *s* still a third, and they
20: 20 they *s* spies, who pretended
22: 8 Jesus *s* Peter and John, saying,
22: 35 "When I *s* you without purse,
23: 7 Herod's jurisdiction, he *s* him
23: 11 in an elegant robe, they *s* him back
23: 15 for he *s* him back to us;
Jn 1: 6 There came a man who was *s*
1: 19 the Jews of Jerusalem *s* priests
1: 22 to take back to those who *s* us.
1: 24 who had been *s* questioned him,
1: 33 that the one who *s* me to baptize
3: 28 'I am not the Christ but am *s* ahead
3: 34 whom God has *s* speaks the words
4: 34 "is to do the will of him who *s* me
4: 38 I *s* you to reap what you have not
5: 23 not honor the Father, who *s* him.
5: 24 believes him who *s* me has eternal
5: 30 to please myself but him who *s* me.
5: 33 "You have *s* to John and he has
5: 36 testifies that the Father has *s* me.
5: 37 the Father who *s* me has himself
5: 38 for you do not believe the one he *s*.
6: 29 to believe in the one he has *s*."
6: 38 but to do the will of him who *s* me.
6: 39 this is the will of him who *s* me,
6: 44 the Father who *s* me draws him,
6: 57 as the living Father *s* me and I live
7: 16 It comes from him who *s* me.
7: 18 of the one who *s* him is a man
7: 28 on my own, but he who *s* me is true
7: 29 I am from him and he *s* me."
7: 32 and the Pharisees *s* temple guards
7: 33 and then I go to the one who *s* me.
8: 16 I stand with the Father who *s* me.
8: 18 witness is the one who *s* me—
8: 26 But he who *s* me is reliable,
8: 29 The one who *s* me is with me;
8: 42 come on my own; but he *s* me.
9: 4 must do the work of him who *s* me.
9: 7 of Siloam" (this word means *S*).

Jn 9: 18 until they *s* for the man's parents.
10: 36 his very own and *s* into the world?
11: 3 So the sisters *s* word to Jesus,
11: 42 that they may believe that you *s* me
12: 44 in me only, but in the one who *s* me
12: 45 at me, he sees the one who *s* me.
12: 49 Father who *s* me commanded me
13: 16 greater than the one who *s* him.
13: 20 me accepts the one who *s* me."
14: 24 they belong to the Father who *s* me
15: 21 do not know the One who *s* me.
16: 5 "Now I am going to him who *s* me,
17: 3 and Jesus Christ, whom you have *s*.
17: 8 and they believed that you *s* me.
17: 18 As you *s* me into the world,
17: 18 I have *s* them into the world.
17: 21 may believe that you have *s* me.
17: 23 to let the world know that you *s* me
17: 25 and they know that you have *s* me.
18: 24 Then Annas *s* him, still bound,
20: 21 As the Father has *s* me, I am
Ac 3: 26 he *s* him first to you to bless you
5: 21 and *s* to the jail for the apostles.
7: 4 God *s* him to this land where you
7: 12 he *s* our fathers on their first visit.
7: 14 Joseph *s* for his father Jacob
7: 35 He was *s* to be their ruler
8: 14 they *s* Peter and John to them.
9: 17 has *s* me so that you may see again
9: 30 him down to Caesarea and *s* him
9: 38 they *s* two men to him
9: 40 Peter *s* them all out of the room;
10: 8 that had happened and *s* them
10: 17 the men *s* by Cornelius found out
10: 20 to go with them, for I have *s* them."
10: 29 May I ask why you *s* for me?"
10: 29 So when I was *s* for, I came
10: 33 So I *s* for you immediately,
10: 36 This is the message God *s*
11: 11 then three men who had been *s*
11: 22 and they *s* Barnabas to Antioch.
12: 11 a doubt that the Lord *s* his angel
13: 3 hands on them and *s* them off.
13: 4 *s* on their way by the Holy Spirit,
13: 7 *s* for Barnabas and Saul
13: 15 the synagogue rulers *s* word
13: 26 message of salvation has been *s*.
15: 3 The church *s* them on their way,
15: 23 With them they *s* the following
15: 30 The men were *s* off and went
15: 33 they were *s* off by the brothers
15: 33 to return to those who had *s* them.
16: 35 the magistrates *s* their officers
17: 10 the brothers *s* Paul and Silas away
17: 14 The brothers immediately *s* Paul
19: 22 He *s* two of his helpers, Timothy
19: 31 *s* him a message begging him not
20: 1 Paul *s* for the disciples and,
20: 17 Paul *s* to Ephesus for the elders
23: 18 *s* for me and asked me
23: 30 out against the man, I *s* him to you
24: 24 He *s* for Paul and listened to him
24: 26 so he *s* for him frequently
28: 28 that God's salvation has been *s*
Ro 10: 15 can they preach unless they are *s*?
2Co 2: 17 with sincerity, like men *s* from God
12: 17 through any of the men I *s* you?
12: 18 and I *s* our brother with him.
Gal 1: 1 *s* not from men nor by man,
4: 4 God *s* his Son, born of a woman,
4: 6 God *s* the Spirit of his Son
Php 2: 25 whom you *s* to take care
4: 16 you *s* me aid again and again
4: 18 from Epaphroditus the gifts you *s*.
1Th 3: 2 We *s* Timothy, who is our brother
3: 5 I *s* to find out about your faith.
2Ti 4: 12 I *s* Tychicus to Ephesus.
Heb 1: 14 not all angels ministering spirits *s*
Jas 2: 25 *s* them off in a different direction?
1Pe 1: 12 by the Holy Spirit *s* from heaven.
2: 14 who are *s* by him to punish those
2Pe 2: 4 when they sinned, but *s* them
1Jn 4: 9 He *s* his one and only Son
4: 10 but that he loved us and *s* his Son
4: 14 testify that the Father has *s* his Son
Rev 5: 6 of God *s* out into all the earth.
22: 6 *s* his angel to show his servants
22: 16 have *s* my angel to give you this

SENTENCE (SENTENCED)

1Ki 20: 40 "That is your *s*," the king
2Ki 25: 6 where *s* was pronounced on him.
Ps 149: 9 to carry out the *s* written
Ecc 8: 11 When the *s* for a crime is not
Jer 39: 5 where he pronounced *s* on him.
52: 9 where he pronounced *s* on him.
Eze 16: 38 I will *s* you to the punishment
23: 45 But righteous men will *s* them
Lk 23: 40 "since you are under the same *s*?
Ac 13: 28 no proper ground for a death *s*,
Ro 9: 28 his *s* on earth with speed
2Co 1: 9 in our hearts we felt the *s* of death.

SENTENCED (SENTENCE)

Jer 26: 11 "This man should be *s* to death
26: 16 This man should not be *s* to death!
Lk 24: 20 him over to be *s* to death,

SENTRIES

Ac 12: 6 and *s* stood guard at the entrance.

SEORIM

1Ch 24: 8 the fourth to *S*, the fifth

SEPARATE (SEPARATED SEPARATES SEPARATION)

Ge 1: 6 the waters to *s* water from water."
1: 14 the expanse of the sky to *s* the day
1: 18 and to *s* light from darkness.
30: 40 Thus he made *s* flocks for himself
Ex 26: 33 The curtain will *s* the Holy Place
Lev 15: 31 " 'You must keep the Israelites *s*
Nu 16: 21 "*S* yourselves from this assembly
Jdg 7: 5 "*S* those who lap the water
2Sa 14: 6 and no one was there to *s* them.
1Ki 5: 9 There I will *s* them and you can
2Ki 15: 5 he died, and he lived in a *s* house.
2Ch 26: 21 He lived in a *s* house—
Ezr 9: 1 have not kept themselves *s*
10: 11 *S* yourselves from the peoples
Est 3: 8 kingdom who keep themselves *s*.
Eze 42: 20 to *s* the holy from the common.
Mt 13: 49 *s* the wicked from the righteous
19: 6 has joined together, let man not *s*."
25: 32 and he will *s* the people one
Mk 10: 9 has joined together, let man not *s*."
Jn 20: 7 up by itself, *s* from the linen.
Ro 8: 35 Who shall *s* us from the love
8: 39 will be able to *s* us from the love
1Co 7: 10 wife must not *s* from her husband.
2Co 6: 17 and be *s*, says the Lord.
Gal 2: 12 and *s* himself from the Gentiles
Eph 2: 12 at that time you were *s* from Christ,

SEPARATED (SEPARATE)

Ge 1: 4 he *s* the light from the darkness.
1: 7 and *s* the water under the expanse
25: 23 peoples from within you will be *s*;
Nu 16: 9 of Israel has *s* you from the rest
1Sa 11: 11 The next day Saul *s* his men
2Ki 2: 11 of fire appeared and *s* the two
25: 5 All his soldiers were *s* from him
1Ch 24: 3 David *s* them into divisions
Ezr 6: 21 with all who had *s* themselves
Ne 4: 19 we are widely *s* from each other
9: 2 Israelite descent had *s* themselves
10: 28 and all who *s* themselves
Isa 59: 2 But your iniquities have *s*
Jer 52: 8 All his soldiers were *s* from him
Eze 46: 18 none of my people will be *s*
Ac 2: 3 seemed to be tongues of fire that *s*
Eph 4: 18 in their understanding and *s*
Phm : 15 Perhaps the reason he was *s*

SEPARATES (SEPARATE)

Ru 1: 17 if anything but death *s* you and me
Pr 16: 28 and a gossip *s* close friends.
17: 9 repeats the matter *s* close friends.
Eze 14: 7 living in Israel *s* himself from me
Mt 25: 32 as a shepherd *s* the sheep

SEPARATION (SEPARATE)

Nu 6: 2 a vow of *s* to the LORD
6: 5 the period of his *s* to the LORD is
6: 5 vow of *s* no razor may be used
6: 6 Throughout the period of his *s*
6: 7 the symbol of his *s* to God is

Nu 6: 8 the period of his *s* he is consecrated
6: 12 he became defiled during his *s*.
6: 12 to the LORD for the period of his *s*
6: 13 when the period of his *s* is over.
6: 21 LORD in accordance with his *s*,

SEPHAR

Ge 10: 30 stretched from Mesha toward *S*,

SEPHARAD

Ob : 20 exiles from Jerusalem who are in *S*

SEPHARVAIM (SEPHARVITES)

2Ki 17: 24 *S* and settled them in the towns
17: 31 and Anammelech, the gods of *S*.
18: 34 Where are the gods of *S*, Hena
19: 13 the king of the city of *S*, or of Hena
Isa 36: 19 of *S*? Have they rescued Samaria
37: 13 the king of the city of *S*, or of Hena

SEPHARVITES (SEPHARVAIM)

2Ki 17: 31 and the *S* burned their children

SERAH

Ge 46: 17 Their sister was *S*.
Nu 26: 46 (Asher had a daughter named *S*.)
1Ch 7: 30 Their sister was *S*.

SERAIAH (SERAIAH'S)

2Sa 8: 17 were priests; *S* was secretary;
2Ki 25: 18 as prisoners *S* the chief priest,
25: 23 *S* son of Tanhumeth
1Ch 4: 13 The sons of Kenaz: Othniel and *S*.
4: 14 *S* was the father of Joab, the father
4: 35 the son of *S*, the son of Asiel,
6: 14 Azariah the father of *S*,
6: 14 and *S* the father of Jehozadak.
Ezr 2: 2 Jeshua, Nehemiah, *S*, Reelaiah,
7: 1 Ezra son of *S*, the son of Azariah,
Ne 10: 2 Zedekiah, *S*, Azariah, Jeremiah,
11: 11 of Joiarib; Jakin; *S* son of Hilkiah,
12: 1 *S*, Jeremiah, Ezra, Amariah,
Jer 36: 26 *S* son of Azriel and Shelemiah son
40: 8 of Kareah, *S* son of Tanhumeth,
51: 59 to the staff officer *S* son of Neriah,
51: 61 He said to *S*, "When you get
52: 24 as prisoners *S* the chief priest,

SERAIAH'S (SERAIAH)

Ne 12: 12 of *S* family, Meraiah; of Jeremiah's

SERAPHS

Isa 6: 2 Above him were *s*, each
6: 6 Then one of the *s* flew to me

SERED (SEREDITE)

Ge 46: 14 The sons of Zebulun: *S*, Elon
Nu 26: 26 through *S*, the Seredite clan;

SEREDITE (SERED)

Nu 26: 26 through Sered, the *S* clan;

SERGIUS PAULUS

Ac 13: 7 an attendant of the proconsul, *S*.

SERIOUS (SERIOUSNESS)

Ge 12: 17 But the LORD inflicted *s* diseases
Ex 21: 22 but there is no *s* injury,
21: 23 But if there is *s* injury, you are
Dt 15: 21 is lame or blind, or has any *s* flaw,
Jer 6: 14 as though it were not *s*.
8: 11 as though it were not *s*.
Ac 18: 14 some misdemeanor or *s* crime,
25: 7 bringing many *s* charges

SERIOUSNESS (SERIOUS)

Tit 2: 7 *s* and soundness of speech that

SERPENT (SERPENT'S SERPENTS)

Ge 3: 1 the *s* was more crafty than any
3: 2 said to the *s*, "We may eat fruit
3: 4 "You will not surely die," the *s* said
3: 13 woman said, "The *s* deceived me,
3: 14 So the LORD God said to the *s*,
49: 17 Dan will be a *s* by the roadside,
Job 26: 13 his hand pierced the gliding *s*.
Ps 91: 13 trample the great lion and the *s*.
Isa 14: 29 fruit will be a darting, venomous *s*.
27: 1 Leviathan the coiling *s*;
Isa 27: 1 Leviathan the gliding *s*,
Jer 46: 22 Egypt will hiss like a fleeing *s*
51: 34 Like a *s* he has swallowed us
Am 9: 3 there I will command the *s*
Rev 12: 9 that ancient *s* called the devil
12: 15 his mouth the *s* spewed water like
20: 2 that ancient *s*, who is the devil,

SERPENT'S (SERPENT)

Ps 140: 3 make their tongues as sharp as a *s*;
Isa 65: 25 but dust will be the *s* food.
2Co 11: 3 Eve was deceived by the *s* cunning,
Rev 12: 14 and half a time, out of the *s* reach.

SERPENTS (SERPENT)

Dt 32: 33 Their wine is the venom of *s*,
Job 20: 14 it will become the venom of *s*
20: 16 He will suck the poison of *s*;

SERUG

Ge 11: 20 he became the father of *S*.
11: 21 And after he became the father of *S*
11: 22 When *S* had lived 30 years,
11: 23 *S* lived 200 years and had other
1Ch 1: 26 Shelah, Eber, Peleg, Reu, *S*, Nahor
Lk 3: 35 the son of *S*, the son of Reu,

SERVANT (MAIDSERVANT MAIDSERVANTS MANSERVANT MENSERVANTS SERVANT'S SERVANTS SERVANTS' WOMENSERVANTS)

Ge 15: 3 so a *s* in my household will be my
16: 5 I put my *s* in your arms,
16: 6 "Your *s* is in your hands,"
16: 8 And he said, "Hagar, *s* of Sarai,
18: 3 my lord, do not pass your *s* by.
18: 5 now that you have come to your *s*."
18: 7 tender calf and gave it to a *s*,
19: 19 Your *s* has found favor in your eyes
24: 2 said to the chief *s* in his household,
24: 5 The *s* asked him, "What
24: 9 the *s* put his hand under the thigh
24: 10 *s* took ten of his master's camels
24: 14 you have chosen for your *s* Isaac.
24: 17 The *s* hurried to meet her and said,
24: 34 So he said, "I am Abraham's *s*.
24: 52 When Abraham's *s* heard what
24: 53 Then the *s* brought out gold
24: 59 and Abraham's *s* and his men.
24: 61 So the *s* took Rebekah and left.
24: 65 from her camel and asked the *s*,
24: 65 "He is my master," the *s* answered.
24: 66 the *s* told Isaac all he had done.
26: 24 for the sake of my *s* Abraham."
29: 24 And Laban gave his *s* girl Zilpah
29: 29 Laban gave his *s* girl Bilhah
30: 4 she gave him her *s* Bilhah as a wife.
30: 7 Rachel's *s* Bilhah conceived again
30: 10 Leah's *s* Zilpah bore Jacob a son.
30: 12 Leah's *s* Zilpah bore Jacob
32: 4 master Esau: 'Your *s* Jacob says,
32: 10 faithfulness you have shown your *s*
32: 18 'They belong to your *s* Jacob.
32: 20 'Your *s* Jacob is coming behind us
33: 5 God has graciously given your *s*."
33: 14 So let my lord go on ahead of his *s*,
41: 12 a *s* of the captain of the guard.
43: 28 "Your *s* our father is still alive
44: 18 Do not be angry with your *s*,
44: 18 let your *s* speak a word to my lord.
44: 24 back to your *s* my father,
44: 27 "Your *s* my father said to us,
44: 30 when I go back to your *s* my father
44: 32 Your *s* guaranteed the boy's safety
44: 33 please let your *s* remain here
Ex 4: 10 since you have spoken to your *s*.
14: 31 trust in him and in Moses his *s*.
21: 2 "If you buy a Hebrew *s*, he is
21: 5 if the *s* declares, 'I love my master
21: 6 Then he will be his *s* for life.
21: 7 "If a man sells his daughter as a *s*,
21: 26 he must let the *s* go free
21: 27 he must let the *s* go free
Nu 11: 11 you brought this trouble on your *s*?
12: 7 But this is not true of my *s* Moses;
12: 8 to speak against my *s* Moses?"
14: 24 my *s* Caleb has a different spirit
Dt 3: 24 to show to your *s* your greatness
Dt 15: 16 if your *s* says to you, "I do not want
15: 17 and he will become your *s* for life.
15: 18 it a hardship to set your *s* free,
34: 5 Moses the *s* of the LORD died
Jos 1: 1 death of Moses the *s* of the LORD,
1: 2 Moses' aide: "Moses my *s* is dead.
1: 7 all the law my *s* Moses gave you;
1: 13 the command that Moses the *s*
1: 15 which Moses the *s*
5: 14 does my Lord have for his *s*?"
8: 31 as Moses the *s* of the LORD had
8: 33 as Moses the *s* of the LORD had
9: 24 God had commanded his *s* Moses
11: 12 as Moses the *s* of the LORD had
11: 15 LORD commanded his *s* Moses,
12: 6 Moses the *s* of the LORD gave
12: 6 Moses, the *s* of the LORD,
13: 8 the *s* of the LORD, had assigned it
14: 7 old when Moses the *s*
18: 7 Moses the *s* of the LORD gave it
22: 2 You have done all that Moses the *s*
22: 4 homes in the land that Moses the *s*
22: 5 and the law that Moses the *s*
24: 29 son of Nun, the *s* of the LORD,
Jdg 2: 8 son of Nun, the *s* of the LORD,
7: 10 to the camp with your *s* Purah
7: 11 his *s* went down to the outposts
9: 54 So his *s* ran him through,
15: 18 have given your *s* this great
16: 26 said to the *s* who held his hand,
19: 3 with him his *s* and two donkeys.
19: 9 with his concubine and his *s*,
19: 11 the *s* said to his master, "Come,
Ru 2: 8 Stay here with my *s* girls.
2: 13 and have spoken kindly to your *s*—
2: 13 the standing of one of your *s* girls."
2: 23 close to the *s* girls of Boaz
3: 2 with whose *s* girls you have been,
3: 9 "I am your *s* Ruth," she said.
1Sa 1: 11 not forget your *s* but give her a son,
1: 16 Do not take your *s*
1: 18 May your *s* find favor in your eyes
2: 13 the *s* of the priest would come
2: 15 the *s* of the priest would come
2: 16 the *s* would then answer, "No,
3: 9 LORD, for your *s* is listening.' "
3: 10 "Speak, for your *s* is listening."
9: 5 Saul said to the *s* who was with him
9: 6 But the *s* replied, "Look,
9: 7 Saul said to his *s*, "If we go,
9: 8 The *s* answered him again.
9: 10 "Good," Saul said to his *s*.
9: 22 Samuel brought Saul and his *s*
9: 27 the *s* did so—"but you stay here
9: 27 "Tell the *s* to go on ahead of us"—
10: 14 Saul's uncle asked him and his *s*,
17: 32 your *s* will go and fight him."
17: 34 "Your *s* has been keeping his
17: 36 Your *s* has killed both the lion
17: 58 son of your *s* Jesse of Bethlehem."
19: 4 the king do wrong to his *s* David;
20: 7 'Very well,' then your *s* is safe.
20: 8 As for you, show kindness to your *s*
22: 8 me that my son has incited my *s*
22: 15 Let not the king accuse your *s*
22: 15 for your *s* knows nothing
23: 10 your *s* has heard definitely that
23: 11 O LORD, God of Israel, tell your *s*
23: 11 as your *s* has heard? O LORD,
25: 24 Please let your *s* speak to you,
25: 24 hear what your *s* has to say.
25: 25 your *s*, I did not see the men my
25: 27 which your *s* has brought
25: 31 master success, remember your *s*."
26: 18 "Why is my lord pursuing his *s*?
27: 5 Why should your *s* live
27: 12 that he will be my *s* forever."
28: 2 for yourself what your *s* can do."
28: 22 Now please listen to your *s*
29: 8 against your *s* from the day I came
2Sa 3: 18 'By my *s* David I will rescue my
7: 5 saying: "Go and tell my *s* David,
7: 8 "Now then, tell my *s* David,
7: 19 the future of the house of your *s*.
7: 20 you know your *s*, O Sovereign
7: 21 and made it known to your *s*.
7: 25 you have made concerning your *s*
7: 26 of your *s* David will be established

2Sa 7:27 So your *s* has found courage
7:27 you have revealed this to your *s*,
7:28 given this good promise to your *s*.
7:29 of your *s* will be blessed forever."
7:29 pleased to bless the house of your *s*,
9: 2 there was a *s* of Saul's household
9: 2 "Are you Ziba?" "Your *s*,"
9: 6 "Mephibosheth!" "Your *s*,"
9: 8 down and said, "What is your *s*,
9: 9 the king summoned Ziba, Saul's *s*,
9:11 my lord the king commands his *s*
9:11 "Your *s* will do whatever my lord
11:21 your *s* Uriah the Hittite is dead.'"
11:24 your *s* Uriah the Hittite is dead."
13:17 He called his personal *s* and said,
13:18 So his *s* put her out and bolted
13:24 "Your *s* has had shearers come.
13:35 it has happened just as your *s* said."
14: 6 I your *s* had two sons.
14: 7 clan has risen up against your *s*;
14:12 "Let your *s* speak a word
14:15 Your *s* thought, 'I will speak
14:15 perhaps he will do what his *s* asks.
14:16 agree to deliver his *s* from the hand
14:17 now your *s* says, 'May the word
14:19 it was your *s* Joab who instructed
14:19 words into the mouth of your *s*.
14:20 Your *s* Joab did this
14:22 "Today your *s* knows that he has
15: 2 "Your *s* is from one of the tribes
15: 8 While your *s* was living at Geshur
15:21 or death, there will your *s* be."
15:34 I was your father's *s* in the past,
15:34 I will be your *s*,' then you can help
15:34 'I will be your *s*, O king; I was your
17:17 A *s* girl was to go and inform them,
18:29 Joab was about to send the king's *s*
18:29 your *s*, but I don't know what it
19:19 remember how your *s* did wrong
19:20 For I your *s* know that I have
19:26 But Ziba my *s* betrayed me.
19:26 since I your *s* am lame, I said,
19:27 And he has slandered your *s*
19:28 but you gave your *s* a place
19:35 Can your *s* taste what he eats
19:35 Why should your *s* be an added
19:36 Your *s* will cross over the Jordan
19:37 But here is your *s* Kimham.
19:37 me in this way? Let your *s* return,
20:17 "Listen to what your *s* has to say."
24:10 take away the guilt of your *s*.
24:21 my lord the king come to his *s*?"
1Ki 1:13 did you not swear to me your *s*:
1:17 to me your *s* by the LORD your
1:19 he has not invited Solomon your *s*.
1:26 me your *s*, and Zadok the priest,
1:26 your *s* Solomon he did not invite.
1:51 me today that he will not put his *s*
2:38 Your *s* will do as my lord the king
3: 6 shown great kindness to your *s*,
3: 7 you have made your *s* king in place
3: 8 Your *s* is here among the people
3: 9 So give your *s* a discerning heart
3:20 side while I your *s* was asleep.
8:24 promise to your *s* David my father;
8:25 keep for your *s* David my father
8:26 you promised your *s* David my
8:28 the prayer that your *s* is praying
8:29 will hear the prayer your *s* prays
8:30 Hear the supplication of your *s*
8:53 through your *s* Moses when you,
8:56 gave through his *s* Moses.
8:59 he may uphold the cause of his *s*
8:66 LORD had done for his *s* David
11:13 tribe for the sake of David my *s*
11:32 But for the sake of my *s* David
11:34 life for the sake of David my *s*,
11:36 that David my *s* may always have
11:38 David my *s* did, I will be with you.
12: 7 "If today you will be a *s*
14: 8 you have not been like my *s* David,
14:18 through his *s* the prophet Ahijah.
15:29 through his *s* Ahijah the Shilonite
18: 9 "that you are handing your *s*
18:12 Yet I your *s* have worshiped
18:36 that I am your *s* and have done all
18:43 look toward the sea," he told his *s*.
18:44 The seventh time the *s* reported,
1Ki 19: 3 in Judah, he left his *s* there,
20: 9 'Your *s* will do all you demanded
20:32 "Your *s* Ben-Hadad says: 'Please
20:39 "Your *s* went into the thick
20:40 While your *s* was busy here
2Ki 4: 1 "Your *s* my husband is dead,
4: 2 "Your *s* has nothing there at all,"
4:12 said to his *s* Gehazi, "Call
4:16 "Don't mislead your *s*, O man
4:19 His father told a *s*, "Carry him
4:20 After the *s* had lifted him up
4:24 the donkey and said to her *s*,
4:25 the man of God said to his *s* Gehazi
4:38 he said to his *s*, "Put
4:43 before a hundred men?" his *s* asked
5: 6 letter I am sending my *s* Naaman
5:15 accept now a gift from your *s*."
5:17 Naaman, "please let me, your *s*,
5:17 for your *s* will never again make
5:18 But may the LORD forgive your *s*
5:18 may the LORD forgive your *s*
5:20 the *s* of Elisha the man of God,
5:25 "Your *s* didn't go anywhere,"
6:15 When the *s* of the man
6:15 what shall we do?" the *s* asked.
8: 4 to Gehazi, the *s* of the man of God,
8:13 "How could your *s*, a mere dog,
8:19 for the sake of his *s* David,
9:36 through his *s* Elijah the Tishbite:
10:10 promised through his *s* Elijah."
14:25 spoken through his *s* Jonah son
16: 7 king of Assyria, "I am your *s*
18:12 all that Moses the *s*
19:34 for the sake of David my *s*."
20: 6 and for the sake of my *s* David.'"
21: 8 Law that my *s* Moses gave them."
1Ch 2:34 He had an Egyptian *s* named Jarha.
2:35 daughter in marriage to his *s* Jarha,
6:49 with all that Moses the *s*
16:13 O descendants of Israel his *s*,
17: 4 saying: "Go and tell my *s* David,
17: 7 "Now then, tell my *s* David,
17:17 the future of the house of your *s*.
17:18 For you know your *s*, O LORD.
17:18 say to you for honoring your *s*?
17:19 the sake of your *s* and according
17:23 you have made concerning your *s*
17:24 of your *s* David will be established
17:25 to your *s* that you will build a house
17:25 your *s* has found courage to pray
17:26 given this good promise to your *s*.
17:27 pleased to bless the house of your *s*,
21: 8 take away the guilt of your *s*.
2Ch 1: 3 Moses the LORD's *s* had made
6:15 promise to your *s* David my father;
6:16 keep for your *s* David my father
6:17 you promised your *s* David come
6:19 the prayer that your *s* is praying
6:20 you hear the prayer your *s* prays
6:21 Hear the supplications of your *s*
6:42 promised to David your *s*."
24: 6 by Moses the *s* of the LORD
24: 9 the LORD the tax that Moses the *s*
32:16 and against his *s* Hezekiah.
Ne 1: 6 to hear the prayer your *s* is praying
1: 7 and laws you gave your *s* Moses.
1: 8 instruction you gave your *s* Moses,
1:11 Give your *s* success today
1:11 to the prayer of this your *s*
2: 5 if your *s* has found favor in his sight
9:14 and laws through your *s* Moses.
10:29 given through Moses the *s* of God
Job 1: 8 "Have you considered my *s* Job?
2: 3 "Have you considered my *s* Job?
19:16 I summon my *s*, but he does not
42: 7 of me what is right, as my *s* Job has.
42: 8 My *s* Job will pray for you,
42: 8 and seven rams and go to my *s* Job
42: 8 of me what is right, as my *s* Job has
Ps 19:11 By them is your *s* warned;
19:13 Keep your *s* also from willful sins;
27: 9 do not turn your *s* away in anger;
31:16 Let your face shine on your *s*;
35:27 delights in the well-being of his *s*."
69:17 Do not hide your face from your *s*;
78:70 He chose David his *s*
86: 2 You are my God; save your *s*
86: 4 Bring joy to your *s*,
Ps 86:16 grant your strength to your *s*
89: 3 I have sworn to David my *s*,
89:20 I have found David my *s*;
89:39 the covenant with your *s*
89:50 Lord, how your *s* has been mocked,
105: 6 O descendants of Abraham his *s*,
105:26 He sent Moses his *s*,
105:42 given to his *s* Abraham.
109:28 but your *s* will rejoice.
116:16 I am your *s*, the son
116:16 O LORD, truly I am your *s*;
119:17 Do good to your *s*, and I will live;
119:23 your *s* will meditate
119:38 Fulfill your promise to your *s*,
119:49 Remember your word to your *s*,
119:65 Do good to your *s*
119:76 to your promise to your *s*.
119:84 How long must your *s* wait?
119:124 Deal with your *s* according
119:125 I am your *s*; give me discernment
119:135 Make your face shine upon your *s*
119:140 and your *s* loves them.
119:176 Seek your *s*,
132:10 For the sake of David your *s*,
136:22 an inheritance to his *s* Israel;
143: 2 Do not bring your *s* into judgment,
143:12 for I am your *s*.
144:10 who delivers his *s* David
Pr 11:29 and the fool will be *s* to the wise.
12: 9 to be a nobody and yet have a *s*
14:35 A king delights in a wise *s*,
14:35 but a shameful *s* incurs his wrath.
17: 2 wise *s* will rule over a disgraceful
22: 7 and the borrower is *s* to the lender.
27:27 and to nourish your *s* girls.
29:19 A *s* cannot be corrected
29:21 If a man pampers his *s* from youth,
30:10 "Do not slander a *s* to his master,
30:22 a *s* who becomes king,
31:15 and portions for her *s* girls.
Ecc 7:21 or you may hear your *s* cursing you
10:16 O land whose king was a *s*
Isa 16:14 a *s* bound by contract would count
20: 3 as my *s* Isaiah has gone stripped
21:16 *s* bound by contract would count it,
22:20 "In that day I will summon my *s*,
24: 2 for master as for *s*,
37:35 for the sake of David my *s*!"
41: 8 "But you, O Israel, my *s*,
41: 9 I said, 'You are my *s*';
42: 1 "Here is my *s*, whom I uphold,
42:19 Who is blind but my *s*,
42:19 blind like the *s* of the LORD?
43:10 "and my *s* whom I have chosen,
44: 1 "But now listen, O Jacob, my *s*,
44: 2 Do not be afraid, O Jacob, my *s*,
44:21 I have made you, you are my *s*;
44:21 for you are my *s*, O Israel.
45: 4 For the sake of Jacob my *s*,
48:20 LORD has redeemed his *s* Jacob."
49: 3 He said to me, "You are my *s*,
49: 5 me in the womb to be his *s*
49: 6 too small a thing for you to be my *s*
49: 7 to the *s* of rulers:
50:10 and obeys the word of his *s*?
52:13 See, my *s* will act wisely;
53:11 my righteous *s* will justify
Jer 2:14 Is Israel a *s*, a slave by birth?
25: 9 and my *s* Nebuchadnezzar king
27: 6 over to my *s* Nebuchadnezzar king
30:10 "'So do not fear, O Jacob my *s*;
33:21 then my covenant with David my *s*
33:22 the descendants of David my *s*
33:26 of Jacob and David my *s*
43:10 for my *s* Nebuchadnezzar king
46:27 "Do not fear, O Jacob my *s*;
46:28 Do not fear, O Jacob my *s*,
Eze 28:25 which I gave to my *s* Jacob.
34:23 my *s* David, and he will tend them;
34:24 and my *s* David will be prince
37:24 My *s* David will be king over them,
37:25 and David my *s* will be their prince
37:25 in the land I gave to my *s* Jacob,
46:17 the *s* may keep it until the year
Da 6:20 "Daniel, *s* of the living God,
9:11 the *s* of God, have been poured out
9:17 the prayers and petitions of your *s*.
10:17 How can I, your *s*, talk with you,

Hag 2:23 my *s* Zerubbabel son of Shealtiel,'
Zec 3:8 going to bring my *s*, the Branch.
Mal 1:6 his father, and a *s* his master.
4:4 Remember the law of my *s* Moses,
Mt 8:6 "my *s* lies at home paralyzed
8:8 the word, and my *s* will be healed.
8:9 I say to my *s*, 'Do this,'
8:13 his *s* was healed at that very hour.
10:24 not above his teacher, nor a *s*
10:25 teacher, and the *s* like his master.
12:18 "Here is my *s* whom I have chosen,
18:26 "The *s* fell on his knees before him.
18:28 "But when that *s* went out,
18:29 "His fellow *s* fell to his knees
18:32 'You wicked *s*,' he said, 'I canceled
18:32 "Then the master called the *s* in.
18:33 mercy on your fellow *s* just
20:26 great among you must be your *s*,
23:11 greatest among you will be your *s*.
24:45 Who then is the faithful and wise *s*,
24:46 for that *s* whose master finds him
24:48 But suppose that *s* is wicked
24:50 The master of that *s* will come
25:21 'Well done, good and faithful *s*!
25:23 'Well done, good and faithful *s*!
25:26 replied, 'You wicked, lazy *s*!
25:30 And throw that worthless *s* outside
26:51 and struck the *s* of the high priest,
26:69 in the courtyard, and a *s* girl came
Mk 9:35 he must be the very last, and the *s*
10:43 great among you must be your *s*,
12:2 At harvest time he sent a *s*
12:4 Then he sent another *s* to them;
14:47 and struck the *s* of the high priest,
14:66 of the *s* girls of the high priest came
14:69 When the *s* girl saw him there,
Lk 1:38 I am the Lord's *s*," Mary answered.
1:48 of the humble state of his *s*.
1:54 He has helped his *s* Israel,
1:69 us in the house of his *s* David
2:29 you now dismiss your *s* in peace.
7:2 There a centurion's *s*, whom his
7:3 asking him to come and heal his *s*.
7:7 the word, and my *s* will be healed.
7:8 I say to my *s*, 'Do this,'
7:10 to the house and found the *s* well.
12:43 for that *s* whom the master finds
12:45 But suppose the *s* says to himself,
12:46 The master of that *s* will come
12:47 That *s* who knows his master's will
14:17 time of the banquet he sent his *s*
14:21 became angry and ordered his *s*,
14:21 "The *s* came back and reported this
14:22 *s* said, 'what you ordered has been
14:23 "Then the master told his *s*,
16:13 "No *s* can serve two masters.
17:7 Suppose one of you had a *s* plowing
17:7 say to the *s* when he comes
17:9 he thank the *s* because he did
19:17 my good *s*!' his master replied.
19:20 Then another *s* came and said, 'Sir,
19:22 you wicked *s*! You knew, did you,
20:10 At harvest time he sent a *s*
20:11 He sent another *s*, but that one
22:50 And one of them struck the *s*
22:56 A *s* girl saw him seated there
Jn 12:26 and where I am, my *s* also will be.
13:16 no *s* is greater than his master,
15:15 a *s* does not know his master's
15:20 'No *s* is greater than his master.'
18:10 and struck the high priest's *s*,
Ac 3:13 fathers, has glorified his *s* Jesus.
3:26 When God raised up his *s*,
4:25 Spirit through the mouth of your *s*,
4:27 conspire against your holy *s* Jesus,
4:30 the name of your holy *s* Jesus."
12:13 and a *s* girl named Rhoda came
12:20 a trusted personal *s* of the king,
26:16 to you to appoint you as a *s*
Ro 1:1 a *s* of Christ Jesus, called
13:4 For he is God's *s* to do you good.
13:4 He is God's *s*, an agent of wrath
14:4 you to judge someone else's *s*?
15:8 tell you that Christ has become a *s*
16:1 a *s* of the church in Cenchrea.
Gal 1:10 I would not be a *s* of Christ.
Eph 3:7 I became a *s* of this gospel
6:21 the dear brother and faithful *s*
Php 2:7 taking the very nature of a *s*,
Col 1:7 it from Epaphras, our dear fellow *s*,
1:23 of which I, Paul, have become a *s*.
1:25 I have become its *s*
4:7 a faithful minister and fellow *s*
4:12 one of you and a *s* of Christ Jesus,
2Ti 2:24 And the Lord's *s* must not quarrel;
Tit 1:1 a *s* of God and an apostle
Heb 3:5 Moses was faithful as a *s*
Jas 1:1 a *s* of God and of the Lord Jesus
2Pe 1:1 a *s* and apostle of Jesus Christ,
Jude :1 a *s* of Jesus Christ and a brother
Rev 1:1 by sending his angel to his *s* John,
15:3 the song of Moses the *s* of God
19:10 I am a fellow *s* with you
22:9 I am a fellow *s* with you

SERVANT'S (SERVANT)

Ge 19:2 "please turn aside to your *s* house.
1Sa 1:11 look upon your *s* misery
25:28 Please forgive your *s* offense,
26:19 lord the king listen to his *s* words.
2Sa 14:22 the king has granted his *s* request."
1Ki 8:28 Yet give attention to your *s* prayer
8:52 your eyes be open to your *s* plea
2Ki 6:17 Then the LORD opened the *s* eyes,
2Ch 6:19 Yet give attention to your *s* prayer
Ps 119:122 Ensure your *s* well-being;
Mt 18:27 The *s* master took pity on him,
Jn 18:10 (The *s* name was Malchus.)

SERVANTS (SERVANT)

Ge 21:25 that Abimelech's *s* had seized.
22:3 He took with him two of his *s*
22:5 He said to his *s*, "Stay here
22:19 Then Abraham returned to his *s*,
26:14 *s* that the Philistines envied him.
26:15 the wells that his father's *s* had dug
26:19 Isaac's *s* dug in the valley
26:25 his tent, and there his *s* dug a well.
26:32 That day Isaac's *s* came
27:37 have made all his relatives his *s*,
32:16 He put them in the care of his *s*,
32:16 and said to his *s*, "Go ahead of me,
39:11 none of the household *s* was inside.
39:14 she called her household *s*.
41:10 Pharaoh was once angry with his *s*,
42:10 "Your *s* have come to buy food.
42:11 Your *s* are honest men, not spies."
42:13 "Your *s* were twelve brothers,
44:7 Far be it from your *s*
44:9 If any of your *s* is found to have it,
44:19 My lord asked his *s*, 'Do you have
44:21 you said to your *s*, 'Bring him
44:23 But you told your *s*, 'Unless your
44:31 Your *s* will bring the gray head
46:34 'Your *s* have tended livestock
47:3 occupation?" "Your *s* are
47:4 please let your *s* settle in Goshen."
50:17 the sins of the *s* of the God
Ex 5:15 have you treated your *s* this way?
5:16 Your *s* are given no straw,
5:16 'Make bricks!' Your *s* are being
5:21 a stench to Pharaoh and his *s*
32:13 Remember your *s* Abraham,
Lev 25:42 Because the Israelites are my *s*,
25:55 They are my *s*, whom I brought out
25:55 for the Israelites belong to me as *s*.
Nu 22:22 and his two *s* were with him.
31:49 "Your *s* have counted the soldiers
32:4 and your *s* have livestock.
32:5 "let this land be given to your *s*
32:25 "We your *s* will do as our lord
32:27 your *s*, every man armed for battle,
32:31 "Your *s* will do what the LORD
Dt 9:27 Remember your *s* Abraham,
32:36 and have compassion on his *s*
32:43 for he will avenge the blood of his *s*
Jos 9:8 We are your *s*," they said to Joshua
9:9 "Your *s* have come
9:11 "We are your *s*; make a treaty
9:24 "Your *s* were clearly told how
10:6 at Gilgal: "Do not abandon your *s*.
Jdg 3:24 the *s* came and found the doors
6:27 So Gideon took ten of his *s* and did
19:19 bread and wine for ourselves your *s*
1Sa 9:3 "Take one of the *s* with you and go
12:19 for your *s* so that we will not die,
16:16 Let our lord command his *s* here
16:18 of the *s* answered, "I have seen
17:8 and are you not the *s* of Saul?
18:24 When Saul's *s* told him what David
21:7 one of Saul's *s* was there that day,
21:11 But the *s* of Achish said to him,
21:14 Achish said to his *s*, "Look
22:14 "Who of all your *s* is as loyal
25:8 Ask your own *s* and they will tell
25:8 Please give your *s* and your son
25:10 Many *s* are breaking away
25:10 Nabal answered David's *s*,
25:14 of the *s* told Nabal's wife Abigail:
25:19 Then she told her *s*, "Go on ahead;
25:40 His *s* went to Carmel and said
25:41 wash the feet of my master's *s*."
29:10 with your master's *s* who have
2Sa 6:20 in the sight of the slave girls of his *s*
9:10 Ziba had fifteen sons and twenty *s*.)
9:10 your *s* are to farm the land for him
9:12 of Ziba's household were *s*
11:9 to the palace with all his master's *s*
11:13 on his mat among his master's *s*;
11:24 arrows at your *s* from the wall,
12:18 David's *s* were afraid
12:19 noticed that his *s* were whispering
12:21 His *s* asked him, "Why are you
13:31 all his *s* stood by with their clothes
13:36 too, and all his *s* wept very bitterly.
14:30 So Absalom's *s* set the field on fire.
14:30 Then he said to his *s*, "Look,
14:31 "Why have your *s* set my field
15:15 "Your *s* are ready to do whatever
19:17 and his fifteen sons and twenty *s*.
1Ki 1:2 So his *s* said to him, "Let us look
1:27 without letting his *s* know who
1:33 "Take your lord's *s* with you
8:23 love with your *s* who continue
8:32 Judge between your *s*, condemning
8:36 and forgive the sin of your *s*,
10:5 the attending *s* in their robes,
12:7 they will always be your *s*."
2Ki 1:13 the lives of these fifty men, your *s*!
2:16 "we your *s* have fifty able men.
4:22 "Please send me one of the *s*
5:13 Naaman's *s* went to him and said,
5:23 He gave them to two of his *s*,
5:24 he took the things from the *s*
6:3 Won't you please come with your *s*
9:7 of all the LORD's *s* shed by Jezebel
9:7 the blood of my *s* the prophets
9:28 His *s* took him by chariot
10:5 "We are your *s* and we will do
10:23 see that no *s* of the LORD are here
17:13 to you through my *s* the prophets."
17:23 through all his *s* the prophets.
18:26 "Please speak to your *s* in Aramaic,
21:10 said through his *s* the prophets:
23:30 Josiah's *s* brought his body
24:2 proclaimed by his *s* the prophets.
1Ch 9:2 priests, Levites and temple *s*.
2Ch 2:10 will give your *s*, the woodsmen
2:15 let my lord send his *s* the wheat
6:14 love with your *s* who continue
6:23 between your *s*, repaying the guilty
6:27 and forgive the sin of your *s*,
9:4 the attending *s* in their robes,
10:7 they will always be your *s*."
36:20 and they became *s* to him
Ezr 2:43 and Shobai 139 The temple *s*:
2:55 descendants of the *s* of Solomon:
2:58 and Ami The temple *s*
2:58 and the descendants of the *s*
2:70 and the temple *s* settled
4:11 From your *s*, the men
5:11 "We are the *s* of the God of heaven
7:7 singers, gatekeepers and temple *s*,
7:24 temple *s* or other workers
8:17 and his kinsmen, the temple *s*
8:20 also brought 220 of the temple *s*—
9:11 gave through your *s* the prophets
Ne 1:6 before you day and night for your *s*
1:10 "They are your *s* and your people,
1:11 to the prayer of your *s* who delight
2:20 We his *s* will start rebuilding,
3:26 and the temple *s* living on the hill
3:31 as the house of the temple *s*
7:46 and Shobai 138 The temple *s*:

Ne 7:57 descendants of the *s* of Solomon:
7:60 and Amon The temple *s*
7:60 and the descendants of the *s*
7:73 the singers and the temple *s*,
10:28 temple *s* and all who separated
11:3 descendants of Solomon's *s* lived
11:3 temple *s* and descendants
11:21 The temple *s* lived on the hill
Job 1:3 and had a large number of *s*.
1:15 They put the *s* to the sword,
1:16 and burned up the sheep and the *s*,
1:17 They put the *s* to the sword,
4:18 If God places no trust in his *s*,
Ps 34:22 The LORD redeems his *s*;
69:36 the children of his *s* will inherit it,
79:2 given the dead bodies of your *s*
79:10 the outpoured blood of your *s*.
90:13 Have compassion on your *s*.
90:16 May your deeds be shown to your *s*
102:14 For her stones are dear to your *s*;
102:28 The children of your *s* will live
103:21 you his *s* who do his will.
104:4 flames of fire his *s*.
105:25 to conspire against his *s*.
113:1 Praise, O *s* of the LORD,
134:1 Praise the LORD, all you *s*
135:1 Praise him, you *s* of the LORD,
135:9 against Pharaoh and all his *s*.
135:14 and have compassion on his *s*.
Isa 36:11 "Please speak to your *s* in Aramaic,
44:26 who carries out the words of his *s*
54:17 the heritage of the *s* of the LORD,
63:17 Return for the sake of your *s*,
65:8 so will I do in behalf of my *s*;
65:9 and there will my *s* live.
65:13 my *s* will drink,
65:13 my *s* will rejoice,
65:13 "My *s* will eat,
65:14 My *s* will sing
65:15 to his *s* he will give another name.
66:14 will be made known to his *s*,
Jer 7:25 again I sent you my *s* the prophets.
14:3 The nobles send their *s* for water;
25:4 sent you all his *s* the prophets again
26:5 to the words of my *s* the prophets,
29:19 and again by my *s* the prophets.
35:15 again I sent all my *s* the prophets
44:4 and again I sent my *s* the prophets,
Eze 38:17 by my *s* the prophets of Israel?
46:17 from his inheritance to one of his *s*,
Da 1:12 "Please test your *s* for ten days:
1:13 and treat your *s* in accordance
2:4 live forever! Tell your *s* the dream,
2:7 "Let the king tell his *s* the dream,
3:26 Abednego, *s* of the Most High God
3:28 sent his angel and rescued his *s*!
9:6 listened to your *s* the prophets,
9:10 us through his *s* the prophets.
Joel 2:29 Even on my *s*, both men
Am 3:7 plan to his *s* the prophets.
Zec 1:6 I commanded my *s* the prophets,
Mt 13:27 The owner's *s* came to him and said
13:28 "The *s* asked him, 'Do you want us
18:23 to settle accounts with his *s*.
18:28 one of his fellow *s* who owed him
18:31 When the other *s* saw what had
21:34 he sent his *s* to the tenants
21:35 tenants seized his *s*; they beat one,
21:36 Then he sent other *s* to them,
22:3 He sent his *s* to those who had been
22:4 Then he sent some more *s* and said,
22:6 rest seized his *s*, mistreated them
22:8 to his *s*, 'The wedding banquet is
22:10 So the *s* went out into the streets
24:45 in charge of the *s* in his household
24:49 he then begins to beat his fellow *s*
25:14 who called his *s* and entrusted his
25:19 the master of those *s* returned
Mk 13:34 leaves his house in charge of his *s*,
Lk 1:2 the first were eyewitnesses and *s*
12:37 for those *s* whose master finds
12:38 for those *s* whose master finds
12:42 of his *s* to give them their food
15:22 But the father said to his *s*, 'Quick!
15:26 So he called one of the *s*
17:10 should say, 'We are unworthy *s*;
19:13 of his *s* and gave them ten minas.
19:15 sent for the *s* to whom he had given
Jn 2:5 to the *s*, "Do whatever he tells you
2:7 Jesus said to the *s*, "Fill the jars
2:9 *s* who had drawn the water knew.
4:51 his *s* met him with the news that his
15:15 longer call you *s*, because a servant
18:18 and the *s* and officials stood
18:26 One of the high priest's *s*, a relative
18:36 my *s* would fight to prevent my
Ac 2:18 Even on my *s*, both men
4:29 enable your *s* to speak your word
10:7 Cornelius called two of his *s*
16:17 "These men are *s* of the Most High
Ro 13:6 for the authorities are God's *s*,
1Co 3:5 And what is Paul? Only *s*,
4:1 ought to regard us as *s* of Christ
2Co 4:5 ourselves as your *s* for Jesus' sake.
6:4 as *s* of God we commend ourselves
11:15 if his *s* masquerade as *s*
11:23 Are they *s* of Christ? (I am out
Php 1:1 Paul and Timothy, *s* of Christ Jesus
Heb 1:7 his *s* flames of fire."
1Pe 2:16 a cover-up for evil; live as *s* of God.
Rev 1:1 to show his *s* what must soon take
2:20 By her teaching she misleads my *s*
6:11 until the number of their fellow *s*
7:3 the foreheads of the *s* of our God."
10:7 he announced to his *s* the prophets
11:18 for rewarding your *s* the prophets
19:2 on her the blood of his *s*."
19:5 all you his *s*,
22:3 in the city, and his *s* will serve him.
22:6 to show his *s* the things that must

SERVANTS' (SERVANT)

Ge 44:16 God has uncovered your *s*' guilt.
47:4 and your *s*' flocks have no pasture.

SERVE (SERVED SERVES SERVICE SERVICES SERVING SERVITUDE)

Ge 1:14 let them *s* as signs to mark seasons
15:14 But I will punish the nation they *s*
25:23 and the older will *s* the younger."
27:29 May nations *s* you
27:40 and you will *s* your brother.
31:44 and let it *s* as a witness between us
43:31 himself, said, "*S* the food."
Ex 14:12 for us to *s* the Egyptians than to die
14:12 us alone; let us *s* the Egyptians"?
18:13 next day Moses took his seat to *s*
18:22 Have them *s* as judges
21:2 he is to *s* you for six years.
28:1 so they may *s* me as priests.
28:3 his consecration, so he may *s* me
28:4 so they may *s* me as priests.
28:41 Consecrate them so they may *s* me
29:1 so they may *s* me as priests:
29:44 and his sons to *s* me as priests.
30:30 consecrate them so they may *s* me
31:10 garments for his sons when they *s*
35:19 garments for his sons when they *s*
40:13 and consecrate him so he may *s* me
40:15 so they may *s* me as priests.
Lev 7:35 were presented to *s* the LORD
Nu 1:3 more who are able to *s* in the army.
1:20 or more who were able to *s*
1:22 or more who were able to *s*
1:24 or more who were able to *s*
1:26 or more who were able to *s*
1:28 or more who were able to *s*
1:30 or more who were able to *s*
1:32 or more who were able to *s*
1:34 or more who were able to *s*
1:36 or more who were able to *s*
1:38 or more who were able to *s*
1:40 or more who were able to *s*
1:42 or more who were able to *s*
1:45 or more who were able to *s*
3:3 who were ordained to *s* as priests.
3:10 and his sons to *s* as priests;
4:3 of age who come to *s* in the work
4:23 of age who come to *s* in the work
4:30 of age who come to *s* in the work
4:35 of age who came to *s* in the work
4:39 of age who came to *s* in the work
4:43 of age who came to *s* in the work
18:7 But only you and your sons may *s*
26:2 more who are able to *s* in the army
Dt 6:13 *s* him only and take your oaths
7:4 from following me to *s* other gods,
7:16 with pity and do not *s* their gods,
10:12 to *s* the LORD your God
10:20 the LORD your God and *s* him.
11:13 and to *s* him with all your heart
12:30 How do these nations *s* their gods?
13:4 *s* him and hold fast to him.
18:7 all his fellow Levites who *s* there
28:47 you did not *s* the LORD your
28:48 you will *s* the enemies the LORD
Jos 4:6 of the tribes of the Israelites, to *s*
9:23 You will never cease to *s*
22:5 and to *s* him with all your heart
23:7 You must not *s* them or bow
23:16 and go and *s* other gods
24:14 and in Egypt, and *s* the LORD.
24:14 and *s* him with all faithfulness.
24:15 my household, we will *s* the LORD
24:15 this day whom you will *s*,
24:16 forsake the LORD to *s* other gods!
24:18 We too will *s* the LORD,
24:19 "You are not able to *s* the LORD.
24:20 the LORD and *s* foreign gods,
24:21 "No! We will *s* the LORD."
24:22 you have chosen to *s* the LORD."
24:24 "We will *s* the LORD our God
Jdg 9:28 Why should we *s* Abimelech?
9:28 isn't Zebul his deputy? *S* the men
18:19 Isn't it better that you *s* a tribe
1Sa 7:3 to the LORD and *s* him only,
8:11 and make them *s* with his chariots
12:10 of our enemies, and we will *s* you.'
12:14 If you fear the LORD and *s*
12:20 but *s* the LORD with all your heart
12:24 *s* him faithfully with all your heart;
17:9 will become our subjects and *s* us."
18:17 only *s* me bravely and fight
25:41 ready to *s* you and wash the feet
26:19 and have said, 'Go, *s* other gods.'
29:6 to have you *s* with me in the army.
2Sa 16:19 I served your father, so I will *s* you
16:19 should I *s*? Should I not *s* the son?
1Ki 9:6 to *s* other gods and worship them,
9:27 *s* in the fleet with Solomon's men.
12:4 put on us, and we will *s* you."
12:7 *s* them and give them a favorable
16:31 began to *s* Baal and worship him.
17:1 the God of Israel, lives, whom I *s*,
18:15 LORD Almighty lives, whom I *s*,
2Ki 3:14 LORD Almighty lives, whom I *s*,
4:41 "*S* it to the people to eat."
5:16 whom I *s*, I will not accept a thing."
10:18 Baal a little; Jehu will *s* him much.
17:35 *s* them or sacrifice to them.
18:7 king of Assyria and did not *s* him.
23:9 priests of the high places did not *s*
25:24 down in the land and *s* the king
1Ch 12:38 fighting men who volunteered to *s*
23:31 to *s* before the LORD regularly
28:9 *s* him with wholehearted devotion
2Ch 7:19 to *s* other gods and worship them,
10:4 put on us, and we will *s* you."
13:10 priests who *s* the LORD are sons
19:9 "You must *s* faithfully
19:11 and the Levites will *s* as officials
29:11 you to stand before him and *s* him,
30:8 *S* the LORD your God,
33:16 and told Judah to *s* the LORD,
34:33 in Israel *s* the LORD their God.
35:3 Now *s* the LORD your God
Ne 4:22 so they can *s* us as guards by night
9:35 they did not *s* you or turn
Est 1:8 to *s* each man what he wished.
Job 21:15 Almighty, that we should *s* him?
36:11 If they obey and *s* him,
39:9 "Will the wild ox consent to *s* you?
Ps 2:11 *S* the LORD with fear
22:30 Posterity will *s* him;
72:11 and all nations will *s* him.
100:2 *S* the LORD with gladness;
119:91 for all things *s* you.
Pr 22:29 He will *s* before kings;
22:29 he will not *s* before obscure men.
Isa 56:6 the LORD to *s* him,
60:7 the rams of Nebaioth will *s* you;
60:10 and their kings will *s* you.
60:12 that will not *s* you will perish;
Jer 2:20 you said, 'I will not *s* you!'

Jer 5: 19 so now you will *s* foreigners
11: 10 followed other gods to *s* them.
13: 10 and go after other gods to *s*
15: 19 that you may *s* me;
16: 13 and there you will *s* other gods day
25: 6 Do not follow other gods to *s*
25: 11 and these nations will *s* the king
27: 7 All nations will *s* him and his son
27: 8 will not *s* Nebuchadnezzar king
27: 9 You will not *s* the king of Babylon.'
27: 10 lies to you that will only *s*
27: 11 of the king of Babylon and *s* him,
27: 12 *s* him and his people, and you will
27: 13 any nation that will not *s* the king
27: 14 'You will never *s* the king
27: 17 *S* the king of Babylon,
28: 14 make them *s* Nebuchadnezzar king
28: 14 of Babylon, and they will *s* him.
30: 9 they will *s* the LORD their God
35: 15 do not follow other gods to *s* them.
35: 19 fail to have a man to *s* me.' "
40: 9 afraid to *s* the Babylonians,"
40: 9 down in the land and *s* the king
Eze 20: 32 peoples of the world, who *s* wood
20: 39 and *s* your idols, every one of you!
20: 40 house of Israel will *s* me,
27: 25 " 'The ships of Tarshish *s*
41: 6 around the wall of the temple to *s*
44: 11 They may *s* in my sanctuary,
44: 11 stand before the people and *s* them.
44: 13 They are not to come near to *s* me
44: 24 the priests are to *s* as judges
45: 5 to the Levites, who *s* in the temple,
47: 12 Their fruit will *s* for food
Da 1: 4 qualified to *s* in the king's palace.
3: 12 They neither *s* your gods
3: 14 that you do not *s* my gods
3: 17 the God we *s* is able to save us
3: 18 that we will not *s* your gods
3: 28 to give up their lives rather than *s*
6: 16 whom you *s* continually, rescue
6: 20 God, whom you *s* continually,
Zep 3: 9 and *s* him shoulder to shoulder.
Zec 4: 14 to *s* the LORD of all the earth."
Mal 3: 14 You have said, 'It is futile to *s* God.
3: 18 between those who *s* God
Mt 4: 10 Lord your God, and *s* him only.' "
6: 24 You cannot *s* both God and Money
6: 24 "No one can *s* two masters.
20: 28 but to *s*, and to give his life
Mk 10: 45 but to *s*, and to give his life
Lk 1: 74 to enable us to *s* him without fear
4: 8 Lord your God and *s* him only.' "
12: 37 the truth, he will dress himself to *s*,
16: 13 You cannot *s* both God and Money
16: 13 "No servant can *s* two masters.
Ac 7: 7 But I will punish the nation they *s*
26: 7 they earnestly *s* God day and night
27: 23 whom I *s* stood beside me and said,
Ro 1: 9 whom I *s* with my whole heart
7: 6 the law so that we *s* in the new way
9: 12 "The older will *s* the younger."
12: 7 If it is serving, let him *s*;
1Co 9: 13 and those who *s* at the altar share
2Co 11: 8 support from them so as to *s* you.
13: 4 live with him to *s* you.
Gal 5: 13 rather, *s* one another in love.
Eph 6: 7 *S* wholeheartedly,
1Th 1: 9 to God from idols to *s* the living
1Ti 3: 10 nothing against them, let them *s*
6: 2 they are to *s* them even better,
2Ti 1: 3 whom I *s*, as my forefathers did,
Heb 1: 14 to *s* those who will inherit salvation
8: 5 They *s* at a sanctuary that is a copy
9: 14 so that we may *s* the living God!
1Pe 4: 10 gift he has received to *s* others,
5: 2 greedy for money, but eager to *s*;
Jude : 7 They *s* as an example
Rev 1: 6 priests to *s* his God and Father—
5: 10 kingdom and priests to *s* our God,
7: 15 *s* him day and night in his temple;
22: 3 and his servants will *s* him.

SERVED (SERVE)

Ge 29: 20 Jacob *s* seven years to get Rachel,
29: 25 I *s* you for Rachel, didn't I?
30: 26 for whom I have *s* you,
43: 32 They *s* him by himself, the brothers
43: 34 When portions were *s* to them
Ex 18: 26 They *s* as judges for the people
38: 8 of the women who *s* at the entrance
Nu 3: 4 so only Eleazar and Ithamar *s*
4: 37 those in the Kohathite clans who *s*
4: 41 in the Gershonite clans who *s*
26: 10 And they *s* as a warning sign.
Jos 24: 15 whether the gods your forefathers *s*
24: 31 Israel *s* the LORD
Jdg 2: 7 The people *s* the LORD
2: 11 eyes of the LORD and *s* the Baals.
2: 13 they forsook him and *s* Baal
3: 6 to their sons, and *s* their gods.
3: 7 and *s* the Baals and the Asherahs.
10: 6 They *s* the Baals
10: 6 the LORD and no longer *s* him,
10: 13 have forsaken me and *s* other gods,
10: 16 among them and *s* the LORD.
1Sa 2: 22 slept with the women who *s*
7: 4 Ashtoreths, and *s* the LORD only.
8: 2 his second was Abijah, and they *s*
12: 10 and *s* the Baals and the Ashtoreths.
2Sa 12: 20 and at his request they *s* him food,
13: 9 took the pan and *s* him the bread,
16: 19 I *s* your father, so I will serve you."
1Ki 11: 17 officials who had *s* his father.
12: 6 the elders who had *s* his father
22: 53 He *s* and worshiped Baal
2Ki 5: 2 Israel, and she *s* Naaman's wife.
10: 18 "Ahab *s* Baal a little; Jehu will
17: 33 also *s* their own gods in accordance
1Ch 6: 10 father of Azariah (it was he who *s*
6: 33 Here are the men who *s*, together
6: 39 Heman's associate Asaph, who *s*
23: 24 or more who *s* in the temple
24: 2 and Ithamar *s* as the priests.
27: 1 who *s* the king in all that concerned
2Ch 10: 6 the elders who had *s* his father
17: 19 These were the men who *s* the king
35: 13 *s* them quickly to all the people.
Ne 12: 26 They *s* in the days of Joiakim son
Est 1: 7 Wine was *s* in goblets of gold,
1: 10 the seven eunuchs who *s* him—
Jer 5: 19 *s* foreign gods in your own land,
8: 2 which they have loved and *s*
16: 11 and *s* and worshiped them.
22: 9 have worshiped and *s* other gods
34: 14 After he has *s* you six years,
52: 12 who *s* the king of Babylon,
Eze 27: 7 and *s* as your banner;
27: 10 *s* as soldiers in your army.
44: 12 they *s* them in the presence
Hos 12: 12 Israel *s* to get a wife,
Mt 20: 28 Son of Man did not come to be *s*,
Mk 10: 45 Son of Man did not come to be *s*,
Jn 12: 2 Martha *s*, while Lazarus was
13: 2 The evening meal was being *s*,
Ac 1: 16 who *s* as guide for those who
13: 36 when David had *s* God's purpose
17: 25 And he is not *s* by human hands,
20: 19 I *s* the Lord with great humility
Ro 1: 25 and *s* created things rather
Php 1: 12 to me has really *s* to advance
2: 22 son with his father he has *s* with me
1Ti 3: 13 Those who have *s* well gain
Heb 7: 13 one from that tribe has ever *s*

SERVES (SERVE)

Dt 15: 12 is sold to you and he *s* you six years
Mal 3: 17 a man spares his son who *s* him.
Lk 22: 26 one who rules like the one who *s*.
22: 27 But I am among you as one who *s*.
22: 27 is at the table or the one who *s*?
Jn 12: 26 Whoever *s* me must follow me;
12: 26 will honor the one who *s* me.
Ro 14: 18 because anyone who *s* Christ
1Co 9: 7 Who *s* as a soldier
Heb 8: 2 and who *s* in the sanctuary,
1Pe 4: 11 If anyone *s*, he should do it

SERVICE (SERVE)

Ge 41: 46 old when he entered the *s*
50: 2 in his *s* to embalm his father Israel.
Ex 27: 19 used in the *s* of the tabernacle,
30: 16 and use it for the *s* of the Tent
35: 21 for all its *s*, and for the sacred
Nu 4: 24 "This is the *s* of the Gershonite
4: 26 and all the equipment used in its *s*.
4: 27 All their *s*, whether carrying
4: 28 This is the *s* of the Gershonite
4: 31 as they perform *s* at the Tent
4: 33 This is the *s* of the Merarite clans
8: 25 retire from their regular *s*
18: 7 I am giving you the *s*
Dt 15: 18 his *s* to you these six years has been
Jos 18: 7 the priestly *s* of the LORD is their
1Sa 14: 52 brave man, he took him into his *s*.
16: 21 came to Saul and entered his *s*.
16: 22 "Allow David to remain in my *s*,
1Ki 8: 11 priests could not perform their *s*
2Ki 25: 14 articles used in the temple *s*.
1Ch 5: 18 men ready for military *s*—
9: 28 of the articles used in the temple *s*;
23: 26 or any of the articles used in its *s*."
23: 28 descendants in the *s* of the temple
23: 32 for the *s* of the temple
25: 1 of the men who performed this *s*:
26: 30 of the LORD and for the king's *s*.
28: 1 of the divisions in the *s* of the king,
28: 13 for all the articles to be used in its *s*.
28: 14 to be used in various kinds of *s*,
28: 14 to be used in various kinds of *s*:
28: 20 the work for the *s* of the temple
2Ch 5: 14 priests could not perform their *s*
17: 16 himself for the *s* of the LORD,
24: 14 for the *s* and for the burnt offerings,
25: 5 thousand men ready for military *s*,
29: 35 So the *s* of the temple
30: 22 of the *s* of the LORD.
31: 21 undertook in the *s* of God's temple
35: 2 and encouraged them in the *s*
35: 10 The *s* was arranged and the priests
35: 16 So at that time the entire *s*
Ezr 6: 18 for the *s* of God at Jerusalem,
Ne 10: 32 for the *s* of the house of our God:
11: 22 for the *s* of the house of God.
12: 45 the *s* of their God and the *s*
13: 10 responsible for the *s* had gone back
Job 7: 1 Does not man have hard *s* on earth
14: 14 All the days of my hard *s*
Isa 40: 2 that her hard *s* has been completed,
41: 2 calling him in righteousness to his *s*
Jer 52: 18 articles used in the temple *s*.
Eze 44: 16 before me and perform my *s*
Da 1: 5 were to enter the king's *s*.
1: 19 so they entered the king's *s*.
Lk 1: 23 When his time of *s* was completed,
9: 62 fit for *s* in the kingdom
12: 35 "Be dressed ready for *s*
Jn 16: 2 kills you will think he is offering a *s*
Ro 15: 17 in Christ Jesus in my *s* to God.
15: 25 way to Jerusalem in the *s*
15: 31 and that my *s* in Jerusalem may be
1Co 12: 5 There are different kinds of *s*,
16: 15 themselves to the *s* of the saints.
2Co 8: 4 of sharing in this *s* to the saints.
8: 18 the churches for his *s* to the gospel.
9: 1 to you about this *s* to the saints.
9: 12 This *s* that you perform is not only
9: 13 of the *s* by which you have proved
Eph 4: 12 God's people for works of *s*,
Php 2: 17 and *s* coming from your faith,
1Ti 1: 12 me faithful, appointing me to his *s*.
6: 2 benefit from their *s* are believers,
Heb 2: 17 and faithful high priest in *s* to God,
Rev 2: 19 and faith, your *s* and perseverance,

SERVICES (SERVE)

Ex 14: 5 Israelites go and have lost their *s*!"
Ne 12: 9 stood opposite them in the *s*.
13: 14 for the house of my God and its *s*.

SERVING (SERVE)

Ex 39: 41 the garments for his sons when *s*
Nu 4: 47 came to do the work of *s*
18: 21 do while *s* at the Tent of Meeting.
Dt 28: 14 following other gods and *s* them.
Jos 20: 6 the death of the high priest who is *s*
24: 15 if *s* the LORD seems undesirable
Jdg 2: 19 and *s* and worshiping them.
10: 10 forsaking our God and *s* the Baals
1Sa 8: 8 forsaking me and *s* other gods,
1Ki 9: 9 gods, worshiping and *s* them—
12: 8 up with him and were *s* him.
2Ki 17: 41 the LORD, they were *s* their idols.
1Ch 28: 13 for all the work of *s* in the temple

2Ch 7:22 gods, worshiping and *s* them—
10: 8 up with him and were *s* him.
12: 8 and *s* the kings of other lands."
12: 8 learn the difference between *s* me
Eze 44:11 of the gates of the temple and *s* in it
48:11 who were faithful in *s* me
Lk 1: 8 and he was *s* as priest before God,
Ro 12: 7 If it is *s*, let him serve;
12:11 your spiritual fervor, *s* the Lord.
16:18 people are not *s* our Lord Christ,
Eph 6: 7 as if you were *s* the Lord, not men,
Col 3:24 It is the Lord Christ you are *s*.
2Ti 2: 4 No one *s* as a soldier gets involved
1Pe 1:12 that they were not *s* themselves
5: 2 *s* as overseers—not because you

SERVITUDE (SERVE)

Ge 47:21 and Joseph reduced the people to *s*,

SETH

Ge 4:25 birth to a son and named him *S*,
4:26 *S* also had a son, and he named him
5: 3 own image; and he named him *S*.
5: 4 After *S* was born, Adam lived 800
5: 6 When *S* had lived 105 years,
5: 7 *S* lived 807 years and had other
5: 8 Altogether, *S* lived 912 years,
1Ch 1: 1 Adam, *S*, Enosh, Kenan, Mahalalel
Lk 3:38 the son of *S*, the son of Adam,

SETHUR

Nu 13:13 tribe of Asher, *S* son of Michael;

SETTLE (RESETTLE RESETTLED SETTLED SETTLEMENT SETTLEMENTS SETTLES)

Ge 34:10 You can *s* among us; the land is
34:16 We'll *s* among you and become one
34:23 and they will *s* among us."
35: 1 "Go up to Bethel and *s* there,
46:34 Then you will be allowed to *s*
47: 4 please let your servants *s*
47: 6 *s* your father and your brothers
Nu 33:53 possession of the land and *s* in it,
Dt 8:12 when you build fine houses and *s*
12:10 *s* in the land the LORD your God
Jdg 18: 1 of their own where they might *s*,
2Ki 25:24 "*S* down in the land and serve
2Ch 19: 8 law of the LORD and to *s* disputes.
Job 3: 5 may a cloud *s* over it;
Ps 69:35 Then people will *s* there
107: 4 to a city where they could *s*.
107: 7 to a city where they could *s*.
107:36 founded a city where they could *s*.
139: 9 if I *s* on the far side of the sea,
Isa 2: 4 will *s* disputes for many peoples.
7:19 They will all come and *s*
14: 1 and will *s* them in their own land.
23: 7 her to *s* in far-off lands?
54: 3 and *s* in their desolate cities.
Jer 29: 5 "Build houses and *s* down;
29:28 Therefore build houses and *s* down
40: 9 "*S* down in the land and serve
42:15 to Egypt and you do go to *s* there,
42:17 to go to Egypt to *s* there will die
42:22 place where you want to go to *s*."
43: 2 go to Egypt to *s* there.'
44:12 to go to Egypt to *s* there.
Eze 32: 4 I will let all the birds of the air *s*
32:14 Then I will let her waters *s*
36:11 I will *s* people on you as in the past
37:14 and I will *s* you in your own land.
Hos 11:11 I will *s* them in their homes,"
Mic 4: 3 will *s* disputes for strong nations far
Na 3:17 that *s* in the walls on a cold day—
Mt 5:25 "*S* matters quickly
18:23 to *s* accounts with his servants.
Ac 18:15 and your own law—*s* the matter
2Th 3:12 in the Lord Jesus Christ to *s* down

SETTLED (SETTLE)

Ge 11: 2 a plain in Shinar and *s* there.
11:31 came to Haran, they *s* there.
19:30 his two daughters left Zoar and *s*
25:18 His descendants *s* in the area
26:17 in the Valley of Gerar and *s* there.
36: 8 Edom) *s* in the hill country of Seir.
47:11 Joseph *s* his father and his brothers
Ge 47:27 Now the Israelites *s* in Egypt
Ex 10: 6 from the day they *s* in this land
10:14 *s* down in every area of the country
16:35 until they came to a land that was *s*
22:11 the issue between them will be *s*
24:16 of the LORD *s* on Mount Sinai.
40:35 because the cloud had *s* upon it,
Nu 9:17 wherever the cloud *s*, the Israelites
11: 9 When the dew *s* on the camp
21:31 Israel *s* in the land of the Amorites.
22: 5 of the land and have *s* next to me.
31:10 towns where the Midianites had *s*,
32:40 of Manasseh, and they *s* there.
Dt 2:12 before them and *s* in their place,
2:21 who drove them out and *s*
2:23 Caphtor destroyed them and *s*
12:29 you have driven them out and *s*
17:14 have taken possession of it and *s*
19: 1 and *s* in their towns and houses,
26: 1 have taken possession of it and *s*
Jos 19:47 They *s* in Leshem and named it
19:50 he built up the town and *s* there.
21:43 took possession of it and *s* there.
Jdg 7:12 all the other eastern peoples had *s*
11: 3 from his brothers and *s* in the land
18:28 Danites rebuilt the city and *s* there.
21:23 rebuilt the towns and *s* in them.
Ru 3:18 rest until the matter is *s* today."
1Sa 12: 8 of Egypt and *s* them in this place.
27: 3 and his men *s* in Gath with Achish.
2Sa 2: 3 and they *s* in Hebron and its towns.
7: 1 After the king was *s* in his palace
20:18 answer at Abel,' and that *s* it.
1Ki 11:24 where they *s* and took control.
2Ki 17: 6 He *s* them in Halah, in Gozan
17:24 and *s* them in the towns of Samaria
17:29 in the several towns where they *s*,
18:11 to Assyria and *s* them in Halah,
1Ch 4:41 Then they *s* in their place,
5: 8 They *s* in the area from Aroer
5:23 they *s* in the land from Bashan
17: 1 After David was *s* in his palace,
2Ch 8: 2 had given him, and *s* Israelites
15: 9 Simeon who had *s* among them,
Ezr 2:70 and the temple servants *s*
2:70 of the Israelites *s* in their towns.
3: 1 the Israelites had *s* in their towns,
4:10 and *s* in the city of Samaria
Ne 7:73 rest of the Israelites, *s* in their own
7:73 the Israelites had *s* in their towns,
11: 1 of the people *s* in Jerusalem,
11: 3 are the provincial leaders who *s*
11:36 the Levites of Judah *s* in Benjamin.
Ps 68:10 Your people *s* in it,
78:55 he *s* the tribes of Israel
Pr 8:25 before the mountains were *s*
Isa 29: 1 the city where David *s*!
Eze 31:13 birds of the air *s* on the fallen tree,
47:22 and for the aliens who have *s*
Zec 7: 7 and the western foothills were *s*?' "
Mt 25:19 and *s* accounts with them.
Ac 7: 4 of the Chaldeans and *s* in Haran.
7:29 where he *s* as a foreigner
19:39 it must be *s* in a legal assembly.
1Co 7:37 But the man who has *s* the matter

SETTLEMENT (SETTLE)

Isa 27:10 an abandoned *s*, forsaken like
Mt 18:24 As he began the *s*, a man who owed

SETTLEMENTS (SETTLE)

Ge 25:16 tribal rulers according to their *s*
36:43 according to their *s*
Nu 21:25 Heshbon and all its surrounding *s*.
21:32 captured its surrounding *s*
32:41 captured their *s* and called them
32:42 Kenath and its surrounding *s*
Jos 13:30 all the *s* of Jair in Bashan, sixty
15:45 with its surrounding *s* and villages;
15:47 and Gaza, its *s* and villages,
15:47 its surrounding *s* and villages;
17:11 with their surrounding *s* (the third
17:16 both those in Beth Shan and its *s*
Jdg 1:27 Megiddo and their surrounding *s*,
11:26 the surrounding *s* and all the towns
1Ki 4:13 in Ramoth Gilead (the *s* of Jair son
1Ch 2:23 as Kenath with its surrounding *s*—
4:33 These were their *s*.
1Ch 6:54 the locations of their *s* allotted
7:28 Their lands and *s* included Bethel
Ne 11:25 Kiriath Arba and its surrounding *s*,
11:25 in Dibon and its *s*, in Jekabzeel
11:27 in Beersheba and its *s*,
11:28 in Meconah and its *s*,
11:30 its fields, and in Azekah and its *s*.
11:31 Aija, Bethel and its *s*, in Anathoth,
Isa 42:11 let the *s* where Kedar lives rejoice.
Eze 26: 6 and her *s* on the mainland will be
26: 8 He will ravage your *s*
34:13 and in all the *s* in the land.

SETTLES (SETTLE)

2Sa 17:12 fall on him as dew *s* on the ground.
Ps 113: 9 He *s* the barren woman
Pr 18:18 Casting the lot *s* disputes
Eze 47:23 In whatever tribe the alien *s*,

SEVEN (SEVENFOLD SEVENS SEVENTH)

Ge 4:15 he will suffer vengeance *s* times
4:24 If Cain is avenged *s* times,
7: 2 Take with you *s* of every kind
7: 3 and also *s* of every kind of bird,
7: 4 *S* days from now I will send rain
7:10 after the *s* days the floodwaters
8:10 He waited *s* more days
8:12 He waited *s* more days
21:28 Abraham set apart *s* ewe lambs
21:29 of these *s* ewe lambs you have set
21:30 "Accept these *s* lambs
29:18 "I'll work for you *s* years in return
29:20 Jacob served *s* years to get Rachel,
29:27 return for another *s* years of work."
29:30 worked for Laban another *s* years.
31:23 he pursued Jacob for *s* days
33: 3 bowed down to the ground *s* times
41: 2 of the river there came up *s* cows,
41: 3 *s* other cows, ugly and gaunt,
41: 4 and gaunt ate up the *s* sleek,
41: 5 *S* heads of grain, healthy and good,
41: 6 *s* other heads of grain sprouted—
41: 7 of grain swallowed up the *s* healthy
41:18 of the river there came up *s* cows,
41:19 After them, *s* other cows came up
41:20 cows ate up the *s* fat cows that
41:22 "In my dreams I also saw *s* heads
41:23 After them, *s* other heads sprouted
41:24 swallowed up the *s* good heads.
41:26 The *s* good cows are *s* years,
41:26 *s* good heads of grain are *s* years;
41:27 The *s* lean, ugly cows that came up
41:27 They are *s* years of famine.
41:27 and so are the *s* worthless heads
41:27 up after they did are *s* years,
41:29 *S* years of great abundance are
41:30 *s* years of famine will follow them.
41:34 during the *s* years of abundance.
41:36 to be used during the *s* years
41:47 During the *s* years
41:48 in those *s* years of abundance
41:53 The *s* years of abundance
41:54 and the *s* years of famine began,
46:25 to his daughter Rachel—*s* in all.
Ex 2:16 a priest of Midian had *s* daughters,
7:25 *S* days passed after the LORD
12:15 For *s* days you are
12:19 For *s* days no yeast is to be found
13: 6 For *s* days eat bread made
13: 7 bread during those *s* days;
22:30 stay with their mothers for *s* days,
23:15 for *s* days eat bread made
25:37 "Then make its *s* lamps
29:30 is to wear them *s* days.
29:35 taking *s* days to ordain them.
29:37 For *s* days make atonement
34:18 For *s* days eat bread made
37:23 They made its *s* lamps, as well
Lev 4: 6 and sprinkle some of it *s* times
4:17 it before the LORD *s* times in front
8:11 some of the oil on the altar *s* times,
8:33 for your ordination will last *s* days.
8:33 to the Tent of Meeting for *s* days,
8:35 for *s* days and do what the LORD
12: 2 be ceremonially unclean for *s* days,
13: 4 person in isolation for *s* days.
13: 5 him in isolation another *s* days.

Lev 13:21 is to put him in isolation for *s* days.
13:26 is to put him in isolation for *s* days.
13:31 person in isolation for *s* days.
13:33 him in isolation another *s* days.
13:50 the affected article for *s* days.
13:54 he is to isolate it for another *s* days.
14: 7 *S* times he shall sprinkle the one
14: 8 stay outside his tent for *s* days.
14:16 of it before the LORD *s* times.
14:27 the oil from his palm *s* times
14:38 close up the house for *s* days.
14:51 and sprinkle the house *s* times.
15:13 he is to count off *s* days
15:19 her monthly period will last *s* days,
15:24 he will be unclean for *s* days;
15:28 she must count off *s* days,
16:14 some of it with his finger *s* times
16:19 with his finger *s* times to cleanse it
22:27 to remain with its mother for *s* days
23: 6 for *s* days you must eat bread made
23: 8 For *s* days present an offering
23:15 offering, count off *s* full weeks.
23:18 with this bread *s* male lambs,
23:34 begins, and it lasts for *s* days.
23:36 For *s* days present offerings made
23:39 festival to the LORD for *s* days;
23:40 the LORD your God for *s* days.
23:41 to the LORD for *s* days each year.
23:42 booths for *s* days: All native-born
25: 8 of years—*s* times *s* years—
25: 8 so that the *s* sabbaths
25: 8 " 'Count off *s* sabbaths of years—
26:18 you for your sins *s* times over.
26:21 multiply your afflictions *s* times
26:24 you for your sins *s* times over.
26:28 you for your sins *s* times over.
Nu 8: 2 'When you set up the *s* lamps,
12:14 been in disgrace for *s* days?
12:14 her outside the camp for *s* days;
12:15 outside the camp for *s* days,
13:22 (Hebron had been built *s* years
19: 4 sprinkle it *s* times toward the front
19:11 of anyone will be unclean for *s* days
19:14 is in it will be unclean for *s* days,
19:16 a grave, will be unclean for *s* days.
23: 1 prepare *s* bulls and *s* rams for me."
23: 1 said, "Build me *s* altars here,
23: 4 said, "I have prepared *s* altars,
23:14 and there he built *s* altars
23:29 prepare *s* bulls and *s* rams for me."
23:29 said, "Build me *s* altars here,
28:11 and *s* male lambs a year old,
28:17 for *s* days eat bread made
28:19 and *s* male lambs a year old,
28:21 and with each of the *s* lambs,
28:24 made by fire every day for *s* days
28:27 and *s* male lambs a year old
28:29 and with each of the *s* lambs,
29: 2 and *s* male lambs a year old,
29: 4 and with each of the *s* lambs,
29: 8 and *s* male lambs a year old,
29:10 and with each of the *s* lambs,
29:12 a festival to the LORD for *s* days.
29:32 On the seventh day prepare *s* bulls,
29:36 and *s* male lambs a year old,
31:19 stay outside the camp *s* days.
Dt 7: 1 *s* nations larger and stronger
15: 1 of every *s* years you must cancel
16: 3 but for *s* days eat unleavened bread
16: 4 in all your land for *s* days.
16: 9 off *s* weeks from the time you begin
16:13 the Feast of Tabernacles for *s* days
16:15 For *s* days celebrate the Feast
28: 7 direction but flee from you in *s*.
28:25 direction but flee from them in *s*,
31:10 "At the end of every *s* years,
Jos 6: 4 Have *s* priests carry trumpets
6: 4 march around the city *s* times,
6: 6 and have *s* priests carry trumpets
6: 8 the *s* priests carrying the *s* trumpets
6:13 carrying the *s* trumpets went
6:13 *s* priests carrying the *s* trumpets
6:15 day they circled the city *s* times.
6:15 marched around the city *s* times
18: 2 but there were still *s* Israelite tribes
18: 5 are to divide the land into *s* parts.
18: 6 of the *s* parts of the land,
18: 9 in *s* parts, and returned to Joshua

Jdg 6: 1 and for *s* years he gave them
6:25 father's herd, the one *s* years old.
12: 9 Ibzan led Israel *s* years.
14:12 within the *s* days of the feast,
14:17 She cried the whole *s* days
16: 7 with *s* fresh thongs that have not
16: 8 brought her *s* fresh thongs
16:13 Delilah took the *s* braids
16:13 "If you weave the *s* braids
16:19 to shave off the *s* braids of his hair,
20:15 addition to *s* hundred chosen men
20:16 there were *s* hundred chosen
Ru 4:15 who is better to you than *s* sons,
1Sa 2: 5 was barren has borne *s* children,
6: 1 in Philistine territory *s* months,
10: 8 you must wait *s* days until I come
11: 3 "Give us *s* days so we can send
13: 8 He waited *s* days, the time set
16:10 Jesse had *s* of his sons pass
31:13 at Jabesh, and they fasted *s* days.
2Sa 2:11 over the house of Judah was *s* years
5: 5 reigned over Judah *s* years
8: 4 *s* thousand charioteers
10:18 and David killed *s* hundred
21: 6 let *s* of his male descendants be
21: 9 All *s* of them fell together;
1Ki 2:11 *s* years in Hebron and thirty-three
6: 6 six cubits and the third floor *s*.
6:38 He had spent *s* years building it.
7:17 top of the pillars, *s* for each capital.
8:65 God for *s* days and *s* days more,
11: 3 He had *s* hundred wives
16:15 Zimri reigned in Tirzah *s* days.
18:43 *S* times Elijah said, "Go back."
19:18 Yet I reserve *s* thousand in Israel—
20:29 For *s* days they camped
2Ki 3: 9 After a roundabout march of *s* days
3:26 with him *s* hundred swordsmen
4:35 The boy sneezed *s* times
5:10 wash yourself *s* times in the Jordan
5:14 himself in the Jordan *s* times,
8: 1 in the land that will last *s* years."
8: 2 in the land of the Philistines *s* years
8: 3 end of the *s* years she came back
11:21 Joash was *s* years old
24:16 force of *s* thousand fighting men,
1Ch 3: 4 where he reigned *s* years
3:24 Delaiah and Anani—*s* in all.
5:13 Jorai, Jacan, Zia and Eber—*s* in all
10:12 in Jabesh, and they fasted *s* days.
11:23 down an Egyptian who was *s*
15:26 *s* bulls and *s* rams were sacrificed.
18: 4 *s* thousand charioteers
19:18 and David killed *s* thousand
29: 4 *s* thousand talents of refined silver,
29:27 *s* in Hebron and thirty-three
2Ch 7: 8 the festival at that time for *s* days,
7: 9 and the festival for *s* days more.
7: 9 dedication of the altar for *s* days
13: 9 and *s* rams may become a priest
15:11 and *s* thousand sheep and goats
15:11 to the LORD *s* hundred head
17:11 and *s* thousand *s* hundred goats.
17:11 *s* thousand *s* hundred rams
24: 1 Joash was *s* years old
29:21 They brought *s* bulls, *s* rams,
29:21 *s* male lambs and *s* male goats
30:21 of Unleavened Bread for *s* days
30:22 For the *s* days they ate their
30:23 celebrate the festival *s* more days;
30:23 for another *s* days they celebrated
30:24 and *s* thousand sheep and goats
35:17 of Unleavened Bread for *s* days.
Ezr 6:22 For *s* days they celebrated
7:14 and his *s* advisers to inquire about
Ne 8:18 They celebrated the feast for *s* days
Est 1: 5 king gave a banquet, lasting *s* days,
1:10 he commanded the *s* eunuchs who
1:14 *s* nobles of Persia and Media who
2: 9 He assigned to her *s* maids selected
Job 1: 2 He had *s* sons and three daughters,
1: 3 and he owned *s* thousand sheep,
2:13 with him for *s* days and *s* nights.
5:19 in *s* no harm will befall you.
42: 8 So now take *s* bulls and *s* rams
42:13 And he also had *s* sons
Ps 12: 6 purified *s* times.
79:12 of our neighbors *s* times

Ps 119:164 *S* times a day I praise you
Pr 6:16 *s* that are detestable to him:
9: 1 she has hewn out its *s* pillars.
24:16 a righteous man falls *s* times,
26:16 than *s* men who answer discreetly.
26:25 for *s* abominations fill his heart.
Ecc 11: 2 Give portions to *s*, yes to eight,
Isa 4: 1 In that day *s* women
11:15 He will break it up into *s* streams
30:26 like the light of *s* full days,
30:26 the sunlight will be *s* times brighter
Jer 15: 9 The mother of *s* will grow faint
52:25 fighting men, and *s* royal advisers.
Eze 3:15 I sat among them for *s* days—
3:16 At the end of *s* days the word
39: 9 For *s* years they will use them
39:12 " 'For *s* months the house
39:14 end of the *s* months they will begin
40:22 *S* steps led up to it, with its portico
40:26 *S* steps led up to it, with its portico
41: 3 of the entrance was *s* cubits.
43:25 "For *s* days you are
43:26 For *s* days they are
44:26 he is cleansed, he must wait *s* days.
45:21 a feast lasting *s* days,
45:23 Every day during the *s* days
45:23 of the Feast he is to provide *s* bulls
45:23 *s* rams without defect as a burnt
45:25 " 'During the *s* days of the Feast,
Da 3:19 the furnace heated *s* times hotter
4:16 till *s* times pass by for him.
4:23 until *s* times pass by for him.'
4:25 *S* times will pass by for you
4:32 *S* times will pass by for you
9:25 comes, there will be *s* 'sevens,'
9:27 a covenant with many for one '*s*,'
9:27 middle of that '*s*' he will put an end
Mic 5: 5 raise against him *s* shepherds,
Zec 3: 9 There are *s* eyes on that one stone,
4: 2 a bowl at the top and *s* lights on it,
4: 2 with *s* channels to the lights.
4:10 These *s* are the eyes of the LORD,
Mt 12:45 with it *s* other spirits more wicked
15:34 "*S*," they replied, "and a few small
15:36 Then he took the *s* loaves
15:37 the disciples picked up *s* basketfuls
16:10 the *s* loaves for the four thousand,
18:21 Up to *s* times?" Jesus answered,
18:22 not *s* times, but seventy-seven
22:25 there were *s* brothers among us.
22:28 whose wife will she be of the *s*,
Mk 8: 5 "*S*," they replied.
8: 6 When he had taken the *s* loaves
8: 8 the disciples picked up *s* basketfuls
8:20 you pick up?" They answered, "*S*."
8:20 "And when I broke the *s* loaves
12:20 Now there were *s* brothers.
12:22 none of the *s* left any children.
12:23 since the *s* were married to her?"
16: 9 of whom he had driven *s* demons.
Lk 2:36 lived with her husband *s* years
8: 2 from whom *s* demons had come
11:26 takes *s* other spirits more wicked
17: 4 and *s* times comes back to you
17: 4 sins against you *s* times in a day,
20:29 Now there were *s* brothers.
20:31 and in the same way the *s* died,
20:33 since the *s* were married to her?"
24:13 about *s* miles from Jerusalem.
Ac 6: 3 choose *s* men from among you who
13:19 He overthrew *s* nations in Canaan
19:14 *S* sons of Sceva, a Jewish chief
20: 6 at Troas, where we stayed *s* days.
21: 4 we stayed with them *s* days.
21: 8 Philip the evangelist, one of the *S*.
21:27 When the *s* days were nearly over,
Ro 11: 4 for myself *s* thousand who have not
Heb 11:30 marched around them for *s* days.
2Pe 2: 5 of righteousness, and *s* others;
Rev 1: 4 To the *s* churches in the province
1: 4 from the *s* spirits before his throne,
1:11 and send it to the *s* churches:
1:12 I turned I saw *s* golden lampstands,
1:16 In his right hand he held *s* stars,
1:20 The *s* stars are the angels
1:20 are the angels of the *s* churches,
1:20 mystery of the *s* stars that you saw
1:20 of the *s* golden lampstands is this:

Rev 1:20 the *s* lampstands are the *s* churches
2: 1 among the *s* golden lampstands:
2: 1 words of him who holds the *s* stars
3: 1 of him who holds the *s* spirits
3: 1 spirits of God and the *s* stars.
4: 5 Before the throne, *s* lamps were
4: 5 These are the *s* spirits of God.
5: 1 both sides and sealed with *s* seals.
5: 5 to open the scroll and its *s* seals."
5: 6 He had *s* horns and *s* eyes,
5: 6 which are the *s* spirits
6: 1 opened the first of the *s* seals.
8: 2 And I saw the *s* angels who stand
8: 2 and to them were given *s* trumpets.
8: 6 the *s* angels who had the *s* trumpets
10: 3 the voices of the *s* thunders spoke.
10: 4 And when the *s* thunders spoke,
10: 4 up what the *s* thunders have said
11:13 *S* thousand people were killed
12: 3 and *s* crowns on his heads.
12: 3 enormous red dragon with *s* heads
13: 1 He had ten horns and *s* heads,
15: 1 *s* angels with the *s* last plagues—
15: 6 angels with the *s* plagues.
15: 6 of the temple came the *s* angels
15: 7 to the *s* angels *s* golden bowls filled
15: 8 of the *s* angels were completed.
15: 8 the temple until the *s* plagues
16: 1 pour out the *s* bowls
16: 1 the temple saying to the *s* angels,
17: 1 angels who had the *s* bowls came
17: 1 of the *s* angels who had the *s* bowls
17: 3 and had *s* heads and ten horns.
17: 7 which has the *s* heads and ten
17: 9 The *s* heads are *s* hills
17: 9 They are also *s* kings.
17:11 He belongs to the *s* and is going
21: 9 full of the *s* last plagues came
21: 9 of the *s* angels who had the *s* bowls

SEVEN-DAY (DAY)

Ge 50:10 there Joseph observed a *s* period
1Ch 9:25 and share their duties for *s* periods.

SEVENFOLD (SEVEN)

Pr 6:31 Yet if he is caught, he must pay *s*,

SEVENS (SEVEN)

Da 9:24 "Seventy '*s*' are decreed
9:25 will be seven '*s*,' and sixty-two '*s*.'
9:26 the sixty-two '*s*,' the Anointed

SEVENTH (SEVEN)

Ge 2: 2 By the *s* day God had finished
2: 2 so on the *s* day he rested
2: 3 And God blessed the *s* day
8: 4 day of the *s* month the ark came
Ex 12:15 day through the *s* must be cut
12:16 and another one on the *s* day.
13: 6 and on the *s* day hold a festival
16:26 but on the *s* day, the Sabbath,
16:27 out on the *s* day to gather it,
16:29 is to stay where he is on the *s* day;
16:30 So the people rested on the *s* day.
20:10 but the *s* day is a Sabbath
20:11 but he rested on the *s* day.
21: 2 But in the *s* year, he shall go free,
23:11 but during the *s* year let the land lie
23:12 but on the *s* day do not work,
24:16 and on the *s* day the LORD called
31:15 but the *s* day is a Sabbath of rest,
31:17 and on the *s* day he abstained
34:21 but on the *s* day you shall rest;
35: 2 but the *s* day shall be your holy day
Lev 13: 5 On the *s* day the priest is
13: 6 On the *s* day the priest is
13:27 On the *s* day the priest is
13:32 On the *s* day the priest is
13:34 On the *s* day the priest is
13:51 On the *s* day he is to examine it,
14: 9 On the *s* day he must shave
14:39 On the *s* day the priest shall return
16:29 day of the *s* month you must deny
23: 3 but the *s* day is a Sabbath of rest,
23: 8 on the *s* day hold a sacred assembly
23:16 up to the day after the *s* Sabbath,
23:24 day of the *s* month you are
23:27 day of this *s* month is the Day
Lev 23:34 of the *s* month the LORD's Feast
23:39 the fifteenth day of the *s* month,
23:41 celebrate it in the *s* month.
25: 4 But in the *s* year the land is
25: 9 on the tenth day of the *s* month;
25:20 "What will we eat in the *s* year
Nu 6: 9 day of his cleansing—the *s* day.
7:48 On the *s* day Elishama son
19:12 himself on the third and *s* days,
19:12 on the third day and on the *s* day;
19:19 and on the *s* day he is to purify him.
19:19 person on the third and *s* days,
28:25 On the *s* day hold a sacred
29: 1 day of the *s* month hold a sacred
29: 7 day of this *s* month hold a sacred
29:12 On the fifteenth day of the *s* month
29:32 " 'On the *s* day prepare seven bulls,
31:19 *s* days you must purify yourselves
31:24 On the *s* day wash your clothes
Dt 5:14 but the *s* day is a Sabbath
15: 9 "The *s* year, the year
15:12 in the *s* year you must let him go
16: 8 and on the *s* day hold an assembly
Jos 6: 4 On the *s* day, march
6:15 On the *s* day, they got up
6:16 *s* time around, when the priests
19:40 The *s* lot came out for the tribe
Jdg 14:17 So on the *s* day he finally told her,
14:18 Before sunset on the *s* day the men
2Sa 12:18 On the *s* day the child died.
1Ki 8: 2 month of Ethanim, the *s* month.
18:44 The *s* time the servant reported,
20:29 on the *s* day the battle was joined.
2Ki 11: 4 In the *s* year Jehoiada sent
12: 1 In the *s* year of Jehu, Joash became
18: 9 which was the *s* year of Hoshea son
25: 8 On the *s* day of the fifth month,
25:25 In the *s* month, however, Ishmael
1Ch 2:15 the sixth Ozem and the *s* David.
12:11 Eliel the *s*, Johanan the eighth,
24:10 sixth to Mijamin, the *s* to Hakkoz,
25:14 and relatives, 12 the *s* to Jesarelah,
26: 3 the sixth and Eliehoenai the *s*.
26: 5 Issachar the *s* and Peullethai
27:10 The *s*, for the *s* month, was Helez
2Ch 5: 3 time of the festival in the *s* month.
7:10 of the *s* month he sent the people
23: 1 In the *s* year Jehoiada showed his
31: 7 and finished in the *s* month.
Ezr 3: 1 When the *s* month came
3: 6 day of the *s* month they began
7: 7 up to Jerusalem in the *s* year
7: 8 month of the *s* year of the king.
Ne 7:73 When the *s* month came
8: 2 day of the *s* month Ezra the priest
8:14 during the feast of the *s* month
10:31 Every *s* year we will forgo working
Est 1:10 On the *s* day, when King Xerxes
2:16 of Tebeth, in the *s* year of his reign.
Jer 28:17 In the *s* month of that same year,
34:14 'Every *s* year each
41: 1 In the *s* month Ishmael son
52:28 in the *s* year, 3,023 Jews;
Eze 20: 1 In the *s* year, in the fifth month
30:20 in the first month on the *s* day,
45:20 the same on the *s* day of the month
45:25 which begins in the *s* month
Hag 2: 1 the twenty-first day of the *s* month,
Zec 7: 5 *s* months for the past seventy years
8:19 *s* and tenth months will become
Mt 22:26 brother, right on down to the *s*.
Jn 4:52 left him yesterday at the *s* hour."
Heb 4: 4 he has spoken about the *s* day
4: 4 "And on the *s* day God rested
Jude :14 the *s* from Adam, prophesied about
Rev 8: 1 When he opened the *s* seal,
10: 7 the days when the *s* angel is about
11:15 The *s* angel sounded his trumpet,
16:17 The *s* angel poured out his bowl
21:20 the sixth carnelian, the *s* chrysolite

SEVERE

Ge 12:10 a while because the famine was *s*.
41:31 famine that follows it will be so *s*.
41:56 for the famine was *s*
41:57 the famine was *s* in all the world.
43: 1 the famine was still *s* in the land.
47: 4 because the famine is *s* in Canaan
Ge 47:13 region because the famine was *s*;
47:20 the famine was too *s* for them.
Nu 11:33 and he struck them with a *s* plague.
Dt 28:59 and *s* and lingering illnesses.
1Ki 18: 2 Now the famine was *s* in Samaria,
2Ki 25: 3 become so *s* that there was no food
2Ch 16:12 Though his disease was *s*,
Jer 52: 6 become so *s* that there was no food
Mt 4:24 those suffering *s* pain,
Lk 4:25 and there was a *s* famine
15:14 there was a *s* famine
Ac 11:28 predicted that a *s* famine would
2Co 8: 2 Out of the most *s* trial, their
1Th 1: 6 of the Lord; in spite of *s* suffering,
Rev 11:13 very hour there was a *s* earthquake
16:18 peals of thunder and a *s* earthquake

SEVERED (SEVERING)

Ecc 12: 6 before the silver cord is *s*,

SEVERING (SEVERED)

Lev 1:17 by the wings, not *s* it completely,
5: 8 from its neck, not *s* it completely,

SEW (SEWED SEWS)

Eze 13:18 to the women who *s* magic charms

SEWED (SEW)

Ge 3: 7 so they *s* fig leaves together
Job 16:15 "I have *s* sackcloth over my skin

SEWS (SEW)

Mt 9:16 No one *s* a patch of unshrunk cloth
Mk 2:21 No one *s* a patch of unshrunk cloth
Lk 5:36 a patch from a new garment and *s* it

SEX (SEXUAL SEXUALLY)

Ge 19: 5 so that we can have *s* with them."
Jdg 19:22 house so we can have *s* with him."

SEXUAL (SEX)

Ex 19:15 Abstain from *s* relations."
22:19 "Anyone who has *s* relations
Lev 18: 6 relative to have *s* relations.
18: 7 father by having *s* relations
18: 8 " 'Do not have *s* relations
18: 9 " 'Do not have *s* relations
18:10 " 'Do not have *s* relations
18:11 " 'Do not have *s* relations
18:12 " 'Do not have *s* relations
18:13 " 'Do not have *s* relations
18:14 wife to have *s* relations;
18:15 " 'Do not have *s* relations
18:16 " 'Do not have *s* relations
18:17 Do not have *s* relations with
18:17 " 'Do not have *s* relations
18:18 and have *s* relations with her
18:19 a woman to have *s* relations
18:23 animal to have *s* relations with it;
18:23 " 'Do not have *s* relations
20:15 " 'If a man has *s* relations
20:16 animal to have *s* relations with it,
20:17 and they have *s* relations, it is
20:18 and has *s* relations with her,
20:19 " 'Do not have *s* relations
Nu 25: 1 began to indulge in *s* immorality
Dt 27:21 is the man who has *s* relations
Mt 15:19 murder, adultery, *s* immorality,
Mk 7:21 come evil thoughts, *s* immorality,
Ac 15:20 by idols, from *s* immorality,
15:29 and from *s* immorality.
21:25 and from *s* immorality."
Ro 1:24 desires of their hearts to *s* impurity
13:13 in *s* immorality and debauchery,
1Co 5: 1 reported that there is *s* immorality
6:13 body is not meant for *s* immorality,
6:18 Flee from *s* immorality.
10: 8 should not commit *s* immorality,
2Co 12:21 *s* sin and debauchery
Gal 5:19 *s* immorality, impurity
Eph 5: 3 even a hint of *s* immorality,
Col 3: 5 *s* immorality, impurity, lust,
1Th 4: 3 that you should avoid *s* immorality
Jude : 7 gave themselves up to *s* immorality
Rev 2:14 and by committing *s* immorality.
2:20 my servants into *s* immorality
9:21 their *s* immorality or their thefts.

SEXUALLY (SEX)
1Co 5: 9 to associate with *s* immoral people
5: 11 but is *s* immoral or greedy,
6: 9 Neither the *s* immoral nor idolaters
6: 18 he who sins *s* sins against his own
Heb 12: 16 See that no one is *s* immoral,
13: 4 the adulterer and all the *s* immoral.
Rev 21: 8 the murderers, the *s* immoral,
22: 15 the *s* immoral, the murderers,

SHAALABBIN
Jos 19: 42 Eshtaol, Ir Shemesh, *S*, Aijalon,

SHAALBIM
Jdg 1: 35 *S*, but when the power of the house
1Ki 4: 9 Ben-Deker—in Makaz, *S*,

SHAALBONITE
2Sa 23: 32 Eliahba the *S*, the sons of Jashen,
1Ch 11: 33 the Baharumite, Eliahba the *S*,

SHAALIM
1Sa 9: 4 They went on into the district of *S*,

SHAAPH
1Ch 2: 47 Geshan, Pelet, Ephah and *S*.
2: 49 also gave birth to *S* the father

SHAARAIM
Jos 15: 36 Adullam, Socoh, Azekah, *S*,
1Sa 17: 52 strewn along the *S* road to Gath
1Ch 4: 31 Hazar Susim, Beth Biri and *S*.

SHAASHGAZ
Est 2: 14 part of the harem to the care of *S*,

SHABBETHAI
Ezr 10: 15 by Meshullam and *S* the Levite,
Ne 8: 7 Jamin, Akkub, *S*, Hodiah,
11: 16 the son of Bunni; *S* and Jozabad,

SHABBY
Jas 2: 2 and a poor man in *s* clothes

SHACKLES
Jdg 16: 21 Binding him with bronze *s*,
2Ki 25: 7 bound him with bronze *s*
2Ch 33: 11 bound him with bronze *s*
36: 6 him with bronze *s* to take him
Job 12: 18 He takes off the *s* put on by kings
13: 27 You fasten my feet in *s*;
33: 11 He fastens my feet in *s*;
Ps 105: 18 They bruised his feet with *s*,
149: 8 their nobles with *s* of iron,
Jer 39: 7 him with bronze *s* to take him
52: 11 bound him with bronze *s*
Na 1: 13 and tear your *s* away."

SHADE
Jdg 9: 15 come and take refuge in my *s*;
Ne 8: 15 palms and *s* trees, to make booths
Ps 80: 10 mountains were covered with its *s*,
121: 5 the LORD is your *s*
SS 2: 3 I delight to sit in his *s*,
Isa 4: 6 and *s* from the heat of the day,
25: 4 and a *s* from the heat.
30: 2 to Egypt's *s* for refuge.
30: 3 Egypt's *s* will bring you disgrace.
Jer 4: 30 Why *s* your eyes with paint?
Eze 17: 23 shelter in the *s* of its branches.
31: 6 lived in its *s*.
31: 12 the earth came out from under its *s*
31: 17 Those who lived in its *s*, its allies
Hos 4: 13 where the *s* is pleasant.
14: 7 Men will dwell again in his *s*.
Jnh 4: 5 sat in its *s* and waited
4: 6 up over Jonah to give *s* for his head
Mk 4: 32 birds of the air can perch in its *s*."

SHADOW (SHADOWS)
2Ki 20: 9 Shall the *s* go forward ten steps,
20: 10 for the *s* to go forward ten steps,"
20: 11 LORD made the *s* go back the ten
1Ch 29: 15 Our days on earth are like a *s*,
Job 3: 5 and deep *s* claim it once more;
8: 9 and our days on earth are but a *s*.
10: 21 to the land of gloom and deep *s*,
10: 22 of deep *s* and disorder,
Job 14: 2 like a fleeting *s*, he does not endure
17: 7 my whole frame is but a *s*.
34: 22 There is no dark place, no deep *s*,
38: 17 Have you seen the gates of the *s*
40: 22 The lotuses conceal him in their *s*;
Ps 17: 8 hide me in the *s* of your wings
23: 4 through the valley of the *s* of death,
36: 7 find refuge in the *s* of your wings.
57: 1 refuge in the *s* of your wings
63: 7 I sing in the *s* of your wings.
91: 1 will rest in the *s* of the Almighty.
102: 11 My days are like the evening *s*;
109: 23 I fade away like an evening *s*;
144: 4 his days are like a fleeting *s*.
Ecc 6: 12 days he passes through like a *s*?
8: 13 their days will not lengthen like a *s*.
Isa 9: 2 living in the land of the *s* of death
16: 3 Make your *s* like night—
25: 5 heat is reduced by the *s* of a cloud,
32: 2 and the *s* of a great rock
34: 15 young under the *s* of her wings;
38: 8 I will make the *s* cast
49: 2 in the *s* of his hand he hid me,
51: 16 covered you with the *s* of my hand
Jer 48: 45 "In the *s* of Heshbon
La 4: 20 We thought that under his *s*
Mt 4: 16 living in the land of the *s* of death
Lk 1: 79 and in the *s* of death,
Ac 5: 15 at least Peter's *s* might fall on some
Col 2: 17 These are a *s* of the things that
Heb 8: 5 and *s* of what is in heaven.
10: 1 The law is only a *s*

SHADOWS (SHADOW)
Jdg 9: 36 You mistake the *s* of the mountains
Ne 13: 19 When evening *s* fell on the gates
Job 7: 2 a slave longing for the evening *s*,
12: 22 and brings deep *s* into the light.
16: 16 deep *s* ring my eyes;
Ps 11: 2 the strings to shoot from the *s*
SS 2: 17 and the *s* flee,
4: 6 and the *s* flee,
Isa 59: 9 brightness, but we walk in deep *s*.
Jer 6: 4 and the *s* of evening grow long.
Jas 1: 17 who does not change like shifting *s*.

SHADRACH
Da 1: 7 to Hananiah, *S*; to Mishael,
2: 49 request the king appointed *S*,
3: 12 *S*, Meshach and Abednego—
3: 13 Nebuchadnezzar summoned *S*,
3: 14 *S*, Meshach and Abednego,
3: 16 *S*, Meshach and Abednego replied
3: 19 was furious with *S*,
3: 20 soldiers in his army to tie up *S*,
3: 22 fire killed the men who took up *S*,
3: 26 come out! Come here!" So *S*,
3: 26 "*S*, Meshach and Abednego,
3: 28 "Praise be to the God of *S*,
3: 29 anything against the God of *S*,
3: 30 Then the king promoted *S*,

SHAFT
Ex 25: 31 base and *s*; its flowerlike cups,
37: 17 base and *s*; its flowerlike cups,
1Sa 17: 7 His spear *s* was like a weaver's rod,
2Sa 5: 8 to use the water *s* to reach those
21: 19 a spear with a *s* like a weaver's rod.
23: 7 uses a tool of iron or the *s* of a spear
1Ch 20: 5 a spear with a *s* like a weaver's rod.
Job 28: 4 from where people dwell he cuts a *s*
Rev 9: 1 the key to the *s* of the Abyss.

SHAGEE
1Ch 11: 34 Jonathan son of *S* the Hararite,

SHAGGY
Da 8: 21 The *s* goat is the king of Greece,

SHAHARAIM
1Ch 8: 8 Sons were born to *S* in Moab

SHAHAZUMAH
Jos 19: 22 The boundary touched Tabor, *S*

SHAKE (SHAKEN SHAKES SHAKING SHOOK)
Jdg 16: 20 as before and *s* myself free."
Ne 5: 13 "In this way may God *s* out
Job 4: 14 and made all my bones *s*.
16: 4 and *s* my head at you.
38: 13 and *s* the wicked out of it?
Ps 10: 6 to himself, "Nothing will *s* me;
44: 14 the peoples *s* their heads at us.
64: 8 all who see them will *s* their heads
99: 1 let the earth *s*.
109: 25 they see me, they *s* their heads.
Isa 2: 19 when he rises to *s* the earth.
2: 21 when he rises to *s* the earth.
5: 25 The mountains *s*,
10: 32 they will *s* their fist
13: 13 and the earth will *s* from its place
24: 18 the foundations of the earth *s*.
52: 2 *S* off your dust;
Jer 18: 16 and will *s* their heads.
48: 27 that you *s* your head in scorn
La 2: 15 they scoff and *s* their heads
Am 9: 1 the pillars so that the thresholds *s*.
9: 9 and I will *s* the house of Israel
Zep 2: 15 and *s* their fists.
Hag 2: 6 I will once more *s* the heavens
2: 7 I will *s* all nations, and the desired
2: 21 of Judah that I will *s* the heavens
Mt 10: 14 *s* the dust off your feet
Mk 6: 11 *s* the dust off your feet
Lk 6: 48 struck that house but could not *s* it,
9: 5 *s* the dust off your feet
Heb 12: 26 "Once more I will *s* not only

SHAKEN (SHAKE)
1Sa 28: 21 and saw that he was greatly *s*,
2Sa 18: 33 The king was *s*.
Ne 5: 13 So may such a man be *s* out
Job 34: 20 the people are *s* and they pass away
Ps 15: 5 will never be *s*.
16: 8 I will not be *s*.
21: 7 he will not be *s*.
30: 6 "I will never be *s*."
60: 2 You have *s* the land and torn it
62: 2 he is my fortress, I will never be *s*.
62: 6 he is my fortress, I will not be *s*.
82: 5 the foundations of the earth are *s*
109: 23 I am *s* off like a locust.
112: 6 Surely he will never be *s*;
125: 1 which cannot be *s* but endures
Isa 7: 2 of Ahaz and his people were *s*.
7: 2 trees of the forest are *s* by the wind.
24: 19 the earth is thoroughly *s*.
54: 10 Though the mountains be *s*
54: 10 love for you will not be *s*
Am 9: 9 as grain is *s* in a sieve,
Na 3: 12 when they are *s*,
Mt 24: 29 and the heavenly bodies will be *s*.'
Mk 13: 25 and the heavenly bodies will be *s*.'
Lk 6: 38 *s* together and running over,
21: 26 for the heavenly bodies will be *s*.
Ac 2: 25 I will not be *s*.
4: 31 where they were meeting was *s*.
16: 26 foundations of the prison were *s*.
Heb 12: 27 that what cannot be *s* may remain.
12: 27 the removing of what can be *s*—
12: 28 a kingdom that cannot be *s*,
Rev 6: 13 tree when *s* by a strong wind.

SHAKES (SHAKE)
Job 9: 6 He *s* the earth from its place
15: 25 because he *s* his fist at God
Ps 29: 8 of the LORD *s* the desert;
29: 8 the LORD *s* the Desert of Kadesh.
Isa 30: 28 He *s* the nations in the sieve
Joel 2: 10 Before them the earth *s*,

SHAKING (SHAKE)
Ps 22: 7 they hurl insults, *s* their heads:
Mt 27: 39 insults at him, *s* their heads
Mk 15: 29 *s* their heads and saying, "So!

SHALISHA
1Sa 9: 4 and through the area around *S*,

SHALLEKETH
1Ch 26: 16 the *S* Gate on the upper road fell

SHALLOW
Mt 13: 5 up quickly, because the soil was *s*.
Mk 4: 5 up quickly, because the soil was *s*.

SHALLUM (SHALLUM'S)

2Ki 15: 10 *S* son of Jabesh conspired
15: 13 *S* son of Jabesh became king
15: 14 He attacked *S* son of Jabesh
22: 14 the wife of *S* son of Tikvah,
1Ch 2: 41 of *S*, *S* the father of Jekamiah,
3: 15 Zedekiah the third, *S* the fourth.
4: 25 Zerah and Shaul; *S* was Shaul's son
6: 13 father of *S*, *S* the father of Hilkiah,
9: 17 The gatekeepers: *S*, Akkub,
9: 17 *S* their chief being stationed
9: 19 *S* son of Kore, the son of Ebiasaph,
9: 31 the firstborn son of *S* the Korahite,
2Ch 28: 12 Jehizkiah son of *S*, and Amasa son
34: 22 the wife of *S* son of Tokhath,
Ezr 2: 42 the descendants of *S*, Ater, Talmon
7: 2 the son of *S*, the son of Zadok,
10: 24 From the gatekeepers: *S*, Telem
10: 42 Azarel, Shelemiah, Shemariah, *S*,
Ne 3: 12 *S* son of Hallohesh, ruler
7: 45 the descendants of *S*, Ater, Talmon
Jer 22: 11 is what the LORD says about *S* son
32: 7 son of *S* your uncle is going
35: 4 son of *S* the doorkeeper.

SHALLUM'S (SHALLUM)

2Ki 15: 15 The other events of *S* reign,

SHALLUN

Ne 3: 15 repaired by *S* son of Col-Hozeh,

SHALMAI

Ezr 2: 46 Akkub, Hagab, *S*, Hanan, Giddel,
Ne 7: 48 Lebana, Hagaba, *S*, Hanan, Giddel,

SHALMAN

Hos 10: 14 as *S* devastated Beth Arbel

SHALMANESER (SHALMANESER'S)

2Ki 17: 3 *S* king of Assyria came up
17: 4 Therefore *S* seized him
18: 9 *S* king of Assyria marched

SHALMANESER'S (SHALMANESER)

2Ki 17: 3 who had been *S* vassal

SHAMA

1Ch 11: 44 *S* and Jeiel the sons

SHAME (ASHAMED SHAMED SHAMEFUL SHAMING)

Ge 2: 25 were both naked, and they felt no *s*.
Dt 32: 5 to their *s* they are no longer his
1Sa 20: 30 to the *s* of the mother who bore you
20: 30 with the son of Jesse to your own *s*
2Ki 19: 26 are dismayed and put to *s*.
Job 8: 22 Your enemies will be clothed in *s*,
10: 15 for I am full of *s*
11: 15 you will lift up your face without *s*;
Ps 4: 2 will you turn my glory into *s*?
25: 2 Do not let me be put to *s*,
25: 3 but they will be put to *s*
25: 3 will ever be put to *s*,
25: 20 let me not be put to *s*,
31: 1 let me never be put to *s*;
31: 17 Let me not be put to *s*, O LORD,
31: 17 but let the wicked be put to *s*
34: 5 their faces are never covered with *s*
35: 4 be disgraced and put to *s*;
35: 26 be clothed with *s* and disgrace.
35: 26 be put to *s* and confusion;
40: 14 be put to *s* and confusion;
40: 15 be appalled at their own *s*.
44: 7 you put our adversaries to *s*.
44: 15 and my face is covered with *s*
53: 5 you put them to *s*,
69: 6 not be put to *s* because of me,
69: 7 and *s* covers my face.
70: 2 be put to *s* and confusion;
70: 3 turn back because of their *s*.
71: 1 let me never be put to *s*.
71: 13 May my accusers perish in *s*;
71: 24 have been put to *s* and confusion.
78: 66 he put them to everlasting *s*.
83: 16 Cover their faces with *s*
86: 17 enemies may see it and be put to *s*,
89: 45 with a mantle of *s*.
97: 7 who worship images are put to *s*,
Ps 109: 28 they attack they will be put to *s*,
109: 29 and wrapped in *s* as in a cloak.
119: 6 Then I would not be put to *s*
119: 31 do not let me be put to *s*.
119: 46 and will not be put to *s*,
119: 78 to *s* for wronging me without cause
119: 80 that I may not be put to *s*.
127: 5 They will not be put to *s*
129: 5 be turned back in *s*.
132: 18 I will clothe his enemies with *s*,
Pr 3: 35 but fools he holds up to *s*.
6: 33 and his *s* will never be wiped away;
13: 5 but the wicked bring *s* and disgrace
13: 18 discipline comes to poverty and *s*,
18: 3 and with *s* comes disgrace.
18: 13 that is his folly and his *s*.
19: 26 is a son who brings *s* and disgrace.
25: 8 end if your neighbor puts you to *s*?
25: 10 or he who hears it may *s* you
Isa 20: 4 with buttocks bared—to Egypt's *s*.
20: 5 in Egypt will be afraid and put to *s*.
26: 11 zeal for your people and be put to *s*;
30: 3 protection will be to your *s*,
30: 5 but only *s* and disgrace."
30: 5 everyone will be put to *s*
37: 27 are dismayed and put to *s*.
42: 17 will be turned back in utter *s*.
44: 9 they are ignorant, to their own *s*.
44: 11 He and his kind will be put to *s*;
45: 16 of idols will be put to *s*
45: 17 you will never be put to *s*
45: 24 will come to him and be put to *s*.
47: 3 and your *s* uncovered.
50: 7 and I know I will not be put to *s*.
54: 4 You will forget the *s* of your youth
54: 4 not be afraid; you will not suffer *s*.
61: 7 Instead of their *s*
65: 13 but you will be put to *s*.
66: 5 Yet they will be put to *s*.
Jer 3: 3 you refuse to blush with *s*.
3: 25 Let us lie down in our *s*,
6: 15 No, they have no *s* at all;
7: 19 to their own *s*? " 'Therefore this is
8: 9 The wise will be put to *s*;
8: 12 No, they have no *s* at all;
9: 19 How great is our *s*!
12: 13 So bear the *s* of your harvest
13: 26 that your *s* may be seen—
17: 13 all who forsake you will be put to *s*.
17: 18 Let my persecutors be put to *s*,
17: 18 but keep me from *s*;
20: 18 and to end my days in *s*?
23: 40 everlasting *s* that will not be
46: 12 The nations will hear of your *s*;
46: 24 of Egypt will be put to *s*,
48: 39 How Moab turns her back in *s*!
50: 2 Bel will be put to *s*,
50: 2 Her images will be put to *s*
51: 51 and *s* covers our faces,
Eze 7: 18 Their faces will be covered with *s*
23: 29 the *s* of your prostitution will be
32: 24 They bear their *s* with those who
32: 25 they bear their *s* with those who go
32: 30 and bear their *s* with those who go
39: 26 They will forget their *s*
44: 13 they must bear the *s*
Da 9: 7 but this day we are covered with *s*
9: 8 and our fathers are covered with *s*
12: 2 to *s* and everlasting contempt.
Hos 4: 19 their sacrifices will bring them *s*.
Am 8: 14 swear by the *s* of Samaria,
Ob : 10 you will be covered with *s*;
Mic 1: 11 Pass on in nakedness and *s*,
7: 10 and will be covered with *s*,
Na 3: 5 and the kingdoms your *s*.
Hab 2: 16 filled with *s* instead of glory.
Zep 3: 5 yet the unrighteous know no *s*.
3: 11 On that day you will not be put to *s*
3: 19 land where they were put to *s*.
Ro 9: 33 trusts in him will never be put to *s*."
10: 11 trusts in him will never be put to *s*."
1Co 1: 27 things of the world to *s* the strong.
1: 27 things of the world to *s* the wise;
4: 14 I am not writing this to *s* you,
6: 5 in the church! I say this to *s* you.
15: 34 of God—I say this to your *s*.
2Co 11: 21 To my *s* I admit that we were too
Php 3: 19 and their glory is in their *s*.
Heb 12: 2 endured the cross, scorning its *s*,
1Pe 2: 6 will never be put to *s*."
Jude : 13 foaming up their *s*; wandering stars

SHAMED (SHAME)

Ps 69: 19 how I am scorned, disgraced and *s*;
Jer 10: 14 every goldsmith is *s* by his idols.
51: 17 every goldsmith is *s* by his idols.
Joel 2: 26 never again will my people be *s*.
2: 27 never again will my people be *s*.

SHAMEFUL (SHAME)

1Sa 20: 34 at his father's *s* treatment of David.
Job 31: 11 For that would have been *s*,
Pr 14: 35 but a *s* servant incurs his wrath.
Jer 3: 24 From our youth *s* gods have
11: 13 incense to that *s* god Baal are
Hos 4: 18 their rulers dearly love *s* ways.
6: 9 committing *s* crimes.
9: 10 themselves to that *s* idol
Zep 2: 1 O *s* nation,
Ro 1: 26 God gave them over to *s* lusts.
2Co 4: 2 have renounced secret and *s* ways;
Eph 5: 12 For it is *s* even to mention what
2Pe 2: 2 Many will follow their *s* ways
Rev 3: 18 so you can cover your *s* nakedness;
21: 27 nor will anyone who does what is *s*

SHAMELESS

Jer 13: 27 your *s* prostitution!

SHAMGAR

Jdg 3: 31 After Ehud came *S* son of Anath,
5: 6 "In the days of *S* son of Anath,

SHAMHUTH

1Ch 27: 8 was the commander *S* the Izrahite.

SHAMING (SHAME)

Hab 2: 10 *s* your own house and forfeiting

SHAMIR

Jos 15: 48 In the hill country: *S*, Jattir, Socoh,
Jdg 10: 1 He lived in *S*, in the hill country
10: 2 then he died, and was buried in *S*.
1Ch 24: 24 Micah; from the sons of Micah: *S*.

SHAMMA

1Ch 7: 37 Imrah, Bezer, Hod, *S*, Shilshah,

SHAMMAH

Ge 36: 13 Nahath, Zerah, *S* and Mizzah.
36: 17 Chiefs Nahath, Zerah, *S*
1Sa 16: 9 Jesse then had *S* pass by,
17: 13 Abinadab; and the third, *S*.
2Sa 23: 11 Next to him was *S* son
23: 12 But *S* took his stand in the middle
23: 25 *S* the Harodite, Elika the Harodite,
23: 33 Jonathan son of *S* the Hararite,
1Ch 1: 37 Nahath, Zerah, *S* and Mizzah.

SHAMMAI (SHAMMAI'S)

1Ch 2: 28 The sons of Onam: *S* and Jada.
2: 28 The sons of *S*: Nadab and Abishur.
2: 44 Rekem was the father of *S*.
2: 45 The son of *S* was Maon,
4: 17 *S* and Ishbah the father

SHAMMAI'S (SHAMMAI)

1Ch 2: 32 The sons of Jada, *S* brother:

SHAMMOTH

1Ch 11: 27 *S* the Harorite, Helez the Pelonite,

SHAMMUA

Nu 13: 4 tribe of Reuben, *S* son of Zaccur;
2Sa 5: 14 *S*, Shobab, Nathan, Solomon,
1Ch 3: 5 *S*, Shobab, Nathan and Solomon.
14: 4 *S*, Shobab, Nathan, Solomon,
Ne 11: 17 and Abda son of *S*, the son of Galal
12: 18 Piltai; of Bilgah's, *S*; of Shemaiah's,

SHAMSHERAI

1Ch 8: 26 *S*, Shehariah, Athaliah, Jaareshiah,

SHAPE (SHAPED SHAPES SHAPING)

Ex 32: 4 it into an idol cast in the *s* of a calf,
32: 8 themselves an idol cast in the *s*
Dt 4: 16 of any *s*, whether formed like

Dt 9: 16 for yourselves an idol cast in the *s*
1Ki 6: 25 were identical in size and *s*.
7: 19 in the portico were in the *s* of lilies,
7: 22 on top were in the *s* of lilies.
7: 23 the Sea of cast metal, circular in *s*,
7: 37 and were identical in size and *s*.
2Ki 17: 16 themselves two idols cast in the *s*
2Ch 4: 2 the Sea of cast metal, circular in *s*,
Job 38: 14 The earth takes *s* like clay

SHAPED (SHAPE)

Ex 25: 33 Three cups *s* like almond flowers
25: 34 be four cups *s* like almond flowers
37: 19 Three cups *s* like almond flowers
37: 20 were four cups *s* like almond
Job 10: 8 "Your hands *s* me and made me.

SHAPES (SHAPE)

Isa 44: 10 Who *s* a god and casts an idol,
44: 12 he *s* an idol with hammers,
44: 13 He *s* it in the form of man,
Jer 10: 3 and a craftsman *s* it with his chisel.

SHAPHAM

1Ch 5: 12 Joel was the chief, *S* the second,

SHAPHAN

2Ki 22: 3 Josiah sent the secretary, *S* son
22: 8 He gave it to *S*, who read it.
22: 8 said to *S* the secretary,
22: 9 *S* the secretary went to the king
22: 10 And *S* read from it in the presence
22: 10 *S* the secretary informed the king,
22: 12 Ahikam son of *S*, Acbor son
22: 12 *S* the secretary and Asaiah
22: 14 *S* and Asaiah went to speak
25: 22 of *S*, to be over the people he had
2Ch 34: 8 he sent *S* son of Azaliah
34: 15 He gave it to *S*.
34: 15 Hilkiah said to *S* the secretary,
34: 16 Then *S* took the book to the king
34: 18 And *S* read from it in the presence
34: 18 *S* the secretary informed the king,
34: 20 Ahikam son of *S*, Abdon son
34: 20 *S* the secretary and Asaiah
Jer 26: 24 son of *S* supported Jeremiah,
29: 3 the letter to Elasah son of *S*
36: 10 of Gemariah son of *S* the secretary,
36: 11 son of Gemariah, the son of *S*,
36: 12 Gemariah son of *S*, Zedekiah son
39: 14 the son of *S*, to take him back
40: 5 son of Ahikam, the son of *S*,
40: 9 son of Ahikam, the son of *S*,
40: 11 the son of *S*, as governor over them
41: 2 the son of *S*, with the sword,
43: 6 son of *S*, and Jeremiah the prophet
Eze 8: 11 Jaazaniah son of *S* was standing

SHAPHAT

Nu 13: 5 the tribe of Simeon, *S* son of Hori;
1Ki 19: 16 and anoint Elisha son of *S*
19: 19 and found Elisha son of *S*.
2Ki 3: 11 answered, "Elisha son of *S* is here.
6: 31 the head of Elisha son of *S* remains
1Ch 3: 22 Bariah, Neariah and *S*— six in all.
5: 12 then Janai and *S*, in Bashan.
27: 29 *S* son of Adlai was in charge

SHAPHIR

Mic 1: 11 you who live in *S*.

SHAPING (SHAPE)

Jer 18: 4 the pot he was *s* from the clay was
18: 4 *s* it as seemed best to him.

SHARAI

Ezr 10: 40 Macnadebai, Shashai, *S*, Azarel,

SHARAR

2Sa 23: 33 Ahiam son of *S* the Hararite,

SHARE (SHARED SHARERS SHARES SHARING)

Ge 14: 24 Let them have their *s*."
14: 24 *s* that belongs to the men who went
21: 10 that slave woman's son will never *s*
31: 14 "Do we still have any *s*
Ex 12: 4 they must *s* one with their nearest
Ex 18: 22 because they will *s* it with you.
29: 26 wave offering, and it will be your *s*.
29: 28 be the regular *s* from the Israelites
Lev 6: 17 their *s* of the offerings made to me
6: 18 It is his regular *s* of the offerings
6: 22 It is the LORD's regular *s*
7: 33 shall have the right thigh as his *s*.
7: 34 as their regular *s* from the Israelites
7: 36 their regular *s* for the generations
8: 29 Moses' *s* of the ordination ram—
10: 13 because it is your *s* and your sons' *s*
10: 14 your *s* of the Israelites' fellowship
10: 15 This will be the regular *s* for you
19: 17 frankly so you will not *s* in his guilt.
24: 9 of their regular *s* of the offerings
25: 51 pay for his redemption a larger *s*
Nu 10: 32 we will *s* with you whatever good
18: 8 as your portion and regular *s*.
18: 11 and daughters as your regular *s*.
18: 19 and daughters as your regular *s*.
18: 20 I am your *s* and your inheritance
18: 20 will you have any *s* among them;
31: 29 Take this tribute from their half *s*
31: 36 The half *s* of those who fought
Dt 10: 9 That is why the Levites have no *s*
18: 3 This is the *s* due the priests
18: 8 He is to *s* equally in their benefits,
21: 17 firstborn by giving him a double *s*
Jos 14: 4 The Levites received no *s*
17: 5 Manasseh's *s* consisted
19: 9 taken from the *s* of Judah,
22: 19 tabernacle stands, and *s* the land
22: 25 You have no *s* in the LORD.'
22: 27 'You have no *s* in the LORD.'
Jdg 8: 24 from your *s* of the plunder."
1Sa 26: 19 me from my *s* in the LORD's
30: 22 we will not *s* with them the plunder
30: 24 All will *s* alike."
30: 24 The *s* of the man who stayed
2Sa 20: 1 "We have no *s* in David,
1Ki 12: 16 "What *s* do we have in David,
1Ch 9: 25 *s* their duties for seven-day periods
2Ch 10: 16 "What *s* do we have in David,
Ne 2: 20 you have no *s* in Jerusalem
Job 39: 17 or give her a *s* of good sense.
Ps 68: 23 tongues of your dogs have their *s*."
69: 27 do not let them *s* in your salvation.
106: 5 that I may *s* in the joy
Pr 1: 14 and we will *s* a common purse"—
14: 10 and no one else can *s* its joy.
16: 19 than to *s* plunder with the proud.
17: 2 and will *s* the inheritance
21: 9 than *s* a house with a quarrelsome
25: 24 than *s* a house with a quarrelsome
Ecc 9: 2 All *s* a common destiny—
Isa 58: 7 Is it not to *s* your food
Jer 37: 12 to get his *s* of the property
Eze 18: 19 'Why does the son not *s* the guilt
18: 20 The son will not *s* the guilt
18: 20 will the father *s* the guilt of the son.
Am 7: 1 locusts after the king's *s* had been
Mt 21: 41 who will give him his *s* of the crop
25: 21 and *s* your master's happiness!'
25: 23 and *s* your master's happiness!'
Lk 3: 11 "The man with two tunics should *s*
15: 12 'Father, give me my *s* of the estate.'
Ac 8: 21 You have no part or *s*
Ro 8: 17 if indeed we *s* in his sufferings
8: 17 in order that we may also *s*
11: 17 and now *s* in the nourishing sap
12: 13 *S* with God's people who are
15: 27 Jews to *s* with them their material
1Co 9: 13 at the altar *s* in what is offered
9: 23 that I may *s* in its blessings.
2Co 1: 7 as you *s* in our sufferings,
1: 7 so also you *s* in our comfort.
2: 3 that you would all *s* my joy.
Gal 4: 30 the slave woman's son will never *s*
6: 6 in the word must *s* all good things
Eph 4: 28 something to *s* with those in need.
Php 1: 7 all of you *s* in God's grace with me.
4: 14 good of you to *s* in my troubles.
Col 1: 12 you to *s* in the inheritance
1Th 2: 8 to *s* with you not only the gospel
2Th 2: 14 that you might *s* in the glory
1Ti 5: 22 and do not *s* in the sins of others.
6: 18 and to be generous and willing to *s*.
2Ti 2: 6 the first to receive a *s* of the crops.
Heb 3: 1 who *s* in the heavenly calling,
3: 14 We have come to *s* in Christ
12: 10 that we may *s* in his holiness.
13: 16 to do good and to *s* with others,
1Pe 5: 1 will *s* in the glory to be revealed:
Jude : 3 to you about the salvation we *s*,
Rev 18: 4 so that you will not *s* in her sins,
22: 19 from him his *s* in the tree of life

SHARED (SHARE)

2Sa 12: 3 It *s* his food, drank from his cup
1Ki 2: 26 and *s* all my father's hardships."
Ps 41: 9 he who *s* my bread,
Pr 5: 17 never to be *s* with strangers.
Lk 1: 58 her great mercy, and they *s* her joy.
Ac 1: 17 one of our number and *s*
4: 32 but they *s* everything they had.
Ro 15: 27 For if the Gentiles have *s*
Php 4: 15 not one church *s* with me
Heb 2: 14 he too *s* in their humanity so that
6: 4 who have *s* in the Holy Spirit,
Rev 18: 9 and *s* her luxury see the smoke

SHARERS (SHARE)

Eph 3: 6 and *s* together in the promise

SHARES (SHARE)

2Sa 19: 43 "We have ten *s* in the king;
Pr 22: 9 for he *s* his food with the poor.
Jn 13: 18 'He who *s* my bread has lifted up
19: 23 them into four *s*, one for each
2Jn : 11 Anyone who welcomes him *s*

SHAREZER

2Ki 19: 37 *S* cut him down with the sword,
Isa 37: 38 *S* cut him down with the sword,
Zec 7: 2 The people of Bethel had sent *S*

SHARING (SHARE)

Job 31: 17 not *s* it with the fatherless—
1Co 9: 10 so in the hope of *s* in the harvest.
2Co 8: 4 for the privilege of *s* in this service
9: 13 for your generosity in *s* with them
Php 3: 10 the fellowship of *s* in his sufferings,
Phm : 6 you may be active in *s* your faith,

SHARON (SHARONITE)

1Ch 5: 16 on all the pasturelands of *S* as far
27: 29 in charge of the herds grazing in *S*.
SS 2: 1 I am a rose of *S*,
Isa 33: 9 *S* is like the Arabah,
35: 2 the splendor of Carmel and *S*;
65: 10 *S* will become a pasture for flocks,
Ac 9: 35 lived in Lydda and *S* saw him

SHARONITE (SHARON)

1Ch 27: 29 Shitrai the *S* was in charge

SHARP (SHARPEN SHARPENED SHARPENING SHARPENS SHARPER)

Ps 45: 5 Let your *s* arrows pierce the hearts
57: 4 whose tongues are *s* swords.
120: 4 you with a warrior's *s* arrows,
140: 3 They make their tongues as *s*
Pr 5: 4 *s* as a double-edged sword.
25: 18 Like a club or a sword or a *s* arrow
Isa 5: 28 Their arrows are *s*,
41: 15 new and *s*, with many teeth.
Eze 5: 1 take a *s* sword and use it
28: 24 who are painful briers and *s* thorns.
Ac 15: 2 and Barnabas into *s* dispute
15: 39 had such a *s* disagreement that
Rev 1: 16 came a *s* double-edged sword.
2: 12 the words of him who has the *s*,
14: 14 gold on his head and a *s* sickle
14: 17 in heaven, and he too had a *s* sickle
14: 18 voice to him who had the *s* sickle,
14: 18 "Take your *s* sickle and gather
19: 15 Out of his mouth comes a *s* sword

SHARPEN (SHARP)

Dt 32: 41 when I *s* my flashing sword
Ps 7: 12 he will *s* his sword;
64: 3 who *s* their tongues like swords
Jer 51: 11 "*S* the arrows,

SHARPENED (SHARP)

1Sa 13: 20 mattocks, axes and sickles *s*.

Ps 52: 2 it is like a *s* razor,
Isa 49: 2 He made my mouth like a *s* sword,
Eze 21: 9 *s* and polished—
21: 10 *s* for the slaughter,
21: 11 it is *s* and polished,

SHARPENING (SHARP)

1Sa 13: 21 and a third of a shekel for *s* forks
13: 21 thirds of a shekel for *s* plowshares

SHARPENS (SHARP)

Pr 27: 17 As iron *s* iron,
27: 17 so one man *s* another.

SHARPER (SHARP)

Heb 4: 12 *S* than any double-edged sword,

SHARUHEN

Jos 19: 6 Beth Lebaoth and *S*—

SHASHAI

Ezr 10: 40 Adaiah, Macnadebai, *S*, Sharai,

SHASHAK

1Ch 8: 14 Ahio, *S*, Jeremoth, Zebadiah, Arad
8: 25 and Penuel were the sons of *S*.

SHATTER (SHATTERED SHATTERING SHATTERS)

Isa 30: 31 of the LORD will *s* Assyria;
Jer 49: 37 I will *s* Elam before their foes,
51: 20 with you I *s* nations,
51: 21 with you I *s* chariot and driver,
51: 21 with you I *s* horse and rider,
51: 22 with you I *s* man and woman,
51: 22 with you I *s* old man and youth,
51: 22 with you I *s* young man
51: 23 with you I *s* farmer and oxen,
51: 23 with you I *s* governors and officials
51: 23 with you I *s* shepherd and flock,
Eze 32: 12 They will *s* the pride of Egypt,
Hag 2: 22 and *s* the power of the foreign

SHATTERED (SHATTER)

Ex 15: 6 *s* the enemy.
Jdg 5: 26 she *s* and pierced his temple.
10: 8 who that year *s* and crushed them.
1Sa 2: 10 who oppose the LORD will be *s*.
1Ki 19: 11 and *s* the rocks before the LORD,
Job 16: 12 All was well with me, but he *s* me;
17: 11 days have passed, my plans are *s*,
Ps 48: 7 *s* by an east wind.
105: 33 and *s* the trees of their country.
Ecc 12: 6 before the pitcher is *s* at the spring,
Isa 7: 8 Ephraim will be too *s* to be a people
8: 9 Prepare for battle, and be *s!*
8: 9 Prepare for battle, and be *s!*
8: 9 the war cry, you nations, and be *s!*
9: 4 you have *s*
21: 9 lie *s* on the ground!' "
30: 14 *s* so mercilessly
Jer 25: 34 will fall and be *s* like fine pottery.
48: 1 stronghold will be disgraced and *s*.
48: 20 Moab is disgraced for she is *s*.
48: 39 "How *s* she is! How they wail!
50: 23 How broken and *s*
Eze 27: 34 Now you are *s* by the sea
Na 1: 6 the rocks are *s* before him.

SHATTERING (SHATTER)

Da 8: 7 the ram and *s* his two horns.

SHATTERS (SHATTER)

Job 34: 24 Without inquiry he *s* the mighty
Ps 46: 9 he breaks the bow and *s* the spear,

SHAUL (SHAUL'S SHAULITE)

Ge 36: 37 *S* from Rehoboth on the river
36: 38 When *S* died, Baal-Hanan son
46: 10 *S* the son of a Canaanite woman.
Ex 6: 15 *S* the son of a Canaanite woman.
Nu 26: 13 through *S*, the Shaulite clan.
1Ch 1: 48 *S* from Rehoboth on the river
1: 49 When *S* died, Baal-Hanan son
4: 24 Jamin, Jarib, Zerah and *S;*
6: 24 Uzziah his son and *S* his son.

SHAUL'S (SHAUL)

1Ch 4: 25 and Shaul; Shallum was *S* son,

SHAULITE (SHAUL)

Nu 26: 13 through Shaul, the *S* clan.

SHAVE (SHAVED)

Lev 14: 8 *s* off all his hair and bathe
14: 9 On the seventh day he must *s*
14: 9 he must *s* his head, his beard,
21: 5 or *s* off the edges of their beards
21: 5 " 'Priests must not *s* their heads
Nu 6: 9 he must *s* his head on the day
6: 18 the Nazirite must *s*
8: 7 then have them *s* their whole
Dt 14: 1 or *s* the front of your heads
21: 12 home and have her *s* her head,
Jdg 16: 19 a man to *s* off the seven braids
Isa 7: 20 to *s* your head and the hair
Jer 16: 6 no one will cut himself or *s* his head
47: 5 Gaza will *s* her head in mourning;
Eze 5: 1 as a barber's razor to *s* your head
27: 31 They will *s* their heads
44: 20 " 'They must not *s* their heads
Am 8: 10 and *s* your heads.
Mic 1: 16 *S* your heads in mourning

SHAVED (SHAVE)

Ge 41: 14 When he had *s* and changed his
Lev 13: 33 must be *s* except for the diseased
Nu 6: 19 After the Nazirite has *s* off the hair
Jdg 16: 17 my head were *s*, my strength would
16: 22 to grow again after it had been *s*.
2Sa 10: 4 *s* off half of each man's beard,
1Ch 19: 4 Hanun seized David's men, *s* them,
Job 1: 20 and tore his robe and *s* his head.
Isa 15: 2 Every head is *s*
Jer 2: 16 have *s* the crown of your head.
41: 5 eighty men who had *s*
48: 37 Every head is *s*
Eze 7: 18 shame and their heads will be *s*.
Ac 21: 24 so that they can have their heads *s*.
1Co 11: 5 it is just as though her head were *s*.
11: 6 woman to have her hair cut or *s* off,

SHAVEH

Ge 14: 17 him in the Valley of *S* (that is,

SHAVEH KIRIATHAIM

Ge 14: 5 the Emites in *S* and the Horites in

SHAVSHA

1Ch 18: 16 were priests; *S* was secretary;

SHAWL (SHAWLS)

Ru 3: 15 "Bring me the *s* you are wearing

SHAWLS (SHAWL)

Isa 3: 23 the linen garments and tiaras and *s*.
Mt 23: 5 the tassels of their prayer *s* long;

SHE-CAMEL (CAMEL)

Jer 2: 23 You are a swift *s*

SHEAF (SHEAVES)

Ge 37: 7 the field when suddenly my *s* rose
Lev 23: 10 bring to the priest a *s*
23: 11 is to wave the *s* before the LORD
23: 12 On the day you wave the *s*,
23: 15 the day you brought the *s*
Dt 24: 19 in your field and you overlook a *s*,

SHEAL

Ezr 10: 29 Adaiah, Jashub, *S* and Jeremoth.

SHEALTIEL

1Ch 3: 17 *S* his son, Malkiram, Pedaiah,
Ezr 3: 2 priests and Zerubbabel son of *S*
3: 8 in Jerusalem, Zerubbabel son of *S*,
5: 2 Then Zerubbabel son of *S*
Ne 12: 1 returned with Zerubbabel son of *S*
Hag 1: 1 Haggai to Zerubbabel son of *S*,
1: 12 Then Zerubbabel son of *S*,
1: 14 the spirit of Zerubbabel son of *S*,
2: 2 "Speak to Zerubbabel son of *S*,
2: 23 my servant Zerubbabel son of *S*,'
Mt 1: 12 Jeconiah was the father of *S*,
1: 12 *S* the father of Zerubbabel,
Lk 3: 27 the son of Zerubbabel, the son of *S*,

SHEAR (SHEARED SHEARER SHEARERS SHEARING SHEEP-SHEARING SHEEPSHEARERS SHORN)

Ge 31: 19 Laban had gone to *s* his sheep,
38: 13 on his way to Timnah to *s* his sheep
Dt 15: 19 do not *s* the firstborn of your sheep.

SHEAR-JASHUB

Isa 7: 3 "Go out, you and your son *S*,

SHEARED (SHEAR)

Isa 22: 25 it will be *s* off and will fall,

SHEARER (SHEAR)

Ac 8: 32 and as a lamb before the *s* is silent,

SHEARERS (SHEAR)

1Sa 25: 11 meat I have slaughtered for my *s*,
2Sa 13: 24 "Your servant has had *s* come.
Isa 53: 7 and as a sheep before her *s* is silent,

SHEARIAH

1Ch 8: 38 Azrikam, Bokeru, Ishmael, *S*,
9: 44 Azrikam, Bokeru, Ishmael, *S*,

SHEARING (SHEAR)

Ge 38: 12 to the men who were *s* his sheep,
Dt 18: 4 wool from the *s* of your sheep,
1Sa 25: 2 which he was *s* in Carmel.
25: 4 he heard that Nabal was *s* sheep.

SHEATH (SHEATHED)

2Sa 20: 8 a belt with a dagger in its *s*.
20: 8 forward, it dropped out of its *s*.
1Ch 21: 27 and he put his sword back into its *s*.

SHEATHED (SHEATH)

Ps 68: 13 wings of ⌞my⌟ dove are *s* with silver,

SHEAVES (SHEAF)

Ge 37: 7 We were binding *s* of grain out
37: 7 while your *s* gathered around mine
Ru 2: 7 and gather among the *s*
2: 15 "Even if she gathers among the *s*,
Job 5: 26 like *s* gathered in season.
24: 10 they carry the *s*, but still go hungry.
Ps 126: 6 carrying *s* with him.
Mic 4: 12 he who gathers them like *s*
Zec 12: 6 like a flaming torch among *s*.

SHEBA

Ge 10: 7 The sons of Raamah: *S* and Dedan.
10: 28 Diklah, Obal, Abimael, *S*, Ophir,
25: 3 Jokshan was the father of *S*
Jos 19: 2 It included: Beersheba (or *S*),
2Sa 20: 1 Now a troublemaker named *S* son
20: 2 David to follow *S* son of Bicri.
20: 6 *S* son of Bicri will do us more harm
20: 7 Jerusalem to pursue *S* son of Bicri.
20: 10 his brother Abishai pursued *S* son
20: 13 with Joab to pursue *S* son of Bicri.
20: 14 *S* passed through all the tribes
20: 15 with Joab came and besieged *S*
20: 21 A man named *S* son of Bicri,
20: 22 cut off the head of *S* son of Bicri
1Ki 10: 1 queen of *S* heard about the fame
10: 4 the queen of *S* saw all the wisdom
10: 10 as those the queen of *S* gave
10: 13 the queen of *S* all she desired
1Ch 1: 9 The sons of Raamah: *S* and Dedan.
1: 22 Diklah, Obal, Abimael, *S*, Ophir,
1: 32 The sons of Jokshan: *S* and Dedan.
5: 13 Michael, Meshullam, *S*, Jorai,
2Ch 9: 1 When the queen of *S* heard
9: 3 the queen of *S* saw the wisdom
9: 9 as those the queen of *S* gave
9: 12 the queen of *S* all she desired
Job 6: 19 the traveling merchants of *S* look
Ps 72: 10 the kings of *S* and Seba
72: 15 May gold from *S* be given him.
Isa 60: 6 And all from *S* will come,
Jer 6: 20 do I care about incense from *S*
Eze 27: 22 " 'The merchants of *S*
27: 23 and Eden and merchants of *S*,
38: 13 *S* and Dedan and the merchants

SHEBANIAH

1Ch 15: 24 *S*, Joshaphat, Nethanel, Amasai,
Ne 9: 4 Bani, Kadmiel, *S*, Bunni, Sherebiah
9: 5 Hodiah, *S* and Pethahiah—
10: 4 Malkijah, Hattush, *S*, Malluch,
10: 10 and their associates: *S*, Hodiah,
10: 12 Zaccur, Sherebiah, *S*, Hodiah,

SHEBAT

Zec 1: 7 the month of *S*, in the second year

SHEBER

1Ch 2: 48 Maacah was the mother of *S*

SHEBNA

2Ki 18: 18 the palace administrator, *S*
18: 26 and *S* and Joah said to the field
18: 37 *S* the secretary and Joah son
19: 2 *S* the secretary and the leading
Isa 22: 15 to *S*, who is in charge of the palace:
36: 3 the palace administrator, *S*
36: 11 *S* and Joah said to the field
36: 22 the palace administrator, *S*
37: 2 the palace administrator, *S*

SHECANIAH (SHECANIAH'S)

1Ch 3: 21 of Arnan, of Obadiah and of *S*.
3: 22 The descendants of *S*: Shemaiah
24: 11 the tenth to *S*, the eleventh
2Ch 31: 15 and *S* assisted him faithfully
Ezr 8: 3 Hattush of the descendants of *S*;
8: 5 of Zattu, *S* son of Jahaziel,
10: 2 Then *S* son of Jehiel, one
Ne 3: 29 Next to him, Shemaiah son of *S*,
6: 18 since he was son-in-law to *S* son
12: 3 Malluch, Hattush, *S*, Rehum,

SHECANIAH'S (SHECANIAH)

Ne 12: 14 Jonathan; of *S*, Joseph; of Harim's,

SHECHEM (SHECHEM'S SHECHEMITE)

Ge 12: 6 site of the great tree of Moreh at *S*.
33: 18 at the city of *S* in Canaan and
33: 19 the father of *S*, the plot
34: 2 When *S* son of Hamor the Hivite,
34: 4 And *S* said to his father Hamor,
34: 7 *S* had done a disgraceful thing
34: 8 "My son *S* has his heart set
34: 11 Then *S* said to Dinah's father
34: 13 spoke to *S* and his father Hamor.
34: 18 good to Hamor and his son *S*.
34: 20 and his son *S* went to the gate
34: 24 agreed with Hamor and his son *S*,
34: 26 They put Hamor and his son *S*
35: 4 them under the oak at *S*.
37: 12 to graze their father's flocks near *S*,
37: 13 are grazing the flocks near *S*.
37: 14 When Joseph arrived at *S*,
Nu 26: 31 through *S*, the Shechemite clan;
Jos 17: 2 Asriel, *S*, Hepher and Shemida.
17: 7 Asher to Micmethath east of *S*.
20: 7 *S* in the hill country of Ephraim,
21: 21 Ephraim they were given *S* (a city
24: 1 all the tribes of Israel at *S*.
24: 25 and there at *S* he drew up
24: 32 the sons of Hamor, the father of *S*.
24: 32 were buried at *S* in the tract
Jdg 8: 31 His concubine, who lived in *S*,
9: 1 went to his mother's brothers in *S*
9: 2 the citizens of *S*, 'Which is better
9: 3 this to the citizens of *S*,
9: 6 Then all the citizens of *S*
9: 6 in *S* to crown Abimelech king.
9: 7 "Listen to me, citizens of *S*,
9: 18 king over the citizens of *S*
9: 20 citizens of *S* and Beth Millo,
9: 20 citizens of *S* and Beth Millo,
9: 23 Abimelech and the citizens of *S*,
9: 24 and on the citizens of *S*,
9: 25 to him these citizens of *S* set men
9: 26 moved with his brothers into *S*,
9: 28 "Who is Abimelech, and who is *S*,
9: 31 and his brothers have come to *S*
9: 34 positions near *S* in four companies.
9: 39 So Gaal led out the citizens of *S*
9: 41 Gaal and his brothers out of *S*.
9: 42 people of *S* went out to the fields,
9: 46 the citizens in the tower of *S* went
Jdg 9: 49 So all the people in the tower of *S*,
9: 57 also made the men of *S* pay
21: 19 the road that goes from Bethel to *S*,
1Ki 12: 1 Rehoboam went to *S*,
12: 25 Then Jeroboam fortified *S*
1Ch 6: 67 Ephraim they were given *S* (a city
7: 19 Ahian, *S*, Likhi and Aniam.
7: 28 and *S* and its villages all the way
2Ch 10: 1 Rehoboam went to *S*,
Ps 60: 6 "In triumph I will parcel out *S*
108: 7 "In triumph I will parcel out *S*
Jer 41: 5 and cut themselves came from *S*,
Hos 6: 9 they murder on the road to *S*,
Ac 7: 16 bodies were brought back to *S*
7: 16 of Hamor at *S* for a certain sum

SHECHEM'S (SHECHEM)

Ge 34: 6 *S* father Hamor went out to talk
34: 26 took Dinah from *S* house and left.
Jdg 9: 28 Serve the men of Hamor, *S* father!

SHECHEMITE (SHECHEM)

Nu 26: 31 through Shechem, the *S* clan;

SHED (SHEDDING SHEDS)

Ge 9: 6 by man shall his blood be *s*;
37: 22 "Don't *s* any blood.
Lev 17: 4 he has *s* blood and must be cut
Nu 35: 33 by the blood of the one who *s* it.
35: 33 the land on which blood has been *s*,
Dt 19: 10 so that innocent blood will not be *s*
21: 7 "Our hands did not *s* this blood,
2Sa 16: 8 you for all the blood you *s*
1Ki 2: 31 of the innocent blood that Joab *s*.
2: 32 him for the blood he *s*,
2Ki 9: 7 blood of all the LORD's servants *s*
21: 16 *s* so much innocent blood that he
1Ch 22: 8 because you have *s* much blood
22: 8 'You have *s* much blood
28: 3 you are a warrior and have *s* blood.'
Ps 97: 11 Light is *s* upon the righteous
106: 38 They *s* innocent blood,
Pr 1: 16 they are swift to *s* blood.
6: 17 hands that *s* innocent blood,
Isa 26: 21 The earth will disclose the blood *s*
59: 7 they are swift to *s* innocent blood.
Jer 7: 6 and do not *s* innocent blood
22: 3 and do not *s* innocent blood
La 4: 13 who *s* within her
Eze 16: 38 commit adultery and who *s* blood;
21: 32 your blood will be *s* in your land,
22: 4 because of the blood you have *s*
22: 6 in you uses his power to *s* blood.
22: 12 In you men accept bribes to *s* blood
22: 13 and at the blood you have *s*
22: 27 they *s* blood and kill people
23: 45 who commit adultery and *s* blood,
24: 7 For the blood she *s* is in her midst:
24: 16 not lament or weep or *s* any tears.
33: 25 and look to your idols and *s* blood,
36: 18 they had *s* blood in the land and
Joel 3: 19 whose land they *s* innocent blood.
Mic 7: 2 All men lie in wait to *s* blood;
Hab 2: 8 For you have *s* man's blood;
2: 17 For you have *s* man's blood;
Mt 23: 35 the righteous blood that has been *s*
Lk 11: 50 of all the prophets that has been *s*
Ac 22: 20 of your martyr Stephen was *s*,
Ro 3: 15 "Their feet are swift to *s* blood;
Col 1: 20 through his blood, *s* on the cross.
Rev 16: 6 for they have *s* the blood

SHEDDING (SHED)

Dt 19: 13 the guilt of *s* innocent blood,
21: 9 the guilt of *s* innocent blood,
Jdg 9: 24 Jerub-Baal's seventy sons, the *s*
1Ki 2: 5 *s* their blood in peacetime
2Ki 24: 4 including the *s* of innocent blood.
Job 15: 33 like an olive tree *s* its blossoms.
Jer 22: 17 on *s* innocent blood
Eze 22: 3 brings on herself doom by *s* blood
22: 9 slanderous men bent on *s* blood;
Mt 23: 30 part with them in *s* the blood
Heb 9: 22 without the *s* of blood there is no
12: 4 to the point of *s* your blood.

SHEDEUR

Nu 1: 5 Elizur son of *S*; from Simeon,
Nu 2: 10 people of Reuben is Elizur son of *S*.
7: 30 On the fourth day Elizur son of *S*,
7: 35 was the offering of Elizur son of *S*.
10: 18 Elizur son of *S* was in command.

SHEDS (SHED)

Ge 9: 6 "Whoever *s* the blood of man,
Eze 18: 10 who *s* blood or does any

SHEEP (SHEEP'S SHEEPSKINS)

Ge 12: 16 and Abram acquired *s* and cattle,
20: 14 Abimelech brought *s* and cattle
21: 27 So Abraham brought *s* and cattle
24: 35 He has given him *s* and cattle,
29: 2 with three flocks of *s* lying near it
29: 3 the well's mouth and water the *s*.
29: 6 his daughter Rachel with the *s*."
29: 7 Water the *s* and take them back
29: 8 Then we will water the *s*."
29: 9 Rachel came with her father's *s*,
29: 10 his mother's brother, and Laban's *s*
29: 10 the well and watered his uncle's *s*.
30: 32 them every speckled or spotted *s*,
31: 19 Laban had gone to shear his *s*,
31: 38 Your *s* and goats have not
32: 5 I have cattle and donkeys, *s*
38: 12 to the men who were shearing his *s*,
38: 13 on his way to Timnah to shear his *s*
47: 17 their *s* and goats, their cattle
Ex 9: 3 and on your cattle and *s* and goats.
12: 5 and you may take them from the *s*
20: 24 your *s* and goats and your cattle.
22: 1 cattle for the ox and four *s* for the *s*.
22: 1 or a *s* and slaughters it or sells it,
22: 4 whether ox or donkey or *s*—
22: 9 a *s*, a garment, or any other lost
22: 10 a *s* or any other animal
22: 30 same with your cattle and your *s*.
Lev 1: 10 from either the *s* or the goats,
7: 23 Do not eat any of the fat of cattle, *s*
22: 19 *s* or goats in order that it may be
22: 23 or a *s* that is deformed or stunted,
22: 27 "When a cow, a *s* or a goat is born,
22: 28 Do not slaughter a cow or a *s*
27: 26 a cow or a *s*, it is the LORD's.
Nu 18: 17 a *s* or a goat; they are holy.
22: 40 Balak sacrificed cattle and *s*,
27: 17 LORD's people will not be like *s*
31: 28 cattle, donkeys, *s* or goats.
31: 30 whether persons, cattle, donkeys, *s*
31: 32 soldiers took was 675,000 *s*,
31: 36 the battle was: 337,500 *s*,
31: 43 was 337,500 *s*, 36,000 cattle,
Dt 14: 4 the ox, the *s*, the goat, the deer,
14: 5 the antelope and the mountain *s*.
14: 26 whatever you like: cattle, *s*,
15: 19 do not shear the firstborn of your *s*.
17: 1 a *s* that has any defect or flaw in it,
18: 3 people who sacrifice a bull or a *s*:
18: 4 wool from the shearing of your *s*,
22: 1 see your brother's ox or *s* straying,
28: 31 Your *s* will be given
Jos 6: 21 and old, cattle, *s* and donkeys.
7: 24 donkeys and *s*, his tent
Jdg 6: 4 neither *s* nor cattle nor donkeys.
1Sa 14: 32 and, taking *s*, cattle and calves,
14: 34 of you bring me your cattle and *s*,
15: 3 cattle and *s*, camels and donkeys
15: 9 and the best of the *s* and cattle,
15: 14 "What then is this bleating of *s*
15: 15 they spared the best of the *s*
15: 21 The soldiers took *s* and cattle
16: 11 answered, "but he is tending the *s*."
16: 19 your son David, who is with the *s*."
17: 15 to tend his father's *s* at Bethlehem.
17: 28 whom did you leave those few *s*
17: 34 and carried off a *s* from the flock,
17: 34 has been keeping his father's *s*.
17: 35 and rescued the *s* from its mouth.
22: 19 and its cattle, donkeys and *s*.
24: 3 He came to the *s* pens
25: 2 goats and three thousand *s*,
25: 4 he heard that Nabal was shearing *s*.
25: 16 all the time we were herding our *s*
25: 18 five dressed *s*, five seahs
27: 9 but took *s* and cattle, donkeys
2Sa 12: 2 man had a very large number of *s*
12: 4 from taking one of his own *s*

2Sa 17: 29 and lentils, honey and curds, *s*,
24: 17 These are but *s*.
1Ki 1: 9 Adonijah then sacrificed *s*,
1: 19 *s*, and has invited all the king's sons
1: 25 of cattle, fattened calves, and *s*.
4: 23 and a hundred *s* and goats,
8: 5 so many *s* and cattle that they
8: 63 and twenty thousand *s* and goats.
22: 17 the hills like *s* without a shepherd,
2Ki 3: 4 Now Mesha king of Moab raised *s*,
1Ch 5: 21 two hundred fifty thousand *s*
12: 40 raisin cakes, wine, oil, cattle and *s*,
21: 17 These are but *s*.
2Ch 5: 6 so many *s* and cattle that they
7: 5 and twenty thousand *s* and goats.
14: 15 carried off droves of *s* and goats
15: 11 and seven thousand *s* and goats
18: 2 Ahab slaughtered many *s*
18: 16 the hills like *s* without a shepherd,
29: 33 and three thousand *s* and goats.
30: 24 and seven thousand *s* and goats
30: 24 and ten thousand *s* and goats.
35: 7 a total of thirty thousand *s*
Ne 3: 1 to work and rebuilt the *S* Gate.
3: 32 and the *S* Gate the goldsmiths
5: 18 six choice *s* and some poultry were
12: 39 of the Hundred, as far as the *S* Gate
Job 1: 3 and he owned seven thousand *s*,
1: 16 burned up the *s* and the servants,
30: 1 disdained to put with my *s* dogs.
31: 20 him with the fleece from my *s*,
42: 12 He had fourteen thousand *s*,
Ps 44: 11 to be devoured like *s*
44: 22 we are considered as *s*
49: 14 Like *s* they are destined
74: 1 against the *s* of your pasture?
78: 52 led them like *s* through the desert.
78: 70 and took him from the *s* pens;
78: 71 from tending the *s* he brought him
79: 13 Then we your people, the *s*
100: 3 we are his people, the *s*
119: 176 I have strayed like a lost *s*.
144: 13 Our *s* will increase by thousands,
SS 1: 7 where you rest your *s* at midday.
1: 8 follow the tracks of the *s*
4: 2 teeth are like a flock of *s* just shorn,
6: 6 Your teeth are like a flock of *s*
Isa 5: 17 *s* will graze as in their own pasture;
7: 25 are turned loose and where *s* run.
13: 14 like *s* without a shepherd,
22: 13 of cattle and killing of *s*,
43: 23 You have not brought me *s*
53: 6 We all, like *s*, have gone astray,
53: 7 as a *s* before her shearers is silent,
Jer 12: 3 them off like *s* to be butchered!
13: 20 the *s* of which you boasted?
23: 1 scattering the *s* of my pasture!"
50: 6 "My people have been lost *s*;
Eze 25: 5 Ammon into a resting place for *s*.
34: 6 My *s* wandered over all
34: 11 I myself will search for my *s*
34: 12 with them, so will I look after my *s*.
34: 15 I myself will tend my *s*
34: 17 I will judge between one *s*
34: 20 between the fat *s* and the lean *s*.
34: 21 butting all the weak *s*
34: 22 I will judge between one *s*
34: 31 You my *s*, the *s* of my pasture,
36: 37 their people as numerous as *s*,
45: 15 Also one *s* is to be taken
Hos 12: 12 and to pay for her he tended *s*.
Joel 1: 18 even the flocks of *s* are suffering.
Mic 2: 12 I will bring them together like *s*
5: 8 like a young lion among flocks of *s*,
Hab 3: 17 though there are no *s* in the pen
Zep 2: 6 for shepherds and *s* pens.
Zec 10: 2 Therefore the people wander like *s*
11: 16 but will eat the meat of the choice *s*
13: 7 and the *s* will be scattered,
Mt 9: 36 helpless, like *s* without a shepherd.
10: 6 Go rather to the lost *s* of Israel.
10: 16 "I am sending you out like *s*
12: 11 "If any of you has a *s* and it falls
12: 12 more valuable is a man than a *s*!
15: 24 I was sent only to the lost *s* of Israel
18: 12 If a man owns a hundred *s*,
18: 13 he is happier about that one *s*
25: 32 as a shepherd separates the *s*
Mt 25: 33 He will put the *s* on his right
26: 31 the *s* of the flock will be scattered.'
Mk 6: 34 they were like *s* without a shepherd
14: 27 and the *s* will be scattered.'
Lk 15: 4 Suppose one of you has a hundred *s*
15: 4 go after the lost *s* until he finds it?
15: 6 with me; I have found my lost *s*.'
17: 7 plowing or looking after the *s*.
Jn 2: 14 he found men selling cattle, *s*
2: 15 all from the temple area, both *s*
5: 2 in Jerusalem near the *S* Gate a pool
10: 1 man who does not enter the *s* pen
10: 2 by the gate is the shepherd of his *s*.
10: 3 He calls his own *s* by name
10: 3 and the *s* listen to his voice.
10: 4 his *s* follow him because they know
10: 7 the truth, I am the gate for the *s*.
10: 8 but the *s* did not listen to them.
10: 11 lays down his life for the *s*.
10: 12 he abandons the *s* and runs away.
10: 12 is not the shepherd who owns the *s*.
10: 13 and cares nothing for the *s*.
10: 14 I know my *s* and my *s* know me—
10: 15 and I lay down my life for the *s*.
10: 16 other *s* that are not of this *s* pen.
10: 26 believe because you are not my *s*.
10: 27 My *s* listen to my voice; I know
21: 16 Jesus said, "Take care of my *s*."
21: 17 Jesus said, "Feed my *s*.
Ac 8: 32 He was led like a *s* to the slaughter,
Ro 8: 36 we are considered as *s*
Heb 13: 20 that great Shepherd of the *s*,
1Pe 2: 25 For you were like *s* going astray,
Rev 18: 13 cattle and *s*; horses and carriages;

SHEEP-SHEARING (SHEAR)

1Sa 25: 7 " 'Now I hear that it is *s* time.

SHEEP'S (SHEEP)

Mt 7: 15 They come to you in *s* clothing,

SHEEPSHEARERS (SHEAR)

2Sa 13: 23 *s* were at Baal Hazor

SHEEPSKINS (SHEEP)

Heb 11: 37 They went about in *s* and goatskins

SHEER

Isa 28: 19 will bring *s* terror.

SHEERAH

1Ch 7: 24 His daughter was *S*, who built

SHEET (SHEETS)

Isa 25: 7 the *s* that covers all nations;
Ac 10: 11 something like a large *s* being let
10: 16 immediately the *s* was taken back
11: 5 something like a large *s* being let

SHEETS (SHEET)

Ex 39: 3 They hammered out thin *s* of gold
Nu 16: 38 Hammer the censers into *s*

SHEHARIAH

1Ch 8: 26 Shamsherai, *S*, Athaliah,

SHEKEL (SHEKELS)

Ex 30: 13 This half *s* is an offering
30: 13 according to the sanctuary *s*,
30: 13 already counted is to give a half *s*,
30: 15 not to give more than a half *s*
30: 24 all according to the sanctuary *s*—
38: 24 according to the sanctuary *s*.
38: 25 according to the sanctuary *s*—
38: 26 according to the sanctuary *s*,
38: 26 half a *s*, according
Lev 5: 15 according to the sanctuary *s*.
27: 3 according to the sanctuary *s*;
27: 25 sanctuary *s*, twenty gerahs to the *s*.
Nu 3: 47 according to the sanctuary *s*,
3: 50 according to the sanctuary *s*.
7: 13 both according to the sanctuary *s*,
7: 19 both according to the sanctuary *s*,
7: 25 both according to the sanctuary *s*,
7: 31 both according to the sanctuary *s*,
7: 37 both according to the sanctuary *s*,
7: 43 both according to the sanctuary *s*,
7: 49 both according to the sanctuary *s*,
Nu 7: 55 both according to the sanctuary *s*,
7: 61 both according to the sanctuary *s*,
7: 67 both according to the sanctuary *s*,
7: 73 both according to the sanctuary *s*,
7: 79 both according to the sanctuary *s*,
7: 85 according to the sanctuary *s*.
7: 86 according to the sanctuary *s*.
18: 16 according to the sanctuary *s*,
1Sa 9: 8 "I have a quarter of a *s* of silver.
13: 21 a third of a *s* for sharpening forks
13: 21 of a *s* for sharpening plowshares
2Ki 7: 1 a seah of flour will sell for a *s*
7: 1 seahs of barley for a *s* at the gate
7: 16 So a seah of flour sold for a *s*,
7: 16 and two seahs of barley sold for a *s*,
7: 18 a seah of flour will sell for a *s*
7: 18 seahs of barley for a *s* at the gate
Ne 10: 32 third of a *s* each year for the service
Eze 45: 12 The *s* is to consist of twenty gerahs.

SHEKELS (SHEKEL)

Ge 20: 16 giving your brother a thousand *s*
23: 15 the land is worth four hundred *s*
23: 16 four hundred *s* of silver, according
24: 22 two gold bracelets weighing ten *s*.
37: 28 and sold him for twenty *s* of silver
45: 22 Benjamin he gave three hundred *s*
Ex 21: 32 the owner must pay thirty *s*
30: 23 250 *s*) of fragrant cinnamon,
30: 23 of fragrant cinnamon, 250 *s*
30: 23 the following fine spices: 500 *s*
30: 24 of fragrant cane, 500 *s* of cassia—
38: 24 sanctuary was 29 talents and 730 *s*,
38: 25 *s*, according to the sanctuary
38: 28 *s* to make the hooks for the posts,
38: 29 offering was 70 talents and 2,400 *s*.
Lev 27: 3 and sixty at fifty *s* of silver,
27: 4 is a female, set her value at thirty *s*.
27: 5 and of a female at ten *s*.
27: 5 set the value of a male at twenty *s*
27: 6 that of a female at three *s* of silver.
27: 6 the value of a male at five *s* of silver
27: 7 and of a female at ten *s*.
27: 7 set the value of a male at fifteen *s*
27: 16 fifty *s* of silver to a homer
Nu 3: 47 collect five *s* for each one,
3: 50 *s*, according to the sanctuary
7: 13 bowl weighing seventy *s*,
7: 13 weighing a hundred and thirty *s*,
7: 14 one gold ladle weighing ten *s*,
7: 19 bowl weighing seventy *s*,
7: 19 weighing a hundred and thirty *s*,
7: 20 one gold ladle weighing ten *s*,
7: 25 bowl weighing seventy *s*,
7: 25 weighing a hundred and thirty *s*,
7: 26 one gold ladle weighing ten *s*,
7: 31 bowl weighing seventy *s*,
7: 31 weighing a hundred and thirty *s*,
7: 32 one gold ladle weighing ten *s*,
7: 37 bowl weighing seventy *s*,
7: 37 weighing a hundred and thirty *s*,
7: 38 one gold ladle weighing ten *s*,
7: 43 bowl weighing seventy *s*,
7: 43 weighing a hundred and thirty *s*,
7: 44 one gold ladle weighing ten *s*,
7: 49 bowl weighing seventy *s*,
7: 49 weighing a hundred and thirty *s*,
7: 50 one gold ladle weighing ten *s*,
7: 55 bowl weighing seventy *s*,
7: 55 weighing a hundred and thirty *s*,
7: 56 one gold ladle weighing ten *s*,
7: 61 bowl weighing seventy *s*,
7: 61 weighing a hundred and thirty *s*,
7: 62 one gold ladle weighing ten *s*,
7: 67 bowl weighing seventy *s*,
7: 67 weighing a hundred and thirty *s*,
7: 68 one gold ladle weighing ten *s*.
7: 73 bowl weighing seventy *s*,
7: 73 weighing a hundred and thirty *s*,
7: 74 one gold ladle weighing ten *s*,
7: 79 bowl weighing seventy *s*,
7: 79 weighing a hundred and thirty *s*,
7: 80 one gold ladle weighing ten *s*,
7: 85 and each sprinkling bowl seventy *s*.
7: 85 two thousand four hundred *s*,
7: 85 weighed a hundred and thirty *s*,
7: 86 weighed a hundred and twenty *s*.
7: 86 with incense weighed ten *s* each,

Nu 18: 16 at the redemption price set at five *s*
31: 52 to the LORD weighed 16,750 *s*.
Dt 22: 19 They shall fine him a hundred *s*
22: 29 he shall pay the girl's father fifty *s*
Jos 7: 21 a wedge of gold weighing fifty *s*,
7: 21 two hundred *s* of silver
Jdg 8: 26 for came to seventeen hundred *s*,
9: 4 They gave him seventy silver *s*
16: 5 of us will give you eleven hundred *s*
17: 2 "The eleven hundred *s*
17: 3 he returned the eleven hundred *s*
17: 4 she took two hundred *s* of silver
17: 10 I'll give you ten *s* of silver a year,
1Sa 17: 5 of bronze weighing five thousand *s*;
17: 7 iron point weighed six hundred *s*.
2Sa 14: 26 and its weight was two hundred *s*
18: 11 had to give you ten *s* of silver
18: 12 if a thousand *s* were weighed out
21: 16 weighed three hundred *s*
24: 24 and paid fifty *s* of silver for them.
1Ki 10: 29 Egypt for six hundred *s* of silver,
2Ki 5: 5 six thousand *s* of gold and ten sets
6: 25 of a cab of seed pods for five *s*.
6: 25 sold for eighty *s* of silver,
15: 20 had to contribute fifty *s* of silver
1Ch 21: 25 David paid Araunah six hundred *s*
2Ch 1: 17 Egypt for six hundred *s* of silver,
3: 9 The gold nails weighed fifty *s*.
Ne 5: 15 and took forty *s* of silver from them
SS 8: 11 a thousand *s* of silver.
8: 12 the thousand *s* are for you,
Isa 7: 23 vines worth a thousand silver *s*,
Jer 32: 9 out for him seventeen *s* of silver.
Eze 4: 10 Weigh out twenty *s* of food
45: 12 Twenty *s* plus twenty-five *s* plus
45: 12 plus fifteen *s* equal one mina.
Hos 3: 2 I bought her for fifteen *s* of silver

SHELAH (SHELANITE)

Ge 10: 24 of *S*, and *S* the father of Eber.
11: 12 he became the father of *S*.
11: 13 And after he became the father of *S*
11: 14 When *S* had lived 30 years,
11: 15 *S* lived 403 years and had other
38: 5 still another son and named him *S*.
38: 11 house until my son *S* grows up."
38: 14 though *S* had now grown up,
38: 26 I wouldn't give her to my son *S*."
46: 12 The sons of Judah: Er, Onan, *S*,
Nu 26: 20 through *S*, the Shelanite clan;
1Ch 1: 18 of *S*, and *S* the father of Eber.
1: 24 Shem, Arphaxad, *S*, Eber, Peleg,
2: 3 The sons of Judah: Er, Onan and *S*.
4: 21 The sons of *S* son of Judah:
Ne 11: 5 of Zechariah, a descendant of *S*
Lk 3: 35 the son of *S*,

SHELANITE (SHELAH)

Nu 26: 20 through Shelah, the *S* clan;

SHELEMIAH

1Ch 26: 14 The lot for the East Gate fell to *S*.
Ezr 10: 39 Shimei, *S*, Nathan, Adaiah,
10: 41 Sharai, Azarel, *S*, Shemariah,
Ne 3: 30 Hananiah son of *S*, and Hanun,
13: 13 I put *S* the priest, Zadok the scribe,
Jer 36: 14 the son of *S*, the son of Cushi,
36: 26 *S* son of Abdeel to arrest Baruch
37: 3 sent Jehucal son of *S*
37: 13 whose name was Irijah son of *S*,
38: 1 son of Pashhur, Jehucal son of *S*,

SHELEPH

Ge 10: 26 *S*, Hazarmaveth, Jerah, Hadoram,
1Ch 1: 20 *S*, Hazarmaveth, Jerah, Hadoram,

SHELESH

1Ch 7: 35 Zophah, Imna, *S* and Amal.

SHELOMI

Nu 34: 27 Ahihud son of *S*, the leader

SHELOMITH

Lev 24: 11 (His mother's name was *S*,
1Ch 3: 19 *S* was their sister.
23: 18 The sons of Izhar: *S* was the first.
26: 25 Zicri his son and *S* his son.
26: 26 *S* and his relatives were in charge
1Ch 26: 28 things were in the care of *S*
2Ch 11: 20 bore him Abijah, Attai, Ziza and *S*.
Ezr 8: 10 of Bani, *S* son of Josiphiah,

SHELOMOTH

1Ch 23: 9 The sons of Shimei: *S*, Haziel
24: 22 *S*; from the sons of *S*:

SHELTER (SHELTERED SHELTERS)

Ex 9: 19 have in the field to a place of *s*,
Dt 32: 38 Let them give you *s*!
Ru 2: 7 except for a short rest in the *s*."
1Ch 28: 18 and *s* the ark of the covenant
Job 24: 8 and hug the rocks for lack of *s*.
Ps 27: 5 me in the *s* of his tabernacle
31: 20 In the *s* of your presence you hide
55: 8 I would hurry to my place of *s*,
61: 4 take refuge in the *s* of your wings.
91: 1 in the *s* of the Most High
Ecc 7: 12 Wisdom is a *s*
7: 12 as money is a *s*,
Isa 1: 8 like a *s* in a vineyard,
4: 6 It will be a *s* and shade
16: 4 be their *s* from the destroyer."
25: 4 a *s* from the storm
32: 2 Each man will be like a *s*
58: 7 the poor wanderer with *s*—
Jer 4: 20 my *s* in a moment.
10: 20 or to set up my *s*.
Eze 17: 23 they will find *s* in the shade
Da 4: 12 the beasts of the field found *s*,
4: 21 giving *s* to the beasts of the field,
Jnh 4: 5 There he made himself a *s*,

SHELTERED (SHELTER)

Zep 2: 3 perhaps you will be *s*

SHELTERS (SHELTER)

Ge 33: 17 and made *s* for his livestock.
Jdg 6: 2 the Israelites prepared *s*
Jer 49: 29 their *s* will be carried off
Mt 17: 4 I will put up three *s*— one for you,
Mk 9: 5 Let us put up three *s*— one for you,
Lk 9: 33 Let us put up three *s*— one for you,

SHELUMIEL

Nu 1: 6 from Simeon, *S* son of Zurishaddai;
2: 12 of Simeon is *S* son of Zurishaddai.
7: 36 On the fifth day *S* son
7: 41 offering of *S* son of Zurishaddai.
10: 19 *S* son of Zurishaddai was

SHEM

Ge 5: 32 he became the father of *S*,
6: 10 Noah had three sons: *S*, Ham
7: 13 that very day Noah and his sons, *S*,
9: 18 who came out of the ark were *S*,
9: 23 But *S* and Japheth took a garment
9: 26 May Canaan be the slave of *S*.
9: 26 be the LORD, the God of *S*!
9: 27 may Japheth live in the tents of *S*,
10: 1 This is the account of *S*, Ham
10: 21 born to *S*, whose older brother was
10: 21 *S* was the ancestor of all the sons
10: 22 The sons of *S*: Elam, Asshur,
10: 31 These are the sons of *S*
11: 10 This is the account of *S*.
11: 10 when *S* was 100 years old,
11: 11 *S* lived 500 years and had other
1Ch 1: 4 The sons of Noah: *S*, Ham
1: 17 The sons of *S*: Elam, Asshur,
1: 24 *S*, Arphaxad, Shelah, Eber, Peleg,
Lk 3: 36 the son of Arphaxad, the son of *S*,

SHEMA

Jos 15: 26 Hazor), Amam, *S*, Moladah,
1Ch 2: 43 Korah, Tappuah, Rekem and *S*.
2: 44 *S* was the father of Raham,
5: 8 the son of *S*, the son of Joel.
8: 13 villages), and Beriah and *S*,
Ne 8: 4 *S*, Anaiah, Uriah, Hilkiah

SHEMAAH

1Ch 12: 3 Joash the sons of *S* the Gibeathite;

SHEMAIAH (SHEMAIAH'S)

1Ki 12: 22 of God came to *S* the man of God:
1Ch 3: 22 The descendants of Shecaniah: *S*
1Ch 4: 37 the son of Shimri, the son of *S*.
5: 4 The descendants of Joel: *S* his son,
9: 14 Of the Levites: *S* son of Hasshub,
9: 16 Obadiah son of *S*, the son of Galal,
15: 8 *S* the leader and 200 relatives;
15: 11 and Uriel, Asaiah, Joel, *S*,
24: 6 The scribe *S* son of Nethanel,
26: 4 also had sons: *S* the firstborn,
26: 6 His son *S* also had sons, who were
26: 7 The sons of *S*: Othni, Rephael,
2Ch 11: 2 came to *S* the man of God:
12: 5 the prophet *S* came to Rehoboam
12: 7 this word of the LORD came to *S*:
12: 15 in the records of *S* the prophet
17: 8 *S*, Nethaniah, Zebadiah, Asahel,
29: 14 the descendants of Jeduthun, *S*
31: 15 Eden, Miniamin, Jeshua, *S*,
35: 9 Also Conaniah along with *S*
Ezr 8: 13 Jeuel and *S*, and with them 60 men;
8: 16 Ariel, *S*, Elnathan, Jarib, Elnathan,
10: 21 Elijah, *S*, Jehiel and Uzziah.
10: 31 Ishijah, Malkijah, *S*, Shimeon,
Ne 3: 29 Next to him, *S* son of Shecaniah,
6: 10 to the house of *S* son of Delaiah,
10: 8 Mijamin, Maaziah, Bilgai and *S*.
11: 15 From the Levites: *S* son
12: 6 Maadiah, Bilgah, *S*, Joiarib,
12: 34 Judah, Benjamin, *S*, Jeremiah,
12: 35 the son of *S*, the son of Mattaniah,
12: 36 and his associates—*S*, Azarel,
12: 42 and also Maaseiah, *S*, Eleazar,
Jer 26: 20 (Now Uriah son of *S*
29: 24 Tell *S* the Nehelamite, "This is
29: 31 Because *S* has prophesied to you,
29: 31 says about *S* the Nehelamite:
29: 32 surely punish *S* the Nehelamite
36: 12 Delaiah son of *S*, Elnathan son

SHEMAIAH'S (SHEMAIAH)

Ne 12: 18 Shammua; of *S*, Jehonathan;

SHEMARIAH

1Ch 12: 5 *S* and Shephatiah the Haruphite;
2Ch 11: 19 She bore him sons: Jeush, *S*
Ezr 10: 32 Benjamin, Malluch and *S*.
10: 41 Azarel, Shelemiah, *S*, Shallum,

SHEMEBER

Ge 14: 2 king of Admah, *S* king of Zeboiim,

SHEMED

1Ch 8: 12 *S* (who built Ono and Lod

SHEMER

1Ki 16: 24 calling it Samaria, after *S*,
16: 24 of Samaria from *S* for two talents
1Ch 6: 46 the son of *S*, the son of Mahli,

SHEMIDA (SHEMIDAITE)

Nu 26: 32 through *S*, the Shemidaite clan;
Jos 17: 2 Asriel, Shechem, Hepher and *S*.
1Ch 7: 19 The sons of *S* were: Ahian,

SHEMIDAITE (SHEMIDA)

Nu 26: 32 through Shemida, the *S* clan;

SHEMINITH

1Ch 15: 21 the harps, directing according to *s*.

SHEMIRAMOTH

1Ch 15: 18 Zechariah, Jaaziel, *S*, Jehiel, Unni,
15: 20 Zechariah, Aziel, *S*, Jehiel, Unni,
16: 5 then Jeiel, *S*, Jehiel, Mattithiah,
2Ch 17: 8 Zebadiah, Asahel, *S*, Jehonathan,

SHEMUEL

Nu 34: 20 tribe of Judah; *S* son of Ammihud,

SHEN

1Sa 7: 12 set it up between Mizpah and *S*.

SHENAZZAR

1Ch 3: 18 Malkiram, Pedaiah, *S*, Jekamiah,

SHEPHAM

Nu 34: 10 run a line from Hazar Enan to *S*.
34: 11 go down from *S* to Riblah

SHEPHATIAH

2Sa 3: 4 the fifth, *S* the son of Abital;
1Ch 3: 3 the fifth, *S* the son of Abital;
9: 8 and Meshullam son of *S*, the son
12: 5 Shemariah and *S* the Haruphite;
27: 16 over the Simeonites: *S* son
2Ch 21: 2 Azariahu, Michael and *S*.
Ezr 2: 4 of *S* 372 of Arah 775
2: 57 Jaala, Darkon, Giddel, *S*, Hattil,
8: 8 the descendants of *S*, Zebadiah son
Ne 7: 9 of *S* 372 of Arah 652
7: 59 Jaala, Darkon, Giddel, *S*, Hattil,
11: 4 the son of *S*, the son of Mahalalel,
Jer 38: 1 *S* son of Mattan, Gedaliah son

SHEPHER

Nu 33: 23 and camped at Mount *S*.
33: 24 They left Mount *S* and camped

SHEPHERD (SHEPHERD'S SHEPHERDED SHEPHERDESS SHEPHERDS)

Ge 48: 15 the God who has been my *S*
49: 24 because of the *S*, the Rock of Israel
Nu 27: 17 will not be like sheep without a *s*.''
1Sa 17: 20 David left the flock with a *s*,
21: 7 Doeg the Edomite, Saul's head *s*.
2Sa 5: 2 'You will *s* my people Israel,
7: 7 commanded to *s* my people Israel,
1Ki 22: 17 on the hills like sheep without a *s*,
1Ch 11: 2 'You will *s* my people Israel,
17: 6 I commanded to *s* my people,
2Ch 18: 16 on the hills like sheep without a *s*,
Ps 23: 1 LORD is my *s*, I shall lack nothing.
28: 9 be their *s* and carry them forever.
78: 71 him to be the *s* of his people Jacob,
80: 1 Hear us, O *S* of Israel,
Ecc 12: 11 embedded nails—given by one *S*.
Isa 13: 14 like sheep without a *s*,
13: 20 no *s* will rest his flocks there.
40: 11 He tends his flock like a *s*:
44: 28 who says of Cyrus, 'He is my *s*
61: 5 Aliens will *s* your flocks;
63: 11 with the *s* of his flock?
Jer 17: 16 away from being your *s*;
31: 10 will watch over his flock like a *s*.'
43: 12 As a *s* wraps his garment
49: 19 And what *s* can stand against me?''
50: 44 And what *s* can stand against me?''
51: 23 with you I shatter *s* and flock,
Eze 34: 5 scattered because there was no *s*,
34: 8 because my flock lacks a *s*
34: 12 As a *s* looks after his scattered
34: 16 I will *s* the flock with justice.
34: 23 I will place over them one *s*,
34: 23 he will tend them and be their *s*.
37: 24 and they will all have one *s*.
Am 3: 12 ''As a *s* saves from the lion's mouth
7: 14 but I was a *s*, and I also took care
Mic 5: 4 He will stand and *s* his flock
7: 14 *S* your people with your staff,
Zec 10: 2 oppressed for lack of a *s*.
11: 9 and said, ''I will not be your *s*.
11: 15 again the equipment of a foolish *s*.
11: 16 to raise up a *s* over the land who
11: 17 ''Woe to the worthless *s*,
13: 7 ''Awake, O sword, against my *s*,
13: 7 ''Strike the *s*,
Mt 2: 6 who will be the *s* of my people
9: 36 and helpless, like sheep without a *s*.
25: 32 as a *s* separates the sheep
26: 31 '' 'I will strike the *s*,
Mk 6: 34 they were like sheep without a *s*.
14: 27 '' 'I will strike the *s*,
Jn 10: 2 by the gate is the *s* of his sheep.
10: 11 The good *s* lays down his life
10: 11 ''I am the good *s*.
10: 12 hand is not the *s* who owns
10: 14 ''I am the good *s*; I know my sheep
10: 16 there shall be one flock and one *s*.
Heb 13: 20 that great *S* of the sheep, equip you
1Pe 2: 25 but now you have returned to the *S*
5: 4 And when the Chief *S* appears,
Rev 7: 17 of the throne will be their *s*;

SHEPHERD'S (SHEPHERD)

Lev 27: 32 that passes under the *s* rod—
1Sa 17: 40 put them in the pouch of his *s* bag
Isa 38: 12 Like a *s* tent my house

SHEPHERDED (SHEPHERD)

Ps 78: 72 David *s* them with integrity

SHEPHERDESS (SHEPHERD)

Ge 29: 9 her father's sheep, for she was a *s*.

SHEPHERDS (SHEPHERD)

Ge 29: 3 the *s* would roll the stone away
29: 4 Jacob asked the *s*, ''My brothers,
46: 32 The men are *s*; they tend livestock,
46: 34 for all *s* are detestable
47: 3 ''Your servants are *s*,'' they replied
Ex 2: 17 Some *s* came along and drove them
2: 19 An Egyptian rescued us from the *s*.
Nu 14: 33 Your children will be *s* here
1Sa 25: 7 When your *s* were with us,
2Ki 10: 12 At Beth Eked of the *S*, he
SS 1: 8 goats by the tents of the *s*.
Isa 31: 4 and though a whole band of *s*
56: 11 They are *s* who lack understanding
Jer 3: 15 I will give you *s* after my own heart
6: 3 *S* with their flocks will come
10: 21 The *s* are senseless
12: 10 Many *s* will ruin my vineyard
22: 22 The wind will drive all your *s* away,
23: 1 ''Woe to the *s* who are destroying
23: 2 says to the *s* who tend my people:
23: 4 I will place *s* over them who will
25: 34 Weep and wail, you *s*;
25: 35 The *s* will have nowhere to flee,
25: 36 Hear the cry of the *s*,
33: 12 pastures for *s* to rest their flocks.
50: 6 their *s* have led them astray
Eze 34: 2 Should not *s* take care of the flock?
34: 2 prophesy against the *s* of Israel;
34: 2 to the *s* of Israel who only take care
34: 7 you *s*, hear the word of the LORD:
34: 8 my *s* did not search for my flock
34: 9 O *s*, hear the word of the LORD:
34: 10 am against the *s* and will hold them
34: 10 so that the *s* can no longer feed
Am 1: 1 of Amos, one of the *s* of Tekoa—
1: 2 the pastures of the *s* dry up,
Mic 5: 5 we will raise against him seven *s*,
Na 3: 18 O king of Assyria, your *s* slumber;
Zep 2: 6 will be a place for *s* and sheep pens.
Zec 10: 3 ''My anger burns against the *s*,
11: 3 Listen to the wail of the *s*;
11: 5 Their own *s* do not spare them.
11: 8 In one month I got rid of the three *s*
Lk 2: 8 there were *s* living out in the fields
2: 15 and gone into heaven, the *s* said
2: 18 amazed at what the *s* said to them.
2: 20 The *s* returned, glorifying
Ac 20: 28 Be *s* of the church of God,
1Pe 5: 2 Be *s* of God's flock that is
Jude : 12 *s* who feed only themselves.

SHEPHO

Ge 36: 23 Manahath, Ebal, *S* and Onam.
1Ch 1: 40 Manahath, Ebal, *S* and Onam.

SHEPHUPHAN

1Ch 8: 5 Ahoah, Gera, *S* and Huram.

SHEREBIAH (SHEREBIAH'S)

Ezr 8: 18 they brought us *S*, a capable man,
8: 24 together with *S*, Hashabiah
Ne 8: 7 Jeshua, Bani, *S*, Jamin, Akkub,
9: 4 Kadmiel, Shebaniah, Bunni, *S*,
9: 5 Bani, Hashabneiah, *S*, Hodiah,
10: 12 Hashabiah, Zaccur, *S*, Shebaniah,
12: 8 Binnui, Kadmiel, *S*, Judah,
12: 24 *S*, Jeshua son of Kadmiel,

SHEREBIAH'S (SHEREBIAH)

Ezr 8: 18 the son of Israel, and *S* sons

SHERESH

1Ch 7: 16 His brother was named *S*,

SHESHACH

Jer 25: 26 the king of *S* will drink it too.
51: 41 ''How *S* will be captured,

SHESHAI

Nu 13: 22 where Ahiman, *S* and Talmai,
Jos 15: 14 *S*, Ahiman and Talmai—
Jdg 1: 10 defeated *S*, Ahiman and Talmai.

SHESHAN

1Ch 2: 31 Ishi, who was the father of *S*.
2: 31 *S* was the father of Ahlai.
2: 34 *S* had no sons—only daughters.
2: 35 *S* gave his daughter in marriage

SHESHBAZZAR

Ezr 1: 8 out to *S* the prince of Judah.
1: 11 *S* brought all these
5: 14 them to a man named *S*,
5: 16 So this *S* came and laid

SHETH

Nu 24: 17 the skulls of all the sons of *S*.

SHETHAR

Est 1: 14 Carshena, *S*, Admatha, Tarshish,

SHETHAR-BOZENAI

Ezr 5: 3 *S* and their associates went to them
5: 6 and *S* and their associates,
6: 6 of Trans-Euphrates, and *S*
6: 13 *S* and their associates carried it out

SHEVA

2Sa 20: 25 was recorder; *S* was secretary;
1Ch 2: 49 and to *S* the father of Macbenah

SHIBAH

Ge 26: 33 We've found water!'' He called it *S*

SHIBBOLETH

Jdg 12: 6 No,'' they said, ''All right, say '*S*.' ''

SHIELD (SHIELDED SHIELDING SHIELDS)

Ge 15: 1 I am your *s*,
Ex 40: 3 and *s* the ark with the curtain.
Dt 13: 8 Do not spare him or *s* him.
33: 29 He is your *s* and helper
Jdg 5: 8 and not a *s* or spear was seen
1Sa 17: 7 His *s* bearer went ahead of him.
17: 41 with his *s* bearer in front of him,
2Sa 1: 21 For there the *s* of the mighty was
1: 21 the *s* of Saul—no longer rubbed
22: 3 my *s* and the horn of my salvation.
22: 31 He is a *s*
22: 36 You give me your *s* of victory;
1Ki 10: 16 bekas of gold went into each *s*.
10: 17 with three minas of gold in each *s*.
2Ki 19: 32 He will not come before it with *s*
1Ch 5: 18 men who could handle *s*
12: 8 and able to handle the *s* and spear.
12: 24 carrying *s* and spear—6,800
2Ch 9: 15 of hammered gold went into each *s*
9: 16 hundred bekas of gold in each *s*.
25: 5 able to handle the spear and *s*.
Job 15: 26 him with a thick, strong *s*.
Ps 3: 3 But you are a *s* around me,
5: 12 with your favor as with a *s*.
7: 10 My *s* is God Most High,
18: 2 He is my *s* and the horn
18: 30 He is a *s*
18: 35 You give me your *s* of victory,
28: 7 LORD is my strength and my *s*;
33: 20 he is our help and our *s*.
35: 2 Take up *s* and buckler;
59: 11 But do not kill them, O Lord our *s*,
84: 9 Look upon our *s*, O God;
84: 11 For the LORD God is a sun and *s*;
89: 18 Indeed, our *s* belongs to the LORD
91: 4 his faithfulness will be your *s*
115: 9 he is their help and *s*.
115: 10 he is their help and *s*.
115: 11 he is their help and *s*.
119:114 You are my refuge and my *s*;
144: 2 my *s*, in whom I take refuge,
Pr 2: 7 he is a *s* to those whose walk is
30: 5 he is a *s* to those who take refuge
Isa 22: 6 Kir uncovers the *s*.
31: 5 he will *s* it and deliver it,
31: 5 LORD Almighty will *s* Jerusalem;
37: 33 He will not come before it with *s*

SHINAR

Ge 10: 10 Erech, Akkad and Calneh, in *S*.
11: 2 they found a plain in *S*
14: 1 At this time Amraphel king of *S*,
14: 9 king of *S* and Arioch king

SHINE (SHINES SHINING SHONE)

Nu 6: 25 the LORD make his face *s*
Ne 9: 19 nor the pillar of fire by night to *s*
Job 3: 4 may no light *s* upon it.
9: 7 to the sun and it does not *s;*
22: 28 and light will *s* on your ways.
33: 30 that the light of life may *s* on him.
Ps 4: 6 Let the light of your face *s* upon us,
31: 16 Let your face *s* on your servant;
37: 6 make your righteousness *s* like
67: 1 and make his face *s* upon us; *Selah*
80: 1 between the cherubim, *s* forth
80: 3 make your face *s* upon us,
80: 7 make your face *s* upon us,
80: 19 make your face *s* upon us,
94: 1 O God who avenges, *s* forth.
104: 15 oil to make his face *s*,
118: 27 and he has made his light *s* upon us.
119:135 your face *s* upon your servant
139: 12 the night will *s* like the day,
Isa 30: 26 The moon will *s* like the sun,
60: 1 "Arise, *s*, for your light has come,
60: 19 brightness of the moon *s* on you,
Jer 31: 35 and stars to *s* by night,
31: 35 the sun to *s* by day,
Da 12: 3 are wise will *s* like the brightness
Joel 2: 10 and the stars no longer *s*.
3: 15 and the stars no longer *s*.
Mt 5: 16 let your light *s* before men,
13: 43 the righteous will *s* like the sun
Lk 1: 79 to *s* on those living in darkness
2Co 4: 6 made his light *s* in our hearts
4: 6 "Let light *s* out of darkness,"
Eph 5: 14 and Christ will *s* on you."
Php 2: 15 in which you *s* like stars
Rev 18: 23 will never *s* in you again.
21: 23 not need the sun or the moon to *s*

SHINES (SHINE)

Ps 50: 2 God *s* forth.
Pr 13: 9 The light of the righteous *s* brightly
Isa 62: 1 till her righteousness *s* out like
Lk 11: 36 as when the light of a lamp *s* on you
Jn 1: 5 The light *s* in the darkness,

SHINING (SHINE)

2Ki 3: 22 the sun was *s* on the water.
Ps 68: 13 its feathers with *s* gold."
148: 3 praise him, all you *s* stars.
Pr 4: 18 *s* ever brighter till the full light
Eze 28: 7 and pierce your *s* splendor.
32: 8 All the *s* lights in the heavens
Lk 23: 45 for the sun stopped *s*.
Ac 10: 30 Suddenly a man in *s* clothes stood
2Pe 1: 19 as to a light *s* in a dark place,
1Jn 2: 8 and the true light is already *s*.
Rev 1: 16 His face was like the sun *s*
15: 6 *s* linen and wore golden sashes

SHION

Jos 19: 19 Shunem, Hapharaim, *S*, Anaharath

SHIP (SHIP'S SHIPS SHIPWRIGHTS)

Pr 30: 19 the way of a *s* on the high seas,
Isa 2: 16 for every trading *s*
33: 21 no mighty *s* will sail them.
Jnh 1: 3 where he found a *s* bound
1: 4 storm arose that the *s* threatened
1: 5 cargo into the sea to lighten the *s*.
Ac 20: 13 We went on ahead to the *s*
20: 38 they accompanied him to the *s*.
21: 2 We found a *s* crossing
21: 3 where our *s* was to unload its cargo.
21: 6 went aboard the *s*, and they
27: 2 a *s* from Adramyttium about
27: 6 found an Alexandrian *s* sailing
27: 10 and bring great loss to *s* and cargo,
27: 11 and of the owner of the *s*.
27: 15 The *s* was caught by the storm
27: 17 and let the *s* be driven along.
27: 17 they passed ropes under the *s* itself
27: 22 only the *s* will be destroyed.
Ac 27: 30 In an attempt to escape from the *s*,
27: 31 "Unless these men stay with the *s*,
27: 38 they lightened the *s*
27: 39 to run the *s* aground if they could.
27: 41 But the *s* struck a sandbar
27: 44 on planks or on pieces of the *s*.
28: 11 It was an Alexandrian *s*
28: 11 out to sea in a *s* that had wintered
Rev 18: 17 and all who travel by *s*, the sailors,

SHIP'S (SHIP)

Ac 27: 19 they threw the *s* tackle overboard

SHIPHI

1Ch 4: 37 and Ziza son of *S*, the son of Allon,

SHIPHMITE

1Ch 27: 27 Zabdi the *S* was in charge

SHIPHRAH

Ex 1: 15 whose names were *S* and Puah,

SHIPHTAN

Nu 34: 24 Kemuel son of *S*, the leader

SHIPS (SHIP)

Ge 49: 13 and become a haven for *s;*
Nu 24: 24 *S* will come from the shores
Dt 28: 68 The LORD will send you back in *s*
Jdg 5: 17 why did he linger by the *s?*
1Ki 9: 26 King Solomon also built *s*
10: 11 Hiram's *s* brought gold from Ophir
10: 22 of trading *s* at sea along with the *s*
22: 48 a fleet of trading *s* to go to Ophir
2Ch 8: 18 And Hiram sent him *s* commanded
9: 21 a fleet of trading *s* manned
20: 36 him to construct a fleet of trading *s*.
20: 37 *s* were wrecked and were not able
Ps 48: 7 You destroyed them like *s*
104: 26 There the *s* go to and fro,
107: 23 Others went out on the sea in *s;*
Pr 31: 14 She is like the merchant *s*,
Isa 23: 1 Wail, O *s* of Tarshish!
23: 14 Wail, you *s* of Tarshish;
43: 14 in the *s* in which they took pride.
60: 9 in the lead are the *s* of Tarshish,
Eze 27: 9 All the *s* of the sea and their sailors
27: 25 " 'The *s* of Tarshish serve
27: 29 will abandon their *s;*
30: 9 from me in *s* to frighten Cush out
Da 11: 30 *S* of the western coastlands will
11: 40 and cavalry and a great fleet of *s*.
Jas 3: 4 Or take *s* as an example.
Rev 8: 9 and a third of the *s* were destroyed.
18: 19 where all who had *s* on the sea

SHIPWRECK (WRECKED)

Eze 27: 27 the sea on the day of your *s*.

SHIPWRECKED (WRECKED)

2Co 11: 25 I was stoned, three times I was *s*,
1Ti 1: 19 and so have *s* their faith.

SHIPWRIGHTS (SHIP)

Eze 27: 9 as *s* to caulk your seams.
27: 27 your mariners, seamen and *s*,

SHISHA

1Ki 4: 3 Elihoreph and Ahijah, sons of *S*—

SHISHAK

1Ki 11: 40 fled to Egypt, to *S* the king,
14: 25 *S* king of Egypt attacked Jerusalem
2Ch 12: 2 *S* king of Egypt attacked Jerusalem
12: 5 in Jerusalem for fear of *S*,
12: 5 therefore, I now abandon you to *S*
12: 7 out on Jerusalem through *S*.
12: 9 When *S* king of Egypt attacked

SHITRAI

1Ch 27: 29 *S* the Sharonite was in charge

SHITTIM

Nu 25: 1 While Israel was staying in *S*,
Jos 2: 1 Nun secretly sent two spies from *S*.
3: 1 and all the Israelites set out from *S*
Mic 6: 5 Remember ⌞your journey⌟ from *S*

SHIZA

1Ch 11: 42 Adina son of *S* the Reubenite,

SHOA

Eze 23: 23 the men of Pekod and *S* and Koa,

SHOBAB

2Sa 5: 14 Shammua, *S*, Nathan, Solomon,
1Ch 2: 18 These were her sons: Jesher, *S*
3: 5 Shammua, *S*, Nathan and Solomon
14: 4 Shammua, *S*, Nathan, Solomon,

SHOBACH

2Sa 10: 16 with *S* the commander
10: 18 also struck down *S* the commander

SHOBAI

Ezr 2: 42 and *S* 139 The temple servants:
Ne 7: 45 and *S* 138 The temple servants:

SHOBAL

Ge 36: 20 Lotan, *S*, Zibeon, Anah, Dishon,
36: 23 The sons of *S:* Alvan, Manahath,
36: 29 Lotan, *S*, Zibeon, Anah, Dishon,
1Ch 1: 38 Lotan, *S*, Zibeon, Anah, Dishon,
1: 40 The sons of *S:* Alvan, Manahath,
2: 50 firstborn of Ephrathah: *S* the father
2: 52 The descendants of *S* the father
4: 1 Perez, Hezron, Carmi, Hur and *S*.
4: 2 Reaiah son of *S* was the father

SHOBEK

Ne 10: 24 Hallohesh, Pilha, *S*, Rehum,

SHOBI

2Sa 17: 27 *S* son of Nahash from Rabbah

SHOCKED (SHOCKING SHOCKS)

Eze 16: 27 who were *s* by your lewd conduct.

SHOCKING (SHOCKED)

Jer 5: 30 "A horrible and *s* thing

SHOCKS (SHOCKED)

Ex 22: 6 so that it burns *s* of grain
Jdg 15: 5 burned up the *s* and standing grain,

SHOHAM

1Ch 24: 27 from Jaaziah: Beno, *S*, Zaccur

SHOMER

2Ki 12: 21 Shimeath and Jehozabad son of *S*.
1Ch 7: 32 *S* and Hotham and of their sister
7: 34 The sons of *S:* Ahi, Rohgah,

SHONE (SHINE)

Dt 33: 2 he *s* forth from Mount Paran.
Job 29: 3 when his lamp *s* upon my head
Mt 17: 2 His face *s* like the sun,
Lk 2: 9 glory of the Lord *s* around them,
Ac 12: 7 of the Lord appeared and a light *s*
Rev 21: 11 It *s* with the glory of God,

SHOOK (SHAKE)

Jdg 5: 4 the earth *s*, the heavens poured,
1Sa 4: 5 a great shout that the ground *s*.
14: 15 raiding parties—and the ground *s*.
2Sa 22: 8 the foundations of the heavens *s;*
1Ki 1: 40 so that the ground *s* with the sound
Ne 5: 13 I also *s* out the folds of my robe
Ps 18: 7 the foundations of the mountains *s;*
68: 8 the earth *s*,
Isa 6: 4 thresholds *s* and the temple was
14: 16 "Is this the man who *s* the earth
Hab 3: 6 He stood, and *s* the earth;
Mt 27: 51 The earth *s* and the rocks split.
28: 4 were so afraid of him that they *s*
Mk 1: 26 The evil spirit *s* the man violently
Ac 13: 51 So they *s* the dust from their feet
18: 6 he *s* out his clothes in protest
28: 5 Paul *s* the snake off into the fire
Heb 12: 26 At that time his voice *s* the earth,

SHOOT (SHOOTING SHOOTS SHOT)

1Sa 20: 20 I will *s* three arrows to the side of it
20: 36 "Run and find the arrows I *s*."
2Sa 11: 20 you know they would *s* arrows
2Ki 13: 17 "*S!*" Elisha said, and he shot.

2Ki 19: 32 or *s* an arrow here.
1Ch 12: 2 and were able to *s* arrows
2Ch 26: 15 on the corner defenses to *s* arrows
Job 41: 19 sparks of fire *s* out.
Ps 11: 2 the strings to *s* from the shadows
64: 4 They *s* from ambush
64: 4 they *s* at him suddenly,
64: 7 But God will *s* them with arrows;
144: 6 *s* your arrows and rout them.
Isa 11: 1 A *s* will come up from the stump
37: 33 or *s* an arrow here.
53: 2 up before him like a tender *s*,
60: 21 They are the *s* I have planted,
Jer 9: 3 like a bow, to *s* lies;
50: 14 *S* at her! Spare no arrows,
Eze 5: 16 When I *s* at you with my deadly
5: 16 of famine, I will *s* to destroy you.
17: 4 he broke off its topmost *s*
17: 22 I myself will take a *s*
Ro 11: 17 and you, though a wild olive *s*,

SHOOTING (SHOOT)

1Sa 20: 20 as though I were *s* at a target.
Pr 26: 18 Like a madman *s*

SHOOTS (SHOOT)

2Ki 19: 26 like tender green *s*,
Job 8: 16 spreading its *s* over the garden;
14: 7 and its new *s* will not fail.
14: 9 and put forth *s* like a plant.
15: 30 a flame will wither his *s*,
Ps 80: 11 its *s* as far as the River.
128: 3 your sons will be like olive *s*
Isa 16: 8 Their *s* spread out
18: 5 cut off the *s* with pruning knives,
37: 27 like tender green *s*,
Eze 17: 22 off a tender sprig from its topmost *s*
Hos 14: 6 his young *s* will grow.

SHOPHACH

1Ch 19: 16 with *S* the commander
19: 18 also killed *S* the commander

SHORE (ASHORE SHORES)

Ex 14: 30 the Egyptians lying dead on the *s*.
1Ki 9: 26 Elath in Edom, on the *s* of the Red
Eze 27: 29 will stand on the *s*.
47: 10 Fishermen will stand along the *s*;
Zep 2: 11 on every *s* will worship him,
Mt 13: 2 while all the people stood on the *s*.
13: 48 the fishermen pulled it up on the *s*.
Mk 4: 1 along the *s* at the water's edge.
Lk 5: 3 asked him to put out a little from *s*.
5: 11 So they pulled their boats up on *s*,
Jn 6: 1 Jesus crossed to the far *s* of the Sea
6: 21 boat reached the *s* where they were
6: 22 that had stayed on the opposite *s*
21: 4 the morning, Jesus stood on the *s*,
21: 8 for they were not far from *s*,
Ac 27: 13 and sailed along the *s* of Crete.
28: 1 on *s*, we found out that the island
Rev 13: 1 the dragon stood on the *s* of the sea

SHORELANDS (LAND)

Eze 27: 28 The *s* will quake

SHORES (SHORE)

Nu 24: 24 come from the *s* of Kittim;
Est 10: 1 the empire, to its distant *s*.
Ps 72: 10 kings of Tarshish and of distant *s*
97: 1 let the distant *s* rejoice.

SHORN (SHEAR)

SS 4: 2 teeth are like a flock of sheep just *s*,

SHORT (SHORTENED)

Nu 11: 23 "Is the LORD's arm too *s*?
Ru 2: 7 except for a *s* rest in the shelter."
1Sa 2: 31 when I will cut *s* your strength
21: 15 Am I so *s* of madmen that you have
2Sa 16: 1 When David had gone a *s* distance
19: 36 with the king for a *s* distance,
Job 17: 1 my days are cut *s*,
Ps 89: 45 You have cut *s* the days
102: 23 he cut *s* my days.
Pr 10: 27 the years of the wicked are cut *s*.
Isa 28: 20 The bed is too *s* to stretch out on,
29: 17 In a very *s* time, will not Lebanon
50: 2 Was my arm too *s* to ransom you?
59: 1 of the LORD is not too *s* to save,
Mic 6: 10 and the *s* ephah, which is accursed?
Mt 13: 21 has no root, he lasts only a *s* time.
24: 22 If those days had not been cut *s*,
Mk 4: 17 no root, they last only a *s* time.
13: 20 If the Lord had not cut *s* those days
Lk 19: 3 but being a *s* man he could not,
Jn 7: 33 "I am with you for only a *s* time,
11: 8 "a *s* while ago the Jews tried
Ac 26: 28 in such a *s* time you can persuade
26: 29 Paul replied, "*S* time or long—
27: 28 A *s* time later they took soundings
Ro 3: 23 and fall *s* of the glory of God,
1Co 7: 29 brothers, is that the time is *s*.
1Th 2: 17 from you for a *s* time (in person,
Heb 4: 1 of you be found to have fallen *s* of it
11: 25 the pleasures of sin for a *s* time.
13: 22 I have written you only a *s* letter.
Rev 12: 12 because he knows that his time is *s*
20: 3 he must be set free for a *s* time.

SHORTCOMINGS

Ge 41: 9 "Today I am reminded of my *s*.

SHORTENED (SHORT)

Mt 24: 22 of the elect those days will be *s*.
Mk 13: 20 whom he has chosen, he has *s* them

SHOT (SHOOT)

Ge 49: 23 they *s* at him with hostility.
Ex 19: 13 He shall surely be stoned or *s*
1Sa 20: 36 he *s* an arrow beyond him.
2Sa 11: 24 Then the archers *s* arrows
22: 15 He *s* arrows and scattered
2Ki 9: 24 *s* Joram between the shoulders.
13: 17 "Shoot!" Elisha said, and he *s*.
2Ch 35: 23 Archers *s* King Josiah,
Ps 18: 14 He *s* his arrows and scattered

SHOULDER (SHOULDERS)

Ge 24: 15 out with her jar on her *s*.
24: 45 with her jar on her *s*.
24: 46 quickly lowered her jar from her *s*
49: 15 he will bend his *s* to the burden
Ex 28: 7 is to have two *s* pieces attached
28: 12 and fasten them on the *s* pieces
28: 25 attaching them to the *s* pieces
28: 27 bottom of the *s* pieces on the front
39: 4 They made *s* pieces for the ephod,
39: 7 them on the *s* pieces of the ephod
39: 18 attaching them to the *s* pieces
39: 20 bottom of the *s* pieces on the front
Nu 6: 19 in his hands a boiled *s* of the ram,
Dt 18: 3 the *s*, the jowls and the inner parts.
Jos 4: 5 of you is to take up a stone on his *s*,
Job 31: 22 then let my arm fall from the *s*,
31: 36 Surely I would wear it on my *s*,
Isa 22: 22 I will place on his *s* the key
Eze 12: 6 on your *s* as they are watching
12: 12 them will put his things on his *s*
24: 4 choice pieces—the leg and the *s*.
29: 18 rubbed bare and every *s* made raw.
34: 21 Because you shove with flank and *s*
Zep 3: 9 and serve him *s* to *s*.

SHOULDERS (SHOULDER)

Ge 9: 23 a garment and laid it across their *s*;
21: 14 them on her *s* and then sent her
Ex 12: 34 and carried it on their *s*
28: 12 Aaron is to bear the names on his *s*
Nu 7: 9 to carry on their *s* the holy things,
Dt 33: 12 LORD loves rests between his *s*."
Jdg 9: 48 branches, which he lifted to his *s*.
16: 3 He lifted them to his *s*
2Ki 6: 31 of Shaphat remains on his *s* today
9: 24 and shot Joram between the *s*.
1Ch 15: 15 of God with the poles on their *s*,
2Ch 35: 3 not to be carried about on your *s*.
Ne 3: 5 their nobles would not put their *s*
Ps 81: 6 I removed the burden from their *s*;
Isa 9: 4 the bar across their *s*,
9: 6 and the government will be on his *s*
10: 27 burden will be lifted from your *s*,
14: 25 his burden removed from their *s*."
46: 7 They lift it to their *s* and carry it;
49: 22 and carry your daughters on their *s*
Eze 12: 7 them on my *s* while they watched.
29: 7 and you tore open their *s*;
Mt 23: 4 loads and put them on men's *s*,
Lk 15: 5 he joyfully puts it on his *s*

SHOUT (SHOUTED SHOUTING SHOUTS)

Nu 23: 21 the *s* of the King is among them.
Jos 6: 5 have all the people give a loud *s*;
6: 10 Then *s*!" So he had the ark
6: 10 a word until the day I tell you to *s*.
6: 16 Joshua commanded the people, "*S*
6: 20 when the people gave a loud *s*,
Jdg 7: 18 around the camp blow yours and *s*,
1Sa 4: 5 such a great *s* that the ground
17: 52 and Judah surged forward with a *s*
1Ki 1: 34 and *s*, 'Long live King Solomon!'
18: 27 "*S* louder!" he said.
Ezr 3: 11 And all the people gave a great *s*
Job 3: 7 may no *s* of joy be heard in it.
3: 18 no longer hear the slave driver's *s*.
39: 7 he does not hear a driver's *s*.
39: 25 the *s* of commanders and the battle
Ps 20: 5 We will *s* for joy when you are
33: 3 play skillfully, and *s* for joy.
35: 27 *s* for joy and gladness;
47: 1 *s* to God with cries of joy.
60: 8 over Philistia I *s* in triumph."
65: 13 they *s* for joy and sing.
66: 1 *S* with joy to God, all the earth!
71: 23 My lips will *s* for joy
81: 1 *s* aloud to the God of Jacob!
95: 1 let us *s* aloud to the Rock
98: 4 *S* for joy to the LORD, all the earth
98: 6 *s* for joy before the LORD,
100: 1 *S* for joy to the LORD, all the earth
108: 9 over Philistia I *s* in triumph."
Isa 12: 6 *S* aloud and sing for joy, people
13: 2 *s* to them;
24: 14 They raise their voices, they *s*
26: 19 wake up and *s* for joy.
35: 2 it will rejoice greatly and *s* for joy.
35: 6 the tongue of the dumb *s* for joy.
40: 9 lift up your voice with a *s*,
42: 2 He will not *s* or cry out,
42: 11 let them *s* from the mountaintops.
42: 13 with a *s* he will raise the battle cry
44: 23 *s* aloud, O earth beneath.
49: 13 *S* for joy, O heavens;
52: 8 together they *s* for joy.
54: 1 burst into song, *s* for joy,
58: 1 "*S* it aloud, do not hold back.
Jer 25: 30 He will *s* like those who tread
25: 30 *s* against all who live on the earth.
31: 7 *s* for the greatest of the nations.
31: 12 and *s* for joy on the heights of Zion;
49: 29 Men will *s* to them,
50: 15 *S* against her on every side!
51: 14 and they will *s* in triumph over you.
51: 39 so that they *s* with laughter—
51: 48 will *s* for joy over Babylon,
La 2: 7 they have raised a *s* in the house
Eze 8: 18 Although they *s* in my ears,
Zep 3: 14 *s* aloud, O Israel!
Zec 2: 10 *S* and be glad, O Daughter of Zion.
9: 9 *S*, Daughter of Jerusalem!
Mk 10: 47 he began to *s*, "Jesus, Son of David,
Rev 10: 3 and he gave a loud *s* like the roar

SHOUTED (SHOUT)

Ge 41: 43 and men *s* before him, "Make way
Lev 9: 24 they *s* for joy and fell facedown.
Jos 6: 20 trumpets sounded, the people *s*,
Jdg 7: 20 they *s*, "A sword for the LORD
9: 7 of Mount Gerizim and *s* to them,
16: 25 they *s*, "Bring out Samson
18: 23 As they *s* after them, the Danites
19: 22 they *s* to the old man who owned
1Sa 10: 24 the people *s*, "Long live the king!"
14: 12 men of the outpost *s* to Jonathan
17: 8 and *s* to the ranks of Israel,
17: 23 his lines and *s* his usual defiance,
20: 38 Then he *s*, "Hurry! Go quickly!
2Sa 20: 1 He sounded the trumpet and *s*
1Ki 1: 39 the trumpet and all the people *s*,
18: 26 "O Baal, answer us!" they *s*.
18: 28 So they *s* louder and slashed
2Ki 7: 11 The gatekeepers *s* the news,
9: 13 Then they blew the trumpet and *s*,
11: 12 people clapped their hands and *s*,

SHOUTING (SHOUT)

SHOUTS (SHOUT)

SHOVE (SHOVES)

SHOVEL (SHOVELS)

SHOVELS (SHOVEL)

SHOVES (SHOVE)

SHOW (SHOWED SHOWING SHOWN SHOWS)

Jn 7: 4 are doing these things, *s* yourself
12: 33 He said this to *s* the kind
14: 8 *s* us the Father and that will be
14: 9 How can you say, '*S* us the Father'?
14: 21 and I too will love him and *s* myself
14: 22 why do you intend to *s* yourself
Ac 1: 24 *S* us which of these two you have
2: 19 I will *s* wonders in the heaven
7: 3 'and go to the land I will *s* you.'
9: 16 I will *s* him how much he must
10: 34 it is that God does not *s* favoritism
26: 16 seen of me and what I will *s* you.
Ro 2: 4 do you *s* contempt for the riches
2: 11 For God does not *s* favoritism.
2: 15 since they *s* that the requirements
9: 22 choosing to *s* his wrath
1Co 11: 19 differences among you to *s* which
12: 31 now I will *s* you the most excellent
2Co 3: 3 You *s* that you are a letter
4: 7 to *s* that this all-surpassing power is
8: 19 and to *s* our eagerness to help.
8: 24 Therefore *s* these men the proof
11: 30 of the things that *s* my weakness.
Eph 2: 7 ages he might *s* the incomparable
Php 4: 10 but you had no opportunity to *s* it.
1Ti 6: 2 not to *s* less respect for them
2Ti 1: 16 May the Lord *s* mercy
Tit 2: 7 In your teaching *s* integrity,
2: 10 to *s* that they can be fully trusted,
3: 2 to *s* true humility toward all men.
Heb 6: 11 each of you to *s* this same diligence
11: 14 who say such things *s* that they are
Jas 2: 1 Jesus Christ, don't *s* favoritism.
2: 3 If you *s* special attention
2: 9 But if you *s* favoritism, you sin
2: 18 I will *s* you my faith by what I do.
2: 18 *S* me your faith without deeds,
3: 13 Let him *s* it by his good life,
1Pe 2: 17 *S* proper respect to everyone:
3Jn : 8 to *s* hospitality to such men
Jude : 23 to others *s* mercy, mixed with fear
Rev 1: 1 to *s* his servants what must soon
4: 1 I will *s* you what must take place
17: 1 I will *s* you the punishment
21: 9 "Come, I will *s* you the bride,
22: 6 to *s* his servants the things that

SHOWED (SHOW)

Ge 39: 21 he *s* him kindness and granted him
Ex 15: 25 the LORD *s* him a piece of wood.
Nu 13: 26 and *s* them the fruit of the land.
20: 13 and where he *s* himself holy
Dt 4: 36 On earth he *s* you his great fire,
34: 1 There the LORD *s* him the whole
Jdg 1: 25 So he *s* them, and they put the city
Ru 3: 10 than that which you *s* earlier:
1Sa 14: 11 So both of them *s* themselves
15: 6 for you *s* kindness
2Sa 10: 2 just as his father *s* kindness to me."
1Ki 3: 3 Solomon *s* his love for the LORD
13: 12 his sons *s* him which road the man
2Ki 6: 6 it fall?" When he *s* him the place,
11: 4 Then he *s* them the king's son.
13: 23 and had compassion and *s* concern
20: 13 and *s* them all that was
1Ch 19: 2 because his father *s* kindness to me
2Ch 23: 1 year Jehoiada *s* his strength.
30: 22 who *s* good understanding
Est 5: 9 that he neither rose nor *s* fear
Job 10: 12 You gave me life and *s* me kindness
13: 10 you if you secretly *s* partiality.
Ps 31: 21 for he *s* his wonderful love to me
85: 1 You *s* favor to your land, O LORD
Isa 39: 2 *s* them what was in his storehouses
40: 14 or *s* him the path of understanding?
47: 6 and you *s* them no mercy.
Jer 11: 18 at that time he *s* me what they were
24: 1 the LORD *s* me two baskets
36: 24 heard all these words *s* no fear,
Eze 35: 11 and jealousy you *s* in your hatred
39: 26 and all the unfaithfulness they *s*
46: 19 and *s* me a place at the western end
Da 2: 29 of mysteries *s* you what is going
Am 7: 1 is what the Sovereign LORD *s* me:
7: 4 is what the Sovereign LORD *s* me:
7: 7 This is what he *s* me: The Lord was
8: 1 is what the Sovereign LORD *s* me:
Mic 6: 8 He has *s* you, O man, what is good.
Zec 1: 20 the LORD *s* me four craftsmen.
3: 1 he *s* me Joshua the high priest
8: 14 and *s* no pity when your fathers
Mt 4: 8 *s* him all the kingdoms of the world
Lk 4: 5 *s* him in an instant all the kingdoms
20: 37 even Moses *s* that the dead rise,
24: 40 he *s* them his hands and feet.
Jn 13: 1 he now *s* them the full extent
20: 20 he *s* them his hands and side.
Ac 1: 3 he *s* himself to these men
15: 8 *s* that he accepted them
15: 14 God at first *s* his concern by taking
18: 17 But Gallio *s* no concern whatever.
20: 35 I *s* you that by this kind
28: 2 The islanders *s* us unusual kindness
1Jn 2: 19 but their going *s* that none
4: 9 This is how God *s* his love
Rev 21: 10 and *s* me the Holy City, Jerusalem,
22: 1 Then the angel *s* me the river

SHOWER (SHOWERING SHOWERS)

Job 37: 6 to the rain *s*, 'Be a mighty
Isa 45: 8 let the clouds *s* it down.

SHOWERING (SHOWER)

2Sa 16: 13 stones at him and *s* him with dirt.

SHOWERS (SHOWER)

Dt 32: 2 like *s* on new grass,
Job 29: 23 They waited for me as for *s*
36: 28 and abundant *s* fall on mankind.
Ps 65: 10 you soften it with *s*
68: 9 You gave abundant *s*, O God;
72: 6 like *s* watering the earth.
Jer 3: 3 Therefore the *s* have been withheld
14: 22 the skies themselves send down *s*?
Eze 22: 24 are a land that has had no rain or *s*
34: 26 I will send down *s* in season;
34: 26 in season; there will be *s* of blessing
Hos 10: 12 and *s* righteousness on you.
Joel 2: 23 He sends you abundant *s*,
Mic 5: 7 like *s* on the grass,
Zec 10: 1 He gives *s* of rain to men,

SHOWING (SHOW)

Ex 20: 6 *s* love to thousands who love me
Dt 5: 10 *s* love to thousands who love me
Jdg 16: 5 him into *s* you the secret
Ru 2: 20 has not stopped *s* his kindness
2Sa 2: 5 you for *s* this kindness
Eze 9: 5 without *s* pity or compassion.
Da 1: 4 *s* aptitude for every kind
Jn 15: 8 *s* yourselves to be my disciples.
Ac 9: 39 crying and *s* him the robes
Ro 12: 8 if it is *s* mercy, let him do it
1Ti 5: 10 bringing up children, *s* hospitality,
Heb 9: 8 The Holy Spirit was *s*
Rev 22: 8 of the angel who had been *s* them

SHOWN (SHOW)

Ge 19: 19 you have *s* great kindness to me
21: 23 an alien the same kindness I have *s*
24: 14 will know that you have *s* kindness
32: 10 you have *s* your servant.
41: 28 God has *s* Pharaoh what he is
Ex 25: 40 according to the pattern *s* you
26: 30 to the plan *s* you on the mountain.
27: 8 as you were *s* on the mountain.
Lev 13: 7 after he has *s* himself to the priest
13: 49 and must be *s* to the priest.
Nu 8: 4 pattern the LORD had *s* Moses.
Dt 4: 35 You were *s* these things
5: 24 LORD our God has *s* us his glory
34: 12 no one has ever *s* the mighty power
Jos 2: 12 because I have *s* kindness to you.
Jdg 13: 23 nor *s* us all these things
Ru 1: 8 as you have *s* to your dead
1Ki 3: 6 "You have *s* great kindness
2Ki 8: 13 "The LORD has *s* me that you will
2Ch 1: 8 "You have *s* great kindness
24: 22 father Jehoiada had *s* him
30: 9 your children will be *s* compassion
32: 25 respond to the kindness *s* him;
Ezr 9: 9 He has *s* us kindness in the sight
Job 38: 12 or *s* the dawn its place,
38: 17 the gates of death been *s* to you?
Ps 48: 3 he has *s* himself to be her fortress.
60: 3 You have *s* your people desperate
Ps 78: 11 the wonders he had *s* them.
90: 16 May your deeds be *s*
111: 6 He has *s* his people the power
Isa 21: 2 A dire vision has been *s* to me:
26: 10 Though grace is *s* to the wicked,
66: 14 but his fury will be *s* to his foes.
Jer 44: 10 themselves or *s* reverence,
44: 25 your wives have *s* by your actions
La 4: 16 The priests are *s* no honor,
5: 12 elders are *s* no respect.
Eze 11: 25 everything the LORD had *s* me.
Da 2: 28 He has *s* King Nebuchadnezzar
2: 45 great God has *s* the king what will
Mal 2: 9 but have *s* partiality in matters
Mt 5: 7 for they will be *s* mercy.
Lk 1: 25 "In these days he has *s* his favor
1: 58 the Lord had *s* her great mercy,
Jn 10: 32 "I have *s* you many great miracles
Ac 4: 9 for an act of kindness *s* to a cripple
10: 28 God has *s* me that I should not call
14: 17 He has *s* kindness by giving you
1Co 3: 13 his work will be *s* for what it is,
1Ti 1: 13 I was *s* mercy because I acted
1: 16 for that very reason I was *s* mercy
Heb 6: 10 and the love you have *s* him
8: 5 according to the pattern *s* you
Jas 2: 13 judgment without mercy will be *s*

SHOWS (SHOW)

Dt 10: 17 who *s* no partiality and accepts no
17: 12 The man who *s* contempt
2Sa 22: 51 he *s* unfailing kindness
1Ki 1: 52 "If he *s* himself to be a worthy man,
Job 34: 19 who *s* no partiality to princes
Ps 18: 50 he *s* unfailing kindness
123: 2 till he *s* us his mercy.
Pr 10: 17 He who heeds discipline *s* the way
11: 22 woman who *s* no discretion.
12: 16 A fool *s* his annoyance at once,
14: 31 who oppresses the poor *s* contempt
15: 5 heeds correction *s* prudence.
17: 5 who mocks the poor *s* contempt
Ecc 10: 3 and *s* everyone how stupid he is.
Isa 27: 11 and their Creator *s* them no favor.
Jn 5: 20 loves the Son and *s* him all he does.

SHREWD

2Sa 13: 3 Jonadab was a very *s* man
22: 27 to the crooked you show yourself *s*.
Ps 18: 26 to the crooked you show yourself *s*.
Mt 10: 16 Therefore be as *s* as snakes and
Lk 16: 8 of this world are more *s* in dealing

SHRIEK (SHRIEKED SHRIEKS)

Mk 1: 26 and came out of him with a *s*.

SHRIEKED (SHRIEK)

Mk 9: 26 spirit *s*, convulsed him violently

SHRIEKS (SHRIEK)

Ac 8: 7 With *s*, evil spirits came out

SHRINE (SHRINES)

Ge 38: 21 hasn't been any *s* prostitute here,"
38: 21 "Where is the *s* prostitute who was
38: 22 hasn't been any *s* prostitute here.'"
Jdg 17: 5 Now this man Micah had a *s*,
1Ki 14: 24 even male *s* prostitutes in the land;
15: 12 He expelled the male *s* prostitutes
22: 46 rest of the male *s* prostitutes who
2Ki 10: 25 and then entered the inner *s*
23: 7 quarters of the male *s* prostitutes,
Isa 16: 12 when she goes to her *s* to pray,
44: 13 that it may dwell in a *s*.
Eze 8: 12 each at the *s* of his own idol?
16: 24 and made a lofty *s* in every public
Am 5: 26 You have lifted up the *s*
Ac 7: 43 You have lifted up the *s* of Moloch

SHRINES (SHRINE)

1Ki 12: 31 Jeroboam built *s* on high places
13: 32 against all the *s* on the high places
2Ki 17: 29 and set them up in the *s* the people
17: 32 as priests in the *s* at the high places.
23: 8 He broke down the *s* at the gates—
23: 19 defiled all the *s* at the high places
Job 36: 14 among male prostitutes of the *s*.
Eze 16: 25 every street you built your lofty *s*

Eze 16: 31 made your lofty *s* in every public
16: 39 mounds and destroy your lofty *s*.
18: 6 He does not eat at the mountain *s*
18: 11 "He eats at the mountain *s*.
18: 15 "He does not eat at the mountain *s*
22: 9 are those who eat at the mountain *s*
Ac 19: 24 who made silver *s* of Artemis,

SHRINK (SHRINKS)

Heb 10: 39 But we are not of those who *s* back
Rev 12: 11 as to *s* from death.

SHRINKS (SHRINK)

Heb 10: 38 And if he *s* back,

SHRIVEL (SHRIVELED)

Isa 64: 6 we all *s* up like a leaf,
Eze 19: 12 The east wind made it *s*,

SHRIVELED (SHRIVEL)

1Ki 13: 4 out toward the man *s* up,
Isa 34: 4 like *s* figs from the fig tree.
La 4: 8 Their skin has *s* on their bones;
Joel 1: 17 The seeds are *s*
Mt 12: 10 and a man with a *s* hand was there.
Mk 3: 1 and a man with a *s* hand was there.
3: 3 said to the man with the *s* hand,
Lk 6: 6 was there whose right hand was *s*.
6: 8 said to the man with the *s* hand,

SHROUD (SHROUDED)

Job 40: 13 *s* their faces in the grave.
Isa 25: 7 the *s* that enfolds all peoples,

SHROUDED (SHROUD)

Job 19: 8 he has *s* my paths in darkness.
Ecc 6: 4 and in darkness its name is *s*.

SHRUB

Ge 2: 5 no *s* of the field had yet appeared

SHUA

Ge 38: 2 of a Canaanite man named *S*.
38: 12 Judah's wife, the daughter of *S*,
1Ch 7: 32 and Hotham and of their sister *S*.

SHUAH

Ge 25: 2 Medan, Midian, Ishbak and *S*.
1Ch 1: 32 Medan, Midian, Ishbak and *S*.

SHUAL

1Sa 13: 17 toward Ophrah in the vicinity of *S*,
1Ch 7: 36 Suah, Harnepher, *S*, Beri, Imrah,

SHUBAEL

1Ch 23: 16 of Gershom: *S* was the first.
24: 20 from the sons of Amram: *S*;
24: 20 from the sons of *S*: Jehdeiah.
25: 4 Mattaniah, Uzziel, *S* and Jerimoth;
25: 20 12 the thirteenth to *S*, his sons
26: 24 Hebronites and the Uzzielites: *S*,

SHUDDER

Isa 19: 16 They will *s* with fear
32: 11 *s*, you daughters who feel secure!
Jer 2: 12 and *s* with great horror,"
Eze 12: 18 *s* in fear as you drink your water.
27: 35 their kings *s* with horror
32: 10 and their kings will *s* with horror
Jas 2: 19 the demons believe that—and *s*.

SHUHAH'S

1Ch 4: 11 *S* brother, was the father of Mehir,

SHUHAM (SHUHAMITE)

Nu 26: 42 through *S*, the Shuhamite clan.

SHUHAMITE (SHUHAM)

Nu 26: 42 through Shuham, the *S* clan.
26: 43 All of them were *S* clans;

SHUHITE

Job 2: 11 Bildad the *S* and Zophar
8: 1 Then Bildad the *S* replied:
18: 1 Then Bildad the *S* replied:
25: 1 Then Bildad the *S* replied:
42: 9 Bildad the *S* and Zophar

SHULAMMITE

SS 6: 13 Come back, come back, O *S*;
6: 13 Why would you gaze on the *S*

SHUMATHITES

1Ch 2: 53 Puthites, *S* and Mishraites.

SHUN (SHUNNED SHUNS)

Job 28: 28 and to *s* evil is understanding.' "
Pr 3: 7 fear the LORD and *s* evil.

SHUNAMMITE

1Ki 1: 3 a *S*, and brought her to the king.
1: 15 where Abishag the *S* was attending
2: 17 to give me Abishag the *S*
2: 21 "Let Abishag the *S* be given
2: 22 Why do you request Abishag the *S*
2Ki 4: 12 to his servant Gehazi, "Call the *S*."
4: 25 There's the *S*! Run to meet her
4: 36 Gehazi and said, "Call the *S*."

SHUNEM

Jos 19: 18 Jezreel, Kesulloth, *S*, Hapharaim,
1Sa 28: 4 and came and set up camp at *S*,
2Ki 4: 8 One day Elisha went to *S*.

SHUNI (SHUNITE)

Ge 46: 16 Zephon, Haggi, *S*, Ezbon, Eri,
Nu 26: 15 through *S*, the Shunite clan;

SHUNITE (SHUNI)

Nu 26: 15 through Shuni, the *S* clan;

SHUNNED (SHUN)

Job 1: 1 upright; he feared God and *s* evil.
Pr 14: 20 poor are *s* even by their neighbors,
19: 7 A poor man is *s* by all his relatives

SHUNS (SHUN)

Job 1: 8 a man who fears God and *s* evil."
2: 3 a man who fears God and *s* evil.
Pr 14: 16 man fears the LORD and *s* evil,
Isa 59: 15 and whoever *s* evil becomes a prey.

SHUPHAM (SHUPHAMITE)

Nu 26: 39 through *S*, the Shuphamite clan;

SHUPHAMITE (SHUPHAM)

Nu 26: 39 through Shupham, the *S* clan;

SHUPPIM

1Ch 26: 16 Gate on the upper road fell to *S*

SHUPPITES

1Ch 7: 12 The *S* and Huppites were
7: 15 from among the Huppites and *S*.

SHUR

Ge 16: 7 is beside the road to *S*.
20: 1 and lived between Kadesh and *S*.
25: 18 in the area from Havilah to *S*,
Ex 15: 22 and they went into the Desert of *S*.
1Sa 15: 7 the way from Havilah to *S*,
27: 8 lived in the land extending to *S*

SHUT (SHUTS)

Ge 7: 16 Then the LORD *s* him in.
19: 6 and *s* the door behind him and said,
19: 10 back into the house and *s* the door.
Dt 11: 17 and he will *s* the heavens
Jos 2: 7 had gone out, the gate was *s*.
6: 1 Now Jericho was tightly *s* up
Jdg 3: 23 he *s* the doors of the upper room
1Sa 12: 3 a bribe to make me *s* my eyes?
1Ki 8: 35 "When the heavens are *s* up
2Ki 4: 4 go inside and *s* the door behind you
4: 5 afterward *s* the door behind her
4: 21 then *s* the door and went out.
4: 33 *s* the door on the two of them
6: 32 *s* the door and hold it *s* against him.
2Ch 6: 26 "When the heavens are *s* up
7: 13 "When I *s* up the heavens
28: 24 He *s* the doors of the LORD's
29: 7 They also *s* the doors of the portico
Ne 6: 10 the son of Mehetabel, who was *s*
7: 3 have them *s* the doors
13: 19 I ordered the doors to be *s*
Job 3: 10 for it did not *s* the doors
24: 16 but by day they *s* themselves in;
38: 8 "Who *s* up the sea behind doors
Ps 107: 42 but all the wicked *s* their mouths.
Isa 22: 22 what he opens no one can *s*,
24: 22 they will be *s* up in prison
26: 20 and *s* the doors behind you;
45: 1 him so that gates will not be *s*:
52: 15 and kings will *s* their mouths
60: 11 they will never be *s*, day or night,
Jer 13: 19 The cities in the Negev will be *s* up,
20: 9 *s* up in my bones.
Eze 3: 24 "Go, *s* yourself inside your house.
22: 26 and they *s* their eyes to the keeping
44: 1 the one facing east, and it was *s*.
44: 2 It is to remain *s* because the LORD
44: 2 to me, "This gate is to remain *s*.
46: 1 is to be *s* on the six working days,
46: 2 the gate will not be *s* until evening.
46: 12 he has gone out, the gate will be *s*.
Da 6: 22 and he *s* the mouths of the lions.
Mal 1: 10 of you would *s* the temple doors,
Mt 23: 13 You *s* the kingdom of heaven
25: 10 And the door was *s*.
Lk 4: 25 when the sky was *s* for three
Ac 21: 30 and immediately the gates were *s*.
2Th 1: 9 *s* out from the presence of the Lord
Heb 11: 33 who *s* the mouths of lions,
Rev 3: 7 no one can *s*; and what he shuts,
3: 8 you an open door that no one can *s*.
11: 6 men have power to *s* up the sky
21: 25 On no day will its gates ever be *s*,

SHUTHELAH (SHUTHELAHITE)

Nu 26: 35 through *S*, the Shuthelahite clan;
26: 36 These were the descendants of *S*:
1Ch 7: 20 The descendants of Ephraim: *S*,
7: 21 Zabad his son and *S* his son.

SHUTHELAHITE (SHUTHELAH)

Nu 26: 35 through Shuthelah, the *S* clan;

SHUTS (SHUT)

Job 5: 16 and injustice *s* its mouth.
Pr 21: 13 If a man *s* his ears to the cry
Isa 22: 22 and what he *s* no one can open.
33: 15 *s* his eyes against contemplating
La 3: 8 he *s* out my prayer.
Rev 3: 7 and what he *s*, no one can open.

SHUTTLE

Job 7: 6 days are swifter than a weaver's *s*,

SHY

Job 39: 22 he does not *s* away from the sword.

SIA

Ne 7: 47 Tabbaoth, Keros, *S*, Padon, Lebana

SIAHA

Ezr 2: 44 Tabbaoth, Keros, *S*, Padon,

SIBBECAI

2Sa 21: 18 At that time *S* the Hushathite
1Ch 11: 29 from Anathoth, *S* the Hushathite,
20: 4 At that time *S* the Hushathite
27: 11 was *S* the Hushathite, a Zerahite.

SIBBOLETH

Jdg 12: 6 *"S,"* because he could not

SIBMAH

Nu 32: 38 (these names were changed) and *S*.
Jos 13: 19 Mephaath, Kiriathaim, *S*,
Isa 16: 8 the vines of *S* also.
16: 9 for the vines of *S*.
Jer 48: 32 O vines of *S*.

SIBRAIM

Eze 47: 16 and *S* (which lies on the border

SICK (SICKNESS SICKNESSES)

Pr 13: 12 Hope deferred makes the heart *s*,
Isa 10: 18 as when a *s* man wastes away.
19: 10 all the wage earners will be *s*
Eze 34: 4 or healed the *s* or bound up
Mt 8: 16 with a word and healed all the *s*.
9: 12 who need a doctor, but the *s*.
10: 8 Heal the *s*, raise the dead, cleanse

Mt 12:15 him, and he healed all their *s*,
14:14 on them and healed their *s*.
14:35 People brought all their *s* to him
14:36 him to let the *s* just touch the edge
25:36 I was *s* and you looked after me,
25:39 When did we see you *s* or in prison
25:43 I was *s* and in prison and you did
25:44 or needing clothes or *s* or in prison,
Mk 1:32 the people brought to Jesus all the *s*
2:17 who need a doctor, but the *s*.
6:5 lay his hands on a few *s* people
6:13 anointed many *s* people with oil
6:55 and carried the *s* on mats
6:56 placed the *s* in the marketplaces.
16:18 will place their hands on *s* people,
Lk 5:17 present for him to heal the *s*.
5:31 who need a doctor, but the *s*.
7:2 his master valued highly, was *s*
9:2 kingdom of God and to heal the *s*.
10:9 Heal the *s* who are there
Jn 4:46 royal official whose son lay *s*
6:2 signs he had performed on the *s*.
11:1 Now a man named Lazarus was *s*.
11:2 whose brother Lazarus now lay *s*,
11:3 "Lord, the one you love is *s*."
11:6 when he heard that Lazarus was *s*,
Ac 5:15 people brought the *s*
5:16 bringing their *s* and those
9:37 About that time she became *s*
19:12 touched him were taken to the *s*,
28:8 His father was *s* in bed, suffering
28:9 the rest of the *s* on the island came
1Co 11:30 many among you are weak and *s*,
2Ti 4:20 and I left Trophimus *s* in Miletus.
Jas 5:14 of you *s*? He should call the elders
5:15 in faith will make the *s* person well;

SICKBED (BED)

Ps 41:3 LORD will sustain him on his *s*

SICKLE (SICKLES)

Dt 16:9 to put the *s* to the standing grain.
23:25 but you must not put a *s*
Jer 50:16 and the reaper with his *s* at harvest.
Joel 3:13 Swing the *s*,
Mk 4:29 he puts the *s* to it,
Rev 14:14 gold on his head and a sharp *s*
14:15 "Take your *s* and reap,
14:16 seated on the cloud swung his *s*
14:17 in heaven, and he too had a sharp *s*.
14:18 voice to him who had the sharp *s*,
14:18 "Take your sharp *s* and gather
14:19 The angel swung his *s* on the earth,

SICKLES (SICKLE)

1Sa 13:20 mattocks, axes and *s* sharpened.

SICKNESS (SICK)

Ex 23:25 I will take away *s* from among you,
Dt 28:61 also bring on you every kind of *s*
Pr 18:14 A man's spirit sustains him in *s*,
Jer 6:7 her *s* and wounds are ever
10:19 This is my *s*, and I must endure it."
Hos 5:13 "When Ephraim saw his *s*,
Mt 4:23 and healing every disease and *s*
9:35 and healing every disease and *s*.
10:1 and to heal every disease and *s*.
Lk 4:40 all who had various kinds of *s*,
Jn 11:4 "This *s* will not end in death.

SICKNESSES (SICK)

Lk 5:15 and to be healed of their *s*.
7:21 cured many who had diseases, *s*

SIDDIM

Ge 14:3 in the Valley of *S* (the Salt Sea).
14:8 of *S* against Kedorlaomer king
14:10 the Valley of *S* was full of tar pits,

SIDE (SIDED SIDES SIDEWALLS SIDING)

Ge 2:14 it runs along the east *s* of Asshur.
3:24 placed on the east *s* of the Garden
6:16 Put a door in the *s* of the ark
31:52 and pillar to my *s* to harm me.
31:52 heap to your *s* to harm you
Ex 3:1 the flock to the far *s* of the desert
14:20 to the one *s* and light to the other *s*;
17:12 one on one *s*, one on the other—
25:12 with two rings on one *s*
25:32 three on one *s* and three
26:18 for the south *s* of the tabernacle
26:20 For the other *s*, the north *s*
26:26 frames on one *s* of the tabernacle,
26:27 five for those on the other *s*,
26:35 on the north *s* of the tabernacle
26:35 opposite it on the south *s*.
27:9 south *s* shall be a hundred cubits
27:11 The north *s* shall also be a hundred
27:14 are to be on one *s* of the entrance,
27:15 are to be on the other *s*,
32:27 'Each man strap a sword to his *s*.
36:23 for the south *s* of the tabernacle
36:25 For the other *s*, the north *s*
36:31 frames on one *s* of the tabernacle,
36:32 five for those on the other *s*,
37:3 with two rings on one *s*
37:18 three on one *s* and three
38:9 south *s* was a hundred cubits long
38:11 north *s* was also a hundred cubits
38:14 were on one *s* of the entrance,
38:15 were on the other *s* of the entrance
40:22 on the north *s* of the tabernacle
40:24 on the south *s* of the tabernacle
Lev 1:11 it at the north *s* of the altar
1:15 out on the *s* of the altar.
1:16 throw it to the east *s* of the altar,
5:9 offering against the *s* of the altar;
13:55 the mildew has affected one *s*
Nu 3:29 on the south *s* of the tabernacle.
3:35 on the north *s* of the tabernacle.
32:19 them on the other *s* of the Jordan,
32:19 to us on the east *s* of the Jordan."
32:32 be on this *s* of the Jordan."
34:3 Your southern *s* will include some
34:11 to Riblah on the east *s* of Ain
34:12 with its boundaries on every *s*.' "
34:15 on the east *s* of the Jordan
35:5 three thousand feet on the east *s*,
35:5 three thousand on the south *s*,
35:14 Give three on this *s* of the Jordan
36:11 cousins on their father's *s*.
Jos 4:11 to the other *s* while the people
7:7 to stay on the other *s* of the Jordan!
12:1 including all the eastern *s*
12:7 on the west *s* of the Jordan,
13:27 king of Heshbon (the east *s*
17:9 of Manasseh was the northern *s*
18:7 on the east *s* of the Jordan.
18:12 On the north *s* their boundary
18:14 This was the western *s*.
18:14 south along the western *s*
18:15 The southern *s* began
18:20 the boundary on the eastern *s*.
20:8 On the east *s* of the Jordan
21:44 LORD gave them rest on every *s*,
22:4 you on the other *s* of the Jordan.
22:7 land on the west *s* of the Jordan
22:11 near the Jordan on the Israelite *s*,
Jdg 8:34 of all their enemies on every *s*.
10:8 on the east *s* of the Jordan
11:18 along the eastern *s* of the country
11:18 on the other *s* of the Arnon.
Ru 2:1 a relative on her husband's *s*,
1Sa 4:13 on his chair by the *s* of the road,
4:18 off his chair by the *s* of the gate.
12:11 hands of your enemies on every *s*,
14:1 Philistine outpost on the other *s*."
14:4 On each *s* of the pass that Jonathan
14:47 against their enemies on every *s*:
20:20 I will shoot three arrows to the *s*
20:21 the arrows are on this *s* of you;
20:41 up from the south *s* of the stone
22:17 the king ordered the guards at his *s*:
23:26 and his men were on the other *s*,
23:26 going along one *s* of the mountain,
26:13 David crossed over to the other *s*
2Sa 2:13 and one group on the other *s*.
2:13 sat down on one *s* of the pool
2:16 dagger into his opponent's *s*,
3:8 "Am I a dog's head—on Judah's *s*?
13:34 coming down the *s* of the hill.
13:34 of Horonaim, on the *s* of the hill."
15:2 stand by the *s* of the road leading
1Ki 3:20 and took my son from my *s*
5:4 has given me peace on every *s*,
6:5 in which there were *s* rooms.
1Ki 6:8 was on the south *s* of the temple;
6:10 And he built the *s* rooms all
7:28 They had *s* panels attached
7:30 cast with wreaths on each *s*.
7:39 He placed the Sea on the south *s*,
7:39 stands on the south *s* of the temple
2Ki 4:4 and as each is filled, put it to one *s*
6:11 of us is on the *s* of the king of Israel
9:32 "Who is on my *s*? Who?" Two
10:6 If you are on my *s* and will obey me
11:11 from the south *s* to the north *s*
12:9 on the right *s* as one enters
16:14 it on the north *s* of the new altar.
16:17 King Ahaz took away the *s* panels
1Ch 18:17 were chief officials at the king's *s*.
22:9 from all his enemies on every *s*.
22:18 he not granted you rest on every *s*?
23:28 of the courtyards, the *s* rooms,
2Ch 4:6 and placed five on the south *s*
4:7 five on the south *s* and five
4:8 five on the south *s* and five
4:10 He placed the Sea on the south *s*,
5:12 stood on the east *s* of the altar,
14:7 he has given us rest on every *s*."
15:15 LORD gave them rest on every *s*.
20:2 from the other *s* of the Sea.
20:30 God had given him rest on every *s*.
23:10 from the south *s* to the north *s*
29:4 them in the square on the east *s*
32:22 He took care of them on every *s*.
32:30 down to the west *s* of the City
Ne 4:3 was at his *s*, said, "What they are
4:18 the builders wore his sword at his *s*
Job 15:10 and the aged are on our *s*,
18:11 Terrors startle him on every *s*
19:10 down on every *s* till I am gone;
21:26 *S* by *s* they lie in the dust,
33:23 "Yet if there is an angel on his *s*
39:23 The quiver rattles against his *s*,
Ps 3:6 drawn up against me on every *s*.
31:13 there is terror on every *s*;
45:3 Gird your sword upon your *s*,
91:7 A thousand may fall at your *s*,
97:3 and consumes his foes on every *s*.
118:11 They surrounded me on every *s*,
124:1 If the LORD had not been on our *s*
124:2 if the LORD had not been on our *s*
139:9 if I settle on the far *s* of the sea,
Pr 8:30 Then I was the craftsman at his *s*.
Ecc 4:1 was on the *s* of their oppressors—
SS 3:8 each with his sword at his *s*,
Jer 6:25 and there is terror on every *s*.
20:10 "Terror on every *s*!
35:2 to one of the *s* rooms of the house
46:5 and there is terror on every *s*,"
49:29 'Terror on every *s*!'
49:32 disaster on them from every *s*,"
50:15 Shout against her on every *s*!
51:2 they will oppose her on every *s*
La 2:22 against me terrors on every *s*.
Eze 1:10 and on the right *s* each had the face
1:11 of another creature on either *s*,
4:4 number of days you lie on your *s*.
4:4 "Then lie on your left *s*
4:6 again, this time on your right *s*,
4:8 turn from one *s* to the other
4:9 the 390 days you lie on your *s*.
9:2 linen who had a writing kit at his *s*.
9:3 who had the writing kit at his *s*
9:11 kit at his *s* brought back word,
10:3 on the south *s* of the temple
10:16 the wheels did not leave their *s*.
21:14 closing in on them from every *s*.
23:22 them against you from every *s*—
23:24 against you on every *s* with large
27:11 manned your walls on every *s*;
28:23 the sword against her on every *s*.
36:3 and hounded you from every *s*
40:2 on whose south *s* were some
40:10 gate were three alcoves on each *s*;
40:10 walls on each *s* had the same
40:19 was a hundred cubits on the east *s*
40:21 Its alcoves—three on each *s*—
40:24 Then he led me to the south *s*
40:26 of the projecting walls on each *s*.
40:27 to the outer gate on the south *s*;
40:32 me to the inner court on the east *s*,
40:34 decorated the jambs on either *s*,

Eze 40: 37 decorated the jambs on either *s*,
40: 39 gateway were two tables on each *s*,
40: 40 on the other *s* of the steps were two
40: 41 tables on one *s* of the gateway
40: 44 another at the *s* of the south gate
40: 44 one at the *s* of the north gate
40: 48 were five cubits wide on either *s*.
40: 48 were three cubits wide on either *s*.
40: 49 pillars on each *s* of the jambs.
41: 1 the jambs was six cubits on each *s*.
41: 2 and the *s* walls on each *s*
41: 5 each *s* room around the temple was
41: 6 The *s* rooms were on three levels,
41: 6 as supports for the *s* rooms,
41: 7 *s* rooms all around the temple were
41: 8 the foundation of the *s* rooms.
41: 9 between the *s* rooms of the temple
41: 9 of the *s* rooms was five cubits thick.
41: 11 were entrances to the *s* rooms
41: 12 on the west *s* was seventy cubits
41: 15 including its galleries on each *s*;
41: 19 man toward the palm tree on one *s*
41: 26 The *s* rooms of the temple
41: 26 with palm trees carved on each *s*.
42: 1 the outer wall on the north *s*.
42: 8 on the *s* nearest the sanctuary was
42: 8 the row of rooms on the *s* next
42: 9 had an entrance on the east *s*
42: 10 On the south *s* along the length
42: 16 He measured the east *s*
42: 17 measured the north *s*; it was five
42: 18 measured the south *s*; it was five
42: 19 Then he turned to the west *s*
45: 7 and eastward from the east *s*,
45: 7 extend westward from the west *s*
45: 7 will have the land bordering each *s*
46: 19 the entrance at the *s* of the gate
47: 1 under the south *s* of the temple,
47: 2 water was flowing from the south *s*.
47: 7 of trees on each *s* of the river.
47: 15 "On the north *s* it will run
47: 18 On the east *s* the boundary will run
47: 19 "On the south *s* it will run
47: 20 "On the west *s*, the Great Sea will
48: 1 border from the east *s* to the west *s*.
48: 10 cubits long on the north *s*, 10,000
48: 10 cubits long on the south *s*.
48: 10 cubits wide on the east *s*
48: 10 cubits wide on the west *s*, 10,000
48: 16 cubits, and the west *s* 4,500 cubits.
48: 16 cubits, the east *s* 4,500 cubits,
48: 16 the north *s* 4,500 cubits, the south *s*
48: 18 and 10,000 cubits on the west *s*.
48: 18 cubits on the east *s* and 10,000
48: 20 a square, 25,000 cubits on each *s*.
48: 23 extend from the east *s* to the west *s*.
48: 30 on the north *s*, which is 4,500
48: 31 gates on the north *s* will be the gate
48: 32 "On the east *s*, which is 4,500
48: 33 "On the south *s*, which measures
48: 34 "On the west *s*, which is 4,500
Joel 3: 11 all you nations from every *s*,
3: 12 to judge all the nations on every *s*.
Zec 3: 1 at his right *s* to accuse him.
5: 3 according to what it says on one *s*,
Mt 8: 18 to cross to the other *s* of the lake.
8: 28 arrived at the other *s* in the region
14: 22 go on ahead of him to the other *s*,
19: 1 Judea to the other *s* of the Jordan.
Mk 4: 35 "Let us go over to the other *s*."
5: 21 by boat to the other *s* of the lake,
8: 13 and crossed to the other *s*.
16: 5 in a white robe sitting on the right *s*
Lk 1: 11 standing at the right *s* of the altar
8: 22 go over to the other *s* of the lake."
10: 31 he passed by on the other *s*.
10: 32 saw him, passed by on the other *s*.
16: 22 angels carried him to Abraham's *s*.
16: 23 with Lazarus by his *s*.
19: 43 and hem you in on every *s*.
Jn 1: 18 is at the Father's *s*, has made him
1: 28 on the other *s* of the Jordan,
3: 26 you on the other *s* of the Jordan—
6: 25 him on the other *s* of the lake,
18: 1 On the other *s* there was an olive
18: 37 Everyone on the *s* of truth listens
19: 18 one on each *s* and Jesus
19: 34 one of the soldiers pierced Jesus' *s*
Jn 20: 20 he showed them his hands and *s*.
20: 25 and put my hand into his *s*,
20: 27 out your hand and put it into my *s*.
21: 6 net on the right *s* of the boat
Ac 12: 7 He struck Peter on the *s*
2Co 4: 8 We are hard pressed on every *s*,
Php 4: 3 at my *s* in the cause of the gospel,
2Ti 4: 17 But the Lord stood at my *s*
Heb 10: 33 at other times you stood *s* by *s*
Rev 22: 2 On each *s* of the river stood

SIDED (SIDE)

1Sa 20: 30 Don't I know that you have *s*
22: 17 because they too have *s* with David
2Ch 11: 13 from all their districts *s* with him.
Ac 14: 4 some *s* with the Jews, others

SIDES (SIDE)

Ex 12: 7 of the blood and put it on the *s*
12: 22 and on both *s* of the doorframe.
12: 23 on the top and *s* of the doorframe
25: 14 into the rings on the *s* of the chest
25: 32 from the *s* of the lampstand—
26: 13 hang over the *s* of the tabernacle so
26: 13 will be a cubit longer on both *s*;
27: 7 so they will be on two *s* of the altar
29: 16 sprinkle it against the altar on all *s*.
29: 20 blood against the altar on all *s*.
30: 3 Overlay the top and all the *s*
30: 4 two on opposite *s*—
32: 15 They were inscribed on both *s*,
37: 5 into the rings on the *s* of the ark
37: 18 from the *s* of the lampstand—
37: 26 and all the *s* and the horns
37: 27 two on opposite *s*—
38: 7 be on the *s* of the altar
Lev 1: 5 the altar on all *s* at the entrance
1: 11 blood against the altar on all *s*.
3: 2 the blood against the altar on all *s*.
3: 8 blood against the altar on all *s*.
3: 13 blood against the altar on all *s*.
7: 2 sprinkled against the altar on all *s*.
8: 19 the blood against the altar on all *s*.
8: 24 blood against the altar on all *s*.
9: 12 it against the altar on all *s*.
9: 18 it against the altar on all *s*.
19: 27 the hair at the *s* of your head
Nu 22: 24 with walls on both *s*.
33: 55 in your eyes and thorns in your *s*.
Jos 8: 22 with Israelites on both *s*.
8: 33 were standing on both *s* of the ark
18: 20 of the clans of Benjamin on all *s*.
Jdg 2: 3 they will be ⌊thorns⌋ in your *s*
1Ki 4: 24 to Gaza, and had peace on all *s*.
5: 3 against my father David from all *s*,
10: 19 On both *s* of the seat were armrests
1Ch 9: 24 The gatekeepers were on the four *s*:
2Ch 9: 18 On both *s* of the seat were armrests
Job 11: 6 for true wisdom has two *s*.
Jer 52: 23 ninety-six pomegranates on the *s*;
Eze 1: 8 on their four *s* they had the hands
2: 10 On both *s* of it were written words
40: 18 It abutted the *s* of the gateways
41: 22 its base and its *s* were of wood.
42: 20 he measured the area on all four *s*.
48: 21 "What remains on both *s*
Da 7: 5 It was raised up on one of its *s*,
Rev 5: 1 a scroll with writing on both *s*

SIDEWALLS (SIDE)

Eze 41: 3 of the *s* of the entrance was seven
41: 26 On the *s* of the portico were

SIDING (SIDE)

Ex 23: 2 justice by *s* with the crowd,

SIDON (SIDONIANS)

Ge 10: 15 was the father of *S* his firstborn,
10: 19 reached from *S* toward Gerar
49: 13 his border will extend toward *S*.
Jos 11: 8 them all the way to Greater *S*,
19: 28 and Kanah, as far as Greater *S*.
Jdg 1: 31 or *S* or Ahlab or Aczib or Helbah
10: 6 the gods of *S*, the gods of Moab,
18: 28 they lived a long way from *S*
2Sa 24: 6 Dan Jaan and around toward *S*.
1Ki 17: 9 "Go at once to Zarephath of *S*
1Ch 1: 13 was the father of *S* his firstborn,
Ezr 3: 7 and oil to the people of *S* and Tyre,
Isa 23: 2 and you merchants of *S*,
23: 4 Be ashamed, O *S*, and you,
23: 12 Daughter of *S*, now crushed!
Jer 25: 22 all the kings of Tyre and *S*;
27: 3 *S* through the envoys who have
47: 4 who could help Tyre and *S*.
Eze 27: 8 of *S* and Arvad were your oarsmen;
28: 21 against *S*; prophesy against her
28: 22 " 'I am against you, O *S*,
Joel 3: 4 *S* and all you regions of Philistia?
Zec 9: 2 and *S*, though they are very skillful.
Mt 11: 21 had been performed in Tyre and *S*,
11: 22 and *S* on the day of judgment
15: 21 to the region of Tyre and *S*.
Mk 3: 8 and around Tyre and *S*.
7: 31 of Tyre and went through *S*,
Lk 4: 26 in Zarephath in the region of *S*.
6: 17 from the seacoast of Tyre and *S*,
10: 13 had been performed in Tyre and *S*,
10: 14 and *S* at the judgment than for you.
Ac 12: 20 with the people of Tyre and *S*;
27: 3 The next day we landed at *S*;

SIDONIANS (SIDON)

Dt 3: 9 (Hermon is called Sirion by the *S*;
Jos 13: 4 from Arah of the *S* as far as Aphek,
13: 6 the *S*, I myself will drive them out
Jdg 3: 3 all the Canaanites, the *S*,
10: 12 Ammonites, the Philistines, the *S*,
18: 7 like the *S*, unsuspecting and secure.
18: 7 they lived a long way from the *S*
1Ki 5: 6 so skilled in felling timber as the *S*
11: 1 Ammonites, Edomites, *S*
11: 5 Ashtoreth the goddess of the *S*,
11: 33 Ashtoreth the goddess of the *S*,
16: 31 daughter of Ethbaal king of the *S*,
2Ki 23: 13 the vile goddess of the *S*,
1Ch 22: 4 for the *S* and Tyrians had brought
Eze 32: 30 of the north and all the *S* are there;

SIEGE (BESIEGE BESIEGED BESIEGES BESIEGING SIEGEWORKS)

Dt 20: 12 you in battle, lay *s* to that city.
20: 19 When you lay *s* to a city
20: 20 and use them to build *s* works
28: 52 They will lay *s* to all the cities
28: 53 inflict on you during the *s*,
28: 55 inflict on you during the *s*
28: 57 to eat them secretly during the *s*
2Sa 11: 16 So while Joab had the city under *s*,
20: 15 They built a *s* ramp up to the city,
1Ki 16: 17 from Gibbethon and laid *s*
2Ki 6: 24 marched up and laid *s* to Samaria.
6: 25 the *s* lasted so long that a donkey's
17: 5 and laid *s* to it for three years.
18: 9 against Samaria and laid *s* to it.
19: 32 or build a *s* ramp against it.
24: 10 on Jerusalem and laid *s* to it,
25: 1 and built *s* works all around it.
25: 2 kept under *s* until the eleventh year
2Ch 32: 1 He laid *s* to the fortified cities,
32: 9 and all his forces were laying *s*
32: 10 remain in Jerusalem under *s*?
Job 19: 12 they build a *s* ramp against me
30: 12 they build their *s* ramps against me.
Isa 1: 8 like a city under *s*.
21: 2 Elam, attack! Media, lay *s*!
23: 13 they raised up their *s* towers,
29: 3 and set up my *s* works against you.
37: 33 or build a *s* ramp against it.
Jer 6: 6 build *s* ramps against Jerusalem.
10: 17 you who live under *s*.
19: 9 the stress of the *s* imposed on them
32: 24 "See how the *s* ramps are built up
33: 4 to be used against the *s* ramps
39: 1 with his whole army and laid *s* to it.
52: 4 and built *s* works all around it.
52: 5 kept under *s* until the eleventh year
Eze 4: 2 lay *s* to it. Erect *s* works against it,
4: 3 be under *s*, and you shall besiege it.
4: 7 face toward the *s* of Jerusalem
4: 8 have finished the days of your *s*.
5: 2 the days of your *s* come to an end,
17: 17 *s* works erected to destroy many
21: 22 to build a ramp and to erect *s* works
24: 2 the king of Babylon has laid *s*
26: 8 he will set up *s* works against you,

Da 11: 15 build up *s* ramps and will capture
Mic 5: 1 for a *s* is laid against us.
Na 3: 14 Draw water for the *s*,

SIEGEWORKS (SIEGE)
Ecc 9: 14 surrounded it and built huge *s*

SIEVE
Isa 30: 28 the nations in the *s* of destruction;
Am 9: 9 as grain is shaken in a *s*,

SIFT
Jdg 7: 4 and I will *s* them for you there.
Lk 22: 31 Satan has asked to *s* you as wheat.

SIGH (SIGHED SIGHING)
Mk 7: 34 and with a deep *s* said to him,

SIGHED (SIGH)
Mk 8: 12 He *s* deeply and said, "Why does

SIGHING (SIGH)
Job 3: 24 For *s* comes to me instead of food;
Ps 5: 1 consider my *s*.
38: 9 my *s* is not hidden from you.
Isa 35: 10 and sorrow and *s* will flee away.
51: 11 and sorrow and *s* will flee away.

SIGHT (SIGHTS)
Ge 6: 11 the earth was corrupt in God's *s*
33: 18 and camped within *s* of the city.
38: 7 was wicked in the LORD's *s*;
38: 10 did was wicked in the LORD's *s*;
43: 30 moved at the *s* of his brother,
Ex 3: 3 I will go over and see this strange *s*
4: 11 Who gives him *s* or makes him
10: 28 said to Moses, "Get out of my *s*!
17: 6 Moses did this in the *s* of the elders
19: 11 Sinai in the *s* of all the people.
40: 38 in the *s* of all the house of Israel
Lev 10: 3 in the *s* of all the people
26: 16 and fever that will destroy your *s*
26: 45 out of Egypt in the *s* of the nations
Nu 20: 12 as holy in the *s* of the Israelites,
20: 27 in the *s* of the whole community.
32: 13 had done evil in his *s* was gone.
Dt 6: 18 and good in the LORD's *s*,
9: 18 what was evil in the LORD's *s*
24: 13 as a righteous act in the *s*
31: 29 evil in the *s* of the LORD
34: 12 did in the *s* of all Israel.
Jos 4: 14 Joshua in the *s* of all Israel;
1Sa 2: 17 was very great in the LORD's *s*,
6: 13 saw the ark, they rejoiced at the *s*.
9: 17 When Samuel caught *s* of Saul,
2Sa 6: 20 disrobing in the *s* of the slave girls
7: 19 as if this were not enough in your *s*,
7: 29 it may continue forever in your *s*;
10: 12 will do what is good in his *s*."
13: 5 the food in my *s* so I may watch her
13: 6 make some special bread in my *s*,
13: 8 made the bread in his *s*
16: 22 concubines in the *s* of all Israel.
22: 25 according to my cleanness in his *s*.
1Ki 14: 4 his *s* was gone because of his age.
2Ki 5: 1 man in the *s* of his master
1Ch 2: 3 was wicked in the LORD's *s*;
17: 17 as if this were not enough in your *s*,
17: 27 it may continue forever in your *s*;
19: 13 will do what is good in his *s*."
21: 7 command was also evil in the *s*
22: 5 splendor in the *s* of all the nations.
22: 8 blood on the earth in my *s*.
28: 8 you in the *s* of all Israel
29: 15 are aliens and strangers in your *s*,
29: 25 Solomon in the *s* of all Israel
Ezr 9: 9 in the *s* of the kings of Persia:
Ne 2: 5 servant has found favor in his *s*,
4: 5 or blot out their sins from your *s*,
9: 28 again did what was evil in your *s*.
Job 11: 4 and I am pure in your *s*.'
18: 3 and considered stupid in your *s*?
41: 9 the mere *s* of him is overpowering.
Ps 18: 24 of my hands in his *s*.
19: 14 be pleasing in your *s*,
31: 19 which you bestow in the *s* of men
31: 22 "I am cut off from your *s*!"
51: 4 and done what is evil in your *s*,
Ps 72: 14 for precious is their blood in his *s*.
78: 12 in the *s* of their fathers
90: 4 For a thousand years in your *s*
116: 15 Precious in the *s* of the LORD
146: 8 the LORD gives *s* to the blind,
Pr 3: 4 in the *s* of God and man.
3: 21 do not let them out of your *s*;
4: 21 Do not let them out of your *s*,
29: 13 The LORD gives *s* to the eyes
Isa 1: 16 out of my *s*!
5: 21 and clever in their own *s*.
31: 9 at *s* of the battle standard their
43: 4 are precious and honored in my *s*,
52: 10 arm in the *s* of all the nations,
59: 12 For our offenses are many in your *s*
65: 12 You did evil in my *s*
66: 4 They did evil in my *s*
Jer 4: 1 your detestable idols out of my *s*
18: 10 evil in my *s* and does not obey me,
18: 23 or blot out their sins from your *s*.
31: 36 if these decrees vanish from my *s*,"
32: 30 but evil in my *s* from their youth;
32: 31 that I must remove it from my *s*.
34: 15 and did what is right in my *s*:
Eze 4: 12 bake it in the *s* of the people,
4: 17 appalled at the *s* of each other
5: 8 on you in the *s* of the nations.
5: 14 in the *s* of all who pass by.
16: 41 on you in the *s* of many women.
20: 9 in whose *s* I had revealed myself
20: 14 in whose *s* I had brought them out.
20: 22 in whose *s* I had brought them out.
20: 41 among you in the *s* of the nations.
28: 18 in the *s* of all who were watching.
28: 25 among them in the *s* of the nations.
36: 17 monthly uncleanness in my *s*.
36: 34 desolate in the *s* of all who pass
38: 23 known in the *s* of many nations.
39: 27 them in the *s* of many nations.
Da 6: 22 I was found innocent in his *s*.
Joel 2: 6 At the *s* of them, nations are
Jnh 2: 4 banished from your *s*;
Hag 2: 14 this people and this nation in my *s*,'
Mt 9: 30 to you"; and their *s* was restored.
11: 5 The blind receive *s*, the lame walk,
16: 23 of my *s*, Satan! You are a stumbling
20: 33 they answered, "we want our *s*."
20: 34 Immediately they received their *s*
Mk 8: 25 were opened, his *s* was restored,
8: 33 "Out of my *s*, Satan!" he said.
10: 52 Immediately he received his *s*
Lk 1: 6 Both of them were upright in the *s*
1: 15 great in the *s* of the Lord.
2: 31 in the *s* of all people,
4: 18 and recovery of *s* for the blind,
7: 21 and gave *s* to many who were blind
7: 22 The blind receive *s*, the lame walk,
16: 15 among men is detestable in God's *s*
18: 42 "Receive your *s*; your faith has
18: 43 Immediately he received his *s*
23: 48 to witness this *s* saw what took
24: 31 and he disappeared from their *s*.
Jn 9: 15 him how he had received his *s*.
9: 18 had received his *s* until they sent
Ac 1: 9 and a cloud hid him from their *s*.
4: 19 right in God's *s* to obey you rather
7: 31 he saw this, he was amazed at the *s*.
9: 12 hands on him to restore his *s*."
22: 13 'Brother Saul, receive your *s*!'
28: 15 At the *s* of these men Paul thanked
Ro 2: 13 law who are righteous in God's *s*,
3: 20 in his *s* by observing the law;
4: 17 He is our father in the *s* of God,
1Co 3: 19 this world is foolishness in God's *s*.
2Co 2: 10 I have forgiven in the *s* of Christ
4: 2 to every man's conscience in the *s*
5: 7 We live by faith, not by *s*.
12: 19 We have been speaking in the *s*
Eph 1: 4 to be holy and blameless in his *s*.
Col 1: 22 death to present you holy in his *s*,
1Ti 5: 21 in the *s* of God and Christ Jesus
6: 13 In the *s* of God, who gives life
Heb 4: 13 all creation is hidden from God's *s*.
12: 21 *s* was so terrifying that Moses said,
1Pe 3: 4 which is of great worth in God's *s*.
Rev 3: 2 complete in the *s* of my God.

SIGHTLESS
Isa 29: 9 blind yourselves and be *s*;

SIGHTS (SIGHT)
Dt 28: 34 The *s* you see will drive you mad.
28: 67 and the *s* that your eyes will see.
Pr 23: 33 Your eyes will see strange *s*

SIGN (SIGNED SIGNS)
Ge 9: 12 "This is the *s* of the covenant I am
9: 13 and it will be the *s* of the covenant
9: 17 "This is the *s* of the covenant I
17: 11 and it will be the *s* of the covenant
49: 3 my might, the first *s* of my strength
Ex 3: 12 this will be the *s* to you that it is I
4: 8 attention to the first miraculous *s*,
8: 23 This miraculous *s* will occur
12: 13 The blood will be a *s* for you
13: 9 be for you like a *s* on your hand
13: 16 And it will be like a *s* on your hand
31: 13 This will be a *s* between me
31: 17 It will be a *s* between me
Nu 16: 38 Let them be a *s* to the Israelites."
17: 10 to be kept as a *s* to the rebellious.
26: 10 And they served as a warning *s*.
Dt 13: 1 announces to you a miraculous *s*
13: 2 if the *s* or wonder of which he has
21: 17 That son is the first *s*
28: 46 They will be a *s* and a wonder
Jos 2: 12 Give me a sure *s* that you will spare
4: 6 to serve as a *s* among you.
Jdg 6: 17 give me a *s* that it is really you
1Sa 2: 34 and Phinehas, will be a *s* to you—
14: 10 that will be our *s* that the LORD
1Ki 13: 3 same day the man of God gave a *s*:
13: 3 "This is the *s* the LORD has
13: 5 to the *s* given by the man of God
20: 33 The men took this as a good *s*
2Ki 19: 29 "This will be the *s* for you,
20: 8 "What will be the *s* that the LORD
20: 9 "This is the LORD's *s*
2Ch 32: 24 and gave him a miraculous *s*.
32: 31 about the miraculous *s* that had
Job 31: 35 I *s* now my defense—let
Ps 86: 17 Give me a *s* of your goodness,
Isa 7: 11 "Ask the LORD your God for a *s*,
7: 14 the Lord himself will give you a *s*:
19: 20 It will be a *s* and witness
20: 3 as a *s* and portent against Egypt
37: 30 "This will be the *s* for you,
38: 7 " 'This is the LORD's *s*
38: 22 "What will be the *s* that I will go up
55: 13 for an everlasting *s*,
66: 19 "I will set a *s* among them,
Jer 44: 29 " 'This will be the *s*
Eze 4: 3 This will be a *s* to the house
12: 6 for I have made you a *s*
12: 11 Say to them, 'I am a *s* to you.'
20: 12 I gave them my Sabbaths as a *s*
20: 20 that they may be a *s* between us.
24: 24 Ezekiel will be a *s* to you; you will
24: 27 So you will be a *s* to them,
Mt 12: 38 to see a miraculous *s* from you."
12: 39 asks for a miraculous *s*!
12: 39 except the *s* of the prophet Jonah.
16: 1 him to show them a *s* from heaven.
16: 4 looks for a miraculous *s*,
16: 4 none will be given it except the *s*
24: 3 what will be the *s* of your coming
24: 30 "At that time the *s* of the Son
Mk 8: 11 they asked him for a *s* from heaven.
8: 12 ask for a miraculous *s*?
8: 12 tell you the truth, no *s* will be given
13: 4 what will be the *s* that they are all
Lk 2: 12 This will be a *s* to you: You will
2: 34 to be a *s* that will be spoken against,
11: 16 him by asking for a *s* from heaven.
11: 29 It asks for a miraculous *s*,
11: 29 none will be given it except the *s*
11: 30 as Jonah was a *s* to the Ninevites,
21: 7 And what will be the *s* that they are
Jn 2: 18 "What miraculous *s* can you show
4: 54 the second miraculous *s* that Jesus
6: 14 saw the miraculous *s* that Jesus did,
6: 30 "What miraculous *s* then will you
10: 41 never performed a miraculous *s*,
12: 18 that he had given this miraculous *s*,

Jn 19:20 Many of the Jews read this *s*,
19:20 and the *s* was written in Aramaic,
Ro 4:11 he received the *s* of circumcision,
1Co 11:10 to have a *s* of authority on her head
14:22 are a *s*, not for believers
Php 1:28 This is a *s* to them that they will be
Rev 12:1 wondrous *s* appeared in heaven:
12:3 Then another *s* appeared in heaven
15:1 another great and marvelous *s*:

SIGNAL (SIGNALED SIGNALING SIGNALS)

Nu 10:6 The blast will be the *s*
10:7 trumpets, but not with the same *s*.
Jer 4:6 Raise the *s* to go to Zion!
6:1 Raise the *s* over Beth Hakkerem!
Zec 10:8 I will *s* for them
Mt 26:48 Now the betrayer had arranged a *s*
Mk 14:44 Now the betrayer had arranged a *s*

SIGNALED (SIGNAL)

Lk 5:7 So they *s* their partners

SIGNALING (SIGNAL)

Nu 31:6 sanctuary and the trumpets for *s*.

SIGNALS (SIGNAL)

Pr 6:13 *s* with his feet

SIGNED (SIGN)

Jer 32:10 I *s* and sealed the deed, had it
32:12 of the witnesses who had *s* the deed
32:44 and deeds will be *s*, sealed

SIGNET

Ge 41:42 Then Pharaoh took his *s* ring
Nu 31:50 armlets, bracelets, *s* rings,
Est 3:10 So the king took the *s* ring
8:2 The king took off his *s* ring,
8:8 and seal it with the king's *s* ring—
8:10 dispatches with the king's *s* ring,
Isa 3:21 the *s* rings and nose rings,
Jer 22:24 were a *s* ring on my right hand,
Da 6:17 it with his own *s* ring
Hag 2:23 'and I will make you like my *s* ring,

SIGNPOST

Eze 21:19 Make a *s* where the road branches

SIGNS (SIGN)

Ge 1:14 let them serve as *s* to mark seasons
Ex 4:9 if they do not believe these two *s*
4:17 so you can perform miraculous *s*
4:28 all the miraculous *s* he had
4:30 performed the *s* before the people,
7:3 though I multiply my miraculous *s*
10:1 I may perform these miraculous *s*
10:2 how I performed my *s* among them
Nu 14:11 all the miraculous *s* I have
14:22 and the miraculous *s* I performed
Dt 4:34 by miraculous *s* and wonders,
6:22 eyes the LORD sent miraculous *s*
7:19 the miraculous *s* and wonders,
11:3 *s* he performed and the things he
26:8 with miraculous *s* and wonders.
29:3 those miraculous *s* and great
34:11 who did all those miraculous *s*
Jos 24:17 and performed those great *s*
1Sa 10:7 Once these *s* are fulfilled, do
10:9 all these *s* were fulfilled that day.
Ne 9:10 You sent miraculous *s*
Ps 74:4 they set up their standards as *s*.
74:9 We are given no miraculous *s*;
78:43 day he displayed his miraculous *s*
105:27 They performed his miraculous *s*
135:9 He sent his *s* and wonders
Isa 8:18 We are *s* and symbols in Israel
44:25 who foils the *s* of false prophets
Jer 10:2 or be terrified by *s* in the sky,
31:21 "Set up road *s*;
32:20 You performed miraculous *s*
32:21 people Israel out of Egypt with *s*
Da 4:2 to tell you about the miraculous *s*
4:3 How great are his *s*,
6:27 he performs *s* and wonders
Mt 16:3 but you cannot interpret the *s*
24:24 and perform great *s* and miracles
Mk 13:22 prophets will appear and perform *s*
Mk 16:17 these *s* will accompany those who
16:20 word by the *s* that accompanied it.
Lk 1:22 for he kept making *s* to them
1:62 Then they made *s* to his father,
21:11 and fearful events and great *s*
21:25 "There will be *s* in the sun,
Jn 2:11 This, the first of his miraculous *s*,
2:23 saw the miraculous *s* he was doing
3:2 perform the miraculous *s* you are
4:48 Unless you people see miraculous *s*
6:2 saw the miraculous *s* he had
6:26 because you saw miraculous *s* but
7:31 will he do more miraculous *s*
9:16 a sinner do such miraculous *s*?"
11:47 performing many miraculous *s*.
12:37 had done all these miraculous *s*
20:30 Jesus did many other miraculous *s*
Ac 2:19 and *s* on the earth below,
2:22 and *s*, which God did among you
2:43 and miraculous *s* were done
4:30 to heal and perform miraculous *s*
5:12 performed many miraculous *s*
6:8 miraculous *s* among the people.
7:36 and miraculous *s* in Egypt,
8:6 and saw the miraculous *s* he did,
8:13 astonished by the great *s*
14:3 them to do miraculous *s*
15:12 Paul telling about the miraculous *s*
Ro 15:19 by the power of *s* and miracles,
1Co 1:22 Jews demand miraculous *s*
2Co 12:12 *s*, wonders and miracles—
2Th 2:9 *s* and wonders, and in every sort
Heb 2:4 God also testified to it by *s*,
Rev 13:13 performed great and miraculous *s*,
13:14 of the *s* he was given power
16:14 of demons performing miraculous *s*
19:20 With these *s* he had deluded those
19:20 had performed the miraculous *s*

SIHON (SIHON'S)

Nu 21:21 to say to *S* king of the Amorites:
21:23 But *S* would not let Israel pass
21:26 the city of *S* king of the Amorites,
21:28 a blaze from the city of *S*.
21:29 captives to *S* king of the Amorites.
21:34 did to *S* king of the Amorites,
32:33 kingdom of *S* king of the Amorites
Dt 1:4 was after he had defeated *S* king
2:24 into your hand *S* the Amorite,
2:26 to *S* king of Heshbon offering
2:30 But *S* king of Heshbon refused
2:31 I have begun to deliver *S*
2:32 When *S* and all his army came out
3:2 did to *S* king of the Amorites,
3:6 done with *S* king of Heshbon,
4:46 the land of *S* king of
29:7 *S* king of Heshbon and Og king
31:4 do to them what he did to *S*
Jos 2:10 and what you did to *S* and Og,
9:10 *S* king of Heshbon, and Og king
12:2 side of the Arabah: *S* king
12:5 to the border of *S* king of Heshbon.
13:10 and all the towns of *S* king
13:21 and the entire realm of *S* king
13:21 princes allied with *S*— who lived
13:27 the rest of the realm of *S* king
Jdg 11:19 Israel sent messengers to *S* king
11:20 *S*, however, did not trust Israel
11:21 gave *S* and all his men
1Ki 4:19 country of *S* king of the Amorites
Ne 9:22 the country of *S* king of Heshbon
Ps 135:11 *S* king of the Amorites,
136:19 *S* king of the Amorites
Jer 48:45 a blaze from the midst of *S*;

SIHON'S (SIHON)

Nu 21:27 let *S* city be restored.

SILAS

Ac 15:22 Judas (called Barsabbas) and *S*,
15:27 and *S* to confirm by word
15:32 *S*, who themselves were prophets,
15:40 sailed for Cyprus, but Paul chose *S*
16:19 they seized Paul and *S*
16:22 in the attack against Paul and *S*,
16:25 midnight Paul and *S* were praying
16:29 fell trembling before Paul and *S*.
16:36 ordered that you and *S* be released.
Ac 16:38 and *S* were Roman citizens,
16:40 and *S* came out of the prison,
17:4 persuaded and joined Paul and *S*,
17:5 and *S* in order to bring them out
17:10 the brothers sent Paul and *S* away
17:14 but *S* and Timothy stayed at Berea.
17:15 and then left with instructions for *S*
18:5 When *S* and Timothy came
2Co 1:19 preached among you by me and *S*
1Th 1:1 *S* and Timothy, To the church
2Th 1:1 *S* and Timothy, To the church
1Pe 5:12 With the help of *S*, whom I regard

SILENCE (SILENCED SILENCES SILENT)

Job 11:3 Will your idle talk reduce men to *s*
29:21 waiting in *s* for my counsel.
Ps 8:2 to *s* the foe and the avenger.
94:17 I would soon have dwelt in the *s*
101:5 him will I put to *s*;
101:8 Every morning I will put to *s*
115:17 those who go down to *s*;
143:12 your unfailing love, *s* my enemies;
Isa 25:5 You *s* the uproar of foreigners;
47:5 "Sit in *s*, go into darkness,
Jer 51:55 he will *s* her noisy din.
La 2:10 sit on the ground in *s*;
3:28 Let him sit alone in *s*,
Am 8:3 flung everywhere! *S*!" Hear this,
Ac 19:33 He motioned for *s* in order
1Pe 2:15 good you should *s* the ignorant talk
Rev 8:1 there was *s* in heaven

SILENCED (SILENCE)

Nu 13:30 Caleb *s* the people before Moses
1Sa 2:9 but the wicked will be *s* in darkness
Job 23:17 Yet I am not *s* by the darkness,
Ps 31:18 Let their lying lips be *s*,
63:11 while the mouths of liars will be *s*.
Jer 47:5 Ashkelon will be *s*.
48:2 You too, O Madmen, will be *s*;
49:26 all her soldiers will be *s* in that day
50:30 all her soldiers will be *s* in that day
Eze 27:32 "Who was ever *s* like Tyre,
Mt 22:34 that Jesus had *s* the Sadducees,
Ro 3:19 so that every mouth may be *s*
Tit 1:11 They must be *s*, because they are

SILENCES (SILENCE)

Job 12:20 He *s* the lips of trusted advisers

SILENT (SILENCE)

Lev 10:3 Aaron remained *s*.
Dt 27:9 "Be *s*, O Israel, and listen!
1Sa 10:27 But Saul kept *s*.
2Ki 18:36 But the people remained *s*
Est 4:14 For if you remain *s* at this time,
Job 7:11 "Therefore I will not keep *s*;
13:5 If only you would be altogether *s*!
13:13 "Keep *s* and let me speak;
13:19 If so, I will be *s* and die.
31:34 that I kept *s* and would not go
32:16 Must I wait, now that they are *s*,
33:31 be *s*, and I will speak.
33:33 be *s*, and I will teach you wisdom."
34:29 if he remains *s*, who can condemn
Ps 4:4 search your hearts and be *s*.
22:2 by night, and am not *s*.
28:1 For if you remain *s*,
30:12 to you and not be *s*.
31:17 and lie *s* in the grave.
32:3 When I kept *s*,
35:22 you have seen this; be not *s*.
39:2 But when I was *s* and still,
39:9 I was *s*; I would not open my
50:3 Our God comes and will not be *s*;
50:21 things you have done and I kept *s*;
83:1 O God, do not keep *s*;
109:1 do not remain *s*,
Pr 17:28 a fool is thought wise if he keeps *s*,
Ecc 3:7 a time to be *s* and a time to speak,
Isa 23:2 Be *s*, you people of the island
24:8 the joyful harp is *s*.
36:21 But the people remained *s*
41:1 "Be *s* before me, you islands!
42:14 "For a long time I have kept *s*,
53:7 as a sheep before her shearers is *s*,
57:11 Is it not because I have long been *s*
62:1 For Zion's sake I will not keep *s*,

Isa 62: 6 they will never be *s* day or night.
64: 12 Will you keep *s* and punish us
65: 6 I will not keep *s* but will pay back
Jer 4: 19 I cannot keep *s*.
Eze 3: 26 of your mouth so that you will be *s*
24: 27 with him and will no longer be *s*.
33: 22 was opened and I was no longer *s*.
Hab 1: 13 Why are you *s* while the wicked
2: 20 let all the earth be *s* before him."
Zep 1: 7 Be *s* before the Sovereign LORD,
Mt 26: 63 against you?" But Jesus remained *s*
Mk 3: 4 or to kill?" But they remained *s*.
14: 61 But Jesus remained *s* and gave no
Lk 1: 20 And now you will be *s*
14: 4 or not?" But they remained *s*.
20: 26 by his answer, they became *s*.
Ac 8: 32 and as a lamb before the shearer is *s*
15: 12 The whole assembly became *s*
18: 9 keep on speaking, do not be *s*.
21: 40 When they were all *s*, he said
1Co 14: 34 women should remain *s*
1Ti 2: 12 over a man; she must be *s*.

SILK

Rev 18: 12 purple, *s* and scarlet cloth;

SILLA

2Ki 12: 20 Beth Millo, on the road down to *S*.

SILOAM

Ne 3: 15 repaired the wall of the Pool of *S*,
Lk 13: 4 when the tower in *S* fell on them—
Jn 9: 7 pool of *S*" (this word means Sent).
9: 11 He told me to go to *S* and wash.

SILVER

Ge 13: 2 wealthy in livestock and in *s*
20: 16 brother a thousand shekels of *s*.
23: 15 is worth four hundred shekels of *s*,
23: 16 four hundred shekels of *s*,
24: 35 *s* and gold, menservants
24: 53 *s* jewelry and articles of clothing
33: 19 For a hundred pieces of *s*,
37: 28 shekels of *s* to the Ishmaelites,
42: 25 to put each man's *s* back in his sack
42: 27 and he saw his *s* in the mouth
42: 28 "My *s* has been returned,"
42: 35 man's sack was his pouch of *s*!
43: 12 Take double the amount of *s*
43: 12 you must return the *s* that was put
43: 15 and double the amount of *s*,
43: 18 because of the *s* that was put back
43: 21 and each of us found his *s*—
43: 22 We don't know who put our *s*
43: 22 also brought additional *s* with us
43: 23 in your sacks; I received your *s*."
44: 1 and put each man's *s* in the mouth
44: 2 Then put my cup, the *s* one,
44: 2 along with the *s* for his grain."
44: 8 So why would we steal *s*
44: 8 the land of Canaan the *s* we found
45: 22 he gave three hundred shekels of *s*
Ex 3: 22 living in her house for articles of *s*
11: 2 ask their neighbors for articles of *s*
12: 35 asked the Egyptians for articles of *s*
20: 23 make for yourselves gods of *s*
21: 32 of *s* to the master of the slave,
22: 7 "If a man gives his neighbor *s*
25: 3 *s* and bronze; blue, purple
26: 19 and make forty *s* bases to go
26: 21 twenty frames and forty *s* bases—
26: 25 eight frames and sixteen *s* bases—
26: 32 and standing on four *s* bases.
27: 10 bronze bases and with *s* hooks
27: 11 bronze bases and with *s* hooks
27: 17 the courtyard are to have *s* bands
31: 4 *s* and bronze, to cut and set stones,
35: 5 *s* and bronze; blue, purple
35: 24 Those presenting an offering of *s*
35: 32 *s* and bronze, to cut and set stones,
36: 24 and made forty *s* bases to go
36: 26 twenty frames and forty *s* bases—
36: 30 eight frames and sixteen *s* bases—
36: 36 and cast their four *s* bases.
38: 10 and with *s* hooks and bands
38: 11 with *s* hooks and bands
38: 12 with *s* hooks and bands
38: 17 and bands on the posts were *s*,
Ex 38: 17 and their tops were overlaid with *s*;
38: 17 posts of the courtyard had *s* bands.
38: 19 Their hooks and bands were *s*,
38: 19 and their tops were overlaid with *s*.
38: 25 The *s* obtained from those
38: 27 The 100 talents of *s* were used
Lev 5: 15 and of the proper value in *s*,
27: 3 and sixty at fifty shekels of *s*,
27: 6 that of a female at three shekels of *s*
27: 6 value of a male at five shekels of *s*
27: 16 fifty shekels of *s* to a homer
Nu 3: 50 he collected *s* weighing 1,365
7: 13 and one *s* sprinkling bowl weighing
7: 13 offering was one *s* plate weighing
7: 19 and one *s* sprinkling bowl weighing
7: 19 brought was one *s* plate weighing
7: 25 and one *s* sprinkling bowl weighing
7: 25 offering was one *s* plate weighing
7: 31 and one *s* sprinkling bowl weighing
7: 31 offering was one *s* plate weighing
7: 37 and one *s* sprinkling bowl weighing
7: 37 offering was one *s* plate weighing
7: 43 and one *s* sprinkling bowl weighing
7: 43 offering was one *s* plate weighing
7: 49 and one *s* sprinkling bowl weighing
7: 49 offering was one *s* plate weighing
7: 55 and one *s* sprinkling bowl weighing
7: 55 offering was one *s* plate weighing
7: 61 and one *s* sprinkling bowl weighing
7: 61 offering was one *s* plate weighing
7: 67 and one *s* sprinkling bowl weighing
7: 67 offering was one *s* plate weighing
7: 73 and one *s* sprinkling bowl weighing
7: 73 offering was one *s* plate weighing
7: 79 and one *s* sprinkling bowl weighing
7: 79 offering was one *s* plate weighing
7: 84 twelve *s* plates, twelve *s* sprinkling
7: 85 Each *s* plate weighed a hundred
7: 85 the *s* dishes weighed two thousand
10: 2 Make two trumpets of hammered *s*
18: 16 set at five shekels of *s*,
22: 18 gave me his palace filled with *s*
24: 13 gave me his palace filled with *s*
31: 22 the LORD gave Moses: Gold, *s*,
Dt 2: 6 them in *s* for the food you eat
2: 28 water to drink for their price in *s*.
7: 25 Do not covet the *s* and gold
8: 13 and your *s* and gold increase
14: 25 and take the *s* with you
14: 25 then exchange your tithe for *s*,
14: 26 Use the *s* to buy whatever you like:
17: 17 not accumulate large amounts of *s*
22: 19 fine him a hundred shekels of *s*
22: 29 the girl's father fifty shekels of *s*.
29: 17 and idols of wood and stone, of *s*
Jos 6: 19 All the *s* and gold and the articles
6: 24 but they put the *s* and gold
7: 21 two hundred shekels of *s*
7: 21 with the *s* underneath."
7: 22 in his tent, with the *s* underneath.
7: 24 the *s*, the robe, the gold wedge,
22: 8 with *s*, gold, bronze and iron,
24: 32 bought for a hundred pieces of *s*
Jdg 5: 19 they carried off no *s*, no plunder.
9: 4 They gave him seventy *s* shekels
16: 5 you eleven hundred shekels of *s*."
16: 18 returned with the *s* in their hands.
17: 2 I have that *s* with me; I took it."
17: 2 shekels of *s* that were taken
17: 3 shekels of *s* to his mother,
17: 3 "I solemnly consecrate my *s*
17: 4 So he returned the *s* to his mother,
17: 4 she took two hundred shekels of *s*
17: 10 I'll give you ten shekels of *s* a year,
1Sa 2: 36 down before him for a piece of *s*
9: 8 "I have a quarter of a shekel of *s*.
2Sa 8: 10 brought with him articles of *s*
8: 11 as he had done with the *s*
18: 11 had to give you ten shekels of *s*
21: 4 "We have no right to demand *s*
24: 24 and paid fifty shekels of *s* for them.
1Ki 7: 51 the *s* and gold and the furnishings
10: 21 Nothing was made of *s*,
10: 21 *s* was considered of little value
10: 22 *s* and ivory, and apes and baboons.
10: 25 articles of *s* and gold, robes,
10: 27 The king made *s* as common
10: 29 Egypt for six hundred shekels of *s*,
1Ki 15: 15 into the temple of the LORD the *s*
15: 18 Asa then took all the *s*
15: 19 I am sending you a gift of *s*
16: 24 from Shemer for two talents of *s*
20: 3 'Your *s* and gold are mine,
20: 5 'I sent to demand your *s* and gold,
20: 7 my *s* and my gold, I did not refuse
20: 39 or you must pay a talent of *s*.'
2Ki 5: 5 taking with him ten talents of *s*,
5: 22 Please give them a talent of *s*
5: 23 and then tied up the two talents of *s*
6: 25 sold for eighty shekels of *s*,
7: 8 and carried away *s*, gold
12: 13 or *s* for the temple of the LORD;
12: 13 spent for making *s* basins,
14: 14 He took all the gold and *s*
15: 19 talents of *s* to gain his support
15: 20 had to contribute fifty shekels of *s*
16: 8 Ahaz took the *s* and gold found
18: 14 of Judah three hundred talents of *s*
18: 15 gave him all the *s* that was found
20: 13 the *s*, the gold, the spices
23: 33 a levy of a hundred talents of *s*
23: 35 he taxed the land and exacted the *s*
23: 35 paid Pharaoh Neco the *s*
25: 15 all that were made of gold or *s*.
1Ch 18: 10 kinds of articles of gold and *s*
18: 11 as he had done with the *s*
19: 6 talents of *s* to hire chariots
22: 14 talents of *s*, quantities of bronze
22: 16 in every kind of work in gold and *s*,
28: 14 the weight of *s* for all the *s* articles
28: 15 weight of *s* for each *s* lampstand
28: 16 the weight of *s* for the *s* tables;
28: 17 the weight of *s* for each *s* dish;
29: 2 gold for the gold work, *s* for the *s*,
29: 3 and *s* for the temple of my God,
29: 4 seven thousand talents of refined *s*,
29: 5 for the gold work and the *s* work,
29: 7 of *s*, eighteen thousand talents
2Ch 1: 15 The king made *s* and gold
1: 17 Egypt for six hundred shekels of *s*,
2: 7 a man skilled to work in gold and *s*,
2: 14 He is trained to work in gold and *s*,
5: 1 *s* and gold and all the furnishings—
9: 14 of the land brought gold and *s*
9: 20 Nothing was made of *s*,
9: 20 *s* was considered of little value
9: 21 carrying gold, *s* and ivory,
9: 24 articles of *s* and gold, and robes,
9: 27 The king made *s* as common
15: 18 into the temple of God the *s*
16: 2 Asa then took the *s* and gold out
16: 3 See, I am sending you *s* and gold.
17: 11 brought Jehoshaphat gifts and *s*
21: 3 had given them many gifts of *s*
24: 14 and other objects of gold and *s*.
25: 6 Israel for a hundred talents of *s*.
25: 24 He took all the gold and *s*
27: 5 paid him a hundred talents of *s*,
32: 27 and he made treasuries for his *s*
36: 3 a levy of a hundred talents of *s*
Ezr 1: 4 are to provide him with *s*
1: 6 assisted them with articles of *s*
1: 9 gold dishes 30 *s* dishes 1,000
1: 9 *s* pans 29 gold bowls 30 matching
1: 10 bowls 30 matching *s* bowls 410
1: 11 were 5,400 articles of gold and of *s*.
2: 69 of *s* and 100 priestly garments.
5: 14 and *s* articles of the house of God,
6: 5 and *s* articles of the house of God,
7: 15 you are to take with you the *s*
7: 16 with all the *s* and gold you may
7: 18 best with the rest of the *s*
7: 22 up to a hundred talents of *s*,
8: 25 out to them the offering of *s*
8: 26 out to them 650 talents of *s*,
8: 26 *s* articles weighing 100 talents,
8: 28 *s* and gold are a freewill offering
8: 30 and Levites received the *s* and gold
8: 33 we weighed out the *s* and gold
Ne 5: 15 took forty shekels of *s* from them
7: 71 of gold and 2,200 minas of *s*.
7: 72 minas of *s* and 67 garments
Est 1: 6 and purple material to *s* rings
1: 6 and *s* on a mosaic pavement
3: 9 talents of *s* into the royal treasury
Job 3: 15 who filled their houses with *s*.

Job 22: 25 the choicest *s* for you.
27: 16 Though he heaps up *s* like dust
27: 17 and the innocent will divide his *s*.
28: 1 "There is a mine for *s*
28: 15 nor can its price be weighed in *s*.
42: 11 and each one gave him a piece of *s*
Ps 12: 6 like *s* refined in a furnace of clay,
66: 10 you refined us like *s*.
68: 13 of ⌞my⌟ dove are sheathed with *s*,
68: 30 Humbled, may it bring bars of *s*.
105: 37 He brought out Israel, laden with *s*
115: 4 But their idols are *s* and gold,
119: 72 than thousands of pieces of *s*
135: 15 The idols of the nations are *s*
Pr 2: 4 and if you look for it as for *s*
3: 14 for she is more profitable than *s*
8: 10 Choose my instruction instead of *s*,
8: 19 what I yield surpasses choice *s*.
10: 20 of the righteous is choice *s*,
16: 16 understanding rather than *s*!
17: 3 The crucible for *s* and the furnace
22: 1 to be esteemed is better than *s*
25: 4 Remove the dross from the *s*,
25: 11 is like apples of gold in settings of *s*.
27: 21 The crucible for *s* and the furnace
Ecc 2: 8 I amassed *s* and gold for myself,
12: 6 before the *s* cord is severed,
SS 1: 11 studded with *s*.
3: 10 Its posts he made of *s*,
8: 9 we will build towers of *s* on her.
8: 11 a thousand shekels of *s*.
Isa 1: 22 Your *s* has become dross,
2: 7 Their land is full of *s* and gold;
2: 20 their idols of *s* and idols of gold,
7: 23 vines worth a thousand *s* shekels,
13: 17 who do not care for *s*
30: 22 defile your idols overlaid with *s*
31: 7 one of you will reject the idols of *s*
39: 2 *s*, the gold, the spices, the fine oil,
40: 19 and fashions *s* chains for it.
46: 6 and weigh out *s* on the scales;
48: 10 I have refined you, though not as *s*;
60: 9 with their *s* and gold,
60: 17 and *s* in place of iron.
Jer 6: 30 They are called rejected *s*,
10: 4 They adorn it with *s* and gold;
10: 9 Hammered *s* is brought
32: 9 out for him seventeen shekels of *s*.
32: 10 and weighed out the *s* on the scales
32: 25 with *s* and have the transaction
32: 44 Fields will be bought for *s*,
52: 19 all that were made of gold or *s*.
Eze 7: 19 Their *s* and gold will not be able
7: 19 They will throw their *s*
16: 13 you were adorned with gold and *s*;
16: 17 the jewelry made of my gold and *s*,
22: 18 They are but the dross of *s*.
22: 20 As men gather *s*, copper, iron,
22: 22 As *s* is melted in a furnace,
27: 12 they exchanged *s*, iron, tin
28: 4 and amassed gold and *s*
38: 13 hordes to loot, to carry off *s*
Da 2: 32 its chest and arms of *s*, its belly
2: 35 the *s* and the gold were broken
2: 45 the *s* and the gold to pieces.
5: 2 *s* goblets that Nebuchadnezzar his
5: 4 they praised the gods of gold and *s*,
5: 23 You praised the gods of *s* and gold,
11: 8 their valuable articles of *s* and gold
11: 38 he will honor with gold and *s*,
11: 43 and *s* and all the riches of Egypt,
Hos 2: 8 who lavished on her the *s* and gold
3: 2 I bought her for fifteen shekels of *s*
8: 4 With their *s* and gold
9: 6 Their treasures of *s* will be taken
13: 2 idols for themselves from their *s*,
Joel 3: 5 For you took my *s* and my gold
Am 2: 6 They sell the righteous for *s*,
8: 6 buying the poor with *s*
Na 2: 9 Plunder the *s*!
Hab 2: 19 It is covered with gold and *s*;
Zep 1: 11 all who trade with *s* will be ruined.
1: 18 Neither their *s* nor their gold
Hag 2: 8 'The *s* is mine and the gold is mine,'
Zec 6: 10 "Take ⌞*s* and gold⌟
6: 11 Take the *s* and gold and make
9: 3 she has heaped up *s* like dust,
11: 12 So they paid me thirty pieces of *s*.
Zec 11: 13 So I took the thirty pieces of *s*
13: 9 I will refine them like *s*
14: 14 great quantities of gold and *s*
Mal 3: 3 and refine them like gold and *s*.
3: 3 as a refiner and purifier of *s*;
Mt 10: 9 or *s* or copper in your belts;
26: 15 out for him thirty *s* coins.
27: 3 and returned the thirty *s* coins
27: 9 "They took the thirty *s* coins,
Lk 10: 35 next day he took out two *s* coins
15: 8 suppose a woman has ten *s* coins
Ac 3: 6 Peter said, "*S* or gold I do not have,
17: 29 the divine being is like gold or *s*
19: 24 who made *s* shrines of Artemis,
20: 33 I have not coveted anyone's *s*
1Co 3: 12 *s*, costly stones, wood, hay or straw
2Ti 2: 20 are articles not only of gold and *s*,
Jas 5: 3 Your gold and *s* are corroded.
1Pe 1: 18 not with perishable things such as *s*
Rev 9: 20 and idols of gold, *s*, bronze,
18: 12 *s*, precious stones and pearls;

SILVERSMITH

Jdg 17: 4 of silver and gave them to a *s*,
Pr 25: 4 and out comes material for the *s*;
Ac 19: 24 A *s* named Demetrius, who made

SIMEON (SIMEONITE SIMEONITES)

Ge 29: 33 So she named him *S*.
34: 25 two of Jacob's sons, *S* and Levi,
34: 30 Then Jacob said to *S* and Levi,
35: 23 Reuben the firstborn of Jacob, *S*,
42: 24 He had *S* taken from them
42: 36 Joseph is no more and *S* is no more,
43: 23 Then he brought *S* out to them.
46: 10 The sons of *S*: Jemuel, Jamin,
48: 5 just as Reuben and *S* are mine.
49: 5 "*S* and Levi are brothers—
Ex 1: 2 Reuben, *S*, Levi and Judah;
6: 15 The sons of *S* were Jemuel, Jamin,
6: 15 These were the clans of *S*.
Nu 1: 6 from *S*, Shelumiel son
1: 22 From the descendants of *S*:
1: 23 from the tribe of *S* was 59,300.
2: 12 The tribe of *S* will camp next
2: 12 of the people of *S* is Shelumiel son
7: 36 the leader of the people of *S*,
10: 19 over the division of the tribe of *S*,
13: 5 from the tribe of *S*, Shaphat son
26: 12 The descendants of *S*
26: 14 These were the clans of *S*;
34: 20 from the tribe of *S*; Elidad son
Dt 27: 12 *S*, Levi, Judah, Issachar, Joseph
Jos 19: 1 lot came out for the tribe of *S*,
21: 4 towns from the tribes of Judah, *S*
21: 9 *S* they allotted the following towns
1Ch 2: 1 Reuben, *S*, Levi, Judah, Issachar,
4: 24 The descendants of *S*: Nemuel,
6: 65 *S* and Benjamin they allotted
12: 25 men of *S*, warriors ready for battle
2Ch 15: 9 *S* who had settled among them,
34: 6 Ephraim and *S*, as far as Naphtali,
Eze 48: 24 "*S* will have one portion; it will
48: 25 the territory of *S* from east to west.
48: 33 will be three gates: the gate of *S*,
Lk 2: 25 a man in Jerusalem called *S*,
2: 28 *S* took him in his arms
2: 34 *S* blessed them and said to Mary,
3: 30 the son of *S*,
Ac 13: 1 *S* called Niger, Lucius of Cyrene,
Rev 7: 7 from the tribe of *S* 12,000,

SIMEONITE (SIMEON)

Nu 25: 14 son of Salu, the leader of a *S* family.

SIMEONITES (SIMEON)

Jos 19: 8 the inheritance of the tribe of the *S*,
19: 9 So the *S* received their inheritance
19: 9 The inheritance of the *S* was taken
Jdg 1: 3 So the *S* went with them.
1: 3 of Judah said to the *S* their brothers
1: 17 went with the *S* their brothers
1Ch 4: 42 And five hundred of these *S*,
27: 16 over the *S*: Shephatiah son

SIMON (SIMON'S)

Mt 4: 18 *S* called Peter and his brother
10: 2 *S* (who is called Peter)
Mt 10: 4 *S* the Zealot and Judas Iscariot,
13: 55 aren't his brothers James, Joseph, *S*
16: 17 "Blessed are you, *S* son of Jonah,
17: 25 "What do you think, *S*?" he asked.
26: 6 of a man known as *S* the Leper,
27: 32 a man from Cyrene, named *S*,
Mk 1: 16 he saw *S* and his brother Andrew
1: 29 John to the home of *S* and Andrew.
1: 36 *S* and his companions went to look
3: 16 *S* (to whom he gave the name Peter
3: 18 *S* the Zealot and Judas Iscariot,
6: 3 *S*? Aren't his sisters here with us?"
14: 3 of a man known as *S* the Leper,
14: 37 *S*," he said to Peter, "are you asleep
15: 21 A certain man from Cyrene, *S*,
Lk 4: 38 and went to the home of *S*.
5: 3 the one belonging to *S*,
5: 4 he said to *S*, "Put out
5: 5 *S* answered, "Master, we've
5: 10 Jesus said to *S*, "Don't be afraid;
6: 14 *S* (whom he named Peter),
6: 15 *S* who was called the Zealot,
7: 40 "*S*, I have something to tell you."
7: 43 will love him more?" *S* replied,
7: 44 toward the woman and said to *S*,
22: 31 "*S*, *S*, Satan has asked to sift you
22: 32 But I have prayed for you, *S*,
23: 26 they seized *S* from Cyrene,
24: 34 has risen and has appeared to *S*."
Jn 1: 40 Andrew, *S* Peter's brother,
1: 41 was to find his brother *S*
1: 42 Then he brought *S* to Jesus,
1: 42 and said, "You are *S* son of John.
6: 8 Andrew, *S* Peter's brother,
6: 71 the son of *S* Iscariot, who,
13: 2 prompted Judas Iscariot, son of *S*,
13: 26 he gave it to Judas Iscariot, son of *S*
21: 15 Jesus said to Simon Peter, "*S*
21: 16 Again Jesus said, "*S* son of John,
21: 17 said to him, "*S* son of John,
Ac 1: 13 son of Alphaeus and *S* the Zealot,
8: 9 a man named *S* had practiced
8: 13 *S* himself believed and was
8: 18 When *S* saw that the Spirit was
8: 24 *S* answered, "Pray to the Lord
9: 43 time with a tanner named *S*.
10: 5 back a man named *S* who is called
10: 6 He is staying with *S* the tanner,
10: 18 asking if *S* who was known
10: 19 "*S*, three men are looking for you.
10: 32 a guest in the home of *S* the tanner,
10: 32 to Joppa for *S* who is called Peter.
11: 13 to Joppa for *S* who is called Peter.
15: 14 *S* has described to us how God

SIMON PETER (PETER)

Mt 16: 16 *S* answered, "You are the Christ,
Lk 5: 8 When *S* saw this, he fell at
Jn 6: 68 *S* answered him, "Lord, to
13: 6 came to *S*, who said to him, "Lord,
13: 9 *S* replied, "not just my feet but
13: 24 *S* motioned to this disciple
13: 36 *S* asked him, "Lord, where are you
18: 10 Then *S*, who had a sword, drew
18: 15 *S* and another disciple
18: 25 As *S* stood warming himself, he
20: 2 So she came running to *S* and
20: 6 Then *S*, who was behind him,
21: 2 *S*, Thomas (called Didymus),
21: 3 "I'm going out to fish," *S* told
21: 7 As soon as *S* heard him say, "It
21: 11 *S* climbed aboard and dragged the
21: 15 Jesus said to *S*, "Simon
2Pe 1: 1 *S*, a servant and apostle of

SIMON'S (SIMON)

Mk 1: 30 *S* mother-in-law was in bed
Lk 4: 38 *S* mother-in-law was suffering
5: 10 the sons of Zebedee, *S* partners.
Ac 10: 17 found out where *S* house was

SIMPLE

Ex 18: 22 *s* cases they can decide themselves.
18: 26 the *s* ones they decided themselves
2Ki 20: 10 "It is a *s* matter for the shadow
Job 5: 2 and envy slays the *s*.
Ps 19: 7 making wise the *s*.
119:130 it gives understanding to the *s*.

Pr 1: 4 for giving prudence to the *s*,
1: 22 will you *s* ones love your *s* ways?
1: 32 of the *s* will kill them,
7: 7 I saw among the *s*,
8: 5 You who are *s*, gain prudence,
9: 4 "Let all who are *s* come in here!"
9: 6 Leave your *s* ways and you will live
9: 16 "Let all who are *s* come in here!"
14: 15 A *s* man believes anything,
14: 18 The *s* inherit folly,
19: 25 and the *s* will learn prudence;
21: 11 is punished, the *s* gain wisdom;
22: 3 the *s* keep going and suffer for it.
27: 12 the *s* keep going and suffer for it.

SIMPLEHEARTED (HEART)

Ps 116: 6 The LORD protects the *s*;

SIN (SIN'S SINFUL SINFULNESS SINNED SINNER SINNER'S SINNERS SINNING SINS)

Ge 4: 7 *s* is crouching at your door;
15: 16 for the *s* of the Amorites has not
18: 20 and their *s* so grievous that I will go
31: 36 "What *s* have I committed that you
39: 9 I do such a wicked thing and *s*
42: 22 not to *s* against the boy?
Ex 10: 17 Now forgive my *s* once more
16: 1 and came to the Desert of *S*,
17: 1 out from the Desert of *S*,
20: 5 the children for the *s* of the fathers
23: 33 they will cause you to *s* against me,
29: 14 It is a *s* offering.
29: 36 as a *s* offering to make atonement.
30: 10 the blood of the atoning *s* offering
32: 21 that you led them into such great *s*
32: 30 I can make atonement for your *s*."
32: 30 "You have committed a great *s*.
32: 31 what a great *s* these people have
32: 32 please forgive their *s*—but if not,
32: 34 I will punish them for their *s*."
34: 7 children for the *s* of the fathers
34: 7 wickedness, rebellion and *s*.
34: 9 forgive our wickedness and our *s*,
Lev 4: 3 as a *s* offering for the *s* he has
4: 8 fat from the bull of the *s* offering—
4: 14 aware of the *s* they committed,
4: 14 bring a young bull as a *s* offering
4: 20 did with the bull for the *s* offering.
4: 21 This is the *s* offering
4: 23 aware of the *s* he committed,
4: 24 It is a *s* offering.
4: 25 of the *s* offering with his finger
4: 26 make atonement for the man's *s*,
4: 28 aware of the *s* he committed,
4: 28 for the *s* he committed a female
4: 29 hand on the head of the *s* offering
4: 32 If he brings a lamb as his *s* offering,
4: 33 and slaughter it for a *s* offering
4: 34 of the *s* offering with his finger
4: 35 for him for the *s* he has committed,
5: 6 goat from the flock as a *s* offering;
5: 6 make atonement for him for his *s*.
5: 6 penalty for the *s* he has committed,
5: 7 one for a *s* offering and the other
5: 7 to the LORD as a penalty for his *s*
5: 8 first offer the one for the *s* offering.
5: 9 It is a *s* offering.
5: 9 of the *s* offering against the side
5: 10 for him for the *s* he has committed,
5: 11 as an offering for his *s* a tenth
5: 11 ephah of fine flour for a *s* offering.
5: 11 on it, because it is a *s* offering.
5: 12 It is a *s* offering.
6: 3 commits any such *s* that people
6: 17 Like the *s* offering and the guilt
6: 25 The *s* offering is to be slaughtered
6: 25 the regulations for the *s* offering:
6: 30 But any *s* offering whose blood is
7: 7 applies to both the *s* offering
7: 37 the grain offering, the *s*
8: 2 oil, the bull for the *s* offering,
8: 14 the bull for the *s* offering,
9: 2 "Take a bull calf for your *s* offering
9: 3 'Take a male goat for a *s* offering,
9: 7 and sacrifice your *s* offering
9: 8 as a *s* offering for himself.
9: 10 of the liver from the *s* offering,
Lev 9: 15 and offered it for a *s* offering
9: 15 the goat for the people's *s* offering
9: 22 having sacrificed the *s* offering,
10: 16 about the goat of the *s* offering
10: 17 "Why didn't you eat the *s* offering
10: 19 if I had eaten the *s* offering today?"
10: 19 they sacrificed their *s* offering
12: 6 or a dove for a *s* offering.
12: 8 and the other for a *s* offering.
14: 13 Like the *s* offering, the guilt
14: 13 the holy place where the *s* offering
14: 19 is to sacrifice the *s* offering
14: 22 one for a *s* offering and the other
14: 31 one as a *s* offering and the other
15: 15 the one for a *s* offering
15: 30 is to sacrifice one for a *s* offering
16: 3 with a young bull for a *s* offering
16: 5 take two male goats for a *s* offering
16: 6 the bull for his own *s* offering
16: 9 and sacrifice it for a *s* offering.
16: 11 the bull for his own *s* offering
16: 11 the bull for his own *s* offering.
16: 15 for the *s* offering for the people
16: 25 the fat of the *s* offering on the altar.
16: 27 and the goat for the *s* offerings,
18: 25 so I punished it for its *s*,
19: 22 committed, and his *s* will be
19: 22 LORD for the *s* he has committed,
23: 19 one male goat for a *s* offering
26: 41 humbled and they pay for their *s*,
Nu 5: 7 and must confess the *s* he has
5: 31 bear the consequences of her *s*.'"
6: 11 as a *s* offering and the other
6: 14 without defect for a *s* offering,
6: 16 make the *s* offering and the burnt
7: 16 one male goat for a *s* offering;
7: 22 one male goat for a *s* offering;
7: 28 one male goat for a *s* offering;
7: 34 one male goat for a *s* offering;
7: 40 one male goat for a *s* offering;
7: 46 one male goat for a *s* offering;
7: 52 one male goat for a *s* offering;
7: 58 one male goat for a *s* offering;
7: 64 one male goat for a *s* offering;
7: 70 one male goat for a *s* offering;
7: 76 one male goat for a *s* offering;
7: 82 one male goat for a *s* offering;
7: 87 goats were used for the *s* offering.
8: 8 a second young bull for a *s* offering.
8: 12 one for a *s* offering to the LORD
9: 13 will bear the consequences of his *s*.
12: 11 hold against us the *s* we have
14: 18 and forgiving *s* and rebellion.
14: 18 the children for the *s* of the fathers
14: 19 forgive the *s* of these people,
15: 24 and a male goat for a *s* offering.
15: 25 made by fire and a *s* offering.
15: 27 female goat for a *s* offering.
18: 9 whether grain or *s* or guilt offerings
18: 22 bear the consequences of their *s*
19: 9 it is for purification from *s*.
27: 3 died for his own *s* and left no sons.
28: 15 to the LORD as a *s* offering.
28: 22 as a *s* offering to make atonement
29: 5 as a *s* offering to make atonement
29: 11 one male goat as a *s* offering,
29: 11 to the *s* offering for atonement
29: 16 one male goat as a *s* offering,
29: 19 one male goat as a *s* offering,
29: 22 one male goat as a *s* offering,
29: 25 one male goat as a *s* offering,
29: 28 one male goat as a *s* offering,
29: 31 one male goat as a *s* offering,
29: 34 one male goat as a *s* offering,
29: 38 one male goat as a *s* offering,
32: 23 be sure that your *s* will find you
33: 11 and camped in the Desert of *S*.
33: 12 They left the Desert of *S*
Dt 5: 9 the children for the *s* of the fathers
9: 18 of all the *s* you had committed,
9: 27 their wickedness and their *s*.
15: 9 and you will be found guilty of *s*.
20: 18 you will *s* against the LORD your
22: 26 committed no *s* deserving death.
23: 21 and you will be guilty of *s*.
24: 4 Do not bring *s* upon the land
24: 15 and you will be guilty of *s*.
24: 16 each is to die for his own *s*.
Jos 22: 17 Was not the *s* of Peor enough for us
22: 17 not cleansed ourselves from that *s*,
22: 20 the only one who died for his *s*.'"
1Sa 2: 17 This *s* of the young men was very
3: 13 because of the *s* he knew about;
12: 23 it from me that I should *s*
14: 34 Do not *s* against the LORD
14: 38 find out what *s* has been
15: 23 For rebellion is like the *s*
15: 25 forgive my *s* and come back
2Sa 12: 13 The LORD has taken away your *s*.
22: 24 and have kept myself from *s*.
1Ki 8: 34 forgive the *s* of your people Israel
8: 35 turn from their *s* because you have
8: 36 and forgive the *s* of your servants,
8: 46 for there is no one who does not *s*
8: 46 "When they *s* against you—
12: 30 And this thing became a *s*;
13: 34 This was the *s* of the house
15: 26 in the ways of his father and in his *s*
15: 34 the ways of Jeroboam and in his *s*,
16: 2 and caused my people Israel to *s*
16: 19 and in the *s* he had committed
16: 26 son of Nebat and in his *s*,
17: 18 come to remind me of my *s*
21: 22 and have caused Israel to *s*.'
22: 52 of Nebat, who caused Israel to *s*.
2Ki 12: 16 and *s* offerings was not brought
17: 21 caused them to commit a great *s*.
21: 11 has led Judah into *s* with his idols.
21: 16 besides the *s* that he had caused
21: 17 including the *s* he committed,
23: 15 who had caused Israel to *s*—
2Ch 6: 25 forgive the *s* of your people Israel
6: 26 turn from their *s* because you have
6: 27 and forgive the *s* of your servants,
6: 36 for there is no one who does not *s*
6: 36 "When they *s* against you—
7: 14 and will forgive their *s* and will heal
19: 10 Do this, and you will not *s*.
19: 10 not to *s* against the LORD;
28: 13 Do you intend to add to our *s*
29: 21 as a *s* offering for the kingdom,
29: 23 for the *s* offering were brought
29: 24 and the *s* offering for all Israel.
29: 24 on the altar for a *s* offering to atone
Ezr 6: 17 and, as a *s* offering for all Israel,
8: 35 as a *s* offering, twelve male goats.
Ne 6: 13 me so that I would commit a *s*
10: 33 for *s* offerings to make atonement
13: 26 he was led into *s* by foreign women
Job 1: 22 Job did not *s* by charging God
2: 10 Job did not *s* in what he said.
8: 4 them over to the penalty of their *s*.
10: 6 and probe after my *s*—
11: 6 forgotten some of your *s*.
11: 14 if you put away the *s* that is
13: 23 Show me my offense and my *s*.
14: 16 but not keep track of my *s*.
14: 17 you will cover over my *s*.
15: 5 Your *s* prompts your mouth;
31: 11 a *s* to be judged.
31: 30 I have not allowed my mouth to *s*
31: 33 if I have concealed my *s* as men do,
33: 9 'I am pure and without *s*;
34: 37 To his *s* he adds rebellion;
35: 6 If you *s*, how does that affect him?
Ps 4: 4 In your anger do not *s*;
17: 3 resolved that my mouth will not *s*.
18: 23 and have kept myself from *s*.
32: 2 whose *s* the LORD does not count
32: 5 Then I acknowledged my *s* to you
32: 5 the guilt of my *s*.
36: 2 too much to detect or hate his *s*.
38: 3 no soundness because of my *s*.
38: 18 I am troubled by my *s*.
39: 1 and keep my tongue from *s*;
39: 11 and discipline men for their *s*;
40: 6 burnt offerings and *s* offerings
51: 2 and cleanse me from my *s*.
51: 3 and my *s* is always before me.
59: 3 me for no offense or *s* of mine,
66: 18 If I had cherished *s* in my heart,
78: 17 But they continued to *s* against him
89: 32 I will punish their *s* with the rod,
106: 43 and they wasted away in their *s*.
109: 14 may the *s* of his mother never be
119: 11 that I might not *s* against you.

Ps 119:133 let no *s* rule over me.
Pr 1:16 for their feet rush into *s*,
5:22 the cords of his *s* hold him fast.
10:19 words are many, *s* is not absent,
14: 9 Fools mock at making amends for *s*
14:34 but *s* is a disgrace to any people.
16: 6 faithfulness *s* is atoned for;
17:19 He who loves a quarrel loves *s;*
20: 9 I am clean and without *s*''?
21: 4 the lamp of the wicked, are *s!*
24: 9 The schemes of folly are *s*,
29: 6 An evil man is snared by his own *s*,
29:16 When the wicked thrive, so does *s*,
Ecc 5: 6 not let your mouth lead you into *s*.
Isa 3: 9 they parade their *s* like Sodom;
5:18 Woe to those who draw *s*
6: 7 is taken away and your *s* atoned
22:14 your dying day this *s* will not be
27: 9 fruitage of the removal of his *s:*
30: 1 heaping *s* upon *s;*
30:13 this *s* will become for you
40: 2 that her *s* has been paid for,
53:12 For he bore the *s* of many,
59: 7 Their feet rush into *s;*
64: 5 But when we continued to *s*
Jer 9: 3 They go from one *s* to another;
9: 7 because of the *s* of my people?
16:10 What *s* have we committed
16:17 is their *s* concealed from my eyes.
16:18 for their wickedness and their *s*,
17: 1 "Judah's *s* is engraved
17: 3 of *s* throughout your country.
31:30 everyone will die for his own *s;*
32:35 thing and so make Judah *s*.
33: 8 from all the *s* they have committed
36: 3 their wickedness and their *s*."
La 2:14 they did not expose your *s*
4:22 of Edom, he will punish your *s*
Eze 3:18 that wicked man will die for his *s*,
3:19 for his *s;* but you will have saved
3:20 not warn him, he will die for his *s*.
3:21 not to *s* and he does not *s*,
4: 4 and put the *s* of the house of Israel
4: 4 are to bear their *s* for the number
4: 5 So for 390 days you will bear the *s*
4: 5 of days as the years of their *s*.
4: 6 bear the *s* of the house of Judah.
4:17 will waste away because of their *s*.
7:19 for it has made them stumble into *s*
9: 9 "The *s* of the house of Israel
16:49 this was the *s* of your sister Sodom:
18:17 He will not die for his father's *s;*
18:17 He withholds his hand from *s*
18:18 But his father will die for his own *s*,
18:24 his righteousness and commits *s*
18:26 his righteousness and commits *s*,
18:26 of the *s* he has committed he will
18:30 then *s* will not be your downfall.
29:16 reminder of their *s* in turning to her
33: 6 will be taken away because of his *s*,
33: 8 that wicked man will die for his *s*,
33: 9 for his *s*, but you will have saved
33:14 but he then turns away from his *s*
39:23 of Israel went into exile for their *s*,
40:39 *s* offerings and guilt offerings were
42:13 *s* offerings and the guilt offerings—
43:19 as a *s* offering to the priests,
43:21 to take the bull for the *s* offering
43:22 goat without defect for a *s* offering,
43:25 a male goat daily for a *s* offering;
44:10 bear the consequences of their *s*.
44:12 bear the consequences of their *s*,
44:12 made the house of Israel fall into *s*,
44:27 he is to offer a *s* offering for himself
44:29 *s* offerings and the guilt offerings;
45:17 He will provide the *s* offerings,
45:19 some of the blood of the *s* offering
45:22 as a *s* offering for himself
45:23 and a male goat for a *s* offering.
45:25 the same provision for *s* offerings,
46:20 the *s* offering and bake the grain
Da 9:20 confessing my *s* and the *s*
9:24 end to *s*, to atone for wickedness,
Hos 5: 5 even Ephraim, stumble in their *s;*
8:11 built many altars for *s* offerings,
10: 8 it is the *s* of Israel.
10:10 them in bonds for their double *s*.
12: 8 any iniquity or *s*."
Hos 13: 2 Now they *s* more and more;
Am 4: 4 go to Gilgal and *s* yet more.
4: 4 "Go to Bethel and *s;*
Mic 1:13 You were the beginning of *s*
3: 8 to Israel his *s*.
6: 7 of my body for the *s* of my soul?
7:18 who pardons *s* and forgives
Zec 3: 4 "See, I have taken away your *s*,
3: 9 'and I will remove the *s* of this land
13: 1 to cleanse them from *s*
Mal 2: 6 and turned many from *s*.
Mt 5:29 If your right eye causes you to *s*,
5:30 if your right hand causes you to *s*,
6:14 men when they *s* against you,
12:31 every *s* and blasphemy will be
13:41 kingdom everything that causes *s*
18: 6 little ones who believe in me to *s*,
18: 7 of the things that cause people to *s!*
18: 8 or your foot causes you to *s*,
18: 9 And if your eye causes you to *s*,
23:32 of the *s* of your forefathers!
Mk 3:29 he is guilty of an eternal *s*."
9:42 little ones who believe in me to *s*,
9:43 If your hand causes you to *s*,
9:45 And if your foot causes you to *s*,
9:47 And if your eye causes you to *s*,
Lk 17: 1 people to *s* are bound to come,
17: 2 to cause one of these little ones to *s*
Jn 1:29 who takes away the *s* of the world!
8: 7 "If any one of you is without *s*,
8:11 "Go now and leave your life of *s*."
8:21 for me, and you will die in your *s*.
8:34 everyone who sins is a slave to *s*.
8:46 Can any of you prove me guilty of *s*
9:34 "You were steeped in *s* at birth;
9:41 you would not be guilty of *s;*
15:22 they have no excuse for their *s*.
15:22 they would not be guilty of *s*.
15:24 they would not be guilty of *s*.
16: 8 the world of guilt in regard to *s*
16: 9 to *s*, because men do not believe
19:11 over to you is guilty of a greater *s*."
Ac 7:60 do not hold this *s* against them."
8:23 full of bitterness and captive to *s*."
Ro 2:12 All who *s* apart from the law will
2:12 and all who *s* under the law will be
3: 9 and Gentiles alike are all under *s*.
3:20 the law we become conscious of *s*.
4: 8 whose *s* the Lord will never count
5:12 as *s* entered the world
5:12 through *s*, and in this way death
5:13 But *s* is not taken into account
5:13 for before the law was given, *s* was
5:14 even over those who did not *s*
5:16 The judgment followed one *s*
5:16 the result of the one man's *s:*
5:20 where *s* increased, grace increased
5:21 so that, just as *s* reigned in death,
6: 2 By no means! We died to *s;*
6: 6 of *s* might be rendered powerless,
6: 6 should no longer be slaves to *s*—
6: 7 who has died has been freed from *s*.
6:10 death he died, he died to *s* once
6:11 count yourselves dead to *s*
6:12 Therefore do not let *s* reign
6:13 offer the parts of your body to *s*,
6:14 For *s* shall not be your master,
6:15 Shall we *s* because we are not
6:16 whether you are slaves to *s*,
6:17 though you used to be slaves to *s*,
6:18 You have been set free from *s*
6:20 When you were slaves to *s*,
6:22 that you have been set free from *s*
6:23 For the wages of *s* is death,
7: 7 I would not have known what *s* was
7: 7 then? Is the law *s?* Certainly not!
7: 8 For apart from law, *s* is dead.
7: 8 *s*, seizing the opportunity afforded
7: 9 the commandment came, *s* sprang
7:11 For *s*, seizing the opportunity
7:13 that *s* might be recognized as *s*,
7:13 the commandment *s* might become
7:14 I am unspiritual, sold as a slave to *s*.
7:17 I myself who do it, but it is *s* living
7:20 but it is *s* living in me that does it.
7:23 a prisoner of the law of *s* at work
7:25 sinful nature a slave to the law of *s*.
8: 2 of life set me free from the law of *s*
Ro 8: 3 of sinful man to be a *s* offering.
8: 3 so he condemned *s* in sinful man,
8:10 your body is dead because of *s*,
14:23 that does not come from faith is *s*.
1Co 8:12 When you *s* against your brothers
8:12 their weak conscience, you *s*
8:13 eat causes my brother to fall into *s*,
15:56 The sting of death is *s*,
15:56 and the power of *s* is the law.
2Co 5:21 God made him who had no *s* to be *s*
11: 7 Was it a *s* for me to lower myself
11:29 into *s*, and I do not inwardly burn?
12:21 sexual *s* and debauchery
Gal 2:17 that mean that Christ promotes *s?*
3:22 the whole world is a prisoner of *s*,
6: 1 if someone is caught in a *s*,
Eph 4:26 your anger do not *s*": Do not let
1Ti 5:20 Those who *s* are to be rebuked
Heb 4:15 just as we are—yet was without *s*.
9:26 to do away with *s* by the sacrifice
9:28 appear a second time, not to bear *s*,
10: 6 with burnt offerings and *s* offerings
10: 8 and *s* offerings you did not desire,
10:18 there is no longer any sacrifice for *s*
11:25 the pleasures of *s* for a short time.
12: 1 and the *s* that so easily entangles,
12: 4 In your struggle against *s*,
13:11 the Most Holy Place as a *s* offering,
Jas 1:15 it gives birth to *s;* and *s*,
2: 9 you *s* and are convicted by the law
1Pe 2:22 "He committed no *s*,
4: 1 suffered in his body is done with *s*.
1Jn 1: 7 his Son, purifies us from all *s*.
1: 8 If we claim to be without *s*,
2: 1 But if anybody does *s*, we have one
2: 1 this to you so that you will not *s*.
3: 4 in fact, *s* is lawlessness.
3: 5 And in him is no *s*.
3: 6 No one who continues to *s* has
3: 9 born of God will continue to *s*,
5:16 There is a *s* that leads to death.
5:16 brother commit a *s* that does not
5:16 refer to those whose *s* does not lead
5:17 All wrongdoing is *s*, and there is *s*
5:18 born of God does not continue to *s;*
Rev 2:14 to *s* by eating food sacrificed

SIN'S (SIN)

Heb 3:13 hardened by *s* deceitfulness.

SINAI

Ex 16: 1 which is between Elim and *S*,
19: 1 they came to the Desert of *S*.
19: 2 they entered the Desert of *S*,
19:11 down on Mount *S* in the sight
19:18 Mount *S* was covered with smoke,
19:20 descended to the top of Mount *S*
19:23 people cannot come up Mount *S*,
24:16 of the LORD settled on Mount *S*.
31:18 speaking to Moses on Mount *S*,
34: 2 and then come up on Mount *S*.
34: 4 up Mount *S* early in the morning,
34:29 came down from Mount *S*
34:32 LORD had given him on Mount *S*.
Lev 7:38 LORD gave Moses on Mount *S*
7:38 to the LORD, in the Desert of *S*.
25: 1 said to Moses on Mount *S*,
26:46 on Mount *S* between himself
27:34 on Mount *S* for the Israelites.
Nu 1: 1 in the Desert of *S* on the first day
1:19 them in the Desert of *S:*
3: 1 talked with Moses on Mount *S*.
3: 4 fire before him in the Desert of *S*.
3:14 said to Moses in the Desert of *S*,
9: 1 in the Desert of *S* in the first month
9: 5 did so in the Desert of *S* at twilight
10:12 out from the Desert of *S*
26:64 the Israelites in the Desert of *S*.
28: 6 offering instituted at Mount *S*
33:15 and camped in the Desert of *S*.
33:16 They left the Desert of *S*
Dt 33: 2 "The LORD came from *S*
Jdg 5: 5 before the LORD, the One of *S*,
Ne 9:13 "You came down on Mount *S;*
Ps 68: 8 before God, the One of *S*,
68:17 from *S* into his sanctuary.
Ac 7:30 bush in the desert near Mount *S*.
7:38 spoke to him on Mount *S;*

Gal 4: 24 One covenant is from Mount *S*
4: 25 stands for Mount *S* in Arabia

SINCERE (SINCERITY)

Da 11: 34 many who are not *s* will join them.
Ac 2: 46 ate together with glad and *s* hearts,
Ro 12: 9 Love must be *s*.
2Co 6: 6 in the Holy Spirit and in *s* love;
11: 3 somehow be led astray from your *s*
1Ti 1: 5 a good conscience and a *s* faith.
3: 8 *s*, not indulging in much wine,
2Ti 1: 5 have been reminded of your *s* faith,
Heb 10: 22 near to God with a *s* heart
Jas 3: 17 and good fruit, impartial and *s*.
1Pe 1: 22 the truth so that you have *s* love

SINCERITY (SINCERE)

1Co 5: 8 bread without yeast, the bread of *s*
2Co 1: 12 in the holiness and *s* that are
2: 17 speak before God with *s*,
8: 8 but I want to test the *s* of your love
Eph 6: 5 and with *s* of heart, just
Col 3: 22 but with *s* of heart and reverence

SINEWS

Job 10: 11 knit me together with bones and *s*?
40: 17 the *s* of his thighs are close-knit.
Isa 48: 4 the *s* of your neck were iron,
Col 2: 19 held together by its ligaments and *s*

SINFUL (SIN)

Dt 9: 21 Also I took that *s* thing of yours,
Ps 36: 4 he commits himself to a *s* course
38: 5 because of my *s* folly.
51: 5 *s* from the time my mother
Pr 12: 13 An evil man is trapped by his *s* talk,
Isa 1: 4 Ah, *s* nation,
31: 7 and gold your *s* hands have made.
57: 17 I was enraged by his *s* greed;
Eze 37: 23 them from all their *s* backsliding,
Hos 9: 15 Because of their *s* deeds,
Am 9: 8 are on the *s* kingdom.
Mk 8: 38 in this adulterous and *s* generation,
Lk 5: 8 from me, Lord; I am a *s* man!''
7: 37 a woman who had lived a *s* life
24: 7 delivered into the hands of *s* men,
Ro 1: 24 over in the *s* desires of their hearts
7: 5 the *s* passions aroused
7: 5 we were controlled by the *s* nature,
7: 13 sin might become utterly *s*.
7: 18 lives in me, that is, in my *s* nature.
7: 25 but in the *s* nature a slave to the law
8: 3 And so he condemned sin in *s* man,
8: 3 Son in the likeness of *s* man
8: 3 it was weakened by the *s* nature,
8: 4 not live according to the *s* nature
8: 5 to the *s* nature have their minds set
8: 6 The mind of *s* man is death,
8: 7 the *s* mind is hostile to God.
8: 8 by the *s* nature cannot please God.
8: 9 are controlled not by the *s* nature
8: 12 but it is not to the *s* nature,
8: 13 if you live according to the *s* nature
13: 14 to gratify the desires of the *s* nature
1Co 5: 5 so that the *s* nature may be
Gal 5: 13 freedom to indulge the *s* nature;
5: 16 gratify the desires of the *s* nature.
5: 17 For the *s* nature desires what is
5: 17 what is contrary to the *s* nature.
5: 19 The acts of the *s* nature are obvious
5: 24 Jesus have crucified the *s* nature
6: 8 sows to please his *s* nature,
Eph 2: 3 the cravings of our *s* nature
Col 2: 11 in the putting off of the *s* nature,
2: 13 uncircumcision of your *s* nature,
1Ti 1: 9 the ungodly and *s*, the unholy
Tit 3: 11 that such a man is warped and *s*;
Heb 3: 12 brothers, that none of you has a *s*,
12: 3 such opposition from *s* men,
1Pe 2: 11 abstain from *s* desires, which war
2Pe 2: 10 the corrupt desire of the *s* nature
2: 18 desires of *s* human nature,
1Jn 2: 16 the world—the cravings of *s* man,
3: 8 He who does what is *s* is

SINFULNESS (SIN)

Ps 36: 1 concerning the *s* of the wicked:

SING (SANG SINGER SINGERS SINGING SINGS SONG SONGS SUNG)

Ex 15: 1 "I will *s* to the LORD,
15: 21 "*S* to the LORD,
Nu 21: 17 *S* about it,
Dt 31: 19 to the Israelites and have them *s* it,
Jdg 5: 3 I will *s* to the LORD, I will *s*;
1Sa 21: 11 Isn't he the one they *s* about
2Sa 22: 50 I will *s* praises to your name.
1Ch 15: 16 as singers to *s* joyful songs,
16: 9 *S* to him, *s* praise to him;
16: 23 *S* to the LORD, all the earth;
16: 33 Then the trees of the forest will *s*,
16: 33 will *s* for joy before the LORD,
2Ch 20: 21 Jehoshaphat appointed men to *s*
20: 22 As they began to *s* and praise,
31: 2 and to *s* praises at the gates
Job 21: 12 They *s* to the music of tambourine
29: 13 I made the widow's heart *s*.
Ps 5: 11 let them ever *s* for joy.
7: 17 will *s* praise to the name
9: 2 I will *s* praise to your name,
9: 11 *S* praises to the LORD, enthroned
13: 6 I will *s* to the LORD,
18: 49 I will *s* praises to your name.
21: 13 we will *s* and praise your might.
27: 6 I will *s* and make music
30: 4 *S* to the LORD, you saints of his;
30: 12 that my heart may *s* to you
32: 11 *s*, all you who are upright in heart!
33: 1 *S* joyfully to the LORD, you
33: 3 *S* to him a new song;
47: 6 *S* praises to God, *s* praises;
47: 6 *s* praises to our King, *s* praises.
47: 7 *s* to him a psalm of praise.
51: 14 tongue will *s* of your righteousness.
57: 7 I will *s* and make music.
57: 9 I will *s* of you among the peoples.
59: 16 But I will *s* of your strength,
59: 16 in the morning I will *s* of your love;
59: 17 O my Strength, I *s* praise to you;
61: 8 will I ever *s* praise to your name
63: 7 I *s* in the shadow of your wings.
65: 13 they shout for joy and *s*.
66: 2 *S* to the glory of his name;
66: 4 they *s* praise to you,
66: 4 they *s* praise to your name."
67: 4 May the nations be glad and *s*
68: 4 *S* to God, *s* praise to his name,
68: 32 *S* to God, O kingdoms of the earth,
68: 32 *s* praise to the Lord, *Selah*
71: 22 I will *s* praise to you with the lyre,
71: 23 joy when I *s* praise to you—
75: 9 I will *s* praise to the God of Jacob.
81: 1 *S* for joy to God our strength;
87: 7 As they make music they will *s*,
89: 1 I will *s* of the LORD's great love
89: 12 Hermon *s* for joy at your name.
90: 14 that we may *s* for joy and be glad
92: 4 I *s* for joy at the works
95: 1 Come, let us *s* for joy to the LORD
96: 1 *S* to the LORD a new song;
96: 1 *s* to the LORD, all the earth.
96: 2 *S* to the LORD, praise his name;
96: 12 the trees of the forest will *s* for joy;
96: 13 they will *s* before the LORD,
98: 1 *S* to the LORD a new song,
98: 8 let the mountains *s* together for joy
98: 9 let them *s* before the LORD,
101: 1 I will *s* of your love and justice;
101: 1 to you, O LORD, I will *s* praise.
104: 12 they *s* among the branches.
104: 33 I will *s* praise to my God as long
104: 33 I will *s* to the LORD all my life;
105: 2 *S* to him, *s* praise to him;
108: 1 I will *s* and make music
108: 3 I will *s* of you among the peoples.
119:172 May my tongue *s* of your word,
132: 9 may your saints *s* for joy."
132: 16 and her saints will ever *s* for joy.
135: 3 *s* praise to his name
137: 3 "*S* us one of the songs of Zion!"
137: 4 How can we *s* the songs
138: 1 the "gods" I will *s* your praise.
138: 5 May they *s* of the ways
144: 9 I will *s* a new song to you, O God;
145: 7 and joyfully *s* of your righteousness
Ps 146: 2 I will *s* praise to my God as long
147: 1 is to *s* praises to our God,
147: 7 *S* to the LORD with thanksgiving;
149: 1 *S* to the LORD a new song,
149: 5 and *s* for joy on their beds.
Pr 29: 6 a righteous one can *s* and be glad.
Isa 5: 1 I will *s* for the one I love
12: 5 *S* to the LORD, for he has done
12: 6 *s* for joy, people of Zion,
23: 16 play the harp well, *s* many a song,
27: 2 "*S* about a fruitful vineyard:
30: 29 And you will *s*
38: 18 death cannot *s* your praise;
38: 20 we will *s* with stringed instruments
42: 10 *S* to the LORD a new song,
42: 11 Let the people of Sela *s* for joy;
44: 23 *S* for joy, O heavens,
54: 1 "*S*, O barren woman,
65: 14 My servants will *s*
Jer 20: 13 *S* to the LORD!
31: 7 "*S* with joy for Jacob;
Hos 2: 15 There she will *s* as in the days
Zep 3: 14 *S*, O Daughter of Zion;
Ro 15: 9 I will *s* hymns to your name."
15: 11 *s* praises to him, all you peoples."
1Co 14: 15 also pray with my mind; I will *s*
14: 15 but I will also *s* with my mind.
Eph 5: 19 *S* and make music in your heart
Col 3: 16 and as you *s* psalms, hymns
Heb 2: 12 congregation I will *s* your praises."
Jas 5: 13 Is anyone happy? Let him *s* songs

SINGED

Da 3: 27 nor was a hair of their heads *s*;

SINGER (SING)

2Sa 23: 1 Israel's *s* of songs:

SINGERS (SING)

Jdg 5: 11 of the *s* at the watering places.
2Sa 19: 35 the voices of men and women *s*?
1Ch 15: 16 to appoint their brothers as *s*
15: 27 and as were the *s*, and Kenaniah,
2Ch 5: 13 The trumpeters and *s* joined
23: 13 *s* with musical instruments were
29: 28 while the *s* sang and the trumpeters
35: 25 and women *s* commemorate Josiah
Ezr 2: 41 the line of Hodaviah) 74 The *s*:
2: 65 also had 200 men and women *s*.
2: 70 The priests, the Levites, the *s*,
7: 7 including priests, Levites, *s*,
7: 24 on any of the priests, Levites, *s*,
10: 24 From the *s*: Eliashib
Ne 7: 1 the gatekeepers and the *s*
7: 44 the line of Hodaviah) 74 The *s*:
7: 67 also had 245 men and women *s*.
7: 73 the *s* and the temple servants,
10: 28 priests, Levites, gatekeepers, *s*,
10: 39 the gatekeepers and the *s* stay.
11: 22 who were the *s* responsible
11: 23 The *s* were under the king's orders,
12: 28 The *s* also were brought together
12: 29 for the *s* had built villages
12: 45 as did also the *s* and gatekeepers,
12: 46 there had been directors for the *s*
12: 47 the daily portions for the *s*
13: 5 and oil prescribed for the Levites, *s*
13: 10 *s* responsible for the service had
Ps 68: 25 In front are the *s*, after them
Ecc 2: 8 I acquired men and women *s*,

SINGING (SING)

Ge 31: 27 and *s* to the music of tambourines
Ex 32: 18 it is the sound of *s* that I hear."
1Sa 18: 6 of Israel to meet King Saul with *s*
1Ch 15: 22 head Levite was in charge of the *s*;
15: 27 was in charge of the *s* of the choirs.
2Ch 23: 18 and *s*, as David had ordered.
29: 27 *s* to the LORD began also,
Ps 63: 5 with *s* lips my mouth will praise
68: 6 he leads forth the prisoners with *s*;
98: 5 with the harp and the sound of *s*,
SS 2: 12 the season of *s* has come,
Isa 14: 7 they break into *s*.
24: 16 of the earth we hear *s*:
35: 10 They will enter Zion with *s*;
51: 3 thanksgiving and the sound of *s*.
51: 11 They will enter Zion with *s*;

Am 8:10 and all your *s* into weeping.
Zep 3:17 he will rejoice over you with *s*."
Ac 16:25 Silas were praying and *s* hymns
Rev 5:13 on the sea, and all that is in them, *s*:

SINGLE (SINGLED SINGLENESS)

Ge 41: 5 were growing on a *s* stalk.
41:22 full and good, growing on a *s* stalk.
Ex 23:29 I will not drive them out in a *s* year,
26:24 into a *s* ring; both shall be like that.
36:29 to the top and fitted into a *s* ring;
Nu 13:23 cut off a branch bearing a *s* cluster
Dt 29:21 The LORD will *s* him out
Jdg 9:18 his seventy sons on a *s* stone,
1Ki 16:11 He did not spare a *s* male,
Est 3:13 and little children—on a *s* day,
Isa 9:14 palm branch and reed in a *s* day;
10:17 in a *s* day it will burn and consume
47: 9 you in a moment, on a *s* day:
Eze 37:19 making them a *s* stick of wood,
Zec 3: 9 the sin of this land in a *s* day.
Mt 6:27 you by worrying can add a *s* hour
23:15 and sea to win a *s* convert,
27:14 even to a *s* charge—to the great
Lk 12:25 you by worrying can add a *s* hour
Jn 12:24 and dies, it remains only a *s* seed.
Ac 27:34 one of you will lose a *s* hair
Gal 5:14 law is summed up in a *s* command:
Heb 12:16 for a *s* meal sold his inheritance
Rev 21:21 each gate made of a *s* pearl.

SINGLED (SINGLE)

1Ki 8:53 For you *s* them out

SINGLENESS (SINGLE)

Jer 32:39 I will give them *s* of heart

SINGS (SING)

Pr 25:20 is one who *s* songs to a heavy heart.
Isa 16:10 no one *s* or shouts in the vineyards;
Eze 33:32 more than one who *s* love songs

SINIM

Isa 49:12 some from the region of *S*."

SINITES

Ge 10:17 Hivites, Arkites, *S*, Arvadites,
1Ch 1:15 Hivites, Arkites, *S*, Arvadites,

SINK (SANK SINKING SINKS SUNK)

Dt 28:43 but you will *s* lower and lower.
Ps 69: 2 I *s* in the miry depths,
69:14 do not let me *s*;
Jer 51:64 'So will Babylon *s* to rise no more
Eze 27:27 will *s* into the heart of the sea
Am 8: 8 it will be stirred up and then *s*
Mt 14:30 beginning to *s*, cried out, "Lord,
Lk 5: 7 boats so full that they began to *s*.

SINKING (SINK)

Ac 20: 9 who was *s* into a deep sleep

SINKS (SINK)

Isa 5:24 as dry grass *s* down in the flames,
Am 9: 5 then *s* like the river of Egypt—

SINNED (SIN)

Ex 9:27 This time I have *s*," he said to them
9:34 he *s* again: He and his officials
10:16 "I have *s* against the LORD your
32:33 "Whoever has *s* against me I will
Lev 5: 5 confess in what way he has *s*
Nu 6:11 he *s* by being in the presence
14:40 "We have *s*," they said.
16:38 of the men who *s* at the cost
21: 7 "We *s* when we spoke
22:34 the angel of the LORD, "I have *s*.
Dt 1:41 "We have *s* against the LORD.
9:16 I saw that you had *s*
Jos 7:11 Israel has *s*; they have violated my
7:20 I have *s* against the LORD,
Jdg 10:10 "We have *s* against you, forsaking
10:15 said to the LORD, "We have *s*.
1Sa 7: 6 "We have *s* against the LORD."
12:10 to the LORD and said, 'We have *s*;
15:24 Then Saul said to Samuel, "I have *s*
15:30 Saul replied, "I have *s*.
26:21 Then Saul said, "I have *s*.
2Sa 12:13 "I have *s* against the LORD."
19:20 I your servant know that I have *s*,
24:10 I have *s* greatly in what I have done
24:17 "I am the one who has *s*
1Ki 8:33 because they have *s* against you,
8:35 your people have *s* against you,
8:47 'We have *s*, we have done wrong,
8:50 forgive your people, who have *s*
16:25 *s* more than all those before him.
2Ki 17: 7 because the Israelites had *s*
1Ch 21: 8 "I have *s* greatly by doing this.
21:17 I am the one who has *s*
2Ch 6:24 because they have *s* against you
6:26 your people have *s* against you,
6:37 'We have *s*, we have done wrong
6:39 forgive your people, who have *s*
Ezr 10:13 we have *s* greatly in this thing.
Ne 9:29 They *s* against your ordinances,
13:26 that Solomon king of Israel *s*?
Job 1: 5 "Perhaps my children have *s*
7:20 If I have *s*, what have I done to you,
8: 4 When your children *s* against him,
10:14 If I *s*, you would be watching me
24:19 snatches away those who have *s*.
33:27 'I *s*, and perverted what was right,
36: 9 that they have *s* arrogantly.
Ps 41: 4 heal me, for I have *s* against you."
51: 4 Against you, you only, have I *s*
106: 6 We have *s*, even as our fathers did;
Isa 42:24 against whom we have *s*?
43:27 Your first father *s*;
Jer 2:35 because you say, 'I have not *s*.'
3:25 We have *s* against the LORD our
8:14 because we have *s* against him.
14: 7 we have *s* against you.
14:20 we have indeed *s* against you.
40: 3 you people *s* against the LORD
44:23 and have *s* against the LORD
50: 7 for they *s* against the LORD,
50:14 for she has *s* against the LORD.
La 1: 8 Jerusalem has *s* greatly
3:42 "We have *s* and rebelled
5: 7 Our fathers *s* and are no more,
5:16 Woe to us, for we have *s*!
Eze 28:16 and you *s*.
Da 9: 5 we have *s* and done wrong.
9: 8 because we have *s* against you.
9:11 because we have *s* against you.
9:15 we have *s*, we have done wrong.
Hos 4: 7 the more they *s* against me;
10: 9 the days of Gibeah, you have *s*,
Mic 7: 9 Because I have *s* against him,
Zep 1:17 they have *s* against the LORD.
Mt 27: 4 "I have *s*," he said,
Lk 15:18 I have *s* against heaven
15:21 I have *s* against heaven
Jn 9: 2 who *s*, this man or his parents,
9: 3 "Neither this man nor his parents *s*
Ro 3:23 for all have *s* and fall short
5:12 all *s*— for before the law was given,
1Co 7:28 and if a virgin marries, she has not *s*
7:28 you have not *s*; and if a virgin
2Co 12:21 over many who have *s* earlier
13: 2 I will not spare those who *s* earlier
Heb 3:17 Was it not with those who *s*,
Jas 5:15 If he has *s*, he will be forgiven.
2Pe 2: 4 did not spare angels when they *s*,
1Jn 1:10 claim we have not *s*, we make him

SINNER (SIN)

Ps 51: 5 Surely I have been a *s* from birth,
Pr 11:31 much more the ungodly and the *s*!
13: 6 but wickedness overthrows the *s*.
13:21 Misfortune pursues the *s*,
Ecc 2:26 but to the *s* he gives the task
7:26 but the *s* she will ensnare.
9: 2 so with the *s*;
9:18 but one *s* destroys much good.
Lk 7:39 of woman she is—that she is a *s*."
15: 7 in heaven over one *s* who repents
15:10 of God over one *s* who repents."
18:13 'God, have mercy on me, a *s*.'
19: 7 "He has gone to be the guest of a '*s*
Jn 9:16 "How can a *s* do such miraculous
9:24 "We know this man is a *s*."
9:25 "Whether he is a *s* or not, I don't
Ro 3: 7 why am I still condemned as a *s*?"
1Co 14:24 convinced by all that he is a *s*
1Ti 2:14 who was deceived and became a *s*.
Jas 5:20 Whoever turns a *s* from the error
1Pe 4:18 become of the ungodly and the *s*?"

SINNER'S (SIN)

Pr 13:22 a *s* wealth is stored up

SINNERS (SIN)

Nu 32:14 "And here you are, a brood of *s*,
Ps 1: 1 or stand in the way of *s*
1: 5 *s* in the assembly of the righteous.
25: 8 therefore he instructs *s* in his ways.
26: 9 not take away my soul along with *s*
37:38 But all *s* will be destroyed;
51:13 and *s* will turn back to you.
104:35 But may *s* vanish from the earth
Pr 1:10 My son, if *s* entice you,
23:17 Do not let your heart envy *s*,
Isa 1:28 *s* will both be broken together,
13: 9 and destroy the *s* within it.
33:14 The *s* in Zion are terrified;
Am 9:10 All the *s* among my people
Mt 9:10 many tax collectors and "*s*" came
9:11 eat with tax collectors and '*s*'?"
9:13 come to call the righteous, but *s*."
11:19 a friend of tax collectors and "*s*." '
26:45 betrayed into the hands of *s*.
Mk 2:15 and "*s*" were eating with him
2:16 eat with tax collectors and '*s*'?"
2:16 saw him eating with the "*s*"
2:17 come to call the righteous, but *s*."
14:41 betrayed into the hands of *s*.
Lk 5:30 drink with tax collectors and '*s*'?"
5:32 come to call the righteous, but *s*
6:32 Even '*s*' love those who love them.
6:33 that to you? Even '*s*' do that.
6:34 Even '*s*' lend to '*s*,' expecting
7:34 a friend of tax collectors and "*s*." '
13: 2 that these Galileans were worse *s*
15: 1 and "*s*" were all gathering
15: 2 "This man welcomes *s*
Jn 9:31 know that God does not listen to *s*.
Ro 5: 8 While we were still *s*, Christ died
5:19 one man the many were made *s*,
Gal 2:15 not 'Gentile *s*' know that a man is
2:17 evident that we ourselves are *s*,
1Ti 1:15 came into the world to save *s*—
1:16 mercy so that in me, the worst of *s*,
Heb 7:26 set apart from *s*, exalted
Jas 4: 8 you *s*, and purify your hearts,
Jude :15 harsh words ungodly *s* have spoken

SINNING (SIN)

Ge 13:13 were *s* greatly against the LORD.
20: 6 you from *s* against me.
Ex 20:20 be with you to keep you from *s*."
Nu 15:28 erred by *s* unintentionally,
32:23 you will be *s* against the LORD;
1Sa 14:33 the men are *s* against the LORD
Job 35: 3 and what do I gain by not *s*?'
Ps 78:32 In spite of all this, they kept on *s*;
Jer 9: 5 they weary themselves with *s*.
Hos 8:11 these have become altars for *s*.
Jn 5:14 Stop *s* or something worse may
Ro 6: 1 go on *s* so that grace may increase?
1Co 7:36 He is not *s*.
11:27 guilty of *s* against the body
15:34 stop *s*; for there are some who are
Heb 10:26 If we deliberately keep on *s*
2Pe 2:14 they never stop *s*; they seduce
1Jn 3: 6 No one who lives in him keeps on *s*
3: 8 because the devil has been *s*
3: 9 go on *s*, because he has been born

SINS (SIN)

Ge 50:17 please forgive the *s* of the servants
50:17 you to forgive your brothers the *s*
Lev 4: 2 'When anyone *s* unintentionally
4: 3 the anointed priest *s*, bringing guilt
4:13 community *s* unintentionally
4:22 " 'When a leader *s* unintentionally
4:27 of the community *s* unintentionally
5: 1 " 'If a person *s* because he does not
5:13 for any of these *s* he has committed
5:15 *s* unintentionally in regard to any
5:17 "If a person *s* and does what is
6: 2 "If anyone *s* and is unfaithful
6: 4 when he thus *s* and becomes guilty,

Lev 16: 16 whatever their *s* have been.
16: 21 all their *s*— and put them
16: 22 on itself all their *s* to a solitary
16: 30 you will be clean from all your *s*.
16: 34 a year for all the *s* of the Israelites.''
26: 18 you for your *s* seven times over.
26: 21 times over, as your *s* deserve.
26: 24 you for your *s* seven times over.
26: 28 you for your *s* seven times over.
26: 39 of their enemies because of their *s*;
26: 39 of their fathers' *s* they will waste
26: 40 and the *s* of their fathers—
26: 40 '' 'But if they will confess their *s*
26: 43 They will pay for their *s*
Nu 14: 34 you will suffer for your *s*
15: 27 if just one person *s* unintentionally,
15: 29 to everyone who *s* unintentionally,
15: 30 '' 'But anyone who *s* defiantly,
16: 22 assembly when only one man *s*?''
16: 26 swept away because of all their *s*.''
Jos 24: 19 forgive your rebellion and your *s*.
1Sa 2: 25 If a man *s* against another man,
2: 25 but if a man *s* against the LORD,
12: 19 to all our other *s* the evil of asking
1Ki 14: 16 of the *s* Jeroboam has committed
14: 22 By the *s* they committed they
15: 3 committed all the *s* his father had
15: 30 of the *s* Jeroboam had committed
16: 2 to provoke me to anger by their *s*.
16: 13 because of all the *s* Baasha
16: 19 because of the *s* he had committed,
16: 31 to commit the *s* of Jeroboam son
2Ki 3: 3 clung to the *s* of Jeroboam son
10: 29 away from the *s* of Jeroboam son
10: 31 away from the *s* of Jeroboam,
13: 2 by following the *s* of Jeroboam son
13: 6 away from the *s* of the house
13: 11 from any of the *s* of Jeroboam son
14: 6 each is to die for his own *s*.''
14: 24 from any of the *s* of Jeroboam son
15: 9 away from the *s* of Jeroboam son
15: 18 away from the *s* of Jeroboam son
15: 24 away from the *s* of Jeroboam son
15: 28 away from the *s* of Jeroboam son
17: 22 persisted in all the *s* of Jeroboam
21: 11 has committed these detestable *s*.
24: 3 of the *s* of Manasseh and all he had
2Ch 25: 4 each is to die for his own *s*.''
28: 10 of *s* against the LORD your God?
33: 19 well as all his *s* and unfaithfulness,
Ezr 9: 6 our *s* are higher than our heads
9: 7 Because of our *s*, we and our kings
9: 13 less than our *s* have deserved
Ne 1: 6 I confess the *s* we Israelites,
4: 5 or blot out their *s* from your sight,
9: 2 and confessed their *s*
9: 37 of our *s*, its abundant harvest goes
Job 7: 21 and forgive my *s*?
13: 23 many wrongs and *s* have I
13: 26 make me inherit the *s* of my youth.
22: 5 Are not your *s* endless?
31: 28 also would be *s* to be judged,
35: 6 If your *s* are many, what does that
Ps 5: 10 Banish them for their many *s*,
19: 13 your servant also from willful *s*;
25: 7 Remember not the *s* of my youth
25: 18 and take away all my *s*.
32: 1 whose *s* are covered.
40: 12 my *s* have overtaken me,
51: 9 Hide your face from my *s*
59: 12 For the *s* of their mouths,
65: 3 When we were overwhelmed by *s*,
68: 21 of those who go on in their *s*.
79: 8 hold against us the *s* of the fathers;
79: 9 deliver us and atone for our *s*
85: 2 and covered all their *s*.
90: 8 our secret *s* in the light
94: 23 He will repay them for their *s*
103: 3 He forgives all my *s*
103: 10 does not treat us as our *s* deserve
109: 15 May their *s* always remain
130: 3 O LORD, kept a record of *s*,
130: 8 from all their *s*.
Pr 14: 21 He who despises his neighbor *s*,
28: 13 who conceals his *s* does not
29: 22 one commits many *s*.
Ecc 7: 20 who does what is right and never *s*.
Isa 1: 18 ''Though your *s* are like scarlet,

Isa 13: 11 the wicked for their *s*.
14: 21 sons for the *s* of their forefathers;
26: 21 of the earth for their *s*.
33: 24 *s* of those who dwell there will be
38: 17 you have put all my *s*
40: 2 double for all her *s*.
43: 24 you have burdened me with your *s*
43: 25 and remembers your *s* no more.
44: 22 your *s* like the morning mist.
50: 1 Because of your *s* you were sold;
58: 1 and to the house of Jacob their *s*.
59: 2 your *s* have hidden his face
59: 12 and our *s* testify against us.
59: 20 in Jacob who repent of their *s*,''
64: 6 like the wind our *s* sweep us away.
64: 7 us waste away because of our *s*.
64: 9 do not remember our *s* forever.
65: 7 both your *s* and the *s*
Jer 2: 13 ''My people have committed two *s*:
5: 25 your *s* have deprived you of good.
11: 10 to the *s* of their forefathers,
13: 22 it is because of your many *s*
14: 7 Although our *s* testify against us,
14: 10 and punish them for their *s*.''
15: 13 because of all your *s*
18: 23 or blot out their *s* from your sight.
30: 14 and your *s* so many.
30: 15 of your great guilt and many *s*
31: 34 and will remember their *s* no more
32: 18 for the fathers' *s* into the laps
33: 8 will forgive all their *s* of rebellion
50: 20 and for the *s* of Judah,
51: 6 not be destroyed because of her *s*.
La 1: 5 because of her many *s*.
1: 14 My *s* have been bound into a yoke;
1: 22 because of all my *s*.
3: 39 complain when punished for his *s*?
4: 13 because of the *s* of her prophets
Eze 7: 13 Because of their *s*, not one
7: 16 of the valleys, each because of his *s*.
14: 11 anymore with all their *s*.
14: 13 if a country *s* against me
16: 51 did not commit half the *s* you did.
16: 52 Because your *s* were more vile
18: 4 soul who *s* is the one who will die.
18: 14 sees all the *s* his father commits,
18: 20 soul who *s* is the one who will die.
18: 21 from all the *s* he has committed
18: 24 because of the *s* he has committed,
21: 24 revealing your *s* in all that you do
23: 49 consequences of your *s* of idolatry.
24: 23 because of your *s* and groan
28: 18 By your many *s* and dishonest
32: 27 The punishment for their *s* rested
33: 10 Our offenses and *s* weigh us down,
33: 12 The righteous man, if he *s*,
33: 16 of the *s* he has committed will be
36: 31 will loathe yourselves for your *s*
36: 33 day I cleanse you from all your *s*,
43: 10 that they may be ashamed of their *s*
45: 20 for anyone who *s* unintentionally
Da 4: 27 Renounce your *s* by doing what is
9: 13 God by turning from our *s*
9: 16 Our *s* and the iniquities
Hos 4: 8 They feed on the *s* of my people
7: 1 the *s* of Ephraim are exposed
7: 2 Their *s* engulf them;
8: 13 and punish their *s*:
9: 7 Because your *s* are so many
9: 9 and punish them for their *s*.
13: 12 his *s* are kept on record.
14: 1 Your *s* have been your downfall!
14: 2 ''Forgive all our *s*
Am 1: 3 ''For three *s* of Damascus,
1: 6 ''For three *s* of Gaza,
1: 9 ''For three *s* of Tyre,
1: 11 ''For three *s* of Edom,
1: 13 ''For three *s* of Ammon,
2: 1 ''For three *s* of Moab,
2: 4 ''For three *s* of Judah,
2: 6 ''For three *s* of Israel,
3: 2 you for all your *s*.''
3: 14 On the day I punish Israel for her *s*,
5: 12 and how great your *s*.
Mic 1: 5 of the *s* of the house of Israel.
6: 13 to ruin you because of your *s*.
7: 19 you will tread our *s* underfoot
Mt 1: 21 he will save his people from their *s*

Mt 3: 6 Confessing their *s*, they were
6: 15 if you do not forgive men their *s*,
6: 15 your Father will not forgive your *s*.
9: 2 Take heart, son; your *s* are forgiven
9: 5 to say, 'Your *s* are forgiven,'
9: 6 authority on earth to forgive *s* . . . . . ''
18: 15 ''If your brother *s* against you,
18: 21 brother when he *s* against me?
26: 28 for many for the forgiveness of *s*.
Mk 1: 4 repentance for the forgiveness of *s*.
1: 5 Confessing their *s*, they were
2: 5 ''Son, your *s* are forgiven.''
2: 7 Who can forgive *s* but God alone?''
2: 9 'Your *s* are forgiven,' or to say,
2: 10 authority on earth to forgive *s*
3: 28 all the *s* and blasphemies
11: 25 in heaven may forgive you your *s*.''
Lk 1: 77 through the forgiveness of their *s*,
3: 3 repentance for the forgiveness of *s*.
5: 20 ''Friend, your *s* are forgiven.''
5: 21 Who can forgive *s* but God alone?''
5: 23 to say, 'Your *s* are forgiven,'
5: 24 authority on earth to forgive *s* . . . . . ''
7: 47 her many *s* have been forgiven—
7: 48 said to her, ''Your *s* are forgiven.''
7: 49 ''Who is this who even forgives *s*?''
11: 4 Forgive us our *s*,
11: 4 forgive everyone who *s* against us.
17: 3 ''If your brother *s*, rebuke him,
17: 4 If he *s* against you seven times
24: 47 forgiveness of *s* will be preached
Jn 8: 24 you that you would die in your *s*;
8: 24 you will indeed die in your *s*.''
8: 34 everyone who *s* is a slave to sin.
20: 23 If you forgive anyone his *s*,
Ac 2: 38 so that your *s* may be forgiven.
3: 19 so that your *s* may be wiped out,
5: 31 and forgiveness of *s* to Israel.
10: 43 forgiveness of *s* through his name.''
13: 38 of *s* is proclaimed to you.
22: 16 be baptized and wash your *s* away,
26: 18 they may receive forgiveness of *s*
Ro 3: 25 left the *s* committed beforehand
4: 7 whose *s* are covered
4: 25 delivered over to death for our *s*
11: 27 when I take away their *s*.''
1Co 6: 18 All other *s* a man commits are
6: 18 but he who *s* sexually *s*
15: 3 died for our *s* according
15: 17 faith is futile; you are still in your *s*.
2Co 5: 19 not counting men's *s* against them.
Gal 1: 4 himself for our *s* to rescue us
Eph 1: 7 his blood, the forgiveness of *s*,
2: 1 dead in your transgressions and *s*,
Col 1: 14 redemption, the forgiveness of *s*.
2: 13 When you were dead in your *s*
2: 13 us all our *s*, having canceled
1Th 2: 16 way they always heap up their *s*
4: 6 Lord will punish men for all such *s*,
1Ti 5: 22 and do not share in the *s* of others.
5: 24 The *s* of some men are obvious,
5: 24 the *s* of others trail behind them.
2Ti 3: 6 who are loaded down with *s*
Heb 1: 3 he had provided purification for *s*,
2: 17 atonement for the *s* of the people,
5: 1 to offer gifts and sacrifices for *s*.
5: 3 as well as for the *s* of the people.
5: 3 has to offer sacrifices for his own *s*,
7: 27 He sacrificed for their *s* once for all
7: 27 and then for the *s* of the people.
7: 27 first for his own *s*, and then
8: 12 and will remember their *s* no more
9: 7 for the *s* the people had committed
9: 15 free from the *s* committed
9: 28 to take away the *s* of many people;
10: 2 longer have felt guilty for their *s*.
10: 3 are an annual reminder of *s*,
10: 4 of bulls and goats to take away *s*.
10: 11 which can never take away *s*.
10: 12 for all time one sacrifice for *s*,
10: 17 ''Their *s* and lawless acts
10: 26 of the truth, no sacrifice for *s* is left,
Jas 4: 17 ought to do and doesn't do it, *s*.
5: 16 Therefore confess your *s*
5: 20 and cover over a multitude of *s*.
1Pe 2: 24 He himself bore our *s* in his body
2: 24 so that we might die to *s*
3: 18 For Christ died for *s* once for all,

1Pe 4: 8 love covers over a multitude of *s*.
2Pe 1: 9 has been cleansed from his past *s*.
1Jn 1: 9 If we confess our *s*, he is faithful
1: 9 and just and will forgive us our *s*
2: 2 He is the atoning sacrifice for our *s*,
2: 2 also for the *s* of the whole world.
2: 12 your *s* have been forgiven
3: 4 Everyone who *s* breaks the law;
3: 5 so that he might take away our *s*.
4: 10 as an atoning sacrifice for our *s*.
Rev 1: 5 has freed us from our *s* by his blood
18: 4 so that you will not share in her *s*,
18: 5 for her *s* are piled up to heaven,

SIPHMOTH

1Sa 30: 28 to those in Aroer, *S*, Eshtemoa

SIPPAI

1Ch 20: 4 Sibbecai the Hushathite killed *S*,

SIRAH

2Sa 3: 26 back from the well of *S*.

SIRION

Dt 3: 9 (Hermon is called *S*
Ps 29: 6 *S* like a young wild ox.

SISERA (SISERA'S)

Jdg 4: 2 The commander of his army was *S*,
4: 7 I will lure *S*, the commander
4: 9 for the LORD will hand *S*
4: 12 When they told *S* that Barak son
4: 13 *S* gathered together his nine
4: 14 is the day the LORD has given *S*
4: 15 and *S* abandoned his chariot
4: 15 LORD routed *S* and all his chariots
4: 16 All the troops of *S* fell by the sword
4: 17 *S*, however, fled on foot to the tent
4: 18 Jael went out to meet *S*
4: 22 Barak came by in pursuit of *S*,
4: 22 and there lay *S* with the tent peg
5: 20 their courses they fought against *S*.
5: 26 She struck *S*, she crushed his head,
5: 30 colorful garments as plunder for *S*,
1Sa 12: 9 so he sold them into the hand of *S*,
Ezr 2: 53 Mehida, Harsha, Barkos, *S*, Temah
Ne 7: 55 Mehida, Harsha, Barkos, *S*, Temah
Ps 83: 9 as you did to *S* and Jabin

SISERA'S (SISERA)

Jdg 5: 28 the window peered *S* mother;

SISMAI

1Ch 2: 40 father of *S*, *S* the father of Shallum,

SISTER (SISTER-IN-LAW SISTER'S SISTERS)

Ge 4: 22 Tubal-Cain's *s* was Naamah.
12: 13 Say you are my *s*, so that I will be
12: 19 Why did you say, 'She is my *s*,'
20: 2 of his wife Sarah, "She is my *s*."
20: 5 She is my *s*,' and didn't she also say
20: 12 Besides, she really is my *s*,
24: 59 So they sent their *s* Rebekah
24: 60 "Our *s*, may you increase
25: 20 and *s* of Laban the Aramean.
26: 7 She is my *s*," because he was afraid
26: 9 She is my *s*'?" Isaac answered him,
28: 9 the *s* of Nebaioth and daughter
30: 1 she became jealous of her *s*.
30: 8 had a great struggle with my *s*,
34: 13 Because their *s* Dinah had been
34: 14 we can't give our *s*
34: 17 to be circumcised, we'll take our *s*
34: 27 city where their *s* had been defiled.
34: 31 have treated our *s* like
36: 3 of Ishmael and *s* of Nebaioth.
36: 22 Timna was Lotan's *s*.
46: 17 Their *s* was Serah.
Ex 2: 4 His *s* stood at a distance
2: 7 his *s* asked Pharaoh's daughter,
6: 20 married his father's *s* Jochebed,
6: 23 of Amminadab and *s* of Nahshon,
15: 20 Miriam the prophetess, Aaron's *s*,
Lev 18: 9 have sexual relations with your *s*,
18: 11 born to your father; she is your *s*.
18: 12 relations with your father's *s*;
18: 13 relations with your mother's *s*,
Lev 18: 18 " 'Do not take your wife's *s*
20: 17 He has dishonored his *s*
20: 17 If a man marries his *s*, the daughter
20: 19 not have sexual relations with the *s*
21: 3 an unmarried *s* who is dependent
Nu 6: 7 or mother or brother or *s* dies,
25: 18 the affair of Peor and their *s* Cozbi,
26: 59 Moses and their *s* Miriam.
Dt 27: 22 is the man who sleeps with his *s*,
Jdg 15: 2 Isn't her younger *s* more attractive
2Sa 13: 1 the beautiful *s* of Absalom son
13: 2 of illness on account of his *s* Tamar
13: 4 my brother Absalom's *s*."
13: 5 'I would like my *s* Tamar to come
13: 6 "I would like my *s* Tamar to come
13: 11 "Come to bed with me, my *s*."
13: 20 Be quiet now, my *s*; he is your
13: 22 he had disgraced his *s* Tamar.
13: 32 the day Amnon raped his *s* Tamar.
17: 25 *s* of Zeruiah the mother of Joab.
1Ki 11: 19 with Hadad that he gave him a *s*
11: 20 The *s* of Tahpenes bore him a son
2Ki 11: 2 of King Jehoram and *s* of Ahaziah,
1Ch 1: 39 Timna was Lotan's *s*.
3: 9 And Tamar was their *s*.
3: 19 Shelomith was their *s*.
4: 3 Their *s* was named Hazzelelponi.
4: 19 of Hodiah's wife, the *s* of Naham:
7: 18 His *s* Hammoleketh gave birth
7: 30 Their *s* was Serah.
7: 32 and Hotham and of their *s* Shua.
2Ch 22: 11 was Ahaziah's *s*, she hid the child
Job 17: 14 to the worm, 'My mother' or 'My *s*
Pr 7: 4 Say to wisdom, "You are my *s*,"
SS 4: 9 You have stolen my heart, my *s*,
4: 10 How delightful is your love, my *s*,
4: 12 You are a garden locked up, my *s*,
5: 1 I have come into my garden, my *s*,
5: 2 "Open to me, my *s*, my darling,
8: 8 What shall we do for our *s*
8: 8 We have a young *s*,
Jer 3: 7 and her unfaithful *s* Judah saw it.
3: 8 that her unfaithful *s* Judah had no
3: 10 her unfaithful *s* Judah did not
22: 18 'Alas, my brother! Alas, my *s*!'
Eze 16: 45 and you are a true *s* of your sisters,
16: 46 Your older *s* was Samaria,
16: 46 and your younger *s*, who lived
16: 48 your *s* Sodom and her daughters
16: 49 this was the sin of your *s* Sodom:
16: 56 mention your *s* Sodom in the day
22: 11 and another violates his *s*,
23: 4 Oholah, and her *s* was Oholibah.
23: 11 she was more depraved than her *s*.
23: 11 "Her *s* Oholibah saw this,
23: 18 just as I had turned away from her *s*
23: 31 You have gone the way of your *s*;
23: 33 the cup of your *s* Samaria.
23: 42 and her *s* and beautiful crowns
44: 25 or unmarried *s*, then he may defile
Mt 12: 50 in heaven is my brother and *s*
Mk 3: 35 does God's will is my brother and *s*
Lk 10: 39 She had a *s* called Mary, who sat
10: 40 don't you care that my *s* has left me
Jn 11: 1 village of Mary and her *s* Martha.
11: 5 Jesus loved Martha and her *s*
11: 28 and called her *s* Mary aside.
11: 39 said Martha, the *s* of the dead man,
19: 25 his mother's *s*, Mary the wife
Ac 23: 16 son of Paul's *s* heard of this plot,
Ro 16: 1 I commend to you our *s* Phoebe,
16: 15 Philologus, Julia, Nereus and his *s*,
Phm : 2 and fellow worker, to Apphia our *s*,
Jas 2: 15 Suppose a brother or *s* is
2Jn : 13 of your chosen *s* send their

SISTER-IN-LAW (SISTER)

Ru 1: 15 "your *s* is going back to her people

SISTER'S (SISTER)

Ge 24: 30 and the bracelets on his *s* arms,
29: 13 his *s* son, he hurried to meet him.
1Ch 7: 15 His *s* name was Maacah.
Eze 23: 32 "You will drink your *s* cup,

SISTERS (SISTER)

Jos 2: 13 and *s*, and all who belong to them,
1Ch 2: 16 Their *s* were Zeruiah and Abigail.
Job 1: 4 and they would invite their three *s*
42: 11 *s* and everyone who had known
Eze 16: 45 and you are a true sister of your *s*,
16: 51 have made your *s* seem righteous
16: 52 have made your *s* appear righteous.
16: 52 some justification for your *s*.
16: 55 your *s*, Sodom with her daughters
16: 61 ashamed when you receive your *s*,
Hos 2: 1 and of your *s*, 'My loved one.'
Mt 13: 56 and Judas? Aren't all his *s* with us?
19: 29 or brothers or *s* or father or mother
Mk 6: 3 Aren't his *s* here with us?"
10: 29 or brothers or *s* or mother or father
10: 30 *s*, mothers, children and fields—
Lk 14: 26 his brothers and *s*— yes,
Jn 11: 3 So the *s* sent word to Jesus, "Lord,
1Ti 5: 2 as *s*, with absolute purity.

SISTRUMS

2Sa 6: 5 lyres, tambourines, *s* and cymbals.

SIT (SAT SITS SITTING)

Ge 27: 19 Please *s* up and eat some
27: 31 *s* up and eat some of my game,
Ex 18: 14 Why do you alone *s* as judge,
Nu 32: 6 go to war while you *s* here?
Dt 6: 7 them when you *s* at home
11: 19 them when you *s* at home
Ru 4: 1 over here, my friend, and *s* down."
4: 2 "*S* here," and they did so.
1Sa 16: 11 we will not *s* down until he arrives
1Ki 1: 13 and he will *s* on my throne"?
1: 17 and he will *s* on my throne.'
1: 20 from you who will *s* on the throne
1: 24 and that he will *s* on your throne?
1: 27 his servants know who should *s*
1: 30 he will *s* on my throne in my place
1: 35 he is to come and *s* on my throne
3: 6 and have given him a son to *s*
8: 20 and now I *s* on the throne of Israel,
8: 25 fail to have a man to *s* before me
2Ki 10: 30 your descendants will *s*
15: 12 "Your descendants will *s*
1Ch 28: 5 to *s* on the throne of the kingdom
2Ch 6: 10 and now I *s* on the throne of Israel,
6: 16 fail to have a man to *s* before me
Ps 1: 1 or *s* in the seat of mockers.
26: 4 I do not *s* with deceitful men,
26: 5 and refuse to *s* with the wicked.
69: 12 Those who *s* at the gate mock me,
80: 1 you who *s* enthroned
102: 12 O LORD, *s* enthroned forever;
110: 1 "*S* at my right hand
119: 23 Though princes *s* together
132: 12 then their sons will *s*
132: 14 here I will *s* enthroned,
139: 2 You know when I *s* and when I rise
Pr 23: 1 When you *s* to dine with a ruler,
SS 2: 3 I delight to *s* in his shade,
Isa 3: 26 destitute, she will *s* on the ground.
14: 13 I will *s* enthroned on the mount
16: 5 in faithfulness a man will *s* on it—
42: 7 from the dungeon those who *s*
47: 1 "Go down, *s* in the dust,
47: 1 *s* on the ground without a throne,
47: 5 "*S* in silence, go into darkness,
47: 14 here is no fire to *s* by.
52: 2 rise up, *s* enthroned, O Jerusalem.
65: 4 who *s* among the graves
Jer 13: 13 including the kings who *s*
16: 8 and *s* down to eat and drink.
17: 25 then kings who *s* on David's throne
22: 2 you who *s* on David's throne—you
22: 4 then kings who *s* on David's throne
22: 30 none will *s* on the throne of David
33: 17 to have a man to *s* on the throne
36: 15 They said to him, "*S* down, please,
36: 30 one to *s* on the throne of David;
48: 18 and *s* on the parched ground,
La 2: 10 *s* on the ground in silence;
3: 28 Let him *s* alone in silence,
Eze 26: 16 Clothed with terror, they will *s*
28: 2 I *s* on the throne of a god
33: 31 *s* before you to listen to your words
44: 3 himself is the only one who may *s*
Da 7: 26 " 'But the court will *s*,
11: 27 will *s* at the same table
Joel 3: 12 for there I will *s*

Am 3: 12 those who *s* in Samaria
Mic 4: 4 Every man will *s* under his own
7: 8 Though I *s* in darkness,
Zec 3: 10 neighbor to *s* under his vine
6: 13 and will *s* and rule on his throne.
8: 4 of ripe old age will *s* in the streets
Mal 3: 3 He will *s* as a refiner and purifier
Mt 14: 19 the people to *s* down on the grass.
15: 35 the crowd to *s* down on the ground.
19: 28 who have followed me will also *s*
20: 21 sons of mine may *s* at your right
20: 23 to *s* at my right or left is not for me
22: 44 "*S* at my right hand
23: 2 and the Pharisees *s* in Moses' seat.
25: 31 he will *s* on his throne
26: 36 "*S* here while I go over there
Mk 6: 39 them to have all the people *s*
8: 6 the crowd to *s* down on the ground.
10: 37 "Let one of us *s* at your right
10: 40 to *s* at my right or left is not for me
12: 36 "*S* at my right hand
14: 32 said to his disciples, "*S* here
Lk 9: 14 "Have them *s* down in groups
14: 28 Will he not first *s* down
14: 31 Will he not first *s* down
16: 6 'Take your bill, *s* down quickly,
17: 7 'Come along now and *s* down to eat
20: 42 "*S* at my right hand
22: 30 in my kingdom and *s* on thrones,
Jn 6: 10 "Have the people *s* down."
9: 8 this the same man who used to *s*
Ac 2: 34 "*S* at my right hand
3: 10 same man who used to *s* begging
8: 31 Philip to come up and *s* with him.
23: 3 You *s* there to judge me according
1Co 9: 3 to those who *s* in judgment on me.
Heb 1: 13 "*S* at my right hand
Jas 2: 3 or "*S* on the floor by my feet,"
Rev 3: 21 right to *s* with me on my throne,
18: 7 'I *s* as queen; I am not a widow,

SITE (SITES)

Ge 12: 6 as the *s* of the great tree of Moreh
23: 4 some property for a burial *s* here
23: 9 as a burial *s* among you.''
23: 20 by the Hittites as a burial *s*.
Nu 21: 15 that lead to the *s* of Ar
1Ki 6: 7 at the temple *s* while it was being
1Ch 17: 5 moved from one tent *s* to another,
21: 22 "Let me have the *s*
21: 25 hundred shekels of gold for the *s*.
Ezr 2: 68 of the house of God on its *s*.
5: 15 rebuild the house of God on its *s*.'
6: 7 rebuild this house of God on its *s*.
Zec 14: 10 Gate to the *s* of the First Gate,

SITES (SITE)

2Ki 23: 14 covered the *s* with human bones.
2Ch 33: 19 and the *s* where he built high places

SITHRI

Ex 6: 22 were Mishael, Elzaphan and *S*.

SITNAH

Ge 26: 21 over that one also; so he named it *S*

SITS (SIT)

Ex 11: 5 of Pharaoh, who *s* on the throne,
Lev 15: 4 anything he *s* on will be unclean.
15: 6 Whoever *s* on anything that
15: 9 " 'Everything the man *s*
15: 20 anything she *s* on will be unclean.
15: 22 Whoever touches anything she *s*
15: 26 anything she *s* on will be unclean,
Est 6: 10 for Mordecai the Jew, who *s*
Ps 29: 10 The LORD *s* enthroned
99: 1 *s* enthroned between the cherubim,
113: 5 the One who *s* enthroned on high,
Pr 9: 14 She *s* at the door of her house,
20: 8 When a king *s* on his throne
Isa 28: 6 justice to him who *s* in judgment,
40: 22 He *s* enthroned above the circle
Jer 29: 16 LORD says about the king who *s*
Mt 19: 28 of Man *s* on his glorious throne,
23: 22 and by the one who *s* on it.
Rev 4: 9 thanks to him who *s* on the throne
4: 10 before him who *s* on the throne,
5: 13 "To him who *s* on the throne
Rev 6: 16 the face of him who *s* on the throne
7: 10 who *s* on the throne,
7: 15 he who *s* on the throne will spread
17: 1 of the great prostitute, who *s*
17: 9 hills on which the woman *s*.
17: 15 where the prostitute *s*, are peoples,

SITTING (SIT)

Ge 18: 1 while he was *s* at the entrance
19: 1 Lot was *s* in the gateway of the city
23: 10 Ephron the Hittite was *s*
31: 34 inside her camel's saddle and was *s*
Lev 15: 23 or anything she was *s* on,
Dt 22: 6 and the mother is *s* on the young
Jdg 3: 20 him while he was *s* alone
5: 10 *s* on your saddle blankets,
1Sa 1: 9 Now Eli the priest was *s* on a chair
4: 13 there was Eli *s* on his chair
19: 9 he was *s* in his house with his spear
2Sa 18: 24 While David was *s*
19: 8 "The king is *s* in the gateway,"
1Ki 13: 14 He found him *s* under an oak tree
13: 20 While they were *s* at the table,
22: 10 of Judah were *s* on their thrones
22: 19 I saw the LORD *s* on his throne
2Ki 1: 9 who was *s* on the top of a hill,
6: 32 Now Elisha was *s* in his house,
6: 32 and the elders were *s* with him.
9: 5 found the army officers *s* together.
18: 27 and not to the men *s* on the wall—
2Ch 18: 9 of Judah were *s* on their thrones
18: 18 I saw the LORD *s* on his throne
Ezr 10: 9 all the people were *s* in the square
Ne 2: 6 with the queen *s* beside him,
Est 2: 19 Mordecai was *s* at the king's gate.
2: 21 During the time Mordecai was *s*
5: 1 The king was *s* on his royal throne
5: 13 as I see that Jew Mordecai *s*
Isa 36: 12 and not to the men *s* on the wall—
Jer 8: 14 "Why are we *s* here?
32: 12 of all the Jews *s* in the courtyard
36: 12 where all the officials were *s*:
36: 22 king was *s* in the winter apartment,
38: 7 While the king was *s*
La 3: 63 Look at them! *S* or standing,
Eze 8: 1 elders of Judah were *s* before me,
8: 1 while I was *s* in my house
8: 14 I saw women *s* there, mourning
Mt 9: 9 he saw a man named Matthew *s*
11: 16 They are like children *s*
20: 30 Two blind men were *s*
24: 3 As Jesus was *s* on the Mount
26: 64 the Son of Man *s* at the right hand
26: 69 Peter was *s* out in the courtyard,
27: 19 While Pilate was *s*
27: 36 And *s* down, they kept watch
27: 61 and the other Mary were *s* there
Mk 2: 6 teachers of the law were *s* there,
2: 14 of Alphaeus *s* at the tax collector's
3: 32 A crowd was *s* around him,
5: 15 *s* there, dressed and in his right
9: 35 *S* down, Jesus called the Twelve
10: 46 was *s* by the roadside begging.
13: 3 As Jesus was *s* on the Mount
14: 62 the Son of Man *s* at the right hand
16: 5 in a white robe *s* on the right side,
Lk 2: 46 him in the temple courts, *s*
5: 17 and Jerusalem, were *s* there.
5: 27 the name of Levi *s* at his tax booth.
7: 32 They are like children *s*
8: 35 *s* at Jesus' feet, dressed
10: 13 would have repented long ago, *s*
18: 35 a blind man was *s* by the roadside
Jn 2: 14 and others *s* at tables exchanging
Ac 2: 2 the whole house where they were *s*.
6: 15 All who were *s* in the Sanhedrin
8: 28 and on his way home was *s*
26: 30 and Bernice and those *s* with them.
1Co 14: 30 comes to someone who is *s* down,
Jas 4: 11 you are not keeping it, but *s*
Rev 4: 2 in heaven with someone *s* on it.
14: 15 to him who was *s* on the cloud,
17: 3 There I saw a woman *s*

SITUATED (SITUATION)

2Ki 2: 19 this town is well *s*, as you can see,
Eze 27: 3 *s* at the gateway to the sea,
Na 3: 8 *s* on the Nile,

SITUATION (SITUATED SITUATIONS)

Ge 31: 40 This was my *s*: The heat consumed
1Sa 13: 6 Israel saw that their *s* was critical
2Sa 14: 20 this to change the present *s*.
Da 2: 9 things, hoping the *s* will change.
6: 17 so that Daniel's *s* might not be
Mt 19: 10 "If this is the *s* between a husband
1Co 7: 20 remain in the *s* which he was
7: 24 remain in the *s* God called him
Php 4: 12 of being content in any and every *s*,

SITUATIONS (SITUATION)

2Ti 4: 5 head in all *s*, endure hardship,

SIVAN

Est 8: 9 of the third month, the month of *S*.

SIYON

Dt 4: 48 Gorge to Mount *S* (that is,

SIZE

Ex 26: 2 All the curtains are to be the same *s*
26: 8 are to be the same *s*—
36: 9 All the curtains were the same *s*—
36: 15 All eleven curtains were the same *s*
Nu 13: 32 people we saw there are of great *s*.
1Ki 6: 25 two cherubim were identical in *s*
7: 9 blocks of high-grade stone cut to *s*
7: 11 cut to *s*, and cedar beams.
7: 37 and were identical in *s* and shape.
2Ki 10: 32 began to reduce the *s* of Israel.
1Ch 23: 29 all measurements of quantity and *s*.
Ps 33: 16 by the *s* of his army;
Eze 45: 11 and the bath are to be the same *s*,
46: 22 in the four corners was the same *s*.
Rev 18: 21 angel picked up a boulder the *s*

SKETCH

2Ki 16: 10 to Uriah the priest a *s* of the altar,

SKIES (SKY)

Dt 28: 24 from the *s* until you are ruined.
Job 26: 7 He spreads out the northern ⌞*s*⌟
26: 13 By his breath the *s* became fair;
37: 18 him in spreading out the *s*,
37: 21 bright as it is in the *s*
Ps 19: 1 the *s* proclaim the work
36: 5 your faithfulness to the *s*.
57: 10 your faithfulness reaches to the *s*.
68: 33 to him who rides the ancient *s*
68: 34 whose power is in the *s*.
71: 19 Your righteousness reaches to the *s*
77: 17 the *s* resounded with thunder;
78: 23 Yet he gave a command to the *s*
89: 6 who in the *s* above can compare
108: 4 your faithfulness reaches to the *s*.
148: 4 and you waters above the *s*.
Jer 14: 22 Do the *s* themselves send
51: 9 for her judgment reaches to the *s*,
Hos 2: 21 "I will respond to the *s*,
Mt 11: 23 will you be lifted up to the *s*? No,
Lk 10: 15 will you be lifted up to the *s*? No,

SKILL (SKILLED SKILLFUL SKILLFULLY SKILLS)

Ex 31: 3 with *s*, ability and knowledge
31: 6 I have given *s* to all the craftsmen
35: 26 and had the *s* spun the goat hair
35: 31 with *s*, ability and knowledge
35: 35 them with *s* to do all kinds
36: 1 to whom the LORD has given *s*
2Ch 2: 13 you Huram-Abi, a man of great *s*,
Ps 137: 5 may my right hand forget ⌞its *s*⌟.
Ecc 2: 19 I have poured my effort and *s*
2: 21 with wisdom, knowledge and *s*,
10: 10 but *s* will bring success.
Eze 28: 5 By your great *s* in trading
Ac 17: 29 made by man's design and *s*.

SKILLED (SKILL)

Ex 26: 1 worked into them by a *s* craftsman.
26: 31 worked into it by a *s* craftsman
28: 3 Tell all the *s* men to whom I have
28: 6 the work of a *s* craftsman.
28: 15 the work of a *s* craftsman.
35: 10 "All who are *s* among you are
35: 25 Every *s* woman spun
36: 1 every *s* person to whom the LORD

Jos 13: 22 In addition to those *s* in battle,
Jdg 16: 24 and multiplied our *s*.''
1Sa 18: 7 ''Saul has *s* his thousands,
21: 11 '' 'Saul has *s* his thousands,
29: 5 '' 'Saul has *s* his thousands,
31: 1 and many fell *s* on Mount Gilboa.
2Sa 1: 19 O Israel, lies *s* on your heights.
1: 22 From the blood of the *s*,
1: 25 Jonathan lies *s* on your heights.
2Ki 11: 20 Athaliah had been *s* with the sword
1Ch 5: 22 and many others fell *s*,
10: 1 and many fell *s* on Mount Gilboa.
2Ch 23: 21 Athaliah had been *s* with the sword
Est 9: 11 number of those *s* in the citadel
Job 39: 30 and where the *s* are, there is he.''
Ps 88: 5 like the *s* who lie in the grave,
89: 10 crushed Rahab like one of the *s*;
Pr 7: 26 her *s* are a mighty throng.
Isa 10: 4 or fall among the *s*.
14: 19 you are covered with the *s*,
22: 2 Your *s* were not killed by the sword
26: 21 she will conceal her *s* no longer.
34: 3 Their *s* will be thrown out,
66: 16 many will be those *s* by the LORD.
Jer 9: 1 and night for the *s* of my people.
14: 18 I see those *s* by the sword;
18: 21 their young men *s* by the sword
25: 33 At that time those *s*
51: 4 They will fall down *s* in Babylon,
51: 47 her *s* will all lie fallen within her.
51: 49 just as the *s* in all the earth
51: 49 must fall because of Israel's *s*,
La 2: 4 Like a foe he has *s*
2: 21 You have *s* them in the day
3: 43 you have *s* without pity.
Eze 6: 7 Your people will fall *s* among you,
6: 13 when their people lie *s*
9: 7 and fill the courts with the *s*.
21: 29 of the wicked who are to be *s*,
28: 23 The *s* will fall within her,
30: 4 When the *s* fall in Egypt,
30: 11 and fill the land with the *s*.
32: 22 by the graves of all her *s*,
32: 23 terror in the land of the living are *s*,
32: 24 All of them are *s*, fallen
32: 25 A bed is made for her among the *s*,
32: 25 to the pit; they are laid among the *s*
32: 30 they went down with the *s*
35: 8 I will fill your mountains with the *s*;
37: 9 into these *s*, that they may live.' ''
Da 5: 30 king of the Babylonians, was *s*,
7: 11 I kept looking until the beast was *s*
Zep 2: 12 will be *s* by my sword.''
Rev 5: 6 as if it had been *s*, standing
5: 9 because you were *s*,
5: 12 ''Worthy is the Lamb, who was *s*,
6: 9 the souls of those who had been *s*
13: 8 belonging to the Lamb that was *s*

SLANDER (SLANDERED SLANDERER SLANDERERS SLANDERING SLANDEROUS SLANDERS)

Lev 19: 16 '' 'Do not go about spreading *s*
Ps 15: 3 and has no *s* on his tongue,
31: 13 For I hear the *s* of many;
38: 20 *s* me when I seek what is good.
41: 6 while his heart gathers *s*;
50: 20 and *s* your own mother's son.
54: 5 Let evil recoil on those who *s* me;
59: 10 gloat over those who *s* me.
119: 23 princes sit together and *s* me,
Pr 10: 18 and whoever spreads *s* is a fool.
30: 10 ''Do not *s* a servant to his master,
Jer 6: 28 going about to *s*.
Eze 36: 3 of people's malicious talk and *s*,
Mt 15: 19 theft, false testimony, *s*.
Mk 7: 22 envy, *s*, arrogance and folly.
2Co 12: 20 outbursts of anger, factions, *s*,
Eph 4: 31 rage and anger, brawling and *s*,
Col 3: 8 *s*, and filthy language
1Ti 5: 14 the enemy no opportunity for *s*.
Tit 3: 2 to *s* no one, to be peaceable
Jas 4: 11 Brothers, do not *s* one another.
1Pe 2: 1 hypocrisy, envy, and *s*
3: 16 in Christ may be ashamed of their *s*
2Pe 2: 10 afraid to *s* celestial beings;
Jude : 8 authority and *s* celestial beings.
Rev 2: 9 I know the *s* of those who say they
13: 6 and to *s* his name and his dwelling

SLANDERED (SLANDER)

Dt 22: 17 Now he has *s* her and said,
2Sa 19: 27 And he has *s* your servant
Ps 35: 15 They *s* me without ceasing.
1Co 4: 13 when we are *s*, we answer kindly.
1Ti 6: 1 and our teaching may not be *s*.

SLANDERER (SLANDER)

Jer 9: 4 and every friend a *s*.
1Co 5: 11 an idolater or a *s*, a drunkard

SLANDERERS (SLANDER)

Ps 56: 2 My *s* pursue me all day long;
140: 11 Let *s* not be established in the land;
Ro 1: 30 They are gossips, *s*, God-haters,
1Co 6: 10 nor the greedy nor drunkards nor *s*
Tit 2: 3 not to be *s* or addicted

SLANDERING (SLANDER)

Jas 2: 7 the ones who are *s* the noble name

SLANDEROUS (SLANDER)

Eze 22: 9 In you are *s* men bent
2Ti 3: 3 unforgiving, *s*, without self-control
2Pe 2: 11 do not bring *s* accusations
Jude : 9 to bring a *s* accusation against him,

SLANDERS (SLANDER)

Dt 22: 14 and *s* her and gives her a bad name,
Ps 101: 5 Whoever *s* his neighbor in secret,

SLAPPED (SLAPS)

1Ki 22: 24 Kenaanah went up and *s* Micaiah
2Ch 18: 23 Kenaanah went up and *s* Micaiah
Mt 26: 67 Others *s* him and said, ''Prophesy

SLAPS (SLAPPED)

2Co 11: 20 or pushes himself forward or *s* you

SLASH (SLASHED)

Eze 21: 16 O sword, *s* to the right,

SLASHED (SLASH)

1Ki 18: 28 and *s* themselves with swords
Jer 48: 37 every hand is *s*

SLAUGHTER (SLAUGHTERED SLAUGHTERING SLAUGHTERS)

Ge 43: 16 *s* an animal and prepare dinner;
Ex 12: 6 of Israel must *s* them at twilight.
12: 21 your families and *s* the Passover
29: 11 *S* it in the LORD's presence
29: 16 *S* it and take the blood
29: 20 *S* it, take some of its blood
Lev 1: 5 He is to *s* the young bull
1: 11 He is to *s* it at the north side
3: 2 and *s* it at the entrance to the Tent
3: 8 *s* it in front of the Tent of Meeting.
3: 13 *s* it in front of the Tent of Meeting.
4: 4 and *s* it before the LORD.
4: 24 *s* it at the place where the burnt
4: 29 and *s* it at the place of the burnt
4: 33 and *s* it for a sin offering
14: 13 He is to *s* the lamb
14: 19 the priest shall *s* the burnt offering
14: 25 He shall *s* the lamb
16: 11 to *s* the bull for his own sin offering
16: 15 ''He shall then *s* the goat
22: 28 Do not *s* a cow or a sheep
Dt 12: 15 you may *s* your animals in any
12: 21 you may *s* animals from the herds
1Sa 4: 10 *s* was very great; Israel lost thirty
14: 30 Would not the *s* of the Philistines
14: 34 and *s* them here and eat them.
2Sa 17: 9 'There has been a *s*
2Ch 35: 6 *S* the Passover lambs, consecrate
Est 7: 4 sold for destruction and *s*
Pr 7: 22 like an ox going to the *s*,
24: 11 back those staggering toward *s*.
Isa 14: 21 Prepare a place to *s* his sons
30: 25 day of great *s*, when the towers fall,
34: 2 he will give them over to *s*.
34: 6 and a great *s* in Edom.
53: 7 he was led like a lamb to the *s*,
65: 12 and you will all bend down for the *s*
Jer 7: 32 Hinnom, but the Valley of *S*,
11: 19 been like a gentle lamb led to the *s*;
12: 3 Set them apart for the day of *s*!
19: 6 Hinnom, but the Valley of *S*.
48: 15 young men will go down in the *s*,''
50: 27 let them go down to the *s*!
51: 40 like lambs to the *s*,
Eze 9: 6 *S* old men, young men
21: 10 sharpened for the *s*,
21: 14 It is a sword for *s*—
21: 14 a sword for great *s*,
21: 15 I have stationed the sword for *s*
21: 15 it is grasped for *s*.
21: 22 to give the command to *s*,
21: 28 drawn for the *s*,
26: 15 and the *s* takes place in you?
34: 3 the wool and *s* the choice animals,
44: 11 they may *s* the burnt offerings
Da 11: 12 and will *s* many thousands,
Hos 5: 2 The rebels are deep in *s*.
Ob : 9 will be cut down in the *s*.
Zec 11: 4 ''Pasture the flock marked for *s*.
11: 5 Their buyers *s* them and go
11: 7 I pastured the flock marked for *s*,
Ac 8: 32 ''He was led like a sheep to the *s*,
Jas 5: 5 fattened yourselves in the day of *s*.

SLAUGHTERED (SLAUGHTER)

Ge 37: 31 *s* a goat and dipped the robe
Lev 4: 15 the bull shall be *s* before the LORD
4: 24 place where the burnt offering is *s*
4: 33 place where the burnt offering is *s*.
6: 25 in the place the burnt offering is *s*
6: 25 is to be *s* before the LORD
7: 2 The guilt offering is to be *s*
7: 2 place where the burnt offering is *s*,
8: 15 Moses *s* the bull and took some
8: 19 Then Moses *s* the ram
8: 23 Moses *s* the ram and took some
9: 8 came to the altar and *s* the calf
9: 12 Then he *s* the burnt offering.
9: 15 *s* it and offered it for a sin offering
9: 18 He *s* the cow and the ram
14: 13 and the burnt offering are *s*.
Nu 11: 22 and herds were *s* for them?
14: 16 so he *s* them in the desert.'
19: 3 taken outside the camp and *s*
Dt 28: 31 Your ox will be *s* before your eyes,
Jdg 15: 8 them viciously and *s* many
1Sa 1: 25 When they had *s* the bull, they
11: 11 *s* them until the heat of the day.
14: 34 his ox that night and *s* it there.
25: 11 the meat I have *s* for my shearers,
1Ki 18: 40 to the Kishon Valley and *s* there.
19: 21 yoke of oxen and *s* them.
2Ki 3: 23 must have fought and *s* each other.
3: 24 the land and *s* the Moabites.
10: 7 took the princes and *s* all seventy
10: 14 *s* them by the well of Beth Eked—
23: 20 Josiah *s* all the priests
2Ch 18: 2 Ahab *s* many sheep and cattle
28: 9 But you have *s* them in a rage that
29: 22 So they *s* the bulls, and the priests
29: 22 next they *s* the rams and sprinkled
29: 22 then they *s* the lambs and sprinkled
29: 24 The priests then *s* the goats
30: 15 They *s* the Passover lamb
35: 1 and the Passover lamb was *s*
35: 11 The Passover lambs were *s*,
Ezr 6: 20 The Levites *s* the Passover lamb
Ps 44: 22 we are considered as sheep to be *s*.
Jer 25: 34 For your time to be *s* has come;
39: 6 of Babylon *s* the sons of Zedekiah
41: 7 the men who were with him *s* them
52: 10 of Babylon *s* the sons of Zedekiah
La 2: 21 you have *s* them without pity.
Eze 16: 21 You *s* my children and sacrificed
40: 39 offerings and guilt offerings were *s*.
40: 41 on which the sacrifices were *s*.
Ro 8: 36 we are considered as sheep to be *s*

SLAUGHTERING (SLAUGHTER)

1Sa 7: 11 *s* them along the way to a point
2Ch 20: 23 After they finished *s* the men
25: 14 returned from *s* the Edomites,
Isa 22: 13 *s* of cattle and killing of sheep,
Eze 40: 42 the utensils for *s* the burnt offerings

SLAUGHTERS (SLAUGHTER)

Ex 22: 1 or a sheep and *s* it or sells it,

SLAVE (ENSLAVE ENSLAVED ENSLAVES ENSLAVING SLAVERY SLAVES SLAVING)

Ge 9:26 May Canaan be the *s* of Shem.
9:27 and may Canaan be his *s*."
20:17 and his *s* girls so they could have
21:10 for that *s* woman's son will never
21:10 "Get rid of that *s* woman
39:17 "That Hebrew *s* you brought us
39:19 "This is how your *s* treated me,"
44:10 found to have it will become my *s*;
44:17 to have the cup will become my *s*.
44:33 as my lord's *s* in place of the boy,
Ex 1:11 So they put *s* masters over them
2: 5 and sent her *s* girl to get it.
3: 7 out because of their *s* drivers,
5: 6 gave this order to the *s* drivers
5:10 *s* drivers and the foremen went out
5:13 The *s* drivers kept pressing them,
5:14 by Pharaoh's *s* drivers were beaten
11: 5 to the firstborn son of the *s* girl,
12:44 Any *s* you have bought may eat
21:20 or female *s* with a rod and the *s* dies
21:21 not to be punished if the *s* gets up
21:21 since the *s* is his property.
21:32 If the bull gores a male or female *s*,
21:32 of silver to the master of the *s*,
23:12 and the *s* born in your household,
Lev 19:20 a woman who is a *s* girl promised
22:11 But if a priest buys a *s* with money,
22:11 in his household, that *s* may eat his
22:11 or if a *s* is born in his household,
25:39 do not make him work as a *s*.
Dt 21:14 must not sell her or treat her as a *s*,
23:15 If a *s* has taken refuge with you,
24: 7 and treats him as a *s* or sells him,
32:36 and no one is left, *s* or free.
Jdg 9:18 Abimelech, the son of his *s* girl,
1Sa 30:13 "I am an Egyptian, the *s*
2Sa 6:20 sight of the *s* girls of his servants
6:22 But by these *s* girls you spoke of,
1Ki 9:21 conscripted for his *s* labor force,
14:10 every last male in Israel—*s*
21:21 Ahab every last male in Israel—*s*
2Ki 9: 8 Ahab every last male in Israel—*s*
14:26 whether *s* or free, was suffering;
2Ch 8: 8 conscripted for his *s* labor force,
Job 3:18 no longer hear the *s* driver's shout.
3:19 and the *s* is freed from his master.
7: 2 Like a *s* longing for the evening
41: 4 for you to take him as your *s* for life
Ps 105: 17 Joseph, sold as a *s*.
Pr 12:24 but laziness ends in *s* labor.
19:10 worse for a *s* to rule over princes!
Jer 2:14 Is Israel a servant, a *s* by birth?
La 1: 1 has now become a *s*.
Na 2: 7 Its *s* girls moan like doves
Mt 20:27 wants to be first must be your *s*—
Mk 10:44 wants to be first must be *s* of all.
Jn 8:34 everyone who sins is a *s* to sin.
8:35 Now a *s* has no permanent place
Ac 7: 9 they sold him as a *s* into Egypt.
16:16 met by a *s* girl who had a spirit
16:19 of the *s* girl realized that their hope
Ro 7:14 I am unspiritual, sold as a *s* to sin.
7:25 in my mind am a *s* to God's law,
7:25 in the sinful nature a *s* to the law
8:15 a spirit that makes you a *s* again
1Co 7:21 Were you a *s* when you were called
7:22 For he who was a *s*
7:22 when he was called is Christ's *s*.
9:19 I make myself a *s* to everyone,
9:27 and make it my *s* so that
12:13 whether Jews or Greeks, *s* or free
Gal 3:28 *s* nor free, male nor female,
4: 1 he is no different from a *s*,
4: 7 So you are no longer a *s*, but a son;
4:22 one by the *s* woman and the other
4:23 His son by the *s* woman was born
4:30 Get rid of the *s* woman and her son
4:30 for the *s* woman's son will never
4:31 we are not children of the *s* woman
Eph 6: 8 good he does, whether he is *s*
Col 3:11 barbarian, Scythian, *s* or free,
1Ti 1:10 for *s* traders and liars and perjurers
Phm :16 no longer as a *s*, but better than a *s*,
2Pe 2:19 a man is a *s* to whatever has
Rev 6:15 and every *s* and every free man hid
13:16 and great, rich and poor, free and *s*,
19:18 free and *s*, small and great."

SLAVERY (SLAVE)

Ex 2:23 The Israelites groaned in their *s*
2:23 because of their *s* went up to God.
13: 3 out of Egypt, out of the land of *s*,
13:14 out of Egypt, out of the land of *s*.
20: 2 out of Egypt, out of the land of *s*.
Dt 5: 6 out of Egypt, out of the land of *s*.
6:12 out of Egypt, out of the land of *s*.
7: 8 redeemed you from the land of *s*,
8:14 out of Egypt, out of the land of *s*.
13: 5 redeemed you from the land of *s*;
13:10 out of Egypt, out of the land of *s*.
Jos 24:17 of *s*, and performed those great
Jdg 6: 8 out of Egypt, out of the land of *s*.
Ne 5: 5 subject our sons and daughters to *s*.
9:17 leader in order to return to their *s*.
Jer 34:13 out of Egypt, out of the land of *s*.
Mic 6: 4 redeemed you from the land of *s*.
Ro 6:19 parts of your body in *s* to impurity
6:19 them in *s* to righteousness leading
Gal 4: 3 were in *s* under the basic principles
4:25 she is in *s* with her children.
5: 1 be burdened again by a yoke of *s*.
1Ti 6: 1 of *s* should consider their masters
Heb 2:15 held in *s* by their fear of death.

SLAVES (SLAVE)

Ge 9:25 The lowest of *s*
15:14 punish the nation they serve as *s*,
20:14 and cattle and male and female *s*
43:18 seize us as *s* and take our donkeys
44: 9 rest of us will become my lord's *s*."
44:16 We are now my lord's *s*—
50:18 "We are your *s*," they said.
Ex 6: 6 I will free you from being *s* to them
9:20 the LORD hurried to bring their *s*
9:21 the word of the LORD left their *s*
Lev 25:42 they must not be sold as *s*.
25:44 and female *s* are to come
25:44 from them you may buy *s*.
25:46 and can make them *s* for life,
26:13 so that you would no longer be *s*
Dt 5:15 Remember that you were *s*
6:21 "We were *s* of Pharaoh in Egypt,
15:15 Remember that you were *s*
16:12 Remember that you were *s*
24:18 Remember that you were *s*
24:22 Remember that you were *s*
28:68 your enemies as male and female *s*,
1Sa 8:17 you yourselves will become his *s*.
1Ki 2:39 and Shimei was told, "Your *s* are
2:39 two of Shimei's *s* ran
2:40 and brought the *s* back from Gath.
2:40 to Achish at Gath in search of his *s*.
9:22 But Solomon did not make *s* of any
2Ki 4: 1 to take my two boys as his *s*."
2Ch 8: 9 But Solomon did not make *s*
28:10 of Judah and Jerusalem your *s*.
Ezr 9: 9 Though we are *s*, our God has not
Ne 9:36 we are *s* today, *s* in the land you
Est 7: 4 been sold as male and female *s*,
Ps 123: 2 As the eyes of *s* look to the hand
Ecc 2: 7 I bought male and female *s*
2: 7 and had other *s* who were born
10: 7 I have seen *s* on horseback,
10: 7 while princes go on foot like *s*.
Jer 34: 8 to proclaim freedom for the *s*.
34: 9 Everyone was to free his Hebrew *s*,
34:10 female *s* and no longer hold them
34:11 and took back the *s* they had freed
34:16 and female *s* you had set free
34:16 them to become your *s* again.
La 5: 8 *S* rule over us,
Eze 27:13 they exchanged *s* and articles
Zec 2: 9 so that their *s* will plunder them.
Jn 8:33 and have never been *s* of anyone.
Ac 7: 7 punish the nation they serve as *s*,'
Ro 6: 6 that we should no longer be *s* to sin
6:16 to someone to obey him as *s*,
6:16 you are *s* to sin, which leads
6:16 you are *s* to the one whom you
Ro 6:17 though you used to be *s* to sin,
6:18 have become *s* to righteousness.
6:20 When you were *s* to sin, you were
6:22 and have become *s* to God,
1Co 7:23 at a price; do not become *s* of men.
Gal 2: 4 in Christ Jesus and to make us *s*.
4: 8 you were *s* to those who
4:24 and bears children who are to be *s*:
Eph 6: 5 *S*, obey your earthly masters
6: 6 but like *s* of Christ, doing the will
6: 9 treat your *s* in the same way.
Col 3:22 *S*, obey your earthly masters
4: 1 provide your *s* with what is right
Tit 2: 9 Teach *s* to be subject
1Pe 2:18 *S*, submit yourselves
2Pe 2:19 while they themselves are *s*

SLAVING (SLAVE)

Lk 15:29 All these years I've been *s* for you

SLAY (SLAIN SLAYER SLAYS SLEW)

Ge 22:10 and took the knife to *s* his son.
Job 13:15 Though he *s* me, yet will I hope
Ps 34:21 Evil will *s* the wicked;
37:14 to *s* those whose ways are upright.
94: 6 They *s* the widow and the alien;
139: 19 If only you would *s* the wicked,
Isa 11: 4 of his lips he will *s* the wicked.
14:30 it will *s* your survivors.
27: 1 he will *s* the monster of the sea.
Jer 33: 5 of the men I will *s* in my anger
Eze 6: 4 and I will *s* your people in front
28: 9 in the hands of those who *s* you.
Hos 2: 3 and *s* her with thirst.
9:16 I will *s* their cherished offspring."
Am 9: 4 will command the sword to *s* them.
Rev 6: 4 and to make men *s* each other.

SLAYER (SLAY)

Eze 21:11 made ready for the hand of the *s*.
Hos 9:13 their children to the *s*."

SLAYS (SLAY)

Job 5: 2 and envy *s* the simple.

SLEDGE (SLEDGES)

Job 41:30 in the mud like a threshing *s*.
Isa 28:27 Caraway is not threshed with a *s*,
41:15 I will make you into a threshing *s*,

SLEDGES (SLEDGE)

2Sa 24:22 and here are threshing *s*
1Ch 21:23 the threshing *s* for the wood,
Am 1: 3 Gilead with *s* having iron teeth,

SLEEK

Ge 41: 2 *s* and fat, and they grazed
41: 4 and gaunt ate up the seven *s*,
41:18 *s*, and they grazed among the reeds
Dt 32:15 with food, he became heavy and *s*.
Jer 5:28 and have grown fat and *s*.
Eze 34:16 the *s* and the strong I will destroy.

SLEEP (ASLEEP SLEEPER SLEEPING SLEEPS SLEEPY SLEPT)

Ge 2:21 the man to fall into a deep *s*;
15:12 Abram fell into a deep *s*,
16: 2 Go, *s* with my maidservant;
28:11 it under his head and lay down to *s*.
28:16 When Jacob awoke from his *s*,
30: 3 *S* with her so that she can bear
30:15 he can *s* with you tonight in return
30:16 "You must *s* with me," she said.
31:40 at night, and *s* fled from my eyes.
38:16 what will you give me to *s* with you
38:16 "Come now, let me *s* with you."
38:26 And he did not *s* with her again.
39:14 He came in here to *s* with me,
Ex 22:27 What else will he *s*
Dt 24:12 do not go to *s* with his pledge
24:13 him by sunset so that he may *s* in it.
Jdg 16:14 from his *s* and pulled up the pin
16:19 Having put him to *s* on her lap,
16:20 He awoke from his *s* and thought,
1Sa 26:12 LORD had put them into a deep *s*.
2Sa 3: 7 "Why did you *s* with my father's
11:13 in the evening Uriah went out to *s*
Est 6: 1 That night the king could not *s*;

Job 4: 13 when deep *s* falls on men,
14: 12 or be roused from their *s*.
31: 10 and may other men *s* with her.
33: 15 when deep *s* falls on men
Ps 3: 5 I lie down and *s*;
4: 8 I will lie down and *s* in peace,
7: 5 and make me *s* in the dust.
13: 3 light to my eyes, or I will *s* in death;
44: 23 Awake, O Lord! Why do you *s*?
68: 13 while you *s* among the campfires,
76: 5 they *s* their last *s*;
78: 65 Then the Lord awoke as from *s*,
90: 5 You sweep men away in the *s*
121: 4 will neither slumber nor *s*.
127: 2 for he grants *s* to those he loves.
132: 4 I will allow no *s* to my eyes,
Pr 3: 24 lie down, your *s* will be sweet.
4: 16 For they cannot *s* till they do evil;
6: 4 Allow no *s* to your eyes,
6: 9 When will you get up from your *s*?
6: 10 A little *s*, a little slumber,
6: 22 when you *s*, they will watch
19: 15 Laziness brings on deep *s*,
20: 13 Do not love *s* or you will grow poor
24: 33 A little *s*, a little slumber,
Ecc 5: 12 The *s* of a laborer is sweet,
5: 12 permits him no *s*.
8: 16 his eyes not seeing *s* day or night—
Isa 29: 10 brought over you a deep *s*:
56: 10 they love to *s*.
Jer 31: 26 My *s* had been pleasant to me.
51: 39 then *s* forever and not awake,"
51: 57 they will *s* forever and not awake,"
Eze 23: 44 As men *s* with a prostitute,
34: 25 and *s* in the forests in safety.
Da 2: 1 was troubled and he could not *s*.
6: 18 And he could not *s*.
8: 18 I was in a deep *s*, with my face
10: 9 I fell into a deep *s*, my face
12: 2 Multitudes who *s* in the dust
Jnh 1: 5 lay down and fell into a deep *s*.
1: 6 "How can you *s*? Get up
Zec 4: 1 as a man is wakened from his *s*.
Jn 11: 13 thought he meant natural *s*.
Ac 20: 9 who was sinking into a deep *s*
1Co 15: 51 We will not all *s*, but we will all be
2Co 11: 27 and have often gone without *s*;
1Th 5: 7 For those who *s*, *s* at night,

SLEEPER (SLEEP)

Eph 5: 14 "Wake up, O *s*,

SLEEPING (SLEEP)

Ge 2: 21 and while he was *s*, he took one
Nu 5: 13 to him by *s* with another man,
5: 20 yourself by *s* with a man other
Dt 22: 22 If a man is found *s*
Jdg 16: 13 So while he was *s*, Delilah took
19: 4 eating and drinking, and *s* there.
1Sa 26: 12 They were all *s*,
1Ki 18: 27 Maybe he is *s* and must be
Pr 23: 34 You will be like one *s*
Mt 8: 24 But Jesus was *s*.
13: 25 But while everyone was *s*,
26: 40 to his disciples and found them *s*.
26: 43 he again found them *s*,
26: 45 "Are you still *s* and resting? Look,
Mk 4: 38 was in the stern, *s* on a cushion.
13: 36 suddenly, do not let him find you *s*.
14: 37 to his disciples and found them *s*.
14: 40 he again found them *s*,
14: 41 Are you still *s* and resting? Enough
Lk 22: 46 "Why are you *s*?" he asked them.
Ac 12: 6 Peter was *s* between two soldiers,
2Pe 2: 3 their destruction has not been *s*.

SLEEPLESS

2Co 6: 5 in hard work, *s* nights and hunger;

SLEEPS (SLEEP)

Ex 22: 16 to be married and *s* with her,
Lev 14: 47 Anyone who *s* or eats
19: 20 " 'If a man *s* with a woman who is
20: 11 " 'If a man *s* with his father's wife,
20: 12 If a man *s* with his daughter-in-law,
20: 20 " 'If a man *s* with his aunt,
Dt 22: 23 to be married and he *s* with her,
27: 20 "Cursed is the man who *s*
27: 22 "Cursed is the man who *s*
27: 23 "Cursed is the man who *s*
Pr 6: 29 is he who *s* with another man's wife
10: 5 he who *s* during harvest is
Isa 5: 27 not one slumbers or *s*;
Mk 4: 27 and day, whether he *s* or gets up,
Jn 11: 12 "Lord, if he *s*, he will get better."

SLEEPY (SLEEP)

Lk 9: 32 and his companions were very *s*,

SLEET

Ps 78: 47 and their sycamore-figs with *s*.

SLEPT (SLEEP)

Ge 16: 4 He *s* with Hagar, and she
19: 8 two daughters who have never *s*
26: 10 One of the men might well have *s*
30: 4 Jacob *s* with her, and she became
30: 16 So he *s* with her that night.
35: 22 and *s* with his father's concubine
38: 18 he gave them to her and *s* with her,
Nu 5: 19 "If no other man has *s* with you
31: 17 And kill every woman who has *s*
31: 18 every girl who has never *s*
31: 35 women who had never *s*
Dt 22: 22 both the man who *s* with her
Jdg 21: 12 young women who had never *s*
1Sa 2: 22 how they *s* with the women who
2Sa 11: 4 She came to him, and he *s* with her.
11: 9 But Uriah *s* at the entrance
12: 3 from his cup and even *s* in his arms.
SS 5: 2 I *s* but my heart was awake.
Eze 23: 8 during her youth men *s* with her,
23: 44 And they *s* with her.
23: 44 so they *s* with those lewd women,

SLEW (SLAY)

Ps 78: 34 Whenever God *s* them, they would

SLIGHTEST

Jude : 12 with you without the *s* qualm—

SLIME (SLIMY)

Job 9: 31 you would plunge me into a *s* pit

SLIMY (SLIME)

Ps 40: 2 He lifted me out of the *s* pit,

SLING (SLINGS SLUNG)

Jdg 20: 16 each of whom could *s* a stone
1Sa 17: 40 with his *s* in his hand, approached
17: 50 over the Philistine with a *s*
25: 29 as from the pocket of a *s*.
1Ch 12: 2 or to *s* stones right-handed
Pr 26: 8 Like tying a stone in a *s*

SLINGS (SLING)

2Ki 3: 25 men armed with *s* surrounded it

SLINGSTONES (STONE)

2Ch 26: 14 bows and *s* for the entire army.
Job 41: 28 *s* are like chaff to him.
Zec 9: 15 and overcome with *s*.

SLIP (SLIPPED SLIPPERY SLIPPING SLIPS)

Dt 4: 9 let them *s* from your heart as long
32: 35 In due time their foot will *s*;
1Sa 27: 1 and I will *s* out of his hand."
2Ki 9: 15 don't let anyone *s* out of the city
Ps 37: 31 his feet do not *s*.
121: 3 He will not let your foot *s*—
Jer 20: 10 are waiting for me to *s*, saying,

SLIPPED (SLIP)

2Sa 4: 6 and his brother Baanah *s* away.
Ps 17: 5 my feet have not *s*.
73: 2 But as for me, my feet had almost *s*;
Jn 5: 13 for Jesus had *s* away
2Co 11: 33 in the wall and *s* through his hands.
Jude : 4 about long ago have secretly *s*

SLIPPERY (SLIP)

Ps 35: 6 may their path be dark and *s*,
73: 18 Surely you place them on *s* ground;
Jer 23: 12 Therefore their path will become *s*;

SLIPPING (SLIP)

Job 12: 5 as the fate of those whose feet are *s*.
Ps 66: 9 and kept our feet from *s*.
94: 18 When I said, "My foot is *s*,"
Jn 8: 59 *s* away from the temple grounds.

SLIPS (SLIP)

Ps 38: 16 over me when my foot *s*."

SLOPE (SLOPES)

Jos 15: 8 Hinnom along the southern *s*
15: 10 ran along the northern *s*
15: 11 It went to the northern *s* of Ekron,
18: 12 passed the northern *s* of Jericho
18: 13 to the south *s* of Luz (that is,
18: 16 Valley along the southern *s*
18: 18 to the northern *s* of Beth Arabah
18: 19 to the northern *s* of Beth Hoglah
Mic 1: 4 like water rushing down a *s*.

SLOPES (SLOPE)

Nu 21: 15 and the *s* of the ravines
34: 11 continue along the *s* east of the Sea
Dt 3: 17 below the *s* of Pisgah.
4: 49 below the *s* of Pisgah.
33: 2 from his mountain *s*.
Jos 7: 5 and struck them down on the *s*.
10: 40 foothills and the mountain *s*,
12: 3 southward below the *s* of Pisgah.
12: 8 the Arabah, the mountain *s*,
13: 20 Beth Peor, the *s* of Pisgah,
Isa 11: 14 down on the *s* of Philistia
Jer 18: 14 ever vanish from its rocky *s*?

SLOW (SLOWNESS)

Ex 4: 10 I am *s* of speech and tongue."
34: 6 and gracious God, *s* to anger,
Nu 14: 18 you have declared: 'The LORD is *s*
Dt 7: 10 he will not be *s* to repay
23: 21 the LORD your God, do not be *s*
2Ki 4: 24 don't *s* down for me unless I tell
Ne 9: 17 *s* to anger and abounding in love.
Ps 86: 15 *s* to anger, abounding in love
103: 8 *s* to anger, abounding in love.
145: 8 *s* to anger and rich in love.
Joel 2: 13 *s* to anger and abounding in love,
Jnh 4: 2 *s* to anger and abounding in love,
Na 1: 3 The LORD is *s* to anger
Lk 24: 25 how *s* of heart to believe all that
Ac 27: 7 We made *s* headway for many days
Heb 5: 11 hard to explain because you are *s*
Jas 1: 19 *s* to speak and *s* to become angry,
2Pe 3: 9 The Lord is not *s* in keeping his

SLOWNESS (SLOW)

2Pe 3: 9 his promise, as some understand *s*.

SLUG

Ps 58: 8 Like a *s* melting away as it moves

SLUGGARD (SLUGGARD'S)

Pr 6: 6 Go to the ant, you *s*;
6: 9 How long will you lie there, you *s*?
10: 26 so is a *s* to those who send him.
13: 4 The *s* craves and gets nothing,
15: 19 The way of the *s* is blocked
19: 24 The *s* buries his hand in the dish;
20: 4 A *s* does not plow in season;
22: 13 The *s* says, "There is a lion outside
24: 30 I went past the field of the *s*,
26: 13 The *s* says, "There is a lion
26: 14 so a *s* turns on his bed.
26: 15 The *s* buries his hand in the dish;
26: 16 The *s* is wiser in his own eyes

SLUGGARD'S (SLUGGARD)

Pr 21: 25 The *s* craving will be the death

SLUMBER (SLUMBERS)

Job 33: 15 as they *s* in their beds,
Ps 121: 3 he who watches over you will not *s*;
121: 4 will neither *s* nor sleep.
132: 4 no *s* to my eyelids,
Pr 4: 16 they are robbed of *s*
6: 4 no *s* to your eyelids.
6: 10 A little sleep, a little *s*,
24: 33 A little sleep, a little *s*,
Na 3: 18 of Assyria, your shepherds *s*;

Ro 13: 11 for you to wake up from your *s*.

SLUMBERS (SLUMBER)

Isa 5: 27 not one *s* or sleeps;

SLUMPED

2Ki 9: 24 and he *s* down in his chariot.

SLUNG (SLING)

1Sa 17: 6 a bronze javelin was *s* on his back.
17: 49 he *s* it and struck the Philistine

SLUR

Ps 15: 3 and casts no *s* on his fellow man,

SLY

Pr 25: 23 so a *s* tongue brings angry looks.
Mt 26: 4 to arrest Jesus in some *s* way
Mk 14: 1 for some *s* way to arrest Jesus

SMASH (SMASHED SMASHES)

Ex 34: 13 *s* their sacred stones and cut
Dt 7: 5 down their altars, *s* their sacred
12: 3 *s* their sacred stones and burn their
Jer 13: 14 I will *s* them one against the other,
19: 11 I will *s* this nation and this city just
48: 12 and *s* her jugs.
Am 6: 11 he will *s* the great house into pieces

SMASHED (SMASH)

Jdg 7: 20 blew the trumpets and *s* the jars.
2Ki 11: 18 They *s* the altars and idols to pieces
18: 4 *s* the sacred stones and cut
23: 12 *s* them to pieces and threw
23: 14 Josiah *s* the sacred stones
2Ch 14: 3 *s* the sacred stones and cut
23: 17 They *s* the altars and idols
31: 1 *s* the sacred stones and cut
34: 4 and *s* the Asherah poles, the idols
Ps 74: 6 They *s* all the carved paneling
Jer 19: 11 this potter's jar is *s* and cannot be
Eze 6: 4 and your incense altars will be *s*;
6: 6 your idols *s* and ruined, your
Da 2: 34 feet of iron and clay and *s* them.

SMASHES (SMASH)

Da 2: 40 for iron breaks and *s* everything—

SMEAR (SMEARED)

Job 13: 4 You, however, *s* me with lies;

SMEARED (SMEAR)

Ps 119: 69 Though the arrogant have *s* me

SMELL (SMELLED)

Ge 27: 27 When Isaac caught the *s*
27: 27 is like the *s* of a field
27: 27 "Ah, the *s* of my son
Ex 16: 20 full of maggots and began to *s*.
Dt 4: 28 which cannot see or hear or eat or *s*
Ps 115: 6 noses, but they cannot *s*;
Ecc 10: 1 As dead flies give perfume a bad *s*,
Da 3: 27 and there was no *s* of fire on them.
Joel 2: 20 its *s* will rise."
1Co 12: 17 where would the sense of *s* be?
2Co 2: 16 To the one we are the *s* of death;

SMELLED (SMELL)

Ge 8: 21 The LORD *s* the pleasing aroma
Ex 7: 21 river *s* so bad that the Egyptians

SMELTED

Job 28: 2 and copper is *s* from ore.

SMILE (SMILED)

Job 9: 27 I will change my expression, and *s*,'
10: 3 while you *s* on the schemes

SMILED (SMILE)

Job 29: 24 When I *s* at them, they scarcely

SMITE (SMITTEN)

Dt 33: 11 *S* the loins of those who rise up

SMITTEN (SMITE)

Isa 53: 4 *s* by him, and afflicted.

SMOKE (SMOKING)

Ge 19: 28 from the land, like *s* from a furnace
19: 28 he saw dense *s* rising from the land,
Ex 19: 18 Mount Sinai was covered with *s*,
19: 18 The *s* billowed up from it like *s*
20: 18 and saw the mountain in *s*,
Lev 16: 13 the *s* of the incense will conceal
Jos 8: 20 and saw the *s* of the city rising
8: 21 that *s* was going up from the city,
Jdg 20: 38 should send up a great cloud of *s*
20: 40 saw the *s* of the whole city going up
20: 40 when the column of *s* began to rise
2Sa 22: 9 *S* rose from his nostrils;
Job 41: 20 *S* pours from his nostrils
Ps 18: 8 *S* rose from his nostrils;
37: 20 they will vanish—vanish like *s*.
68: 2 As *s* is blown away by the wind,
102: 3 For my days vanish like *s*;
104: 32 touches the mountains, and they *s*.
119: 83 I am like a wineskin in the *s*,
144: 5 touch the mountains, so that they *s*
Pr 10: 26 to the teeth and *s* to the eyes,
SS 3: 6 like a column of *s*,
Isa 4: 5 who assemble there a cloud of *s*
6: 4 and the temple was filled with *s*.
9: 18 it rolls upward in a column of *s*.
14: 31 A cloud of *s* comes from the north,
30: 27 anger and dense clouds of *s*;
34: 10 its *s* will rise forever.
51: 6 the heavens will vanish like *s*,
65: 5 Such people are *s* in my nostrils,
Hos 13: 3 like *s* escaping through a window.
Joel 2: 30 blood and fire and billows of *s*.
Na 2: 13 "I will burn up your chariots in *s*,
Ac 2: 19 blood and fire and billows of *s*.
Rev 8: 4 The *s* of the incense, together
9: 2 darkened by the *s* from the Abyss.
9: 2 *s* rose from it like the *s*
9: 3 And out of the *s* locusts came
9: 17 and out of their mouths came fire, *s*
9: 18 *s* and sulfur that came out
14: 11 the *s* of their torment rises for ever
15: 8 filled with *s* from the glory
18: 9 and shared her luxury see the *s*
18: 18 When they see the *s* of her burning,
19: 3 The *s* from her goes up for ever

SMOKING (SMOKE)

Ge 15: 17 a *s* fire pot with a blazing torch

SMOLDER (SMOLDERING SMOLDERS)

Ps 74: 1 Why does your anger *s*
80: 4 how long will your anger *s*

SMOLDERING (SMOLDER)

Nu 16: 37 the censers out of the *s* remains
Isa 7: 4 of these two *s* stubs of firewood—
42: 3 and a *s* wick he will not snuff out.
Mt 12: 20 and a *s* wick he will not snuff out,

SMOLDERS (SMOLDER)

Hos 7: 6 Their passion *s* all night;

SMOOTH-SKINNED (SKIN)

Isa 18: 2 to a people tall and *s*,
18: 7 Almighty from a people tall and *s*,

SMYRNA

Rev 1: 11 to Ephesus, *S*, Pergamum,
2: 8 the angel of the church in *S* write:

SNAKE (SNAKES)

Ex 4: 3 it on the ground and it became a *s*,
4: 4 reached out and took hold of the *s*
7: 9 Pharaoh,' and it will become a *s*."
7: 10 and his officials, and it became a *s*.
7: 12 down his staff and it became a *s*.
7: 15 the staff that was changed into a *s*.
Nu 21: 8 "Make a *s* and put it up on a pole;
21: 9 So Moses made a bronze *s*
21: 9 and looked at the bronze *s*,
21: 9 when anyone was bitten by a *s*
2Ki 18: 4 pieces the bronze *s* Moses had
Ps 58: 4 venom is like the venom of a *s*,
Pr 23: 32 In the end it bites like a *s*
30: 19 the way of a *s* on a rock,
Ecc 10: 8 through a wall may be bitten by a *s*.
10: 11 If a *s* bites before it is charmed,
Isa 14: 29 root of that *s* will spring up a viper,
Am 5: 19 only to have a *s* bite him.
Mic 7: 17 They will lick dust like a *s*,
Mt 7: 10 will give him a *s*? If you, then,
Lk 11: 11 will give him a *s* instead?
Jn 3: 14 Moses lifted up the *s* in the desert,
Ac 28: 4 the islanders saw the *s* hanging
28: 5 Paul shook the *s* off into the fire

SNAKES (SNAKE)

Nu 21: 6 Then the LORD sent venomous *s*
21: 7 that the LORD will take the *s* away
Dt 8: 15 with its venomous *s* and scorpions.
Isa 30: 6 of adders and darting *s*,
Jer 8: 17 I will send venomous *s* among you,
Mt 10: 16 as shrewd as *s* and as innocent
23: 33 "You *s*! You brood of vipers!
Mk 16: 18 they will pick up *s* with their hands;
Lk 10: 19 given you authority to trample on *s*
1Co 10: 9 of them did—and were killed by *s*.
Rev 9: 19 their tails were like *s*, having heads

SNAPPED (SNAPS)

Jdg 16: 9 But he *s* the thongs as easily
16: 12 But he *s* the ropes off his arms
Jer 10: 20 all its ropes are *s*.

SNAPS (SNAPPED)

Jdg 16: 9 of string *s* when it comes close

SNARE (ENSNARE ENSNARED SNARED SNARES)

Ex 10: 7 How long will this man be a *s* to us?
23: 33 gods will certainly be a *s*
34: 12 or they will be a *s* among you.
Dt 7: 16 for that will be a *s* to you.
Jdg 2: 3 and their gods will be a *s* to you."
8: 27 and it became a *s* to Gideon
1Sa 18: 21 "so that she may be a *s* to him
Job 18: 9 a *s* holds him fast.
Ps 25: 15 he will release my feet from the *s*.
69: 22 before them become a *s*;
91: 3 from the fowler's *s*
106: 36 which became a *s* to them.
119: 110 The wicked have set a *s* for me,
124: 7 out of the fowler's *s*;
124: 7 the *s* has been broken,
140: 5 Proud men have hidden a *s* for me;
142: 3 men have hidden a *s* for me.
Pr 6: 5 like a bird from the *s* of the fowler.
7: 23 like a bird darting into a *s*,
18: 7 and his lips are a *s* to his soul.
21: 6 is a fleeting vapor and a deadly *s*.
29: 25 Fear of man will prove to be a *s*,
Ecc 7: 26 the woman who is a *s*,
9: 12 or birds are taken in a *s*,
Isa 8: 14 a trap and a *s*.
24: 17 Terror and pit and *s* await you,
24: 18 will be caught in a *s*.
Jer 5: 26 who lie in wait like men who *s* birds
48: 43 Terror and pit and *s* await you,
48: 44 will be caught in a *s*;
Eze 12: 13 and he will be caught in my *s*;
17: 20 and he will be caught in my *s*.
Hos 5: 1 You have been a *s* at Mizpah,
Am 3: 5 where no *s* has been set?
Ro 11: 9 "May their table become a *s*

SNARED (SNARE)

Pr 3: 26 will keep your foot from being *s*.
29: 6 An evil man is *s* by his own sin,
Isa 8: 15 they will be *s* and captured."
28: 13 be injured and *s* and captured.

SNARES (SNARE)

Jos 23: 13 they will become *s* and traps
2Sa 22: 6 the *s* of death confronted me.
Job 22: 10 That is why *s* are all around you,
30: 12 they lay *s* for my feet,
34: 30 from laying *s* for the people.
Ps 18: 5 the *s* of death confronted me.
64: 5 they talk about hiding their *s*;
141: 9 Keep me from the *s* they have laid
Pr 13: 14 turning a man from the *s* of death.
14: 27 turning a man from the *s* of death.
22: 5 of the wicked lie thorns and *s*,
Jer 18: 22 and have hidden *s* for my feet.
Hos 9: 8 yet *s* await him on all his paths,

Lk 14: 35 It is fit neither for the *s*

SOILED (SOIL)

Rev 3: 4 Sardis who have not *s* their clothes.

SOLD (SELL)

Ge 31: 15 as foreigners? Not only has he *s* us,
37: 28 *s* him for twenty shekels of silver
37: 36 the Midianites *s* Joseph in Egypt
41: 56 and *s* grain to the Egyptians,
42: 6 the one who *s* grain to all its people
45: 4 the one you *s* into Egypt! And now
47: 20 one and all, *s* their fields,
Ex 22: 3 he must be *s* to pay for his theft.
Lev 25: 23 land must not be *s* permanently,
25: 25 redeem what his countryman has *s*.
25: 27 balance to the man to whom he *s* it;
25: 27 the value for the years since he *s* it
25: 28 what he *s* will remain
25: 33 a house *s* in any town they hold—
25: 34 to their towns must not be *s;*
25: 42 they must not be *s* as slaves.
25: 48 redemption after he has *s* himself.
25: 50 time from the year he *s* himself up
27: 20 or if he has *s* it to someone else,
27: 27 is to be *s* at its set value.
27: 28 or family land—may be *s*
Dt 15: 12 is *s* to you and he serves you six
32: 30 unless their Rock had *s* them,
Jdg 2: 14 He *s* them to their enemies all
3: 8 so that he *s* them into the hands
4: 2 the LORD *s* them into the hands
10: 7 He *s* them into the hands
1Sa 12: 9 so he *s* them into the hand of Sisera
1Ki 21: 20 you have *s* yourself to do evil
21: 25 who *s* himself to do evil in the eyes
2Ki 6: 25 so long that a donkey's head *s*
7: 16 So a seah of flour *s* for a shekel,
7: 16 two seahs of barley *s* for a shekel,
17: 17 *s* themselves to do evil in the eyes
Ne 5: 8 only for them to be *s* back to us!"
5: 8 our Jewish brothers who were *s*
Est 7: 4 If we had merely been *s* as male
7: 4 and my people have been *s*
Ps 44: 12 You *s* your people for a pittance,
105: 17 Joseph, *s* as a slave.
Isa 50: 1 Because of your sins you were *s;*
52: 3 "You were *s* for nothing,
Jer 34: 14 fellow Hebrew who has *s* himself
Eze 7: 13 will not recover the land he has *s*
Hos 8: 9 Ephraim has *s* herself to lovers.
8: 10 Although they have *s* themselves
Joel 3: 3 they *s* girls for wine
3: 6 You *s* the people of Judah
3: 7 of the places to which you *s* them,
Am 1: 6 and *s* them to Edom,
1: 9 Because she *s* whole communities
Mt 10: 29 Are not two sparrows *s* for a penny
13: 44 then in his joy went and *s* all he had
13: 46 went away and *s* everything he had
18: 25 and all that he had be *s*
26: 9 "This perfume could have been *s*
Mk 14: 5 It could have been *s* for more
Lk 12: 6 Are not five sparrows *s*
Jn 2: 16 To those who *s* doves he said,
12: 5 "Why wasn't this perfume *s*
Ac 4: 34 who owned lands or houses *s* them,
4: 37 *s* a field he owned and brought
5: 1 his wife Sapphira, also *s* a piece
5: 4 after it was *s*, wasn't the money
5: 4 belong to you before it was *s?*
7: 9 they *s* him as a slave into Egypt.
Ro 7: 14 I am unspiritual, *s* as a slave to sin.
1Co 10: 25 Eat anything *s* in the meat market
Heb 12: 16 a single meal *s* his inheritance
Rev 18: 15 The merchants who *s* these things

SOLDIER (SOLDIERS)

Nu 31: 53 Each *s* had taken plunder
1Sa 13: 22 day of the battle not a *s* with Saul
2Sa 17: 10 the bravest *s*, whose heart is like
2Ki 5: 1 He was a valiant *s*, but he had
2Ch 17: 17 Eliada, a valiant *s*, with 200,000
Am 2: 15 the fleet-footed *s* will not get away,
Ac 28: 16 by himself, with a *s* to guard him.
1Co 9: 7 as a *s* at his own expense?
Php 2: 25 fellow worker and fellow *s*,
2Ti 2: 3 with us like a good *s* of Christ Jesus
2Ti 2: 4 a *s* gets involved in civilian affairs
Phm : 2 to Archippus our fellow *s*

SOLDIERS (SOLDIER)

Nu 31: 21 to the *s* who had gone into battle,
31: 27 spoils between the *s* who took part
31: 28 From the *s* who fought in the battle
31: 32 spoils that the *s* took was 675,000
31: 49 "Your servants have counted the *s*
Jos 8: 13 They had the *s* take up their
17: 1 because the Makirites were great *s*.
Jdg 9: 35 his *s* came out from their hiding
20: 2 four hundred thousand *s* armed
20: 16 Among all these *s* there were seven
1Sa 4: 3 When the *s* returned to camp,
4: 10 Israel lost thirty thousand foot *s*.
13: 5 and *s* as numerous as the sand
14: 28 Then one of the *s* told him,
15: 4 two hundred thousand foot *s*
15: 15 "The *s* brought them
15: 21 The *s* took sheep and cattle
26: 7 and the *s* were lying around him.
2Sa 3: 23 and all the *s* with him arrived,
8: 4 and twenty thousand foot *s*.
10: 6 twenty thousand Aramean foot *s*
10: 18 and forty thousand of their foot *s*.
11: 7 how the *s* were and how the war
1Ki 20: 29 on the Aramean foot *s* in one day.
2Ki 13: 7 chariots and ten thousand foot *s*,
25: 5 All his *s* were separated from him
1Ch 12: 33 experienced *s* prepared for battle
12: 36 experienced *s* prepared for battle—
18: 4 and twenty thousand foot *s*.
19: 18 and forty thousand of their foot *s*.
2Ch 28: 6 and twenty thousand *s* in Judah—
28: 14 So the *s* gave up the prisoners
Ezr 8: 22 I was ashamed to ask the king for *s*
Jer 38: 4 is discouraging the *s* who are left
39: 4 of Judah and all the *s* saw them,
41: 3 the Babylonian *s* who were there.
41: 16 the *s*, women, children
49: 26 all her *s* will be silenced in that day
50: 30 all her *s* will be silenced in that day
51: 32 and the *s* terrified."
52: 8 All his *s* were separated from him
Eze 27: 10 served as *s* in your army.
27: 27 your merchants and all your *s*,
39: 20 mighty men and *s* of every kind,'
Da 3: 20 some of the strongest *s* in his army
Joel 2: 7 they scale walls like *s*.
Na 2: 3 The shields of his *s* are red;
Mt 8: 9 under authority, with *s* under me.
27: 27 Then the governor's *s* took Jesus
27: 27 gathered the whole company of *s*
28: 12 they gave the *s* a large sum
28: 15 So the *s* took the money and did
Mk 15: 16 The *s* led Jesus away
15: 16 together the whole company of *s*.
Lk 3: 14 Then some *s* asked him,
7: 8 under authority, with *s* under me.
23: 11 Then Herod and his *s* ridiculed
23: 36 *s* also came up and mocked him.
Jn 18: 3 guiding a detachment of *s*
18: 12 Then the detachment of *s*
19: 2 The *s* twisted together a crown
19: 16 So the *s* took charge of Jesus.
19: 23 When the *s* crucified Jesus,
19: 24 So this is what the *s* did.
19: 32 *s* therefore came and broke the legs
19: 34 one of the *s* pierced Jesus' side
Ac 10: 7 one of his *s* who was a devout man.
12: 4 by four squads of four *s* each.
12: 6 Peter was sleeping between two *s*,
12: 18 a great commotion among the *s*.
21: 32 and *s* and ran down to the crowd.
21: 32 saw the commander and his *s*,
21: 35 had to be carried by the *s*.
21: 37 As the *s* were about to take Paul
23: 23 a detachment of two hundred *s*,
23: 31 So the *s*, carrying out their orders,
27: 31 Paul said to the centurion and the *s*
27: 32 So the *s* cut the ropes that held
27: 42 The *s* planned to kill the prisoners

SOLE (SOLES)

Dt 28: 56 the ground with the *s* of her foot—
28: 65 place for the *s* of your foot.
2Sa 14: 25 the top of his head to the *s*
Isa 1: 6 From the *s* of your foot to the top

SOLEMN

Ge 50: 11 are holding a *s* ceremony
Jos 6: 26 Joshua pronounced this *s* oath:
Jdg 21: 5 they had taken a *s* oath that anyone
Eze 16: 8 I gave you my *s* oath and entered
Ac 23: 14 "We have taken a *s* oath not

SOLES (SOLE)

Dt 28: 35 spreading from the *s* of your feet
2Ki 19: 24 With the *s* of my feet
Job 2: 7 sores from the *s* of his feet
13: 27 marks on the *s* of my feet.
Isa 37: 25 With the *s* of my feet
Eze 43: 7 and the place for the *s* of my feet.
Mal 4: 3 ashes under the *s* of your feet

SOLID

Nu 4: 6 spread a cloth of *s* blue over that
2Ch 4: 21 lamps and tongs (they were *s* gold);
Zec 4: 2 "I see a *s* gold lampstand
1Co 3: 2 I gave you milk, not *s* food,
2Ti 2: 19 God's *s* foundation stands firm,
Heb 5: 12 You need milk, not *s* food!
5: 14 But *s* food is for the mature,

SOLITARY

Lev 16: 22 on itself all their sins to a *s* place;
Mt 14: 13 by boat privately to a *s* place.
Mk 1: 35 the house and went off to a *s* place,
6: 32 by themselves in a boat to a *s* place.
Lk 4: 42 Jesus went out to a *s* place.
8: 29 driven by the demon into *s* places.

SOLOMON (SOLOMON'S)

2Sa 5: 14 Shobab, Nathan, *S*, Ibhar, Elishua,
12: 24 to a son, and they named him *S*.
1Ki 1: 10 the special guard or his brother *S*.
1: 12 own life and the life of your son *S*.
1: 13 "Surely *S* your son shall be king
1: 17 '*S* your son shall be king after me,
1: 19 he has not invited *S* your servant.
1: 21 I and my son *S* will be treated
1: 26 your servant *S* he did not invite.
1: 30 *S* your son shall be king after me,
1: 33 and set *S* my son on my own mule
1: 34 and shout, 'Long live King *S!*'
1: 37 be with *S* to make his throne
1: 38 and put *S* on King David's mule
1: 39 the sacred tent and anointed *S*.
1: 39 "Long live King *S!*" And all
1: 43 lord King David has made *S* king.
1: 46 *S* has taken his seat
1: 50 But Adonijah, in fear of *S*,
1: 51 'Let King *S* swear to me today that
1: 51 *S* was told, "Adonijah is afraid
1: 51 "Adonijah is afraid of King *S*
1: 52 *S* replied, "If he shows himself
1: 53 Then King *S* sent men,
1: 53 and bowed down to King *S*,
1: 53 and *S* said, "Go to your home."
2: 1 he gave a charge to *S* his son.
2: 12 So *S* sat on the throne
2: 17 "Please ask King *S*— he will not
2: 19 went to King *S* to speak to him
2: 22 King *S* answered his mother,
2: 23 Then King *S* swore by the LORD:
2: 25 King *S* gave orders to Benaiah son
2: 27 So *S* removed Abiathar
2: 29 King *S* was told that Joab had fled
2: 29 *S* ordered Benaiah son of Jehoiada,
2: 41 When *S* was told that Shimei had
2: 45 But King *S* will be blessed,
3: 1 *S* made an alliance
3: 3 *S* showed his love for the LORD
3: 4 and *S* offered a thousand burnt
3: 5 appeared to *S* during the night
3: 6 *S* answered, "You have shown
3: 10 Lord was pleased that *S* had asked
3: 15 *S* awoke—and he realized it had
4: 1 So King *S* ruled over all Israel.
4: 7 *S* also had twelve district
4: 11 married to Taphath daughter of *S);*
4: 15 married Basemath daughter of *S);*
4: 21 And *S* ruled over all the kingdoms
4: 26 *S* had four thousand stalls
4: 27 supplied provisions for King *S*

1Ki 4:29 God gave *S* wisdom and very great
5: 1 Tyre heard that *S* had been
5: 1 he sent his envoys to *S*,
5: 2 *S* sent back this message to Hiram:
5: 8 to *S*: "I have received the message
5:10 In this way Hiram kept *S* supplied
5:11 and *S* gave Hiram twenty thousand
5:11 *S* continued to do this
5:12 The LORD gave *S* wisdom,
5:12 relations between Hiram and *S*,
5:13 King *S* conscripted laborers
5:15 *S* had seventy thousand carriers
5:18 The craftsmen of *S* and Hiram
6: 2 The temple that King *S* built
6:11 The word of the LORD came to *S*:
6:14 *S* built the temple and completed it
6:21 *S* covered the inside of the temple
7: 1 It took *S* thirteen years, however,
7: 8 *S* also made a palace like this hall
7:13 King *S* sent to Tyre and brought
7:14 to King *S* and did all the work
7:40 for King *S* in the temple
7:45 made for King *S* for the temple
7:47 *S* left all these things unweighed,
7:48 *S* also made all the furnishings that
7:51 When all the work King *S* had done
8: 1 Then King *S* summoned
8: 2 together to King *S* at the time
8: 5 and King *S* and, with him,
8:12 *S* said, "The LORD has said that
8:22 Then *S* stood before the altar
8:54 When *S* had finished all these
8:63 *S* offered a sacrifice
8:65 *S* observed the festival at that time,
9: 1 When *S* had finished building
9:10 during which *S* built these two
9:11 King *S* gave twenty towns
9:12 see the towns that *S* had given him,
9:15 forced labor King *S* conscripted
9:17 And *S* rebuilt Gezer.)
9:21 these *S* conscripted
9:22 But *S* did not make slaves of any
9:24 to the palace *S* had built for her,
9:25 times a year *S* sacrificed burnt
9:26 King *S* also built ships
9:28 which they delivered to King *S*.
10: 1 of Sheba heard about the fame of *S*
10: 2 she came to *S* and talked
10: 3 *S* answered all her questions;
10: 4 of Sheba saw all the wisdom of *S*
10:10 the queen of Sheba gave to King *S*.
10:13 King *S* gave the queen
10:14 the gold that *S* received yearly was
10:16 King *S* made two hundred large
10:23 King *S* was greater in riches
10:24 world sought audience with *S*
10:26 *S* accumulated chariots and horses;
11: 1 King *S*, however, loved many
11: 2 *S* held fast to them in love.
11: 4 As *S* grew old, his wives turned his
11: 6 *S* did evil in the eyes of the LORD;
11: 7 *S* built a high place
11: 9 The LORD became angry with *S*
11:10 Although he had forbidden *S*
11:10 *S* did not keep the LORD's
11:11 to *S*, "Since this is your attitude
11:14 up against *S* an adversary,
11:23 up against *S* another adversary,
11:25 adversary as long as *S* lived,
11:27 *S* had built the supporting terraces
11:28 when *S* saw how well the young
11:40 *S* tried to kill Jeroboam,
11:41 in the book of the annals of *S*?
11:42 *S* reigned in Jerusalem
12: 2 where he had fled from King *S*),
12: 6 elders who had served his father *S*
12:21 kingdom for Rehoboam son of *S*.
12:23 son of *S* king of Judah,
14:21 Rehoboam son of *S* was king
14:26 all the gold shields *S* had made.
2Ki 21: 7 said to David and to his son *S*,
23:13 the ones *S* king of Israel had built
24:13 all the gold articles that *S* king
25:16 which *S* had made for the temple
1Ch 3: 5 Shammua, Shobab, Nathan and *S*.
6:10 in the temple *S* built in Jerusalem),
6:32 until *S* built the temple
14: 4 Shobab, Nathan, *S*, Ibhar, Elishua,
1Ch 18: 8 which *S* used to make the bronze
22: 5 "My son *S* is young
22: 6 Then he called for his son *S*
22: 7 David said to *S*: "My son,
22: 9 His name will be *S*, and I will grant
22:17 leaders of Israel to help his son *S*.
23: 1 he made his son *S* king over Israel.
28: 5 he has chosen my son *S* to sit
28: 6 '*S* your son is the one who will
28: 9 my son *S*, acknowledge the God
28:11 David gave his son *S* the plans
28:20 David also said to *S* his son,
29: 1 "My son *S*, the one whom God has
29:19 give my son *S* the wholehearted
29:22 they acknowledged *S* son of David
29:23 *S* sat on the throne of the LORD
29:24 pledged their submission to King *S*.
29:25 The LORD highly exalted *S*
29:28 His son *S* succeeded him as king.
2Ch 1: 1 *S* son of David established himself
1: 2 Then *S* spoke to all Israel—
1: 3 and *S* and the whole assembly went
1: 5 so *S* and the assembly inquired
1: 6 *S* went up to the bronze altar
1: 7 That night God appeared to *S*
1: 8 *S* answered God, "You have
1:11 said to *S*, "Since this is your heart's
1:13 Then *S* went to Jerusalem
1:14 *S* accumulated chariots and horses;
2: 1 *S* gave orders to build a temple
2: 3 *S* sent this message to Hiram king
2:11 king of Tyre replied by letter to *S*:
2:17 *S* took a census of all the aliens
3: 1 Then *S* began to build the temple
3: 3 The foundation *S* laid
4:11 for King *S* in the temple of God:
4:16 made for King *S* for the temple
4:18 these things that *S* made amounted
4:19 *S* also made all the furnishings that
5: 1 When all the work *S* had done
5: 2 Then *S* summoned to Jerusalem
5: 6 and King *S* and the entire assembly
6: 1 *S* said, "The LORD has said that
6:12 Then *S* stood before the altar
7: 1 When *S* finished praying, fire came
7: 5 And King *S* offered a sacrifice
7: 7 *S* consecrated the middle part
7: 8 *S* observed the festival at that time
7:10 and *S* and for his people Israel.
7:11 When *S* had finished the temple
8: 1 during which *S* built the temple
8: 2 *S* rebuilt the villages that Hiram
8: 3 *S* then went to Hamath Zobah
8: 8 these *S* conscripted
8: 9 But *S* did not make slaves
8:11 *S* brought Pharaoh's daughter up
8:12 *S* sacrificed burnt offerings
8:17 Then *S* went to Ezion Geber
8:18 which they delivered to King *S*.
9: 1 she came to *S* and talked
9: 2 *S* answered all her questions;
9: 3 of Sheba saw the wisdom of *S*,
9: 9 the queen of Sheba gave to King *S*.
9:10 and the men of *S* brought gold
9:12 King *S* gave the queen
9:13 the gold that *S* received yearly was
9:14 land brought gold and silver to *S*.
9:15 King *S* made two hundred large
9:22 King *S* was greater in riches
9:23 of the earth sought audience with *S*
9:25 *S* had four thousand stalls
9:30 *S* reigned in Jerusalem
10: 2 where he had fled from King *S*),
10: 6 elders who had served his father *S*
11: 3 son of *S* king of Judah
11:17 Rehoboam son of *S* three years,
11:17 of David and *S* during this time.
12: 9 the gold shields *S* had made.
13: 6 an official of *S* son of David,
13: 7 and opposed Rehoboam son of *S*
30:26 for since the days of *S* son
33: 7 said to David and to his son *S*,
35: 3 ark in the temple that *S* son
35: 4 king of Israel and by his son *S*.
Ezr 2:55 descendants of the servants of *S*:
2:58 of *S* 392 The following came up
Ne 7:57 descendants of the servants of *S*:
7:60 of *S* 392 The following came up
Ne 12:45 commands of David and his son *S*.
13:26 of marriages like these that *S* king
Pr 1: 1 The proverbs of *S* son of David,
10: 1 The proverbs of *S*:
25: 1 These are more proverbs of *S*,
SS 1: 5 like the tent curtains of *S*.
3: 9 King *S* made for himself
3:11 look at King *S* wearing the crown,
8:11 *S* had a vineyard in Baal Hamon;
8:12 thousand shekels are for you, O *S*,
Jer 52:20 which King *S* had made
Mt 1: 6 David was the father of *S*,
1: 7 *S* the father of Rehoboam,
6:29 *S* in all his splendor was dressed
12:42 and now one greater than *S* is here.
Lk 11:31 and now one greater than *S* is here.
12:27 *S* in all his splendor was dressed
Ac 7:47 it was *S* who built the house for him

SOLOMON'S (SOLOMON)

1Ki 1:11 Nathan asked Bathsheba, *S* mother
1:47 your God make *S* name more
2:13 went to Bathsheba, *S* mother.
2:46 now firmly established in *S* hands.
4:21 and were *S* subjects all his life.
4:22 *S* daily provisions were thirty cors
4:25 During *S* lifetime Judah and Israel,
4:30 *S* wisdom was greater
4:34 came to listen to *S* wisdom,
5: 7 When Hiram heard *S* message,
6: 1 year of *S* reign over Israel,
9:16 gift to his daughter, *S* wife.
9:23 officials in charge of *S* projects—
9:27 to serve in the fleet with *S* men.
10:21 All King *S* goblets were gold,
10:21 considered of little value in *S* days.
10:28 *S* horses were imported
11:26 one of *S* officials, an Ephraimite
11:31 to tear the kingdom out of *S* hand
11:33 and laws as David, *S* father,
11:34 the whole kingdom out of *S* hand;
11:40 and stayed there until *S* death.
11:41 As for the other events of *S* reign—
1Ch 3:10 *S* son was Rehoboam, Abijah his
2Ch 1:16 *S* horses were imported
8:10 also King *S* chief officials—
8:16 All *S* work was carried out,
8:18 with *S* men, sailed to Ophir
9: 1 queen of Sheba heard of *S* fame,
9:20 All King *S* goblets were gold,
9:20 considered of little value in *S* day.
9:28 *S* horses were imported
9:29 As for the other events of *S* reign,
Ne 11: 3 and descendants of *S* servants lived
SS 1: 1 *S* Song of Songs.
3: 7 Look! It is *S* carriage,
Mt 12:42 of the earth to listen to *S* wisdom,
Lk 11:31 of the earth to listen to *S* wisdom,
Jn 10:23 area walking in *S* Colonnade.
Ac 3:11 in the place called *S* Colonnade.
5:12 to meet together in *S* Colonnade.

SOLVE (SOLVED)

Da 5:12 riddles and *s* difficult problems.
5:16 and to *s* difficult problems

SOLVED (SOLVE)

Jdg 14:18 you would not have *s* my riddle."

SOMBER

Mt 6:16 do not look *s* as the hypocrites do,

SON (GRANDSON GRANDSONS SON'S SONS SONS' SONSHIP)

Ge 4:17 and he named it after his *s* Enoch.
4:22 Zillah also had a *s*, Tubal-Cain,
4:25 birth to a *s* and named him Seth,
4:26 had a *s*, and he named him Enosh.
5: 3 he had a *s* in his own likeness,
5:28 had lived 182 years, he had a *s*.
9:24 out what his youngest *s* had done
11:31 Sarai, the wife of his *s* Abram,
11:31 Terah took his *s* Abram, his
11:31 his grandson Lot *s* of Haran,
15: 4 *s* coming from your own body will
16:11 and you will have a *s*.
16:15 Ishmael to the *s* she had borne.
16:15 So Hagar bore Abram a *s*,

Ge 17: 16 and will surely give you a *s* by her.
17: 17 "Will a *s* be born to a man
17: 19 your wife Sarah will bear you a *s*,
17: 23 day Abraham took his *s* Ishmael
17: 25 and his *s* Ishmael was thirteen;
17: 26 and his *s* Ishmael were both
18: 10 and Sarah your wife will have a *s*."
18: 14 next year and Sarah will have a *s*."
19: 37 The older daughter had a *s*,
19: 38 The younger daughter also had a *s*,
21: 2 bore a *s* to Abraham in his old age,
21: 3 Isaac to the *s* Sarah bore him.
21: 4 When his *s* Isaac was eight days old
21: 5 when his *s* Isaac was born to him.
21: 7 Yet I have borne him a *s*
21: 9 Sarah saw that the *s* whom Hagar
21: 10 in the inheritance with my *s* Isaac."
21: 10 rid of that slave woman and her *s*,
21: 10 that slave woman's *s* will never
21: 11 greatly because it concerned his *s*.
21: 13 will make the *s* of the maidservant
22: 2 "Take your *s*, your only *s* Isaac,
22: 3 two of his servants and his *s* Isaac.
22: 6 and placed it on his *s* Isaac,
22: 7 "Yes, my *s*?" Abraham replied.
22: 8 lamb for the burnt offering, my *s*."
22: 9 He bound his *s* Isaac and laid him
22: 10 and took the knife to slay his *s*.
22: 12 from me your *s*, your only *s*."
22: 13 as a burnt offering instead of his *s*.
22: 16 not withheld your *s*, your only *s*,
23: 8 intercede with Ephron *s* of Zohar
24: 3 a wife for my *s* from the daughters
24: 4 and get a wife for my *s* Isaac."
24: 5 Shall I then take your *s* back
24: 6 you do not take my *s* back there,"
24: 7 a wife for my *s* from there.
24: 8 Only do not take my *s* back there."
24: 15 daughter of Bethuel *s* of Milcah,
24: 24 the *s* that Milcah bore to Nahor."
24: 36 wife Sarah has borne him a *s*
24: 37 a wife for my *s* from the daughters
24: 38 own clan, and get a wife for my *s*.'
24: 40 a wife for my *s* from my own clan
24: 44 chosen for my master's *s*.'
24: 47 The daughter of Bethuel *s* of Nahor
24: 48 of my master's brother for his *s*.
24: 51 the wife of your master's *s*,
25: 6 away from his *s* Isaac to the land
25: 9 of Ephron *s* of Zohar the Hittite,
25: 11 death, God blessed his *s* Isaac,
25: 12 account of Abraham's *s* Ishmael,
25: 19 the account of Abraham's *s* Isaac.
27: 1 his older *s* and said to him, "My *s*."
27: 5 as Isaac spoke to his *s* Esau.
27: 6 Rebekah said to her *s* Jacob, "Look
27: 8 my *s*, listen carefully and do what I
27: 13 His mother said to him, "My *s*,
27: 15 clothes of Esau her older *s*,
27: 15 put them on her younger *s* Jacob.
27: 17 to her *s* Jacob the tasty food
27: 18 "Yes, my *s*," he answered.
27: 20 Isaac asked his *s*, "How did you
27: 20 my *s*?" "The LORD your God
27: 21 near so I can touch you, my *s*,
27: 21 you really are my *s* Esau or not."
27: 24 "Are you really my *s* Esau?"
27: 25 My *s*, bring me some of your game
27: 26 "Come here, my *s*, and kiss me."
27: 27 "Ah, the smell of my *s*
27: 32 "I am your *s*," he answered,
27: 37 my *s*?" Esau said to his father,
27: 42 she sent for her younger *s* Jacob
27: 42 told what her older *s* Esau had said,
27: 43 Now then, my *s*, do what I say:
28: 9 daughter of Ishmael *s* of Abraham,
29: 12 of her father and a *s* of Rebekah.
29: 13 his sister's *s*, he hurried
29: 32 pregnant and gave birth to a *s*.
29: 33 when she gave birth to a *s* she said,
29: 34 when she gave birth to a *s* she said,
29: 35 when she gave birth to a *s* she said,
30: 5 became pregnant and bore him a *s*.
30: 6 to my plea and given me a *s*."
30: 7 and bore Jacob a second *s*.
30: 10 servant Zilpah bore Jacob a *s*.

Ge 30: 12 Zilpah bore Jacob a second *s*.
30: 17 pregnant and bore Jacob a fifth *s*.
30: 19 again and bore Jacob a sixth *s*.
30: 23 and gave birth to a *s* and said,
30: 24 the LORD add to me another *s*."
34: 2 When Shechem *s* of Hamor
34: 8 "My *s* Shechem has his heart set
34: 18 good to Hamor and his *s* Shechem.
34: 20 and his *s* Shechem went to the gate
34: 24 with Hamor and his *s* Shechem,
34: 26 and his *s* Shechem to the sword
35: 17 for you have another *s*."
35: 18 she named her *s* Ben-Oni.
36: 10 Eliphaz, the *s* of Esau's wife Adah,
36: 10 the *s* of Esau's wife Basemath.
36: 12 Esau's *s* Eliphaz also had
36: 17 The sons of Esau's *s* Reuel:
36: 32 Bela *s* of Beor became king
36: 33 *s* of Zerah from Bozrah succeeded
36: 35 When Husham died, Hadad *s*
36: 38 Baal-Hanan *s* of Acbor succeeded
36: 39 When Baal-Hanan *s* of Acbor died,
37: 34 and mourned for his *s* many days.
37: 35 go down to the grave to my *s*."
38: 3 pregnant and gave birth to a *s*,
38: 4 birth to a *s* and named him Onan.
38: 5 She gave birth to still another *s*
38: 11 house until my *s* Shelah grows up."
38: 26 wouldn't give her to my *s* Shelah."
41: 52 The second *s* he named Ephraim
42: 38 "My *s* will not go down there
43: 29 his own mother's *s*, he asked,
43: 29 "God be gracious to you, my *s*."
44: 20 and there is a young *s* born to him
45: 9 'This is what your *s* Joseph says:
45: 28 "I'm convinced! My *s* Joseph is
46: 10 Shaul the *s* of a Canaanite woman.
46: 23 The *s* of Dan: Hushim.
47: 29 he called for his *s* Joseph
48: 2 "Your *s* Joseph has come to you,"
48: 19 refused and said, "I know, my *s*,
49: 9 you return from the prey, my *s*.
50: 23 Also the children of Makir *s*
Ex 2: 2 pregnant and gave birth to a *s*.
2: 10 daughter and he became her *s*.
2: 22 Zipporah gave birth to a *s*,
4: 22 Israel is my firstborn *s*,
4: 23 and I told you, "Let my *s* go,
4: 23 so I will kill your firstborn *s*.'"
6: 14 The sons of Reuben the firstborn *s*
6: 15 Shaul the *s* of a Canaanite woman.
6: 25 Eleazar *s* of Aaron married one
11: 5 Every firstborn *s* in Egypt will die,
11: 5 from the firstborn *s* of Pharaoh,
11: 5 to the firstborn *s* of the slave girl,
13: 8 On that day tell your *s*, 'I do this
13: 14 to come, when your *s* asks you,
18: 3 One *s* was named Gershom,
20: 10 neither you, nor your *s* or daughter
21: 9 her for his *s*, he must grant her
21: 31 also applies if the bull gores a *s*
29: 30 The *s* who succeeds him as priest
31: 2 See, I have chosen Bezalel *s* of Uri,
31: 2 the *s* of Hur, of the tribe of Judah,
31: 6 I have appointed Oholiab *s*
33: 11 but his young aide Joshua *s*
35: 30 the LORD has chosen Bezalel *s*
35: 30 the *s* of Hur, of the tribe of Judah,
35: 34 and Oholiab *s* of Ahisamach,
38: 21 direction of Ithamar *s* of Aaron,
38: 22 (Bezalel *s* of Uri, the *s* of Hur,
38: 23 with him was Oholiab *s*
Lev 6: 22 The *s* who is to succeed him
7: 33 *s* of Aaron who offers the blood
12: 2 to a *s* will be ceremonially unclean
12: 6 the days of her purification for a *s*
21: 2 his *s* or daughter, his brother,
24: 10 Now the *s* of an Israelite mother
24: 11 The *s* of the Israelite woman
Nu 1: 5 from Reuben, Elizur *s* of Shedeur,
1: 6 Shelumiel *s* of Zurishaddai;
1: 7 Nahshon *s* of Amminadab;
1: 8 from Issachar, Nethanel *s* of Zuar;
1: 9 from Zebulun, Eliab *s* of Helon;
1: 10 from Ephraim, Elishama *s*
1: 10 from Manasseh, Gamaliel *s*
1: 11 from Benjamin, Abidan *s*
1: 12 Ahiezer *s* of Ammishaddai;

Nu 1: 13 from Asher, Pagiel *s* of Ocran;
1: 14 from Gad, Eliasaph *s* of Deuel;
1: 15 from Naphtali, Ahira *s* of Enan."
1: 20 of Reuben the firstborn *s* of Israel:
2: 3 the people of Judah is Nahshon *s*
2: 5 of Issachar is Nethanel *s* of Zuar.
2: 7 of Zebulun is Eliab *s* of Helon.
2: 10 of Reuben is Elizur *s* of Shedeur.
2: 12 the people of Simeon is Shelumiel *s*
2: 14 of Gad is Eliasaph *s* of Deuel.
2: 18 people of Ephraim is Elishama *s*
2: 20 people of Manasseh is Gamaliel *s*
2: 22 of Benjamin is Abidan *s* of Gideoni
2: 25 the people of Dan is Ahiezer *s*
2: 27 of Asher is Pagiel *s* of Ocran.
2: 29 of Naphtali is Ahira *s* of Enan.
3: 24 of the Gershonites was Eliasaph *s*
3: 30 Kohathite clans was Elizaphan *s*
3: 32 leader of the Levites was Eleazar *s*
3: 35 of the Merarite clans was Zuriel *s*
4: 16 "Eleazar *s* of Aaron, the priest,
4: 28 direction of Ithamar *s* of Aaron,
4: 33 direction of Ithamar *s* of Aaron,
7: 8 direction of Ithamar *s* of Aaron,
7: 12 on the first day was Nahshon *s*
7: 17 of Nahshon *s* of Amminadab.
7: 18 On the second day Nethanel *s*
7: 23 the offering of Nethanel *s* of Zuar.
7: 24 On the third day, Eliab *s* of Helon,
7: 29 the offering of Eliab *s* of Helon.
7: 30 On the fourth day Elizur *s*
7: 35 the offering of Elizur *s* of Shedeur.
7: 36 On the fifth day Shelumiel *s*
7: 41 of Shelumiel *s* of Zurishaddai.
7: 42 On the sixth day Eliasaph *s*
7: 47 the offering of Eliasaph *s* of Deuel.
7: 48 On the seventh day Elishama *s*
7: 53 of Elishama *s* of Ammihud.
7: 54 On the eighth day Gamaliel *s*
7: 59 offering of Gamaliel *s* of Pedahzur.
7: 60 On the ninth day Abidan *s*
7: 65 offering of Abidan *s* of Gideoni.
7: 66 On the tenth day Ahiezer *s*
7: 71 of Ahiezer *s* of Ammishaddai.
7: 72 On the eleventh day Pagiel *s*
7: 77 the offering of Pagiel *s* of Ocran.
7: 78 On the twelfth day Ahira *s* of Enan
7: 83 the offering of Ahira *s* of Enan.
10: 14 Nahshon *s* of Amminadab was
10: 15 Nethanel *s* of Zuar was
10: 16 and Eliab *s* of Helon was
10: 18 Elizur *s* of Shedeur was
10: 19 Shelumiel *s* of Zurishaddai was
10: 20 and Eliasaph *s* of Deuel was
10: 22 Elishama *s* of Ammihud was
10: 23 Gamaliel *s* of Pedahzur was
10: 24 and Abidan *s* of Gideoni was
10: 25 Ahiezer *s* of Ammishaddai was
10: 26 Pagiel *s* of Ocran was
10: 27 and Ahira *s* of Enan was
10: 29 Now Moses said to Hobab *s*
11: 28 Joshua *s* of Nun, who had been
13: 4 of Reuben, Shammua *s* of Zaccur;
13: 5 tribe of Simeon, Shaphat *s* of Hori;
13: 6 of Judah, Caleb *s* of Jephunneh;
13: 7 tribe of Issachar, Igal *s* of Joseph;
13: 8 tribe of Ephraim, Hoshea *s* of Nun;
13: 9 tribe of Benjamin, Palti *s* of Raphu;
13: 10 tribe of Zebulun, Gaddiel *s* of Sodi;
13: 11 Gaddi *s* of Susi; from the tribe
13: 12 tribe of Dan, Ammiel *s* of Gemalli;
13: 13 tribe of Asher, Sethur *s* of Michael;
13: 14 of Naphtali, Nahbi *s* of Vophsi;
13: 15 the tribe of Gad, Geuel *s* of Maki.
13: 16 (Moses gave Hoshea *s*
14: 6 Joshua *s* of Nun and Caleb *s*
14: 30 except Caleb *s* of Jephunneh
14: 30 of Jephunneh and Joshua *s* of Nun.
14: 38 and Caleb *s* of Jephunneh survived.
14: 38 only Joshua *s* of Nun and Caleb
16: 1 Korah *s* of Izhar, the *s* of Kohath,
16: 1 sons of Eliab, and On *s* of Peleth—
16: 1 the *s* of Kohath, the *s* of Levi,
16: 37 Tell Eleazar *s* of Aaron, the priest,
18: 15 you must redeem every firstborn *s*
20: 25 Get Aaron and his *s* Eleazar
20: 26 and put them on his *s* Eleazar,
20: 28 and put them on his *s* Eleazar.

Nu 22: 2 Balak *s* of Zippor saw all that Israel
22: 4 So Balak *s* of Zippor, who was king
22: 5 to summon Balaam *s* of Beor,
22: 10 said to God, "Balak *s* of Zippor,
22: 16 This is what Balak *s* of Zippor says:
23: 18 hear me, *s* of Zippor.
23: 19 *s* of man, that he should change his
24: 3 "The oracle of Balaam *s* of Beor,
24: 15 "The oracle of Balaam *s* of Beor,
25: 7 *s* of Eleazar, the *s* of Aaron,
25: 11 *s* of Eleazar, the *s* of Aaron,
25: 14 the Midianite woman was Zimri *s*
26: 1 to Moses and Eleazar *s* of Aaron,
26: 5 the firstborn *s* of Israel, were:
26: 8 The *s* of Pallu was Eliab,
26: 33 (Zelophehad *s* of Hepher had no
26: 65 Caleb *s* of Jephunneh and Joshua
26: 65 of Jephunneh and Joshua *s* of Nun.
27: 1 of Zelophehad *s* of Hepher,
27: 1 the clans of Manasseh *s* of Joseph.
27: 1 the *s* of Gilead, the *s* of Makir,
27: 1 the *s* of Makir, the *s* of Manasseh,
27: 4 from his clan because he had no *s*?
27: 8 'If a man dies and leaves no *s*,
27: 18 to Moses, "Take Joshua *s* of Nun,
31: 6 along with Phinehas *s* of Eleazar,
31: 8 also killed Balaam *s* of Beor
32: 12 Caleb *s* of Jephunneh the Kenizzite
32: 12 the Kenizzite and Joshua *s*
32: 28 to Eleazar the priest and Joshua *s*
32: 33 and the half-tribe of Manasseh *s*
32: 39 of Makir *s* of Manasseh went
34: 17 Eleazar the priest and Joshua *s*
34: 19 These are their names: Caleb *s*
34: 20 of Judah; Shemuel *s* of Ammihud,
34: 21 tribe of Simeon; Elidad *s* of Kislon,
34: 22 tribe of Benjamin; Bukki *s* of Jogli,
34: 23 the tribe of Manasseh *s* of Joseph;
34: 23 tribe of Dan; Hanniel *s* of Ephod,
34: 24 of Joseph, Kemuel *s* of Shiphtan,
34: 24 the tribe of Ephraim *s* of Joseph;
34: 25 Elizaphan *s* of Parnach, the leader
34: 26 tribe of Zebulun, Paltiel *s* of Azzan,
34: 27 of Issachar; Ahihud *s* of Shelomi,
34: 28 of Asher; Pedahel *s* of Ammihud,
36: 1 *s* of Makir, the *s* of Manasseh,
36: 12 of Manasseh *s* of Joseph,
Dt 1: 31 father carries his *s*, all the way you
1: 36 except Caleb *s* of Jephunneh.
1: 38 But your assistant, Joshua *s* of Nun
5: 14 neither you, nor your *s* or daughter
6: 20 In the future, when your *s* asks you,
8: 5 as a man disciplines his *s*,
10: 6 and Eleazar his *s* succeeded him
13: 6 If your very own brother, or your *s*
18: 10 among you who sacrifices his *s*
21: 15 but the firstborn is the *s*
21: 16 the rights of the firstborn to the *s*
21: 16 the *s* of the wife he does not love.
21: 17 He must acknowledge the *s*
21: 17 That *s* is the first sign
21: 18 rebellious *s* who does not obey his
21: 20 "This *s* of ours is stubborn
23: 4 and they hired Balaam *s* of Beor
25: 5 and one of them dies without a *s*,
25: 6 The first *s* she bears shall carry
28: 56 and her own *s* or daughter
31: 23 command to Joshua *s* of Nun:
32: 44 Moses came with Joshua *s* of Nun
34: 9 Now Joshua *s* of Nun was filled
Jos 1: 1 the LORD said to Joshua *s* of Nun,
2: 1 Joshua *s* of Nun secretly sent two
2: 23 and came to Joshua *s* of Nun
6: 6 Joshua *s* of Nun called the priests
6: 26 "At the cost of his firstborn *s*
7: 1 Achan *s* of Carmi, the *s* of Zimri,
7: 1 the *s* of Zerah, of the tribe
7: 18 Achan *s* of Carmi, the *s* of Zimri,
7: 18 the *s* of Zerah, of the tribe
7: 19 "My *s*, give glory to the LORD,
7: 24 took Achan *s* of Zerah, the silver,
13: 22 put to the sword Balaam *s* of Beor,
13: 31 of Makir *s* of Manasseh—
14: 1 Joshua *s* of Nun and the heads
14: 6 Caleb *s* of Jephunneh the Kenizzite
14: 13 Then Joshua blessed Caleb *s*
14: 14 So Hebron has belonged to Caleb *s*
15: 6 to the Stone of Bohan *s* of Reuben.
Jos 15: 13 Joshua gave to Caleb *s*
15: 17 Othniel *s* of Kenaz, Caleb's brother
17: 2 of Manasseh *s* of Joseph
17: 3 the *s* of Makir, the *s* of Manasseh,
17: 3 *s* of Hepher, the *s* of Gilead,
17: 4 went to Eleazar the priest, Joshua *s*
18: 17 to the Stone of Bohan *s* of Reuben.
19: 49 the Israelites gave Joshua *s*
19: 51 Joshua *s* of Nun and the heads
21: 1 Eleazar the priest, Joshua *s*
21: 12 given to Caleb *s* of Jephunneh
22: 13 So the Israelites sent Phinehas *s*
22: 20 When Achan *s* of Zerah acted
22: 31 And Phinehas *s* of Eleazar,
22: 32 Then Phinehas *s* of Eleazar,
24: 9 When Balak *s* of Zippor, the king
24: 9 he sent for Balaam *s* of Beor
24: 29 After these things, Joshua *s* of Nun
24: 33 And Eleazar *s* of Aaron died
24: 33 to his *s* Phinehas in the hill country
Jdg 1: 13 Othniel *s* of Kenaz, Caleb's
2: 8 Joshua *s* of Nun, the servant
3: 9 Othniel *s* of Kenaz, Caleb's
3: 11 until Othniel *s* of Kenaz died.
3: 15 the *s* of Gera the Benjamite.
3: 31 After Ehud came Shamgar *s*
4: 6 She sent for Barak *s* of Abinoam
4: 12 When they told Sisera that Barak *s*
5: 1 Barak *s* of Abinoam sang this song:
5: 6 In the days of Shamgar *s* of Anath,
5: 12 Take captive your captives, O *s*
6: 11 where his *s* Gideon was threshing
6: 29 "Gideon *s* of Joash did it."
6: 30 of Joash, "Bring out your *s*.
7: 14 the sword of Gideon *s* of Joash,
8: 13 Gideon *s* of Joash then returned
8: 20 his oldest *s*, he said, "Kill them!"
8: 22 you, your *s* and your grandson—
8: 23 nor will my *s* rule over you.
8: 29 Jerub-Baal *s* of Joash went back
8: 31 also bore him a *s*, whom he named
8: 32 Gideon *s* of Joash died
9: 1 Abimelech *s* of Jerub-Baal went
9: 5 the youngest *s* of Jerub-Baal,
9: 18 and made Abimelech, the *s*
9: 26 Now Gaal *s* of Ebed moved
9: 28 Isn't he Jerub-Baal's *s*,
9: 28 Then Gaal *s* of Ebed said, "Who is
9: 30 of the city heard what Gaal *s*
9: 31 "Gaal *s* of Ebed and his brothers
9: 35 Now Gaal *s* of Ebed had gone out
9: 57 of Jotham *s* of Jerub-Baal came
10: 1 Tola *s* of Puah, the *s* of Dodo,
11: 2 you are the *s* of another woman."
11: 25 better than Balak *s* of Zippor,
11: 34 Except for her he had neither *s*
12: 13 After him, Abdon *s* of Hillel,
12: 15 Then Abdon *s* of Hillel died,
13: 3 going to conceive and have a *s*.
13: 5 will conceive and give birth to a *s*.
13: 7 will conceive and give birth to a *s*.
17: 2 "The LORD bless you, my *s*!"
17: 3 silver to the LORD for my *s*
18: 30 *s* of Gershom, the *s* of Moses,
20: 28 the *s* of Aaron, ministering
20: 28 with Phinehas *s* of Eleazar,
Ru 4: 13 conceive, and she gave birth to a *s*.
4: 17 living there said, "Naomi has a *s*."
1Sa 1: 1 the *s* of Elihu, the *s* of Tohu,
1: 1 the *s* of Zuph, an Ephraimite.
1: 1 whose name was Elkanah *s*
1: 11 forget your servant but give her a *s*,
1: 20 conceived and gave birth to a *s*.
1: 23 nursed her *s* until she had weaned
3: 6 "My *s*," Eli said, "I did not call;
3: 16 him and said, "Samuel, my *s*."
4: 16 Eli asked, "What happened, my *s*
4: 20 you have given birth to a *s*."
7: 1 and consecrated Eleazar his *s*
9: 1 the *s* of Aphiah of Benjamin.
9: 1 the *s* of Zeror, the *s* of Becorath,
9: 1 whose name was Kish *s* of Abiel,
9: 2 He had a *s* named Saul,
9: 3 and Kish said to his *s* Saul,
10: 2 "What shall I do about my *s*?" '
10: 11 is this that has happened to the *s*
10: 21 Finally Saul *s* of Kish was chosen.
13: 16 Saul and his *s* Jonathan
1Sa 13: 22 and his *s* Jonathan had them.
14: 1 One day Jonathan *s* of Saul said
14: 3 a *s* of Ichabod's brother Ahitub *s*
14: 3 the *s* of Eli, the LORD's priest
14: 39 even if it lies with my *s* Jonathan,
14: 40 Jonathan my *s* will stand over here
14: 42 between me and Jonathan my *s*."
14: 50 of Saul's army was Abner *s* of Ner,
16: 18 "I have seen a *s* of Jesse
16: 19 "Send me your *s* David, who is
16: 20 sent them with his *s* David to Saul.
17: 12 David was the *s* of an Ephrathite
17: 17 Now Jesse said to his *s* David,
17: 55 "Abner, whose *s* is that young man
17: 56 Find out whose *s* this young man is
17: 58 "I am the *s* of your servant Jesse
17: 58 "Whose *s* are you, young man?"
19: 1 Saul told his *s* Jonathan
20: 27 Then Saul said to his *s* Jonathan,
20: 27 "Why hasn't the *s* of Jesse come
20: 30 sided with the *s* of Jesse
20: 30 "You *s* of a perverse and rebellious
20: 31 as the *s* of Jesse lives on this earth,
22: 7 Will the *s* of Jesse give all
22: 8 a covenant with the *s* of Jesse.
22: 8 me when my *s* makes a covenant
22: 8 or tells me that my *s* has incited my
22: 9 to Ahimelech *s* of Ahitub at Nob.
22: 9 "I saw the *s* of Jesse come
22: 11 sent for the priest Ahimelech *s*
22: 12 "Listen now, *s* of Ahitub."
22: 13 against me, you and the *s* of Jesse,
22: 20 a *s* of Ahimelech *s* of Ahitub,
23: 6 (Now Abiathar *s* of Ahimelech had
23: 16 Saul's *s* Jonathan went to David
24: 16 David my *s*?" And he wept aloud.
25: 8 and your *s* David whatever you can
25: 10 "Who is this David? Who is this *s*
25: 44 David's wife, to Paltiel *s* of Laish,
26: 5 He saw where Saul and Abner *s*
26: 6 the Hittite and Abishai *s*
26: 14 to the army and to Abner *s* of Ner,
26: 17 David my *s*?" David replied,
26: 21 Come back, David my *s*.
26: 25 "May you be blessed, my *s* David;
27: 2 over to Achish *s* of Maoch king
30: 7 the *s* of Ahimelech, "Bring me
2Sa 1: 4 Saul and his *s* Jonathan are dead."
1: 5 and his *s* Jonathan are dead?"
1: 12 for Saul and his *s* Jonathan,
1: 13 I am the *s* of an alien, an Amalekite
1: 17 Saul and his *s* Jonathan,
2: 8 Meanwhile, Abner *s* of Ner,
2: 8 had taken Ish-Bosheth *s* of Saul
2: 10 Ish-Bosheth *s* of Saul was forty
2: 12 Abner *s* of Ner, together
2: 12 the men of Ish-Bosheth *s* of Saul,
2: 13 Joab *s* of Zeruiah and David's men
2: 15 and Ish-Bosheth *s* of Saul,
3: 2 His firstborn was Amnon the *s*
3: 3 Absalom the *s* of Maacah daughter
3: 3 Kileab the *s* of Abigail the widow
3: 4 Adonijah the *s* of Haggith;
3: 4 the fifth, Shephatiah the *s* of Abital
3: 5 Ithream the *s* of David's wife Eglah
3: 14 to Ish-Bosheth *s* of Saul,
3: 15 from her husband Paltiel *s* of Laish.
3: 23 he was told that Abner *s*
3: 25 You know Abner *s* of Ner;
3: 28 the blood of Abner *s* of Ner.
3: 37 in the murder of Abner *s* of Ner.
4: 1 When Ish-Bosheth *s*
4: 2 Saul's *s* had two men who were
4: 4 *s* of Saul had a *s* who was lame
4: 8 the head of Ish-Bosheth *s* of Saul,
7: 14 be his father, and he will be my *s*.
8: 3 David fought Hadadezer *s*
8: 10 he sent his *s* Joram to King David
8: 12 taken from Hadadezer *s* of Rehob,
8: 16 Jehoshaphat *s* of Ahilud was
8: 16 Joab *s* of Zeruiah was
8: 17 Zadok *s* of Ahitub and Ahimelech
8: 17 and Ahimelech *s* of Abiathar were
8: 18 Benaiah *s* of Jehoiada was
9: 3 "There is still a *s* of Jonathan;
9: 4 house of Makir *s* of Ammiel in Lo
9: 5 the house of Makir *s* of Ammiel.
9: 6 When Mephibosheth *s* of Jonathan

2Sa 9: 6 the *s* of Saul, came to David,
9: 12 had a young *s* named Mica,
10: 1 and his *s* Hanun succeeded him
10: 2 kindness to Hanun *s* of Nahash,
11: 21 Who killed Abimelech *s*
11: 27 became his wife and bore him a *s*.
12: 14 the *s* born to you will die."
12: 24 birth to a *s*, and they named him
13: 1 Amnon *s* of David fell in love
13: 1 sister of Absalom *s* of David.
13: 3 had a friend named Jonadab *s*
13: 4 "Why do you, the king's *s*,
13: 25 "No, my *s*," the king replied.
13: 32 But Jonadab *s* of Shimeah,
13: 37 and went to Talmai *s* of Ammihud,
13: 37 mourned for his *s* every day.
14: 1 Joab *s* of Zeruiah knew that
14: 11 so that my *s* will not be destroyed."
14: 13 not brought back his banished *s?*
14: 16 and my *s* from the inheritance God
15: 27 and Jonathan *s* of Abiathar.
15: 27 with your *s* Ahimaaz and Jonathan
15: 36 Ahimaaz *s* of Zadok and Jonathan
15: 36 and Jonathan *s* of Abiathar,
16: 5 His name was Shimei *s* of Gera,
16: 8 kingdom over to your *s* Absalom.
16: 9 Then Abishai *s* of Zeruiah said
16: 11 "My *s*, who is of my own flesh,
16: 19 Should I not serve the *s?* Just
17: 25 Amasa was the *s* of a man named
17: 27 Shobi *s* of Nahash from Rabbah
17: 27 and Makir *s* of Ammiel from Lo
18: 2 under Joab's brother Abishai *s*
18: 12 hand against the king's *s*.
18: 18 I have no *s* to carry on the memory
18: 19 Now Ahimaaz *s* of Zadok said,
18: 20 because the king's *s* is dead."
18: 22 Ahimaaz *s* of Zadok again said
18: 22 "My *s*, why do you want to go?
18: 27 the first one runs like Ahimaaz *s*
18: 33 my *s*, my *s!*" Joab was told,
18: 33 *s* Absalom! My *s*, my *s* Absalom!
19: 2 "The king is grieving for his *s*."
19: 4 O Absalom, my *s*, my *s!*"
19: 4 "O my *s* Absalom! O Absalom,
19: 16 Shimei *s* of Gera, the Benjamite
19: 18 When Shimei *s* of Gera crossed
19: 21 Then Abishai *s* of Zeruiah said,
20: 1 a troublemaker named Sheba *s*
20: 1 no part in Jesse's *s!*
20: 2 David to follow Sheba *s* of Bicri.
20: 6 Sheba *s* of Bicri will do us more
20: 7 to pursue Sheba *s* of Bicri.
20: 10 brother Abishai pursued Sheba *s*
20: 13 with Joab to pursue Sheba *s* of Bicri
20: 21 A man named Sheba *s* of Bicri,
20: 22 cut off the head of Sheba *s* of Bicri
20: 23 Benaiah *s* of Jehoiada was
20: 24 Jehoshaphat *s* of Ahilud was
21: 7 between David and Jonathan *s*
21: 7 *s* of Jonathan, the *s* of Saul,
21: 8 borne to Adriel *s* of Barzillai
21: 12 his *s* Jonathan from the citizens
21: 13 and his *s* Jonathan from there,
21: 14 and his *s* Jonathan in the tomb
21: 17 But Abishai *s* of Zeruiah came
21: 19 Elhanan *s* of Jaare-Oregim
21: 21 Jonathan *s* of Shimeah, David's
23: 1 "The oracle of David *s* of Jesse,
23: 9 Next to him was Eleazar *s*
23: 11 Next to him was Shammah *s*
23: 18 of Joab *s* of Zeruiah was chief
23: 20 Benaiah *s* of Jehoiada was a valiant
23: 22 exploits of Benaiah *s* of Jehoiada;
23: 24 Elhanan *s* of Dodo
23: 26 Ira *s* of Ikkesh from Tekoa,
23: 29 Heled *s* of Baanah
23: 29 Ithai *s* of Ribai from Gibeah
23: 33 Ahiam *s* of Sharar the Hararite,
23: 33 Jonathan *s* of Shammah
23: 34 Eliam *s* of Ahithophel the Gilonite,
23: 34 Eliphelet *s* of Ahasbai
23: 36 Igal *s* of Nathan from Zobah,
23: 36 *s* of Hagri, Zelek the Ammonite,
23: 37 armor-bearer of Joab *s* of Zeruiah,
1Ki 1: 7 conferred with Joab *s* of Zeruiah
1: 8 But Zadok the priest, Benaiah *s*
1: 11 you not heard that Adonijah, the *s*

1Ki 1: 12 and the life of your *s* Solomon.
1: 13 "Surely Solomon your *s* shall be
1: 17 'Solomon your *s* shall be king
1: 21 I and my *s* Solomon will be treated
1: 26 and Benaiah *s* of Jehoiada,
1: 30 Solomon your *s* shall be king
1: 32 and Benaiah *s* of Jehoiada."
1: 33 set Solomon my *s* on my own mule
1: 36 Benaiah *s* of Jehoiada answered
1: 38 Nathan the prophet, Benaiah *s*
1: 42 Jonathan *s* of Abiathar the priest
1: 44 Nathan the prophet, Benaiah *s*
2: 1 he gave a charge to Solomon his *s*.
2: 5 Abner *s* of Ner and Amasa *s*
2: 5 you yourself know what Joab *s*
2: 8 have with you Shimei *s* of Gera,
2: 13 Now Adonijah, the *s* of Haggith,
2: 22 for Abiathar the priest and Joab *s*
2: 25 orders to Benaiah *s* of Jehoiada,
2: 29 Then Solomon ordered Benaiah *s*
2: 32 Both of them—Abner *s* of Ner,
2: 32 of Israel's army, and Amasa *s*
2: 34 So Benaiah *s* of Jehoiada went up
2: 35 The king put Benaiah *s* of Jehoiada
2: 39 ran off to Achish *s* of Maacah,
2: 46 the order to Benaiah *s* of Jehoiada,
3: 6 and have given him a *s* to sit
3: 19 the night this woman's *s* died
3: 20 and put her dead *s* by my breast.
3: 20 and took my *s* from my side
3: 21 I got up to nurse my *s*—
3: 21 that it wasn't the *s* I had borne."
3: 22 living one is my *s;* the dead one is
3: 23 Your *s* is dead and mine is alive.' "
3: 23 'My *s* is alive and your *s* is dead,'
3: 26 filled with compassion for her *s*
3: 26 woman whose *s* was alive was filled
4: 2 Azariah *s* of Zadok—the priest;
4: 3 Jehoshaphat *s* of Ahilud—
4: 4 recorder; Benaiah *s* of Jehoiada—
4: 5 of the district officers; Zabud *s*
4: 5 priests; Azariah *s* of Nathan—
4: 6 of the palace; Adoniram *s* of Abda
4: 12 Baana *s* of Ahilud—in Taanach
4: 13 settlements of Jair *s* of Manasseh
4: 14 Ahinadab *s* of Iddo—
4: 16 Baana *s* of Hushai—in Asher
4: 17 Jehoshaphat *s* of Paruah—
4: 18 in Issachar; Shimei *s* of Ela—
4: 19 in Benjamin; Geber *s* of Uri—
5: 5 'Your *s* whom I will put
5: 7 for he has given David a wise *s*
8: 19 but your *s*, who is your own flesh
11: 12 out of the hand of your *s*.
11: 20 bore him a *s* named Genubath,
11: 23 Rezon *s* of Eliada, who had fled
11: 26 Also, Jeroboam *s* of Nebat rebelled
11: 36 I will give one tribe to his *s*
11: 43 Rehoboam his *s* succeeded him
12: 2 When Jeroboam *s*
12: 15 spoken to Jeroboam *s* of Nebat
12: 16 what part in Jesse's *s?*
12: 21 for Rehoboam *s* of Solomon.
12: 23 "Say to Rehoboam *s*
13: 2 'A *s* named Josiah will be born
14: 1 At that time Abijah *s*
14: 5 coming to ask you about her *s*,
14: 20 And Nadab his *s* succeeded him
14: 21 Rehoboam *s* of Solomon was king
14: 31 And Abijah his *s* succeeded him
15: 1 of the reign of Jeroboam *s* of Nebat
15: 4 by raising up a *s* to succeed him
15: 8 And Asa his *s* succeeded him
15: 18 the *s* of Hezion, the king of Aram,
15: 18 to Ben-Hadad *s* of Tabrimmon,
15: 24 Jehoshaphat his *s* succeeded him
15: 25 Nadab *s* of Jeroboam became king
15: 27 Baasha *s* of Ahijah of the house
15: 33 Baasha *s* of Ahijah became king
16: 1 to Jehu *s* of Hanani against Baasha:
16: 3 that of Jeroboam *s* of Nebat.
16: 6 And Elah his *s* succeeded him
16: 7 came through the prophet Jehu *s*
16: 8 Elah *s* of Baasha became king
16: 13 and his *s* Elah had committed
16: 21 half supported Tibni *s* of Ginath
16: 22 than those of Tibni *s* of Ginath.
16: 26 the ways of Jeroboam *s* of Nebat

1Ki 16: 28 And Ahab his *s* succeeded him
16: 29 Ahab *s* of Omri became king
16: 30 Ahab *s* of Omri did more evil
16: 31 the sins of Jeroboam *s* of Nebat,
16: 34 at the cost of his firstborn *s* Abiram
16: 34 at the cost of his youngest *s* Segub,
16: 34 spoken by Joshua *s* of Nun.
17: 12 make a meal for myself and my *s*,
17: 13 something for yourself and your *s*.
17: 17 Some time later the *s*
17: 18 me of my sin and kill my *s?*"
17: 19 "Give me your *s*," Elijah replied.
17: 20 with, by causing her *s* to die?"
17: 23 your *s* is alive!" Then the woman
19: 16 Also, anoint Jehu *s* of Nimshi king
19: 16 and anoint Elisha *s* of Shaphat
19: 19 and found Elisha *s* of Shaphat.
21: 22 and that of Baasha *s* of Ahijah,
21: 22 that of Jeroboam *s* of Nebat
21: 29 it on his house in the days of his *s*."
22: 8 He is Micaiah *s* of Imlah."
22: 9 Bring Micaiah *s* of Imlah at once."
22: 11 Zedekiah *s* of Kenaanah had made
22: 24 Zedekiah *s* of Kenaanah went up
22: 26 and to Joash the king's *s* and say,
22: 40 And Ahaziah his *s* succeeded him
22: 41 Jehoshaphat *s* of Asa became king
22: 49 At that time Ahaziah *s*
22: 50 And Jehoram his *s* succeeded him.
22: 51 Ahaziah *s* of Ahab became king
22: 52 in the ways of Jeroboam *s* of Nebat
2Ki 1: 17 Because Ahaziah had no *s*,
1: 17 of Jehoram *s* of Jehoshaphat king
3: 1 Joram *s* of Ahab became king
3: 3 to the sins of Jeroboam *s* of Nebat,
3: 11 "Elisha *s* of Shaphat is here.
3: 27 Then he took his firstborn *s*,
4: 6 to her *s*, "Bring me another one."
4: 14 she has no *s* and her husband is old
4: 16 "you will hold a *s* in your arms."
4: 17 that same time she gave birth to a *s*,
4: 28 "Did I ask you for a *s*, my lord?"
4: 36 she came, he said, "Take your *s*."
4: 37 Then she took her *s* and went out.
6: 28 and tomorrow we'll eat my *s*.'
6: 28 'Give up your *s* so we may eat him
6: 29 So we cooked my *s* and ate him.
6: 29 'Give up your *s* so we may eat him,'
6: 31 of Elisha *s* of Shaphat remains
8: 1 the woman whose *s* he had
8: 5 this is her *s* whom Elisha restored
8: 5 woman whose *s* Elisha had brought
8: 9 "Your *s* Ben-Hadad king
8: 16 Jehoram *s* of Jehoshaphat began
8: 16 of Joram *s* of Ahab king of Israel,
8: 24 And Ahaziah his *s* succeeded him
8: 25 Ahaziah *s* of Jehoram king
8: 25 of Joram *s* of Ahab king of Israel,
8: 28 went with Joram *s* of Ahab
8: 29 Then Ahaziah *s* of Jehoram king
8: 29 to Jezreel to see Joram *s* of Ahab,
9: 2 look for Jehu *s* of Jehoshaphat,
9: 2 of Jehoshaphat, the *s* of Nimshi.
9: 9 like the house of Baasha *s* of Ahijah
9: 9 the house of Jeroboam *s* of Nebat
9: 14 So Jehu *s* of Jehoshaphat,
9: 14 the *s* of Nimshi, conspired
9: 20 that of Jehu *s* of Nimshi—
9: 29 year of Joram *s* of Ahab,
10: 15 came upon Jehonadab *s* of Recab,
10: 23 and Jehonadab *s* of Recab went
10: 29 the sins of Jeroboam *s* of Nebat,
10: 35 And Jehoahaz his *s* succeeded him
11: 1 of Ahaziah saw that her *s* was dead,
11: 2 took Joash *s* of Ahaziah
11: 4 Then he showed them the king's *s*.
11: 12 Jehoiada brought out the king's *s*
12: 21 And Amaziah his *s* succeeded him
12: 21 and Jehozabad *s* of Shomer.
12: 21 who murdered him were Jozabad *s*
13: 1 Jehoahaz *s* of Jehu became king
13: 1 of Joash *s* of Ahaziah king of Judah
13: 2 the sins of Jeroboam *s* of Nebat,
13: 3 king of Aram and Ben-Hadad his *s*.
13: 9 And Jehoash his *s* succeeded him
13: 10 Jehoash *s* of Jehoahaz became king
13: 11 of the sins of Jeroboam *s* of Nebat,
13: 24 Ben-Hadad his *s* succeeded him

2Ki 13: 25 Jehoash *s* of Jehoahaz recaptured
13: 25 recaptured from Ben-Hadad *s*
14: 1 Amaziah *s* of Joash king
14: 1 year of Jehoash *s* of Jehoahaz king
14: 8 the *s* of Jehu, king of Israel,
14: 8 to Jehoash *s* of Jehoahaz,
14: 9 daughter to my *s* in marriage.'
14: 13 the *s* of Joash, the *s* of Ahaziah,
14: 16 And Jeroboam his *s* succeeded him
14: 17 Amaziah *s* of Joash king
14: 17 of Jehoash *s* of Jehoahaz king
14: 23 Jeroboam *s* of Jehoash king
14: 23 year of Amaziah *s* of Joash king
14: 24 of the sins of Jeroboam *s* of Nebat,
14: 25 spoken through his servant Jonah *s*
14: 27 the hand of Jeroboam *s* of Jehoash.
14: 29 Zechariah his *s* succeeded him
15: 1 Azariah *s* of Amaziah king
15: 5 Jotham the king's *s* had charge
15: 7 And Jotham his *s* succeeded him
15: 8 Zechariah *s* of Jeroboam became
15: 9 the sins of Jeroboam *s* of Nebat,
15: 10 Shallum *s* of Jabesh conspired
15: 13 Shallum *s* of Jabesh became king
15: 14 He attacked Shallum *s* of Jabesh
15: 14 Then Menahem *s* of Gadi went
15: 17 Menahem *s* of Gadi became king
15: 18 the sins of Jeroboam *s* of Nebat,
15: 22 And Pekahiah his *s* succeeded him
15: 23 Pekahiah *s* of Menahem became
15: 24 the sins of Jeroboam *s* of Nebat,
15: 25 Pekah *s* of Remaliah, conspired
15: 27 Pekah *s* of Remaliah became king
15: 28 the sins of Jeroboam *s* of Nebat,
15: 30 Then Hoshea *s* of Elah conspired
15: 30 against Pekah *s* of Remaliah.
15: 30 year of Jotham *s* of Uzziah.
15: 32 Jotham *s* of Uzziah king
15: 32 year of Pekah *s* of Remaliah king
15: 37 Pekah *s* of Remaliah against Judah
15: 38 And Ahaz his *s* succeeded him
16: 1 Ahaz *s* of Jotham king
16: 1 year of Pekah *s* of Remaliah,
16: 3 and even sacrificed his *s* in the fire,
16: 5 and Pekah *s* of Remaliah king
16: 20 And Hezekiah his *s* succeeded him
17: 1 Hoshea *s* of Elah became king
17: 21 they made Jeroboam *s*
18: 1 Hezekiah *s* of Ahaz king
18: 1 of Hoshea *s* of Elah king of Israel,
18: 9 of Hoshea *s* of Elah king of Israel,
18: 18 Joah *s* of Asaph the recorder went
18: 18 and Eliakim *s* of Hilkiah the palace
18: 26 Then Eliakim *s* of Hilkiah,
18: 37 Eliakim *s* of Hilkiah the palace
18: 37 Joah *s* of Asaph the recorder went
19: 2 to the prophet Isaiah *s* of Amoz.
19: 20 Isaiah *s* of Amoz sent a message
19: 37 Esarhaddon his *s* succeeded him
20: 1 The prophet Isaiah *s* of Amoz went
20: 12 At that time Merodach-Baladan *s*
20: 21 Manasseh his *s* succeeded him
21: 6 He sacrificed his own *s* in the fire,
21: 7 said to David and to his *s* Solomon,
21: 18 And Amon his *s* succeeded him
21: 24 and they made Josiah his *s* king
21: 26 And Josiah his *s* succeeded him
22: 3 *s* of Azaliah, the *s* of Meshullam,
22: 12 Ahikam *s* of Shaphan, Acbor *s*
22: 14 the wife of Shallum *s* of Tikvah,
22: 14 the *s* of Harhas, keeper
23: 10 no one could use it to sacrifice his *s*
23: 15 made by Jeroboam *s* of Nebat,
23: 30 people of the land took Jehoahaz *s*
23: 34 Pharaoh Neco made Eliakim *s*
24: 6 Jehoiachin his *s* succeeded him
25: 22 *s* of Ahikam, the *s* of Shaphan,
25: 23 Ishmael *s* of Nethaniah, Johanan
25: 23 Jaazaniah the *s* of the Maacathite,
25: 23 Seraiah *s* of Tanhumeth
25: 23 of Nethaniah, Johanan *s* of Kareah,
25: 25 however, Ishmael *s* of Nethaniah,
25: 25 of Nethaniah, the *s* of Elishama,
1Ch 1: 41 The *s* of Anah: Dishon.
1: 43 Bela *s* of Beor, whose city was
1: 44 *s* of Zerah from Bozrah succeeded
1: 46 When Husham died, Hadad *s*
1: 49 Baal-Hanan *s* of Acbor succeeded

1Ch 2: 7 *s* of Carmi: Achar, who brought
2: 8 The *s* of Ethan: Azariah.
2: 13 the second *s* was Abinadab,
2: 18 Caleb *s* of Hezron had children
2: 31 The *s* of Appaim: Ishi, who was
2: 42 his *s* Mareshah, who was the father
2: 45 The *s* of Shammai was Maon,
3: 1 Daniel the *s* of Abigail of Carmel;
3: 1 The firstborn was Amnon the *s*
3: 2 Absalom the *s* of Maacah daughter
3: 2 Adonijah the *s* of Haggith;
3: 3 the fifth, Shephatiah the *s* of Abital
3: 10 Asa his *s*, Jehoshaphat his *s*,
3: 10 *s* was Rehoboam, Abijah his *s*,
3: 11 Jehoram his *s*, Ahaziah his *s*,
3: 11 Joash his *s*, Amaziah his *s*,
3: 12 Azariah his *s*, Jotham his *s*,
3: 13 Ahaz his *s*, Hezekiah his *s*,
3: 14 his *s*, Amon his *s*, Josiah his *s*.
3: 15 Jehoiakim the second *s*, Zedekiah
3: 16 Jehoiachin his *s*, and Zedekiah.
3: 17 Shealtiel his *s*, Malkiram, Pedaiah,
4: 2 Reaiah *s* of Shobal was the father
4: 8 of the clans of Aharhel *s* of Harum.
4: 15 The sons of Caleb *s* of Jephunneh:
4: 15 The *s* of Elah: Kenaz.
4: 21 The sons of Shelah *s* of Judah:
4: 25 Mibsam his *s* and Mishma his *s*.
4: 25 and Shaul; Shallum was Shaul's *s*,
4: 26 Zaccur his *s* and Shimei his *s*.
4: 26 of Mishma: Hammuel his *s*,
4: 35 the *s* of Asiel, also Elioenai,
4: 35 *s* of Amaziah, Joel, Jehu *s*
4: 37 the *s* of Allon, the *s* of Jedaiah,
4: 37 the *s* of Shimri, the *s* of Shemaiah.
5: 1 to the sons of Joseph *s* of Israel;
5: 4 Shemaiah his *s*, Gog his *s*,
5: 5 Baal his *s*, and Beerah his *s*,
5: 5 his *s*, Micah his *s*, Reaiah his *s*,
5: 8 Zechariah, and Bela *s* of Azaz,
5: 8 the *s* of Shema, the *s* of Joel.
5: 14 the sons of Abihail *s* of Huri,
5: 14 the *s* of Jahdo, the *s* of Buz.
5: 14 the *s* of Jaroah, the *s* of Gilead,
5: 14 the *s* of Michael, the *s* of Jeshishai,
5: 15 Ahi *s* of Abdiel, the *s* of Guni,
6: 20 Gershon: Libni his *s*, Jehath his *s*,
6: 21 Zerah his *s* and Jeatherai his *s*.
6: 21 Zimmah his *s*, Joah his *s*, Iddo his *s*,
6: 22 Amminadab his *s*, Korah his *s*,
6: 22 Assir his *s*, Elkanah his *s*,
6: 23 Ebiasaph his *s*, Assir his *s*,
6: 24 Tahath his *s*, Uriel his *s*,
6: 24 Uzziah his *s* and Shaul his *s*.
6: 26 Elkanah his *s*, Zophai his *s*,
6: 27 Elkanah his *s* and Samuel his *s*.
6: 27 his *s*, Eliab his *s*, Jeroham his *s*,
6: 28 firstborn and Abijah the second *s*.
6: 29 Mahli, Libni his *s*, Shimei his *s*,
6: 29 Uzzah his *s*, Shimea his *s*,
6: 30 Haggiah his *s* and Asaiah his *s*.
6: 33 the *s* of Joel, the *s* of Samuel,
6: 34 the *s* of Eliel, the *s* of Toah,
6: 34 the *s* of Elkanah, the *s* of Jeroham,
6: 35 the *s* of Mahath, the *s* of Amasai,
6: 35 the *s* of Zuph, the *s* of Elkanah,
6: 36 the *s* of Azariah, the *s* of Zephaniah
6: 36 the *s* of Elkanah, the *s* of Joel,
6: 37 the *s* of Ebiasaph, the *s* of Korah,
6: 37 the *s* of Tahath, the *s* of Assir,
6: 38 the *s* of Izhar, the *s* of Kohath,
6: 38 the *s* of Levi, the *s* of Israel;
6: 39 *s* of Berekiah, the *s* of Shimea,
6: 40 the *s* of Michael, the *s* of Baaseiah,
6: 41 the *s* of Malkijah, the *s* of Ethni,
6: 41 the *s* of Zerah, the *s* of Adaiah,
6: 42 the *s* of Ethan, the *s* of Zimmah,
6: 43 the *s* of Gershon, the *s* of Levi;
6: 43 the *s* of Shimei, the *s* of Jahath,
6: 44 Ethan *s* of Kishi, the *s* of Abdi,
6: 45 the *s* of Amaziah, the *s* of Hilkiah,
6: 45 *s* of Malluch, the *s* of Hashabiah,
6: 46 the *s* of Amzi, the *s* of Bani,
6: 47 Merari, the *s* of Levi.
6: 47 the *s* of Mushi, the *s* of Merari,
6: 47 the *s* of Shemer, the *s* of Mahli,
6: 50 Phinehas his *s*, Abishua his *s*,
6: 50 of Aaron: Eleazar his *s*,

1Ch 6: 51 Bukki his *s*, Uzzi his *s*,
6: 52 Amariah his *s*, Ahitub his *s*,
6: 52 Zerahiah his *s*, Meraioth his *s*,
6: 53 Zadok his *s* and Ahimaaz his *s*.
6: 56 given to Caleb *s* of Jephunneh.
7: 3 The *s* of Uzzi: Izrahiah.
7: 10 The *s* of Jediael: Bilhan.
7: 16 wife Maacah gave birth to a *s*
7: 17 The *s* of Ulam: Bedan.
7: 17 *s* of Makir, the *s* of Manasseh.
7: 20 Eleadah his *s*, Tahath his *s*,
7: 20 Shuthelah, Bered his *s*, Tahath his *s*
7: 21 Zabad his *s* and Shuthelah his *s*.
7: 23 pregnant and gave birth to a *s*.
7: 25 Rephah was his *s*, Resheph his *s*,
7: 25 Telah his *s*, Tahan his *s*, Ladan his *s*
7: 26 Ammihud his *s*, Elishama his *s*,
7: 27 Nun his *s* and Joshua his *s*.
7: 29 of Joseph *s* of Israel lived
8: 1 Ashbel the second *s*, Aharah
8: 30 and his firstborn *s* was Abdon,
8: 34 The *s* of Jonathan: Merib-Baal,
8: 37 Eleasah his *s* and Azel his *s*.
8: 37 father of Binea; Raphah was his *s*,
8: 39 Jeush the second *s* and Eliphelet
9: 4 Uthai *s* of Ammihud, the *s* of Omri,
9: 4 a descendant of Perez *s* of Judah.
9: 4 the *s* of Imri, the *s* of Bani,
9: 7 Of the Benjamites: Sallu *s*
9: 7 of Meshullam, the *s* of Hodaviah,
9: 8 Elah *s* of Uzzi, the *s* of Micri;
9: 8 and Meshullam *s* of Shephatiah,
9: 8 the *s* of Hassenuah; Ibneiah *s*
9: 8 the *s* of Reuel, the *s* of Ibnijah.
9: 11 the *s* of Zadok, the *s* of Meraioth,
9: 11 *s* of Hilkiah, the *s* of Meshullam,
9: 12 Maasai *s* of Adiel, the *s* of Jahzerah
9: 12 of Meshillemith, the *s* of Immer.
9: 12 of Pashhur, the *s* of Malkijah;
9: 12 the *s* of Meshullam, the *s*
9: 12 *s* of Jeroham, the *s* of Pashhur,
9: 14 the *s* of Hashabiah, a Merarite;
9: 14 *s* of Hasshub, the *s* of Azrikam,
9: 15 Galal and Mattaniah *s* of Mica,
9: 15 the *s* of Zicri, the *s* of Asaph;
9: 16 Berekiah *s* of Asa, the *s* of Elkanah,
9: 16 of Asaph; Obadiah *s* of Shemaiah,
9: 16 the *s* of Galal, the *s* of Jeduthun;
9: 19 Shallum *s* of Kore,
9: 19 the *s* of Ebiasaph, the *s* of Korah,
9: 20 In earlier times Phinehas *s*
9: 21 Zechariah *s* of Meshelemiah was
9: 31 firstborn *s* of Shallum the Korahite,
9: 36 and his firstborn *s* was Abdon,
9: 40 The *s* of Jonathan: Merib-Baal,
9: 43 Binea; Rephaiah was his *s*,
9: 43 Eleasah his *s* and Azel his *s*.
10: 14 kingdom over to David *s* of Jesse.
11: 6 Joab *s* of Zeruiah went up first,
11: 12 Next to him was Eleazar *s*
11: 22 Benaiah *s* of Jehoiada was a valiant
11: 24 exploits of Benaiah *s* of Jehoiada;
11: 26 Elhanan *s* of Dodo
11: 28 Ira *s* of Ikkesh from Tekoa,
11: 30 Heled *s* of Baanah
11: 31 Ithai *s* of Ribai from Gibeah
11: 34 Jonathan *s* of Shagee the Hararite,
11: 35 Ahiam *s* of Sacar the Hararite,
11: 35 Eliphal *s* of Ur, Hepher
11: 37 Hezro the Carmelite, Naarai *s*
11: 38 Mibhar *s* of Hagri, Zelek
11: 39 armor-bearer of Joab *s* of Zeruiah,
11: 41 Uriah the Hittite, Zabad *s* of Ahlai,
11: 42 Adina *s* of Shiza the Reubenite,
11: 43 Hanan *s* of Maacah, Joshaphat
11: 45 Jediael *s* of Shimri, his brother
12: 1 of Saul *s* of Kish (they were
12: 18 We are with you, O *s* of Jesse!
15: 17 So the Levites appointed Heman *s*
15: 17 brothers the Merarites, Ethan *s*
15: 17 from his brothers, Asaph *s*
16: 38 Obed-Edom *s* of Jeduthun,
17: 13 be his father, and he will be my *s*.
18: 10 he sent his *s* Hadoram
18: 12 Abishai *s* of Zeruiah struck
18: 15 Jehoshaphat *s* of Ahilud was
18: 15 Joab *s* of Zeruiah was
18: 16 Zadok *s* of Ahitub and Ahimelech

1Ch 18: 16 and Ahimelech *s* of Abiathar were
18: 17 Benaiah *s* of Jehoiada was
19: 1 and his *s* succeeded him as king.
19: 2 kindness to Hanun *s* of Nahash,
20: 5 Elhanan *s* of Jair killed Lahmi
20: 7 Jonathan *s* of Shimea, David's
22: 5 "My *s* Solomon is young
22: 6 Then he called for his *s* Solomon
22: 7 David said to Solomon: "My *s*,
22: 9 you will have a *s* who will be a man
22: 10 He will be my *s*, and I will be his
22: 11 Now, my *s*, the LORD be with you
22: 17 of Israel to help his *s* Solomon.
23: 1 he made his *s* Solomon king
24: 6 Ahimelech *s* of Abiathar
24: 6 The scribe Shemaiah *s* of Nethanel
24: 24 The *s* of Uzziel: Micah;
24: 26 The *s* of Jaaziah: Beno.
24: 29 Kish: the *s* of Kish: Jerahmeel.
26: 1 the Korahites: Meshelemiah *s*
26: 6 His *s* Shemaiah also had sons,
26: 14 lots were cast for his *s* Zechariah,
26: 24 of Gershom *s* of Moses,
26: 25 Joram his *s*,
26: 25 Rehabiah his *s*, Jeshaiah his *s*,
26: 25 Zicri his *s* and Shelomith his *s*.
26: 28 Abner *s* of Ner and Joab *s*
26: 28 by Samuel the seer and by Saul *s*
27: 2 was Jashobeam *s* of Zabdiel.
27: 5 was Benaiah *s* of Jehoiada
27: 6 His *s* Ammizabad was in charge
27: 7 his *s* Zebadiah was his successor.
27: 9 was Ira the *s* of Ikkesh the Tekoite.
27: 16 over the Reubenites: Eliezer *s*
27: 16 over the Simeonites: Shephatiah *s*
27: 17 over Levi: Hashabiah *s* of Kemuel;
27: 18 over Issachar: Omri *s* of Michael;
27: 19 over Naphtali: Jerimoth *s* of Azriel
27: 19 over Zebulun: Ishmaiah *s*
27: 20 of Manasseh: Joel *s* of Pedaiah;
27: 20 over the Ephraimites: Hoshea *s*
27: 21 Iddo *s* of Zechariah; over Benjamin
27: 21 over Benjamin: Jaasiel *s* of Abner;
27: 22 over Dan: Azarel *s* of Jeroham.
27: 24 Joab *s* of Zeruiah began
27: 25 Azmaveth *s* of Adiel was in charge
27: 25 Jonathan *s* of Uzziah was in charge
27: 26 Ezri *s* of Kelub was in charge
27: 29 Shaphat *s* of Adlai was in charge
27: 32 Jehiel *s* of Hacmoni took care
27: 34 by Jehoiada *s* of Benaiah
28: 5 he has chosen my *s* Solomon to sit
28: 6 for I have chosen him to be my *s*,
28: 6 'Solomon your *s* is the one who will
28: 9 "And you, my *s* Solomon,
28: 11 David gave his *s* Solomon the plans
28: 20 David also said to Solomon his *s*,
29: 1 "My *s* Solomon, the one whom
29: 19 And give my *s* Solomon
29: 22 they acknowledged Solomon *s*
29: 26 David *s* of Jesse was king
29: 28 His *s* Solomon succeeded him
2Ch 1: 1 Solomon *s* of David established
1: 5 *s* of Uri, the *s* of Hur,
2: 12 He has given King David a wise *s*,
6: 9 but your *s*, who is your own flesh
9: 29 the seer concerning Jeroboam *s*
9: 31 Rehoboam his *s* succeeded him
10: 2 When Jeroboam *s*
10: 15 spoken to Jeroboam *s* of Nebat
10: 16 what part in Jesse's *s*?
11: 3 "Say to Rehoboam *s*
11: 17 and supported Rehoboam *s*
11: 18 the daughter of David's *s* Jerimoth
11: 18 the daughter of Jesse's *s* Eliab.
11: 22 Rehoboam appointed Abijah *s*
12: 16 And Abijah his *s* succeeded him
13: 6 Yet Jeroboam *s* of Nebat,
13: 6 an official of Solomon *s* of David,
13: 7 opposed Rehoboam *s* of Solomon
14: 1 Asa his *s* succeeded him as king,
15: 1 came upon Azariah *s* of Oded.
15: 8 and the prophecy of Azariah *s*
17: 1 Jehoshaphat his *s* succeeded him
17: 16 with 280,000; next, Amasiah *s*
18: 7 He is Micaiah *s* of Imlah."
18: 8 Bring Micaiah *s* of Imlah at once."
18: 10 Zedekiah *s* of Kenaanah had made
2Ch 18: 23 Zedekiah *s* of Kenaanah went up
18: 25 of the city and to Joash the king's *s*,
19: 2 Jehu the seer, the *s* of Hanani,
19: 11 and Zebadiah *s* of Ishmael,
20: 14 came upon Jahaziel *s* of Zechariah,
20: 14 the *s* of Benaiah, the *s* of Jeiel,
20: 14 the *s* of Mattaniah, a Levite
20: 34 in the annals of Jehu *s* of Hanani,
20: 37 Eliezer *s* of Dodavahu
21: 1 And Jehoram his *s* succeeded him
21: 3 because he was his firstborn *s*.
21: 17 Not a *s* was left to him
22: 1 Jehoram's youngest *s*, king
22: 1 So Ahaziah *s* of Jehoram king
22: 5 went with Joram *s* of Ahab king
22: 6 Then Ahaziah *s* of Jehoram king
22: 6 to Jezreel to see Joram *s* of Ahab
22: 7 Joram to meet Jehu *s* of Nimshi,
22: 9 "He was a *s* of Jehoshaphat,
22: 10 of Ahaziah saw that her *s* was dead,
22: 11 took Joash *s* of Ahaziah
23: 1 Azariah *s* of Jeroham, Ishmael *s*
23: 1 of Jehohanan, Azariah *s* of Obed,
23: 1 *s* of Adaiah, and Elishaphat *s*
23: 3 to them, "The king's *s* shall reign,
23: 11 his sons brought out the king's *s*
24: 20 came upon Zechariah *s* of Jehoiada
24: 22 had shown him but killed his *s*,
24: 25 him for murdering the *s*
24: 26 *s* of Shimeath an Ammonite
24: 26 *s* of Shimrith a Moabite woman.
24: 27 And Amaziah his *s* succeeded him
25: 17 challenge to Jehoash *s* of Jehoahaz,
25: 17 the *s* of Jehu, king of Israel: "Come
25: 18 daughter to my *s* in marriage.'
25: 23 the *s* of Joash, the *s* of Ahaziah,
25: 25 Amaziah *s* of Joash king
25: 25 of Jehoash *s* of Jehoahaz king
26: 21 Jotham his *s* had charge
26: 22 by the prophet Isaiah *s* of Amoz.
26: 23 And Jotham his *s* succeeded him
27: 9 And Ahaz his *s* succeeded him
28: 6 In one day Pekah *s*
28: 7 killed Maaseiah the king's *s*,
28: 12 Azariah *s* of Jehohanan, Berekiah
28: 12 of Shallum, and Amasa *s* of Hadlai
28: 12 *s* of Meshillemoth, Jehizkiah *s*
28: 27 And Hezekiah his *s* succeeded him
29: 12 Joah *s* of Zimmah and Eden *s*
29: 12 Kish *s* of Abdi and Azariah *s*
29: 12 Mahath *s* of Amasai and Joel *s*
30: 26 days of Solomon *s* of David king
31: 14 Kore *s* of Imnah the Levite,
32: 20 and the prophet Isaiah *s*
32: 32 of the prophet Isaiah *s* of Amoz
32: 33 Manasseh his *s* succeeded him
33: 7 said to David and to his *s* Solomon,
33: 20 And Amon his *s* succeeded him
33: 25 and they made Josiah his *s* king
34: 8 he sent Shaphan *s* of Azaliah
34: 8 with Joah *s* of Joahaz, the recorder,
34: 20 *s* of Shaphan, Abdon *s* of Micah,
34: 22 the wife of Shallum *s* of Tokhath,
34: 22 the *s* of Hasrah, keeper
35: 3 ark in the temple that Solomon *s*
35: 4 king of Israel and by his *s* Solomon.
36: 1 people of the land took Jehoahaz *s*
36: 8 Jehoiachin his *s* succeeded him
Ezr 3: 2 Then Jeshua *s* of Jozadak
3: 2 and Zerubbabel *s* of Shealtiel
3: 8 God in Jerusalem, Zerubbabel *s*
3: 8 Jeshua *s* of Jozadak and the rest
5: 2 Then Zerubbabel *s* of Shealtiel
5: 2 and Jeshua *s* of Jozadak set to work
7: 1 Ezra *s* of Seraiah, the *s* of Azariah,
7: 2 the *s* of Hilkiah, the *s* of Shallum,
7: 2 the *s* of Zadok, the *s* of Ahitub,
7: 3 the *s* of Amariah, the *s* of Azariah,
7: 4 the *s* of Meraioth, the *s* of Zerahiah
7: 4 the *s* of Uzzi, the *s* of Bukki,
7: 5 Phinehas, the *s* of Eleazar,
7: 5 the *s* of Aaron the chief priest—
7: 5 the *s* of Abishua, the *s* of Phinehas,
8: 4 of Pahath-Moab, Eliehoenai *s*
8: 5 of Zattu, Shecaniah *s* of Jahaziel,
8: 6 of Adin, Ebed *s* of Jonathan,
8: 7 of Elam, Jeshaiah *s* of Athaliah,
8: 8 of Shephatiah, Zebadiah *s*
Ezr 8: 9 of Joab, Obadiah *s* of Jehiel,
8: 10 of Bani, Shelomith *s* of Josiphiah,
8: 11 of Bebai, Zechariah *s* of Bebai,
8: 12 of Azgad, Johanan *s* of Hakkatan,
8: 18 the descendants of Mahli *s* of Levi,
8: 18 the *s* of Israel, and Sherebiah's sons
8: 33 Eleazar *s* of Phinehas was with him
8: 33 and so were the Levites Jozabad *s*
8: 33 of Jeshua and Noadiah *s* of Binnui.
8: 33 the hands of Meremoth *s* of Uriah,
10: 2 Then Shecaniah *s* of Jehiel,
10: 6 room of Jehohanan *s* of Eliashib.
10: 15 Only Jonathan *s* of Asahel
10: 15 of Asahel and Jahzeiah *s* of Tikvah,
10: 18 of Jeshua *s* of Jozadak,
Ne 1: 1 words of Nehemiah *s* of Hacaliah:
3: 2 Zaccur *s* of Imri built next to them.
3: 4 Meremoth *s* of Uriah, the *s*
3: 4 and next to him Zadok *s* of Baana
3: 4 the *s* of Meshezabel, made repairs,
3: 4 to him Meshullam *s* of Berekiah,
3: 6 and Meshullam *s* of Besodeiah.
3: 6 repaired by Joiada *s* of Paseah
3: 8 Uzziel *s* of Harhaiah, one
3: 9 Rephaiah *s* of Hur, ruler
3: 10 Hattush *s* of Hashabneiah made
3: 10 Jedaiah *s* of Harumaph made
3: 11 Malkijah *s* of Harim and Hasshub
3: 11 *s* of Pahath-Moab repaired
3: 12 Shallum *s* of Hallohesh, ruler
3: 14 repaired by Malkijah *s* of Recab,
3: 15 by Shallun *s* of Col-Hozeh,
3: 16 Beyond him, Nehemiah *s* of Azbuk
3: 17 the Levites under Rehum *s* of Bani.
3: 18 under Binnui *s* of Henadad,
3: 19 Next to him, Ezer *s* of Jeshua,
3: 20 Baruch *s* of Zabbai zealously
3: 21 *s* of Uriah, the *s* of Hakkoz,
3: 23 *s* of Maaseiah, the *s* of Ananiah,
3: 24 Binnui *s* of Henadad repaired
3: 25 Pedaiah *s* of Parosh and the temple
3: 25 and Palal *s* of Uzai worked
3: 29 Zadok *s* of Immer made repairs
3: 29 to him, Shemaiah *s* of Shecaniah,
3: 30 Hananiah *s* of Shelemiah,
3: 30 Meshullam *s* of Berekiah made
3: 30 and Hanun, the sixth *s* of Zalaph,
6: 10 house of Shemaiah *s* of Delaiah,
6: 10 the *s* of Mehetabel, who was shut
6: 18 and his *s* Jehohanan had married
6: 18 of Meshullam *s* of Berekiah.
6: 18 son-in-law to Shecaniah *s* of Arah,
8: 17 From the days of Joshua *s* of Nun
10: 1 Nehemiah the governor, the *s*
10: 9 The Levites: Jeshua *s* of Azaniah,
11: 4 of Amariah, the *s* of Shephatiah,
11: 4 of Judah: Athaiah *s* of Uzziah,
11: 4 of Shephatiah, the *s* of Mahalalel,
11: 4 *s* of Zechariah, the *s* of Amariah,
11: 5 the *s* of Hazaiah, the *s* of Adaiah,
11: 5 the *s* of Joiarib, the *s* of Zechariah,
11: 5 *s* of Baruch, the *s* of Col-Hozeh,
11: 7 of Benjamin: Sallu *s* of Meshullam,
11: 7 the *s* of Ithiel, the *s* of Jeshaiah,
11: 7 the *s* of Joed, the *s* of Pedaiah,
11: 7 the *s* of Kolaiah, the *s* of Maaseiah,
11: 9 Joel *s* of Zicri was their chief
11: 9 and Judah *s* of Hassenuah was
11: 10 Jedaiah; the *s* of Joiarib; Jakin;
11: 11 Jakin; Seraiah *s* of Hilkiah,
11: 11 the *s* of Meraioth, the *s* of Ahitub,
11: 11 the *s* of Meshullam, the *s* of Zadok,
11: 12 the *s* of Amzi, the *s* of Zechariah,
11: 12 the *s* of Pashhur, the *s* of Malkijah,
11: 12 *s* of Jeroham, the *s* of Pelaliah,
11: 13 of Ahzai, the *s* of Meshillemoth,
11: 13 of Meshillemoth, the *s* of Immer,
11: 13 *s* of Azarel, the *s* of Ahzai,
11: 14 Their chief officer was Zabdiel *s*
11: 15 the *s* of Hashabiah, the *s* of Bunni;
11: 15 *s* of Hasshub, the *s* of Azrikam,
11: 17 Mattaniah *s* of Mica,
11: 17 among his associates; and Abda *s*
11: 17 the *s* of Galal, the *s* of Jeduthun.
11: 17 the *s* of Zabdi, the *s* of Asaph,
11: 22 Bani, the *s* of Hashabiah,
11: 22 in Jerusalem was Uzzi *s* of Bani,
11: 22 the *s* of Mattaniah, the *s* of Mica.

Eze 11: 4 against them; prophesy, *s* of man."
11: 13 Pelatiah *s* of Benaiah died.
11: 15 "*S* of man, your brothers—
12: 2 word of the LORD came to me: "*S*
12: 3 *s* of man, pack your belongings
12: 9 "*S* of man, did not that rebellious house
12: 18 "*S* of man, tremble as you eat
12: 22 "*S* of man, what is this proverb
12: 27 "*S* of man, the house of Israel
13: 2 "*S* of man, prophesy against the
13: 17 "Now, *s* of man, set your face
14: 3 "*S* of man, these men have set up
14: 13 "*S* of man, if a country sins
14: 20 they could save neither *s*
15: 2 "*S* of man, how is the wood of a vine
16: 2 "*S* of man, confront Jerusalem
17: 2 "*S* of man, set forth an allegory
18: 4 the father as well as the *s*—
18: 10 "Suppose he has a violent *s*,
18: 14 suppose this *s* has a *s* who sees all
18: 19 Since the *s* has done what is just
18: 19 'Why does the *s* not share the guilt
18: 20 The *s* will not share the guilt
18: 20 the father share the guilt of the *s*.
20: 3 "*S* of man, speak to the elders
20: 4 Will you judge them, *s* of man?
20: 27 *s* of man, speak to the people
20: 46 "*S* of man, set your face toward
21: 2 "*S* of man, set your face against
21: 6 "Therefore groan, *s* of man!
21: 9 "*S* of man prophesy and say,
21: 10 my *s*, have despised the rod
21: 12 Cry out and wail, *s* of man,
21: 14 "So prophesy, *s* of man.
21: 19 "*S* of man, mark out two roads
21: 28 *s* of man, prophesy and say,
22: 2 "*S* of man, will you judge her?
22: 18 "*S* of man, the house of Israel
22: 24 "*S* of man, say to the land,
23: 2 "*S* of man, there were two women,
23: 36 The LORD said to me: "*S* of man,
24: 2 "*S* of man, record this date,
24: 16 "*S* of man, with one blow
24: 25 *s* of man, on the day I take away
25: 2 "*S* of man, set your face against the
26: 2 "*S* of man, because Tyre
27: 2 "*S* of man, take up a lament
28: 2 "*S* of man, say to the ruler of Tyre,
28: 12 "*S* of man, take up a lament
28: 21 "*S* of man, set your face against Sidon;
29: 2 "*S* of man, set your face against
29: 18 "*S* of man, Nebuchadnezzar king
30: 2 "*S* of man, prophesy and say:
30: 21 "*S* of man, I have broken the arm
31: 2 "*S* of man, say to Pharaoh
32: 2 "*S* of man, take up a lament concerning
32: 18 "*S* of man, wail for the hordes of Egypt
33: 2 "*S* of man, speak to your countrymen
33: 7 "*S* of man, I have made you
33: 10 *S* of man, say to the house of Israel,
33: 12 of Israel?' "Therefore, *s* of man,
33: 24 "*S* of man, the people living
33: 30 *s* of man, your countrymen are
34: 2 "*S* of man, prophesy against the
35: 2 "*S* of man, set your face against Mount
36: 1 "*S* of man, prophesy
36: 17 "*S* of man, when the people of Israel
37: 3 "*S* of man, can these bones live?"
37: 9 to the breath; prophesy, *s* of man,
37: 11 Then he said to me: "*S* of man,
37: 16 "*S* of man, take a stick of wood
38: 2 *S* of man, set your face against Gog
38: 14 *s* of man, prophesy and say to Gog:
39: 1 "*S* of man, prophesy against Gog
39: 17 "*S* of man, this is what
40: 4 The man said to me, "*S* of man,
43: 7 "*S* of man, this is the place
43: 10 "*S* of man, describe the temple
43: 18 Then he said to me, "*S* of man,
44: 5 The LORD said to me, "*S* of man,
44: 25 *s* or daughter, brother
47: 6 "*S* of man, do you see this?"
Da 3: 25 the fourth looks like a *s* of the gods
5: 22 "But you his *s*, O Belshazzar,
7: 13 before me was one like a *s* of man,
8: 17 "*S* of man," he said to me,
9: 1 year of Darius *s* of Xerxes (a Mede
Hos 1: 1 came to Hosea *s* of Beeri
Hos 1: 1 of Jeroboam *s* of Jehoash king
1: 3 and she conceived and bore him a *s*
1: 8 Gomer had another *s*.
11: 1 and out of Egypt I called my *s*.
Joel 1: 1 came to Joel *s* of Pethuel.
Am 1: 1 Jeroboam *s* of Jehoash was king
2: 7 Father and *s* use the same girl
7: 14 neither a prophet nor a prophet's *s*,
8: 10 time like mourning for an only *s*
Jnh 1: 1 came to Jonah *s* of Amittai:
Mic 6: 5 what Balaam *s* of Beor answered.
7: 6 For a *s* dishonors his father,
Zep 1: 1 came to Zephaniah *s* of Cushi,
1: 1 of Amariah, the *s* of Hezekiah,
1: 1 the reign of Josiah *s* of Amon king
1: 1 the *s* of Gedaliah, the *s* of Amariah,
Hag 1: 1 and to Joshua *s* of Jehozadak,
1: 1 to Zerubbabel *s* of Shealtiel,
1: 12 Joshua *s* of Jehozadak, the high
1: 12 Then Zerubbabel *s* of Shealtiel,
1: 14 spirit of Zerubbabel *s* of Shealtiel,
1: 14 the spirit of Joshua *s* of Jehozadak,
2: 2 Speak to Zerubbabel *s* of Shealtiel,
2: 2 of Judah, to Joshua *s* of Jehozadak,
2: 4 Be strong, O Joshua *s* of Jehozadak
2: 23 my servant Zerubbabel *s*
Zec 1: 1 came to the prophet Zechariah *s*
1: 1 *s* of Iddo: "The LORD was very
1: 7 *s* of Berekiah, the *s* of Iddo.
6: 10 the house of Josiah *s* of Zephaniah.
6: 11 head of the high priest, Joshua *s*
6: 14 Jedaiah and Hen *s* of Zephaniah
12: 10 as one grieves for a firstborn *s*.
Mal 1: 6 of Israel!' "A *s* honors his father,
3: 17 a man spares his *s* who serves him.
Mt 1: 1 of Jesus Christ the *s* of David,
1: 1 the *s* of Abraham: Abraham was
1: 20 Joseph *s* of David, do not be afraid
1: 21 She will give birth to a *s*,
1: 23 with child and will give birth to a *s*,
1: 25 with her until she gave birth to a *s*.
2: 15 "Out of Egypt I called my *s*."
3: 17 "This is my *S*, whom I love;
4: 3 "If you are the *S* of God, tell these
4: 6 "If you are the *S* of God," he said,
4: 21 James *s* of Zebedee and his brother
7: 9 Which of you, if his *s* asks for bread
8: 20 but the *S* of Man has no place
8: 29 want with us, *S* of God?"
9: 2 "Take heart, *s*; your sins are
9: 6 so that you may know that the *S*
9: 27 "Have mercy on us, *S* of David!"
10: 2 James *s* of Zebedee, and his
10: 3 James *s* of Alphaeus,
10: 23 of Israel before the *S* of Man comes
10: 37 anyone who loves his *s*
11: 19 The *S* of Man came eating
11: 27 and those to whom the *S* chooses
11: 27 one knows the Father except the *S*
11: 27 one knows the *S* except the Father,
12: 8 For the *S* of Man is Lord
12: 23 "Could this be the *S* of David?"
12: 32 a word against the *S* of Man will be
12: 40 so the *S* of Man will be three days
13: 37 who sowed the good seed is the *S*
13: 41 *S* of Man will send out his angels,
13: 55 "Isn't this the carpenter's *s*?
14: 33 "Truly you are the *S* of God."
15: 22 crying out, "Lord, *S* of David,
16: 13 Who do people say the *S* of Man is
16: 16 "You are the Christ, the *S*
16: 17 Blessed are you, Simon *s* of Jonah,
16: 27 For the *S* of Man is going to come
16: 28 death before they see the *S*
17: 5 "This is my *S*, whom I love;
17: 9 until the *S* of Man has been raised
17: 12 In the same way the *S*
17: 15 have mercy on my *s*," he said.
17: 22 "The *S* of Man is going
19: 28 when the *S* of Man sits
20: 18 and the *S* of Man will be betrayed
20: 28 as the *S* of Man did not come
20: 30 they shouted, "Lord, *S* of David,
20: 31 Lord, *S* of David, have mercy on us
21: 9 "Hosanna to the *S* of David!"
21: 15 "Hosanna to the *S* of David,"
21: 28 He went to the first and said, '*S*,
21: 30 the father went to the other *s*
Mt 21: 37 Last of all, he sent his *s* to them.
21: 37 'They will respect my *s*,' he said.
21: 38 "But when the tenants saw the *s*,
22: 2 a wedding banquet for his *s*.
22: 42 Whose *s* is he?" "The *s* of David,"
22: 45 can he be his *s*?" No one could say
23: 15 as much a *s* of hell as you are.
23: 35 blood of Zechariah *s* of Berakiah,
24: 27 so will be the coming of the *S*
24: 30 They will see the *S* of Man coming
24: 30 the sign of the *S* of Man will appear
24: 36 nor the *S*, but only the Father.
24: 37 be at the coming of the *S* of Man.
24: 39 be at the coming of the *S* of Man.
24: 44 the *S* of Man will come at an hour
25: 31 "When the *S* of Man comes
26: 2 and the *S* of Man will be handed
26: 24 The *S* of Man will go just
26: 24 woe to that man who betrays the *S*
26: 45 and the *S* of Man is betrayed
26: 63 if you are the Christ, the *S* of God."
26: 64 In the future you will see the *S*
27: 40 if you are the *S* of God!"
27: 43 for he said, 'I am the *S* of God.'"
27: 54 "Surely he was the *S* of God!"
28: 19 and of the *S* and of the Holy Spirit,
Mk 1: 1 the gospel about Jesus Christ, the *S*
1: 11 "You are my *S*, whom I love;
1: 19 he saw James *s* of Zebedee
2: 5 "*S*, your sins are forgiven."
2: 10 But that you may know that the *S*
2: 14 he saw Levi *s* of Alphaeus sitting
2: 28 So the *S* of Man is Lord
3: 11 cried out, "You are the *S* of God."
3: 17 he gave the name Peter); James *s*
3: 18 Thomas, James *s* of Alphaeus,
5: 7 Jesus, *S* of the Most High God?
6: 3 Isn't this Mary's *s* and the brother
8: 31 began to teach them that the *S*
8: 38 the *S* of Man will be ashamed
9: 7 "This is my *S*, whom I love.
9: 9 seen until the *S* of Man had risen
9: 12 Why then is it written that the *S*
9: 17 "Teacher, I brought you my *s*,
9: 31 "The *S* of Man is going
10: 33 "and the *S* of Man will be betrayed
10: 45 even the *S* of Man did not come
10: 46 Bartimaeus (that is, the *S*
10: 47 began to shout, "Jesus, *S* of David,
10: 48 but he shouted all the more, "*S*
12: 6 saying, 'They will respect my *s*.'
12: 6 "He had one left to send, a *s*,
12: 35 the law say that the Christ is the *s*
12: 37 How then can he be his *s*?"
13: 26 "At that time men will see the *S*
13: 32 nor the *S*, but only the Father.
14: 21 The *S* of Man will go just
14: 21 woe to that man who betrays the *S*
14: 41 the *S* of Man is betrayed
14: 61 the *S* of the Blessed One?"
14: 62 you will see the *S* of Man sitting
15: 39 Surely this man was the *S* of God!"
Lk 1: 13 wife Elizabeth will bear you a *s*,
1: 31 be with child and give birth to a *s*,
1: 32 and will be called the *S*
1: 35 one to be born will be called the *S*
1: 57 have her baby, she gave birth to a *s*.
2: 7 she gave birth to her firstborn, a *s*.
2: 48 His mother said to him, "*S*,
3: 2 came to John *s* of Zechariah
3: 22 "You are my *S*, whom I love;
3: 23 He was the *s*, so it was thought,
3: 23 the *s* of Heli,
3: 24 the *s* of Jannai, the *s* of Joseph,
3: 24 the *s* of Levi, the *s* of Melki,
3: 24 the *s* of Matthat,
3: 25 the *s* of Mattathias, the *s* of Amos,
3: 25 the *s* of Naggai,
3: 25 the *s* of Nahum, the *s* of Esli,
3: 26 the *s* of Josech, the *s* of Joda,
3: 26 the *s* of Maath,
3: 26 the *s* of Mattathias, the *s* of Semein
3: 27 the *s* of Joanan, the *s* of Rhesa,
3: 27 the *s* of Neri,
3: 27 the *s* of Zerubbabel, the *s*
3: 28 the *s* of Addi, the *s* of Cosam,
3: 28 the *s* of Elmadam, the *s* of Er,
3: 28 the *s* of Melki,

Lk 3: 29 the *s* of Jorim, the *s* of Matthat,
3: 29 the *s* of Joshua, the *s* of Eliezer,
3: 29 the *s* of Levi,
3: 30 the *s* of Jonam, the *s* of Eliakim,
3: 30 the *s* of Judah, the *s* of Joseph,
3: 30 the *s* of Simeon,
3: 31 the *s* of David,
3: 31 the *s* of Mattatha, the *s* of Nathan,
3: 31 the *s* of Melea, the *s* of Menna,
3: 32 the *s* of Jesse,
3: 32 the *s* of Obed, the *s* of Boaz,
3: 32 the *s* of Salmon, the *s* of Nahshon,
3: 33 the *s* of Amminadab, the *s* of Ram,
3: 33 the *s* of Hezron, the *s* of Perez,
3: 33 the *s* of Judah,
3: 34 the *s* of Isaac, the *s* of Abraham,
3: 34 the *s* of Jacob,
3: 34 the *s* of Terah, the *s* of Nahor,
3: 35 the *s* of Peleg, the *s* of Eber,
3: 35 the *s* of Serug, the *s* of Reu,
3: 35 the *s* of Shelah,
3: 36 the *s* of Arphaxad, the *s* of Shem,
3: 36 the *s* of Cainan,
3: 36 the *s* of Noah, the *s* of Lamech,
3: 37 the *s* of Cainan,
3: 37 the *s* of Jared, the *s* of Mahalaleel,
3: 37 the *s* of Methuselah, the *s* of Enoch
3: 38 the *s* of Enos,
3: 38 the *s* of God.
3: 38 the *s* of Seth, the *s* of Adam,
4: 3 "If you are the *S* of God, tell this
4: 9 "If you are the *S* of God," he said,
4: 22 "Isn't this Joseph's *s*?" they asked.
4: 41 shouting, "You are the *S* of God!"
5: 24 But that you may know that the *S*
6: 5 "The *S* of Man is Lord
6: 15 Thomas, James *s* of Alphaeus,
6: 16 Judas *s* of James, and Judas
6: 22 because of the *S* of Man.
7: 12 the only *s* of his mother,
7: 34 The *S* of Man came eating
8: 28 Jesus, *S* of the Most High God?
9: 22 *S* of Man must suffer many things
9: 26 the *S* of Man will be ashamed
9: 35 This is my *S*, whom I have chosen;
9: 38 at my *s*, for he is my only child.
9: 41 put up with you? Bring your *s* here.
9: 44 The *S* of Man is going
9: 58 but the *S* of Man has no place
10: 22 No one knows who the *S* is
10: 22 and those to whom the *S* chooses
10: 22 who the Father is except the *S*
11: 11 if your *s* asks for a fish,
11: 30 also will the *S* of Man be
12: 8 the *S* of Man will also acknowledge
12: 10 a word against the *S* of Man will be
12: 40 the *S* of Man will come at an hour
12: 53 father against *s* and *s* against father
14: 5 one of you has a *s* or an ox that falls
15: 13 younger *s* got together all he had,
15: 19 worthy to be called your *s*;
15: 20 he ran to his *s*, threw his arms
15: 21 worthy to be called your *s*.'
15: 21 "The *s* said to him, 'Father,
15: 24 For this *s* of mine was dead
15: 25 the older *s* was in the field.
15: 30 But when this *s* of yours who has
15: 31 calf for him!" 'My *s*,'
16: 25 "But Abraham replied, '*S*,
17: 22 one of the days of the *S* of Man,
17: 24 For the *S* of Man in his day will be
17: 26 be in the days of the *S* of Man.
17: 30 on the day the *S* of Man is revealed
18: 8 when the *S* of Man comes,
18: 31 written by the prophets about the *S*
18: 38 He called out, "Jesus, *S* of David,
18: 39 but he shouted all the more, "*S*
19: 9 this man, too, is a *s* of Abraham.
19: 10 For the *S* of Man came to seek
20: 13 I will send my *s*, whom I love;
20: 41 is it that they say the Christ is the *S*
20: 44 How then can he be his *s*?"
21: 27 At that time they will see the *S*
21: 36 able to stand before the *S* of Man."
22: 22 The *S* of Man will go as it has been
22: 48 are you betraying the *S* of Man
22: 69 the *S* of Man will be seated
22: 70 "Are you then the *S* of God?"
Lk 24: 7 'The *S* of Man must be delivered
Jn 1: 14 the glory of the one and only *S*,
1: 18 but God the only *S*, who is
1: 34 I testify that this is the *S* of God."
1: 42 "You are Simon *s* of John.
1: 45 Jesus of Nazareth, the *s* of Joseph."
1: 49 "Rabbi, you are the *S* of God;
1: 51 and descending on the *S* of Man."
3: 13 came from heaven—the *S* of Man.
3: 14 so the *S* of Man must be lifted up,
3: 16 that he gave his one and only *S*,
3: 17 For God did not send his *S*
3: 18 the name of God's one and only *S*.
3: 35 The Father loves the *S*
3: 36 believes in the *S* has eternal life,
3: 36 whoever rejects the *S* will not see
4: 5 Jacob had given to his *s* Joseph.
4: 46 royal official whose *s* lay sick
4: 47 begged him to come and heal his *s*,
4: 50 Your *s* will live."
4: 52 as to the time when his *s* got better,
4: 53 said to him, "Your *s* will live."
5: 19 the *S* can do nothing by himself;
5: 19 whatever the Father does the *S*
5: 20 For the Father loves the *S*
5: 21 so the *S* gives life to whom he is
5: 22 has entrusted all judgment to the *S*,
5: 23 not honor the *S* does not honor
5: 23 that all may honor the *S* just
5: 25 the dead will hear the voice of the *S*
5: 26 so he has granted the *S* to have life
5: 27 to judge because he is the *S* of Man.
6: 27 which the *S* of Man will give you.
6: 40 is that everyone who looks to the *S*
6: 42 "Is this not Jesus, the *s* of Joseph,
6: 53 you eat the flesh of the *S* of Man
6: 62 if you see the *S* of Man ascend
6: 71 (He meant Judas, the *s* of Simon
8: 28 "When you have lifted up the *S*
8: 35 but a *s* belongs to it forever.
8: 36 So if the *S* sets you free, you will be
9: 19 "Is this your *s*?" they asked.
9: 20 he is our *s*," the parents answered,
9: 35 "Do you believe in the *S* of Man?"
10: 36 'I am God's *S*'? Do not believe me
11: 4 so that God's *S* may be glorified
11: 27 that you are the Christ, the *S*
12: 23 for the *S* of Man to be glorified.
12: 34 Who is this '*S* of Man'?"
12: 34 'The *S* of Man must be lifted up'?
13: 2 *s* of Simon, to betray Jesus.
13: 26 it to Judas Iscariot, *s* of Simon.
13: 31 "Now is the *S* of Man glorified
13: 32 God will glorify the *S* in himself,
14: 13 so that the *S* may bring glory
17: 1 Glorify your *S*, that your *S* may
19: 7 he claimed to be the *S* of God."
19: 26 here is your *s*," and to the disciple,
20: 31 the *S* of God, and that
21: 15 Simon Peter, "Simon *s* of John,
21: 16 Again Jesus said, "Simon *s* of John,
21: 17 Simon *s* of John, do you love me?"
Ac 1: 13 James *s* of Alphaeus and Simon
1: 13 and Simon the Zealot, and Judas *s*
4: 36 called Barnabas (which means *S*
7: 21 and brought him up as her own *s*.
7: 56 and the *S* of Man standing
9: 20 the synagogues that Jesus is the *S*
13: 21 and he gave them Saul *s* of Kish,
13: 22 'I have found David *s*
13: 33 " 'You are my *S*;
20: 4 by Sopater *s* of Pyrrhus from Berea
23: 6 I am a Pharisee, the *s* of a Pharisee.
23: 16 when the *s* of Paul's sister heard
Ro 1: 3 Holy Scriptures regarding his *S*,
1: 4 with power to be the *S* of God
1: 9 in preaching the gospel of his *S*,
5: 10 to him through the death of his *S*,
8: 3 did by sending his own *S*
8: 29 conformed to the likeness of his *S*,
8: 32 He who did not spare his own *S*,
9: 9 return, and Sarah will have a *s*."
1Co 1: 9 with his *S* Jesus Christ our Lord,
4: 17 my *s* whom I love, who is faithful
15: 28 then the *S* himself will be made
2Co 1: 19 For the *S* of God, Jesus Christ,
Gal 1: 16 was pleased to reveal his *S* in me
2: 20 I live by faith in the *S* of God,
Gal 4: 4 God sent his *S*, born of a woman,
4: 6 the Spirit of his *S* into our hearts,
4: 7 but a *s*; and since you are a *s*,
4: 23 His *s* by the slave woman was born
4: 23 his *s* by the free woman was born
4: 29 At that time the *s* born
4: 29 ordinary way persecuted the *s* born
4: 30 rid of the slave woman and her *s*,
4: 30 the slave woman's *s* will never
4: 30 with the free woman's *s*."
Eph 4: 13 in the knowledge of the *S* of God
Php 2: 22 as a *s* with his father he has served
Col 1: 13 into the kingdom of the *S* he loves,
1Th 1: 10 and to wait for his *S* from heaven,
1Ti 1: 2 To Timothy my true *s* in the faith:
1: 18 my *s*, I give you this instruction
2Ti 1: 2 To Timothy, my dear *s*: Grace,
2: 1 my *s*, be strong in the grace that is
Tit 1: 4 my true *s* in our common faith:
Phm : 10 I appeal to you for my *s* Onesimus,
: 10 who became my *s* while I was
Heb 1: 2 days he has spoken to us by his *S*,
1: 3 The *S* is the radiance
1: 5 and he will be my *S*"?
1: 5 "You are my *S*;
1: 8 But about the *S* he says,
2: 6 the *s* of man that you care for him?
3: 6 But Christ is faithful as a *s*
4: 14 Jesus the *S* of God, let us hold
5: 5 "You are my *S*;
5: 8 he was a *s*, he learned obedience
6: 6 their loss they are crucifying the *S*
7: 3 like the *S* of God he remains
7: 28 appointed the *S*, who has been
10: 29 punished who has trampled the *S*
11: 17 to sacrifice his one and only *s*,
11: 24 as the *s* of Pharaoh's daughter.
12: 5 "My *s*, do not make light
12: 6 everyone he accepts as a *s*."
12: 7 For what *s* is not disciplined
12: 16 inheritance rights as the oldest *s*.
Jas 2: 21 did when he offered his *s* Isaac
1Pe 5: 13 and so does my *s* Mark.
2Pe 1: 17 saying, "This is my *S*, whom I love;
2: 15 the way of Balaam *s* of Beor,
1Jn 1: 3 is with the Father and with his *S*
1: 7 his *S*, purifies us from all sin.
2: 22 he denies the Father and the *S*.
2: 23 who denies the *S* has the Father;
2: 23 whoever acknowledges the *S* has
2: 24 also will remain in the *S*
3: 8 reason the *S* of God appeared was
3: 23 to believe in the name of his *S*,
4: 9 only *S* into the world that we might
4: 10 but that he loved us and sent his *S*
4: 14 that the Father has sent his *S*
4: 15 acknowledges that Jesus is the *S*
5: 5 he who believes that Jesus is the *S*
5: 9 which he has given about his *S*.
5: 10 Anyone who believes in the *S*
5: 10 God has given about his *S*.
5: 11 eternal life, and this life is in his *S*.
5: 12 He who has the *S* has life; he who
5: 12 he who does not have the *S*
5: 13 believe in the name of the *S* of God
5: 20 also that the *S* of God has come
5: 20 even in his *S* Jesus Christ.
2Jn : 3 the Father's *S*, will be with us
: 9 has both the Father and the *S*.
Rev 1: 13 lampstands was someone "like a *s*
2: 18 These are the words of the *S*
12: 5 She gave birth to a *s*, a male child,
14: 14 on the cloud was one "like a *s*
21: 7 will be his God and he will be my *s*.

SON'S (SON)

Ge 30: 14 some of your *s* mandrakes."
30: 15 Will you take my *s* mandrakes too
30: 15 in return for your *s* mandrakes."
30: 16 you with my *s* mandrakes."
37: 32 it to see whether it is your *s* robe."
37: 33 "It is my *s* robe! Some ferocious
Ex 4: 25 cut off her *s* foreskin and touched
Lev 18: 10 relations with your *s* daughter
18: 15 She is your *s* wife; do not have
18: 17 her *s* daughter or her daughter's
2Sa 14: 11 not one hair of your *s* head will fall
1Ki 11: 35 take the kingdom from his *s* hands

SONG (SING)

Ex 15: 1 and the Israelites sang this *s*
15: 2 LORD is my strength and my *s;*
Nu 21: 17 Then Israel sang this *s:*
Dt 31: 19 write down for yourselves this *s*
31: 21 this *s* will testify against them,
31: 22 Moses wrote down this *s* that day
31: 30 of this *s* from beginning to end
32: 44 the words of this *s* in the hearing
Jdg 5: 1 Barak son of Abinoam sang this *s:*
5: 12 Wake up, wake up, break out in *s!*
2Sa 22: 1 of this *s* when the LORD delivered
1Ch 16: 42 the other instruments for sacred *s*.
Job 30: 9 "And now their sons mock me in *s;*
36: 24 which men have praised in *s*.
Ps 28: 7 and I will give thanks to him in *s*.
33: 3 Sing to him a new *s;*
40: 3 He put a new *s* in my mouth,
42: 8 at night his *s* is with me—
69: 12 and I am the *s* of the drunkards.
69: 30 I will praise God's name in *s*
95: 2 and extol him with music and *s*.
96: 1 Sing to the LORD a new *s;*
98: 1 Sing to the LORD a new *s*,
98: 4 burst into jubilant *s* with music;
118: 14 LORD is my strength and my *s;*
119: 54 Your decrees are the theme of my *s*
144: 9 I will sing a new *s* to you, O God;
149: 1 Sing to the LORD a new *s*,
Ecc 7: 5 than to listen to the *s* of fools.
SS 1: 1 Solomon's *S* of Songs.
Isa 5: 1 a *s* about his vineyard:
12: 2 LORD, is my strength and my *s;*
23: 15 as in the *s* of the prostitute:
23: 16 play the harp well, sing many a *s*,
24: 9 longer do they drink wine with a *s;*
25: 5 so the *s* of the ruthless is stilled.
26: 1 In that day this *s* will be sung
42: 10 Sing to the LORD a new *s*,
44: 23 Burst into *s*, you mountains,
49: 13 burst into *s*, O mountains!
54: 1 burst into *s*, shout for joy,
55: 12 will burst into *s* before you,
La 3: 14 they mock me in *s* all day long.
Jnh 2: 9 But I, with a *s* of thanksgiving,
Mic 2: 4 you with this mournful *s:*
Rev 5: 9 And they sang a new *s:*
14: 3 No one could learn the *s*
14: 3 they sang a new *s* before the throne
15: 3 and sang the *s* of Moses the servant
15: 3 of God and the *s* of the Lamb:

SONGS (SING)

1Sa 18: 6 with joyful *s* and with tambourines
2Sa 6: 5 with *s* and with harps, lyres,
23: 1 Israel's singer of *s:*
1Ki 4: 32 his *s* numbered a thousand and five
1Ch 13: 8 with *s* and with harps, lyres,
15: 16 as singers to sing joyful *s*,
Ne 12: 8 in charge of the *s* of thanksgiving.
12: 27 dedication with *s* of thanksgiving
12: 46 for the *s* of praise and thanksgiving
Job 35: 10 who gives *s* in the night,
Ps 32: 7 surround me with *s* of deliverance.
65: 8 you call forth *s* of joy.
77: 6 I remembered my *s* in the night.
78: 63 their maidens had no wedding *s;*
100: 2 come before him with joyful *s*.
107: 22 and tell of his works with *s* of joy.
126: 2 our tongues with *s* of joy.
126: 5 will reap with *s* of joy.
126: 6 will return with *s* of joy,
137: 3 for there our captors asked us for *s*,
137: 3 our tormentors demanded *s* of joy;
137: 3 "Sing us one of the *s* of Zion!"
137: 4 How can we sing the *s*
Pr 25: 20 is one who sings *s* to a heavy heart.
Ecc 12: 4 but all their *s* grow faint;
SS 1: 1 Solomon's Song of *S*.
Isa 52: 9 Burst into *s* of joy together,
Jer 30: 19 From them will come *s*
La 3: 63 they mock me in their *s*.
Eze 26: 13 I will put an end to your noisy *s*,
33: 32 more than one who sings love *s*
Am 5: 23 Away with the noise of your *s!*
8: 3 "the *s* in the temple will turn
Eph 5: 19 with psalms, hymns and spiritual *s*.
Col 3: 16 and spiritual *s* with gratitude
Jas 5: 13 Is anyone happy? Let him sing *s*

SONS (SON)

Ge 5: 4 and had other *s* and daughters.
5: 7 and had other *s* and daughters.
5: 10 and had other *s* and daughters.
5: 13 and had other *s* and daughters.
5: 16 and had other *s* and daughters.
5: 19 and had other *s* and daughters.
5: 22 and had other *s* and daughters.
5: 26 and had other *s* and daughters.
5: 30 and had other *s* and daughters.
6: 2 the *s* of God saw that the daughters
6: 4 when the *s* of God went
6: 10 Noah had three *s:* Shem, Ham
6: 18 you and your *s* and your wife
7: 7 And Noah and his *s* and his wife
7: 13 On that very day Noah and his *s*,
7: 13 and the wives of his three *s*,
8: 16 and your *s* and their wives.
8: 18 together with his *s* and his wife
9: 1 Then God blessed Noah and his *s*,
9: 8 said to Noah and to his *s* with him:
9: 18 The *s* of Noah who came out
9: 19 These were the three *s* of Noah,
10: 1 Ham and Japheth, Noah's *s*,
10: 1 who themselves had *s*
10: 2 The *s* of Japheth: Gomer, Magog,
10: 3 The *s* of Gomer: Ashkenaz,
10: 4 The *s* of Javan: Elishah, Tarshish,
10: 6 The *s* of Ham: Cush, Mizraim,
10: 7 The *s* of Cush: Seba, Havilah,
10: 7 The *s* of Raamah: Sheba
10: 21 *S* were also born to Shem,
10: 21 the ancestor of all the *s* of Eber.
10: 22 The *s* of Shem: Elam, Asshur,
10: 23 The *s* of Aram: Uz, Hul, Gether
10: 25 Two *s* were born to Eber: One was
10: 29 All these were *s* of Joktan.
10: 31 These are the *s* of Shem
10: 32 These are the clans of Noah's *s*,
11: 11 and had other *s* and daughters.
11: 13 and had other *s* and daughters.
11: 15 and had other *s* and daughters.
11: 17 and had other *s* and daughters.
11: 19 and had other *s* and daughters.
11: 21 and had other *s* and daughters.
11: 23 and had other *s* and daughters.
11: 25 and had other *s* and daughters.
19: 12 sons-in-law, *s* or daughters,
22: 20 she has borne *s* to your brother
22: 23 Milcah bore these eight *s*
22: 24 also had *s:* Tebah, Gaham,
25: 4 The *s* of Midian were Ephah,
25: 6 gifts to the *s* of his concubines
25: 9 His *s* Isaac and Ishmael buried him
25: 13 the names of the *s* of Ishmael,
25: 16 These were the *s* of Ishmael,
27: 29 and may the *s* of your mother bow
29: 34 because I have borne him three *s*."
30: 20 because I have borne him six *s*."
30: 35 he placed them in the care of his *s*.
31: 1 heard that Laban's *s* were saying,
32: 22 two maidservants and his eleven *s*
33: 19 he bought from the *s* of Hamor,
34: 5 his *s* were in the fields
34: 7 Now Jacob's *s* had come
34: 13 Jacob's *s* replied deceitfully
34: 25 two of Jacob's *s*, Simeon and Levi,
34: 27 The *s* of Jacob came
35: 22 Jacob had twelve *s:*
35: 23 The *s* of Leah:
35: 24 The *s* of Rachel: Joseph
35: 25 *s* of Rachel's maidservant Bilhah:
35: 26 The *s* of Leah's maidservant Zilpah
35: 26 These were the *s* of Jacob,
35: 29 his *s* Esau and Jacob buried him.
36: 5 These were the *s* of Esau, who were
36: 6 Esau took his wives and *s*
36: 10 These are the names of Esau's *s:*
36: 11 The *s* of Eliphaz: Teman, Omar,
36: 13 The *s* of Reuel: Nahath, Zerah,
36: 14 The *s* of Esau's wife Oholibamah
36: 15 The *s* of Eliphaz the firstborn
36: 17 The *s* of Esau's son Reuel:
36: 18 The *s* of Esau's wife Oholibamah:
36: 19 These were the *s* of Esau (that is,
Ge 36: 20 These were the *s* of Seir the Horite,
36: 21 These *s* of Seir in Edom were
36: 22 The *s* of Lotan: Hori and Homam.
36: 23 The *s* of Shobal: Alvan, Manahath,
36: 24 The *s* of Zibeon: Aiah and Anah.
36: 26 The *s* of Dishon: Hemdan, Eshban,
36: 27 The *s* of Ezer: Bilhan, Zaavan
36: 28 The *s* of Dishan: Uz and Aran.
37: 2 the *s* of Bilhah and the *s* of Zilpah,
37: 3 more than any of his other *s*,
37: 35 All his *s* and daughters came
41: 50 two *s* were born to Joseph
42: 1 said to his *s*, "Why do you just keep
42: 5 So Israel's *s* were among those who
42: 11 We are all the *s* of one man.
42: 13 were twelve brothers, the *s*
42: 32 We were twelve brothers, *s*
42: 37 You may put both of my *s* to death
44: 20 one of his mother's *s* left,
44: 27 know that my wife bore me two *s*.
45: 21 So the *s* of Israel did this.
46: 5 Israel's *s* took their father Jacob
46: 7 He took with him to Egypt his *s*
46: 9 The *s* of Reuben: Hanoch, Pallu,
46: 10 The *s* of Simeon: Jemuel, Jamin,
46: 11 The *s* of Levi: Gershon, Kohath
46: 12 The *s* of Judah: Er, Onan, Shelah,
46: 12 The *s* of Perez: Hezron and Hamul.
46: 13 The *s* of Issachar: Tola, Puah,
46: 14 The *s* of Zebulun: Sered, Elon
46: 15 These were the *s* Leah bore
46: 15 These *s* and daughters
46: 16 The *s* of Gad: Zephon, Haggi,
46: 17 The *s* of Asher: Imnah, Ishvah,
46: 17 The *s* of Beriah: Heber and Malkiel
46: 19 The *s* of Jacob's wife Rachel:
46: 21 The *s* of Benjamin: Bela, Beker,
46: 22 These were the *s* of Rachel who
46: 24 The *s* of Naphtali: Jahziel, Guni,
46: 25 These were the *s* born to Jacob
46: 27 With the two *s* who had been born
48: 1 So he took his two *s* Manasseh
48: 5 your two *s* born to you in Egypt
48: 8 When Israel saw the *s* of Joseph,
48: 9 "They are the *s* God has given me
48: 10 Joseph brought his *s* close to him,
49: 1 Then Jacob called for his *s* and said
49: 2 "Assemble and listen, *s* of Jacob;
49: 8 your father's *s* will bow
49: 33 finished giving instructions to his *s*,
50: 12 Jacob's *s* did as he had commanded
50: 25 And Joseph made the *s*
Ex 1: 1 of the *s* of Israel who entered
3: 22 which you will put on your *s*
4: 20 So Moses took his wife and *s*,
6: 14 The *s* of Reuben the firstborn son
6: 15 The *s* of Simeon were Jemuel,
6: 16 names of the *s* of Levi according
6: 17 The *s* of Gershon, by clans,
6: 18 The *s* of Kohath were Amram,
6: 19 The *s* of Merari were Mahli
6: 21 The *s* of Izhar were Korah,
6: 22 The *s* of Uzziel were Mishael,
6: 24 The *s* of Korah were Assir,
10: 9 with our *s* and daughters,
13: 13 every firstborn among your *s*.
13: 15 and redeem each of my firstborn *s*.'
13: 19 because Joseph had made the *s*
18: 3 Jethro received her and her two *s*.
18: 5 together with Moses' *s* and wife,
18: 6 to you with your wife and her two *s*
21: 4 and she bears him *s* or daughters,
22: 29 give me the firstborn of your *s*.
27: 21 his *s* are to keep the lamps burning
28: 1 along with his *s* Nadab and Abihu,
28: 4 for your brother Aaron and his *s*,
28: 9 names of the *s* of Israel in the order
28: 11 Engrave the names of the *s*
28: 12 memorial stones for the *s* of Israel.
28: 21 each of the names of the *s* of Israel,
28: 29 of the *s* of Israel over his heart
28: 40 sashes and headbands for Aaron's *s*
28: 41 on your brother Aaron and his *s*,
28: 43 his *s* must wear them whenever
29: 4 his *s* to the entrance to the Tent
29: 8 Bring his *s* and dress them in tunics
29: 9 Then tie sashes on Aaron and his *s*.
29: 9 you shall ordain Aaron and his *s*.

Ex 29:10 and his *s* shall lay their hands
29:15 and his *s* shall lay their hands
29:19 and his *s* shall lay their hands
29:20 of the right ears of Aaron and his *s*,
29:21 and his *s* and their garments will be
29:21 and on his *s* and their garments.
29:24 and his *s* and wave them
29:27 belong to Aaron and his *s*:
29:28 the Israelites for Aaron and his *s*.
29:32 his *s* are to eat the meat of the ram
29:35 and his *s* everything I have
29:44 and will consecrate Aaron and his *s*
30:19 and his *s* are to wash their hands
30:30 and his *s* and consecrate them
31:10 garments for his *s* when they serve
32: 2 your *s* and your daughters are
32:29 for you were against your own *s*
34:16 for your *s* and those daughters
34:16 they will lead your *s* to do the same
34:20 Redeem all your firstborn *s*.
35:19 garments for his *s* when they serve
39: 6 with the names of the *s* of Israel.
39: 7 memorial stones for the *s* of Israel,
39:14 each of the names of the *s* of Israel,
39:27 his *s*, they made tunics of fine linen
39:41 the garments for his *s* when serving
40:12 his *s* to the entrance to the Tent
40:14 Bring his *s* and dress them in tunics
40:31 his *s* used it to wash their hands
Lev 1: 5 and then Aaron's *s* the priests shall
1: 7 The *s* of Aaron the priest are
1: 8 Aaron's *s* the priests shall arrange
1:11 Aaron's *s* the priests shall sprinkle
2: 2 and take it to Aaron's *s* the priests.
2: 3 belongs to Aaron and his *s*;
2:10 belongs to Aaron and his *s*;
3: 2 Aaron's *s* the priests shall sprinkle
3: 5 Aaron's *s* are to burn it on the altar
3: 8 Aaron's *s* shall sprinkle its blood
3:13 Aaron's *s* shall sprinkle its blood
6: 9 Aaron and his *s* this command:
6:14 Aaron's *s* are to bring it
6:16 and his *s* shall eat the rest of it,
6:20 and his *s* are to bring to the LORD
6:25 his *s*: 'These are the regulations
7:10 equally to all the *s* of Aaron.
7:31 belongs to Aaron and his *s*.
7:34 and his *s* as their regular share
7:35 and his *s* on the day they were
8: 2 Aaron and his *s*, their garments,
8: 6 brought Aaron and his *s* forward
8:13 Then he brought Aaron's *s* forward
8:14 his *s* laid their hands on its head.
8:18 his *s* laid their hands on its head.
8:22 his *s* laid their hands on its head.
8:24 also brought Aaron's *s* forward
8:27 and his *s* and waved them
8:30 and his *s* and their garments.
8:30 and on his *s* and their garments.
8:31 Moses then said to Aaron and his *s*,
8:31 saying, 'Aaron and his *s* are to eat it
8:36 and his *s* did everything the LORD
9: 1 and his *s* and the elders of Israel.
9: 9 His *s* brought the blood to him,
9:12 His *s* handed him the blood,
9:18 His *s* handed him the blood,
10: 1 Aaron's *s* Nadab and Abihu took
10: 4 *s* of Aaron's uncle Uzziel,
10: 6 and his *s* Eleazar and Ithamar,
10: 9 and your *s* are not to drink wine
10:12 said to Aaron and his remaining *s*,
10:14 your *s* and your daughters may eat
10:16 Aaron's remaining *s*, and asked,
13: 2 or to one of his *s* who is a priest.
16: 1 of the two *s* of Aaron who died
17: 2 "Speak to Aaron and his *s*
21: 1 Speak to the priests, the *s* of Aaron,
21:24 and his *s* and to all the Israelites.
22: 2 and his *s* to treat with respect
22:18 "Speak to Aaron and his *s*
24: 9 It belongs to Aaron and his *s*,
26:29 You will eat the flesh of your *s*
Nu 1:10 from the *s* of Joseph: from Ephraim
1:32 From the *s* of Joseph: From
3: 2 The names of the *s*
3: 3 Those were the names of Aaron's *s*,
3: 4 They had no *s*, so only Eleazar
3: 9 Give the Levites to Aaron and his *s*
Nu 3:10 Appoint Aaron and his *s* to serve
3:17 These were the names of the *s*
3:38 and his *s* were to camp to the east
3:48 Israelites to Aaron and his *s*."
3:51 money to Aaron and his *s*,
4: 5 Aaron and his *s* are to go in
4:15 and his *s* have finished covering
4:19 his *s* are to go into the sanctuary
4:27 the direction of Aaron and his *s*.
6:23 to Moses, "Tell Aaron and his *s*,
8:13 and his *s* and then present them
8:18 place of all the firstborn *s* in Israel.
8:19 and his *s* to do the work at the Tent
8:22 the supervision of Aaron and his *s*.
10: 8 "The *s* of Aaron, the priests,
16: 1 Dathan and Abiram, *s* of Eliab,
16:12 and Abiram, the *s* of Eliab.
18: 1 and your *s* alone are to bear
18: 1 your *s* and your father's family are
18: 2 and your *s* minister before the Tent
18: 7 But only you and your *s* may serve
18: 8 and your *s* as your portion
18: 9 that part belongs to you and your *s*.
18:11 and your *s* and daughters as your
18:19 and your *s* and daughters as your
21:29 He has given up his *s* as fugitives
21:35 with his *s* and his whole army,
24:17 the skulls of all the *s* of Sheth.
26: 9 and the *s* of Eliab were Nemuel,
26:19 Er and Onan were *s* of Judah,
26:33 son of Hepher had no *s*;
27: 3 he died for his own sin and left no *s*
Dt 2:33 with his *s* and his whole army.
7: 3 not give your daughters to their *s*
7: 3 or take their daughters for your *s*,
7: 4 for they will turn your *s* away
11: 6 Abiram, *s* of Eliab the Reubenite,
12:12 you, your *s* and daughters,
12:18 you, your *s* and daughters,
12:31 They even burn their *s*
16:11 you, your *s* and daughters,
16:14 you, your *s* and daughters,
21: 5 the *s* of Levi, shall step forward,
21:15 both bear him *s* but the firstborn is
21:16 when he wills his property to his *s*,
28:32 Your *s* and daughters will be given
28:41 You will have *s* and daughters
28:53 of the *s* and daughters the LORD
31: 9 the *s* of Levi, who carried the ark
32: 8 to the number of the *s* of Israel.
32:19 he was angered by his *s*
33:24 "Most blessed of *s* is Asher;
Jos 5: 7 So he raised up their *s* in their place
7:24 the gold wedge, his *s* and daughters
13:31 for half of the *s* of Makir, clan
14: 4 for the *s* of Joseph had become two
17: 3 had no *s* but only daughters,
17: 6 an inheritance among the *s*.
24: 4 and his *s* went down to Egypt.
24:32 of silver from the *s* of Hamor,
Jdg 1:20 drove from it the three *s* of Anak.
3: 6 gave their own daughters to their *s*,
8:19 "Those were my brothers, the *s*
8:30 He had seventy *s* of his own,
9: 2 of Jerub-Baal's *s* rule over you,
9: 5 his seventy brothers, the *s*
9:18 murdered his seventy *s*
9:24 against Jerub-Baal's seventy *s*,
10: 4 He had thirty *s*, who rode thirty
11: 2 Gilead's wife also bore him *s*,
12: 9 He had thirty *s* and thirty
12: 9 and for his *s* he brought
12:14 He had forty *s* and thirty
17: 5 installed one of his *s* as his priest.
17:11 was to him like one of his *s*.
18:30 and his *s* were priests for the tribe
Ru 1: 1 together with his wife and two *s*,
1: 2 names of his two *s* were Mahlon
1: 3 and she was left with her two *s*.
1: 5 Naomi was left without her two *s*
1:11 Am I going to have any more *s*,
1:12 tonight and then gave birth to *s*—
4:15 who is better to you than seven *s*,
1Sa 1: 3 and Phinehas, the two *s* of Eli,
1: 4 and to all her *s* and daughters.
1: 8 more to you than ten *s*?"
2: 5 who has had many *s* pines away.
2:12 Eli's *s* were wicked men; they had
1Sa 2:21 birth to three *s* and two daughters.
2:22 about everything his *s* were doing
2:24 my *s*; it is not a good report that I
2:25 who will intercede for him?" His *s*,
2:29 Why do you honor your *s* more
2:34 " 'And what happens to your two *s*,
3:13 his *s* made themselves
4: 4 And Eli's two *s*, Hophni
4:11 and Eli's two *s*, Hophni
4:17 Also your two *s*, Hophni
8: 1 he appointed his *s* as judges
8: 3 But his *s* did not walk in his ways.
8: 5 your *s* do not walk in your ways;
8:11 He will take your *s* and make them
12: 2 and my *s* are here with you.
14:49 Saul's *s* were Jonathan, Ishvi
14:51 Abner's father Ner were *s* of Abiel.
16: 1 one of his *s* to be king."
16: 5 he consecrated Jesse and his *s*
16:10 seven of his *s* pass before Samuel,
16:11 "Are these all the *s* you have?"
17:12 Jesse had eight *s*, and in Saul's time
17:13 Jesse's three oldest *s* had followed
28:19 and your *s* will be with me.
30: 3 and *s* and daughters taken captive.
30: 6 because of his *s* and daughters.
31: 2 and they killed his *s* Jonathan,
31: 2 hard after Saul and his *s*,
31: 6 three of his *s* and his armor-bearer
31: 7 and that Saul and his *s* had died,
31: 8 his three *s* fallen on Mount Gilboa.
31:12 his *s* from the wall of Beth Shan
2Sa 2:18 The three *s* of Zeruiah were there;
3: 2 *S* were born to David in Hebron:
3:39 these *s* of Zeruiah are too strong
4: 2 they were *s* of Rimmon
4: 5 the *s* of Rimmon the Beerothite,
4: 9 the *s* of Rimmon the Beerothite,
5:13 more *s* and daughters were born
6: 3 Uzzah and Ahio, *s* of Abinadab,
8:18 and David's *s* were royal advisers.
9:10 and your *s* and your servants are
9:10 (Now Ziba had fifteen *s* and twenty
9:11 table like one of the king's *s*.
13:23 invited all the king's *s* to
13:27 and the rest of the king's *s*.
13:29 Then all the king's *s* got up,
13:30 struck down all the king's *s*;
13:33 report that all the king's *s* are dead.
13:35 "See, the king's *s* are here;
13:36 the king's *s* came in, wailing loudly.
14: 6 I your servant had two *s*.
14:27 Three *s* and a daughter were born
15:27 Abiathar take your two *s* with you.
15:36 Their two *s*, Ahimaaz son of Zadok
16:10 I have in common, you *s* of Zeruiah
19: 5 the lives of your *s* and daughters
19:17 his fifteen *s* and twenty servants.
19:22 I have in common, you *s* of Zeruiah
21: 8 together with the five *s*
21: 8 two *s* of Aiah's daughter Rizpah,
23:32 Eliahba the Shaalbonite, the *s*
1Ki 1: 9 invited all his brothers, the king's *s*,
1:19 and has invited all the king's *s*,
1:25 He has invited all the king's *s*,
2: 7 show kindness to the *s* of Barzillai
4: 3 Elihoreph and Ahijah, *s* of Shisha
4:31 Calcol and Darda, the *s* of Mahol.
8:25 if only your *s* are careful
9: 6 if you or your *s* turn away from me
13:11 whose *s* came and told him all that
13:12 And his *s* showed him which road
13:13 he said to his *s*, "Saddle the donkey
13:27 said to his *s*, "Saddle the donkey
13:31 he said to his *s*, "When I die,
20:35 one of the *s* of the prophets said
2Ki 4: 4 the door behind you and your *s*.
4: 5 the door behind her and her *s*.
4: 7 and your *s* can live on what is left."
9:26 of Naboth and the blood of his *s*,
10: 1 in Samaria seventy *s* of the house
10: 2 since your master's *s* are with you
10: 3 and most worthy of your master's *s*
10: 6 take the heads of your master's *s*
14: 6 Yet he did not put the *s*
17:17 They sacrificed their *s*
19:37 his *s* Adrammelech and Sharezer
25: 7 They killed the *s* of Zedekiah

1Ch 1: 4 The *s* of Noah: Shem, Ham
1: 5 The *s* of Japheth: Gomer, Magog,
1: 6 The *s* of Gomer: Ashkenaz,
1: 7 The *s* of Javan: Elishah, Tarshish,
1: 8 The *s* of Ham: Cush, Mizraim,
1: 9 The *s* of Cush: Seba, Havilah, Sabta
1: 9 The *s* of Raamah: Sheba
1: 17 The *s* of Aram: Uz, Hul, Gether
1: 17 The *s* of Shem: Elam, Asshur,
1: 19 Two *s* were born to Eber: One was
1: 23 All these were *s* of Joktan.
1: 28 The *s* of Abraham: Isaac
1: 31 These were the *s* of Ishmael.
1: 32 The *s* born to Keturah, Abraham's
1: 32 The *s* of Jokshan: Sheba
1: 33 The *s* of Midian: Ephah, Epher,
1: 34 The *s* of Isaac: Esau and Israel.
1: 35 The *s* of Esau: Eliphaz, Reuel,
1: 36 The *s* of Eliphaz: Teman, Omar,
1: 37 The *s* of Reuel: Nahath, Zerah,
1: 38 The *s* of Seir: Lotan, Shobal,
1: 39 The *s* of Lotan: Hori and Homam.
1: 40 The *s* of Shobal: Alvan, Manahath,
1: 40 The *s* of Zibeon: Aiah and Anah.
1: 41 The *s* of Dishon: Hemdan, Eshban,
1: 42 The *s* of Dishan: Uz and Aran.
1: 42 The *s* of Ezer: Bilhan, Zaavan
2: 1 These were the *s* of Israel: Reuben,
2: 3 The *s* of Judah: Er, Onan
2: 4 Judah had five *s* in all.
2: 5 The *s* of Perez: Hezron and Hamul.
2: 6 The *s* of Zerah: Zimri, Ethan,
2: 9 The *s* born to Hezron were:
2: 16 Zeruiah's three *s* were Abishai,
2: 18 These were her *s:* Jesher, Shobab
2: 25 The *s* of Jerahmeel the firstborn
2: 27 The *s* of Ram the firstborn
2: 28 The *s* of Onam: Shammai and Jada.
2: 28 The *s* of Shammai: Nadab
2: 30 The *s* of Nadab: Seled and Appaim.
2: 32 The *s* of Jada, Shammai's brother:
2: 33 The *s* of Jonathan: Peleth and Zaza
2: 34 Sheshan had no *s*— only daughters
2: 42 The *s* of Caleb the brother
2: 43 The *s* of Hebron: Korah, Tappuah,
2: 47 The *s* of Jahdai: Regem, Jotham,
2: 50 The *s* of Hur the firstborn
3: 1 These were the *s* of David born
3: 9 All these were the *s* of David,
3: 9 besides his *s* by his concubines.
3: 15 *s* of Josiah: Johanan the firstborn,
3: 19 The *s* of Pedaiah: Zerubbabel
3: 19 The *s* of Zerubbabel: Meshullam
3: 21 and the *s* of Rephaiah, of Arnan,
3: 22 Shemaiah and his *s:* Hattush, Igal,
3: 23 The *s* of Neariah: Elioenai,
3: 24 The *s* of Elioenai: Hodaviah,
4: 3 These were the *s* of Etam: Jezreel,
4: 7 The *s* of Helah: Zereth, Zohar,
4: 13 The *s* of Kenaz: Othniel
4: 13 The *s* of Othniel: Hathath
4: 15 The *s* of Caleb son of Jephunneh:
4: 16 The *s* of Jehallelel: Ziph, Ziphah,
4: 17 The *s* of Ezrah: Jether, Mered,
4: 19 The *s* of Hodiah's wife, the sister
4: 20 The *s* of Shimon: Amnon, Rinnah,
4: 21 The *s* of Shelah son of Judah:
4: 27 Shimei had sixteen *s* and six
4: 42 Rephaiah and Uzziel, the *s* of Ishi,
5: 1 The *s* of Reuben the firstborn
5: 1 given to the *s* of Joseph son
5: 3 the *s* of Reuben the firstborn
5: 14 These were the *s* of Abihail son
6: 1 The *s* of Levi: Gershon, Kohath
6: 2 The *s* of Kohath: Amram, Izhar,
6: 3 The *s* of Aaron: Nadab, Abihu,
6: 16 The *s* of Levi: Gershon, Kohath
6: 17 the names of the *s* of Gershon:
6: 18 The *s* of Kohath: Amram, Izhar,
6: 19 The *s* of Merari: Mahli and Mushi.
6: 28 The *s* of Samuel: Joel the firstborn
6: 33 with their *s:* From the Kohathites:
7: 1 The *s* of Issachar: Tola, Puah,
7: 2 The *s* of Tola: Uzzi, Rephaiah,
7: 3 The *s* of Izrahiah: Michael,
7: 6 Three *s* of Benjamin: Bela,
7: 7 The *s* of Bela: Ezbon, Uzzi, Uzziel,
7: 8 All these were the *s* of Beker.

1Ch 7: 8 The *s* of Beker: Zemirah, Joash,
7: 10 The *s* of Bilhan: Jeush, Benjamin,
7: 11 All these *s* of Jediael were heads
7: 13 Jezer and Shillem—his *s* by Bilhah
7: 13 The *s* of Naphtali: Jahziel, Guni,
7: 16 and his *s* were Ulam and Rakem.
7: 17 These were the *s* of Gilead son
7: 19 The *s* of Shemida were: Ahian,
7: 30 The *s* of Asher: Imnah, Ishvah,
7: 31 The *s* of Beriah: Heber and Malkiel
7: 33 The *s* of Japhlet: Pasach, Bimhal
7: 33 These were Japhlet's *s*.
7: 34 The *s* of Shomer: Ahi, Rohgah,
7: 35 The *s* of his brother Helem:
7: 36 The *s* of Zophah: Suah, Harnepher,
7: 38 The *s* of Jether: Jephunneh,
7: 39 The *s* of Ulla: Arah, Hanniel
8: 3 The *s* of Bela were: Addar, Gera,
8: 8 *S* were born to Shaharaim in Moab
8: 10 These were his *s*, heads of families.
8: 12 The *s* of Elpaal: Eber, Misham,
8: 16 and Joha were the *s* of Beriah.
8: 18 and Jobab were the *s* of Elpaal.
8: 21 and Shimrath were the *s* of Shimei.
8: 25 and Penuel were the *s* of Shashak.
8: 27 and Zicri were the *s* of Jeroham.
8: 35 The *s* of Micah: Pithon, Melech,
8: 38 All these were the *s* of Azel.
8: 38 Azel had six *s*, and these were their
8: 39 The *s* of his brother Eshek:
8: 40 They had many *s* and grandsons—
8: 40 *s* of Ulam were brave warriors who
9: 5 Asaiah the firstborn and his *s*.
9: 41 The *s* of Micah: Pithon, Melech,
9: 44 Azel had six *s*, and these were their
9: 44 These were the *s* of Azel.
10: 2 and they killed his *s* Jonathan,
10: 2 hard after Saul and his *s*,
10: 6 So Saul and three of his *s* died,
10: 7 and that Saul and his *s* had died,
10: 8 and his *s* fallen on Mount Gilboa.
10: 12 his *s* and brought them to Jabesh.
11: 34 the *s* of Hashem the Gizonite,
11: 44 Jeiel the *s* of Hotham the Aroerite,
11: 46 and Joshaviah the *s* of Elnaam,
12: 3 Jeziel and Pelet the *s* of Azmaveth;
12: 3 and Joash the *s* of Shemaah
12: 7 and Zebadiah the *s* of Jeroham
14: 3 and became the father of more *s*
16: 13 O *s* of Jacob, his chosen ones.
16: 42 The *s* of Jeduthun were stationed
17: 11 of your own *s*, and I will establish
18: 17 and David's *s* were chief officials
21: 20 his four *s* who were
23: 6 into groups corresponding to the *s*
23: 8 The *s* of Ladan: Jehiel the first,
23: 9 The *s* of Shimei: Shelomoth,
23: 10 And the *s* of Shimei: Jahath, Ziza,
23: 10 These were the *s* of Shimei—
23: 11 and Beriah did not have many *s;*
23: 12 The *s* of Kohath: Amram, Izhar,
23: 13 The *s* of Amram: Aaron and Moses
23: 14 The *s* of Moses the man
23: 15 The *s* of Moses: Gershom
23: 17 Eliezer had no other *s*,
23: 17 *s* of Rehabiah were very numerous.
23: 18 *s* of Izhar: Shelomith was the first.
23: 19 The *s* of Hebron: Jeriah the first,
23: 20 The *s* of Uzziel: Micah the first
23: 21 The *s* of Mahli: Eleazar and Kish.
23: 21 The *s* of Merari: Mahli and Mushi.
23: 22 Eleazar died without having *s:*
23: 22 Their cousins, the *s* of Kish,
23: 23 The *s* of Mushi: Mahli, Eder
24: 1 The *s* of Aaron were Nadab, Abihu
24: 1 These were the divisions of the *s*
24: 2 and they had no *s;* so Eleazar
24: 20 Shubael; from the *s* of Shubael:
24: 20 from the *s* of Amram: Shubael;
24: 21 from his *s:* Isshiah was the first.
24: 22 from the *s* of Shelomoth:
24: 23 The *s* of Hebron: Jeriah the first,
24: 24 Micah; from the *s* of Micah:
24: 25 Isshiah; from the *s* of Isshiah:
24: 26 The *s* of Merari: Mahli and Mushi.
24: 27 The *s* of Merari: from Jaaziah:
24: 28 From Mahli: Eleazar, who had no *s*
24: 30 And the *s* of Mushi: Mahli,

1Ch 25: 1 set apart some of the *s* of Asaph,
25: 2 From the *s* of Asaph: Zaccur,
25: 2 The *s* of Asaph were
25: 3 from his *s:* Gedaliah, Zeri, Jeshaiah
25: 4 from his *s:* Bukkiah, Mattaniah,
25: 5 All these were *s* of Heman
25: 5 God gave Heman fourteen *s*
25: 9 and *s*, 12 the third to Zaccur,
25: 9 fell to Joseph, his *s* and relatives,
25: 10 the third to Zaccur, his *s*
25: 11 the fourth to Izri, his *s*
25: 12 the fifth to Nethaniah, his *s*
25: 13 the sixth to Bukkiah, his *s*
25: 14 the seventh to Jesarelah, his *s*
25: 15 the eighth to Jeshaiah, his *s*
25: 16 the ninth to Mattaniah, his *s*
25: 17 the tenth to Shimei, his *s*
25: 18 the eleventh to Azarel, his *s*
25: 19 the twelfth to Hashabiah, his *s*
25: 20 the thirteenth to Shubael, his *s*
25: 21 the fourteenth to Mattithiah, his *s*
25: 22 the fifteenth to Jerimoth, his *s*
25: 23 the sixteenth to Hananiah, his *s*
25: 24 seventeenth to Joshbakashah, his *s*
25: 25 the eighteenth to Hanani, his *s*
25: 26 the nineteenth to Mallothi, his *s*
25: 27 the twentieth to Eliathah, his *s*
25: 28 the twenty-first to Hothir, his *s*
25: 29 twenty-second to Giddalti, his *s*
25: 30 twenty-third to Mahazioth, his *s*
25: 31 to Romamti-Ezer, his *s*
26: 1 son of Kore, one of the *s* of Asaph.
26: 2 Meshelemiah had *s:* Zechariah
26: 4 also had *s:* Shemaiah the firstborn,
26: 6 His son Shemaiah also had *s*,
26: 7 The *s* of Shemaiah: Othni, Rephael
26: 8 and their *s* and their relatives were
26: 9 Meshelemiah had *s* and relatives,
26: 10 Hosah the Merarite had *s:*
26: 11 The *s* and relatives
26: 15 lot for the storehouse fell to his *s*.
26: 22 were Jehieli, the *s* of Jehieli,
26: 29 and his *s* were assigned duties away
27: 32 Hacmoni took care of the king's *s*.
28: 1 belonging to the king and his *s*,
28: 4 from my father's *s* he was pleased
28: 5 Of all my *s*— and the LORD has
29: 24 as well as all of King David's *s*,
2Ch 5: 12 Jeduthun and their *s* and relatives
6: 16 if only your *s* are careful
11: 14 and his *s* had rejected them
11: 19 She bore him *s:* Jeush, Shemariah
11: 21 twenty-eight *s* and sixty daughters.
11: 23 of his *s* throughout the districts
13: 9 the *s* of Aaron, and the Levites,
13: 10 priests who serve the LORD are *s*
13: 21 and had twenty-two *s* and sixteen
21: 2 Jehoram's brothers, the *s*
21: 2 these were *s* of Jehoshaphat king
21: 14 your *s*, your wives and everything
21: 17 together with his *s* and wives.
22: 1 the camp, had killed all the older *s*.
22: 8 and the *s* of Ahaziah's relatives,
23: 11 and his *s* brought out the king's son
24: 3 and he had *s* and daughters.
24: 7 *s* of that wicked woman Athaliah
24: 27 of his *s*, the many prophecies about
25: 4 Yet he did not put their *s* to death,
28: 3 and sacrificed his *s* in the fire,
28: 8 two hundred thousand wives, *s*
29: 9 and why our *s* and daughters
29: 11 My *s*, do not be negligent now,
31: 18 and the *s* and daughters
32: 21 some of his *s* cut him
33: 6 He sacrificed his *s* in the fire
36: 20 and his *s* until the kingdom
Ezr 3: 9 Jeshua and his *s* and brothers
3: 9 and the *s* of Henadad and their *s*
3: 9 his *s* (descendants of Hodaviah)
3: 10 and the Levites (the *s* of Asaph)
6: 10 the well-being of the king and his *s*.
7: 23 the realm of the king and of his *s?*
8: 18 and Sherebiah's *s* and brothers,
9: 2 as wives for themselves and their *s*,
9: 12 daughters in marriage to their *s*
9: 12 or take their daughters for your *s*.
Ne 3: 3 rebuilt by the *s* of Hassenaah.
4: 14 your *s* and your daughters,

Ne 5: 2 our *s* and daughters are numerous;
5: 5 and though our *s* are as good
5: 5 yet we have to subject our *s*
9: 23 You made their *s* as numerous
9: 24 Their *s* went in and took possession
10: 9 Binnui of the *s* of Henadad,
10: 28 with their wives and all their *s*
10: 30 or take their daughters for our *s*.
10: 36 we will bring the firstborn of our *s*
13: 25 daughters in marriage for your *s*
13: 25 daughters in marriage to their *s*,
13: 28 One of the *s* of Joiada son
Est 5: 11 about his vast wealth, his many *s*,
9: 10 the ten *s* of Haman son
9: 12 the ten *s* of Haman in the citadel
9: 13 and let Haman's ten *s* be hanged
9: 14 they hanged the ten *s* of Haman.
9: 25 and his *s* should be hanged
Job 1: 2 He had seven *s* and three daughters
1: 4 His *s* used to take turns holding
1: 13 when Job's *s* and daughters were
1: 18 Your *s* and daughters were feasting
14: 21 If his *s* are honored, he does not
21: 19 up a man's punishment for his *s*.'
30: 9 "And now their *s* mock me in song;
35: 8 and your righteousness only the *s*
42: 13 had seven *s* and three daughters.
Ps 11: 4 He observes the *s* of men;
14: 2 heaven on the *s* of men
17: 14 their *s* have plenty,
45: 16 Your *s* will take the place
53: 2 heaven on the *s* of men
69: 8 an alien to my own mother's *s*;
82: 6 you are all *s* of the Most High.'
89: 30 "If his *s* forsake my law
90: 3 "Return to dust, O *s* of men."
105: 6 O *s* of Jacob, his chosen ones.
106: 37 They sacrificed their *s*
106: 38 the blood of their *s* and daughters,
127: 3 *S* are a heritage from the LORD,
127: 4 are *s* born in one's youth.
128: 3 your *s* will be like olive shoots
132: 12 if your *s* keep my covenant
132: 12 then their *s* will sit
144: 12 Then our *s* in their youth
Pr 4: 1 my *s*, to a father's instruction;
5: 7 Now then, my *s*, listen to me;
7: 24 Now then, my *s*, listen to me;
8: 32 "Now then, my *s*, listen to me;
SS 1: 6 My mother's *s* were angry with me
Isa 14: 21 Prepare a place to slaughter his *s*
23: 4 I have neither reared *s*
37: 38 his *s* Adrammelech and Sharezer
43: 6 Bring my *s* from afar
49: 17 Your *s* hasten back,
49: 18 all your *s* gather and come to you.
49: 22 they will bring your *s* in their arms
51: 12 the *s* of men, who are but grass,
51: 18 Of all the *s* she bore
51: 18 of all the *s* she reared
51: 20 Your *s* have fainted;
54: 13 All your *s* will be taught
56: 5 better than *s* and daughters;
57: 3 come here, you *s* of a sorceress,
60: 4 your *s* come from afar,
60: 9 bringing your *s* from afar,
60: 14 The *s* of your oppressors will come
62: 5 so will your *s* marry you;
63: 8 *s* who will not be false to me";
Jer 3: 19 gladly would I treat you like *s*
3: 24 their *s* and daughters.
5: 17 devour your *s* and daughters;
6: 21 and *s* alike will stumble over them;
7: 31 of Ben Hinnom to burn their *s*
10: 20 My *s* are gone from me
11: 22 their *s* and daughters by famine.
13: 14 and *s* alike, declares the LORD.
14: 16 or their wives, their *s* or their
16: 2 have *s* or daughters in this place."
16: 3 is what the LORD says about the *s*
19: 5 of Baal to burn their *s* in the fire
19: 9 make them eat the flesh of their *s*
29: 6 Marry and have *s* and daughters;
29: 6 for your *s* and give your daughters
29: 6 so that they too may have *s*
32: 35 of Ben Hinnom to sacrifice their *s*
33: 26 his *s* to rule over the descendants
35: 3 and his brothers and all his *s*—
Jer 35: 4 into the room of the *s* of Hanan son
35: 8 nor our *s* and daughters have ever
35: 14 son of Recab ordered his *s* not
39: 6 king of Babylon slaughtered the *s*
40: 8 and Jonathan the *s* of Kareah,
40: 8 the *s* of Ephai the Netophathite,
48: 46 your *s* are taken into exile
49: 1 "Has Israel no *s*?
52: 10 king of Babylon slaughtered the *s*
La 4: 2 How the precious *s* of Zion,
Eze 14: 16 they could not save their own *s*
14: 18 they could not save their own *s*
14: 22 *s* and daughters who will be
16: 20 " 'And you took your *s*
20: 31 the sacrifice of your *s* in the fire—
23: 4 and gave birth to *s* and daughters.
23: 10 took away her *s* and daughters
23: 25 They will take away your *s*
23: 47 they will kill their *s* and daughters
24: 21 The *s* and daughters you left
24: 25 and their *s* and daughters as well—
40: 46 These are the *s* of Zadok, who are
46: 16 from his inheritance to one of his *s*,
46: 17 inheritance belongs to his *s* only;
46: 18 is to give his *s* their inheritance out
Da 11: 10 His *s* will prepare for war
Hos 1: 10 they will be called '*s*
Joel 2: 28 Your *s* and daughters will prophesy
3: 8 I will sell your *s* and daughters
Am 2: 11 from among your *s*
7: 17 and your *s* and daughters will fall
Zep 1: 8 and the king's *s*
Zec 9: 13 I will rouse your *s*, O Zion,
9: 13 against your *s*, O Greece,
Mt 5: 9 for they will be called *s* of God.
5: 45 that you may be *s* of your Father
13: 38 The weeds are the *s* of the evil one,
13: 38 stands for the *s* of the kingdom.
17: 25 from their own *s* or from others?"
17: 26 the *s* are exempt," Jesus said
20: 20 came to Jesus with her *s*
20: 20 of Zebedee's *s* came to Jesus
20: 21 one of these two *s* of mine may sit
21: 28 There was a man who had two *s*.
26: 37 and the two *s* of Zebedee
27: 56 and the mother of Zebedee's *s*.
Mk 3: 17 which means *S* of Thunder);
10: 35 James and John, the *s* of Zebedee,
Lk 5: 10 the *s* of Zebedee, Simon's partners.
6: 35 and you will be *s* of the Most High,
15: 11 "There was a man who had two *s*.
Jn 4: 12 as did also his *s* and his flocks
12: 36 so that you may become *s* of light."
21: 2 Cana in Galilee, the *s* of Zebedee,
Ac 2: 17 Your *s* and daughters will prophesy
7: 16 from the *s* of Hamor at Shechem
7: 29 as a foreigner and had two *s*.
19: 14 Seven *s* of Sceva, a Jewish chief
Ro 8: 14 by the Spirit of God are *s* of God.
8: 19 waits in eager expectation for the *s*
8: 23 eagerly for our adoption as *s*,
9: 4 Theirs is the adoption as *s*;
9: 26 they will be called '*s*
2Co 6: 18 and you will be my *s* and daughters
Gal 3: 26 You are all *s* of God through faith
4: 5 we might receive the full rights of *s*.
4: 6 Because you are *s*, God sent
4: 22 is written that Abraham had two *s*,
Eph 1: 5 as his *s* through Jesus Christ,
1Th 5: 5 *s* of the light and *s* of the day.
Heb 2: 10 In bringing many *s* to glory,
11: 21 blessed each of Joseph's *s*,
12: 5 that addresses you as *s*:
12: 7 discipline; God is treating you as *s*.
12: 8 illegitimate children and not true *s*.

SONS' (SON)

Ge 6: 18 and your *s'* wives with you.
7: 7 and his *s'* wives entered the ark
8: 18 and his wife and his *s'* wives.
46: 26 not counting his *s'* wives—
Lev 10: 13 your *s'* share of the offerings made

SONSHIP (SON)

Ro 8: 15 but you received the Spirit of *s*.

SOOT

Ex 9: 8 "Take handfuls of *s* from a furnace
Ex 9: 10 So they took *s* from a furnace
La 4: 8 But now they are blacker than *s*;

SOOTHED (SOOTHES SOOTHING)

Isa 1: 6 or *s* with oil.

SOOTHES (SOOTHED)

Pr 21: 14 A gift given in secret *s* anger,

SOOTHING (SOOTHED)

Ps 55: 21 his words are more *s* than oil,

SOOTHSAYER (SOOTHSAYERS')

Isa 3: 2 the *s* and elder,

SOOTHSAYERS' (SOOTHSAYER)

Jdg 9: 37 from the direction of the *s'* tree."

SOPATER

Ac 20: 4 accompanied by *S* son of Pyrrhus

SOPHERETH

Ne 7: 57 the descendants of Sotai, *S*, Perida,

SORCERER (SORCERY)

Ac 13: 6 There they met a Jewish *s*
13: 8 Elymas the *s* (for that is what his

SORCERERS (SORCERY)

Ex 7: 11 then summoned wise men and *s*,
Jer 27: 9 mediums or your *s* who tell you,
Da 2: 2 *s* and astrologers to tell him what
Mal 3: 5 I will be quick to testify against *s*,

SORCERESS (SORCERY)

Ex 22: 18 "Do not allow a *s* to live.
Isa 57: 3 come here, you sons of a *s*,

SORCERIES (SORCERY)

Isa 47: 9 in spite of your many *s*
47: 12 and with your many *s*,
Na 3: 4 alluring, the mistress of *s*,

SORCERY (SORCERER SORCERERS SORCERESS SORCERIES)

Lev 19: 26 " 'Do not practice divination or *s*.
Nu 23: 23 There is no *s* against Jacob,
24: 1 resort to *s* as at other times,
Dt 18: 10 who practices divination or *s*,
18: 14 listen to those who practice *s*
2Ki 17: 17 They practiced divination and *s*
21: 6 practiced *s* and divination,
2Ch 33: 6 practiced *s*, divination
Ac 8: 9 man named Simon had practiced *s*
19: 19 who had practiced *s* brought their

SORE (SORES)

Lev 13: 3 and the *s* appears to be more
13: 3 if the hair in the *s* has turned white
13: 3 is to examine the *s* on his skin,
13: 5 if he sees that the *s* is unchanged
13: 6 and if the *s* has faded and has not
13: 29 or woman has a *s* on the head
13: 30 the priest is to examine the *s*,
13: 31 the priest examines this kind of *s*,
13: 32 day the priest is to examine the *s*,
13: 42 But if he has a reddish-white *s*
13: 43 and, if the swollen *s* on his head
13: 44 because of the *s* on his head.
2Sa 3: 29 someone who has a running *s*
Jer 30: 13 no remedy for your *s*,

SOREK

Jdg 16: 4 of *S* whose name was Delilah.

SORES (SORE)

Lev 13: 17 and if the *s* have turned white,
21: 20 or running *s* or damaged testicles.
22: 22 or festering or running *s*.
Dt 28: 27 festering *s* and the itch,
Job 2: 7 Job with painful *s* from the soles
Isa 1: 6 and open *s*,
3: 17 Therefore the Lord will bring *s*
Hos 5: 13 and Judah his *s*,
5: 13 not able to heal your *s*.
Lk 16: 20 covered with *s* and longing
16: 21 the dogs came and licked his *s*.
Rev 16: 2 and painful *s* broke out
16: 11 because of their pains and their *s*,

SORROW (SORROWFUL SORROWS)

Ge 42: 38 head down to the grave in *s*.''
44: 31 of our father down to the grave in *s*.
48: 7 to my *s* Rachel died in the land
Est 9: 22 the month when their *s* was turned
Ps 6: 7 My eyes grow weak with *s;*
13: 2 and every day have *s* in my heart?
31: 9 my eyes grow weak with *s*,
90: 10 yet their span is but trouble and *s*,
107: 39 by oppression, calamity and *s;*
116: 3 I was overcome by trouble and *s*.
119: 28 My soul is weary with *s;*
Pr 23: 29 Who has woe? Who has *s?*
Ecc 1: 18 with much wisdom comes much *s;*
7: 3 *S* is better than laughter,
Isa 35: 10 and *s* and sighing will flee away.
51: 11 and *s* and sighing will flee away.
60: 20 and your days of *s* will end.
Jer 8: 18 O my Comforter in *s*,
20: 18 the womb to see trouble and *s*
31: 12 and they will *s* no more.
31: 13 them comfort and joy instead of *s*.
45: 3 The LORD has added *s* to my pain;
Eze 23: 33 filled with drunkenness and *s*,
Mt 26: 38 overwhelmed with *s* to the point
Mk 14: 34 overwhelmed with *s* to the point
Lk 22: 45 them asleep, exhausted from *s*.
Ro 9: 2 I have great *s* and unceasing
2Co 2: 7 be overwhelmed by excessive *s*.
7: 7 your deep *s*, your ardent concern
7: 8 Even if I caused you *s* by my letter,
7: 9 your *s* led you to repentance.
7: 10 Godly *s* brings repentance that
7: 10 but worldly *s* brings death.
7: 11 See what this godly *s* has produced
Php 2: 27 also on me, to spare me *s* upon *s*.

SORROWFUL (SORROW)

Mt 26: 37 and he began to be *s* and troubled.
2Co 6: 10 and yet not killed; *s*, yet always
7: 9 For you became *s* as God intended

SORROWS (SORROW)

Ps 16: 4 The *s* of those will increase
Isa 53: 3 a man of *s*, and familiar
53: 4 and carried our *s*,
Zep 3: 18 ''The *s* for the appointed feasts

SORRY

Ex 2: 6 He was crying, and she felt *s*
2Co 7: 9 not because you were made *s*,

SORT (SORTS)

2Ki 9: 11 and the *s* of things he says,''
Ecc 10: 5 the *s* of error that arises
2Th 2: 10 and in every *s* of evil that deceives
Rev 18: 12 and scarlet cloth; every *s*

SORTS (SORT)

1Ki 12: 31 priests from all *s* of people,
13: 33 places from all *s* of people.
2Ki 17: 32 appointed all *s* of their own people
Pr 1: 13 we will get all *s* of valuable things
1Co 14: 10 Undoubtedly there are all *s*

SOSIPATER

Ro 16: 21 Jason and *S*, my relatives.

SOSTHENES

Ac 18: 17 turned on *S* the synagogue ruler
1Co 1: 1 and our brother *S*, To the church

SOTAI

Ezr 2: 55 descendants of *S*, Hassophereth,
Ne 7: 57 the descendants of *S*, Sophereth,

SOUGHT (SEEK)

Ex 32: 11 Moses *s* the favor of the LORD his
1Sa 7: 2 the people of Israel mourned and *s*
13: 12 and I have not *s* the LORD's favor
13: 14 the LORD has *s* out a man
2Sa 21: 1 so David *s* the face of the LORD.
1Ki 10: 24 The whole world *s* audience
2Ki 13: 4 Then Jehoahaz *s* the LORD's favor
2Ch 9: 23 the kings of the earth *s* audience
14: 7 we have *s* the LORD our God;
14: 7 we *s* him and he has given us rest
15: 4 the God of Israel, and *s* him,
2Ch 15: 15 They *s* God eagerly, and he was
17: 4 but *s* the God of his father
22: 9 who *s* the LORD with all his heart
25: 20 because they *s* the gods of Edom.
26: 5 As long as he *s* the LORD,
26: 5 He *s* God during the days
31: 21 he *s* his God and worked
33: 12 In his distress he *s* the favor
Ne 12: 27 the Levites were *s* out
Ps 34: 4 I *s* the LORD, and he answered me
77: 2 When I was in distress, I *s* the Lord
119: 45 for I have *s* out your precepts.
119: 58 I have *s* your face with all my heart;
119: 94 I have *s* out your precepts.
Isa 9: 13 have they *s* the LORD Almighty.
62: 12 and you will be called *S* After,
Jer 26: 21 the king *s* to put him to death.
Eze 25: 15 and with ancient hostility *s*
26: 21 You will be *s*, but you will never
Da 4: 36 My advisers and nobles *s* me out,
9: 13 yet we have not *s* the favor
Ac 12: 20 and *s* an audience with him.
Ro 10: 3 and *s* to establish their own,
11: 7 What Israel *s* so earnestly it did not
Heb 8: 7 no place would have been *s*
12: 17 though he *s* the blessing with tears.

SOUL (SOULS)

Dt 4: 29 all your heart and with all your *s*.
6: 5 with all your *s* and with all your
10: 12 all your heart and with all your *s*,
11: 13 all your heart and with all your *s*—
13: 3 all your heart and with all your *s*.
26: 16 all your heart and with all your *s*.
30: 2 and with all your *s* according
30: 6 all your heart and with all your *s*,
30: 10 all your heart and with all your *s*.
Jos 22: 5 with all your heart and all your *s*.''
23: 14 and *s* that not one of all the good
Jdg 5: 21 March on, my *s;* be strong!
1Sa 1: 10 bitterness of *s* Hannah wept much
1: 15 I was pouring out my *s*
14: 7 I am with you heart and *s*.''
1Ki 2: 4 before me with all their heart and *s*,
8: 48 *s* in the land of their enemies who
2Ki 23: 3 with all his heart and all his *s*,
23: 25 and with all his *s* and with all his
1Ch 22: 19 *s* to seeking the LORD your God.
2Ch 6: 38 and *s* in the land of their captivity
15: 12 with all their heart and *s*.
34: 31 with all his heart and all his *s*,
Job 3: 20 and life to the bitter of *s*,
7: 11 complain in the bitterness of my *s*.
10: 1 speak out in the bitterness of my *s*.
21: 25 Another man dies in bitterness of *s*,
27: 2 has made me taste bitterness of *s*,
30: 25 Has not my *s* grieved for the poor?
33: 18 to preserve his *s* from the pit,
33: 20 and his *s* loathes the choicest meal.
33: 22 His *s* draws near to the pit,
33: 28 He redeemed my *s* from going
33: 30 to turn back his *s* from the pit,
Ps 6: 3 My *s* is in anguish.
11: 5 his *s* hates.
19: 7 reviving the *s*.
23: 3 he restores my *s*.
24: 4 who does not lift up his *s* to an idol
25: 1 I lift up my *s;* in you I trust,
26: 9 Do not take away my *s*
31: 7 and knew the anguish of my *s*.
31: 9 my *s* and my body with grief.
34: 2 My *s* will boast in the LORD;
35: 3 Say to my *s*,
35: 9 my *s* will rejoice in the LORD
35: 12 and leave my *s* forlorn.
42: 1 so my *s* pants for you, O God.
42: 2 My *s* thirsts for God,
42: 4 as I pour out my *s:*
42: 5 Why are you downcast, O my *s?*
42: 6 My *s* is downcast within me;
42: 11 Why are you downcast, O my *s?*
43: 5 Why are you downcast, O my *s?*
49: 15 God will redeem my *s*
56: 13 For you have delivered my *s*
57: 1 for in you my *s* takes refuge.
57: 8 Awake, my *s!*
62: 1 My *s* finds rest in God alone;
62: 5 Find rest, O my *s*, in God alone;
Ps 63: 1 my *s* thirsts for you,
63: 5 My *s* will be satisfied
77: 2 and my *s* refused to be comforted.
84: 2 My *s* yearns, even faints
86: 4 I lift up my *s*.
86: 13 you have delivered my *s*
88: 3 For my *s* is full of trouble
94: 19 consolation brought joy to my *s*.
103: 1 Praise the LORD, O my *s;*
103: 2 Praise the LORD, O my *s*,
103: 22 Praise the LORD, O my *s*.
104: 1 Praise the LORD, O my *s*.
104: 35 Praise the LORD, O my *s*.
108: 1 make music with all my *s*.
116: 7 Be at rest once more, O my *s*,
116: 8 have delivered my *s* from death,
119: 20 My *s* is consumed with longing
119: 28 My *s* is weary with sorrow;
119: 81 My *s* faints with longing
130: 5 I wait for the LORD, my *s* waits,
130: 6 My *s* waits for the Lord
131: 2 But I have stilled and quieted my *s;*
131: 2 like a weaned child is my *s*
143: 6 my *s* thirsts for you like a parched
143: 8 for to you I lift up my *s*.
146: 1 Praise the LORD, O my *s*.
Pr 1: 11 let's waylay some harmless *s;*
2: 10 will be pleasant to your *s*.
13: 3 He who guards his lips guards his *s*,
13: 19 A longing fulfilled is sweet to the *s*,
16: 17 he who guards his way guards his *s*.
16: 24 sweet to the *s* and healing
18: 7 and his lips are a snare to his *s*.
19: 8 who gets wisdom loves his own *s;*
19: 16 obeys instructions guards his *s*,
22: 5 he who guards his *s* stays far
23: 14 and save his *s* from death.
24: 14 also that wisdom is sweet to your *s;*
25: 25 Like cold water to a weary *s*
29: 17 he will bring delight to your *s*.
Isa 1: 14 my *s* hates.
26: 9 My *s* yearns for you in the night;
38: 15 because of this anguish of my *s*.
53: 11 After the suffering of his *s*,
55: 2 your *s* will delight in the richest
55: 3 hear me, that your *s* may live.
61: 10 my *s* rejoices in my God.
Jer 32: 41 in this land with all my heart and *s*.
La 3: 20 and my *s* is downcast within me.
3: 51 What I see brings grief to my *s*
Eze 18: 4 For every living *s* belongs to me,
18: 4 *s* who sins is the one who will die.
18: 20 *s* who sins is the one who will die.
27: 31 weep over you with anguish of *s*
Mic 6: 7 of my body for the sin of my *s?*
Mt 10: 28 kill the body but cannot kill the *s*.
10: 28 of the one who can destroy both *s*
16: 26 give in exchange for his *s?*
16: 26 yet forfeits his *s?* Or what can
22: 37 with all your *s* and with all your
26: 38 ''My *s* is overwhelmed with sorrow
Mk 8: 36 yet forfeit his *s?* Or what can a man
8: 37 give in exchange for his *s?*
12: 30 with all your *s* and with all your
14: 34 ''My *s* is overwhelmed with sorrow
Lk 1: 46 ''My *s* praises the Lord
2: 35 a sword will pierce your own *s* too
10: 27 with all your *s* and with all your
1Th 5: 23 *s* and body be kept blameless
Heb 4: 12 even to dividing *s* and spirit,
6: 19 this hope as an anchor for the *s*,
1Pe 2: 11 desires, which war against your *s*.
2Pe 2: 8 was tormented in his righteous *s*
3Jn : 2 even as your *s* is getting along well.

SOULS (SOUL)

Job 24: 12 the *s* of the wounded cry out
Pr 11: 30 and he who wins *s* is wise.
Isa 66: 3 *s* delight in their abominations;
Jer 6: 16 and you will find rest for your *s*.
Mt 11: 29 and you will find rest for your *s*.
1Pe 1: 9 of your faith, the salvation of your *s*
2: 25 Shepherd and Overseer of your *s*.
Rev 6: 9 I saw under the altar the *s*
18: 13 carriages; and bodies and *s* of men.
20: 4 I saw the *s* of those who had been

SOUND (FINE-SOUNDING SOUNDED SOUNDING SOUNDINGS SOUNDNESS SOUNDS)

Ge 3: 8 and his wife heard the *s*
Ex 19: 19 the *s* of the trumpet grew louder
28: 35 The *s* of the bells will be heard
32: 17 "There is the *s* of war in the camp."
32: 18 it is not the *s* of defeat;
32: 18 it is the *s* of singing that I hear."
32: 18 "It is not the *s* of victory,
Lev 25: 9 Day of Atonement *s* the trumpet
26: 36 the lands of their enemies that the *s*
Nu 10: 9 who is oppressing you, *s* a blast
10: 10 you are to *s* the trumpets
29: 1 It is a day for you to *s* the trumpets.
Dt 4: 12 You heard the *s* of words
Jos 6: 5 When you hear them *s* a long blast
6: 20 and at the *s* of the trumpet,
Jdg 11: 34 dancing to the *s* of tambourines!
1Sa 20: 12 I will surely *s* out my father
2Sa 5: 24 as you hear the *s* of marching
6: 15 with shouts and the *s* of trumpets.
15: 10 as you hear the *s* of the trumpets,
1Ki 1: 40 so that the ground shook with the *s*
1: 41 On hearing the *s* of the trumpet,
14: 6 So when Ahijah heard the *s*
18: 41 for there is the *s* of a heavy rain."
2Ki 4: 31 but there was no *s* or response.
6: 32 Is not the *s* of his master's footsteps
7: 6 Arameans to hear the *s* of chariots
7: 10 not a *s* of anyone—only tethered
1Ch 14: 15 as you hear the *s* of marching
15: 19 were to *s* the bronze cymbals;
16: 5 Asaph was to *s* the cymbals,
2Ch 13: 12 their trumpets will *s* the battle cry
13: 15 At the *s* of their battle cry,
Ezr 3: 13 And the *s* was heard far away.
3: 13 No one could distinguish the *s*
3: 13 shouts of joy from the *s* of weeping,
Ne 4: 20 Wherever you hear the *s*
12: 43 *s* of rejoicing in Jerusalem could be
Job 21: 12 to the *s* of the flute.
30: 31 and my flute to the *s* of wailing.
37: 4 After that comes the *s* of his roar;
Ps 66: 8 let the *s* of his praise be heard;
81: 3 *S* the ram's horn at the New Moon,
98: 5 with the harp and the *s* of singing,
104: 7 at the *s* of your thunder they took
115: 7 can they utter a *s* with their throats
Pr 3: 21 preserve *s* judgment
4: 2 I give you *s* learning,
8: 14 Counsel and *s* judgment are mine;
18: 1 he defies all *s* judgment
22: 21 so that you can give *s* answers
Ecc 12: 4 and the *s* of grinding fades;
12: 4 when men rise up at the *s* of birds,
Isa 6: 4 At the *s* of their voices
24: 18 Whoever flees at the *s* of terror
27: 13 in that day a great trumpet will *s*.
51: 3 thanksgiving and the *s* of singing.
65: 19 the *s* of weeping and of crying
66: 6 It is the *s* of the LORD
Jer 2: 21 of *s* and reliable stock.
4: 5 '*S* the trumpet throughout the land
4: 19 For I have heard the *s*
4: 21 and hear the *s* of the trumpet?
4: 29 At the *s* of horsemen and archers
6: 1 *S* the trumpet in Tekoa!
6: 17 'Listen to the *s* of the trumpet!'
6: 23 They *s* like the roaring sea
9: 19 The *s* of wailing is heard from Zion:
25: 10 the *s* of millstones and the light
30: 19 and the *s* of rejoicing.
47: 3 wail at the *s* of the hoofs
48: 34 "The *s* of their cry rises
49: 2 "when I will *s* the battle cry
49: 21 At the *s* of their fall the earth will
50: 42 They *s* like the roaring sea
50: 46 At the *s* of Babylon's capture
51: 54 The *s* of a cry comes from Babylon,
51: 54 the *s* of great destruction
Eze 1: 24 I heard the *s* of their wings,
3: 12 I heard behind me a loud rushing *s*
3: 13 beside them, a loud rushing *s*.
3: 13 the *s* of the wheels beside them,
3: 13 the *s* of the wings of the living
10: 5 The *s* of the wings
Eze 21: 22 to slaughter, to *s* the battle cry,
26: 15 tremble at the *s* of your fall,
31: 16 I made the nations tremble at the *s*
33: 5 Since he heard the *s* of the trumpet
37: 7 a rattling *s*, and the bones came
Da 3: 5 as you hear the *s* of the horn,
3: 7 soon as they heard the *s* of the horn
3: 10 that everyone who hears the *s*
3: 15 when you hear the *s* of the horn,
10: 6 his voice like the *s* of a multitude.
Hos 5: 8 "*S* the trumpet in Gibeah,
Joel 2: 1 *s* the alarm on my holy hill.
Hab 3: 16 my lips quivered at the *s*;
Zec 8: 16 and *s* judgment in your courts;
9: 14 LORD will *s* the trumpet;
Mt 12: 13 it was completely restored, just as *s*
Lk 1: 44 *s* of your greeting reached my ears,
15: 27 he has him back safe and *s*.'
Jn 3: 8 You hear its *s*, but you cannot tell
Ac 2: 2 Suddenly a *s* like the blowing
2: 6 they heard this *s*, a crowd came
9: 7 they heard the *s* but did not see
20: 9 When he was *s* asleep, he fell
1Co 14: 8 if the trumpet does not *s* a clear call
15: 52 the trumpet will *s*, the dead will
1Ti 1: 10 to the *s* doctrine that conforms
6: 3 does not agree to the *s* instruction
2Ti 1: 13 keep as the pattern of *s* teaching,
4: 3 men will not put up with *s* doctrine.
Tit 1: 9 can encourage others by *s* doctrine
1: 13 so that they will be *s* in the faith
2: 1 is in accord with *s* doctrine.
2: 2 self-controlled, and *s* in faith,
Rev 1: 15 and his voice was like the *s*
8: 6 seven trumpets prepared to *s* them.
9: 9 and the *s* of their wings was like
10: 7 angel is about to *s* his trumpet,
14: 2 And I heard a *s* from heaven like
14: 2 The *s* I heard was like that
18: 22 The *s* of a millstone

SOUNDED (SOUND)

Lev 25: 9 have the trumpet *s* everywhere
Nu 10: 3 When both are *s*, the whole
10: 4 If only one is *s*, the leaders—
10: 5 When a trumpet blast is *s*,
Jos 6: 16 when the priests *s* the trumpet blast
6: 20 When the trumpets *s*, the people
Jdg 7: 22 the three hundred trumpets *s*,
2Sa 18: 16 Then Joab *s* the trumpet,
20: 1 He *s* the trumpet and shouted,
20: 22 So he *s* the trumpet, and his men
1Ki 1: 39 Then they *s* the trumpet
Ne 4: 18 the man who *s* the trumpet stayed
Rev 8: 6 Then I heard what *s* like a voice
8: 7 The first angel *s* his trumpet,
8: 8 The second angel *s* his trumpet,
8: 10 The third angel *s* his trumpet,
8: 12 The fourth angel *s* his trumpet,
8: 13 to be *s* by the other three angels!"
9: 1 The fifth angel *s* his trumpet,
11: 15 The seventh angel *s* his trumpet,
19: 1 this I heard what *s* like the roar
19: 6 Then I heard what *s* like a great

SOUNDING (SOUND)

Nu 10: 6 At the *s* of a second blast,
Jos 6: 9 All this time the trumpets were *s*.
6: 13 while the trumpets kept *s*.
1Ch 15: 28 with the *s* of rams' horns
16: 42 for the *s* of the trumpets
2Ch 5: 12 by 120 priests *s* trumpets.
Ps 47: 5 the LORD amid the *s* of trumpets.
150: 3 him with the *s* of the trumpet,

SOUNDINGS (SOUND)

Ac 27: 28 A short time later they took *s* again
27: 28 They took *s* and found that

SOUNDNESS (SOUND)

Ps 38: 3 my bones have no *s*
Isa 1: 6 there is no *s*—
Tit 2: 8 and *s* of speech that cannot be

SOUNDS (SOUND)

Ex 19: 13 when the ram's horn *s* a long blast
Job 15: 21 Terrifying *s* fill his ears;
39: 24 when the trumpet *s*.
Isa 18: 3 and when a trumpet *s*,
Jer 7: 34 I will bring an end to the *s* of joy
16: 9 days I will bring an end to the *s*
25: 10 I will banish from them the *s* of joy
33: 11 there will be heard once more the *s*
Am 3: 6 When a trumpet *s* in a city,
1Co 14: 7 case of lifeless things that make *s*,

SOUR

Job 20: 14 yet his food will turn *s*
Jer 31: 29 'The fathers have eaten *s* grapes,
31: 30 own sin; whoever eats *s* grapes—
Eze 18: 2 " 'The fathers eat *s* grapes,
Rev 10: 9 It will turn your stomach *s*,
10: 10 had eaten it, my stomach turned *s*.

SOURCE (SOURCES)

Ge 26: 35 They were a *s* of grief to Isaac
Lev 20: 18 he has exposed the *s* of her flow,
Ps 80: 6 You have made us a *s* of contention
Isa 28: 6 a *s* of strength
Eze 29: 16 Egypt will no longer be a *s*
Heb 5: 9 became the *s* of eternal salvation

SOURCES (SOURCE)

Job 28: 11 He searches the *s* of the rivers
Jer 18: 14 Do its cool waters from distant *s*

SOUTH (SOUTHERN SOUTHERNMOST SOUTHLAND SOUTHWARD)

Ge 13: 14 you are and look north and *s*,
28: 14 to the east, to the north and to the *s*
Ex 26: 18 for the *s* side of the tabernacle
26: 35 lampstand opposite it on the *s* side.
27: 9 The *s* side shall be a hundred cubits
36: 23 for the *s* side of the tabernacle
38: 9 *s* side was a hundred cubits long
40: 24 table on the *s* side of the tabernacle
Nu 2: 10 On the *s* will be the divisions
3: 29 were to camp on the *s* side
10: 6 the camps on the *s* are to set out.
34: 4 cross *s* of Scorpion Pass, continue
34: 4 to Zin and go *s* of Kadesh Barnea.
35: 5 three thousand on the *s* side,
Dt 3: 27 look west and north and *s* and east.
33: 2 ones from the *s*, from his mountain
Jos 11: 2 in the Arabah *s* of Kinnereth,
13: 4 that of the Avvites); from the *s*,
15: 1 the Desert of Zin in the extreme *s*.
15: 3 and went over to the *s* of Kadesh
15: 3 crossed *s* of Scorpion Pass,
15: 7 Pass of Adummim *s* of the gorge.
17: 9 Then the boundary continued *s*
17: 10 On the *s* the land belonged
18: 5 is to remain in its territory on the *s*
18: 13 the hill *s* of Lower Beth Horon.
18: 13 to the *s* slope of Luz (that is,
18: 14 on the *s* the boundary turned *s*
18: 19 at the mouth of the Jordan in the *s*.
19: 34 It touched Zebulun on the *s*,
Jdg 21: 19 and to the *s* of Lebonah."
1Sa 14: 5 the other to the *s* toward Geba.
20: 41 up from the *s* side of the stone
23: 19 the hill of Hakilah, *s* of Jeshimon?
23: 24 in the Arabah *s* of Jeshimon.
2Sa 24: 5 *s* of the town in the gorge,
1Ki 6: 8 was on the *s* side of the temple;
7: 21 The pillar to the *s* he named Jakin
7: 25 three facing *s* and three facing east.
7: 39 He placed the Sea on the *s* side,
7: 39 stands on the *s* side of the temple
2Ki 11: 11 from the *s* side to the north side
23: 13 of Jerusalem on the *s* of the Hill
1Ch 9: 24 four sides: east, west, north and *s*.
26: 15 The lot for the *S* Gate fell
26: 17 four a day on the *s* and two
2Ch 3: 17 The one to the *s* he named Jakin
3: 17 one to the *s* and one to the north.
4: 4 three facing *s* and three facing east.
4: 6 and placed five on the *s* side
4: 7 five on the *s* side and five
4: 8 five on the *s* side and five
4: 10 He placed the Sea on the *s* side,
23: 10 from the *s* side to the north side
Job 9: 9 the constellations of the *s*.
23: 9 to the *s*, I catch no glimpse
37: 17 land lies hushed under the *s* wind,
39: 26 and spread his wings toward the *s*?

Ps 78: 26 led forth the *s* wind by his power.
89: 12 You created the north and the *s;*
107: 3 and west, from north and *s*.
Ecc 1: 6 The wind blows to the *s*
11: 3 Whether a tree falls to the *s*
SS 4: 16 and come, *s* wind!
Isa 43: 6 to the *s*, 'Do not hold them back.'
Eze 10: 3 standing on the *s* side of the temple
16: 46 who lived to the *s* of you
20: 46 preach against the *s* and prophesy
20: 46 set your face toward the *s;*
20: 47 from *s* to north will be scorched
21: 4 against everyone from *s* to north.
40: 2 on whose *s* side were some
40: 24 the *s* side and I saw a gate facing *s*.
40: 27 gate to the outer gate on the *s* side;
40: 27 inner court also had a gate facing *s*,
40: 28 and he measured the *s* gate;
40: 28 court through the *s* gate,
40: 44 and another at the side of the *s* gate
40: 44 side of the north gate and facing *s*,
40: 45 "The room facing *s* is
41: 11 on the north and another on the *s;*
42: 10 On the *s* side along the length
42: 12 doorways of the rooms on the *s*.
42: 13 and *s* rooms facing the temple
42: 18 He measured the *s* side; it was five
46: 9 and whoever enters by the *s* gate is
46: 9 to worship is to go out the *s* gate;
47: 1 coming down from under the *s* side
47: 1 side of the temple, *s* of the altar.
47: 2 water was flowing from the *s* side.
47: 19 This will be the *s* boundary.
47: 19 "On the *s* side it will run
48: 10 25,000 cubits long on the *s* side.
48: 16 cubits, the *s* side 4,500 cubits,
48: 17 250 cubits on the *s*, 250 cubits
48: 28 of Gad will run *s* from Tamar
48: 33 "On the *s* side, which measures
Da 8: 4 the west and the north and the *s*.
8: 9 but grew in power to the *s*
11: 5 king of the *S* will become strong,
11: 6 daughter of the king of the *S* will go
11: 9 the realm of the king of the *S*
11: 11 the king of the *S* will march out
11: 12 the king of the *S* will be filled
11: 14 rise against the king of the *S*.
11: 15 forces of the *S* will be powerless
11: 17 an alliance with the king of the *S*.
11: 25 The king of the *S* will wage war
11: 25 courage against the king of the *S*.
11: 29 time he will invade the *S* again,
11: 40 of the *S* will engage him in battle,
Zec 6: 6 the dappled horses toward the *s*."
9: 14 he will march in the storms of the *s*,
14: 4 moving north and half moving *s*.
14: 10 Geba to Rimmon, *s* of Jerusalem,
Mt 12: 42 The Queen of the *S* will rise
Lk 11: 31 The Queen of the *S* will rise
12: 55 And when the *s* wind blows,
13: 29 from east and west and north and *s*,
Ac 8: 26 "Go *s* to the road—the desert road
21: 3 Cyprus and passing to the *s*
27: 13 When a gentle *s* wind began
28: 13 The next day the *s* wind came up,
Rev 21: 13 three on the *s* and three on the west

SOUTHEAST (EAST)

1Ki 7: 39 at the *s* corner of the temple.
2Ch 4: 10 on the south side, at the *s* corner.

SOUTHERN (SOUTH)

Nu 34: 3 your *s* boundary will start
34: 3 " 'Your *s* side will include some
Jos 15: 2 Their *s* boundary started
15: 2 started from the bay at the *s* end
15: 4 This is their *s* boundary.
15: 8 of Ben Hinnom along the *s* slope
18: 15 The *s* side began at the outskirts
18: 16 along the *s* slope of the Jebusite
18: 19 This was the *s* boundary.
Eze 20: 47 Say to the *s* forest: 'Hear the word
48: 28 *s* boundary of Gad will run south

SOUTHERNMOST (SOUTH)

Jos 15: 21 The *s* towns of the tribe of Judah

SOUTHLAND (SOUTH)

Isa 21: 1 whirlwinds sweeping through the *s*,
Eze 20: 46 prophesy against the forest of the *s*.

SOUTHWARD (SOUTH)

Dt 33: 23 he will inherit *s* to the lake."
Jos 12: 3 then *s* below the slopes of Pisgah.
17: 7 The boundary ran *s* from there

SOUTHWEST (WEST)

Ac 27: 12 facing both *s* and northwest.

SOVEREIGN (SOVEREIGNTY)

Ge 15: 2 But Abram said, "O *S* LORD,
15: 8 But Abram said, "O *S* LORD,
Ex 23: 17 are to appear before the *S* LORD.
34: 23 are to appear before the *S* LORD,
Dt 3: 24 with the LORD: "O *S* LORD,
9: 26 "O *S* LORD, do not destroy your
Jos 7: 7 And Joshua said, "Ah, *S* LORD,
Jdg 6: 22 he exclaimed, "Ah, *S* LORD!
16: 28 "O *S* LORD, remember me.
2Sa 7: 18 O *S* LORD, and what is my family,
7: 19 O *S* LORD? "What more can
7: 19 enough in your sight, O *S* LORD,
7: 20 know your servant, O *S* LORD.
7: 22 "How great you are, O *S* LORD!
7: 28 O *S* LORD, you are God!
7: 29 for you, O *S* LORD, have spoken,
1Ki 2: 26 of the *S* LORD before my father
8: 53 O *S* LORD, brought our fathers
Ps 68: 20 from the *S* LORD comes escape
71: 5 have been my hope, O *S* LORD,
71: 16 your mighty acts, O *S* LORD;
73: 28 have made the *S* LORD my refuge;
109: 21 But you, O *S* LORD,
140: 7 O *S* LORD, my strong deliverer,
141: 8 on you, O *S* LORD;
Isa 7: 7 Yet this is what the *S* LORD says:
25: 8 *S* LORD will wipe away the tears
28: 16 So this is what the *S* LORD says:
30: 15 This is what the *S* LORD,
40: 10 the *S* LORD comes with power,
48: 16 And now the *S* LORD has sent me,
49: 22 This is what the *S* LORD says:
50: 4 *S* LORD has given me
50: 5 The *S* LORD has opened my ears,
50: 7 Because the *S* LORD helps me,
50: 9 It is the *S* LORD who helps me.
51: 22 This is what your *S* LORD says,
52: 4 For this is what the *S* LORD says:
56: 8 The *S* LORD declares—
61: 1 The Spirit of the *S* LORD is on me,
61: 11 so the *S* LORD will make
65: 13 this is what the *S* LORD says:
65: 15 the *S* LORD will put you to death,
Jer 1: 6 *S* LORD," I said, "I do not know
2: 22 declares the *S* LORD.
4: 10 Then I said, "Ah, *S* LORD,
7: 20 this is what the *S* LORD says:
14: 13 But I said, "Ah, *S* LORD,
32: 17 to the LORD: "Ah, *S* LORD,
32: 25 you, O *S* LORD, say to me,
44: 26 "As surely as the *S* LORD lives."
50: 25 for the *S* LORD Almighty has
Eze 2: 4 'This is what the *S* LORD says.'
3: 11 'This is what the *S* LORD says,'
3: 27 'This is what the *S* LORD says.'
4: 14 Then I said, "Not so, *S* LORD!
5: 5 "This is what the *S* LORD says:
5: 7 this is what the *S* LORD says:
5: 8 this is what the *S* LORD says:
5: 11 as I live, declares the *S* LORD,
6: 3 This is what the *S* LORD says
6: 3 hear the word of the *S* LORD.
6: 11 " 'This is what the *S* LORD says:
7: 2 this is what the *S* LORD says
7: 5 "This is what the *S* LORD says:
8: 1 the hand of the *S* LORD came
9: 8 crying out, "Ah, *S* LORD!
11: 7 this is what the *S* LORD says:
11: 8 against you, declares the *S* LORD.
11: 13 *S* LORD! Will you completely
11: 16 'This is what the *S* LORD says:
11: 17 'This is what the *S* LORD says:
11: 21 have done, declares the *S* LORD."
12: 10 'This is what the *S* LORD says:
Eze 12: 19 is what the *S* LORD says about
12: 23 'This is what the *S* LORD says:
12: 25 I say, declares the *S* LORD.' "
12: 28 fulfilled, declares the *S* LORD.' "
12: 28 'This is what the *S* LORD says:
13: 3 This is what the *S* LORD says:
13: 8 against you, declares the *S* LORD.
13: 8 this is what the *S* LORD says:
13: 9 will know that I am the *S* LORD.
13: 13 this is what the *S* LORD says:
13: 16 no peace, declares the *S* LORD." '
13: 18 'This is what the *S* LORD says:
13: 20 this is what the *S* LORD says:
14: 4 'This is what the *S* LORD says:
14: 6 'This is what the *S* LORD says:
14: 11 God, declares the *S* LORD.' "
14: 14 declares the *S* LORD.
14: 16 as I live, declares the *S* LORD,
14: 18 as I live, declares the *S* LORD,
14: 20 declares the *S* LORD,
14: 21 "For this is what the *S* LORD says:
14: 23 cause, declares the *S* LORD."
15: 6 this is what the *S* LORD says:
15: 8 unfaithful, declares the *S* LORD."
16: 3 'This is what the *S* LORD says
16: 8 declares the *S* LORD,
16: 14 perfect, declares the *S* LORD.
16: 19 happened, declares the *S* LORD.
16: 23 Woe to you, declares the *S* LORD.
16: 30 you are, declares the *S* LORD,
16: 36 This is what the *S* LORD says:
16: 43 have done, declares the *S* LORD.
16: 48 as I live, declares the *S* LORD,
16: 59 " 'This is what the *S* LORD says:
16: 63 declares the *S* LORD.' "
17: 3 'This is what the *S* LORD says:
17: 9 'This is what the *S* LORD says:
17: 16 declares the *S* LORD, he shall die
17: 19 this is what the *S* LORD says:
17: 22 " 'This is what the *S* LORD says:
18: 3 as I live, declares the *S* LORD,
18: 9 declares the *S* LORD.
18: 23 the wicked? declares the *S* LORD.
18: 30 to his ways, declares the *S* LORD.
18: 32 of anyone, declares the *S* LORD.
20: 3 of me, declares the *S* LORD.'
20: 3 'This is what the *S* LORD says:
20: 5 'This is what the *S* LORD says:
20: 27 'This is what the *S* LORD says:
20: 30 'This is what the *S* LORD says:
20: 31 as I live, declares the *S* LORD,
20: 33 as I live, declares the *S* LORD,
20: 36 judge you, declares the *S* LORD.
20: 39 this is what the *S* LORD says:
20: 40 of Israel, declares the *S* LORD,
20: 44 of Israel, declares the *S* LORD.' "
20: 47 This is what the *S* LORD says:
20: 49 Then I said, "Ah, *S* LORD!
21: 7 take place, declares the *S* LORD."
21: 13 succeed! declares the *S* LORD.'
21: 24 this is what the *S* LORD says:
21: 26 this is what the *S* LORD says:
21: 28 is what the *S* LORD says about
22: 3 'This is what the *S* LORD says:
22: 12 me, declares the *S* LORD.
22: 19 this is what the *S* LORD says:
22: 28 'This is what the *S* LORD says'—
22: 31 have done, declares the *S* LORD."
23: 22 this is what the *S* LORD says:
23: 28 "For this is what the *S* LORD says:
23: 32 "This is what the *S* LORD says:
23: 34 spoken, declares the *S* LORD.
23: 35 this is what the *S* LORD says:
23: 46 "This is what the *S* LORD says:
23: 49 will know that I am the *S* LORD."
24: 3 'This is what the *S* LORD says:
24: 6 For this is what the *S* LORD says:
24: 9 this is what the *S* LORD says:
24: 14 your actions, declares the *S* LORD
24: 21 'This is what the *S* LORD says:
24: 24 will know that I am the *S* LORD.'
25: 3 This is what the *S* LORD says:
25: 3 'Hear the word of the *S* LORD.
25: 6 For this is what the *S* LORD says:
25: 8 "This is what the *S* LORD says:
25: 12 "This is what the *S* LORD says:
25: 13 this is what the *S* LORD says:
25: 14 declares the *S* LORD.' "

Eze 25: 15 "This is what the *S* LORD says:
25: 16 this is what the *S* LORD says:
26: 3 this is what the *S* LORD says:
26: 5 spoken, declares the *S* LORD.
26: 7 "For this is what the *S* LORD says:
26: 14 spoken, declares the *S* LORD.
26: 15 "This is what the *S* LORD says
26: 19 "This is what the *S* LORD says:
26: 21 be found, declares the *S* LORD."
27: 3 'This is what the *S* LORD says:
28: 2 'This is what the *S* LORD says:
28: 6 this is what the *S* LORD says:
28: 10 spoken, declares the *S* LORD.' "
28: 12 'This is what the *S* LORD says:
28: 22 'This is what the *S* LORD says:
28: 24 will know that I am the *S* LORD.
28: 25 " 'This is what the *S* LORD says:
29: 3 'This is what the *S* LORD says:
29: 8 this is what the *S* LORD says:
29: 13 Yet this is what the *S* LORD says:
29: 16 know that I am the *S* LORD.' "
29: 19 this is what the *S* LORD says:
29: 20 it for me, declares the *S* LORD.
30: 2 'This is what the *S* LORD says:
30: 6 declares the *S* LORD.
30: 10 " 'This is what the *S* LORD says:
30: 13 " 'This is what the *S* LORD says:
30: 22 this is what the *S* LORD says:
31: 10 this is what the *S* LORD says:
31: 15 " 'This is what the *S* LORD says:
31: 18 hordes, declares the *S* LORD.' "
32: 3 " 'This is what the *S* LORD says:
32: 8 declares the *S* LORD.
32: 11 For this is what the *S* LORD says:
32: 14 declares the *S* LORD.
32: 16 chant it, declares the *S* LORD."
32: 31 the sword, declares the *S* LORD.
32: 32 the sword, declares the *S* LORD."
33: 11 as I live, declares the *S* LORD,
33: 25 'This is what the *S* LORD says:
33: 27 'This is what the *S* LORD says:
34: 2 'This is what the *S* LORD says:
34: 8 as I live, declares the *S* LORD,
34: 10 This is what the *S* LORD says:
34: 11 For this is what the *S* LORD says:
34: 15 lie down, declares the *S* LORD.
34: 17 this is what the *S* LORD says:
34: 20 this is what the *S* LORD says
34: 30 my people, declares the *S* LORD.
34: 31 your God, declares the *S* LORD.' "
35: 3 'This is what the *S* LORD says:
35: 6 as I live, declares the *S* LORD,
35: 11 as I live, declares the *S* LORD,
35: 14 This is what the *S* LORD says:
36: 2 This is what the *S* LORD says:
36: 3 'This is what the *S* LORD says:
36: 4 This is what the *S* LORD says
36: 4 hear the word of the *S* LORD:
36: 5 this is what the *S* LORD says:
36: 6 'This is what the *S* LORD says:
36: 7 this is what the *S* LORD says:
36: 13 " 'This is what the *S* LORD says:
36: 14 childless, declares the *S* LORD.
36: 15 to fall, declares the *S* LORD.' "
36: 22 'This is what the *S* LORD says:
36: 23 declares the *S* LORD,
36: 32 your sake, declares the *S* LORD.
36: 33 " 'This is what the *S* LORD says:
36: 37 "This is what the *S* LORD says:
37: 3 "O *S* LORD, you alone know."
37: 5 This is what the *S* LORD says
37: 9 'This is what the *S* LORD says:
37: 12 'This is what the *S* LORD says:
37: 19 'This is what the *S* LORD says:
37: 21 'This is what the *S* LORD says:
38: 3 'This is what the *S* LORD says:
38: 10 " 'This is what the *S* LORD says:
38: 14 'This is what the *S* LORD says:
38: 17 " 'This is what the *S* LORD says:
38: 18 be aroused, declares the *S* LORD.
38: 21 mountains, declares the *S* LORD.
39: 1 'This is what the *S* LORD says:
39: 5 spoken, declares the *S* LORD.
39: 8 take place, declares the *S* LORD.
39: 10 looted them, declares the *S* LORD.
39: 13 for them, declares the *S* LORD.
39: 17 this is what the *S* LORD says:
39: 20 every kind,' declares the *S* LORD.
Eze 39: 25 this is what the *S* LORD says:
39: 29 of Israel, declares the *S* LORD."
43: 18 this is what the *S* LORD says:
43: 19 before me, declares the *S* LORD.
43: 27 accept you, declares the *S* LORD."
44: 6 'This is what the *S* LORD says:
44: 9 This is what the *S* LORD says:
44: 12 of their sin, declares the *S* LORD.
44: 15 and blood, declares the *S* LORD.
44: 27 for himself, declares the *S* LORD.
45: 9 my people, declares the *S* LORD.
45: 9 " 'This is what the *S* LORD says:
45: 15 the people, declares the *S* LORD.
45: 18 " 'This is what the *S* LORD says:
46: 1 " 'This is what the *S* LORD says:
46: 16 " 'This is what the *S* LORD says:
47: 13 This is what the *S* LORD says:
47: 23 declares the *S* LORD.
48: 29 portions," declares the *S* LORD.
Da 4: 17 may know that the Most High is *s*
4: 25 that the Most High is *s*
4: 32 that the Most High is *s*
5: 21 that the Most High God is *s*
7: 14 glory and *s* power; all peoples,
Am 1: 8 says the *S* LORD.
3: 7 Surely the *S* LORD does nothing
3: 8 The *S* LORD has spoken—
3: 11 this is what the *S* LORD says:
4: 2 The *S* LORD has sworn
4: 5 declares the *S* LORD.
5: 3 This is what the *S* LORD says:
6: 8 The *S* LORD has sworn by himself
7: 1 is what the *S* LORD showed me:
7: 2 I cried out, "*S* LORD, forgive!
7: 4 The *S* LORD was calling
7: 4 is what the *S* LORD showed me:
7: 5 Then I cried out, "*S* LORD,
7: 6 happen either," the *S* LORD said.
8: 1 is what the *S* LORD showed me:
8: 3 In that day," declares the *S* LORD,
8: 9 In that day," declares the *S* LORD,
8: 11 coming," declares the *S* LORD,
9: 8 "Surely the eyes of the *S* LORD
Ob : 1 is what the *S* LORD says about
Mic 1: 2 that the *S* LORD may witness
Hab 3: 19 The *S* LORD is my strength;
Zep 1: 7 Be silent before the *S* LORD,
Zec 9: 14 *S* LORD will sound the trumpet;
Lk 2: 29 "*S* Lord, as you have promised,
Ac 4: 24 "*S* Lord," they said, "you made
2Pe 2: 1 denying the *s* Lord who bought
Jude : 4 and deny Jesus Christ our only *S*
Rev 6: 10 "How long, *S* Lord, holy and true,

SOVEREIGNTY (SOVEREIGN)

Da 5: 18 your father Nebuchadnezzar *s*
7: 27 Then the *s*, power and greatness

SOW (SOWED SOWER SOWING SOWN SOWS)

Ex 23: 10 six years you are to *s* your fields
23: 16 of the crops you *s* in your field.
Lev 25: 3 For six years *s* your fields,
25: 4 Do not *s* your fields or prune your
25: 11 do not *s* and do not reap what
Dt 28: 38 You will *s* much seed in the field
2Ki 19: 29 But in the third year *s* and reap,
Job 4: 8 and those who *s* trouble reap it.
Ps 126: 5 Those who *s* in tears
126: 6 carrying seed to *s*,
Ecc 11: 6 *S* your seed in the morning,
Isa 28: 25 does he not *s* caraway
30: 23 for the seed you *s* in the ground,
37: 30 But in the third year *s* and reap,
Jer 4: 3 and do not *s* among thorns.
12: 13 They will *s* wheat but reap thorns;
35: 7 must never build houses, *s* seed
Hos 8: 7 "They *s* the wind
10: 12 *S* for yourselves righteousness,
Mt 6: 26 they do not *s* or reap or store away
13: 3 "A farmer went out to *s* his seed.
13: 27 didn't you *s* good seed in your field
Mk 4: 3 A farmer went out to *s* his seed.
Lk 8: 5 "A farmer went out to *s* his seed.
12: 24 Consider the ravens: They do not *s*
19: 21 and reap what you did not *s*.'
19: 22 and reaping what I did not *s*?
1Co 15: 36 What you *s* does not come to life
1Co 15: 37 When you *s*, you do not plant
Jas 3: 18 Peacemakers who *s*
2Pe 2: 22 and, "A *s* that is washed goes back

SOWED (SOW)

Ps 107: 37 They *s* fields and planted vineyards
Mt 13: 24 is like a man who *s* good seed
13: 25 and *s* weeds among the wheat,
13: 37 one who *s* the good seed is the Son

SOWER (SOW)

Isa 55: 10 so that it yields seed for the *s*
Jer 50: 16 Cut off from Babylon the *s*,
Mt 13: 18 to what the parable of the *s* means:
Jn 4: 36 so that the *s* and the reaper may be
2Co 9: 10 Now he who supplies seed to the *s*

SOWING (SOW)

Isa 32: 20 *s* your seed by every stream,

SOWN (SOW)

Job 31: 8 then may others eat what I have *s*,
Isa 19: 7 Every *s* field along the Nile
40: 24 no sooner are they *s*,
Jer 2: 2 through a land not *s*.
Eze 36: 9 you will be plowed and *s*,
Mt 13: 8 sixty or thirty times what was *s*.
13: 19 This is the seed *s* along the path.
13: 19 and snatches away what was *s*
13: 20 What was *s* on rocky places is
13: 22 What was *s* among the thorns is
13: 23 sixty or thirty times what was *s*."
13: 23 what was *s* on good soil is the man
25: 24 harvesting where you have not *s*
25: 26 that I harvest where I have not *s*
Mk 4: 15 along the path, where the word is *s*.
4: 15 and takes away the word that was *s*
4: 16 Others, like seed *s* on rocky places,
4: 18 Still others, like seed *s*
4: 20 Others, like seed *s* on good soil,
4: 20 even a hundred times what was *s*."
Lk 8: 8 a hundred times more than was *s*."
1Co 9: 11 If we have *s* spiritual seed
15: 42 The body that is *s* is perishable,
15: 43 it is raised imperishable; it is *s*
15: 43 raised in glory; it is *s* in weakness,
15: 44 in power; it is *s* a natural body,

SOWS (SOW)

Pr 11: 18 he who *s* righteousness reaps a sure
22: 8 He who *s* wickedness reaps trouble
Mt 13: 39 the enemy who *s* them is the devil.
Mk 4: 14 parable? The farmer *s* the word.
Jn 4: 37 Thus the saying 'One *s*
2Co 9: 6 Whoever *s* sparingly will
9: 6 and whoever *s* generously will
Gal 6: 7 A man reaps what he *s*.
6: 8 The one who *s* to please his sinful
6: 8 the one who *s* to please the Spirit,

SPACE (SPACIOUS)

Ge 32: 16 and keep some *s* between the herds
Ex 25: 37 so that they light the *s* in front of it.
1Sa 26: 13 there was a wide *s* between them.
1Ki 7: 36 in every available *s*,
Job 26: 7 the northern skies over empty *s*;
Isa 5: 8 field till no *s* is left
49: 20 give us more *s* to live in.'
Eze 41: 17 *s* above the outside of the entrance
42: 5 for the galleries took more *s*
42: 6 in floor *s* than those on the lower

SPACIOUS (SPACE)

Ex 3: 8 of that land into a good and *s* land,
Jdg 18: 10 and a *s* land that God has put
2Sa 22: 20 He brought me out into a *s* place;
1Ch 4: 40 the land was *s*, peaceful and quiet.
Ne 7: 4 Now the city was large and *s*,
9: 35 great goodness to them in the *s*
Job 36: 16 to a *s* place free from restriction,
Ps 18: 19 He brought me out into a *s* place;
31: 8 but have set my feet in a *s* place.
104: 25 There is the sea, vast and *s*,
Jer 22: 14 with *s* upper rooms.'

SPAIN

Ro 15: 24 I plan to do so when I go to *S*.
15: 28 I will go to *S* and visit you

SPAN

Ex 23:26 I will give you a full life *s*.
28:16 a *s* long and a *s* wide—
39: 9 a *s* long and a *s* wide—
Ps 39: 5 the *s* of my years is as nothing
90:10 yet their *s* is but trouble and sorrow
Isa 23:15 for seventy years, the *s*
Eze 43:13 with a rim of one *s* around the edge

SPARE (SPARED SPARES SPARING)

Ge 18:24 and not *s* the place for the sake
18:26 I will *s* the whole place
Dt 13: 8 Do not *s* him or shield him.
Jos 2:13 a sure sign that you will *s* the lives
22:22 to the LORD, do not *s* us this day.
Jdg 6: 4 did not *s* a living thing for Israel,
1Sa 15: 3 Do not *s* them; put to death men
2Sa 21: 2 Israelites had sworn to *s* them,
1Ki 16:11 He did not *s* a single male,
20:31 Perhaps he will *s* your life.''
2Ki 7: 4 If they *s* us, we live; if they kill us,
2Ch 31:10 enough to eat and plenty to *s*,
Est 4:11 scepter to him and *s* his life.
7: 3 *s* my people—this is my request.
Job 2: 6 hands; but you must *s* his life.''
33:24 '*S* him from going down to the pit;
Ps 78:50 he did not *s* them from death
Pr 20:13 you will have food to *s*.
Isa 9:19 no one will *s* his brother.
47: 3 I will *s* no one.''
Jer 50:14 Shoot at her! *S* no arrows,
50:20 for I will forgive the remnant I *s*.
51: 3 Do not *s* her young men;
Eze 5:11 look on you with pity or *s* you.
6: 8 '' 'But I will *s* some, for some
7: 4 look on you with pity or *s* you;
7: 9 look on you with pity or *s* you;
8:18 look on them with pity or *s* them.
9:10 look on them with pity or *s* them,
12:16 But I will *s* a few of them
Da 5:19 those he wanted to *s*, he spared;
Joel 2:17 Let them say, ''*S* your people,
Am 7: 8 Israel; I will *s* them no longer.
8: 2 Israel; I will *s* them no longer.
Zec 11: 5 Their own shepherds do not *s* them
Mal 3:17 I will *s* them, just as in compassion
Lk 15:17 father's hired men have food to *s*,
Ac 20:29 among you and will not *s* the flock.
27:43 centurion wanted to *s* Paul's life
Ro 8:32 He who did not *s* his own Son,
11:21 God did not *s* the natural branches,
11:21 natural branches, he will not *s* you
1Co 7:28 in this life, and I want to *s* you this.
2Co 1:23 order to *s* you that I did not return
13: 2 return I will not *s* those who sinned
Php 2:27 to *s* me sorrow upon sorrow.
2Pe 2: 4 For if God did not *s* angels
2: 5 if he did not *s* the ancient world

SPARED (SPARE)

Ge 12:13 my life will be *s* because of you.''
19:20 isn't it? Then my life will be *s*.''
32:30 face to face, and yet my life was *s*.''
Ex 12:27 and *s* our homes when he struck
Nu 22:33 by now, but I would have *s* her.''
Jos 6:17 are with her in her house shall be *s*,
6:25 But Joshua *s* Rahab the prostitute,
Jdg 1:25 but *s* the man and his whole family.
8:19 if you had *s* their lives, I would not
21:14 Jabesh Gilead who had been *s*.
1Sa 2:33 off from my altar will be *s* only
15: 9 But Saul and the army *s* Agag
15:15 they *s* the best of the sheep
24:10 me to kill you, but I *s* you;
2Sa 21: 7 The king *s* Mephibosheth son
2Ki 23:18 So they *s* his bones and those
2Ch 36:17 and *s* neither young man
Job 21:30 that the evil man is *s* from the day
Ps 30: 3 you *s* me from going
Isa 57: 1 away to be *s* from evil.
Jer 38:17 your life will be *s* and this city will
38:20 with you, and your life will be *s*.
Eze 6:12 he that survives and is *s* will die
13:19 have *s* those who should not live.
Da 5:19 he *s*; those he wanted to promote,
Ac 27:21 you would have *s* yourselves this

SPARES (SPARE)

Pr 13:24 He who *s* the rod hates his son,
Mal 3:17 in compassion a man *s* his son who

SPARING (SPARE)

Ge 19:19 great kindness to me in *s* my life.
Jos 11:11 not *s* anything that breathed,
11:14 not *s* anyone that breathed.
Pr 21:26 but the righteous give without *s*.

SPARK (SPARKS)

Isa 1:31 and his work a *s*;
Jas 3: 5 set on fire by a small *s*.

SPARKLE (SPARKLED SPARKLES SPARKLING)

Zec 9:16 They will *s* in his land

SPARKLED (SPARKLE)

Eze 1:16 They *s* like chrysolite,
10: 9 the wheels *s* like chrysolite.

SPARKLES (SPARKLE)

Pr 23:31 when it *s* in the cup,

SPARKLING (SPARKLE)

Isa 54:12 your gates of *s* jewels,
Eze 1:22 looked like an expanse, *s* like ice

SPARKS (SPARK)

Job 5: 7 as surely as *s* fly upward.
41:19 *s* of fire shoot out.

SPARROW (SPARROWS)

Ps 84: 3 Even the *s* has found a home,
Pr 26: 2 Like a fluttering *s* or a darting

SPARROWS (SPARROW)

Mt 10:29 Are not two *s* sold for a penny?
10:31 you are worth more than many *s*.
Lk 12: 6 Are not five *s* sold for two pennies?
12: 7 you are worth more than many *s*.

SPATTERED

Lev 6:27 if any of the blood is *s* on a garment
2Ki 9:33 and some of her blood *s* the wall
Isa 63: 3 their blood *s* my garments,

SPEAR (SPEARHEAD SPEARMEN SPEARS)

Nu 25: 7 took a *s* in his hand and followed
25: 8 He drove the *s* through both
Jdg 5: 8 and not a shield or *s* was seen
1Sa 13:22 and Jonathan had a sword or *s*
17: 7 His *s* shaft was like a weaver's rod,
17:45 come against me with sword and *s*
17:47 or *s* that the LORD saves;
18:10 Saul had a *s* in his hand
19: 9 in his house with his *s* in his hand.
19:10 as Saul drove the *s* into the wall.
19:10 to pin him to the wall with his *s*,
20:33 Saul hurled his *s* at him to kill him.
21: 8 Don't you have a *s* or a sword here?
22: 6 *s* in hand, was seated
26: 7 camp with his *s* stuck in the ground
26: 8 the ground with one thrust of my *s*;
26:11 get the *s* and water jug that are
26:12 So David took the *s* and water jug
26:16 Where are the king's *s*
26:22 is the king's *s*,'' David answered.
2Sa 1: 6 and there was Saul, leaning on his *s*
2:23 butt of his *s* into Asahel's stomach,
2:23 the *s* came out through his back.
21:19 who had a *s* with a shaft like
23: 7 uses a tool of iron or the shaft of a *s*;
23: 8 raised his *s* against eight hundred
23:18 raised his *s* against three hundred
23:21 Although the Egyptian had a *s*
23:21 He snatched the *s*
23:21 and killed him with his own *s*.
1Ch 11:11 raised his *s* against three hundred
11:20 raised his *s* against three hundred
11:23 He snatched the *s*
11:23 and killed him with his own *s*.
11:23 the Egyptian had a *s* like a weaver's
12: 8 and able to handle the shield and *s*.
12:24 carrying shield and *s*— 6,800
20: 5 who had a *s* with a shaft like
2Ch 25: 5 able to handle the *s* and shield.
Job 39:23 along with the flashing *s* and lance.
41:26 nor does the *s* or the dart
Ps 35: 3 Brandish *s* and javelin
46: 9 breaks the bow and shatters the *s*,
Jer 6:23 They are armed with bow and *s*;
Hab 3:11 at the lightning of your flashing *s*.
3:14 With his own *s* you pierced his
Jn 19:34 soldiers pierced Jesus' side with a *s*,

SPEARHEAD (SPEAR)

2Sa 21:16 whose bronze *s* weighed three

SPEARMEN (SPEAR)

Ac 23:23 two hundred *s* to go to Caesarea

SPEARS (SPEAR)

1Sa 13:19 Hebrews will make swords or *s*!''
1Ki 18:28 themselves with swords and *s*,
2Ki 11:10 he gave the commanders the *s*
1Ch 12:34 men carrying shields and *s*;
2Ch 11:12 He put shields and *s* in all the cities
14: 8 with large shields and with *s*,
23: 9 of units of a hundred the *s*
26:14 Uzziah provided shields, *s*, helmets
Ne 4:13 with their swords, *s* and bows.
4:16 other half were equipped with *s*,
4:21 work with half the men holding *s*,
Job 41: 7 or his head with fishing *s*?
Ps 57: 4 men whose teeth are *s* and arrows,
Isa 2: 4 and their *s* into pruning hooks.
Jer 46: 4 Polish your *s*,
50:42 They are armed with bows and *s*;
Eze 39: 9 and arrows, the war clubs and *s*.
Joel 3:10 and your pruning hooks into *s*.
Mic 4: 3 and their *s* into pruning hooks.
Na 2: 3 the *s* of pine are brandished.
3: 3 and glittering *s*!

SPECIAL

Ge 47: 6 of any among them with *s* ability,
Lev 22:21 to the LORD to fulfill a *s* vow
27: 2 'If anyone makes a *s* vow
Nu 6: 2 or woman wants to make a *s* vow,
15: 3 for *s* vows or freewill offerings
15: 8 for a *s* vow or a fellowship offering
Dt 12: 6 sacrifices, your tithes and *s* gifts,
12:11 sacrifices, your tithes and *s* gifts,
12:17 or your freewill offerings or *s* gifts.
Jos 15:19 She replied, ''Do me a *s* favor.
Jdg 1:15 She replied, ''Do me a *s* favor.
2Sa 13: 6 and make some *s* bread in my sight,
16: 6 the *s* guard were on David's right
1Ki 1: 8 and David's *s* guard did not join
1:10 or Benaiah or the *s* guard
Est 1:14 Media who had *s* access to the king
2: 9 her beauty treatments and *s* food.
Jer 13:21 those you cultivated as your *s* allies
Eze 44:30 and of all your *s* gifts will belong
45:13 '' 'This is the *s* gift you are to offer:
45:16 participate in this *s* gift for the use
48: 8 are to present as a *s* gift.
48: 9 ''The *s* portion you are to offer
48:12 It will be a *s* gift to them
48:20 As a *s* gift you will set
Jn 19:31 the next day was to be a *s* Sabbath.
Ro 14: 6 He who regards one day as *s*,
1Co 12:23 are treated with *s* modesty,
12:23 honorable we treat with *s* honor.
12:24 parts need no *s* treatment.
Gal 4:10 You are observing *s* days
2Th 3:14 in this letter, take *s* note of him.
Jas 2: 3 If you show *s* attention

SPECIFIC (SPECIFY)

Nu 4:32 to each man the *s* things he is

SPECIFICATIONS (SPECIFY)

1Ki 6:38 in all its details according to its *s*.
2Ch 4: 7 gold lampstands according to the *s*

SPECIFIED (SPECIFY)

Lev 27: 8 poor to pay the *s* amount,
Nu 29: 6 offerings and drink offerings as *s*.
29:18 according to the number *s*.
29:21 according to the number *s*.
29:24 according to the number *s*.
29:27 according to the number *s*.

Nu 29: 30 according to the number *s*.
29: 33 according to the number *s*.
29: 37 according to the number *s*.

SPECIFY (SPECIFIC SPECIFICATIONS SPECIFIED SPECIFYING)

1Ki 5: 9 in rafts by sea to the place you *s*.

SPECIFYING (SPECIFY)

Ac 25: 27 on a prisoner without *s* the charges

SPECK (SPECKLED)

Mt 7: 3 look at the *s* of sawdust
7: 4 'Let me take the *s* out of your eye,'
7: 5 remove the *s* from your brother's
Lk 6: 41 look at the *s* of sawdust
6: 42 let me take the *s* out of your eye,'
6: 42 remove the *s* from your brother's

SPECKLED (SPECK)

Ge 30: 32 and every spotted or *s* goat.
30: 32 and remove from them every *s*
30: 33 goat in my possession that is not *s*
30: 35 all the *s* or spotted female goats (all
30: 39 bore young that were streaked or *s*
31: 8 all the flocks gave birth to *s* young;
31: 8 'The *s* ones will be your wages,'
31: 10 with the flock were streaked, *s*
31: 12 *s* or spotted, for I have seen all that
Jer 12: 9 like a *s* bird of prey

SPECTACLE

Eze 28: 17 I made a *s* of you before kings.
Na 3: 6 and make you a *s*.
1Co 4: 9 We have been made a *s*
Col 2: 15 he made a public *s* of them,

SPED (SPEED)

Eze 1: 14 The creatures *s* back and forth like

SPEECH (SPEECHES)

Ge 11: 1 had one language and a common *s*.
Ex 4: 10 I am slow of *s* and tongue.''
Ps 19: 2 Day after day they pour forth *s*;
19: 3 There is no *s* or language
55: 9 wicked, O Lord, confound their *s*,
55: 21 His *s* is smooth as butter,
Pr 1: 21 of the city she makes her *s*:
5: 3 and her *s* is smoother than oil;
8: 13 evil behavior and perverse *s*.
12: 6 the *s* of the upright rescues them.
16: 27 and his *s* is like a scorching fire.
22: 11 pure heart and whose *s* is gracious
26: 25 Though his *s* is charming, do not
Ecc 5: 3 so the *s* of a fool when there are
Isa 18: 2 an aggressive nation of strange *s*,
18: 7 an aggressive nation of strange *s*,
29: 4 out of the dust your *s* will whisper.
29: 4 your *s* will mumble out of the dust.
33: 19 those people of an obscure *s*,
Jer 5: 15 whose *s* you do not understand.
Eze 3: 5 sent to a people of obscure *s*
3: 6 not to many peoples of obscure *s*
Mk 9: 17 by a spirit that has robbed him of *s*.
Jn 10: 6 Jesus used this figure of *s*,
16: 29 and without figures of *s*.
Ac 5: 40 His *s* persuaded them.
7: 22 and was powerful in *s* and action.
2Co 6: 7 in truthful *s* and in the power
8: 7 in faith, in *s*, in knowledge,
1Ti 4: 12 set an example for the believers in *s*
Tit 2: 8 of *s* that cannot be condemned,
1Pe 3: 10 and his lips from deceitful *s*.
2Pe 2: 16 a beast without *s*— who spoke

SPEECHES (SPEECH)

Job 15: 3 with *s* that have no value?
16: 3 Will your long-winded *s* never end
16: 4 I could make fine *s* against you
18: 2 ''When will you end these *s*?

SPEECHLESS

Da 10: 15 face toward the ground and was *s*.
Mt 22: 12 wedding clothes?' The man was *s*.
Ac 9: 7 traveling with Saul stood there *s*;

SPEED (SPED SPEEDS)

Ro 9: 28 his sentence on earth with *s*
2Pe 3: 12 to the day of God and *s* its coming.

SPEEDS (SPEED)

Isa 16: 5 and *s* the cause of righteousness.

SPELL (SPELLS)

Rev 18: 23 By your magic *s* all the nations

SPELLS (SPELL)

Dt 18: 11 engages in witchcraft, or casts *s*,
Isa 47: 9 and all your potent *s*.
47: 12 ''Keep on, then, with your magic *s*
Mic 5: 12 and you will no longer cast *s*.

SPELT

Ex 9: 32 The wheat and *s*, however,
Isa 28: 25 and *s* in its field?
Eze 4: 9 beans and lentils, millet and *s*;

SPEND (SPENDING SPENT)

Ge 19: 2 can wash your feet and *s* the night
19: 2 ''we will *s* the night in the square.''
24: 23 house for us to *s* the night?''
24: 25 well as room for you to *s* the night
Nu 22: 8 ''*S* the night here,'' Balaam said
Dt 32: 23 and *s* my arrows against them.
Jdg 16: 1 He went in to *s* the night with her.
19: 9 *S* the night here; the day is nearly
19: 11 of the Jebusites and *s* the night.''
19: 13 *s* the night in one of those places.''
19: 15 There they stopped to *s* the night.
19: 20 Only don't *s* the night in the square
20: 4 Gibeah in Benjamin to *s* the night.
2Sa 17: 8 he will not *s* the night
17: 16 'Do not *s* the night at the fords
1Ch 9: 27 They would *s* the night stationed
Ne 13: 21 Why do you *s* the night by the wall
Job 21: 13 They *s* their years in prosperity
24: 7 Lacking clothes, they *s* the night
31: 32 but no stranger had to *s* the night
36: 11 they will *s* the rest of their days
Ps 25: 13 He will *s* his days in prosperity,
Pr 31: 3 do not *s* your strength on women,
SS 7: 11 let us *s* the night in the villages.
Isa 55: 2 Why *s* money on what is not bread,
58: 10 and if you *s* yourselves in behalf
65: 4 *s* their nights keeping secret vigil;
Eze 6: 12 So will I *s* my wrath upon them.
7: 8 and *s* my anger against you;
13: 15 I will *s* my wrath against the wall
20: 8 *s* my anger against them in Egypt.
20: 21 and *s* my anger against them
Joel 1: 13 Come, *s* the night in sackcloth,
Mk 6: 37 we to go and *s* that much on bread
Lk 21: 37 evening he went out to *s* the night
Ac 18: 20 him to *s* more time with them,
28: 14 us to *s* a week with them.
1Co 16: 6 you awhile, or even *s* the winter,
16: 7 I hope to *s* some time with you,
2Co 12: 15 So I will very gladly *s*
Jas 4: 3 that you may *s* what you get
4: 13 *s* a year there, carry on business

SPENDING (SPEND)

Ac 15: 33 After *s* some time there, they were
18: 23 After *s* some time in Antioch,
20: 16 to avoid *s* time in the province
25: 6 After *s* eight or ten days with them,
25: 14 Since they were *s* many days there,

SPENT (SPEND)

Ge 24: 54 and drank and *s* the night there.
31: 54 had eaten, they *s* the night there.
32: 13 He *s* the night there,
32: 21 he himself *s* the night in the camp.
Lev 26: 20 Your strength will be *s* in vain,
Dt 1: 46 days—all the time you *s* there.
Jos 6: 11 to camp and *s* the night there.
8: 9 Joshua *s* that night with the people.
Jdg 18: 2 of Micah, where they *s* the night.
2Sa 12: 16 *s* the nights lying on the ground.
14: 2 a woman who has *s* many days
1Ki 5: 11 so that they *s* one month
6: 38 He had *s* seven years building it.
19: 9 went into a cave and *s* the night.
2Ki 12: 13 brought into the temple was not *s*
1Ch 12: 39 The men *s* three days there
Ne 9: 3 and *s* another fourth in confession
13: 20 kinds of goods *s* the night
Pr 5: 11 when your flesh and body are *s*.
Isa 49: 4 I have *s* my strength in vain
Eze 5: 13 when I have *s* my wrath upon them
Da 6: 18 and *s* the night without eating
Mt 21: 17 to Bethany, where he *s* the night.
Mk 5: 26 many doctors and had *s* all she had,
Lk 6: 12 and *s* the night praying to God.
15: 14 After he had *s* everything,
Jn 1: 39 he was staying, and *s* that day
3: 22 where he *s* some time with them,
Ac 9: 19 Saul *s* several days
14: 3 Barnabas *s* considerable time there
17: 21 who lived there *s* their time doing
2Co 11: 25 I *s* a night and a day in the open sea
1Pe 4: 3 For you have *s* enough time

SPEW (SPEWED)

Ps 59: 7 See what they *s* from their mouths
59: 7 they *s* out swords from their lips,
Jer 51: 44 make him *s* out what he has

SPEWED (SPEW)

Jer 51: 34 and then has *s* us out.
Rev 12: 15 his mouth the serpent *s* water like
12: 16 the river that the dragon had *s* out

SPICE (SPICED SPICES)

SS 4: 10 of your perfume than any *s*!
5: 1 gathered my myrrh with my *s*
5: 13 His cheeks are like beds of *s*
Rev 18: 13 cargoes of cinnamon and *s*,

SPICE-LADEN (LOAD)

SS 8: 14 stag on the *s* mountains.

SPICED (SPICE)

SS 8: 2 I would give you *s* wine to drink,

SPICES (SPICE)

Ge 37: 25 Their camels were loaded with *s*,
43: 11 some *s* and myrrh, some pistachio
Ex 25: 6 *s* for the anointing oil
30: 23 ''Take the following fine *s*:
30: 34 ''Take fragrant *s*— gum resin,
35: 8 *s* for the anointing oil
35: 28 brought *s* and olive oil for the light
1Ki 10: 2 camels carrying *s*, large quantities
10: 10 quantities of *s*, and precious stones.
10: 10 were so many *s* brought in
10: 25 weapons and *s*, and horses
2Ki 20: 13 the gold, the *s* and the fine oil—
1Ch 9: 29 wine, and the oil, incense and *s*.
9: 30 priests took care of mixing the *s*.
2Ch 9: 1 camels carrying *s*, large quantities
9: 9 There had never been such *s*
9: 9 quantities of *s*, and precious stones.
9: 24 and robes, weapons and *s*,
16: 14 him on a bier covered with *s*
32: 27 *s*, shields and all kinds of valuables.
Ps 75: 8 full of foaming wine mixed with *s*;
SS 3: 6 made from all the *s* of the merchant
4: 14 and all the finest *s*.
6: 2 to the beds of *s*,
Isa 39: 2 the gold, the *s*, the fine oil,
Eze 24: 10 mixing in the *s*;
27: 22 the finest of all kinds of *s*
Mt 23: 23 You give a tenth of your *s*— mint,
Mk 16: 1 Salome bought *s* so that they might
Lk 23: 56 and prepared *s* and perfumes.
24: 1 the women took the *s* they had
Jn 19: 40 with the *s*, in strips of linen.

SPIDER'S

Job 8: 14 what he relies on is a *s* web.
Isa 59: 5 and spin a *s* web.

SPIED (SPY)

Jos 6: 22 two men who had *s* out the land,
7: 2 So the men went up and *s* out Ai.
Jdg 18: 14 the five men who had *s* out the land
18: 17 five men who had *s* out the land

SPIES (SPY)

Ge 42: 9 ''You are *s*! You have come
42: 11 servants are honest men, not *s*.''
42: 14 You are *s*! And this is how you will
42: 16 surely as Pharaoh lives, you are *s*!''

Ge 42: 31 'We are honest men; we are not *s*.
42: 34 me so I will know that you are not *s*
Nu 21: 32 After Moses had sent *s* to Jazer,
Jos 2: 1 son of Nun secretly sent two *s*
2: 7 of the *s* on the road that leads
2: 8 Before the *s* lay down for the night,
6: 17 because she hid the *s* we sent.
6: 25 hid the men Joshua had sent as *s*
Jdg 1: 24 the *s* saw a man coming out
Lk 20: 20 they sent *s*, who pretended
20: 21 So the *s* questioned him: "Teacher,
Heb 11: 31 because she welcomed the *s*,
Jas 2: 25 did when she gave lodging to the *s*

SPILLED (SPILLS)

Ge 38: 9 he *s* his seed on the ground to keep
2Sa 14: 14 Like water *s* on the ground,
20: 10 his intestines *s* out on the ground.
Ac 1: 18 and all his intestines *s* out.

SPILLS (SPILLED)

Job 16: 13 and *s* my gall on the ground.

SPIN (SPUN)

Isa 59: 5 and *s* a spider's web.
Mt 6: 28 They do not labor or *s*.
Lk 12: 27 They do not labor or *s*.

SPINDLE

Pr 31: 19 and grasps the *s* with her fingers.

SPIRIT (SPIRIT'S SPIRITIST SPIRITISTS SPIRITS SPIRITUAL SPIRITUALLY)

Ge 1: 2 and the *S* of God was hovering
6: 3 "My *S* will not contend
41: 38 one in whom is the *s* of God?"
45: 27 the *s* of their father Jacob revived.
Ex 31: 3 I have filled him with the *S* of God,
35: 31 he has filled him with the *S* of God,
Nu 11: 17 I will take of the *S* that is on you
11: 17 is on you and put the *S* on them.
11: 25 When the *S* rested on them,
11: 25 and put the *S* on the seventy elders.
11: 25 he took of the *S* that was on him
11: 26 Yet the *S* also rested on them,
11: 29 that the LORD would put his *S*
14: 24 my servant Caleb has a different *s*
24: 2 the *S* of God came upon him
27: 18 a man in whom is the *s*,
Dt 2: 30 your God had made his *s* stubborn
34: 9 filled with the *s* of wisdom
Jdg 3: 10 The *S* of the LORD came
6: 34 Then the *S* of the LORD came
9: 23 sent an evil *s* between Abimelech
11: 29 Then the *S* of the LORD came
13: 25 and the *S* of the LORD began
14: 6 The *S* of the LORD came
14: 19 the *S* of the LORD came upon him
15: 14 The *S* of the LORD came
1Sa 10: 6 The *S* of the LORD will come
10: 10 the *S* of God came upon him
11: 6 the *S* of God came upon him
16: 13 day on the *S* of the LORD came
16: 14 evil *s* from the LORD tormented
16: 14 the *S* of the LORD had departed
16: 15 evil *s* from God is tormenting you.
16: 16 when the evil *s* from God comes
16: 23 Whenever the *s* from God came
16: 23 and the evil *s* would leave him.
18: 1 Jonathan became one in *s*
18: 10 The next day an evil *s*
19: 9 But an evil *s* from the LORD came
19: 20 the *S* of God came upon Saul's men
19: 23 But the *S* of God came
28: 8 "Consult a *s* for me," he said,
28: 13 "I see a *s* coming up out
30: 6 each one was bitter in *s*
2Sa 13: 39 And the *s* of the king longed to go
23: 2 "The *S* of the LORD spoke
1Ki 18: 12 I don't know where the *S*
22: 21 Finally, a *s* came forward,
22: 22 and be a lying *s* in the mouths
22: 23 now the LORD has put a lying *s*
22: 24 "Which way did the *s*
2Ki 2: 9 inherit a double portion of your *s*,"
2: 15 "The *s* of Elijah is resting on Elisha
2: 16 Perhaps the *S* of the LORD has
5: 26 "Was not my *s* with you
2Ki 19: 7 going to put such a *s* in him that
1Ch 5: 26 of Israel stirred up the *s* of Pul king
12: 18 Then the *S* came upon Amasai,
28: 12 of all that the *S* had put in his mind
2Ch 15: 1 The *S* of God came
18: 20 Finally, a *s* came forward,
18: 21 and be a lying *s* in the mouths
18: 22 now the LORD has put a lying *s*
18: 23 "Which way did the *s*
20: 14 Then the *S* of the LORD came
24: 20 Then the *S* of God came
Ne 9: 20 You gave your good *S*
9: 30 By your *S* you admonished them
Job 4: 15 A *s* glided past my face,
6: 4 my *s* drinks in their poison;
7: 11 out in the anguish of my *s*,
10: 12 providence watched over my *s*.
17: 1 My *s* is broken,
26: 4 whose *s* spoke from your mouth?
31: 39 or broken the *s* of its tenants,
32: 8 But it is the *s* in a man,
32: 18 and the *s* within me compels me;
33: 4 The *S* of God has made me;
34: 14 and he withdrew his *s* and breath,
Ps 31: 5 Into your hands I commit my *s*;
32: 2 and in whose *s* is no deceit.
34: 18 saves those who are crushed in *s*.
51: 10 and renew a steadfast *s* within me.
51: 11 or take your Holy *S* from me.
51: 12 grant me a willing *s*, to sustain me.
51: 17 sacrifices of God are a broken *s*;
73: 21 and my *s* embittered,
76: 12 He breaks the *s* of rulers;
77: 3 I mused, and my *s* grew faint.
77: 6 My heart mused and my *s* inquired
104: 30 When you send your *S*,
106: 33 rebelled against the *S* of God,
139: 7 Where can I go from your *S*?
142: 3 When my *s* grows faint within me,
143: 4 So my *s* grows faint within me;
143: 7 my *s* faints with longing.
143: 10 may your good *S*
146: 4 When their *s* departs, they return
Pr 15: 4 but a deceitful tongue crushes the *s*
15: 13 but heartache crushes the *s*.
16: 18 a haughty *s* before a fall.
16: 19 in *s* and among the oppressed
17: 22 but a crushed *s* dries up the bones.
18: 14 A man's *s* sustains him in sickness,
18: 14 but a crushed *s* who can bear?
20: 27 of the LORD searches the *s*
25: 13 he refreshes the *s* of his masters.
29: 23 but a man of lowly *s* gains honor.
Ecc 3: 21 Who knows if the *s*
3: 21 and if the *s* of the animal goes
7: 9 not be quickly provoked in your *s*,
12: 7 the *s* returns to God who gave it.
Isa 4: 4 by a *s* of judgment and a *s* of fire.
11: 2 The *S* of the LORD will rest
11: 2 *S* of wisdom and of understanding,
11: 2 the *S* of counsel and of power,
11: 2 the *S* of knowledge and of the fear
19: 14 a *s* of dizziness;
26: 9 in the morning my *s* longs for you.
28: 6 He will be a *s* of justice
29: 24 in *s* will gain understanding;
30: 1 an alliance, but not by my *S*,
31: 3 their horses are flesh and not *s*.
32: 15 till the *S* is poured upon us
34: 16 and his *S* will gather them together.
37: 7 I am going to put a *s* in him so that
38: 16 and my *s* finds life in them too.
40: 13 Who has understood the *S*
42: 1 I will put my *S* on him
44: 3 I will pour out my *S*
48: 16 with his *S*.
54: 6 wife deserted and distressed in *s*—
57: 15 him who is contrite and lowly in *s*,
57: 15 to revive the *s* of the lowly
57: 16 for then the *s* of man would grow
59: 21 "My *S*, who is on you,
61: 1 The *S* of the Sovereign LORD is
61: 3 instead of a *s* of despair.
63: 10 and grieved his Holy *S*.
63: 11 his Holy *S* among them,
63: 14 rest by the *S* of the LORD.
65: 14 and wail in brokenness of *s*.
66: 2 he who is humble and contrite in *s*,
Jer 51: 1 I will stir up the *s* of a destroyer
La 1: 16 no one to restore my *s*.
Eze 1: 12 Wherever the *s* would go, they
1: 20 Wherever the *s* would go, they
1: 20 the *s* of the living creatures was
1: 21 the *s* of the living creatures was
2: 2 the *S* came into me and raised me
3: 12 Then the *S* lifted me up,
3: 14 The *S* then lifted me up
3: 14 and in the anger of my *s*,
3: 24 Then the *S* came into me
8: 3 The *S* lifted me up between earth
10: 17 the *s* of the living creatures was
11: 1 Then the *S* lifted me up
11: 5 the *S* of the LORD came upon me,
11: 19 an undivided heart and put a new *s*
11: 24 The *S* lifted me up and brought me
11: 24 in the vision given by the *S* of God.
13: 3 prophets who follow their own *s*
18: 31 and get a new heart and a new *s*.
21: 7 every *s* will become faint
36: 26 you a new heart and put a new *s*
36: 27 And I will put my *S* in you
37: 1 out by the *S* of the LORD
37: 14 I will put my *S* in you and you will
39: 29 for I will pour out my *S*
43: 5 Then the *S* lifted me up
Da 4: 8 and the *s* of the holy gods is in him
4: 9 I know that the *s* of the holy gods is
4: 18 the *s* of the holy gods is in you."
5: 11 man in your kingdom who has the *s*
5: 14 I have heard that the *s*
7: 15 "I, Daniel, was troubled in *s*,
Hos 4: 12 *s* of prostitution leads them astray;
5: 4 A *s* of prostitution is in their heart;
Joel 2: 28 I will pour out my *S* on all people.
2: 29 I will pour out my *S* in those days.
Mic 2: 7 "Is the *S* of the LORD angry?
3: 8 with the *S* of the LORD,
Hag 1: 14 So the LORD stirred up the *s*
1: 14 and the *s* of the whole remnant
1: 14 the *s* of Joshua son of Jehozadak,
2: 5 And my *S* remains among you.
Zec 4: 6 but by my *S*,' says the LORD
6: 8 north country have given my *S* rest
7: 12 sent by his *S* through the earlier
12: 1 who forms the *s* of man within him,
12: 10 of Jerusalem a *s* of grace
13: 2 and the *s* of impurity from the land.
Mal 2: 15 In flesh and *s* they are his.
2: 15 So guard yourself in your *s*,
2: 16 So guard yourself in your *s*,
Mt 1: 18 to be with child through the Holy *S*
1: 20 in her is from the Holy *S*.
3: 11 will baptize you with the Holy *S*
3: 16 he saw the *S* of God descending
4: 1 led by the *S* into the desert
5: 3 saying: "Blessed are the poor in *s*,
10: 20 but the *S* of your Father speaking
12: 18 I will put my *S* on him,
12: 28 But if I drive out demons by the *S*
12: 31 against the *S* will not be forgiven.
12: 32 against the Holy *S* will not be
12: 43 When an evil *s* comes out of a man,
22: 43 speaking by the *S*, calls him 'Lord'?
26: 41 *s* is willing, but the body is weak."
27: 50 in a loud voice, he gave up his *s*.
28: 19 and of the Son and of the Holy *S*,
Mk 1: 8 he will baptize you with the Holy *S*
1: 10 *S* descending on him like a dove.
1: 12 At once the *S* sent him out
1: 23 possessed by an evil *s* cried out,
1: 26 The evil *s* shook the man violently
2: 8 in his *s* that this was what they
3: 29 against the Holy *S* will never be
3: 30 they were saying, "He has an evil *s*
5: 2 with an evil *s* came from the tombs
5: 8 you evil *s*!" Then Jesus asked him,
7: 25 was possessed by an evil *s* came
9: 17 by a *s* that has robbed him
9: 18 your disciples to drive out the *s*,
9: 20 When the *s* saw Jesus, it
9: 25 to the scene, he rebuked the evil *s*.
9: 25 "You deaf and dumb *s*," he said,
9: 26 *s* shrieked, convulsed him violently
12: 36 speaking by the Holy *S*, declared:
13: 11 is not you speaking, but the Holy *S*.
14: 38 *s* is willing, but the body is weak."

Lk 1:15 he will be filled with the Holy *S*
1:17 in the *s* and power of Elijah,
1:35 "The Holy *S* will come upon you,
1:41 was filled with the Holy *S*.
1:47 and my *s* rejoices in God my Savior
1:67 was filled with the Holy *S*
1:80 child grew and became strong in *s*;
2:25 and the Holy *S* was upon him.
2:26 by the Holy *S* that he would not die
2:27 Moved by the *S*, he went
3:16 will baptize you with the Holy *S*
3:22 and the Holy *S* descended on him
4: 1 and was led by the *S* in the desert,
4: 1 full of the Holy *S*, returned
4:14 to Galilee in the power of the *S*,
4:18 "The *S* of the Lord is on me,
4:33 possessed by a demon, an evil *s*.
8:29 Jesus had commanded the evil *s*
8:55 "My child, get up!" Her *s* returned,
9:39 A *s* seizes him and he suddenly
9:42 But Jesus rebuked the evil *s*,
10:21 full of joy through the Holy *S*, said,
11:13 Father in heaven give the Holy *S*
11:24 When an evil *s* comes out of a man,
12:10 against the Holy *S* will not be
12:12 for the Holy *S* will teach you
13:11 crippled by a *s* for eighteen years.
23:46 into your hands I commit my *s*."
Jn 1:32 "I saw the *S* come
1:33 on whom you see the *S* come down
1:33 who will baptize with the Holy *S*.'
3: 5 a man is born of water and the *S*,
3: 6 but the Spirit gives birth to *s*.
3: 6 but the *S* gives birth to spirit.
3: 8 So it is with everyone born of the *S*
3:34 to him God gives the *S*
4:23 will worship the Father in *s*
4:24 God is *s*, and his worshipers must
4:24 his worshipers must worship in *s*
6:63 The *S* gives life; the flesh counts
6:63 words I have spoken to you are *s*
7:39 Up to that time the *S* had not been
7:39 he meant the *S*, whom those who
11:33 he was deeply moved in *s*
13:21 Jesus was troubled in *s*
14:17 with you forever—the *S* of truth.
14:26 But the Counselor, the Holy *S*,
15:26 the *S* of truth who goes out
16:13 But when he, the *S* of truth, comes,
16:15 That is why I said the *S* will take
19:30 bowed his head and gave up his *s*.
20:22 and said, "Receive the Holy *S*.
Ac 1: 2 instructions through the Holy *S*
1: 5 will be baptized with the Holy *S*."
1: 8 when the Holy *S* comes on you;
1:16 which the Holy *S* spoke long ago
2: 4 of them were filled with the Holy *S*
2: 4 tongues as the *S* enabled them.
2:17 I will pour out my *S* on all people.
2:18 I will pour out my *S* in those days,
2:33 the Father the promised Holy *S*
2:38 will receive the gift of the Holy *S*.
4: 8 filled with the Holy *S*, said to them:
4:25 by the Holy *S* through the mouth
4:31 they were all filled with the Holy *S*
5: 3 that you have lied to the Holy *S*
5: 9 agree to test the *S* of the Lord?
5:32 so is the Holy *S*, whom God has
6: 3 who are known to be full of the *S*
6: 5 a man full of faith and of the Holy *S*
6:10 or the *S* by which he spoke.
7:51 You always resist the Holy *S*!
7:55 But Stephen, full of the Holy *S*,
7:59 "Lord Jesus, receive my *s*."
8:15 that they might receive the Holy *S*,
8:16 the Holy *S* had not yet come
8:17 and they received the Holy *S*.
8:18 Simon saw that the *S* was given
8:19 my hands may receive the Holy *S*."
8:29 The *S* told Philip, "Go
8:39 *S* of the Lord suddenly took Philip
9:17 and be filled with the Holy *S*."
9:31 and encouraged by the Holy *S*,
10:19 the *S* said to him, "Simon,
10:38 Jesus of Nazareth with the Holy *S*
10:44 the Holy *S* came on all who heard
10:45 of the Holy *S* had been poured out
10:47 They have received the Holy *S* just

Ac 11:12 The *S* told me to have no hesitation
11:15 the Holy *S* came on them
11:16 will be baptized with the Holy *S*.'
11:24 full of the Holy *S* and faith,
11:28 and through the *S* predicted that
13: 2 and fasting, the Holy *S* said,
13: 4 sent on their way by the Holy *S*,
13: 9 with the Holy *S*, looked straight
13:52 filled with joy and with the Holy *S*.
15: 8 them by giving the Holy *S* to them,
15:28 It seemed good to the Holy *S*
16: 6 kept by the Holy *S* from preaching
16: 7 *S* of Jesus would not allow them
16:16 met by a slave girl who had a *s*
16:18 At that moment the *s* left her.
16:18 turned around and said to the *s*,
19: 2 even heard that there is a Holy *S*."
19: 2 "Did you receive the Holy *S*
19: 6 the Holy *S* came on them,
19:15 The evil *s* answered them,
19:16 the man who had the evil *s* jumped
20:22 "And now, compelled by the *S*,
20:23 city the Holy *S* warns me that
20:28 of which the Holy *S* has made you
21: 4 Through the *S* they urged Paul not
21:11 and said, "The Holy *S* says,
23: 9 "What if a *s* or an angel has spoken
28:25 "The Holy *S* spoke the truth
Ro 1: 4 and who through the *S*
2:29 by the *S*, not by the written code.
5: 5 love into our hearts by the Holy *S*,
7: 6 serve in the new way of the *S*,
8: 2 the law of the *S* of life set me free
8: 4 nature but according to the *S*.
8: 5 set on what the *S* desires.
8: 5 with the *S* have their minds set
8: 6 the mind controlled by the *S* is life
8: 9 And if anyone does not have the *S*
8: 9 by the sinful nature but by the *S*,
8: 9 if the *S* of God lives in you.
8:10 yet your *s* is alive
8:11 if the *S* of him who raised Jesus
8:11 to your mortal bodies through his *S*
8:13 but if by the *S* you put
8:14 led by the *S* of God are sons
8:15 but you received the *S* of sonship.
8:15 did not receive a *s* that makes you
8:16 The *S* himself testifies
8:16 with our *s* that we are God's
8:23 who have the firstfruits of the *S*,
8:26 but the *S* himself intercedes for us
8:26 the *S* helps us in our weakness.
8:27 our hearts knows the mind of the *S*,
8:27 the *S* intercedes for the saints
9: 1 confirms it in the Holy *S*—
11: 8 "God gave them a *s* of stupor,
14:17 peace and joy in the Holy *S*,
15: 5 and encouragement give you a *s*
15:13 hope by the power of the Holy *S*.
15:16 to God, sanctified by the Holy *S*.
15:19 through the power of the *S*.
15:30 and by the love of the *S*,
1Co 2:10 God has revealed it to us by his *S*.
2:10 The *S* searches all things,
2:11 except the man's *s* within him?
2:11 of God except the *S* of God.
2:12 We have not received the *s*
2:12 but the *S* who is from God,
2:13 but in words taught by the *S*,
2:14 come from the *S* of God,
2:14 man without the *S* does not accept
3:16 and that God's *S* lives in you?
4:21 or in love and with a gentle *s*?
5: 3 present, I am with you in *s*.
5: 4 Lord Jesus and I am with you in *s*,
5: 5 his *s* saved on the day of the Lord.
6:11 and by the *S* of our God.
6:17 with the Lord is one with him in *s*.
6:19 body is a temple of the Holy *S*,
7:34 to the Lord in both body and *s*.
7:40 I think that I too have the *S* of God.
12: 3 is Lord," except by the Holy *S*.
12: 3 speaking by the *S* of God says,
12: 4 kinds of gifts, but the same *S*.
12: 7 of the *S* is given for the common
12: 8 given through the *S* the message
12: 8 knowledge by means of the same *S*,
12: 9 gifts of healing by that one *S*,

1Co 12: 9 to another faith by the same *S*,
12:11 the work of one and the same *S*,
12:13 baptized by one *S* into one body—
12:13 we were all given the one *S* to drink
14: 2 he utters mysteries with his *s*.
14:14 my *s* prays, but my mind is
14:15 I will pray with my *s*, but I will
14:15 I will sing with my *s*, but I will
14:16 If you are praising God with your *s*,
15:45 the last Adam, a life-giving *s*.
16:18 For they refreshed my *s* and yours
2Co 1:22 and put his *S* in our hearts
3: 3 but with the *S* of the living God,
3: 6 not of the letter but of the *S*;
3: 6 the letter kills, but the *S* gives life.
3: 8 will not the ministry of the *S* be
3:17 Now the Lord is the *S*,
3:17 and where the *S* of the Lord is,
3:18 comes from the Lord, who is the *S*.
4:13 With that same *s* of faith we
5: 5 and has given us the *S* as a deposit,
6: 6 in the Holy *S* and in sincere love;
7: 1 that contaminates body and *s*,
7:13 his *s* has been refreshed by all
11: 4 or if you receive a different *s*
12:18 Did we not act in the same *s*
13:14 of the Holy *S* be with you all.
Gal 3: 2 Did you receive the *S*
3: 3 After beginning with the *S*,
3: 5 Does God give you his *S*
3:14 might receive the promise of the *S*.
4: 6 God sent the *S* of his Son
4: 6 the *S* who calls out, "*Abba*, Father
4:29 born by the power of the *S*.
5: 5 through the *S* the righteousness
5:16 by the *S*, and you will not gratify
5:17 and the *S* what is contrary
5:17 desires what is contrary to the *S*,
5:18 But if you are led by the *S*,
5:22 But the fruit of the *S* is love, joy,
5:25 Since we live by the *S*, let us keep
5:25 let us keep in step with the *S*.
6: 8 from the *S* will reap eternal life.
6: 8 the one who sows to please the *S*,
6:18 Lord Jesus Christ be with your *s*,
Eph 1:13 with a seal, the promised Holy *S*,
1:17 may give you the *S* of wisdom
2: 2 the *s* who is now at work
2:18 access to the Father by one *S*.
2:22 in which God lives by his *S*.
3: 5 by the *S* to God's holy apostles
3:16 you with power through his *S*
4: 3 of the *S* through the bond of peace.
4: 4 There is one body and one *S*—
4:30 do not grieve the Holy *S* of God,
5:18 Instead, be filled with the *S*.
6:17 of salvation and the sword of the *S*,
6:18 And pray in the *S* on all occasions
Php 1:19 given by the *S* of Jesus Christ,
1:27 know that you stand firm in one *s*,
2: 1 if any fellowship with the *S*,
2: 2 being one in *s* and purpose.
3: 3 we who worship by the *S* of God,
4:23 Lord Jesus Christ be with your *s*.
Col 1: 8 also told us of your love in the *S*.
2: 5 I am present with you in *s*
1Th 1: 5 Holy *S* and with deep conviction.
1: 6 with the joy given by the Holy *S*.
4: 8 who gives you his Holy *S*.
5:23 May your whole *s*, soul
2Th 2:13 the sanctifying work of the *S*
1Ti 3:16 was vindicated by the *S*,
4: 1 The *S* clearly says that
2Ti 1: 7 For God did not give us a *s*
1: 7 but a *s* of power, of love
1:14 help of the Holy *S* who lives in us.
4:22 The Lord be with your *s*.
Tit 3: 5 and renewal by the Holy *S*,
Phm :25 Lord Jesus Christ be with your *s*.
Heb 2: 4 of the Holy *S* distributed according
3: 7 So, as the Holy *S* says:
4:12 even to dividing soul and *s*,
6: 4 who have shared in the Holy *S*,
9: 8 The Holy *S* was showing
9:14 the eternal *S* offered himself
10:15 The Holy *S* also testifies
10:29 and who has insulted the *S* of grace
Jas 2:26 As the body without the *s* is dead,

Jas 4: 5 without reason that the *s* he caused
1Pe 1: 2 the sanctifying work of the *S*,
1: 11 to which the *S* of Christ
1: 12 by the Holy *S* sent from heaven.
3: 4 beauty of a gentle and quiet *s*,
3: 18 in the body but made alive by the *S*
4: 6 according to God in regard to the *s*.
4: 14 for the *S* of glory and of God rests
2Pe 1: 21 carried along by the Holy *S*.
1Jn 3: 24 We know it by the *S* he gave us.
4: 1 Dear friends, do not believe every *s*
4: 2 Every *s* that acknowledges that
4: 2 is how you can recognize the *S*
4: 3 This is the *s* of the antichrist,
4: 3 every *s* that does not acknowledge
4: 6 This is how we recognize the *S*
4: 6 of truth and the *s* of falsehood.
4: 13 because he has given us of his *S*.
5: 6 And it is the *S* who testifies,
5: 6 testifies, because the *S* is the truth.
5: 8 the *S*, the water and the blood;
Jude : 19 instincts and do not have the *S*.
: 20 holy faith and pray in the Holy *S*.
Rev 1: 10 On the Lord's Day I was in the *S*,
2: 7 let him hear what the *S* says
2: 11 let him hear what the *S* says
2: 17 let him hear what the *S* says
2: 29 let him hear what the *S* says
3: 6 let him hear what the *S* says
3: 13 let him hear what the *S* says
3: 22 let him hear what the *S* says
4: 2 At once I was in the *S*,
14: 13 says the *S*, "they will rest
17: 3 away in the *S* into a desert.
18: 2 and a haunt for every evil *s*,
19: 10 of Jesus is the *s* of prophecy."
21: 10 away in the *S* to a mountain great
22: 17 The *S* and the bride say, "Come!"

SPIRIT'S (SPIRIT)

1Co 2: 4 a demonstration of the *S* power,
1Th 5: 19 not put out the *S* fire; do not treat

SPIRITIST (SPIRIT)

Lev 20: 27 *s* among you must be put to death.
Dt 18: 11 or *s* or who consults the dead.

SPIRITISTS (SPIRIT)

Lev 19: 31 turn to mediums or seek out *s*,
20: 6 and *s* to prostitute himself
1Sa 28: 3 had expelled the mediums and *s*
28: 9 cut off the mediums and *s*
2Ki 21: 6 and consulted mediums and *s*.
23: 24 Josiah got rid of the mediums and *s*
2Ch 33: 6 and consulted mediums and *s*,
Isa 8: 19 you to consult mediums and *s*,
19: 3 the mediums and the *s*.

SPIRITS (SPIRIT)

Nu 16: 22 O God, God of the *s* of all mankind
27: 16 the God of the *s* of all mankind,
Jdg 16: 25 While they were in high *s*,
Ru 3: 7 and drinking and was in good *s*,
1Sa 25: 36 He was in high *s* and very drunk.
2Sa 13: 28 is in high *s* from drinking wine
Est 1: 10 was in high *s* from wine,
5: 9 out that day happy and in high *s*.
Ps 78: 8 whose *s* were not faithful to him.
Pr 2: 18 and her paths to the *s* of the dead.
Isa 14: 9 it rouses the *s* of the departed
19: 3 they will consult the idols and the *s*
26: 14 those departed *s* do not rise.
Zec 6: 5 "These are the four *s* of heaven,
Mt 8: 16 and he drove out the *s* with a word
10: 1 them authority to drive out evil *s*
12: 45 with it seven other *s* more wicked
Mk 1: 27 to evil *s* and they obey him."
3: 11 Whenever the evil *s* saw him,
5: 13 and the evil *s* came out
6: 7 gave them authority over evil *s*.
Lk 4: 36 and power he gives orders to evil *s*
6: 18 Those troubled by evil *s* were cured
7: 21 and evil *s*, and gave sight
8: 2 who had been cured of evil *s*
10: 20 do not rejoice that the *s* submit
11: 26 takes seven other *s* more wicked
Ac 5: 16 and those tormented by evil *s*,
8: 7 With shrieks, evil *s* came out
19: 12 were cured and the evil *s* left them.
19: 13 went around driving out evil *s* tried
23: 8 that there are neither angels nor *s*,
1Co 12: 10 the ability to distinguish between *s*,
14: 32 The *s* of prophets are subject
1Ti 4: 1 and follow deceiving *s* and things
Heb 1: 14 not all angels ministering *s* sent
12: 9 submit to the Father of our *s*
12: 23 to the *s* of righteous men made
1Pe 3: 19 to the *s* in prison who disobeyed
1Jn 4: 1 test the *s* to see whether they are
Rev 1: 4 from the seven *s* before his throne,
3: 1 words of him who holds the seven *s*
4: 5 These are the seven *s* of God.
5: 6 which are the seven *s*
16: 13 I saw three evil *s* that looked like
16: 14 They are *s* of demons performing
22: 6 the God of the *s* of the prophets,

SPIRITUAL (SPIRIT)

Ro 1: 11 to you some *s* gift to make you
7: 14 We know that the law is *s*;
12: 1 to God—which is your *s* worship.
12: 11 but keep your *s* fervor, serving
15: 27 shared in the Jews' *s* blessings,
1Co 1: 7 you do not lack any *s* gift
2: 13 expressing *s* truths in *s* words.
2: 15 *s* man makes judgments about all
3: 1 I could not address you as *s* but
9: 11 If we have sown *s* seed among you,
10: 3 They all ate the same *s* food
10: 4 and drank the same *s* drink;
10: 4 from the *s* rock that accompanied
12: 1 Now about *s* gifts, brothers,
14: 1 of love and eagerly desire *s* gifts,
14: 12 Since you are eager to have *s* gifts,
15: 44 a natural body, it is raised a *s* body.
15: 44 natural body, there is also a *s* body.
15: 46 The *s* did not come first,
15: 46 but the natural, and after that the *s*.
Gal 6: 1 you who are *s* should restore him
Eph 1: 3 with every *s* blessing in Christ.
5: 19 with psalms, hymns and *s* songs.
6: 12 and against the *s* forces of evil
Col 1: 9 of his will through all *s* wisdom
3: 16 and *s* songs with gratitude
1Pe 2: 2 newborn babies, crave pure *s* milk,
2: 5 are being built into a *s* house
2: 5 offering *s* sacrifices acceptable

SPIRITUALLY (SPIRIT)

1Co 2: 14 because they are *s* discerned.
14: 37 thinks he is a prophet or *s* gifted,

SPIT (SPITS SPITTING)

Nu 12: 14 "If her father had *s* in her face,
Dt 25: 9 off one of his sandals, *s* in his face
Job 17: 6 a man in whose face people *s*.
20: 15 He will *s* out the riches he
30: 10 they do not hesitate to *s* in my face.
Mt 26: 67 Then they *s* in his face
27: 30 They *s* on him, and took the staff
Mk 7: 33 he *s* and touched the man's tongue.
8: 23 When he had *s* on the man's eyes
10: 34 who will mock him and *s* on him,
14: 65 Then some began to *s* at him;
15: 19 the head with a staff and *s* on him.
Lk 18: 32 They will mock him, insult him, *s*
Jn 9: 6 Having said this, he *s*
Rev 3: 16 I am about to *s* you out

SPITE

Lev 26: 23 " 'If in *s* of these things you do not
26: 27 If in *s* of this you still do not listen
26: 44 Yet in *s* of this, when they are
Nu 14: 11 in *s* of all the miraculous signs I
Dt 1: 32 In *s* of this, you did not trust
Ezr 10: 2 But in *s* of this, there is still hope
Ne 5: 18 In *s* of all this, I never demanded
Job 23: 2 in *s* of my groaning.
Ps 78: 32 In *s* of all this, they kept on sinning;
78: 32 in *s* of his wonders, they did not
Isa 47: 9 in *s* of your many sorceries
Jer 2: 34 Yet in *s* of all this
3: 10 In *s* of all this, her unfaithful sister
1Th 1: 6 of the Lord; in *s* of severe suffering,
2: 2 gospel in *s* of strong opposition.

SPITS (SPIT)

Lev 15: 8 the man with the discharge *s*

SPITTING (SPIT)

Isa 50: 6 face from mocking and *s*.

SPLENDID (SPLENDOR)

Isa 22: 18 there your *s* chariots will remain—
Eze 17: 8 bear fruit and become a *s* vine.'
17: 23 bear fruit and become a *s* cedar.

SPLENDOR (SPLENDID)

1Ch 16: 27 *S* and majesty are before him;
16: 29 the LORD in the *s* of his holiness.
22: 5 and *s* in the sight of all the nations.
29: 11 the glory and the majesty and the *s*,
29: 25 and bestowed on him royal *s* such
2Ch 20: 21 him for the *s* of his holiness
Est 1: 4 and the *s* and glory of his majesty.
Job 13: 11 Would not his *s* terrify you?
31: 23 of his *s* I could not do such things.
31: 26 or the moon moving in *s*,
37: 22 of the north he comes in golden *s*;
40: 10 adorn yourself with glory and *s*,
Ps 21: 5 you have bestowed on him *s*
29: 2 in the *s* of his holiness.
45: 3 clothe yourself with *s* and majesty.
49: 16 when the *s* of his house increases;
49: 17 his *s* will not descend with him.
71: 8 declaring your *s* all day long.
78: 61 his *s* into the hands of the enemy.
89: 44 You have put an end to his *s*
90: 16 your *s* to their children.
96: 6 *S* and majesty are before him;
96: 9 in the *s* of his holiness;
104: 1 you are clothed with *s* and majesty.
145: 5 of the glorious *s* of your majesty,
145: 12 and the glorious *s* of your kingdom.
148: 13 his *s* is above the earth
Pr 4: 9 and present you with a crown of *s*."
16: 31 Gray hair is a crown of *s*;
20: 29 gray hair the *s* of the old.
Isa 2: 10 and the *s* of his majesty!
2: 19 and the *s* of his majesty,
2: 21 and the *s* of his majesty,
10: 18 The *s* of his forests and fertile fields
16: 14 Moab's *s* and all her many people
35: 2 the *s* of Carmel and Sharon;
35: 2 the *s* of our God.
46: 13 my *s* to Israel.
49: 3 in whom I will display my *s*."
52: 1 Put on your garments of *s*,
55: 5 for he has endowed you with *s*."
60: 9 for he has endowed you with *s*.
60: 21 for the display of my *s*.
61: 3 the LORD for the display of his *s*.
62: 3 of *s* in the LORD's hand,
63: 1 Who is this, robed in *s*,
Jer 22: 18 'Alas, my master! Alas, his *s*!'
La 1: 6 All the *s* has departed
2: 1 He has hurled down the *s* of Israel
3: 18 So I say, "My *s* is gone
Eze 16: 14 *s* I had given you made your beauty
27: 10 bringing you *s*.
28: 7 and pierce your shining *s*.
28: 17 because of your *s*.
31: 18 can be compared with you in *s*
Da 4: 36 *s* were returned to me for the glory
5: 18 and greatness and glory and *s*.
11: 20 collector to maintain the royal *s*.
Hos 10: 5 those who had rejoiced over its *s*,
14: 6 His *s* will be like an olive tree,
Na 2: 2 The LORD will restore the *s*
2: 2 like the *s* of Israel,
Hab 3: 4 His *s* was like the sunrise;
Mt 4: 8 kingdoms of the world and their *s*.
6: 29 in all his *s* was dressed like one
Lk 4: 6 give you all their authority and *s*,
9: 31 appeared in glorious *s*, talking
12: 27 in all his *s* was dressed like one
1Co 15: 40 the *s* of the heavenly bodies is one
15: 40 *s* of the earthly bodies is another.
15: 41 The sun has one kind of *s*,
15: 41 and star differs from star in *s*.
2Th 2: 8 and destroy by the *s* of his coming.
Rev 18: 1 the earth was illuminated by his *s*.
18: 14 All your riches and *s* have vanished

Rev 21: 24 of the earth will bring their *s* into it.

SPLINT

Eze 30: 21 or put in a *s* so as to become strong

SPLINTERED

2Ki 18: 21 on Egypt, that *s* reed of a staff,
Isa 36: 6 on Egypt, that *s* reed of a staff,
Eze 29: 7 you *s* and you tore open their

SPLIT (SPLITS)

Lev 11: 3 that has a *s* hoof completely
11: 4 chew the cud or only have a *s* hoof,
11: 4 does not have a *s* hoof; it is
11: 5 does not have a *s* hoof; it is unclean
11: 6 does not have a *s* hoof; it is unclean
11: 7 it has a *s* hoof completely divided,
11: 26 that has a *s* hoof not completely
Nu 16: 31 the ground under them *s* apart
Dt 14: 6 animal that has a *s* hoof divided
14: 7 do not have a *s* hoof; they are
14: 7 or that have a *s* hoof completely
14: 8 it has a *s* hoof, it does not chew
1Ki 13: 3 The altar will be *s* apart
13: 5 the altar was *s* apart and its ashes
16: 21 of Israel were *s* into two factions;
Ps 74: 13 It was you who *s* open the sea
78: 15 He *s* the rocks in the desert
Isa 24: 19 the earth is *s* asunder,
48: 21 he *s* the rock
Mic 1: 4 and the valleys *s* apart,
Hab 3: 9 You *s* the earth with rivers;
Zec 14: 4 of Olives will be *s* in two from east
Mt 27: 51 The earth shook and the rocks *s*.
Rev 16: 19 The great city *s* into three parts,

SPLITS (SPLIT)

Ecc 10: 9 whoever *s* logs may be endangered

SPOIL (DESPOIL SPOILS)

Ps 119: 162 like one who finds great *s*.
Jer 30: 16 all who make *s* of you I will despoil.
1Pe 1: 4 *s* or fade—kept in heaven for you,

SPOILS (SPOIL)

Ex 15: 9 I will divide the *s*;
Nu 31: 11 They took all the plunder and *s*,
31: 12 *s* and plunder to Moses
31: 27 Divide the *s* between the soldiers
31: 32 from the *s* that the soldiers took
Jdg 5: 30 they not finding and dividing the *s*:
Isa 33: 23 an abundance of *s* will be divided
53: 12 he will divide the *s* with the strong,
Lk 11: 22 man trusted and divides up the *s*.
Jn 6: 27 Do not work for food that *s*,

SPOKESMAN (SPOKESMEN)

Jer 15: 19 you will be my *s*.

SPOKESMEN (SPOKESMAN)

Isa 43: 27 your *s* rebelled against me.

SPONGE

Mt 27: 48 one of them ran and got a *s*.
Mk 15: 36 filled a *s* with wine vinegar,
Jn 19: 29 put the *s* on a stalk
19: 29 so they soaked a *s* in it,

SPONTANEOUS

Phm : 14 so that any favor you do will be *s*

SPORT

Ge 39: 14 brought to us to make *s* of us!
39: 17 came to me to make *s* of me.
Ps 69: 11 people make *s* of me.

SPOT (SPOTS SPOTTED)

Lev 13: 2 or a bright *s* on his skin that may
13: 4 If the *s* on his skin is white
13: 19 or reddish-white *s* appears,
13: 23 But if the *s* is unchanged
13: 24 or white *s* appears in the raw flesh
13: 25 the priest is to examine the *s*,
13: 26 and there is no white hair in the *s*
13: 28 *s* is unchanged and has not spread
14: 56 or a bright *s*, to determine
Jos 4: 9 at the *s* where the priests who
2Sa 2: 23 He fell there and died on the *s*.
2Ki 5: 11 wave his hand over the *s*
Job 8: 18 But when it is torn from its *s*,
Isa 28: 8 and there is not a *s* without filth.
46: 7 From that *s* it cannot move.
Lk 19: 5 When Jesus reached the *s*,
1Ti 6: 14 keep this commandment without *s*

SPOTLESS

Da 11: 35 made *s* until the time of the end,
12: 10 Many will be purified, made *s*
2Pe 3: 14 make every effort to be found *s*,

SPOTS (SPOT)

Lev 13: 38 or woman has white *s* on the skin,
13: 39 and if the *s* are dull white,
Jer 13: 23 or the leopard its *s*?

SPOTTED (SPOT)

Ge 30: 32 and every *s* or speckled goat.
30: 32 them every speckled or *s* sheep,
30: 33 possession that is not speckled or *s*,
30: 35 male goats that were streaked or *s*,
30: 35 or *s* female goats (all that had white
30: 39 that were streaked or speckled or *s*.
31: 10 flock were streaked, speckled or *s*.
31: 12 *s*, for I have seen all that Laban has

SPRANG (SPRING)

Jnh 4: 10 It *s* up overnight and died
Mt 13: 5 It *s* up quickly, because the soil was
Mk 4: 5 It *s* up quickly, because the soil was
Ro 7: 9 the commandment came, sin *s*

SPREAD (SPREADING SPREADS WIDESPREAD)

Ge 10: 5 these the maritime peoples *s* out
10: 32 From these the nations *s* out
28: 14 and you will *s* out to the west
41: 56 When the famine had *s*
Ex 1: 12 the more they multiplied and *s*;
9: 29 I will *s* out my hands in prayer
9: 33 He *s* out his hands
10: 21 so that darkness will *s* over Egypt
23: 1 "Do not *s* false reports.
25: 20 are to have their wings *s* upward,
29: 2 with oil, and wafers *s* with oil.
37: 9 had their wings *s* upward,
40: 19 he *s* the tent over the tabernacle
Lev 2: 4 made without yeast and *s* with oil.
7: 12 made without yeast and *s* with oil,
13: 5 the sore is unchanged and has not *s*
13: 6 if the sore has faded and has not *s*
13: 7 But if the rash does *s* in his skin
13: 8 and if the rash has *s* in the skin,
13: 23 spot is unchanged and has not *s*,
13: 28 has not *s* in the skin but has faded,
13: 32 and if the itch has not *s*
13: 34 and if it has not *s* in the skin
13: 35 But if the itch does *s* in the skin
13: 36 and if the itch has *s* in the skin,
13: 51 if the mildew has *s* in the clothing,
13: 53 the mildew has not *s* in the clothing
13: 55 though it has not *s*, it is unclean.
14: 39 If the mildew has *s* on the walls,
14: 44 if the mildew has *s* in the house,
14: 48 and the mildew has not *s*
Nu 4: 6 *s* a cloth of solid blue over that
4: 7 Presence they are to *s* a blue cloth
4: 8 are to *s* a scarlet cloth,
4: 11 gold altar they are to *s* a blue cloth
4: 13 and *s* a purple cloth over it.
4: 14 are to *s* a covering of hides
6: 15 with oil, and wafers *s* with oil.
11: 32 Then they *s* them out all
13: 32 they *s* among the Israelites a bad
24: 6 "Like valleys they *s* out,
Jos 6: 27 and his fame *s* throughout the land.
7: 23 and *s* them out before the LORD.
Jdg 8: 25 So they *s* out a garment,
20: 37 *s* out and put the whole city
Ru 3: 9 "*S* the corner of your garment
1Sa 4: 2 as the battle *s*, Israel was defeated
2Sa 5: 18 and *s* out in the Valley of Rephaim;
5: 22 and *s* out in the Valley of Rephaim;
17: 19 *s* it out over the opening of the well
18: 8 The battle *s* out over the whole
21: 10 and *s* it out for herself on a rock.
1Ki 4: 31 his fame *s* to all the surrounding
1Ki 6: 27 with their wings *s* out.
8: 7 The cherubim *s* their wings
8: 22 *s* out his hands toward heaven
8: 54 with his hands *s* out toward heaven
22: 36 As the sun was setting, a cry *s*
2Ki 8: 15 and *s* it over the king's face,
9: 13 *s* them under him on the bare steps.
19: 14 and *s* it out before the LORD.
1Ch 14: 17 fame *s* throughout every land,
28: 18 cherubim of gold that *s* their wings
2Ch 5: 8 The cherubim *s* their wings
6: 12 of Israel and *s* out his hands.
6: 13 and *s* out his hands toward heaven.
26: 8 and his fame *s* as far as the border
26: 15 His fame *s* far and wide,
Ezr 9: 5 on my knees with my hands *s* out
Ne 4: 19 "The work is extensive and *s* out,
8: 15 and *s* it throughout their towns
Est 9: 4 *s* throughout the provinces,
Job 1: 10 herds are *s* throughout the land.
15: 29 will his possessions *s* over the land.
17: 13 if I *s* out my bed in darkness,
39: 26 and *s* his wings toward the south?
Ps 5: 11 *S* your protection over them,
44: 20 or *s* out our hands to a foreign god,
57: 6 They *s* a net for my feet—
78: 19 "Can God *s* a table in the desert?
88: 9 I *s* out my hands to you.
105: 39 He *s* out a cloud as a covering,
136: 6 who *s* out the earth
140: 5 they have *s* out the cords
143: 6 I *s* out my hands to you;
Pr 1: 17 How useless to *s* a net
15: 7 The lips of the wise *s* knowledge;
SS 1: 12 my perfume *s* its fragrance.
2: 13 blossoming vines *s* their fragrance.
4: 16 that its fragrance may *s* abroad.
Isa 1: 15 When you *s* out your hands
14: 11 maggots are *s* out beneath you
16: 8 Their shoots *s* out
16: 8 and *s* toward the desert.
21: 5 they *s* the rugs,
25: 11 They will *s* out their hands in it,
30: 24 *s* out with fork and shovel
33: 23 the sail is not *s*.
37: 14 and *s* it out before the LORD.
42: 5 who *s* out the earth and all that
44: 24 who *s* out the earth by myself,
48: 13 my right hand *s* out the heavens;
54: 3 For you will *s* out to the right
65: 11 who *s* a table for Fortune
Jer 23: 15 has *s* throughout the land."
43: 10 he will *s* his royal canopy
48: 32 Your branches *s* as far as the sea;
La 1: 13 He *s* a net for my feet
Eze 1: 11 Their wings were *s* out upward;
1: 22 *S* out above the heads
5: 4 A fire will *s* from there
10: 16 when the cherubim *s* their wings
10: 19 the cherubim *s* their wings
11: 22 wheels beside them, *s* their wings,
12: 13 I will *s* my net for him,
16: 8 I *s* the corner of my garment
16: 14 your fame *s* among the nations
17: 20 I will *s* my net for him,
19: 8 They *s* their net for him,
19: 14 Fire *s* from one of its main
23: 41 with a table *s* before it
26: 5 will become a place to *s* fishnets,
26: 14 will become a place to *s* fishnets.
30: 13 I will *s* fear throughout the land.
32: 5 I will *s* your flesh on the mountains
32: 23 All who had *s* terror in the land
32: 24 All who had *s* terror in the land
32: 25 Because their terror had *s*
32: 26 they *s* their terror in the land
32: 32 Although I had him *s* terror
Hos 5: 1 a net *s* out on Tabor.
Mal 2: 3 I will *s* on your faces the offal
Mt 4: 24 News about him *s* all over Syria,
9: 26 of this *s* through all that region.
9: 31 and *s* the news about him all
21: 8 A very large crowd *s* their cloaks
21: 8 branches from the trees and *s* them
Mk 1: 28 News about him *s* quickly
11: 8 Many people *s* their cloaks
11: 8 while others *s* branches they had
Lk 2: 17 they *s* the word concerning what

Lk 4: 14 about him *s* through the whole
4: 37 And the news about him *s*
5: 15 the news about him *s* all the more,
7: 17 This news about Jesus *s*
19: 36 people *s* their cloaks on the road.
Jn 12: 17 to *s* the word that he had called
21: 23 rumor *s* among the brothers that
Ac 6: 7 So the word of God *s*.
11: 28 that a severe famine would *s*
12: 24 of God continued to increase and *s*.
13: 49 of the Lord *s* through the whole
19: 20 the word of the Lord *s* widely
2Th 3: 1 message of the Lord may *s* rapidly
2Ti 2: 17 Their teaching will *s* like gangrene.
Rev 7: 15 sits on the throne will *s* his tent

SPREADING (SPREAD)

Lev 13: 22 If it is *s* in the skin, the priest shall
13: 27 if it is *s* in the skin, the priest shall
13: 49 it is a *s* mildew and must be shown
13: 57 or in the leather article, it is *s*,
14: 34 and I put a *s* mildew in a house
19: 16 " 'Do not go about *s* slander
Nu 14: 36 him by *s* a bad report about it—
14: 37 for *s* the bad report about the land
Dt 12: 2 and under every *s* tree where
28: 35 *s* from the soles of your feet
Jdg 15: 9 camped in Judah, *s* out near Lehi.
1Sa 2: 24 it is not a good report that I hear *s*
1Ki 8: 38 *s* out his hands toward this temple
14: 23 and under every *s* tree.
2Ki 16: 4 and under every *s* tree.
17: 10 and under every *s* tree.
2Ch 6: 29 *s* out his hands toward this temple
28: 4 and under every *s* tree.
Job 8: 16 *s* its shoots over the garden;
26: 9 *s* his clouds over it.
37: 18 can you join him in *s* out the skies,
Pr 29: 5 is *s* a net for his feet.
Isa 18: 5 and take away the *s* branches.
57: 5 and under every *s* tree;
Jer 2: 20 and under every *s* tree
3: 6 and under every *s* tree and has
3: 13 gods under every *s* tree,
17: 2 poles beside the *s* trees
25: 32 "Look! Disaster is *s*
48: 40 *s* its wings over Moab.
49: 22 *s* its wings over Bozrah.
Eze 6: 13 under every *s* tree and every leafy
17: 6 sprouted and became a low, *s* vine.
31: 5 *s* because of abundant waters.
31: 7 with its *s* boughs,
47: 10 there will be places for *s* nets.
Hos 10: 1 Israel was a *s* vine;
Joel 2: 2 Like dawn *s* across the mountains
Mk 1: 45 and began to talk freely, *s* the news.
Ac 4: 17 to stop this thing from *s* any further
1Th 3: 2 God's fellow worker in *s* the gospel

SPREADS (SPREAD)

Ex 22: 6 and *s* into thornbushes
Dt 32: 11 that *s* its wings to catch them
Job 26: 7 He *s* out the northern ⌊skies⌋
36: 29 understand how he *s* out
39: 18 Yet when she *s* her feathers to run,
Ps 41: 6 then he goes out and *s* it abroad.
147: 16 He *s* the snow like wool
Pr 10: 18 and whoever *s* slander is a fool.
Isa 25: 11 a swimmer *s* out his hands to swim.
32: 6 and *s* error concerning the LORD;
40: 22 and *s* them out like a tent to live in.
2Co 2: 14 and through us *s* everywhere

SPRIG

Eze 17: 22 off a tender *s* from its topmost

SPRING (SPRANG SPRINGING SPRINGS SPRINGTIME SPRUNG WELLSPRING)

Ge 16: 7 Hagar near a *s* in the desert;
16: 7 it was the *s* that is beside the road
24: 13 See, I am standing beside this *s*,
24: 16 went down to the *s*, filled her jar
24: 29 he hurried out to the man at the *s*.
24: 30 standing by the camels near the *s*.
24: 42 When I came to the *s* today, I said,
24: 43 See, I am standing beside this *s*;
24: 45 She went down to the *s*
49: 22 a fruitful vine near a *s*,
Lev 11: 36 A *s*, however, or a cistern
Nu 21: 17 "*S* up, O well!
Dt 11: 14 and *s* rains, so that you may gather
33: 28 Jacob's *s* is secure
Jos 15: 9 headed toward the *s* of the Waters
18: 15 at the *s* of the Waters of Nephtoah.
Jdg 7: 1 and all his men camped at the *s*
15: 19 So the *s* was called En Hakkore,
1Sa 29: 1 Israel camped by the *s* in Jezreel.
2Sa 11: 1 In the *s*, at the time when kings go
1Ki 20: 22 next *s* the king of Aram will attack
20: 26 The next *s* Ben-Hadad mustered
2Ki 2: 21 Then he went out to the *s*
13: 20 used to enter the country every *s*.
1Ch 20: 1 In the *s*, at the time when kings go
2Ch 32: 30 the upper outlet of the Gihon *s*
33: 14 west of the Gihon *s* in the valley,
Job 5: 6 For hardship does not *s*
29: 23 and drank in my words as the *s* rain
Ps 92: 7 though the wicked *s* up like grass
Pr 16: 15 his favor is like a rain cloud in *s*.
25: 26 Like a muddied *s* or a polluted well
Ecc 4: 4 all achievement *s* from man's envy
12: 6 the pitcher is shattered at the *s*,
SS 4: 12 you are a *s* enclosed, a sealed
Isa 14: 29 root of that snake will *s* up a viper,
42: 9 before they *s* into being
44: 4 They will *s* up like grass
45: 8 let salvation *s* up,
58: 11 like a *s* whose waters never fail.
61: 11 *s* up before all nations.
Jer 2: 13 the *s* of living water,
3: 3 and no *s* rains have fallen.
5: 24 who gives autumn and *s* rains
9: 1 Oh, that my head were a *s* of water
15: 18 like a *s* that fails?
17: 13 the *s* of living water.
Hos 6: 3 like the *s* rains that water the earth
10: 4 therefore lawsuits *s* up
13: 15 his *s* will fail
Joel 2: 23 both autumn and *s* rains, as before.
Am 3: 5 Does a trap *s* up from the earth
Jn 4: 14 in him a *s* of water welling up
Ro 15: 12 "The root of Jesse will *s* up,
Col 1: 5 love that *s* from the hope that is
1Th 2: 3 For the appeal we make does not *s*
Jas 3: 11 salt water flow from the same *s*?
3: 12 can a salt *s* produce fresh water.
5: 7 is for the autumn and *s* rains.
Rev 21: 6 without cost from the *s* of the water

SPRINGING (SPRING)

Dt 33: 22 *s* out of Bashan."

SPRINGS (SPRING)

Ge 7: 11 on that day all the *s*
8: 2 Now the *s* of the deep
36: 24 the Anah who discovered the hot *s*
Ex 15: 27 where there were twelve *s*
Nu 33: 9 where there were twelve *s*
Dt 8: 7 with *s* flowing in the valleys
Jos 15: 19 gave her the upper and lower *s*.
15: 19 land in the Negev, give me also *s*
Jdg 1: 15 gave her the upper and lower *s*.
1: 15 land in the Negev, give me also *s*
1Ki 18: 5 "Go through the land to all the *s*
2Ki 3: 19 stop up all the *s*, and ruin every
3: 25 They stopped up all the *s*
19: 29 the second year what *s* from that.
2Ch 32: 3 water from the *s* outside the city,
32: 4 and they blocked all the *s*
Job 14: 2 He *s* up like a flower and withers
38: 16 "Have you journeyed to the *s*
Ps 74: 15 It was you who opened up *s*
84: 6 they make it a place of *s*;
85: 11 Faithfulness *s* forth from the earth,
90: 6 though in the morning it *s* up new,
104: 10 He makes *s* pour water
107: 33 flowing *s* into thirsty ground,
107: 35 the parched ground into flowing *s*;
114: 8 the hard rock into *s* of water.
Pr 5: 16 Should your *s* overflow
8: 24 when there were no *s* abounding
27: 9 of one's friend *s* from his earnest
Isa 35: 7 the thirsty ground bubbling *s*.
37: 30 the second year what *s* from that.
41: 18 and the parched ground into *s*.
41: 18 and *s* within the valleys.
Isa 43: 19 Now it *s* up; do you not perceive it?
49: 10 and lead them beside *s* of water.
Jer 51: 36 and make her *s* dry.
Eze 31: 4 deep *s* made it grow tall;
31: 15 to the grave I covered the deep *s*
2Pe 2: 17 These men are *s* without water
Rev 7: 17 to *s* of living water.
8: 10 of the rivers and on the *s* of water
14: 7 the earth, the sea and the *s* of water
16: 4 bowl on the rivers and *s* of water,

SPRINGTIME (SPRING)

Zec 10: 1 Ask the LORD for rain in the *s*;

SPRINKLE (SPRINKLED SPRINKLES SPRINKLING)

Ex 29: 16 *s* it against the altar on all sides.
29: 20 *s* blood against the altar on all sides
29: 21 some of the anointing oil and *s* it
Lev 1: 5 and *s* it against the altar on all sides
1: 11 sons the priests shall *s* its blood
3: 2 sons the priests shall *s* the blood
3: 8 Then Aaron's sons shall *s* its blood
3: 13 Then Aaron's sons shall *s* its blood
4: 6 and *s* some of it seven times
4: 17 *s* it before the LORD seven times
5: 9 and is to *s* some of the blood
14: 7 Seven times he shall *s* the one
14: 16 and with his finger *s* some of it
14: 27 and with his right forefinger *s* some
14: 51 and *s* the house seven times.
16: 14 and with his finger *s* it on the front
16: 14 then he shall *s* some of it
16: 15 He shall *s* it on the atonement
16: 19 He shall *s* some of the blood on it
17: 6 The priest is to *s* the blood
Nu 8: 7 *S* the water of cleansing on them;
18: 17 *S* their blood on the altar
19: 4 *s* it seven times toward the front
19: 18 dip it in the water and *s* the tent
19: 18 *s* anyone who has touched a human
19: 19 to *s* the unclean person on the third
2Ki 16: 15 *S* on the altar all the blood
Isa 52: 15 so will he *s* many nations,
Eze 27: 30 they will *s* dust on their heads
36: 25 I will *s* clean water on you,
43: 24 and the priests are to *s* salt on them

SPRINKLED (SPRINKLE)

Ex 24: 6 and the other half he *s* on the altar.
24: 8 *s* it on the people and said,
Lev 7: 2 its blood is to be *s* against the altar
8: 11 He *s* some of the oil
8: 19 and *s* the blood against the altar
8: 24 Then he *s* blood against the altar
8: 30 *s* them on Aaron and his garments
9: 12 he *s* it against the altar on all sides.
9: 18 he *s* it against the altar on all sides.
Nu 19: 13 of cleansing has not been *s* on him,
19: 20 of cleansing has not been *s* on him,
Jos 7: 6 of Israel did the same, and *s* dust
2Ki 16: 13 and *s* the blood of his fellowship
2Ch 29: 22 and *s* their blood on the altar;
29: 22 and *s* their blood on the altar.
29: 22 the priests took the blood and *s* it
30: 16 The priests *s* the blood handed
35: 11 and the priests *s* the blood handed
Job 2: 12 and they tore their robes and *s* dust
La 2: 10 they have *s* dust on their heads
Hos 7: 9 His hair is *s* with gray,
Heb 9: 13 and the ashes of a heifer *s*
9: 19 and *s* the scroll and all the people.
9: 21 he *s* with the blood both
10: 22 having our hearts *s* to cleanse us
12: 24 to the *s* blood that speaks a better

SPRINKLES (SPRINKLE)

Lev 7: 14 to the priest who *s* the blood
Nu 19: 21 "The man who *s* the water

SPRINKLING (SPRINKLE)

Ex 27: 3 *s* bowls, meat forks and firepans.
38: 3 *s* bowls, meat forks and firepans.
Nu 4: 14 meat forks, shovels and *s* bowls.
7: 13 one silver *s* bowl weighing seventy
7: 19 one silver *s* bowl weighing seventy
7: 25 one silver *s* bowl weighing seventy
7: 31 one silver *s* bowl weighing seventy

Nu 7: 37 one silver *s* bowl weighing seventy
7: 43 one silver *s* bowl weighing seventy
7: 49 one silver *s* bowl weighing seventy
7: 55 one silver *s* bowl weighing seventy
7: 61 one silver *s* bowl weighing seventy
7: 67 one silver *s* bowl weighing seventy
7: 73 one silver *s* bowl weighing seventy
7: 79 one silver *s* bowl weighing seventy
7: 84 twelve silver *s* bowls and twelve
7: 85 and each *s* bowl seventy shekels.
1Ki 7: 40 the basins and shovels and *s* bowls.
7: 45 the pots, shovels and *s* bowls.
7: 50 *s* bowls, ladles and censers;
2Ki 12: 13 basins, wick trimmers, *s* bowls,
25: 15 away the censers and *s* bowls—
1Ch 28: 17 of pure gold for the forks, *s* bowls
2Ch 4: 8 also made a hundred gold *s* bowls.
4: 11 the pots and shovels and *s* bowls.
4: 22 *s* bowls, ladles and censers;
Jer 52: 18 shovels, wick trimmers, *s* bowls,
52: 19 censers, *s* bowls, pots, lampstands,
Eze 43: 18 and *s* blood upon the altar
Zec 9: 15 used for *s* the corners of the altar.
Heb 11: 28 faith he kept the Passover and the *s*
1Pe 1: 2 to Jesus Christ and *s* by his blood:

SPROUT (SPROUTED SPROUTING SPROUTS)

Nu 17: 5 to the man I choose will *s*,
Job 5: 6 nor does trouble *s* from the ground.
14: 7 If it is cut down, it will *s* again,
38: 27 and make it *s* with grass?
Pr 23: 5 for they will surely *s* wings
Isa 61: 11 For as the soil makes the *s* come up
Jer 33: 15 I will make a righteous Branch *s*
Lk 21: 30 When they *s* leaves, you can see

SPROUTED (SPROUT)

Ge 41: 6 seven other heads of grain *s*—
41: 23 After them, seven other heads *s*—
Nu 17: 8 had not only *s* but had budded,
Eze 17: 6 and it *s* and became a low,
Mt 13: 26 When the wheat *s* and formed

SPROUTING (SPROUT)

Dt 29: 23 nothing planted, nothing *s*,
2Ki 19: 26 like grass *s* on the housetops,
Isa 37: 27 like grass *s* on the housetops,

SPROUTS (SPROUT)

Mk 4: 27 or gets up, the seed *s* and grows,

SPRUNG (SPRING)

Ge 2: 5 no plant of the field had yet *s* up;

SPUN (SPIN)

Ex 35: 25 Every skilled woman *s*
35: 25 and brought what she had *s*—
35: 26 and had the skill *s* the goat hair.

SPUR (SPURRED SPURS)

Heb 10: 24 how we may *s* one another

SPURN (SPURNED SPURNS)

Job 10: 3 to *s* the work of your hands,

SPURNED (SPURN)

Ps 89: 38 But you have rejected, you have *s*,
Pr 1: 30 and *s* my rebuke,
5: 12 How my heart *s* correction!
Isa 1: 4 they have *s* the Holy One of Israel
5: 24 and *s* the word of the Holy One
La 2: 6 in his fierce anger he has *s*

SPURNS (SPURN)

Pr 15: 5 A fool *s* his father's discipline,

SPURRED (SPUR)

Est 3: 15 *S* on by the king's command,
8: 14 *s* on by the king's command.
Isa 9: 11 and has *s* their enemies on.

SPURS (SPUR)

Isa 41: 7 *s* on him who strikes the anvil.

SPY (SPIED SPIES SPYING)

Dt 1: 22 ahead to *s* out the land for us
Jos 2: 2 tonight to *s* out the land."
2: 3 come to *s* out the whole land."
Jos 7: 2 "Go up and *s* out the region."
Jdg 1: 23 to *s* out Bethel (formerly called
18: 2 and Eshtaol to *s* out the land
2Sa 10: 3 and *s* it out and overthrow it?"
1Ch 19: 3 *s* out the country and overthrow it
Gal 2: 4 ranks to *s* on the freedom we have

SPYING (SPY)

Ge 42: 30 as though we were *s* on the land.
Jos 6: 23 men who had done the *s* went

SQUADS

Ac 12: 4 by four *s* of four soldiers each.

SQUALL

Mk 4: 37 A furious *s* came up, and the waves
Lk 8: 23 A *s* came down on the lake,

SQUANDERED (SQUANDERS)

Lk 15: 13 there *s* his wealth in wild living.
15: 30 of yours who has *s* your property

SQUANDERS (SQUANDERED)

Pr 29: 3 of prostitutes *s* his wealth.

SQUARE (SQUARES)

Ge 19: 2 "we will spend the night in the *s*."
Ex 27: 1 three cubits high; it is to be *s*,
28: 16 It is to be *s*— a span long
30: 2 It is to be *s*, a cubit long
37: 25 It was *s*, a cubit long and a cubit
38: 1 three cubits high; it was *s*,
39: 9 It was *s*— a span long and a span
Dt 13: 16 town into the middle of the public *s*
Jdg 19: 15 They went and sat in the city *s*,
19: 17 and saw the traveler in the city *s*,
19: 20 Only don't spend the night in the *s*
2Sa 21: 12 secretly from the public *s* at Beth
1Ki 7: 31 The panels of the stands were *s*,
2Ch 29: 4 assembled them in the *s*
32: 6 before him in the *s* at the city gate
Ezr 10: 9 in the *s* before the house of God,
Ne 8: 1 in the *s* before the Water Gate.
8: 3 as he faced the *s* before the Water
8: 16 and in the *s* by the Water Gate
Est 4: 6 Mordecai in the open *s* of the city
Job 29: 7 and took my seat in the public *s*,
Eze 16: 24 a lofty shrine in every public *s*
16: 31 your lofty shrines in every public *s*,
40: 12 and the alcoves were six cubits *s*.
40: 47 he measured the court: It was *s*—
41: 22 three cubits high and two cubits *s*;
43: 16 altar hearth is *s*, twelve cubits long
43: 17 also is *s*, fourteen cubits long
45: 2 a section 500 cubits *s* is to be
48: 20 The entire portion will be a *s*,
Am 5: 16 cries of anguish in every public *s*.
Rev 21: 16 The city was laid out like a *s*,

SQUARES (SQUARE)

Pr 1: 20 she raises her voice in the public *s*;
5: 16 streams of water in the public *s*?
7: 12 now in the street, now in the *s*,
SS 3: 2 through its streets and *s*;
Isa 15: 3 on the roofs and in the public *s*
Jer 5: 1 search through her *s*.
9: 21 the young men from the public *s*.
48: 38 and in the public *s*
Na 2: 4 back and forth through the *s*.

SQUEEZED

Ge 40: 11 *s* them into Pharaoh's cup
Jdg 6: 38 he *s* the fleece and wrung out

STAB (STABBED)

Zec 13: 3 his own parents will *s* him.

STABBED (STAB)

2Sa 3: 27 Joab *s* him in the stomach,
4: 6 and they *s* him in the stomach.
4: 7 After they *s* and killed him,
20: 10 Without being *s* again, Amasa died

STABILITY

Pr 29: 4 By justice a king gives a country *s*,

STACHYS

Ro 16: 9 in Christ, and my dear friend *S*.

STADIA

Rev 14: 20 bridles for a distance of 1,600 *s*.
21: 16 *s* in length, and as wide and high

STAFF (STAFFS)

Ge 32: 10 I had only my *s* when I crossed this
38: 18 the *s* in your hand," she answered.
38: 25 seal and cord and *s* these are."
47: 31 as he leaned on the top of his *s*.
49: 10 the ruler's *s* from between his feet,
Ex 4: 2 What is that in your hand?" "A *s*,"
4: 4 it turned back into a *s* in his hand.
4: 17 But take this *s* in your hand
4: 20 he took the *s* of God in his hand.
7: 9 'Take your *s* and throw it
7: 10 Aaron threw his *s* down in front
7: 12 Aaron's *s* swallowed up their staffs.
7: 12 Each one threw down his *s*
7: 15 your hand the *s* that was changed
7: 17 With the *s* that is in my hand I will
7: 19 'Take your *s* and stretch out your
7: 20 He raised his *s* in the presence
8: 5 hand with your *s* over the streams
8: 16 'Stretch out your *s* and strike
8: 17 stretched out his hand with the *s*
9: 23 When Moses stretched out his *s*
10: 13 So Moses stretched out his *s*
12: 11 sandals on your feet and your *s*
14: 16 Raise your *s* and stretch out your
17: 5 and take in your hand the *s*
17: 9 top of the hill with the *s* of God
21: 19 walks around outside with his *s*;
Nu 17: 2 the name of each man on his *s*.
17: 3 On the *s* of Levi write Aaron's
17: 3 for there must be one *s* for the head
17: 5 *s* belonging to the man I choose
17: 6 and Aaron's *s* was among them.
17: 8 Testimony and saw that Aaron's *s*,
17: 9 and each man took his own *s*.
17: 10 "Put back Aaron's *s* in front
20: 8 said to Moses, "Take the *s*,
20: 9 Moses took the *s* from the LORD's
20: 11 struck the rock twice with his *s*.
22: 27 was angry and beat her with his *s*.
Jdg 5: 14 those who bear a commander's *s*.
6: 21 With the tip of the *s* that was
1Sa 14: 27 the end of the *s* that was in his hand
14: 43 honey with the end of my *s*.
17: 40 Then he took his *s* in his hand,
2Ki 4: 29 Lay my *s* on the boy's face."
4: 29 take my *s* in your hand and run.
4: 31 and laid the *s* on the boy's face,
18: 21 that splintered reed of a *s*,
2Ch 32: 3 and military *s* about blocking
Ps 23: 4 your rod and your *s*,
Isa 36: 6 that splintered reed of a *s*,
Jer 48: 17 how broken the glorious *s*!'
51: 59 gave to the *s* officer Seraiah son
Eze 12: 14 those around him—his *s*
20: 37 note of you as you pass under my *s*,
29: 6 " 'You have been a *s* of reed
Mic 7: 14 Shepherd your people with your *s*,
Zec 11: 10 Then I took my *s* called Favor
11: 14 I broke my second *s* called Union,
Mt 10: 10 or extra tunic, or sandals or a *s*;
27: 29 They put a *s* in his right hand
27: 30 and took the *s* and struck him
Mk 6: 8 for the journey except a *s*—
15: 19 him on the head with a *s*
Lk 9: 3 nothing for the journey—no *s*,
Heb 11: 21 as he leaned on the top of his *s*.

STAFFS (STAFF)

Ex 7: 12 Aaron's staff swallowed up their *s*.
Nu 17: 2 and get twelve *s* from them,
17: 6 and their leaders gave him twelve *s*
17: 7 Moses placed the *s*
17: 9 Then Moses brought out all the *s*
21: 18 the nobles with scepters and *s*."
Zec 11: 7 I took two *s* and called one Favor

STAG

SS 2: 9 lover is like a gazelle or a young *s*.
2: 17 or like a young *s*
8: 14 or like a young *s*

STAGE (STAGES)

Jos 3: 15 is at flood *s* all during harvest.

Jos 4:18 and ran at flood *s* as before.

STAGES (STAGE)

Nu 33: 1 Here are the *s* in the journey
33: 2 command Moses recorded the *s*
33: 2 journey by *s:* The Israelites set out
Eze 41: 7 the temple was built in ascending *s*,

STAGGER (STAGGERED STAGGERING STAGGERS)

Job 12:25 he makes them *s* like drunkards.
Ps 60: 3 have given us wine that makes us *s*.
Isa 19:14 they make Egypt *s*
28: 7 And these also *s* from wine
28: 7 Priests and prophets *s* from beer
28: 7 they *s* when seeing visions,
29: 9 *s*, but not from beer.
51:17 the goblet that makes men *s*.
51:22 the cup that made you *s;*
Jer 25:16 they will *s* and go mad
La 5:13 boys *s* under loads of wood.
Am 8:12 Men will *s* from sea to sea

STAGGERED (STAGGER)

Ps 107: 27 They reeled and *s* like drunken
Isa 21: 3 I am *s* by what I hear,
Am 4: 8 People *s* from town to town

STAGGERING (STAGGER)

1Sa 25:31 on his conscience the *s* burden
Pr 24:11 hold back those *s* toward slaughter.

STAGGERS (STAGGER)

Isa 3: 8 Jerusalem *s*,
19:14 as a drunkard *s* around in his vomit

STAIN (STAINED)

Jer 2:22 the *s* of your guilt is still before me
Eph 5:27 without *s* or wrinkle or any other

STAINED (STAIN)

1Ki 2: 5 and with that blood *s* the belt
Isa 59: 3 For your hands are *s* with blood,
63: 1 with his garments *s* crimson?
63: 3 and I *s* all my clothing.
Hos 6: 8 *s* with footprints of blood.
Jude :23 the clothing *s* by corrupted flesh.

STAIRS (DOWNSTAIRS STAIRWAY UPSTAIRS)

Ne 9: 4 Standing on the *s* were the Levites
Eze 40:49 It was reached by a flight of *s*,

STAIRWAY (STAIRS)

Ge 28:12 a dream in which he saw a *s* resting
1Ki 6: 8 a *s* led up to the middle level
2Ki 20:11 gone down on the *s* of Ahaz.
Isa 38: 8 gone down on the *s* of Ahaz.' "
Eze 41: 7 A *s* went up from the lowest floor

STAKE (STAKES)

Job 6:29 reconsider, for my integrity is at *s*.

STAKES (STAKE)

Isa 33:20 its *s* will never be pulled up,
54: 2 strengthen your *s*.

STALK (STALKED STALKS)

Ge 41: 5 were growing on a single *s*.
41:22 full and good, growing on a single *s*
Job 10:16 my head high, you *s* me like a lion
Hos 8: 7 The *s* has no head;
Mk 4:28 the soil produces grain—first the *s*,
Jn 19:29 sponge on a *s* of the hyssop plant,

STALKED (STALK)

La 4:18 Men *s* us at every step
Eze 32:27 the terror of these warriors had *s*

STALKS (STALK)

Jos 2: 6 and hidden them under the *s*
Ru 2:16 pull out some *s* for her
Ps 91: 6 nor the pestilence that *s*

STALL (STALLS)

Ps 50: 9 I have no need of a bull from your *s*
Mal 4: 2 leap like calves released from the *s*.
Lk 13:15 donkey from the *s* and lead it out

STALL-FED (FEED)

1Ki 4:23 ten head of *s* cattle, twenty

STALLIONS

Jer 5: 8 They are well-fed, lusty *s*,
8:16 at the neighing of their *s*
50:11 and neigh like *s*,

STALLS (STALL)

1Ki 4:26 Solomon had four thousand *s*
2Ch 9:25 Solomon had four thousand *s*
32:28 and he made *s* for various kinds
Hab 3:17 and no cattle in the *s*,

STAMMERING

Isa 32: 4 and the *s* tongue will be fluent

STAMP (STAMPED)

Eze 6:11 your hands together and *s* your feet

STAMPED (STAMP)

Eze 25: 6 clapped your hands and *s* your feet,

STAND (STANDING STANDS STOOD)

Ge 31:35 that I cannot *s* up in your presence;
Ex 9:11 The magicians could not *s*
14:13 *S* firm and you will see
17: 6 I will *s* there before you by the rock
17: 9 Tomorrow I will *s* on top of the hill
18:14 while all these people *s* around you
18:23 you will be able to *s* the strain,
30:18 with its bronze *s*, for washing.
30:28 its utensils, and the basin with its *s*.
31: 9 the basin with its *s*— and
33:21 near me where you may *s* on a rock
35:16 the bronze basin with its *s;*
38: 8 and its bronze *s* from the mirrors
39:39 all its utensils; the basin with its *s;*
40:11 and its *s* and consecrate them.
Lev 8:11 its utensils and the basin with its *s*,
26:37 able to *s* before your enemies.
Nu 5:16 and have her *s* before the LORD.
5:18 the priest has had the woman *s*
5:30 is to have her *s* before the LORD
8:13 Have the Levites *s* in front
11:16 that they may *s* there with you.
11:24 and had them *s* around the tent.
16: 9 and to *s* before the community
27:19 Have him *s* before Eleazar
27:21 He is to *s* before Eleazar the priest,
27:22 had him *s* before Eleazar the priest
30: 4 which she obligated herself will *s*.
30: 5 which she obligated herself will *s;*
30: 7 which she obligated herself will *s*.
30:11 which she obligated herself will *s*.
30:12 came from her lips will *s*.
Dt 7:24 able to *s* up against you;
9: 2 Who can *s* up against the Anakites
10: 8 to *s* before the LORD to minister
11:25 No man will be able to *s*
18: 5 out of all your tribes to *s*
19:16 If a malicious witness takes the *s*
19:17 involved in the dispute must *s*
27:12 these tribes shall *s*
27:13 these tribes shall *s* on Mount Ebal
Jos 1: 5 No one will be able to *s* up
3: 8 of the Jordan's waters, go and *s*
3:13 cut off and *s* up in a heap."
7:10 The LORD said to Joshua, "*S* up!
7:12 That is why the Israelites cannot *s*
7:13 You cannot *s* against your enemies
10:12 "O sun, *s* still over Gibeon,
20: 4 he is to *s* in the entrance
Jdg 4:20 "*S* in the doorway of the tent,"
1Sa 6:20 "Who can *s* in the presence
12: 3 Here I *s*.
12: 7 *s* here, because I am going
12:16 *s* still and see this great thing
14:40 Jonathan my son will *s* over here."
14:40 said to all the Israelites, "You *s*
17:16 and evening and took his *s*.
19: 3 *s* with my father in the field where
2Sa 1: 9 "Then he said to me, '*S* over me
2:25 and took their *s* on top of a hill.
15: 2 *s* by the side of the road leading
18:30 The king said, "*S* aside
22:34 he enables me to *s* on the heights.
23:12 Shammah took his *s* in the middle
1Ki 7:30 Each *s* had four bronze wheels
7:31 of the *s* there was an opening that
7:32 the wheels were attached to the *s*.
7:34 Each *s* had four handles, one
7:34 each corner, projecting from the *s*.
7:35 attached to the top of the *s*.
7:35 of the *s* there was a circular band
10: 8 who continually *s* before you
19:11 *s* on the mountain in the presence
2Ki 5:11 and *s* and call on the name
1Ch 11:14 But they took their *s* in the middle
23:30 also to *s* every morning to thank
2Ch 9: 7 who continually *s* before you
20: 9 we will *s* in your presence
20:17 *s* firm and see the deliverance
29:11 for the LORD has chosen you to *s*
35: 5 "*S* in the holy place with a group
Ezr 9:15 one of us can *s* in your presence."
10:13 so we cannot *s* outside.
Ne 9: 5 "*S* up and praise the LORD your
Est 6:13 you cannot *s* against him—
9: 2 No one could *s* against them,
Job 11:15 you will *s* firm and without fear.
19:25 in the end he will *s* upon the earth.
21:16 so I *s* aloof from the counsel
22:18 so I *s* aloof from the counsel
30:20 I *s* up, but you merely look at me.
30:28 I *s* up in the assembly and cry
32:16 now that they *s* there with no reply
38:14 its features *s* out like those
39:24 he cannot *s* still when the trumpet
40:12 crush the wicked where they *s*.
41:10 Who then is able to *s* against me?
Ps 1: 1 or *s* in the way of sinners
1: 5 Therefore the wicked will not *s*
2: 2 The kings of the earth take their *s*
5: 5 The arrogant cannot *s*
10: 1 Why, O LORD, do you *s* far off?
18:33 he enables me to *s* on the heights.
20: 8 but we rise up and *s* firm.
24: 3 Who may *s* in his holy place?
26:12 My feet *s* on level ground;
30: 7 you made my mountain *s* firm;
33:11 of the LORD *s* firm forever,
40: 2 and gave me a firm place to *s*.
76: 7 Who can *s* before you
78:13 he made the water *s* firm like a wall
93: 5 Your statutes *s* firm;
94:16 Who will take a *s* for me
101: 7 will *s* in my presence.
109: 6 let an accuser *s* at his right hand.
119:120 I *s* in awe of your laws.
122: 5 There the thrones for judgment *s*,
127: 1 the watchmen *s* guard in vain.
130: 3 O Lord, who could *s?*
Pr 8: 2 the paths meet, she takes her *s;*
10:25 but the righteous *s* firm forever.
27: 4 but who can *s* before jealousy?
Ecc 5: 7 Therefore *s* in awe of God.
8: 3 Do not *s* up for a bad cause,
Isa 7: 9 If you do not *s* firm in your faith,
7: 9 you will not *s* at all.' "
8:10 propose your plan, but it will not *s*,
11:10 In that day the Root of Jesse will *s*
14:24 and as I have purposed, so it will *s*.
21: 8 my lord, I *s* on the watchtower;
28:18 with the grave will not *s*.
29:23 will *s* in awe of the God of Israel.
44:11 all come together and take their *s;*
46:10 I say: My purpose will *s*,
48:13 they all *s* up together.
60:11 Your gates will always *s* open,
Jer 1:17 *S* up and say to them whatever I
1:18 wall to *s* against the whole land—
6:16 "*S* at the crossroads and look;
7: 2 "*S* at the gate of the LORD's house
7:10 and *s* before me in this house,
14: 6 Wild donkeys *s* on the barren
15: 1 and Samuel were to *s* before me,
17:19 "Go and *s* at the gate of the people,
17:19 *s* also at all the other gates
26: 2 *S* in the courtyard
30:18 the palace will *s* in its proper place.
33:18 a man to *s* before me continually
44:28 will know whose word will *s*—
44:29 of harm against you will surely *s*.'
46:15 They cannot *s*, for the LORD will
46:21 they will not *s* their ground,

Jer 48: 19 *S* by the road and watch,
48: 45 the fugitives *s* helpless,
49: 19 what shepherd can *s* against me?''
50: 44 what shepherd can *s* against me?''
51: 29 purposes against Babylon *s*—
Eze 2: 1 *s* up on your feet and I will speak
13: 5 so that it will *s* firm in the battle
22: 30 *s* before me in the gap on behalf
27: 29 will *s* on the shore.
44: 11 and sacrifices for the people and *s*
44: 15 they are to *s* before me
46: 2 the portico of the gateway and *s*
47: 10 Fishermen will *s* along the shore;
Da 8: 4 No animal could *s* against him,
8: 7 The ram was powerless to *s*
8: 25 and take his *s* against the Prince
10: 11 and *s* up, for I have now been sent
11: 1 I took my *s* to support
11: 15 will not have the strength to *s*.
11: 16 no one will be able to *s* against him.
11: 25 but he will not be able to *s*
Am 2: 15 The archer will not *s* his ground,
5: 21 I cannot *s* your assemblies.
Mic 5: 4 He will *s* and shepherd his flock
6: 1 "*S* up, plead your case
Hab 2: 1 I will *s* at my watch
3: 2 I *s* in awe of your deeds, O LORD.
Zep 3: 8 "for the day I will *s* up to testify.
Zec 14: 4 On that day his feet will *s*
Mal 3: 2 Who can *s* when he appears?
Mt 4: 5 and had him *s* on the highest point
5: 15 Instead they put it on its *s*,
12: 25 divided against itself will not *s*.
12: 26 How then can his kingdom *s*?
12: 41 The men of Nineveh will *s* up
18: 2 and had him *s* among them.
Mk 3: 3 "*S* up in front of everyone."
3: 24 itself, that kingdom cannot *s*.
3: 25 against itself, that house cannot *s*.
3: 26 he cannot *s*; his end has come.
4: 21 Instead, don't you put it on its *s*?
9: 36 and had him *s* among them.
11: 25 And when you *s* praying,
13: 9 of me you will *s* before governors
Lk 1: 19 I *s* in the presence of God,
4: 9 and had him *s* on the highest point
6: 8 Get up and *s* in front of everyone."
8: 16 it on a *s*, so that those who come
9: 47 took a little child and had him *s*
11: 18 himself, how can his kingdom *s*?
11: 32 The men of Nineveh will *s* up
11: 33 it on its *s*, so that those who come
13: 25 you will *s* outside knocking
21: 28 *s* up and lift up your heads,
21: 36 able to *s* before the Son of Man."
Jn 8: 3 They made her *s* before the group
8: 16 I *s* with the Father who sent me.
Ac 1: 11 "why do you *s* here looking
4: 26 The kings of the earth take their *s*
5: 20 Go, *s* in the temple courts," he said
6: 10 but they could not *s* up
10: 26 "*S* up," he said, "I am only a man
14: 10 "*S* up on your feet!" At that,
22: 30 and had him *s* before them.
23: 6 I *s* on trial because of my hope
25: 9 and *s* trial before me there
25: 20 and *s* trial there on these charges
26: 2 fortunate to *s* before you today
26: 16 'Now get up and *s* on your feet.
26: 22 and so I *s* here and testify to small
27: 24 You must *s* trial before Caesar;
Ro 5: 2 into this grace in which we now *s*.
9: 11 purpose in election might *s*:
11: 20 of unbelief, and you *s* by faith.
14: 4 And he will *s*, for the Lord is able
14: 4 for the Lord is able to make him *s*.
14: 10 we will all *s* before God's judgment
1Co 10: 13 out so that you can *s* up under it.
15: 1 on which you have taken your *s*.
15: 58 Therefore, my dear brothers, *s* firm
16: 13 Be on your guard; *s* firm in the faith
2Co 1: 21 who makes both us and you *s* firm
1: 24 because it is by faith you *s* firm.
2: 9 was to see if you would *s* the test
Gal 5: 1 *S* firm, then, and do not let
Eph 6: 11 God so that you can take your *s*
6: 13 you have done everything, to *s*.
6: 13 you may be able to *s* your ground,
Eph 6: 14 *S* firm then, with the belt
Php 1: 27 I will know that you *s* firm
4: 1 that is how you should *s* firm
Col 4: 12 that you may *s* firm in all the will
1Th 3: 1 So when we could *s* it no longer,
3: 5 when I could *s* it no longer,
2Th 2: 15 *s* firm and hold to the teachings we
Jas 2: 3 "You *s* there" or "Sit on the floor
5: 8 You too, be patient and *s* firm,
1Pe 5: 12 *S* fast in it.
Rev 3: 20 Here I am! I *s* at the door
6: 17 wrath has come, and who can *s*?"
8: 2 And I saw the seven angels who *s*
11: 4 and the two lampstands that *s*
18: 10 at her torment, they will *s* far off
18: 15 wealth from her will *s* far off,
18: 17 living from the sea, will *s* far off.

STANDARD (STANDARDS)

Nu 1: 52 in his own camp under his own *s*.
2: 2 man under his *s* with the banners
2: 3 are to encamp under their *s*.
2: 10 the camp of Reuben under their *s*.
2: 17 each in his own place under his *s*.
2: 18 the camp of Ephraim under their *s*.
2: 25 of the camp of Dan, under their *s*.
10: 14 of Judah went first, under their *s*.
10: 18 of Reuben went next, under their *s*.
10: 22 Ephraim went next, under their *s*.
10: 25 camp of Dan set out, under their *s*.
2Sa 14: 26 two hundred shekels by the royal *s*.
2Ch 3: 3 wide (using the cubit of the old *s*).
Isa 31: 9 of the battle *s* their commanders
Jer 4: 21 How long must I see the battle *s*
Eze 45: 11 is to be the *s* measure for both.

STANDARDS (STANDARD)

Lev 19: 35 " 'Do not use dishonest *s*
Nu 2: 31 They will set out last, under their *s*.
2: 34 way they encamped under their *s*,
Ps 74: 4 they set up their *s* as signs.
Eze 5: 7 conformed to the *s* of the nations
7: 27 by their own *s* I will judge them.
11: 12 conformed to the *s* of the nations
23: 24 punish you according to their *s*.
Jn 8: 15 judge by human *s*; I pass judgment
1Co 1: 26 many of you were wise by human *s*;
3: 18 wise by the *s* of this age,
2Co 10: 2 live by the *s* of this world.

STANDING (STAND)

Ge 18: 2 and saw three men *s* nearby.
18: 22 but Abraham remained *s*
24: 13 See, I am *s* beside this spring,
24: 30 and found him *s* by the camels
24: 31 "Why are you *s* out here? I have
24: 43 See, I am *s* beside this spring;
41: 1 Pharaoh had a dream: He was *s*
41: 17 "In my dream I was *s* on the bank
Ex 3: 5 where you are *s* is holy ground."
22: 6 or *s* grain or the whole field,
26: 32 with gold and *s* on four silver bases.
33: 10 the pillar of cloud *s* at the entrance
Nu 16: 27 and were *s* with their wives,
22: 23 angel of the LORD *s* in the road
22: 31 angel of the LORD *s* in the road
22: 34 I did not realize you were *s*
23: 6 and found him *s* beside his offering,
23: 17 and found him *s* beside his offering,
32: 14 *s* in the place of your fathers
Dt 16: 9 to put the sickle to the *s* grain.
23: 25 must not put a sickle to his *s* grain.
29: 10 All of you are *s* today
29: 12 You are *s* here in order to enter
29: 15 only with you who are *s* here
Jos 4: 10 who carried the ark remained *s*
5: 13 and saw a man *s* in front of him
5: 15 the place where you are *s* is holy."
8: 33 were *s* on both sides of the ark
20: 9 the avenger of blood prior to *s* trial
Jdg 9: 35 and was *s* at the entrance
15: 5 burned up the shocks and *s* grain,
15: 5 in the *s* grain of the Philistines.
Ru 2: 1 a man of *s*, whose name was Boaz.
2: 13 though I do not have the *s* of one
4: 11 May you have *s* in Ephratah
1Sa 9: 1 There was a Benjamite, a man of *s*,
17: 26 David asked the men *s* near him,
1Sa 19: 20 with Samuel *s* there as their leader,
22: 6 with all his officials *s* around him.
22: 9 who was *s* with Saul's officials, said
2Sa 13: 34 Now the man *s* watch looked up
1Ki 8: 14 assembly of Israel was *s* there,
10: 19 with a lion *s* beside each of them.
11: 28 Now Jeroboam was a man of *s*,
13: 1 as Jeroboam was *s* by the altar
13: 24 with both the donkey and the lion *s*
13: 25 with the lion *s* beside the body,
13: 28 with the donkey and the lion *s*
22: 19 of heaven *s* around him on his right
2Ki 9: 17 When the lookout *s* on the tower
11: 14 there was the king, *s* by the pillar,
13: 6 Also, the Asherah pole remained *s*
1Ch 21: 15 The angel of the LORD was then *s*
21: 16 of the LORD *s* between heaven
2Ch 6: 3 assembly of Israel was *s* there,
7: 6 and all the Israelites were *s*.
9: 18 with a lion *s* beside each of them.
18: 18 the host of heaven *s* on his right
23: 13 *s* by his pillar at the entrance.
Ne 8: 5 could see him because he was *s*
8: 7 Law while the people were *s* there.
9: 4 *S* on the stairs were the Levites—
Est 5: 2 When he saw Queen Esther *s*
6: 5 "Haman is *s* in the court."
Ps 122: 2 Our feet are *s*
Isa 17: 5 as when a reaper gathers the *s* grain
27: 9 will be left *s*.
Jer 28: 5 and all the people who were *s*
36: 21 and all the officials *s* beside him.
La 3: 63 Look at them! Sitting or *s*,
Eze 3: 23 the glory of the LORD was *s* there,
8: 11 son of Shaphan was *s* among them.
10: 3 Now the cherubim were *s*
40: 3 he was *s* in the gateway
43: 6 While the man was *s* beside me,
Da 7: 16 I approached one of those *s* there
8: 3 *s* beside the canal, and the horns
8: 6 the two-horned ram I had seen *s*
8: 17 came near the place where I was *s*,
10: 4 as I was *s* on the bank
10: 16 I said to the one *s* before me,
Am 7: 7 Lord was *s* by a wall that had been
9: 1 I saw the Lord *s* by the altar,
Zec 1: 8 He was *s* among the myrtle trees
1: 10 the man *s* among the myrtle trees
1: 11 who was *s* among the myrtle trees,
3: 1 and Satan *s* at his right side
3: 1 showed me Joshua the high priest *s*
3: 4 to those who were *s* before him,
3: 7 a place among these *s* here.
6: 5 going out from *s* in the presence
14: 12 while they are still *s* on their feet,
Mt 6: 5 love to pray *s* in the synagogues
12: 47 and brothers are *s* outside,
16: 28 some who are *s* here will not taste
20: 3 saw others *s* in the marketplace
20: 6 and found still others *s* around.
20: 6 'Why have you been *s* here all day
24: 15 when you see *s* in the holy place
26: 73 those *s* there went up to Peter
27: 47 some of those *s* there heard this,
Mk 3: 31 *S* outside, they sent someone
9: 1 some who are *s* here will not taste
11: 5 some people *s* there asked,
13: 14 that causes desolation' *s* where it
14: 47 one of those *s* near drew his sword
14: 69 she said again to those *s* around,
14: 70 while, those *s* near said to Peter,
15: 35 some of those *s* near heard this,
Lk 1: 11 *s* at the right side of the altar
5: 1 as Jesus was *s* by the Lake
8: 20 and brothers are *s* outside,
9: 27 some who are *s* here will not taste
9: 32 and the two men *s* with him.
19: 24 "Then he said to those *s* by,
21: 19 By *s* firm you will save yourselves.
23: 10 the teachers of the law were *s* there
Jn 8: 9 with the woman still *s* there.
11: 42 for the benefit of the people *s* here,
18: 5 (And Judas the traitor was *s* there
18: 18 Peter also was *s* with them,
19: 26 and the disciple whom he loved *s*
20: 14 around and saw Jesus *s* there,
Ac 4: 14 man who had been healed *s* there
5: 23 with the guards *s* at the doors;

Ac 5: 25 The men you put in jail are *s*
7: 33 where you are *s* is holy ground.
7: 55 Jesus *s* at the right hand of God.
7: 56 the Son of Man *s* at the right hand
13: 16 *S* up, Paul motioned with his hand
13: 50 the God-fearing women of high *s*
16: 9 a vision of a man of Macedonia *s*
22: 25 Paul said to the centurion *s* there,
23: 2 high priest Ananias ordered those *s*
23: 4 Those who were *s* near Paul said,
25: 10 "I am now *s* before Caesar's court,
1Co 10: 12 So, if you think you are *s* firm,
1Th 3: 8 since you are *s* firm in the Lord.
1Ti 3: 13 have served well gain an excellent *s*
Heb 9: 8 as the first tabernacle was still *s*.
Jas 5: 9 The Judge is *s* at the door! Brothers
1Pe 5: 9 Resist him, *s* firm in the faith,
Rev 4: 1 there before me was a door *s* open
5: 6 *s* in the center of the throne,
7: 1 After this I saw four angels *s*
7: 9 *s* before the throne and in front
7: 11 All the angels were *s*
10: 5 the angel I had seen *s* on the sea
10: 8 of the angel who is *s* on the sea
14: 1 there before me was the Lamb, *s*
15: 2 with fire and, *s* beside the sea,
19: 11 I saw heaven *s* open and there
19: 17 And I saw an angel *s* in the sun,
20: 12 great and small, *s* before the throne

STANDS (STAND)

Nu 35: 12 he *s* trial before the assembly.
Dt 17: 12 the priest who *s* ministering there
Jos 22: 19 where the LORD's tabernacle *s*,
22: 29 altar of the LORD our God that *s*
Jdg 6: 24 To this day it *s* in Ophrah
1Sa 16: 6 Surely the LORD's anointed *s* here
1Ki 7: 27 also made ten movable *s* of bronze;
7: 28 This is how the *s* were made:
7: 31 The panels of the *s* were square,
7: 37 This is the way he made the ten *s*.
7: 38 one basin to go on each of the ten *s*.
7: 39 five of the *s* on the south side
7: 43 the ten *s* with their ten basins;
2Ki 16: 17 the basins from the movable *s*.
25: 13 movable *s* and the bronze Sea that
25: 16 the Sea and the movable *s*,
2Ch 4: 14 top of the pillars); the *s*
Est 7: 9 "A gallows seventy-five feet high *s*
Job 9: 35 but as it now *s* with me, I cannot.
23: 13 he *s* alone, and who can oppose
Ps 89: 2 that your love *s* firm forever,
109: 31 For he *s* at the right hand
119: 89 it *s* firm in the heavens.
Pr 12: 7 the house of the righteous *s* firm.
SS 2: 9 Look! There he *s* behind our wall,
Isa 27: 10 The fortified city *s* desolate,
32: 8 and by noble deeds he *s*.
40: 8 but the word of our God *s* forever."
46: 7 in its place, and there it *s*.
59: 14 and righteousness *s* at a distance;
65: 6 "See, it *s* written before me:
Jer 27: 19 the movable *s* and the other
52: 17 movable *s* and the bronze Sea that
52: 20 movable *s*, which King Solomon
Da 6: 12 The king answered, "The decree *s*
Mt 10: 22 but he who *s* firm to the end will be
13: 38 and the good seed *s* for the sons
24: 13 but he who *s* firm to the end will be
Mk 13: 13 but he who *s* firm to the end will be
Lk 8: 14 among thorns *s* for those who hear,
8: 15 the seed on good soil *s* for those
Jn 1: 26 among you *s* one you do not know.
3: 18 not believe *s* condemned already
16: 11 of this world now *s* condemned.
Ac 4: 10 this man *s* before you completely
Ro 14: 4 To his own master he *s* or falls.
Gal 4: 25 Hagar *s* for Mount Sinai in Arabia
2Ti 2: 19 God's solid foundation *s* firm,
Heb 4: 1 promise of entering his rest still *s*,
10: 11 Day after day every priest *s*
1Pe 1: 25 but the word of the Lord *s* forever
Rev 19: 8 (Fine linen *s* for the righteous acts

STANDSTILL

Ezr 4: 24 came to a *s* until the second year

STAR (STARGAZERS STARRY STARS)

Nu 24: 17 A *s* will come out of Jacob;
Isa 14: 12 O morning *s*, son of the dawn!
Am 5: 26 the *s* of your god—
Mt 2: 2 We saw his *s* in the east
2: 7 the exact time the *s* had appeared.
2: 9 and the *s* they had seen
2: 10 they saw the *s*, they were
Ac 7: 43 and the *s* of your god Rephan,
1Co 15: 41 and *s* differs from *s* in splendor.
2Pe 1: 19 the morning *s* rises in your hearts.
Rev 2: 28 I will also give him the morning *s*.
8: 10 and a great *s*, blazing like a torch,
8: 11 the name of the *s* is Wormwood.
9: 1 The *s* was given the key to the shaft
9: 1 and I saw a *s* that had fallen
22: 16 and the bright Morning *S*."

STARE (STARED STARES)

Ps 22: 17 people *s* and gloat over me.
SS 1: 6 Do not *s* at me because I am dark,
Isa 14: 16 Those who see you *s* at you,
Ac 3: 12 Why do you *s* at us as

STARED (STARE)

2Ki 8: 11 He *s* at him with a fixed gaze
Jn 13: 22 His disciples *s* at one another,
Ac 10: 4 "Cornelius!" Cornelius *s* at him

STARES (STARE)

Ps 55: 3 at the *s* of the wicked;

STARGAZERS (STAR)

Isa 47: 13 those *s* who make predictions

STARRY (STAR)

2Ki 17: 16 They bowed down to all the *s* hosts
21: 3 He bowed down to all the *s* hosts
21: 5 he built altars to all the *s* hosts.
23: 4 and Asherah and all the *s* hosts.
23: 5 constellations and to all the *s* hosts.
2Ch 33: 3 He bowed down to all the *s* hosts
33: 5 he built altars to all the *s* hosts.
Ne 9: 6 heavens, and all their *s* host,
Ps 33: 6 their *s* host by the breath
Isa 34: 4 all the *s* host will fall
40: 26 He who brings out the *s* host one
45: 12 I marshaled their *s* hosts.
Jer 19: 13 on the roofs to all the *s* hosts
Da 8: 10 and it threw some of the *s* host
Zep 1: 5 housetops to worship the *s* host,

STARS (STAR)

Ge 1: 16 He also made the *s*.
15: 5 up at the heavens and count the *s*—
22: 17 as numerous as the *s* in the sky and
26: 4 as numerous as the *s* in the sky
37: 9 eleven *s* were bowing down to me."
Ex 32: 13 as numerous as the *s* in the sky
Dt 1: 10 as many as the *s* in the sky.
4: 19 the *s*— all the heavenly array—
10: 22 as numerous as the *s* in the sky.
17: 3 or the moon or the *s* of the sky,
28: 62 as the *s* in the sky will be left
Jdg 5: 20 From the heavens the *s* fought,
1Ch 27: 23 as numerous as the *s* in the sky.
Ne 4: 21 light of dawn till the *s* came out.
9: 23 as numerous as the *s* in the sky,
Job 3: 9 May its morning *s* become dark;
9: 7 he seals off the light of the *s*.
22: 12 And see how lofty are the highest *s*
25: 5 and the *s* are not pure in his eyes,
38: 7 while the morning *s* sang together
Ps 8: 3 the moon and the *s*,
136: 9 the moon and *s* to govern the night;
147: 4 He determines the number of the *s*
148: 3 praise him, all you shining *s*.
Ecc 12: 2 and the moon and the *s* grow dark,
SS 6: 10 majestic as the *s* in procession?
Isa 13: 10 *s* of heaven and their constellations
14: 13 throne above the *s* of God;
34: 4 All the *s* of the heavens will be
Jer 8: 2 and all the *s* of the heavens,
31: 35 who decrees the moon and *s*
33: 22 as countless as the *s* of the sky and
Eze 32: 7 and darken their *s*;
Da 12: 3 like the *s* for ever and ever.
Joel 2: 10 and the *s* no longer shine.
Joel 3: 15 and the *s* no longer shine.
Ob : 4 and make your nest among the *s*,
Na 3: 16 more than the *s* of the sky,
Mt 24: 29 the *s* will fall from the sky,
Mk 13: 25 the *s* will fall from the sky,
Lk 21: 25 signs in the sun, moon and *s*.
Ac 27: 20 nor *s* appeared for many days
1Co 15: 41 moon another and the *s* another;
Php 2: 15 in which you shine like *s*
Heb 11: 12 as numerous as the *s* in the sky and
Jude : 13 up their shame; wandering *s*,
Rev 1: 16 In his right hand he held seven *s*,
1: 20 The seven *s* are the angels
1: 20 mystery of the seven *s* that you saw
2: 1 words of him who holds the seven *s*
3: 1 spirits of God and the seven *s*.
6: 13 and the *s* in the sky fell to earth,
8: 12 and a third of the *s*, so that a third
12: 1 a crown of twelve *s* on her head.
12: 4 a third of the *s* out of the sky

START (STARTED STARTING)

Nu 34: 3 your southern boundary will *s*
1Sa 9: 5 the donkeys and *s* worrying about
1Ki 20: 14 "And who will *s* the battle?"
Ne 2: 18 They replied, "Let us *s* rebuilding."
2: 20 We his servants will *s* rebuilding,

STARTED (START)

Ge 33: 16 So that day Esau *s* on his way back
Ex 4: 20 on a donkey and *s* back to Egypt.
22: 6 the one who *s* the fire must make
Nu 11: 4 and again the Israelites *s* wailing
16: 46 from the LORD; the plague has *s*."
16: 47 The plague had already *s*
Jos 2: 23 Then the two men *s* back.
15: 2 Their southern boundary *s*
15: 5 The northern boundary *s*
18: 8 As the men *s* on their way
Est 6: 13 before whom your downfall has *s*,
Jer 37: 12 Jeremiah *s* to leave the city to go
Da 8: 9 which *s* small but grew in power
Jnh 3: 4 Jonah *s* into the city, going a day's
Mk 10: 17 As Jesus *s* on his way, a man ran up
Lk 9: 46 An argument *s* among the disciples
23: 5 He *s* in Galilee and has come all
Jn 8: 6 and *s* to write on the ground
20: 3 the other disciple *s* for the tomb.
Ac 8: 27 So he *s* out, and on his way he met
10: 23 The next day Peter *s* out with them
17: 5 formed a mob and *s* a riot
21: 38 you the Egyptian who *s* a revolt

STARTING (START)

2Ki 15: 16 At that time Menahem, *s* out
Pr 17: 14 *S* a quarrel is like breaching a dam;
Eze 21: 19 both *s* from the same country.
Mt 27: 24 but that instead an uproar was *s*,

STARTLE (STARTLED)

Job 18: 11 Terrors *s* him on every side

STARTLED (STARTLE)

Ru 3: 8 of the night something *s* the man,
Lk 1: 12 he was *s* and was gripped with fear.
24: 37 They were *s* and frightened,

STARVATION (STARVE)

Jer 15: 2 those for *s*, to *s*;

STARVE (STARVATION STARVING)

Ex 16: 3 desert to *s* this entire assembly
Jer 38: 9 where he will *s* to death

STARVING (STARVE)

Ge 42: 19 back for your *s* households.
42: 33 take food for your *s* households
2Ki 7: 12 They know we are *s*;
Pr 6: 30 to satisfy his hunger when he is *s*.
Lk 15: 17 to spare, and here I am *s* to death!

STATE (STATED STATEMENT STATEMENTS)

Jos 20: 4 and *s* his case before the elders
Job 23: 4 I would *s* my case before him
33: 26 restored by God to his righteous *s*.
Isa 14: 18 All the kings of the nations lie in *s*,
43: 26 *s* the case for your innocence.

Lk 1: 48 of the humble *s* of his servant.
Ac 24: 20 are here should *s* what crime they

STATED (STATE)

Ac 13: 34 never to decay, is *s* in these words:
13: 35 So it is *s* elsewhere:
Ro 9: 9 For this was how the promise was *s*

STATELY

Pr 30: 29 four that move with *s* bearing:
30: 29 "There are three things that are *s*
Isa 2: 16 and every *s* vessel.
Zec 11: 2 the *s* trees are ruined!

STATEMENT (STATE)

Ac 20: 38 most was his *s* that they would
28: 25 after Paul had made this final *s*:

STATEMENTS (STATE)

Mk 14: 56 him, but their *s* did not agree.

STATION (STATIONED)

2Ki 11: 8 *S* yourselves around the king,
2Ch 23: 7 The Levites are to *s* themselves
Jer 51: 12 *s* the watchmen,
Hab 2: 1 and *s* myself on the ramparts;

STATIONED (STATION)

Jdg 20: 22 where they had *s* themselves
2Ki 3: 21 could bear arms was called up and *s*
11: 11 *s* themselves around the king—
1Ch 9: 18 Shallum their chief being *s*
9: 27 They would spend the night *s*
16: 42 sons of Jeduthun were *s* at the gate.
2Ch 17: 2 He *s* troops in all the fortified cities
17: 19 besides those he *s* in the fortified
23: 10 He *s* all the men, each
23: 19 also *s* doorkeepers at the gates
29: 25 He *s* the Levites in the temple
33: 14 He *s* military commanders
Ne 4: 13 Therefore I *s* some of the people
13: 11 I called them together and *s* them
13: 19 I *s* some of my own men
Eze 21: 15 I have *s* the sword for slaughter

STATUE

Da 2: 31 and there before you stood a large *s*
2: 31 dazzling *s*, awesome in appearance
2: 32 The head of the *s* was made
2: 34 It struck the *s* on its feet of iron
2: 35 that struck the *s* became a huge

STATURE

1Sa 2: 26 boy Samuel continued to grow in *s*
SS 7: 7 Your *s* is like that of the palm,
Lk 2: 52 And Jesus grew in wisdom and *s*,

STATUTE (STATUTES)

1Sa 30: 25 David made this a *s* and ordinance
Ps 81: 5 He established it as a *s* for Joseph
122: 4 according to the *s* given to Israel.

STATUTES (STATUTE)

1Ki 3: 3 to the *s* of his father David,
3: 14 and obey my *s* and commands
11: 33 nor kept my *s* and laws as David,
11: 34 who observed my commands and *s*
11: 38 right in my eyes by keeping my *s*
Ps 19: 7 *s* of the LORD are trustworthy,
78: 5 He decreed *s* for Jacob
78: 56 they did not keep his *s*.
89: 30 and do not follow my *s*,
93: 5 Your *s* stand firm;
99: 7 they kept his *s* and the decrees he
119: 2 Blessed are they who keep his *s*
119: 14 I rejoice in following your *s*
119: 22 for I keep your *s*.
119: 24 Your *s* are my delight;
119: 31 I hold fast to your *s*, O LORD;
119: 36 Turn my heart toward your *s*
119: 46 I will speak of your *s* before kings
119: 59 and have turned my steps to your *s*.
119: 79 those who understand your *s*.
119: 88 and I will obey the *s* of your mouth.
119: 95 but I will ponder your *s*.
119: 99 for I meditate on your *s*.
119:111 Your *s* are my heritage forever;
119:119 therefore I love your *s*.
Ps 119:125 that I may understand your *s*.
119:129 Your *s* are wonderful;
119:138 The *s* you have laid
119:144 Your *s* are forever right;
119:146 and I will keep your *s*.
119:152 Long ago I learned from your *s*
119:157 but I have not turned from your *s*.
119:167 I obey your *s*,
119:168 I obey your precepts and your *s*,
132: 12 and the *s* I teach them,
Isa 24: 5 violated the *s*
Eze 20: 18 Do not follow the *s* of your fathers
20: 25 them over to *s* that were not good
Mic 6: 16 You have observed the *s* of Omri

STEADFAST (STEADFASTLY)

Ps 51: 10 and renew a *s* spirit within me.
57: 7 My heart is *s*, O God,
57: 7 my heart is *s*;
108: 1 My heart is *s*, O God;
111: 8 They are *s* for ever and ever,
112: 7 his heart is *s*, trusting in the LORD
119: 5 Oh, that my ways were *s*
Isa 26: 3 him whose mind is *s*,
1Pe 5: 10 and make you strong, firm and *s*.

STEADFASTLY (STEADFAST)

2Ch 27: 6 he walked *s* before the LORD his

STEADY

Ge 49: 24 But his bow remained *s*,
Ex 17: 12 so that his hands remained *s*
1Ch 13: 9 reached out his hand to *s* the ark,
Isa 35: 3 *s* the knees that give way;

STEAL (STEALING STEALS STOLE STOLEN)

Ge 31: 30 But why did you *s* my gods?"
44: 8 So why would we *s* silver
Ex 20: 15 "You shall not *s*.
Lev 19: 11 " 'Do not *s*.
Dt 5: 19 "You shall not *s*.
2Sa 19: 3 as men *s* in who are ashamed
19: 41 *s* the king away and bring him
Ps 69: 4 what I did not *s*.
104: 22 The sun rises, and they *s* away;
Pr 30: 9 Or I may become poor and *s*,
Jer 7: 9 " 'Will you *s* and murder, commit
23: 30 am against the prophets who *s*
49: 9 would they not *s* only as much
Ob : 5 would they not *s* only as much
Mt 6: 19 and where thieves break in and *s*.
6: 20 where thieves do not break in and *s*
19: 18 do not *s*, do not give false
27: 64 disciples may come and *s* the body
Mk 10: 19 do not *s*, do not give false
Lk 18: 20 do not *s*, do not give false
Jn 10: 10 The thief comes only to *s* and kill
Ro 2: 21 preach against stealing, do you *s*?
13: 9 "Do not *s*," "Do not covet,"
Eph 4: 28 has been stealing must *s* no longer,
Tit 2: 10 to them, and not to *s* from them,

STEALING (STEAL)

Hos 4: 2 *s* and adultery;
Ro 2: 21 You who preach against *s*,
Eph 4: 28 He who has been *s* must steal no

STEALS (STEAL)

Ex 22: 1 "If a man *s* an ox or a sheep
Job 24: 14 in the night he *s* forth like a thief.
Pr 6: 30 Men do not despise a thief if he *s*

STEEDS

Jdg 5: 22 galloping, galloping go his mighty *s*
Jer 46: 4 mount the *s*!
47: 3 sound of the hoofs of galloping *s*,

STEEP (STEEPED)

Isa 7: 19 all come and settle in the *s* ravines
Mt 8: 32 down the *s* bank into the lake
Mk 5: 13 rushed down the *s* bank
Lk 8: 33 down the *s* bank into the lake

STEEPED (STEEP)

Jn 9: 34 "You were *s* in sin at birth;

STEERED

Jas 3: 4 they are *s* by a very small rudder

STENCH (STINK)

Ge 34: 30 by making me a *s* to the Canaanites
Ex 5: 21 You have made us a *s* to Pharaoh
1Sa 13: 4 and now Israel has become a *s*
2Sa 10: 6 realized that they had become a *s*
16: 21 that you have made yourself a *s*
1Ch 19: 6 realized that they had become a *s*
Isa 3: 24 of fragrance there will be a *s*;
34: 3 their dead bodies will send up a *s*;
Joel 2: 20 And its *s* will go up;
Am 4: 10 nostrils with the *s* of your camps,

STEP (FOOTSTEPS OVERSTEP STEPPED STEPPING STEPS)

Dt 21: 5 the sons of Levi, shall *s* forward,
1Sa 5: 5 at Ashdod *s* on the threshold.
20: 3 there is only a *s* between me
1Ki 10: 20 one at either end of each *s*.
2Ch 9: 19 one at either end of each *s*.
Job 18: 7 The vigor of his *s* is weakened;
18: 11 and dog his every *s*.
31: 4 and count my every *s*?
31: 37 give him an account of my every *s*;
34: 21 he sees their every *s*.
Ps 89: 51 which they have mocked every *s*
La 4: 18 Men stalked us at every *s*
Eze 26: 16 the princes of the seacoast will *s*
Gal 5: 25 let us keep in *s* with the Spirit.

STEPHANAS

1Co 1: 16 I also baptized the household of *S*;
16: 15 of *S* were the first converts
16: 17 I was glad when *S*, Fortunatus

STEPHEN

Ac 6: 5 They chose *S*, a man full of faith
6: 8 Now *S*, a man full of God's grace
6: 9 These men began to argue with *S*,
6: 11 "We have heard *S* speak words
6: 12 They seized *S* and brought him
6: 15 the Sanhedrin looked intently at *S*,
7: 55 But *S*, full of the Holy Spirit,
7: 59 they were stoning him, *S* prayed,
8: 2 Godly men buried *S* and mourned
11: 19 in connection with *S* traveled
22: 20 blood of your martyr *S* was shed,

STEPPED (STEP)

Lev 9: 22 the fellowship offering, he *s* down.
Nu 12: 5 When both of them *s* forward,
Jdg 8: 21 Gideon *s* forward and killed them,
19: 27 and *s* out to continue on his way,
1Sa 17: 23 *s* out from his lines and shouted his
2Sa 18: 30 So he *s* aside and stood there.
20: 8 As he *s* forward, it dropped out
1Ki 14: 17 as she *s* over the threshold
18: 36 the prophet Elijah *s* forward
Job 29: 8 the young men saw me and *s* aside
Jer 26: 17 of the elders of the land *s* forward
Mt 9: 1 Jesus *s* into a boat, crossed over
26: 50 the men *s* forward, seized Jesus
Lk 8: 27 When Jesus *s* ashore, he was met

STEPPING (STEP)

Pr 7: 22 like a deer *s* into a noose
Zep 1: 9 all who avoid *s* on the threshold,

STEPS (STEP)

Ex 20: 26 And do not go up to my altar on *s*,
2Sa 6: 13 ark of the LORD had taken six *s*,
1Ki 10: 19 throne had six *s*, and its back had
10: 20 Twelve lions stood on the six *s*,
2Ki 9: 13 them under him on the bare *s*.
20: 9 Shall the shadow go forward ten *s*,
20: 9 or shall it go back ten *s*?"
20: 10 for the shadow to go forward ten *s*
20: 10 "Rather, have it go back ten *s*."
20: 11 go back the ten *s* it had gone
2Ch 9: 11 to make *s* for the temple
9: 18 throne had six *s*, and a footstool
9: 19 Twelve lions stood on the six *s*,
Ne 3: 15 as the *s* going down from the City
12: 37 they continued directly up the *s*
Job 14: 16 Surely then you will count my *s*
23: 11 My feet have closely followed his *s*

Job 31: 7 if my *s* have turned from the path,
Ps 17: 5 My *s* have held to your paths;
37: 23 whose *s* he has made firm;
56: 6 they watch my *s*,
85: 13 and prepares the way for his *s*.
119: 59 have turned my *s* to your statutes.
Pr 4: 12 your *s* will not be hampered;
5: 5 her *s* lead straight to the grave.
14: 15 prudent man gives thought to his *s*.
16: 9 but the LORD determines his *s*.
20: 24 A man's *s* are directed
Ecc 5: 1 Guard your *s* when you go
Isa 3: 16 tripping along with mincing *s*,
38: 8 sun go back the ten *s* it has gone
38: 8 went back the ten *s* it had gone
Jer 10: 23 it is not for man to direct his *s*.
Eze 40: 6 He climbed its *s* and measured
40: 22 Seven *s* led up to it, with its portico
40: 26 Seven *s* led up to it, with its portico
40: 31 its jambs, and eight *s* led up
40: 34 either side, and eight *s* led up to it.
40: 37 either side, and eight *s* led up to it.
40: 40 near the *s* at the entrance
40: 40 side of the *s* were two tables.
43: 17 The *s* of the altar face east."
Hab 3: 5 pestilence followed his *s*.
Ac 21: 35 Paul reached the *s*, the violence
21: 40 Paul stood on the *s* and motioned
1Pe 2: 21 that you should follow in his *s*.

STERILE

Jdg 13: 2 a wife who was *s* and remained
13: 3 and said, "You are *s* and childless,

STERN (STERNNESS)

Pr 15: 10 *S* discipline awaits him who leaves
Mk 4: 38 Jesus was in the *s*, sleeping
Ac 27: 29 dropped four anchors from the *s*
27: 41 and the *s* was broken to pieces

STERN-FACED (FACE)

Da 8: 23 a *s* king, a master of intrigue,

STERNNESS (STERN)

Ro 11: 22 and *s* of God: *s* to those who fell,

STEW

Ge 25: 29 when Jacob was cooking some *s*,
25: 30 let me have some of that red *s!*
25: 34 Esau some bread and some lentil *s*.
2Ki 4: 38 and cook some *s* for these men."
4: 39 he cut them up into the pot of *s*,
4: 40 The *s* was poured out for the men,
Hag 2: 12 that fold touches some bread or *s*,

STEWARD (STEWARDS)

Ge 43: 16 he said to the *s* of his house,
43: 19 So they went up to Joseph's *s*
43: 24 The *s* took the men
44: 1 instructions to the *s* of his house:
44: 4 the city when Joseph said to his *s*,
44: 12 Then the *s* proceeded to search,
2Sa 16: 1 there was Ziba, the *s*
19: 17 with Ziba, the *s* of Saul's household
Isa 22: 15 "Go, say to this *s*,

STEWARDS (STEWARD)

Est 1: 8 the king instructed all the wine *s*

STICK (STICKING STICKS STUCK)

2Ki 6: 6 Elisha cut a *s* and threw it there,
Job 33: 21 his bones, once hidden, now *s* out.
38: 38 and the clods of earth *s* together?
Isa 28: 27 and cummin with a *s*.
57: 4 and *s* out your tongue?
La 4: 8 it has become as dry as a *s*.
Eze 3: 26 I will make your tongue *s*
29: 4 of your streams *s* to your scales.
37: 16 Then take another *s* of wood,
37: 16 and write on it, 'Ephraim's *s*,
37: 16 take a *s* of wood and write on it,
37: 17 Join them together into one *s*
37: 19 I am going to take the *s* of Joseph—
37: 19 making them a single *s* of wood,
37: 19 to Judah's *s*, making them a single
Hos 4: 12 and are answered by a *s* of wood.
Am 4: 11 You were like a burning *s* snatched
Zec 3: 2 not this man a burning *s* snatched
Mt 27: 48 put it on a *s*, and offered it to Jesus
Mk 15: 36 put it on a *s*, and offered it to Jesus

STICKING (STICK)

Eze 29: 4 with all the fish *s* to your scales.

STICKS (STICK)

1Sa 17: 43 that you come at me with *s?*"
1Ki 17: 10 a widow was there gathering *s*.
17: 12 I am gathering a few *s* to take home
Ps 22: 15 and my tongue *s* to the roof
Pr 18: 24 there is a friend who *s* closer
La 4: 4 *s* to the roof of its mouth;
Eze 37: 20 their eyes the *s* you have written
Lk 10: 11 the dust of your town that *s*

STIFF-NECKED (NECK)

Ex 32: 9 to Moses, "and they are a *s* people.
33: 3 because you are a *s* people
33: 5 the Israelites, 'You are a *s* people.
34: 9 Although this is a *s* people,
Dt 9: 6 to possess, for you are a *s* people.
9: 13 and they are a *s* people indeed!
10: 16 and do not be *s* any longer.
31: 27 know how rebellious and *s* you are.
2Ki 17: 14 and were as *s* as their fathers,
2Ch 30: 8 Do not be *s*, as your fathers were;
36: 13 He became *s* and hardened his
Ne 9: 16 forefathers, became arrogant and *s*,
9: 17 became *s* and in their rebellion
9: 29 became *s* and refused to listen.
Pr 29: 1 A man who remains *s*
Jer 7: 26 They were *s* and did more evil
17: 23 they were *s* and would not listen
19: 15 they were *s* and would not listen
Ac 7: 51 *s* people, with uncircumcised

STIFLING

Am 1: 11 *s* all compassion,

STILL (STILLED)

Ex 14: 14 for you; you need only to be *s*."
15: 16 they will be as *s* as a stone—
Jos 10: 12 "O sun, stand *s* over Gibeon,
10: 13 So the sun stood *s*,
1Sa 12: 16 stand *s* and see this great thing
Ne 8: 11 "Be *s*, for this is a sacred day.
Ps 17: 14 You *s* the hunger of those you
37: 7 Be *s* before the LORD
39: 2 But when I was silent and *s*,
46: 10 "Be *s*, and know that I am God;
76: 6 both horse and chariot lie *s*.
83: 1 be not quiet, O God, be not *s*.
89: 9 its waves mount up, you *s* them.
Jer 47: 6 cease and be *s*.'
Eze 1: 21 creatures stood *s*, they also stood *s;*
1: 24 When they stood *s*, they lowered
10: 17 When the cherubim stood *s*,
10: 17 stood *s;* and when the cherubim
Hab 3: 11 and moon stood *s* in the heavens
Zec 2: 13 Be *s* before the LORD, all mankind
Mk 4: 39 said to the waves, "Quiet! Be *s!*"
Lk 7: 14 and those carrying it stood *s*.
24: 17 They stood *s*, their faces downcast.

STILLBORN (BEAR)

Nu 12: 12 not let her be like a *s* infant coming
Job 3: 16 hidden in the ground like a *s* child,
Ps 58: 8 like a *s* child, may they not see
Ecc 6: 3 I say that a *s* child is better

STILLED (STILL)

Ps 65: 7 who *s* the roaring of the seas,
107: 29 He *s* the storm to a whisper;
131: 2 But I have *s* and quieted my soul;
Isa 16: 9 and over your harvests have been *s*.
24: 8 The gaiety of the tambourines is *s*,
25: 5 so the song of the ruthless is *s*.
1Co 13: 8 they will be *s;* where there is

STIMULATE

2Pe 3: 1 as reminders to *s* you

STING (STINGING STINGS)

1Co 15: 55 Where, O death, is your *s?*"
15: 56 The *s* of death is sin, and the power
Rev 9: 5 that of the *s* of a scorpion

STINGING (STING)

Eze 5: 15 and in wrath and with *s* rebuke.

STINGS (STING)

Rev 9: 10 They had tails and *s* like scorpions,

STINGY

Pr 23: 6 Do not eat the food of a *s* man,
28: 22 A *s* man is eager to get rich

STINK (STENCH)

Ex 7: 18 river will *s;* the Egyptians will not
16: 24 and it did not *s* or get maggots in it.
Isa 19: 6 The canals will *s;*

STIPULATIONS

Dt 4: 45 These are the *s*, decrees
6: 17 the *s* and decrees he has given you.
6: 20 "What is the meaning of the *s*,
Jer 44: 23 his law or his decrees or his *s*,

STIR (STIRRED STIRRING STIRS)

Jdg 13: 25 began to *s* him while he was
Ne 4: 8 and *s* up trouble against it.
Ps 78: 38 and did not *s* up his full wrath.
140: 2 and *s* up war every day.
Pr 29: 8 Mockers *s* up a city,
Isa 13: 17 I will *s* up against them the Medes,
19: 2 "I will *s* up Egyptian
42: 13 like a warrior he will *s* up his zeal;
Jer 50: 9 For I will *s* up and bring
51: 1 I will *s* up the spirit of a destroyer
Eze 23: 22 I will *s* up your lovers against you,
24: 8 To *s* up wrath and take revenge
Da 11: 2 he will *s* up everyone
11: 25 large army he will *s* up his strength
Hos 7: 4 whose fire the baker need not *s*
Am 6: 14 "I will *s* up a nation against you,
Php 1: 17 that they can *s* up trouble

STIRRED (STIR)

Ru 1: 19 the whole town was *s*
1Ki 14: 22 they committed they *s* up his
1Ch 5: 26 So the God of Israel *s* up the spirit
Ps 45: 1 My heart is *s* by a noble theme
107: 25 For he spoke and *s* up a tempest
Ecc 12: 5 and desire no longer is *s*.
Isa 41: 2 "Who has *s* up one from the east,
41: 25 "I have *s* up one from the north,
Jer 6: 22 a great nation is being *s* up
50: 41 are being *s* up from the ends
51: 11 The LORD has *s* up the kings
Eze 32: 13 no longer to be *s* by the foot of man
Am 8: 8 it will be *s* up and then sink
Hag 1: 14 So the LORD *s* up the spirit
Mt 21: 10 the whole city was *s* and asked,
Mk 15: 11 But the chief priests *s* up the crowd
Jn 5: 7 into the pool when the water is *s*.
Ac 6: 12 So they *s* up the people
13: 50 They *s* up persecution against Paul
14: 2 refused to believe *s* up the Gentiles
21: 27 They *s* up the whole crowd
2Co 9: 2 and your enthusiasm has *s* most

STIRRING (STIR)

Jdg 9: 31 and are *s* up the city against you.
Ne 13: 18 Now you are *s* up more wrath
Pr 30: 33 so *s* up anger produces strife."
Ac 17: 13 agitating the crowds and *s* them up.
24: 5 *s* up riots among the Jews all
24: 12 or *s* up a crowd in the synagogues

STIRS (STIR)

Dt 32: 11 like an eagle that *s* up its nest
Job 41: 31 *s* up the sea like a pot of ointment
Ps 147: 18 he *s* up his breezes, and the waters
Pr 6: 14 he always *s* up dissension.
6: 19 and a man who *s* up dissension
10: 12 Hatred *s* up dissension,
15: 1 but a harsh word *s* up anger.
15: 18 hot-tempered man *s* up dissension,
16: 28 A perverse man *s* up dissension,
28: 25 A greedy man *s* up dissension,
29: 22 An angry man *s* up dissension,
Jer 31: 35 who *s* up the sea
Lk 23: 5 "He *s* up the people all over Judea

STOCK (STOCKS)
Job 5:24 you will take *s* of your property
Jer 2:21 of sound and reliable *s*.

STOCKS (STOCK)
Jer 20: 2 and put in the *s* at the Upper Gate
20: 3 Pashhur released him from the *s*,
29:26 who acts like a prophet into the *s*
Ac 16:24 and fastened their feet in the *s*.

STOIC
Ac 17:18 *S* philosophers began to dispute

STOLE (STEAL)
Ge 31:19 Rachel *s* her father's household
2Sa 15: 6 and so he *s* the hearts of the men
19: 3 The men *s* into the city that day
2Ki 11: 2 *s* him away from among the royal
2Ch 22:11 *s* him away from among the royal
Mt 28:13 *s* him away while we were asleep.'

STOLEN (STEAL)
Ge 30:33 dark-colored will be considered *s*."
31:32 know that Rachel had *s* the gods.
31:39 from me for whatever was *s* by day
Ex 22: 4 "If the *s* animal is found alive
22: 7 and they are *s* from the neighbor's
22:12 But if the animal was *s*
Lev 6: 2 to him or left in his care or *s*,
6: 4 he must return what he has *s*
Jos 7:11 they have *s*, they have lied,
Job 24: 2 they pasture flocks they have *s*.
Ps 62:10 or take pride in *s* goods;
Pr 9:17 "*S* water is sweet;
SS 4: 9 You have *s* my heart, my sister,
4: 9 you have *s* my heart
Eze 33:15 what he has *s*, follows the decrees
Hab 2: 6 " 'Woe to him who piles up *s* goods

STOMACH (STOMACHS)
2Sa 2:23 the butt of his spear into Asahel's *s*,
3:27 Joab stabbed him in the *s*,
4: 6 and they stabbed him in the *s*.
Job 20:14 yet his food will turn sour in his *s*;
20:15 God will make his *s* vomit them up.
Pr 13:25 but the *s* of the wicked goes hungry
18:20 of his mouth a man's *s* is filled;
Jer 30: 6 hands on his *s* like a woman
51:34 and filled his *s* with our delicacies,
Eze 3: 3 I am giving you and fill your *s*
Mic 6:14 your *s* will still be empty.
Mt 15:17 enters the mouth goes into the *s*
Mk 7:19 go into his heart but into his *s*,
Lk 15:16 He longed to fill his *s*
1Co 6:13 Food for the *s* and the *s* for food"—
Php 3:19 their god is their *s*, and their glory
1Ti 5:23 of your *s* and your frequent
Rev 10: 9 It will turn your *s* sour,
10:10 I had eaten it, my *s* turned sour.

STOMACHS (STOMACH)
Eze 7:19 satisfy their hunger or fill their *s*
Am 4: 6 "I gave you empty *s* in every city

STONE (CAPSTONE CORNERSTONE CORNERSTONES FIELDSTONES MILLSTONE MILLSTONES SLINGSTONES STONE'S STONECUTTERS STONED STONEMASONS STONES STONING TOMBSTONE)
Ge 11: 3 They used brick instead of *s*,
28:18 Jacob took the *s* he had placed
28:22 This *s* that I have set up
29: 2 The *s* over the mouth
29: 3 shepherds would roll the *s* away
29: 3 they would return the *s* to its place
29: 8 and the *s* has been rolled away
29:10 rolled the *s* away from the mouth
31:45 So Jacob took a *s* and set it up
35:14 Jacob set up a *s* pillar
Ex 7:19 in the wooden buckets and *s* jars."
8:26 in their eyes, will they not *s* us?
15: 5 they sank to the depths like a *s*.
15:16 they will be as still as a *s*—
17: 4 They are almost ready to *s* me."
17:12 they took a *s* and put it under him
21:18 and one hits the other with a *s*
Ex 24: 4 set up twelve *s* pillars representing
24:12 and I will give you the tablets of *s*,
28:10 on one *s* and the remaining six
31:18 the tablets of *s* inscribed
34: 1 "Chisel out two *s* tablets like
34: 4 and he carried the two *s* tablets
34: 4 chiseled out two *s* tablets like
Lev 20: 2 of the community are to *s* him.
20:27 are to *s* them; their blood will be
24:14 and the entire assembly is to *s* him.
24:16 The entire assembly must *s* him.
26: 1 do not place a carved *s* in your land
26: 1 or a sacred *s* for yourselves,
Nu 15:35 The whole assembly must *s* him
35:17 if anyone has a *s* in his hand that
35:23 drops a *s* on him that could kill him
Dt 4:13 then wrote them on two *s* tablets.
4:28 man-made gods of wood and *s*,
5:22 he wrote them on two *s* tablets
9: 9 to receive the tablets of *s*,
9:10 gave me two *s* tablets inscribed
9:11 LORD gave me the two *s* tablets,
10: 1 "Chisel out two *s* tablets like
10: 3 and chiseled out two *s* tablets like
13:10 *S* him to death, because he tried
16:22 and do not erect a sacred *s*,
17: 5 and *s* that person to death.
19:14 your neighbor's boundary *s* set up
21:21 of his town shall *s* him to death.
22:21 of her town shall *s* her to death.
22:24 of that town and *s* them to death—
27:17 moves his neighbor's boundary *s*."
28:36 other gods, gods of wood and *s*.
28:64 of wood and *s*, which neither you
29:17 images and idols of wood and *s*,
Jos 4: 5 is to take up a *s* on his shoulder,
7: 5 as the *s* quarries and struck them
15: 6 the *S* of Bohan son of Reuben.
18:17 and ran down to the *S* of Bohan son
24:26 Then he took a large *s*
24:27 "This *s* will be a witness against us.
Jdg 9: 5 and on one *s* murdered his seventy
9:18 his seventy sons on a single *s*,
20:16 of whom could sling a *s* at a hair
1Sa 7:12 Then Samuel took a *s* and set it up
14:33 "Roll a large *s* over here at once."
17:49 The *s* sank into his forehead,
17:49 into his bag and taking out a *s*,
17:50 the Philistine with a sling and a *s*;
20:19 began, and wait by the *s* Ezel.
20:41 up from the south side of the *s*
25:37 failed him and he became like a *s*.
1Ki 1: 9 fattened calves at the *S* of Zoheleth
5:17 of dressed *s* for the temple.
5:17 of quality *s* to provide a foundation
5:18 and *s* for the building of the temple.
6:18 Everything was cedar; no *s* was
6:36 of three courses of dressed *s*
7: 9 of blocks of high-grade *s* cut to size
7:12 a wall of three courses of dressed *s*
8: 9 two *s* tablets that Moses had placed
21:10 take him out and *s* him to death."
2Ki 3: 2 He got rid of the sacred *s*
3:25 and each man threw a *s*
10:26 They brought the sacred *s* out
10:27 They demolished the sacred *s*
12:12 and dressed *s* for the repair
16:17 supported it and set it on a *s* base.
19:18 were not gods but only wood and *s*,
19:25 cities into piles of *s*.
22: 6 and dressed *s* to repair the temple.
1Ch 22: 2 stonecutters to prepare dressed *s*
22:14 to be weighed, and wood and *s*.
29: 2 and all kinds of fine *s* and marble—
2Ch 2:14 bronze and iron, *s* and wood,
34:11 and builders to purchase dressed *s*,
Ne 9:11 like a *s* into mighty waters.
Job 6:12 Do I have the strength of *s*?
38:30 when the waters become hard as *s*,
Ps 91:12 will not strike your foot against a *s*.
118:22 The *s* the builders rejected
Pr 22:28 not move an ancient boundary *s*
23:10 not move an ancient boundary *s*
24:31 and the *s* wall was in ruins.
26: 8 Like tying a *s* in a sling
26:27 if a man rolls a *s*, it will roll back
27: 3 *S* is heavy and sand a burden,
Isa 8:14 a *s* that causes men to stumble
Isa 9:10 but we will rebuild with dressed *s*;
28:16 a tested *s*,
28:16 "See, I lay a *s* in Zion,
37:19 were not gods but only wood and *s*,
37:26 cities into piles of *s*.
Jer 2:27 and to *s*, 'You gave me birth.'
3: 9 and committed adultery with *s*
5: 3 made their faces harder than *s*
51:26 nor any *s* for a foundation,
51:63 tie a *s* to it and throw it
La 3: 9 has barred my way with blocks of *s*;
Eze 3: 9 your forehead like the hardest *s*,
11:19 remove from them their heart of *s*
16:40 who will *s* you and hack you
20:32 of the world, who serve wood and *s*
23:47 The mob will *s* them and cut them
28:13 every precious *s* adorned you:
36:26 remove from you your heart of *s*
40:42 also four tables of dressed *s*
46:23 of the four courts was a ledge of *s*,
Da 5: 4 of bronze, iron, wood and *s*.
5:23 of bronze, iron, wood and *s*,
6:17 A *s* was brought and placed
Am 5:11 though you have built *s* mansions,
Hab 2:19 Or to lifeless *s*, 'Wake up!'
Hag 2:15 before one *s* was laid on another
Zec 3: 9 There are seven eyes on that one *s*,
3: 9 the *s* I have set in front of Joshua!
Mt 4: 6 not strike your foot against a *s*.' "
7: 9 will give him a *s*? Or if he asks
21:42 " 'The *s* the builders rejected
21:44 falls on this *s* will be broken
23:37 kill the prophets and *s* those sent
24: 2 not one *s* here will be left
27:60 He rolled a big *s* in front
27:66 secure by putting a seal on the *s*
28: 2 rolled back the *s* and sat on it.
Mk 12:10 " 'The *s* the builders rejected
13: 2 "Not one *s* here will be left
15:46 he rolled a *s* against the entrance
16: 3 "Who will roll the *s* away
16: 4 they saw that the *s*, which was very
Lk 4: 3 tell this *s* to become bread."
4:11 not strike your foot against a *s*.' "
13:34 kill the prophets and *s* those sent
19:44 They will not leave one *s*
20: 6 'From men,' all the people will *s* us,
20:17 " 'The *s* the builders rejected
20:18 falls on that *s* will be broken
21: 6 come when not one *s* will be left
24: 2 They found the *s* rolled away
Jn 2: 6 Nearby stood six *s* water jars,
8: 5 commanded us to *s* such women.
8: 7 the first to throw a *s* at her."
8:59 they picked up stones to *s* him,
10:31 the Jews picked up stones to *s* him,
10:32 For which of these do you *s* me?"
11: 8 while ago the Jews tried to *s* you,
11:38 with a *s* laid across the entrance.
11:39 "Take away the *s*," he said.
11:41 of God?" So they took away the *s*.
19:13 as The *S* Pavement (which
20: 1 saw that the *s* had been removed
Ac 4:11 " 'the *s* you builders rejected,
5:26 that the people would *s* them.
7:58 out of the city and began to *s* him.
14: 5 to mistreat them and *s* them.
17:29 being is like gold or silver or *s*—
Ro 9:32 stumbled over the "stumbling *s*."
9:33 I lay in Zion a *s* that causes men
2Co 3: 3 not on tablets of *s* but on tablets
3: 7 which was engraved in letters on *s*,
Heb 9: 4 and the *s* tablets of the covenant.
1Pe 2: 4 As you come to him, the living *S*—
2: 6 "See, I lay a *s* in Zion,
2: 7 you who believe, this *s* is precious.
2: 7 "The *s* the builders rejected
2: 8 "A *s* that causes men to stumble
Rev 2:17 also give him a white *s*
9:20 silver, bronze, *s* and wood—
21:19 with every kind of precious *s*.

STONE'S (STONE)
Lk 22:41 He withdrew about a *s* throw

STONECUTTERS (STONE)
1Ki 5:15 and eighty thousand *s* in the hills,
2Ki 12:12 and builders, the masons and *s*.

1Ch 22: 2 from among them he appointed *s*
22: 15 *s*, masons and carpenters,
2Ch 2: 2 and eighty thousand as *s* in the hills
2: 18 to be *s* in the hills, with 3,600

STONED (STONE)

Ex 19: 13 He shall surely be *s* or shot
21: 28 the bull must be *s* to death,
21: 29 the bull must be *s* and the owner
21: 32 of the slave, and the bull must be *s*.
Lev 24: 23 outside the camp and *s* him.
Nu 15: 36 him outside the camp and *s* him
Jos 7: 25 all Israel *s* him, and after they had
7: 25 and after they had *s* the rest,
1Ki 12: 18 but all Israel *s* him to death.
21: 13 outside the city and *s* him to death.
21: 14 "Naboth has been *s* and is dead."
21: 15 heard that Naboth had been *s*
2Ch 10: 18 but the Israelites *s* him to death.
24: 21 of the king they *s* him to death
Mt 21: 35 killed another, and *s* a third.
Ac 14: 19 They *s* Paul and dragged him
2Co 11: 25 once I was *s*, three times I was
Heb 11: 37 They were *s*; they were sawed
12: 20 the mountain, it must be *s*."

STONEMASONS (STONE)

2Sa 5: 11 cedar logs and carpenters and *s*,
1Ch 14: 1 *s* and carpenters to build a palace

STONES (STONE)

Ge 28: 11 Taking one of the *s* there, he put it
31: 46 So they took *s* and piled them
31: 46 to his relatives, "Gather some *s*."
Ex 20: 25 If you make an altar of *s* for me,
20: 25 do not build it with dressed *s*,
23: 24 and break their sacred *s* to pieces.
25: 7 and onyx *s* and other gems
28: 9 "Take two onyx *s* and engrave
28: 11 mount the *s* in gold filigree settings
28: 11 on the two *s* the way a gem cutter
28: 12 as memorial *s* for the sons of Israel.
28: 17 mount four rows of precious *s* on it.
28: 21 are to be twelve *s*, one for each
31: 5 to cut and set *s*, to work in wood,
34: 13 smash their sacred *s* and cut
35: 9 and onyx *s* and other gems
35: 27 The leaders brought onyx *s*
35: 33 silver and bronze, to cut and set *s*,
39: 6 They mounted the onyx *s*
39: 7 as memorial *s* for the sons of Israel,
39: 10 rows of precious *s* on it.
39: 14 There were twelve *s*, one for each
Lev 14: 40 that the contaminated *s* be torn out
14: 42 are to take other *s* to replace these
14: 43 house after the *s* have been torn out
14: 45 its *s*, timbers and all the plaster—
Dt 7: 5 their altars, smash their sacred *s*,
12: 3 smash their sacred *s* and burn their
27: 2 set up some large *s* and coat them
27: 4 set up these *s* on Mount Ebal,
27: 5 the LORD your God, an altar of *s*.
27: 8 law on these *s* you have set up."
Jos 4: 3 to take up twelve *s* from the middle
4: 6 ask you, 'What do these *s* mean?'
4: 7 These *s* are to be a memorial
4: 8 They took twelve *s*
4: 9 set up the twelve *s* that had been
4: 20 Gilgal the twelve *s* they had taken
4: 21 'What do these *s* mean?' tell them,
8: 31 an altar of uncut *s*,
8: 32 Joshua copied on *s* the law
1Sa 17: 40 chose five smooth *s*
2Sa 12: 30 and it was set with precious *s*—
16: 6 and all the king's officials with *s*,
16: 13 as he went and throwing *s* at him
1Ki 7: 10 laid with large *s* of good quality,
7: 11 Above were high-grade *s*, cut
10: 2 quantities of gold, and precious *s*—
10: 10 quantities of spices, and precious *s*.
10: 11 of almugwood and precious *s*.
10: 27 as common in Jerusalem as *s*,
14: 23 sacred *s* and Asherah poles
15: 22 away from Ramah the *s*
18: 31 Elijah took twelve *s*, one for each
18: 32 With the *s* he built an altar
18: 38 the wood, the *s* and the soil,
2Ki 3: 19 and ruin every good field with *s*."
2Ki 3: 25 Kir Hareseth was left with its *s*
17: 10 set up sacred *s* and Asherah poles
18: 4 smashed the sacred *s* and cut
23: 14 Josiah smashed the sacred *s*
1Ch 12: 2 or to sling *s* right-handed
20: 2 and it was set with precious *s*—
29: 2 turquoise, *s* of various colors,
29: 8 Any who had precious *s* gave them
2Ch 1: 15 gold as common in Jerusalem as *s*,
3: 6 the temple with precious *s*.
9: 1 quantities of gold, and precious *s*—
9: 9 quantities of spices, and precious *s*.
9: 10 brought algumwood and precious *s*
9: 27 as common in Jerusalem as *s*,
14: 3 smashed the sacred *s* and cut
16: 6 away from Ramah the *s*
26: 15 to shoot arrows and hurl large *s*.
31: 1 smashed the sacred *s* and cut
32: 27 and gold and for his precious *s*,
Ezr 5: 8 people are building it with large *s*
6: 4 with three courses of large *s*
Ne 4: 2 Can they bring the *s* back to life
4: 3 he would break down their wall of *s*
Est 1: 6 mother-of-pearl and other costly *s*.
Job 5: 23 with the *s* of the field,
8: 17 and looks for a place among the *s*.
14: 19 as water wears away *s*
24: 2 Men move boundary *s*;
Ps 102: 14 For her *s* are dear to your servants;
Ecc 3: 5 a time to scatter *s* and a time
10: 9 Whoever quarries *s* may be injured
Isa 5: 2 He dug it up and cleared it of *s*
14: 19 those who descend to the *s*
27: 9 When he makes all the altar *s*
27: 9 to be like chalk *s* crushed to pieces,
54: 11 I will build you with *s* of turquoise,
54: 12 and all your walls of precious *s*.
57: 6 ⌊The idols⌋ among the smooth *s*
60: 17 and iron in place of *s*.
62: 10 Remove the *s*.
Jer 43: 9 take some large *s* with you
43: 10 over these *s* I have buried here;
La 3: 53 and threw *s* at me;
Eze 26: 12 your fine houses and throw your *s*,
27: 22 of all kinds of spices and precious *s*,
28: 14 you walked among the fiery *s*.
28: 16 from among the fiery *s*.
Da 11: 38 with precious *s* and costly gifts.
Hos 3: 4 without sacrifice or sacred *s*,
5: 10 who move boundary *s*.
10: 1 he adorned his sacred *s*.
10: 2 and destroy their sacred *s*.
12: 11 Their altars will be like piles of *s*
Mic 1: 6 I will pour her *s* into the valley
5: 13 and your sacred *s* from among you;
Hab 2: 11 The *s* of the wall will cry out,
Zec 5: 4 both its timbers and its *s*.' "
Mt 3: 9 out of these *s* God can raise up
4: 3 tell these *s* to become bread."
Mk 5: 5 cry out and cut himself with *s*.
13: 1 Teacher! What massive *s*!
Lk 3: 8 out of these *s* God can raise up
19: 40 if they keep quiet, the *s* will cry out
21: 5 was adorned with beautiful *s*
Jn 8: 59 they picked up *s* to stone him,
10: 31 Again the Jews picked up *s*
1Co 3: 12 silver, costly *s*, wood, hay or straw,
1Pe 2: 5 also, like living *s*, are being built
Rev 17: 4 was glittering with gold, precious *s*
18: 12 silver, precious *s* and pearls;
18: 16 and glittering with gold, precious *s*

STONING (STONE)

Nu 14: 10 assembly talked about *s* them.
1Sa 30: 6 the men were talking of *s* him;
Jn 10: 33 We are not *s* you for any of these,"
Ac 7: 59 While they were *s* him, Stephen

STOOD (STAND)

Ge 18: 8 he *s* near them under a tree.
19: 27 to the place where he had *s*
28: 13 There above it *s* the LORD,
37: 7 my sheaf rose and *s* upright,
41: 3 *s* beside those on the riverbank.
Ex 2: 4 His sister *s* at a distance
9: 10 soot from a furnace and *s*
14: 19 from in front and *s* behind them,
15: 8 surging waters *s* firm like a wall;
Ex 18: 13 they *s* around him from morning
19: 17 they *s* at the foot of the mountain.
32: 26 So he *s* at the entrance to the camp
33: 8 *s* at the entrances to their tents,
33: 10 they all *s* and worshiped, each
34: 5 *s* there with him and proclaimed
Lev 9: 5 came near and *s* before the LORD.
Nu 12: 5 he *s* at the entrance to the Tent
12: 10 there *s* Miriam—leprous,
16: 18 and *s* with Moses and Aaron
16: 48 He *s* between the living
22: 22 angel of the LORD *s* in the road
22: 24 of the LORD *s* in a narrow path
22: 26 *s* in a narrow place where there was
27: 2 of Meeting and *s* before Moses,
Dt 4: 10 Remember the day you *s*
4: 11 and *s* at the foot of the mountain
5: 5 At that time I *s* between the LORD
31: 15 and the cloud *s* over the entrance
Jos 3: 17 of the LORD *s* firm on dry ground
4: 3 from right where the priests *s*
4: 9 the ark of the covenant had *s*.
8: 33 Half of the people *s* in front
10: 13 So the sun *s* still,
20: 6 he has *s* trial before the assembly
Jdg 16: 25 When they *s* him among the pillars,
16: 29 pillars on which the temple *s*.
18: 16 *s* at the entrance to the gate.
18: 17 and the six hundred armed men *s*
1Sa 1: 9 drinking in Shiloh, Hannah *s* up.
1: 26 I am the woman who *s* here
3: 10 The LORD came and *s* there,
10: 23 as he *s* among the people he was
12: 18 So all the people *s* in awe
14: 5 One cliff *s* to the north
17: 8 Goliath *s* and shouted to the ranks
17: 51 David ran and *s* over him.
26: 13 *s* on top of the hill some distance
2Sa 1: 10 "So I *s* over him and killed him,
2: 15 So they *s* up and were counted off
12: 17 of his household *s* beside him
13: 31 The king *s* up, tore his clothes
13: 31 his servants *s* by with their clothes
18: 4 So the king *s* beside the gate
18: 30 So he stepped aside and *s* there.
20: 11 One of Joab's men *s* beside Amasa
20: 15 it *s* against the outer fortifications.
23: 10 but he *s* his ground and struck
1Ki 1: 28 came into the king's presence and *s*
2: 7 They *s* by me when I fled
2: 19 him for Adonijah, the king *s* up
3: 15 *s* before the ark of the Lord's
3: 16 came to the king and *s* before him.
7: 25 Sea *s* on twelve bulls, three facing
8: 22 Then Solomon *s* before the altar
8: 55 He *s* and blessed the whole
10: 20 Twelve lions *s* on the six steps,
19: 13 and *s* at the mouth of the cave.
20: 38 *s* by the road waiting for the king.
22: 21 *s* before the LORD and said,
2Ki 2: 7 of the prophets went and *s*
2: 13 and *s* on the bank of the Jordan.
4: 12 he called her, and she *s* before him.
4: 15 So he called her, and she *s*
5: 15 He *s* before him and said,
5: 25 and *s* before his master Elisha.
8: 9 He went in and *s* before him,
10: 9 He *s* before all the people and said,
13: 21 came to life and *s* up on his feet.
16: 14 The bronze altar that *s*
18: 28 Then the commander *s*
23: 3 The king *s* by the pillar
2Ch 3: 13 They *s* on their feet, facing
4: 4 Sea *s* on twelve bulls, three facing
5: 12 *s* on the east side of the altar,
6: 12 Then Solomon *s* before the altar
6: 13 He *s* on the platform and then
9: 19 Twelve lions *s* on the six steps,
13: 4 Abijah *s* on Mount Zemaraim,
18: 20 *s* before the LORD and said,
20: 5 Jehoshaphat *s* up in the assembly
20: 13 *s* there before the LORD.
20: 14 of Asaph, as he *s* in the assembly.
20: 19 and Korahites *s* up and praised
20: 20 As they set out, Jehoshaphat *s*
24: 20 He *s* before the people and said,
29: 26 So the Levites *s* ready
30: 27 the Levites *s* to bless the people,

2Ch 34: 31 The king *s* by his pillar
35: 10 and the priests *s* in their places
Ezr 10: 10 Then Ezra the priest *s* up
Ne 4: 14 I *s* up and said to the nobles,
8: 4 Ezra the scribe *s* on a high wooden
8: 4 him on his right *s* Mattithiah,
8: 5 as he opened it, the people all *s* up.
9: 2 They *s* in their places
9: 3 They *s* where they were
12: 9 *s* opposite them in the services.
12: 24 who *s* opposite them to give praise
Est 5: 1 *s* in the inner court of the palace,
8: 4 and she arose and *s* before him.
Job 4: 15 and the hair on my body *s* on end.
4: 16 A form *s* before my eyes,
Ps 33: 9 he commanded, and it *s* firm.
104: 6 the waters *s* above the mountains.
106: 23 *s* in the breach before him
106: 30 But Phinehas *s* up and intervened,
Isa 36: 13 Then the commander *s*
Jer 18: 20 Remember that I *s* before you
19: 14 and *s* in the court of the LORD's
23: 18 which of them has *s* in the council
23: 22 But if they had *s* in my council,
Eze 1: 21 the creatures *s* still, they also *s* still;
1: 24 When they *s* still, they lowered
1: 25 as they *s* with lowered wings.
8: 3 the idol that provokes to jealousy *s*.
8: 11 In front of them *s* seventy elders
9: 2 and *s* beside the bronze altar.
10: 6 went in and *s* beside a wheel.
10: 17 When the cherubim *s* still,
10: 17 *s* still; and when the cherubim rose,
37: 10 came to life and *s* up on their feet—
Da 2: 2 came in and *s* before the king,
2: 31 there before you *s* a large statue—
3: 3 had set up, and they *s*
4: 10 and there before me *s* a tree
7: 4 lifted from the ground so that it *s*
7: 10 ten thousand times ten thousand *s*
8: 15 before me *s* one who looked like
10: 11 this to me, I *s* up trembling.
12: 5 and there before me *s* two others,
Ob : 11 On the day you *s* aloof
Hab 3: 6 He *s*, and shook the earth;
3: 11 Sun and moon *s* still in the heavens
Zec 3: 3 dressed in filthy clothes as he *s*
3: 5 while the angel of the LORD *s* by.
Mal 2: 5 and he revered me and *s* in awe
Mt 12: 46 his mother and brothers *s* outside,
13: 2 while all the people *s* on the shore.
26: 62 Then the high priest *s* up
27: 11 Meanwhile Jesus *s*
Mk 5: 42 Immediately the girl *s* up
9: 27 lifted him to his feet, and he *s* up.
14: 57 Then some *s* up and gave this false
14: 60 the high priest *s* up before them
15: 39 who *s* there in front of Jesus,
Lk 4: 16 And he *s* up to read.
5: 25 Immediately he *s* up in front
6: 8 So he got up and *s* there.
6: 17 went down with them and *s*
7: 14 and those carrying it *s* still
7: 38 and as she *s* behind him at his feet
8: 55 returned, and at once she *s* up.
10: 25 expert in the law *s* up to test Jesus.
17: 12 They *s* at a distance and called out
18: 11 Pharisee *s* up and prayed about
18: 13 But the tax collector *s* at a distance.
19: 8 But Zacchaeus *s* up and said
22: 28 You are those who have *s* by me
23: 35 The people *s* watching,
23: 49 *s* at a distance, watching these
24: 4 that gleamed like lightning *s*
24: 17 They *s* still, their faces downcast.
24: 36 Jesus himself *s* among them
Jn 2: 6 Nearby *s* six stone water jars,
7: 37 Jesus *s* and said in a loud voice,
11: 56 as they *s* in the temple area they
18: 18 officials *s* around a fire they had
18: 25 As Simon Peter *s* warming himself,
19: 25 the cross of Jesus *s* his mother,
20: 11 but Mary *s* outside the tomb crying
20: 19 Jesus came and *s* among them
20: 26 Jesus came and *s* among them
21: 4 Early in the morning, Jesus *s*
Ac 1: 10 dressed in white *s* beside them.
1: 15 In those days Peter *s* up
Ac 2: 14 Then Peter *s* up with the Eleven,
5: 34 *s* up in the Sanhedrin and ordered
9: 7 with Saul *s* there speechless;
9: 39 All the widows *s* around him,
10: 30 man in shining clothes *s* before me
11: 28 *s* up and through the Spirit
12: 6 and sentries *s* guard at the entrance
15: 5 to the party of the Pharisees *s* up
17: 22 Paul then *s* up in the meeting
21: 40 Paul *s* on the steps and motioned
22: 13 He *s* beside me and said, 'Brother
22: 20 I *s* there giving my approval
23: 9 of the law who were Pharisees *s* up
23: 11 The following night the Lord *s*
24: 20 when I *s* before the Sanhedrin—
24: 21 it was this one thing I shouted as I *s*
25: 7 down from Jerusalem *s* around him
27: 21 Paul *s* up before them and said:
27: 23 whom I serve *s* beside me and said,
2Co 13: 7 will see that we have *s* the test
Col 2: 14 against us and that *s* opposed to us;
2Ti 4: 17 But the Lord *s* at my side
Heb 10: 32 when you *s* your ground
10: 33 at other times you *s* side by side
Jas 1: 12 because when he has *s* the test,
Rev 8: 3 had a golden censer, came and *s*
11: 11 and they *s* on their feet,
12: 4 The dragon *s* in front
13: 1 the dragon *s* on the shore of the sea
22: 2 side of the river *s* the tree of life,

STOOL (FOOTSTOOL)

Ex 1: 16 and observe them on the delivery *s*,

STOOP (STOOPED STOOPS)

2Sa 22: 36 you *s* down to make me great.
Ps 18: 35 you *s* down to make me great.
Ecc 12: 3 and the strong men *s*,
Isa 46: 2 They *s* and bow down together;
Mk 1: 7 whose sandals I am not worthy to *s*

STOOPED (STOOP)

Jn 8: 8 Again he *s* down and wrote

STOOPS (STOOP)

Ps 113: 6 who *s* down to look
Isa 46: 1 Bel bows down, Nebo *s* low;

STOP (STOPPED STOPPING STOPS)

Ge 19: 17 and don't *s* anywhere in the plain!
Ex 9: 29 thunder will *s* and there will be no
Nu 11: 28 "Moses, my lord, *s* them!"
Jos 10: 19 But don't *s!* Pursue your enemies,
22: 25 ours to *s* fearing the LORD.
Jdg 15: 7 I won't *s* until I get my revenge
19: 11 let's *s* at this city of the Jebusites
1Sa 7: 8 "Do not *s* crying out
9: 5 or my father will *s* thinking about
15: 16 "*S!*" Samuel said to Saul.
20: 38 "Hurry! Go quickly! Don't *s!*"
2Sa 2: 21 Asahel would not *s* chasing him.
2: 22 warned Asahel, "*S* chasing me!
2: 26 men to *s* pursuing their brothers?"
2Ki 3: 19 cut down every good tree, *s* up all
2Ch 25: 16 *S!* Why be struck down?"
35: 21 so *s* opposing God, who is with me,
Ezr 4: 21 an order to these men to *s* work,
4: 23 and compelled them by force to *s*.
6: 8 so that the work will not *s*.
Ne 5: 10 But let the exacting of usury *s!*
6: 3 Why should the work *s*
Job 9: 12 If he snatches away, who can *s* him
13: 21 *s* frightening me with your terrors.
37: 14 *s* and consider God's wonders.
Pr 19: 27 *S* listening to instruction, my son,
Isa 1: 13 *S* bringing meaningless offerings!
1: 16 *S* doing wrong,
2: 22 *S* trusting in man,
28: 22 Now *s* your mocking,
30: 11 and *s* confronting us
33: 1 When you *s* destroying,
33: 1 when you *s* betraying,
Jer 15: 5 Who will *s* to ask how you are?
32: 40 I will never *s* doing good to them,
44: 5 or *s* burning incense to other gods.
Eze 16: 41 I will put a *s* to your prostitution,
21: 21 king of Babylon will *s* at the fork
23: 27 So I will put a *s* to the lewdness
Eze 45: 9 *S* dispossessing my people,
Hos 2: 11 I will *s* all her celebrations:
Am 7: 5 *s!* How can Jacob survive?
7: 16 and *s* preaching against the house
Na 2: 8 "*S! S!*" they cry,
Mk 9: 38 in your name and we told him to *s*,
9: 39 "Do not *s* him," Jesus said.
Lk 6: 29 do not *s* him from taking your tunic
8: 52 "*S* wailing," Jesus said.
9: 49 in your name and we tried to *s* him,
9: 50 "Do not *s* him," Jesus said,
Jn 5: 14 *S* sinning or something worse may
6: 43 "*S* grumbling among yourselves,"
7: 24 *S* judging by mere appearances,
20: 27 *S* doubting and believe."
Ac 4: 17 to *s* this thing from spreading any
5: 39 you will not be able to *s* these men;
8: 38 And he ordered the chariot to *s*.
13: 10 Will you never *s* perverting
Ro 14: 13 Therefore let us *s* passing judgment
1Co 14: 20 Brothers, *s* thinking like children.
14: 30 down, the first speaker should *s*.
15: 34 as you ought, and *s* sinning;
2Co 11: 10 of Achaia will *s* this boasting
1Ti 5: 23 *S* drinking only water,
2Pe 2: 14 they never *s* sinning; they seduce
Rev 4: 8 Day and night they never *s* saying:
9: 20 they did not *s* worshiping demons,

STOPPED (STOP)

Ge 8: 2 the rain had *s* falling from the sky.
11: 8 and they *s* building the city.
26: 15 the Philistines *s* up, filling them
26: 18 which the Philistines had *s* up
28: 11 he *s* for the night because the sun
29: 35 Then she *s* having children.
30: 9 saw that she had *s* having children,
41: 49 so much that he *s* keeping records
42: 27 At the place where they *s*
43: 21 But at the place where we *s*
Ex 9: 33 the thunder and hail *s*,
9: 34 and hail and thunder had *s*.
Nu 16: 48 and the dead, and the plague *s*.
16: 50 of Meeting, for the plague had *s*.
25: 8 plague against the Israelites was *s*;
Jos 3: 16 the water from upstream *s* flowing
5: 12 The manna *s* the day
10: 13 The sun *s* in the middle of the sky
10: 13 and the moon *s*,
Jdg 19: 15 There they *s* to spend the night.
Ru 1: 18 to go with her, she *s* urging her.
2: 20 "The LORD has not *s* showing his
1Sa 6: 14 and there it *s* beside a large rock.
10: 2 your father has *s* thinking about
10: 13 After Saul *s* prophesying, he went
14: 46 Saul *s* pursuing the Philistines,
2Sa 2: 23 And every man *s* when he came
18: 16 and the troops *s* pursuing Israel,
20: 12 everyone who came up to Amasa *s*,
24: 21 the plague on the people may be *s*."
24: 25 and the plague on Israel was *s*.
1Ki 15: 21 he *s* building Ramah and withdrew
17: 17 and worse, and finally *s* breathing.
22: 33 king of Israel and *s* pursuing him.
2Ki 2: 7 and Elisha had *s* at the Jordan.
3: 25 They *s* up all the springs
4: 6 Then the oil *s* flowing.
4: 8 came by, he *s* there to eat.
5: 9 and *s* at the door of Elisha's house.
6: 23 bands from Aram *s* raiding Israel's
13: 18 He struck it three times and *s*.
18: 17 *s* at the aqueduct of the Upper Pool
1Ch 21: 22 the plague on the people may be *s*.
2Ch 16: 5 he *s* building Ramah
18: 32 king of Israel, they *s* pursuing him.
25: 16 So the prophet *s* but said,
Ezr 5: 5 they were not *s* until a report could
Ne 12: 39 At the Gate of the Guard they *s*.
Job 4: 16 It *s*,
32: 1 So these three men *s* answering Job
Ps 58: 4 that of a cobra that has *s* its ears,
Isa 24: 8 the noise of the revelers has *s*,
36: 2 When the commander *s*
Jer 44: 18 But ever since we *s* burning incense
48: 33 I have *s* the flow of wine
51: 30 Babylon's warriors have *s* fighting;
La 5: 14 the young men have *s* their music.
Eze 10: 18 and *s* above the cherubim.

Eze 10: 19 They *s* at the entrance
11: 23 and *s* above the mountain east of it.
Zec 7: 11 their backs and *s* up their ears.
Mt 2: 9 them until it *s* over the place where
20: 32 have mercy on us!'' Jesus *s*
Mk 5: 29 Immediately her bleeding *s*
10: 49 Jesus *s* and said, ''Call him.''
Lk 7: 45 I entered, has not *s* kissing my feet.
8: 44 and immediately her bleeding *s*.
18: 40 Jesus *s* and ordered the man
23: 45 for the sun *s* shining.
Ac 5: 42 they never *s* teaching
10: 17 out where Simon's house was and *s*
11: 11 sent to me from Caesarea *s*
20: 31 three years I never *s* warning each
21: 32 his soldiers, they *s* beating Paul.
Eph 1: 16 I have not *s* giving thanks for you,
Col 1: 9 we have not *s* praying for you
1Th 2: 18 again and again—but Satan *s* us.
Heb 10: 2 they not have *s* being offered?

STOPPING (STOP)

Ex 5: 5 and you are *s* them from working.''
Jer 41: 17 *s* at Geruth Kimham

STOPS (STOP)

1Ki 18: 44 go down before the rain *s* you.' ''
Job 18: 5 the flame of his fire *s* burning.
30: 27 The churning inside me never *s*;
37: 7 he *s* every man from his labor.
Isa 33: 15 who *s* his ears against plots
44: 19 No one *s* to think,
Ac 6: 13 ''This fellow never *s* speaking
3Jn : 10 He also *s* those who want to do so

STORAGE (STORE)

Jer 40: 10 and put them in your *s* jars,
Eze 4: 9 put them in a *s* jar and use them

STORE (STORAGE STORED STORES STORING)

Ge 6: 21 and *s* it away as food for you
41: 35 *s* up the grain under the authority
Ex 1: 11 Rameses as *s* cities for Pharaoh.
Dt 14: 28 of that year's produce and *s* it
1Ki 9: 19 as well as all his *s* cities
2Ch 8: 4 and all the *s* cities he had built
8: 6 as well as Baalath and all his *s* cities
16: 4 and all the *s* cities of Naphtali.
17: 12 he built forts and *s* cities in Judah
32: 28 also made buildings to *s* the harvest
Ne 13: 5 used to *s* the grain offerings
Job 23: 14 many such plans he still has in *s*.
Ps 17: 14 they *s* up wealth for their children.
Pr 2: 1 and *s* up my commands within you,
2: 7 victory in *s* for the upright,
7: 1 and *s* up my commands within you.
10: 14 Wise men *s* up knowledge,
30: 25 yet they *s* up their food
Isa 2: 12 LORD Almighty has a day in *s*
10: 28 they *s* supplies at Micmash.
33: 6 a rich *s* of salvation and wisdom
Mic 6: 14 You will *s* up but save nothing,
Mt 6: 19 not *s* up for yourselves treasures
6: 20 But *s* up for yourselves treasures
6: 26 or reap or *s* away in barns,
Lk 12: 17 I have no place to *s* my crops.'
12: 18 and there I will *s* all my grain
2Co 9: 10 supply and increase your *s* of seed
2Ti 4: 8 Now there is in *s* for me the crown

STORED (STORE)

Ge 41: 48 in Egypt and *s* it in the cities.
41: 49 Joseph *s* up huge quantities of grain
2Ki 20: 17 and all that your fathers have *s* up
Ezr 6: 1 in the archives *s* in the treasury
Job 15: 20 through all the years *s* up for him.
Ps 31: 19 which you have *s* up
Pr 13: 22 a sinner's wealth is *s* up
SS 7: 13 that I have *s* up for you, my lover.
Isa 15: 7 wealth they have acquired and *s* up
22: 9 you *s* up water
23: 18 they will not be *s* up or hoarded.
39: 6 and all that your fathers have *s* up
45: 3 riches *s* in secret places,
Hos 13: 12 The guilt of Ephraim is *s* up,
Mt 12: 35 out of the evil *s* up in him.
12: 35 out of the good *s* up in him,
Lk 6: 45 out of the evil *s* up in his heart.
6: 45 out of the good *s* up in his heart,
Col 1: 5 from the hope that is *s* up for you

STOREHOUSE (HOUSE)

Dt 28: 12 LORD will open the heavens, the *s*
1Ch 26: 15 and the lot for the *s* fell to his sons.
26: 17 the south and two at a time at the *s*.
Hos 13: 15 His *s* will be plundered
Mal 3: 10 Bring the whole tithe into the *s*,

STOREHOUSES (HOUSE)

Ge 41: 56 Joseph opened the *s* and sold grain
2Ki 20: 13 showed them all that was in his *s*—
1Ch 27: 25 of the *s* in the outlying districts,
27: 25 was in charge of the royal *s*.
Job 38: 22 or seen the *s* of the hail,
38: 22 ''Have you entered the *s*
Ps 33: 7 he puts the deep into *s*.
135: 7 and brings out the wind from his *s*.
Isa 39: 2 showed them what was in his *s*—
Jer 10: 13 and brings out the wind from his *s*.
51: 16 and brings out the wind from his *s*.
Joel 1: 17 The *s* are in ruins,

STOREROOM (ROOM)

Mt 13: 52 out of his *s* new treasures
Lk 12: 24 they have no *s* or barn; yet God

STOREROOMS (ROOM)

1Ch 28: 11 its buildings, its *s*, its upper parts,
2Ch 31: 11 orders to prepare *s* in the temple
Ne 10: 37 we will bring to the *s* of the house
10: 38 of our God, to the *s* of the treasury.
10: 39 and oil to the *s* where the articles
12: 25 gatekeepers who guarded the *s*
12: 44 into the *s* the portions required
12: 44 of the *s* for the contributions,
13: 4 put in charge of the *s* of the house
13: 12 new wine and oil into the *s*.
13: 13 named Pedaiah in charge of the *s*

STORES (STORE)

Job 21: 19 'God *s* up a man's punishment
Pr 6: 8 yet it *s* its provisions in summer
21: 20 of the wise are *s* of choice food
Lk 12: 21 be with anyone who *s* up things

STORIES (STORY)

2Pe 1: 16 did not follow cleverly invented *s*
2: 3 you with *s* they have made up.

STORING (STORE)

Ecc 2: 26 and *s* up wealth to hand it
Ro 2: 5 you are *s* up wrath against yourself

STORK

Lev 11: 19 the osprey, the *s*, any kind of heron
Dt 14: 18 the cormorant, the *s*, any kind
Job 39: 13 the pinions and feathers of the *s*.
Ps 104: 17 the *s* has its home in the pine trees.
Jer 8: 7 Even the *s* in the sky
Zec 5: 9 They had wings like those of a *s*,

STORM (STORMED STORMS STORMY THUNDERSTORM WINDSTORM)

Ex 9: 24 It was the worst *s* in all the land
Job 9: 17 He would crush me with a *s*
30: 22 you toss me about in the *s*.
36: 33 thunder announces the coming *s*;
38: 1 LORD answered Job out of the *s*.
40: 6 the LORD spoke to Job out of the *s*
Ps 55: 8 far from the tempest and *s*.''
83: 15 and terrify them with your *s*.
107: 29 He stilled the *s* to a whisper;
Pr 1: 27 calamity overtakes you like a *s*,
10: 25 When the *s* has swept
Isa 4: 6 hiding place from the *s* and rain.
25: 4 a shelter from the *s*
25: 4 is like a *s* driving against a wall
32: 2 and a refuge from the *s*,
Jer 11: 16 But with the roar of a mighty *s*
23: 19 See, the *s* of the LORD
25: 32 a mighty *s* is rising
30: 23 See, the *s* of the LORD
Eze 30: 16 Thebes will be taken by *s*;
38: 9 advancing like a *s*; you will be like
Da 11: 40 of the North will *s* out against him
Jnh 1: 4 such a violent *s* arose that the ship
1: 12 my fault that this great *s* has come
Na 1: 3 is in the whirlwind and the *s*,
2: 4 The chariots *s* through the streets,
Zec 10: 1 LORD who makes the *s* clouds.
Mt 8: 24 a furious *s* came up on the lake,
Lk 8: 24 the *s* subsided, and all was calm.
Ac 27: 15 The ship was caught by the *s*
27: 18 from the *s* that the next day they
27: 20 and the *s* continued raging,
Heb 12: 18 gloom and *s*; to a trumpet blast
2Pe 2: 17 water and mists driven by a *s*.

STORMED (STORM)

Jdg 9: 52 went to the tower and *s* it.
Hab 3: 14 head when his warriors *s* out

STORMS (STORM)

Isa 54: 11 lashed by *s* and not comforted,
Zec 9: 14 he will march in the *s* of the south,

STORMY (STORM)

Ps 148: 8 *s* winds that do his bidding,
Am 1: 14 amid violent winds on a *s* day.
Mt 16: 3 'Today it will be *s*, for the sky is red

STORY (STORIES)

Ge 39: 17 told him this *s*: ''That Hebrew slave
39: 19 his master heard the *s* his wife told
Mt 28: 15 this *s* has been widely circulated
Ac 20: 9 fell to the ground from the third *s*

STOUTHEARTED (HEART)

Ps 138: 3 you made me bold and *s*.

STRAGGLER

Isa 14: 31 and there is not a *s* in its ranks.

STRAIGHT (STRAIGHTEN STRAIGHTENED)

Jos 6: 5 the people will go up, every man *s*
6: 20 so every man charged *s* in,
1Sa 6: 12 Then the cows went *s* up
2Sa 5: 23 and he answered, ''Do not go *s* up,
1Ch 14: 14 answered him, ''Do not go *s* up,
Job 10: 19 had been carried *s* from the womb
Ps 5: 8 make *s* your way before me.
27: 11 lead me in a *s* path
107: 7 He led them by a *s* way
Pr 2: 13 who leave the *s* paths
3: 6 and he will make your paths *s*.
4: 11 and lead you along *s* paths.
4: 25 Let your eyes look *s* ahead,
5: 5 her steps lead *s* to the grave.
9: 15 who go *s* on their way.
11: 5 of the blameless makes a *s* way
15: 21 of understanding keeps a *s* course.
SS 7: 9 May the wine go *s* to my lover,
Isa 40: 3 make *s* in the wilderness
45: 13 I will make all his ways *s*.
Jer 31: 39 from there *s* to the hill of Gareb
Eze 1: 7 Their legs were *s*; their feet were
1: 9 Each one went *s* ahead; they did
1: 12 Each one went *s* ahead.
10: 22 Each one went *s* ahead.
Joel 2: 8 each marches *s* ahead.
Am 4: 3 You will each go *s* out
Mt 3: 3 make *s* paths for him.' ''
Mk 1: 3 make *s* paths for him.' ''
Lk 3: 4 make *s* paths for him.
3: 5 The crooked roads shall become *s*,
22: 61 The Lord turned and looked *s*
Jn 1: 23 'Make *s* the way for the Lord.' ''
Ac 3: 4 Peter looked *s* at him, as did John.
9: 11 to the house of Judas on *S* Street
13: 9 looked *s* at Elymas and said,
16: 11 and sailed *s* for Samothrace,
21: 1 out to sea and sailed *s* to Cos.
23: 1 Paul looked *s* at the Sanhedrin
2Pe 2: 15 They have left the *s* way

STRAIGHTEN (STRAIGHT)

Ecc 7: 13 Who can *s*
Lk 13: 11 bent over and could not *s* up at all.
Tit 1: 5 was that you might *s* out what was

STRAIGHTENED (STRAIGHT)

Ecc 1:15 What is twisted cannot be *s;*
Lk 13:13 and immediately she *s* up
Jn 8:7 kept on questioning him, he *s* up
8:10 Jesus *s* up and asked her, "Woman,

STRAIN (STRAINING)

Ex 18:23 you will be able to stand the *s,*
Mt 23:24 You *s* out a gnat but swallow

STRAINING (STRAIN)

Zec 6:7 were *s* to go throughout the earth.
Mk 6:48 He saw the disciples *s* at the oars,
Php 3:13 and *s* toward what is ahead,

STRANDS

Ex 39:3 cut *s* to be worked into the blue,
Ecc 4:12 of three *s* is not quickly broken.
Eze 5:3 But take a few *s* of hair

STRANGE (STRANGER STRANGER'S STRANGERS)

Ex 3:3 I will go over and see this *s* sight—
Pr 23:33 Your eyes will see *s* sights
Isa 18:2 an aggressive nation of *s* speech,
18:7 an aggressive nation of *s* speech,
28:11 with foreign lips and *s* tongues
28:21 to do his work, his *s* work,
33:19 with their *s,* incomprehensible
Ac 17:20 You are bringing some *s* ideas
1Co 14:21 "Through men of *s* tongues
Heb 13:9 away by all kinds of *s* teachings.
1Pe 4:4 They think it *s* that you do not
4:12 something *s* were happening to you

STRANGER (STRANGE)

Ge 23:4 "I am an alien and a *s* among you.
42:7 to be a *s* and spoke harshly
Job 19:15 my maidservants count me a *s;*
29:16 I took up the case of the *s.*
31:32 but no *s* had to spend the night
Ps 39:12 a *s,* as all my fathers were.
69:8 I am a *s* to my brothers,
119:19 I am a *s* on earth;
Pr 20:16 of one who puts up security for a *s;*
27:13 of one who puts up security for a *s;*
Ecc 6:2 and a *s* enjoys them instead.
Jer 14:8 why are you like a *s* in the land,
Mt 25:35 I was a *s* and you invited me in,
25:38 When did we see you a *s*
25:43 I was a *s* and you did not invite me
25:44 or thirsty or a *s* or needing clothes
Jn 10:5 But they will never follow a *s;*
Heb 11:9 home in the promised land like a *s*

STRANGER'S (STRANGE)

Jn 10:5 they do not recognize a *s* voice."

STRANGERS (STRANGE)

Ge 15:13 that your descendants will be *s*
1Ch 16:19 few indeed, and *s* in it,
29:15 We are aliens and *s* in your sight,
Ps 54:3 *S* are attacking me;
105:12 few indeed, and *s* in it,
109:11 may *s* plunder the fruits of his labor
Pr 5:10 lest *s* feast on your wealth
5:17 never to be shared with *s.*
Isa 1:7 laid waste as when overthrown by *s*
Eze 16:32 You prefer *s* to your own husband!
Ob :11 aloof while *s* carried off his wealth
Zec 7:14 all the nations, where they were *s.*
Ac 7:6 'Your descendants will be *s*
Heb 11:13 that they were aliens and *s*
13:2 Do not forget to entertain *s,*
1Pe 1:1 To God's elect, *s* in the world,
1:17 as *s* here in reverent fear.
2:11 as aliens and *s* in the world,
3Jn :5 even though they are *s* to you.

STRANGLED (STRANGLING)

Na 2:12 and *s* the prey for his mate,
Ac 15:20 from the meat of *s* animals
15:29 from the meat of *s* animals
21:25 from the meat of *s* animals

STRANGLING (STRANGLED)

Job 7:15 so that I prefer *s* and death,

STRAP (STRAPPED STRAPS)

Ex 32:27 'Each man *s* a sword to his side.

STRAPPED (STRAP)

Jdg 3:16 which he *s* to his right thigh
2Sa 20:8 and *s* over it at his waist was a belt

STRAPS (STRAP)

Jer 27:2 Make a yoke out of *s* and crossbars

STRATEGY

2Ki 18:20 say you have *s* and military
Isa 8:10 Devise your *s,* but it will be
36:5 say you have *s* and military

STRAW

Ge 24:25 "We have plenty of *s* and fodder,
24:32 *S* and fodder were brought
Ex 5:7 let them go and gather their own *s.*
5:7 people with *s* for making bricks;
5:10 'I will not give you any more *s.*
5:11 get your own *s* wherever you can
5:12 Egypt to gather stubble to use for *s.*
5:13 each day, just as when you had *s.*"
5:16 Your servants are given no *s,*
5:18 You will not be given any *s,*
Jdg 19:19 We have both *s* and fodder
1Ki 4:28 and *s* for the chariot horses
Job 21:18 How often are they like *s*
41:27 Iron he treats like *s*
41:29 A club seems to him but a piece of *s*
Isa 5:24 as tongues of fire lick up *s*
11:7 and the lion will eat *s* like the ox.
25:10 *s* is trampled down in the manure.
33:11 you give birth to *s;*
65:25 and the lion will eat *s* like the ox,
Jer 23:28 For what has *s* to do with grain?"
1Co 3:12 silver, costly stones, wood, hay or *s*

STRAY (STRAYED STRAYING STRAYS)

Ex 22:5 or vineyard and lets them *s*
1Ki 22:43 ways of his father Asa and did not *s*
2Ch 20:32 ways of his father Asa and did not *s*
Ps 119:10 not let me *s* from your commands.
119:21 and who *s* from your commands.
119:118 You reject all who *s*
Pr 7:25 or *s* into her paths.
19:27 you will *s* from the words
Eze 14:11 of Israel will no longer *s* from me,

STRAYED (STRAY)

Ps 44:18 our feet had not *s* from your path.
119:110 but I have not *s* from your precepts
119:176 I have *s* like a lost sheep.
Jer 2:5 that they *s* so far from me?
31:19 After I *s,*
Hos 7:13 because they have *s* from me!

STRAYING (STRAY)

Dt 22:1 see your brother's ox or sheep *s,*

STRAYS (STRAY)

Pr 21:16 A man who *s* from the path
27:8 Like a bird that *s* from its nest
27:8 is a man who *s* from his home.
Eze 34:4 You have not brought back the *s*
34:16 for the lost and bring back the *s.*

STREAKED

Ge 30:35 all the male goats that were *s*
30:39 And they bore young that were *s*
30:40 but made the rest face the *s*
31:8 'The *s* ones will be your wages,'
31:8 then all the flocks bore *s* young.
31:10 mating with the flock were *s,*
31:12 mating with the flock are *s,*

STREAM (DOWNSTREAM HEADSTREAMS STREAMING STREAMS UPSTREAM)

Ge 32:23 After he had sent them across the *s*
Dt 9:21 threw the dust into a *s* that flowed
21:4 and where there is a flowing *s.*
1Sa 17:40 five smooth stones from the *s,*
2Ch 32:4 the *s* that flowed through the land.
Job 30:6 to live in the dry *s* beds,
40:22 the poplars by the *s* surround him.
41:19 Firebrands *s* from his mouth;
Isa 2:2 and all nations will *s* to it.
30:33 like a *s* of burning sulfur,
32:20 sowing your seed by every *s,*
66:12 wealth of nations like a flooding *s;*
Jer 17:8 that sends out its roots by the *s.*
51:44 The nations will no longer *s* to him.
Am 5:24 righteousness like a never-failing *s!*
Mic 4:1 and peoples will *s* to it.

STREAMING (STREAM)

SS 4:15 *s* down from Lebanon.

STREAMS (STREAM)

Ge 2:6 but *s* came up from the earth
Ex 7:19 over the *s* and canals,
8:5 hand with your staff over the *s*
Lev 11:9 in the water of the seas and the *s,*
11:10 or *s* that do not have fins
Dt 8:7 a land with *s* and pools of water,
10:7 to Jotbathah, a land with *s* of water.
2Ki 19:24 I have dried up all the *s* of Egypt."
Job 6:15 as the *s* that overflow
6:15 as undependable as intermittent *s,*
20:17 He will not enjoy the *s,*
29:6 out for me *s* of olive oil.
36:27 which distill as rain to the *s;*
Ps 1:3 He is like a tree planted by *s*
42:1 As the deer pants for *s* of water,
46:4 is a river whose *s* make glad
65:9 The *s* of God are filled with water
74:15 you who opened up springs and *s;*
78:16 he brought *s* out of a rocky crag
78:20 and *s* flowed abundantly.
78:44 they could not drink from their *s.*
119:136 *S* of tears flow from my eyes,
126:4 like *s* in the Negev.
Pr 5:16 your *s* of water in the public
Ecc 1:7 All *s* flow into the sea,
1:7 To the place the *s* come from,
SS 5:12 doves by the water *s,*
Isa 7:18 for flies from the distant *s* of Egypt
11:15 He will break it up into seven *s*
19:6 the *s* of Egypt will dwindle
30:25 *s* of water will flow
32:2 like *s* of water in the desert
33:21 of broad rivers and *s.*
34:9 Edom's *s* will be turned into pitch,
35:6 and *s* in the desert
37:25 I have dried up all the *s* of Egypt.'
43:19 and *s* in the wasteland.
43:20 and *s* in the wasteland,
44:3 and *s* on the dry ground;
44:4 like poplar trees by flowing *s.*
44:27 and I will dry up your *s,'*
47:2 and wade through the *s.*
Jer 9:18 and water *s* from our eyelids.
31:9 I will lead them beside *s* of water
La 3:48 *S* of tears flow from my eyes
Eze 29:3 great monster lying among your *s.*
29:4 of your *s* stick to your scales.
29:4 out from among your *s,*
29:5 you and all the fish of your *s.*
29:10 I am against you and against your *s*
30:12 I will dry up the *s* of the Nile
31:4 their *s* flowed
31:15 I held back its *s,* and its abundant
32:2 and muddying the *s.*
32:2 thrashing about in your *s,*
32:14 and make her *s* flow like oil,
Joel 1:20 the *s* of water have dried up
Hab 3:8 Was your wrath against the *s?*
Mt 7:25 The rain came down, the *s* rose,
7:27 The rain came down, the *s* rose,
Jn 7:38 *s* of living water will flow

STREET (STREETS)

Dt 32:25 In the *s* the sword will make them
Jos 2:19 goes outside your house into the *s,*
2Ch 28:24 at every *s* corner in Jerusalem.
Job 31:32 had to spend the night in the *s,*
Ps 31:11 me on the *s* flee from me.
Pr 1:20 Wisdom calls aloud in the *s,*
7:8 going down the *s* near her corner,
7:12 now in the *s,* now in the squares,
Ecc 12:4 when the doors to the *s* are closed
Isa 51:20 they lie at the head of every *s,*
51:23 like a *s* to be walked over."
Jer 6:11 "Pour it out on the children in the *s*

Rev 14:10 which has been poured full *s*

STRENGTHEN (STRONG)

Dt 3:28 Joshua, and encourage and *s* him,
Jdg 16:28 O God, please *s* me just once more,
1Ki 20:22 "*S* your position and see what must
2Ki 15:19 and *s* his own hold on the kingdom.
2Ch 16:9 to *s* those whose hearts are fully
Ne 6:9 ⌞But I prayed,⌟ "Now *s* my hands."
Job 8:20 or *s* the hands of evildoers.
Ps 89:21 surely my arm will *s* him.
119:28 *s* me according to your word.
SS 2:5 *S* me with raisins,
Isa 22:10 and tore down houses to *s* the wall.
35:3 *S* the feeble hands,
41:10 I will *s* you and help you;
45:5 I will *s* you,
54:2 *s* your stakes.
58:11 and will *s* your frame.
Jer 23:14 They *s* the hands of evildoers,
Eze 30:24 I will *s* the arms of the king
30:25 I will *s* the arms of the king
34:16 bind up the injured and *s* the weak,
Na 3:14 *s* your defenses!
Zec 10:6 I will *s* the house of Judah
10:12 I will *s* them in the LORD
Lk 22:32 have turned back, *s* your brothers."
Ac 15:32 to encourage and *s* the brothers.
Eph 3:16 of his glorious riches he may *s* you
1Th 3:2 to *s* and encourage you
3:13 May he *s* your hearts
2Th 2:17 and *s* you in every good deed
3:3 and he will *s* and protect you
Heb 12:12 *s* your feeble arms and weak knees.
Rev 3:2 *S* what remains and is about to die,

STRENGTHENED (STRONG)

2Sa 16:21 of everyone with you will be *s*."
1Ki 19:8 *S* by that food, he traveled forty
2Ch 11:11 He *s* their defenses and put
11:17 They *s* the kingdom of Judah
17:1 as king and *s* himself against Israel.
Job 4:3 how you have *s* feeble hands.
4:4 you have *s* faltering knees.
Isa 9:11 the LORD has *s* Rezin's foes
Eze 34:4 You have not *s* the weak
Da 10:19 I was *s* and said, "Speak, my lord,
Hos 7:15 I trained them and *s* them,
Lk 22:43 heaven appeared to him and *s* him.
Ac 9:31 It was *s;* and encouraged
16:5 So the churches were *s* in the faith
Ro 4:20 but was *s* in his faith and gave glory
Col 1:11 being *s* with all power according
2:7 *s* in the faith as you were taught,
Heb 13:9 good for our hearts to be *s* by grace,

STRENGTHENING (STRONG)

2Sa 3:6 Abner had been *s* his own position
Ac 14:22 *s* the disciples and encouraging
15:41 and Cilicia, *s* the churches.
18:23 and Phrygia, *s* all the disciples.
1Co 14:3 speaks to men for their *s*,
14:26 done for the *s* of the church.
2Co 12:19 we do, dear friends, is for your *s*.

STRENGTHENS (STRONG)

Ps 147:13 for he *s* the bars of your gates

STRESS

Jer 19:9 during the *s* of the siege imposed
Tit 3:8 And I want you to *s* these things,

STRETCH (OUTSTRETCHED STRETCHED STRETCHES STRETCHING)

Ex 3:20 So I will *s* out my hand
7:5 the LORD when I *s* out my hand
7:19 *s* out your hand over the waters
8:5 '*S* out your hand with your staff
8:16 '*S* out your staff and strike the dust
9:22 "*S* out your hand toward the sky
10:12 "*S* out your hand over Egypt
10:21 "*S* out your hand toward the sky
14:16 and *s* out your hand over the sea
14:26 "*S* out your hand over the sea
2Ki 21:13 I will *s* out over Jerusalem
Job 1:11 But *s* out your hand and strike
2:5 *s* out your hand and strike his flesh
11:13 and *s* out your hands to him,
Ps 138:7 you *s* out your hand
Isa 28:20 The bed is too short to *s* out on,
34:11 God will *s* out over Edom
54:2 *s* your tent curtains wide,
Jer 6:12 when I *s* out my hand
31:39 The measuring line will *s*
51:25 "I will *s* out my hand against you,
Eze 6:14 I will *s* out my hand against them
14:9 I will *s* out my hand against him
14:13 I *s* out my hand against it to cut
25:7 I will *s* out my hand against you
25:13 I will *s* out my hand against Edom
25:16 I am about to *s* out my hand
35:3 I will *s* out my hand against you
Zep 1:4 "I will *s* out my hand against Judah
2:13 He will *s* out his hand
Mt 12:13 said to the man, "*S* out your hand."
Mk 3:5 said to the man, "*S* out your hand."
Lk 6:10 said to the man, "*S* out your hand."
Jn 21:18 are old you will *s* out your hands,
Ac 4:30 *S* out your hand to heal

STRETCHED (STRETCH)

Ge 10:30 The region where they lived *s*
Ex 8:6 So Aaron *s* out his hand
8:17 and when Aaron *s* out his hand
9:15 by now I could have *s* out my hand
9:23 When Moses *s* out his staff
10:13 So Moses *s* out his staff over Egypt
10:22 So Moses *s* out his hand
14:21 Moses *s* out his hand over the sea,
14:27 Moses *s* out his hand over the sea,
15:12 You *s* out your right hand
2Sa 24:16 When the angel *s* out his hand
1Ki 13:4 he *s* out his hand from the altar
13:4 the hand he *s* out toward the man
17:21 he *s* himself out on the boy three
2Ki 4:34 As he *s* himself out upon him,
4:35 and *s* out upon him once more.
Job 38:5 Who *s* a measuring line across it?
Ps 77:2 at night I *s* out untiring hands
Pr 1:24 heed when I *s* out my hand,
Isa 14:26 this is the hand *s* out
14:27 His hand is *s* out, and who can turn
23:11 The LORD has *s* out his hand
42:5 the heavens and *s* them out,
44:24 who alone *s* out the heavens,
45:12 My own hands *s* out the heavens;
51:13 who *s* out the heavens
Jer 10:12 and *s* out the heavens by his
51:15 and *s* out the heavens by his
La 2:8 He *s* out a measuring line
Eze 1:23 expanse their wings were *s* out one
2:9 and I saw a hand *s* out to me.
8:3 He *s* out what looked like a hand
16:27 So I *s* out my hand against you
17:7 *s* out its branches to him for water.
Zec 1:16 the measuring line will be *s* out
Mt 12:13 So he *s* it out and it was completely
Mk 3:5 He *s* it out, and his hand was
Ac 22:25 As they *s* him out to flog him,

STRETCHES (STRETCH)

Job 9:8 He alone *s* out the heavens
Ps 104:2 he *s* out the heavens like a tent
Isa 31:3 When the LORD *s* out his hand,
33:17 and view a land that *s* afar.
40:22 He *s* out the heavens like a canopy,
La 1:17 Zion *s* out her hands,
Zec 12:1 The LORD, who *s* out the heavens,

STRETCHING (STRETCH)

Est 1:1 over 127 provinces *s* from India
8:9 of the 127 provinces *s* from India
Jer 4:31 *s* out her hands and saying,

STREWN

1Sa 17:52 dead were *s* along the Shaaraim
2Ki 7:15 and they found the whole road *s*

STRICKEN (STRIKE)

Isa 53:4 yet we considered him *s* by God,
53:8 of my people he was *s*.
Zec 14:13 On that day men will be *s*

STRICT (STRICTEST)

1Sa 14:28 bound the army under a *s* oath,
Mk 3:12 But he gave them *s* orders not
Mk 5:43 He gave *s* orders not
Ac 5:28 "We gave you *s* orders not to teach
1Co 9:25 in the games goes into *s* training.

STRICTEST (STRICT)

Ac 26:5 that according to the *s* sect

STRIDE (STRIDING STRODE)

Pr 30:29 things that are stately in their *s*,

STRIDING (STRIDE)

Isa 63:1 *s* forward in the greatness

STRIFE (STRIVE)

Ps 31:20 safe from the *s* of tongues.
55:9 for I see violence and *s* in the city.
Pr 17:1 than a house full of feasting, with *s*.
18:6 A fool's lips bring him *s*,
20:3 It is to a man's honor to avoid *s*,
22:10 out the mocker, and out goes *s;*
23:29 Who has *s?* Who has complaints?
26:21 a quarrelsome man for kindling *s*.
30:33 so stirring up anger produces *s*."
Isa 58:4 in quarreling and *s*,
Hab 1:3 there is *s*, and conflict abounds.
Ro 1:29 murder, *s*, deceit and malice.

STRIKE (STRICKEN STRIKES STRIKING STROKE STRUCK)

Ge 3:15 and you will *s* his heel."
Ex 3:20 and *s* the Egyptians with all
5:3 or he may *s* us with plagues
7:17 is in my hand I will *s* the water
8:16 and *s* the dust of the ground,'
12:12 and *s* down every firstborn—
12:13 will touch you when I *s* Egypt.
12:23 the land to *s* down the Egyptians,
12:23 to enter your houses and *s* you
17:6 *S* the rock, and water will come out
Nu 8:19 that no plague will *s* the Israelites
14:12 I will *s* them down with a plague
Dt 28:22 The LORD will *s* you
33:11 *s* his foes till they rise no more."
Jdg 6:16 and you will *s* down the Midianites
1Sa 17:46 and I'll *s* you down and cut
22:17 to raise a hand to *s* the priests
22:18 "You turn and *s* down the priests."
26:8 of my spear; I won't *s* him twice."
26:10 "the LORD himself will *s* him;
2Sa 1:15 *s* him down!" So he struck him
2:22 Why should I *s* you down?
5:24 of you to *s* the Philistine army."
13:28 '*S* Amnon down,' then kill him.
17:2 I would *s* down only the king
17:2 I would *s* him with terror,
18:11 Why didn't you *s* him
1Ki 2:29 of Jehoiada, "Go, *s* him down!"
2:31 *S* him down and bury him,
14:15 And the LORD will *s* Israel,
20:35 "*S* me with your weapon,"
20:37 another man and said, "*S* me,
2Ki 6:18 "*S* these people with blindness."
13:18 Elisha told him, "*S* the ground."
1Ch 14:15 of you to *s* the Philistine army."
2Ch 21:14 LORD is about to *s* your people,
Job 1:11 your hand and *s* everything he has,
2:5 out your hand and *s* his flesh
16:10 they *s* my cheek in scorn
36:32 and commands it to *s* its mark.
Ps 9:20 *S* them with terror, O LORD;
81:2 Begin the music, *s* the tambourine,
89:23 and *s* down his adversaries.
91:12 so that you will not *s* your foot
141:5 Let a righteous man *s* me—
Pr 11:15 whoever refuses to *s* hands
Isa 11:4 He will *s* the earth with the rod
13:18 Their bows will *s* down the young
19:22 The LORD will *s* Egypt
19:22 he will *s* them and heal them.
30:31 with his scepter he will *s* them
Jer 21:6 I will *s* down those who live
La 3:30 to one who would *s* him,
Eze 5:2 and *s* it with the sword all
6:11 *S* your hands together
21:14 Let the sword *s* twice,
21:14 and *s* your hands together.
21:17 I too will *s* my hands together,
22:13 " 'I will surely *s* my hands together

Da 4: 20 and *s*, with its top touching the sky,
4: 22 You have become great and *s*;
8: 24 He will become very *s*,
10: 19 "Peace! Be *s* now; be *s*."
11: 5 king of the South will become *s*,
Joel 3: 10 "I am *s*!"
Am 2: 9 and *s* as the oaks.
2: 14 the *s* will not muster their strength,
5: 3 city that marches out a thousand *s*
5: 3 town that marches out a hundred *s*
8: 13 young women and *s* young men
Mic 4: 3 will settle disputes for *s* nations far
4: 7 those driven away a *s* nation.
Hag 2: 4 Be *s*, all you people of the land,'
2: 4 But now be *s*, O Zerubbabel,'
2: 4 'Be *s*, O Joshua son of Jehozadak,
Zec 8: 9 let your hands be *s*
8: 13 be afraid, but let your hands be *s*."
12: 5 'The people of Jerusalem are *s*,
Mt 12: 29 can anyone enter a *s* man's house
12: 29 unless he first ties up the *s* man?
Mk 1: 43 away at once with a *s* warning:
3: 27 no one can enter a *s* man's house
3: 27 unless he first ties up the *s* man.
5: 4 No one was *s* enough
Lk 1: 80 And the child grew and became *s*
2: 40 And the child grew and became *s*;
11: 21 "When a *s* man, fully armed,
16: 3 I'm not *s* enough to dig,
Jn 6: 18 *s* wind was blowing and the waters
Ac 3: 7 the man's feet and ankles became *s*.
3: 16 you see and know was made *s*.
Ro 1: 11 some spiritual gift to make you *s*—
15: 1 We who are *s* ought to bear
1Co 1: 8 He will keep you *s* to the end,
1: 27 things of the world to shame the *s*.
4: 10 but you are *s*! You are honored,
16: 13 in the faith; be men of courage; be *s*
2Co 12: 10 For when I am weak, then I am *s*.
13: 9 we are weak but you are *s*;
Eph 6: 10 be *s* in the Lord and in his mighty
1Th 2: 2 gospel in spite of *s* opposition.
2Ti 2: 1 be *s* in the grace that is
Jas 3: 4 so large and are driven by *s* winds,
1Pe 5: 10 restore you and make you *s*,
1Jn 2: 14 because you are *s*,
Rev 6: 13 tree when shaken by a *s* wind.
12: 8 But he was not *s* enough,

STRONGER (STRONG)

Ge 25: 23 one people will be *s* than the other,
30: 41 Whenever the *s* females were
Nu 13: 31 attack those people; they are *s*
14: 12 you into a nation greater and *s*
Dt 1: 28 'The people are *s* and taller
4: 38 before you nations greater and *s*
7: 1 seven nations larger and *s* than you
7: 17 "These nations are *s* than we are.
9: 1 dispossess nations greater and *s*
9: 14 And I will make you into a nation *s*
11: 23 will dispossess nations larger and *s*
Jos 17: 13 when the Israelites grew *s*,
Jdg 4: 24 hand of the Israelites grew *s* and *s*
14: 18 What is *s* than a lion?"
2Sa 1: 23 they were *s* than lions.
3: 1 David grew *s* and *s*,
13: 14 and since he was *s* than she,
1Ki 16: 22 But Omri's followers proved *s*
20: 23 surely we will be *s* than they
20: 25 Then surely we will be *s* than they
Job 17: 9 those with clean hands will grow *s*.
Ecc 6: 10 contend with one who is *s* than he.
Jer 31: 11 from the hand of those *s* than they.
Da 11: 5 commanders will become even *s*
Lk 11: 22 But when someone *s* attacks
1Co 1: 25 of God is *s* than man's strength.
10: 22 Are we *s* than he? "Everything is
2Pe 2: 11 they are *s* and more powerful,

STRONGEST (STRONG)

2Sa 11: 16 he knew the *s* defenders were.
1Ch 5: 2 Judah was the *s* of his brothers
Da 3: 20 commanded some of the *s* soldiers

STRONGHOLD (STRONGHOLDS)

Jdg 9: 46 went into the *s* of the temple
9: 49 They piled them against the *s*
1Sa 22: 4 as long as David was in the *s*.
22: 5 to David, "Do not stay in the *s*.
24: 22 David and his men went up to the *s*
2Sa 5: 17 about it and went down to the *s*.
22: 3 He is my *s*, my refuge and my
23: 14 At that time David was in the *s*,
1Ch 11: 16 At that time David was in the *s*,
12: 8 to David at his *s* in the desert.
12: 16 also came to David in his *s*.
Job 39: 28 a rocky crag is his *s*.
Ps 9: 9 a *s* in times of trouble.
18: 2 the horn of my salvation, my *s*.
27: 1 The LORD is the *s* of my life—
37: 39 he is their *s* in time of trouble.
43: 2 You are God my *s*.
52: 7 who did not make God his *s*
144: 2 my *s* and my deliverer,
Pr 21: 22 pulls down the *s* in which they trust
Isa 25: 2 the foreigners' *s* a city no more;
31: 9 Their *s* will fall because of terror;
Jer 48: 1 the *s* will be disgraced
51: 53 and fortifies her lofty *s*,
Eze 24: 21 the *s* in which you take pride,
24: 25 on the day I take away their *s*,
30: 15 the *s* of Egypt,
Joel 3: 16 a *s* for the people of Israel.
Am 5: 9 he flashes destruction on the *s*
Mic 4: 8 O *s* of the Daughter of Zion,
Zec 9: 3 Tyre has built herself a *s*;

STRONGHOLDS (STRONGHOLD)

Jdg 6: 2 in mountain clefts, caves and *s*.
1Sa 23: 14 David stayed in the desert *s*
23: 19 hiding among us in the *s* at Horesh,
23: 29 from there and lived in the *s* of En
2Sa 22: 46 they come trembling from their *s*.
Ps 18: 45 they come trembling from their *s*.
89: 40 and reduced his *s* to ruins.
Isa 13: 22 Hyenas will howl in her *s*,
34: 13 nettles and brambles her *s*.
Jer 48: 41 and the *s* taken.
51: 30 they remain in their *s*.
La 2: 2 the *s* of the Daughter of Judah.
2: 5 and destroyed her *s*.
Eze 19: 7 He broke down their *s*
33: 27 and those in *s* and caves will die
Am 3: 11 he will pull down your *s*
Mic 5: 11 and tear down all your *s*.
Zep 3: 6 their *s* are demolished.
2Co 10: 4 have divine power to demolish *s*.

STRUCK (STRIKE)

Ge 19: 11 Then they *s* the men who were
Ex 7: 20 and *s* the water of the Nile,
7: 25 passed after the LORD *s* the Nile
8: 17 and *s* the dust of the ground,
9: 15 stretched out my hand and *s* you
9: 25 Egypt hail *s* everything
12: 27 when he *s* down the Egyptians.' "
12: 29 At midnight the LORD *s*
17: 5 the staff with which you *s* the Nile,
21: 19 one who *s* the blow will not be held
22: 2 breaking in and is *s* so that he dies,
32: 35 And the LORD *s* the people
Nu 3: 13 When I *s* down all the firstborn
8: 17 When I *s* down all the firstborn
11: 33 and he *s* them with a severe plague.
14: 37 bad report about the land were *s*
20: 11 and *s* the rock twice with his staff.
21: 35 So they *s* him down, together
24: 10 He *s* his hands together
31: 16 that a plague *s* the LORD's people.
33: 4 whom the LORD had *s*
Dt 2: 33 him over to us and we *s* him down,
3: 3 We *s* them down, leaving no
Jos 7: 5 and *s* them down on the slopes.
10: 26 Then Joshua *s* and killed the kings
11: 17 captured all their kings and *s* them
Jdg 1: 4 and they *s* down ten thousand men
3: 29 At that time they *s*
3: 31 who *s* down six hundred Philistines
5: 26 She *s* Sisera, she crushed his head,
7: 13 It *s* the tent with such force that
9: 44 in the fields and *s* them down.
12: 4 The Gileadites *s* them down
14: 19 *s* down thirty of their men,
15: 15 and *s* down a thousand men.
20: 35 and on that day the Israelites *s*
20: 45 and *s* down two thousand more.
1Sa 4: 8 are the gods who *s* the Egyptians
6: 4 the same plague has *s* both you
6: 9 that it was not his hand that *s* us
6: 19 But God *s* down some of the men
14: 15 Then panic *s* the whole army—
14: 31 after the Israelites had *s*
17: 35 I seized it by its hair, *s* it
17: 35 *s* it and rescued the sheep
17: 49 *s* the Philistine on the forehead.
17: 50 in his hand he *s* down the Philistine
19: 8 He *s* them with such force that
22: 18 the Edomite turned and *s* them
25: 38 the LORD *s* Nabal and he died.
2Sa 1: 15 him down!" So he *s* him down,
5: 25 and he *s* down the Philistines all
6: 7 therefore God *s* him down
8: 5 *s* down twenty-two thousand
10: 18 *s* down Shobach the commander
11: 15 from him so he will be *s* down
12: 9 You *s* down Uriah the Hittite
12: 15 LORD *s* the child that Uriah's wife
13: 30 "Absalom has *s* down all the king's
14: 6 One *s* the other and killed him.
14: 7 over the one who *s* his brother
18: 15 surrounded Absalom, *s* him
21: 12 after they *s* Saul down on Gilboa.)
21: 17 he *s* the Philistine down
23: 10 and *s* down the Philistines
23: 12 and *s* the Philistines down,
23: 20 He *s* down two of Moab's best men
23: 21 And he *s* down a huge Egyptian.
1Ki 2: 25 and he *s* down Adonijah
2: 34 and *s* down Joab and killed him,
2: 46 and he went out and *s* Shimei down
11: 15 had *s* down all the men in Edom
15: 27 and he *s* him down at Gibbethon,
16: 10 *s* him down and killed him
20: 20 and each one *s* down his opponent.
20: 37 the man *s* him and wounded him.
2Ki 2: 8 rolled it up and *s* the water with it.
2: 14 When he *s* the water, it divided
2: 14 from him and *s* the water with it.
6: 18 So he *s* them with blindness,
13: 18 He *s* it three times and stopped.
13: 19 "You should have *s* the ground five
1Ch 11: 14 and *s* the Philistines down,
11: 22 He *s* down two of Moab's best men
11: 23 he *s* down an Egyptian who was
13: 10 he *s* him down because he had put
14: 16 they *s* down the Philistine army,
18: 5 *s* down twenty-two thousand
18: 12 Abishai son of Zeruiah *s*
2Ch 13: 20 And the LORD *s* him down
14: 12 The LORD *s* down the Cushites
25: 16 Why be *s* down?" So the prophet
Est 9: 5 The Jews *s* down all their enemies
Job 1: 19 and *s* the four corners of the house.
19: 21 for the hand of God has *s* me.
Ps 3: 7 For you have *s* all my enemies
64: 7 suddenly they will be *s* down.
78: 20 When he *s* the rock, water gushed
78: 51 He *s* down all the firstborn
105: 33 he *s* down their vines and fig trees
105: 36 he *s* down all the firstborn
135: 8 He *s* down the firstborn of Egypt,
135: 10 He *s* down many nations
136: 10 to him who *s* down the firstborn
136: 17 who *s* down great kings,
Pr 6: 1 if you have *s* hands in pledge
Isa 9: 13 to him who *s* them,
10: 20 who *s* them down
10: 26 when he *s* down Midian at the rock
14: 6 which in anger *s* down peoples
14: 29 that the rod that *s* you is broken;
27: 7 Has ⌊the LORD⌋ *s* her
27: 7 as he *s* down those who *s* her?
60: 10 Though in anger I *s* you,
Jer 5: 3 You *s* them, but they felt no pain;
26: 23 who had him *s* down with a sword
30: 14 I have *s* you as an enemy would
41: 2 *s* down Gedaliah son of Ahikam,
Da 2: 34 It *s* the statue on its feet of iron
2: 35 the rock that *s* the statue became
Am 4: 9 I *s* them with blight and mildew.
4: 9 "Many times I *s* your gardens
Hag 2: 17 I *s* all the work of your hands
Zec 13: 8 "two-thirds will be *s* down
Mt 26: 51 and *s* the servant of the high priest,

Mt 26: 67 in his face and *s* him with their fists
27: 30 and *s* him on the head again
Mk 12: 4 they *s* this man on the head
14: 47 and *s* the servant of the high priest,
14: 65 they blindfolded him, *s* him
15: 19 and again they *s* him on the head
Lk 6: 48 the torrent *s* that house
6: 49 moment the torrent *s* that house,
22: 50 And one of them *s* the servant
Jn 18: 10 and *s* the high priest's servant,
18: 22 one of the officials nearby *s* him
19: 3 And they *s* him in the face.
Ac 7: 11 "Then a famine *s* all Egypt
12: 7 He *s* Peter on the side
12: 23 an angel of the Lord *s* him down,
23: 3 law by commanding that I be *s!*"
27: 41 But the ship *s* a sandbar
2Co 4: 9 but not abandoned; *s* down,
Rev 8: 12 and a third of the sun was *s,*
11: 11 and terror *s* those who saw them.

STRUCTURE (STRUCTURES)

1Ki 6: 5 and inner sanctuary he built a *s*
1Ch 29: 1 this palatial *s* is not for man
29: 19 everything to build the palatial *s*
Ezr 5: 3 this temple and restore this *s?*"
5: 9 this temple and restore this *s?*"
Eze 1: 16 This was the appearance and *s*
41: 7 *s* surrounding the temple was built

STRUCTURES (STRUCTURE)

1Ki 7: 9 All these *s,* from the

STRUGGLE (STRUGGLED STRUGGLES STRUGGLING)

Ge 30: 8 I have had a great *s* with my sister,
Jdg 12: 2 in a great *s* with the Ammonites,
Job 9: 29 why should I *s* in vain?
41: 8 you will remember the *s*
Ro 15: 30 me in my *s* by praying to God
Eph 6: 12 For our *s* is not against flesh
Php 1: 30 through the same *s* you saw I had,
Heb 12: 4 In your *s* against sin, you have not

STRUGGLED (STRUGGLE)

Ge 32: 28 because you have *s* with God
Hos 12: 3 as a man he *s* with God.
12: 4 He *s* with the angel and overcame

STRUGGLES (STRUGGLE)

Ps 73: 4 They have no *s;*

STRUGGLING (STRUGGLE)

Col 1: 29 To this end I labor, *s*
2: 1 to know how much I am *s* for you

STRUM

Am 6: 5 You *s* away on your harps like

STRUNG (STRING)

Isa 5: 28 all their bows are *s;*
La 2: 4 Like an enemy he has *s* his bow;

STRUT (STRUTTING)

Ps 12: 8 The wicked freely *s* about

STRUTTING (STRUT)

Pr 30: 31 a *s* rooster, a he-goat,

STUBBLE

Ex 5: 12 all over Egypt to gather *s* to use
15: 7 it consumed them like *s.*
Isa 47: 14 Surely they are like *s;*
Joel 2: 5 like a crackling fire consuming *s,*
Ob : 18 the house of Esau will be *s,*
Na 1: 10 they will be consumed like dry *s.*
Mal 4: 1 and every evildoer will be *s,*

STUBBORN (STUBBORNNESS)

Lev 26: 19 I will break down your *s* pride
Dt 2: 30 your God had made his spirit *s*
21: 18 a man has a *s* and rebellious son
21: 20 This son of ours is *s* and rebellious.
Jdg 2: 19 up their evil practices and *s* ways.
Ps 78: 8 a *s* and rebellious generation,
81: 12 I gave them over to their *s* hearts
Isa 48: 4 For I knew how *s* you were;
Jer 5: 23 these people have *s* and rebellious
7: 24 they followed the *s* inclinations
Eze 2: 4 am sending you are obstinate and *s.*
Hos 4: 16 The Israelites are *s,*
4: 16 like a *s* heifer.
Mk 3: 5 deeply distressed at their *s* hearts,
16: 14 their *s* refusal to believe those who

STUBBORN-HEARTED (HEART)

Isa 46: 12 Listen to me, you *s,*

STUBBORNNESS (STUBBORN)

Dt 9: 27 Overlook the *s* of this people,
Jer 3: 17 No longer will they follow the *s*
9: 14 they have followed the *s*
11: 8 they followed the *s*
13: 10 who follow the *s* of their hearts
16: 12 each of you is following the *s*
18: 12 each of us will follow the *s*
23: 17 And to all who follow the *s*
Ro 2: 5 of your *s* and your unrepentant

STUBS

Isa 7: 4 because of these two smoldering *s*

STUCK (STICK)

1Sa 26: 7 camp with his spear *s* in the ground
Job 29: 10 and their tongues *s* to the roof
Ac 27: 41 The bow *s* fast and would not move

STUDDED

SS 1: 11 *s* with silver.

STUDENT (STUDY)

1Ch 25: 8 well as *s,* cast lots for their duties.
Mt 10: 24 "A *s* is not above his teacher,
10: 25 It is enough for the *s*
Lk 6: 40 A *s* is not above his teacher,

STUDIED (STUDY)

Jn 7: 15 learning without having *s?*"

STUDY (STUDENT STUDIED)

Ezr 7: 10 Ezra had devoted himself to the *s*
Ecc 1: 13 myself to *s* and to explore
12: 12 and much *s* wearies the body.
Jn 5: 39 You diligently *s* the Scriptures

STUMBLE (STUMBLED STUMBLES STUMBLING)

Lev 26: 37 They will *s* over one another as
Ps 9: 3 they *s* and perish before you.
27: 2 they will *s* and fall.
37: 24 though he *s,* he will not fall,
119:165 and nothing can make them *s.*
Pr 3: 23 and your foot will not *s;*
4: 12 when you run, you will not *s.*
4: 19 do not know what makes them *s.*
Isa 8: 14 a stone that causes men to *s*
8: 15 Many of them will *s;*
28: 7 they *s* when rendering decisions.
31: 3 he who helps will *s,*
40: 30 and young men *s* and fall;
59: 10 At midday we *s* as if it were
63: 13 they did not *s;*
Jer 6: 21 and sons alike will *s* over them;
12: 5 If you *s* in safe country,
13: 16 before your feet *s*
18: 15 which made them *s* in their ways
20: 11 so my persecutors will *s*
31: 9 a level path where they will not *s,*
46: 6 they *s* and fall.
46: 12 One warrior will *s* over another;
46: 16 They will *s* repeatedly;
50: 32 The arrogant one will *s* and fall
Eze 7: 19 for it has made them *s* into sin.
Da 11: 19 of his own country but will *s*
11: 35 Some of the wise will *s,*
Hos 4: 5 You *s* day and night,
4: 5 and the prophets *s* with you.
5: 5 even Ephraim, *s* in their sin;
14: 9 but the rebellious *s* in them.
Na 2: 5 yet they *s* on their way.
Mal 2: 8 teaching have caused many to *s;*
Jn 11: 9 A man who walks by day will not *s,*
Ro 9: 33 in Zion a stone that causes men to *s*
11: 11 Did they *s* so as to fall
14: 20 that causes someone else to *s.*
1Co 10: 32 Do not cause anyone to *s,*
Jas 3: 2 We all *s* in many ways.
1Pe 2: 8 They *s* because they disobey
2: 8 and, "A stone that causes men to *s*
1Jn 2: 10 nothing in him to make him *s.*

STUMBLED (STUMBLE)

1Sa 2: 4 those who *s* are armed
2Sa 6: 6 the ark of God, because the oxen *s.*
1Ch 13: 9 steady the ark, because the oxen *s.*
Job 4: 4 words have supported those who *s;*
Ps 35: 15 But when I *s,* they gathered in glee;
107: 12 they *s,* and there was no one
Isa 59: 14 truth has *s* in the streets,
Ro 9: 32 They *s* over the "stumbling stone."

STUMBLES (STUMBLE)

Pr 24: 17 when he *s,* do not let your heart
Isa 5: 27 Not one of them grows tired or *s,*
Hos 5: 5 Judah also *s* with them.
Jn 11: 10 is when he walks by night that he *s,*
Jas 2: 10 and yet *s* at just one point is guilty

STUMBLING (STUMBLE)

Lev 19: 14 put a *s* block in front of the blind,
Ps 56: 13 and my feet from *s,*
116: 8 my feet from *s,*
Eze 3: 20 and I put a *s* block before him,
14: 3 and put wicked *s* blocks
14: 4 and puts a wicked *s* block
14: 7 and puts a wicked *s* block
Na 3: 3 people *s* over the corpses—
Mt 16: 23 Satan! You are a *s* block to me;
Ro 9: 32 They stumbled over the "*s* stone."
11: 9 a *s* block and a retribution for them
14: 13 up your mind not to put any *s* block
1Co 1: 23 a *s* block to Jews and foolishness
8: 9 freedom does not become a *s* block
2Co 6: 3 We put no *s* block in anyone's path,

STUMP (STUMPS)

Job 14: 8 and its *s* die in the soil,
Isa 6: 13 so the holy seed will be the *s*
11: 1 up from the *s* of Jesse;
Da 4: 15 But let the *s* and its roots, bound
4: 23 but leave the *s,* bound with iron
4: 26 command to leave the *s* of the tree

STUMPS (STUMP)

Isa 6: 13 leave *s* when they are cut down,

STUNNED

Ge 45: 26 Jacob was *s;* he did not believe
Isa 29: 9 Be *s* and amazed,

STUNTED

Lev 22: 23 or a sheep that is deformed or *s,*

STUPID (STUPIDITY)

Job 18: 3 and considered *s* in your sight?
Pr 12: 1 but he who hates correction is *s.*
Ecc 10: 3 and shows everyone how *s* he is.
2Ti 2: 23 to do with foolish and *s* arguments,

STUPIDITY (STUPID)

Ecc 7: 25 to understand the *s* of wickedness

STUPOR

Ps 78: 65 as a man wakes from the *s* of wine.
Ro 11: 8 "God gave them a spirit of *s,*

STURDIEST (STURDY)

Ps 78: 31 he put to death the *s* among them,

STURDY (STURDIEST)

Isa 10: 16 disease upon his *s* warriors;

SUAH

1Ch 7: 36 *S,* Harnepher, Shual, Beri,

SUBDIVISION (DIVIDE)

2Ch 35: 5 of Levites for each *s* of the families

SUBDIVISIONS (DIVIDE)

2Ch 35: 12 to give them to the *s* of the families

SUBDUE (SUBDUED SUBDUES SUBDUING)

Ge 1: 28 in number; fill the earth and *s* it.
Nu 24: 24 they will *s* Asshur and Eber,

Dt 9: 3 will destroy them; he will *s* them
Jdg 16: 5 so we may tie him up and *s* him.
16: 19 of his hair, and so began to *s* him.
1Ch 17: 10 I will also *s* all your enemies.
Ps 81: 14 quickly would I *s* their enemies
Isa 45: 1 of to *s* nations before him
Da 7: 24 earlier ones; he will *s* three kings.
Mk 5: 4 No one was strong enough to *s* him

SUBDUED (SUBDUE)

Nu 32: 4 the land the LORD *s*
32: 22 the land is *s* before the LORD,
32: 29 then when the land is *s* before you,
Jos 10: 40 So Joshua *s* the whole region,
10: 41 *s* them from Kadesh Barnea
Jdg 4: 23 that day God *s* Jabin,
8: 28 Thus Midian was *s*
11: 33 Thus Israel *s* Ammon.
16: 6 and how you can be tied up and *s*."
1Sa 7: 13 So the Philistines were *s*
2Sa 8: 1 the Philistines and *s* them,
8: 11 gold from all the nations he had *s*:
1Ch 18: 1 the Philistines and *s* them,
2Ch 13: 18 of Israel were *s* on that occasion,
Ne 9: 24 You *s* before them the Canaanites,
Ps 47: 3 He *s* nations under us,
Isa 10: 13 like a mighty one I *s* their kings.
14: 6 and in fury *s* nations
Zec 10: 11 the surging sea will be *s*

SUBDUES (SUBDUE)

Ps 18: 47 who *s* nations under me,
144: 2 who *s* peoples under me.
Isa 41: 2 and *s* kings before him.

SUBDUING (SUBDUE)

Job 41: 9 Any hope of *s* him is false;

SUBJECT (SUBJECTED SUBJECTING SUBJECTS)

Ge 14: 4 For twelve years they had been *s*
Dt 20: 11 in it shall be *s* to forced labor
Jdg 1: 30 but they did *s* them to forced labor.
3: 8 to whom the Israelites were *s*
3: 14 The Israelites were *s* to Eglon king
3: 30 That day Moab was made *s*
9: 28 that we should be *s* to him?
9: 38 is Abimelech that we should be *s*
1Sa 4: 9 or you will be *s* to the Hebrews,
11: 1 with us, and we will be *s* to you."
2Sa 8: 2 So the Moabites became *s* to David
8: 6 and the Arameans became *s* to him
8: 14 all the Edomites became *s* to David
10: 19 with the Israelites and became *s*
22: 44 People I did not know are *s* to me,
1Ch 18: 2 and they became *s* to him
18: 6 and the Arameans became *s* to him
18: 13 all the Edomites became *s* to David
19: 19 with David and became *s* to him.
22: 18 and the land is *s* to the LORD
2Ch 12: 8 however, become *s* to him,
Ne 5: 5 yet we have to *s* our sons
Ps 18: 43 people I did not know are *s* to me.
89: 22 No enemy will *s* him to tribute;
Isa 11: 14 the Ammonites will be *s* to them.
Jer 27: 6 even the wild animals *s* to him.
Mt 5: 21 and anyone who murders will be *s*
5: 22 angry with his brother will be *s*
9: 20 Just then a woman who had been *s*
Mk 5: 25 a woman was there who had been *s*
Lk 8: 43 a woman was there who had been *s*
Ac 17: 32 We want to hear you again on this *s*
1Co 2: 15 he himself is not *s* to any man's
14: 32 of prophets are *s* to the control
15: 28 then the Son himself will be made *s*
Gal 4: 2 He is *s* to guardians and trustees
Tit 2: 5 and to be *s* to their husbands,
2: 9 slaves to be *s* to their masters
3: 1 Remind the people to be *s* to rulers
Heb 2: 8 God left nothing that is not *s*
2: 8 present we do not see everything *s*
5: 2 since he himself is *s* to weakness.

SUBJECTED (SUBJECT)

Jos 17: 13 they *s* the Canaanites
Ezr 9: 7 and our priests have been *s*
Ps 106: 42 and *s* them to their power
107: 12 So he *s* them to bitter labor;
Ro 8: 20 For the creation was *s*
8: 20 but by the will of the one who *s* it,
Heb 2: 5 to angels that he has *s* the world

SUBJECTING (SUBJECT)

Heb 6: 6 and *s* him to public disgrace.

SUBJECTS (SUBJECT)

1Sa 17: 9 we will become your *s*;
17: 9 you will become our *s* and serve us
1Ki 4: 21 and were Solomon's *s* all his life.
1Ch 21: 3 are they not all my lord's *s*?
Pr 14: 28 but without *s* a prince is ruined.
Mt 8: 12 the *s* of the kingdom will be thrown
Lk 19: 14 "But his *s* hated him and sent

SUBJUGATE (SUBJUGATED)

Jer 27: 7 nations and great kings will *s* him.

SUBJUGATED (SUBJUGATE)

1Ch 20: 4 and the Philistines were *s*.

SUBMISSION (SUBMIT)

1Ch 29: 24 pledged their *s* to King Solomon.
Da 11: 43 with the Libyans and Nubians in *s*.
1Co 14: 34 but must be in *s*, as the Law says.
1Ti 2: 11 learn in quietness and full *s*.
Heb 5: 7 heard because of his reverent *s*.
1Pe 3: 22 authorities and powers in *s* to him.

SUBMISSIVE (SUBMIT)

Jas 3: 17 then peace loving, considerate, *s*,
1Pe 3: 1 in the same way be *s*
3: 5 They were *s* to their own husbands,
5: 5 in the same way be *s*

SUBMIT (SUBMISSION SUBMISSIVE SUBMITS SUBMITTED)

Ge 16: 9 back to your mistress and *s* to her."
41: 40 are to *s* to your orders.
49: 15 and *s* to forced labor.
2Ch 30: 8 your fathers were; *s* to the LORD.
Job 22: 21 *S* to God and be at peace with him;
Ps 68: 31 Cush will *s* herself to God.
81: 11 Israel would not *s* to me.
Lk 10: 17 the demons *s* to us in your name."
10: 20 do not rejoice that the spirits *s*
Ro 8: 7 It does not *s* to God's law,
10: 3 did not *s* to God's righteousness.
13: 1 Everyone must *s* himself
13: 5 necessary to *s* to the authorities,
1Co 16: 16 to *s* to such as these
Eph 5: 21 *S* to one another out of reverence
5: 22 *s* to your husbands as to the Lord.
5: 24 wives should *s* to their husbands
Col 2: 20 do you *s* to its rules: "Do not
3: 18 Wives, *s* to your husbands,
Heb 12: 9 How much more should we *s*
13: 17 Obey your leaders and *s*
Jas 4: 7 *S* yourselves, then, to God.
1Pe 2: 13 *S* yourselves for the Lord's sake
2: 18 *s* yourselves to your masters

SUBMITS (SUBMIT)

Eph 5: 24 Now as the church *s* to Christ,

SUBMITTED (SUBMIT)

La 5: 6 We *s* to Egypt and Assyria

SUBORDINATES

1Ki 11: 11 and give it to one of your *s*.

SUBSIDE (SUBSIDED SUBSIDES)

Eze 5: 13 and my wrath against them will *s*,
16: 42 Then my wrath against you will *s*
21: 17 and my wrath will *s*.

SUBSIDED (SUBSIDE)

Jdg 8: 3 their resentment against him *s*.
Est 2: 1 the anger of King Xerxes had *s*,
7: 10 Then the king's fury *s*.
Eze 24: 13 until my wrath against you has *s*.
Lk 8: 24 the storm *s*, and all was calm.

SUBSIDES (SUBSIDE)

Ge 27: 44 a while until your brother's fury *s*.

SUBSTANCE

Da 7: 1 He wrote down the *s* of his dream.

SUBSTITUTE (SUBSTITUTION)

Lev 27: 10 both it and the *s* become holy.
27: 10 if he should *s* one animal
27: 10 or *s* a good one for a bad one,
27: 33 the animal and its *s* become holy

SUBSTITUTION (SUBSTITUTE)

Lev 27: 33 good from the bad or make any *s*.
27: 33 he does make a *s*, both the animal

SUBTRACT

Dt 4: 2 what I command you and do not *s*

SUBVERTING

Lk 23: 2 have found this man *s* our nation.

SUCATHITES

1Ch 2: 55 the Tirathites, Shimeathites and *S*.

SUCCEED (SUCCEEDED SUCCEEDS SUCCESS SUCCESSFUL SUCCESSIVE SUCCESSOR SUCCESSORS)

Lev 6: 22 The son who is to *s* him
16: 32 and ordained to *s* his father
Nu 14: 41 This will not *s*! Do not go up,
1Sa 30: 8 will certainly overtake them and *s*
2Sa 7: 12 raise up your offspring to *s* you,
1Ki 5: 1 king to *s* his father David,
15: 4 by raising up a son to *s* him
19: 16 to *s* you as prophet.
22: 22 " 'You will *s* in luring him,'
2Ki 3: 27 his firstborn son, who was to *s* him
1Ch 17: 11 raise up your offspring to *s* you,
2Ch 13: 12 of your fathers, for you will not *s*."
18: 21 " 'You will *s* in luring him,'
Job 30: 13 they *s* in destroying me—
Ps 20: 4 and make all your plans *s*.
21: 11 wicked schemes, they cannot *s*;
37: 7 fret when men *s* in their ways,
140: 8 do not let their plans *s*,
Pr 15: 22 but with many advisers they *s*.
16: 3 and your plans will *s*.
21: 30 that can *s* against the LORD.
Ecc 11: 6 for you do not know which will *s*,
Isa 47: 12 Perhaps you will *s*,
48: 15 and he will *s* in his mission.
Jer 32: 5 the Babylonians, you will not *s*.' "
Eze 17: 15 Will he *s*? Will he who does such
21: 13 It will not *s*! declares the Sovereign
Da 8: 24 and will *s* in whatever he does.
11: 17 but his plans will not *s* or help him.

SUCCEEDED (SUCCEED)

Ge 36: 33 son of Zerah from Bozrah *s* him
36: 34 the land of the Temanites *s* him
36: 35 in the country of Moab, *s* him
36: 36 Samlah from Masrekah *s* him
36: 37 from Rehoboth on the river *s* him
36: 38 Baal Hanan son of Acbor *s* him
36: 39 son of Acbor died, Hadad *s* him
Dt 10: 6 and Eleazar his son *s* him as priest.
2Sa 10: 1 and his son Hanun *s* him as king.
1Ki 8: 20 I have *s* David my father
11: 43 Rehoboam his son *s* him as king.
14: 20 And Nadab his son *s* him as king.
14: 31 And Abijah his son *s* him as king.
15: 8 And Asa his son *s* him as king.
15: 24 Jehoshaphat his son *s* him as king.
15: 28 year of Asa king of Judah and *s* him
16: 6 And Elah his son *s* him as king
16: 10 Then he *s* him as king.
16: 28 And Ahab his son *s* him as king.
22: 40 And Ahaziah his son *s* him as king.
22: 50 And Jehoram his son *s* him.
2Ki 1: 17 Joram *s* him as king
8: 15 Then Hazael *s* him as king.
8: 24 And Ahaziah his son *s* him as king.
10: 35 And Jehoahaz his son *s* him as king
12: 21 And Amaziah his son *s* him as king
13: 9 And Jehoash his son *s* him as king.
13: 13 and Jeroboam *s* him on the throne.
13: 24 Ben-Hadad his son *s* him as king.
14: 16 Jeroboam his son *s* him as king.
14: 29 Zechariah his son *s* him as king.
15: 7 And Jotham his son *s* him as king.
15: 10 assassinated him and *s* him as king.
15: 14 assassinated him and *s* him as king.
15: 22 And Pekahiah his son *s* him as king

2Ki 15:25 Pekah killed Pekahiah and *s* him
15:30 and then *s* him as king
15:38 And Ahaz his son *s* him as king.
16:20 And Hezekiah his son *s* him as king
19:37 Esarhaddon his son *s* him as king.
20:21 Manasseh his son *s* him as king.
21:18 And Amon his son *s* him as king.
21:26 And Josiah his son *s* him as king.
24: 6 Jehoiachin his son *s* him as king.
1Ch 1:44 son of Zerah from Bozrah *s* him
1:45 the land of the Temanites *s* him
1:46 in the country of Moab, *s* him
1:47 Samlah from Masrekah *s* him
1:48 from Rehoboth on the river *s* him
1:49 Baal-Hanan son of Acbor *s* him
1:50 Baal-Hanan died, Hadad *s* him
19: 1 Ammonites died, and his son *s* him
27:34 Ahithophel was *s* by Jehoiada son
29:28 His son Solomon *s* him as king.
2Ch 6:10 I have *s* David my father
7:11 and had *s* in carrying out all he had
9:31 Rehoboam his son *s* him as king.
12:16 And Abijah his son *s* him as king.
14: 1 Asa his son *s* him as king,
17: 1 Jehoshaphat his son *s* him as king
21: 1 And Jehoram his son *s* him as king.
24:27 And Amaziah his son *s* him as king
26:23 And Jotham his son *s* him as king.
27: 9 And Ahaz his son *s* him as king.
28:27 And Hezekiah his son *s* him as king
32:30 He *s* in everything he undertook.
32:33 Manasseh his son *s* him as king.
33:20 And Amon his son *s* him as king.
36: 8 Jehoiachin his son *s* him as king.
Isa 37:38 Esarhaddon his son *s* him as king.
Jer 22:11 who *s* his father as king of Judah
Da 11:21 "He will be *s* by a contemptible
Ac 24:27 two years had passed, Felix was *s*

SUCCEEDS (SUCCEED)

Ex 29:30 The son who *s* him as priest
Pr 17: 8 wherever he turns, he *s*.

SUCCESS (SUCCEED)

Ge 24:12 master Abraham, give me *s* today,
24:40 and make your journey a *s*,
24:42 please grant *s* to the journey
24:56 now that the LORD has granted *s*
27:20 "The LORD your God gave me *s*,"
39: 3 and that the LORD gave him *s*
39:23 and gave him *s* in whatever he did.
1Sa 18:14 In everything he did he had great *s*,
18:30 met with more *s* than the rest
25:31 LORD has brought my master *s*,
1Ki 22:13 the other prophets are predicting *s*
1Ch 12:18 *S*, *s* to you, and *s*
22:11 may you have *s* and build the house
22:13 you will have *s* if you are careful
2Ch 18:12 the other prophets are predicting *s*
26: 5 the LORD, God gave him *s*.
Ne 1:11 Give your servant *s* today
2:20 "The God of heaven will give us *s*.
Job 5:12 so that their hands achieve no *s*.
6:13 now that *s* has been driven from me
Ps 118:25 O LORD, grant us *s*.
Ecc 10:10 but skill will bring *s*.
Da 11:14 of the vision, but without *s*.

SUCCESSFUL (SUCCEED)

Ge 24:21 the LORD had made his journey *s*.
Jos 1: 7 that you may be *s* wherever you go.
1: 8 Then you will be prosperous and *s*.
Jdg 18: 5 whether our journey will be *s*."
1Sa 18:15 When Saul saw how *s* he was,
2Ki 18: 7 he was *s* in whatever he undertook.
2Ch 20:20 in his prophets and you will be *s*."
Da 11:36 He will be *s* until the time

SUCCESSIVE (SUCCEED)

2Sa 21: 1 there was a famine for three *s* years
Eze 41: 7 temple were wider at each *s* level.

SUCCESSOR (SUCCEED)

1Ki 1:48 to see a *s* on my throne today.' "
1Ch 27: 7 his son Zebadiah was his *s*.
Ecc 2:12 What more can the king's *s* do
4:15 followed the youth, the king's *s*.
4:16 later were not pleased with the *s*.

Da 11:20 "His *s* will send out a tax collector

SUCCESSORS (SUCCEED)

1Ch 3:16 *s* of Jehoiakim: Jehoiachin his son,

SUCCOTH

Ge 33:17 Jacob, however, went to *S*,
33:17 That is why the place is called *S*.
Ex 12:37 journeyed from Rameses to *S*.
13:20 After leaving *S* they camped
Nu 33: 5 left Rameses and camped at *S*.
33: 6 They left *S* and camped at Etham,
Jos 13:27 *S* and Zaphon with the rest
Jdg 8: 5 of *S*, "Give my troops some bread;
8: 6 of *S* said, "Do you already have
8: 8 they answered as the men of *S* had.
8:14 He caught a young man of *S*
8:14 of the seventy-seven officials of *S*,
8:15 came and said to the men of *S*,
8:16 and taught the men of *S* a lesson
1Ki 7:46 the plain of the Jordan between *S*
2Ch 4:17 the plain of the Jordan between *S*
Ps 60: 6 and measure off the Valley of *S*.
108: 7 and measure off the Valley of *S*.

SUCCOTH BENOTH

2Ki 17:30 The men from Babylon made *S*,

SUCK (SUCKLING)

Job 20:16 He will *s* the poison of serpents;

SUCKLING (SUCK)

1Sa 7: 9 Then Samuel took a *s* lamb

SUDDEN

Lev 26:16 I will bring upon you *s* terror,
Dt 28:20 are destroyed and come to *s* ruin
Jdg 20:37 been in ambush made a *s* dash
Job 9:23 When a scourge brings *s* death,
22:10 why *s* peril terrifies you,
Ps 6:10 may they turn back in *s* disgrace.
Pr 3:25 Have no fear of *s* disaster
24:22 those two will send *s* destruction
Isa 17:14 In the evening, *s* terror!
Zep 1:18 for he will make a *s* end
Jn 19:34 bringing a *s* flow of blood

SUE

Mt 5:40 And if someone wants to *s* you

SUFFER (LONG-SUFFERING SUFFERED SUFFERING SUFFERINGS SUFFERS)

Ge 4:15 he will *s* vengeance seven times
Nu 14:34 you will *s* for your sins
Dt 26: 6 mistreated us and made us *s*,
Ezr 4:13 and the royal revenues will *s*.
Job 24:11 tread the winepresses, yet *s* thirst.
36:15 those who *s* he delivers
Ps 42:10 My bones *s* mortal agony
Pr 9:12 are a mocker, you alone will *s*."
11:15 for another will surely *s*,
22: 3 the simple keep going and *s* for it.
27:12 the simple keep going and *s* for it.
Isa 47: 8 or *s* the loss of children.'
53:10 to crush him and cause him to *s*,
54: 4 not be afraid; you will not *s* shame.
Jer 14:13 will not see the sword or *s* famine.
15:15 think of how I *s* reproach
Eze 23:49 You will *s* the penalty
36: 7 around you will also *s* scorn.
36:15 and no longer will you *s* the scorn
36:30 that you will no longer *s* disgrace
Da 6: 2 so that the king might not *s* loss.
Mt 16:21 and *s* many things at the hands
17:12 of Man is going to *s* at their hands
Mk 8:31 the Son of Man must *s* many things
9:12 the Son of Man must *s* much
Lk 9:22 Son of Man must *s* many things
17:25 But first he must *s* many things
22:15 Passover with you before I *s*.
24:26 the Christ have to *s* these things
24:46 The Christ will *s* and rise
Ac 3:18 saying that his Christ would *s*.
9:16 will show him how much he must *s*
17: 3 and proving that the Christ had to *s*
26:23 that the Christ would *s* and,
1Co 3:15 he will *s* loss; he himself will be
2Co 1: 6 of the same sufferings we *s*.

Php 1:29 to *s* for him, since you are going
1Th 5: 9 God did not appoint us to *s* wrath
Heb 9:26 would have had to *s* many times
1Pe 1: 6 had to *s* grief in all kinds
2:20 But if you *s* for doing good
3:14 if you should *s* for what is right,
3:17 to *s* for doing good
4:15 If you *s*, it should not be
4:16 However, if you *s* as a Christian,
4:19 those who *s* according
Jude : 7 of those who *s* the punishment
Rev 2:10 afraid of what you are about to *s*.
2:10 you will *s* persecution for ten days.
2:22 adultery with her *s* intensely,

SUFFERED (SUFFER)

1Sa 4:17 and the army has *s* heavy losses.
Ps 88:15 I have *s* your terrors and am
107: 17 *s* affliction because of their
119:107 I have *s* much;
Isa 38:17 that I *s* such anguish.
Jer 14:17 has *s* a grievous wound,
44:17 and were well off and *s* no harm.
La 3:47 We have *s* terror and pitfalls,
Eze 36: 6 you have *s* the scorn of the nations.
Mt 27:19 for I have *s* a great deal today
Mk 5:26 She had *s* a great deal
Lk 13: 2 Galileans because they *s* this way?
Ac 28: 5 off into the fire and *s* no ill effects.
2Co 1: 8 about the hardships we *s*
Gal 3: 4 Have you *s* so much for nothing—
Col 1:24 Now I rejoice in what was *s* for you
1Th 2: 2 We had previously *s* and been
2:14 You *s* from your own countrymen
2:14 the same things those churches *s*
Heb 2: 9 and honor because he *s* death,
2:18 Because he himself *s*
5: 8 learned obedience from what he *s*
13:12 also *s* outside the city gate
1Pe 2:21 Christ *s* for you, leaving you
2:23 when he *s*, he made no threats.
4: 1 Therefore, since Christ *s*
4: 1 he who has *s* in his body is done
5:10 after you have *s* a little while,
Rev 9: 5 And the agony they *s* was like that

SUFFERING (SUFFER)

Ge 16: 5 responsible for the wrong I am *s*.
41:52 fruitful in the land of my *s*."
Ex 3: 7 and I am concerned about their *s*.
Nu 5:24 will enter her and cause bitter *s*.
5:27 it will go into her and cause bitter *s*;
14:33 years, *s* for your unfaithfulness,
Dt 28:53 of the *s* that your enemy will inflict
28:55 of the *s* your enemy will inflict
2Ki 13:14 Now Elisha was *s* from the illness
14:26 whether slave or free, was *s*;
Ne 9: 9 "You saw the *s* of our forefathers
Job 2:13 they saw how great his *s* was.
30:16 days of *s* grip me.
30:27 days of *s* confront me.
36:15 who suffer he delivers in their *s*;
Ps 22:24 the *s* of the afflicted one;
55: 3 for they bring down *s* upon me
107: 10 prisoners *s* in iron chains,
119: 50 My comfort in my *s* is this:
119:153 Look upon my *s* and deliver me,
Isa 14: 3 the LORD gives you relief from *s*
53: 3 of sorrows, and familiar with *s*.
53:11 After the *s* of his soul,
La 1:12 Is any *s* like my *s*
1:18 look upon my *s*.
Joel 1:18 even the flocks of sheep are *s*.
Mt 4:24 those *s* severe pain,
8: 6 at home paralyzed and in terrible *s*
15:22 My daughter is *s* terribly
17:15 "He is an epileptic and is *s* greatly.
Mk 5:29 body that she was freed from her *s*.
5:34 and be freed from your *s*."
Lk 4:38 Now Simon's mother-in-law was *s*
14: 2 of him was a man *s* from dropsy.
Ac 1: 3 After his *s*, he showed himself
5:41 worthy of *s* disgrace for the Name.
7:11 bringing great *s*, and our fathers
28: 8 *s* from fever and dysentery.
Ro 5: 3 know that *s* produces
1Th 1: 6 spite of severe *s*, you welcomed
2Th 1: 5 of God, for which you are *s*.

2Ti 1: 8 But join with me in *s* for the gospel,
1: 12 That is why I am *s* as I am.
2: 9 for which I am *s* even to the point
Heb 2: 10 of their salvation perfect through *s*.
10: 32 in a great contest in the face of *s*.
13: 3 as if you yourselves were *s*.
Jas 5: 10 example of patience in the face of *s*,
1Pe 2: 19 up under the pain of unjust *s*
4: 12 at the painful trial you are *s*,
Rev 1: 9 companion in the *s* and kingdom
2: 22 So I will cast her on a bed of *s*,

SUFFERINGS (SUFFER)

Job 9: 28 I still dread all my *s*,
Ro 5: 3 but we also rejoice in our *s*,
8: 17 share in his *s* in order that we may
8: 18 that our present *s* are not worth
2Co 1: 5 as the *s* of Christ flow
1: 6 endurance of the same *s* we suffer.
1: 7 know that just as you share in our *s*,
Eph 3: 13 to be discouraged because of my *s*
Php 3: 10 the fellowship of sharing in his *s*,
2Ti 3: 11 love, endurance, persecutions, *s*—
1Pe 1: 11 when he predicted the *s* of Christ
4: 13 rejoice that you participate in the *s*
5: 1 a witness of Christ's *s* and one who
5: 9 are undergoing the same kind of *s*.

SUFFERS (SUFFER)

Job 15: 20 his days the wicked man *s* torment,
Pr 13: 20 but a companion of fools *s* harm.
1Co 12: 26 If one part *s*, every part *s* with it;

SUFFICIENT

Lev 25: 26 and acquires *s* means to redeem it,
Isa 40: 16 Lebanon is not *s* for altar fires,
2Co 2: 6 on him by the majority is *s* for him.
12: 9 said to me, "My grace is *s* for you,
Php 1: 20 but will have *s* courage so that now

SUGGEST (SUGGESTED SUGGESTION)

Ru 4: 4 *s* that you buy it in the presence

SUGGESTED (SUGGEST)

1Ki 22: 20 "One *s* this, and another that.
2Ch 18: 19 "One *s* this, and another that.
Ezr 10: 5 under oath to do what had been *s*.
Est 2: 15 was in charge of the harem, *s*.
6: 10 you have *s* for Mordecai the Jew,

SUGGESTION (SUGGEST)

Est 5: 14 This *s* delighted Haman,

SUIT (SUITABLE)

2Ti 4: 3 Instead, to *s* their own desires,

SUITABLE (SUIT)

Ge 2: 18 I will make a helper *s* for him."
2: 20 for Adam no *s* helper was found.
Nu 32: 1 and Gilead were *s* for livestock.
32: 4 are *s* for livestock, and your

SUKKITES

2Ch 12: 3 *S* and Cushites that came with him

SULFUR

Ge 19: 24 rained down burning *s* on Sodom
Dt 29: 23 be a burning waste of salt and *s*—
Job 18: 15 burning *s* is scattered
Ps 11: 6 fiery coals and burning *s*;
Isa 30: 33 like a stream of burning *s*,
34: 9 her dust into burning *s*;
Eze 38: 22 hailstones and burning *s* on him
Lk 17: 29 fire and *s* rained down from heaven
Rev 9: 17 dark blue, and yellow as *s*.
9: 17 mouths came fire, smoke and *s*.
9: 18 *s* that came out of their mouths.
14: 10 with burning *s* in the presence
19: 20 into the fiery lake of burning *s*.
20: 10 thrown into the lake of burning *s*,
21: 8 be in the fiery lake of burning *s*.

SULKING

1Ki 21: 4 lay on his bed *s* and refused to eat.

SULLEN

1Ki 20: 43 *S* and angry, the king of Israel went
21: 4 *s* and angry because Naboth

1Ki 21: 5 you so *s*? Why won't you eat?"

SUM (SUMMED SUMS)

Ps 139: 17 How vast is the *s* of them!
Mt 28: 12 they gave the soldiers a large *s*
Ac 7: 16 Shechem for a certain *s* of money.
1Co 16: 2 set aside a *s* of money in keeping

SUMMED (SUM)

Ro 13: 9 there may be, are *s* up
Gal 5: 14 The entire law is *s* up

SUMMER

Ge 8: 22 *s* and winter,
Jdg 3: 20 in the upper room of his *s* palace
Ps 32: 4 as in the heat of *s*.
74: 17 you made both *s* and winter.
Pr 6: 8 yet it stores its provisions in *s*
10: 5 who gathers crops in *s* is a wise son,
26: 1 Like snow in *s* or rain in harvest,
30: 25 yet they store up their food in the *s*;
Isa 18: 6 the birds will feed on them all *s*,
Jer 8: 20 the *s* has ended,
40: 10 you are to harvest the wine, *s* fruit
40: 12 an abundance of wine and *s* fruit.
Da 2: 35 chaff on a threshing floor in the *s*.
Am 3: 15 house along with the *s* house;
Mic 7: 1 I am like one who gathers *s* fruit
Zec 14: 8 and half to the western sea, in *s*
Mt 24: 32 leaves come out, you know that *s* is
Mk 13: 28 leaves come out, you know that *s* is
Lk 21: 30 for yourselves and know that *s* is

SUMMIT

2Sa 15: 32 When David arrived at the *s*,
16: 1 gone a short distance beyond the *s*,
SS 4: 8 the top of Senir, the *s* of Hermon,
Jer 22: 6 like the *s* of Lebanon,

SUMMON (SUMMONED SUMMONING SUMMONS)

Nu 22: 5 sent messengers to *s* Balaam son
22: 20 these men have come to *s* you,
Dt 25: 8 the elders of his town shall *s* him
33: 19 They will *s* peoples
2Sa 17: 5 "*S* also Hushai the Arkite,
20: 4 "*S* the men of Judah to come to me
20: 5 But when Amasa went to *s* Judah,
1Ki 18: 19 *s* the people from all over Israel
22: 13 gone to *s* Micaiah said to him,
2Ki 10: 19 Now *s* all the prophets of Baal,
2Ch 18: 12 gone to *s* Micaiah said to him,
Job 9: 19 a matter of justice, who will *s* him?
13: 22 Then *s* me and I will answer,
19: 16 I *s* my servant, but he does not
Ps 68: 28 *S* your power, O God;
Isa 22: 20 "In that day I will *s* my servant,
46: 11 From the east I *s* a bird of prey;
48: 13 when I *s* them,
55: 5 Surely you will *s* nations you know
Jer 1: 15 I am about to *s* all the peoples
25: 9 I will *s* all the peoples of the north
50: 29 "*S* archers against Babylon,
51: 27 *s* against her these kingdoms:
La 2: 22 "As you *s* to a feast day,
Eze 38: 21 I will *s* a sword against Gog
Joel 1: 14 *S* the elders

SUMMONED (SUMMON)

Ge 12: 18 So Pharaoh *s* Abram.
20: 8 next morning Abimelech *s* all his
26: 9 So Abimelech *s* Isaac and said,
Ex 1: 18 the king of Egypt *s* the midwives
7: 11 Pharaoh then *s* wise men
8: 8 Pharaoh *s* Moses and Aaron
8: 25 Then Pharaoh *s* Moses and Aaron
9: 27 Then Pharaoh *s* Moses and Aaron.
10: 16 Pharaoh quickly *s* Moses
10: 24 Then Pharaoh *s* Moses and said,
12: 21 Moses *s* all the elders of Israel
12: 31 During the night Pharaoh *s* Moses
19: 7 and *s* the elders of the people
36: 2 Then Moses *s* Bezalel and Oholiab
Lev 9: 1 On the eighth day Moses *s* Aaron
10: 4 Moses *s* Mishael and Elzaphan,
Nu 12: 5 entrance to the Tent and *s* Aaron
16: 12 Then Moses *s* Dathan and Abiram,
24: 10 "I *s* you to curse my enemies,

Dt 5: 1 Moses *s* all Israel and said: Hear,
29: 2 Moses *s* all the Israelites
31: 7 Moses *s* Joshua and said to him
Jos 9: 22 Then Joshua *s* the Gibeonites
10: 24 he *s* all the men of Israel
22: 1 Then Joshua *s* the Reubenites,
23: 2 *s* all Israel—their elders, leaders,
24: 1 He *s* the elders, leaders, judges
Jdg 4: 10 where he *s* Zebulun and Naphtali.
1Sa 10: 17 Samuel *s* the people of Israel
13: 4 And the people were *s* to join Saul
15: 4 Saul *s* the men and mustered them
2Sa 9: 9 Then the king *s* Ziba, Saul's servant
14: 33 Then the king *s* Absalom,
21: 2 The king *s* the Gibeonites
1Ki 2: 42 the king *s* Shimei and said to him,
8: 1 King Solomon *s* into his presence
18: 3 and Ahab had *s* Obadiah, who was
20: 7 The king of Israel *s* all the elders
20: 15 So Ahab *s* the young officers
2Ki 4: 36 Elisha *s* Gehazi and said, "Call
6: 11 He *s* his officers and demanded
9: 1 The prophet Elisha *s* a man
12: 7 Therefore King Joash *s* Jehoiada
1Ch 15: 11 Then David *s* Zadok and Abiathar
28: 1 David *s* all the officials of Israel
2Ch 5: 2 Solomon *s* to Jerusalem the elders
24: 6 Therefore the king *s* Jehoiada
Ezr 8: 16 So I *s* Eliezer, Ariel, Shemaiah,
Ne 5: 12 I *s* the priests and made the nobles
Est 2: 14 with her and *s* her by name.
3: 12 month the royal secretaries were *s*.
4: 5 Then Esther *s* Hathach, one
4: 11 court without being *s* the king has
8: 9 once the royal secretaries were *s*—
Job 9: 16 Even if I *s* him and he responded,
Isa 13: 3 I have *s* my warriors
La 1: 15 he has *s* an army against me
2: 22 so you *s* against me terrors
Da 2: 2 So the king *s* the magicians,
3: 2 He then *s* the satraps, prefects,
3: 13 Nebuchadnezzar *s* Shadrach,
Am 5: 16 The farmers will be *s* to weep
Jn 9: 24 A second time they *s* the man who
18: 33 back inside the palace, *s* Jesus

SUMMONING (SUMMON)

Jdg 6: 34 *s* the Abiezrites to follow him.
Mk 15: 44 *S* the centurion, he asked him

SUMMONS (SUMMON)

Nu 22: 37 "Did I not send you an urgent *s*?
Ps 50: 1 speaks and *s* the earth
50: 4 He *s* the heavens above,
Na 2: 5 He *s* his picked troops,

SUMS (SUM)

Mt 7: 12 for this *s* up the Law

SUN (SUNDOWN SUNRISE SUNSET SUNSHINE)

Ge 15: 12 As the *s* was setting, Abram fell
15: 17 When the *s* had set and darkness
19: 23 the *s* had risen over the land.
28: 11 for the night because the *s* had set.
29: 7 "Look," he said, "the *s* is still high;
32: 31 The *s* rose above him as he passed
37: 9 and this time the *s* and moon
Ex 16: 21 and when the *s* grew hot, it melted
Lev 22: 7 When the *s* goes down, he will be
Dt 4: 19 up to the sky and see the *s*,
11: 30 toward the setting *s*,
16: 6 *s* goes down, on the anniversary
17: 3 bowing down to them or to the *s*
33: 14 with the best the *s* brings forth
Jos 10: 12 "O *s*, stand still over Gibeon,
10: 13 So the *s* stood still,
10: 13 The *s* stopped in the middle
Jdg 5: 31 may they who love you be like the *s*
19: 14 and the *s* set as they neared Gibeah
1Sa 11: 9 'By the time the *s* is hot tomorrow,
2Sa 2: 24 Abner, and as the *s* was setting,
3: 35 or anything else before the *s* sets!"
1Ki 22: 36 As the *s* was setting, a cry spread
2Ki 3: 22 the *s* was shining on the water.
23: 5 burned incense to Baal, to the *s*
23: 11 of Judah had dedicated to the *s*.
23: 11 the chariots dedicated to the *s*.

Ne 7: 3 not to be opened until the *s* is hot.
Job 9: 7 to the *s* and it does not shine;
30: 28 about blackened, but not by the *s;*
31: 26 if I have regarded the *s*
37: 21 Now no one can look at the *s,*
Ps 19: 4 he has pitched a tent for the *s,*
37: 6 of your cause like the noonday *s.*
50: 1 the earth from the rising of the *s*
58: 8 child, may they not see the *s.*
72: 5 He will endure as long as the *s,*
72: 17 may it continue as long as the *s.*
74: 16 you established the *s* and moon.
84: 11 For the LORD God is a *s*
89: 36 endure before me like the *s;*
104: 19 and the *s* knows when to go down.
104: 22 The *s* rises, and they steal away;
113: 3 From the rising of the *s*
121: 6 the *s* will not harm you by day,
136: 8 the *s* to govern the day,
148: 3 Praise him, *s* and moon,
Ecc 1: 3 labor at which he toils under the *s?*
1: 5 The *s* rises and the *s* sets,
1: 9 there is nothing new under the *s.*
1: 14 things that are done under the *s;*
2: 11 nothing was gained under the *s.*
2: 17 under the *s* was grievous to me.
2: 18 things I had toiled for under the *s,*
2: 19 my effort and skill under the *s.*
2: 20 all my toilsome labor under the *s.*
2: 22 with which he labors under the *s?*
3: 16 I saw something else under the *s:*
4: 1 that was taking place under the *s:*
4: 3 that is done under the *s.*
4: 7 meaningless under the *s:*
4: 15 under the *s* followed the youth,
5: 13 seen a grievous evil under the *s:*
5: 18 under the *s* during the few days
6: 1 I have seen another evil under the *s*
6: 5 Though it never saw the *s*
6: 12 under the *s* after he is gone?
7: 11 and benefits those who see the *s.*
8: 9 to everything done under the *s.*
8: 15 for a man under the *s* than to eat
8: 15 life God has given him under the *s.*
8: 17 what goes on under the *s.*
9: 3 that happens under the *s:*
9: 6 anything that happens under the *s.*
9: 9 God has given you under the *s*—
9: 9 in your toilsome labor under the *s.*
9: 11 seen something else under the *s:*
9: 13 also saw under the *s* this example
10: 5 is an evil I have seen under the *s,*
11: 7 and it pleases the eyes to see the *s.*
12: 2 before the *s* and the light
SS 1: 6 because I am darkened by the *s.*
6: 10 fair as the moon, bright as the *s,*
Isa 13: 10 The rising *s* will be darkened
24: 23 will be abashed, the *s* ashamed;
30: 26 The moon will shine like the *s,*
38: 8 by the *s* go back the ten steps it has
41: 25 one from the rising *s* who calls
45: 6 so that from the rising of the *s*
49: 10 will the desert heat or the *s* beat
59: 19 and from the rising of the *s,*
60: 19 The *s* will no more be your light
60: 20 Your *s* will never set again,
Jer 8: 2 They will be exposed to the *s*
15: 9 Her *s* will set while it is still day;
31: 35 he who appoints the *s*
43: 13 There in the temple of the *s*
Eze 8: 16 bowing down to the *s* in the east.
32: 7 I will cover the *s* with a cloud,
Hos 6: 3 As surely as the *s* rises,
Joel 2: 10 the *s* and moon are darkened,
2: 31 The *s* will be turned to darkness
3: 15 The *s* and moon will be darkened,
Am 8: 9 "I will make the *s* go down at noon
Jnh 4: 8 When the *s* rose, God provided
4: 8 and the *s* blazed on Jonah's head
Mic 3: 6 The *s* will set for the prophets,
Na 3: 17 when the *s* appears they fly away,
Hab 3: 11 *S* and moon stood still
Mal 1: 11 the rising to the setting of the *s.*
4: 2 the *s* of righteousness will rise
Mt 5: 45 He causes his *s* to rise on the evil
13: 6 But when the *s* came up, the plants
13: 43 the righteous will shine like the *s*
17: 2 His face shone like the *s,*
24: 29 " 'the *s* will be darkened,
Mk 4: 6 But when the *s* came up, the plants
13: 24 " 'the *s* will be darkened,
Lk 1: 78 by which the rising *s* will come
4: 40 When the *s* was setting, the people
21: 25 "There will be signs in the *s,*
23: 45 for the *s* stopped shining.
Ac 2: 20 The *s* will be turned to darkness
13: 11 unable to see the light of the *s.*"
26: 13 brighter than the *s,* blazing
27: 20 When neither *s* nor stars appeared
1Co 15: 41 The *s* has one kind of splendor,
Eph 4: 26 Do not let the *s* go
Jas 1: 11 For the *s* rises with scorching heat
Rev 1: 16 His face was like the *s* shining
6: 12 *s* turned black like sackcloth made
7: 16 The *s* will not beat upon them,
8: 12 and a third of the *s* was struck,
9: 2 The *s* and sky were darkened
10: 1 his face was like the *s,*
12: 1 a woman clothed with the *s,*
16: 8 and the *s* was given power
16: 8 angel poured out his bowl on the *s,*
19: 17 I saw an angel standing in the *s,*
21: 23 The city does not need the *s*
22: 5 light of a lamp or the light of the *s,*

SUN-SCORCHED (SCORCH)

Ps 68: 6 but the rebellious live in a *s* land.
Isa 58: 11 will satisfy your needs in a *s* land

SUNDOWN (SUN)

Da 6: 14 effort until *s* to save him.

SUNG (SING)

Isa 26: 1 In that day this song will be *s*
Mt 26: 30 When they had *s* a hymn, they
Mk 14: 26 When they had *s* a hymn, they

SUNK (SINK)

Jer 38: 22 Your feet are *s* in the mud;
La 2: 9 Her gates have *s* into the ground;
Hos 9: 9 They have *s* deep into corruption,

SUNLIGHT (LIGHT)

Isa 30: 26 the *s* will be seven times brighter,
38: 8 the *s* went back the ten steps it had

SUNRISE (SUN)

Ex 22: 3 but if it happens after *s,* he is guilty
27: 13 On the east end, toward the *s,*
38: 13 The east end, toward the *s,*
Nu 2: 3 toward the *s,* the divisions
3: 38 toward the *s,* in front of the Tent
21: 11 that faces Moab toward the *s.*
34: 15 Jordan of Jericho, toward the *s.*"
Jos 1: 15 east of the Jordan toward the *s.*"
19: 12 Sarid toward the *s* to the territory
Jdg 9: 33 In the morning at *s,* advance
2Sa 23: 4 he is like the light of morning at *s*
Hab 3: 4 His splendor was like the *s;*
Mk 16: 2 day of the week, just after *s,*

SUNSET (SUN)

Ex 17: 12 his hands remained steady till *s.*
22: 26 by *s,* because his cloak is the only
Dt 23: 11 and at *s* he may return to the camp.
24: 13 to him by *s* so that he may sleep
24: 15 him his wages each day before *s,*
Jos 8: 29 At *s,* Joshua ordered them
10: 27 At *s* Joshua gave the order
Jdg 14: 18 Before *s* on the seventh day
2Ch 18: 34 Then at *s* he died.
Mk 1: 32 evening after *s* the people brought

SUNSHINE (SUN)

Job 8: 16 is like a well-watered plant in the *s,*
Isa 18: 4 like shimmering heat in the *s,*

SUPER-APOSTLES (APOSTLE)

2Co 11: 5 in the least inferior to those "*s.*"
12: 11 not in the least inferior to the "*s,*"

SUPERIOR

Da 8: 25 and he will consider himself *s.*
Ro 2: 18 of what is *s* because you are
1Co 2: 1 come with eloquence or *s* wisdom
Heb 1: 4 as the name he has inherited is *s*
1: 4 he became as much *s* to the angels
8: 6 ministry Jesus has received is as *s*
8: 6 of which he is mediator is *s*

SUPERSTITIONS

Isa 2: 6 They are full of *s* from the East;

SUPERVISE (SUPERVISED SUPERVISING SUPERVISION SUPERVISOR SUPERVISORS)

2Ki 12: 11 to the men appointed to *s* the work
22: 5 to the men appointed to *s* the work
1Ch 23: 4 thousand are to *s* the work
2Ch 34: 10 to the men appointed to *s* the work
Ezr 3: 8 older to *s* the building of the house

SUPERVISED (SUPERVISE)

1Ki 5: 16 hundred foremen who *s* the project
2Ch 34: 13 *s* all the workers from job to job.

SUPERVISING (SUPERVISE)

1Ki 9: 23 550 officials *s* the men who did
2Ch 8: 10 and fifty officials *s* the men.
Ezr 3: 9 joined together in *s* those working

SUPERVISION (SUPERVISE)

Nu 8: 22 of Meeting under the *s* of Aaron
1Ch 25: 2 were under the *s* of Asaph,
25: 2 who prophesied under the king's *s.*
25: 3 under the *s* of their father Jeduthun
25: 6 were under the *s* of the king.
25: 6 were under the *s* of their fathers
Gal 3: 25 longer under the *s* of the law.

SUPERVISOR (SUPERVISE)

Ne 11: 11 the son of Ahitub, *s* in the house

SUPERVISORS (SUPERVISE)

2Ki 22: 9 to the workers and *s* at the temple
2Ch 31: 13 Benaiah were *s* under Conaniah
34: 17 and have entrusted it to the *s*
Ne 3: 5 shoulders to the work under their *s.*

SUPH

Dt 1: 1 in the Arabah—opposite *S,*

SUPHAH

Nu 21: 14 ". . . . Waheb in *S*

SUPPER

Lk 17: 8 he not rather say, 'Prepare my *s,*
22: 20 after the *s* he took the cup, saying,
Jn 21: 20 back against Jesus at the *s*
1Co 11: 20 it is not the Lord's *S* you eat,
11: 25 after *s* he took the cup,
Rev 19: 9 to the wedding *s* of the Lamb!' "
19: 17 together for the great *s* of God,

SUPPLICATION (SUPPLICATIONS)

1Ki 8: 30 Hear the *s* of your servant
8: 33 and making *s* to you in this temple,
2Ch 6: 24 making *s* before you in this temple,
Ps 119: 170 May my *s* come before you;
Zec 12: 10 of Jerusalem a spirit of grace and *s.*

SUPPLICATIONS (SUPPLICATION)

1Ki 8: 54 had finished all these prayers and *s*
2Ch 6: 21 Hear the *s* of your servant

SUPPLIED (SUPPLY)

Nu 31: 5 were *s* from the clans of Israel.
1Ki 4: 7 who *s* provisions for the king
4: 27 *s* provisions for King Solomon
5: 10 In this way Hiram kept Solomon *s*
9: 11 Hiram had *s* him with all the cedar
18: 4 and had *s* them with food
18: 13 and *s* them with food and water.
1Ch 12: 39 for their families had *s* provisions
Isa 33: 16 His bread will be *s,*
Jer 5: 7 I *s* all their needs,
Ac 20: 34 of mine have *s* my own needs
1Co 16: 17 they have *s* what was lacking
2Co 11: 9 from Macedonia *s* what I needed.
Php 4: 18 and even more; I am amply *s,*

SUPPLIES (SUPPLY)

Jos 1: 11 tell the people, 'Get your *s* ready.
1Sa 17: 22 things with the keeper of *s,*
25: 13 two hundred stayed with the *s.*

1Sa 30: 24 stayed with the *s* is to be the same
1Ki 4: 7 had to provide *s* for one month
1Ch 12: 40 There were plentiful *s* of flour,
27: 28 was in charge of the *s* of olive oil.
2Ch 11: 11 with *s* of food, olive oil and wine.
17: 13 had large *s* in the towns of Judah.
Ne 13: 13 responsible for distributing the *s*
Ps 105: 16 and destroyed all their *s* of food;
147: 8 he *s* the earth with rain
Pr 31: 24 and *s* the merchants with sashes.
Isa 3: 1 all *s* of food and all *s* of water,
10: 28 they store *s* at Micmash.
Ac 28: 10 us with the *s* we needed.
2Co 9: 10 Now he who *s* seed to the sower

SUPPLY (SUPPLIED SUPPLIES SUPPLYING)

Ex 5: 7 longer to *s* the people with straw
Lev 26: 26 When I cut off your *s* of bread,
Nu 4: 9 and all its jars for the oil used to *s* it
Dt 15: 14 *S* him liberally from your flock,
Jos 9: 5 the bread of their food *s* was dry
Jdg 19: 20 "Let me *s* whatever you need.
2Sa 12: 27 Rabbah and taken its water *s*.
1Ki 17: 9 in that place to *s* you with food."
2Ki 3: 4 and he had to *s* the king of Israel
Ezr 7: 20 that you may have occasion to *s*,
Ne 5: 18 and every ten days an abundant *s*
Ps 78: 20 Can he *s* meat for his people?"
Isa 3: 1 both *s* and support:
Eze 4: 16 cut off the *s* of food in Jerusalem.
5: 16 upon you and cut off your *s* of food.
14: 13 hand against it to cut off its food *s*
48: 18 Its produce will *s* food
Na 2: 9 The *s* is endless,
Ac 12: 20 the king's country for their food *s*.
2Co 8: 14 their plenty will *s* what you need.
8: 14 your plenty will *s* what they need,
9: 10 and bread for food will also *s*
1Th 3: 10 and *s* what is lacking in your faith.

SUPPLYING (SUPPLY)

2Co 9: 12 you perform is not only *s* the needs

SUPPORT (SUPPORTED SUPPORTING SUPPORTS)

Ge 13: 6 But the land could not *s* them
36: 7 were staying could not *s* them both
Lev 25: 35 is unable to *s* himself among you,
Jdg 16: 26 feel the pillars that *s* the temple,
2Sa 18: 3 for you to give us *s* from the city."
22: 19 but the LORD was my *s*.
1Ki 1: 7 and they gave him their *s*.
2Ki 15: 19 talents of silver to gain his *s*
1Ch 11: 10 gave his kingship strong *s*
2Ch 26: 13 a powerful force to *s* the king
Ezr 10: 4 We will *s* you, so take courage
Ps 18: 18 but the LORD was my *s*.
20: 2 and grant you *s* from Zion.
Pr 28: 17 let no one *s* him.
Isa 3: 1 both supply and *s*:
63: 5 I was appalled that no one gave *s*;
Jer 37: 7 which has marched out to *s* you,
Da 11: 1 stand to *s* and protect him.)
Lk 8: 3 women were helping to *s* them out
Ac 12: 20 Having secured the *s* of Blastus,
Ro 11: 18 consider this: You do not *s* the root
1Co 9: 12 If others have this right of *s*
2Co 11: 8 by receiving *s* from them so
2Ti 4: 16 to my *s*, but everyone deserted me.

SUPPORTED (SUPPORT)

1Ki 16: 21 and the other half *s* Omri.
16: 21 half *s* Tibni son of Ginath for king,
2Ki 16: 17 Sea from the bronze bulls that *s* it
2Ch 11: 17 *s* Rehoboam son of Solomon three
Ezr 10: 15 *s* by Meshullam and Shabbethai
Job 4: 4 Your words have *s* those who
Ps 89: 43 and have not *s* him in battle.
94: 18 your love, O LORD, *s* me.
Jer 26: 24 Ahikam son of Shaphan *s* Jeremiah
Da 11: 6 her father and the one who *s* her.
Col 2: 19 *s* and held together by its ligaments

SUPPORTING (SUPPORT)

2Sa 5: 9 from the *s* terraces inward.
1Ki 7: 2 of cedar columns *s* trimmed cedar
9: 15 his own palace, the *s* terraces,
9: 24 he constructed the *s* terraces.
11: 27 Solomon had built the *s* terraces
1Ch 11: 8 from the *s* terraces
2Ch 32: 5 reinforced the *s* terraces of the City
Eph 4: 16 held together by every *s* ligament,

SUPPORTS (SUPPORT)

1Ki 7: 30 each had a basin resting on four *s*,
7: 35 The *s* and panels were attached
7: 36 palm trees on the surfaces of the *s*
10: 12 to make *s* for the temple
Eze 41: 6 so that the *s* were not inserted
41: 6 to serve as *s* for the side rooms,
Da 10: 21 (No one *s* me against them
Ro 11: 18 support the root, but the root *s* you.

SUPPOSE (SUPPOSED SUPPOSING)

Ex 3: 13 "*S* I go to the Israelites
Nu 36: 3 Now *s* they marry men from other
Jdg 11: 9 "*S* you take me back
Job 34: 31 "*S* a man says to God,
Eze 18: 5 "*S* there is a righteous man
18: 10 "*S* he has a violent son, who sheds
18: 14 *s* this son has a son who sees all
Mt 10: 34 "Do not *s* that I have come
24: 48 But *s* that servant is wicked
Lk 7: 43 "I *s* the one who had the bigger
11: 5 "*S* one of you has a friend,
12: 45 But *s* the servant says to himself,
14: 28 *S* one of you wants to build a tower.
14: 31 "Or *s* a king is about to go to war
15: 4 "*S* one of you has a hundred sheep
15: 8 "Or *s* a woman has ten silver coins
17: 7 *S* one of you had a servant plowing
Jn 21: 25 I *s* that even the whole world
Ac 2: 15 These men are not drunk, as you *s*.
Jas 2: 2 *S* a man comes into your meeting
2: 15 *S* a brother or sister is

SUPPOSED (SUPPOSE)

1Sa 20: 5 and I am *s* to dine with the king;
2Th 2: 2 or letter *s* to have come from us,

SUPPOSING (SUPPOSE)

Jn 11: 31 *s* she was going to the tomb
Php 1: 17 *s* that they can stir up trouble

SUPPRESS

Ro 1: 18 wickedness of men who *s* the truth

SUPREMACY (SUPREME)

Col 1: 18 in everything he might have the *s*.

SUPREME (SUPREMACY)

2Ki 18: 17 of Assyria sent his *s* commander,
Pr 4: 7 Wisdom is *s*; therefore get wisdom.
Ecc 8: 4 a king's word is *s*, who can say
Isa 20: 1 In the year that the *s* commander,
1Pe 2: 13 as the *s* authority, or to governors,

SUR

2Ki 11: 6 a third at the *S* Gate, and a third

SURE

Ge 20: 7 you may be *s* that you
24: 6 "Make *s* that you do not take my
32: 20 be *s* to say, 'Your servant Jacob is
Ex 8: 29 Only be *s* that Pharaoh does not
10: 28 Make *s* you do not appear
17: 14 and make *s* that Joshua hears it,
23: 4 be *s* to take it back to him.
23: 5 not leave it there; be *s* you help him
Nu 26: 55 Be *s* that the land is distributed
28: 31 Be *s* the animals are without defect
32: 23 you may be *s* that your sin will find
Dt 5: 1 Learn them and be *s* to follow them
6: 17 Be *s* to keep the commands
11: 32 be *s* that you obey all the decrees
12: 23 But be *s* you do not eat the blood,
14: 22 Be *s* to set aside a tenth
17: 15 be *s* to appoint over you the king
21: 23 Be *s* to bury him that same day,
22: 1 but be *s* to take it back to him.
22: 7 but be *s* to let the mother go,
23: 23 your lips utter you must be *s*
28: 66 and day, never *s* of your life.
29: 18 Make *s* there is no man or woman,
29: 18 make *s* there is no root
31: 29 that after my death you are *s*
Jos 2: 12 Give me a *s* sign that you will spare
13: 6 Be *s* to allocate this land to Israel
23: 13 then you may be *s* that the LORD
Jdg 15: 2 I was so *s* you thoroughly hated her
1Sa 12: 24 But be *s* to fear the LORD
20: 7 you can be *s* that he is determined
22: 22 I knew he would be *s* to tell Saul.
1Ki 2: 37 you can be *s* you will die; your
2: 42 you can be *s* you will die'?
Ezr 7: 17 With this money be *s* to buy bulls,
Ps 19: 9 The ordinances of the LORD are *s*
69: 13 answer me with your *s* salvation.
132: 11 a *s* oath that he will not revoke:
Pr 11: 14 but many advisers make victory *s*.
11: 18 righteousness reaps a *s* reward.
11: 21 Be *s* of this: The wicked will not go
16: 5 Be *s* of this: They will not go
27: 23 Be *s* you know the condition
Isa 28: 16 cornerstone for a *s* foundation;
33: 6 He will be the *s* foundation
Jer 42: 19 Be *s* of this: I warn you today that
42: 22 be *s* of this: You will die
Eze 30: 9 of Egypt's doom, for it is *s* to come.
Mt 17: 11 "To be *s*, Elijah comes
Mk 9: 12 "To be *s*, Elijah does come first,
Lk 1: 18 asked the angel, "How can I be *s*
10: 11 Yet be *s* of this: The kingdom
Ac 13: 34 *s* blessings promised to David.'
Ro 15: 28 and have made *s* that they have
2Co 13: 4 For to be *s*, he was crucified
Eph 5: 5 of this you can be *s*: No immoral,
1Th 5: 15 Make *s* that nobody pays back
Tit 3: 11 You may be *s* that such a man is
Heb 6: 11 in order to make your hope *s*.
11: 1 faith is being *s* of what we hope for
13: 18 We are *s* that we have a clear
2Pe 1: 10 to make your calling and election *s*.

SURF

Ac 27: 41 to pieces by the pounding of the *s*.

SURFACE (SURFACES)

Ge 1: 2 darkness was over the *s* of the deep
2: 6 watered the whole *s* of the ground.
7: 18 the ark floated on the *s* of the water
8: 8 receded from the *s* of the ground.
8: 9 water over all the *s* of the earth;
8: 13 saw that the *s* of the ground was
Lev 14: 37 to be deeper than the *s* of the wall,
Job 24: 18 foam on the *s* of the water;
38: 30 when the *s* of the deep is frozen?
Isa 28: 25 When he has leveled the *s*,
Hos 10: 7 like a twig on the *s* of the waters.
2Co 10: 7 You are looking only on the *s*

SURFACES (SURFACE)

1Ki 7: 36 palm trees on the *s* of the supports

SURGE (SURGED SURGING)

Job 40: 23 the Jordan should *s*
Isa 54: 8 In a *s* of anger

SURGED (SURGE)

1Sa 17: 52 and Judah *s* forward with a shout

SURGING (SURGE)

Ex 15: 8 The *s* waters stood firm like a wall;
Ps 46: 3 the mountains quake with their *s*
89: 9 You rule over the *s* sea;
Isa 17: 13 roar like the roar of *s* waters,
Jer 46: 7 like rivers of *s* waters?
46: 8 like rivers of *s* waters.
Zec 10: 11 the *s* sea will be subdued

SURLY

1Sa 25: 3 was *s* and mean in his dealings.

SURMOUNTED

Eze 40: 16 walls inside the gateway were *s*

SURPASS (ALL-SURPASSING SURPASSED SURPASSES SURPASSING)

Pr 31: 29 but you *s* them all."

SURPASSED (SURPASS)

Jn 1: 15 'He who comes after me has *s* me
1: 30 man who comes after me has *s* me

SURPASSES (SURPASS)

Pr 8: 19 what I yield *s* choice silver.
Mt 5: 20 unless your righteousness *s* that
Eph 3: 19 to know this love that *s* knowledge

SURPASSING (SURPASS)

Ps 150: 2 praise him for his *s* greatness.
2Co 3: 10 in comparison with the *s* glory.
9: 14 of the *s* grace God has given you.
Php 3: 8 the *s* greatness of knowing Christ

SURPRISE (SURPRISED SURPRISING)

Jos 10: 9 from Gilgal, Joshua took them by *s*
Ps 35: 8 may ruin overtake them by *s*—
55: 15 Let death take my enemies by *s*;
Jer 14: 9 Why are you like a man taken by *s*,
Ac 3: 12 Men of Israel, why does this *s* you?
1Th 5: 4 that this day should *s* you like

SURPRISED (SURPRISE)

Ecc 5: 8 and rights denied, do not be *s*
Mk 15: 44 Pilate was *s* to hear that he was
Lk 11: 38 wash before the meal, was *s*.
Jn 3: 7 You should not be *s* at my saying,
4: 27 and were *s* to find him talking
1Pe 4: 12 do not be *s* at the painful trial you
1Jn 3: 13 Do not be *s*, my brothers,

SURPRISING (SURPRISE)

2Co 11: 15 It is not *s*, then, if his servants

SURRENDER (SURRENDERED SURRENDERS)

Jos 20: 5 they must not *s* the one accused,
Jdg 20: 13 *s* those wicked men of Gibeah
1Sa 11: 3 to rescue us, we will *s* to you."
11: 10 "Tomorrow we will *s* to you,
23: 11 the citizens of Keilah *s* me to him?
23: 12 "Will the citizens of Keilah *s* me
2Ki 7: 4 to the camp of the Arameans and *s*.
Ps 41: 2 not *s* him to the desire of his foes.
Isa 54: 15 whoever attacks you will *s* to you.
Jer 38: 17 'If you *s* to the officers of the king
38: 18 But if you will not *s* to the officers
38: 21 to *s*, this is what the LORD has
Da 8: 13 and the *s* of the sanctuary
1Co 13: 3 and *s* my body to the flames,

SURRENDERED (SURRENDER)

2Ki 24: 12 and his officials all *s* to him.
Lk 23: 25 asked for, and *s* Jesus to their will.

SURRENDERS (SURRENDER)

Jer 21: 9 and *s* to the Babylonians who are
50: 15 She *s*, her towers fall,

SURROUND (SURROUNDED SURROUNDING SURROUNDS)

Jos 7: 9 and they will *s* us and wipe out our
Job 16: 13 his archers *s* me.
17: 2 Surely mockers *s* me;
40: 22 the poplars by the stream *s* him.
Ps 5: 12 you *s* them with your favor
17: 9 from my mortal enemies who *s* me.
17: 11 down, they now *s* me,
22: 12 Many bulls *s* me;
27: 6 above the enemies who *s* me;
32: 7 and *s* me with songs of deliverance.
40: 12 For troubles without number *s* me;
49: 5 when wicked deceivers *s* me—
88: 17 All day long they *s* me like a flood;
89: 7 awesome than all who *s* him.
97: 2 Clouds and thick darkness *s* him;
109: 3 With words of hatred they *s* me;
125: 2 As the mountains *s* Jerusalem,
140: 9 Let the heads of those who *s* me
Jer 4: 17 They *s* her like men guarding
12: 9 that other birds of prey *s* and attack
31: 22 a woman will *s* a man."

SURROUNDED (SURROUND)

Ge 19: 4 both young and old—*s* the house.
Jdg 16: 2 So they *s* the place and lay in wait
19: 22 men of the city *s* the house.
20: 5 came after me and *s* the house,
20: 43 They *s* the Benjamites, chased
2Sa 18: 15 of Joab's armor-bearers *s* Absalom,
1Ki 7: 12 The great courtyard was *s* by a wall
2Ki 3: 25 but men armed with slings *s* it
6: 14 They went by night and *s* the city.
6: 15 and chariots had *s* the city.
8: 21 The Edomites *s* him and his chariot
1Ch 29: 30 and the circumstances that *s* him
2Ch 21: 9 The Edomites *s* him and his chariot
Ps 22: 16 Dogs have *s* me;
118: 10 All the nations *s* me,
118: 11 They *s* me on every side,
Ecc 9: 14 *s* it and built huge siegeworks
La 3: 5 He has besieged me and *s* me
Eze 1: 4 cloud with flashing lightning and *s*
1: 27 like fire; and brilliant light *s* him.
27: 32 *s* by the sea?"
32: 22 she is *s* by the graves of all her slain
Hos 11: 12 Ephraim has *s* me with lies,
Jnh 2: 5 the deep *s* me;
Lk 21: 20 "When you see Jerusalem *s*
Jn 5: 2 and which is *s* by five covered
Heb 12: 1 since we are *s* by such a great cloud
Rev 20: 9 and *s* the camp of God's people,

SURROUNDING (SURROUND)

Ge 41: 48 put the food grown in the fields *s* it.
Ex 38: 20 and of the *s* courtyard were bronze.
38: 31 and those for the *s* courtyard.
38: 31 the bases for the *s* courtyard
Nu 3: 26 to the courtyard *s* the tabernacle
3: 37 as the posts of the *s* courtyard
4: 26 of the courtyard *s* the tabernacle
4: 32 as the posts of the *s* courtyard
21: 25 Heshbon and all its *s* settlements.
21: 32 Israelites captured its *s* settlements
32: 42 Kenath and its *s* settlements
Jos 15: 45 with its *s* settlements and villages;
15: 47 its *s* settlements and villages;
17: 11 with their *s* settlements (the third
21: 11 Hebron), with its *s* pastureland,
21: 42 of these towns had pasturelands *s* it
Jdg 1: 27 Megiddo and their *s* settlements,
11: 26 the *s* settlements and all the towns
1Ki 4: 31 his fame spread to all the *s* nations.
2Ki 25: 4 the Babylonians were *s* the city.
1Ch 2: 23 as Kenath with its *s* settlements—
4: 32 Their *s* villages were Etam, Ain,
6: 55 in Judah with its *s* pasturelands.
7: 28 included Bethel and its *s* villages,
8: 12 and Lod with its *s* villages),
11: 8 supporting terraces to the *s* wall,
18: 1 and its *s* villages from the control
28: 12 of the LORD and all the *s* rooms,
2Ch 13: 19 and Ephron, with their *s* villages.
17: 10 the kingdoms of the lands *s* Judah,
28: 18 and Gimzo, with their *s* villages.
Ne 3: 22 by the priests from the *s* region.
5: 17 came to us from the *s* nations.
6: 16 and all the *s* nations saw it,
11: 25 Kiriath Arba and its *s* settlements,
Jer 1: 15 come against all her *s* walls
25: 9 and against all the *s* nations.
34: 1 Jerusalem and all its *s* towns,
49: 2 and its *s* villages will be set on fire.
52: 7 the Babylonians were *s* the city.
52: 23 above the *s* network was a hundred
Eze 34: 26 bless them and the places *s* my hill.
40: 5 a wall completely *s* the temple
41: 7 structure *s* the temple was built
43: 12 All the *s* area on top
Zec 7: 7 and its *s* towns were at rest
12: 2 that sends all the *s* peoples reeling.
12: 6 right and left all the *s* peoples,
14: 14 of all the *s* nations will be collected
Mt 14: 35 they sent word to all the *s* country.
Mk 6: 36 so they can go to the *s* countryside
Lk 4: 37 spread throughout the *s* area.
7: 17 Judea and the *s* country.
9: 12 so they can go to the *s* villages
Ac 14: 6 and Derbe and to the *s* country,
Jude : 7 and the *s* towns gave themselves up
Rev 4: 4 *S* the throne were twenty-four

SURROUNDS (SURROUND)

Ps 32: 10 *s* the man who trusts in him.
89: 8 and your faithfulness *s* you.
125: 2 so the LORD *s* his people

SURVEY (SURVEYED)

Jos 18: 4 out to make a *s* of the land
18: 8 "Go and make a *s* of the land

SURVEYED (SURVEY)

Ecc 2: 11 Yet when I *s* all that my hands had

SURVIVE (SURVIVED SURVIVES SURVIVING SURVIVOR SURVIVORS)

Dt 4: 27 few of you will *s* among the nations
Jos 11: 22 Gath and Ashdod did any *s*.
2Sa 1: 10 after he had fallen he could not *s*.
Job 27: 15 plague will bury those who *s* him,
Isa 66: 19 of those who *s* to the nations—
Jer 21: 7 people in this city who *s* the plague,
31: 2 "The people who *s* the sword
42: 17 of them will *s* or escape the disaster
44: 14 or *s* to return to the land of Judah,
Eze 7: 16 All who *s* and escape will be
Am 7: 2 forgive! How can Jacob *s*?
7: 5 How can Jacob *s*? He is so small!"
Zec 10: 9 They and their children will *s*,
Mt 24: 22 not been cut short, no one would *s*,
Mk 13: 20 short those days, no one would *s*.
Ac 27: 34 You need it to *s*.

SURVIVED (SURVIVE)

Ex 14: 28 Not one of them *s*.
Nu 14: 38 and Caleb son of Jephunneh *s*.
Dt 5: 26 and *s*? Go near and listen
Jos 13: 12 and had *s* as one of the last
1Sa 11: 11 Those who *s* were scattered,
Ne 1: 2 the Jewish remnant that *s* the exile,
1: 3 "Those who *s* the exile
Ps 106: 11 not one of them *s*.
La 2: 22 no one escaped or *s*;

SURVIVES (SURVIVE)

2Ki 19: 4 pray for the remnant that still *s*."
Isa 37: 4 pray for the remnant that still *s*."
Eze 6: 12 and he that *s* and is spared will die
1Co 3: 14 what he has built *s*, he will receive

SURVIVING (SURVIVE)

Dt 28: 54 the wife he loves or his *s* children,
Jer 29: 1 sent from Jerusalem to the *s* elders
Eze 17: 14 *s* only by keeping his treaty.

SURVIVOR (SURVIVE)

Jdg 12: 5 and whenever a *s* of Ephraim said,
2Ki 10: 11 and his priests, leaving him no *s*.
10: 14 He left no *s*.
Ezr 9: 14 leaving us no remnant or *s*?
Job 18: 19 no *s* where once he lived.

SURVIVORS (SURVIVE)

Nu 21: 35 his whole army, leaving them no *s*.
24: 19 and destroy the *s* of the city."
Dt 2: 34 We left no *s*.
3: 3 We struck them down, leaving no *s*
7: 20 *s* who hide from you have perished.
Jos 8: 22 leaving them neither *s* nor fugitives
10: 28 He left no *s*.
10: 30 He left no *s* there.
10: 33 and his army—until no *s* were left.
10: 37 They left no *s*.
10: 39 They left no *s*.
10: 40 He left no *s*.
11: 8 the east, until no *s* were left.
23: 12 and ally yourselves with the *s*
Jdg 21: 17 The Benjamite *s* must have heirs,"
2Sa 21: 2 but were *s* of the Amorites;
2Ki 19: 31 and out of Mount Zion a band of *s*.
Ezr 1: 4 of any place where *s* may now be
Ps 76: 10 the *s* of your wrath are restrained.
Isa 1: 9 had left us some *s*,
4: 2 glory of the *s* in Israel.
10: 20 the *s* of the house of Jacob,
14: 22 off from Babylon her name and *s*,
14: 30 it will slay your *s*.
16: 14 and her *s* will be very few
21: 17 The *s* of the bowmen, the warriors
37: 32 and out of Mount Zion a band of *s*.
Jer 8: 3 all the *s* of this evil nation will
15: 9 I will put the *s* to the sword
24: 8 his officials and the *s*
41: 16 were with him led away all the *s*
47: 4 and to cut off all *s*
Eze 5: 10 will scatter all your *s* to the winds.
14: 22 Yet there will be some *s*—

Eze 17: 21 the *s* will be scattered to the winds.
Joel 2: 32 among the *s*
Ob : 14 nor hand over their *s*
: 18 There will be no *s*
Zep 2: 9 the *s* of my nation will inherit their
Zec 14: 16 the *s* from all the nations that have
Rev 11: 13 and the *s* were terrified

SUSA

Ezr 4: 9 and Babylon, the Elamites of *S*,
Ne 1: 1 while I was in the citadel of *S*,
Est 1: 2 throne in the citadel of *S*,
1: 5 who were in the citadel of *S*.
2: 3 into the harem at the citadel of *S*.
2: 5 in the citadel of *S* a Jew of the tribe
2: 8 were brought to the citadel of *S*
3: 15 but the city of *S* was bewildered.
3: 15 issued in the citadel of *S*.
4: 8 which had been published in *S*,
4: 16 together all the Jews who are in *S*,
8: 14 also issued in the citadel of *S*.
8: 15 city of *S* held a joyous celebration.
9: 6 In the citadel of *S*, the Jews killed
9: 11 in the citadel of *S* was reported
9: 12 sons of Haman in the citadel of *S*.
9: 13 "give the Jews in *S* permission
9: 14 An edict was issued in *S*,
9: 15 The Jews in *S* came together
9: 15 to death in *S* three hundred men,
9: 18 Jews in *S*, however, had assembled
Da 8: 2 in the citadel of *S* in the province

SUSANNA

Lk 8: 3 manager of Herod's household; *S*;

SUSI

Nu 13: 11 Gaddi son of *S*; from the tribe

SUSPECTS (SUSPICIONS)

Nu 5: 14 he *s* his wife and she is impure—
5: 14 or if he is jealous and *s* her even
5: 30 over a man because he *s* his wife.

SUSPENDS

Job 26: 7 he *s* the earth over nothing.

SUSPENSE

Dt 28: 66 You will live in constant *s*,
Jn 10: 24 "How long will you keep us in *s*?
Ac 27: 33 "you have been in constant *s*

SUSPICIONS (SUSPECTS)

1Ti 6: 4 evil *s* and constant friction

SUSTAIN (SUSTAINED SUSTAINING SUSTAINS)

Ru 4: 15 He will renew your life and *s* you
Job 36: 19 *s* you so you would not be
Ps 41: 3 The LORD will *s* him
51: 12 grant me a willing spirit, to *s* me.
55: 22 and he will *s* you;
89: 21 My hand will *s* him;
119:116 *S* me according to your promise,
119:175 and may your laws *s* me.
Isa 46: 4 I am he, I am he who will *s* you.
46: 4 I will *s* you and I will rescue you.

SUSTAINED (SUSTAIN)

Ge 27: 37 and I have *s* him with grain
Ne 9: 21 For forty years you *s* them
Isa 59: 16 and his own righteousness *s* him.
63: 5 and my own wrath *s* me.

SUSTAINING (SUSTAIN)

Heb 1: 3 *s* all things by his powerful word.

SUSTAINS (SUSTAIN)

Ps 3: 5 again, because the LORD *s* me.
18: 35 and your right hand *s* me;
54: 4 the Lord is the one who *s* me.
104: 15 and bread that *s* his heart.
146: 9 and *s* the fatherless and the widow,
147: 6 The LORD *s* the humble
Pr 18: 14 A man's spirit *s* him in sickness,
Isa 50: 4 to know the word that *s* the weary.

SWALLOW (SWALLOWED SWALLOWING SWALLOWS)

Nu 14: 9 because we will *s* them up.
16: 34 "The earth is going to *s* us too!"
2Sa 20: 19 to *s* up the LORD's inheritance?"
20: 20 Far be it from me to *s* up or destroy
Ps 21: 9 wrath the LORD will *s* them up,
69: 15 or the depths *s* me up
84: 3 and the *s* a nest for herself,
Pr 1: 12 let's *s* them alive, like the grave,
26: 2 a fluttering sparrow or a darting *s*,
Isa 25: 8 he will *s* up death forever.
Hos 8: 7 foreigners would *s* it up.
Jnh 1: 17 provided a great fish to *s* Jonah,
Hab 1: 13 *s* up those more righteous
Mt 23: 24 You strain out a gnat but *s* a camel.

SWALLOWED (SWALLOW)

Ge 41: 7 of grain *s* up the seven healthy,
41: 24 of grain *s* up the seven good heads.
Ex 7: 12 But Aaron's staff *s* up their staffs.
15: 12 and the earth *s* them.
Nu 16: 32 earth opened its mouth and *s* them,
26: 10 and *s* them along with Korah,
Dt 11: 6 *s* them up with their households,
2Sa 17: 16 all the people with him will be *s* up
Job 20: 15 He will spit out the riches he *s*;
37: 20 Would any man ask to be *s* up?
Ps 35: 25 or say, "We have *s* him up."
106: 17 The earth opened up and *s* Dathan;
124: 3 they would have *s* us alive;
Jer 51: 34 Like a serpent he has *s* us
51: 44 make him spew out what he has *s*.
La 2: 2 Without pity the Lord has *s* up
2: 5 He has *s* up all her palaces
2: 5 he has *s* up Israel.
2: 16 and say, "We have *s* her up.
Hos 8: 8 Israel is *s* up;
1Co 15: 54 "Death has been *s* up in victory."
2Co 5: 4 so that what is mortal may be *s* up

SWALLOWING (SWALLOW)

Rev 12: 16 and *s* the river that the dragon had

SWALLOWS (SWALLOW)

Nu 16: 30 earth opens its mouth and *s* them,
Isa 28: 4 he *s* it.

SWAMPED (SWAMPLAND SWAMPS)

Mk 4: 37 so that it was nearly *s*.
Lk 8: 23 so that the boat was being *s*,

SWAMPLAND (SWAMPED)

Isa 14: 23 and into *s*;

SWAMPS (SWAMPED)

Eze 47: 11 the *s* and marshes will not become

SWARM (SWARMED SWARMING SWARMS)

Ge 7: 21 all the creatures that *s*
Ex 10: 12 so that locusts will *s* over the land
Dt 1: 44 they chased you like a *s* of bees
14: 19 All flying insects that *s* are unclean
Jdg 14: 8 In it was a *s* of bees and some
Isa 33: 4 like a *s* of locusts men pounce on it.
Jer 12: 12 destroyers will *s*,
51: 14 with men, as with a *s* of locusts,
51: 27 send up horses like a *s* of locusts.
Joel 1: 4 What the locust *s* has left
2: 25 the other locusts and the locust *s*—

SWARMED (SWARM)

Ps 118: 12 They *s* around me like bees,

SWARMING (SWARM)

Lev 11: 10 whether among all the *s* things

SWARMS (SWARM)

Ex 8: 21 I will send *s* of flies on you
8: 22 where my people live; no *s*
8: 24 Dense *s* of flies poured
Dt 28: 42 *S* of locusts will take
Jdg 6: 5 and their tents like *s* of locusts.
Ps 78: 45 He sent *s* of flies that devoured
105: 31 He spoke, and there came *s* of flies,
Eze 47: 9 *S* of living creatures will live
Am 7: 1 He was preparing *s* of locusts

Na 3: 17 your officials like *s* of locusts

SWAY (SWAYED SWAYING SWAYS)

Ps 72: 16 on the tops of the hills may it *s*.

SWAYED (SWAY)

Mt 11: 7 A reed *s* by the wind? If not,
22: 16 You aren't *s* by men, because you
Mk 12: 14 You aren't *s* by men, because you
Lk 7: 24 A reed *s* by the wind? If not,
2Ti 3: 6 are *s* by all kinds of evil desires,

SWAYING (SWAY)

1Ki 14: 15 so that it will be like a reed *s*
Jer 4: 24 all the hills were *s*.

SWAYS (SWAY)

Job 28: 4 far from men he dangles and *s*.
40: 17 His tail *s* like a cedar;
Isa 24: 20 it *s* like a hut in the wind;

SWEAR (SWEARING SWEARS SWORE SWORN)

Ge 21: 23 *s* to me here before God that you
21: 24 Abraham said, "I *s* it."
22: 16 "I *s* by myself, declares the LORD,
24: 3 I want you to *s* by the LORD,
24: 37 And my master made me *s* an oath,
25: 33 But Jacob said, "*S* to me first."
47: 31 "*S* to me," he said.
50: 5 'My father made me *s* an oath
50: 6 bury your father, as he made you *s*
50: 25 made the sons of Israel *s* an oath
Ex 13: 19 the sons of Israel *s* an oath.
Lev 5: 4 one might carelessly *s* about—
19: 12 " 'Do not *s* falsely by my name
Jos 2: 12 please *s* to me by the LORD that
2: 17 oath you made us *s* will not be
2: 20 from the oath you made us *s*."
23: 7 names of their gods or *s* by them.
Jdg 15: 12 "*S* to me that you won't kill me
1Sa 24: 21 *s* to me by the LORD that you will
30: 15 "*S* to me before God that you will
2Sa 19: 7 I *s* by the LORD that
1Ki 1: 13 did you not *s* to me your servant:
1: 51 'Let King Solomon *s*
2: 42 Did I not make you *s* by the LORD
18: 10 he made them *s* they could not find
22: 16 many times must I make you *s*
2Ch 18: 15 many times must I make you *s*
Ps 24: 4 or *s* by what is false.
63: 11 all who *s* by God's name will praise
Isa 19: 18 and *s* allegiance to the LORD
45: 23 by me every tongue will *s*.
65: 16 will *s* by the God of truth.
Jer 4: 2 you *s*, 'As surely as the LORD
12: 16 as they once taught my people to *s*
12: 16 of my people and *s* by my name,
22: 5 I *s* by myself that this palace will
44: 26 ever again invoke my name or *s*,
44: 26 in Egypt: 'I *s* by my great name,'
49: 13 I *s* by myself," declares the LORD,
Eze 36: 7 I *s* with uplifted hand that
Da 12: 7 and I heard him *s* by him who lives
Hos 4: 15 And do not *s*, 'As surely
Am 8: 14 They who *s* by the shame
Zep 1: 5 and who also *s* by Molech,
1: 5 bow down and *s* by the LORD
Zec 8: 17 and do not love to *s* falsely.
Mt 5: 34 Do not *s* at all: either by heaven,
5: 36 And do not *s* by your head,
Mk 5: 7 *S* to God that you won't torture me
Heb 3: 18 to whom did God *s* that they would
6: 13 was no one greater for him to *s*
6: 16 Men *s* by someone greater
Jas 5: 12 Above all, my brothers, do not *s*—

SWEARING (SWEAR)

Jer 5: 2 still they are *s* falsely."

SWEARS (SWEAR)

Lev 6: 3 if he *s* falsely, or if he commits any
1Ki 8: 31 and *s* the oath before your altar
2Ch 6: 22 and *s* the oath before your altar
Zec 5: 3 everyone who *s* falsely will be
5: 4 of him who *s* falsely by my name.
Mt 23: 16 You say, 'If anyone *s* by the temple
23: 16 but if anyone *s* by the gold

Mt 23: 18 also say, 'If anyone *s* by the altar,
23: 18 but if anyone *s* by the gift on it,
23: 20 he who *s* by the altar *s* by it
23: 21 And he who *s* by the temple *s* by it
23: 22 And he who *s* by heaven *s*

SWEAT

Ge 3: 19 By the *s* of your brow
Lk 22: 44 his *s* was like drops of blood falling

SWEEP (SWEEPING SWEEPINGS SWEEPS SWEPT)

Ge 18: 23 "Will you *s* away the righteous
18: 24 Will you really *s* it away
Ps 90: 5 You *s* men away in the sleep
Isa 8: 8 and *s* on into Judah, swirling over it
11: 15 a scorching wind he will *s* his hand
14: 23 I will *s* her with the broom
28: 17 hail will *s* away your refuge, the lie,
28: 19 it will *s* through."
43: 2 they will not *s* over you.
64: 6 and like the wind our sins *s* us away
Eze 5: 17 and bloodshed will *s* through you,
Da 11: 10 which will *s* on like an irresistible
11: 40 and *s* through them like a flood.
Hos 4: 19 A whirlwind will *s* them away,
Am 5: 6 or he will *s* through the house
Hab 1: 6 who *s* across the whole earth
1: 11 Then they *s* past like the wind
Zep 1: 2 of Judah: "I will *s* away everything
1: 3 I will *s* away both men and animals;
1: 3 I will *s* away the birds of the air
Lk 15: 8 *s* the house and search carefully
Rev 12: 15 and *s* her away with the torrent.

SWEEPING (SWEEP)

Isa 21: 1 Like whirlwinds *s*

SWEEPINGS (SWEEP)

Am 8: 6 selling even the *s* with the wheat.

SWEEPS (SWEEP)

Job 27: 21 it *s* him out of his place.
Pr 1: 27 when disaster *s* over you like
13: 23 but injustice *s* it away.
Isa 28: 15 When an overwhelming scourge *s*
28: 18 When the overwhelming scourge *s*
40: 24 a whirlwind *s* them away like chaff.
Zep 2: 2 and that day *s* on like chaff,

SWEET (SWEETER SWEETNESS)

Ex 15: 25 the water, and the water became *s*.
Jdg 9: 11 and *s*, to go waving over the trees?'
14: 14 out of the strong, something *s*."
Ne 8: 10 and enjoy choice food and *s* drinks,
Job 20: 12 "Though evil is *s* in his mouth
21: 33 The soil in the valley is *s* to him;
Ps 55: 14 whom I once enjoyed *s* fellowship
119:103 How *s* are your promises
Pr 3: 24 lie down, your sleep will be *s*.
9: 17 "Stolen water is *s*;
13: 19 A longing fulfilled is *s* to the soul,
16: 24 *s* to the soul and healing
20: 17 by fraud tastes *s* to a man,
24: 13 from the comb is *s* to your taste.
24: 14 also that wisdom is *s* to your soul;
27: 7 hungry even what is bitter tastes *s*.
Ecc 5: 12 The sleep of a laborer is *s*,
11: 7 Light is *s*,
SS 2: 3 and his fruit is *s* to my taste.
2: 14 for your voice is *s*,
Isa 5: 20 and *s* for bitter.
5: 20 who put bitter for *s*
Jer 6: 20 or *s* calamus from a distant land?
Eze 3: 3 it tasted as *s* as honey in my mouth.
Rev 10: 9 but in your mouth it will be as *s*
10: 10 It tasted as *s* as honey in my mouth

SWEETER (SWEET)

Jdg 14: 18 "What is *s* than honey?
Ps 19: 10 they are *s* than honey,
119:103 *s* than honey to my mouth!

SWEETNESS (SWEET)

SS 4: 11 Your lips drop *s* as the honeycomb,
5: 16 His mouth is *s* itself;

SWELL (SWELLING SWELLS SWOLLEN)

Nu 5: 21 waste away and your abdomen to *s*.
5: 27 her abdomen will *s* and her thigh
Dt 8: 4 and your feet did not *s*
Isa 60: 5 your heart will throb and *s* with joy
Ac 28: 6 The people expected him to *s* up

SWELLING (SWELL)

Lev 13: 2 "When anyone has a *s* or a rash
13: 10 and if there is a white *s*
13: 10 and if there is raw flesh in the *s*,
13: 19 a white *s* or reddish-white spot
13: 28 it is a *s* from the burn,
14: 56 and for a *s*, a rash or a bright spot,

SWELLS (SWELL)

Nu 5: 22 body so that your abdomen *s*

SWELTER

Job 37: 17 You who *s* in your clothes

SWEPT (SWEEP)

Ge 19: 15 or you will be *s* away
19: 17 mountains or you will be *s* away!"
Ex 14: 27 and the LORD *s* them into the sea.
Nu 16: 26 or you will be *s* away
Jdg 5: 21 The river Kishon *s* them away,
1Sa 12: 25 and your king will be *s* away."
1Ch 21: 12 three months of being *s* away
Job 1: 17 and *s* down on your camels
1: 19 when suddenly a mighty wind *s*
5: 13 the schemes of the wily are *s* away.
21: 18 like chaff *s* away by a gale?
37: 21 after the wind has *s* them clean.
Ps 42: 7 have *s* over me.
58: 9 the wicked will be *s* away.
73: 19 completely *s* away by terrors!
88: 16 Your wrath has *s* over me;
124: 4 the torrent would have *s* over us,
124: 5 waters would have *s* us away.
136: 15 *s* Pharaoh and his army
Pr 10: 25 When the storm has *s*
Isa 44: 22 I have *s* away your offenses like
Da 2: 35 The wind *s* them away
11: 22 overwhelming army will be *s* away
11: 26 his army will be *s* away,
Jnh 2: 3 *s* over me.
Mic 7: 2 The godly have been *s*
Hab 3: 10 Torrents of water *s* by;
Mt 8: 24 so that the waves *s* over the boat.
12: 44 finds the house unoccupied, *s* clean
Lk 11: 25 it finds the house *s* clean
Ac 27: 14 called the "Northeaster," *s*
Rev 12: 4 His tail *s* a third of the stars out

SWERVE (SWERVING)

Pr 4: 5 do not forget my words or *s*
4: 27 Do not *s* to the right or the left;

SWERVING (SWERVE)

Joel 2: 7 not *s* from their course.

SWIFT (SWIFTER)

1Ch 12: 8 as *s* as gazelles in the mountains.
Pr 1: 16 they are *s* to shed blood.
Ecc 9: 11 The race is not to the *s*
Isa 18: 2 Go, *s* messengers,
19: 1 See, the LORD rides on a *s* cloud
30: 16 Therefore your pursuers will be *s*!
30: 16 'We will ride off on *s* horses.'
38: 14 I cried like a *s* or thrush,
59: 7 they are *s* to shed innocent blood.
Jer 2: 23 You are a *s* she-camel
8: 7 and the dove, the *s* and the thrush
46: 6 "The *s* cannot flee
Da 9: 21 to me in *s* flight about the time
Am 2: 14 The *s* will not escape,
Ro 3: 15 "Their feet are *s* to shed blood;
2Pe 2: 1 bringing *s* destruction

SWIFTER (SWIFT)

2Sa 1: 23 They were *s* than eagles,
Job 7: 6 "My days are *s* than a weaver's
9: 25 "My days are *s* than a runner;
Jer 4: 13 his horses are *s* than eagles.
La 4: 19 Our pursuers were *s*
Hab 1: 8 Their horses are *s* than leopards,

SWIM (SWIMMER SWIMMING)

Ps 8: 8 all that *s* the paths of the seas.
Isa 25: 11 spreads out his hands to *s*.
Eze 47: 5 and was deep enough to *s* in—
Ac 27: 43 He ordered those who could *s*

SWIMMER (SWIM)

Isa 25: 11 as a *s* spreads out his hands to swim

SWIMMING (SWIM)

Ac 27: 42 to prevent any of them from *s* away

SWINDLER (SWINDLERS)

1Co 5: 11 or a slanderer, a drunkard or a *s*.

SWINDLERS (SWINDLER)

1Co 5: 10 or the greedy and *s*, or idolaters.
6: 10 *s* will inherit the kingdom of God.

SWING (SWINGS SWUNG)

Ex 28: 28 that the breastpiece will not *s* out
39: 21 the breastpiece would not *s* out
Joel 3: 13 *S* the sickle,

SWINGS (SWING)

Dt 19: 5 and as he *s* his ax to fell a tree,
Isa 10: 15 itself above him who *s* it,

SWIRL (SWIRLED SWIRLING)

Job 37: 12 At his direction they *s* around

SWIRLED (SWIRL)

2Sa 22: 5 "The waves of death *s* about me;
Jnh 2: 3 and the currents *s* about me;

SWIRLING (SWIRL)

Isa 8: 8 and sweep on into Judah, *s* over it,
Jer 23: 19 a whirlwind *s* down
30: 23 a driving wind *s* down
Hos 13: 3 like chaff *s* from a threshing floor,

SWOLLEN (SWELL)

Lev 13: 43 and, if the *s* sore on his head
Ne 9: 21 nor did their feet become *s*.
Job 6: 16 and *s* with melting snow,

SWOOP (SWOOPING)

Isa 11: 14 They will *s* down on the slopes
Jer 49: 22 An eagle will soar and *s* down,

SWOOPING (SWOOP)

Dt 28: 49 of the earth, like an eagle *s* down,
Job 9: 26 like eagles *s* down on their prey.
Jer 48: 40 "Look! An eagle is *s* down,
Hab 1: 8 They fly like a vulture *s* to devour;

SWORD (SWORDS SWORDSMEN)

Ge 3: 24 and a flaming *s* flashing back
27: 40 You will live by the *s*
34: 26 and his son Shechem to the *s*
48: 22 took from the Amorites with my *s*
Ex 5: 3 us with plagues or with the *s*."
5: 21 have put a *s* in their hand to kill us
15: 9 I will draw my *s*
17: 13 the Amalekite army with the *s*.
18: 4 he saved me from the *s* of Pharaoh
22: 24 and I will kill you with the *s*;
32: 27 says: 'Each man strap a *s* to his side
Lev 26: 6 the *s* will not pass through your
26: 7 they will fall by the *s* before you.
26: 8 fall by the *s* before you.
26: 25 And I will bring the *s* upon you
26: 33 will draw out my *s* and pursue you.
26: 36 as though fleeing from the *s*.
26: 37 as though fleeing from the *s*,
Nu 14: 3 only to let us fall by the *s*?
14: 43 with you and you will fall by the *s*."
19: 16 who has been killed with a *s*
20: 18 and attack you with the *s*."
21: 24 put him to the *s* and took
22: 23 the road with a drawn *s* in his hand,
22: 29 If I had a *s* in my hand, I would kill
22: 31 in the road with his *s* drawn.
31: 8 son of Beor with the *s*.
Dt 13: 15 put to the *s* all who live
20: 13 put to the *s* all the men in it.
32: 25 In the street the *s* will make them
32: 41 when I sharpen my flashing *s*

Dt 32:42 while my *s* devours flesh:
33:29 and your glorious *s*.
Jos 5:13 of him with a drawn *s* in his hand.
6:21 with the *s* every living thing
8:24 one of them had been put to the *s*,
10:28 king to the *s* and totally destroyed
10:30 everyone in it Joshua put to the *s*.
10:32 and everyone in it he put to the *s*,
10:35 it to the *s* and totally destroyed
10:37 took the city and put it to the *s*,
10:39 its villages, and put them to the *s*.
11:10 Hazor and put its king to the *s*.
11:11 Everyone in it they put to the *s*.
11:12 their kings and put them to the *s*.
11:14 put to the *s* until they completely
13:22 put to the *s* Balaam son of Beor,
19:47 put it to the *s* and occupied it.
24:12 You did not do it with your own *s*
Jdg 1:8 They put the city to the *s*
1:25 and they put the city to the *s*
3:16 made a double-edged *s* about a foot
3:21 drew the *s* from his right thigh
3:22 Ehud did not pull the *s* out,
4:15 all his chariots and army by the *s*,
4:16 All the troops of Sisera fell by the *s*;
7:14 than the *s* of Gideon son of Joash,
7:20 "A *s* for the LORD and for Gideon
8:20 But Jether did not draw his *s*,
9:54 "Draw your *s* and kill me,
18:27 They attacked them with the *s*
20:37 and put the whole city to the *s*.
20:48 and put all the towns to the *s*,
21:10 and put to the *s* those living there,
1Sa 13:22 and Jonathan had a *s* or spear
15:8 he totally destroyed with the *s*.
15:33 "As your *s* has made women
17:39 fastened on his *s* over the tunic
17:45 "You come against me with *s*
17:47 here will know that it is not by *s*
17:50 without a *s* in his hand he struck
17:51 He took hold of the Philistine's *s*
17:51 he cut off his head with the *s*.
18:4 and even his *s*, his bow and his belt.
21:8 Don't you have a spear or a *s* here?
21:8 I haven't brought my *s*
21:9 there is no *s* here but that one."
21:9 "The *s* of Goliath the Philistine,
22:10 and the *s* of Goliath the Philistine.
22:13 giving him bread and a *s*
22:19 also put to the *s* Nob, the town
31:4 so Saul took his own *s* and fell on it.
31:4 "Draw your *s* and run me through,
31:5 fell on his *s* and died with him.
2Sa 1:12 because they had fallen by the *s*.
1:22 *s* of Saul did not return unsatisfied.
2:26 "Must the *s* devour forever?
3:29 who falls by the *s* or who lacks food
11:25 the *s* devours one as well
12:9 down Uriah the Hittite with the *s*
12:9 him with the *s* of the Ammonites.
12:10 therefore, the *s* will never depart
15:14 upon us and put the city to the *s*."
18:8 more lives that day than the *s*.
21:16 was armed with a new *s*,
23:10 hand grew tired and froze to the *s*.
24:9 men who could handle a *s*.
1Ki 1:51 servant to death with the *s*.' "
2:8 I will not put you to death by the *s*.'
2:32 and killed them with the *s*.
3:24 So they brought a *s* for the king.
3:24 Then the king said, "Bring me a *s*."
19:1 killed all the prophets with the *s*.
19:10 prophets to death with the *s*.
19:14 prophets to death with the *s*.
19:17 put to death any who escape the *s*
19:17 put to death any who escape the *s*
2Ki 6:22 you have captured with your own *s*
8:12 kill their young men with the *s*,
10:25 So they cut them down with the *s*.
11:15 put to the *s* anyone who follows her
11:20 slain with the *s* at the palace.
19:7 cut down with the *s*.' "
19:37 Sharezer cut him down with the *s*,
1Ch 5:18 who could handle shield and *s*,
10:4 so Saul took his own *s* and fell on it.
10:4 "Draw your *s* and run me through,
10:5 he too fell on his *s* and died.
21:5 men who could handle a *s*,
1Ch 21:12 or three days of the *s* of the LORD
21:16 with a drawn *s* in his hand
21:27 and he put his *s* back into its sheath
21:30 he was afraid of the *s* of the angel
2Ch 20:9 whether the *s* of judgment,
21:4 brothers to the *s* along with some
23:14 put to the *s* anyone who follows her
23:21 Athaliah had been slain with the *s*.
29:9 why our fathers have fallen by the *s*
32:21 of his sons cut him down with the *s*.
36:17 men with the *s* in the sanctuary,
36:20 remnant, who escaped from the *s*,
Ezr 9:7 priests have been subjected to the *s*
Ne 4:18 of the builders wore his *s* at his side
Est 9:5 down all their enemies with the *s*,
Job 1:15 They put the servants to the *s*,
1:17 They put the servants to the *s*,
5:15 from the *s* in their mouth;
5:20 in battle from the stroke of the *s*.
15:22 he is marked for the *s*.
19:29 will bring punishment by the *s*,
19:29 you should fear the *s* yourselves;
27:14 his children, their fate is the *s*;
33:18 his life from perishing by the *s*.
36:12 they will perish by the *s*
39:22 he does not shy away from the *s*.
40:19 can approach him with his *s*.
41:26 *s* that reaches him has no effect,
Ps 7:12 he will sharpen his *s*;
17:13 from the wicked by your *s*.
22:20 Deliver my life from the *s*,
37:14 The wicked draw the *s*
44:3 by their *s* that they won the land,
44:6 my *s* does not bring me victory;
45:3 Gird your *s* upon your side,
63:10 They will be given over to the *s*
78:62 He gave his people over to the *s*;
78:64 their priests were put to the *s*,
89:43 have turned back the edge of his *s*
144:10 David from the deadly *s*.
149:6 and a double-edged *s* in their hands
Pr 5:4 sharp as a double-edged *s*.
12:18 Reckless words pierce like a *s*,
25:18 Like a club or a *s* or a sharp arrow
SS 3:8 all of them wearing the *s*,
3:8 each with his *s* at his side,
Isa 1:20 you will be devoured by the *s*."
2:4 Nation will not take up *s*
3:25 Your men will fall by the *s*,
13:15 all who are caught will fall by the *s*.
14:19 with those pierced by the *s*,
21:15 They flee from the *s*,
21:15 from the drawn *s*,
22:2 Your slain were not killed by the *s*,
27:1 his fierce, great and powerful *s*,
27:1 the LORD will punish with his *s*,
31:8 They will flee before the *s*
31:8 "Assyria will fall by a *s* that is not
31:8 *s*, not of mortals, will devour them.
34:5 My *s* has drunk its fill
34:6 The *s* of the LORD is bathed
37:7 cut down with the *s*.' "
37:38 Sharezer cut him down with the *s*,
41:2 He turns them to dust with his *s*,
49:2 made my mouth like a sharpened *s*,
51:19 ruin and destruction, famine and *s*
65:12 I will destine you for the *s*,
66:16 For with fire and with his *s*
Jer 2:30 Your *s* has devoured your prophets
4:10 when the *s* is at our throats."
5:12 we will never see *s* or famine.
5:17 With the *s* they will destroy
6:25 for the enemy has a *s*,
9:16 with the *s* until I have destroyed
11:22 Their young men will die by the *s*,
12:12 for the *s* of the LORD will devour
14:12 I will destroy them with the *s*,
14:13 'You will not see the *s*
14:15 'No *s* or famine will touch this land
14:15 same prophets will perish by *s*
14:16 because of the famine and *s*.
14:18 I see those slain by the *s*;
15:2 those for the *s*, to the *s*;
15:3 "the *s* to kill and the dogs
15:9 I will put the survivors to the *s*
16:4 They will perish by *s* and famine,
18:21 over to the power of the *s*.
18:21 their young men slain by the *s*
Jer 19:7 fall by the *s* before their enemies,
20:4 fall by the *s* of their enemies.
20:4 to Babylon or put them to the *s*.
21:7 them to the *s*; he will show them no
21:7 this city who survive the plague, *s*
21:9 stays in this city will die by the *s*,
24:10 I will send the *s*, famine
25:16 of the *s* I will send among them."
25:27 of the *s* I will send among you.'
25:29 calling down a *s* upon all who live
25:31 and put the wicked to the *s*,' "
25:38 because of the *s* of the oppressor
26:23 who had him struck down with a *s*
27:8 I will punish that nation with the *s*,
27:13 and your people die by the *s*,
29:17 Almighty says: "I will send the *s*,
29:18 I will pursue them with the *s*,
31:2 "The people who survive the *s*
32:24 Because of the *s*, famine and plague
32:36 are saying about this city, 'By the *s*,
33:4 *s* in the fight with the Babylonians:
34:4 die by the *s*; you will die peacefully.
34:17 'freedom' to fall by the *s*, plague
38:2 stays in this city will die by the *s*,
39:18 you will not fall by the *s*
41:2 the son of Shaphan, with the *s*,
42:16 then the *s* you fear will overtake
42:17 to settle there will die by the *s*,
42:22 be sure of this: You will die by the *s*
43:11 and the *s* to those destined for the *s*
44:12 fall by the *s* or die from famine.
44:12 they will die by *s* or famine.
44:13 live in Egypt with the *s*,
44:18 and have been perishing by *s*
44:27 the Jews in Egypt will perish by *s*
44:28 Those who escape the *s*
46:10 The *s* will devour till it is satisfied,
46:14 for the *s* devours those around you
46:16 away from the *s* of the oppressor.'
47:6 " 'Ah, *s* of the LORD,' you cry,
48:2 the *s* will pursue you.
48:10 A curse on him who keeps his *s*
49:37 "I will pursue them with the *s*
50:16 Because of the *s* of the oppressor
50:35 "A *s* against the Babylonians!"
50:36 A *s* against her false prophets!
50:36 A *s* against her warriors!
50:37 A *s* against her horses and chariots
50:37 A *s* against her treasures!
51:50 You who have escaped the *s*,
La 1:20 Outside, the *s* bereaves;
2:21 have fallen by the *s*.
4:9 Those killed by the *s* are better off
5:9 because of the *s* in the desert.
Eze 5:1 take a sharp *s* and use it
5:2 I will pursue them with drawn *s*.
5:2 and strike it with the *s* all
5:12 fall by the *s* outside your walls;
5:12 the winds and pursue with drawn *s*.
5:17 and I will bring the *s* against you.
6:3 I am about to bring a *s* against you,
6:8 some of you will escape the *s*
6:11 for they will fall by the *s*, famine
6:12 and he that is near will fall by the *s*,
7:15 in the country will die by the *s*,
7:15 "Outside is the *s*, inside are plague
11:8 You fear the *s*, and the *s* is what I
11:10 fall by the *s*, and I will execute
12:14 I will pursue them with drawn *s*.
12:16 I will spare a few of them from the *s*
14:17 Let the *s* pass throughout the land,'
14:17 if I bring a *s* against that country
14:21 *s* and famine and wild beasts
17:21 his fleeing troops will fall by the *s*,
21:3 I will draw my *s* from its scabbard
21:4 my *s* will be unsheathed
21:5 that I the LORD have drawn my *s*
21:9 " 'A *s*, a *s*,
21:11 The *s* is appointed to be polished,
21:12 They are thrown to the *s*
21:14 It is a *s* for slaughter—
21:14 Let the *s* strike twice,
21:14 a *s* for great slaughter,
21:15 I have stationed the *s* for slaughter
21:16 O *s*, slash to the right,
21:19 for the *s* of the king of Babylon
21:20 for the *s* to come against Rabbah
21:28 " 'A *s*, a *s*, drawn for the slaughter,

SWORDS (SWORD)

SWORDSMEN (SWORD)

SWORE (SWEAR)

SWORN (SWEAR)

SWUNG (SWING)

SYCAMORE-FIG (FIG)

SYCAMORE-FIGS (FIG)

SYCHAR

SYMBOL (SYMBOLIC SYMBOLIZES SYMBOLS)

Ex 13: 16 *s* on your forehead that the LORD
Nu 6: 7 the *s* of his separation to God is

SYMBOLIC (SYMBOL)

Zec 3: 8 who are men *s* of things to come:

SYMBOLIZES (SYMBOL)

1Pe 3: 21 this water *s* baptism that now saves

SYMBOLS (SYMBOL)

Dt 6: 8 Tie them as *s* on your hands
11: 18 tie them as *s* on your hands
Isa 8: 18 and *s* in Israel from the LORD
57: 8 you have put your pagan *s*.

SYMPATHETIC (SYMPATHY)

1Pe 3: 8 in harmony with one another; be *s*,

SYMPATHIZE (SYMPATHY)

Job 2: 11 and *s* with him and comfort him.
Heb 4: 15 unable to *s* with our weaknesses,

SYMPATHIZED (SYMPATHY)

Heb 10: 34 You *s* with those in prison

SYMPATHY (SYMPATHETIC SYMPATHIZE SYMPATHIZED)

2Sa 10: 2 express his *s* to Hanun concerning
10: 3 by sending men to you to express *s*
1Ch 19: 2 express his *s* to Hanun concerning
19: 2 the Ammonites to express *s* to him,
19: 3 by sending men to you to express *s*
Ps 69: 20 I looked for *s*, but there was none,
Jer 16: 5 do not go to mourn or show *s*,
Da 1: 9 to show favor and *s* to Daniel,

SYNAGOGUE (SYNAGOGUES)

Mt 12: 9 that place, he went into their *s*,
13: 54 teaching the people in their *s*,
Mk 1: 21 Jesus went into the *s* and began
1: 23 a man in their *s* who was possessed
1: 29 as they left the *s*, they went
3: 1 Another time he went into the *s*,
5: 22 one of the *s* rulers, named Jairus,
5: 35 from the house of Jairus, the *s* ruler
5: 36 Jesus told the *s* ruler, "Don't be
5: 38 came to the home of the *s* ruler,
6: 2 he began to teach in the *s*,
Lk 4: 16 the Sabbath day he went into the *s*,
4: 20 of everyone in the *s* were fastened
4: 28 All the people in the *s* were furious
4: 33 In the *s* there was a man possessed
4: 38 Jesus left the *s* and went
6: 6 another Sabbath he went into the *s*
7: 5 our nation and has built our *s*."
8: 41 a ruler of the *s*, came and fell
8: 49 from the house of Jairus, the *s* ruler
13: 14 the *s* ruler said to the people,
Jn 6: 59 teaching in the *s* in Capernaum.
9: 22 Christ would be put out of the *s*.
12: 42 fear they would be put out of the *s*;
16: 2 They will put you out of the *s*;
Ac 6: 9 members of the *S* of the Freedmen
13: 14 On the Sabbath they entered the *s*
13: 15 the *s* rulers sent word to them,
13: 42 and Barnabas were leaving the *s*,
14: 1 as usual into the Jewish *s*.
17: 1 where there was a Jewish *s*.
17: 2 custom was, Paul went into the *s*,
17: 10 they went to the Jewish *s*.
17: 17 he reasoned in the *s* with the Jews
18: 4 Every Sabbath he reasoned in the *s*
18: 7 Paul left the *s* and went next door
18: 8 *s* ruler, and his entire household
18: 17 turned on Sosthenes the *s* ruler
18: 19 He himself went into the *s*
18: 26 He began to speak boldly in the *s*.
19: 8 Paul entered the *s* and spoke boldly
22: 19 from one *s* to another to imprison
26: 11 went from one *s* to another
Rev 2: 9 and are not, but are a *s* of Satan.
3: 9 I will make those who are of the *s*

SYNAGOGUES (SYNAGOGUE)

Mt 4: 23 Galilee, teaching in their *s*,
6: 2 as the hypocrites do in the *s*
6: 5 love to pray standing in the *s*
9: 35 and villages, teaching in their *s*,
10: 17 councils and flog you in their *s*.
23: 6 the most important seats in the *s*;
23: 34 others you will flog in your *s*
Mk 1: 39 in their *s* and driving out demons.
12: 39 the most important seats in the *s*
13: 9 local councils and flogged in the *s*.
Lk 4: 15 in their *s*, and everyone praised
4: 44 kept on preaching in the *s* of Judea.
11: 43 the most important seats in the *s*
12: 11 "When you are brought before *s*,
13: 10 Jesus was teaching in one of the *s*,
20: 46 the most important seats in the *s*
21: 12 They will deliver you to *s*
Jn 18: 20 I always taught in *s* or at the temple
Ac 9: 2 for letters to the *s* in Damascus,
9: 20 preach in the *s* that Jesus is the Son
13: 5 the word of God in the Jewish *s*.
15: 21 is read in the *s* on every Sabbath."
24: 12 or stirring up a crowd in the *s*

SYNTYCHE

Php 4: 2 and I plead with *S* to agree

SYRACUSE

Ac 28: 12 in at *S* and stayed there three days.

SYRIA (SYRIAN)

Mt 4: 24 News about him spread all over *S*,
Lk 2: 2 while Quirinius was governor of *S*.)
Ac 15: 23 the Gentile believers in Antioch, *S*
15: 41 He went through *S* and Cilicia,
18: 18 he left the brothers and sailed for *S*
20: 3 as he was about to sail for *S*,
21: 3 to the south of it, we sailed on to *S*.
Gal 1: 21 Later I went to *S* and Cilicia.

SYRIAN (SYRIA)

Mk 7: 26 was a Greek, born in *S* Phoenicia.
Lk 4: 27 cleansed—only Naaman the *S*."

SYRTIS

Ac 27: 17 aground on the sandbars of *S*,

TAANACH

Jos 12: 21 one the king of *T* one the king
17: 11 and the people of Dor, Endor, *T*
21: 25 tribe of Manasseh they received *T*
Jdg 1: 27 or *T* or Dor or Ibleam or Megiddo
5: 19 at *T* by the waters of Megiddo,
1Ki 4: 12 Baana son of Ahilud—in *T*
1Ch 7: 29 *T*, Megiddo and Dor, together

TAANATH SHILOH

Jos 16: 6 the north it curved eastward to *T*,

TABALIAH

1Ch 26: 11 *T* the third and Zechariah

TABBAOTH

Ezr 2: 43 Hasupha, *T*, Keros, Siaha, Padon,
Ne 7: 46 Hasupha, *T*, Keros, Sia, Padon,

TABBATH

Jdg 7: 22 border of Abel Meholah near *T*.

TABEEL

Ezr 4: 7 *T* and the rest of his associates
Isa 7: 6 and make the son of *T* king over it

TABERAH

Nu 11: 3 So that place was called *T*,
Dt 9: 22 also made the LORD angry at *T*,

TABERNACLE (TABERNACLES)

Ex 25: 9 Make this *t* and all its furnishings
26: 1 "Make the *t* with ten curtains
26: 6 together so that the *t* is a unit.
26: 7 of goat hair for the tent over the *t*—
26: 12 is to hang down at the rear of the *t*.
26: 13 hang over the sides of the *t* so
26: 15 frames of acacia wood for the *t*.
26: 17 the frames of the *t* in this way.
26: 18 frames for the south side of the *t*
26: 20 side of the *t*, make twenty frames
26: 22 that is, the west end of the *t*,
26: 26 for the frames on one side of the *t*,
26: 27 on the west, at the far end of the *t*.
Ex 26: 30 "Set up the *t* according
26: 35 curtain on the north side of the *t*
27: 9 "Make a courtyard for the *t*.
27: 19 used in the service of the *t*,
35: 11 the *t* with its tent and its covering,
35: 15 doorway at the entrance to the *t*;
35: 18 pegs for the *t* and for the courtyard,
36: 8 among the workmen made the *t*
36: 13 together so that the *t* was a unit.
36: 14 of goat hair for the tent over the *t*—
36: 20 frames of acacia wood for the *t*.
36: 22 the frames of the *t* in this way.
36: 23 frames for the south side of the *t*
36: 25 of the *t*, they made twenty frames
36: 27 that is, the west end of the *t*,
36: 28 the corners of the *t* at the far end.
36: 31 for the frames on one side of the *t*,
36: 32 on the west, at the far end of the *t*.
38: 20 All the tent pegs of the *t*
38: 21 for the *t*, the *t* of the Testimony,
38: 31 and all the tent pegs for the *t*
39: 32 work on the *t*, the Tent of Meeting,
39: 33 Then they brought the *t* to Moses:
39: 40 all the furnishings for the *t*,
40: 2 "Set up the *t*, the Tent of Meeting,
40: 5 the curtain at the entrance to the *t*.
40: 6 in front of the entrance to the *t*,
40: 9 anoint the *t* and everything in it;
40: 17 So the *t* was set up on the first day
40: 18 Moses set up the *t*, he put the bases
40: 19 Then he spread the tent over the *t*
40: 21 Then he brought the ark into the *t*
40: 22 side of the *t* outside the curtain
40: 24 the table on the south side of the *t*
40: 28 the curtain at the entrance to the *t*.
40: 29 offering near the entrance to the *t*,
40: 33 set up the courtyard around the *t*
40: 34 the glory of the LORD filled the *t*.
40: 35 the glory of the LORD filled the *t*.
40: 36 the cloud lifted from above the *t*,
40: 38 of the LORD was over the *t* by day
Lev 8: 10 anointed the *t* and everything in it,
17: 4 in front of the *t* of the LORD—
Nu 1: 50 They are to carry the *t*
1: 50 in charge of the *t* of the Testimony
1: 51 Whenever the *t* is to move,
1: 51 and whenever the *t* is to be set up,
1: 53 tents around the *t* of the Testimony
1: 53 the care of the *t* of the Testimony."
3: 7 Meeting by doing the work of the *t*.
3: 8 by doing the work of the *t*.
3: 23 to camp on the west, behind the *t*.
3: 25 responsible for the care of the *t*
3: 26 to the courtyard surrounding the *t*
3: 29 to camp on the south side of the *t*.
3: 35 to camp on the north side of the *t*.
3: 36 to take care of the frames of the *t*,
3: 38 were to camp to the east of the *t*,
4: 16 He is to be in charge of the entire *t*
4: 25 are to carry the curtains of the *t*,
4: 26 of the courtyard surrounding the *t*
4: 31 to carry the frames of the *t*,
5: 17 dust from the *t* floor into the water.
7: 1 Moses finished setting up the *t*,
7: 3 These they presented before the *t*.
9: 15 On the day the *t*, the Tent
9: 15 cloud above the *t* looked like fire.
9: 18 as the cloud stayed over the *t*,
9: 19 remained over the *t* a long time,
9: 20 was over the *t* only a few days;
9: 22 stayed over the *t* for two days
10: 11 from above the *t* of the Testimony.
10: 17 Then the *t* was taken down,
10: 21 The *t* was to be set up
16: 9 to do the work at the LORD's *t*
17: 13 near the *t* of the LORD will die.
19: 13 himself defiles the LORD's *t*.
31: 30 for the care of the LORD's *t*."
31: 47 for the care of the LORD's *t*.
Jos 22: 19 where the LORD's *t* stands,
22: 29 our God that stands before his *t*."
1Ch 6: 32 with music before the *t*—
6: 48 to all the other duties of the *t*,
16: 39 priests before the *t* of the LORD
21: 29 *t* of the LORD, which Moses had
23: 26 no longer need to carry the *t*
2Ch 1: 5 in front of the *t* of the LORD;
Ps 27: 5 me in the shelter of his *t*

Ps 27: 6 at his *t* will I sacrifice with shouts
78: 60 He abandoned the *t* of Shiloh,
Ac 7: 44 "Our forefathers had the *t*
7: 45 Having received the *t*, our fathers
Heb 8: 2 the true *t* set up by the Lord,
8: 5 when he was about to build the *t*:
9: 2 A *t* was set up.
9: 8 long as the first *t* was still standing.
9: 11 and more perfect *t* that is not
9: 21 sprinkled with the blood both the *t*
13: 10 at the *t* have no right to eat.
Rev 15: 5 that is, the *t* of Testimony,

TABERNACLES (TABERNACLE)

Lev 23: 34 the LORD's Feast of *T* begins,
Dt 16: 13 the Feast of *T* for seven days
16: 16 Feast of Weeks and the Feast of *T*.
31: 10 during the Feast of *T*,
2Ch 8: 13 Feast of Weeks and the Feast of *T*.
Ezr 3: 4 of *T* with the required number
Zec 14: 16 and to celebrate the Feast of *T*.
14: 18 up to celebrate the Feast of *T*.
14: 19 up to celebrate the Feast of *T*.
Jn 7: 2 when the Jewish Feast of *T* was

TABITHA

Ac 9: 36 was a disciple named *T* (which,
9: 40 the dead woman, he said, "*T*,

TABLE (TABLES)

Ge 43: 34 served to them from Joseph's *t*,
Ex 25: 23 "Make a *t* of acacia wood—
25: 26 Make four gold rings for the *t*
25: 27 the poles used in carrying the *t*.
25: 28 and carry the *t* with them.
25: 30 Presence on this *t* to be before me
26: 35 Place the *t* outside the curtain
30: 27 the ark of the Testimony, the *t*
31: 8 other furnishings of the tent—the *t*
35: 13 *t* with its poles and all its articles
37: 10 They made the *t* of acacia wood—
37: 13 They cast four gold rings for the *t*
37: 14 the poles used in carrying the *t*.
37: 15 poles for carrying the *t* were made
37: 16 from pure gold the articles for the *t*
39: 36 the *t* with all its articles
40: 4 in the *t* and set out what belongs
40: 22 Moses placed the *t* in the Tent
40: 24 the Tent of Meeting opposite the *t*
Lev 24: 6 on the *t* of pure gold
Nu 3: 31 the *t*, the lampstand, the altars,
4: 7 Over the *t* of the Presence they are
Jdg 1: 7 have picked up scraps under my *t*.
1Sa 20: 29 he has not come to the king's *t*."
20: 34 up from the *t* in fierce anger;
2Sa 9: 7 and you will always eat at my *t*."
9: 10 master, will always eat at my *t*."
9: 11 ate at David's *t* like one
9: 13 he always ate at the king's *t*,
19: 28 among those who sat at your *t*.
1Ki 2: 7 be among those who eat at your *t*.
4: 27 and all who came to the king's *t*.
7: 48 golden *t* on which was the bread
10: 5 the food on his *t*, the seating
13: 20 While they were sitting at the *t*,
18: 19 of Asherah, who eat at Jezebel's *t*."
2Ki 4: 10 the roof and put in it a bed and a *t*,
25: 29 his life ate regularly at the king's *t*.
1Ch 9: 32 Sabbath the bread set out on the *t*.
23: 29 charge of the bread set out on the *t*,
28: 16 for each *t* for consecrated bread;
2Ch 9: 4 the food on his *t*, the seating
13: 11 bread on the ceremonially clean *t*
29: 18 *t* for setting out the consecrated
Ne 5: 17 fifty Jews and officials ate at my *t*,
10: 33 for the bread set out on the *t*;
Job 36: 16 of your *t* laden with choice food.
Ps 23: 5 You prepare a *t* before me
69: 22 May the *t* set before them become
78: 19 "Can God spread a *t* in the desert?
128: 3 shoots around your *t*.
Pr 9: 2 she has also set her *t*.
SS 1: 12 While the king was at his *t*,
Isa 65: 11 who spread a *t* for Fortune
Jer 52: 33 his life ate regularly at the king's *t*.
Eze 23: 41 with a *t* spread before it
39: 20 At my *t* you will eat your fill
41: 22 "This is the *t* that is
Eze 44: 16 are to come near my *t* to minister
Da 1: 5 and wine from the king's *t*.
11: 27 will sit at the same *t* and lie
Mal 1: 7 that the LORD's *t* is contemptible.
1: 12 it by saying of the Lord's *t*,
Mt 15: 27 fall from their masters' *t*."
26: 7 as he was reclining at the *t*.
26: 20 reclining at the *t* with the Twelve.
Mk 7: 28 dogs under the *t* eat the children's
14: 3 reclining at the *t* in the home
14: 18 they were reclining at the *t* eating,
Lk 7: 36 house and reclined at the *t*.
11: 37 so he went in and reclined at the *t*.
12: 37 will have them recline at the *t*
14: 7 picked the places of honor at the *t*,
14: 15 of those at the *t* with him heard this
16: 21 fell from the rich man's *t*.
22: 14 and his apostles reclined at the *t*.
22: 21 to betray me is with mine on the *t*.
22: 27 Is it not the one who is at the *t*?
22: 27 the one who is at the *t*
22: 30 and drink at my *t* in my kingdom
24: 30 When he was at the *t* with them,
Jn 12: 2 was among those reclining at the *t*
Ro 11: 9 "May their *t* become a snare
1Co 10: 21 a part in both the Lord's *t* and the *t*
Heb 9: 2 the *t* and the consecrated bread;

TABLES (TABLE)

1Ch 28: 16 the weight of silver for the silver *t*;
2Ch 4: 8 He made ten *t* and placed them
4: 19 the *t* on which was the bread
Est 9: 1 but now the *t* were turned
Isa 21: 5 They set the *t*,
28: 8 All the *t* are covered with vomit
Eze 40: 39 portico of the gateway were two *t*
40: 40 side of the steps were two *t*.
40: 40 to the north gateway were two *t*,
40: 41 So there were four *t* on one side
40: 41 eight *t* in all—on which
40: 42 also four *t* of dressed stone
40: 43 The *t* were for the flesh
Mt 21: 12 He overturned the *t*
Mk 11: 15 He overturned the *t*
Jn 2: 14 sitting at *t* exchanging money.
2: 15 changers and overturned their *t*.
Ac 6: 2 word of God in order to wait on *t*.

TABLET (TABLETS)

Pr 3: 3 write them on the *t* of your heart.
7: 3 write them on the *t* of your heart.
Isa 30: 8 Go now, write it on a *t* for them,
Eze 4: 1 "Now, son of man, take a clay *t*,
Lk 1: 63 He asked for a writing *t*,

TABLETS (TABLET)

Ex 24: 12 and I will give you the *t* of stone,
31: 18 he gave him the two *t*
31: 18 the *t* of stone inscribed
32: 15 with the two *t* of the Testimony
32: 16 The *t* were the work of God;
32: 16 writing of God, engraved on the *t*.
32: 19 and he threw the *t* out of his hands,
34: 1 out two stone *t* like the first
34: 1 the words that were on the first *t*,
34: 4 and he carried the two stone *t*
34: 4 out two stone *t* like the first
34: 28 And he wrote on the *t* the words
34: 29 with the two *t* of the Testimony
Dt 4: 13 then wrote them on two stone *t*.
5: 22 Then he wrote them on two stone *t*
9: 9 mountain to receive the *t* of stone,
9: 9 *t* of the covenant that the LORD
9: 10 gave me two stone *t* inscribed
9: 11 gave me the two stone *t*, the *t*
9: 15 And the two *t* of the covenant were
9: 17 So I took the two *t* and threw them
10: 1 out two stone *t* like the first
10: 2 the words that were on the first *t*,
10: 2 write on the *t* the words that were
10: 3 out two stone *t* like the first
10: 3 with the two *t* in my hands.
10: 4 on these *t* what he had written
10: 5 and put the *t* in the ark I had made,
1Ki 8: 9 two stone *t* that Moses had placed
2Ch 5: 10 the two *t* that Moses had placed
Jer 17: 1 on the *t* of their hearts
Hab 2: 2 and make it plain on *t*
2Co 3: 3 not on *t* of stone but on *t*
Heb 9: 4 and the stone *t* of the covenant.

TABOR

Jos 19: 22 boundary touched *T*, Shahazumah
Jdg 4: 6 and lead the way to Mount *T*.
4: 12 Abinoam had gone up to Mount *T*,
4: 14 So Barak went down Mount *T*,
8: 18 What kind of men did you kill at *T*
1Sa 10: 3 until you reach the great tree of *T*.
1Ch 6: 77 *T*, together with their pasturelands;
Ps 89: 12 *T* and Hermon sing for joy
Jer 46: 18 "one will come who is like *T*
Hos 5: 1 a net spread out on *T*.

TABRIMMON

1Ki 15: 18 sent them to Ben-Hadad son of *T*,

TACKLE

Ac 27: 19 they threw the ship's *t* overboard

TACT

Da 2: 14 spoke to him with wisdom and *t*.

TADMOR

1Ki 9: 18 Baalath, and *T* in the desert,
2Ch 8: 4 He also built up *T* in the desert

TAHAN (TAHANITE)

Nu 26: 35 through *T*, the Tahanite clan.
1Ch 7: 25 Telah his son, *T* his son, Ladan his

TAHANITE (TAHAN)

Nu 26: 35 through Tahan, the *T* clan.

TAHASH

Ge 22: 24 Tebah, Gaham, *T* and Maacah.

TAHATH

Nu 33: 26 left Makheloth and camped at *T*.
33: 27 They left *T* and camped at Terah.
1Ch 6: 24 Assir his son, *T* his son, Uriel his
6: 37 the son of *T*, the son of Assir,
7: 20 Shuthelah, Bered his son, *T* his son
7: 21 Eleadah his son, *T* his son,

TAHKEMONITE

2Sa 23: 8 a *T*, was chief of the Three;

TAHPANHES

Jer 2: 16 Also, the men of Memphis and *T*
43: 7 to the LORD and went as far as *T*.
43: 8 In *T* the word of the LORD came
43: 9 entrance to Pharaoh's palace in *T*.
44: 1 in Migdol, *T* and Memphis—
46: 14 proclaim it also in Memphis and *T*:
Eze 30: 18 Dark will be the day at *T*

TAHPENES

1Ki 11: 19 a sister of his own wife, Queen *T*,
11: 20 sister of *T* bore him a son named
11: 20 whom *T* brought up

TAHREA

1Ch 9: 41 Pithon, Melech, *T* and Ahaz.

TAHTIM HODSHI

2Sa 24: 6 went to Gilead and the region of *T*,

TAIL (TAILS)

Ex 4: 4 out your hand and take it by the *t*."
29: 22 fat *t*, the fat around the inner parts,
Lev 3: 9 the entire fat *t* cut off close
7: 3 the fat *t* and the fat that covers
8: 25 the fat *t*, all the fat
9: 19 of the cow and the ram—the fat *t*,
Dt 28: 13 will make you the head, not the *t*.
28: 44 be the head, but you will be the *t*.
Jdg 15: 4 and tied them *t* to *t* in pairs.
Job 40: 17 His *t* sways like a cedar;
Isa 9: 14 cut off from Israel both head and *t*,
9: 15 prophets who teach lies are the *t*.
19: 15 head or *t*, palm branch or reed.
Rev 12: 4 His *t* swept a third of the stars out

TAILS (TAIL)

Jdg 15: 4 fastened a torch to every pair of *t*,
Rev 9: 10 They had *t* and stings like
9: 10 and in their *t* they had power

Rev 9: 19 for their *t* were like snakes,
9: 19 was in their mouths and in their *t;*

TAKE (RETAKE TAKEN TAKES TAKING TOOK)

Ge 2: 15 of Eden to work it and *t* care of it.
3: 22 *t* also from the tree of life and eat,
6: 21 You are to *t* every kind
7: 2 *T* with you seven of every kind
12: 19 *T* her and go!" Then Pharaoh gave
15: 7 land to *t* possession of it."
19: 15 *T* your wife and your two
21: 18 Lift the boy up and *t* him
22: 2 Then God said, "*T* your son,
22: 17 Your descendants will *t* possession
24: 5 Shall I then *t* your son back
24: 6 that you do not *t* my son back
24: 8 Only do not *t* my son back there."
24: 51 Here is Rebekah; *t* her and go,
27: 10 Then *t* it to your father to eat,
28: 2 *T* a wife for yourself there,
28: 4 so that you may *t* possession
28: 6 him to Paddan Aram to *t* a wife
29: 7 and *t* them back to pasture."
30: 15 Will you *t* my son's mandrakes too
31: 31 you would *t* your daughters
31: 32 of yours here with me; and if so, *t* it
31: 50 *t* any wives besides my daughters,
34: 9 and *t* our daughters for yourselves.
34: 16 and *t* your daughters for ourselves.
34: 17 to be circumcised, we'll *t* our sister
37: 21 "Let's not *t* his life," he said.
37: 22 and *t* him back to his father.
37: 25 were on their way to *t* them
41: 34 over the land to *t* a fifth
42: 19 and *t* grain back for your starving
42: 33 *t* food for your starving households
42: 36 and now you want to *t* Benjamin.
43: 11 *t* them down to the man as a gift—
43: 12 *T* double the amount of silver
43: 13 *T* your brother also and go back
43: 16 "*T* these men to my house,
43: 18 seize us as slaves and *t* our donkeys
44: 29 If you *t* this one from me too
45: 19 *T* some carts from Egypt
48: 21 and *t* you back to the land
50: 24 and *t* you up out of this land
Ex 2: 9 "*T* this baby and nurse him for me,
3: 5 "*T* off your sandals,
3: 18 Let us *t* a three-day journey
4: 4 "Reach out your hand and *t* it
4: 9 The water you *t* from the river will
4: 9 *t* some water from the Nile
4: 17 But *t* this staff in your hand
5: 3 Now let us *t* a three-day journey
6: 7 I will *t* you as my own people,
7: 9 '*T* your staff and throw it
7: 15 *t* in your hand the staff that was
7: 19 '*T* your staff and stretch out your
7: 23 and did not *t* even this to heart.
8: 8 to the LORD to *t* the frogs away
8: 27 We must *t* a three-day journey
9: 8 "*T* handfuls of soot from a furnace
10: 17 God to *t* this deadly plague away
12: 3 is to *t* a lamb for his family,
12: 5 and you may *t* them from the sheep
12: 6 *T* care of them until the fourteenth
12: 7 they are to *t* some of the blood
12: 22 *T* a bunch of hyssop, dip it
12: 32 *T* your flocks and herds,
12: 46 *t* none of the meat
12: 48 then he may *t* part like one born
16: 16 *T* an omer for each person you
16: 32 '*T* an omer of manna and keep it
16: 33 "*T* a jar and put an omer of manna
17: 5 and *t* in your hand the staff
17: 5 *T* with you some of the elders
21: 6 He shall *t* him to the door
21: 6 then his master must *t* him
21: 14 *t* him away from my altar
21: 23 you are to *t* life for life, eye for eye,
22: 22 "Do not *t* advantage of a widow
22: 26 If you *t* your neighbor's cloak
23: 4 be sure to *t* it back to him.
23: 25 I will *t* away sickness
23: 30 enough to *t* possession of the land.
28: 9 "*T* two onyx stones and engrave
29: 1 *T* a young bull and two rams
Ex 29: 5 *T* the garments and dress Aaron
29: 7 *T* the anointing oil and anoint him
29: 12 *T* some of the bull's blood
29: 13 *t* all the fat around the inner parts,
29: 15 "*T* one of the rams, and Aaron
29: 16 Slaughter it and *t* the blood
29: 19 "*T* the other ram, and Aaron
29: 20 *t* some of its blood and put it
29: 21 *t* some of the blood on the altar
29: 22 *T* from this ram the fat, the fat tail,
29: 23 which is before the LORD, *t* a loaf,
29: 25 Then *t* them from their hands
29: 26 After you *t* the breast of the ram
29: 31 "*T* the ram for the ordination
30: 12 "When you *t* a census
30: 23 "*T* the following fine spices:
30: 34 "*T* fragrant spices—gum resin,
32: 2 "*T* off the gold earrings that your
32: 24 'Whoever has any gold jewelry, *t* it
33: 5 Now *t* off your ornaments
33: 7 Now Moses used to *t* a tent
34: 9 and *t* us as your inheritance."
35: 5 *t* an offering for the LORD.
40: 9 "*T* the anointing oil and anoint
Lev 2: 2 The priest shall *t* a handful
2: 2 and *t* it to Aaron's sons the priests.
2: 8 it to the priest, who shall *t* it
2: 9 He shall *t* out the memorial portion
4: 5 the anointed priest shall *t* some
4: 12 he must *t* outside the camp
4: 16 the anointed priest is to *t* some
4: 21 he shall *t* the bull outside the camp
4: 25 the priest shall *t* some of the blood
4: 30 the priest is to *t* some of the blood
4: 34 the priest shall *t* some of the blood
5: 12 who shall *t* a handful of it
6: 11 Then he is to *t* off these clothes
6: 15 The priest is to *t* a handful
9: 2 "*T* a bull calf for your sin offering
9: 3 '*T* a male goat for a sin offering,
10: 12 "*T* the grain offering left
10: 17 given to you to *t* away the guilt
14: 6 He is then to *t* the live bird
14: 12 "Then the priest is to *t* one
14: 14 The priest is to *t* some of the blood
14: 15 The priest shall then *t* some
14: 21 he must *t* one male lamb
14: 24 The priest is to *t* the lamb
14: 25 for the guilt offering and *t* some
14: 42 Then they are to *t* other stones
14: 42 *t* new clay and plaster the house.
14: 49 purify the house he is to *t* two birds
14: 51 Then he is to *t* the cedar wood,
15: 14 the eighth day he must *t* two doves
15: 29 eighth day she must *t* two doves
16: 5 is to *t* two male goats
16: 7 Then he is to *t* the two goats
16: 12 He is to *t* a censer full
16: 12 and *t* them behind the curtain.
16: 14 He is to *t* some of the bull's blood
16: 15 and *t* its blood behind the curtain
16: 18 He shall *t* some of the bull's blood
16: 23 and *t* off the linen garments he put
18: 18 " 'Do not *t* your wife's sister
23: 40 are to *t* choice fruit from the trees,
24: 5 *T* fine flour and bake twelve loaves
24: 14 *T* the blasphemer outside the camp
25: 14 do not *t* advantage of each other.
25: 17 Do not *t* advantage of each other,
25: 36 Do not *t* interest of any kind
26: 31 I will *t* no delight in the pleasing
Nu 1: 2 "*T* a census of the whole Israelite
1: 50 they are to *t* care of it and encamp
1: 51 the Levites are to *t* it down,
3: 8 are to *t* care of all the furnishings
3: 36 appointed to *t* care of the frames
3: 41 *T* the Levites for me in place
3: 45 "*T* the Levites in place
4: 2 *T* a census of the Kohathite branch
4: 5 and *t* down the shielding curtain
4: 9 "They are to *t* a blue cloth
4: 12 "They are to *t* all the articles used
4: 22 "*T* a census also of the Gershonites
5: 15 then he is to *t* his wife to the priest.
5: 15 *t* an offering of a tenth of an ephah
5: 17 Then he shall *t* some holy water
5: 25 is to *t* from her hands the grain
5: 26 The priest is then to *t* a handful
Nu 6: 18 He is to *t* the hair and put it
8: 6 "*T* the Levites
8: 8 Have them *t* a young bull
8: 8 are to *t* a second young bull
8: 24 or more shall come to *t* part
11: 17 I will *t* of the Spirit that is on you
13: 30 and *t* possession of the land,
16: 6 *T* censers and tomorrow put fire
16: 17 Each man is to *t* his censer
16: 37 to *t* the censers out
16: 46 *T* your censer and put incense in it,
19: 4 is to *t* some of its blood
19: 6 The priest is to *t* some cedar wood,
19: 18 clean is to *t* some hyssop,
20: 8 said to Moses, "*T* the staff,
20: 25 and *t* them up Mount Hor.
21: 7 the LORD will *t* the snakes away
23: 27 let me *t* you to another place.
25: 4 "*T* all the leaders of these people,
26: 2 "*T* a census of the whole Israelite
26: 4 "*T* a census of the men twenty
27: 18 to Moses, "*T* Joshua son of Nun,
31: 2 "*T* vengeance on the Midianites
31: 29 *T* this tribute from their half share
33: 53 *T* possession of the land
35: 8 *T* many towns from a tribe that has
Dt 1: 8 and *t* possession of the land that
1: 21 Go up and *t* possession of it
1: 22 a report about the route we are to *t*
1: 39 and they will *t* possession of it.
2: 24 Begin to *t* possession of it
3: 4 of the sixty cities that we did not *t*
3: 18 land to *t* possession of it.
4: 1 and *t* possession of the land that
4: 5 entering to *t* possession of it.
4: 22 and *t* possession of that good land.
4: 34 tried to *t* for himself one nation out
4: 39 *t* to heart this day that the LORD
6: 13 and *t* your oaths in his name.
6: 18 and *t* over the good land that
7: 3 or *t* their daughters for your sons,
7: 11 *t* care to follow the commands,
7: 25 and do not *t* it for yourselves,
9: 4 here to *t* possession of this land
9: 5 in to *t* possession of their land;
9: 23 and *t* possession of the land I have
9: 28 the LORD was not able to *t* them
10: 20 and *t* your oaths in his name.
11: 8 and *t* over the land that you are
11: 10 The land you are entering to *t*
11: 11 Jordan to *t* possession of is a land
11: 31 *t* possession of the land the LORD
12: 26 But *t* your consecrated things
12: 32 do not add to it or *t* away from it.
14: 25 and *t* the silver with you
15: 17 then *t* an awl and push it
17: 5 *t* the man or woman who has done
17: 8 *t* them to the place the LORD your
17: 17 He must not *t* many wives,
18: 22 of the LORD does not *t* place
20: 14 you may *t* these as plunder
21: 3 the body shall *t* a heifer that
21: 10 into your hands and you *t* captives,
21: 11 you may *t* her as your wife.
21: 19 and mother shall *t* hold of him
22: 1 but be sure to *t* it back to him.
22: 2 *t* it home with you and keep it
22: 6 do not *t* the mother with the young
22: 7 You may *t* the young, but be sure
22: 18 and the elders shall *t* the man
22: 24 you shall *t* both of them to the gate
24: 6 Do not *t* a pair of millstones—
24: 14 Do not *t* advantage
24: 17 or *t* the cloak of the widow
25: 1 they are to *t* it to court
25: 5 Her husband's brother shall *t* her
25: 9 *t* off one of his sandals, spit
26: 2 *t* some of the firstfruits
26: 4 The priest shall *t* the basket
28: 30 another will *t* her and ravish her.
28: 42 Swarms of locusts will *t*
30: 1 and you *t* them to heart wherever
30: 5 and you will *t* possession of it.
31: 3 you will *t* possession of their land.
31: 26 "*T* this Book of the Law
32: 41 will *t* vengeance on my adversaries
32: 43 he will *t* vengeance on his enemies
32: 46 "*T* to heart all the words I have

Jos 1: 11 *t* possession of the land the LORD
3: 6 "*T* up the ark of the covenant
4: 3 and tell them to *t* up twelve stones
4: 5 Each of you is to *t* up a stone
5: 15 of the LORD's army replied, "*T*
6: 6 "*T* up the ark of the covenant
7: 3 or three thousand men to *t* it
8: 1 *T* the whole army with you,
8: 7 up from ambush and *t* the city.
8: 13 had the soldiers *t* up their
8: 29 Joshua ordered them to *t* his body
9: 11 '*T* provisions for your journey;
18: 3 before you begin to *t* possession
23: 5 you will *t* possession of their land,
Jdg 2: 6 they went to *t* possession
4: 6 *t* with you ten thousand men
5: 2 the princes in Israel *t* the lead,
5: 12 *T* captive your captives, O son
6: 20 "*T* the meat and the unleavened
6: 25 "*T* the second bull
7: 4 *T* them down to the water,
9: 15 come and *t* refuge in my shade;
11: 9 "Suppose you *t* me back
11: 15 Israel did not *t* the land of Moab
11: 23 what right have you to *t* it over?
11: 24 Will you not *t* what your god
15: 2 more attractive? *T* her instead."
15: 10 come to *t* Samson prisoner,"
18: 9 hesitate to go there and *t* it over.
20: 10 We'll *t* ten men out
Ru 1: 7 on the road that would *t* them back
2: 12 wings you have come to *t* refuge."
1Sa 1: 16 Do not *t* your servant
1: 22 I will *t* him and present him
2: 14 priest would *t* for himself whatever
2: 16 and then *t* whatever you want,"
2: 16 if you don't, I'll *t* it by force."
2: 20 by this woman to *t* the place
6: 7 but *t* their calves away
6: 8 *T* the ark of the LORD
6: 21 Come down and *t* it up
8: 11 He will *t* your sons and make them
8: 13 He will *t* your daughters
8: 14 He will *t* the best of your fields
8: 15 He will *t* a tenth of your grain
8: 16 donkeys he will *t* for his own use.
8: 17 He will *t* a tenth of your flocks,
9: 3 "*T* one of the servants with you
9: 6 he will tell us what way to *t*."
9: 7 We have no gift to *t* to the man
9: 8 so that he will tell us what way to *t*
16: 2 "*T* a heifer with you and say,
16: 23 David would *t* his harp and play.
17: 17 "*T* this ephah of roasted grain
17: 18 *T* along these ten cheeses
18: 25 to *t* revenge on his enemies.' "
20: 1 that he is trying to *t* my life?"
21: 9 *t* it; there is no sword here
23: 15 that Saul had come out to *t* his life.
24: 11 are hunting me down to *t* my life.
25: 11 Why should I *t* my bread and water
25: 29 is pursuing you to *t* your life,
25: 40 to you to *t* you to become his wife."
30: 15 and I will *t* you down to them."
30: 22 each man may *t* his wife
2Sa 2: 21 *t* on one of the young men
4: 8 enemy, who tried to *t* your life.
6: 10 He was not willing to *t* the ark
12: 11 your very eyes I will *t* your wives
12: 28 Otherwise I will *t* the city,
13: 20 Don't *t* this thing to heart."
14: 14 But God does not *t* away life;
15: 5 *t* hold of him and kiss him.
15: 16 concubines to *t* care of the palace.
15: 20 Go back, and *t* your countrymen.
15: 25 *T* the ark of God back into the city.
15: 27 Abiathar *t* your two sons with you.
16: 11 my own flesh, is trying to *t* my life.
16: 21 left to *t* care of the palace.
18: 19 and *t* the news to the king that
18: 20 the one to *t* the news today,"
18: 20 "You may *t* the news another time,
19: 18 at the ford to *t* the king's household
19: 30 to the king, "Let him *t* everything,
20: 3 left to *t* care of the palace
20: 6 *T* your master's men and pursue
22: 3 in whom I *t* refuge,
22: 31 a shield for all who *t* refuge in him.
2Sa 24: 10 *t* away the guilt of your servant.
24: 22 lord the king *t* whatever pleases
1Ki 1: 2 to attend the king and *t* care of him
1: 33 son on my own mule and *t* him
1: 33 "*T* your lord's servants with you
5: 9 them and you can *t* them away.
8: 31 and is required to *t* an oath
11: 31 "*T* ten pieces for yourself,
11: 34 I will not *t* the whole kingdom out
11: 35 I will *t* the kingdom
11: 37 However, as for you, I will *t* you,
14: 3 *T* ten loaves of bread with you,
17: 12 am gathering a few sticks to *t* home
19: 4 "*T* my life; I am no better
20: 18 out for peace, *t* them alive;
20: 18 out for war, *t* them alive."
21: 10 *t* him out and stone him to death."
21: 15 and *t* possession of the vineyard
21: 16 and went down to *t* possession
21: 18 gone to *t* possession of it.
22: 26 "*T* Micaiah and send him back
2Ki 2: 1 about to *t* Elijah up to heaven
2: 3 to *t* your master from you today?"
2: 5 to *t* your master from you today?"
4: 1 creditor is coming to *t* my two boys
4: 29 *t* my staff in your hand and run.
4: 36 she came, he said, "*T* your son."
5: 23 "By all means, *t* two talents,"
5: 26 Is this the time to *t* money,
7: 12 and then we will *t* them alive
7: 13 "Have some men *t* five
8: 8 "*T* a gift with you and go
9: 1 *t* this flask of oil with you
9: 2 and *t* him into an inner room.
9: 3 Then *t* the flask and pour the oil
9: 34 "*T* care of that cursed woman,"
10: 6 *t* the heads of your master's sons
10: 14 "*T* them alive!" he ordered.
11: 6 who *t* turns guarding the temple—
12: 7 *T* no more money
13: 16 "*T* the bow in your hands,"
13: 18 Then he said, "*T* the arrows,"
18: 32 and *t* you to a land like your own,
19: 30 will *t* root below and bear fruit
1Ch 9: 29 Others were assigned to *t* care
13: 13 He did not *t* the ark to be with him
17: 13 I will never *t* my love away
21: 1 incited David to *t* a census of Israel
21: 8 *t* away the guilt of your servant.
21: 11 the LORD says: '*T* your choice:
21: 23 Araunah said to David, "*T* it!
21: 24 I will not *t* for the LORD what is
27: 23 David did not *t* the number
2Ch 2: 16 You can then *t* them up
6: 22 and is required to *t* an oath
18: 25 "*T* Micaiah and send him back
20: 17 *T* up your positions; stand firm
20: 25 more than they could *t* away.
25: 13 and had not allowed to *t* part
35: 23 he told his officers, "*T* me away;
36: 6 shackles to *t* him to Babylon.
36: 13 who had made him *t* an oath
Ezr 5: 15 '*T* these articles and go
7: 15 you are to *t* with you the silver
9: 12 or *t* their daughters for your sons.
10: 4 We will support you, so *t* courage
Ne 2: 6 "How long will your journey *t*,
5: 12 officials *t* an oath to do what they
9: 12 light on the way they were to *t*.
9: 15 *t* possession of the land you had
9: 19 to shine on the way they were to *t*.
10: 30 or *t* their daughters for our sons.
13: 25 I made them *t* an oath
13: 25 nor are you to *t* their daughters
Est 2: 13 her to *t* with her from the harem
Job 1: 4 used to *t* turns holding feasts
5: 24 you will *t* stock of your property
11: 11 he sees evil, does he not *t* note?
11: 18 will look about you and *t* your rest
13: 14 and *t* my life in my hands?
13: 17 let your ears *t* in what I say.
23: 10 But he knows the way that I *t*;
24: 3 and *t* the widow's ox in pledge.
32: 22 my Maker would soon *t* me away.
35: 15 and he does not *t* the least notice
36: 7 He does not *t* his eyes
37: 8 The animals *t* cover;
38: 13 that it might *t* the earth
Job 38: 20 Can you *t* them to their places?
39: 26 "Does the hawk *t* flight
41: 4 you for you to *t* him as your slave
42: 8 now *t* seven bulls and seven rams
Ps 2: 2 The kings of the earth *t* their stand
2: 12 Blessed are all who *t* refuge in him.
5: 11 let all who *t* refuge in you be glad;
7: 1 O LORD my God, I *t* refuge in you
10: 14 you consider it to *t* it in hand.
11: 1 In the LORD I *t* refuge.
16: 1 for in you I *t* refuge.
16: 4 or *t* up their names on my lips.
17: 7 those who *t* refuge in you
18: 2 in whom I *t* refuge.
18: 30 a shield for all who *t* refuge in him.
25: 18 and *t* away all my sins.
25: 20 for I *t* refuge in you.
26: 9 Do not *t* away my soul
27: 14 be strong and *t* heart
31: 13 and plot to *t* my life.
31: 19 men on those who *t* refuge in you.
31: 24 Be strong and *t* heart,
35: 2 *T* up shield and buckler;
37: 40 because they *t* refuge in him.
40: 14 May all who seek to *t* my life
45: 16 Your sons will *t* the place
49: 15 he will surely *t* me to himself.
49: 17 for he will *t* nothing with him
50: 16 or *t* my covenant on your lips?
51: 11 or *t* your Holy Spirit from me.
51: 16 you do not *t* pleasure
55: 15 Let death *t* my enemies by surprise
56: 6 eager to *t* my life.
57: 1 I will *t* refuge in the shadow
61: 4 *t* refuge in the shelter of your wings
62: 4 they *t* delight in lies.
62: 10 or *t* pride in stolen goods;
64: 10 and *t* refuge in him;
72: 13 He will *t* pity on the weak
73: 9 their tongues *t* possession
73: 24 afterward you will *t* me into glory.
74: 11 *T* it from the folds of your garment
83: 12 who said, "Let us *t* possession
89: 33 but I will not *t* my love from him,
94: 8 *T* heed, you senseless ones
94: 16 Who will *t* a stand for me
94: 22 in whom I *t* refuge.
102: 24 "Do not *t* me away, O my God,
104: 29 when you *t* away their breath,
109: 8 may another *t* his place
109: 12 or *t* pity on his fatherless children.
118: 8 It is better to *t* refuge in the LORD
118: 9 It is better to *t* refuge in the LORD
119: 39 *T* away the disgrace I dread,
119: 109 Though I constantly *t* my life
141: 4 to *t* part in wicked deeds
141: 8 in you I *t* refuge—do not give me
144: 2 my shield, in whom I *t* refuge,
Pr 4: 26 and *t* only ways that are firm.
13: 10 in those who *t* advice.
16: 13 Kings *t* pleasure in honest lips;
20: 16 *T* the garment of one who puts up
22: 23 for the LORD will *t* up their case
23: 11 he will *t* up their case against you.
27: 12 prudent see danger and *t* refuge,
27: 13 *T* the garment of one who puts up
30: 5 shield to those who *t* refuge in him.
Ecc 4: 13 no longer knows how to *t* warning.
7: 2 the living should *t* this to heart.
9: 2 as it is with those who *t* oaths,
9: 2 with those who are afraid to *t* them
SS 1: 4 *T* me away with you—let us hurry!
1: 6 made me *t* care of the vineyards;
7: 8 I will *t* hold of its fruit."
Isa 1: 16 *T* your evil deeds
2: 4 Nation will not *t* up sword
3: 1 is about to *t* from Jerusalem
3: 6 *t* charge of this heap of ruins!"
4: 1 *T* away our disgrace!"
4: 1 will *t* hold of one man
5: 5 I will *t* away its hedge,
7: 7 " 'It will not *t* place,
7: 20 and to *t* off your beards also.
8: 1 "*T* a large scroll and write on it
9: 17 the Lord will *t* no pleasure
10: 31 the people of Gebim *t* cover.
14: 2 Nations will *t* them
14: 4 you will *t* up this taunt

Isa 18: 5 and *t* away the spreading branches.
20: 2 *T* off the sackcloth from your body
22: 17 about to *t* firm hold of you
23: 16 *T* up a harp, walk through the city,
27: 6 In days to come Jacob will *t* root,
31: 2 he does not *t* back his words.
36: 17 and *t* you to a land like your own—
37: 31 will *t* root below and bear fruit
40: 24 no sooner do they *t* root
42: 6 I will *t* hold of your hand.
42: 25 but they did not *t* it to heart.
44: 5 and will *t* the name Israel.
44: 11 all come together and *t* their stand;
45: 1 whose right hand I *t* hold of
45: 21 let them *t* counsel together.
46: 8 *t* it to heart, you rebels.
47: 2 *T* millstones and grind flour;
47: 2 *t* off your veil.
47: 3 I will *t* vengeance;
48: 1 you who *t* oaths in the name
51: 18 there was none to *t* her by the hand
62: 4 for the LORD will *t* delight in you,
65: 19 and *t* delight in my people;
Jer 6: 8 *T* warning, O Jerusalem,
7: 29 *t* up a lament on the barren heights,
8: 13 " 'I will *t* away their harvest,
9: 10 *t* up a lament concerning the desert
13: 4 "*T* the belt you bought
15: 15 long-suffering—do not *t* me away;
19: 1 *T* along some of the elders
20: 5 They will *t* it away as plunder
20: 10 and *t* our revenge on him."
25: 15 "*T* from my hand this cup filled
25: 28 But if they refuse to *t* the cup
27: 20 king of Babylon did not *t* away
31: 4 Again you will *t* up your
31: 21 *T* note of the highway,
31: 21 the road that you *t*.
32: 5 He will *t* Zedekiah to Babylon,
32: 14 of Israel, says: *T* these documents,
32: 24 ramps are built up to *t* the city.
34: 22 They will fight against it, *t* it
36: 2 "*T* a scroll and write
36: 28 "*T* another scroll and write
38: 10 "*T* thirty men from here with you
39: 7 shackles to *t* him to Babylon.
39: 12 "*T* him and look after him;
39: 14 to *t* him back to his home.
40: 14 son of Nethaniah to *t* your life?"
40: 15 Why should he *t* your life
43: 9 *t* some large stones with you
43: 12 their temples and *t* their gods
44: 12 I will *t* away the remnant
46: 4 *T* your positions
46: 14 '*T* your positions and get ready,
50: 9 They will *t* up their positions
50: 14 "*T* up your positions
50: 15 *t* vengeance on her;
51: 11 The LORD will *t* vengeance,
51: 11 *t* up the shields!
Eze 3: 10 and *t* to heart all the words I speak
4: 1 "Now, son of man, *t* a clay tablet,
4: 3 Then *t* an iron pan, place it
4: 9 "*T* wheat and barley, beans
5: 1 Then *t* a set of scales and divide up
5: 1 *t* a sharp sword and use it
5: 2 *T* a third and strike it
5: 3 But *t* a few strands of hair
5: 4 *t* a few of these and throw them
7: 24 of the nations to *t* possession
10: 6 "*T* fire from among the wheels,
12: 5 *t* your belongings out through it.
16: 39 *t* your fine jewelry and leave you
17: 9 It will not *t* a strong arm
17: 22 I myself will *t* a shoot
18: 8 or *t* excessive interest.
18: 23 Do I *t* any pleasure in the death
18: 32 For I *t* no pleasure in the death
19: 1 "*T* up a lament concerning
20: 37 I will *t* note of you as you pass
21: 7 It will surely *t* place, declares
21: 19 sword of the king of Babylon to *t*
21: 23 of their guilt and *t* them captive.
21: 26 *T* off the turban, remove the crown
22: 12 you *t* usury and excessive interest
22: 25 *t* treasures and precious things
23: 24 they will *t* up positions against you
23: 25 They will *t* away your sons
Eze 23: 26 your clothes and *t* your fine
23: 29 and *t* away everything you have
23: 48 that all women may *t* warning
24: 5 *t* the pick of the flock.
24: 8 To stir up wrath and *t* revenge
24: 16 to *t* away from you the delight
24: 21 the stronghold in which you *t* pride
24: 25 the day I *t* away their stronghold,
25: 14 I will *t* vengeance on Edom
25: 17 when I *t* vengeance on them.' "
26: 16 *t* off their embroidered garments.
26: 17 they will *t* up a lament concerning
26: 20 *t* your place in the land of the living
27: 2 *t* up a lament concerning Tyre.
27: 26 Your oarsmen *t* you
27: 32 they will *t* up a lament concerning
28: 12 *t* up a lament concerning the king
30: 9 Anguish will *t* hold of them
32: 2 *t* up a lament concerning Pharaoh
33: 4 does not *t* warning and the sword
33: 5 the trumpet but did not *t* warning,
33: 11 I *t* no pleasure in the death
34: 2 Should not shepherds *t* care
34: 2 shepherds of Israel who only *t* care
34: 3 but you do not *t* care of the flock.
35: 10 and we will *t* possession of them,"
36: 24 For I will *t* you out of the nations;
37: 16 Then *t* another stick of wood,
37: 16 *t* a stick of wood and write on it,
37: 19 I am going to *t* the stick of Joseph
37: 21 I will *t* the Israelites out
38: 7 about you, and *t* command
38: 13 to *t* away livestock and goods
38: 14 in safety, will you not *t* notice of it?
39: 8 It will surely *t* place, declares
43: 20 You are to *t* some of its blood
43: 21 You are to *t* the bull
44: 19 to *t* off the clothes they have been
45: 18 are to *t* a young bull without defect
45: 19 The priest is to *t* some of the blood
46: 18 The prince must not *t* any
Da 2: 24 *T* me to the king, and I will
2: 45 shown the king what will *t* place
8: 13 "How long will it *t* for the vision
8: 14 "It will *t* 2,300 evenings
8: 25 and *t* his stand against the Prince
11: 7 family line will arise to *t* her place.
11: 18 to the coastlands and will *t* many
11: 28 He will *t* action against it
11: 36 has been determined must *t* place.
Hos 1: 2 *t* to yourself an adulterous wife
2: 9 I will *t* back my wool and my linen,
2: 9 "Therefore I will *t* away my grain
2: 10 no one will *t* her out of my hands.
4: 11 which *t* away the understanding
10: 4 *t* false oaths
14: 2 *T* words with you
Joel 2: 18 and *t* pity on his people.
Am 5: 1 this lament I *t* up concerning you:
5: 12 oppress the righteous and *t* bribes
6: 13 "Did we not *t* Karnaim
9: 2 from there my hand will *t* them.
Jnh 1: 6 Maybe he will *t* notice of us,
4: 3 Now, O LORD, *t* away my life,
Mic 2: 2 and houses, and *t* them.
2: 9 You *t* away my blessing
4: 3 Nation will not *t* up sword
5: 15 I will *t* vengeance in anger
Zep 3: 17 He will *t* great delight in you,
Hag 1: 8 so that I may *t* pleasure in it
2: 23 the LORD Almighty, 'I will *t* you,
Zec 3: 4 before him, "*T* off his filthy clothes
6: 10 "*T* silver and gold
6: 11 *T* the silver and gold and make
8: 23 nations will *t* firm hold of one Jew
9: 4 LORD will *t* away her possessions
9: 7 I will *t* the blood from their mouths
9: 10 I will *t* away the chariots
11: 15 "*T* again the equipment
14: 18 people do not go up and *t* part,
14: 21 to sacrifice will *t* some of the pots
Mt 1: 20 do not be afraid to *t* Mary home
2: 13 "*t* the child and his mother
2: 20 trying to *t* the child's life are dead."
2: 20 *t* the child and his mother
5: 40 wants to sue you and *t* your tunic,
7: 4 Let me *t* the speck out of your eye,'
7: 5 first *t* the plank out
Mt 8: 11 and will *t* their places at the feast
9: 2 he said to the paralytic, "*T* heart,
9: 6 "Get up, *t* your mat and go home."
9: 22 "*T* heart, daughter," he said,
10: 9 Do not *t* along any gold or silver
10: 10 *t* no bag for the journey,
10: 38 anyone who does not *t* his cross
11: 29 *T* my yoke upon you and learn
12: 11 will you not *t* hold of it
14: 27 said to them: "*T* courage!
15: 26 right to *t* the children's bread
16: 5 the disciples forgot to *t* bread.
16: 24 deny himself and *t* up his cross
17: 27 *T* it and give it to them for my tax
17: 27 *T* the first fish you catch; open its
18: 16 But if he will not listen, *t* one
20: 14 to work for a denarius? *T* your pay
21: 38 let's kill him and *t* his inheritance.'
24: 17 go down to *t* anything out
24: 20 that your flight will not *t* place
25: 3 but did not *t* any oil with them.
25: 28 " '*T* the talent from him
25: 34 by my Father; *t* your inheritance,
26: 26 saying, "*T* and eat; this is my body
27: 65 "*T* a guard," Pilate answered.
Mk 2: 9 'Get up, *t* your mat and walk'?
2: 11 get up, *t* your mat and go home."
3: 21 they went to *t* charge of him,
6: 8 "*T* nothing for the journey
6: 37 "That would *t* eight months
6: 50 to them and said, "*T* courage!
7: 27 right to *t* the children's bread
8: 34 deny himself and *t* up his cross
9: 22 if you can do anything, *t* pity on us
13: 15 enter the house to *t* anything out.
13: 18 Pray that this will not *t* place
14: 22 saying, "*T* it; this is my body."
14: 36 *T* this cup from me.
15: 23 with myrrh, but he did not *t* it.
15: 36 see if Elijah comes to *t* him down,"
Lk 1: 15 to *t* wine or other fermented drink,
5: 18 and tried to *t* him into the house
5: 24 get up, *t* your mat and go home."
6: 42 first *t* the plank out of your eye,
6: 42 let me *t* the speck out of your eye,'
9: 3 "*T* nothing for the journey—
9: 23 deny himself and *t* up his cross
10: 4 Do not *t* a purse or bag or sandals;
12: 19 *T* life easy; eat, drink and be merry
13: 29 and will *t* their places at the feast
14: 8 do not *t* the place of honor,
14: 9 have to *t* the least important place.
14: 10 you are invited, *t* the lowest place,
16: 6 The manager told him, '*T* your bill,
16: 7 '*T* your bill and make it eight
19: 17 in a very small matter, *t* charge
19: 19 'You *t* charge of five cities.'
19: 21 You *t* out what you did not put in
19: 24 '*T* his mina away from him
21: 7 sign that they are about to *t* place?"
21: 28 When these things begin to *t* place,
22: 17 "*T* this and divide it among you.
22: 36 "But now if you have a purse, *t* it,
22: 42 if you are willing, *t* this cup
Jn 1: 22 Give us an answer to *t* back
2: 8 *t* it to the master of the banquet."
6: 21 Then they were willing to *t* him
7: 1 there were waiting to *t* his life.
10: 17 down my life—only to *t* it up again
10: 18 and authority to *t* it up again.
11: 39 "*T* away the stone," he said.
11: 44 "*T* off the grave clothes
11: 48 will come and *t* away both our
11: 53 day on they plotted to *t* his life.
14: 3 and *t* you to be with me that you
16: 15 That is why I said the Spirit will *t*
16: 22 and no one will *t* away your joy.
16: 33 *t* heart! I have overcome the world
17: 15 prayer is not that you *t* them out
18: 31 "*T* him yourselves and judge him
19: 6 "You *t* him and crucify him.
19: 15 "*T* him away! *T* him away!
21: 16 Jesus said, "*T* care of my sheep."
Ac 1: 20 and, " 'May another *t* his place
1: 25 to *t* over this apostolic ministry,
4: 26 The kings of the earth *t* their stand
7: 33 said to him, '*T* off your sandals;
9: 2 he might *t* them as prisoners

Ac 9:21 And hasn't he come here to *t* them
9:34 Get up and *t* care of your mat."
13:40 *T* care that what the prophets have
15:37 Barnabas wanted to *t* John,
15:38 Paul did not think it wise to *t* him,
16:3 Paul wanted to *t* him
20:13 we were going to *t* Paul aboard.
21:24 *T* these men, join in their
21:37 about to *t* Paul into the barracks,
23:10 and *t* him away from them by force
23:11 "*T* courage! As you have testified
23:17 "*T* this young man
24:23 and permit his friends to *t* care
27:34 Now I urge you to *t* some food.
Ro 2:16 This will *t* place on the day
11:27 when I *t* away their sins."
12:19 Do not *t* revenge, my friends,
1Co 4:6 you will not *t* pride in one man
6:1 dare he *t* it before the ungodly
6:15 Shall I then *t* the members
9:5 the right to *t* a believing wife
10:30 If I *t* part in the meal
2Co 5:12 you an opportunity to *t* pride
5:12 you can answer those who *t* pride
7:4 in you; I *t* great pride in you.
10:5 and we *t* captive every thought
11:16 I repeat: Let no one *t* me for a fool.
12:8 with the Lord to *t* it away from me.
Gal 3:15 let me *t* an example
5:10 Lord that you will *t* no other view.
6:4 Then he can *t* pride in himself,
Eph 6:11 of God so that you can *t* your stand
6:16 addition to all this, *t* up the shield
6:17 *T* the helmet of salvation
Php 2:25 whom you sent to *t* care
3:12 but I press on to *t* hold of that
3:15 are mature should *t* such a view
3:17 *t* note of those who live according
1Th 4:6 wrong his brother or *t* advantage
2Th 3:14 in this letter, *t* special note of him.
1Ti 3:5 how can he *t* care of God's church
5:20 so that the others may *t* warning.
6:7 and we can *t* nothing out of it.
6:12 *T* hold of the eternal life
6:19 so that they may *t* hold
Phm :13 me so that he could *t* your place
Heb 5:5 did not *t* upon himself the glory
6:18 we who have fled to *t* hold
9:28 sacrificed once to *t* away the sins
10:4 of bulls and goats to *t* away sins.
10:11 which can never *t* away sins.
Jas 1:9 circumstances ought to *t* pride
1:10 the one who is rich should *t* pride
1:19 My dear brothers, *t* note of this:
3:4 Or *t* ships as an example.
5:10 *t* the prophets who spoke
1Jn 3:5 so that he might *t* away our sins.
2Jn :10 do not *t* him into your house
Rev 1:1 servants what must soon *t* place.
1:3 and *t* to heart what is written in it,
1:19 and what will *t* place later.
3:11 so that no one will *t* your crown.
4:1 I will show you what must *t* place
5:9 "You are worthy to *t* the scroll
6:4 power to *t* peace from the earth
10:8 *t* the scroll that lies open
10:9 He said to me, "*T* it and eat it.
14:15 "*T* your sickle and reap,
14:18 "*T* your sharp sickle and gather
22:6 the things that must soon *t* place."
22:17 let him *t* the free gift of the water
22:19 God will *t* away from him his share

TAKEN (TAKE)

Ge 2:22 from the rib he had *t* out of the man
2:23 for she was *t* out of man."
3:19 since from it you were *t*;
3:23 ground from which he had been *t*.
12:15 and she was *t* into his palace.
14:14 that his relative had been *t* captive,
14:22 have *t* an oath that I will accept
20:3 because of the woman you have *t*;
27:36 and now he's *t* my blessing!"
30:23 "God has *t* away my disgrace."
31:1 "Jacob has *t* everything our father
31:9 So God has *t* away your father's
31:34 Rachel had *t* the household gods
39:1 Ishmaelites who had *t* him there.
Ge 39:1 Joseph had been *t* down to Egypt.
42:24 He had Simeon *t* from them
43:18 when they were *t* to his house.
Ex 12:4 having *t* into account the number
22:10 or is *t* away while no one is looking,
Lev 6:4 must return what he has stolen or *t*
7:34 I have *t* the breast that is waved
10:18 Since its blood was not *t*
14:45 and *t* out of the town to an unclean
16:27 must be *t* outside the camp;
25:12 eat only what is *t* directly
Nu 3:12 "I have *t* the Levites
8:16 I have *t* them as my own in place
8:18 And I have *t* the Levites in place
10:17 Then the tabernacle was *t* down,
14:3 and children will be *t* as plunder.
14:31 children that you said would be *t*
16:15 I have not *t* so much as a donkey
19:3 it is to be *t* outside the camp
21:26 had *t* from him all his land as far
30:9 or obligation *t* by a widow
31:53 Each soldier had *t* plunder
36:3 allotted to us will be *t* away.
36:3 then their inheritance will be *t*
36:4 and their property will be *t*
Dt 1:39 that you said would be *t* captive,
3:20 they too have *t* over the land that
11:31 When you have *t* it over
17:14 and have *t* possession of it
17:18 *t* from that of the priests, who are
23:15 If a slave has *t* refuge with you,
26:1 and have *t* possession of it
28:31 Your donkey will be forcibly *t*
Jos 1:15 until they too have *t* possession
2:4 But the woman had *t* the two men
2:6 (But she had *t* them up to the roof
4:20 the twelve stones they had *t* out
7:11 They have *t* some of the devoted
7:16 forward by tribes, and Judah was *t*.
7:17 by families, and Zimri was *t*.
7:18 of the tribe of Judah, was *t*.
8:8 When you have *t* the city,
8:12 Joshua had *t* about five thousand
8:21 saw that the ambush had *t* the city
10:1 heard that Joshua had *t* Ai
13:1 areas of land to be *t* over.
13:12 Moses had defeated them and *t*
19:9 inheritance of the Simeonites was *t*
Jdg 14:9 tell them that he had *t* the honey
17:2 of silver that were *t* from you
19:18 No one has *t* me into his house.
21:1 of Israel had *t* an oath at Mizpah:
21:5 For they had *t* a solemn oath that
21:7 since we have *t* an oath
21:18 since we Israelites have *t* this oath:
1Sa 12:3 donkey have I *t*? Whom have I
12:3 ox have I *t*? Whose donkey have
12:4 "You have not *t* anything
14:41 Jonathan and Saul were *t* by lot,
14:42 And Jonathan was *t*.
21:6 bread on the day it was *t* away.
30:2 and had *t* captive the women
30:3 and sons and daughters *t* captive.
30:16 of plunder they had *t* from the land
30:18 everything the Amalekites had *t*,
30:19 plunder or anything else they had *t*
2Sa 2:8 had *t* Ish-Bosheth son of Saul
3:15 had her *t* away from her husband
6:13 ark of the LORD had *t* six steps,
7:15 But my love will never be *t* away
8:12 also dedicated the plunder *t*
12:13 "The LORD has *t* away your sin.
12:27 against Rabbah and *t* its water
18:18 his lifetime Absalom had *t* a pillar
19:24 He had not *t* care of his feet
19:40 troops of Israel had *t* the king over.
19:42 Have we *t* anything for ourselves?"
21:12 (They had *t* them secretly
1Ki 1:46 Solomon has *t* his seat
13:12 the man of God from Judah had *t*.
16:18 When Zimri saw that the city was *t*
18:4 Obadiah had *t* a hundred prophets
2Ki 2:9 do for you before I am *t* from you?"
2:10 if you see me when I am *t* from you
5:2 and had *t* captive a young girl
13:16 When he had *t* it, Elisha put his
13:25 son of Hazael the towns he had *t*
17:23 Israel were *t* from their homeland
2Ki 20:18 born to you, will be *t* away,
24:7 of Babylon had *t* all his territory,
25:6 He was *t* to the king of Babylon
1Ch 9:1 of Judah were *t* captive to Babylon
9:28 in and when they were *t* out.
18:11 gold he had *t* from all these nations
22:14 "I have *t* great pains to provide
24:6 one family being *t* from Eleazar
26:27 Some of the plunder *t*
2Ch 2:17 the census his father David had *t*;
6:38 of their captivity where they were *t*
28:11 your fellow countrymen you have *t*
34:14 out the money that had been *t*
Ezr 2:1 king of Babylon had *t* captive
5:14 which Nebuchadnezzar had *t*
8:30 out to be *t* to the house of our God
9:2 have *t* some of their daughters
10:13 this matter cannot be *t* care
Ne 7:6 king of Babylon had *t* captive (they
Est 1:15 Xerxes that the eunuchs have *t*
2:6 among those *t* captive
2:7 and Mordecai had *t* her
2:8 also was *t* to the king's palace
2:16 She was *t* to King Xerxes
Job 1:21 and the LORD has *t* away;
28:2 Iron is *t* from the earth,
33:6 I too have been *t* from clay.
36:17 justice have *t* hold of you.
Ps 31:1 In you, O LORD, I have *t* refuge;
71:1 In you, O LORD, I have *t* refuge;
78:54 hill country his right hand had *t*.
88:8 You have *t* from me my closest
88:18 You have *t* my companions
102:10 for you have *t* me up and thrown
119:106 I have *t* an oath and confirmed it,
Pr 27:14 it will be *t* as a curse.
Ecc 3:14 added to it and nothing *t* from it.
5:9 increase from the land is *t* by all;
9:12 or birds are *t* in a snare,
SS 2:4 He has *t* me to the banquet hall,
5:3 I have *t* off my robe—
Isa 6:6 which he had *t* with tongs
6:7 your guilt is *t* away and your sin
14:25 His yoke will be *t* from my people,
16:10 and gladness are *t* away
22:3 caught were *t* prisoner together,
23:7 whose feet have *t* her
28:9 to those just *t* from the breast?
38:12 down and *t* from me.
39:7 born to you, will be *t* away,
42:9 See, the former things have *t* place,
49:24 Can plunder be *t* from warriors,
49:25 captives will be *t* from warriors,
51:22 "See, I have *t* out of your hand
52:5 "For my people have been *t* away
53:8 and judgment, he was *t* away.
57:1 devout men are *t* away,
57:1 that the righteous are *t* away
Jer 8:13 will be *t* from them.' "
12:2 planted them, and they have *t* root;
13:17 the LORD's flock will be *t* captive.
14:9 Why are you like a man *t*
27:18 in Jerusalem not be *t* to Babylon.
27:22 'They will be *t* to Babylon
34:16 each of you has *t* back the male
39:1 This is how Jerusalem was *t*:
39:14 had Jeremiah *t* out of the courtyard
40:10 live in the towns you have *t* over."
41:14 the people Ishmael had *t* captive
48:7 you too will be *t* captive,
48:41 and the strongholds *t*.
48:46 your sons are *t* into exile
49:1 Why then has Molech *t* possession
49:29 Their tents and their flocks will be *t*
50:28 LORD our God has *t* vengeance,
51:26 No rock will be *t* from you
52:9 He was *t* to the king of Babylon
52:30 year, 745 Jews *t* into exile
Eze 15:3 Is wood ever *t* from it
21:24 done this, you will be *t* captive.
30:16 Thebes will be *t* by storm;
33:5 If he had *t* warning, he would have
33:6 that man will be *t* away
45:15 is to be *t* from every flock
Da 4:31 Your royal authority has been *t*
5:2 Nebuchadnezzar his father had *t*
5:3 in the gold goblets that had been *t*
7:26 and his power will be *t* away

Hos 9: 6 of silver will be *t* over by briers,
10: 5 because it is *t* from them into exile.
Am 2: 8 on garments *t* in pledge.
2: 8 they drink wine *t* as fines.
4: 2 come when you will be *t* away
Mic 1: 11 its protection is *t* from you.
Na 3: 10 Yet she was *t* captive
Zep 3: 15 The LORD has *t* away your
Zec 3: 4 "See, I have *t* away your sin,
14: 2 the rest of the people will not be *t*
Mt 9: 15 when the bridegroom will be *t*
13: 12 even what he has will be *t* from him
21: 43 of God will be *t* away from you
23: 30 we would not have *t* part with them
24: 40 one will be *t* and the other left.
24: 41 one will be *t* and the other left.
25: 29 even what he has will be *t* from him
26: 39 may this cup be *t* from me.
26: 42 possible for this cup to be *t* away
26: 56 this has all *t* place that the writings
Mk 2: 20 when the bridegroom will be *t*
4: 25 even what he has will be *t* from him
8: 6 When he had *t* the seven loaves
16: 19 he was *t* up into heaven
Lk 1: 25 and *t* away my disgrace
2: 1 a decree that a census should be *t*
5: 9 at the catch of fish they had *t*,
5: 35 when the bridegroom will be *t*
8: 18 even what he thinks he has will be *t*
9: 51 for him to be *t* up to heaven,
10: 42 and it will not be *t* away from her."
11: 52 because you have *t* away the key
17: 34 one will be *t* and the other left.
17: 35 one will be *t* and the other left."
19: 26 even what he has will be *t* away.
21: 24 and will be *t* as prisoners
24: 51 he left them and was *t* up
Jn 2: 20 "It has *t* forty-six years
13: 30 As soon as Judas had *t* the bread,
18: 40 Barabbas had *t* part in a rebellion.
19: 31 the legs broken and the bodies *t*
20: 2 "They have *t* the Lord out
20: 13 "They have *t* my Lord away,"
21: 7 around him (for he had *t* it off)
Ac 1: 2 until the day he was *t* up to heaven,
1: 9 he was *t* up before their very eyes,
1: 11 who has been *t* from you
1: 22 time when Jesus was *t* up from us.
8: 33 For his life was *t* from the earth."
9: 39 when he arrived he was *t* upstairs
10: 16 immediately the sheet was *t* back
18: 18 because of a vow he had *t*.
19: 12 that had touched him were *t*
21: 34 he ordered that Paul be *t*
22: 24 Paul to be *t* into the barracks.
23: 14 "We have *t* a solemn oath not
23: 21 They have *t* an oath not to eat
23: 24 Paul so that he may be *t* safely
27: 21 you should have *t* my advice not
Ro 5: 13 But sin is not *t* into account
1Co 15: 1 on which you have *t* your stand.
2Co 3: 14 because only in Christ is it *t* away.
3: 16 turns to the Lord, the veil is *t* away.
Gal 4: 24 These things may be *t* figuratively,
Php 3: 13 yet to have *t* hold of it.
Col 3: 9 since you have *t* off your old self
2Th 2: 7 to do so till he is *t* out of the way.
1Ti 3: 16 was *t* up in glory.
2Ti 2: 18 resurrection has already *t* place,
2: 26 who has *t* them captive
Heb 11: 5 By faith Enoch was *t* from this life,
11: 5 For before he was *t*, he was
11: 5 because God had *t* him away.
Jude :11 They have *t* the way of Cain;
Rev 5: 8 when he had *t* it, the four living
11: 17 you have *t* your great power
12: 6 where she might be *t* care
12: 14 where she would be *t* care

TAKES (TAKE)

Ge 27: 46 *t* a wife from among the women
Lev 5: 4 if a person thoughtlessly *t* an oath
24: 17 " 'If anyone *t* the life
24: 18 Anyone who *t* the life
Nu 24: 22 when Asshur *t* you captive."
30: 2 or *t* an oath to obligate himself
Dt 1: 2 (It *t* eleven days to go from Horeb
13: 2 of which he has spoken *t* place,
Dt 17: 18 When he *t* the throne
19: 16 If a malicious witness *t* the stand
22: 13 If a man *t* a wife and, after lying
Jos 7: 14 that the LORD *t* shall come
7: 14 that the LORD *t* shall come
7: 14 that the LORD *t* shall come
2Sa 15: 8 'If the LORD *t* me back
1Ki 8: 46 who *t* them captive to his own land
20: 11 should not boast like one who *t* it
2Ch 6: 36 who *t* them captive
Job 12: 18 He *t* off the shackles put
12: 20 *t* away the discernment of elders.
27: 8 when God *t* away his life?
34: 25 Because he *t* note of their deeds,
38: 14 The earth *t* shape like clay
Ps 5: 4 You are not a God who *t* pleasure
34: 8 blessed is the man who *t* refuge
34: 22 no one who *t* refuge
57: 1 for in you my soul *t* refuge.
149: 4 For the LORD *t* delight
Pr 1: 19 it *t* away the lives of those who get
3: 32 *t* the upright into his confidence.
6: 34 mercy when he *t* revenge.
8: 2 the paths meet, she *t* her stand;
10: 9 he who *t* crooked paths will be
16: 32 than one who *t* a city.
21: 12 The Righteous One *t* note
22: 3 man sees danger and *t* refuge,
25: 20 Like one who *t* away a garment
31: 23 where he *t* his seat
Ecc 5: 15 He *t* nothing from his labor
Isa 3: 13 The LORD *t* his place in court;
21: 2 traitor betrays, the looter *t* loot.
22: 6 Elam *t* up the quiver,
28: 4 someone sees it and *t* it in his hand,
41: 13 who *t* hold of your right hand
44: 12 The blacksmith *t* a tool
44: 15 some of it he *t* and warms himself,
65: 16 he who *t* an oath in the land
Jer 4: 29 every town *t* to flight.
Eze 18: 13 at usury and *t* excessive interest.
18: 17 and *t* no usury or excessive interest
26: 15 and the slaughter *t* place in you?
33: 4 and the sword comes and *t* his life,
33: 6 and *t* the life of one of them,
Mic 2: 4 He *t* it from me!
Na 1: 2 The LORD *t* vengeance on his foes
1: 2 the LORD *t* vengeance
Hab 2: 5 and *t* captive all the peoples.
Mt 12: 45 *t* with it seven other spirits more
Mk 4: 15 and *t* away the word that was sown
Lk 6: 29 If someone *t* your cloak, do not
6: 30 and if anyone *t* what belongs to you
8: 12 *t* away the word from their hearts,
11: 22 he *t* away the armor
11: 26 *t* seven other spirits more wicked
Jn 1: 29 who *t* away the sin of the world!
10: 18 No one *t* it from me, but I lay it
2Co 11: 20 exploits you or *t* advantage of you
Php 2: 20 who *t* a genuine interest
Col 2: 8 See to it that no one *t* you captive
Heb 5: 4 No one *t* this honor upon himself;
9: 17 it never *t* effect while the one who
Rev 22: 19 And if anyone *t* words away

TAKING (TAKE)

Ge 8: 20 and, *t* some of all the clean animals
24: 10 *t* with him all kinds of good things
28: 11 *T* one of the stones there, he put it
28: 20 over me on this journey I am *t*
31: 23 *T* his relatives with him, he
34: 29 *t* as plunder everything
42: 38 to him on the journey you are *t*,
50: 3 physicians embalmed him, *t* a full
Ex 5: 4 why are you *t* the people away
22: 11 settled by the *t* of an oath
29: 35 *t* seven days to ordain them.
Nu 15: 18 the land to which I am *t* you
22: 7 *t* with them the fee for divination.
Dt 1: 25 *T* with them some of the fruit
24: 6 that would be *t* a man's livelihood
Jos 6: 18 your own destruction by *t* any
19: 47 Danites had difficulty *t* possession
Jdg 3: 28 and, *t* possession of the fords
1Sa 14: 32 on the plunder and, *t* sheep,
17: 49 into his bag and *t* out a stone,
29: 4 than by *t* the heads of our own men
2Sa 4: 5 while he was *t* his noonday rest.
2Sa 4: 7 *T* it with them, they traveled all
12: 4 the rich man refrained from *t* one
1Ki 11: 18 Then *t* men from Paran with them,
2Ki 5: 5 *t* with him ten talents of silver,
8: 9 *t* with him as a gift forty
15: 25 *T* fifty men of Gilead with him,
1Ch 2: 7 the ban on *t* devoted things.
2Ch 17: 9 *t* with them the Book of the Law
Job 5: 3 I myself have seen a fool *t* root,
5: 5 *t* it even from among thorns,
Ecc 4: 1 all the oppression that was *t* place
Isa 30: 14 found for *t* coals from a hearth
Eze 17: 3 *T* hold of the top of a cedar,
Hos 11: 3 *t* them by the arms;
Jnh 1: 14 die for *t* this man's life.
Zec 5: 10 "Where are they *t* the basket?"
Mt 5: 25 with your adversary who is *t* you
14: 19 *T* the five loaves and the two fish
Mk 6: 41 *T* the five loaves and the two fish
9: 36 *T* him in his arms, he said to them,
Lk 6: 4 and *t* the consecrated bread,
6: 29 do not stop him from *t* your tunic.
9: 16 *T* the five loaves and the two fish
12: 45 'My master is *t* a long time
14: 4 So *t* hold of the man, he healed him
16: 3 My master is *t* away my job.
19: 22 *t* out what I did not put in,
20: 35 worthy of *t* part in that age
22: 17 After *t* the cup, he gave thanks
Jn 16: 14 glory to me by *t* from what is mine
19: 40 *T* Jesus' body, the two
Ac 3: 7 *T* him by the right hand, he helped
9: 19 after *t* some food, he regained his
12: 25 from Jerusalem, *t* with them John,
15: 14 by *t* from the Gentiles a people
2Co 8: 21 For we are *t* pains
Php 2: 7 *t* the very nature of a servant,

TALENT (TALENTS)

Ex 25: 39 A *t* of pure gold is to be used
37: 24 accessories from one *t* of pure gold.
38: 27 bases from the 100 talents, one *t*
2Sa 12: 30 its weight was a *t* of gold,
1Ki 20: 39 or you must pay a *t* of silver.'
2Ki 5: 22 Please give them a *t* of silver
23: 33 talents of silver and a *t* of gold
1Ch 20: 2 its weight was found to be a *t*
2Ch 36: 3 talents of silver and a *t* of gold.
Mt 25: 15 to another one *t*, each according
25: 18 who had received the one *t* went
25: 24 who had received the one *t* came.
25: 25 and hid your *t* in the ground.
25: 28 " 'Take the *t* from him

TALENTS (TALENT)

Ex 38: 24 the work on the sanctuary was 29 *t*
38: 25 counted in the census was 100 *t*
38: 27 The 100 *t* of silver were used
38: 27 bases from the 100 *t*, one talent
38: 29 from the wave offering was 70 *t*
1Ki 9: 14 sent to the king 120 *t* of gold.
9: 28 and brought back 420 *t* of gold,
10: 10 And she gave the king 120 *t* of gold
10: 14 received yearly was 666 *t*,
16: 24 from Shemer for two *t* of silver
2Ki 5: 5 taking with him ten *t* of silver,
5: 23 and then tied up the two *t* of silver
5: 23 take two *t*," said Naaman.
15: 19 Menahem gave him a thousand *t*
18: 14 *t* of silver and thirty *t* of gold.
23: 33 a levy of a hundred *t* of silver
1Ch 19: 6 the Ammonites sent a thousand *t*
22: 14 a million *t* of silver, quantities
22: 14 of the LORD a hundred thousand *t*
29: 4 seven thousand *t* of refined silver,
29: 4 three thousand *t* of gold (gold
29: 7 and a hundred thousand *t* of iron.
29: 7 eighteen thousand *t* of bronze
29: 7 ten thousand *t* of silver, eighteen
29: 7 the temple of God five thousand *t*
2Ch 3: 8 with six hundred *t* of fine gold.
8: 18 back four hundred and fifty *t*
9: 9 she gave the king 120 *t* of gold,
9: 13 received yearly was 666 *t*,
25: 6 from Israel for a hundred *t* of silver
25: 9 what about the hundred *t* I paid
27: 5 Ammonites paid him a hundred *t*
36: 3 a levy of a hundred *t* of silver

Ezr 7: 22 up to a hundred *t* of silver,
8: 26 out to them 650 *t* of silver,
8: 26 silver articles weighing 100 *t*, 100 *t*
Est 3: 9 I will put ten thousand *t* of silver
Mt 18: 24 him ten thousand *t* was brought
25: 15 To one he gave five *t* of money,
25: 15 another two *t*, and to another one
25: 16 who had received the five *t* went
25: 17 with the two *t* gained two more.
25: 20 received the five *t* brought
25: 20 'you entrusted me with five *t*.
25: 22 "The man with the two *t* also came.
25: 22 'you entrusted me with two *t*; see,
25: 28 give it to the one who has the ten *t*.

TALES

1Ti 4: 7 with godless myths and old wives' *t*

TALITHA

Mk 5: 41 "*T koum!*" (which means,

TALL (TALLER TALLEST)

Dt 2: 10 numerous, and as *t* as the Anakites.
2: 21 numerous, and as *t* as the Anakites.
9: 2 The people are strong and *t*—
1Sa 17: 4 He was over nine feet *t*.
1Ch 11: 23 who was seven and a half feet *t*.
Job 8: 11 Can papyrus grow *t* where there is
Isa 2: 13 for all the cedars of Lebanon, *t*
10: 33 the *t* ones will be brought low.
18: 2 to a people *t* and smooth-skinned,
18: 7 a people *t* and smooth-skinned,
45: 14 and those *t* Sabeans—
Eze 17: 24 I the LORD bring down the *t* tree
17: 24 and make the low tree grow *t*.
31: 4 deep springs made it grow *t*;
Am 2: 9 though he was *t* as the cedars

TALLER (TALL)

Dt 1: 28 'The people are stronger and *t*
1Sa 9: 2 a head *t* than any of the others.
10: 23 among the people he was a head *t*

TALLEST (TALL)

2Ki 19: 23 I have cut down its *t* cedars,
Isa 37: 24 I have cut down its *t* cedars,

TALMAI

Nu 13: 22 where Ahiman, Sheshai and *T*,
Jos 15: 14 Sheshai, Ahiman and *T*—
Jdg 1: 10 defeated Sheshai, Ahiman and *T*.
2Sa 3: 3 daughter of *T* king of Geshur;
13: 37 and went to *T* son of Ammihud,
1Ch 3: 2 daughter of *T* king of Geshur;

TALMON

1Ch 9: 17 gatekeepers: Shallum, Akkub, *T*,
Ezr 2: 42 descendants of Shallum, Ater, *T*,
Ne 7: 45 descendants of Shallum, Ater, *T*,
11: 19 Akkub, *T* and their associates,
12: 25 *T* and Akkub were gatekeepers

TAMAR

Ge 38: 6 his firstborn, and her name was *T*.
38: 11 said to his daughter-in-law *T*,
38: 11 *T* went to live in her father's house.
38: 13 When *T* was told, "Your
38: 24 "Your daughter-in-law *T* is guilty
Ru 4: 12 of Perez, whom *T* bore to Judah."
2Sa 13: 1 son of David fell in love with *T*,
13: 2 of illness on account of his sister *T*,
13: 4 love with *T*, my brother Absalom's
13: 5 'I would like my sister *T* to come
13: 6 "I would like my sister *T* to come
13: 7 David sent word to *T* at the palace:
13: 8 So *T* went to the house
13: 10 said to *T*, "Bring the food here
13: 10 *T* took the bread she had prepared
13: 19 *T* put ashes on her head
13: 20 *T* lived in her brother Absalom's
13: 22 he had disgraced his sister *T*.
13: 32 the day Amnon raped his sister *T*.
14: 27 The daughter's name was *T*,
1Ch 2: 4 *T*, Judah's daughter-in-law,
3: 9 And *T* was their sister.
Eze 47: 18 to the eastern sea and as far as *T*.
47: 19 On the south side it will run from *T*
48: 28 Gad will run south from *T*

Mt 1: 3 whose mother was *T*, Perez

TAMARISK

Ge 21: 33 Abraham planted a *t* tree
1Sa 22: 6 was seated under the *t* tree
31: 13 them under a *t* tree at Jabesh,

TAMBOURINE (TAMBOURINES)

Ex 15: 20 Aaron's sister, took a *t* in her hand,
Job 21: 12 They sing to the music of *t*
Ps 81: 2 Begin the music, strike the *t*,
149: 3 make music to him with *t* and harp.
150: 4 praise him with *t* and dancing,

TAMBOURINES (TAMBOURINE)

Ge 31: 27 singing to the music of *t* and harps?
Ex 15: 20 all the women followed her, with *t*
Jdg 11: 34 dancing to the sound of *t*!
1Sa 10: 5 *t*, flutes and harps being played
18: 6 with joyful songs and with *t*
2Sa 6: 5 lyres, *t*, sistrums and cymbals.
1Ch 13: 8 lyres, *t*, cymbals and trumpets.
Ps 68: 25 them are the maidens playing *t*.
Isa 5: 12 *t* and flutes and wine,
24: 8 The gaiety of the *t* is stilled,
30: 32 will be to the music of *t* and harps,
Jer 31: 4 Again you will take up your *t*

TAME (TAMED)

Jas 3: 8 but no man can *t* the tongue.

TAMED (TAME)

Jas 3: 7 the sea are being *t* and have been *t*

TAMMUZ

Eze 8: 14 sitting there, mourning for *T*.

TANHUMETH

2Ki 25: 23 Seraiah son of *T* the Netophathite,
Jer 40: 8 Seraiah son of *T*, the sons

TANNER

Ac 9: 43 time with a *t* named Simon.
10: 6 He is staying with Simon the *t*,
10: 32 a guest in the home of Simon the *t*,

TAPESTRY

SS 7: 5 Your hair is like royal *t*;

TAPHATH

1Ki 4: 11 to *T* daughter of Solomon);

TAPPUAH

Jos 12: 17 one the king of *T* one the king
15: 34 En Gannim, *T*, Enam, Jarmuth,
16: 8 From *T* the border went west
17: 8 but *T* itself, on the boundary
17: 8 (Manasseh had the land of *T*,
1Ch 2: 43 Korah, *T*, Rekem and Shema.

TAR

Ge 11: 3 of stone, and *t* instead of mortar.
14: 10 Valley of Siddim was full of *t* pits,
Ex 2: 3 and coated it with *t* and pitch.

TARALAH

Jos 18: 27 Rekem, Irpeel, *T*, Zelah, Haeleph,

TAREA

1Ch 8: 35 Pithon, Melech, *T* and Ahaz.

TARGET

1Sa 20: 20 as though I were shooting at a *t*.
Job 7: 20 Why have you made me your *t*?
16: 12 He has made me his *t*;
La 3: 12 and made me the *t* for his arrows.

TARSHISH

Ge 10: 4 The sons of Javan: Elishah, *T*,
1Ch 1: 7 The sons of Javan: Elishah, *T*,
7: 10 Zethan, *T* and Ahishahar.
Est 1: 14 Shethar, Admatha, *T*, Meres,
Ps 48: 7 You destroyed them like ships of *T*
72: 10 kings of *T* and of distant shores
Isa 23: 1 Wail, O ships of *T*!
23: 6 Cross over to *T*;
23: 10 the Daughter of *T*, like the Nile,
23: 14 Wail, you ships of *T*;
60: 9 in the lead are the ships of *T*,

Isa 66: 19 to *T*, to the Libyans and Lydians
Jer 10: 9 Hammered silver is brought from *T*
Eze 27: 12 " '*T* did business with you
27: 25 " 'The ships of *T* serve
38: 13 and Dedan and the merchants of *T*
Jnh 1: 3 from the LORD and headed for *T*.
1: 3 sailed for *T* to flee from the LORD.
4: 2 was so quick to flee to *T*.

TARSUS

Ac 9: 11 ask for a man from *T* named Saul,
9: 30 to Caesarea and sent him off to *T*.
11: 25 Barnabas went to *T* to look for Saul
21: 39 "I am a Jew, from *T* in Cilicia,
22: 3 "I am a Jew, born in *T* of Cilicia,

TARTAK

2Ki 17: 31 the Avvites made Nibhaz and *T*,

TASK (TASKS)

Ge 31: 36 was angry and took Laban to *t*.
Lev 16: 21 care of a man appointed for the *t*.
1Ch 29: 1 The *t* is great, because this palatial
2Ch 29: 34 them until the *t* was finished
Ne 13: 30 them duties, each to his own *t*.
Ecc 2: 26 but to the sinner he gives the *t*
Isa 28: 21 and perform his *t*, his alien *t*.
Mk 13: 34 each with his assigned *t*,
Ac 20: 24 complete the *t* the Lord Jesus has
20: 24 the *t* of testifying to the gospel
Ro 15: 28 So after I have completed this *t*
1Co 3: 5 the Lord has assigned to each his *t*.
2Co 2: 16 And who is equal to such a *t*?
Gal 2: 7 as Peter had been given the *t*
2: 7 they saw that I had been given the *t*
1Ti 3: 1 an overseer, he desires a noble *t*.

TASKS (TASK)

2Ch 31: 16 the daily duties of their various *t*,
Pr 31: 17 her arms are strong for her *t*.

TASSEL (TASSELS)

Nu 15: 38 with a blue cord on each *t*.

TASSELS (TASSEL)

Nu 15: 38 are to make *t* on the corners
15: 39 You will have these *t* to look at
Dt 22: 12 Make *t* on the four corners
Mt 23: 5 the *t* of their prayer shawls long;

TASTE (TASTED TASTES TASTING TASTY)

Ge 25: 28 Isaac, who had a *t* for wild game,
2Sa 3: 35 if I *t* bread or anything else
19: 35 Can your servant *t* what he eats
Job 27: 2 who has made me *t* bitterness
Ps 34: 8 *T* and see that the LORD is good;
119: 103 sweet are your promises to my *t*,
Pr 24: 13 from the comb is sweet to your *t*.
SS 2: 3 and his fruit is sweet to my *t*.
4: 16 and *t* its choice fruits.
Jnh 3: 7 *t* anything; do not let them eat
Mt 16: 28 are standing here will not *t* death
Mk 9: 1 are standing here will not *t* death
Lk 9: 27 are standing here will not *t* death
14: 24 men who were invited will get a *t*
Jn 8: 52 your word, he will never *t* death.
Col 2: 21 Do not *t*! Do not touch!"?
Heb 2: 9 the grace of God he might *t* death

TASTED (TASTE)

Ex 16: 31 and *t* like wafers made with honey.
Nu 11: 8 And it *t* like something made
1Sa 14: 24 So none of the troops *t* food.
14: 29 when I *t* a little of this honey.
14: 43 "I merely *t* a little honey
Eze 3: 3 it *t* as sweet as honey in my mouth.
Jn 2: 9 of the banquet *t* the water that had
Heb 6: 4 who have *t* the heavenly gift,
6: 5 who have *t* the goodness
1Pe 2: 3 now that you have *t* that the Lord
Rev 10: 10 It *t* as sweet as honey in my mouth,

TASTELESS

Job 6: 6 Is *t* food eaten without salt,

TASTES (TASTE)

Job 12: 11 as the tongue *t* food?

Job 34: 3 as the tongue *t* food.
Pr 20: 17 Food gained by fraud *t* sweet
27: 7 hungry even what is bitter *t* sweet.
Jer 48: 11 So she *t* as she did,

TASTING (TASTE)

Mt 27: 34 mixed with gall; but after *t* it,

TASTY (TASTE)

Ge 27: 4 Prepare me the kind of *t* food I like
27: 7 and prepare me some *t* food to eat,
27: 9 so I can prepare some *t* food
27: 14 and she prepared some *t* food,
27: 17 handed to her son Jacob the *t* food
27: 31 He too prepared some *t* food

TATTENAI

Ezr 5: 3 At that time *T,* governor
5: 6 This is a copy of the letter that *T,*
6: 6 *T,* governor of Trans-Euphrates,
6: 13 *T,* governor of Trans-Euphrates,

TATTOO

Lev 19: 28 or put *t* marks on yourselves.

TAUGHT (TEACH)

Dt 4: 5 I have *t* you decrees and laws
31: 22 down this song that day and *t* it
Jdg 8: 16 and *t* the men of Succoth a lesson
2Sa 1: 18 the men of Judah be *t* this lament
1Ki 4: 33 He also *t* about animals and birds,
2Ki 17: 28 *t* them how to worship the LORD.
2Ch 17: 9 They *t* throughout Judah,
17: 9 towns of Judah and *t* the people.
Ps 71: 17 my youth, O God, you have *t* me,
119:102 for you yourself have *t* me.
Pr 4: 4 he *t* me and said,
31: 1 an oracle his mother *t* him:
SS 8: 2 she who has *t* me.
Isa 29: 13 is made up only of rules *t* by men.
40: 14 Who was it that *t* him knowledge
40: 14 and who *t* him the right way?
50: 4 ear to listen like one being *t.*
54: 13 All your sons will be *t*
Jer 9: 5 They have *t* their tongues to lie;
9: 14 the Baals, as their fathers *t* them."
10: 8 they are *t* by worthless wooden
12: 16 as they once *t* my people to swear
32: 33 though I *t* them again and again,
Hos 11: 3 It was I who *t* Ephraim to walk,
Mt 7: 29 he *t* as one who had authority,
15: 9 their teachings are but rules *t*
Mk 1: 22 he *t* them as one who had authority
4: 2 He *t* them many things by parables,
6: 30 to him all they had done and *t.*
7: 7 their teachings are but rules *t*
10: 1 and as was his custom, he *t* them.
11: 17 And as he *t* them, he said,
12: 38 As he *t,* Jesus said, "Watch out
Lk 1: 4 of the things you have been *t.*
4: 15 He *t* in their synagogues,
5: 3 and *t* the people from the boat.
11: 1 just as John *t* his disciples."
13: 26 with you, and you *t* in our streets.'
Jn 6: 45 'They will all be *t* by God.'
8: 28 speak just what the Father has *t* me
18: 20 "I always *t* in synagogues
Ac 11: 26 and *t* great numbers of people.
15: 1 to the custom *t* by Moses,
15: 35 where they and many others *t*
18: 25 and *t* about Jesus accurately,
20: 20 have *t* you publicly and from house
28: 31 and *t* about the Lord Jesus Christ.
1Co 2: 13 but in words *t* by the Spirit,
2: 13 not in words *t* us by human wisdom
Gal 1: 12 nor was I *t* it; rather, I received it
Eph 4: 21 and were *t* in him in accordance
4: 22 You were *t,* with regard
Col 2: 7 in the faith as you were *t,*
1Th 4: 9 for you yourselves have been *t*
1Ti 1: 20 to Satan to be *t* not to blaspheme.
4: 1 deceiving spirits and things *t*
Tit 1: 9 message as it has been *t,*
1Jn 2: 27 just as it has *t* you, remain in him.
Rev 2: 14 who *t* Balak to entice the Israelites

TAUNT (TAUNTED TAUNTS)

Dt 32: 27 but I dreaded the *t* of the enemy,
1Ki 18: 27 At noon Elijah began to *t* them.
Ps 42: 10 as my foes *t* me,
102: 8 All day long my enemies *t* me;
Isa 14: 4 you will take up this *t*
Eze 5: 15 You will be a reproach and a *t,*
Mic 2: 4 they will *t* you with this mournful
Hab 2: 6 all of them *t* him with ridicule

TAUNTED (TAUNT)

Jdg 8: 15 about whom you *t* me by saying,
2Sa 21: 21 When he *t* Israel, Jonathan son
23: 9 David when they *t* the Philistines
1Ch 20: 7 When he *t* Israel, Jonathan son

TAUNTS (TAUNT)

Ps 44: 16 at the *t* of those who reproach
89: 50 in my heart the *t* of all the nations,
89: 51 *t* with which your enemies have
119: 42 then I will answer the one who *t* me
Eze 36: 15 longer will I make you hear the *t*
Zep 2: 8 and the *t* of the Ammonites,

TAVERNS

Ac 28: 15 and the Three *T* to meet us.

TAX (TAXED TAXES)

2Ch 24: 6 and Jerusalem the *t* imposed
24: 9 to the LORD the *t* that Moses
Ne 5: 4 to pay the king's *t* on our fields
Da 11: 20 successor will send out a *t* collector
Mt 5: 46 even the *t* collectors doing that?
9: 9 sitting at the *t* collector's booth.
9: 10 many *t* collectors and "sinners"
9: 11 your teacher eat with *t* collectors
10: 3 and Matthew the *t* collector;
11: 19 a friend of *t* collectors and "sinners
17: 24 of the two-drachma *t* came to Peter
17: 24 your teacher pay the temple *t?*"
17: 27 give it to them for my *t* and yours."
18: 17 you would a pagan or a *t* collector.
21: 31 *t* collectors and the prostitutes are
21: 32 *t* collectors and the prostitutes did.
22: 19 me the coin used for paying the *t.*"
Mk 2: 14 sitting at the *t* collector's booth.
2: 15 many *t* collectors and "sinners"
2: 16 with the "sinners" and *t* collectors,
2: 16 "Why does he eat with *t* collectors
Lk 3: 12 *T* collectors also came
5: 27 and saw a *t* collector by the name
5: 27 name of Levi sitting at his *t* booth.
5: 29 and a large crowd of *t* collectors
5: 30 drink with *t* collectors and 'sinners
7: 29 the people, even the *t* collectors,
7: 34 a friend of *t* collectors and "sinners
15: 1 *t* collectors and "sinners" were all
18: 10 and the other a *t* collector.
18: 11 or even like this *t* collector.
18: 13 the *t* collector stood at a distance.
19: 2 he was a chief *t* collector

TAXED (TAX)

2Ki 23: 35 he *t* the land and exacted the silver

TAXES (TAX)

1Sa 17: 25 exempt his father's family from *t*
Ezr 4: 13 no more *t,* tribute or duty will be
4: 20 and *t,* tribute and duty were paid
7: 24 you have no authority to impose *t,*
Mt 17: 25 of the earth collect duty and *t*—
22: 17 Is it right to pay *t* to Caesar or not
Mk 12: 14 Is it right to pay *t* to Caesar or not?
Lk 20: 22 Is it right for us to pay *t* to Caesar
23: 2 He opposes payment of *t* to Caesar
Ro 13: 6 This is also why you pay *t,*
13: 7 If you owe *t,* pay *t;* if revenue,

TEACH (TAUGHT TEACHER TEACHERS TEACHES TEACHING TEACHINGS)

Ex 4: 12 and will *t* you what to say."
4: 15 of you speak and will *t* you what
18: 20 *T* them the decrees and laws,
33: 13 *t* me your ways so I may know you
35: 34 tribe of Dan, the ability to *t* others.
Lev 10: 11 and you must *t* the Israelites all
Dt 4: 1 and laws I am about to *t* you.
4: 9 *T* them to your children
4: 10 and may *t* them to their children."
4: 14 me at that time to *t* you the decrees
Dt 5: 31 laws you are to *t* them to follow
6: 1 me to *t* you to observe
8: 3 to *t* you that man does not live
11: 19 *T* them to your children, talking
17: 11 Act according to the law they *t* you
20: 18 they will *t* you to follow all
31: 19 for yourselves this song and *t* it
Jdg 3: 2 to *t* warfare to the descendants
13: 8 sent to us come again to *t* us how
1Sa 12: 23 I will *t* you the way that is good
14: 12 up to us and we'll *t* you a lesson."
1Ki 8: 36 *T* them the right way to live,
2Ki 17: 27 and *t* the people what the god
2Ch 6: 27 *T* them the right way to live,
15: 3 without a priest to *t*
17: 7 Micaiah to *t* in the towns of Judah.
Ezr 7: 25 are to *t* any who do not know them.
Job 6: 24 "*T* me, and I will be quiet;
12: 7 ask the animals, and they will *t* you
12: 8 speak to the earth, and it will *t* you,
21: 22 "Can anyone *t* knowledge to God,
27: 11 I will *t* you about the power of God
32: 7 advanced years should *t* wisdom.'
33: 33 be silent, and I will *t* you wisdom."
34: 32 *T* me what I cannot see;
Ps 25: 4 *t* me your paths;
25: 5 guide me in your truth and *t* me,
27: 11 *T* me your way, O LORD;
32: 8 *t* you in the way you should go;
34: 11 I will *t* you the fear of the LORD.
51: 6 you *t* me wisdom in the inmost
51: 13 I will *t* transgressors your ways,
78: 5 forefathers to *t* their children,
86: 11 *T* me your way, O LORD,
90: 12 *T* us to number our days aright,
94: 12 the man you *t* from your law;
105: 22 and *t* his elders wisdom.
119: 12 *t* me your decrees.
119: 26 *t* me your decrees.
119: 33 *T* me, O LORD, to follow your
119: 64 *t* me your decrees.
119: 66 *T* me knowledge and good
119: 68 *t* me your decrees.
119:108 and *t* me your laws.
119:124 and *t* me your decrees.
119:135 and *t* me your decrees.
119:171 for you *t* me your decrees.
132: 12 and the statutes I *t* them,
143: 10 *T* me to do your will,
Pr 9: 9 *t* a righteous man and he will add
22: 17 apply your heart to what I *t,*
22: 19 I *t* you today, even you.
Isa 2: 3 He will *t* us his ways,
9: 15 the prophets who *t* lies are the tail.
28: 9 "Who is it he is trying to *t?*
Jer 9: 20 *T* your daughters how to wail;
9: 20 *t* one another a lament.
16: 21 this time I will *t* them
16: 21 "Therefore I will *t* them—
31: 34 No longer will a man *t* his neighbor
Eze 22: 26 they *t* that there is no difference
44: 23 are to *t* my people the difference
Da 1: 4 He was to *t* them the language
Mic 3: 11 her priests *t* for a price,
4: 2 He will *t* us his ways,
Mt 5: 2 and he began to *t* them, saying:
11: 1 he went on from there to *t*
22: 16 and that you *t* the way of God
Mk 1: 21 into the synagogue and began to *t.*
2: 13 to him, and he began to *t* them.
4: 1 another occasion Jesus began to *t*
6: 2 he began to *t* in the synagogue,
8: 31 began to *t* them that the Son
12: 14 but you *t* the way of God
Lk 4: 31 the Sabbath began to *t* the people.
11: 1 said to him, "Lord, *t* us to pray,
12: 12 for the Holy Spirit will *t* you
20: 21 but *t* the way of God in accordance
20: 21 that you speak and *t* what is right,
Jn 7: 14 to the temple courts and begin to *t.*
7: 35 *t* the Greeks? What did he mean
8: 2 and he sat down to *t* them.
14: 26 will *t* you all things and will remind
Ac 1: 1 to *t* until the day he was taken up
4: 18 or *t* at all in the name of Jesus.
5: 21 and began to *t* the people.
5: 28 not to *t* in this name,"
21: 21 informed that you *t* all the Jews

Ro 2:21 who *t* others, do you not *t* yourself?
12: 7 let him *t*; if it is encouraging,
15: 4 in the past was written to *t* us,
1Co 4:17 agrees with what I *t* everywhere
11:14 nature of things *t* you that
Col 3:16 as you *t* and admonish one another
1Ti 1: 3 not to *t* false doctrines any longer
2:12 I do not permit a woman to *t*
3: 2 respectable, hospitable, able to *t*,
4:11 Command and *t* these things.
6: 2 These are the things you are to *t*
2Ti 2: 2 also be qualified to *t* others.
2:24 kind to everyone, able to *t*,
Tit 1:11 things they ought not to *t*—
2: 1 You must *t* what is in accord
2: 2 *T* the older men to be temperate,
2: 3 to much wine, but to *t* what is good
2: 3 *t* the older women to be reverent
2: 9 *T* slaves to be subject
2:15 then, are the things you should *t*.
Heb 5:12 to *t* you the elementary truths
8:11 No longer will a man *t* his neighbor
Jas 3: 1 know that we who *t* will be judged
1Jn 2:27 you do not need anyone to *t* you.

TEACHER (TEACH)

1Ch 25: 8 Young and old alike, *t* as well
Ezr 7: 6 He was a *t* well versed in the Law
7:11 given to Ezra the priest and *t*,
7:12 a *t* of the Law of the God of heaven
7:21 a *t* of the Law of the God of heaven
Job 36:22 Who is a *t* like him?
Ecc 1: 1 The words of the *T*, son of David,
1: 2 Meaningless!" says the *T*.
1:12 the *T*, was king over Israel
7:27 says the *T*, "this is what I have
12: 8 Meaningless!" says the *T*.
12: 9 Not only was the *T* wise, but
12:10 *T* searched to find just the right
Joel 2:23 a *t* for righteousness.
Mt 8:19 Then a *t* of the law came to him
8:19 "*T*, I will follow you wherever you
9:11 "Why does your *t* eat
10:24 "A student is not above his *t*,
10:25 for the student to be like his *t*,
12:38 *T*, we want to see a miraculous sign
13:52 "Therefore every *t*
17:24 "Doesn't your *t* pay the temple tax
19:16 up to Jesus and asked, "*T*,
22:16 "*T*," they said, "we know you are
22:24 "*T*," they said, "Moses told us that
22:36 tested him with this question: "*T*,
23:10 Nor are you to be called '*t*,'
23:10 for you have one *T*, the Christ.
26:18 'The *T* says: My appointed time is
Mk 4:38 "*T*, don't you care if we drown?"
5:35 "Why bother the *t* any more?"
9:17 "*T*, I brought you my son,
9:38 "*T*," said John, "we saw a man
10:17 Good *t*," he asked, "what must I do
10:20 "*T*," he declared, "all these I have
10:35 "*T*," they said, "we want you to do
12:14 They came to him and said, "*T*,
12:19 "*T*," they said, "Moses wrote
12:32 "Well said, *t*," the man replied.
13: 1 "Look, *T*! What massive stones!
14:14 *T* asks: Where is my guest room,
Lk 3:12 *T*," they asked, "what should we do
6:40 A student is not above his *t*,
6:40 is fully trained will be like his *t*.
7:40 "Tell me, *t*," he said.
8:49 "Don't bother the *t* any more."
9:38 A man in the crowd called out, "*T*,
10:25 "*T*," he asked, "what must I do
11:45 "*T*, when you say these things,
12:13 in the crowd said to him, "*T*,
18:18 A certain ruler asked him, "Good *t*
19:39 "*T*, rebuke your disciples!"
20:21 So the spies questioned him: "*T*,
20:28 "*T*," they said, "Moses wrote
20:39 of the law responded, "Well said, *t*
21: 7 "*T*," they asked, "when will these
22:11 *T* asks: Where is the guest room,
Jn 1:38 "Rabbi" (which means *T*),
3: 2 we know you are a *t* who has come
3:10 "You are Israel's *t*," said Jesus,
8: 4 "*T*, this woman was caught
11:28 "The *T* is here," she said,
Jn 13:13 "You call me '*T*' and 'Lord,'
13:14 and *T*, have washed your feet,
20:16 "Rabboni!" (which means *T*).
Ac 5:34 But a Pharisee named Gamaliel, a *t*
Ro 2:20 of the foolish, a *t* of infants,
1Ti 2: 7 a *t* of the true faith to the Gentiles.
2Ti 1:11 a herald and an apostle and a *t*.

TEACHERS (TEACH)

Ps 119: 99 I have more insight than all my *t*,
Pr 5:13 I would not obey my *t*
Isa 30:20 your *t* will be hidden no more;
Mt 2: 4 all the people's chief priests and *t*
5:20 of the Pharisees and the *t* of the law
7:29 and not as their *t* of the law.
9: 3 some of the *t* of the law said
12:38 and *t* of the law said to him,
15: 1 and *t* of the law came to Jesus
16:21 chief priests and *t* of the law,
17:10 "Why then do the *t*
20:18 to the chief priests and the *t*
21:15 the *t* of the law saw the wonderful
23: 2 *t* of the law and the Pharisees sit
23:13 *t* of the law and Pharisees,
23:15 *t* of the law and Pharisees,
23:23 *t* of the law and Pharisees,
23:25 *t* of the law and Pharisees,
23:27 *t* of the law and Pharisees,
23:29 *t* of the law and Pharisees,
23:34 you prophets and wise men and *t*.
26:57 where the *t* of the law
27:41 *t* of the law and the elders mocked
Mk 1:22 one who had authority, not as the *t*
2: 6 some *t* of the law were sitting there
2:16 When the *t* of the law who were
3:22 And the *t* of the law who came
7: 1 of the *t* of the law who had come
7: 5 and *t* of the law asked Jesus,
8:31 chief priests and *t* of the law,
9:11 "Why do the *t* of the law say that
9:14 the *t* of the law arguing with them.
10:33 to the chief priests and *t* of the law.
11:18 and the *t* of the law heard this
11:27 the *t* of the law and the elders came
12:28 One of the *t* of the law came
12:35 "How is it that the *t*
12:38 "Watch out for the *t* of the law.
14: 1 and the *t* of the law were looking
14:43 sent from the chief priests, the *t*
14:53 and *t* of the law came together.
15: 1 the *t* of the law and the whole
15:31 and the *t* of the law mocked him
Lk 2:46 sitting among the *t*, listening
5:17 Pharisees and *t* of the law,
5:21 and the *t* of the law began thinking
5:30 and the *t* of the law who belonged
6: 7 and the *t* of the law were looking
9:22 chief priests and *t* of the law,
11:53 and the *t* of the law began
15: 2 and the *t* of the law muttered,
19:47 the *t* of the law and the leaders
20: 1 the chief priests and the *t* of the law
20:19 *t* of the law and the chief priests
20:39 Some of the *t* of the law responded,
20:46 "Beware of the *t* of the law.
22: 2 and the *t* of the law were looking
22:66 both the chief priests and *t*
23:10 the *t* of the law were standing there
Jn 8: 3 The *t* of the law and the Pharisees
Ac 4: 5 and *t* of the law met in Jerusalem.
6:12 and the elders and the *t* of the law.
13: 1 Antioch there were prophets and *t*:
23: 9 some of the *t* of the law who were
1Co 12:28 third *t*, then workers of miracles,
12:29 Are all *t*? Do all work miracles?
Eph 4:11 and some to be pastors and *t*,
1Ti 1: 7 They want to be *t* of the law,
2Ti 4: 3 around them a great number of *t*
Heb 5:12 by this time you ought to be *t*,
Jas 3: 1 of you should presume to be *t*,
2Pe 2: 1 as there will be false *t* among you.
2: 3 their greed these *t* will exploit you

TEACHES (TEACH)

Dt 33:10 He *t* your precepts to Jacob
Job 35:11 who *t* more to us than to the beasts
Ps 25: 9 and *t* them his way.
94:10 Does he who *t* man lack
Pr 15:33 of the LORD *t* a man wisdom,
Isa 28:26 and *t* him the right way.
48:17 who *t* you what is best for you,
Hab 2:18 Or an image that *t* lies?
Mt 5:19 and *t* others to do the same will be
5:19 *t* these commands will be called
Ac 21:28 the man who *t* all men everywhere
1Ti 6: 3 If anyone *t* false doctrines
Tit 2:12 It *t* us to say "No" to ungodliness
1Jn 2:27 his anointing *t* you about all things

TEACHING (TEACH)

Dt 32: 2 Let my *t* fall like rain
Ezr 7:10 to *t* its decrees and laws in Israel.
Ps 78: 1 O my people, hear my *t*;
119: 27 Let me understand the *t*
Pr 1: 8 and do not forsake your mother's *t*.
3: 1 My son, do not forget my *t*,
4: 2 so do not forsake my *t*.
6:20 and do not forsake your mother's *t*.
6:23 this *t* is a light,
13:14 The *t* of the wise is a fountain of life
22:21 *t* you true and reliable words,
Jer 18:18 for the *t* of the law
Eze 7:26 the *t* of the law by the priest will be
Mal 2: 8 and by your *t* have caused many
Mt 4:23 went throughout Galilee, *t*
7:28 the crowds were amazed at his *t*,
9:35 and villages, *t* in their synagogues,
13:54 he began *t* the people
16:12 but against the *t* of the Pharisees
19:11 "Not everyone can accept this *t*,
21:23 temple courts, and, while he was *t*,
22:33 they were astonished at his *t*.
26:55 sat in the temple courts *t*,
28:20 *t* them to obey everything I have
Mk 1:22 The people were amazed at his *t*,
1:27 A new *t*—and with authority!
4: 2 things by parables, and in his *t* said:
6: 6 Jesus went around *t* from village
6:34 So he began *t* them many things.
9:31 because he was *t* his disciples.
11:18 whole crowd was amazed at his *t*.
12:35 While Jesus was *t* in the temple
14:49 with you, *t* in the temple courts,
Lk 4:32 They were amazed at his *t*,
4:36 said to each other, "What is this *t*?
5:17 One day as he was *t*, Pharisees
6: 6 went into the synagogue and was *t*,
13:10 On a Sabbath Jesus was *t* in one
13:22 *t* as he made his way to Jerusalem.
19:47 Every day he was *t* at the temple.
20: 1 as he was *t* the people
21:37 Each day Jesus was *t* at the temple,
23: 5 all over Judea by his *t*.
Jn 6:59 this while *t* in the synagogue
6:60 his disciples said, "This is a hard *t*.
7:16 Jesus answered, "My *t* is not my
7:17 whether my *t* comes from God or
7:28 still *t* in the temple courts,
8:20 words while *t* in the temple area
8:31 to my *t*, you are really my disciples.
14:23 loves me, he will obey my *t*.
14:24 not love me will not obey my *t*.
15:20 If they obeyed my *t*, they will obey
18:19 Jesus about his disciples and his *t*.
Ac 2:42 themselves to the apostles' *t*
4: 2 the apostles were *t* the people
5:25 in the temple courts *t* the people."
5:28 have filled Jerusalem with your *t*
5:42 never stopped *t* and proclaiming
13:12 amazed at the *t* about the Lord.
15: 1 to Antioch and were *t* the brothers:
17:19 know what this new *t* is that you
18:11 and a half, *t* them the word of God.
Ro 6:17 of *t* to which you were entrusted.
12: 7 let him serve; if it is *t*, let him teach;
16:17 contrary to the *t* you have learned.
Eph 4:14 and there by every wind of *t*
Col 1:28 and *t* everyone with all wisdom,
2Th 3: 6 to the *t* you received from us.
1Ti 4: 6 and of the good *t* that you have
4:13 of Scripture, to preaching and to *t*.
5:17 whose work is preaching and *t*.
6: 1 and our *t* may not be slandered.
6: 3 Lord Jesus Christ and to godly *t*,
2Ti 1:13 keep as the pattern of sound *t*,
2:17 Their *t* will spread like gangrene.

2Ti 3: 10 know all about my *t*, my way of life
3: 16 is God-breathed and is useful for *t*,
Tit 1: 11 by *t* things they ought not
2: 7 In your *t* show integrity,
2: 10 they will make the *t* about God our
Heb 5: 13 with the *t* about righteousness.
2Jn : 9 and does not continue in the *t*
: 9 in the *t* has both the Father
: 10 to you and does not bring this *t*,
Rev 2: 14 hold to the *t* of Balaam,
2: 15 hold to the *t* of the Nicolaitans.
2: 20 By her *t* she misleads my servants
2: 24 to you who do not hold to her *t*

TEACHINGS (TEACH)

Pr 7: 2 guard my *t* as the apple of your eye.
Mt 15: 9 their *t* are but rules taught by men
Mk 7: 7 their *t* are but rules taught by men.'
1Co 11: 2 and for holding to the *t*,
Col 2: 22 based on human commands and *t*.
2Th 2: 15 hold to the *t* we passed on to you,
1Ti 4: 2 *t* come through hypocritical liars,
Heb 6: 1 leave the elementary *t* about Christ
13: 9 away by all kinds of strange *t*.

TEAM (TEAMS)

Isa 21: 9 with a *t* of horses.
Mic 1: 13 harness the *t* to the chariot.

TEAMS (TEAM)

Isa 21: 7 chariots with *t* of horses,

TEAR (TEARING TEARS TORE TORN)

Ex 28: 32 so that it will not *t*.
39: 23 so that it would not *t*.
Lev 1: 17 He shall *t* it open by the wings,
10: 6 and do not *t* your clothes,
13: 56 he is to *t* the contaminated part out
21: 10 become unkempt or *t* his clothes.
Jdg 6: 25 *T* down your father's altar to Baal
8: 7 will *t* your flesh with desert thorns
8: 9 in triumph, I will *t* down this tower
2Sa 3: 31 "*T* your clothes and put
1Ki 11: 11 will most certainly *t* the kingdom
11: 12 I will *t* it out of the hand
11: 13 Yet I will not *t* the whole kingdom
11: 31 I am going to *t* the kingdom out
Job 18: 4 You who *t* yourself to pieces
Ps 7: 2 or they will *t* me like a lion
28: 5 he will *t* them down
50: 22 or I will *t* you to pieces, with none
52: 5 He will snatch you up and *t* you
58: 6 *t* out, O LORD, the fangs
137: 7 "*T* it down," they cried,
137: 7 "*t* it down to its foundations!"
Ecc 3: 3 a time to *t* down and a time to build
3: 7 a time to *t* and a time to mend,
Isa 7: 6 let us *t* it apart and divide it
22: 12 to *t* out your hair and put
Jer 1: 10 kingdoms to uproot and *t* down,
5: 6 to *t* to pieces any who venture out,
24: 6 I will build them up and not *t* them
30: 8 and will *t* off their bonds;
31: 28 over them to uproot and *t* down,
36: 24 nor did they *t* their clothes.
42: 10 I will build you up and not *t* you
La 2: 8 The LORD determined to *t* down
Eze 13: 14 I will *t* down the wall you have
13: 20 and I will *t* them from your arms;
13: 21 I will *t* off your veils and save my
16: 39 and they will *t* down your mounds
19: 3 He learned to *t* the prey
19: 6 He learned to *t* the prey
23: 34 and *t* your breasts.
Hos 5: 14 I will *t* them to pieces and go away;
13: 8 a wild animal will *t* them apart.
Am 3: 15 I will *t* down the winter house
Mic 3: 2 who *t* the skin from my people
5: 11 and *t* down all your strongholds.
Na 1: 13 and *t* your shackles away."
Mt 7: 6 and then turn and *t* you to pieces.
9: 16 the garment, making the *t* worse.
Mk 2: 21 from the old, making the *t* worse.
Lk 12: 18 I will *t* down my barns
Jn 19: 24 "Let's not *t* it," they said
Rev 7: 17 God will wipe away every *t*
21: 4 He will wipe every *t*

TEARING (TEAR)

Dt 33: 20 *t* at arm or head.
Ps 22: 13 Roaring lions *t* their prey
Eze 22: 25 her like a roaring lion *t* its prey;
22: 27 her are like wolves *t* their prey;
Zec 11: 16 the meat of the choice sheep, *t*
2Co 13: 10 for building you up, not for *t* you

TEARS (TEAR)

1Sa 2: 33 only to blind your eyes with *t*
2Ki 20: 5 heard your prayer and seen your *t*;
Job 12: 14 What he *t* down cannot be rebuilt;
16: 9 God assails me and *t* me
16: 20 as my eyes pour out *t* to God;
19: 10 He *t* me down on every side
31: 38 and all its furrows are wet with *t*,
Ps 6: 6 and drench my couch with *t*.
42: 3 My *t* have been my food
56: 8 list my *t* on your scroll—
80: 5 them with the bread of *t*;
80: 5 you have made them drink *t*
102: 9 and mingle my drink with *t*
116: 8 my eyes from *t*,
119:136 Streams of *t* flow from my eyes,
126: 5 Those who sow in *t*
Pr 14: 1 own hands the foolish one *t* hers
15: 25 LORD *t* down the proud man's
29: 4 for bribes *t* it down.
Ecc 4: 1 I saw the *t* of the oppressed—
Isa 16: 9 I drench you with *t*!
25: 8 LORD will wipe away the *t*
38: 5 heard your prayer and seen your *t*;
Jer 9: 1 and my eyes a fountain of *t*!
9: 18 us till our eyes overflow with *t*
13: 17 overflowing with *t*,
14: 17 " 'Let my eyes overflow with *t*
31: 16 and your eyes from *t*,
50: 4 in *t* to seek the LORD their God.
La 1: 2 *t* are upon her cheeks.
1: 16 and my eyes overflow with *t*.
2: 18 let your *t* flow like a river
3: 48 Streams of *t* flow from my eyes
Eze 24: 16 not lament or weep or shed any *t*.
Mal 2: 13 You flood the LORD's altar with *t*.
Lk 5: 36 "No one *t* a patch
7: 38 she began to wet his feet with her *t*.
7: 44 but she wet my feet with her *t*
Ac 20: 19 with great humility and with *t*,
20: 31 each of you night and day with *t*.
2Co 2: 4 anguish of heart and with many *t*,
Php 3: 18 and now say again even with *t*,
2Ti 1: 4 Recalling your *t*, I long to see you,
Heb 5: 7 *t* to the one who could save him
12: 17 he sought the blessing with *t*.

TEBAH

Ge 22: 24 *T*, Gaham, Tahash and Maacah.
2Sa 8: 8 From *T* and Berothai, towns that
1Ch 18: 8 From *T* and Cun, towns that

TEBETH

Est 2: 16 the month of *T*, in the seventh year

TEEM (TEEMED TEEMING TEEMS)

Ge 1: 20 the water *t* with living creatures,
Ex 8: 3 The Nile will *t* with frogs.

TEEMED (TEEM)

Ps 105: 30 Their land *t* with frogs,

TEEMING (TEEM)

Ps 104: 25 *t* with creatures beyond number—

TEEMS (TEEM)

Ge 1: 21 thing with which the water *t*,

TEETH (TOOTH)

Ge 49: 12 his *t* whiter than milk.
Nu 11: 33 the meat was still between their *t*
Job 4: 10 yet the *t* of the great lions are
16: 9 and gnashes his *t* at me;
19: 20 with only the skin of my *t*
29: 17 snatched the victims from their *t*.
41: 14 ringed about with his fearsome *t*?
Ps 3: 7 you have broken the *t*
35: 16 they gnashed their *t* at me.
37: 12 and gnash their *t* at them;
57: 4 men whose *t* are spears and arrows,
58: 6 Break the *t* in their mouths, O God
112: 10 he will gnash his *t* and waste away;
124: 6 who has not let us be torn by their *t*
Pr 10: 26 As vinegar to the *t* and smoke
30: 14 those whose *t* are swords
SS 4: 2 Your *t* are like a flock
6: 6 Your *t* are like a flock of sheep
7: 9 flowing gently over lips and *t*.
Isa 41: 15 new and sharp, with many *t*.
Jer 31: 29 and the children's *t* are set on edge
31: 30 his own *t* will be set on edge.
La 2: 16 they scoff and gnash their *t*
3: 16 He has broken my *t* with gravel;
Eze 18: 2 and the children's *t* are set on edge
Da 7: 5 ribs in its mouth between its *t*.
7: 7 It had large iron *t*; it crushed
7: 19 with its iron *t* and bronze claws—
Joel 1: 6 it has the *t* of a lion,
Am 1: 3 Gilead with sledges having iron *t*,
Zec 9: 7 from between their *t*.
Mt 8: 12 will be weeping and gnashing of *t*."
13: 42 will be weeping and gnashing of *t*.
13: 50 will be weeping and gnashing of *t*."
22: 13 will be weeping and gnashing of *t*.'
24: 51 will be weeping and gnashing of *t*.
25: 30 will be weeping and gnashing of *t*.'
Mk 9: 18 gnashes his *t* and becomes rigid.
Lk 13: 28 of *t*, when you see Abraham,
Ac 7: 54 and gnashed their *t* at him.
Rev 9: 8 and their *t* were like lions' *t*.

TEHINNAH

1Ch 4: 12 *T* the father of Ir Nahash.

TEKEL

Da 5: 25 MENE, MENE, *T*, PARSIN
5: 27 *T*: You have been weighed

TEKOA (TEKOITE)

2Sa 14: 2 So Joab sent someone to *T*
14: 4 When the woman from *T* went
14: 9 But the woman from *T* said to him,
23: 26 son of Ikkesh from *T*, Abiezer
1Ch 2: 24 bore him Ashhur the father of *T*.
4: 5 the father of *T* had two wives,
11: 28 son of Ikkesh from *T*, Abiezer
2Ch 11: 6 Bethlehem, Etam, *T*, Beth Zur,
20: 20 left for the Desert of *T*.
Ne 3: 5 was repaired by the men of *T*,
3: 27 men of *T* repaired another section,
Jer 6: 1 Sound the trumpet in *T*!
Am 1: 1 one of the shepherds of *T*—

TEKOITE (TEKOA)

1Ch 27: 9 was Ira the son of Ikkesh the *T*.

TEL ASSAR

2Ki 19: 12 the people of Eden who were in *T*?
Isa 37: 12 the people of Eden who were in *T*?

TEL AVIV

Eze 3: 15 lived at *T* near the Kebar River.

TEL HARSHA

Ezr 2: 59 *T*, Kerub, Addon and Immer,
Ne 7: 61 *T*, Kerub, Addon and Immer,

TEL MELAH

Ezr 2: 59 up from the towns of *T*,
Ne 7: 61 up from the towns of *T*,

TELAH

1Ch 7: 25 Resheph his son, *T* his son,

TELAIM

1Sa 15: 4 and mustered them at *T*—

TELEM

Jos 15: 24 Ithnan, Ziph, *T*, Bealoth,
Ezr 10: 24 From the gatekeepers: Shallum, *T*

TEMA

Ge 25: 15 Dumah, Massa, Hadad, *T*, Jetur,
1Ch 1: 30 Dumah, Massa, Hadad, *T*, Jetur,
Job 6: 19 The caravans of *T* look for water,
Isa 21: 14 you who live in *T*,
Jer 25: 23 *T*, Buz and all who are

TEMAH

Ezr 2:53 Mehida, Harsha, Barkos, Sisera, *T*,
Ne 7:55 Mehida, Harsha, Barkos, Sisera, *T*,

TEMAN (TEMANITE TEMANITES)

Ge 36:11 The sons of Eliphaz: *T*, Omar,
36:15 Chiefs *T*, Omar, Zepho, Kenaz,
36:42 Elah, Pinon, Kenaz, *T*, Mibzar,
1Ch 1:36 The sons of Eliphaz: *T*, Omar,
1:53 Elah, Pinon, Kenaz, *T*, Mibzar,
Jer 49:7 "Is there no longer wisdom in *T*?
49:20 against those who live in *T*:
Eze 25:13 and from *T* to Dedan they will fall
Am 1:12 I will send fire upon *T*
Ob :9 Your warriors, O *T*, will be
Hab 3:3 God came from *T*,

TEMANITE (TEMAN)

Job 2:11 Job's three friends, Eliphaz the *T*,
4:1 Then Eliphaz the *T* replied:
15:1 Then Eliphaz the *T* replied:
22:1 Then Eliphaz the *T* replied:
42:7 said to Eliphaz the *T*, "I am angry
42:9 Eliphaz the *T*, Bildad the Shuhite

TEMANITES (TEMAN)

Ge 36:34 the land of the *T* succeeded him
1Ch 1:45 the land of the *T* succeeded him

TEMENI

1Ch 4:6 Hepher, *T* and Haahashtari.

TEMPER (EVEN-TEMPERED HOT-TEMPERED ILL-TEMPERED QUICK-TEMPERED)

1Sa 20:7 But if he loses his *t*, you can be sure
Pr 16:32 a man who controls his *t*

TEMPERATE

1Ti 3:2 *t*, self-controlled, respectable,
3:11 not malicious talkers but *t*
Tit 2:2 Teach the older men to be *t*,

TEMPEST

Job 27:20 a *t* snatches him away in the night.
37:9 The *t* comes out from its chamber,
Ps 50:3 and around him a *t* rages.
55:8 far from the *t* and storm."
83:15 so pursue them with your *t*
107:25 For he spoke and stirred up a *t*
Isa 29:6 *t* and flames of a devouring fire.

TEMPLE (TEMPLES)

Dt 23:17 woman is to become a *t* prostitute.
Jdg 4:21 peg through his *t* into the ground,
4:22 with the tent peg through his *t*—
5:26 she shattered and pierced his *t*.
9:4 shekels from the *t* of Baal-Berith,
9:27 a festival in the *t* of their god.
9:46 the stronghold of the *t* of El-Berith.
16:26 feel the pillars that support the *t*,
16:27 Now the *t* was crowded with men
16:29 pillars on which the *t* stood.
16:30 and down came the *t* on the rulers
1Sa 1:9 by the doorpost of the Lord's *t*.
3:3 lying down in the *t* of the Lord,
5:2 they carried the ark into Dagon's *t*
5:5 nor any others who enter Dagon's *t*
31:9 the news in the *t* of their idols
31:10 armor in the *t* of the Ashtoreths
2Sa 22:7 From his *t* he heard my voice;
1Ki 3:1 building his palace and the *t*
3:2 because a *t* had not yet been built
5:3 he could not build a *t* for the Name
5:5 therefore, to build a *t* for the Name
5:5 throne in your place will build the *t*
5:17 of dressed stone for the *t*.
5:18 and stone for the building of the *t*.
6:1 began to build the *t* of the Lord.
6:2 The *t* that King Solomon built
6:3 cubits from the front of the *t*.
6:3 of the *t* extended the width of the *t*,
6:4 clerestory windows in the *t*.
6:6 ledges around the outside of the *t*
6:6 would be inserted into the *t* walls.
6:7 In building the *t*, only blocks
6:7 at the *t* site while it was being built.
6:8 was on the south side of the *t*;
1Ki 6:9 So he built the *t* and completed it,
6:10 attached to the *t* by beams of cedar.
6:10 built the side rooms all along the *t*.
6:12 "As for this *t* you are building,
6:14 Solomon built the *t* and completed
6:15 floor of the *t* with planks of pine.
6:15 from the floor of the *t* to the ceiling
6:16 the rear of the *t* with cedar boards
6:16 within the *t* an inner sanctuary,
6:18 The inside of the *t* was cedar,
6:19 sanctuary within the *t* to set the ark
6:21 the inside of the *t* with pure gold,
6:27 inside the innermost room of the *t*,
6:29 On the walls all around the *t*,
6:30 and outer rooms of the *t* with gold.
6:37 The foundation of the *t*
6:38 the *t* was finished in all its details
7:12 courtyard of the *t* of the Lord
7:21 the pillars at the portico of the *t*.
7:39 at the southeast corner of the *t*.
7:39 the stands on the south side of the *t*
7:40 Solomon in the *t* of the Lord:
7:45 for the *t* of the Lord were
7:48 that were in the Lord's *t*:
7:50 the doors of the main hall of the *t*.
7:51 for the *t* of the Lord was finished,
7:51 in the treasuries of the Lord's *t*.
8:6 in the inner sanctuary of the *t*,
8:10 the cloud filled the *t* of the Lord.
8:11 the glory of the Lord filled his *t*.
8:13 I have indeed built a magnificent *t*
8:16 Israel to have a *t* built for my Name
8:17 heart to build a *t* for the Name
8:18 heart to build a *t* for my Name,
8:19 he is the one who will build the *t*
8:19 you are not the one to build the *t*,
8:20 and I have built the *t* for the Name
8:27 How much less this *t* I have built!
8:29 open toward this *t* night
8:31 the oath before your altar in this *t*,
8:33 making supplication to you in this *t*
8:38 out his hands toward this *t*—
8:42 he comes and prays toward this *t*,
8:44 the *t* I have built for your Name,
8:48 the *t* I have built for your Name;
8:63 all the Israelites dedicated the *t*
8:64 in front of the *t* of the Lord,
9:1 had finished building the *t*
9:3 have consecrated this *t*, which you
9:7 will reject this *t* I have consecrated
9:8 And though this *t* is now imposing,
9:8 a thing to this land and to this *t*?'
9:10 the *t* of the Lord and the royal
9:15 conscripted to build the Lord's *t*,
9:25 and so fulfilled the *t* obligations.
10:5 made at the *t* of the Lord,
10:12 supports for the *t* of the Lord
12:27 sacrifices at the *t* of the Lord
14:26 the treasures of the *t* of the Lord
14:28 the king went to the Lord's *t*,
15:15 He brought into the *t*
15:18 in the treasuries of the Lord's *t*
16:32 an altar for Baal in the *t* of Baal
2Ki 5:18 When my master enters the *t*
5:18 bow down in the *t* of Rimmon,
10:21 They crowded into the *t* of Baal
10:23 of Recab went into the *t* of Baal.
10:25 entered the inner shrine of the *t*
10:26 the sacred stone out of the *t*
10:27 and tore down the *t* of Baal,
11:3 with his nurse at the *t* of the Lord
11:4 to him at the *t* of the Lord.
11:4 under oath at the *t* of the Lord.
11:6 who take turns guarding the *t*—
11:7 all to guard the *t* for the king.
11:10 that were in the *t* of the Lord.
11:11 near the altar and the *t*,
11:11 side to the north side of the *t*.
11:13 to the people at the *t* of the Lord.
11:15 put to death in the *t* of the Lord."
11:18 guards at the *t* of the Lord.
11:18 of the land went to the *t* of Baal
11:19 king down from the *t* of the Lord
12:4 money brought voluntarily to the *t*.
12:4 offerings to the *t* of the Lord—
12:5 damage is found in the *t*."
12:6 priests still had not repaired the *t*.
12:7 but hand it over for repairing the *t*
2Ki 12:7 the damage done to the *t*?
12:8 would not repair the *t* themselves.
12:9 as one enters the *t* of the Lord.
12:9 brought to the *t* of the Lord.
12:10 brought into the *t* of the Lord
12:11 to supervise the work on the *t*.
12:11 worked on the *t* of the Lord—
12:12 for the repair of the *t* of the Lord,
12:12 other expenses of restoring the *t*.
12:13 brought into the *t* was not spent
12:13 or silver for the *t* of the Lord;
12:14 who used it to repair the *t*.
12:16 brought into the *t* of the Lord;
12:18 the treasuries of the *t* of the Lord
14:14 found in the *t* of the Lord
15:35 Gate of the *t* of the Lord.
16:8 gold found in the *t* of the Lord
16:14 between the new altar and the *t*
16:14 brought from the front of the *t*—
16:18 canopy that had been built at the *t*
16:18 outside the *t* of the Lord,
18:15 found in the *t* of the Lord
18:16 doorposts of the *t* of the Lord,
19:1 and went into the *t* of the Lord.
19:14 he went up to the *t* of the Lord
19:37 in the *t* of his god Nisroch,
20:5 up to the *t* of the Lord.
20:8 up to the *t* of the Lord
21:4 altars in the *t* of the Lord,
21:5 courts of the *t* of the Lord,
21:7 he had made and put it in the *t*,
21:7 "In this *t* and in Jerusalem,
22:3 to the *t* of the Lord.
22:4 brought into the *t* of the Lord,
22:5 pay the workers who repair the *t*
22:5 to supervise the work on the *t*.
22:6 and dressed stone to repair the *t*.
22:8 of the Law in the *t* of the Lord."
22:9 was in the *t* of the Lord
22:9 workers and supervisors at the *t*."
23:2 He went up to the *t* of the Lord
23:2 found in the *t* of the Lord.
23:4 doorkeepers to remove from the *t*
23:6 pole from the *t* of the Lord
23:7 which were in the *t* of the Lord
23:11 removed from the entrance to the *t*
23:12 courts of the *t* of the Lord.
23:24 discovered in the *t* of the Lord.
23:27 and this *t*, about which I said,
24:13 made for the *t* of the Lord.
24:13 treasures from the *t* of the Lord
25:9 He set fire to the *t* of the Lord,
25:13 were at the *t* of the Lord
25:14 articles used in the *t* service.
25:16 made for the *t* of the Lord,
1Ch 6:10 as priest in the *t* Solomon built
6:32 until Solomon built the *t*
9:2 priests, Levites and *t* servants.
9:28 of the articles used in the *t* service;
9:33 stayed in the rooms of the *t*
10:10 armor in the *t* of their gods
10:10 hung up his head in the *t* of Dagon.
22:14 pains to provide for the *t*
22:19 to God into the *t* that will be built
23:4 the work of the *t* of the Lord
23:24 served in the *t* of the Lord.
23:28 in the service of the *t* of the Lord:
23:32 the service of the *t* of the Lord.
24:19 when they entered the *t*
25:6 for the music of the *t* of the Lord,
26:12 ministering in the *t* of the Lord,
26:22 treasuries of the *t* of the Lord.
26:27 for the repair of the *t* of the Lord.
26:29 assigned duties away from the *t*,
28:10 Lord has chosen you to build a *t*
28:11 the plans for the portico of the *t*,
28:12 for the courts of the *t* of the Lord
28:12 for the treasuries of the *t* of God
28:13 of serving in the *t* of the Lord,
28:20 the work for the service of the *t*
28:21 for all the work on the *t* of God,
29:2 provided for the *t* of my God—
29:3 I have provided for this holy *t*:
29:3 and silver for the *t* of my God,
29:3 in my devotion to the *t*
29:7 gave toward the work on the *t*
29:8 the treasury of the *t* of the Lord
29:16 provided for building you a *t*

2Ch 2: 1 orders to build a *t* for the Name
2: 4 about to build a *t* for the Name
2: 5 *t* I am going to build will be great,
2: 6 But who is able to build a *t* for him,
2: 6 Who then am I to build a *t* for him,
2: 9 because the *t* I build must be large
2: 12 who will build a *t* for the LORD
3: 1 began to build the *t* of the LORD
3: 3 for building the *t* of God was sixty
3: 4 of the *t* was twenty cubits long
3: 6 adorned the *t* with precious stones.
3: 7 walls and doors of the *t* with gold,
3: 8 to the width of the *t*—
3: 11 cubits long and touched the *t* wall,
3: 12 and touched the other *t* wall,
3: 15 front of the *t* he made two pillars,
3: 17 the pillars in the front of the *t*,
4: 7 for them and placed them in the *t*,
4: 8 ten tables and placed them in the *t*,
4: 11 for King Solomon in the *t* of God:
4: 16 for the *t* of the LORD were
4: 19 furnishings that were in God's *t*:
4: 22 and the gold doors of the *t*:
5: 1 for the *t* of the LORD was finished,
5: 1 them in the treasuries of God's *t*.
5: 7 in the inner sanctuary of the *t*,
5: 13 Then the *t* of the LORD was filled
5: 14 of the LORD filled the *t* of God.
6: 2 I have built a magnificent *t* for you,
6: 5 Israel to have a *t* built for my Name
6: 7 heart to build a *t* for the Name
6: 8 heart to build a *t* for my Name,
6: 9 he is the one who will build the *t*
6: 9 you are not the one to build the *t*,
6: 10 and I have built the *t* for the Name
6: 18 How much less this *t* I have built!
6: 20 your eyes be open toward this *t* day
6: 22 the oath before your altar in this *t*,
6: 24 supplication before you in this *t*,
6: 29 out his hands toward this *t*—
6: 32 he comes and prays toward this *t*,
6: 34 the *t* I have built for your Name,
6: 38 and toward the *t* I have built
7: 1 the glory of the LORD filled the *t*.
7: 2 The priests could not enter the *t*
7: 3 the glory of the LORD above the *t*,
7: 5 and all the people dedicated the *t*
7: 7 in front of the *t* of the LORD,
7: 11 When Solomon had finished the *t*
7: 11 in mind to do in the *t* of the LORD
7: 12 place for myself as a *t* for sacrifices.
7: 16 consecrated this *t* so that my Name
7: 20 will reject this *t* I have consecrated
7: 21 a thing to this land and to this *t*?'
7: 21 though this *t* is now so imposing,
8: 1 during which Solomon built the *t*
8: 16 So the *t* of the LORD was finished.
8: 16 of the *t* of the LORD was laid
9: 4 made at the *t* of the LORD,
9: 11 steps for the *t* of the LORD
12: 9 the treasures of the *t* of the LORD
12: 11 the king went to the LORD's *t*,
15: 8 of the portico of the LORD's *t*.
15: 18 He brought into the *t*
16: 2 of the treasuries of the LORD's *t*
20: 5 Jerusalem at the *t* of the LORD
20: 9 before this *t* that bears your Name
20: 28 and went to the *t* of the LORD
22: 12 hidden with them at the *t* of God
23: 3 with the king at the *t* of God.
23: 5 courtyards of the *t* of the LORD.
23: 6 is to enter the *t* of the LORD
23: 7 who enters the *t* must be put
23: 9 and that were in the *t* of God.
23: 10 near the altar and the *t*,
23: 10 side to the north side of the *t*.
23: 12 went to them at the *t* of the LORD.
23: 14 her to death at the *t* of the LORD."
23: 17 All the people went to the *t* of Baal
23: 18 had made assignments in the *t*,
23: 18 the oversight of the *t* of the LORD
23: 19 at the gates of the LORD's *t*
23: 20 down from the *t* of the LORD.
24: 4 to restore the *t* of the LORD.
24: 5 to repair the *t* of your God.
24: 7 Athaliah had broken into the *t*
24: 8 at the gate of the *t* of the LORD.
24: 12 carpenters to restore the LORD's *t*
2Ch 24: 12 in iron and bronze to repair the *t*.
24: 12 required for the *t* of the LORD.
24: 13 rebuilt the *t* of God according
24: 14 articles for the LORD's *t*:
24: 14 continually in the *t* of the LORD.
24: 16 done in Israel for God and his *t*.
24: 18 They abandoned the *t*
24: 21 in the courtyard of the LORD's *t*.
24: 27 of the *t* of God are written
25: 24 found in the *t* of God that had been
26: 16 and entered the *t* of the LORD
26: 19 the incense altar in the LORD's *t*,
26: 21 and excluded from the *t* of the
27: 2 unlike him he did not enter the *t*
27: 3 Gate of the *t* of the LORD
28: 21 the things from the *t* of the LORD
28: 24 He shut the doors of the LORD's *t*
28: 24 together the furnishings from the *t*
29: 3 the doors of the *t* of the LORD
29: 5 and consecrate the *t* of the LORD,
29: 15 in to purify the *t* of the LORD,
29: 16 found in the *t* of the LORD,
29: 16 the LORD's *t* everything unclean
29: 17 more days they consecrated the *t*
29: 18 "We have purified the entire *t*
29: 20 and went up to the *t* of the LORD.
29: 25 in the *t* of the LORD with cymbals,
29: 31 offerings to the *t* of the LORD."
29: 35 So the service of the *t*
30: 1 them to come to the *t* of the LORD
30: 15 offerings to the *t* of the LORD.
31: 10 to the *t* of the LORD,
31: 11 storerooms in the *t* of the LORD,
31: 13 official in charge of the *t* of God.
31: 16 all who would enter the *t*
31: 21 undertook in the service of God's *t*
32: 21 when he went into the *t* of his god,
33: 4 altars in the *t* of the LORD,
33: 5 courts of the *t* of the LORD,
33: 7 he had made and put it in God's *t*,
33: 7 "In this *t* and in Jerusalem,
33: 15 the altars he had built on the *t* hill
33: 15 the image from the *t* of the LORD,
34: 8 to purify the land and the *t*,
34: 8 to repair the *t* of the LORD his
34: 9 that had been brought into the *t*
34: 10 the work on the LORD's *t*.
34: 10 who repaired and restored the *t*.
34: 14 taken into the *t* of the LORD,
34: 15 of the Law in the *t* of the LORD."
34: 17 was in the *t* of the LORD
34: 30 He went up to the *t* of the LORD
34: 30 found in the *t* of the LORD.
35: 2 in the service of the LORD's *t*.
35: 3 ark in the *t* that Solomon son
35: 8 the administrators of God's *t*,
35: 20 when Josiah had set the *t* in order,
36: 7 and put them in his *t* there.
36: 7 articles from the *t* of the LORD
36: 10 of value from the *t* of the LORD,
36: 14 and defiling the *t* of the LORD,
36: 18 and the treasures of the LORD's *t*
36: 18 the articles from the *t* of God,
36: 19 They set fire to God's *t*
36: 23 me to build a *t* for him at Jerusalem
Ezr 1: 2 me to build a *t* for him at Jerusalem
1: 3 and build the *t* of the LORD,
1: 4 for the *t* of God in Jerusalem.' "
1: 7 and had placed in the *t* of his god
1: 7 belonging to the *t* of the LORD,
2: 42 128 The gatekeepers of the *t*:
2: 43 and Shobai 139 The *t* servants:
2: 58 and Ami The *t* servants
2: 70 and the *t* servants settled
3: 6 of the LORD's *t* had not yet been
3: 10 foundation of the *t* of the LORD,
3: 12 the foundation of this *t* being laid,
3: 12 who had seen the former *t*,
4: 1 that the exiles were building a *t*
4: 3 with us in building a *t* to our God.
5: 3 authorized you to rebuild this *t*
5: 8 of Judah, to the *t* of the great God.
5: 9 authorized you to rebuild this *t*
5: 11 are rebuilding the *t* that was built
5: 12 who destroyed this *t* and deported
5: 14 and brought to the *t* in Babylon.
5: 14 even removed from the *t*
5: 14 taken from the *t* in Jerusalem
Ezr 5: 15 deposit them in the *t* in Jerusalem.
6: 3 Let the *t* be rebuilt as a place
6: 3 issued a decree concerning the *t*
6: 5 to their places in the *t* in Jerusalem;
6: 5 took from the *t* in Jerusalem
6: 7 with the work on this *t* of God.
6: 12 or to destroy this *t* in Jerusalem.
6: 14 finished building the *t* according
6: 15 The *t* was completed
7: 7 singers, gatekeepers and *t* servants,
7: 16 and priests for the *t* of their God
7: 17 on the altar of the *t* of your God
7: 19 for worship in the *t* of your God.
7: 20 And anything else needed for the *t*
7: 23 with diligence for the *t* of the God
7: 24 *t* servants or other workers
8: 17 the *t* servants in Casiphia,
8: 20 brought 220 of the *t* servants—
Ne 2: 8 for the gates of the citadel by the *t*
3: 26 and the *t* servants living on the hill
3: 31 as the house of the *t* servants
6: 10 and let us close the *t* doors,
6: 10 inside the *t*, and let us close
6: 11 go into the *t* to save his life?
7: 46 and Shobai 138 The *t* servants:
7: 60 and Amon The *t* servants
7: 73 the singers and the *t* servants,
10: 28 *t* servants and all who separated
11: 3 *t* servants and descendants
11: 12 who carried on work for the *t*—
11: 21 The *t* servants lived on the hill
13: 5 offerings and incense and *t* articles,
Ps 5: 7 down toward your holy *t*.
11: 4 The LORD is in his holy *t*;
18: 6 From his *t* he heard my voice;
27: 4 and to seek him in his *t*.
29: 9 And in his *t* all cry, "Glory!"
48: 9 Within your *t*, O God,
65: 4 of your holy *t*.
66: 13 come to your *t* with burnt offerings
68: 29 Because of your *t* at Jerusalem
79: 1 they have defiled your holy *t*,
138: 2 I will bow down toward your holy *t*
Ecc 5: 6 do not protest to the *t* messenger,
Isa 2: 2 of the LORD's *t* will be established
6: 1 and the train of his robe filled the *t*.
6: 4 and the *t* was filled with smoke.
15: 2 Dibon goes up to its *t*,
37: 1 and went into the *t* of the LORD.
37: 14 he went up to the *t* of the LORD
37: 38 in the *t* of his god Nisroch,
38: 20 lives in the *t* of the LORD.
38: 22 up to the *t* of the LORD?"
43: 28 disgrace the dignitaries of your *t*,
44: 28 of the *t*, "Let its foundations be laid
56: 5 to them I will give within my *t*
60: 7 and I will adorn my glorious *t*.
64: 11 and glorious *t*, where our fathers
66: 6 hear that noise from the *t*!
66: 20 to the *t* of the LORD
Jer 7: 4 of the LORD, the *t* of the LORD,
7: 4 of the LORD, the *t* of the LORD!"
7: 4 "This is the *t* of the LORD,
7: 14 the *t* you trust in, the place I gave
11: 15 "What is my beloved doing in my *t*
19: 14 stood in the court of the LORD's *t*
20: 1 officer in the *t* of the LORD,
20: 2 Gate of Benjamin at the LORD's *t*
23: 11 in my *t* I find their wickedness,"
24: 1 in front of the *t* of the LORD.
26: 18 the *t* hill a mound overgrown
36: 5 I cannot go to the LORD's *t*.
36: 8 at the LORD's *t* he read the words
36: 10 entrance of the New Gate of the *t*,
36: 10 people at the LORD's *t* the words
38: 14 entrance to the *t* of the LORD.
43: 13 There in the *t* of the sun
50: 28 vengeance for his *t*.
51: 11 vengeance for his *t*.
52: 13 He set fire to the *t* of the LORD,
52: 17 were at the *t* of the LORD
52: 18 articles used in the *t* service.
52: 20 made for the *t* of the LORD,
Eze 8: 16 and there at the entrance to the *t*,
8: 16 backs toward the *t* of the LORD
9: 3 and moved to the threshold of the *t*
9: 6 elders who were in front of the *t*.
9: 7 "Defile the *t* and fill the courts

Eze 10: 3 side of the *t* when the man went in,
10: 4 cloud filled the *t*, and the court was
10: 4 moved to the threshold of the *t*.
10: 18 from over the threshold of the *t*
40: 5 completely surrounding the *t* area.
40: 7 the portico facing the *t* was one rod
40: 9 portico of the gateway faced the *t*.
40: 45 priests who have charge of the *t*,
40: 47 And the altar was in front of the *t*.
40: 48 me to the portico of the *t*
41: 5 Then he measured the wall of the *t*;
41: 5 around the *t* was four cubits wide.
41: 6 all around the wall of the *t* to serve
41: 6 inserted into the wall of the *t*.
41: 7 all around the *t* were wider
41: 7 surrounding the *t* was built
41: 8 I saw that the *t* had a raised base all
41: 9 between the side rooms of the *t*
41: 10 twenty cubits wide all around the *t*.
41: 12 The building facing the *t* courtyard
41: 13 he measured the *t*; it was a hundred
41: 13 the *t* courtyard and the building
41: 14 The width of the *t* courtyard
41: 14 including the front of the *t*,
41: 15 the courtyard at the rear of the *t*,
41: 19 all around the whole *t*.
41: 26 The side rooms of the *t*
42: 1 the rooms opposite the *t* courtyard
42: 10 adjoining the *t* courtyard
42: 13 rooms facing the *t* courtyard are
42: 15 what was inside the *t* area,
43: 4 glory of the LORD entered the *t*
43: 5 the glory of the LORD filled the *t*.
43: 6 speaking to me from inside the *t*.
43: 10 describe the *t* to the people
43: 11 to them the design of the *t*—
43: 12 Such is the law of the *t*.
43: 12 of the *t*: All the surrounding area
43: 21 of the *t* area outside the sanctuary.
44: 4 gate to the front of the *t*.
44: 4 the glory of the LORD filling the *t*
44: 5 attention to the entrance of the *t*
44: 5 regarding the *t* of the LORD.
44: 7 desecrating my *t* while you offered
44: 11 having charge of the gates of the *t*
44: 14 them in charge of the duties of the *t*
44: 17 of the inner court or inside the *t*.
45: 5 serve in the *t*, as their possession
45: 19 and put it on the doorposts of the *t*,
45: 20 are to make atonement for the *t*.
46: 24 at the *t* will cook the sacrifices
47: 1 back to the entrance to the *t*,
47: 1 from under the south side of the *t*,
47: 1 threshold of the *t* toward the east
47: 1 toward the east (for the *t* faced east
48: 21 portion with the *t* sanctuary will be
Da 1: 2 of the articles from the *t* of God.
1: 2 off to the *t* of his god in Babylonia
5: 2 taken from the *t* in Jerusalem,
5: 3 from the *t* of God in Jerusalem,
5: 23 goblets from his *t* brought to you,
9: 27 abominations on a wing ⌊of the *t*⌋
11: 31 up to desecrate the *t* fortress
Hos 4: 14 and sacrifice with *t* prostitutes—
9: 4 come into the *t* of the LORD.
Joel 2: 17 weep between the *t* porch
Am 7: 13 and the *t* of the kingdom.''
8: 3 ''the songs in the *t* will turn
Jnh 2: 4 again toward your holy *t*.'
2: 7 to your holy *t*.
Mic 1: 2 the Lord from his holy *t*.
1: 7 all her *t* gifts will be burned
3: 12 the *t* hill a mound overgrown
4: 1 of the LORD's *t* will be established
Na 1: 14 that are in the *t* of your gods.
Hab 2: 20 But the LORD is in his holy *t*;
Zep 1: 9 who fill the *t* of their gods
Hag 2: 15 laid on another in the LORD's *t*.
2: 18 of the LORD's *t* was laid.
Zec 4: 9 have laid the foundation of this *t*;
6: 12 and build the *t* of the LORD.
6: 13 It is he who will build the *t*
6: 14 a memorial in the *t* of the LORD.
6: 15 help to build the *t* of the LORD,
8: 9 strong so that the *t* may be built.
Mal 1: 10 one of you would shut the *t* doors,
3: 1 you are seeking will come to his *t*;
Mt 4: 5 stand on the highest point of the *t*.

Mt 12: 5 priests in the *t* desecrate the day
12: 6 that one greater than the *t* is here.
17: 24 ''Doesn't your teacher pay the *t* tax
21: 12 Jesus entered the *t* area
21: 14 and the lame came to him at the *t*,
21: 15 the children shouting in the *t* area,
21: 23 Jesus entered the *t* courts, and,
23: 16 'If anyone swears by the *t*,
23: 16 swears by the gold of the *t*,
23: 17 or the *t* that makes the gold sacred?
23: 21 he who swears by the *t* swears by it
23: 35 whom you murdered between the *t*
24: 1 Jesus left the *t* and was walking
26: 55 sat in the *t* courts teaching,
26: 61 'I am able to destroy the *t* of God
27: 5 Judas threw the money into the *t*
27: 40 You who are going to destroy the *t*
27: 51 of the *t* was torn in two from top
Mk 11: 11 Jerusalem and went to the *t*.
11: 15 Jesus entered the *t* area
11: 16 merchandise through the *t* courts.
11: 27 Jesus was walking in the *t* courts,
12: 35 Jesus was teaching in the *t* courts,
12: 41 money into the *t* treasury.
13: 1 As he was leaving the *t*, one
13: 3 the Mount of Olives opposite the *t*,
14: 49 teaching in the *t* courts,
14: 58 'I will destroy this man-made *t*
15: 29 You who are going to destroy the *t*
15: 38 The curtain of the *t* was torn in two
Lk 1: 9 to go into the *t* of the Lord
1: 21 why he stayed so long in the *t*.
1: 22 he had seen a vision in the *t*,
2: 27 the Spirit, he went into the *t* courts.
2: 37 never left the *t* but worshiped night
2: 46 days they found him in the *t* courts,
4: 9 stand on the highest point of the *t*.
18: 10 ''Two men went up to the *t* to pray,
19: 45 Then he entered the *t* area
19: 47 Every day he was teaching at the *t*.
20: 1 teaching the people in the *t* courts
21: 1 gifts into the *t* treasury.
21: 5 about how the *t* was adorned
21: 37 day Jesus was teaching at the *t*,
21: 38 in the morning to hear him at the *t*.
22: 4 and the officers of the *t* guard
22: 52 the officers of the *t* guard,
22: 53 was with you in the *t* courts,
23: 45 the curtain of the *t* was torn in two.
24: 53 they stayed continually at the *t*,
Jn 2: 14 In the *t* courts he found men selling
2: 15 and drove all from the *t* area,
2: 19 answered them, ''Destroy this *t*,
2: 20 taken forty-six years to build this *t*,
2: 21 the *t* he had spoken of was his body
5: 14 Later Jesus found him at the *t*
7: 14 Feast did Jesus go up to the *t* courts
7: 28 still teaching in the *t* courts,
7: 32 and the Pharisees sent *t* guards
7: 45 Finally the *t* guards went back
8: 2 he appeared again in the *t* courts,
8: 20 words while teaching in the *t* area
8: 59 slipping away from the *t* grounds.
10: 23 and Jesus was in the *t* area walking
11: 56 stood in the *t* area they asked one
18: 20 taught in synagogues or at the *t*,
Ac 2: 46 to meet together in the *t* courts.
3: 1 up to the *t* at the time of prayer—
3: 2 from those going into the *t* courts.
3: 2 to the *t* gate called Beautiful,
3: 8 he went with them into the *t* courts
3: 10 at the *t* gate called Beautiful,
4: 1 and the captain of the *t* guard
5: 20 ''Go, stand in the *t* courts,'' he said,
5: 21 daybreak they entered the *t* courts,
5: 24 the captain of the *t* guard
5: 25 in the *t* courts teaching the people
5: 42 in the *t* courts and from house
14: 13 whose *t* was just outside the city,
19: 27 also that the *t* of the great goddess
19: 35 of the *t* of the great Artemis
21: 26 Then he went to the *t* to give notice
21: 27 province of Asia saw Paul at the *t*.
21: 28 has brought Greeks into the *t* area
21: 29 had brought him into the *t* area.)
21: 30 they dragged him from the *t*,
22: 17 Jerusalem and was praying at the *t*,
24: 6 and even tried to desecrate the *t*;

Ac 24: 12 arguing with anyone at the *t*,
24: 18 me in the *t* courts doing this.
25: 8 or against the *t* or against Caesar.''
26: 21 the Jews seized me in the *t* courts
Ro 9: 4 the *t* worship and the promises.
1Co 3: 16 that you yourselves are God's *t*
3: 17 If anyone destroys God's *t*,
3: 17 *t* is sacred, and you are that *t*.
6: 19 you not know that your body is a *t*
8: 10 this knowledge eating in an idol's *t*,
9: 13 in the *t* get their food from the *t*,
2Co 6: 16 For we are the *t* of the living God.
6: 16 there between the *t* of God
Eph 2: 21 rises to become a holy *t* in the Lord
2Th 2: 4 and even sets himself up in God's *t*,
Rev 3: 12 a pillar in the *t* of my God.
7: 15 and serve him day and night in his *t*
11: 1 ''Go and measure the *t* of God
11: 19 God's *t* in heaven was opened,
11: 19 and within his *t* was seen the ark
14: 15 another angel came out of the *t*
14: 17 out of the *t* in heaven,
15: 5 this I looked and in heaven the *t*,
15: 6 Out of the *t* came the seven angels
15: 8 And the *t* was filled with smoke
15: 8 and no one could enter the *t*
16: 1 voice from the *t* saying to the seven
16: 17 and out of the *t* came a loud voice
21: 22 Almighty and the Lamb are its *t*.
21: 22 I did not see a *t* in the city,

TEMPLES (TEMPLE)

SS 4: 3 Your *t* behind your veil
6: 7 Your *t* behind your veil
Jer 43: 12 fire to the *t* of the gods of Egypt;
43: 12 he will burn their *t* and take their
43: 13 will burn down the *t* of the gods
Joel 3: 5 off my finest treasures to your *t*.
Ac 17: 24 does not live in *t* built by hands.
19: 37 though they have neither robbed *t*
Ro 2: 22 do you rob *t*? You who brag about

TEMPORARY

Ex 12: 45 a *t* resident and a hired worker may
Lev 25: 6 and *t* resident who live among you,
25: 35 you would an alien or a *t* resident,
25: 40 or a *t* resident among you;
25: 45 buy some of the *t* residents living
25: 47 *t* resident among you becomes rich
2Co 4: 18 what is seen is *t*, but what is unseen

TEMPT (TEMPTATION TEMPTED TEMPTER TEMPTING)

1Co 7: 5 again so that Satan will not *t* you
Jas 1: 13 does he *t* anyone; but each one is

TEMPTATION (TEMPT)

Mt 6: 13 And lead us not into *t*,
26: 41 pray so that you will not fall into *t*.
Mk 14: 38 pray so that you will not fall into *t*.
Lk 11: 4 And lead us not into *t*.' ''
22: 40 ''Pray that you will not fall into *t*.''
22: 46 pray so that you will not fall into *t*
1Co 10: 13 No *t* has seized you except what is
1Ti 6: 9 want to get rich fall into *t*

TEMPTED (TEMPT)

Mt 4: 1 into the desert to be *t* by the devil.
Mk 1: 13 was in the desert forty days, being *t*
Lk 4: 2 for forty days he was *t* by the devil.
1Co 10: 13 But when you are *t*, he will
10: 13 he will not let you be *t*
Gal 6: 1 yourself, or you also may be *t*.
1Th 3: 5 way the tempter might have *t* you
Heb 2: 18 able to help those who are being *t*.
2: 18 he himself suffered when he was *t*,
4: 15 but we have one who has been *t*
Jas 1: 13 For God cannot be *t* by evil,
1: 13 When *t*, no one should say,
1: 14 each one is *t* when, by his own evil

TEMPTER (TEMPT)

Mt 4: 3 The *t* came to him and said,
1Th 3: 5 some way the *t* might have

TEMPTING (TEMPT)

Lk 4: 13 the devil had finished all this *t*,
Jas 1: 13 no one should say, ''God is *t* me.''

TEN (ONE-TENTH TENS TENTH TITHE TITHES)

Ge 16: 3 living in Canaan *t* years,
18: 32 What if only *t* can be found there?"
18: 32 the sake of *t*, I will not destroy it."
24: 10 the servant took *t* of his master's
24: 22 gold bracelets weighing *t* shekels.
24: 55 "Let the girl remain with us *t* days
31: 7 me by changing my wages *t* times.
31: 41 and you changed my wages *t* times.
32: 15 donkeys and *t* male donkeys.
32: 15 their young, forty cows and *t* bulls,
42: 3 Then *t* of Joseph's brothers went
45: 23 *t* donkeys loaded with the best
45: 23 *t* female donkeys loaded with grain
50: 22 He lived a hundred and *t* years
50: 26 died at the age of a hundred and *t*.
Ex 26: 1 the tabernacle with *t* curtains
26: 16 Each frame is to be *t* cubits long
27: 12 with *t* posts and *t* bases.
34: 28 covenant—the *T* Commandments.
36: 8 with *t* curtains of finely twisted
36: 21 Each frame was *t* cubits long
38: 12 with *t* posts and *t* bases,
Lev 26: 8 of you will chase *t* thousand,
26: 26 *t* women will be able
27: 5 and of a female at *t* shekels.
27: 7 and of a female at *t* shekels.
Nu 7: 14 one gold ladle weighing *t* shekels,
7: 20 one gold ladle weighing *t* shekels,
7: 26 one gold ladle weighing *t* shekels,
7: 32 one gold ladle weighing *t* shekels,
7: 38 one gold ladle weighing *t* shekels,
7: 44 one gold ladle weighing *t* shekels,
7: 50 one gold ladle weighing *t* shekels,
7: 56 one gold ladle weighing *t* shekels,
7: 62 one gold ladle weighing *t* shekels,
7: 68 one gold ladle weighing *t* shekels,
7: 74 one gold ladle weighing *t* shekels,
7: 80 one gold ladle weighing *t* shekels,
7: 86 incense weighed *t* shekels each,
11: 19 two days, or five, *t* or twenty days,
11: 32 No one gathered less than *t* homers
14: 22 me and tested me *t* times—
29: 23 On the fourth day prepare *t* bulls,
Dt 4: 13 covenant, the *T* Commandments,
10: 4 The *T* Commandments he had
32: 30 or two put *t* thousand to flight,
33: 17 Such are the *t* thousands
Jos 15: 57 *t* towns and their villages.
17: 5 share consisted of *t* tracts
21: 5 descendants were allotted *t* towns
21: 26 All these *t* towns and their
22: 14 With him they sent *t*
24: 29 died at the age of a hundred and *t*.
Jdg 1: 4 they struck down *t* thousand men
2: 8 died at the age of a hundred and *t*.
3: 29 down about *t* thousand Moabites,
4: 6 take with you *t* thousand men
4: 10 *T* thousand men followed him,
4: 14 followed by *t* thousand men.
6: 27 So Gideon took *t* of his servants
7: 3 while *t* thousand remained.
12: 11 the Zebulunite led Israel *t* years.
17: 10 and I'll give you *t* shekels
20: 10 We'll take *t* men out
20: 10 and a thousand from *t* thousand,
20: 34 *t* thousand of Israel's finest men
Ru 1: 4 they had lived there about *t* years,
4: 2 Boaz took *t* of the elders
1Sa 1: 8 more to you than *t* sons?"
15: 4 and *t* thousand men from Judah.
17: 17 and these *t* loaves of bread
17: 18 Take along these *t* cheeses
25: 5 So he sent *t* young men
25: 38 About *t* days later, the LORD
2Sa 15: 16 but he left *t* concubines to take care
18: 3 but you are worth *t* thousand of us.
18: 11 had to give you *t* shekels of silver
18: 15 And *t* of Joab's armor-bearers
19: 43 "We have *t* shares in the king;
20: 3 he took the *t* concubines he had
1Ki 4: 23 and sixty cors of meal, *t* head
5: 14 in shifts of *t* thousand a month,
6: 3 projected *t* cubits from the front
6: 23 of olive wood, each *t* cubits high.
6: 24 *t* cubits from wing tip to wing tip.
6: 25 cherub also measured *t* cubits,
6: 26 height of each cherub was *t* cubits.
7: 10 some measuring *t* cubits
7: 23 measuring *t* cubits from rim to rim
7: 24 gourds encircled it—*t* to a cubit.
7: 27 made *t* movable stands of bronze;
7: 37 is the way he made the *t* stands.
7: 38 He then made *t* bronze basins,
7: 38 basin to go on each of the *t* stands.
7: 43 the *t* stands with their *t* basins;
11: 31 hand and give you *t* tribes.
11: 31 "Take *t* pieces for yourself,
11: 35 son's hands and give you *t* tribes.
14: 3 Take *t* loaves of bread with you,
2Ki 5: 5 of gold and *t* sets of clothing.
5: 5 taking with him *t* talents of silver,
13: 7 *t* chariots and *t* thousand foot
14: 7 who defeated *t* thousand Edomites
15: 17 and he reigned in Samaria *t* years.
20: 9 Shall the shadow go forward *t* steps
20: 9 or shall it go back *t* steps?"
20: 10 the shadow to go forward *t* steps,"
20: 10 "Rather, have it go back *t* steps."
20: 11 shadow go back the *t* steps it had
24: 14 artisans—a total of *t* thousand.
25: 25 came with *t* men and assassinated
1Ch 6: 61 descendants were allotted *t* towns
29: 7 and *t* thousand darics of gold,
29: 7 *t* thousand talents of silver,
2Ch 4: 1 cubits wide and *t* cubits high.
4: 2 measuring *t* cubits from rim to rim
4: 3 of bulls encircled it—*t* to a cubit.
4: 6 He then made *t* basins for washing
4: 7 He made *t* gold lampstands
4: 8 He made *t* tables and placed them
14: 1 was at peace for *t* years.
25: 11 where he killed *t* thousand men
25: 12 also captured *t* thousand men alive,
27: 5 and *t* thousand cors of barley.
27: 5 *t* thousand cors of wheat
30: 24 and *t* thousand sheep and goats.
36: 9 Jerusalem three months and *t* days.
Ezr 8: 24 Hashabiah and *t* of their brothers,
Ne 4: 12 near them came and told us *t* times
5: 18 every *t* days an abundant supply
11: 1 out of every *t* to live in Jerusalem,
Est 3: 9 and I will put *t* thousand talents
9: 10 the *t* sons of Haman son
9: 12 the *t* sons of Haman in the citadel
9: 13 and let Haman's *t* sons be hanged
9: 14 they hanged the *t* sons of Haman.
Job 19: 3 *T* times now you have reproached
Ps 91: 7 *t* thousand at your right hand,
Ecc 7: 19 than *t* rulers in a city.
SS 5: 10 outstanding among *t* thousand.
Isa 38: 8 sun go back the *t* steps it has gone
38: 8 went back the *t* steps it had
Jer 41: 1 came with *t* men to Gedaliah son
41: 2 and the *t* men who were
41: 8 But *t* of them said to Ishmael,
42: 7 *T* days later the word
Eze 40: 11 it was *t* cubits and its length was
41: 2 The entrance was *t* cubits wide,
42: 4 an inner passageway *t* cubits wide
45: 14 each cor (which consists of *t* baths
45: 14 for *t* baths are equivalent
Da 1: 12 Please test your servants for *t* days:
1: 14 and tested them for *t* days.
1: 15 of the *t* days they looked healthier
1: 20 he found them *t* times better
7: 7 former beasts, and it had *t* horns.
7: 10 *t* thousand times *t* thousand stood
7: 20 wanted to know about the *t* horns
7: 24 *t* horns are *t* kings who will come
Am 5: 3 will have only *t* left."
6: 9 If *t* men are left in one house,
Mic 6: 7 with *t* thousand rivers of oil?
Hag 2: 16 measures, there were only *t*.
Zec 8: 23 "In those days *t* men
Mt 18: 24 who owed him *t* thousand talents
20: 24 When the *t* heard about this,
25: 1 will be like *t* virgins who took
25: 28 it to the one who has the *t* talents.
Mk 10: 41 When the *t* heard about this,
Lk 14: 31 he is able with *t* thousand men
15: 8 suppose a woman has *t* silver coins
17: 12 *t* men who had leprosy met him.
17: 17 asked, "Were not all *t* cleansed?
Lk 19: 13 So he called *t* of his servants
19: 13 his servants and gave them *t* minas.
19: 16 'Sir, your mina has earned *t* more.'
19: 17 matter, take charge of *t* cities.'
19: 24 give it to the one who has *t* minas.'
19: 25 'he already has *t*!' "He replied,
Ac 25: 6 After spending eight or *t* days
1Co 4: 15 you have *t* thousand guardians
14: 19 others than *t* thousand words
Rev 2: 10 will suffer persecution for *t* days.
5: 11 and *t* thousand times *t* thousand.
12: 3 and *t* horns and seven crowns
13: 1 He had *t* horns and seven heads,
13: 1 with *t* crowns on his horns,
17: 3 and had seven heads and *t* horns.
17: 7 has the seven heads and *t* horns.
17: 12 *t* horns you saw are *t* kings who
17: 16 and the *t* horns you saw will hate

TEN-ACRE (ACRE)

Isa 5: 10 *t* vineyard will produce only a bath

TEN-STRINGED (STRING)

Ps 33: 2 make music to him on the *t* lyre.
92: 3 to the music of the *t* lyre
144: 9 on the *t* lyre I will make music

TENANTS

Lev 25: 23 and you are but aliens and my *t*.
Job 31: 39 or broken the spirit of its *t*,
SS 8: 11 he let out his vineyard to *t*.
Mt 21: 34 servants to the *t* to collect his fruit.
21: 35 "The *t* seized his servants;
21: 36 the *t* treated them the same way.
21: 38 "But when the *t* saw the son,
21: 40 what will he do to those *t*?"
21: 41 he will rent the vineyard to other *t*,
Mk 12: 2 to the *t* to collect from them some
12: 7 "But the *t* said to one another,
12: 9 He will come and kill those *t*
Lk 20: 10 the *t* beat him and sent him away
20: 10 to the *t* so they would give him
20: 14 when the *t* saw him, they talked
20: 16 He will come and kill those *t*

TEND (TENDED TENDING TENDS)

Ge 30: 36 while Jacob continued to *t* the rest
46: 32 are shepherds; they *t* livestock,
Lev 24: 3 Aaron is to *t* the lamps
1Sa 17: 15 from Saul to *t* his father's sheep
SS 8: 12 are for those who *t* its fruit.
Jer 23: 2 to the shepherds who *t* my people:
23: 4 over them who will *t* them,
Eze 34: 14 I will *t* them in a good pasture,
34: 15 I myself will *t* my sheep
34: 23 he will *t* them and be their
34: 23 servant David, and he will *t* them;
Jnh 4: 10 though you did not *t* it

TENDED (TEND)

Ge 46: 34 'Your servants have *t* livestock
Lev 24: 4 the LORD must be *t* continually.
Hos 12: 12 and to pay for her he *t* sheep.

TENDER (TENDERNESS)

Ge 18: 7 *t* calf and gave it to a servant,
33: 13 lord knows that the children are *t*
Dt 32: 2 like abundant rain on *t* plants.
2Ki 19: 26 like *t* green shoots,
Pr 4: 3 still *t*, and an only child
Isa 37: 27 like *t* green shoots,
47: 1 *t* or delicate.
53: 2 up before him like a *t* shoot,
Eze 17: 22 I will break off a *t* sprig
Mt 24: 32 its twigs get *t* and its leaves come
Mk 13: 28 its twigs get *t* and its leaves come
Lk 1: 78 because of the *t* mercy of our God,

TENDERNESS (TENDER)

Isa 63: 15 Your *t* and compassion are
Php 2: 1 fellowship with the Spirit, if any *t*

TENDING (TEND)

Ge 30: 31 I will go on *t* your flocks
37: 2 was *t* the flocks with his brothers,
Ex 3: 1 Now Moses was *t* the flock
1Sa 16: 11 answered, "but he is *t* the sheep."
Ps 78: 71 from *t* the sheep he brought him

Jer 6: 3 each *t* his own portion."
Eze 34: 10 I will remove them from *t* the flock
Am 7: 15 LORD took me from *t* the flock
Mt 8: 33 Those *t* the pigs ran off, went
Mk 5: 14 Those *t* the pigs ran off
Lk 8: 34 When those *t* the pigs saw what

TENDON (TENDONS)

Ge 32: 32 Israelites do not eat the *t* attached
32: 32 Jacob's hip was touched near the *t*.

TENDONS (TENDON)

Eze 37: 6 I will attach *t* to you and make
37: 8 and *t* and flesh appeared on them

TENDS (TEND)

Ex 30: 7 morning when he *t* the lamps.
Pr 27: 18 He who *t* a fig tree will eat its fruit,
Isa 40: 11 He *t* his flock like a shepherd:
1Co 9: 7 Who *t* a flock and does not drink
Jas 4: 5 caused to live in us *t* toward envy,

TENS (TEN)

Ex 18: 21 thousands, hundreds, fifties and *t*.
18: 25 thousands, hundreds, fifties and *t*.
Dt 1: 15 and of *t* and as tribal officials.
1Sa 18: 7 and David his *t* of thousands."
18: 8 David with *t* of thousands,"
21: 11 and David his *t* of thousands'?"
29: 5 and David his *t* of thousands'?"
Ps 3: 6 I will not fear the *t* of thousands
68: 17 chariots of God are *t* of thousands
144: 13 by *t* of thousands in our fields;

TENT (TENTMAKER TENTS)

Ge 9: 21 and lay uncovered inside his *t*.
12: 8 east of Bethel and pitched his *t*,
13: 3 and Ai where his *t* had been earlier
18: 1 at the entrance to his *t* in the heat
18: 2 the entrance of his *t* to meet them
18: 6 hurried into the *t* to Sarah.
18: 9 "There, in the *t*," he said.
18: 10 listening at the entrance to the *t*,
24: 67 her into the *t* of his mother Sarah,
26: 25 There he pitched his *t*,
31: 25 Jacob had pitched his *t*
31: 33 into Jacob's *t* and into Leah's *t*
31: 33 into the *t* of the two maidservants,
31: 33 of Leah's *t*, he entered Rachel's *t*.
31: 34 through everything in the *t*
33: 19 of ground where he pitched his *t*.
35: 21 and pitched his *t* beyond Migdal
Ex 16: 16 for each person you have in your *t*
18: 7 other and then went into the *t*.
26: 7 hair for the *t* over the tabernacle—
26: 9 double at the front of the *t*.
26: 11 in the loops to fasten the *t* together
26: 12 additional length of the *t* curtains,
26: 13 The *t* curtains will be a cubit longer
26: 14 Make for the *t* a covering
26: 36 entrance to the *t* make a curtain
27: 19 including all the *t* pegs for it
27: 21 In the *T* of Meeting,
28: 43 them whenever they enter the *T*
29: 4 to the entrance to the *T* of Meeting
29: 10 to the front of the *T* of Meeting
29: 11 at the entrance to the *T* of Meeting
29: 30 and comes to the *T* of Meeting
29: 32 the entrance to the *T* of Meeting,
29: 42 at the entrance to the *T* of Meeting
29: 44 I will consecrate the *T* of Meeting
30: 16 for the service of the *T* of Meeting.
30: 18 Place it between the *T* of Meeting
30: 20 Whenever they enter the *T*
30: 26 use it to anoint the *T* of Meeting,
30: 36 the Testimony in the *T* of Meeting,
31: 7 all the other furnishings of the *t*—
31: 7 the *T* of Meeting, the ark
33: 7 Now Moses used to take a *t*
33: 7 calling it the "*t* of meeting."
33: 7 go to the *t* of meeting
33: 8 Moses until he entered the *t*.
33: 8 whenever Moses went out to the *t*,
33: 9 As Moses went into the *t*,
33: 10 each at the entrance to his *t*.
33: 10 standing at the entrance to the *t*,
33: 11 son of Nun did not leave the *t*.
35: 11 the tabernacle with its *t*
Ex 35: 18 the *t* pegs for the tabernacle
35: 21 for the work on the *T* of Meeting,
36: 14 hair for the *t* over the tabernacle—
36: 18 clasps to fasten the *t* together
36: 19 they made for the *t* a covering
36: 37 to the *t* they made a curtain
38: 8 at the entrance to the *T* of Meeting
38: 20 All the *t* pegs of the tabernacle
38: 30 the entrance to the *T* of Meeting,
38: 31 and all the *t* pegs for the tabernacle
39: 32 the *T* of Meeting, was completed.
39: 33 the *t* and all its furnishings,
39: 38 the curtain for the entrance to the *t*
39: 40 and *t* pegs for the courtyard;
39: 40 for the tabernacle, the *T*
40: 2 "Set up the tabernacle, the *T*
40: 6 to the tabernacle, the *T* of Meeting;
40: 7 the basin between the *T* of Meeting
40: 12 to the entrance to the *T* of Meeting
40: 19 and put the covering over the *t*,
40: 19 he spread the *t* over the tabernacle
40: 22 the table in the *T* of Meeting
40: 24 the lampstand in the *T* of Meeting
40: 26 altar in the *T* of Meeting in front
40: 29 the *T* of Meeting, and offered
40: 30 the basin between the *T* of Meeting
40: 32 whenever they entered the *T*
40: 34 the cloud covered the *T* of Meeting
40: 35 Moses could not enter the *T*
Lev 1: 1 to him from the *T* of Meeting.
1: 3 at the entrance to the *T* of Meeting
1: 5 at the entrance to the *T* of Meeting
3: 2 at the entrance to the *T* of Meeting
3: 8 it in front of the *T* of Meeting.
3: 13 it in front of the *T* of Meeting.
4: 4 at the entrance to the *T* of Meeting
4: 5 and carry it into the *T* of Meeting.
4: 7 at the entrance to the *T* of Meeting
4: 7 the LORD in the *T* of Meeting.
4: 14 present it before the *T* of Meeting.
4: 16 blood into the *T* of Meeting.
4: 18 at the entrance to the *T* of Meeting
4: 18 the LORD in the *T* of Meeting.
6: 16 the courtyard of the *T* of Meeting.
6: 26 the courtyard of the *T* of Meeting.
6: 30 brought into the *T* of Meeting
8: 3 at the entrance to the *T* of Meeting
8: 4 at the entrance to the *T* of Meeting
8: 31 at the entrance to the *T* of Meeting
8: 33 to the *T* of Meeting for seven days,
8: 35 entrance to the *T* of Meeting day
9: 5 to the front of the *T* of Meeting,
9: 23 went into the *T* of Meeting.
10: 7 the entrance to the *T* of Meeting
10: 9 go into the *T* of Meeting,
12: 6 the priest at the entrance to the *T*
14: 8 stay outside his *t* for seven days.
14: 11 at the entrance to the *T* of Meeting
14: 23 at the entrance to the *T* of Meeting
15: 14 to the entrance to the *T* of Meeting
15: 29 at the entrance to the *T* of Meeting
16: 7 at the entrance to the *T* of Meeting
16: 16 to do the same for the *T* of Meeting
16: 17 No one is to be in the *T* of Meeting
16: 20 the *T* of Meeting and the altar,
16: 23 is to go into the *T* of Meeting
16: 33 for the *T* of Meeting and the altar,
17: 4 to the entrance to the *T* of Meeting
17: 5 at the entrance to the *T* of Meeting
17: 6 at the entrance to the *T* of Meeting
17: 9 to the entrance to the *T* of Meeting
19: 21 to the entrance to the *T* of Meeting
24: 3 the Testimony in the *T* of Meeting,
Nu 1: 1 spoke to Moses in the *T* of Meeting
2: 2 are to camp around the *T*
2: 17 Then the *T* of Meeting
3: 7 community at the *T* of Meeting
3: 8 the furnishings of the *T* of Meeting,
3: 25 At the *T* of Meeting
3: 25 at the entrance to the *T* of Meeting
3: 25 for the care of the tabernacle and *t*,
3: 37 courtyard with their bases, *t* pegs
3: 38 in front of the *T* of Meeting.
4: 3 in the work in the *T* of Meeting.
4: 4 the Kohathites in the *T* of Meeting:
4: 15 are in the *T* of Meeting.
4: 23 in the work at the *T* of Meeting.
4: 25 of the tabernacle, the *T* of Meeting,
Nu 4: 25 the entrance to the *T* of Meeting,
4: 28 clans at the *T* of Meeting.
4: 30 in the work at the *T* of Meeting.
4: 31 service at the *T* of Meeting:
4: 32 *t* pegs, ropes, all their equipment
4: 33 as they work at the *T* of Meeting
4: 35 in the work in the *T* of Meeting,
4: 37 served in the *T* of Meeting.
4: 39 in the work at the *T* of Meeting,
4: 41 served at the *T* of Meeting.
4: 43 in the work at the *T* of Meeting,
4: 47 the *T* of Meeting numbered
6: 10 at the entrance to the *T* of Meeting
6: 13 to the entrance to the *T* of Meeting
6: 18 at the entrance to the *T* of Meeting
7: 5 in the work at the *T* of Meeting.
7: 89 When Moses entered the *T*
8: 9 to the front of the *T* of Meeting
8: 15 work at the *T* of Meeting.
8: 19 work at the *T* of Meeting on behalf
8: 22 work at the *T* of Meeting
8: 24 in the work at the *T* of Meeting,
8: 26 duties at the *T* of Meeting,
9: 15 On the day the tabernacle, the *T*
9: 17 the cloud lifted from above the *T*,
10: 3 at the entrance to the *T* of Meeting
11: 10 each at the entrance to his *t*.
11: 16 come to the *T* of Meeting,
11: 24 and had them stand around the *t*.
11: 26 but did not go out to the *t*.
12: 4 "Come out to the *T* of Meeting,
12: 5 he stood at the entrance to the *T*
12: 10 the cloud lifted from above the *T*,
14: 10 appeared at the *T* of Meeting
16: 18 at the entrance to the *T* of Meeting
16: 19 at the entrance to the *T* of Meeting
16: 42 turned toward the *T* of Meeting,
16: 43 to the front of the *T* of Meeting,
16: 50 at the entrance to the *T* of Meeting
17: 4 Place them in the *T* of Meeting
17: 7 LORD in the *T* of the Testimony.
17: 8 The next day Moses entered the *T*
18: 2 before the *T* of the Testimony.
18: 3 to perform all the duties of the *T*,
18: 4 all the work at the *T*—
18: 4 for the care of the *T* of Meeting—
18: 6 to do the work at the *T* of Meeting.
18: 21 while serving at the *T* of Meeting.
18: 22 go near the *T* of Meeting,
18: 23 to do the work at the *T* of Meeting
18: 31 for your work at the *T* of Meeting.
19: 4 the front of the *T* of Meeting.
19: 14 Anyone who enters the *t*
19: 14 applies when a person dies in a *t*:
19: 18 and sprinkle the *t* and all
20: 6 to the entrance to the *T* of Meeting
25: 6 at the entrance to the *T* of Meeting
25: 8 followed the Israelite into the *t*.
27: 2 the entrance to the *T* of Meeting
31: 54 brought it into the *T* of Meeting
Dt 31: 14 themselves at the *T* of Meeting.
31: 14 yourselves at the *T* of Meeting,
31: 15 Then the LORD appeared at the *T*
31: 15 stood over the entrance to the *T*.
Jos 7: 21 hidden in the ground inside my *t*,
7: 22 hidden in his *t*, with the silver
7: 22 they ran to the *t*, and there it was,
7: 23 They took the things from the *t*,
7: 24 donkeys and sheep, his *t*
18: 1 and set up the *T* of Meeting there.
19: 51 at the entrance to the *T* of Meeting
Jdg 4: 11 and pitched his *t* by the great tree
4: 17 fled on foot to the *t* of Jael,
4: 18 So he entered her *t*, and she put
4: 20 "Stand in the doorway of the *t*,"
4: 21 picked up a *t* peg and a hammer
4: 22 with the *t* peg through his temple—
5: 26 Her hand reached for the *t* peg,
7: 13 It struck the *t* with such force that
7: 13 such force that the *t* overturned
1Sa 2: 22 at the entrance to the *T* of Meeting
4: 10 and every man fled to his *t*.
17: 54 Philistine's weapons in his own *t*.
2Sa 6: 17 inside the *t* that David had pitched
7: 2 while the ark of God remains in a *t*
7: 6 moving from place to place with a *t*
16: 22 So they pitched a *t* for Absalom
20: 1 Every man to his *t*, O Israel!"

1Ki 1:39 the horn of oil from the sacred *t*
2:28 he fled to the *t* of the LORD
2:29 fled to the *t* of the LORD
2:30 Benaiah entered the *t* of the LORD
8:4 the *T* of Meeting and all the sacred
2Ki 7:8 returned and entered another *t*
1Ch 6:32 before the tabernacle—the *T*
9:19 guarding the thresholds of the *t* just
9:21 at the entrance to the *T* of Meeting
9:23 LORD—the house called the *T*.
15:1 ark of God and pitched a *t* for it.
16:1 inside the *t* that David had pitched
17:1 of the LORD is under a *t*."
17:5 moved from one *t* site to another,
23:32 for the *T* of Meeting,
2Ch 1:3 for God's *T* of Meeting was there,
1:4 because he had pitched a *t* for it
1:6 the LORD in the *T* of Meeting
1:13 from before the *T* of Meeting.
5:5 they brought up the ark and the *T*
24:6 of Israel for the *T* of the Testimony
Job 4:21 the cords of their *t* pulled up,
5:24 You will know that your *t* is secure;
11:14 and allow no evil to dwell in your *t*,
18:6 The light in his *t* becomes dark;
18:14 He is torn from the security of his *t*
18:15 Fire resides in his *t*;
19:12 and encamp around my *t*.
20:26 and devour what is left in his *t*.
22:23 remove wickedness far from your *t*
Ps 19:4 In the heavens he has pitched a *t*
52:5 you up and tear you from your *t*;
61:4 I long to dwell in your *t* forever
76:2 His *t* is in Salem,
78:60 the *t* he had set up among men.
91:10 no disaster will come near your *t*.
104:2 he stretches out the heavens like a *t*
Pr 14:11 but the *t* of the upright will flourish
SS 1:5 like the *t* curtains of Solomon.
Isa 13:20 no Arab will pitch his *t* there,
33:20 a *t* that will not be moved;
38:12 Like a shepherd's *t* my house
40:22 spreads them out like a *t* to live in.
54:2 stretch your *t* curtains wide,
54:2 "Enlarge the place of your *t*,
Jer 10:20 My *t* is destroyed;
10:20 no one is left now to pitch my *t*
La 2:4 on the *t* of the Daughter of Zion.
Am 9:11 David's fallen *t*.
Zec 10:4 from him the *t* peg,
Ac 15:16 and rebuild David's fallen *t*.
2Co 5:1 that if the earthly *t* we live
5:4 For while we are in this *t*, we groan
2Pe 1:13 as long as I live in the *t* of this body,
Rev 7:15 sits on the throne will spread his *t*

TENT-DWELLING (DWELL)

Jdg 5:24 most blessed of *t* women.

TENTH (TEN)

Ge 8:5 day of the *t* month the tops
8:5 to recede until the *t* month,
14:20 Abram gave him a *t* of everything.
28:22 you give me I will give you a *t*."
Ex 12:3 of Israel that on the *t* day
16:36 (An omer is one *t* of an ephah.)
29:40 With the first lamb offer a *t*
Lev 5:11 offering for his sin a *t* of an ephah
6:20 a *t* of an ephah of fine flour
14:21 together with a *t* of an ephah
16:29 On the *t* day of the seventh month
23:27 "The *t* day of this seventh month is
25:9 on the *t* day of the seventh month;
27:32 every *t* animal that passes
Nu 5:15 take an offering of a *t* of an ephah
7:66 On the *t* day Ahiezer son
15:4 of a *t* of an ephah of fine flour
18:26 you must present a *t* of that tithe
28:5 together with a grain offering of a *t*
28:13 a grain offering of a *t* of an ephah
29:7 " 'On the *t* day of this seventh
Dt 14:22 Be sure to set aside a *t*
23:2 even down to the *t* generation.
23:3 even down to the *t* generation.
26:12 setting aside a *t* of all your produce
Jos 4:19 On the *t* day of the first month
1Sa 8:15 He will take a *t* of your grain
8:17 He will take a *t* of your flocks,
2Ki 25:1 on the *t* day of the *t* month,
1Ch 12:13 Jeremiah the *t* and Macbannai
24:11 ninth to Jeshua, the *t* to Shecaniah,
25:17 and relatives, 12 the *t* to Shimei,
27:13 *t*, for the *t* month, was Maharai
Ezr 10:16 day of the *t* month they sat
Ne 10:38 are to bring a *t* of the tithes up
Est 2:16 the royal residence in the *t* month,
Isa 6:13 And though a *t* remains in the land,
Jer 32:1 in the *t* year of Zedekiah king
39:1 king of Judah, in the *t* month,
52:4 on the *t* day of the *t* month,
52:12 On the *t* day of the fifth month,
Eze 20:1 in the fifth month on the *t* day,
24:1 in the *t* month on the *t* day,
29:1 In the *t* year, in the *t* month
33:21 in the *t* month on the fifth day,
40:1 of the year, on the *t* of the month,
45:11 and the ephah a *t* of a homer;
45:11 the bath containing a *t* of a homer
45:14 is a *t* of a bath from each cor (which
Zec 8:19 and *t* months will become joyful
Mt 23:23 You give a *t* of your spices—mint,
Lk 11:42 you give God a *t* of your mint,
18:12 I fast twice a week and give a *t*
Jn 1:39 It was about the *t* hour.
Heb 7:2 and Abraham gave him a *t*
7:4 patriarch Abraham gave him a *t*
7:5 to collect a *t* from the people—
7:6 yet he collected a *t* from Abraham
7:8 the *t* is collected by men who die;
7:9 who collects the *t*, paid the *t*
Rev 11:13 and a *t* of the city collapsed.
21:20 the ninth topaz, the *t* chrysoprase,

TENTMAKER (TENT)

Ac 18:3 and because he was a *t* as they were

TENTS (TENT)

Ge 4:20 the father of those who live in *t*
9:27 may Japheth live in the *t* of Shem,
13:5 also had flocks and herds and *t*.
13:12 and pitched his *t* near Sodom.
13:18 So Abram moved his *t*
25:27 a quiet man, staying among the *t*.
Ex 33:8 stood at the entrances to their *t*.
Nu 1:52 are to set up their *t* by divisions,
1:53 set up their *t* around the tabernacle
16:24 'Move away from the *t* of Korah,
16:26 "Move back from the *t*
16:27 away from the *t* of Korah,
16:27 little ones at the entrances to their *t*
24:5 How beautiful are your *t*, O Jacob,
Dt 1:27 You grumbled in your *t* and said,
5:30 "Go, tell them to return to their *t*.
11:6 their *t* and every living thing that
16:7 in the morning return to your *t*.
33:18 and you, Issachar, in your *t*.
Jdg 6:5 and their *t* like swarms of locusts.
7:8 the rest of the Israelites to their *t*
2Sa 11:11 Israel and Judah are staying in *t*,
1Ki 12:16 To your *t*, O Israel!
20:12 the kings were drinking in their *t*,
20:16 were in their *t* getting drunk.
2Ki 7:7 abandoned their *t* and their horses
7:8 the camp and entered one of the *t*.
7:10 and the *t* left just as they were."
2Ch 10:16 To your *t*, O Israel!
Job 8:22 the *t* of the wicked will be no more
12:6 The *t* of marauders are undisturbed
15:34 fire will consume the *t*
21:28 the *t* where wicked men lived?'
Ps 69:25 there be no one to dwell in their *t*.
78:28 all around their *t*.
78:51 of manhood in the *t* of Ham.
78:67 Then he rejected the *t* of Joseph,
83:6 the *t* of Edom and the Ishmaelites,
84:10 than dwell in the *t* of the wicked.
106:25 They grumbled in their *t*
118:15 resound in the *t* of the righteous:
120:5 that I live among the *t* of Kedar!
SS 1:5 dark like the *t* of Kedar,
1:8 goats by the *t* of the shepherds.
Jer 4:20 In an instant my *t* are destroyed,
6:3 they will pitch their *t* around her,
30:18 restore the fortunes of Jacob's *t*
35:7 things, but must always live in *t*.
35:10 lived in *t* and have fully obeyed
Jer 37:10 wounded men were left in their *t*,
49:29 Their *t* and their flocks will be
Eze 25:4 and pitch their *t* among you;
Da 11:45 He will pitch his royal *t*
Hos 9:6 and thorns will overrun their *t*.
12:9 I will make you live in *t* again,
Hab 3:7 I saw the *t* of Cushan in distress,
Mal 2:12 him off from the *t* of Jacob—
Heb 11:9 he lived in *t*, as did Isaac and Jacob

TERAH

Ge 11:24 he became the father of *T*.
11:25 after he became the father of *T*,
11:26 After *T* had lived 70 years,
11:27 This is the account of *T*.
11:27 *T* became the father of Abram,
11:28 While his father *T* was still alive,
11:31 *T* took his son Abram, his
11:32 *T* lived 205 years, and he died
Nu 33:27 They left Tahath and camped at *T*.
33:28 They left *T* and camped at Mithcah
Jos 24:2 including *T* the father of Abraham
1Ch 1:26 Nahor, *T* and Abram (that is,
Lk 3:34 the son of *T*, the son of Nahor,

TEREBINTH

Isa 6:13 But as the *t* and oak
Hos 4:13 under oak, poplar and *t*,

TERESH

Est 2:21 *T*, two of the king's officers who
6:2 had exposed Bigthana and *T*,

TERMS

Ge 23:16 Abraham agreed to Ephron's *t*
Dt 29:1 These are the *t* of the covenant
29:9 Carefully follow the *t*
1Sa 11:4 and reported these *t* to the people,
1Ki 5:1 been on friendly *t* with David.
Job 34:33 God then reward you on your *t*,
Jer 11:2 "Listen to the *t* of this covenant
11:3 is the man who does not obey the *t*
11:4 *t* I commanded your forefathers
11:6 'Listen to the *t* of this covenant
32:11 the sealed copy containing the *t*
34:18 and have not fulfilled the *t*
Lk 14:32 way off and will ask for *t* of peace.
Ro 6:19 in human *t* because you are weak

TERRACES

2Sa 5:9 from the supporting *t* inward.
1Ki 9:15 the supporting *t*, the wall
9:24 he constructed the supporting *t*.
11:27 Solomon had built the supporting *t*
1Ch 11:8 from the supporting *t*
2Ch 32:5 and reinforced the supporting *t*
Job 24:11 They crush olives among the *t*;
Jer 31:40 all the *t* out to the Kidron Valley

TERRIBLE (TERROR)

Ex 9:3 of the LORD will bring a *t* plague
Nu 20:5 out of Egypt to this *t* place?
Dt 6:22 great and *t*— upon Egypt
Ne 13:27 too are doing all this *t* wickedness
Jer 4:6 even *t* destruction."
6:1 even *t* destruction.
21:6 and they will die of a *t* plague.
26:19 to bring a *t* disaster on ourselves!"
Mt 8:6 home paralyzed and in *t* suffering."
2Ti 3:1 There will be *t* times
Rev 16:21 because the plague was so *t*.

TERRIFIED (TERROR)

Ge 45:3 because they were *t* at his presence
Ex 14:10 They were *t* and cried out
15:15 The chiefs of Edom will be *t*,
Nu 22:3 and Moab was *t* because there were
Dt 1:29 "Do not be *t*; do not be afraid
7:21 Do not be *t* by them,
20:3 do not be *t* or give way to panic
31:6 Do not be afraid or *t*
Jos 1:9 Do not be *t*; do not be discouraged,
Jdg 20:41 and the men of Benjamin were *t*,
1Sa 17:11 the Israelites were dismayed and *t*.
31:4 But his armor-bearer was *t*
2Ki 10:4 they were *t* and said, "If two kings
1Ch 10:4 But his armor-bearer was *t*
Est 7:6 Then Haman was *t* before the king

Job 21: 6 When I think about this, I am *t;*
23: 15 That is why I am *t* before him;
23: 16 the Almighty has *t* me.
41: 25 When he rises up, the mighty are *t;*
Ps 90: 7 and *t* by your indignation.
104: 29 they are *t;*
Isa 19: 17 whom Judah is mentioned will be *t,*
33: 14 The sinners in Zion are *t;*
51: 7 or be *t* by their insults.
Jer 1: 17 Do not be *t* by them, or I will
10: 2 or be *t* by signs in the sky,
10: 2 though the nations are *t* by them.
17: 18 let them be *t,*
23: 4 they will no longer be afraid or *t,*
46: 5 They are *t,*
51: 32 and the soldiers *t.*''
Eze 2: 6 of what they say or *t* by them,
3: 9 afraid of them or *t* by them,
19: 7 were *t* by his roaring.
26: 18 are *t* at your collapse.'
Da 4: 5 passed through my mind *t* me.
5: 9 Belshazzar became even more *t*
8: 17 place where I was standing, I was *t*
Ob : 9 Your warriors, O Teman, will be *t,*
Jnh 1: 10 This *t* them and they asked,
Mt 14: 26 walking on the lake, they were *t.*
17: 6 they fell facedown to the ground, *t.*
27: 54 they were *t,* and exclaimed,
Mk 4: 41 They were *t* and asked each other,
6: 50 they all saw him and were *t.*
Lk 2: 9 around them, and they were *t.*
Jn 6: 19 on the water; and they were *t.*
Rev 11: 13 and the survivors were *t*
18: 10 *T* at her torment, they will stand
18: 15 far off, *t* at her torment.

TERRIFIES (TERROR)

Job 22: 10 why sudden peril *t* you,
Ps 2: 5 and *t* them in his wrath, saying,

TERRIFY (TERROR)

2Ch 32: 18 to *t* them and make them afraid
Job 7: 14 and *t* me with visions,
13: 11 Would not his splendor *t* you?
33: 16 and *t* them with warnings,
Ps 10: 18 who is of the earth, may *t* no more.
83: 15 and *t* them with your storm.
Jer 1: 17 or I will *t* you before them.
Hab 2: 17 of animals will *t* you.
Zec 1: 21 the craftsmen have come to *t* them

TERRIFYING (TERROR)

Job 15: 21 *T* sounds fill his ears;
Da 7: 7 *t* and frightening and very
7: 19 from all the others and most *t,*
Heb 12: 21 The sight was so *t* that Moses said,

TERRITORIES (TERRITORY)

Ge 10: 5 out into their *t* by their clans
10: 20 languages, in their *t* and nations.
10: 31 languages, in their *t* and nations.
Jos 19: 51 These are the *t* that Eleazar
1Ch 13: 2 brothers throughout the *t* of Israel,

TERRITORY (TERRITORIES)

Ge 9: 27 May God extend the *t* of Japheth;
14: 7 they conquered the whole *t* of
48: 6 in the *t* they inherit they will be
Ex 34: 24 before you and enlarge your *t,*
Nu 20: 16 a town on the edge of your *t.*
20: 17 we have passed through your *t.*''
20: 21 to let them go through their *t,*
21: 13 desert extending into Amorite *t.*
21: 22 we have passed through your *t.*''
21: 23 not let Israel pass through his *t.*
22: 36 at the edge of his *t.*
32: 33 land with its cities and the *t*
Dt 1: 5 East of the Jordan in the *t* of Moab,
2: 4 about to pass through the *t*
3: 8 kings of the Amorites the *t* east
3: 12 the Gadites the *t* north of Aroer
3: 16 the Gadites I gave the *t* extending
11: 30 in the *t* of those Canaanites living
12: 20 your God has enlarged your *t*
19: 8 LORD your God enlarges your *t,*
34: 2 the *t* of Ephraim and Manasseh,
Jos 1: 4 Your *t* will extend from the desert
11: 22 No Anakites were left in Israelite *t;*
Jos 12: 1 and whose *t* they took over east
12: 4 And the *t* of Og king of Bashan,
13: 3 as Canaanite (the *t* of the five
13: 3 the east of Egypt to the *t* of Ekron
13: 11 the *t* of the people of Geshur
13: 16 The *t* from Aroer on the rim
13: 25 clan by clan: The *t* of Jazer,
13: 26 Mahanaim to the *t* of Debir; and
13: 27 the *t* up to the end of the Sea
13: 30 The *t* extending from Mahanaim
15: 1 extended down to the *t* of Edom,
16: 2 crossed over to the *t* of the Arkites
16: 3 westward to the *t* of the Japhletites
16: 5 This was the *t* of Ephraim,
17: 7 The *t* of Manasseh extended
17: 10 The *t* of Manasseh reached the sea
18: 5 is to remain in its *t* on the south
18: 5 of Joseph in its *t* on the north.
18: 11 Their allotted *t* lay
19: 1 lay within the *t* of Judah.
19: 9 inheritance within the *t* of Judah.
19: 12 Sarid toward the sunrise to the *t*
19: 18 Their *t* included: Jezreel, Kesulloth
19: 25 Their *t* included: Helkath, Hali,
19: 41 The *t* of their inheritance included:
19: 47 taking possession of their *t,*
21: 41 towns of the Levites in the *t* held
Jdg 1: 3 up with us into the *t* allotted to us,
1: 18 and Ekron—each city with its *t.*
11: 18 They did not enter the *t* of Moab,
11: 20 Israel to pass through his *t.*
1Sa 6: 1 been in Philistine *t* seven months,
6: 9 its own *t,* toward Beth Shemesh,
7: 13 and did not invade Israelite *t* again.
7: 14 Israel delivered the neighboring *t*
9: 4 passed through the *t* of Benjamin,
27: 7 David lived in Philistine *t* a year
27: 11 as long as he lived in Philistine *t.*
30: 14 and the *t* belonging to Judah
1Ki 9: 19 and throughout all the *t* he ruled.
15: 17 entering the *t* of Asa king of Judah.
2Ki 6: 23 Aram stopped raiding Israel's *t.*
10: 32 Israelites throughout their *t* east
18: 8 Philistines, as far as Gaza and its *t.*
24: 7 king of Babylon had taken all his *t,*
1Ch 4: 10 would bless me and enlarge my *t!*
6: 54 as their *t* (they were assigned
6: 66 as their *t* towns from the tribe
2Ch 8: 6 and throughout all the *t* he ruled.
16: 1 entering the *t* of Asa king of Judah.
20: 10 whose *t* you would not allow Israel
34: 33 idols from all the *t* belonging
Jer 1: 1 at Anathoth in the *t* of Benjamin.
17: 26 from the *t* of Benjamin
32: 8 at Anathoth in the *t* of Benjamin.
32: 44 and witnessed in the *t* of Benjamin,
33: 13 of the Negev, in the *t* of Benjamin,
37: 12 the city to go to the *t* of Benjamin
Eze 16: 27 against you and reduced your *t;*
48: 2 it will border the *t* of Dan from east
48: 3 it will border the *t* of Asher
48: 4 it will border the *t* of Naphtali
48: 5 it will border the *t* of Manasseh
48: 6 it will border the *t* of Ephraim
48: 7 it will border the *t* of Reuben
48: 8 ''Bordering the *t* of Judah from east
48: 12 bordering the *t* of the Levites.
48: 13 ''Alongside the *t* of the priests,
48: 24 it will border the *t* of Benjamin
48: 25 it will border the *t* of Simeon
48: 26 it will border the *t* of Issachar
48: 27 it will border the *t* of Zebulun
2Co 10: 16 done in another man's *t.*

TERROR (TERRIBLE TERRIFIED TERRIFIES TERRIFY TERRIFYING TERRORISTS TERRORS)

Ge 35: 5 the *t* of God fell upon the towns all
Ex 15: 16 *t* and dread will fall upon them.
23: 27 ''I will send my *t* ahead of you
Lev 26: 16 I will bring upon you sudden *t,*
Dt 2: 25 very day I will begin to put the *t*
11: 25 will put the *t* and fear of you
26: 8 great *t* and with miraculous signs
28: 67 of the *t* that will fill your hearts
32: 25 in their homes *t* will reign.
1Sa 11: 7 Then the *t* of the LORD fell
28: 5 he was afraid; *t* filled his heart.
2Sa 17: 2 I would strike him with *t,*
2Ch 14: 14 for the *t* of the LORD had fallen
Job 9: 34 so that his *t* would frighten me no
15: 24 Distress and anguish fill him with *t;*
39: 20 striking *t* with his proud snorting?
Ps 9: 20 Strike them with *t,* O LORD;
31: 13 there is *t* on every side;
48: 5 they fled in *t.*
78: 33 and their years in *t.*
91: 5 You will not fear the *t* of night,
Pr 21: 15 but *t* to evildoers.
Isa 13: 8 *T* will seize them,
17: 14 In the evening, sudden *t!*
19: 17 And the land of Judah will bring *t*
21: 1 from a land of *t.*
22: 5 a day of tumult and trampling and *t*
24: 17 *T* and pit and snare await you,
24: 18 Whoever flees at the sound of *t*
28: 19 will bring sheer *t.*
31: 9 stronghold will fall because of *t;*
33: 18 you will ponder the former *t:*
44: 11 they will be brought down to *t*
47: 12 perhaps you will cause *t.*
51: 13 live in constant *t* every day
54: 14 *T* will be far removed;
Jer 6: 25 and there is *t* on every side.
8: 15 but there was only *t.*
14: 19 but there is only *t.*
15: 8 anguish and *t.*
17: 17 Do not be a *t* to me;
17: 18 but keep me from *t.*
20: 4 'I will make you a *t* to yourself
20: 10 ''*T* on every side!
30: 5 *t,* not peace.
32: 21 outstretched arm and with great *t.*
46: 5 and there is *t* on every side,''
48: 43 *T* and pit and snare await you,
48: 44 ''Whoever flees from the *t*
49: 5 I will bring *t* on you
49: 16 The *t* you inspire
49: 29 '*T* on every side!'
50: 2 Marduk filled with *t.*
50: 2 and her idols filled with *t.*'
50: 36 They will be filled with *t.*
50: 38 idols that will go mad with *t.*
La 3: 47 We have suffered *t* and pitfalls,
Eze 7: 18 on sackcloth and be clothed with *t.*
7: 25 When *t* comes, they will seek peace
23: 46 give them over to *t* and plunder.
26: 16 Clothed with *t,* they will sit
26: 17 you put your *t*
32: 23 All who had spread *t* in the land
32: 24 All who had spread *t* in the land
32: 25 Because their *t* had spread
32: 26 they spread their *t* in the land
32: 27 the *t* of these warriors had stalked
32: 30 in disgrace despite the *t* caused
32: 32 Although I had him spread *t*
Da 10: 7 but such *t* overwhelmed them that
Am 6: 3 and bring near a reign of *t.*
Lk 21: 26 Men will faint from *t,* apprehensive
Ro 13: 3 For rulers hold no *t*
Rev 11: 11 and *t* struck those who saw them.

TERRORISTS (TERROR)

Ac 21: 38 and led four thousand *t* out

TERRORS (TERROR)

Job 6: 4 God's *t* are marshaled against me.
13: 21 and stop frightening me with your *t*
18: 11 *T* startle him on every side
18: 14 and marched off to the king of *t.*
20: 25 *T* will come over him;
24: 17 with the *t* of darkness.
27: 20 *T* overtake him like a flood;
30: 15 *T* overwhelm me;
Ps 55: 4 the *t* of death assail me.
73: 19 completely swept away by *t!*
88: 15 I have suffered your *t* and am
88: 16 your *t* have destroyed me.
SS 3: 8 prepared for the *t* of the night.
La 2: 22 against me *t* on every side.

TERTIUS

Ro 16: 22 I, *T,* who wrote down this letter,

TERTULLUS

Ac 24: 1 of the elders and a lawyer named *T*

Ac 24: 2 *T* presented his case before Felix:

TEST (TESTED TESTER TESTING TESTINGS TESTS)

Ex 16: 4 In this way I will *t* them and see
17: 2 Why do you put the LORD to the *t*
20: 20 God has come to *t* you,
Dt 6: 16 Do not *t* the LORD your God
8: 2 to *t* you in order to know what was
8: 16 to *t* you so that in the end it might
Jdg 2: 22 I will use them to *t* Israel and see
3: 1 to *t* all those Israelites who had not
3: 4 They were left to *t* the Israelites
6: 39 Allow me one more *t*
1Ki 10: 1 came to *t* him with hard questions.
1Ch 29: 17 that you *t* the heart and are pleased
2Ch 9: 1 came to Jerusalem to *t* him
32: 31 God left him to *t* him
Job 7: 18 and *t* him every moment?
12: 11 Does not the ear *t* words
Ps 17: 3 you *t* me, you will find nothing;
26: 2 *T* me, O LORD, and try me,
78: 18 They willfully put God to the *t*
78: 41 and again they put God to the *t;*
78: 56 But they put God to the *t*
106: 14 wasteland they put God to the *t*.
139: 23 *t* me and know my anxious
Ecc 2: 1 I will *t* you with pleasure
Isa 7: 12 I will not put the LORD to the *t*.''
Jer 6: 27 and *t* their ways.
9: 7 "See, I will refine and *t* them,
11: 20 and *t* the heart and mind,
12: 3 *t* my thoughts about you.
La 3: 40 us examine our ways and *t* them,
Da 1: 12 Please *t* your servants for ten days:
Zec 13: 9 and *t* them like gold.
Mal 3: 10 *T* me in this,'' says the LORD
Mt 4: 7 put the Lord your God to the *t*.' ''
19: 3 Pharisees came to him to *t* him.
Mk 8: 11 To *t* him, they asked him for a sign
Lk 4: 12 put the Lord your God to the *t*.' ''
10: 25 in the law stood up to *t* Jesus.
Jn 6: 6 He asked this only to *t* him,
Ac 5: 9 How could you agree to *t* the Spirit
15: 10 why do you try to *t* God by putting
Ro 12: 2 Then you will be able to *t*
1Co 3: 13 and the fire will *t* the quality
10: 9 We should not *t* the Lord,
2Co 2: 9 was to see if you would stand the *t*
8: 8 but I want to *t* the sincerity
13: 5 unless, of course, you fail the *t?*
13: 5 you are in the faith; *t* yourselves.
13: 6 that we have not failed the *t*.
13: 7 will see that we have stood the *t*
Gal 6: 4 Each one should *t* his own actions.
1Th 5: 21 *T* everything.
Jas 1: 12 because when he has stood the *t*,
1Jn 4: 1 *t* the spirits to see whether they are
Rev 2: 10 some of you in prison to *t* you,
3: 10 world to *t* those who live

TESTED (TEST)

Ge 22: 1 Some time later God *t* Abraham.
42: 15 And this is how you will be *t:*
42: 16 so that your words may be *t* to see
Ex 15: 25 a law for them, and there he *t* them.
17: 7 because they *t* the LORD saying,
Nu 14: 22 disobeyed me and *t* me ten times—
Dt 33: 8 You *t* him at Massah;
Job 23: 10 when he has *t* me, I will come forth
28: 27 he confirmed it and *t* it.
34: 36 that Job might be *t* to the utmost
Ps 66: 10 For you, O God, *t* us;
81: 7 I *t* you at the waters of Meribah.
95: 9 where your fathers *t* and tried me,
119:140 promises have been thoroughly *t*,
Pr 27: 21 man is *t* by the praise he receives.
Ecc 7: 23 All this I *t* by wisdom and I said,
Isa 28: 16 a *t* stone,
48: 10 I have *t* you in the furnace
Da 1: 14 to this and *t* them for ten days.
Mt 16: 1 and *t* him by asking him
22: 35 in the law, *t* him with this question:
Mk 10: 2 Some Pharisees came and *t* him
Lk 11: 16 Others *t* him by asking for a sign
Ac 20: 19 I was severely *t* by the plots
Ro 16: 10 Greet Apelles, *t* and approved
1Ti 3: 10 They must first be *t;* and then
Heb 3: 9 where your fathers *t* and tried me
11: 17 By faith Abraham, when God *t* him
Rev 2: 2 that you have *t* those who claim

TESTER (TEST)

Jer 6: 27 "I have made you a *t* of metals

TESTICLES

Lev 21: 20 or running sores or damaged *t*.
22: 24 an animal whose *t* are bruised,

TESTIFIED (TESTIFY)

2Sa 1: 16 Your own mouth *t* against you
2Ch 24: 19 and though they *t* against them,
Mk 14: 56 Many *t* falsely against him,
Jn 3: 26 the one you *t* about—well,
5: 33 to John and he has *t* to the truth.
5: 37 me has himself *t* concerning me.
13: 21 Jesus was troubled in spirit and *t*,
Ac 6: 13 produced false witnesses, who *t*,
8: 25 When they had *t* and proclaimed
13: 22 He *t* concerning him: 'I have found
23: 11 As you have *t* about me
1Co 15: 15 for we have *t* about God that he
Heb 2: 4 God also *t* to it by signs, wonders
2: 6 is a place where someone has *t:*

TESTIFIES (TESTIFY)

Job 16: 8 my gauntness rises up and *t*
Isa 3: 9 look on their faces *t* against them;
Hos 5: 5 Israel's arrogance *t* against them;
7: 10 Israel's arrogance *t* against him,
Jn 1: 15 John *t* concerning him.
3: 32 He *t* to what he has seen and heard,
5: 32 There is another who *t* in my favor,
5: 36 *t* that the Father has sent me.
8: 18 I am one who *t* for myself;
19: 35 he *t* so that you also may believe.
21: 24 This is the disciple who *t*
Ro 8: 16 The Spirit himself *t*
2Co 1: 12 Our conscience *t* that we have
Heb 10: 15 The Holy Spirit also *t*
1Jn 5: 6 And it is the Spirit who *t*,
Rev 1: 2 who *t* to everything he saw—
22: 20 He who *t* to these things says, "Yes

TESTIFY (TESTIFIED TESTIFIES TESTIFYING TESTIMONY)

Ge 30: 33 And my honesty will *t* for me
Lev 5: 1 to *t* regarding something he has
Dt 8: 19 I *t* against you today that you will
31: 21 this song will *t* against them,
31: 28 and earth to *t* against them.
1Sa 12: 3 *T* against me in the presence
1Ki 21: 10 have them *t* that he has cursed both
Job 15: 6 your own lips *t* against you.
Ps 50: 7 O Israel, and I will *t* against you:
Pr 24: 28 Do not *t* against your neighbor
29: 24 he is put under oath and dare not *t*.
Isa 59: 12 and our sins *t* against us.
Jer 14: 7 Although our sins *t* against us,
Am 3: 13 and *t* against the house of Jacob,"
Zep 3: 8 "for the day I will stand up to *t*.
Mal 3: 5 I will be quick to *t* against sorcerers
Mt 23: 31 you *t* against yourselves that you
Lk 11: 48 So you *t* that you approve
Jn 1: 7 a witness to *t* concerning that light,
1: 34 and I *t* that this is the Son of God."
3: 11 and we *t* to what we have seen
3: 28 You yourselves can *t* that I said,
5: 31 "If I *t* about myself, my testimony
5: 39 are the Scriptures that *t* about me,
7: 7 because I *t* that what it does is evil.
8: 14 "Even if I *t* on my own behalf,
15: 26 he will *t* about me; but you
15: 27 about me; but you also must *t*,
18: 23 Jesus replied, "*t* as to what is
18: 37 into the world, to *t* to the truth.
Ac 4: 33 continued to *t* to the resurrection
10: 42 to *t* that he is the one whom God
10: 43 All the prophets *t* about him that
22: 5 priest and all the council can *t*.
23: 11 so you must also *t* in Rome."
26: 5 me for a long time and can *t*,
26: 22 and so I stand here and *t* to small
Ro 3: 21 which the Law and the Prophets *t*.
10: 2 For I can *t* about them that they
2Co 8: 3 For I *t* that they gave as much
Gal 4: 15 I can *t* that, if you could have done
Php 1: 8 God can *t* how I long for all of you
2Ti 1: 8 ashamed to *t* about our Lord,
Jas 5: 3 Their corrosion will *t* against you
1Jn 1: 2 we have seen it and *t* to it,
4: 14 *t* that the Father has sent his Son
5: 7 For there are three that *t:* the Spirit

TESTIFYING (TESTIFY)

Ac 18: 5 *t* to the Jews that Jesus was
20: 24 the task of *t* to the gospel
1Ti 6: 13 while *t* before Pontius Pilate made
Heb 3: 5 *t* to what would be said
1Pe 5: 12 *t* that this is the true grace of God.

TESTIMONY (TESTIFY)

Ex 16: 34 put the manna in front of the *T*,
20: 16 "You shall not give false *t*
23: 2 When you give *t* in a lawsuit,
25: 16 in the ark the *T*, which I will give
25: 21 of the ark and put in the ark the *T*,
25: 22 are over the ark of the *T*,
26: 33 the ark of the *T* behind the curtain.
26: 34 cover on the ark of the *T*
27: 21 the curtain that is in front of the *T*,
30: 6 cover that is over the *T*—
30: 6 is before the ark of the *T*—
30: 26 the ark of the *T*, the table
30: 36 it in front of the *T* in the Tent
31: 7 of the *T* with the atonement cover
31: 18 gave him the two tablets of the *T*,
32: 15 tablets of the *T* in his hands.
34: 29 tablets of the *T* in his hands,
38: 21 tabernacle, the tabernacle of the *T*,
39: 35 the ark of the *T* with its poles
40: 3 Place the ark of the *T* in it
40: 5 incense in front of the ark of the *T*
40: 20 He took the *T* and placed it
40: 21 and shielded the ark of the *T*,
Lev 16: 13 the atonement cover above the *T*,
24: 3 the curtain of the *T* in the Tent
Nu 1: 50 in charge of the tabernacle of the *T*
1: 53 around the tabernacle of the *T*
1: 53 the care of the tabernacle of the *T*."
4: 5 and cover the ark of the *T* with it.
7: 89 cover on the ark of the *T*.
9: 15 the Tent of the *T*, was set up,
10: 11 from above the tabernacle of the *T*.
17: 4 Tent of Meeting in front of the *T*,
17: 7 the LORD in the Tent of the *T*.
17: 8 Moses entered the Tent of the *T*
17: 10 back Aaron's staff in front of the *T*,
18: 2 minister before the Tent of the *T*.
35: 30 death on the *t* of only one witness.
35: 30 only on the *t* of witnesses.
Dt 5: 20 "You shall not give false *t*
17: 6 On the *t* of two or three witnesses
17: 6 death on the *t* of only one witness.
19: 15 matter must be established by the *t*
19: 18 giving false *t* against his brother,
Jos 4: 16 the ark of the *T* to come up out
2Ch 24: 6 of Israel for the Tent of the *T?*"
Pr 12: 17 A truthful witness gives honest *t*,
25: 18 is the man who gives false *t*
Isa 8: 16 Bind up the *t*
8: 20 and to the *t!* If they do not speak
29: 21 with false *t* deprive the innocent
Mt 8: 4 the gift Moses commanded, as a *t*
15: 19 sexual immorality, theft, false *t*
18: 16 matter may be established by the *t*
19: 18 not give false *t*, honor your father
24: 14 preached in the whole world as a *t*
26: 62 What is this *t* that these men are
Mk 1: 44 for your cleansing, as a *t* to them."
6: 11 when you leave, as a *t* against them
10: 19 do not give false *t*, do not defraud,
14: 57 and gave this false *t* against him:
14: 59 Yet even then their *t* did not agree.
14: 60 What is this *t* that these men are
Lk 5: 14 for your cleansing, as a *t* to them."
9: 5 when you leave their town, as a *t*
18: 20 not give false *t*, honor your father
22: 71 "Why do we need any more *t?*
Jn 1: 19 this was John's *t* when the Jews
1: 32 John gave this *t:* "I saw the Spirit
2: 25 He did not need man's *t* about man
3: 11 still you people do not accept our *t*.
3: 32 and heard, but no one accepts his *t*.

Jn 4: 39 in him because of the woman's *t*,
5: 31 about myself, my *t* is not valid.
5: 32 I know that his *t* about me is valid.
5: 34 Not that I accept human *t*;
5: 36 I have *t* weightier than that of John
8: 13 own witness; your *t* is not valid."
8: 14 on my own behalf, my *t* is valid,
8: 17 own Law it is written that the *t*
19: 35 saw it has given *t*, and his *t* is true.
21: 24 We know that his *t* is true.
Ac 7: 44 of *T* with them in the desert.
14: 17 he has not left himself without *t*:
22: 18 will not accept your *t* about me.'
1Co 1: 6 our *t* about Christ was confirmed
2: 1 proclaimed to you the *t* about God.
2Co 13: 1 matter must be established by the *t*
2Th 1: 10 because you believed our *t* to you.
1Ti 2: 6 the *t* given in its proper time.
Tit 1: 13 This *t* is true.
Heb 10: 28 died without mercy on the *t* of two
1Jn 5: 9 We accept man's *t*, but God's
5: 9 but God's *t* is greater because it is
5: 9 is greater because it is the *t*
5: 10 Son of God has this *t* in his heart.
5: 10 not believed the *t* God has given
5: 11 And this is the *t*: God has given us
3Jn : 12 and you know that our *t* is true.
Rev 1: 2 of God and the *t* of Jesus Christ.
1: 9 the word of God and the *t* of Jesus.
6: 9 and the *t* they had maintained.
11: 7 when they have finished their *t*,
12: 11 and by the word of their *t*;
12: 17 commandments and hold to the *t*
15: 5 the tabernacle of *T*, was opened.
17: 6 blood of those who bore *t* to Jesus.
19: 10 For the *t* of Jesus is the spirit
19: 10 your brothers who hold to the *t*
20: 4 because of their *t* for Jesus and
22: 16 to give you this *t* for the churches.

TESTING (TEST)

Dt 13: 3 The LORD your God is *t* you
Eze 21: 13 " '*T* will surely come.
Lk 8: 13 but in the time of *t* they fall away.
Heb 3: 8 during the time of *t* in the desert,
Jas 1: 3 because you know that the *t*

TESTINGS (TEST)

Dt 4: 34 by *t*, by miraculous signs

TESTS (TEST)

Job 34: 3 For the ear *t* words
Pr 17: 3 but the LORD *t* the heart.
Ecc 3: 18 God *t* them so that they may see
1Th 2: 4 but God, who *t* our hearts.

TETHER (TETHERED)

Ge 49: 11 He will *t* his donkey to a vine,

TETHERED (TETHER)

2Ki 7: 10 only *t* horses and donkeys,

TETRARCH

Mt 14: 1 time Herod the *t* heard the reports
Lk 3: 1 and Lysanias *t* of Abilene—
3: 1 his brother Philip *t* of Iturea
3: 1 of Judea, Herod *t* of Galilee,
3: 19 when John rebuked Herod the *t*
9: 7 Herod the *t* heard about all that
Ac 13: 1 been brought up with Herod the *t*)

TEXT

Est 3: 14 A copy of the *t* of the edict was
4: 8 gave him a copy of the *t* of the edict
8: 13 A copy of the *t* of the edict was
Jer 29: 1 This is the *t* of the letter that

THADDAEUS

Mt 10: 3 James son of Alphaeus, and *T*;
Mk 3: 18 Thomas, James son of Alphaeus, *T*,

THANK (THANKED THANKFUL THANKFULNESS THANKING THANKS THANKSGIVING)

Dt 24: 13 Then he will *t* you, and it will be
1Ch 23: 30 also to stand every morning to *t*
2Ch 29: 31 and *t* offerings to the temple
29: 31 brought sacrifices and *t* offerings,
2Ch 33: 16 fellowship and *t* offerings
Ps 50: 14 Sacrifice *t* offerings to God,
50: 23 who sacrifices *t* offerings honors
56: 12 I will present my *t* offerings to you.
107: 22 Let them sacrifice *t* offerings
116: 17 I will sacrifice a *t* offering to you
Jer 17: 26 and *t* offerings to the house
33: 11 of those who bring *t* offerings
Da 2: 23 I *t* and praise you, O God
Am 4: 5 Burn leavened bread as a *t* offering
Lk 17: 9 Would he *t* the servant
18: 11 I *t* you that I am not like all other
Jn 11: 41 I *t* you that you have heard me.
Ro 1: 8 I *t* my God through Jesus Christ
1Co 1: 4 I always *t* God for you
10: 30 because of something I *t* God for?
14: 18 I *t* God that I speak
2Co 8: 16 I *t* God, who put into the heart
Php 1: 3 I *t* my God every time I remember
Col 1: 3 We always *t* God, the Father
1Th 1: 2 We always *t* God for all of you,
2: 13 And we also *t* God continually
3: 9 How can we *t* God enough for you
2Th 1: 3 We ought always to *t* God for you,
2: 13 we ought always to *t* God for you,
1Ti 1: 12 I *t* Christ Jesus our Lord, who has
2Ti 1: 3 I *t* God, whom I serve,
Phm : 4 I always *t* my God as I remember

THANKED (THANK)

Lk 17: 16 himself at Jesus' feet and *t* him—
Ac 28: 15 the sight of these men Paul *t* God

THANKFUL (THANK)

1Co 1: 14 I am *t* that I did not baptize any
Col 3: 15 And be *t*.
4: 2 to prayer, being watchful and *t*.
Heb 12: 28 let us be *t*, and so worship God

THANKFULNESS (THANK)

Lev 7: 12 If he offers it as an expression of *t*,
1Co 10: 30 If I take part in the meal with *t*,
Col 2: 7 taught, and overflowing with *t*.

THANKING (THANK)

1Ch 25: 3 harp in *t* and praising the LORD.

THANKS (THANK)

1Ch 16: 4 to make petition, to give *t*,
16: 7 of *t* to the LORD:
16: 8 Give *t* to the LORD, call
16: 34 Give *t* to the LORD, for he is good;
16: 35 that we may give *t*
16: 41 by name to give *t* to the LORD,
29: 13 Now, our God, we give you *t*,
2Ch 5: 13 to give praise and *t* to the LORD.
7: 3 and they worshiped and gave *t*
7: 6 which were used when he gave *t*,
20: 21 "Give *t* to the LORD,
31: 2 to give *t* and to sing praises
Ne 12: 31 assigned two large choirs to give *t*.
12: 40 choirs that gave *t* then took their
Ps 7: 17 I will give *t* to the LORD
28: 7 and I will give *t* to him in song.
30: 12 my God, I will give you *t* forever.
35: 18 I will give you *t* in the great
75: 1 We give *t* to you, O God,
75: 1 we give *t*, for your Name is near;
100: 4 give *t* to him and praise his name.
105: 1 Give *t* to the LORD, call
106: 1 Give *t* to the LORD, for he is good;
106: 47 that we may give *t*
107: 1 Give *t* to the LORD, for he is good;
107: 8 Let them give *t* to the LORD
107: 15 Let them give *t* to the LORD
107: 21 Let them give *t* to the LORD
107: 31 Let them give *t* to the LORD
118: 1 Give *t* to the LORD, for he is good;
118: 19 I will enter and give *t* to the LORD
118: 21 I will give you *t*, for you answered
118: 28 are my God, and I will give you *t*;
118: 29 Give *t* to the LORD, for he is good;
119: 62 At midnight I rise to give you *t*
136: 1 Give *t* to the LORD, for he is good.
136: 2 Give *t* to the God of gods.
136: 3 Give *t* to the Lord of lords:
136: 26 Give *t* to the God of heaven.
Isa 12: 4 "Give *t* to the LORD, call
Jer 33: 11 "Give *t* to the LORD Almighty,
Da 6: 10 giving *t* to his God, just
Mt 14: 19 he gave *t* and broke the loaves.
15: 36 he had given *t*, he broke them
26: 26 Jesus took bread, gave *t*
26: 27 gave *t* and offered it to them,
Mk 6: 41 he gave *t* and broke the loaves.
8: 6 taken the seven loaves and given *t*,
8: 7 he gave *t* for them also
14: 22 Jesus took bread, gave *t*
14: 23 gave *t* and offered it to them,
Lk 2: 38 she gave *t* to God and spoke about
9: 16 he gave *t* and broke them.
22: 17 After taking the cup, he gave *t*
22: 19 he took bread, gave *t* and broke it,
24: 30 gave *t*, broke it and began to give it
Jn 6: 11 Jesus then took the loaves, gave *t*,
6: 23 bread after the Lord had given *t*.
Ac 27: 35 gave *t* to God in front of them all.
Ro 1: 21 as God nor gave *t* to him,
6: 17 leads to righteousness? But *t* be
7: 25 *T* be to God—through Jesus
14: 6 for he gives *t* to God; and he who
14: 6 so to the Lord and gives *t* to God.
1Co 10: 16 for which we give *t* a participation
11: 24 when he had given *t*, he broke it
14: 17 You may be giving *t* well enough,
15: 57 *t* be to God! He gives us the victory
2Co 1: 11 Then many will give *t* on our behalf
2: 14 *t* be to God, who always leads us
9: 12 in many expressions of *t* to God.
9: 15 *T* be to God for his indescribable
Eph 1: 16 I have not stopped giving *t* for you,
5: 20 always giving *t* to God the Father
Col 1: 12 and joyfully giving *t* to the Father,
3: 17 giving *t* to God the Father
1Th 5: 18 give *t* in all circumstances,
Rev 4: 9 and *t* to him who sits on the throne
7: 12 and wisdom and *t* and honor
11: 17 "We give *t* to you, Lord God

THANKSGIVING (THANK)

Lev 7: 12 along with this sacrifice of *t* he is
7: 13 his fellowship offering of *t* he is
7: 15 fellowship offering of *t* must be
22: 29 an offering of *t* to the LORD,
Ezr 3: 11 and *t* they sang to the LORD:
Ne 11: 17 the director who led in *t* and prayer
12: 8 was in charge of the songs of *t*.
12: 24 opposite them to give praise and *t*,
12: 27 the dedication with songs of *t*
12: 46 for the songs of praise and *t* to God
Ps 42: 4 with shouts of joy and *t*
69: 30 and glorify him with *t*.
95: 2 Let us come before him with *t*
100: 4 Enter his gates with *t*
147: 7 Sing to the LORD with *t*;
Isa 51: 3 *t* and the sound of singing.
Jer 30: 19 From them will come songs of *t*
Jnh 2: 9 But I, with a song of *t*,
1Co 10: 16 cup of *t* for which we give thanks
14: 16 understand say "Amen" to your *t*,
2Co 4: 15 and more people may cause *t*
9: 11 us your generosity will result in *t*
Eph 5: 4 which are out of place, but rather *t*.
Php 4: 6 by prayer and petition, with *t*,
1Ti 2: 1 and *t* be made for everyone—
4: 3 created to be received with *t*
4: 4 to be rejected if it is received with *t*

THAWING

Job 6: 16 overflow when darkened by *t* ice

THEATER

Ac 19: 29 and rushed as one man into the *t*.
19: 31 not to venture into the *t*.

THEBES

Jer 46: 25 punishment on Amon god of *T*,
Eze 30: 14 and inflict punishment on *T*.
30: 15 and cut off the hordes of *T*.
30: 16 *T* will be taken by storm;
Na 3: 8 Are you better than *T*,

THEBEZ

Jdg 9: 50 Next Abimelech went to *T*
2Sa 11: 21 died in *T*? Why did you get

THEFT (THIEF)
Ex 22: 3 he must be sold to pay for his *t*.
Mt 15: 19 sexual immorality, *t*, false
Mk 7: 21 sexual immorality, *t*, murder,

THEFTS (THIEF)
Rev 9: 21 their sexual immorality or their *t*.

THEME
Ps 45: 1 My heart is stirred by a noble *t*
119: 54 Your decrees are the *t* of my song

THEOPHILUS
Lk 1: 3 most excellent *T*, so that you may
Ac 1: 1 *T*, I wrote about all that Jesus

THESSALONIANS (THESSALONICA)
Ac 17: 11 of more noble character than the *T*,
1Th 1: 1 church of the *T* in God the Father
2Th 1: 1 church of the *T* in God our Father

THESSALONICA (THESSALONIANS)
Ac 17: 1 to *T*, where there was a Jewish
17: 13 the Jews in *T* learned that Paul was
20: 4 Aristarchus and Secundus from *T*,
27: 2 a Macedonian from *T*, was with us.
Php 4: 16 you only; for even when I was in *T*,
2Ti 4: 10 has deserted me and has gone to *T*.

THEUDAS
Ac 5: 36 Some time ago *T* appeared,

THICKET (THICKETS)
Ge 22: 13 there in a *t* he saw a ram caught
Job 38: 40 or lie in wait in a *t*?
Ps 74: 5 to cut through a *t* of trees.
Hos 2: 12 I will make them a *t*,
Am 3: 4 Does a lion roar in the *t*
Zec 11: 3 the lush *t* of the Jordan is ruined!

THICKETS (THICKET)
1Sa 13: 6 in caves and *t*, among the rocks,
Isa 9: 18 it sets the forest *t* ablaze,
10: 34 down the forest *t* with an ax;
17: 9 will be like places abandoned to *t*
21: 13 who camp in the *t* of Arabia,
Jer 4: 29 Some go into the *t*;
12: 5 manage in the *t* by the Jordan?
26: 18 hill a mound overgrown with *t*.'
49: 19 a lion coming up from Jordan's *t*
50: 44 a lion coming up from Jordan's *t*
Mic 3: 12 hill a mound overgrown with *t*.

THIEF (THEFT THEFTS THIEVES)
Ex 22: 2 "If a *t* is caught breaking in
22: 3 A *t* must certainly make restitution
22: 7 the *t*, if he is caught, must pay back
22: 8 But if the *t* is not found, the owner
Job 24: 14 in the night he steals forth like a *t*.
Ps 50: 18 When you see a *t*, you join
Pr 6: 30 Men do not despise a *t* if he steals
29: 24 of a *t* is his own enemy;
Jer 2: 26 "As a *t* is disgraced
Zec 5: 3 one side, every *t* will be banished,
5: 4 and it will enter the house of the *t*
Mt 24: 43 time of night the *t* was coming,
Lk 12: 33 where no *t* comes near
12: 39 at what hour the *t* was coming,
Jn 10: 1 climbs in by some other way, is a *t*
10: 10 The *t* comes only to steal and kill
12: 6 the poor but because he was a *t*;
1Th 5: 2 day of the Lord will come like a *t*
5: 4 day should surprise you like a *t*.
1Pe 4: 15 or *t* or any other kind of criminal,
2Pe 3: 10 day of the Lord will come like a *t*.
Rev 3: 3 do not wake up, I will come like a *t*,
16: 15 I come like a *t*! Blessed is he who

THIEVES (THIEF)
Job 30: 5 shouted at as if they were *t*.
Isa 1: 23 companions of *t*;
Jer 48: 27 Was she caught among *t*,
49: 9 If *t* came during the night,
Hos 7: 1 *t* break into houses,
Joel 2: 9 *t* they enter through the windows.
Ob : 5 "If *t* came to you,
Mt 6: 19 and where *t* break in and steal.
6: 20 and where *t* do not break in
Jn 10: 8 who ever came before me were *t*
1Co 6: 10 nor homosexual offenders nor *t*

THIGH (THIGHS)
Ge 24: 2 "Put your hand under my *t*.
24: 9 under the *t* of his master Abraham
47: 29 put your hand under my *t*
Ex 28: 42 reaching from the waist to the *t*.
29: 22 fat around them, and the right *t*.
29: 27 and the *t* that was presented.
Lev 7: 32 give the right *t* of your fellowship
7: 33 offering shall have the right *t*
7: 34 is waved and the *t* that is presented
8: 25 and their fat and the right *t*.
8: 26 the fat portions and on the right *t*.
9: 21 and the right *t* before the LORD
10: 14 and the *t* that was presented.
10: 15 The *t* that was presented
Nu 5: 21 causes your *t* to waste away
5: 22 swells and your *t* wastes away."
5: 27 will swell and her *t* waste away,
6: 20 and the *t* that was presented.
18: 18 offering and the right *t* are yours.
Jdg 3: 16 to his right *t* under his clothing.
3: 21 drew the sword from his right *t*
Rev 19: 16 on his *t* he has this name written:

THIGHS (THIGH)
Job 40: 17 the sinews of his *t* are close-knit.
Da 2: 32 and *t* of bronze, its legs of iron,

THINK (THINKING THINKS THOUGHT THOUGHTS)
Ge 16: 6 "Do with her whatever you *t* best."
Ex 14: 3 Pharaoh will *t*, 'The Israelites are
Jdg 9: 17 to *t* that my father fought for you,
10: 15 Do with us whatever you *t* best,
19: 30 *T* about it! Consider it! Tell us
1Sa 18: 23 "Do you *t* it is a small matter
25: 17 *t* it over and see what you can do,
2Sa 10: 3 "Do you *t* David is honoring your
13: 32 lord should not *t* that they killed
24: 13 *t* it over and decide how I should
1Ki 20: 28 the Arameans *t* the LORD
2Ki 10: 5 you do whatever you *t* best."
1Ch 19: 3 "Do you *t* David is honoring your
Est 4: 13 "Do not *t* that because you are
Job 4: 3 *T* how you have instructed many,
7: 4 When I lie down I *t*, 'How long
7: 13 When I *t* my bed will comfort me
21: 6 When I *t* about this, I am terrified;
23: 15 when I *t* of all this, I fear him.
35: 2 Elihu said: "Do you *t* this is just?
41: 32 one would *t* the deep had white
Ps 35: 25 Do not let them *t*, "Aha, just what
40: 17 may the Lord *t* of me.
63: 6 I *t* of you through the watches
144: 3 the son of man that you *t* of him?
Isa 29: 15 do their work in darkness and *t*,
44: 19 No one stops to *t*,
Jer 15: 15 *t* of how I suffer reproach
23: 27 They *t* the dreams they tell one
26: 14 do with me whatever you *t* is good
44: 21 and *t* about the incense burned
51: 50 and *t* on Jerusalem."
Eze 28: 2 though you *t* you are as wise
28: 6 " 'Because you *t* you are wise,
Zep 1: 12 who *t*, 'The LORD will do nothing,
Zec 7: 10 In your hearts do not *t* evil
11: 12 I told them, "If you *t* it best,
Mt 3: 9 do not *t* you can say to yourselves,
5: 17 "Do not *t* that I have come
6: 7 for they *t* they will be heard
17: 25 "What do you *t*, Simon?" he asked.
18: 12 "What do you *t*? If a man owns
21: 28 "What do you *t*? There was a man
22: 42 "What do you *t* about the Christ?
26: 53 Do you *t* I cannot call
26: 66 What do you *t*?" "He is worthy
Mk 14: 64 What do you *t*?" They all
Lk 10: 36 these three do you *t* was a neighbor
12: 51 Do you *t* I came to bring peace
13: 2 "Do you *t* that these Galileans
13: 4 do you *t* they were more guilty
Jn 5: 39 you *t* that by them you possess
5: 45 "But do not *t* I will accuse you
8: 53 Who do you *t* you are?" Jesus
11: 56 "What do you *t*? Isn't he coming
16: 2 who kills you will *t* he is offering
18: 35 "Do you *t* I am a Jew?" Pilate
Ac 5: 4 What made you *t* of doing such
11: 17 I to *t* that I could oppose God!"
13: 25 he said: 'Who do you *t* I am?
15: 38 Paul did not *t* it wise to take him,
17: 29 we should not *t* that the divine
25: 27 For I *t* it is unreasonable to send
26: 28 "Do you *t* that in such a short time
Ro 1: 28 since they did not *t* it worthwhile
2: 3 do you *t* you will escape God's
12: 3 Do not *t* of yourself more highly
12: 3 but rather *t* of yourself
13: 14 and do not *t* about how
1Co 1: 26 *t* of what you were
7: 26 I *t* that it is good for you to remain
7: 40 I *t* that I too have the Spirit of God.
8: 7 when they eat such food they *t* of it
10: 12 So, if you *t* you are standing firm,
12: 23 parts that we *t* are less honorable
2Co 10: 2 some people who *t* that we live
11: 5 I do not *t* I am in the least inferior
12: 6 so no one will *t* more of me
Php 2: 25 But I *t* it is necessary to send back
3: 15 if on some point you *t* differently,
4: 8 praiseworthy—*t* about such things
1Ti 6: 5 and who *t* that godliness is a means
Heb 7: 4 Just *t* how great he was: Even
10: 29 severely do you *t* a man deserves
Jas 1: 7 man should not *t* he will receive
4: 5 Or do you *t* Scripture says
1Pe 4: 4 They *t* it strange that you do not
2Pe 1: 13 I *t* it is right to refresh your

THINKING (THINK)
Ex 2: 14 Are you *t* of killing me
Dt 1: 41 *t* it easy to go up into the hill
1Sa 9: 5 father will stop *t* about the donkeys
10: 2 father has stopped *t* about them
15: 32 Agag came to him confidently, *t*,
2Ki 7: 12 *t*, 'They will surely come out,
2Ch 32: 1 *t* to conquer them for himself.
Ne 6: 9 were all trying to frighten us, *t*,
Job 1: 5 *t*, "Perhaps my children have
21: 27 "I know full well what you are *t*,
Pr 23: 7 who is always *t* about the cost.
Jer 37: 9 Do not deceive yourselves, *t*,
Da 7: 8 "While I was *t* about the horns,
8: 5 As I was *t* about this, suddenly
Mk 2: 6 of the law were sitting there, *t*
2: 8 spirit that this was what they were *t*
2: 8 "Why are you *t* these things?
Lk 2: 44 *T* he was in their company,
5: 21 of the law began *t* to themselves,
5: 22 Jesus knew what they were *t*
5: 22 "Why are you *t* these things
6: 8 But Jesus knew what they were *t*
24: 37 and frightened, *t* they saw a ghost.
Jn 20: 15 *T* he was the gardener, she said,
Ac 10: 19 Peter was still *t* about the vision,
14: 19 him outside the city, *t* he was dead.
Ro 1: 21 but their *t* became futile
1Co 14: 20 Brothers, stop *t* like children.
14: 20 but in your *t* be adults.
2Co 12: 19 Have you been *t* all
Eph 4: 17 in the futility of their *t*.
Heb 11: 15 If they had been *t* of the country
2Pe 3: 1 to stimulate you to wholesome *t*.

THINKS (THINK)
Dt 29: 19 blessing on himself and therefore *t*,
2Sa 16: 3 staying in Jerusalem, because he *t*,
Est 8: 5 and *t* it the right thing to do,
Job 24: 15 he *t*, 'No eye will see me,'
Lk 8: 18 even what he *t* he has will be taken
1Co 3: 18 If any one of you *t* he is wise
7: 36 If anyone *t* he is acting improperly
8: 2 man who *t* he knows something
14: 37 If anybody *t* he is a prophet
Gal 6: 3 If anyone *t* he is something
Php 3: 4 If anyone else *t* he has reasons

THIRST (THIRSTS THIRSTY)
Ex 17: 3 our children and livestock die of *t*
Dt 28: 48 in hunger and *t*, in nakedness
Jdg 15: 18 Must I now die of *t* and fall
2Ch 32: 11 to let you die of hunger and *t*.
Ne 9: 15 in their *t* you brought them water

Ps 92: 5 how profound your *t*!
94: 11 The LORD knows the *t* of man;
139: 2 you perceive my *t* from afar
139: 17 How precious to me are your *t*,
139: 23 test me and know my anxious *t*.
Pr 1: 23 and made my *t* known to you.
15: 26 The LORD detests the *t*
Ecc 2: 12 I turned my *t* to consider wisdom,
10: 20 not revile the king even in your *t*,
Isa 33: 18 In your *t* you will ponder
55: 7 and the evil man his *t*.
55: 8 "For my *t* are not your *t*,
55: 9 and my *t* than your *t*.
59: 7 Their *t* are evil *t*;
Jer 4: 14 How long will you harbor wicked *t*
12: 3 you see me and test my *t* about you
Eze 38: 10 On that day *t* will come
Da 4: 19 for a time, and his *t* alarmed him.
7: 28 was deeply troubled by my *t*,
Am 4: 13 and reveals his *t* to man,
Mic 4: 12 the *t* of the LORD;
Mt 9: 4 Knowing their *t*, Jesus said,
9: 4 "Why do you entertain evil *t*
12: 25 Jesus knew their *t* and said to them
15: 19 For out of the heart come evil *t*,
Mk 7: 21 come evil *t*, sexual immorality,
Lk 1: 51 who are proud in their inmost *t*.
2: 35 so that the *t* of many hearts will be
9: 47 knowing their *t*, took a little child
11: 17 Jesus knew their *t* and said to them
Ro 2: 15 and their *t* now accusing, now
1Co 2: 11 among men knows the *t* of a man
2: 11 the same way no one knows the *t*
3: 20 "The Lord knows that the *t*
Eph 2: 3 and following its desires and *t*.
Heb 3: 1 in the heavenly calling, fix your *t*
4: 12 it judges the *t* and attitudes
Jas 2: 4 and become judges with evil *t*?

THRASHING

Job 41: 25 they retreat before his *t*.
Eze 32: 2 *t* about in your streams,

THREAD (THREADS)

Ge 14: 23 not even a *t* or the thong of a sandal
38: 28 so the midwife took a scarlet *t*
38: 30 who had the scarlet *t* on his wrist,

THREADS (THREAD)

Jdg 16: 12 ropes off his arms as if they were *t*.

THREAT (THREATEN THREATENED THREATS)

Ezr 4: 22 Why let this *t* grow,
Ne 4: 9 guard day and night to meet this *t*.
Ps 64: 1 from the *t* of the enemy.
Pr 13: 8 but a poor man hears no *t*.
Isa 30: 17 at the *t* of five
30: 17 flee at the *t* of one;

THREATEN (THREAT)

Ps 73: 8 their arrogance they *t* oppression.
Eze 6: 10 I did not *t* in vain to bring this
Eph 6: 9 Do not *t* them, since you know that

THREATENED (THREAT)

Ex 32: 14 on his people the disaster he had *t*.
Jos 23: 15 bring on you all the evil he has *t*,
Jer 27: 13 the LORD has *t* any nation that
Jnh 1: 4 a violent storm arose that the ship *t*
2: 5 The engulfing waters *t* me,
3: 10 upon them the destruction he had *t*

THREATS (THREAT)

Ps 10: 7 of curses and lies and *t*;
55: 11 *t* and lies never leave its streets.
Jer 44: 29 'so that you will know that my *t*
Zep 2: 8 and made *t* against their land.
Ac 4: 21 After further *t* they let them go.
4: 29 consider their *t* and enable your
9: 1 was still breathing out murderous *t*
1Pe 2: 23 when he suffered, he made no *t*.

THREE

Ge 6: 10 Noah had *t* sons: Shem, Ham
7: 13 and the wives of his *t* sons,
9: 19 These were the *t* sons of Noah,
15: 9 a goat and a ram, each *t* years old,
18: 2 and saw *t* men standing nearby.
18: 6 get *t* seahs of fine flour and knead it
29: 2 with *t* flocks of sheep lying near it
29: 34 because I have borne him *t* sons."
34: 25 *T* days later, while all
38: 24 About *t* months later Judah was
40: 10 and on the vine were *t* branches.
40: 12 "The *t* branches are *t* days.
40: 13 Within *t* days Pharaoh will lift up
40: 16 On my head were *t* baskets
40: 18 "The *t* baskets are *t* days.
40: 19 Within *t* days Pharaoh will lift
42: 17 all in custody for *t* days.
45: 22 he gave *t* hundred shekels
Ex 2: 2 child, she hid him for *t* months.
10: 22 covered all Egypt for *t* days.
10: 23 or leave his place for *t* days.
15: 22 For *t* days they traveled
21: 11 her with these *t* things,
23: 14 "*T* times a year you are
23: 17 "*T* times a year all the men are
25: 32 *t* on one side and *t* on the other.
25: 33 *T* cups shaped like almond flowers
25: 33 *t* on the next branch, and the same
27: 1 altar of acacia wood, *t* cubits high;
27: 14 with *t* posts and *t* bases,
27: 15 with *t* posts and *t* bases.
32: 28 and that day about *t* thousand
34: 23 *T* times a year all your men are
34: 24 when you go up *t* times each year
37: 18 *t* on one side and *t* on the other.
37: 19 *T* cups shaped like almond flowers
37: 19 *t* on the next branch and the same
38: 1 *t* cubits high; it was square,
38: 14 with *t* posts and *t* bases,
38: 15 with *t* posts and *t* bases.
Lev 19: 23 For *t* years you are
25: 21 land will yield enough for *t* years.
27: 6 of a female at *t* shekels of silver.
Nu 10: 33 before them during those *t* days
10: 33 the LORD and traveled for *t* days.
11: 31 to about *t* feet above the ground,
12: 4 So the *t* of them came out.
12: 4 to the Tent of Meeting, all *t* of you
22: 28 to make you beat me these *t* times
22: 32 beaten your donkey these *t* times?
22: 33 turned away from me these *t* times.
24: 10 have blessed them these *t* times.
33: 8 traveled for *t* days in the Desert
35: 5 and *t* thousand on the north,
35: 5 measure *t* thousand feet
35: 5 *t* thousand on the south side,
35: 5 *t* thousand on the west
35: 14 Give *t* on this side of the Jordan
35: 14 and *t* in Canaan as cities of refuge.
Dt 4: 41 Then Moses set aside *t* cities east
14: 28 At the end of every *t* years,
16: 16 *T* times a year all your men must
17: 6 or *t* witnesses a man shall be put
19: 2 for yourselves *t* cities centrally
19: 3 into *t* parts the land the LORD
19: 7 to set aside for yourselves *t* cities.
19: 9 are to set aside *t* more cities.
19: 15 the testimony of two or *t* witnesses.
Jos 1: 11 *T* days from now you will cross
2: 16 Hide yourselves there *t* days
2: 22 the hills and stayed there *t* days,
3: 2 After *t* days the officers went
7: 3 or *t* thousand men to take it
7: 4 So about *t* thousand men went up;
9: 16 *T* days after they made the treaty
15: 14 Caleb drove out the *t* Anakites—
18: 4 Appoint *t* men from each tribe.
21: 32 with their pasturelands—*t* towns.
Jdg 1: 20 drove from it the *t* sons of Anak.
7: 6 *T* hundred men lapped
7: 7 "With the *t* hundred men that
7: 8 their tents but kept the *t* hundred,
7: 16 Dividing the *t* hundred men
7: 16 hundred men into *t* companies,
7: 20 The *t* companies blew the trumpets
7: 22 When the *t* hundred trumpets
8: 4 Gideon and his *t* hundred men,
9: 22 had governed Israel *t* years,
9: 43 divided them into *t* companies
11: 26 For *t* hundred years Israel
14: 14 For *t* days they could not give
15: 4 and caught *t* hundred foxes
15: 11 *t* thousand men from Judah went
16: 27 roof were about *t* thousand men
19: 4 so he remained with him *t* days,
1Sa 2: 21 birth to *t* sons and two daughters.
9: 20 for the donkeys you lost *t* days ago,
10: 3 *T* men going up to God
10: 3 *t* young goats, another *t* loaves
11: 8 Israel numbered *t* hundred
11: 11 separated his men into *t* divisions;
13: 2 Saul chose *t* thousand men
13: 5 with *t* thousand chariots, six
13: 17 Philistine camp in *t* detachments.
17: 13 Jesse's *t* oldest sons had followed
17: 14 The *t* oldest followed Saul,
20: 20 I will shoot *t* arrows to the side of it
20: 41 down before Jonathan *t* times,
24: 2 Saul took *t* thousand chosen men
25: 2 goats and *t* thousand sheep,
26: 2 with his *t* thousand chosen men
30: 12 water for *t* days and *t* nights.
30: 13 me when I became ill *t* days ago.
31: 6 So Saul and *t* of his sons
31: 8 his *t* sons fallen on Mount Gilboa.
2Sa 2: 18 The *t* sons of Zeruiah were there:
2: 31 David's men had killed *t* hundred
6: 11 the Gittite for *t* months,
13: 38 to Geshur, he stayed there *t* years.
14: 27 *T* sons and a daughter were born
18: 14 So he took *t* javelins in his hand
20: 4 Judah to come to me within *t* days,
21: 1 a famine for *t* successive years;
21: 16 spearhead weighed *t* hundred
23: 8 a Tahkemonite, was chief of the *T*;
23: 9 As one of the *t* mighty men,
23: 13 *t* of the thirty chief men came
23: 16 So the *t* mighty men broke
23: 17 the exploits of the *t* mighty men.
23: 18 so he became as famous as the *T*.
23: 18 son of Zeruiah was chief of the *T*.
23: 18 spear against *t* hundred men,
23: 19 held in greater honor than the *T*?
23: 22 as famous as the *t* mighty men.
23: 23 he was not included among the *T*.
24: 12 says: I am giving you *t* options.
24: 13 Or *t* days of plague in your land?
24: 13 Or *t* months of fleeing
24: 13 come upon you *t* years of famine
1Ki 2: 39 *t* years later, two of Shimei's slaves
4: 32 He spoke *t* thousand proverbs
6: 36 of *t* courses of dressed stone
7: 4 were placed high in sets of *t*,
7: 5 were in the front part in sets of *t*,
7: 12 surrounded by a wall of *t* courses
7: 25 *t* facing north, *t* facing west,
7: 25 *t* facing south and *t* facing east.
7: 27 cubits long, four wide and *t* high.
9: 25 *T* times a year Solomon sacrificed
10: 17 also made *t* hundred small shields
10: 17 with *t* minas of gold in each shield.
10: 22 Once every *t* years it returned
11: 3 and *t* hundred concubines,
12: 5 for *t* days and then come back
12: 12 *T* days later Jeroboam
12: 12 "Come back to me in *t* days."
15: 2 and he reigned in Jerusalem *t* years
17: 21 out on the boy *t* times
22: 1 For *t* years there was no war
2Ki 2: 17 who searched for *t* days
3: 10 LORD called us *t* kings together
3: 13 who called us *t* kings together
9: 32 or *t* eunuchs looked down at him.
11: 5 in the *t* companies that are going
13: 18 He struck it *t* times and stopped.
13: 19 now you will defeat it only *t* times
13: 25 *T* times Jehoash defeated him,
17: 5 and laid siege to it for *t* years.
18: 10 end of *t* years the Assyrians took it.
18: 14 of Judah *t* hundred talents of silver
23: 31 he reigned in Jerusalem *t* months.
24: 1 became his vassal for *t* years.
24: 8 he reigned in Jerusalem *t* months.
25: 18 next in rank and the *t* doorkeepers.
1Ch 2: 3 These *t* were born to him
2: 16 Zeruiah's *t* sons were Abishai,
3: 23 Hizkiah and Azrikam—*t* in all.
7: 6 *T* sons of Benjamin: Bela, Beker
10: 6 So Saul and *t* of his sons died,
11: 11 spear against *t* hundred men,

1Ch 11: 12 one of the *t* mighty men.
11: 15 *T* of the thirty chiefs came
11: 18 the *T* broke through the Philistine
11: 19 the exploits of the *t* mighty men.
11: 20 brother of Joab was chief of the *T*.
11: 20 so he became as famous as the *T*.
11: 20 spear against *t* hundred men,
11: 21 was doubly honored above the *T*
11: 24 as famous as the *t* mighty men.
11: 25 he was not included among the *T*.
12: 39 The men spent *t* days there
13: 14 in his house for *t* months,
21: 10 says: I am giving you *t* options.
21: 12 Take your choice: *t* years of famine
21: 12 or *t* days of the sword of the LORD
21: 12 *t* months of being swept away
23: 8 Zetham and Joel—*t* in all.
23: 9 Haziel and Haran—*t* in all.
23: 23 Eder and Jeremoth—*t* in all.
25: 5 fourteen sons and *t* daughters.
29: 4 *t* thousand talents of gold (gold
2Ch 4: 4 *t* facing north, *t* facing west,
4: 4 *t* facing south and *t* facing east.
4: 5 It held *t* thousand baths.
6: 13 five cubits wide and *t* cubits high,
8: 13 New Moons and the *t* annual feasts
9: 16 also made *t* hundred small shields
9: 16 with *t* hundred bekas of gold
9: 21 Once every *t* years it returned,
10: 5 "Come back to me in *t* days."
10: 12 *T* days later Jeroboam
10: 12 "Come back to me in *t* days."
11: 17 son of Solomon *t* years,
13: 2 and he reigned in Jerusalem *t* years
14: 8 army of *t* hundred thousand men
14: 9 a vast army and *t* hundred chariots,
20: 25 so much plunder that it took *t* days
25: 5 that there were *t* hundred thousand
25: 13 They killed *t* thousand people
29: 33 and *t* thousand sheep and goats.
31: 16 distributed to the males *t* years old
35: 7 and also *t* thousand cattle—
35: 8 offerings and *t* hundred cattle.
36: 2 he reigned in Jerusalem *t* months.
36: 9 he reigned in Jerusalem *t* months
Ezr 6: 4 with *t* courses of large stones
8: 15 and we camped there *t* days.
8: 32 Jerusalem, where we rested *t* days.
10: 8 within *t* days would forfeit all his
10: 9 Within the *t* days, all the men
Ne 2: 11 after staying there *t* days I set out
Est 4: 16 Do not eat or drink for *t* days,
9: 15 to death in Susa *t* hundred men,
Job 1: 2 He had seven sons and *t* daughters,
1: 3 thousand sheep, *t* thousand
1: 4 and they would invite their *t* sisters
1: 17 Chaldeans formed *t* raiding parties
2: 11 When Job's *t* friends, Eliphaz
32: 1 these *t* men stopped answering Job
32: 3 also angry with the *t* friends,
32: 5 he saw that the *t* men had nothing
33: 29 twice, even *t* times—
42: 13 had seven sons and *t* daughters.
Pr 30: 15 "There are *t* things that are never
30: 18 "There are *t* things that are too
30: 21 "Under *t* things the earth trembles,
30: 29 "There are *t* things that are stately
Ecc 4: 12 of *t* strands is not quickly broken.
Isa 16: 14 the LORD says: "Within *t* years,
17: 6 *t* olives on the topmost branches,
20: 3 stripped and barefoot for *t* years,
Jer 36: 23 Whenever Jehudi had read *t*
52: 24 next in rank and the *t* doorkeepers.
Eze 14: 14 even if these *t* men—Noah,
14: 16 even if these *t* men were in it,
14: 18 even if these *t* men were in it,
21: 14 even *t* times.
40: 10 Inside the east gate were *t* alcoves
40: 10 the *t* had the same measurements,
40: 21 Its alcoves—*t* on each side—
40: 48 projecting walls were *t* cubits wide
41: 6 The side rooms were on *t* levels,
41: 16 galleries around the *t* of them—
41: 22 was a wooden altar *t* cubits high
42: 3 gallery faced gallery at the *t* levels.
48: 31 The *t* gates on the north side will be
48: 32 cubits long, will be *t* gates:
48: 33 will be *t* gates: the gate of Simeon,
Eze 48: 34 cubits long, will be *t* gates:
Da 1: 5 They were to be trained for *t* years,
3: 23 and these *t* men, firmly tied,
3: 24 "Wasn't it *t* men that we tied up
6: 2 with *t* administrators over them,
6: 10 *T* times a day he got
6: 13 He still prays *t* times a day."
7: 5 and it had *t* ribs in its mouth
7: 8 *t* of the first horns were uprooted
7: 20 before which *t* of them fell—
7: 24 earlier ones; he will subdue *t* kings.
10: 2 Daniel, mourned for *t* weeks.
10: 3 at all until the *t* weeks were over.
11: 2 *T* more kings will appear in Persia,
Am 1: 3 "For *t* sins of Damascus,
1: 6 "For *t* sins of Gaza,
1: 9 "For *t* sins of Tyre,
1: 11 "For *t* sins of Edom,
1: 13 "For *t* sins of Ammon,
2: 1 "For *t* sins of Moab,
2: 4 "For *t* sins of Judah,
2: 6 "For *t* sins of Israel,
4: 4 your tithes every *t* years.
4: 7 harvest was still *t* months away.
Jnh 1: 17 inside the fish *t* days and *t* nights.
3: 3 it took *t* days to go all through it.
Zec 11: 8 rid of the *t* shepherds.
Mt 12: 40 For as Jonah was *t* days
12: 40 so the Son of Man will be *t* days
12: 40 *t* nights in the belly of a huge fish,
12: 40 *t* nights in the heart of the earth.
15: 32 have already been with me *t* days
17: 4 I will put up *t* shelters—one
18: 16 testimony of two or *t* witnesses.'
18: 20 or *t* come together in my name,
26: 34 you will disown me *t* times."
26: 61 of God and rebuild it in *t* days.' "
26: 75 you will disown me *t* times."
27: 40 the temple and build it in *t* days,
27: 63 'After *t* days I will rise again.'
Mk 8: 2 have already been with me *t* days
8: 31 and after *t* days rise again.
9: 5 Let us put up *t* shelters—one
9: 31 and after *t* days he will rise."
10: 34 *T* days later he will rise."
14: 30 yourself will disown me *t* times."
14: 58 and in *t* days will build another,
14: 72 twice you will disown me *t* times."
15: 29 the temple and build it in *t* days,
Lk 1: 56 with Elizabeth for about *t* months
2: 46 After *t* days they found him
4: 25 when the sky was shut for *t*
9: 33 Let us put up *t* shelters—one
10: 36 "Which of these *t* do you think was
11: 5 'Friend, lend me *t* loaves of bread,
12: 52 *t* against two and two against *t*.
13: 7 'For *t* years now I've been coming
22: 34 you will deny *t* times that you
22: 61 you will disown me *t* times."
Jn 2: 19 and I will raise it again in *t* days."
2: 20 you are going to raise it in *t* days?"
6: 19 When they had rowed *t* or *t*
13: 38 you will disown me *t* times!
Ac 2: 41 and about *t* thousand were added
3: 1 of prayer—at *t* in the afternoon.
5: 7 About *t* hours later his wife came
7: 20 For *t* months he was cared
9: 9 For *t* days he was blind,
10: 3 One day at about *t*
10: 16 This happened *t* times,
10: 19 "Simon, *t* men are looking for you.
10: 30 at this hour, at *t* in the afternoon.
11: 10 This happened *t* times,
11: 11 "Right then *t* men who had been
17: 2 and on *t* Sabbath days he reasoned
19: 8 spoke boldly there for *t* months,
20: 3 where he stayed *t* months.
20: 31 for *t* years I never stopped warning
25: 1 *T* days after arriving
28: 7 for *t* days entertained us hospitably
28: 11 After *t* months we put out to sea
28: 12 at Syracuse and stayed there *t* days
28: 15 and the *T* Taverns to meet us.
28: 17 *T* days later he called together
1Co 13: 13 And now these *t* remain: faith,
14: 27 or at the most *t*—should speak,
14: 29 Two or *t* prophets should speak,
2Co 11: 25 *T* times I was beaten with rods,
2Co 11: 25 *t* times I was shipwrecked,
12: 8 *T* times I pleaded with the Lord
13: 1 testimony of two or *t* witnesses."
Gal 1: 18 Then after *t* years, I went up
1Ti 5: 19 it is brought by two or *t* witnesses.
Heb 10: 28 the testimony of two or *t* witnesses.
11: 23 him for *t* months after he was born,
Jas 5: 17 and it did not rain on the land for *t*
1Jn 5: 7 For there are *t* that testify:
5: 8 and the *t* are in agreement.
Rev 6: 6 *t* quarts of barley for a day's wages,
8: 13 to be sounded by the other *t* angels
9: 18 killed by the *t* plagues of fire,
11: 9 For *t* and a half days men
11: 11 after the *t* and a half days a breath
16: 13 I saw *t* evil spirits that looked like
16: 19 The great city split into *t* parts,
21: 13 There were *t* gates on the east,
21: 13 gates on the east, *t* on the north,
21: 13 *t* on the south and *t* on the west.

THREE-DAY (DAY)

Ge 30: 36 he put a *t* journey between himself
Ex 3: 18 Let us take a *t* journey
5: 3 Now let us take a *t* journey
8: 27 We must take a *t* journey

THRESH (THRESHED THRESHER THRESHES THRESHING)

Isa 27: 12 In that day the LORD will *t*
41: 15 You will *t* the mountains
Hos 10: 11 that loves to *t*;
Mic 4: 13 "Rise and *t*, O Daughter of Zion,

THRESHED (THRESH)

Ru 2: 17 she *t* the barley she had gathered,
Isa 28: 27 Caraway is not *t* with a sledge,
Am 1: 3 Because she *t* Gilead
Hab 3: 12 and in anger you *t* the nations.

THRESHER (THRESH)

1Co 9: 10 plowman plows and the *t* threshes,

THRESHES (THRESH)

1Co 9: 10 plowman plows and the thresher *t*,

THRESHING (THRESH)

Ge 50: 10 When they reached the *t* floor
50: 11 the mourning at the *t* floor of Atad,
Lev 26: 5 Your *t* will continue
Nu 15: 20 as an offering from the *t* floor.
18: 27 as grain from the *t* floor or juice
18: 30 as the product of the *t* floor
Dt 15: 14 your *t* floor and your winepress.
16: 13 the produce of your *t* floor
Jdg 6: 11 where his son Gideon was *t* wheat
6: 37 place a wool fleece on the *t* floor.
Ru 3: 2 be winnowing barley on the *t* floor.
3: 3 Then go down to the *t* floor,
3: 6 So she went down to the *t* floor
3: 14 that a woman came to the *t* floor."
1Sa 23: 1 and are looting the *t* floors,"
2Sa 6: 6 came to the *t* floor of Nacon,
24: 16 then at the *t* floor of Araunah
24: 18 an altar to the LORD on the *t* floor
24: 21 "To buy your *t* floor," David
24: 22 and here are *t* sledges and ox yokes
24: 24 So David bought the *t* floor
1Ki 22: 10 at the *t* floor by the entrance
2Ki 6: 27 From the *t* floor? From
13: 7 made them like the dust at *t* time.
1Ch 13: 9 came to the *t* floor of Kidon,
21: 15 standing at the *t* floor of Araunah
21: 18 an altar to the LORD on the *t* floor
21: 20 While Araunah was *t* wheat,
21: 21 he left the *t* floor and bowed
21: 22 Let me have the site of your *t* floor
21: 23 the *t* sledges for the wood,
21: 28 him on the *t* floor of Araunah
2Ch 3: 1 It was on the *t* floor
18: 9 at the *t* floor by the entrance
Job 39: 12 and gather it to your *t* floor?
41: 30 in the mud like a *t* sledge.
Pr 20: 26 he drives the *t* wheel over them.
Isa 21: 10 O my people, crushed on the *t* floor
28: 28 so one does not go on *t* it forever.
28: 28 the wheels of his *t* cart over it,
41: 15 I will make you into a *t* sledge,

Jer 50: 11 you frolic like a heifer *t* grain
51: 33 of Babylon is like a *t* floor
Da 2: 35 chaff on a *t* floor in the summer.
Hos 9: 1 a prostitute at every *t* floor.
9: 2 *T* floors and winepresses will not
13: 3 like chaff swirling from a *t* floor,
Joel 2: 24 The *t* floors will be filled with grain
Mic 4: 12 them like sheaves to the *t* floor.
Mt 3: 12 and he will clear his *t* floor,
Lk 3: 17 is in his hand to clear his *t* floor

THRESHOLD (THRESHOLDS)

Jdg 19: 27 with her hands on the *t*.
1Sa 5: 4 broken off and were lying on the *t*;
5: 5 temple at Ashdod step on the *t*.
1Ki 14: 17 she stepped over the *t* of the house,
Eze 9: 3 and moved to the *t* of the temple.
10: 4 and moved to the *t* of the temple.
10: 18 from over the *t* of the temple
40: 6 and measured the *t* of the gate;
40: 7 And the *t* of the gate next
41: 16 and including the *t* was covered
43: 8 they placed their *t* next to my *t*
46: 2 is to worship at the *t* of the gateway
47: 1 out from under the *t* of the temple
Zep 1: 9 all who avoid stepping on the *t*,

THRESHOLDS (THRESHOLD)

1Ch 9: 19 for guarding the *t* of the tent just
9: 22 gatekeepers at the *t* numbered 212.
Isa 6: 4 *t* shook and the temple was filled
Eze 41: 16 as the *t* and the narrow windows
Am 9: 1 the pillars so that the *t* shake.

THREW (THROW)

Ge 33: 4 he *t* his arms around his neck
37: 24 and they took him and *t* him
44: 14 they *t* themselves to the ground
45: 14 he *t* his arms around his brother
46: 29 he *t* his arms around his father
50: 1 Joseph *t* himself upon his father
50: 18 and *t* themselves down before him.
Ex 4: 3 Moses *t* it on the ground
7: 10 Aaron *t* his staff down in front
7: 12 Each one *t* down his staff
14. 24 cloud at the Egyptian army and *t* it
15: 7 you *t* down those who opposed you
15: 25 He *t* it into the water,
32: 19 he *t* the tablets out of his hands,
32: 24 they gave me the gold, and I *t* it
Dt 9: 17 and *t* them out of my hands,
9: 21 *t* the dust into a stream that flowed
Jos 10: 10 The LORD *t* them into confusion
10: 27 *t* them into the cave where they
Jdg 8: 25 each man *t* a ring from his plunder
14: 16 Samson's wife *t* herself on him,
15: 17 finished speaking, he *t* away
1Sa 7: 10 *t* them into such a panic that they
2Sa 18: 17 *t* him into a big pit in the forest
20: 12 road into a field and *t* a garment
20: 22 son of Bicri and *t* it to Joab.
1Ki 19: 19 and *t* his cloak around him.
2Ki 2: 21 to the spring and *t* the salt into it,
3: 25 and each man *t* a stone
6: 6 Elisha cut a stick and *t* it there,
9: 33 So they *t* her down, and some
10: 25 and officers *t* the bodies out
13: 21 so they *t* the man's body
23: 12 *t* the rubble into the Kidron Valley.
2Ch 25: 12 and *t* them down so that all were
30: 14 and *t* them into the Kidron Valley.
33: 15 and he *t* them out of the city.
Ne 13: 8 *t* all Tobiah's household goods out
Jer 36: 23 and *t* them into the firepot,
41: 7 him slaughtered them and *t* them
41: 9 the cistern where he *t* all the bodies
La 3: 53 and *t* stones at me;
Eze 28: 17 So I *t* you to the earth;
Da 3: 24 it three men that we tied up and *t*
6: 16 and *t* him into the lions' den.
8: 10 and it *t* some of the starry host
Jnh 1: 5 And they *t* the cargo into the sea
1: 15 took Jonah and *t* him overboard,
Zec 11: 13 *t* them into the house of the LORD
Mt 13: 48 fish in baskets, but *t* the bad away.
21: 39 and *t* him out of the vineyard
27: 5 Judas *t* the money into the temple
Mk 9: 20 it immediately *t* the boy
11: 7 to Jesus and *t* their cloaks over it,
12: 8 and *t* him out of the vineyard.
12: 41 Many rich people *t*
Lk 4: 35 Then the demon *t* the man
9: 42 the demon *t* him to the ground
15: 20 *t* his arms around him
17: 16 He *t* himself at Jesus' feet
19: 35 *t* their cloaks on the colt
20: 12 they wounded him and *t* him out.
20: 15 So they *t* him out of the vineyard
Jn 9: 34 lecture us!'' And they *t* him out.
Ac 16: 37 we are Roman citizens, and *t* us
20: 10 *t* himself on the young man
27: 19 they *t* the ship's tackle overboard
Rev 14: 19 and *t* them into the great winepress
18: 21 the size of a large millstone and *t* it
20: 3 He *t* him into the Abyss,

THRIVE (THRIVES THRIVING)

Dt 31: 20 and when they eat their fill and *t*,
Job 8: 11 Can reeds *t* without water?
39: 4 Their young *t* and grow strong
Ps 72: 16 let it *t* like the grass of the field.
Pr 11: 28 the righteous will *t* like a green leaf.
28: 28 the wicked perish, the righteous *t*.
29: 2 When the righteous *t*, the people
29: 16 When the wicked *t*, so does sin,
Eze 17: 9 Sovereign LORD says: Will it *t*?
17: 10 Even if it is transplanted, will it *t*?
Zec 9: 17 Grain will make the young men *t*,

THRIVES (THRIVE)

Hos 13: 15 though he *t* among his brothers.

THRIVING (THRIVE)

Jer 11: 16 The LORD called you a *t* olive tree

THROAT (THROATS)

Ps 5: 9 Their *t* is an open grave;
69: 3 my *t* is parched.
Pr 23: 2 and put a knife to your *t*
Jer 2: 25 and your *t* is dry.

THROATS (THROAT)

Ps 115: 7 can they utter a sound with their *t*.
Jer 4: 10 when the sword is at our *t*.''
Ro 3: 13 "Their *t* are open graves;

THROB

Isa 60: 5 your heart will *t* and swell with joy;

THROES

2Sa 1: 9 in the *t* of death, but I'm still alive.'

THRONE (ENTHRONED ENTHRONES THRONES)

Ge 41: 40 respect to the *t* will I be greater
Ex 11: 5 sits on the *t*, to the firstborn son
12: 29 who sat on the *t*, to the firstborn
17: 16 up to the *t* of the LORD.
Dt 17: 18 When he takes the *t* of his kingdom
1Sa 2: 8 and has them inherit a *t* of honor.
2Sa 3: 10 and establish David's *t* over Israel
7: 13 and I will establish the *t*
7: 16 your *t* will be established forever
14: 9 and his *t* be without guilt.''
1Ki 1: 13 on my *t*''? Why then has Adonijah
1: 17 after me, and he will sit on my *t*.'
1: 20 sit on the *t* of my lord the king
1: 24 and that he will sit on your *t*?
1: 27 sit on the *t* of my lord the king
1: 30 and he will sit on my *t* in my place
1: 35 sit on my *t* and reign in my place.
1: 37 be with Solomon to make his *t*
1: 37 than the *t* of my lord King David!''
1: 46 has taken his seat on the royal *t*.
1: 47 and his *t* greater than yours!'
1: 48 to see a successor on my *t* today.' ''
2: 4 to have a man on the *t* of Israel.'
2: 12 So Solomon sat on the *t*
2: 19 He had a *t* brought
2: 19 down to her and sat down on his *t*.
2: 24 on the *t* of my father David
2: 33 his *t*, may there be the LORD's
2: 45 and David's *t* will remain secure
3: 6 a son to sit on his *t* this very day.
5: 5 put on the *t* in your place will build
7: 7 He built the *t* hall, the Hall
8: 20 and now I sit on the *t* of Israel,
8: 25 to sit before me on the *t* of Israel,
9: 5 I will establish your royal *t*
9: 5 to have a man on the *t* of Israel.'
10: 9 and placed you on the *t* of Israel.
10: 18 Then the king made a great *t* inlaid
10: 19 *t* had six steps, and its back had
16: 11 to reign and was seated on the *t*,
22: 19 sitting on his *t* with all the host
2Ki 10: 3 and set him on his father's *t*.
10: 30 your descendants will sit on the *t*
11: 19 then took his place on the royal *t*,
13: 13 Jeroboam succeeded him on the *t*.
15: 12 "Your descendants will sit on the *t*
1Ch 17: 12 and I will establish his *t* forever.
17: 14 his *t* will be established forever.' ''
22: 10 I will establish the *t* of his kingdom
28: 5 to sit on the *t* of the kingdom
29: 23 Solomon sat on the *t* of the LORD
2Ch 6: 10 and now I sit on the *t* of Israel,
6: 16 to sit before me on the *t* of Israel,
7: 18 I will establish your royal *t*,
9: 8 placed you on his *t* as king to rule
9: 17 Then the king made a great *t* inlaid
9: 18 The *t* had six steps, and a footstool
18: 18 sitting on his *t* with all the host
23: 20 and seated the king on the royal *t*,
Est 1: 2 from his royal *t* in the citadel
5: 1 sitting on his royal *t* in the hall,
Ps 9: 4 on your *t*, judging righteously.
9: 7 he has established his *t*
11: 4 the LORD is on his heavenly *t*.
45: 6 Your *t*, O God, will last for ever
47: 8 God is seated on his holy *t*.
89: 4 *t* firm through all generations.' ''
89: 14 justice are the foundation of your *t*;
89: 29 his *t* as long as the heavens endure.
89: 36 his *t* endure before me like the sun;
89: 44 and cast his *t* to the ground.
93: 2 Your *t* was established long ago;
94: 20 Can a corrupt *t* be allied with you
97: 2 justice are the foundation of his *t*.
103: 19 The LORD has established his *t*
123: 1 to you whose *t* is in heaven.
132: 11 I will place on your *t*—
132: 12 sit on your *t* for ever and ever.''
Pr 16: 12 for a *t* is established
20: 8 When a king sits on his *t* to judge,
20: 28 through love his *t* is made secure.
25: 5 and his *t* will be established
29: 14 his *t* will always be secure.
Isa 6: 1 I saw the Lord seated on a *t*,
9: 7 He will reign on David's *t*
14: 13 I will raise my *t*
16: 5 In love a *t* will be established;
47: 1 sit on the ground without a *t*,
63: 15 from your lofty *t*, holy and glorious
66: 1 "Heaven is my *t*
Jer 3: 17 time they will call Jerusalem The *T*
13: 13 the kings who sit on David's *t*,
14: 21 do not dishonor your glorious *t*.
17: 12 A glorious *t*, exalted
17: 25 sit on David's *t* will come
22: 2 you who sit on David's *t*— you,
22: 4 sit on David's *t* will come
22: 30 none will sit on the *t* of David
29: 16 the king who sits on David's *t*
33: 17 to sit on the *t* of the house of Israel,
33: 21 have a descendant to reign on his *t*.
36: 30 one to sit on the *t* of David;
43: 10 I will set his *t* over these stones I
49: 38 I will set my *t* in Elam
La 5: 19 your *t* endures from generation
Eze 1: 26 above on the *t* was a figure like that
1: 26 their heads was what looked like a *t*
10: 1 I saw the likeness of a *t* of sapphire
17: 16 of the king who put him on the *t*,
28: 2 I sit on the *t* of a god
43: 7 this is the place of my *t*
Da 4: 36 I was restored to my *t* and became
5: 20 he was deposed from his royal *t*
7: 9 His *t* was flaming with fire,
Jnh 3: 6 he rose from his *t*, took
Zec 6: 13 And he will be a priest on his *t*.
6: 13 and will sit and rule on his *t*.
Mt 5: 34 for it is God's *t*; or by the earth,
19: 28 Son of Man sits on his glorious *t*,
23: 22 by heaven swears by God's *t*

Mt 25: 31 he will sit on his *t* in heavenly glory
Lk 1: 32 The Lord God will give him the *t*
Ac 2: 30 one of his descendants on his *t*.
7: 49 prophet says: " 'Heaven is my *t*,
12: 21 sat on his *t* and delivered a public
Heb 1: 8 "Your *t*, O God, will last for ever
4: 16 Let us then approach the *t* of grace
8: 1 of the *t* of the Majesty in heaven,
12: 2 at the right hand of the *t* of God.
Rev 1: 4 from the seven spirits before his *t*,
2: 13 you live—where Satan has his *t*.
3: 21 sat down with my Father on his *t*.
3: 21 the right to sit with me on my *t*,
4: 2 there before me was a *t* in heaven
4: 3 an emerald, encircled the *t*.
4: 4 Surrounding the *t* were
4: 5 Before the *t*, seven lamps were
4: 5 From the *t* came flashes
4: 6 around the *t*, were four living
4: 6 before the *t* there was what looked
4: 9 and thanks to him who sits on the *t*
4: 10 They lay their crowns before the *t*
4: 10 down before him who sits on the *t*,
5: 1 sat on the *t* a scroll with writing
5: 6 standing in the center of the *t*,
5: 7 hand of him who sat on the *t*.
5: 11 They encircled the *t* and the living
5: 13 "To him who sits on the *t*
6: 16 the face of him who sits on the *t*
7: 9 standing before the *t* and in front
7: 10 who sits on the *t*,
7: 11 angels were standing around the *t*
7: 11 fell down on their faces before the *t*
7: 15 sits on the *t* will spread his tent
7: 15 "they are before the *t* of God
7: 17 of the *t* will be their shepherd;
8: 3 on the golden altar before the *t*.
12: 5 up to God and to his *t*.
13: 2 and his *t* and great authority.
14: 3 they sang a new song before the *t*
16: 10 bowl on the *t* of the beast,
16: 17 came a loud voice from the *t*,
19: 4 God, who was seated on the *t*.
19: 5 Then a voice came from the *t*,
20: 11 Then I saw a great white *t*
20: 12 before the *t*, and books were
21: 3 a loud voice from the *t* saying,
21: 5 He who was seated on the *t* said,
22: 1 flowing from the *t* of God
22: 3 *t* of God and of the Lamb will be

THRONES (THRONE)

1Ki 22: 10 on their *t* at the threshing floor
2Ch 18: 9 on their *t* at the threshing floor
Ps 122: 5 There the *t* for judgment stand,
122: 5 the *t* of the house of David.
Isa 14: 9 it makes them rise from their *t*—
Jer 1: 15 kings will come and set up their *t*
13: 18 "Come down from your *t*,
Eze 26: 16 seacoast will step down from their *t*
Da 7: 9 "*t* were set in place,
Hag 2: 22 I will overturn royal *t* and shatter
Mt 19: 28 me will also sit on twelve *t*,
Lk 1: 52 down rulers from their *t*
22: 30 table in my kingdom and sit on *t*,
Col 1: 16 whether *t* or powers or rulers
Rev 4: 4 throne were twenty-four other *t*,
11: 16 seated on their *t* before God,
20: 4 I saw *t* on which were seated those

THRONG (THRONGED THRONGS)

Job 21: 33 and a countless *t* goes before him.
Ps 42: 4 thanksgiving among the festive *t*.
55: 14 we walked with the *t* at the house
68: 27 there the great *t* of Judah's princes,
109: 30 in the great *t* I will praise him.
Pr 7: 26 her slain are a mighty *t*.
Jer 31: 8 a great *t* will return.
Eze 23: 24 and wagons and with a *t* of people;
32: 3 " 'With a great *t* of people
Mic 2: 12 the place will *t* with people.

THRONGED (THRONG)

Jer 5: 7 and *t* to the houses of prostitutes.

THRONGS (THRONG)

Ps 35: 18 among *t* of people I will praise you.

THROW (THREW THROWING THROWN THROWS)

Ge 27: 40 you will *t* his yoke
37: 20 and *t* him into one of these cisterns
37: 22 *T* him into this cistern here
Ex 1: 22 "Every boy that is born you must *t*
4: 3 The LORD said, "*T* it
7: 9 and *t* it down before Pharaoh,'
22: 31 torn by wild beasts; *t* it to the dogs.
23: 27 *t* into confusion every nation you
Lev 1: 16 and *t* it to the east side of the altar,
Nu 19: 6 and *t* them onto the burning heifer.
Jos 8: 29 and *t* it down at the entrance
24: 14 *T* away the gods your forefathers
24: 23 "*t* away the foreign gods that are
2Sa 11: 21 Didn't a woman *t* an upper
2Ki 9: 25 *t* him on the field that belonged
9: 26 pick him up and *t* him on that plot,
9: 33 "*T* her down!" Jehu said.
Job 18: 7 his own schemes *t* him down.
30: 11 they *t* off restraint in my presence.
Ps 2: 3 "and *t* off their fetters."
17: 11 with eyes alert, to *t* me
50: 18 you *t* in your lot with adulterers.
62: 3 Would all of you *t* him down—
Pr 1: 14 *t* in your lot with us,
Ecc 3: 6 a time to keep and a time to *t* away,
Isa 2: 20 In that day men will *t* away
19: 8 those who *t* nets on the water
22: 18 and *t* you into a large country.
28: 2 he will *t* it forcefully to the ground.
30: 22 you will *t* them away like
Jer 7: 29 Cut off your hair and *t* it away;
16: 13 So I will *t* you out of this land
22: 7 and *t* them into the fire.
51: 63 and *t* it into the Euphrates.
Eze 5: 4 few of these and *t* them into the fire
7: 19 They will *t* their silver
26: 12 your fine houses and *t* your stones,
32: 4 I will *t* you on the land
Da 3: 20 *t* them into the blazing furnace.
Hos 7: 12 When they go, I will *t* my net
8: 5 *T* out your calf-idol, O Samaria!
Jnh 1: 12 "Pick me up and *t* me into the sea,"
Zec 1: 21 and *t* down these horns
11: 13 said to me, "*T* it to the potter"—
Mal 3: 10 if I will not *t* open the floodgates
Mt 4: 6 of God," he said, "*t* yourself down.
5: 29 gouge it out and *t* it away.
5: 30 you to sin, cut it off and *t* it away.
7: 6 do not *t* your pearls to pigs.
13: 42 They will *t* them into the fiery
13: 50 and *t* them into the fiery furnace,
17: 27 go to the lake and *t* out your line.
18: 8 you to sin, cut it off and *t* it away.
18: 9 gouge it out and *t* it away.
21: 21 'Go, *t* yourself into the sea,'
22: 13 *t* him outside, into the darkness,
25: 30 *t* that worthless servant outside,
Mk 11: 23 'Go, *t* yourself into the sea,'
Lk 4: 9 he said, "*t* yourself down from here
4: 29 in order to *t* him down the cliff.
12: 5 has power to *t* you into hell.
12: 58 and the officer *t* you into prison.
22: 41 He withdrew about a stone's *t*
Jn 8: 7 the first to *t* a stone at her."
21: 6 "*T* your net on the right side
Ac 7: 19 them to *t* out their newborn babies
27: 18 began to *t* the cargo overboard.
Heb 10: 35 So do not *t* away your confidence;
12: 1 let us *t* off everything that hinders
Rev 18: 19 They will *t* dust on their heads,

THROWING (THROW)

Dt 7: 23 *t* them into great confusion
1Sa 5: 9 was against that city, *t* it
2Sa 16: 13 as he went and *t* stones at him
Ezr 10: 1 *t* himself down before the house
Mk 10: 50 *T* his cloak aside, he jumped
Ac 16: 20 and are *t* our city into an uproar
22: 4 and women and *t* them into prison,
22: 23 As they were shouting and *t*
27: 38 lightened the ship by *t* the grain
Gal 1: 7 Evidently some people are *t* you
5: 10 The one who is *t* you

THROWN (THROW)

Lev 4: 12 where the ashes are *t*, and burn it
14: 40 and *t* into an unclean place
2Sa 20: 21 "His head will be *t* to you
1Ki 13: 24 his body was *t* down on the road,
13: 25 by saw the body *t* down there,
13: 28 found the body *t* down on the road,
2Ki 7: 15 the Arameans had *t* away
19: 18 They have *t* their gods into the fire
Ne 4: 5 for they have *t* insults in the face
Job 16: 11 *t* me into the clutches
Ps 36: 12 *t* down, not able to rise!
102: 10 for you have taken me up and *t* me
140: 10 may they be *t* into the fire,
141: 6 their rulers will be *t*
Isa 34: 3 Their slain will be *t* out,
37: 19 They have *t* their gods into the fire
Jer 14: 16 to will be *t* out into the streets
22: 19 dragged away and *t*
26: 23 and his body *t* into the burial place
31: 40 where dead bodies and ashes are *t*,
36: 30 his body will be *t* out and exposed
38: 9 They have *t* him into a cistern,
51: 34 he has *t* us into confusion,
Eze 11: 7 The bodies you have *t* there are
15: 4 And after it is *t* on the fire as fuel
16: 5 you were *t* out into the open field,
19: 12 and *t* to the ground.
21: 12 They are *t* to the sword
Da 3: 6 and worship will immediately be *t*
3: 11 and worship will be *t* into a blazing
3: 15 you will be *t* immediately
3: 17 If we are *t* into the blazing furnace,
3: 21 and *t* into the blazing furnace.
6: 7 O king, shall be *t* into the lions' den
6: 12 would be *t* into the lions' den?"
6: 24 brought in and *t* into the lions' den,
7: 11 and its body destroyed and *t*
8: 12 and truth was *t* to the ground.
Joel 1: 7 and *t* it away,
Na 2: 6 The river gates are *t* open
Mt 3: 10 cut down and *t* into the fire.
5: 13 to be *t* out and trampled by men.
5: 25 and you may be *t* into prison.
5: 29 than for your whole body to be *t*
6: 30 and tomorrow is *t* into the fire,
7: 19 cut down and *t* into the fire.
8: 12 of the kingdom will be *t* outside,
18: 8 two feet and be *t* into eternal fire.
18: 9 and be *t* into the fire of hell.
18: 30 and had the man *t* into prison
24: 2 every one will be *t* down."
Mk 9: 22 "It has often *t* him into fire
9: 42 better for him to be *t* into the sea
9: 45 to have two feet and be *t* into hell.
9: 47 to have two eyes and be *t* into hell,
13: 2 every one will be *t* down."
Lk 3: 9 cut down and *t* into the fire."
12: 28 and tomorrow is *t* into the fire,
13: 28 of God, but you yourselves *t* out.
14: 35 nor for the manure pile; it is *t* out.
17: 2 better for him to be *t* into the sea
21: 6 every one of them will be *t* down."
23: 19 (Barabbas had been *t* into prison
23: 25 released the man who had been *t*
Jn 9: 35 Jesus heard that they had *t* him out
15: 6 he is like a branch that is *t* away
15: 6 such branches are picked up, *t*
Ac 16: 23 been severely flogged, they were *t*
17: 8 the city officials were *t* into turmoil
Rev 8: 8 all ablaze, was *t* into the sea.
18: 21 city of Babylon will be *t* down,
19: 20 The two of them were *t* alive
20: 10 and the false prophet had been *t*.
20: 10 was *t* into the lake of burning sulfur
20: 14 Hades were *t* into the lake of fire.
20: 15 he was *t* into the lake of fire.

THROWS (THROW)

Nu 35: 20 or *t* something at him intentionally
35: 22 *t* something at him unintentionally
Job 30: 19 He *t* me into the mud,
41: 18 His sneezing *t* out flashes of light;
Mk 9: 18 Whenever it seizes him, it *t* him
Lk 9: 39 it *t* him into convulsions

THRUSH
Isa 38:14 I cried like a swift or *t*,
Jer 8: 7 and the dove, the swift and the *t*

THRUST (THRUSTING)
Dt 29:28 and *t* them into another land,
1Sa 26: 8 the ground with one *t* of my spear;
2Sa 2:16 and *t* his dagger into his opponent's
2:23 so Abner *t* the butt of his spear
1Ki 14: 9 and *t* me behind your back.
2Ki 17:20 until he *t* them from his presence.
24:20 and in the end he *t* them
Job 18: 8 His feet *t* him into a net
24: 4 They *t* the needy from the path
SS 5: 4 My lover *t* his hand
Isa 8:22 they will be *t* into utter darkness.
13:15 Whoever is captured will be *t*
Jer 7:15 I will *t* you from my presence,
52: 3 and in the end he *t* them
Eze 23:35 and *t* me behind your back,

THRUSTING (THRUST)
Dt 6:19 *t* out all your enemies before you,

THUMB (THUMBS)
Lev 8:23 on the *t* of his right hand
14:14 on the *t* of his right hand
14:17 on the *t* of his right hand
14:25 on the *t* of his right hand
14:28 on the *t* of his right hand

THUMBS (THUMB)
Ex 29:20 on the *t* of their right hands,
Lev 8:24 on the *t* of their right hands
Jdg 1: 6 and cut off his *t* and big toes.
1: 7 "Seventy kings with their *t*

THUMMIM
Ex 28:30 and the *T* in the breastpiece,
Lev 8: 8 and put the Urim and *T*
Dt 33: 8 "Your *T* and Urim belong
Ezr 2:63 ministering with the Urim and *T*.
Ne 7:65 ministering with the Urim and *T*.

THUNDER (THUNDERED THUNDERING THUNDERS)
Ex 9:23 the LORD sent *t* and hail,
9:28 for we have had enough *t* and hail.
9:29 The *t* will stop and there will be no
9:33 hands toward the LORD; the *t*
9:34 and hail and *t* had stopped,
19:16 of the third day there was *t*
20:18 When the people saw the *t*
1Sa 2:10 He will *t* against them from heaven
7:10 with loud *t* against the Philistines
12:17 I will call upon the LORD to send *t*
12:18 that same day the LORD sent *t*
Job 26:14 Who then can understand the *t*
36:33 His *t* announces the coming storm;
40: 9 and can your voice *t* like his?
Ps 77:17 the skies resounded with *t*;
77:18 Your *t* was heard in the whirlwind,
93: 4 Mightier than the *t*
104: 7 sound of your *t* they took to flight;
Isa 29: 6 come with *t* and earthquake
33: 3 At the *t* of your voice, the peoples
Joel 3:16 and *t* from Jerusalem;
Mk 3:17 which means Sons of *T*); Andrew,
Rev 4: 5 lightning, rumblings and peals of *t*.
6: 1 living creatures say in a voice like *t*,
8: 5 there came peals of *t*, rumblings,
11:19 peals of *t*, an earthquake
14: 2 waters and like a loud peal of *t*.
16:18 peals of *t* and a severe earthquake.
19: 6 waters and like loud peals of *t*,

THUNDERCLOUD (CLOUD)
Ps 81: 7 I answered you out of a *t*;

THUNDERED (THUNDER)
Jdg 5:22 Then *t* the horses' hoofs—
1Sa 7:10 But that day the LORD *t*
2Sa 22:14 The LORD *t* from heaven;
Ps 18:13 The LORD *t* from heaven;
Jn 12:29 was there and heard it said it had *t*;

THUNDERING (THUNDER)
Rev 9: 9 sound of their wings was like the *t*

THUNDERS (THUNDER)
Job 36:29 how he *t* from his pavilion?
37: 4 he *t* with his majestic voice.
37: 5 God's voice *t* in marvelous ways;
Ps 29: 3 LORD *t* over the mighty waters.
29: 3 the God of glory *t*,
68:33 who *t* with mighty voice.
Jer 10:13 When he *t*, the waters
51:16 When he *t*, the waters
Joel 2:11 The LORD *t*
Am 1: 2 and *t* from Jerusalem;
Rev 10: 3 the voices of the seven *t* spoke.
10: 4 And when the seven *t* spoke,
10: 4 "Seal up what the seven *t* have said

THUNDERSTORM (STORM)
Job 28:26 and a path for the *t*,
38:25 and a path for the *t*,
Isa 30:30 with cloudburst, *t* and hail.

THWART (THWARTED THWARTS)
Isa 14:27 has purposed, and who can *t* him?

THWARTED (THWART)
Job 42: 2 no plan of yours can be *t*.
Isa 8:10 your strategy, but it will be *t*;

THWARTS (THWART)
Job 5:12 He *t* the plans of the crafty,
Ps 33:10 he *t* the purposes of the peoples.
Pr 10: 3 but he *t* the craving of the wicked.

THYATIRA
Ac 16:14 in purple cloth from the city of *T*,
Rev 1:11 Smyrna, Pergamum, *T*, Sardis,
2:18 the angel of the church in *T* write:
2:24 Now I say to the rest of you in *T*,

TIARAS
Isa 3:23 and the linen garments and *t*

TIBERIAS
Jn 6: 1 of Galilee (that is, the Sea of *T*),
6:23 Then some boats from *T* landed
21: 1 to his disciples by the Sea of *T*.

TIBERIUS
Lk 3: 1 year of the reign of *T* Caesar—

TIBNI
1Ki 16:21 half supported *T* son of Ginath
16:22 So *T* died and Omri became king.
16:22 than those of *T* son of Ginath.

TIDAL
Ge 14: 1 and *T* king of Goiim went to war
14: 9 *T* king of Goiim, Amraphel king

TIDINGS
Isa 40: 9 You who bring good *t* to Jerusalem
40: 9 You who bring good *t* to Zion,
41:27 to Jerusalem a messenger of good *t*.
52: 7 who bring good *t*,

TIE (TIED TIES TYING)
Ex 29: 9 Then *t* sashes on Aaron
Lev 16: 4 he is to *t* the linen sash around him
Dt 6: 8 *T* them as symbols on your hands
11:18 *t* them as symbols on your hands
Jdg 15:12 "We've come to *t* you up
15:13 "We will only *t* you up
16: 5 him so we may *t* him up
Job 41: 1 or *t* down his tongue with a rope?
Jer 51:63 *t* a stone to it and throw it
Eze 3:25 son of man, they will *t* with ropes;
4: 8 I will *t* you up with ropes
Da 3:20 in his army to *t* up Shadrach,
Mt 13:30 and *t* them in bundles to be burned,
22:13 told the attendants, '*T* him hand
23: 4 They *t* up heavy loads

TIED (TIE)
Ge 38:28 and *t* it on his wrist and said,
Ex 28:28 are to be *t* to the rings
39:21 They *t* the rings of the breastpiece
Lev 8: 7 also *t* the ephod to him
8: 7 on Aaron, *t* the sash around him,
8:13 *t* sashes around them and put
Jos 2:18 you have *t* this scarlet cord
2:21 she *t* the scarlet cord in the window
Jdg 15: 4 and *t* them tail to tail in pairs.
16: 6 how you can be *t* up and subdued."
16: 8 had not been dried, and she *t* him
16:10 tell me how you can be *t*."
16:12 Delilah took new ropes and *t* him
16:13 Tell me how you can be *t*."
2Ki 5:23 then *t* up the two talents of silver
Ps 109:19 like a belt *t* forever around him.
Da 3:23 and these three men, firmly *t*,
3:24 "Wasn't it three men that we *t* up
Mt 21: 2 once you will find a donkey *t* there,
Mk 9:42 the sea with a large millstone *t*
11: 2 you will find a colt *t* there,
11: 4 outside in the street, *t* at a doorway
Lk 17: 2 with a millstone *t* around his neck
19:30 you will find a colt *t* there,
Ac 21:11 *t* his own hands and feet with it

TIES (TIE)
Jdg 16: 7 "If anyone *t* me with seven fresh
16:11 "If anyone *t* me securely
Job 12:18 and *t* a loincloth around their waist
Hos 11: 4 with *t* of love;
Mt 12:29 unless he first *t* up the strong man?
Mk 3:27 unless he first *t* up the strong man.

TIGHT (TIGHTEN TIGHTENED)
Jas 1:26 and yet does not keep a *t* rein

TIGHTEN (TIGHT)
Jdg 16:13 and *t* it with the pin,

TIGHTENED (TIGHT)
Jdg 16:14 into the fabric and *t* it with the pin.

TIGHTFISTED (FIST)
Dt 15: 7 or *t* toward your poor brother.

TIGLATH-PILESER
2Ki 15:29 *T* king of Assyria came
16: 7 to say to *T* king of Assyria,
16:10 to meet *T* king of Assyria.
1Ch 5: 6 whom *T* king of Assyria took
5:26 *T* king of Assyria), who took
2Ch 28:20 *T* king of Assyria came to him,

TIGRIS
Ge 2:14 The name of the third river is the *T*
Da 10: 4 on the bank of the great river, the *T*

TIKVAH
2Ki 22:14 the wife of Shallum son of *T*,
Ezr 10:15 of Asahel and Jahzeiah son of *T*,

TILES
Lk 5:19 mat through the *t* into the middle

TILON
1Ch 4:20 Amnon, Rinnah, Ben-Hanan and *T*

TILTING
Jer 1:13 "I see a boiling pot, *t* away

TIMAEUS
Mk 10:46 Bartimaeus (that is, the Son of *T*),

TIMBER (TIMBERS)
1Ki 5: 6 one so skilled in felling *t*
5:18 of Gebal cut and prepared the *t*
15:22 and *t* Baasha had been using there.
2Ki 12:12 They purchased *t* and dressed
22: 6 Also have them purchase *t*
2Ch 2: 8 men are skilled in cutting *t* there.
2:10 the woodsmen who cut the *t*,
16: 6 and *t* Baasha had been using.
34:11 and *t* for joists and beams
Ne 2: 8 so he will give me *t* to make beams
Eze 26:12 and throw your stones, *t* and rubble
Hag 1: 8 bring down *t* and build the house,

TIMBERS (TIMBER)
Lev 14:45 its stones, *t* and all the plaster—
Ezr 5: 8 and placing the *t* in the walls.
6: 4 courses of large stones and one of *t*.
Eze 27: 5 They made all your *t*
Zec 5: 4 both its *t* and its stones.'"

TIME (TIMES)

Ge 4: 3 the course of *t* Cain brought some
4: 26 At that *t* men began to call
5: 2 at the *t* they were created,
6: 5 of his heart was only evil all the *t*.
6: 9 blameless among the people of his *t*
8: 12 but this *t* it did not return to him.
10: 25 in his *t* the earth was divided;
13: 7 also living in the land at that *t*.
14: 1 At this *t* Amraphel king of Shinar,
17: 21 bear to you by this *t* next year."
18: 10 return to you about this *t* next year,
18: 14 to you at the appointed *t* next year
19: 23 By the *t* Lot reached Zoar,
21: 2 at the very *t* God had promised
21: 22 At that *t* Abimelech and Phicol
21: 34 land of the Philistines for a long *t*.
22: 1 Some *t* later God tested Abraham.
22: 15 Abraham from heaven a second *t*
22: 20 Some *t* later Abraham was told,
24: 11 the *t* the women go out
25: 24 When the *t* came for her
26: 1 earlier famine of Abraham's *t*—
26: 8 When Isaac had been there a long *t*
26: 15 dug in the *t* of his father Abraham,
26: 18 dug in the *t* of his father Abraham,
29: 7 it is not *t* for the flocks
29: 21 My *t* is completed, and I want to lie
29: 35 "This *t* I will praise the LORD."
30: 20 This *t* my husband will treat me
30: 21 Some *t* later she gave birth
34: 19 lost no *t* in doing what they said,
37: 9 and this *t* the sun and moon
38: 1 At that *t*, Judah left his brothers
38: 12 After a long *t* Judah's wife,
38: 27 When the *t* came for her
39: 5 From the *t* he put him in charge
40: 1 Some *t* later, the cupbearer
40: 4 been in custody for some *t*,
43: 18 back into our sacks the first *t*.
43: 20 down here the first *t* to buy food.
46: 29 his father and wept for a long *t*.
47: 29 When the *t* drew near for Israel
48: 1 Some *t* later Joseph was told,
50: 3 for that was the *t* required
Ex 4: 26 (At that *t* she said "bridegroom
8: 9 of setting the *t* for me to pray
8: 32 this *t* also Pharaoh hardened his
9: 5 The LORD set a *t* and said,
9: 14 or this *t* I will send the full force
9: 18 at this *t* tomorrow I will send
9: 27 "This *t* I have sinned," he said
12: 39 and did not have *t* to prepare food
12: 40 length of *t* the Israelite people lived
13: 10 at the appointed *t* year after year.
21: 19 man for the loss of his *t*
23: 15 this at the appointed *t* in the month
30: 12 for his life at the *t* he is counted.
32: 34 when the *t* comes for me to punish,
34: 18 this at the appointed *t* in the month
Lev 14: 2 at the *t* of his ceremonial cleansing,
15: 25 blood for many days at a *t* other
16: 17 of Meeting from the *t* Aaron goes
19: 10 go over your vineyard a second *t*
25: 29 During that *t* he may redeem it.
25: 50 and his buyer are to count the *t*
26: 34 sabbath years all the *t* that it lies
26: 35 All the *t* that it lies desolate,
Nu 3: 1 Moses at the *t* the LORD talked
9: 2 the Passover at the appointed *t*.
9: 3 Celebrate it at the appointed *t*,
9: 7 Israelites at the appointed *t*?"
9: 13 offering at the appointed *t*.
9: 19 over the tabernacle a long *t*,
10: 13 this first *t*, at the LORD's
14: 15 people to death all at one *t*,
14: 19 from the *t* they left Egypt until now
22: 4 who was king of Moab at that *t*,
28: 2 to me at the appointed *t* the food
30: 15 he nullifies them some *t*
Dt 1: 9 At that *t* I said to you, "You are too
1: 16 And I charged your judges at that *t*
1: 18 at that *t* I told you everything you
1: 46 days—all the *t* you spent there.
2: 1 For a long *t* we made our way
2: 14 from the *t* we left Kadesh Barnea
2: 34 At that *t* we took all his towns
Dt 3: 4 At that *t* we took all his cities.
3: 8 So at that *t* we took from these two
3: 12 the land that we took over at that *t*,
3: 18 I commanded you at that *t*:
3: 21 At that *t* I commanded Joshua:
3: 23 At that *t* I pleaded with the LORD:
4: 14 at that *t* to teach you the decrees
4: 25 have lived in the land a long *t*—
4: 32 the former days, long before your *t*,
4: 40 your God gives you for all *t*.
5: 5 that *t* I stood between the LORD
9: 20 but at that *t* I prayed for Aaron too.
10: 1 At that *t* the LORD said to me,
10: 8 At that *t* the LORD set apart
10: 10 as I did the first *t*, and the LORD
10: 10 the LORD listened to me at this *t*
15: 2 LORD's *t* for canceling debts has
16: 3 your life you may remember the *t*
16: 9 weeks from the *t* you begin
17: 9 the judge who is in office at that *t*.
17: 20 his descendants will reign a long *t*
19: 17 the judges who are in office at the *t*.
20: 19 siege to a city for a long *t*,
24: 20 go over the branches a second *t*.
26: 3 say to the priest in office at the *t*,
28: 47 and gladly in the *t* of prosperity,
32: 35 In due *t* their foot will slip;
34: 8 until the *t* of weeping
Jos 2: 5 when it was *t* to close the city gate,
5: 2 At that *t* the LORD said to Joshua,
6: 9 All this *t* the trumpets were
6: 16 seventh *t* around, when the priests
6: 26 At that *t* Joshua pronounced this
11: 6 by this *t* tomorrow I will hand all
11: 10 At that *t* Joshua turned back
11: 18 against all these kings for a long *t*.
11: 21 At that *t* Joshua went
14: 10 years since the *t* he said this
20: 6 high priest who is serving at that *t*.
22: 3 For a long *t* now—to this very day
23: 1 After a long *t* had passed
24: 7 you lived in the desert for a long *t*.
Jdg 3: 29 At that *t* they struck
4: 4 was leading Israel at that *t*.
6: 39 This *t* make the fleece dry
10: 1 After the *t* of Abimelech a man
11: 4 Some *t* later, when the Ammonites
11: 26 you retake them during that *t*?
12: 6 Ephraimites were killed at that *t*.
14: 4 for at that *t* they were ruling
14: 8 Some *t* later, when he went back
15: 1 Later on, at the *t* of wheat harvest,
15: 3 "This *t* I have a right to get
16: 4 Some *t* later, he fell in love
16: 15 This is the third *t* you have made
18: 30 of Dan until the *t* of the captivity
18: 31 all the *t* the house of God was
20: 25 This *t*, when the Benjamites came
21: 14 the Benjamites returned at that *t*
21: 24 At that *t* the Israelites left that
1Sa 1: 20 the course of *t* Hannah conceived
2: 31 *t* is coming when I will cut short
3: 8 The LORD called Samuel a third *t*,
3: 12 At that *t* I will carry out
4: 19 and near the *t* of delivery.
7: 2 It was a long *t*, twenty years in all,
9: 13 you should find him about this *t*."
9: 16 "About this *t* tomorrow I will send
9: 24 from the *t* I said, 'I have invited
11: 9 'By the *t* the sun is hot tomorrow,
13: 8 He waited seven days, the *t* set
13: 11 that you did not come at the set *t*,
13: 13 kingdom over Israel for all *t*.
14: 18 At that *t* it was with the Israelites.)
14: 35 it was the first *t* he had done this.
17: 12 and in Saul's *t* he was old
18: 9 from that *t* on Saul kept a jealous
18: 19 So when the *t* came for Merab,
18: 26 So before the allotted *t* elapsed,
19: 21 Saul sent men a third *t*, and they
20: 12 by this *t* the day after tomorrow!
22: 15 Was that day the first *t* I inquired
25: 7 I hear that it is sheep-shearing *t*.
25: 7 and the whole *t* they were
25: 8 since we come at a festive *t*.
25: 15 and the whole *t* we were out
25: 16 around us all the *t* we were herding
25: 18 Abigail lost no *t*.
1Sa 26: 10 his *t* will come and he will die,
2Sa 2: 1 In the course of *t*, David inquired
2: 11 The length of *t* David was king
3: 1 the house of David lasted a long *t*.
3: 17 "For some *t* you have wanted
7: 11 ever since the *t* I appointed leaders
8: 1 of *t*, David defeated the Philistines
10: 1 In the course of *t*, the king
11: 1 at the *t* when kings go off to war,
11: 27 After the *t* of mourning was over,
13: 1 In the course of *t*, Amnon son
14: 26 he used to cut his hair from *t* to *t*
14: 29 he sent a second *t*, but he refused
15: 1 of *t*, Absalom provided himself
17: 7 has given is not good this *t*.
18: 20 "You may take the news another *t*,
20: 5 longer than the *t* the king had set
21: 18 At that *t* Sibbecai the Hushathite
21: 18 of *t*, there was another battle
23: 13 During harvest *t*, three
23: 14 At that *t* David was
24: 15 until the end of the *t* designated,
1Ki 2: 1 When the *t* drew near for David
2: 38 stayed in Jerusalem for a long *t*.
2: 42 you will die'? At that *t* you said
8: 2 Solomon at the *t* of the festival
8: 40 they will fear you all the *t* they live
8: 61 obey his commands, as at this *t*."
8: 65 observed the festival at that *t*,
9: 2 LORD appeared to him a second *t*,
11: 29 About that *t* Jeroboam was going
14: 1 At that *t* Abijah son
16: 9 Elah was in Tirzah at the *t*,
16: 34 In Ahab's *t*, Hiel of Bethel rebuilt
17: 7 Some *t* later the brook dried up
17: 17 Some *t* later the son
18: 1 After a long *t*, in the third year,
18: 29 until the *t* for the evening sacrifice.
18: 34 and they did it the third *t*.
18: 34 "Do it a third *t*," he ordered,
18: 36 At the *t* of sacrifice, the prophet
18: 44 The seventh *t* the servant reported,
19: 2 if by this *t* tomorrow I do not make
19: 7 of the LORD came back a second *t*
20: 6 about this *t* tomorrow I am going
20: 9 will do all you demanded the first *t*,
21: 1 Some *t* later there was an incident
22: 49 At that *t* Ahaziah son of Ahab said
2Ki 3: 6 So at that *t* King Joram set out
3: 20 about the *t* for offering the sacrifice
4: 16 About this *t* next year," Elisha said
4: 17 about that same *t* she gave birth
5: 26 Is this the *t* to take money,
6: 10 *T* and again Elisha warned the king
6: 24 Some *t* later, Ben-Hadad king
7: 1 says: About this *t* tomorrow,
7: 18 the king: "About this *t* tomorrow,
8: 20 In the *t* of Jehoram, Edom rebelled
8: 22 Libnah revolted at the same *t*.
10: 6 to me in Jezreel by this *t* tomorrow
10: 36 The *t* that Jehu reigned over Israel
12: 17 About this *t* Hazael king
13: 3 and for a long *t* he kept them
13: 7 them like the dust at threshing *t*.
15: 16 At that *t* Menahem, starting out
15: 29 In the *t* of Pekah king of Israel,
16: 6 At that *t*, Rezin king
18: 4 up to that *t* the Israelites had been
18: 16 At this *t* Hezekiah king
20: 12 At that *t* Merodach-Baladan son
20: 17 The *t* will surely come
24: 10 At that *t* the officers
1Ch 1: 19 in his *t* the earth was divided;
9: 18 on the east, up to the present *t*.
9: 25 had to come from *t* to *t*
11: 16 At that *t* David was
15: 13 it up the first *t* that the LORD our
17: 10 ever since the *t* I appointed leaders
18: 1 of *t*, David defeated the Philistines
19: 1 In the course of *t*, Nahash king
20: 1 at the *t* when kings go off to war,
20: 4 At that *t* Sibbecai the Hushathite
20: 4 In the course of *t*, war broke out
21: 28 At that *t*, when David saw that
21: 29 were at that *t* on the high place
26: 17 and two at a *t* at the storehouse.
28: 7 and laws, as is being done at this *t*.'
29: 22 son of David as king a second *t*,

2Ch 5: 3 to the king at the *t* of the festival
6: 31 walk in your ways all the *t* they live
7: 8 the festival at that *t* for seven days,
11: 17 and Solomon during this *t*.
13: 20 power during the *t* of Abijah.
15: 3 For a long *t* Israel was
15: 11 At that *t* they sacrificed
16: 7 At that *t* Hanani the seer came
16: 10 At the same *t* Asa brutally
21: 8 In the *t* of Jehoram, Edom rebelled
21: 10 Libnah revolted at the same *t*,
21: 19 In the course of *t*, at the end
24: 4 Some *t* later Joash decided
25: 27 From the *t* that Amaziah turned
28: 16 At that *t* King Ahaz sent
28: 22 In his *t* of trouble King Ahaz
30: 3 able to celebrate it at the regular *t*
35: 16 So at that *t* the entire service
35: 17 celebrated the Passover at that *t*
35: 21 It is not you I am attacking at this *t*,
36: 21 all the *t* of its desolation it rested,
Ezr 4: 2 him since the *t* of Esarhaddon king
5: 3 At that *t* Tattenai, governor
8: 34 weight was recorded at that *t*.
9: 12 their welfare or prosperity at any *t*,
10: 14 a foreign woman come at a set *t*,
Ne 2: 6 the king to send me; so I set a *t*.
4: 22 At that *t* I also said to the people,
6: 1 up to that *t* I had not set the doors
6: 4 each *t* I gave them the same answer
6: 5 the fifth *t*, Sanballat sent his aide
9: 28 you delivered them *t* after *t*.
12: 23 of Levi up to the *t* of Johanan son
12: 44 At that *t* men were appointed to be
13: 6 Some *t* later I asked his permission
13: 21 From that *t* on they no longer came
Est 1: 1 happened during the *t* of Xerxes,
1: 2 At that *t* King Xerxes reigned
2: 19 virgins were assembled a second *t*,
2: 21 During the *t* Mordecai was sitting
4: 14 For if you remain silent at this *t*,
4: 14 come to royal position for such a *t*
8: 16 For the Jews it was a *t* of happiness
9: 22 as the *t* when the Jews got relief
9: 27 and at the *t* appointed.
Job 9: 3 he could not answer him one *t* out
14: 6 in his *t* like a hired man.
14: 13 If only you would set me a *t*
15: 32 Before his *t* he will be paid in full,
22: 16 They were carried off before their *t*
39: 2 Do you know the *t* they give birth?
Ps 21: 9 At the *t* of your appearing
37: 39 he is their stronghold in *t* of trouble
51: 5 from the *t* my mother conceived
69: 13 in the *t* of your favor;
75: 2 You say, "I choose the appointed *t*;
77: 8 Has his promise failed for all *t*?
78: 38 *T* after *t* he restrained his anger
102: 13 for it is *t* to show favor to her;
102: 13 the appointed *t* has come.
104: 27 them their food at the proper *t*.
119: 126 It is *t* for you to act, O LORD;
145: 15 them their food at the proper *t*.
Pr 20: 4 so at harvest *t* he looks
25: 13 the coolness of snow at harvest *t*
Ecc 1: 10 it was here before our *t*.
3: 1 There is a *t* for everything,
3: 2 a *t* to be born and a *t* to die,
3: 2 a *t* to plant and a *t* to uproot,
3: 3 a *t* to kill and a *t* to heal,
3: 3 a *t* to tear down and a *t* to build,
3: 4 a *t* to mourn and a *t* to dance,
3: 4 a *t* to weep and a *t* to laugh,
3: 5 a *t* to embrace and a *t* to refrain,
3: 5 a *t* to scatter stones and a *t*
3: 6 a *t* to keep and a *t* to throw away,
3: 6 a *t* to search and a *t* to give up,
3: 7 a *t* to be silent and a *t* to speak,
3: 7 a *t* to tear and a *t* to mend,
3: 8 a *t* for war and a *t* for peace.
3: 8 a *t* to love and a *t* to hate,
3: 11 made everything beautiful in its *t*.
3: 17 a *t* for every deed."
3: 17 for there will be a *t*
7: 17 why die before your *t*?
8: 5 wise heart will know the proper *t*
8: 6 there is a proper *t* and procedure
8: 8 As no one is discharged in *t* of war,
Ecc 8: 9 There is a *t* when a man lords it
8: 12 crimes and still lives a long *t*,
9: 11 *t* and chance happen to them all.
10: 17 and whose princes eat at a proper *t*
Isa 7: 17 house of your father a *t* unlike any
9: 7 from that *t* on and forever.
11: 11 will reach out his hand a second *t*
13: 22 Her *t* is at hand,
18: 7 At that *t* gifts will be brought
20: 2 at that *t* the LORD spoke
23: 15 At that *t* Tyre will be forgotten
29: 17 In a very short *t*, will not Lebanon
33: 2 our salvation in *t* of distress.
39: 1 At that *t* Merodach-Baladan son
39: 6 The *t* will surely come
42: 14 "For a long *t* I have kept silent,
42: 23 or pay close attention in *t* to come?
48: 16 at the *t* it happens, I am there."
49: 8 "In the *t* of my favor I will answer
59: 21 of their descendants from this *t* on
60: 22 in its *t* I will do this swiftly."
Jer 2: 24 at mating *t* they will find her.
3: 17 At that *t* they will call Jerusalem
4: 11 At that *t* this people and Jerusalem
7: 25 From the *t* your forefathers left
8: 1 " 'At that *t*, declares the LORD,
8: 7 observe the *t* of their migration.
8: 15 for a *t* of healing
10: 18 "At this *t* I will hurl out
11: 7 From the *t* I brought your
11: 14 call to me in the *t* of their distress.
11: 18 at that *t* he showed me what they
13: 3 the LORD came to me a second *t*:
14: 19 for a *t* of healing
16: 19 my refuge in *t* of distress,
16: 21 this *t* I will teach them
18: 7 If at any *t* I announce that a nation
18: 9 And if at another *t* I announce that
18: 23 with them in the *t* of your anger.
25: 33 At that *t* those slain
25: 34 For your *t* to be slaughtered has
27: 7 and his grandson until the *t*
29: 28 to us in Babylon: It will be a long *t*.
30: 7 It will be a *t* of trouble for Jacob,
31: 1 "At that *t*," declares the LORD,
31: 31 *t* is coming," declares the LORD,
31: 33 after that *t*," declares the LORD.
32: 14 in a clay jar so they will last a long *t*
33: 1 the LORD came to him a second *t*:
33: 15 " 'In those days and at that *t*
33: 20 come at their appointed *t*,
35: 7 Then you will live a long *t*
36: 2 from the *t* I began speaking to you
36: 9 a *t* of fasting before the LORD was
37: 16 where he remained a long *t*.
39: 10 at that *t* he gave them vineyards
39: 16 At that *t* they will be fulfilled
44: 17 At that *t* we had plenty of food
46: 21 the *t* for them to be punished.
49: 8 Esau at the *t* I punish him.
50: 4 "In those days, at that *t*,"
50: 20 In those days, at that *t*,"
50: 27 the *t* for them to be punished.
50: 31 the *t* for you to be punished.
51: 6 It is *t* for the LORD's vengeance;
51: 13 the *t* for you to be cut off
51: 33 floor at the *t* it is trampled;
51: 33 the *t* to harvest her will soon come
51: 47 For the *t* will surely come
Eze 4: 6 lie down again, this *t*
7: 7 The *t* has come, the day is near;
7: 12 The *t* has come, the day has arrived
11: 3 Will it not soon be *t* to build houses
21: 25 whose *t* of punishment has reached
21: 29 whose *t* of punishment has reached
23: 38 At that same *t* they defiled my
24: 14 The *t* has come for me to act.
24: 27 At that *t* your mouth will be
30: 3 a *t* of doom for the nations.
35: 5 the sword at the *t* of their calamity,
35: 5 the *t* their punishment reached its
38: 17 At that *t* they prophesied
38: 19 that at that *t* there shall be a great
48: 35 of the city from that *t* on will be:
Da 1: 18 At the end of the *t* set by the king
2: 8 certain that you are trying to gain *t*,
2: 16 went in to the king and asked for *t*,
2: 35 broken to pieces at the same *t*
Da 2: 44 "In the *t* of those kings, the God
3: 8 At this *t* some astrologers came
4: 19 was greatly perplexed for a *t*,
4: 34 end of that *t*, I, Nebuchadnezzar
4: 36 At the same *t* that my sanity was
5: 11 In the *t* of your father he was found
7: 12 allowed to live for a period of *t*.)
7: 22 the *t* came when they possessed
7: 25 to him for a *t*, times and half a *t*.
8: 17 that the vision concerns the *t*
8: 19 the vision concerns the appointed *t*
8: 19 you what will happen later in the *t*
9: 21 me in swift flight about the *t*
10: 2 At that *t* I, Daniel, mourned
10: 14 for the vision concerns a *t* yet
11: 24 of fortresses—but only for a *t*.
11: 27 come at the appointed *t*.
11: 29 this *t* the outcome will be different
11: 29 "At the appointed *t* he will invade
11: 33 for a *t* they will fall by the sword
11: 35 come at the appointed *t*.
11: 35 made spotless until the *t* of the end,
11: 36 until the *t* of wrath is completed,
11: 40 "At the *t* of the end the king
12: 1 But at that *t* your people—
12: 1 There will be a *t* of distress such
12: 1 "At that *t* Michael, the great
12: 4 of the scroll until the *t* of the end.
12: 7 "It will be for a *t*, times and half a *t*.
12: 9 and sealed until the *t* of the end.
12: 11 "From the *t* that the daily sacrifice
Hos 10: 12 for it is *t* to seek the LORD,
13: 13 when the *t* arrives,
Joel 3: 1 "In those days and at that *t*,
Am 4: 2 "The *t* will surely come
8: 2 "The *t* is ripe for my people Israel;
8: 10 I will make that *t* like mourning
Jnh 3: 1 came to Jonah a second *t*:
Mic 2: 3 for it will be a *t* of calamity.
3: 4 At that *t* he will hide his face
5: 3 until the *t* when she who is
7: 4 Now is the *t* of their confusion.
Na 1: 9 trouble will not come a second *t*.
Hab 2: 3 revelation awaits an appointed *t*;
3: 2 in our *t* make them known;
Zep 1: 12 At that *t* I will search Jerusalem
2: 2 before the appointed *t* arrives
3: 19 At that *t* I will deal
3: 20 At that *t* I will gather you;
3: 20 at that *t* I will bring you home.
Hag 1: 2 'The *t* has not yet come
1: 4 "Is it a *t* for you yourselves
2: 20 came to Haggai a second *t*
Zec 8: 6 the remnant of this people at that *t*,
8: 10 Before that *t* there were no wages
Mal 3: 7 since the *t* of your forefathers you
Mt 1: 11 and his brothers at the *t* of the exile
2: 1 during the *t* of King Herod,
2: 7 from them the exact *t* the star had
2: 16 with the *t* he had learned
4: 17 From that *t* on Jesus began
7: 4 when all the *t* there is a plank
8: 29 to torture us before the appointed *t*
9: 15 *t* will come when the bridegroom
10: 19 At that *t* you will be given what
11: 25 At that *t* Jesus said, "I praise you,
12: 1 At that *t* Jesus went
13: 21 has no root, he lasts only a short *t*.
13: 30 At that *t* I will tell the harvesters:
14: 1 At that *t* Herod the tetrarch heard
16: 21 From that *t* on Jesus began
18: 1 At that *t* the disciples came
21: 34 When the harvest *t* approached,
21: 36 than the first *t*, and the tenants
21: 41 share of the crop at harvest *t*."
24: 10 At that *t* many will turn away
24: 23 At that *t* if anyone says to you,
24: 25 See, I have told you ahead of *t*.
24: 30 "At that *t* the sign of the Son
24: 43 at what *t* of night the thief was
24: 45 them their food at the proper *t*?
24: 48 'My master is staying away a long *t*
25: 1 "At that *t* the kingdom
25: 5 The bridegroom was a long *t*
25: 19 "After a long *t* the master
26: 18 Teacher says: My appointed *t* is
26: 42 He went away a second *t*
26: 44 once more and prayed the third *t*,

Mt 26: 55 At that *t* Jesus said to the crowd,
27: 16 At that *t* they had a notorious
Mk 1: 9 At that *t* Jesus came
1: 15 "The *t* has come," he said.
2: 20 *t* will come when the bridegroom
3: 1 Another *t* he went
4: 17 no root, they last only a short *t*.
6: 21 Finally the opportune *t* came.
6: 35 By this *t* it was late in the day,
12: 2 At harvest *t* he sent a servant
13: 11 say whatever is given you at the *t*,
13: 21 At that *t* if anyone says to you,
13: 23 told you everything ahead of *t*.
13: 26 "At that *t* men will see the Son
13: 33 know when that *t* will come.
14: 7 you can help them any *t* you want.
14: 41 Returning the third *t*, he said
14: 72 the rooster crowed the second *t*.—
Lk 1: 5 In the *t* of Herod king
1: 10 And when the *t* for the burning
1: 20 will come true at their proper *t*."
1: 23 When his *t* of service was
1: 39 At that *t* Mary got ready
1: 57 When it was *t* for Elizabeth
2: 6 the *t* came for the baby to be born,
2: 21 when it was *t* to circumcise him,
2: 22 When the *t* of their purification
4: 13 he left him until an opportune *t*.
4: 25 widows in Israel in Elijah's *t*,
4: 27 Israel with leprosy in the *t*
5: 35 *t* will come when the bridegroom
7: 21 At that very *t* Jesus cured many
7: 45 this woman, from the *t* I entered,
8: 13 but in the *t* of testing they fall away
8: 27 For a long *t* this man had not worn
9: 36 one at that *t* what they had seen.
9: 51 As the *t* approached for him
10: 21 At that *t* Jesus, full of joy
12: 12 you at that *t* what you should say."
12: 42 food allowance at the proper *t*?
12: 45 'My master is taking a long *t*
12: 56 how to interpret this present *t*?
13: 1 at that *t* who told Jesus about
13: 31 At that *t* some Pharisees came
14: 17 At the *t* of the banquet he sent his
16: 16 Since that *t*, the good news
16: 22 "The *t* came when the beggar died
17: 22 The *t* is coming when you will long
18: 4 "For some *t* he refused.
19: 44 because you did not recognize the *t*
20: 9 and went away for a long *t*.
20: 10 At harvest *t* he sent a servant
21: 6 *t* will come when not one stone will
21: 8 'I am he,' and, 'The *t* is near.'
21: 22 For this is the *t* of punishment
21: 27 At that *t* they will see the Son
23: 7 who was also in Jerusalem at that *t*.
23: 8 for a long *t* he had been wanting
23: 22 For the third *t* he spoke to them:
23: 29 For the *t* will come
Jn 2: 4 Jesus replied, "My *t* has not yet
2: 13 When it was almost *t*
3: 4 "Surely he cannot enter a second *t*
3: 22 where he spent some *t* with them,
4: 21 *t* is coming when you will worship
4: 23 Yet a *t* is coming and has now
4: 52 as to the *t* when his son got better,
4: 53 realized that this was the exact *t*
5: 1 Some *t* later, Jesus went up
5: 6 been in this condition for a long *t*,
5: 25 a *t* is coming and has now come
5: 28 for a *t* is coming when all who are
5: 35 you chose for a *t* to enjoy his light.
6: 1 to believe what I say?" Some *t*
6: 66 From this *t* many of his disciples
7: 6 The right *t* for me has not yet come
7: 6 for you any *t* is right.
7: 8 for me the right *t* has not yet come
7: 30 because his *t* had not yet come.
7: 33 "I am with you for only a short *t*,
7: 39 Up to that *t* the Spirit had not been
8: 9 began to go away one at a *t*,
8: 20 because his *t* had not yet come.
9: 24 second *t* they summoned the man
11: 39 "by this *t* there is a bad odor,
11: 55 When it was almost *t*
12: 31 is the *t* for judgment on this world;
12: 42 Yet at the same *t* many
Jn 13: 1 Jesus knew that the *t* had come
14: 9 been among you such a long *t*?
16: 2 *t* is coming when anyone who kills
16: 4 that when the *t* comes you will
16: 21 has pain because her *t* has come;
16: 22 So with you: Now is your *t* of grief,
16: 25 a *t* is coming when I will no longer
16: 32 "But a *t* is coming, and has come,
17: 1 prayed: "Father, the *t* has come.
18: 39 prisoner at the *t* of the Passover.
19: 27 From that *t* on, this disciple took
21: 14 was now the third *t* Jesus appeared
21: 17 Jesus asked him the third *t*,
21: 17 The third *t* he said to him,
Ac 1: 6 are you at this *t* going
1: 21 with us the whole *t* the Lord Jesus
1: 22 from John's baptism to the *t*
3: 1 to the temple at the *t* of prayer—
3: 21 in heaven until the *t* comes for God
4: 34 from *t* to *t* those who owned lands
5: 36 Some *t* ago Theudas appeared,
7: 5 at that *t* Abraham had no child.
7: 17 "As the *t* drew near for God
7: 20 "At that *t* Moses was born,
7: 41 That was the *t* they made an idol
7: 45 in the land until the *t* of David,
8: 9 for some *t* a man named Simon had
8: 11 them for a long *t* with his magic.
9: 31 and Samaria enjoyed a *t* of peace.
9: 37 About that *t* she became sick
9: 43 stayed in Joppa for some *t*
10: 15 The voice spoke to him a second *t*,
11: 9 spoke from heaven a second *t*,
11: 27 During this *t* some prophets came
12: 1 It was about this *t* that King Herod
13: 11 and for a *t* you will be unable
13: 20 until the *t* of Samuel the prophet.
14: 3 spent considerable *t* there,
14: 28 And they stayed there a long *t*
15: 7 know that some *t* ago God made
15: 33 After spending some *t* there,
15: 36 Some *t* later Paul said to Barnabas,
17: 21 there spent their *t* doing nothing
18: 18 stayed on in Corinth for some *t*.
18: 20 him to spend more *t* with them,
18: 23 After spending some *t* in Antioch,
19: 23 About that *t* there arose a great
20: 16 to avoid spending *t* in the province
20: 18 know how I lived the whole *t* I was
21: 5 But when our *t* was up, we left
21: 38 out into the desert some *t* ago?"
24: 26 At the same *t* he was hoping that
26: 5 They have known me for a long *t*
26: 11 a *t* I went from one synagogue
26: 28 in such a short *t* you can persuade
26: 29 Paul replied, "Short *t* or long—
27: 9 Much *t* had been lost,
27: 21 After the men had gone a long *t*
27: 28 A short *t* later they took soundings
27: 40 at the same *t* untied the ropes that
28: 6 but after waiting a long *t*
Ro 3: 26 his justice at the present *t*,
5: 6 at just the right *t*, when we were
5: 14 the *t* of Adam to the *t* of Moses,
6: 21 What benefit did you reap at that *t*
8: 22 childbirth right up to the present *t*.
9: 9 "At the appointed *t* I will return,
11: 5 at the present *t* there is a remnant
11: 30 you who were at one *t* disobedient
13: 6 who give their full *t* to governing.
13: 11 understanding the present *t*.
1Co 2: 7 for our glory before *t* began.
4: 5 At that *t* each will receive his
4: 5 nothing before the appointed *t*;
7: 5 by mutual consent and for a *t*,
7: 29 brothers, is that the *t* is short.
14: 27 at a *t*, and someone must interpret.
15: 6 of the brothers at the same *t*,
16: 7 I hope to spend some *t* with you,
2Co 6: 2 now is the *t* of God's favor,
6: 2 "In the *t* of my favor I heard you,
8: 14 At the present *t* your plenty will
12: 14 ready to visit you for the third *t*,
13: 2 when I was with you the second *t*.
Gal 2: 1 to Jerusalem, this *t* with Barnabas.
4: 2 trustees until the *t* set by his father.
4: 4 But when the *t* had fully come,
4: 29 At that *t* the son born
Gal 6: 9 for at the proper *t* we will reap
Eph 2: 3 also lived among them at one *t*,
2: 12 that at that *t* you were separate
Php 1: 3 my God every *t* I remember you.
1Th 2: 17 from you for a short *t* (in person,
2Th 2: 6 he may be revealed at the proper *t*.
1Ti 2: 6 the testimony given in its proper *t*.
6: 15 God will bring about in his own *t*—
2Ti 1: 9 Jesus before the beginning of *t*,
4: 3 For the *t* will come
4: 6 the *t* has come for my departure.
Tit 1: 2 promised before the beginning of *t*,
3: 3 At one *t* we too were foolish,
3: 10 and then warn him a second *t*.
Heb 3: 8 during the *t* of testing in the desert,
4: 7 when a long *t* later he spoke
4: 16 grace to help us in our *t* of need.
5: 12 by this *t* you ought to be teachers,
8: 8 The *t* is coming, declares the Lord,
8: 10 after that *t*, declares the Lord.
9: 9 is an illustration for the present *t*,
9: 10 until the *t* of the new order.
9: 28 and he will appear a second *t*,
10: 12 for all *t* one sacrifice for sins,
10: 13 Since that *t* he waits
10: 16 after that *t*, says the Lord.
11: 25 the pleasures of sin for a short *t*.
11: 32 I do not have *t* to tell about Gideon
12: 11 discipline seems pleasant at the *t*,
12: 26 At that *t* his voice shook the earth,
1Pe 1: 5 ready to be revealed in the last *t*.
1: 11 trying to find out the *t*
4: 3 For you have spent enough *t*
4: 17 For it is *t* for judgment to begin
5: 6 that he may lift you up in due *t*.
2Pe 3: 6 also the world of that *t* was deluged
Rev 1: 3 written in it, because the *t* is near.
2: 21 I have given her *t* to repent
3: 3 know at what *t* I will come to you.
11: 6 during the *t* they are prophesying;
11: 18 *t* has come for judging the dead,
12: 12 because he knows that his *t* is short
12: 14 half a *t*, out of the serpent's reach.
12: 14 she would be taken care of for a *t*,
14: 15 because the *t* to reap has come,
20: 3 he must be set free for a short *t*.
22: 10 of this book, because the *t* is near.

TIMES (TIME)

Ge 4: 15 he will suffer vengeance seven *t*
4: 24 If Cain is avenged seven *t*,
4: 24 then Lamech seventy-seven *t*."
27: 36 He has deceived me these two *t*:
31: 7 me by changing my wages ten *t*.
31: 41 and you changed my wages ten *t*.
33: 3 bowed down to the ground seven *t*
43: 34 Benjamin's portion was five *t*
Ex 18: 22 as judges for the people at all *t*,
18: 26 as judges for the people at all *t*.
23: 14 "Three *t* a year you are
23: 17 "Three *t* a year all the men are
25: 30 on this table to be before me at all *t*.
34: 23 Three *t* a year all your men are
34: 24 when you go up three *t* each year
Lev 4: 6 of it seven *t* before the LORD,
4: 17 it before the LORD seven *t* in front
8: 11 some of the oil on the altar seven *t*,
14: 7 Seven *t* he shall sprinkle the one
14: 16 of it before the LORD seven *t*.
14: 27 the oil from his palm seven *t*
14: 51 and sprinkle the house seven *t*.
16: 14 it with his finger seven *t*
16: 19 with his finger seven *t* to cleanse it
23: 4 to proclaim at their appointed *t*:
25: 8 of years—seven *t* seven years—
26: 18 you for your sins seven *t* over.
26: 21 multiply your afflictions seven *t*
26: 24 you for your sins seven *t* over.
26: 28 you for your sins seven *t* over.
Nu 10: 10 Also at your *t* of rejoicing—
14: 22 me and tested me ten *t*—
19: 4 sprinkle it seven *t* toward the front
22: 28 to make you beat me these three *t*
22: 32 beaten your donkey these three *t*?
22: 33 turned away from me these three *t*.
24: 1 resort to sorcery as at other *t*,
24: 10 have blessed them these three *t*.
Dt 1: 11 increase you a thousand *t*

Dt 16: 16 Three *t* a year all your men must
Jos 6: 4 march around the city seven *t*,
6: 15 day they circled the city seven *t*.
6: 15 marched around the city seven *t*
Ru 4: 7 (Now in earlier *t* in Israel,
1Sa 3: 10 calling as at the other *t*, "Samuel!
20: 41 down before Jonathan three *t*,
27: 8 (From ancient *t* these peoples had
2Sa 12: 6 pay for that lamb four *t* over,
24: 3 multiply the troops a hundred *t*
1Ki 9: 25 Three *t* a year Solomon sacrificed
17: 21 himself out on the boy three *t*
18: 43 Seven *t* Elijah said, "Go back."
22: 16 "How many *t* must I make you
2Ki 4: 35 The boy sneezed seven *t*
5: 10 wash yourself seven *t* in the Jordan
5: 14 himself in the Jordan seven *t*,
13: 18 He struck it three *t* and stopped.
13: 19 have struck the ground five or six *t*;
13: 19 now you will defeat it only three *t*."
13: 25 Three *t* Jehoash defeated him,
1Ch 4: 22 (These records are from ancient *t*.)
9: 20 In earlier *t* Phinehas son
12: 32 who understood the *t* and knew
21: 3 multiply his troops a hundred *t*
2Ch 18: 15 "How many *t* must I make you
Ezr 4: 15 a place of rebellion from ancient *t*.
Ne 4: 12 near them came and told us ten *t*
6: 4 Four *t* they sent me the same
10: 34 at set *t* each year a contribution
13: 31 of wood at designated *t*,
Est 9: 31 days of Purim at their designated *t*,
9: 31 in regard to their *t* of fasting
Job 19: 3 Ten *t* now you have reproached me
24: 1 "Why does the Almighty not set *t*
27: 10 Will he call upon God at all *t*?
33: 29 twice, even three *t*—
38: 23 which I reserve for *t* of trouble,
Ps 9: 9 a stronghold in *t* of trouble.
10: 1 Why do you hide yourself in *t*
12: 6 purified seven *t*.
31: 15 My *t* are in your hands;
34: 1 I will extol the LORD at all *t*;
37: 19 In *t* of disaster they will not wither;
41: 1 the LORD delivers him in *t*
59: 16 my refuge in *t* of trouble.
60: 3 shown your people desperate *t*;
62: 8 Trust in him at all *t*, O people;
79: 12 of our neighbors seven *t*
106: 43 Many *t* he delivered them,
119: 20 for your laws at all *t*.
119: 164 Seven *t* a day I praise you
Pr 17: 17 A friend loves at all *t*,
24: 10 If you falter in *t* of trouble,
24: 16 a righteous man falls seven *t*,
25: 19 on the unfaithful in *t* of trouble.
Ecc 7: 14 When *t* are good, be happy;
7: 14 but when *t* are bad, consider:
7: 22 that many *t* you yourself have
9: 12 so men are trapped by evil *t*
Isa 30: 26 the sunlight will be seven *t* brighter
33: 6 be the sure foundation for your *t*,
46: 10 from ancient *t*, what is still to come
64: 4 Since ancient *t* no one has heard,
Jer 14: 8 its Savior in *t* of distress,
15: 11 you in *t* of disaster and *t* of distress.
21: 2 as in *t* past so that he will withdraw
28: 8 early *t* the prophets who preceded
46: 26 Egypt will be inhabited as in *t* past
Eze 4: 10 to eat each day and eat it at set *t*.
4: 11 of a hin of water and drink it at set *t*
21: 14 even three *t*.
Da 1: 20 he found them ten *t* better
2: 21 He changes *t* and seasons;
3: 19 the furnace heated seven *t* hotter
4: 16 till seven *t* pass by for him.
4: 23 until seven *t* pass by for him.'
4: 25 Seven *t* will pass by for you
4: 32 Seven *t* will pass by for you
6: 10 Three *t* a day he got
6: 13 He still prays three *t* a day."
7: 10 ten thousand *t* ten thousand stood
7: 25 handed over to him for a time, *t*
7: 25 try to change the set *t* and the laws.
9: 25 and a trench, but in *t* of trouble.
11: 14 "In those *t* many will rise
12: 7 "It will be for a time, *t*
Am 4: 9 "Many *t* I struck your gardens
5: 13 for the *t* are evil.
5: 13 prudent man keeps quiet in such *t*,
Mic 5: 2 from ancient *t*."
Na 1: 7 a refuge in *t* of trouble.
Mt 13: 8 sixty or thirty *t* what was sown.
13: 23 sixty or thirty *t* what was sown."
16: 3 cannot interpret the signs of the *t*.
18: 21 Up to seven *t*?" Jesus answered,
18: 21 how many *t* shall I forgive my
18: 22 not seven *t*, but seventy-seven *t*.
19: 29 my sake will receive a hundred *t*
26: 34 you will disown me three *t*."
26: 75 you will disown me three *t*."
Mk 4: 8 sixty, or even a hundred *t*."
4: 20 even a hundred *t* what was sown."
10: 30 fail to receive a hundred *t*
14: 30 yourself will disown me three *t*."
14: 72 twice you will disown me three *t*."
Lk 8: 8 a hundred *t* more than was sown."
8: 29 Many *t* it had seized him, and
17: 4 and seven *t* comes back to you
17: 4 sins against you seven *t* in a day,
18: 30 of God will fail to receive many *t*
19: 8 I will pay back four *t* the amount."
21: 24 on by the Gentiles until the *t*
22: 34 will deny three *t* that you know
22: 61 you will disown me three *t*."
Jn 13: 38 you will disown me three *t*!
Ac 1: 7 "It is not for you to know the *t*
3: 19 that *t* of refreshing may come
10: 16 This happened three *t*,
11: 10 This happened three *t*,
15: 21 in every city from the earliest *t*
17: 26 he determined the *t* set for them
Ro 1: 10 you in my prayers at all *t*;
1: 13 that I planned many *t* to come
2Co 9: 8 so that in all things at all *t*,
11: 24 Five *t* I received from the Jews
11: 25 Three *t* I was beaten with rods,
11: 25 three *t* I was shipwrecked,
12: 8 Three *t* I pleaded with the Lord
Eph 1: 10 when the *t* will have reached their
1Th 5: 1 about *t* and dates we do not need
2Th 3: 16 himself give you peace at all *t*
1Ti 4: 1 that in later *t* some will abandon
2Ti 3: 1 There will be terrible *t*
Heb 1: 1 through the prophets at many *t*
9: 26 to suffer many *t* since the creation
10: 33 at other *t* you stood side by side
1Pe 1: 20 in these last *t* for your sake.
Jude : 18 "In the last *t* there will be scoffers
Rev 5: 11 and ten thousand *t* ten thousand.
12: 14 *t* and half a time, out

TIMID (TIMIDITY)

2Co 10: 1 who am "*t*" when face to face
1Th 5: 14 encourage the *t*, help the weak,

TIMIDITY (TIMID)

2Ti 1: 7 For God did not give us a spirit of *t*

TIMNA

Ge 36: 12 also had a concubine named *T*,
36: 22 *T* was Lotan's sister.
36: 40 *T*, Alvah, Jetheth, Oholibamah,
1Ch 1: 36 Gatam and Kenaz; by *T*: Amalek.
1: 39 *T* was Lotan's sister.
1: 51 *T*, Alvah, Jetheth, Oholibamah,

TIMNAH (TIMNITE'S)

Ge 38: 12 to *T*, to the men who were shearing
38: 13 on his way to *T* to shear his sheep,"
38: 14 to Enaim, which is on the road to *T*
Jos 15: 10 to Beth Shemesh and crossed to *T*.
15: 57 Zanoah, Kain, Gibeah and *T*—
19: 43 Ithlah, Elon, *T*, Ekron, Eltekeh,
Jdg 14: 1 Samson went down to *T*
14: 2 I have seen a Philistine woman in *T*
14: 5 Samson went down to *T* together
14: 5 approached the vineyards of *T*,
2Ch 28: 18 as well as Soco, *T* and Gimzo,

TIMNATH HERES

Jdg 2: 9 at *T* in the hill country of Ephraim,

TIMNATH SERAH

Jos 19: 50 *T* in the hill country of Ephraim.
24: 30 at *T* in the hill country of Ephraim,

TIMNITE'S (TIMNAH)

Jdg 15: 6 "Samson, the *T* son-in-law,

TIMON

Ac 6: 5 Procorus, Nicanor, *T*, Parmenas,

TIMOTHY

Ac 16: 1 where a disciple named *T* lived,
17: 14 but Silas and *T* stayed at Berea.
17: 15 for Silas and *T* to join him
18: 5 and *T* came from Macedonia,
19: 22 *T* and Erastus, to Macedonia,
20: 4 Gaius from Derbe, *T* also,
Ro 16: 21 *T*, my fellow worker, sends his
1Co 4: 17 this reason I am sending to you *T*,
16: 10 If *T* comes, see to it that he has
2Co 1: 1 and *T* our brother, To the church
1: 19 among you by me and Silas and *T*,
Php 1: 1 Paul and *T*, servants of Christ Jesus
2: 19 Jesus to send *T* to you soon,
2: 22 But you know that *T* has proved
Col 1: 1 the will of God, and *T* our brother,
1Th 1: 1 and *T*, To the church
3: 2 We sent *T*, who is our brother
3: 6 *T* has just now come to us from you
2Th 1: 1 and *T*, To the church
1Ti 1: 2 To *T* my true son in the faith:
1: 18 *T*, my son, I give you this
6: 20 *T*, guard what has been entrusted
2Ti 1: 2 To *T*, my dear son: Grace,
Phm : 1 of Christ Jesus, and *T* our brother,
Heb 13: 23 that our brother *T* has been

TIN

Nu 31: 22 Gold, silver, bronze, iron, *t*,
Eze 22: 18 all of them are the copper, *t*,
22: 20 and *t* into a furnace to melt it
27: 12 *t* and lead for your merchandise.

TINDER

Isa 1: 31 The mighty man will become *t*

TINGLE

1Sa 3: 11 ears of everyone who hears of it *t*.
2Ki 21: 12 of everyone who hears of it will *t*.
Jer 19: 3 ears of everyone who hears of it *t*.

TIP

Jdg 6: 21 With the *t* of the staff that was
1Ki 6: 24 ten cubits from wing *t* to wing *t*.
Est 5: 2 and touched the *t* of the scepter.
Job 33: 2 my words are on the *t* of my tongue
38: 37 Who can *t* over the water jars
Lk 16: 24 Lazarus to dip the *t* of his finger

TIPHSAH

1Ki 4: 24 from *T* to Gaza, and had peace
2Ki 15: 16 He sacked *T* and ripped open all
15: 16 attacked *T* and everyone in the city

TIRAS

Ge 10: 2 Javan, Tubal, Meshech and *T*.
1Ch 1: 5 Javan, Tubal, Meshech and *T*.

TIRATHITES

1Ch 2: 55 the *T*, Shimeathites and Sucathites,

TIRE (TIRED)

Jer 2: 24 pursue her need not *t* themselves;
2Th 3: 13 never *t* of doing what is right.

TIRED (TIRE)

Ex 17: 12 When Moses' hands grew *t*,
Jdg 16: 16 after day until he was *t* to death.
2Sa 17: 29 and *t* and thirsty in the desert."
23: 10 the Philistines till his hand grew *t*
Isa 5: 27 Not one of them grows *t*
40: 28 He will not grow *t* or weary,
40: 30 Even youths grow *t* and weary,
Jn 4: 6 *t* as he was from the journey,

TIRHAKAH

2Ki 19: 9 received a report that *T*,
Isa 37: 9 received a report that *T*,

TIRHANAH

1Ch 2: 48 was the mother of Sheber and *T*.

TIRIA

1Ch 4: 16 Ziph, Ziphah, *T* and Asarel.

TIRZAH

Nu 26: 33 Noah, Hoglah, Milcah and *T*.)
27: 1 Noah, Hoglah, Milcah and *T*.
36: 11 daughters—Mahlah, *T*,
Jos 12: 24 of *T* one thirty-one kings in all.
17: 3 Noah, Hoglah, Milcah and *T*.
1Ki 14: 17 wife got up and left and went to *T*.
15: 21 Ramah and withdrew to *T*.
15: 33 became king of all Israel in *T*,
16: 6 with his fathers and was buried in *T*
16: 8 and he reigned in *T* two years.
16: 9 man in charge of the palace at *T*.
16: 9 was in *T* at the time, getting drunk
16: 15 Zimri reigned in *T* seven days.
16: 17 from Gibbethon and laid siege to *T*
16: 23 twelve years, six of them in *T*.
2Ki 15: 14 of Gadi went from *T* up to Samaria.
15: 16 Menahem, starting out from *T*,
SS 6: 4 You are beautiful, my darling, as *T*,

TISHBE (TISHBITE)

1Ki 17: 1 Now Elijah the Tishbite, from *T*

TISHBITE (TISHBE)

1Ki 17: 1 Elijah the *T*, from Tishbe in Gilead
21: 17 of the LORD came to Elijah the *T*:
21: 28 of the LORD came to Elijah the *T*:
2Ki 1: 3 of the LORD said to Elijah the *T*,
1: 8 king said, "That was Elijah the *T*."
9: 36 through his servant Elijah the *T*:

TITHE (TEN)

Lev 27: 30 " 'A *t* of everything from the land,
27: 31 If a man redeems any of his *t*,
27: 32 The entire *t* of the herd and flock—
Nu 18: 26 from the Israelites the *t* I give you
18: 26 you must present a tenth of that *t*
Dt 12: 17 eat in your own towns the *t*
14: 23 Eat the *t* of your grain, new wine
14: 24 your God and cannot carry your *t*
14: 25 then exchange your *t* for silver,
26: 12 the year of the *t*, you shall give it
2Ch 31: 5 They brought a great amount, a *t*
31: 6 also brought a *t* of their herds
31: 6 and a *t* of the holy things dedicated
Ne 10: 37 And we will bring a *t* of our crops
Mal 3: 10 the whole *t* into the storehouse,

TITHES (TEN)

Nu 18: 21 give to the Levites all the *t* in Israel
18: 24 as their inheritance the *t* that
18: 28 From these *t* you must give
18: 28 LORD from all the *t* you receive
Dt 12: 6 sacrifices, your *t* and special gifts,
12: 11 sacrifices, your *t* and special gifts,
14: 28 bring all the *t* of that year's
2Ch 31: 12 brought in the contributions, *t*
Ne 10: 37 it is the Levites who collect the *t*
10: 38 Levites when they receive the *t*,
10: 38 a tenth of the *t* up to the house
12: 44 the contributions, firstfruits and *t*.
13: 5 and also the *t* of grain, new wine
13: 12 All Judah brought the *t* of grain,
Am 4: 4 your *t* every three years.
Mal 3: 8 'How do we rob you?' "In *t*

TITIUS JUSTUS

Ac 18: 7 went next door to the house of *T*,

TITLE

Isa 45: 4 and bestow on you a *t* of honor,
Eph 1: 21 and every *t* that can be given,
Rev 17: 5 This *t* was written on her forehead:

TITUS

2Co 2: 13 I did not find my brother *T* there.
7: 6 comforted us by the coming of *T*,
7: 13 delighted to see how happy *T* was,
7: 14 you to *T* has proved to be true
8: 6 So we urged *T*, since he had earlier
8: 16 heart of *T* the same concern I have
8: 17 For *T* not only welcomed our
8: 23 As for *T*, he is my partner
12: 18 I urged *T* to go to you and I sent
12: 18 *T* did not exploit you, did he?
Gal 2: 1 I took *T* along also.
2: 3 Yet not even *T*, who was with me,
2Ti 4: 10 gone to Galatia, and *T* to Dalmatia.
Tit 1: 4 To *T*, my true son

TIZITE

1Ch 11: 45 brother Joha the *T*, Eliel

TOAH

1Ch 6: 34 the son of *T*, the son of Zuph,

TOB

Jdg 11: 3 and settled in the land of *T*,
11: 5 to get Jephthah from the land of *T*.
2Sa 10: 6 also twelve thousand men from *T*.
10: 8 and Rehob and the men of *T*

TOB-ADONIJAH

2Ch 17: 8 Adonijah, Tobijah and *T*—

TOBIAH (TOBIAH'S)

Ezr 2: 60 *T* and Nekoda 652 And
Ne 2: 10 and *T* the Ammonite official heard
2: 19 *T* the Ammonite official
4: 3 as they are?" *T* the Ammonite,
4: 7 But when Sanballat, *T*, the Arabs,
6: 1 When word came to Sanballat, *T*,
6: 12 *T* and Sanballat had hired him.
6: 14 Remember *T* and Sanballat,
6: 17 replies from *T* kept coming to them
6: 17 were sending many letters to *T*,
6: 19 And *T* sent letters to intimidate me
7: 62 *T* and Nekoda 642 And
13: 4 He was closely associated with *T*,
13: 7 in providing *T* a room in the courts

TOBIAH'S (TOBIAH)

Ne 13: 8 threw all *T* household goods out

TOBIJAH

2Ch 17: 8 Adonijah, *T* and Tob-Adonijah—
Zec 6: 10 *T* and Jedaiah, who have arrived
6: 14 crown will be given to Heldai, *T*,

TODAY (TODAY'S)

Ge 4: 14 *T* you are driving me from the land,
19: 37 he is the father of the Moabites of *t*.
19: 38 the father of the Ammonites of *t*.
21: 26 and I heard about it only *t*."
24: 12 give me success *t*, and show
24: 42 When I came to the spring *t*, I said,
30: 32 Let me go through all your flocks *t*
31: 43 can I do *t* about these daughters
31: 48 a witness between you and me *t*."
40: 7 "Why are your faces so sad *t*?"
41: 9 "*T* I am reminded
47: 23 and your land *t* for Pharaoh,
47: 26 still in force *t*— that a fifth
Ex 2: 18 "Why have you returned so early *t*
5: 14 quota of bricks yesterday or *t*,
13: 4 *T*, in the month of Abib, you are
14: 13 Egyptians you see *t* you will never
14: 13 the LORD will bring you *t*.
16: 25 any of it on the ground *t*.
16: 25 "Eat it *t*," Moses said,
16: 25 *t* is a Sabbath to the LORD.
19: 10 consecrate them *t* and tomorrow.
32: 29 have been set apart to the LORD *t*,
34: 11 Obey what I command you *t*.
Lev 8: 34 has been done *t* was commanded
9: 4 For *t* the LORD will appear to you
10: 19 if I had eaten the sin offering *t*?"
10: 19 "*T* they sacrificed their sin offering
Dt 1: 10 your numbers so that *t* you are
2: 18 "*T* you are to pass by the region
4: 4 LORD your God are still alive *t*.
4: 8 of laws I am setting before you *t*?
4: 38 to you for your inheritance, as it is *t*
4: 40 which I am giving you *t*,
5: 1 laws I declare in your hearing *t*.
5: 3 with all of us who are alive here *t*.
5: 24 *T* we have seen that a man can live
6: 6 that I give you *t* are
6: 24 and be kept alive, as is the case *t*.
7: 11 decrees and laws I give you *t*.
8: 1 every command I am giving you *t*,
8: 18 swore to your forefathers, as it is *t*.
8: 19 against you *t* that you will surely be
Dt 9: 3 be assured *t* that the LORD your
10: 8 in his name, as they still do *t*.
10: 13 and decrees that I am giving you *t*
10: 15 above all the nations, as it is *t*.
11: 2 Remember *t* that your children
11: 8 all the commands I am giving you *t*
11: 13 the commands I am giving you *t*—
11: 26 I am setting before you *t* a blessing
11: 27 your God that I am giving you *t*;
11: 28 from the way that I command you *t*
11: 32 and laws I am setting before you *t*.
12: 8 You are not to do as we do here *t*,
13: 18 commands that I am giving you *t*
15: 5 these commands I am giving you *t*.
15: 15 is why I give you this command *t*.
19: 9 all these laws I command you *t*—
20: 3 *t* you are going into battle
26: 3 "I declare *t* to the LORD your
27: 1 these commands that I give you *t*.
27: 4 as I command you *t*, and coat them
27: 10 and decrees that I give you *t*."
28: 1 all his commands I give you *t*,
28: 14 any of the commands I give you *t*,
28: 15 and decrees I am giving you *t*,
29: 10 All of you are standing *t*
29: 15 also with those who are not here *t*.
29: 15 here with us *t* in the presence
29: 18 among you *t* whose heart turns
30: 2 to everything I command you *t*,
30: 8 all his commands I am giving you *t*.
30: 11 I am commanding you *t* is not too
30: 15 set before you *t* life and prosperity,
30: 16 For I command you *t*
Jos 3: 7 "*T* I will begin to exalt you
5: 9 "*T* I have rolled away the reproach
7: 25 will bring disaster on you *t*."
14: 10 So here I am *t*, eighty-five years old
14: 11 strong *t* as the day Moses sent me
22: 18 " 'If you rebel against the LORD *t*,
22: 29 and turn away from him *t*
22: 31 "*T* we know that the LORD is
Jdg 9: 18 (but *t* you have revolted
9: 19 toward Jerub-Baal and his family *t*,
12: 3 Now why have you come up *t*
21: 3 one tribe be missing from Israel *t*?"
21: 6 "*T* one tribe is cut off from Israel,"
Ru 2: 19 did you glean *t*? Where did you
2: 19 of the man I worked with *t* is Boaz
3: 18 rest until the matter is settled *t*."
4: 9 "*T* you are witnesses that I have
4: 10 *T* you are witnesses!"
1Sa 4: 3 upon us *t* before the Philistines?
9: 9 because the prophet of *t* used
9: 12 he has just come to our town *t*,
9: 19 for *t* you are to eat with me,
10: 2 you leave me *t*, you will meet
11: 13 "No one shall be put to death *t*,
14: 28 Cursed be any man who eats food *t*
14: 30 been if the men had eaten *t* some
14: 38 out what sin has been committed *t*.
14: 45 for he did this *t* with God's help."
15: 28 the kingdom of Israel from you *t*
17: 46 *T* I will give the carcasses
20: 27 or *t*?" Jonathan answered,
21: 5 How much more so *t*!"
22: 8 to lie in wait for me, as he does *t*."
22: 13 he does *t*?" Ahimelech answered
24: 19 well for the way you treated me *t*.
25: 32 who has sent you *t* to meet me.
26: 8 "*T* God has delivered your enemy
26: 21 you considered my life precious *t*,
26: 23 delivered you into my hands *t*,
26: 24 As surely as I valued your life *t*,
27: 10 "Where did you go raiding *t*?"
28: 18 the LORD has done this to you *t*.
2Sa 3: 39 *t*, though I am the anointed king,
6: 20 of Israel has distinguished himself *t*
14: 22 "*T* your servant knows that he has
15: 20 *t* shall I make you wander about
16: 3 '*T* the house of Israel will give me
16: 12 for the cursing I am receiving *t*."
18: 20 but you must not do so *t*,
18: 20 the one to take the news *t*,"
18: 31 The LORD has delivered you *t*
19: 5 "*T* you have humiliated all your
19: 6 made it clear *t* that
19: 6 pleased if Absalom were alive *t*
19: 20 but *t* I have come here

2Sa 19: 22 Do I not know that *t* I am king
19: 22 put to death in Israel *t?*
1Ki 1: 25 *T* he has gone down and sacrificed
1: 30 will surely carry out *t* what I swore
1: 48 to see a successor on my throne *t*
1: 51 to me *t* that he will not put his
2: 24 Adonijah shall be put to death *t!*''
5: 7 ''Praise be to the LORD *t*,
8: 8 Place; and they are still there *t*.
8: 24 you have fulfilled it—as it is *t*.
12: 7 ''If *t* you will be a servant
18: 15 surely present myself to Ahab *t*.''
18: 36 let it be known *t* that you are God
20: 13 I will give it into your hand *t*,
2Ki 2: 3 to take your master from you *t?*''
2: 5 to take your master from you *t?*''
4: 23 ''Why go to him *t?*'' he asked.
6: 28 son so we may eat him *t*,
6: 31 remains on his shoulders *t!*''
1Ch 29: 5 willing to consecrate himself *t*
2Ch 5: 9 Place; and they are still there *t*.
6: 15 you have fulfilled it—as it is *t*.
Ezr 9: 7 the hand of foreign kings, as it is *t*.
Ne 1: 11 Give your servant success *t*
9: 32 days of the kings of Assyria until *t*.
9: 36 we are slaves *t*, slaves
Est 5: 4 come *t* to a banquet I have
Job 23: 2 ''Even *t* my complaint is bitter;
Ps 2: 7 *t* I have become your Father.
95: 7 *T*, if you hear his voice,
Pr 7: 14 *t* I fulfilled my vows
22: 19 I teach you *t*, even you.
Isa 38: 19 as I am doing *t*;
48: 7 have not heard of them before *t*.
56: 12 And tomorrow will be like *t*,
58: 4 You cannot fast as you do *t*
Jer 1: 10 *t* I appoint you over nations
1: 18 *T* I have made you a fortified city,
11: 5 honey'—the land you possess *t*.''
11: 7 up from Egypt until *t*,
25: 18 they are *t*; Pharaoh king of Egypt,
40: 4 *t* I am freeing you from the chains
42: 19 I warn you *t* that you made a fatal
42: 21 I have told you *t*, but you still have
44: 2 *T* they lie deserted and in ruins
44: 6 them the desolate ruins they are *t*.
44: 22 waste without inhabitants, as it is *t*.
Mt 6: 11 Give us *t* our daily bread.
6: 30 which is here *t* and tomorrow is
16: 3 in the morning, '*T* it will be stormy,
21: 28 'Son, go and work *t* in the vineyard
27: 19 for I have suffered a great deal *t*
Mk 14: 30 Jesus answered, ''*t*— yes, tonight
Lk 2: 11 *T* in the town of David a Savior has
4: 21 ''*T* this scripture is fulfilled
5: 26 ''We have seen remarkable things *t*
12: 28 which is here *t*, and tomorrow is
13: 32 and heal people *t* and tomorrow,
13: 33 I must keep going *t* and tomorrow
19: 5 I must stay at your house *t*.''
19: 9 *T* salvation has come to this house,
22: 34 Peter, before the rooster crows *t*,
22: 61 ''Before the rooster crows *t*,
23: 43 *t* you will be with me in paradise.''
Ac 4: 9 called to account *t* for an act
13: 33 *t* I have become your Father.'
20: 26 declare to you *t* that I am innocent
22: 3 zealous for God as any of you are *t*.
24: 21 am on trial before you *t*.' ''
26: 2 fortunate to stand before you *t*
26: 6 our fathers that I am on trial *t*.
26: 29 to me *t* may become what I am,
Heb 1: 5 *t* I have become your Father''?
3: 7 ''*T*, if you hear his voice,
3: 13 daily, as long as it is called *T*,
3: 15 ''*T*, if you hear his voice,
4: 7 again set a certain day, calling it *T*,
4: 7 ''*T*, if you hear his voice,
5: 5 *t* I have become your Father.''
13: 8 Christ is the same yesterday and *t*
Jas 4: 13 ''*T* or tomorrow we will go to this

TODAY'S (TODAY)

Ac 19: 40 with rioting because of *t* events.

TOE (TOES)

Lev 8: 23 and on the big *t* of his right foot.
14: 14 and on the big *t* of his right foot.
14: 17 and on the big *t* of his right foot,
14: 25 and on the big *t* of his right foot.
14: 28 and on the big *t* of his right foot.

TOES (TOE)

Ex 29: 20 and on the big *t* of their right feet.
Lev 8: 24 and on the big *t* of their right feet.
Jdg 1: 6 and cut off his thumbs and big *t*.
1: 7 big *t* cut off have picked up scraps
2Sa 21: 20 on each hand and six *t* on each foot
1Ch 20: 6 on each hand and six *t* on each foot
Da 2: 41 and *t* were partly of baked clay
2: 42 As the *t* were partly iron

TOGARMAH

Ge 10: 3 Ashkenaz, Riphath and *T*.
1Ch 1: 6 Ashkenaz, Riphath and *T*.

TOHU

1Sa 1: 1 the son of *T*, the son of Zuph,

TOIL (TOILED TOILING TOILS TOILSOME)

Ge 3: 17 through painful *t* you will eat of it
5: 29 and painful *t* of our hands caused
31: 42 has seen my hardship and the *t*
Dt 26: 7 saw our misery, *t* and oppression.
Jos 24: 13 a land on which you did not *t*
Pr 5: 10 your *t* enrich another man's house.
Ecc 2: 22 What does a man get for all the *t*
3: 9 does the worker gain from his *t?*
3: 13 and find satisfaction in all his *t*—
4: 6 than two handfuls with *t*
4: 8 There was no end to his *t*,
Isa 65: 23 They will not *t* in vain
La 5: 13 Young men *t* at the millstones;
1Th 2: 9 brothers, our *t* and hardship;

TOILED (TOIL)

Job 20: 18 What he *t* for he must give back
Ps 105: 44 heir to what others had *t* for—
Ecc 2: 11 and what I had *t* to achieve,
2: 18 I hated all the things I had *t*
Isa 62: 8 wine for which you have *t*;
2Co 11: 27 and *t* and have often gone

TOILING (TOIL)

Ps 127: 2 *t* for food to eat—
Ecc 4: 8 ''For whom am I *t*,'' he asked,
2Th 3: 8 *t* so that we would not be a burden

TOILS (TOIL)

Ecc 1: 3 labor at which he *t* under the sun?
5: 16 since he *t* for the wind?

TOILSOME (TOIL)

Ecc 2: 20 over all my *t* labor under the sun.
5: 18 in his *t* labor under the sun
9: 9 and in your *t* labor under the sun.

TOKEN

1Ch 4: 32 Ain, Rimmon, *T* and Ashan—

TOKHATH

2Ch 34: 22 the wife of Shallum son of *T*,

TOLA (TOLAITE)

Ge 46: 13 The sons of Issachar: *T*, Puah,
Nu 26: 23 through *T*, the Tolaite clan;
Jdg 10: 1 *T* son of Puah, the son of Dodo,
1Ch 7: 1 The sons of Issachar: *T*, Puah,
7: 2 The sons of *T:* Uzzi, Rephaiah,
7: 2 the descendants of *T* listed

TOLAD

1Ch 4: 29 Bilhah, Ezem, *T*, Bethuel,

TOLAITE (TOLA)

Nu 26: 23 through Tola, the *T* clan;

TOLERANCE (TOLERATE)

Ro 2: 4 for the riches of his kindness, *t*

TOLERATE (TOLERANCE TOLERATED)

Est 3: 8 in the king's best interest to *t* them.
Hab 1: 3 Why do you *t* wrong?
1: 13 Why then do you *t* the treacherous
1: 13 you cannot *t* wrong.
Rev 2: 2 that you cannot *t* wicked men,
2: 20 You *t* that woman Jezebel,

TOLERATED (TOLERATE)

Est 3: 4 Mordecai's behavior would be *t*,

TOMB (TOMBS)

Ge 23: 6 None of us will refuse you his *t*
35: 20 Over her *t* Jacob set up a pillar,
35: 20 day that pillar marks Rachel's *t*.
50: 5 bury me in the *t* I dug for myself
Jdg 8: 32 and was buried in the *t*
16: 31 in the *t* of Manoah his father.
1Sa 10: 2 will meet two men near Rachel's *t*,
2Sa 2: 32 him in his father's *t* at Bethlehem.
3: 32 the king wept aloud at Abner's *t*.
4: 12 buried it in Abner's *t* at Hebron.
17: 23 and was buried in his father's *t*.
19: 37 town near the *t* of my father
21: 14 in the *t* of Saul's father Kish,
1Ki 13: 22 buried in the *t* of your fathers.' ''
13: 30 Then he laid the body in his own *t*,
2Ki 9: 28 with his fathers in his *t* in the City
13: 21 the man's body into Elisha's *t*.
23: 17 ''It marks the *t* of the man
23: 30 and buried him in his own *t*.
2Ch 16: 14 him in the *t* that he had cut out
Job 21: 32 and watch is kept over his *t*.
Isa 14: 18 each in his own *t*.
14: 19 But you are cast out of your *t*
Mt 27: 60 in front of the entrance to the *t*
27: 60 in his own new *t* that he had cut out
27: 61 were sitting there across from the *t*.
27: 64 order for the *t* to be made secure
27: 65 make the *t* as secure as you know
27: 66 made the *t* secure by putting a seal
28: 1 other Mary went to look at the *t*.
28: 2 going to the *t*, rolled back the stone
28: 8 the women hurried away from the *t*
Mk 6: 29 and took his body and laid it in a *t*.
15: 46 and placed it in a *t* cut out of rock.
15: 46 stone against the entrance of the *t*.
16: 2 they were on their way to the *t*
16: 3 away from the entrance of the *t?*''
16: 5 As they entered the *t*, they saw
16: 8 went out and fled from the *t*.
Lk 23: 53 and placed it in a *t* cut in the rock,
23: 55 saw the *t* and how his body was laid
24: 1 had prepared and went to the *t*.
24: 2 the stone rolled away from the *t*,
24: 9 When they came back from the *t*,
24: 12 however, got up and ran to the *t*.
24: 22 went to the *t* early this morning
24: 24 of our companions went to the *t*
Jn 11: 17 been in the *t* for four days.
11: 31 going to the *t* to mourn there.
11: 38 more deeply moved, came to the *t*.
12: 17 he had called Lazarus from the *t*,
19: 41 and in the garden a new *t*,
19: 42 and since the *t* was nearby,
20: 1 Mary of Magdala went to the *t*
20: 2 have taken the Lord out of the *t*,
20: 3 the other disciple started for the *t*.
20: 4 Peter and reached the *t* first.
20: 6 arrived and went into the *t*.
20: 8 who had reached the *t* first,
20: 11 but Mary stood outside the *t* crying
20: 11 she bent over to look into the *t*
Ac 2: 29 and his *t* is here to this day.
7: 16 in the *t* that Abraham had bought
13: 29 from the tree and laid him in a *t*.

TOMBS (TOMB)

Ge 23: 6 dead in the choicest of our *t*.
2Ki 23: 16 when he saw the *t* that were there
2Ch 21: 20 but not in the *t* of the kings.
24: 25 but not in the *t* of the kings.
28: 27 in the *t* of the kings of Israel.
32: 33 buried on the hill where the *t*
35: 24 He was buried in the *t* of his fathers
Ne 3: 16 a point opposite the *t* of David, as
Ps 49: 11 Their *t* will remain their houses
Mt 8: 28 coming from the *t* met him.
23: 27 You are like whitewashed *t*,
23: 29 You build *t* for the prophets
27: 52 The *t* broke open and the bodies
27: 53 They came out of the *t*,
Mk 5: 2 came from the *t* to meet him.
5: 3 This man lived in the *t*,

Mk 5: 5 Night and day among the *t*
Lk 8: 27 in a house, but had lived in the *t*.
11: 47 you build *t* for the prophets,
11: 48 the prophets, and you build their *t*.

TOMBSTONE (STONE)

2Ki 23: 17 king asked, "What is that *t* I see?"

TOMORROW

Ex 8: 10 "*T*," Pharaoh said.
8: 23 This miraculous sign will occur *t*
8: 29 and *t* the flies will leave Pharaoh
9: 5 "*T* the LORD will do this
9: 18 at this time *t* I will send the worst
10: 4 locusts into your country *t*.
16: 23 what the LORD commanded: '*T* is
17: 9 *T* I will stand on top of the hill
19: 10 and consecrate them today and *t*.
32: 5 "*T* there will be a festival
Nu 11: 18 yourselves in preparation for *t*,
14: 25 turn back *t* and set out
16: 7 Take censers and *t* put fire
16: 16 are to appear before the LORD *t*—
Jos 3: 5 for *t* the LORD will do amazing
7: 13 yourselves in preparation for *t*;
11: 6 by this time *t* I will hand all of them
22: 18 *t* he will be angry with the whole
Jdg 19: 9 Early *t* morning you can get up
20: 28 for *t* I will give them
1Sa 9: 16 "About this time *t* I will send you
11: 9 'By the time the sun is hot *t*,
11: 10 "*T* we will surrender to you,
19: 2 Be on your guard *t* morning;
19: 11 your life tonight, *t* you'll be killed."
20: 5 until the evening of the day after *t*.
20: 5 "Look, *t* is the New Moon festival,
20: 12 father by this time the day after *t*!
20: 18 "*T* is the New Moon festival.
20: 19 The day after *t*, toward evening,
28: 19 *t* you and your sons will be with me
2Sa 11: 12 and *t* I will send you back."
1Ki 19: 2 if by this time *t* I do not make your
20: 6 But about this time *t* I am going
2Ki 6: 28 eat him today, and *t* we'll eat my
7: 1 the LORD says: About this time *t*,
7: 18 said to the king: "About this time *t*,
10: 6 come to me in Jezreel by this time *t*
2Ch 20: 16 *T* march down against them.
20: 17 Go out to face them *t*,
Est 5: 8 Haman come *t* to the banquet I will
5: 12 me along with the king *t*.
9: 13 to carry out this day's edict *t*
Pr 3: 28 "Come back later; I'll give it *t*"—
27: 1 Do not boast about *t*,
Isa 22: 13 "for *t* we die!"
56: 12 And *t* will be like today,
Mt 6: 30 and *t* is thrown into the fire,
6: 34 Therefore do not worry about *t*,
6: 34 for *t* will worry about itself.
Lk 12: 28 and *t* is thrown into the fire,
13: 32 and heal people today and *t*,
13: 33 I must keep going today and *t*
Ac 23: 20 Paul before the Sanhedrin *t*
25: 22 He replied, "*T* you will hear him."
1Co 15: 32 for *t* we die."
Jas 4: 13 "Today or *t* we will go to this
4: 14 even know what will happen *t*.

TONE

Gal 4: 20 be with you now and change my *t*,

TONGS

1Ki 7: 49 gold floral work and lamps and *t*;
2Ch 4: 21 lamps and *t* (they were solid gold);
Isa 6: 6 taken with *t* from the altar.

TONGUE (TONGUES)

Ex 4: 10 I am slow of speech and *t*."
2Sa 23: 2 his word was on my *t*.
Est 1: 22 in each people's *t* that every man
Job 5: 21 from the lash of the *t*,
12: 11 as the *t* tastes food?
15: 5 you adopt the *t* of the crafty.
20: 12 and he hides it under his *t*,
27: 4 and my *t* will utter no deceit.
33: 2 my words are on the tip of my *t*.
34: 3 as the *t* tastes food.
41: 1 or tie down his *t* with a rope?
Ps 5: 9 with their *t* they speak deceit.
10: 7 trouble and evil are under his *t*.
12: 3 and every boastful *t*
15: 3 and has no slander on his *t*,
16: 9 my heart is glad and my *t* rejoices;
22: 15 my *t* sticks to the roof of my mouth
34: 13 keep your *t* from evil
35: 28 *t* will speak of your righteousness
37: 30 and his *t* speaks what is just.
39: 1 and keep my *t* from sin;
39: 3 then I spoke with my *t*:
45: 1 my *t* is the pen of a skillful writer.
50: 19 and harness your *t* to deceit.
51: 14 my *t* will sing of your righteousness
52: 2 Your *t* plots destruction;
52: 4 O you deceitful *t*!
66: 17 his praise was on my *t*.
71: 24 My *t* will tell of your righteous acts
114: 1 of Jacob from a people of foreign *t*,
119: 172 May my *t* sing of your word,
120: 3 what more besides, O deceitful *t*?
137: 6 May my *t* cling to the roof
139: 4 Before a word is on my *t*
Pr 6: 17 a lying *t*,
6: 24 from the smooth *t*
10: 19 but he who holds his *t* is wise.
10: 20 *t* of the righteous is choice silver,
10: 31 but a perverse *t* will be cut out.
11: 12 a man of understanding holds his *t*.
12: 18 but the *t* of the wise brings healing.
12: 19 but a lying *t* lasts only a moment.
15: 2 *t* of the wise commends
15: 4 The *t* that brings healing is a tree
15: 4 but a deceitful *t* crushes the spirit.
16: 1 LORD comes the reply of the *t*.
17: 4 a liar pays attention to a malicious *t*
17: 20 he whose *t* is deceitful falls
17: 28 and discerning if he holds his *t*.
18: 21 The *t* has the power of life
21: 6 A fortune made by a lying *t*
21: 23 He who guards his mouth and his *t*
25: 15 and a gentle *t* can break a bone.
25: 23 so a sly *t* brings angry looks.
26: 28 A lying *t* hates those it hurts,
28: 23 than he who has a flattering *t*.
31: 26 and faithful instruction is on her *t*.
SS 4: 11 milk and honey are under your *t*.
Isa 30: 27 and his *t* is a consuming fire.
32: 4 and the stammering *t* will be fluent
33: 19 their strange, incomprehensible *t*.
35: 6 and the *t* of the dumb shout for joy.
45: 23 by me every *t* will swear.
50: 4 has given me an instructed *t*,
54: 17 will refute every *t* that accuses you.
57: 4 and stick out your *t*?
59: 3 and your *t* mutters wicked things.
Jer 9: 3 "They make ready their *t*
9: 8 Their *t* is a deadly arrow;
La 4: 4 Because of thirst the infant's *t*
Eze 3: 26 I will make your *t* stick to the roof
Mk 7: 33 he spit and touched the man's *t*.
7: 35 his *t* was loosened and he began
Lk 1: 64 was opened and his *t* was loosed,
16: 24 of his finger in water and cool my *t*,
Ac 2: 26 my heart is glad and my *t* rejoices;
Ro 14: 11 every *t* will confess to God.' "
1Co 14: 2 speaks in a *t* does not speak to men
14: 4 He who speaks in a *t* edifies himself
14: 9 intelligible words with your *t*,
14: 13 in a *t* should pray that he may
14: 14 For if I pray in a *t*, my spirit prays,
14: 19 than ten thousand words in a *t*.
14: 26 revelation, a *t* or an interpretation.
14: 27 If anyone speaks in a *t*, two—
Php 2: 11 every *t* confess that Jesus Christ is
Jas 1: 26 does not keep a tight rein on his *t*,
3: 5 Likewise the *t* is a small part
3: 6 The *t* also is a fire, a world of evil
3: 8 but no man can tame the *t*.
3: 9 With the *t* we praise our Lord
1Pe 3: 10 must keep his *t* from evil
1Jn 3: 18 or *t* but with actions and in truth.

TONGUES (TONGUE)

Jdg 7: 5 the water with their *t* like a dog
Job 29: 10 and their *t* stuck to the roof
Ps 12: 4 "We will triumph with our *t*;
31: 20 safe from the strife of *t*.
Ps 57: 4 whose *t* are sharp swords.
64: 3 who sharpen their *t* like swords
64: 8 He will turn their own *t*
68: 23 while the *t* of your dogs have their
73: 9 their *t* take possession of the earth.
78: 36 lying to him with their *t*;
109: 2 spoken against me with lying *t*.
120: 2 and from deceitful *t*.
126: 2 our *t* with songs of joy.
140: 3 They make their *t* as sharp
Isa 5: 24 Therefore, as *t* of fire lick up straw
28: 11 with foreign lips and strange *t*
41: 17 their *t* are parched with thirst.
66: 18 and gather all nations and *t*,
Jer 9: 5 They have taught their *t* to lie;
18: 18 let's attack him with our *t*
23: 31 the prophets who wag their own *t*
Mic 6: 12 and their *t* speak deceitfully.
Zec 14: 12 and their *t* will rot in their mouths.
Mk 16: 17 in new *t*; they will pick up snakes
Ac 2: 3 to be *t* of fire that separated
2: 4 and began to speak in other *t*
2: 11 the wonders of God in our own *t*!"
10: 46 For they heard them speaking in *t*
19: 6 and they spoke in *t* and prophesied
Ro 3: 13 their *t* practice deceit."
1Co 12: 10 still another the interpretation of *t*.
12: 10 to speak in different kinds of *t*,
12: 28 speaking in different kinds of *t*.
12: 30 Do all speak in *t*? Do all interpret?
13: 1 If I speak in the *t* of men
13: 8 where there are *t*, they will be
14: 5 greater than one who speaks in *t*,
14: 5 one of you to speak in *t*,
14: 6 if I come to you and speak in *t*,
14: 18 speak in *t* more than all of you.
14: 21 "Through men of strange *t*
14: 22 *T*, then, are a sign, not for believers
14: 23 together and everyone speaks in *t*,
14: 39 and do not forbid speaking in *t*.
Rev 16: 10 Men gnawed their *t* in agony

TONIGHT

Ge 19: 5 are the men who came to you *t*?
19: 34 Let's get him to drink wine again *t*,
30: 15 "he can sleep with you *t* in return
Nu 22: 19 Now stay here *t* as the others did,
Jos 2: 2 of the Israelites have come here *t*
4: 3 down at the place where you stay *t*
Jdg 19: 6 "Please stay *t* and enjoy yourself."
Ru 1: 12 even if I had a husband *t*
3: 2 *T* he will be winnowing barley
1Sa 19: 11 "If you don't run for your life *t*,
2Sa 17: 1 and set out *t* in pursuit of David.
Mk 14: 30 Jesus answered, "today—yes, *t*—
Ac 23: 23 to go to Caesarea at nine *t*.

TOOK (TAKE)

Ge 2: 15 The LORD God *t* the man
2: 21 he *t* one of the man's ribs
3: 6 for gaining wisdom, she *t* some
5: 24 no more, because God *t* him away.
8: 9 out his hand and *t* the dove
9: 23 But Shem and Japheth *t* a garment
11: 31 Terah *t* his son Abram, his
12: 5 He *t* his wife Sarai, his nephew Lot,
12: 19 so that I *t* her to be my wife?
15: 5 He *t* him outside and said,
16: 3 Sarai his wife *t* her Egyptian
17: 23 very day Abraham *t* his son
20: 2 of Gerar sent for Sarah and *t* her.
21: 14 morning Abraham *t* some food
22: 3 He *t* with him two of his servants
22: 6 Abraham *t* the wood
22: 10 and *t* the knife to slay his son.
22: 13 He went over and *t* the ram
24: 10 servant *t* ten of his master's camels
24: 22 man *t* out a gold nose ring weighing
24: 61 So the servant *t* Rebekah and left.
24: 65 she *t* her veil and covered herself.
25: 1 Abraham *t* another wife, whose
27: 15 Then Rebekah *t* the best clothes
27: 35 deceitfully and *t* your blessing."
27: 36 two times: He *t* my birthright,
28: 18 next morning Jacob *t* the stone he
29: 23 he *t* his daughter Leah
30: 9 she *t* her maidservant Zilpah
30: 15 enough that you *t* away my

Ge 30:37 *t* fresh-cut branches from poplar,
31:16 all the wealth that God *t* away
31:36 Jacob was angry and *t* Laban
31:45 So Jacob *t* a stone and set it up
31:46 So they *t* stones and piled them
31:53 So Jacob *t* an oath in the name
32:22 Jacob got up and *t* his two wives,
34: 2 saw her, he *t* her and violated her.
34:25 *t* their swords and attacked
34:26 and *t* Dinah from Shechem's house
36: 2 Esau *t* his wives from the women
36: 6 Esau *t* his wives and sons
37:24 and they *t* him and threw him
37:28 silver to the Ishmaelites, who *t* him
37:32 They *t* the ornamented robe back
38:14 she *t* off her widow's clothes,
38:19 she *t* off her veil and put
38:28 so the midwife *t* a scarlet thread
39: 7 a while his master's wife *t* notice
39:20 Joseph's master *t* him and put him
40:11 was in my hand, and I *t* the grapes,
41:42 Then Pharaoh *t* his signet ring
43:15 So the men *t* the gifts and double
43:17 and *t* the men to Joseph's house.
43:24 The steward *t* the men
46: 5 Israel's sons *t* their father Jacob
46: 6 also *t* with them their livestock
46: 7 He *t* with him to Egypt his sons
48: 1 So he *t* his two sons Manasseh
48:13 And Joseph *t* both of them,
48:17 so he *t* hold of his father's hand
48:22 ridge of land I *t* from the Amorites
Ex 2: 9 So the woman *t* the baby
2:10 she *t* him to Pharaoh's daughter
4: 4 So Moses reached out and *t* hold
4: 6 and when he *t* it out, it was leprous,
4: 7 when he *t* it out, it was restored,
4:20 So Moses *t* his wife and sons,
4:20 he *t* the staff of God in his hand.
4:25 But Zipporah *t* a flint knife,
9:10 So they *t* soot from a furnace
12:34 So the people *t* their dough
13:19 Moses *t* the bones of Joseph
14: 6 chariot made ready and *t* his army
14: 7 He *t* six hundred of the best
15:20 *t* a tambourine in her hand,
17:12 they *t* a stone and put it under him
18:13 The next day Moses *t* his seat
24: 6 Moses *t* half of the blood
24: 7 he *t* the Book of the Covenant
24: 8 Moses then *t* the blood, sprinkled
32: 3 So all the people *t* off their earrings
32: 4 He *t* what they handed him
32:20 And he *t* the calf they had made
40:20 He *t* the Testimony and placed it
Lev 8:10 Then Moses *t* the anointing oil
8:15 slaughtered the bull and *t* some
8:16 *t* all the fat around the inner parts,
8:23 slaughtered the ram and *t* some
8:25 He *t* the fat, the fat tail, all the fat
8:26 was before the LORD, he *t* a cake
8:28 Moses *t* them from their hands
8:29 also *t* the breast—Moses' share
8:30 Moses *t* some of the anointing oil
9: 5 They *t* the things Moses
9:15 He *t* the goat for the people's sin
9:17 *t* a handful of it and burned it
10: 1 Nadab and Abihu *t* their censers,
24:23 and they *t* the blasphemer
Nu 1:17 Aaron *t* these men whose names
7: 6 So Moses *t* the carts and oxen
11:25 he *t* of the Spirit that was on him
15:36 So the assembly *t* him
16:18 So each man *t* his censer, put fire
17: 9 and each man *t* his own staff.
20: 9 Moses *t* the staff from the LORD's
21:24 and *t* over his land from the Arnon
21:35 And they *t* possession of his land.
22:41 next morning Balak *t* Balaam up
23:14 So he *t* him to the field of Zophim
23:28 Balak *t* Balaam to the top of Peor,
25: 7 *t* a spear in his hand and followed
27:22 He *t* Joshua and had him stand
31: 6 who *t* with him articles
31: 9 and *t* all the Midianite herds,
31:11 They *t* all the plunder and spoils,
31:27 between the soldiers who *t* part
31:32 that the soldiers *t* was 675,000

Dt 1:15 I *t* the leading men of your tribes,
2:34 At that time we *t* all his towns
3: 4 At that time we *t* all his cities.
3: 8 So at that time we *t* from these two
3:10 We *t* all the towns on the plateau,
3:12 Of the land that we *t*
3:14 *t* the whole region of Argob as far
4:20 LORD *t* you and brought you out
4:47 They *t* possession of his land
9:17 I *t* the two tablets and threw them
9:21 Also I *t* that sinful thing of yours,
29: 8 We *t* their land and gave it
32:37 the rock they *t* refuge in,
Jos 3: 6 they *t* it up and went ahead of them
4: 8 They *t* twelve stones
6:12 and the priests *t* up the ark
6:20 straight in, and they *t* the city.
7: 1 the tribe of Judah, *t* some of them.
7:17 forward, and he *t* the Zerahites.
7:21 I coveted them and *t* them.
7:23 They *t* the things from the tent,
7:24 with all Israel, *t* Achan son
8:23 But they *t* the king of Ai alive
10: 5 and *t* up positions against Gibeon
10: 9 Joshua *t* them by surprise.
10:27 they *t* them down from the trees
10:28 That day Joshua *t* Makkedah.
10:31 he *t* up positions against it
10:32 and Joshua *t* it on the second day.
10:34 they *t* up positions against it
10:37 They *t* the city and put it
10:39 They *t* the city, its king
11:12 Joshua *t* all these royal cities
11:16 So Joshua *t* this entire land.
11:19 with the Israelites, who *t* them all
11:23 So Joshua *t* the entire land,
12: 1 whose territory they *t* over east
15:17 son of Kenaz, Caleb's brother, *t* it;
19:47 and attacked Leshem, *t* it,
21:43 and they *t* possession of it
24: 3 But I *t* your father Abraham
24: 8 and you *t* possession of their land.
24:26 Then he *t* a large stone
Jdg 1: 8 attacked Jerusalem also and *t* it.
1:13 Caleb's younger brother, *t* it;
1:18 The men of Judah also *t* Gaza,
1:19 They *t* possession
3: 6 They *t* their daughters in marriage
3:13 and they *t* possession of the City
3:25 they *t* a key and unlocked them.
5: 6 travelers *t* to winding paths.
6:27 So Gideon *t* ten of his servants
7: 5 *t* the men down to the water.
7: 8 who *t* over the provisions
7:24 and they *t* the waters of the Jordan
8:16 He *t* the elders of the town
8:21 *t* the ornaments off their camels'
9:34 and *t* up concealed positions
9:43 So he *t* his men, divided them
9:48 He *t* an ax and cut
11:13 they *t* away my land
11:21 Israel *t* over all the land
12: 3 I *t* my life in my hands
13:19 Then Manoah *t* a young goat,
15: 1 Samson *t* a young goat
16: 3 *t* hold of the doors of the city gate,
16:12 So Delilah *t* new ropes
16:13 Delilah *t* the seven braids
16:21 gouged out his eyes and *t* him
17: 2 I have that silver with me; I *t* it."
17: 4 she *t* two hundred shekels of silver
18:17 went inside and *t* the carved image,
18:18 Micah's house and *t* the carved
18:20 He *t* the ephod, the other
18:24 He replied, "You *t* the gods I made
18:27 Then they *t* what Micah had made,
19: 1 country of Ephraim *t* a concubine
19: 3 She *t* him into her father's house,
19:15 but no one *t* them into his home
19:21 So he *t* him into his house
19:25 So the man *t* his concubine
19:29 he *t* a knife and cut up his
20: 2 of the tribes of Israel *t* their places
20: 6 I *t* my concubine, cut her
20:20 *t* up battle positions against them
20:22 again *t* up their positions where
20:30 and *t* up positions against Gibeah
20:33 from their places and *t* up positions

Jdg 21:12 they *t* them to the camp at Shiloh
Ru 2:19 Blessed be the man who *t* notice
4: 2 Boaz *t* ten of the elders of the town
4: 7 one party *t* off his sandal
4:13 So Boaz *t* Ruth and she became his
4:16 Then Naomi *t* the child, laid him
1Sa 1:24 After he was weaned, she *t* the boy
2:19 and *t* it to him when she went up
5: 1 they *t* it from Ebenezer to Ashdod.
5: 3 They *t* Dagon and put him back
6:10 They *t* two such cows and hitched
6:15 The Levites *t* down the ark
7: 1 They *t* it to Abinadab's house
7: 1 and *t* up the ark of the LORD.
7: 9 Then Samuel *t* a suckling lamb
7:12 Then Samuel *t* a stone
9:24 the cook *t* up the leg with what was
10: 1 Then Samuel *t* a flask of oil
11: 7 He *t* a pair of oxen, cut them
14:30 some of the plunder they *t*
14:52 brave man, he *t* him into his service
15: 8 He *t* Agag king of the Amalekites
15:21 The soldiers *t* sheep and cattle
16:13 So Samuel *t* the horn of oil
16:20 Jesse *t* a donkey loaded with bread,
17:16 and evening and *t* his stand.
17:39 So he *t* them off.
17:40 Then he *t* his staff in his hand,
17:51 He *t* hold of the Philistine's sword
17:54 David *t* the Philistine's head
17:57 Abner *t* him and brought him
18: 4 Jonathan *t* off the robe he was
19: 5 He *t* his life in his hands
19: 6 to Jonathan and *t* this oath:
19:13 Then Michal *t* an idol
20: 3 But David *t* an oath and said,
21:12 David *t* these words to heart
24: 2 Saul *t* three thousand chosen men
25:18 She *t* two hundred loaves of bread,
26:12 So David *t* the spear and water jug
27: 9 but *t* sheep and cattle, donkeys
28:21 I *t* my life in my hands
28:24 She *t* some flour, kneaded it
30:20 He *t* all the flocks and herds,
31: 4 so Saul *t* his own sword
31:12 They *t* down the bodies of Saul
31:13 Then they *t* their bones
2Sa 1:10 I *t* the crown that was on his head
1:11 with him *t* hold of their clothes
1:17 David *t* up this lament concerning
2: 3 also *t* the men who were with him,
2:25 and *t* their stand on top of a hill.
2:32 They *t* Asahel and buried him
3:27 Joab *t* him aside into the gateway,
3:35 but David *t* an oath, saying,
3:36 All the people *t* note and were
4:12 But they *t* the head of Ish-Bosheth
5: 9 David then *t* up residence
5:13 David *t* more concubines
6: 6 and *t* hold of the ark of God,
6:10 he *t* it aside to the house
7: 8 I *t* you from the pasture
7:15 as I *t* it away from Saul, whom I
8: 1 and he *t* Metheg Ammah
8: 7 David *t* the gold shields that
8: 8 King David *t* a great quantity
12: 4 he *t* the ewe lamb that belonged
12: 9 and *t* his wife to be your own.
12:10 and *t* the wife of Uriah the Hittite
12:30 He *t* a great quantity of plunder
12:30 He *t* the crown from the head
13: 8 She *t* some dough, kneaded it,
13: 9 Then she *t* the pan and served him
13:10 And Tamar *t* the bread she had
13:11 But when she *t* it to him to eat,
15:29 and Abiathar *t* the ark of God back
17:19 His wife *t* a covering and spread it
18: 6 and the battle *t* place in the forest
18:14 So he *t* three javelins in his hand
18:17 They *t* Absalom, threw him
19: 8 and *t* his seat in the gateway.
20: 3 he *t* the ten concubines he had left
20: 5 he *t* longer than the time the king
20: 9 Then Joab *t* Amasa by the beard
21: 8 But the king *t* Armoni
21:10 daughter of Aiah *t* sackcloth
21:12 he went and *t* the bones of Saul
21:20 In still another battle, which *t* place

Mt 26:27 Then he *t* the cup, gave thanks
26:37 He *t* Peter and the two sons
26:57 who had arrested Jesus *t* him
27: 9 "They *t* the thirty silver coins,
27:24 he *t* water and washed his hands
27:27 the governor's soldiers *t* Jesus
27:30 and *t* the staff and struck him
27:31 they *t* off the robe and put his own
27:59 Joseph *t* the body, wrapped it
28:15 So the soldiers *t* the money and did
Mk 1:31 *t* her hand and helped her up.
2:12 *t* his mat and walked out
4:36 crowd behind, they *t* him along,
5:40 he *t* the child's father and mother
5:41 He *t* her by the hand and said
6: 3 And they *t* offense at him.
6:29 disciples came and *t* his body
7:33 After he *t* him aside, away
8:23 He *t* the blind man by the hand
8:32 and Peter *t* him aside and began
9: 2 After six days Jesus *t* Peter,
9:27 But Jesus *t* him by the hand
9:36 He *t* a little child and had him
10:16 And he *t* the children in his arms,
10:32 Again he *t* the Twelve aside
12: 8 So they *t* him and killed him,
14:22 they were eating, Jesus *t* bread,
14:23 Then he *t* the cup, gave thanks
14:33 He *t* Peter, James and John
14:53 They *t* Jesus to the high priest,
14:65 And the guards *t* him and beat him.
15:20 they *t* off the purple robe
15:46 Joseph bought some linen cloth, *t*
Lk 2: 2 was the first census that *t* place
2:22 and Mary *t* him to Jerusalem
2:28 Simeon *t* him in his arms
4:29 and *t* him to the brow of the hill
5:25 *t* what he had been lying on
8:54 But he *t* her by the hand and said,
9:10 Then he *t* them with him
9:28 after Jesus said this, he *t* Peter,
9:47 *t* a little child and had him stand
10:33 when he saw him, he *t* pity on him.
10:34 *t* him to an inn and *t* care of him.
10:35 next day he *t* out two silver coins
13: 7 said to the man who *t* care
13:19 which a man *t* and planted
13:21 It is like yeast that a woman *t*
18:31 Jesus *t* the Twelve aside
22:19 And he *t* bread, gave thanks
22:20 after the supper he *t* the cup, saying
22:54 and *t* him into the house
23:48 witness this sight saw what *t* place,
23:53 Then he *t* it down, wrapped it
24: 1 the women *t* the spices they had
24:21 day since all this *t* place.
24:30 at the table with them, he *t* bread,
24:43 he *t* it and ate it in their presence.
Jn 2: 1 On the third day a wedding *t* place
4:50 The man *t* Jesus at his word
5: 9 on which this *t* place was a Sabbath
6:11 Jesus then *t* the loaves, gave thanks
11:41 So they *t* away the stone.
12: 3 Mary *t* about a pint of pure nard,
12:13 They *t* palm branches
13: 4 up from the meal, *t* off his outer
13:27 As soon as Judas *t* the bread,
19: 1 Pilate *t* Jesus and had him flogged.
19:16 So the soldiers *t* charge of Jesus.
19:23 crucified Jesus, they *t* his clothes,
19:27 this disciple *t* her into his home.
19:38 he came and *t* the body.
21:13 *t* the bread and gave it to them,
Ac 4:13 and they *t* note that these men had
7:21 Pharaoh's daughter *t* him
7:45 it with them when they *t* the land
8:39 of the Lord suddenly *t* Philip away,
9:25 But his followers *t* him by night
9:27 Barnabas *t* him and brought him
9:30 they *t* him down to Caesarea
9:41 He *t* her by the hand and helped
13:20 All this *t* about 450 years.
13:29 they *t* him down from the tree
15:39 Barnabas *t* Mark and sailed
16:33 hour of the night the jailer *t* them
17:19 Then they *t* him and brought him
19: 1 Paul *t* the road through the interior
19: 9 He *t* the disciples with him
Ac 20:12 people *t* the young man home alive
20:14 we *t* him aboard and went
21:11 Coming over to us, he *t* Paul's belt,
21:26 The next day Paul *t* the men
21:32 He at once *t* some officers
23:18 So he *t* him to the commander.
23:19 The commander *t* the young man
23:31 *t* Paul with them during the night
27:18 We *t* such a violent battering
27:28 They *t* soundings and found that
27:28 time later they *t* soundings again
27:35 he *t* some bread and gave thanks
1Co 11:23 the night he was betrayed, *t* bread,
11:25 after supper he *t* the cup, saying,
Gal 2: 1 I *t* Titus along also.
Php 3:12 for which Christ Jesus *t* hold of me.
Col 2:14 he *t* it away, nailing it to the cross.
Heb 8: 9 when I *t* them by the hand
9:19 he *t* the blood of calves, together
Rev 5: 7 and *t* the scroll from the right hand
8: 5 Then the angel *t* the censer,
10:10 I *t* the little scroll from the angel's

TOOL (TOOLS)

Ex 20:25 it if you use a *t* on it.
32: 4 of a calf, fashioning it with a *t*.
Dt 27: 5 Do not use any iron *t* upon them.
Jos 8:31 on which no iron *t* had been used.
2Sa 23: 7 uses a *t* of iron or the shaft
1Ki 6: 7 or any other iron *t* was heard
Job 19:24 inscribed with an iron *t* on lead,
Isa 44:12 The blacksmith takes a *t*
Jer 17: 1 sin is engraved with an iron *t*,

TOOLS (TOOL)

Ge 4:22 who forged all kinds of *t* out

TOOTH (TEETH)

Ex 21:24 eye for eye, *t* for *t*, hand for hand,
21:27 And if he knocks out the *t*
21:27 free to compensate for the *t*.
Lev 24:20 for fracture, eye for eye, *t* for *t*.
Dt 19:21 eye for eye, *t* for *t*, hand for hand,
Pr 25:19 Like a bad *t* or a lame foot
Mt 5:38 'Eye for eye, and *t* for *t*.'

TOP

Ge 6:16 the ark to within 18 inches of the *t*.
22: 9 him on the altar, on *t* of the wood.
28:12 with its *t* reaching to heaven,
28:18 as a pillar and poured oil on *t* of it.
40:17 In the *t* basket were all kinds
47:31 as he leaned on the *t* of his staff.
Ex 12:22 and put some of the blood on the *t*
12:23 he will see the blood on the *t*
17: 9 Tomorrow I will stand on *t*
17:10 and Hur went to the *t* of the hill.
19:20 Moses to the *t* of the mountain.
19:20 descended to the *t* of Mount Sinai
24:17 fire on *t* of the mountain.
25:21 Place the cover on *t* of the ark
26:24 from the bottom all the way to the *t*
30: 3 Overlay the *t* and all the sides
34: 2 to me there on *t* of the mountain.
36:29 from the bottom all the way to the *t*
37:26 They overlaid the *t* and all
Lev 3: 5 on *t* of the burnt offering that is
4:35 the altar on *t* of the offerings made
5:12 the altar on *t* of the offerings made
8:28 the altar on *t* of the burnt offering
9:14 them on *t* of the burnt offering
14:17 on *t* of the blood of the guilt
Nu 20:28 there on *t* of the mountain.
21:20 the valley in Moab where the *t*
23:14 field of Zophim on the *t* of Pisgah,
23:28 Balak took Balaam to the *t* of Peor,
Dt 3:27 Go up to the *t* of Pisgah
28:13 you will always be at the *t*,
28:35 of your feet to the *t* of your head.
34: 1 plains of Moab to the *t* of Pisgah,
Jos 15: 8 climbed to the *t* of the hill west
Jdg 6:26 God on the *t* of this bluff.
9: 7 up on the *t* of Mount Gerizim
16: 3 and carried them to the *t*
1Sa 26:13 on *t* of the hill some distance away;
28:12 she cried out at the *t* of her voice
2Sa 2:25 and took their stand on *t* of a hill.
14:25 From the *t* of his head to the sole
1Ki 7:17 chains festooned the capitals on *t*
7:18 to decorate the capitals on *t*
7:19 The capitals on *t* of the pillars
7:22 The capitals on *t* were in the shape
7:25 The Sea rested on *t* of them,
7:35 At the *t* of the stand there was
7:35 attached to the *t* of the stand.
7:41 the two bowl-shaped capitals on *t*
7:41 the two bowl-shaped capitals on *t*
7:42 capitals on *t* of the pillars);
10:19 and its back had a rounded *t*.
18:42 Elijah climbed to the *t* of Carmel,
2Ki 1: 9 who was sitting on the *t* of a hill,
25:17 The bronze capital on *t*
2Ch 3:15 a capital on *t* measuring five cubits.
3:16 and put them on *t* of the pillars.
4: 4 The Sea rested on *t* of them,
4:12 the two bowl-shaped capitals on *t*
4:12 the two bowl-shaped capitals on *t*
4:13 capitals on *t* of the pillars);
25:12 took them to the *t* of a cliff
Ne 12:31 One was to proceed on *t* of the wall
12:31 of Judah go up on *t* of the wall.
12:38 I followed them on *t* of the wall,
Job 2: 7 soles of his feet to the *t* of his head.
Pr 23:34 lying on *t* of the rigging.
SS 4: 8 from the *t* of Senir, the summit
Isa 1: 6 of your foot to the *t* of your head
Jer 52:22 The bronze capital on *t*
Eze 17: 3 Taking hold of the *t* of a cedar,
17:22 a shoot from the very *t* of a cedar
31: 3 its *t* above the thick foliage.
31:10 lifting its *t* above the thick foliage,
40:13 alcove to the *t* of the opposite one;
40:13 gateway from the *t* of the rear wall
41: 7 to the *t* floor through the middle
43:12 All the surrounding area on *t*
Da 4:11 strong and its *t* touched the sky;
4:20 with its *t* touching the sky,
Am 1: 2 and the *t* of Carmel withers."
9: 3 on the *t* of Carmel,
Zec 4: 2 lampstand with a bowl at the *t*
Mt 27:51 torn in two from *t* to bottom.
Mk 5: 7 He shouted at the *t* of his voice,
15:38 torn in two from *t* to bottom.
Lk 4:33 He cried out at the *t* of his voice,
8:28 shouting at the *t* of his voice,
Jn 19:23 in one piece from *t* to bottom.
Ac 7:57 and, yelling at the *t* of their voices,
Heb 11:21 as he leaned on the *t* of his staff.

TOPAZ

Ex 28:17 a *t* and a beryl; in the second row
39:10 In the first row there was a ruby, a *t*
Job 28:19 The *t* of Cush cannot compare
Eze 28:13 ruby, *t* and emerald,
Rev 21:20 the ninth *t*, the tenth chrysoprase,

TOPHEL

Dt 1: 1 between Paran and *T*, Laban,

TOPHETH

2Ki 23:10 He desecrated *T*, which was
Isa 30:33 *T* has long been prepared;
Jer 7:31 of *T* in the Valley of Ben Hinnom
7:32 in *T* until there is no more room.
7:32 when people will no longer call it *T*
19: 6 will no longer call this place *T*
19:11 They will bury the dead in *T*
19:12 I will make this city like *T*.
19:13 will be defiled like this place, *T*—
19:14 Jeremiah then returned from *T*,

TOPPLE

Ps 62: 4 They fully intend to *t* him
Isa 40:20 to set up an idol that will not *t*.
41: 7 down the idol so it will not *t*.

TORCH (TORCHES)

Ge 15:17 pot with a blazing *t* appeared
Jdg 15: 4 He then fastened a *t* to every pair
Isa 62: 1 her salvation like a blazing *t*.
Zec 12: 6 like a flaming *t* among sheaves.
Rev 8:10 and a great star, blazing like a *t*,

TORCHES (TORCH)

Jdg 7:16 hands of all of them, with *t* inside.
7:20 Grasping the *t* in their left hands

Jdg 15: 5 lit the *t* and let the foxes loose
Isa 50: 11 and of the *t* you have set ablaze.
50: 11 provide yourselves with flaming *t*,
Eze 1: 13 like burning coals of fire or like *t*.
Da 10: 6 lightning, his eyes like flaming *t*,
Na 2: 4 They look like flaming *t*;
Jn 18: 3 They were carrying *t*, lanterns

TORE (TEAR)

Ge 37: 29 was not there, he *t* his clothes.
37: 34 Then Jacob *t* his clothes, put
44: 13 At this, they *t* their clothes.
Nu 14: 6 *t* their clothes and said
Jos 7: 6 Then Joshua *t* his clothes
Jdg 11: 35 When he saw her, he *t* his clothes
14: 6 in power so that he *t* the lion apart
16: 3 and *t* them loose, bar and all.
1Sa 15: 27 of the edge of his robe, and it *t*.
2Sa 1: 11 hold of their clothes and *t* them.
13: 19 and *t* the ornamented robe she was
13: 31 *t* his clothes and lay
1Ki 11: 30 and *t* it into twelve pieces.
14: 8 I *t* the kingdom away
19: 11 and powerful wind *t* the mountains
21: 27 heard these words, he *t* his clothes,
2Ki 2: 12 of his own clothes and *t* them apart
5: 7 he *t* his robes and said, "Am I God?
6: 30 the woman's words, he *t* his robes.
10: 27 and *t* down the temple of Baal,
11: 14 Then Athaliah *t* her robes
11: 18 to the temple of Baal and *t* it down.
17: 21 When he *t* Israel away
19: 1 he *t* his clothes and put
22: 11 the Book of the Law, he *t* his robes.
22: 19 and because you *t* your robes
23: 7 also *t* down the quarters
2Ch 23: 13 Then Athaliah *t* her robes
23: 17 to the temple of Baal and *t* it down.
34: 7 he *t* down the altars
34: 19 words of the Law, he *t* his robes.
34: 27 yourself before me and *t* your robes
Ezr 9: 3 When I heard this, I *t* my tunic
Est 4: 1 he *t* his clothes, put on sackcloth
Job 1: 20 Job got up and *t* his robe
2: 12 they *t* their robes and sprinkled
Isa 22: 10 *t* down houses to strengthen
37: 1 he *t* his clothes and put
Jer 2: 20 and *t* off your bonds;
Eze 29: 7 and you *t* open their shoulders;
Mt 26: 65 Then the high priest *t* his clothes
Mk 5: 4 but he *t* the chains apart
14: 63 The high priest *t* his clothes.
Ac 14: 14 they *t* their clothes and rushed out

TORMENT (TORMENTED TORMENTING TORMENTORS)

Job 13: 25 Will you *t* a wind-blown leaf?
15: 20 his days the wicked man suffers *t*,
19: 2 replied: "How long will you *t* me
Isa 50: 11 You will lie down in *t*.
La 1: 20 I am in *t* within,
2: 11 I am in *t* within,
Lk 16: 23 where he was in *t*, he looked up
16: 28 also come to this place of *t*.'
2Co 12: 7 a messenger of Satan, to *t* me.
Rev 9: 10 power to *t* people for five months.
14: 11 the smoke of their *t* rises for ever
18: 10 at her *t*, they will stand far
18: 15 far off, terrified at her *t*.

TORMENTED (TORMENT)

1Sa 16: 14 an evil spirit from the LORD *t* him
Pr 28: 17 A man *t* by the guilt of murder
Ac 5: 16 bringing their sick and those *t*
2Pe 2: 8 was *t* in his righteous soul
Rev 11: 10 two prophets had *t* those who live
14: 10 He will be *t* with burning sulfur
20: 10 They will be *t* day and night

TORMENTING (TORMENT)

1Sa 16: 15 See, an evil spirit from God is *t* you

TORMENTORS (TORMENT)

Ps 137: 3 our *t* demanded songs of joy;
Isa 51: 23 I will put it into the hands of your *t*,

TORN (TEAR)

Ge 31: 39 I did not bring you animals *t*
37: 33 Joseph has surely been *t* to pieces."
44: 28 "He has surely been *t* to pieces."
Ex 22: 13 If it was *t* to pieces by a wild animal
22: 13 required to pay for the *t* animal.
22: 31 meat of an animal *t* by wild beasts;
Lev 7: 24 or *t* by wild animals may be used
13: 45 disease must wear *t* clothes,
14: 40 the contaminated stones be *t* out
14: 43 after the stones have been *t* out
14: 45 It must be *t* down—its stones,
17: 15 or *t* by wild animals must wash his
22: 8 not eat anything found dead or *t*
22: 24 testicles are bruised, crushed, *t*
Jdg 14: 6 as he might have *t* a young goat.
1Sa 4: 12 his clothes *t* and dust on his head.
15: 28 "The LORD has *t* the kingdom
28: 17 The LORD has *t* the kingdom out
2Sa 1: 2 with his clothes *t* and with dust
13: 31 stood by with their clothes *t*.
15: 32 his robe *t* and dust on his head.
2Ki 5: 8 the king of Israel had *t* his robes,
5: 8 "Why have you *t* your robes?
18: 37 with their clothes *t*, and told him
2Ch 34: 4 the altars of the Baals were *t* down;
Ezr 9: 5 with my tunic and cloak *t*,
Job 8: 18 But when it is *t* from its spot,
18: 14 He is *t* from the security of his tent
Ps 60: 2 have shaken the land and *t* it open;
124: 6 who has not let us be *t*
Pr 2: 22 and the unfaithful will be *t* from it.
Isa 36: 22 with their clothes *t*, and told him
Jer 5: 5 and *t* off the bonds.
13: 22 that your skirts have been *t* off
18: 7 *t* down and destroyed,
33: 4 palaces of Judah that have been *t*
41: 5 *t* their clothes and cut themselves
50: 15 her walls are *t* down.
La 2: 2 in his wrath he has *t* down
Eze 4: 14 eaten anything found dead or *t*
30: 4 and her foundations *t* down.
44: 31 found dead or *t* by wild animals.
Da 7: 4 I watched until its wings were *t* off
Hos 6: 1 He has *t* us to pieces
Mt 27: 51 of the temple was *t* in two from top
Mk 1: 10 he saw heaven being *t* open
15: 38 of the temple was *t* in two from top
Lk 5: 36 he will have *t* the new garment,
23: 45 curtain of the temple was *t* in two.
Jn 21: 11 with so many the net was not *t*.
Ac 21: 1 After we had *t* ourselves away
23: 10 was afraid Paul would be *t*
Ro 11: 3 have killed your prophets and *t*
Gal 4: 15 you would have *t* out your eyes
Php 1: 23 I do not know! I am *t*
1Th 2: 17 when we were *t* away from you

TORRENT (TORRENTS)

Ps 124: 4 the *t* would have swept over us,
Isa 30: 28 His breath is like a rushing *t*,
Jer 47: 2 they will become an overflowing *t*.
Lk 6: 48 the *t* struck that house
6: 49 moment the *t* struck that house,
Rev 12: 15 and sweep her away with the *t*.

TORRENTS (TORRENT)

2Sa 22: 5 *t* of destruction overwhelmed me.
Job 14: 19 and *t* wash away the soil,
38: 25 Who cuts a channel for the *t* of rain
Ps 18: 4 *t* of destruction overwhelmed me.
Eze 13: 11 in *t*, and I will send hailstones
13: 13 *t* of rain will fall with destructive
38: 22 and bloodshed; I will pour down *t*
Hab 3: 10 *T* of water swept by;

TORTURE (TORTURED)

Mt 8: 29 "Have you come here to *t* us
Mk 5: 7 Swear to God that you won't *t* me
Lk 8: 28 High God? I beg you, don't *t* me!"
Rev 9: 5 but only to *t* them for five months.
18: 7 Give her as much *t* and grief

TORTURED (TORTURE)

Heb 11: 35 Others were *t* and refused

TOSS (TOSSED TOSSES TOSSING)

Ex 9: 8 and have Moses *t* it into the air
Job 7: 4 on, and I *t* till dawn.
30: 22 you *t* me about in the storm.
Ps 60: 8 upon Edom I *t* my sandal;
108: 9 upon Edom I *t* my sandal;
Mt 15: 26 to take the children's bread and *t* it
Mk 7: 27 to take the children's bread and *t* it

TOSSED (TOSS)

Ex 9: 10 Moses *t* it into the air,
Eph 4: 14 *t* back and forth by the waves,
Jas 1: 6 of the sea, blown and *t* by the wind.

TOSSES (TOSS)

2Ki 19: 21 *t* her head as you flee.
Isa 37: 22 *t* her head as you flee.

TOSSING (TOSS)

Isa 57: 20 But the wicked are like the *t* sea,
Lk 21: 25 at the roaring and *t* of the sea.

TOTTER (TOTTERING)

Jer 10: 4 and nails so it will not *t*.

TOTTERING (TOTTER)

Ps 62: 3 this leaning wall, this *t* fence?

TOU

2Sa 8: 9 When *T* king of Hamath heard that
8: 10 who had been at war with *T*.
1Ch 18: 9 When *T* king of Hamath heard that
18: 10 who had been at war with *T*.

TOUCH (TOUCHED TOUCHES TOUCHING)

Ge 3: 3 you must not *t* it, or you will die.' "
20: 6 That is why I did not let you *t* her.
27: 21 "Come near so I can *t* you, my son,
Ex 12: 13 No destructive plague will *t* you
19: 12 go up the mountain or *t* the foot
Lev 11: 8 eat their meat or *t* their carcasses;
12: 4 She must not *t* anything sacred
Nu 4: 15 But they must not *t* the holy things
16: 26 Do not *t* anything belonging
Dt 14: 8 eat their meat or *t* their carcasses.
28: 56 to *t* the ground with the sole
Jos 9: 19 and we cannot *t* them now.
Ru 2: 9 I have told the men not to *t* you.
1Sa 24: 12 but my hand will not *t* you.
24: 13 so my hand will not *t* you.
2Sa 21: 10 the birds of the air *t* them by day
1Ch 16: 22 "Do not *t* my anointed ones;
Job 6: 7 I refuse to *t* it;
Ps 105: 15 "Do not *t* my anointed ones;
144: 5 *t* the mountains, so that they
Isa 28: 15 it cannot *t* us,
52: 11 *T* no unclean thing!
Jer 13: 1 waist, but do not let it *t* water."
14: 15 'No sword or famine will *t* this land
La 4: 14 dares to *t* their garments.
4: 15 "Away! Away! Don't *t* us!"
Eze 9: 6 do not *t* anyone who has the mark.
Mt 9: 21 If I only *t* his cloak, I will be healed
14: 36 him to let the sick just *t* the edge
Mk 3: 10 were pushing forward to *t* him.
5: 28 she thought, "If I just *t* his clothes,
6: 56 They begged him to let them *t*
8: 22 and begged Jesus to *t* him.
10: 13 to Jesus to have him *t* them,
Lk 6: 19 and the people all tried to *t* him,
18: 15 babies to Jesus to have him *t* them.
24: 39 It is I myself! *T* me and see;
2Co 6: 17 *T* no unclean thing,
Col 2: 21 Do not taste! Do not *t*!"?
Heb 11: 28 firstborn would not *t* the firstborn
1Jn 5: 18 and the evil one does not *t* him.

TOUCHED (TOUCH)

Ge 27: 22 close to his father Isaac, who *t* him
32: 25 he *t* the socket of Jacob's hip
32: 32 the socket of Jacob's hip was *t*
Ex 4: 25 son's foreskin and *t* ⌊Moses'⌋ feet
Nu 19: 18 anyone who has *t* a human bone
31: 19 *t* anyone who was killed must stay
Jos 3: 15 and their feet *t* the water's edge,
16: 7 *t* Jericho and came out
19: 11 ran to Maralah, *t* Dabbesheth,
19: 22 boundary *t* Tabor, Shahazumah
19: 26 On the west the boundary *t* Carmel
19: 27 *t* Zebulun and the Valley
19: 34 It *t* Zebulun on the south, Asher

Jdg 6: 21 the angel of the LORD *t* the meat
1Sa 10: 26 men whose hearts God had *t*.
1Ki 6: 27 The wing of one cherub *t* one wall,
6: 27 and their wings *t* each other
6: 27 wing of the other *t* the other wall,
19: 5 All at once an angel *t* him and said,
19: 7 came back a second time and *t* him
2Ki 13: 21 When the body *t* Elisha's bones,
2Ch 3: 11 cubits long and *t* the temple wall,
3: 11 *t* the wing of the other cherub.
3: 12 and *t* the other temple wall,
3: 12 *t* the wing of the first cherub.
Est 5: 2 and *t* the tip of the scepter.
Isa 6: 7 With it he *t* my mouth and said,
6: 7 and said, "See, this has *t* your lips;
Jer 1: 9 and *t* my mouth and said to me,
Eze 1: 9 and their wings *t* one another.
Da 4: 11 and strong and its top *t* the sky;
8: 18 he *t* me and raised me to my feet.
10: 3 no meat or wine *t* my lips;
10: 10 A hand *t* me and set me trembling
10: 16 who looked like a man *t* my lips,
10: 18 the one who looked like a man *t* me
Mt 8: 3 out his hand and *t* the man.
8: 15 He *t* her hand and the fever left her
9: 20 and *t* the edge of his cloak.
9: 29 Then he *t* their eyes and said,
14: 36 and all who *t* him were healed.
17: 7 But Jesus came and *t* them.
20: 34 on them and *t* their eyes.
Mk 1: 41 out his hand and *t* the man.
5: 27 him in the crowd and *t* his cloak,
5: 30 and asked, "Who *t* my clothes?"
5: 31 and yet you can ask, 'Who *t* me?' "
6: 56 and all who *t* him were healed.
7: 33 he spit and *t* the man's tongue.
Lk 5: 13 out his hand and *t* the man.
7: 14 Then he went up and *t* the coffin,
8: 44 and *t* the edge of his cloak,
8: 45 "Who *t* me?" Jesus asked.
8: 46 But Jesus said, "Someone *t* me;
8: 47 she told why she had *t* him
22: 51 And he *t* the man's ear
Ac 19: 12 aprons that had *t* him were taken
Heb 12: 18 come to a mountain that can be *t*
1Jn 1: 1 looked at and our hands have *t*—

TOUCHES (TOUCH)

Ge 27: 12 if my father *t* me? I would appear
Ex 19: 12 Whoever *t* the mountain shall
29: 37 and whatever *t* it will be holy.
30: 29 and whatever *t* them will be holy.
Lev 5: 2 if a person *t* anything ceremonially
5: 3 " 'Or if he *t* human uncleanness—
6: 18 Whatever *t* it will become holy.' "
6: 27 Whatever *t* any of the flesh will
7: 19 " 'Meat that *t* anything
7: 21 If anyone *t* something unclean—
11: 24 whoever *t* their carcasses will be
11: 26 whoever *t* the carcass of any
11: 27 whoever *t* their carcasses will be
11: 31 Whoever *t* them when they are
11: 36 but anyone who *t* one
11: 39 anyone who *t* the carcass will be
15: 5 Anyone who *t* his bed must wash
15: 7 " 'Whoever *t* the man who has
15: 10 whoever *t* any of the things that
15: 11 a discharge *t* without rinsing his
15: 12 pot that the man *t* must be broken,
15: 19 anyone who *t* her will be unclean
15: 21 Whoever *t* her bed must wash his
15: 22 Whoever *t* anything she sits
15: 23 when anyone *t* it, he will be
15: 24 and her monthly flow *t* him,
15: 27 Whoever *t* them will be unclean;
22: 4 unclean if he *t* something defiled
22: 5 or if he *t* any crawling thing that
22: 6 one who *t* any such thing will be
Nu 19: 11 "Whoever *t* the dead body
19: 13 Whoever *t* the dead body
19: 16 or anyone who *t* a human bone
19: 16 the open who *t* someone who has
19: 21 and anyone who *t* the water
19: 22 anyone who *t* it becomes unclean
19: 22 unclean person *t* becomes unclean,
2Sa 23: 7 Whoever *t* thorns
Job 20: 6 and his head *t* the clouds,
Ps 104: 32 he *t* the mountains, and they
Pr 6: 29 no one who *t* her will go
Am 9: 5 he who *t* the earth and it melts,
Hag 2: 12 and that fold *t* some bread or stew,
2: 13 contact with a dead body *t* one
Zec 2: 8 for whoever *t* you *t* the apple
Heb 12: 20 "If even an animal *t* the mountain,

TOUCHING (TOUCH)

Eze 1: 11 one *t* the wing of another creature
Da 4: 20 with its top *t* the sky, visible
8: 5 earth without *t* the ground.
Lk 7: 39 he would know who is *t* him

TOWEL

Jn 13: 4 and wrapped a *t* around his waist.
13: 5 them with the *t* that was wrapped

TOWER (TOWERED TOWERING TOWERS WATCHTOWER WATCHTOWERS)

Ge 11: 4 with a *t* that reaches to the heavens
11: 5 the *t* that the men were building.
Jdg 8: 9 in triumph, I will tear down this *t*."
8: 17 He also pulled down the *t* of Peniel
9: 46 citizens in the *t* of Shechem went
9: 49 all the people in the *t* of Shechem,
9: 51 and climbed up on the *t* roof.
9: 51 the city, however, was a strong *t*,
9: 52 Abimelech went to the *t*
9: 52 entrance to the *t* to set it on fire,
2Ki 9: 17 When the lookout standing on the *t*
Ne 3: 1 and as far as the *T* of Hananel.
3: 1 as far as the *T* of the Hundred,
3: 11 repaired another section and the *T*
3: 25 *t* projecting from the upper palace
3: 26 toward the east and the projecting *t*
3: 27 from the great projecting *t*
12: 38 past the *T* of the Ovens
12: 39 the *T* of Hananel and the *T*
Ps 61: 3 a strong *t* against the foe.
Pr 18: 10 of the LORD is a strong *t*;
SS 4: 4 Your neck is like the *t* of David,
7: 4 Your neck is like an ivory *t*.
7: 4 Your nose is like the *t* of Lebanon
Isa 2: 15 for every lofty *t*
Jer 31: 38 for me from the *T* of Hananel
Eze 31: 14 ever to *t* proudly on high,
Zec 14: 10 and from the *T* of Hananel
Lk 13: 4 when the *t* in Siloam fell on them—
14: 28 one of you wants to build a *t*.

TOWERED (TOWER)

Eze 19: 11 It *t* high
31: 3 it *t* on high,
31: 5 So it *t* higher
31: 10 Because it *t* on high, lifting its top

TOWERING (TOWER)

Isa 2: 14 for all the *t* mountains

TOWERS (TOWER)

2Ch 14: 7 "and put walls around them, with *t*,
26: 9 Uzziah built *t* in Jerusalem
26: 10 He also built *t* in the desert
26: 15 by skillful men for use on the *t*
27: 4 forts and *t* in the wooded areas.
32: 5 of the wall and building *t* on it.
Ps 48: 12 count her *t*,
SS 8: 9 we will build *t* of silver on her.
8: 10 and my breasts are like *t*.
Isa 23: 13 they raised up their siege *t*,
29: 3 I will encircle you with *t*
30: 25 of great slaughter, when the *t* fall,
33: 18 the officer in charge of the *t*?"
Jer 50: 15 She surrenders, her *t* fall,
La 4: 17 from our *t* we watched
Eze 26: 4 walls of Tyre and pull down her *t*;
26: 9 demolish your *t* with his weapons.
27: 11 were in your *t*.
Zep 1: 16 and against the corner *t*.

TOWING

Jn 21: 8 in the boat, *t* the net full of fish,

TOWN (TOWNS TOWNSMEN TOWNSPEOPLE)

Ge 19: 20 here is a *t* near enough to run to,
19: 21 will not overthrow the *t* you speak
19: 22 (That is why the *t* was called Zoar.)
24: 10 made his way to the *t* of Nahor.
24: 11 down near the well outside the *t*;
26: 33 name of the *t* has been Beersheba.
Lev 14: 40 into an unclean place outside the *t*.
14: 41 into an unclean place outside the *t*.
14: 45 out of the *t* to an unclean place.
14: 53 bird in the open fields outside the *t*.
25: 33 a house sold in any *t* they hold—
Nu 20: 16 a *t* on the edge of your territory.
22: 36 him at the Moabite *t* on the Arnon
35: 4 hundred feet from the *t* wall.
35: 5 Outside the *t*, measure three
35: 5 with the *t* in the center.
Dt 2: 36 Gorge, and from the *t* in the gorge,
2: 36 not one *t* was too strong for us.
13: 13 have led the people of their *t* astray
13: 15 to the sword all who live in that *t*.
13: 16 completely burn the *t* and all its
13: 16 the plunder of the *t* into the middle
16: 5 in any *t* the LORD your God gives
16: 18 in every *t* the LORD your God is
19: 12 the elders of his *t* shall send for him
21: 3 of the *t* nearest the body shall take
21: 6 of the *t* nearest the body shall wash
21: 19 to the elders at the gate of his *t*.
21: 21 all the men of his *t* shall stone him
22: 15 a virgin to the *t* elders at the gate.
22: 17 the cloth before the elders of the *t*,
22: 21 the men of her *t* shall stone her
22: 23 to meet in a *t* a virgin pledged
22: 24 both of them to the gate of that *t*
22: 24 she was in a *t* and did not scream
23: 16 and in whatever *t* he chooses.
25: 7 go to the elders at the *t* gate
25: 8 elders of his *t* shall summon him
Jos 3: 16 at a *t* called Adam in the vicinity
13: 9 and from the *t* in the middle
13: 16 and from the *t* in the middle
18: 9 its description on a scroll, *t* by *t*,
18: 14 a *t* of the people of Judah.
19: 50 They gave him the *t* he asked for—
19: 50 he built up the *t* and settled there.
20: 6 home in the *t* from which he fled."
Jdg 6: 27 of his family and the men of the *t*,
6: 28 when the men of the *t* got up,
6: 30 men of the *t* demanded of Joash,
8: 14 of Succoth, the elders of the *t*.
8: 16 He took the elders of the *t*
8: 17 and killed the men of the *t*.
8: 27 which he placed in Ophrah, his *t*.
12: 7 and was buried in a *t* in Gilead.
14: 18 the men of the *t* said to him,
17: 8 left that *t* in search
Ru 1: 19 the whole *t* was stirred
2: 18 She carried it back to *t*,
3: 15 Then he went back to *t*.
4: 1 Boaz went up to the *t* gate
4: 2 Boaz took ten of the elders of the *t*
4: 10 or from the *t* records.
1Sa 1: 3 up from his *t* to worship
4: 13 When the man entered the *t*
4: 13 had happened, the whole *t* sent up
8: 22 "Everyone go back to his *t*."
9: 6 in this *t* there is a man of God;
9: 10 out for the *t* where the man
9: 11 they were going up the hill to the *t*,
9: 12 he has just come to our *t* today,
9: 13 As soon as you enter the *t*,
9: 14 They went up to the *t*, and
9: 25 down from the high place to the *t*,
9: 27 going down to the edge of the *t*,
10: 5 you approach the *t*, you will meet
16: 4 the elders of the *t* trembled
20: 6 to hurry to Bethlehem, his home *t*,
20: 29 is observing a sacrifice in the *t*
20: 40 "Go, carry them back to *t*."
20: 42 and Jonathan went back to the *t*.
22: 19 also put to the sword Nob, the *t*
23: 7 himself by entering a *t* with gates
23: 10 and destroy the *t* on account of me.
28: 3 buried him in his own *t* of Ramah.
2Sa 12: 1 "There were two men in a certain *t*,
15: 2 "What *t* are you from?" He would
15: 12 to come from Giloh, his home *t*.
17: 23 set out for his house in his home *t*.
19: 37 die in my own *t* near the tomb
24: 5 south of the *t* in the gorge,

1Ki 15:27 a Philistine *t*, while Nadab
16:15 near Gibbethon, a Philistine *t*.
17:10 When he came to the *t* gate,
22:36 "Every man to his *t*; everyone
2Ki 2:19 our lord, this *t* is well situated,
2:23 some youths came out of the *t*
3:19 fortified city and every major *t*.
2Ch 14:5 incense altars in every *t* in Judah,
20:4 they came from every *t* in Judah
28:25 In every *t* in Judah he built high
30:10 The couriers went from *t* to *t*
Ezr 2:1 each to his own *t*, in company
10:14 with the elders and judges of each *t*
Ne 7:6 each to his own *t*, in company
Job 39:7 at the commotion in the *t*;
Ecc 10:15 he does not know the way to *t*.
Isa 22:2 O *t* full of commotion,
25:2 the fortified *t* a ruin,
Jer 3:14 one of you from every *t*
4:29 every *t* takes to flight.
48:8 and not a *t* will escape.
48:8 will come against every *t*,
49:25 the *t* in which I delight?
Eze 39:16 a *t* called Hamonah will be there.)
Am 4:6 and lack of bread in every *t*,
4:7 I sent rain on one *t*,
4:8 staggered from *t* to *t* for water
5:3 the *t* that marches out a hundred
Mic 1:14 The *t* of Aczib will prove deceptive
Hab 2:12 and establishes a *t* by crime!
Mt 2:23 and lived in a *t* called Nazareth.
8:33 went into the *t* and reported all this
8:34 the whole *t* went out to meet Jesus.
9:1 crossed over and came to his own *t*.
10:5 or enter any *t* of the Samaritans.
10:11 "Whatever *t* or village you enter,
10:14 feet when you leave that home or *t*.
10:15 the day of judgment than for that *t*.
13:54 to his home *t*, he began teaching
13:57 "Only in his home *t*
23:34 synagogues and pursue from *t* to *t*.
Mk 1:33 The whole *t* gathered at the door,
1:45 could no longer enter a *t* openly
5:14 this in the *t* and countryside,
6:1 left there and went to his home *t*,
6:4 said to them, "Only in his home *t*,
6:10 stay there until you leave that *t*.
Lk 1:26 Gabriel to Nazareth, a *t* in Galilee,
1:39 hurried to a *t* in the hill country
2:3 went to his own *t* to register.
2:4 to Bethlehem the *t* of David,
2:4 went up from the *t* of Nazareth
2:11 in the *t* of David a Savior has been
2:39 Galilee to their own *t* of Nazareth.
4:23 in your home *t* what we have heard
4:24 prophet is accepted in his home *t*.
4:29 They got up, drove him out of the *t*,
4:29 of the hill on which the *t* was built,
4:31 down to Capernaum, a *t* in Galilee,
7:11 Jesus went to a *t* called Nain,
7:12 As he approached the *t* gate,
7:12 crowd from the *t* was with her.
7:37 life in that *t* learned that Jesus was
8:1 Jesus traveled about from one *t*
8:4 coming to Jesus from *t* after *t*,
8:27 a demon-possessed man from the *t*.
8:34 this in the *t* and countryside,
8:39 all over *t* how much Jesus had done
9:4 stay there until you leave that *t*.
9:5 off your feet when you leave their *t*
9:10 themselves to a *t* called Bethsaida,
10:1 two by two ahead of him to every *t*
10:8 you enter a *t* and are welcomed,
10:10 But when you enter a *t* and are not
10:11 'Even the dust of your *t* that sticks
10:12 day for Sodom than for that *t*.
14:21 alleys of the *t* and bring in the poor,
18:2 "In a certain *t* there was a judge
18:3 in that *t* who kept coming to him
23:51 from the Judean *t* of Arimathea
Jn 1:44 was from the *t* of Bethsaida.
4:5 to a *t* in Samaria called Sychar,
4:8 gone into the *t* to buy food.)
4:28 the woman went back to the *t*
4:30 They came out of the *t*
4:39 from that *t* believed in him
7:42 the *t* where David lived?"
Ac 16:4 As they traveled from *t* to *t*,
Ac 27:8 near the *t* of Lasea.
Tit 1:5 and appoint elders in every *t*,

TOWNS (TOWN)

Ge 35:5 fell upon the *t* all around them
Lev 25:32 their houses in the Levitical *t*,
25:33 because the houses in the *t*
25:34 to their *t* must not be sold;
Nu 13:19 What kind of *t* do they live in?
21:3 destroyed them and their *t*;
31:10 burned all the *t* where
35:2 them pasturelands around the *t*.
35:2 to give the Levites *t* to live
35:3 Then they will have *t* to live in
35:4 around the *t* that you give
35:5 this area as pastureland for the *t*.
35:6 give them forty-two other *t*.
35:6 of the *t* you give the Levites will be
35:7 must give the Levites forty-eight *t*,
35:8 Take many *t* from a tribe that has
35:8 The *t* you give the Levites
35:11 select some *t* to be your cities
35:13 These six *t* you give will be your
35:15 These six *t* will be a place of refuge
Dt 1:22 and the *t* we will come to."
2:34 At that time we took all his *t*
2:35 from the *t* we had captured we
2:37 nor that around the *t* in the hills.
3:10 We took all the *t* on the plateau,
3:10 *t* of Og's kingdom in Bashan.
3:12 of Gilead, together with its *t*.
3:19 stay in the *t* I have given you,
12:12 and the Levites from your *t*,
12:15 your animals in any of your *t*
12:17 eat in your own *t* the tithe
12:18 and the Levites from your *t*—
12:21 and in your own *t* you may eat
13:12 one of the *t* the LORD your God is
14:21 it to an alien living in any of your *t*,
14:27 neglect the Levites living in your *t*,
14:28 produce and store it in your *t*,
14:29 live in your *t* may come
15:7 among your brothers in any of the *t*
15:22 You are to eat it in your own *t*.
16:11 the Levites in your *t*, and the aliens
16:14 and the widows who live in your *t*.
17:2 one of the *t* the LORD gives you is
18:6 from one of your *t* anywhere
19:1 and settled in their *t* and houses,
21:2 from the body to the neighboring *t*.
24:14 or an alien living in one of your *t*.
26:12 so that they may eat in your *t*
31:12 and the aliens living in your *t*—
Jos 11:21 totally destroyed them and their *t*.
13:10 and all the *t* of Sihon king
13:17 and all its *t* on the plateau,
13:21 all the *t* on the plateau and the
13:23 These *t* and their villages were
13:25 all the *t* of Gilead and half
13:28 These *t* and their villages were
13:30 of Jair in Bashan, sixty *t*,
14:4 of the land but only *t* to live in,
15:9 came out at the *t* of Mount Ephron
15:21 The southernmost *t* of the tribe
15:32 a total of twenty-nine *t*
15:36 fourteen *t* and their villages.
15:41 sixteen *t* and their villages.
15:44 and Mareshah—nine *t* and their
15:51 eleven *t* and their villages.
15:54 and Zior—nine *t* and their villages.
15:57 Timnah—ten *t* and their villages.
15:59 Eltekon—six *t* and their villages.
15:60 Rabbah—two *t* and their villages.
15:62 six *t* and their villages.
16:9 It also included all the *t*
17:9 There were *t* belonging
17:9 lying among the *t* of Manasseh,
17:12 were not able to occupy these *t*,
18:24 twelve *t* and their villages.
18:28 fourteen *t* and their villages.
19:6 thirteen *t* and their villages;
19:7 Ashan—four *t* and their villages—
19:8 all the villages around these *t* as far
19:15 There were twelve *t* and their
19:16 These *t* and their villages were
19:22 There were sixteen *t* and their
19:23 These *t* and their villages were
19:30 There were twenty-two *t*
Jos 19:31 These *t* and their villages were
19:38 There were nineteen *t*
19:39 These *t* and their villages were
19:48 These *t* and their villages were
21:2 through Moses that you give us *t*
21:3 gave the Levites the following *t*
21:4 the priest were allotted thirteen *t*
21:5 descendants were allotted ten *t*
21:6 of Gershon were allotted thirteen *t*
21:7 received twelve *t* from the tribes
21:8 allotted to the Levites these *t*
21:9 they allotted the following *t*
21:10 by name (these *t* were assigned
21:16 nine *t* from these two tribes.
21:18 with their pasturelands—four *t*.
21:19 All the *t* for the priests,
21:20 clans of the Levites were allotted *t*
21:22 with their pasturelands—four *t*.
21:24 with their pasturelands—four *t*.
21:25 with their pasturelands—two *t*.
21:26 All these ten *t* and their
21:27 with their pasturelands—two *t*;
21:29 four *t*; from the tribe of Asher,
21:31 with their pasturelands—four *t*;
21:32 with their pasturelands—three *t*.
21:33 All the *t* of the Gershonite clans
21:35 with their pasturelands—four *t*;
21:37 with their pasturelands—four *t*;
21:39 with their pasturelands—four *t*
21:40 All the *t* allotted to the Merarite
21:41 The *t* of the Levites
21:42 Each of these *t* had pasturelands
21:42 this was true for all these *t*.
Jdg 10:4 They controlled thirty *t* in Gilead,
11:26 and all the *t* along the Arnon.
11:33 He devastated twenty *t* from Aroer
20:14 From their *t* they came together
20:15 thousand swordsmen from their *t*,
20:42 out of the *t* cut them down there.
20:48 All the *t* they came across they set
20:48 and put all the *t* to the sword,
21:23 rebuilt the *t* and settled in them.
1Sa 6:18 number of Philistine *t* belonging
6:18 the fortified *t* with their country
7:14 The *t* from Ekron to Gath that
18:6 out from all the *t* of Israel
27:5 to me in one of the country *t*,
30:29 those in the *t* of the Jerahmeelites
31:7 they abandoned their *t* and fled.
2Sa 2:1 up to one of the *t* of Judah?"
2:3 and they settled in Hebron and its *t*
8:8 *t* that belonged to Hadadezer,
12:31 He did this to all the Ammonite *t*.
24:7 and all the *t* of the Hivites
1Ki 9:11 King Solomon gave twenty *t*
9:12 to see the *t* that Solomon had given
9:13 of *t* are these you have given me,
9:19 as all his store cities and the *t*
12:17 Israelites who were living in the *t*
13:32 shrines on the high places in the *t*
15:20 of his forces against the *t* of Israel.
2Ki 3:25 They destroyed the *t*, and each
13:25 and so he recovered the Israelite *t*.
13:25 son of Hazael the *t* he had taken
17:6 and in the *t* of the Medes.
17:9 high places in all their *t*.
17:24 settled them in the *t* of Samaria
17:24 took over Samaria and lived in its *t*.
17:26 in the *t* of Samaria do not know
17:29 in the several *t* where they settled,
18:11 Gozan on the Habor River and in *t*
23:5 on the high places of the *t* of Judah
23:8 the priests from the *t* of Judah
23:19 the kings of Israel had built in the *t*
1Ch 2:22 who controlled twenty-three *t*
2:23 surrounding settlements—sixty *t*.)
4:31 These were their *t* until the reign
4:32 Token and Ashan—five *t*—
4:33 all the villages around these *t* as far
6:60 These *t*, which were distributed
6:61 descendants were allotted ten *t*
6:62 were allotted thirteen *t*
6:63 were allotted twelve *t*
6:64 Israelites gave the Levites these *t*
6:65 allotted the previously named *t*.
6:66 as their territory *t* from the tribe
7:29 son of Israel lived in these *t*.
9:2 in their own *t* were some Israelites,

1Ch 10: 7 they abandoned their *t* and fled.
13: 2 are with them in their *t*
18: 8 *t* that belonged to Hadadezer,
19: 7 were mustered from their *t*
20: 3 this to all the Ammonite *t*.
27: 25 in the *t*, the villages
2Ch 10: 17 Israelites who were living in the *t*
11: 5 and built up *t* for defense in Judah:
13: 19 and took from him the *t* of Bethel,
14: 7 "Let us build up these *t*," he said
15: 8 and from the *t* he had captured
16: 4 of his forces against the *t* of Israel.
17: 2 in the *t* of Ephraim that his father
17: 7 Micaiah to teach in the *t* of Judah.
17: 9 went around to all the *t* of Judah
17: 13 had large supplies in the *t* of Judah.
23: 2 of Israelite families from all the *t*.
24: 5 "Go to the *t* of Judah and collect
25: 13 part in the war raided Judean *t*
26: 6 He then rebuilt *t* near Ashdod
27: 4 He built *t* in the Judean hills
28: 18 while the Philistines had raided *t*
31: 1 Israelites returned to their own *t*
31: 1 who were there went out to the *t*
31: 6 Judah who lived in the *t* of Judah
31: 15 faithfully in the *t* of the priests,
31: 19 around their *t* or in any other *t*,
34: 6 In the *t* of Manasseh, Ephraim
Ezr 2: 59 The following came up from the *t*
2: 70 of the Israelites settled in their *t*.
2: 70 servants settled in their own *t*,
3: 1 the Israelites had settled in their *t*,
10: 14 in our *t* who has married a foreign
Ne 7: 61 The following came up from the *t*
7: 73 the Israelites had settled in their *t*,
7: 73 the Israelites, settled in their own *t*.
8: 15 and spread it throughout their *t*
10: 37 tithes in all the *t* where we work.
11: 1 were to stay in their own *t*.
11: 3 his own property in the various *t*,
11: 3 of Solomon's servants lived in the *t*
11: 20 were in all the *t* of Judah, each
12: 44 around the *t* they were to bring
Job 15: 28 he will inhabit ruined *t*
Isa 40: 9 say to the *t* of Judah,
42: 11 its *t* raise their voices;
44: 26 of the *t* of Judah, 'They shall be
Jer 1: 15 and against all the *t* of Judah.
2: 15 his *t* are burned and deserted.
2: 28 as you have *t*, O Judah.
4: 7 Your *t* will lie in ruins
4: 26 all its *t* lay in ruins
4: 29 All the *t* are deserted;
5: 6 a leopard will lie in wait near their *t*
7: 17 not see what they are doing in the *t*
7: 34 and bridegroom in the *t* of Judah
9: 11 and I will lay waste the *t* of Judah
10: 22 It will make the *t* of Judah desolate
11: 6 "Proclaim all these words in the *t*
11: 12 The *t* of Judah and the people
11: 13 as many gods as you have *t*,
17: 26 come from the *t* of Judah
20: 16 May that man be like the *t*
22: 6 like *t* not inhabited.
25: 18 Jerusalem and the *t* of Judah,
26: 2 people of the *t* of Judah who come
31: 21 return to your *t*.
31: 23 in its *t* will once again use these
31: 24 together in Judah and all its *t*—
32: 44 in the *t* of Judah and in the *t*
33: 10 Yet in the *t* of Judah and the streets
33: 12 in all its *t* there will again be
33: 13 In the *t* of the hill country,
33: 13 around Jerusalem and in the *t*
34: 1 Jerusalem and all its surrounding *t*,
34: 22 And I will lay waste the *t* of Judah
36: 6 of Judah who come in from their *t*.
36: 9 come from the *t* of Judah.
40: 5 appointed over the *t* of Judah,
40: 10 live in the *t* you have taken over."
44: 2 and on all the *t* of Judah.
44: 6 it raged against the *t* of Judah
44: 17 our officials did in the *t* of Judah
44: 21 about the incense burned in the *t*
47: 2 the *t* and those who live in them.
48: 9 her *t* will become desolate,
48: 15 be destroyed and her *t* invaded;
48: 24 to all the *t* of Moab, far and near.
Jer 48: 28 Abandon your *t* and dwell
49: 1 Why do his people live in its *t*?
49: 13 and all its *t* will be in ruins forever
49: 18 along with their neighboring *t*,"
50: 32 I will kindle a fire in her *t*
50: 40 along with their neighboring *t*,"
51: 43 Her *t* will be desolate,
La 5: 11 and virgins in the *t* of Judah.
Eze 6: 6 the *t* will be laid waste
12: 20 The inhabited *t* will be laid waste
19: 7 and devastated their *t*.
25: 9 beginning at its frontier *t*—
35: 4 I will turn your *t* into ruins
35: 9 your *t* will not be inhabited.
36: 4 and the deserted *t* that have been
36: 10 The *t* will be inhabited
36: 33 I will resettle your *t*, and the ruins
39: 9 " 'Then those who live in the *t*
45: 5 as their possession for *t* to live in.
Hos 8: 14 Judah has fortified many *t*.
13: 10 Where are your rulers in all your *t*,
Ob : 20 will possess the *t* of the Negev.
Zec 1: 12 and from the *t* of Judah,
1: 17 'My *t* will again overflow
7: 7 and its surrounding *t* were at rest
Mt 9: 35 Jesus went through all the *t*
11: 1 and preach in the *t* of Galilee.
14: 13 him on foot from the *t*.
Mk 6: 33 and ran on foot from all the *t*
6: 56 into villages, *t* or countryside
Lk 4: 43 the kingdom of God to the other *t*
5: 12 While Jesus was in one of the *t*,
13: 22 Then Jesus went through the *t*
Ac 5: 16 also from the *t* around Jerusalem,
8: 40 gospel in all the *t* until he reached
15: 36 in all the *t* where we preached
Jude : 7 surrounding *t* gave themselves up

TOWNSMEN (TOWN)

Ge 34: 20 city to speak to their fellow *t*.
Ru 3: 11 All my fellow *t* know that you are

TOWNSPEOPLE (TOWN)

Ge 24: 13 daughters of the *t* are coming out

TRACE (TRACED TRACING)

Da 2: 35 away without leaving a *t*.
Heb 7: 6 did not *t* his descent from Levi,

TRACED (TRACE)

Ro 9: 5 from them is *t* the human ancestry

TRACING (TRACE)

Ro 11: 33 and his paths beyond *t* out!

TRACK (TRACKED TRACKS)

1Sa 23: 23 I will *t* him down among all
Job 14: 16 but not keep *t* of my sin.

TRACKED (TRACK)

Ps 17: 11 They have *t* me down, they now

TRACKLESS

Job 12: 24 through a *t* waste.
Ps 107: 40 made them wander in a *t* waste.

TRACKS (TRACK)

SS 1: 8 follow the *t* of the sheep

TRACONITIS

Lk 3: 1 Philip tetrarch of Iturea and *T*,

TRACT (TRACTS)

Jos 24: 32 buried at Shechem in the *t*

TRACTS (TRACT)

Jos 17: 5 of ten *t* of land besides Gilead

TRADE (TRADED TRADERS TRADES TRADING)

Ge 34: 10 *t* in it, and acquire property in it."
34: 21 Let them live in our land and *t* in it;
42: 34 and you can *t* in the land.' "
2Ch 20: 37 and were not able to set sail to *t*.
Isa 23: 17 will ply her *t* with all the kingdoms
Eze 27: 9 came alongside to *t* for your wares.
28: 16 Through your widespread *t*
28: 18 By your many sins and dishonest *t*
Zep 1: 11 all who *t* with silver will be ruined.
Ac 19: 27 not only that our *t* will lose its good
Rev 18: 22 No workman of any *t*

TRADED (TRADE)

Eze 27: 13 Tubal and Meshech *t* with you;
27: 15 " 'The men of Rhodes *t* with you,
27: 17 " 'Judah and Israel *t* with you;
27: 20 " 'Dedan *t* in saddle blankets
27: 22 of Sheba and Raamah *t* with you;
27: 23 Asshur and Kilmad *t* with you.
27: 24 In your marketplace they *t*
Joel 3: 3 and *t* boys for prostitutes;

TRADERS (TRADE)

1Ki 10: 15 *t* and from all the Arabian kings
2Ch 9: 14 brought in by merchants and *t*.
Job 41: 6 Will *t* barter for him?
Isa 23: 8 whose *t* are renowned in the earth?
Eze 17: 4 where he planted it in a city of *t*.
1Ti 1: 10 for slave *t* and liars and perjurers—

TRADES (TRADE)

Ac 19: 25 with the workmen in related *t*,

TRADING (TRADE)

1Ki 10: 22 The king had a fleet of *t* ships at sea
22: 48 Jehoshaphat built a fleet of *t* ships
2Ch 9: 21 of *t* ships manned by Hiram's men.
20: 36 him to construct a fleet of *t* ships.
Job 20: 18 will not enjoy the profit from his *t*.
Pr 31: 18 She sees that her *t* is profitable,
Isa 2: 16 for every *t* ship
Eze 28: 5 By your great skill in *t*

TRADITION (TRADITIONS)

2Ch 35: 25 These became a *t* in Israel
Mt 15: 2 "Why do your disciples break the *t*
15: 3 of God for the sake of your *t*?
15: 6 word of God for the sake of your *t*.
Mk 7: 3 holding to the *t* of the elders.
7: 5 to the *t* of the elders instead
7: 13 by your *t* that you have handed
Col 2: 8 which depends on human *t*

TRADITIONS (TRADITION)

Mic 6: 16 and you have followed their *t*.
Mk 7: 4 And they observe many other *t*,
7: 8 are holding on to the *t* of men."
7: 9 in order to observe your own *t*!
Gal 1: 14 zealous for the *t* of my fathers.

TRAFFICKED

Isa 47: 15 and *t* with since childhood.

TRAGEDY

1Ki 17: 20 have you brought *t*

TRAIL

Job 41: 30 leaving a *t* in the mud like
1Ti 5: 24 the sins of others *t* behind them.

TRAIN (TRAINED TRAINING TRAINS WELL-TRAINED)

Ps 68: 18 you led captives in your *t*;
Pr 22: 6 *T* a child in the way he should go,
Isa 2: 4 nor will they *t* for war anymore.
6: 1 the *t* of his robe filled the temple.
Mic 4: 3 nor will they *t* for war anymore.
Eph 4: 8 he led captives in his *t*
1Ti 4: 7 rather, *t* yourself to be godly.
Tit 2: 4 they can *t* the younger women

TRAINED (TRAIN)

Ge 14: 14 he called out the 318 *t* men born
1Ch 5: 18 could use a bow, and who were *t*
25: 7 all of them *t* and skilled in music
2Ch 2: 14 He is *t* to work in gold and silver,
26: 13 an army of 307,500 men *t* for war,
Da 1: 5 They were to be *t* for three years,
Hos 7: 15 I *t* them and strengthened them,
10: 11 Ephraim is a *t* heifer
Lk 6: 40 everyone who is fully *t* will be like
Ac 22: 3 Under Gamaliel I was thoroughly *t*
2Co 11: 6 I may not be a *t* speaker,
Heb 5: 14 by constant use have *t* themselves
12: 11 for those who have been *t* by it.

TRAINING (TRAIN)

1Co 9: 25 in the games goes into strict *t*.
Eph 6: 4 up in the *t* and instruction
1Ti 4: 8 For physical *t* is of some value,
2Ti 3: 16 correcting and *t* in righteousness,

TRAINS (TRAIN)

2Sa 22: 35 He *t* my hands for battle;
Ps 18: 34 He *t* my hands for battle;
144: 1 who *t* my hands for war,

TRAITOR (TREASON)

2Ki 17: 4 discovered that Hoshea was a *t*,
Isa 21: 2 The *t* betrays, the looter takes loot.
33: 1 Woe to you, O *t*,
Lk 6: 16 and Judas Iscariot, who became a *t*.
Jn 18: 5 Judas the *t* was standing there

TRAITORS (TREASON)

Ps 59: 5 show no mercy to wicked *t*.
Mic 2: 4 He assigns our fields to *t*.' "

TRAMPLE (TRAMPLED TRAMPLING)

Dt 33: 29 you will *t* down their high places."
Job 39: 15 that some wild animal may *t* them.
Ps 7: 5 let him *t* my life to the ground
44: 5 through your name we *t* our foes.
60: 12 and he will *t* down our enemies.
91: 13 you will *t* the great lion
108: 13 and he will *t* down our enemies.
Isa 10: 6 and to *t* them down like mud
14: 25 on my mountains I will *t* him down
26: 6 Feet *t* it down—
Jer 12: 10 and *t* down my field;
Eze 26: 11 of his horses will *t* all your streets;
34: 18 also *t* the rest of your pasture
Joel 3: 13 Come, *t* the grapes,
Am 2: 7 They *t* on the heads of the poor
5: 11 You *t* on the poor
8: 4 Hear this, you who *t* the needy
Mal 4: 3 Then you will *t* down the wicked;
Mt 7: 6 they may *t* them under their feet,
Lk 10: 19 I have given you authority to *t*
Rev 11: 2 They will *t* on the holy city

TRAMPLED (TRAMPLE)

2Sa 22: 43 *t* them like mud in the streets.
2Ki 7: 17 the people *t* him in the gateway,
7: 20 for the people *t* him in the gateway,
9: 33 the horses as they *t* her underfoot.
14: 9 and *t* the thistle underfoot.
2Ch 25: 18 and *t* the thistle underfoot.
Isa 5: 5 and it will be *t*.
14: 19 Like a corpse *t* underfoot,
16: 8 have *t* down the choicest vines,
25: 10 as straw is *t* down in the manure.
25: 10 but Moab will be *t* under him
28: 3 will be *t* underfoot.
63: 3 I *t* them in my anger
63: 6 I *t* the nations in my anger;
63: 18 now our enemies have *t*
Jer 51: 33 floor at the time it is *t*;
La 1: 15 In his winepress the Lord has *t*
3: 16 he has *t* me in the dust.
Eze 34: 19 feed on what you have *t*
Da 7: 7 and *t* underfoot whatever was left.
7: 19 and *t* underfoot whatever was left.
8: 7 him to the ground and *t* on him,
8: 10 down to the earth and *t* on them.
8: 13 of the host that will be *t* underfoot
Hos 5: 11 *t* in judgment,
Mic 7: 10 even now she will be *t* underfoot
Hab 3: 15 You *t* the sea with your horses,
Mt 5: 13 to be thrown out and *t* by men.
Lk 8: 5 some fell along the path; it was *t* on
21: 24 Jerusalem will be *t*
Heb 10: 29 to be punished who has *t* the Son
Rev 14: 20 They were *t* in the winepress

TRAMPLING (TRAMPLE)

Isa 1: 12 this *t* of my courts?
22: 5 a day of tumult and *t* and terror
Da 7: 23 will devour the whole earth, *t* it
Zec 10: 5 *t* the muddy streets in battle.
Lk 12: 1 so that they were *t* on one another,

TRANCE

Ac 10: 10 was being prepared, he fell into a *t*.
11: 5 and in a *t* I saw a vision.
22: 17 into a *t* and saw the Lord speaking.

TRANQUILLITY

Ecc 4: 6 Better one handful with *t*

TRANS-EUPHRATES (EUPHRATES)

Ezr 4: 10 city of Samaria and elsewhere in *T*.
4: 11 From your servants, the men of *T*:
4: 16 you will be left with nothing in *T*.
4: 17 in Samaria and elsewhere in *T*:
4: 20 ruling over the whole of *T*,
5: 3 that time Tattenai, governor of *T*,
5: 6 of *T*, and Shethar-Bozenai
5: 6 the officials of *T*, sent
6: 6 of *T*, and Shethar-Bozenai
6: 8 from the revenues of *T*,
6: 13 of *T*, and Shethar-Bozenai
7: 21 order all the treasurers of *T*
7: 25 justice to all the people of *T*—
8: 36 and to the governors of *T*,
Ne 2: 7 letters to the governors of *T*,
2: 9 So I went to the governors of *T*
3: 7 the authority of the governor of *T*.

TRANSACTION (TRANSACTIONS)

Jer 32: 25 and have the *t* witnessed.' "

TRANSACTIONS (TRANSACTION)

Ru 4: 7 method of legalizing *t* in Israel.)

TRANSCENDS

Php 4: 7 which *t* all understanding,

TRANSFER (TRANSFERRED)

Ru 4: 7 and *t* of property to become final,
2Sa 3: 10 and *t* the kingdom from the house

TRANSFERRED (TRANSFER)

Ac 25: 3 to have Paul *t* to Jerusalem,

TRANSFIGURED

Mt 17: 2 There he was *t* before them.
Mk 9: 2 There he was *t* before them.

TRANSFORM (TRANSFORMED)

Php 3: 21 will *t* our lowly bodies

TRANSFORMED (TRANSFORM)

Job 28: 5 is *t* below as by fire;
Ro 12: 2 be *t* by the renewing of your mind.
2Co 3: 18 are being *t* into his likeness

TRANSGRESSED (TRANSGRESSION)

Da 9: 11 All Israel has *t* your law

TRANSGRESSION (TRANSGRESSED TRANSGRESSIONS TRANSGRESSORS)

Ps 19: 13 innocent of great *t*.
Isa 53: 8 for the *t* of my people he was
Da 9: 24 and your holy city to finish *t*,
Mic 1: 5 All this is because of Jacob's *t*,
1: 5 What is Jacob's *t*?
3: 8 to declare to Jacob his *t*,
6: 7 Shall I offer my firstborn for my *t*,
7: 18 who pardons sin and forgives the *t*
Ro 4: 15 where there is no law there is no *t*.
11: 11 Rather, because of their *t*,
11: 12 if their *t* means riches for the world

TRANSGRESSIONS (TRANSGRESSION)

Ps 32: 1 whose *t* are forgiven,
32: 5 my *t* to the LORD"—
39: 8 Save me from all my *t*;
51: 1 blot out my *t*.
51: 3 For I know my *t*,
65: 3 you atoned for our *t*.
103: 12 so far has he removed our *t* from us
Isa 43: 25 your *t*, for my own sake,
50: 1 of your *t* your mother was sent
53: 5 But he was pierced for our *t*,
Mic 1: 13 for the *t* of Israel
Ro 4: 7 whose *t* are forgiven,
Gal 3: 19 because of *t* until the Seed to whom
Eph 2: 1 you were dead in your *t* and sins,
2: 5 even when we were dead in *t*—

TRANSGRESSORS (TRANSGRESSION)

Ps 51: 13 Then I will teach *t* your ways,
Isa 53: 12 and made intercession for the *t*.
53: 12 and was numbered with the *t*.
Lk 22: 37 'And he was numbered with the *t*';

TRANSLATED

Ezr 4: 18 you sent us has been read and *t*
Jn 1: 42 be called Cephas" (which, when *t*,
Ac 9: 36 named Tabitha (which, when *t*,

TRANSPARENT

Rev 21: 21 was of pure gold, like *t* glass.

TRANSPLANTED (PLANT)

Eze 17: 10 Even if it is *t*, will it thrive?

TRANSPORT

Ge 46: 5 that Pharaoh had sent to *t* him.

TRAP (TRAPPED TRAPS)

1Sa 28: 9 Why have you set a *t* for my life
Job 18: 9 A *t* seizes him by the heel;
18: 10 a *t* lies in his path.
40: 24 or *t* him and pierce his nose?
Ps 31: 4 Free me from the *t* that is set
69: 22 may it become retribution and a *t*.
Pr 20: 25 a *t* for a man to dedicate something
28: 10 will fall into his own *t*,
Ecc 7: 26 whose heart is a *t*
Isa 8: 14 a *t* and a snare.
Jer 9: 8 but in his heart he sets a *t* for him.
50: 24 I set a *t* for you, O Babylon,
Am 3: 5 Does a *t* spring up from the earth
3: 5 fall into a *t* on the ground
Ob : 7 who eat your bread will set a *t*
Mt 22: 15 and laid plans to *t* him in his words.
22: 18 why are you trying to *t* me?
Mk 12: 15 "Why are you trying to *t* me?"
Lk 20: 26 They were unable to *t* him
21: 34 close on you unexpectedly like a *t*.
Jn 8: 6 They were using this question as a *t*
Ro 11: 9 their table become a snare and a *t*,
1Ti 3: 7 into disgrace and into the devil's *t*.
6: 9 and a *t* and into many foolish
2Ti 2: 26 and escape from the *t* of the devil,

TRAPPED (TRAP)

Pr 6: 2 if you have been *t* by what you said
11: 6 the unfaithful are *t* by evil desires.
12: 13 An evil man is *t* by his sinful talk,
Ecc 9: 12 so men are *t* by evil times
Isa 42: 22 all of them *t* in pits
Jer 8: 9 they will be dismayed and *t*.
Eze 19: 4 and he was *t* in their pit.
19: 8 and he was *t* in their pit.

TRAPS (TRAP)

Jos 23: 13 they will become snares and *t*
Ps 38: 12 Those who seek my life set their *t*,
140: 5 have set *t* for me along my path.
141: 9 from the *t* set by evildoers.
Jer 5: 26 like those who set *t* to catch men.
La 4: 20 was caught in their *t*.

TRAVEL (TRAVELED TRAVELER TRAVELERS TRAVELING TRAVELS)

Ex 13: 21 so that they could *t* by day or night.
Nu 20: 17 We will *t* along the king's highway
21: 22 We will *t* along the king's highway
2Ch 15: 5 days it was not safe to *t* about,
Job 21: 29 you never questioned those who *t*?
Pr 4: 15 Avoid it, do not *t* on it;
Eze 39: 11 of those who *t* east toward the Sea.
Mt 23: 15 You *t* over land and sea
Rev 18: 17 and all who *t* by ship, the sailors,

TRAVELED (TRAVEL)

Ge 12: 6 Abram *t* through the land as far
41: 46 out from Pharaoh's presence and *t*
Ex 15: 22 For three days they *t* in the desert
Nu 10: 12 and *t* from place to place
10: 33 of the LORD and *t* for three days.
11: 35 the people *t* to Hazeroth
21: 4 They *t* from Mount Hor
22: 1 Then the Israelites *t* to the plains
33: 8 and when they had *t* for three days
Dt 2: 8 *t* along the desert road of Moab.

Dt 10: 6 (The Israelites *t* from the wells
10: 7 From there they *t* to Gudgodah
Jos 24: 17 the nations through which we *t*.
Jdg 11: 18 "Next they *t* through the desert,
2Sa 4: 7 they *t* all night by way
1Ki 19: 8 he *t* forty days and forty nights
2Ki 5: 19 After Naaman had *t* some distance
Isa 41: 3 by a path his feet have not *t* before.
Mk 1: 39 So he *t* throughout Galilee,
Lk 2: 44 was in their company, they *t*
8: 1 Jesus *t* about from one town
10: 33 as he *t*, came where the man was;
17: 11 Jesus *t* along the border
Ac 8: 36 As they *t* along the road, they
8: 40 appeared at Azotus and *t* about,
9: 32 As Peter *t* about the country,
11: 19 in connection with Stephen *t*
13: 6 They *t* through the whole island
13: 31 seen by those who had *t* with him
15: 3 and as they *t* through Phoenicia
16: 4 As they *t* from town to town,
16: 6 *t* throughout the region
16: 12 From there we *t* to Philippi,
18: 23 and *t* from place to place
20: 2 He *t* through that area, speaking
28: 15 and they *t* as far as the Forum

TRAVELER (TRAVEL)

Jdg 19: 17 and saw the *t* in the city square,
2Sa 12: 4 for the *t* who had come to him.
12: 4 "Now a *t* came to the rich man,
Job 31: 32 door was always open to the *t*—
Jer 14: 8 like a *t* who stays only a night?

TRAVELERS (TRAVEL)

Jdg 5: 6 *t* took to winding paths.
Isa 33: 8 no *t* are on the roads.
Jer 9: 2 a lodging place for *t*,
Eze 39: 11 It will block the way of *t*,

TRAVELING (TRAVEL)

Ex 14: 19 who had been *t* in front
17: 1 *t* from place to place as the LORD
1Ki 18: 27 deep in thought, or busy, or *t*.
Job 6: 19 the *t* merchants of Sheba look
Isa 60: 15 with no one *t* through,
Lk 14: 25 Large crowds were *t* with Jesus,
Ac 9: 7 The men *t* with Saul stood there
19: 29 Paul's *t* companions

TRAVELS (TRAVEL)

Ex 40: 36 In all the *t* of the Israelites,
40: 38 house of Israel during all their *t*.
Jer 2: 6 a land where no one *t* and no one
51: 43 through which no man *t*.

TRAYS

Ex 25: 38 and *t* are to be of pure gold.
37: 23 as well as its wick trimmers and *t*,
Nu 4: 9 its lamps, its wick trimmers and *t*,

TREACHEROUS (TREASON)

Ps 25: 3 who are *t* without excuse.
Isa 24: 16 The *t* betray!
24: 16 With treachery the *t* betray!"
48: 8 Well do I know how *t* you are;
Hab 1: 13 Why then do you tolerate the *t*?
Zep 3: 4 they are *t* men.
2Ti 3: 4 not lovers of the good, *t*, rash,

TREACHERY (TREASON)

Lev 26: 40 their *t* against me and their
2Ki 9: 23 calling out to Ahaziah, "*T*,
Isa 24: 16 With *t* the treacherous betray!"
59: 13 rebellion and *t* against the LORD,

TREAD (TREADING TREADS TROD TRODDEN)

Job 24: 11 they *t* the winepresses, yet suffer
Ps 91: 13 You will *t* upon the lion
Jer 25: 30 shout like those who *t* the grapes,
Mic 7: 19 you will *t* our sins underfoot
Na 3: 14 *t* the mortar

TREADING (TREAD)

Dt 25: 4 an ox while it is *t* out the grain.
Ne 13: 15 men in Judah *t* winepresses
Isa 41: 25 as if he were a potter *t* the clay.
63: 2 like those of one *t* the winepress?
Am 9: 13 and the planter by the one *t* grapes.
1Co 9: 9 an ox while it is *t* out the grain."
1Ti 5: 18 the ox while it is *t* out the grain,"

TREADS (TREAD)

Job 9: 8 and *t* on the waves of the sea.
Isa 16: 10 no one *t* out wine at the presses,
41: 25 He *t* on rulers as if they were
Jer 48: 33 no one *t* them with shouts of joy.
Am 4: 13 and *t* the high places of the earth—
Mic 1: 3 *t* the high places of the earth.
Rev 19: 15 He *t* the winepress of the fury

TREASON (TRAITOR TRAITORS TREACHEROUS TREACHERY)

2Ki 11: 14 her robes and called out, "*T! T!*"
2Ch 23: 13 her robes and shouted, "*T! T!*"

TREASURE (TREASURED TREASURER TREASURERS TREASURES TREASURIES TREASURY)

Ge 43: 23 God of your father has given you *t*
Job 3: 21 for it more than for hidden *t*,
20: 20 he cannot save himself by his *t*.
Pr 2: 4 and search for it as for hidden *t*,
15: 6 of the righteous contains great *t*,
Ecc 2: 8 and the *t* of kings and provinces.
Isa 33: 6 of the LORD is the key to this *t*.
44: 9 and the things they *t* are worthless
Da 1: 2 and put in the *t* house of his god.
Mt 6: 21 For where your *t* is, there your
13: 44 of heaven is like *t* hidden in a field.
19: 21 and you will have *t* in heaven.
Mk 10: 21 and you will have *t* in heaven.
Lk 12: 33 a *t* in heaven that will not be
12: 34 For where your *t* is, there your
18: 22 and you will have *t* in heaven.
2Co 4: 7 But we have this *t* in jars of clay
1Ti 6: 19 In this way they will lay up *t*

TREASURED (TREASURE)

Ex 19: 5 you will be my *t* possession.
Dt 7: 6 to be his people, his *t* possession.
14: 2 you to be his *t* possession.
26: 18 his *t* possession as he promised,
Job 23: 12 I have *t* the words
Ps 135: 4 Israel to be his *t* possession.
Isa 64: 11 and all that we *t* lies in ruins.
Eze 7: 22 and they will desecrate my *t* place;
Mal 3: 17 when I make up my *t* possession.
Lk 2: 19 But Mary *t* up all these things
2: 51 But his mother *t* all these things

TREASURER (TREASURE)

Ezr 1: 8 brought by Mithredath the *t*,

TREASURERS (TREASURE)

2Ki 12: 5 the money from one of the *t*,
12: 7 Take no more money from your *t*,
Ezr 7: 21 order all the *t* of Trans-Euphrates
Da 3: 2 governors, advisers, *t*, judges,
3: 3 governors, advisers, *t*, judges,

TREASURES (TREASURE)

Dt 33: 19 on the *t* hidden in the sand."
1Ki 14: 26 He carried off the *t* of the temple
14: 26 and the *t* of the royal palace.
2Ki 20: 13 and everything found among his *t*.
20: 15 among my *t* that I did not show
24: 13 Nebuchadnezzar removed all the *t*
1Ch 29: 3 my God I now give my personal *t*
2Ch 12: 9 and the *t* of the royal palace.
12: 9 he carried off the *t* of the temple
25: 24 together with the palace *t*
36: 18 and the *t* of the LORD's temple
36: 18 the *t* of the king and his officials
Job 20: 26 total darkness lies in wait for his *t*.
28: 10 his eyes see all its *t*.
Pr 10: 2 Ill-gotten *t* are of no value,
24: 4 filled with rare and beautiful *t*.
Isa 2: 7 there is no end to their *t*.
10: 13 I plundered their *t*,
30: 6 their *t* on the humps of camels,
39: 2 and everything found among his *t*.
39: 4 among my *t* that I did not show
45: 3 I will give you the *t* of darkness,
Jer 15: 13 Your wealth and your *t*
17: 3 and your wealth and all your *t*
20: 5 and all the *t* of the kings of Judah.
50: 37 A sword against her *t*!
51: 13 and are rich in *t*,
La 1: 7 Jerusalem remembers all the *t*
1: 10 hands on all her *t*;
1: 11 they barter their *t* for food
Eze 22: 25 take *t* and precious things
Da 11: 43 He will gain control of the *t* of gold
Hos 9: 6 Their *t* of silver will be taken
13: 15 plundered of all its *t*.
Joel 3: 5 off my finest *t* to your temples.
Ob : 6 his hidden *t* pillaged!
Mic 6: 10 your ill-gotten *t*
Na 2: 9 the wealth from all its *t*!
Mt 2: 11 Then they opened their *t*
6: 19 up for yourselves *t* on earth,
6: 20 store up for yourselves *t* in heaven,
13: 52 out of his storeroom new *t*
Col 2: 3 in whom are hidden all the *t*
Heb 11: 26 of greater value than the *t* of Egypt,

TREASURIES (TREASURE)

1Ki 7: 51 in the *t* of the LORD's temple.
15: 18 left in the *t* of the LORD's temple
2Ki 12: 18 found in the *t* of the temple
14: 14 and in the *t* of the royal palace.
16: 8 and in the *t* of the royal palace
18: 15 and in the *t* of the royal palace.
1Ch 9: 26 for the rooms and *t* in the house
26: 20 and the *t* for the dedicated things.
26: 20 were in charge of the *t* of the house
26: 22 in charge of the *t* of the temple
26: 24 was the officer in charge of the *t*.
26: 26 of all the *t* for the things dedicated
28: 12 for the *t* for the dedicated things.
28: 12 for the *t* of the temple of God
2Ch 5: 1 them in the *t* of God's temple.
8: 15 any matter, including that of the *t*.
16: 2 out of the *t* of the LORD's temple
32: 27 and he made *t* for his silver
Pr 8: 21 and making their *t* full.
Eze 28: 4 and silver in your *t*.

TREASURY (TREASURE)

Jos 6: 19 to the LORD and must go into his *t*
6: 24 into the *t* of the LORD's house.
1Ch 29: 8 to the *t* of the temple of the LORD
Ezr 2: 69 gave to the *t* for this work 61,000
6: 1 stored in the *t* at Babylon.
6: 4 are to be paid by the royal *t*.
6: 8 to be fully paid out of the royal *t*.
7: 20 you may provide from the royal *t*.
Ne 7: 70 The governor gave to the *t* 1,000
7: 71 gave to the *t* for the work 20,000
10: 38 to the storerooms of the *t*.
Est 3: 9 talents of silver into the royal *t*
4: 7 into the royal *t* for the destruction
Jer 38: 11 to a room under the *t* in the palace.
Mt 27: 6 against the law to put this into the *t*
Mk 12: 41 their money into the temple *t*.
12: 43 more into the *t* than all the others.
Lk 21: 1 putting their gifts into the temple *t*.
Ac 8: 27 in charge of all the *t* of Candace,

TREAT (TREATED TREATING TREATMENT TREATMENTS TREATS)

Ge 19: 9 We'll *t* you worse than them."
30: 20 This time my husband will *t* me
Lev 22: 2 sons to *t* with respect the sacred
Nu 10: 29 with us and we will *t* you well,
11: 15 If this is how you are going to *t* me,
14: 11 "How long will these people *t* me
25: 17 "*T* the Midianites as enemies
Dt 20: 15 are to *t* all the cities that are
21: 14 You must not sell her or *t* her
Jos 2: 14 we will *t* you kindly and faithfully
2Sa 19: 43 So why do you *t* us with contempt?
Job 6: 26 *t* the words of a despairing man
Ps 103: 10 he does not *t* us as our sins deserve
Jer 3: 19 gladly would I *t* you like sons
29: 22 'The LORD *t* you like Zedekiah
34: 18 I will *t* like the calf they cut in two
Eze 15: 6 so will I *t* the people living
35: 11 I will *t* you in accordance
35: 15 desolate, that is how I will *t* you.
Da 1: 13 and *t* your servants in accordance
Hos 11: 8 How can I *t* you like Admah?

Na 3: 6 I will *t* you with contempt
Mt 18: 17 *t* him as you would a pagan
18: 35 my heavenly Father will *t* each
Jn 15: 21 They will *t* you this way
1Co 12: 23 we think are less honorable we *t*
Gal 4: 14 you did not *t* me with contempt
Eph 6: 9 *t* your slaves in the same way.
1Th 5: 20 do not *t* prophecies with contempt.
1Ti 5: 1 *T* younger men as brothers,
1Pe 3: 7 and *t* them with respect

TREATED (TREAT)

Ge 12: 13 so that I will be *t* well for your sake
12: 16 He *t* Abram well for her sake,
26: 29 molest you but always *t* you well
34: 31 "Should he have *t* our sister like
39: 19 "This is how your slave *t* me,"
42: 30 and *t* us as though we were spying
Ex 5: 15 "Why have you *t* your servants this
18: 11 those who had *t* Israel arrogantly."
Lev 19: 34 The alien living with you must be *t*
25: 40 He is to be *t* as a hired worker
25: 53 He is to be *t* as a man hired
Nu 14: 23 No one who has *t* me
16: 30 that these men have *t* the LORD
25: 18 because they *t* you as enemies
Jdg 1: 24 and we will see that you are *t* well."
8: 1 "Why have you *t* us like this?
9: 16 if you have *t* him as he deserves—
1Sa 2: 14 This is how they *t* all the Israelites
6: 6 did? When he *t* them harshly,
24: 17 me well, but I have *t* you badly.
24: 17 "You have *t* me well, but I have
24: 19 well for the way you *t* me today.
1Ki 1: 21 and my son Solomon will be *t*
1Ch 24: 31 the oldest brother were *t* the same
Ne 9: 10 arrogantly the Egyptians *t* them.
La 2: 20 Whom have you ever *t* like this?
Eze 22: 7 In you they have *t* father
Mt 21: 36 the tenants *t* them the same way.
Mk 12: 4 on the head and *t* him shamefully.
Lk 2: 48 "Son, why have you *t* us like this?
6: 23 is how their fathers *t* the prophets.
6: 26 how their fathers *t* the false
20: 11 also they beat and *t* shamefully
1Co 4: 11 we are brutally *t*, we are homeless.
12: 23 parts that are unpresentable are *t*
Heb 10: 29 who has *t* as an unholy thing
10: 33 by side with those who were so *t*.
Rev 18: 20 her for the way she *t* you.' "

TREATING (TREAT)

Ge 18: 25 *t* the righteous and the wicked
50: 17 wrongs they committed in *t* you
Lev 22: 9 and die for *t* them with contempt.
1Sa 2: 17 for they were *t* the LORD's
25: 39 cause against Nabal for *t* me
Heb 12: 7 as discipline; God is *t* you as sons.

TREATMENT (TREAT)

1Sa 20: 34 at his father's shameful *t* of David.
Isa 66: 4 also will choose harsh *t* for them
1Co 12: 24 presentable parts need no special *t*.
Col 2: 23 and their harsh *t* of the body,

TREATMENTS (TREAT)

Est 2: 3 and let beauty *t* be given to them.
2: 9 he provided her with her beauty *t*
2: 12 months of beauty *t* prescribed

TREATS (TREAT)

Dt 24: 7 and *t* him as a slave or sells him,
Job 39: 16 She *t* her young harshly,
41: 27 Iron he *t* like straw
Pr 27: 11 then I can answer anyone who *t* me

TREATY

Ge 21: 27 and the two men made a *t*.
21: 32 After the *t* had been made
26: 28 Let us make a *t* with you that you
Ex 34: 12 not to make a *t* with those who live
34: 15 not to make a *t* with those who live
Dt 7: 2 Make no *t* with them, and show
Jos 9: 6 from a distant country; make a *t*
9: 7 How then can we make a *t*
9: 11 "We are your servants; make a *t*
9: 15 Joshua made a *t* of peace with them
9: 16 days after they made the *t*
Jos 10: 1 of Gibeon had made a *t* of peace
11: 19 not one city made a *t* of peace
1Sa 11: 1 "Make a *t* with us, and we will be
11: 2 "I will make a *t* with you only
1Ki 5: 12 and the two of them made a *t*.
15: 19 Now break your *t* with Baasha king
15: 19 "Let there be a *t* between me
20: 34 On the basis of a *t* I will set you free
20: 34 So he made a *t* with him,
2Ch 16: 3 Now break your *t* with Baasha king
16: 3 "Let there be a *t* between me
Isa 33: 8 The *t* is broken,
Eze 17: 13 of the royal family and made a *t*
17: 14 surviving only by keeping his *t*.
17: 15 Will he break the *t* and yet escape?
17: 16 he despised and whose *t* he broke.
Hos 12: 1 He makes a *t* with Assyria
Am 1: 9 disregarding a *t* of brotherhood,

TREE (TREES)

Ge 1: 29 every *t* that has fruit with seed in it.
2: 9 and the *t* of the knowledge of good
2: 9 of the garden were the *t* of life
2: 16 free to eat from any *t* in the garden;
2: 17 eat from the *t* of the knowledge
3: 1 eat from any *t* in the garden'?"
3: 3 fruit from the *t* that is in the middle
3: 6 the fruit of the *t* was good for food
3: 11 from the *t* that I commanded you
3: 12 she gave me some fruit from the *t*,
3: 17 and ate from the *t* about which I
3: 22 take also from the *t* of life and eat,
3: 24 to guard the way to the *t* of life.
12: 6 of the great *t* of Moreh at Shechem
18: 4 your feet and rest under this *t*.
18: 8 he stood near them under a *t*.
21: 33 Abraham planted a tamarisk *t*
40: 19 off your head and hang you on a *t*.
Ex 9: 25 in the fields and stripped every *t*.
10: 5 including every *t* that is growing
10: 15 Nothing green remained on *t*
Lev 19: 23 and plant any kind of fruit *t*,
Dt 12: 2 and under every spreading *t* where
19: 5 and as he swings his ax to fell a *t*,
21: 22 and his body is hung on a *t*,
21: 23 body on the *t* overnight.
21: 23 hung on a *t* is under God's curse.
22: 6 either in a *t* or on the ground,
Jos 8: 29 He hung the king of Ai on a *t*
8: 29 them to take his body from the *t*
19: 33 and the large *t* in Zaanannim,
Jdg 4: 11 tent by the great *t* in Zaanannim
9: 6 beside the great *t* at the pillar
9: 8 said to the olive *t*, 'Be our king.'
9: 9 "But the olive *t* answered,
9: 10 the trees said to the fig *t*, 'Come
9: 11 fig *t* replied, 'Should I give up my
9: 37 the direction of the soothsayers' *t*."
1Sa 10: 3 until you reach the great *t* of Tabor.
14: 2 under a pomegranate *t* in Migron.
22: 6 under the tamarisk *t* on the hill
31: 13 them under a tamarisk *t* at Jabesh,
2Sa 18: 9 Absalom's head got caught in the *t*.
18: 10 saw Absalom hanging in an oak *t*."
18: 14 Absalom was still alive in the oak *t*.
1Ki 4: 25 man under his own vine and fig *t*.
13: 14 found him sitting under an oak *t*
14: 23 and under every spreading *t*.
19: 4 to a broom *t*, sat down under it
19: 5 Then he lay down under the *t*
2Ki 3: 19 You will cut down every good *t*,
3: 25 and cut down every good *t*.
6: 5 one of them was cutting down a *t*,
16: 4 and under every spreading *t*.
17: 10 and under every spreading *t*.
18: 31 and fig *t* and drink water
1Ch 10: 12 bones under the great *t* in Jabesh,
2Ch 3: 5 and decorated it with palm *t*
28: 4 and under every spreading *t*.
Ne 10: 35 of our crops and of every fruit *t*.
Job 14: 7 "At least there is hope for a *t*:
15: 33 like an olive *t* shedding its
19: 10 he uproots my hope like a *t*.
24: 20 but are broken like a *t*.
30: 4 food was the root of the broom *t*.
Ps 1: 3 He is like a *t* planted by streams
37: 35 flourishing like a green *t*
52: 8 But I am like an olive *t*
Ps 92: 12 righteous will flourish like a palm *t*,
120: 4 with burning coals of the broom *t*.
Pr 3: 18 She is a *t* of life to those who
11: 30 of the righteous is a *t* of life,
13: 12 but a longing fulfilled is a *t* of life.
15: 4 tongue that brings healing is a *t*
27: 18 He who tends a fig *t* will eat its fruit
Ecc 11: 3 Whether a *t* falls to the south
12: 5 when the almond *t* blossoms
SS 2: 3 Like an apple *t*
2: 13 The fig *t* forms its early fruit;
4: 14 with every kind of incense *t*,
7: 8 I said, "I will climb the palm *t*;
8: 5 Under the apple *t* I roused you;
Isa 17: 6 as when an olive *t* is beaten,
24: 13 as when an olive *t* is beaten,
34: 4 like shriveled figs from the fig *t*.
36: 16 and fig *t* and drink water
55: 13 the thornbush will grow the pine *t*,
56: 3 "I am only a dry *t*."
57: 5 and under every spreading *t*;
65: 22 For as the days of a *t*,
Jer 1: 11 "I see the branch of an almond *t*,"
2: 20 and under every spreading *t*
3: 6 and under every spreading *t*
3: 13 gods under every spreading *t*,
8: 13 There will be no figs on the *t*,
10: 3 they cut a *t* out of the forest,
11: 16 LORD called you a thriving olive *t*
11: 19 "Let us destroy the *t* and its fruit;
17: 8 He will be like a *t* planted
Eze 6: 13 under every spreading *t*
17: 24 I the LORD bring down the tall *t*
17: 24 and make the dry *t* flourish.
17: 24 and make the low *t* grow tall.
17: 24 dry up the green *t* and make
20: 28 they saw any high hill or any leafy *t*
31: 8 no *t* in the garden of God
31: 13 of the air settled on the fallen *t*,
40: 22 its palm *t* decorations had the same
40: 26 it had palm *t* decorations
41: 19 lion toward the palm *t* on the other.
41: 19 man toward the palm *t* on one side
Da 4: 10 before me stood a *t* in the middle
4: 11 The *t* grew large and strong
4: 14 'Cut down the *t* and trim
4: 20 The *t* you saw, which grew large
4: 22 are that *t*! You have become great
4: 23 'Cut down the *t* and destroy it,
4: 26 to leave the stump of the *t*
Hos 9: 10 the early fruit on the fig *t*.
14: 6 His splendor will be like an olive *t*,
14: 8 I am like a green pine *t*;
Joel 1: 12 and the fig *t* is withered;
1: 12 the palm and the apple *t*—
2: 22 fig *t* and the vine yield their riches.
Mic 4: 4 and under his own fig *t*,
Hab 3: 17 Though the fig *t* does not bud
Hag 2: 19 Until now, the vine and the fig *t*,
2: 19 and the olive *t* have not borne fruit.
Zec 3: 10 to sit under his vine and fig *t*,'
11: 2 O pine *t*, for the cedar has fallen;
Mt 3: 10 every *t* that does not produce good
7: 17 Likewise every good *t* bears good
7: 17 but a bad *t* bears bad fruit.
7: 18 A good *t* cannot bear bad fruit,
7: 18 and a bad *t* cannot bear good fruit.
7: 19 Every *t* that does not bear good
12: 33 for a *t* is recognized by its fruit.
12: 33 or make a *t* bad and its fruit will be
12: 33 "Make a *t* good and its fruit will be
13: 32 of garden plants and becomes a *t*,
21: 19 Immediately the *t* withered.
21: 19 Seeing a fig *t* by the road, he went
21: 20 How did the fig *t* wither so quickly
21: 21 you do what was done to the fig *t*,
24: 32 Now learn this lesson from the fig *t*
Mk 11: 13 Seeing in the distance a fig *t* in leaf,
11: 14 to the *t*, "May no one ever eat fruit
11: 20 they saw the fig *t* withered
11: 21 The fig *t* you cursed has withered!"
13: 28 Now learn this lesson from the fig *t*
Lk 3: 9 every *t* that does not produce good
6: 43 nor does a bad *t* bear good fruit.
6: 43 "No good *t* bears bad fruit,
6: 44 Each *t* is recognized
13: 6 "A man had a fig *t*, planted
13: 7 coming to look for fruit on this fig *t*

Lk 13: 19 became a *t*, and the birds
17: 6 you can say to this mulberry *t*,
19: 4 climbed a sycamore-fig *t* to see him
21: 29 "Look at the fig *t* and all the trees.
23: 31 things when the *t* is green,
Jn 1: 48 under the fig *t* before Philip called
1: 50 I told you I saw you under the fig *t*.
Ac 5: 30 killed by hanging him on a *t*.
10: 39 him by hanging him on a *t*,
13: 29 they took him down from the *t*
Ro 11: 24 be grafted into their own olive *t!*
11: 24 grafted into a cultivated olive *t*,
11: 24 of an olive *t* that is wild by nature,
Gal 3: 13 is everyone who is hung on a *t*."
Jas 3: 12 My brothers, can a fig *t* bear olives,
1Pe 2: 24 sins in his body on the *t*,
Rev 2: 7 the right to eat from the *t* of life,
6: 13 drop from a fig *t* when shaken
7: 1 or on the sea or on any *t*.
9: 4 grass of the earth or any plant or *t*,
22: 2 And the leaves of the *t* are
22: 2 side of the river stood the *t* of life,
22: 14 they may have the right to the *t*
22: 19 from him his share in the *t* of life

TREES (TREE)

Ge 1: 11 and *t* on the land that bear fruit
1: 12 and *t* bearing fruit with seed
2: 9 kinds of *t* grow out of the ground—
2: 9 *t* that were pleasing to the eye
3: 2 fruit from the *t* in the garden,
3: 8 God among the *t* of the garden.
13: 18 live near the great *t* of Mamre
14: 13 living near the great *t* of Mamre
18: 1 near the great *t* of Mamre
23: 17 and all the *t* within the borders
30: 37 and plane *t* and made white stripes
Ex 10: 15 in the fields and the fruit on the *t*.
15: 27 twelve springs and seventy palm *t*,
Lev 23: 40 are to take choice fruit from the *t*,
26: 4 and the *t* of the field their fruit.
26: 20 nor will the *t* of the land yield their
27: 30 from the soil or fruit from the *t*,
Nu 13: 20 or poor? Are there *t* on it or not?
33: 9 twelve springs and seventy palm *t*,
Dt 8: 8 vines and fig *t*, pomegranates,
11: 30 near the great *t* of Moreh,
20: 19 Are the *t* of the field people,
20: 19 do not destroy its *t* by putting an ax
20: 20 *t* that you know are not fruit *t*
24: 20 you beat the olives from your *t*,
28: 40 You will have olive *t*
28: 42 of locusts will take over all your *t*
Jos 10: 26 hanging on the *t* until evening.
10: 26 the kings and hung them on five *t*,
10: 27 they took them down from the *t*
Jdg 9: 8 One day the *t* went out
9: 9 to go waving over the *t?*' "Next,
9: 10 "Next, the *t* said to the fig tree,
9: 11 to go waving over the *t?*'
9: 12 "Then the *t* said to the vine,
9: 13 over the *t?*' "Finally all the *t* said
9: 15 "The thornbush said to the *t*,
2Sa 5: 23 attack them in front of the balsam *t*
5: 24 in the tops of the balsam *t*,
1Ki 6: 29 he carved cherubim, palm *t*
6: 32 and palm *t* with beaten gold.
6: 32 doors he carved cherubim, palm *t*
6: 35 palm *t* and open flowers on them
7: 36 and palm *t* on the surfaces
10: 27 as sycamore-fig *t* in the foothills.
2Ki 6: 4 Jordan and began to cut down *t*.
18: 32 a land of olive *t* and honey.
1Ch 14: 14 attack them in front of the balsam *t*
14: 15 in the tops of the balsam *t*,
16: 33 Then the *t* of the forest will sing,
27: 28 and sycamore-fig *t* in the western
2Ch 1: 15 as sycamore-fig *t* in the foothills.
9: 27 as sycamore-fig *t* in the foothills.
Ne 8: 15 from olive and wild olive *t*,
8: 15 palms and shade *t*, to make booths
9: 25 olive groves and fruit *t*
10: 37 of all our *t* and of our new wine
Ps 74: 5 to cut through a thicket of *t*.
96: 12 Then all the *t* of the forest will sing
104: 16 *t* of the LORD are well watered,
104: 17 the stork has its home in the pine *t*.
105: 33 and shattered the *t* of their country
Ps 105: 33 he struck down their vines and fig *t*
148: 9 fruit *t* and all cedars,
Ecc 2: 5 planted all kinds of fruit *t* in them.
2: 6 to water groves of flourishing *t*.
SS 2: 3 among the *t* of the forest
6: 11 I went down to the grove of nut *t*
Isa 7: 2 as the *t* of the forest are shaken
9: 10 the fig *t* have been felled,
10: 19 remaining *t* of his forests will be
10: 33 The lofty *t* will be felled,
14: 8 Even the pine *t* and the cedars
44: 4 like poplar *t* by flowing streams.
44: 14 grow among the *t* of the forest,
44: 23 you forests and all your *t*,
55: 12 and all the *t* of the field
Jer 5: 17 devour your vines and fig *t*.
6: 6 "Cut down the *t*
7: 20 on the *t* of the field and on the fruit
17: 2 poles beside the spreading *t*
46: 22 like men who cut down *t*.
Eze 15: 2 branch on any of the *t* in the forest?
15: 6 the vine among the *t* of the forest
17: 24 All the *t* of the field will know that
20: 47 and it will consume all your *t*,
27: 5 timbers of pine *t* from Senir;
31: 4 channels to all the *t* of the field.
31: 5 higher than all the *t* of the field;
31: 8 nor could the pine *t*
31: 8 nor could the plane *t*
31: 9 the envy of all the *t* of Eden
31: 14 No other *t* so well-watered are ever
31: 14 Therefore no other *t*
31: 15 all the *t* of the field withered away.
31: 16 Then all the *t* of Eden, the choicest
31: 16 all the *t* that were well-watered,
31: 18 brought down with the *t* of Eden
31: 18 of the *t* of Eden can be compared
34: 27 *t* of the field will yield their fruit
36: 30 I will increase the fruit of the *t*
40: 16 walls were decorated with palm *t*.
40: 31 palm *t* decorated its jambs,
40: 34 palm *t* decorated the jambs on
40: 37 palm *t* decorated the jambs on
41: 18 Palm *t* alternated with cherubim.
41: 18 were carved cherubim and palm *t*.
41: 20 and palm *t* were carved on the wall
41: 25 and palm *t* like those carved
41: 26 with palm *t* carved on each side.
47: 7 I saw a great number of *t*
47: 12 Fruit *t* of all kinds will grow
Hos 2: 12 I will ruin her vines and her fig *t*,
Joel 1: 7 and ruined my fig *t*.
1: 12 all the *t* of the field are dried up.
1: 19 and flames have burned up all the *t*
2: 22 The *t* are bearing their fruit;
Am 4: 9 devoured your fig and olive *t*,
7: 14 I also took care of sycamore-fig *t*.
Na 3: 12 All your fortresses are like fig *t*
Zec 1: 8 among the myrtle *t* in a ravine.
1: 10 among the myrtle *t* explained,
1: 11 standing among the myrtle *t*,
4: 3 Also there are two olive *t* by it,
4: 11 "What are these two olive *t*
11: 2 the stately *t* are ruined!
Mt 3: 10 The ax is already at the root of the *t*
21: 8 others cut branches from the *t*
Mk 8: 24 they look like *t* walking around."
Lk 3: 9 The ax is already at the root of the *t*
21: 29 "Look at the fig tree and all the *t*.
Jude : 12 autumn *t*, without fruit
Rev 7: 3 or the *t* until we put a seal
8: 7 a third of the *t* were burned up,
11: 4 These are the two olive *t*

TREMBLE (TREMBLED TREMBLES TREMBLING)

Ex 15: 14 The nations will hear and *t;*
Dt 2: 25 and will *t* and be in anguish
1Ch 16: 30 *T* before him, all the earth!
Job 9: 6 and makes its pillars *t*.
Ps 96: 9 *t* before him, all the earth.
99: 1 let the nations *t;*
114: 7 *T*, O earth, at the presence
Ecc 12: 3 when the keepers of the house *t*,
Isa 13: 13 Therefore I will make the heavens *t*
14: 16 and made kingdoms *t*,
19: 1 The idols of Egypt *t* before him,
21: 4 fear makes me *t;*
Isa 23: 11 and made its kingdoms *t*.
32: 10 you who feel secure will *t;*
32: 11 *T*, you complacent women;
41: 5 the ends of the earth *t*.
41: 8 Do not *t*, do not be afraid.
64: 1 that the mountains would *t*
66: 5 you who *t* at his word:
Jer 5: 22 "Should you not *t* in my presence?
23: 9 all my bones *t*.
33: 9 will *t* at the abundant prosperity
49: 21 of their fall the earth will *t;*
50: 46 Babylon's capture the earth will *t;*
Eze 7: 27 of the people of the land will *t*.
12: 18 Son of man, *t* as you eat your food,
26: 10 Your walls will *t* at the noise
26: 15 Will not the coastlands *t*
26: 18 Now the coastlands *t*
31: 16 I made the nations *t* at the sound
32: 10 each of them will *t*
38: 20 of the earth will *t* at my presence.
Joel 2: 1 Let all who live in the land *t*,
3: 16 the earth and the sky will *t*.
Am 3: 6 do not the people *t?*
8: 8 "Will not the land *t* for this,
Na 2: 10 bodies *t*, every face grows pale.
Hab 2: 7 they not wake up and make you *t?*
3: 6 he looked, and made the nations *t*.

TREMBLED (TREMBLE)

Ge 27: 33 Isaac *t* violently and said, "Who
Ex 19: 16 Everyone in the camp *t*.
19: 18 the whole mountain *t* violently,
20: 18 in smoke, they *t* with fear.
1Sa 16: 4 of the town *t* when they met him.
21: 1 Ahimelech *t* when he met him,
2Sa 22: 8 they *t* because he was angry.
22: 8 "The earth *t* and quaked,
Ezr 9: 4 Then everyone who *t* at the words
Ps 18: 7 The earth *t* and quaked,
18: 7 they *t* because he was angry.
77: 18 the earth *t* and quaked.
Isa 64: 3 and the mountains *t* before you.
Hos 13: 1 When Ephraim spoke, men *t;*
Hab 3: 16 and my legs *t*.
Ac 7: 32 Moses *t* with fear and did not dare

TREMBLES (TREMBLE)

Jdg 7: 3 'Anyone who *t* with fear may turn
Ps 97: 4 the earth sees and *t*.
104: 32 He looks at the earth, and it *t;*
119:120 My flesh *t* in fear of you;
119:161 but my heart *t* at your word.
Pr 30: 21 "Under three things the earth *t*,
Isa 10: 29 Ramah *t;*
66: 2 and *t* at my word.
Jer 8: 16 the whole land *t*.
10: 10 When he is angry, the earth *t;*
51: 29 The land *t* and writhes,
Joel 2: 10 the sky *t*,
Na 1: 5 The earth *t* at his presence,

TREMBLING (TREMBLE)

Ge 42: 28 and they turned to each other *t*
Ex 15: 15 of Moab will be seized with *t*,
2Sa 22: 46 they come *t* from their strongholds
Job 4: 14 fear and *t* seized me
21: 6 *t* seizes my body.
Ps 2: 11 and rejoice with *t*.
18: 45 they come *t* from their strongholds
48: 6 *T* seized them there,
55: 5 Fear and *t* have beset me;
Isa 33: 14 *t* grips the godless:
Eze 26: 16 *t* every moment, appalled at you.
Da 10: 10 set me *t* on my hands and knees.
10: 11 this to me, I stood up *t*.
Hos 3: 5 They will come *t* to the LORD
11: 10 his children will come *t*
11: 11 They will come *t*
Mic 7: 17 They will come *t* out of their dens;
Mk 5: 33 and fell at his feet and, *t* with fear,
16: 8 *T* and bewildered, the women went
Lk 8: 47 she could not go unnoticed, came *t*
Ac 16: 29 rushed in and fell *t* before Paul
1Co 2: 3 and fear, and with much *t*.
2Co 7: 15 receiving him with fear and *t*.
Php 2: 12 out your salvation with fear and *t*,
Heb 12: 21 terrifying that Moses said, "I am *t*

TREMENDOUS

Rev 16: 18 been on earth, so *t* was the quake.

TRENCH

1Ki 18: 32 he dug a *t* around it large enough
18: 35 the altar and even filled the *t*.
18: 38 and also licked up the water in the *t*
Da 9: 25 It will be rebuilt with streets and a *t*

TRESPASS (TRESPASSES)

Ro 5: 15 But the gift is not like the *t*.
5: 15 died by the *t* of the one man,
5: 17 For if, by the *t* of the one man,
5: 18 result of one *t* was condemnation
5: 20 added so that the *t* might increase.

TRESPASSES (TRESPASS)

Ro 5: 16 but the gift followed many *t*

TRESSES

SS 7: 5 the king is held captive by its *t*.

TRIAL (TRIALS)

Nu 35: 12 he stands *t* before the assembly.
Jos 20: 6 city until he has stood *t*
20: 9 to standing *t* before the assembly.
Ps 37: 33 condemned when brought to *t*.
Mk 13: 11 you are arrested and brought to *t*,
Ac 12: 4 out for public *t* after the Passover.
12: 6 before Herod was to bring him to *t*,
16: 37 "They beat us publicly without a *t*,
23: 6 I stand on *t* because of my hope
24: 21 am on *t* before you today.' "
25: 9 and stand *t* before me there
25: 20 and stand *t* there on these charges.
26: 6 our fathers that I am on *t* today.
27: 24 You must stand *t* before Caesar;
2Co 8: 2 most severe *t*, their overflowing
Gal 4: 14 though my illness was a *t* to you,
Jas 1: 12 is the man who perseveres under *t*,
1Pe 4: 12 at the painful *t* you are suffering,
Rev 3: 10 you from the hour of *t* that is going

TRIALS (TRIAL)

Dt 7: 19 saw with your own eyes the great *t*,
29: 3 own eyes you saw those great *t*,
Lk 22: 28 who have stood by me in my *t*.
1Th 3: 3 one would be unsettled by these *t*.
2Th 1: 4 the persecutions and *t* you are
Jas 1: 2 whenever you face *t* of many kinds,
1Pe 1: 6 had to suffer grief in all kinds of *t*.
2Pe 2: 9 how to rescue godly men from *t*

TRIBAL (TRIBE)

Ge 25: 16 of the twelve *t* rulers according
Nu 4: 18 that the Kohathite *t* clans are not
7: 2 of families who were the *t* leaders
25: 15 a *t* chief of a Midianite family.
36: 4 taken from the *t* inheritance
36: 6 as they marry within the *t* clan
36: 7 shall keep the *t* land inherited
36: 8 someone in her father's *t* clan,
Dt 1: 15 and of tens and as *t* officials.
Jos 11: 23 according to their *t* divisions.
12: 7 according to their *t* divisions—
14: 1 and the heads of the *t* clans
18: 10 according to their *t* divisions.
19: 51 and the heads of the *t* clans
21: 1 of the other *t* families of Israel
Eze 45: 7 parallel to one of the *t* portions.
48: 8 will equal one of the *t* portions;
48: 21 length of the *t* portions will belong

TRIBE (HALF-TRIBE TRIBAL TRIBES)

Ex 31: 2 the son of Hur, of the *t* of Judah,
31: 6 of the *t* of Dan, to help him.
35: 30 the son of Hur, of the *t* of Judah,
35: 34 of the *t* of Dan, the ability
38: 22 the son of Hur, of the *t* of Judah,
38: 23 of the *t* of Dan—a craftsman
Nu 1: 4 man from each *t*, each the head
1: 21 The number from the *t*
1: 23 The number from the *t*
1: 25 The number from the *t*
1: 27 The number from the *t*
1: 29 The number from the *t*
1: 31 The number from the *t*
1: 33 The number from the *t*
Nu 1: 35 The number from the *t*
1: 37 The number from the *t*
1: 39 The number from the *t*
1: 41 The number from the *t*
1: 43 The number from the *t*
1: 47 The families of the *t* of Levi,
1: 49 "You must not count the *t* of Levi
2: 5 The *t* of Issachar will camp next
2: 7 The *t* of Zebulun will be next.
2: 12 The *t* of Simeon will camp next
2: 14 The *t* of Gad will be next.
2: 20 The *t* of Manasseh will be next
2: 22 The *t* of Benjamin will be next.
2: 27 The *t* of Asher will camp next
2: 29 The *t* of Naphtali will be next.
3: 6 "Bring the *t* of Levi and present
7: 12 of Amminadab of the *t* of Judah.
10: 15 the division of the *t* of Issachar,
10: 16 the division of the *t* of Zebulun.
10: 19 over the division of the *t* of Simeon
10: 20 over the division of the *t* of Gad.
10: 23 the division of the *t* of Manasseh,
10: 24 the division of the *t* of Benjamin.
10: 26 over the division of the *t* of Asher,
10: 27 the division of the *t* of Naphtali.
13: 2 From each ancestral *t* send one
13: 4 from the *t* of Reuben,
13: 5 of Zaccur; from the *t* of Simeon,
13: 6 son of Hori; from the *t* of Judah,
13: 7 from the *t* of Issachar,
13: 8 of Joseph; from the *t* of Ephraim,
13: 9 of Nun; from the *t* of Benjamin,
13: 10 of Raphu; from the *t* of Zebulun,
13: 11 the *t* of Manasseh (a *t* of Joseph),
13: 12 son of Susi; from the *t* of Dan,
13: 13 of Gemalli; from the *t* of Asher,
13: 14 of Michael; from the *t* of Naphtali,
13: 15 son of Vophsi; from the *t* of Gad,
17: 3 for the head of each ancestral *t*.
18: 2 from your ancestral *t* to join you
24: 2 and saw Israel encamped *t* by *t*,
26: 55 to the names for its ancestral *t*.
31: 5 from each *t*, were supplied
31: 6 a thousand from each *t*,
34: 14 the families of the *t* of Reuben,
34: 14 the *t* of Gad and the half-tribe
34: 18 appoint one leader from each *t*
34: 19 of Jephunneh, from the *t* of Judah;
34: 20 of Ammihud, from the *t* of Simeon;
34: 21 of Kislon, from the *t* of Benjamin;
34: 22 the leader from the *t* of Dan;
34: 23 leader from the *t* of Manasseh son
34: 24 leader from the *t* of Ephraim son
34: 25 the leader from the *t* of Zebulun;
34: 26 the leader from the *t* of Issachar;
34: 27 the leader from the *t* of Asher;
34: 28 the leader from the *t* of Naphtali."
35: 8 to the inheritance of each *t*:
35: 8 towns from a *t* that has many,
36: 3 to that of the *t* they marry into.
36: 4 that of the *t* into which they marry,
36: 5 "What the *t* of the descendants
36: 7 in Israel is to pass from *t* to *t*,
36: 8 land in any Israelite *t* must marry
36: 9 No inheritance may pass from *t* to *t*
36: 9 for each Israelite *t* is
36: 12 in their father's clan and *t*.
Dt 1: 23 of you, one man from each *t*.
3: 13 I gave to the half *t* of Manasseh.
10: 8 that time the LORD set apart the *t*
18: 1 indeed the whole *t* of Levi—
29: 18 or *t* among you today whose heart
Jos 3: 12 the tribes of Israel, one from each *t*.
4: 2 among the people, one from each *t*,
4: 4 one from each *t*, and said to them,
7: 1 the son of Zerah, of the *t* of Judah,
7: 14 morning, present yourselves *t* by *t*.
7: 14 *t* that the LORD takes shall come
7: 18 of the *t* of Judah, was taken.
13: 7 and half of the *t* of Manasseh."
13: 14 But to the *t* of Levi he gave no
13: 15 given to the *t* of Reuben,
13: 24 is what Moses had given to the *t*
13: 33 to the *t* of Levi, Moses had given
15: 1 The allotment for the *t* of Judah,
15: 20 This is the inheritance of the *t*
15: 21 The southernmost towns of the *t*
16: 8 of the *t* of the Ephraimites,
Jos 17: 1 the allotment for the *t* of Manasseh
17: 6 because the daughters of the *t*
18: 4 Appoint three men from each *t*.
18: 11 up for the *t* of Benjamin,
18: 21 The *t* of Benjamin, clan by clan,
19: 1 out for the *t* of Simeon,
19: 8 of the *t* of the Simeonites,
19: 23 the inheritance of the *t* of Issachar,
19: 24 The fifth lot came out for the *t*
19: 31 were the inheritance of the *t*
19: 39 the inheritance of the *t* of Naphtali,
19: 40 The seventh lot came out for the *t*
19: 48 were the inheritance of the *t*
20: 8 Ramoth in Gilead in the *t* of Gad,
20: 8 in Bashan in the *t* of Manasseh.
20: 8 on the plateau in the *t* of Reuben,
21: 17 from the *t* of Benjamin they gave
21: 20 towns from the *t* of Ephraim:
21: 23 from the *t* of Dan they received
21: 25 From half the *t* of Manasseh they
21: 28 from the *t* of Issachar, Kishion,
21: 30 from the *t* of Asher, Mishal,
21: 32 four towns; from the *t* of Naphtali,
21: 34 from the *t* of Zebulun, Jokneam,
21: 36 from the *t* of Reuben, Bezer,
21: 38 four towns; from the *t* of Gad,
22: 7 half of the *t* Joshua gave land
Jdg 18: 1 And in those days the *t*
18: 19 Isn't it better that you serve a *t*
18: 30 for the *t* of Dan until the time
20: 12 men throughout the *t* of Benjamin,
21: 3 Why should one *t* be missing
21: 6 Today one *t* is cut off from Israel,"
21: 17 "so that a *t* of Israel will not be
1Sa 9: 21 from the smallest *t* of Israel,
9: 21 of all the clans of the *t* of Benjamin
10: 20 the *t* of Benjamin was chosen.
10: 21 Then he brought forward the *t*
2Sa 4: 2 from the *t* of Benjamin—
1Ki 7: 14 a widow from the *t* of Naphtali
8: 16 in any *t* of Israel to have a temple
11: 13 but will give him one *t* for the sake
11: 32 tribes of Israel, he will have one *t*.
11: 36 I will give one *t* to his son
12: 20 Only the *t* of Judah remained loyal
12: 21 of Judah and the *t* of Benjamin—
2Ki 17: 18 Only the *t* of Judah was left,
1Ch 6: 60 from the *t* of Benjamin they were
6: 61 the clans of half the *t* of Manasseh.
6: 62 the part of the *t* of Manasseh that is
6: 66 towns from the *t* of Ephraim.
6: 70 And from half the *t* of Manasseh
6: 72 from the *t* of Issachar they received
6: 74 from the *t* of Asher they received
6: 76 and from the *t* of Naphtali they
6: 77 From the *t* of Zebulun they
6: 78 from the *t* of Reuben
6: 80 from the *t* of Gad they received
12: 2 of Saul from the *t* of Benjamin):
12: 31 men of half the *t* of Manasseh,
23: 14 God were counted as part of the *t*
27: 20 over half the *t* of Manasseh:
2Ch 6: 5 in any *t* of Israel to have a temple
11: 16 Those from every *t*
19: 11 the leader of the *t* of Judah,
Est 2: 5 of Susa a Jew of the *t* of Benjamin,
Job 30: 12 On my right the *t* attacks;
Ps 68: 27 There is the little *t* of Benjamin,
74: 2 the *t* you redeemed as your
78: 67 he did not choose the *t* of Ephraim;
78: 68 but he chose the *t* of Judah,
Jer 10: 16 including Israel, the *t*
51: 19 including the *t* of his inheritance—
Eze 47: 23 In whatever *t* the alien settles,
Lk 2: 36 of Phanuel, of the *t* of Asher.
Ac 13: 21 of the *t* of Benjamin, who ruled
Ro 11: 1 from the *t* of Benjamin.
Php 3: 5 of the *t* of Benjamin, a Hebrew
Heb 7: 13 are said belonged to a different *t*,
7: 13 no one from that *t* has ever served
7: 14 to that *t* Moses said nothing about
Rev 5: 5 See, the Lion of the *t* of Judah,
5: 9 God from every *t* and language
7: 5 From the *t* of Judah 12,000
7: 5 from the *t* of Gad 12,000,
7: 5 from the *t* of Reuben 12,000,
7: 6 from the *t* of Asher 12,000,
7: 6 from the *t* of Manasseh 12,000,

Rev 7: 6 from the *t* of Naphtali 12,000,
7: 7 from the *t* of Issachar 12,000,
7: 7 from the *t* of Levi 12,000,
7: 7 from the *t* of Simeon 12,000,
7: 8 from the *t* of Benjamin 12,000.
7: 8 from the *t* of Joseph 12,000,
7: 8 from the *t* of Zebulun 12,000,
7: 9 from every nation, *t*, people
11: 9 men from every people, *t*,
13: 7 he was given authority over every *t*
14: 6 to every nation, *t*, language

TRIBES (TRIBE)

Ge 49: 16 as one of the *t* of Israel.
49: 28 All these are the twelve *t* of Israel,
Ex 24: 4 pillars representing the twelve *t*
28: 21 the name of one of the twelve *t*.
39: 14 the name of one of the twelve *t*.
Nu 1: 16 the leaders of their ancestral *t*.
10: 5 the *t* camping on the east are
17: 2 leader of each of their ancestral *t*.
17: 6 leader of each of their ancestral *t*,
30: 1 said to the heads of the *t* of Israel:
31: 4 men from each of the *t* of Israel."
32: 28 to the family heads of the Israelite *t*
33: 54 according to your ancestral *t*.
34: 13 given to the nine and a half *t*,
34: 15 and a half *t* have received their
36: 3 men from other Israelite *t*;
Dt 1: 13 respected men from each of your *t*,
1: 15 So I took the leading men of your *t*,
5: 23 all the leading men of your *t*
12: 5 choose from among all your *t*
12: 14 LORD will choose in one of your *t*,
16: 18 and officials for each of your *t*
18: 5 out of all your *t* to stand
27: 12 these *t* shall stand
27: 13 these *t* shall stand on Mount Ebal
29: 21 from all the *t* of Israel for disaster,
31: 28 before me all the elders of your *t*
33: 5 along with the *t* of Israel.
Jos 3: 12 men from the *t* of Israel,
4: 5 number of the *t* of the Israelites,
4: 8 number of the *t* of the Israelites,
7: 16 had Israel come forward by *t*,
12: 7 to the *t* of Israel according
13: 7 as an inheritance among the nine *t*
14: 2 by lot to the nine-and-a-half *t*,
14: 3 the two-and-a-half *t* their
14: 4 sons of Joseph had become two *t*—
18: 2 still seven Israelite *t* who had not
18: 11 lay between the *t* of Judah
21: 4 towns from the *t* of Judah,
21: 5 from the clans of the *t* of Ephraim,
21: 6 from the clans of the *t* of Issachar,
21: 7 towns from the *t* of Reuben,
21: 9 From the *t* of Judah and Simeon
21: 16 nine towns from these two *t*.
22: 14 one for each of the *t* of Israel,
23: 4 inheritance for your *t* all the land
24: 1 Joshua assembled all the *t* of Israel
Jdg 18: 1 inheritance among the *t* of Israel.
20: 2 of the *t* of Israel took their places
20: 10 hundred from all the *t* of Israel,
20: 12 The *t* of Israel sent men
21: 5 "Who from all the *t*
21: 8 "Which one of the *t* of Israel failed
21: 15 the LORD had made a gap in the *t*
21: 24 and went home to their *t* and clans,
1Sa 2: 28 of all the *t* of Israel to be my priest,
10: 19 before the LORD by your *t*
10: 20 When Samuel brought all the *t*
15: 17 you not become the head of the *t*
2Sa 5: 1 All the *t* of Israel came to David
15: 2 is from one of the *t* of Israel."
15: 10 throughout the *t* of Israel to say,
19: 9 Throughout the *t* of Israel,
20: 14 passed through all the *t* of Israel
24: 2 "Go throughout the *t* of Israel
1Ki 8: 1 all the heads of the *t* and the chiefs
11: 31 Solomon's hand and give you ten *t*.
11: 32 out of all the *t* of Israel,
11: 35 his son's hands and give you ten *t*.
14: 21 out of all the *t* of Israel in which
18: 31 of the *t* descended from Jacob,
2Ki 21: 7 out of all the *t* of Israel,
1Ch 6: 62 towns from the *t* of Issachar,
6: 63 towns from the *t* of Reuben,
1Ch 6: 65 From the *t* of Judah, Simeon
27: 16 The officers over the *t* of Israel:
27: 22 the officers over the *t* of Israel.
28: 1 over the *t*, the commanders
29: 6 the officers of the *t* of Israel,
2Ch 5: 2 all the heads of the *t* and the chiefs
12: 13 out of all the *t* of Israel in which
33: 7 out of all the *t* of Israel,
Ezr 6: 17 one for each of the *t* of Israel.
Ps 72: 9 The desert *t* will bow before him
78: 55 he settled the *t* of Israel
105: 37 from among their *t* no one faltered.
122: 4 That is where the *t* go up,
122: 4 the *t* of the LORD,
Isa 49: 6 servant to restore the *t* of Jacob
63: 17 the *t* that are your inheritance.
Eze 37: 19 and of the Israelite *t* associated
45: 8 the land according to their *t*.
47: 13 among the twelve *t* of Israel,
47: 21 yourselves according to the *t*
47: 22 inheritance among the *t* of Israel.
48: 1 "These are the *t*, listed by name:
48: 19 come from all the *t* of Israel.
48: 23 of the *t*: Benjamin will have one
48: 29 as an inheritance to the *t* of Israel,
48: 31 named after the *t* of Israel.
Hos 5: 9 Among the *t* of Israel
Zec 9: 1 eyes of men and all the *t* of Israel
Mt 19: 28 judging the twelve *t* of Israel.
Lk 22: 30 judging the twelve *t* of Israel.
Ac 26: 7 the promise our twelve *t* are hoping
Jas 1: 1 To the twelve *t* scattered
Rev 7: 4 from all the *t* of Israel.
21: 12 the names of the twelve *t* of Israel.

TRIBULATION

Rev 7: 14 who have come out of the great *t*;

TRIBUTE

Nu 31: 28 as *t* for the LORD one out
31: 29 Take this *t* from their half share
31: 37 of which the *t* for the LORD was
31: 38 of which the *t* for the LORD was
31: 39 of which the *t* for the LORD was
31: 40 of which the *t* for the LORD was
31: 41 Moses gave the *t* to Eleazar
Jdg 3: 15 him with *t* to Eglon king
3: 17 He presented the *t* to Eglon king
3: 18 After Ehud had presented the *t*,
2Sa 8: 2 subject to David and brought *t*.
8: 6 subject to him and brought *t*.
1Ki 4: 21 These countries brought *t*
2Ki 17: 3 vassal and had paid him *t*.
17: 4 and he no longer paid *t* to the king
1Ch 18: 2 subject to him and brought *t*.
18: 6 subject to him and brought *t*.
2Ch 17: 11 Jehoshaphat gifts and silver as *t*,
26: 8 The Ammonites brought *t*
Ezr 4: 13 no more taxes, *t* or duty will be
4: 20 *t* and duty were paid to them.
7: 24 *t* or duty on any of the priests,
Est 10: 1 King Xerxes imposed *t*
Ps 72: 10 will bring *t* to him;
89: 22 No enemy will subject him to *t*;
Isa 16: 1 Send lambs as *t*
Hos 10: 6 as *t* for the great king.

TRICK (TRICKERY TRICKING)

1Th 2: 3 nor are we trying to *t* you.

TRICKERY (TRICK)

Ac 13: 10 full of all kinds of deceit and *t*.
2Co 12: 16 fellow that I am, I caught you by *t*!

TRICKING (TRICK)

Ge 27: 12 I would appear to be *t* him

TRIED (TRY)

Ge 37: 21 he *t* to rescue him from their hands
Ex 2: 15 heard of this, he *t* to kill Moses,
8: 18 But when the magicians *t*
Dt 4: 34 Has any god ever *t* to take
13: 5 he has *t* to turn you
13: 10 because he *t* to turn you away
1Sa 17: 39 sword over the tunic and *t* walking
19: 10 Saul *t* to pin him to the wall
2Sa 4: 8 your enemy, who *t* to take your life
21: 2 Judah had *t* to annihilate them.)
1Ki 11: 40 Solomon *t* to kill Jeroboam,
Ps 73: 16 When I *t* to understand all this,
95: 9 where your fathers tested and *t* me,
109: 7 When he is *t*, let him be found
Ecc 2: 3 I *t* cheering myself with wine,
La 3: 53 They *t* to end my life in a pit
Eze 24: 13 Because I *t* to cleanse you
Da 6: 4 and the satraps *t* to find grounds
Mt 3: 14 But John *t* to deter him, saying,
Lk 4: 42 they *t* to keep him
5: 18 and *t* to take him into the house
6: 19 and the people all *t* to touch him,
9: 9 I hear such things about?" And he *t*
9: 49 in your name and we *t* to stop him,
Jn 5: 18 this reason the Jews *t* all the harder
7: 30 At this they *t* to seize him,
10: 39 Again they *t* to seize him,
11: 8 while ago the Jews *t* to stone you,
19: 12 From then on, Pilate *t*
Ac 7: 26 He *t* to reconcile them by saying,
9: 26 came to Jerusalem, he *t* to join
9: 29 with the Grecian Jews, but they *t*
13: 8 and *t* to turn the proconsul
16: 7 of Mysia, they *t* to enter Bithynia,
19: 13 around driving out evil spirits *t*
24: 6 and even *t* to desecrate the temple;
25: 10 court, where I ought to be *t*.
26: 11 and I *t* to force them to blaspheme.
26: 21 in the temple courts and *t* to kill me
28: 23 and *t* to convince them about Jesus
Gal 1: 13 church of God and *t* to destroy it.
1: 23 is now preaching the faith he once *t*
Heb 3: 9 where your fathers tested and *t* me
11: 29 but when the Egyptians *t* to do so,

TRIES (TRY)

Job 34: 9 when he *t* to please God.'
Lk 17: 33 Whoever *t* to keep his life will lose
Rev 11: 5 If anyone *t* to harm them, fire

TRIFLING

Ne 9: 32 do not let all this hardship seem *t*

TRIM (TRIMMED TRIMMERS TRIMS)

Dt 21: 12 *t* her nails and put
Da 4: 14 down the tree and *t* off its branches

TRIMMED (TRIM)

2Sa 19: 24 care of his feet or *t* his mustache
1Ki 6: 36 and one course of *t* cedar beams.
7: 2 columns supporting *t* cedar beams.
7: 9 and *t* with a saw on their inner
7: 12 and one course of *t* cedar beams,
Eze 44: 20 are to keep the hair of their heads *t*.
Mt 25: 7 virgins woke up and *t* their lamps.

TRIMMERS (TRIM)

Ex 25: 38 Its wick *t* and trays are to be
37: 23 as well as its wick *t* and trays,
Nu 4: 9 together with its lamps, its wick *t*
1Ki 7: 50 the pure gold dishes, wick *t*,
2Ki 12: 13 for making silver basins, wick *t*,
25: 14 took away the pots, shovels, wick *t*,
2Ch 4: 22 pure gold wick *t*, sprinkling bowls,
Jer 52: 18 shovels, wick *t*, sprinkling bowls,

TRIMS (TRIM)

Jn 15: 2 that does bear fruit he *t* clean

TRIP (TRIPPING)

Ps 140: 4 who plan to *t* my feet.

TRIPOLIS

Ezr 4: 9 and officials over the men from *T*,

TRIPPING (TRIP)

Isa 3: 16 *t* along with mincing steps,

TRIUMPH (TRIUMPHAL TRIUMPHANT TRIUMPHED TRIUMPHING TRIUMPHS)

Jdg 8: 9 "When I return in *t*, I will tear
11: 31 to meet me when I return in *t*
1Sa 26: 25 will do great things and surely *t*."
Job 17: 4 therefore you will not let them *t*.
Ps 9: 19 Arise, O LORD, let not man *t*;
12: 4 "We will *t* with our tongues;
13: 2 How long will my enemy *t* over me
25: 2 nor let my enemies *t* over me.

Ps 41: 11 for my enemy does not *t* over me.
54: 7 my eyes have looked in *t*
60: 6 "In *t* I will parcel out Shechem
60: 8 over Philistia I shout in *t*."
108: 7 "In *t* I will parcel out Shechem
108: 9 over Philistia I shout in *t*."
112: 8 in the end he will look in *t*
118: 7 I will look in *t* on my enemies.
Pr 28: 12 When the righteous *t*, there is great
Isa 13: 3 those who rejoice in my *t*.
42: 13 and will *t* over his enemies.
Jer 9: 3 that they *t* in the land.
51: 14 and they will shout in *t* over you.
Mic 5: 9 in *t* over your enemies,

TRIUMPHAL (TRIUMPH)

Isa 60: 11 their kings led in *t* procession.
2Co 2: 14 us in *t* procession in Christ

TRIUMPHANT (TRIUMPH)

Da 11: 12 thousands, yet he will not remain *t*.

TRIUMPHED (TRIUMPH)

Dt 32: 27 and say, 'Our hand has *t*;
1Sa 17: 50 So David *t* over the Philistine
La 1: 9 for the enemy has *t*."
Rev 5: 5 of Judah, the Root of David, has *t*.

TRIUMPHING (TRIUMPH)

Col 2: 15 of them, *t* over them by the cross.

TRIUMPHS (TRIUMPH)

Jas 2: 13 Mercy *t* over judgment! What

TROAS

Ac 16: 8 by Mysia and went down to *T*.
16: 11 From *T* we put out to sea
20: 5 on ahead and waited for us at *T*.
20: 6 days later joined the others at *T*,
2Co 2: 12 went to *T* to preach the gospel
2Ti 4: 13 cloak that I left with Carpus at *T*,

TROD (TREAD)

Job 22: 15 that evil men have *t*?
Isa 63: 3 and *t* them down in my wrath;

TRODDEN (TREAD)

Jdg 9: 27 gathered the grapes and *t* them,
Isa 63: 3 "I have *t* the winepress alone;

TROOP (TROOPS)

2Sa 22: 30 your help I can advance against a *t*;
Ps 18: 29 your help I can advance against a *t*;

TROOPS (TROOP)

Ex 14: 9 and chariots, horsemen and *t*—
Jos 10: 5 They moved up with all their *t*
11: 4 They came out with all their *t*
Jdg 4: 7 and his *t* to the Kishon River
4: 16 All the *t* of Sisera fell by the sword;
8: 5 "Give my *t* some bread; they are
8: 6 should we give bread to your *t*?"
9: 34 and all his *t* set out by night
1Sa 13: 7 and all the *t* with him were quaking
14: 24 So none of the *t* tasted food.
18: 13 David led the *t* in their campaigns.
2Sa 10: 9 some of the best *t* in Israel
10: 13 and the *t* with him advanced
12: 28 Now muster the rest of the *t*
16: 6 all the *t* and the special guard were
17: 8 will not spend the night with the *t*.
17: 9 If he should attack your *t* first,
17: 9 among the *t* who follow Absalom.'
18: 2 David sent the *t* out—a third
18: 2 king told the *t*, "I myself will surely
18: 5 And all the *t* heard the king giving
18: 16 and the *t* stopped pursuing Israel,
19: 2 on that day the *t* heard it said,
19: 40 All the *t* of Judah and half
19: 40 and half the *t* of Israel had taken
20: 12 and the man saw that all the *t* came
20: 15 All the *t* with Joab came
23: 10 The *t* returned to Eleazar,
23: 11 of lentils, Israel's *t* fled from them.
24: 3 God multiply the *t* a hundred times
2Ki 9: 17 he called out, "I see some *t* coming
9: 17 in Jezreel saw Jehu's *t* approaching
11: 15 who were in charge of the *t*:
1Ch 11: 13 the *t* fled from the Philistines.
19: 7 as the king of Maacah with his *t*,
19: 10 some of the best *t* in Israel
19: 14 and the *t* with him advanced
21: 2 and the commanders of the *t*,
21: 3 the LORD multiply his *t* a hundred
2Ch 12: 3 and the innumerable *t* of Libyans,
13: 3 with eight hundred thousand able *t*
13: 13 Now Jeroboam had sent *t*
17: 2 He stationed *t* in all the fortified
23: 14 who were in charge of the *t*,
25: 7 these *t* from Israel must not march
25: 9 paid for these Israelite *t*?"
25: 10 Amaziah dismissed the *t* who had
25: 13 Meanwhile the *t* that Amaziah had
Job 19: 12 His *t* advance in force;
29: 25 I dwelt as a king among his *t*;
Ps 110: 3 Your *t* will be willing
SS 6: 4 majestic as *t* with banners.
Eze 12: 14 his staff and all his *t*—
17: 21 All his fleeing *t* will fall
38: 6 from the far north with all its *t*—
38: 6 helmets, also Gomer with all its *t*,
38: 9 and all your *t* and the many nations
38: 22 burning sulfur on him and on his *t*
39: 4 all your *t* and the nations with you.
Da 11: 15 even their best *t* will not have
Mic 5: 1 Marshal your *t*, O city of *t*,
Na 2: 5 He summons his picked *t*,
3: 13 Look at your *t*—
Ac 21: 31 of the Roman *t* that the whole city
23: 10 He ordered the *t* to go down
23: 27 I came with my *t* and rescued him,
Rev 9: 16 of the mounted *t* was two hundred

TROPHIMUS

Ac 20: 4 province of Asia Tychicus and *T*.
21: 29 previously seen *T* the Ephesian
2Ti 4: 20 and I left *T* sick in Miletus.

TROUBLE (TROUBLED TROUBLEMAKER TROUBLEMAKERS TROUBLER TROUBLES TROUBLESOME TROUBLING)

Ge 34: 30 "You have brought *t* on me
41: 51 God has made me forget all my *t*
43: 6 "Why did you bring this *t* on me
Ex 5: 19 were in *t* when they were told,
5: 22 why have you brought *t*
5: 23 he has brought *t* upon this people,
Nu 11: 11 "Why have you brought this *t*
33: 55 They will give you *t*
Jdg 10: 14 you when you are in *t*!"
11: 7 when you're in *t*?" The elders
1Sa 4: 7 "We're in *t*! Nothing like this has
14: 29 "My father has made *t*
20: 19 hid when this *t* began,
26: 24 and deliver me from all *t*."
2Sa 4: 9 who has delivered me out of all *t*,
1Ki 1: 29 has delivered me out of every *t*,
11: 25 adding to the *t* caused by Hadad.
18: 18 "I have not made *t* for Israel,"
20: 7 "See how this man is looking for *t*!
2Ki 4: 13 'You have gone to all this *t* for us.
14: 10 for *t* and cause your own downfall
2Ch 25: 19 for *t* and cause your own downfall
28: 20 but he gave him *t* instead of help.
28: 22 In his time of *t* King Ahaz became
Ne 1: 3 back in the province are in great *t*
2: 17 "You see the *t* we are
4: 8 fight against Jerusalem and stir up *t*
Job 2: 10 good from God, and not *t*?"
3: 10 me to hide *t* from my eyes.
4: 5 But now *t* comes to you,
4: 8 and those who sow *t* reap it.
5: 6 nor does *t* sprout from the ground.
5: 7 Yet man is born to *t*
11: 16 You will surely forget your *t*,
14: 1 is of few days and full of *t*.
15: 35 They conceive *t* and give birth
19: 28 since the root of the *t* lies in him,'
30: 25 Have I not wept for those in *t*?
31: 29 gloated over the *t* that came to him
38: 23 which I reserve for times of *t*,
42: 11 him over all the *t* the LORD had
Ps 7: 14 conceives *t* gives birth
7: 16 The *t* he causes recoils on himself;
9: 9 a stronghold in times of *t*.
Ps 10: 1 do you hide yourself in times of *t*?
10: 6 always be happy and never have *t*."
10: 7 *t* and evil are under his tongue.
10: 14 But you, O God, do see *t* and grief;
22: 11 for *t* is near
27: 5 For in the day of *t*
32: 7 you will protect me from *t*
37: 39 he is their stronghold in time of *t*.
41: 1 LORD delivers him in times of *t*.
46: 1 an ever present help in *t*.
50: 15 and call upon me in the day of *t*;
55: 2 My thoughts *t* me and I am
59: 16 my refuge in times of *t*.
66: 14 spoke when I was in *t*.
69: 17 answer me quickly, for I am in *t*.
86: 7 In the day of my *t* I will call to you,
88: 3 For my soul is full of *t*
90: 10 yet their span is but *t* and sorrow,
90: 15 for as many years as we have seen *t*
91: 15 I will be with him in *t*,
94: 13 you grant him relief from days of *t*,
106: 32 *t* came to Moses because of them;
107: 6 to the LORD in their *t*,
107: 13 they cried to the LORD in their *t*,
107: 19 they cried to the LORD in their *t*,
107: 28 to the LORD in their *t*,
116: 3 I was overcome by *t* and sorrow.
119:143 *T* and distress have come upon me,
138: 7 Though I walk in the midst of *t*,
140: 9 with the *t* their lips have caused.
142: 2 before him I tell my *t*.
143: 11 righteousness, bring me out of *t*.
Pr 10: 22 and he adds no *t* to it.
11: 8 righteous man is rescued from *t*,
11: 29 He who brings *t* on his family will
12: 13 but a righteous man escapes *t*.
12: 21 but the wicked have their fill of *t*.
13: 17 A wicked messenger falls into *t*,
15: 6 of the wicked brings them *t*.
15: 27 A greedy man brings *t* to his family
17: 20 tongue is deceitful falls into *t*.
19: 23 one rests content, untouched by *t*.
22: 8 He who sows wickedness reaps *t*,
24: 2 and their lips talk about making *t*.
24: 10 If you falter in times of *t*,
25: 19 on the unfaithful in times of *t*.
28: 14 he who hardens his heart falls into *t*
Ecc 12: 1 before the days of *t* come
Isa 59: 4 they conceive *t* and give birth
Jer 2: 27 yet when they are in *t*, they say,
2: 28 you when you are in *t*!
20: 18 the womb to see *t* and sorrow
30: 7 It will be a time of *t* for Jacob,
Eze 32: 9 " 'I will *t* the hearts
Da 9: 25 and a trench, but in times of *t*.
Ob : 12 much in the day of their *t*.
: 14 survivors in the day of their *t*.
Jnh 1: 8 for making all this *t* for us?
Na 1: 7 a refuge in times of *t*.
1: 9 *t* will not come a second time.
Zep 1: 15 a day of *t* and ruin,
Zec 10: 11 They will pass through the sea of *t*;
Mt 6: 34 Each day has enough *t* of its own.
13: 21 When *t* or persecution comes
28: 14 satisfy him and keep you out of *t*."
Mk 4: 17 When *t* or persecution comes
Lk 7: 6 don't *t* yourself, for I do not
Jn 16: 33 In this world you will have *t*.
Ac 17: 6 "These men who have caused *t* all
Ro 2: 9 There will be *t* and distress
8: 35 Shall *t* or hardship or persecution
1Co 7: 21 Don't let it *t* you—
2Co 1: 4 those in any *t* with the comfort we
Gal 6: 17 Finally, let no one cause me *t*,
Php 1: 17 supposing that they can stir up *t*
3: 1 It is no *t* for me to write the same
2Th 1: 6 *t* to those who *t* you
1Ti 5: 10 those in *t* and devoting herself
Heb 12: 15 no bitter root grows up to cause *t*
Jas 5: 13 one of you in *t*? He should pray.

TROUBLED (TROUBLE)

Ge 41: 8 In the morning his mind was *t*,
Nu 11: 10 angry, and Moses was *t*.
1Sa 1: 15 "I am a woman who is deeply *t*.
15: 11 Samuel was *t*, and he cried out
Job 20: 2 "My *t* thoughts prompt me
Ps 38: 18 I am *t* by my sin.

Ps 77: 4 I was too *t* to speak.
Isa 38: 14 I am *t;* O Lord, come to my aid!"
Jer 49: 23 *t* like the restless sea.
Da 2: 1 his mind was *t* and he could not
7: 15 was *t* in spirit, and the visions that
7: 28 was deeply *t* by my thoughts,
Mt 26: 37 and he began to be sorrowful and *t.*
Mk 14: 33 began to be deeply distressed and *t.*
Lk 1: 29 Mary was greatly *t* at his words
6: 18 Those *t* by evil spirits were cured,
24: 38 He said to them, "Why are you *t,*
Jn 11: 33 he was deeply moved in spirit and *t*
12: 27 my heart is *t,* and what shall I say?
13: 21 Jesus was *t* in spirit and testified,
14: 1 "Do not let your hearts be *t.*
14: 27 Do not let your hearts be *t*
Ac 16: 18 became so *t* that he turned
2Th 1: 7 and give relief to you who are *t,*

TROUBLEMAKER (TROUBLE)

2Sa 20: 1 Now a *t* named Sheba son of Bicri,
Ac 24: 5 "We have found this man to be a *t,*

TROUBLEMAKERS (TROUBLE)

1Sa 10: 27 some *t* said, "How can this fellow
30: 22 *t* among David's followers said,

TROUBLER (TROUBLE)

1Ki 18: 17 "Is that you, you *t* of Israel?"

TROUBLES (TROUBLE)

Job 2: 11 heard about all the *t* that had come
Ps 25: 17 The *t* of my heart have multiplied;
25: 22 from all their *t!*
34: 6 he saved him out of all his *t.*
34: 17 he delivers them from all their *t.*
34: 19 A righteous man may have many *t,*
40: 12 For *t* without number surround me
54: 7 he has delivered me from all my *t,*
71: 20 Though you have made me see *t,*
Pr 1: 27 when distress and *t* overwhelm you
Ecc 11: 10 and cast off the *t* of your body,
Isa 22: 1 What *t* you now,
46: 7 it cannot save him from his *t.*
65: 16 For the past *t* will be forgotten
Da 2: 3 "I have had a dream that *t* me
Ac 7: 10 and rescued him from all his *t.*
1Co 7: 28 those who marry will face many *t*
2Co 1: 4 who comforts us in all our *t,*
4: 17 and momentary *t* are achieving
6: 4 in *t,* hardships and distresses;
7: 4 in all our *t* my joy knows no bounds
Php 4: 14 good of you to share in my *t.*

TROUBLESOME (TROUBLE)

Ezr 4: 15 *t* to kings and provinces, a place

TROUBLING (TROUBLE)

2Sa 14: 5 "What is *t* you?" She said,
2Ch 15: 6 God was *t* them with every kind
Est 4: 5 to find out what was *t* Mordecai
Ac 15: 24 *t* your minds by what they said.

TROUGH (TROUGHS)

Ge 24: 20 quickly emptied her jar into the *t,*
Dt 28: 5 your kneading *t* will be blessed.
28: 17 and your kneading *t* will be cursed.

TROUGHS (TROUGH)

Ge 30: 38 branches in all the watering *t,*
30: 41 in the *t* in front of the animals
Ex 2: 16 fill the *t* to water their father's flock
8: 3 and into your ovens and kneading *t*
12: 34 in kneading *t* wrapped in clothing.

TROUSERS

Da 3: 21 *t,* turbans and other clothes,

TRUDGE

Isa 45: 14 they will *t* behind you,

TRUE (TRUTH)

Nu 11: 23 not what I say will come *t* for you."
12: 7 this is not *t* of my servant Moses;
Dt 13: 14 if it is *t* and it has been proved that
17: 4 If it is *t* and it has been proved that
18: 22 does not take place or come *t,*
22: 20 the charge is *t* and no proof
Jos 7: 20 "It is *t!* I have sinned
21: 42 this was *t* for all these towns.
23: 15 of the LORD your God has come *t*
Jdg 13: 17 you when your word comes *t?*"
Ru 3: 12 Although it is *t* that I am
1Sa 9: 6 and everything he says comes *t.*
1Ki 8: 26 servant David my father come *t.*
10: 6 and your wisdom is *t.*
13: 32 of Samaria will certainly come *t.*"
2Ki 9: 12 "That's not *t!*" they said.
19: 17 "It is *t,* O LORD, that the Assyrian
2Ch 6: 17 your servant David come *t.*
9: 5 and your wisdom is *t.*
15: 3 was without the *t* God,
Ne 6: 6 and Geshem says it is *t*— that you
Est 2: 23 was investigated and found to be *t,*
Job 5: 27 "We have examined this, and it is *t.*
9: 2 "Indeed, I know that this is *t.*
11: 6 for *t* wisdom has two sides.
19: 4 If it is *t* that I have gone astray,
Ps 33: 4 of the LORD is right and *t;*
105: 19 word of the LORD proved him *t.*
119:142 and your law is *t.*
119:151 and all your commands are *t.*
119:160 All your words are *t;*
144: 15 are the people of whom this is *t;*
Pr 8: 7 My mouth speaks what is *t,*
22: 21 teaching you *t* and reliable words,
Ecc 12: 10 what he wrote was upright and *t.*
Isa 37: 18 "It is *t,* O LORD, that the Assyrian
43: 9 others may hear and say, "It is *t.*"
Jer 10: 10 But the LORD is the *t* God;
28: 9 only if his prediction comes *t.*"
37: 14 "That's not *t!*" Jeremiah said.
40: 16 are saying about Ishmael is not *t.*"
42: 5 "May the LORD be a *t*
50: 7 against the LORD, their *t* pasture,
Eze 16: 45 You are a *t* daughter
16: 45 and you are a *t* sister of your sisters
33: 33 "When all this comes *t*—
Da 2: 45 dream is *t* and the interpretation is
3: 14 "Is it *t,* Shadrach, Meshach
7: 16 asked him the *t* meaning of all this.
7: 19 I wanted to know the *t* meaning
8: 26 that has been given you is *t,*
10: 1 Its message was *t* and it concerned
Am 2: 11 Is this not *t,* people of Israel?"
7: 7 by a wall that had been built *t*
Mic 7: 20 You will be *t* to Jacob,
Zec 7: 9 says: 'Administer *t* justice;
8: 16 and render *t* and sound judgment
Mal 2: 6 *T* instruction was in his mouth
Lk 1: 20 which will come *t* at their proper
16: 11 who will trust you with *t* riches?
24: 34 together and saying, "It is *t!*
Jn 1: 9 The *t* light that gives light
1: 47 he said of him, "Here is a *t* Israelite
4: 18 What you have just said is quite *t.*"
4: 23 when the *t* worshipers will worship
4: 37 'One sows and another reaps' is *t.*
6: 32 Father who gives you the *t* bread
7: 28 on my own, but he who sent me is *t*
10: 41 John said about this man was *t.*"
15: 1 "I am the *t* vine and my Father is
17: 3 the only *t* God, and Jesus Christ,
19: 35 testimony, and his testimony is *t.*
21: 24 We know that his testimony is *t.*
Ac 7: 1 "Are these charges *t?*" To this he
10: 34 "I now realize how *t* it is that God
11: 23 all to remain *t* to the Lord
14: 22 them to remain *t* to the faith.
17: 11 day to see if what Paul said was *t.*
24: 9 asserting that these things were *t.*
25: 11 against me by these Jews are not *t,*
26: 25 "What I am saying is *t*
Ro 3: 4 Let God be *t,* and every man a liar.
1Co 15: 54 saying that is written will come *t:*
2Co 7: 14 as everything we said to you was *t,*
7: 14 you to Titus has proved to be *t*
Eph 4: 24 to be like God in *t* righteousness
Php 1: 15 It is *t* that some preach Christ out
1: 18 whether from false motives or *t,*
4: 8 whatever is *t,* whatever is noble,
1Th 1: 9 idols to serve the living and *t* God,
1Ti 1: 2 To Timothy my *t* son in the faith:
2: 7 and a teacher of the *t* faith
Tit 1: 4 my *t* son in our common faith:
1: 13 This testimony is *t.*
Tit 3: 2 to show *t* humility toward all men.
Heb 8: 2 the *t* tabernacle set up by the Lord,
9: 24 that was only a copy of the *t* one;
12: 8 illegitimate children and not *t* sons.
1Pe 5: 12 testifying that this is the *t* grace
2Pe 2: 10 This is especially *t*
2: 22 Of them the proverbs are *t:*
1Jn 2: 8 and the *t* light is already shining.
5: 20 And we are in him who is *t*—
5: 20 He is the *t* God and eternal life.
5: 20 so that we may know him who is *t.*
3Jn : 12 you know that our testimony is *t.*
Rev 2: 13 Yet you remain *t* to my name.
3: 7 the words of him who is holy and *t,*
3: 14 and *t* witness, the ruler
6: 10 Sovereign Lord, holy and *t,*
15: 3 Just and *t* are your ways,
16: 7 *t* and just are your judgments."
19: 2 for *t* and just are his judgments.
19: 9 "These are the *t* words of God."
19: 11 whose rider is called Faithful and *T*
21: 5 words are trustworthy and *t.*"
22: 6 These words are trustworthy and *t.*

TRUMPET (TRUMPETERS TRUMPETS)

Ex 19: 16 mountain, and a very loud *t* blast.
19: 19 and the sound of the *t* grew louder
20: 18 and lightning and heard the *t*
Lev 23: 24 commemorated with *t* blasts.
25: 9 have the *t* sounded everywhere
25: 9 the Day of Atonement sound the *t*
Nu 10: 5 When a *t* blast is sounded,
Jos 6: 16 the priests sounded the *t* blast,
6: 20 and at the sound of the *t,*
Jdg 3: 27 he blew a *t* in the hill country
6: 34 and he blew a *t,* summoning
1Sa 13: 3 Then Saul had the *t* blown
2Sa 2: 28 So Joab blew the *t,* and all the men
18: 16 Then Joab sounded the *t,*
20: 1 He sounded the *t* and shouted,
20: 22 So he sounded the *t,* and his men
1Ki 1: 34 Blow the *t* and shout, 'Long live
1: 39 Then they sounded the *t*
1: 41 On hearing the sound of the *t,*
2Ki 9: 13 Then they blew the *t* and shouted,
Ne 4: 18 the man who sounded the *t* stayed
4: 20 you hear the sound of the *t,*
Job 39: 24 when the *t* sounds.
39: 25 At the blast of the *t* he snorts, 'Aha
Ps 150: 3 him with the sounding of the *t,*
Isa 18: 3 and when a *t* sounds,
27: 13 And in that day a great *t* will sound
58: 1 Raise your voice like a *t.*
Jer 4: 5 'Sound the *t* throughout the land!'
4: 19 For I have heard the sound of the *t,*
4: 21 and hear the sound of the *t?*
6: 1 Sound the *t* in Tekoa!
6: 17 'Listen to the sound of the *t!*'
42: 14 hear the *t* or be hungry for bread,'
51: 27 Blow the *t* among the nations!
Eze 7: 14 Though they blow the *t*
33: 3 and blows the *t* to warn the people,
33: 4 then if anyone hears the *t*
33: 5 Since he heard the sound of the *t*
33: 6 and does not blow the *t*
Hos 5: 8 "Sound the *t* in Gibeah,
8: 1 "Put the *t* to your lips!
Joel 2: 1 Blow the *t* in Zion;
2: 15 Blow the *t* in Zion,
Am 2: 2 amid war cries and the blast of the *t*
3: 6 When a *t* sounds in a city,
Zep 1: 16 a day of *t* and battle cry
Zec 9: 14 Sovereign LORD will sound the *t;*
Mt 24: 31 send his angels with a loud *t* call,
1Co 14: 8 if the *t* does not sound a clear call,
15: 52 For the *t* will sound, the dead will
15: 52 twinkling of an eye, at the last *t.*
1Th 4: 16 and with the *t* call of God,
Heb 12: 19 to a *t* blast or to such a voice
Rev 1: 10 behind me a loud voice like a *t,*
4: 1 speaking to me like a *t* said,
8: 7 The first angel sounded his *t,*
8: 8 The second angel sounded his *t,*
8: 10 The third angel sounded his *t,*
8: 12 The fourth angel sounded his *t,*
8: 13 of the *t* blasts about to be sounded
9: 1 The fifth angel sounded his *t,*
9: 13 The sixth angel blew his *t,*

Rev 9: 14 to the sixth angel who had the *t*,
10: 7 angel is about to sound his *t*,
11: 15 The seventh angel sounded his *t*,

TRUMPETERS (TRUMPET)

2Ki 11: 14 and the *t* were beside the king,
2Ch 5: 13 The *t* and singers joined in unison,
23: 13 and the *t* were beside the king,
29: 28 the singers sang and the *t* played.
Rev 18: 22 musicians, flute players and *t*,

TRUMPETS (TRUMPET)

Nu 10: 2 "Make two *t* of hammered silver,
10: 7 To gather the assembly, blow the *t*,
10: 8 the priests, are to blow the *t*.
10: 9 you, sound a blast on the *t*.
10: 10 are to sound the *t* over your burnt
29: 1 It is a day for you to sound the *t*.
31: 6 from the sanctuary and the *t*
Jos 6: 4 Have seven priests carry *t*
6: 4 with the priests blowing the *t*.
6: 5 them sound a long blast on the *t*,
6: 6 have seven priests carry *t* in front
6: 8 blowing their *t*, and the ark
6: 8 seven priests carrying the seven *t*
6: 9 All this time the *t* were sounding.
6: 9 ahead of the priests who blew the *t*,
6: 13 carrying the seven *t* went forward,
6: 13 of the LORD and blowing the *t*.
6: 13 while the *t* kept sounding.
6: 20 When the *t* sounded, the people
Jdg 7: 8 took over the provisions and *t*
7: 16 he placed *t* and empty jars
7: 18 and all who are with me blow our *t*,
7: 19 They blew their *t* and broke the jars
7: 20 The three companies blew the *t*
7: 20 in their right hands the *t* they were
7: 22 When the three hundred *t* sounded
2Sa 6: 15 with shouts and the sound of *t*.
15: 10 as you hear the sound of the *t*,
2Ki 11: 14 land were rejoicing and blowing *t*.
12: 13 *t* or any other articles of gold
1Ch 13: 8 lyres, tambourines, cymbals and *t*.
15: 24 to blow *t* before the ark of God.
15: 28 the sounding of rams' horns and *t*,
16: 6 were to blow the *t* regularly
16: 42 for the sounding of the *t*
2Ch 5: 12 by 120 priests sounding *t*.
5: 13 Accompanied by *t*, cymbals
7: 6 the priests blew their *t*,
13: 12 with their *t* will sound the battle
13: 14 The priests blew their *t*
15: 14 with shouting and with *t* and horns.
20: 28 LORD with harps and lutes and *t*.
23: 13 land were rejoicing and blowing *t*,
29: 26 and the priests with their *t*.
29: 27 by *t* and the instruments
Ezr 3: 10 in their vestments and with *t*,
Ne 12: 35 as well as some priests with *t*,
12: 41 and Hananiah with their *t*—
Ps 47: 5 the LORD amid the sounding of *t*.
98: 6 with *t* and the blast
Mt 6: 2 do not announce it with *t*,
Rev 8: 2 and to them were given seven *t*.
8: 6 who had the seven *t* prepared

TRUST (ENTRUST ENTRUSTED TRUSTED TRUSTEES TRUSTFULLY TRUSTING TRUSTS TRUSTWORTHY)

Ex 14: 31 put their *t* in him and in Moses his
19: 9 and will always put their *t* in you."
Nu 20: 12 "Because you did not *t*
Dt 1: 32 you did not *t* in the LORD your
9: 23 You did not *t* him or obey him.
28: 52 walls in which you *t* fall down.
Jdg 11: 20 did not *t* Israel to pass
2Ki 17: 14 who did not *t* in the LORD their
18: 30 to *t* in the LORD when he says,
1Ch 9: 22 to their positions of *t* by David
Job 4: 18 If God places no *t* in his servants,
15: 15 If God places no *t* in his holy ones,
31: 24 "If I have put my *t* in gold
39: 12 Can you *t* him to bring
Ps 4: 5 and *t* in the LORD.
9: 10 Those who know your name will *t*
13: 5 But I *t* in your unfailing love;
20: 7 Some *t* in chariots and some
20: 7 we *t* in the name of the LORD our
Ps 22: 4 In you our fathers put their *t*;
22: 9 you made me *t* in you
25: 2 I lift up my soul; in you I *t*,
31: 6 I *t* in the LORD.
31: 14 But I *t* in you, O LORD;
33: 21 for we *t* in his holy name.
37: 3 *T* in the LORD and do good;
37: 5 *t* in him and he will do this:
40: 3 and put their *t* in the LORD.
40: 4 who makes the LORD his *t*,
44: 6 I do not *t* in my bow,
49: 6 those who *t* in their wealth
49: 13 of those who *t* in themselves,
52: 8 I *t* in God's unfailing love
55: 23 But as for me, I *t* in you.
56: 3 I will *t* in you.
56: 4 in God I *t*; I will not be afraid.
56: 11 in God I *t*; I will not be afraid.
62: 8 *T* in him at all times, O people;
62: 10 Do not *t* in extortion
78: 7 Then they would put their *t* in God
78: 22 or *t* in his deliverance.
91: 2 my God, in whom I *t*."
115: 8 and so will all who *t* in them.
115: 9 O house of Israel, *t* in the LORD—
115: 10 O house of Aaron, *t* in the LORD—
115: 11 You who fear him, *t* in the LORD—
118: 8 than to *t* in man.
118: 9 than to *t* in princes.
119: 42 for I *t* in your word.
125: 1 Those who *t* in the LORD are like
135: 18 and so will all who *t* in them.
143: 8 for I have put my *t* in you.
146: 3 Do not put your *t* in princes,
Pr 3: 5 *T* in the LORD with all your heart
21: 22 the stronghold in which they *t*.
22: 19 So that your *t* may be in the LORD
Isa 8: 17 I will put my *t* in him.
12: 2 I will *t* and not be afraid.
26: 4 *T* in the LORD forever,
30: 15 in quietness and *t* is your strength,
31: 1 who *t* in the multitude
36: 15 to *t* in the LORD when he says,
42: 17 But those who *t* in idols,
50: 10 *t* in the name of the LORD
Jer 2: 37 LORD has rejected those you *t*;
5: 17 the fortified cities in which you *t*.
7: 4 Do not *t* in deceptive words
7: 14 the temple you *t* in, the place I gave
9: 4 do not *t* your brothers.
12: 6 Do not *t* them,
28: 15 you have persuaded this nation to *t*
39: 18 you *t* in me, declares the LORD.' "
48: 7 Since you *t* in your deeds
49: 4 you *t* in your riches and say,
49: 11 Your widows too can *t* in me."
Mic 7: 5 Do not *t* a neighbor;
Na 1: 7 He cares for those who *t* in him,
Zep 3: 2 She does not *t* in the LORD,
3: 12 who *t* in the name of the LORD.
Lk 16: 11 who will *t* you with true riches?
Jn 12: 36 Put your *t* in the light
14: 1 *T* in God; *t* also in me.
Ac 14: 23 Lord in whom they had put their *t*.
Ro 15: 13 you with all joy and peace as you *t*
1Co 4: 2 been given a *t* must prove faithful.
9: 17 discharging the *t* committed
2Co 13: 6 I *t* that you will discover that we
Heb 2: 13 "I will put my *t* in him."

TRUSTED (TRUST)

1Sa 27: 12 Achish *t* David and said to himself,
2Ki 18: 5 Hezekiah *t* in the LORD, the God
1Ch 5: 20 their prayers, because they *t*
Job 12: 20 He silences the lips of *t* advisers
Ps 5: 9 from their mouth can be *t*;
22: 4 they *t* and you delivered them.
22: 5 in you they *t* and were not
26: 1 I have *t* in the LORD
41: 9 Even my close friend, whom I *t*,
52: 7 but *t* in his great wealth
Isa 20: 5 Those who *t* in Cush and boasted
25: 9 This is the LORD, we *t* in him;
25: 9 we *t* in him, and he saved us.
47: 10 You have *t* in your wickedness
Jer 13: 25 and *t* in false gods.
38: 22 those *t* friends of yours.
48: 13 ashamed when they *t* in Bethel.
Eze 16: 15 " 'But you *t* in your beauty
Da 3: 28 They *t* in him and defied the king's
6: 23 because he had *t* in his God.
Lk 11: 22 the armor in which the man *t*
16: 10 *t* with very little can also be *t*
Ac 12: 20 a *t* personal servant of the king,
Tit 2: 10 but to show that they can be fully *t*,
3: 8 so that those who have *t*

TRUSTEES (TRUST)

Gal 4: 2 *t* until the time set by his father.

TRUSTFULLY (TRUST)

Pr 3: 29 who lives *t* near you.

TRUSTING (TRUST)

Job 15: 31 by *t* what is worthless,
Ps 112: 7 his heart is steadfast, *t*
Isa 2: 22 Stop *t* in man,
Jer 7: 8 you are *t* in deceptive words that

TRUSTS (TRUST)

Job 8: 14 What he *t* in is fragile;
Ps 21: 7 For the king *t* in the LORD;
22: 8 "He *t* in the LORD;
28: 7 my heart *t* in him, and I am helped.
32: 10 surrounds the man who *t* in him.
84: 12 blessed is the man who *t* in you.
86: 2 who *t* in you.
Pr 11: 28 Whoever *t* in his riches will fall,
16: 20 blessed is he who *t* in the LORD.
28: 25 he who *t* in the LORD will prosper.
28: 26 He who *t* in himself is a fool,
29: 25 whoever *t* in the LORD is kept safe
Isa 26: 3 because he *t* in you.
28: 16 one who *t* will never be dismayed.
Jer 17: 5 "Cursed is the one who *t* in man,
17: 7 blessed is the man who *t*
Eze 33: 13 but then he *t* in his righteousness
Hab 2: 18 For he who makes it *t*
Mt 27: 43 He *t* in God.
Ro 4: 5 but *t* God who justifies the wicked,
9: 33 one who *t* in him will never be put
10: 11 "Everyone who *t* in him will never
1Co 13: 7 always protects, always *t*,
1Pe 2: 6 and the one who *t* in him

TRUSTWORTHY (TRUST)

Ex 18: 21 *t* men who hate dishonest gain—
2Sa 7: 28 you are God! Your words are *t*,
Ne 13: 13 these men were considered *t*.
Ps 19: 7 The statutes of the LORD are *t*,
111: 7 all his precepts are *t*.
119: 86 All your commands are *t*;
119: 138 they are fully *t*.
Pr 11: 13 but a *t* man keeps a secret.
13: 17 but a *t* envoy brings healing.
25: 13 is a *t* messenger to those who send
Da 2: 45 and the interpretation is *t*."
6: 4 he was *t* and neither corrupt
Lk 16: 11 So if you have not been *t*
16: 12 And if you have not been *t*
19: 17 'Because you have been *t*
1Co 7: 25 one who by the Lord's mercy is *t*.
1Ti 1: 15 Here is a *t* saying that deserves full
3: 1 Here is a *t* saying: If anyone sets his
3: 11 but temperate and *t* in everything.
4: 9 This is a *t* saying that deserves full
2Ti 2: 11 Here is a *t* saying:
Tit 1: 9 must hold firmly to the *t* message
3: 8 This is a *t* saying.
Rev 21: 5 for these words are *t* and true."
22: 6 "These words are *t* and true.

TRUTH (TRUE TRUTHFUL TRUTHFULNESS TRUTHS)

Ge 42: 16 tested to see if you are telling the *t*.
1Ki 17: 24 LORD from your mouth is the *t*."
22: 16 the *t* in the name of the LORD?"
2Ch 18: 15 the *t* in the name of the LORD?"
Ps 15: 2 who speaks the *t* from his heart
25: 5 guide me in your *t* and teach me,
26: 3 and I walk continually in your *t*.
31: 5 redeem me, O LORD, the God of *t*
40: 10 do not conceal your love and your *t*
40: 11 your *t* always protect me.
43: 3 Send forth your light and your *t*,
45: 4 victoriously in behalf of *t*, humility

Ps 51: 6 Surely you desire t
52: 3 than speaking the t.
86: 11 and I will walk in your t;
96: 13 and the peoples in his t.
119: 30 I have chosen the way of t;
119: 43 of t from my mouth,
145: 18 to all who call on him in t.
Pr 16: 13 they value a man who speaks the t.
23: 23 Buy the t and do not sell it;
Isa 45: 19 I, the LORD, speak the t;
48: 1 but not in t or righteousness—
59: 14 t has stumbled in the streets,
59: 15 T is nowhere to be found,
65: 16 will do so by the God of t;
65: 16 will swear by the God of t.
Jer 5: 1 who deals honestly and seeks the t,
5: 3 do not your eyes look for t?
7: 28 T has perished; it has vanished
9: 3 it is not by t
9: 5 and no one speaks the t.
26: 15 for in t the LORD has sent me
Da 8: 12 and t was thrown to the ground.
9: 13 and giving attention to your t.
10: 21 what is written in the Book of T.
11: 2 "Now then, I tell you the t:
Am 5: 10 and despise him who tells the t.
Zec 8: 3 will be called The City of T,
8: 16 are to do: Speak the t to each other,
8: 19 Therefore love t and peace."
Mt 5: 18 I tell you the t, until heaven
5: 26 I tell you the t, you will not get out
6: 2 I tell you the t, they have received
6: 5 I tell you the t, they have received
6: 16 I tell you the t, they have received
8: 10 "I tell you the t, I have not found
10: 15 I tell you the t, it will be more
10: 23 I tell you the t, you will not finish
10: 42 I tell you the t, he will certainly not
11: 11 I tell you the t: Among those born
13: 17 For I tell you the t, many prophets
16: 28 I tell you the t, some who are
17: 20 I tell you the t, if you have faith
18: 3 And he said: "I tell you the t,
18: 13 And if he finds it, I tell you the t,
18: 18 "I tell you the t, whatever you bind
19: 23 to his disciples, "I tell you the t,
19: 28 "I tell you the t, at the renewal
21: 21 Jesus replied, "I tell you the t,
21: 31 Jesus said to them, "I tell you the t,
22: 16 of God in accordance with the t.
23: 36 I tell you the t, all this will come
24: 2 "I tell you the t, not one stone here
24: 34 I tell you the t, this generation will
24: 47 I tell you the t, he will put him
25: 12 'I tell you the t, I don't know you.'
25: 40 The King will reply, 'I tell you the t
25: 45 "He will reply, 'I tell you the t,
26: 13 tell you the t, wherever this gospel
26: 21 "I tell you the t, one
26: 34 "I tell you the t," Jesus answered,
Mk 3: 28 I tell you the t, all the sins
5: 33 with fear, told him the whole t.
8: 12 I tell you the t, no sign will be given
9: 1 he said to them, "I tell you the t,
9: 41 I tell you the t, anyone who gives
10: 15 I tell you the t, anyone who will not
10: 29 "I tell you the t," Jesus replied,
11: 23 "I tell you the t, if anyone says
12: 14 of God in accordance with the t.
12: 43 Jesus said, "I tell you the t,
13: 30 I tell you the t, this generation will
14: 9 I tell you the t, wherever the gospel
14: 18 "I tell you the t, one
14: 25 "I tell you the t, I will not drink
14: 30 "I tell you the t," Jesus answered,
Lk 4: 24 "I tell you the t," he continued,
9: 27 I tell you the t, some who are
12: 37 I tell you the t, he will dress himself
12: 44 I tell you the t, he will put him
18: 17 I tell you the t, anyone who will not
18: 29 I tell you the t," Jesus said to them,
20: 21 of God in accordance with the t.
21: 3 "I tell you the t," he said, "this
21: 32 tell you the t, this generation will
23: 43 answered him, "I tell you the t,
Jn 1: 14 from the Father, full of grace and t.
1: 17 and t came through Jesus Christ.
1: 51 "I tell you the t, you shall see
Jn 3: 3 "I tell you the t, unless a man is
3: 5 Jesus answered, "I tell you the t,
3: 11 I tell you the t, we speak
3: 21 But whoever lives by the t comes
4: 23 worship the Father in spirit and t,
4: 24 must worship in spirit and in t."
5: 19 "I tell you the t, the Son can do
5: 24 "I tell you the t, whoever hears my
5: 25 I tell you the t, a time is coming
5: 33 and he has testified to the t.
6: 26 "I tell you the t, you are looking
6: 32 Jesus said to them, "I tell you the t,
6: 47 I tell you the t, he who believes has
6: 53 Jesus said to them, "I tell you the t,
7: 18 the one who sent him is a man of t;
8: 32 Then you will know the t,
8: 32 and the t will set you free."
8: 34 Jesus replied, "I tell you the t,
8: 40 who has told you the t that I heard
8: 44 to the t, for there is no t in him.
8: 45 I tell the t, you do not believe me!
8: 46 I am telling the t, why don't you
8: 51 I tell you the t, if a man keeps my
8: 58 "I tell you the t," Jesus answered,
10: 1 "I tell you the t, the man who does
10: 7 "I tell you the t, I am the gate
12: 24 I tell you the t, unless a kernel
13: 16 I tell you the t, no servant is greater
13: 20 tell you the t, whoever accepts
13: 21 "I tell you the t, one of you is going
13: 38 I tell you the t, before the rooster
14: 6 I am the way and the t and the life.
14: 12 I tell you the t, anyone who has
14: 17 with you forever—the Spirit of t.
15: 26 the Spirit of t who goes out
16: 7 But I tell you the t: It is
16: 13 But when he, the Spirit of t, comes,
16: 13 comes, he will guide you into all t.
16: 20 I tell you the t, you will weep
16: 23 I tell you the t, my Father will give
17: 17 them by the t; your word is t.
18: 23 if I spoke the t, why did you strike
18: 37 into the world, to testify to the t.
18: 37 on the side of t listens to me."
18: 38 "What is t?" Pilate asked.
19: 35 He knows that he tells the t,
21: 18 I tell you the t, when you were
Ac 20: 30 and distort the t in order
21: 24 everybody will know there is no t
21: 34 commander could not get at the t
24: 8 able to learn the t about all these
28: 25 "The Holy Spirit spoke the t
Ro 1: 18 of men who suppress the t
1: 25 They exchanged the t of God
2: 2 who do such things is based on t.
2: 8 who reject the t and follow evil,
2: 20 embodiment of knowledge and t—
9: 1 I speak the t in Christ—I am not
15: 8 of the Jews on behalf of God's t,
1Co 5: 8 the bread of sincerity and t.
13: 6 in evil but rejoices with the t.
2Co 4: 2 setting forth the t plainly we
11: 10 As surely as the t of Christ is in me,
12: 6 because I would be speaking the t.
13: 8 against the t, but only for the t.
Gal 2: 5 so that the t of the gospel might
2: 14 in line with the t of the gospel,
4: 16 enemy by telling you the t?
5: 7 and kept you from obeying the t?
Eph 1: 13 when you heard the word of t,
4: 15 Instead, speaking the t in love,
4: 21 him in accordance with the t that is
5: 9 and t) and find out what pleases
6: 14 with the belt of t buckled
Col 1: 5 heard about in the word of t,
1: 6 understood God's grace in all its t.
2Th 2: 10 because they refused to love the t
2: 12 who have not believed the t
2: 13 and through belief in the t.
1Ti 2: 4 to come to a knowledge of the t.
2: 7 I am telling the t, I am not lying—
3: 15 the pillar and foundation of the t.
4: 3 who believe and who know the t.
6: 5 who have been robbed of the t
2Ti 2: 15 correctly handles the word of t.
2: 18 have wandered away from the t.
2: 25 them to a knowledge of the t,
3: 7 never able to acknowledge the t.
2Ti 3: 8 so also these men oppose the t—
4: 4 will turn their ears away from the t
Tit 1: 1 the knowledge of the t that leads
1: 14 of those who reject the t.
Heb 10: 26 received the knowledge of the t,
Jas 1: 18 birth through the word of t,
3: 14 do not boast about it or deny the t.
5: 19 of you should wander from the t
1Pe 1: 22 by obeying the t so that you have
2Pe 1: 12 established in the t you now have.
2: 2 the way of t into disrepute.
1Jn 1: 6 we lie and do not live by the t.
1: 8 deceive ourselves and the t is not
2: 4 commands is a liar, and the t is not
2: 8 its t is seen in him and you,
2: 20 and all of you know the t.
2: 21 because no lie comes from the t.
2: 21 because you do not know the t,
3: 18 or tongue but with actions and in t.
3: 19 we know that we belong to the t,
4: 6 is how we recognize the Spirit of t
5: 6 testifies, because the Spirit is the t.
2Jn : 1 whom I love in the t—
: 2 who know the t— because of the t,
: 3 will be with us in t and love.
: 4 of your children walking in the t,
3Jn : 1 friend Gaius, whom I love in the t.
: 3 how you continue to walk in the t.
: 3 tell about your faithfulness to the t
: 4 my children are walking in the t.
: 8 we may work together for the t.
: 12 everyone—and even by the t itself.

TRUTHFUL (TRUTH)

Pr 12: 17 A t witness gives honest testimony,
12: 19 T lips endure forever,
12: 22 but he delights in men who are t.
14: 5 A t witness does not deceive,
14: 25 A t witness saves lives,
Jer 4: 2 and if in a t, just and righteous way
Jn 3: 33 it has certified that God is t.
2Co 6: 7 in t speech and in the power

TRUTHFULNESS (TRUTH)

Ro 3: 7 "If my falsehood enhances God's t

TRUTHS (TRUTH)

1Co 2: 13 expressing spiritual t
1Ti 3: 9 hold of the deep t of the faith
4: 6 brought up in the t of the faith
Heb 5: 12 to teach you the elementary t

TRY (TRIED TRIES TRYING)

Nu 20: 18 pass through here; if you t,
Jdg 19: 13 let's t to reach Gibeah or Ramah
Ru 3: 1 should I not t to find a home
1Sa 26: 21 I will not t to harm you again.
Job 17: 10 "But come on, all of you, t again!
Ps 26: 2 Test me, O LORD, and t me,
Isa 7: 13 Will you t the patience of my God
7: 13 enough to t the patience of men?
22: 4 Do not t to console me
Eze 7: 26 They will t to get a vision
Da 7: 25 and t to change the set times
11: 26 eat from the king's provisions will t
Zec 12: 3 All who t to move it will injure
Mal 1: 8 T offering them to your governor!
Lk 12: 58 t hard to be reconciled to him
13: 24 will t to enter and will not be able
14: 19 and I'm on my way to t them out.
Ac 15: 10 why do you t to test God
1Co 10: 33 even as I t to please everybody
14: 12 t to excel in gifts that build up
2Co 5: 11 is to fear the Lord, we t
1Th 5: 15 always t to be kind to each other
Tit 2: 9 to t to please them, not to talk back

TRYING (TRY)

Nu 16: 10 now you are t to get the priesthood
Jdg 6: 31 to plead Baal's cause? Are you t
1Sa 20: 1 that he is t to take my life?" "Never
2Sa 14: 16 the hand of the man who is t to cut
16: 11 of my own flesh, is t to take my life.
20: 19 You are t to destroy a city that is
1Ki 19: 10 and now they are t to kill me too."
19: 14 and now they are t to kill me too."
2Ki 5: 7 See how he is t to pick a quarrel
Ne 6: 9 They were all t to frighten us,

Ne 6: 14 of the prophets who have been t
Isa 28: 9 "Who is it he is t to teach?
Da 2: 8 "I am certain that you are t
8: 15 was watching the vision and t
Mt 2: 20 for those who were t
22: 18 "You hypocrites, why are you t
23: 13 will you let those enter who are t to
Mk 12: 15 "Why are you t to trap me?"
Lk 19: 47 among the people were t to kill him
Jn 5: 7 While I am t to get
7: 19 Why are you t to kill me?"
7: 20 "Who is t to kill you?" Jesus said
7: 25 Isn't this the man they are t to kill?
Ac 17: 18 "What is this babbler t to say?"
18: 4 t to persuade Jews and Greeks.
21: 31 While they were t to kill him,
Ro 11: 3 and they are t to kill me"?
1Co 10: 22 Are we t to arouse the Lord's
2Co 5: 12 We are not t to commend ourselves
10: 9 want to seem to be t to frighten you
Gal 1: 7 are t to pervert the gospel of Christ.
1: 10 Am I now t to win the approval
1: 10 If I were still t to please men,
1: 10 or of God? Or am I t to please men?
3: 3 are you now t to attain your goal
5: 4 You who are t to be justified
6: 12 a good impression outwardly are t
1Th 2: 3 or impure motives, nor are we t
2: 4 We are not t to please men but God
1Pe 1: 11 t to find out the time
1Jn 2: 26 things to you about those who are t

TRYPHENA

Ro 16: 12 Greet T and Tryphosa, those

TRYPHOSA

Ro 16: 12 T, those women who work hard

TUBAL

Ge 10: 2 Javan, T, Meshech and Tiras.
1Ch 1: 5 Javan, T, Meshech and Tiras.
Isa 66: 19 as archers), to T and Greece,
Eze 27: 13 T and Meshech traded with you;
32: 26 "Meshech and T are there,
38: 2 the chief prince of Meshech and T;
38: 3 chief prince of Meshech and T.
39: 1 chief prince of Meshech and T.

TUBAL-CAIN (TUBAL-CAIN'S)

Ge 4: 22 T, who forged all kinds of tools out

TUBAL-CAIN'S (TUBAL-CAIN)

Ge 4: 22 T sister was Naamah.

TUBES

Job 40: 18 His bones are t of bronze,

TUCK (TUCKED TUCKING)

2Ki 4: 29 "T your cloak into your belt,
9: 1 "T your cloak into your belt,
Eze 5: 3 and t them away in the folds

TUCKED (TUCK)

Ex 12: 11 with your cloak t into your belt,

TUCKING (TUCK)

1Ki 18: 46 and, t his cloak into his belt,

TUMBLES (TUMBLING)

Ge 49: 17 heels so that its rider t backward.

TUMBLEWEED

Ps 83: 13 Make them like t, O my God,
Isa 17: 13 like t before a gale.

TUMBLING (TUMBLES)

Jdg 7: 13 loaf of barley bread came t

TUMORS

Dt 28: 27 with the boils of Egypt and with t,
1Sa 5: 6 them and afflicted them with t.
5: 9 and old, with an outbreak of t.
5: 12 did not die were afflicted with t,
6: 4 "Five gold t and five gold rats,
6: 5 Make models of the t
6: 11 gold rats and the models of the t.
6: 17 are the gold t the Philistines sent

TUMULT

1Sa 14: 19 t in the Philistine camp increased
Isa 22: 2 O city of t and revelry?
22: 5 a day of t and trampling and terror
Jer 25: 31 The t will resound to the ends
Eze 1: 24 voice of the Almighty, like the t
Am 2: 2 Moab will go down in great t

TUNE (TUNED)

Ps 58: 5 that will not heed the t
1Co 14: 7 anyone know what t is being

TUNED (TUNE)

Job 30: 31 My harp is t to mourning,

TUNIC (TUNICS)

Ex 28: 4 a woven t, a turban and a sash.
28: 39 "Weave the t of fine linen
29: 5 and dress Aaron with the t,
Lev 8: 7 He put the t on Aaron, tied
16: 4 He is to put on the sacred linen t,
1Sa 17: 38 Saul dressed David in his own t.
17: 39 fastened on his sword over the t
18: 4 with his t, and even his sword,
2Sa 20: 8 Joab was wearing his military t,
Ezr 9: 3 When I heard this, I tore my t
9: 5 from my self-abasement, with my t
Mt 5: 40 wants to sue you and take your t,
10: 10 or extra t, or sandals or a staff;
Mk 6: 9 Wear sandals but not an extra t.
Lk 6: 29 do not stop him from taking your t.
9: 3 no bread, no money, no extra t.

TUNICS (TUNIC)

Ex 28: 40 Make t, sashes and headbands
29: 8 dress them in t and put headbands
39: 27 they made t of fine linen—
40: 14 Bring his sons and dress them in t.
Lev 8: 13 Aaron's sons forward, put t
10: 5 still in their t, outside the camp,
Lk 3: 11 "The man with two t should share

TUNNEL (TUNNELS)

2Ki 20: 20 the t by which he brought water

TUNNELS (TUNNEL)

Job 28: 10 He t through the rock;

TURBAN (TURBANS)

Ex 28: 4 a robe, a woven tunic, a t and a sash
28: 37 cord to it to attach it to the t;
28: 37 it is to be on the front of the t.
28: 39 and make the t of fine linen.
29: 6 Put the t on his head and attach
29: 6 attach the sacred diadem to the t.
39: 28 of a weaver—and the t of fine linen
39: 31 cord to it to attach it to the t,
Lev 8: 9 he placed the t on Aaron's head
16: 4 around him and put on the linen t.
Job 29: 14 justice was my robe and my t.
Eze 21: 26 Take off the t, remove the crown.
24: 17 Keep your t fastened and your
Zec 3: 5 So they put a clean t on his head
3: 5 "Put a clean t on his head."

TURBANS (TURBAN)

Eze 23: 15 and flowing t on their heads;
24: 23 You will keep your t on your heads
44: 18 are to wear linen t on their heads
Da 3: 21 trousers, t and other clothes,

TURBULENT

Ge 49: 4 T as the waters, you will no longer

TURMOIL

2Ch 15: 5 of the lands were in great t.
Job 3: 17 There the wicked cease from t,
3: 26 I have no rest, but only t."
Ps 65: 7 and the t of the nations.
Pr 15: 16 than great wealth with t.
Isa 14: 3 relief from suffering and t
Eze 22: 5 you, O infamous city, full of t.
Ac 17: 8 the city officials were thrown into t

TURN (TURNED TURNING TURNS)

Ge 19: 2 "please t aside to your servant's
24: 49 so I may know which way to t."
37: 30 Where can I t now?" Then they got
Ex 7: 19 all the reservoirs'—and they will t
14: 2 "Tell the Israelites to t back
23: 27 make all your enemies t their backs
32: 8 They have been quick to t away
32: 12 T from your fierce anger; relent
34: 22 of Ingathering at the t of the year.
Lev 13: 16 the raw flesh change and t white,
19: 4 " 'Do not t to idols or make gods
19: 29 or the land will t to prostitution
19: 31 " 'Do not t to mediums
26: 31 I will t your cities into ruins
Nu 6: 26 the LORD t his face toward you
14: 25 t back tomorrow and set out
20: 17 along the king's highway and not t
21: 22 We will not t aside into any field
22: 26 where there was no room to t,
25: 4 LORD's fierce anger may t away
27: 7 and t their father's inheritance
27: 8 t his inheritance over to his
32: 15 If you t away from following him,
34: 5 it will t, join the Wadi of
Dt 1: 40 t around and set out
2: 3 country long enough; now t north.
2: 27 we will not t aside to the right
5: 32 do not t aside to the right
7: 4 for they will t your sons away
11: 16 or you will be enticed to t away
11: 28 t from the way that I command you
13: 5 he has tried to t you
13: 10 because he tried to t you away
13: 17 so that the LORD will t
17: 11 Do not t aside from what they tell
17: 20 and t from the law to the right
23: 14 you anything indecent and t away
28: 14 Do not t aside from any
28: 24 The LORD will t the rain
30: 10 and t to the LORD your God
31: 20 they will t to other gods
31: 29 and to t from the way I have
Jos 1: 7 do not t from it to the right
7: 12 they t their backs and run
22: 16 How could you t away
22: 23 altar to t away from the LORD
22: 29 and t away from him today
23: 12 if you t away and ally yourselves
24: 20 he will t and bring disaster on you
Jdg 1: 3 We in t will go with you into yours
7: 3 trembles with fear may t back
7: 22 the men throughout the camp to t
14: 17 She in t explained the riddle
20: 39 men of Israel would t in the battle.
Ru 1: 16 to leave you or to t back from you.
1Sa 6: 12 they did not t to the right
12: 20 yet do not t away from the LORD,
12: 21 Do not t away after useless idols.
22: 17 T and kill the priests of the LORD,
22: 18 You t and strike down the priests."
29: 4 or he will t against us
29: 7 T back and go in peace; do nothing
2Sa 1: 22 the bow of Jonathan did not t back,
2: 21 "T aside to the right or to the left;
14: 19 no one can t to the right
15: 31 t Ahithophel's counsel
22: 37 so that my ankles do not t.
22: 38 I did not t back till they were
22: 41 made my enemies t their backs
1Ki 8: 33 and when they t back to you
8: 35 and confess your name and t
8: 48 and if they t back to you
8: 58 May he t our hearts to him,
9: 6 if you or your sons t away from me
11: 2 they will surely t your hearts
12: 15 for this t of events was
13: 16 "I cannot t back and go with you,
17: 3 t eastward and hide in the Kerith
2Ki 3: 3 he did not t away from them.
10: 29 he did not t away from the sins
10: 31 He did not t away from the sins
13: 2 and he did not t away from them.
13: 6 they did not t away from the sins
13: 11 did not t away from any of the sins
14: 24 did not t away from any of the sins
15: 9 He did not t away from the sins
15: 18 his entire reign he did not t away
15: 24 He did not t away from the sins
15: 28 He did not t away from the sins
17: 13 and seers: "T from your evil ways.
17: 22 and did not t away from them

2Ki 23: 26 the LORD did not *t* away
1Ch 12: 23 at Hebron to *t* Saul's kingdom
2Ch 6: 24 when they *t* back and confess your
6: 26 and confess your name and *t*
6: 38 and if they *t* back to you
7: 14 and *t* from their wicked ways,
7: 19 "But if you *t* away and forsake
10: 15 for this *t* of events was from God,
24: 23 At the *t* of the year, the army
29: 10 so that his fierce anger will *t* away
30: 8 so that his fierce anger will *t* away
30: 9 He will not *t* his face from you
35: 22 would not *t* away from him,
36: 10 At the *t* of the year, King
36: 13 and would not *t* to the LORD,
Ne 4: 4 *T* their insults back
4: 12 Wherever you *t*, they will attack us
9: 26 in order to *t* them back to you;
9: 35 or *t* from their evil ways.
Est 2: 12 Before a girl's *t* came to go
2: 15 When the *t* came for Esther
2: 22 who in *t* reported it to the king,
Job 3: 4 That day—may it *t* to darkness;
5: 1 which of the holy ones will you *t*?
6: 18 Caravans *t* aside from their routes;
10: 8 Will you now *t* and destroy me?
10: 9 Will you now *t* me to dust again?
10: 20 *T* away from me so I can have
13: 9 Would it *t* out well
13: 16 this might *t* out for my deliverance,
17: 12 These men *t* night into day;
20: 14 yet his food will *t* sour
30: 21 You *t* on me ruthlessly;
33: 17 to *t* man from wrongdoing
33: 30 to *t* back his soul from the pit,
36: 18 do not let a large bribe *t* you aside.
Ps 4: 2 will you *t* my glory into shame?
6: 4 *T*, O LORD, and deliver me;
6: 10 may they *t* back in sudden disgrace
9: 3 My enemies *t* back;
18: 36 so that my ankles do not *t*.
18: 37 I did not *t* back till they were
18: 40 made my enemies *t* their backs
21: 12 you will make them *t* their backs
22: 27 will remember and *t* to the LORD,
25: 16 *T* to me and be gracious to me,
27: 9 do not *t* your servant away in anger
27: 12 Do not *t* me over to the desire
28: 1 do not *t* a deaf ear to me.
31: 2 *T* your ear to me,
34: 14 *T* from evil and do good;
37: 8 from anger and *t* from wrath;
37: 27 *T* from evil and do good;
40: 4 to those who *t* aside to false gods.
49: 4 I will *t* my ear to a proverb;
51: 13 and sinners will *t* back to you.
56: 9 Then my enemies will *t* back
64: 8 He will *t* their own tongues
69: 16 in your great mercy *t* to me.
70: 3 *t* back because of their shame.
71: 2 *t* your ear to me and save me.
73: 10 Therefore their people *t* to them
78: 6 they in *t* would tell their children.
80: 18 Then we will not *t* away from you;
81: 14 and *t* my hand against their foes!
86: 16 *T* to me and have mercy on me;
88: 2 *t* your ear to my cry.
90: 3 You *t* men back to dust,
102: 2 *T* your ear to me;
119: 36 *T* my heart toward your statutes
119: 37 *T* my eyes away from worthless
119: 51 but I do not *t* from your law.
119: 79 May those who fear you *t* to me,
119:132 *T* to me and have mercy on me,
125: 5 But those who *t* to crooked ways
Pr 1: 26 I in *t* will laugh at your disaster;
4: 15 *t* from it and go on your way.
5: 7 do not *t* aside from what I say.
7: 25 Do not let your heart *t* to her ways
22: 6 when he is old he will not *t* from it.
24: 18 and *t* his wrath away from him.
29: 8 but wise men *t* away anger.
SS 2: 17 *t*, my lover,
6: 1 Which way did your lover *t*,
6: 5 *T* your eyes from me;
Isa 1: 25 I will *t* my hand against you;
3: 12 they *t* you from the path.
6: 10 and *t* and be healed."

Isa 9: 21 together they will *t* against Judah.
14: 23 "I will *t* her into a place for owls
14: 27 out, and who can *t* it back?
17: 7 *t* their eyes to the Holy One
19: 22 They will *t* to the LORD,
22: 4 Therefore I said, "*T* away from me;
28: 6 to those who *t* back the battle
29: 16 You *t* things upside down,
30: 21 Whether you *t* to the right
41: 18 I will *t* the desert into pools
42: 15 I will *t* rivers into islands
42: 16 I will *t* the darkness into light
45: 22 "*T* to me and be saved,
49: 11 I will *t* all my mountains into roads,
50: 2 I *t* rivers into a desert;
55: 7 Let him *t* to the LORD,
56: 11 they all *t* to their own way,
58: 7 not to *t* away from your own flesh
Jer 2: 21 How then did you *t* against me
3: 19 and not *t* away from following me.
4: 28 I have decided and will not *t* back."
6: 8 or I will *t* away from you
8: 5 Why does Jerusalem always *t* away
12: 10 they will *t* my pleasant field
13: 16 but he will *t* it to thick darkness
15: 19 Let this people *t* to you,
15: 19 but you must not *t* to them.
17: 13 Those who *t* away
18: 11 So *t* from your evil ways, each one
18: 20 to *t* your wrath away from them
21: 4 about to *t* against you the weapons
23: 20 anger of the LORD will not *t* back
25: 5 They said, "*T* now, each of you,
26: 3 and each will *t* from his evil way.
30: 24 anger of the LORD will not *t* back
31: 13 I will *t* their mourning
31: 39 hill of Gareb and then *t* to Goah.
32: 40 so that they will never *t* away
35: 15 "Each of you must *t*
36: 3 each of them will *t*
36: 7 each will *t* from his wicked ways,
44: 5 did not *t* from their wickedness
46: 21 They too will *t* and flee together,
47: 3 Fathers will not *t* to help their
49: 8 *T* and flee, hide in deep caves,
50: 5 and *t* their faces toward it.
Eze 1: 9 they did not *t* as they moved.
1: 17 the wheels did not *t* about
3: 19 he does not *t* from his wickedness
4: 3 the city and *t* your face toward it.
4: 7 *T* your face toward the siege
4: 8 so that you cannot *t* from one side
7: 20 Therefore I will *t* these
7: 22 I will *t* my face away from them,
10: 11 the wheels did not *t* about
13: 22 not to *t* from their evil ways
14: 6 *T* from your idols and renounce all
16: 42 and my jealous anger will *t* away
18: 23 when they *t* from their ways
18: 30 *T* away from all your offenses;
23: 24 I will *t* you over to them
25: 5 I will *t* Rabbah into a pasture
33: 9 if you do warn the wicked man to *t*
33: 11 rather that they *t* from their ways
33: 11 *T*! *T* from your evil ways!
35: 4 I will *t* your towns into ruins
38: 4 I will *t* you around, put hooks
38: 12 and *t* my hand against the resettled
39: 2 I will *t* you around and drag you
Da 9: 16 *t* away your anger and your wrath
11: 18 Then he will *t* his attention
11: 18 will *t* his insolence back upon him.
11: 19 he will *t* back toward the fortresses
11: 30 he will *t* back and vent his fury
Hos 2: 3 *t* her into a parched land,
3: 1 though they *t* to other gods
4: 13 Therefore your daughters *t*
4: 14 when they *t* to prostitution,
7: 14 but *t* away from me.
7: 16 They do not *t* to the Most High;
9: 12 them when I *t* away from them!
11: 7 My people are determined to *t*
Joel 2: 14 Who knows? He may *t*
Am 1: 3 I will not *t* back ⌊my wrath⌋.
1: 6 I will not *t* back ⌊my wrath⌋.
1: 8 I will *t* my hand against Ekron
1: 9 I will not *t* back ⌊my wrath⌋.
1: 11 I will not *t* back ⌊my wrath⌋.

Am 1: 13 I will not *t* back ⌊my wrath⌋.
2: 1 I will not *t* back ⌊my wrath⌋.
2: 4 I will not *t* back ⌊my wrath⌋.
2: 6 I will not *t* back ⌊my wrath⌋.
5: 7 You who *t* justice into bitterness
8: 3 in the temple will *t* to wailing.
8: 10 I will *t* your religious feasts
Jnh 3: 9 and with compassion *t*
Mic 7: 17 they will *t* in fear to the LORD our
Hab 2: 16 Now it is your *t*! Drink
Zep 1: 6 those who *t* back from following
Hag 2: 17 yet you did not *t* to me,' declares
Zec 1: 4 '*T* from your evil ways
13: 7 I will *t* my hand against the little
Mal 4: 6 He will *t* the hearts of the fathers
Mt 5: 39 you on the right cheek, *t*
5: 42 do not *t* away from the one who
7: 6 and then *t* and tear you to pieces.
10: 35 For I have come to *t*
13: 15 and *t*, and I would heal them.'
15: 36 and they in *t* to the people.
20: 19 and will *t* him over to the Gentiles
24: 10 At that time many will *t* away
Mk 4: 12 otherwise they might *t*
Lk 1: 17 to *t* the hearts of the fathers
6: 29 on one cheek, *t* to him the other
12: 58 the judge *t* you over to the officer,
Jn 2: 16 How dare you *t* my Father's house
12: 22 Andrew and Philip in *t* told Jesus.
12: 40 nor *t*— and I would heal them."
16: 20 but your grief will *t* to joy.
Ac 3: 19 Repent, then, and *t* to God,
6: 3 We will *t* this responsibility
13: 8 and tried to *t* the proconsul
13: 46 worthy of eternal life, we now *t*
14: 15 to *t* from these worthless things
20: 21 Greeks that they must *t* to God
21: 21 the Gentiles to *t* away from Moses,
26: 18 and *t* them from darkness to light,
26: 20 that they should repent and *t*
28: 27 and *t* and I would heal them.'
Ro 11: 26 he will *t* godlessness away
1Co 14: 31 For you can all prophesy in *t*
15: 23 But each in his own *t*: Christ,
2Co 7: 5 but we were harassed at every *t*—
8: 14 in *t* their plenty will supply what
Php 1: 19 to me will *t* out for my deliverance.
Col 4: 16 and that you in *t* read the letter
1Ti 6: 20 *T* away from godless chatter
2Ti 2: 19 the name of the Lord must *t* away
4: 4 They will *t* their ears away
4: 4 from the truth and *t* aside to myths.
Heb 12: 25 if we *t* away from him who warns
Jas 3: 3 we can *t* the whole animal.
1Pe 3: 11 He must *t* from evil and do good;
2Pe 2: 21 and then to *t* their backs
Rev 10: 9 It will *t* your stomach sour,
11: 6 they have power to *t* the waters

TURNED (TURN)

Ge 9: 23 Their faces were *t* the other way
14: 7 *t* back and went to En Mishpat
18: 22 The men *t* away and went
41: 13 And things *t* out exactly
42: 24 He *t* away from them and began
42: 24 but then *t* back and spoke
42: 28 and they *t* to each other trembling
Ex 4: 4 and it *t* back into a staff in his hand.
7: 23 he *t* and went into his palace,
10: 6 Then Moses *t* and left Pharaoh.
14: 21 with a strong east wind and *t* it
32: 15 *t* and went down the mountain
Lev 13: 3 if the hair in the sore has *t* white
13: 4 and the hair in it has not *t* white,
13: 10 in the skin that has *t* the hair white
13: 13 Since it has all *t* white, he is clean.
13: 17 and if the sores have *t* white,
13: 20 and the hair in it has *t* white,
13: 25 and if the hair in it has *t* white,
Nu 12: 10 Aaron *t* toward her and saw that
14: 43 Because you have *t* away
16: 42 and *t* toward the Tent of Meeting,
20: 21 their territory, Israel *t* away
21: 33 they *t* and went up along the road
22: 23 she *t* off the road into a field.
22: 33 If she had not *t* away, I would
22: 33 *t* away from me these three times.
24: 1 but *t* his face toward the desert.

Nu 25: 11 has *t* my anger away
33: 7 left Etham, *t* back to Pi Hahiroth,
Dt 1: 45 to your weeping and *t* a deaf ear
2: 1 Then we *t* back and set out
2: 8 We *t* from the Arabah road,
3: 1 Next we *t* and went up
9: 12 They have *t* away quickly
9: 15 *t* and went
9: 16 You had *t* aside quickly
23: 5 *t* the curse into a blessing for you,
26: 13 not *t* aside from your commands
Jos 7: 26 the LORD *t* from his fierce anger.
8: 20 toward the desert had *t* back
8: 21 they *t* around and attacked
10: 38 and all Israel with him *t* around
11: 10 At that time Joshua *t* back
15: 7 of Achor and *t* north to Gilgal,
15: 11 of Ekron, *t* toward Shikkeron,
18: 14 on the south the boundary *t* south
19: 12 It *t* east from Sarid
19: 13 out at Rimmon and *t* toward Neah.
19: 27 It then *t* east toward Beth Dagon,
19: 29 The boundary then *t* back
19: 29 *t* toward Hosah and came out
Jdg 2: 17 they quickly *t* from the way
3: 19 idols near Gilgal he himself *t* back
6: 14 The LORD *t* to him and said,
14: 8 he *t* aside to look at the lion's
18: 3 so they *t* in there and asked him,
18: 15 So they *t* in there and went
18: 21 in front of them, they *t* away
18: 23 the Danites *t* and said to Micah,
18: 26 *t* around and went back home.
20: 40 Benjamites *t* and saw the smoke
20: 41 Then the men of Israel *t* on them,
20: 45 they *t* and fled toward the desert
20: 47 But six hundred men *t*
Ru 2: 3 As it *t* out, she found herself
3: 8 he *t* and discovered a woman lying
1Sa 8: 3 They *t* aside after dishonest gain
9: 20 to whom is all the desire of Israel *t*,
10: 9 As Saul *t* to leave Samuel,
11: 7 and they *t* out as one man.
13: 17 One *t* toward Ophrah
14: 47 Wherever he *t*, he inflicted
15: 11 because he has *t* away from me
15: 12 has *t* and gone on down to Gilgal."
15: 27 As Samuel *t* to leave, Saul caught
17: 30 He then *t* away to someone else
17: 35 When it *t* on me, I seized it
17: 51 saw that their hero was dead, they *t*
22: 18 So Doeg the Edomite *t*
25: 12 David's men *t* around
28: 15 and God has *t* away from me.
28: 16 now that the LORD has *t* away
2Sa 1: 7 When he *t* around and saw me,
19: 2 army the victory that day was *t*
22: 23 I have not *t* away from his decrees.
1Ki 6: 34 each having two leaves that *t*
8: 14 the king *t* around and blessed them
11: 4 his wives *t* his heart
11: 9 because his heart had *t* away
22: 32 So they *t* to attack him,
2Ki 2: 24 you baldhead!" He *t* around,
4: 35 Elisha *t* away and walked back
5: 12 So he *t* and went off in a rage.
9: 23 Joram *t* about and fled, calling out
12: 17 Then he *t* to attack Jerusalem.
19: 25 that you have *t* fortified cities
20: 2 Hezekiah *t* his face to the wall
23: 25 was there a king like him who *t*
1Ch 10: 14 *t* the kingdom over to David son
21: 20 Araunah was threshing wheat, he *t*
2Ch 6: 3 the king *t* around and blessed them
11: 4 and *t* back from marching
12: 12 the LORD's anger *t* from him,
13: 14 Judah *t* and saw that they were
15: 4 But in their distress they *t*
18: 31 So they *t* to attack him,
19: 4 and *t* them back to the LORD,
20: 10 so they *t* away from them
25: 27 the time that Amaziah *t* away
29: 6 They *t* their faces away
29: 6 dwelling place and *t* their backs
Ezr 10: 14 in this matter is *t* away from us."
Ne 2: 15 I *t* back and reentered
9: 29 Stubbornly they *t* their backs
13: 2 however, *t* the curse into a blessing
Est 9: 1 but now the tables were *t*
9: 22 when their sorrow was *t* into joy
Job 16: 11 God has *t* me over to evil men
19: 19 those I love have *t* against me.
31: 7 if my steps have *t* from the path,
34: 27 because they *t* from following him
Ps 14: 3 All have *t* aside,
18: 22 I have not *t* away from his decrees.
22: 14 My heart has *t* to wax;
30: 11 You *t* my wailing into dancing;
35: 4 be *t* back in dismay.
40: 1 he *t* to me and heard my cry.
40: 14 be *t* back in disgrace.
44: 18 Our hearts had not *t* back;
53: 3 Everyone has *t* away,
66: 6 He *t* the sea into dry land,
70: 2 be *t* back in disgrace.
78: 9 *t* back on the day of battle;
78: 30 before they *t* from the food they
78: 34 they eagerly *t* to him again.
78: 44 He *t* their rivers to blood;
85: 3 and *t* from your fierce anger.
89: 43 You have *t* back the edge
105: 25 whose hearts he *t* to hate his people
105: 29 He *t* their waters into blood,
105: 32 He *t* their rain into hail,
107: 33 He *t* rivers into a desert,
107: 35 He *t* the desert into pools of water
114: 3 the Jordan *t* back;
114: 5 O Jordan, that you *t* back,
114: 8 who *t* the rock into a pool,
116: 2 Because he *t* his ear to me,
119: 59 have *t* my steps to your statutes.
119:157 but I have not *t* from your statutes.
129: 5 be *t* back in shame.
Ecc 2: 12 I *t* my thoughts to consider wisdom
7: 25 So I *t* my mind to understand,
Isa 1: 4 and *t* their backs on him.
5: 25 for all this, his anger is not *t* away,
7: 25 places where cattle are *t* loose
9: 12 for all this, his anger is not *t* away,
9: 17 for all this, his anger is not *t* away,
9: 21 for all this, his anger is not *t* away,
10: 4 for all this, his anger is not *t* away,
12: 1 your anger has *t* away
23: 13 and *t* it into a ruin.
29: 17 will not Lebanon be *t*
34: 9 Edom's streams will be *t* into pitch,
37: 26 that you have *t* fortified cities
38: 2 Hezekiah *t* his face to the wall
42: 17 will be *t* back in utter shame.
53: 6 each of us has *t* to his own way;
59: 8 have *t* them into crooked roads;
63: 10 So he *t* and became their enemy
Jer 2: 27 They have *t* their backs to me
4: 8 has not *t* away from us.
5: 23 they have *t* aside and gone away.
6: 12 Their houses will be *t*
8: 5 Why then have these people *t* away
23: 22 and would have *t* them
30: 6 every face *t* deathly pale?
32: 33 They *t* their backs to me
34: 16 But now you have *t* around
39: 14 They *t* him over to Gedaliah son
40: 5 However, before Jeremiah *t* to go,
41: 14 had taken captive at Mizpah *t*
49: 24 she has *t* to flee
La 1: 13 and *t* me back.
3: 3 he has *t* his hand against me
4: 6 without a hand *t* to help her.
5: 2 Our inheritance has been *t*
5: 15 our dancing has *t* to mourning.
Eze 6: 9 which have *t* away from me,
17: 6 Its branches *t* toward him,
21: 16 wherever your blade is *t*.
23: 17 she *t* away from them in disgust.
23: 18 I *t* away from her in disgust,
23: 18 just as I had *t* away from her sister.
23: 22 those you *t* away from in disgust,
23: 28 to those you *t* away from in disgust.
42: 19 Then he *t* to the west side
Da 2: 5 your houses *t* into piles of rubble.
2: 29 your mind *t* to things to come,
3: 29 their houses be *t* into piles of rubble
5: 6 His face *t* pale and he was
7: 28 and my face *t* pale, but I kept
9: 3 So I *t* to the Lord God
9: 5 have *t* away from your commands
Da 9: 11 transgressed your law and *t* away,
10: 8 my face *t* deathly pale
Hos 5: 3 you have now *t* to prostitution;
5: 13 then Ephraim *t* to Assyria,
7: 8 Ephraim is a flat cake not *t* over.
14: 4 for my anger has *t* away from them.
Joel 2: 31 The sun will be *t* to darkness
Am 6: 12 But you have *t* justice into poison
Jnh 3: 10 how they *t* from their evil ways,
Zep 3: 15 he has *t* back your enemy.
Hag 1: 9 but see, it *t* out to be little.
Zec 7: 11 stubbornly they *t* their backs
8: 10 for I had *t* every man
Mal 1: 3 and I have *t* his mountains
2: 6 uprightness, and *t* many from sin.
2: 8 But you have *t* from the way
3: 7 of your forefathers you have *t* away
Mt 9: 22 Jesus *t* and saw her.
16: 23 shall never happen to you!" Jesus *t*
18: 34 In anger his master *t* him
Mk 5: 30 He *t* around in the crowd
8: 33 But when Jesus *t* and looked
Lk 7: 44 Then he *t* toward the woman
9: 55 But Jesus *t* and rebuked them,
10: 23 Then he *t* to his disciples
22: 32 And when you have *t* back,
22: 61 The Lord *t* and looked straight
23: 28 *t* and said to them, "Daughters
Jn 2: 9 tasted the water that had been *t*
4: 46 where he had *t* the water into wine.
6: 66 many of his disciples *t* back
9: 17 Finally they *t* again
20: 14 she *t* around and saw Jesus
20: 16 She *t* toward him and cried out
21: 20 Peter *t* and saw that the disciple
Ac 2: 20 The sun will be *t* to darkness
7: 39 and in their hearts *t* back to Egypt.
7: 42 But God *t* away and gave them
9: 35 Sharon saw him and *t* to the Lord.
11: 21 number of people believed and *t*
16: 18 so troubled that he *t* around
18: 17 Then they all *t* on Sosthenes
Ro 3: 12 All have *t* away,
1Th 1: 9 They tell how you *t* to God
3: 4 it *t* out that way, as you well know.
1Ti 1: 6 these and *t* to meaningless talk.
5: 15 have in fact already *t* away
Heb 8: 9 and I *t* away from them, declares
11: 34 whose weakness was *t* to strength;
Rev 1: 12 And when I *t* I saw seven golden
1: 12 I *t* around to see the voice that was
6: 12 sun *t* black like sackcloth made
6: 12 the whole moon *t* blood red,
8: 8 A third of the sea *t* into blood,
8: 11 A third of the waters *t* bitter,
8: 12 so that a third of them *t* dark.
10: 10 I had eaten it, my stomach *t* sour.
16: 3 and it *t* into blood like that

TURNING (TURN)

Nu 31: 16 the means of *t* the Israelites away
Dt 31: 18 because of all their wickedness in *t*
Jos 22: 18 And are you now *t* away
23: 6 without *t* aside to the right
Jdg 8: 20 *T* to Jether, his oldest son, he said,
11: 8 Nevertheless, we are *t* to you now;
2Sa 2: 19 *t* neither to the right nor to the left
22: 22 by *t* from my God.
1Ki 18: 37 and that you are *t* their hearts back
2Ki 21: 13 wiping it and *t* it upside down.
22: 2 not *t* aside to the right or to the left.
2Ch 34: 2 not *t* aside to the right or to the left.
Job 23: 11 to his way without *t* aside.
36: 21 Beware of *t* to evil,
Ps 18: 21 by *t* from my God.
Pr 2: 2 *t* your ear to wisdom
13: 14 *t* a man from the snares of death.
13: 19 but fools detest *t* from evil.
14: 27 *t* a man from the snares of death.
Isa 59: 13 *t* our backs on our God,
Eze 1: 12 they would go, without *t*
10: 11 direction the head faced, without *t*
29: 16 of their sin in *t* to her for help.
Da 9: 13 favor of the LORD our God by *t*
Hos 7: 11 now *t* to Assyria.
Lk 7: 9 and *t* to the crowd following him,
14: 25 with Jesus, and *t* to them he said:
Jn 1: 38 *T* around, Jesus saw them

Ac 3: 26 to you to bless you by *t* each of you
9: 40 *T* toward the dead woman, he said,
15: 19 for the Gentiles who are *t* to God.
Gal 1: 6 and are *t* to a different gospel—
4: 9 how is it that you are *t* back

TURNS (TURN)

Lev 20: 6 face against the person who *t*
Dt 29: 18 you today whose heart *t* away
30: 17 But if your heart *t* away
2Sa 22: 29 the LORD *t* my darkness into light
2Ki 11: 6 who take *t* guarding the temple—
Job 1: 4 used to take *t* holding feasts
23: 9 when he *t* to the south, I catch no
Ps 18: 28 my God *t* my darkness into light.
Pr 15: 1 A gentle answer *t* away wrath,
17: 8 wherever he *t*, he succeeds.
26: 14 As a door *t* on its hinges,
26: 14 so a sluggard *t* on his bed.
28: 9 If anyone *t* a deaf ear to the law,
Ecc 1: 6 and *t* to the north;
7: 7 Extortion *t* a wise man into a fool,
Isa 24: 11 all joy *t* to gloom,
41: 2 He *t* them to dust with his sword,
44: 25 and *t* it into nonsense,
Jer 8: 4 When a man *t* away, does he not
17: 5 and whose heart *t* away
23: 14 that no one *t* from his wickedness.
48: 39 How Moab *t* her back in shame!
La 1: 8 and *t* away.
Eze 3: 20 when a righteous man *t*
18: 21 "But if a wicked man *t* away
18: 24 "But if a righteous man *t*
18: 26 If a righteous man *t*
18: 27 But if a wicked man *t* away
18: 28 he has committed and *t* away
33: 12 him to fall when he *t* from it.
33: 14 but he then *t* away from his sin
33: 18 If a righteous man *t*
33: 19 And if a wicked man *t* away
Joel 2: 6 every face *t* pale.
Am 4: 13 he who *t* dawn to darkness,
5: 8 who *t* blackness into dawn
Na 2: 8 but no one *t* back.
2Co 3: 16 But whenever anyone *t* to the Lord
Heb 3: 12 unbelieving heart that *t* away
Jas 5: 20 Whoever *t* a sinner from the error

TURQUOISE

Ex 28: 18 in the second row a *t*, a sapphire
39: 11 in the second row a *t*, a sapphire
1Ch 29: 2 *t*, stones of various colors,
Isa 54: 11 I will build you with stones of *t*,
Eze 27: 16 they exchanged *t*, purple fabric,
28: 13 sapphire, *t* and beryl.

TUSKS

Eze 27: 15 they paid you with ivory *t*

TWELFTH (TWELVE)

Nu 7: 78 On the *t* day Ahira son of Enan,
1Ki 19: 19 he himself was driving the *t* pair.
2Ki 8: 25 In the *t* year of Joram son
17: 1 In the *t* year of Ahaz king of Judah,
25: 27 twenty-seventh day of the *t* month.
1Ch 24: 12 eleventh to Eliashib, the *t* to Jakim,
25: 19 relatives, 12 the *t* to Hashabiah,
27: 15 The *t*, for the *t* month, was Heldai
2Ch 34: 3 In his *t* year he began
Ezr 8: 31 On the *t* day of the first month we
Est 3: 7 And the lot fell on the *t* month,
3: 7 In the *t* year of King Xerxes,
3: 13 the thirteenth day of the *t* month,
8: 12 the thirteenth day of the *t* month,
9: 1 the thirteenth day of the *t* month,
Jer 52: 31 the twenty-fifth day of the *t* month.
Eze 29: 1 in the tenth month on the *t* day,
32: 1 In the *t* year, in the *t* month
32: 17 In the *t* year, on the fifteenth day
33: 21 In the *t* year of our exile,
Rev 21: 20 jacinth, and the *t* amethyst.

TWELVE (TWELFTH 12 12,000 144,000)

Ge 14: 4 For *t* years they had been subject
17: 20 He will be the father of *t* rulers,
25: 16 of the *t* tribal rulers according
35: 22 Jacob had *t* sons: The sons of Leah:
42: 13 "Your servants were *t* brothers,
42: 32 We were *t* brothers, sons
49: 28 All these are the *t* tribes of Israel,
Ex 15: 27 where there were *t* springs
24: 4 pillars representing the *t* tribes
24: 4 set up *t* stone pillars representing
28: 21 There are to be *t* stones, one
28: 21 with the name of one of the *t* tribes.
39: 14 There were *t* stones, one for each
39: 14 with the name of one of the *t* tribes.
Lev 24: 5 and bake *t* loaves of bread,
Nu 1: 44 Aaron and the *t* leaders of Israel,
7: 3 six covered carts and *t* oxen—
7: 84 sprinkling bowls and *t* gold ladles.
7: 84 *t* silver plates, *t* silver sprinkling
7: 86 The *t* gold ladles filled
7: 87 offering came to *t* young bulls,
7: 87 *T* male goats were used
7: 87 *t* rams and *t* male lambs a year old,
17: 2 and get *t* staffs from them,
17: 6 and their leaders gave him *t* staffs,
29: 17 second day prepare *t* young bulls,
31: 5 So *t* thousand men armed for battle
33: 9 where there were *t* springs
Dt 1: 23 so I selected *t* of you, one man
Jos 3: 12 choose *t* men from the tribes
4: 2 *t* men from among the people,
4: 3 to take up *t* stones from the middle
4: 4 called together the *t* men he had
4: 8 They took *t* stones from the middle
4: 9 Joshua set up the *t* stones that had
4: 20 up at Gilgal the *t* stones they had
8: 25 *T* thousand men and women fell
18: 24 *t* towns and their villages.
19: 15 There were *t* towns and their
21: 7 received *t* towns from the tribes
21: 40 the rest of the Levites, were *t*.
Jdg 19: 29 into *t* parts and sent them
21: 10 assembly sent *t* thousand fighting
2Sa 2: 15 son of Saul, and *t* for David.
2: 15 *t* men for Benjamin
10: 6 and also *t* thousand men from Tob.
17: 1 "I would choose *t* thousand men
1Ki 4: 7 also had *t* district governors
4: 26 horses, and *t* thousand horses.
7: 15 eighteen cubits high and *t* cubits
7: 25 stood on *t* bulls, three facing north,
7: 44 the Sea and the *t* bulls under it;
10: 20 *T* lions stood on the six steps,
10: 26 chariots and *t* thousand horses,
11: 30 wearing and tore it into *t* pieces.
16: 23 and he reigned *t* years, six of them
18: 31 Elijah took *t* stones, one for each
19: 19 plowing with *t* yoke of oxen,
2Ki 3: 1 of Judah, and he reigned *t* years.
21: 1 Manasseh was *t* years old
1Ch 6: 63 were allotted *t* towns
2Ch 1: 14 chariots and *t* thousand horses,
4: 4 stood on *t* bulls, three facing north,
4: 15 the Sea and the *t* bulls under it;
9: 19 *T* lions stood on the six steps,
9: 25 chariots, and *t* thousand horses,
12: 3 With *t* hundred chariots
33: 1 Manasseh was *t* years old
Ezr 6: 17 offering for all Israel, *t* male goats,
8: 24 I set apart *t* of the leading priests,
8: 35 and as a sin offering, *t* male goats.
8: 35 *t* bulls for all Israel, ninety-six rams
Ne 5: 14 his thirty-second year—*t* years—
Est 2: 12 she had to complete *t* months
Jer 52: 20 and the *t* bronze bulls under it,
52: 21 and *t* cubits in circumference;
Eze 40: 49 and *t* cubits from front to back.
43: 16 *t* cubits long and *t* cubits wide.
47: 13 among the *t* tribes of Israel,
Da 4: 29 *T* months later, as the king was
Mt 9: 20 to bleeding for *t* years came up
10: 1 He called his *t* disciples to him
10: 2 are the names of the *t* apostles:
10: 5 These *t* Jesus sent out
11: 1 finished instructing his *t* disciples,
14: 20 the disciples picked up *t* basketfuls
19: 28 judging the *t* tribes of Israel.
19: 28 me will also sit on *t* thrones,
20: 17 he took the *t* disciples aside
26: 14 one of the *T*— the one called Judas
26: 20 reclining at the table with the *T*.
26: 47 Judas, one of the *T*, arrived.
26: 53 more than *t* legions of angels?
Mk 3: 14 He appointed *t*— designating them
3: 16 These are the *t* he appointed:
4: 10 the *T* and the others
5: 25 subject to bleeding for *t* years.
5: 42 walked around (she was *t* years old
6: 7 Calling the *T* to him, he sent them
6: 43 the disciples picked up *t* basketfuls
8: 19 of pieces did you pick up?" "*T*,"
9: 35 Jesus called the *T* and said,
10: 32 Again he took the *T* aside
11: 11 he went out to Bethany with the *T*.
14: 10 Then Judas Iscariot, one of the *T*,
14: 17 came, Jesus arrived with the *T*.
14: 20 "It is one of the *T*," he replied,
14: 43 Judas, one of the *T*, appeared.
Lk 2: 42 When he was *t* years old, they went
6: 13 to him and chose *t* of them,
8: 1 The *T* were with him, and
8: 42 a girl of about *t*, was dying.
8: 43 subject to bleeding for *t* years,
9: 1 Jesus had called the *T* together,
9: 12 in the afternoon the *T* came to him
9: 17 the disciples picked up *t* basketfuls
18: 31 Jesus took the *T* aside
22: 3 called Iscariot, one of the *T*.
22: 30 judging the *t* tribes of Israel.
22: 47 one of the *T*, was leading them.
Jn 6: 13 and filled *t* baskets with the pieces
6: 67 do you?" Jesus asked the *T*.
6: 70 "Have I not chosen you, the *T*?
6: 71 who, though one of the *T*,
11: 9 "Are there not *t* hours of daylight?
20: 24 (called Didymus), one of the *T*,
Ac 6: 2 So the *T* gathered all the disciples
7: 8 the father of the *t* patriarchs.
19: 7 There were about *t* men in all.
24: 11 more than *t* days ago I went up
26: 7 the promise our *t* tribes are hoping
1Co 15: 5 to Peter, and then to the *T*.
Jas 1: 1 To the *t* tribes scattered
Rev 12: 1 and a crown of *t* stars on her head.
21: 12 It had a great, high wall with *t* gates
21: 12 and with *t* angels at the gates.
21: 12 the names of the *t* tribes of Israel.
21: 14 of the *t* apostles of the Lamb.
21: 14 wall of the city had *t* foundations,
21: 21 The *t* gates were *t* pearls, each gate
22: 2 bearing *t* crops of fruit, yielding its

TWIG (TWIGS)

Hos 10: 7 like a *t* on the surface of the waters.

TWIGS (TWIG)

Isa 27: 11 When its *t* are dry, they are broken
64: 2 As when fire sets *t* ablaze
Mt 24: 32 As soon as its *t* get tender
Mk 13: 28 As soon as its *t* get tender

TWILIGHT

Ex 12: 6 of Israel must slaughter them at *t*.
16: 12 Tell them, 'At *t* you will eat meat,
29: 39 in the morning and the other at *t*.
29: 41 Sacrifice the other lamb at *t*
30: 8 at *t* so incense will burn regularly
Lev 23: 5 begins at *t* on the fourteenth day
Nu 9: 3 at *t* on the fourteenth day
9: 5 of Sinai at *t* on the fourteenth day
9: 11 day of the second month at *t*.
28: 4 in the morning and the other at *t*,
28: 8 Prepare the second lamb at *t*,
Pr 7: 9 house at *t*, as the day was fading,
Isa 21: 4 the *t* I longed for
59: 10 midday we stumble as if it were *t*;

TWIN (TWINS)

Ge 25: 24 there were *t* boys in her womb.
38: 27 there were *t* boys in her womb.
SS 4: 2 Each has its *t*;
4: 5 like *t* fawns of a gazelle
6: 6 Each has its *t*,
Ac 28: 11 the figurehead of the *t* gods Castor

TWINKLING

1Co 15: 52 in a flash, in the *t* of an eye,

TWINS (TWIN)

SS 7: 3 *t* of a gazelle.
Ro 9: 11 before the *t* were born

UNCHANGING (UNCHANGED)

Heb 6: 17 wanted to make the *u* nature

UNCHECKED

Am 1: 11 and his fury flamed *u*,

UNCIRCUMCISED

Ge 17: 14 Any *u* male, who has not been
Ex 12: 48 No *u* male may eat of it.
Lev 26: 41 when their *u* hearts are humbled
Jos 5: 7 They were still *u* because they had
Jdg 14: 3 Must you go to the *u* Philistines
15: 18 and fall into the hands of the *u*?"
1Sa 14: 6 to the outpost of those *u* fellows.
17: 26 Who is this *u* Philistine that he
17: 36 this *u* Philistine will be like one
31: 4 or these *u* fellows will come
2Sa 1: 20 lest the daughters of the *u* rejoice.
1Ch 10: 4 or these *u* fellows will come
Isa 52: 1 The *u* and defiled
Jer 9: 26 For all these nations are really *u*,
9: 26 house of Israel is *u* in heart."
Eze 28: 10 You will die the death of the *u*
31: 18 lie among the *u*, with those killed
32: 19 Go down and be laid among the *u*.'
32: 21 come down and they lie with the *u*,
32: 24 went down *u* to the earth below.
32: 25 All of them are *u*, killed
32: 26 All of them are *u*, killed
32: 27 with the other *u* warriors who have
32: 28 be broken and will lie among the *u*,
32: 29 They lie with the *u*,
32: 30 They lie *u* with those killed
32: 32 his hordes will be laid among the *u*,
44: 7 you brought foreigners *u* in heart
44: 9 No foreigner *u* in heart
Ac 7: 51 stiff-necked people, with *u* hearts
11: 3 "You went into the house of *u* men
Ro 3: 30 and the *u* through that same faith.
4: 9 the circumcised, or also for the *u*?
4: 11 had by faith while he was still *u*.
1Co 7: 18 Was a man *u* when he was called?
7: 18 called? He should not become *u*.
Eph 2: 11 and called "*u*" by those who call
Col 3: 11 circumcised or *u*, barbarian,

UNCIRCUMCISION

1Co 7: 19 is nothing and *u* is nothing.
Gal 5: 6 neither circumcision nor *u* has any
6: 15 circumcision nor *u* means
Col 2: 13 and in the *u* of your sinful nature,

UNCLE (UNCLE'S)

Lev 10: 4 sons of Aaron's *u* Uzziel,
20: 20 his aunt, he has dishonored his *u*.
25: 49 *u* or a cousin or any blood relative
1Sa 10: 14 Now Saul's *u* asked him
10: 15 Saul's *u* said, "Tell me what
10: 16 did not tell his *u* what Samuel had
14: 50 son of Ner, and Ner was Saul's *u*.
2Ki 24: 17 made Mattaniah, Jehoiachin's *u*,
1Ch 27: 32 David's *u*, was a counselor,
2Ch 36: 10 and he made Jehoiachin's *u*,
Est 2: 15 the daughter of his *u* Abihail) to go
Jer 32: 7 of Shallum your *u* is going to come

UNCLE'S (UNCLE)

Ge 29: 10 of the well and watered his *u* sheep

UNCLEAN (UNCLEANNESS)

Ge 7: 2 and two of every kind of *u* animal,
7: 8 Pairs of clean and *u* animals,
Lev 5: 2 he has become *u* and is guilty.
5: 2 or of *u* creatures that move
5: 2 the carcasses of *u* wild animals
5: 2 touches anything ceremonially *u*—
5: 2 wild animals or of *u* livestock
5: 3 anything that would make him *u*—
7: 19 anything ceremonially *u* must not
7: 20 if anyone who is *u* eats any meat
7: 21 If anyone touches something *u*—
7: 21 or an *u* animal or any *u*,
10: 10 between the *u* and the clean,
11: 4 it is ceremonially *u* for you.
11: 5 does not have a split hoof; it is *u*
11: 6 does not have a split hoof; it is *u*
11: 7 does not chew the cud; it is *u*
11: 8 or touch their carcasses; they are *u*
Lev 11: 24 touches their carcasses will be *u*
11: 24 " 'You will make yourselves *u*
11: 25 and he will be *u* till evening.
11: 26 carcass of any of them will be *u*.
11: 26 or that does not chew the cud is *u*
11: 27 touches their carcasses will be *u*
11: 27 walk on their paws are *u* for you;
11: 28 They are *u* for you.
11: 28 and he will be *u* till evening.
11: 29 these are *u* for you: the weasel,
11: 31 move along the ground, these are *u*
11: 31 them when they are dead will be *u*
11: 32 it in water; it will be *u* till evening,
11: 32 whatever its use, will be *u*,
11: 33 everything in it will be *u*,
11: 34 has water on it from such a pot is *u*,
11: 34 that could be drunk from it is *u*.
11: 35 They are *u*, and you are
11: 35 and you are to regard them as *u*.
11: 35 their carcasses falls on becomes *u*;
11: 36 one of these carcasses is *u*.
11: 38 a carcass falls on it, it is *u* for you.
11: 39 who touches the carcass will be *u*
11: 40 and he will be *u* till evening.
11: 40 and he will be *u* till evening.
11: 43 Do not make yourselves *u*
11: 43 of them or be made *u* by them.
11: 44 Do not make yourselves *u*
11: 47 must distinguish between the *u*
12: 2 she is *u* during her monthly period.
12: 2 to a son will be ceremonially *u*
12: 5 for two weeks the woman will be *u*,
13: 3 pronounce him ceremonially *u*.
13: 8 he shall pronounce him *u*;
13: 11 in isolation, because he is already *u*
13: 11 the priest shall pronounce him *u*.
13: 14 appears on him, he will be *u*.
13: 15 he shall pronounce him *u*.
13: 15 raw flesh is *u*; he has an infectious
13: 20 the priest shall pronounce him *u*.
13: 22 the priest shall pronounce him *u*;
13: 25 The priest shall pronounce him *u*;
13: 27 the priest shall pronounce him *u*.
13: 30 shall pronounce that person *u*;
13: 36 for yellow hair; the person is *u*.
13: 44 The priest shall pronounce him *u*
13: 44 the man is diseased and is *u*.
13: 45 part of his face and cry out, '*U*!
13: 45 *U*!' As long as he has the infection
13: 46 he has the infection he remains *u*.
13: 51 destructive mildew; the article is *u*.
13: 55 though it has not spread, it is *u*.
13: 59 for pronouncing them clean or *u*.
14: 36 in the house will be pronounced *u*.
14: 40 and thrown into an *u* place
14: 41 scraped off dumped into an *u* place
14: 44 destructive mildew; the house is *u*.
14: 45 taken out of the town to an *u* place.
14: 46 house while it is closed up will be *u*
14: 57 when something is clean or *u*.
15: 2 discharge, the discharge is *u*.
15: 3 or is blocked, it will make him *u*.
15: 4 and anything he sits on will be *u*.
15: 4 with a discharge lies on will be *u*,
15: 5 and he will be *u* till evening.
15: 6 and he will be *u* till evening.
15: 7 and he will be *u* till evening.
15: 8 and he will be *u* till evening.
15: 9 sits on when riding will be *u*,
15: 10 and he will be *u* till evening.
15: 10 under him will be *u* till evening;
15: 11 and he will be *u* till evening.
15: 16 and he will be *u* till evening.
15: 17 and it will be *u* till evening.
15: 18 and they will be *u* till evening.
15: 19 anyone who touches her will be *u*
15: 20 and anything she sits on will be *u*.
15: 20 lies on during her period will be *u*,
15: 21 and he will be *u* till evening.
15: 22 and he will be *u* till evening.
15: 23 anyone touches it, he will be *u*
15: 24 any bed he lies on will be *u*.
15: 24 he will be *u* for seven days,
15: 25 she will be *u* as long as she has
15: 26 and anything she sits on will be *u*,
15: 26 her discharge continues will be *u*,
15: 27 Whoever touches them will be *u*;
15: 27 and he will be *u* till evening.
Lev 15: 31 from things that make them *u*,
15: 32 for anyone made *u* by an emission
15: 33 a woman who is ceremonially *u*.
17: 15 and he will be *u* till evening;
20: 25 and *u* animals and between *u*
20: 25 those which I have set apart as *u*
21: 1 not make himself ceremonially *u*
21: 3 for her he may make himself *u*.
21: 4 He must not make himself *u*
21: 11 He must not make himself *u*,
22: 3 your descendants is ceremonially *u*
22: 4 also be *u* if he touches something
22: 5 crawling thing that makes him *u*,
22: 5 or any person who makes him *u*,
22: 6 touches any such thing will be *u*
22: 8 and so become *u* through it.
27: 11 is a ceremonially *u* animal—
27: 27 If it is one of the *u* animals,
Nu 5: 2 or who is ceremonially *u*
6: 7 not make himself ceremonially *u*
9: 6 because they were ceremonially *u*
9: 7 "We have become *u*
9: 10 or your descendants are *u*
18: 15 every firstborn male of *u* animals.
19: 7 but he will be ceremonially *u*
19: 8 and he too will be *u* till evening.
19: 10 and he too will be *u* till evening.
19: 11 of anyone will be *u* for seven days.
19: 13 he is *u*; his uncleanness remains
19: 14 is in it will be *u* for seven days,
19: 15 a lid fastened on it will be *u*.
19: 16 or a grave, will be *u* for seven days.
19: 17 "For the *u* person, put some ashes
19: 19 is to sprinkle the *u* person
19: 20 a person who is *u* does not purify
19: 20 sprinkled on him, and he is *u*.
19: 21 of cleansing will be *u* till evening.
19: 22 an *u* person touches becomes *u*,
19: 22 anyone who touches it becomes *u*
Dt 12: 15 Both the ceremonially *u*
12: 22 Both the ceremonially *u*
14: 7 they are ceremonially *u* for you.
14: 8 also *u*; although it has a split hoof,
14: 10 you may not eat; for you it is *u*.
14: 19 All flying insects that swarm are *u*
15: 22 Both the ceremonially *u*
23: 10 If one of your men is *u*
26: 14 any of it while I was *u*,
Jdg 13: 4 and that you do not eat anything *u*,
13: 7 and do not eat anything *u*,
13: 14 drink nor eat anything *u*
1Sa 20: 26 ceremonially *u*— surely he is *u*."
2Ch 23: 19 was in any way *u* might enter.
29: 16 temple everything *u* that they
Ezr 2: 62 excluded from the priesthood as *u*.
6: 21 themselves from the *u* practices
Ne 7: 64 excluded from the priesthood as *u*.
Ecc 9: 2 and the bad, the clean and the *u*,
Isa 6: 5 and I live among a people of *u* lips,
6: 5 ruined! For I am a man of *u* lips,
35: 8 The *u* will not journey on it;
52: 11 Touch no *u* thing!
64: 6 us have become like one who is *u*,
65: 4 whose pots hold broth of *u* meat;
Jer 13: 27 How long will you be *u*?"
La 1: 8 and so has become *u*.
1: 17 an *u* thing among them.
4: 15 You are *u*!" men cry to them.
Eze 4: 14 No *u* meat has ever entered my
7: 19 and their gold will be an *u* thing.
7: 20 these into an *u* thing for them.
22: 10 when they are ceremonially *u*.
22: 26 is no difference between the *u*
44: 23 how to distinguish between the *u*
Hos 9: 3 and eat *u* food in Assyria.
9: 4 all who eat them will be *u*.
Mt 15: 11 mouth does not make him '*u*,'
15: 11 that is what makes him '*u*.' "
15: 18 and these make a man '*u*.'
15: 20 These are what make a man '*u*';
15: 20 hands does not make him '*u*.' "
23: 27 men's bones and everything *u*.
Mk 7: 2 of his disciples eating food with "*u*
7: 5 of eating their food with '*u*' hands
7: 15 out of a man that makes him '*u*.' "
7: 15 outside a man can make him '*u*'
7: 18 from the outside can make him '*u*'?
7: 20 out of a man is what makes him '*u*.'

Mk 7: 23 from inside and make a man '*u*.' "
Ac 10: 14 never eaten anything impure or *u*."
10: 28 not call any man impure or *u*.
11: 8 or *u* has ever entered my mouth.'
Ro 14: 14 fully convinced that no food is *u*
14: 14 something as *u*, then for him it is *u*.
1Co 7: 14 your children would be *u*,
2Co 6: 17 Touch no *u* thing,
Heb 9: 13 are ceremonially *u* sanctify them
Rev 18: 2 for every *u* and detestable bird.

UNCLEANNESS (UNCLEAN)

Lev 5: 3 " 'Or if he touches human *u*—
7: 21 human *u* or an unclean animal
14: 19 the one to be cleansed from his *u*.
15: 3 his discharge will bring about *u*:
15: 30 LORD for the *u* of her discharge.
15: 31 in their *u* for defiling my dwelling
16: 16 among them in the midst of their *u*.
16: 16 because of the *u* and rebellion
16: 19 it from the *u* of the Israelites.
18: 19 during the *u* of her monthly period.
22: 5 unclean, whatever the *u* may be.
Nu 19: 13 he is unclean; his *u* remains on him
2Sa 11: 4 She had purified herself from her *u*
Eze 22: 15 and I will put an end to your *u*.
36: 17 was like a woman's monthly *u*
36: 29 I will save you from all your *u*.
39: 24 with them according to their *u*
Jn 18: 28 to avoid ceremonial *u* the Jews did

UNCLOTHED

2Co 5: 4 because we do not wish to be *u*

UNCONCERNED

Eze 16: 49 were arrogant, overfed and *u*;

UNCOVER (UNCOVERED UNCOVERS)

Ru 3: 4 Then go and *u* his feet and lie down
Jer 49: 10 I will *u* his hiding places,

UNCOVERED (UNCOVER)

Ge 9: 21 he became drunk and lay *u*
44: 16 God has *u* your servants' guilt.
Lev 20: 18 of her flow, and she has also *u* it.
Ru 3: 7 Ruth approached quietly, *u* his feet
Job 26: 6 Destruction lies *u*.
Isa 47: 3 and your shame *u*.
57: 8 Forsaking me, you *u* your bed,
Eze 16: 57 before your wickedness was *u*.
Hab 3: 9 You *u* your bow,
1Co 11: 5 with her head *u* dishonors her head
11: 13 to pray to God with her head *u*?
Heb 4: 13 Everything is *u* and laid bare

UNCOVERS (UNCOVER)

Ex 21: 33 "If a man *u* a pit or digs one
Isa 22: 6 Kir *u* the shield.

UNCUT

Jos 8: 31 an altar of *u* stones,
Job 8: 12 While still growing and *u*,

UNDENIABLE

Ac 19: 36 Therefore, since these facts are *u*,

UNDEPENDABLE

Job 6: 15 as *u* as intermittent streams,

UNDERBRUSH

Job 30: 7 and huddled in the *u*.
Isa 17: 9 abandoned to thickets and *u*.

UNDERFOOT (FOOT)

2Ki 9: 33 the horses as they trampled her *u*.
14: 9 and trampled the thistle *u*.
2Ch 25: 18 and trampled the thistle *u*.
Isa 14: 19 Like a corpse trampled *u*,
28: 3 will be trampled *u*.
La 3: 34 To crush *u*
Da 7: 7 and trampled *u* whatever was left.
7: 19 and trampled *u* whatever was left.
8: 13 of the host that will be trampled *u*
Mic 7: 10 even now she will be trampled *u*
7: 19 you will tread our sins *u*

UNDERGARMENT (GARMENT)

Jn 19: 23 of them, with the *u* remaining.

UNDERGARMENTS (GARMENT)

Ex 28: 42 "Make linen *u* as a covering
39: 28 and the *u* of finely twisted linen.
Lev 6: 10 with linen *u* next to his body,
16: 4 with linen *u* next to his body;
Eze 44: 18 and linen *u* around their waists.

UNDERGO (UNDERGOES UNDERGOING)

Ge 17: 11 You are to *u* circumcision,
Lk 12: 50 But I have a baptism to *u*,

UNDERGOES (UNDERGO)

Heb 12: 8 (and everyone *u* discipline),

UNDERGOING (UNDERGO)

1Pe 5: 9 the world are *u* the same kind

UNDERLINGS

2Ki 19: 6 words with which the *u* of the king
Isa 37: 6 words with which the *u* of the king

UNDERMINE

Job 15: 4 But you even *u* piety

UNDERSIDES

Job 41: 30 His *u* are jagged potsherds,

UNDERSTAND (UNDERSTANDING UNDERSTANDS UNDERSTOOD)

Ge 11: 7 so they will not *u* each other."
42: 23 realize that Joseph could *u* them,
Dt 9: 6 *U*, then, that it is not
28: 49 whose language you will not *u*,
32: 29 they were wise and would *u* this
1Sa 24: 11 Now *u* and recognize that I am not
28: 1 "You must *u* that you
2Ki 18: 26 servants in Aramaic, since we *u* it.
Ne 8: 2 women and all who were able to *u*.
8: 3 women and others who could *u*.
8: 8 the people could *u* what was being
10: 28 and daughters who are able to *u*—
Job 26: 14 Who then can *u* the thunder
32: 9 only the aged who *u* what is right.
36: 29 Who can *u* how he spreads out
38: 4 Tell me, if you *u*.
42: 3 Surely I spoke of things I did not *u*,
Ps 14: 2 men to see if there are any who *u*,
53: 2 men to see if there are any who *u*,
73: 16 When I tried to *u* all this,
81: 5 we heard a language we did not *u*.
82: 5 know nothing, they *u* nothing.
92: 6 fools do not *u*,
119: 27 Let me *u* the teaching
119: 79 those who *u* your statutes.
119:125 that I may *u* your statutes.
Pr 2: 5 then you will *u* the fear
2: 9 Then you will *u* what is right
20: 24 then can anyone *u* his own way?
28: 5 Evil men do not *u* justice,
28: 5 who seek the LORD *u* it fully.
30: 18 four that I do not *u*:
Ecc 7: 25 So I turned my mind to *u*,
7: 25 to *u* the stupidity of wickedness
11: 5 so you cannot *u* the work of God,
Isa 1: 3 my people do not *u*."
6: 10 *u* with their hearts,
32: 4 of the rash will know and *u*,
36: 11 servants in Aramaic, since we *u* it.
41: 20 may consider and *u*,
42: 25 them in flames, yet they did not *u*;
43: 10 and *u* that I am he.
44: 18 know nothing, they *u* nothing;
44: 18 minds closed so they cannot *u*.
52: 15 they have not heard, they will *u*.
Jer 5: 15 whose speech you do not *u*.
9: 12 What man is wise enough to *u* this?
15: 15 You *u*, O LORD;
17: 9 Who can *u* it?
23: 20 you will *u* it clearly.
30: 24 you will *u* this.
31: 19 after I came to *u*,
Eze 3: 6 whose words you cannot *u*.
12: 3 Perhaps they will *u*, though they
Da 1: 4 well informed, quick to *u*,
1: 17 And Daniel could *u* visions
2: 30 and that you may *u* what went
5: 23 which cannot see or hear or *u*.
8: 15 the vision and trying to *u* it,
8: 17 *u* that the vision concerns the time
9: 23 the message and *u* the vision:
9: 25 and *u* this: From the issuing
12: 8 I heard, but I did not *u*.
12: 10 None of the wicked will *u*,
12: 10 but those who are wise will *u*.
Hos 14: 9 Who is discerning? He will *u* them.
Mic 4: 12 they do not *u* his plan,
Mt 13: 13 hearing, they do not hear or *u*.
13: 15 *u* with their hearts
13: 19 the kingdom and does not *u* it,
15: 10 to him and said, "Listen and *u*.
16: 9 you still not *u*? Don't you
16: 11 How is it you don't *u* that I was not
24: 15 Daniel—let the reader *u*—
24: 43 But *u* this: If the owner
Mk 4: 13 How then will you *u* any parable?
4: 13 "Don't you *u* this parable?
4: 33 as much as they could *u*.
7: 14 Listen to me, everyone, and *u* this.
8: 17 or *u*? Are your hearts hardened?
8: 21 "Do you still not *u*?" They came
9: 32 But they did not *u* what he meant
13: 14 let the reader *u*— then let those
14: 68 or *u* what you're talking about,"
Lk 2: 50 they did not *u* what he was saying
8: 10 though hearing, they may not *u*.'
9: 45 But they did not *u* what this meant.
12: 39 But *u* this: If the owner
18: 34 The disciples did not *u* any of this.
24: 45 so they could *u* the Scriptures.
Jn 3: 10 "and do you not *u* these things?
8: 27 They did not *u* that he was telling
10: 6 they did not *u* what he was telling
10: 38 and *u* that the Father is in me,
12: 16 first his disciples did not *u* all this.
12: 40 nor *u* with their hearts,
13: 7 I am doing, but later you will *u*."
13: 12 Do you *u* what I have done for you
16: 18 We don't *u* what he is saying."
20: 9 (They still did not *u*
Ac 8: 30 "Do you *u* what you are reading?"
22: 9 but they did not *u* the voice
28: 27 *u* with their hearts
Ro 7: 15 I do not *u* what I do.
10: 19 did Israel not *u*? First, Moses says,
15: 21 those who have not heard will *u*."
1Co 2: 12 that we may *u* what God has freely
2: 14 and he cannot *u* them,
14: 16 those who do not *u* say "Amen"
14: 23 and some who do not *u*
14: 24 or someone who does not *u* comes
2Co 1: 13 you anything you cannot read or *u*.
1: 14 come to *u* fully that you can boast
Gal 3: 7 *U*, then, that those who believe are
Eph 3: 4 you will be able to *u* my insight
5: 17 but *u* what the Lord's will is.
Heb 11: 3 By faith we *u* that the universe was
2Pe 1: 20 you must *u* that no prophecy
2: 12 in matters they do not *u*.
3: 3 you must *u* that in the last days
3: 9 his promise, as some *u* slowness.
3: 16 some things that are hard to *u*,
Jude : 10 against whatever they do not *u*;
: 10 what things they do *u* by instinct,

UNDERSTANDING (UNDERSTAND)

Dt 1: 13 *u* and respected men from each
4: 6 nation is a wise and *u* people."
4: 6 this will show your wisdom and *u*
32: 21 angry by a nation that has no *u*.
Jdg 13: 18 you ask my name? It is beyond *u*."
1Ki 4: 29 and a breadth of *u* as measureless
1Ch 22: 12 *u* when he puts you in command
28: 19 and he gave me *u* in all the details
2Ch 30: 22 who showed good *u* of the service
Job 8: 10 not bring forth words from their *u*?
12: 12 Does not long life bring *u*?
12: 13 counsel and *u* are his.
17: 4 You have closed their minds to *u*;
20: 3 and my *u* inspires me to reply.
28: 12 Where does *u* dwell?
28: 20 Where does *u* dwell?
28: 28 and to shun evil is *u*.' "
32: 8 of the Almighty, that gives him *u*.

Job 34: 10 "So listen to me, you men of *u*.
34: 16 "If you have *u*, hear this;
34: 34 "Men of *u* declare,
36: 26 How great is God—beyond our *u*!
37: 5 he does great things beyond our *u*
38: 36 or gave *u* to the mind?
Ps 32: 9 which have no *u*
49: 3 from my heart will give *u*.
49: 20 A man who has riches without *u*
111: 10 follow his precepts have good *u*.
119: 34 Give me *u*, and I will keep your law
119: 73 give me *u* to learn your commands.
119:100 I have more *u* than the elders,
119:104 I gain *u* from your precepts;
119:130 it gives *u* to the simple.
119:144 give me *u* that I may live.
119:169 give me *u* according to your word.
136: 5 who by his *u* made the heavens,
147: 5 his *u* has no limit.
Pr 1: 2 for *u* words of insight;
1: 6 for *u* proverbs and parables,
2: 2 and applying your heart to *u*,
2: 3 and cry aloud for *u*,
2: 6 his mouth come knowledge and *u*.
2: 11 and *u* will guard you.
3: 5 and lean not on your own *u*;
3: 13 the man who gains *u*,
3: 19 by *u* he set the heavens in place;
4: 1 pay attention and gain *u*.
4: 5 Get wisdom, get *u*;
4: 7 Though it cost all you have, get *u*.
7: 4 and call *u* your kinsman;
8: 1 Does not *u* raise her voice?
8: 5 you who are foolish, gain *u*.
8: 14 I have *u* and power.
9: 6 walk in the way of *u*.
9: 10 knowledge of the Holy One is *u*.
10: 23 but a man of *u* delights in wisdom.
11: 12 but a man of *u* holds his tongue.
13: 15 Good *u* wins favor,
14: 29 A patient man has great *u*,
15: 21 a man of *u* keeps a straight course.
15: 32 whoever heeds correction gains *u*.
16: 16 to choose *u* rather than silver!
16: 22 *U* is a fountain of life
17: 27 and a man of *u* is even-tempered.
18: 2 A fool finds no pleasure in *u*
19: 8 he who cherishes *u* prospers.
20: 5 but a man of *u* draws them out.
21: 16 from the path of *u*
23: 23 get wisdom, discipline and *u*.
24: 3 and through *u* it is established;
28: 2 of *u* and knowledge maintains
30: 2 I do not have a man's *u*.
Ecc 1: 17 I applied myself to the *u* of wisdom
Isa 5: 13 exile for lack of *u*;
6: 9 " 'Be ever hearing, but never *u*;
10: 13 by my wisdom, because I have *u*.
11: 2 the Spirit of wisdom and of *u*,
27: 11 For this is a people without *u*;
28: 19 The *u* of this message
29: 24 in spirit will gain *u*;
40: 14 or showed him the path of *u*?
40: 28 and his *u* no one can fathom.
44: 19 no one has the knowledge or *u*
56: 11 They are shepherds who lack *u*;
Jer 3: 15 you with knowledge and *u*.
4: 22 they have no *u*.
10: 12 stretched out the heavens by his *u*.
51: 15 stretched out the heavens by his *u*.
Eze 28: 4 By your wisdom and *u*
Da 1: 17 and *u* of all kinds of literature
1: 20 *u* about which the king questioned
5: 12 a keen mind and knowledge and *u*,
8: 27 by the vision; it was beyond *u*.
9: 22 come to give you insight and *u*.
10: 1 The *u* of the message came to him
10: 12 that you set your mind to gain *u*
Hos 4: 11 which take away the *u*
4: 14 a people without *u* will come
Ob : 8 men of *u* in the mountains of Esau?
Mt 13: 14 will be ever hearing but never *u*;
Mk 4: 12 and ever hearing but never *u*;
12: 33 with all your *u* and with all your
Lk 2: 47 who heard him was amazed at his *u*
Ac 28: 26 will be ever hearing but never *u*;
Ro 10: 19 angry by a nation that has no *u*."
13: 11 And do this, *u* the present time.
2Co 6: 6 in purity, *u*, patience and kindness;
Eph 1: 8 on us with all wisdom and *u*.
4: 18 They are darkened in their *u*
Php 4: 7 of God, which transcends all *u*,
Col 1: 9 through all spiritual wisdom and *u*.
2: 2 have the full riches of complete *u*,
Phm : 6 so that you will have a full *u*
Jas 3: 13 Who is wise and *u* among you?
1Jn 5: 20 God has come and has given us *u*,

UNDERSTANDS (UNDERSTAND)

Dt 29: 4 has not given you a mind that *u*
1Ch 28: 9 and *u* every motive
Job 28: 23 God *u* the way to it
Pr 29: 19 though he *u*, he will not respond.
Isa 57: 1 and no one *u*
Jer 9: 24 that he *u* and knows me,
Mt 13: 23 man who hears the word and *u* it.
Ro 3: 11 there is no one who *u*,
1Co 14: 2 no one *u* him; he utters mysteries
1Ti 6: 4 he is conceited and *u* nothing.

UNDERSTOOD (UNDERSTAND)

1Ch 12: 32 who *u* the times and knew what
Ne 8: 12 they now *u* the words that had
Est 1: 13 with the wise men who *u* the laws
Job 13: 1 my ears have heard and *u* it.
Ps 73: 17 then I *u* their final destiny.
Isa 40: 13 Who has *u* the Spirit of the LORD,
40: 21 Have you not *u* since the earth was
48: 8 You have neither heard nor *u*;
Da 9: 2 I, Daniel, *u* from the Scriptures,
Mt 13: 51 "Have you *u* all these things?"
16: 12 they *u* that he was not telling them
17: 13 the disciples *u* that he was talking
Mk 6: 52 for they had not *u* about the loaves;
Jn 1: 5 but the darkness has not *u* it.
13: 28 at the meal *u* why Jesus said this
Ro 1: 20 being *u* from what has been made,
1Co 2: 8 None of the rulers of this age *u* it,
2Co 1: 14 I hope that, as you have *u* us in part
Col 1: 6 and *u* God's grace in all its truth.

UNDERTAKEN (UNDERTOOK)

1Ki 7: 40 finished all the work he had *u*
2Ch 4: 11 Huram finished the work he had *u*
Lk 1: 1 Many have *u* to draw up

UNDERTAKES (UNDERTOOK)

Jos 6: 26 before the LORD is the man who *u*

UNDERTOOK (UNDERTAKEN UNDERTAKES)

2Ki 18: 7 he was successful in whatever he *u*.
2Ch 31: 21 In everything that he *u*
32: 30 He succeeded in everything he *u*.
Ecc 2: 4 I *u* great projects: I built houses

UNDESERVED

Pr 26: 2 an *u* curse does not come to rest.

UNDESIRABLE

Jos 24: 15 But if serving the LORD seems *u*

UNDETECTED

Nu 5: 13 her impurity is *u* (since there is no

UNDIGNIFIED

2Sa 6: 22 I will become even more *u*

UNDISCIPLINED

Pr 9: 13 she is *u* and without knowledge.

UNDISTURBED

Job 12: 6 The tents of marauders are *u*,
Isa 32: 18 in *u* places of rest.

UNDIVIDED

1Ch 12: 33 to help David with *u* loyalty—
Ps 86: 11 give me an *u* heart,
Eze 11: 19 I will give them an *u* heart
1Co 7: 35 way in *u* devotion to the Lord.

UNDOING (UNDONE)

2Ch 22: 4 they became his advisers, to his *u*.
Pr 18: 7 A fool's mouth is his *u*,

UNDONE (UNDOING)

Jos 11: 15 he left nothing *u* of all that
Lk 11: 42 latter without leaving the former *u*.

UNDYING

Eph 6: 24 Lord Jesus Christ with an *u* love.

UNEATEN

Job 20: 18 for he must give back *u*;

UNENDING

Jer 15: 18 Why is my pain *u*

UNEQUALED

Mt 24: 21 *u* from the beginning of the world
Mk 13: 19 of distress *u* from the beginning,

UNFADING

1Pe 3: 4 the *u* beauty of a gentle

UNFAILING

Ex 15: 13 "In your *u* love you will lead
1Sa 20: 14 But show me *u* kindness like that
2Sa 22: 51 he shows *u* kindness
Ps 6: 4 save me because of your *u* love.
13: 5 But I trust in your *u* love;
18: 50 he shows *u* kindness
21: 7 through the *u* love
31: 16 save me in your *u* love.
32: 10 but the LORD's *u* love
33: 5 the earth is full of his *u* love.
33: 18 those whose hope is in his *u* love,
33: 22 May your *u* love rest upon us,
36: 7 How priceless is your *u* love!
44: 26 redeem us because of your *u* love.
48: 9 we meditate on your *u* love.
51: 1 according to your *u* love;
52: 8 I trust in God's *u* love
77: 8 Has his *u* love vanished forever?
85: 7 Show us your *u* love, O LORD,
90: 14 in the morning with your *u* love,
107: 8 thanks to the LORD for his *u* love
107: 15 thanks to the LORD for his *u* love
107: 21 to the LORD for his *u* love
107: 31 to the LORD for his *u* love
119: 41 May your *u* love come to me,
119: 76 May your *u* love be my comfort,
130: 7 for with the LORD is *u* love
143: 8 bring me word of your *u* love,
143: 12 In your *u* love, silence my enemies;
147: 11 who put their hope in his *u* love.
Pr 19: 22 What a man desires is *u* love;
20: 6 Many a man claims to have *u* love,
Isa 54: 10 yet my *u* love for you will not be
La 3: 32 so great is his *u* love.
Hos 10: 12 reap the fruit of *u* love,

UNFAIR

Mt 20: 13 'Friend, I am not being *u* to you.

UNFAITHFUL (UNFAITHFULLY UNFAITHFULNESS)

Lev 6: 2 is *u* to the LORD by deceiving his
Nu 5: 6 and so is *u* to the LORD,
5: 12 and is *u* to him by sleeping
5: 27 and been *u* to her husband,
Dt 32: 20 children who are *u*.
Jdg 19: 2 But she was *u* to him.
1Ch 5: 25 But they were *u* to the God
10: 13 because he was *u* to the LORD;
2Ch 12: 2 Because they had been *u*
26: 16 He was *u* to the LORD his God,
26: 18 for you have been *u*;
28: 19 and had been most *u* to the LORD.
28: 22 even more *u* to the LORD.
29: 6 Our fathers were *u*; they did evil
30: 7 who were *u* to the LORD,
36: 14 people became more and more *u*,
Ezr 10: 2 "We have been *u* to our God
10: 10 "You have been *u*; you have
Ne 1: 8 'If you are *u*, I will scatter you
13: 27 and are being *u* to our God
Job 31: 28 for I would have been *u* to God
Ps 73: 27 you destroy all who are *u* to you.
Pr 2: 22 and the *u* will be torn from it.
11: 3 the *u* are destroyed
11: 6 the *u* are trapped by evil desires.
13: 2 the *u* have a craving for violence.
13: 15 but the way of the *u* is hard.
21: 18 and the *u* for the upright.

Pr 22: 12 but he frustrates the words of the *u*.
23: 28 and multiplies the *u* among men.
25: 19 is reliance on the *u* in times
Jer 3: 7 and her *u* sister Judah saw it.
3: 8 I saw that her *u* sister Judah had no
3: 10 her *u* sister Judah did not return
3: 11 is more righteous than *u* Judah.
3: 20 But like a woman *u* to her husband,
3: 20 so you have been *u* to me,
5: 11 have been utterly *u* to me,"
9: 2 a crowd of *u* people.
31: 22 O *u* daughter?
49: 4 O *u* daughter,
Eze 14: 13 sins against me by being *u*
15: 8 desolate because they have been *u*,
17: 20 upon him there because he was *u*
39: 23 because they were *u* to me.
Hos 2: 5 Their mother has been *u*
4: 12 they are *u* to their God.
5: 7 They are *u* to the LORD;
6: 7 they were *u* to me there.
9: 1 For you have been *u* to your God;

UNFAITHFULLY (UNFAITHFUL)

Jos 7: 1 But the Israelites acted *u* in regard
22: 20 acted *u* regarding the devoted
22: 31 because you have not acted *u*

UNFAITHFULNESS (UNFAITHFUL)

Nu 14: 33 suffering for your *u*, until the last
1Ch 9: 1 to Babylon because of their *u*.
2Ch 29: 19 removed in his *u* while he was king.
33: 19 as well as all his sins and *u*,
Ezr 9: 2 officials have led the way in this *u*
9: 4 because of this *u* of the exiles.
10: 6 to mourn over the *u* of the exiles.
Eze 18: 24 Because of the *u* he is guilty of and
39: 26 all the *u* they showed toward me
Da 9: 7 have scattered us because of our *u*
Hos 1: 2 adulterous wife and children of *u*,
2: 2 and the *u* from between her breasts
Mt 5: 32 except for marital *u*, causes her
19: 9 for marital *u*, and marries another

UNFAMILIAR

Isa 42: 16 along *u* paths I will guide them;

UNFANNED

Job 20: 26 A fire *u* will consume him

UNFAVORABLE

Jer 42: 6 Whether it is favorable or *u*,

UNFEELING

Ps 119: 70 Their hearts are callous and *u*,

UNFILLED

Jer 14: 3 They return with their jars *u*;

UNFINISHED

Tit 1: 5 straighten out what was left *u*

UNFIT

Tit 1: 16 and *u* for doing anything good.

UNFORGIVING

2Ti 3: 3 unholy, without love, *u*, slanderous

UNFORMED

Ps 139: 16 your eyes saw my *u* body.

UNFRIENDLY

Pr 18: 1 An *u* man pursues selfish ends;

UNFRUITFUL

Mt 13: 22 of wealth choke it, making it *u*.
Mk 4: 19 and choke the word, making it *u*.
1Co 14: 14 my spirit prays, but my mind is *u*.

UNFULFILLED

Eze 19: 5 " 'When she saw her hope *u*,

UNFURLED

Ps 60: 4 to be *u* against the bow.

UNGODLINESS (UNGODLY)

Isa 32: 6 He practices *u*
Jer 23: 15 *u* has spread throughout the land."
Tit 2: 12 It teaches us to say "No" to *u*

UNGODLY (UNGODLINESS)

Job 17: 8 innocent are aroused against the *u*.
Ps 35: 16 Like the *u* they maliciously
43: 1 plead my cause against an *u* nation;
Pr 11: 31 how much more the *u*
Isa 9: 17 for everyone is *u* and wicked,
Ro 5: 6 powerless, Christ died for the *u*.
1Co 6: 1 it before the *u* for judgment instead
1Ti 1: 9 the *u* and sinful, the unholy
2Ti 2: 16 in it will become more and more *u*.
1Pe 4: 18 what will become of the *u*
2Pe 2: 5 brought the flood on its *u* people,
2: 6 of what is going to happen to the *u*;
3: 7 and destruction of *u* men.
Jude : 15 acts they have done in the *u* way,
: 15 and to convict all the *u*
: 15 of all the *u* acts they have done
: 15 the harsh words *u* sinners have
: 18 will follow their own *u* desires."

UNGRATEFUL

Lk 6: 35 he is kind to the *u* and wicked.
2Ti 3: 2 disobedient to their parents, *u*,

UNHARMED

1Sa 24: 19 does he let him get away *u*?
2Sa 17: 3 of all; all the people will be *u*."
Ps 55: 18 He ransoms me *u*
Da 3: 25 *u*, and the fourth looks like a son

UNHEALTHY

1Ti 6: 4 He has an *u* interest

UNHEARD-OF

Eze 7: 5 Disaster! An *u* disaster is coming.
Da 11: 36 will say *u* things against the God

UNHOLY

1Ti 1: 9 and sinful, the *u* and irreligious;
2Ti 3: 2 ungrateful, *u*, without love,
Heb 10: 29 as an *u* thing the blood

UNIMPRESSIVE

2Co 10: 10 in person he is *u* and his speaking

UNINFORMED

2Co 1: 8 We do not want you to be *u*,

UNINTENTIONAL (UNINTENTIONALLY)

Nu 15: 26 were involved in the *u* wrong.

UNINTENTIONALLY (UNINTENTIONAL)

Lev 4: 2 'When anyone sins *u* and does
4: 13 whole Israelite community sins *u*
4: 22 " 'When a leader sins *u*
4: 27 a member of the community sins *u*
5: 15 and sins *u* in regard to any
5: 18 for the wrong he has committed *u*,
Nu 15: 22 " 'Now if you *u* fail to keep any
15: 24 is done *u* without the community
15: 27 " 'But if just one person sins *u*,
15: 28 for the one who erred by sinning *u*,
15: 29 applies to everyone who sins *u*,
35: 22 or throws something at him *u* or,
Dt 4: 42 flee if he had *u* killed his neighbor
19: 4 one who kills his neighbor *u*,
Jos 20: 3 person accidentally and *u* may flee
20: 5 because he killed his neighbor *u*
Eze 45: 20 of the month for anyone who sins *u*

UNION (UNITE)

Zec 11: 7 called one Favor and the other *U*,
11: 14 I broke my second staff called *U*,
Mt 1: 25 But he had no *u* with her

UNIQUE

SS 6: 9 but my dove, my perfect one, is *u*,
Zec 14: 7 It will be a *u* day, without daytime

UNISON (UNITE)

2Ch 5: 13 trumpeters and singers joined in *u*,
Ac 19: 34 they all shouted in *u*

UNIT (UNITS)

Ex 26: 6 so that the tabernacle is a *u*.
26: 11 to fasten the tent together as a *u*.
36: 13 so that the tabernacle was a *u*.
36: 18 to fasten the tent together as a *u*.

1Sa 17: 18 to the commander of their *u*.
1Co 12: 12 body is a *u*, though it is made up

UNITE (REUNITED UNION UNISON UNITED UNITES UNITY)

1Ch 12: 17 I am ready to have you *u* with me.
Job 16: 10 and *u* together against me.
Isa 14: 1 and *u* with the house of Jacob.
1Co 6: 15 and *u* them with a prostitute?

UNITED (UNITE)

Ge 2: 24 and mother and be *u* to his wife,
Jdg 20: 11 and *u* as one man against the city.
Da 2: 43 be a mixture and will not remain *u*,
Mt 19: 5 and mother and be *u* to his wife,
Mk 10: 7 and mother and be *u* to his wife,
Ac 18: 12 the Jews made a *u* attack on Paul
Ro 6: 5 If we have been *u* with him
6: 5 be *u* with him in his resurrection.
1Co 1: 10 and that you may be perfectly *u*
Eph 5: 31 and mother and be *u* to his wife,
Php 2: 1 from being *u* with Christ,
Col 2: 2 encouraged in heart and *u* in love,

UNITES (UNITE)

1Co 6: 16 not know that he who *u* himself
6: 17 he who *u* himself with the Lord is

UNITS (UNIT)

Nu 10: 25 as the rear guard for all the *u*,
31: 48 were over the *u* of the army—
1Sa 29: 2 marched with their *u* of hundreds
2Sa 18: 4 while all the men marched out in *u*
2Ki 11: 4 sent for the commanders of *u*
11: 9 The commanders of *u*
11: 15 ordered the commanders of *u*
1Ch 12: 20 leaders of *u* of a thousand
15: 25 and the commanders of *u*
2Ch 17: 14 commanders of *u* of 1,000:
23: 1 with the commanders of *u*
23: 9 Then he gave the commanders of *u*
23: 14 sent out the commanders of *u*

UNITY (UNITE)

2Ch 30: 12 the people to give them *u* of mind
Ps 133: 1 is when brothers live together in *u*!
Jn 17: 23 May they be brought to complete *u*
Ro 15: 5 a spirit of *u* among yourselves
Eph 4: 3 effort to keep the *u* of the Spirit
4: 13 up until we all reach *u* in the faith
Col 3: 14 them all together in perfect *u*.

UNIVERSE

1Co 4: 9 made a spectacle to the whole *u*,
Eph 4: 10 in order to fill the whole *u*.)
Php 2: 15 which you shine like stars in the *u*
Heb 1: 2 and through whom he made the *u*.
11: 3 understand that the *u* was formed

UNJUST

Job 6: 29 Relent, do not be *u*;
27: 7 my adversaries like the *u*!
Ps 82: 2 "How long will you defend the *u*
Isa 10: 1 Woe to those who make *u* laws,
Jer 17: 11 man who gains riches by *u* means.
Eze 18: 25 Is it not your ways that are *u*?
18: 25 O house of Israel: Is my way *u*?
18: 29 Are my ways *u*, O house of Israel?
18: 29 Is it not your ways that are *u*?
22: 12 make *u* gain from your neighbors
22: 13 at the *u* gain you have made
22: 27 and kill people to make *u* gain.
33: 31 their hearts are greedy for *u* gain.
Hab 2: 9 him who builds his realm by *u* gain
Lk 18: 6 "Listen to what the *u* judge says.
Ro 3: 5 That God is *u* in bringing his wrath
9: 14 What then shall we say? Is God *u*?
Heb 6: 10 God is not *u*; he will not forget
1Pe 2: 19 up under the pain of *u* suffering

UNKEMPT

Lev 10: 6 "Do not let your hair become *u*,
13: 45 let his hair be *u*, cover the lower
21: 10 must not let his hair become *u*

UNKNOWN

Dt 28: 36 set over you to a nation *u* to you
Isa 48: 6 of hidden things *u* to you.

Da 11: 38 a god *u* to his fathers he will honor
Ac 17: 23 as something *u* I am going
17: 23 TO AN *U* GOD.
2Co 6: 9 known, yet regarded as *u;* dying,
Gal 1: 22 I was personally *u* to the churches

UNLAWFUL

Mt 12: 2 Your disciples are doing what is *u*
Mk 2: 24 why are they doing what is *u*
Lk 6: 2 "Why are you doing what is *u*
Ac 16: 21 an uproar by advocating customs *u*

UNLEASH (UNLEASHED UNLEASHES)

Job 40: 11 *U* the fury of your wrath,
Eze 7: 3 and I will *u* my anger against you.
13: 13 In my wrath I will *u* a violent wind,

UNLEASHED (UNLEASH)

Ex 15: 7 You *u* your burning anger;
Ps 78: 49 He *u* against them his hot anger,

UNLEASHES (UNLEASH)

Job 37: 3 He *u* his lightning

UNLEAVENED

Ex 12: 17 "Celebrate the Feast of *U* Bread,
12: 20 you live, you must eat *u* bread."
12: 39 they baked cakes of *u* bread.
13: 7 Eat *u* bread during those seven
23: 15 "Celebrate the Feast of *U* Bread;
34: 18 "Celebrate the Feast of *U* Bread.
Lev 23: 6 Feast of *U* Bread begins;
Nu 6: 17 is to present the basket of *u* bread
9: 11 with *u* bread and bitter herbs.
Dt 16: 3 but for seven days eat *u* bread,
16: 8 For six days eat *u* bread
16: 16 at the Feast of *U* Bread, the Feast
Jos 5: 11 *u* bread and roasted grain.
Jdg 6: 20 "Take the meat and the *u* bread,
6: 21 touched the meat and the *u* bread.
2Ki 23: 9 they ate *u* bread with their fellow
1Ch 23: 29 the *u* wafers, the baking
2Ch 8: 13 feasts—the Feast of *U* Bread,
30: 13 to celebrate the Feast of *U* Bread
30: 21 the Feast of *U* Bread for seven days
35: 17 and observed the Feast of *U* Bread
Ezr 6: 22 with joy the Feast of *U* Bread,
Mt 26: 17 day of the Feast of *U* Bread,
Mk 14: 1 of *U* Bread were only two days
14: 12 day of the Feast of *U* Bread,
Lk 22: 1 Now the Feast of *U* Bread,
22: 7 Then came the day of *U* Bread
Ac 12: 3 during the Feast of *U* Bread.
20: 6 Philippi after the Feast of *U* Bread,

UNLIKE

2Ch 27: 2 *u* him he did not enter the temple
33: 23 But *u* his father Manasseh,
Isa 7: 17 house of your father a time *u* any
Eze 16: 31 you were *u* a prostitute,

UNLIMITED

1Ti 1: 16 Jesus might display his *u* patience

UNLOAD (UNLOADED)

Ac 21: 3 where our ship was to *u* its cargo.

UNLOADED (UNLOAD)

Ge 24: 32 the house, and the camels were *u*.

UNLOCKED

Jdg 3: 25 they took a key and *u* them.

UNLOVED

Dt 21: 17 acknowledge the son of his *u* wife
Pr 30: 23 an *u* woman who is married,

UNMARKED

Lk 11: 44 because you are like *u* graves,

UNMARRIED

Lev 21: 3 or an *u* sister who is dependent
Ru 1: 13 Would you remain *u* for them? No,
Eze 44: 25 son or daughter, brother or *u* sister,
Ac 21: 9 He had four *u* daughters who
1Co 7: 8 It is good for them to stay *u*,
7: 8 Now to the *u* and the widows I say:
7: 11 she must remain *u* or else be
7: 27 Are you *u?* Do not look for a wife.
7: 32 An *u* man is concerned about
7: 34 An *u* woman or virgin is concerned

UNMINDFUL

Job 39: 15 *u* that a foot may crush them,

UNNATURAL

Ro 1: 26 natural relations for *u* ones.

UNNI

1Ch 15: 18 Shemiramoth, Jehiel, *U*, Eliab,
15: 20 Shemiramoth, Jehiel, *U*, Eliab,
Ne 12: 9 Bakbukiah and *U*, their associates,

UNNOTICED

1Sa 24: 4 Then David crept up *u*
Job 4: 20 *u*, they perish forever.
Lk 8: 47 seeing that she could not go *u*,

UNOCCUPIED

Mt 12: 44 it finds the house *u*, swept clean

UNPLOWED

Ex 23: 11 the seventh year let the land lie *u*
Jer 4: 3 "Break up your *u* ground
Hos 10: 12 and break up your *u* ground;

UNPREPARED

2Co 9: 4 come with me and find you *u*,

UNPRESENTABLE

1Co 12: 23 And the parts that are *u* are treated

UNPRODUCTIVE

2Ki 2: 19 the water is bad and the land is *u*."
2: 21 cause death or make the land *u*.' "
Tit 3: 14 necessities and not live *u* lives.
2Pe 1: 8 and *u* in your knowledge

UNPROFITABLE

Isa 30: 6 to that *u* nation,
Tit 3: 9 because these are *u* and useless.

UNPROTECTED

Ge 42: 9 come to see where our land is *u*."
42: 12 come to see where our land is *u*."

UNPUNISHED

Ex 34: 7 Yet he does not leave the guilty *u;*
Nu 14: 18 Yet he does not leave the guilty *u;*
Job 10: 14 and would not let my offense go *u*.
Pr 6: 29 no one who touches her will go *u*.
11: 21 of this: The wicked will not go *u*,
16: 5 Be sure of this: They will not go *u*.
17: 5 over disaster will not go *u*.
19: 5 A false witness will not go *u*,
19: 9 A false witness will not go *u*,
28: 20 one eager to get rich will not go *u*.
Jer 25: 29 indeed go *u?* You will not go *u*,
30: 11 I will not let you go entirely *u*.'
46: 28 I will not let you go entirely *u*."
49: 12 You will not go *u*, but must drink it
49: 12 why should you go *u?* You will not
Na 1: 3 LORD will not leave the guilty *u*.
Zec 11: 5 buyers slaughter them and go *u*.
Ro 3: 25 sins committed beforehand *u*—

UNQUENCHABLE (UNQUENCHED)

Jer 17: 27 then I will kindle an *u* fire
Mt 3: 12 burning up the chaff with *u* fire."
Lk 3: 17 he will burn up the chaff with *u* fire

UNQUENCHED (UNQUENCHABLE)

Isa 29: 8 he awakens faint, with his thirst *u*.

UNREASONABLE

Ac 25: 27 For I think it is *u* to send

UNREASONING

Jude : 10 by instinct, like *u* animals—

UNRELENTING

Job 6: 10 my joy in *u* pain—

UNRELIABLE

Ps 78: 57 as *u* as a faulty bow.

UNREPENTANT

Ro 2: 5 stubbornness and your *u* heart,

UNREST

Jer 50: 34 but *u* to those who live in Babylon.
Am 3: 9 see the great *u* within her

UNRIGHTEOUS (UNRIGHTEOUSNESS)

Zep 3: 5 yet the *u* know no shame.
Mt 5: 45 rain on the righteous and the *u*.
1Pe 3: 18 the righteous for the *u*, to bring you
2Pe 2: 9 and to hold the *u* for the day

UNRIGHTEOUSNESS (UNRIGHTEOUS)

Jer 22: 13 to him who builds his palace by *u*,
Ro 3: 5 But if our *u* brings out God's
1Jn 1: 9 us our sins and purify us from all *u*.

UNRIPE

Job 15: 33 like a vine stripped of its *u* grapes,

UNROLLED (UNROLLING)

Eze 2: 10 In it was a scroll, which he *u*

UNROLLING (UNROLLED)

Lk 4: 17 *U* it, he found the place where it is

UNRULY

Jer 31: 18 'You disciplined me like an *u* calf,
Eze 5: 7 You have been more *u*
Hos 11: 12 And Judah is *u* against God,

UNSANDALED

Dt 25: 10 in Israel as The Family of the *U*.

UNSATISFIED

2Sa 1: 22 the sword of Saul did not return *u*.

UNSCALABLE

Pr 18: 11 they imagine it an *u* wall.

UNSCATHED

Job 9: 4 has resisted him and come out *u?*
Isa 41: 3 He pursues them and moves on *u*,
Jer 43: 12 himself and depart from there *u*.
Na 1: 12 Although they are *u* and numerous

UNSCHOOLED

Ac 4: 13 John and realized that they were *u*,

UNSEALED

Ne 6: 5 and in his hand was an *u* letter
Jer 32: 11 as well as the *u* copy—
32: 14 *u* copies of the deed of purchase,

UNSEARCHABLE

Pr 25: 3 so the hearts of kings are *u*.
Jer 33: 3 and *u* things you do not know.'
Ro 11: 33 How *u* his judgments,
Eph 3: 8 preach to the Gentiles the *u* riches

UNSEEN

Mt 6: 6 and pray to your Father, who is *u*.
6: 18 who is *u;* and your Father,
2Co 4: 18 on what is seen, but on what is *u*.
4: 18 temporary, but what is *u* is eternal.

UNSETTLED

1Th 3: 3 so that no one would be *u*
2Th 2: 2 not to become easily *u*

UNSHARPENED

Ecc 10: 10 and its edge *u*,

UNSHEATHED

Eze 21: 4 my sword will be *u*

UNSHRUNK

Mt 9: 16 patch of *u* cloth on an old garment,
Mk 2: 21 patch of *u* cloth on an old garment.

UNSPIRITUAL

Ro 7: 14 but I am *u*, sold as a slave to sin.
Col 2: 18 and his *u* mind puffs him up
Jas 3: 15 down from heaven but is earthly, *u*,

UNSTABLE

Jas 1: 8 he is a double-minded man, *u*
2Pe 2: 14 they seduce the *u;* they are experts
3: 16 ignorant and *u* people distort,

UNSTOPPED

Isa 35: 5 and the ears of the deaf *u*.

UNSTRUNG

Job 30: 11 Now that God has *u* my bow

UNSUCCESSFUL

Dt 28: 29 You will be *u* in everything you do;

UNSUITABLE (UNSUITED)

Ac 27: 12 Since the harbor was *u* to winter in,

UNSUITED (UNSUITABLE)

Pr 17: 7 Arrogant lips are *u* to a fool—

UNSUSPECTING

Ge 34: 25 swords and attacked the *u* city,
Jdg 8: 11 Jogbehah and fell upon the *u* army.
18: 7 like the Sidonians, *u* and secure.
18: 10 you will find an *u* people
18: 27 against a peaceful and *u* people.
Eze 38: 11 attack a peaceful and *u* people—

UNSWERVING

1Ch 28: 7 forever if he is *u* in carrying out my

UNTENDED

Lev 25: 5 harvest the grapes of your *u* vines.
25: 11 of itself or harvest the *u* vines.

UNTHINKABLE

Job 34: 12 It is *u* that God would do wrong,

UNTIE (UNTIED UNTYING)

Isa 58: 6 and *u* the cords of the yoke,
Mt 21: 2 *U* them and bring them to me.
Mk 1: 7 worthy to stoop down and *u*.
11: 2 *U* it and bring it here.
Lk 3: 16 sandals I am not worthy to *u*.
13: 15 each of you on the Sabbath *u* his ox
19: 30 *U* it and bring it here.
Jn 1: 27 sandals I am not worthy to *u*."
Ac 13: 25 whose sandals I am not worthy to *u*

UNTIED (UNTIE)

Job 39: 5 Who *u* his ropes?
Mk 11: 4 As they *u* it, some people standing
Ac 27: 40 at the same time *u* the ropes that

UNTIRING

Ps 77: 2 at night I stretched out *u* hands

UNTOUCHED

Pr 19: 23 one rests content, *u* by trouble.

UNTRAVELED

Jer 9: 10 They are desolate and *u*,

UNTRUE

Jos 24: 27 you if you are *u* to your God."

UNTYING (UNTIE)

Mk 11: 5 "What are you doing, *u* that colt?"
Lk 19: 31 'Why are you *u* it?' tell him,
19: 33 As they were *u* the colt, its owners
19: 33 "Why are you *u* the colt?"

UNUSED

Ex 23: 11 let the land lie unplowed and *u*.

UNUSUAL

Ac 28: 2 islanders showed us *u* kindness.
28: 6 seeing nothing *u* happen to him,

UNVEILED

2Co 3: 18 with *u* faces all reflect the Lord's

UNWALLED

Nu 13: 19 Are they *u* or fortified? How is
Dt 3: 5 also a great many *u* villages.
Eze 38: 11 "I will invade a land of *u* villages;

UNWASHED

Mt 15: 20 with *u* hands does not make him
Mk 7: 2 that is, ceremonially *u*— hands.

UNWEIGHED

1Ki 7: 47 Solomon left all these things *u*,

UNWHOLESOME

Eph 4: 29 Do not let any *u* talk come out

UNWILLING

Ge 24: 5 if the woman is *u* to come back
24: 8 If the woman is *u* to come back
Dt 1: 26 you were *u* to go up; you rebelled
Jdg 19: 10 But, *u* to stay another night,
1Sa 15: 9 These they were *u*
2Ki 13: 23 To this day he has been *u*
Isa 30: 9 children *u* to listen
1Co 16: 12 He was quite *u* to go now,
Rev 2: 21 of her immorality, but she is *u*.

UNWISE

Dt 32: 6 O foolish and *u* people?
Eph 5: 15 how you live—not as *u* but as wise,

UNWORTHY

Ge 32: 10 I am *u* of all the kindness
Job 40: 4 "I am *u*— how can I reply to you?
Lk 17: 10 should say, 'We are *u* servants;
1Co 11: 27 Lord in an *u* manner will be guilty

UNYIELDING

Ex 7: 14 "Pharaoh's heart is *u;* he refuses
9: 7 Yet his heart was *u* and he would
Pr 18: 19 An offended brother is more *u*
SS 8: 6 its jealousy *u* as the grave.
Eze 3: 8 I will make you as *u* and hardened

UPHAZ

Jer 10: 9 and gold from *U*.

UPHELD (UPHOLD)

1Sa 25: 39 who has *u* my cause against Nabal
2Ch 20: 20 your God and you will be *u;*
Ps 9: 4 For you have *u* my right
Isa 46: 3 you whom I have *u*

UPHOLD (UPHELD UPHOLDING UPHOLDS)

Dt 27: 26 the man who does not *u* the words
32: 51 because you did not *u* my holiness
1Sa 24: 15 May he consider my cause and *u* it;
1Ki 8: 45 and their plea, and *u* their cause.
8: 49 and their plea, and *u* their cause.
8: 59 that he may *u* the cause
2Ch 6: 35 and their plea, and *u* their cause.
6: 39 and their pleas, and *u* their cause.
9: 8 and his desire to *u* them forever,
Ps 41: 12 In my integrity you *u* me
119:117 *U* me, and I will be delivered;
Isa 34: 8 of retribution, to *u* Zion's cause.
41: 10 I will *u* you with my righteous right
42: 1 "Here is my servant, whom I *u*,
La 3: 59 *U* my cause!
Ro 3: 31 Not at all! Rather, we *u* the law.

UPHOLDING (UPHOLD)

Isa 9: 7 establishing and *u* it

UPHOLDS (UPHOLD)

Ps 37: 17 but the LORD *u* the righteous.
37: 24 for the LORD *u* him with his hand.
63: 8 your right hand *u* me.
140: 12 and *u* the cause of the needy.
145: 14 The LORD *u* all those who fall
146: 7 He *u* the cause of the oppressed

UPHOLSTERED

SS 3: 10 Its seat was *u* with purple,

UPLIFTED (LIFT)

Ex 6: 8 with *u* hand to give to Abraham,
Nu 14: 30 with *u* hand to make your home,
Ne 9: 15 sworn with *u* hand to give them.
Ps 106: 26 So he swore to them with *u* hand
Isa 19: 16 fear at the *u* hand that the LORD
Eze 20: 5 I swore with *u* hand
20: 5 With *u* hand I said to them,
20: 15 Also with *u* hand I swore to them
20: 23 Also with *u* hand I swore to them
20: 42 sworn with *u* hand to give
36: 7 swear with *u* hand that the nations
44: 12 with *u* hand that they must bear
47: 14 Because I swore with *u* hand

UPRAISED (RISE)

Job 38: 15 and their *u* arm is broken.
Isa 5: 25 his hand is still *u*.
9: 12 his hand is still *u*.
9: 17 his hand is still *u*.
9: 21 his hand is still *u*.
10: 4 his hand is still *u*.

UPRIGHT (UPRIGHTLY UPRIGHTNESS UPRIGHTS)

Ge 37: 7 my sheaf rose and stood *u*,
Ex 26: 15 "Make *u* frames of acacia wood
36: 20 They made *u* frames
Dt 32: 4 *u* and just is he.
1Ki 2: 32 were better men and more *u*
3: 6 and righteous and *u* in heart.
Job 1: 1 This man was blameless and *u;*
1: 8 and *u*, a man who fears God
2: 3 and *u*, a man who fears God
4: 7 Where were the *u* ever destroyed?
8: 6 if you are pure and *u*,
17: 8 *U* men are appalled at this;
23: 7 There an *u* man could present his
33: 3 My words come from an *u* heart;
Ps 7: 10 who saves the *u* in heart.
11: 2 the shadows at the *u* in heart.
11: 7 *u* men will see his face.
25: 8 Good and *u* is the LORD;
32: 11 sing, all you who are *u* in heart!
33: 1 it is fitting for the *u* to praise him.
36: 10 your righteousness to the *u* in heart
37: 14 to slay those whose ways are *u*.
37: 37 the blameless, observe the *u;*
49: 14 The *u* will rule over them
64: 10 let all the *u* in heart praise him!
92: 15 proclaiming, "The LORD is *u;*
94: 15 and all the *u* in heart will follow it.
97: 11 and joy on the *u* in heart.
107: 42 The *u* see and rejoice,
111: 1 heart in the council of the *u*
112: 2 of the *u* will be blessed.
112: 4 in darkness light dawns for the *u*,
119: 7 I will praise you with an *u* heart
125: 4 to those who are *u* in heart.
140: 13 and the *u* will live before you.
Pr 2: 7 He holds victory in store for the *u*,
2: 21 For the *u* will live in the land,
3: 32 but takes the *u* into his confidence.
11: 3 The integrity of the *u* guides them,
11: 6 of the *u* delivers them,
11: 11 of the *u* a city is exalted,
12: 6 the speech of the *u* rescues them.
14: 2 whose walk is *u* fears the LORD,
14: 9 but good will is found among the *u*.
14: 11 but the tent of the *u* will flourish.
15: 8 but the prayer of the *u* pleases him.
15: 19 but the path of the *u* is a highway.
16: 17 The highway of the *u* avoids evil;
21: 8 but the conduct of the innocent is *u*
21: 18 and the unfaithful for the *u*.
21: 29 an *u* man gives thought to his ways.
28: 10 He who leads the *u*
29: 10 and seek to kill the *u*.
29: 27 the wicked detest the *u*.
Ecc 7: 28 I found one ⌊*u*⌋ man
7: 28 not one ⌊*u*⌋ woman among them all.
7: 29 God made mankind *u*,
12: 10 and what he wrote was *u* and true.
Isa 26: 7 O *u* One, you make the way
Mic 2: 7 good to him whose ways are *u?*
7: 2 not one *u* man remains.
7: 4 most *u* worse than a thorn hedge.
Hab 2: 4 his desires are not *u*—
Lk 1: 6 Both of them were *u* in the sight
23: 50 of the Council, a good and *u* man,
Tit 1: 8 who is self-controlled, *u*, holy
2: 12 *u* and godly lives in this present

UPRIGHTLY (UPRIGHT)

Ps 58: 1 Do you judge *u* among men?
75: 2 it is I who judge *u*.
Isa 57: 2 Those who walk *u*

UPRIGHTNESS (UPRIGHT)

1Ki 9: 4 me in integrity of heart and *u*,
Ps 25: 21 May integrity and *u* protect me,
111: 8 done in faithfulness and *u*.

Isa 26: 10 in a land of *u* they go on doing evil
Mal 2: 6 He walked with me in peace and *u*,

UPRIGHTS (UPRIGHT)

1Ki 7: 28 They had side panels attached to *u*
7: 29 cherubim—and on the *u* as well.
7: 29 panels between the *u* were lions,

UPRISING (RISE)

Mk 15: 7 had committed murder in the *u*.

UPROAR

1Sa 4: 6 Hearing the *u*, the Philistines
4: 14 "What is the meaning of this *u*?"
Ps 46: 6 Nations are in *u*, kingdoms fall;
74: 23 *u* of your enemies, which rises
Isa 13: 4 Listen, an *u* among the kingdoms,
17: 12 Oh, the *u* of the peoples—
25: 5 You silence the *u* of foreigners;
66: 6 Hear that *u* from the city,
Mt 27: 24 but that instead an *u* was starting,
Ac 16: 20 into an *u* by advocating customs
19: 29 Soon the whole city was in an *u*.
20: 1 When the *u* had ended, Paul sent
21: 31 city of Jerusalem was in an *u*.
21: 34 get at the truth because of the *u*,
23: 9 There was a great *u*, and some

UPROOT (UPROOTED UPROOTS)

1Ki 14: 15 He will *u* Israel from this good land
2Ch 7: 20 then I will *u* Israel from my land,
Ps 52: 5 he will *u* you from the land
Ecc 3: 2 a time to plant and a time to *u*,
Jer 1: 10 and kingdoms to *u* and tear down,
12: 14 I will *u* them from their lands
12: 14 and I will *u* the house of Judah
12: 15 But after I *u* them, I will again have
12: 17 I will completely *u* and destroy it,"
24: 6 I will plant them and not *u* them.
31: 28 as I watched over them to *u*
42: 10 I will plant you and not *u* you,
45: 4 and *u* what I have planted,
Mic 5: 14 I will *u* from among you your

UPROOTED (UPROOT)

Dt 28: 63 You will be *u* from the land you are
29: 28 in great wrath the LORD *u* them
Job 31: 8 and may my crops be *u*.
31: 12 it would have *u* my harvest.
Ps 9: 6 you have *u* their cities;
Pr 10: 30 The righteous will never be *u*,
12: 3 but the righteous cannot be *u*.
Jer 18: 7 that a nation or kingdom is to be *u*,
31: 40 The city will never again be *u*
Eze 17: 9 Will it not be *u* and stripped
19: 12 But it was *u* in fury
Da 7: 8 of the first horns were *u* before it.
11: 4 his empire will be *u* and given
Am 9: 15 never again to be *u*
Zep 2: 4 and Ekron *u*.
Lk 17: 6 'Be *u* and planted in the sea,'
Jude : 12 without fruit and *u*— twice dead.

UPROOTS (UPROOT)

Job 19: 10 he *u* my hope like a tree.

UPSET

2Sa 11: 25 this to Joab: 'Don't let this *u* you;
Lk 10: 41 are worried and *u* about many

UPSIDE

2Ki 21: 13 wiping it and turning it *u* down.
Isa 29: 16 You turn things *u* down,

UPSTAIRS (STAIRS)

Da 6: 10 to his *u* room where the windows
Ac 1: 13 they went *u* to the room where
9: 37 washed and placed in an *u* room.
9: 39 when he arrived he was taken *u*
20: 8 lamps in the *u* room where we were
20: 11 he went *u* again and broke bread

UPSTREAM (STREAM)

Jos 3: 16 the water from *u* stopped flowing.

UR

Ge 11: 28 Haran died in *U* of the Chaldeans,
11: 31 out from *U* of the Chaldeans
Ge 15: 7 out of *U* of the Chaldeans
1Ch 11: 35 son of *U*, Hepher the Mekerathite,
Ne 9: 7 out of *U* of the Chaldeans

URBANUS

Ro 16: 9 Greet *U*, our fellow worker

URGE (URGED URGENT URGING)

Ru 1: 16 "Don't *u* me to leave you
Est 4: 8 and he told him to *u* her to go
Ac 27: 22 But now I *u* you to keep up your
27: 34 Now I *u* you to take some food.
Ro 12: 1 Therefore, I *u* you, brothers,
15: 30 I *u* you, brothers, by our Lord
16: 17 I *u* you, brothers, to watch out
1Co 4: 16 Therefore I *u* you to imitate me.
16: 15 I *u* you, brothers, to submit to such
2Co 2: 8 I *u* you, therefore, to reaffirm your
6: 1 God's fellow workers we *u* you not
9: 5 it necessary to *u* the brothers
Eph 4: 1 I *u* you to live a life worthy
1Th 4: 1 and *u* you in the Lord Jesus
4: 10 Yet we *u* you, brothers, to do
5: 14 we *u* you, brothers, warn those
2Th 3: 12 *u* in the Lord Jesus Christ to settle
1Ti 2: 1 I *u*, then, first of all, that requests,
6: 2 are to teach and *u* on them.
Heb 13: 19 I particularly *u* you to pray
13: 22 I *u* you to bear with my word
1Pe 2: 11 I *u* you, as aliens and strangers
Jude : 3 *u* you to contend for the faith that

URGED (URGE)

Ge 19: 15 the angels *u* Lot, saying, "Hurry!
Ex 12: 33 The Egyptians *u* the people
Jos 15: 18 she *u* him to ask her father
Jdg 1: 14 she *u* him to ask her father
1Sa 24: 10 Some *u* me to kill you,
2Sa 3: 35 and *u* David to eat something
13: 25 Although Absalom *u* him,
13: 27 go with you?" But Absalom *u* him,
1Ki 21: 25 of the LORD, *u* on by Jezebel his
2Ki 4: 8 who *u* him to stay for a meal.
5: 16 And even though Naaman *u* him,
5: 23 He *u* Gehazi to accept them,
2Ch 18: 2 and *u* him to attack Ramoth
Jer 36: 25 and Gemariah *u* the king not
Da 2: 18 He *u* them to plead for mercy
Mt 15: 23 disciples came to him and *u* him,
Lk 24: 29 they *u* him strongly, "Stay with us,
Jn 4: 31 Meanwhile his disciples *u* him,
4: 40 they *u* him to stay with them,
Ac 9: 38 sent two men to him and *u* him,
13: 43 and *u* them to continue in the grace
21: 4 Through the Spirit they *u* Paul not
27: 33 Just before dawn Paul *u* them all
1Co 16: 12 I strongly *u* him to go to you
2Co 8: 6 So we *u* Titus, since he had earlier
12: 18 I *u* Titus to go to you and I sent our
1Ti 1: 3 As I *u* you when I went

URGENT (URGE)

Nu 22: 37 Did I not send you an *u* summons?
1Sa 21: 8 because the king's business was *u*."
Da 3: 22 The king's command was so *u*

URGING (URGE)

Ru 1: 18 to go with her, she stopped *u* her.
1Sa 28: 23 his men joined the woman in *u* him
1Th 2: 12 *u* you to live lives worthy of God,

URI

Ex 31: 2 I have chosen Bezalel son of *U*,
35: 30 has chosen Bezalel son of *U*,
38: 22 (Bezalel son of *U*, the son of Hur,
1Ki 4: 19 in Benjamin; Geber son of *U*—
1Ch 2: 20 Hur was the father of *U*,
2: 20 and *U* the father of Bezalel.
2Ch 1: 5 bronze altar that Bezalel son of *U*,
Ezr 10: 24 Shallum, Telem and *U*.

URIAH (URIAH'S)

2Sa 11: 3 and the wife of *U* the Hittite?"
11: 6 to Joab: "Send me *U* the Hittite."
11: 7 When *U* came to him, David asked
11: 8 So *U* left the palace, and a gift
11: 8 Then David said to *U*, "Go
11: 9 But *U* slept at the entrance
2Sa 11: 10 David was told, "*U* did not go
11: 11 Why didn't you go home?" *U* said
11: 12 *U* remained in Jerusalem that day
11: 13 in the evening *U* went out to sleep
11: 14 a letter to Joab and sent it with *U*.
11: 16 he put *U* at a place where he knew
11: 17 moreover, *U* the Hittite was dead.
11: 21 your servant *U* the Hittite is dead
11: 24 your servant *U* the Hittite is dead."
12: 9 You struck down *U* the Hittite
12: 10 and took the wife of *U* the Hittite
23: 39 Gareb the Ithrite and *U* the Hittite.
1Ki 15: 5 except in the case of *U* the Hittite.
2Ki 16: 10 and sent to *U* the priest a sketch
16: 11 So *U* the priest built an altar
16: 15 gave these orders to *U* the priest:
16: 16 And *U* the priest did just
1Ch 11: 41 Gareb the Ithrite, *U* the Hittite,
Ezr 8: 33 the hands of Meremoth son of *U*,
Ne 3: 4 Meremoth son of *U*, the son
3: 21 Meremoth son of *U*, the son
8: 4 Anaiah, *U*, Hilkiah and Maaseiah;
Isa 8: 2 And I will call in *U* the priest
Jer 26: 20 (Now *U* son of Shemaiah
26: 21 But *U* heard of it and fled in fear
26: 23 They brought *U* out of Egypt

URIAH'S (URIAH)

2Sa 11: 26 When *U* wife heard that her
12: 15 the child that *U* wife had borne
Mt 1: 6 whose mother had been *U* wife,

URIEL

1Ch 6: 24 Tahath his son, *U* his son,
15: 5 *U* the leader and 120 relatives;
15: 11 and *U*, Asaiah, Joel, Shemaiah,
2Ch 13: 2 a daughter of *U* of Gibeah.

URIM

Ex 28: 30 Also put the *U* and the Thummim
Lev 8: 8 and put the *U* and Thummim
Nu 27: 21 of the *U* before the LORD.
Dt 33: 8 "Your Thummim and *U* belong
1Sa 28: 6 did not answer him by dreams or *U*
Ezr 2: 63 was a priest ministering with the *U*
Ne 7: 65 be a priest ministering with the *U*

URINE

2Ki 18: 27 own filth and drink their own *u*?"
Isa 36: 12 own filth and drink their own *u*?"

USEFUL

Eze 15: 3 taken from it to make anything *u*?
15: 4 is it then *u* for anything? If it was
15: 5 If it was not *u* for anything
15: 5 into something *u* when the fire has
Eph 4: 28 doing something *u*
2Ti 2: 21 *u* to the Master and prepared
3: 16 Scripture is God-breathed and is *u*
Phm : 11 now he has become *u* both to you
Heb 6: 7 and that produces a crop *u* to those

USELESS

1Sa 12: 21 Do not turn away after *u* idols.
12: 21 rescue you, because they are *u*.
25: 21 David had just said, "It's been *u*—
Job 15: 3 Would he argue with *u* words,
Pr 1: 17 How *u* to spread a net
Isa 30: 5 because of a people *u* to them,
30: 7 to Egypt, whose help is utterly *u*.
59: 6 Their cobwebs are *u* for clothing;
Jer 13: 7 it was ruined and completely *u*.
13: 10 will be like this belt—completely *u*
Mal 1: 10 so that you would not light *u* fires
1Co 15: 14 our preaching is *u*
1Th 3: 5 and our efforts might have been *u*.
Tit 3: 9 these are unprofitable and *u*.
Phm : 11 Formerly he was *u* to you,
Heb 7: 18 *u* (for the law made nothing perfect
Jas 2: 20 faith without deeds is *u*?

USHERS

Pr 18: 16 *u* him into the presence of the great

USURY

Ne 5: 7 "You are exacting *u*
5: 10 But let the exacting of *u* stop!
5: 11 also the *u* you are charging them—

Ps 15: 5 who lends his money without *u*
Eze 18: 8 He does not lend at *u*
18: 13 at *u* and takes excessive interest.
18: 17 and takes no *u* or excessive interest
22: 12 you take *u* and excessive interest

UTENSILS

Ex 27: 3 Make all its *u* of bronze—
30: 28 altar of burnt offering and all its *u*,
31: 9 altar of burnt offering and all its *u*,
35: 16 and all its *u;* the bronze basin
38: 3 They made all its *u* of bronze—
38: 30 with its bronze grating and all its *u*,
39: 39 all its *u;* the basin with its stand;
40: 10 altar of burnt offering and all its *u;*
Lev 8: 11 anointing the altar and all its *u*
Nu 4: 14 on it all the *u* used for ministering
7: 1 consecrated the altar and all its *u*.
2Ch 29: 18 altar of burnt offering with all its *u*,
Eze 40: 42 On them were placed the *u*

UTHAI

1Ch 9: 4 *U* son of Ammihud, the son
Ezr 8: 14 of the descendants of Bigvai, *U*

UTMOST

2Ki 19: 23 the *u* heights of Lebanon.
Job 34: 36 that Job might be tested to the *u*
Ps 48: 2 Like the *u* heights
Isa 14: 13 on the *u* heights of the sacred
37: 24 the *u* heights of Lebanon.

UTTER (UTTERANCE UTTERED UTTERING UTTERS)

Nu 30: 6 or after her lips *u* a rash promise
Dt 23: 23 Whatever your lips *u* you must be
Jdg 17: 2 about which I heard you *u* a curse
2Sa 12: 14 of the LORD show *u* contempt,
Job 26: 4 Who has helped you *u* these words
27: 4 and my tongue will *u* no deceit.
Ps 31: 11 I am the *u* contempt
59: 12 For the curses and lies they *u*,
78: 2 I will *u* things hidden from of old—
115: 7 nor can they *u* a sound
Pr 5: 14 I have come to the brink of *u* ruin
Ecc 5: 2 heart to *u* anything before God.
Isa 8: 22 they will be thrust into *u* darkness.
42: 17 will be turned back in *u* shame.
Jer 15: 19 if you *u* worthy, not worthless,
Eze 13: 9 visions and *u* lying divinations.
14: 9 is persuaded to *u* a prophecy,
Mt 13: 35 I will *u* things hidden
Rev 13: 5 given a mouth to *u* proud words

UTTERANCE (UTTER)

Ps 49: 3 the *u* from my heart will give

UTTERED (UTTER)

Nu 23: 7 Then Balaam *u* his oracle:
23: 18 LORD say?" Then he *u* his oracle:
24: 3 came upon him and he *u* his oracle:
24: 15 Then he *u* his oracle:
24: 20 saw Amalek and *u* his oracle:
24: 21 he saw the Kenites and *u* his oracle
24: 23 Then he *u* his oracle:
Jos 10: 21 one *u* a word against the Israelites.
Ps 89: 34 or alter what my lips have *u*.
Isa 45: 23 my mouth has *u* in all integrity
Eze 13: 7 *u* lying divinations when you say,

UTTERING (UTTER)

Isa 59: 13 *u* lies our hearts have conceived.

UTTERS (UTTER)

Ps 37: 30 of the righteous man *u* wisdom,
1Co 14: 2 he *u* mysteries with his spirit.

UZ

Ge 10: 23 The sons of Aram: *U*, Hul,
22: 21 *U* the firstborn, Buz his brother,
36: 28 The sons of Dishan: *U* and Aran.
1Ch 1: 17 The sons of Aram: *U*, Hul,
1: 42 The sons of Dishan: *U* and Aran.
Job 1: 1 of *U* there lived a man whose name
Jer 25: 20 all the kings of *U;* all the kings
La 4: 21 you who live in the land of *U*.

UZAI

Ne 3: 25 and Palal son of *U* worked

UZAL

Ge 10: 27 Jerah, Hadoram, *U*, Diklah, Obal,
1Ch 1: 21 Jerah, Hadoram, *U*, Diklah, Obal,
Eze 27: 19 from *U* bought your merchandise;

UZZA

2Ki 21: 18 his palace garden, the garden of *U*.
21: 26 in his grave in the garden of *U*.
1Ch 8: 7 and who was the father of *U*
Ezr 2: 49 Nekoda, Gazzam, *U*, Paseah, Besai
Ne 7: 51 Nekoda, Gazzam, *U*, Paseah, Besai

UZZAH

2Sa 6: 3 *U* and Ahio, sons of Abinadab,
6: 6 *U* reached out and took hold
6: 7 LORD's anger burned against *U*
6: 8 wrath had broken out against *U*,
1Ch 6: 29 *U* his son, Shimea his son,
13: 7 with *U* and Ahio guiding it.
13: 9 *U* reached out his hand
13: 10 LORD's anger burned against *U*,
13: 11 wrath had broken out against *U*,

UZZEN SHEERAH

1Ch 7: 24 Upper Beth Horon as well as *U*.

UZZI

1Ch 6: 6 of *U*, *U* the father of Zerahiah,
6: 51 *U* his son, Zerahiah his son,
7: 2 *U*, Rephaiah, Jeriel, Jahmai,
7: 3 The son of *U:* Izrahiah.
7: 7 Ezbon, *U*, Uzziel, Jerimoth and Iri,
9: 8 Elah son of *U*, the son of Micri;
Ezr 7: 4 the son of *U*, the son of Bukki,
Ne 11: 22 in Jerusalem was *U* son of Bani,
11: 22 *U* was one of Asaph's descendants,
12: 19 Mattenai; of Jedaiah's, *U;* of Sallu's
12: 42 Shemaiah, Eleazar, *U*, Jehohanan,

UZZIA

1Ch 11: 44 the Mithnite, *U* the Ashterathite,

UZZIAH (UZZIAH'S)

2Ki 15: 13 year of *U* king of Judah,
15: 30 year of Jotham son of *U*.
15: 32 Jotham son of *U* king
15: 34 just as his father *U* had done.
1Ch 6: 24 *U* his son and Shaul his son.
27: 25 Jonathan son of *U* was in charge
2Ch 26: 1 all the people of Judah took *U*,
26: 3 *U* was sixteen years old
26: 8 Ammonites brought tribute to *U*,
26: 9 *U* built towers in Jerusalem
26: 11 *U* had a well-trained army,
26: 14 *U* provided shields, spears, helmets
26: 16 But after *U* became powerful,
26: 18 *U*, to burn incense to the LORD.
26: 19 *U*, who had a censer
26: 21 King *U* had leprosy
26: 23 *U* rested with his fathers
27: 2 just as his father *U* had done,
Ezr 10: 21 Elijah, Shemaiah, Jehiel and *U*.
Ne 11: 4 Athaiah son of *U*, the son
Isa 1: 1 of Amoz saw during the reigns of *U*
6: 1 In the year that King *U* died,
7: 1 the son of *U*, was king of Judah,
Hos 1: 1 son of Beeri during the reigns of *U*,
Am 1: 1 when *U* was king of Judah
Zec 14: 5 in the days of *U* king of Judah.
Mt 1: 9 father of *U*, *U* the father of Jotham,

UZZIAH'S (UZZIAH)

2Ch 26: 22 The other events of *U* reign,

UZZIEL (UZZIELITES)

Ex 6: 18 Amram, Izhar, Hebron and *U*.
6: 22 The sons of *U* were Mishael,
Lev 10: 4 sons of Aaron's uncle *U*,
Nu 3: 19 Amram, Izhar, Hebron and *U*.
3: 30 clans was Elizaphan son of *U*.
1Ch 4: 42 Neariah, Rephaiah and *U*,
6: 2 Amram, Izhar, Hebron and *U*.
6: 18 Amram, Izhar, Hebron and *U*.
7: 7 Ezbon, Uzzi, *U*, Jerimoth and Iri,
15: 10 from the descendants of *U*,
23: 12 Izhar, Hebron and *U*— four in all.
23: 20 The sons of *U:* Micah the first
24: 24 The son of *U:* Micah; from the sons
25: 4 Mattaniah, *U*, Shubael
2Ch 29: 14 of Jeduthun, Shemaiah and *U*.
Ne 3: 8 *U* son of Harhaiah, one

UZZIELITES (UZZIEL)

Nu 3: 27 Izharites, Hebronites and *U;*
1Ch 26: 23 the Hebronites and the *U:* Shubael,

VAIN

Lev 26: 16 You will plant seed in *v*.
26: 20 Your strength will be spent in *v*,
Job 3: 9 may it wait for daylight in *v*
9: 29 why should I struggle in *v?*
24: 1 look in *v* for such days?
39: 16 she cares not that her labor was in *v*
Ps 2: 1 and the peoples plot in *v?*
33: 17 A horse is a *v* hope for deliverance;
39: 6 He bustles about, but only in *v;*
73: 13 in *v* have I kept my heart pure;
73: 13 in *v* have I washed my hands
119:118 for their deceitfulness is in *v*.
127: 1 its builders labor in *v*.
127: 1 the watchmen stand guard in *v*.
127: 2 In *v* you rise early
Isa 45: 19 'Seek me in *v*.'
49: 4 I have spent my strength in *v*
65: 23 They will not toil in *v*
Jer 2: 30 "In *v* I punished your people;
4: 30 You adorn yourself in *v*.
6: 29 but the refining goes on in *v;*
46: 11 But you multiply remedies in *v;*
La 4: 17 looking in *v* for help;
Eze 6: 10 threaten in *v* to bring this calamity
Zec 10: 2 they give comfort in *v*.
Mt 15: 9 They worship me in *v;*
Mk 7: 7 They worship me in *v;*
Ac 4: 25 and the peoples plot in *v?*
1Co 15: 2 Otherwise, you have believed in *v*.
15: 58 labor in the Lord is not in *v*.
2Co 6: 1 not to receive God's grace in *v*.
Gal 2: 2 running or had run my race in *v*.
Php 2: 3 out of selfish ambition or *v* conceit,

VAIZATHA

Est 9: 9 Parmashta, Arisai, Aridai and *V*,

VALIANT

Jdg 20: 44 all of them *v* fighters.
20: 46 all of them *v* fighters.
1Sa 10: 26 by *v* men whose hearts God had
31: 12 all their *v* men journeyed
2Sa 23: 20 son of Jehoiada was a *v* fighter
2Ki 5: 1 He was a *v* soldier, but he had
1Ch 10: 12 all their *v* men went and took
11: 22 son of Jehoiada was a *v* fighter
2Ch 17: 17 Eliada, a *v* soldier, with 200,000
Ps 76: 5 *V* men lie plundered,
Jer 48: 14 men *v* in battle'?

VALID

2Sa 15: 3 Look, your claims are *v* and proper,
Jn 5: 31 myself, my testimony is not *v*.
5: 32 that his testimony about me is *v*.
8: 13 witness; your testimony is not *v*."
8: 14 my own behalf, my testimony is *v*,
8: 17 that the testimony of two men is *v*.

VALLEY (VALLEYS)

Ge 14: 3 in the *V* of Siddim (the Salt Sea).
14: 8 lines in the *V* of Siddim
14: 10 the *V* of Siddim was full of tar pits,
14: 17 him in the *V* of Shaveh (that is,
14: 17 of Shaveh (that is, the King's *V)*.
26: 17 and encamped in the *V* of Gerar
26: 19 Isaac's servants dug in the *v*
37: 14 him off from the *V* of Hebron.
Nu 13: 23 When they reached the *V*
13: 24 That place was called the *V*
21: 12 and camped in the Zered *V*.
21: 20 and from Bamoth to the *v*
32: 9 up to the *V* of Eshcol
Dt 1: 24 and came to the *V* of Eshcol
2: 13 So we crossed the *v*.
2: 13 "Now get up and cross the Zered *V*
2: 14 until we crossed the Zered *V*.

Dt 3: 29 we stayed in the *v* near Beth Peor.
4: 46 and were in the *v* near Beth Peor
21: 4 There in the *v* they are
21: 4 to a *v* that has not been plowed
21: 6 whose neck was broken in the *v*,
34: 3 region from the *V* of Jericho,
34: 6 in Moab, in the *v* opposite Beth
Jos 7: 24 all that he had, to the *V* of Achor.
7: 26 that place has been called the *V*
8: 11 with the *v* between them
8: 13 That night Joshua went into the *v*.
10: 12 O moon, over the *V* of Aijalon."
11: 8 and to the *V* of Mizpah on the east,
11: 17 to Baal Gad in the *V* of Lebanon
12: 7 Baal Gad in the *V* of Lebanon
13: 19 Zereth Shahar on the hill in the *v*,
13: 27 the territory of Debir; and in the *v*,
15: 7 up to Debir from the *V* of Achor
15: 8 end of the *V* of Rephaim.
15: 8 it ran up the *V* of Ben Hinnom
15: 8 of the Hinnom *V* at the northern
17: 16 and those in the *V* of Jezreel."
18: 16 continued down the Hinnom *V*
18: 16 foot of the hill facing the *V* of Ben
18: 16 north of the *V* of Rephaim.
19: 14 and ended at the *V* of Iphtah
19: 27 Zebulun and the *V* of Iphtah El,
Jdg 5: 15 rushing after him into the *v*.
6: 33 and camped in the *V* of Jezreel.
7: 1 north of them in the *v* near the hill
7: 8 of Midian lay below him in the *v*.
7: 12 eastern peoples had settled in the *v*,
16: 4 love with a woman in the *V*
18: 28 The city was in a *v*
1Sa 6: 13 harvesting their wheat in the *v*,
13: 18 the borderland overlooking the *V*
17: 2 and camped in the *V* of Elah
17: 3 with the *v* between them.
17: 19 the men of Israel in the *V* of Elah,
21: 9 whom you killed in the *V* of Elah,
31: 7 When the Israelites along the *v*
2Sa 5: 18 spread out in the *V* of Rephaim;
5: 22 spread out in the *V* of Rephaim;
8: 13 thousand Edomites in the *V*
15: 23 The king also crossed the Kidron *V*
17: 13 it down to the *v* until not
18: 18 and erected it in the King's *V*
23: 13 encamped in the *V* of Rephaim.
1Ki 2: 37 you leave and cross the Kidron *V*,
15: 13 and burned it in the Kidron *V*.
18: 40 brought down to the Kishon *V*
2Ki 2: 16 on some mountain or in some *v*."
3: 16 Make this *v* full of ditches.
3: 17 yet this *v* will be filled with water,
14: 7 ten thousand Edomites in the *V*
23: 4 in the fields of the Kidron *V*
23: 6 to the Kidron *V* outside Jerusalem
23: 10 which was in the *V* of Ben Hinnom,
23: 12 threw the rubble into the Kidron *V*.
1Ch 4: 39 the east of the *v* in search of pasture
10: 7 in the *v* saw that the army had fled
11: 15 encamped in the *V* of Rephaim.
14: 9 and raided the *V* of Rephaim;
14: 13 more the Philistines raided the *v*;
18: 12 thousand Edomites in the *V*
2Ch 14: 10 positions in the *V* of Zephathah
15: 16 and burned it in the Kidron *V*.
20: 26 This is why it is called the *V*
20: 26 assembled in the *V* of Beracah,
25: 11 and led his army to the *V* of Salt,
26: 9 at the *V* Gate and at the angle
28: 3 sacrifices in the *V* of Ben Hinnom
29: 16 and carried it out to the Kidron *V*.
30: 14 and threw them into the Kidron *V*.
33: 6 sons in the fire in the *V* of Ben
33: 14 west of the Gihon spring in the *v*,
Ne 2: 13 out through the *V* Gate
2: 15 and reentered through the *V*
2: 15 so I went up the *v* by night,
3: 13 The *V* Gate was repaired by Hanun
11: 30 Beersheba to the *V* of Hinnom.
11: 35 and in the *V* of the Craftsmen.
Job 21: 33 The soil in the *v* is sweet to him;
Ps 23: 4 walk through the *v* of the shadow
60: 6 and measure off the *V* of Succoth.
84: 6 As they pass through the *V* of Baca
108: 7 and measure off the *V* of Succoth.
Pr 30: 17 out by the ravens of the *v*,
SS 6: 11 to look at the new growth in the *v*,
Isa 17: 5 grain in the *V* of Rephaim.
22: 1 An oracle concerning the *V*
22: 5 and terror in the *V* of Vision,
28: 1 set on the head of a fertile *v*—
28: 4 set on the head of a fertile *v*,
28: 21 as in the *V* of Gibeon—
40: 4 Every *v* shall be raised up,
65: 10 and the *V* of Achor a resting place
Jer 2: 23 See how you behaved in the *v*;
7: 31 Topheth in the *V* of Ben Hinnom
7: 32 Hinnom, but the *V* of Slaughter,
7: 32 no longer call it Topheth or the *V*
19: 2 and go out to the *V* of Ben
19: 6 Hinnom, but the *V* of Slaughter.
19: 6 call this place Topheth or the *V*
21: 13 you who live above this *v*
31: 40 The whole *v* where dead bodies
31: 40 out to the Kidron *V* on the east
32: 35 for Baal in the *V* of Ben Hinnom
48: 8 The *v* will be ruined
Eze 37: 1 and set me in the middle of a *v*;
37: 2 bones on the floor of the *v*,
39: 11 called the *V* of Hamon Gog.
39: 11 in the *v* of those who travel east
39: 15 it in the *V* of Hamon
Hos 1: 5 bow in the *V* of Jezreel."
2: 15 will make the *V* of Achor a door
Joel 3: 2 down to the *V* of Jehoshaphat.
3: 12 advance into the *V* of Jehoshaphat,
3: 14 multitudes in the *v* of decision!
3: 14 near in the *v* of decision.
3: 18 and will water the *v* of acacias.
Am 1: 5 destroy the king who is in the *V*
6: 14 to the *v* of the Arabah."
Mic 1: 6 I will pour her stones into the *v*
Zec 14: 4 forming a great *v*, with half
14: 5 You will flee by my mountain *v*,
Lk 3: 5 Every *v* shall be filled in,
Jn 18: 1 and crossed the Kidron *V*.

VALLEYS (VALLEY)

Nu 14: 25 and Canaanites are living in the *v*,
24: 6 "Like *v* they spread out,
Dt 8: 7 with springs flowing in the *v*
11: 11 and *v* that drinks rain from heaven.
2Sa 22: 16 The *v* of the sea were exposed
1Ki 18: 5 the land to all the springs and *v*.
20: 28 of the hills and not a god of the *v*,
1Ch 12: 15 to flight everyone living in the *v*,
27: 29 was in charge of the herds in the *v*.
Job 39: 10 Will he till the *v* behind you?
Ps 18: 15 The *v* of the sea were exposed
65: 13 and the *v* are mantled with grain;
104: 8 they went down into the *v*,
SS 2: 1 a lily of the *v*.
Isa 22: 7 Your choicest *v* are full of chariots,
41: 18 and springs within the *v*.
Jer 49: 4 Why do you boast of your *v*,
49: 4 boast of your *v* so fruitful?
Eze 6: 3 and *v*: I am about to bring a sword
7: 16 moaning like doves of the *v*,
31: 12 on the mountains and in all the *v*;
32: 5 and fill the *v* with your remains.
35: 8 in your *v* and in all your ravines.
36: 4 and hills, to the ravines and *v*,
36: 6 and *v*: 'This is what the Sovereign
Mic 1: 4 and the *v* split apart,

VALUABLE (VALUE)

2Ch 32: 23 *v* gifts for Hezekiah king of Judah.
Ezr 1: 6 and livestock, and with *v* gifts,
Pr 1: 13 we will get all sorts of *v* things
Da 11: 8 and their *v* articles of silver
Mt 6: 26 Are you not much more *v*
12: 12 How much more *v* is a man
Lk 12: 24 And how much more *v* you are
Jas 5: 7 waits for the land to yield its *v* crop

VALUABLES (VALUE)

2Ch 32: 27 spices, shields and all kinds of *v*.
Jer 20: 5 all its *v* and all the treasures

VALUE (VALUABLE VALUABLES VALUED VALUES)

Lev 5: 15 and of the proper *v* in silver,
5: 16 add a fifth of the *v* to that
5: 18 without defect and of the proper *v*.
6: 5 add a fifth of the *v* to it
6: 6 without defect and of the proper *v*.
22: 14 and add a fifth of the *v* to it.
25: 27 is to determine the *v* for the years
27: 3 set the *v* of a male between the ages
27: 4 and if it is a female, set her *v*
27: 5 the *v* of a male at twenty shekels
27: 6 set the *v* of a male at five shekels
27: 7 set the *v* of a male at fifteen shekels
27: 8 will set the *v* for him according
27: 12 Whatever *v* the priest then sets,
27: 13 he must add a fifth to its *v*.
27: 14 Whatever *v* the priest then sets,
27: 15 he must add a fifth to its *v*,
27: 16 its *v* is to be set according
27: 17 the *v* that has been set remains.
27: 18 and its set *v* will be reduced.
27: 18 will determine the *v* according
27: 19 he must add a fifth to its *v*,
27: 23 the man must pay its *v* on that day
27: 23 the priest will determine its *v* up
27: 25 Every *v* is to be set according
27: 27 adding a fifth of the *v* to it.
27: 27 he may buy it back at its set *v*,
27: 27 is to be sold at its set *v*.
27: 31 he must add a fifth of the *v* to it.
1Sa 26: 24 so may the LORD *v* my life
1Ki 10: 21 of little *v* in Solomon's days.
20: 6 They will seize everything you *v*
2Ch 9: 20 of little *v* in Solomon's day.
20: 25 clothing and also articles of *v*—
21: 3 of silver and gold and articles of *v*,
36: 10 with articles of *v* from the temple
36: 19 destroyed everything of *v* there.
Job 15: 3 with speeches that have no *v*?
Pr 10: 2 Ill-gotten treasures are of no *v*,
10: 20 the heart of the wicked is of little *v*.
16: 13 they *v* a man who speaks the truth.
31: 11 and lacks nothing of *v*.
Eze 7: 11 crowd—no wealth, nothing of *v*.
Hab 2: 18 "Of what *v* is an idol,
Mt 13: 46 When he found one of great *v*,
Ac 19: 19 When they calculated the *v*
Ro 2: 25 Circumcision has *v*
3: 1 or what *v* is there in circumcision?
4: 14 faith has no *v* and the promise is
Gal 5: 2 Christ will be of no *v* to you at all.
5: 6 nor uncircumcision has any *v*.
Col 2: 23 lack any *v* in restraining sensual
1Ti 4: 8 For physical training is of some *v*,
4: 8 but godliness has *v* for all things,
2Ti 2: 14 is of no *v*, and only ruins those who
Heb 4: 2 the message they heard was of no *v*
11: 26 as of greater *v* than the treasures
13: 9 are of no *v* to those who eat them.

VALUED (VALUE)

1Sa 26: 24 As surely as I *v* your life today,
Ezr 8: 27 20 bowls of gold *v* at 1,000 darics,
Lk 7: 2 whom his master *v* highly,
16: 15 What is highly *v* among men is

VALUES (VALUE)

Lev 27: 2 the LORD by giving equivalent *v*,

VANIAH

Ezr 10: 36 Bedeiah, Keluhi, *V*, Meremoth,

VANISH (VANISHED VANISHES)

Job 6: 17 in the heat *v* from their channels.
Ps 37: 20 they will *v*— *v* like smoke.
58: 7 Let them *v* like water that flows
102: 3 For my days *v* like smoke;
104: 35 But may sinners *v* from the earth
Isa 11: 13 Ephraim's jealousy will *v*,
16: 4 the aggressor will *v* from the land.
29: 14 of the intelligent will *v*."
29: 20 The ruthless will *v*,
34: 12 all her princes will *v* away.
51: 6 the heavens will *v* like smoke,
Jer 18: 14 ever *v* from its rocky slopes?
31: 36 if these decrees *v* from my sight,"

VANISHED (VANISH)

Ps 12: 1 the faithful have *v*
77: 8 Has his unfailing love *v* forever?
Ecc 9: 6 and their jealousy have long since *v*
Jer 7: 28 Truth has perished; it has *v*

Rev 18: 14 All your riches and splendor have *v*

VANISHES (VANISH)

Job 7: 9 As a cloud *v* and is gone,
30: 15 my safety *v* like a cloud.
Jas 4: 14 appears for a little while and then *v*.

VAPOR

Pr 21: 6 is a fleeting *v* and a deadly snare.

VASHTI

Est 1: 9 Queen *V* also gave a banquet
1: 11 to bring before him Queen *V*,
1: 12 Queen *V* refused to come.
1: 15 what must be done to Queen *V*?"
1: 16 "Queen *V* has done wrong,
1: 17 King Xerxes commanded Queen *V*
1: 19 that *V* is never again
2: 1 he remembered *V* and what she
2: 4 the king be queen instead of *V*."
2: 17 and made her queen instead of *V*.

VASSAL (VASSALS)

2Ki 16: 7 Assyria, "I am your servant and *v*.
17: 3 who had been Shalmaneser's *v*
24: 1 and Jehoiakim became his *v*

VASSALS (VASSAL)

2Sa 10: 19 When all the kings who were *v*
1Ch 19: 19 When the *v* of Hadadezer saw that

VAST

Ge 2: 1 completed in all their *v* array.
Dt 1: 19 of the Amorites through all that *v*
2: 7 journey through this *v* desert.
8: 15 He led you through the *v*
1Ki 8: 65 all Israel with him—a *v* assembly,
20: 13 'Do you see this *v* army? I will give
20: 28 I will deliver this *v* army
2Ch 7: 8 all Israel with him—a *v* assembly,
13: 8 You are indeed a *v* army
14: 9 out against them with a *v* army
14: 11 come against this *v* army.
20: 2 "A *v* army is coming against you
20: 12 to face this *v* army that is attacking
20: 15 discouraged because of this *v* army.
20: 24 and looked toward the *v* army,
32: 7 of Assyria and the *v* army with him
Est 1: 4 he displayed the *v* wealth
1: 20 throughout all his *v* realm,
5: 11 boasted to them about his *v* wealth,
Job 9: 4 wisdom is profound, his power is *v*.
38: 18 you comprehended the *v* expanses
Ps 104: 25 There is the sea, *v* and spacious,
139: 17 How *v* is the sum of them!
Eze 26: 19 and its *v* waters cover you,
37: 10 stood up on their feet—a *v* army.

VAT (VATS)

Hag 2: 16 to a wine *v* to draw fifty measures,

VATS (VAT)

Ex 22: 29 from your granaries or your *v*.
1Ch 27: 27 of the vineyards for the wine *v*.
Pr 3: 10 *v* will brim over with new wine.
Joel 2: 24 the *v* will overflow with new wine
3: 13 and the *v* overflow—

VAULTED (VAULT)

Job 22: 14 as he goes about in the *v* heavens.'
Jer 37: 16 put into a *v* cell in a dungeon,

VAULTS (VAULTED)

Dt 32: 34 and sealed it in my *v*?

VAUNTS

Job 15: 25 and *v* himself against the Almighty

VEGETABLE (VEGETABLES)

Dt 11: 10 irrigated it by foot as in a *v* garden.
1Ki 21: 2 vineyard to use for a *v* garden,

VEGETABLES (VEGETABLE)

Pr 15: 17 of *v* where there is love
Da 1: 12 Give us nothing but *v* to eat
1: 16 to drink and gave them *v* instead.
Ro 14: 2 whose faith is weak, eats only *v*.

VEGETATION

Ge 1: 11 God said, "Let the land produce *v*:
1: 12 land produced *v*: plants bearing
19: 25 living in the cities—and also the *v*
Dt 29: 23 nothing sprouting, no *v* growing
Isa 15: 6 the *v* is gone
42: 15 and dry up all their *v*;

VEIL (VEILED VEILS)

Ge 24: 65 she took her *v* and covered herself.
38: 14 herself with a *v* to disguise herself,
38: 19 she took off her *v* and put
Ex 34: 33 to them, he put a *v* over his face.
34: 34 he removed the *v* until he came out
34: 35 Then Moses would put the *v* back
Job 22: 14 Thick clouds *v* him,
SS 4: 1 Your eyes behind your *v* are doves.
4: 3 Your temples behind your *v*
6: 7 Your temples behind your *v*
Isa 47: 2 take off your *v*.
La 3: 65 Put a *v* over their hearts,
2Co 3: 13 who would put a *v* over his face
3: 14 for to this day the same *v* remains
3: 15 is read, a *v* covers their hearts.
3: 16 to the Lord, the *v* is taken away.

VEILED (VEIL)

SS 1: 7 Why should I be like a *v* woman
2Co 4: 3 And even if our gospel is *v*,
4: 3 it is *v* to those who are perishing.

VEILS (VEIL)

Isa 3: 19 the earrings and bracelets and *v*,
Eze 13: 18 and make *v* of various lengths
13: 21 tear off your *v* and save my people

VENGEANCE (AVENGE AVENGED AVENGER AVENGES AVENGING REVENGE)

Ge 4: 15 he will suffer *v* seven times over."
Nu 31: 2 "Take *v* on the Midianites
31: 3 to carry out the LORD's *v* on them
Dt 32: 41 I will take *v* on my adversaries
32: 43 he will take *v* on his enemies
Ps 149: 7 to inflict *v* on the nations
Isa 34: 8 For the LORD has a day of *v*,
35: 4 he will come with *v*;
47: 3 I will take *v*;
59: 17 he put on the garments of *v*
61: 2 and the day of *v* of our God,
63: 4 For the day of *v* was in my heart,
Jer 11: 20 let me see your *v* upon them,
20: 12 let me see your *v* upon them,
46: 10 a day of *v*, for *v* on his foes.
50: 15 Since this is the *v* of the LORD,
50: 15 take *v* on her;
50: 28 the LORD our God has taken *v*,
50: 28 *v* for his temple.
51: 6 It is time for the LORD's *v*;
51: 11 The LORD will take *v*,
51: 11 *v* for his temple.
La 3: 60 You have seen the depth of their *v*,
Eze 16: 38 upon you the blood *v* of my wrath
25: 14 I will take *v* on Edom by the hand
25: 14 will know my *v*, declares
25: 15 'Because the Philistines acted in *v*
25: 17 I will carry out great *v* on them
25: 17 when I take *v* on them.' "
Mic 5: 15 I will take *v* in anger and wrath
Na 1: 2 The LORD takes *v* on his foes
1: 2 the LORD takes *v* and is filled

VENOM (VENOMOUS)

Dt 32: 24 the *v* of vipers that glide in the dust
32: 33 Their wine is the *v* of serpents,
Job 20: 14 it will become the *v* of serpents
Ps 58: 4 Their *v* is like the *v* of a snake,

VENOMOUS (VENOM)

Nu 21: 6 Then the LORD sent *v* snakes
Dt 8: 15 with its *v* snakes and scorpions.
Isa 14: 29 its fruit will be a darting, *v* serpent.
Jer 8: 17 I will send *v* snakes among you,

VENT

Job 15: 13 so that you *v* your rage against God
20: 23 God will *v* his burning anger
Pr 29: 11 A fool gives full *v* to his anger,

La 4: 11 The LORD has given full *v*
Da 11: 30 *v* his fury against the holy covenant

VENTURE (VENTURES)

Dt 28: 56 and gentle that she would not *v*
Jer 5: 6 to tear to pieces any who *v* out,
Ac 19: 31 not to *v* into the theater.
Ro 15: 18 I will not *v* to speak of anything

VENTURES (VENTURE)

Job 4: 2 "If someone *v* a word with you,

VERDANT

SS 1: 16 And our bed is *v*.

VERDICT

Dt 17: 9 and they will give you the *v*.
Jdg 20: 7 speak up and give your *v*."
1Ki 3: 28 all Israel heard the *v* the king had
2Ch 19: 6 is with you whenever you give a *v*.
Da 4: 17 the holy ones declare the *v*,
Jn 3: 19 This is the *v*: Light has come

VERIFIED (VERIFY)

Ge 42: 20 so that your words may be *v*

VERIFY (VERIFIED)

Ac 24: 11 You can easily *v* that no more

VERSED

Ezr 7: 6 He was a teacher well *v* in the Law

VERSES

Ps 45: 1 as I recite my *v* for the king;

VESSEL (VESSELS)

Isa 2: 16 and every stately *v*.

VESSELS (VESSEL)

Isa 22: 24 and offshoots—all its lesser *v*,
52: 11 you who carry the *v* of the LORD.
66: 20 the LORD in ceremonially clean *v*.

VESTMENTS

Ezr 3: 10 priests in their *v* and with trumpets,

VETERAN

Eze 27: 9 *V* craftsmen of Gebal were

VEXED

Ps 78: 41 they *v* the Holy One of Israel.
112: 10 The wicked man will see and be *v*,

VICINITY

Dt 11: 30 in the Arabah in the *v* of Gilgal.
Jos 3: 16 Adam in the *v* of Zarethan,
15: 46 all that were in the *v* of Ashdod,
Jdg 11: 33 from Aroer to the *v* of Minnith,
20: 43 and easily overran them in the *v*
1Sa 5: 6 the people of Ashdod and its *v*;
13: 17 toward Ophrah in the *v* of Shual,
2Ki 15: 16 and everyone in the city and its *v*,
Mt 2: 16 and its *v* who were two years old
15: 22 woman from that *v* came to him,
15: 39 and went to the *v* of Magadan.
Mk 7: 24 left that place and went to the *v*
7: 31 Then Jesus left the *v* of Tyre
Lk 24: 50 out to the *v* of Bethany,

VICTIM (VICTIMS)

Ps 10: 14 The *v* commits himself to you;
Hab 2: 7 Then you will become their *v*.

VICTIMS (VICTIM)

Nu 23: 24 and drinks the blood of his *v*."
31: 8 Among their *v* were Evi, Rekem,
Job 29: 17 and snatched the *v* from their teeth
Ps 10: 8 watching in secret for his *v*.
10: 10 His *v* are crushed, they collapse;
Pr 7: 26 Many are the *v* she has brought
Eze 34: 29 they will no longer be *v* of famine
Da 7: 7 it crushed and devoured its *v*
7: 19 and devoured its *v* and trampled
Na 3: 1 never without *v*!

VICTOR'S (VICTORY)

2Ti 2: 5 he does not receive the *v* crown

VICTORIES (VICTORY)

2Sa 22:51 He gives his king great *v;*
Ps 18:50 He gives his king great *v;*
21: 1 great is his joy in the *v* you give!
21: 5 Through the *v* you gave, his glory is
44: 4 who decrees *v* for Jacob.

VICTORIOUS (VICTORY)

1Ki 22:12 "Attack Ramoth Gilead and be *v,*"
22:15 "Attack and be *v,*" he answered,
2Ch 13:18 and the men of Judah were *v*
18:11 "Attack Ramoth Gilead and be *v,*"
18:14 "Attack and be *v,*" he answered,
Ps 20: 5 for joy when you are *v*
Da 11: 7 he will fight against them and be *v.*
Hab 3: 8 and your *v* chariots?
Rev 15: 2 those who had been *v*

VICTORIOUSLY (VICTORY)

Ps 45: 4 In your majesty ride forth *v*

VICTORY (VICTOR'S VICTORIES VICTORIOUS VICTORIOUSLY)

Ex 32:18 "It is not the sound of *v,*
Dt 20: 4 against your enemies to give you *v*
Jos 10:10 them in a great *v* at Gibeon.
Jdg 12: 3 and the LORD gave me the *v*
15:18 given your servant this great *v.*
1Sa 19: 5 The LORD won a great *v*
2Sa 8: 6 gave David *v* everywhere he
8:10 congratulate him on his *v* in battle
8:14 gave David *v* everywhere he
19: 2 the whole army the *v* that day was
22:36 You give me your shield of *v;*
23:10 brought about a great *v* that day.
23:12 the LORD brought about a great *v.*
2Ki 5: 1 him the LORD had given *v*
13:17 The LORD's arrow of *v,* the arrow
13:17 the arrow of *v* over Aram!"
14:10 Glory in your *v,* but stay at home!
1Ch 11:14 the LORD brought about a great *v.*
18: 6 gave David *v* everywhere he
18:10 congratulate him on his *v* in battle
18:13 gave David *v* everywhere he
Job 12:16 To him belong strength and *v;*
Ps 18:35 You give me your shield of *v,*
44: 3 nor did their arm bring them *v;*
44: 6 my sword does not bring me *v;*
44: 7 but you give us *v* over our enemies,
60:12 With God we will gain the *v,*
108:13 With God we will gain the *v,*
118:15 Shouts of joy and *v*
129: 2 they have not gained the *v* over me.
144:10 to the One who gives *v* to kings,
Pr 2: 7 He holds *v* in store for the upright,
11:14 but many advisers make *v* sure.
21:31 but *v* rests with the LORD.
24: 6 and for *v* many advisers.
Mt 12:20 till he leads justice to *v.*
1Co 15:54 "Death has been swallowed up in *v*
15:55 "Where, O death, is your *v?*
15:57 He gives us the *v* through our Lord
1Jn 5: 4 This is the *v* that has overcome

VIEW (VIEWED VIEWPOINT VIEWS)

Nu 23: 9 from the heights I *v* them.
33: 3 boldly in full *v* of all the Egyptians,
Dt 32:49 across from Jericho, and *v* Canaan,
Ne 9:38 "In *v* of all this, we are making
Ps 48:13 *v* her citadels,
68:24 Your procession has come into *v,*
Pr 1:17 a net in full *v* of all the birds!
5:21 are in full *v* of the LORD,
17:24 discerning man keeps wisdom in *v,*
Isa 33:17 and *v* a land that stretches afar.
Mk 2:12 and walked out in full *v* of them all.
Ro 12: 1 brothers, in *v* of God's mercy,
1Co 9: 8 merely from a human point of *v?*
2Co 5:16 one from a worldly point of *v.*
Gal 5:10 Lord that you will take no other *v.*
Php 3:15 are mature should take such a *v*
2Ti 4: 1 and in *v* of his appearing
Rev 13:13 heaven to earth in full *v* of men.

VIEWED (VIEW)

Nu 32: 9 the Valley of Eshcol and *v* the land,
Ps 102:19 from heaven he *v* the earth,

VIEWPOINT (VIEW)

1Jn 4: 5 speak from the *v* of the world,

VIEWS (VIEW)

Job 28:24 for he *v* the ends of the earth
Ac 28:22 we want to hear what your *v* are,

VIGIL

Ex 12:42 are to keep *v* to honor the LORD
12:42 the LORD kept *v* that night
Isa 65: 4 spend their nights keeping secret *v;*

VIGOR (VIGOROUS)

Job 5:26 You will come to the grave in full *v,*
18: 7 The *v* of his step is weakened;
20:11 The youthful *v* that fills his bones
21:23 One man dies in full *v,*
30: 2 since their *v* had gone from them?
Pr 31: 3 your *v* on those who ruin kings.
Ecc 11:10 for youth and *v* are meaningless.

VIGOROUS (VIGOR)

Ex 1:19 they are *v* and give birth
Jos 14:11 I'm just as *v* to go out to battle now
Jdg 3:29 all *v* and strong; not a man escaped.
Ps 38:19 are those who are my *v* enemies;

VILE (VILENESS VILEST)

Jdg 19:23 "No, my friends, don't be so *v.*
2Ki 23:13 built for Ashtoreth the *v* goddess
23:13 for Chemosh the *v* god of Moab,
Est 7: 6 and enemy is this *v* Haman."
Job 15:16 how much less man, who is *v*
Ps 12: 8 when what is *v* is honored
14: 1 They are corrupt, their deeds are *v;*
15: 4 who despises a *v* man
41: 8 "A *v* disease has beset him;
53: 1 are corrupt, and their ways are *v;*
101: 3 no *v* thing.
Jer 16:18 the lifeless forms of their *v* images
Eze 5:11 sanctuary with all your *v* images
7:20 their detestable idols and *v* images.
11:18 and remove all its *v* images
11:21 hearts are devoted to their *v* images
16:52 Because your sins were more *v*
20: 7 of the *v* images you have set your
20: 8 of the *v* images they had set their
20:30 and lust after their *v* images?
37:23 and *v* images or with any
Hos 9:10 became as *v* as the thing they loved
Na 1:14 for you are *v.*"
Rev 21: 8 unbelieving, the *v,* the murderers,
22:11 let him who is *v* continue to be *v;*

VILENESS (VILE)

Jdg 20:10 for all this *v* done in Israel."
Isa 9:17 every mouth speaks *v.*

VILEST (VILE)

1Ki 21:26 behaved in the *v* manner by going
Hos 1: 2 guilty of the *v* adultery in departing

VILLAGE (VILLAGES)

Jdg 5: 7 *V* life in Israel ceased,
Mt 10:11 "Whatever town or *v* you enter,
21: 2 "Go to the *v* ahead of you,
Mk 6: 6 went around teaching from *v* to *v.*
8:23 the hand and led him outside the *v.*
8:26 saying, "Don't go into the *v.*"
11: 2 "Go to the *v* ahead of you,
Lk 5:17 come from every *v* of Galilee
8: 1 from one town and *v* to another,
9: 6 they set out and went from *v* to *v,*
9:52 went into a Samaritan *v*
9:56 and they went to another *v.*
10:38 came to a *v* where a woman named
17:12 into a *v,* ten men who had leprosy
19:30 "Go to the *v* ahead of you,
24:13 going to a *v* called Emmaus,
24:28 As they approached the *v*
Jn 11: 1 *v* of Mary and her sister Martha.
11:30 Jesus had not yet entered the *v,*
11:54 to a *v* called Ephraim, where he

VILLAGES (VILLAGE)

Lev 25:31 But houses in *v* without walls
Dt 2:23 for the Avvites who lived in *v* as far
3: 5 also a great many unwalled *v.*
Jos 10:37 together with its king, its *v*
10:39 its *v,* and put them to the sword.
13:23 and their *v* were the inheritance
13:28 and their *v* were the inheritance
15:32 of twenty-nine towns and their *v.*
15:36 fourteen towns and their *v.*
15:41 sixteen towns and their *v.*
15:44 Mareshah—nine towns and their *v*
15:45 its surrounding settlements and *v;*
15:46 together with their *v;* Ashdod,
15:47 and Gaza, its settlements and *v,*
15:47 its surrounding settlements and *v;*
15:51 Giloh—eleven towns and their *v.*
15:54 and Zior—nine towns and their *v.*
15:57 Timnah—ten towns and their *v.*
15:59 Eltekon—six towns and their *v.*
15:60 Rabbah—two towns and their *v.*
15:62 six towns and their *v.*
16: 9 and their *v* that were set
18:24 Geba—twelve towns and their *v.*
18:28 fourteen towns and their *v.*
19: 6 thirteen towns and their *v;*
19: 7 Ashan—four towns and their *v*—
19: 8 and all the *v* around these towns
19:15 were twelve towns and their *v.*
19:16 and their *v* were the inheritance
19:22 were sixteen towns and their *v.*
19:23 and their *v* were the inheritance
19:30 were twenty-two towns and their *v.*
19:31 and their *v* were the inheritance
19:38 were nineteen towns and their *v.*
19:39 and their *v* were the inheritance
19:48 and their *v* were the inheritance
21:12 *v* around the city they had given
1Sa 6:18 towns with their country *v.*
1Ch 4:32 Their surrounding *v* were Etam,
4:33 and all the *v* around these towns
5:16 in Bashan and its outlying *v,*
6:56 and *v* around the city were given
7:28 Bethel and its surrounding *v,*
7:28 Gezer and its *v* to the west,
7:28 and its *v* all the way to Ayyah
7:28 the way to Ayyah and its *v.*
7:29 and Dor, together with their *v.*
8:12 and Lod with its surrounding *v),*
9:16 lived in the *v* of the Netophathites
9:22 registered by genealogy in their *v.*
9:25 brothers in their *v* had to come
18: 1 its surrounding *v* from the control
27:25 the *v* and the watchtowers.
2Ch 8: 2 Solomon rebuilt the *v* that Hiram
13:19 Ephron, with their surrounding *v.*
14:14 They destroyed all the *v*
14:14 They plundered all these *v,*
28:18 Gimzo, with their surrounding *v.*
32:29 He built *v* and acquired great
Ne 6: 2 in one of the *v* on the plain of Ono
11:25 As for the *v* with their fields,
11:25 in Jekabzeel and its *v,* in Jeshua,
11:30 Zanoah, Adullam and their *v,*
12:28 from the *v* of the Netophathites,
12:29 for the singers had built *v*
Est 9:19 rural Jews—those living in *v*—
Ps 10: 8 He lies in wait near the *v;*
48:11 the *v* of Judah are glad
97: 8 and the *v* of Judah are glad
SS 7:11 let us spend the night in the *v.*
Jer 17:26 and the *v* around Jerusalem,
19:15 and the *v* around it every disaster I
32:44 in the *v* around Jerusalem,
33:13 in the *v* around Jerusalem
49: 2 its surrounding *v* will be set on fire.
Eze 30:18 and her *v* will go into captivity.
38:11 "I will invade a land of unwalled *v;*
38:13 and all her *v* will say to you,
Mt 9:35 went through all the towns and *v,*
14:15 so they can go to the *v*
Mk 1:38 nearby *v*—so I can preach there
6:36 *v* and buy themselves something
6:56 into *v,* towns or countryside—
8:27 went on to the *v* around Caesarea
Lk 9:12 so they can go to the surrounding *v*
13:22 Jesus went through the towns and *v*
Ac 8:25 the gospel in many Samaritan *v.*

VILLAIN

Pr 6:12 A scoundrel and *v,*

2Ki 18: 12 but had v his covenant—all that
Isa 24: 5 v the statutes
Jer 34: 18 The men who have v my covenant
Da 11: 32 those who have v the covenant,
Mal 2: 8 you have v the covenant with Levi

VIOLATES (VIOLATE)

Ps 55: 20 he v his covenant.
Eze 22: 11 and another v his sister, his own

VIOLATING (VIOLATE)

1Ch 2: 7 disaster on Israel by v the ban

VIOLATION (VIOLATE)

Lev 5: 15 "When a person commits a v
Dt 17: 2 God in v of his covenant,
Heb 2: 2 every v and disobedience received

VIOLENCE (VIOLENT)

Ge 6: 11 in God's sight and was full of v.
6: 13 for the earth is filled with v
49: 5 their swords are weapons of v.
1Ch 12: 17 when my hands are free from v,
Job 16: 17 yet my hands have been free of v
Ps 7: 9 bring to an end the v of the wicked
7: 16 his v comes down on his own head.
11: 5 the wicked and those who love v
27: 12 breathing out v.
55: 9 for I see v and strife in the city.
58: 2 your hands mete out v on the earth.
72: 14 from oppression and v,
73: 6 they clothe themselves with v.
74: 20 haunts of v fill the dark places
140: 1 protect me from men of v,
140: 4 protect me from men of v
140: 11 may disaster hunt down men of v.
Pr 4: 17 and drink the wine of v.
10: 6 v overwhelms the mouth
10: 11 v overwhelms the mouth
13: 2 the unfaithful have a craving for v.
21: 7 v of the wicked will drag them
24: 2 for their hearts plot v,
26: 6 off one's feet or drinking v
Isa 42: 25 the v of war.
53: 9 though he had done no v,
59: 6 and acts of v are in their hands.
60: 18 No longer will v be heard
Jer 6: 7 V and destruction resound in her;
20: 8 proclaiming v and destruction.
22: 3 Do no wrong or v to the alien,
51: 35 May the v done to our flesh be
51: 46 rumors of v in the land
Eze 7: 11 V has grown into a rod
7: 23 of bloodshed and the city is full of v
8: 17 with v and continually provoke me
12: 19 of the v of all who live there.
22: 26 Her priests do v to my law
28: 16 you were filled with v,
45: 9 Give up your v and oppression
Hos 12: 1 and multiplies lies and v.
Joel 3: 19 of v done to the people of Judah,
Ob : 10 of the v against your brother Jacob,
Jnh 3: 8 give up their evil ways and their v.
Hab 1: 2 Or cry out to you, "V!"
1: 3 Destruction and v are before me;
1: 9 they all come bent on v.
2: 17 The v you have done
Zep 1: 9 gods with v and deceit.
3: 4 and do v to the law.
Mal 2: 16 a man's covering himself with v
Ac 21: 35 the v of the mob was
Rev 18: 21 "With such v

VIOLENT (VIOLENCE)

2Sa 22: 3 from v men you save me.
22: 49 from v men you rescued me.
Ps 17: 4 myself from the ways of the v.
18: 48 from v men you rescued me.
Pr 3: 31 Do not envy a v man
16: 29 A v man entices his neighbor
Eze 13: 11 and v winds will burst forth.
13: 13 In my wrath I will unleash a v wind,
18: 10 "Suppose he has a v son, who sheds
28: 8 and you will die a v death
Da 11: 14 v men among your own people will
Am 1: 14 amid v winds on a stormy day.
Jnh 1: 4 such a v storm arose that the ship
Mic 6: 12 Her rich men are v;

Mt 8: 28 so v that no one could pass that
28: 2 There was a v earthquake,
Ac 2: 2 of a v wind came from heaven
16: 26 there was such a v earthquake that
23: 10 so v that the commander was afraid
27: 18 We took such a v battering
1Ti 1: 13 and a persecutor and a v man,
3: 3 not v but gentle, not quarrelsome,
Tit 1: 7 not v, not pursuing dishonest gain.

VIPER (VIPER'S VIPERS)

Ge 49: 17 a v along the path,
Pr 23: 32 and poisons like a v.
Isa 14: 29 root of that snake will spring up a v,
Ac 28: 3 a v, driven out by the heat,

VIPER'S (VIPER)

Isa 11: 8 child put his hand into the v nest.

VIPERS (VIPER)

Dt 32: 24 the venom of v that glide
Ps 140: 3 the poison of v is on their lips.
Isa 59: 5 They hatch the eggs of v
Jer 8: 17 v that cannot be charmed,
Mt 3: 7 he said to them: "You brood of v!
12: 34 of v, how can you who are evil say
23: 33 "You snakes! You brood of v!
Lk 3: 7 "You brood of v! Who warned you
Ro 3: 13 "The poison of v is on their lips."

VIRGIN (VIRGIN'S VIRGINITY VIRGINS)

Ge 24: 16 The girl was very beautiful, a v;
Ex 22: 16 a man seduces a v who is not
Lev 21: 13 The woman he marries must be a v.
21: 14 but only a v from his own people,
Dt 22: 15 shall bring proof that she was a v
22: 17 not find your daughter to be a v.'
22: 19 has given an Israelite v a bad name.
22: 23 in a town a v pledged to be married
22: 28 to meet a v who is not pledged
Jdg 11: 39 And she was a v.
19: 24 Look, here is my v daughter,
21: 11 and every woman who is not a v."
2Sa 13: 2 for she was a v, and it seemed
13: 18 kind of garment the v daughters
1Ki 1: 2 for a young v to attend the king
2Ki 19: 21 " 'The V Daughter of Zion
Ps 45: 14 her v companions follow her
Isa 7: 14 The v will be with child
23: 12 O V Daughter of Sidon, now
37: 22 "The V Daughter of Zion
47: 1 V Daughter of Babylon;
Jer 14: 17 for my v daughter—my people—
18: 13 done by V Israel.
31: 4 and you will be rebuilt, O V Israel.
31: 21 Return, O V Israel,
46: 11 O V Daughter of Egypt.
La 1: 15 the V Daughter of Judah.
2: 13 O V Daughter of Zion?
Eze 23: 3 and their v bosoms caressed.
23: 8 caressed her v bosom and poured
Joel 1: 8 Mourn like a v in sackcloth
Am 5: 2 concerning you: "Fallen is V Israel,
Mt 1: 23 "The v will be with child
Lk 1: 27 to a v pledged to be married
1: 34 I am a v?" The angel answered,
1Co 7: 28 if a v marries, she has not sinned.
7: 34 or v is concerned about the Lord's
7: 36 toward the v he is engaged to,
7: 37 up his mind not to marry the v—
7: 38 he who marries the v does right,
2Co 11: 2 that I might present you as a pure v

VIRGIN'S (VIRGIN)

Lk 1: 27 The v name was Mary.

VIRGINITY (VIRGIN)

Dt 22: 14 I did not find proof of her v,"
22: 17 here is the proof of my daughter's v
22: 20 no proof of the girl's v can be found

VIRGINS (VIRGIN)

Ex 22: 17 must still pay the bride-price for v.
Est 2: 2 for beautiful young v for the king.
2: 17 more than any of the other v.
2: 19 When the v were assembled
SS 6: 8 and v beyond number;
La 5: 11 and v in the towns of Judah.

Eze 44: 22 they may marry only v
Mt 25: 1 will be like ten v who took their
25: 7 "Then all the v woke up
25: 10 The v who were ready went
1Co 7: 25 Now about v: I have no command

VIRTUES

Col 3: 14 And over all these v put on love,

VISIBLE

Ge 8: 5 tops of the mountains became v.
Da 4: 11 it was v to the ends of the earth.
4: 20 with its top touching the sky, v
Eph 5: 13 exposed by the light becomes v,
5: 14 it is light that makes everything v.
Col 1: 16 and on earth, v and invisible,
Heb 11: 3 was not made out of what was v.

VISION (VISIONS)

Ge 15: 1 of the LORD came to Abram in a v
46: 2 God spoke to Israel in a v at night
Nu 24: 4 who sees a v from the Almighty,
24: 16 who sees a v from the Almighty,
1Sa 3: 15 He was afraid to tell Eli the v,
2Ch 32: 32 in the v of the prophet Isaiah son
Job 20: 8 banished like a v of the night.
33: 15 In a dream, in a v of the night,
Ps 89: 19 Once you spoke in a v,
Isa 1: 1 The v concerning Judah
21: 2 A dire v has been shown to me:
22: 1 oracle concerning the Valley of V:
22: 5 and terror in the Valley of V,
29: 7 with a v in the night—
29: 11 For you this whole v is nothing
Eze 7: 13 for the v concerning the whole
7: 26 try to get a v from the prophet;
8: 4 as in the v I had seen in the plain.
11: 24 exiles in Babylonia in the v given
11: 24 the v I had seen went up from me,
12: 22 and every v comes to nothing'?
12: 23 near when every v will be fulfilled
12: 27 'The v he sees is for many years
43: 3 v I saw was like the v I had seen
Da 2: 19 was revealed to Daniel in a v.
2: 45 meaning of the v of the rock cut out
7: 2 "In my v at night I looked,
7: 7 After that, in my v at night I looked
7: 13 "In my v at night I looked,
8: 1 had a v, after the one that had
8: 2 In my v I saw myself in the citadel
8: 2 in the v I was beside the Ulai Canal.
8: 13 take for the v to be fulfilled—
8: 13 the v concerning the daily sacrifice,
8: 15 was watching the v and trying
8: 16 tell this man the meaning of the v."
8: 17 "understand that the v concerns
8: 19 the v concerns the appointed time
8: 26 but seal up the v, for it concerns
8: 26 "The v of the evenings
8: 27 appalled by the v; it was
9: 21 the man I had seen in the earlier v,
9: 23 the message and understand the v:
9: 24 to seal up v and prophecy
10: 1 of the message came to him in a v.
10: 7 was the only one who saw the v;
10: 8 at this great v; I had no strength left
10: 14 for the v concerns a time yet
10: 16 with anguish because of the v,
11: 14 rebel in fulfillment of the v,
Ob : 1 The v of Obadiah.
Mic 1: 1 the v he saw concerning Samaria
Na 1: 1 of the v of Nahum the Elkoshite.
Zec 1: 8 During the night I had a v—
13: 4 ashamed of his prophetic v.
Lk 1: 22 They realized he had seen a v
24: 23 and told us that they had seen a v
Ac 9: 10 The Lord called to him in a v,
9: 12 In a v he has seen a man named
10: 3 three in the afternoon he had a v.
10: 17 about the meaning of the v,
10: 19 Peter was still thinking about the v,
11: 5 and in a trance I saw a v.
12: 9 he thought he was seeing a v.
16: 9 During the night Paul had a v
16: 10 After Paul had seen the v,
18: 9 night the Lord spoke to Paul in a v:
26: 19 disobedient to the v from heaven.
Rev 9: 17 riders I saw in my v looked like this

VISIONS (VISION)

Nu 12: 6 I reveal myself to him in v,
1Sa 3: 1 was rare; there were not many v.
2Ch 9: 29 in the v of Iddo the seer concerning
Job 7: 14 and terrify me with v,
Isa 28: 7 they stagger when seeing v,
30: 10 Give us no more v of what is right!
30: 10 "See no more v!"
Jer 14: 14 They are prophesying to you false v
23: 16 They speak v from their own minds
La 2: 9 v from the LORD.
2: 14 The v of your prophets
Eze 1: 1 heavens were opened and I saw v
8: 3 and in v of God he took me
12: 24 For there will be no more false v
13: 6 Their v are false and their
13: 7 Have you not seen false v
13: 8 of your false words and lying v,
13: 9 against the prophets who see false v
13: 16 and saw v of peace for her
13: 23 you will no longer see false v
21: 29 Despite false v concerning you
22: 28 deeds for them by false v
40: 2 In v of God he took me to the land
43: 3 and like the v I had seen
Da 1: 17 And Daniel could understand v
2: 28 v that passed through your mind
4: 5 and v that passed through my mind
4: 10 These are the v I saw while lying
4: 13 In the v I saw while lying in my bed
7: 1 and v passed through his mind
7: 15 the v that passed through my mind
Hos 12: 10 gave them many v
Joel 2: 28 your young men will see v.
Mic 3: 6 over you, without v,
Zec 10: 2 diviners see v that lie;
Ac 2: 17 your young men will see v,
2Co 12: 1 I will go on to v and revelations

VISIT (VISITED VISITORS VISITS)

Ge 34: 1 went out to v the women
Jdg 15: 1 a young goat and went to v his wife.
2Ch 18: 2 went down to v Ahab in Samaria.
22: 7 Through Ahaziah's v to Joram,
Mt 25: 36 in prison and you came to v me.'
25: 39 or in prison and go to v you?'
Jn 11: 45 the Jews who had come to v Mary,
Ac 7: 12 he sent our fathers on their first v.
7: 13 On their second v, Joseph told his
7: 23 he decided to v his fellow Israelites.
9: 32 he went to v the saints in Lydda.
10: 28 to associate with a Gentile or v him
15: 36 and v the brothers in all the towns
19: 21 he said, "I must v Rome also."
Ro 15: 24 I hope to v you while passing
15: 28 go to Spain and v you on the way.
1Co 16: 7 and make only a passing v;
2Co 1: 15 I planned to v you first
1: 16 I planned to v you on my way
2: 1 I would not make another painful v
9: 5 the brothers to v you in advance
12: 14 Now I am ready to v you
13: 1 This will be my third v to you.
1Th 2: 1 that our v to you was not a failure.
2Jn : 12 I hope to v you and talk

VISITED (VISIT)

Jn 4: 46 Once more he v Cana in Galilee,
19: 39 the man who earlier had v Jesus

VISITORS (VISIT)

Ac 2: 10 v from Rome (both Jews

VISITS (VISIT)

Mic 7: 4 the day God v you.
1Pe 2: 12 and glorify God on the day he v us.

VOICE (VOICES)

Ge 27: 22 and said, "The v is the v of Jacob,
Ex 15: 26 to the v of the LORD your God
19: 19 and the v of God answered him.
24: 3 they responded with one v,
Nu 7: 89 he heard the v speaking to him
Dt 4: 12 saw no form; there was only a v.
4: 33 Has any other people heard the v
4: 36 heaven he made you hear his v
5: 22 in a loud v to your whole assembly
5: 23 When you heard the v out
Dt 5: 24 we have heard his v from the fire.
5: 25 and we will die if we hear the v
5: 26 mortal man has ever heard the v
18: 16 "Let us not hear the v
26: 7 and the LORD heard our v
27: 14 to all the people of Israel in a loud v
30: 20 listen to his v, and hold fast to him.
Jdg 5: 11 the v of the singers
18: 3 they recognized the v
1Sa 1: 13 moving but her v was not heard.
15: 22 as in obeying the v of the LORD?
24: 16 "Is that your v, David my son?"
26: 17 Saul recognized David's v and said,
26: 17 "Is that your v, David my son?"
28: 12 she cried out at the top of her v
2Sa 22: 7 From his temple he heard my v;
22: 14 the v of the Most High resounded.
1Ki 8: 55 assembly of Israel in a loud v,
19: 13 v said to him, "What are you doing
2Ki 19: 22 whom have you raised your v
2Ch 5: 13 as with one v, to give praise
20: 19 the God of Israel, with very loud v.
Ezr 10: 12 assembly responded with a loud v:
Job 4: 16 and I heard a hushed v:
37: 2 Listen! Listen to the roar of his v,
37: 4 When his v resounds,
37: 4 he thunders with his majestic v.
37: 5 v thunders in marvelous ways;
38: 34 "Can you raise your v to the clouds
40: 9 and can your v thunder like his?
Ps 5: 3 morning, O LORD, you hear my v;
18: 6 From his temple he heard my v;
18: 13 the v of the Most High resounded.
19: 3 where their v is not heard.
19: 4 Their v goes out into all the earth,
27: 7 Hear my v when I call, O LORD;
29: 3 The v of the LORD is
29: 4 The v of the LORD is powerful;
29: 4 the v of the LORD is majestic.
29: 5 v of the LORD breaks the cedars;
29: 7 The v of the LORD strikes
29: 8 v of the LORD shakes the desert;
29: 9 The v of the LORD twists the oaks
46: 6 he lifts his v, the earth melts.
55: 3 distraught at the v of the enemy,
55: 17 and he hears my v.
64: 1 O God, as I v my complaint;
66: 19 and heard my v in prayer.
68: 33 who thunders with mighty v.
93: 3 the seas have lifted up their v;
95: 7 Today, if you hear his v,
116: 1 for he heard my v;
119: 149 Hear my v in accordance
130: 2 O LORD; O Lord, hear my v.
141: 1 Hear my v when I call to you.
142: 1 I lift up my v to the LORD
Pr 1: 20 she raises her v in the public
8: 1 Does not understanding raise her v
8: 4 I raise my v to all mankind.
SS 2: 14 for your v is sweet,
2: 14 let me hear your v;
8: 13 let me hear your v!
Isa 6: 8 I heard the v of the Lord saying,
28: 23 Listen and hear my v;
29: 4 Your v will come ghostlike
30: 21 your ears will hear a v behind you,
30: 30 men to hear his majestic v
30: 31 v of the LORD will shatter
33: 3 of your v, the peoples flee;
37: 23 whom have you raised your v
40: 3 A v of one calling:
40: 6 A v says, "Cry out."
40: 9 lift up your v with a shout,
42: 2 or raise his v in the streets.
58: 1 Raise your v like a trumpet.
58: 4 expect your v to be heard on high.
Jer 4: 15 A v is announcing from Dan,
22: 20 let your v be heard in Bashan,
25: 30 he will lift his v from his holy
31: 15 "A v is heard in Ramah,
31: 16 "Restrain your v from weeping
Eze 1: 24 like the v of the Almighty,
1: 25 came a v from above the expanse
1: 28 and I heard the v of one speaking.
9: 1 I heard him call out in a loud v,
10: 5 like the v of God Almighty
11: 13 facedown and cried out in a loud v,
27: 30 They will raise their v
Eze 33: 32 sings love songs with a beautiful v
43: 2 His v was like the roar
Da 4: 14 in a loud v: 'Cut down the tree
4: 31 lips when a v came from heaven,
6: 20 called to Daniel in an anguished v,
8: 16 I heard a man's v from the Ulai
10: 6 his v like the sound of a multitude.
Hag 1: 12 remnant of the people obeyed the v
Mt 2: 18 was fulfilled: "A v is heard
3: 3 "A v of one calling in the desert,
3: 17 And a v from heaven said,
12: 19 no one will hear his v in the streets.
17: 5 and a v from the cloud said,
27: 46 hour Jesus cried out in a loud v,
27: 50 had cried out again in a loud v,
Mk 1: 3 "a v of one calling in the desert,
1: 11 And a v came from heaven:
5: 7 He shouted at the top of his v,
9: 7 and a v came from the cloud:
15: 34 hour Jesus cried out in a loud v,
Lk 1: 42 In a loud v she exclaimed:
3: 4 "A v of one calling in the desert,
3: 22 And a v came from heaven:
4: 33 He cried out at the top of his v, "Ha
8: 28 shouting at the top of his v,
9: 35 A v came from the cloud, saying,
9: 36 When the v had spoken, they found
17: 13 distance and called out in a loud v,
17: 15 came back, praising God in a loud v
23: 18 With one v they cried out,
23: 46 Jesus called out with a loud v,
Jn 1: 23 "I am the v of one calling
3: 29 when he hears the bridegroom's v.
5: 25 come when the dead will hear the v
5: 28 are in their graves will hear his v
5: 37 You have never heard his v
7: 37 Jesus stood and said in a loud v,
10: 3 and the sheep listen to his v.
10: 4 him because they know his v.
10: 5 they do not recognize a stranger's v
10: 16 They too will listen to my v,
10: 27 listen to my v; I know them,
11: 43 Jesus called in a loud v, "Lazarus,
12: 28 Then a v came from heaven,
12: 30 "This v was for your benefit,
Ac 2: 14 raised his v and addressed
7: 31 he heard the Lord's v: 'I am
9: 4 fell to the ground and heard a v say
10: 13 Then a v told him, "Get up, Peter.
10: 15 The v spoke to him a second time,
11: 7 Then I heard a v telling me, 'Get up
11: 9 v spoke from heaven a second time,
12: 14 When she recognized Peter's v,
12: 22 They shouted, "This is the v
22: 7 fell to the ground and heard a v say
22: 9 but they did not understand the v
26: 14 I heard a v saying to me in Aramaic
Ro 10: 18 "Their v has gone out
1Th 4: 16 with the v of the archangel
Heb 3: 7 "Today, if you hear his v,
3: 15 "Today, if you hear his v,
4: 7 "Today, if you hear his v,
12: 19 or to such a v speaking words,
12: 26 At that time his v shook the earth,
2Pe 1: 17 the Father when the v came to him
1: 18 ourselves heard this v that came
2: 16 who spoke with a man's v
Rev 1: 10 behind me a loud v like a trumpet,
1: 12 to see the v that was speaking
1: 15 and his v was like the sound
3: 20 If anyone hears my v and opens
4: 1 the v I had first heard speaking
5: 2 angel proclaiming in a loud v,
5: 11 and heard the v of many angels,
5: 12 In a loud v they sang:
6: 1 say in a v like thunder,
6: 6 Then I heard what sounded like a v
6: 7 I heard the v of the fourth living
6: 10 They called out in a loud v,
7: 2 He called out in a loud v
7: 10 And they cried out in a loud v:
8: 13 flying in midair call out in a loud v:
9: 13 I heard a v coming from the horns
10: 4 but I heard a v from heaven say,
10: 8 Then the v that I had heard
11: 12 Then they heard a loud v
12: 10 Then I heard a loud v in heaven say
14: 7 He said in a loud v, "Fear God

Rev 14: 9 followed them and said in a loud *v:*
14: 13 Then I heard a *v* from heaven say,
14: 15 in a loud *v* to him who was sitting
14: 18 called in a loud *v* to him who had
16: 1 I heard a loud *v* from the temple
16: 17 and out of the temple came a loud *v*
18: 2 With a mighty *v* he shouted:
18: 4 I heard another *v* from heaven say:
18: 23 The *v* of bridegroom and bride
19: 5 Then a *v* came from the throne,
19: 17 who cried in a loud *v*
21: 3 I heard a loud *v* from the throne

VOICES (VOICE)

Nu 14: 1 of the community raised their *v*
Jos 6: 10 give a war cry, do not raise your *v,*
Jdg 21: 2 raising their *v* and weeping bitterly.
2Sa 19: 35 Can I still hear the *v* of men
2Ch 5: 13 they raised their *v* in praise
Ne 9: 4 who called with loud *v*
Job 29: 10 the *v* of the nobles were hushed,
Isa 6: 4 the sound of their *v* the doorposts
15: 4 their *v* are heard all the way
24: 14 They raise their *v,* they shout
42: 11 desert and its towns raise their *v;*
52: 8 Your watchmen lift up their *v;*
Jer 7: 34 and gladness and to the *v* of bride
16: 9 and gladness and to the *v* of bride
25: 10 the *v* of bride and bridegroom,
33: 11 and the *v* of those who bring thank
33: 11 the *v* of bride and bridegroom,
51: 55 the roar of their *v* will resound.
Da 5: 10 hearing the *v* of the king
Na 2: 13 The *v* of your messengers
Lk 19: 37 to praise God in loud *v*
Ac 4: 24 they raised their *v* together
7: 57 and, yelling at the top of their *v,*
22: 22 they raised their *v* and shouted,
Rev 10: 3 the *v* of the seven thunders spoke.
11: 15 and there were loud *v* in heaven,

VOLUNTEERED (VOLUNTEERS)

1Ch 12: 38 All these were fighting men who *v*
2Ch 17: 16 who *v* himself for the service
Ne 11: 2 commended all the men who *v*

VOLUNTEERS (VOLUNTEERED)

Jdg 5: 9 the willing *v* among the people.

VOMIT (VOMITED)

Lev 18: 28 it will *v* you out as it vomited out
20: 22 you to live may not *v* you out.
Job 20: 15 will make his stomach *v* them up.
Pr 23: 8 You will *v* up the little you have
25: 16 too much of it, and you will *v.*
26: 11 As a dog returns to its *v,*
Isa 19: 14 a drunkard staggers around in his *v.*
28: 8 All the tables are covered with *v*
Jer 25: 27 says: Drink, get drunk and *v,*
48: 26 Let Moab wallow in her *v;*
2Pe 2: 22 "A dog returns to its *v,*" and,

VOMITED (VOMIT)

Lev 18: 25 and the land *v* out its inhabitants.
18: 28 as it *v* out the nations that were
Jnh 2: 10 and it *v* Jonah onto dry land.

VOPHSI

Nu 13: 14 Nahbi son of *V;* from the tribe

VOTE

Ac 26: 10 to death, I cast my *v* against them.

VOUCH

Col 4: 13 I *v* for him that he is working hard

VOW (VOWED VOWS)

Ge 28: 20 Then Jacob made a *v,* saying,
31: 13 and where you made a *v* to me.
Lev 7: 16 his offering is the result of a *v*
22: 18 to fulfill a *v* or as a freewill offering,
22: 21 to the LORD to fulfill a special *v*
22: 23 accepted in fulfillment of a *v*
27: 2 'If anyone makes a special *v*
27: 8 If anyone making the *v* is too poor
27: 8 the man making the *v* can afford.
Nu 6: 2 a *v* of separation to the LORD
6: 2 woman wants to make a special *v,*
Nu 6: 5 " 'During the entire period of his *v*
6: 21 He must fulfill the *v* he has made,
15: 8 for a special *v* or a fellowship
21: 2 Israel made this *v* to the LORD:
29: 39 " 'In addition to what you *v*
30: 2 When a man makes a *v*
30: 3 in her father's house makes a *v*
30: 4 and her father hears about her *v*
30: 6 "If she marries after she makes a *v*
30: 8 he nullifies the *v* that obligates her
30: 9 "Any *v* or obligation taken
30: 10 living with her husband makes a *v*
30: 13 or nullify any *v* she makes
Dt 23: 18 the LORD your God to pay any *v,*
23: 21 If you make a *v* to the LORD your
23: 22 But if you refrain from making a *v,*
23: 23 because you made your *v* freely
Jdg 11: 30 Jephthah made a *v* to the LORD:
11: 35 I have made a *v* to the LORD that I
Ru 3: 13 But if he is not willing, I *v* that,
1Sa 1: 11 And she made a *v,* saying,
1: 21 to the LORD and to fulfill his *v,*
2Sa 15: 7 and fulfill a *v* I made to the LORD.
15: 8 I made this *v:* 'If the LORD takes
Ps 132: 2 and made a *v* to the Mighty One
Ecc 5: 4 When you make a *v* to God,
5: 4 pleasure in fools; fulfill your *v.*
5: 5 It is better not to *v* than to make a *v*
5: 6 the ⌊temple⌋ messenger, "My *v* was
Ac 18: 18 because of a *v* he had taken.
21: 23 men with us who have made a *v.*

VOWED (VOW)

Lev 23: 38 your gifts and whatever you have *v*
27: 9 " 'If what he *v* is an animal that is
27: 11 If what he *v* is a ceremonially
Dt 12: 6 what you have *v* to give
12: 11 the choice possessions you have *v*
12: 17 or whatever you have *v* to give,
12: 26 and whatever you have *v* to give,
Jdg 11: 39 and he did to her as he had *v.*
Jnh 2: 9 What I have *v* I will make good.

VOWS (VOW)

Nu 6: 21 of the Nazirite who *v* his offering
15: 3 for special *v* or freewill offerings
30: 4 then all her *v* and every pledge
30: 5 none of her *v* or the pledges
30: 7 then her *v* or the pledges
30: 11 then all her *v* or the pledges
30: 12 none of the *v* or pledges that came
30: 14 then he confirms all her *v*
2Ki 12: 4 money received from personal *v*
Job 22: 27 and you will fulfill your *v.*
Ps 22: 25 who fear you will I fulfill my *v.*
50: 14 fulfill your *v* to the Most High,
56: 12 I am under *v* to you, O God;
61: 5 For you have heard my *v,* O God;
61: 8 and fulfill my *v* day after day.
65: 1 to you our *v* will be fulfilled.
66: 13 and fulfill my *v* to you—
66: 14 *v* my lips promised and my mouth
76: 11 Make *v* to the LORD your God
116: 14 I will fulfill my *v* to the LORD
116: 18 I will fulfill my *v* to the LORD
Pr 7: 14 today I fulfilled my *v.*
20: 25 and only later to consider his *v.*
31: 2 O son of my *v,*
Isa 19: 21 they will make *v* to the LORD
Jer 44: 25 certainly carry out the *v* we made
44: 25 what you promised! Keep your *v!*
Jnh 1: 16 to the LORD and made *v* to him.
Na 1: 15 and fulfill your *v.*
Mal 1: 14 male in his flock and *v* to give it,

VOYAGE

Ac 21: 7 We continued our *v* from Tyre
27: 10 I can see that our *v* is going

VULGAR

2Sa 6: 20 servants as any *v* fellow would!"

VULTURE (VULTURES)

Lev 11: 13 the eagle, the *v,* the black *v,*
Dt 14: 12 the eagle, the *v,* the black *v,*
Mic 1: 16 make yourselves as bald as the *v,*
Hab 1: 8 They fly like a *v* swooping

VULTURES (VULTURE)

Job 15: 23 He wanders about—food for *v;*
Pr 30: 17 will be eaten by the *v.*
Mt 24: 28 is a carcass, there the *v* will gather.
Lk 17: 37 dead body, there the *v* will gather."

WADE

Isa 47: 2 and *w* through the streams.

WADI

Nu 34: 5 join the *W* of Egypt and end
Jos 15: 4 and joined the *W* of Egypt,
15: 47 as far as the *W* of Egypt
1Ki 8: 65 Lebo Hamath to the *W* of Egypt.
2Ki 24: 7 from the *W* of Egypt
2Ch 7: 8 Lebo Hamath to the *W* of Egypt.
Isa 27: 12 Euphrates to the *W* of Egypt,
Eze 47: 19 then along the *W* ⌊of Egypt⌋
48: 28 then along the *W* ⌊of Egypt⌋

WAFER (WAFERS)

Ex 29: 23 and a cake made with oil, and a *w.*
Lev 8: 26 and one made with oil, and a *w;*
Nu 6: 19 and a cake and a *w* from the basket,

WAFERS (WAFER)

Ex 16: 31 and tasted like *w* made with honey.
29: 2 with oil, and *w* spread with oil.
Lev 2: 4 or *w* made without yeast
7: 12 *w* made without yeast
Nu 6: 15 with oil, and *w* spread with oil.
1Ch 23: 29 the unleavened *w,* the baking

WAG

Jer 23: 31 the prophets who *w* their own

WAGE (WAGED WAGES WAGING)

Jos 11: 20 hearts to *w* war against Israel,
Pr 20: 18 if you *w* war, obtain guidance.
Isa 19: 10 all the *w* earners will be sick
41: 12 Those who *w* war against you
Da 11: 25 of the South will *w* war with a large
Mic 3: 5 they prepare to *w* war against him.
2Co 10: 3 we do not *w* war as the world does.

WAGED (WAGE)

Jos 11: 18 Joshua *w* war against all these
1Ki 5: 3 of the wars *w* against my father
1Ch 5: 10 During Saul's reign they *w* war
5: 19 They *w* war against the Hagrites,
Ps 55: 18 from the battle *w* against me,

WAGES (WAGE)

Ge 29: 15 Tell me what your *w* should be."
30: 28 He added, "Name your *w,*
30: 32 They will be my *w.*
30: 33 check on the *w* you have paid me.
31: 7 me by changing my *w* ten times.
31: 8 'The speckled ones will be your *w,*'
31: 8 'The streaked ones will be your *w,*'
31: 41 and you changed my *w* ten times.
Lev 19: 13 " 'Do not hold back the *w*
Nu 18: 31 for it is your *w* for your work
Dt 24: 15 Pay him his *w* each day
1Ki 5: 6 for your men whatever *w* you set.
Job 7: 2 man waiting eagerly for his *w,*
Pr 10: 16 *w* of the righteous bring them life
11: 18 The wicked man earns deceptive *w*
Hos 9: 1 you love the *w* of a prostitute
Mic 1: 7 gifts from the *w* of prostitutes,
1: 7 *w* of prostitutes they will again be
Hag 1: 6 You earn *w,* only to put them
Zec 8: 10 Before that time there were no *w*
Mal 3: 5 who defraud laborers of their *w,*
Mt 20: 8 the workers and pay them their *w,*
Mk 6: 37 take eight months of a man's *w!*
14: 5 sold for more than a year's *w*
Lk 10: 7 for the worker deserves his *w.*
Jn 4: 36 Even now the reaper draws his *w,*
6: 7 "Eight months' *w* would not buy
12: 5 to the poor? It was worth a year's *w*
Ro 4: 4 his *w* are not credited to him
6: 23 For the *w* of sin is death,
1Ti 5: 18 and "The worker deserves his *w.*"
Jas 5: 4 *w* you failed to pay the workmen
2Pe 2: 15 who loved the *w* of wickedness.
Rev 6: 6 three quarts of barley for a day's *w,*
6: 6 "A quart of wheat for a day's *w,*

WAGING (WAGE)

Jdg 11: 27 wrong by *w* war against me.
Pr 24: 6 for *w* war you need guidance,
Da 7: 21 this horn was *w* war
Ro 7: 23 *w* war against the law of my mind

WAGONS

Isa 66: 20 on horses, in chariots and *w*,
Eze 23: 24 and *w* and with a throng of people;
26: 10 *w* and chariots when he enters your

WAHEB

Nu 21: 14 " . . . *W* in Suphah and the ravines,

WAIL (WAILED WAILING WAILS)

Isa 13: 6 *W*, for the day of the LORD is near
14: 31 *W*, O gate! Howl, O city!
15: 3 they all *w*,
16: 7 Therefore the Moabites *w*,
16: 7 they *w* together for Moab.
22: 12 day to weep and to *w*,
23: 1 *W*, O ships of Tarshish!
23: 6 *w*, you people of the island.
23: 14 *W*, you ships of Tarshish;
65: 14 and *w* in brokenness of spirit.
Jer 4: 8 lament and *w*,
9: 10 will weep and *w* for the mountains
9: 18 and *w* over us
9: 20 Teach your daughters how to *w*;
14: 2 they *w* for the land,
25: 34 Weep and *w*, you shepherds;
47: 2 all who dwell in the land will *w*
48: 20 *W* and cry out!
48: 31 Therefore I *w* over Moab,
48: 39 How shattered she is! How they *w!*
49: 3 *W*, O Heshbon, for Ai is destroyed
51: 8 *W* over her!
Eze 21: 12 Cry out and *w*, son of man,
27: 32 As they *w* and mourn over you,
30: 2 " '*W* and say,
32: 18 *w* for the hordes of Egypt
Hos 7: 14 but *w* upon their beds.
Joel 1: 5 *W*, all you drinkers of wine;
1: 5 *w* because of the wine,
1: 11 *w*, you vine growers;
1: 13 *w*, you who minister
Am 5: 16 and the mourners to *w*.
Mic 1: 8 Because of this I will weep and *w*;
Zep 1: 11 *W*, you who live in the market
Zec 11: 2 *W*, O pine tree, for the cedar has
11: 2 *W*, oaks of Bashan;
11: 3 Listen to the *w* of the shepherds;
Mal 2: 13 and *w* because he no longer pays
Jas 4: 9 Grieve, mourn and *w*.
5: 1 and *w* because of the misery that is

WAILED (WAIL)

Nu 11: 18 The LORD heard you when you *w*,
11: 20 and have *w* before him, saying,
Lk 23: 27 women who mourned and *w*

WAILING (WAIL)

Ex 11: 6 There will be loud *w*
12: 30 and there was loud *w* in Egypt,
Nu 11: 4 and again the Israelites started *w*
11: 10 the people of every family *w*,
11: 13 They keep *w* to me, 'Give us meat
2Sa 13: 36 the king's sons came in, *w* loudly.
Est 4: 1 and went out into the city, *w* loudly
4: 3 with fasting, weeping and *w*.
Job 30: 31 and my flute to the sound of *w*.
Ps 30: 11 You turned my *w* into dancing;
Isa 15: 8 their *w* reaches as far as Eglaim,
Jer 6: 26 mourn with bitter *w*
9: 17 Call for the *w* women to come;
9: 19 The sound of *w* is heard from Zion:
20: 16 May he hear *w* in the morning,
25: 36 the *w* of the leaders of the flock,
Am 5: 16 "There will be *w* in all the streets
5: 17 There will be *w* in all the vineyards,
8: 3 songs in the temple will turn to *w*.
Zep 1: 10 *w* from the New Quarter,
Mk 5: 38 with people crying and *w* loudly.
5: 39 "Why all this commotion and *w?*
Lk 8: 52 the people were *w* and mourning
8: 52 "Stop *w*," Jesus said.

WAILS (WAIL)

Isa 15: 2 Moab *w* over Nebo and Medeba.

WAIST (WAISTS)

Ex 28: 42 reaching from the *w* to the thigh.
2Sa 20: 8 strapped over it at his *w* was a belt
1Ki 2: 5 blood stained the belt around his *w*
12: 10 thicker than my father's *w*.
2Ki 1: 8 and a leather belt around his *w*."
2Ch 10: 10 thicker than my father's *w*.
Job 12: 18 and ties a loincloth around their *w*.
15: 27 and his *w* bulges with flesh,
SS 7: 2 Your *w* is a mound of wheat
Isa 5: 27 not a belt is loosened at the *w*,
11: 5 faithfulness the sash around his *w*.
Jer 13: 1 linen belt and put it around your *w*,
13: 2 directed, and put it around my *w*.
13: 4 and are wearing around your *w*,
13: 11 as a belt is bound around a man's *w*,
48: 37 every *w* is covered with sackcloth.
Eze 1: 27 to be his *w* up he looked like
8: 2 to be his *w* down he was like fire,
47: 4 through water that was up to the *w*.
Da 10: 5 belt of the finest gold around his *w*.
Mt 3: 4 he had a leather belt around his *w*.
Mk 1: 6 with a leather belt around his *w*,
Jn 13: 4 and wrapped a towel around his *w*.
Eph 6: 14 of truth buckled around your *w*,

WAISTBAND

Ex 28: 8 Its skillfully woven *w* is to be like it
28: 27 just above the *w* of the ephod.
28: 28 connecting it to the *w*,
29: 5 on him by its skillfully woven *w*.
39: 5 Its skillfully woven *w* was like it—
39: 20 just above the *w* of the ephod.
39: 21 connecting it to the *w*
Lev 8: 7 to him by its skillfully woven *w*;

WAISTS (WAIST)

1Ki 20: 31 Israel with sackcloth around our *w*
20: 32 Wearing sackcloth around their *w*
Isa 32: 11 put sackcloth around your *w*.
Eze 23: 15 with belts around their *w*
44: 18 undergarments around their *w*.

WAIT (AWAIT AWAITS WAITED WAITING WAITS)

Ex 7: 15 *W* on the bank of the Nile
24: 14 "*W* here for us until we come back
Lev 12: 4 woman must *w* thirty-three days
12: 5 Then she must *w* sixty-six days
Nu 9: 8 "*W* until I find out what the LORD
Dt 19: 11 hates his neighbor and lies in *w*
Jos 8: 9 lay in *w* between Bethel and Ai,
18: 3 "How long will you *w*
Jdg 6: 18 "I will *w* until you return."
9: 32 your men should come and lie in *w*
16: 2 and lay in *w* for him all night
19: 8 *W* till afternoon!" So the two
Ru 1: 13 would you *w* until they grew up?
3: 18 Naomi said, "*W*, my daughter,
1Sa 10: 8 you must *w* seven days until I come
14: 9 '*W* there until we come to you,'
20: 19 hid when this trouble began, and *w*
22: 8 has incited my servant to lie in *w*
22: 13 against me and lies in *w* for me,
2Sa 15: 28 I will *w* at the fords in the desert
18: 14 "I'm not going to *w* like this for you
18: 30 "Stand aside and *w* here."
2Ki 6: 33 Why should I *w* for the LORD any
7: 9 If we *w* until daylight, punishment
Job 3: 9 may it *w* for daylight in vain
14: 14 I will *w* for my renewal to come.
20: 26 in *w* for his treasures.
32: 16 Must I *w*, now that they are silent,
35: 14 and you must *w* for him,
38: 40 or lie in *w* in a thicket?
Ps 5: 3 and *w* in expectation.
10: 8 He lies in *w* near the villages;
10: 9 He lies in *w* like a lion in cover;
10: 9 he lies in *w* to catch the helpless;
27: 14 and *w* for the LORD.
27: 14 *W* for the LORD;
33: 20 We *w* in hope for the LORD;
37: 7 before the LORD and *w* patiently
37: 32 lie in *w* for the righteous,
37: 34 *W* for the LORD
Ps 38: 15 I *w* for you, O LORD;
59: 3 See how they lie in *w* for me!
71: 10 those who *w* to kill me conspire
106: 13 and did not *w* for his counsel.
119: 84 How long must your servant *w?*
119: 166 I *w* for your salvation, O LORD,
130: 5 I *w* for the LORD, my soul waits,
130: 6 more than watchmen *w*
130: 6 more than watchmen *w*
Pr 1: 11 let's lie in *w* for someone's blood,
1: 18 These men lie in *w*
12: 6 of the wicked lie in *w* for blood,
20: 22 *W* for the LORD, and he will
23: 28 Like a bandit she lies in *w*,
24: 15 Do not lie in *w* like an outlaw
Isa 8: 17 I will *w* for the LORD,
26: 8 we *w* for you;
30: 18 Blessed are all who *w* for him!
51: 5 and *w* in hope for my arm.
64: 4 on behalf of those who *w* for him.
Jer 5: 6 lie in *w* near their towns
5: 26 lie in *w* like men who snare birds
La 3: 10 Like a bear lying in *w*,
3: 24 therefore I will *w* for him."
3: 26 it is good to *w* quietly
4: 19 and lay in *w* for us in the desert.
Eze 44: 26 is cleansed, he must *w* seven days.
Hos 12: 6 and *w* for your God always.
Ob : 14 You should not *w* at the crossroads
Mic 5: 7 which do not *w* for man
7: 2 All men lie in *w* to shed blood;
7: 7 I *w* for God my Savior;
Hab 2: 3 Though it linger, *w* for it;
3: 16 Yet I will *w* patiently for the day
Zep 3: 8 Therefore *w* for me," declares
Mt 8: 15 she got up and began to *w* on him.
Mk 1: 31 and she began to *w* on them.
Lk 4: 39 up at once and began to *w* on them.
12: 37 and will come and *w* on them.
17: 8 get yourself ready and *w* on me
Jn 18: 16 Peter had to *w* outside at the door.
Ac 1: 4 *w* for the gift my Father promised,
6: 2 of God in order to *w* on tables.
Ro 8: 23 as we *w* eagerly for our adoption
8: 25 for what we do not yet have, we *w*
1Co 1: 7 as you eagerly *w* for our Lord Jesus
4: 5 before the appointed time; *w*
11: 33 together to eat, *w* for each other.
1Th 1: 10 and to *w* for his Son from heaven,
Tit 2: 13 while we *w* for the blessed hope—
Jude : 21 as you *w* for the mercy
Rev 6: 11 they were told to *w* a little longer,

WAITED (WAIT)

Ge 8: 10 He *w* seven more days
8: 12 He *w* seven more days
Jdg 3: 25 They *w* to the point
3: 26 While they *w*, Ehud got away.
1Sa 13: 8 He *w* seven days, the time set
25: 9 Then they *w*.
1Ki 1: 4 care of the king and *w* on him,
Job 29: 23 They *w* for me as for showers
32: 4 Elihu had *w* before speaking to Job
32: 11 I *w* while you spoke,
Ps 40: 1 I *w* patiently for the LORD;
Isa 38: 13 I *w* patiently till dawn,
La 2: 16 This is the day we have *w* for;
Jnh 4: 5 and *w* to see what would happen
Ac 20: 5 on ahead and *w* for us at Troas.
1Pe 3: 20 when God *w* patiently in the days

WAITING (WAIT)

Ex 5: 20 and Aaron *w* to meet them,
2Sa 16: 1 of Mephibosheth, *w* to meet him.
1Ki 20: 38 stood by the road *w* for the king.
Job 7: 2 a hired man *w* eagerly for his wages
29: 21 *w* in silence for my counsel.
Ps 119: 95 The wicked are *w* to destroy me,
Pr 8: 34 *w* at my doorway.
Jer 3: 2 By the roadside you sat *w*
20: 10 are *w* for me to slip, saying,
Mic 1: 12 *w* for relief,
Mk 15: 43 who was himself *w* for the kingdom
Lk 1: 21 the people were *w* for Zechariah
2: 25 He was *w* for the consolation
3: 15 The people were *w* expectantly
11: 54 *w* to catch him in something he
12: 36 like men *w* for their master

Lk 23:51 he was *w* for the kingdom of God.
Jn 7: 1 because the Jews there were *w*
Ac 17:16 While Paul was *w* for them
22:16 And now what are you *w* for?
23:21 of them are *w* in ambush for him.
23:21 *w* for your consent to their request
28: 6 but after *w* a long time
1Co 11:21 ahead without *w* for anybody else.
Heb 6:15 And so after *w* patiently, Abraham
9:28 to those who are *w* for him.

WAITS (WAIT)

Ps 130: 5 I wait for the LORD, my soul *w*,
130: 6 My soul *w* for the Lord
Da 12:12 Blessed is the one who *w* for
Jn 3:29 who attends the bridegroom *w*
Ro 8:19 creation *w* in eager expectation
Heb 10:13 Since that time he *w*
Jas 5: 7 See how the farmer *w* for the land

WAKE (AWAKE AWAKEN AWAKENED AWAKENS AWAKES AWOKE WAKENED WAKENS WAKES WOKE)

Jdg 5:12 *W* up, *w* up, break out in song!
5:12 "*W* up, *w* up, Deborah!
1Sa 26:12 knew about it, nor did anyone *w* up
Job 41:32 Behind him he leaves a glistening *w*
Ps 3: 5 I *w* again, because the LORD
Pr 23:35 When will I *w* up
Isa 26:19 *w* up and shout for joy.
Joel 1: 5 *W* up, you drunkards, and weep!
Hab 2: 7 Will they not *w* up and make you
2:19 Or to lifeless stone, '*W* up!'
Jn 11:11 but I am going there to *w* him up."
Ro 13:11 for you to *w* up from your slumber,
Eph 5:14 "*W* up, O sleeper,
Rev 3: 2 *W* up! Strengthen what remains
3: 3 if you do not *w* up, I will come like

WAKENED (WAKE)

Zec 4: 1 as a man is *w* from his sleep.
4: 1 talked with me returned and *w* me,

WAKENS (WAKE)

Isa 50: 4 He *w* me morning by morning,
50: 4 *w* my ear to listen like one being

WAKES (WAKE)

Ps 78:65 as a man *w* from the stupor of wine.

WALK (WALKED WALKING WALKS)

Ge 13:17 *w* through the length and breadth
17: 1 *w* before me and be blameless.
Ex 17: 5 "*W* on ahead of the people.
Lev 11:20 " 'All flying insects that *w*
11:21 some winged creatures that *w*
11:27 Of all the animals that *w*
11:27 those that *w* on their paws are
26:12 I will *w* among you and be your
26:13 you to *w* with heads held high.
Nu 11:31 as far as a day's *w* in any direction.
Dt 5:33 *W* in all the way that the LORD
6: 7 and when you *w* along the road,
10:12 to *w* in all his ways, to love him,
11:19 and when you *w* along the road,
11:22 to *w* in all his ways and to hold fast
19: 9 and to *w* always in his ways—
26:17 and that you will *w* in his ways,
28: 9 of the LORD your God and *w*
30:16 to *w* in his ways, and to keep his
Jos 22: 5 to *w* in all his ways,
Jdg 2:22 and *w* in it as their forefathers did."
5:10 and you who *w* along the road,
1Sa 8: 3 But his sons did not *w* in his ways.
8: 5 your sons do not *w* in your ways;
2Sa 3:31 *w* in mourning in front of Abner."
1Ki 2: 3 the LORD your God requires: *W*
2: 4 and if they *w* faithfully before me
3:14 And if you *w* in my ways
8:25 in all they do to *w* before me
8:58 to *w* in all his ways
9: 4 if you *w* before me in integrity
11:38 do whatever I command you and *w*
2Ki 21:22 did not *w* in the way of the LORD.
2Ch 6:16 do to *w* before me according
6:31 *w* in your ways all the time they
7:17 if you *w* before me as David your
Ne 5: 9 Shouldn't you *w* in the fear
Ps 1: 1 who does not *w* in the counsel
15: 2 He whose *w* is blameless
23: 4 Even though I *w*
26: 3 and I *w* continually in your truth.
48:12 *W* about Zion, go around her,
56:13 that I may *w* before God
82: 5 They *w* about in darkness;
84:11 from those whose *w* is blameless.
86:11 and I will *w* in your truth;
89:15 who *w* in the light of your presence
101: 2 I will *w* in my house
101: 6 he whose *w* is blameless
115: 7 feet, but they cannot *w*;
116: 9 that I may *w* before the LORD
119: 1 who *w* according to the law
119: 3 they *w* in his ways.
119:45 I will *w* about in freedom,
128: 1 who *w* in his ways.
138: 7 Though I *w* in the midst of trouble,
142: 3 In the path where I *w*
Pr 2: 7 to those whose *w* is blameless,
2:13 paths to *w* in dark ways,
2:20 Thus you will *w* in the ways
4:12 When you *w*, your steps will not be
4:14 or *w* in the way of evil men.
6:22 When you *w*, they will guide you;
6:28 Can a man *w* on hot coals
8:20 I *w* in the way of righteousness,
9: 6 *w* in the way of understanding.
14: 2 He whose *w* is upright fears
19: 1 a poor man whose *w* is blameless
28: 6 a poor man whose *w* is blameless
28:18 He whose *w* is blameless is kept
Isa 2: 3 so that we may *w* in his paths."
2: 5 let us *w* in the light of the LORD.
23:16 Take up a harp, *w* through the city,
30:21 saying, "This is the way; *w* in it."
35: 8 be for those who *w* in that Way;
35: 9 But only the redeemed will *w* there
38:15 I will *w* humbly all my years
40:31 they will *w* and not be faint.
42: 5 and life to those who *w* on it:
43: 2 When you *w* through the fire,
50:11 go, *w* in the light of your fires
51:23 'Fall prostrate that we may *w*
57: 2 Those who *w* uprightly
59: 9 but we *w* in deep shadows.
65: 2 who *w* in ways not good,
Jer 6:16 But you said, 'We will not *w* in it.'
6:16 ask where the good way is, and *w*
6:25 or *w* on the roads,
7:23 *W* in all the ways I command you,
10: 5 because they cannot *w*.
18:15 They made them *w* in bypaths
La 3: 2 driven me away and made me *w*
4:18 so we could not *w* in our streets.
Eze 36:12 my people Israel, to *w* upon you.
Da 4:37 And those who *w* in pride he is able
Hos 11: 3 It was I who taught Ephraim to *w*,
14: 9 the righteous *w* in them,
Am 3: 3 Do two *w* together
Mic 2: 3 You will no longer *w* proudly,
4: 2 so that we may *w* in his paths."
4: 5 All the nations may *w*
4: 5 we will *w* in the name of the LORD
6: 8 and to *w* humbly with your God.
Zep 1:17 and they will *w* like blind men,
Zec 3: 7 'If you will *w* in my ways
10:12 and in his name they will *w*,"
Mt 9: 5 or to say, 'Get up and *w*'?
11: 5 The blind receive sight, the lame *w*,
Mk 2: 9 'Get up, take your mat and *w*'?
12:38 like to *w* around in flowing robes
Lk 5:23 or to say, 'Get up and *w*'?
7:22 The blind receive sight, the lame *w*,
11:44 men *w* over without knowing it."
20:46 like to *w* around in flowing robes
24:17 you discussing together as you *w*
Jn 5: 8 "Get up! Pick up your mat and *w*."
5:11 'Pick up your mat and *w*.' "
5:12 you to pick it up and *w*?"
8:12 Whoever follows me will never *w*
12:35 *W* while you have the light,
Ac 1:12 a Sabbath day's *w* from the city.
3: 6 of Jesus Christ of Nazareth, *w*."
3: 8 jumped to his feet and began to *w*.
3:12 godliness we had made this man *w*
14:10 the man jumped up and began to *w*.
Ro 4:12 *w* in the footsteps of the faith that
2Co 6:16 live with them and *w* among them,
Col 3: 7 You used to *w* in these ways,
1Jn 1: 6 with him yet *w* in the darkness,
1: 7 But if we *w* in the light,
2: 6 claims to live in him must *w*
2Jn : 6 his command is that you *w* in love.
: 6 that we *w* in obedience
3Jn : 3 how you continue to *w* in the truth.
Rev 3: 4 They will *w* with me, dressed
9:20 idols that cannot see or hear or *w*.
21:24 The nations will *w* by its light,

WALKED (WALK)

Ge 5:22 Enoch *w* with God 300 years
5:24 Enoch *w* with God; then he was no
6: 9 of his time, and he *w* with God.
9:23 then they *w* in backward
18:16 and Abraham *w* along with them
24:40 The LORD, before whom I have *w*,
48:15 Abraham and Isaac *w*,
Ex 15:19 but the Israelites *w* through the sea
Jos 14: 9 which your feet have *w* will be your
Jdg 2:17 way in which their fathers had *w*,
1Sa 19:23 and he *w* along prophesying
2Sa 3:31 King David himself *w*
11: 2 *w* around on the roof of the palace.
1Ki 11:33 and have not *w* in my ways,
16: 2 but you *w* in the ways of Jeroboam
16:26 He *w* in all the ways
22:43 In everything he *w* in the ways
22:52 he *w* in the ways of his father
2Ki 2: 6 So the two of them *w* on.
4:35 Elisha turned away and *w* back
8:18 He *w* in the ways of the kings
8:27 He *w* in the ways of the house
16: 3 He *w* in the ways of the kings
20: 3 how I have *w* before you faithfully
21:21 He *w* in all the ways of his father;
22: 2 and *w* in all the ways of his father
2Ch 17: 3 because in his early years he *w*
20:32 He *w* in the ways of his father Asa
21: 6 He *w* in the ways of the kings
21:12 'You have not *w* in the ways
21:13 you have *w* in the ways of the kings
22: 3 He too *w* in the ways of the house
27: 6 he *w* steadfastly before the LORD
28: 2 He *w* in the ways of the kings
34: 2 *w* in the ways of his father David,
Est 2:11 Every day he *w* back and forth
Job 29: 3 by his light I *w* through darkness!
31: 5 "If I have *w* in falsehood
38:16 or *w* in the recesses of the deep?
Ps 55:14 we *w* with the throng at the house
Ecc 4:15 *w* under the sun followed the youth
Isa 38: 3 how I have *w* before you faithfully
51:23 like a street to be *w* over."
Jer 34:18 and then *w* between its pieces.
34:19 the land who *w* between the pieces
Eze 16:47 You not only *w* in their ways
28:14 you *w* among the fiery stones.
Mal 2: 6 He *w* with me in peace
Mt 14:29 and *w* on the water to Jesus.
Mk 1:16 As Jesus *w* beside the Sea
2:12 and *w* out in full view of them all.
2:14 As he *w* along, he saw Levi son
2:23 and as his disciples *w* along,
5:42 *w* around (she was twelve years old
Lk 4:30 But he *w* right through the crowd
24:15 Jesus himself came up and *w*
Jn 5: 9 he picked up his mat and *w*.
Ac 12:10 When they had *w* the length
14: 8 lame from birth and had never *w*.
17:23 as I *w* around and observed your

WALKING (WALK)

Ge 3: 8 he was *w* in the garden in the cool
Ex 2: 5 and her attendants were *w*
Dt 8: 6 *w* in his ways and revering him.
1Sa 17:39 over the tunic and tried *w* around,
2Sa 6: 4 and Ahio was *w* in front of it.
1Ki 3: 3 love for the LORD by *w* according
15:26 *w* in the ways of his father
15:34 *w* in the ways of Jeroboam
16:19 and *w* in the ways of Jeroboam
18: 7 As Obadiah was *w*
2Ki 2:11 As they were *w* along and talking
2:23 As he was *w* along the road,

2Ch 11: 17 *w* in the ways of David
Pr 7: 8 *w* along in the direction
Isa 3: 16 *w* along with outstretched necks,
9: 2 along the Jordan—The people *w*
26: 8 LORD, *w* in the way of your laws,
Da 3: 25 I see four men *w* around in the fire,
4: 29 as the king was *w* on the roof
Mt 4: 18 As Jesus was *w* beside the Sea
14: 25 out to them, *w* on the lake.
14: 26 When the disciples saw him *w*
15: 31 the lame *w* and the blind seeing.
24: 1 and was *w* away when his disciples
Mk 6: 48 out to them, *w* on the lake.
6: 49 when they saw him *w* on the lake,
8: 24 they look like trees *w* around.''
11: 27 while Jesus was *w* in the temple
16: 12 while they were *w* in the country.
Lk 9: 57 As they were *w* along the road,
Jn 6: 19 saw Jesus approaching the boat, *w*
10: 23 was in the temple area *w*
Ac 3: 8 *w* and jumping, and praising God.
3: 9 When all the people saw him *w*
2Jn : 4 of your children *w* in the truth,
3Jn : 4 than to hear that my children are *w*

WALKS (WALK)

Ex 21: 19 and *w* around outside with his staff;
Lev 11: 42 moves on its belly or *w* on all fours
Pr 10: 9 The man of integrity *w* securely,
13: 20 He who *w* with the wise grows wise
28: 26 he who *w* in wisdom is kept safe.
Ecc 2: 14 while the fool *w* in the darkness;
10: 3 Even as he *w* along the road,
Isa 33: 15 He who *w* righteously
50: 10 Let him who *w* in the dark,
59: 8 no one who *w* in them will know
Jn 11: 9 A man who *w* by day will not
11: 10 is when he *w* by night that he
12: 35 man who *w* in the dark does not
1Jn 2: 11 and *w* around in the darkness;
Rev 2: 1 and *w* among the seven golden

WALL (WALLED WALLS)

Ge 49: 22 whose branches climb over a *w*.
Ex 14: 22 with a *w* of water on their right
14: 29 with a *w* of water on their right
15: 8 surging waters stood firm like a *w*;
Lev 11: 30 the monitor lizard, the *w* lizard,
14: 37 deeper than the surface of the *w*,
Nu 22: 25 she pressed close to the *w*,
35: 4 hundred feet from the town *w*.
Jos 2: 15 lived in was part of the city *w*.
6: 5 then the *w* of the city will collapse
6: 20 *w* collapsed; so every man charged
1Sa 18: 11 to himself, "I'll pin David to the *w*
19: 10 as Saul drove the spear into the *w*.
19: 10 to pin him to the *w* with his spear,
20: 25 sat in his customary place by the *w*.
25: 16 and day they were a *w*
31: 10 fastened his body to the *w* of Beth
31: 12 from the *w* of Beth Shan
2Sa 11: 20 would shoot arrows from the *w*?
11: 21 Why did you get so close to the *w*?'
11: 21 millstone on him from the *w*,
11: 24 arrows at your servants from the *w*,
18: 24 to the roof of the gateway by the *w*.
20: 15 While they were battering the *w*
20: 21 thrown to you from the *w*.''
22: 30 with my God I can scale a *w*.
1Ki 3: 1 and the *w* around Jerusalem.
6: 27 of the other touched the other *w*,
6: 27 wing of one cherub touched one *w*,
7: 12 surrounded by a *w* of three courses
9: 15 the supporting terraces, the *w*
11: 27 filled in the gap in the *w* of the city
20: 30 where the *w* collapsed
21: 23 Jezebel by the *w* of Jezreel.'
2Ki 3: 27 as a sacrifice on the city *w*.
6: 26 of Israel was passing by on the *w*,
6: 30 along the *w*, the people looked,
9: 33 some of her blood spattered the *w*
14: 13 and broke down the *w* of Jerusalem
18: 26 hearing of the people on the *w*.''
18: 27 and not to the men sitting on the *w*
20: 2 Hezekiah turned his face to the *w*
25: 4 the city *w* was broken through,
1Ch 11: 8 terraces to the surrounding *w*,
2Ch 3: 11 and touched the temple *w*,
2Ch 3: 12 and touched the other temple *w*,
25: 23 and broke down the *w* of Jerusalem
26: 9 and at the angle of the *w*,
27: 3 work on the *w* at the hill
32: 5 He built another *w* outside that one
32: 5 all the broken sections of the *w*
32: 18 of Jerusalem who were on the *w*,
33: 14 Afterward he rebuilt the outer *w*
36: 19 broke down the *w* of Jerusalem;
Ezr 9: 9 he has given us a *w* of protection
Ne 1: 3 The *w* of Jerusalem is broken down
2: 8 for the city *w* and for the residence
2: 15 valley by night, examining the *w*.
2: 17 let us rebuild the *w* of Jerusalem,
3: 8 Jerusalem as far as the Broad *W*.
3: 13 five hundred yards of the *w*
3: 15 also repaired the *w* of the Pool
3: 27 tower to the *w* of Ophel.
4: 1 that we were rebuilding the *w*,
4: 2 they restore their *w*? Will they
4: 3 break down their *w* of stones!''
4: 6 So we rebuilt the *w* till all
4: 10 that we cannot rebuild the *w*.''
4: 13 of the *w* at the exposed places,
4: 15 we all returned to the *w*, each
4: 17 of Judah who were building the *w*.
4: 19 from each other along the *w*.
5: 16 myself to the work on this *w*.
6: 1 our enemies that I had rebuilt the *w*
6: 6 therefore you are building the *w*.
6: 15 So the *w* was completed
7: 1 After the *w* had been rebuilt
12: 27 dedication of the *w* of Jerusalem,
12: 30 the people, the gates and the *w*.
12: 31 of Judah go up on top of the *w*.
12: 31 on top of the *w* to the right,
12: 37 of David on the ascent to the *w*
12: 38 I followed them on top of the *w*,
12: 38 of the Ovens to the Broad *W*,
13: 21 do you spend the night by the *w*?
Ps 18: 29 with my God I can scale a *w*.
62: 3 this leaning *w*, this tottering fence?
78: 13 made the water stand firm like a *w*.
Pr 18: 11 they imagine it an unscalable *w*.
24: 31 and the stone *w* was in ruins.
Ecc 10: 8 through a *w* may be bitten
SS 2: 9 There he stands behind our *w*,
8: 9 If she is a *w*,
8: 10 I am a *w*,
Isa 2: 15 and every fortified *w*,
5: 5 I will break down its *w*,
22: 10 down houses to strengthen the *w*.
25: 4 is like a storm driving against a *w*
30: 13 like a high *w*, cracked and bulging,
36: 11 hearing of the people on the *w*.''
36: 12 and not to the men sitting on the *w*
38: 2 Hezekiah turned his face to the *w*
59: 10 the blind we grope along the *w*,
Jer 1: 18 and a bronze *w* to stand
15: 20 I will make you a *w* to this people,
15: 20 a fortified *w* of bronze;
21: 4 are outside the *w* besieging you.
39: 2 the city *w* was broken through.
51: 44 And the *w* of Babylon will fall.
51: 58 "Babylon's thick *w* will be leveled
52: 7 the city *w* was broken through,
La 2: 8 the *w* around the Daughter of Zion.
2: 18 O *w* of the Daughter of Zion,
Eze 4: 3 place it as an iron *w* between you
8: 7 I looked, and I saw a hole in the *w*.
8: 8 into the *w* and saw a doorway there
8: 8 "Son of man, now dig into the *w*."
12: 5 dig through the *w* and take your
12: 7 dug through the *w* with my hands.
12: 12 dug in the *w* for him to go through.
13: 5 up to the breaks in the *w* to repair it
13: 10 because, when a flimsy *w* is built,
13: 12 When the *w* collapses, will people
13: 14 tear down the *w* you have covered
13: 15 I will spend my wrath against the *w*
13: 15 *w* is gone and so are those who
22: 30 them who would build up the *w*
23: 14 She saw men portrayed on a *w*,
38: 20 and every *w* will fall to the ground.
40: 5 He measured the *w*; it was one
40: 5 I saw a *w* completely surrounding
40: 12 each alcove was a *w* one cubit high,
40: 13 the top of the rear *w* of one alcove
Eze 40: 40 By the outside *w* of the portico
40: 43 were attached to the *w* all around.
41: 5 he measured the *w* of the temple;
41: 6 around the *w* of the temple to serve
41: 6 inserted into the *w* of the temple.
41: 9 outer *w* of the side rooms was five
41: 12 *w* of the building was five cubits
41: 16 The floor, the *w* up to the windows,
41: 20 on the *w* of the outer sanctuary.
42: 1 and opposite the outer *w*
42: 7 There was an outer *w* parallel
42: 10 and opposite the outer *w*,
42: 10 length of the *w* of the outer court,
42: 12 the corresponding *w* extending
42: 20 It had a *w* around it, five hundred
43: 8 with only a *w* between me
Da 5: 5 and wrote on the plaster of the *w*,
Hos 2: 6 I will *w* her in so that she cannot
Joel 2: 9 they run along the *w*.
Am 4: 3 out through breaks in the *w*,
5: 19 and rested his hand on the *w*
7: 7 by a *w* that had been built true
Na 2: 5 They dash to the city *w*;
3: 8 the waters her *w*.
Hab 2: 11 The stones of the *w* will cry out,
Zec 2: 5 I myself will be a *w* of fire around it
Mt 21: 33 He put a *w* around it, dug
Mk 12: 1 He put a *w* around it, dug a pit
Ac 9: 25 through an opening in the *w*.
23: 3 strike you, you whitewashed *w*!
2Co 11: 33 in a basket from a window in the *w*
Eph 2: 14 the dividing *w* of hostility,
Rev 21: 12 It had a great, high *w*
21: 14 The *w* of the city had twelve
21: 15 the city, its gates and its *w*.
21: 17 He measured its *w* and it was 144
21: 18 The *w* was made of jasper,

WALLED (WALL)

Lev 25: 29 " 'If a man sells a house in a *w* city,
25: 30 the house in the *w* city shall belong
1Ki 4: 13 and its sixty large *w* cities
La 3: 7 He has *w* me in so I cannot escape;

WALLOW (WALLOWING)

Jer 48: 26 Let Moab *w* in her vomit;

WALLOWING (WALLOW)

2Sa 20: 12 Amasa lay *w* in his blood
2Pe 2: 22 back to her *w* in the mud."

WALLS (WALL)

Lev 14: 37 is to examine the mildew on the *w*,
14: 39 If the mildew has spread on the *w*,
14: 41 the inside *w* of the house scraped
25: 31 But houses in villages without *w*
Nu 22: 24 with *w* on both sides.
Dt 1: 28 with *w* up to the sky.
3: 5 cities were fortified with high *w*
9: 1 with large cities that have *w* up
28: 52 land until the high fortified *w*
1Ki 4: 33 to the hyssop that grows out of *w*.
6: 5 Against the *w* of the main hall
6: 6 inserted into the temple *w*.
6: 15 He lined its interior *w*
6: 29 On the *w* all around the temple,
2Ki 25: 4 the gate between the two *w*
25: 10 down the *w* around Jerusalem.
1Ch 29: 4 of the *w* of the buildings,
2Ch 3: 7 and he carved cherubim on the *w*.
3: 7 *w* and doors of the temple
8: 5 *w* and with gates and bars, as
14: 7 put *w* around them, with towers,
26: 6 and broke down the *w* of Gath,
Ezr 4: 12 They are restoring the *w*
4: 13 city is built and its *w* are restored,
4: 16 city is built and its *w* are restored,
5: 8 and placing the timbers in the *w*.
Ne 2: 13 examining the *w* of Jerusalem,
4: 7 to Jerusalem's *w* had gone ahead
Ps 51: 18 build up the *w* of Jerusalem.
55: 10 night they prowl about on its *w*;
80: 12 Why have you broken down its *w*
89: 40 You have broken through all his *w*
122: 7 May there be peace within your *w*
144: 14 There will be no breaching of *w*,
Pr 25: 28 Like a city whose *w* are broken
SS 5: 7 those watchmen of the *w*!

Isa 22: 5 a day of battering down *w*
22: 11 a reservoir between the two *w*
25: 12 bring down your high fortified *w*
26: 1 its *w* and ramparts.
49: 16 your *w* are ever before me.
54: 12 and all your *w* of precious stones.
56: 5 give within my temple and its *w*
58: 12 be called Repairer of Broken *W*,
60: 10 "Foreigners will rebuild your *w*,
60: 18 but you will call your *w* Salvation
62: 6 I have posted watchmen on your *w*,
Jer 1: 15 come against all her surrounding *w*
39: 4 the gate between the two *w*,
39: 8 broke down the *w* of Jerusalem.
49: 3 rush here and there inside the *w*,
49: 27 I will set fire to the *w* of Damascus;
50: 15 her *w* are torn down.
51: 12 a banner against the *w* of Babylon!
52: 7 the gate between the two *w*
52: 14 down all the *w* around Jerusalem.
La 2: 7 the *w* of her palaces;
2: 8 He made ramparts and *w* lament;
Eze 5: 12 fall by the sword outside your *w*;
8: 10 all over the *w* all kinds
26: 4 They will destroy the *w* of Tyre
26: 8 build a ramp up to your *w*
26: 9 of his battering rams against your *w*
26: 10 Your *w* will tremble at the noise
26: 10 a city whose *w* have been broken
26: 12 they will break down your *w*
27: 10 shields and helmets on your *w*,
27: 11 hung their shields around your *w*;
27: 11 manned your *w* on every side;
33: 30 talking together about you by the *w*
38: 11 all of them living without *w*
40: 7 projecting *w* between the alcoves
40: 10 and the faces of the projecting *w*
40: 14 of the projecting *w* all around the
40: 16 of the projecting *w* were decorated
40: 16 the projecting *w* inside the gateway
40: 21 its projecting *w* and its portico had
40: 26 of the projecting *w* on each side.
40: 29 its projecting *w* and its portico had
40: 33 its projecting *w* and its portico had
40: 36 its projecting *w* and its portico,
40: 48 its projecting *w* were three cubits
41: 2 and the side *w* on each side
41: 13 and the building with its *w* were
41: 17 and on the *w* at regular intervals all
41: 25 trees like those carved on the *w*,
Joel 2: 7 they scale *w* like soldiers.
Am 1: 7 I will send fire upon the *w* of Gaza
1: 10 I will send fire upon the *w* of Tyre
1: 14 I will set fire to the *w* of Rabbah
Mic 7: 11 for building your *w* will come,
Na 3: 17 that settle in the *w* on a cold day—
Zec 2: 4 'Jerusalem will be a city without *w*
Lk 19: 44 you and the children within your *w*
Heb 11: 30 By faith the *w* of Jericho fell,
Rev 21: 19 of the city *w* were decorated

WANDER (WANDERED WANDERER WANDERERS WANDERING WANDERS)

Ge 20: 13 And when God had me *w*
Nu 32: 13 he made them *w* in the desert forty
2Sa 15: 20 today shall I make you *w* about
2Ki 21: 8 of the Israelites *w* from the land I
Job 38: 41 and *w* about for lack of food?
Ps 59: 11 In your might make them *w* about,
59: 15 They *w* about for food
107: 40 made them *w* in a trackless waste.
Pr 17: 24 a fool's eyes *w* to the ends
Isa 63: 17 do you make us *w* from your ways
Jer 14: 10 "They greatly love to *w*;
31: 22 How long will you *w*,
La 4: 15 When they flee and *w* about,
Am 8: 12 and *w* from north to east,
Zec 10: 2 Therefore the people *w* like sheep
Mt 18: 13 the ninety-nine that did not *w*
Jas 5: 19 one of you should *w* from the truth

WANDERED (WANDER)

Ge 21: 14 and *w* in the desert of Beersheba.
1Ch 16: 20 they *w* from nation to nation,
Ps 105: 13 they *w* from nation to nation,
107: 4 Some *w* in desert wastelands,
Jer 50: 6 They *w* over mountain and hill
Eze 34: 6 My sheep *w* over all the mountains
Eze 44: 10 who *w* from me after their idols
Mt 18: 12 go to look for the one that *w* off?
1Ti 1: 6 Some have *w* away from these
6: 10 have *w* from the faith and pierced
6: 21 in so doing have *w* from the faith.
2Ti 2: 18 who have *w* away from the truth.
Heb 11: 38 They *w* in deserts and mountains,
2Pe 2: 15 and *w* off to follow the way

WANDERER (WANDER)

Ge 4: 12 You will be a restless *w*
4: 14 I will be a restless *w* on the earth,
Isa 58: 7 to provide the poor *w* with shelter

WANDERERS (WANDER)

Hos 9: 17 they will be *w* among the nations.

WANDERING (WANDER)

Ge 37: 15 a man found him *w*
Ex 14: 3 'The Israelites are *w*
23: 4 your enemy's ox or donkey *w*
Dt 26: 5 "My father was a *w* Aramean,
Job 12: 24 sends them *w* through a trackless
Ps 109: 10 May his children be *w* beggars;
La 1: 7 In the days of her affliction and *w*
3: 19 I remember my affliction and my *w*
Hos 8: 9 like a wild donkey *w* alone.
Jude : 13 foaming up their shame; *w* stars,

WANDERS (WANDER)

Job 15: 23 He *w* about—food for vultures;
18: 8 and he *w* into its mesh.
Mt 18: 12 sheep, and one of them *w* away,

WANE

Isa 60: 20 and your moon will *w* no more;

WANT (WANTED WANTING WANTS)

Ge 24: 3 I *w* you to swear by the LORD,
29: 21 My time is completed, and I *w*
42: 36 and now you *w* to take Benjamin.
Ex 16: 8 all the bread you *w* in the morning,
16: 23 So bake what you *w* to bake
16: 23 and boil what you *w* to boil.
21: 5 children and do not *w* to go free,'
Lev 26: 5 and you will eat all the food you *w*
Nu 16: 13 now you also *w* to lord it over us?
20: 19 We only *w* to pass through on foot
Dt 12: 15 eat as much of the meat as you *w*,
12: 20 you may eat as much of it as you *w*.
12: 21 as much of them as you *w*.
15: 16 "I do not *w* to leave you,"
23: 24 you may eat all the grapes you *w*,
25: 7 if a man does not *w*
25: 8 "I do not *w* to marry her,"
Jdg 9: 15 'If you really *w* to anoint me king
1Sa 2: 16 and then take whatever you *w*,"
8: 19 "We *w* a king over us.
12: 12 'No, we *w* a king to rule over us'—
20: 4 "Whatever you *w* me to do,
21: 9 If you *w* it, take it; there is no
2Sa 14: 32 Now then, I *w* to see the king's face
18: 22 "My son, why do you *w* to go?
18: 23 "Come what may, I *w* to run."
20: 19 Why do you *w* to swallow up
21: 4 "What do you *w* me to do for you?"
24: 3 But why does my lord the king *w*
1Ki 1: 16 "What is it you *w*?" the king asked.
3: 5 "Ask for whatever you *w* me
5: 8 and will do all you *w* in providing
11: 22 have you lacked here that you *w*
1Ch 21: 3 Why does my lord *w* to do this?
2Ch 1: 7 "Ask for whatever you *w* me
Ne 2: 4 "What is it you *w*?" Then I prayed
Job 24: 16 they *w* nothing to do with the light.
30: 3 Haggard from *w* and hunger,
33: 32 speak up, for I *w* you to be cleared.
37: 20 Should he be told that I *w* to speak?
Ps 71: 13 may those who *w* to harm me
Jer 40: 4 if you do not *w* to, then don't come.
42: 22 in the place where you *w* to go
Eze 20: 32 "We *w* to be like the nations,
36: 32 I *w* you to know that I am not
Da 2: 3 and I *w* to know what it means."
3: 18 we *w* you to know, O king,
Mt 1: 19 and did not *w* to expose her
8: 29 What do you *w* with us, Son of God
12: 38 we *w* to see a miraculous sign
Mt 13: 28 Do you *w* us to go and pull them up
15: 32 I do not *w* to send them away
19: 17 If you *w* to enter life, obey
19: 21 Jesus answered, "If you *w*
20: 14 I *w* to give the man who was hired
20: 15 to do what I *w* with my own money
20: 21 "What is it you *w*?" he asked.
20: 32 "What do you *w* me to do for you?"
20: 33 they answered, "we *w* our sight."
26: 17 "Where do you *w* us
27: 17 "Which one do you *w* me to release
27: 21 of the two do you *w* me to release
Mk 1: 24 "What do you *w* with us, Jesus
5: 7 "What do you *w* with me, Jesus,
6: 22 "Ask me for anything you *w*,
6: 25 "I *w* you to give me right now
6: 26 he did not *w* to refuse her.
7: 24 and did not *w* anyone to know it;
7: 27 "First let the children eat all they *w*
9: 30 Jesus did not *w* anyone
10: 35 "we *w* you to do for us whatever we
10: 36 "What do you *w* me to do for you?"
10: 51 The blind man said, "Rabbi, I *w*
10: 51 "What do you *w* me to do for you?"
14: 7 you can help them any time you *w*.
14: 12 "Where do you *w* us to go
15: 9 "Do you *w* me to release
Lk 4: 6 and I can give it to anyone I *w* to.
4: 34 "Ha! What do you *w* with us,
8: 28 "What do you *w* with me, Jesus,
9: 54 do you *w* us to call fire
16: 26 so that those who *w* to go from here
18: 41 "Lord, I *w* to see," he replied.
18: 41 "What do you *w* me to do for you?"
19: 14 'We don't *w* this man to be our king
19: 27 enemies of mine who did not *w* me
22: 9 Where do you *w* us to prepare for it
Jn 1: 38 "What do you *w*?" They said,
4: 27 But no one asked, "What do you *w*
5: 6 "Do you *w* to get well?" "Sir,"
6: 67 "You do not *w* to leave too, do you
8: 44 you *w* to carry out your father's
9: 27 Do you *w* to become his disciples,
9: 27 Why do you *w* to hear it again?
17: 24 I *w* those you have given me to be
18: 4 "Who is it you *w*?" "Jesus
18: 7 "Who is it you *w*?" And they said,
18: 39 Do you *w* me to release 'the king
19: 31 the Jews did not *w* the bodies left
21: 18 lead you where you do not *w* to go
21: 22 "If I *w* him to remain alive
21: 23 "If I *w* him to remain alive
Ac 7: 26 why do you *w* to hurt each other?'
7: 28 Do you *w* to kill me as you killed
13: 22 he will do everything I *w* him to do
13: 38 I *w* you to know that
16: 37 And now do they *w* to get rid
17: 20 and we *w* to know what they mean
17: 32 "We *w* to hear you again
19: 39 If there is anything further you *w*
23: 19 "What is it you *w* to tell me?"
28: 22 we *w* to hear what your views are,
28: 28 "Therefore I *w* you
Ro 1: 13 I do not *w* you to be unaware,
7: 15 For what I *w* to do I do not do,
7: 16 And if I do what I do not *w* to do,
7: 19 For what I do is not the good I *w*
7: 19 no, the evil I do not *w* to do—
7: 20 Now if I do what I do not *w* to do,
7: 21 law at work: When I *w* to do good,
11: 25 I do not *w* you to be ignorant
13: 3 Do you *w* to be free from fear
16: 19 but I *w* you to be wise about what is
1Co 4: 8 Already you have all you *w*!
7: 28 in this life, and I *w* to spare you this
10: 1 For I do not *w* you to be ignorant
10: 20 I do not *w* you to be participants
10: 27 you to a meal and you *w* to go,
11: 3 I *w* you to realize that the head
12: 1 I do not *w* you to be ignorant.
14: 35 If they *w* to inquire about
15: 1 I *w* to remind you of the gospel I
16: 7 I do not *w* to see you now
2Co 1: 8 We do not *w* you to be uninformed,
8: 1 we *w* you to know about the grace
8: 8 I *w* to test the sincerity of your love
8: 20 We *w* to avoid any criticism
10: 9 I do not *w* to seem to be trying

2Co 10: 16 For we do not *w* to boast about
11: 12 under those who *w* an opportunity
12: 14 what I *w* is not your possessions
12: 20 come I may not find you as I *w* you
12: 20 you may not find me as you *w* me
Gal 1: 11 I *w* you to know, brothers,
4: 17 What they *w* is to alienate you
4: 21 you who *w* to be under the law,
5: 17 so that you do not do what you *w*.
6: 12 Those who *w* to make a good
6: 13 yet they *w* you to be circumcised
Php 1: 12 Now I *w* you to know, brothers,
3: 10 I *w* to know Christ and the power
4: 12 whether living in plenty or in *w*.
Col 2: 1 I *w* you to know how much I am
1Th 4: 13 we do not *w* you to be ignorant
1Ti 1: 7 They *w* to be teachers of the law,
2: 8 I *w* men everywhere
2: 9 I also *w* women to dress modestly,
5: 11 to Christ, they *w* to marry.
6: 9 People who *w* to get rich fall
2Ti 4: 3 to say what their itching ears *w*
Tit 3: 8 And I *w* you to stress these things,
Phm : 14 But I did not *w* to do anything
Heb 6: 11 We *w* each of you to show this
6: 12 We do not *w* you to become lazy,
13: 23 I *w* you to know that our brother
Jas 2: 20 do you *w* evidence that faith
4: 2 You *w* something but don't get it.
4: 2 but you cannot have what you *w*.
2Pe 3: 2 I *w* you to recall the words spoken
2Jn : 12 but I do not *w* to use paper and ink.
3Jn : 10 He also stops those who *w* to do so
: 13 but I do not *w* to do so with pen
Jude : 5 I *w* to remind you that the Lord
Rev 11: 6 kind of plague as often as they *w*.

WANTED (WANT)

Ex 4: 19 for all the men who *w*
16: 3 of meat and ate all the food we *w*,
Ru 2: 14 She ate all she *w* and had some left
2Sa 3: 17 "For some time you have *w*
3: 19 house of Benjamin *w* to do.
1Ki 5: 10 all the cedar and pine logs he *w*,
9: 11 the cedar and pine and gold he *w*.
13: 33 Anyone who *w* to become a priest
Est 2: 13 Anything she *w* was given her
Ps 35: 25 think, "Aha, just what we *w!*"
71: 24 for those who *w* to harm me
Ecc 2: 3 I *w* to see what was worthwhile
Jer 49: 9 not steal only as much as they *w?*
Da 5: 19 Those the king *w* to put to death,
5: 19 and those he *w* to humble,
5: 19 he spared; those he *w* to promote,
5: 19 those he *w* to spare, he spared;
7: 19 I *w* to know the true meaning
7: 20 also *w* to know about the ten horns
Ob : 5 not steal only as much as they *w?*
Jnh 4: 8 He *w* to die, and said, "It would be
Mt 14: 5 Herod *w* to kill John, but he was
18: 23 of heaven is like a king who *w*
21: 31 of the two did what his father *w?*"
Mk 3: 13 and called to him those he *w*,
6: 19 against John and *w* to kill him.
Lk 10: 24 and kings *w* to see what you see
10: 29 But he *w* to justify himself,
19: 3 He *w* to see who Jesus was,
Jn 6: 11 were seated as much as they *w*.
7: 44 Some *w* to seize him, but no one
16: 19 Jesus saw that they *w*
18: 28 they *w* to be able to eat
21: 18 yourself and went where you *w;*
Ac 5: 33 and *w* to put them to death.
10: 10 became hungry and *w* something
13: 7 he *w* to hear the word of God.
14: 13 and the crowd *w* to offer sacrifices
15: 37 Barnabas *w* to take John,
16: 3 Paul *w* to take him
18: 27 When Apollos *w* to go to Achaia,
19: 30 Paul *w* to appear before the crowd,
22: 30 since the commander *w*
23: 28 I *w* to know why they were
24: 27 Felix *w* to grant a favor to the Jews,
27: 13 they had obtained what they *w;*
27: 38 they had eaten as much as they *w*,
27: 43 the centurion *w* to spare Paul's life
28: 18 They examined me and *w*
1Co 12: 18 of them, just as he *w* them to be.

1Th 2: 18 For we *w* to come to you—
Heb 6: 17 Because God *w* to make
12: 17 when he *w* to inherit this blessing,

WANTING (WANT)

Da 5: 27 weighed on the scales and found *w*.
Mt 12: 46 brothers stood outside, *w* to speak
12: 47 standing outside, *w* to speak
Mk 15: 15 "Crucify him!" *W*
Lk 8: 20 standing outside, *w* to see you."
23: 8 for a long time he had been *w*
23: 20 *W* to release Jesus, Pilate appealed
Ac 23: 15 of *w* more accurate information
23: 20 of *w* more accurate information
2Pe 3: 9 with you, not *w* anyone to perish,

WANTON

Isa 47: 8 "Now then, listen, you *w* creature,
Na 3: 4 all because of the *w* lust of a harlot,

WANTS (WANT)

Ge 19: 9 and now he *w* to play the judge!
43: 18 He *w* to attack us and overpower us
Ex 12: 48 "An alien living among you who *w*
Nu 6: 2 or woman *w* to make a special vow,
9: 14 An alien living among you who *w*
Ru 3: 13 in the morning if he *w* to redeem,
1Sa 18: 25 'The king *w* no other price
Jer 22: 28 an object no one *w?*
48: 38 like a jar that no one *w*,"
Eze 46: 7 and with the lambs as much as he *w*
Mt 5: 40 And if someone *w* to sue you
5: 42 from the one who *w* to borrow
16: 25 For whoever *w* to save his life will
20: 26 whoever *w* to become great
20: 27 whoever *w* to be first must be your
27: 43 God rescue him now if he *w* him,
Mk 8: 35 For whoever *w* to save his life will
9: 35 and said, "If anyone *w* to be first,
10: 43 whoever *w* to become great
10: 44 whoever *w* to be first must be slave
Lk 5: 39 after drinking old wine *w* the new,
9: 24 For whoever *w* to save his life will
12: 47 do what his master *w* will be beaten
13: 31 Herod *w* to kill you."
14: 28 "Suppose one of you *w*
Jn 7: 4 No one who *w* to become a public
Ro 9: 18 he hardens whom he *w* to harden.
9: 18 on whom he *w* to have mercy,
1Co 7: 36 to marry, he should do as he *w*.
11: 16 If anyone *w* to be contentious
1Ti 2: 4 who *w* all men to be saved
2Ti 2: 4 he *w* to please his commanding
3: 12 everyone who *w* to live a godly life
Jas 3: 4 small rudder wherever the pilot *w*
1Pe 5: 2 you are willing, as God *w* you to be;
Rev 11: 5 This is how anyone who *w*

WAR (WARFARE WARRIOR WARRIOR'S WARRIORS WARS)

Ge 14: 2 went to *w* against Bera king
31: 26 off my daughters like captives in *w*.
Ex 1: 10 and, if *w* breaks out, will join our
13: 17 For God said, "If they face *w*,
17: 16 be at *w* against the Amalekites
32: 17 There is the sound of *w* in the camp
Nu 31: 3 to go to *w* against the Midianites
32: 6 go to *w* while you sit here?
Dt 2: 5 Do not provoke them to *w*,
2: 9 Moabites or provoke them to *w*,
2: 19 harass them or provoke them to *w*,
4: 34 signs and wonders, by *w*,
20: 1 go to *w* against your enemies
20: 20 until the city at *w* with you falls.
21: 10 go to *w* against your enemies
24: 5 he must not be sent to *w*
Jos 4: 13 to the plains of Jericho for *w*.
6: 10 "Do not give a *w* cry, do not raise
9: 2 together to make *w* against Joshua
11: 18 Joshua waged *w* against all these
11: 20 hearts to wage *w* against Israel,
11: 23 Then the land had rest from *w*.
14: 15 Then the land had rest from *w*.
22: 12 at Shiloh to go to *w* against them.
22: 33 talked no more about going to *w*
Jdg 3: 10 Israel's judge and went to *w*.
5: 8 *w* came to the city gates,
11: 4 when the Ammonites made *w*

Jdg 11: 27 wrong by waging *w* against me.
21: 22 wives for them during the *w*,
1Sa 8: 12 still others to make weapons of *w*
14: 52 the days of Saul there was bitter *w*
15: 18 make *w* on them until you have
17: 1 gathered their forces for *w*
17: 13 sons had followed Saul to the *w:*
17: 20 positions, shouting the *w* cry.
19: 8 Once more *w* broke out,
2Sa 1: 27 The weapons of *w* have perished!"
3: 1 The *w* between the house of Saul
3: 6 During the *w* between the house
8: 10 who had been at *w* with Tou.
11: 1 at the time when kings go off to *w*,
11: 7 were and how the *w* was going.
1Ki 8: 44 go to *w* against their enemies,
12: 21 to make *w* against the house
15: 6 There was *w* between Rehoboam
15: 7 There was *w* between Abijah
15: 16 There was *w* between Asa
15: 32 There was *w* between Asa
20: 18 if they have come out for *w*,
22: 1 For three years there was no *w*
22: 6 go to *w* against Ramoth Gilead,
22: 15 shall we go to *w* against Ramoth
2Ki 6: 8 king of Aram was at *w* with Israel.
8: 28 of Ahab to *w* against Hazael king
13: 12 his *w* against Amaziah king
14: 15 his *w* against Amaziah king
24: 16 fit for *w*, and a thousand craftsmen
1Ch 5: 10 During Saul's reign they waged *w*
5: 19 They waged *w* against the Hagrites
7: 11 fighting men ready to go out to *w*.
18: 10 who had been at *w* with Tou.
20: 1 at the time when kings go off to *w*,
20: 4 *w* broke out with the Philistines,
2Ch 6: 34 go to *w* against their enemies,
11: 1 to make *w* against Israel
13: 2 There was *w* between Abijah
14: 6 No one was at *w* with him
15: 19 There was no more *w*
16: 9 and from now on you will be at *w*."
17: 10 so that they did not make *w*
18: 3 we will join you in the *w*."
18: 5 go to *w* against Ramoth Gilead,
18: 14 go to *w* against Ramoth Gilead,
20: 1 came to make *w* on Jehoshaphat.
22: 5 of Israel to *w* against Hazael king
25: 13 part in the *w* raided Judean towns
26: 6 went to *w* against the Philistines
26: 13 men trained for *w*, a powerful force
27: 5 Jotham made *w* on the king
28: 12 who were arriving from the *w*.
32: 2 intended to make *w* on Jerusalem,
35: 21 but the house with which I am at *w*.
Job 38: 23 for days of *w* and battle?
Ps 27: 3 though *w* break out against me,
55: 21 yet *w* is in his heart;
68: 30 the nations who delight in *w*.
76: 3 the swords, the weapons of *w*.
120: 7 but when I speak, they are for *w*.
140: 2 and stir up *w* every day.
144: 1 who trains my hands for *w*,
Pr 20: 18 if you wage *w*, obtain guidance.
24: 6 for waging *w* you need guidance,
Ecc 3: 8 a time for *w* and a time for peace.
8: 8 no one is discharged in time of *w*,
9: 18 than weapons of *w*,
Isa 2: 4 nor will they train for *w* anymore.
8: 9 Raise the *w* cry, you nations,
13: 4 an army for *w*.
41: 12 Those who wage *w* against you
42: 25 the violence of *w*.
Jer 4: 16 raising a *w* cry against the cities
21: 4 you the weapons of *w* that are
28: 8 and me have prophesied *w*,
42: 14 where we will not see *w*
51: 20 "You are my *w* club,
Eze 17: 17 be of no help to him in *w*,
26: 10 at the noise of the *w* horses,
27: 14 *w* horses and mules
32: 27 the grave with their weapons of *w*,
38: 8 a land that has recovered from *w*,
39: 9 and arrows, the *w* clubs and spears.
Da 7: 21 this horn was waging *w*
9: 26 *W* will continue until the end,
10: 1 and it concerned a great *w*.
11: 10 His sons will prepare for *w*

Na 2: 3 the *w* are clad in scarlet.
Hab 3: 14 head when his *w* stormed out

WARS (WAR)

Nu 21: 14 Book of the *W* of the LORD says:
Jdg 3: 1 of the *w* in Canaan (he did this only
1Ki 5: 3 of the *w* waged against my father
14: 19 events of Jeroboam's reign, his *w*
1Ch 22: 8 blood and have fought many *w*.
2Ch 27: 7 including all his *w* and the other
Ps 46: 9 He makes *w* cease to the ends
Mt 24: 6 You will hear of *w* and rumors of *w*,
Mk 13: 7 hear of *w* and rumors of *w*,
Lk 21: 9 hear of *w* and revolutions,

WARTS

Lev 22: 22 or anything with *w* or festering

WASH (WASHED WASHERMAN'S WASHING WASHINGS WHITEWASH WHITEWASHED)

Ge 18: 4 and then you may all *w* your feet
19: 2 You can *w* your feet and spend
24: 32 and his men to *w* their feet.
43: 24 gave them water to *w* their feet
49: 11 he will *w* his garments in wine,
Ex 19: 10 Have them *w* their clothes
29: 4 of Meeting and *w* them with water.
29: 17 into pieces and *w* the inner parts
30: 19 and his sons are to *w* their hands
30: 20 they shall *w* with water
30: 21 they shall *w* their hands
40: 12 of Meeting and *w* them with water.
40: 31 his sons used it to *w* their hands
Lev 1: 9 He is to *w* the inner parts
1: 13 He is to *w* the inner parts
6: 27 you must *w* it in a holy place.
11: 25 their carcasses must *w* his clothes,
11: 28 their carcasses must *w* his clothes,
11: 40 of the carcass must *w* his clothes,
11: 40 up the carcass must *w* his clothes,
13: 6 The man must *w* his clothes,
13: 34 He must *w* his clothes,
14: 8 to be cleansed must *w* his clothes,
14: 9 He must *w* his clothes
14: 47 eats in the house must *w* his clothes
15: 5 touches his bed must *w* his clothes
15: 6 sat on must *w* his clothes
15: 7 has a discharge must *w* his clothes
15: 8 that person must *w* his clothes
15: 10 up those things must *w* his clothes
15: 11 with water must *w* his clothes
15: 13 he must *w* his clothes and bathe
15: 21 touches her bed must *w* his clothes
15: 22 sits on must *w* his clothes
15: 27 he must *w* his clothes and bathe
16: 26 as a scapegoat must *w* his clothes
16: 28 who burns them must *w* his clothes
17: 15 by wild animals must *w* his clothes
17: 16 But if he does not *w* his clothes
Nu 5: 23 and then *w* them off into the bitter
8: 7 whole bodies and *w* their clothes,
19: 7 the priest must *w* his clothes
19: 8 *w* his clothes and bathe with water,
19: 10 of the heifer must also *w* his clothes
19: 19 being cleansed must *w* his clothes
19: 21 of cleansing must also *w* his clothes
31: 24 On the seventh day *w* your clothes
Dt 21: 6 the body shall *w* their hands
23: 11 approaches he is to *w* himself,
Ru 3: 3 *W* and perfume yourself,
1Sa 25: 41 *w* the feet of my master's servants
2Sa 11: 8 to your house and *w* your feet."
2Ki 5: 10 *w* yourself seven times
5: 12 Couldn't I *w* in them and be
5: 13 he tells you, '*W* and be cleansed'!"
Job 14: 19 and torrents *w* away the soil,
Ps 26: 6 I *w* my hands in innocence,
51: 2 *W* away all my iniquity
51: 7 *w* me, and I will be whiter
SS 8: 7 rivers cannot *w* it away.
Isa 1: 16 *w* and make yourselves clean.
4: 4 The Lord will *w* away the filth
Jer 2: 22 Although you *w* yourself with soda
4: 14 *w* the evil from your heart
Mt 6: 17 oil on your head and *w* your face,
15: 2 They don't *w* their hands
Mk 7: 4 they do not eat unless they *w*.
Lk 11: 38 noticing that Jesus did not first *w*
Jn 9: 7 "*w* in the pool of Siloam" (this
9: 11 He told me to go to Siloam and *w*.
13: 5 and began to *w* his disciples' feet,
13: 6 are you going to *w* my feet?"
13: 8 Jesus answered, "Unless I *w* you,
13: 8 "you shall never *w* my feet."
13: 10 had a bath needs only to *w* his feet;
13: 14 also should *w* one another's feet.
Ac 22: 16 be baptized and *w* your sins away,
Jas 4: 8 *W* your hands, you sinners,
Rev 22: 14 Blessed are those who *w* their robes

WASHBASIN

Ps 60: 8 Moab is my *w*,
108: 9 Moab is my *w*,

WASHED (WASH)

Ge 43: 31 After he had *w* his face, he came
Ex 19: 14 them, and they *w* their clothes.
40: 32 They *w* whenever they entered
Lev 8: 6 and his sons forward and *w* them
8: 21 He *w* the inner parts and the legs
9: 14 He *w* the inner parts and the legs
13: 54 that the contaminated article be *w*.
13: 55 the affected article has been *w*,
13: 56 faded after the article has been *w*,
13: 58 any leather article that has been *w*
13: 58 must be *w* again, and it will be
15: 17 semen on it must be *w* with water,
Nu 8: 21 themselves and *w* their clothes.
Jdg 19: 21 After they had *w* their feet,
2Sa 12: 20 After he had *w*, put on lotions
19: 24 *w* his clothes from the day the king
1Ki 22: 38 They *w* the chariot at a pool
Job 9: 30 Even if I *w* myself with soap
22: 16 their foundations *w* away
Ps 73: 13 in vain have I *w* my hands
SS 5: 3 I have *w* my feet—
5: 12 *w* in milk,
Eze 16: 4 nor were you *w* with water
16: 9 you with water and *w* the blood
40: 38 where the burnt offerings were *w*.
Mt 27: 24 *w* his hands in front of the crowd.
Jn 9: 7 and *w*, and came home seeing.
9: 11 I went and *w*, and then I could see
9: 15 the man replied, "and I *w*,
13: 14 and Teacher, have *w* your feet,
Ac 9: 37 and her body was *w* and placed
16: 33 took them and *w* their wounds;
1Co 6: 11 you were *w*, you were sanctified,
Heb 10: 22 and having our bodies *w*
2Pe 2: 22 and, "A sow that is *w* goes back
Rev 7: 14 they have *w* their robes

WASHERMAN'S (WASH)

2Ki 18: 17 on the road to the *W* Field.
Isa 7: 3 on the road to the *W* Field.
36: 2 on the road to the *W* Field,

WASHING (WASH)

Ex 30: 18 with its bronze stand, for *w*.
40: 30 the altar and put water in it for *w*,
2Ch 4: 6 He then made ten basins for *w*
4: 6 was to be used by the priests for *w*.
Job 9: 30 and my hands with *w* soda,
SS 4: 2 coming up from the *w*.
6: 6 coming up from the *w*.
Mk 7: 3 give their hands a ceremonial *w*,
7: 4 such as the *w* of cups, pitchers
Lk 5: 2 fishermen, who were *w* their nets.
Jn 2: 6 used by the Jews for ceremonial *w*,
3: 25 over the matter of ceremonial *w*.
13: 12 When he had finished *w* their feet,
Eph 5: 26 cleansing her by the *w* with water
1Ti 5: 10 showing hospitality, *w* the feet
Tit 3: 5 us through the *w* of rebirth

WASHINGS (WASH)

Heb 9: 10 drink and various ceremonial *w*—

WASTE (WASTED WASTES WASTING)

Lev 26: 31 and lay *w* your sanctuaries,
26: 32 I will lay *w* the land,
26: 33 Your land will be laid *w*,
26: 39 of you who are left will *w* away
26: 39 their fathers' sins they will *w* away.
Nu 5: 21 he causes your thigh to *w* away
Nu 5: 27 will swell and her thigh *w* away,
Dt 29: 23 The whole land will be a burning *w*
32: 10 in a barren and howling *w*.
Jdg 16: 24 the one who laid *w* our land
2Ki 19: 17 kings have laid *w* these nations
22: 19 would become accursed and laid *w*,
1Ch 20: 1 He laid *w* the land
Job 12: 24 through a trackless *w*.
Ps 107: 34 and fruitful land into a salt *w*,
107: 40 made them wander in a trackless *w*
112: 10 he will gnash his teeth and *w* away;
Isa 1: 7 laid *w* as when overthrown
6: 13 it will again be laid *w*.
7: 16 two kings you dread will be laid *w*.
17: 4 the fat of his body will *w* away.
24: 1 LORD is going to lay *w* the earth
24: 3 The earth will be completely laid *w*
24: 16 But I said, "I *w* away, I *w* away!
37: 18 kings have laid *w* all these peoples
42: 15 I will lay *w* the mountains and hills
49: 17 those who laid you *w* depart
49: 19 and your land laid *w*,
64: 7 made us *w* away because of our sins
Jer 2: 15 They have laid *w* his land;
4: 7 place to lay *w* your land.
9: 11 and I will lay *w* the towns of Judah
9: 12 laid *w* like a desert that no one can
12: 11 the whole land will be laid *w*
18: 16 Their land will be laid *w*,
25: 37 peaceful meadows will be laid *w*
32: 43 'It is a desolate *w*, without men
33: 10 "It is a desolate *w*, without men
34: 22 And I will lay *w* the towns of Judah
44: 22 a desolate *w* without inhabitants,
46: 19 for Memphis will be laid *w*
48: 9 for she will be laid *w*;
50: 3 and lay *w* her land.
51: 29 to lay *w* the land of Babylon
La 2: 6 He has laid *w* his dwelling like
4: 9 racked with hunger, they *w* away
Eze 4: 17 will *w* away because of their sin.
6: 6 so that your altars will be laid *w*
6: 6 the towns will be laid *w*
6: 14 and make the land a desolate *w*
12: 20 The inhabited towns will be laid *w*
24: 23 will *w* away because of your sins
25: 3 the land of Israel when it was laid *w*
25: 13 I will lay it *w*, and from Teman
29: 10 and a desolate *w* from Migdol
30: 12 I will lay *w* the land and everything
30: 14 I will lay Pathros *w*,
33: 28 I will make the land a desolate *w*,
33: 29 I have made the land a desolate *w*
35: 3 and make you a desolate *w*.
35: 7 will make Mount Seir a desolate *w*
35: 12 "They have been laid *w*
36: 35 that was laid *w* has become like
Hos 4: 3 and all who live in it *w* away;
5: 9 Ephraim will be laid *w*
8: 10 They will begin to *w* away
Joel 1: 7 It has laid *w* my vines
2: 3 behind them, a desert *w*—
3: 19 Edom a desert *w*,
Na 2: 2 destroyers have laid them *w*
Mt 26: 8 "Why this *w*?" they asked.
Mk 14: 4 to one another, "Why this *w*

WASTED (WASTE)

Ge 47: 13 both Egypt and Canaan *w* away
Ps 32: 3 my bones *w* away
106: 43 and they *w* away in their sin.
Pr 23: 8 and will have *w* your compliments.
La 2: 8 together they *w* away.
Jn 6: 12 Let nothing be *w*."
Gal 4: 11 that somehow I have *w* my efforts

WASTELAND (LAND)

Nu 21: 20 the top of Pisgah overlooks the *w*.
23: 28 the top of Peor, overlooking the *w*.
2Sa 2: 24 on the way to the *w* of Gibeon.
Job 6: 18 they go up into the *w* and perish.
24: 5 the *w* provides food
38: 27 to satisfy a desolate *w*
39: 6 I gave him the *w* as his home,
Ps 68: 7 when you marched through the *w*,
78: 40 and grieved him in the *w*!
106: 14 in the *w* they put God to the test.
Isa 5: 6 I will make it a *w*,

Isa 32: 14 will become a *w* forever,
41: 19 I will set pines in the *w*,
43: 19 and streams in the *w*.
43: 20 and streams in the *w*,
Jer 12: 10 field into a desolate *w*.
12: 11 It will be made a *w*,
25: 11 country will become a desolate *w*,
Eze 29: 9 Egypt will become a desolate *w*.
Zep 2: 9 a *w* forever.
Mal 1: 3 have turned his mountains into a *w*

WASTELANDS (LAND)

Job 30: 3 land in desolate *w* at night.
Ps 107: 4 Some wandered in desert *w*,
Isa 51: 3 her *w* like the garden of the LORD.
Jer 17: 6 He will be like a bush in the *w*;

WASTES (WASTE)

Nu 5: 22 swells and your thigh *w* away."
Job 13: 28 man *w* away like something rotten,
33: 21 His flesh *w* away to nothing,
Isa 10: 18 as when a sick man *w* away.
33: 9 The land mourns and *w* away,

WASTING (WASTE)

Lev 26: 16 *w* diseases and fever that will
Dt 28: 22 will strike you with *w* disease,
32: 24 I will send *w* famine against them,
Ps 106: 15 but sent a *w* disease upon them.
Isa 10: 16 will send a *w* disease
Eze 33: 10 and we are *w* away because of them
Lk 16: 1 accused of *w* his possessions.
2Co 4: 16 Though outwardly we are *w* away,

WATCH (WATCHED WATCHER WATCHES WATCHFUL WATCHING WATCHMAN WATCHMEN)

Ge 21: 16 thought, "I cannot *w* the boy die."
28: 15 will *w* over you wherever you go,
28: 20 will *w* over me on this journey I am
31: 49 "May the LORD keep *w*
Ex 14: 24 In the morning *w* the LORD
Dt 4: 9 and *w* yourselves closely
4: 15 Therefore *w* yourselves very
Jdg 7: 17 "*W* me," he told them.
7: 19 at the beginning of the middle *w*.
21: 21 Go and hide in the vineyards and *w*
Ru 2: 9 *W* the field where the men are
1Sa 11: 11 during the last *w* of the night they
17: 28 you came down only to *w* the battle
19: 11 men to David's house to *w* it
2Sa 13: 5 the food in my sight so I may *w* her
13: 34 Now the man standing *w* looked up
1Ki 2: 4 'If your descendants *w* how they
2Ch 23: 4 are to keep *w* at the doors,
Ne 11: 19 who kept *w* at the gates—172 men.
Job 13: 27 you keep close *w* on all my paths
21: 32 and *w* is kept over his tomb.
33: 11 he keeps close *w* on all my paths.'
39: 1 Do you *w* when the doe bears her
Ps 32: 8 I will counsel you and *w* over you.
39: 1 I said, "I will *w* my ways
56: 6 they *w* my steps,
59: 9 O my Strength, I *w* for you;
66: 7 his eyes *w* the nations—
80: 14 *W* over this vine,
90: 4 or like a *w* in the night.
121: 7 he will *w* over your life;
121: 8 LORD will *w* over your coming
141: 3 keep *w* over the door of my lips.
Pr 4: 6 love her, and she will *w* over you.
6: 22 when you sleep, they will *w*
15: 3 keeping *w* on the wicked
22: 12 of the LORD keep *w*
Isa 27: 3 I, the LORD, *w* over it;
Jer 24: 6 My eyes will *w* over them
31: 10 will *w* over his flock like a shepherd
31: 28 so I will *w* over them to build
48: 19 Stand by the road and *w*,
Eze 12: 3 and in the daytime, as they *w*,
12: 4 During the daytime, while they *w*,
12: 5 While they *w*, dig through the wall
Da 7: 11 "Then I continued to *w*
Mic 7: 7 I *w* in hope for the LORD,
Na 2: 1 *w* the road,
Hab 1: 5 "Look at the nations and *w*—
2: 1 I will stand at my *w*
Zec 9: 8 for now I am keeping *w*.
Mt 7: 15 "*W* out for false prophets.
14: 25 During the fourth *w*
24: 4 "*W* out that no one deceives you.
24: 42 "Therefore keep *w*, because you do
24: 43 would have kept *w* and would not
25: 13 "Therefore keep *w*, because you do
26: 38 Stay here and keep *w* with me."
26: 40 Could you men not keep *w* with me
26: 41 *W* and pray so that you will not fall
27: 36 they kept *w* over him there.
Mk 6: 48 About the fourth *w*
8: 15 *W* out for the yeast of the Pharisees
12: 38 "*W* out for the teachers of the law.
13: 5 "*W* out that no one deceives you.
13: 34 tells the one at the door to keep *w*.
13: 35 "Therefore keep *w* because you do
13: 37 to you, I say to everyone: '*W!*' "
14: 34 "Stay here and keep *w*."
14: 37 Could you not keep *w* for one hour
14: 38 *W* and pray so that you will not fall
Lk 2: 8 keeping *w* over their flocks at night
12: 15 Then he said to them, "*W* out!
12: 38 comes in the second or third *w*
17: 3 So *w* yourselves.
20: 20 Keeping a close *w* on him,
21: 8 "*W* out that you are not deceived.
21: 36 on the *w*, and pray that you may be
Ac 9: 24 and night they kept close *w*
20: 28 Keep *w* over yourselves
Ro 16: 17 to *w* out for those who cause
Gal 5: 15 *w* out or you will be destroyed
6: 1 But *w* yourself, or you
Php 3: 2 *W* out for those dogs, those men
1Ti 4: 16 *W* your life and doctrine closely.
Heb 13: 17 They keep *w* over you
2Jn : 8 *W* out that you do not lose what

WATCHED (WATCH)

Ge 24: 21 the man *w* her closely to learn
Ex 2: 11 and *w* them at their hard labor.
3: 16 I have *w* over you and have seen
Dt 2: 7 He has *w* over your journey
33: 9 but he *w* over your word
Jos 4: 11 to the other side while the people *w*
Jdg 13: 19 thing while Manoah and his wife *w*:
1Sa 17: 55 As Saul *w* David going out
2Sa 6: 16 daughter of Saul *w* from a window.
1Ch 15: 29 daughter of Saul *w* from a window.
Job 10: 12 and in your providence *w*
29: 2 for the days when God *w* over me,
Jer 31: 28 Just as I *w* over them to uproot
La 4: 17 from our towers we *w*
Eze 10: 2 And as I *w*, he went in.
10: 19 While I *w*, the cherubim spread
12: 7 on my shoulders while they *w*.
Da 5: 5 The king *w* the hand as it wrote.
7: 4 I *w* until its wings were torn off
7: 21 As I *w*, this horn was waging war
8: 4 I *w* the ram as he charged
Mt 26: 16 then on Judas *w* for an opportunity
Mk 3: 2 so they *w* him closely to see
12: 41 *w* the crowd putting their money
14: 11 So he *w* for an opportunity
Lk 6: 7 so they *w* him closely to see
14: 1 Pharisee, he was being carefully *w*.
22: 6 *w* for an opportunity to hand Jesus
Rev 6: 1 I *w* as the Lamb opened the first
6: 12 I *w* as he opened the sixth seal.
8: 13 As I *w*, I heard an eagle that was

WATCHER (WATCH)

Job 7: 20 O *w* of men?

WATCHES (WATCH)

Nu 19: 5 While he *w*, the heifer is
Job 24: 15 The eye of the adulterer *w* for dusk;
Ps 1: 6 For the LORD *w* over the way
33: 14 from his dwelling place he *w*
63: 6 of you through the *w* of the night.
119:148 through the *w* of the night,
121: 3 he who *w* over you will not slumber
121: 4 indeed, he who *w* over Israel
121: 5 The LORD *w* over you—
127: 1 Unless the LORD *w* over the city,
145: 20 LORD *w* over all who love him,
146: 9 The LORD *w* over the alien
Pr 31: 27 She *w* over the affairs
Ecc 11: 4 Whoever *w* the wind will not plant;
La 2: 19 as the *w* of the night begin;
4: 16 he no longer *w* over them.

WATCHFUL (WATCH)

Zec 12: 4 "I will keep a *w* eye over the house
Col 4: 2 yourselves to prayer, being *w*

WATCHING (WATCH)

Ge 30: 31 go on tending your flocks and *w*
Ex 33: 8 *w* Moses until he entered the tent.
Dt 28: 32 and you will wear out your eyes *w*
Jdg 16: 27 and women *w* Samson perform.
1Sa 4: 13 *w*, because his heart feared
6: 9 Send it on its way, but keep *w* it.
25: 21 all my *w* over this fellow's property
2Ki 2: 15 from Jericho, who were *w*,
Ezr 5: 5 of their God was *w* over the elders
Job 10: 14 If I sinned, you would be *w* me
Ps 10: 8 *w* in secret for his victims.
Pr 8: 34 *w* daily at my doors,
Jer 1: 12 for I am *w* to see that my word is
7: 11 I have been *w*! declares the LORD.
19: 10 while those who go with you are *w*,
43: 9 to Jeremiah: "While the Jews are *w*
44: 27 For I am *w* over them for harm,
Eze 12: 4 in the evening, while they are *w*,
12: 6 as they are *w* and carry them out
28: 18 in the sight of all who were *w*.
Da 2: 34 While you were *w*, a rock was cut
8: 15 was *w* the vision and trying
Zec 11: 11 the flock who were *w* me knew it
Mt 27: 55 Many women were there, *w*
Mk 15: 40 Some women were *w*
Lk 12: 37 whose master finds them *w*
23: 35 The people stood *w*, and the rulers
23: 49 stood at a distance, *w* these things.
Jn 7: 11 Now at the Feast the Jews were *w*

WATCHMAN (WATCH)

2Sa 13: 34 The *w* went and told the king,
18: 24 the *w* went up to the roof
18: 25 The *w* called out to the king
18: 26 the *w* saw another man running,
18: 27 The *w* said, "It seems
Job 27: 18 like a hut made by a *w*.
Isa 21: 11 *W*, what is left of the night?"
21: 11 "*W*, what is left of the night?
21: 12 The *w* replies,
Eze 3: 17 I have made you a *w* for the house
33: 2 of their men and make him their *w*,
33: 6 But if the *w* sees the sword coming
33: 6 but I will hold the *w* accountable
33: 7 I have made you a *w* for the house
Hos 9: 8 is the *w* over Ephraim,
Jn 10: 3 The *w* opens the gate for him,

WATCHMEN (WATCH)

Ps 127: 1 the *w* stand guard in vain.
130: 6 more than *w* wait for the morning.
130: 6 more than *w* wait for the morning,
SS 3: 3 The *w* found me
5: 7 The *w* found me
5: 7 those *w* of the walls!
Isa 52: 8 Listen! Your *w* lift up their voices;
56: 10 Israel's *w* are blind,
62: 6 I have posted *w* on your walls,
Jer 6: 17 I appointed *w* over you and said,
31: 6 There will be a day when *w* cry out
51: 12 station the *w*,
Mic 7: 4 The day of your *w* has come,

WATCHTOWER (TOWER)

2Ki 17: 9 From *w* to fortified city they built
18: 8 From *w* to fortified city, he
Isa 5: 2 He built a *w* in it
21: 8 after day, my lord, I stand on the *w*;
32: 14 *w* will become a wasteland forever,
Mic 4: 8 As for you, O *w* of the flock,
Mt 21: 33 dug a winepress in it and built a *w*.
Mk 12: 1 pit for the winepress and built a *w*.

WATCHTOWERS (TOWER)

1Ch 27: 25 in the towns, the villages and the *w*.

WATER (WATER'S WATERCOURSE WATERED WATERFALLS WATERING WATERS WATERY WELL-WATERED)

Ge 1: 6 the waters to separate *w* from *w*."

Ge 1: 7 separated the *w* under the expanse
1: 7 the expanse from the *w* above it.
1: 9 "Let the *w* under the sky be
1: 20 the *w* teem with living creatures,
1: 21 thing with which the *w* teems,
1: 22 in number and fill the *w* in the seas,
7: 18 floated on the surface of the *w*.
8: 3 The *w* receded steadily
8: 3 fifty days the *w* had gone down,
8: 7 and forth until the *w* had dried up
8: 8 a dove to see if the *w* had receded
8: 9 there was *w* over all the surface
8: 11 Noah knew that the *w* had receded
8: 13 the *w* had dried up from the earth.
18: 4 Let a little *w* be brought,
21: 14 a skin of *w* and gave them to Hagar.
21: 15 When the *w* in the skin was gone,
21: 19 her eyes and she saw a well of *w*.
21: 19 with *w* and gave the boy a drink.
21: 25 of *w* that Abimelech's servants had
24: 11 time the women go out to draw *w*.
24: 13 are coming out to draw *w*.
24: 14 'Drink, and I'll *w* your camels too
24: 17 "Please give me a little *w*
24: 19 "I'll draw *w* for your camels too,
24: 20 back to the well to draw more *w*,
24: 32 and *w* for him and his men
24: 43 if a maiden comes out to draw *w*
24: 43 "Please let me drink a little *w*
24: 44 and I'll draw *w* for your camels too
24: 45 down to the spring and drew *w*,
24: 46 'Drink, and I'll *w* your camels too.'
26: 19 discovered a well of fresh *w* there.
26: 20 *w* is ours!" So he named the well
26: 32 They said, "We've found *w!*"
29: 3 the well's mouth and *w* the sheep.
29: 7 *W* the sheep and take them back
29: 8 Then we will *w* the sheep."
37: 24 cistern was empty; there was no *w*
43: 24 gave them *w* to wash their feet
Ex 2: 10 saying, "I drew him out of the *w*."
2: 16 and they came to draw *w*
2: 16 troughs to *w* their father's flock.
2: 19 He even drew *w* for us
4: 9 The *w* you take from the river will
4: 9 take some *w* from the Nile
7: 15 morning as he goes out to the *w*.
7: 17 is in my hand I will strike the *w*
7: 18 will not be able to drink its *w*.' "
7: 20 all the *w* was changed into blood.
7: 20 and struck the *w* of the Nile,
7: 21 Egyptians could not drink its *w*.
7: 24 along the Nile to get drinking *w*,
7: 24 because they could not drink the *w*
8: 20 as he goes to the *w* and say to him,
12: 9 eat the meat raw or cooked in *w*,
14: 16 hand over the sea to divide the *w*
14: 22 with a wall of *w* on their right
14: 28 The *w* flowed back and covered
14: 29 with a wall of *w* on their right
15: 22 in the desert without finding *w*.
15: 23 they could not drink its *w*
15: 25 into the *w*, and the *w* became sweet
15: 27 and they camped there near the *w*.
17: 1 but there was no *w* for the people
17: 2 and said, "Give us *w* to drink."
17: 3 the people were thirsty for *w* there,
17: 6 *w* will come out of it for the people
23: 25 be on your food and *w*.
29: 4 of Meeting and wash them with *w*.
30: 18 and the altar, and put *w* in it.
30: 19 to wash their hands and feet with *w*
30: 20 they shall wash with *w*
32: 20 it on the *w* and made the Israelites
34: 28 without eating bread or drinking *w*.
40: 7 and the altar and put *w* in it.
40: 12 of Meeting and wash them with *w*.
40: 30 the altar and put *w* in it for washing
Lev 1: 9 the inner parts and the legs with *w*,
1: 13 the inner parts and the legs with *w*,
6: 28 is to be scoured and rinsed with *w*.
8: 6 forward and washed them with *w*.
8: 21 with *w* and burned the whole ram
11: 9 living in the *w* of the seas
11: 10 other living creatures in the *w*—
11: 12 in the *w* that does not have fins
11: 32 Put it in *w;* it will be unclean
11: 34 but has *w* on it from such a pot is
Lev 11: 36 for collecting *w* remains clean,
11: 38 But if *w* has been put on the seed
11: 46 living thing that moves in the *w*
14: 5 killed over fresh *w* in a clay pot.
14: 6 that was killed over the fresh *w*.
14: 8 off all his hair and bathe with *w;*
14: 9 clothes and bathe himself with *w*,
14: 50 the birds over fresh *w* in a clay pot.
14: 51 of the dead bird and the fresh *w*,
14: 52 the fresh *w*, the live bird, the cedar
15: 5 wash his clothes and bathe with *w*,
15: 6 wash his clothes and bathe with *w*,
15: 7 wash his clothes and bathe with *w*,
15: 8 wash his clothes and bathe with *w*,
15: 10 wash his clothes and bathe with *w*,
15: 11 hands with *w* must wash his clothes
15: 11 wash his clothes and bathe with *w*,
15: 12 is to be rinsed with *w*.
15: 13 and bathe himself with fresh *w*,
15: 16 must bathe his whole body with *w*,
15: 17 on it must be washed with *w*,
15: 18 both must bathe with *w*,
15: 21 wash his clothes and bathe with *w*,
15: 22 wash his clothes and bathe with *w*,
15: 27 wash his clothes and bathe with *w*,
16: 4 with *w* before he puts them on.
16: 24 himself with *w* in a holy place
16: 26 clothes and bathe himself with *w;*
16: 28 clothes and bathe himself with *w;*
17: 15 wash his clothes and bathe with *w*,
22: 6 he has bathed himself with *w*.
Nu 5: 17 Then he shall take some holy *w*
5: 17 from the tabernacle floor into the *w*
5: 18 holds the bitter *w* that brings
5: 19 may this bitter *w* that brings a curse
5: 22 May this *w* that brings a curse
5: 23 them off into the bitter *w*.
5: 24 and this *w* will enter her
5: 24 drink the bitter *w* that brings
5: 26 is to have the woman drink the *w*.
5: 27 to drink the *w* that brings a curse,
8: 7 Sprinkle the *w* of cleansing
19: 7 clothes and bathe himself with *w*.
19: 8 wash his clothes and bathe with *w*,
19: 9 for use in the *w* of cleansing;
19: 12 himself with the *w* on the third day
19: 13 Because the *w* of cleansing has not
19: 17 and pour fresh *w* over them.
19: 18 dip it in the *w* and sprinkle the tent
19: 19 wash his clothes and bathe with *w*,
19: 20 The *w* of cleansing has not been
19: 21 and anyone who touches the *w*
19: 21 "The man who sprinkles the *w*
20: 2 there was no *w* for the community,
20: 5 And there is no *w* to drink!"
20: 8 You will bring *w* out of the rock
20: 8 their eyes and it will pour out its *w*.
20: 10 must we bring you *w* out
20: 11 *W* gushed out, and the community
20: 17 vineyard, or drink *w* from any well.
20: 19 our livestock drink any of your *w*,
21: 5 There is no *w!* And we detest this
21: 16 together and I will give them *w*."
21: 22 vineyard, or drink *w* from any well.
24: 7 their seed will have abundant *w*.
24: 7 *W* will flow from their buckets;
31: 23 be purified with the *w* of cleansing.
31: 23 fire must be put through that *w*.
33: 14 where there was no *w*
Dt 2: 6 you eat and the *w* you drink.' "
2: 28 *w* to drink for their price in silver.
4: 18 or any fish in the *w* below.
8: 7 a land with streams and pools of *w*,
8: 15 He brought you *w* out of hard rock.
9: 9 I ate no bread and drank no *w*.
9: 18 I ate no bread and drank no *w*,
10: 7 a land with streams of *w*
12: 16 pour it out on the ground like *w*.
12: 24 pour it out on the ground like *w*.
14: 9 Of all the creatures living in the *w*,
15: 23 pour it out on the ground like *w*.
23: 4 *w* on your way when you came out
29: 11 chop your wood and carry your *w*.
Jos 2: 10 how the LORD dried up the *w*
3: 13 *w* flowing downstream will be cut
3: 16 while the *w* flowing
3: 16 *w* from upstream stopped flowing.
7: 5 people melted and became like *w*.
Jos 9: 21 and *w* carriers for the entire
9: 23 *w* carriers for the house of my God
9: 27 and *w* carriers for the community
15: 19 give me also springs of *w*."
Jdg 1: 15 give me also springs of *w*."
4: 19 "Please give me some *w*."
5: 4 the clouds poured down *w*.
5: 25 for *w*, and she gave him milk;
6: 38 wrung out the dew—a bowlful of *w*
7: 4 Take them down to the *w*,
7: 5 took the men down to the *w*.
7: 5 "Separate those who lap the *w*
15: 19 place in Lehi, and *w* came out of it.
Ru 2: 9 from the *w* jars the men have filled
1Sa 7: 6 they drew *w* and poured it out
9: 11 some girls coming out to draw *w*,
25: 11 Why should I take my bread and *w*,
26: 11 and *w* jug that are near his head,
26: 12 and *w* jug near Saul's head,
26: 16 and *w* jug that were near his head?"
30: 11 They gave him *w* to drink
30: 12 or drunk any *w* for three days
2Sa 5: 8 to use the *w* shaft to reach those
12: 27 Rabbah and taken its *w* supply.
14: 14 Like *w* spilled on the ground,
23: 15 David longed for *w* and said, "Oh,
23: 15 of *w* from the well near the gate
23: 16 drew *w* from the well near the gate
1Ki 13: 8 would I eat bread or drink *w* here.
13: 9 'You must not eat bread or drink *w*
13: 16 or drink *w* with you in this place.
13: 17 must not eat bread or drink *w* there
13: 18 he may eat bread and drink *w*.' "
13: 22 drank *w* in the place where he told
14: 15 will be like a reed swaying in the *w*.
17: 10 "Would you bring me a little *w*
18: 4 had supplied them with food and *w*
18: 13 and supplied them with food and *w*
18: 33 "Fill four large jars with *w*
18: 35 The *w* ran down around the altar
18: 38 also licked up the *w* in the trench.
19: 6 baked over hot coals, and a jar of *w*.
22: 27 bread and *w* until I return safely.' "
2Ki 2: 8 The *w* divided to the right
2: 8 rolled it up and struck the *w* with it.
2: 14 When he struck the *w*, it divided
2: 14 from him and struck the *w* with it.
2: 19 but the *w* is bad and the land is
2: 21 LORD says: 'I have healed this *w*.
2: 22 the *w* has remained wholesome
3: 9 the army had no more *w*
3: 11 He used to pour *w* on the hands
3: 17 yet this valley will be filled with *w*,
3: 20 And the land was filled with *w*.
3: 20 *w* flowing from the direction
3: 22 the sun was shining on the *w*.
3: 22 the *w* looked red—like blood.
6: 5 the iron axhead fell into the *w*.
6: 22 *w* before them so that they may eat
8: 15 soaked it in *w* and spread it
18: 31 and drink *w* from his own cistern,
19: 24 and drunk the *w* there.
20: 20 by which he brought *w* into the city
1Ch 11: 17 David longed for *w* and said, "Oh,
11: 17 of *w* from the well near the gate
11: 18 drew *w* from the well near the gate
2Ch 18: 26 bread and *w* until I return safely.' "
32: 3 blocking off the *w* from the springs
32: 4 come and find plenty of *w?*"
32: 30 channeled the *w* down to the west
Ezr 10: 6 he ate no food and drank no *w*,
Ne 3: 26 a point opposite the *W* Gate
4: 23 even when he went for *w*.
8: 1 in the square before the *W* Gate.
8: 3 before the *W* Gate in the presence
8: 16 and in the square by the *W* Gate
9: 15 in their thirst you brought them *w*
9: 20 you gave them *w* for their thirst.
12: 37 of David to the *W* Gate on the east.
13: 2 met the Israelites with food and *w*
Job 3: 24 my groans pour out like *w*.
5: 10 he sends *w* upon the countryside.
6: 19 The caravans of Tema look for *w*,
8: 11 Can reeds thrive without *w?*
14: 9 yet at the scent of *w* it will bud
14: 11 As *w* disappears from the sea
14: 19 as *w* wears away stones
15: 16 who drinks up evil like *w!*

Job 22: 7 You gave no *w* to the weary
22: 11 and why a flood of *w* covers you.
24: 18 foam on the surface of the *w;*
29: 19 My roots will reach to the *w,*
34: 7 who drinks scorn like *w?*
36: 27 "He draws up the drops of *w,*
37: 13 or to *w* his earth and show his love.
38: 26 to *w* a land where no man lives,
38: 34 cover yourself with a flood of *w?*
38: 37 tip over the *w* jars of the heavens
Ps 1: 3 like a tree planted by streams of *w,*
22: 14 I am poured out like *w,*
42: 1 As the deer pants for streams of *w,*
58: 7 them vanish like *w* that flows away;
63: 1 where there is no *w.*
65: 9 You care for the land and *w* it;
65: 9 streams of God are filled with *w*
66: 12 we went through fire and *w,*
77: 17 The clouds poured down *w,*
78: 13 he made the *w* stand firm like
78: 15 and gave them *w* as abundant
78: 16 and made *w* flow down like rivers.
78: 20 he struck the rock, *w* gushed out,
79: 3 They have poured out blood like *w*
104: 10 He makes springs pour *w*
104: 11 They give *w* to all the beasts
105: 41 opened the rock, and *w* gushed out;
107: 35 turned the desert into pools of *w*
109: 18 it entered into his body like *w,*
114: 8 the hard rock into springs of *w.*
Pr 5: 15 Drink *w* from your own cistern,
5: 15 running *w* from your own well.
5: 16 streams of *w* in the public squares?
8: 24 were no springs abounding with *w;*
9: 17 "Stolen *w* is sweet;
25: 21 if he is thirsty, give him *w* to drink.
25: 25 Like cold *w* to a weary soul
27: 19 As *w* reflects a face,
30: 16 which is never satisfied with *w,*
Ecc 2: 6 I made reservoirs to *w* groves
11: 3 If clouds are full of *w,*
SS 4: 15 a well of flowing *w*
5: 12 doves by the *w* streams,
Isa 1: 22 your choice wine is diluted with *w.*
1: 30 like a garden without *w.*
3: 1 of food and all supplies of *w,*
7: 19 thornbushes and at all the *w* holes.
12: 3 With joy you will draw *w*
18: 2 sea in papyrus boats over the *w.*
19: 8 those who throw nets on the *w*
21: 14 bring *w* for the thirsty;
22: 9 you stored up *w*
22: 11 walls for the *w* of the Old Pool,
27: 3 I *w* it continually
28: 17 *w* will overflow your hiding place.
30: 14 or scooping *w* out of a cistern."
30: 20 of adversity and the *w* of affliction,
30: 25 streams of *w* will flow
32: 2 like streams of *w* in the desert
32: 6 from the thirsty he withholds *w.*
33: 16 and *w* will not fail him.
35: 6 *W* will gush forth in the wilderness
36: 16 and drink *w* from his own cistern,
37: 25 and drunk the *w* there.
41: 17 "The poor and needy search for *w,*
41: 18 I will turn the desert into pools of *w*
43: 20 because I provide *w* in the desert
44: 3 For I will pour *w* on the thirsty land
44: 12 he drinks no *w* and grows faint.
48: 21 and *w* gushed out.
48: 21 he made *w* flow for them
49: 10 and lead them beside springs of *w.*
50: 2 their fish rot for lack of *w*
64: 2 and causes *w* to boil,
Jer 2: 13 broken cisterns that cannot hold *w.*
2: 13 the spring of living *w,*
2: 18 Assyria to drink *w* from the River?
2: 18 Egypt to drink *w* from the Shihor?
6: 7 As a well pours out its *w,*
8: 14 and given us poisoned *w* to drink,
9: 1 that my head were a spring of *w*
9: 15 bitter food and drink poisoned *w.*
9: 18 and *w* streams from our eyelids.
13: 1 but do not let it touch *w.*"
14: 3 but find no *w.*
14: 3 nobles send their servants for *w;*
17: 8 will be like a tree planted by the *w*
17: 13 the spring of living *w.*
Jer 23: 15 and drink poisoned *w,*
31: 9 I will lead them beside streams of *w*
38: 6 it had no *w* in it, only mud,
La 2: 19 pour out your heart like *w*
5: 4 We must buy the *w* we drink;
Eze 4: 11 measure out a sixth of a hin of *w*
4: 16 and drink rationed *w* in despair,
4: 17 for food and *w* will be scarce.
7: 17 knee will become as weak as *w.*
12: 18 shudder in fear as you drink your *w*
12: 19 and drink their *w* in despair,
16: 4 nor were you washed with *w*
16: 9 " 'I bathed you with *w*
17: 5 it like a willow by abundant *w,*
17: 7 out its branches to him for *w.*
17: 8 planted in good soil by abundant *w*
19: 10 because of abundant *w.*
19: 10 planted by the *w;*
21: 7 every knee become as weak as *w.*'
24: 3 and pour *w* into it.
32: 2 churning the *w* with your feet
34: 18 enough for you to drink clear *w?*
36: 25 I will sprinkle clean *w* on you,
47: 1 The *w* was coming down
47: 1 and I saw *w* coming out
47: 2 *w* was flowing from the south side.
47: 3 me through *w* that was ankle-deep.
47: 4 and led me through *w* that was up
47: 4 me through *w* that was knee-deep.
47: 5 because the *w* had risen
47: 8 the *w* there becomes fresh.
47: 8 "This *w* flows toward the eastern
47: 9 and makes the salt *w* fresh;
47: 9 because this *w* flows there
47: 12 the *w* from the sanctuary flows
Da 1: 12 vegetables to eat and *w* to drink.
Hos 2: 5 who give me my food and my *w,*
5: 10 like a flood of *w.*
6: 3 the spring rains that *w* the earth."
Joel 1: 20 the streams of *w* have dried up
3: 18 and will *w* the valley of acacias.
3: 18 ravines of Judah will run with *w.*
Am 4: 8 staggered from town to town for *w*
8: 11 a famine of food or a thirst for *w,*
Mic 1: 4 like *w* rushing down a slope.
Na 2: 8 and its *w* is draining away.
3: 8 with *w* around her?
3: 14 Draw *w* for the siege,
Hab 3: 10 Torrents of *w* swept by;
Zec 14: 8 On that day living *w* will flow out
Mt 3: 11 I baptize you with *w* for repentance
3: 16 baptized, he went up out of the *w.*
8: 32 into the lake and died in the *w.*
10: 42 of cold *w* to one of these little ones
14: 28 "tell me to come to you on the *w.*"
14: 29 and walked on the *w* to Jesus.
17: 15 falls into the fire or into the *w.*
27: 24 he took *w* and washed his hands
Mk 1: 8 you with *w,* but he will baptize you
1: 10 Jesus was coming up out of the *w,*
9: 22 him into fire or *w* to kill him.
9: 41 anyone who gives you a cup of *w*
14: 13 a jar of *w* will meet you.
Lk 3: 16 them all, "I baptize you with *w.*
5: 4 to Simon, "Put out into deep *w,*
7: 44 You did not give me any *w*
8: 25 even the winds and the *w,*
13: 15 and lead it out to give it *w?*
16: 24 to dip the tip of his finger in *w*
22: 10 a jar of *w* will meet you.
Jn 1: 26 "I baptize with *w,*" John replied,
1: 31 with *w* was that he might be
1: 33 me to baptize with *w* told me,
2: 6 Nearby stood six stone *w* jars,
2: 7 "Fill the jars with *w*";
2: 9 banquet tasted the *w* that had been
2: 9 who had drawn the *w* knew.
3: 5 a man is born of *w* and the Spirit,
3: 23 because there was plenty of *w,*
4: 7 Samaritan woman came to draw *w,*
4: 10 he would have given you living *w.*"
4: 11 Where can you get this living *w?*
4: 13 who drinks this *w* will be thirsty
4: 14 in him a spring of *w* welling up
4: 14 the *w* I give him will become
4: 14 whoever drinks the *w* I give him
4: 15 give me this *w* so that I won't get
4: 15 to keep coming here to draw *w.*"
Jn 4: 28 with her?" Then, leaving her *w* jar,
4: 46 where he had turned the *w*
5: 7 into the pool when the *w* is stirred.
6: 19 on the *w,* and they were terrified.
7: 38 streams of living *w* will flow
13: 5 he poured *w* into a basin
19: 34 a sudden flow of blood and *w.*
21: 7 it off) and jumped into the *w.*
Ac 1: 5 For John baptized with *w,*
8: 36 the eunuch said, "Look, here is *w.*
8: 36 to some *w* and the eunuch said,
8: 38 the eunuch went down into the *w*
8: 39 When they came up out of the *w,*
10: 47 from being baptized with *w?*
11: 16 'John baptized with *w,*
27: 28 found that the *w* was a hundred
Eph 5: 26 washing with *w* through the word,
1Ti 5: 23 Stop drinking only *w,* and use
Heb 9: 19 together with *w,* scarlet wool
10: 22 our bodies washed with pure *w.*
Jas 3: 11 Can both fresh *w* and salt *w* flow
3: 12 can a salt spring produce fresh *w.*
1Pe 3: 20 eight in all, were saved through *w,*
3: 21 this *w* symbolizes baptism that now
2Pe 2: 17 These men are springs without *w*
3: 5 was formed out of *w* and with *w.*
3: 6 By *w* also the world
1Jn 5: 6 This is the one who came by *w*
5: 6 come by *w* only, but by *w*
5: 8 the Spirit, the *w* and the blood;
Rev 7: 17 to springs of living *w.*
8: 10 of the rivers and on the springs of *w*
12: 15 the serpent spewed *w* like a river,
14: 7 the sea and the springs of *w.*"
16: 4 bowl on the rivers and springs of *w,*
16: 12 and its *w* was dried up to prepare
21: 6 cost from the spring of the *w* of life.
22: 1 angel showed me the river of the *w*
22: 17 let him take the free gift of the *w*

WATER'S (WATER)

Jos 3: 15 and their feet touched the *w* edge,
Mk 4: 1 were along the shore at the *w* edge.
Lk 5: 2 he saw at the *w* edge two boats,

WATERCOURSE (WATER)

Pr 21: 1 it like a *w* wherever he pleases.

WATERED (WATER)

Ge 2: 6 *w* the whole surface of the ground.
13: 10 plain of the Jordan was well *w,*
24: 46 and she *w* the camels also.
29: 2 the flocks were *w* from that well.
29: 10 of the well and *w* his uncle's sheep.
Ex 2: 17 to their rescue and *w* their flock.
2: 19 drew water for us and *w* the flock."
Dt 29: 19 will bring disaster on the *w* land
Ps 104: 16 The trees of the LORD are well *w,*
1Co 3: 6 I planted the seed, Apollos *w* it,

WATERFALLS (WATER)

Ps 42: 7 deep in the roar of your *w;*

WATERING (WATER)

Ge 2: 10 A river *w* the garden flowed
30: 38 branches in all the *w* troughs,
Jdg 5: 11 voice of the singers at the *w* places.
Ps 72: 6 like showers *w* the earth.
Isa 55: 10 it without *w* the earth

WATERLESS

Dt 8: 15 *w* land, with its venomous snakes
Zec 9: 11 free your prisoners from the *w* pit.

WATERS (WATER)

Ge 1: 2 of God was hovering over the *w.*
1: 6 between the *w* to separate water
1: 10 and the gathered *w* he called "seas
7: 7 the ark to escape the *w* of the flood.
7: 17 *w* increased they lifted the ark high
7: 18 The *w* rose and increased greatly
7: 20 *w* rose and covered the mountains
7: 24 The *w* flooded the earth
8: 1 over the earth and the *w* receded.
8: 5 The *w* continued to recede
9: 11 cut off by the *w* of a flood;
9: 15 again will the *w* become a flood
49: 4 as the *w,* you will no longer excel,

Ex 7: 19 hand over the *w* of Egypt—
8: 6 hand over the *w* of Egypt,
14: 21 *w* were divided, and the Israelites
14: 26 the sea so that the *w* may flow back
15: 5 The deep *w* have covered them;
15: 8 The surging *w* stood firm like a wall
15: 8 the deep *w* congealed in the heart
15: 8 the *w* piled up.
15: 10 lead in the mighty *w*.
15: 19 the LORD brought the *w*
20: 4 earth beneath or in the *w* below.
Nu 20: 13 These were the *w* of Meribah,
20: 24 command at the *w* of Meribah.
24: 6 like cedars beside the *w*.
27: 14 at the *w* in the Desert of Zin,
27: 14 (These were the *w* of Meribah
Dt 5: 8 earth beneath or in the *w* below.
11: 4 them with the *w* of the Red Sea
32: 51 at the *w* of Meribah Kadesh
33: 8 with him at the *w* of Meribah.
33: 13 and with the deep *w* that lie below;
Jos 3: 8 reach the edge of the Jordan's *w*,
4: 7 the *w* of the Jordan were cut off.
4: 18 than the *w* of the Jordan returned
11: 5 together at the *W* of Merom,
11: 7 suddenly at the *W* of Merom
15: 7 the *W* of En Shemesh
15: 9 the spring of the *W* of Nephtoah,
16: 1 of Jericho, east of the *w* of Jericho,
18: 15 at the spring of the *W* of Nephtoah.
Jdg 5: 19 at Taanach by the *w* of Megiddo,
7: 24 and seize the *w* of the Jordan ahead
7: 24 they took the *w* of the Jordan as far
2Sa 5: 20 "As *w* break out, the LORD has
22: 17 he drew me out of deep *w*.
2Ki 5: 12 better than any of the *w* of Israel?
1Ch 14: 11 "As *w* break out, God has broken
Ne 9: 11 like a stone into mighty *w*.
Job 11: 16 recalling it only as *w* gone by.
12: 15 holds back the *w*, there is drought;
20: 28 rushing *w* on the day
26: 5 beneath the *w* and all that live
26: 8 He wraps up the *w* in his clouds,
26: 10 on the face of the *w*
28: 25 and measured out the *w*,
37: 10 and the broad *w* become frozen.
38: 30 when the *w* become hard as stone,
Ps 18: 16 he drew me out of deep *w*.
23: 2 he leads me beside quiet *w*,
24: 2 and established it upon the *w*.
29: 3 thunders over the mighty *w*.
29: 3 voice of the LORD is over the *w*;
32: 6 surely when the mighty *w* rise,
33: 7 He gathers the *w* of the sea into jars
46: 3 though its *w* roar and foam
69: 1 for the *w* have come up to my neck.
69: 2 I have come into the deep *w*;
69: 14 from the deep *w*.
73: 10 and drink up *w* in abundance.
74: 13 of the monster in the *w*.
77: 16 The *w* saw you, O God,
77: 16 the *w* saw you and writhed;
77: 19 your way through the mighty *w*,
81: 7 I tested you at the *w* of Meribah.
93: 4 than the thunder of the great *w*,
104: 3 of his upper chambers on their *w*.
104: 6 the *w* stood above the mountains.
104: 7 But at your rebuke the *w* fled,
104: 12 The birds of the air nest by the *w*;
104: 13 He *w* the mountains
105: 29 He turned their *w* into blood,
106: 11 The *w* covered their adversaries;
106: 32 By the *w* of Meribah they angered
107: 23 were merchants on the mighty *w*.
124: 5 the raging *w* would have swept us
136: 6 spread out the earth upon the *w*,
144: 7 me from the mighty *w*,
147: 18 stirs up his breezes, and the *w* flow.
148: 4 and you *w* above the skies.
Pr 8: 29 so the *w* would not overstep his
18: 4 of a man's mouth are deep *w*,
20: 5 of a man's heart are deep *w*,
30: 4 Who has wrapped up the *w*
Ecc 11: 1 Cast your bread upon the *w*,
SS 8: 7 Many *w* cannot quench love;
Isa 8: 6 the gently flowing *w* of Shiloah
8: 7 the mighty flood *w* of the River—
10: 26 and he will raise his rod over the *w*,
Isa 11: 9 as the *w* cover the sea.
15: 6 The *w* of Nimrim are dried up
15: 9 Dimon's *w* are full of blood,
17: 12 they roar like the roaring of great *w*
17: 13 roar like the roar of surging *w*,
19: 5 The *w* of the river will dry up,
23: 3 On the great *w*
40: 12 Who has measured the *w*
43: 2 When you pass through the *w*,
43: 16 a path through the mighty *w*,
51: 10 the *w* of the great deep,
54: 9 when I swore that the *w*
55: 1 come to the *w*;
58: 11 like a spring whose *w* never fail.
63: 12 who divided the *w* before them,
Jer 10: 13 When he thunders, the *w*
18: 14 Do its cool *w* from distant sources
46: 7 like rivers of surging *w*?
46: 8 like rivers of surging *w*.
47: 2 "See how the *w* are rising
48: 34 even the *w* of Nimrim are dried up.
50: 38 A drought on her *w*!
51: 13 You who live by many *w*
51: 16 When he thunders, the *w*
51: 55 ⌊of enemies⌋ will rage like great *w*;
La 3: 54 the *w* closed over my head,
Eze 1: 24 the roar of rushing *w*, like the voice
26: 19 over you and its vast *w* cover you,
27: 34 the sea in the depths of the *w*;
31: 4 The *w* nourished it,
31: 5 spreading because of abundant *w*.
31: 7 down to abundant *w*.
31: 14 by the *w* are ever to tower proudly
31: 15 and its abundant *w* were restrained
32: 13 cattle from beside abundant *w*
32: 14 Then I will let her *w* settle
43: 2 was like the roar of rushing *w*,
47: 19 the *w* of Meribah Kadesh,
48: 28 to the *w* of Meribah Kadesh,
Da 12: 6 who was above the *w* of the river,
12: 7 who was above the *w* of the river,
Hos 10: 7 like a twig on the surface of the *w*.
Am 5: 8 who calls for the *w* of the sea
9: 6 who calls for the *w* of the sea
Jnh 2: 5 The engulfing *w* threatened me,
Na 3: 8 the *w* her wall.
Hab 2: 14 as the *w* cover the sea.
3: 15 churning the great *w*.
Lk 8: 24 rebuked the wind and the raging *w*;
Jn 6: 18 was blowing and the *w* grew rough.
1Co 3: 7 plants nor he who *w* is anything,
3: 8 the man who *w* have one purpose,
Rev 1: 15 was like the sound of rushing *w*.
8: 11 A third of the *w* turned bitter,
8: 11 from the *w* that had become bitter.
11: 6 power to turn the *w* into blood
14: 2 heaven like the roar of rushing *w*
16: 5 the angel in charge of the *w* say:
17: 1 prostitute, who sits on many *w*.
17: 15 *w* you saw, where the prostitute
19: 6 like the roar of rushing *w*

WATERY (WATER)

Isa 44: 27 who says to the *w* deep, 'Be dry,

WAVE (WAVED WAVES WAVING WAVY)

Ex 29: 24 and *w* them before the LORD
29: 24 before the LORD as a *w* offering.
29: 26 it before the LORD as a *w* offering,
29: 26 *w* it before the LORD
35: 22 as a *w* offering to the LORD.
38: 24 the gold from the *w* offering used
38: 29 from the *w* offering was 70 talents
Lev 7: 30 and *w* the breast before the LORD
7: 30 before the LORD as a *w* offering.
8: 27 before the LORD as a *w* offering
8: 29 it before the LORD as a *w* offering,
9: 21 before the LORD as a *w* offering,
10: 15 before the LORD as a *w* offering.
14: 12 before the LORD as a *w* offering.
14: 12 he shall *w* them before the LORD
14: 24 and *w* them before the LORD
14: 24 before the LORD as a *w* offering.
23: 11 He is to *w* the sheaf
23: 11 the priest is to *w* it on the day
23: 12 On the day you *w* the sheaf,
23: 15 brought the sheaf of the *w* offering,
Lev 23: 17 as a *w* offering of firstfruits
23: 20 The priest is to *w* the two lambs
23: 20 before the LORD as a *w* offering,
Nu 5: 25 *w* it before the LORD
6: 20 The priest shall then *w* them
6: 20 before the LORD as a *w* offering;
8: 11 as a *w* offering from the Israelites,
8: 13 as a *w* offering to the LORD.
8: 15 and presented them as a *w* offering,
8: 21 as a *w* offering before the LORD
18: 11 the gifts of all the *w* offerings
18: 18 just as the breast of the *w* offering
2Ki 5: 11 *w* his hand over the spot
Job 10: 17 come against me *w* upon *w*.
Jas 1: 6 he who doubts is like a *w* of the sea,

WAVED (WAVE)

Ex 29: 27 breast that was *w* and the thigh that
Lev 7: 34 I have taken the breast that is *w*
8: 27 and *w* them before the LORD
8: 29 and *w* it before the LORD
9: 21 Aaron *w* the breasts and the right
10: 14 may eat the breast that was *w*
10: 15 breast that was *w* must be brought
10: 15 to be *w* before the LORD
14: 21 offering to be *w* to make atonement
Nu 6: 20 together with the breast that was *w*

WAVER (WAVERING)

1Ki 18: 21 "How long will you *w*
Ro 4: 20 Yet he did not *w* through unbelief

WAVERING (WAVER)

Ps 26: 1 the LORD without *w*.

WAVES (WAVE)

2Sa 22: 5 "The *w* of death swirled about me;
Job 9: 8 and treads on the *w* of the sea.
38: 11 here is where your proud *w* halt'?
Ps 42: 7 all your *w* and breakers
65: 7 the roaring of their *w*,
88: 7 overwhelmed me with all your *w*.
89: 9 when its *w* mount up, you still
93: 3 have lifted up their pounding *w*.
107: 25 that lifted high the *w*.
107: 29 the *w* of the sea were hushed.
Isa 48: 18 your righteousness like the *w*
51: 15 the sea so that its *w* roar—
57: 20 whose *w* cast up mire and mud.
Jer 5: 22 *w* may roll, but they cannot prevail;
31: 35 the sea so that its *w* roar—
51: 42 its roaring *w* will cover her.
51: 55 *W* ⌊of enemies⌋ will rage like great
Eze 26: 3 like the sea casting up its *w*.
Jnh 2: 3 all your *w* and breakers
Hab 3: 10 and lifted its *w* on high.
Mt 8: 24 so that the *w* swept over the boat.
8: 26 and rebuked the winds and the *w*,
8: 27 Even the winds and the *w* obey him
14: 24 by the *w* because the wind was
Mk 4: 37 and the *w* broke over the boat,
4: 39 rebuked the wind and said to the *w*,
4: 41 Even the wind and the *w* obey him
Eph 4: 14 tossed back and forth by the *w*,
Jude : 13 They are wild *w* of the sea,

WAVING (WAVE)

Jdg 9: 9 to go *w* over the trees?' "Next,
9: 11 and sweet, to go *w* over the trees?'
9: 13 and men, to go *w* over the trees?'

WAVY (WAVE)

SS 5: 11 his hair is *w*

WAX

Ps 22: 14 My heart has turned to *w*;
68: 2 as *w* melts before the fire,
97: 5 The mountains melt like *w*
Mic 1: 4 like *w* before the fire,

WAY (WAYS)

Ge 3: 24 and forth to guard the *w* to the tree
9: 23 faces were turned the other *w*
12: 20 and they sent him on his *w*,
18: 5 refreshed and then go on your *w*—
18: 16 with them to see them on their *w*.
18: 19 him to keep the *w* of the LORD
19: 2 and then go on your *w*

Ge 19: 9 "Get out of our *w*," they replied.
21: 14 She went on her *w* and wandered
24: 1 LORD had blessed him in every *w*.
24: 10 made his *w* to the town of Nahor.
24: 49 so I may know which *w* to turn."
24: 50 we can say nothing to you one *w*
24: 54 "Send me on my *w* to my master."
24: 56 Send me on my *w* so I may go
24: 59 sent their sister Rebekah on her *w*,
26: 31 Then Isaac sent them on their *w*,
27: 9 for your father, just the *w* he likes it
27: 14 just the *w* his father liked it.
28: 5 Then Isaac sent Jacob on his *w*,
30: 25 "Send me on my *w* so I can go back
30: 26 served you, and I will be on my *w*.
30: 43 In this *w* the man grew exceedingly
32: 1 Jacob also went on his *w*,
33: 12 be on our *w*; I'll accompany you."
33: 16 started on his *w* back to Seir.
35: 19 and was buried on the *w*
37: 25 they were on their *w* to take them
38: 13 is on his *w* to Timnah
41: 43 men shouted before him, "Make *w*
44: 3 sent on their *w* with their donkeys.
45: 24 "Don't quarrel on the *w*!"
48: 7 while we were still on the *w*,
Ex 2: 12 Glancing this *w* and that
3: 9 I have seen the *w* the Egyptians are
4: 14 He is already on his *w* to meet you,
4: 24 At a lodging place on the *w*,
5: 15 you treated your servants this *w*?
13: 21 of cloud to guide them on their *w*
16: 4 In this *w* I will test them and see
18: 8 hardships they had met along the *w*
18: 20 and show them the *w* to live
18: 27 sent his father-in-law on his *w*,
19: 21 people so they do not force their *w*
19: 24 the people must not force their *w*
23: 20 of you to guard you along the *w*
23: 28 and Hittites out of your *w*.
26: 17 frames of the tabernacle in this *w*.
26: 24 from the bottom all the *w* to the top
28: 11 the two stones the *w* a gem cutter
29: 9 In this *w* you shall ordain Aaron
33: 3 and I might destroy you on the *w*."
36: 22 frames of the tabernacle in this *w*.
36: 29 from the bottom all the *w* to the top
Lev 4: 20 In this *w* the priest will make
4: 26 In this *w* the priest will make
4: 31 In this *w* the priest will make
4: 35 In this *w* the priest will make
5: 5 confess in what *w* he has sinned
5: 10 a burnt offering in the prescribed *w*
5: 13 In this *w* the priest will make
5: 18 In this *w* the priest will make
6: 7 In this *w* the priest will make
9: 16 and offered it in the prescribed *w*.
12: 8 In this *w* the priest will make
14: 31 In this *w* the priest will make
14: 53 In this *w* he will make atonement
15: 15 In this *w* he will make atonement
15: 30 In this *w* he will make atonement
16: 16 In this *w* he will make atonement
19: 5 in such a *w* that it will be accepted
19: 25 In this *w* your harvest will be
22: 29 in such a *w* that it will be accepted
Nu 2: 34 and that is the *w* they set out,
2: 34 that is the *w* they encamped
5: 6 or woman wrongs another in any *w*
8: 14 In this *w* you are to set the Levites
14: 45 them down all the *w* to Hormah.
15: 13 in this *w* when he brings an offering
18: 28 In this *w* you also will present
21: 4 the people grew impatient on the *w*
21: 30 Heshbon is destroyed all the *w*
24: 25 and Balak went his own *w*.
28: 24 In this *w* prepare the food
Dt 1: 31 all the *w* you went
1: 33 to show you the *w* you should go.
1: 44 from Seir all the *w* to Hormah.
2: 1 For a long time we made our *w*
2: 3 "You have made your *w*
4: 7 near them the *w* the LORD our
5: 33 in all the *w* that the LORD your
8: 2 LORD your God led you all the *w*
9: 16 from the *w* that the LORD had
10: 11 "and lead the people on their *w*,
11: 28 from the *w* that I command you

Dt 12: 4 the LORD your God in their *w*.
12: 31 the LORD your God in their *w*,
13: 5 from the *w* the LORD your God
16: 17 to the *w* the LORD your God has
17: 16 You are not to go back that *w* again
20: 3 or give *w* to panic before them.
23: 4 on your *w* when you came out
24: 9 did to Miriam along the *w*
25: 17 did to you along the *w*
29: 16 the countries on the *w* here.
29: 19 though I persist in going my own *w*
31: 29 from the *w* I have commanded you.
32: 6 Is this the *w* you repay the LORD,
Jos 2: 5 I don't know which *w* they went.
2: 16 return, and then go on your *w*."
3: 4 Then you will know which *w* to go,
3: 4 since you have never been this *w*
5: 4 desert on the *w* after leaving Egypt.
5: 7 had not been circumcised on the *w*.
9: 22 'We live a long *w* from you,'
10: 10 cut them down all the *w* to Azekah
11: 8 and pursued them all the *w*
18: 8 on their *w* to map out the land,
23: 5 will drive them out of your *w*.
23: 14 about to go the *w* of all the earth.
Jdg 2: 17 the *w* of obedience
2: 17 they quickly turned from the *w*
2: 22 they will keep the *w* of the LORD
3: 18 on their *w* the men who had carried
4: 6 and lead the *w* to Mount Tabor.
4: 9 of the *w* you are going about this,
6: 4 ruined the crops all the *w* to Gaza
9: 40 all the *w* to the entrance to the gate
11: 13 the Arnon to the Jabbok, all the *w*
17: 8 On his *w* he came to Micah's house
18: 7 Also, they lived a long *w*
18: 12 On their *w* they set up camp
18: 26 So the Danites went their *w*,
18: 28 they lived a long *w* from Sidon
19: 9 and be on your *w* home."
19: 18 "We are on our *w* from Bethlehem
19: 27 stepped out to continue on his *w*,
20: 36 Now the men of Israel had given *w*
1Sa 1: 18 she went her *w* and ate something,
6: 6 out so they could go on their *w*?
6: 8 it on its *w*, but keep watching it
6: 12 on the road and lowing all the *w*;
7: 11 them along the *w* to a point
9: 6 Perhaps he will tell us what *w*
9: 8 so that he will tell us what *w* to take
9: 14 coming toward them on his *w* up
9: 26 and I will send you on your *w*."
12: 23 I will teach you the *w* that is good
15: 7 attacked the Amalekites all the *w*
16: 1 horn with oil and be on your *w*;
19: 24 He lay that *w* all that day and night
24: 3 to the sheep pens along the *w*;
24: 7 Saul left the cave and went his *w*.
24: 19 for the *w* you treated me today.
26: 25 on his *w*, and Saul returned home.
28: 22 have the strength to go on your *w*."
30: 2 them off as they went on their *w*.
2Sa 2: 24 Giah on the *w* to the wasteland
3: 16 behind her all the *w* to Bahurim.
4: 7 night by *w* of the Arabah.
5: 25 down the Philistines all the *w*
7: 19 Is this your usual *w* of dealing
12: 21 "Why are you acting this *w*?
13: 30 While they were on their *w*,
15: 6 Absalom behaved in this *w*
18: 23 Ahimaaz ran by *w* of the plain
19: 31 to send him on his *w* from there.
19: 36 the king reward me in this *w*?
20: 2 stayed by their king all the *w*
22: 31 "As for God, his *w* is perfect;
22: 33 and makes my *w* perfect.
1Ki 2: 2 about to go the *w* of all the earth,"
5: 10 In this *w* Hiram kept Solomon
6: 33 In the same *w* he made four-sided
7: 37 This is the *w* he made the ten
8: 23 wholeheartedly in your *w*.
8: 36 Teach them the right *w* to live,
11: 29 of Shiloh met him on the *w*,
13: 9 or return by the *w* you came.'"
13: 10 return by the *w* he had come
13: 12 asked them, "Which *w* did he go?"
13: 17 or return by the *w* you came.'"
13: 24 As he went on his *w*, a lion met him

1Ki 18: 46 ahead of Ahab all the *w* to Jezreel.
19: 15 "Go back the *w* you came,
22: 24 "Which *w* did the spirit
2Ki 2: 1 Elisha were on their *w* from Gilgal.
3: 22 To the Moabites across the *w*,
4: 9 who often comes our *w* is a holy
8: 7 of God has come all the *w* up here
9: 15 Jehu said, "If this is the *w* you feel,
9: 27 in his chariot on the *w* up to Gur
10: 15 who was on his *w* to meet him.
11: 19 entering by *w* of the gate
19: 28 return by the *w* you came.'
19: 33 By the *w* that he came he will
21: 22 did not walk in the *w* of the LORD.
1Ch 7: 28 and its villages all the *w* to Ayyah
14: 16 all the *w* from Gibeon to Gezer.
15: 13 how to do it in the prescribed *w*."
23: 31 and in the *w* prescribed for them.
2Ch 6: 14 wholeheartedly in your *w*.
6: 27 Teach them the right *w* to live,
18: 23 "Which *w* did the spirit
23: 19 was in any *w* unclean might enter.
29: 25 lyres in the *w* prescribed by David
Ezr 7: 27 of the LORD in Jerusalem in this *w*
8: 31 enemies and bandits along the *w*.
9: 2 and officials have led the *w*
Ne 5: 13 "In this *w* may God shake out
9: 12 light on the *w* they were to take.
9: 19 to shine on the *w* they were to take.
11: 30 So they were living all the *w*
Est 1: 8 allowed to drink in his own *w*,
1: 18 all the king's nobles in the same *w*.
3: 6 Instead Haman looked for a *w*
9: 27 in the *w* prescribed
Job 3: 23 whose *w* is hidden,
8: 15 He leans on his web, but it gives *w*;
19: 8 He has blocked my *w*
22: 21 in this *w* prosperity will come
23: 10 But he knows the *w* that I take;
23: 11 to his *w* without turning aside.
28: 23 God understands the *w* to it
29: 25 I chose the *w* for them and sat
32: 3 they had found no *w* to refute Job,
33: 14 now one *w*, now another—
36: 31 This is the *w* he governs the nations
38: 19 What is the *w* to the abode of light?
38: 24 What is the *w* to the place where
38: 35 send the lightning bolts on their *w*?
Ps 1: 1 or stand in the *w* of sinners
1: 6 but the *w* of the wicked will perish.
1: 6 over the *w* of the righteous,
2: 12 and you be destroyed in your *w*,
5: 8 make straight your *w* before me.
18: 30 As for God, his *w* is perfect;
18: 32 and makes my *w* perfect.
25: 9 and teaches them his *w*.
25: 12 in the *w* chosen for him.
27: 11 Teach me your *w*, O LORD;
32: 8 teach you in the *w* you should go;
37: 5 Commit your *w* to the LORD;
37: 23 delights in the *w* of the man
37: 34 and keep his *w*.
46: 2 not fear, though the earth give *w*
50: 23 and he prepares the *w*
74: 3 your *w* through these everlasting
77: 19 your *w* through the mighty waters,
85: 13 and prepares the *w* for his steps.
86: 11 Teach me your *w*, O LORD,
107: 4 finding no *w* to a city where they
107: 7 He led them by a straight *w*
109: 24 My knees give *w* from fasting;
110: 7 from a brook beside the *w*;
119: 9 can a young man keep his *w* pure?
119: 30 I have chosen the *w* of truth;
139: 24 See if there is any offensive *w* in me
139: 24 and lead me in the *w* everlasting.
142: 3 it is you who know my *w*.
143: 8 Show me the *w* I should go,
Pr 2: 8 protects the *w* of his faithful ones.
3: 23 you will go on your *w* in safety,
4: 11 I guide you in the *w* of wisdom
4: 14 or walk in the *w* of evil men.
4: 15 turn from it and go on your *w*.
4: 19 *w* of the wicked is like deep
5: 6 She gives no thought to the *w*
6: 23 are the *w* to life,
8: 2 On the heights along the *w*,
8: 20 I walk in the *w* of righteousness,

Pr 9: 6 walk in the *w* of understanding.
9: 15 who go straight on their *w*.
10: 17 who heeds discipline shows the *w*
10: 29 The *w* of the LORD is a refuge
11: 5 of the blameless makes a straight *w*
12: 15 The *w* of a fool seems right to him,
12: 26 *w* of the wicked leads them astray.
12: 28 In the *w* of righteousness there is
13: 15 but the *w* of the unfaithful is hard.
14: 12 There is a *w* that seems right
15: 9 The LORD detests the *w*
15: 19 The *w* of the sluggard is blocked
16: 17 he who guards his *w* guards his soul
16: 25 There is a *w* that seems right
18: 16 A gift opens the *w* for the giver
19: 2 nor to be hasty and miss the *w*.
20: 24 can anyone understand his own *w?*
21: 8 The *w* of the guilty is devious,
22: 6 Train a child in the *w* he should go,
25: 26 is a righteous man who gives *w*
30: 19 and the *w* of a man with a maiden.
30: 19 the *w* of a ship on the high seas,
30: 19 the *w* of a snake on a rock,
30: 19 the *w* of an eagle in the sky,
30: 20 "This is the *w* of an adulteress:
Ecc 10: 15 he does not know the *w* to town.
SS 6: 1 Which *w* did your lover turn,
Isa 8: 11 not to follow the *w* of this people.
9: 1 by the *w* of the sea,
15: 4 their voices are heard all the *w*
15: 5 They go up the *w* to Luhith,
22: 25 into the firm place will give *w;*
26: 7 you make the *w* of the righteous
26: 8 walking in the *w* of your laws,
28: 26 and teaches him the right *w*.
30: 11 Leave this *w*,
30: 21 saying, "This is the *w;* walk in it."
35: 3 steady the knees that give *w;*
35: 8 be for those who walk in that *W;*
35: 8 it will be called the *W* of Holiness.
37: 29 return by the *w* you came.
37: 34 By the *w* that he came he will
40: 3 the *w* for the LORD;
40: 14 and who taught him the right *w?*
40: 27 "My *w* is hidden from the LORD;
43: 16 he who made a *w* through the sea,
43: 19 I am making a *w* in the desert
48: 17 you in the *w* you should go.
51: 5 my salvation is on the *w*,
53: 6 each of us has turned to his own *w;*
55: 7 Let the wicked forsake his *w*
56: 11 they all turn to their own *w*,
57: 14 out of the *w* of my people."
58: 13 it by not going your own *w*
59: 8 The *w* of peace they do not know;
59: 10 feeling our *w* like men without eyes
62: 10 Prepare the *w* for the people.
Jer 2: 17 God when he led you in the *w?*
4: 2 if in a truthful, just and righteous *w*
5: 4 for they do not know the *w*
5: 5 surely they know the *w*
5: 31 and my people love it this *w*.
6: 16 ask where the good *w* is,
12: 1 Why does the *w* of the wicked
13: 9 'In the same *w* I will ruin the pride
21: 8 the *w* of life and the *w* of death.
22: 21 This has been your *w*
26: 3 and each will turn from his evil *w*.
28: 11 'In the same *w* will I break the yoke
28: 11 prophet Jeremiah went on his *w*.
36: 3 of them will turn from his wicked *w*
39: 4 at night by *w* of the king's garden,
41: 17 Bethlehem on their *w* to Egypt
48: 5 They go up the *w* to Luhith,
50: 5 They will ask the *w* to Zion
La 2: 15 All who pass your *w*
3: 9 He has barred my *w* with blocks
Eze 4: 13 "In this *w* the people
18: 25 O house of Israel: Is my *w* unjust?
18: 25 'The *w* of the Lord is not just.'
18: 29 'The *w* of the Lord is not just.'
20: 30 defile yourselves the *w* your fathers
23: 13 both of them went the same *w*.
23: 31 You have gone the *w* of your sister;
32: 6 all the *w* to the mountains,
33: 17 But it is their *w* that is not just.
33: 17 'The *w* of the Lord is not just.'
33: 20 'The *w* of the Lord is not just.'
Eze 39: 11 It will block the *w* of travelers,
44: 3 He is to enter by *w* of the portico
44: 3 gateway and go out the same *w*."
44: 4 me by *w* of the north gate
46: 8 and he is to come out the same *w*.
Da 1: 8 not to defile himself this *w*.
3: 29 for no other god can save in this *w*
5: 6 together and his legs gave *w*.
12: 9 He replied, "Go your *w*, Daniel,
12: 13 "As for you, go your *w* till the end.
Hos 2: 6 in so that she cannot find her *w*.
Am 6: 14 that will oppress you all the *w*
Mic 2: 13 who breaks open the *w* will go up
Na 1: 3 His *w* is in the whirlwind
2: 5 yet they stumble on their *w*.
2: 10 Hearts melt, knees give *w*,
Mal 2: 8 But you have turned from the *w*
3: 1 who will prepare the *w* before me.
Mt 2: 9 the king, they went on their *w*,
3: 3 'Prepare the *w* for the Lord,
4: 15 the *w* to the sea, along the Jordan,
5: 12 for in the same *w* they persecuted
5: 16 In the same *w*, let your light shine
5: 25 still with him on the *w*,
7: 2 For in the same *w* you judge others,
8: 28 that no one could pass that *w*.
11: 10 who will prepare your *w* before you
15: 32 or they may collapse on the *w*."
17: 12 In the same *w* the Son
18: 14 In the same *w* your Father
19: 8 was not this *w* from the beginning.
19: 12 because they were born that *w;*
19: 12 others were made that *w* by men;
21: 18 as he was on his *w* back to the city,
21: 32 to show you the *w* of righteousness,
21: 36 tenants treated them the same *w*.
21: 46 They looked for a *w* to arrest him,
22: 16 and that you teach the *w* of God
23: 28 same *w*, on the outside you appear
25: 10 were on their *w* to buy the oil,
26: 4 to arrest Jesus in some sly *w*
26: 54 that say it must happen in this *w?*"
27: 41 In the same *w* the chief priests,
27: 44 In the same *w* the robbers who
28: 11 While the women were on their *w*,
Mk 1: 2 who will prepare your *w*"—
1: 3 'Prepare the *w* for the Lord,
7: 9 "You have a fine *w* of setting
8: 3 they will collapse on the *w*,
8: 27 On the *w* he asked them, "Who do
9: 34 on the *w* they had argued about
10: 17 started on his *w*, a man ran up
10: 32 were on their *w* up to Jerusalem,
10: 32 with Jesus leading the *w*,
11: 18 began looking for a *w* to kill him,
12: 12 they looked for a *w* to arrest him
12: 14 but you teach the *w* of God
14: 1 for some sly *w* to arrest Jesus
15: 21 by on his *w* in from the country,
15: 31 In the same *w* the chief priests
16: 2 they were on their *w* to the tomb
Lk 1: 76 the Lord to prepare the *w* for him,
3: 4 'Prepare the *w* for the Lord,
4: 30 the crowd and went on his *w*.
5: 19 When they could not find a *w*
7: 27 who will prepare your *w* before you
7: 29 that God's *w* was right,
8: 14 they go on their *w* they are choked
8: 42 was on his *w*, the crowds almost
10: 38 and his disciples were on their *w*,
12: 58 to be reconciled to him on the *w*,
13: 2 because they suffered this *w?*
13: 22 as he made his *w* to Jerusalem.
14: 19 and I'm on my *w* to try them out.
14: 32 while the other is still a long *w* off
14: 33 In the same *w*, any
15: 7 that in the same *w* there is more
15: 10 In the same *w*, I tell you, there is
15: 20 "But while he was still a long *w* off,
16: 16 and everyone is forcing his *w* into it
17: 11 Now on his *w* to Jerusalem,
18: 39 Those who led the *w* rebuked him
19: 4 since Jesus was coming that *w*.
19: 48 Yet they could not find any *w*
20: 19 for a *w* to arrest him immediately,
20: 21 teach the *w* of God in accordance
20: 31 and in the same *w* the seven died,
22: 2 for some *w* to get rid of Jesus,
Lk 22: 20 In the same *w*, after the supper he
23: 5 and has come all the *w* here."
23: 26 was on his *w* in from the country,
24: 35 told what had happened on the *w*,
Jn 1: 23 'Make straight the *w* for the Lord
4: 30 and made their *w* toward him.
4: 51 While he was still on the *w*,
7: 46 ever spoke the *w* this man does,"
10: 1 but climbs in by some other *w*,
12: 12 was on his *w* to Jerusalem.
14: 4 You know the *w* to the place where
14: 5 so how can we know the *w?*"
14: 6 "I am the *w* and the truth
15: 21 They will treat you this *w*
18: 22 "Is that any *w* to answer the high
21: 1 It happened this *w:* Simon
Ac 1: 11 in the same *w* you have seen him go
7: 6 God spoke to him in this *w:*
8: 27 and on his *w* he met an Ethiopian
8: 28 and on his *w* home was sitting
8: 39 but went on his *w* rejoicing.
9: 2 any there who belonged to the *W*,
13: 4 sent on their *w* by the Holy Spirit,
14: 16 he let all nations go their own *w*.
15: 3 The church sent them on their *w*,
16: 17 who are telling you the *w*
17: 22 in every *w* you are very religious.
18: 25 instructed in the *w* of the Lord,
18: 26 and explained to him the *w*
19: 9 and publicly maligned the *W*.
19: 20 In this *w* the word
19: 23 a great disturbance about the *W*.
21: 5 we left and continued on our *w*.
21: 11 'In this *w* the Jews
22: 4 followers of this *W* to their death,
24: 3 Everywhere and in every *w*,
24: 14 of the *W*, which they call a sect.
24: 22 was well acquainted with the *W*,
25: 3 an ambush to kill him along the *w*.
26: 4 Jews all know the *w* I have lived
27: 15 so we gave *w* to it and were driven
27: 44 In this *w* everyone reached land
Ro 1: 10 by God's will the *w* may be opened
1: 27 In the same *w* the men
3: 2 Much in every *w!* First of all,
3: 17 the *w* of peace they do not know."
5: 12 and in this *w* death came to all men
6: 11 In the same *w*, count yourselves
7: 6 not in the old *w* of the written code.
7: 6 serve in the new *w* of the Spirit,
8: 26 In the same *w*, the Spirit helps us
10: 5 in this *w* the righteousness that is
14: 13 or obstacle in your brother's *w*.
14: 18 Christ in this *w* is pleasing to God
15: 19 So from Jerusalem all the *w*
15: 25 I am on my *w* to Jerusalem
15: 28 go to Spain and visit you on the *w*.
16: 2 the Lord in a *w* worthy of the saints
16: 17 in your *w* that are contrary
1Co 1: 5 have been enriched in every *w*—
2: 11 In the same *w* no one knows
4: 17 you of my *w* of life in Christ Jesus,
7: 4 In the same *w*, the husband's body
7: 35 in a right *w* in undivided devotion
8: 12 sin against your brothers in this *w*
9: 14 In the same *w*, the Lord has
9: 24 Run in such a *w* as to get the prize.
10: 13 also provide a *w* out so that you can
10: 33 try to please everybody in every *w*.
11: 25 In the same *w*, after supper he took
12: 31 will show you the most excellent *w*.
14: 1 Follow the *w* of love and eagerly
14: 40 done in a fitting and orderly *w*.
16: 11 Send him on his *w* in peace
2Co 1: 16 me on my *w* to Judea.
1: 16 to visit you on my *w* to Macedonia
5: 16 we once regarded Christ in this *w*,
6: 4 we commend ourselves in every *w:*
7: 9 so were not harmed in any *w* by us.
8: 20 of the *w* we administer this liberal
9: 11 rich in every *w* so that you can be
11: 6 perfectly clear to you in every *w*.
11: 9 being a burden to you in any *w*,
11: 18 boasting in the *w* the world does,
Gal 1: 13 of my previous *w* of life in Judaism,
4: 23 woman was born in the ordinary *w;*
4: 29 born in the ordinary *w* persecuted
5: 12 I wish they would go the whole *w*

Gal 6: 2 and in this *w* you will fulfill the law
Eph 1: 23 who fills everything in every *w*.
4: 20 did not come to know Christ that *w*
4: 22 with regard to your former *w* of life
5: 28 In this same *w*, husbands ought
6: 9 treat your slaves in the same *w*.
Php 1: 7 for me to feel this *w* about all of you
1: 18 important thing is that in every *w*,
1: 20 hope that I will in no *w* be ashamed
1: 28 without being frightened in any *w*
Col 1: 10 and may please him in every *w*:
4: 5 Be wise in the *w* you act
1Th 2: 16 In this *w* they always heap up their
3: 4 it turned out that *w*, as you well
3: 5 in some *w* the tempter might have
3: 11 our Lord Jesus clear the *w* for us
4: 4 his own body in a *w* that is holy
2Th 2: 3 let anyone deceive you in any *w*,
2: 7 to do so till he is taken out of the *w*.
3: 16 peace at all times and in every *w*.
1Ti 3: 11 In the same *w*, their wives are
5: 25 In the same *w*, good deeds are
6: 19 In this *w* they will lay up treasure
2Ti 3: 6 are the kind who worm their *w*
3: 10 my *w* of life, my purpose, faith,
Tit 2: 3 to be reverent in the *w* they live,
2: 10 that in every *w* they will make
3: 13 on their *w* and see that they have
Heb 2: 17 made like his brothers in every *w*,
4: 15 who has been tempted in every *w*,
9: 8 was showing by this that the *w*
9: 21 In the same *w*, he sprinkled
9: 25 *w* the high priest enters the Most
10: 20 and living *w* opened for us
13: 7 Consider the outcome of their *w*
13: 18 desire to live honorably in every *w*.
Jas 1: 11 In the same *w*, the rich man will
2: 17 In the same *w*, faith by itself,
2: 25 In the same *w*, was not
5: 20 the error of his *w* will save him
1Pe 1: 18 from the empty *w* of life handed
3: 1 in the same *w* be submissive
3: 5 For this is the *w* the holy women
3: 6 do what is right and do not give *w*
3: 7 in the same *w* be considerate
5: 5 in the same *w* be submissive
2Pe 2: 2 and will bring the *w* of truth
2: 15 They have left the straight *w*
2: 15 off to follow the *w* of Balaam son
2: 21 not to have known the *w*
3: 11 will be destroyed in this *w*,
3: 16 He writes the same *w*
3Jn : 6 on their *w* in a manner worthy
Jude : 7 In a similar *w*, Sodom
: 8 the very same *w*, these dreamers
: 11 They have taken the *w* of Cain;
: 15 they have done in the ungodly *w*,
Rev 16: 12 up to prepare the *w* for the kings
18: 20 her for the *w* she treated you.' "

WAYLAID (WAYLAY)

1Sa 15: 2 did to Israel when they *w* them

WAYLAY (WAYLAID)

Pr 1: 11 let's *w* some harmless soul;
1: 18 they *w* only themselves!

WAYS (WAY)

Ge 6: 12 on earth had corrupted their *w*.
Ex 33: 13 teach me your *w* so I may know
Lev 5: 5 anyone is guilty in any of these *w*,
18: 24 defile yourselves in any of these *w*,
25: 54 is not redeemed in any of these *w*,
Dt 8: 6 walking in his *w* and revering him.
10: 12 to walk in all his *w*, to love him,
11: 22 to walk in all his *w* and to hold fast
18: 9 learn to imitate the detestable *w*
19: 9 and to walk always in his *w*—
26: 17 and that you will walk in his *w*,
28: 9 your God and walk in his *w*.
30: 16 in his *w*, and to keep his commands
32: 4 and all his *w* are just.
Jos 22: 5 in all his *w*, to obey his commands,
Jdg 2: 19 the people returned to *w*
2: 19 their evil practices and stubborn *w*.
1Sa 8: 3 But his sons did not walk in his *w*.
8: 5 your sons do not walk in your *w*;
2Sa 14: 14 he devises *w* so that a banished
2Sa 22: 22 For I have kept the *w* of the LORD
1Ki 2: 3 Walk in his *w*, and keep his decrees
3: 14 walk in my *w* and obey my statutes
8: 58 to walk in all his *w*
11: 33 and have not walked in my *w*,
11: 38 I command you and walk in my *w*
13: 33 Jeroboam did not change his evil *w*
15: 26 walking in the *w* of his father
15: 34 walking in the *w* of Jeroboam
16: 2 you walked in the *w* of Jeroboam
16: 19 and walking in the *w* of Jeroboam
16: 26 walked in all the *w* of Jeroboam son
22: 43 walked in the *w* of his father Asa
22: 52 he walked in the *w* of his father
22: 52 in the *w* of Jeroboam son of Nebat,
2Ki 8: 18 He walked in the *w* of the kings
8: 27 He walked in the *w* of the house
16: 3 He walked in the *w* of the kings
16: 3 following the detestable *w*
17: 13 and seers: "Turn from your evil *w*.
21: 21 He walked in all the *w* of his father;
22: 2 and walked in all the *w*
2Ch 6: 31 walk in your *w* all the time they live
7: 14 and turn from their wicked *w*,
11: 17 walking in the *w* of David
17: 3 in the *w* his father David had
17: 6 devoted to the *w* of the LORD;
20: 32 He walked in the *w*
21: 6 He walked in the *w* of the kings
21: 12 in the *w* of your father Jehoshaphat
21: 13 walked in the *w* of the kings
22: 3 walked in the *w* of the house
28: 2 He walked in the *w* of the kings
28: 3 following the detestable *w*
28: 26 events of his reign and all his *w*,
34: 2 walked in the *w* of his father David,
Ne 9: 35 or turn from their evil *w*.
Est 5: 11 all the *w* the king had honored him
Job 4: 6 and your blameless *w* your hope?
13: 15 I will surely defend my *w*
17: 9 the righteous will hold to their *w*,
21: 14 We have no desire to know your *w*.
22: 3 gain if your *w* were blameless?
22: 28 and light will shine on your *w*.
24: 13 who do not know its *w*
24: 23 but his eyes are on their *w*.
27: 11 the *w* of the Almighty I will not
31: 4 Does he not see my *w*
34: 21 "His eyes are on the *w* of men;
34: 27 and had no regard for any of his *w*.
36: 23 Who has prescribed his *w* for him,
37: 5 voice thunders in marvelous *w*;
Ps 10: 5 His *w* are always prosperous;
17: 4 myself from the *w* of the violent.
18: 21 For I have kept the *w* of the LORD
25: 4 Show me your *w*, O LORD,
25: 7 and my rebellious *w*;
25: 8 he instructs sinners in his *w*.
25: 10 All the *w* of the LORD are loving
37: 7 fret when men succeed in their *w*,
37: 14 to slay those whose *w* are upright.
39: 1 I said, "I will watch my *w*
51: 13 I will teach transgressors your *w*,
53: 1 are corrupt, and their *w* are vile;
55: 19 men who never change their *w*
67: 2 may your *w* be known on earth,
77: 13 Your *w*, O God, are holy.
81: 13 if Israel would follow my *w*,
91: 11 you to guard you in all your *w*,
95: 10 and they have not known my *w*."
103: 7 He made known his *w* to Moses,
107: 17 through their rebellious *w*
119: 1 are they whose *w* are blameless,
119: 3 they walk in his *w*.
119: 5 Oh, that my *w* were steadfast
119: 15 and consider your *w*.
119: 26 I recounted my *w* and you
119: 29 Keep me from deceitful *w*;
119: 59 I have considered my *w*
119:168 for all my *w* are known to you.
125: 5 But those who turn to crooked *w*
128: 1 who walk in his *w*.
138: 5 of the *w* of the LORD,
139: 3 you are familiar with all my *w*.
145: 17 The LORD is righteous in all his *w*
146: 9 he frustrates the *w* of the wicked.
Pr 1: 22 simple ones love your simple *w*?
1: 31 they will eat the fruit of their *w*
Pr 2: 12 you from the *w* of wicked men,
2: 13 paths to walk in dark *w*,
2: 15 and who are devious in their *w*.
2: 20 in the *w* of good men
3: 6 in all your *w* acknowledge him,
3: 17 Her *w* are pleasant *w*,
3: 31 or choose any of his *w*,
4: 26 and take only *w* that are firm.
5: 21 For a man's *w* are in full view
6: 6 consider its *w* and be wise!
7: 25 Do not let your heart turn to her *w*
8: 32 blessed are those who keep my *w*.
9: 6 Leave your simple *w* and you will
11: 20 in those whose *w* are blameless.
14: 2 he whose *w* are devious despises
14: 8 to give thought to their *w*,
14: 14 will be fully repaid for their *w*,
16: 2 All a man's *w* seem innocent
16: 7 When a man's *w* are pleasing
19: 16 is contemptuous of his *w* will die.
21: 2 All a man's *w* seem right to him,
21: 29 upright man gives thought to his *w*.
22: 25 or you may learn his *w*
23: 26 and let your eyes keep to my *w*,
28: 6 a rich man whose *w* are perverse.
28: 18 he whose *w* are perverse will
Ecc 11: 9 Follow the *w* of your heart
Isa 2: 3 He will teach us his *w*,
42: 16 blind by *w* they have not known,
42: 24 For they would not follow his *w*;
45: 13 I will make all his *w* straight.
55: 8 neither are your *w* my *w*,"
55: 9 so are my *w* higher than your *w*
57: 10 You were wearied by all your *w*,
57: 17 yet he kept on in his willful *w*.
57: 18 I have seen his *w*, but I will heal
58: 2 they seem eager to know my *w*,
59: 7 ruin and destruction mark their *w*.
63: 17 you make us wander from your *w*
64: 5 who remember your *w*.
65: 2 who walk in *w* not good,
66: 3 They have chosen their own *w*,
Jer 2: 33 of women can learn from your *w*.
2: 36 changing your *w*?
3: 21 they have perverted their *w*
6: 27 and test their *w*
7: 3 Reform your *w* and your actions,
7: 5 If you really change your *w*
7: 23 Walk in all the *w* I command you,
10: 2 "Do not learn the *w* of the nations
12: 16 And if they learn well the *w*
15: 7 for they have not changed their *w*.
16: 17 My eyes are on all their *w*;
18: 11 So turn from your evil *w*, each one
18: 11 reform your *w* and your actions.'
18: 15 made them stumble in their *w*
23: 22 have turned them from their evil *w*
25: 5 from your evil *w* and your evil
26: 13 reform your *w* and your actions
32: 19 open to all the *w* of men;
35: 15 turn from your wicked *w*
36: 7 each will turn from his wicked *w*,
La 3: 40 Let us examine our *w* and test them
Eze 3: 18 him from his evil *w* in order
3: 19 his wickedness or from his evil *w*,
13: 22 not to turn from their evil *w*
16: 47 You not only walked in their *w*
16: 47 but in all your *w* you soon became
16: 61 Then you will remember your *w*
18: 23 when they turn from their *w*
18: 25 Is it not your *w* that are unjust?
18: 29 Are my *w* unjust, O house of Israel
18: 29 Is it not your *w* that are unjust?
18: 30 each one according to his *w*,
20: 44 and not according to your evil *w*
28: 15 You were blameless in your *w*
33: 8 out to dissuade him from his *w*,
33: 9 the wicked man to turn from his *w*
33: 11 from your evil *w*! Why will you die
33: 11 rather that they turn from their *w*
33: 20 of you according to his own *w*."
36: 31 you will remember your evil *w*
Da 4: 37 does is right and all his *w* are just.
5: 23 in his hand your life and all your *w*.
Hos 4: 9 both of them for their *w*
4: 18 their rulers dearly love shameful *w*.
12: 2 punish Jacob according to his *w*
14: 9 The *w* of the LORD are right;

Jnh 3: 8 Let them give up their evil *w*
3: 10 how they turned from their evil *w*,
Mic 2: 7 good to him whose *w* are upright?
4: 2 He will teach us his *w*,
Hab 3: 6 His *w* are eternal.
Hag 1: 5 "Give careful thought to your *w*.
1: 7 "Give careful thought to your *w*.
Zec 1: 4 'Turn from your evil *w*
1: 6 has done to us what our *w*
3: 7 'If you will walk in my *w*
Mal 2: 9 you have not followed my *w*
Lk 3: 5 the rough *w* smooth.
Ac 3: 26 each of you from your wicked *w*."
13: 10 never stop perverting the right *w*
18: 13 to worship God in *w* contrary
28: 10 They honored us in many *w*
Ro 1: 30 they invent *w* of doing evil;
3: 16 ruin and misery mark their *w*,
1Co 13: 11 I put childish *w* behind me.
2Co 4: 2 renounced secret and shameful *w*;
8: 22 to us in many *w* that he is zealous,
Eph 2: 2 live when you followed the *w*
Col 3: 7 You used to walk in these *w*,
2Ti 1: 18 well in how many *w* he helped me
Heb 1: 1 at many times and in various *w*,
3: 10 and they have not known my *w*.'
Jas 3: 2 We all stumble in many *w*.
2Pe 2: 2 Many will follow their shameful *w*
Rev 2: 22 unless they repent of her *w*.
15: 3 Just and true are your *w*,

WAYWARD (WAYWARDNESS)

Ps 58: 3 from the womb they are *w*
Pr 2: 16 from the *w* wife with her seductive
6: 24 the smooth tongue of the *w* wife.
7: 5 from the *w* wife with her seductive
20: 16 if he does it for a *w* woman.
23: 27 and a *w* wife is a narrow well.
27: 13 if he does it for a *w* woman.
Isa 29: 24 Those who are *w* in spirit will gain

WAYWARDNESS (WAYWARD)

Pr 1: 32 For the *w* of the simple will kill
Hos 14: 4 "I will heal their *w*

WEAK (WEAKENED WEAKENING WEAKER WEAKEST WEAKLING WEAKNESS WEAKNESSES)

Ge 27: 1 so *w* that he could no longer see,
29: 17 Leah had *w* eyes, but Rachel was
30: 42 So the *w* animals went to Laban
30: 42 if the animals were *w*, he would not
Nu 13: 18 who live there are strong or *w*,
Dt 34: 7 yet his eyes were not *w*
Jdg 16: 7 I'll become as *w* as any other man."
16: 11 I'll become as *w* as any other man."
16: 13 I'll become as *w* as any other man."
16: 17 I would become as *w* as any other
1Sa 3: 2 so *w* that he could barely see,
15: 9 and *w* they totally destroyed.
2Sa 3: 39 I am the anointed king, I am *w*,
17: 2 him when he is weary and *w*.
2Ch 28: 15 All those who were *w* they put
Ne 6: 9 "Their hands will get too *w*
Ps 6: 7 My eyes grow *w* with sorrow;
10: 2 the wicked man hunts down the *w*,
12: 5 of the oppression of the *w*
31: 9 my eyes grow *w* with sorrow,
31: 10 and my bones grow *w*.
34: 10 The lions may grow *w* and hungry,
41: 1 is he who has regard for the *w*;
72: 13 He will take pity on the *w*
82: 3 Defend the cause of the *w*
82: 4 Rescue the *w* and needy;
Isa 14: 10 You also have become *w*, as we are;
38: 14 My eyes grew *w* as I looked
40: 29 and increases the power of the *w*.
Eze 7: 17 and every knee will become as *w*
21: 7 every knee become as *w* as water.'
29: 15 it so *w* that it will never again rule
34: 4 You have not strengthened the *w*
34: 16 the injured and strengthen the *w*,
34: 21 butting all the *w* sheep
Mt 26: 41 spirit is willing, but the body is *w*."
Mk 14: 38 spirit is willing, but the body is *w*."
Ac 20: 35 of hard work we must help the *w*,
Ro 6: 19 you are *w* in your natural selves.
14: 1 Accept him whose faith is *w*,

Ro 14: 2 whose faith is *w*, eats only
15: 1 to bear with the failings of the *w*
1Co 1: 27 God chose the *w* things
4: 10 We are *w*, but you are strong!
8: 7 and since their conscience is *w*,
8: 9 become a stumbling block to the *w*.
8: 10 with a *w* conscience sees you who
8: 11 So this *w* brother, for whom Christ
8: 12 and wound their *w* conscience,
9: 22 To the *w* I became *w*, to win the *w*.
11: 30 That is why many among you are *w*
2Co 11: 21 shame I admit that we were too *w*
11: 29 Who is *w*, and I do not feel *w*?
12: 10 For when I am *w*, then I am strong.
13: 3 He is not *w* in dealing with you,
13: 4 Likewise, we are *w* in him,
13: 9 We are glad whenever we are *w*
Gal 4: 9 you are turning back to those *w*
1Th 5: 14 help the *w*, be patient
Heb 7: 18 because it was *w* and useless
7: 28 as high priests men who are *w*;
12: 12 your feeble arms and *w* knees.

WEAK-WILLED (WILL)

Eze 16: 30 " 'How *w* you are, declares
2Ti 3: 6 and gain control over *w* women,

WEAKENED (WEAK)

Job 18: 7 The vigor of his step is *w*;
Ro 8: 3 in that it was *w* by the sinful nature,

WEAKENING (WEAK)

Ro 4: 19 Without *w* in his faith, he faced

WEAKER (WEAK)

2Sa 3: 1 the house of Saul grew *w* and *w*.
1Co 12: 22 seem to be *w* are indispensable,
1Pe 3: 7 them with respect as the *w* partner

WEAKEST (WEAK)

Jdg 6: 15 My clan is the *w* in Manasseh,

WEAKLING (WEAK)

Joel 3: 10 Let the *w* say,

WEAKNESS (WEAK)

La 1: 6 in *w* they have fled
Ro 8: 26 the Spirit helps us in our *w*.
1Co 1: 25 and the *w* of God is stronger
2: 3 I came to you in *w* and fear,
15: 43 it is sown in *w*, it is raised in power;
2Co 11: 30 boast of the things that show my *w*.
12: 9 for my power is made perfect in *w*
13: 4 he was crucified in *w*, yet he lives
Heb 5: 2 since he himself is subject to *w*.
11: 34 whose *w* was turned to strength;

WEAKNESSES (WEAK)

2Co 12: 5 about myself, except about my *w*.
12: 9 all the more gladly about my *w*,
12: 10 I delight in *w*, in insults,
Heb 4: 15 unable to sympathize with our *w*,

WEALTH (WEALTHY)

Ge 26: 13 and his *w* continued to grow
31: 1 and has gained all this *w*
31: 16 Surely all the *w* that God took
34: 29 They carried off all their *w*
Dt 8: 17 of my hands have produced this *w*
8: 18 gives you the ability to produce *w*,
Jos 22: 8 to your homes with your great *w*—
1Sa 2: 7 The LORD sends poverty and *w*;
17: 25 The king will give great *w*
1Ki 3: 11 not for long life or *w* for yourself,
10: 7 *w* you have far exceeded the report
1Ch 29: 12 *W* and honor come from you;
29: 28 having enjoyed long life, *w*
2Ch 1: 11 and you have not asked for *w*,
1: 12 And I will also give you *w*,
17: 5 so that he had great *w* and honor.
18: 1 Now Jehoshaphat had great *w*
Est 1: 4 he displayed the vast *w*
5: 11 boasted to them about his vast *w*,
Job 5: 5 and the thirsty pant after his *w*.
6: 22 pay a ransom for me from your *w*,
15: 29 be rich and his *w* will not endure,
20: 10 his own hands must give back his *w*
22: 20 and fire devours their *w*.'

Job 31: 25 if I have rejoiced over my great *w*,
36: 19 Would your *w*
Ps 17: 14 they store up *w* for their children.
37: 16 have than the *w* of many wicked;
39: 6 he heaps up *w*, not knowing who
39: 11 you consume their *w* like a moth—
45: 12 men of *w* will seek your favor.
49: 6 those who trust in their *w*
49: 10 and leave their *w* to others.
52: 7 but trusted in his great *w*
73: 12 always carefree, they increase in *w*.
112: 3 *W* and riches are in his house,
Pr 3: 9 Honor the LORD with your *w*,
5: 10 lest strangers feast on your *w*
6: 31 it costs him all the *w* of his house.
8: 18 enduring *w* and prosperity.
8: 21 bestowing *w* on those who love me
10: 4 but diligent hands bring *w*.
10: 15 *w* of the rich is their fortified city,
10: 22 The blessing of the LORD brings *w*
11: 4 *W* is worthless in the day of wrath,
11: 16 but ruthless men gain only *w*.
13: 7 to be poor, yet has great *w*.
13: 22 a sinner's *w* is stored up
14: 24 The *w* of the wise is their crown,
15: 16 than great *w* with turmoil.
18: 11 *w* of the rich is their fortified city;
19: 4 *W* brings many friends,
19: 14 *w* are inherited from parents,
22: 4 bring *w* and honor and life.
22: 16 the poor to increase his *w*
28: 8 He who increases his *w*
29: 3 of prostitutes squanders his *w*.
Ecc 2: 26 and storing up *w* to hand it
4: 8 eyes were not content with his *w*.
5: 10 whoever loves *w* is never satisfied
5: 13 *w* hoarded to the harm of its owner,
5: 14 or *w* lost through some misfortune,
5: 19 when God gives any man *w*
6: 2 God gives a man *w*, possessions
9: 11 or *w* to the brilliant
SS 8: 7 all the *w* of his house for love,
Isa 8: 4 the *w* of Damascus and the plunder
10: 14 reached for the *w* of the nations;
15: 7 So the *w* they have acquired
60: 5 the *w* on the seas will be brought
60: 11 so that men may bring you the *w*
61: 6 You will feed on the *w* of nations,
66: 12 *w* of nations like a flooding stream;
Jer 15: 13 Your *w* and your treasures
17: 3 and your *w* and all your treasures
20: 5 over to their enemies all the *w*
48: 36 The *w* they acquired is gone.
Eze 7: 11 none of that crowd—no *w*,
16: 36 Because you poured out your *w*
26: 12 They will plunder your *w*
27: 12 because of your great *w* of goods;
27: 18 of your many products and great *w*
27: 27 Your *w*, merchandise and wares,
27: 33 with your great *w* and your wares
28: 4 you have gained *w* for yourself
28: 5 and because of your *w*
28: 5 you have increased your *w*,
29: 19 Babylon, and he will carry off its *w*.
30: 4 her *w* will be carried away
Da 11: 2 When he has gained power by his *w*
11: 24 loot and *w* among his followers.
11: 28 to his own country with great *w*,
Hos 12: 8 With all my *w* they will not find
Ob : 11 while strangers carried off his *w*
: 13 nor seize their *w*
Mic 4: 13 their *w* to the Lord of all the earth.
Na 2: 9 the *w* from all its treasures!
Zep 1: 13 Their *w* will be plundered,
Zec 14: 14 *w* of all the surrounding nations
Mt 13: 22 and the deceitfulness of *w* choke it,
19: 22 away sad, because he had great *w*.
Mk 4: 19 deceitfulness of *w* and the desires
10: 22 away sad, because he had great *w*.
12: 44 They all gave out of their *w*; but she
Lk 15: 13 and there squandered his *w*
16: 9 use worldly *w* to gain friends
16: 11 trustworthy in handling worldly *w*,
18: 23 because he was a man of great *w*.
21: 4 gave their gifts out of their *w*;
1Ti 6: 17 nor to put their hope in *w*,
Jas 5: 2 Your *w* has rotted, and moths have
5: 3 You have hoarded *w*

Rev 3: 17 I have acquired *w* and do not need
5: 12 to receive power and *w*
18: 15 gained their *w* from her will stand
18: 17 hour such great *w* has been brought
18: 19 became rich through her *w!*

WEALTHY (WEALTH)

Ge 13: 2 Abram had become very *w*
24: 35 abundantly, and he has become *w*.
26: 13 to grow until he became very *w*.
1Sa 25: 2 there at Carmel, was very *w*.
2Sa 19: 32 for he was a very *w* man.
2Ki 15: 20 *w* man had to contribute fifty
Job 27: 19 He lies down *w*, but will do
Hos 12: 8 "I am very rich; I have become *w*.
Hab 2: 6 and makes himself *w* by extortion!
Lk 19: 2 was a chief tax collector and was *w*.

WEANED

Ge 21: 8 The child grew and was *w*,
21: 8 the day Isaac was *w* Abraham held
1Sa 1: 22 to her husband, "After the boy is *w*
1: 23 nursed her son until she had *w* him.
1: 23 "Stay here until you have *w* him;
1: 24 After he was *w*, she took the boy
Ps 131: 2 like a *w* child is my soul within me.
131: 2 like a *w* child with its mother,
Isa 28: 9 To children *w* from their milk,
Hos 1: 8 After she had *w* Lo-Ruhamah,

WEAPON (WEAPONS)

1Sa 21: 8 brought my sword or any other *w*,
1Ki 20: 35 "Strike me with your *w*,"
2Ki 11: 8 each man with his *w* in his hand.
11: 11 each with his *w* in his hand,
1Ch 12: 33 for battle with every type of *w*,
12: 37 armed with every type of *w*—
2Ch 23: 10 each with his *w* in his hand,
Ne 4: 17 work with one hand and held a *w*
4: 23 each had his *w*, even when he went
Job 20: 24 Though he flees from an iron *w*,
Isa 54: 16 and forges a *w* fit for its work.
54: 17 no *w* forged against you will prevail
Jer 51: 20 my *w* for battle—
Eze 9: 1 each with a *w* in his hand."
9: 2 each with a deadly *w* in his hand.

WEAPONS (WEAPON)

Ge 27: 3 get your *w*— your quiver and bow
49: 5 their swords are *w* of violence.
Dt 1: 41 So every one of you put on his *w*,
1Sa 8: 12 and still others to make *w* of war
17: 54 and he put the Philistine's *w*
20: 40 Jonathan gave his *w* to the boy
2Sa 1: 27 The *w* of war have perished!"
2: 21 young men and strip him of his *w*."
1Ki 10: 25 and gold, robes, *w* and spices,
2Ki 10: 2 and horses, a fortified city and *w*,
2Ch 9. 24 *w* and spices, and horses and mules
23: 7 each man with his *w* in his hand.
32: 5 also made large numbers of *w*
Ps 7: 13 He has prepared his deadly *w;*
76: 3 the swords, the *w* of war.
Ecc 9: 18 Wisdom is better than *w* of war,
Isa 13: 5 the LORD and the *w* of his wrath
22. 8 to the *w* in the Palace of the Forest;
Jer 21: 4 against you the *w* of war that are
22: 7 each man with his *w*,
50: 25 and brought out the *w* of his wrath,
Eze 23: 24 They will come against you with *w*,
26: 9 demolish your towers with his *w*.
32: 27 to the grave with their *w* of war,
39: 9 use the *w* for fuel and burn them up
39: 10 because they will use the *w* for fuel.
Jn 18: 3 carrying torches, lanterns and *w*.
2Co 6: 7 with *w* of righteousness
10: 4 The *w* we fight with are not
10: 4 with are not the *w* of the world.

WEAR (WEARING WEARS WORE WORN WORN-OUT)

Ge 28: 20 clothes to *w* so that I return safely
Ex 18: 18 to you will only *w* yourselves out.
28: 35 Aaron must *w* it when he ministers.
28: 43 his sons must *w* them whenever
29: 30 is to *w* them seven days.
Lev 13: 45 disease must *w* torn clothes,
19: 19 " 'Do not *w* clothing woven
Lev 21: 10 to *w* the priestly garments,
Dt 8: 4 Your clothes did not *w* out
22: 5 nor a man *w* women's clothing,
22: 5 woman must not *w* men's clothing,
22: 11 Do not *w* clothes of wool
22: 12 corners of the cloak you *w*.
28: 32 you will *w* out your eyes watching
29: 5 your clothes did not *w* out,
Jdg 8: 24 the Ishmaelites to *w* gold earrings.)
1Sa 2: 28 and to *w* an ephod in my presence.
1Ki 22: 30 but you *w* your royal robes."
2Ch 18: 29 but you *w* your royal robes."
Ne 9: 21 their clothes did not *w* out
Job 27: 17 what he lays up the righteous will *w*
31: 36 Surely I would *w* it on my shoulder,
Ps 102: 26 they will all *w* out like a garment.
Pr 23: 4 Do not *w* yourself out to get rich;
Isa 15: 3 In the streets they *w* sackcloth;
49: 18 "you will *w* them all as ornaments;
50: 9 They will all *w* out like a garment;
51: 6 the earth will *w* out like a garment
Jer 12: 13 they will *w* themselves out
Eze 44: 17 they are to *w* linen clothes;
44: 17 they must not *w* any woolen
44: 18 They are to *w* linen turbans
44: 18 They must not *w* anything that
Am 8: 10 I will make all of you *w* sackcloth
Mt 6: 25 about your body, what you will *w*.
6: 31 'What shall we *w?*' For the pagans
11: 8 those who *w* fine clothes are
Mk 6: 9 *W* sandals but not an extra tunic.
Lk 7: 25 those who *w* expensive clothes
12: 22 about your body, what you will *w*.
12: 33 for yourselves that will not *w* out,
18: 5 that she won't eventually *w* me out
Heb 1: 11 they will all *w* out like a garment.
Rev 3: 18 and white clothes to *w*,
19: 8 was given her to *w*."

WEARIED (WEARY)

Isa 43: 22 you have not *w* yourselves for me,
43: 23 *w* you with demands for incense.
43: 24 and *w* me with your offenses.
57: 10 You were *w* by all your ways,
Mal 2: 17 You have *w* the LORD
2: 17 "How have we *w* him?" you ask.

WEARIES (WEARY)

Ecc 10: 15 A fool's work *w* him;
12: 12 and much study *w* the body.

WEARING (WEAR)

Ge 37: 23 richly ornamented robe he was *w*—
Ex 32: 2 your sons and your daughters are *w*
Dt 21: 13 and put aside the clothes she was *w*
Ru 3: 15 "Bring me the shawl you are *w*
1Sa 2: 18 LORD—a boy *w* a linen ephod.
14: 3 was Ahijah, who was *w* an ephod.
18: 4 took off the robe he was *w*
28: 14 "An old man *w* a robe is coming up
2Sa 6: 14 *w* a linen ephod, danced
13: 18 She was *w* a richly ornamented
13: 19 the ornamented robe she was *w*.
20: 8 Joab was *w* his military tunic,
1Ki 11: 29 him on the way, *w* a new cloak.
11: 30 hold of the new cloak he was *w*
20: 32 *W* sackcloth around their waists
2Ki 19: 2 the leading priests, all *w* sackcloth,
Ne 9: 1 fasting and *w* sackcloth
Est 1: 11 him Queen Vashti, *w* her royal
8: 15 king's presence *w* royal garments
SS 3: 8 all of them *w* the sword,
3: 11 look at King Solomon *w* the crown,
Isa 37: 2 the leading priests, all *w* sackcloth,
Jer 13: 4 and are *w* around your waist,
Da 3: 21 So these men, *w* their robes,
Mt 22: 11 who was not *w* wedding clothes.
Mk 14: 51 *w* nothing but a linen garment,
Jn 19: 5 When Jesus came out *w* the crown
Ac 12: 21 appointed day Herod, *w* his royal
Jas 2: 2 into your meeting *w* a gold ring
2: 3 attention to the man *w* fine clothes
1Pe 3: 3 as braided hair and the *w*
Rev 7: 9 They were *w* white robes

WEARISOME (WEARY)

Ecc 1: 8 All things are *w*,

WEARS (WEAR)

Job 14: 19 as water *w* away stones
Ps 119:139 My zeal *w* me out,
Isa 16: 12 she only *w* herself out;

WEARY (WEARIED WEARIES WEARISOME)

Dt 25: 18 When you were *w* and worn out,
28: 65 eyes *w* with longing,
Jos 7: 3 and do not *w* all the people,
2Sa 17: 2 I would attack him when he is *w*
Job 3: 17 and there the *w* are at rest.
22: 7 You gave no water to the *w*
31: 16 or let the eyes of the widow grow *w*
Ps 63: 1 in a dry and *w* land
68: 9 you refreshed your *w* inheritance.
119: 28 My soul is *w* with sorrow;
Pr 25: 25 Like cold water to a *w* soul
Isa 1: 14 I am *w* of bearing them.
28: 12 is the resting place, let the *w* rest";
40: 28 He will not grow tired or *w*,
40: 29 He gives strength to the *w*
40: 30 Even youths grow tired and *w*,
40: 31 they will run and not grow *w*,
46: 1 a burden for the *w*.
50: 4 know the word that sustains the *w*.
Jer 9: 5 they *w* themselves with sinning.
20: 9 I am *w* of holding it in;
31: 25 I will refresh the *w* and satisfy
La 5: 5 we are *w* and find no rest.
Zec 11: 8 and I grew *w* of them and said,
Mt 11: 28 all you who are *w* and burdened,
Ac 24: 4 But in order not to *w* you further,
Gal 6: 9 Let us not become *w* in doing good,
Heb 12: 3 so that you will not grow *w*
Rev 2: 3 my name, and have not grown *w*.

WEASEL

Lev 11: 29 these are unclean for you: the *w*,

WEATHER

Mt 16: 2 'It will be fair *w*, for the sky is red,'

WEAVE (INTERWOVEN WEAVER WEAVER'S WEAVERS WEAVING WOVE WOVEN)

Ex 28: 39 "*W* the tunic of fine linen
Jdg 16: 13 "If you *w* the seven braids

WEAVER (WEAVE)

Ex 39: 22 of blue cloth—the work of a *w*
39: 27 the work of a *w*— and the turban
Isa 38: 12 Like a *w* I have rolled up my life,

WEAVER'S (WEAVE)

1Sa 17: 7 His spear shaft was like a *w* rod,
2Sa 21: 19 a spear with a shaft like a *w* rod.
1Ch 11: 23 Egyptian had a spear like a *w* rod
20: 5 a spear with a shaft like a *w* rod.
Job 7: 6 days are swifter than a *w* shuttle,

WEAVERS (WEAVE)

Ex 35: 35 *w*— all of them master craftsmen
Isa 19: 9 the *w* of fine linen will lose hope.

WEAVING (WEAVE)

2Ki 23: 7 where women did *w* for Asherah.

WEB (COBWEBS)

Job 8: 14 what he relies on is a spider's *w*.
8: 15 He leans on his *w*, but it gives way;
Isa 59: 5 and spin a spider's *w*.

WEDDING

Jdg 14: 20 who had attended him at his *w*.
1Ki 9: 16 as a *w* gift to his daughter,
Ps 78: 63 and their maidens had no *w* songs;
SS 3: 11 him on the day of his *w*,
Jer 2: 32 a bride her *w* ornaments?
Mt 22: 2 a king who prepared a *w* banquet
22: 4 Come to the *w* banquet.'
22: 8 his servants, 'The *w* banquet is
22: 10 the *w* hall was filled with guests.
22: 11 who was not wearing *w* clothes.
22: 12 get in here without *w* clothes?'
25: 10 went in with him to the *w* banquet.
Lk 12: 36 master to return from a *w* banquet,
14: 8 someone invites you to a *w* feast,

Jn 2: 1 On the third day a *w* took place
2: 2 had also been invited to the *w*.
Rev 19: 7 For the *w* of the Lamb has come,
19: 9 to the *w* supper of the Lamb!' "

WEDGE

Jos 7: 21 a *w* of gold weighing fifty shekels,
7: 24 the gold *w*, his sons and daughters,

WEED (SEAWEED WEEDS)

Mt 13: 41 and they will *w* out of his kingdom

WEEDS (WEED)

Job 31: 40 and *w* instead of barley."
Pr 24: 31 the ground was covered with *w*,
Hos 10: 4 like poisonous *w* in a plowed field.
Zep 2: 9 a place of *w* and salt pits,
Mt 13: 25 and sowed *w* among the wheat,
13: 26 and formed heads, then the *w*
13: 27 Where then did the *w* come from?'
13: 29 because while you are pulling the *w*
13: 30 First collect the *w* and tie them
13: 36 the parable of the *w* in the field."
13: 38 The *w* are the sons of the evil one,
13: 40 "As the *w* are pulled up

WEEK (WEEKS)

Ge 29: 27 Finish out this daughter's bridal *w;*
29: 28 He finished out the *w* with Leah,
Mt 28: 1 at dawn on the first day of the *w*,
Mk 16: 2 Very early on the first day of the *w*,
16: 9 rose early on the first day of the *w*,
Lk 18: 12 I fast twice a *w* and give a tenth
24: 1 of the *w*, very early in the morning,
Jn 19: 14 day of Preparation of Passover *W*,
20: 1 Early on the first day of the *w*,
20: 19 evening of that first day of the *w*,
20: 26 A *w* later his disciples were
Ac 20: 7 day of the *w* we came together
28: 14 us to spend a *w* with them.
1Co 16: 2 On the first day of every *w*,

WEEKS (WEEK)

Ex 34: 22 the Feast of *W* with the firstfruits
Lev 12: 5 for two *w* the woman will be
23: 15 offering, count off seven full *w*.
Nu 28: 26 of new grain during the Feast of *W*,
Dt 16: 9 Count off seven *w*
16: 10 Then celebrate the Feast of *W*
16: 16 the Feast of *W* and the Feast
2Ch 8: 13 the Feast of *W* and the Feast
Jer 5: 24 us of the regular *w* of harvest.'
Da 10: 2 Daniel, mourned for three *w*.
10: 3 at all until the three *w* were over.

WEEP (WEEPING WEEPS WEPT)

Ge 23: 2 mourn for Sarah and to *w* over her.
29: 11 Rachel and began to *w* aloud.
42: 24 away from them and began to *w*,
43: 30 and looked for a place to *w*.
Jdg 11: 37 months to roam the hills and *w*
1Sa 30: 4 until they had no strength left to *w*.
2Sa 1: 24 *w* for Saul,
2Ki 8: 11 Then the man of God began to *w*.
Ne 8: 9 Do not mourn or *w*."
Job 2: 12 him; they began to *w* aloud,
27: 15 their widows will not *w* for them.
Ps 69: 10 When I *w* and fast,
78: 64 and their widows could not *w*.
Ecc 3: 4 a time to *w* and a time to laugh,
Isa 15: 2 to its high places to *w;*
16: 9 So I *w*, as Jazer weeps,
22: 4 let me *w* bitterly.
22: 12 day to *w* and to wail,
30: 19 in Jerusalem, you will *w* no more.
33: 7 the envoys of peace *w* bitterly.
Jer 9: 1 I would *w* day and night
9: 10 I will *w* and wail for the mountains
13: 17 I will *w* in secret
13: 17 my eyes will *w* bitterly,
22: 10 Do not *w* for the dead king
22: 10 *w* bitterly for him who is exiled,
25: 34 *W* and wail, you shepherds;
48: 32 I *w* for you, as Jazer weeps,
La 1: 16 "This is why I *w*
Eze 24: 16 Yet do not lament or *w*
24: 23 You will not mourn or *w*
27: 31 They will *w* over you with anguish
Joel 1: 5 Wake up, you drunkards, and *w!*
2: 17 *w* between the temple porch
Am 5: 16 farmers will be summoned to *w*
Mic 1: 8 Because of this I will *w* and wail;
1: 10 *w* not at all.
Mal 2: 13 You *w* and wail because he no
Lk 6: 21 Blessed are you who *w* now,
6: 25 for you will mourn and *w*.
23: 28 of Jerusalem, do not *w* for me;
23: 28 *w* for yourselves and for your
Jn 16: 20 you will *w* and mourn
Jas 5: 1 *w* and wail because of the misery
Rev 5: 5 Do not *w!* See, the Lion of the tribe
18: 9 they will *w* and mourn over her.
18: 11 "The merchants of the earth will *w*
18: 15 They will *w* and mourn and cry out

WEEPING (WEEP)

Ge 45: 14 and Benjamin embraced him, *w*.
Nu 25: 6 while they were *w* at the entrance
Dt 1: 45 but he paid no attention to your *w*
34: 8 the time of *w* and mourning was
Jdg 20: 26 there they sat *w* before the LORD.
21: 2 raising their voices and *w* bitterly.
1Sa 1: 8 "Hannah, why are you *w?*
11: 5 with the people? Why are they *w?"*
2Sa 3: 16 *w* behind her all the way
13: 19 went away, *w* aloud as she went.
15: 30 and were *w* as they went up.
15: 30 up the Mount of Olives, *w*
19: 1 "The king is *w* and mourning
2Ki 8: 12 Why is my lord *w?"* asked Hazael.
Ezr 3: 13 shouts of joy from the sound of *w*,
10: 1 *w* and throwing himself
Ne 8: 9 For all the people had been *w*
Est 4: 3 with fasting, *w* and wailing.
8: 3 the king, falling at his feet and *w*.
Job 16: 16 My face is red with *w*,
Ps 6: 6 all night long I flood my bed with *w*
6: 8 for the LORD has heard my *w*.
30: 5 *w* may remain for a night,
35: 14 as though *w* for my mother.
39: 12 be not deaf to my *w*.
126: 6 He who goes out *w*,
Isa 15: 3 prostrate with *w*.
15: 5 *w* as they go;
65: 19 the sound of *w* and of crying
Jer 3: 21 the *w* and pleading of the people
31: 9 They will come with *w;*
31: 15 Rachel *w* for her children
31: 15 mourning and great *w*,
31: 16 "Restrain your voice from *w*
41: 6 out from Mizpah to meet them, *w*
48: 5 *w* bitterly as they go;
La 2: 11 My eyes fail from *w*,
Joel 2: 12 with fasting and *w* and mourning."
Am 8: 10 and all your singing into *w*.
Zec 12: 11 On that day the *w*
12: 11 like the *w* of Hadad Rimmon
Mt 2: 18 Rachel *w* for her children
2: 18 *w* and great mourning,
8: 12 where there will be *w* and gnashing
13: 42 where there will be *w* and gnashing
13: 50 where there will be *w* and gnashing
22: 13 where there will be *w* and gnashing
24: 51 where there will be *w* and gnashing
25: 30 where there will be *w* and gnashing
Mk 16: 10 and who were mourning and *w*.
Lk 7: 38 she stood behind him at his feet *w*,
13: 28 "There will be *w* there,
Jn 11: 33 When Jesus saw her *w*,
11: 33 come along with her also *w*,
Ac 21: 13 "Why are you *w* and breaking my
Rev 18: 19 and with *w* and mourning cry out:

WEEPS (WEEP)

Isa 16: 9 So I weep, as Jazer *w*,
Jer 48: 32 I weep for you, as Jazer *w*,
La 1: 2 Bitterly she *w* at night,

WEIGH (OUTWEIGH OUTWEIGHS WEIGHED WEIGHING WEIGHS WEIGHT WEIGHTIER WEIGHTS WEIGHTY)

2Sa 14: 26 he would *w* it, and its weight was
Ezr 8: 29 carefully until you *w* them out
Job 31: 6 let God *w* me in honest scales
Isa 46: 6 and *w* out silver on the scales;
Eze 4: 10 *W* out twenty shekels of food
Eze 33: 10 "Our offenses and sins *w* us down,
1Co 14: 29 others should *w* carefully what is

WEIGHED (WEIGH)

Ge 23: 16 and *w* out for him the price he had
Nu 7: 85 Each silver plate *w* a hundred
7: 85 silver dishes *w* two thousand four
7: 86 the gold ladles *w* a hundred
7: 86 with incense *w* ten shekels each,
31: 52 as a gift to the LORD *w* 16,750
1Sa 2: 3 and by him deeds are *w*.
17: 7 its iron point *w* six hundred shekels
2Sa 18: 12 if a thousand shekels were *w* out
21: 16 bronze spearhead *w* three hundred
2Ki 25: 16 was more than could be *w*.
1Ch 22: 3 and more bronze than could be *w*.
22: 14 and iron too great to be *w*,
2Ch 3: 9 The gold nails *w* fifty shekels.
Ezr 8: 25 and I *w* out to them the offering
8: 26 I *w* out to them 650 talents of silver
8: 30 sacred articles that had been *w* out
8: 33 we *w* out the silver and gold
Job 6: 2 "If only my anguish could be *w*
28: 15 nor can its price be *w* in silver.
Ps 62: 9 if *w* on a balance, they are nothing;
Pr 16: 2 but motives are *w* by the LORD.
Isa 40: 12 or *w* the mountains on the scales
Jer 6: 11 the old, those *w* down with years.
32: 9 *w* out for him seventeen shekels
32: 10 and *w* out the silver on the scales.
52: 20 was more than could be *w*.
La 3: 7 he has *w* me down with chains.
Da 5: 27 You have been *w* on the scales
Lk 21: 34 or your hearts will be *w*
Ac 27: 13 so they *w* anchor and sailed

WEIGHING (WEIGH)

Ge 24: 22 took out a gold nose ring *w* a beka
24: 22 two gold bracelets *w* ten shekels.
Nu 3: 50 he collected silver *w* 1,365
7: 13 sprinkling bowl *w* seventy shekels,
7: 13 was one silver plate *w* a hundred
7: 14 one gold ladle *w* ten shekels,
7: 19 sprinkling bowl *w* seventy shekels,
7: 19 was one silver plate *w* a hundred
7: 20 one gold ladle *w* ten shekels,
7: 25 sprinkling bowl *w* seventy shekels,
7: 25 was one silver plate *w* a hundred
7: 26 one gold ladle *w* ten shekels,
7: 31 sprinkling bowl *w* seventy shekels,
7: 31 was one silver plate *w* a hundred
7: 32 one gold ladle *w* ten shekels,
7: 37 sprinkling bowl *w* seventy shekels,
7: 37 was one silver plate *w* a hundred
7: 38 one gold ladle *w* ten shekels,
7: 43 sprinkling bowl *w* seventy shekels,
7: 43 was one silver plate *w* a hundred
7: 44 one gold ladle *w* ten shekels,
7: 49 sprinkling bowl *w* seventy shekels,
7: 49 was one silver plate *w* a hundred
7: 50 one gold ladle *w* ten shekels,
7: 55 sprinkling bowl *w* seventy shekels,
7: 55 was one silver plate *w* a hundred
7: 56 one gold ladle *w* ten shekels,
7: 61 sprinkling bowl *w* seventy shekels,
7: 61 was one silver plate *w* a hundred
7: 62 one gold ladle *w* ten shekels,
7: 67 sprinkling bowl *w* seventy shekels,
7: 67 was one silver plate *w* a hundred
7: 68 one gold ladle *w* ten shekels,
7: 73 sprinkling bowl *w* seventy shekels,
7: 73 was one silver plate *w* a hundred
7: 74 one gold ladle *w* ten shekels,
7: 79 sprinkling bowl *w* seventy shekels,
7: 79 was one silver plate *w* a hundred
7: 80 one gold ladle *w* ten shekels,
Jos 7: 21 and a wedge of gold *w* fifty shekels,
1Sa 17: 5 of bronze *w* five thousand shekels;
Ezr 8: 26 silver articles *w* 100 talents,

WEIGHS (WEIGH)

Ex 30: 13 shekel, which *w* twenty gerahs.
Nu 3: 47 shekel, which *w* twenty gerahs.
18: 16 shekel, which *w* twenty gerahs.
Pr 12: 25 An anxious heart *w* a man down,
15: 28 of the righteous *w* its answers,
21: 2 but the LORD *w* the heart.
24: 12 not he who *w* the heart perceive

Ecc 6: 1 and it *w* heavily on men: God gives
8: 6 a man's misery *w* heavily upon him
Isa 40: 15 he *w* the islands as though they

WEIGHT (WEIGH)

Ge 23: 16 according to the *w* current
43: 21 the exact *w*— in the mouth
Lev 19: 35 when measuring length, *w*
26: 26 they will dole out the bread by *w*.
Jdg 8: 26 The *w* of the gold rings he asked
2Sa 12: 30 of their king—its *w* was a talent
14: 26 and its *w* was two hundred shekels
1Ki 7: 47 the *w* of the bronze was not
10: 14 The *w* of the gold that Solomon
1Ch 20: 2 its *w* was found to be a talent
28: 14 He designated the *w* of gold
28: 14 *w* of silver for all the silver articles
28: 15 and the *w* of silver for each silver
28: 15 with the *w* for each lampstand
28: 15 *w* of gold for the gold lampstands
28: 16 the *w* of gold for each table
28: 16 the *w* of silver for the silver tables;
28: 17 the *w* of gold for each gold dish;
28: 17 the *w* of pure gold for the forks,
28: 17 the *w* of silver for each silver dish;
28: 18 and the *w* of the refined gold
2Ch 4: 18 amounted to so much that the *w*
9: 13 The *w* of the gold that Solomon
Ezr 8: 34 accounted for by number and *w*,
8: 34 and the entire *w* was recorded
Job 26: 8 clouds do not burst under their *w*.
La 4: 2 once worth their *w* in gold,

WEIGHTIER (WEIGH)

Jn 5: 36 "I have testimony *w* than that

WEIGHTS (WEIGH)

Lev 19: 36 Use honest scales and honest *w*,
Dt 25: 13 Do not have two differing *w*
25: 15 and honest *w* and measures,
Pr 11: 1 but accurate *w* are his delight.
16: 11 all the *w* in the bag are
20: 10 Differing *w* and differing measures
20: 23 The LORD detests differing *w*,
Mic 6: 11 with a bag of false *w*?

WEIGHTY (WEIGH)

2Co 10: 10 "His letters are *w* and forceful,

WELCOME (WELCOMED WELCOMES)

Jdg 19: 20 "You are *w* at my house,"
Mt 10: 14 If anyone will not *w* you
Mk 6: 11 And if any place will not *w* you
9: 37 welcomes me does not *w* me
Lk 9: 5 If people do not *w* you, shake
9: 53 but the people there did not *w* him,
16: 4 people will *w* me into their houses.'
Ac 18: 27 to the disciples there to *w* him.
Php 2: 29 *W* him in the Lord with great joy,
Col 4: 10 if he comes to you, *w* him.)
Phm : 17 *w* him as you would *w* me.
2Pe 1: 11 and you will receive a rich *w*
2Jn : 10 him into your house or *w* him.
3Jn : 10 he refuses to *w* the brothers.

WELCOMED (WELCOME)

Jdg 19: 3 father saw him, he gladly *w* him.
Ps 21: 3 You *w* him with rich blessings
Lk 8: 40 Jesus returned, a crowd *w* him,
9: 11 He *w* them and spoke
10: 8 "When you enter a town and are *w*,
10: 10 you enter a town and are not *w*,
16: 9 you will be *w* into eternal dwellings
19: 6 down at once and *w* him gladly.
Jn 4: 45 in Galilee, the Galileans *w* him.
Ac 15: 4 they were *w* by the church
17: 7 Jason has *w* them into his house.
28: 2 They built a fire and *w* us all
28: 7 He *w* us to his home
28: 30 and *w* all who came to see him.
2Co 8: 17 For Titus not only *w* our appeal,
Gal 4: 14 you *w* me as if I were an angel
1Th 1: 6 you *w* the message
Heb 11: 13 and *w* them from a distance.
11: 31 Rahab, because she *w* the spies,

WELCOMES (WELCOME)

Mt 18: 5 this in my name *w* me.
Mt 18: 5 whoever *w* a little child like this
Mk 9: 37 children in my name *w* me;
9: 37 whoever *w* me does not welcome
9: 37 "Whoever *w* one of these little
Lk 9: 48 child in my name *w* me;
9: 48 whoever *w* me *w* the one who sent
9: 48 "Whoever *w* this little child
15: 2 "This man *w* sinners and eats
2Jn : 11 Anyone who *w* him shares

WELDING

Isa 41: 7 He says of the *w*, "It is good."

WELFARE

Ezr 9: 12 Do not further their *w*
Ne 2: 10 to promote the *w* of the Israelites.
Est 10: 3 spoke up for the *w* of all the Jews.
Php 2: 20 takes a genuine interest in your *w*.

WELL (WELL'S WELLED WELLING WELLS)

Ge 16: 14 the *w* was called Beer Lahai Roi;
21: 19 opened her eyes and she saw a *w*
21: 25 to Abimelech about a *w*
21: 30 as a witness that I dug this *w*."
24: 11 down near the *w* outside the town;
24: 20 back to the *w* to draw more water,
26: 19 discovered a *w* of fresh water there.
26: 20 So he named the *w* Esek,
26: 21 Then they dug another *w*,
26: 22 on from there and dug another *w*,
26: 25 and there his servants dug a *w*
26: 32 told him about the *w* they had dug.
29: 2 There he saw a *w* in the field,
29: 2 flocks were watered from that *w*.
29: 2 over the mouth of the *w* was large.
29: 3 to its place over the mouth of the *w*
29: 6 "Is he *w*?" "Yes, he is," they said,
29: 8 away from the mouth of the *w*.
29: 10 away from the mouth of the *w*
Ex 2: 15 where he sat down by a *w*.
Nu 20: 17 or drink water from any *w*.
21: 16 the *w* where the LORD said
21: 17 "Spring up, O *w*!
21: 18 about the *w* that the princes dug,
21: 22 or drink water from any *w*.
2Sa 3: 26 back from the *w* of Sirah
17: 18 He had a *w* in his courtyard,
17: 19 out over the opening of the *w*
17: 21 the two climbed out of the *w*
23: 15 of water from the *w* near the gate
23: 16 water from the *w* near the gate
2Ki 10: 14 by the *w* of Beth Eked—
1Ch 11: 17 of water from the *w* near the gate
11: 18 water from the *w* near the gate
Ne 2: 13 Gate toward the Jackal *W*
Pr 5: 15 running water from your own *w*.
23: 27 and a wayward wife is a narrow *w*.
25: 26 a muddied spring or a polluted *w*
Ecc 12: 6 or the wheel broken at the *w*,
SS 4: 15 a *w* of flowing water
Jer 6: 7 As a *w* pours out its water,
Hos 13: 15 and his *w* dry up.
Mt 15: 31 crippled made *w*, the lame walking
Mk 16: 18 on sick people, and they will get *w*
Lk 7: 10 the house and found the servant *w*.
14: 5 falls into a *w* on the Sabbath day,
17: 19 your faith has made you *w*."
Jn 4: 6 Jacob's *w* was there, and Jesus,
4: 6 the journey, sat down by the *w*.
4: 11 to draw with and the *w* is deep.
4: 12 who gave us the *w* and drank
5: 6 "Do you want to get *w*?" "Sir,"
5: 11 "The man who made me *w* said
5: 14 said to him, "See, you are *w* again.
5: 15 it was Jesus who had made him *w*.
Jas 5: 15 in faith will make the sick person *w*

WELL-BEING

Ezr 6: 10 and pray for the *w* of the king
Ps 35: 27 who delights in the *w* of his servant
119: 122 Ensure your servant's *w*;
Jer 14: 11 Do not pray for the *w* of this people

WELL-BUILT (BUILD)

Ge 39: 6 Now Joseph was *w* and handsome,

WELL-DRESSED (DRESS)

Isa 3: 24 instead of *w* hair, baldness;

WELL-FED (FEED)

Jer 5: 8 They are *w*, lusty stallions,

WELL-KNEADED (KNEAD)

Lev 7: 12 and cakes of fine flour *w* and mixed

WELL-KNOWN (KNOW)

Nu 16: 2 *w* community leaders who had

WELL-MIXED (MIX)

Lev 6: 21 bring it *w* and present the grain

WELL-NOURISHED (NOURISH)

Ne 9: 25 They ate to the full and were *w*;

WELL-NURTURED (NURTURED)

Ps 144: 12 will be like *w* plants,

WELL-TO-DO

2Ki 4: 8 And a *w* woman was there,

WELL-TRAINED (TRAIN)

2Ch 26: 11 Uzziah had a *w* army, ready

WELL-WATERED (WATER)

Job 8: 16 He is like a *w* plant in the sunshine,
Isa 58: 11 You will be like a *w* garden,
Jer 31: 12 They will be like a *w* garden,
Eze 31: 14 No other trees so *w* are ever
31: 16 trees that were *w*, were consoled
45: 15 from the *w* pastures of Israel.

WELL'S (WELL)

Ge 29: 3 away from the *w* mouth

WELLED (WELL)

2Co 8: 2 and their extreme poverty *w* up

WELLING (WELL)

Jn 4: 14 of water *w* up to eternal life."

WELLS (WELL)

Ge 26: 15 all the *w* that his father's servants
26: 18 Isaac reopened the *w* that had been
Dt 6: 11 you did not provide, *w* you did not
10: 6 from the *w* of the Jaakanites
2Ki 19: 24 I have dug *w* in foreign lands
Ne 9: 25 *w* already dug, vineyards, olive
Isa 12: 3 from the *w* of salvation.
37: 25 I have dug *w* in foreign lands

WELLSPRING (SPRING)

Pr 4: 23 for it is the *w* of life.

WELTS

Isa 1: 6 only wounds and *w*

WEPT (WEEP)

Ge 27: 38 my father!" Then Esau *w* aloud.
33: 4 And they *w*.
37: 35 So his father *w* for him.
43: 30 into his private room and *w* there.
45: 2 he *w* so loudly that the Egyptians
45: 14 around his brother Benjamin and *w*
45: 15 he kissed all his brothers and *w*
46: 29 arms around his father and *w*
50: 1 and *w* over him and kissed him.
50: 17 message came to him, Joseph *w*.
Nu 14: 1 raised their voices and *w* aloud.
Dt 1: 45 You came back and *w*
Jdg 2: 4 the people *w* aloud, and they called
11: 38 *w* because she would never marry.
20: 23 *w* before the LORD until evening,
Ru 1: 9 she kissed them and they *w* aloud
1: 14 against me!" At this they *w* again.
1Sa 1: 7 her rival provoked her till she *w*
1: 10 bitterness of soul Hannah *w* much
11: 4 to the people, they all *w* aloud.
20: 41 kissed each other and *w* together—
20: 41 together—but David *w* the most.
24: 16 David my son?" And he *w* aloud.
30: 4 his men *w* aloud until they had no
2Sa 1: 12 *w* and fasted till evening for Saul
3: 32 All the people *w* also.
3: 32 the king *w* aloud at Abner's tomb.

2Sa 3:34 all the people *w* over him again.
12:21 *w*, but now that the child is dead,
12:22 child was still alive, I fasted and *w*.
13:36 and all his servants *w* very bitterly.
15:23 The whole countryside *w* aloud
18:33 the room over the gateway and *w*.
2Ki 13:14 down to see him and *w* over him.
20: 3 And Hezekiah *w* bitterly.
22:19 because you tore your robes and *w*
2Ch 34:27 and tore your robes and *w*
Ezr 3:12 *w* aloud when they saw
10: 1 They too *w* bitterly.
Ne 1: 4 these things, I sat down and *w*.
Job 30:25 Have I not *w* for those in trouble?
Ps 137: 1 of Babylon we sat and *w*
Isa 38: 3 And Hezekiah *w* bitterly.
Hos 12: 4 he *w* and begged for his favor.
Mt 26:75 And he went outside and *w* bitterly
Mk 14:72 And he broke down and *w*.
Lk 19:41 he *w* over it and said, "If you,
22:62 And he went outside and *w* bitterly
Jn 11:35 Jesus *w*.
20:11 As she *w*, she bent over to look
Ac 20:37 They all *w* as they embraced him
Rev 5: 4 I *w* and *w* because no one was

WEST (NORTHWEST SOUTHWEST WESTERN WESTWARD)

Ge 12: 8 with Bethel on the *w* and Ai
13:14 look north and south, east and *w*.
28:14 and you will spread out to the *w*
Ex 10:19 the wind to a very strong *w* wind,
26:22 that is, the *w* end of the tabernacle,
26:27 and five for the frames on the *w*,
27:12 *w* end of the courtyard shall be fifty
36:27 that is, the *w* end of the tabernacle,
36:32 and five for the frames on the *w*,
38:12 The *w* end was fifty cubits wide
Nu 2:18 On the *w* will be the divisions
3:23 clans were to camp on the *w*,
34: 6 will be your boundary on the *w*.
35: 5 three thousand on the *w*
Dt 3:27 and look *w* and north and south
11:30 across the Jordan, *w* of the road,
Jos 1: 4 and to the Great Sea on the *w*.
5: 1 Now when all the Amorite kings *w*
8: 9 to the *w* of Ai—but Joshua spent
8:12 and Ai, to the *w* of the city.
8:13 and the ambush to the *w* of it.
9: 1 Now when all the kings *w*
11: 2 and in Naphoth Dor on the *w*;
11: 3 to the Canaanites in the east and *w*;
12: 7 on the *w* side of the Jordan,
15: 8 of the hill *w* of the Hinnom Valley
15:46 settlements and villages; *w*
16: 8 From Tappuah the border went *w*
18:12 and headed *w* into the hill country,
18:15 Kiriath Jearim on the *w*,
19:11 Going *w* it ran to Maralah,
19:26 On the *w* the boundary touched
19:34 Asher on the *w* and the Jordan
19:34 The boundary ran *w*
22: 7 land on the *w* side of the Jordan
23: 4 and the Great Sea in the *w*.
Jdg 18:12 This is why the place *w*
20:33 of its place on the *w* of Gibeah.
2Sa 13:34 people on the road *w* of him,
1Ki 4:24 ruled over all the kingdoms *w*
7:25 three facing north, three facing *w*,
1Ch 7:28 Gezer and its villages to the *w*,
9:24 were on the four sides: east, *w*,
12:15 to the east and to the *w*.
26:16 The lots for the *W* Gate
26:18 the court to the *w*, there were four
26:30 in Israel *w* of the Jordan
2Ch 4: 4 three facing north, three facing *w*,
32:30 down to the *w* side of the City
33:14 *w* of the Gihon spring in the valley,
Job 18:20 Men of the *w* are appalled
23: 8 if I go to the *w*, I do not find him.
Ps 75: 6 No one from the east or the *w*
103: 12 as far as the east is from the *w*,
107: 3 from east and *w*, from north
Isa 9:12 Philistines from the *w*
11:14 on the slopes of Philistia to the *w*;
24:14 from the *w* they acclaim
43: 5 and gather you from the *w*.
49:12 from the north, some from the *w*,
59:19 From the *w*, men will fear the name
Eze 41:12 on the *w* side was seventy cubits
42:19 Then he turned to the *w* side
45: 7 extend westward from the *w* side
47:20 This will be the *w* boundary.
47:20 "On the *w* side, the Great Sea will
48: 1 from the east side to the *w* side.
48: 2 the territory of Dan from east to *w*.
48: 3 territory of Asher from east to *w*.
48: 4 of Naphtali from east to *w*.
48: 5 of Manasseh from east to *w*.
48: 6 of Ephraim from east to *w*.
48: 7 territory of Reuben from east to *w*.
48: 8 east to *w* will be the portion you are
48: 8 length from east to *w* will equal one
48:10 cubits wide on the *w* side, 10,000
48:16 cubits, and the *w* side 4,500 cubits.
48:17 on the east, and 250 cubits on the *w*
48:18 and 10,000 cubits on the *w* side.
48:23 from the east side to the *w* side.
48:24 of Benjamin from east to *w*.
48:25 territory of Simeon from east to *w*.
48:26 territory of Issachar from east to *w*.
48:27 territory of Zebulun from east to *w*.
48:34 "On the *w* side, which is 4,500
Da 8: 4 as he charged toward the *w*
8: 5 between his eyes came from the *w*,
Hos 11:10 will come trembling from the *w*.
Zec 6: 6 with the white horses toward the *w*
8: 7 the countries of the east and the *w*.
14: 4 split in two from east to *w*,
Mt 8:11 come from the east and the *w*,
24:27 from the east and flashes to the *w*,
Lk 12:54 you see a cloud rising in the *w*,
13:29 and *w* and north and south,
Rev 21:13 on the south and three on the *w*.

WESTERN (WEST)

Nu 34: 6 Your *w* boundary will be the coast
Dt 1: 7 in the mountains, in the *w* foothills,
3:17 Its *w* border was the Jordan
11:24 the Euphrates River to the *w* sea.
34: 2 land of Judah as far as the *w* sea,
Jos 9: 1 the hill country, in the *w* foothills,
10:40 the *w* foothills and the mountain
11: 2 *w* foothills and in Naphoth Dor
11:16 region of Goshen, the *w* foothills,
12: 8 the *w* foothills, the Arabah,
15:12 The *w* boundary is the coastline
15:33 In the *w* foothills: Eshtaol, Zorah,
18:14 This was the *w* side.
18:14 turned south along the *w* side
Jdg 1: 9 the Negev and the *w* foothills.
1Ch 27:28 trees in the *w* foothills.
Jer 17:26 of Benjamin and the *w* foothills,
32:44 of the *w* foothills and of the Negev,
33:13 of the *w* foothills and of the Negev,
Eze 45: 7 running lengthwise from the *w*
46:19 showed me a place at the *w* end.
48:21 the 25,000 cubits to the *w* border.
Da 11:30 of the *w* coastlands will oppose him
Joel 2:20 and those in the rear into the *w* sea.
Zec 7: 7 and the *w* foothills were settled?' "
14: 8 eastern sea and half to the *w* sea,

WESTWARD (WEST)

Jos 15:10 Then it curved *w* from Baalah
16: 3 descended *w* to the territory
Eze 45: 7 It will extend *w* from the west side
48:21 and *w* from the 25,000 cubits

WET

Job 31:38 and all its furrows are *w* with tears,
Lk 7:38 she began to *w* his feet
7:44 but she *w* my feet with her tears

WHEAT

Ge 30:14 During *w* harvest, Reuben went
Ex 9:32 The *w* and spelt, however,
29: 2 from fine *w* flour, without yeast,
34:22 with the firstfruits of the *w* harvest,
Dt 8: 8 a land with *w* and barley, vines
32:14 and the finest kernels of *w*.
Jdg 6:11 his son Gideon was threshing *w*
15: 1 Later on, at the time of *w* harvest,
Ru 2:23 and *w* harvests were finished.
1Sa 6:13 were harvesting their *w*
12:17 Is it not *w* harvest now? I will call
2Sa 4: 6 of the house as if to get some *w*,
17:28 They also brought *w* and barley,
1Ki 5:11 Hiram twenty thousand cors of *w*
1Ch 21:20 While Araunah was threshing *w*,
21:23 and the *w* for the grain offering.
2Ch 2:10 twenty thousand cors of ground *w*,
2:15 let my lord send his servants the *w*
27: 5 ten thousand cors of *w*
Ezr 6: 9 to the God of heaven, and *w*,
7:22 cors of *w*, a hundred baths
Job 31:40 then let briers come up instead of *w*
Ps 81:16 with the finest of *w*;
147: 14 satisfies you with the finest of *w*.
SS 7: 2 Your waist is a mound of *w*
Isa 28:25 Does he not plant *w* in its place,
Jer 12:13 They will sow *w* but reap thorns;
41: 8 "Don't kill us! We have *w*
Eze 4: 9 "Take *w* and barley, beans
27:17 they exchanged *w* from Minnith
45:13 of an ephah from each homer of *w*
Joel 1:11 grieve for the *w* and the barley,
Am 8: 5 that we may market *w*?"—
8: 6 even the sweepings with the *w*.
Mt 3:12 gathering the *w* into his barn
13:25 and sowed weeds among the *w*,
13:26 When the *w* sprouted and formed
13:29 you may root up the *w* with them.
13:30 then gather the *w* and bring it
Lk 3:17 and to gather the *w* into his barn,
16: 7 " 'A thousand bushels of *w*,'
22:31 Satan has asked to sift you as *w*.
Jn 12:24 a kernel of *w* falls to the ground
1Co 15:37 perhaps of *w* or of something else.
Rev 6: 6 "A quart of *w* for a day's wages,
18:13 of fine flour and *w*; cattle and sheep

WHEEL (WHEELS)

1Ki 7:32 The diameter of each *w* was a cubit
22:34 "*W* around and get me out
2Ch 18:33 "*W* around and get me out
Pr 20:26 he drives the threshing *w*
Ecc 12: 6 or the *w* broken at the well,
Jer 18: 3 and I saw him working at the *w*.
Eze 1:15 I saw a *w* on the ground
1:16 to be made like a *w* intersecting a *w*
10: 6 went in and stood beside a *w*.
10:10 each was like a *w* intersecting a *w*.

WHEELS (WHEEL)

Ex 14:25 He made the *w* of their chariots
1Ki 7:30 Each stand had four bronze *w*
7:32 The four *w* were under the panels,
7:32 the axles of the *w* were attached
7:33 The *w* were made like chariot *w*;
Isa 5:28 their chariot *w* like a whirlwind.
28:28 Though he drives the *w*
Jer 47: 3 and the rumble of their *w*.
Eze 1:16 appearance and structure of the *w*:
1:17 the *w* did not turn about
1:19 rose from the ground, the *w*
1:19 the *w* beside them moved;
1:20 of the living creatures was in the *w*.
1:20 the *w* would rise along with them,
1:21 of the living creatures was in the *w*.
1:21 the *w* rose along with them,
3:13 the sound of the *w* beside them,
10: 2 among the *w* beneath the cherubim
10: 6 "Take fire from among the *w*,
10: 9 I saw beside the cherubim four *w*,
10: 9 the *w* sparkled like chrysolite.
10:11 the *w* did not turn about
10:12 full of eyes, as were their four *w*.
10:13 I heard the *w* being called
10:13 being called "the whirling *w*."
10:16 the *w* beside them moved;
10:16 the *w* did not leave their side.
10:19 as they went, the *w* went with them
11:22 with the *w* beside them,
Da 7: 9 and its *w* were all ablaze.
Na 3: 2 the clatter of *w*,

WHIP (WHIPS)

Pr 26: 3 A *w* for the horse, a halter
Isa 10:26 Almighty will lash them with a *w*,
Jn 2:15 So he made a *w* out of cords,
1Co 4:21 Shall I come to you with a *w*,

WHIPS (WHIP)

Jos 23: 13 *w* on your backs and thorns
1Ki 12: 11 My father scourged you with *w;*
12: 14 My father scourged you with *w;*
2Ch 10: 11 My father scourged you with *w;*
10: 14 My father scourged you with *w;*
Na 3: 2 The crack of *w,*

WHIRLING

Eze 10: 13 being called "the *w* wheels."

WHIRLWIND (WIND)

2Ki 2: 1 to take Elijah up to heaven in a *w,*
2: 11 and Elijah went up to heaven in a *w*
Ps 77: 18 Your thunder was heard in the *w,*
Pr 1: 27 disaster sweeps over you like a *w,*
Isa 5: 28 their chariot wheels like a *w.*
40: 24 a *w* sweeps them away like chaff.
66: 15 and his chariots are like a *w;*
Jer 4: 13 his chariots come like a *w,*
23: 19 a *w* swirling down
Hos 4: 19 A *w* will sweep them away,
8: 7 and reap the *w.*
Na 1: 3 His way is in the *w* and the storm,
Zec 7: 14 with a *w* among all the nations,

WHIRLWINDS (WIND)

Isa 21: 1 *w* sweeping through the southland,

WHIRRING

Isa 18: 1 Woe to the land of *w* wings

WHISPER (WHISPERED WHISPERING)

1Ki 19: 12 And after the fire came a gentle *w.*
Job 4: 12 my ears caught a *w* of it.
26: 14 how faint the *w* we hear of him!
Ps 41: 7 All my enemies *w* together
107: 29 He stilled the storm to a *w;*
Isa 8: 19 and spiritists, who *w* and mutter,
26: 16 they could barely *w* a prayer.
29: 4 out of the dust your speech will *w.*
La 3: 62 what my enemies *w* and mutter

WHISPERED (WHISPER)

Mt 10: 27 speak in the daylight; what is *w*
Lk 12: 3 and what you have *w* in the ear

WHISPERING (WHISPER)

2Sa 12: 19 noticed that his servants were *w*
Jer 20: 10 I hear many *w,*
Jn 7: 12 there was widespread *w* about him.
7: 32 heard the crowd *w* such things

WHISTLE (WHISTLES WHISTLING)

Isa 7: 18 In that day the LORD will *w*

WHISTLES (WHISTLE)

Isa 5: 26 he *w* for those at the ends

WHISTLING (WHISTLE)

Jdg 5: 16 to hear the *w* for the flocks?

WHITE (REDDISH-WHITE WHITER)

Ge 30: 35 spotted female goats (all that had *w*
30: 37 and exposing the *w* inner wood
30: 37 and made *w* stripes on them
Ex 16: 31 It was *w* like coriander seed
Lev 11: 18 the great owl, the *w* owl, the desert
13: 3 if the hair in the sore has turned *w*
13: 4 If the spot on his skin is *w*
13: 4 and the hair in it has not turned *w,*
13: 10 and if there is a *w* swelling
13: 10 the skin that has turned the hair *w*
13: 13 Since it has all turned *w,* he is clean
13: 16 the raw flesh change and turn *w,*
13: 17 and if the sores have turned *w,*
13: 19 a *w* swelling or reddish-white spot
13: 20 and the hair in it has turned *w,*
13: 21 there is no *w* hair in it and it is not
13: 24 or *w* spot appears in the raw flesh
13: 25 and if the hair in it has turned *w,*
13: 26 and there is no *w* hair in the spot
13: 38 or woman has *w* spots on the skin,
13: 39 and if the spots are dull *w,*
Dt 14: 16 the great owl, the *w* owl, the desert
Jdg 5: 10 "You who ride on *w* donkeys,
2Ki 5: 27 and he was leprous, as *w* as snow.
Est 1: 6 The garden had hangings of *w*
Est 1: 6 fastened with cords of *w* linen
8: 15 royal garments of blue and *w,*
Job 6: 6 or is there flavor in the *w* of an egg?
41: 32 would think the deep had *w* hair.
Ecc 9: 8 Always be clothed in *w,*
Isa 1: 18 they shall be as *w* as snow;
Da 7: 9 His clothing was as *w* as snow;
7: 9 the hair of his head was *w* like wool
Joel 1: 7 leaving their branches *w.*
Zec 1: 8 him were red, brown and *w* horses.
6: 3 the third *w,* and the fourth dappled
6: 6 the one with the *w* horses
Mt 5: 36 you cannot make even one hair *w*
17: 2 his clothes became as *w* as the light
28: 3 and his clothes were *w* as snow.
Mk 9: 3 His clothes became dazzling *w,*
16: 5 in a *w* robe sitting on the right side,
Jn 20: 12 the tomb and saw two angels in *w,*
Ac 1: 10 dressed in *w* stood beside them.
Rev 1: 14 hair were *w* like wool, as *w* as snow,
2: 17 also give him a *w* stone
3: 4 dressed in *w,* for they are worthy.
3: 5 like them, be dressed in *w.*
3: 18 you can become rich; and *w* clothes
4: 4 They were dressed in *w*
6: 2 and there before me was a *w* horse!
6: 11 each of them was given a *w* robe,
7: 9 They were wearing *w* robes
7: 13 "These in *w* robes—who are they,
7: 14 and made them *w* in the blood
14: 14 and there before me was a *w* cloud,
19: 11 and there before me was a *w* horse,
19: 14 dressed in fine linen, *w* and clean.
19: 14 riding on *w* horses and dressed
20: 11 Then I saw a great *w* throne

WHITER (WHITE)

Ge 49: 12 his teeth *w* than milk.
Ps 51: 7 and I will be *w* than snow.
La 4: 7 and *w* than milk,
Mk 9: 3 *w* than anyone in the world could

WHITEWASH (WASH)

Eze 13: 10 wall is built, they cover it with *w,*
13: 11 it with *w* that it is going
13: 12 Where is the *w* you covered it with
13: 14 the wall you have covered with *w*
13: 15 those who covered it with *w.*
22: 28 Her prophets *w* these deeds

WHITEWASHED (WASH)

Eze 13: 15 and so are those who *w* it,
Mt 23: 27 hypocrites! You are like *w* tombs,
Ac 23: 3 "God will strike you, you *w* wall!

WHOLE

Ge 1: 29 plant on the face of the *w* earth
2: 6 and watered the *w* surface
7: 1 into the ark, you and your *w* family
11: 1 Now the *w* world had one language
11: 4 over the face of the *w* earth."
11: 9 the language of the *w* world.
11: 9 them over the face of the *w* earth.
13: 9 Is not the *w* land before you?
13: 10 and saw that the *w* plain
13: 11 chose for himself the *w* plain
14: 7 and they conquered the *w* territory
17: 8 *w* land of Canaan, where you are
18: 26 I will spare the *w* place
18: 28 Will you destroy the *w* city
25: 25 his *w* body was like a hairy garment
29: 14 stayed with him for a *w* month,
41: 41 in charge of the *w* land of Egypt."
41: 43 in charge of the *w* land of Egypt.
41: 54 in the *w* land of Egypt there was
41: 56 spread over the *w* country,
47: 13 in the *w* region because the famine
Ex 8: 2 I will plague your *w* country
9: 9 dust over the *w* land of Egypt,
12: 3 Tell the *w* community of Israel that
12: 4 is too small for a *w* lamb,
12: 47 The *w* community
16: 1 The *w* Israelite community set out
16: 2 desert the *w* community grumbled
16: 10 to the *w* Israelite community,
17: 1 The *w* Israelite community set out
19: 5 Although the *w* earth is mine,
19: 18 the *w* mountain trembled violently,
Ex 22: 6 or standing grain or the *w* field,
35: 1 assembled the *w* Israelite
35: 4 said to the *w* Israelite community,
35: 20 *w* Israelite community withdrew
Lev 4: 13 " 'If the *w* Israelite community sins
8: 21 and burned the *w* ram on the altar
10: 6 angry with the *w* community.
13: 13 the disease has covered his *w* body,
15: 16 he must bathe his *w* body
16: 17 and the *w* community of Israel.
Nu 1: 2 of the *w* Israelite community
1: 18 called the *w* community together
3: 7 for the *w* community at the Tent
8: 7 have them shave their *w* bodies
8: 9 and assemble the *w* Israelite
8: 20 and the *w* Israelite community did
10: 3 the *w* community is to assemble
11: 20 twenty days, but for a *w* month—
11: 21 meat to eat for a *w* month!'
13: 26 and the *w* Israelite community
13: 26 to them and to the *w* assembly
14: 2 and the *w* assembly said to them,
14: 5 front of the *w* Israelite assembly
14: 10 *w* assembly talked about stoning
14: 21 of the LORD fills the *w* earth,
14: 35 to this *w* wicked community,
14: 36 made the *w* community grumble
15: 24 then the *w* community is
15: 25 for the *w* Israelite community,
15: 26 The *w* Israelite community
15: 33 and Aaron and the *w* assembly,
15: 35 The *w* assembly must stone him
16: 3 The *w* community is holy,
16: 41 next day the *w* Israelite community
20: 1 month the *w* Israelite community
20: 22 The *w* Israelite community set out
20: 27 in the sight of the *w* community.
20: 29 when the *w* community learned
21: 33 and his *w* army marched out
21: 34 with his *w* army and his land.
21: 35 with his sons and his *w* army,
25: 6 and the *w* assembly of Israel
26: 2 of the *w* Israelite community
27: 2 the leaders and the *w* assembly,
27: 20 so the *w* Israelite community will
27: 22 the priest and the *w* assembly
32: 13 until the *w* generation
32: 33 the *w* land with its cities
Dt 2: 33 with his sons and his *w* army.
3: 1 with his *w* army marched out
3: 2 him over to you with his *w* army
3: 4 *w* region of Argob, Og's kingdom
3: 13 (The *w* region of Argob
3: 14 took the *w* region of Argob as far
5: 22 voice to your *w* assembly there
6: 22 and Pharaoh and his *w* household.
11: 3 king of Egypt and to his *w* country;
11: 25 and fear of you on the *w* land,
13: 16 *w* burnt offering to the LORD your
18: 1 indeed the *w* tribe of Levi—
19: 8 gives you the *w* land he promised
29: 23 The *w* land will be a burning waste
31: 30 hearing of the *w* assembly of Israel:
33: 10 and *w* burnt offerings on your altar.
34: 1 LORD showed him the *w* land—
34: 3 and the *w* region from the Valley
34: 11 to all his officials and to his *w* land.
Jos 2: 3 come to spy out the *w* land."
2: 24 LORD has surely given the *w* land
3: 17 until the *w* nation had completed
4: 1 When the *w* nation had finished
5: 8 And after the *w* nation had been
6: 24 Then they burned the *w* city
8: 1 Take the *w* army with you,
8: 3 the *w* army moved out to attack Ai.
8: 35 read to the *w* assembly of Israel,
9: 18 The *w* assembly grumbled
9: 24 Moses to give you the *w* land
10: 21 The *w* army then returned safely
10: 40 So Joshua subdued the *w* region,
10: 41 and from the *w* region of Goshen
11: 7 *w* army came against them
11: 16 all the Negev, the *w* region
13: 9 included the *w* plateau of Medeba
13: 12 the *w* kingdom of Og in Bashan,
13: 16 and the *w* plateau past Medeba
18: 1 The *w* assembly of the Israelites
22: 12 the *w* assembly of Israel gathered

Jos 22: 16 The *w* assembly of the LORD says:
22: 18 with the *w* community of Israel.
22: 20 upon the *w* community of Israel?
Jdg 1: 25 spared the man and his *w* family.
2: 10 After that *w* generation had been
7: 14 and the *w* camp into his hands.''
9: 29 'Call out your *w* army!' ''
14: 17 She cried the *w* seven days
16: 31 and his father's *w* family went
20: 37 and put the *w* city to the sword.
20: 40 the smoke of the *w* city going up
Ru 1: 19 the *w* town was stirred
1Sa 1: 28 For his *w* life he will be given
4: 13 had happened, the *w* town sent up
7: 3 said to the *w* house of Israel,
7: 9 as a *w* burnt offering to the LORD.
13: 19 found in the *w* land of Israel,
14: 15 Then panic struck the *w* army—
17: 46 the *w* world will know that there is
19: 7 and told him the *w* conversation.
20: 6 is being made there for his *w* clan.'
22: 11 of Ahitub and his father's *w* family,
22: 15 nothing at all about this *w* affair.''
22: 16 you and your father's *w* family.''
22: 22 the death of your father's *w* family.
25: 7 and the *w* time they were
25: 15 the *w* time we were out in the fields
25: 17 our master and his *w* household.
2Sa 2: 29 continued through the *w* Bithron
3: 19 the *w* house of Benjamin wanted
6: 5 *w* house of Israel were celebrating
6: 19 person in the *w* crowd of Israelites,
11: 1 men and the *w* Israelite army.
14: 7 Now the *w* clan has risen up
15: 23 The *w* countryside wept aloud
18: 8 out over the *w* countryside,
19: 2 for the *w* army the victory that day
19: 20 as the first of the *w* house of Joseph
1Ki 6: 22 he overlaid the *w* interior with gold
8: 14 While the *w* assembly
8: 22 in front of the *w* assembly of Israel,
8: 55 blessed the *w* assembly of Israel
10: 24 The *w* world sought audience
11: 13 Yet I will not tear the *w* kingdom
11: 28 him in charge of the *w* labor force
11: 34 I will not take the *w* kingdom out
12: 3 and the *w* assembly of Israel went
12: 21 he mustered the *w* house of Judah
12: 23 to the *w* house of Judah
15: 29 he killed Jeroboam's *w* family.
16: 11 he killed off Baasha's *w* family.
16: 12 So Zimri destroyed the *w* family
2Ki 7: 15 and they found the *w* road strewn
9: 8 The *w* house of Ahab will perish.
11: 1 to destroy the *w* royal family.
21: 8 and will keep the *w* Law that my
25: 1 against Jerusalem with his *w* army.
25: 4 and the *w* army fled at night
25: 10 The *w* Babylonian army,
1Ch 11: 10 to extend it over the *w* land,
13: 2 said to the *w* assembly of Israel,
13: 4 The *w* assembly agreed to do this,
28: 4 chose me from my *w* family
29: 1 King David said to the *w* assembly:
29: 10 in the presence of the *w* assembly,
29: 20 Then David said to the *w* assembly,
2Ch 1: 3 and the *w* assembly went
6: 3 While the *w* assembly
6: 12 in front of the *w* assembly of Israel
6: 13 knelt down before the *w* assembly
15: 8 idols from the *w* land of Judah
22: 10 to destroy the *w* royal family
23: 3 the *w* assembly made a covenant
29: 28 The *w* assembly bowed in worship,
30: 2 *w* assembly in Jerusalem decided
30: 4 to the king and to the *w* assembly.
30: 23 The *w* assembly then agreed
31: 18 of the *w* community listed
Ezr 2: 64 The *w* company numbered 42,360,
4: 20 over the *w* of Trans-Euphrates,
10: 12 The *w* assembly responded
10: 14 act for the *w* assembly.
Ne 5: 13 At this the *w* assembly said,
7: 66 The *w* company numbered 42,360,
8: 17 The *w* company that had returned
Est 3: 6 throughout the *w* kingdom
Job 17: 7 my *w* frame is but a shadow.
34: 13 him in charge of the *w* world?

Job 37: 3 beneath the *w* heaven
37: 12 around over the face of the *w* earth
Ps 35: 10 My *w* being will exclaim,
48: 2 the joy of the *w* earth.
51: 19 *w* burnt offerings to delight you;
72: 19 may the *w* earth be filled
110: 6 crushing the rulers of the *w* earth.
Pr 1: 12 and *w*, like those who go
4: 22 and health to a man's *w* body.
5: 14 in the midst of the *w* assembly.''
8: 31 rejoicing in his *w* world
Ecc 12: 13 for this is the *w* duty of man.
Isa 1: 5 Your *w* head is injured,
1: 5 your *w* heart afflicted.
6: 3 the *w* earth is full of his glory.''
10: 23 decreed upon the *w* land.
13: 5 to destroy the *w* country.
14: 26 plan determined for the *w* world;
28: 22 decreed against the *w* land.
29: 11 For you this *w* vision is nothing
31: 4 and though a *w* band of shepherds
Jer 1: 18 wall to stand against the *w* land—
4: 20 the *w* land lies in ruins.
4: 27 ''The *w* land will be ruined,
8: 16 the *w* land trembles.
9: 26 *w* house of Israel is uncircumcised
12: 11 the *w* land will be laid waste
13: 11 and the *w* house of Judah to me,'
13: 11 so I bound the *w* house of Israel
15: 10 man with whom the *w* land strives
25: 11 This *w* country will become
31: 40 The *w* valley where dead bodies
35: 3 the *w* family of the Recabites.
39: 1 against Jerusalem with his *w* army
40: 4 Look, the *w* country lies before you
44: 28 the *w* remnant of Judah who came
50: 23 is the hammer of the *w* earth!
51: 7 she made the *w* earth drunk.
51: 25 you who destroy the *w* earth,''
51: 41 the boast of the *w* earth seized!
51: 47 her *w* land will be disgraced
52: 4 against Jerusalem with his *w* army.
52: 7 through, and the *w* army fled.
52: 14 The *w* Babylonian army
La 2: 15 the joy of the *w* earth?''
Eze 3: 7 for the *w* house of Israel is
5: 4 from there to the *w* house of Israel.
7: 12 for wrath is upon the *w* crowd.
7: 13 vision concerning the *w* crowd will
7: 14 for my wrath is upon the *w* crowd.
11: 15 and the *w* house of Israel—
12: 10 the *w* house of Israel who are there
15: 5 useful for anything when it was *w*,
32: 22 ''Assyria is there with her *w* army;
34: 6 were scattered over the *w* earth,
35: 14 While the *w* earth rejoices,
36: 10 even the *w* house of Israel.
37: 11 these bones are the *w* house
38: 4 bring you out with your *w* army—
41: 19 all around the *w* temple.
43: 11 its *w* design and all its regulations
45: 6 belong to the *w* house of Israel.
Da 1: 20 and enchanters in his *w* kingdom.
2: 35 mountain and filled the *w* earth.
2: 39 of bronze, will rule over the *w* earth
4: 20 visible to the *w* earth,
6: 3 to set him over the *w* kingdom.
7: 23 and will devour the *w* earth,
7: 27 under the *w* heaven will be handed
8: 5 crossing the *w* earth
9: 12 Under the *w* heaven nothing has
Am 1: 6 she took captive *w* communities
1: 9 Because she sold *w* communities
3: 1 against the *w* family I brought up
8: 8 The *w* land will rise like the Nile;
9: 5 the *w* land rises like the Nile,
Hab 1: 6 who sweep across the *w* earth
Zep 1: 18 the *w* world will be consumed,
3: 8 The *w* world will be consumed
Hag 1: 12 *w* remnant of the people obeyed
1: 14 and the spirit of the *w* remnant
Zec 1: 11 and found the *w* world at rest
5: 3 that is going out over the *w* land;
6: 5 of the Lord of the *w* world.
13: 8 In the *w* land,'' declares the LORD
14: 9 will be king over the *w* earth.
14: 10 The *w* land, from Geba to Rimmon
Mal 3: 9 under a curse—the *w* nation of you

Mal 3: 10 the *w* tithe into the storehouse,
Mt 3: 5 and the *w* region of the Jordan.
5: 29 than for your *w* body to be thrown
5: 30 than for your *w* body to go into hell
6: 22 your *w* body will be full of light.
6: 23 your *w* body will be full of darkness
8: 32 and the *w* herd rushed
8: 34 the *w* town went out to meet Jesus.
16: 26 for a man if he gains the *w* world,
21: 10 the *w* city was stirred and asked,
24: 14 will be preached in the *w* world
26: 59 and the *w* Sanhedrin were looking
27: 27 gathered the *w* company of soldiers
Mk 1: 5 The *w* Judean countryside
1: 28 over the *w* region of Galilee.
1: 33 The *w* town gathered at the door,
5: 33 with fear, told him the *w* truth.
6: 55 They ran throughout that *w* region
8: 36 it for a man to gain the *w* world,
11: 18 because the *w* crowd was amazed
14: 55 and the *w* Sanhedrin were looking
15: 1 of the law and the *w* Sanhedrin,
15: 16 and called together the *w* company
15: 33 over the *w* land until the ninth hour
Lk 4: 14 spread through the *w* countryside.
9: 25 it for a man to gain the *w* world,
11: 34 your *w* body also is full of light.
11: 36 if your *w* body is full of light,
15: 14 a severe famine in that *w* country,
19: 37 *w* crowd of disciples began joyfully
21: 35 live on the face of the *w* earth.
23: 1 Then the *w* assembly rose
23: 44 and darkness came over the *w* land
Jn 7: 23 me for healing the *w* man
11: 50 than that the *w* nation perish.''
12: 19 Look how the *w* world has gone
13: 10 to wash his feet; his *w* body is clean
21: 25 the *w* world would not have room
Ac 1: 21 with us the *w* time the Lord Jesus
2: 2 filled the *w* house where they were
5: 11 Great fear seized the *w* church
6: 5 This proposal pleased the *w* group.
7: 14 his father Jacob and his *w* family,
11: 26 So for a *w* year Barnabas
13: 6 They traveled through the *w* island
13: 44 Sabbath almost the *w* city gathered
13: 49 spread through the *w* region.
15: 12 The *w* assembly became silent
15: 22 and elders, with the *w* church,
16: 34 and the *w* family was filled with joy
17: 26 they should inhabit the *w* earth;
19: 26 and in practically the *w* province
19: 29 Soon the *w* city was in an uproar.
20: 18 know how I lived the *w* time I was
20: 27 proclaim to you the *w* will of God.
21: 27 They stirred up the *w* crowd
21: 30 The *w* city was aroused,
21: 31 of the Roman troops that the *w* city
25: 24 The *w* Jewish community has
28: 30 For two *w* years Paul stayed there
Ro 1: 9 whom I serve with my *w* heart
3: 19 and the *w* world held accountable
8: 22 know that the *w* creation has been
11: 16 then the *w* batch is holy;
16: 23 and the *w* church here enjoy,
1Co 4: 9 made a spectacle to the *w* universe,
5: 6 through the *w* batch of dough?
12: 17 If the *w* body were an ear,
12: 17 If the *w* body were an eye,
14: 23 So if the *w* church comes together
Gal 3: 22 declares that the *w* world is
4: 1 although he owns the *w* estate.
5: 3 obligated to obey the *w* law.
5: 9 through the *w* batch of dough.''
5: 12 I wish they would go the *w* way
Eph 2: 21 In him the *w* building is joined
3: 15 from whom his *w* family in heaven
4: 10 in order to fill the *w* universe.)
4: 13 attaining to the *w* measure
4: 16 From him the *w* body, joined
Php 1: 13 throughout the *w* palace guard
Col 2: 19 from whom the *w* body,
1Th 5: 23 May your *w* spirit, soul
Tit 1: 11 they are ruining *w* households
Jas 2: 10 For whoever keeps the *w* law
3: 2 able to keep his *w* body in check.
3: 3 obey us, we can turn the *w* animal.
3: 6 It corrupts the *w* person, sets

Jas 3: 6 sets the *w* course of his life on fire,
1Jn 2: 2 but also for the sins of the *w* world.
5: 19 and that the *w* world is
Rev 3: 10 going to come upon the *w* world
6: 12 the *w* moon turned blood red,
12: 9 who leads the *w* world astray.
13: 3 The *w* world was astonished
16: 14 out to the kings of the *w* world,

WHOLEHEARTED (HEART)

2Ki 20: 3 you faithfully and with *w* devotion
1Ch 28: 9 and serve him with *w* devotion
29: 19 my son Solomon the *w* devotion
Isa 38: 3 you faithfully and with *w* devotion

WHOLEHEARTEDLY (HEART)

Nu 14: 24 a different spirit and follows me *w*,
32: 11 they have not followed me *w*,
32: 12 for they followed the LORD *w*.'
Dt 1: 36 because he followed the LORD *w*
Jos 14: 8 followed the LORD my God *w*.
14: 9 followed the LORD my God *w*.'
14: 14 the LORD, the God of Israel, *w*.
1Ki 8: 23 with your servants who continue *w*
1Ch 29: 9 for they had given freely and *w*
2Ch 6: 14 with your servants who continue *w*
15: 15 oath because they had sworn it *w*.
19: 9 and *w* in the fear of the LORD.
25: 2 in the eyes of the LORD, but not *w*
31: 21 he sought his God and worked *w*.
Ro 6: 17 you *w* obeyed the form of teaching
Eph 6: 7 Serve *w*, as if you were serving

WHOLESOME

2Ki 2: 22 And the water has remained *w*
2Pe 3: 1 to stimulate you to *w* thinking.

WICK

Ex 25: 38 Its *w* trimmers and trays are to be
37: 23 as well as its *w* trimmers and trays,
Nu 4: 9 with its lamps, its *w* trimmers
1Ki 7: 50 *w* trimmers, sprinkling bowls,
2Ki 12: 13 *w* trimmers, sprinkling bowls,
25: 14 the pots, shovels, *w* trimmers,
2Ch 4: 22 the pure gold *w* trimmers,
Isa 42: 3 a smoldering *w* he will not snuff out
43: 17 extinguished, snuffed out like a *w*:
Jer 52: 18 *w* trimmers, sprinkling bowls,
Mt 12: 20 a smoldering *w* he will not snuff out

WICKED (OVERWICKED WICKEDNESS)

Ge 13: 13 Now the men of Sodom were *w*
18: 23 away the righteous with the *w*?
18: 25 the righteous and the *w* alike.
18: 25 to kill the righteous with the *w*,
19: 7 Don't do this *w* thing.
38: 7 was *w* in the LORD's sight;
38: 10 What he did was *w*
39: 9 How then could I do such a *w* thing
44: 5 This is a *w* thing you have done.' "
Ex 23: 1 Do not help a *w* man
Lev 20: 14 a woman and her mother, it is *w*.
Nu 14: 27 will this *w* community grumble
14: 35 things to this whole *w* community,
16: 26 from the tents of these *w* men!
Dt 13: 13 to live in that *w* men have arisen
15: 9 not to harbor this *w* thought:
Jdg 19: 22 some of the *w* men
20: 13 surrender those *w* men of Gibeah
1Sa 1: 16 take your servant for a *w* woman;
2: 9 the *w* will be silenced in darkness.
2: 12 Eli's sons were *w* men; they had no
2: 23 all the people about these *w* deeds
15: 18 completely destroy those *w* people,
17: 28 you are and how *w* your heart is;
25: 17 He is such a *w* man that no one can
25: 25 attention to that *w* man Nabal.
2Sa 3: 34 You fell as one falls before *w* men.''
4: 11 when *w* men have killed
7: 10 *W* people will not oppress them
13: 12 in Israel! Don't do this *w* thing.
13: 13 one of the *w* fools in Israel.
2Ki 17: 11 They did *w* things that provoked
1Ch 2: 3 was *w* in the LORD's sight;
17: 9 *W* people will not oppress them
2Ch 7: 14 and turn from their *w* ways,
19: 2 "Should you help the *w*
24: 7 sons of that *w* woman Athaliah had

Ezr 4: 12 that rebellious and *w* city.
Ne 13: 17 "What is this *w* thing you are doing
Job 3: 17 There the *w* cease from turmoil,
8: 22 the tents of the *w* will be no more.''
9: 22 both the blameless and the *w*.'
9: 24 into the hands of the *w*,
10: 3 smile on the schemes of the *w*?
11: 20 But the eyes of the *w* will fail,
15: 20 his days the *w* man suffers torment,
16: 11 into the clutches of the *w*.
18: 5 "The lamp of the *w* is snuffed out;
20: 5 that the mirth of the *w* is brief,
20: 29 Such is the fate God allots the *w*,
21: 7 Why do the *w* live on,
21: 16 aloof from the counsel of the *w*.
21: 17 the lamp of the *w* snuffed out?
21: 28 the tents where *w* men lived?'
22: 18 aloof from the counsel of the *w*.
24: 6 and glean in the vineyards of the *w*.
27: 7 "May my enemies be like the *w*,
27: 13 Here is the fate God allots to the *w*,
29: 17 I broke the fangs of the *w*
31: 3 Is it not ruin for the *w*,
34: 8 he associates with *w* men.
34: 18 and to nobles, 'You are *w*,'
34: 36 utmost for answering like a *w* man!
35: 12 because of the arrogance of the *w*.
36: 6 He does not keep the *w* alive
36: 17 with the judgment due the *w*;
38: 13 and shake the *w* out of it?
38: 15 The *w* are denied their light,
40: 12 crush the *w* where they stand.
Ps 1: 1 walk in the counsel of the *w*
1: 4 Not so the *w*!
1: 5 Therefore the *w* will not stand
1: 6 but the way of the *w* will perish.
3: 7 you have broken the teeth of the *w*.
5: 4 with you the *w* cannot dwell.
7: 9 to an end the violence of the *w*
9: 5 the nations and destroyed the *w*;
9: 16 the *w* are ensnared by the work
9: 17 The *w* return to the grave,
10: 2 In his arrogance the *w* man hunts
10: 4 In his pride the *w* does not seek
10: 13 Why does the *w* man revile God?
10: 15 Break the arm of the *w*
11: 2 For look, the *w* bend their bows;
11: 5 the *w* and those who love violence
11: 6 On the *w* he will rain
12: 8 The *w* freely strut about
17: 9 wings from the *w* who assail me,
17: 13 from the *w* by your sword.
21: 11 and devise *w* schemes, they cannot
26: 5 and refuse to sit with the *w*.
26: 10 in whose hands are *w* schemes,
28: 3 Do not drag me away with the *w*,
31: 17 but let the *w* be put to shame
32: 10 Many are the woes of the *w*,
34: 21 Evil will slay the *w*;
36: 1 concerning the sinfulness of the *w*:
36: 3 The words of his mouth are *w*
36: 11 the hand of the *w* drive me away.
37: 7 they carry out their *w* schemes.
37: 10 and the *w* will be no more;
37: 12 The *w* plot against the righteous
37: 13 but the Lord laughs at the *w*,
37: 14 The *w* draw the sword
37: 16 have than the wealth of many *w*;
37: 17 the power of the *w* will be broken,
37: 20 But the *w* will perish:
37: 21 The *w* borrow and do not repay,
37: 28 the offspring of the *w* will be cut off
37: 32 The *w* lie in wait for the righteous,
37: 34 when the *w* are cut
37: 35 I have seen a *w* and ruthless man
37: 38 the future of the *w* will be cut off.
37: 40 he delivers them from the *w*
39: 1 as long as the *w* are in my presence
43: 1 me from deceitful and *w* men.
49: 5 when *w* deceivers surround me—
50: 16 But to the *w*, God says:
55: 3 at the stares of the *w*;
55: 9 Confuse the *w*, O Lord, confound
55: 23 O God, will bring down the *w*
58: 3 Even from birth the *w* go astray;
58: 9 dry—the *w* will be swept away.
58: 10 in the blood of the *w*.
59: 5 show no mercy to *w* traitors.

Ps 64: 2 me from the conspiracy of the *w*,
68: 2 may the *w* perish before God.
71: 4 O my God, from the hand of the *w*,
73: 3 when I saw the prosperity of the *w*.
73: 12 This is what the *w* are like—
75: 4 to the *w*, 'Do not lift up your horns.
75: 8 he pours it out, and all the *w*
75: 10 I will cut off the horns of all the *w*,
82: 2 and show partiality to the *w*? *Selah*
82: 4 from the hand of the *w*.
84: 10 than dwell in the tents of the *w*.
89: 22 no *w* man will oppress him.
91: 8 and see the punishment of the *w*.
92: 7 though the *w* spring up like grass
92: 11 have heard the rout of my *w* foes.
94: 3 How long will the *w*, O LORD,
94: 3 how long will the *w* be jubilant?
94: 13 till a pit is dug for the *w*.
94: 16 up for me against the *w*?
97: 10 them from the hand of the *w*.
101: 8 all the *w* in the land;
104: 35 and the *w* be no more.
106: 18 a flame consumed the *w*.
106: 29 LORD to anger by their *w* deeds,
107: 42 but all the *w* shut their mouths.
109: 2 for *w* and deceitful men
112: 10 The *w* man will see and be vexed,
112: 10 the longings of the *w* will come
119: 53 grips me because of the *w*,
119: 61 Though the *w* bind me with ropes,
119: 95 The *w* are waiting to destroy me,
119:110 The *w* have set a snare for me,
119:119 All the *w* of the earth you discard
119:150 Those who devise *w* schemes are
119:155 Salvation is far from the *w*,
125: 3 scepter of the *w* will not remain
129: 4 from the cords of the *w*.
139: 19 If only you would slay the *w*,
140: 4 O LORD, from the hands of the *w*;
140: 8 do not grant the *w* their desires,
141: 4 to take part in *w* deeds
141: 6 *w* will learn that my words were
141: 10 Let the *w* fall into their own nets,
145: 20 but all the *w* he will destroy
146: 9 but he frustrates the ways of the *w*.
147: 6 but casts the *w* to the ground.
Pr 2: 12 you from the ways of *w* men,
2: 22 the *w* will be cut off from the land,
3: 25 or of the ruin that overtakes the *w*,
3: 33 on the house of the *w*,
4: 14 Do not set foot on the path of the *w*
4: 19 of the *w* is like deep darkness;
5: 22 of a *w* man ensnare him;
6: 18 a heart that devises *w* schemes,
9: 7 whoever rebukes a *w* man incurs
10: 3 but he thwarts the craving of the *w*.
10: 6 overwhelms the mouth of the *w*.
10: 7 but the name of the *w* will rot.
10: 11 overwhelms the mouth of the *w*.
10: 16 of the *w* brings them punishment.
10: 20 the heart of the *w* is of little value.
10: 24 What the *w* dreads will overtake
10: 25 by, the *w* are gone,
10: 27 but the years of the *w* are cut short.
10: 28 the hopes of the *w* come to nothing
10: 30 the *w* will not remain in the land.
10: 32 of the *w* only what is perverse.
11: 5 *w* are brought down by their own
11: 7 When a *w* man dies, his hope
11: 8 and it comes on the *w* instead.
11: 10 when the *w* perish, there are shouts
11: 11 of the *w* it is destroyed.
11: 18 The *w* man earns deceptive wages,
11: 21 The *w* will not go unpunished,
11: 23 but the hope of the *w* only in wrath.
12: 5 but the advice of the *w* is deceitful.
12: 6 The words of the *w* lie in wait
12: 7 *W* men are overthrown
12: 10 the kindest acts of the *w* are cruel.
12: 12 The *w* desire the plunder
12: 21 but the *w* have their fill of trouble.
12: 26 the way of the *w* leads them astray.
13: 5 but the *w* bring shame and disgrace
13: 9 but the lamp of the *w* is snuffed out.
13: 17 A *w* messenger falls into trouble,
13: 25 the stomach of the *w* goes hungry.
14: 11 of the *w* will be destroyed,
14: 19 the *w* at the gates of the righteous.

Pr 14: 32 calamity comes, the *w* are brought
15: 3 keeping watch on the *w*
15: 6 of the *w* brings them trouble.
15: 8 detests the sacrifice of the *w*,
15: 9 Lord detests the way of the *w*
15: 26 detests the thoughts of the *w*,
15: 28 but the mouth of the *w* gushes evil.
15: 29 The Lord is far from the *w*
16: 4 even the *w* for a day of disaster.
17: 4 A *w* man listens to evil lips;
17: 23 A *w* man accepts a bribe in secret
18: 5 It is not good to be partial to the *w*
19: 28 the mouth of the *w* gulps down evil.
20: 26 A wise king winnows out the *w*;
21: 4 the lamp of the *w*, are sin!
21: 7 of the *w* will drag them away,
21: 10 The *w* man craves evil;
21: 12 and brings the *w* to ruin.
21: 12 of the house of the *w*
21: 18 The *w* become a ransom
21: 27 The sacrifice of the *w* is detestable
21: 29 A *w* man puts up a bold front,
22: 5 In the paths of the *w* lie thorns
24: 1 Do not envy *w* men,
24: 16 *w* are brought down by calamity.
24: 19 or be envious of the *w*,
24: 20 lamp of the *w* will be snuffed out.
25: 5 remove the *w* from the king's
25: 26 man who gives way to the *w*.
28: 1 *w* man flees though no one pursues,
28: 4 who forsake the law praise the *w*,
28: 12 but when the *w* rise to power,
28: 15 is a *w* man ruling over a helpless
28: 28 When the *w* rise to power,
28: 28 when the *w* perish, the righteous
29: 2 when the *w* rule, the people groan.
29: 7 but the *w* have no such concern.
29: 12 all his officials become *w*.
29: 16 When the *w* thrive, so does sin,
29: 27 the *w* detest the upright.
Ecc 3: 17 both the righteous and the *w*,
7: 15 and a *w* man living long
8: 10 Then too, I saw the *w* buried—
8: 12 Although a *w* man commits
8: 13 Yet because the *w* do not fear God,
8: 14 men who get what the *w* deserve,
8: 14 *w* men who get what the righteous
9: 2 the righteous and the *w*, the good
10: 13 at the end they are *w* madness—
Isa 3: 11 Woe to the *w*!
9: 17 for everyone is ungodly and *w*,
11: 4 breath of his lips he will slay the *w*.
13: 11 the *w* for their sins.
14: 5 Lord has broken the rod of the *w*,
14: 20 The offspring of the *w*
26: 10 Though grace is shown to the *w*,
31: 2 up against the house of the *w*,
32: 7 The scoundrel's methods are *w*,
35: 8 *w* fools will not go about on it.
48: 22 says the Lord, "for the *w*."
53: 9 He was assigned a grave with the *w*
55: 7 Let the *w* forsake his way
57: 20 But the *w* are like the tossing sea,
57: 21 says my God, "for the *w*."
58: 4 in striking each other with *w* fists.
59: 3 and your tongue mutters *w* things.
Jer 4: 14 long will you harbor *w* thoughts?
5: 26 "Among my people are *w* men
6: 29 the *w* are not purged out.
12: 1 Why does the way of the *w* prosper
12: 4 Because those who live in it are *w*,
12: 14 for all my *w* neighbors who seize
13: 10 These *w* people, who refuse
15: 21 from the hands of the *w*
20: 13 the needy from the hands of the *w*.
23: 19 down on the heads of the *w*.
25: 31 and put the *w* to the sword,' "
30: 23 down on the heads of the *w*.
35: 15 of you must turn from your *w* ways
36: 3 of them will turn from his *w* way;
36: 7 and each will turn from his *w* ways,
44: 22 no longer endure your *w* actions
Eze 3: 18 that *w* man will die for his sin,
3: 18 to a *w* man, 'You will surely die,'
3: 19 But if you do warn the *w* man
6: 11 of all the *w* and detestable practices
7: 21 and as loot to the *w* of the earth,
7: 24 I will bring the most *w*

Eze 8: 9 and see the *w* and detestable things
11: 2 and giving *w* advice in this city.
13: 22 you encouraged the *w* not to turn
14: 3 and put *w* stumbling blocks
14: 4 and puts a *w* stumbling block
14: 7 and puts a *w* stumbling block
18: 20 of the *w* will be charged
18: 21 "But if a *w* man turns away
18: 23 pleasure in the death of the *w*?
18: 24 detestable things the *w* man does,
18: 27 But if a *w* man turns away
21: 3 you both the righteous and the *w*.
21: 4 to cut off the righteous and the *w*,
21: 25 " 'O profane and *w* prince of Israel,
21: 29 necks of the *w* who are to be slain,
33: 8 When I say to the *w*, 'O *w* man,
33: 8 that *w* man will die for his sin,
33: 9 if you do warn the *w* man to turn
33: 11 pleasure in the death of the *w*,
33: 12 of the *w* man will not cause him
33: 14 to the *w* man, 'You will surely die,'
33: 19 And if a *w* man turns away
36: 31 your evil ways and *w* deeds,
Da 2: 9 to tell me misleading and *w* things,
8: 23 rebels have become completely *w*,
9: 5 We have been *w* and have rebelled;
12: 10 None of the *w* will understand,
12: 10 but the *w* will continue to be *w*.
Hos 6: 8 Gilead is a city of *w* men,
12: 11 Is Gilead *w*?
Mic 6: 10 Am I still to forget, O *w* house,
Na 1: 15 No more will the *w* invade you;
Hab 1: 4 The *w* hem in the righteous,
1: 13 Why are you silent while the *w*
1: 15 The *w* foe pulls all of them up
Zep 1: 3 The *w* will have only heaps
Mal 1: 4 They will be called The *W* Land,
3: 18 between the righteous and the *w*,
4: 3 Then you will trample down the *w*;
Mt 12: 39 *w* and adulterous generation asks
12: 45 be with this *w* generation."
12: 45 with it seven other spirits more *w*
13: 49 separate the *w* from the righteous
16: 4 *w* and adulterous generation looks
18: 32 'You *w* servant,' he said, 'I
24: 48 But suppose that servant is *w*
25: 26 "His master replied, 'You *w*,
Lk 6: 35 he is kind to the ungrateful and *w*.
11: 26 takes seven other spirits more *w*
11: 29 Jesus said, "This is a *w* generation.
19: 22 you *w* servant! You knew, did you,
Ac 2: 23 and you, with the help of *w* men,
3: 26 each of you from your *w* ways."
24: 15 of both the righteous and the *w*.
Ro 4: 5 but trusts God who justifies the *w*,
1Co 5: 13 "Expel the *w* man from among you
6: 9 not know that the *w* will not inherit
2Th 3: 2 that we may be delivered from *w*
2Jn : 11 him shares in his *w* work.
Rev 2: 2 that you cannot tolerate *w* men,

WICKEDNESS (WICKED)

Ge 6: 5 The Lord saw how great man's *w*
Ex 34: 7 and forgiving *w*, rebellion and sin.
34: 9 a stiff-necked people, forgive our *w*
Lev 16: 21 and confess over it all the *w*
18: 17 That is *w*.
19: 29 to prostitution and be filled with *w*.
20: 14 so that no *w* will be among you.
Dt 9: 4 it is on account of the *w*
9: 5 account of the *w* of these nations,
9: 27 stubbornness of this people, their *w*
31: 18 because of all their *w* in turning
Jdg 9: 56 God repaid the *w* that Abimelech
9: 57 men of Shechem pay for all their *w*.
2Ch 20: 35 king of Israel, who was guilty of *w*.
28: 19 for he had promoted *w* in Judah
Ne 9: 2 and confessed their sins and the *w*
13: 27 you too are doing all this terrible *w*
Job 6: 30 Is there any *w* on my lips?
22: 5 Is not your *w* great?
22: 23 If you remove *w* far from your tent
27: 4 my lips will not speak *w*,
34: 26 He punishes them for their *w*
35: 8 Your *w* affects only a man like
35: 15 does not take the least notice of *w*.
Ps 10: 15 call him to account for his *w*
45: 7 You love righteousness and hate *w*;

Ps 92: 15 he is my Rock, and there is no *w*
94: 23 and destroy them for their *w*;
107: 34 of the *w* of those who lived there.
Pr 4: 17 They eat the bread of *w*
8: 7 for my lips detest *w*,
11: 5 down by their own *w*.
12: 3 cannot be established through *w*,
13: 6 but *w* overthrows the sinner.
18: 3 When *w* comes, so does contempt,
22: 8 He who sows *w* reaps trouble,
26: 26 his *w* will be exposed
Ecc 3: 16 place of judgment—*w* was there,
3: 16 the place of justice—*w* was there.
7: 15 a wicked man living long in his *w*.
7: 25 to understand the stupidity of *w*
8: 8 so *w* will not release those who
Isa 5: 18 and *w* as with cart ropes,
9: 18 Surely *w* burns like a fire;
47: 10 You have trusted in your *w*
Jer 1: 16 because of their *w* in forsaking me,
2: 19 Your *w* will punish you;
3: 2 land with your prostitution and *w*.
6: 7 so she pours out her *w*.
7: 12 of the *w* of my people Israel.
8: 6 No one repents of his *w*,
11: 15 When you engage in your *w*,
14: 10 he will now remember their *w*
14: 20 O Lord, we acknowledge our *w*
16: 18 I will repay them double for their *w*
22: 22 because of all your *w*.
23: 11 even in my temple I find their *w*,"
23: 14 so that no one turns from his *w*.
31: 34 "For I will forgive their *w*
33: 5 from this city because of all its *w*.
36: 3 then I will forgive their *w*
36: 31 and his attendants for their *w*;
44: 5 they did not turn from their *w*
44: 9 and the *w* committed by you
44: 9 you forgotten the *w* committed
La 1: 22 "Let all their *w* come before you;
4: 22 and expose your *w*.
Eze 3: 19 and he does not turn from his *w*
5: 6 Yet in her *w* she has rebelled
7: 11 grown into a rod to punish *w*;
16: 23 In addition to all your other *w*,
16: 57 before your *w* was uncovered.
18: 20 the *w* of the wicked will be charged
18: 27 away from the *w* he has committed
28: 15 created till *w* was found in you.
31: 11 him to deal with according to its *w*.
33: 12 *w* of the wicked man will not cause
33: 19 wicked man turns away from his *w*
Da 4: 27 and your *w* by being kind
9: 24 to atone for *w*, to bring
Hos 4: 8 and relish their *w*.
7: 3 They delight the king with their *w*,
8: 13 Now he will remember their *w*
9: 9 God will remember their *w*
9: 15 "Because of all their *w* in Gilgal,
10: 8 of *w* will be destroyed—
10: 13 But you have planted *w*,
10: 15 because your *w* is great.
Joel 3: 13 so great is their *w*!"
Jnh 1: 2 its *w* has come up before me."
Mic 3: 10 and Jerusalem with *w*.
Na 1: 11 and counsels *w*.
Hab 3: 13 crushed the leader of the land of *w*,
Zec 5: 8 sat a woman! He said, "This is *w*,"
Mt 23: 28 full of hypocrisy and *w*.
24: 12 Because of the increase of *w*,
Lk 11: 39 inside you are full of greed and *w*.
Ac 1: 18 (With the reward he got for his *w*,
8: 22 Repent of this *w* and pray
Ro 1: 18 who suppress the truth by their *w*,
1: 18 *w* of men who suppress the truth
1: 29 filled with every kind of *w*,
6: 13 of *w*, but rather offer yourselves
6: 19 and to ever-increasing *w*,
1Co 5: 8 the yeast of malice and *w*,
2Co 6: 14 what do righteousness and *w* have
2Th 2: 12 the truth but have delighted in *w*.
2Ti 2: 19 of the Lord must turn away from *w*
Tit 2: 14 for us to redeem us from all *w*
Heb 1: 9 loved righteousness and hated *w*;
8: 12 For I will forgive their *w*
2Pe 2: 15 who loved the wages of *w*.

WIDE (WIDENED WIDER WIDTH)

Ge 6: 15 75 feet *w* and 45 feet high.
Ex 25: 10 a cubit and a half *w*, and a cubit
25: 17 cubits long and a cubit and a half *w*.
25: 23 a cubit *w* and a cubit and a half high
25: 25 around it a rim a handbreadth *w*
26: 2 cubits long and four cubits *w*.
26: 8 thirty cubits long and four cubits *w*.
26: 16 cubits long and a cubit and a half *w*,
27: 1 five cubits long and five cubits *w*.
27: 12 the courtyard shall be fifty cubits *w*
27: 13 shall also be fifty cubits *w*.
27: 18 cubits long and fifty cubits *w*,
28: 16 a span long and a span *w*—
30: 2 a cubit long and a cubit *w*,
36: 9 cubits long and four cubits *w*.
36: 15 thirty cubits long and four cubits *w*.
36: 21 cubits long and a cubit and a half *w*,
37: 1 a cubit and a half *w*, and a cubit
37: 6 cubits long and a cubit and a half *w*.
37: 10 two cubits long, a cubit *w*,
37: 12 around it a rim a handbreadth *w*
37: 25 a cubit long and a cubit *w*,
38: 1 five cubits long and five cubits *w*.
38: 12 The west end was fifty cubits *w*
38: 13 the sunrise, was also fifty cubits *w*.
39: 9 a span long and a span *w*—
Dt 3: 11 thirteen feet long and six feet *w*.
1Sa 26: 13 there was a *w* space between them.
1Ki 6: 2 was sixty cubits long, twenty *w*
6: 6 The lowest floor was five cubits *w*,
6: 20 twenty *w* and twenty high
7: 2 fifty *w* and thirty high,
7: 6 fifty cubits long and thirty *w*.
7: 27 each was four cubits long, four *w*
1Ch 13: 2 and *w* to the rest of our brothers
2Ch 3: 3 twenty cubits *w* (using the cubit
3: 8 cubits long and twenty cubits *w*.
4: 1 twenty cubits *w* and ten cubits high
6: 13 five cubits *w* and three cubits high,
26: 15 His fame spread far and *w*,
Ezr 6: 3 ninety feet high and ninety feet *w*,
Ps 22: 13 open their mouths *w* against me.
81: 10 Open *w* your mouth and I will fill it
Isa 18: 2 to a people feared far and *w*,
18: 7 from a people feared far and *w*,
30: 33 fire pit has been made deep and *w*,
45: 8 Let the earth open *w*,
54: 2 stretch your tent curtains *w*,
57: 8 you climbed into it and opened it *w*
La 2: 16 *w* against you;
3: 46 *w* against us.
Eze 40: 7 were one rod long and one rod *w*,
40: 18 and was as *w* as they were long;
40: 21 long and twenty-five cubits *w*.
40: 25 long and twenty-five cubits *w*.
40: 29 long and twenty-five cubits *w*.
40: 30 court were twenty-five cubits *w*
40: 33 long and twenty-five cubits *w*.
40: 36 long and twenty-five cubits *w*.
40: 42 a cubit and a half *w* and a cubit high
40: 47 cubits long and a hundred cubits *w*.
40: 48 they were five cubits *w* on
40: 48 walls were three cubits *w*
40: 49 The portico was twenty cubits *w*,
41: 2 The entrance was ten cubits *w*,
41: 2 cubits long and twenty cubits *w*.
41: 2 on each side of it were five cubits *w*
41: 3 The entrance was six cubits *w*,
41: 3 entrance; each was two cubits *w*.
41: 5 the temple was four cubits *w*.
41: 10 rooms was twenty cubits *w* all
41: 11 the open area was five cubits *w* all
41: 12 the west side was seventy cubits *w*.
42: 2 cubits long and fifty cubits *w*.
42: 4 an inner passageway ten cubits *w*
42: 20 and five hundred cubits *w*,
43: 13 gutter is a cubit deep and a cubit *w*,
43: 14 it is four cubits high and a cubit *w*.
43: 14 it is two cubits high and a cubit *w*,
43: 16 cubits long and twelve cubits *w*.
43: 17 cubits long and fourteen cubits *w*,
45: 1 cubits long and 20,000 cubits *w*;
45: 3 cubits long and 10,000 cubits *w*.
45: 5 cubits *w* will belong to the Levites,
45: 6 cubits *w* and 25,000 cubits long,
46: 22 cubits long and thirty cubits *w*;
Eze 48: 8 cubits *w*, and its length from east
48: 9 cubits long and 10,000 cubits *w*.
48: 10 10,000 cubits *w* on the west side,
48: 10 cubits *w* on the east side
48: 13 cubits long and 10,000 cubits *w*.
48: 15 5,000 cubits *w* and 25,000
Da 3: 1 ninety feet high and nine feet *w*,
Mic 4: 3 for strong nations far and *w*.
Na 3: 13 are *w* open to your enemies;
Zec 2: 2 to find out how *w* and how long it is
5: 2 thirty feet long and fifteen feet *w*."
Mt 7: 13 For *w* is the gate and broad is
23: 5 They make their phylacteries *w*
2Co 6: 11 and opened *w* our hearts to you.
6: 13 my children—open *w* your hearts
Eph 3: 18 to grasp how *w* and long and high
Rev 21: 16 and as *w* and high as it is long.
21: 16 like a square, as long as it was *w*.

WIDENED (WIDE)

Eze 41: 7 so that the rooms *w* as one went

WIDER (WIDE)

Job 11: 9 and *w* than the sea.
Eze 41: 7 all around the temple were *w*

WIDESPREAD (SPREAD)

Eze 28: 16 Through your *w* trade
Jn 7: 12 there was *w* whispering about

WIDOW (WIDOW'S WIDOWHOOD WIDOWS WIDOWS')

Ge 38: 11 as a *w* in your father's house
Ex 22: 22 "Do not take advantage of a *w*
Lev 21: 14 not marry a *w*, a divorced woman,
22: 13 if a priest's daughter becomes a *w*
Nu 30: 9 Any vow or obligation taken by a *w*
Dt 10: 18 cause of the fatherless and the *w*,
24: 17 take the cloak of the *w* as a pledge.
24: 19 the alien, the fatherless and the *w*,
24: 20 the alien, the fatherless and the *w*.
24: 21 the alien, the fatherless and the *w*.
25: 5 his *w* must not marry
25: 9 his brother's *w* shall go up to him
26: 12 the alien, the fatherless and the *w*,
26: 13 and the *w*, according to all you
27: 19 the alien, the fatherless or the *w*."
Ru 4: 5 you acquire the dead man's *w*,
4: 10 Ruth the Moabitess, Mahlon's *w*,
1Sa 27: 3 Abigail of Carmel, the *w* of Nabal.
30: 5 the *w* of Nabal of Carmel.
2Sa 2: 2 the *w* of Nabal of Carmel.
3: 3 of Abigail the *w* of Nabal of Carmel
14: 5 "I am indeed a *w*; my husband is
1Ki 7: 14 whose mother was a *w*
11: 26 his mother was a *w* named Zeruah.
17: 9 I have commanded a *w*
17: 10 a *w* was there gathering sticks.
17: 20 also upon this *w* I am staying with,
Job 24: 21 and to the *w* show no kindness.
31: 16 or let the eyes of the *w* grow weary,
31: 18 and from my birth I guided the *w*—
Ps 94: 6 They slay the *w* and the alien;
109: 9 and his wife a *w*.
146: 9 sustains the fatherless and the *w*,
Isa 1: 17 plead the case of the *w*.
47: 8 I will never be a *w*
Jer 7: 6 the fatherless or the *w*
22: 3 the fatherless or the *w*,
La 1: 1 How like a *w* is she,
Eze 22: 7 mistreated the fatherless and the *w*.
Zec 7: 10 not oppress the *w* or the fatherless,
Mt 22: 24 his brother must marry the *w*
Mk 12: 19 the man must marry the *w*
12: 21 The second one married the *w*,
12: 42 But a poor *w* came and put
12: 43 this poor *w* has put more
Lk 2: 37 and then was a *w* until she was
4: 26 to a *w* in Zarephath in the region
7: 12 son of his mother, and she was a *w*.
18: 3 there was a *w* in that town who
18: 5 because this *w* keeps bothering me,
20: 28 the man must marry the *w*
21: 2 saw a poor *w* put in two very small
21: 3 "this poor *w* has put in more
1Ti 5: 4 But if a *w* has children
5: 5 The *w* who is really in need
5: 6 the *w* who lives for pleasure is dead
1Ti 5: 9 No *w* may be put on the list
Rev 18: 7 'I sit as queen; I am not a *w*,

WIDOW'S (WIDOW)

Ge 38: 14 she took off her *w* clothes,
38: 19 and put on her *w* clothes again.
Job 24: 3 and take the *w* ox in pledge.
29: 13 I made the *w* heart sing.
Pr 15: 25 he keeps the *w* boundaries intact.
Isa 1: 23 the *w* case does not come

WIDOWHOOD (WIDOW)

Isa 47: 9 loss of children and *w*.
54: 4 no more the reproach of your *w*.

WIDOWS (WIDOW)

Ex 22: 24 your wives will become *w*
Dt 14: 29 the *w* who live in your towns may
16: 11 and the *w* living among you.
16: 14 and the *w* who live in your towns.
2Sa 20: 3 the day of their death, living as *w*.
Job 22: 9 you sent *w* away empty-handed
27: 15 and their *w* will not weep for them.
Ps 68: 5 to the fatherless, a defender of *w*,
78: 64 and their *w* could not weep.
Isa 9: 17 nor will he pity the fatherless and *w*
10: 2 making *w* their prey
Jer 15: 8 I will make their *w* more numerous
18: 21 wives be made childless and *w*;
49: 11 Your *w* too can trust in me."
La 5: 3 our mothers like *w*.
Eze 22: 25 and make many *w* within her.
44: 22 They must not marry *w*
44: 22 of Israelite descent or *w* of priests.
Mal 3: 5 who oppress the *w*
Lk 4: 25 assure you that there were many *w*
Ac 6: 1 their *w* were being overlooked
9: 39 All the *w* stood around him,
9: 41 he called the believers and the *w*
1Co 7: 8 to the unmarried and the *w* I say:
1Ti 5: 3 to those *w* who are really
5: 9 widow may be put on the list of *w*
5: 11 As for younger *w*, do not put them
5: 14 So I counsel younger *w* to marry,
5: 16 any woman who is a believer has *w*
5: 16 can help those *w* who are really
Jas 1: 27 look after orphans and *w*

WIDOWS' (WIDOW)

Mk 12: 40 They devour *w*' houses
Lk 20: 47 They devour *w*' houses

WIDTH (WIDE)

1Ki 6: 3 hall of the temple extended the *w*
2Ch 3: 4 long across the *w* of the building
3: 8 to the *w* of the temple—
Eze 40: 11 he measured the *w* of the entrance
40: 20 and *w* of the gate facing north,
40: 48 The *w* of the entrance was fourteen
41: 1 the *w* of the jambs was six cubits
41: 3 and the *w* of the sidewalls
41: 4 and its *w* was twenty cubits
41: 14 The *w* of the temple courtyard
42: 11 they had the same length and *w*,
48: 13 cubits and its *w* 10,000 cubits.

WIELD (WIELDING)

Isa 10: 15 were to *w* him who lifts it up,

WIELDING (WIELD)

Ps 74: 5 They behaved like men *w* axes

WIFE (WIFE'S WIVES WIVES')

Ge 2: 24 and mother and be united to his *w*,
2: 25 and his *w* were both naked,
3: 8 and his *w* heard the sound
3: 17 "Because you listened to your *w*
3: 20 Adam named his *w* Eve,
3: 21 and his *w* and clothed them.
4: 1 Adam lay with his *w* Eve,
4: 17 lay with his *w*, and she became
4: 25 Adam lay with his *w* again,
6: 18 you and your sons and your *w*
7: 7 And Noah and his sons and his *w*
7: 13 together with his *w* and the wives
8: 16 you and your *w* and your sons
8: 18 and his *w* and his sons' wives.
11: 29 The name of Abram's *w* was Sarai,

Ge 11:29 the name of Nahor's *w* was Milcah;
11:31 his daughter-in-law Sarai, the *w*
12: 5 He took his *w* Sarai, his nephew
12:11 said to his *w* Sarai, "I know what
12:12 they will say, 'This is his *w*.'
12:17 because of Abram's *w* Sarai.
12:18 didn't you tell me she was your *w?*
12:19 Now then, here is your *w*.
12:19 so that I took her to be my *w?*
12:20 with his *w* and everything he had.
13: 1 with his *w* and everything he had,
16: 1 Abram's *w*, had borne him no
16: 3 Sarai his *w* took her Egyptian
16: 3 gave her to her husband to be his *w*.
17:15 for Sarai your *w*, you are no longer
17:19 your *w* Sarah will bear you a son,
18: 9 "Where is your *w* Sarah?"
18:10 and Sarah your *w* will have a son."
19:15 Take your *w* and your two
19:16 and the hands of his *w*
19:26 But Lot's *w* looked back
20: 2 there Abraham said of his *w* Sarah,
20: 7 Now return the man's *w*,
20:11 they will kill me because of my *w*.'
20:12 my mother; and she became my *w*.
20:14 and he returned Sarah his *w* to him.
20:17 his *w* and his slave girls
20:18 because of Abraham's *w* Sarah.
21:21 his mother got a *w* for him
23: 3 rose from beside his dead *w*
23:19 Abraham buried his *w* Sarah
24: 3 that you will not get a *w* for my son
24: 4 and get a *w* for my son Isaac."
24: 7 so that you can get a *w* for my son
24:15 was the *w* of Abraham's brother
24:36 My master's *w* Sarah has borne
24:37 'You must not get a *w* for my son
24:38 and to my own clan, and get a *w*
24:40 so that you can get a *w* for my son
24:51 and let her become the *w*
24:67 she became his *w*, and he loved her;
25: 1 Abraham took another *w*,
25:10 was buried with his *w* Sarah.
25:21 his *w* Rebekah became pregnant.
25:21 to the LORD on behalf of his *w*,
26: 7 he was afraid to say, "She is my *w*."
26: 7 of that place asked him about his *w*,
26: 8 saw Isaac caressing his *w* Rebekah.
26: 9 "She is really your *w!* Why did you
26:10 might well have slept with your *w*,
26:11 his *w* shall surely be put to death."
27:46 takes a *w* from among the women
28: 2 Take a *w* for yourself there,
28: 6 him to Paddan Aram to take a *w*
29:21 said to Laban, "Give me my *w*.
29:28 his daughter Rachel to be his *w*.
30: 4 gave him her servant Bilhah as a *w*.
30: 9 and gave her to Jacob as a *w*.
34: 4 "Get me this girl as my *w*."
34: 8 Please give her to him as his *w*.
34:12 Only give me the girl as my *w*."
36:10 the son of Esau's *w* Adah,
36:10 the son of Esau's *w* Basemath.
36:12 grandsons of Esau's *w* Adah.
36:13 grandsons of Esau's *w* Basemath.
36:14 of Esau's *w* Oholibamah daughter
36:17 grandsons of Esau's *w* Basemath.
36:18 The sons of Esau's *w* Oholibamah:
36:18 from Esau's *w* Oholibamah
38: 6 Judah got a *w* for Er, his firstborn,
38: 8 "Lie with your brother's *w*
38: 9 lay with his brother's *w*,
38:12 After a long time Judah's *w*,
38:14 had not been given to him as his *w*.
39: 7 a while his master's *w* took notice
39: 9 except you, because you are his *w*.
39:19 heard the story his *w* told him,
41:45 priest of On, to be his *w*.
44:27 'You know that my *w* bore me two
46:19 The sons of Jacob's *w* Rachel:
49:31 and his *w* Rebekah were buried,
49:31 and his *w* Sarah were buried,
Ex 4:20 So Moses took his *w* and sons,
18: 2 had sent away his *w* Zipporah,
18: 5 together with Moses' sons and *w*,
18: 6 am coming to you with your *w*
20:17 shall not covet your neighbor's *w*,
21: 3 but if he has a *w* when he comes,
Ex 21: 4 If his master gives him a *w*
21: 5 'I love my master and my *w*
22:16 bride-price, and she shall be his *w*.
Lev 18: 8 relations with your father's *w;*
18:11 the daughter of your father's *w*,
18:14 brother by approaching his *w*
18:15 She is your son's *w;* do not have
18:16 relations with your brother's *w;*
18:18 take your wife's sister as a rival *w*
18:18 with her while your *w* is living.
18:20 intercourse with your neighbor's *w*
20:10 adultery with another man's *w*—
20:10 with the *w* of his neighbor—
20:11 If a man sleeps with his father's *w*,
20:21 " 'If a man marries his brother's *w*,
Nu 5:12 'If a man's *w* goes astray
5:14 he suspects his *w* and she is impure
5:15 then he is to take his *w* to the priest
5:30 a man because he suspects his *w*.
12: 1 Moses because of his Cushite *w*,
26:59 name of Amram's *w* was Jochebed,
30:16 between a man and his *w*,
Dt 5:21 shall not covet your neighbor's *w*.
13: 6 or daughter, or the *w* you love,
21:11 you may take her as your *w*.
21:13 husband and she shall be your *w*.
21:15 the son of the *w* he does not love,
21:16 son of the *w* he loves in preference
21:16 the son of the *w* he does not love.
21:17 the son of his unloved *w*
22:13 If a man takes a *w* and, after lying
22:19 She shall continue to be his *w;*
22:22 sleeping with another man's *w*,
22:24 he violated another man's *w*.
22:30 not to marry his father's *w;*
24: 2 leaves his house she becomes the *w*
24: 5 happiness to the *w* he has married.
25: 7 want to marry his brother's *w*,
25:11 and the *w* of one of them comes
27:20 sleeps with his father's *w*,
28:54 or the *w* he loves or his surviving
Jdg 4: 4 a prophetess, the *w* of Lappidoth,
4:17 the *w* of Heber the Kenite,
4:21 Heber's *w*, picked up a tent peg
5:24 the *w* of Heber the Kenite,
11: 2 Gilead's *w* also bore him sons,
13: 2 had a *w* who was sterile
13:11 Manoah got up and followed his *w*.
13:11 you the one who talked to my *w?*"
13:13 "Your *w* must do all that I have
13:19 while Manoah and his *w* watched:
13:20 and his *w* fell with their faces
13:21 again to Manoah and his *w*,
13:22 doomed to die!" he said to his *w*.
13:23 seen God!" But his *w* answered,
14: 2 now get her for me as my *w*."
14: 3 Philistines to get a *w?*"
14:15 day, they said to Samson's *w*,
14:16 Samson's *w* threw herself on him,
14:20 And Samson's *w* was given
15: 1 young goat and went to visit his *w*.
15: 6 his *w* was given to his friend."
21:18 'Cursed be anyone who gives a *w*
21:21 each of you seize a *w* from the girls
21:23 and carried her off to be his *w*.
Ru 1: 1 together with his *w* and two sons,
4:10 Mahlon's widow, as my *w*,
4:13 took Ruth and she became his *w*.
1Sa 1: 4 of the meat to his *w* Peninnah
1:19 Elkanah lay with Hannah his *w*,
2:20 Eli would bless Elkanah and his *w*,
4:19 His daughter-in-law, the *w*
19:11 Michal, David's *w*, warned him,
25:14 servants told Nabal's *w* Abigail:
25:37 his *w* told him all these things,
25:39 asking her to become his *w*.
25:40 to you to take you to become his *w*
25:42 messengers and became his *w*.
25:44 David's *w*, to Paltiel son of Laish,
30:22 each man may take his *w*
2Sa 3: 5 Ithream the son of David's *w* Eglah
3:14 "Give me my *w* Michal,
11: 3 and the *w* of Uriah the Hittite?"
11:11 and drink and lie with my *w?*
11:26 When Uriah's *w* heard that her
11:27 and she became his *w* and bore him
12: 9 and took his *w* to be your own.
12:10 and took the *w* of Uriah the Hittite
2Sa 12:15 the child that Uriah's *w* had borne
12:24 David comforted his *w* Bathsheba,
17:19 His *w* took a covering and spread it
1Ki 2:17 the Shunammite as my *w*."
9:16 gift to his daughter, Solomon's *w*.
11:19 he gave him a sister of his own *w*,
14: 2 and Jeroboam said to his *w*, "Go,
14: 2 you won't be recognized as the *w*
14: 4 So Jeroboam's *w* did what he said
14: 5 "Jeroboam's *w* is coming
14: 6 he said, "Come in, *w* of Jeroboam.
14:17 Then Jeroboam's *w* got up and left
21: 5 His *w* Jezebel came in
21: 7 Jezebel his *w* said, "Is this how you
21:25 urged on by Jezebel his *w*.
2Ki 4: 1 The *w* of a man from the company
5: 2 and she served Naaman's *w*.
22:14 who was the *w* of Shallum son
1Ch 2:18 had children by his *w* Azubah
2:24 Abijah the *w* of Hezron bore him
2:26 Jerahmeel had another *w*,
2:29 Abishur's *w* was named Abihail,
3: 3 the sixth, Ithream, by his *w* Eglah.
4:18 (His Judean *w* gave birth
4:19 The sons of Hodiah's *w*, the sister
7:15 took a *w* from among the Huppites
7:16 Makir's *w* Maacah gave birth
7:23 Then he lay with his *w* again,
8: 9 By his *w* Hodesh he had Jobab,
2Ch 8:11 "My *w* must not live in the palace
22:11 and *w* of the priest Jehoiada,
34:22 who was the *w* of Shallum son
Est 5:10 his friends and Zeresh, his *w*,
5:14 His *w* Zeresh and all his friends
6:13 and his *w* Zeresh said to him,
6:13 told Zeresh his *w* and all his friends
Job 2: 9 His *w* said to him, "Are you still
19:17 My breath is offensive to my *w;*
31:10 then may my *w* grind another
Ps 109: 9 and his *w* a widow.
128: 3 Your *w* will be like a fruitful vine
Pr 2:16 from the wayward *w*
5:18 in the *w* of your youth.
5:20 the bosom of another man's *w?*
6:24 tongue of the wayward *w*.
6:29 sleeps with another man's *w;*
7: 5 from the wayward *w*
12: 4 a disgraceful *w* is like decay
12: 4 *w* of noble character is her
18:22 He who finds a *w* finds what is
19:13 quarrelsome *w* is like a constant
19:14 but a prudent *w* is from the LORD.
21: 9 with a quarrelsome *w*.
21:19 a quarrelsome and ill-tempered *w*.
23:27 and a wayward *w* is a narrow well.
25:24 with a quarrelsome *w*.
27:15 A quarrelsome *w* is like
31:10 *w* of noble character who can find?
Ecc 9: 9 life with your *w*, whom you love,
Isa 54: 6 a *w* who married young,
54: 6 as if you were a *w* deserted
Jer 3: 1 "If a man divorces his *w*
5: 8 each neighing for another man's *w*.
6:11 both husband and *w* will be caught
Eze 16:32 " 'You adulterous *w!* You prefer
18: 6 He does not defile his neighbor's *w*
18:11 He defiles his neighbor's *w*.
18:15 He does not defile his neighbor's *w*.
22:11 offense with his neighbor's *w*,
24:18 and in the evening my *w* died.
33:26 each of you defiles his neighbor's *w*
Hos 1: 2 take to yourself an adulterous *w*
2: 2 for she is not my *w*,
3: 1 Go, show your love to your *w* again
12:12 Israel served to get a *w*,
Am 7:17 " 'Your *w* will become a prostitute
Mal 2:14 the witness between you and the *w*
2:14 the *w* of your marriage covenant.
2:15 faith with the *w* of your youth.
Mt 1: 6 whose mother had been Uriah's *w*,
1:20 to take Mary home as your *w*,
1:24 and took Mary home as his *w*.
5:31 who divorces his *w* must give her
5:32 that anyone who divorces his *w*,
14: 3 his brother Philip's *w*,
18:25 master ordered that he and his *w*
19: 3 for a man to divorce his *w* for any
19: 5 and mother and be united to his *w*,

Mt 19: 7 that a man give his *w* a certificate
19: 9 that anyone who divorces his *w*,
19: 10 situation between a husband and *w*,
22: 25 he left his *w* to his brother.
22: 28 whose *w* will she be of the seven,
27: 19 his *w* sent him this message:
Mk 6: 17 his brother Philip's *w*, whom he
6: 18 for you to have your brother's *w*.”
10: 2 lawful for a man to divorce his *w*?”
10: 7 and mother and be united to his *w*,
10: 11 “Anyone who divorces his *w*
12: 19 and leaves a *w* but no children,
12: 23 the resurrection whose *w* will she
Lk 1: 5 his *w* Elizabeth was
1: 13 Your *w* Elizabeth will bear you
1: 18 and my *w* is well along in years.”
1: 24 After this his *w* Elizabeth became
3: 19 his brother's *w*, and all the other
8: 3 Joanna the *w* of Cuza, the manager
14: 26 his *w* and children, his brothers
16: 18 “Anyone who divorces his *w*
17: 32 Remember Lot's *w*! Whoever tries
18: 29 or *w* or brothers or parents
20: 28 and leaves a *w* but no children,
20: 33 the resurrection whose *w* will she
Jn 19: 25 his mother's sister, Mary the *w*
Ac 5: 1 together with his *w* Sapphira,
5: 7 About three hours later his *w* came
18: 2 from Italy with his *w* Priscilla,
24: 24 came with his *w* Drusilla,
1Co 5: 1 pagans: A man has his father's *w*.
7: 2 each man should have his own *w*,
7: 3 and likewise the *w* to her husband.
7: 3 fulfill his marital duty to his *w*,
7: 4 to him alone but also to his *w*.
7: 10 A *w* must not separate
7: 11 a husband must not divorce his *w*.
7: 12 If any brother has a *w* who is not
7: 14 has been sanctified through his *w*,
7: 14 unbelieving *w* has been sanctified
7: 16 whether you will save your *w*?
7: 16 *w*, whether you will save your
7: 27 unmarried? Do not look for a *w*.
7: 33 how he can please his *w*—
9: 5 to take a believing *w* along with us,
Eph 5: 23 the husband is the head of the *w*
5: 28 He who loves his *w* loves himself.
5: 31 and mother and be united to his *w*,
5: 33 must love his *w* as he loves himself,
5: 33 the *w* must respect her husband.
1Ti 3: 2 husband of but one *w*, temperate,
3: 12 but one *w* and must manage his
Tit 1: 6 the husband of but one *w*,
Rev 21: 9 I will show you the bride, the *w*

WIFE'S (WIFE)

Ge 36: 39 and his *w* name was Mehetabel
Lev 18: 18 “ 'Do not take your *w* sister
Jdg 15: 1 “I'm going to my *w* room.”
Ru 1: 2 was Elimelech, his *w* name Naomi,
1Sa 14: 50 His *w* name was Ahinoam
25: 3 and his *w* name was Abigail.
1Ch 1: 50 and his *w* name was Mehetabel
8: 29 His *w* name was Maacah,
9: 35 His *w* name was Maacah,
Ac 5: 2 With his *w* full knowledge he kept
1Co 7: 4 The *w* body does not belong

WILD (WILDER WILDERNESS WILDS)

Ge 1: 24 and *w* animals, each according
1: 25 God made the *w* animals according
3: 1 of the *w* animals the LORD God
3: 14 and all the *w* animals!
7: 14 them every *w* animal according
7: 21 birds, livestock, *w* animals,
8: 1 Noah and all the *w* animals
9: 10 the livestock and all the *w* animals,
16: 12 He will be a *w* donkey of a man;
25: 28 who had a taste for *w* game,
27: 3 to hunt some *w* game for me.
31: 39 bring you animals torn by *w* beasts;
Ex 22: 13 torn to pieces by a *w* animal,
22: 31 meat of an animal torn by *w* beasts;
23: 11 *w* animals may eat what they leave.
23: 29 and the *w* animals too numerous
32: 25 saw that the people were running *w*
Lev 5: 2 the carcasses of unclean *w* animals
7: 24 or torn by *w* animals may be used
17: 15 by *w* animals must wash his clothes
22: 8 found dead or torn by *w* animals,
25: 7 and the *w* animals in your land.
26: 22 I will send *w* animals against you,
Nu 23: 22 they have the strength of a *w* ox.
24: 8 they have the strength of a *w* ox.
Dt 7: 22 or the *w* animals will multiply
14: 5 the roe deer, the *w* goat, the ibex,
32: 24 against them the fangs of *w* beasts,
33: 17 his horns are the horns of a *w* ox,
1Sa 24: 2 near the Crags of the *W* Goats.
2Sa 2: 18 as fleet-footed as a *w* gazelle.
17: 8 as a *w* bear robbed of her cubs.
21: 10 or the *w* animals by night.
2Ki 4: 39 to gather herbs and found a *w* vine.
14: 9 a *w* beast in Lebanon came along
2Ch 25: 18 a *w* beast in Lebanon came along
Ne 8: 15 from olive and *w* olive trees,
Job 5: 23 the *w* animals will be at peace
6: 5 Does a *w* donkey bray
11: 12 than a *w* donkey's colt can be born
24: 5 Like *w* donkeys in the desert,
39: 5 “Who let the *w* donkey go free?
39: 9 Will the *w* ox consent to serve you?
39: 15 that some *w* animal may trample
40: 20 and all the *w* animals play nearby.
Ps 22: 21 from the horns of the *w* oxen.
29: 6 Sirion like a young *w* ox.
74: 19 of your dove to *w* beasts;
92: 10 exalted my horn like that of a *w* ox;
104: 11 the *w* donkeys quench their thirst.
104: 18 mountains belong to the *w* goats;
148: 10 *w* animals and all cattle,
Isa 13: 21 there the *w* goats will leap about.
18: 6 and to the *w* animals;
18: 6 the *w* animals all winter.
34: 7 And the *w* oxen will fall with them,
34: 14 and *w* goats will bleat to each other
43: 20 The *w* animals honor me,
Jer 2: 21 me into a corrupt, *w* vine?
2: 24 a *w* donkey accustomed
12: 9 Go and gather all the *w* beasts;
14: 6 *W* donkeys stand on the barren
27: 6 even the *w* animals subject to him.
28: 14 control over the *w* animals.' ”
Eze 4: 14 found dead or torn by *w* animals.
5: 17 I will send famine and *w* beasts
14: 15 send *w* beasts through that country
14: 21 famine and *w* beasts and plague—
33: 27 to the *w* animals to be devoured,
34: 5 food for all the *w* animals.
34: 8 food for all the *w* animals,
34: 25 and rid the land of *w* beasts
34: 28 nor will *w* animals devour them.
39: 4 carrion birds and to the *w* animals.
39: 17 kind of bird and all the *w* animals:
44: 31 found dead or torn by *w* animals.
Da 4: 23 let him live like *w* animals,
4: 25 and will live with the *w* animals;
4: 32 and will live with the *w* animals;
5: 21 he lived with the *w* donkeys
Hos 2: 12 and *w* animals will devour them.
8: 9 like a *w* donkey wandering alone.
13: 8 a *w* animal will tear them apart.
Joel 1: 20 Even the *w* animals pant for you;
2: 22 Be not afraid, O *w* animals,
Zep 2: 15 a lair for *w* beasts!
Mt 3: 4 His food was locusts and *w* honey.
Mk 1: 6 and he ate locusts and *w* honey.
1: 13 He was with the *w* animals,
Lk 15: 13 squandered his wealth in *w* living.
Ac 11: 6 *w* beasts, reptiles, and birds
Ro 11: 17 and you, though a *w* olive shoot,
11: 24 of an olive tree that is *w* by nature,
1Co 15: 32 If I fought *w* beasts in Ephesus
Tit 1: 6 open to the charge of being *w*
Jas 1: 10 he will pass away like a *w* flower.
Jude : 13 They are *w* waves of the sea,
Rev 6: 8 and by the *w* beasts of the earth.

WILDER (WILD)

Jnh 1: 13 for the sea grew even *w* than before

WILDERNESS (WILD)

Isa 35: 1 the *w* will rejoice and blossom.
35: 6 Water will gush forth in the *w*
40: 3 make straight in the *w*
Jer 2: 6 and led us through the barren *w*,
50: 12 a *w*, a dry land, a desert.

WILDS (WILD)

Job 39: 4 thrive and grow strong in the *w*,

WILL (FREEWILL WEAK-WILLED WILLFUL WILLFULLY WILLING WILLINGNESS WILLS)

Ge 23: 13 hearing, “Listen to me, if you *w*.
24: 42 of my master Abraham, if you *w*,
Ex 18: 15 come to me to seek God's *w*.
Lev 24: 12 until the *w* of the LORD
25: 46 You can *w* them to your children
Dt 10: 10 It was not his *w* to destroy you.
15: 9 so that you do not show ill *w*
33: 21 out the LORD's righteous *w*,
1Sa 2: 25 for it was the LORD's *w*
2Sa 7: 21 word and according to your *w*,
1Ch 13: 2 if it is the *w* of the LORD our God,
Ezr 7: 18 with the *w* of your God.
10: 11 God of your fathers, and do his *w*.
Est 9: 30 words of good *w* and assurance—
Job 5: 1 “Call if you *w*, but who
Ps 40: 8 I desire to do your *w*, O my God;
103: 21 you his servants who do his *w*.
143: 10 Teach me to do your *w*,
Pr 11: 27 He who seeks good finds good *w*,
14: 9 good *w* is found among the upright.
Isa 53: 10 Yet it was the LORD's *w*
53: 10 the *w* of the LORD will prosper
Mt 6: 10 your *w* be done
7: 21 who does the *w* of my Father
10: 29 apart from the *w* of your Father.
12: 50 does the *w* of my Father
26: 39 Yet not as I *w*, but as you *w*.”
26: 42 I drink it, may your *w* be done.”
Mk 3: 35 Whoever does God's *w* is my
14: 36 Yet not what I *w*, but what you *w*.”
Lk 12: 47 servant who knows his master's *w*
22: 42 yet not my *w*, but yours be done.”
23: 25 and surrendered Jesus to their *w*.
Jn 1: 13 of human decision or a husband's *w*
4: 34 “is to do the *w* of him who sent me
6: 38 but to do the *w* of him who sent me.
6: 38 down from heaven not to do my *w*
6: 39 this is the *w* of him who sent me,
6: 40 For my Father's *w* is that everyone
7: 17 If any one chooses to do God's *w*,
9: 31 to the godly man who does his *w*.
Ac 4: 28 what your power and *w* had decided
18: 21 come back if it is God's *w*.”
20: 27 to you the whole *w* of God.
21: 14 and said, “The Lord's *w* be done.”
22: 14 has chosen you to know his *w*
Ro 1: 10 by God's *w* the way may be opened
2: 18 if you know his *w* and approve
8: 20 by the *w* of the one who subjected
8: 27 saints in accordance with God's *w*.
9: 19 For who resists his *w*?”
12: 2 and approve what God's *w* is—
12: 2 his good, pleasing and perfect *w*.
15: 32 so that by God's *w* I may come
1Co 1: 1 of Christ Jesus by the *w* of God,
7: 37 but has control over his own *w*,
2Co 1: 1 of Christ Jesus by the *w* of God,
8: 5 then to us in keeping with God's *w*.
Gal 1: 4 according to the *w* of our God
Eph 1: 1 of Christ Jesus by the *w* of God,
1: 5 with his pleasure and *w*—
1: 9 the mystery of his *w* according
1: 11 with the purpose of his *w*,
5: 17 understand what the Lord's *w* is.
6: 6 doing the *w* of God
Php 1: 15 rivalry, but others out of good *w*.
2: 13 for it is God who works in you to *w*
Col 1: 1 of Christ Jesus by the *w* of God,
1: 9 knowledge of his *w* through all
4: 12 firm in all the *w* of God,
1Th 4: 3 God's *w* that you should be holy;
5: 18 for this is God's *w* for you
2Ti 1: 1 of Christ Jesus by the *w* of God,
2: 26 has taken them captive to do his *w*.
Heb 2: 4 distributed according to his *w*.
9: 16 In the case of a *w*, it is necessary
9: 17 because a *w* is in force only
10: 7 I have come to do your *w*, O God
10: 9 I have come to do your *w*.”
10: 10 by that *w*, we have been made holy

Heb 10: 36 when you have done the *w* of God,
13: 21 everything good for doing his *w*,
Jas 4: 15 "If it is the Lord's *w*,
1Pe 2: 15 For it is God's *w* that
3: 17 It is better, if it is God's *w*,
4: 2 but rather for the *w* of God.
4: 19 to God's *w* should commit
2Pe 1: 21 never had its origin in the *w*
1Jn 2: 17 but the man who does the *w*
5: 14 we ask anything according to his *w*,
Rev 2: 26 who overcomes and does my *w*
4: 11 and by your *w* they were created

WILLFUL (WILL)

Ps 19: 13 Keep your servant also from *w* sins;
Isa 10: 12 the king of Assyria for the *w* pride
57: 17 yet he kept on in his *w* ways.

WILLFULLY (WILL)

Ps 78: 18 They *w* put God to the test

WILLING (WILL)

Ge 23: 8 If you are *w* to let me bury my dead
Ex 10: 27 and he was not *w* to let them go.
35: 5 Everyone who is *w* is to bring
35: 21 and everyone who was *w*
35: 22 All who were *w*, men and women
35: 26 And all the women who were *w*
35: 29 and women who were *w* brought
36: 2 and who was *w* to come and do
Dt 29: 20 The LORD will never be *w*
Jdg 5: 9 with the *w* volunteers
Ru 3: 13 But if he is not *w*, I vow that,
1Sa 22: 17 But the king's officials were not *w*
2Sa 6: 10 He was not *w* to take the ark
2Ki 8: 19 the LORD was not *w*
24: 4 the LORD was not *w* to forgive.
1Ch 19: 19 So the Arameans were not *w*
28: 9 devotion and with a *w* mind,
28: 21 and every *w* man skilled
29: 5 who is *w* to consecrate himself
29: 9 at the *w* response of their leaders,
2Ch 21: 7 the LORD was not *w*
29: 31 whose hearts were *w* brought burnt
Job 6: 9 that God would be *w* to crush me,
Ps 51: 12 grant me a *w* spirit, to sustain me.
110: 3 Your troops will be *w*
119:108 the *w* praise of my mouth,
Pr 11: 26 blessing crowns him who is *w*
19: 18 do not be a *w* party to his death.
Isa 1: 19 If you are *w* and obedient,
Eze 3: 7 of Israel is not *w* to listen to you
3: 7 they are not *w* to listen to me,
Da 3: 28 were *w* to give up their lives rather
Mt 8: 2 if you are *w*, you can make me
8: 3 "I am *w*," he said.
11: 14 And if you are *w* to accept it,
18: 14 Father in heaven is not *w* that any
23: 4 but they themselves are not *w*
23: 37 her wings, but you were not *w*.
26: 15 "What are you *w* to give me
26: 41 The spirit is *w*, but the body is weak
Mk 1: 40 "If you are *w*, you can make me
1: 41 "I am *w*," he said.
14: 38 The spirit is *w*, but the body is weak
Lk 5: 12 if you are *w*, you can make me
5: 13 "I am *w*," he said.
13: 34 but you were not *w*! Look,
22: 42 if you are *w*, take this cup from me;
Jn 6: 21 Then they were *w* to take him
Ac 25: 9 "Are you *w* to go up to Jerusalem
25: 20 if he would be *w* to go to Jerusalem
26: 5 if they are *w*, that according
Ro 12: 16 but be *w* to associate with people
1Co 4: 19 to you very soon, if the Lord is *w*,
7: 12 and she is *w* to live with him,
7: 13 and he is *w* to live with her,
1Ti 6: 18 and to be generous and *w* to share.
1Pe 5: 2 but because you are *w*,

WILLINGNESS (WILL)

2Co 8: 11 so that your eager *w*
8: 12 For if the *w* is there, the gift is

WILLOW

Eze 17: 5 He planted it like a *w*

WILLS (WILL)

Dt 21: 16 when he *w* his property to his sons,

WILY

Job 5: 13 of the *w* are swept away.

WIN (WINNING WINS WON)

Pr 3: 4 Then you will *w* favor
Jer 5: 28 the case of the fatherless to *w* it,
Mt 23: 15 and sea to *w* a single convert,
1Co 9: 19 myself a slave to everyone, to *w*
9: 20 I became like a Jew, to *w* the Jews.
9: 20 so as to *w* those under the law.
9: 21 so as to *w* those not having the law.
9: 22 I became weak, to *w* the weak.
Gal 1: 10 trying to *w* the approval of men,
4: 17 Those people are zealous to *w* you
Eph 6: 6 them not only to *w* their favor
Php 3: 14 on toward the goal to *w* the prize
Col 3: 22 is on you and to *w* their favor,
1Th 4: 12 your daily life may *w* the respect

WIND (WHIRLWIND WHIRLWINDS WINDS)

Ge 8: 1 and he sent a *w* over the earth
41: 6 thin and scorched by the east *w*.
41: 23 thin and scorched by the east *w*.
41: 27 of grain scorched by the east *w*:
Ex 10: 13 By morning the *w* had brought
10: 13 the LORD made an east *w* blow
10: 19 the *w* to a very strong west *w*,
14: 21 back with a strong east *w*
Nu 11: 31 Now a *w* went out from the LORD
2Sa 22: 11 he soared on the wings of the *w*.
1Ki 18: 45 black with clouds, the *w* rose,
19: 11 After the *w* there was
19: 11 and powerful *w* tore the mountains
19: 11 but the LORD was not in the *w*.
2Ki 3: 17 You will see neither *w* nor rain,
Job 1: 19 when suddenly a mighty *w* swept
6: 26 words of a despairing man as *w*?
8: 2 Your words are a blustering *w*.
15: 2 or fill his belly with the hot east *w*?
21: 18 are they like straw before the *w*,
27: 21 The east *w* carries him off,
28: 25 he established the force of the *w*
30: 15 dignity is driven away as by the *w*,
30: 22 drive me before the *w*;
37: 17 hushed under the south *w*,
37: 21 after the *w* has swept them clean.
Ps 1: 4 that the *w* blows away.
11: 6 a scorching *w* will be their lot.
18: 10 he soared on the wings of the *w*.
18: 42 fine as dust borne on the *w*;
35: 5 May they be like chaff before the *w*
48: 7 shattered by an east *w*.
68: 2 As smoke is blown away by the *w*,
78: 26 He let loose the east *w*
78: 26 led forth the south *w* by his power.
83: 13 like chaff before the *w*.
103: 16 the *w* blows over it and it is gone,
104: 3 and rides on the wings of the *w*.
135: 7 out the *w* from his storehouses.
Pr 11: 29 on his family will inherit only *w*,
25: 14 Like clouds and *w* without rain
25: 23 As a north *w* brings rain,
27: 16 her is like restraining the *w*
30: 4 Who has gathered up the *w*
Ecc 1: 6 The *w* blows to the south
1: 14 meaningless, a chasing after the *w*.
1: 17 too, is a chasing after the *w*.
2: 11 meaningless, a chasing after the *w*;
2: 17 meaningless, a chasing after the *w*.
2: 26 meaningless, a chasing after the *w*.
4: 4 meaningless, a chasing after the *w*.
4: 6 and chasing after the *w*.
4: 16 meaningless, a chasing after the *w*.
5: 16 since he toils for the *w*?
6: 9 a chasing after the *w*.
8: 8 power over the *w* to contain it;
11: 4 Whoever watches the *w* will not
11: 5 you do not know the path of the *w*,
SS 4: 16 and come, south *w*!
4: 16 Awake, north *w*,
Isa 7: 2 of the forest are shaken by the *w*.
11: 15 with a scorching *w* he will sweep
17: 13 driven before the *w* like chaff
24: 20 it sways like a hut in the *w*;
26: 18 but we gave birth to *w*.
27: 8 as on a day the east *w* blows.
28: 2 a hailstorm and a destructive *w*,
32: 2 will be like a shelter from the *w*
41: 16 winnow them, the *w* will pick them
41: 29 their images are but *w*
57: 13 The *w* will carry all of them off,
64: 6 like the *w* our sins sweep us away.
Jer 2: 24 sniffing the *w* in her craving—
4: 11 "A scorching *w* from the barren
4: 12 a *w* too strong for that comes
5: 13 The prophets are but *w*
10: 13 out the *w* from his storehouses.
13: 24 driven by the desert *w*.
18: 17 Like a *w* from the east,
22: 22 *w* will drive all your shepherds
30: 23 a driving *w* swirling down
51: 16 out the *w* from his storehouses.
Eze 5: 2 And scatter a third to the *w*.
13: 13 my wrath I will unleash a violent *w*,
17: 10 when the east *w* strikes it—
19: 12 The east *w* made it shrivel,
27: 26 the east *w* will break you to pieces
Da 2: 35 The *w* swept them away
Hos 8: 7 "They sow the *w*
12: 1 Ephraim feeds on the *w*;
12: 1 he pursues the east *w* all day
13: 15 east *w* from the LORD will come,
Am 4: 13 creates the *w*,
Jnh 1: 4 the LORD sent a great *w* on the sea
4: 8 God provided a scorching east *w*,
Hab 1: 9 hordes advance like a desert *w*
1: 11 they sweep past like the *w*
Zec 5: 9 with the *w* in their wings!
Mt 11: 7 A reed swayed by the *w*? If not,
14: 24 by the waves because the *w* was
14: 30 when he saw the *w*, he was afraid
14: 32 into the boat, the *w* died down.
Mk 4: 39 Then the *w* died down
4: 39 rebuked the *w* and said
4: 41 Even the *w* and the waves obey
6: 48 because the *w* was against them.
6: 51 with them, and the *w* died down.
Lk 7: 24 A reed swayed by the *w*? If not,
8: 24 and rebuked the *w* and the raging
12: 55 And when the south *w* blows,
Jn 3: 8 The *w* blows wherever it pleases.
6: 18 A strong *w* was blowing
Ac 2: 2 of a violent *w* came from heaven
27: 7 When the *w* did not allow us
27: 13 When a gentle south *w* began
27: 14 Before very long, a *w*
27: 15 and could not head into the *w*;
27: 40 they hoisted the foresail to the *w*
28: 13 The next day the south *w* came up,
Eph 4: 14 and there by every *w* of teaching
Jas 1: 6 blown and tossed by the *w*.
Jude : 12 blown along by the *w*; autumn trees
Rev 6: 13 tree when shaken by a strong *w*.
7: 1 to prevent any *w* from blowing

WIND-BLOWN (BLOW)

Lev 26: 36 of a *w* leaf will put them to flight.
Job 13: 25 Will you torment a *w* leaf?

WINDBLOWN (BLOW)

Isa 41: 2 to *w* chaff with his bow.

WINDING (WOUND)

Jdg 5: 6 travelers took to *w* paths.

WINDOW (WINDOWS)

Ge 8: 6 Noah opened the *w* he had made
26: 8 Philistines looked down from a *w*
Jos 2: 15 down by a rope through the *w*,
2: 18 in the *w* through which you let us
2: 21 she tied the scarlet cord in the *w*.
Jdg 5: 28 "Through the *w* peered Sisera's
1Sa 19: 12 David down through a *w*,
2Sa 6: 16 daughter of Saul watched from a *w*.
2Ki 9: 30 her hair and looked out of a *w*.
9: 32 He looked up at the *w*
13: 17 "Open the east *w*," he said,
1Ch 15: 29 daughter of Saul watched from a *w*.
Pr 7: 6 At the *w* of my house
Hos 13: 3 like smoke escaping through a *w*.
Ac 20: 9 in a *w* was a young man named
2Co 11: 33 in a basket from a *w* in the wall

WINDOWS (WINDOW)

1Ki 6: 4 He made narrow clerestory *w*
7: 4 Its *w* were placed high in sets
Ecc 12: 3 looking through the *w* grow dim;
SS 2: 9 gazing through the *w*,
Jer 9: 21 has climbed in through our *w*
22: 14 So he makes large *w* in it,
Eze 41: 16 as the thresholds and the narrow *w*
41: 16 to the *w*, and the *w* were covered.
41: 26 of the portico were narrow *w*
Da 6: 10 upstairs room where the *w* opened
Joel 2: 9 thieves they enter through the *w*.
Zep 2: 14 Their calls will echo through the *w*,

WINDS (WIND WOUND)

Ge 2: 11 it *w* through the entire land
2: 13 it *w* through the entire land of Cush
Job 37: 9 the cold from the driving *w*.
38: 24 where the east *w* are scattered
Ps 104: 4 He makes *w* his messengers,
148: 8 stormy *w* that do his bidding,
Jer 49: 32 I will scatter to the *w* those who are
49: 36 I will bring against Elam the four *w*
49: 36 I will scatter them to the four *w*,
Eze 5: 10 scatter all your survivors to the *w*.
5: 12 and a third I will scatter to the *w*
12: 14 to the *w* all those around him—
13: 11 and violent *w* will burst forth.
17: 21 survivors will be scattered to the *w*.
37: 9 Come from the four *w*, O breath,
Da 7: 2 there before me were the four *w*
8: 8 up toward the four *w* of heaven.
11: 4 out toward the four *w* of heaven.
Am 1: 14 amid violent *w* on a stormy day.
Zec 2: 6 you to the four *w* of heaven,"
Mt 7: 25 and the *w* blew and beat
7: 27 and the *w* blew and beat
8: 26 and rebuked the *w* and the waves,
8: 27 Even the *w* and the waves obey
24: 31 gather his elect from the four *w*,
Mk 13: 27 gather his elect from the four *w*,
Lk 8: 25 He commands even the *w*
Ac 27: 4 because the *w* were against us.
Heb 1: 7 "He makes his angels *w*,
Jas 3: 4 and are driven by strong *w*,
Rev 7: 1 holding back the four *w*

WINDSTORM (STORM)

Isa 29: 6 with *w* and tempest and flames
Eze 1: 4 I saw a *w* coming out of the north—

WINE (WINES)

Ge 9: 21 When he drank some of its *w*,
9: 24 When Noah awoke from his *w*
14: 18 of Salem brought out bread and *w*.
19: 32 Let's get our father to drink *w*
19: 33 they got their father to drink *w*,
19: 34 him to drink *w* again tonight,
19: 35 father to drink *w* that night
27: 25 he brought some *w* and he drank.
27: 28 an abundance of grain and new *w*.
27: 37 him with grain and new *w*.
49: 11 he will wash his garments in *w*,
49: 12 His eyes will be darker than *w*,
Ex 29: 40 of a hin of *w* as a drink offering.
Lev 10: 9 and your sons are not to drink *w*
23: 13 offering of a fourth of a hin of *w*.
Nu 6: 3 he must abstain from *w*
6: 3 not drink vinegar made from *w*
6: 20 the Nazirite may drink *w*.
15: 5 prepare a fourth of a hin of *w*
15: 7 of a hin of *w* as a drink offering.
15: 10 a hin of *w* as a drink offering.
18: 12 all the finest new *w* and grain they
28: 14 a drink offering of half a hin of *w*;
Dt 7: 13 your grain, new *w* and oil—
11: 14 gather in your grain, new *w*
12: 17 the tithe of your grain and new *w*
14: 23 Eat the tithe of your grain, new *w*
14: 26 sheep, *w* or other fermented drink,
18: 4 the firstfruits of your grain, new *w*
28: 39 but you will not drink the *w*
28: 51 will leave you no grain, new *w*
29: 6 and drank no *w* or other fermented
32: 33 Their *w* is the venom of serpents,
32: 38 drank the *w* of their drink offerings
33: 28 secure in a land of grain and new *w*,
Jdg 9: 13 I give up my *w*, which cheers both
13: 4 Now see to it that you drink no *w*
13: 7 drink no *w* or other fermented
13: 14 nor drink any *w* or other fermented
19: 19 *w* for ourselves your servants—
Ru 2: 14 and dip it in the *w* vinegar."
1Sa 1: 14 on getting drunk? Get rid of your *w*
1: 15 I have not been drinking *w* or beer;
1: 24 an ephah of flour and a skin of *w*,
10: 3 of bread, and another a skin of *w*.
16: 20 a skin of *w* and a young goat
25: 18 two skins of *w*, five dressed sheep,
2Sa 13: 28 is in high spirits from drinking *w*
16: 1 cakes of figs and a skin of *w*.
16: 2 *w* is to refresh those who become
2Ki 18: 32 a land of grain and new *w*,
1Ch 9: 29 well as the flour and *w*, and the oil,
12: 40 fig cakes, raisin cakes, *w*, oil,
27: 27 of the vineyards for the *w* vats.
2Ch 2: 10 twenty thousand baths of *w*
2: 15 the olive oil and *w* he promised,
11: 11 supplies of food, olive oil and *w*.
31: 5 new *w*, oil and honey and all that
32: 28 to store the harvest of grain, new *w*
Ezr 6: 9 and wheat, salt, *w* and oil,
7: 22 baths of *w*, a hundred baths
Ne 2: 1 I took the *w* and gave it to the king.
2: 1 when *w* was brought for him,
5: 11 part of the money, grain, new *w*
5: 15 them in addition to food and *w*.
5: 18 ten days an abundant supply of *w*
10: 37 of all our trees and of our new *w*
10: 39 new *w* and oil to the storerooms
13: 5 new *w* and oil prescribed
13: 12 new *w* and oil into the storerooms.
13: 15 together with *w*, grapes, figs
Est 1: 7 and the royal *w* was abundant,
1: 7 *W* was served in goblets of gold,
1: 8 king instructed all the *w* stewards
1: 10 was in high spirits from *w*,
5: 6 they were drinking *w*, the king
7: 2 and as they were drinking *w*
7: 7 left his *w* and went out
Job 1: 13 drinking *w* at the oldest brother's
1: 18 drinking *w* at the oldest brother's
32: 19 inside I am like bottled-up *w*,
Ps 4: 7 their grain and new *w* abound
60: 3 you have given us *w* that makes us
75: 8 full of foaming *w* mixed with spices
78: 65 a man wakes from the stupor of *w*.
104: 15 *w* that gladdens the heart of man,
Pr 3: 10 vats will brim over with new *w*.
4: 17 and drink the *w* of violence.
9: 2 her meat and mixed her *w*;
9: 5 and drink the *w* I have mixed.
20: 1 *W* is a mocker and beer a brawler;
21: 17 whoever loves *w* and oil will never
23: 20 join those who drink too much *w*
23: 30 Those who linger over *w*,
23: 30 who go to sample bowls of mixed *w*
23: 31 Do not gaze at *w* when it is red,
31: 4 not for kings to drink *w*,
31: 6 *w* to those who are in anguish;
Ecc 2: 3 I tried cheering myself with *w*,
9: 7 drink your *w* with a joyful heart,
10: 19 and *w* makes life merry,
SS 1: 2 your love is more delightful than *w*.
1: 4 will praise your love more than *w*.
4: 10 more pleasing is your love than *w*,
5: 1 I have drunk my *w* and my milk.
7: 2 that never lacks blended *w*.
7: 9 May the *w* go straight to my lover,
7: 9 and your mouth like the best *w*.
8: 2 I would give you spiced *w* to drink,
Isa 1: 22 your choice *w* is diluted with water
5: 10 will produce only a bath of *w*,
5: 11 night till they are inflamed with *w*.
5: 12 tambourines and flutes and *w*,
5: 22 those who are heroes at drinking *w*
16: 10 no one treads out *w* at the presses,
22: 13 eating of meat and drinking of *w*!
24: 7 new *w* dries up and the vine
24: 9 No longer do they drink *w*
24: 11 In the streets they cry out for *w*;
25: 6 a banquet of aged *w*—
28: 1 the pride of those laid low by *w*!
28: 7 And these also stagger from *w*
28: 7 and are befuddled with *w*;
Isa 29: 9 be drunk, but not from *w*,
36: 17 a land of grain and new *w*,
49: 26 on their own blood, as with *w*.
51: 21 made drunk, but not with *w*.
55: 1 Come, buy *w* and milk
56: 12 each one cries, "let me get *w*!
62: 8 will foreigners drink the new *w*
65: 11 fill bowls of mixed *w* for Destiny,
Jer 13: 12 wineskin should be filled with *w*.'
13: 12 wineskin should be filled with *w*?'
23: 9 like a man overcome by *w*,
25: 15 filled with the *w* of my wrath
31: 12 the grain, the new *w* and the oil,
35: 2 and give them *w* to drink."
35: 5 Then I set bowls full of *w*
35: 5 and said to them, "Drink some *w*."
35: 6 descendants must ever drink *w*.
35: 6 they replied, "We do not drink *w*,
35: 8 and daughters have ever drunk *w*
35: 14 To this day they do not drink *w*,
35: 14 ordered his sons not to drink *w*
40: 10 but you are to harvest the *w*,
40: 12 they harvested an abundance of *w*
48: 11 like *w* left on its dregs,
48: 33 the flow of *w* from the presses;
51: 7 The nations drank her *w*;
La 2: 12 "Where is bread and *w*?"
Eze 27: 18 with you in *w* from Helbon
44: 21 No priest is to drink *w*
Da 1: 5 and *w* from the king's table.
1: 8 himself with the royal food and *w*,
1: 16 and the *w* they were to drink
5: 1 thousand of his nobles and drank *w*
5: 2 Belshazzar was drinking his *w*,
5: 4 As they drank the *w*, they praised
5: 23 and your concubines drank *w*
10: 3 no meat or *w* touched my lips;
Hos 2: 8 who gave her the grain, the new *w*
2: 9 and my new *w* when it is ready.
2: 22 the new *w* and oil,
4: 11 to old *w* and new,
7: 5 princes become inflamed with *w*,
7: 14 together for grain and new *w*
9: 2 the new *w* will fail them.
9: 4 They will not pour out *w* offerings
14: 7 and his fame will be like the *w*
Joel 1: 5 Wail, all you drinkers of *w*;
1: 5 wail because of the *w*,
1: 10 the new *w* is dried up,
2: 19 "I am sending you grain, new *w*
2: 24 the vats will overflow with new *w*
3: 3 they sold girls for *w*
3: 18 day the mountains will drip new *w*,
Am 2: 8 they drink *w* taken as fines.
2: 12 you made the Nazirites drink *w*
5: 11 you will not drink their *w*.
6: 6 You drink *w* by the bowlful
9: 13 *w* will drip from the mountains
9: 14 plant vineyards and drink their *w*;
Mic 2: 11 'I will prophesy for you plenty of *w*
6: 15 crush grapes but not drink the *w*.
Na 1: 10 and drunk from their *w*;
Hab 2: 5 indeed, *w* betrays him;
Zep 1: 12 who are like *w* left on its dregs,
1: 13 but not drink the *w*.
Hag 1: 11 the new *w*, the oil and whatever
2: 12 some *w*, oil or other food, does it
2: 16 When anyone went to a *w* vat
Zec 9: 15 They will drink and roar as with *w*;
9: 17 and new *w* the young women.
10: 7 their hearts will be glad as with *w*.
Mt 9: 17 Neither do men pour new *w*
9: 17 pour new *w* into new wineskins,
9: 17 *w* will run out and the wineskins
27: 34 There they offered him *w* to drink,
27: 48 He filled it with *w* vinegar,
Mk 2: 22 And no one pours new *w*
2: 22 If he does, the *w* will burst the skins
2: 22 both the *w* and the wineskins will
2: 22 he pours new *w* into new wineskins
15: 23 Then they offered him *w* mixed
15: 36 filled a sponge with *w* vinegar,
Lk 1: 15 to take *w* or other fermented drink,
5: 37 And no one pours new *w*
5: 37 the new *w* will burst the skins,
5: 37 *w* will run out and the wineskins
5: 38 new *w* must be poured
5: 39 after drinking old *w* wants the new,

Lk 7:33 eating bread nor drinking *w*,
10:34 his wounds, pouring on oil and *w*.
23:36 They offered him *w* vinegar
Jn 2:3 When the *w* was gone, Jesus'
2:3 to him, "They have no more *w*."
2:9 water that had been turned into *w*.
2:10 and then the cheaper *w*
2:10 brings out the choice *w* first
4:46 he had turned the water into *w*.
19:29 A jar of *w* vinegar was there,
Ac 2:13 "They have had too much *w*."
Ro 14:21 not to eat meat or drink *w*
Eph 5:18 on *w*, which leads to debauchery.
1Ti 3:3 not given to much *w*, not violent
3:8 sincere, not indulging in much *w*,
5:23 a little *w* because of your stomach
Tit 1:7 not given to much *w*, not violent,
2:3 slanderers or addicted to much *w*,
Rev 6:6 do not damage the oil and the *w*!"
14:8 the nations drink the maddening *w*
14:10 will drink of the *w* of God's fury,
16:19 with the *w* of the fury of his wrath.
17:2 with the *w* of her adulteries."
18:3 the maddening *w* of her adulteries.
18:13 frankincense, of *w* and olive oil,

WINEPRESS (WINEPRESSES)

Nu 18:27 threshing floor or juice from the *w*.
18:30 of the threshing floor or the *w*.
Dt 15:14 your threshing floor and your *w*.
16:13 of your threshing floor and your *w*.
Jdg 6:11 a *w* to keep it from the Midianites.
7:25 and Zeeb at the *w* of Zeeb.
2Ki 6:27 From the *w*?" Then he asked her,
Isa 5:2 and cut out a *w* as well.
63:2 like those of one treading the *w*?
63:3 "I have trodden the *w* alone;
La 1:15 In his *w* the Lord has trampled
Joel 3:13 for the *w* is full
Mt 21:33 dug a *w* in it and built a watchtower
Mk 12:1 for the *w* and built a watchtower.
Rev 14:19 into the great *w* of God's wrath.
14:20 trampled in the *w* outside the city,
19:15 He treads the *w* of the fury

WINEPRESSES (WINEPRESS)

Ne 13:15 in Judah treading *w* on the Sabbath
Job 24:11 they tread the *w*, yet suffer thirst.
Hos 9:2 *w* will not feed the people;
Zec 14:10 Tower of Hananel to the royal *w*.

WINES (WINE)

Isa 25:6 best of meats and the finest of *w*.

WINESKIN (WINESKINS)

Ps 119:83 Though I am like a *w* in the smoke,
Jer 13:12 Every *w* should be filled with wine
13:12 know that every *w* should be filled
Hab 2:15 pouring it from the *w*

WINESKINS (WINESKIN)

Jos 9:4 with worn-out sacks and old *w*,
9:13 these *w* that we filled were new,
Job 32:19 like new *w* ready to burst.
Mt 9:17 do men pour new wine into old *w*.
9:17 run out and the *w* will be ruined.
9:17 they pour new wine into new *w*,
Mk 2:22 he pours new wine into new *w*."
2:22 no one pours new wine into old *w*.
2:22 the wine and the *w* will be ruined.
Lk 5:37 no one pours new wine into old *w*.
5:37 run out and the *w* will be ruined.
5:38 wine must be poured into new *w*.

WING (WINGED WINGS WINGSPAN)

1Ki 6:24 One *w* of the first cherub was five
6:24 and the other *w* five cubits—
6:24 ten cubits from *w* tip to *w* tip.
6:27 while the *w* of the other touched
6:27 *w* of one cherub touched one wall,
2Ch 3:11 One *w* of the first cherub was five
3:11 touched the *w* of the other cherub.
3:11 while its other *w*, also five cubits
3:12 Similarly one *w* of the second
3:12 and its other *w*, also five cubits long
3:12 touched the *w* of the first cherub.
Ecc 10:20 on the *w* may report what you say.
Isa 10:14 not one flapped a *w*,
Eze 1:11 one touching the *w*
Da 9:27 abominations on a *w* ⌊of the temple⌋

WINGED (WING)

Ge 1:21 every *w* bird according to its kind.
Lev 11:21 some *w* creatures that walk
11:23 all other *w* creatures that have four
Dt 14:20 any *w* creature that is clean you

WINGS (WING)

Ge 7:14 to its kind, everything with *w*.
Ex 19:4 and how I carried you on eagles' *w*
25:20 are to have their *w* spread upward,
37:9 had their *w* spread upward,
Lev 1:17 He shall tear it open by the *w*,
Dt 32:11 that spreads its *w* to catch them
Ru 2:12 under whose *w* you have come
2Sa 22:11 he soared on the *w* of the wind.
1Ki 6:27 and their *w* touched each other
6:27 with their *w* spread out.
8:6 it beneath the *w* of the cherubim.
8:7 The cherubim spread their *w*
1Ch 28:18 of gold that spread their *w*
2Ch 3:13 The *w* of these cherubim extended
5:7 it beneath the *w* of the cherubim.
5:8 The cherubim spread their *w*
Job 39:13 "The *w* of the ostrich flap joyfully,
39:26 and spread his *w* toward the south?
Ps 17:8 hide me in the shadow of your *w*
18:10 he soared on the *w* of the wind.
36:7 find refuge in the shadow of your *w*
55:6 "Oh, that I had the *w* of a dove!
57:1 refuge in the shadow of your *w*
61:4 take refuge in the shelter of your *w*.
63:7 I sing in the shadow of your *w*.
68:13 the *w* of ⌊my⌋ dove are sheathed
91:4 under his *w* you will find refuge;
104:3 and rides on the *w* of the wind.
139:9 If I rise on the *w* of the dawn,
Pr 23:5 for they will surely sprout *w*
Isa 6:2 With two *w* they covered their
6:2 him were seraphs, each with six *w*:
8:8 Its outspread *w* will cover
18:1 Woe to the land of whirring *w*
34:15 young under the shadow of her *w*;
40:31 They will soar on *w* like eagles;
Jer 48:40 spreading its *w* over Moab.
49:22 spreading its *w* over Bozrah.
Eze 1:6 of them had four faces and four *w*.
1:8 All four of them had faces and *w*,
1:8 Under their *w* on their four sides
1:9 and their *w* touched one another.
1:11 Their *w* were spread out upward;
1:11 and two *w* covering its body.
1:11 out upward; each had two *w*,
1:23 each had two *w* covering its body.
1:23 the expanse their *w* were stretched
1:24 I heard the sound of their *w*,
1:24 stood still, they lowered their *w*.
1:25 as they stood with lowered *w*.
3:13 the sound of the *w*
10:5 The sound of the *w*
10:8 (Under the *w* of the cherubim
10:12 and their *w*, were completely full
10:16 when the cherubim spread their *w*
10:19 the cherubim spread their *w*
10:21 Each had four faces and four *w*,
10:21 under their *w* was what looked like
11:22 wheels beside them, spread their *w*,
17:3 A great eagle with powerful *w*,
17:7 great eagle with powerful *w*
Da 7:4 I watched until its *w* were torn off
7:4 and it had the *w* of an eagle.
7:6 on its back it had four *w* like those
Zec 5:9 in their *w*! They had *w* like those
Mal 4:2 rise with healing in its *w*.
Mt 23:37 hen gathers her chicks under her *w*,
Lk 13:34 hen gathers her chicks under her *w*,
Rev 4:8 all around, even under his *w*.
4:8 the four living creatures had six *w*
9:9 of their *w* was like the thundering
12:14 The woman was given the two *w*

WINGSPAN (WING)

2Ch 3:11 total *w* of the cherubim was twenty

WINK (WINKS)

Ps 35:19 maliciously *w* the eye.

WINKS (WINK)

Pr 6:13 who *w* with his eye,
10:10 He who *w* maliciously causes grief,
16:30 He who *w* with his eye is plotting

WINNING (WIN)

Ex 17:11 Israelites were *w*, but whenever he
17:11 his hands, the Amalekites were *w*.

WINNOW (WINNOWING WINNOWS)

Isa 41:16 You will *w* them, the wind will pick
Jer 4:11 to *w* or cleanse; a wind too strong
15:7 I will *w* them with a winnowing
51:2 to *w* her and to devastate her land;

WINNOWING (WINNOW)

Ru 3:2 Tonight he will be *w* barley
Jer 15:7 I will winnow them with a *w* fork
Mt 3:12 His *w* fork is in his hand,
Lk 3:17 His *w* fork is in his hand

WINNOWS (WINNOW)

Pr 20:8 he *w* out all evil with his eyes.
20:26 A wise king *w* out the wicked;

WINS (WIN)

Pr 11:30 and he who *w* souls is wise.
13:15 Good understanding *w* favor,

WINTER (WINTERED)

Ge 8:22 summer and *w*,
Ps 74:17 you made both summer and *w*.
SS 2:11 See! The *w* is past;
Isa 18:6 the wild animals all *w*.
Jer 36:22 sitting in the *w* apartment,
Hos 6:3 he will come to us like the *w* rains,
Am 3:15 I will tear down the *w* house
Zec 14:8 in summer and in *w*.
Mt 24:20 your flight will not take place in *w*
Mk 13:18 that this will not take place in *w*,
Jn 10:22 It was *w*, and Jesus was
Ac 27:12 the harbor was unsuitable to *w*
27:12 to reach Phoenix and *w* there.
1Co 16:6 spend the *w*, so that you can help
2Ti 4:21 Do your best to get here before *w*.
Tit 3:12 because I have decided to *w* there.

WINTERED (WINTER)

Ac 28:11 in a ship that had *w* in the island.

WIPE (WIPED WIPES WIPING)

Ge 6:7 "I will *w* mankind, whom I have
7:4 and I will *w* from the face
Ex 23:23 Jebusites, and I will *w* them out.
32:12 to *w* them off the face of the earth'?
Dt 7:24 and you will *w* out their names
12:3 and *w* out their names from those
Jos 7:9 and *w* out our name from the earth.
9:24 and to *w* out all its inhabitants
1Sa 24:21 or *w* out my name from my father's
2Ki 21:13 I will *w* out Jerusalem
Isa 25:8 The Sovereign LORD will *w* away
Lk 10:11 to our feet we *w* off against you.
Rev 7:17 God will *w* away every tear
21:4 He will *w* every tear

WIPED (WIPE)

Ge 7:23 of the air were *w* from the earth.
7:23 on the face of the earth was *w* out;
Ex 9:15 a plague that would have *w* you
Jdg 21:17 a tribe of Israel will not be *w* out.
1Sa 15:18 on them until you have *w* them out
Ps 119:87 They almost *w* me from the earth,
Pr 6:33 and his shame will never be *w* away
Isa 26:14 you *w* out all memory of them.
Eze 6:6 and what you have made *w* out.
Zep 1:11 all your merchants will be *w* out,
Lk 7:38 Then she *w* them with her hair,
7:44 feet with her tears and *w* them
Jn 11:2 and *w* his feet with her hair.
12:3 and *w* his feet with her hair.
Ac 3:19 so that your sins may be *w* out,

WIPES (WIPE)

2Ki 21:13 wipe out Jerusalem as one *w* a dish,
Pr 30:20 She eats and *w* her mouth

WIPING (WIPE)

2Ki 21: 13 *w* it and turning it upside down.

WISDOM (WISE)

Ge 3: 6 and also desirable for gaining *w*,
Ex 28: 3 men to whom I have given *w*
Dt 4: 6 for this will show your *w*
34: 9 filled with the spirit of *w*
2Sa 14: 20 My lord has *w* like that of an angel
1Ki 2: 6 Deal with him according to your *w*,
2: 9 a man of *w*; you will know what
3: 28 they saw that he had *w* from God
4: 29 God gave Solomon *w* and very
4: 30 Solomon's *w* was greater
4: 30 and greater than all the *w* of Egypt.
4: 30 greater than the *w* of all the men
4: 34 came to listen to Solomon's *w*,
4: 34 the world, who had heard of his *w*.
5: 12 The LORD gave Solomon *w*,
10: 4 of Sheba saw all the *w* of Solomon
10: 6 achievements and your *w* is true.
10: 7 in *w* and wealth you have far
10: 8 stand before you and hear your *w*!
10: 23 and *w* than all the other kings
10: 24 to hear the *w* God had put
11: 41 all he did and the *w* he displayed—
2Ch 1: 10 Give me *w* and knowledge,
1: 11 asked for a long life but for *w*
1: 12 *w* and knowledge will be given you.
9: 3 of Sheba saw the *w* of Solomon,
9: 5 achievements and your *w* is true.
9: 6 greatness of your *w* was told me;
9: 7 stand before you and hear your *w*!
9: 22 and *w* than all the other kings
9: 23 to hear the *w* God had put
Ezr 7: 25 with the *w* of your God,
Job 4: 21 so that they die without *w*?'
9: 4 His *w* is profound, his power is vast
11: 6 and disclose to you the secrets of *w*
11: 6 for true *w* has two sides.
12: 2 and *w* will die with you!
12: 12 Is not *w* found among the aged?
12: 13 "To God belong *w* and power;
13: 5 For you, that would be *w*.
15: 8 Do you limit *w* to yourself?
26: 3 you have offered to one without *w*!
26: 12 by his *w* he cut Rahab to pieces.
28: 12 "But where can *w* be found?
28: 18 the price of *w* is beyond rubies.
28: 20 "Where then does *w* come from?
28: 27 looked at *w* and appraised it;
28: 28 'The fear of the Lord—that is *w*,
32: 7 advanced years should teach *w*.'
32: 13 Do not say, 'We have found *w*;
33: 33 be silent, and I will teach you *w*."
38: 36 Who endowed the heart with *w*
38: 37 Who has the *w* to count the clouds?
39: 17 for God did not endow her with *w*
39: 26 the hawk take flight by your *w*
Ps 37: 30 of the righteous man utters *w*,
49: 3 My mouth will speak words of *w*;
51: 6 you teach me *w* in the inmost place
90: 12 that we may gain a heart of *w*.
104: 24 In *w* you made them all;
105: 22 and teach his elders *w*.
111: 10 of the LORD is the beginning of *w*;
Pr 1: 2 for attaining *w* and discipline;
1: 7 but fools despise *w* and discipline.
1: 20 *W* calls aloud in the street,
2: 2 turning your ear to *w*
2: 6 For the LORD gives *w*,
2: 10 For *w* will enter your heart,
2: 12 *W* will save you from the ways
3: 13 Blessed is the man who finds *w*,
3: 19 By *w* the LORD laid the earth's
4: 5 Get *w*, get understanding;
4: 6 Do not forsake *w*, and she will
4: 7 is supreme; therefore get *w*.
4: 7 *W* is supreme; therefore get
4: 11 I guide you in the way of *w*
5: 1 My son, pay attention to my *w*,
7: 4 Say to *w*, "You are my sister,"
8: 1 Does not *w* call out?
8: 11 for *w* is more precious than rubies,
8: 12 I, *w*, dwell together with prudence;
9: 1 *W* has built her house;
9: 10 of the LORD is the beginning of *w*,
Pr 9: 12 are wise, your *w* will reward you;
10: 13 *W* is found on the lips
10: 23 of understanding delights in *w*.
10: 31 of the righteous brings forth *w*,
11: 2 but with humility comes *w*.
12: 8 A man is praised according to his *w*
13: 10 *w* is found in those who take advice
14: 6 The mocker seeks *w* and finds none
14: 8 The *w* of the prudent is
14: 33 *W* reposes in the heart
15: 33 of the LORD teaches a man *w*,
16: 16 better to get *w* than gold,
17: 16 since he has no desire to get *w*?
17: 24 A discerning man keeps *w* in view,
18: 4 of *w* is a bubbling brook.
19: 8 He who gets *w* loves his own soul;
19: 11 A man's *w* gives him patience;
21: 11 is punished, the simple gain *w*;
21: 30 There is no *w*, no insight, no plan
23: 4 have the *w* to show restraint.
23: 9 for he will scorn the *w*
23: 23 get *w*, discipline and understanding
24: 3 By *w* a house is built,
24: 7 *W* is too high for a fool;
24: 14 also that *w* is sweet to your soul;
28: 26 but he who walks in *w* is kept safe.
29: 3 A man who loves *w* brings joy
29: 15 The rod of correction imparts *w*,
30: 3 I have not learned *w*,
31: 26 She speaks with *w*,
Ecc 1: 13 and to explore by *w* all that is done
1: 16 I have experienced much of *w*
1: 16 and increased in *w* more
1: 17 myself to the understanding of *w*,
1: 18 with much *w* comes much sorrow;
2: 3 my mind still guiding me with *w*.
2: 9 In all this my *w* stayed with me.
2: 12 I turned my thoughts to consider *w*
2: 13 I saw that *w* is better than folly,
2: 21 For a man may do his work with *w*,
2: 26 God gives *w*, knowledge
7: 11 *W*, like an inheritance, is a good
7: 12 that *w* preserves the life
7: 12 *W* is a shelter
7: 19 *W* makes one wise man more
7: 23 All this I tested by *w* and I said,
7: 24 Whatever *w* may be,
7: 25 and to search out *w* and the scheme
8: 1 *W* brightens a man's face
8: 16 I applied my mind to know *w*
9: 10 nor planning nor knowledge nor *w*.
9: 13 of *w* that greatly impressed me:
9: 15 and he saved the city by his *w*.
9: 16 But the poor man's *w* is despised,
9: 16 "*W* is better than strength."
9: 18 *W* is better than weapons of war,
10: 1 so a little folly outweighs *w*
Isa 10: 13 and by my *w*, because I have
11: 2 Spirit of *w* and of understanding,
28: 29 in counsel and magnificent in *w*.
29: 14 the *w* of the wise will perish,
33: 6 a rich store of salvation and *w*
47: 10 Your *w* and knowledge mislead
Jer 8: 9 what kind of *w* do they have?
9: 23 not the wise man boast of his *w*
10: 12 he founded the world by his *w*
49: 7 Has their *w* decayed?
49: 7 "Is there no longer *w* in Teman?
51: 15 he founded the world by his *w*
Eze 28: 4 By your *w* and understanding
28: 7 swords against your beauty and *w*
28: 12 full of *w* and perfect in beauty.
28: 17 and you corrupted your *w*
Da 1: 20 of *w* and understanding about
2: 14 Daniel spoke to him with *w*
2: 20 *w* and power are his.
2: 21 He gives *w* to the wise
2: 23 You have given me *w* and power,
2: 30 I have greater *w* than other living
5: 11 and *w* like that of the gods.
5: 14 intelligence and outstanding *w*.
Hos 13: 13 but he is a child without *w*;
Mic 6: 9 and to fear your name is *w*—
Mt 11: 19 But *w* is proved right by her actions
12: 42 the earth to listen to Solomon's *w*,
13: 54 "Where did this man get this *w*
Mk 6: 2 "What's this *w* that has been given
Lk 1: 17 to the *w* of the righteous—
Lk 2: 40 he was filled with *w*, and the grace
2: 52 And Jesus grew in *w* and stature,
7: 35 *w* is proved right by all her children
11: 31 the earth to listen to Solomon's *w*,
11: 49 Because of this, God in his *w* said,
21: 15 *w* that none of your adversaries
Ac 6: 3 known to be full of the Spirit and *w*.
6: 10 could not stand up against his *w*
7: 10 He gave Joseph *w* and enabled him
7: 22 in all the *w* of the Egyptians
Ro 11: 33 the depth of the riches of the *w*
1Co 1: 17 not with words of human *w*,
1: 19 "I will destroy the *w* of the wise;
1: 20 Has not God made foolish the *w*
1: 21 For since in the *w* of God the world
1: 21 through its *w* did not know him,
1: 22 signs and Greeks look for *w*,
1: 24 power of God and the *w* of God.
1: 25 of God is wiser than man's *w*,
1: 30 who has become for us *w* from God
2: 1 come with eloquence or superior *w*
2: 5 faith might not rest on men's *w*,
2: 6 a message of *w* among the mature,
2: 6 but not the *w* of this age
2: 7 No, we speak of God's secret *w*,
2: 7 a *w* that has been hidden
2: 13 not in words taught us by human *w*
3: 19 For the *w* of this world is
12: 8 through the Spirit the message of *w*
2Co 1: 12 done so not according to worldly *w*
Eph 1: 8 that he lavished on us with all *w*
1: 17 may give you the Spirit of *w*
3: 10 manifold *w* of God should be made
Col 1: 9 of his will through all spiritual *w*
1: 28 and teaching everyone with all *w*,
2: 3 are hidden all the treasures of *w*
2: 23 indeed have an appearance of *w*,
3: 16 admonish one another with all *w*,
Jas 1: 5 of you lacks *w*, he should ask God,
3: 13 in the humility that comes from *w*.
3: 15 Such "*w*" does not come
3: 17 *w* that comes from heaven is first
2Pe 3: 15 you with the *w* that God gave him.
Rev 5: 12 and wealth and *w* and strength
7: 12 and *w* and thanks and honor
13: 18 This calls for *w*.
17: 9 "This calls for a mind with *w*.

WISE (OVERWISE WISDOM WISER WISEST)

Ge 41: 8 for all the magicians and *w* men
41: 33 look for a discerning and *w* man
41: 39 there is no one so discerning and *w*
Ex 7: 11 Pharaoh then summoned *w* men
Dt 1: 13 Choose some *w*, understanding
1: 15 the leading men of your tribes, *w*
4: 6 "Surely this great nation is a *w*
16: 19 for a bribe blinds the eyes of the *w*
32: 29 only they were *w* and would
2Sa 14: 2 had a *w* woman brought from there
20: 16 a *w* woman called from the city,
20: 22 to all the people with her *w* advice,
1Ki 3: 12 give you a *w* and discerning heart,
5: 7 for he has given David a *w* son
1Ch 26: 14 his son Zechariah, a *w* counselor,
2Ch 2: 12 He has given King David a *w* son,
Est 1: 13 with the *w* men who understood
Job 5: 13 He catches the *w* in their craftiness
11: 12 witless man can no more become *w*
15: 2 "Would a *w* man answer
15: 18 what *w* men have declared,
17: 10 I will not find a *w* man among you.
22: 2 Can even a *w* man benefit him?
32: 9 It is not only the old who are *w*,
34: 2 "Hear my words, you *w* men;
34: 34 *w* men who hear me say to me,
37: 24 for all the *w* in heart?"
Ps 2: 10 Therefore, you kings, be *w*;
19: 7 making *w* the simple.
36: 3 to be *w* and to do good.
49: 10 For all can see that *w* men die;
94: 8 when will you become *w*?
107: 43 Whoever is *w*, let him heed these
Pr 1: 5 let the *w* listen and add
1: 6 the sayings and riddles of the *w*.
3: 7 Do not be *w* in your own eyes;
3: 35 The *w* inherit honor,
6: 6 consider its ways and be *w*!

Pr 8: 33 Listen to my instruction and be *w;*
9: 8 rebuke a *w* man and he will love
9: 9 Instruct a *w* man and he will be
9: 12 If you are *w,* your wisdom will
10: 1 A *w* son brings joy to his father,
10: 5 in summer is a *w* son,
10: 8 The *w* in heart accept commands,
10: 14 *W* men store up knowledge,
10: 19 but he who holds his tongue is *w.*
11: 29 and the fool will be servant to the *w*
11: 30 and he who wins souls is *w.*
12: 15 but a *w* man listens to advice.
12: 18 the tongue of the *w* brings healing.
13: 1 A *w* son heeds his father's
13: 14 The teaching of the *w* is a fountain
13: 20 He who walks with the *w* grows *w,*
14: 1 The *w* woman builds her house,
14: 3 but the lips of the *w* protect them.
14: 16 A *w* man fears the LORD
14: 24 The wealth of the *w* is their crown,
14: 35 A king delights in a *w* servant,
15: 2 of the *w* commends knowledge,
15: 7 The lips of the *w* spread knowledge
15: 12 he will not consult the *w.*
15: 20 A *w* son brings joy to his father,
15: 24 path of life leads upward for the *w*
15: 31 will be at home among the *w.*
16: 14 but a *w* man will appease it.
16: 21 *w* in heart are called discerning,
16: 23 A *w* man's heart guides his mouth,
17: 2 A *w* servant will rule
17: 28 Even a fool is thought *w*
18: 15 the ears of the *w* seek it out.
19: 20 and in the end you will be *w.*
20: 1 is led astray by them is not *w.*
20: 26 A *w* king winnows out the wicked;
21: 11 when a *w* man is instructed,
21: 20 In the house of the *w* are stores
21: 22 A *w* man attacks the city
22: 17 and listen to the sayings of the *w;*
23: 15 My son, if your heart is *w,*
23: 19 Listen, my son, and be *w,*
23: 24 he who has a *w* son delights in him.
24: 5 A *w* man has great power,
24: 23 These also are sayings of the *w:*
25: 12 is a *w* man's rebuke
26: 5 or he will be *w* in his own eyes.
26: 12 Do you see a man *w*
27: 11 Be *w,* my son, and bring joy
28: 11 A rich man may be *w*
29: 8 but *w* men turn away anger.
29: 9 If a *w* man goes to court with a fool,
29: 11 a *w* man keeps himself
30: 24 yet they are extremely *w:*
Ecc 2: 14 The *w* man has eyes in his head,
2: 15 What then do I gain by being *w?"*
2: 16 For the *w* man, like the fool,
2: 16 Like the fool, the *w* man too must
2: 19 he will be a *w* man or a fool?
4: 13 Better a poor but *w* youth
6: 8 What advantage has a *w* man
7: 4 The heart of the *w* is in the house
7: 5 to heed a *w* man's rebuke
7: 7 Extortion turns a *w* man into a fool,
7: 10 For it is not *w* to ask such questions
7: 19 Wisdom makes one *w* man more
7: 23 "I am determined to be *w*"—
8: 1 Who is like the *w* man?
8: 5 *w* heart will know the proper time
8: 17 Even if a *w* man claims he knows,
9: 1 that the righteous and the *w*
9: 11 nor does food come to the *w*
9: 15 lived in that city a man poor but *w,*
9: 17 The quiet words of the *w* are more
10: 2 The heart of the *w* inclines
10: 12 from a *w* man's mouth are gracious,
12: 9 Not only was the Teacher *w,*
12: 11 The words of the *w* are like goads,
Isa 5: 21 to those who are *w*
19: 11 "I am one of the *w* men,
19: 11 *w* counselors of Pharaoh give
19: 12 Where are your *w* men now?
29: 14 the wisdom of the *w* will perish,
31: 2 Yet he too is *w* and can bring
44: 25 overthrows the learning of the *w*
Jer 8: 8 " 'How can you say, "We are *w,*
8: 9 The *w* will be put to shame;
9: 12 What man is *w* enough
Jer 9: 23 "Let not the *w* man boast
10: 7 Among all the *w* men
18: 18 nor will counsel from the *w,*
50: 35 and against her officials and *w* men
51: 57 her officials and *w* men drunk,
Eze 28: 2 you think you are as *w* as a god.
28: 6 as *w* as a god,
28: 6 " 'Because you think you are *w,*
Da 2: 12 of all the *w* men of Babylon.
2: 13 issued to put the *w* men to death,
2: 14 put to death the *w* men of Babylon,
2: 18 the rest of the *w* men of Babylon.
2: 21 He gives wisdom to the *w*
2: 24 to execute the *w* men of Babylon,
2: 24 "Do not execute the *w* men
2: 27 Daniel replied, "No *w* man,
2: 48 him in charge of all its *w* men.
4: 6 So I commanded that all the *w* men
4: 18 for none of the *w* men
5: 7 said to these *w* men of Babylon,
5: 8 Then all the king's *w* men came in,
5: 15 The *w* men and enchanters were
11: 33 "Those who are *w* will instruct
11: 35 Some of the *w* will stumble,
12: 3 Those who are *w* will shine like
12: 10 those who are *w* will understand.
Hos 14: 9 Who is *w?* He will realize these
Ob : 8 "will I not destroy the *w* men
Mt 7: 24 practice is like a *w* man who built
11: 25 hidden these things from the *w*
23: 34 sending you prophets and *w* men
24: 45 then is the faithful and *w* servant,
25: 2 them were foolish and five were *w.*
25: 4 The *w,* however, took oil in jars
25: 8 The foolish ones said to the *w,*
Lk 10: 21 hidden these things from the *w*
12: 42 then is the faithful and *w* manager,
Ac 15: 38 Paul did not think it *w* to take him,
Ro 1: 14 both to the *w* and the foolish.
1: 22 Although they claimed to be *w,*
16: 19 you to be *w* about what is good,
16: 27 to the only *w* God be glory forever
1Co 1: 19 I will destroy the wisdom of the *w;*
1: 20 Where is the *w* man? Where is
1: 26 of you were *w* by human standards;
1: 27 things of the world to shame the *w;*
2: 4 and my preaching were not with *w*
3: 18 one of you thinks he is *w*
3: 18 so that he may become *w.*
3: 19 He catches the *w* in their craftiness
3: 20 the thoughts of the *w* are futile."
4: 10 but you are so *w* in Christ!
6: 5 nobody among you *w* enough
2Co 10: 12 with themselves, they are not *w.*
11: 19 up with fools since you are so *w!*
Eph 5: 15 but as *w,* making the most
Col 4: 5 Be *w* in the way you act
2Ti 3: 15 able to make you *w* for salvation
Jas 3: 13 Who is *w* and understanding

WISER (WISE)

1Ki 4: 31 He was *w* than any other man,
4: 31 including Ethan the Ezrahite—*w*
Job 35: 11 makes us *w* than the birds of the air
Ps 119: 98 Your commands make me *w*
Pr 9: 9 a wise man and he will be *w* still;
26: 16 The sluggard is *w* in his own eyes
Eze 28: 3 Are you *w* than Daniel?
1Co 1: 25 of God is *w* than man's wisdom,

WISEST (WISE)

Jdg 5: 29 The *w* of her ladies answer her;

WISH (WISHED WISHES WISHING)

Ex 4: 18 Jethro said, "Go, and I *w* you well
Nu 11: 29 I *w* that all the LORD's people
Dt 14: 26 drink, or anything you *w.*
Jdg 19: 24 and do to them whatever you *w.*
1Sa 24: 4 for you to deal with as you *w.*' "
1Ki 5: 9 to grant my *w* by providing food
Ezr 7: 13 who *w* to go to Jerusalem with you,
Job 10: 18 I *w* I had died before any eye saw
11: 5 Oh, how I *w* that God would speak,
Mt 17: 4 If you *w,* I will put up three shelters
Lk 12: 49 how I *w* it were already kindled!
Jn 15: 7 ask whatever you *w,* and it will be
Ro 9: 3 For I could *w* that I myself were
1Co 4: 8 How I *w* that you really had
1Co 7: 7 I *w* that all men were as I am.
2Co 5: 4 we do not *w* to be unclothed
Gal 4: 9 Do you *w* to be enslaved
4: 20 how I *w* I could be with you now
5: 12 I *w* they would go the whole way
Phm : 20 I do *w,* brother, that I may have
Jas 2: 16 I *w* you well; keep warm
Rev 3: 15 I *w* you were either one

WISHED (WISH)

2Sa 19: 18 over and to do whatever he *w.*
Est 1: 8 to serve each man what he *w.*
Job 9: 3 Though one *w* to dispute with him,
Jer 34: 16 free to go where they *w.*
Mt 17: 12 done to him everything they *w.*
Mk 9: 13 done to him everything they *w,*

WISHES (WISH)

Lev 27: 13 If the owner *w* to redeem
27: 19 the man who dedicates the field *w*
Dt 21: 14 let her go wherever she *w.*
Da 4: 17 and gives them to anyone he *w*
4: 25 and gives them to anyone he *w.*
4: 32 and gives them to anyone he *w.*"
5: 21 and sets over them anyone he *w.*
1Co 7: 39 she is free to marry anyone she *w,*
Rev 22: 17 let him come; and whoever *w,*

WISHING (WISH)

Ac 25: 9 Festus, *w* to do the Jews a favor,

WITCHCRAFT

Dt 18: 10 engages in *w,* or casts spells,
2Ki 9: 22 *w* of your mother Jezebel abound?"
2Ch 33: 6 practiced sorcery, divination and *w*
Mic 5: 12 I will destroy your *w*
Na 3: 4 and peoples by her *w.*
Gal 5: 20 idolatry and *w;* hatred, discord,

WITHDRAW (WITHDRAWN WITHDRAWS WITHDREW)

Lev 26: 25 When you *w* into your cities,
1Sa 14: 19 said to the priest, "*W* your hand."
2Sa 11: 15 *w* from him so he will be struck
20: 21 Hand over this one man, and I'll *w*
24: 16 people, "Enough! *W* your hand."
1Ki 15: 19 of Israel so he will *w* from me."
2Ki 18: 14 *W* from me, and I will pay
1Ch 21: 15 people, "Enough! *W* your hand."
2Ch 16: 3 of Israel so he will *w* from me."
Job 13: 21 *W* your hand far from me,
Jer 21: 2 past so that he will *w* from us."
Eze 5: 11 I myself will *w* my favor; I will not
Ac 4: 15 them to *w* from the Sanhedrin

WITHDRAWN (WITHDRAW)

Jer 16: 5 because I have *w* my blessing,
34: 21 of Babylon, which has *w* from you.
37: 11 After the Babylonian army had *w*
La 2: 3 He has *w* his right hand
Hos 5: 6 he has *w* himself from them.

WITHDRAWS (WITHDRAW)

2Sa 17: 13 If he *w* into a city, then all Israel

WITHDREW (WITHDRAW)

Ex 14: 19 in front of Israel's army, *w*
35: 20 the whole Israelite community *w*
1Sa 14: 46 and they *w* to their own land.
1Ki 8: 10 When the priests *w*
15: 21 he stopped building Ramah and *w*
16: 17 with him *w* from Gibbethon
2Ki 3: 27 they *w* and returned
12: 18 who then *w* from Jerusalem.
15: 20 So the king of Assyria *w*
19: 8 he *w* and found the king fighting
19: 36 king of Assyria broke camp and *w.*
2Ch 5: 11 The priests then *w*
24: 25 When the Arameans *w,* they left
32: 21 So he *w* to his own land in disgrace.
Ezr 10: 6 Then Ezra *w* from before the house
Job 34: 14 and he *w* his spirit and breath,
Isa 37: 8 he *w* and found the king fighting
37: 37 king of Assyria broke camp and *w.*
Jer 37: 5 the report about them, they *w*
Mt 2: 22 he *w* to the district of Galilee,
12: 15 of this, Jesus *w* from that place.
14: 13 he *w* by boat privately

Mt 15: 21 Jesus *w* to the region of Tyre
Mk 3: 7 Jesus *w* with his disciples
Lk 5: 16 But Jesus often *w* to lonely places
9: 10 and they *w* by themselves
22: 41 He *w* about a stone's throw
Jn 6: 15 *w* again into the hills by himself.
11: 54 Instead he *w* to a region
Ac 22: 29 to question him *w* immediately.

WITHER (WITHERED WITHERS)

Job 8: 12 they *w* more quickly than grass.
15: 30 a flame will *w* his shoots,
18: 16 and his branches *w* above.
Ps 1: 3 and whose leaf does not *w*.
37: 2 for like the grass they will soon *w*,
37: 19 In times of disaster they will not *w*;
102: 11 I *w* away like grass.
Isa 16: 8 The fields of Heshbon *w*,
19: 6 The reeds and rushes will *w*,
40: 24 than he blows on them and they *w*,
Jer 8: 13 and their leaves will *w*.
Eze 17: 9 withers? All its new growth will *w*.
17: 10 Will it not *w* completely
17: 10 *w* away in the plot where it grew
47: 12 Their leaves will not *w*,
Na 1: 4 Bashan and Carmel *w*
Zec 9: 5 and Ekron too, for her hope will *w*.
Mt 21: 20 How did the fig tree *w* so quickly?"

WITHERED (WITHER)

Ge 41: 23 *w* and thin and scorched
Ps 90: 6 by evening it is dry and *w*.
102: 4 heart is blighted and *w* like grass;
Isa 15: 6 and the grass is *w*;
34: 4 like *w* leaves from the vine,
Jer 12: 4 and the grass in every field be *w*?
23: 10 and the pastures in the desert are *w*
Eze 19: 12 its strong branches *w*
31: 15 and all the trees of the field *w* away
Hos 9: 16 their root is *w*,
Joel 1: 12 and the fig tree is *w*;
1: 12 is *w* away.
Jnh 4: 7 which chewed the vine so that it *w*.
Zec 11: 17 May his arm be completely *w*,
Mt 13: 6 they *w* because they had no root.
21: 19 again!" Immediately the tree *w*.
Mk 4: 6 they *w* because they had no root.
11: 20 they saw the fig tree *w*
11: 21 The fig tree you cursed has *w*!"
Lk 8: 6 the plants *w* because they had no

WITHERS (WITHER)

Job 8: 19 Surely its life *w* away,
14: 2 up like a flower and *w* away;
Ps 129: 6 which *w* before it can grow;
Isa 24: 4 The earth dries up and *w*,
24: 4 the world languishes and *w*,
24: 7 new wine dries up and the vine *w*;
33: 9 Lebanon is ashamed and *w*;
40: 7 The grass *w* and the flowers fall,
40: 8 The grass *w* and the flowers fall,
Eze 17: 9 and stripped of its fruit so that it *w*?
Am 1: 2 and the top of Carmel *w*."
Jn 15: 6 branch that is thrown away and *w*;
Jas 1: 11 scorching heat and *w* the plant;
1Pe 1: 24 the grass *w* and the flowers fall,

WITHHELD (WITHHOLD)

Ge 22: 12 you have not *w* from me your son,
22: 16 done this and have not *w* your son,
39: 9 My master has *w* nothing from me
Job 22: 7 and you *w* food from the hungry,
Ps 21: 2 have not *w* the request of his lips.
66: 20 or *w* his love from me!
77: 9 Has he in anger *w* his compassion
Isa 63: 15 and compassion are *w* from us.
Jer 3: 3 Therefore the showers have been *w*
Eze 20: 22 But I *w* my hand, and for the sake
Joel 1: 13 are *w* from the house of your God.
Am 4: 7 but *w* it from another.
4: 7 "I also *w* rain from you
Hag 1: 10 you the heavens have *w* their dew

WITHHOLD (WITHHELD WITHHOLDING WITHHOLDS)

Ne 9: 20 You did not *w* your manna
Ps 40: 11 Do not *w* your mercy from me,
84: 11 no good thing does he *w*
Pr 3: 27 Do not *w* good from those who
23: 13 Do not *w* discipline from a child;
La 2: 8 did not *w* his hand from destroying
Zec 1: 12 how long will you *w* mercy

WITHHOLDING (WITHHOLD)

2Co 6: 12 We are not *w* our affection
6: 12 but you are *w* yours from us.

WITHHOLDS (WITHHOLD)

Dt 27: 19 "Cursed is the man who *w* justice
Pr 11: 24 another *w* unduly, but comes
Isa 32: 6 and from the thirsty he *w* water.
Eze 18: 8 He *w* his hand from doing wrong
18: 17 He *w* his hand from sin

WITHSTAND (WITHSTOOD)

Nu 31: 23 else that can *w* fire must be
31: 23 whatever cannot *w* fire must be put
Jos 10: 8 one of them will be able to *w* you."
23: 9 day no one has been able to *w* you.
2Ch 20: 6 in your hand, and no one can *w* you
Ps 147: 17 Who can *w* his icy blast?
La 1: 14 over to those I cannot *w*.
Na 1: 6 Who can *w* his indignation?

WITHSTOOD (WITHSTAND)

Jos 21: 44 Not one of their enemies *w* them;

WITLESS

Job 11: 12 a *w* man can no more become wise

WITNESS (EYEWITNESSES WITNESSED WITNESSES)

Ge 21: 30 as a *w* that I dug this well."
31: 44 and let it serve as a *w* between us."
31: 48 "This heap is a *w* between you
31: 50 remember that God is a *w*
31: 52 heap is a *w*, and this pillar is a *w*,
Ex 23: 1 man by being a malicious *w*.
Nu 5: 13 (since there is no *w* against her
35: 30 on the testimony of only one *w*.
Dt 17: 6 on the testimony of only one *w*.
19: 15 One *w* is not enough
19: 16 If a malicious *w* takes the stand
19: 18 and if the *w* proves to be a liar,
31: 19 so that it may be a *w* for me
31: 26 There it will remain as a *w*
Jos 22: 27 it is to be a *w* between us and you
22: 28 but as a *w* between us and you.'
22: 34 W BETWEEN US THAT THE LORD
24: 27 It will be a *w* against you
24: 27 "This stone will be a *w* against us.
Jdg 11: 10 LORD is our *w*; we will certainly
1Sa 6: 18 is a *w* to this day in the field
12: 5 and also his anointed is *w* this day,
12: 5 "He is *w*," they said.
12: 5 "The LORD is *w* against you,
20: 23 the LORD is *w* between you
20: 42 'The LORD is *w* between you
Job 16: 8 bound me—and it has become a *w*;
16: 19 Even now my *w* is in heaven;
Ps 89: 37 the faithful *w* in the sky."
Pr 6: 19 a false *w* who pours out lies
12: 17 but a false *w* tells lies.
12: 17 truthful *w* gives honest testimony,
14: 5 A truthful *w* does not deceive,
14: 5 but a false *w* pours out lies.
14: 25 A truthful *w* saves lives,
14: 25 but a false *w* is deceitful.
19: 5 A false *w* will not go unpunished,
19: 9 A false *w* will not go unpunished,
19: 28 A corrupt *w* mocks at justice,
21: 28 A false *w* will perish,
Isa 19: 20 and *w* to the LORD Almighty
30: 8 it may be an everlasting *w*.
55: 4 I have made him a *w* to the peoples,
Jer 29: 23 I know it and am a *w* to it,"
42: 5 and faithful *w* against us
Mic 1: 2 that the Sovereign LORD may *w*
Mal 2: 14 the LORD is acting as the *w*
Lk 23: 48 to *w* this sight saw what took place,
Jn 1: 7 a *w* to testify concerning that light,
1: 8 he came only as a *w* to the light.
8: 13 your own *w*; your testimony is not
8: 18 my other *w* is the one who sent me
Ac 1: 22 of these must become a *w* with us
22: 15 You will be his *w* to all men
Ac 26: 16 as a *w* of what you have seen of me
Ro 1: 9 is my *w* how constantly I
2: 15 their consciences also bearing *w*,
2Co 1: 23 as my *w* that it was in order
1Th 2: 5 to cover up greed—God is our *w*.
1Pe 5: 1 a *w* of Christ's sufferings
Rev 1: 5 who is the faithful *w*, the firstborn
2: 13 the days of Antipas, my faithful *w*,
3: 14 true *w*, the ruler of God's creation.

WITNESSED (WITNESS)

Jer 32: 10 and sealed the deed, had it *w*,
32: 25 and have the transaction *w*.' "
32: 44 and *w* in the territory of Benjamin,

WITNESSES (WITNESS)

Nu 35: 30 only on the testimony of *w*.
Dt 4: 26 *w* against you this day that you will
17: 6 three *w* a man shall be put to death,
17: 7 The hands of the *w* must be the first
19: 15 by the testimony of two or three *w*.
30: 19 as *w* against you that I have set
Jos 24: 22 "Yes, we are *w*," they replied.
24: 22 "You are *w* against yourselves that
Ru 4: 9 Today you are *w* that I have bought
4: 10 Today you are *w*!" Then the elders
4: 11 all those at the gate said, "We are *w*
Job 10: 17 You bring new *w* against me
Ps 27: 12 for false *w* rise up against me,
35: 11 Ruthless *w* come forward;
Isa 8: 2 of Jeberekiah as reliable *w* for me."
33: 8 its *w* are despised,
43: 9 Let them bring in their *w*
43: 10 "You are my *w*," declares
43: 12 You are my *w*," declares
44: 8 You are my *w*.
Jer 6: 18 observe, O *w*,
32: 12 of the *w* who had signed the deed
Mt 10: 18 as *w* to them and to the Gentiles.
18: 16 by the testimony of two or three *w*.'
26: 60 though many false *w* came forward
26: 65 Why do we need any more *w*?
Mk 13: 9 before governors and kings as *w*
14: 63 "Why do we need any more *w*?"
Lk 21: 13 result in your being *w* to them.
24: 48 You are *w* of these things.
Ac 1: 8 and you will be my *w* in Jerusalem,
2: 32 and we are all *w* of the fact.
3: 15 We are *w* of this.
5: 32 We are *w* of these things,
6: 13 produced false *w*, who testified,
7: 58 the *w* laid their clothes at the feet
10: 39 "We are *w* of everything he did
10: 41 but by *w* whom God had already
13: 31 They are now his *w* to our people.
1Co 15: 15 found to be false *w* about God,
2Co 13: 1 by the testimony of two or three *w*
1Th 2: 10 You are *w*, and so is God,
1Ti 5: 19 it is brought by two or three *w*.
6: 12 in the presence of many *w*.
2Ti 2: 2 in the presence of many *w* entrust
Heb 10: 28 on the testimony of two or three *w*.
12: 1 by such a great cloud of *w*,
Rev 11: 3 And I will give power to my two *w*,

WITS'

Ps 107: 27 they were at their *w*' end.

WIVES (WIFE)

Ge 4: 23 Lamech said to his *w*,
4: 23 *w* of Lamech, hear my words.
6: 18 and your sons' *w* with you.
7: 7 and his sons' *w* entered the ark
7: 13 and the *w* of his three sons,
8: 16 and your sons and their *w*.
8: 18 and his wife and his sons' *w*.
28: 9 in addition to the *w* he already had.
30: 26 Give me my *w* and children,
31: 17 Jacob put his children and his *w*
31: 50 take any *w* besides my daughters,
32: 22 Jacob got up and took his two *w*,
36: 2 Esau took his *w* from the women
36: 6 Esau took his *w* and sons
37: 2 his father's *w*, and he brought their
45: 19 for your children and your *w*,
46: 5 their *w* in the carts that Pharaoh
46: 26 not counting his sons' *w*—
Ex 22: 24 your *w* will become widows

Ex 32: 2 off the gold earrings that your *w*,
34: 16 some of their daughters as *w*
Nu 14: 3 Our *w* and children will be taken
16: 27 and were standing with their *w*,
32: 26 Our children and *w*, our flocks
Dt 3: 19 your *w*, your children and your
17: 17 He must not take many *w*,
21: 15 a man has two *w*, and he loves one
29: 11 with your children and your *w*,
Jos 1: 14 Your *w*, your children
Jdg 8: 30 sons of his own, for he had many *w*.
12: 9 as *w* from outside his clan.
21: 7 "How can we provide *w*
21: 16 how shall we provide *w*
21: 18 can't give them our daughters as *w*,
21: 22 because we did not get *w* for them
1Sa 1: 2 He had two *w*; one was called
25: 43 Jezreel, and they both were his *w*.
27: 3 and David had his two *w*: Ahinoam
30: 3 and their *w* and sons and daughters
30: 5 David's two *w* had been captured
30: 18 had taken, including his two *w*.
2Sa 2: 2 David went up there with his two *w*
5: 13 David took more concubines and *w*
12: 8 and your master's *w* into your arms
12: 11 lie with your *w* in broad daylight.
12: 11 your very eyes I will take your *w*
19: 5 the lives of your *w* and concubines.
1Ki 11: 3 He had seven hundred *w*
11: 3 concubines, and his *w* led him
11: 4 his *w* turned his heart
11: 8 the same for all his foreign *w*,
20: 3 of your *w* and children are mine.' "
20: 5 your *w* and your children.
20: 7 When he sent for my *w*
2Ki 24: 15 his *w*, his officials and the leading
1Ch 4: 5 the father of Tekoa had two *w*,
4: 17 One of Mered's *w* gave birth
7: 4 for they had many *w* and children.
8: 8 after he had divorced his *w* Hushim
14: 3 In Jerusalem David took more *w*
2Ch 11: 21 he had eighteen *w* and sixty
11: 21 more than any of his other *w*
11: 23 and took many *w* for them.
13: 21 He married fourteen *w*
20: 13 with their *w* and children
21: 14 your *w* and everything that is yours
21: 17 together with his sons and *w*.
24: 3 Jehoiada chose two *w* for him,
28: 8 kinsmen two hundred thousand *w*,
29: 9 and our *w* are in captivity.
31: 18 included all the little ones, the *w*,
Ezr 9: 2 as *w* for themselves and their sons,
10: 11 and from your foreign *w*."
10: 19 in pledge to put away their *w*,
10: 44 of them had children by these *w*.
Ne 4: 14 and your daughters, your *w*
5: 1 and their *w* raised a great outcry
10: 28 with their *w* and all their sons
Isa 13: 16 will be looted and their *w* ravished.
Jer 6: 12 with their fields and their *w*,
8: 10 Therefore I will give their *w*
14: 16 one to bury them or their *w*,
18: 21 Let their *w* be made childless
29: 6 find *w* for your sons and give your
29: 23 adultery with their neighbors' *w*
35: 8 Neither we nor our *w* nor our sons
38: 23 "All your *w* and children will be
44: 9 and your *w* in the land of Judah
44: 15 knew that their *w* were burning
44: 25 and your *w* have shown
Da 5: 2 his *w* and his concubines might
5: 3 his *w* and his concubines drank
5: 23 your *w* and your concubines drank
6: 24 along with their *w* and children.
Zec 12: 12 of the house of David and their *w*,
12: 12 of the house of Nathan and their *w*,
12: 12 with their *w* by themselves:
12: 13 of the house of Levi and their *w*,
12: 13 the clan of Shimei and their *w*,
12: 14 all the rest of the clans and their *w*.
Mt 19: 8 permitted you to divorce your *w*
Ac 21: 5 All the disciples and their *w*
1Co 7: 29 on those who have *w* should live
Eph 5: 22 *W*, submit to your husbands
5: 24 *w* should submit to their husbands
5: 25 love your *w*, just as Christ loved
5: 28 husbands ought to love their *w*
Col 3: 18 *W*, submit to your husbands,
3: 19 love your *w* and do not be harsh
1Ti 3: 11 their *w* are to be women worthy
1Pe 3: 1 talk by the behavior of their *w*,
3: 1 *W*, in the same way be submissive
3: 7 as you live with your *w*,

WIVES' (WIFE)

1Ti 4: 7 with godless myths and old *w*' tales

WOE (WOES)

Nu 21: 29 *W* to you, O Moab!
1Sa 4: 8 *W* to us! Who will deliver us
Job 10: 15 If I am guilty—*w* to me!
Ps 120: 5 *W* to me that I dwell in Meshech,
Pr 23: 29 Who has *w*? Who has sorrow?
Ecc 10: 16 *W* to you, O land whose king was
Isa 3: 9 *W* to them!
3: 11 *W* to the wicked!
5: 8 *W* to you who add house to house
5: 11 *W* to those who rise
5: 18 *W* to those who draw sin
5: 20 *W* to those who call evil good
5: 21 *W* to those who are wise
5: 22 *W* to those who are heroes
6: 5 "*W* to me!" I cried.
10: 1 *W* to those who make unjust laws,
10: 5 "*W* to the Assyrian, the rod
18: 1 *W* to the land of whirring wings
24: 16 *W* to me!
28: 1 *W* to that wreath, the pride
29: 1 *W* to you, Ariel, Ariel,
29: 15 *W* to those who go to great depths
30: 1 "*W* to the obstinate children,"
31: 1 *W* to those who go down to Egypt
33: 1 *W* to you, O destroyer,
33: 1 *W* to you, O traitor,
45: 9 "*W* to him who quarrels
45: 10 *W* to him who says to his father,
Jer 4: 13 *W* to us! We are ruined!
10: 19 *W* to me because of my injury!
13: 27 *W* to you, O Jerusalem!
22: 13 "*W* to him who builds his palace
23: 1 "*W* to the shepherds who are
45: 3 Baruch: You said, '*W* to me!
48: 1 "*W* to Nebo, for it will be ruined.
48: 46 *W* to you, O Moab!
50: 27 *W* to them! For their day has come
La 5: 16 *W* to us, for we have sinned!
Eze 2: 10 of lament and mourning and *w*.
13: 3 *W* to the foolish prophets who
13: 18 *W* to the women who sew magic
16: 23 " '*W*! *W* to you, declares
24: 6 " '*W* to the city of bloodshed,
24: 9 " '*W* to the city of bloodshed!
34: 2 *W* to the shepherds
Hos 7: 13 *W* to them,
9: 12 *W* to them
Am 5: 18 *W* to you who long
6: 1 *W* to you who are complacent
Mic 2: 1 *W* to those who plan iniquity,
Na 3: 1 *W* to the city of blood,
Hab 2: 6 " '*W* to him who piles up stolen
2: 9 "*W* to him who builds his realm
2: 12 "*W* to him who builds a city
2: 15 "*W* to him who gives drink
2: 19 *W* to him who says to wood,
Zep 2: 5 *W* to you who live by the sea,
3: 1 *W* to the city of oppressors,
Zec 11: 17 "*W* to the worthless shepherd,
Mt 11: 21 "*W* to you, Korazin! *W* to you,
18: 7 *W* to the world
18: 7 *w* to the man through whom they
23: 13 "*W* to you, teachers of the law
23: 15 "*W* to you, teachers of the law
23: 16 "*W* to you, blind guides! You say,
23: 23 "*W* to you, teachers of the law
23: 25 "*W* to you, teachers of the law
23: 27 "*W* to you, teachers of the law
23: 29 "*W* to you, teachers of the law
26: 24 *w* to that man who betrays the Son
Mk 14: 21 *w* to that man who betrays the Son
Lk 6: 24 "But *w* to you who are rich,
6: 25 *W* to you who are well fed now,
6: 25 *W* to you who laugh now,
6: 26 *W* to you when all men speak well
10: 13 "*W* to you, Korazin! *W* to you,
11: 42 "*W* to you Pharisees, because you
Lk 11: 43 "*W* to you Pharisees, because you
11: 44 "*W* to you, because you are like
11: 46 you experts in the law, *w* to you,
11: 47 *W* to you, because you build tombs
11: 52 "*W* to you experts in the law,
17: 1 but *w* to that person through whom
22: 22 but *w* to that man who betrays him
1Co 9: 16 *W* to me if I do not preach
Jude : 11 *W* to them! They have taken
Rev 8: 13 "*W*! *W*! *W* to the inhabitants
9: 12 first *w* is past; two other woes are
11: 14 second *w* has passed; the third *w* is
12: 12 But *w* to the earth and the sea,
18: 10 " '*W*! *W*, O great city,
18: 16 " '*W*! *W*, O great city,
18: 19 " '*W*! *W*, O great city,

WOES (WOE)

Ps 32: 10 Many are the *w* of the wicked,
Rev 9: 12 two other *w* are yet to come.

WOKE (WAKE)

Ge 41: 4 Then Pharaoh *w* up.
41: 7 Pharaoh *w* up; it had been a dream.
41: 21 Then I *w* up.
Mt 1: 24 When Joseph *w* up, he did what
8: 25 The disciples went and *w* him,
25: 7 "Then all the virgins *w* up
Mk 4: 38 The disciples *w* him and said
Lk 8: 24 The disciples went and *w* him,
Ac 12: 7 Peter on the side and *w* him up.
16: 27 The jailer *w* up, and when he saw

WOLF (WOLVES)

Ge 49: 27 "Benjamin is a ravenous *w*;
Isa 11: 6 The *w* will live with the lamb,
65: 25 *w* and the lamb will feed together,
Jer 5: 6 *w* from the desert will ravage them,
Jn 10: 12 So when he sees the *w* coming,
10: 12 Then the *w* attacks the flock

WOLVES (WOLF)

Eze 22: 27 her are like *w* tearing their prey;
Hab 1: 8 fiercer than *w* at dusk.
Zep 3: 3 her rulers are evening *w*,
Mt 7: 15 but inwardly they are ferocious *w*.
10: 16 you out like sheep among *w*.
Lk 10: 3 you out like lambs among *w*.
Ac 20: 29 savage *w* will come in among you

WOMB (WOMBS)

Ge 20: 18 the LORD had closed up every *w*
25: 23 "Two nations are in your *w*,
25: 24 there were twin boys in her *w*.
29: 31 he opened her *w*, but Rachel was
30: 22 he listened to her and opened her *w*
38: 27 there were twin boys in her *w*.
49: 25 blessings of the breast and *w*.
Ex 13: 2 of every *w* among the Israelites
13: 12 the first offspring of every *w*.
13: 15 the first male offspring of every *w*
34: 19 offspring of every *w* belongs to me,
Nu 12: 12 coming from its mother's *w*
18: 15 The first offspring of every *w*,
Dt 7: 13 He will bless the fruit of your *w*,
28: 4 The fruit of your *w* will be blessed,
28: 11 in the fruit of your *w*, the young
28: 18 The fruit of your *w* will be cursed,
28: 53 you will eat the fruit of the *w*,
28: 57 daughter the afterbirth from her *w*
30: 9 and in the fruit of your *w*,
1Sa 1: 5 and the LORD had closed her *w*.
1: 6 the LORD had closed her *w*,
Job 1: 21 Naked I came from my mother's *w*,
3: 10 it did not shut the doors of the *w*
3: 11 and die as I came from the *w*?
10: 18 then did you bring me out of the *w*?
10: 19 straight from the *w* to the grave!
15: 35 their *w* fashions deceit."
24: 20 The *w* forgets them,
31: 15 me in the *w* make them?
38: 8 when it burst forth from the *w*,
38: 29 From whose *w* comes the ice?
Ps 22: 9 Yet you brought me out of the *w*;
22: 10 from my mother's *w* you have been
58: 3 from the *w* they are wayward
71: 6 from my mother's *w*.
110: 3 from the *w* of the dawn

Ps 139: 13 in my mother's *w*.
Pr 30: 16 the grave, the barren *w*,
31: 2 "O my son, O son of my *w*,
Ecc 5: 15 from his mother's *w*,
11: 5 the body is formed in a mother's *w*.
Isa 44: 2 you, who formed you in the *w*,
44: 24 who formed you in the *w*:
49: 5 me in the *w* to be his servant
66: 9 "Do I close up the *w*
Jer 1: 5 you in the *w* I knew you,
20: 17 For he did not kill me in the *w*,
20: 17 her *w* enlarged forever.
20: 18 Why did I ever come out of the *w*
Hos 12: 3 In the *w* he grasped his brother's
13: 13 come to the opening of the *w*.
Lk 1: 41 the baby leaped in her *w*,
1: 44 the baby in my *w* leaped for joy.
Jn 3: 4 into his mother's *w* to be born!"
Ro 4: 19 and that Sarah's *w* was also dead.

WOMBS (WOMB)

Hos 9: 14 Give them *w* that miscarry
Lk 23: 29 *w* that never bore and the breasts

WOMENSERVANTS (SERVANT)

Lk 12: 45 and *w* and to eat and drink

WON (WIN)

Ge 30: 8 with my sister, and I have *w*."
1Sa 19: 5 The LORD *w* a great victory
2Sa 19: 14 He *w* over the hearts of all the men
Est 2: 9 girl pleased him and *w* his favor.
2: 15 And Esther *w* the favor
2: 17 she *w* his favor and approval more
Ps 44: 3 by their sword that they *w* the land,
Mt 18: 15 you have *w* your brother over.
Ac 14: 19 and Iconium and *w* the crowd over.
14: 21 and *w* a large number of disciples.
1Pe 3: 1 they may be *w* over without talk

WONDER (WONDERED WONDERFUL WONDERING WONDERS WONDROUS)

Dt 13: 1 to you a miraculous sign or *w*,
13: 2 or *w* of which he has spoken takes
28: 46 a *w* to you and your descendants
Job 6: 3 no *w* my words have been
Ps 17: 7 Show the *w* of your great love,
SS 1: 3 No *w* the maidens love you!
Isa 29: 14 people with *w* upon *w*;
Mk 9: 15 they were overwhelmed with *w*
Ac 3: 10 and they were filled with *w*
13: 41 *w* and perish,
2Co 11: 14 And no *w*, for Satan himself

WONDERED (WONDER)

Lk 1: 29 *w* what kind of greeting this might
1: 66 Everyone who heard this *w* about it

WONDERFUL (WONDER)

2Sa 1: 26 Your love for me was *w*,
1: 26 more *w* than that of women.
1Ch 16: 9 tell of all his *w* acts.
Job 42: 3 things too *w* for me to know.
Ps 26: 7 and telling of all your *w* deeds.
31: 21 for he showed his *w* love to me
75: 1 men tell of your *w* deeds.
105: 2 tell of all his *w* acts.
107: 8 and his *w* deeds for men,
107: 15 and his *w* deeds for men,
107: 21 and his *w* deeds for men.
107: 24 his *w* deeds in the deep.
107: 31 and his *w* deeds for men.
119: 18 *w* things in your law.
119:129 Your statutes are *w*;
131: 1 or things too *w* for me.
139: 6 Such knowledge is too *w* for me,
139: 14 your works are *w*,
145: 5 I will meditate on your *w* works.
Isa 9: 6 *W* Counselor, Mighty God,
28: 29 *w* in counsel and magnificent
Mt 21: 15 of the law saw the *w* things he did
Lk 13: 17 with all the *w* things he was doing.
1Pe 2: 9 out of darkness into his *w* light.

WONDERING (WONDER)

Lk 1: 21 and *w* why he stayed so long
3: 15 and were all *w* in their hearts
24: 4 While they were *w* about this,
Lk 24: 12 *w* to himself what had happened.
Ac 5: 24 *w* what would come of this.
10: 17 While Peter was *w* about

WONDERS (WONDER)

Ex 3: 20 with all the *w* that I will perform
4: 21 Pharaoh all the *w* I have given
7: 3 my miraculous signs and *w*
11: 9 so that my *w* may be multiplied
11: 10 and Aaron performed all these *w*
15: 11 working *w*?
34: 10 all your people I will do *w* never
Dt 4: 34 by miraculous signs and *w*, by war,
6: 22 sent miraculous signs and *w*—
7: 19 the miraculous signs and *w*,
10: 21 and awesome *w* you saw
26: 8 and with miraculous signs and *w*.
29: 3 those miraculous signs and great *w*.
34: 11 and *w* the LORD sent him to do
Jdg 6: 13 Where are all his *w* that our fathers
2Sa 7: 23 awesome *w* by driving out nations
1Ch 16: 12 Remember the *w* he has done,
17: 21 awesome *w* by driving out nations
Ne 9: 10 You sent miraculous signs and *w*
Job 5: 9 He performs *w* that cannot be
9: 10 He performs *w* that cannot be
37: 14 stop and consider God's *w*.
37: 16 those *w* of him who is perfect
Ps 9: 1 I will tell of all your *w*.
40: 5 are the *w* you have done.
65: 8 Those living far away fear your *w*;
78: 4 his power, and the *w* he has done.
78: 11 the *w* he had shown them.
78: 32 of his *w*, they did not believe.
78: 43 his *w* in the region of Zoan.
88: 10 Do you show your *w* to the dead?
88: 12 Are your *w* known in the place
89: 5 The heavens praise your *w*,
105: 5 Remember the *w* he has done,
105: 27 his *w* in the land of Ham.
111: 4 He has caused his *w*
119: 27 then I will meditate on your *w*.
135: 9 He sent his signs and *w*
136: 4 to him who alone does great *w*,
Jer 21: 2 Perhaps the LORD will perform *w*
32: 20 performed miraculous signs and *w*
32: 21 out of Egypt with signs and *w*,
Da 4: 2 and *w* that the Most High God has
4: 3 how mighty his *w*!
6: 27 he performs signs and *w*
Joel 2: 26 who has worked *w* for you;
2: 30 I will show *w* in the heavens
Mic 7: 15 I will show them my *w*."
Jn 4: 48 see miraculous signs and *w*,"
Ac 2: 11 we hear them declaring the *w*
2: 19 I will show *w* in the heaven above
2: 22 *w* and signs, which God did
2: 43 many *w* and miraculous signs were
4: 30 and *w* through the name
5: 12 many miraculous signs and *w*
6: 8 did great *w* and miraculous signs
7: 36 and did *w* and miraculous signs
14: 3 them to do miraculous signs and *w*.
15: 12 and *w* God had done
2Co 12: 12 that mark an apostle—signs, *w*
2Th 2: 9 and *w*, and in every sort
Heb 2: 4 also testified to it by signs, *w*

WONDROUS (WONDER)

Rev 12: 1 and *w* sign appeared in heaven:

WOOD (BRUSHWOOD WOODED WOODEN WOODPILE WOODS WOODWORK)

Ge 6: 14 make yourself an ark of cypress *w*;
22: 3 When he had cut enough *w*
22: 6 Abraham took the *w*
22: 7 The fire and *w* are here," Isaac said
22: 9 an altar there and arranged the *w*
22: 9 him on the altar, on top of the *w*.
30: 37 and exposing the white inner *w*
Ex 15: 25 LORD showed him a piece of *w*.
25: 5 acacia *w*; olive oil for the light;
25: 10 them make a chest of acacia *w*—
25: 13 Then make poles of acacia *w*
25: 23 "Make a table of acacia *w*—
25: 28 Make the poles of acacia *w*,
26: 15 of acacia *w* for the tabernacle.
Ex 26: 26 "Also make crossbars of acacia *w*:
26: 32 posts of acacia *w* overlaid with gold
26: 37 of acacia *w* overlaid with gold.
27: 1 "Build an altar of acacia *w*,
27: 6 Make poles of acacia *w* for the altar
30: 1 of acacia *w* for burning incense.
30: 5 Make the poles of acacia *w*
31: 5 to cut and set stones, to work in *w*,
35: 7 acacia *w*; olive oil for the light;
35: 24 and everyone who had acacia *w*
35: 33 to work in *w* and to engage
36: 20 of acacia *w* for the tabernacle.
36: 31 also made crossbars of acacia *w*:
36: 36 They made four posts of acacia *w*
37: 1 Bezalel made the ark of acacia *w*—
37: 4 Then he made poles of acacia *w*
37: 10 They made the table of acacia *w*—
37: 15 the table were made of acacia *w*
37: 25 the altar of incense out of acacia *w*.
37: 28 They made the poles of acacia *w*
38: 1 altar of burnt offering of acacia *w*,
38: 6 They made the poles of acacia *w*
Lev 1: 7 fire on the altar and arrange *w*
1: 8 on the burning *w* that is on the altar
1: 12 on the burning *w* that is on the altar
1: 17 it on the *w* that is on the fire
3: 5 offering that is on the burning *w*,
4: 12 burn it in a *w* fire on the ash heap.
11: 32 whether it is made of *w*, cloth,
14: 4 live clean birds and some cedar *w*,
14: 6 together with the cedar *w*,
14: 49 to take two birds and some cedar *w*
14: 51 Then he is to take the cedar *w*,
14: 52 the cedar *w*, the hyssop
Nu 15: 32 a man was found gathering *w*
15: 33 him gathering *w* brought him
19: 6 The priest is to take some cedar *w*,
31: 20 made of leather, goat hair or *w*."
Dt 4: 28 will worship man-made gods of *w*
10: 3 So I made the ark out of acacia *w*
19: 5 forest with his neighbor to cut *w*,
28: 36 will worship other gods, gods of *w*
28: 64 worship other gods—gods of *w*
29: 11 in your camps who chop your *w*
29: 17 detestable images and idols of *w*
Jdg 6: 26 Using the *w* of the Asherah pole
1Sa 6: 14 The people chopped up the *w*
2Sa 24: 22 sledges and ox yokes for the *w*.
1Ki 6: 23 a pair of cherubim of olive *w*,
6: 31 of olive *w* with five-sided jambs.
6: 32 on the two olive *w* doors he carved
6: 33 jambs of olive *w* for the entrance
18: 23 put it on the *w* but not set fire to it.
18: 23 put it on the *w* but not set fire to it.
18: 33 He arranged the *w*, cut the bull
18: 33 bull into pieces and laid it on the *w*.
18: 33 pour it on the offering and on the *w*
18: 38 the *w*, the stones and the soil,
2Ki 19: 18 for they were not gods but only *w*
1Ch 21: 23 the threshing sledges for the *w*,
22: 14 iron too great to be weighed, and *w*
29: 2 iron for the iron and *w* for the *w*,
2Ch 2: 14 bronze and iron, stone and *w*,
Ne 10: 34 of *w* to burn on the altar
13: 31 provision for contributions of *w*
Job 41: 27 and bronze like rotten *w*.
Pr 26: 20 Without *w* a fire goes out;
26: 21 to embers and as *w* to fire,
SS 3: 9 he made it of *w* from Lebanon.
Isa 10: 15 or a club brandish him who is not *w*
30: 33 with an abundance of fire and *w*;
37: 19 for they were not gods but only *w*
40: 20 selects *w* that will not rot.
44: 16 Half of the *w* he burns in the fire;
44: 19 Shall I bow down to a block of *w*?"
45: 20 those who carry about idols of *w*,
60: 17 Instead of *w* I will bring you bronze
Jer 2: 27 They say to *w*, 'You are my father,'
3: 9 adultery with stone and *w*.
5: 14 and these people the *w* it consumes
7: 18 children gather *w*, the fathers light
La 5: 4 our *w* can be had only at a price.
5: 13 boys stagger under loads of *w*.
Eze 15: 2 how is the *w* of a vine better
15: 3 Is *w* ever taken from it
15: 6 As I have given the *w* of the vine
20: 32 peoples of the world, who serve *w*
24: 5 Pile *w* beneath it for the bones;

Eze 24: 9 I, too, will pile the *w* high.
24: 10 So heap on the *w*
27: 6 of cypress *w* from the coasts
37: 16 Then take another stick of *w*,
37: 16 take a stick of *w* and write on it,
37: 19 making them a single stick of *w*,
39: 10 need to gather *w* from the fields
41: 16 the threshold was covered with *w*.
41: 22 its base and its sides were of *w*.
Da 5: 4 of bronze, iron, *w* and stone.
5: 23 of bronze, iron, *w* and stone,
Hos 4: 12 and are answered by a stick of *w*.
Hab 2: 19 Woe to him who says to *w*,
1Co 3: 12 costly stones, *w*, hay or straw,
2Ti 2: 20 but also of *w* and clay; some are
Rev 9: 20 silver, bronze, stone and *w*—
18: 12 costly *w*, bronze, iron and marble;
18: 12 scarlet cloth; every sort of citron *w*,

WOODCUTTERS

Jos 9: 21 let them be *w* and water carriers
9: 23 You will never cease to serve as *w*
9: 27 That day he made the Gibeonites *w*

WOODED (WOOD)

2Ch 27: 4 and forts and towers in the *w* areas.

WOODEN (WOOD)

Ex 7: 19 in the *w* buckets and stone jars."
Lev 15: 12 and any *w* article is to be rinsed
Nu 35: 18 Or if anyone has a *w* object
Dt 10: 1 Also make a *w* chest.
16: 21 Do not set up any *w* Asherah pole
Ne 8: 4 stood on a high *w* platform built
Isa 48: 5 my *w* image and metal god
Jer 10: 8 by worthless *w* idols.
28: 13 You have broken a *w* yoke,
Eze 41: 22 There was a *w* altar three cubits
41: 25 and there was a *w* overhang
Hos 4: 12 They consult a *w* idol
10: 6 Israel will be ashamed of its *w* idols

WOODPILE (WOOD)

Zec 12: 6 of Judah like a firepot in a *w*,

WOODS (WOOD)

1Sa 14: 25 The entire army entered the *w*,
14: 26 When they went into the *w*,
2Ki 2: 24 Then two bears came out of the *w*

WOODSMAN (WOODSMEN)

Isa 14: 8 no *w* comes to cut us down."

WOODSMEN (WOODSMAN)

2Ch 2: 10 give your servants, the *w* who cut

WOODWORK (WOOD)

Hab 2: 11 and the beams of the *w* will echo it.

WOOING

Job 36: 16 "He is *w* you from the jaws

WOOL (WOOLEN)

Lev 13: 48 or knitted material of linen or *w*,
13: 52 or knitted material of *w* or linen,
Nu 19: 6 and scarlet *w* and throw them
Dt 18: 4 and the first *w* from the shearing
22: 11 Do not wear clothes of *w*
Jdg 6: 37 I will place a *w* fleece
2Ki 3: 4 with the *w* of a hundred thousand
Ps 147: 16 He spreads the snow like *w*
Pr 31: 13 She selects *w* and flax
Isa 1: 18 they shall be like *w*.
51: 8 the worm will devour them like *w*.
Eze 27: 18 from Helbon and *w* from Zahar.
34: 3 clothe yourselves with the *w*
Da 7: 9 hair of his head was white like *w*.
Hos 2: 5 my *w* and my linen, my oil
2: 9 I will take back my *w* and my linen,
Heb 9: 19 scarlet *w* and branches of hyssop,
Rev 1: 14 and hair were white like *w*,

WOOLEN (WOOL)

Lev 13: 47 with mildew—any *w*
13: 59 contamination by mildew in *w*
Eze 44: 17 they must not wear any *w* garment

WORD (BYWORD WORDS)

Ge 15: 1 the *w* of the LORD came to Abram
15: 4 the *w* of the LORD came to him:
24: 21 Without saying a *w*, the man
27: 45 I'll send *w* for you to come back
31: 4 So Jacob sent *w* to Rachel
37: 4 could not speak a kind *w* to him.
37: 14 with the flocks, and bring *w* back
41: 44 but without your *w* no one will lift
44: 18 let your servant speak a *w*
50: 16 So they sent *w* to Joseph, saying,
Ex 9: 20 of Pharaoh who feared the *w*
9: 21 But those who ignored the *w*
18: 6 Jethro had sent *w* to him, "I,
36: 6 sent this *w* throughout the camp:
Nu 3: 16 by the *w* of the LORD.
3: 51 by the *w* of the LORD.
15: 31 he has despised the LORD's *w*
30: 2 he must not break his *w*
Dt 5: 5 declare to you the *w* of the LORD,
8: 3 but on every *w* that comes
30: 14 No, the *w* is very near you;
33: 9 but he watched over your *w*
Jos 1: 18 Whoever rebels against your *w*
6: 10 do not say a *w* until the day I tell
8: 35 There was not a *w*
10: 6 The Gibeonites then sent *w*
10: 21 and no one uttered a *w*
11: 1 he sent *w* to Jobab king of Madon,
Jdg 11: 36 "you have given your *w*
12: 6 not pronounce the *w* correctly,
13: 17 you when your *w* comes true?"
16: 18 she sent *w* to the rulers
18: 19 him, "Be quiet! Don't say a *w*.
1Sa 1: 23 may the LORD make good his *w*."
3: 1 In those days the *w*
3: 7 *w* of the LORD had not yet been
3: 21 himself to Samuel through his *w*.
4: 1 And Samuel's *w* came to all Israel.
14: 39 But not one of the men said a *w*.
15: 10 Then the *w* of the LORD came
15: 23 Because you have rejected the *w*
15: 26 You have rejected the *w*
16: 22 Then Saul sent *w* to Jesse, saying,
19: 19 *W* came to Saul: "David is
20: 12 I not send you *w* and let you know?
25: 12 arrived, they reported every *w*.
25: 39 Then David sent *w* to Abigail,
2Sa 3: 11 dare to say another *w* to Abner,
7: 4 That night the *w* of the LORD
7: 21 For the sake of your *w*
11: 5 The woman conceived and sent *w*
11: 6 So David sent this *w* to Joab:
12: 9 Why did you despise the *w*
12: 25 he sent *w* through Nathan
13: 7 David sent *w* to Tamar
13: 22 Absalom never said a *w* to Amnon,
14: 12 "Let your servant speak a *w*
14: 17 'May the *w* of my lord the king
14: 32 "Look, I sent *w* to you and said,
15: 28 the desert until *w* comes from you
19: 14 They sent *w* to the king, "Return,
22: 31 the *w* of the LORD is flawless.
23: 2 his *w* was on my tongue.
24: 4 king's *w*, however, overruled Joab
24: 11 the *w* of the LORD had come
1Ki 2: 27 fulfilling the *w* the LORD had
5: 8 So Hiram sent *w* to Solomon:
6: 11 The *w* of the LORD came
8: 26 let your *w* that you promised your
8: 56 Not one *w* has failed
12: 15 to fulfill the *w* the LORD had
12: 22 But this *w* of God came
12: 24 So they obeyed the *w* of the LORD
13: 1 By the *w* of the LORD a man
13: 2 the altar by the *w* of the LORD:
13: 5 man of God by the *w* of the LORD.
13: 9 by the *w* of the LORD:
13: 17 told by the *w* of the LORD:
13: 18 said to me by the *w* of the LORD:
13: 20 the *w* of the LORD came
13: 21 'You have defied the *w*
13: 26 the man of God who defied the *w*
13: 26 *w* of the LORD had warned him."
13: 32 declared by the *w* of the LORD
15: 29 according to the *w*
16: 1 Then the *w* of the LORD came
1Ki 16: 7 the *w* of the LORD came
16: 12 in accordance with the *w*
16: 34 in accordance with the *w*
17: 1 the next few years except at my *w*."
17: 2 the *w* of the LORD came to Elijah:
17: 8 the *w* of the LORD came to him:
17: 16 in keeping with the *w*
17: 24 and that the *w* of the LORD
18: 1 the *w* of the LORD came to Elijah:
18: 20 Ahab sent *w* throughout all Israel
18: 31 to whom the *w* of the LORD had
19: 9 the *w* of the LORD came to him:
20: 33 and were quick to pick up his *w*.
20: 35 By the *w* of the LORD one
21: 14 Then they sent *w* to Jezebel:
21: 17 Then the *w* of the LORD came
21: 28 Then the *w* of the LORD came
22: 13 Let your *w* agree with theirs,
22: 19 Therefore hear the *w* of the LORD:
22: 38 as the *w* of the LORD had declared
2Ki 1: 17 according to the *w*
2: 22 to the *w* Elisha had spoken.
3: 12 "The *w* of the LORD is with him."
4: 44 according to the *w* of the LORD.
6: 9 The man of God sent *w* to the king
7: 1 "Hear the *w* of the LORD.
9: 26 with the *w* of the LORD."
9: 36 "This is the *w* of the LORD that he
10: 10 that not a *w* the LORD has spoken
10: 17 according to the *w*
10: 21 Then he sent *w* throughout Israel,
14: 25 with the *w* of the LORD,
15: 12 So the *w* of the LORD spoken
18: 25 place without *w* from the LORD?
18: 28 "Hear the *w* of the great king,
19: 9 to Hezekiah with this *w*:
19: 21 This is the *w* that the LORD has
20: 4 the *w* of the LORD came to him:
20: 16 "Hear the *w* of the LORD:
20: 19 *w* of the LORD you have spoken is
23: 16 in accordance with the *w*
24: 2 in accordance with the *w*
1Ch 10: 13 he did not keep the *w* of the LORD
13: 2 let us send *w* far and wide
15: 15 with the *w* of the LORD.
16: 15 the *w* he commanded,
17: 3 That night the *w* of God came
21: 4 king's *w*, however, overruled Joab;
21: 19 to the *w* that Gad had spoken
22: 8 this *w* of the LORD came to me:
2Ch 6: 17 let your *w* that you promised your
10: 15 to fulfill the *w* the LORD had
11: 2 But this *w* of the LORD came
12: 7 this *w* of the LORD came
18: 12 Let your *w* agree with theirs,
18: 18 Therefore hear the *w* of the LORD:
29: 15 following the *w* of the LORD.
30: 1 Hezekiah sent *w* to all Israel
30: 12 following the *w* of the LORD.
34: 21 our fathers have not kept the *w*
36: 12 who spoke the *w* of the LORD.
36: 15 *w* to them through his messengers
36: 21 completed in fulfillment of the *w*
36: 22 to fulfill the *w* of the LORD spoken
Ezr 1: 1 to fulfill the *w* of the LORD spoken
Ne 6: 1 When *w* came to Sanballat, Tobiah,
8: 15 that they should proclaim this *w*
Est 7: 8 as the *w* left the king's mouth,
9: 26 were called Purim, from the *w pur*.)
Job 2: 13 No one said a *w* to him,
4: 2 "If someone ventures a *w* with you,
4: 12 "A *w* was secretly brought to me,
Ps 5: 9 Not a *w* from their mouth can be
17: 4 by the *w* of your lips
18: 30 the *w* of the LORD is flawless.
33: 4 For the *w* of the LORD is right
33: 6 By the *w* of the LORD were
52: 4 You love every harmful *w*,
56: 4 In God, whose *w* I praise,
56: 10 In God, whose *w* I praise,
56: 10 in the LORD, whose *w* I praise—
68: 11 The Lord announced the *w*,
103: 20 who obey his *w*.
105: 8 the *w* he commanded,
105: 19 till the *w* of the LORD proved him
107: 20 sent forth his *w* and healed them;
119: 9 By living according to your *w*.
119: 11 I have hidden your *w* in my heart

Ps 119: 16 I will not neglect your *w*.
119: 17 I will obey your *w*.
119: 25 renew my life according to your *w*.
119: 28 strengthen me according to your *w*.
119: 37 renew my life according to your *w*.
119: 42 for I trust in your *w*.
119: 43 Do not snatch the *w* of truth
119: 49 Remember your *w* to your servant,
119: 65 according to your *w*, O LORD.
119: 67 but now I obey your *w*.
119: 74 for I have put my hope in your *w*.
119: 81 but I have put my hope in your *w*.
119: 89 Your *w*, O LORD, is eternal;
119:101 so that I might obey your *w*.
119:105 Your *w* is a lamp to my feet
119:107 O LORD, according to your *w*.
119:114 I have put my hope in your *w*.
119:133 my footsteps according to your *w*;
119:147 I have put my hope in your *w*.
119:158 for they do not obey your *w*.
119:161 but my heart trembles at your *w*.
119:169 according to your *w*.
119:172 May my tongue sing of your *w*,
130: 5 and in his *w* I put my hope.
138: 2 your name and your *w*.
139: 4 Before a *w* is on my tongue
143: 8 Let the morning bring me *w*
147: 15 his *w* runs swiftly.
147: 18 He sends his *w* and melts them;
147: 19 He has revealed his *w* to Jacob,
Pr 12: 25 but a kind *w* cheers him up.
15: 1 but a harsh *w* stirs up anger.
15: 23 and how good is a timely *w*!
25: 11 A *w* aptly spoken
30: 5 "Every *w* of God is flawless;
Ecc 7: 21 attention to every *w* people say,
8: 4 Since a king's *w* is supreme,
Isa 1: 10 Hear the *w* of the LORD,
2: 3 the *w* of the LORD from Jerusalem
5: 24 and spurned the *w* of the Holy One
8: 20 do not speak according to this *w*,
16: 13 This is the *w* the LORD has
23: 1 *w* has come to them.
23: 5 When *w* comes to Egypt,
24: 3 The LORD has spoken this *w*.
28: 13 the *w* of the LORD
28: 14 Therefore hear the *w* of the LORD,
29: 21 those who with a *w* make a man out
37: 9 to Hezekiah with this *w*:
37: 22 this is the *w* the LORD has spoken
38: 4 the *w* of the LORD came to Isaiah:
39: 5 Hear the *w* of the LORD Almighty
39: 8 *w* of the LORD you have spoken is
40: 8 but the *w* of our God stands forever
45: 23 a *w* that will not be revoked.
50: 4 to know the *w* that sustains
50: 10 and obeys the *w* of his servant?
55: 11 so is my *w* that goes out
66: 2 and trembles at my *w*.
66: 5 Hear the *w* of the LORD,
66: 5 you who tremble at his *w*:
Jer 1: 2 The *w* of the LORD came to him
1: 4 The *w* of the LORD came to me,
1: 11 The *w* of the LORD came to me:
1: 12 to see that my *w* is fulfilled."
1: 13 The *w* of the LORD came
2: 1 The *w* of the LORD came to me:
2: 4 Hear the *w* of the LORD, O house
2: 31 consider the *w* of the LORD:
5: 13 and the *w* is not in them;
6: 10 The *w* of the LORD is offensive
7: 1 This is the *w* that came to Jeremiah
7: 2 " 'Hear the *w* of the LORD,
8: 9 Since they have rejected the *w*
9: 20 O women, hear the *w* of the LORD
11: 1 This is the *w* that came to Jeremiah
13: 3 Then the *w* of the LORD came
13: 8 the *w* of the LORD came to me:
14: 1 This is the *w* of the LORD
14: 17 "Speak this *w* to them:
16: 1 the *w* of the LORD came to me:
17: 15 "Where is the *w* of the LORD?
17: 20 'Hear the *w* of the LORD,
18: 1 This is the *w* that came to Jeremiah
18: 5 the *w* of the LORD came to me:
18: 18 nor the *w* from the prophets.
19: 3 and say, 'Hear the *w* of the LORD,
20: 8 the *w* of the LORD has brought me
Jer 20: 9 his *w* is in my heart like a burning
21: 1 The *w* came to Jeremiah
21: 11 'Hear the *w* of the LORD;
22: 2 'Hear the *w* of the LORD,
22: 29 hear the *w* of the LORD!
23: 18 Who has listened and heard his *w*?
23: 18 the LORD to see or to hear his *w*?
23: 28 who has my *w* speak it faithfully.
23: 29 "Is not my *w* like fire," declares
23: 36 every man's own *w* becomes his
24: 4 the *w* of the LORD came to me:
25: 1 *w* came to Jeremiah concerning all
25: 3 the *w* of the LORD has come to me
26: 1 this *w* came from the LORD:
26: 2 I command you; do not omit a *w*.
27: 1 this *w* came to Jeremiah
27: 3 Then send *w* to the kings of Edom,
27: 18 and have the *w* of the LORD,
28: 12 the *w* of the LORD came
29: 20 Therefore, hear the *w* of the LORD
29: 30 Then the *w* of the LORD came
30: 1 This is the *w* that came to Jeremiah
31: 10 "Hear the *w* of the LORD,
32: 1 This is the *w* that came to Jeremiah
32: 6 "The *w* of the LORD came to me:
32: 8 "I knew that this was the *w*
32: 26 Then the *w* of the LORD came
33: 1 the *w* of the LORD came
33: 19 The *w* of the LORD came
33: 23 The *w* of the LORD came
34: 1 this *w* came to Jeremiah
34: 8 The *w* came to Jeremiah
34: 12 Then the *w* of the LORD came
35: 1 This is the *w* that came to Jeremiah
35: 12 Then the *w* of the LORD came
36: 1 this *w* came to Jeremiah
36: 27 the *w* of the LORD came
37: 6 Then the *w* of the LORD came
37: 17 "Is there any *w* from the LORD?"
39: 15 the *w* of the LORD came to him:
40: 1 The *w* came to Jeremiah
42: 7 Ten days later the *w*
42: 15 then hear the *w* of the LORD,
43: 8 In Tahpanhes the *w*
44: 1 *w* came to Jeremiah concerning
44: 24 "Hear the *w* of the LORD,
44: 26 But hear the *w* of the LORD,
44: 28 will know whose *w* will stand—
46: 1 This is the *w* of the LORD that
47: 1 This is the *w* of the LORD that
49: 34 This is the *w* of the LORD that
50: 1 This is the *w* the LORD spoke
La 2: 17 he has fulfilled his *w*,
Eze 1: 3 the *w* of the LORD came
3: 16 the end of seven days the *w*
3: 17 so hear the *w* I speak and give them
6: 1 The *w* of the LORD came to me:
6: 3 hear the *w* of the Sovereign LORD
7: 1 The *w* of the LORD came to me:
9: 11 kit at his side brought back *w*,
11: 14 The *w* of the LORD came to me:
12: 1 The *w* of the LORD came to me:
12: 8 In the morning the *w*
12: 17 The *w* of the LORD came to me:
12: 21 The *w* of the LORD came to me:
12: 26 The *w* of the LORD came to me:
13: 1 The *w* of the LORD came to me:
13: 2 'Hear the *w* of the LORD!
14: 2 the *w* of the LORD came to me:
14: 12 The *w* of the LORD came to me:
15: 1 The *w* of the LORD came to me:
16: 1 The *w* of the LORD came to me:
16: 35 you prostitute, hear the *w*
17: 1 The *w* of the LORD came to me:
17: 11 the *w* of the LORD came to me:
18: 1 The *w* of the LORD came to me:
20: 2 the *w* of the LORD came to me:
20: 45 The *w* of the LORD came to me:
20: 47 'Hear the *w* of the LORD.
21: 1 The *w* of the LORD came to me:
21: 8 The *w* of the LORD came to me:
21: 18 The *w* of the LORD came to me:
22: 1 The *w* of the LORD came to me:
22: 17 the *w* of the LORD came to me:
22: 23 Again the *w* of the LORD came
23: 1 The *w* of the LORD came to me:
24: 1 the *w* of the LORD came to me:
24: 15 The *w* of the LORD came to me:
Eze 24: 20 "The *w* of the LORD came to me:
25: 1 The *w* of the LORD came to me:
25: 3 'Hear the *w* of the Sovereign
26: 1 the *w* of the LORD came to me:
27: 1 The *w* of the LORD came to me:
28: 1 The *w* of the LORD came to me:
28: 11 The *w* of the LORD came to me:
28: 20 The *w* of the LORD came to me:
29: 1 the *w* of the LORD came to me:
29: 17 the *w* of the LORD came to me:
30: 1 The *w* of the LORD came to me:
30: 20 the *w* of the LORD came to me:
31: 1 the *w* of the LORD came to me:
32: 1 the *w* of the LORD came to me:
32: 17 the *w* of the LORD came to me:
33: 1 The *w* of the LORD came to me:
33: 7 so hear the *w* I speak and give them
33: 23 the *w* of the LORD came to me:
34: 1 The *w* of the LORD came to me:
34: 7 you shepherds, hear the *w*
34: 9 therefore, O shepherds, hear the *w*
35: 1 The *w* of the LORD came to me:
36: 1 of Israel, hear the *w* of the LORD.
36: 4 hear the *w* of the Sovereign LORD
36: 16 Again the *w* of the LORD came
37: 4 'Dry bones, hear the *w*
37: 15 The *w* of the LORD came to me:
38: 1 The *w* of the LORD came to me:
Da 9: 2 according to the *w*
Hos 1: 1 The *w* of the LORD that came
4: 1 Hear the *w* of the LORD, you
Joel 1: 1 The *w* of the LORD that came
Am 3: 1 Hear this *w* the LORD has spoken
4: 1 Hear this *w*, you cows of Bashan
5: 1 Hear this *w*, O house of Israel,
7: 16 Now then, hear the *w* of the LORD
8: 12 searching for the *w* of the LORD,
Jnh 1: 1 The *w* of the LORD came
3: 1 Then the *w* of the LORD came
3: 3 Jonah obeyed the *w* of the LORD
Mic 1: 1 The *w* of the LORD given
4: 2 the *w* of the LORD from Jerusalem
Zep 1: 1 The *w* of the LORD that came
2: 5 the *w* of the LORD is against you,
Hag 1: 1 the *w* of the LORD came
1: 3 Then the *w* of the LORD came
2: 1 the *w* of the LORD came
2: 10 the *w* of the LORD came
2: 20 The *w* of the LORD came
Zec 1: 1 the *w* of the LORD came
1: 7 the *w* of the LORD came
1: 14 "Proclaim this *w*: This is what
4: 6 "This is the *w* of the LORD
4: 8 the *w* of the LORD came to me:
6: 9 The *w* of the LORD came to me:
7: 1 the *w* of the LORD came
7: 4 the *w* of the LORD Almighty came
7: 8 the *w* of the LORD came again
8: 1 Again the *w* of the LORD
8: 18 Again the *w* of the LORD
9: 1 The *w* of the LORD is
11: 11 watching me knew it was the *w*
12: 1 An Oracle This is the *w*
Mal 1: 1 The *w* of the LORD to Israel
Mt 4: 4 but on every *w* that comes
8: 8 just say the *w*, and my servant will
8: 16 he drove out the spirits with a *w*
12: 32 Anyone who speaks a *w*
12: 36 for every careless *w* they have
13: 20 places is the man who hears the *w*
13: 21 comes because of the *w*,
13: 22 thorns is the man who hears the *w*,
13: 23 soil is the man who hears the *w*
14: 35 they sent *w* to all the surrounding
15: 6 Thus you nullify the *w* of God
15: 23 Jesus did not answer a *w*.
22: 46 No one could say a *w* in reply,
26: 75 Peter remembered the *w* Jesus had
Mk 2: 2 and he preached the *w* to them.
4: 14 parable? The farmer sows the *w*.
4: 15 along the path, where the *w* is sown
4: 15 takes away the *w* that was sown
4: 16 hear the *w* and at once receive it
4: 17 comes because of the *w*,
4: 18 hear the *w*; but the worries
4: 19 come in and choke the *w*,
4: 20 hear the *w*, accept it, and produce
4: 33 similar parables Jesus spoke the *w*

Mk 7: 13 Thus you nullify the *w* of God
14: 72 Peter remembered the *w* Jesus had
16: 20 confirmed his *w* by the signs that
Lk 1: 2 eyewitnesses and servants of the *w*.
2: 17 they spread the *w* concerning what
3: 2 the *w* of God came to John son
5: 1 and listening to the *w* of God,
7: 7 say the *w*, and my servant will be
8: 11 of the parable: The seed is the *w*
8: 12 takes away the *w* from their hearts,
8: 13 are the ones who receive the *w*
8: 15 who hear the *w*, retain it,
8: 21 are those who hear God's *w*
11: 28 rather are those who hear the *w*
12: 10 And everyone who speaks a *w*
22: 61 Peter remembered the *w* the Lord
24: 19 powerful in *w* and deed before God
Jn 1: 1 was the *W*, and the *W* was
1: 1 was with God, and the *W* was God.
1: 14 The *W* became flesh and lived for a
4: 50 The man took Jesus at his *w*
5: 24 whoever hears my *w* and believes
5: 38 nor does his *w* dwell in you,
7: 26 and they are not saying a *w* to him.
8: 37 you have no room for my *w*.
8: 51 a man keeps my *w*, he will never
8: 52 that if a man keeps your *w*,
8: 55 but I do know him and keep his *w*.
9: 7 of Siloam'' (this *w* means Sent).
10: 35 to whom the *w* of God came—
11: 3 So the sisters sent *w* to Jesus,
12: 17 to spread the *w* that he had called
12: 38 to fulfill the *w* of Isaiah the prophet
12: 48 that very *w* which I spoke will
15: 3 of the *w* I have spoken to you.
17: 6 and they have obeyed your *w*.
17: 14 I have given them your *w*
17: 17 them by the truth; your *w* is truth.
Ac 4: 29 speak your *w* with great boldness.
4: 31 and spoke the *w* of God boldly.
6: 2 ministry of the *w* of God in order
6: 4 and the ministry of the *w*.''
6: 7 So the *w* of God spread.
8: 4 preached the *w* wherever they
8: 14 that Samaria had accepted the *w*
8: 25 and proclaimed the *w* of the Lord,
11: 1 also had received the *w* of God.
12: 24 the *w* of God continued to increase
13: 5 they proclaimed the *w* of God
13: 7 he wanted to hear the *w* of God.
13: 15 the synagogue rulers sent *w*
13: 44 gathered to hear the *w* of the Lord.
13: 46 ''We had to speak the *w* of God
13: 48 and honored the *w* of the Lord;
13: 49 The *w* of the Lord spread
14: 25 and when they had preached the *w*
15: 27 and Silas to confirm by *w*
15: 35 and preached the *w* of the Lord.
15: 36 towns where we preached the *w*
16: 6 Spirit from preaching the *w*
16: 32 Then they spoke the *w* of the Lord
17: 13 that Paul was preaching the *w*
18: 11 teaching them the *w* of God.
19: 10 of Asia heard the *w* of the Lord.
19: 20 In this way the *w* of the Lord
20: 32 to God and to the *w* of his grace,
Ro 9: 6 as though God's *w* had failed.
10: 8 But what does it say? ''The *w* is
10: 8 the *w* of faith we are proclaiming:
10: 17 heard through the *w* of Christ.
1Co 14: 6 or prophecy or *w* of instruction?
14: 26 or a *w* of instruction, a revelation,
14: 36 Did the *w* of God originate
15: 2 firmly to the *w* I preached to you.
2Co 2: 17 we do not peddle the *w* of God
4: 2 nor do we distort the *w* of God.
Gal 6: 6 in the *w* must share all good things
Eph 1: 13 when you heard the *w* of truth,
5: 26 washing with water through the *w*,
6: 17 of the Spirit, which is the *w* of God.
Php 1: 14 to speak the *w* of God more
2: 16 as you hold out the *w* of life—
Col 1: 5 have already heard about in the *w*
1: 25 me to present to you the *w* of God
3: 16 Let the *w* of Christ dwell
3: 17 whatever you do, whether in *w*
1Th 2: 13 but as it actually is, the *w* of God,
2: 13 when you received the *w* of God,
1Th 2: 13 you accepted it not as the *w* of men
4: 15 According to the Lord's own *w*,
2Th 2: 15 whether by *w* of mouth or by letter.
2: 17 you in every good deed and *w*.
1Ti 4: 5 it is consecrated by the *w* of God
2Ti 2: 9 But God's *w* is not chained.
2: 15 and who correctly handles the *w*
4: 2 give you this charge: Preach the *W*;
Tit 1: 3 appointed season he brought his *w*
2: 5 so that no one will malign the *w*
Heb 1: 3 things by his powerful *w*.
4: 12 For the *w* of God is living
5: 12 truths of God's *w* all over again.
6: 5 have tasted the goodness of the *w*
12: 5 And you have forgotten that *w*
12: 19 begged that no further *w* be spoken
12: 24 blood that speaks a better *w*
13: 7 who spoke the *w* of God to you.
13: 22 to bear with my *w* of exhortation,
Jas 1: 18 birth through the *w* of truth,
1: 21 and humbly accept the *w* planted
1: 22 Do not merely listen to the *w*,
1: 23 Anyone who listens to the *w*
1Pe 1: 23 through the living and enduring *w*
1: 25 And this is the *w* that was preached
1: 25 the *w* of the Lord stands forever.''
3: 1 if any of them do not believe the *w*,
2Pe 1: 19 And we have the *w* of the prophets
3: 5 ago by God's *w* the heavens existed
3: 7 By the same *w* the present heavens
1Jn 1: 1 this we proclaim concerning the *W*
1: 10 and his *w* has no place in our lives.
2: 5 But if anyone obeys his *w*,
2: 14 and the *w* of God lives in you,
Rev 1: 2 the *w* of God and the testimony
1: 9 of the *w* of God and the testimony
3: 8 yet you have kept my *w*
6: 9 of the *w* of God and the testimony
12: 11 and by the *w* of their testimony;
19: 13 and his name is the *W* of God.
20: 4 and because of the *w* of God.

WORDS (WORD)

Ge 4: 23 wives of Lamech, hear my *w*.
27: 34 When Esau heard his father's *w*,
42: 16 so that your *w* may be tested to see
42: 20 so that your *w* may be verified
44: 6 he repeated these *w* to them.
Ex 4: 15 to him and put *w* in his mouth;
19: 6 These are the *w* you are to speak
19: 7 them all the *w* the LORD had
20: 1 And God spoke all these *w*:
23: 8 and twists the *w* of the righteous.
24: 3 told the people all the LORD's *w*
24: 8 in accordance with all these *w*.''
33: 4 people heard these distressing *w*,
34: 1 I will write on them the *w* that were
34: 27 to Moses, ''Write down these *w*,
34: 27 with these *w* I have made
34: 28 on the tablets the *w* of the covenant
Nu 12: 6 forward, he said, ''Listen to my *w*:
24: 4 of one who hears the *w* of God,
24: 16 of one who hears the *w* of God,
Dt 1: 1 These are the *w* Moses spoke
4: 10 the people before me to hear my *w*
4: 12 You heard the sound of *w*
4: 36 you heard his *w* from out of the fire
10: 2 write on the tablets the *w* that were
11: 18 Fix these *w* of mine in your hearts
13: 3 listen to the *w* of that prophet
16: 19 and twists the *w* of the righteous.
17: 19 follow carefully all the *w* of this law
18: 18 I will put my *w* in his mouth,
18: 19 to my *w* that the prophet speaks
27: 3 Write on them all the *w* of this law
27: 8 shall write very clearly all the *w*
27: 26 the man who does not uphold the *w*
28: 58 do not carefully follow all the *w*
29: 19 When such a person hears the *w*
29: 29 that we may follow all the *w*
31: 1 and spoke these *w* to all Israel:
31: 12 follow carefully all the *w* of this law
31: 24 writing in a book the *w* of this law
31: 28 so that I can speak these *w*
31: 30 Moses recited the *w* of this song
32: 1 hear, O earth, the *w* of my mouth.
32: 2 and my *w* descend like dew,
32: 44 and spoke all the *w* of this song
Dt 32: 45 Moses finished reciting all these *w*
32: 46 children to obey carefully all the *w*
32: 46 to heart all the *w* I have solemnly
32: 47 They are not just idle *w* for you—
Jos 1: 18 and does not obey your *w*,
3: 9 to the *w* of the LORD your God.
8: 34 Joshua read all the *w* of the law—
24: 27 has heard all the *w* the LORD has
Jdg 11: 11 And he repeated all his *w*
13: 12 ''When your *w* are fulfilled,
1Sa 3: 19 none of his *w* fall to the ground.
8: 10 Samuel told all the *w* of the LORD
11: 6 When Saul heard their *w*, the Spirit
17: 11 On hearing the Philistine's *w*,
18: 23 They repeated these *w* to David.
21: 12 David took these *w* to heart
24: 7 With these *w* David rebuked his
25: 35 have heard your *w* and granted
26: 19 the king listen to his servant's *w*.
28: 20 with fear because of Samuel's *w*.
2Sa 7: 17 to David all the *w* of this entire
7: 28 are God! Your *w* are trustworthy,
14: 3 And Joab put the *w* in her mouth.
14: 3 and speak these *w* to him.''
14: 19 who put all these *w* into the mouth
22: 1 to the LORD the *w* of this song
23: 1 These are the last *w* of David:
1Ki 8: 59 And may these *w* of mine,
21: 27 When Ahab heard these *w*,
22: 28 ''Mark my *w*, all you people!''
2Ki 6: 12 king of Israel the very *w* you speak
6: 30 the king heard the woman's *w*,
18: 20 but you speak only empty *w*.
19: 4 for the *w* the LORD your God has
19: 4 LORD your God will hear all the *w*
19: 6 those *w* with which the underlings
19: 16 to the *w* Sennacherib has sent
22: 11 When the king heard the *w*
22: 13 our fathers have not obeyed the *w*
22: 18 says concerning the *w* you heard:
23: 2 read in their hearing all the *w*
23: 3 confirming the *w* of the covenant
1Ch 17: 15 to David all the *w* of this entire
2Ch 11: 4 So they obeyed the *w* of the LORD
15: 8 When Asa heard these *w*
18: 27 ''Mark my *w*, all you people!''
29: 30 the LORD with the *w* of David
32: 6 and encouraged them with these *w*:
33: 18 and the *w* the seers spoke to him
34: 19 When the king heard the *w*
34: 26 says concerning the *w* you heard:
34: 30 read in their hearing all the *w*
34: 31 and to obey the *w* of the covenant
36: 16 despised his *w* and scoffed
Ezr 9: 4 trembled at the *w* of the God
Ne 1: 1 The *w* of Nehemiah son
8: 9 they listened to the *w* of the Law.
8: 12 now understood the *w* that had
8: 13 attention to the *w* of the Law.
Est 4: 12 When Esther's *w* were reported
9: 30 *w* of good will and assurance—
Job 4: 4 Your *w* have supported those who
6: 3 no wonder my *w* have been
6: 10 that I had not denied the *w*
6: 25 How painful are honest *w*!
6: 26 and treat the *w* of a despairing man
8: 2 Your *w* are a blustering wind.
8: 10 Will they not bring forth *w*
9: 14 How can I find *w* to argue with him
11: 2 ''Are all these *w* to go unanswered?
12: 11 Does not the ear test *w*
13: 17 Listen carefully to my *w*;
15: 3 Would he argue with useless *w*,
15: 11 *w* spoken gently to you?
15: 13 pour out such *w* from your mouth?
19: 2 and crush me with *w*?
19: 23 ''Oh, that my *w* were recorded,
21: 2 ''Listen carefully to my *w*;
22: 22 and lay up his *w* in your heart.
23: 12 I have treasured the *w*
24: 25 and reduce my *w* to nothing?''
26: 4 Who has helped you utter these *w*?
29: 22 my *w* fell gently on their ears.
29: 23 drank in my *w* as the spring rain.
31: 40 The *w* of Job are ended.
32: 11 while you were searching for *w*,
32: 14 Job has not marshaled his *w*
32: 15 *w* have failed them.

Job 32: 18 For I am full of *w*,
33: 1 "But now, Job, listen to my *w*;
33: 2 my *w* are on the tip of my tongue.
33: 3 My *w* come from an upright heart;
33: 8 I heard the very *w*—
33: 13 that he answers none of man's *w*?
34: 2 "Hear my *w*, you wise men;
34: 3 For the ear tests *w*
34: 35 his *w* lack insight.'
34: 37 and multiplies his *w* against God."
35: 16 without knowledge he multiplies *w*
36: 4 Be assured that my *w* are not false;
38: 2 with *w* without knowledge?
41: 3 Will he speak to you with gentle *w*?
Ps 5: 1 Give ear to my *w*, O LORD,
12: 6 the *w* of the LORD are flawless,
19: 4 their *w* to the ends of the world.
19: 14 May the *w* of my mouth
22: 1 so far from the *w* of my groaning?
36: 3 The *w* of his mouth are wicked
49: 3 My mouth will speak *w* of wisdom;
50: 17 and cast my *w* behind you.
54: 2 listen to the *w* of my mouth.
55: 21 his *w* are more soothing than oil,
56: 5 All day long they twist my *w*;
59: 12 for the *w* of their lips,
64: 3 and aim their *w* like deadly arrows.
78: 1 listen to the *w* of my mouth.
94: 4 They pour out arrogant *w*;
105: 28 they not rebelled against his *w*?
106: 33 and rash *w* came from Moses' lips.
107: 11 rebelled against the *w* of God
109: 3 With *w* of hatred they surround me
119: 57 I have promised to obey your *w*.
119:130 The entrance of your *w* gives light;
119:139 for my enemies ignore your *w*.
119:160 All your *w* are true;
138: 4 when they hear the *w*
141: 6 learn that my *w* were well spoken.
Pr 1: 2 for understanding *w* of insight;
2: 1 My son, if you accept my *w*
2: 12 from men whose *w* are perverse,
2: 16 wife with her seductive *w*,
4: 4 "Lay hold of my *w*
4: 5 do not forget my *w* or swerve
4: 20 listen closely to my *w*.
5: 1 listen well to my *w* of insight,
6: 2 ensnared by the *w* of your mouth,
7: 1 My son, keep my *w*
7: 5 wife with her seductive *w*.
7: 21 With persuasive *w* she led him
8: 8 All the *w* of my mouth are just;
10: 19 When *w* are many, sin is not absent
12: 6 The *w* of the wicked lie in wait
12: 18 Reckless *w* pierce like a sword,
16: 21 and pleasant *w* promote instruction
16: 24 Pleasant *w* are a honeycomb,
17: 27 of knowledge uses *w* with restraint,
18: 4 *w* of a man's mouth are deep
18: 8 *w* of a gossip are like choice
19: 27 from the *w* of knowledge.
22: 12 he frustrates the *w* of the unfaithful
22: 21 teaching you true and reliable *w*,
23: 9 he will scorn the wisdom of your *w*.
23: 12 and your ears to *w* of knowledge.
26: 22 *w* of a gossip are like choice
29: 19 cannot be corrected by mere *w*;
30: 6 Do not add to his *w*,
Ecc 1: 1 The *w* of the Teacher, son of David
5: 2 so let your *w* be few.
5: 3 of a fool when there are many *w*.
5: 7 and many *w* are meaningless.
6: 11 The more the *w*,
9: 16 and his *w* are no longer heeded.
9: 17 The quiet *w* of the wise are more
10: 12 *W* from a wise man's mouth are
10: 13 At the beginning his *w* are folly;
10: 14 and the fool multiplies *w*.
10: 20 a bird of the air may carry your *w*,
12: 10 searched to find just the right *w*,
12: 11 The *w* of the wise are like goads,
Isa 3: 8 their *w* and deeds are
29: 11 vision is nothing but *w* sealed
29: 18 In that day the deaf will hear the *w*
31: 2 he does not take back his *w*.
36: 5 but you speak only empty *w*.
36: 13 "Hear the *w* of the great king,
37: 4 for the *w* the LORD your God has

Isa 37: 4 LORD your God will hear the *w*
37: 6 those *w* with which the underlings
37: 17 to all the *w* Sennacherib has sent
41: 26 no one heard any *w* from you.
44: 26 who carries out the *w*
51: 16 I have put my *w* in your mouth
58: 13 as you please or speaking idle *w*,
59: 21 and my *w* that I have put
Jer 1: 1 The *w* of Jeremiah son of Hilkiah,
1: 9 I have put my *w* in your mouth.
5: 14 I will make my *w* in your mouth
5: 14 the people have spoken these *w*,
6: 19 they have not listened to my *w*
7: 4 Do not trust in deceptive *w* and say
7: 8 in deceptive *w* that are worthless.
9: 20 to the *w* of his mouth.
11: 6 "Proclaim all these *w* in the towns
11: 10 who refused to listen to my *w*.
13: 10 who refuse to listen to my *w*,
15: 16 When your *w* came, I ate them;
15: 19 you utter worthy, not worthless, *w*,
19: 2 There proclaim the *w* I tell you,
19: 15 and would not listen to my *w*.' "
23: 9 and his holy *w*.
23: 22 they would have proclaimed my *w*
23: 30 from one another *w* supposedly
23: 36 and so you distort the *w*
23: 38 You used the *w*, 'This is the oracle
25: 8 you have not listened to my *w*,
25: 30 prophesy all these *w* against them
26: 5 listen to the *w* of my servants
26: 7 heard Jeremiah speak these *w*
26: 15 to speak all these *w* in your hearing
26: 21 officers and officials heard his *w*,
27: 14 Do not listen to the *w*
28: 6 the LORD fulfill the *w* you have
29: 19 For they have not listened to my *w*
29: 19 "*w* that I sent to them again
30: 2 in a book all the *w* I have spoken
30: 4 These are the *w* the LORD spoke
31: 23 towns will once again use these *w*:
35: 13 not learn a lesson and obey my *w*?'
36: 2 write on it all the *w* I have spoken
36: 4 dictated all the *w* the LORD had
36: 6 the people from the scroll the *w*
36: 8 the LORD's temple he read the *w*
36: 10 people at the LORD's temple the *w*
36: 11 heard all the *w* of the LORD
36: 16 When they heard all these *w*,
36: 16 "We must report all these *w*
36: 18 "he dictated all these *w* to me,
36: 24 heard all these *w* showed no fear,
36: 27 scroll containing the *w* that Baruch
36: 28 and write on it all the *w* that were
36: 32 And many similar *w* were added
36: 32 Baruch wrote on it all the *w*
37: 2 to the *w* the LORD had spoken
39: 16 to fulfill my *w* against this city
43: 1 finished telling the people all the *w*
45: 1 on a scroll the *w* Jeremiah was then
51: 61 see that you read all these *w* aloud.
51: 64 The *w* of Jeremiah end here.
Eze 2: 6 do not be afraid of them or their *w*.
2: 7 You must speak my *w* to them,
2: 10 sides of it were written *w* of lament
3: 4 of Israel and speak my *w* to them.
3: 6 whose *w* you cannot understand.
3: 10 to heart all the *w* I speak to you.
12: 28 of my *w* will be delayed any longer;
13: 6 yet they expect their *w*
13: 8 Because of your false *w*
33: 31 sit before you to listen to your *w*,
33: 32 for they hear your *w* but do not put
Da 4: 31 The *w* were still on his lips
5: 26 "This is what these *w* mean:
7: 11 of the boastful *w* the horn was
9: 12 You have fulfilled the *w* spoken
10: 11 consider carefully the *w* I am about
10: 12 your *w* were heard, and I have
12: 4 and seal the *w* of the scroll
12: 9 because the *w* are closed up
Hos 6: 5 you with the *w* of my mouth;
7: 16 because of their insolent *w*.
14: 2 Take *w* with you
Am 1: 1 dwells in Zion! The *w* of Amos,
7: 10 The land cannot bear all his *w*.
8: 11 of hearing the *w* of the LORD.
Mic 2: 7 "Do not my *w* do good

Mic 7: 5 be careful of your *w*.
Zec 1: 6 But did not my *w* and my decrees,
1: 13 and comforting *w* to the angel who
7: 7 these not the *w* the LORD
7: 12 to the *w* that the LORD Almighty
8: 9 You who now hear these *w* spoken
Mal 2: 17 wearied the LORD with your *w*.
Mt 6: 7 be heard because of their many *w*.
7: 24 everyone who hears these *w*
7: 26 But everyone who hears these *w*
10: 14 welcome you or listen to your *w*,
12: 7 had known what these *w* mean,
12: 37 For by your *w* you will be acquitted
12: 37 by your *w* you will be condemned."
22: 15 and laid plans to trap him in his *w*.
24: 35 but my *w* will never pass away.
Mk 8: 38 and my *w* in this adulterous
10: 24 The disciples were amazed at his *w*.
12: 13 to Jesus to catch him in his *w*.
13: 31 but my *w* will never pass away.
Lk 1: 20 because you did not believe my *w*,
1: 29 Mary was greatly troubled at his *w*
3: 4 book of the *w* of Isaiah the prophet:
3: 18 with many other *w* John exhorted
4: 22 amazed at the gracious *w* that came
6: 47 and hears my *w* and puts them
6: 49 But the one who hears my *w*
7: 29 when they heard Jesus' *w*,
9: 26 is ashamed of me and my *w*,
19: 22 'I will judge you by your own *w*,
19: 48 all the people hung on his *w*.
21: 15 I will give you *w* and wisdom that
21: 33 but my *w* will never pass away.
24: 8 Then they remembered his *w*.
24: 11 their *w* seemed to them like
Jn 1: 23 John replied in the *w*
2: 22 and the *w* that Jesus had spoken.
3: 34 whom God has sent speaks the *w*
4: 41 of his *w* many more became
6: 63 The *w* I have spoken
6: 68 You have the *w* of eternal life.
7: 40 On hearing his *w*, some
8: 20 He spoke these *w* while teaching
10: 19 At these *w* the Jews were again
12: 47 "As for the person who hears my *w*
12: 48 and does not accept my *w*;
14: 10 *w* I say to you are not just my own
14: 24 These *w* you hear are not my own;
15: 7 in me and my *w* remain in you,
15: 20 Remember the *w* I spoke to you:
17: 8 For I gave them the *w* you gave me
18: 9 so that the *w* he had spoken would
18: 32 so that the *w* Jesus had spoken
Ac 2: 40 With many other *w* he warned
6: 11 "We have heard Stephen speak *w*
7: 35 they had rejected with the *w*,
7: 38 and he received living *w* to pass
10: 44 Peter was still speaking these *w*,
13: 27 him they fulfilled the *w*
13: 34 never to decay, is stated in these *w*:
14: 18 with these *w*, they had difficulty
15: 15 The *w* of the prophets are
18: 15 since it involves questions about *w*
20: 2 speaking many *w*
20: 35 remembering the *w* the Lord Jesus
22: 14 and to hear *w* from his mouth.
Ro 3: 2 entrusted with the very *w* of God.
3: 4 you may be proved right in your *w*
4: 23 The *w* "it was credited
8: 26 with groans that *w* cannot express.
9: 8 In other *w*, it is not the natural
10: 18 their *w* to the ends of the world."
1Co 1: 17 not with *w* of human wisdom,
2: 4 not with wise and persuasive *w*,
2: 13 but in *w* taught by the Spirit,
2: 13 in *w* taught us by human wisdom
2: 13 spiritual truths in spiritual *w*.
14: 9 Unless you speak intelligible *w*
14: 19 rather speak five intelligible *w*
14: 19 than ten thousand *w* in a tongue.
Gal 5: 2 Mark my *w*! I, Paul, tell you that
Eph 5: 6 no one deceive you with empty *w*,
6: 19 *w* may be given me
1Th 1: 5 came to you not simply with *w*,
4: 18 encourage each other with these *w*.
2Ti 2: 14 God against quarreling about *w*;
Heb 4: 4 about the seventh day in these *w*:
12: 19 or to such a voice speaking *w*,

Heb 12: 27 The *w* "once more" indicate
1Pe 4: 11 as one speaking the very *w* of God.
2Pe 2: 18 For they mouth empty, boastful *w*
3: 2 to recall the *w* spoken in the past
1Jn 3: 18 let us not love with *w* or tongue
Jude : 15 all the harsh *w* ungodly sinners
Rev 1: 3 Blessed is the one who reads the *w*
2: 1 These are the *w* of him who holds
2: 8 These are the *w* of him who is
2: 12 These are the *w* of him who has
2: 18 These are the *w* of the Son of God,
3: 1 These are the *w* of him who holds
3: 7 These are the *w* of him who is holy
3: 14 These are the *w* of the Amen,
13: 5 was given a mouth to utter proud *w*
17: 17 until God's *w* are fulfilled.
19: 9 "These are the true *w* of God."
21: 5 for these *w* are trustworthy
22: 6 "These *w* are trustworthy and true.
22: 7 Blessed is he who keeps the *w*
22: 9 of all who keep the *w* of this book.
22: 10 "Do not seal up the *w*
22: 18 I warn everyone who hears the *w*
22: 19 And if anyone takes *w* away

WORE (WEAR)

Jos 9: 5 on their feet and *w* old clothes.
1Sa 17: 5 and *w* a coat of scale armor
17: 6 on his legs he *w* bronze greaves,
22: 18 eighty-five men who *w* the linen
2Sa 13: 18 the virgin daughters of the king *w*.
1Ch 15: 27 David also *w* a linen ephod.
Ne 4: 18 each of the builders *w* his sword
Ps 109: 18 He *w* cursing as his garment;
Mk 1: 6 John *w* clothing made
Rev 9: 7 their heads they *w* something like
15: 6 and *w* golden sashes around their

WORK (HARDWORKING WORKED WORKER WORKERS WORKING WORKMAN WORKMAN'S WORKMANSHIP WORKMEN WORKS)

Ge 2: 2 day he rested from all his *w*.
2: 2 had finished the *w* he had been
2: 3 from all the *w* of creating that he
2: 5 there was no man to *w* the ground,
2: 15 him in the Garden of Eden to *w* it
3: 23 Garden of Eden to *w* the ground
4: 12 When you *w* the ground, it will no
29: 15 should you *w* for me for nothing?
29: 18 "I'll *w* for you seven years in return
29: 27 for another seven years of *w*."
30: 26 You know how much *w* I've done
Ex 1: 14 and with all kinds of *w* in the fields;
5: 4 to your *w*!" Then Pharaoh said,
5: 9 Make the *w* harder for the men
5: 11 your *w* will not be reduced at all.' "
5: 13 "Complete the *w* required of you
5: 18 Now get to *w*.
12: 16 Do no *w* at all on these days,
18: 18 The *w* is too heavy for you;
20: 9 you shall labor and do all your *w*,
20: 10 On it you shall not do any *w*,
23: 12 but on the seventh day do not *w*,
23: 12 "Six days do your *w*,
26: 36 and finely twisted linen—the *w*
27: 16 the *w* of an embroiderer—
28: 6 the *w* of a skilled craftsman.
28: 15 the *w* of a skilled craftsman.
28: 39 is to be the *w* of an embroiderer.
30: 25 a fragrant blend, the *w*
30: 35 of incense, the *w* of a perfumer.
31: 4 to make artistic designs for *w*
31: 5 to cut and set stones, to *w* in wood,
31: 14 whoever does any *w*
31: 15 For six days *w* is to be done,
31: 15 Whoever does any *w*
31: 17 seventh day he abstained from *w*
32: 16 The tablets were the *w* of God;
34: 10 see how awesome is the *w* that I,
35: 2 For six days, *w* is to be done,
35: 2 Whoever does any *w*
35: 21 to the LORD for the *w* on the Tent
35: 24 for any part of the *w* brought it.
35: 29 offerings for all the *w* the LORD
35: 32 to make artistic designs for *w*
35: 33 to *w* in wood and to engage
35: 35 them with skill to do all kinds of *w*
Ex 36: 1 how to carry out all the *w*
36: 1 the sanctuary are to do the *w* just
36: 2 willing to come and do the *w*.
36: 3 to carry out the *w* of constructing
36: 4 the *w* on the sanctuary left their *w*
36: 5 enough for doing the *w* the LORD
36: 7 more than enough to do all the *w*.
36: 37 and finely twisted linen—the *w*
37: 29 fragrant incense—the *w*
38: 18 and finely twisted linen—the *w*
38: 24 for all the *w* on the sanctuary was
39: 3 the *w* of a skilled craftsman.
39: 8 the *w* of a skilled craftsman.
39: 22 of blue cloth—the *w* of a weaver—
39: 27 of fine linen—the *w* of a weaver—
39: 29 the *w* of an embroiderer—
39: 32 So all the *w* on the tabernacle,
39: 42 Israelites had done all the *w* just
39: 43 Moses inspected the *w*
40: 33 And so Moses finished the *w*.
Lev 16: 29 yourselves and not do any *w*—
23: 3 There are six days when you may *w*
23: 3 not to do any *w*; wherever you live,
23: 7 assembly and do no regular *w*.
23: 8 assembly and do no regular *w*.' "
23: 21 assembly and do no regular *w*.
23: 25 Do no regular *w*, but present
23: 28 Do no *w* on that day, because it is
23: 30 his people anyone who does any *w*
23: 31 You shall do no *w* at all.
23: 35 a sacred assembly; do no regular *w*.
23: 36 closing assembly; do no regular *w*.
25: 39 do not make him *w* as a slave.
25: 40 he is to *w* for you until the Year
Nu 3: 7 by doing the *w* of the tabernacle.
3: 8 by doing the *w* of the tabernacle.
4: 3 come to serve in the *w* in the Tent
4: 4 "This is the *w* of the Kohathites
4: 19 and assign to each man his *w*
4: 23 come to serve in the *w* at the Tent
4: 24 as they *w* and carry burdens:
4: 27 whether carrying or doing other *w*,
4: 30 come to serve in the *w* at the Tent
4: 33 as they *w* at the Tent of Meeting
4: 35 came to serve in the *w* in the Tent
4: 39 came to serve in the *w* at the Tent
4: 43 came to serve in the *w* at the Tent
4: 47 came to do the *w* of serving
4: 49 each was assigned his *w*
7: 5 as each man's *w* requires."
7: 5 in the *w* at the Tent of Meeting.
7: 7 Gershonites, as their *w* required,
7: 8 the Merarites, as their *w* required.
8: 11 ready to do the *w* of the LORD.
8: 15 to come to do their *w* at the Tent
8: 19 and his sons to do the *w* at the Tent
8: 22 came to do their *w* at the Tent
8: 24 to take part in the *w* at the Tent
8: 25 regular service and *w* no longer.
8: 26 they themselves must not do the *w*.
16: 9 himself to do the *w* at the LORD's
18: 4 all the *w* at the Tent—
18: 6 to do the *w* at the Tent of Meeting.
18: 21 in return for the *w* they do
18: 23 to do the *w* at the Tent of Meeting
18: 31 for your *w* at the Tent of Meeting.
28: 18 assembly and do no regular *w*.
28: 25 assembly and do no regular *w*.
28: 26 assembly and do no regular *w*.
29: 1 assembly and do no regular *w*.
29: 7 must deny yourselves and do no *w*.
29: 12 assembly and do no regular *w*.
29: 35 an assembly and do no regular *w*.
Dt 2: 7 you in all the *w* of your hands.
5: 13 you shall labor and do all your *w*,
5: 14 On it you shall not do any *w*,
14: 29 you in all the *w* of your hands.
15: 10 God will bless you in all your *w*
15: 19 the firstborn of your oxen to *w*,
16: 8 the LORD your God and do no *w*.
16: 15 and in all the *w* of your hands,
20: 11 to forced labor and shall *w* for you.
24: 19 you in all the *w* of your hands.
27: 15 the *w* of the craftsman's hands—
28: 12 and to bless all the *w* of your hands.
30: 9 in all the *w* of your hands
33: 11 be pleased with the *w* of his hands.
Jdg 13: 12 the rule for the boy's life and *w*?"
Jdg 19: 16 came in from his *w* in the fields.
Ru 2: 19 glean today? Where did you *w*?
2Sa 12: 31 he made them *w* at brickmaking.
1Ki 5: 6 My men will *w* with yours,
7: 14 and did all the *w* assigned to him.
7: 14 in all kinds of bronze *w*.
7: 22 And so the *w* on the pillars was
7: 29 bulls were wreaths of hammered *w*.
7: 40 finished all the *w* he had
7: 49 the gold floral *w* and lamps
7: 51 When all the *w* King Solomon had
9: 23 supervising the men who did the *w*.
11: 28 how well the young man did his *w*,
2Ki 12: 11 to supervise the *w* on the temple.
22: 5 to supervise the *w* on the temple.
25: 12 of the land to *w* the vineyards
1Ch 9: 33 they were responsible for the *w* day
22: 15 skilled in every kind of *w* in gold
22: 16 begin the *w*, and the LORD be
23: 4 are to supervise the *w* of the temple
26: 8 with the strength to do the *w*—
26: 30 Jordan for all the *w* of the LORD
28: 10 Be strong and do the *w*."
28: 13 and for all the *w* of serving
28: 20 and courageous, and do the *w*.
28: 20 you until all the *w* for the service
28: 21 any craft will help you in all the *w*.
28: 21 for all the *w* on the temple of God,
29: 2 gold for the gold *w*, silver
29: 5 and for all the *w* to be done
29: 5 for the gold *w* and the silver *w*,
29: 6 of the king's *w* gave willingly.
29: 7 gave toward the *w* on the temple
2Ch 2: 7 a man skilled to *w* in gold and silver
2: 7 to *w* in Judah and Jerusalem
2: 8 My men will *w* with yours
2: 14 He is trained to *w* in gold and silver
2: 14 He will *w* with your craftsmen
4: 11 So Huram finished the *w* he had
4: 21 the gold floral *w* and lamps
5: 1 When all the *w* Solomon had done
8: 9 slaves of the Israelites for his *w*;
8: 16 All Solomon's *w* was carried out,
15: 7 for your *w* will be rewarded."
16: 5 Ramah and abandoned his *w*.
24: 12 who carried out the *w* required
24: 13 in charge of the *w* were diligent,
27: 3 and did extensive *w* on the wall
29: 12 Then these Levites set to *w*:
32: 19 peoples of the world—the *w*
34: 10 appointed to supervise the *w*
34: 12 The men did the *w* faithfully.
Ezr 2: 69 to the treasury for this *w* 61,000
3: 8 to Jerusalem) began the *w*,
4: 5 They hired counselors to *w*
4: 21 an order to these men to stop *w*,
4: 24 Thus the *w* on the house of God
5: 2 son of Jozadak set to *w*
5: 8 The *w* is being carried
6: 7 interfere with the *w* on this temple
6: 8 so that the *w* will not stop.
6: 22 them in the *w* on the house of God,
Ne 2: 16 others who would be doing the *w*.
2: 18 So they began this good *w*.
3: 1 and his fellow priests went to *w*
3: 5 to the *w* under their supervisors.
4: 11 kill them and put an end to the *w*."
4: 15 to the wall, each to his own *w*.
4: 16 half of my men did the *w*,
4: 17 who carried materials did their *w*
4: 19 "The *w* is extensive and spread out,
4: 21 So we continued the *w*
5: 16 myself to the *w* on this wall.
5: 16 were assembled there for the *w*;
6: 3 Why should the *w* stop
6: 9 hands will get too weak for the *w*,
6: 16 realized that this *w* had been done
7: 70 of the families contributed to the *w*
7: 71 to the treasury for the *w* 20,000
10: 37 tithes in all the towns where we *w*.
11: 12 who carried on *w* for the temple—
11: 16 of the outside *w* of the house
Job 1: 10 You have blessed the *w*
10: 3 to spurn the *w* of your hands,
23: 9 When he is at *w* in the north,
34: 19 for they are all the *w* of his hands?
36: 24 Remember to extol his *w*,
37: 7 men he has made may know his *w*,

Job 39: 11 Will you leave your heavy *w* to him
Ps 8: 3 the *w* of your fingers,
9: 16 by the *w* of their hands.
19: 1 the skies proclaim the *w*
28: 4 and for their evil *w*;
55: 11 Destructive forces are at *w*
90: 17 establish the *w* of our hands for us
90: 17 yes, establish the *w* of our hands.
102: 25 the heavens are the *w*
104: 13 by the fruit of his *w*.
104: 23 Then man goes out to his *w*,
Pr 8: 22 me at the beginning of his *w*,
12: 14 the *w* of his hands rewards him.
14: 23 All hard *w* brings a profit,
18: 9 One who is slack in his *w*
21: 25 because his hands refuse to *w*.
22: 29 Do you see a man skilled in his *w*?
24: 27 Finish your outdoor *w*
31: 17 She sets about her *w* vigorously;
Ecc 2: 10 My heart took delight in all my *w*,
2: 17 *w* that is done under the sun was
2: 19 over all the *w* into which I have
2: 21 For a man may do his *w*
2: 23 All his days his *w* is pain and grief;
2: 24 drink and find satisfaction in his *w*.
3: 22 for a man than to enjoy his *w*,
4: 9 they have a good return for their *w*:
5: 6 and destroy the *w* of your hands?
5: 19 his lot and be happy in his *w*—
8: 15 him in his *w* all the days
10: 15 A fool's *w* wearies him;
11: 5 so you cannot understand the *w*
SS 7: 1 the *w* of a craftsman's hands.
Isa 1: 31 and his *w* a spark;
2: 8 bow down to the *w* of their hands,
5: 12 no respect for the *w* of his hands.
5: 19 let him hasten his *w*
10: 12 the Lord has finished all his *w*
17: 8 the *w* of their hands,
19: 9 Those who *w* with combed flax will
28: 21 to do his *w*, his strange *w*,
29: 15 who do their *w* in darkness
29: 23 the *w* of my hands,
30: 24 and donkeys that *w* the soil will eat
45: 9 Does your *w* say,
45: 11 or give me orders about the *w*
54: 16 and forges a weapon fit for its *w*.
54: 16 created the destroyer to *w* havoc;
60: 21 the *w* of my hands,
61: 5 foreigners will *w* your fields
64: 8 we are all the *w* of your hand.
Jer 17: 22 or do any *w* on the Sabbath,
17: 24 holy by not doing any *w* on it,
22: 13 making his countrymen *w*
25: 14 according to their deeds and the *w*
31: 16 for your *w* will be rewarded,"
48: 10 lax in doing the LORD's *w*!
50: 25 Sovereign LORD Almighty has *w*
52: 16 of the land to *w* the vineyards
La 4: 2 the *w* of a potter's hands!
Eze 27: 14 exchanged *w* horses,
27: 16 embroidered *w*, fine linen,
27: 24 embroidered *w* and multicolored
44: 14 and all the *w* that is to be done in it.
Hos 13: 2 all of them the *w* of craftsmen.
Mic 5: 13 down to the *w* of your hands.
Na 3: 14 *W* the clay,
Hag 1: 14 and began to *w* on the house
2: 4 declares the LORD, 'and *w*.
2: 17 I struck all the *w* of your hands
Mt 14: 2 is why miraculous powers are at *w*
20: 1 to hire men to *w* in his vineyard.
20: 4 'You also go and *w* in my vineyard,
20: 7 You also go and *w* in my vineyard.'
20: 12 have borne the burden of the *w*
20: 13 agree to *w* for a denarius?
21: 28 go and *w* today in the vineyard.'
25: 16 money to *w* and gained five more.
Mk 6: 14 is why miraculous powers are at *w*
Lk 10: 40 me to do the *w* by myself?
13: 14 people, "There are six days for *w*.
19: 13 'Put this money to *w*,' he said,
Jn 4: 34 who sent me and to finish his *w*.
4: 38 Others have done the hard *w*,
5: 17 always at his *w* to this very day,
5: 36 For the very *w* that the Father has
6: 27 Do not *w* for food that spoils,
6: 29 Jesus answered, "The *w*
Jn 9: 3 "but this happened so that the *w*
9: 4 we must do the *w* of him who sent
9: 4 when no one can *w*.
14: 10 living in me, who is doing his *w*.
17: 4 by completing the *w* you gave me
Ac 13: 2 for the *w* to which I have called
13: 25 As John was completing his *w*,
14: 26 for the *w* they had now completed.
15: 38 continued with them in the *w*.
20: 35 of hard *w* we must help the weak,
Ro 4: 5 to the man who does not *w*
7: 5 by the law were at *w* in our bodies,
7: 21 So I find this law at *w*: When I want
7: 23 law at *w* in the members
7: 23 law of sin at *w* within my members.
14: 20 Do not destroy the *w* of God
15: 23 place for me to *w* in these regions,
16: 12 those women who *w* hard
1Co 3: 13 his *w* will be shown for what it is,
3: 13 test the quality of each man's *w*.
4: 12 We *w* hard with our own hands.
9: 1 the result of my *w* in the Lord?
9: 6 Barnabas who must *w* for a living?
9: 13 Don't you know that those who *w*
12: 11 All these are the *w* of one
12: 29 Are all teachers? Do all *w* miracles
15: 58 fully to the *w* of the Lord,
16: 9 for effective *w* has opened to me,
16: 10 carrying on the *w* of the Lord,
16: 16 and to everyone who joins in the *w*,
2Co 1: 24 but we *w* with you for your joy,
4: 12 is at *w* in us, but life is at *w* in you.
6: 5 in hard *w*, sleepless nights
8: 11 finish the *w*, so that your eager
9: 8 you will abound in every good *w*.
10: 15 by boasting of *w* done by others.
10: 16 want to boast about *w* already done
Gal 2: 8 was also at *w* in my ministry
2: 8 who was at *w* in the ministry
3: 5 and *w* miracles among you
Eph 2: 2 at *w* in those who are disobedient.
3: 20 to his power that is at *w* within us,
4: 16 up in love, as each part does its *w*.
4: 28 but must *w*, doing something useful
Php 1: 6 that he who began a good *w*
2: 12 continue to *w* out your salvation
2: 22 with me in the *w* of the gospel.
2: 30 he almost died for the *w* of Christ,
Col 1: 10 bearing fruit in every good *w*,
3: 23 Whatever you do, *w* at it
4: 17 you complete the *w* you have
1Th 1: 3 Father your *w* produced by faith,
2: 13 which is at *w* in you who believe.
4: 11 and to *w* with your hands,
5: 12 to respect those who *w* hard
5: 13 regard in love because of their *w*.
2Th 2: 7 of lawlessness is already at *w*;
2: 9 with the *w* of Satan displayed
2: 13 saved through the sanctifying *w*
3: 10 If a man will not *w*, he shall not eat
1Ti 1: 4 rather than God's *w*—
5: 17 those whose *w* is preaching
2Ti 2: 21 and prepared to do any good *w*.
3: 17 equipped for every good *w*.
4: 5 endure hardship, do the *w*
Tit 1: 7 overseer is entrusted with God's *w*,
Heb 1: 10 and the heavens are the *w*
4: 3 And yet his *w* has been finished
4: 4 day God rested from all his *w*."
4: 10 rest also rests from his own *w*,
6: 10 he will not forget your *w*
13: 17 them so that their *w* will be a joy,
13: 21 and may he *w* in us what is pleasing
Jas 1: 4 Perseverance must finish its *w*
1Pe 1: 2 through the sanctifying *w*
1: 17 judges each man's *w* impartially,
1Jn 3: 8 was to destroy the devil's *w*.
2Jn : 11 him shares in his wicked *w*.
3Jn : 8 men so that we may *w* together
Rev 2: 2 your hard *w* and your perseverance
9: 20 repent of the *w* of their hands;

WORKED (WORK)

Ge 4: 2 kept flocks, and Cain *w* the soil.
29: 30 he *w* for Laban another seven years
30: 29 "You know how I have *w* for you
31: 6 You know that I've *w*
31: 41 I *w* for you fourteen years
Ex 1: 13 Israelites and *w* them ruthlessly.
26: 1 with cherubim *w* into them
26: 31 with cherubim *w* into it
36: 8 with cherubim *w* into them
36: 35 with cherubim *w* into it
39: 3 cut strands to be *w* into the blue,
Dt 21: 3 take a heifer that has never been *w*
Ru 2: 7 and has *w* steadily from morning
2: 19 of the man I *w* with today is Boaz,"
2Ki 12: 11 With it they paid those who *w*
1Ch 4: 23 they stayed there and *w*
2Ch 3: 14 fine linen, with cherubim *w* into it.
25: 20 God so *w* that he might hand them
31: 21 his God and *w* wholeheartedly.
32: 5 he *w* hard repairing all the broken
Ne 3: 25 son of Uzai *w* opposite the angle
4: 6 for the people *w* with all their heart
4: 18 sword at his side as he *w*.
Est 10: 3 he *w* for the good of his people
Ps 98: 1 have *w* salvation for him.
Ecc 2: 21 to someone who has not *w* for it.
Isa 59: 16 so his own arm *w* salvation for him,
63: 5 so my own arm *w* salvation for me,
Eze 23: 29 take away everything you have *w*
Joel 2: 26 who has *w* wonders for you;
Mt 13: 33 amount of flour until it *w* all
20: 12 were hired last *w* only one hour,'
Mk 16: 20 and the Lord *w* with them
Lk 5: 5 we've *w* hard all night
13: 21 amount of flour until it *w* all
Jn 4: 38 to reap what you have not *w* for.
Ac 18: 3 he stayed and *w* with them.
Ro 16: 6 Greet Mary, who *w* very hard
16: 12 woman who has *w* very hard
1Co 15: 10 No, I *w* harder than all of them—
2Co 11: 23 I have *w* much harder, been
1Th 2: 9 we *w* night and day in order not
2Th 3: 8 On the contrary, we *w* night
2Jn : 8 you do not lose what you have *w*

WORKER (WORK)

Ex 12: 45 and a hired *w* may not eat of it.
Lev 22: 10 of a priest or his hired *w* eat it.
25: 6 the hired *w* and temporary resident
25: 40 a hired *w* or a temporary resident
Ecc 3: 9 What does the *w* gain from his toil?
Mt 10: 10 for the *w* is worth his keep.
Lk 10: 7 for the *w* deserves his wages.
Ro 16: 9 Greet Urbanus, our fellow *w*
16: 21 my fellow *w*, sends his greetings
2Co 8: 23 he is my partner and fellow *w*
Php 2: 25 fellow *w* and fellow soldier,
1Th 3: 2 and God's fellow *w* in spreading
1Ti 5: 18 and "The *w* deserves his wages."
Phm : 1 our dear friend and fellow *w*,

WORKERS (WORK)

Ru 2: 21 'Stay with my *w* until they finish
2Ki 12: 15 they gave the money to pay the *w*,
22: 5 these men pay the *w* who repair
22: 9 and have entrusted it to the *w*
1Ch 4: 21 and the clans of the linen *w*
23: 24 the *w* twenty years old
27: 26 of the field *w* who farmed the land.
2Ch 24: 12 and also *w* in iron and bronze
34: 10 These men paid the *w* who repaired
34: 13 supervised all the *w* from job to job.
34: 17 it to the supervisors and *w*."
Ezr 7: 24 or other *w* at this house of God.
Isa 19: 10 The *w* in cloth will be dejected,
58: 3 and exploit all your *w*.
Jer 10: 9 all made by skilled *w*.
Eze 48: 18 food for the *w* of the city.
48: 19 *w* from the city who farm it will
Mt 9: 37 is plentiful but the *w* are few.
9: 38 to send out *w* into his harvest field
20: 8 'Call the *w* and pay them their
20: 9 "The *w* who were hired about
Lk 10: 2 is plentiful, but the *w* are few.
10: 2 to send out *w* into his harvest field.
Ro 16: 3 my fellow *w* in Christ Jesus.
1Co 3: 9 For we are God's fellow *w*;
12: 28 third teachers, then *w* of miracles,
2Co 6: 1 As God's fellow *w* we urge you not
Php 4: 3 and the rest of my fellow *w*,
Col 4: 11 Jews among my fellow *w*
Phm : 24 Demas and Luke, my fellow *w*.

Ro 1: 20 of the *w* God's invisible qualities—
3: 6 how could God judge the *w?*
3: 19 and the whole *w* held accountable
4: 13 that he would be heir of the *w*,
5: 12 sin entered the *w* through one man,
5: 13 the law was given, sin was in the *w*.
10: 18 their words to the ends of the *w*.''
11: 12 means riches for the *w*,
11: 15 is the reconciliation of the *w*,
12: 2 longer to the pattern of this *w*,
1Co 1: 20 made foolish the wisdom of the *w?*
1: 21 since in the wisdom of God the *w*
1: 27 things of the *w* to shame the strong.
1: 27 things of the *w* to shame the wise;
1: 28 He chose the lowly things of this *w*
2: 12 not received the spirit of the *w*
3: 19 the wisdom of this *w* is foolishness
3: 22 or Cephas or the *w* or life or death
4: 13 of the earth, the refuse of the *w*.
5: 10 people of this *w* who are immoral,
5: 10 you would have to leave this *w*.
6: 2 And if you are to judge the *w*,
6: 2 that the saints will judge the *w?*
7: 31 For this *w* in its present form is
7: 31 those who use the things of the *w*,
7: 33 about the affairs of this *w*—
7: 34 about the affairs of this *w*—
8: 4 that an idol is nothing at all in the *w*
11: 32 will not be condemned with the *w*.
14: 10 sorts of languages in the *w*,
2Co 1: 12 have conducted ourselves in the *w*,
5: 19 that God was reconciling the *w*
10: 2 live by the standards of this *w*.
10: 3 For though we live in the *w*,
10: 3 we do not wage war as the *w* does.
10: 4 with are not the weapons of the *w*.
11: 18 boasting in the way the *w* does,
Gal 3: 22 that the whole *w* is a prisoner
4: 3 under the basic principles of the *w*.
6: 14 crucified to me, and I to the *w*.
6: 14 through which the *w* has been
Eph 1: 4 the creation of the *w* to be holy
2: 2 you followed the ways of this *w*
2: 12 and without God in the *w*.
6: 12 against the powers of this dark *w*
Col 1: 6 over the *w* this gospel is producing
2: 8 of this *w* rather than on Christ.
2: 20 to the basic principles of this *w*,
1Ti 1: 15 came into the *w* to save sinners—
3: 16 was believed on in the *w*,
6: 7 For we brought nothing into the *w*,
6: 17 in this present *w* not to be arrogant
2Ti 4: 10 for Demas, because he loved this *w*
Heb 1: 6 God brings his firstborn into the *w*,
2: 5 angels that he has subjected the *w*
4: 3 finished since the creation of the *w*.
9: 26 times since the creation of the *w*.
10: 5 when Christ came into the *w*,
11: 7 By his faith he condemned the *w*
11: 38 the *w* was not worthy of them.
Jas 1: 27 from being polluted by the *w*.
2: 5 poor in the eyes of the *w* to be rich
3: 6 a *w* of evil among the parts
4: 4 of the *w* becomes an enemy of God
4: 4 with the *w* is hatred toward God?
1Pe 1: 1 strangers in the *w*, scattered
1: 20 before the creation of the *w*,
2: 11 as aliens and strangers in the *w*,
5: 9 throughout the *w* are undergoing
2Pe 1: 4 in the *w* caused by evil desires.
2: 5 if he did not spare the ancient *w*
2: 20 of the *w* by knowing our Lord
3: 6 also the *w* of that time was deluged
1Jn 2: 2 but also for the sins of the whole *w*.
2: 15 If anyone loves the *w*, the love
2: 15 not love the *w* or anything in the *w*.
2: 16 For everything in the *w*—
2: 16 not from the Father but from the *w*.
2: 17 The *w* and its desires pass away,
3: 1 reason the *w* does not know us is
3: 13 my brothers, if the *w* hates you.
4: 1 prophets have gone out into the *w*.
4: 3 and even now is already in the *w*.
4: 4 than the one who is in the *w*.
4: 5 They are from the *w* and
4: 5 of the *w*, and the *w* listens to them.
4: 9 Son into the *w* that we might live
4: 14 Son to be the Savior of the *w*.
1Jn 4: 17 because in this *w* we are like him.
5: 4 born of God overcomes the *w*.
5: 4 victory that has overcome the *w*,
5: 5 Who is it that overcomes the *w?*
5: 19 and that the whole *w* is
2Jn : 7 the flesh, have gone out into the *w*.
Rev 3: 10 going to come upon the whole *w*
11: 15 of the *w* has become the kingdom
12: 9 who leads the whole *w* astray.
13: 3 The whole *w* was astonished
13: 8 slain from the creation of the *w*.
16: 14 out to the kings of the whole *w*,
17: 8 creation of the *w* will be astonished

WORLD'S (WORLD)

La 4: 12 nor did any of the *w* people,
Jn 11: 9 for he sees by this *w* light.
Rev 18: 23 merchants were the *w* great men.

WORLDLY (WORLD)

Lk 16: 9 use *w* wealth to gain friends
16: 11 trustworthy in handling *w* wealth,
1Co 3: 1 address you as spiritual but as *w*—
3: 3 You are still *w*.
3: 3 are you not *w?* Are you not acting
2Co 1: 12 done so not according to *w* wisdom
1: 17 plans in a *w* manner so that
5: 16 one from a *w* point of view.
7: 10 but *w* sorrow brings death.
Tit 2: 12 to ungodliness and *w* passions,

WORM (WORMS)

Job 17: 14 and to the *w*, 'My mother'
24: 20 the *w* feasts on them;
25: 6 a son of man, who is only a *w!*''
Ps 22: 6 But I am a *w* and not a man,
Isa 41: 14 Do not be afraid, O *w* Jacob,
51: 8 the *w* will devour them like wool.
66: 24 their *w* will not die, nor will their
Jnh 4: 7 the next day God provided a *w*,
Mk 9: 48 '' 'their *w* does not die,
2Ti 3: 6 They are the kind who *w* their way

WORMS (WORM)

Dt 28: 39 the grapes, because *w* will eat
Job 7: 5 My body is clothed with *w*
21: 26 and *w* cover them both.
Isa 14: 11 and *w* cover you.
Ac 12: 23 and he was eaten by *w* and died.

WORMWOOD

Rev 8: 11 water—the name of the star is *W*.

WORN (WEAR)

Ge 18: 12 ''After I am *w* out and my master is
Ex 35: 19 the woven garments *w*
39: 26 of the robe to be *w* for ministering,
39: 41 and the woven garments *w*
Dt 21: 3 has never *w* a yoke and lead her
25: 18 When you were weary and *w* out,
Jos 9: 5 men put *w* and patched sandals
9: 13 sandals are *w* out by the very long
Jdg 8: 5 troops some bread; they are *w* out,
8: 26 the purple garments *w* by the kings
Est 6: 8 bring a royal robe the king has *w*
Job 16: 7 Surely, O God, you have *w* me out;
Ps 6: 6 I am *w* out from groaning;
69: 3 I am *w* out calling for help;
Isa 47: 13 have received has only *w* you out!
Jer 12: 5 and they have *w* you out,
45: 3 I am *w* out with groaning
Eze 23: 43 Then I said about the one *w* out
Lk 8: 27 time this man had not *w* clothes

WORN-OUT (WEAR)

Jos 9: 4 donkeys were loaded with *w* sacks
Jer 38: 11 took some old rags and *w* clothes
38: 12 and *w* clothes under your arms

WORRIED (WORRY)

1Sa 10: 2 about them and is *w* about you.
Lk 10: 41 ''you are *w* and upset about many

WORRIES (WORRY)

Jer 17: 8 It has no *w* in a year of drought
Mt 13: 22 *w* of this life and the deceitfulness
Mk 4: 19 hear the word; but the *w* of this life,
Lk 8: 14 way they are choked by life's *w*,

WORRY (WORRIED WORRIES WORRYING)

1Sa 9: 20 do not *w* about them; they have
Mt 6: 25 I tell you, do not *w* about your life,
6: 28 ''And why do you *w* about clothes?
6: 31 So do not *w*, saying, 'What shall we
6: 34 do not *w* about tomorrow,
6: 34 for tomorrow will *w* about itself.
10: 19 do not *w* about what to say
Mk 13: 11 do not *w* beforehand about what
Lk 12: 11 do not *w* about how you will
12: 22 I tell you, do not *w* about your life,
12: 26 why do you *w* about the rest?
12: 29 or drink; do not *w* about it.
21: 14 not to *w* beforehand how you will

WORRYING (WORRY)

1Sa 9: 5 the donkeys and start *w* about us.''
Mt 6: 27 of you by *w* can add a single hour
Lk 12: 25 of you by *w* can add a single hour

WORSHIP (WORSHIPED WORSHIPER WORSHIPERS WORSHIPING WORSHIPS)

Ge 22: 5 We will *w* and then we will come
Ex 3: 12 you will *w* God on this mountain.''
4: 23 ''Let my son go, so he may *w* me.''
7: 16 so that they may *w* me in the desert
8: 1 so that they may *w* me.
8: 20 so that they may *w* me.
9: 1 so that they may *w* me.''
9: 13 so that they may *w* me,
10: 3 so that they may *w* me.
10: 7 so that they may *w* the LORD their
10: 8 ''Go, *w* the LORD your God,''
10: 11 only the men go; and *w* the LORD,
10: 24 and said, ''Go, *w* the LORD.
10: 26 are to use to *w* the LORD.''
12: 31 *w* the LORD as you have
20: 5 bow down to them or *w* them;
23: 24 or *w* them or follow their practices.
23: 25 *W* the LORD your God,
23: 33 the *w* of their gods
24: 1 You are to *w* at a distance,
34: 14 Do not *w* any other god,
Dt 4: 28 There you will *w* man-made gods
5: 9 bow down to them or *w* them;
8: 19 and follow other gods and *w*
11: 16 and *w* other gods and bow
12: 2 you are dispossessing *w* their gods.
12: 4 You must not *w* the LORD your
12: 31 You must not *w* the LORD your
13: 2 not known) ''and let us *w* them,''
13: 6 *w* other gods'' (gods that neither
13: 13 *w* other gods'' (gods you have not
28: 36 There you will *w* other gods,
28: 64 There you will *w* other gods—
29: 18 and *w* the gods of those nations;
30: 17 down to other gods and *w* them,
31: 20 turn to other gods and *w* them,
Jos 22: 27 that we will *w* the LORD
Jdg 6: 10 do not *w* the gods of the Amorites,
1Sa 1: 3 up from his town to *w*
15: 25 so that I may *w* the LORD.''
15: 30 so that I may *w* the LORD your
2Sa 15: 8 I will *w* the LORD in Hebron.' ''
15: 32 where people used to *w* God,
1Ki 1: 47 the king bowed in *w* on his bed
9: 6 off to serve other gods and *w* them,
12: 30 as far as Dan to *w* the one there.
16: 31 and began to serve Baal and *w* him.
2Ki 10: 28 So Jehu destroyed Baal *w* in Israel.
10: 29 the *w* of the golden calves at Bethel
17: 25 they did not *w* the LORD;
17: 28 taught them how to *w* the LORD.
17: 34 They neither *w* the LORD
17: 35 ''Do not *w* any other gods
17: 36 arm, is the one you must *w*.
17: 37 Do not *w* other gods.
17: 38 with you, and do not *w* other gods.
17: 39 Rather, *w* the LORD your God;
18: 22 ''You must *w* before this altar
1Ch 16: 29 *w* the LORD in the splendor
2Ch 7: 19 off to serve other gods and *w* them,
20: 18 fell down in *w* before the LORD.
29: 28 The whole assembly bowed in *w*,
32: 12 'You must *w* before one altar
Ezr 7: 19 to you for *w* in the temple

Ne 9: 6 the multitudes of heaven *w* you.
Job 1: 20 he fell to the ground in *w* and said:
Ps 22: 29 rich of the earth will feast and *w*;
29: 2 *w* the LORD in the splendor
86: 9 will come and *w* before you,
95: 6 Come, let us bow down in *w*,
96: 9 *W* the LORD in the splendor
97: 7 All who *w* images are put to shame,
97: 7 *w* him, all you gods!
99: 5 and *w* at his footstool;
99: 9 and *w* at his holy mountain,
102: 22 assemble to *w* the LORD.
132: 7 let us *w* at his footstool—
Isa 2: 20 which they made to *w*.
19: 21 They will *w* with sacrifices
19: 23 and Assyrians will *w* together.
27: 13 *w* the LORD on the holy mountain
29: 13 Their *w* of me
36: 7 "You must *w* before this altar"?
46: 6 and they bow down and *w* it.
56: 6 and to *w* him,
Jer 7: 2 these gates to *w* the LORD.
13: 10 gods to serve and *w* them,
23: 27 forgot my name through Baal *w*.
25: 6 gods to serve and *w* them;
26: 2 the towns of Judah who come to *w*
Eze 46: 2 He is to *w* at the threshold
46: 3 of the land are to *w* in the presence
46: 9 enters by the north gate to *w* is
Da 3: 5 and *w* the image of gold that King
3: 6 and *w* will immediately be thrown
3: 10 fall down and *w* the image of gold,
3: 11 and *w* will be thrown into a blazing
3: 12 *w* the image of gold you have set up
3: 14 *w* the image of gold I have set up?
3: 15 But if you do not *w* it, you will be
3: 15 fall down and *w* the image I made,
3: 18 *w* the image of gold you have set up
3: 28 *w* any god except their own God.
7: 27 and all rulers will *w* and obey him.'
Hos 13: 1 he became guilty of Baal *w*
Jnh 1: 9 I am a Hebrew and I *w* the LORD,
Zep 1: 5 the housetops to *w* the starry host,
2: 11 nations on every shore will *w* him,
Zec 14: 16 year after year to *w* the King,
14: 17 up to Jerusalem to *w* the King,
Mt 2: 2 and have come to *w* him."
2: 8 so that I too may go and *w* him."
4: 9 "if you will bow down and *w* me."
4: 10 For it is written: '*W* the Lord your
15: 9 They *w* me in vain;
Mk 7: 7 They *w* me in vain;
Lk 4: 7 So if you *w* me, it will all be yours."
4: 8 '*W* the Lord your God
Jn 4: 20 that the place where we must *w* is
4: 21 when you will *w* the Father neither
4: 22 You Samaritans *w* what you do not
4: 22 do not know; we *w* what we do
4: 23 true worshipers will *w* the Father
4: 24 and his worshipers must *w* in spirit
12: 20 among those who went up to *w*
Ac 7: 7 out of that country and *w* me
7: 42 to the *w* of the heavenly bodies.
7: 43 the idols you made to *w*.
8: 27 gone to Jerusalem to *w*,
13: 16 and you Gentiles who *w* God,
17: 23 and observed your objects of *w*,
17: 23 what you *w* as something unknown
18: 13 people to *w* God in ways contrary
24: 11 up to Jerusalem to *w*.
24: 14 I admit that I *w* the God
Ro 9: 4 the temple *w* and the promises.
12: 1 to God—which is your spiritual *w*.
1Co 14: 25 So he will fall down and *w* God,
Php 3: 3 we who *w* by the Spirit of God,
Col 2: 18 and the *w* of angels disqualify you
2: 23 with their self-imposed *w*,
1Ti 2: 10 for women who profess to *w* God.
Heb 1: 6 "Let all God's angels *w* him."
9: 1 first covenant had regulations for *w*
10: 1 perfect those who draw near to *w*.
12: 28 and so *w* God acceptably
Rev 4: 10 and *w* him who lives for ever
13: 8 of the earth will *w* the beast—
13: 12 and its inhabitants *w* the first beast,
13: 15 all who refused to *w* the image
14: 7 *W* him who made the heavens,
14: 11 or night for those who *w* the beast
Rev 15: 4 and *w* before you,
19: 10 At this I fell at his feet to *w* him.
19: 10 *W* God! For the testimony
22: 8 I fell down to *w* at the feet
22: 9 *W* God!" Then he told me,

WORSHIPED (WORSHIP)

Ge 24: 26 bowed down and *w* the LORD,
24: 48 I bowed down and *w* the LORD.
47: 31 and Israel *w* as he leaned on the top
Ex 4: 31 misery, they bowed down and *w*.
12: 27 the people bowed down and *w*.
33: 10 *w*, each at the entrance to his tent.
34: 8 bowed to the ground at once and *w*.
Dt 17: 3 to my command has *w* other gods,
29: 26 They went off and *w* other gods
Jos 24: 2 beyond the River and *w* other gods
24: 14 away the gods your forefathers *w*
Jdg 2: 12 and *w* various gods of the peoples
2: 17 to other gods and *w* them.
7: 15 and its interpretation, he *w* God.
1Sa 1: 19 the next morning they arose and *w*
1: 28 And he *w* the LORD there.
15: 31 with Saul, and Saul *w* the LORD.
2Sa 12: 20 into the house of the LORD and *w*.
1Ki 11: 33 and *w* Ashtoreth the goddess
18: 12 I your servant have *w* the LORD
22: 53 *w* Baal and provoked the LORD,
2Ki 17: 7 They *w* other gods and followed
17: 12 They *w* idols, though the LORD
17: 16 the starry hosts, and they *w* Baal.
17: 32 They *w* the LORD, but they
17: 33 They *w* the LORD, but they
21: 3 to all the starry hosts and *w* them.
21: 21 he *w* the idols his father had
21: 21 the idols his father had *w*,
2Ch 7: 3 and they *w* and gave thanks
24: 18 and *w* Asherah poles and idols.
29: 29 with him knelt down and *w*.
29: 30 and bowed their heads and *w*.
33: 3 to all the starry hosts and *w* them.
33: 22 Amon *w* and offered sacrifices
Ne 8: 6 and *w* the LORD with their faces
Ps 74: 8 every place where God was *w*
106: 19 and *w* an idol cast from metal.
106: 36 They *w* their idols,
Jer 8: 2 followed and consulted and *w*.
16: 11 other gods and served and *w* them.
22: 9 have *w* and served other gods.' "
Da 3: 7 and *w* the image of gold that King
7: 14 and men of every language *w* him.
Mt 2: 11 and they bowed down and *w* him.
14: 33 those who were in the boat *w* him,
28: 9 clasped his feet and *w* him.
28: 17 they *w* him; but some doubted.
Mk 15: 19 Falling on their knees, they *w* him.
Lk 2: 37 never left the temple but *w* night
24: 52 Then they *w* him and returned
Jn 4: 20 Our fathers *w* on this mountain,
9: 38 "Lord, I believe," and he *w* him.
Ac 19: 27 who is *w* throughout the province
Ro 1: 25 *w* and served created things rather
2Th 2: 4 that is called God or is *w*,
Heb 11: 21 and *w* as he leaned on the top
Rev 5: 14 and the elders fell down and *w*.
7: 11 faces before the throne and *w* God,
11: 16 fell on their faces and *w* God,
13: 4 Men *w* the dragon because he had
13: 4 and they also *w* the beast and asked
16: 2 mark of the beast and *w* his image.
19: 4 creatures fell down and *w* God,
19: 20 mark of the beast and *w* his image.
20: 4 They had not *w* the beast

WORSHIPER (WORSHIP)

Ac 16: 14 of Thyatira, who was a *w* of God.
18: 7 Titius Justus, a *w* of God.
Heb 9: 9 to clear the conscience of the *w*.

WORSHIPERS (WORSHIP)

Zep 3: 10 my *w*, my scattered people,
Lk 1: 10 all the assembled *w* were praying
Jn 4: 23 come when the true *w* will worship
4: 23 the kind of *w* the Father seeks.
4: 24 and his *w* must worship in spirit
Heb 10: 2 For the *w* would have been
Rev 11: 1 the altar, and count the *w* there.

WORSHIPING (WORSHIP)

Ex 10: 26 of them in *w* the LORD our God,
Nu 25: 3 Israel joined in *w* the Baal of Peor.
25: 5 joined in *w* the Baal of Peor."
Dt 4: 19 *w* things the LORD your God has
12: 31 in *w* their gods, they do all kinds
20: 18 things they do in *w* their gods,
Jdg 2: 19 other gods and serving and *w* them.
8: 27 themselves by *w* it there,
1Ki 9: 9 and have embraced other gods, *w*
2Ki 17: 41 these people were *w* the LORD,
19: 37 while he was *w* in the temple
2Ch 7: 22 and have embraced other gods, *w*
28: 2 also made cast idols for *w* the Baals
Ne 9: 3 and in *w* the LORD their God.
Isa 37: 38 while he was *w* in the temple
Jer 1: 16 in *w* what their hands have made.
44: 3 by *w* other gods that neither they
Ac 13: 2 While they were *w* the Lord
Rev 9: 20 they did not stop *w* demons,

WORSHIPS (WORSHIP)

Isa 44: 15 But he also fashions a god and *w* it;
44: 17 he bows down to it and *w*.
66: 3 like one who *w* an idol.
Rev 14: 9 If anyone *w* the beast and his image

WORTH (WORTHY)

Ge 23: 15 the land is *w* four hundred shekels
27: 46 my life will not be *w* living."
Dt 15: 18 these six years has been *w* twice
2Sa 18: 3 but you are *w* ten thousand of us.
1Ki 21: 2 I will pay you whatever it is *w*."
Job 28: 13 Man does not comprehend its *w*;
Pr 31: 10 She is *w* far more than rubies.
Isa 7: 23 a thousand vines *w* a thousand
La 4: 2 once *w* their weight in gold,
Mt 10: 10 for the worker is *w* his keep.
10: 31 are *w* more than many sparrows.
Mk 12: 42 *w* only a fraction of a penny.
Lk 12: 7 are *w* more than many sparrows.
Jn 12: 5 to the poor? It was *w* a year's wages
Ac 20: 24 I consider my life *w* nothing to me,
Ro 8: 18 sufferings are not *w* comparing
1Pe 1: 7 of greater *w* than gold,
3: 4 which is of great *w* in God's sight.

WORTHLESS

Ge 41: 27 and so are the seven *w* heads
Dt 32: 21 and angered me with their *w* idols.
1Ki 16: 13 of Israel to anger by their *w* idols.
16: 26 of Israel, to anger by their *w* idols.
2Ki 17: 15 They followed *w* idols
17: 15 and themselves became *w*.
2Ch 13: 7 Some *w* scoundrels gathered
Job 13: 4 you are *w* physicians, all of you!
15: 31 by trusting what is *w*,
34: 18 says to kings, 'You are *w*,'
Ps 31: 6 I hate those who cling to *w* idols;
60: 11 for the help of man is *w*.
108: 12 for the help of man is *w*.
119: 37 Turn my eyes away from *w* things;
Pr 11: 4 Wealth is *w* in the day of wrath,
Isa 40: 17 they are regarded by him as *w*
41: 24 and your works are utterly *w*;
44: 9 and the things they treasure are *w*.
Jer 2: 5 They followed *w* idols
2: 5 and became *w* themselves.
2: 8 following *w* idols.
2: 11 Glory for *w* idols.
7: 8 in deceptive words that are *w*.
8: 19 with their *w* foreign idols?"
10: 3 the customs of the peoples are *w*;
10: 8 they are taught by *w* wooden idols.
10: 15 They are *w*, the objects of mockery
14: 22 Do any of the *w* idols
15: 19 if you utter worthy, not *w*, words,
16: 19 *w* idols that did them no good.
18: 15 they burn incense to *w* idols,
51: 18 They are *w*, the objects of mockery
La 2: 14 were false and *w*;
Hos 8: 8 like a *w* thing.
12: 11 Its people are *w*!
Jnh 2: 8 "Those who cling to *w* idols
Zec 11: 17 "Woe to the *w* shepherd,
Mt 25: 30 And throw that *w* servant outside,
Ac 14: 15 you to turn from these *w* things

Ro 3: 12 they have together become *w;*
4: 14 has no value and the promise is *w,*
Heb 6: 8 produces thorns and thistles is *w*
Jas 1: 26 himself and his religion is *w.*

WORTHWHILE

Ecc 2: 3 to see what was *w* for men to do
Ro 1: 28 since they did not think it *w*

WORTHY (WORTH)

2Sa 22: 4 to the LORD, who is *w* of praise,
1Ki 1: 42 A *w* man like you must be bringing
1: 52 "If he shows himself to be a *w* man,
2Ki 10: 3 and most *w* of your master's sons
1Ch 16: 25 For great is the LORD and most *w*
Job 28: 18 jasper are not *w* of mention;
Ps 18: 3 to the LORD, who is *w* of praise,
48: 1 Great is the LORD, and most *w*
96: 4 For great is the LORD and most *w*
145: 3 Great is the LORD and most *w*
Pr 8: 6 Listen, for I have *w* things to say;
Jer 15: 19 if you utter *w*, not worthless, words
Mt 10: 11 search for some *w* person there
10: 37 more than me is not *w* of me;
10: 37 more than me is not *w* of me;
10: 38 and follow me is not *w* of me.
26: 66 "He is *w* of death," they answered.
Mk 1: 7 thongs of whose sandals I am not *w*
14: 64 They all condemned him as *w*
Lk 3: 16 thongs of whose sandals I am not *w*
7: 7 consider myself *w* to come to you.
15: 19 I am no longer *w* to be called your
15: 21 I am no longer *w* to be called your
20: 35 But those who are considered *w*
Jn 1: 27 thongs of whose sandals I am not *w*
Ac 5: 41 because they had been counted *w*
13: 25 whose sandals I am not *w* to untie.'
13: 46 and do not consider yourselves *w*
Ro 16: 2 in the Lord in a way *w* of the saints
Eph 4: 1 to live a life *w* of the calling you
Php 1: 27 in a manner *w* of the gospel
Col 1: 10 in order that you may live a life *w*
1Th 2: 12 urging you to live lives *w* of God,
2Th 1: 5 as a result you will be counted *w*
1: 11 that our God may count you *w*
1Ti 3: 8 are to be men *w* of respect, sincere,
3: 11 are to be women *w* of respect,
5: 17 the affairs of the church well are *w*
6: 1 should consider their masters *w*
Tit 2: 2 *w* of respect, self-controlled,
Heb 3: 3 Jesus has been found *w*
11: 38 the world was not *w* of them.
3Jn : 6 on their way in a manner *w* of God
Rev 3: 4 dressed in white, for they are *w.*
4: 11 "You are *w*, our Lord and God,
5: 2 "Who is *w* to break the seals
5: 4 no one was found who was *w*
5: 9 "You are *w* to take the scroll
5: 12 "*W* is the Lamb, who was slain,

WOUND (WOUNDED WOUNDING WOUNDS)

Ex 21: 25 burn for burn, *w* for *w*, bruise
1Ki 22: 35 The blood from his *w* ran
Job 34: 6 his arrow inflicts an incurable *w.*'
Ps 69: 26 For they persecute those you *w*
Jer 6: 14 They dress the *w* of my people
8: 11 They dress the *w* of my people
8: 22 healing for the *w* of my people?
10: 19 My *w* is incurable!
14: 17 has suffered a grievous *w,*
15: 18 and my *w* grievous and incurable?
30: 12 " 'Your *w* is incurable,
30: 15 Why do you cry out over your *w,*
La 2: 13 Your *w* is as deep as the sea.
Da 6: 23 lifted from the den, no *w* was found
Mic 1: 9 For her *w* is incurable;
Na 3: 19 Nothing can heal your *w;*
1Co 8: 12 and *w* their weak conscience,
Rev 13: 3 but the fatal *w* had been healed.
13: 3 seemed to have had a fatal *w,*
13: 12 whose fatal *w* had been healed.

WOUNDED (WOUND)

Dt 32: 39 I have *w* and I will heal,
Jdg 9: 40 and many fell *w* in the flight—
1Sa 31: 3 him, they *w* him critically.
1Ki 20: 37 So the man struck him and *w* him.
1Ki 22: 34 I've been *w.*"
2Ki 8: 28 The Arameans *w* Joram;
8: 29 of Ahab, because he had been *w.*
9: 27 They *w* him in his chariot
1Ch 10: 3 archers overtook him, they *w* him.
2Ch 18: 33 I've been *w.*"
22: 5 The Arameans *w* Joram;
22: 6 of Ahab because he had been *w.*
24: 25 they left Joash severely *w.*
35: 23 "Take me away; I am badly *w.*"
Job 24: 12 the souls of the *w* cry out for help.
Ps 109: 22 and my heart is *w* within me.
Jer 37: 10 only *w* men were left in their tents,
51: 4 fatally *w* in her streets.
51: 52 the *w* will groan.
La 2: 12 as they faint like *w* men
Eze 26: 15 when the *w* groan and the slaughter
30: 24 before him like a mortally *w* man.
Lk 20: 12 and they *w* him and threw him out.
Rev 13: 14 honor of the beast who was *w*

WOUNDING (WOUND)

Ge 4: 23 I have killed a man for *w* me,

WOUNDS (WOUND)

2Ki 8: 29 from the *w* the Arameans had
9: 15 from the *w* the Arameans had
18: 21 and *w* him if he leans on it!
2Ch 22: 6 from the *w* they had inflicted
Job 5: 18 For he *w*, but he also binds up;
9: 17 and multiply my *w* for no reason.
Ps 38: 5 My *w* fester and are loathsome
38: 11 avoid me because of my *w;*
147: 3 and binds up their *w.*
Pr 20: 30 Blows and *w* cleanse away evil,
26: 10 Like an archer who *w* at random
27: 6 but faithful are the *w* of a friend.
Isa 1: 6 only *w* and welts
30: 26 and heals the *w* he inflicted.
36: 6 and *w* him if he leans on it!
53: 5 and by his *w* we are healed.
Jer 6: 7 her sickness and *w* are ever
19: 8 and will scoff because of all its *w.*
30: 17 and heal your *w,*'
49: 17 because of all its *w.*
50: 13 because of all her *w.*
Hos 6: 1 but he will bind up our *w.*
Zec 13: 6 'The *w* I was given at the house
13: 6 'What are these *w* on your body?'
Lk 10: 34 went to him and bandaged his *w,*
Ac 16: 33 took them and washed their *w;*
1Pe 2: 24 by his *w* you have been healed.

WOVE (WEAVE)

Jdg 16: 13 *w* them into the fabric
Mt 27: 29 and then *w* a crown of thorns
Mk 15: 17 then *w* a crown of thorns

WOVEN (WEAVE)

Ex 28: 4 an ephod, a robe, a *w* tunic,
28: 8 Its skillfully *w* waistband is
28: 32 There shall be a *w* edge like a collar
29: 5 on him by its skillfully *w* waistband
31: 10 stand—and also the *w* garments,
35: 19 the *w* garments worn
39: 1 scarlet yarn they made *w* garments
39: 5 Its skillfully *w* waistband was like it
39: 41 and the *w* garments worn
Lev 8: 7 to him by its skillfully *w* waistband;
13: 48 any *w* or knitted material of linen
13: 49 or leather, or *w* or knitted material,
13: 51 or the *w* or knitted material,
13: 52 or the *w* or knitted material of wool
13: 53 or the *w* or knitted material,
13: 56 or the *w* or knitted material.
13: 57 or in the *w* or knitted material,
13: 58 or the *w* or knitted material,
13: 59 *w* or knitted material, or any
19: 19 " 'Do not wear clothing *w*
Dt 22: 11 of wool and linen *w* together.
Ps 139: 15 When I was *w* together
La 1: 14 by his hands they were *w* together.
Jn 19: 23 *w* in one piece from top to bottom.

WRAP (WRAPPED WRAPS)

Nu 4: 10 are to *w* it and all its accessories
4: 12 in the sanctuary, *w* them
Isa 28: 20 the blanket too narrow to *w*
Jer 43: 12 so will he *w* Egypt around himself
Ac 12: 8 "*W* your cloak around you

WRAPPED (WRAP)

Ex 12: 34 in kneading troughs *w* in clothing.
1Sa 21: 9 it is *w* in a cloth behind the ephod.
Job 38: 9 and *w* it in thick darkness,
Ps 109: 19 May it be like a cloak *w* about him,
109: 29 and *w* in shame as in a cloak.
Pr 30: 4 Who has *w* up the waters
Isa 59: 17 and *w* himself in zeal as in a cloak.
Eze 16: 4 rubbed with salt or *w* in cloth.
Jnh 2: 5 seaweed was *w* around my head.
Mt 27: 59 Joseph took the body, *w* it
Mk 15: 46 took down the body, *w* it
Lk 2: 7 She *w* him in cloths and placed him
2: 12 You will find a baby *w* in strips
23: 53 *w* it in linen cloth and placed it
Jn 11: 44 and feet *w* with strips of linen,
13: 4 and *w* a towel around his waist.
13: 5 them with the towel that was *w*
19: 40 the two of them *w* it,
21: 7 he *w* his outer garment around him
Ac 5: 6 men came forward, *w* up his body,

WRAPS (WRAP)

Job 26: 8 He *w* up the waters in his clouds,
Ps 104: 2 He *w* himself in light
Jer 43: 12 As a shepherd *w* his garment

WRATH

Nu 1: 53 Testimony so that *w* will not fall
16: 46 *W* has come out from the LORD;
18: 5 so that *w* will not fall
Dt 9: 8 Horeb you aroused the LORD's *w*
9: 19 I feared the anger and *w*
29: 20 his *w* and zeal will burn
29: 28 and in great *w* the LORD uprooted
32: 22 For a fire has been kindled by my *w*
Jos 9: 20 so that *w* will not fall on us
22: 20 did not *w* come upon the whole
1Sa 28: 18 or carry out his fierce *w*
2Sa 6: 8 the LORD's *w* had broken out
1Ch 13: 11 the LORD's *w* had broken out
27: 24 *W* came on Israel on account
2Ch 12: 7 My *w* will not be poured out
19: 2 the *w* of the LORD is upon you.
19: 10 otherwise his *w* will come on you
32: 25 the LORD's *w* was on him
32: 26 the LORD's *w* did not come
36: 16 scoffed at his prophets until the *w*
Ezr 7: 23 Why should there be *w*
Ne 13: 18 Now you are stirring up more *w*
Job 19: 29 for *w* will bring punishment
20: 28 on the day of God's *w.*
21: 20 drink of the *w* of the Almighty.
21: 30 delivered from the day of *w?*
40: 11 Unleash the fury of your *w,*
Ps 2: 5 and terrifies them in his *w*, saying,
2: 12 for his *w* can flare up in a moment.
6: 1 or discipline me in your *w.*
7: 11 who expresses his *w* every day.
21: 9 In his *w* the LORD will swallow
37: 8 from anger and turn from *w;*
38: 1 or discipline me in your *w.*
38: 3 of your *w* there is no health
59: 13 consume them in *w,*
69: 24 Pour out your *w* on them;
76: 10 Surely your *w* against men brings
76: 10 of your *w* are restrained.
78: 21 and his *w* rose against Israel,
78: 38 and did not stir up his full *w.*
78: 49 his *w*, indignation and hostility—
79: 6 Pour out your *w* on the nations
85: 3 You set aside all your *w*
88: 7 Your *w* lies heavily upon me;
88: 16 Your *w* has swept over me;
89: 46 How long will your *w* burn like fire
90: 9 our days pass away under your *w;*
90: 11 For your *w* is as great as the fear
102: 10 because of your great *w,*
106: 23 to keep his *w* from destroying them
110: 5 on the day of his *w.*
Pr 11: 4 Wealth is worthless in the day of *w,*
11: 23 the hope of the wicked only in *w.*
14: 35 but a shameful servant incurs his *w.*
15: 1 A gentle answer turns away *w,*
16: 14 A king's *w* is a messenger of death,

Pr 20: 2 A king's *w* is like the roar of a lion;
21: 14 in the cloak pacifies great *w*.
22: 14 under the LORD's *w* will fall into it
24: 18 and turn his *w* away from him.
Isa 9: 19 By the *w* of the LORD Almighty
10: 5 in whose hand is the club of my *w*!
10: 25 my *w* will be directed
13: 3 warriors to carry out my *w*—
13: 5 and the weapons of his *w*—
13: 9 a cruel day, with *w* and fierce
13: 13 at the *w* of the LORD Almighty,
26: 20 while until his *w* has passed by.
30: 27 his lips are full of *w*,
34: 2 his *w* is upon all their armies.
48: 9 my own name's sake I delay my *w*;
51: 13 For where is the *w* of the oppressor
51: 13 because of the *w* of the oppressor,
51: 17 the cup of his *w*,
51: 20 filled with the *w* of the LORD
51: 22 from that cup, the goblet of my *w*,
59: 18 *w* to his enemies
63: 3 and trod them down in my *w*;
63: 5 and my own *w* sustained me.
63: 6 in my *w* I made them drunk
Jer 3: 5 Will your *w* continue forever?'
4: 4 or my *w* will break out
6: 11 But I am full of the *w* of the LORD,
7: 20 and my *w* will be poured out
7: 29 this generation that is under his *w*.
10: 10 the nations cannot endure his *w*.
10: 25 Pour out your *w* on the nations
18: 20 to turn your *w* away from them.
21: 5 arm in anger and fury and great *w*.
21: 12 or my *w* will break out
23: 19 will burst out in *w*,
25: 15 filled with the wine of my *w*
30: 23 will burst out in *w*,
32: 31 and *w* that I must remove it
32: 37 in my furious anger and great *w*;
33: 5 slay in my anger and *w*.
36: 7 *w* pronounced against this people
42: 18 and *w* have been poured out
42: 18 so will my *w* be poured out on you
50: 25 brought out the weapons of his *w*,
La 2: 2 in his *w* he has torn down
2: 4 he has poured out his *w* like fire
3: 1 affliction by the rod of his *w*.
4: 11 LORD has given full vent to his *w*;
Eze 5: 13 my *w* against them will subside,
5: 13 when I have spent my *w* upon them
5: 15 and in *w* and with stinging rebuke.
6: 12 So will I spend my *w* upon them.
7: 8 I am about to pour out my *w* on you
7: 12 for *w* is upon the whole crowd.
7: 14 for my *w* is upon the whole crowd.
7: 19 them in the day of the LORD's *w*.
9: 8 of your *w* on Jerusalem?"
13: 13 In my *w* I will unleash a violent
13: 15 I will spend my *w* against the wall
14: 19 and pour out my *w* upon it
16: 38 you the blood vengeance of my *w*
16: 42 Then my *w* against you will subside
20: 8 So I said I would pour out my *w*
20: 13 So I said I would pour out my *w*
20: 21 So I said I would pour out my *w*
20: 33 and with outpoured *w*.
20: 34 and with outpoured *w*.
21: 17 and my *w* will subside.
21: 31 I will pour out my *w* upon you
22: 20 my *w* and put you inside the city
22: 21 I will blow on you with my fiery *w*,
22: 22 I the LORD have poured out my *w*
22: 24 or showers in the day of *w*.'
22: 31 So I will pour out my *w* on them
24: 8 To stir up *w* and take revenge
24: 13 again until my *w* against you has
25: 14 with my anger and my *w*;
25: 17 on them and punish them in my *w*.
30: 15 I will pour out my *w* on Pelusium,
36: 6 I speak in my jealous *w*
36: 18 So I poured out my *w* on them
38: 19 and fiery *w* I declare that
Da 8: 19 will happen later in the time of *w*,
9: 16 and your *w* from Jerusalem,
11: 36 until the time of *w* is completed,
Hos 5: 10 I will pour out my *w* on them
11: 9 I will not come in *w*.
13: 11 and in my *w* I took him away.
Am 1: 3 I will not turn back ⌞my *w*⌟.
1: 6 I will not turn back ⌞my *w*⌟.
1: 9 I will not turn back ⌞my *w*⌟.
1: 11 I will not turn back ⌞my *w*⌟.
1: 13 I will not turn back ⌞my *w*⌟.
2: 1 I will not turn back ⌞my *w*⌟.
2: 4 I will not turn back ⌞my *w*⌟.
2: 6 I will not turn back ⌞my *w*⌟.
Mic 5: 15 will take vengeance in anger and *w*
7: 9 I will bear the LORD's *w*,
Na 1: 2 maintains his *w* against his enemies
1: 2 vengeance and is filled with *w*.
1: 6 His *w* is poured out like fire;
Hab 3: 2 in *w* remember mercy.
3: 8 Was your *w* against the streams?
3: 12 In *w* you strode through the earth
Zep 1: 15 That day will be a day of *w*,
1: 18 them on the day of the LORD's *w*.
2: 2 of the LORD's *w* comes upon you.
3: 8 and to pour out my *w* on them—
Mal 1: 4 always under the *w* of the LORD.
Mt 3: 7 you to flee from the coming *w*?
Lk 3: 7 you to flee from the coming *w*?
21: 23 the land and *w* against this people.
Jn 3: 36 for God's *w* remains on him."
Ro 1: 18 The *w* of God is being revealed
2: 5 you are storing up *w*
2: 5 yourself for the day of God's *w*,
2: 8 and follow evil, there will be *w*
3: 5 unjust in bringing his *w* on us?
4: 15 is worthless, because law brings *w*.
5: 9 saved from God's *w* through him!
9: 22 choosing to show his *w*
9: 22 patience the objects of his *w*—
12: 19 but leave room for God's *w*,
13: 4 an agent of *w* to bring punishment
Eph 2: 3 we were by nature objects of *w*.
5: 6 of such things God's *w* comes
Col 3: 6 Because of these, the *w*
1Th 1: 10 who rescues us from the coming *w*.
2: 16 The *w* of God has come upon them
5: 9 God did not appoint us to suffer *w*
Rev 6: 16 and from the *w* of the Lamb!
6: 17 day of their *w* has come,
11: 18 and your *w* has come.
14: 10 strength into the cup of his *w*.
14: 19 into the great winepress of God's *w*
15: 1 with them God's *w* is completed.
15: 7 filled with the *w* of God,
16: 1 bowls of God's *w* on the earth."
16: 19 with the wine of the fury of his *w*.
19: 15 the fury of the *w* of God Almighty.

WREATH (WREATHS)

Isa 28: 1 Woe to that *w*, the pride
28: 3 *w*, the pride of Ephraim's
28: 5 a beautiful *w*

WREATHS (WREATH)

1Ki 7: 29 bulls were *w* of hammered work.
7: 30 cast with *w* on each side.
7: 36 with *w* all around.
Ac 14: 13 brought bulls and *w*

WRECKED (SHIPWRECK SHIPWRECKED)

1Ki 22: 48 they never set sail—they were *w*
2Ch 20: 37 The ships were *w* and were not able

WRENCHED

Ge 32: 25 of Jacob's hip so that his hip was *w*
Eze 29: 7 you broke and their backs were *w*.

WRESTLE (WRESTLED WRESTLING)

Ps 13: 2 How long must I *w*

WRESTLED (WRESTLE)

Ge 32: 24 and a man *w* with him till daybreak
32: 25 that his hip was wrenched as he *w*

WRESTLING (WRESTLE)

Col 4: 12 He is always *w* in prayer for you,

WRETCHED (WRETCHES)

Jdg 11: 35 have made me miserable and *w*,
Pr 15: 15 All the days of the oppressed are *w*,
Hab 3: 14 the *w* who were in hiding.
Mt 21: 41 bring those wretches to a *w* end,"
Ro 7: 24 What a *w* man I am! Who will
Rev 3: 17 you do not realize that you are *w*,

WRETCHES (WRETCHED)

Mt 21: 41 "He will bring those *w*

WRING

Lev 1: 15 *w* off the head and burn it
5: 8 He is to *w* its head from its neck,

WRINKLE

Eph 5: 27 or *w* or any other blemish,

WRIST (WRISTS)

Ge 38: 28 and tied it on his *w* and said,
38: 30 who had the scarlet thread on his *w*

WRISTS (WRIST)

Jer 40: 4 you from the chains on your *w*.
Eze 13: 18 sew magic charms on all their *w*
Ac 12: 7 and the chains fell off Peter's *w*.

WRITE (WRITER WRITES WRITING WRITINGS WRITTEN WROTE)

Ex 17: 14 "*W* this on a scroll as something
34: 1 and I will *w* on them the words that
34: 27 to Moses, "*W* down these words,
Nu 5: 23 " 'The priest is to *w* these curses
17: 2 *W* the name of each man
17: 3 the staff of Levi *w* Aaron's name,
Dt 6: 9 *W* them on the doorframes
10: 2 I will *w* on the tablets the words
11: 20 *W* them on the doorframes
17: 18 he is to *w* for himself
27: 3 *W* on them all the words of this law
27: 8 And you shall *w* very clearly all
31: 19 *w* down for yourselves this song
Jos 18: 4 and to *w* a description of it,
18: 8 of the land and *w* a description of it
Ezr 5: 10 so that we could *w* down the names
Est 8: 8 Now *w* another decree in the king's
Job 13: 26 For you *w* down bitter things
Ps 87: 6 The LORD will *w* in the register
Pr 3: 3 *w* them on the tablet of your heart.
7: 3 *w* them on the tablet of your heart.
Isa 8: 1 and *w* on it with an ordinary pen:
10: 19 that a child could *w* them down.
30: 8 Go now, *w* it on a tablet for them,
44: 5 still another will *w* on his hand,
Jer 30: 2 '*W* in a book all the words I have
31: 33 and *w* it on their hearts.
36: 2 *w* on it all the words I have spoken
36: 17 how did you come to *w* all this?
36: 28 and *w* on it all the words that were
36: 29 "Why did you *w* on it that the king
Eze 37: 16 and *w* on it, 'Ephraim's stick,
37: 16 take a stick of wood and *w* on it,
43: 11 *W* these down before them
Hab 2: 2 "*W* down the revelation
Mk 10: 4 a man to *w* a certificate of divorce
Lk 1: 3 also to me to *w* an orderly account
Jn 8: 6 and started to *w* on the ground
19: 21 "Do not *w* 'The King of the Jews,'
Ac 15: 20 Instead we should *w* to them,
25: 26 But I have nothing definite to *w*
25: 26 I may have something to *w*.
1Co 16: 21 *w* this greeting in my own hand.
2Co 1: 13 For we do not *w* you anything you
9: 1 me to *w* to you about this service
13: 10 This is why I *w* these things
Gal 6: 11 as I *w* to you with my own hand!
Php 3: 1 trouble for me to *w* the same things
Col 4: 18 *w* this greeting in my own hand.
1Th 4: 9 brotherly love we do not need to *w*
5: 1 dates we do not need to *w* to you,
2Th 3: 17 This is how I *w*.
3: 17 *w* this greeting in my own hand,
Phm : 21 of your obedience, I *w* to you,
Heb 8: 10 and *w* them on their hearts.
10: 16 and I will *w* them on their minds."
1Jn 1: 4 We *w* this to make our joy
2: 1 I *w* this to you so that you will not
2: 12 I *w* to you, dear children,
2: 13 I *w* to you, dear children,
2: 13 I *w* to you, fathers,
2: 13 I *w* to you, young men,
2: 14 I *w* to you, fathers,
2: 14 I *w* to you, young men,

1Jn 2: 21 I do not *w* to you because you do
5: 13 I *w* these things to you who believe
2Jn : 12 I have much to *w* to you,
3Jn : 13 I have much to *w* you,
Jude : 3 I felt I had to *w* and urge you
: 3 although I was very eager to *w*
Rev 1: 11 "*W* on a scroll what you see
1: 19 "*W*, therefore, what you have seen,
2: 1 angel of the church in Ephesus *w:*
2: 8 angel of the church in Smyrna *w:*
2: 12 of the church in Pergamum *w:*
2: 18 angel of the church in Thyatira *w:*
3: 1 the angel of the church in Sardis *w:*
3: 7 of the church in Philadelphia *w:*
3: 12 I will also *w* on him my new name.
3: 12 I will *w* on him the name
3: 14 angel of the church in Laodicea *w:*
10: 4 about to *w;* but I heard a voice
10: 4 thunders have said and do not *w* it
14: 13 a voice from heaven say, "*W:*
19: 9 Then the angel said to me, "*W:*
21: 5 Then he said, "*W* this down,

WRITER (WRITE)

Ps 45: 1 my tongue is the pen of a skillful *w.*

WRITES (WRITE)

Dt 24: 1 he *w* her a certificate of divorce,
24: 3 and *w* her a certificate of divorce,
2Pe 3: 16 He *w* the same way in all his letters,

WRITHE (WRITHED WRITHES)

Isa 13: 8 they will *w* like a woman in labor.
Jer 4: 19 I *w* in pain.
Eze 30: 16 Pelusium will *w* in agony.
Mic 1: 12 Those who live in Maroth *w* in pain
4: 10 *W* in agony, O Daughter of Zion,
Zec 9: 5 Gaza will *w* in agony,

WRITHED (WRITHE)

Ps 77: 16 the waters saw you and *w;*
Isa 26: 18 We were with child, we *w* in pain,
Hab 3: 10 the mountains saw you and *w.*

WRITHES (WRITHE)

Isa 26: 17 *w* and cries out in her pain,
Jer 51: 29 The land trembles and *w,*

WRITING (WRITE)

Ex 32: 16 the *w* was the *w* of God, engraved
Dt 31: 24 After Moses finished *w*
1Ch 28: 19 "All this is in *w,*" David said,
2Ch 36: 22 his realm and to put it in *w:*
Ezr 1: 1 his realm and to put it in *w:*
Ne 9: 38 putting it in *w,* and our leaders,
Job 31: 35 my accuser put his indictment in *w.*
Isa 38: 9 A *w* of Hezekiah king of Judah
Eze 9: 2 in linen who had a *w* kit at his side.
9: 3 clothed in linen who had the *w* kit
9: 11 the man in linen with the *w* kit
Da 5: 7 "Whoever reads this *w*
5: 8 but they could not read the *w*
5: 12 he will tell you what the *w* means."
5: 15 brought before me to read this *w*
5: 16 you can read this *w* and tell me
5: 17 I will read the *w* for the king
6: 8 it in *w* so that it cannot be altered—
6: 9 So King Darius put the decree in *w.*
6: 13 or to the decree you put in *w.*
Lk 1: 63 He asked for a *w* tablet,
Ac 15: 27 by word of mouth what we are *w.*
1Co 4: 14 I am not *w* this to shame you,
5: 11 now I am *w* you that you must not
9: 15 I am not *w* this in the hope that you
14: 37 him acknowledge that what I am *w*
Gal 1: 20 God that what I am *w* you is no lie.
1Ti 3: 14 I am *w* you these instructions
Phm : 19 Paul, am *w* this with my own hand.
1Jn 2: 7 I am not *w* you a new command
2: 8 Yet I am *w* you a new command;
2: 26 I am *w* these things
2Jn : 5 I am not *w* you a new command
Rev 5: 1 a scroll with *w* on both sides

WRITINGS (WRITE)

Mt 26: 56 this has all taken place that the *w*
Ro 16: 26 known through the prophetic *w*

WRITTEN (WRITE)

Ge 5: 1 This is the *w* account
Ex 24: 12 and commands I have *w*
32: 32 out of the book you have *w.*"
Dt 10: 4 on these tablets what he had *w*
28: 58 which are *w* in this book,
29: 20 All the curses *w* in this book will
29: 21 of the covenant *w* in this Book
29: 27 on it all the curses *w* in this book.
30: 10 and decrees that are *w* in this Book
Jos 1: 8 careful to do everything *w* in it.
8: 31 to what is *w* in the Book of the Law
8: 32 the law of Moses, which he had *w.*
8: 34 as it is *w* in the Book of the Law.
10: 13 as it is *w* in the Book of Jashar.
18: 6 After you have *w* descriptions
23: 6 to obey all that is *w* in the Book
2Sa 1: 18 of the bow (it is *w* in the Book
1Ki 2: 3 as *w* in the Law of Moses,
11: 41 are they not *w* in the book
14: 19 are *w* in the book of the annals
14: 29 are they not *w* in the book
15: 7 are they not *w* in the book
15: 23 are they not *w* in the book
15: 31 are they not *w* in the book
16: 5 are they not *w* in the book
16: 14 are they not *w* in the book
16: 20 are they not *w* in the book
16: 27 are they not *w* in the book
21: 11 in the letters she had *w* to them.
22: 39 are they not *w* in the book
22: 45 are they not *w* in the book
2Ki 1: 18 are they not *w* in the book
8: 23 are they not *w* in the book
10: 34 are they not *w* in the book
12: 19 are they not *w* in the book
13: 8 are they not *w* in the book
13: 12 are they not *w* in the book
14: 6 with what is *w* in the Book
14: 15 are they not *w* in the book
14: 18 are they not *w* in the book
14: 28 are they not *w* in the book
15: 6 are they not *w* in the book
15: 11 events of Zechariah's reign are *w*
15: 15 are *w* in the book of the annals
15: 21 are they not *w* in the book
15: 26 are *w* in the book of the annals
15: 31 are they not *w* in the book
15: 36 are they not *w* in the book
16: 19 are they not *w* in the book
20: 20 are they not *w* in the book
21: 17 are they not *w* in the book
21: 25 are they not *w* in the book
22: 13 all that is *w* there concerning us."
22: 13 and for all Judah about what is *w*
22: 16 according to everything *w*
23: 3 of the covenant *w* in this book.
23: 21 it is *w* in this Book of the Covenant
23: 24 fulfill the requirements of the law *w*
23: 28 are they not *w* in the book
24: 5 are they not *w* in the book
1Ch 16: 40 with everything *w* in the Law
29: 29 they are *w* in the records
2Ch 9: 29 are they not *w* in the records
12: 15 are they not *w* in the records
13: 22 are *w* in the annotations
16: 11 are *w* in the book of the kings
20: 34 are *w* in the annals of Jehu son
23: 18 as *w* in the Law of Moses,
24: 27 of God are *w* in the annotations
25: 4 with what is *w* in the Law,
25: 26 are they not *w* in the book
27: 7 are *w* in the book of the kings
28: 26 are *w* in the book of the kings
30: 5 numbers according to what was *w.*
30: 18 Passover, contrary to what was *w.*
31: 3 as *w* in the Law of the LORD.
32: 32 acts of devotion are *w* in the vision
33: 18 are *w* in the annals of the kings
33: 19 all are *w* in the records of the seers.
34: 21 and Judah about what is *w*
34: 21 with all that is *w* in this book."
34: 24 all the curses *w* in the book that has
34: 31 of the covenant *w* in this book.
35: 4 to the directions *w* by David king
35: 12 as is *w* in the Book of Moses.
35: 25 in Israel and are *w* in the Laments.
2Ch 35: 26 according to what is *w* in the Law
35: 27 are *w* in the book of the kings
36: 8 are *w* in the book of the kings
Ezr 3: 2 with what is *w* in the Law
3: 4 Then in accordance with what is *w,*
4: 7 The letter was *w* in Aramaic script
5: 5 and his *w* reply be received.
6: 2 and this was *w* on it: Memorandum
6: 18 according to what is *w* in the Book
Ne 6: 6 an unsealed letter in which was *w:*
7: 5 This is what I found *w* there:
8: 14 They found *w* in the Law, which
8: 15 to make booths"—as it is *w.*
10: 34 of the LORD our God, as it is *w*
10: 36 "As it is also *w* in the Law,
13: 1 it was found *w* that no Ammonite
Est 1: 19 and let it be *w* in the laws of Persia
3: 12 These were *w* in the name
8: 5 an order be *w* overruling
8: 8 for no document *w*
8: 9 These orders were *w* in the script
9: 23 doing what Mordecai had *w*
9: 25 he issued *w* orders that the evil
9: 26 Because of everything *w*
9: 32 and it was *w* down in the records.
10: 2 are they not *w* in the book
Job 19: 23 that they were *w* on a scroll,
Ps 40: 7 it is *w* about me in the scroll.
102: 18 Let this be *w* for a future
139: 16 were *w* in your book
149: 9 to carry out the sentence *w*
Pr 22: 20 Have I not *w* thirty sayings for you,
Isa 65: 6 "See, it stands *w* before me:
Jer 17: 13 away from you will be *w* in the dust
25: 13 all that are *w* in this book
36: 27 the words that Baruch had *w*
45: 1 after Baruch had *w*
51: 60 Jeremiah had *w* on a scroll about
Eze 2: 10 sides of it were *w* words of lament
37: 20 their eyes the sticks you have *w*
Da 5: 25 "This is the inscription that was *w:*
9: 11 and sworn judgments *w* in the Law
9: 13 Just as it is *w* in the Law of Moses,
10: 21 but first I will tell you what is *w*
12: 1 everyone whose name is found *w*
Mal 3: 16 A scroll of remembrance was *w*
Mt 2: 5 "for this is what the prophet has *w:*
4: 4 "It is *w:* 'Man does not live
4: 6 For it is *w:*
4: 7 Jesus answered him, "It is also *w:*
4: 10 For it is *w:* 'Worship the Lord your
11: 10 This is the one about whom it is *w:*
21: 13 "It is *w,*" he said to them, " 'My
26: 24 will go just as it is *w* about him.
26: 31 away on account of me, for it is *w:*
27: 37 his head they placed the *w* charge
Mk 1: 2 It is *w* in Isaiah the prophet:
7: 6 about you hypocrites; as it is *w:*
9: 12 Why then is it *w* that the Son
9: 13 wished, just as it is *w* about him."
11: 17 he taught them, he said, "Is it not *w*
14: 21 will go just as it is *w* about him.
14: 27 Jesus told them, "for it is *w:*
15: 26 The *w* notice of the charge
Lk 2: 23 (as it is *w* in the Law of the Lord,
3: 4 As is *w* in the book of the words
4: 4 "It is *w:* 'Man does not live
4: 8 "It is *w:* 'Worship the Lord your
4: 10 For it is *w:*
4: 17 he found the place where it is *w:*
7: 27 This is the one about whom it is *w:*
10: 20 but rejoice that your names are *w*
10: 26 "What is *w* in the Law?" he replied.
18: 31 and everything that is *w*
19: 46 "It is *w,*" he said to them, " 'My
20: 17 the meaning of that which is *w:*
21: 22 in fulfillment of all that has been *w.*
22: 37 It is *w:* 'And he was numbered
22: 37 what is *w* about me is reaching its
23: 38 There was a *w* notice above him,
24: 44 must be fulfilled that is *w* about me
24: 46 He told them, "This is what is *w:*
Jn 2: 17 disciples remembered that it is *w:*
6: 31 as it is *w:* 'He gave them bread
6: 45 It is *w* in the Prophets: 'They will
8: 17 own Law it is *w* that the testimony
10: 34 Jesus answered them, "Is it not *w*
12: 14 as it is *w,* "Do not be afraid,

Jn 12: 16 these things had been *w* about him
15: 25 is to fulfill what is *w* in their Law:
19: 20 and the sign was *w* in Aramaic,
19: 22 "What I have *w*, I have *w*."
20: 31 these are *w* that you may believe
21: 25 If every one of them were *w* down,
21: 25 for the books that would be *w*.
Ac 1: 20 "it is *w* in the book of Psalms,
7: 42 agrees with what is *w* in the book
13: 29 out all that was *w* about him,
13: 33 As it is *w* in the second Psalm:
15: 15 as it is *w:* " 'After this I will return
21: 25 we have *w* to them our decision
23: 5 for it is *w:* 'Do not speak evil about
24: 14 and that is *w* in the Prophets,
Ro 1: 17 as it is *w:* "The righteous will live
2: 15 of the law are *w* on their hearts,
2: 24 As it is *w:* "God's name is
2: 27 even though you have the *w* code
2: 29 by the Spirit, not by the *w* code.
3: 4 As it is *w:*
3: 10 As it is *w:*
4: 17 As it is *w:* "I have made you
4: 23 to him" were *w* not for him alone,
7: 6 not in the old way of the *w* code.
8: 36 or danger or sword? As it is *w:*
9: 13 Just as it is *w:* "Jacob I loved,
9: 33 As it is *w:*
10: 15 As it is *w*, "How beautiful are
11: 8 others were hardened, as it is *w:*
11: 26 so all Israel will be saved, as it is *w:*
12: 19 for it is *w:* "It is mine to avenge;
14: 11 It is *w:*
15: 3 not please himself but, as it is *w:*
15: 4 For everything that was *w*
15: 4 in the past was *w* to teach us,
15: 9 God for his mercy, as it is *w:*
15: 15 I have *w* you quite boldly
15: 21 Rather, as it is *w:*
1Co 1: 19 For it is *w:*
1: 31 it is *w:* "Let him who boasts boast
2: 9 However, as it is *w:*
3: 19 As it is *w:* "He catches the wise
4: 6 "Do not go beyond what is *w*."
5: 9 I have *w* you in my letter not
9: 9 For it is *w* in the Law of Moses:
9: 10 doesn't he? Yes, this was *w* for us,
10: 7 as some of them were; as it is *w:*
10: 11 as examples and were *w* down
14: 21 In the Law it is *w:*
15: 45 So it is *w:* "The first man Adam
15: 54 the saying that is *w* will come true:
2Co 3: 2 You yourselves are our letter, *w*
3: 3 *w* not with ink but with the Spirit
4: 13 It is *w:* "I believed; therefore I have
8: 15 there will be equality, as it is *w:*
9: 9 As it is *w:*
Gal 3: 10 are under a curse, for it is *w:*
3: 10 to do everything *w* in the Book
3: 13 for it is *w:* "Cursed is everyone who
4: 22 For it is *w* that Abraham had two
4: 27 For it is *w:*
Eph 3: 3 as I have already *w* briefly.
Col 2: 14 having canceled the *w* code,
Heb 10: 7 it is *w* about me in the scroll—
12: 23 whose names are *w* in heaven.
13: 22 for I have *w* you only a short letter.
1Pe 1: 16 for it is *w:* "Be holy, because I am
5: 12 as a faithful brother, I have *w*
2Pe 3: 1 I have *w* both of them as reminders
Jude : 4 condemnation was *w* about long
Rev 1: 3 and take to heart what is *w* in it,
2: 17 stone with a new name *w* on it,
13: 8 all whose names have not been *w*
14: 1 and his Father's name *w*
17: 5 This title was *w* on her forehead:
17: 8 whose names have not been *w*
19: 12 He has a name *w* on him that no
19: 16 on his thigh he has this name *w:*
20: 15 If anyone's name was not found *w*
21: 12 On the gates were *w* the names
21: 27 but only those whose names are *w*

WRONG (WRONGDOER WRONGDOING WRONGDOINGS WRONGED WRONGING WRONGS)

Ge 16: 5 for the *w* I am suffering.
Ex 2: 13 He asked the one in the *w*,
Ex 9: 27 and I and my people are in the *w*.
23: 2 Do not follow the crowd in doing *w*
Lev 5: 18 him for the *w* he has committed
Nu 5: 7 must make full restitution for his *w*,
5: 8 restitution can be made for the *w*,
15: 25 LORD for their *w* an offering made
15: 26 involved in the unintentional *w*.
Dt 32: 4 A faithful God who does no *w*,
Jdg 11: 27 you are doing me *w* by waging war
1Sa 11: 5 "What is *w* with the people?
19: 4 "Let not the king do *w*
19: 5 Why then would you do *w*
25: 39 He has kept me from doing *w*
26: 18 and what *w* am I guilty of?
2Sa 7: 14 When he does *w*, I will punish him
13: 16 me away would be a greater *w*
19: 19 remember how your servant did *w*
24: 17 one who has sinned and done *w*.
1Ki 2: 44 in your heart all the *w* you did
3: 9 to distinguish between right and *w*.
8: 47 we have done *w*, we have acted
18: 9 have I done *w*," asked Obadiah,
2Ki 18: 14 Assyria at Lachish: "I have done *w*.
1Ch 21: 17 one who has sinned and done *w*.
2Ch 6: 37 we have done *w* and acted
22: 3 encouraged him in doing *w*.
Ne 9: 33 acted faithfully, while we did *w*.
Est 1: 16 "Queen Vashti has done *w*,
Job 6: 24 show me where I have been *w*.
21: 27 by which you would *w* me.
31: 3 disaster for those who do *w?*
32: 12 not one of you has proved Job *w;*
34: 10 from the Almighty to do *w*.
34: 12 unthinkable that God would do *w*,
34: 32 if I have done *w*, I will not do
36: 23 or said to him, 'You have done *w*'?
Ps 5: 5 you hate all who do *w*.
15: 3 who does his neighbor no *w*
36: 4 and does not reject what is *w*.
37: 1 or be envious of those who do *w;*
59: 4 I have done no *w*, yet they are
106: 6 we have done *w* and acted
119: 3 They do nothing *w;*
119:104 therefore I hate every *w* path.
119:128 I hate every *w* path.
Pr 2: 14 who delight in doing *w*
20: 22 "I'll pay you back for this *w!*"
28: 21 yet a man will do *w* for a piece
28: 24 and says, "It's not *w*"—
30: 20 and says, 'I've done nothing *w*.'
Ecc 5: 1 who do not know that they do *w*.
8: 11 filled with schemes to do *w*.
Isa 1: 16 Stop doing *w*,
7: 15 he knows enough to reject the *w*
7: 16 boy knows enough to reject the *w*
Jer 16: 10 against us? What *w* have we done?
22: 3 Do no *w* or violence to the alien,
51: 24 for all the *w* they have done
La 3: 59 O LORD, the *w* done to me.
Eze 18: 8 withholds his hand from doing *w*
18: 18 did what was *w* among his people.
Da 6: 22 Nor have I ever done any *w*
9: 5 we have sinned and done *w*.
9: 15 we have sinned, we have done *w*.
Hab 1: 3 Why do you tolerate *w?*
1: 13 you cannot tolerate *w*.
Zep 3: 5 he does no *w*.
3: 13 The remnant of Israel will do no *w;*
Mal 1: 8 is that not *w?* Try offering them
1: 8 is that not *w?* When you sacrifice
Lk 23: 41 But this man has done nothing *w*."
Jn 18: 23 I said something *w*," Jesus replied,
18: 23 replied, "testify as to what is *w*.
Ac 23: 9 We find nothing *w* with this man,"
25: 5 if he has done anything *w*."
25: 8 "I have done nothing *w*
25: 10 I have not done any *w* to the Jews,
Ro 13: 3 but for those who do *w*.
13: 4 But if you do *w*, be afraid,
14: 20 but it is *w* for a man to eat anything
1Co 6: 8 you yourselves cheat and do *w*,
2Co 7: 12 account of the one who did the *w*
12: 13 Forgive me this *w!* Now I am
13: 7 that you will not do anything *w*.
Gal 2: 11 to his face, because he was in the *w*.
4: 12 You have done me no *w*.
Col 3: 25 who does *w* will be repaid for his *w*,
1Th 4: 6 matter no one should *w* his brother
1Th 5: 15 that nobody pays back *w* for *w*,
Phm : 18 If he has done you any *w*
Heb 8: 7 For if there had been nothing *w*
Jas 4: 3 because you ask with *w* motives,
1Pe 2: 12 though they accuse you of doing *w*,
2: 14 by him to punish those who do *w*
2: 20 if you receive a beating for doing *w*
Rev 22: 11 him who does *w* continue to do *w;*

WRONGDOER (WRONG)

Ro 13: 4 to bring punishment on the *w*.

WRONGDOING (WRONG)

Lev 5: 19 guilty of *w* against the LORD."
Nu 5: 31 husband will be innocent of any *w*,
1Sa 24: 11 recognize that I am not guilty of *w*
25: 28 Let no *w* be found in you as long
25: 39 and has brought Nabal's *w*
1Ki 2: 44 LORD will repay you for your *w*.
Job 1: 22 sin by charging God with *w*.
24: 12 But God charges no one with *w*.
33: 17 to turn man from *w*
Pr 16: 12 Kings detest *w*,
2Pe 2: 16 rebuked for his *w* by a donkey—
1Jn 5: 17 All *w* is sin, and there is sin that

WRONGDOINGS (WRONG)

Jer 5: 25 Your *w* have kept these away;

WRONGED (WRONG)

Ge 20: 9 How have I *w* you that you have
Nu 5: 7 give it all to the person he has *w*.
16: 15 nor have I *w* any of them."
Jdg 11: 27 during that time? I have not *w* you,
1Sa 19: 4 he has not *w* you, and what he has
20: 1 How have I *w* your father,
24: 11 I have not *w* you, but you are
Job 19: 6 then know that God has *w* me
19: 7 'I've been *w!*' I get no response;
1Co 6: 7 not rather be *w?* Why not rather
2Co 7: 2 We have *w* no one, we have

WRONGING (WRONG)

Ps 119: 78 to shame for *w* me without cause;

WRONGS (WRONG)

Ge 50: 15 back for all the *w* we did to him?"
50: 17 and the *w* they committed
Nu 5: 6 or woman *w* another in any way
1Sa 24: 12 the LORD avenge the *w* you have
1Ki 8: 31 "When a man *w* his neighbor
2Ch 6: 22 "When a man *w* his neighbor
Job 13: 23 How many *w* and sins have I
Pr 10: 12 but love covers over all *w*.
Zep 3: 11 for all the *w* you have done to me,
1Co 13: 5 angered, it keeps no record of *w*.

WROTE (WRITE)

Ex 24: 4 Moses then *w* down everything
34: 28 And he *w* on the tablets the words
Dt 4: 13 then *w* them on two stone tablets.
5: 22 he *w* them on two stone tablets
10: 4 LORD *w* on these tablets what he
31: 9 So Moses *w* down this law
31: 22 Moses *w* down this song that day
Jos 18: 9 They *w* its description on a scroll,
Jdg 8: 14 and the young man *w* down for him
1Sa 10: 25 He *w* them down on a scroll
2Sa 11: 14 In the morning David *w* a letter
11: 15 he *w*, "Put Uriah in the front line
1Ki 21: 8 So she *w* letters in Ahab's name,
21: 9 those letters she *w:* "Proclaim
2Ki 10: 1 So Jehu *w* letters and sent them
10: 6 Then Jehu *w* them a second letter,
17: 37 and commands he *w* for you.
2Ch 30: 1 and also *w* letters to Ephraim
32: 17 also *w* letters insulting the LORD,
Ezr 4: 7 the rest of his associates *w* a letter
4: 8 Shimshai the secretary *w* a letter
Est 3: 12 They *w* out in the script
8: 5 and *w* to destroy the Jews
8: 9 They *w* out all Mordecai's orders
8: 10 Mordecai *w* in the name
9: 22 He *w* them to observe the days
9: 29 *w* with full authority
Ecc 12: 10 and what he *w* was upright and true
Jer 36: 4 Baruch *w* them on the scroll.
36: 6 the words of the LORD that you *w*

Jer 36: 18 and I *w* them in ink on the scroll.''
36: 32 Baruch *w* on it all the words
Da 5: 5 The king watched the hand as it *w*.
5: 5 and *w* on the plaster of the wall,
5: 24 the hand that *w* the inscription.
6: 25 King Darius *w* to all the peoples,
7: 1 He *w* down the substance
Hos 8: 12 I *w* for them the many things
Mk 10: 5 hard that Moses *w* you this law,''
12: 19 "Moses *w* for us that
Lk 1: 63 to everyone's astonishment he *w*,
20: 28 "Moses *w* for us that
Jn 1: 45 about whom the prophets also *w*—
1: 45 have found the one Moses *w* about
5: 46 for he *w* about me.
5: 47 since you do not believe what he *w*,
8: 8 down and *w* on the ground.
21: 24 to these things and who *w* them
Ac 1: 1 I *w* about all that Jesus began to do
18: 27 and *w* to the disciples there
23: 25 He *w* a letter as follows: Claudius
Ro 16: 22 I, Tertius, who *w* down this letter,
1Co 7: 1 Now for the matters you *w* about:
2Co 2: 3 I *w* as I did so that
2: 4 For I *w* you out of great distress
2: 9 The reason I *w* you was to see
7: 12 So even though I *w* to you,
2Pe 3: 15 *w* you with the wisdom that God
3Jn : 9 I *w* to the church, but Diotrephes,

WROUGHT

Eze 27: 19 they exchanged *w* iron, cassia

WRUNG

Jdg 6: 38 the fleece and *w* out the dew—

XERXES

Ezr 4: 6 At the beginning of the reign of *X*,
Est 1: 1 happened during the time of *X*,
1: 1 *X* who ruled over 127 provinces
1: 2 At that time King *X* reigned
1: 9 in the royal palace of King *X*.
1: 10 when King *X* was in high spirits
1: 15 of King *X* that the eunuchs have
1: 16 of all the provinces of King *X*.
1: 17 'King *X* commanded Queen Vashti
1: 19 to enter the presence of King *X*.
2: 1 the anger of King *X* had subsided,
2: 12 came to go in to King *X*,
2: 16 to King *X* in the royal residence
2: 21 conspired to assassinate King *X*.
3: 1 King *X* honored Haman son
3: 6 the whole kingdom of *X*.
3: 7 In the twelfth year of King *X*,
3: 8 Then Haman said to King *X*,
3: 12 in the name of King *X* himself
6: 2 conspired to assassinate King *X*.
7: 5 King *X* asked Queen Esther,
8: 1 same day King *X* gave Queen
8: 7 King *X* replied to Queen Esther
8: 10 wrote in the name of King *X*,
8: 12 of King *X* was the thirteenth day
9: 2 cities in all the provinces of King *X*
9: 20 the provinces of King *X*,
9: 30 provinces of the kingdom of *X*—
10: 1 King *X* imposed tribute
10: 3 Jew was second in rank to King *X*,
Da 9: 1 year of Darius son of *X* (a Mede

YAHWEH (LORD)

YARDS

Jos 3: 4 of about a thousand *y* between you
Ne 3: 13 repaired five hundred *y* of the wall
Jn 21: 8 far from shore, about a hundred *y*.

YARN

Ex 25: 4 purple and scarlet *y* and fine linen;
26: 1 scarlet *y*, with cherubim worked
26: 31 scarlet *y* and finely twisted linen,
26: 36 scarlet *y* and finely twisted linen—
27: 16 scarlet *y* and finely twisted linen—
28: 5 purple and scarlet *y*, and fine linen.
28: 6 and scarlet *y*, and of finely twisted
28: 8 scarlet *y*, and with finely twisted
28: 15 and scarlet *y*, and of finely twisted
28: 33 and scarlet *y* around the hem
35: 6 purple and scarlet *y* and fine linen;
Ex 35: 23 purple or scarlet *y* or fine linen,
35: 25 purple or scarlet *y* or fine linen.
35: 35 purple and scarlet *y* and fine linen,
36: 8 scarlet *y*, with cherubim worked
36: 35 scarlet *y* and finely twisted linen,
36: 37 scarlet *y* and finely twisted linen—
38: 18 scarlet *y* and finely twisted linen—
38: 23 purple and scarlet *y* and fine linen.)
39: 1 and scarlet *y* they made woven
39: 2 and scarlet *y*, and of finely twisted
39: 3 purple and scarlet *y* and fine linen
39: 5 scarlet *y*, and with finely twisted
39: 8 and scarlet *y*, and of finely twisted
39: 24 scarlet *y* and finely twisted linen
39: 29 and scarlet *y*— the work
Lev 14: 4 scarlet *y* and hyssop be brought
14: 6 the scarlet *y* and the hyssop,
14: 49 and some cedar wood, scarlet *y*
14: 51 the scarlet *y* and the live bird,
14: 52 the hyssop and the scarlet *y*.
2Ch 2: 7 and in purple, crimson and blue *y*,
2: 14 blue and crimson *y* and fine linen.
3: 14 purple and crimson *y* and fine linen

YAUDI

2Ki 14: 28 Hamath, which had belonged to *Y*,

YEAR (YEAR-OLD YEAR'S YEARLING YEARLY YEARS)

Ge 7: 11 In the six hundredth *y*
8: 13 of Noah's six hundred and first *y*,
14: 4 in the thirteenth *y* they rebelled.
14: 5 In the fourteenth *y*, Kedorlaomer
17: 21 bear to you by this time next *y*.''
18: 10 to you about this time next *y*,
18: 14 to you at the appointed time next *y*
26: 12 the same *y* reaped a hundredfold,
47: 17 them through that *y* with food
47: 18 When that *y* was over, they came
47: 18 they came to him the following *y*
Ex 12: 2 month, the first month of your *y*.
13: 10 at the appointed time *y* after *y*.
21: 2 in the seventh *y*, he shall go free,
23: 11 during the seventh *y* let the land lie
23: 14 "Three times a *y* you are
23: 16 of Ingathering at the end of the *y*,
23: 17 "Three times a *y* all the men are
23: 29 not drive them out in a single *y*,
29: 38 each day: two lambs a *y* old.
30: 10 Once a *y* Aaron shall make
34: 22 of Ingathering at the turn of the *y*.
34: 23 Three times a *y* all your men are
34: 24 when you go up three times each *y*
40: 17 of the first month in the second *y*.
Lev 9: 3 both a *y* old and without defect—
14: 10 lambs and one ewe lamb a *y* old,
16: 34 to be made once a *y* for all the sins
19: 24 In the fourth *y* all its fruit will be
19: 25 in the fifth *y* you may eat its fruit.
23: 12 to the LORD a lamb a *y* old
23: 18 each a *y* old and without defect,
23: 19 each a *y* old, for a fellowship
23: 41 to the LORD for seven days each *y*
25: 4 But in the seventh *y* the land is
25: 5 The land is to have a *y* of rest.
25: 6 during the sabbath *y* will be food
25: 10 Consecrate the fiftieth *y*
25: 11 The fiftieth *y* shall be a jubilee
25: 13 " 'In this *Y* of Jubilee everyone is
25: 20 in the seventh *y* if we do not plant
25: 21 in the sixth *y* that the land will
25: 22 plant during the eighth *y*,
25: 22 the harvest of the ninth *y* comes in.
25: 28 of the buyer until the *Y* of Jubilee.
25: 29 of redemption a full *y* after its sale.
25: 30 before a full *y* has passed,
25: 40 work for you until the *Y* of Jubilee.
25: 50 time from the *y* he sold himself up
25: 50 up to the *Y* of Jubilee.
25: 52 remain until the *Y* of Jubilee,
25: 53 as a man hired from *y* to *y*;
25: 54 to be released in the *Y* of Jubilee,
27: 17 field during the *Y* of Jubilee,
27: 18 remain until the next *Y* of Jubilee,
27: 23 up to the *Y* of Jubilee,
27: 24 In the *Y* of Jubilee the field will
Nu 1: 1 of the second *y* after the Israelites
7: 15 one ram and one male lamb a *y* old,
Nu 7: 17 and five male lambs a *y* old,
7: 21 one ram and one male lamb a *y* old,
7: 23 and five male lambs a *y* old,
7: 27 one ram and one male lamb a *y* old,
7: 29 and five male lambs a *y* old,
7: 33 one ram and one male lamb a *y* old,
7: 35 and five male lambs a *y* old,
7: 39 one ram and one male lamb a *y* old,
7: 41 and five male lambs a *y* old,
7: 45 one ram and one male lamb a *y* old,
7: 47 and five male lambs a *y* old,
7: 51 one ram and one male lamb a *y* old,
7: 53 and five male lambs a *y* old,
7: 57 one ram and one male lamb a *y* old,
7: 59 and five male lambs a *y* old,
7: 63 one ram and one male lamb a *y* old,
7: 65 and five male lambs a *y* old,
7: 69 one ram and one male lamb a *y* old,
7: 71 and five male lambs a *y* old,
7: 75 one ram and one male lamb a *y* old,
7: 77 and five male lambs a *y* old,
7: 81 one ram and one male lamb a *y* old,
7: 83 and five male lambs a *y* old,
7: 87 and twelve male lambs a *y* old,
7: 88 and sixty male lambs a *y* old.
9: 1 of the second *y* after they came out
9: 22 for two days or a month or a *y*,
10: 11 the second month of the second *y*,
14: 34 one *y* for each of the forty days you
28: 3 two lambs a *y* old without defect,
28: 9 of two lambs a *y* old without defect
28: 11 and seven male lambs a *y* old,
28: 14 at each new moon during the *y*.
28: 19 and seven male lambs a *y* old,
28: 27 and seven male lambs a *y* old
29: 2 and seven male lambs a *y* old,
29: 8 and seven male lambs a *y* old,
29: 13 and fourteen male lambs a *y* old,
29: 17 and fourteen male lambs a *y* old,
29: 20 and fourteen male lambs a *y* old,
29: 23 and fourteen male lambs a *y* old,
29: 26 and fourteen male lambs a *y* old,
29: 29 and fourteen male lambs a *y* old,
29: 32 and fourteen male lambs a *y* old,
29: 36 and seven male lambs a *y* old,
33: 38 of the fortieth *y* after the Israelites
36: 4 When the *Y* of Jubilee
Dt 1: 3 In the fortieth *y*, on the first day
11: 12 it from the beginning of the *y*
14: 22 all that your fields produce each *y*.
15: 9 "The seventh *y*, the *y*
15: 12 in the seventh *y* you must let him
15: 20 Each *y* you and your family are
16: 16 Three times a *y* all your men must
24: 5 For one *y* he is to be free to stay
26: 12 of all your produce in the third *y*,
26: 12 the *y* of the tithe, you shall give it
31: 10 in the *y* for canceling debts,
Jos 5: 12 but that *y* they ate of the produce
Jdg 10: 8 who that *y* shattered and crushed
11: 40 custom that each *y* the young
17: 10 I'll give you ten shekels of silver a *y*
1Sa 1: 3 *Y* after *y* this man went up
1: 7 This went on *y* after *y*.
2: 19 Each *y* his mother made him
7: 16 From *y* to *y* he went on a circuit
27: 7 lived in Philistine territory a *y*
29: 3 been with me for over a *y*,
1Ki 4: 7 supplies for one month in the *y*.
5: 11 to do this for Hiram *y* after *y*.
6: 1 eightieth *y* after the Israelites had
6: 1 in the fourth *y* of Solomon's reign
6: 37 the LORD was laid in the fourth *y*,
6: 38 In the eleventh *y* in the month
9: 25 Three times a *y* Solomon sacrificed
10: 25 *Y* after *y*, everyone who came
14: 25 In the fifth *y* of King Rehoboam,
15: 1 In the eighteenth *y* of the reign
15: 9 In the twentieth *y*
15: 25 Israel in the second *y* of Asa king
15: 28 in the third *y* of Asa king of Judah
15: 33 In the third *y* of Asa king of Judah,
16: 8 In the twenty-sixth *y* of Asa king
16: 10 him in the twenty-seventh *y*
16: 15 In the twenty-seventh *y*
16: 23 In the thirty-first *y* of Asa king
16: 29 In the thirty-eighth *y* of Asa king
18: 1 After a long time, in the third *y*,

1Ki 22: 2 But in the third *y* Jehoshaphat king
22: 41 Judah in the fourth *y* of Ahab king
22: 51 Samaria in the seventeenth *y*
2Ki 1: 17 in the second *y* of Jehoram son
3: 1 Samaria in the eighteenth *y*
4: 16 this time next *y*,'' Elisha said,
4: 17 the next *y* about that same time she
8: 16 In the fifth *y* of Joram son
8: 25 In the twelfth *y* of Joram son
8: 26 and he reigned in Jerusalem one *y*.
9: 29 (In the eleventh *y* of Joram son
11: 4 In the seventh *y* Jehoiada sent
12: 1 In the seventh *y* of Jehu, Joash
12: 6 But by the twenty-third *y*
13: 1 In the twenty-third *y* of Joash son
13: 10 In the thirty-seventh *y*
14: 1 In the second *y* of Jehoash son
14: 23 In the fifteenth *y* of Amaziah son
15: 1 In the twenty-seventh *y*
15: 8 In the thirty-eighth *y*
15: 13 in the thirty-ninth *y* of Uzziah king
15: 17 In the thirty-ninth *y*
15: 23 In the fiftieth *y* of Azariah king
15: 27 In the fifty-second *y*
15: 30 in the twentieth *y* of Jotham son
15: 32 In the second *y* of Pekah son
16: 1 In the seventeenth *y* of Pekah son
17: 1 In the twelfth *y* of Ahaz king
17: 4 of Assyria, as he had done *y* by *y*.
17: 6 In the ninth *y* of Hoshea, the king
18: 1 In the third *y* of Hoshea son
18: 9 In King Hezekiah's fourth *y*,
18: 9 which was the seventh *y*
18: 10 captured in Hezekiah's sixth *y*,
18: 10 which was the ninth *y*
18: 13 In the fourteenth *y*
19: 29 But in the third *y* sow and reap,
19: 29 This *y* you will eat what grows
19: 29 and the second *y* what springs
22: 3 In the eighteenth *y* of his reign,
23: 23 in the eighteenth *y* of King Josiah,
24: 12 In the eighth *y* of the reign
25: 1 in the ninth *y* of Zedekiah's reign,
25: 2 siege until the eleventh *y*
25: 8 in the nineteenth *y*
25: 27 In the thirty-seventh *y* of the exile
25: 27 in the *y* Evil-Merodach became
1Ch 26: 31 In the fortieth *y* of David's reign
27: 1 month by month throughout the *y*.
2Ch 3: 2 month in the fourth *y* of his reign.
9: 24 *Y* after *y*, everyone who came
12: 2 in the fifth *y* of King Rehoboam.
13: 1 In the eighteenth *y* of the reign
15: 10 of the fifteenth *y* of Asa's reign.
15: 19 war until the thirty-fifth *y*
16: 1 In the thirty-sixth *y*
16: 12 In the thirty-ninth *y*
16: 13 in the forty-first *y* of his reign Asa
17: 7 In the third *y* of his reign he sent
21: 19 at the end of the second *y*,
22: 2 and he reigned in Jerusalem one *y*.
23: 1 In the seventh *y* Jehoiada showed
24: 23 At the turn of the *y*, the army
27: 5 That *y* the Ammonites paid him
29: 3 month of the first *y* of his reign,
34: 3 In his twelfth *y* he began
34: 3 In the eighth *y* of his reign,
34: 8 In the eighteenth *y*
35: 19 in the eighteenth *y* of Josiah's reign
36: 10 of the *y*, King Nebuchadnezzar
36: 22 In the first *y* of Cyrus king of Persia
Ezr 1: 1 In the first *y* of Cyrus king of Persia
3: 8 of the second *y* after their arrival
4: 24 until the second *y* of the reign
5: 13 in the first *y* of Cyrus king
6: 3 In the first *y* of King Cyrus,
6: 15 in the sixth *y* of the reign
7: 7 in the seventh *y* of King Artaxerxes
7: 8 month of the seventh *y* of the king.
Ne 1: 1 month of Kislev in the twentieth *y*,
2: 1 the twentieth *y* of King Artaxerxes,
5: 14 from the twentieth *y*
5: 14 until his thirty-second *y*—
10: 31 Every seventh *y* we will forgo
10: 32 of a shekel each *y* for the service
10: 34 at set times each *y* a contribution
10: 35 of the LORD each *y* the firstfruits
13: 6 for in the thirty-second *y*

Est 1: 3 in the third *y* of his reign he gave
2: 16 in the seventh *y* of his reign.
3: 7 In the twelfth *y* of King Xerxes,
9: 27 fail observe these two days every *y*,
Job 3: 6 included among the days of the *y*
Ps 65: 11 You crown the *y* with your bounty,
Isa 6: 1 In the *y* that King Uzziah died,
14: 28 came in the *y* King Ahaz died:
20: 1 In the *y* that the supreme
21: 16 "Within one *y*, as a servant bound
29: 1 Add *y* to *y*
32: 10 In little more than a *y*
34: 8 *y* of retribution, to uphold Zion's
36: 1 In the fourteenth *y*
37: 30 But in the third *y* sow and reap,
37: 30 and the second *y* what springs
37: 30 "This *y* you will eat what grows
61: 2 to proclaim the *y* of the LORD's
63: 4 the *y* of my redemption has come.
Jer 1: 2 him in the thirteenth *y* of the reign
1: 3 of the eleventh *y* of Zedekiah son
11: 23 in the *y* of their punishment.' "
17: 8 It has no worries in a *y* of drought
23: 12 them in the *y* they are punished,"
25: 1 in the fourth *y* of Jehoiakim son
25: 1 which was the first *y*
25: 3 from the thirteenth *y* of Josiah son
28: 1 In the fifth month of that same *y*,
28: 1 the fourth *y*, early in the reign
28: 16 This very *y* you are going to die,
28: 17 the seventh month of that same *y*,
32: 1 in the tenth *y* of Zedekiah king
32: 1 which was the eighteenth *y*
34: 14 'Every seventh *y* each
36: 1 In the fourth *y* of Jehoiakim son
36: 9 of the fifth *y* of Jehoiakim son
39: 1 In the ninth *y* of Zedekiah king
39: 2 month of Zedekiah's eleventh *y*,
45: 1 in the fourth *y* of Jehoiakim son
46: 2 in the fourth *y* of Jehoiakim son
48: 44 the *y* of her punishment,"
51: 46 rumor comes this *y*, another
51: 59 of Judah in the fourth *y* of his reign.
52: 4 in the ninth *y* of Zedekiah's reign,
52: 5 siege until the eleventh *y*
52: 12 in the nineteenth *y*
52: 28 in the seventh *y*, 3,023 Jews;
52: 29 in Nebuchadnezzar's eighteenth *y*,
52: 30 in his twenty-third *y*,
52: 31 In the thirty-seventh *y* of the exile
52: 31 in the *y* Evil-Merodach became
Eze 1: 1 In the thirtieth *y*, in the fourth
1: 2 it was the fifth *y* of the exile
4: 6 you 40 days, a day for each *y*.
8: 1 In the sixth *y*, in the sixth month
20: 1 In the seventh *y*, in the fifth month
24: 1 In the ninth *y*, in the tenth month
26: 1 In the eleventh *y*, on the first day
29: 1 In the tenth *y*, in the tenth month
29: 17 In the twenty-seventh *y*,
30: 20 In the eleventh *y*, in the first month
31: 1 In the eleventh *y*, in the third
32: 1 In the twelfth *y*, in the twelfth
32: 17 In the twelfth *y*, on the fifteenth
33: 21 In the twelfth *y* of our exile,
40: 1 In the twenty-fifth *y* of our exile,
40: 1 in the fourteenth *y* after the fall
40: 1 the beginning of the *y*, on the tenth
46: 17 it until the *y* of freedom;
Da 1: 1 In the third *y* of the reign
1: 21 until the first *y* of King Cyrus.
2: 1 In the second *y* of his reign,
7: 1 In the first *y* of Belshazzar king
8: 1 In the third *y* of King Belshazzar's
9: 1 In the first *y* of Darius son
9: 2 in the first *y* of his reign, I, Daniel,
10: 1 In the third *y* of Cyrus king
11: 1 in the first *y* of Darius the Mede,
Mic 6: 6 with calves a *y* old?
Hag 1: 1 In the second *y* of King Darius,
1: 15 in the second *y* of King Darius.
2: 10 in the second *y* of Darius,
Zec 1: 1 month of the second *y* of Darius,
1: 7 of Shebat, in the second *y* of Darius
7: 1 In the fourth *y* of King Darius,
14: 16 *y* after *y* to worship the King,
Lk 2: 41 Every *y* his parents went
3: 1 In the fifteenth *y* of the reign

Lk 4: 19 to proclaim the *y* of the Lord's
13: 8 'leave it alone for one more *y*,
13: 9 If it bears fruit next *y*, fine! If not,
Jn 11: 49 who was high priest that *y*,
11: 51 as high priest that *y* he prophesied
18: 13 of Caiaphas, the high priest that *y*.
Ac 11: 26 So for a whole *y* Barnabas
18: 11 So Paul stayed for a *y* and a half,
2Co 8: 10 Last *y* you were the first not only
9: 2 telling them that since last *y* you
Heb 9: 7 and that only once a *y*, and never
9: 25 enters the Most Holy Place every *y*
10: 1 repeated endlessly *y* after *y*,
Jas 4: 13 spend a *y* there, carry on business
Rev 9: 15 and *y* were released to kill a third

YEAR-OLD (YEAR)

Ex 12: 5 you choose must be *y* males
Lev 12: 6 the Tent of Meeting a *y* lamb
Nu 6: 12 and must bring a *y* male lamb
6: 14 a *y* ewe lamb without defect
6: 14 a *y* male lamb without defect
15: 27 he must bring a *y* female goat
Eze 46: 13 to provide a *y* lamb without defect

YEAR'S (YEAR)

Lev 26: 10 will still be eating last *y* harvest
Dt 14: 28 all the tithes of that *y* produce
Mk 14: 5 sold for more than a *y* wages
Jn 12: 5 to the poor? It was worth a *y* wages

YEARLING (YEAR)

Isa 11: 6 and the lion and the *y* together;

YEARLY (YEAR)

1Ki 10: 14 that Solomon received *y* was 666
2Ch 9: 13 that Solomon received *y* was 666
Hos 2: 11 her *y* festivals, her New Moons,

YEARNS

Job 19: 27 How my heart *y* within me!
Ps 84: 2 My soul *y*, even faints
Isa 26: 9 My soul *y* for you in the night;
Jer 31: 20 Therefore my heart *y* for him;

YEARS (YEAR)

Ge 1: 14 to mark seasons and days and *y*,
5: 3 When Adam had lived 130 *y*,
5: 4 Adam lived 800 *y* and had other
5: 5 Altogether, Adam lived 930 *y*,
5: 6 When Seth had lived 105 *y*,
5: 7 Seth lived 807 *y* and had other sons
5: 8 Altogether, Seth lived 912 *y*,
5: 9 When Enosh had lived 90 *y*,
5: 10 Enosh lived 815 *y* and had other
5: 11 Altogether, Enosh lived 905 *y*,
5: 12 When Kenan had lived 70 *y*,
5: 13 Kenan lived 840 *y* and had other
5: 14 Altogether, Kenan lived 910 *y*,
5: 15 When Mahalalel had lived 65 *y*,
5: 16 Mahalalel lived 830 *y* and had
5: 17 Altogether, Mahalalel lived 895 *y*,
5: 18 When Jared had lived 162 *y*,
5: 19 Jared lived 800 *y* and had other
5: 20 Altogether, Jared lived 962 *y*,
5: 21 When Enoch had lived 65 *y*,
5: 22 Enoch walked with God 300 *y*
5: 23 Altogether, Enoch lived 365 *y*.
5: 25 When Methuselah had lived 187 *y*,
5: 26 Methuselah lived 782 *y*
5: 27 Methuselah lived 969 *y*,
5: 28 When Lamech had lived 182 *y*,
5: 30 Lamech lived 595 *y* and had other
5: 31 Altogether, Lamech lived 777 *y*,
5: 32 After Noah was 500 *y* old,
6: 3 will be a hundred and twenty *y*."
7: 6 Noah was six hundred *y* old
9: 28 After the flood Noah lived 350 *y*.
9: 29 Altogether, Noah lived 950 *y*,
11: 10 Two *y* after the flood,
11: 10 when Shem was 100 *y* old,
11: 11 Shem lived 500 *y* and had other
11: 12 When Arphaxad had lived 35 *y*,
11: 13 Arphaxad lived 403 *y* and had
11: 14 When Shelah had lived 30 *y*,
11: 15 Shelah lived 403 *y* and had other
11: 16 When Eber had lived 34 *y*,
11: 17 Eber lived 430 *y* and had other

Ge 11:18 When Peleg had lived 30 *y*,
11:19 Peleg lived 209 *y* and had other
11:20 When Reu had lived 32 *y*,
11:21 Reu lived 207 *y* and had other sons
11:22 When Serug had lived 30 *y*,
11:23 Serug lived 200 *y* and had other
11:24 When Nahor had lived 29 *y*,
11:25 Nahor lived 119 *y* and had other
11:26 After Terah had lived 70 *y*,
11:32 Terah lived 205 *y*, and he died
12:4 Abram was seventy-five *y* old
14:4 For twelve *y* they had been subject
15:9 a goat and a ram, each three *y* old,
15:13 and mistreated four hundred *y*.
16:3 had been living in Canaan ten *y*,
16:16 Abram was eighty-six *y* old
17:1 Abram was ninety-nine *y* old,
17:17 born to a man a hundred *y* old?
17:24 Abraham was ninety-nine *y* old
18:11 already old and well advanced in *y*,
21:5 Abraham was a hundred *y* old
23:1 a hundred and twenty-seven *y* old.
24:1 now old and well advanced in *y*,
25:7 lived a hundred and seventy-five *y*.
25:8 an old man and full of *y*;
25:17 lived a hundred and thirty-seven *y*.
25:20 and Isaac was forty *y* old
25:26 Isaac was sixty *y* old
26:34 When Esau was forty *y* old,
29:18 "I'll work for you seven *y* in return
29:20 Jacob served seven *y* to get Rachel,
29:27 for another seven *y* of work."
29:30 worked for Laban another seven *y*.
31:38 been with you for twenty *y* now.
31:41 for your two daughters and six *y*
31:41 this for the twenty *y* I was
31:41 worked for you fourteen *y*
35:28 Isaac lived a hundred and eighty *y*.
35:29 to his people, old and full of *y*.
41:1 When two full *y* had passed,
41:26 The seven good cows are seven *y*,
41:26 heads of grain are seven *y*;
41:27 They are seven *y* of famine.
41:27 up after they did are seven *y*,
41:29 Seven *y* of great abundance are
41:30 seven *y* of famine will follow them.
41:34 during the seven *y* of abundance.
41:35 of these good *y* that are coming
41:36 used during the seven *y*
41:46 Joseph was thirty *y* old
41:47 During the seven *y*
41:48 in those seven *y* of abundance
41:50 Before the *y* of famine came,
41:53 The seven *y* of abundance
41:54 and the seven *y* of famine began,
45:6 For two *y* now there has been
45:6 for the next five *y* there will not be
45:11 five *y* of famine are still to come.
47:9 My *y* have been few and difficult,
47:9 and they do not equal the *y*
47:9 *y* of my pilgrimage are a hundred
47:28 Jacob lived in Egypt seventeen *y*,
47:28 and the *y* of his life were a hundred
50:22 He lived a hundred and ten *y*
Ex 6:16 Levi lived 137 *y*.
6:18 Kohath lived 133 *y*.
6:20 Amram lived 137 *y*.
7:7 Moses was eighty *y* old
12:40 lived in Egypt was 430 *y*.
12:41 end of the 430 *y*, to the very day,
16:35 The Israelites ate manna forty *y*,
21:2 he is to serve you for six *y*.
23:10 For six *y* you are to sow your fields
30:14 those twenty *y* old or more,
38:26 twenty *y* old or more, a total
Lev 19:23 For three *y* you are
25:3 For six *y* sow your fields,
25:3 and for six *y* prune your vineyards
25:8 amount to a period of forty-nine *y*.
25:8 of *y*— seven times seven *y*—
25:8 sabbaths of *y* amount to a period
25:15 of the number of *y* since the Jubilee
25:15 the basis of the number of *y* left
25:16 When the *y* are many, you are
25:16 and when the *y* are few, you are
25:21 land will yield enough for three *y*.
25:27 the value for the *y* since he sold it
25:50 to a hired man for that number of *y*.
Lev 25:51 If many *y* remain, he must pay
25:52 If only a few *y* remain
26:34 will enjoy its sabbath *y* all the time
27:6 between one month and five *y*,
27:7 If it is a person sixty *y* old or more,
27:18 to the number of *y* that remain
Nu 1:3 the men in Israel twenty *y* old
1:18 and the men twenty *y* old
1:20 All the men twenty *y* old
1:22 All the men twenty *y* old
1:24 All the men twenty *y* old
1:26 All the men twenty *y* old
1:28 All the men twenty *y* old
1:30 All the men twenty *y* old
1:32 All the men twenty *y* old
1:34 All the men twenty *y* old
1:36 All the men twenty *y* old
1:38 All the men twenty *y* old
1:40 All the men twenty *y* old
1:42 All the men twenty *y* old
1:45 All the Israelites twenty *y* old
4:3 the men from thirty to fifty *y*
4:23 the men from thirty to fifty *y*
4:30 the men from thirty to fifty *y*
4:35 the men from thirty to fifty *y*
4:39 the men from thirty to fifty *y*
4:43 the men from thirty to fifty *y*
4:47 the men from thirty to fifty *y*
8:24 Men twenty-five *y* old
13:22 (Hebron had been built seven *y*
14:29 every one of you twenty *y* old
14:33 will be shepherds here for forty *y*,
14:34 For forty *y*— one year for each
20:15 and we lived there many *y*.
26:2 all those twenty *y* old or more who
26:4 a census of the men twenty *y* old
32:11 not one of the men twenty *y* old
32:13 wander in the desert forty *y*,
33:39 twenty-three *y* old when he died
Dt 2:7 These forty *y* the LORD your God
2:14 Thirty-eight *y* passed
8:2 the way in the desert these forty *y*,
8:4 swell during these forty *y*.
14:28 At the end of every three *y*,
15:1 of every seven *y* you must cancel
15:12 sold to you and he serves you six *y*,
15:18 to you these six *y* has been worth
29:5 During the forty *y* that I led you
30:20 and he will give you many *y*
31:2 now a hundred and twenty *y* old
31:10 "At the end of every seven *y*,
34:7 and twenty *y* old when he died,
Jos 5:6 about in the desert forty *y*
13:1 was old and well advanced in *y*,
14:7 I was forty *y* old when Moses
14:10 for forty-five *y* since the time he
14:10 here I am today, eighty-five *y* old!
23:1 by then old and well advanced in *y*,
23:2 "I am old and well advanced in *y*.
Jdg 3:8 Israelites were subject for eight *y*.
3:11 So the land had peace for forty *y*,
3:14 king of Moab for eighteen *y*.
3:30 and the land had peace for eighty *y*
4:3 the Israelites for twenty *y*,
5:31 Then the land had peace forty *y*.
6:1 and for seven *y* he gave them
6:25 father's herd, the one seven *y* old.
8:28 the land enjoyed peace forty *y*.
9:22 had governed Israel three *y*,
10:2 He led Israel twenty-three *y*;
10:3 who led Israel twenty-two *y*.
10:8 For eighteen *y* they oppressed all
11:26 three hundred *y* Israel occupied
12:7 Jephthah led Israel six *y*.
12:9 Ibzan led Israel seven *y*.
12:11 Elon the Zebulunite led Israel ten *y*
12:14 He led Israel eight *y*.
13:1 hands of the Philistines for forty *y*.
15:20 Israel for twenty *y* in the days
16:31 He had led Israel twenty *y*.
Ru 1:4 they had lived there about ten *y*,
1Sa 4:15 who was ninety-eight *y* old
4:18 He had led Israel forty *y*.
7:2 It was a long time, twenty *y* in all,
13:1 Saul was ⌊thirty⌋ *y* old
13:1 he reigned over Israel ⌊forty-⌋ two *y*
17:12 he was old and well advanced in *y*.
2Sa 2:10 over Israel, and he reigned two *y*.
2Sa 2:10 son of Saul was forty *y* old
2:11 the house of Judah was seven *y*
4:4 He was five *y* old when the news
5:4 David was thirty *y* old
5:4 king, and he reigned forty *y*.
5:5 all Israel and Judah thirty-three *y*.
5:5 reigned over Judah seven *y*
13:23 *y* later, when Absalom's
13:38 to Geshur, he stayed there three *y*.
14:28 Absalom lived two *y* in Jerusalem
15:7 At the end of four *y*, Absalom said
19:32 was a very old man, eighty *y*
19:34 "How many more *y* will I live,
19:35 the king? I am now eighty *y* old.
21:1 a famine for three successive *y*;
24:13 come upon you three *y* of famine
1Ki 1:1 was old and well advanced in *y*,
2:11 He had reigned forty *y* over Israel
2:11 seven *y* in Hebron and thirty-three
2:39 three *y* later, two of Shimei's slaves
6:38 He had spent seven *y* building it.
7:1 It took Solomon thirteen *y*,
9:10 At the end of twenty *y*,
10:22 Once every three *y* it returned
11:42 in Jerusalem over all Israel forty *y*.
14:20 He reigned for twenty-two *y*
14:21 He was forty-one *y* old
14:21 and he reigned seventeen *y*
15:2 and he reigned in Jerusalem three *y*
15:10 he reigned in Jerusalem forty-one *y*
15:25 and he reigned over Israel two *y*.
15:33 and he reigned twenty-four *y*.
16:8 and he reigned in Tirzah two *y*.
16:23 he reigned twelve *y*, six of them
16:29 Samaria over Israel twenty-two *y*.
17:1 the next few *y* except at my word."
22:1 For three *y* there was no war
22:42 Jehoshaphat was thirty-five *y* old
22:42 reigned in Jerusalem twenty-five *y*.
22:51 and he reigned over Israel two *y*.
2Ki 3:1 of Judah, and he reigned twelve *y*.
8:1 in the land that will last seven *y*."
8:2 the land of the Philistines seven *y*.
8:3 end of the seven *y* she came back
8:17 He was thirty-two *y* old
8:17 and he reigned in Jerusalem eight *y*
8:26 Ahaziah was twenty-two *y* old
10:36 in Samaria was twenty-eight *y*.
11:3 the temple of the LORD for six *y*
11:21 Joash was seven *y* old
12:1 and he reigned in Jerusalem forty *y*
12:2 LORD all the *y* Jehoiada the priest
13:1 and he reigned seventeen *y*.
13:10 Samaria, and he reigned sixteen *y*.
14:2 He was twenty-five *y* old
14:2 in Jerusalem twenty-nine *y*.
14:17 lived for fifteen *y* after the death
14:21 Azariah, who was sixteen *y* old,
14:23 and he reigned forty-one *y*.
15:2 He was sixteen *y* old
15:2 he reigned in Jerusalem fifty-two *y*.
15:17 and he reigned in Samaria ten *y*.
15:23 in Samaria, and he reigned two *y*.
15:27 Samaria, and he reigned twenty *y*.
15:33 He was twenty-five *y* old
15:33 he reigned in Jerusalem sixteen *y*.
16:2 Ahaz was twenty *y* old
16:2 he reigned in Jerusalem sixteen *y*.
17:1 in Samaria, and he reigned nine *y*.
17:5 and laid siege to it for three *y*.
18:2 He was twenty-five *y* old
18:2 in Jerusalem twenty-nine *y*.
18:10 of three *y* the Assyrians took it.
20:6 I will add fifteen *y* to your life.
21:1 Manasseh was twelve *y* old
21:1 he reigned in Jerusalem fifty-five *y*.
21:19 Amon was twenty-two *y* old
21:19 and he reigned in Jerusalem two *y*.
22:1 Josiah was eight *y* old
22:1 reigned in Jerusalem thirty-one *y*.
23:31 Jehoahaz was twenty-three *y* old
23:36 Jehoiakim was twenty-five *y* old
23:36 he reigned in Jerusalem eleven *y*.
24:1 became his vassal for three *y*.
24:8 Jehoiachin was eighteen *y* old
24:18 Zedekiah was twenty-one *y* old
24:18 he reigned in Jerusalem eleven *y*.
1Ch 2:21 her when he was sixty *y* old),

1Ch 3: 4 reigned in Jerusalem thirty-three y,
3: 4 where he reigned seven y
21: 12 Take your choice: three y of famine
23: 1 When David was old and full of y,
23: 3 The Levites thirty y old
23: 24 the workers twenty y old
23: 27 counted from those twenty y old
27: 23 number of the men twenty y old
29: 27 He ruled over Israel forty y—
2Ch 8: 1 At the end of twenty y,
9: 21 Once every three y it returned,
9: 30 in Jerusalem over all Israel forty y.
11: 17 son of Solomon three y,
12: 13 He was forty-one y old
12: 13 and he reigned seventeen y
13: 2 and he reigned in Jerusalem three y
14: 1 the country was at peace for ten y.
14: 6 was at war with him during those y,
17: 3 because in his early y he walked
18: 2 Some y later he went
20: 31 He was thirty-five y old
20: 31 reigned in Jerusalem twenty-five y.
21: 5 Jehoram was thirty-two y old
21: 5 and he reigned in Jerusalem eight y
21: 20 Jehoram was thirty-two y old
21: 20 and he reigned in Jerusalem eight y
22: 2 Ahaziah was twenty-two y old
22: 12 God for six y while Athaliah ruled
24: 1 Joash was seven y old
24: 1 and he reigned in Jerusalem forty y
24: 2 the eyes of the LORD all the y
24: 15 Now Jehoiada was old and full of y,
25: 1 Amaziah was twenty-five y old
25: 1 in Jerusalem twenty-nine y.
25: 5 then mustered those twenty y old
25: 25 lived for fifteen y after the death
26: 1 Uzziah, who was sixteen y old,
26: 3 Uzziah was sixteen y old
26: 3 he reigned in Jerusalem fifty-two y.
27: 1 Jotham was twenty-five y old
27: 1 he reigned in Jerusalem sixteen y.
27: 5 also in the second and third y.
27: 8 He was twenty-five y old
27: 8 he reigned in Jerusalem sixteen y.
28: 1 Ahaz was twenty y old
28: 1 he reigned in Jerusalem sixteen y.
29: 1 Hezekiah was twenty-five y old
29: 1 in Jerusalem twenty-nine y.
31: 16 distributed to the males three y old
31: 17 likewise to the Levites twenty y old
33: 1 Manasseh was twelve y old
33: 1 he reigned in Jerusalem fifty-five y.
33: 21 Amon was twenty-two y old
33: 21 and he reigned in Jerusalem two y.
34: 1 Josiah was eight y old
34: 1 reigned in Jerusalem thirty-one y.
36: 2 Jehoahaz was twenty-three y old
36: 5 Jehoiakim was twenty-five y old
36: 5 he reigned in Jerusalem eleven y.
36: 9 Jehoiachin was eighteen y old
36: 11 Zedekiah was twenty-one y old
36: 11 he reigned in Jerusalem eleven y.
36: 21 until the seventy y were completed
Ezr 3: 8 appointing Levites twenty y of age
5: 11 temple that was built many y ago,
Ne 5: 14 thirty-second year—twelve y—
9: 21 For forty y you sustained them
9: 30 For many y you were patient
Job 10: 5 or your y like those of a man,
15: 20 through all the y stored up for him.
16: 22 "Only a few y will pass
21: 13 They spend their y in prosperity
32: 6 "I am young in y,
32: 7 advanced y should teach wisdom.'
36: 11 and their y in contentment.
36: 26 of his y is past finding out.
38: 21 You have lived so many y!
42: 16 Job lived a hundred and forty y;
42: 17 And so he died, old and full of y.
Ps 31: 10 and my y by groaning;
39: 5 the span of my y is as nothing
61: 6 his y for many generations.
77: 5 the y of long ago;
77: 10 the y of the right hand
78: 33 and their y in terror.
90: 4 For a thousand y in your sight
90: 9 we finish our y with a moan.
90: 10 The length of our days is seventy y
Ps 90: 15 many y as we have seen trouble.
95: 10 For forty y I was angry
102: 24 y go on through all generations.
102: 27 and your y will never end.
Pr 3: 2 they will prolong your life many y
4: 10 and the y of your life will be many.
5: 9 and your y to one who is cruel,
9: 11 and y will be added to your life.
10: 27 the y of the wicked are cut short.
Ecc 6: 3 hundred children and live many y;
6: 6 if he lives a thousand y twice over
11: 8 However many y a man may live,
12: 1 the y approach when you will say,
Isa 7: 8 Within sixty-five y
16: 14 the LORD says: "Within three y,
20: 3 stripped and barefoot for three y,
23: 15 But at the end of these seventy y,
23: 15 will be forgotten for seventy y,
23: 17 of seventy y, the LORD will deal
38: 5 I will add fifteen y to your life.
38: 10 and be robbed of the rest of my y?"
38: 15 I will walk humbly all my y
65: 20 man who does not live out his y;
Jer 6: 11 those weighed down with y.
25: 3 For twenty-three y—
25: 11 the king of Babylon seventy y.
25: 12 But when the seventy y are fulfilled
28: 3 Within two y I will bring back
28: 11 of all the nations within two y.' "
29: 10 "When seventy y are completed
34: 14 After he has served you six y,
52: 1 Zedekiah was twenty-one y old
52: 1 he reigned in Jerusalem eleven y.
Eze 4: 5 number of days as the y of their sin.
12: 27 is for many y from now,
22: 4 and the end of your y has come.
29: 11 no one will live there for forty y.
29: 12 her cities will lie desolate forty y
29: 13 the end of forty y I will gather
38: 8 In future y you will invade a land
38: 17 for y that I would bring you
39: 9 For seven y they will use them
Da 1: 5 They were to be trained for three y,
9: 2 of Jerusalem would last seventy y.
11: 6 After some y, they will become
11: 8 For some y he will leave the king
11: 13 than the first; and after several y,
11: 20 In a few y, however, he will be
Joel 2: 25 for the y the locusts have eaten—
Am 1: 1 he saw concerning Israel two y
2: 10 and I led you forty y in the desert
4: 4 your tithes every three y.
5: 25 forty y in the desert, O house
Zec 1: 12 angry with these seventy y?"
7: 3 as I have done for so many y?"
7: 5 months for the past seventy y,
Mal 3: 4 as in days gone by, as in former y.
Mt 2: 16 and its vicinity who were two y old
9: 20 to bleeding for twelve y came up
Mk 5: 25 subject to bleeding for twelve y.
5: 42 around (she was twelve y old).
Lk 1: 7 and they were both well along in y.
1: 18 and my wife is well along in y."
2: 36 lived with her husband seven y
2: 42 When he was twelve y old,
3: 23 Jesus himself was about thirty y old
4: 25 and a half y and there was a severe
8: 43 subject to bleeding for twelve y,
12: 19 of good things laid up for many y.
13: 7 'For three y now I've been coming
13: 11 crippled by a spirit for eighteen y.
13: 16 bound for eighteen long y,
15: 29 All these y I've been slaving
Jn 2: 20 "It has taken forty-six y
5: 5 been an invalid for thirty-eight y.
8: 57 "You are not yet fifty y old,"
Ac 4: 22 healed was over forty y old.
7: 6 and mistreated four hundred y.
7: 23 "When Moses was forty y old,
7: 30 "After forty y had passed,
7: 36 and for forty y in the desert.
7: 42 forty y in the desert, O house
9: 33 had been bedridden for eight y.
13: 18 and endured their conduct forty y
13: 20 All this took about 450 y.
13: 21 of Benjamin, who ruled forty y.
19: 10 This went on for two y,
20: 31 for three y I never stopped warning
Ac 24: 10 number of y you have been a judge
24: 17 "After an absence of several y,
24: 27 When two y had passed, Felix was
28: 30 For two whole y Paul stayed there
Ro 4: 19 since he was about a hundred y old
15: 23 longing for many y to see you,
1Co 7: 36 and if she is getting along in y
2Co 12: 2 Christ who fourteen y ago was
Gal 1: 18 Then after three y, I went up
2: 1 Fourteen y later I went up again
3: 17 The law, introduced 430 y later,
4: 10 and months and seasons and y!
Heb 1: 12 and your y will never end."
3: 9 and for forty y saw what I did.
3: 17 with whom was he angry for forty y
Jas 5: 17 on the land for three and a half y.
2Pe 3: 8 and a thousand y are like a day.
3: 8 the Lord a day is like a thousand y,
Rev 20: 2 and bound him for a thousand y.
20: 3 until the thousand y were ended.
20: 4 reigned with Christ a thousand y.
20: 5 until the thousand y were ended.)
20: 6 will reign with him for a thousand y
20: 7 When the thousand y are over,

YEAST

Ge 19: 3 baking bread without y,
Ex 12: 8 and bread made without y.
12: 15 On the first day remove the y
12: 15 are to eat bread made without y.
12: 15 for whoever eats anything with y
12: 18 are to eat bread made without y,
12: 19 And whoever eats anything with y
12: 19 For seven days no y is to be found
12: 20 Eat nothing made with y.
12: 34 dough before the y was added,
12: 39 The dough was without y
13: 3 Eat nothing containing y.
13: 6 days eat bread made without y
13: 7 nor shall any y be seen anywhere
13: 7 nothing with y in it is to be seen
23: 15 days eat bread made without y,
23: 18 along with anything containing y.
29: 2 from fine wheat flour, without y,
29: 23 basket of bread made without y,
34: 18 days eat bread made without y,
34: 25 along with anything containing y,
Lev 2: 4 cakes made without y
2: 4 or wafers made without y
2: 5 mixed with oil, and without y.
2: 11 for you are not to burn any y
2: 11 LORD must be made without y,
6: 16 is to be eaten without y
6: 17 It must not be baked with y;
7: 12 cakes of bread made without y
7: 12 wafers made without y
7: 13 with cakes of bread made with y.
8: 2 containing bread made without y,
8: 26 basket of bread made without y,
10: 12 prepared without y beside the altar,
23: 6 must eat bread made without y.
23: 17 baked with y, as a wave offering
Nu 6: 15 a basket of bread made without y—
6: 19 the basket, both made without y.
28: 17 days eat bread made without y.
Dt 16: 3 it with bread made with y,
16: 4 no y be found in your possession
Jdg 6: 19 of flour he made bread without y.
1Sa 28: 24 and baked bread without y.
Eze 45: 21 you shall eat bread made without y.
Mt 13: 33 of heaven is like y that a woman
16: 6 guard against the y of the Pharisees
16: 11 guard against the y of the Pharisees
16: 12 to guard against the y used in bread
Mk 8: 15 out for the y of the Pharisees
Lk 12: 1 against the y of the Pharisees,
13: 21 It is like y that a woman took
1Co 5: 6 you know that a little y works
5: 7 may be a new batch without y—
5: 7 of the old y that you may be a new
5: 8 but with bread without y, the bread
5: 8 not with the old y, the y of malice
Gal 5: 9 little y works through the whole

YELLING

Ac 7: 57 and, y at the top of their voices,

YELLOW

Lev 13: 30 and the hair in it is *y* and thin,
13: 32 not spread and there is no *y* hair
13: 36 does not need to look for *y* hair;
Rev 9: 17 were fiery red, dark blue, and *y*

YESTERDAY

Ex 5: 14 you met your quota of bricks *y*
1Sa 20: 27 *y* or today?" Jonathan answered,
2Sa 15: 20 You came only *y*.
2Ki 9: 26 '*Y* I saw the blood of Naboth
Job 8: 9 for we were born only *y*
Jn 4: 52 "The fever left him *y*
Ac 7: 28 as you killed the Egyptian *y*?'
Heb 13: 8 Jesus Christ is the same *y*

YIELD (YIELDED YIELDING YIELDS)

Ge 4: 12 it will no longer *y* its crops for you.
Lev 25: 19 Then the land will *y* its fruit,
25: 21 year that the land will *y* enough
26: 4 and the ground will *y* its crops
26: 20 the trees of the land *y* their fruit.
26: 20 your soil will not *y* its crops,
Dt 11: 17 and the ground will *y* no produce,
13: 8 do not *y* to him or listen to him.
33: 14 and the finest the moon can *y*;
Jos 24: 23 and *y* your hearts to the LORD,
2Sa 1: 21 nor fields that *y* offerings
Job 31: 39 if I have devoured its *y*
Ps 67: 6 Then the land will *y* its harvest,
85: 12 and our land will *y* its harvest.
Pr 8: 19 what I *y* surpasses choice silver.
Isa 5: 4 why did it *y* only bad?
48: 11 I will not *y* my glory to another.
Eze 34: 27 and the ground will *y* its crops;
34: 27 trees of the field will *y* their fruit
36: 37 Once again I will *y* to the plea
Hos 8: 7 Were it to *y* grain,
9: 16 they *y* no fruit.
Joel 2: 22 and the vine *y* their riches.
Zec 8: 12 grow well, the vine will *y* its fruit,
Jas 5: 7 for the land to *y* its valuable crop

YIELDED (YIELD)

Ps 107: 37 that *y* a fruitful harvest;
Isa 5: 2 but it *y* only bad fruit.
Lk 8: 8 and *y* a crop, a hundred times more

YIELDING (YIELD)

SS 5: 13 *y* perfume.
Mt 13: 23 He produces a crop, *y* a hundred,
Rev 22: 2 of fruit, *y* its fruit every month.

YIELDS (YIELD)

Lev 25: 6 Whatever the land *y*
Ps 1: 3 which *y* its fruit in season
Pr 3: 14 and *y* better returns than gold.
14: 24 but the folly of fools *y* folly.
Isa 55: 10 so that it *y* seed for the sower

YOKE (YOKED YOKEFELLOW YOKES)

Ge 27: 40 you will throw his *y*
Ex 6: 6 from under the *y* of the Egyptians.
6: 7 from under the *y* of the Egyptians.
Lev 26: 13 I broke the bars of your *y*
Nu 19: 2 and that has never been under a *y*.
Dt 21: 3 has never worn a *y* and lead her
28: 48 He will put an iron *y* on your neck
1Ki 12: 4 and the heavy *y* he put on us,
12: 4 "Your father put a heavy *y* on us,
12: 9 'Lighten the *y* your father put on us
12: 10 but make our *y* lighter'—tell them,
12: 10 'Your father put a heavy *y* on us,
12: 11 My father laid on you a heavy *y*;
12: 14 "My father made your *y* heavy;
19: 19 plowing with twelve *y* of oxen,
19: 21 He took his *y* of oxen
2Ch 10: 4 and the heavy *y* he put on us,
10: 4 "Your father put a heavy *y* on us,
10: 9 'Lighten the *y* your father put on us
10: 10 but make our *y* lighter'—tell them,
10: 10 'Your father put a heavy *y* on us,
10: 11 My father laid on you a heavy *y*;
10: 14 "My father made your *y* heavy;
Job 1: 3 five hundred *y* of oxen
42: 12 thousand *y* of oxen and a thousand
Isa 9: 4 the *y* that burdens them,
10: 27 the *y* will be broken
10: 27 their *y* from your neck;
14: 25 His *y* will be taken from my people,
47: 6 you laid a very heavy *y*.
58: 6 and break every *y*?
58: 6 and untie the cords of the *y*,
58: 9 away with the *y* of oppression,
Jer 2: 20 "Long ago you broke off your *y*
5: 5 they too had broken off the *y*
27: 2 "Make a *y* out of straps
27: 8 or bow its neck under his *y*,
27: 11 under the *y* of the king of Babylon
27: 12 neck under the *y* of the king
28: 2 'I will break the *y* of the king
28: 4 'for I will break the *y* of the king
28: 10 the prophet Hananiah took the *y*
28: 11 'In the same way will I break the *y*
28: 12 Hananiah had broken the *y*
28: 13 You have broken a wooden *y*,
28: 13 in its place you will get a *y* of iron.
28: 14 I will put an iron *y* on the necks
30: 8 'I will break the *y* off their necks
La 1: 14 "My sins have been bound into a *y*;
3: 27 It is good for a man to bear the *y*
Eze 30: 18 when I break the *y* of Egypt;
34: 27 when I break the bars of their *y*
Hos 10: 11 so I will put a *y*
11: 4 I lifted the *y* from their neck
Na 1: 13 I will break their *y* from your neck
Mt 11: 29 Take my *y* upon you and learn
11: 30 For my *y* is easy and my burden is
Lk 14: 19 'I have just bought five *y* of oxen,
Ac 15: 10 of the disciples a *y* that neither we
Gal 5: 1 be burdened again by a *y*
1Ti 6: 1 All who are under the *y*

YOKED (YOKE)

Dt 22: 10 with an ox and a donkey *y* together
1Sa 6: 7 have calved and have never been *y*.
Ps 106: 28 They *y* themselves to the Baal
2Co 6: 14 Do not be *y* together

YOKEFELLOW (YOKE)

Php 4: 3 Yes, and I ask you, loyal *y*,

YOKES (YOKE)

2Sa 24: 22 here are threshing sledges and ox *y*

YOUNG (YOUNGER YOUNGEST YOUTH YOUTHFUL YOUTHS)

Ge 4: 23 a *y* man for injuring me.
15: 9 along with a dove and a *y* pigeon."
19: 4 both *y* and old—surrounded
19: 11 *y* and old, with blindness
27: 9 and bring me two choice *y* goats,
30: 39 And they bore *y* that were streaked
30: 40 Jacob set apart the *y* of the flock
31: 8 the flocks gave birth to speckled *y*;
31: 8 then all the flocks bore streaked *y*.
32: 15 thirty female camels with their *y*,
33: 13 and cows that are nursing their *y*.
34: 19 *y* man, who was the most honored
37: 2 Joseph, a *y* man of seventeen,
38: 17 I'll send you a *y* goat from my flock
38: 20 Meanwhile Judah sent the *y* goat
38: 23 I did send her this *y* goat,
41: 12 Now a *y* Hebrew was there with us,
44: 20 and there is a *y* son born to him
Ex 10: 9 "We will go with our *y* and old,
23: 19 "Do not cook a *y* goat
24: 5 Then he sent *y* Israelite men,
24: 5 offerings and sacrificed *y* bulls
29: 1 Take a *y* bull and two rams
33: 11 but his *y* aide Joshua son
34: 26 "Do not cook a *y* goat
Lev 1: 5 is to slaughter the *y* bull
1: 14 he is to offer a dove or a *y* pigeon.
4: 3 bring to the LORD a *y* bull
4: 14 the assembly must bring a *y* bull
5: 7 or two *y* pigeons to the LORD
5: 11 afford two doves or two *y* pigeons,
12: 6 and a *y* pigeon or a dove
12: 8 to bring two doves or two *y* pigeons
14: 22 and two doves or two *y* pigeons,
14: 30 the doves or the *y* pigeons,
15: 14 take two doves or two *y* pigeons
15: 29 take two doves or two *y* pigeons
16: 3 with a *y* bull for a sin offering
22: 28 a sheep and its *y* on the same day.
Lev 23: 18 and without defect, one *y* bull
Nu 6: 10 or two *y* pigeons to the priest
7: 15 filled with incense; one *y* bull,
7: 21 filled with incense; one *y* bull,
7: 27 filled with incense; one *y* bull,
7: 33 filled with incense; one *y* bull,
7: 39 filled with incense; one *y* bull,
7: 45 filled with incense; one *y* bull,
7: 51 filled with incense; one *y* bull,
7: 57 filled with incense; one *y* bull,
7: 63 filled with incense; one *y* bull,
7: 69 filled with incense; one *y* bull,
7: 75 filled with incense; one *y* bull,
7: 81 filled with incense; one *y* bull,
7: 87 offering came to twelve *y* bulls,
8: 8 Have them take a *y* bull
8: 8 are to take a second *y* bull
11: 27 A *y* man ran and told Moses,
15: 8 " 'When you prepare a *y* bull
15: 11 or ram, each lamb or *y* goat,
15: 24 to offer a *y* bull for a burnt offering
28: 11 a burnt offering of two *y* bulls,
28: 19 a burnt offering of two *y* bulls,
28: 27 a burnt offering of two *y* bulls,
29: 2 a burnt offering of one *y* bull,
29: 8 a burnt offering of one *y* bull,
29: 13 a burnt offering of thirteen *y* bulls,
29: 17 second day prepare twelve *y* bulls,
30: 3 "When a *y* woman still living
30: 16 and his *y* daughter still living
Dt 7: 14 nor any of your livestock without *y*
14: 21 Do not cook a *y* goat
22: 6 and the mother is sitting on the *y*
22: 6 do not take the mother with the *y*.
22: 7 You may take the *y*, but be sure
28: 4 and the *y* of your livestock—
28: 11 the *y* of your livestock
28: 50 respect for the old or pity for the *y*.
28: 51 They will devour the *y*
30: 9 the *y* of your livestock
32: 11 and hovers over its *y*,
32: 25 Young men and *y* women will
32: 25 *Y* men and young women will
Jos 6: 21 men and women, *y* and old, cattle,
6: 23 the *y* men who had done the spying
Jdg 6: 19 Gideon went in, prepared a *y* goat,
8: 14 He caught a *y* man of Succoth
8: 14 and the *y* man wrote down for him
11: 40 custom that each year the *y* women
12: 9 brought in thirty *y* women
13: 15 until we prepare a *y* goat for you."
13: 19 Then Manoah took a *y* goat,
14: 1 saw there a *y* Philistine woman,
14: 5 suddenly a *y* lion came roaring
14: 6 as he might have torn a *y* goat.
15: 1 Samson took a *y* goat and went
17: 7 A *y* Levite from Bethlehem
17: 11 and the *y* man was to him like one
17: 12 and the *y* man became his priest
18: 3 the voice of the *y* Levite;
18: 15 of the *y* Levite at Micah's place
19: 19 your maidservant, and the *y* man
21: 12 four hundred *y* women who had
Ru 2: 5 "Whose *y* woman is that?"
4: 12 LORD gives you by this *y* woman,
1Sa 1: 24 she took the boy with her, *y*
2: 17 sin of the *y* men was very great
5: 9 both *y* and old, with an outbreak
9: 2 an impressive *y* man without equal
10: 3 One will be carrying three *y* goats,
14: 1 to the *y* man bearing his armor,
14: 6 Jonathan said to his *y* armor-bearer
16: 20 a skin of wine and a *y* goat
17: 55 whose son is that *y* man?"
17: 56 Find out whose son this *y* man is."
17: 58 "Whose son are you, *y* man?"
25: 5 he sent ten *y* men and said to them,
25: 8 favorable toward my *y* men,
26: 22 "Let one of your *y* men come over
30: 2 all who were in it, both *y* and old.
30: 17 four hundred *y* men who rode
30: 19 Nothing was missing: *y* or old,
2Sa 1: 5 said to the *y* man who brought him
1: 6 the *y* man said, "and there was Saul
1: 13 said to the *y* man who brought him
2: 14 some of the *y* men get up
2: 21 take on one of the *y* men
9: 12 Mephibosheth had a *y* son named

2Sa 14:21 bring back the y man Absalom."
17:18 But a y man saw them
18: 5 Be gentle with the y man Absalom
18:12 'Protect the y man Absalom
18:29 "Is the y man Absalom safe?"
18:32 up to harm you be like that y man."
18:32 "Is the y man Absalom safe?"
1Ki 1: 2 "Let us look for a y virgin
11:28 saw how well the y man did his
12: 8 and consulted the y men who had
12:10 The y men who had grown up
12:14 he followed the advice of the y men
20:14 'The y officers of the provincial
20:15 So Ahab summoned the y officers
20:17 The y officers of the provincial
20:19 The y officers of the provincial
2Ki 3:21 y and old, who could bear arms was
5: 2 and had taken captive a y girl
5:14 became clean like that of a y boy.
5:22 'Two y men from the company
8:12 kill their y men with the sword,
9: 4 So the y man, the prophet,
1Ch 12:28 men, and Zadok, a brave y warrior,
22: 5 "My son Solomon is y
25: 8 Y and old alike, teacher as well
26:13 according to their families, y
29: 1 the one whom God has chosen, is y
2Ch 10: 8 and consulted the y men who had
10:10 The y men who had grown up
10:14 he followed the advice of the y men
13: 7 son of Solomon when he was y
13: 9 to consecrate himself with a y bull
31:15 to their divisions, old and y alike.
34: 3 while he was still y, he began
36:17 spared neither y man nor y woman,
36:17 who killed their y men
Ezr 6: 9 Whatever is needed—y bulls, rams
Est 2: 2 for beautiful y virgins for the king.
3:13 annihilate all the Jews—y and old,
Job 29: 8 the y men saw me and stepped
32: 6 "I am y in years,
38:41 the raven when its y cry out to God
39: 3 down and bring forth their y;
39: 4 Their y thrive and grow strong
39:16 She treats her y harshly,
39:30 His y ones feast on blood,
Ps 29: 6 Sirion like a y wild ox.
37:25 I was y and now I am old,
78:31 cutting down the y men of Israel.
78:63 Fire consumed their y men,
84: 3 where she may have her y—
89:19 I have exalted a y man
119: 9 How can a y man keep his way
147: 9 and for the y ravens when they call.
148: 12 y men and maidens,
Pr 1: 4 knowledge and discretion to the y
7: 7 I noticed among the y men,
20:29 The glory of y men is their strength
Ecc 11: 9 Be happy, y man, while you are y,
SS 1: 8 and graze your y goats
2: 3 is my lover among the y men.
2: 9 My lover is like a gazelle or a y stag
2:17 or like a y stag
8: 8 We have a y sister,
8:14 or like a y stag
Isa 3: 5 The y will rise up against the old,
5:29 they roar like y lions;
7:21 a man will keep alive a y cow
9:17 will take no pleasure in the y men,
11: 7 their y will lie down together,
11: 8 the y child put his hand
13:18 bows will strike down the y men;
20: 4 y and old, with buttocks bared—
31: 8 and their y men will be put
33: 4 is harvested as by y locusts;
34:15 care for her y under the shadow
40:11 he gently leads those that have y.
40:30 and y men stumble and fall;
54: 6 a wife who married y,
60: 6 y camels of Midian and Ephah.
62: 5 As a y man marries a maiden,
Jer 6:11 on the y men gathered together;
9:21 the y men from the public squares.
11:22 Their y men will die by the sword,
15: 8 against the mothers of their y men;
18:21 their y men slain by the sword
31:12 the y of the flocks and herds.
31:13 y men and old as well.
Jer 48:15 her finest y men will go
49:20 y of the flock will be dragged away;
49:26 her y men will fall in the streets;
50:27 Kill all her y bulls;
50:30 her y men will fall in the streets;
50:45 y of the flock will be dragged away;
51: 3 Do not spare her y men;
51:22 with you I shatter y man
51:38 Her people all roar like y lions,
La 1:15 me to crush my y men.
1:18 My y men and maidens
2:10 The y women of Jerusalem
2:21 my y men and maidens
2:21 "Y and old lie together
3:27 while he is y.
4: 3 breasts to nurse their y,
5:13 Y men toil at the millstones;
5:14 the y men have stopped their music
Eze 9: 6 Slaughter old men, y men
19: 2 She lay down among the y lions
23: 6 all of them handsome y men,
23:12 horsemen, all handsome y men.
23:21 and your y breasts fondled.
23:23 with them, handsome y men,
30:17 The y men of Heliopolis
43:19 You are to give a y bull
43:23 you are to offer a y bull
43:25 you are also to provide a y bull
45:18 are to take a y bull without defect
46: 6 New Moon he is to offer a y bull,
Da 1: 4 y men without any physical defect,
1:10 than the other y men your age?
1:13 of the y men who eat the royal food
1:15 of the y men who ate the royal food
1:17 To these four y men God gave
Hos 14: 6 his y shoots will grow.
Joel 1: 4 the y locusts have eaten;
1: 4 what the y locusts have left
2:25 the great locust and the y locust,
2:28 your y men will see visions.
Am 2:11 Nazirites from among your y men.
4:10 I killed your y men with the sword,
8:13 lovely y women and strong y men
Mic 5: 8 like a y lion among flocks of sheep,
Na 2:11 the place where they fed their y,
2:13 the sword will devour your y lions.
Zec 2: 4 said to him: "Run, tell that y man,
9:17 Grain will make the y men thrive,
9:17 and new wine the y women.
11:16 or seek the y, or heal the injured,
Mt 19:20 these I have kept," the y man said.
19:22 When the y man heard this,
Mk 14:51 A y man, wearing nothing
16: 5 they saw a y man dressed
Lk 2:24 "a pair of doves or two y pigeons."
7:14 He said, "Y man, I say to you,
15:29 even a y goat so I could celebrate
Jn 12:14 Jesus found a y donkey
Ac 2:17 your y men will see visions,
5: 6 Then the y men came forward,
5:10 Then the y men came in and,
7:58 at the feet of a y man named Saul.
20: 9 a window was a y man named
20:10 threw himself on the y man
20:12 people took the y man home alive
23:17 Take this y man to the commander;
23:18 asked me to bring this y man to you
23:19 The commander took the y man
23:22 commander dismissed the y man
1Ti 4:12 down on you because you are y,
Tit 2: 6 encourage the y men
1Pe 5: 5 Y men, in the same way be
1Jn 2:13 I write to you, y men,
2:14 I write to you, y men,

YOUNGER (YOUNG)

Ge 19:31 the older daughter said to the y,
19:34 the older daughter said to the y,
19:35 also, and the y daughter went
19:38 The y daughter also had a son,
25:23 and the older will serve the y."
27:15 and put them on her y son Jacob.
27:42 she sent for her y son Jacob
29:16 and the name of the y was Rachel.
29:18 for your y daughter Rachel."
29:26 to give the y daughter in marriage
29:27 then we will give you the y one also
48:14 he was the y, and crossing his arms,
Ge 48:19 his y brother will be greater than he
Jdg 1:13 son of Kenaz, Caleb's y brother,
3: 9 Caleb's y brother, who saved them.
15: 2 Isn't her y sister more attractive?
Ru 3:10 You have not run after the y men,
1Sa 14:49 and that of the y was Michal.
Job 30: 1 men y than I,
Eze 16:46 and your y sister, who lived
16:61 than you and those who are y.
Mk 15:40 Mary the mother of James the y
Lk 15:12 The y one said to his father, 'Father
15:13 the y son got together all he had,
Jn 21:18 when you were y you dressed
Ro 9:12 "The older will serve the y."
1Ti 5: 1 Treat y men as brothers, older
5: 2 as mothers, and y women as sisters,
5:11 As for y widows, do not put them
5:14 So I counsel y widows to marry,
Tit 2: 4 Then they can train the y women

YOUNGEST (YOUNG)

Ge 9:24 found out what his y son had done
42:13 The y is now with our father,
42:15 unless your y brother comes here.
42:20 But you must bring your y brother
42:32 and the y is now with our father
42:34 But bring your y brother to me
43:29 he asked, "Is this your y brother,
43:33 from the firstborn to the y;
44: 2 in the mouth of the y one's sack,
44:12 the oldest and ending with the y.
44:23 'Unless your y brother comes
44:26 Only if our y brother is
44:26 unless our y brother is with us.'
Jos 6:26 at the cost of his y
Jdg 9: 5 Jotham, the y son of Jerub-Baal,
1Sa 16:11 There is still the y," Jesse answered
17:14 David was the y.
1Ki 16:34 gates at the cost of his y son Segub,
1Ch 24:31 treated the same as those of the y.
2Ch 21:17 left to him except Ahaziah, the y.
22: 1 Jehoram's y son, king in his place,
Lk 22:26 among you should be like the y,

YOUTH (YOUNG)

Lev 22:13 in her father's house as in her y,
Nu 11:28 who had been Moses' aide since y,
1Sa 12: 2 leader from my y until this day.
17:33 been a fighting man from his y."
2Sa 19: 7 upon you from your y till now."
1Ki 18:12 worshiped the LORD since my y.
Job 13:26 make me inherit the sins of my y.
31:18 but from my y I reared him
33:25 it is restored as in the days of his y.
36:14 They die in their y,
Ps 25: 7 Remember not the sins of my y
71: 5 my confidence since my y.
71:17 Since my y, O God, you have
88:15 From my y I have been afflicted
89:45 have cut short the days of his y;
103: 5 so that my y is renewed like
110: 3 you will receive the dew of your y.
127: 4 are sons born in one's y.
129: 1 greatly oppressed me from my y—
129: 2 greatly oppressed me from my y,
144: 12 Then our sons in their y
Pr 2:17 who has left the partner of her y
5:18 in the wife of your y.
7: 7 a y who lacked judgment.
29:21 a man pampers his servant from y,
Ecc 4:13 Better a poor but wise y than an old
4:14 The y may have come from prison
4:15 under the sun followed the y,
11: 9 in the days of your y.
11:10 for y and vigor are meaningless.
12: 1 Creator in the days of your y,
Isa 54: 4 You will forget the shame of your y
65:20 will be thought a mere y;
Jer 2: 2 I remember the devotion of your y,
3: 4 'My Father, my friend from my y,
3:24 From our y shameful gods have
3:25 from our y till this day
22:21 has been your way from your y;
31:19 because I bore the disgrace of my y
32:30 but evil in my sight from their y;
48:11 "Moab has been at rest from y,
51:22 with you I shatter old man and y,
Eze 4:14 From my y until now I have never

Eze 16: 22 not remember the days of your *y*,
16: 43 not remember the days of your *y*
16: 60 with you in the days of your *y*,
23: 3 in prostitution from their *y*.
23: 8 when during her *y* men slept
23: 19 as she recalled the days of her *y*,
23: 21 longed for the lewdness of your *y*,
Hos 2: 15 as in the days of her *y*,
Joel 1: 8 grieving for the husband of her *y*.
Zec 13: 5 has been my livelihood since my *y*.'
Mal 2: 14 between you and the wife of your *y*
2: 15 faith with the wife of your *y*.
2Ti 2: 22 Flee the evil desires of *y*,

YOUTHFUL (YOUNG)

Job 20: 11 The *y* vigor that fills his bones

YOUTHS (YOUNG)

2Ki 2: 23 some *y* came out of the town
2: 24 and mauled forty-two of the *y*.
Isa 3: 12 *Y* oppress my people,
40: 30 Even *y* grow tired and weary,

ZAANAN

Mic 1: 11 Those who live in *Z*

ZAANANNIM

Jos 19: 33 from Heleph and the large tree in *Z*
Jdg 4: 11 by the great tree in *Z* near Kedesh.

ZAAVAN

Ge 36: 27 The sons of Ezer: Bilhan, *Z*
1Ch 1: 42 The sons of Ezer: Bilhan, *Z*

ZABAD

1Ch 2: 37 father of *Z*, *Z* the father of Ephlal,
7: 21 *Z* his son and Shuthelah his son.
11: 41 Uriah the Hittite, *Z* son of Ahlai,
2Ch 24: 26 conspired against him were *Z*,
Ezr 10: 27 Mattaniah, Jeremoth, *Z* and Aziza.
10: 33 Mattenai, Mattattah, *Z*, Eliphelet,
10: 43 Jeiel, Mattithiah, *Z*, Zebina, Jaddai

ZABBAI

Ezr 10: 28 Jehohanan, Hananiah, *Z*
Ne 3: 20 of *Z* zealously repaired another

ZABDI

1Ch 8: 19 Jakim, Zicri, *Z*, Elienai, Zillethai,
27: 27 *Z* the Shiphmite was in charge
Ne 11: 17 the son of *Z*, the son of Asaph,

ZABDIEL

1Ch 27: 2 month, was Jashobeam son of *Z*.
Ne 11: 14 Their chief officer was *Z* son

ZABUD

1Ki 4: 5 *Z* son of Nathan—a priest

ZACCAI

Ezr 2: 9 of Zattu 945 of *Z* 760 of Bani 642
Ne 7: 14 of Zattu 845 of *Z* 760 of Binnui 648

ZACCHAEUS

Lk 19: 2 A man was there by the name of *Z*;
19: 5 "*Z*, come down immediately.
19: 8 *Z* stood up and said to the Lord,

ZACCUR

Nu 13: 4 Shammua son of *Z*; from the tribe
1Ch 4: 26 *Z* his son and Shimei his son.
24: 27 Beno, Shoham, *Z* and Ibri.
25: 2 *Z*, Joseph, Nethaniah
25: 10 the third to *Z*, his sons
Ezr 8: 14 and *Z*, and with them 70 men.
Ne 3: 2 *Z* son of Imri built next to them.
10: 12 Rehob, Hashabiah, *Z*, Sherebiah,
12: 35 the son of *Z*, the son of Asaph,
13: 13 and made Hanan son of *Z*,

ZADOK (ZADOKITES)

2Sa 8: 17 *Z* son of Ahitub and Ahimelech
15: 24 *Z* was there, too, and all
15: 25 the king said to *Z*, "Take the ark
15: 27 The king also said to *Z* the priest,
15: 29 So *Z* and Abiathar took the ark
15: 35 Won't the priests *Z* and Abiathar
15: 36 son of *Z* and Jonathan son
17: 15 Hushai told *Z* and Abiathar,
18: 19 Now Ahimaaz son of *Z* said,
18: 22 Ahimaaz son of *Z* again said
18: 27 one runs like Ahimaaz son of *Z*."
19: 11 King David sent this message to *Z*
20: 25 *Z* and Abiathar were priests;
1Ki 1: 8 But *Z* the priest, Benaiah son
1: 26 me your servant, and *Z* the priest,
1: 32 David said, "Call in *Z* the priest,
1: 34 There have *Z* the priest
1: 38 *Z* the priest, Nathan the prophet,
1: 39 *Z* the priest took the horn of oil
1: 44 sent with him *Z* the priest,
1: 45 and *Z* the priest and Nathan
2: 35 replaced Abiathar with *Z* the priest
4: 2 Azariah son of *Z*— the priest;
4: 4 commander in chief; *Z*
2Ki 15: 33 name was Jerusha daughter of *Z*.
1Ch 6: 8 of *Z*, *Z* the father of Ahimaaz,
6: 12 of *Z*, *Z* the father of Shallum,
6: 53 *Z* his son and Ahimaaz his son.
9: 11 the son of *Z*, the son of Meraioth,
12: 28 men, and *Z*, a brave young warrior,
15: 11 Then David summoned *Z*
16: 39 David left *Z* the priest
18: 16 *Z* son of Ahitub and Ahimelech
24: 3 With the help of *Z* a descendant
24: 6 and of the officials: *Z* the priest,
24: 31 presence of King David and of *Z*,
27: 17 over Aaron: *Z*; over Judah: Elihu,
29: 22 to be ruler and *Z* to be priest.
2Ch 27: 1 name was Jerusha daughter of *Z*.
31: 10 from the family of *Z*, answered,
Ezr 7: 2 the son of *Z*, the son of Ahitub,
Ne 3: 4 and next to him *Z* son of Baana
3: 29 *Z* son of Immer made repairs
10: 21 Hezir, Meshezabel, *Z*, Jaddua,
11: 11 the son of *Z*, the son of Meraioth,
13: 13 Shelemiah the priest, *Z* the scribe,
Eze 40: 46 of *Z*, who are the only Levites who
43: 19 who are Levites, of the family of *Z*,
44: 15 are Levites and descendants of *Z*
Mt 1: 14 father of *Z*, *Z* the father of Akim,

ZADOKITES (ZADOK)

Eze 48: 11 for the consecrated priests, the *Z*,

ZAHAM

2Ch 11: 19 him sons: Jeush, Shemariah and *Z*.

ZAHAR

Eze 27: 18 from Helbon and wool from *Z*.

ZAIR

2Ki 8: 21 So Jehoram went to *Z*

ZALAPH

Ne 3: 30 son of *Z*, repaired another section.

ZALMON

Jdg 9: 48 and all his men went up Mount *Z*.
2Sa 23: 28 the Hushathite, *Z* the Ahohite,
Ps 68: 14 it was like snow fallen on *Z*.

ZALMONAH

Nu 33: 41 left Mount Hor and camped at *Z*.
33: 42 They left *Z* and camped at Punon.

ZALMUNNA

Jdg 8: 5 I am still pursuing Zebah and *Z*,
8: 6 of Zebah and *Z* in your possession?
8: 7 the LORD has given Zebah and *Z*
8: 10 and *Z* were in Karkor with a force
8: 12 and *Z*, the two kings of Midian,
8: 15 of Zebah and *Z* in your possession?
8: 15 *Z*, about whom you taunted me
8: 18 Then he asked Zebah and *Z*,
8: 21 Zebah and *Z* said, "Come,
Ps 83: 11 all their princes like Zebah and *Z*,

ZAMZUMMITES

Dt 2: 20 but the Ammonites called them *Z*.

ZANOAH

Jos 15: 34 Eshtaol, Zorah, Ashnah, *Z*,
15: 56 Juttah, Jezreel, Jokdeam, *Z*, Kain,
1Ch 4: 18 and Jekuthiel the father of *Z*.)
Ne 3: 13 by Hanun and the residents of *Z*.
11: 30 *Z*, Adullam and their villages,

ZAPHENATH-PANEAH

Ge 41: 45 Pharaoh gave Joseph the name *Z*

ZAPHON

Jos 13: 27 *Z* with the rest of the realm of
Jdg 12: 1 crossed over to *Z* and said
Ps 48: 2 heights of *Z* is Mount Zion,

ZAREPHATH

1Ki 17: 9 "Go at once to *Z* of Sidon
17: 10 So he went to *Z*.
Ob : 20 will possess ⌊the land⌋ as far as *Z*;
Lk 4: 26 but to a widow in *Z* in the region

ZARETHAN

Jos 3: 16 Adam in the vicinity of *Z*,
1Ki 4: 12 Beth Shan next to *Z* below Jezreel,
7: 46 Jordan between Succoth and *Z*.
2Ch 4: 17 Jordan between Succoth and *Z*.

ZATTU

Ezr 2: 8 of *Z* 945 of Zaccai 760 of Bani 642
8: 5 descendants of *Z*, Shecaniah son
10: 27 From the descendants of *Z*:
Ne 7: 13 of *Z* 845 of Zaccai 760
10: 14 Pahath-Moab, Elam, *Z*, Bani,

ZAZA

1Ch 2: 33 The sons of Jonathan: Peleth and *Z*

ZEAL (ZEALOUS)

Nu 25: 11 so that in my *z* I did not put an end
Dt 29: 20 and *z* will burn against that man.
2Sa 21: 2 but Saul in his *z* for Israel
2Ki 10: 16 and see my *z* for the LORD."
19: 31 The *z* of the LORD Almighty will
Ps 69: 9 for *z* for your house consumes me,
119:139 My *z* wears me out,
Pr 19: 2 to have *z* without knowledge,
Isa 9: 7 The *z* of the LORD Almighty
26: 11 Let them see your *z* for your people
37: 32 The *z* of the LORD Almighty
42: 13 like a warrior he will stir up his *z*;
59: 17 and wrapped himself in *z*
63: 15 Where are your *z* and your might?
Eze 5: 13 I the LORD have spoken in my *z*.
36: 5 In my burning *z* I have spoken
38: 19 In my *z* and fiery wrath I declare
Jn 2: 17 "*Z* for your house will consume me
Ro 10: 2 their *z* is not based on knowledge.
12: 11 Never be lacking in *z*,
Php 3: 6 as for *z*, persecuting the church;

ZEALOT

Mt 10: 4 Simon the *Z* and Judas Iscariot,
Mk 3: 18 Simon the *Z* and Judas Iscariot,
Lk 6: 15 Simon who was called the *Z*,
Ac 1: 13 son of Alphaeus and Simon the *Z*,

ZEALOUS (ZEAL)

Nu 25: 11 *z* as I am for my honor among them
25: 13 he was *z* for the honor of his God
1Ki 19: 10 "I have been very *z*
19: 14 "I have been very *z*
Pr 23: 17 always be *z* for the fear
Eze 39: 25 and I will be *z* for my holy name.
Ac 21: 20 and all of them are *z* for the law.
22: 3 *z* for God as any of you are today.
Ro 10: 2 testify about them that they are *z*
2Co 8: 22 to us in many ways that he is *z*,
Gal 1: 14 was extremely *z* for the traditions
4: 17 Those people are *z* to win you over,
4: 17 so that you may be *z* for them.
4: 18 fine to be *z*, provided the purpose is

ZEBADIAH

1Ch 8: 15 Shashak, Jeremoth, *Z*, Arad, Eder,
8: 17 *Z*, Meshullam, Hizki, Heber,
12: 7 *Z* the sons of Jeroham from Gedor.
26: 2 Jediael the second, *Z* the third,
27: 7 his son *Z* was his successor.
2Ch 17: 8 Shemaiah, Nethaniah, *Z*, Asahel,
19: 11 and *Z* son of Ishmael, the leader
Ezr 8: 8 of Shephatiah, *Z* son of Michael,
10: 20 of Immer: Hanani and *Z*.

ZEBAH

Jdg 8: 5 I am still pursuing *Z* and Zalmunna

Jdg 8: 6 you already have the hands of *Z*
8: 7 when the LORD has given *Z*
8: 10 *Z* and Zalmunna were in Karkor
8: 12 *Z* and Zalmunna, the two kings
8: 15 you already have the hands of *Z*
8: 15 "Here are *Z* and Zalmunna,
8: 18 Then he asked *Z* and Zalmunna,
8: 21 *Z* and Zalmunna said, "Come,
Ps 83: 11 all their princes like *Z*

ZEBEDEE (ZEBEDEE'S)

Mt 4: 21 son of *Z* and his brother John.
4: 21 were in a boat with their father *Z*,
10: 2 son of *Z*, and his brother John;
26: 37 the two sons of *Z* along with him,
Mk 1: 19 he saw James son of *Z*
1: 20 they left their father *Z* in the boat
3: 17 the name Peter); James son of *Z*,
10: 35 the sons of *Z*, came to him.
Lk 5: 10 the sons of *Z*, Simon's partners.
Jn 21: 2 of *Z*, and two other disciples were

ZEBEDEE'S (ZEBEDEE)

Mt 20: 20 the mother of *Z* sons came to Jesus
27: 56 and the mother of *Z* sons.

ZEBIDAH

2Ki 23: 36 His mother's name was *Z* daughter

ZEBINA

Ezr 10: 43 Jeiel, Mattithiah, Zabad, *Z*, Jaddai,

ZEBOIIM

Ge 10: 19 Gomorrah, Admah and *Z*,
14: 2 of Admah, Shemeber king of *Z*,
14: 8 the king of *Z* and the king
Dt 29: 23 *Z*, which the LORD overthrew
Hos 11: 8 How can I make you like *Z*?

ZEBOIM

1Sa 13: 18 the Valley of *Z* facing the desert.
Ne 11: 34 in Hadid, *Z* and Neballat,

ZEBUL

Jdg 9: 28 son, and isn't *Z* his deputy?
9: 30 When *Z* the governor
9: 36 When Gaal saw them, he said to *Z*,
9: 36 tops of the mountains!" *Z* replied,
9: 38 *Z* said to him, "Where is your big
9: 41 *Z* drove Gaal and his brothers out

ZEBULUN (ZEBULUNITE)

Ge 30: 20 So she named him *Z*.
35: 23 Levi, Judah, Issachar and *Z*.
46: 14 The sons of *Z*: Sered, Elon
49: 13 "*Z* will live by the seashore
Ex 1: 3 Issachar, *Z* and Benjamin;
Nu 1: 9 from *Z*, Eliab son of Helon;
1: 30 From the descendants of *Z*:
1: 31 from the tribe of *Z* was 57,400.
2: 7 The tribe of *Z* will be next.
2: 7 of the people of *Z* is Eliab son
7: 24 the leader of the people of *Z*,
10: 16 over the division of the tribe of *Z*.
13: 10 from the tribe of *Z*, Gaddiel son
26: 26 The descendants of *Z*
26: 27 These were the clans of *Z*;
34: 25 the leader from the tribe of *Z*;
Dt 27: 13 Gad, Asher, *Z*, Dan and Naphtali.
33: 18 About *Z* he said:
33: 18 "Rejoice, *Z*, in your going out,
Jos 19: 10 The third lot came up for *Z*,
19: 16 villages were the inheritance of *Z*,
19: 27 *Z* and the Valley of Iphtah El,
19: 34 It touched *Z* on the south,
21: 7 the tribes of Reuben, Gad and *Z*.
21: 34 from the tribe of *Z*, Jokneam,
Jdg 1: 30 Neither did *Z* drive out
4: 6 and *Z* and lead the way
4: 10 where he summoned *Z*
5: 14 from *Z* those who bear
5: 18 of *Z* risked their very lives;
6: 35 also into Asher, *Z* and Naphtali,
12: 12 buried in Aijalon in the land of *Z*.
1Ch 2: 1 Judah, Issachar, *Z*, Dan, Joseph,
6: 63 the tribes of Reuben, Gad and *Z*.
6: 77 tribe of *Z* they received Jokneam,
12: 33 under their command; men of *Z*,
1Ch 12: 40 *Z* and Naphtali came bringing food
27: 19 over *Z*: Ishmaiah son of Obadiah;
2Ch 30: 10 as far as *Z*, but the people scorned
30: 11 and *Z* humbled themselves
30: 18 and *Z* had not purified themselves,
Ps 68: 27 the princes of *Z* and of Naphtali.
Isa 9: 1 the past he humbled the land of *Z*
Eze 48: 26 "*Z* will have one portion; it will
48: 27 the territory of *Z* from east to west.
48: 33 gate of Issachar and the gate of *Z*.
Mt 4: 13 was by the lake in the area of *Z*
4: 15 "Land of *Z* and land of Naphtali,
Rev 7: 8 from the tribe of *Z* 12,000,

ZEBULUNITE (ZEBULUN)

Jdg 12: 11 Elon the *Z* led Israel ten years.

ZECHARIAH (ZECHARIAH'S)

2Ki 14: 29 And *Z* his son succeeded him
15: 8 *Z* son of Jeroboam became king
15: 10 son of Jabesh conspired against *Z*.
18: 2 name was Abijah daughter of *Z*.
1Ch 5: 7 Jeiel the chief, *Z*, and Bela son
9: 21 *Z* son of Meshelemiah was
9: 37 Gedor, Ahio, *Z* and Mikloth.
15: 18 *Z*, Jaaziel, Shemiramoth, Jehiel,
15: 20 *Z*, Aziel, Shemiramoth, Jehiel,
15: 24 Joshaphat, Nethanel, Amasai, *Z*,
16: 5 Asaph was the chief, *Z* second,
24: 25 Isshiah; from the sons of Isshiah: *Z*
26: 2 had sons: *Z* the firstborn,
26: 11 Tabaliah the third and *Z* the fourth
26: 14 Then lots were cast for his son *Z*,
27: 21 Iddo son of *Z*; over Benjamin:
2Ch 17: 7 *Z*, Nethanel and Micaiah to teach
20: 14 came upon Jahaziel son of *Z*,
21: 2 were Azariah, Jehiel, *Z*, Azariahu,
24: 20 the Spirit of God came upon *Z* son
26: 5 God during the days of *Z*,
29: 1 name was Abijah daughter of *Z*.
29: 13 from the descendants of Asaph, *Z*
34: 12 descended from Merari, and *Z*
35: 8 *Z* and Jehiel, the administrators
Ezr 5: 1 the prophet and *Z* the prophet,
6: 14 of Haggai the prophet and *Z*,
8: 3 of the descendants of Parosh, *Z*,
8: 11 of Bebai, *Z* son of Bebai,
8: 16 Nathan, *Z* and Meshullam,
10: 26 Mattaniah, *Z*, Jehiel, Abdi,
Ne 8: 4 Hashbaddanah, *Z* and Meshullam.
11: 4 the son of *Z*, the son of Amariah,
11: 5 the son of *Z*, a descendant
11: 12 the son of *Z*, the son of Pashhur,
12: 16 of Iddo's, *Z*; of Ginnethon's,
12: 35 and also *Z* son of Jonathan,
12: 41 *Z* and Hananiah with their
Isa 8: 2 call in Uriah the priest and *Z* son
Zec 1: 1 to the prophet *Z* son of Berekiah,
1: 7 to the prophet *Z* son of Berekiah,
7: 1 came to *Z* on the fourth day
7: 8 of the LORD came again to *Z*:
Mt 23: 35 to the blood of *Z* son of Berakiah,
Lk 1: 5 Judea there was a priest named *Z*,
1: 12 When *Z* saw him, he was startled
1: 13 *Z*; your prayer has been heard.
1: 18 *Z* asked the angel, "How can I be
1: 21 the people were waiting for *Z*
1: 59 to name him after his father *Z*,
1: 67 His father *Z* was filled
3: 2 to John son of *Z* in the desert.
11: 51 the blood of Abel to the blood of *Z*,

ZECHARIAH'S (ZECHARIAH)

2Ki 15: 11 events of *Z* reign are written
2Ch 24: 22 the kindness *Z* father Jehoiada
Lk 1: 8 Once when *Z* division was on duty
1: 40 where she entered *Z* home

ZEDAD

Nu 34: 8 Then the boundary will go to *Z*,
Eze 47: 15 past Lebo Hamath to *Z*,

ZEDEKIAH (ZEDEKIAH'S)

1Ki 22: 11 *Z* son of Kenaanah had made iron
22: 24 Then *Z* son of Kenaanah went up
2Ki 24: 17 and changed his name to *Z*.
24: 18 *Z* was twenty-one years old
24: 20 Now *Z* rebelled against the king
2Ki 25: 2 until the eleventh year of King *Z*.
25: 7 the sons of *Z* before his eyes.
1Ch 3: 15 the second son, *Z* the third,
3: 16 Jehoiachin his son, and *Z*.
2Ch 18: 10 *Z* son of Kenaanah had made iron
18: 23 Then *Z* son of Kenaanah went up
36: 10 and he made Jehoiachin's uncle, *Z*,
36: 11 *Z* was twenty-one years old
Ne 10: 1 *Z*, Seraiah, Azariah, Jeremiah,
Jer 1: 3 year of *Z* son of Josiah king
21: 1 from the LORD when King *Z* sent
21: 3 Jeremiah answered them, "Tell *Z*,
21: 7 I will hand over *Z* king of Judah,
24: 8 'so will I deal with *Z* king of Judah,
27: 1 in the reign of *Z* son of Josiah king
27: 3 to Jerusalem to *Z* king of Judah.
27: 12 message to *Z* king of Judah.
28: 1 in the reign of *Z* king of Judah,
29: 3 whom *Z* king of Judah sent
29: 21 of Kolaiah and *Z* son of Maaseiah,
29: 22 'The LORD treat you like *Z*
32: 1 in the tenth year of *Z* king of Judah
32: 3 *Z* king of Judah had imprisoned
32: 4 *Z* king of Judah will not escape out
32: 5 He will take *Z* to Babylon,
34: 2 Go to *Z* king of Judah and tell him,
34: 4 of the LORD, O *Z* king of Judah.
34: 6 this to *Z* king of Judah,
34: 8 after King *Z* had made a covenant
34: 21 "I will hand *Z* king of Judah
36: 12 of Shaphan, *Z* son of Hananiah,
37: 1 *Z* son of Josiah was made king
37: 3 King *Z*, however, sent Jehucal son
37: 17 Then King *Z* sent for him
37: 18 Then Jeremiah said to King *Z*,
37: 21 King *Z* then gave orders
38: 5 in your hands," King *Z* answered.
38: 14 Then King *Z* sent for Jeremiah
38: 15 said to *Z*, "If I give you an answer,
38: 16 But King *Z* swore this oath secretly
38: 17 to *Z*, "This is what the LORD God
38: 19 King *Z* said to Jeremiah, "I am
38: 24 *Z* said to Jeremiah, "Do not let
39: 1 In the ninth year of *Z* king of Judah
39: 4 When *Z* king of Judah
39: 5 overtook *Z* in the plains of Jericho.
39: 6 the sons of *Z* before his eyes
44: 30 as I handed *Z* king of Judah
49: 34 in the reign of *Z* king of Judah:
51: 59 to Babylon with *Z* king of Judah
52: 1 *Z* was twenty-one years old
52: 3 Now *Z* rebelled against the king
52: 5 until the eleventh year of King *Z*.
52: 8 Babylonian army pursued King *Z*
52: 10 the sons of *Z* before his eyes;

ZEDEKIAH'S (ZEDEKIAH)

2Ki 25: 1 So in the ninth year of *Z* reign,
Jer 39: 2 month of *Z* eleventh year,
39: 7 Then he put out *Z* eyes
52: 4 So in the ninth year of *Z* reign,
52: 11 Then he put out *Z* eyes, bound him

ZEEB

Jdg 7: 25 and *Z* at the winepress of *Z*.
7: 25 heads of Oreb and *Z* to Gideon,
7: 25 the Midianite leaders, Oreb and *Z*.
8: 3 and *Z*, the Midianite leaders,
Ps 83: 11 Make their nobles like Oreb and *Z*,

ZEKER

1Ch 8: 31 Gedor, Ahio, *Z* and Mikloth,

ZELA

2Sa 21: 14 at *Z* in Benjamin, and did

ZELAH

Jos 18: 28 Irpeel, Taralah, *Z*, Haeleph,

ZELEK

2Sa 23: 37 the son of Hagri, *Z* the Ammonite,
1Ch 11: 39 son of Hagri, *Z* the Ammonite,

ZELOPHEHAD (ZELOPHEHAD'S)

Nu 26: 33 (*Z* son of Hepher had no sons;
27: 1 The daughters of *Z* son of Hepher,
36: 2 of our brother *Z* to his daughters.
Jos 17: 3 *Z* son of Hepher, the son of Gilead,

1Ch 7: 15 Another descendant was named *Z*,

ZELOPHEHAD'S (ZELOPHEHAD)

Nu 27: 7 "What *Z* daughters are saying is
36: 6 commands for *Z* daughters:
36: 10 So *Z* daughters did as the LORD
36: 11 *Z* daughters—Mahlah, Tirzah,

ZELZAH

1Sa 10: 2 at *Z* on the border of Benjamin.

ZEMARAIM

Jos 18: 22 *Z*, Bethel, Avvim, Parah,
2Ch 13: 4 Abijah stood on Mount *Z*,

ZEMARITES

Ge 10: 18 Arvadites, *Z* and Hamathites.
1Ch 1: 16 Arvadites, *Z* and Hamathites.

ZEMIRAH

1Ch 7: 8 *Z*, Joash, Eliezer, Elioenai,

ZENAN

Jos 15: 37 *Z*, Hadashah, Migdal Gad, Dilean,

ZENAS

Tit 3: 13 can to help *Z* the lawyer

ZEPHANIAH

2Ki 25: 18 *Z* the priest next in rank
1Ch 6: 36 the son of *Z*, the son of Tahath,
Jer 21: 1 and the priest *Z* son of Maaseiah.
29: 25 to *Z* son of Maaseiah the priest,
29: 25 to *Z*, 'The LORD has appointed
29: 29 *Z* the priest, however, read
37: 3 with the priest *Z* son of Maaseiah
52: 24 *Z* the priest next in rank
Zep 1: 1 came to *Z* son of Cushi,
Zec 6: 10 day to the house of Josiah son of *Z*.
6: 14 Jedaiah and Hen son of *Z*

ZEPHATH

Jdg 1: 17 attacked the Canaanites living in *Z*

ZEPHATHAH

2Ch 14: 10 in the Valley of *Z* near Mareshah.

ZEPHO

Ge 36: 11 Omar, *Z*, Gatam and Kenaz.
36: 15 Chiefs Teman, Omar, *Z*, Kenaz,
1Ch 1: 36 Omar, *Z*, Gatam and Kenaz;

ZEPHON (ZEPHONITE)

Ge 46: 16 The sons of Gad: *Z*, Haggi, Shuni,
Ex 14: 2 by the sea, directly opposite Baal *Z*
14: 9 near Pi Hahiroth, opposite Baal *Z*.
Nu 26: 15 through *Z*, the Zephonite clan;
33: 7 *Z*, and camped near Migdol.

ZEPHONITE (ZEPHON)

Nu 26: 15 through Zephon, the *Z* clan;

ZER

Jos 19: 35 *Z*, Hammath, Rakkath, Kinnereth,

ZERAH (ZERAHITE ZERAHITES)

Ge 36: 13 Nahath, *Z*, Shammah and Mizzah.
36: 17 *Z*, Shammah and Mizzah.
36: 33 of *Z* from Bozrah succeeded him
38: 30 and he was given the name *Z*.
46: 12 and *Z* (but Er and Onan had died
Nu 26: 13 through *Z*, the Zerahite clan;
26: 20 through *Z*, the Zerahite clan.
Jos 7: 1 the son of *Z*, of the tribe of Judah,
7: 18 the son of *Z*, of the tribe of Judah,
7: 24 took Achan son of *Z*, the silver,
22: 20 son of *Z* acted unfaithfully
1Ch 1: 37 Nahath, *Z*, Shammah and Mizzah.
1: 44 of *Z* from Bozrah succeeded him
2: 4 bore him Perez and *Z*.
2: 6 The sons of *Z*: Zimri, Ethan,
4: 24 Nemuel, Jamin, Jarib, *Z* and Shaul;
6: 21 *Z* his son and Jeatherai his son.
6: 41 the son of *Z*, the son of Adaiah,
2Ch 14: 9 *Z* the Cushite marched out
Ne 11: 24 the descendants of *Z* son of Judah,
Mt 1: 3 Judah the father of Perez and *Z*,

ZERAHIAH

1Ch 6: 6 of *Z*, *Z* the father of Meraioth,
6: 51 Bukki his son, Uzzi his son, *Z*
Ezr 7: 4 the son of *Z*, the son of Uzzi,
8: 4 Eliehoenai son of *Z*,

ZERAHITE (ZERAH)

Nu 26: 13 through Zerah, the *Z* clan;
26: 20 through Zerah, the *Z* clan.
1Ch 27: 11 was Sibbecai the Hushathite, a *Z*.
27: 13 was Maharai the Netophathite, a *Z*

ZERAHITES (ZERAH)

Jos 7: 17 came forward, and he took the *Z*.
7: 17 of the *Z* come forward by families,
1Ch 9: 6 Of the *Z*: Jeuel.

ZERED

Nu 21: 12 and camped in the *Z* Valley.
Dt 2: 13 Now get up and cross the *Z* Valley
2: 14 until we crossed the *Z* Valley.

ZEREDAH

1Ki 11: 26 an Ephraimite from *Z*,

ZERERAH

Jdg 7: 22 fled to Beth Shittah toward *Z*

ZERESH

Est 5: 10 Calling together his friends and *Z*,
5: 14 His wife *Z* and all his friends said
6: 13 and his wife *Z* said to him,
6: 13 told *Z* his wife and all his friends

ZERETH

1Ch 4: 7 The sons of Helah: *Z*, Zohar,

ZERETH SHAHAR

Jos 13: 19 Sibmah, *Z* on the hill in the valley,

ZERI

1Ch 25: 3 Gedaliah, *Z*, Jeshaiah, Shimei,

ZEROR

1Sa 9: 1 the son of *Z*, the son of Becorath,

ZERUAH

1Ki 11: 26 his mother was a widow named *Z*.

ZERUBBABEL

1Ch 3: 19 The sons of Pedaiah: *Z* and Shimei.
3: 19 The sons of *Z*: Meshullam
Ezr 2: 2 in company with *Z*, Jeshua,
3: 2 and his fellow priests and *Z* son
3: 8 in Jerusalem, *Z* son of Shealtiel,
4: 2 they came to *Z* and to the heads
4: 3 *Z*, Jeshua and the rest of the heads
5: 2 Then *Z* son of Shealtiel
Ne 7: 7 in company with *Z*, Jeshua,
12: 1 returned with *Z* son of Shealtiel
12: 47 in the days of *Z* and of Nehemiah,
Hag 1: 1 Haggai to *Z* son of Shealtiel,
1: 12 Then *Z* son of Shealtiel, Joshua son
1: 14 the spirit of *Z* son of Shealtiel,
2: 2 "Speak to *Z* son of Shealtiel,
2: 4 O *Z*,' declares the LORD.
2: 21 "Tell *Z* governor of Judah that I
2: 23 my servant *Z* son of Shealtiel,'
Zec 4: 6 This is the word of the LORD to *Z*:
4: 7 Before *Z* you will become level
4: 9 of *Z* have laid the foundation
4: 10 see the plumb line in the hand of *Z*.
Mt 1: 13 father of *Z*, *Z* the father of Abiud,
Lk 3: 27 the son of *Z*, the son of Shealtiel,

ZERUIAH (ZERUIAH'S)

1Sa 26: 6 the Hittite and Abishai son of *Z*,
2Sa 2: 13 son of *Z* and David's men went out
2: 18 The three sons of *Z* were there:
3: 39 and these sons of *Z* are too strong
8: 16 Joab son of *Z* was over the army;
14: 1 son of *Z* knew that the king's heart
16: 9 Abishai son of *Z* said to the king,
16: 10 you sons of *Z*? If he is cursing
17: 25 and sister of *Z* the mother of Joab.
18: 2 Joab's brother Abishai son of *Z*,
19: 21 Then Abishai son of *Z* said,
19: 22 of *Z*? This day you have become
21: 17 But Abishai son of *Z* came
23: 18 brother of Joab son of *Z* was chief
23: 37 the armor-bearer of Joab son of *Z*,
1Ki 1: 7 conferred with Joab son of *Z*
2: 5 know what Joab son of *Z* did
2: 22 the priest and Joab son of *Z*!"
1Ch 2: 16 Their sisters were *Z* and Abigail.
11: 6 Joab son of *Z* went up first,
11: 39 the armor-bearer of Joab son of *Z*,
18: 12 Abishai son of *Z* struck
18: 15 Joab son of *Z* was over the army;
26: 28 son of Ner and Joab son of *Z*,
27: 24 Joab son of *Z* began

ZERUIAH'S (ZERUIAH)

1Ch 2: 16 *Z* three sons were Abishai,

ZETHAM

1Ch 23: 8 Jehiel the first, *Z* and Joel—
26: 22 of Jehieli, *Z* and his brother Joel.

ZETHAN

1Ch 7: 10 Benjamin, Ehud, Kenaanah, *Z*,

ZETHAR

Est 1: 10 Bigtha, Abagtha, *Z* and Carcas—

ZEUS

Ac 14: 12 Barnabas they called *Z*,
14: 13 priest of *Z*, whose temple was just

ZIA

1Ch 5: 13 Sheba, Jorai, Jacan, *Z* and Eber—

ZIBA (ZIBA'S)

2Sa 9: 2 of Saul's household named *Z*.
9: 2 "Are you *Z*?" "Your servant,"
9: 3 *Z* answered the king, "There is still
9: 4 *Z* answered, "He is at the house
9: 9 Then the king summoned *Z*,
9: 10 (Now *Z* had fifteen sons
9: 11 *Z* said to the king, "Your servant
16: 1 there was *Z*, the steward
16: 2 The king asked *Z*, "Why have you
16: 2 you brought these?" *Z* answered,
16: 3 is your master's grandson?" *Z* said
16: 4 said to *Z*, "All that belonged
16: 4 "I humbly bow," *Z* said.
19: 17 along with *Z*, the steward
19: 26 But *Z* my servant betrayed me.
19: 29 and *Z* to divide the fields."

ZIBA'S (ZIBA)

2Sa 9: 12 of *Z* household were servants

ZIBEON

Ge 36: 2 granddaughter of *Z* the Hivite—
36: 14 of Anah and granddaughter of *Z*,
36: 20 Lotan, Shobal, *Z*, Anah, Dishon,
36: 24 The sons of *Z*: Aiah and Anah.
36: 24 the donkeys of his father *Z*.
36: 29 Lotan, Shobal, *Z*, Anah, Dishon,
1Ch 1: 38 Lotan, Shobal, *Z*, Anah, Dishon,
1: 40 The sons of *Z*: Aiah and Anah.

ZIBIA

1Ch 8: 9 *Z*, Mesha, Malcam, Jeuz, Sakia

ZIBIAH

2Ki 12: 1 His mother's name was *Z*;
2Ch 24: 1 His mother's name was *Z*;

ZICRI

Ex 6: 21 Izhar were Korah, Nepheg and *Z*.
1Ch 8: 19 Jakim, *Z*, Zabdi, Elienai, Zillethai,
8: 23 Eliel, Abdon, *Z*, Hanan, Hananiah,
8: 27 and *Z* were the sons of Jeroham.
9: 15 the son of *Z*, the son of Asaph;
26: 25 *Z* his son and Shelomith his son.
27: 16 son of *Z*; over the Simeonites:
2Ch 17: 16 next, Amasiah son of *Z*,
23: 1 of Adaiah, and Elishaphat son of *Z*
28: 7 *Z*, an Ephraimite warrior,
Ne 11: 9 Joel son of *Z* was their chief officer
12: 17 Meshullam; of Abijah's, *Z*;

ZIDDIM

Jos 19: 35 The fortified cities were *Z*, Zer,

ZIHA

Ezr 2:43 the descendants of Z, Hasupha,
Ne 7:46 the descendants of Z, Hasupha,
11:21 and Z and Gishpa were in charge

ZIKLAG

Jos 15:31 Kesil, Hormah, Z, Madmannah,
19:5 Eltolad, Bethul, Hormah, Z,
1Sa 27:6 So on that day Achish gave him Z,
30:1 They had attacked Z and burned it,
30:1 had raided the Negev and Z.
30:1 his men reached Z on the third day
30:3 David and his men came to Z,
30:14 And we burned Z."
30:26 When David arrived in Z,
2Sa 1:1 and stayed in Z two days.
4:10 and put him to death in Z.
1Ch 4:30 Tolad, Bethuel, Hormah, Z,
12:1 the men who came to David at Z,
12:20 went to Z, these were the men
Ne 11:28 in Z, in Meconah and its

ZILLAH

Ge 4:19 one named Adah and the other Z.
4:22 Z also had a son, Tubal-Cain,
4:23 "Adah and Z, listen to me;

ZILLETHAI

1Ch 8:20 Zabdi, Elienai, Z, Eliel, Adaiah,
12:20 Michael, Jozabad, Elihu and Z,

ZILPAH

Ge 29:24 And Laban gave his servant girl Z
30:9 she took her maidservant Z
30:10 Leah's servant Z bore Jacob a son.
30:12 Leah's servant Z bore Jacob
35:26 The sons of Leah's maidservant Z:
37:2 sons of Bilhah and the sons of Z,
46:18 the children born to Jacob by Z,

ZIMMAH

1Ch 6:20 Jehath his son, Z his son, Joah his
6:42 the son of Z, the son of Shimei,
2Ch 29:12 Joah son of Z and Eden son of Joah

ZIMRAN

Ge 25:2 She bore him Z, Jokshan, Medan,
1Ch 1:32 Abraham's concubine: Z, Jokshan,

ZIMRI (ZIMRI'S)

Nu 25:14 the Midianite woman was Z son
Jos 7:1 the son of Z, the son of Zerah,
7:17 by families, and Z was taken.
7:18 the son of Z, the son of Zerah,
1Ki 16:9 Z, one of his officials, who had
16:10 Z came in, struck him down
16:12 So Z destroyed the whole family
16:15 Z reigned in Tirzah seven days.
16:16 the camp heard that Z had plotted
16:18 When Z saw that the city was
2Ki 9:31 "Have you come in peace, Z,
1Ch 2:6 The sons of Zerah: Z, Ethan,
8:36 Z, and Z was the father of Moza.
9:42 Z, and Z was the father of Moza.
Jer 25:25 all the kings of Z, Elam and Media;

ZIMRI'S (ZIMRI)

1Ki 16:20 As for the other events of Z reign,

ZIN

Nu 13:21 the land from the Desert of Z
20:1 arrived at the Desert of Z,
27:14 at the waters in the Desert of Z,
27:14 in Kadesh, in the Desert of Z.)
33:36 at Kadesh, in the Desert of Z.
34:3 of the Desert of Z along the border
34:4 continue on to Z and go south
Dt 32:51 Meribah Kadesh in the Desert of Z
Jos 15:1 to the Desert of Z
15:3 continued on to Z and went

ZION (ZION'S)

2Sa 5:7 David captured the fortress of Z,
1Ki 8:1 of the LORD's covenant from Z,
2Ki 19:21 " 'The Virgin Daughter of Z
19:31 out of Mount Z a band of survivors
1Ch 11:5 David captured the fortress of Z,
2Ch 5:2 of the LORD's covenant from Z,
Ps 2:6 King on Z, my holy hill."
9:11 to the LORD, enthroned in Z;
9:14 in the gates of the Daughter of Z
14:7 for Israel would come out of Z!
20:2 and grant you support from Z.
48:2 heights of Zaphon is Mount Z,
48:11 Mount Z rejoices,
48:12 Walk about Z, go around her,
50:2 From Z, perfect in beauty,
51:18 good pleasure make Z prosper;
53:6 for Israel would come out of Z!
65:1 Praise awaits you, O God, in Z;
69:35 for God will save Z
74:2 Mount Z, where you dwelt.
76:2 his dwelling place in Z.
78:68 Mount Z, which he loved.
84:7 till each appears before God in Z.
87:2 the LORD loves the gates of Z
87:4 'This one was born in Z.' "
87:5 Indeed, of Z it will be said,
87:6 "This one was born in Z."
97:8 Z hears and rejoices
99:2 Great is the LORD in Z;
102:13 and have compassion on Z,
102:16 For the LORD will rebuild Z
102:21 of the LORD will be declared in Z
110:2 your mighty scepter from Z;
125:1 in the LORD are like Mount Z,
126:1 brought back the captives to Z,
128:5 May the LORD bless you from Z
129:5 May all who hate Z
132:13 For the LORD has chosen Z,
133:3 were falling on Mount Z.
134:3 bless you from Z.
135:21 Praise be to the LORD from Z,
137:1 when we remembered Z.
137:3 "Sing us one of the songs of Z!"
146:10 your God, O Z, for all generations.
147:12 praise your God, O Z,
149:2 let the people of Z be glad
SS 3:11 Come out, you daughters of Z,
Isa 1:8 The Daughter of Z is left
1:27 Z will be redeemed with justice,
2:3 The law will go out from Z,
3:16 "The women of Z are haughty,
3:17 on the heads of the women of Z;
3:26 The gates of Z will lament
4:3 left in Z, who remain in Jerusalem,
4:4 the filth of the women of Z;
4:5 create over all of Mount Z
8:18 who dwells on Mount Z.
10:12 all his work against Mount Z
10:24 "O my people who live in Z,
10:32 at the mount of the Daughter of Z,
12:6 sing for joy, people of Z,
14:32 "The LORD has established Z,
16:1 to the mount of the Daughter of Z.
18:7 gifts will be brought to Mount Z,
24:23 on Mount Z and in Jerusalem,
28:16 "See, I lay a stone in Z,
29:8 that fight against Mount Z.
30:19 O people of Z, who live
31:4 down to do battle on Mount Z
31:9 whose fire is in Z,
33:5 he will fill Z with justice
33:14 The sinners in Z are terrified;
33:20 Look upon Z, the city
33:24 No one living in Z will say,
35:10 They will enter Z with singing;
37:22 "The Virgin Daughter of Z
37:32 out of Mount Z a band of survivors
40:9 You who bring good tidings to Z,
41:27 I was the first to tell Z, 'Look,
46:13 I will grant salvation to Z,
49:14 Z said, "The LORD has forsaken
51:3 The LORD will surely comfort Z
51:11 They will enter Z with singing;
51:16 who say to Z, 'You are my people
52:1 Awake, awake, O Z,
52:2 O captive Daughter of Z.
52:7 who say to Z,
52:8 When the LORD returns to Z,
59:20 "The Redeemer will come to Z,
60:14 Z of the Holy One of Israel.
61:3 provide for those who grieve in Z
62:11 "Say to the Daughter of Z,
64:10 Z is a desert, Jerusalem
66:8 Yet no sooner is Z in labor
Jer 3:14 from every clan and bring you to Z.
4:6 Raise the signal to go to Z!
4:31 Daughter of Z gasping for breath,
6:2 I will destroy the Daughter of Z,
6:23 to attack you, O Daughter of Z."
8:19 "Is the LORD not in Z?
9:19 sound of wailing is heard from Z:
14:19 Do you despise Z?
26:18 " 'Z will be plowed like a field,
30:17 Z for whom no one cares.'
31:6 'Come, let us go up to Z,
31:12 shout for joy on the heights of Z;
50:5 They will ask the way to Z
50:28 declaring in Z
51:10 come, let us tell in Z
51:24 all the wrong they have done in Z,"
51:35 say the inhabitants of Z.
La 1:4 The roads to Z mourn,
1:6 from the Daughter of Z.
1:17 Z stretches out her hands,
2:1 has covered the Daughter of Z
2:4 on the tent of the Daughter of Z.
2:6 The LORD has made Z forget
2:8 the wall around the Daughter of Z.
2:10 The elders of the Daughter of Z
2:13 O Virgin Daughter of Z?
2:18 O wall of the Daughter of Z,
4:2 How the precious sons of Z,
4:11 He kindled a fire in Z
4:22 of Z, your punishment will end;
5:11 Women have been ravished in Z,
5:18 for Mount Z, which lies desolate,
Joel 2:1 Blow the trumpet in Z;
2:15 Blow the trumpet in Z,
2:23 Be glad, O people of Z,
2:32 for on Mount Z and in Jerusalem
3:16 The LORD will roar from Z
3:17 dwell in Z, my holy hill.
3:21 The LORD dwells in Z! The words
Am 1:2 "The LORD roars from Z
6:1 to you who are complacent in Z,
Ob :17 on Mount Z will be deliverance;
:21 Deliverers will go up on Mount Z
Mic 1:13 sin to the Daughter of Z,
3:10 who build Z with bloodshed,
3:12 Z will be plowed like a field,
4:2 The law will go out from Z,
4:7 rule over them in Mount Z
4:8 O stronghold of the Daughter of Z,
4:10 Writhe in agony, O Daughter of Z,
4:11 let our eyes gloat over Z!"
4:13 "Rise and thresh, O Daughter of Z,
Zep 3:14 Sing, O Daughter of Z;
3:16 "Do not fear, O Z;
Zec 1:14 jealous for Jerusalem and Z,
1:17 the LORD will again comfort Z
2:7 O Z! Escape, you who live
2:10 and be glad, O Daughter of Z.
8:2 jealous for Z; I am burning
8:3 "I will return to Z and dwell
9:9 Rejoice greatly, O Daughter of Z!
9:13 I will rouse your sons, O Z,
Mt 21:5 "Say to the Daughter of Z,
Jn 12:15 Do not be afraid, O Daughter of Z;
Ro 9:33 I lay in Z a stone that causes men
11:26 "The deliverer will come from Z;
Heb 12:22 But you have come to Mount Z,
1Pe 2:6 "See, I lay a stone in Z,
Rev 14:1 standing on Mount Z,

ZION'S (ZION)

Isa 34:8 of retribution, to uphold Z cause.
62:1 For Z sake I will not keep silent,

ZIOR

Jos 15:54 Hebron) and Z—nine towns

ZIPH (ZIPHITES)

Jos 15:24 Hazor, Ithnan, Z, Telem, Bealoth,
15:55 Maon, Carmel, Z, Juttah, Jezreel,
1Sa 23:14 and in the hills of the Desert of Z.
23:15 was at Horesh in the Desert of Z,
23:24 and went to Z ahead of Saul.
26:2 Saul went down to the Desert of Z,
1Ch 2:42 who was the father of Z,
4:16 The sons of Jehallelel: Z, Ziphah,
2Ch 11:8 Gath, Mareshah, Z, Adoraim,

ZIPHAH

1Ch 4: 16 Ziph, *Z,* Tiria and Asarel.

ZIPHITES (ZIPH)

1Sa 23: 19 The *Z* went up to Saul at Gibeah
26: 1 The *Z* went to Saul at Gibeah

ZIPHRON

Nu 34: 9 to *Z* and end at Hazar Enan.

ZIPPOR

Nu 22: 2 of *Z* saw all that Israel had done
22: 4 So Balak son of *Z,* who was king
22: 10 "Balak son of *Z,* king of Moab,
22: 16 "This is what Balak son of *Z* says:
23: 18 hear me, son of *Z.*
Jos 24: 9 When Balak son of *Z,* the king
Jdg 11: 25 Are you better than Balak son of *Z,*

ZIPPORAH

Ex 2: 21 who gave his daughter *Z* to Moses
2: 22 *Z* gave birth to a son, and Moses
4: 25 But *Z* took a flint knife, cut
18: 2 Moses had sent away his wife *Z,*

ZITHER

Da 3: 5 *z,* lyre, harp, pipes and all kinds
3: 7 *z,* lyre, harp and all kinds of music,
3: 10 the sound of the horn, flute, *z,*
3: 15 *z,* lyre, harp, pipes and all kinds

ZIV

1Ki 6: 1 the month of *Z,* the second month,
6: 37 in the month of *Z.*

ZIZ

2Ch 20: 16 be climbing up by the Pass of *Z,*

ZIZA

1Ch 4: 37 Benaiah, and *Z* son of Shiphi,
23: 10 Jahath, *Z,* Jeush and Beriah.
23: 11 was the first and *Z* the second,
2Ch 11: 20 who bore him Abijah, Attai, *Z*

ZOAN

Nu 13: 22 years before *Z* in Egypt.)
Ps 78: 12 of Egypt, in the region of *Z.*
78: 43 his wonders in the region of *Z.*
Isa 19: 11 The officials of *Z* are nothing
19: 13 officials of *Z* have become fools,
30: 4 Though they have officials in *Z,*
Eze 30: 14 set fire to *Z*

ZOAR

Ge 13: 10 like the land of Egypt, toward *Z.*
14: 2 and the king of Bela (that is, *Z).*
14: 8 *Z)* marched out and drew up their
19: 22 That is why the town was called *Z.)*
19: 23 By the time Lot reached *Z,*
19: 30 and his two daughters left *Z*
19: 30 for he was afraid to stay in *Z.*
Dt 34: 3 the City of Palms, as far as *Z.*
Isa 15: 5 her fugitives flee as far as *Z,*
Jer 48: 34 from *Z* as far as Horonaim

ZOBAH

1Sa 14: 47 the kings of *Z,* and the Philistines.
2Sa 8: 3 son of Rehob, king of *Z,*
8: 5 came to help Hadadezer king of *Z,*
8: 12 son of Rehob, king of *Z.*
10: 6 from Beth Rehob and *Z,*
10: 8 while the Arameans of *Z*
23: 36 Igal son of Nathan from *Z,*
1Ki 11: 23 his master, Hadadezer king of *Z.*
11: 24 David destroyed the forces of *Z;*
1Ch 18: 3 David fought Hadadezer king of *Z,*
18: 5 came to help Hadadezer king of *Z,*
18: 9 army of Hadadezer king of *Z,*
19: 6 Aram Maacah and *Z.*

ZOHAR

Ge 23: 8 with Ephron son of *Z* on my behalf
25: 9 of Ephron son of *Z* the Hittite,
46: 10 *Z* and Shaul the son
Ex 6: 15 *Z* and Shaul the son
1Ch 4: 7 Zereth, *Z,* Ethnan, and Koz,

ZOHELETH

1Ki 1: 9 calves at the Stone of *Z* near En

ZOHETH

1Ch 4: 20 The descendants of Ishi: *Z*

ZOPHAH

1Ch 7: 35 *Z,* Imna, Shelesh and Amal.
7: 36 The sons of *Z:* Suah, Harnepher,

ZOPHAI

1Ch 6: 26 Elkanah his son, *Z* his son,

ZOPHAR

Job 2: 11 the Shuhite and *Z* the Naamathite,
11: 1 Then *Z* the Naamathite replied:
20: 1 Then *Z* the Naamathite replied:
42: 9 and *Z* the Naamathite did what

ZOPHIM

Nu 23: 14 him to the field of *Z* on the top

ZORAH

Jos 15: 33 Eshtaol, *Z,* Ashnah, Zanoah,
19: 41 inheritance included: *Z,*
Jdg 13: 2 man of *Z,* named Manoah,
13: 25 was in Mahaneh Dan, between *Z*
16: 31 and buried him between *Z*
18: 2 Danites sent five warriors from *Z*
18: 8 When they returned to *Z*
18: 11 set out from *Z* and Eshtaol.
2Ch 11: 10 Adoraim, Lachish, Azekah, *Z,*
Ne 11: 29 in En Rimmon, in *Z,* in Jarmuth,

ZORATHITES

1Ch 2: 53 From these descended the *Z*
4: 2 These were the clans of the *Z.*

ZORITES

1Ch 2: 54 half the Manahathites, the *Z,*

ZUAR

Nu 1: 8 Nethanel son of *Z;* from Zebulun,
2: 5 of Issachar is Nethanel son of *Z.*
7: 18 the second day Nethanel son of *Z,*
7: 23 the offering of Nethanel son of *Z.*
10: 15 Nethanel son of *Z* was

ZUPH (ZUPHITE)

1Sa 1: 1 the son of *Z,* an Ephraimite.
9: 5 they reached the district of *Z,*
1Ch 6: 35 the son of *Z,* the son of Elkanah,

ZUPHITE (ZUPH)

1Sa 1: 1 a *Z* from the hill country

ZUR

Nu 25: 15 to death was Cozbi daughter of *Z,*
31: 8 Rekem, *Z,* Hur and Reba—
Jos 13: 21 Evi, Rekem, *Z,* Hur and Reba—
1Ch 8: 30 followed by *Z,* Kish, Baal, Ner,
9: 36 followed by *Z,* Kish, Baal, Ner,

ZURIEL

Nu 3: 35 of the Merarite clans was *Z* son

ZURISHADDAI

Nu 1: 6 Shelumiel son of *Z;* from Judah,
2: 12 of Simeon is Shelumiel son of *Z.*
7: 36 On the fifth day Shelumiel son of *Z*
7: 41 the offering of Shelumiel son of *Z.*
10: 19 Shelumiel son of *Z* was

ZUZITES

Ge 14: 5 Karnaim, the *Z* in Ham, the Emites

12 (TWELVE)

1Ch 25: 9 Joseph, his sons . . . *12*
25: 9 Gedaliah, he and his relatives . . . *12*
25: 10 Zaccur, his sons . . . *12*
25: 11 Izri, his sons . . . *12*
25: 12 Nethaniah, his sons . . . *12*
25: 13 Bukkiah, his sons . . . *12*
25: 14 Jesarelah, his sons . . . *12*
25: 15 Jeshaiah, his sons . . . *12*
25: 16 Mattaniah, his sons . . . *12*
25: 17 Shimei, his sons . . . *12*
25: 18 Azarel, his sons . . . *12*
1Ch 25: 19 Hashabiah, his sons . . . *12*
25: 20 Shubael, his sons . . . *12*
25: 21 Mattithiah, his sons . . . *12*
25: 22 Jerimoth, his sons . . . *12*
25: 23 Hananiah, his sons . . . *12*
25: 24 Joshbakashah, his sons . . . *12*
25: 25 Hanani, his sons . . . *12*
25: 26 Mallothi, his sons . . . *12*
25: 27 Eliathah, his sons . . . *12*
25: 28 Hothir, his sons . . . *12*
25: 29 Giddalti, his sons . . . *12*
25: 30 Mahazioth, his sons . . . *12*
25: 31 Romamti-Ezer, his sons . . . *12*

12,000 (TWELVE)

Rev 7: 5 From the tribe of Judah *12,000*
7: 5 from the tribe of Gad *12,000,*
7: 5 from the tribe of Reuben *12,000,*
7: 6 from the tribe of Asher *12,000,*
7: 6 from the tribe of Manasseh *12,000,*
7: 6 from the tribe of Naphtali *12,000,*
7: 7 from the tribe of Issachar *12,000,*
7: 7 from the tribe of Levi *12,000,*
7: 7 from the tribe of Simeon *12,000,*
7: 8 from the tribe of Benjamin *12,000.*
7: 8 from the tribe of Joseph *12,000,*
7: 8 from the tribe of Zebulun *12,000,*
21: 16 the rod and found it to be *12,000*

144,000 (TWELVE)

Rev 7: 4 *144,000* from all the tribes of Israel
14: 1 Mount Zion, and with him *144,000*
14: 3 learn the song except the *144,000*

40 (FORTY)

Eze 4: 6 I have assigned you *40* days,

APPENDIX

WORDS OMITTED IN THE NIV COMPLETE CONCORDANCE

a
abnormally
about
above
absolutely
abundantly
abusively
acceptably
accidentally
accordance
according
accordingly
across
actual
actually
adequately
adjoining
afar
affair
affairs
aforethought
after
afterward
again
against
ago
ah
aha
ahead
aimlessly
alas
alike
all
almost
alone
along
alongside
already
also
although
altogether
am
amid
among
amply
an
and
anew
another
another's
answer
answerable
answered
answering
answers
anxiously
any
anybody
anymore
anyone
anyone's
anything
anywhere
apart
aptly
are
aren't
around
arrogantly
article
articles
as
aside
ask
asked
asking
asks
assuredly
at
attentively
away
awhile
back
backward
bad
badly
barely
be
beautifully
became
because
become
becomes
becoming
been
before
beforehand
began
begin
begins
begun
behalf
beheld
behind
behold
being
beings
below
beneath
beside
besides
best
better
between
beyond
bitterly
boastfully
boldly
both
bottom
boy
boyhood
boys
boy's
bravely
briefly
brightly
bring
bringing
brings
brought
brutally
but
by
came
can
cannot
can't
carefully
carelessly
centrally
certainly
cheerfully
clear
cleared
clearly
cleverly
closely
closest
come
comes
coming
completely
concerning
confidently
consequently
constantly
contemptuously
continually
continously
cordially
correctly
corruptly
could
couldn't
courageously
critically
cruelly
customary
daily
daughter
daughters
daughters-in-law
daughter-in-law
daughter's
dearly
deceitfully
deceptively
deeply
definitely
deliberately
descendant
descendants
despite
did
didn't
differently
diligently
directly
discreetly
dishonestly
distance

distant
distinctly
do
does
doesn't
doing
done
don't
doubly
doubtless
down
duly
during
each
eagerly
earlier
earliest
early
earnestly
easily
effectively
eight
eighteen
eighteenth
eighth
eightieth
eighty
eighty-five
eighty-four
eighty-six
eighty-three
either
eleven
eleventh
else
elsewhere
else's
emphatically
encouragingly
endlessly
enough
entirely
equally
especially
even
evenly
events
eventually
every
everybody
everybody's
everyday
everyone
everyone's
everything
everywhere
evidently
exactly
exceedingly
except
exclusively
extremely
fairly
far
faraway
farther
farthest
far-off
fatally
favorably
fearlessly
fellow
fellowman
fellows
fellow's
few
fewest
fiercely
fifteen
fifteenth
fifth
fifties
fiftieth
fifty
fifty-five
fifty-second
fifty-two
figuratively
finally
finely
firmly
five
five-sided
for
forcefully
forcibly
foremost
former
formerly
forth
forty-
forty-eight
forty-first
forty-five
forty-nine
forty-one
forty-seven
forty-six
forty-two
forward
four
fours
fourteen
fourteenth
fourth
four-fifths
four-sided
frankly
freely
frequent
frequently
freshly
fro
from
front
frontal
furiously
further
furthermore
generously
gently
girl
girls
girl's
gladly
go
goes
going
gone
graciously
greatly
grudgingly
had
handsomely
happen
happened
happening
happens
hardly
harshly
ha
has
hasn't
hastily
have
haven't
having
he
heavily
her
here
hereby
here's
hers
herself
he's
high
higher
highest
highly
him
himself
his
honestly
hotly
how
however
humbly
hurriedly
I
if
I'll
I'm
immeasurably
immediately
impartially
improperly
in
inasmuch
include
included
includes
including
incomparably
indeed
indignantly
individually
indoors
inmost
inner
innermost
innocently
inside
insistently
instantly
instead
intensely
intently
into
inward
inwardly
is
isn't
it
its
itself
it's
I've
joyfully
kindly
ladies
lady
large
larger
largest
late
lately
later
latest
least
leave
leaving
less
lesser
lest
let
lets
letting
let's
liberally
lightly
like
liked
likely
liken
likes
likewise
little
longer
loud
louder
loudly

lovingly
low
lowest
lustfully
maliciously
man
manhood
manifold
manned
many
man's
material
materials
matter
mattered
matters
may
maybe
me
meanwhile
meekly
men
men's
mercilessly
mere
merely
middle
midst
mightily
miraculously
modestly
more
moreover
most
mournfully
much
must
my
myself
namely
naught
near
nearby
neared
nearer
nearest
nearly
neither
never
nevertheless
newly
next
nine
nineteen
nineteenth
ninety
ninety-eight
ninety-nine
ninety-six
nine-and-a-half
ninth
no
nobody
none
nor
normally
not
nothing
now
nowhere
number
numbered
numbering
numberless
numbers
numerous
O
of
off
often
Oh
old
older
oldest
on
once
one
ones
oneself
one-third
one's
only
onto
open
opened
opening
openings
openly
opens
opposite
or
other
others
otherwise
other's
ought
our
ours
ourselves
out
outdoor
outer
outside
outward
outwardly
over
part
parted
particularly
partly
parts
peaceably
peacefully
people
peopled
peoples
people's
per
perfectly
perhaps
permanently
person
personal
personally
persons
person's
persuasively
pertaining
place
placed
places
placing
plainly
plentifully
possibly
powerfully
practically
precisely
prematurely
presumptously
previously
prior
privately
properly
proudly
purposely
put
puts
putting
quick
quickly
quietly
quite
rapidly
rarely
rashly
rather
reach
reached
reaches
reaching
readily
ready
really
rear
reared
rearing
recent
recently
regarding
regardless
region
regions
regularly
reluctantly
reopened
repeatedly
replied
replies
reply
resolutely
richly
rightfully
rightly
roundabout
ruthlessly
safely
said
same
saw
say
saying
sayings
says
scarcely
scornfully
second
securely
see
seeing
seem
seemed
seems
seen
sees
seldom
self
selves
set
sets
setting
settings
seventeen
seventeenth
seventy
seventy-five
seventy-seven
seventy-two
several
severely
shall
shamefully
shamelessly
sharply
she
she's
shorter
shortly
should
shouldn't
shrewdly
sighting
similar
similarly
simply
since
sincerely
sir
Sirs
six
sixteen
sixteenth

sixth
sixty
sixty-eight
sixty-five
sixty-six
sixty-two
slanderously
slowly
small
smaller
smallest
smooth
smoother
smoothly
smooths
so
solemnly
some
somebody
somehow
someone
someone's
something
sometimes
somewhat
somewhere
sons-in-law
son-in-law
soon
sooner
sparingly
speak
speaker
speaking
speaks
speedily
spoke
spoken
spokes
stay
stayed
staying
stays
stead
steadily
sternly
strictly
strongly
stubbornly
successfully
such
suddenly
supposedly
surely
surpassingly
swiftly
talk
talked
talker
talkers
talking
talks
tell
telling
tells
tenderly
terribly
than
that
that's
the
their
theirs
them
themselves
then
there
therefore
there's
these
they
thick
thicker
thickness
thin
thing
things
things'
third
thirds
thirteen
thirteenth
thirtieth
thirty
thirty-eight
thirty-eighth
thirty-fifth
thirty-first
thirty-five
thirty-ninth
thirty-one
thirty-second
thirty-seven
thirty-seventh
thirty-six
thirty-sixth
thirty-three
thirty-two
this
thorough
thoroughly
those
though
thoughtlessly
thousand
thousands
three-pronged
three-tenths
three-year-old
through
throughout
thus
tightly
till
timely
to
together
told
too
topmost
tops
total
totaled
totally
toward
treacherously
trivial
truly
truthfully
twentieth
twenty
twenty-eight
twenty-fifth
twenty-first
twenty-five
twenty-four
twenty-fourth
twenty-nine
twenty-one
twenty-second
twenty-seven
twenty-seventh
twenty-six
twenty-sixth
twenty-third
twenty-three
twenty-two
twice
two
two-and-a-half
two-tenths
two-thirds
unanswered
unceasingly
under
underneath
undoubtedly
unduly
unexpectedly
unjustly
unless
unlike
unswervingly
until
unto
up
upon
upper
upward
urgently
us
use
used
uses
using
usual
usually
utterly
valiantly
varied
various
vehemently
very
viciously
vigorously
violently
visibly
voluntarily
warmly
was
wasn't
we
went
were
we'll
we're
we've
what
what's
whatever
when
whenever
where
wherever
whether
which
while
who
whoever
wholly
whom
whose
why
wickedly
widely
willingly
wisely
with
within
without
woman
woman's
women
women's
wonderfully
won't
worse
worst
would
wouldn't
yes
yet
you
your
yours
yourself
yourselves
you'll
you're
you've
zealously